D1265526

Acronyms, Initialisms & Abbreviations Dictionary

ISSN 0270-4404

Acronyms, Initialisms & Abbreviations Dictionary

A Guide to Acronyms, Abbreviations,
Contractions, Alphabetic Symbols, and Similar Condensed Appellations

Covering: Aerospace, Associations, Banking, Biochemistry, Business, Data Processing,
Domestic and International Affairs, Economics, Education, Electronics, Genetics,
Government, Information Technology, Internet, Investment, Labor, Law, Medicine, Military Affairs,
Pharmacy, Physiology, Politics, Religion, Science, Societies, Sports, Technical
Drawings and Specifications, Telecommunications, Trade, Transportation, and Other Fields

27th Edition

Volume 1

Part 2

G-O

Mary Rose Bonk,
Editor

Pamela Dear,
Associate Editor

Detroit
San Francisco
London
Boston
Woodbridge, CT

Editor:	Mary Rose Bonk
Associate Editor:	Pamela Dear
Assistant Editor:	Phyllis Spinelli
Data Capture Manager:	Ronald D. Montgomery
Project Administrator:	Gwendolyn S. Tucker
Data Capture Specialists:	Beverly Jendrowski, Constance Wells
Manufacturing Manager:	Dorothy Maki
Buyer:	Nekita McKee
Graphic Services Manager:	Barbara J. Yarrow
Graphic Artist:	Gary Leach
Manager, Technical Support Services:	Theresa A. Rocklin
Programmer:	Charles Beaumont

Library of Congress Catalog Card Number 84-643188
ISBN 0-7876-2857-3 (Volume 1 Complete)
ISBN 0-7876-2858-1 (Part 1: A-F only)
ISBN 0-7876-2859-X (Part 2: G-O only)
ISBN 0-7876-2860-3 (Part 3: P-Z only)
ISSN 0270-4404

Printed in the United States of America

Contents

Volume 1

Part 1 A-F

Volume 1

Part 2 G-O

Volume 1

Part 3 P-Z

Gale's publications in the acronyms and abbreviations field include:

Acronyms, Initialisms & Abbreviations Dictionary series:

Acronyms, Initialisms & Abbreviations Dictionary (Volume 1). A guide to acronyms, initialisms, abbreviations, and similar contractions, arranged alphabetically by abbreviation.

Acronyms, Initialisms & Abbreviations Dictionary Supplement (Volume 2). An interedition supplement in which terms are arranged alphabetically both by abbreviation and by meaning.

Reverse Acronyms, Initialisms & Abbreviations Dictionary (Volume 3). A companion to Volume 1 in which terms are arranged alphabetically by meaning of the acronym, initialism, or abbreviation.

Acronyms, Initialisms & Abbreviations Dictionary Subject Guide series:

Computer & Telecommunications Acronyms (Volume 1). A guide to acronyms, initialisms, abbreviations, and similar contractions used in the field of computers and telecommunications in which terms are arranged alphabetically both by abbreviation and by meaning.

Business Acronyms (Volume 2). A guide to business-oriented acronyms, initialisms, abbreviations, and similar contractions in which terms are arranged alphabetically both by abbreviation and by meaning.

International Acronyms, Initialisms & Abbreviations Dictionary series:

International Acronyms, Initialisms & Abbreviations Dictionary (Volume 1). A guide to foreign and international acronyms, initialisms, abbreviations, and similar contractions, arranged alphabetically by abbreviation.

Reverse International Acronyms, Initialisms & Abbreviations Dictionary (Volume 2). A companion to Volume 1, in which terms are arranged alphabetically by meaning of the acronym, initialism, or abbreviation.

Periodical Title Abbreviations series:

Periodical Title Abbreviations: By Abbreviation (Volume 1). A guide to abbreviations commonly used for periodical titles, arranged alphabetically by abbreviation.

Periodical Title Abbreviations: By Title (Volume 2). A guide to abbreviations commonly used for periodical titles, arranged alphabetically by title.

User's Guide

The following examples illustrate possible elements of entries in *AIAD:*

```
      ①            ②                    ③              ④      ⑤
    FATAC... Force Aerienne Tactique [Tactical Air Force] [French] (NATG)

                                       ⑥              ⑦
    MMT... Multiple-Mirror Telescope [Mount Hopkins, AZ] [Jointly operated by
    Smithsonian Institution and the University of Arizona] [Astronomy]
                                          ⑧
```

① Acronym, Initialism, or Abbreviation

② Meaning or Phrase

③ English Translation

④ Language (for non-English entries)

⑤ Source code (Allows you to verify entries or find additional information. Decoded in the List of Selected Sources)

⑥ Location or Country of origin (Provides geographic identifiers for airports, colleges and universities, libraries, military bases, political parties, radio and television stations, and others)

⑦ Sponsoring organization

⑧ Subject category (Clarifies entries by providing appropriate context)

The completeness of a listing is dependent upon both the nature of the term and the amount of information provided by the source. If additional information becomes available during future research, an entry is revised.

Arrangement of Entries

Acronyms, initialisms, and abbreviations are arranged alphabetically in letter-by-letter sequence. Spacing, punctuation, and capitalization are not considered. If the same term has more than one meaning, the various meanings are subarranged in word-by-word sequence.

Should you wish to eliminate the guesswork from acronym formation and usage, a companion volume could help. *Reverse Acronyms, Initialisms and Abbreviations Dictionary* contains essentially the same entries as *AIAD,* but arranges them alphabetically by meaning, rather than by acronym or initialism.

List of Selected Sources

Each of the sources included in the following list contributed at least 50 terms. It would be impossible to cite a source for every entry because the majority of terms are sent by outside contributors, are uncovered through independent research by the editorial staff, or surface as miscellaneous broadcast or print media references.

For sources used on an ongoing basis, only the latest edition is listed. For most of the remaining sources, the edition that was used is cited. The editors will provide further information about these sources upon request.

Unless further described in an annotation, the publications listed here contain no additional information about the acronym, initialism, or abbreviation cited.

(AABC) *Catalog of Abbreviations and Brevity Codes*. Washington, DC: U.S. Department of the Army, 1981. [Use of source began in 1969]

(AAEL) *Common Abbreviations and Acronyms in Electronics*. By Gunham Kaytaz. <http://www.seas.smu.edu/~kaytaz/menu.html> (27 April 1999)

(AAG) *Aerospace Abbreviations Glossary*. Report Number AG60-0014. Prepared by General Dynamics/Astronautics. San Diego, CA: 1962.

(AAGC) *Acronyms and Abbreviations in Government Contracting*. 2d ed. By Patricia A. Tobin and Joan Nelson Phillips. Washington, DC: George Washington University, 1997.

(AAMN) *Abbreviations and Acronyms in Medicine and Nursing*. By Solomon Garb, Eleanor Krakauer, and Carson Justice. New York, NY: Springer Publishing Co., 1976.

(ABBR) *Abbreviations: The Comprehensive Dictionary of Abbreviations and Letter Symbols*. Vol. 1 C. By Edward Wall. Ann Arbor, MI: The Pierian Press, 1984.

(AC) *Associations Canada 1995/96*. Edited by Ward McBurney. Toronto, Canada: Canadian Almanac & Directory Publishing Co. Ltd., 1995.

(ACII) *"Acronym and Initials Index."* 7 February 1996. <http://www.ioi.ie/~readout/cl.html> (7 November 1996)

(AD) *Abbreviations Dictionary*. 8thed. By Ralph De Sola. Boca Raton, FL: CRC Press, 1992.

(ADA) *The Australian Dictionary of Acronyms and Abbreviations*. 2nd ed. Compiled by David J. Jones. Leura, NSW, Australia: Second Back Row Press Pty. Ltd., 1981.

(ADDR) *Army Dictionary and Desk Reference*. By Tim Zurick. Harrisburg, PA: Stackpole Books, 1992.

(AEBS) *Acronyms in Education and the Behavioral Sciences*. By Toyo S. Kawakami. Chicago, IL: American Library Association, 1971.

(AEE) *American Educators' Encyclopedia*. By Edward L. Dejnozka and David E. Kapel. Westport, CT: Greenwood Press, 1991.

(AEPA)   U.S. Environmental Protection Agency. *ACCESS EPA.* 1995/96 ed. Washington, DC: Office of Information Resources Management, 1996.

(AF)   *Reference Aid: Abbreviations in the African Press.* Arlington, VA: Joint Publications Research Service, 1979.

(AFIT)   *Compendium of Authenticated Systems and Logistics.* Washington, DC: Air Force Institute of Technology, 1984.

(AFM)   *Air Force Manual of Abbreviations.* Washington, DC: U.S. Department of the Air Force, 1975. [Use of source began in 1969]

(AIA)   *Aviation Insurance Abbreviations, Organisations and Institutions.* By M.J. Spurway. London, England: Witherby & Co. Ltd., 1983.

(AIE)   *Acronyms and Initialisms in Education.* 6th ed. Compiled by John Hutchins. Norwich, England: Librarians of Institutes and Schools of Education, 1995.

(AL)   *"Acronyms & Abbreviations."* American Library Association. <http://www.ala.org/> (2 December 1997)

(ANA)   *"Abbreviations" - U.S. Navy Dictionary.* 3rd revision. Washington, DC: DCP, 1989.

(APTA)   *Australian Periodical Title Abbreviations.* Compiled by David J. Jones. Leura, NSW, Australia: Second Back Row Press Pty. Ltd., 1985.

(ARC)   *Agricultural Research Centres: A World Directory of Organizations and Programmes.* 2 vols. Edited by Nigel Harvey. Harlow, Essex, England: Longman Group, 1983.
         A world guide to official, educational, industrial, and independent research centers which support research in the fields of agriculture, veterinary medicine, horticulture, aquaculture, food science, forestry, zoology, and botany.

(ARCH)   *Dictionary of Architecture and Construction.* Edited by Cyril M. Harris. New York, NY: McGraw-Hill, Inc., 1975.

(ASF)   *Guide to Names and Acronyms of Organizations, Activities, and Projects.* By Food and Agriculture Organization of the United Nations. Fishery Information, Data, and Statistics Service and U.S. National Oceanic and Atmospheric Administration. Aquatic Sciences and Fisheries Information System Reference Series, Number 10, 1982. n.p.

(BABM)   *Bailliere's Abbreviations in Medicine.* 5th ed. By Edwin B. Steen. London, England: Bailliere Tindall, 1984.

(BARN)   *The Barnhart Abbreviations Dictionary.* Edited by Robert K. Barnhart. New York, NY: John Wiley & Sons, Inc., 1995.

(BCP)   *BCP Guidebook.* <http://www.dtic.dla.mil/environdod/> (Fall 1995)

(BI)   *British Initials and Abbreviations.* 3rd ed. By Ian H. Wilkes. London, England: Leonard Hill Books, 1971.

(BIB)   *Bibliotech.* Ottawa, Canada: National Library of Canada, 1988-89.

(BJA) *Biblical and Judaic Acronyms*. By Lawrence Marwick. New York, NY: Ktav Publishing House, Inc., 1979.

(BRI) *Book Review Index*. 1997 Cumulation. Edited by Beverly Baer. Detroit, MI: Gale Research, 1998.

(BROA) *Broadcasting and Cable Yearbook 1998*. 2 vol. New Providence, NJ: Reed Elsevier, Inc., 1998.

(BTTJ) *Breaking Through Technical Jargon: A Dictionary of Computer and Automation Acronyms*. By Mark S. Merkow. New York, NY: Van Nostrand Reinhold, 1990.

(BUAC) *Buttress's World Guide to Abbreviations of Organizations*. 11th ed. Revised by L.M. Pitman. London, England: Blackie Academic and Professional, 1997.

(BUR) *Computer Acronyms and Abbreviations Handbook*. Tokyo, Japan: Burroughs Co. Ltd., 1978.

(BYTE) *Byte: The Small Systems Journal*. Peterborough, NH: McGraw-Hill Information Systems, Inc., 1987-89.

(CAAL) *CAAL COMOPTEVFOR Acronym and Abbreviation List*. Norfolk, VA: (CAAL-U) Operational Test and Evaluation Force, 1981.

(CB) *Centres & Bureaux: A Directory of Concentrations of Effort, Information and Expertise*. Edited by Lindsay Sellar. Beckenham, Kent, England: CBD Research Ltd., 1987.
A guide to British organizations which include the words "centre" or "bureau" in their names. Entries include name and address; telephone and telex numbers; chief official; and a description of the purposes, activities, and services of the organization.

(CDAI) *Concise Dictionary of Acronyms and Initialisms*. By Stuart W. Miller. New York, NY: Facts on File Publications, 1988.

(CDE) *The Computer Desktop Encyclopedia*. By Alan Freedman. New York, NY: AMACOM, 1996.

(CDI) *The Cancer Dictionary*. By Roberta Altman and Michael Sarg, M.D. New York, NY: Facts on File, 1992.

(CED) *Current European Directories*. 2nd ed. Edited by G.P. Henderson. Beckenham, Kent, England: CBD Research, 1981.

(CET) *Communications-Electronics Terminology*. AFM 11-1. Vol. 3. U.S. Department of the Air Force, 1973.

(CINC) *A CINCPAC Glossary of Commonly Used Abbreviations and Short Titles*. By Ltc. J.R. Johnson. Washington, DC: 1968.

(CIST) *Computer & Information Science & Technology Abbreviations & Acronyms Dictionary*. Edited by David W. South, ed. Boca Raton, FL: CRC Press, Inc., 1994.

(CMD) *Complete Multilingual Dictionary of Computer Terminology*. Compiled by Georges Nania. Chicago, IL: National Textbook Co., 1984.
Computer-related terms in Spanish, French, Italian, Portuguese, and English.
Indexes in French, Italian, Spanish, and Portuguese are also provided.

(CNC)   *American National Standard Codes for the Representation of Names of Countries, Dependencies, and Areas of Special Sovereignty for Information Interchange.* U.S. National Bureau of Standards. Washington, DC: Government Printing Office, 1986. [Use of source began in 1977]
> These standard codes, approved by the International Organization for Standardization and the American National Standards Institute, are used in the international interchange of data in many fields.

(COE)   *Cooper's Comprehensive Environmental Desk Reference.* Edited by Andre R. Cooper. New York, NY: John Wiley & Sons, 1990.

(CPH)   *The Charles Press Handbook of Current Medical Abbreviations.* 3rd ed. Philadelphia, PA: The Charles Press Publishers, Inc., 1991.

(CRD)   *Computer-Readable Databases: A Directory and Data Sourcebook.* 6th ed. Edited by Kathleen Young Marcaccio. Detroit, MI: Gale Research, 1990.
> A guide to online databases, offline files available in various magnetic formats, and CD-ROM files. Entries include producer name, address, telephone number, description of coverage, vendors, and contact person.

(CROSS)   *Cross-Border Links: A Directory of Organizations in Canada, Mexico, and the United States.* Edited by Ricardo Hernandez and Edith Sanchez. Albuquerque, NM: Inter-Hemispheric Education Resource Center, 1992.

(CSR)   *Computer Science Resources: A Guide to Professional Literature.* Edited by Darlene Myers. White Plains, NY: Knowledge Industry Publications, Inc., 1981.
> Covers several types of computer-related literature including journals, technical reports, directories, dictionaries, handbooks, and university computer center newsletters. Five appendices cover career and salary trends in the computer industry, user group acronyms, university computer libraries, and trade fairs and shows.

(CTT)   *Corporate TrendTrac.* Edited by A. Dale Timpe. Detroit, MI: Gale Research, 1988-89.
> Covers mergers and acquisitions, stock exchange listings and suspensions, company name changes, bankruptcies, liquidations, and reorganizations.

(DA)   *Dictionary of Aviation.* By R. J. Hall and R. D. Campbell. Chicago, IL: St. James Press, 1991.

(DAS)   *Dictionary of Abbreviations and Symbols.* By Edward Frank Allen. London, England: Cassell and Co. Ltd., 1949.

(DAVI)   *The Davis Book of Medical Abbreviations: A Deciphering Guide.* By Sarah Lu Mitchell-Hatton. Philadelphia, PA: F. A. Davis Co., 1991.

(DB)   *Dictionary of Biomedical Acronyms and Abbreviations.* 2nd ed. By Jacques Dupayrat. New York, NY: John Wiley & Sons, 1990.

(DBA)   *Directory of British Associations.* Edited by G. P. Henderson and S. P. A. Henderson. Beckenham, Kent, England: CBD Research, Ltd., 1990.

(DBQ)   *A Dictionary of British Qualifications.* London, England: Kogan Page Ltd., 1985.

(DCTA)   *Dictionary of Commercial Terms and Abbreviations.* By Alan E. Branch. London, England: Witherby & Co. Ltd., 1984.

(DD)   *The Financial Post Directory of Directors 1997*. Toronto, Canada: The Financial Post, 1996.

(DDC)   *The International Dictionary of Data Communications*. By Robert A. Saigh. Chicago, IL: The Glenlake Publishing Company, Ltd., 1998.

(DDSO)   *D & D Standard Oil Abbreviator*. 4th ed. Compiled by the Association of Desk and Derrick Clubs. Tulsa, OK: PennWell Books, 1994.

(DEN)   *Dictionary of Electronics and Nucleonics*. By L.E.C. Hughes, R.W.B. Stephens and L. D. Brown. New York, NY: Barnes & Noble, 1969.

(DET)   *Dictionary of Educational Terms*. Edited by David Blake and Vincent Hanley. Brookfield, VT: Ashgate Publishing Co., 1995.

(DFIT)   *Dictionary of Finance and Investment Terms*. 4th ed. Edited by John Downes and Jordan Elliot Goodman. Hauppauge, NY: Barron's Educational Series, 1995.

(DGA)   *Dictionary of Graphic Arts Abbreviations*. By L. W. Wallis. Rockport, MA: Rockport Publishers, Inc., 1986.

(DHP)   *Dictionary of Abbreviations and Acronyms in Helping Professions*. By John W. Hollis. Muncie, IN: Accelerated Development, Inc., 1987.

(DHSM)   *Dictionary of Health Services Management*. 2nd ed. By Thomas C. Timmreck. Owings Mills, MD: Rynd Communications, 1987.

(DI)   *The Dictionary of Initials--What They Mean*. Compiled and edited by Harriette Lewis. Kingswood, Surrey, England: Paper Fronts Elliot Right Way Books, 1983.

(DICI)   *The Dictionary of Initials*. By Betsy M. Parks. Secaucus, NJ: Citadel Press, 1981.

(DIT)   *Dictionary of Informatics Terms in Russian and English*. By G.S. Zhdanov, E.S. Kolobrodov, V.A. Polushkin, and A.I. Cherny. Moscow: Nauka, 1971.

(DLA)   *Bieber's Dictionary of Legal Abbreviations*. 3rd ed. By Mary Miles Prince. Buffalo, NY: William S. Hein & Co., 1988.

(DMA)   *Dictionary of Military Abbreviations: British, Empire, Commonwealth*. By B.K.C. Scott. Hastings, East Sussex, England: Tamarisk Books, 1982.

(DMAA)   *Dictionary of Medical Acronyms and Abbreviations*. 3rd ed. Edited by Stanley Jablonski. Philadelphia, PA: Hanley & Belfus, Inc., 1998.

(DMC)   *Webster's New World Dictionary of Media and Communications*. Revised ed. By Richard Weiner. New York, NY: Macmillan, 1996.

(DNAB)   *Dictionary of Naval Abbreviations*. 3rd ed. Compiled and edited by Bill Wedertz. Annapolis, MD: Naval Institute Press, 1984.

(DOAD)   *The Dictionary of Advertising*. Edited by Laurence Urdang. Lincolnwood, IL: NTC Business Books, 1986.

(DOG)   *A Dictionary of Genetics*. 5th ed. By Robert C. King and William D. Stansfield. New York, NY: Oxford University Press, 1997.

(DOGT)   *"List of Acronyms."* <http://www.em.doe.gov/rtc1994/loa.html> (5 March 1997)

(DOM)   *The Dictionary of Multimedia: Terms & Acronyms.* By Brad Hansen. Wilsonvillee, OR: Franklin, Beedle & Associates, 1997.

(DOMA)   *Dictionary of Military Abbreviations.* By Norman Polmar, Mark Warren, and Eric Wertheim. Annapolis, MD: Naval Institute Press, 1994.

(DS)   *Dictionary of Shipping International Trade Terms and Abbreviations.* 3rd ed. By Alan E. Branch. London, England: Witherby & Co. Ltd., 1986.

(DSA)   *Dictionary of Sigla and Abbreviations to and in Law Books before 1607.* By William Hamilton Bryson. Charlottesville, VA: University Press of Virginia, 1975.

(DSUE)   *A Dictionary of Slang and Unconventional English.* 8th ed. By Eric Partridge. New York, NY: Macmillan Publishing Co., 1984.

(DUND)   *Directory of United Nations Databases and Information Services.* 4th ed. Compiled by the Advisory Committee for the Coordination of Information Systems. New York, NY: United Nations, 1990.
           A guide to computerized databases and information systems/services. Entries include sponsoring organization, year established, type, scope, coverage, timespan, and contact information.

(DWSG)   *Defense Weapon Systems Glossary.* By David Trotz. Piscataway, NJ: Target Marketing, 1992.

(EA)   *Encyclopedia of Associations.* 34th ed. Vol. 1, National Oranizations of the U.S. Edited by Christine Maurer and Tara E. Sheets. Farmington Hills, MI: Gale Group, 1999.
           [Use of source began in 1960]
           A guide to trade, professional, and other nonprofit associations that are national and international in scope and membership and that are headquartered in the United States. Entries include name and address; telephone and telex number; chief official; and a description of the purpose, activities, and structure of the organization.

(EAAP)   *Encyclopedia of Associations: Association Periodicals.* 3 vols. Edited by Denise M. Allard and Robert C. Thomas. Detroit, MI: Gale Research, 1987.
           A directory of publications issued by all types of national nonprofit organizations in the United States. Entries include title and organization name, address, telephone number; description of periodical, frequency of publication, and price.

(EAIO)   *Encyclopedia of Associations: International Organizations.* 29th ed. Edited by Linda Irvin. Detroit, MI: Gale Research, 1995. [Use of source began in 1985]
           A guide to trade, professional, and other nonprofit associations that are national or international in scope and membership and that are headquartered outside the United States. Entries include name and address; principal foreign language name; telephone and telex number; chief official; and a description of the purpose, activities, and structure of the organization.

(EBF)   *Encyclopedia of Banking and Finance.* 10th ed. Edited by Charles J. Woelfel. Chicago, IL: Probus Publishing Co., 1994.

(ECED)   *The European Communities Encyclopedia and Directory 1992.* London, England: Europa Publications Ltd., 1991; distributed in U.S. by Gale Research, Detroit, MI.

A comprehensive guide to the European Communities. Entries explain widely-used acronyms and include address, telephone, telex, fax numbers and chief officers for EC-level organizations.

(ECII)   *Electronics, Computers and Industrial Instrumentation Abbreviations and Acronyms.* Edited by Sergio Sobredo. Miami, FL: Sergio Sobredo Technical Services, 1986.

(ECON)   *The Economist.* London, England: The Economist Newspaper Ltd., 1997. [Use of source began in 1988]

(EDAC)   *Dictionary of Educational Acronyms, Abbreviations, and Initialisms.* 2nd ed. Edited by James C. Palmer and Anita Y. Colby. Phoenix, AZ: Oryx Press, 1985.

(EDCT)   *Encyclopedic Dictionary of Chemical Technology.* By Dorit Noether and Herman Noether. New York, NY: VCH Publishers, Inc., 1993.

(EE)   *Eastern Europe and the Commonwealth of Independent States 1992.* London, England: Europa Publications Ltd., 1992; distributed in U.S. by Gale Research, Detroit, MI.

(EECA)   *Dictionary of Electrical, Electronics, and Computer Abbreviations.* By Phil Brown. London, England: Buttersworth, 1985.

(EES)   *A Dictionary of Ecology, Evolution and Systematics.* 2nd edition. Edited by Roger Lincoln, Geoff Boxshall and Paul Clark. New York, NY: Cambridge University Press, 1998.

(EFIS)   *Corporate Acronym Resource Guide, 1800s-1995.* Seattle, WA: Environmental Financial Information Services, Inc. (EFIS), 1996.

(EG)   *Environmental Glossary.* 4th ed. Edited by G. William Frick and Thomas F.P. Sullivan. Rockville, MD: Government Institutes, Inc., 1986.

(EGAO)   *Encyclopedia of Governmental Advisory Organizations.* 9th ed. Edited by Donna Batten. Detroit, MI: Gale Research, 1994-95 (and supplement, 1995). [Use of source began in 1975]
A reference guide to permanent, continuing, and ad hoc U.S. presidential advisory committees, interagency committees, and other government-related boards, panels, task forces, commissions, conferences, and other similar bodies serving in a consultative, coordinating, advisory, research, or investigative capacity. Entries include name and address, telephone number, designated federal employee, history, recommendation and findings of the committee, staff size, publications, and subsidiaries. Also includes indexes to personnel, reports, federal agencies, presidential administration, and an alphabetical and keyword index.

(EMRF)   *The St. James Encyclopedia of Mortgage & Real Estate Finance.* By James Newell, Albert Santi, and Chip Mitchell. Chicago, IL: St. James Press, 1991.

(EPA)   *Glossary of EPA Acronyms.* Washington, DC: Environmental Protection Agency, 1987.

(ERG)   *Environmental Regulatory Glossary.* 5th ed. Edited by G. William Frick and Thomas F.P. Sullivan. Rockville, MD: Government Institutes, Inc., 1990.

(EY)   *The Europa World Year Book 1992.* London: Europa Publications Ltd., 1992. distributed in U.S. by Gale Research, Detroit, MI.
An annual survey containing detailed information about the political, economic, statistical, and commercial situation of the regions and countries covered.

(FAAC) *Contractions Handbook*. Changes. U.S. Department of Transportation. Federal Aviation Administration, 1993. [Use of source began in 1969]

(FAAL) *Location Identifiers*. U.S. Department of Transportation. Federal Aviation Administration. Air Traffic Service, 1982.

(FEA) *The Far East and Australasia 1987*. 18th ed. London, England: Europa Publications Ltd., 1986; distributed in U.S. by Gale Research, Detroit, MI.
>   An annual survey containing detailed information about the political, economic, statistical, and commercial situation of the regions and countries covered.

(FFDE) *The Facts on File Dictionary of Environmental Science*. By L. Harold Stevenson and Bruce Wyman. New York, NY: Facts on File, 1991.
>   Defines terms from disciplines as diverse as biology, chemistry, geology, physics, engineering, meteorology, social science, medicine, and economics.

(GAAI) *"Glossary of Abbreviations, Acronyms, and Initialisms."*
   <http://www.em.doe.gov/idb97/acropdf.html> (17 February 1998)

(GAVI) *"Glossary of Aviation Acronyms and Abbreviations."*
   <http://olias.arc.nasa.gov/AFO_Acronyms_.html> (5 March 1997)

(GEA) *Government Economic Agencies of the World: An International Directory of Governmental Organisations Concerned with Economic Development and Planning*. A Keesing's Reference Publication. Edited by Alan J. Day. Harlow, Essex, England: Longman Group Ltd., 1985.
>   Covers over 170 countries and territories. Two introductory sections for each area cover economic data and prevailing economic and political conditions. Individual entries provide title, address, and names of chief officials of each agency. Current activities and financial structure of each agency are also detailed. An index of agency officials is provided.

(GFGA) *Guide to Federal Government Acronyms*. Edited by William R. Evinger. Phoenix, AZ: The Oryx Press, 1989.

(GNE) *The Green Encyclopedia*. By Irene Franck and David Brownstone. New York, NY: Prentice Hall General Reference, 1992.

(GPO) *Style Manual*. Washington, DC: Government Printing Office, 1984.[Terms are included in Chapter 24, Foreign Languages]

(GRD) *Government Research Directory*. 8th ed. Edited by Joseph M. Palmisano. Detroit, MI: Gale Research, 1994. (and supplement, 1994).
>   A descriptive guide to U.S. government research and development centers, institutes, laboratories, bureaus, test facilities, experiment stations, data collection and analysis centers, and grants management and research coordinating offices in agriculture, business, education, energy, engineering, environment, the humanities, medicine, military science, and basic applied sciences.

(HCT) *Health Care Terms*. 2nd ed. By Vergil N. Slee and Debora A. Slee. St. Paul, MN: Tringa Press, 1991.

(HGAA) *The Handy Guide to Abbreviations and Acronyms for the Automated Office*. By Mark W. Greenia. Seattle, WA: Self-Counsel Press, Inc., 1986.

(HGEN)   *Human Genome Acronym List.* <http://www.ornl.gov/hgmis/acronym.html> (2 December 1998)

(HRG)   *The Human Resources Glossary: The Complete Desk Reference for HR Executives, Managers, and Practitioners.* 2nd ed. By William R. Tracey. Boca Raton, FL: St. Lucie Press, 1998.

(IAA)   *Index of Acronyms and Abbreviations in Electrical and Electronic Engineering.* Compiled by Buro Scientia. New York, NY: VCH Publishers, 1989.

(IBMDP)   *IBM Data Processing Glossary.* 6th ed. White Plains, NY: IBM Corp., 1977.

(ICAO)   *Aircraft Type Designators.* 13th ed. International Civil Aviation Organization, August, 1981.

(ICDA)   *Designators for Aircraft Operating Agencies, Aeronautical Authorities and Services.* 49th ed. International Civil Aviation Organization, June, 1982.
             Document also includes telephony designators and postal and telegraphic addresses of government civil aviation authorities.

(ICLI)   *Location Indicators.* 51st ed. International Civil Aviation Organization, February, 1987.
             Document also contains addresses of flight information centers.

(IDOE)   *The Illustrated Dictionary of Electronics.* 6th ed. By Stan Gibilisco. New York, NY: TAB Books, 1994.

(IEEE)   *IEEE Standard Dictionary of Electrical and Electronics Terms.* Edited by Frank Jay. New York, NY: The Institute of Electrical and Electronics Engineers, Inc., 1977, 1984.
             Includes definitions for thousands of electrical and electronics terms. Each entry includes a numeric source code.

(IGQR)   *The Internet Glossary & Quick Reference Guide.* By Alan Freedman, Alfred Glossbrenner and Emily Glossbrenner. New York, NY: AMACOM, 1998.

(IIA)   *Index of Initials and Acronyms.* Compiled by Richard Kleiner. New York, NY: Auerbach Publishers, 1971.

(IID)   *Information Industry Directory.* 15th ed. Edited by Annette Novallo. Detroit, MI: Gale Research, 1995. (and supplement, 1995).
             An international guide to computer-readable databases, database producers, and publishers, online vendors and time-sharing companies, telecommunications networks, and many other information systems and services. Entries include name and address, telephone number, chief official, and a detailed description of the purpose and function of the system or service.

(ILCA)   *Index to Legal Citations and Abbreviations.* By Donald Raistrick. Abingdon, Oxfordshire, England: Professional Books Ltd., 1981.

(IMH)   *International Marketing Handbook.* 2nd ed. Edited by Frank Bair. Detroit, MI: Gale Research, 1985.
             An in-depth guide to commercial and trade data on 142 countries of the world. Features include a list of European trade fairs and a report on growth markets in Western Europe.

(INF)   *Infantry.* Fort Benning, GA: U.S. Army Infantry Training School, 1996. [Use of source began in 1983]

(IRC) *International Research Centers Directory 1992-93.* 6th ed. Edited by Annette Piccirelli. Detroit, MI: Gale Research, 1991.
    A world guide to government, university, independent, nonprofit, and commercial research and development centers, institutes, laboratories, bureaus, test facilities, experiment stations, and data collection and analysis centers, as well as foundations, councils, and other organizations which support research.

(IRUK) *Industrial Research in the United Kingdom.* 12th ed. Harlow, Essex, England: Longman Group UK Ltd., 1987.
    A guide to all groups conducting or funding research relevant to British industrial development. Entries include name, address, telephone and telex numbers; chief officials; and scope of activities.

(IT) *Information Today: The Newspaper for Users and Producers of Electronic Information Services.* Medford, NJ: Learned Information, Inc., 1988-89.

(ITD) *International Tradeshow Directory.* 5th ed. Frankfurt, Germany: M + A Publishers for Fairs, Exhibitions and Conventions Ltd., 1989.
    A guide to trade fairs and exhibitions throughout the world. Entries include event name, dates, frequency, location, description of purpose, profile of exhibitors and attendees.

(IYR) *The 1989-92 International Yacht Racing Rules.* London, England: International Yacht Racing Union, 1989.

(KSC) *A Selective List of Acronyms and Abbreviations.* Compiled by the Documents Department, Kennedy Space Center Library, 1971, 1973.

(LAIN) *Latest Intelligence: An International Directory of Codes Used by Government, Law Enforcement, Military, and Surveillance Agencies.* By James E. Tunnell. Blue Ridge Summit, PA: TAB BOOKS, 1990.

(LCCP) *MARC Formats for Bibliographic Data.* Appendix II. Washington, DC: Library of Congress, 1982.

(LCLS) *Symbols of American Libraries.* 14th ed. Edited by the Enhanced Cataloging Division. Washington, DC: Library of Congress, 1992. [Use of source began in 1980]

(LWAP) *Legal Words and Phrases: Speed Abbreviations.* By Joel Larus. Boston, MA: Aurico Publishing, 1965.

(MAE) *Medical Abbreviations and Eponyms.* By Sheila B. Sloane. Philadelphia, PA: W.B. Saunders Co., 1985.

(MAH) *Medical Abbreviations Handbook.* 2nd ed. Oradell, NJ: Medical Economics Co., Inc., 1983.

(MCD) *Acronyms, Abbreviations, and Initialisms.* Compiled by Carl Lauer. St. Louis, MO: McDonnell Douglas Corp., 1989. [Use of source began in 1969]

(MDG) *Microcomputer Dictionary and Guide.* By Charles J. Sippl. Champaign, IL: Matrix Publishers, Inc., 1975.
    A listing of definitions for over 5,000 microelectronics terms. Seven appendices.

(ME) *The Marine Encyclopaedic Dictionary.* 5th ed. By Eric Sullivan. London, England: LLP Ltd., 1996.

(MEC) *Macmillan Encyclopedia of Chemistry.* Vol. 1. Edited by Joseph J. Lagowski. New York, NY:

Macmillan Reference USA, 1997.

(MED)   *McGraw-Hill Electronic Dictionary.* 5th ed. Edited by John Markus and Neil Sclater. New York, NY: McGraw-Hill, Inc., 1994.

(MEDA)   *Medical Acronyms.* 2nd ed. By Marilyn Fuller Delong. Oradell, NJ: Medical Economic Books, 1989.

(MELL)   *Melloni's Illustrated Dictionary of Medical Abbreviations.* By John Melloni and Ida G. Dox. Pearl River, NY: Parthenon Publishing Group, Inc., 1998.

(MENA)   *The Middle East and North Africa 1987.* 33rd ed. London, England: Europa Publications Ltd., 1986; distributed in U.S. by Gale Research, Detroit, MI.
           An annual survey containing detailed information about the political, economic, statistical, and commercial situation of the regions and countries covered.

(MHDB)   *McGraw-Hill Dictionary of Business Acronyms, Initials, and Abbreviations.* By Jerry M. Rosenberg. New York, NY: McGraw-Hill, Inc., 1992.

(MHDI)   *McGraw-Hill Dictionary of Information Technology and Computer Acronyms, Initials, and Abbreviations.* By Jerry M. Rosenberg. New York, NY: McGraw-Hill, Inc., 1992.

(MHDW)   *McGraw-Hill Dictionary of Wall Street Acronyms, Initials, and Abbreviations.* By Jerry M. Rosenberg. New York, NY: McGraw-Hill, Inc., 1992.

(MSA)   *Military Standard Abbreviations for Use on Drawings, and in Specifications, Standards, and Technical Documents.* MIL-STD-12D. U.S. Department of Defense, 1981. [Use of source began in 1975]

(MSC)   *Annotated Acronyms and Abbreviations of Marine Science Related Activities.* 3rd ed. Revised by Charlotte M. Ashby and Alan R. Flesh. Washington, DC: U.S. Department of Commerce. National Oceanographic and Atmospheric Administration. Environmental Data Service. National Oceanographic Data Center, 1976, 1981.

(MUGU)   *The Mugu Book of Acronyms and Abbreviations.* Missile Range, CA: Management Engineering Office, 1963, 1964.

(MUSM)   *Dictionary of Modern United States Military.* By S.F. Tomajczyk. Jefferson, NC: McFarland and Co., Inc., 1996.

(NADA)   *The New American Dictionary of Abbreviations.* By Mary A. De Vries. New York, NY: Signet, 1991.

(NAKS)   *"NASA/KSC Aronym List."* <http://www.ksc.nasa.gov/facts/acronyms.html> (27 May 1999)

(NASA)   *Space Transportation System and Associated Payloads: Glossary, Acronyms, and Abbreviations.* Washington, DC: U.S. National Aeronautics and Space Administration, 1985.

(NATG)   *Glossary of Abbreviations Used in NATO Documents.* AAP 15(B), n.p., 1979. [Use of source began in 1976]

(NCC)   *NCC The National Centre for Information Technology. Guide to Computer Aided Engineering, Manufacturing and Construction Software.* Manchester, England: NCC Publications, The National Computing Centre Ltd., 1985.

Includes software classifications and descriptions, names and addresses of suppliers, processor manufacturers, and operating systems.

(NFD)   *The NSFRE Fund-Raising Dictionary*. Edited by Barbara R. Levy. New York, NY: John Wiley & Sons, Inc., 1996.

(NFPA)   *Standard for Fire Safety Symbols/NFPA170*. Quincy, MA: National Fire Protection Association, 1994.

(NG)   *NAVAIR Glossary of Unclassified Common-Use Abbreviated Titles and Phrases*. NAVAIRNOTE 5216 AIR-6031, n.p., July, 1969.

(NGC)   *Catalogue of the National Gallery of Canada*. Compiled by National Gallery of Canada. Ottawa, Canada: National Gallery of Canada, 1998.

(NHD)   *The New Hacker's Dictionary*. Edited by Eric Raymond. Cambridge, MA: MIT Press, 1991.

(NITA)   *Dictionary of New Information Technology Acronyms*. 2nd ed. By Michael Gordon, Alan Singleton, and Clarence Rickards. London, England: Kogan Page, Ltd., 1986.

(NLC)   *Symbols of Canadian Libraries*. 12th ed. National Library of Canada. Minister of Supply and Services Canada, 1987.

(NOAA)   *NOAA Directives Manual*. 66-13 Acronyms. 1977.

(NQ)   *NASDAQ Company Directory*. New York, NY: National Association of Securities Dealers, Inc., 1990. [Use of source began in 1983]

(NRCH)   *A Handbook of Acronyms and Initialisms*. Washington, DC: U.S. Nuclear Regulatory Commission. Division of Technical Information and Document Control, 1985.

(NTCM)   *NTC's Mass Media Dictionary*. R. Terry Ellmore. Lincolnwood, IL: National Textbook Co., 1991.

(NTPA)   *NTPA '97: National Trade and Professional Associations of the United States*. 32nd ed. Edited by John J. Russell. Washington, DC: Columbia Books, Inc., 1997.

(NUCP)   *A Dictionary of Nuclear Power and Waste Management with Abbreviations and Acronyms*. Foo-Sun Lau. Letchworth, England: Research Studies Press Ltd., 1987.

(NUMA)   *The Numa Dictionary of Derivatives Acronyms*. <http://www.numa.com/ref/acronym.html> (24 February 1999)

(NVT)   *Naval Terminology*. NWP3. Rev. B. U.S. Department of the Navy. Office of the Chief of Naval Operations, 1980. [Use of source began in 1974]

(OA)   *Ocran's Acronyms: A Dictionary of Abbreviations and Acronyms Used in Scientific and Technical Writing*. By Emanuel Benjamin Ocran. London, England: Routledge & Kegan Paul Ltd., 1978.

(OAG)   *Official Airline Guide Worldwide Edition*. Oak Brook, IL: Official Airlines Guide, Inc., 1984. [Use of source began in 1975]

(OCD)   *Oxford Classical Dictionary*. 2nd ed. Edited by N.G. Hammond and H.H. Scullard. London, England: Oxford University Press, 1970.

(OCLC)   *OCLC Participating Institutions Arranged by OCLC Symbol*. Dublin, OH: OCLC, 1981.

(ODBW)   *The Oxford Dictionary for the Business World*. New York, NY: Oxford University Press, Inc., 1993.

(ODCC)   *The Oxford Dictionary of the Christian Church*. Edited by F.L. Cross and E.A. Livingstone. New York, NY: Oxford University Press, 1997.

(OICC)   *Abbreviations and Acronyms*. Des Moines, IA: Iowa State Occupational Information Coordinating Committee, 1986.

(OLDSS)   *Online Database Search Services Directory*. 2nd ed. Edited by Doris Morris Maxfield. Detroit, MI: Gale Research, 1988.
> Provides detailed descriptions of the online information retrieval services offered by libraries, private information firms, and other organizations in the United States and Canada. Entries include name and address, telephone number, and key contact, as well as online systems accessed, frequently searched databases, and access hardware.

(OPSA)   *"Official Postal Service Abbreviations."* <http://www.usps.gov/ncsc/lookups/abbr_suffix.txt> (17 December 1996)

(OSI)   *OSI Standards and Acronyms*. 3rd ed. Compiled by Adrian V. Stokes. United Kingdom: Stokes, 1991.

(OTD)   *Official Telecommunications Dictionary*. Edited by Thomas F.P. Sullivan. Rockille, MD: Government Institutes, Inc., 1997.

(PA)   *Planning Acronyms*. <http://www.planning.org/info/acronyms/html> (24 February 1999)

(PAZ)   *Parenting A to Z*. By Irene M. Franck and David M. Brownstone. New York, NY: HarperCollins Publishers, Inc., 1996.

(PCM)   *PC Magazine*. New York, NY: Ziff-Davis Publishing Co., 1997. [Use of source began in 1987]

(PD)   *Political Dissent: An International Guide to Dissident, Extra-Parliamentary, Guerrilla and Illegal Political Movements*. A Keesing's Reference Publication. Compiled by Henry W. Degenhardt. Edited by Alan J. Day. Harlow, Essex, England: Longman Group, 1983.
> Includes the history and aims of approximately 1,000 organizations, with details of their leaderships.

(PDAA)   *Pugh's Dictionary of Acronyms and Abbreviations: Abbreviations in Management, Technology and Information Science*. 5th ed. By Eric Pugh. Chicago, IL: American Library Association, 1987.

(PGP)   *Peterson's Graduate Programs in the Humanities, Arts & Social Sciences*. 31st ed. Princeton, NJ: Peterson's 1997.

(PHSD)   *1998/1999 Public Human Services Directory*. Vol 59. Washinton, DC: American Public Human Services Association, 1998.

(PPE)   *Political Parties of Europe*. 2 vols. Edited by Vincent E. McHale. The Greenwood Historical Encyclopedia of the World's Political Parties. Westport, CT: Greenwood Press, 1983.
> One of a series of reference guides to the world's significant political parties. Each guide provides concise histories of the political parties of a region and attempts to detail the evolution of ideology, changes in organization, membership, leadership, and each party's impact upon society.

(PPW)   *Political Parties of the World.* 2nd ed. A Keesing's Reference Publication. Compiled and edited by Alan J. Day and Henry W. Degenhardt. Harlow, Essex, England: Longman Group, 1980, 1984.
          Covers historical development, structure, leadership, membership, policy, publications, and international affiliations. For each country, an overview of the current political situation and constitutional structure is provided.

(PS)   *Popular Science.* New York, NY: Times-Mirror Magazines, Inc., 1995. [Use of source began in 1992]

(PSS)   *Peterson's Sports Scholarships & College Athletic Programs.* 3rd ed. Edited by Ron Walker. Princeton, NJ: Peterson's, 1998.

(RCD)   *Research Centers Directory.* 19th ed. Edited by Thomas J. Cichonski. Detroit, MI: Gale Research, 1994. [Use of source began in 1986]
          A guide to university-related and other nonprofit research organizations carrying on research in agriculture, astronomy and space sciences, behavioral and social sciences, computers and mathematics, engineering and technology, physical and earth sciences and regional and area studies.

(RDA)   *Army RD and A Magazine.* Alexandria, VA: Development, Engineering, and Acquisition Directorate, Army Materiel Command, 1997. [Use of source began in 1979]

(REAL)   *Abbreviations.* <http://www.reboc.on.ca/abbreviations.html> (24 February 1999)

(ROG)   *Dictionary of Abbreviations.* By Walter T. Rogers. London, England: George Allen & Co. Ltd., 1913; reprinted by Gale Research, 1969.

(SAA)   *Space-Age Acronyms, Abbreviations and Designations.* 2nd ed. By Reta C. Moser. New York, NY: IFI/Plenum, 1969.

(SAG)   *Stock Abbreviation Guide.* New York, NY: Associated Press. [Database]

(SDI)   *Report to the Congress on the Strategic Defense Initiative.* U.S. Department of Defense. Strategic Defense Initiative Organization, April, 1987.

(SEIS)   *Seismograph Station Codes and Characteristics.* Geological Survey. Circular 791. By Barbara B. Poppe, Debbi A. Naab, and John S. Derr. Washington, DC: U.S. Department of the Interior, 1978.

(SG)   *Standard & Poor's Stock Guide.* New York, NY: Standard & Poor's, 1999.

(SLS)   *World Guide to Scientific Associations and Learned Societies/Internationales Verzeichnis Wissenschaftlicher Verbande und Gesellschaften.* 4th ed. Edited by Barbara Verrel. New York, NY: K.G. Saur, 1984.
          A directory of more than 22,000 societies and associations in all fields of science, culture, and technology. International, national, and regional organizations from 150 countries are also included.

(SPSG)   *Security Owner's Stock Guide.* New York, NY: Standard & Poor's Corp., 1994. [Use of source began in 1988]

(SRA)   *State and Regional Associations of the United States.* 9th ed. Edited by Tracey E. Chirico, Buck J. Downs and John J. Russell. Washington, DC: Columbia Books, Inc., 1997.

(SSD)   *Space Station Directory and Program Guide.* Edited and compiled by Melinda Gipson, Jane Glass, and Mary Linden. Arlington, VA: Pasha Publications, Inc., 1988.

(STED)   *Stedman's Abbreviations, Acronyms and Symbols.* Edited by William R. Hensyl. Baltimore, MD: Williams & Wilkins, 1992.

(TAD)   *The AIDS Dictionary.* By Sarah Barbara Watstein and Karen Chandler. New York, NY: Facts on File, Inc., 1998.

(TAG)   *Transportation Acronym Guide 1996.* U.S. Department of Transportation. Washington, DC: Bureau of Transportation Statistics, 1996.

(TBD)   *Thomson Bank Directory.* Skokie, IL: Thomson Financial Publishing, 1991.

(TDOB)   *The Dictionary of Banking.* By Charles J. Woelfel. Chicago, IL: Probus Publishing Company, 1994.

(TEL)   *Telephony's Dictionary.* 2nd ed. By Graham Langley. Chicago, IL: Telephony Publishing Corp., 1986.
               Includes definitions for U.S. and international telecommunications terms. Ten
               appendices.

(TELE)   *List of Libraries Abbreviations Encountered in the Context of EU R&D.*
           <http://www2.echo.lu/libraries/en/acronym.html> (24 February 1999)

(TES)   *Tests: A Comprehensive Reference for Assessments in Psychology, Education, and Business.* 3rd ed. Austin, TX: PRO-ED, Inc., 1991.

(TMMY)   *The Thirteenth Mental Measurements Yearbook.* Edited by James C. Impara and Barbara S. Plake. Lincoln: NE: The Buros Institute of Mental Measurements of the University of Nebraska-Lincoln, 1998.

(TNIG)   *Telecommunications, Networking and Internet Glossary.* By George S. Machovec. Chicago, IL: American Library Association, 1993.

(TOCD)   *The Official Catholic Directory 1997.* New Providence, NJ: P.J. Kennedy & Sons, 1997.

(TSPED)   *Trade Shows and Professional Exhibits Directory.* 2nd ed. Edited by Robert J. Elster. Detroit, MI: Gale Research, 1987. [Use of source began in 1986]
               A guide to scheduled events providing commercial display facilities including
               conferences, conventions, meetings, fairs and festivals, etc. Entries include name
               of trade show; sponsor name, address, and telephone number; attendance figures;
               principal exhibits; special features; publications; and date and location of shows.

(TSSD)   *Telecommunications Systems and Services Directory.* 4th ed. (and supplement). Edited by John Krol. Detroit, MI: Gale Research, 1989. [Use of source began in 1985]
               An international descriptive guide to telecommunications organizations, systems,
               and services. Entries include name and address, telephone number, chief official,
               and a description of the purposes, technical structure, and background of the service
               or system.

(USDC)   *"Glossary of Acronyms."* U.S. Department of Commerce.
           <http://www.pmel.noaa.gov/pubs/acronym.html> (5 March 1997)

(USGC)   *"U.S. Government Commonly Used Abbreviations and Acronyms."* <http://www.fed.gov/hptext/infohwy/gov_acro.html> (5 March 1997)

(USMO)   *The Military Online: A Directory for Internet Access to the Development of Defense.* Edited by William M. Arkin. Washington, DC: Brassey's, 1997.

(VERA)   *VERA-Virtual Entity of Relevant Acronyms.* <http://www.thphy.uni~duesseldorf.de/~gnu/info/VERA/vera_2.html#SEC3> (1 December 1998)

(VNW)   *Words of the Vietnam War.* By Gregory R. Clark. Jefferson, NC: McFarland and Co., Inc., 1990.

(VRA)   *VRA Special Bulletin. No. 2, 1987: Standard Abbreviations for Image Descriptions for Use in Fine Arts Visual Resources Collections.* Compiled by Nancy S. Schuller. Austin, TX: Visual Resources Association, 1987.

(WDAA)   *Webster's New World Dictionary of Acronyms and Abbreviations.* By Auriel Douglas and Michael Strumpf. New York, NY: Webster's New World, 1989.

(WDMC)   *Webster's New World Dictionary of Media and Communications.* Revised and updated ed. By Richard Weiner. New York, NY: Webster's New World, 1996.

(WGA)   *Webster's Guide to Abbreviations.* Springfield, MA: Merriam-Webster, Inc., 1985.

(WPI)   *Selected Acronyms and Abbreviations for Wood Products, Forest Industry and Governmental Affairs.* <http://www.ari.net/awpi/acronyms.html> (3 March 1999)

(WYGK)   *HR Words you Gotta Know!* By William R. Tracey. New York, NY: AMACOM, 1994.

G
By Acronym

G .... Acceleration Force (DMAA)
g .... Acceleration of Free Fall [Symbol]
G .... Air Force Training Category [12 training periods and zero days active duty training per year]
G .... Application for Writ of Error Granted [Legal term] (DLA)
G .... Chicago [Branch in the Federal Reserve regional banking system] (BARN)
G .... Ciba-Geigy AG [Switzerland] [Research code symbol]
G .... Conductance [Symbol] [IUPAC]
G .... Dividends and Earnings in Canadian Dollars [Investment term] (DFIT)
G .... Federal Republic of Germany [IYRU nationality code] (IYR)
G .... Fire Control [JETDS nomenclature]
G .... Force [Pull of gravity] (STED)
G .... Gage (IAA)
G .... Gain
G .... Gale [Meteorology]
G .... Gale's English Exchequer Reports [A publication] (DLA)
G .... Galliot [Ship's rigging] (ROG)
G .... Gallop [Cardiology] (DAVI)
G .... Gambia [Country in West Africa] (ROG)
G .... Game
G .... Games Played [Sports statistics]
G .... Gamma
G .... Gamut [Music] (ROG)
G .... Gandulphus [Flourished, 1160-85] [Authority cited in pre-1607 legal work] (DSA)
G .... Ganglion [Medicine]
G .... Ganz [White Blot] [Rorschach] [Psychology]
G .... Gaon (BJA)
G .... Gap in Cell Cycle [Cytology]
G .... Garage
(g) .... Gas [Chemistry]
G .... Gas (STED)
G .... Gas Oil
G .... Gas Shutoff [NFPA pre-fire planning symbol] (NFPA)
g .... Gastralia [Osteology]
G .... Gastrin [Biochemistry]
G .... Gate [Electronics]
g .... Gate (IDOE)
g .... Gauche [Chemical conformation]
G .... Gauche [Left] [French]
g .... Gauge (WDMC)
G .... Gauge [Of needle] (STED)
G .... Gauss [Unit of magnetic flux density] [Preferred unit is T, Telsa]
G .... Gear (AAG)
G .... Ge'ez (BJA)
G .... Gelaendegaengig [Having cross-country mobility] [German military - World War II]
G .... Gelding [Thoroughbred racing]
g .... Gemeisamer Faktor [General Factor] [Rorschach] [Psychology]
G .... Gemini Airline [British]
G .... Gender
G .... General
G .... General Audiences [All ages admitted] [Movie rating]
G .... General Duties [Ranking title] [British Women's Royal Naval Service]
G .... General Factor (ADA)
G .... General Intelligence
G .... Generalist [Ecology]
G .... Generalized Feeder [Ichthyology]
G .... General List [Navy British]
G .... Generally Labeled [Radioactive compounds]
G .... General Procedures
G .... General-Purpose Freight Container (DCTA)
G .... General Staff Branch [Army British]
G .... Generating Item [Military]
g .... Generator (IDOE)
G .... Generators, Power [JETDS nomenclature] [Military] (CET)
G .... Genitive [Case] [Grammar]
g .... Genome [Genetics]
G .... Geography [Secondary school course] [British]
G .... Geometric Efficiency (DMAA)
G .... Geonic (BJA)
G .... George [Phonetic alphabet] [Royal Navy World War I Pre-World War II] [World War II] (DSUE)
G .... George (King of England) (DLA)

G .... Georgia State Library, Atlanta, GA [Library symbol Library of Congress] (LCLS)
G .... Georgics [of Vergil] [Classical studies] (OCD)
G .... Gericht [Court] [German] (ILCA)
G .... German [or Germanic]
G .... Germanischer Lloyd [Shipping] (ROG)
G .... Germany (WDAA)
G .... Gerontology [American Occupational Therapy Association]
G .... Geschichte [History] [German] (ILCA)
G .... Gesetz [Law] [German] (ILCA)
G .... Ghost
G .... Giant Slalom [In Olympics event, Super-G]
G .... Gibbs Energy [Symbol] [IUPAC]
G .... Gibbs Free Energy (STED)
G .... Gibbs Function [Preferred term is Gibbs Energy]
G .... Giemsa [Method] [Chromosome stain]
g .... GIF [Graphics Interchange Format] [Computer science] [Telecommunications]
G .... Gift Tax (DLA)
G .... Giga [A prefix meaning multiplied by 10^9] [SI symbol]
G .... Gigabyte
G .... Gilbert [A unit of magnetomotive force]
G .... Gilbertus [Flourished, 13th century] [Authority cited in pre-1607 legal work] (DSA)
G .... Gillette Co. [NYSE symbol] (SAG)
G .... Gilt [Bookbinding]
G .... Gingiva (DMAA)
G .... Gingival [Dentistry]
G .... Girder [Technical drawings]
G .... Girls School [British]
G .... Givenchy [Couturier]
G .... Glabella [Medicine] (DMAA)
G .... Gladstonian [Politics, 1868-1894] [British] (ROG)
G .... Glasgow [Postcode] (ODBW)
G .... Glass (AAG)
G .... Glider
G .... Glimpse [Optics]
G .... Globular [Referring to proteins] [Biochemistry] (DAVI)
G .... Globulin
G .... Gloom
G .... Glucinium [Also, Gl] [Old name for chemical element beryllium]
G .... Glucose [Also, Glc, GLUC] [A sugar]
G .... Glycine [One-letter symbol; see Gly] [An amino acid]
G .... Glycogen [Biochemistry]
g .... Go [to] [Computer science] [Telecommunications]
G .... Goal [A position in lacrosse, soccer, hockey, etc.]
G .... Goalkeeper [Sports] (BARN)
G .... Goat [Veterinary medicine]
G .... Gofredus de Trano [Deceased, 1245] [Authority cited in pre-1607 legal work] (DSA)
G .... Gold
G .... Goldcorp Investments Ltd. [Toronto Stock Exchange symbol]
G .... Gold Inlay [Dentistry]
G .... Golf [Phonetic alphabet] [International] (DSUE)
G .... Gonidial [With reference to colonies of bacteria]
G .... Good [Condition] [Antiquarian book trade, numismatics, etc.]
g .... Good (WDMC)
G .... Good Skiing Conditions
G .... Goose (STED)
g .... G-Orbital (MEC)
G .... Gourde [Monetary unit] [Haiti]
G .... Government
G .... Government Expenditure [Economics]
G .... Government Purchases
G .... Grade (ADA)
G .... Grafenberg Spot [Medicine] (DMAA)
g .... Graft (Polymer) [Organic chemistry]
G .... Grain
g .... Gram
G .... Gram [Stain] (STED)
G .... Grammar School [British]
g% .... Gram Percent [Meaning grams per deciliter] [Measurement] (DAVI)
G .... Grand [Slang term for 1,000 dollars]
G .... Grand-Orgue [Great Organ] [Music]
G .... Granite
G .... Granted [Legal term] (ILCA)

G	Granular
G	Graph (OA)
G	Graphed [Quilting]
G	Graphite
G	Grass [Botany]
G	Gravel
G	Gravida [Obstetrics]
G	Gravitational Constant [or Newtonian Constant] [Physics] (DAVI)
G	Gravity [or the force or acceleration produced by it]
g	Gravity (IDOE)
G	Great
G	Greek
G	Green
G	Greenhouse Plant [Botany]
G	Greenwich Meridian [Upper branch]
g	Greenwich Meridian [Lower branch]
G	Greenwich Time
G	Gregarious [Biology]
G	Gregorowski's Reports of the High Court [A publication] (DLA)
G	Grid [Electronics]
g	Grid (IDOE)
G	Grog [i.e., entitled to draw a daily rum ration and doing so] [See also, T, UA] [Obsolete] [Navy] [British]
G	Grondwet [Constitution] [Netherlands] (ILCA)
G	Gros [Large] [French]
G	Groschen [Monetary unit] [Austria]
G	Gross [Leukemia antigen] [Immunochemistry]
G	Groszy [Monetary unit] [Poland]
G	Ground
G	Ground Control [Aviation] (DA)
G	Grounded [Electronics]
G	Ground Foraging [Ecology]
G	Ground, General [JETDS nomenclature]
G	Ground Swell
G	Group
G	Growth [Business term]
G	Grumman American Aviation [ICAO aircraft manufacturer identifier] (ICAO)
G	Gruppenfuehrer [Squad Leader] [German military - World War II]
G	Guanidine [Biochemistry] (DAVI)
G	Guanine [Also, Gua] [Biochemistry]
G	Guanosine [One-letter symbol; see Guo]
G	Guarani [Monetary unit] [Paraguay]
G	Guard [Position in football, basketball, etc.]
G	Guardian
G	Guarnerius [Irnerius] [Flourished, 1113-18] [Authority cited in pre-1607 legal work] (DSA)
G	Gucci [Designer]
G	Guide
G	Guided Tour [On a bus] [British]
G	Guido de Baysio [Deceased, 1313] [Authority cited in pre-1607 legal work] (DSA)
G	Guido de Suzaria [Deceased, 1293] [Authority cited in pre-1607 legal work] (DSA)
G	Guilder [Modification of gulden] [Monetary unit] [Netherlands]
G	Guillelmus de Tocco [Authority cited in pre-1607 legal work] (DSA)
G	Guilty
G	Guinea [Monetary unit] [Obsolete British]
G	Guirsh [Monetary unit] [Saudi Arabia]
G	Guitar [Music]
G	Guizzardinus [Deceased, 1222] [Authority cited in pre-1607 legal work] (DSA)
G	Gulden [Monetary unit] [Netherlands]
G	Gules [Heraldry]
G	Gulf [Maps and charts]
G	Gun
g	Gunnery [Navy British]
G	Guttae [Drops of liquid] [Pharmacy] (CPH)
G	Gutter Ball [Bowling]
G	Gynecology (STED)
G	Gynoecium [Botany]
G	Gyromagnetic Ratio
G	Halls (Noncommercial) [Public-performance tariff class] [British]
G	HMV [His Master's Voice], Gramophone Co. [Record label] [Great Britain, Europe, etc.]
G	Immunoglobulin G (STED)
G	Longitude
G	Obstetrics and Gynaecology [Medical Officer designation] [British]
G	Permanently Grounded [Aircraft classification letter]
G	Promoted to Glory [Salvation Army]
G	Ranger [Army skill qualification identifier] (INF)
G	Reports of the High Court of Griqualand [1882-1910] [South Africa] [A publication] (DLA)
G	Shear Modulus [Symbol] [IUPAC]
g	Statistical Weight [Symbol] [IUPAC]
G	Surface Attack [Missile mission symbol]
G	Telegraph [JETDS nomenclature]
G	Teletype [JETDS nomenclature]
G	Unit of Acceleration [Military]
G	Unit of Force of Acceleration (STED)
G	Unit of Gravitational Force (NASA)
G	Weight [Symbol] [IUPAC]
G	Workout from Starting Gate [Horse racing]
G1	Government Current Expenditure [Economics]

G-1	Personnel Section [of an Army or Marine Corps division general staff, or Marine brigade or aircraft wing general staff; also, the officer in charge of this section]
G^1	Staff Officer for Personnel [Army] [Marine Corps] (DOMA)
G1P	Glucose-1-phosphate [Biochemistry]
G-2	Army Intelligence Network [Guatemala] (BUAC)
G-2	Army Intelligence Unit [Panama] (BUAC)
G2	Government Capital Expenditure [Economics]
G-2	Group of Two (BUAC)
G-2	Military Intelligence Section [of an Army or Marine Corps division general staff, or Marine brigade or aircraft wing general staff; also, the officer in charge of this section]
G^2	Staff Officer for Intelligence [Army] [Marine Corps] (DOMA)
G2W	Glaube in der 2. Welt [Faith in the Second World - FSW] [An association Switzerland] (EAIO)
G3	Gadolinium, Gallium, Garnet
G3	[The] Godfather Part III [Motion picture]
G-3	Group of Three (BUAC)
G-3	Operations and Training Section [of an Army or Marine Corps division general staff or Marine brigade or aircraft wing general staff; also, the officer in charge of this section]
G^3	Staff Officer for Operations [Army] [Marine Corps] (DOMA)
G-3	Treaty of the Group of Three among the United States of Mexico, the Republic of Colombia, and the Republic of Venezuela
G-3-P	Glyceraldehyde-3-Phosphate [Biochemistry] (DAVI)
G-4	Logistics Section [of an Army or Marine Corps division general staff, or Marine brigade or aircraft wing general staff; also, the officer in charge of this section]
G^4	Staff Officer for Supply/Logistics [Army] [Marine Corps] (DOMA)
G-5	Civil Affairs Section [of an Army division or brigade general staff; the officer in charge of this section]
G5	Group of Five [United States, Japan, West Germany, France, and Britain]
G^5	Staff Officer for Planning [Army] [Marine Corps] (DOMA)
G-6	Group of Six (BUAC)
G6P	Glucose-6-Phosphate (LDT)
G-6-Pase	Glucose-6-Phosphatase [Organic chemistry] (DAVI)
G6PD	Glucose-6-phosphate Dehydrogenase [Also, GPD, G6PDH] [An enzyme]
G6PD	Glucose-6-Phosphate Dehydrogenase Deficiency [Inherited enzyme deficiency] [Medicine] (TAD)
G6PDA	Glucose-6-Phosphate Dehydrogenase, Varient A (STED)
G6PDH	Glucose-6-phosphate Dehydrogenase [Also, GPD, G6PD] [An enzyme]
G-6-PDHA	Glucose-6-Phosphate Dehydrogenase Enzyme Variant A [Organic chemistry] (DAVI)
G-7	Group of Seven [United States, Japan, West Germany, France, Britain, Italy, and Canada]
G7	Grumpy Seven [Facetious translation for the Group of Seven: United States, Japan West Germany, France, Britain, Italy, and Canada] (ECON)
G-8	Group of Eight [Nations] (EERA)
G-9	Group of Nine (BUAC)
G10	Group of Ten [United States, Japan, West Germany, France, Britain, Italy, Canada, Sweden, Holland, Belgium, and Switzerland] [There are actually eleven member countries]
G-11	Gulfstream 11 [Shuttle Training Aircraft] (NAKS)
G18 IYRA	Geary 18 International Yacht Racing Association (EA)
G24	Group of 24 [A clearinghouse for monetary aid to Eastern Europe] (ECON)
G30	Group of Thirty [Financial think-tank] (ECON)
G-33	Group of Thirty-Three (BUAC)
G-77	Group of 77 [Coalition of environmentalists representing developing countries]
Ga	Airway Conductance [Medicine] (DAVI)
GA	Atlanta Public Library, Atlanta, GA [Library symbol Library of Congress] (LCLS)
GA	Decisions of General Appraisers [United States] [A publication] (DLA)
GA	Gabon [ANSI two-letter standard code] (CNC)
GA	Gage
GA	Gain of Antenna (IEEE)
GA	Galatians [New Testament book]
Ga	Galatians [New Testament book]
Ga	Galileo Number
GA	Gallic
Ga	Gallium [Chemical element]
GA	Galvanizers Association [British] (EAIO)
GA	Gamblers Anonymous (EA)
GA	Games Abroad [Baseball]
GA	Games Ahead [Baseball]
Ga	Gandulphus [Flourished, 1160-85] [Authority cited in pre-1607 legal work] (DSA)
GA	Gardens for All [Later, National Association for Gardening] (EA)
GA	Garin Arava (EA)
GA	Garrison Adjutant [Military British]
GA	Garrison Artillery [British military] (DMA)
GA	Garuda Indonesia [Airline flight code] (ODBW)
GA	Garuda Indonesian Airways [ICAO designator] (AD)
GA	Gas Amplification
GA	Gas Analysis (NRCH)
GA	Gasoline Stowage and Fuel System Man [Navy]
GA	Gas or Air [Transportation]
GA	Gastric Analysis
GA	Gastric Antrum [Medicine] (DMAA)

GA	Gate
GA	Gated Attenuation [*Computer science*]
GA	Gauge (AAG)
ga	Gauge [*of needles*] [*Measurement*] (DAVI)
GA	Gauge Man [*Navy*]
GA	Gear Assembly
GA	Gelbray Association [*Later, GI*] (EA)
GA	Gemini Agena [*NASA*] (KSC)
GA	Gemmological Association [*British*] (DBA)
GA	Gemmological Association of Great Britain (BUAC)
GA	General Accident [*British insurance organization*]
GA	General Accounting (AAG)
GA	General Activities (ADA)
GA	General Agent [*Insurance*]
GA	General Aircraft Ltd.
GA	General Alert (NATG)
GA	General American [*A type of spoken American English*] (BARN)
GA	General Anesthesia [*Medicine*]
GA	General Appearance [*On physical examination*] [*Medicine*] (DAVI)
GA	General Appraisers' Decisions [*A publication*] (DLA)
GA	General Arrangement (MCD)
GA	General Assembly
GA	General Assembly of the United Nations (BUAC)
GA	General Assignment (ADA)
GA	General Assistance [*A form of public charity*]
GA	General Atomics [*Division of General Dynamics Corp.*]
GA	General Atomics Corporation
GA	General Attention [*Medicine*]
GA	General Automation, Inc. [*AMEX symbol*]
GA	General Average [*Insurance*]
GA	General Avia SpA [*Italy ICAO aircraft manufacturer identifier*] (ICAO)
GA	General Aviation (EA)
GA	General of the Army (AABC)
GA	Genetic Algorithm [*Computer science*]
GA	Genl Automation [*NYSE symbol*] (TTSB)
GA	Gentisic Acid [*Analgesic drug*]
GA	Geographical Association [*British*] (DBA)
GA	Geological Abstracts
GA	Geologic Associates (EFIS)
GA	Geologists' Association [*British*]
GA	Geometrical Acoustics
GA	Georgia [*Postal code*] (AFM)
Ga	Georgia (ODBW)
GA	Georgia Railroad Co. [*AAR code*]
GA	Georgia Supreme Court Reports [*A publication*] (DLA)
GA	Geriatric Authority (DICI)
GA	German Army (NATG)
GA	Germanium Alloy (IAA)
GA	Gesammelte Abhandlungen [*A publication*] (BJA)
GA	Gesellschaft fuer Arzneipflanzenforschung [*Society for Medicinal Plant Research*] (EA)
GA	Gestational Age [*Medicine*]
GA	Getting Along [*Psychological testing*]
GA	Giant Axon [*Neurology*]
GA	Gibberellic Acid [*Also, GA₃*] [*Plant growth hormone*]
GA	Giftware Association (BUAC)
GA	Gimbal Angle (KSC)
GA	Gimbal Assembly
ga	Ginger Ale
GA	Gingivoaxial [*Dentistry*]
GA	Gland Anlage
GA	Glide Angle [*Aviation*]
GA	Global Address
GA	Global Assessment [*Psychiatric evaluation test*]
GA	Global Auto [*Computer science*]
G/A	Globulin/Albumin [*Ratio*] [*Medicine*] (DMAA)
GA	Glucoamylase [*An enzyme*]
GA	Glucose/Acetone [*Biochemistry*] (DAVI)
GA	Glucuronic Acid [*Also, GlcUA*] [*Biochemistry*]
GA	Glutamic Acid [*See also Glu*] [*An amino acid*]
GA	Glutaraldehyde [*Biochemistry*]
GA	Glyoxylic Acid [*Biochemistry*] (OA)
GA	Gnomes Anonymous [*New Malden, Surrey, England*] (EA)
GA	Go Ahead [*or resume sending*] [*Communications*]
GA	Goal Attack [*Netball*]
GA	Goals Against [*Hockey*]
GA	Go Around (MCD)
GA	Golgi Apparatus [*Medicine*] (DMAA)
GA	Good Afternoon [*Amateur radio shorthand*] (WDAA)
GA	Government Actuary [*Australia*]
GA	Government Agency (AAG)
GA	Governmental Affairs (DLA)
GA	Government Architect (ADA)
GA	Grade Age [*Education*]
GA	Graduate Assistant
GA	Graduate in Agriculture
G/A	Grains per Anther [*Botany*]
GA	Gramicidin A [*Antibiotic*]
GA	Grand Admiral [*Freemasonry*] (ROG)
GA	Grand Almoner [*Freemasonry*]
GA	Grand Architect [*Freemasonry*]
GA	Grand Award [*Record label*]
GA	Grands Arrets de la Jurisprudence Civile [*A publication*] (ILCA)
GA	Grant Agreement (COE)
GA	Grant Aid [*Military*] (AFM)
GA	Grant Application [*Job Training and Partnership Act*] (OICC)
GA	Grant Award [*Job Training and Partnership Act*] (OICC)
GA	Granulocyte Adherence (DB)
Ga	Granulocyte Agglutination (STED)
GA	Granulocyte Agglutination [*Hematology*]
GA	Granulomatous Angiitis [*Medicine*]
GA	Graphic Ammeter (MSA)
GA	Graphic Artists Guild (EA)
GA	Graphics and Administration [*Military*] (GFGA)
GA	Grapple Adapter [*Nuclear energy*] (NRCH)
GA	Great Artists [*A publication*]
GA	Great Attractor [*Galactic science*]
GA	Green Alliance (BUAC)
GA	Green Alliance Senate - New South Wales [*Political party Australia*]
GA	Greenhouse Annual [*Horticulture*] (ROG)
GA	Greening Australia (EERA)
GA	Gross Asset [*Business term*]
GA	Ground Attack [*Military*]
GA	Ground Attacker Aircraft
G-A	Ground-to-Air [*Communications, weapons*] (MSA)
GA	Group Atmosphere (PDAA)
GA	Guanosine Triphosphatase Activating [*Biochemistry*]
GA	Guardian Angels (EA)
GA	Guardian Association (EA)
GA	Guessed Average
GA	Guidance Amplifier (IAA)
GA	Gunlayer Armourer [*British military*] (DMA)
GA	Gut-Associated [*Medicine*]
GA	Gypsum Association (EA)
GA	Gyrate Atrophy [*Medicine*]
GA	Gyro Assembly (NASA)
GA	L-Glutamic [*acid*] and L-Alanine [*Copolymer*]
GA	Tabun [*Nerve gas*] [*Army symbol*]
GA₃	Gibberellin A₃ [*Also, GA*] [*Plant growth hormone*]
GAA	Atlanta College of Art Library, Atlanta, GA [*OCLC symbol*] (OCLC)
GAA	Atlanta School of Art, Atlanta, GA [*Library symbol Library of Congress*] (LCLS)
GAA	Business Express [*ICAO designator*] (FAAC)
GAA	Gaelic Athletic Association
GAA	Gaelic Athletic Association of Australia
GAA	Gain Adjuster Adapter
GAA	Gale Auto Annual [*A publication*]
GaA	Gallium Arsenide [*Semiconductor*]
GAA	Gay AA (EA)
GAA	Gay Activists' Alliance [*Defunct*]
GAA	General Account of Advances
GAA	General Agency Agreement [*Navy*] (AABC)
GAA	General Aviation Authority [*FAA*] (TAG)
GAA	Geographic Areas of Affinity (TAD)
GAA	Georgia Apartment Association (SRA)
GaA	Georgia Appeals Reports [*A publication*] (DLA)
GAA	Gift Association of America (EA)
GAA	Girls Athletic Association [*Local school affiliates of National Girls Athletic Association*] [*Defunct*]
GAA	Glacial Acrylic Acid [*Organic chemistry*]
GAA	Gospel and the Age Series [*A publication*]
GAA	Gossypol Acetic Acid (DMAA)
GAA	Government Administrators Association (SRA)
GAA	Government Advertising Agency [*New South Wales, Australia*]
GAA	Grand National Resources, Inc. [*Vancouver Stock Exchange symbol*]
GAA	Grandparents Association of America
GAA	Grants for Aboriginal Advancement [*Australia*]
GAA	Graphic Arts Association (SRA)
GAA	Gravure Association of America (EA)
GAA	Grease, Artillery/Automotive [*Military*] (INF)
GAA	Greenhouse Action Australia (EERA)
GAA	Greening Australia Action
GAA	Grenfell Association of America (EA)
GAA	Gross Average Audience [*Nielsen rating*] [*Television*] (WDMC)
GAA	Ground-Aided Acquisition
GAA	Ground Area Attainable
GAA	GTO [*Gran Turismo Omologato*] Association of America (EA)
GAA	Guanine Adenine Adenine [*A triplet of bases coding for the amino acid, glutamic acid*] (EES)
GAAA	General Aviation Activity and Avionics [*FAA*] (TAG)
GAAA	General Aviation Association Australia
GAAA	Greek Advertising Agencies Association (BUAC)
GAAB	Alston & Bird, Law Library, Atlanta, GA [*Library symbol*] [*Library of Congress*] (LCLS)
GAAC	Graphic Arts Advertisers Council [*Later, GAAEC*]
GA Admin Comp	Official Compilation of the Rules and Regulations of the State of Georgia [*A publication*] (DLA)
GAAE	Graphic Arts Association Executives [*Defunct*] (EA)
GAAEC	Graphic Arts Advertisers and Exhibitors Council [*Defunct*] (EA)
GAAEF	Grupo de Abogados Argentinos en el Exilio en Francia
GAAG	Guerrilla Art Action Group
GAAI	Atlanta Art Institute, Atlanta, GA [*Library symbol*] [*Library of Congress*] (LCLS)
GaAIAs	Gallium Aluminum Arsenide (SSD)
GAAM	Ghana Association for the Advancement of Mangement (BUAC)
GAAM	Guided Antiaircraft Missile [*Military*] (IAA)
GA & CS	Ground Acquisition and Command Station (MCD)
GAAO	Ansongo [*Mali*] [*ICAO location identifier*] (ICLI)
GAAP	Gateway Army Ammunition Plant
GAAP	Generally Accepted Accounting Principles [*or Procedures*]

GA App	Georgia Appeals Reports [*A publication*] (DLA)
Ga App	Georgia Court of Appeals Reports [*A publication*] (AAGC)
GA App (NS)	Georgia Appeals Reports [*A publication*] (DLA)
GAARD	General Automation Automatic Recovery Device (IAA)
GAARS	Global Atmospheric and Aerosol Radiation Study
GAART	Government Astronomy Administration Round Table
GaAs	Gallium Arsenide [*Semiconductor*] (IEEE)
GAAS	Generally Accepted Auditing Standards
GAAS	German Association for American Studies (EAIO)
GAAS	Goldberg Anorectic Attitude Scale [*Medicine*] (DMAA)
GAAS	Guangdong Academy of Agricultural Sciences [*China*] (BUAC)
GAAS	Guangxi Academy of Agricultural Sciences [*China*] (BUAC)
GAASD	Gallium Arsenide [*Phosphide Semiconductor*]
GaAs FET	Gallium Arsenide Field-Effect Transistor [*Electronics*] (LAIN)
GaAsP	Gallium Arsenide Phosphide [*Semiconductor*] (IEEE)
GAASS	Government Agency Arbitrage and Swap System (MHDW)
GAAT	Gunner-Assisted Autotracking
GAATS	Gander Automated Air Traffic System
GAATV	Gemini Atlas/Agena Target Vehicle [*NASA*] (MCD)
GAB	Gabbs [*Nevada*] [*Seismograph station code, US Geological Survey Closed*] (SEIS)
GAB	Gabbs, NV [*Location identifier FAA*] (FAAL)
GAB	Gabbs Resources Ltd. [*Vancouver Stock Exchange symbol*]
GAB	Gabelli Equity Trust, Inc. [*NYSE symbol*] (SPSG)
GAB	Gable
GAB	Gabon [*ANSI three-letter standard code*] (CNC)
GAB	Gendall Air Ltd. [*Canada ICAO designator*] (FAAC)
GAB	General Adjustment Bureau [*Insurance*]
GAB	General Agreements to Borrow [*International Monetary Fund*] (EBF)
GAB	General Agreement to Borrow [*Business term*] (EBF)
GAB	General Arrangements to Borrow [*United Nations*] (EY)
GAB	Georgia Association of Broadcasters (SRA)
GAB	Gospel Association for the Blind (EA)
GAB	Government Affairs Branch [*European Theater of Operations*] [*World War II*]
GAB	Graphic Adapter Board
GAB	Great Artesian Basin [*Australia*]
GAB	Great Australian Bight [*Region*] (EERA)
GAB	Great Australian Bight Trawl Fishery (EERA)
GAB	Group Announcement Bulletin [*Defense Documentation Center*]
GAB	Guardianship and Administration Board [*Victoria, Australia*]
GABA	Gambling and Betting Addiction
GABA	Gamma-Aminobutyric Acid [*Biochemistry*]
GABA	German American Business Association (NTPA)
GABA	Global Agricultural Biotechnology Association (BUAC)
GABA-Ch	Gamma-Aminobutyrylcholine (DB)
GA Back	Great American Backrub Store, Inc. [*Associated Press*] (SAG)
GABA-T	Gamma-Aminobutyric Acid Transaminase [*Pharmacology*] (DMAA)
Gabb Cr Law	Gabbett's Criminal Law [*A publication*] (DLA)
Gabb Stat L	Gabbett. Abridgment of Statute Law [1812-18] [*A publication*] (ILCA)
GABC	GAB Bancorp [*NASDAQ symbol*] (SAG)
GABC	German Amer Bancorp [*NASDAQ symbol*] (TTSB)
GABC	German American Bancorp [*NASDAQ symbol*] (SAG)
GABCC	Great Australian Bight Consultative Committee
GA Bcp	Great American Bancorp, Inc. [*Associated Press*] (SAG)
GabCv	Gabelli Convertible Securities Fund [*Associated Press*] (SAG)
GABD	Bandiagara [*Mali*] [*ICAO location identifier*] (ICLI)
GABD	Gauge Board
Gabeli	Gabelli Equity Trust [*Associated Press*] (SAG)
Gabelli	Gabelli Equity Trust, Inc. [*Associated Press*] (SAG)
GABF	Bafoulabe [*Mali*] [*ICAO location identifier*] (ICLI)
GABG	Bougouni [*Mali*] [*ICAO location identifier*] (ICLI)
GabGloM	Gabelli Global Multimedia Trust, Inc. [*Associated Press*] (SAG)
GabGM	Gabelli Global Multimedia Trust, Inc. [*Associated Press*] (SAG)
GABH	Georgia Baptist Hospital, Medical Library, Atlanta, GA [*Library symbol Library of Congress*] (LCLS)
GABH-N	Georgia Baptist Hospital, School of Nursing, Atlanta, GA [*Library symbol Library of Congress*] (LCLS)
GABHS	Group A Beta-Hemolytic Streptococcus [*Pathology*]
GABIA	Great Australian Bight Industry Association (EERA)
GabIRsd	Gables Residential Trust [*Associated Press*] (SAG)
GABN	Ground-to-Air Broadcast Network
GaBnd	Georgia Bonded Fibers, Inc. [*Associated Press*] (SAG)
GABOA	Gamma-Amino-Beta-Hydroxybutyric Acid (DMAA)
GABOB	Gamma-Amino-beta-hydroxybutyric Acid [*Pharmacology*]
GABR	Bourem [*Mali*] [*ICAO location identifier*] (ICLI)
GABRA	Gamma-Aminobutyric Acid Alpha Receptor (DMAA)
GABRIELA	General Assembly Binding Women for Reforms, Integrity, Equality, Leadership and Action [*Philippines*] (BUAC)
GABS	Bamako/Senou [*Mali*] [*ICAO location identifier*] (ICLI)
GABS	Group A Beta-Hemolytic Streptococcus (STED)
GA Bus Law	Georgia Business Lawyer (DLA)
GABV	Bamako [*Mali*] [*ICAO location identifier*] (ICLI)
GABVX	Gabelli Value Fund [*Mutual fund ticker symbol*] (SG)
GAC	Armstrong State College, Savannah, GA [*OCLC symbol*] (OCLC)
GAC	Clark College, Atlanta, GA [*Library symbol Library of Congress*] (LCLS)
GAC	Galvanized Aircraft
GAC	Geac Computer Corp. Ltd. [*Toronto Stock Exchange symbol*]
GAC	General Acceptance Corp. (MHDW)
GAC	General Access Copy (MHDI)
GAC	General Advisory Committee [*to the AEC, later, the Energy Research and Development Administration*]
GAC	General Agency Check [*Army*]
GAC	General Air Cargo [*Venezuela*] [*ICAO designator*] (FAAC)

GAC	General Areas of Competence [*Education*] (AIE)
GAC	General Average Certificate [*Business term*] (DS)
GAC	Geological Association of Canada (BUAC)
GAC	Georgia Athletic Conference (PSS)
GAC	Ghost in Addition to Crew [*Sailing*]
GAC	Gimbal Angle Change
GAC	Gimbal Angle Controller
GAC	Giordano Automation Corp.
GAC	Gippsland Agriculture Centre [*Australia*]
GAC	Global Area Coverage [*Meteorology*]
GAC	Goodyear Aerospace Corp.
GAC	Government Advisory Committee on International Book and Library Programs [*Terminated, 1977*] (EGAO)
GAC	Government Art Collection (BUAC)
GAC	Grand Assistant Conductor [*Freemasonry*] (ROG)
GAC	Granular Activated Carbon
GAC	Granular Activated Carbon Absorption
GAC	Graphic Art Club, Toronto [*c.1903, SGA from 1912, CSGA from 1923*] [*Canada*] (NGC)
GAC	Grilled American Cheese Sandwich
GAC	Gross Available Capacity [*Electronics*] (IEEE)
GAC	Ground Attitude Control (MCD)
GAC	Groundwater Activated Carbon (EPA)
GAC	Group Access Capabilities [*Library automation*]
GAC	Grumman Aerospace Corp. [*of Grumman Corp.*]
GAC	Guangxi Agricultural College [*China*] (BUAC)
GAC	Guanine Adenine Cytosine [*A triplet of bases coding for the amino acid, aspartic acid*] (EES)
GAC	Guidance and Control [*Military*] (IAA)
G Ac	Guillelmus de Accursio [*Deceased, 1314*] [*Authority cited in pre-1607 legal work*] (DSA)
GAC	Gustavus Adolphus College [*St. Peter, MN*]
GACA	American College of Applied Arts, Atlanta, GA [*Library symbol*] [*Library of Congress*] (LCLS)
GACAC	Gateway Collegiate Athletic Conference (PSS)
GACC	Atlanta Chamber of Commerce, Atlanta, GA [*Library symbol Library of Congress*] (LCLS)
GACC	General Acceptance Corp. [*NASDAQ symbol*] (SAG)
GACC	Genl Acceptance [*NASDAQ symbol*] (TTSB)
GACC	German American Chamber of Commerce (NTPA)
GACC	Guidance Alignment and Checkout Console (IAA)
GACC	Guidance and Control Coupler (IAA)
GACCC	Coca-Cola Co., Technical Information Services, Atlanta, GA [*Library symbol Library of Congress*] (LCLS)
GACCLC	Cooperative College Library Center, Inc., Atlanta, GA [*Library symbol Library of Congress*] (LCLS)
GACCP	Georgia Agricultural Commodity Commission for Peanuts (SRA)
GACDC	Center for Disease Control, Main Library, Atlanta, GA [*Library symbol Library of Congress*] (LCLS)
GACDC-FP	Center for Disease Control, Family Planning Evaluation Division, Atlanta, GA [*Library symbol Library of Congress*] (LCLS)
GACDL	Georgia Association of Criminal Defense Lawyers (SRA)
GACEP	Guidance and Control Equipment Performance (IAA)
GACHA	Georgia Automated Clearing House Association
GACI	Geographic Area Code Index [*Bureau of Census*]
GACIA	Guidance and Control Information [*DoD*] (MCD)
GACIAC	Guidance and Control Information Analysis Center [*Chicago, IL DoD Also, an information service or system*]
GACIC	German Australian Chamber of Industry and Commerce [*Australia*]
GACL	Crawford W. Long Memorial Hospital, Atlanta, GA [*Library symbol Library of Congress*] (LCLS)
GACNA	Graphic Arts Council of North America (EA)
GACo	Coca-Cola Co., Marketing Information Center, Atlanta, GA [*Library symbol Library of Congress*] (LCLS)
GACOA	Groupe Commercial Africain [*Central Africa*] (BUAC)
GA Code	Code of Georgia [*A publication*] (DLA)
GA Code Ann	Georgia Code, Annotated [*A publication*] (DLA)
G/A COMM	Ground-to-Air Communications (MCD)
G/A Con	General Average Contribution [*Marine insurance*] (DS)
GA Const	Georgia Constitution [*A publication*] (DLA)
GACP	Gunner's Accuracy Control Panel (MCD)
GACRI	Guangdong Arts and Crafts Research Institute [*China*] (BUAC)
GACS	Georgia Association of Christian Schools (SRA)
GACS	Georgia Association of Convenience Stores (SRA)
GACS	Gun Alignment and Control System (MCD)
GACSC	Contel Service Corp., Atlanta, GA [*Library symbol*] [*Library of Congress*] (LCLS)
GACSU	Singapore Government Administrative and Clerical Services' Union
GACT	Generally Available Control Technology [*Environmental chemistry*]
GACT	Graphic Analysis and Correlation Terminal (MCD)
GACT	Greenwich Apparent Civil Time [*Astronomy*] (IAA)
GACTAI	General Arbitration Council of the Textile and Apparel Industries (EA)
GACTFOSIF	Graphic Analysis and Correlation Terminal Fleet Ocean Surveillance Information Facility (DNAB)
GACTI	General Arbitration Council of the Textile Industry [*Later, GACTAI*] (EA)
GACU	Ground Air Conditioning Unit (MCD)
GACU	Ground Avionics Cooling Unit
GAD	Gadabout (DSUE)
GAD	Gadsden [*Alabama*] [*Airport symbol*] (OAG)
GAD	Gallium Arsenide Diode
GAD	Galvanized and Dipped Metal (IAA)
GAD	General Anthropology Division (EA)
GAD	General Assembly Data
GAD	Generalized Anxiety Disorder [*Medicine*] (DMAA)

GAD .... Germanium Alloy Diffused (IAA)
GAD .... Germersheim Army Depot (MCD)
GAD .... Gladstone Resources [*Vancouver Stock Exchange symbol*]
GAD .... Glutamate Acid Decarboxylase [*An enzyme*]
GAD .... Glutamate Decarboxylase [*An enzyme*]
GAD .... Government Actuary's Department
GAD .... Government Archives Division [*National Archives of Canada*]
　　　　　　　[*Information service or system*] (IID)
GAD .... Graduate Assistantship Directory [*A publication*]
GAD .... Grand Alliance for Democracy [*Philippines*] [*Political party*]
GAD .... Grants Administration Division [*Environmental Protection Agency*]
GAD .... Graphic Active Device [*Computer science*] (MHDI)
GAD .... Great American Dream
GAD .... Guards' Armoured Division [*Military unit*] [*British*]
GAD .... Guards Artillery Division [*British*]
GAD .... Guide to American Directories [*A publication*]
GADA .... Dioila [*Mali*] [*ICAO location identifier*] (ICLI)
GADAR........ Guild of Antique Dealers and Restorers [*British*] (DBA)
GADC .... General Audio and Data Communications Ltd. (NITA)
GA Dec .... Georgia Decisions [*A publication*] (DLA)
GA Dec (Dudley)... Dudley's Georgia Reports [*A publication*] (DLA)
GADEF .... Groupement des Associations Dentaires Francophones [*Group of*
　　　　　　　Francophone Dentists' Associations] [*Paris, France*] (EAIO)
G/A Dep .... General Average Deposit [*Marine insurance*] (DS)
GADES........ Gun Air Defense Effectiveness Study (MCD)
GADH.......... Gastric Alcohol Dehydrogenase [*An enzyme*]
GADL .... Ground-to-Air Data Link
GADNA........ Gduei Noar [*Youth Battalions*] [*Israel*]
GADNPH ...... Glycolic Aldehyde Dinitrophenylhydrazone [*Organic chemistry*]
GADO .... General Aviation District Office [*FAA*]
GADPET .... Graphic Data Presentation and Edit (PDAA)
GADPS........ Graphic Automatic Data Processing System (MCD)
GADR .... Guided Air Defense Rocket
GADS .... Gate-Assignment and Display System [*United Air Lines, Inc.*]
GADS .... Geographic and Alphanumeric Display System (MCD)
GADS .... Gonococcal Arthritis/Dermatitis Syndrome [*Medicine*]
GADS .... Goose Air Defense Sector
GADSCO ...... Gages Documentation Scheduling Committee
GADT .... Graded Assessment in Design and Technology (AIE)
GADT .... Ground/Air Defense Threat (MCD)
GADZ .... Douentza [*Mali*] [*ICAO location identifier*] (ICLI)
GADZ .... Gadzooks, Inc. [*NASDAQ symbol*] (SAG)
Gadzks........ Gadzooks, Inc. [*Associated Press*]
gae .... Gaelic (Scots) [*MARC language code Library of Congress*] (LCCP)
GAE............. Gale Environmental Almanac [*A publication*]
GAE............. Gallic Acid Equivalent [*Wine analysis*]
GAE............. GAO [*General Accounting Office*] Denver Regional Office, Denver,
　　　　　　　CO [*OCLC symbol*] (OCLC)
GAE............. Gaslite Petroleum [*Vancouver Stock Exchange symbol*]
GAE............. General Administrative Expense [*A budget appropriation title*]
GAE............. General Air Express
GAE............. General American English
GAE............. General Analytical Evaluation
GAE............. General Classification Test/Arithmetic Test/Electronics Technician
　　　　　　　Selection Test [*Military*] (DNAB)
GAE............. Gibbs Adsorption Equation [*Physical chemistry*]
GAE............. Graphic Arts Employers of America (EA)
GAE............. Grupos Armados Espanoles [*Armed Spanish Groups*] [*Political
　　　　　　　party*] (PD)
GAE............. Gummed All Edges [*Envelopes*] (DGA)
GAE............. Gunner Aiming Error (MCD)
GAE-BPH..... Georgia State Department of Education, Division of Public Library,
　　　　　　　Library for the Blind and Physically Handicapped, Atlanta, GA
　　　　　　　[*Library symbol Library of Congress*] (LCLS)
GAEC .... Ghana Atomic Energy Commission (BUAC)
GAEC .... Goodyear Aircraft and Engineering Corp.
GAEC .... Greek Atomic Energy Commission
GAEC .... Grumman Aircraft Engineering Corp. [*Later, Grumman Corp.*]
GAEI .... Equifax, Inc., Atlanta, GA [*Library symbol Library of Congress*]
GAEL .... Gaelic [*Language, etc.*]
GAEL .... Georgia Association of Educational Leaders (SRA)
GAELIC .... Gauteng and Environs Library Consortium
GAELIC .... Grumman Aerospace Engineering Language for Instructional
　　　　　　　Checkout
GAEO .... Galileo Electro-Optics [*NASDAQ symbol*] (TTSB)
GAEO .... Galileo Electro-Optics Corp. [*NASDAQ symbol*] (NQ)
GAE-P .... Georgia State Department of Education, Division of Public Library
　　　　　　　Services, Atlanta, GA [*Library symbol Library of Congress*]
　　　　　　　(LCLS)
GAERF .... Graphic Arts Education and Research Foundation (DGA)
GAES .... Gas Appliance Engineers Society [*Later, ASGE*] (EA)
GAESDA....... Graphic Arts Equipment and Supply Dealers Association [*Defunct*]
　　　　　　　(EA)
GAESRE....... Genealogical Association of English-Speaking Researchers in
　　　　　　　Europe (EAIO)
GAF............. GA Financial [*AMEX symbol*] (TTSB)
GAF............. GA Financial, Inc. [*AMEX symbol*] (SAG)
GAF............. Gamma-Activated Factor [*Biochemistry*]
GAF............. GAO [*General Accounting Office*] Boston Regional Office, Boston,
　　　　　　　MA [*OCLC symbol*] (OCLC)
GAF............. German Air Force [*ICAO designator*] (FAAC)
GAF............. German Air Force [*German Luftwaffe*]
GAF............. Giant Axon Formation (STED)
GAF............. Government Affairs Foundation [*Defunct*] (EA)

GAF............. Government Aircraft Facilities
GAF............. Grafton, ND [*Location identifier FAA*] (FAAL)
GAF............. Growth of the American Family [*A study*]
GAFA .... German-American Football Association [*Later, CSL*]
GAFADS ...... German Air Force Air Defense School (MCD)
GAFB .... George Air Force Base [*California*] (MCD)
GAFB .... Goodfellow Air Force Base [*Texas*]
GAFB .... Griffiss Air Force Base [*New York*]
GAFC .... Fulton County Court House, Atlanta, GA [*Library symbol Library of
　　　　　　　Congress*] (LCLS)
GAFCOR...... Gas and Fuel Corp. [*Victoria, Australia*] [*Commercial firm*]
GAFD .... Faladie [*Mali*] [*ICAO location identifier*] (ICLI)
GAFD .... Guild of American Funeral Directors [*Defunct*]
GAFD .... United States Food and Drug Administration, Atlanta, GA [*Library
　　　　　　　symbol Library of Congress*] (LCLS)
GAFET .... Gallium Arsenide Field-Effect Transistor (MCD)
GAFG .... General Aviation Flight Guide [*British*] (AIA)
GAFG .... Goal Attainment Follow-Up Guide (DMAA)
GAFIA .... German Armed Forces Intelligence Agency (MCD)
GAFL .... Fulton County Law Library, Atlanta, GA [*Library symbol Library of
　　　　　　　Congress*] (LCLS)
GAFM.......... Fulton County Medical Society, Atlanta, GA [*Library symbol Library of
　　　　　　　Congress*] (LCLS)
GA Fncl .... GA Financial, Inc. [*Associated Press*] (SAG)
GAFPG .... General Aviation Facilities Planning Group
GAFR .... Federal Reserve Bank of Atlanta, Research Library, Atlanta, GA
　　　　　　　[*Library symbol Library of Congress*] (LCLS)
GAFRO .... Ghana Association for Research on Women (BUAC)
GAFS .... Gentile Air Force Station [*Ohio*]
GAFS .... United States Forest Service, Atlanta, GA [*Library symbol Library of
　　　　　　　Congress*] (LCLS)
GAFSC .... Fernbank Science Center, Atlanta, GA [*Library symbol Library of
　　　　　　　Congress*] (LCLS)
GAFSC .... German Air Force Southern Command (MCD)
GAFTA .... Grain and Feed Trade Association (BUAC)
GAFTA .... Grain and Food Trade Association [*British*]
GAFTAC ...... German Air Force Tactical Air Command (MCD)
GAFTO .... Germany Air Force Technical Order (MCD)
GAFW .... United States Fish and Wildlife Service, Atlanta, GA [*Library symbol
　　　　　　　Library of Congress*] (LCLS)
GAG .... Cologne Air Transport [*Germany*] [*FAA designator*] (FAAC)
GAG .... Gage, OK [*Location identifier FAA*] (FAAL)
GAG .... Gallant Gold Mines Ltd. [*Vancouver Stock Exchange symbol*]
GAG .... GAO [*General Accounting Office*] Philadelphia Regional Office,
　　　　　　　Philadelphia, PA [*OCLC symbol*] (OCLC)
GAG .... Gays Against Genocide [*An association*] (BUAC)
GAG .... Glycosaminoglycan [*Biochemistry*]
GAG .... Glyoxal Bis(guanylhydrazone) [*Organic chemistry*]
GAG .... Grand Aleph Godol (BJA)
GAG .... Graphic Artists Guild (EA)
GAG .... Gross Available Generation [*Electronics*] (IEEE)
GAG .... Gross Gradability [*Truck specification*]
GAG .... Ground-to-Air-to-Ground [*Aviation*]
GAG .... Group-Specific Antigen Gene (DMAA)
GAG .... Guanine Adenine Guanine [*A triplet of bases coding for the amino
　　　　　　　acid, glutamic acid*] (EES)
GAGAS........ Generally Accepted Government Auditing Standards [*A publication*]
　　　　　　　(AAGC)
GAGB .... Gemmological Association of Great Britain (BI)
GAGB .... General Association of General Baptists (EA)
GAGDT .... Ground-to-Air-to-Ground Data Terminal [*Air Force*] (MCD)
GAGE .... Global Atmosphere Gases Experiment (EERA)
GAGE .... Global Atmospheric Gases Experiment [*Environmental science*]
GAGF .... Graphic Artists Guild Foundation (EA)
GAGI .... Goethe Institute, German Culture Institute, Atlanta, GA [*Library
　　　　　　　symbol Library of Congress*] (LCLS)
GAGK .... Graphic Arts Guidance Kit
GAGL .... Aguelhoc [*Mali*] [*ICAO location identifier*] (ICLI)
GAGM .... Georgia Mental Health Institute, Atlanta, GA [*Library symbol Library
　　　　　　　of Congress*] (LCLS)
GAGM .... Goundam [*Mali*] [*ICAO location identifier*] (ICLI)
GAGN .... Graphic Artists Guild National (NTPA)
GAGO .... Gao [*Mali*] [*ICAO location identifier*] (ICLI)
GAGP .... Georgia Power Co., Atlanta, GA [*Library symbol Library of
　　　　　　　Congress*] (LCLS)
GAGR .... Courma-Rharous [*Mali*] [*ICAO location identifier*] (ICLI)
GAGR .... Georgia Retardation Center, Atlanta, GA [*Library symbol Library of
　　　　　　　Congress*] (LCLS)
GAGTh .... Gammon Theological Seminary, Atlanta, GA [*Library symbol Library
　　　　　　　of Congress*] (LCLS)
GAGTL .... Gemmological Association and Gem Testing Laboratory of Great
　　　　　　　Britain (BUAC)
GaGulf .... Georgia Gulf Corp. [*Associated Press*] (SAG)
GAH .... Games at Home [*Baseball*]
GAH .... Gayndah [*Australia Airport symbol*] (OAG)
GAH .... Grand American Handicap [*Shooting competition*]
GAH .... Wren's Nest [*Joel Chandler Harris Home*], Atlanta, GA [*Library
　　　　　　　symbol Library of Congress*] (LCLS)
GAHB .... Hombori [*Mali*] [*ICAO location identifier*] (ICLI)
GAHF .... Grapple Adapter Handling Fixture [*Nuclear energy*] (NRCH)
GAHH .... Good American Helping Hands (EA)
GAHi .... Atlanta Historical Society, Atlanta, GA [*Library symbol Library of
　　　　　　　Congress*] (LCLS)
GAHM .... High Museum of Art, Atlanta, GA [*Library symbol Library of
　　　　　　　Congress*] (LCLS)

GAHoM .... Home Mission Board of the Southern Baptist Convention, Atlanta, GA [*Library symbol*] [*Library of Congress*] (LCLS)

GAHR .... Georgia Department of Human Resources, Atlanta, GA [*Library symbol Library of Congress*] (LCLS)

GAHSC .... Georgia Association of Homes and Services for Children (SRA)

GAHu .... Hurt, Richardson, Garner, Law Library, Atlanta, GA [*Library symbol*] [*Library of Congress*] (LCLS)

GAI .... Gaithersburg, MD [*Location identifier FAA*] (FAAL)

GAI .... Gate Alarm Indicator [*RADAR*]

GAI .... Gay American Indians (EA)

GAI .... General Accounting Instructions

GAI .... Generalized Area of Intersection (OA)

GAI .... Geophysical Associates International

GAI .... Gibbs Adsorption Isotherm [*Physical chemistry*]

GAI .... Gilbert Associates, Inc.

GAI .... [*A*] Glossary of the Aramaic Inscriptions [*A publication*] (BJA)

GAI .... Governmental Affairs Institute [*Later, VPS*] (EA)

GAI .... Guaranteed Annual Income

GAI .... Guild of Architectural Ironmongers [*British*] (BI)

GAI .... Gurr & Associates, Inc. (EFIS)

GAIA .... Graphic Arts Industries Association

GAIC .... Gallium Arsenide Integrated Circuit [*Computer chip*]

GAICO .... Gilbert Associates, Inc. (EFIS)

GAIF .... General Arab Insurance Federation [*Egypt*] (BUAC)

GAIF .... General Assembly of International Sports Federations [*Later, GAISF*] (EA)

GAIF .... Gimbal Angle Information Failure

GAIFC .... Gene Autry International Fan Club (EA)

Gaii .... Gaii Institutionum Commentarii [*Gaius' Institutes*] [*A publication*] (DLA)

GAIIA .... Global Alliance of International Information Industry Associations (BUAC)

Gai Inst ...... Gaius, Institutiones [*Second century AD*] [*Classical studies*] (OCD)

GAIL .... Gas Authority of India Ltd. (ECON)

GAIL .... Gate Array Interface Language [*NITA*]

GAIL .... General Atomic In-Pool Loop (SAA)

GAIL .... Glide Angle Indicator Light [*Aviation*] (DNAB)

GAILL .... Groupement des Allergologistes et Immunologistes de Langues Latines [*Latin Languages Speaking Allergists - LLSA*] (EAIO)

GAIM .... Global Analyses, Interpretation, and Modeling [*Task Force*] [*Marine science*] (OSRA)

GAIM .... Global Analysis, Interpretation and Modelling [*Climate*] (EERA)

GAIM .... Group Achievement Identification Measure [*Test*] [*Sylvia B. Rimm*] (TES)

GAIN .... Federal and State Governments Assistance Programs [*Database*] [*Australia*]

GAIN .... Gas Appliance Improvement Network

GAIN .... Gifted Advocacy Information Network [*Defunct*] (EA)

GAIN .... Giftware Associates Interchange (NTPA)

GAIN .... Global Automation Information Network [*An association*]

GAIN .... Graphic Aids for Investigating Networks [*NASA*] (NASA)

GainAs .... Gallium Indium Arsenide (MED)

GainP .... Gallium Indium Phosphide (MED)

GAINS .... Gimballess Analytic Inertial Navigation System

GAINS .... Global Airborne Integrated Navigation System [*Military*] (IAA)

GAINS .... Graphic Administrative Information System (DNAB)

GAINS .... Growth and Income Security [*Finance*]

GAINS .... Guaranteed Annual Income System

Gainsco ...... Gainsco, Inc. [*Associated Press*] (SAG)

GAInv .... General American Investors Co., Inc. [*Associated Press*] (SAG)

GAIS .... Gallium Arsenide Illuminator System

GAIS .... General Aviation Inspection Aids Summary [*FAA*]

GAISF .... General Association of International Sports Federations [*Formerly, GAIF*] (EA)

GAISO .... Gam-Anon International Service Office (EA)

GAISSAR ..... Gilbert Associates, Incorporated, Standard Safety Analysis Report [*Nuclear energy*] (NRCH)

GAIT .... Government and Industry Team

G/AIT .... Ground/Airborne Integrated Terminal [*Air Force*] (DOMA)

GAIT .... Langer Biomechanics Group [*NASDAQ symbol*] (SAG)

GAIT .... Langer Biomechanics Grp [*NASDAQ symbol*] (TTSB)

GAITh .... Interdenominational Theological Center, Atlanta, GA [*Library symbol Library of Congress*] (LCLS)

GAIU .... Graphic Arts International Union [*Later, GCIU*]

Gaius .... Gaius' Institutes [*A publication*] (DLA)

Gaius Inst .... Gaius' Institutes [*A publication*] (DLA)

GAJ .... Atlanta Junior College, Atlanta, GA [*Library symbol Library of Congress*] (LCLS)

GAJ .... Gaseous Axisymmetric Jet

GAJ .... Guild of Agricultural Journalists

GAJ .... Yamagata [*Japan*] [*Airport symbol*] (OAG)

GAJC .... Jimmy Carter Library, Atlanta, GA [*Library symbol Library of Congress*] (LCLS)

GAK .... Gakona, AK [*Location identifier FAA*] (FAAL)

GAK .... Galactokinase [*Also, GALK*] [*An enzyme*]

GAKA .... Kenieba [*Mali*] [*ICAO location identifier*] (ICLI)

GAKL .... Kidal [*Mali*] [*ICAO location identifier*] (ICLI)

GAKM .... Ke-Macina [*Mali*] [*ICAO location identifier*] (ICLI)

GAKN .... Kolokani [*Mali*] [*ICAO location identifier*] (ICLI)

GAKO .... Koutiala [*Mali*] [*ICAO location identifier*] (ICLI)

GAKT .... Kita [*Mali*] [*ICAO location identifier*] (ICLI)

GAKY .... Kayes [*Mali*] [*ICAO location identifier*] (ICLI)

GAl .... Albany Public Library, Albany, GA [*Library symbol Library of Congress*] (LCLS)

GAL .... Anti-Terrorist Liberation Group [*Undercover anti-Basque terrorist interior-ministry network*] [*Acronym is based on foreign phrase Spain*] (ECON)

GAL .... Galactic (KSC)

Gal .... Galactose [*A sugar*]

Gal .... Galactosyl [*Biochemistry*] (DAVI)

Gal .... Galatians [*New Testament book*]

Gal .... Galen [*Second century AD*] [*Classical studies*] (OCD)

GAL .... Galena [*Alaska*] [*Airport symbol*] (OAG)

GAL .... Galerazamba [*Colombia*] [*Seismograph station code, US Geological Survey*] (SEIS)

gal .... Galileo [*Unit of acceleration*]

gal .... Galla [*MARC language code Library of Congress*] (LCCP)

GAL .... Gallery

Gal .... Gallery (WDAA)

Gal .... Gallison's United States Circuit Court Reports [*A publication*] (DLA)

GAL .... Gallium Arsenide LASER

GAL .... Gallon (AAG)

gal .... Gallon (ODBW)

GAL .... Gallons of Fuel [*"Energy equivalent" abbreviation - biomass agriculture and conversion*] [*Fuel chemistry*]

GAL .... Gallop [*Music*] (ROG)

GAL .... Gallup Public Library, Gallup, NM [*OCLC symbol*] (OCLC)

GAL .... Gallus-adeno-like [*Avian virus*]

GAL .... Galoob (Lewis) Toys [*NYSE symbol*] (TTSB)

GAL .... Galoob [*Lewis*] Toys, Inc. [*NYSE symbol*] (SPSS)

gal .... Galvanized Iron (ADA)

GAL .... Galveston-Houston [*Diocesan abbreviation*] [*Texas*] (TOCD)

GAL .... Galveston Resources Ltd. [*Toronto Stock Exchange symbol Vancouver Stock Exchange symbol*]

GAL .... Galway [*County in Ireland*] (ROG)

GAL .... Gas-Analysis Laboratory [*NASA*]

GAL .... Gate Array Logic (AAEL)

GAL .... Gemini Airlines Ltd. [*Ghana*] [*ICAO designator*] (FAAC)

GAL .... General Administration Letter (OICC)

GAL .... General George A. Lincoln [*World War II*]

GAL .... Generalized Assembly Language [*Computer science*] (MHDB)

GAL .... Generic Array Logic [*Computer science*]

GA L .... Georgia Lawyer [*A publication*] (DLA)

GA L .... Georgia Sessions Laws [*A publication*] (DLA)

GAL .... German Atlantic Line [*Steamship*] (MHDB)

GAL .... Get a Life

GAL .... Gimbal Angle Loss

GAL .... Glucuronic Acid Lactone (DB)

GAL .... Graphics Application Language (BYTE)

GAL .... Greening Australia Limited (EERA)

GAL .... Grupos Armados Libertarios [*Armed Libertarian Groups*] [*Spain Political party*] (PD)

Gal .... Gualcosius [*Flourished, 11th-12th century*] [*Authority cited in pre-1607 legal work*] (DSA)

GAL .... Guaranteed Access Level [*Foreign Trade*]

GAL .... Guardian Ad Litem [*Social services*] (PAZ)

GAL .... Guggenheim Aeronautical Laboratory [*California Institute of Technology*]

GAL .... Guild of American Luthiers (EA)

GAL .... Guinea Airways Ltd.

gal-1-P .... Galactose-1-Phosphate [*Organic chemistry*] (DAVI)

GALA .... Gallium Aluminum Arsenide (CIST)

GALA .... Gay and Lesbian Atheists [*Defunct*] (EA)

GALA .... Graduated Audio Level Adjustment

GALA .... Graphic Arts Literature Abstracts [*A publication*]

GALA .... Greek Applied Linguistics Association (BUAC)

GALA .... Grupo de Artistas Latino Americanos [*An association*]

GALA .... Guidance and Learner Autonomy [*Project*] (AIE)

GALAC .... Gay and Lesbian Association of Choruses (EA)

GalaGen ...... GalaGen, Inc. [*Associated Press*] (SAG)

Gal & Dav ... Gale and Davison's English Queen's Bench Reports [*1841-43*] [*A publication*] (DLA)

GA Law Reporter... Georgia Law Reporter [*A publication*] (DLA)

GALAXY ...... General Automatic Luminosity and X-Y [*Engine technology*] (PDAA)

GALB .... Galbanum [*Agum*] [*Pharmacology*] (ROG)

Galb .... Galbraith's Reports [*9-11 Florida*] [*A publication*] (DLA)

G-ALB .... Globulin-Albumin [*Biochemistry*] (DAVI)

Galb & M..... Galbraith and Meek's Reports [*9-12 Florida*] [*A publication*] (DLA)

Galb & M (Fla)... Galbraith and Meek's Reports [*9-12 Florida*] [*A publication*] (DLA)

Galbraith ..... Galbraith's Reports [*9-12 Florida*] [*A publication*] (DLA)

GALC .... European Booksellers Association (BUAC)

GalC .... Galactocerebroside [*Biochemistry*]

GALC .... Galactosylceramidase [*An enzyme*]

GALC .... Groupement des Associations de Librairies de la CEE [*Group of Booksellers Associations in the EEC*] (ECED)

GAL CAP ..... Gallon Capacity (WDAA)

GALCIT .... Graduate Aeronautical Laboratories - California Institute of Technology [*Research center*] (RCD)

GALCIT .... Guggenheim Aeronautical Laboratory, California Institute of Technology (MCD)

GAID .... Dougherty County Court House, Albany, GA [*Library symbol Library of Congress*] (LCLS)

GALD .... Greatest Axial Linear Dimension

GAIDC .... Darton College, Albany, GA [*Library symbol*] [*Library of Congress*] (LCLS)

Gale .... Gale on Easements [*A publication*] (DLA)

GALE .... Galerias de Arte y Salas de Exposiciones [*Ministerio de Cultura*] [*Spain Information service or system*] (CRD)

Gale............. Gale's English Exchequer Reports [*A publication*] (DLA)
Gale............. Gale's New Forest Decisions [*England*] [*A publication*] (DLA)
GALE.......... Gaseous and Liquid Effluent [*Nuclear energy*] (NRCH)
GALE.......... Genesis of Atlantic Lows Experiment (USDC)
GALE.......... Genesis of Atlantic Tropical Lows Experiment [*National Oceanic and Atmospheric Administration*]
Gale & D ..... Gale and Davison's English Queen's Bench Reports [*1841-43*] [*A publication*] (DLA)
Gale & Dav... Gale and Davison's English Queen's Bench Reports [*1841-43*] [*A publication*] (DLA)
Gale & D (Eng)... Gale and Davison's English Queen's Bench Reports [*1841-43*] [*A publication*] (DLA)
Gale & Whatley Easem... Gale and Whatley [*later, Gale*] on Easements [*A publication*] (DLA)
Gale & Wh Eas... Gale and Whatley [*later, Gale*] on Easements [*A publication*] (ILCA)
Gale Eas...... Gale on Easements [*A publication*] (ILCA)
Gale's St .... Gale's Statutes [*A publication*] (DLA)
Gale Stat .... Gale's Statutes [*A publication*] (DLA)
GaleyL........ Galey & Lord, Inc. [*Associated Press*] (SAG)
GALF.......... Groupement des Acousticiens de Langue Francaise [*Group of French-Speaking Acousticians*] (EA)
GAL/(FT² D)... Gallons per Square-Foot per Day
GAL/(FT D)... Gallons per Foot per Day
GAL/H .... Gallons per Hour (MCD)
GALH .... General Association of Ladies Hairdressers [*British*] (BI)
GALHA .... Gay and Lesbian Humanist Association (BUAC)
GAL/(HP H)... Gallons per Horsepower-Hour
GALIC .... General American Life Insurance Co.
Galileo........ Galileo Electro-Optics Corp. [*Associated Press*] (SAG)
GA LJ .... Georgia Law Journal [*A publication*] (DLA)
GAIJC.......... Albany Junior College, Albany, GA [*Library symbol Library of Congress*] (LCLS)
GALK .... Galactokinase [*Also, GAK*] [*An enzyme*]
GALL.......... Gallae [*Nut Galls*] [*Pharmacology*] (ROG)
GALL.......... Gallery (MSA)
gall .... Gallery (VRA)
Gall............ Gallison's United States Circuit Court Reports [*A publication*] (DLA)
GALL.......... Gallon
gall .... Gallon (ODBW)
GALL.......... Galloway [*District in Scotland*] (ROG)
Gallagr .... Gallagher [*Arthur J.*] & Co. [*Associated Press*] (SAG)
Gallaudet U... Gallaudet University (GAGS)
Gall CCR..... Gallison's United States Circuit Court Reports [*A publication*] (DLA)
Gall Cr Cas... Gallick's Reports (French Criminal Cases) [*A publication*] (DLA)
GALLEX....... Gallium Experiment
GallHist .... Gallery of History, Inc. [*Associated Press*] (SAG)
Gall Int L .... Gallaudet on International Law [*A publication*] (DLA)
Gallison....... Gallison's United States Circuit Court Reports [*A publication*] (DLA)
Gallison's Rep... Gallison's United States Circuit Court Reports [*A publication*] (DLA)
GALLSMIN... Gallons per Minute (IAA)
GALLY .... Gallery (ROG)
GAL/MIN ...... Gallons per Minute
GalN .... Galactosamine [*Biochemistry*]
GalNac........ N-Acetylgalactosamine
Galob......... Galoob [*Lewis*] Toys, Inc. [*Associated Press*] (SAG)
Galoob........ Galoob [*Lewis*] Toys, Inc. [*Associated Press*] (SAG)
GALOP........ Gay London Policing (BUAC)
GALOVAL..... Grappling and Lock-On Validation
GALP .... Good Automated Laboratory Practice [*Environmental Protection Agency*]
GALPAT ...... Galloping Pattern Memory
GA L Rep .... Georgia Law Reporter [*A publication*] (DLA)
GAL/S .... Gallons per Second
GALS .... General Aerodynamic Lifting Surface (KSC)
GALS .... Generalized Assembly Line Simulator [*General Motors Corp.*]
GALS .... Geographic Adjustment by Least Squares (PDAA)
GAISC .... Albany State College, Albany, GA [*Library symbol Library of Congress*] (LCLS)
GALSFC .... Ginger Alden ™Lady Superstar∫Fan Club (EA)
GALT........... Galactotransferase [*Cell strain deficient in galactose-1-phosphate uridyltransferase*]
GALT........... Gut-Associated Lymphoid Tissue [*Medicine*]
GALTS .... Generated Author Language Teaching System (EDAC)
GALV .... Galvanic [*or Galvanized*]
galv .... Galvanized (VRA)
GALV .... Galvanometer
GALV .... Galveston [*Texas*]
GALV .... Gibbon Ape Leukemia Virus
GALVI .... Galvanized Iron
GALVND...... Galvannealed
GALVNM...... Galvanometer
galvo .... Galvanometer [*An instrument for detecting and measuring an electric current*] (WDMC)
GALVS .... Galvanized Steel
GALV TND ... Galvanized or Tinned [*Freight*]
GALVWG...... Gemini Agena Launch Vehicle Working Group [*NASA*] (KSC)
GALW .... Galway [*County in Ireland*]
GALX .... Galaxy Foods [*NASDAQ symbol*] (TTSB)
GALX .... Galaxy Foods Co. [*NASDAQ symbol*] (SAG)
GalxCbl........ Galaxy Cablevision Ltd. [*Associated Press*] (SAG)
GALXY .... Galaxy
GALY .... Galley (MSA)
GALZ........... Gays and Lesbians of Zimbabwe [*An association*]

GAM............ Gambell [*Alaska*] [*Airport symbol*] (OAG)
GAM............ Gambia
GAM............ Gameness (DSUE)
GAM............ Gamin Resources, Inc. [*Vancouver Stock Exchange symbol*]
GAM............ Gamma (NASA)
Gam............ Gamma Biologicals, Inc.
GAM............ Gamut [*Music*] (ROG)
GAM............ General Accounting Material (DNAB)
GAM............ General Accounting Office, Los Angeles Region, Los Angeles, CA [*OCLC symbol*] (OCLC)
GAM............ General Aeronautical Material
GAM............ General American Investors Co., Inc. [*NYSE symbol*] (SPSG)
GAM............ General Audit Manual
GAM............ Genl Amer Investors [*NYSE symbol*] (TTSB)
GAM............ Georgia Motor Trucking Association [*STAC*]
GAM............ German Army [*ICAO designator*] (FAAC)
GAM............ Global Asset Management [*Commercial firm British*] (ECON)
GAM............ Globe and Mail [*Newspaper databank*] [*Canada*] (NITA)
GAM............ Globe and Mail Data Base [*Info Globe*] [*Information service or system*] (CRD)
GAM............ Golf Association of Michigan (SRA)
GAM............ Graduate Aerospace Mechanical Engineering
GAM............ Grants Administration Manual [*HEW*]
GAM............ Graphic Arts Monthly [*A publication*] (DGA)
GAM............ Graphics Access Method (BUR)
GAM............ Ground-to-Air Missile (AAG)
GAM............ Groupement des Associations Meunieres des Pays de la CEE [*Flour Milling Associations Group of the EEC Countries*] (EAIO)
GAM............ Grupo de Apoyo Mutuo [*Group for Mutual Support*] [*Mexico Political party*]
GAM............ Guaranteed Annual Minimum
GAM............ Guest Aerovias Mexico, SA
GAM............ Guided Aircraft Missile [*Obsolete*]
GAM............ Guided Air Missile (AAGC)
GAM............ Morehouse College, Atlanta, GA [*Library symbol Library of Congress*] (LCLS)
GAMA .... Game Manufacturers Association (EA)
GAMA .... Gas Appliance Manufacturers Association (EA)
GAMA .... General Agents & Managers Association [*Insurance*]
GAMA .... General Aviation Manufacturers Association (EA)
GAMA .... Graphic-Arts Machinery Association (DGA)
GAMA .... Graphics-Assisted Management Application [*Computer science*] (BUR)
GAMA .... Groupe d'Analyse Macroeconomique Appliquee [*Group for Applied Macroeconomic Analysis*] [*University of Paris - Nanterre*] [*Information service or system*] (IID)
GAMA .... Guitar and Accessory Manufacturers Association [*Formerly, NAMMM*]
GAMA .... Guitar and Accessory Manufacturers Association of America (BUAC)
GAMA .... Markala [*Mali*] [*ICAO location identifier*] (ICLI)
GAMAA .... Graphic Arts Merchants' Association of Australia
GamaB........ Gamma Biologicals, Inc. [*Associated Press*] (SAG)
Gam-Anon ... Gamblers (WDAA)
GAMARTA... Metropolitan Atlanta Rapid Transit Authority, Atlanta, GA [*Library symbol Library of Congress*] (LCLS)
GAMAS .... Gamma Activation Materials Assay System [*Mobile laboratory*]
GAMAS .... General Atomic Material Assay System [*Nuclear energy*] (NRCH)
GAMAS .... Gulf Atomic Mobile Assay System
GAMAST ..... Girls and Mathematics and Science Teaching
GAMB .... Gambro [*A.B.*], Inc. [*NASDAQ symbol*] (NQ)
GAMB .... Mopti/Barbe [*Mali*] [*ICAO location identifier*] (ICLI)
GAMB .... Morris Brown College, Atlanta, GA [*Library symbol Library of Congress*] (LCLS)
Gamb & Barl... Gamble and Barlow's Digest [*Ireland*] [*A publication*] (DLA)
GAMBICA..... Association for the Instrumentation Control and Automation Industry in the United Kingdom (BUAC)
GAMBICA..... Group of Association of Manufacturers of British Instrumentation, Control and Automation (ECII)
GAMBICA..... Group of Association of Manufacturers of British, Instruments, Control and Automation (ACII)
GAMBIT ...... Gate-Modulated Bipolar Transistor (MCD)
Gamboa ...... Gamboa's Introduction to Philippine Law [*A publication*] (DLA)
Gamboa Philippine Law... Gamboa's Introduction to Philippine Law [*A publication*] (DLA)
GAMBOG..... Gambogia [*Gamboge*] [*Pharmacology*] (ROG)
Gambro....... Gambro [*A. B.*], Inc. [*Associated Press*] (SAG)
GAMC .... General Agents and Managers Conference of NALU [*Washington, DC*] (EA)
GAMD .... Gallium Arsenide Microwave Diode
GAME......... Gametek, Inc. [*NASDAQ symbol*] (SAG)
GAME......... GEWEX [*Global Energy and Water Cycle Experiment*] [*Marine science*] (OSRA)
GAMECOIN... Game Conservation International (EA)
Game Coin... Game Conservation International (BUAC)
GameFn...... Game Financial Corp. [*Associated Press*] (SAG)
GAMET .... Gyro Accelerometer Misalignment Erection Test
GAMETAG ... Global Atmospheric Measurements Experiment on Tropospheric Aerosols and Gases [*National Science Foundation*]
Gametek...... Gametek, Inc. [*Associated Press*] (SAG)
GAmG .... Georgia Southwestern College, Americus, GA [*Library symbol Library of Congress*] (LCLS)
GAMG .... Goat Anti-Mouse Immunoglobulin G (STED)
GAMHTE ..... General Association of Municipal Health and Technical Experts (EA)
GAMI .... Great American Management & Investment, Inc. [*NASDAQ symbol*] (NQ)
GAMIC......... Gamma Incomplete [*Chemistry*] (IAA)

GAMIg .... Goat Anti-Mouse Immunoglobulin [*Immunology*]

GAMIN .... General Activity, Ascendence-Submission, Masculinity-Femininity, Inferiority Feelings, Nervousness [*Psychology*] (AEBS)

GamingW .... Gaming World International, Inc. [*Associated Press*] (SAG)

GAMIS .... General Analytical Methods Information Service [*Laboratory of the Government Chemist*] [*British*] (NITA)

GAMIS .... Graphic Arts Marketing Information Service (EA)

GAMK .... Martin Luther King, Jr., Memorial Center, Atlanta, GA [*Library symbol Library of Congress*] (LCLS)

GAMK .... Menaka [*Mali*] [*ICAO location identifier*] (ICLI)

GAMLOGS.... Gamma Ray Logs (IEEE)

GamLott....... Gaming Lottery Corp. [*Associated Press*] (SAG)

GAMM .... German Association for Applied Mathematics and Mechanics

GAMM .... Gimbal Angle Matching Monitor

GAM-M .... Morehouse College, School of Medicine, Atlanta, GA [*Library symbol Library of Congress*] (LCLS)

GAMMA ...... Gender and Mathematics Association (BUAC)

GAMMA .... Generalized Automatic Method of Matrix Assembly [*Computer science*] (IAA)

GAMMA ...... Graphically-Aided Mathematical Machine

GAMMA ...... Guitar and Accesories Music Marketing Association (EA)

GAMMA ...... Guns and Magnetic Material Alarm [*Weapon-detecting device to prevent skyjacking*]

GAMMA .... Institute of Advanced Research Long-Range Planning (BUAC)

GAMNA .... Gambia News Agency (EY)

Gamng .... Gaming Corporation of America [*Associated Press*] (SAG)

GamngCp.... Gaming Corporation of America [*Associated Press*] (SAG)

GAMO .... German Army Material Office

GAMO .... Ground and Amphibious Military Operations [*Army*]

GAMP .... Global Atmospheric Measurements Program [*National Science Foundation*]

GAMP .... Guided Antiarmor Mortar Projectile (INF)

GAMPS .... Gander Automated Message Processing System [*ICAO*] (DA)

GAMRA .... Graphic Arts Manufacturers' Representative Association

GAMS .... Gas Analysis Modeling System [*Department of Energy*] (GFGA)

GAMS .... Groupement pour l'Avancement des Methodes Spectroscopiques et Physio-Chimiques d'Analyse [*Group for the Advancement of Spectroscopic Methods and Physicochemical Analysis*] [*Information service or system*] (IID)

GAMS .... Group for the Advancement of Spectroscopic and Physiochemical Analysis Methods (BUAC)

GAMSA .... Glutamylaminomethylsulfonic Acid [*Biochemistry*]

GAMSA .... Management Science America, Inc., Atlanta, GA [*Library symbol Library of Congress*] (LCLS)

GAM/SP ...... Graphics Access Method/System Product [*IBM Corp.*]

GAMTA .... General Aviation Manufacturers' and Traders' Association [*British*] (DA)

GAMU .... Mercer University, Atlanta, GA [*Library symbol Library of Congress*] (LCLS)

GAMU-P...... Mercer University, Southern School of Pharmacy, Atlanta, GA [*Library symbol Library of Congress*] (LCLS)

GAMV .... Galinsoga Mosaic Virus [*Plant pathology*]

GamW .... Gaming World International, Inc. [*Associated Press*] (SAG)

GaN .... Gallium Nitride (AAEL)

GAN .... Gandalf Technologies, Inc. [*Toronto Stock Exchange symbol*]

GAN .... Gander Aviation Ltd. [*Canada ICAO designator*] (FAAC)

Gan............. Gandulphus [*Flourished, 1160-85*] [*Authority cited in pre-1607 legal work*] (DSA)

GAN .... GAO [*General Accounting Office*] Norfolk Regional Office, Virginia Beach, VA [*OCLC symbol*] (OCLC)

GAN .... Garan, Inc. [*AMEX symbol*] (SPSG)

GAN .... Gaseous Nitrogen (PDAA)

GAN .... Generalized Activity Network (IEEE)

GAN .... Generating and Analyzing Networks [*Computer science*]

GAN .... Generating and Assembly Networks (NITA)

GAN .... Giant Axon Neuropathy [*Medicine*] (DMAA)

GAN .... Global Area Network (IAA)

GAN .... Goldfields Air Navigation [*Australia*]

GAN .... Grant Anticipation Note (EBF)

GAN .... Green Academic Network (BUAC)

GAN .... Greenwich Apparent Noon (ROG)

GAN .... Ground Attack Night (MCD)

GAN .... Guidance and Navigation

GAN .... Gyro-Compass Automatic Navigation [*System*] (RDA)

GAN .... Net Gradability [*Truck specification*]

GANA .... Glass Association of North America (NTPA)

Ganatra....... Ganatra's Criminal Cases [*India*] [*A publication*] (DLA)

Gand........... Gandulphus [*Flourished, 1160-85*] [*Authority cited in pre-1607 legal work*] (DSA)

G and A ...... Gas and Air [*Medicine*]

G & A .... General and Administrative

GANDALF.... General Alpha-Numeric Direct Access Library Facility [*Search system*]

G & B .... Gloucester and Bristol [*Diocese*] (ROG)

G & B .... Gordon & Breach [*Publisher*] [*British*]

G and B ...... Grafton and Belington Railroad [*Initialism refers to a settlement of Indians who lived near this railroad*]

G&C .... Glass & Ceramic Division (ACII)

G & C .... Gonville and Caius College [*Cambridge University*] (ROG)

G & C .... Goodrich and Clincher (ROG)

G & C .... Guidance and Control [*Military*] (CAAL)

G & CC .... Guidance and Control Coupler (KSC)

G & CEP ...... Guidance and Control Equipment Performance (KSC)

G & CS .... Guidance and Control System

G & D .... Gale and Davison's English Queen's Bench Reports [*1841-43*] [*A publication*] (DLA)

G & D.......... Grosset & Dunlap [*Publisher*]

G & D.......... Growth and Development [*Pediatrics*] (DAVI)

G and D....... Growth and Development (STED)

G and D....... Guts and Determination (DSUE)

G&E............ Gift and Exchange

G & E.......... Ground and Environmental (KSC)

Gander........ Gander Mountain, Inc. [*Associated Press*] (SAG)

GANDER ...... Guidance and Navigation Development and Evaluation Routine (PDAA)

GANDF........ Gandalf Technologies [*NASDAQ symbol*] (TTSB)

GANDF........ Gandalf Technologies, Inc. [*NASDAQ symbol*] (NQ)

G & F.......... Georgia & Florida R. R.

G & G.......... Gems & Gemology [*A publication*] (EAAP)

G & G.......... Goldsmith and Guthrie's Appeals Reports [*Missouri*] [*A publication*] (DLA)

G & G.......... Gyandoh and Griffiths. Sourcebook of the Constitutional Law of Ghana [*A publication*] (ILCA)

G & G (MO)... Goldsmith and Guthrie's Appeals Reports [*Missouri*] [*A publication*] (DLA)

G & H.......... Gavin and Hord's Indiana Statutes [*A publication*] (DLA)

G & H.......... Gibbs & Hill, Inc. (NRCH)

G & J.......... Gill and Johnson's Maryland Court of Appeals Reports [*1829-42*] [*A publication*] (DLA)

G & J.......... Glyn and Jameson's English Bankruptcy Reports [*1821-28*] [*A publication*] (DLA)

G & J.......... Gruner & Jahr AG & Co. [*Magazine publisher*] [*Germany*]

G & J (MD)... Gill and Johnson's Maryland Reports [*A publication*] (DLA)

G & Jo........ Gill and Johnson's Maryland Reports [*A publication*] (DLA)

G & John...... Gill and Johnson's Maryland Reports [*A publication*] (DLA)

G & K.......... G & K Services, Inc. [*Associated Press*] (SAG)

Gandlf......... Gandalf Technologies, Inc. [*Associated Press*] (SAG)

G & L Rty .... G & L Realty Corp. [*Associated Press*] (SAG)

G & M .... General and Municipal

G & M .... Geraghty & Miller, Inc.

G & M .... Girth and Mirth (EA)

G & M .... Gulf & Mississippi Railroad

G & N .... Greenville & Northern Railway Co. (IIA)

G & N .... Guidance and Navigation [*System*] [*Apollo*] [*NASA*]

G&NS.......... Guidance and Navigation Subsystem [*Aerospace*] (NAKS)

G & O .... Gas and Oxygen [*Medicine*]

G & OA........ Glycerine and Oleochemicals Association (EA)

G & PA........ Girls and Physical Activity National Newsletter [*A publication*]

G & P RR Laws... Gregg and Pond's Railroad Laws of the New England States [*A publication*] (DLA)

G & R.......... Geldert and Russell's Nova Scotia Reports [*A publication*] (DLA)

G & RS........ Guidance and Reporting System [*Army*]

G & S .... Gilbert and Sullivan

G & Sh RR... Godefroi and Shortt's Law of Railway Companies [*A publication*] (DLA)

G & SI .... Gulf & Ship Island Railroad Co.

G & SS .... Gilbert and Sullivan Society [*Australia*]

G & SW........ Glasgow & South-Western [*Railway*] [*Scotland*]

G & SWR..... Glasgow & South-Western Railway [*Scotland*]

G & T.......... Gin and Tonic

G&T............ Goals and Timetables (AAGC)

G & T.......... Gould and Tucker's Notes on Revised Statutes of United States [*A publication*] (DLA)

G & T.......... Gowns and Towels [*Medicine*] (DMAA)

G & U .... Grafe & Unzer [*Publisher*] [*German*]

G & W......... Genesee & Western Railroad (IIA)

G&W.......... Glycerine and Water (STED)

G & W .... Gulf & Western Industries, Inc.

G & Wh Eas... Gale and Whatley [*later, Gale*] on Easements [*A publication*] (ILCA)

G & WI........ Gulf & Western Industries, Inc.

G & W New Tr... Graham and Waterman on New Trials [*A publication*] (DLA)

Gane........... Eastern District Court Reports [*South Africa*] [*A publication*] (DLA)

GANEFO....... Games of the New Emerging Forces [*A counter-attraction to the Olympic Games*] [*Indonesia*]

GANF .... Ganfield [*England*]

GANF .... Niafunke [*Mali*] [*ICAO location identifier*] (ICLI)

GANG.......... Ganglion [*Medicine*]

gang........... Ganglion (STED)

gangl .... Ganglion [*or Ganglionic*] [*Neurology*] (DAVI)

GANH.......... Northside Hospital, Atlanta, GA [*Library symbol Library of Congress*] (LCLS)

GANIP......... Graphic Approach to Numerical Information Processing (IAA)

GANK.......... Nara/Keibane [*Mali*] [*ICAO location identifier*] (ICLI)

GANNET....... General Administrative Network [*Computer linkup*] [*British*]

Gannett....... Gannett Co., Inc. [*Associated Press*] (SAG)

Gannon U .... Gannon University (GAGS)

GANO.......... [*The*] Georgia Northern Railway Co. [*AAR code*]

GA-NOC....... General Assembly, National Olympic Committees (BUAC)

GANPAC...... German American National Political Action Committee (EA)

GANR.......... Nioro [*Mali*] [*ICAO location identifier*] (ICLI)

GANS.......... Granulomatous Angiitis of the Nervous System [*Medicine*] (DMAA)

GANS.......... Guidance and Navigation System [*Apollo*] [*NASA*] (IAA)

GANSAT....... Gannett Satellite Information Network

Gantos........ Gantos, Inc. [*Associated Press*] (SAG)

Gantt Dig .... Gantt's Digest of Arkansas Statutes [*A publication*] (DLA)

Gantts Dig ... Gantt's Digest of Arkansas Statutes [*A publication*] (DLA)

ganz........... Ganzlich [*Complete*] (BARN)

GAO .... GARP Activities Office [*Marine science*] (MSC)

GAO .... General Accounting Office [*of the US government*]

GAO .... General Accounting Office, Technical Information Sources and Service, Washington, DC [*OCLC symbol*] (OCLC)
GAO .... General Administrative Order
GAO .... General Agricultural Officer [*Ministry of Agriculture, Fisheries, and Food*] [*British*]
GAO .... General Alert Order (NATG)
GAO .... German Army Office
GAO .... Glycolic Acid Oxidase [*An enzyme*]
GAO .... Golden Air Commuter AB [*Sweden ICAO designator*] (FAAC)
GAO .... Government Accounting Office (MCD)
GAO .... Guantanamo [*Cuba*] [*Airport symbol*] (OAG)
GAO .... Gummed All Over [*Envelopes*] (DGA)
GAOC .... Oglethorpe University, Atlanta, GA [*Library symbol Library of Congress*] (LCLS)
GAO/CED ...... General Accounting Office/Community and Economic Development Division
GAOF .... Gummed All Over Flap [*Envelopes*]
GAO/FGMSD ... General Accounting Office/Financial and General Management Studies Division
GAO/FPCD ... General Accounting Office/Federal Personnel and Compensation Division
GAO/GGD ..... General Accounting Office General Government Division
GAOHP .... General Alliance of Operative House Painters [*A union*] [*British*]
GAO/HRD ..... General Accounting Office Human Resources Division
GAO/LCD ..... General Accounting Office/Logistics and Communications Division
GAO Let Rep... General Accounting Office Letter Report [*A publication*] (DLA)
GAO/MASAD... General Accounting Office Mission Analysis and Systems Acquisition Division
GAO NOTE ... General Accounting Office, Notice of Execution (DNAB)
GAO/NSIAD... General Accounting Office National Security and International Affairs Division
GAO/PAD ..... General Accounting Office Program Analysis Division
GAO/PEMD... General Accounting Office Program Evaluation and Methodology Division
GAO/PSAD ... General Accounting Office/Procurement and Systems Acquisition Division
GAOR .... General Accounting Office Review
GAOR.......... General Assembly Official Record [*United Nations*] [*A publication*] (DLA)
GAOTU .... Grand Architect of the Universe [*Freemasonry*] (ROG)
GAOW .... General Accounting Office, Washington
GAP .... Atlanta Public Library, Atlanta, GA [*OCLC symbol*] (OCLC)
GAP .... Atlanta Public Schools, Professional Library, Atlanta, GA [*Library symbol Library of Congress*] (LCLS)
GAP .... Gadolinium Aluminium Perovskite [*Inorganic chemistry*]
GaP .... Gallium Phosphide (AAEL)
Gap .... Gap, Inc. [*Formerly, Gap Stores, Inc.*] [*Associated Press*] (SAG)
GAP .... Gardner Analysis of Personality [*Survey*] [*Medicine*] (STED)
GAP .... Garmisch-Partenkirchen [*Federal Republic of Germany*] [*Seismograph station code, US Geological Survey*] (SEIS)
GAP .... Gastric and Peptic Ulcer [*A laboratory test kit*] [*Medicine*]
GAP .... General Accounting Package (IAA)
GAP .... General and Practical Energy Information Data Base (MCD)
GAP .... General Antenna Package [*COMSAT*]
GAP .... General Application Plan (AFIT)
GAPS .... General Assembly Program [*Computer science*]
GAP .... Generic Address Parameter [*Computer science*] (DDC)
GAP .... Geographic Applications Program [*United States Geological Survey*] (IID)
GaP.......... Georgia Power [*Associated Press*] (SAG)
GAP .... Ghetto Arts Program [*Later, Urban Arts Corps*] (EA)
GAP .... Girls Alone Project (BUAC)
GAP .... Global Action Plan for the Earth (BUAC)
GAP .... Glyceraldehyde Phosphate [*Biochemistry*]
GAP .... Glycidyl Azide Polymer [*Chemistry*]
GAP .... GnRH [*Gonadotropin Releasing Hormone*] Associated Peptide [*Endocrinology*]
GAP .... GOAL [*Ground Operations Aerospace Language*] Automatic Procedure [*NASA*] (NASA)
GAP .... Good Agricultural Practice [*Toxicology*]
GAP .... Goodyear Associative Processor [*Computer science*]
GAP .... Government Accountability Project (EA)
GAP .... Government Aircraft Plant
GAP .... Government of Alberta Publications [*Alberta Public Affairs Bureau*] [*Canada Information service or system*] (CRD)
GAP .... Grand Anatolia Project [*Dam system*] [*Turkey*] (ECON)
GAP .... Grant Air Program [*DoD*] (MCD)
GAP .... Graphical Automatic Programming [*Computer science*]
GAP .... Graphic Arts Professionals (NTPA)
GAP .... Graphics Adapter Processor [*Baytec*]
GAP .... Graphics Application Program
GAP .... Great Atl & Pac Tea [*NYSE symbol*] (TTSB)
GAP .... Great Atlantic & Pacific Tea Co., Inc. [*NYSE symbol*] (SPSG)
GAP .... Greater Access to Publishing [*British*]
GAP .... Greenwood, Archer, and Pine [*Major streets in Tulsa, OK*] [*In musical group "The GAP Band"*]
GAP .... Gross Agricultural Product (WDAA)
GAP .... Group Attainment Program
GAP .... Group for Aquatic Primary Productivity [*ICSU*]
GAP .... Group for the Advancement of Psychiatry (EA)
GAP .... Growth-Associated Protein [*Cytochemistry*]
GAP .... Grupo de Auto-Defensa [*Self-Defense Group*] [*Uruguay*] [*Political party*] (PD)
GAP .... Guanosine Triphosphatase Activating Protein [*Biochemistry*]
GAP .... Guided Antitank Projectile (MCD)

GAP .... Guildhall Automation Project (TELE)
GAP .... Gusap [*Papua New Guinea*] [*Airport symbol Obsolete*] (OAG)
GAP .... Southeast Anatolia Project [*Turkey*] (BUAC)
GAPA .... Greek American Progressive Association (EA)
GAPA .... Ground-to-Air Pilotless Aircraft [*Early US test missiles*]
GaPac .... Georgia-Pacific Corp. [*Associated Press*] (SAG)
GAPAN .... Guide to Air Pilots and Air Navigation [*A publication*]
GAPAN .... Guild of Air Pilots and Air Navigators (MCD)
GAPB .... General Aptitude Test Battery (DNAB)
GaPC .... Georgia Power Capital Ltd. [*Associated Press*] (SAG)
GaPC .... Georgia Power Capital Trust I [*Associated Press*] (SAG)
GAPCE .... General Assembly of the Presbyterian Church of England (DAS)
GAP CON ..... Gap Conductance (GAAI)
Ga-PD .... Gallium Arsenide Phosphide Photodiode
GAPD .... Garrett Auxiliary Power Division [*Military contractor*] (RDA)
GAPD .... Glyceraldehyde-3-Phosphate Dehydrogenase (STED)
GAPD .... Glyceraldehyde Phosphate Dehydrogenase [*Organic chemistry*] (MAH)
GAPD .... Government and Aeronautical Products Division [*Honeywell, Inc.*]
GAPDH........ Glyceraldehydephosphate Dehydrogenase [*Also, GPDH*] [*An enzyme*]
GAPE .... General Aviation Pilot Education [*Safety project*]
GAPE .... Geographical Association Package Exchange (AIE)
GAPE .... Graphic Acids to Packaging Equipment (PDAA)
GAPE .... Ground Anchor Placement Equipment
GAPEA .... Graphic Arts Platemakers Employers' Federation (DGA)
GAPEX .... General Agricultural Products Export Corp. [*Tanzania*] (BUAC)
GAPh .... Southern School of Pharmacy, Mercer University, Atlanta, GA [*Library symbol Library of Congress*] (LCLS)
GAPHYOR .... Gaz-Physique-Orsay Database [*Universite de Paris-Sud*] [*Information service or system*]
GAPie .... Piedmont Hospital, Atlanta, GA [*Library symbol Library of Congress*] (LCLS)
GAPL .... Group Assembly Parts List (MCD)
GAPL .... Group Assembly Provisioning List (MCD)
GAPM .... Generalized Access Path Method [*Computer science*] (MHDB)
GAPMB .... Ghana Agricultural Produce Marketing Board (BUAC)
GAPO .... Growth Retardation, Alopecia, Pseudoanodontia, and Optic Atrophy [*Syndrome*] [*Medicine*] (STED)
GAPO .... Growth Retardation, Alopecia, Pseudo-Anodontia, and Optic Atrophy Syndrome [*Medicine*] (DMAA)
GAPP .... Geometric Arithmetic Parallel Processor [*Computer science*]
GAPR .... Grant Application Request (WDAA)
GA Prac ...... Stand's Georgia Practice [*A publication*] (DLA)
GAPS .... Geo-Assimilated Positioning System [*Navigation systems*]
GAPS .... German Association for Political Science (BUAC)
GAPS .... Government Accountability Property System (MCD)
GAPSALS .... Give a Pint, Save a Life Society [*World War II organization which encouraged donating blood*]
GAPSAT ...... Gap-Filler Satellite [*RADAR*] (NVT)
GAPSATCOM... Gap-Filler Satellite Communication System (MCD)
GA PSC ...... Georgia Public Service Commission Reports [*A publication*] (DLA)
GAPSF .... Government Agricultural Policy and Services for Farmers [*British*]
GAPSFAS .... Graduate and Professional School Financial Aid Service (GAGS)
GAPSS .... Graphical Analysis Procedures for System Simulation (PDAA)
GAPT .... Generalized Atomic Polar Tensor [*Physical chemistry*]
GAPT .... Graphical Automatically Programmed Tools [*Computer science*]
GAPT .... Guild of Anatomical Pathology Technicians (BUAC)
GAP UK ...... Global Action Plan [*United Kingdom*] (BUAC)
GaPw .... Georgia Power Co. [*Associated Press*] (SAG)
GAQ .... Gao [*Mali*] [*Airport symbol*] (OAG)
GAQ .... Golfe Air Quebec Ltd. [*Canada ICAO designator*] (FAAC)
GAQ .... Good Average Quality (ADA)
GAQ .... Graphic Arts Quality (DGA)
GAQA .... Government Acquisition Quality Assurance (MCD)
GAR .... Commodore Aviation [*Australia ICAO designator*] (FAAC)
GAR .... GAO [*General Accounting Office*] San Francisco Regional Office, San Francisco, CA [*OCLC symbol*] (OCLC)
GAR .... Garage [*Classified advertising*]
GAR .... Garaina [*Papua New Guinea*] [*Airport symbol*] (OAG)
GAR .... Garamond [*Typography*] (DGA)
GAR .... Garden Lake Resources [*Vancouver Stock Exchange symbol*]
GAR .... Garm [*Former USSR Seismograph station code, US Geological Survey*] (SEIS)
GAR .... Garrison (MUGU)
GAR .... General Adverse Reaction [*Noise*]
GAR .... Genitoanorectal [*Syndrome*] [*Medicine*] (DB)
GaR .... Georgia Reports [*A publication*] (DLA)
Ga R .... Georgia Review [*A publication*] (BRI)
G-Ar.......... Georgia State Department of Archives and History, Atlanta, GA [*Library symbol Library of Congress*] (LCLS)
GAR .... German Army
GAR .... Gimbal Angle Rate
GAR .... Gimbal Angle Readout
GAR .... Glass Accumulation Rate [*Oceanography*]
GAR .... Global Atmospheric Research (NOAA)
GAR .... Go-Around (GAVI)
GAR .... Goat Anti-Rabbit [*Also, GARb*] [*Immunology*]
GAR .... Golden Age Records [*Record label*]
GAR .... Government Authorized Representative
GAR .... Grand Army of the Republic (GPO)
GAR .... Graphics Action Request (MCD)
GAR .... Ground Accident Report (MCD)
GAR .... Growth Analysis and Review (BUR)

GAR .... Gruppi Armati Radicali per il Comunismo [*Armed Radical Groups for Communism*] [*Italy*] (PD)
GAR .... Guangxi Research and Design Institute of Architectural Science [*China*] (BUAC)
GAR .... Guided Aerial Rocket
GAR .... Guided Aircraft Rocket
GAR .... Guided Antiarmor Rocket
GAR .... Gummed All Round [*Envelopes*] (DGA)
GARA .... Garamond [*Typography*] (WDAA)
Garan .... Garan, Inc. [*Associated Press*] (SAG)
garb .... Garbage (BARN)
GARb .... Goat Anti-Rabbit [*Also, GAR*] [*Immunology*]
GARB .... Green, Amber, Red, Blue [*Priority of the airways*]
GARB .... Guided Antiradiation Bomb
Garbage .... Garbage: The Independent Environmental Quarterly [*A publication*] (BRI)
GARBC .... General Association of Regular Baptist Churches (EA)
GARBD .... Garboard [*Naval architecture*]
GARC .... Graphic Arts Research Center [*Later, T & E Center*] [*Rochester Institute of Technology*]
GARC .... Great Atlantic Radio Conspiracy (EA)
GARC .... Retail Credit Co., Atlanta, GA [*Library symbol Library of Congress*] (LCLS)
GARCH .... Generalized Auto-Regressive Conditional Heteroskedacity [*Business term*] (ECON)
G Arch .... Graduate in Architecture
GARD .... Gamma Atomic Radiation Detector
gard .... Garden (VRA)
GARD .... Gardener (ROG)
Gard .... Gardens (BARN)
GARD .... General Address Reading Devices [*Computer science*]
GARD .... General Aviation Recovery Device
GARD .... Gimbal Angle Runaway Detector
GARD .... Graphic Analyzer of Resistance Defects
GARD .... Grumman-Alderson Research Dummy [*Aircraft ejection seats*]
GARDAE .... Gathers Alarms, Reports, Displays, and Evaluates
GardDen ...... Gardner Denver Machinery, Inc. [*Associated Press*] (SAG)
GARDE .... Gather, Alarm, Report, Display, and Evaluate (IAA)
GARDEN ...... Garden [*Commonly used*] (OPSA)
GARDENEX ... Federation of Garden and Leisure Equipment Exporters (BUAC)
Gardenhire ... Gardenhire's Reports [*14, 15 Missouri*] [*A publication*] (DLA)
GARDENS .... Gardens [*Commonly used*] (OPSA)
Gard Ev .... Garde on Evidence [*1830*] [*A publication*] (DLA)
GARDN .... Garden [*Commonly used*] (OPSA)
GardnFr .... Garden Fresh Restaurant Corp. [*Associated Press*] (SAG)
Gardn PC .... Gardner's Peerage Case, Reported by Le Marchant [*A publication*] (DLA)
GardnR .... Garden Ridge Corp. [*Associated Press*] (SAG)
Gard NY Rep... Gardenier's New York Reporter [*A publication*] (DLA)
Gard NY Rept... Gardenier's New York Reporter [*A publication*] (DLA)
Gard NY Rptr... Gardenier's New York Reporter [*A publication*] (DLA)
Gard Pl .... Garde's First Principles of Pleading [*A publication*] (DLA)
GardStat ...... Garden State Bancshares [*Associated Press*] (SAG)
GARDTRAK... Gamma Absorption and Radiation Detection Tracking (IAA)
GARE .... Guidelines for Authority and Reference Entries [*Cataloguing*] [*Association for Library Collections and Technical Services*]
GA Rep .... Georgia Reports [*A publication*] (DLA)
GA Rep Ann... Georgia Reports, Annotated [*A publication*] (DLA)
GAREX .... Ground Aviation Radio Exchange System (MCD)
GARF .... Graphic Arts Research Foundation (EA)
GARF .... Ground Approach Radio Fuse (IAA)
GARF .... Guam Acoustic Range Facility [*Military*] (CAAL)
GARG .... Gargarisma [*Gargle*] [*Pharmacy*]
Garg .... Gargle (STED)
GarG .... Garment Graphics, Inc. [*Associated Press*] (SAG)
GARGAR ...... Gargarisma [*Gargle*] [*Pharmacy*] (ROG)
GARGD .... Garaged [*Automotive advertising*]
GARGG .... Goat Anti-Rabbit Gamma Globulin (STED)
GARGG .... Goat Antiserum to Rabbit Gamma-Globulin [*Immunology*]
GARH .... Georgia Regional Hospital at Atlanta, Atlanta, GA [*Library symbol Library of Congress*] (LCLS)
GARI .... Goat Anti-Rabbit Immunoglobulin [*Immunochemistry*]
GARI .... Groupe d'Action Revolutionnaire Internationaliste [*International Revolutionary Action Group*] [*France Political party*] (PD)
GARI .... Grupo de Accion Revolucionaria Internacional [*International Revolutionary Action Group*] [*Spain Political party*]
GARIOA .... Government and Relief in Occupied Areas [*Post-World War II*]
Garkreba ...... Garantie- und Kreditbank [*Guaranty and Credit Bank*] [*Germany*] (EG)
GARL .... Group Action Request Lists
GarmGph ..... Garment Graphics, Inc. [*Associated Press*] (SAG)
GARMI .... General Aviation Radio Magnetic Indicator
GArmO .... Group Armaments Officer [*British military*] (DMA)
GARN .... Garnet Resources [*NASDAQ symbol*] (TTSB)
GARN .... Garnet Resources Corp. [*NASDAQ symbol*] (NQ)
GARN .... Garnish [*Automotive engineering*]
GARN .... Garnishee Order (DCTA)
GARNEE .... Garnishee [*Legal shorthand*] (LWAP)
Garnet .... Garnet Resources Corp. [*Associated Press*] (SAG)
GARNOR ...... Garnishor [*Legal shorthand*] (LWAP)
GARP .... Global Atmospheric Research Program [*Terminated National Science Foundation*]
GARP .... Growth at the Right Price
GARS .... Generic Airborne RADAR System (DWSG)
GARS .... Geological Applications of Remote Sensing

GARS .... Gilliam Autism Rating Scale [*Test*] (TMMY)
GARS .... Glycine Amide Phosphoribosyl Synthetase (DMAA)
GARS .... Grand Assistant Recording Scribe [*Freemasonry*] (ROG)
GART .... Gartner Group'A' [*NASDAQ symbol*] (TTSB)
GART .... Gartner Group, Inc. [*NASDAQ symbol*] (NQ)
GARTEur ..... Group for Aeronautical Research and Technology in Europe (BUAC)
Gartner .... Gartner Group, Inc. [*Associated Press*] (SAG)
GAS .... Autonomous Anarchist Groups [*Spanish*] (PD)
GAS .... Gach Saran [*Iran*] [*Airport symbol*] (AD)
GAS .... Galactorrhea-Amenorrhea Syndrome [*Medicine*] (DMAA)
GAS .... Galena Air Services, Inc. [*ICAO designator*] (FAAC)
GAS .... Gallipolis, OH [*Location identifier FAA*] (FAAL)
GAS .... Gallium Arsenide [*Semiconductor*]
GAS .... Gamma-Activated Site [*Biochemistry*]
GAS .... Garissa [*Kenya*] [*Airport symbol*] (OAG)
GAS .... Gas Acquisition System
GAS .... Gas Anti-Solvent [*Chemical engineering*]
GAS .... Gas-Insulated Switchgear
GAS .... Gasoline (AFM)
GAS .... Gastric Acid Secretion [*Medicine*] (DMAA)
GAS .... Gastroenterology [*Medicine*]
GAS .... Gauss [*Later, GTT*] [*Federal Republic of Germany*] [*Geomagnetic observatory code*]
GAS .... General Adaptation Syndrome [*Medicine*]
GAS .... General Air Staff (NATG)
GAS .... General Aptitude Series [*Test*]
GAS .... General Automotive Support
GAS .... General Aviation Services [*Canada*] (BUAC)
GAS .... General Aviation Simulator [*Computer science NASA*]
GAS .... Generalized Arteriosclerosis [*Medicine*]
GAS .... Generalized Audit Software [*Computer science*]
GAS .... Genome Automation System (HGEN)
GAS .... Get Away Special (MCD)
GAS .... Giant Air Shower
GAS .... Giant Attribute Survey
GAS .... Glasgow Archaeological Society [*Scotland*] (BUAC)
GAS .... Glass Art Society (EA)
GAS .... Global Address Space (MHDI)
GAS .... Global Analysis Systems [*Information service or system*] (IID)
GAS .... Global Anxiety Score [*Medicine*] (DMAA)
GAS .... Global Assessment Scale [*Psychiatric evaluation test*]
GAS .... Goal Attainment Scale
GAS .... Goilala Air Services [*Australia*]
GAS .... Government Accounting Service [*British*]
GAS .... Government-Assisted Students
GAS .... Government of American Samoa (MUGU)
GAS .... Grand Annual Sojourner [*Freemasonry*] (ROG)
GAS .... Graphics Application Program [*Computer science*] (MHDI)
GAS .... Graphics Attachment Support (IAA)
GAS .... Gray Area Systems (MCD)
GAS .... Group Analytic Society (BUAC)
GAS .... Group A Streptococci [*Medicine*]
GAS .... Growth Arrest-Specific Gene [*Medicine*] (DMAA)
GAS .... Guild of All Saints [*British*] (ROG)
GAS .... Guild of All Souls [*British*]
GAS .... Gun Accessory System (MCD)
GAS .... Gun Aiming Sensor (MCD)
GAS .... Gunner's Auxiliary Sight (MCD)
GAS .... Gust Alleviation System [*Aviation*] (MCD)
GAS .... NICOR, Inc. [*Formerly, Northern Illinois Gas Co.*] [*NYSE symbol*] (SPSG)
GAS .... Southern Technical Institute, Marietta, GA [*OCLC symbol*] (OCLC)
GASA .... German Australian Society of Australia
GASA .... Graphic Arts Suppliers Association (EA)
GASA .... Growth-Adjusted Sonographic Age [*Obstetrics*] (DMAA)
GASAC .... Garden State Athletic Conference (PSS)
GASAD .... Gate and Source and Drain (AAEL)
GASANSW ... Graphic Arts Services Association of New South Wales [*Australia*]
GASAV .... Graphic Arts Services Association of Victoria [*Australia*]
GASB .... Governmental Accounting Standards Board [*Stamford, CT*] (EA)
GASBIINDO... Gabungan Serikat Buruh Islam Indonesia [*Federation of Indonesian Islamic Trade Unions*]
GASC .... Gas-Analysis Sample Container [*Apollo*] [*NASA*]
GASC .... Georgia, Ashburn, Sylvester & Camilla R. R. [*AAR code*]
GASC .... German-American Securities Corp. (BARN)
GASC .... Graphic Arts Show Co., Inc. (DGA)
GASC .... Gurkha Army Service Corps [*British military*] (DMA)
GAS Can ...... Get-Away-Special Cannister [*NASA*]
GASCO .... Abu Dhabi Gas Industries Ltd. (BUAC)
GASCO .... General Aviation Safety Committee (BUAC)
GASD .... Government Aerospace Systems Division [*Harris Corp.*]
GASDA .... Gasoline and Automotive Service Dealers Association (EA)
Gas de Cal ... Gaspar de Calderinis [*Deceased, 1390*] [*Authority cited in pre-1607 legal work*] (DSA)
Gas de Cald... Gaspar de Calderinis [*Deceased, 1390*] [*Authority cited in pre-1607 legal work*] (DSA)
GASDSAS .... Gust Alleviation and Structural Dynamic Stability Augmentation [*Aviation*]
GASEQ .... Graziers' Association of South East Queensland [*Australia*]
GASER .... Gamma Ray LASER (NATG)
GASERBUN... Gabungan SB2 Non-Vakcentral [*Federation of Non-Affiliated Trade Unions*] [*Indonesia*]
GASERC .... Gulf Arab States Educational Research Center [*Kuwait*] (BUAC)
GASES .... Gravity-Anchored Space Experiments Satellite (MCD)

GAS-EUROSOUD... European Committee of Manufacturers of Gas-Welding Equipment (BUAC)

GASF .... Graphic Arts Sales Foundation (EA)

GASFET .... Gallium Arsenide Field-Effect Transistor

GASG .... Segou [Mali] [ICAO location identifier] (ICLI)

GASGA .... Group for Assistance on Systems Relating to Grain Afterharvest [Netherlands] (BUAC)

GASGASGAS... Gild of Ancient Suppliers of Gas Appliances, Skills, Gins, Accessories, and Substances (EA)

GASH .... Guanidine Aluminum Sulfate Hexahydrate [Insecticide]

GASH .... Guanidine Aluminum Sulfate Hydrate [Ferroelectrics]

GASHA .... Golden American Saddlebred Horse Association (EA)

GASI .... Greenwich Air Services, Inc. [NASDAQ symbol] (SAG)

GASIA .... Greenwich Air Services 'A' [NASDAQ symbol] (TTSB)

GASIB .... Greenwich Air Svcs'B' [NASDAQ symbol] (TTSB)

GASJ .... Saint Joseph's Infirmary, Atlanta, GA [Library symbol Library of Congress] (LCLS)

GASK .... Sikasso [Mali] [ICAO location identifier] (ICLI)

GASKET ...... Graphic Surface Kinetics [Computer program] (KSC)

GASL .... General Activity Simulation Language [Computer science]

GASL .... General Applied Science Laboratory

GASL .... Southeastern Library Network [SOLINET], Atlanta, GA [Library symbol] [Library of Congress] (LCLS)

GASLAB ...... Global Atmospheric Sampling Laboratory (EERA)

GASM .... Graphic Arts Spray Manufacturers [Defunct] (EA)

GAS-MOP .... Gulf of Alaska Mesoscale Oceanographic Processes

GASN .... San [Mali] [ICAO location identifier] (ICLI)

GASO .... Gasoline

GASOHOL .... Gasoline/Ethanol [Automotive fuel]

Gasonics ..... Gasonics International Corp. [Associated Press] (SAG)

GASP .... Galloping Acronyms Save Paper

GASP .... Gas Annulus Sizing Program

GASP .... Gas Plasma Display (HGAA)

GASP .... Gas Properties [NASA computer program]

GASP .... General Activity Simulation Program [Programming language] [1970] [Computer science] (BUR)

GASP .... General All-Purpose Simulation Package [McDonnell Douglas Automation Co.] (MCD)

GASP .... General Analysis of System Performance (IAA)

GASP .... General Assembly to Stop the Powerline (EA)

GASP .... Generalized Academic Simulation Program [Computer science] (IEEE)

GASP .... Generalized Aerospace Program (KSC)

GASP .... Generalized Antisymmetric Potential

GASP .... Generalized Audit Software Package [Computer science] (MHDI)

GASP .... Gevic Arithmetic Simulation Program

GASP .... Global Assimilation and Prognosis System (EERA)

GASP .... Global Atmospheric Sampling Program [NASA]

GASP .... Goldfields Against Serious Pollution [Australia]

GASP .... Graded Assessment in Science Project (AIE)

GASP .... Grand Accelerated Space Platform

GASP .... Graphic Applications Subroutine Package [Computer science] (BUR)

GASP .... Gravity-Assisted Space Probe [NASA]

GASP .... Greater [name of city] Alliance to Stop Pollution

GASP .... Grip, Aim, Stance, and Posture [Golf]

GASP .... Ground Avoidance Simulation Program (MCD)

GASP .... Group Against Smokers' Pollution (EA)

GASP .... Group Against Steroid Prescription (WDAA)

GASP .... Groups Against Sewage Pollution [Australia]

Gaspar .... Gaspar's Small Cause Court Reports [Bengal] [A publication] (DLA)

Gasp de Cald... Gaspar de Calderinis [Deceased, 1390] [Authority cited in pre-1607 legal work] (DSA)

GASPE .... Gated Spin Echo [Nuclear magnetic resonance]

GASPI .... Guidance Attitude Space Position Indicator (MCD)

GASPT .... Generalized Axially-Symmetrical Potential Theory (PDAA)

GASR .... Guided Air-to-Surface Rocket (IAA)

GASS .... American Resources, Inc. [NASDAQ symbol] (SAG)

GASS .... Amer Resources Del [NASDAQ symbol] (TTSB)

GASS .... Generalized Assembly System [Computer science] (IEEE)

GASS .... Geomagnetic Airborne Survey System

GASS .... Gimbal Assembly Storage System

GASS .... Great American Shoe Store [Advertising slogan of Kinney Shoe Corp.]

GASS .... Great Analog Signal Saver

GASS .... Guidance Accuracy Study for SPRINT [Missile] [Army] (AABC)

GASSAR ...... Gilbert Associates [or General Atomic] Standard Safety Analysis Report [Nuclear energy] (NRCH)

GASSER .... Geographic Aerospace Search RADAR

GASSP .... Gas Source Seismic Section Profiler

GASSW .... Amer Res Del Wrrt [NASDAQ symbol] (TTSB)

GAST .... Gastric (WDAA)

GAST .... Gastronomia Espanola [Ministerio de Cultura] [Spain Information service or system] (CRD)

GAST .... Geraeteausgabestelle [Equipment distributing point] [German military - World War II]

GAST .... Globally Averaged Surface Temperature (EERA)

GAST .... Greenwich Apparent Sidereal Time (PDAA)

GASTA .... Gimbal Angle Sequencing Transformation Assembly (KSC)

GASTRN ...... Gastrin [Gastroenterology] (DAVI)

GASTRNTRLGST... Gastroenterologist

GASTRNTRLY... Gastroenterology

Gastro .... Gastroenterology (DAVI)

Gastro .... Gastrointestinal [Gastroenterology] (DAVI)

GASTROC .... Gastrocnemius [Muscle] [Anatomy]

GASU .... Georgia State University, Atlanta, GA [Library symbol Library of Congress] (LCLS)

GASU-D .... Georgia State University, Documents Library, Atlanta, GA [Library symbol] [Library of Congress] (LCLS)

GASU-I .... Georgia State University, Instructional Resource Center, Atlanta, GA [Library symbol] [Library of Congress] (LCLS)

GASU-L .... Georgia State University, Law Library, Atlanta, GA [Library symbol Library of Congress] (LCLS)

GA Sup .... Georgia Reports, Supplement [A publication] (DLA)

GA Supp ...... Georgia Reports, Supplement [A publication] (DLA)

GAS/W .... Gas Weld

GASWOA ..... Great American Station Wagon Owner's Association [Defunct] (EA)

GAt .... Athens Regional Library, Athens, GA [Library symbol Library of Congress] (LCLS)

GAT .... Gabon Air Transport (BUAC)

GAT .... Gate-Associated Transistor (MCD)

GAT .... Gelatin-Agglutination Test [Clinical chemistry]

GAT .... Gemini Agena Target [NASA]

GAT .... General Air Traffic [Europe-Asia]

GAT .... General Air Training

GAT .... General Analysis Technique

GAT .... General Aptitude Test [Psychometrics]

GAT .... General Aviation Trainer

GAT .... General Aviation Transponder

GAT .... Generalized Algebraic Translator [Computer science]

GAT .... Georgetown Automatic Translator [Computer science]

GAT .... Georgia Institute of Technology, Atlanta, GA [Library symbol Library of Congress OCLC symbol] (LCLS)

GAT .... Geriatric Assessment Team [Medicine] (DMAA)

GAT .... Gerontological Apperception Test [Medicine] (DMAA)

GAT .... Gonorrhea Antibody Test [Medicine] (DB)

GAT .... Goodyear Atomic Corp. (KSC)

GAT .... Government Acceptance Test (MCD)

GAT .... Graphic Arts Terminal [Phototypesetting] (NITA)

GAT .... Great American Trials [A publication]

GAT .... Greenwich Apparent Time

GAT .... Ground Attack Tactics [for air delivery of weapons against a ground target]

GAT .... Ground-to-Air Transmitter

GAT .... Ground-to-Air Transmitter Gate (MCD)

GAT .... Group Adjustment Therapy [Psychology] (DAVI)

GAT .... Gulf Air, Inc. [ICAO designator] (FAAC)

GAT .... Guyane Air Transport [Airline] [French Guiana]

GAT₁₀ .... Glutamic Acid-Alanine-Tyrosine [Biopolymer]

GATA .... Glass and Allied Traders' Association [British] (DBA)

GATA .... Glass and Allied Trades Association (BUAC)

GATAC .... General Assessment Tridimensional Analog Computer (IEEE)

GATAE .... Graphic Arts Trade Association Executives [Later, GAAE]

GATaR .... United States Department of Agriculture, Russell Agriculture Research Center, Athens, GA [Library symbol Library of Congress] (LCLS)

GATB .... General Aptitude Test Battery

GATB .... General Avionics Testbed [Military]

GATB .... Graphical Articulted Total Body

GATB .... Tombouctou [Mali] [ICAO location identifier] (ICLI)

GATBY .... General Aptitude Test Battery

GATCO .... Guild of Air Traffic Control Officers [British]

GATD .... Graphic Analysis of Three-Dimensional Data

GATE .... GARP [Global Atmospheric Research Program] Atlantic Tropical Experiment [National Oceanic and Atmospheric Administration]

GATE .... Gateway 2000 [NASDAQ symbol] (TTSB)

GATE .... Gateway 2000, Inc. [NASDAQ symbol] (SAG)

GATE .... General Access Transportation Extention [Telecommunications] (TSSD)

GATE .... Generalized Algebraic Translator Extended [Computer science]

GATE .... General-Purpose Automatic Test Equipment [Army] (RDA)

GATE .... Germany Appropriate Technology Exchange (BUAC)

GATE .... Gifted and Taleted Education Program [California] (EDAC)

GATE .... Graduate Aid to Employment (OICC)

Gate2000 .... Gateway 2000, Inc. [Associated Press] (SAG)

GATEC .... Government Acquisition through Electronic Commerce

GATEOR ...... Gas-Assisted Thermal-Enhanced Oil Recovery

GATERS ...... Ground-Air Telerobotic Systems [Marine Corps] (DOMA)

GATEWAY .... Gateway [Commonly used] (OPSA)

Gateway ..... National Federation of Gateway Clubs (BUAC)

GATEWY ..... Gateway [Commonly used] (OPSA)

GATF .... Graphic Arts Technical Foundation (EA)

GATH .... Gatha [Language, etc.] (ROG)

GAThS .... Theosophical Society, Atlanta, GA [Library symbol Library of Congress] (LCLS)

GAtL .... Athens Regional Library, Athens, GA [Library symbol] [Library of Congress] (LCLS)

GATN .... Taoudenni [Mali] [ICAO location identifier] (ICLI)

GAT-NUMERICAL... General Ability Tests: Numerical (TES)

GATP .... Ground Acceptance [or Article] Test Procedure (MCD)

GAT PERCEPTUAL... General Ability Tests: Perceptual (TES)

GATPRO-CO... German-American Trade Promotion Company (BUAC)

GATR .... Great American Truck Racing (EA)

GATR .... Gross Average Tax Rate

GATR .... Ground-to-Air Transmitting-Receiving [Station]

GATRI .... Gamma Technology Research Irradiator (ADA)

GATS .... General Acceptance Test Software

GATS .... General Agreement on Trade in Services

GATS .... GPS [Global Positioning System] Aided Targeting System [Army] (DOMA)

GATS .... Guidance Acceptance Test Set
GATS .... Tessalit [*Mali*] [*ICAO location identifier*] (ICLI)
GAtT............ Athens Are Technical Institute, Athens, GA [*Library symbol*] [*Library of Congress*] (LCLS)
GATT............ Gate Assisted Turnoff Thyristor [*NASA*] (NASA)
GATT............ General Agreement on Tariffs and Trade [*Organization, and the concept it represents, concerned with adjustment of tariffs among 73 member nations*] [*See also AGTDC*] [*Switzerland*] [*Also, an information service or system*]
GATT............ Ground-to-Air Transmitter Terminal
GATTC .... General Aviation Technical Training Conference
GATTIS .... Georgia Institute of Technology and Technical Information Science (HGAA)
GATTIS .... Georgia Institute of Technology Technical Information Service (NITA)
GATTS .... General Area Time-Based Train Simulator (PDAA)
GATU .... Geophysical Automatic Tracker Unit
GATV .... Gemini Agena Target Vehicle [*NASA*]
GAT VERBAL... General Ability Test: Verbal (TES)
GATWAY ..... Gateway [*Commonly used*] (OPSA)
G AT WT...... Gram Atomic Weight (WDAA)
GATX .... GATX Corp. [*Formerly, General American Transportation Corp.*] [*Associated Press*] (SAG)
GAU .... Atlanta University, Atlanta, GA [*Library symbol Library of Congress*] (LCLS)
GAu .... Augusta-Richmond County Library, Augusta, GA [*Library symbol Library of Congress*] (LCLS)
GAU .... Gauhati [*India*] [*Airport symbol*] (OAG)
Gau............. Gauss [*Unit of magnetic flux density*]
GAU .... Gay Academic Union [*Defunct*] (EA)
gau .... Georgia [*MARC country of publication code Library of Congress*] (LCCP)
GAU .... Geriatric Assessment Unit [*Australia*]
GAU .... Glen Auden Resources Ltd. [*Toronto Stock Exchange symbol*]
GAU .... Glucoamylase Unit [*Of hydrolytic enzyme activity*]
GAU .... Grupos de Accion Unificadora [*Groups for Unified Action*] [*Uruguay*] (PD)
GAU .... Guanine Adenine Uracil [*A triplet of bases coding for the amino acid, aspartic acid*] (EES)
GAU .... Gun Automatic (MCD)
GAuA .... Augusta College, Augusta, GA [*Library symbol Library of Congress*] (LCLS)
GAuACH....... Augusta Chronicle-Herald, Augusta, GA [*Library symbol Library of Congress*] (LCLS)
GAuAH........ Aquinas High School, Augusta, GA [*Library symbol Library of Congress*] (LCLS)
GAuAR........ Academy of Richmond County, Augusta, GA [*Library symbol Library of Congress*] (LCLS)
GAuBH........ Butler High School, Augusta, GA [*Library symbol Library of Congress*] (LCLS)
GAuCL .... Augusta-Richmond County Library, Augusta, GA [*Library symbol*] [*Library of Congress*] (LCLS)
GAUFCC ...... General Assembly of Unitarian and Free Christian Churches (BUAC)
GAUGE........ General Automation Users Group Exchange [*Defunct*] (EA)
GAuJ .... T. W. Josey High School, Augusta, GA [*Library symbol Library of Congress*] (LCLS)
GAUK .... Gamekeepers' Association of the United Kingdom (BI)
Gaul............ Gaulish [*Language*] (BARN)
GAuL .... Lucey C. Laney High School, Augusta, GA [*Library symbol Library of Congress*] (LCLS)
GAuM .... Medical College of Georgia, Augusta, GA [*Library symbol Library of Congress*] (LCLS)
GA (UN)....... General Assembly of the United Nations
GAuP .... Paine College, Augusta, GA [*Library symbol Library of Congress*] (LCLS)
GAuRC .... Richmond County Law Library, Augusta, GA [*Library symbol Library of Congress*] (LCLS)
GAUSA........ Georgian Association in USA (EA)
GAUSS .... Gravity Association for Universal Scientific Study
GAuT .... Augusta Technical Institute, Augusta, GA [*Library symbol*] [*Library of Congress*] (LCLS)
GAuU .... University Hospital, Augusta, GA [*Library symbol Library of Congress*] (LCLS)
GAuV-F .... United States Veterans Administration Hospital, Forest Hills Division, Augusta, GA [*Library symbol Library of Congress*] (LCLS)
GAuV-L .... United States Veterans Administration Hospital, Lenwood Division, Augusta, GA [*Library symbol Library of Congress*] (LCLS)
G/AV .... General Average (WDAA)
GAV .... Geschichte des Alten Vorderasien [*A publication*] (BJA)
GAV .... Glen Avon [*California*] [*Seismograph station code, US Geological Survey*] (SEIS)
GAV .... Granada Aviacion [*Spain ICAO designator*] (FAAC)
GAV .... Gross Annual Value [*Accounting*] (ODBW)
GAV .... Gustavus, AK [*Location identifier FAA*] (FAAL)
GAVA .... Gavotto [*Gavotte*] [*Music*] (ROG)
GAvA .... Guild of Aviation Artists [*British*] (DBA)
GAVA .... United States Veterans Administration Hospital, Atlanta, GA [*Library symbol Library of Congress*]
Gav & H Rev St... Gavin and Hord's Revised Indiana Statutes [*A publication*] (DLA)
GAVRS........ Ground Attitude Vertical Reference System [*Aviation*]
GAW .... Airway Conductance [*The reciprocal of airway resistance*] [*Medicine*] (DAVI)
GAW .... Gambia Airways [*ICAO designator*] (FAAC)
GAW .... Gangaw [*Myanmar*] [*Airport symbol*] (OAG)
GAW .... Gay Authors Workshop (BUAC)

GAW .... Global Atmosphere Watch [*Marine science*] (OSRA)
GAW .... Global Atmospheric Watch (EERA)
GAW .... Gram Atomic Weight [*Chemistry*]
GAW .... Guaranteed Annual Wage
GAW .... Guided Atomic Warhead
GAWA .... Geographical Association of Western Australia
GAWAM .... Great American Wife and Mother [*Slang*]
GAWBS .... Guided Acoustic Wave Brillouin Scattering [*Physics*]
GAWF .... General Arab Women Federation (EA)
GAWF .... Greek Animal Welfare Fund (BUAC)
GAWR .... Gross Axle Weight Rating [*Auto safety*]
GAWRF........ Gross Axle Weight Rating Front [*Auto safety*]
GAWRR........ Gross Axle Weight Rating Rear [*Auto safety*]
GAWS .... German American World Society (EA)
GAWS .... Grandmothers of America in War Service [*World War II*]
GAWS .... Westminster School, Carlyle Fraser Library, Atlanta, GA [*Library symbol*] [*Library of Congress*] (LCLS)
GAWTS .... Genetic Amplification with Transverse Sequencing [*Genetics*]
GAWTS .... Genomic Amplification with Transcript Sequencing [*Genetics*]
GAWU .... General Agricultural Workers' Union [*Kenya*]
GAWU .... Guyana Agricultural Workers Union (BUAC)
GAW/V₁....... Specific Conductance [*Expressed per liter of lung volume at which G is measured*] [*Medicine*] (DAVI)
GAWW .... Woodrow Wilson College of Law, Atlanta, GA [*Library symbol Library of Congress*] (LCLS)
GAX .... Gamba [*Gabon*] [*Airport symbol*] (OAG)
GAX .... GAO [*General Accounting Office*] Seattle Regional Office, Seattle, WA [*OCLC symbol*] (OCLC)
GAY .... Galvasay [*Former USSR Seismograph station code, US Geological Survey Closed*] (SEIS)
GAY .... Gaylord [*Diocesan abbreviation*] [*Michigan*] (TOCD)
GAY .... Government Accumulation Yard
Gayarre........ Gayarre's Annual Reports [*25-28 Louisiana*] [*A publication*] (DLA)
GAYE .... Yelimane [*Mali*] [*ICAO location identifier*] (ICLI)
GAYIG .... Gallium Substituted Yttrium Iron Garnet
Gay (LA)...... Gayarre's Annual Reports [*25-28 Louisiana*] [*A publication*] (DLA)
GaylC.......... Gaylord Container Corp. [*Associated Press*] (SAG)
GaylCn........ Gaylord Container Corp. [*Associated Press*] (SAG)
GaylEnt........ Gaylord Entertainment [*Associated Press*] (SAG)
Gaylord........ Gaylord Companies, Inc. [*Associated Press*] (SAG)
Gaylrd......... Gaylord Companies, Inc. [*Associated Press*] (SAG)
GAZ............. GAO [*General Accounting Office*] Atlanta Regional Office, Atlanta, GA [*OCLC symbol*] (OCLC)
gaz............. Gazeteer (WDAA)
GAZ............. Gazette [*or Gazetteer*]
GAZ............. General Allied Oil [*Vancouver Stock Exchange symbol*]
GAZ............. Gesamtverzeichnis Auslaendischer Zeitschriften [*Cumulative List of Foreign Periodicals*]
GAZ............. Globe, AZ [*Location identifier FAA*] (FAAL)
GAZ............. Gruene Aktion Zukunft [*Green Action for the Future*] [*Germany*] (PPW)
Gaz............. Weekly Law Gazette [*Ohio*] [*A publication*] (DLA)
Gaz & BC Rep... Gazette and Bankrupt Court Reporter [*New York*] [*A publication*] (DLA)
GAZ B .... Gazette of Bankruptcy [*A publication*] (ROG)
Gaz Bank .... Gazette of Bankruptcy [*A publication*] (DLA)
Gaz Bank Dig... Gazzam's Digest of Bankruptcy Decisions [*A publication*] (DLA)
Gaz Bankr .... Gazette of Bankruptcy [*A publication*] (DLA)
Gaz LR .... Gazette Law Reports [*New Zealand*] [*A publication*] (DLA)
Gaz LR (NZ).... New Zealand Gazette Law Reports [*A publication*] (DLA)
Gaz L Soc of Upper Can... Gazette. Law Society of Upper Canada [*A publication*] (DLA)
GAZS .... Gesamtverzeichnis Auslaendischer Zeitschriften und Serien [*Cumulative List of Foreign Periodicals and Serials*]
Gaz Zan EA... Gazette for Zanzibar and East Africa [*A publication*] (ILCA)
GB.............. Air Inter Gabon [*ICAO designator*] (AD)
GB.............. Der Grosse Brockhaus [*A publication*]
GB.............. Gain Bandwidth (DEN)
GB.............. Galaxy Books [*Oxford University Press*]
GB.............. Gall Bladder [*or a patient with an affliction of this organ*] [*Medicine*]
GB.............. Games Behind [*Baseball*]
GB.............. G & B Automated Equipment Ltd. [*Toronto Stock Exchange symbol*]
GB.............. Ganzer Bogen [*Full Bow*] [*Music*]
GB.............. Garanti Bankasi [*Guarantee Bank*] [*Turkey*]
GB.............. Gardner's Books Ltd. [*British*]
GB.............. Gemeinde Berlin (BJA)
GB.............. Gemini B
GB.............. General Background
GB.............. General Board [*Military judicial or investigative body*]
GB.............. General Bronze Corp. (MCD)
GB.............. General Business (MHDI)
GB.............. Generation Breakdown
GB.............. Geschichtsbetrachtung und Geschichtliche Ueberlieferung bei den Vorexilischen Propheten [*A publication*] (BJA)
Gb.............. Gibbsite [*A mineral*]
Gb.............. GigaBIT [*Binary Digit*] [10^9 BITs]
GB.............. Gigabyte [10^9 bytes]
GB.............. Giga Byte (AAEL)
Gb.............. Gigabyte [*Computer science*] (EERA)
Gb.............. Gilbert [*A unit of magnetomotive force*] (CET)
GB.............. Gilbert-Behcet [*Syndrome*] [*Medicine*] (DB)
gb.............. Gilbert Islands [*gn (Gilbert and Ellice Islands) used in records cataloged before October 1978*] [*MARC country of publication code Library of Congress*] (LCCP)

GB.............. Ginzburg's Bible [*New Massoretico-Critical Text of the Hebrew Bible*] [*A publication*] (BJA)
GB.............. Girls Brigade [*British*] (BI)
GB.............. Glass Block (DAC)
GB.............. Glass Bowl
GB.............. Glial Bundle [*Medicine*] (DMAA)
GB.............. Glide Bomb [*Air Force*]
GB.............. Gold Black [*Ultrafine gold metal particles*]
GB.............. Gold Bond [*Bond payable in gold coin*]
GB.............. [*The*] Golden Bough [*A publication*] (OCD)
GB.............. Good-By [*Amateur radio*]
GB.............. Goofball [*Barbiturate pill*]
GB.............. Gougerot-Blum [*Syndrome*] [*Medicine*] (DB)
GB.............. Gould Belt [*Galactic science*]
GB.............. Governing Body
G/B.............. Government Boat
GB.............. Government Bunkers
GB.............. Grab Bar [*Technical drawings*]
GB.............. Grand Bounce [*Suspension or dismissal*] [*Slang*]
GB.............. Grassland Biome [*Ecological biogeographic study*]
GB.............. Great Barrier Airlines [*Airline code*] [*Australia*]
GB.............. Great Books
GB.............. Great Britain [*International automobile identification tag*]
GB.............. Green Bay [*Diocesan abbreviation*] [*Wisconsin*] (TOCD)
GB.............. Green Belt Act [*Town planning*] [*British*]
GB.............. Greenhouse Biennial [*Horticulture*] (ROG)
GB.............. Greenish Blue
GB.............. Greif Bros. (EFIS)
GB.............. Grid Base [*Electronics*] (EECA)
GB.............. Grid Bearing [*Navigation*]
GB.............. Grid Bias (DEN)
GB.............. Griffiths & Bedell's [*System of stud tramways*] [*British*] (ROG)
GB.............. Ground Beacon [*Navigation*] (IAA)
GB.............. Grounded Base
GB.............. Group Buffer (COE)
GB.............. Grundbuch [*Land Register*] [*German*] (ILCA)
GB.............. Guaranteed Bond [*Business term*]
GB.............. Guard Book (DGA)
GB.............. Guardbridge Papers [*Manufacturer*] [*British*]
GB.............. Guardian Bancorp [*AMEX symbol*] (SPSG)
GB.............. Guardianship Board [*Tasmania, Australia*]
GB.............. Guidebook
GB.............. Guild of Bricklayers [*British*] (BI)
GB.............. Guillain-Barre [*Syndrome*] [*Medicine*]
GB.............. Gun Board [*British*]
GB.............. Gunboat [*Naval*]
GB.............. Gun Branch [*Electronics*] (OA)
GB.............. Gun-Bus [*Gun-carrying plane*] [*Air Force British*]
GB.............. Sarin [*Nerve gas*] [*Army symbol*]
GB.............. United Kingdom [*ANSI two-letter standard code*] (CNC)
GBA .... Alderney [*International vehicle registration*] (ODBW)
GBA .... Ganglionic-Blocking Agent [*Medicine*]
GBA .... Gauribidanur Array [*India*] [*Seismograph station code, US Geological Survey*] (SEIS)
GBA .... George Butler Associates, Inc. (EFIS)
GBA .... Georgian Bay Airways [*Canada ICAO designator*] (FAAC)
GBA .... Gingivobuccoaxial [*Dentistry*]
GBA .... Girls' Brigade Australia
GBA .... Give Better Address [*Communications*]
GBA .... Global Alert System [*Vancouver Stock Exchange symbol*]
GBA .... Global Biodiversity Assessment [*Book*] (EERA)
GBA .... Governing Bodies Association [*Organization of school officials*] [*British*]
GBA .... Grammatik des Biblische-Aramaeischen [*A publication*] (BJA)
GBA .... Gross Building Area (ADA)
GBA .... Grundbuchamt [*Land Registry*] [*German*] (ILCA)
GBA .... Gurkha Brigade Associatin (WDAA)
GBaB .... Bainbridge Junior College, Bainbridge, GA [*Library symbol Library of Congress*] (LCLS)
GB & A .... Grosvenor Barber and Associates (IID)
GB & I .... Great Britain and Ireland
GB & W .... Green Bay & Western Railroad Co.
GBAO .... Graham Bond Appreciators Organization [*Defunct*] (EA)
GBAPS .... Governing Bodies Association of Public Schools [*British*]
GBARC .... Great Britain Aeronautical Research Committee (BUAC)
GBaS .... Southwest Georgia Regional Library, Bainbridge, GA [*Library symbol Library of Congress*] (LCLS)
GBASE .... Genome Database of the Mouse (HGEN)
GBAT .... Graduate Business Administration Test (WDAA)
GBAT .... Graduate Business Admission Test
GBB .... General Banner Bearer [*Freemasonry*] (ROG)
GBB .... Guild of British Butlers [*British*] (EAIO)
GBBA .... Glass Bottle Blowers Association of the United States and Canada [*Later, GPPAW*]
GBBHS .... Group B Beta-Hemolytic Streptococcus [*Bacteriology*] (DAVI)
GBBS .... Group B Beta-Hemolytic Streptococcus [*Medicine*] (MEDA)
GBC .... Berry College, Mount Berry, GA [*OCLC symbol*] (OCLC)
GBC .... General Binding Corp.
GBC .... Ghana Broadcasting Corp. (BUAC)
GBC .... Gibraltar Broadcasting Corp. (BUAC)
GBC .... Globe Air Cargo [*Antigua and Barbuda*] [*ICAO designator*] (FAAC)
GBC .... Gold-Braid Chaser [*Refers to a woman who dates only officers*] [*Slang British*] (DSUE)
GBC .... Greenland Base Command
GBC .... Ground-Based Computer

GBC .... Guantanamo Bay [*Cuba*] [*Seismograph station code, US Geological Survey Closed*] (SEIS)
GBCB .... GBC Bancorp [*NASDAQ symbol*] (NQ)
GBC Bc .... GBC Bancorp [*Associated Press*] (SAG)
GBCC .... Beijing Computer Center [*China*] (BUAC)
GBCC .... Great Britain Collectors Club (EA)
GBCI .... Glacier Bancorp, Inc. [*NASDAQ symbol*] (SPSG)
GBCL .... Glacier Bancorp [*NASDAQ symbol*] (TTSB)
GBCO .... Greif Brothers Corp. [*NASDAQ symbol*] (SAG)
GBCOA .... Grief Bros CI'A' [*NASDAQ symbol*] (TTSB)
GBCOB .... Greif Bros 'B' [*NASDAQ symbol*] (TTSB)
GBCRMWU... Grand Bahama Construction, Refinery, and Maintenance Workers' Union (BUAC)
GBCS .... General Board of Church and Society of the United Methodist Church (EA)
GBCS .... Global Casinos [*NASDAQ symbol*] (SAG)
GBCS .... Ground-Based Common Sensor
GBCSCMC.... General Board of Christian Social Concerns of the Methodist Church (EA)
GBCS-L/H .... Ground Based Common Sensor-Light/Heavy [*Military*]
GBCT .... GBC Technologies, Inc. [*NASDAQ symbol*] (SAG)
GBCT .... Guild of British Camera Technicians (DBA)
GBC Tch ...... GBC Technologies, Inc. [*Associated Press*] (SAG)
GBCW .... Governing Body of the Church in Wales (DAS)
GBD .... Gale's Business Directory [*A publication*]
GBD .... Gallbladder Disease [*Gastroenterology*] (DAVI)
GBD .... Gamma Ray Burst Detector [*Instrumentation*]
GBD .... General Board
GBD .... Geometric Data Base (DOMA)
GBD .... Glass-Blowers' Disease [*Medicine*] (DB)
GBD .... Global Burden of Disease
GBD .... Grain Boundary Dislocation
GBD .... Great Bear Development [*Vancouver Stock Exchange symbol*]
GBD .... Great Bend [*Kansas*] [*Airport symbol*] (OAG)
GBDO .... Guild of British Dispensing Opticians (BI)
GBDV .... Gate Breakdown Voltage
GBE .... Dame Grand Cross of the Order of the British Empire (ADA)
GBE .... Gaborone [*Botswana*] [*Airport symbol*] (OAG)
GBE .... Gilt Beveled Edges [*Bookbinding*]
GBE .... Ginkgo Biloba Extract [*Biochemistry*]
GBE .... Goal-Based Evaluation
GBE .... Groupement Belge des Banques d'Epargne [*Banking association*] [*Belgium*] (EY)
GBE .... Grubb & Ellis [*NYSE symbol*] (TTSB)
GBE .... Grubb & Ellis Co. [*NYSE symbol*] (SPSG)
GBE .... Knight Grand Cross of the [*Order of the*] British Empire
GBERL .... Gulf Breeze Environmental Research Laboratory [*Environmental Protection Agency*] (MSC)
GBEU .... Grand Bahama Entertainers' Union (BUAC)
GBF .... Gay Black Female [*Classified advertising*] (CDAI)
GBF .... Geographic Base File [*Civil Defense*]
GBF .... Grand Ballon [*France*] [*Seismograph station code, US Geological Survey Closed*] (SEIS)
GBF .... Great Bear Foundation (EA)
GBF .... Great Books Foundation (EA)
GBF .... Ground-Based Field
GBFC .... GB Foods [*NASDAQ symbol*] (TTSB)
GBFC .... GB Foods Corp. [*NASDAQ symbol*] (SAG)
GBF/DIME .... Geographic Base File/Dual Independent Map Encoding [*BTS*] (TAG)
GB Fds........ GB Foods [*Associated Press*] (SAG)
GBFE .... Golden Books Family Ent [*NASDAQ symbol*] (TTSB)
GBFE .... Golden Books Family Entertainment [*NASDAQ symbol*] [*Formerly, Western Publishing*] (SG)
GBFE .... Golden Books Family Entertainment, Inc. [*NASDAQ symbol*] (SAG)
GBFE .... Guild of British Film Editors (BUAC)
GBFEL.......... Ground Based Free Electron LASER Proposal
GBG .... Galesburg [*Illinois*] [*Airport symbol*] (OAG)
GBG .... Garbage (MSA)
GBG .... Glycine-Rich Beta-Globulin [*Immunology*]
GBG .... Gonadal Steroid-Binding Globulin [*Medicine*] (DMAA)
GBG .... Gordon Junior College, Barnesville, GA [*Library symbol*] [*Library of Congress*] (LCLS)
GBG .... Governor's Bodyguard [*British military*] (DMA)
GBG .... Greensboro [*Georgia*] [*Seismograph station code, US Geological Survey*] (SEIS)
GBG .... Greensburg [*Diocesan abbreviation*] [*Pennsylvania*] (TOCD)
GBG .... Guernsey [*International vehicle registration*] (ODBW)
GBGSA........ Governing Body of Girls' Schools Association [*British*]
GBH .... Galbraith Lake, AK [*Location identifier FAA*] (FAAL)
GBH .... Gamma Benzene Hexachloride [*Also, BHC, HCH*] [*Insecticide*]
GBH .... Garbell Holdings Ltd. [*Toronto Stock Exchange symbol*]
GBH .... Gas Bath Heater [*Classified advertising*] (ADA)
GBH .... Girth Breast Height (WGA)
gbh .... Grams per Brake Horsepower Hour (COE)
GBH .... Graphite-Benzalkonium-Heparin [*Medicine*] (MAE)
GBH .... Great British Holiday [*Television movie*]
GBH .... Grievous Body Harm
GBH .... Group Busy Hour [*Telecommunications*] (TEL)
GBHA .... Glyoxal Bis(o-hydroxyanil) [*An indicator*] [*Chemistry*]
GBHP .... Gross Brake Horsepower (MCD)
GBHRG........ Ground-Based Hypervelocity Rail Gun [*Military*] (SDI)
GBHRS........ Granite Belt Horticultural Research Station [*Australia*]
GBI.............. Blufete Industrial S.A. ADS [*NYSE symbol*] (TTSB)
GBI.............. Bufete Industrial SA [*NYSE symbol*] (SPSG)
GBI.............. Buffalo, NY [*Location identifier FAA*] (FAAL)

GBI............ Gabriel Resources, Inc. [*Vancouver Stock Exchange symbol*]
GBI............ Gained by Inventory (DNAB)
GBI............ Gesellschaft fuer Betriebswirtschaftliche Information mbH [*Society for Business Information*] [*Germany Database producer*]
GBI............ Global Brain Ischemia
GBI............ Globulin-Binding Insulin [*Medicine*] (DMAA)
GBI............ Globulin-Bound Insulin [*Medicine*] (STED)
GBI............ Governesses Benevolent Institute [*British*] (AIE)
GBI............ Grace Bible Institute [*Nebraska*]
GBI............ Grand Bahama Island (KSC)
GBI............ Gridlays Bank International Zambia Ltd.
GBI............ Ground Backup Instrument (MUGU)
GBI............ Ground-Based Interceptor [*Army*] (DOMA)
GBI............ Guanidinebenzimidazole [*Biochemistry*]
GBIA.......... Guthrie Bacterial Inhibition Assay [*Medicine*] (MAE)
GBIGAS........ Institute of Geochemistry, Guangzhou Branch, Academia Sinica [*China*] (BUAC)
GBII........... Ground-Based Infrared Instrumentation
GBIIS......... Ground-Based Infrared Instrumentation System
GBiP.......... German Books in Print [*A publication*]
GBIT.......... Gigabit (MHDB)
GBIT.......... Global Intellicom [*NASDAQ symbol*] (TTSB)
GBIT.......... Global Intellicom, Inc. [*NASDAQ symbol*] (SAG)
GBIU.......... Geoballistic Input Unit
GBIX.......... Globix Corp. [*NASDAQ symbol*] [*Formerly, Bell Tech Group Ltd.*]
GBI-X......... Ground-Based Interceptor-Experiment [*US Army Strategic Defense Command*] (RDA)
GBIZ.......... Grow Biz International [*NASDAQ symbol*] (TTSB)
GBIZ.......... Grow Biz International, Inc. [*NASDAQ symbol*] (SAG)
GBJ........... Glass Bell Jar
GBJ........... Jersey [*Great Britain*]
GBJ........... Marie Galante [*French Antilles*] [*Airport symbol*] (OAG)
GBK........... Gbangbatok [*Sierra Leone*] [*Airport symbol*] (OAG)
GBL........... Gable Mountain [*Washington*] [*Seismograph station code, US Geological Survey*] (SEIS)
GBL........... Games behind Leader [*Baseball*]
GBL........... Gamma Biologicals [*AMEX symbol*] (TTSB)
GBL........... Gamma Biologicals, Inc. [*AMEX symbol*] (SPSG)
GBL........... Gamma-Butyrolactone [*Organic chemistry*]
GBL........... GB Airways Ltd. [*British ICAO designator*] (FAAC)
GBL........... General Bearing Line [*Navy*] (NVT)
GBL........... Gesetzblatt [*Gazette*] [*German*] (DLA)
GBL........... Glomerular Basal Lamina [*Medicine*] (DAVI)
GBL........... Goldenbell Resources, Inc. [*Toronto Stock Exchange symbol Vancouver Stock Exchange symbol*]
GBL........... Goulburn Island [*Australia Airport symbol Obsolete*] (OAG)
GBL........... Government Bill of Lading
GBL........... Ground-Based LASER (MCD)
GBL........... Guide to Baseball Literature [*A publication*]
GBLADING ... Government Bill of Lading
GBLE.......... Green Barley Leaf Extract (TAD)
GBLIC........ Gaussian Band Limited Channel (NITA)
GBLOC........ Government Bill of Lading Office Code (AFIT)
GBLV.......... Grapevine Bulgarian Latent Virus [*Plant pathology*]
GBM........... Gain Band Merit
GBM........... Galilean Baptist Mission (EA)
GBM........... Gay Black Male [*Classified advertising*] (CDAI)
GBM........... Gesellschaft Fuer Biochemie Und Molekularbiologie [*Germany*]
GBM........... Gibraltar Mines Ltd. [*Toronto Stock Exchange symbol Vancouver Stock Exchange symbol*]
GBM........... Glass-Bonded Mica
GBM........... Glomerular Basement Membrane [*Medicine*] (STED)
GBM........... Glycerine Ball Memory
GBM........... Granite Butte [*Montana*] [*Seismograph station code, US Geological Survey Closed*] (SEIS)
GBM........... Grape Berry Moth
GBM........... Greater Britain Movement [*British*]
GBM........... Ground-Based Measurement (MCD)
GBM........... Gulf Building Materials (BUAC)
GBM........... Isle Of Man (Great Britain)
GBMA .... Garden Building Manufacturers Association (BUAC)
GBMA .... Golf Ball Manufacturers Association (EA)
GBMA .... Great Britain Ministry of Aviation
GBMC........ Golf Ball Manufacturers' Conference [*British*] (BI)
GBMC........ Grain Bin Manufacturers Council [*Later, GEMC*] (EA)
GBMD........ Global Ballistic Missile Defense
GBMI......... Ground-Based Midcourse Interceptor [*Military*] (SDI)
GBMI......... Guilty-but-Mentally-Ill [*Legal term*]
GBMP........ General Benchmark Program (MHDB)
GBMPC....... Great Britain Map Postcard Club (BUAC)
GBM-rAb..... Glomerular Basement Membrane-Reactive Antibodies [*Immunology*]
GBN.......... Gila Bend, AZ [*Location identifier FAA*] (FAAL)
GBN.......... Golden Band Resources [*Vancouver Stock Exchange symbol*]
GBND........ General Binding Corp. [*NASDAQ symbol*] (NQ)
GBND........ Genl Binding [*NASDAQ symbol*] (TTSB)
GBNE........ Guild of British Newspapers Editors (BI)
GBO.......... Gissel Bargaining Order [*Labor relations*] (WYGK)
GBO.......... Goods in Bad Order
GBO.......... Ogooue Air Cargo [*Gabon*] [*ICAO designator*] (FAAC)
GBOA........ Gale Book of Averages [*A publication*]
GboSidek.... Grupo Sidek SA de CV [*Associated Press*] (SAG)
GBOT........ Garden Botanika [*NASDAQ symbol*] (TTSB)
GBowdC...... Bowdon College, Bowdon, GA [*Library symbol Library of Congress Obsolete*] (LCLS)
GBP .... Gables Residential Trust [*NYSE symbol*] (SPSG)

GBP .... Gain-Bandwidth Product
GBP .... Galactose-Binding Protein [*Biochemistry*]
GBP .... Gas Bearing Part
GBP .... Gastric Bypass [*Surgery*]
GBP .... Gated Blood Pool [*Hematology*] (DMAA)
GBP .... Gay Bereavement Project (BUAC)
GBP .... Glutamate-Binding Protein [*Biochemistry*]
GBP .... Glycophorin Binding Protein [*Biochemistry*]
GBP .... Great Britain Pound [*Banking*]
GBP .... Great British Public
GBP .... Guanylate-Binding Protein [*Biochemistry*]
GBP .... Guinea-Bissau Peso [*Monetary unit*]
GBPA .... Gettysburg Battlefield Preservation Association [*Defunct*] (EA)
GBPC .... Gold Bondholders Protective Council (EA)
GBPR .... Grain-Burning Pattern Regulation (MCD)
GBPS .... Gallbladder Pigment Stones [*Medicine*] (STED)
GBPS .... Gemini B Procedures Simulator (MCD)
GBPS .... GigaBIT [*Binary Digits*] per Second [*Transmission rate*] [*Computer science*] (TSSD)
Gbps .... Gigabits per Second (EERA)
GBPW .... Great Bay Power [*NASDAQ symbol*] (TTSB)
GBPW .... Great Bay Power Corp. [*NASDAQ symbol*] (SAG)
GBq .... Gigabecquerel (NUCP)
GBR .... Gas-Cooled Breeder Reactor [*Nuclear energy*] (NRCH)
GBR .... Give Better Reference [*Communications*]
GBR .... Glass Bead Rating (MCD)
GBR .... Glutathione Bicarbonate Ringer [*Solution mixture*]
GBR .... Golden Bear Resources Ltd. [*Vancouver Stock Exchange symbol*]
GBR .... Grain Boundary Relaxation
GBR .... Great Barrier Reef (EERA)
GBR .... Great Barrington, MA [*Location identifier FAA*] (FAAL)
GBR .... Greenbriar Corp. [*AMEX symbol*] (SAG)
GBR .... Ground-Based RADAR [*Military*]
GBR .... Ground-Based Radiometer
GBR .... Gun, Bomb, and Rocket
GBR .... Rader Aviation, Inc. [*ICAO designator*] (FAAC)
GBR .... United Kingdom [*ANSI three-letter standard code*] (CNC)
GBRA .... Gas Breeder Reactor Association (BUAC)
GBRCC........ Great Barrier Reef Consultative Committee [*Australia*]
GBRF .... Great Britain Racquetball Federation (BUAC)
GBRMP .... Great Barrier Reef Marine Park [*Region*] (EERA)
GBRMPA...... Great Barrier Reef Marine Park Authority [*Commonwealth*] (EERA)
GBRP .... General Bending Response Program [*Computer*] [*Navy*]
GBR-P........ Ground-Based RADAR Prototype [*Military*]
GBR-PO....... Ground-Based RADAR Project Office [*Military*] (RDA)
GBru .... Brunswick Regional Library, Brunswick, GA [*Library symbol Library of Congress*] (LCLS)
GBruJC....... Brunswick Junior College, Brunswick, GA [*Library symbol Library of Congress*] (LCLS)
GBruM .... MAP International, Brunswick, GA [*Library symbol*] [*Library of Congress*] (LCLS)
GBR-X........ Ground Based RADAR-Experimental [*Army*]
GBS .... British Guillain Barre Syndrome Support Group (BUAC)
GBS .... Gall Bladder Series [*Radiography*]
GBS .... Gallbladder Stone [*Medicine*]
GBS .... Gas Bearing System (KSC)
GBS .... Gas Bioassay System [*NASA*]
GBS .... Gastric Bypass Surgery (STED)
GBS .... General Business System (MHDW)
GBS .... George Bernard Shaw [*Irish-born playwright, 1856-1950*]
GBS .... GigaBIT [*Binary Digit*] per Second [*Computer science*] (IAA)
GBS .... Glycerine-Buffered Saline [*Medicine*] (STED)
GBS .... Glycine-Buffered Saline [*Microbiology*]
GBS .... Government Bureau of Standards
GBS .... Grain Boundary Segregation [*Metallurgy*]
GBS .... Granular Boundary Segregation [*Petrology*]
GBS .... Great Big Star [*in the movies*]
GBS .... Ground-Based Scanner
GBS .... Ground Based Sensor [*Radar*]
GBS .... Ground-Based Software (MCD)
GBS .... Ground Beacon System (MCD)
GBS .... Group B Streptococci [*Medicine*]
GBS .... Guidance Test Battery for Secondary Pupils (TES)
GBS .... Guillain-Barre Syndrome [*Medicine*]
GBSAS .... Ground-Based Scanning Antenna System (IAA)
GBSCA .... Greater Blouse and Skirt Contractors Association [*Later, GBSUA*] (EA)
GBSE .... Gibbs Construction [*NASDAQ symbol*] (TTSB)
GBSE .... Gibbs Construction, Inc. [*NASDAQ symbol*] (SAG)
GBSEW .... Gibbs Construction Wrrt [*NASDAQ symbol*] (TTSB)
GBSFI .... Guillain-Barre Syndrome Foundation International (EA)
GBSM .... Graduate of the Birmingham School of Music [*British*] (DBQ)
GBSM .... Guild of Better Shoe Manufacturers
GBSR .... Graphite-Moderated Boiling and Superheating Reactor
GBSS .... Gey's Balanced Salt Solution [*Medium*] [*Cell culture*]
GBSS .... Governesses' Benevolent Society of Scotland (BUAC)
GBSS .... Grey's Balanced Saline Solution [*Medicine*] (STED)
GBSS .... Guillain-Barre-Strohl Syndrome [*Medicine*] (STED)
GBSSG .... Guillain-Barre Syndrome Support Group [*Later, GBSFI*] (EA)
GBSSGI ...... Guillain-Barre Syndrome Support Group International [*Later, GBSFI*] (EA)
GBST .... Global Blood Safety Initiative [*Switzerland*] (BUAC)
GBST .... Grassi Block Substitution Test [*Psychology*]
GBSUA........ Greater Blouse, Skirt, and Undergarment Association (EA)

GBSVC	General Broadcast Signaling Virtual Channel [*Telecommunications*] (ACRL)
GBT	Der Babylonische Talmud [*Goldschmidt*] [*A publication*] (BJA)
GBT	Generalized Burst Trapping
GBT	Global Ballistic Transport [*Military*]
GBT	Gold Belt Air Transport, Inc. [*Canada ICAO designator*] (FAAC)
GBT	Graded Base Transistor
GBT	Great Bustard Trust [*An association*] (EA)
GBT	Ground-Based Telemetry
GBT	Gunboat
GBTA	Guild of Business Travel Agents [*British*] (DBA)
GBTBC	Graham Brothers Truck and Bus Club (EA)
GBTC	Generalized Burst Trapping Code (PDAA)
GBTCU	Grand Bahama Telephone and Telecommunications Union (BUAC)
GBTI	Gray-Body Temperature Index [*for thermal ecology of lizards*]
GBTS	General Banking Terminal System (MHDW)
GBTS	Gold Beaters' Trade Society [*A union*] [*British*]
GBTSF	Great Britain Target Shooting Federation (BUAC)
GBTV	Granite Broadcasting Corp. [*NASDAQ symbol*] (SPSG)
GBTVK	Granite Broadcasting [*NASDAQ symbol*] (TTSB)
GBTVP	Granite Brdcst $1.9375 Cv Pfd [*NASDAQ symbol*] (TTSB)
GBU	Geschichtsbetrachtung und Geschichtliche Ueberlieferung bei den Vorexilischen Propheten [*A publication*] (BJA)
GBU	Glide Bomb Unit [*Air Force*] (MCD)
GBU	Ground Backup (DNAB)
GBU	Groupes Bibliques Universitaires [*University Biblical Groups*] [*Canada*]
GBU	Guided Bomb Unit (MCD)
GBU	Khasm el Girba [*Sudan*] [*Airport symbol*] (AD)
GBU	Transports Aeriens de la Guinee-Bissau [*Guinea-Bissau*] [*ICAO designator*] (FAAC)
GBUR	Gardenburger, Inc. [*NASDAQ symbol*] [*Formerly, Wholesome & Hearty Foods*] (SG)
GBV	Gate Breakdown Voltage
GBV	Gibb River [*Australia Airport symbol Obsolete*] (OAG)
GBV	Globe Ball Valve
GBV	Green Bank [*West Virginia*] [*Seismograph station code, US Geological Survey*] (SEIS)
GBviz	Gall Bladder Visualization [*Medicine*]
GBW	Gain Bandwidth
GBW	Good Bears of the World (EA)
GBW	Green Bay & Western Railroad Co. [*AAR code*]
GBW	Guild of Book Workers (EA)
GBWA	Georgia Beer Wholesalers Association (SRA)
GBX	GBX Resources [*Vancouver Stock Exchange symbol*]
GBX	Ginkgo Biloba Extract [*Biochemistry*]
GBX	[*The*] Greenbrier Companies, Inc. [*NYSE symbol*] (SAG)
GBX	Greenbrier Cos. [*NYSE symbol*] (TTSB)
GBX	Ground Branch Exchange (DNAB)
GBY	Giant Bay Resources Ltd. [*Toronto Stock Exchange symbol*]
G-B-Y	God Bless You
GBY	Greate Bay Casino [*AMEX symbol*] (SAG)
GBYD	Banjul [*Gambia*] [*ICAO location identifier*] (ICLI)
G by Pos	Games by Position [*Baseball*]
GBZ	Gibraltar
GBZ	Glass-Bonded Zeolite
GBZ	Great Barrier [*New Zealand*] [*Seismograph station code, US Geological Survey*] (SEIS)
GBZ	Great Barrier Island [*Australia Airport symbol*] (OAG)
GBZ	Tampa, FL [*Location identifier FAA*] (FAAL)
GC	Gain Control
GC	Galactic Center
GC	Galactocerebroside [*Biochemistry*]
GC	Galvanized Corrugated [*Metal industry*]
GC	Game Conservancy [*British*]
GC	Game Conservancy Trust (BUAC)
GC	Ganglion Cell [*Medicine*]
GC	Garbage Collection [*Slang Computer science*]
GC	Garrison Co. [*British military*] (DMA)
GC	Gas Chromatograph [*or Chromatography*]
GC	Gas Council [*British*]
G/C	Gas-to-Cloth [*Ratio*] (FFDE)
GC	Gastrocnemius [*A muscle*]
GC	Gavel Clubs (EA)
GC	Geiger-Mueller Counter [*Nucleonics*] (IAA)
GC	Gel Chromatography
GC	General Cable (IAA)
GC	General Cinema Theatres, Inc. (EFIS)
GC	General Circular
GC	General Code [*A publication*] (DLA)
GC	General Condition [*Medicine*]
GC	General Contractor [*Technical drawings*]
GC	General Control
GC	General Council (IAA)
GC	General Counsel
GC	General Cover [*Insurance*]
GC	General Cueing
GC	Generative Cell [*Botany*]
GC	Generic Code (AFM)
GC	Geneva Convention (COE)
GC	Geneva Convention Relative to Protection of Civilian Persons in Time of War [*Army*] (AABC)
GC	Gentleman Cadet [*British*]
GC	Geopolitical Code [*Military*] (AFIT)
GC	George Cross [*British*]
GC	Geriatric Care
GC	Geriatric Chair (DAVI)
GC	Germinal Center [*Immunochemistry*]
Gc	Gigacycle [*Measurement*]
GC	Gigacycles (NAKS)
GC	Gimbal Case (KSC)
GC	Gin Cocktail [*Slang*]
GC	Girls' College (ADA)
GC	Glass Capillary
GC	Glassy Carbon
GC	Gliding Club [*British*] (ADA)
GC	Global Control (IAA)
GC	Globular Cluster [*Astrophysics*]
GC	Glucocorticoid [*Endocrinology*]
GC	Gnome Club (EA)
GC	Gold Coast [*Later, Ghana*] (ROG)
GC	Gold Corp. [*Western Australia*] [*Commercial firm*]
GC	Golden Companions [*An association*] (EA)
GC	Goldsmith's College [*London, England*]
GC	Golf Club
GC	Gonococcal [*Clinical chemistry*]
GC	Gonorrhea Case [*Medical slang*]
gc	Good Condition [*Doll collecting*]
GC	Good Conduct [*Military decoration*]
GC	Gougerot-Carteaud [*Syndrome*] [*Medicine*] (DB)
GC	Governing Council (EERA)
GC	Government Communications (TEL)
GC	Government Contractor
GC	Government Contribution
GC	Governors' Conference
Gc	Gradational, Calcareous [*Soil*]
GC	Graham Center [*An association*] (EA)
GC	Graham County Railroad Co. [*AAR code*]
GC	Grain Count [*Measurement of cell labeling*]
GC	Grain Cubic (DS)
G-C	Gram-Negative Cocci [*Clinical chemistry*] (DAVI)
G+C	Gram-Positive Cocci [*Clinical chemistry*] (DAVI)
GC	GranCare, Inc. [*NYSE symbol*] (SPSG)
GC	Grand Canyon [*Arizona*]
GC	Grand Chancellor
GC	Grand Chaplain
GC	Grand Chapter
GC	Grand Commander
GC	Grand Conductor
GC	Grand Council [*Freemasonry*] (ROG)
GC	Grand Cross
GC	Grantsmanship Center (EA)
GC	Granular Cast [*Medicine*]
GC	Granular Cyst [*Medicine*] (MAE)
GC	Granulocyte Cytotoxic [*Hematology*]
GC	Granulomatous Colitis [*Medicine*] (DB)
GC	Granulosa Cells [*Cytology*]
GC	Graphics Conferencing (MCD)
GC	Gravimetric Calibrator (AAEL)
GC	Grazing Capacity [*Agriculture*]
GC	Great Central Railway [*British*] (ROG)
GC	Great Churchmen [*A publication*]
GC	Great Circle
GC	Greek Church (ROG)
GC	Green Currency [*EEC*]
GC	Greenhouse Corps [*Australia*]
GC	Greenland Cruiser
GC	Grid Course [*Navigation*]
GC	Grolier Club (EA)
GC	Ground Control (AFM)
GC	Grounded Collector
GC	Group Captain
GC	Group Code [*Dialog*] [*Searchable field*] [*Information service or system*] (NITA)
GC	Group Cohesiveness [*Psychological testing*]
GC	Groupe de Chasse [*French aircraft fighter unit*] [*World War II*]
Gc	Group-Specific Component [*A serum group*]
GC	Guanine, Cytosine [*Type*] [*Biochemistry*]
GC	Guanylcyclase (DB)
GC	Guidance Computer
GC	Guidance Control [*NASA*] (NASA)
GC	Gun Camera (MCD)
GC	Gun Capital (DNAB)
GC	Gun Captain
GC	Gun Carriage
GC	Gun Control
GC	Gyro Compass
GC	Gyrocompassing [*Aerospace*] (NAKS)
GC	Gyro Control
GC	Lina-Congo [*ICAO designator*] (AD)
GCA	Gain Control Amplifier
GCA	Garden Centers of America (EA)
GCA	Garden Centre Association (BUAC)
GCA	Garden Centres of Australia
GCA	Garden Club of America (EA)
GCA	Garden Club of Australia
GCA	Gasket Cutters' Association (BUAC)
GCA	Gastric Cancer Area [*Medicine*] (DMAA)
GCA	Gauge Control Analyzer
GCA	Genealogy Club of America [*Defunct*] (EA)

GCA	General Claim Agent
GCA	General Combining Ability
GCA	General Control Approach
GCA	Geophysics Corp. of America
GCA	Giant Cell Arteritis [*Medicine*]
GCA	Girls Clubs of America [*Later, GI*] (EA)
GCA	Glass Crafts of America [*Defunct*] (EA)
GCA	Glen Canyon [*Arizona*] [*Seismograph station code, US Geological Survey*] (SEIS)
GCA	Global Citizens Association [*Quebec, PQ*] (EAIO)
GCA	Gold Clause Agreement [*Shipping*] (DS)
GCA	Golf Course Association (EA)
GCA	Government Contract Advisor [*CD-ROM*] [*Published by Clark Boardman*] (AAGC)
GCA	Grains Council of Australia (EERA)
GCA	Graphic Communications Association (EA)
GCA	Great China Airlines [*Taiwan*] [*ICAO designator*] (FAAC)
GCA	Green Coffee Association of New York City (EA)
GCA	Greeting Card Association (EA)
GCA	Greyhound Club of America (EA)
GCA	Ground Communication Activity (IAA)
GCA	Ground-Controlled Aircraft (AFM)
GCA	Ground-Controlled Apparatus [*RADAR*]
GCA	Ground-Controlled Approach [*for lateral and vertical guidance of landing aircraft through use of ground RADAR and radio communications*]
GCA	Grounded Cathode Amplifier
GCA	Group Capacity Analysis [*or Assessment*]
GCA	Guacamayas [*Colombia*] [*Airport symbol*] (OAG)
GCA	Guanine Cytosine Adenine [*A triplet of bases coding for the amino acid, alanine*] (EES)
GCA	Guidance and Control Assembly (NG)
GCA	Guidance Control and Adapter Section (MCD)
GCA	Gun Control Act [*1968*]
GCA	Gun Control Australia
GCA	Gunite Contractors Association (EA)
GCA	Gyro Control Assembly
GCAA	Golf Coaches Association of America (EA)
GCAA	Guidance, Control, and Airframe (IAA)
GCABY	General Cable PLC [*NASDAQ symbol*] (SAG)
GCABY	Genl Cable plc.ADS [*NASDAQ symbol*] (TTSB)
GCAC	Gulf Coast Athletic Conference (PSS)
GCA-CTS	Ground-Controlled Approach - Controller Training System (MCD)
GCAD	Granite City Army Depot (AABC)
GCai	Roddenbery Memorial Library, Cairo, GA [*Library symbol Library of Congress*] (LCLS)
GCAL	Gram Calorie
g-cal	Gram-Calorie (IDOE)
GCAM	Gaming Corp. of America [*NASDAQ symbol*] (SAG)
GCAM	Groupement de la Caisse des Depots Automatisation pour le Management [*Bank Group for Automation in Management*] [*Information service or system*] (IID)
GC & A	Guidance, Control, and Airframe
GC & O	Guidance, Control, and Ordnance
GC & SF	Gulf, Colorado & Santa Fe Railway Co.
GCanS	Sequoyah Regional Library, Canton, GA [*Library symbol Library of Congress*] (LCLS)
GCA of NO	Green Coffee Association of New Orleans (EA)
GCAP	Generalized Circuit Analysis Program (IEEE)
GCAP	Germ-Cell Alkaline Phosphatase (DMAA)
GCAPEF	Grace Contrino Abrams Peace Education Foundation (EA)
G/Capt	Group Captain [*British military*] (DMA)
GCarrS	Southwire Co., Carrollton, GA [*Library symbol Library of Congress*] (LCLS)
GCarrWG	West Georgia College, Carrollton, GA [*Library symbol Library of Congress*] (LCLS)
GCAS	Ground Collision Avoidance System [*Army*]
GCAT	Guidance and Control Analysis Team [*Space Flight Operations, NASA*]
GCatO	Group Catering Officer [*British military*] (DMA)
GCAU	Grain-Consuming Animal Unit [*Agricultural Statistics*] (BARN)
GCAutrey	Grupo Casa Autrey [*Associated Press*] (SAG)
GCB	Dame Grand Cross of the Order of the Bath [*British*] (ADA)
GCB	General Circuit Breaker (MHDI)
GCB	Generator Control Breaker
GCB	German Convention Bureau (EA)
GCB	Ghana Commercial Bank
GCB	Ghanian Cocoa Butter
GCB	Gonococcal Base [*Broth*] [*Growth medium*]
GCB	Good Conduct Badge [*British*]
GCB	Graphitized Carbon Black
GCB	Gravity Cutback (NRCH)
GCB	Great-Circle Bearing [*Navigation*] (IAA)
GCB	Greyhound Consultative Body (BUAC)
GCB	Guernsey Cattle Breeders' Association (BUAC)
GCB	Guthrie, C. B., Tariff Bureau Inc., Washington DC [*STAC*]
GCB	Knight Grand Cross of the [*Order of the*] Bath [*British*]
GCB	Lignes Nationales Aeriennes - Linacongo [*Congo*] [*ICAO designator*] (FAAC)
GCBA	Golf Course Builders of America (EA)
GCBAA	Golf Course Builders Association of America (NTPA)
GCBC	Goucher College Babylonian Collection (BJA)
GCBK	Great Country Bank [*NASDAQ symbol*] (NQ)
GCBM	Gas Chromatography in Biology and Medicine [*British*]
GCBR	Gas-Cooled Breeder Reactor [*Nuclear energy*]

GCBS	General Council of British Shipping
GCBS	Ground-Control Bombing System (NG)
GCBW	General Committee for Bahrain Workers (BUAC)
GCBW	Global Cooperation for a Better World [*Australia*]
GCC	Coca-Cola Co., Business Information, Atlanta, GA [*OCLC symbol*] (OCLC)
GCC	Game Conservancy Council (BUAC)
GCC	Garden Cat Club (EA)
GCC	Gas Consumers Council (BUAC)
GCC	General Cinema Corp. [*Chestnut Hill, MA*]
GCC	General Commission on Chaplains and Armed Forces Personnel [*Later, NCMAF*] (EA)
GCC	Generic Cell Controller (AAEL)
GCC	Georgian Court College [*Lakewood, NJ*]
GCC	Giannini Controls Corp. (AAG)
GCC	Gillette [*Wyoming*] [*Airport symbol*] (OAG)
GCC	Girton College [*Cambridge University*] (DAS)
GCC	Global Climate Coalition [*A US lobby group*]
GCC	Global Climatic Change [*Marine science*] (OSRA)
GCC	Global Competitiveness Council [*Defunct*] (EA)
GCC	Glove Collector Club (EA)
GCC	Goddard Communications Center [*NASA*]
GCC	Goddard Computing Center [*NASA*]
GCC	Goebel Collectors' Club [*Later, MIHC*] (EA)
GCC	Gogebic Community College [*Ironwood, MI*]
GCC	Golden Concord Mining [*Vancouver Stock Exchange symbol*]
GCC	Gonville and Caius College [*Cambridge University*] (ROG)
GCC	Good Counsel College [*New York*]
GCC	Government Contract Committee [*Later, OFCCP*] [*Department of Labor*]
GCC	Graduated Combat Capability [*Military*]
GCC	Grand Canyon College [*Phoenix, AZ*]
GCC	Granite Creek [*California*] [*Seismograph station code, US Geological Survey*] (SEIS)
GCC	Graphic Control Center [*Touch-activated CRT display*]
GCC	Great Council of Chiefs [*Fiji*] (BUAC)
GCC	Greenfield Community College [*Massachusetts*]
GCC	Grid Cooperating Centre (EERA)
GCC	Ground Calcium Carbonate [*Inorganic chemistry*]
GCC	Ground Communications Controller
GCC	Ground Communications Coordinator [*NASA*] (NASA)
GCC	Ground Computer Controller
GCC	Ground-Control Center
GCC	Group Change Control
GCC	Group Control Center (MCD)
GCC	Grove City College [*Pennsylvania*]
GCC	Guanine Cytosine Cytosine [*A triplet of bases coding for the amino acid, alanine*] (EES)
GCC	Guidance and Control Computer
GCC	Guidance Checkout Computer
GCC	Gulf Cooperation Council [*Consists of Saudi Arabia, Bahrain, Kuwait, Oman, Qatar, and the United Arab Emirates*]
GCC	Gulf Cooperative Council (EERA)
GCC	Gun Control Console [*Military*] (CAAL)
GCCA	Gambling Chip Collectors Association (EA)
GCCA	G-Cat Class Association (EA)
GCCA	Graphic Communications Computer Association [*Printing Industries of America*] [*Later, GCA*]
GCCA	Greater Clothing Contractors Association (EA)
GCCA	Greeting Card and Calendar Association [*British*]
GCCC	Canarias [*Canary Islands*] [*ICAO location identifier*] (ICLI)
GCCC	General Council of County Councils [*Eire*] (BUAC)
GCCC	Ground Control Computer Center [*Aerospace*] (NAKS)
GCCC	Ground-Control Computer Center (MCD)
GCCEA	General Committee of the Comite Europeen des Assurances [*France*] (EAIO)
GCCF	Governing Council of the Cat Fancy [*British*] (BI)
GCCG	German Colonies Collectors Group (EA)
GCCIP	Global Climate Change Information Programme (BUAC)
GCCNI	General Consumer Council for Northern Ireland (BUAC)
GCCNPIP	General Conference Committee of the National Poultry Improvement Plan [*Department of Agriculture*] (EGAO)
GCCO	Granite Construction [*NASDAQ symbol*] (TTSB)
GCCO	Granite Construction, Inc. [*NASDAQ symbol*] (SAG)
GCCO	Ground-Control Checkout (MCD)
GC Cos	GC Companies [*Associated Press*] (SAG)
GCCS	Geneva Convention on the Continental Shelf (NOAA)
GCCS	Global Command and Control System
GCCS	Government Code and Cypher School [*Later, GCHQ*] [*Sometimes facetiously translated as Golf, Chess, and Cheese Society*] [*British*]
GCCS-A	Global Command and Control System-Army
GCCW	United Gas, Coke, and Chemical Workers of America [*Later, OCAW*]
GCD	DeKalb Community College, Clarkston, GA [*OCLC symbol*] (OCLC)
GCD	Gain Control Driver (CET)
GCD	Gas Chromatography Distillation (AAEL)
GCD	Gate-Controlled Diode (IAA)
GCD	General and Complete Disarmament
GCD	Gold Coupling Dendrite
GCD	Golden Cadillac Resources Ltd. [*Vancouver Stock Exchange symbol*]
GCD	Good Conduct Discharge
GCD	Graft Coronary Disease [*Cardiology*] (DMAA)
GCD	Graphic Codepoint Definition [*Telecommunications*]
GCD	Great Circle Distance
GCD	Greatest Common Denominator

GCD	Greatest Common Divisor
GCD	Gyro-Compass, Desired Cluster Orientation (MCD)
GCDC	Gold Coast Divisional Court Reports [*A publication*] (DLA)
GCDC	Grace Cancer Drug Center [*Roswell Park Memorial Institute*] [*Research center*] (RCD)
GCDC	Ground Checkout Display and Control [*NASA*] (NASA)
GCDCS	Ground Checkout Display and Control System (MCD)
GCDFP	Gross Cystic Disease Fluid Protein (DAVI)
GCDI	Galacticomm Custom Device Interface [*Galacticomm, Inc.*] [*Telecommunications*]
GCDIS	Global Change Data and Information System [*Marine science*] (OSRA)
GC Div C	Selected Judgments of the Divisional Courts [*Ghana*] [*A publication*] (DLA)
GC Div Ct.	Gold Coast Selected Judgments of the Divisional Courts [*A publication*] (DLA)
GCDP	Global Change Database Project (EERA)
GCDP	Gunner's Control and Display Panel [*Military*] (RDA)
GCDU	Grupo de Convergencia Democratica en Uruguay [*Group of Democratic Convergence in Uruguay*] (EA)
GCE	Commission for Geographical Education (EA)
GCE	General Certificate of Education [*British*]
GCE	General Consumers Electronics (NITA)
GCE	Glassy Carbon Electrode
GCE	Government Capital Expenditure [*Finance*]
GCE	Government Computer Expo (HGAA)
GCE	Great Canadian Cider [*Vancouver Stock Exchange symbol*]
GCE	Greenwood Cotton Exchange (EA)
GCE	Ground Checkout Equipment [*Aerospace*] (AAG)
GCE	Ground Combat Element [*Marine Corps*] (DOMA)
GCE	Ground Communications Equipment
GCE	Ground-Control Equipment
GCE	Gun Control Equipment (DNAB)
GCEBT	Galveston Cotton Exchange and Board of Trade (EA)
GC-EC	Gas Chromatography with Electron Capture
GCEC	Gold Coast Environment Centre (EERA)
GC/ECD	Gas Chromatograph with Electron Capture Detector [*Chemical analysis*]
GCECEE	Groupement des Caisses d'Epargne de la CEE [*Savings Bank Group of the European Economic Community*]
GCEG	Grid-Controlled Electron Gun
GCEOS	Group Contribution Equation of State
GCEP	Gas Centrifuge Enrichment Plant [*Department of Energy*]
GCEP	Governing Council for Environmental Programs [*United Nations*]
GCER	Growth Environmental, Inc. [*NASDAQ symbol*] (SAG)
GCertClinInstr...	Graduate Certificate in Clinical Instruction [*Australia*]
GCertEd	Graduate Certificate in Education [*Australia*]
GCertEdStudies...	Graduate Certificate in Educational Studies [*Australia*]
GCertMaths & MathEd...	Graduate Certificate in Mathematics and Mathematics Education [*Australia*]
GCertMusMgmt...	Graduate Certificate of Museum Management [*Australia*]
GCertSc & TechWriting...	Graduate Certificate of Scientific and Technical Writing [*Australia*]
GCertSocAdmin...	Graduate Certificate in Social Administration [*Australia*]
GCES	Generalized Constant Elasticity of Substitution (PDAA)
GCES	Glen Canyon Environmental Studies [*Department of the Interior*]
GCESq	Geodetic Communications and Electronics Squadron [*Air Force*] (AFM)
G-CEU	General Certified End User [*Department of Commerce export license*]
GCF	Generation Control Function [*Telecommunications*] (TEL)
GCF	Greatest Common Factor
GCF	Greenhouse Crisis Foundation (EA)
GCF	Gross Capacity Factor (IEEE)
GCF	Ground Command Facility
GCF	Ground Communications Facility [*NASA*]
GCF	Growth-Rate-Controlling Factor [*Medicine*] (DMAA)
GCFA	Gridded Crossed Field Amplifier (IAA)
GCFAP	Guidance and Control Flight Analysis Program [*Aerospace*]
GCFBR	Gas Cooled Fast Breeder (EDCT)
GCFBR	Gas-Cooled Fast Breeder Reactor
GCFC	Glen Campbell Fan Club (EA)
GCFC	Gold Coast Full Court Selected Judgments [*A publication*] (DLA)
GCFC	Gulf Coast Fisheries Center
GCF-CS	Ground Communications Facility - Communications Switcher [*NASA*]
GCFI	Gulf and Caribbean Fisheries Institute (EA)
GC-FID	Gas Chromatography with Flame Ionization Detection
GCFLH	Grand Cross of the French Legion of Honour
GCFR	Gas-Cooled Fast Reactor
GCFRE	Gas-Cooled Fast Reactor Experiment (IEEE)
GCFT	Gonorrhea Complement Fixation Test [*Medicine*]
GC/FTIR	Gas Chromatography plus Fourier Transform Infrared Spectrometry
GCFU	Germinal Center-Forming Unit (DNAB)
GC Full Ct.	Gold Coast Full Court Selected Judgments [*A publication*] (DLA)
GCFV	Puerto Del Rosario/Fuerteventura [*Canary Islands*] [*ICAO location identifier*] (ICLI)
GCG	General Electric Capital Exchange [*AMEX symbol*] (SAG)
GCG	Genl Chemical Group [*NYSE symbol*] (TTSB)
GCG	Glucagon (DMAA)
GCG	Gorham Collectors' Guild [*Defunct*] (EA)
GCG	Grand Captain General [*Freemasonry*]
GCG	Grand Captain of the Guard [*Freemasonry*]
GCG	Gravity-Controlled Gyro
GCG	Greenhouse Coordinating Group [*Australia*]
GCG	Ground Command Guidance

GCG	Guanine Cytosine Guanine [*A triplet of bases coding for the amino acid, alanine*] (EES)
GCG	Guardian Capital Group Ltd. [*Toronto Stock Exchange symbol*]
GCG	Guatemala City [*Guatemala*] [*Seismograph station code, US Geological Survey Closed*] (SEIS)
GCG	Guidance Control Group [*Military*]
GCG	Gyro Control Gunsight
GCGLD	Grants, Contracts, and General Law Division [*Environmental Protection Agency*] (GFGA)
GCGR	Glucagon Receptor (DMAA)
GCGR	Glucocorticoid Receptor (DMAA)
GCGS	Gravity-Controlled Gyro System
G CH	[*The*] Gardeners' Chronicle [*A publication*] (ROG)
GCH	Gas Collection Header (NRCH)
GCH	Generalized Continuum Hypothesis [*Logic*]
GCH	Germinal Center Hyperplasia [*Medicine*]
GCH	Gigacharacters
GCH	Global Community Health
GCH	Glucocorticoid Hormone [*Endocrinology*]
GCH	Golden Chance Resources, Inc. [*Vancouver Stock Exchange symbol*]
GCH	Grand Captain of the Host [*Freemasonry*]
GCH	Grand Chapter of Harodim [*Freemasonry*]
GCH	[*The*] Greater China Fund [*NYSE symbol*] (SAG)
GCH	Guidance Capsule Handling
GCH	Knight Grand Cross of the Guelphic Order of Hanover [*British*]
GCHC	Gulf Coast Hydroscience Center [*Department of the Interior*] [*National Space Technology Laboratories Station, MS*] (GRD)
GCHI	Giant Cement Holding [*NASDAQ symbol*] (TTSB)
GCHI	Giant Cement Holding, Inc. [*NASDAQ symbol*] (SAG)
GCHI	Hierro [*Canary Islands*] [*ICAO location identifier*] (ICLI)
GCHQ	Government Code Headquarters [*Formerly, GCCS*] [*British*] (INF)
GCHQ	Government Communications Headquarters [*British*]
GCHR	Guatemala Committee for Human Rights (EAIO)
GCHWR	Gas-Cooled, Heavy-Water-Moderated Reactor [*Nuclear energy*] (NRCH)
GCHX	Ground Cooling Heat Exchanger [*NASA*] (NASA)
GCI	Gannett Co. [*NYSE symbol*] (TTSB)
GCI	Gannett Co., Inc. [*NYSE symbol*] (SPSG)
GCI	Gas Chromatograph Intoximeter [*Measure-of-intoxication test for drunk drivers*]
GCI	General Capital Increase [*Banking*]
GCI	General Cognitive Index [*Medicine*] (DMAA)
GCI	General Communication, Inc. [*Anchorage, AK*] [*Telecommunications*] (TSSD)
GCI	Generalized Communication Interface
GCI	Genie Climatique International (EA)
GCI	Getty Conservation Institute [*Database producer*] (IID)
GCI	Gnostic Concepts, Inc. [*San Mateo, CA*] [*Database producer*] [*Information service or system*] [*Telecommunications*] (TSSD)
GCI	Gossman Consulting, Inc. (EFIS)
GCI	Grand China Resources Ltd. [*Vancouver Stock Exchange symbol*]
GCI	Graphic Communications, Inc. [*Computer science*]
GCI	Graphic Converter Interface [*Computer science*] (DGA)
GCI	Graphics Command Interpreter (IAA)
GCI	Gray Cast Iron
GCI	Green Chemistry Institute
GCI	Ground Clearance Intercept [*System similar to US commercial RADAR for ground control of aircraft*] [*North Vietnam*]
GCI	Ground Control Intercept [*Military*] (MUSM)
GCI	Ground-Controlled Interception [*RADAR*]
GCI	Groupe des Communications Informatiques [*Computer Communications Group*] [*Canada*]
GCI	Guernsey [*Channel Islands*] [*Airport symbol*] (OAG)
GCI	Gulf Communications, Inc. [*Melbourne, FL*] [*Telecommunications service*] (TSSD)
GCIA	Granite Cutters' International Association [*Later, Tile, Marble, Terrazzo, Finishers, Shopworkers, and Granite Cutters International Union*]
GCIAA	Granite Cutters' International Association of America (DICI)
GCI/ADC	Ground-Controlled Intercept/Air Defense Center (DNAB)
GCIC	Gifted Children's Information Centre [*British*] (CB)
GCIC	Groupement Cinematographique International de Conciliation (EA)
GCICU	German Chamber of Industry and Commerce in the United Kingdom (EAIO)
GCIE	Knight Grand Commander of the [*Order of the*] Indian Empire [*British*]
GCIIG	Glass and Ceramics Industry Instrumentation Group (ACII)
GCIIS	Glucose Controlled Insulin Infusion System [*Medicine*] (DMAA)
GCIL	Ground Command Interface Logic (NAKS)
GCIL	Ground-Control Interface Logic (MCD)
GCILC	Ground-Control Interface Logic Controller (MCD)
GCILU	Ground-Control Interface Logic Unit (MCD)
GCIP	GEWEX [*Global Energy and Water Cycle Experiment*] Continental-Scale International Project [*World Climate Research Program*] [*Geoscience*]
GCIP	Guidance Correction Input Panel
GC/IR	Gas Chromatography/Infrared
GCIRC	Glass Container Industry Research Corp. [*An association*] (EA)
GCIRC	Groupe Consultatif International de Recherche sur le Colza [*International Consultative Research Group on Rape Seed*] (EAIO)
GC-IRMS	Gas Chromatography - Isotope-Ratio Mass Spectrometry [*Chemistry*]
GCIS	Grade Crossing Inventory System [*BTS*] (TAG)
GCIS	Ground-Control Intercept Squadron
GCISD	Guidance, Control, and Information Systems Division [*NASA*]

GCIT............ Ground Control Interception Team (IAA)
GCITING...... Ground-Control Intercept Training [Navy] (ANA)
GCITNG....... Ground-Control Intercept Training (NVT)
GCIU .... Graphic Communications International Union (EA)
GCJB........... Guidance Checkout Junction Box
GCK .... Garden City [Kansas] [Airport symbol] (OAG)
GCK .... Glomerulocystic Kidney [Nephrology]
GCK .... Grid-Controlled Klystron
GCK .... Grocka [Yugoslavia] [Geomagnetic observatory code]
GCKP .... Grand Commander of the Knights of Saint Patrick
GCL .... Columbia Theological Seminary, Decatur, GA [OCLC symbol]
                (OCLC)
GCL .... Galactic Center Lobe
GCL .... Ganglion Cell Layer [Neuroanatomy]
GCL .... Gas-Cooled Loop [Nuclear energy] (NRCH)
GCL .... Generic Control Language [Computer science] (TEL)
GCL .... Globoid Cell Leukodystrophy [Medicine] (DMAA)
GCL .... Golden Circle Ltd. [Australia Commercial firm]
GCL .... Grand Cross (of the Order) of Leopold (ROG)
GCL .... Great Cameron Lake Resources, Inc. [Vancouver Stock Exchange
                symbol]
GCL .... Greenclose Aviation Services Ltd. [British ICAO designator] (FAAC)
GCL .... Ground-Control Landing
GCL .... Ground Coolant Loop (MCD)
GCL .... Guidance Control Laboratory (AAG)
GCL .... Guide to Computing Literature [A publication] (IT)
GCL .... Guild of Catholic Lawyers (EA)
GCL .... Guild of Cleaners and Launderers [British] (DBA)
GCL .... Gulf Canada Ltd. [UTLAS symbol]
GCLA .... Group Carry Look-Ahead (MHDI)
GCLA .... La Palma [Canary Islands] [ICAO location identifier] (ICLI)
GCLC .... Greater Cincinnati Library Consortium [Library network]
GCLC .... Guidance Control Launch Console (IAA)
GCLCS .... Groundcrew Liquid Cooling System
GCLH .... Knight Grand Cross of the Legion of Honour [British]
GC LISP ...... Golden Common LISP [List Processor] [Artificial intelligence
                language]
GCLJ .... Grand Cross, St. Lazarus of Jerusalem (DD)
GCLLM .... Groupement Canadien des Locataires des Logements Municipaux
                [Canadian Organization of Public Housing Tenants]
GCLP .... Gran Canaria [Canary Islands] [ICAO location identifier] (ICLI)
GC/LRMS ..... Gas Chromatography/Low Resolution Mass Spectrometry
GCLWD .... Gulf Coast Low Water Datum
GCM .... Gaussian Cosine Modulation (PDAA)
GCM .... Gay Christian Movement [British]
GCM .... General Circulation Model [Meteorology] [Computer science]
GCM .... General Counsel's Memorandum [Internal Revenue Service]
GCM .... General Court-Martial
GCM .... General George C. Marshall [World War II]
GCM .... Generator Coordinate Method [Physics]
GCM .... Geriatric-Care Manager
GCM .... Glazed Ceramic Mosaic (DICI)
GCM .... Global Circulation Model [National Center for Atmospheric Research]
GCM .... Global Circulation Models [Climate] (EERA)
GCM .... Global Climate Model
GCM .... Good Company Man [Theater term] (DSUE)
GCM .... Good Conduct Medal [Military decoration]
g-cm .... Gram-Centimeter (AAMN)
GCM .... Grand Cayman [West Indies] [Airport symbol] (OAG)
GCM .... Great Central Mines [Vancouver Stock Exchange symbol]
GCM .... Greatest Common Measure
GCM .... Greatest Common Multiple (ADA)
GCM .... Greenwich Street California Municipal Fund, Inc. [AMEX symbol]
                (SAG)
GCM .... Greenwich Street CA Muni Fd [AMEX symbol] (TTSB)
GCM .... Ground-Control Message (MCD)
GCM .... Groupement Carte a Memoire [Group promoting use of 'smart' credit
                cards] [France] (NITA)
GCM² .... Guild of Church Musicians [British] (DBA)
G/CM² .... Grams per Square Centimeter
G/CM³ .... Grams per Cubic Centimeter
GCMA .... General Court-Martial Authority
GCMA .... Glazed Cement Manufacturers Association Ltd. [British] (BI)
GCMA .... Government Contract Management Association (AAGC)
GCMA .... Government Contract Management Association of America (EA)
GCMAPA...... Gay Caucus of Members of the American Psychiatric Association
                [Later, AGLP] (EA)
gc-mass spec... Gas Chromatography-Mass Spectrometry (MEC)
GCMC .... Good Conduct Medal Clasp
GCMCA .... General Court-Martial Convening Authority [DoD]
GCMD .... Global Change Master Director (EERA)
GCMDL .... Good Conduct Medal [Military decoration] (AABC)
GCMF.......... George C. Marshall Foundation (EA)
GCMG .... Dame Grand Cross of the Order of Saint Michael and Saint George
                [British] (ADA)
GCMG .... Knight Grand Cross of St. Michael and St. George [Facetiously
                translated "God Calls Me God"] [British]
GCMI .... Glass Container Manufacturers Institute [Later, GPI] (EA)
GCMJ.......... General Court-Martial Jurisdiction
GCMO .... General Court-Martial Order
GCMP .... General Court-Martial Prisoner
GCMP .... Greater Cleveland Mathematics Program [Education]
GCMPC .... General Chairman-Member Pickwick Club [From "The Pickwick
                Papers" by Charles Dickens]
GCMPS .... Gyro Compass

GCMR .... Ground-Control Message Request (MCD)
GCMRF .... George C. Marshall Research Foundation (EA)
GCMRGlc.... Global Cerebral Metabolic Rate for Glucose [Brain research]
GCMRJS ..... Great Central Midland [or Metropolitan] Joint Stock [Railroad]
                [British] (ROG)
GCMS .... Gas Chromatography and Mass Spectroscopy
GC/MS .... Gas Chromatography/Mass Spectrometry
GCMSC .... George C. Marshall Space Flight Center [Also known as MSFC]
                [NASA]
GCMSFC ..... George C. Marshall Space Flight Center [Also known as MSFC]
                [NASA]
GCMTW .... Guild of Canadian Musical Theatre Writers [Canada] (WWLA)
GCMU .... Glazed Concrete Masonry Units [Technical drawings]
GCMV .... Grapevine Chrome Mosaic Virus [Plant pathology]
GCN .... Gamma-Ray Burst Coordinates Network
GCN .... Gauge Code Number
GCN .... Geometric Constraint Network (DMAA)
GCN .... Giant Cerebral Neuron [Brain anatomy]
GCN .... Gold Canyon Mines, Inc. [Vancouver Stock Exchange symbol]
GCN .... Government Computer News
GCN .... Grand Canyon [Arizona] [Airport symbol] (OAG)
GCN .... Greenwich Civil Noon
GCN .... Ground Communications Network
GCN .... Ground-Control Network [NASA] (NASA)
GCN .... Gulf Central Airlines, Inc. [ICAO designator] (FAAC)
GCNA .... Guild of Carillonneurs in North America (EA)
GcNM .... GCN/Microfilm, Boston, MA [Library symbol Library of Congress]
                (LCLS)
GC-NPD .... Gas Chromatography-Nitrogen Phosphorus Detector
GCNPP........ Gay Community News Prisoner Project [An association] (EA)
GCNPP........ Greene County Nuclear Power Plant (NRCH)
GCNR .... Gas Core Nuclear Rocket
GCNSW .... Gas Council of New South Wales [Australia]
GCO .... Columbus College, Library, Columbus, GA [OCLC symbol] (OCLC)
GCO .... GC Optronics, Inc.
GCO .... GENESCO, Inc. [NYSE symbol] (SPSG)
GCO .... Georgetown College Observatory (MCD)
GCO .... Glenco International Corp. [Vancouver Stock Exchange symbol]
GCO .... Government Concept of Operations (RDA)
GCO .... Governor's Commissioned Officer [British military] (DMA)
GCO .... Ground Checkout [NASA] (NASA)
GCO .... Ground Cutout
GCO .... Guidance Control Officer (AAG)
GCO .... Gun Control Officer [Navy]
gCO2 .... Grams of Carbon Dioxide Equivalent (EERA)
GCOC .... General Conditions of Contract
GCOC .... Gun Control Officer Console [Military] (CAAL)
GCocM .... Middle Georgia College, Cochran, GA [Library symbol Library of
                Congress] (LCLS)
GCOE .... Ground-Control Operational Equipment (IAA)
GColu.......... W. C. Bradley Memorial Library, Columbus, GA [Library symbol
                Library of Congress] (LCLS)
GColuC .... Columbus College, Columbus, GA [Library symbol Library of
                Congress] (LCLS)
GColuGS ...... Church of Jesus Christ of Latter-Day Saints, Genealogical Society
                Library, MaconBranch, Columbus, GA [Library symbol Library of
                Congress] (LCLS)
GCom .... Grand Commander [or Commandery] [Freemasonry]
GCON.......... Grand Cross, Order of the Niger [British]
GConT .... Monastery of the Holy Ghost, Conyers, GA [Library symbol Library of
                Congress] (LCLS)
GCOR .... Gencor Industries, Inc. [NASDAQ symbol] (NQ)
GCOS .... General Comprehensive Operating Supervisor [Computer science]
GCOS .... General Comprehensive Operating System (NITA)
GCOS .... General Computer Operational System [NASA]
GCOS .... Global Climate Observing System [Marine science] (OSRA)
GCOS .... Great Canadian Oil Sands Ltd.
GCOS .... Ground Computer Operating System [NASA] (NASA)
GCP .... Gain Control Pulse (IAA)
GCP .... Gaining Command Program (MCD)
GCP .... Generalized Computer Program
GCP .... Generator Control Panel (DNAB)
GCP .... Gift Coupon Programme [Later, Co-Action] [UNESCO]
GCP .... Golden CommPass [Front-end computer processor] (PCM)
GCP .... Good Clinical Practice [Medicine]
GCP .... Government Contracts Program [George Washington University Law
                Center] (DLA)
GCP .... Grancamp Resources [Vancouver Stock Exchange symbol]
GCP .... Graphics Control Program [IBM Corp.] (PCM)
GCP .... Green Circle Program (EA)
GCP .... Gross Criminal Product
GCP .... Ground Control Point
GCP .... Guidance Checkout [or Control] Package (NG)
GCP .... Guild of Catholic Psychiatrists [Later, National Guild of Catholic
                Psychiatrists] (EA)
GCP .... Guild of Computer Practitioners [British] (DBA)
GCPA .... Grammatik des Christlich-Palaestinischen Aramaeisch
                [A publication] (BJA)
GCPD .... Grade Crossing Protection Device
GCPPD .... Global Committee of Parliamentarians on Population and
                Development (EA)
GCPPI........ Gifted Children's Pen Pals International (EA)
GCPR .... General Ceiling Price Regulation (DLA)
GCPS .... Gigacycles per Second (MUGU)
GCPS .... Global Climate Perspectives System [Marine science] (OSRA)

GCPS .... Greig Cephalopolysyndactyly Syndrome [*Medicine*]
GCPS .... Ground Claims Processing System
GCPS .... Group Claims Processing System [*McAuto*]
GCQ .... Group Climate Questionnaire [*Occupational therapy*]
GCR .... Gain Control Range
GCR .... Galactic Cosmic Radiation [*or Ray*]
GCR .... Galvanocutaneous Reaction
GCR .... Gamma Cosmic Ray [*Geophysics*]
GCR .... Gas Cooled Power Reactor (EDCT)
GCR .... Gas-Cooled Reactor
GCR .... Gaylord Container 'A' [*AMEX symbol*] (TTSB)
GCR .... Gaylord Container Corp. Class A [*AMEX symbol*] (SPSG)
GCR .... General Cargo Rates [*Business term*]
GCR .... General Commodity Rate [*Shipping*] (DS)
GCR .... General Component Reference (IEEE)
GCR .... Generator Control Relay [*Electronics*] (OA)
GCR .... Geneva Consultants Registry [*Alpha Systems Resource*] [*Database*]
GCR .... Ghost Canceling Reference [*Television technology*]
GCR .... Glencair Resources, Inc. [*Toronto Stock Exchange symbol*]
GCR .... Glomerular Complement Receptor [*Immunology*]
GCR .... Glucocorticoid Receptor (DMAA)
GCR .... Glucose Consumption Rate
GCR .... Glucuronidase [*An enzyme*]
GCR .... Glycinecresol Red [*An indicator*] [*Chemistry*]
GCR .... Gold Coast Regiment [*British military*] (DMA)
GCR .... Government Contracts Reporter [*A publication*] (AAGC)
GCR .... Grand Central Rocket Co. (AAG)
GCR .... Grandparents'/Children's Rights (EA)
GCR .... Graphics Code Recording [*Computer science*]
GCR .... Gray-Component Replacement [*Color reproduction technology*]
GCR .... Grayling Creek [*Montana*] [*Seismograph station code, US Geological Survey*] (SEIS)
GCR .... Great Central Railway [*British*]
GCR .... Great Circle Route (WDAA)
GCR .... Grignard's Chemical Reaction
GCR .... Ground-Controlled RADAR
GCR .... Group Coded Recording [*Computer science*] (BUR)
GCR .... Group Code Recording [*Data storage method*] (NITA)
GCR .... Group Conformity Rate (DB)
GCR .... Group Conformity Rating (DMAA)
GCR .... Group Encoded Recording (NITA)
GCR .... Guerrilleros de Cristo Rey [*Warriors of Christ and King*] [*Revolutionary Group Spain*]
GCRA .... Gas-Cooled Reactor Associates (NRCH)
GCRA .... Giant Chinchilla Rabbit Association (EA)
GCRA .... Global Coral Reef Alliance (EA)
GCRC .... General Clinical Research Center [*University of Virginia*] (RCD)
GCRC .... General Clinical Research Center [*University of Alabama in Birmingham*] (RCD)
GCRC .... General Clinical Research Center [*Stanford University*] (RCD)
GCRC .... General Clinical Research Center [*Scripps Clinic and Research Foundation*]
GCRCH .... General Council and Register of Consultant Herbalists [*British*] (DBA)
GCRCPB .... General Clinical Research Center Program Branch [*National Institutes of Health*]
GCRE .... Gas-Cooled Reactor Experiment (NRCH)
GCREF .... GCR Hldgs Ltd [*NASDAQ symbol*] (TTSB)
GCRES .... Ground Combat-Readiness Evaluation Squadron
GCRF .... Greensboro Civil Rights Fund [*Defunct*] (EA)
GCRG .... Giant Cell Reparative Granuloma [*Oncology*]
GCRG .... Gun Carriage
GCRI .... Georgetown Clinical Research Institute [*FAA*]
GCRI .... German Carpet Research Institute [*See also TFI*] (EAIO)
GCRI .... Gillette Co. Research Institute
GCRL .... Glass House Crops Research Institute [*Agricultural Research Council*] (PDAA)
GCRL .... Gulf Coast Research Laboratory [*Ocean Springs, MS*]
GCRN .... General Council and Register of Naturopaths [*British*] (DBA)
GCRO .... General Council and Register of Osteopaths Ltd. [*British*]
GCRP .... Galactic Cosmic Ray Particle
GCRP .... Global Change Research Plan [*Program*] [*Marine science*] (OSRA)
GCRP .... Global Change Research Plan/Program (USDC)
GCRP .... Global Change Research Program (EERA)
GCRR .... Arrecife/Lanzarote [*Canary Islands*] [*ICAO location identifier*] (ICLI)
GCRV .... Ground Cruising Recreational Vehicle [*Owosso Motor Car Co.*] [*Owosso, MI*]
GCRWS .... Gaylord Container Wrrt [*AMEX symbol*] (TTSB)
GCS .... Gas Cleaning System [*Combustion technology*]
GCS .... Gas Cylinder System
GCS .... Gate-Controlled Switch
GCS .... General Clinical Service (MAE)
GCS .... General Communications System [*Sperry Univac*] (NITA)
GCS .... General Communication Subsystem [*Computer science*]
GCS .... General Computer Systems (NITA)
GCS .... General Computer Systems, Inc.
GCS .... Generalized Contentment Scale (STED)
GCS .... Generator Control Switch (MCD)
GCS .... Geo-Common Subsystem [*Environmental Protection Agency*] (AEPA)
GCS .... Geostationary Communications Satellite [*WARC*]
GCS .... Gifted Child Society (EA)
Gc/s .... Gigacycles per Second [*IEEE*]
GCS .... Glasgow Coma Scale [*Medicine*] (WDAA)
GCS .... Glasgow Coma Score [*Medicine*]
GCS .... Glucocorticosteroid [*Biochemistry*] (DB)
GCS .... Glutamylcysteine Synthetase (STED)

GCS .... Golden Crown Resources Ltd. [*Vancouver Stock Exchange symbol*]
GCS .... Golf Collectors' Society (EA)
GCS .... Government Contractors Subcontractors
GCS .... Grand Commander (of the Order) of Spain (ROG)
GCS .... Graphic Compatibility System [*US Military Academy*] (NITA)
GCS .... Graphics Compatibility Standard [*For image processing*]
GCS .... Gray Communications Systems [*NYSE symbol*] (SAG)
GCS .... Ground Command System
GCS .... Ground Communications System
GCS .... Ground-Control Station (MCD)
GCS .... Guidance Cutoff Signal [*NASA*] (NASA)
GCS .... Gyroless Control System
GCS .... Portland, ME [*Location identifier FAA*] (FAAL)
GCSA .... Galloway Cattle Society of America (EA)
GCSA .... Gross Cell-Surface Antigen [*Immunology*]
GCSAA .... Golf Course Superintendents Association of America (EA)
GCSA/NJ ...... Golf Course Superintendents Association of New Jersey (SRA)
GCSC .... Guidance Control and Sequencing Computer
GCSE .... General Certificate of Secondary Education [*British*]
GCSE .... Generalized Convulsive Status Epilepticus [*Medicine*] (CPH)
Gc/sec .... Gigacycles per Second [*AIP*]
GCSF .... Granulocyte Cell-Stimulating Factor (STED)
G-CSF .... Granulocyte-Colony Stimulating Factor [*Hematology*]
GCSF .... Gulf, Colorado & Santa Fe Railway Co. [*AAR code*]
GCSG .... Graphic Communications Societies Group [*British*] (NITA)
GCSG .... Knight Grand Cross of St. Gregory the Great [*British*]
GCSI .... Knight Grand Commander of the [*Order of the*] Star of India [*British*]
GC-SICM ...... Gas Chromatography - Single Ion Current Monitoring (PDAA)
GCSM .... Glandless Cottonseed Meal [*Animal feed*]
GCSM .... Ground Composite Signal Mixer
GCSOLAR ..... Green Cross Solar (AEPA)
GCSP .... Guidance and Control Set Processor
GCSRW - UMC... General Commission on the Status and Role of Women - United Methodist Church (EA)
GCSS .... GEWEX [*Global Energy and Water Cycle Experiment*] Cloud System Study (EERA)
GCSS .... Global Communications Satellite System
GCSS .... Ground-Controlled Space System
GCSS .... Knight Grand Cross of St. Sylvester [*British*]
GCStJ .... Bailiff Grand Cross of [*the Order of*] Saint John of Jerusalem [*British*] (ADA)
GCStJ .... Dame Grand Cross of [*the Order of*] Saint John of Jerusalem [*British*] (ADA)
GCStJ .... Knight Grand Cross of [*the Order of*] St. John of Jerusalem [*British*]
GCSU .... Government Clerical Services' Union [*Ceylon*]
GCSV .... Groundnut Chlorotic Spot Virus
GCSW .... Graduate Certificate of Social Work
GCT .... Coca-Cola Co., Technical Information Services, Atlanta, GA [*OCLC symbol*] (OCLC)
GCT .... Galactic Center Transient [*Astronomy*]
GCT .... General Care and Treatment (STED)
GCT .... General Classification Test [*Military*]
GCT .... General Clerical Test (TES)
GCT .... Gesture Comprehension Test [*Occupational therapy*]
GCT .... Giant Cell Thyroiditis [*Medicine*] (DB)
GCT .... Giant Cell Tumor [*Oncology*]
GCT .... Giro [*Money Order*] Credit Transfer (DI)
GCT .... Glasgow College of Technology (AIE)
GCT .... Glass Cloth Tape
GCT .... Government Competitive Testing
GCT .... Grand Cadence de Tir [*Self-propelled howitzer*] (RDA)
GCT .... Graphics Communications Terminal
GCT .... Great Circle Track
GCT .... Greenwich Central Time [*Astronomy*] (IAA)
GCT .... Greenwich Civil Time
GCT .... Greenwich Conservatory Time
GCT .... Ground Checkout and Test [*Aerospace*]
GCT .... Guidance Command Test
GCT .... Guidance Computer Test
GCT .... Gun Compatibility Test
GCT .... Gun Control Tower [*British military*] (DMA)
GCT .... Gyro-Compass Trial (IAA)
GCTA .... Ground Commanded [*or Controlled*] Television Assembly [*Apollo*] [*NASA*]
GCTC .... Giant Cell Tumor Cells [*A cell line*]
GCTE .... Global Change and Terrestrial Ecosystems [*Marine science*] (OSRA)
GCTE .... Guidance Computer Test Equipment
GCTEV .... Garland Chrysanthemum Temperate Virus [*Plant pathology*]
GCTF .... Gold Coast Territorial Force [*British military*] (DMA)
GCTM .... Global Chemical Transport Model [*Marine science*] (OSRA)
GCTOA .... Greek Cultural and Theatrical Organisation of Australia
GCtryB .... Great Country Bank [*Associated Press*] (SAG)
GCTS .... Gas Component Test Stand (MCD)
GCTS .... Ground Communications Tracking Systems
GCTS .... Tenerife-Reina Sofia [*Canary Islands*] [*ICAO location identifier*] (ICLI)
GCTW .... Gross Combination Test Weight [*Automotive engineering*]
GCU .... Gas-Cooled Unit
GCU .... General Control Unit (MCD)
GCU .... Generator Control Unit [*Aviation*] (NASA)
GCU .... Generator/Converter Unit
GCU .... Gold Canyon Resources [*Vancouver Stock Exchange symbol*]
GCU .... Gonococcal Urethritis [*Medicine*] (DMAA)
GCU .... Ground Checkout Unit [*Aerospace*] (MCD)
GCU .... Ground-Control Unit (AAG)
GCU .... Ground Cooling Unit [*NASA*] (NASA)

GCU .... Guidance and Control Unit (NATG)
GCU .... Guidance Coupler Unit
GCU .... Gunner's Control Unit
GCU .... Gyro Coupling Unit (KSC)
GCuA .... Andrew College, Cuthbert, GA [*Library symbol Library of Congress*] (LCLS)
GCUGA .... Grounded Current Unity-Gain Amplifier
GCUUSA ...... Greek Catholic Union of the USA (EA)
GCV .... Chattahoochee Valley Regional Library, Columbus, GA [*OCLC symbol*] (OCLC)
GCV .... Gabelli Convertible Securities Fund [*NYSE symbol*] (SAG)
GCV .... Gabelli Conv Securities Fd [*NYSE symbol*] (TTSB)
GCV .... Gaseous Oxygen Control Valve (NASA)
GCV .... Great Cardiac Vein [*Medicine*] (DMAA)
GCV .... Gross Caloric Value
GCV .... Leakesville, MS [*Location identifier FAA*] (FAAL)
GCVF .... Great Cardiac Vein Flow [*Medicine*] (DMAA)
GCVO .... Dame Grand Cross of the Royal Victorian Order [*British*] (ADA)
GCVO .... Knight Grand Cross of the Royal Victorian Order [*British*]
GCVS .... General Catalog of Variable Stars [*Astronomy*] (OA)
GCVW .... Gross Combination Vehicle Weight [*Automotive engineering*]
GCW .... Coca-Cola Co., Law Library, Atlanta, GA [*OCLC symbol*] (OCLC)
GCW .... [*The*] Garden City Western Railway Co. [*AAR code*]
GCW .... General Continuous Wave (IAA)
GCW .... Generative Cell Wall [*Botany*]
GCW .... Global Chart of the World [*Air Force*]
GCW .... Glomerular Capillary Wall [*Anatomy*]
GCW .... Grand Coulee [*Washington*] [*Seismograph station code, US Geological Survey Closed*] (SEIS)
GCW .... Gridiron Club of Washington, DC (EA)
GCW .... Gross Combination Weight [*for tractor and loaded trailer*]
GCWDA .... Gulf Coast Waste Disposal Authority [*Governmental industrial waste disposal system*]
GCWIU .... General Cigarette Workers' Industrial Union [*British*]
GCWM .... General Conference on Weights and Measures
GCWR .... Global Congress of the World's Religions (EA)
GCWR .... Gross Combination Weight Rating [*Environmental Protection Agency*]
GCX .... GC Companies [*NYSE symbol*] (SAG)
GCXO .... Tenerife [*Canary Islands*] [*ICAO location identifier*] (ICLI)
GCY .... Gastroscopy [*Medicine*] (DMAA)
GCY .... General Cybernetics Corp. [*Vancouver Stock Exchange symbol*]
GCY .... Glen Cove [*New York*] [*Seismograph station code, US Geological Survey*] (SEIS)
GCY .... Greeneville, TN [*Location identifier FAA*] (FAAL)
GCYF .... Grantmakers for Children, Youth, and Families (NFD)
GD .... Air Antilles [*Airline*] (MHDB)
GD .... Air North [*ICAO designator*] (AD)
GD .... DeKalb County Library System, Regional Service-Rockdale and Newton Counties, Decatur, GA [*Library symbol Library of Congress*] (LCLS)
GD .... Diganglioside [*Chemistry*]
Gd .... Gadolinium [*Chemical element*]
GD .... Gaol Delivery [*Legal*] [*British*] (ROG)
GD .... Gap Detector
GD .... Gas Dragster [*Class of racing cars*]
GD .... Gas Drainage
GD .... Gastroduodenal (STED)
GD .... Gate Driver
GD .... Gave Delivery
GD .... Gear Down [*Aviation*]
GD .... Gel Destainer [*Analytical chemistry*]
GD .... Gel Dryer [*Chromatography*]
GD .... General Delivery
GD .... General Design (AAG)
GD .... General Development
GD .... General Diagnostics [*Medicine*] (STED)
GD .... General Diagram
GD .... General Discharge
GD .... General Dispensary [*Military*]
GD .... General Duties (STED)
GD .... General Duty
GD .... General Dynamics Corp. [*NYSE symbol*] (SPSG)
GD .... Genl Dynamics [*NYSE symbol*] (TTSB)
GD .... Geographic Digest [*A publication British*]
GD .... Geographic Distribution
GD .... Gestational Day
GD .... Gianotti Disease [*Medicine*] (STED)
GD .... Glass Door (ADA)
GD .... Global Data Systems [*Vancouver Stock Exchange symbol*]
GD .... Glow Discharge [*Photovoltaic energy systems*]
GD .... Glutamate Dehydrogenase [*An enzyme*]
GD .... Glutaraldehyde-Dichromate [*Fixative*]
GD .... Glyceryl Distearate [*Organic chemistry*]
GD .... Goal Defence [*Netball*]
GD .... God Damn
GD .... Golden Dawn [*In occult society name, Hermetic Order of the Golden Dawn*]
GD .... Gonadal Dysgenesis [*Endocrinology*]
GD .... Good [*Track condition*] [*Thoroughbred racing*]
GD .... Good Day [*Amateur radio shorthand*] (WDAA)
GD .... Good Delivery [*Business term*]
GD .... Good for the Day [*Investment term*] (NUMA)
Gd .... Government Expenditure [*Economics*]
GD .... Grade [*Technical drawings*]
GD .... Graduate Diploma

GD .... Graduate in Divinity
GD .... Granddaughter
GD .... Grand Deacon [*Freemasonry*]
GD .... Grand Division
GD .... Grand Duchess [*or Duke*]
GD .... Grand Duchy
GD .... Grand Duke (WGA)
GD .... Grandes Decisions de la Jurisprudence Administrative [*A publication*] (ILCA)
GD .... Graphic Demand Meter
GD .... Graphic Display
GD .... Grave's Disease [*Endocrinology*]
GD .... Gravimetric Density
Gd .... Greenside Darter [*Ichthyology*]
GD .... Greenwich Date
GD .... Grenada [*ANSI two-letter standard code*] (CNC)
gd .... Grenada [*MARC country of publication code Library of Congress*] (LCCP)
GD .... Gross Debt [*Business term*]
GD .... Ground
GD .... Ground Detector (MSA)
GD .... Ground Directional (IAA)
GD .... Group Delay Distortion (LAIN)
GD .... Grouping Distance [*Industrial engineering*]
GD .... Grove Dictionary of Music and Musicians [*A publication*]
GD .... Grown Diffused
GD .... Growth and Development (STED)
GD .... Guard (AABC)
GD .... Gudermannian Amplitude
GD .... Gundeck
GD .... Gunnery Division [*British military*] (DMA)
GD .... Guntersville Dam [*TVA*]
GD .... Nerve Gas [*US Chemical Corps symbol*]
GD .... Soman [*Nerve gas*] [*Army symbol*]
GDA .... Galvo-Drive Amplifier
GDA .... General Disposal Authority
GDA .... General Dynamics Astronautics
GDA .... Germine Diacetate [*Medicine*] (DMAA)
GDA .... Gimbal Drive Actuator [*or Assembly*] (KSC)
GDA .... Global Data Administrator (MHDI)
GDA .... Global Data Area
GDA .... Global Directory Agent
GDA .... Glycidyldiisopropylidenearabitol [*Organic chemistry*]
GDA .... Goat Dairymen's Association [*Australia*]
GDA .... Goldera Resources, Inc. [*Vancouver Stock Exchange symbol*]
GDA .... Graduate Diploma in Administration
Gda .... Granddaughter
GDA .... Guide Dogs of America (EA)
GDA .... Gun Damage Assessment (NVT)
GDA .... Gun-Defended Area
GDAA .... Gift and Decorative Accessories Association of America [*Later, GAA*] (EA)
GDahN .... North Georgia College, Dahlonega, GA [*Library symbol Library of Congress*] (LCLS)
GDAIS .... Atlanta Information Services, Decatur, GA [*Library symbol Library of Congress*] (LCLS)
GDal .... Dalton Regional Library, Dalton, GA [*Library symbol Library of Congress*] (LCLS)
GDalC .... Dalton College, Dalton, GA [*Library symbol*] [*Library of Congress*] (LCLS)
GDAM .... Graduate Division of Applied Mathematics
GD & R .... Grinning, Ducking, and Running (CDE)
GD & T .... Geometric Dimensioning and Tolerancing
GDanH .... Heritage Papers, Danielsville, GA [*Library symbol Library of Congress*] (LCLS)
GDAP .... GEOS [*Geodetic Earth-Orbiting Satellite*] Data Adjustment Program
GDAP .... Government Document Application Profile [*Telecommunications*] (OSI)
GDAS .... Geokinetic Data Acquisition System (PDAA)
GDAS .... Ground Data Acquisition System
GDAU .... General Data Acquisition Unit (MCD)
GDB .... Gas Density Balance [*Medicine*] (DMAA)
GDB .... Genome Data Base [*Genetics*]
GDB .... Geometric Database (MCD)
GDB .... Global Database
GDB .... Government Development Bank of Puerto Rico
GDB .... Guide Dogs for the Blind (EA)
GDBA .... Guide Dogs for the Blind Association [*British*] (EAIO)
GDBMS .... Generalized Data Base Management Systems [*Air Force*]
GDB/OMIM... Genome Database/Onlin Mendelian Inheritance in Man (HGEN)
GDBS .... Generalized Database System (NASA)
GDBusAd .... Graduate Diploma in Business Administration
GDC .... Columbia Theological Seminary, Decatur, GA [*Library symbol Library of Congress*] (LCLS)
GDC .... Garage Door Council (EA)
GDC .... Gas Discharge Counter
GDC .... Gas Displacement Chromatography
GDC .... Gel Dryer with Clamps [*Chromatography*]
GDC .... Gel Drying Cart [*Chromatography*]
GDC .... General Data Comm (NITA)
GDC .... General DataComm Industries, Inc. [*NYSE symbol*] (SPSG)
GDC .... General Dental Council [*British*]
GDC .... General Design Criteria (NRCH)
GDC .... General Development Corp. (AAG)
GDC .... General [*Purpose*] Digital Computer

GDC .... General Dynamics, Convair
GDC .... General Dynamics Corp.
GDC .... Genl DataComm Ind [*NYSE symbol*] (TTSB)
GDC .... Geocentric Dust Cloud
GDC .... Geodetic Data Center [*Environmental Science Services Administration*]
GDC .... Geological Data Center [*University of California, San Diego*] (IID)
GDC .... Geomagnetic Data Center [*National Oceanic and Atmospheric Administration*]
GDC .... Geophysical Data Center
GDC .... Gettysburg College, Gettysburg, PA [*OCLC symbol*] (OCLC)
GDC .... Giant Dopamine-Containing Cell [*Medicine*] (DMAA)
GDC .... Good Door Closer
GDC .... Governmental Defence Council [*British*]
GDC .... Grand-Dad's Day Council [*Defunct*] (EA)
GDC .... Grand Deacon of Ceremonies [*Freemasonry*] (ROG)
GDC .... Granduc Mines Ltd. [*Toronto Stock Exchange symbol Vancouver Stock Exchange symbol*]
GDC .... Graphic Display Console (MCD)
GDC .... Gravity Die-Cast [*Automotive engineering*]
GDC .... Gross Dependable Capacity [*Electronics*] (IEEE)
GDC .... Ground Digit Control (IAA)
GDC .... Guidance Data Converter [*Aerospace*] (AAG)
GDC .... Guidance Display Computer (DNAB)
GDC .... Guild of Dyers and Cleaners [*British*] (BI)
GDC .... Gun Direction Computer
GDC .... Gyro Display Coupler (MCD)
GDC .... Society of Graphic Designers of Canada (EAIO)
GDCA .... Great Dane Club of America (EA)
GDCH .... Glycerol Dichlorohydrin [*Organic chemistry*]
GDCH .... Graduate Diploma in Community Health
GDCI .... Gypsum Drywall Contractors International [*Later, AWCI*]
GDCR .... Glacial Debris Conjugate Region [*Oceanography*]
GDCS .... Government Documents Catalog Service [*Information service or system*] (IID)
GDCS .... Ground Distributed Control System (SSD)
GD/CV .... General Dynamics/Convair Division (MCD)
GDD .... DeKalb Historical Society, Decatur, GA [*Library symbol Library of Congress*] (LCLS)
GDD .... Gas Discharge Display (IAA)
GDD .... Gay Disaster Disease [*Also called AIDS*] (DAVI)
GDD .... Geddes Resources Ltd. [*Toronto Stock Exchange symbol*]
GDD .... General Design Document [*Computer science*] (MHDI)
GD/D .... General Dynamics/Daingerfield (SAA)
GDD .... Global Developmental Delay
GDD .... Group Display Device (MCD)
GDD .... Growing Degree Day [*Agriculture*] (PDAA)
GDDL .... Graphical Data Definition Language
GDDM .... Graphical Data Display Manager [*Computer science*]
GDDQ .... Group Dimensions Descriptions Questionnaire [*Psychology*]
GDDS .... DeKalb County School System, Decatur, GA [*Library symbol*] [*Library of Congress*] (LCLS)
GDDS .... Gamma Dose Detector System
GD/DS .... Generalized Dictionary/Directory System [*Computer science*] (MHDB)
GDE .... Beaumont, TX [*Location identifier FAA*] (FAAL)
GD/E .... General Dynamics/Electronics (SAA)
GDE .... Generalized Data Entry (ADA)
GDE .... Gibbs-Duhem Equation [*Physical chemistry*]
GDE .... Gilt Deckled Edge [*Bookbinding*]
GDE .... Gode [*Ethiopia*] [*Airport symbol*] (OAG)
GDE .... Golden Dawn Explorations Ltd. [*Vancouver Stock Exchange symbol*]
GDE .... Gourde [*Monetary unit*] [*Haiti*]
GDE .... Graduate Diploma in Educational Studies
GDE .... Graduate Diploma in Extension (ADA)
GDE .... Granular Diatomaceous Earth (DB)
GDE .... Gross Domestic Expenditure (WDAA)
GDE .... Ground Data Equipment [*Electronics*]
GDE .... Guide [*or Guided*] (MSA)
GDE .... Servicios Aereos Gadel SA de CV [*Mexico ICAO designator*] (FAAC)
GD/EB .... General Dynamics/Electric Boat Division (KSC)
G de Bay ...... Guido de Baysio [*Deceased, 1313*] [*Authority cited in pre-1607 legal work*] (DSA)
G de Ca .... Guillelmus de Cabriano [*Deceased, 1201*] [*Authority cited in pre-1607 legal work*] (DSA)
G de Cal ...... Gaspar de Calderinis [*Deceased, 1390*] [*Authority cited in pre-1607 legal work*] (DSA)
G de Cu .... Guillelmus de Cuneo [*Deceased, 1335*] [*Authority cited in pre-1607 legal work*] (DSA)
G de Fr .... Guillelmus de Ferreriis [*Deceased, 1295*] [*Authority cited in pre-1607 legal work*] (DSA)
G de Mon .... Guillelmus de Monte Lauduno [*Deceased, 1343*] [*Authority cited in pre-1607 legal work*] (DSA)
G de Mon Lau... Guillelmus de Monte Lauduno [*Deceased, 1343*] [*Authority cited in pre-1607 legal work*] (DSA)
G de Mon Laud... Guillelmus de Monte Lauduno [*Deceased, 1343*] [*Authority cited in pre-1607 legal work*] (DSA)
GDemP .... Piedmont College, Demorest, GA [*Library symbol Library of Congress*] (LCLS)
G-Dest .... General Destination
G de Suz ...... Guido de Suzaria [*Deceased, 1293*] [*Authority cited in pre-1607 legal work*] (DSA)
GDEU .... Guidance Digital Evaluation Unit
GDF .... Gas Dynamic Facility [*Air Force*]
GDF .... Geographic Data File [*LPC, Inc.*] [*Information service or system*] (IID)

GDF .... Gibraltar Defence Force [*British military*] (DMA)
GDF .... Global Partners Income Fd [*NYSE symbol*] (TTSB)
GDF .... Global Partners Income Fund [*NYSE symbol*] (SPSG)
GDF .... Goldfarb Corp. [*Toronto Stock Exchange symbol*]
GDF .... Granular Diffusion Flame (MCD)
GDF .... Ground Decommutation Facility
GDF .... Ground Defense Forces
GDF .... Ground Diverted Force [*Military*] (CINC)
GDF .... Group Distributing Frames
GDF .... Group Distribution Frame [*Telecommunications*] (NITA)
GDF .... Growth Differentiation Factor [*Embryology*]
GDF .... Guyanese Defense Force
GDFB .... Guide Dog Foundation for the Blind [*Also known as Second Sight Guiding Eyes - Guide Dog Foundation*] (EA)
GDFCF .... Gross Domestic Fixed Capital Formation (EERA)
GDFF .... Geographic Distribution of Federal Funds Information System [*Comptroller General of the United States*]
GD/FW .... General Dynamics/Fort Worth (KSC)
GDG .... Gas Discharge Gauge
GD(G) .... General Duties (Ground) [*British military*] (DMA)
GDG .... Generation Data Group [*Computer science*] (BUR)
GDG .... Golden Glory [*Vancouver Stock Exchange symbol*]
GDG .... Group Display Generator
GDG .... Guarding [*Bookbinding*] (DGA)
GDGA .... Garment Dyers Guild of America (EA)
GD/GA .... General Dynamics/General Atomic (KSC)
GDGIP .... Gas-Driven Gyro Inertial Platform [*Aerospace*] (AAG)
GDGS .... Guidance Digital Ground Station (IAA)
GDH .... DeKalb General Hospital, Decatur, GA [*Library symbol Library of Congress*] (LCLS)
GDH .... Glutamate Dehydrogenase [*An enzyme*]
GDH .... Glycerophosphate Dehydrogenase (MAE)
GDH .... Glycol Dehydrogenase (DB)
GDH .... Godhavn [*Greenland*] [*Seismograph station code, US Geological Survey*] (SEIS)
GDH .... Goldsearch, Inc. [*Vancouver Stock Exchange symbol*]
GDH .... Gonadotropic Hormone [*Endocrinology*]
GDH .... Goods on Hand (DS)
GDH .... Grand Ducal Highness (ROG)
GDH .... Ground Data Handling
GDH .... Growth and Differentiation Hormone [*Endocrinology*]
GDH .... Sargodha [*Pakistan*] [*Airport symbol*] (AD)
GDHA .... Garage Door Hardware Association (NTPA)
GDHC .... Ground Data Handling Centre [*Canada*]
GDHS .... Ground Data Handling System (MCD)
GDHSE .... Guardhouse (AABC)
GDHSWT ..... General Dynamics High-Speed Wind Tunnel
GDI .... Gas-Driven Intensifier Pump (MCD)
GDI .... Gasoline Direct Injection
GDI .... Generalized Database Interface [*Computer science*] (MHDB)
GDI .... God Damned Independent [*College slang for student not affiliated with a fraternity or sorority*]
GDI .... Gordon Diagnostic System (TES)
GDI .... Graphic Display Interface (MCD)
GDI .... Graphics Device Interface
GDI .... Ground Detector Indicator
GDI .... New York, NY [*Location identifier FAA*] (FAAL)
GDI .... Sammlung der Griechischen Dialektinschriften [*A publication*] (OCD)
GDIAN .... Guardian (ROG)
GDIFS .... Gray and Ductile Iron Founders' Society [*Later, Iron Castings Society - ICS*]
GdIG .... Gadolinium Iron Garnet (IEEE)
GDIM .... Graduate Diploma in Industrial Management [*Australia*]
GDIP .... Gale Directory of International Publications [*A publication*]
GDIP .... General Defense Intelligence Program [*DoD*]
GDip .... Graduate Diploma (DD)
GDipA(Couns)... Graduate Diploma in Arts (Counselling)
GDipCD .... Graduate Diploma in Child Development
GDipCh .... Graduate Diploma in Chiropractic
GDipClinSc... Graduate Diploma in Clinical Science
GDipCompSt... Graduate Diploma in Computer Studies
GDipEc .... Graduate Diploma in Economics
GDipErg .... Graduate Diploma in Ergonomics
GDipExerSpSc... Graduate Diploma in Exercise and Sport Science
GDipHA .... Graduate Diploma in Health Administration
GDipHC .... Graduate Diploma in Health Counselling
GDipHSM ..... Graduate Diploma in Health Services Management
GDipHumNut... Graduate Diploma in Human Nutrition
GDipLS .... Graduate Diploma in Legal Studies
GDipM .... Graduate Diploma in Management
GDipMLS ..... Graduate Diploma in Medical Laboratory Science
GDIPP .... General Defense Intelligence Proposed Program [*DoD*] (MCD)
GDipPEC ...... Graduate Diploma in Parent Education and Counselling
GDipPHC ...... Graduate Diploma in Primary Health
GDipPrfMgt... Graduate Diploma in Professional Management
GDipPubL ..... Graduate Diploma in Public Law
GDIS .... Gier-Dunkle Integrating Sphere
Gdk .... Gdansk [*Poland*] (BARN)
GDL .... Gas Discharge Lamp
GDL .... Gas Dynamic LASER
GDL .... Gas Dynamics Laboratory
GDL .... Gladstone-Dale Law
GDL .... Glass Delay Line
GDL .... Glass Development LASER
GDL .... Global Data Link

GDL .... Glow-Discharge Lamp [Spectrometry]
GDL .... Glucono-delta-Lactone [Organic chemistry]
GDL .... Graphic Display Library
GDL .... Graphic Drawing Library [Graphic Data Ltd.] [Software package] (NCC)
GDL .... Graphics Display List [Graphic Data Ltd.] [Software package] (NCC)
GDL .... Guadalajara [Mexico] [Airport symbol] (OAG)
GDLB .... Glendale Federal Bank FSB [NASDAQ symbol] (SAG)
GDLE .... Graduate Diploma in Land Economy
GDLEW ...... Glendale Fed Bk FSB Wrrt [NASDAQ symbol] (TTSB)
GDLK .... Grid Leak
GDLP .... Grenada Democratic Labour Party [Political party] (EY)
GDLP .... Ground Data Link Processor (GAVI)
GDLS .... General Dynamics [Corp.] Land Systems Division
GDLS .... General Dynamics Land Systems Inc. [A publication] (AAGC)
GDLS .... Glow-Discharge Lamp Source [Spectrometry]
GDLS .... Graduate Diploma in Library Science (ADA)
GDM .... Gardner, MA [Location identifier FAA] (FAAL)
GDM .... General Design Memorandum [US Army Corps of Engineers]
GDM .... General Development Map [or Model]
GDM .... Geodetic Distance Measurement
GDM .... Gestational Diabetes Mellitus [Medicine]
GDM .... Ghana Democratic Movement [Political party] (EY)
GDM .... Gibraltar Democratic Movement [Political party] (PPE)
GDM .... Global Data Manager
GDM .... Gravitational Dipole Moment (PDAA)
GDM .... Grenada Democratic Movement [Political party] (EAIO)
GDM .... Grid-Dip Meter (IAA)
GDM .... Grid-Dip Modulator
GDM .... Guidance Design Manager (MCD)
GDMA .... Glycol Dimethacrylate (MCD)
GDManTher... Graduate Diploma in Manipulative Therapy
GdmCl .... Guanidinium Chloride [Biochemistry]
GDMCN ...... Ground Data Management and Communications Network (MCD)
GDME .... Glycol Dimethyl Ether [Organic chemistry]
GDMI .... Gardner Denver Machinery [NASDAQ symbol] (TTSB)
GDMI .... Gardner Denver Machinery, Inc. [NASDAQ symbol] (SAG)
GDMK .... GoodMark Foods [NASDAQ symbol] (TTSB)
GDMK .... GoodMark Foods, Inc. [NASDAQ symbol] (NQ)
GDML .... Gas Dynamic Mixing LASER [Navy]
GDMO .... General Duties Medical Officer
GDMS .... Generalized Data Management System [Computer science] (BUR)
GDMS .... Geographic Data Management System [Computer science]
GDMS .... Global Data Management System
GDMS .... Glow-Discharge Mass Spectroscopy [or Spectrometry]
GDMS .... Graphics Display Management System (MCD)
GDMT .... Gemini Detailed Maneuver Table (IAA)
GDN .... Garden
GDN .... Gdansk [Poland] [Airport symbol] (OAG)
GDN .... Giant Descending Neuron [Neurology]
GDN .... Glycol Dinitrate [Organic chemistry]
GDN .... Golden News Resources Corp. [Vancouver Stock Exchange symbol]
GDN .... Government Data Network [Telecommunications] (OSI)
Gdn .... Guanidine [Biochemistry]
GDN .... Guardian
GDNC .... Guidance (MSA)
GDNCE .... Guidance (AFM)
GDNF .... Glial-Derived Growth Factor [Biochemistry]
GdNPF .... Glia-Derived Neurite-Promoting Factor (DB)
Gdns .... Gardens (DD)
GDNS .... Gardens (MCD)
GDO .... Garage Door Opener (NG)
gdo .... Gate-Dip Oscillator (IDOE)
GDO .... General Development Order [Town and country planning] [British]
GDO .... Grid-Dip Oscillator
gdo .... Grid-Dip Oscillator (IDOE)
GDO .... Gross Domestic Output [Economics]
GDO .... Guasdualito [Venezuela] [Airport symbol] (OAG)
GDO .... Guidance Officer (KSC)
GDO .... Gun Direction Officer (NATG)
GDO .... Gunn Diode Oscillator [Electronics] (PDAA)
GDOA .... Graphic Data Output Area (CMD)
GDO(A) .... Guild of Dispensing Opticians (Australia)
GDOC .... University of Guelph Document Holdings [Database] [No longer available online]
GDOccHlth ... Graduate Diploma in Occupational Health
GDOES .... Glow-Discharge Optical Emission Spectroscopy
GDOFA .... Guide Dog Owners and Friends' Association [Australia]
GDOP .... Geometric Degradation of Position [Aerospace]
GDOP .... Geometric Dilution of Precision
GDoS .... South Georgia College, Douglas, GA [Library symbol Library of Congress] (LCLS)
GDP .... Gaede Diffusion Pump
GDP .... Gale Directory of Publications [Later, GDPBM] [A publication]
GDP .... Gallium Photo Diode
GDP .... Gaseous Diffusion Plant [Nuclear energy] (NUCP)
GDP .... Gaseous Discharge Principle
GDP .... Gel Diffusion Precipitin [Biochemistry] (DAVI)
GDP .... General Defense Plan [Formerly, EDP] [NATO] (NATG)
GDP .... General Development Plan (MUGU)
GDP .... Generalized Data Base Processor [Computer science] (MHDI)
GDP .... Generalized Distributor Program [Computer science]
GDP .... Generalized Documentation Processor (NASA)
GDP .... Generalized Drawing Primitive
GDP .... Gesamtdeutsche Partei [All-German Party] [Political party] (PPE)

GDP .... Giant Depolarizing Potential [Neurophysiology]
GDP .... Giant Depolarizing Synaptic Potential [Neurochemistry]
GDP .... Gloria Dei Press [An association] (EA)
GDP .... Goal-Directed Programming
GDP .... Golden Pond Resources [Vancouver Stock Exchange symbol]
GDP .... Good Design Practice (DB)
GDP .... Goodrich Petroleum [NYSE symbol] (SAG)
GDP .... Government Data Publications [Information service or system] (IID)
GDP .... Government Development Platform [Marine science] (OSRA)
GDP .... Graphic Display Processor
GDP .... Grid Driving Power
GDP .... Gross Domestic Product [Economics]
GDP .... Grounded into Double Plays [Baseball]
GDP .... Groupe des Democrates Patriotes [Burkina Faso] [Political party] (EY)
GDP .... Guadalupe Pass, TX [Location identifier FAA] (FAAL)
GDP .... Guanosine Diphosphate [Biochemistry]
GDP .... Guanosine Dyphosphate [Biochemistry]
GDP .... Gun Defence Position [Navy British]
GDP .... Gun Director Pointer [Naval gunnery]
GDPA .... General Dental Practitioner's Association [British]
GDPA .... Graduate Diploma in Public Accountancy (DD)
GDPA .... Graduate Diploma in Public Accounting (DD)
GDPA .... Graduate Diploma in Public Administration (PGP)
GDP (A) ...... Gross Domestic Product (Average) [Economics]
GDPAP .... Goodrich Petrol 8% Cv'A'Pfd [NASDAQ symbol] (TTSB)
GDPAP .... Goodrich Petroleum [NASDAQ symbol] (SAG)
GDPBM .... Gale Directory of Publications and Broadcast Media [Formerly, GDP] [A publication]
GDP(CL) ...... Gun Director Pointer (Cross Leveler) [Naval gunnery]
GD/PD .... General Dynamics, Pomona Division
GDP (E) ...... Gross Domestic Product (Expenditure) [Economics]
GDPGM .... Ground Delay Program [Aviation] (FAAC)
GDP (I) .... Gross Domestic Product (Income) [Economics]
GDP(L) .... Gun Director Pointer (Leveler) [Naval gunnery]
GDPMan ...... Guanosine Diphosphomannose [Biochemistry]
GDP (P) ...... Gross Domestic Product (Production) [Economics]
GDP(P) .... Gun Director Pointer (Pointer) [Naval gunnery]
GDPS .... General Disk Programming System [Computer science] (IAA)
GDPS .... Global Data Processing System [World Meteorological Organization]
GDPS .... Government Document Publishing Service
GDP(SS) ...... Gun Director Pointer (Sight Setter) [Naval gunnery]
GDP(T) .... Gun Director Pointer (Trainer) [Naval gunnery]
GDQ .... Golden Dragon Resources [Vancouver Stock Exchange symbol]
GDQ .... Gondar [Ethiopia] [Airport symbol] (OAG)
GDQ .... Lincoln, Nebraska Air National Guard [FAA designator] (FAAC)
GDQF .... Graphical Display and Query Facility [IBM Corp.]
GDR .... Gaol Delivery Roll (ROG)
GDR .... Gaucher's Disease Registry [National Gaucher Foundation - NGF] [Superseded by] (EA)
GDR .... Geodetic Data Reduction
GDR .... Geophysical Data Record
GDR .... German Democratic Republic [East Germany]
GDR .... Giant Dipole Resonance
GDR .... Graphic Depth Recorder
GDR .... Grid Dead Reckon [Military] (CAAL)
GDR .... Ground Delay Response [Telecommunications] (OA)
GDR .... Group Delay Response (IAA)
GDR .... Groupement des Democrates Revolutionnaires [Burkina Faso] [Political party] (EY)
GDR .... Guard Rail (AAG)
GDRC .... Gyro Drift Rate Compensation
GdrcCa. ...... Goodrich, BF Capital [Associated Press] (SAG)
GDRDA .... Genetically Directed Representational Difference Analysis
GDRE .... Graduate Diploma in Religious Education (PGP)
Gdrich .... [The] Goodrich [B.F.] Co. [Associated Press] (SAG)
GDS .... Agnes Scott College, Decatur, GA [Library symbol Library of Congress] (LCLS)
GDS .... Gas Deployed Skirt (MCD)
GDS .... Gas Dynamic System
GDS .... GDP [Guanosine Diphosphate] Dissociation Stimulator [Biochemistry]
GDS .... Gel Drying System [Chromatography]
GDS .... Gendis, Inc. [Toronto Stock Exchange symbol]
GDS .... General Data Stream [Computer science]
GDS .... General Declassification Schedule (MCD)
GDS .... General Drafting System [Applied Research of Cambridge Ltd.] [Software package] (NCC)
GDS .... Geodetic Data Site
GDS .... Geriatric Depression Scale [Medicine] (DMAA)
GDS .... Gesell Developmental Schedules [Education]
GDS .... Global Deterioration Scale [Medicine]
GDS .... Global Directory Service
GDS .... Global Distribution Systems
GDS .... Glow-Discharge Spectrometry
GDS .... GNC [Guidance and Navigation Computer] Dynamic Simulator [NASA] (NASA)
GDS .... Goldstone, CA [Spaceflight tracking and data network] [NASA] (NASA)
GDS .... Goods
gds. .... Goods (WDAA)
GDS .... Gordon Diagnostic System (EDAC)
GDS .... Government Disclosure Service [A publication] (AAGC)
GDS .... Gradual Dosage Schedule [Medicine] (DMAA)
GDS .... Graphical Design Software (AAEL)

GDS	Graphical Display System [*Station control and data acquisition*] (IEEE)
GDS	Graphic Data System
GDS	Graphic Design System
GDS	Graphic Display Segment
GDS	Great Dark Spot [*Image on Neptune*] [*Astronomy*]
GDS	Great Dark Spot on Neptune [*Astronomy*]
GDS	Ground Data System
GDS	Ground Display System
Gds	Guards [*British military*] (DMA)
GDS	Gun Display System (MCD)
GDSA	Goal-Directed Serial Alternation
GDSafH	Graduate Diploma in Safety and Health
GDSafS	Graduate Diploma in Safety Science
GDSBFC	Good Day Sunshine Beatles Fan Club (EA)
GDSC	Gateway Data Sciences [*NASDAQ symbol*] (TTSB)
GDSC	Gateway Data Sciences Corp. [*NASDAQ symbol*] (SAG)
GDSC	Geodesic
GDSC	Graduate Diploma in Social Communication (ADA)
GDSCC	Goldstone Deep Space Communications Complex [*NASA*]
GDSD	Ground Data Systems Divsion [*NASA*] (NASA)
GDSDF	Generalized Data Structure Definition Facility [*Computer science*] (MHDB)
GDSIB	Global Digital Sea Ice Data Bank (USDC)
GDSIDB	Global Digital Sea Ice Data Bank [*Marine science*] (OSRA)
GDSL	Graduate Diploma in School Librarianship (ADA)
GDSM	Ground Data Systems Manager (MCD)
GDSM	Guardsman [*Military*]
GDSN	Global Digital Seismic Network
GDSN	Global Digital Seismograph Network [*Earthquake study*]
GDSO	Ground Data Systems Officer (MCD)
GDSS	Global Decision Support System (MCD)
GDSSc	Graduate Diploma in Sport Science
GDSSR	GDSD [*Ground Data Systems Division*] Staff Support Room [*NASA*] (NASA)
GDT	Gas Decay Tank (NRCH)
GDT	Gas Discharge Tube
GD/T	General Dynamics/Telecommunications
GDT	Generator Development Tools [*Silicon Design Laboratories*] (NITA)
GDT	Geographic Data Technology, Inc. [*Information service or system*] (IID)
GDT	Global Descriptor Table [*Computer science*]
GDT	Golden Diamond Travel and Tourism Agency [*Saudi Arabia*]
GDT	Graduate Diploma in Taxation (PGP)
GDT	Graduate Diploma in Theology (PGP)
GDT	Grand Turk [*British West Indies*] [*Airport symbol*] (OAG)
GDT	Graphic Display Terminal
GDT	Ground Data Terminal
GDT	Ground Delay Time (IAA)
GDT	Guidant Corp. [*NYSE symbol*] (SAG)
GDTE	Graduate Diploma in Technological Entrepreneurship (PGP)
GDTL	Graduate Diploma in Teacher Librarianship (ADA)
GDTR	Global Descriptor Table Register [*Computer science*] (PCM)
GDTS	Gliding Deceleration Technology System
GDU	Gamo Democratic Union [*Ethiopia*]
GDU	Garbage Disposal Unit (ADA)
GDU	Gastroduodenal Ulcer [*Medicine*] (DMAA)
GDU	Glendale Resources, Inc. [*Vancouver Stock Exchange symbol*]
GDU	Graphic Display Unit
GDU	Guide Dog Users (EA)
GDUI	Guide Dog Users, Inc. (EA)
GDunGS	Church of Jesus Christ of Latter-Day Saints, Genealogical Society Library, SandySprings Georgia Branch, Dunwoody, GA [*Library symbol Library of Congress*] (LCLS)
G Dur	Guillelmus Durandi [*Deceased, 1296*] [*Authority cited in pre-1607 legal work*] (DSA)
G Duran	Guillelmus Durandi [*Deceased, 1296*] [*Authority cited in pre-1607 legal work*] (DSA)
GDurng	Grupo Industrial Durango SA de CV [*Associated Press*] (SAG)
GDuV	United States Veterans Administration Center, Dublin, GA [*Library symbol Library of Congress*] (LCLS)
GDV	Gastric Dilatation Volvulus
GDV	Geomagnetic Daily Variations
GDV	Glendive [*Montana*] [*Airport symbol*] (OAG)
GdVP	Grossdeutsche Volkspartei [*Pan-German People's Party*] [*Austria Political party*] (PPE)
GDVS	Greater Delaware Valley Savings Bank [*NASDAQ symbol*] (SAG)
GDVS	Greater Del Valley Svgs [*NASDAQ symbol*] (TTSB)
GDW	Gladwin, MI [*Location identifier FAA*] (FAAL)
GDW	Glass-Distilled Water [*Medicine*] (DMAA)
GDW	Golden West Financial Corp. [*NYSE symbol*] (SPSG)
GDW	Golden West Finl [*NYSE symbol*] (TTSB)
GDW	Goldwest Resources Ltd. [*Vancouver Stock Exchange symbol*]
GDWND	Gradient Wind (NOAA)
GDX	Gated-Diode Crosspoint [*Electronics*] (PDAA)
GDX	Genovese Drug Stores, Inc. [*AMEX symbol*] (SPSG)
GDX	Glycidydiisopropylidenexylitol [*Organic chemistry*]
GDX	Goldstone, California [*Spaceflight Tracking and Data Network*] [*NASA*]
GDX	Grandex Resources Ltd. [*Vancouver Stock Exchange symbol*]
GDX	Gun Direction Exercise [*British military*] (DMA)
GDX	Upperville, VA [*Location identifier FAA*] (FAAL)
GDXA	Genovese Drug Str'A' [*AMEX symbol*] (TTSB)
GDY	Grundy, VA [*Location identifier FAA*] (FAAL)
GdyFam	Goody's Family Clothing [*Associated Press*] (SAG)

GDYL	Great Dictionary of the Yiddish Language [*Columbia University Department of Linguistics*] [*Information service or system*] (IID)
GDYN	Geodynamics Corp. [*NASDAQ symbol*] (NQ)
GDYS	Goody's Family Clothing [*NASDAQ symbol*] (SPSG)
GE	Federal Republic of Germany [*NATO*]
GE	Gaensslen-Erb [*Syndrome*] [*Medicine*] (DB)
GE	Gamma-Endorphin (DB)
GE	Garrison Engineer [*British military*] (DMA)
GE	Garrison Extracts [*Army*]
GE	Gas Ejection [*Opening*] [*Technical drawings*]
GE	Gas Examiner [*British*]
GE	Gastric Emptying [*Medicine*] (DB)
GE	Gastroemotional [*Medicine*] (MAE)
GE	Gastroenteritis [*Medicine*] (DB)
GE	Gastroenterology [*Medicine*]
GE	Gastroenterostomy [*Medicine*]
GE	Gastroesophageal [*Medicine*] (CPH)
GE	Gateway Exchange [*Telecommunications*]
GE	Gauge
GE	Gaussian Elimination (IEEE)
Ge	Gecelinus [*Zenzelinus de Cassanis*] [*Deceased, 1334*] [*Authority cited in pre-1607 legal work*] (DSA)
GE	Gel Electrophoresis [*Analytical chemistry*]
GE	General Election
GE	General Electric (NITA)
GE	General Electric Co. [*NYSE symbol*] (SPSG)
GE	General Electric Vallecitos Nuclear Center (DOGT)
GE	General Emergency (COE)
GE	General Examination
GE	General Expenses
GE	Generator of Excitation [*Medicine*] (DMAA)
GE	Gentamicin [*Antibacterial compound*] [*Generic form*]
GE	Georgia [*Internet country code*]
GE	Geoscience Electronics (MCD)
Ge	Gerbich [*Red cell antigen*] (STED)
Ge	Germanium [*Chemical element*]
GE	Germany (NATG)
ge	Germany, East [*MARC country of publication code Library of Congress*] (LCCP)
GE	Gilbert Islands [*ANSI two-letter standard code Obsolete*] (CNC)
GE	[*The*] Gilgamesh Epic and Old Testament Parallels [*A publication*] (BJA)
ge	Gilt-Edge (WDMC)
GE	Gilt Edges [*Bookbinding*]
GE	Gimbal Electronics
GE	Gnome Engine [*Hovercraft*]
GE	Good Evening [*Amateur radio*]
GE	Grand Earl [*Freemasonry*] (ROG)
GE	Grand East [*Freemasonry*] (ROG)
GE	Grand Encampment [*Freemasonry*]
GE	Grand Expert [*Freemasonry*] (ROG)
GE	Grand Ezra [*Freemasonry*] (ROG)
G/E	Granulocyte-Erythroid (Ratio) [*Hematology*]
G/E	Graphite Epoxy (NASA)
GE	Gravissimam Educationis [*Declaration on Christian Education*] [*Vatican II document*]
G-E	Gravity Eliminated (DAVI)
GE	Great Educators [*A publication*]
GE	Greater than or Equal To [*FORTRAN*]
GE	Great Exuma [*Bahama Islands*]
GE	Gripper Edge [*Bookbinding*] (DGA)
GE	Gross Earnings [*Business term*]
GE	Grounded Emitter
GE	Ground Equipment
GE	Group Engineer
GE	Group of Experts (NATG)
GE	Gsell-Erdheim [*Syndrome*] [*Medicine*] (DB)
GE	Guernsey Airlines [*ICAO designator*] (AD)
GE	Gyro Error
GEA	Farbenfabriken Bayer [*Germany*] [*Research code symbol*]
GEA	Gale Environmental Almanac [*A publication*]
GEA	Gamma Energy Analysis [*Nuclear energy*] (NUCP)
GEA	Garage Equipment Association (EAIO)
GEA	Gas Evolution Analysis (DICI)
GEA	Gastric Electrical Activity [*Medicine*] (DMAA)
GEA	General Electric-ARSD, Sunnyvale, CA [*OCLC symbol*] (OCLC)
GEA	Georgia Air [*Czechoslovakia*] [*ICAO designator*] (FAAC)
GEA	Geothermal Energy Association (NTPA)
GEA	German East Africa [*Obsolete*] (ROG)
GEA	Gigabit Ethernet Alliance [*Telecommunications*] (ACRL)
GEA	Global Education Associates (EA)
GEA	Glossary of EPA [*Environmental Protection Agency*] Acronyms [*A publication*] (EPA)
GEA	Gravure Engravers Association (EA)
GEA	Greater East Asia [*Used by Japanese in such terms as War of Greater East Asia and Greater East Asia Co-Prosperity Sphere*] [*World War II*]
GEA	Greater Ecosystem Alliance (EA)
GEA	Gross External Area
GEA	Grupo de Economistas y Asociados [*Provides economic analysis in Mexico and abroad*] (CROSS)
GEA	Noumea [*New Caledonia*] Magenta Airport [*Airport symbol*] (OAG)
GEAAE	Groupement Europeen des Artistes des Ardennes et de l'Eifel [*European Group of Artists of the Ardennes and the Eifel*] (EAIO)
GEAB	Geophysical Abstracts [*A publication*]

GEADGE...... German Air Defense Ground Environment

GEAG.......... General Electric Airborne Guidance (AAG)

GEAMR....... Groupement Europeen des Associations des Maisons de Reforme [EC] (ECED)

GE & JR ..... Great Eastern & Joint Railway [British] (ROG)

GE-ANPD .... General Electric Aircraft Nuclear Propulsion Department (SAA)

GEANS........ Gimbaled Electrostatic-Gyro Aircraft Navigation System [Air Force]

GEaO .... Ocmulgee Regional Library System, Eastman, GA [Library symbol] [Library of Congress] (LCLS)

GEAP .... General Electric Atomic Power [or Products]

GEAP .... Groupe d'Administration Publique [European Group of Public Administration - EGPA] [Brussels, Belgium] (EAIO)

GEAPS .... Grain Elevator and Processing Society (EA)

GEAR .... Great Eastern Australian Rally [Cycling]

GEAR .... Growth, Employment & Redistribution [Economic program] [South Africa]

Gear Landl & T... Gear on Landlord and Tenant [A publication] (DLA)

GEAR UP ..... Gaining Early Awareness and Readiness for Undergraduate Programs [U.S. Department of Education]

GEASCOP..... General Asymptotic Composition Program [Computer science]

GE/ASD........ General Electric/Apollo Support Division (KSC)

GEAU .... Groupe d'Etudes et d'Actions Urbaines [Canada]

GEAV .... Guidance Error Analysis Vehicles [Air Force]

GEB............. Geboren [Born] [German]

GEB............. Gebrueder [Brothers] [German]

GEB............. Gebunden [Bound] [Publishing] [German]

GEB............. General Engine Bulletin

GEB............. Guiding Eyes for the Blind (EA)

GEBA .... Global Energy Balance Archive [A publication]

GEBA .... Government Excess Baggage Authorization

GEBCO .... General Bathymetric Chart of the Oceans [International Hydrographic Bureau]

GEC............. Galactose Elimination Capacity

GEC............. Gaseous Electronics Conference

GEC............. Geauga County Public Library, Chardon, OH [OCLC symbol] (OCLC)

GEC............. GEICO Corp. [NYSE symbol] (SPSG)

GEC............. General Electric Capital Exchange [Associated Press] (SAG)

GEC............. General Electric Co.

GEC............. General Electrodynamics Corp. (MCD)

GEC............. General Equipment Command [Army]

GEC............. Generalized Equivalent Cylinder (OA)

GEC............. Geneva Executives Club (EA)

GEC............. German Cargo Services [ICAO designator] (FAAC)

GEC............. Global Environmental Change [Marine science] (OSRA)

GEC............. Glomerular Epithelial Cell [Medicine Medicine] (DMAA)

GEC............. Government Employees Council [Later, PED] (EA)

GEC............. Graphic Export Center [Netherlands]

GEC............. Grolier Educational Corp. (AEBS)

GEC............. Ground Environment Complex (MCD)

GEC............. Guyana Electricity Corp.

GEC............. Lufthansa Cargo, AG [Germany] [FAA designator] (FAAC)

GECA .... Government Employees' Compensation Act [1908]

GECAL .... General Electric Caliber [Gatling Gun]

GECAL .... General Electric Credit Auto Lease, Inc.

GECC .... Gasoline Engine, Close-Coupled

GECC .... General Electric Capital Corp.

GECC .... Government Employees Clinic Center [British]

GECCMSEF... Group to Establish Criteria for Certifying Munitions Systems to Electromagnetic Fields [DoD] (RDA)

GECCS .... General Electric Company Computer Services [British] (NITA)

GECE .... Groupement Europeen des Caisses d'Epargne [European Savings Bank Group] [EC] (ECED)

GECECS ...... General Electric Chemical Engineering Calculation System

Gecel .... Gecelinus [Zenzelinus de Cassanis] [Deceased, 1334] [Authority cited in pre-1607 legal work] (DSA)

GECEP .... General Civil Engineering Package (IAA)

GECM.......... GENICOM Corp. [NASDAQ symbol] (NQ)

GECO .... Guidance Engine Cutoff [NASA] (KSC)

GECOM .... General Compiler (NITA)

GECOM .... Generalized Compiler [Computer science]

GECOR .... General Communication Routine (IAA)

GECOS........ General Comprehensive Operating Supervisor [Computer science]

GECOS........ General Comprehensive Operating System

GECOS........ General Electric Comprehensive Operating System [Computer science] (NHD)

GECR .... Global Environment Change Report (EERA)

GECS .... Graphite-Epoxy Composite Structure (PDAA)

GECS .... Ground Environmental Control System (IAA)

GED............. Gasoline Engine Driven

GED............. Gas-Phase Electron Diffraction [Physics]

Ged............. Gedaagde [Defendant] [Netherlands] (ILCA)

GED............. Gedampft [Muted] [Music]

GED............. Gedeh [Java] [Seismograph station code, US Geological Survey Closed] (SEIS)

GED............. General Educational Development [Test]

GED............. General Equivalency Diploma [For nongraduates]

GED............. Geo-Data International [Vancouver Stock Exchange symbol]

GED............. Georgetown [Delaware] [Airport symbol] (AD)

GED............. Georgetown, DE [Location identifier FAA] (FAAL)

GED............. Global Engineering Documents [Santa Ana, CA] [Information service or system]

GED............. Gluten-Free Diet (DB)

GED............. Government Electronics Division

GED............. Gross Earnings Deflator [Economics] (BARN)

GED............. Group on Electronic Devices

GED .... Gunn Effect Device

GEDA .... Goldfields Esperance Development Authority [Australia]

GEDA .... Goodyear Electronic Differential Analyzer (IAA)

GEDAC .... General Electric Detection and Automatic Correction (NASA)

GEDAN........ General Data Analyzer (IAA)

GEDCOM...... Genealogical Data Communications [Computer science]

GED-GB........ Gulf Ecology Division-Gulf Breeze [Environmental Protection Agency] (AEPA)

GEDI .... General Educational Development Institute (EA)

GEDI .... Groupe d'Etudes en Developpement International [International Development Studies Group] [Canada]

GEDIS .... Geological, Exploration and Development Information System [Australia]

GEDIS .... Groupement Europeen des Enterprises de Distribution Integrees [European Multiple Retailers Association] [Belgium EC] (ECED)

GEDIT .... General-Purpose Text Editor [Computer science] (MHDB)

GEdO .... Group Education Officer [British military] (DMA)

GEDP .... General Educational Development Program [Army] (AABC)

GEDPD........ Gallaudet Encyclopedia of Deaf People and Deafness [A publication]

GEDRT........ Group Europeen d'Echange d'Experience sur la Direction de la Recherche Textil e [European Group for the Exchange of Information on Textile Research] (PDAA)

GEDS .... Gaseous Emissions Data System [Environmental Protection Agency] (GFGA)

GEDT .... General Educational Development Test

GEDU .... Gun Elevation Displacement Unit (DNAB)

GEE............. Geehi [Australia Seismograph station code, US Geological Survey Closed] (SEIS)

GEE............. Geeseair [Canada ICAO designator] (FAAC)

GEE............. General Estimating Equation [Mathematics]

GEE............. General Evaluation Equipment

GEE............. Generalized Estimating Equation (DMAA)

GEE............. Geneseo, NY [Location identifier FAA] (FAAL)

GEE............. Glycine Ethyl Ester (MAE)

GEE............. Gross Ecosystem Exchange [Biology]

GEE............. Group for Environmental Education

GEE............. Group of Economic Experts (EERA)

GEEB .... Geerlings & Wade [NASDAQ symbol] (TTSB)

GE economic forecasts... General Economic Forecasts [Databank] (NITA)

GEEIA.......... Ground Electronics Engineering Installation Agency [Air Force]

GEEK .... Geomagnetic Electrokinetograph [Equipment for exploring ocean depths]

GEEL .... General Election Expenditure Limit [Federal Election Commission]

GE ENG ...... Geological Engineer (WDAA)

Ge Engr ...... Geological Engineer

GEEP .... General Electric Electronic Processor

GEEP .... Group of Experts on Environmental Pollutants (EERA)

GEER .... Geerlings & Wade, Inc. [NASDAQ symbol] (SAG)

GeerlWd ...... Geerlings & Wade, Inc. [Associated Press] (SAG)

GEESE........ General Electric Electronic System Evaluator

GEF............. Air GEFCO [France ICAO designator] (FAAC)

GEF............. Gauss Error Function [Mathematics]

GEF............. Gel Electrofocusing [Analytical chemistry]

GEF............. General Electric Co. and Fanuc Automation Corp.

GEF............. Global Environment Facility [Implemented jointly by the World Bank, the United Nations Environment Program, and the United Nations Development Program]

GEF............. Global Environment Fund [of the World Bank] (EERA)

GEF............. Glossoepiglottic Fold (STED)

GEF............. Gonadotropin Enhancing Factor [Endocrinology]

GEF............. Gradient Elution Fractionation

GEF............. Gravure Education Foundation (EA)

GEF............. Greenville, FL [Location identifier FAA] (FAAL)

GEF............. Ground Equipment Failure [Air Force]

GEF............. Guanine-Nucleotide-Exchange Factor [Biochemistry]

GEF............. Guanine-Nucleoxide Exchange Factor [Biochemistry]

GEFA.......... Gulf-European Freight Association [Defunct] (EA)

GEFACS ...... Groupement des Fabricants d'Appariels Sanitaires en Ceramique de la CEE [Group of Manufacturers of Ceramic Sanitary Ware of the European Economic Community] (PDAA)

GEFAP .... Groupement Europeen des Associations Nationales des Fabricants de Pesticides [European Group of National Pesticide Manufacturer' Associations] [Common Market]

GEFDU........ Groupe Europeen des Femmes Diplomees des Universites [University Women of Europe - UWE] (EA)

GEFFEN...... Gay Extremists Fighting Fascistic Entertainment Normalcy [Focus group of Queer Nation]

GEFP.......... Guild of Ethical Funeral Practice (EA)

GEFRC........ General File/Record Control [Honeywell, Inc.]

GEFS........... General Electric Financial Services [Australia Commercial firm]

GEFS........... General Electric Flame Site (MUGU)

GEFT........... Group Embedded Figure Test [Education]

GEG............ Gamma Eta Gamma [Fraternity]

GEG............ Gegechkori [Former USSR Seismograph station code, US Geological Survey Closed] (SEIS)

GEG............ Generalized Euclidian Geometry (OA)

GEG............ Grace Energy Corp. (EFIS)

GEG............ Grange Gold Corp. [Vancouver Stock Exchange symbol]

GEG............ Gravure Engraving Group [British] (DBA)

GEG............ Gun Evaluation Group [Military] (CAAL)

GEG............ Spokane [Washington] [Airport symbol] (OAG)

GEGAS........ General Electric Gas [Process]

GEGB.......... General Electricity-Generating Board (OA)

GEGID......... Global Spill Mgmt [NASDAQ symbol] (TTSB)

GE-GLOSS ... Group of Experts on the Global Sea-Level Observing System [*Marine science*] (OSRA)
GEGP .... Golden Eagle Group [*NASDAQ symbol*] (TTSB)
GEGP .... Golden Eagle Group, Inc. [*NASDAQ symbol*] (SAG)
GEGPW .... Golden Eagle Group Wrrt [*NASDAQ symbol*] (TTSB)
GEGR .... General Grant National Memorial
GEGS .... General Electric Guidance System [*Aerospace*] (AAG)
Geh .... Gehalt [*Contents*] [*German*] (ILCA)
Geh .... Geheimrat [*Privy Councillor*] [*German*] (ILCA)
GEH .... George Eastman House [*Rochester, NY*]
GEH .... Glycerol Ester Hydrolase (DB)
GE-HAPO ..... General Electric Hanford Atomic Products Operation (SAA)
GEHL .... Gehl Co. [*NASDAQ symbol*] (NQ)
GEHME .... General Electric Heavy Military Electronics (IAA)
GEI .... Geisinger Medical Center, Medical Library, Danville, PA [*OCLC symbol*] (OCLC)
GEI .... Gender Equality Indicator [*Australia*]
GEI .... Geographic Enforcement Initiative [*Environmental Protection Agency*] (EPA)
GEI .... Geotechnical Engineers, Inc. (EFIS)
GEI .... Graphics Engine Interface [*Computer science*]
GEI .... Graymoor Ecumenical Institute (EA)
GEI .... Grenlock Energy, Inc. [*Vancouver Stock Exchange symbol*]
GEI .... Gruppo Esponenti Italiani (EA)
GEICO .... GEICO Corp. [*Associated Press*] (SAG)
GEICO .... Government Employees Insurance Co.
GEIDC .... Greater Erie Industrial Development Corp. [*Pennsylvania*]
GEII .... Graymoor Ecumenical and Interreligious Institute (EA)
GEIL .... Greenfield Industries [*NASDAQ symbol*] (TTSB)
GEIMS .... General Electric Inventory Management System (IAA)
GEIP .... Greenhouse Education and Information Program (EERA)
GEIPS .... General Electric Industrial and Power Systems [*Australia Commercial firm*]
GEIR .... GPETE End Item Replacement (NVT)
GEIS .... GE [*General Electric Co.*] Information Services [*Information service or system*] (IID)
GEIS .... Generalized Environmental Impact Statement
GEIS .... Generic Environmental Impact Statement [*or Study*] [*Nuclear energy*] (NRCH)
GEISA .... Gestion et Etude des Informations Spectroscopiques Atmospheriques [*Database*] [*Laboratoire de Meteorologie Dynamique du CNRS*] [*French*] [*Information service or system*] (CRD)
GEISCO .... General Electric Information Services Co. [*General Electric Co.*] [*Software manufacturer*] [*Information service or system Telecommunications*] (IID)
GEISHA .... Geodetic Inertial Survey and Horizontal Alignment (IEEE)
GEISHA .... Gun Electron-Induced Semiconductor Hybrid Amplifier
GEJ .... Gaseous Ejection (KSC)
GEJ .... Gastroesophageal Junction [*Anatomy*] (DAVI)
GEK .... Ganes Creek, AK [*Location identifier FAA*] (FAAL)
GEK .... Geomagnetic Electrokinetograph [*Equipment for exploring ocean depths*]
GEL .... Gambcrest Enterprises Ltd. [*Gambia*] [*ICAO designator*] (FAAC)
GEL .... Gelatin
gel .... Gelatin [*Theatrical lighting*] (WDMC)
GEL .... General Electric Laboratory
GEL .... General Electric Lighting [*Australia Commercial firm*]
GEL .... General Emulation Language
GEL .... Genesis Energy LP [*NYSE symbol*] (SAG)
GEL .... Gilbert Islands [*ANSI three-letter standard code Obsolete*] (CNC)
GEL .... Goldenlode Resources Ltd. [*Vancouver Stock Exchange symbol*]
GEL .... Groupement Europeen de Lymphologie [*European Lymphology Group - ELG*] [*Brussels, Belgium*] (EAIO)
GEL .... Guaranteed Employment Level
GEL .... Santo Angelo [*Brazil*] [*Airport symbol*] (OAG)
GELAC .... Georgia Division, Lockheed Aircraft Corp.
GELAP .... General Electric Computer Analysis Program
GELC .... Groupe des Editeurs de Livres de la CEE [*Book Publishers Group of EEC*] (EAIO)
Gelcap .... Gelatin-Coated Capsule [*Pharmacy*]
GELCINA ...... German Evangelical Lutheran Conference in North America (EA)
GELCO .... General Electric Co. (EFIS)
Geld & M. ...... Geldart and Maddock's English Chancery Reports [*6 Maddock's Reports*] [*A publication*] (DLA)
Geld & O. ...... Nova Scotia Decisions, by Geldert and Oxley [*A publication*] (DLA)
Geld & Ox. ... Nova Scotia Decisions, by Geldert and Oxley [*A publication*] (DLA)
Geld & R. ...... Geldert and Russell's Nova Scotia Reports [*A publication*] (DLA)
Geldart .... Geldart and Maddock's English Chancery Reports [*6 Maddock's Reports*] [*A publication*] (DLA)
GElektr. .... Grupo Elektra SA de CV [*Associated Press*] (SAG)
GELFAC .... Gel Frontal Analysis Chromatography
GELIS .... Ground Emitter Location and Identification System [*Army*]
GELIS-H .... Ground Emitter Location and Identification System - High [*Army*]
GELME .... General Electric Light Military Electronics (IAA)
GelmSci. .... Gelman Sciences, Inc. [*Associated Press*] (SAG)
GELOAD .... General Loader [*Honeywell*] (NITA)
GELOC .... Geolocation (DOMA)
GEL QUAV ..... Gelatina Quavis [*In Any Kind of Jelly*] [*Pharmacy*] (ROG)
GelTex .... GelTex Pharmaceuticals, Inc. [*Associated Press*] (SAG)
GELTSPAP .... Group of Experts on Long-Term Scientific Policy and Planning [*UNESCO*]
GELX .... GelTex Pharmaceuticals [*NASDAQ symbol*] (TTSB)
GELX .... GelTex Pharmaceuticals, Inc. [*NASDAQ symbol*] (SAG)
GEM .... Bristol BAE [*British ICAO designator*] (FAAC)
GEM .... Gamma-Electron-Muon [*Particle detector*]

GEM .... Gas Energy Management
GEM .... Gas Engine Management [*Alternative fuel conversion equipment*]
GEM .... Gas Equipment Manufacturers' Group (IIA)
GEM .... Gas Exchange Module [*Cell culture*]
GEM .... Gateway to Educational Materials
Gem .... Gemara (BJA)
Gem .... Geminatae (BJA)
gem .... Geminate [*Chemistry*]
Gem .... Gemini [*Constellation*]
GEM .... General Effectiveness Model (DNAB)
GEM .... General Electric Motors [*Australia Commercial firm*]
GEM .... General Enrollment Manual
GEM .... General Epitaxial Monolith (IEEE)
GEM .... Generic Electronic Module (SSD)
GEM .... Generic Equipment Model [*Electronics*] (AAEL)
GEM .... Generic Experiment Module
GEM .... Genetically Engineered Microorganism
GEM .... Genetically Modified Organism
gem .... Germanic [*MARC language code Library of Congress*] (LCCP)
GEM .... GeV Electron Microtron [*Atomic accelerator*] [*Proposed*]
GEM .... Giant Earth Mover [*Machine*]
GEM .... Giotto Extended Mission [*European Space Agency*]
GEM .... Goddard Earth Model [*NASA*]
GEM .... Government-Education-Medical
GEM .... Government Electronics Market (IAA)
GEM .... Graduated [*or Growing*] Equity Mortgage
GEM .... Graff Electronic Machines Ltd. [*British*]
GEM .... Graphic Engine Monitor (DA)
GEM .... Graphics Environment Manager [*Computer science*]
GEM .... Graphite Electrode Contouring Machine (PDAA)
GEM .... Graphite Epoxy Motor (MCD)
GEM .... Grey Entertainment & Media (EFIS)
GEM .... Ground Effect Machine (NG)
GEM .... Ground Electronics Maintenance
GEM .... Ground Elevation Meter (PDAA)
GEM .... Ground Exploitation Module
GEM .... Groupes Evangile et Mission [*Institute of the Heart of Jesus - IHJ*] [*France*] (EA)
GEM .... Growing Equity Mortgage
GEM .... Growth with Equity in Mindano [*A USAID backed organization*] [*Philippines*]
GEM .... Grupo Embotellador de Mexico [*NYSE symbol*] (SAG)
GEM .... Grupo Embotellador Mex GDS [*NYSE symbol*] (TTSB)
GEM .... Guidance Evaluation Missile
GEM .... Guild of Experienced Motorists [*British*] (DBA)
GEM .... Gulf Energy & Minerals Co.
GEM .... Gun Effectiveness Model
GEM .... Gunn Effect Material
GEM .... Gyro Energy & Minerals Corp. [*Vancouver Stock Exchange symbol*]
GEM .... Miami, FL [*Location identifier FAA*] (FAAL)
GEM .... National Consortium for Graduate Degrees for Minorities in Engineering (EA)
GEMA .... Gale Encyclopedia of Multicultural America [*A publication*]
GEMA .... Grain Equipment Manufacturers Association (EA)
GEMA .... Gymnastic Equipment Manufacturers' Association [*British*] (BI)
GE/MAC .... General Electric Measurement and Control
GEMAGS .... General Electric Magnetically Anchored Gravity System
GEMAS .... Groupement Europeen des Maisons d'Alimentation et d'Approvisionnement a Succursales [*European Group of Food and Provision Chain Stores*] [*Common Market Brussels, Belgium*]
GEmbMx .... Grupo Embotellador de Mexico [*Associated Press*] (SAG)
GEMC .... Geriatric & Medical Companies [*NASDAQ symbol*] (NQ)
GEMC .... Geriatric & Medl Cos. [*NASDAQ symbol*] (TTSB)
GEMCO .... Global Electronic Markets Co. [*Joint venture of Citicorp and McGraw-Hill, In c. to provide computerized buying, selling, shipping, and insuring services for commodities traders*]
GEMCO .... Groote Eylandt Mining Co. [*Australia Commercial firm*]
GEMCOS .... Generalized Message Control System (BUR)
Gemi .... Gemini [*Constellation*]
Gemi .... Geminiano [*Flourished, 1407-09*] [*Authority cited in pre-1607 legal work*] (DSA)
GEMI .... Global Environmental Management Initiative [*Environmental science*]
GemII .... Gemini II Fund, Inc. [*Associated Press*] (SAG)
GEMIM .... Group of Experts on Marine Information Management [*Marine science*] (OSRA)
GEML .... Melilla [*Spain ICAO location identifier*] (ICLI)
GEMM .... Generalized Electronics Maintenance Model
GEMM .... Generic Missile Model (MCD)
GEMM .... Gilt-Edged Market Maker [*London Stock Exchange*] [*England*]
GEMM .... Granulocyte, Erythroid, Macrophage, Megakaryocyte [*Hematology*]
GEMMA .... Gilt-Edged Market Makers' Association [*London Stock Exchange*] [*England*]
GEMMS .... Geophysical Exploration Manned Mobile Submersible
GEMMSS .... Ground Emplaced Mine Scattering System [*Military*] (RDA)
GEMO .... Ground Electronic Maintenance Officer [*NASA*] (NG)
GEMP .... Government Energy Management Program [*Australia*]
GEMS .... Gender Equality in Mathematics and Science
GEMS .... General Education Management System [*Computer science*] (IEEE)
GEMS .... General Electrical and Mechanical Systems (IAA)
GEMS .... General Electric Manufacturing Simulator (IEEE)
GEMS .... General Electric Medical Systems [*Australia Commercial firm*]
GEMS .... General Energy and Materials Balance System [*Chemical engineering*] [*Computer science*]
GEMS .... General Engine Management System

GEMS........... General Equipment Maintenance System [*Software*] [*Diagonal Data Corp.*] [*Automotive engineering*]
GEMS........... Generalized Evaluation Model Simulator [*NASA*]
GEMS........... Geostationary European Meteorological Satellite
GEMS........... German Mass Spectrometer
GEMS........... Glass with Embedded Metal and Sulphide [*In interplanetary dust particles*]
GEMS........... Glenayre Technologies [*NASDAQ symbol*] (TTSB)
GEMS........... Glenayre Techs, Inc. [*NASDAQ symbol*] (SAG)
GEMS........... Global Environment Monitoring System [*UNEP*] [*Database producer*] (IID)
GEMS........... Good Emergency Mother Substitute [*Pediatrics*] (DAVI)
GEMS........... Government Expenditure Management System [*Australia*]
GEMS........... Graphical Exposure Modeling System [*For estimating pollutants*]
GEMS........... Graphics Engineering and Mapping System [*Navy*] (GFGA)
GEMS........... Ground Emplaced Mine Scattering System [*Military*] (AABC)
GEMS........... Ground Equipment Maintenance Squadron
GEMS........... Growth, Economy, Management, and Customer Satisfaction [*Procedure for establishing management goals*]
GEMSA .... Guanidinoethylmercaptosuccinic Acid [*Biochemistry*]
GeMSAEC .... General Medical Sciences and Atomic Energy Commission
GEMSAT ...... Girls' Education in Mathematics, Science, and Technology (AIE)
GEMSERVICE... Global Electronic Mail Service [*Electronic Mail Corp. of America*] [*Old Greenwich, CT*] [*Telecommunications*] (TSSD)
GEMSI .... Group of Experts on Methods, Standards, and Intercalibration [*Oceanography*] (MSC)
GEMSIP .... Gemini Stability Improvement Program [*NASA*]
GEMSS .... Ground Emplaced Mine Scattering System [*Military*] (RDA)
Gemstr......... Gemstar International Group Ltd. [*Associated Press*] (SAG)
GEMSVD ..... General Electric Missile and Space Vehicle Department [*Military*] (IAA)
GEMT .... Group of European Metallurgical Thermodynamicists [*National Physical Laboratory*] [*Databank*] (NITA)
GEMU .... German Economic and Monetary Union
GEMVS .... Generic Equipment Model Verification System [*Electronics*] (AAEL)
GEMx .... German Equity Market Index (NUMA)
GEN .... Business Operations Support Services [*British*] [*FAA designator*] (FAAC)
Gen.............. Gecelinus [*Zenzelinus de Cassanis*] [*Deceased, 1334*] [*Authority cited in pre-1607 legal work*] (DSA)
GEN .... Genavco Air Ltd. [*British ICAO designator*] (FAAC)
GEN .... Gender
GEN .... Genealogy
GEN .... General (AABC)
Gen.............. General (ODBW)
gen .... General (VRA)
GEN .... General Electric Network [*Computer science*]
GEN .... Generate
gen .... Generate [*News media*] (WDMC)
GEN .... Generation (MSA)
GEN .... Generator [*Computer science*] (AAG)
gen .... Generator (IDOE)
GEN .... Generic
Gen.............. Genesis [*Old Testament book*]
GEN .... Genetics
GEN .... Geneva [*City in Switzerland*]
GEN .... Genital
gen .... Genital [*Medicine*] (DMAA)
GEN .... Genitive [*Case*] [*Grammar*]
GEN .... Genoa [*Italy*] [*Seismograph station code, US Geological Survey Closed*] (SEIS)
GEN .... GenRad, Inc. [*NYSE symbol*] (SPSG)
GEN .... Genuine (ADA)
GEN .... Genus [*Biology*]
GEN .... Gerin, Inc. [*Toronto Stock Exchange symbol*]
GEN .... Gilgamesh, Enkidu, and the Netherworld (BJA)
GEN .... Greater Lenora Resources Corp. [*Toronto Stock Exchange symbol Vancouver Stock Exchange symbol*]
GEN .... Oslo [*Norway*] Ardermoen Airport [*Airport symbol*] (OAG)
GENA .... Ground Environment and Navigational Aid (PDAA)
Gen Abr Cas Eq... General Abridgment of Cases in Equity [*Equity Cases Abridged*] [*1677-1744*] [*A publication*] (DLA)
Gen AF .... General of the Air Force (WGA)
Gen An .... De Generatione Animalium [*of Aristotle*] [*Classical studies*] (OCD)
GEN AV....... General Average (WDAA)
GENB .... [*The*] Genesee Brewing Co., Inc. [*NASDAQ symbol*] (NQ)
GENB .... Genessee Brewing [*NASDAQ symbol*] (SAG)
GENBANK ... Genetic Sequences Databank [*Intelligenetics, Inc.*] [*Information service or system*] (IID)
GENBB......... Genesee Corp. 'B' [*NASDAQ symbol*] (TTSB)
GENC .... General Electric Nose Cone [*Aerospace*] (AAG)
GEN CAR .... General Cargo [*Shipping*] (DS)
GENCHEM... General Chemical Indicators [*Database*] [*Probe Economics, Inc.*] [*Information service or system*] (CRD)
Gen Con ...... General Counsel (AAGC)
GENCONV ... Geneva Conventions [*Military*] (NVT)
Gencor......... Gencor Industries, Inc. [*Associated Press*] (SAG)
Gen Corr...... De Generatione et Corruptione [*of Aristotle*] [*Classical studies*] (OCD)
GenCrp .... GenCorp, Inc. [*Associated Press*] (SAG)
GEND .... Generated Data File [*Computer science*]
GENDA .... General Data Analysis and Simulation (IAA)
GENDARME.. Generalized Data Reduction, Manipulation, Evaluation
GEN DEL...... General Delivery
GENDEP....... General Depot [*Military*]

GENDET ...... General Detail [*Coast Guard*]
Gen Dig .... General Digest [*A publication*] (DLA)
Gen Dig NS... General Digest, New Series [*A publication*] (DLA)
GENDIS........ General Distribution [*Pentagon security classification code*]
GENDISP...... General Dispensary [*Military*]
GENDYN ..... General Dynamics
GENE .... Genome Therapeutics [*NASDAQ symbol*] (TTSB)
GENE .... Genome Therapeutics Corp [*NASDAQ symbol*] (SAG)
GENEAL ...... Genealogy
GenEl........... General Electric Co. [*Associated Press*] (SAG)
GeneLTc....... GeneLabs Technologies, Inc. [*Associated Press*] (SAG)
GeneMed ..... GeneMedicine, Inc. [*Associated Press*] (SAG)
GENENG ..... Generalized Engine [*Computer science*]
Genentc........ Genentech, Inc. [*Associated Press*] (SAG)
Generation... Generations [*A publication*] (BRI)
GENESCO.... General Shoe Corp. [*Acronym now official name of firm*]
GenesCp ...... [*The*] Genessee Brewing Company, Inc. [*Associated Press*] (SAG)
GENESIS ..... Generation Simulation System [*Power systems*]
Genesis .... Genesis Health Ventures, Inc. [*Associated Press*] (SAG)
GenesisH ..... Genesis Health Ventures, Inc. [*Associated Press*] (SAG)
GENESSIS.... Generic Scene Simulation Software (EERA)
GENESYS.... General Engineering System
GENESYS.... Generalized System [*Computer program*] (NITA)
GENESYS.... Graduate Engineering Education System
GENET........ Genetics
Genetl.......... Genetics Institute, Inc. [*Associated Press*] (SAG)
GenetInst...... Genetics Institute, Inc. [*Associated Press*] (SAG)
GENETOX .... Genetic Toxicity [*Database*] [*Environmental Protection Agency Information service or system*] (CRD)
gen et sp nov... Genus et Species Nova [*New Genus and Species*] [*Latin*] (DMAA)
GENFAP ...... General Nonlinear Frame Analysis Program [*Structures & Computers Ltd.*] [*Software package*] (NCC)
GENG .... Gasoline Engine
GENI .... Genetics Institute, Inc. [*NASDAQ symbol*] (NQ)
GENI .... Global Energy Network International
Genicm......... GENICOM Corp. [*Associated Press*] (SAG)
GEnie .... General Electric Network for Information Exchange [*General Electric Co.*] [*Online information service*] (IID)
GENIE .... General Information Environment [*Data Dynamics, Inc.*] [*Portland, OR*] [*Telecommunications service*] (TSSD)
GENIE .... General Information Extractor
GENIP .... Geographic Education National Implementation Project [*National Geographic Society*]
GENIRAS.... General Information Retrieval and Application System (PDAA)
GENISYS.... General Inferencing System
GENIT .... Genitalia [*Medicine*]
GENIT .... Genitive [*Case*] [*Grammar*]
GENIZ .... Genetics Institute Dep Shrs [*NASDAQ symbol*] (TTSB)
GenKinet...... General Kinetics, Inc. [*Associated Press*] (SAG)
GENL .... General
GEN L .... General Licence [*British*] (ROG)
GENLED ...... General Ledger
Gen Led ...... General Ledger (EBF)
genlock........ Generator Lock (CDE)
GenlRe .... General Re Corp. [*Associated Press*] (SAG)
GENLY .... Generally (ROG)
Genlyte .... Genlyte Group, Inc. [*Associated Press*] (SAG)
GenManCert... General Management Certificate
GEN MGR .... General Manager (WDAA)
GENMISH.... US Military Mission with the Iranian Gendarmerie
GENMO....... Generalissimo [*Commander-in-Chief*] [*Spanish*] (ROG)
GENMOD...... General Model (RDA)
Gen Mtge..... General Mortgage [*Bond*] (MHDW)
gen nov .... Genus Novum [*New Genus*] [*Latin*] (DAVI)
GenNutr....... General Nutrition Co. [*Associated Press*] (SAG)
Genome....... Genome Therapeutics Corp. [*Associated Press*] (SAG)
GENOPAUSE... Geodetic Satellite in Polar Geosynchronous Orbit (NAKS)
Gen Ord Ch... General Orders of the English High Court of Chancery [*A publication*] (DLA)
GENOS .... Generate Operating System [*Computer program*]
GENOT .... General Notice
GENP .... Gentamicin Peak [*Level*] [*Immunology*] (DAVI)
GEN PRAC ... General Practice (WDAA)
GENPRL....... General Precision Laboratory
GEN PROC ... General Procedure (BABM)
GENPS .... Genital Neoplasm-Papilloma Syndrome [*Medicine*] (DMAA)
GENR .... Generate (AABC)
genr............. Generation (BARN)
GenR .... Genesis Rabbah (BJA)
GenRabb...... Genesis Rabbah (BJA)
GENREP....... General Reports [*Military*]
GENS .... General Soviet [*Later, A Group*] [*Division of National Security Agency*]
GENSAL ...... Generic Structure Language
GenScan...... General Scanning, Inc. [*Associated Press*] (SAG)
Gensco .... Genesco, Inc. [*Associated Press*] (SAG)
GENSER ...... General Service [*Military*] (MCD)
GENSER ...... General Services Intelligence [*Military*] (CAAL)
GENSESS..... General Sessions (ADA)
GENSH .... Generate Shell [*Computer science*] (PCM)
Gensia .... Gensia Pharmaceuticals, Inc. [*Associated Press*] (SAG)
GenSignl...... General Signal Corp. [*Associated Press*] (SAG)
GensisE .... Genesis Energy LP [*Associated Press*] (SAG)
GENSIT .... General Situation [*Military*] (NVT)
GENSPECS... General Specifications (DNAB)

GENSTAN..... Generalized Data Standardizer [Bureau of the Census] (GFGA)
GENSUP....... General Support [Army]
GENSURG ... General Surgery (AABC)
GenSurg ...... General Surgical Innovations, Inc. [Associated Press] (SAG)
GENSV .... General Service [Military]
GENSYM ...... Generated Symbol [Computer science] (NHD)
Gen T.......... General Term (DLA)
GENT .... Gentamicin [Antibacterial compound]
GENT .... Gentamicin Trough [Level] [Immunology] (DAVI)
GENT .... Gentleman
Genta.......... Genta, Inc. [Associated Press] (SAG)
GENTEL....... General Telephone & Electronics Corp.
GENTEX ...... General Telegraph Exchange (IAA)
Gentex .... Gentex Corp. [Associated Press] (SAG)
GENTEXT ..... General Text (COE)
GENTN .... Gentleman [or Gentlemen] (ROG)
Gentnr .... Gentner Communications Corp. [Associated Press] (SAG)
GENTRAS ..... General Training System (MHDB)
GenuPrt .... Genuine Parts Co. [Associated Press] (SAG)
Genus .... Genus, Inc. [Associated Press] (SAG)
GenvDr .... Genovese Drug Stores, Inc. [Associated Press] (SAG)
Gen View Cr L... Stephen's General View of the Criminal Law [2nd ed.] [1890] [A publication] (DLA)
GENVST .... General Public Visiting [Navy] (NVT)
GenWyo .... Genessee and Wyoming, Inc. [Associated Press] (SAG)
GENY .... Generally
GENZ .... Genzyme Corp. [NASDAQ symbol] (NQ)
GENZ .... Genzyme Corp.-Genl Div [NASDAQ symbol] (TTSB)
GENZL .... Genzyme Corp.-Tissue Repair [NASDAQ symbol] (TTSB)
Genzy .... Genzyme Corp. [Associated Press] (SAG)
Genzym .... Genzyme Corp. [Associated Press] (SAG)
GenzyT........ Genzyme Corp. [Associated Press] (SAG)
GenzyTis ...... Genzyme Corp. [Associated Press] (SAG)
GenzyTr .... Genzyme Transgenics Corp. [Associated Press] (SAG)
GENZZ .... Genzyme Corp. Wrrt [NASDAQ symbol] (TTSB)
GEO .... Air Georgia [Former USSR] [FAA designator] (FAAC)
GEO .... Genetically Engineered Organism
GEO .... Geographic
GEO .... Geographic Division [Census] (OICC)
GEO .... Geologist
GEO .... Geomaque Explorations [TS, exchange symbol] (TTSB)
GEO .... Geometry
GEO .... Geophysical Report [Oil industry term] (DSUE)
GEO .... Georgetown [District of Columbia] [Seismograph station code, US Geological Survey] (SEIS)
GEO .... Georgetown [Guyana] [Airport symbol] (OAG)
GEO .... Georgetown, OH [Location identifier FAA] (FAAL)
GEO .... Georgia [Obsolete] (ROG)
geo .... Georgian [MARC language code Library of Congress] (LCCP)
Geo .... Georgia Reports [A publication] (DLA)
Geo .... Geoscience Electronics (MCD)
GEO .... Geostationary Earth Orbit
GEO .... Geosynchronous [Satellite orbit] (CDE)
GEO .... Geosynchronous Earth Orbit
GEO .... Geotech Capital [Vancouver Stock Exchange symbol]
GEO .... Glosa Education Organisation (EAIO)
GEOARCHIVE... Geology Archive [Database on earth science] [British] (NITA)
GEOBASE..... Geographic Cross-Reference Data [Claritas LP] [Information service or system] (CRD)
GEOC .... GeoTel Communications Corp. [NASDAQ symbol] (SAG)
GEOCEIVER... Geodetic Receiver
GEOCHEM.... Geochemical
GEOCODES... Geographic Codes (COE)
GEOD .... Geodesy [Science of measuring the earth] (ROG)
GEOD .... Geodetic
GEODAS....... Geophysical Data System (EERA)
Geod E........ Geodetic Engineer
Geo Dec ...... Georgia Decisions [A publication] (DLA)
GEODES....... Ground-based Electro-Optical Deep Space Surveillance (DICI)
GEODIAL...... Geoscience Data Index for Alberta [Alberta Research Council] [Information service or system] (IID)
Geo Dig ...... George's Mississippi Digest [A publication] (DLA)
GEODIS........ Geographic Design and Implementation System [Australian Capital Territory] (EERA)
GeoDIS .... Geographic Districting Information System for Maryland [Maryland State Department of State Planning] [Baltimore] [Information service or system] (IID)
GEODSS....... Ground-Based Electro-Optical Deep Space Surveillance [Satellite-tracking network]
Geodyn .... Geodynamics Corp. [Associated Press] (SAG)
GEO-EAS...... Geostatistical Environmental Assessment Software [US Environmental Protection Agency]
GEOFILE ..... Geographic File [DoD]
GEOFILE ..... Geographic Location File (COE)
GEOFIZ .... Geosciences Information Center [Federal Institute for Geosciences and NaturalResources] [Information service or system] (IID)
Geog........... Geographia [of Ptolemy] [Classical studies] (OCD)
Geog........... Geographical [A publication] (BRI)
Geog........... Geography (AL)
GEOG .... Geographer [or Geographer] (AFM)
GEOGNOS.... Geognosy [A knowledge of the structure of the earth] (ROG)
GEOGRAPHY... George Emerson's Old Grandmother Rode a Pig Home Yesterday [Mnemonic guide for spelling "geography"]
Geogr Ed ..... Geographical Education [A publication]
Geogrph....... Geographics, Inc. [Associated Press] (SAG)

GEOG T........ Geographical Teacher [A publication] (ROG)
GEOI .... Georesources, Inc. [NASDAQ symbol] (NQ)
GEOIS .... Geographic Information System [Computer science]
GEOL .... Geologist
GEOL .... Geology [or Geologist] (AFM)
GEOL .... Georesources Inc. [NASDAQ symbol] (TTSB)
Geol E .... Geological Engineer
GEOLGCL..... Geological
GEOLGY....... Geology
Geo Lib....... George on Libel [1812] [A publication] (DLA)
GEOLOC...... Geographical Location [Military] (AABC)
GEOLOC...... Geographic Location Code (COE)
GeolSci........ Geological Science (DD)
GEOM .... Geometry [or Geometric]
GEOMAG...... Geomagnetism
GEOMAN...... Global Energy Operations & Management Co.
Geo Mason U... George Mason University (GAGS)
GEOMOD...... Geometric Modeller [GE CAE International] [Software package] (NCC)
GEON .... Gyro Erected Optical Navigation
GEONAMES... Geologic Names of the United States [US Geological Survey] [Information service or system] (IID)
GEONAV...... Geographic Navigation [Navy] (CAAL)
Geon Co ...... [The] Geon Co. [Associated Press] (SAG)
GEOP .... General Emergency Operations Plan (CINC)
GEOPAUSE... Geodetic Satellite in Polar Geosynchronous Orbit [NASA] (NASA)
GE-OPC....... Group of Experts on Ocean Processes and Climate [Marine science] (OSRA)
Geo Peabody C... George Peabody College for Teachers of Vanderbilt University (GAGS)
Geoph .... Geophysics (DD)
GEOPHYS .... Geophysical
geopol .... Geopolitics (BARN)
Geopp......... Geopposserde [Defendant] [Netherlands Legal term] (DLA)
GEOPS .... Geodetic Estimates from Orbital Perturbation of Satellites (IAA)
GEOPS .... Geodetic Estimates from Orbital Perturbations of Satellites
GEOREF ...... Geographic Reference System [Civil Defense]
GEOREF .... Geological Reference File [American Geological Institute] [Bibliographic database] [Information service or system] (IID)
Geo Rep ...... Georgia Reports [A publication] (DLA)
GEOREQ...... Relocation Request [Code] [Military] (MCD)
Geores......... Georesources, Inc. [Associated Press] (SAG)
GEORG........ Georgics [Poetry] (ROG)
GEORGE....... General Organizational Environment [Computer science] (BUR)
George........ George's Reports [30-39 Mississippi] [A publication] (DLA)
George Partn... George on Partnership [A publication] (DLA)
GEORGETN... Georgetown (ROG)
Georgetown C... Georgetown College (Kentucky) (GAGS)
Georgetown U... Georgetown University (District of Columbia) (GAGS)
George Washington U... [The] George Washington University (GAGS)
Georgia........ Georgia Reports [A publication] (DLA)
Georgia C Milledgeville... Georgia College of Milledgeville (GAGS)
Georgia Inst Tech... Georgia Institute of Technology (GAGS)
Georgia Rep... Georgia Reports [A publication] (DLA)
Georgia So U... Georgia Southern University (GAGS)
Georgia St U... Georgia State University (GAGS)
Georg Nat.... Georgius Natta [Flourished, 1477-95] [Authority cited in pre-1607 legal work] (DSA)
GEOS .... Geodetic Earth-Orbiting Satellite
GEOS .... Geodetic Observation Satellite
GEOS .... Geodynamic Experimental Ocean Satellite
GEOS .... Geological (Research) Satellite
GEOS .... Geosynchronous Earth Observation System (IEEE)
GEOS .... Geosynchronous Earth Orbit Satellites (ACRL)
GEOS .... Graphic Environment Operating System [Commodore 64]
GEOSAR....... Geosynchronous Synthetic Aperture RADAR (IEEE)
Geosat........ Geodesy Satellite
Geosat........ Geodesy Satellite [Instrument] (EERA)
Geosat......... Geodetic Satellite
GEOSAT .... Geodynamic Experimental Ocean Satellite (MCD)
GEOSCAN ... Ground-Based Electronic Omnidirectional Satellite Communications Antenna
GEOSECS ..... Geochemical Ocean Sections Study [Submarine ocean exploration by US for International Decade of Ocean Exploration]
GEOSECS ..... Geochemical Sections Study (USDC)
GEOSEPS .... General Summary Edit Program (NAKS)
GEOSEPS .... Geosynchronous Solar Electric Propulsion Stage [NASA] (NASA)
GEO/SIT .... Geographical Situation (MCD)
GEOSS .... Geophysical Survey System [Naval Oceanographic Office]
GeoSSR .... Georgian Soviet Socialist Republic
Geosynchron... Geosynchronous Operational Environmental Satellite (NAKS)
GeoTk........ Geotek Communications, Inc. [Associated Press] (SAG)
GeoTICo....... GeoTel Communications Corp. [Associated Press] (SAG)
GEOU .... Graphics Entity and Operation Unification [Computer science]
GEOW .... GeoWaste, Inc. [NASDAQ symbol] (SPSG)
Geo Williams C... George Williams College (GAGS)
Geoworks..... GeoWorks [Associated Press] (SAG)
GeoWste...... GeoWaste, Inc. [Associated Press] (SAG)
GEP........... Gastroenteropancreatic System [Medicine]
GEP........... General Electric Plastics [Australia Commercial firm]
GEP........... General Enrollment Plan [Insurance]
GEP........... General Entry Permit
GEP........... Geological Echo Profiler [Oceanography] (MSC)
GEP........... Goddard Experimental Package [NASA]
GEP........... Good Engineering Practice (EG)

GEP............	Grasslands Ecology Program (EERA)
GEP............	Great Pacific Resources [*Vancouver Stock Exchange symbol*]
GEP............	Grolier Electronic Publishing, Inc. [*Information service or system*] (IID)
GEP............	Gross Energy Product
GEP............	Ground Effects Phenomenon
GEP............	Ground Entry Point (NVT)
GEP............	Group Employment Plan (MCD)
GEP............	Grupos Especiais de Paraquedistas [*Mozambique*]
GEP............	Gulf Environmental Measurements Program (MCD)
GEP............	Gustatory Evoked Potential [*Medicine*] (DMAA)
GEP............	Minneapolis, MN [*Location identifier FAA*] (FAAL)
GEPA.........	General Education Provisions Act [*1970*]
GEPAC.......	General Electric Process Automation Computer
GEPAC.......	General Electric Programmable Automatic Comparator [*or Computer*]
GEPB.........	Grievance and Employment Policy Board [*Army*]
GEPC	German External Property Control Commission [*Minden*] [*Allied German Occupation Forces*]
GEPDS.......	General Electric Process Design System
GEPE.........	GATE [*GARP Atlantic Tropical Experiment*] Equatorial Profiling Experiment [*Marine science*] (MSC)
GEPE.........	Groupe d'Etudes Politiques Europeennes (EA)
GEPEXS	General Electric Parts Explosion System
GEpFAR	Federal Archives and Records Center, General Services Administration, Atlanta Region, East Point, GA [*Library symbol Library of Congress*] (LCLS)
GEPI...........	Gestioni e Partecipazioni Industriali [*Industrial Management and Participation*] [*Italian government-sponsored agency to aid ailing companies*]
GEPL.........	General Equipment and Packaging Laboratory [*Army*]
GEPLACEA ...	Grupo de Paises Latinoamericanos y del Caribe Exportadores de Azucar [*Group of Latin American and Caribbean Sugar Exporting Countries - GLACSEC*] (EAIO)
GEPOL........	Generalized Processor for Command-Oriented Language (DNAB)
GEPURS	General Electric General Purpose
GEPVP........	Groupement Europeen des Producteurs de Verre Plat [*European Group of Flat Glass Manufacturers*] (EAIO)
GEQ	Moline, IL [*Location identifier FAA*] (FAAL)
GEQUIV.......	Gram Equivalent [*Chemistry*] (IAA)
GER	Gardiner Resources [*Vancouver Stock Exchange symbol*]
GER	Gastroesophageal Reflux [*See also GERD*] [*Medicine*]
GER	General Engineering Research
GER	Geomagnetic Electrorinetograph
Ger.............	Gerard Pucelle [*Deceased, 1184*] [*Authority cited in pre-1607 legal work*] (DSA)
GER	Geriatrics
Ger.............	Gerim (BJA)
GER	German [*Language, etc.*]
ger.............	German [*MARC language code Library of Congress*] (LCCP)
Ger.............	German (ODCC)
GER	Germany
Ger.............	Germany (VRA)
GER	Germany Fund [*NYSE symbol*] (TTSB)
GER	Germany Fund, Inc. [*NYSE symbol*] (SPSG)
GER	Gerontology [*American Occupational Therapy Association*]
GER	Gerund
GER	Goodyear Engineering Report (MCD)
GER	Gran Enciclopedia Rialp [*A publication*]
GER	Granular Endoplasmic Reticulum (DB)
GER	Great Eastern Railway [*British*]
GER	Guernsey Airlines Ltd. [*British ICAO designator*] (FAAC)
GER	Guilde Europeenne du Raid [*European Expedition Guild - EEG*] (EAIO)
GER	Nueva Gerona [*Cuba*] [*Airport symbol*] (OAG)
GERA	Guard's Expense in Returning Absentee [*Army*]
GerABcp	German American Bancorp [*Associated Press*] (SAG)
GerAE	German Antarctic Expedition [*1901-03,1911-12,1938-39*]
GERBIL	Great Education Reform Bill [*British*]
GerbSc........	Gerber Scientific, Inc. [*Associated Press*] (SAG)
GERD	Gastroesophageal Reflux Disease [*Gastroenterology*] (DAVI)
GERD	Gross Expenditure on Research Development
GERDAT......	Groupement d'Etudes et de Recherche pour le Developpement de l'Agronomie Tropicale [*Group for the Study and Research of Tropical Agronomy*] [*International Cooperation Center of Agricultural Research for Development*] [*Information service or system*] (IID)
GER DEM REP...	German Democratic Republic (WDAA)
GERD/GDP ...	Gross Expenditure on Research and Development/Gross Domestic Product [*Ratio*]
GEREP	Generalized Equipment Reliability Evaluation Procedure
Gereq.........	Gerequireerde [*Defendant*] [*Netherlands*] (ILCA)
GerFd..........	Germany Fund, Inc. [*Associated Press*] (SAG)
GERG	Groupe Europeen de Recherches Gazieres [*European Gas Research Group*] (EAIO)
GERI	Geriatric
geri.............	Geriatrics [*Medicine*] (DAVI)
GERIACT......	Great Education Reform Act [*1988*] (AIE)
GERIAT	Geriatrics
GeriMed	Geriatric & Medical Companies, Inc. [*Associated Press*] (SAG)
GERIS	Graphic Expression Reading Improvement System
GERL	Golgi-Associated Endoplasmic Reticulum Lysosomes
GERM	Generalized Entity-Relationship Model (HGAA)
GERM	German [*Language, etc.*] (ROG)
Germ	Germania [*of Tacitus*] [*Classical studies*] (OCD)
Germ	Germany (CMD)

GERM	Ground Effect Research Machine
GERMA	Groupe d'Etude des Ressources Maritimes [*Universite du Quebec a Rimouski*] [*Canada Research center*]
German........	Germanicus [*15BC-19AD*] [*Classical studies*] (OCD)
German Yb Int'l L ..	German Yearbook of International Law [*A publication*] (DLA)
GERMDF......	German Ministry of Defense
GERME	Groupe d'Etude en Regulation Metabolique [*University of Quebec at Rimouski*] [*Research center*] (RCD)
Germfask....	Grant, Edge, Robinson, Mead, French, Ackley, Shephard, and Knaggs [*Founders of a town in Michigan's Upper Peninsula that derived its name from the initial letters of their surnames*]
GermJud......	Germania Judaica [*A publication*] (BJA)
GERN..........	Geron Corp. [*NASDAQ symbol*] (SAG)
GerNew.......	Germany Fund New [*Associated Press*] (SAG)
GERNORSEA...	German Naval Forces, North Sea Subarea [*NATO*] (NATG)
GERO	George Rogers Clark National Historical Park
GERO	GE [*General Electric Co.*] Robot
GERO	Global Environmental Research Organization
GeronCp	Geron Corp. [*Associated Press*] (SAG)
Gerontol	Gerontology [*or Gerontologist*] [*Geriatrics*] (DAVI)
GEROS	General Routing Optimization System (IAA)
GERPAT	German Patent (IAA)
Ger Q..........	German Quarterly [*A publication*] (BRI)
GERRI	Geriatric Evaluation by Relative Rating Instrument [*Medicine*] (DMAA)
GERRI	Geriatric Evaluation by Relative's Rating Instrument
Gerrity.........	Gerrity Oil & Gas [*Associated Press*] (SAG)
GERSAL	General Electric Symbolic Assembly Language (IAA)
GERSIS	General Electric Range Safety Instrumentation System [*Aerospace*]
GERT	Graphical Evaluation and Review Technique
GERTIE	GEORGE [*General Organizational Environment*] Remote Terminal Interrogative Environment [*Computer science*] (IAA)
Ger Tit	Gerard's Titles to Real Estate [*A publication*] (DLA)
GERTS	General Electric Radio [*or Range*] Tracking System [*Aerospace*]
GERTS	General Electric Remote Terminal Supervisor
GERTS	General Electric Remote Terminal System (IEEE)
GERTS	General Remote Terminal System (NITA)
GERV	General Electric Reentry Vehicle [*Aerospace*] (AAG)
GES	Gale Environmental Sourcebook [*A publication*]
GES	Gamma European System (IAA)
GES	General Edit System [*Computer science*] (IAA)
GES	General Educational Services Corp.
GES	General Electric Semiconductor
GES	General Electric Silicones [*Australia Commercial firm*]
GES	General Engineering Squadron
GES	General Estimates System [*NHTSA*] (TAG)
GES	General Santos [*Philippines*] [*Airport symbol*] (OAG)
GES	Generic Environmental Statement [*Nuclear energy*] (NRCH)
GES	Generic Equipment Simulator [*Electronics*] (AAEL)
GES	Genesis Resource Corp. [*Vancouver Stock Exchange symbol*]
GES	Gesellschaft [*Company*] [*German*]
Ges	Gesellschaft [*Company*] [*German*] (ODBW)
ges.............	Gesso (VRA)
GES	Gestair Executive Jet [*Spain ICAO designator*] (FAAC)
GES	Gilt-Edged Securities [*Business term*]
GES	Glucose Electrolyte Solution [*Medicine*]
GES	Goddard Experiment Support System [*NASA*] (MCD)
GES	Gold Exchange Standard
GES	Goliath Edison Screw
GES	Goode Environmental Services (EFIS)
GES	Gordon, E. S., Joplin MO [*STAC*]
GES	Government Economic Service [*British*]
GES	Government Evacuation Scheme [*British World War II*]
GES	Green Extension System [*Traffic signal*] (DICI)
GES	Grips Strong and Equal [*Medicine*] (MEDA)
GES	Ground Earth Station [*Telecommunications*]
GES	Ground Electronic System
GES	Ground Entry Station (MCD)
GES	Ground Equipment System
GES	Groupe d'Etudes Sartriennes (EAIO)
GES	Group Encounter Survey
GES	Group Environment Scale [*Personality development test*] [*Psychology*]
GESAANP/NW...	GE [*General Electric Co.*] Stockholders' Alliance Against Nuclear Power/Nuclear Weapons (EA)
Ges Abh	Gesammelte Abhandlungen zur Roemischen Religions- und Stadtgeschichte [*A publication*] (OCD)
GESAC	General Electric Self-Adaptive Control System
GESAL	General Electric Symbolic Assembly Language (IAA)
GESAMP	Group of Experts on the Scientific Aspects of Marine Environmental Protection [*Marine science*] (OSRA)
GESAMP	Group of Experts on the Scientific Aspects of Marine Pollution [*ICSU*] (EAIO)
GESASA	Greek Ex-Servicemen's Association of South Australia
GESASNFF...	General Electric Stockholders' Alliance for a Sustainable Nuclear-Free Future (EA)
GESB	General Export Services Branch [*Department of Trade*] [*British*]
GesB...........	Hebraeisches und Aramaeisches Handwoerterbuch ueber das Alte Testament [*W. Gesenius and F. Buhl*] [*A publication*] (BJA)
GESBT	Generic Expert System Building Tool
GESC	Government EDP [*Electronic Data Processing*] Standards Committee [*Canada*]
GESCH........	Geschichte [*History*] [*German*]
Gesch	Geschichte [*of Germanicus*] [*Classical studies*] (OCD)
GESCO	General Electric Supply Corp.
GESCOM........	General Electric Scientific Color Matching (IAA)

GESEM.........	Groupement Europeen des Sources d'Eaux Minerales Naturelles [*European Group ofNatural Mineral Water Sources*] (EAIO)
GESH	Grain Effect Screenless Halftone [*Printing technique*]
GESHUA......	General Electric Six Hundred Users' Association [*Later, HLSUA*] [*Computer science*]
GESMAR	Geodetic Survey Marks Register [*of Western Australia*] [*State*] (EERA)
GESMO	General Environmental Statement for Mixed Oxide Fuel
GESO	Group Equipment Staff Officer [*British military*] (DMA)
GESOC	General Electric Satellite Orbit Control [*Aerospace*]
GESP	General Extrasensory Perception [*Parapsychology*]
G-ESP	Greens-Ecological Social Party [*Slovenia*] [*Political party*] (BUAC)
GESPL	General Edit System Programming Language (IAA)
GESPL	Generalized Edit System Programming Language [*Computer science*] (PDAA)
GESS	Generator Exhaust Signature Suppression (PDAA)
Ges Schr......	Gesammelte Schriften [*A publication*] (OCD)
GesStud.......	Gesammelte Studien [*A publication*] (BJA)
GEST...........	Gas Explosive Simulation Technique [*Air Force*]
GEST...........	Gemini Slowscan Television [*NASA*]
GEST...........	General Systems Theory
gest............	Gestation (STED)
GEST...........	Gestational [*Pediatrics*]
GEST...........	Gestorben [*Died*] [*German*]
gest............	Gesture [*Theater*] (WDMC)
GEST...........	Grants for Education Support and Training [*British*] (DET)
GEST...........	Guest Supply [*NASDAQ symbol*] (TTSB)
GEST...........	Guest Supply, Inc. [*NASDAQ symbol*] (NQ)
GESTA	Gesetzgebungsstand [*Database*] [*Deutscher Bundestag*] [*German*] [*Information service or system*] (CRD)
GESTAPO....	Geheime Staats Polizei [*Secret State Police*] [*Germany*]
GESTAPU....	Gerkang, September, Tigapuluh [*See also GESTOK*] [*Plot against the government of Indonesia beginning on September 30, 1965*]
GESTEC.......	Genome Science and Technology Center (HGEN)
GESTOK	Gerkang Oktober [*See also GESTAPU*] [*Plot against the government of Indonesia which began on September 30, 1965 and continued into October*]
GET.............	Gaming Entertainment Television [*Interactive-gambling TV station*] (ECON)
GET.............	Gas, Electric, Telephones [*of GET, Inc., a consumer group*]
GET.............	Gastric Emptying Time [*Medicine*]
GET.............	Gaylord Entertainment [*NYSE symbol*] (SPSG)
GET.............	Gaylord Entertainment 'A' [*NYSE symbol*] (TTSB)
GET.............	General Employee Training (COE)
GET.............	Generator Environmental Tester
GET.............	Geraldton [*Australia Airport symbol*] (OAG)
GET.............	Germanium Transistor [*Electronics*] (IAA)
Get.............	Geteilt [*Divided*] [*Music*]
GET.............	Graded Treadmill Exercise Test [*Medicine*] (DMAA)
GET.............	Graduate Employment and Training [*British*]
GET.............	Graduate Employment and Training Survey (AIE)
GET.............	Gross Error Test (PDAA)
GET.............	Ground Elapsed Time [*Aerospace*]
GET.............	Ground Entry Terminal (MCD)
GET$_{1/2}$	Gastric Emptying Half-Time [*Gastroenterology*] (DAVI)
GETA...........	GeneralEndotracheal Anesthesia [*Medicine*] (DAVI)
GETA...........	General Equipment Test Activity [*Army*]
GETA...........	Government Employees Training Act [*1966*]
GETAB	General Electric BWR [*Boiling Water Reactor*] Thermal Analysis Branch (NRCH)
GETAC........	General Electric Telemetering and Control
GetchGld......	Getchell Gold Corp. [*Associated Press*] (SAG)
GETEL.........	General Electric Test Engineering Language [*Computer science*] (IEEE)
GETF..........	Global Environmental Trust Fund [*GEF-Core Fund*] (EERA)
GETh..........	[*The*] Epic of Gilgamesh [*R. C. Thompson*] [*A publication*] (BJA)
GETI..........	Ground Elapsed Time of Ignition [*Aerospace*] (KSC)
GETIL.........	Ground Elapsed Time of Landing
GETIS.........	Ground Environment Technical Installation System [*NATO*] (NATG)
GETL..........	Ground Elapsed Time of Landing [*NASA*] (GFGA)
GETLO........	Obtain by Local Purchase [*Military*]
GETMA........	Obtain by Local Manufacture [*Military*]
GETO	Ground Equipment Turn Off (KSC)
GETOL........	General Electric Training Operational Language (MCD)
GETOL........	General Electric Training Operational Logic [*Computer science*] (IEEE)
GETOL	Ground Effect Takeoff and Landing
GETR	General Electric Test Reactor
GETS..........	General Electric Transportation Systems [*Australia Commercial firm*]
GETS..........	Generalized Electronic Troubleshooting (IAA)
GETS..........	General Track Simulation [*NASA*] (KSC)
GETS..........	Ground Equipment Test Set
GETS..........	Groundwater Extraction and Treatment System [*Environmental science*] (BCP)
GETSC	General Electric Technical Services Company
GETSCO	General Electric Technical Services Co. (NRCH)
GETSS	General Electric Time Sharing System (IAA)
GETT	German Tactical Truck (MCD)
GETT..........	Gettysburg National Military Park
GETT..........	Grants Equal to Taxes
GETTY.........	Getty Communications [*NASDAQ symbol*] (SAG)
Getty.........	Getty Petroleum Corp. [*Associated Press*] (SAG)
GettyCo.......	Getty Communications [*Associated Press*] (SAG)
Getuig.........	Getuigenis [*Roermond/Maaseik*] (BJA)
GETY..........	Gettysburg Railroad Co. [*AAR code*]

Getz F.........	Getz's Forms in Conveyancing [*A publication*] (DLA)
GEU	Emory University, Atlanta, GA [*Library symbol Library of Congress*] (LCLS)
GEU	Genetic Evaluation and Utilization (PDAA)
GEU	Geothermal Energy Update [*A publication*]
GEU	Geriatric Evaluation Unit [*Veterans Administration*] (GFGA)
GEU	Gestation, Extrauterine (STED)
GEU	Grossesse Extra-Uterine [*Medicine*]
GEU	Ground Electro-Optic Unit
GEU-B.........	Emory University, School of Business Administration, Atlanta, GA [*Library symbol Library of Congress*] (LCLS)
GEU-D.........	Emory University, School of Dentistry, Atlanta, GA [*Library symbol Library of Congress*] (LCLS)
GEU-L.........	Emory University, Lamar School of Law, Atlanta, GA [*Library symbol Library of Congress*] (LCLS)
GEU-LS........	Emory University, Division of Librarianship, Atlanta, GA [*Library symbol Library of Congress*] (LCLS)
GEU-M.........	Emory University, A. W. Calhoun Medical Library, Atlanta, GA [*Library symbol Library of Congress*] (LCLS)
GEU-S.........	Emory University, Special Collections Department, Atlanta, GA [*Library symbol*] [*Library of Congress*] (LCLS)
GEU-T.........	Emory University, Candler School of Theology, Atlanta, GA [*Library symbol Library of Congress*] (LCLS)
GEU-Y.........	Emory University, Yerkes Primate Research Center, Atlanta, GA [*Library symbol Library of Congress*] (LCLS)
GEV............	Gallivare [*Sweden*] [*Airport symbol*] (OAG)
GeV............	Giga Electron Volt
Gev............	Giga Electron Volt (STED)
GEV............	Ground Effect Vehicle
GEV............	Groundnut Eyespot Virus
GEVIC.........	General Electric Variable Increment Computer
GEVNC........	General Electric Vallecitos Nuclear Center [*Vallecitos, CA*] (GAAI)
GEVST	Gordon Environmental Studies Laboratory [*University of Montana*] [*Research center*] (RCD)
GEW...........	Gas, Electricity, Water [*Department of Employment*] [*British*]
GEW...........	Gewoya [*Papua New Guinea*] [*Airport symbol*] (OAG)
GEW...........	Glazed Earthenware
GEW...........	Gram Equivalent Weight
GEW...........	Ground Effect Wing (PDAA)
GEWA	George Washington Birthplace National Monument
GEWEX	Global Energy and Water Cycle Experiment [*World Climate Research Program*] [*Geo science*]
GEWP	George Washington Memorial Parkway [*National Park Service designation*]
GEX...........	Gas Exchange
GEX...........	Government Employees Exchange
GEX...........	Granges Exploration Ltd. [*Toronto Stock Exchange symbol*]
GEY...........	Getty Resources Ltd. [*Toronto Stock Exchange symbol*]
GEY...........	Geuserland Airways Ltd. [*New Zealand*] [*ICAO designator*] (FAAC)
GEY...........	Greybull, WY [*Location identifier FAA*] (FAAL)
GEZ...........	Garretson - Elmendorf - Zinov, Architects and Engineers [*San Francisco, CA*] [*Telecommunications service*] (TSSD)
GEZ...........	General Electric Canada, Inc. [*Toronto Stock Exchange symbol*]
GEZ...........	Gosudarstvennoe Knigoizdatelstvo [*State Publishing House*] [*Former USSR*]
GEZERD	Alfarbandishe Gezelshaft far Ainordenen Yidn af Erd in FSSR [*A publication*] (BJA)
GF.............	French Guiana [*ANSI two-letter standard code*] (CNC)
GF.............	Gage Factor [*Aerospace*] (NAKS)
GF.............	Gain Factor [*Computer science*]
GF.............	Galois Field [*Mathematics*] (IAA)
GF.............	Galvanized Steel Fastenings
GF.............	Games Finished [*Baseball*]
GF.............	G and A Factor
GF.............	Gap Filler [*RADAR*]
GF.............	Garage Forecourts [*Public-performance tariff class*] [*British*]
GF.............	Gas Filled (MSA)
GF.............	Gas-Freeing System
GF.............	Gasoline-Fueled [*Automotive engineering*]
GF.............	Gastric Fistula [*Gastroenterology*] (DAVI)
GF.............	Gastric Fluid [*Medicine*] (MAE)
GF.............	Gaudeamus Foundation [*Netherlands*] (EAIO)
GF.............	Gauge Factor (MCD)
GF.............	Gelatinous Fiber [*Botany*]
GF.............	General File (COE)
GF.............	General Foods Corp. (CDAI)
G/F............	General within Families (DICI)
GF.............	Generator Field
GF.............	Generic Failure
GF.............	Gentleman Friend
GF.............	Georgia & Florida R. R. [*AAR code*]
GF.............	Germfree [*Medicine*]
GF.............	Giant Food, Inc. (EFIS)
GF.............	Girl Friend [*Slang*]
GF.............	Girl Friends (EA)
GF.............	Glaciofluvial Soil [*Agronomy*]
GF.............	Glass Factor [*Tissue culture*]
GF.............	Glass Fiber
GF.............	Globular-Fibrous [*Biochemistry*]
G-F............	Globular-Fibrous [*Protein*] (STED)
GF.............	Globule Fibril (STED)
GF.............	Glomerular Filtrate [*Medicine*]
GF.............	Glomerular Filtration (STED)
GF.............	Gluten-Free [*Diet*]
GF.............	Goals For [*Hockey*]

GF	Gold Field
GF	Goldfinch [*Ornithology*]
GF	Goldflow (AFM)
GF	Gonococcus Filus [*A microorganism*]
GF	Good Faith [*Legal shorthand*] (LWAP)
GF	Gordon Fraser [*Publisher*] [*British*]
GF	Gorilla Foundation (EA)
GF	Government Form
GF	Government Funded (BABM)
GF	Gram Force (IAA)
gf	Gram-Force (DMAA)
GF	Grandfather
GF	Grand Fleet [*British military*] (DMA)
GF	Grand Format [*Graphic arts*] (DGA)
GF	Grayson Foundation [*Later, GJC*] (EA)
GF	Great Falls-Billings [*Diocesan abbreviation*] [*Montana*] (TOCD)
GF	Great Fire [*of London, 1666*]
GF	Greensward Foundation (EA)
GF	Grief Facilitation [*Psychology*] (DHP)
GF	Grinding Fixture (MCD)
GF	Griseofulvin (STED)
GF	Ground Face [*Technical drawings*]
G/F	Ground/Flight Test
GF	Ground Fog [*Meteorology*]
GF	Ground Foraging [*Ecology*]
GF	Ground Forces [*Military*]
GF	Group of Fourteen [*NATO countries minus France*] (NATG)
GF	Growth Factor [*Endocrinology*] (DAVI)
GF	Growth Failure (STED)
GF	Growth Fraction [*Endocrinology*]
GF	Guggenheim Foundation (BARN)
GF	Guinean Franc [*Monetary unit*] (ODBW)
GF	Gulf Air [*ICAO designator*] (AD)
GF	Gunnery Flight
GF	New Germany Fund [*NYSE symbol*] (SPSG)
GFA	Federal Aviation Administration, Southern Region, East Point, GA [*OCLC symbol*] (OCLC)
GFA	Gasket Fabricators Association (EA)
GFA	General Fitness Assessment
GFA	General Forestry Assistance
GFA	General Freight Agent
GFA	Georgia Foestry Association (WPI)
GFA	Giddens Family Associates (EA)
GFA	Gideon Family Association (EA)
GFA	Glial Fibrillary Acidic Protein [*Also, GFAP*] [*Biochemistry*]
GFA	Gloucester Fisheries Association (EA)
GFA	Gold Filled Association [*Defunct*] (EA)
GFA	Goodenow Family Association (EA)
GFA	Good Fair Average [*Insurance*]
GFA	Government-Furnished Ammunition (MCD)
GFA	Government-Furnished Articles (KSC)
GFA	Grain Futures Administration [*Superseded by Commodity Exchange Administration, 1936*]
GFA	Graves Family Association
GFA	Great Falls, MT [*Location identifier FAA*] (FAAL)
GFA	Gross Floor Area (ADA)
GFA	Group Feedback Analysis
GFA	Guitar Foundation of America (EA)
GFA	Gulf Air [*United Arab Emirates*] [*ICAO designator*] (FAAC)
GFA	Gunfire Area
GFA	Gust Front Algorithm (USDC)
GFAA	Game Fishing Association of Australia (EERA)
GFAA	Graphite-Furnace Atomic Absorption [*Spectroscopy*] [*Physics*]
GFAAS	Graphite Furnace Atomic Absorption Spectrometry (AAEL)
GFAAS	Graphite Furnace Atomic Absorption Spectroscopy [*Physics*]
GFAC	Ground Forward Air Controller (MCD)
GFADS	Grand Forks Air Defense Sector [*North Dakota*] (SAA)
GFAE	Government-Furnished Accessory Equipment
GFAE	Government-Furnished Aeronautical Equipment (AFM)
GFAE	Government-Furnished Aerospace Equipment
GFAE	Government-Furnished Aircraft Equipment
GFAEL	Government-Furnished Aeronautical Equipment List (MCD)
GFAM	Graphics Flutter Analysis Methods [*Computer science*]
GF & A	Gulf Florida & Alabama Railway
GF & P	Gases, Fluids, and Propellants [*NASA*] (NASA)
GFAP	Glial Fibrillary Acidic Protein [*Also, GFA*] [*Biochemistry*]
GFB	Go for Broke [*Slang*]
GFB	Government Facilities Brochure
GFB	Government-Furnished Baseline
GFBA	Graduate Fellowships for Black Americans (EA)
GFBI	Grand Fleet Battle Instructions [*British military*] (DMA)
GFbIS	United States Army, Infantry School, Fort Benning, GA [*Library symbol Library of Congress*] (LCLS)
GFBN	Bonthe [*Sierra Leone*] [*ICAO location identifier*] (ICLI)
GFBO	Grand Fleet Battle Orders [*British military*] (DMA)
GfBV	Gesellschaft fuer Bedrohte Voelker [*Society for Threatened Peoples*] (EAIO)
GFC	Gas-Filled Counter
GFC	Gas Filter Correlation [*NASA*] (KSC)
GFC	Gas Frontal Chromatography
GFC	Gateway Football Conference (PSS)
GFC	Gel Filtration Chromatography
GFC	General Failure Criteria
GFC	Generic Flow Control [*Telecommunications*] (ACRL)
GFC	Genstar Financial Corp. [*Toronto Stock Exchange symbol*]

GFC	George Fox College [*Oregon*]
GFC	Get Fresh Crew [*Rap recording group*]
GFC	Glass Filter Covers
GFC	Global Forcing Contribution [*Environmental science*]
GFC	Going for Coffee [*Computer hacker terminology*]
GFC	Goldwing Flyers Club (EA)
GFC	Grand Falls Central Railway Co. Ltd. [*AAR code*]
GFC	Graphite Fiber Composite
GFC	Gun Feed Control (MCD)
GFC	Gunfire Control (DOMA)
GFCB	Ground Fault Circuit Breaker [*Electronics*]
GFCC	Gun Fire Control Computer [*Military*] (CAAL)
GFCE	Government-Furnished Capital Equipment (MCD)
GFCE	Gross Fixed Capital Expenditure
GFCES	Glider Flight Control Electronics Subsystem
GFCF	Gross Fixed Capital Formation
GFCG	Government Fluidic Coordinating Group
GFCI	Gay Fathers Coalition International [*Later, GLPCI*] (EA)
GFCI	Ground Fault Circuit Interrupter [*Electronics*]
GFCM	General Fisheries Council for the Mediterranean [*ICSU*]
GF/CM²	Gram Force per Square Centimeter
GFCO	Glenway Financial Corp. [*NASDAQ symbol*] (SAG)
GFCO	Glenway Fin'l [*NASDAQ symbol*] (TTSB)
GFCO	Good Faith Charitable Organization (EA)
GFCO	Group Fire Control Officer (WDAA)
GFCR	Gas Filter Correlation Radiometer [*NASA*]
GFCRP	Gap-Filler Control and Reporting Post [*RADAR*] (IAA)
GFCS	Gaseous Flowmeter Calibration Stand
GFCS	Gunfire Control System
GFCS-B	Gunfire Control System-Backup (DNAB)
GFCSMT	Generalized Fire-Control System Maintenance Trainer [*Spacecraft*] [*Navy*]
GFCSS	Gunfire Control Subsystem (DNAB)
GFCS SATSIM	Gun Fire Control System Satellite Simulation [*Military*] (CAAL)
GFCV	Gas and Fuel Corp. of Victoria [*Australia*]
GFD	Gallons per Square-Foot per Day
GFD	Gap-Filler Data [*RADAR*]
GFD	Gemini Food Corp. [*Toronto Stock Exchange symbol*]
GFD	General Freight Department
GFD	General Functional Description [*Military*] (AABC)
GFD	Geophysical Fluid Dynamics Laboratory [*National Oceanic and Atmospheric Administration*]
GFD	Gesellschaft fur Flugzieldarstellung GmbH [*Germany ICAO designator*] (FAAC)
GFD	Gingival Fibromatosis-Progressive Deafness Syndrome [*Medicine*] (DMAA)
GFD	Glucose-Free Dialysate [*Nephrology*]
GFD	Gluten-Free Diet
GFD	Gone for the Day
GFD	Goodenough Figure Drawing [*Psychology*] (DAVI)
GFD	Government-Furnished Data (NASA)
GFD	Government-Furnished Documentation (KSC)
GFD	Greenfield, IN [*Location identifier FAA*] (FAAL)
GFD	Ground Forces Training Devices (Provisional) [*Army*] (RDA)
GFD	Group Finance Department
GFD	Guilford Mills [*NYSE symbol*] (SAG)
GFDA	Gust Front Detection Algorithm (USDC)
GFDC	Group Fire Distribution Center [*Army*] (AABC)
GFDD	Gunfire Detection Device
GFDL	Geophysical Fluid Dynamics Laboratory [*Princeton, NJ*] [*National Oceanic and Atmospheric Administration*]
GFDNA	Grain and Feed Dealers National Association [*Later, NGFA*] (EA)
GFDP	Geophysical Fluid Dynamics Program [*National Oceanic and Atmospheric Administration*] (GFGA)
GFE	Gays for Equality
GFE	Gibbs Free Energy [*Physical chemistry*]
GFE	Goal-Free Evaluation [*Education*] (AEE)
GFE	Government-Furnished Equipment
GFE	Greater Fuel Economy
GFE	Gross Feasibility Estimator (MCD)
GFEAM	Government-Furnished Equipment and Material (IAA)
GFE & D	Government-Furnished Equipment and Data
GFE & M	Government-Furnished Equipment and Material (NRCH)
GFEC	Graphite-Fiber Epoxy-Composite
GFED	Guaranty Federal Savings Bank [*NASDAQ symbol*] (SAG)
GFED	Guaranty Fedl Svgs [*NASDAQ symbol*] (TTSB)
GFE/GFAE	Government-Furnished Equipment / Government-Furnished Aircraft Equipment (SAA)
GFE/I	Government-Furnished Equipment/Information (AAGC)
GFEL	Government-Furnished Equipment List (MCD)
GFEM	Graphics Finite Element Module [*McDonnell-Douglas Automation Corp.*]
GFER	Government-Furnished Equipment Records
GFERC	Grand Forks Energy Research Center [*Energy Research and Development Administration*]
GFERR	Government-Furnished Equipment Requirements Request
GFETC	Grand Forks Energy Technology Center [*Later, University of North Dakota Energy Research Center*] [*Department of Energy*] (GRD)
GFF	Glass-Fiber Filter [*Separation technology*]
GFF	Government-Furnished Facilities (MCD)
GFF	Granolithic Finish Floor [*Technical drawings*]
GFF	Graphic Firing Fan [*Weaponry*] (INF)
GFF	Griffith [*Australia Airport symbol*] (OAG)
GFF	Griffon Corp. [*NYSE symbol*] (SAG)
GFFAR	Guided Folding-Fin Aircraft Rocket

GFFC........... Geophysical Fluid Flow Cell [*Instrumentation*]
GFFC........... Gibb Family Friendship Club (EA)
GFFD .... Gross Failed Fuel Detector [*Nuclear energy*] (NRCH)
GFFIL........... Groupement Francais des Fournisseurs d'Information en Ligne [*French Association of Online Information Providers*] [*Paris*] [*Information service or system*] (IID)
GFFPrl .... Griffon Corp. 2nd Cv Pfd [*NYSE symbol*] (TTSB)
GFFS........... Glycogen and Fat-Free Solid (DMAA)
GFG .... Geographical Field Group [*British*]
GFG .... Glare Free Gloss [*Paper*]
GFG .... [*The*] Good Food Guide [*A publication British*]
GFG .... Governor's Foot Guard
GFG .... Grafton Group Ltd. [*Toronto Stock Exchange symbol*]
GFG .... Leesburg, VA [*Location identifier FAA*] (FAAL)
GFGA .... Gippsland Fruit Growers' Association [*Australia*]
GFgC........... United States Army, Civil Affairs School, Fort Gordon, GA [*Library symbol Library of Congress*] (LCLS)
GFGCA .... Gympie Fruit Growers' Cooperative Association [*Australia*]
GFGF .... Group Fore Golf Foundation (EA)
GFGK .... Gbangbatok [*Sierra Leone*] [*ICAO location identifier*] (ICLI)
GFgML........ United States Army, Medical Library, Fort Gordon, GA [*Library symbol Library of Congress*] (LCLS)
GFgMP........ United States Army, Military Police School, Fort Gordon, GA [*Library symbol Library of Congress*] (LCLS)
GFgS........... United States Army, Special Services Library, Fort Gordon, GA [*Library symbol Library of Congress*] (LCLS)
GFgSS .... United States Army, Southeastern Signal School, Fort Gordon, GA [*Library symbol Library of Congress*] (LCLS)
GFH .... Glucose-Free Hanks [*Solution*] [*Cell incubation medium*]
GFHA .... Gaelic Football and Hurling Association [*Australia*]
GFHA .... Hastings [*Sierra Leone*] [*ICAO location identifier*] (ICLI)
GFHR .... Gas-Filled Hydrophobic Region
GFI .... Gap-Filler Input [*RADAR*]
GFI .... Gas Flow Indicator [*NASA*]
GFI .... General Format Identifier [*Computer science*] (TNIG)
GFI .... Global Finance Information [*Information service or system*] (IID)
GFI .... Glucagon-Free Insulin [*Medicine*] (DMAA)
GFI .... Gmelin Formula Index [*Gmelin-Institut fuer Anorganische Chemie und Grenzgebiete*] [*Germany Information service or system*] (CRD)
GFI .... Government Final Inspection
GFI .... Government Free Issue (AABC)
GFI .... Government-Furnished Information
GFI .... Government-Furnished Items [*DoD*]
GFI .... Government-Owned Financial Institution (ADA)
GFI .... Graham-Field Health [*NYSE symbol*] (TTSB)
GFI .... Graham Field Health Products [*NYSE symbol*] (SAG)
GFI .... Greyvest Financial Services, Inc. [*Toronto Stock Exchange symbol*]
GFI .... Ground Fault Interrupter [*Electronics*]
gfi .... Ground-Fault Interrupter (IDOE)
GFI .... Group Fuel Injection [*Automotive engineering*]
GFI .... Guided Fault Isolation
GFII .... Greenfield Industries, Inc. [*NASDAQ symbol*] (SAG)
GFIN .... Game Financial Corp. [*NASDAQ symbol*] (SAG)
GFIN .... Gam Financial [*NASDAQ symbol*] (TTSB)
GFinSerf ...... Grupo Fnanciero Serfin SA [*Associated Press*] (SAG)
GFIP........... Gross Fault Indicator Panel (SAA)
GFIT .... Glass-Fiber Insulation Tubing
GFK........... Grand Forks [*North Dakota*] [*Airport symbol*] (OAG)
GFK........... Grand Forks Mines [*Vancouver Stock Exchange symbol*]
GFKB .... Kabala [*Sierra Leone*] [*ICAO location identifier*] (ICLI)
GFKE .... Kenema [*Sierra Leone*] [*ICAO location identifier*] (ICLI)
GFL........... Geoffrion, Leclerc, Inc. [*Toronto Stock Exchange symbol*]
GFL........... Giant Follicular Lymphoma [*Medicine*] (DMAA)
GFL........... Glens Falls [*New York*] [*Airport symbol*] (AD)
GFL........... Glens Falls, NY [*Location identifier FAA*] (FAAL)
GFL........... Glossary Function List
GFL........... Government-Furnished List
GFL........... Green Forest Lumber Ltd. [*Canada ICAO designator*] (FAAC)
GFL........... Ground Fire Locator
GFL........... Guide to Football Literature [*A publication*]
GFLAAL........ Gesellschaft zur Foerderung der Literatur aus Afrika, Asien, und Lateinamerika (EAIO)
GFLD .... Generator Field
GFLL .... Freetown/Lungi [*Sierra Leone*] [*ICAO location identifier*] (ICLI)
GFLOPS .... Giga Floating Operations per Second [*Computer science*]
GFLOPS ...... One Billion Floating Point Operations per Second (ACRL)
GFLS........... Ground Fire Locating System
GFLU .... General Federation of Labor Unions [*Syria*]
GFLV.......... Grapevine Fan Leaf Virus [*Plant pathology*]
GFM........... Glass-Fiber Material
GFM........... Goldfinch Mineral Ltd. [*Vancouver Stock Exchange symbol*]
GFM........... Government-Furnished Material
GFM........... Government-Furnished Missile
GFM........... Graphics Function Monitor [*Tektronix*] (NITA)
GFM........... Gravitational Field Measurements (SAA)
GFM........... Greyhound Food Management
GFMA .... Gold-Filled Manufacturers Association [*Later, GFA*] (EA)
GFmA........ United States Army, Fort McPherson Post Library, Fort McPherson, GA [*Library symbol Library of Congress*] (LCLS)
GFMD .... Gold Film Mercury Detector [*Spectrometry*]
GFME .... Government-Furnished Missile Equipment (AAG)
GFMM .... Gaussian Fast Multipole Method [*Physics*]
GFMP.......... Marampa [*Sierra Leone*] [*ICAO location identifier*] (ICLI)
GFMS.......... Gaseous Flow Measuring System
GFMS.......... Generalized File Maintenance System (ADA)

GFMVT........ General Foods Moisture Vapor Transmission
GFN .... Global Futures Network [*India*] [*India*] (EAIO)
GFN .... Grafton [*New York*] [*Seismograph station code, US Geological Survey Closed*] (SEIS)
GFN .... Grafton [*Australia Airport symbol*] (OAG)
GFNL .... Granite Financial, Inc. [*NASDAQ symbol*] (SAG)
GFO .... Bartica [*Guyana*] [*Airport symbol*] (OAG)
GFO .... Gap-Filler Output [*RADAR*]
GFO .... Gas-Fired Oven
GFO .... General Freight Office
GFO .... GEOSAT [*Geodetic Satellite*] Follow On [*Marine science*] (OSRA)
GFO .... German Foreign Office [*British World War II*]
GFO .... Goodwin Family Organization (EA)
GFO .... Gulf, Mobile & Ohio [*Railroad*] (MHDB)
GFO .... Gulf, Mobile & Ohio Railroad [*Later, Illinois Central Gulf Railroad*] (IIA)
GFOA .... Government Finance Officers Association of United States and Canada (EA)
GFOAR........ Global Family of Operational [*Plan*] Assessment Report (DOMA)
GFoF .... Fort Valley State College, Fort Valley, GA [*Library symbol Library of Congress*] (LCLS)
GFOF .... Geared Futures and Options Fund [*Investment term*] (NUMA)
GForsT........ Tift College, Forsyth, GA [*Library symbol Library of Congress*] (LCLS)
GFP .... Gamma-Fetoprotein (DB)
GFP .... Gas Flow Programmer [*Chromatography*]
GFP .... Geheime Feldpolizei [*Secret Police*] [*German*]
GFP .... General Forecasting Program (BUR)
GFP .... General Foreign Policy [*A publication*]
GFP .... Generalized File Processor
GFP .... Generations for Peace (EA)
GFP .... Glass-Fiber Pulling [*Materials processing*]
GFP .... Government-Funded Procurement
GFP .... Government-Funded Program
GFP .... Government-Furnished Parts (AFM)
GFP .... Government-Furnished Property
GFP .... Green Fluorescent Protein [*Biochemistry*]
GFP .... Ground Fault Protector (PDAA)
GFP .... Ground Fine Pitch (AIA)
GFP & S ..... Government-Furnished Property and Services (MSA)
GFPBBD .... Groupement Francais des Producteurs de Bases et Banques de Donnees [*French Federation of Data Base Producers*] [*Information service or system*] (IID)
GF-PET .... Glass-Fiber Polyethylene Terephthalate [*Plastics technology*]
GFPL .... Government-Furnished Property List (MCD)
GFPM.......... Gas Fission Products Monitor
GFPM.......... Gate Frequency Position Modulation (IAA)
GFP/M......... Government-Furnished Property and Material
GFPO .... Grand Forks Project Office [*Grand Forks, ND*] [*Terminated Department of Energy*] (GRD)
GFPO .... Port Loko [*Sierra Leone*] [*ICAO location identifier*] (ICLI)
GFQ .... Austin, TX [*Location identifier FAA*] (FAAL)
GFR .... Federal Reserve Bank of Atlanta, Atlanta, GA [*OCLC symbol*] (OCLC)
GFR .... Gap-Filler RADAR
GFR .... Gas-Filled Rectifier
GFR .... General Flight Rules [*CAB*] [*A publication*] (DLA)
GFR .... General Functional Requirements
GFR .... Generator Field Regulator (IAA)
GFR .... Geotechnical Fabrics Report [*A publication*] (EAAP)
GFR .... German Federal Republic [*West Germany*]
GFR .... Glass and Fiber Resin
GFR .... Glass-Fiber Reinforced
GFR .... Glomerular Filtration Rate [*Nephrology*]
GFR .... Government Facilities Request (AAG)
GFR .... Government Flight Representative
GFR .... Granville [*France*] [*Airport symbol*] (AD)
GFR .... Grim File Reaper [*Computer hacker terminology*] (NHD)
GFRC .... Gas Flow Radiation Counter [*Nucleonics*] (IAA)
GFRC .... General File/Record Control [*Honeywell, Inc.*] (IAA)
GFRC .... Glass Fiber Reinforced Concrete
GFRHS........ Germans-from-Russia Heritage Society (EA)
GF/RP .... Gap-Filler/Reporting Post [*RADAR*]
GFRP .... Glass-Fiber-Reinforced Plastic [*Also, GIFRP*]
GFRP .... Government Furnished Repair Parts
GFRP .... Graphite-Fiber-Reinforced Plastic [*Also, GrFRP*] (NASA)
GFRS .... Ground Forces Replacement Service [*World War II*]
GFRT .... Gas-Filled Rectifying Tube
GFRTP .... Glass-Fiber-Reinforced Thermoplastic (MCD)
GFS .... Fernbank Science Center, Atlanta, GA [*OCLC symbol*] (OCLC)
GFS .... Giant Foods [*AMEX symbol*] (SAG)
GFS .... Girls' Friendly Society of the USA (EA)
GFS .... Global Financial Studies
GFS .... Global Focal Sclerosis [*Medicine*] (DMAA)
GFS .... Goffs, CA [*Location identifier FAA*] (FAAL)
GFS .... Government Finance Statistics (NITA)
GFS .... Government-Furnished Services (KSC)
GFS .... Government-Furnished Software (NASA)
GFS .... Gower Federal Service [*Rocky Mountain Mineral Law Foundation*] [*Information service or system*] (CRD)
GFS .... Grandfather-Father-Son [*Computer science*] (PCM)
GFS .... Grand Financial Scribe [*Freemasonry*] (ROG)
GFS .... Group Final Selector (IAA)
GFS .... Guernsey Freight Services [*British*]
GFS .... Gulfstream Airlines, Inc. [*ICAO designator*] (FAAC)

GFS............. Gunfire Support (NVT)
GFSA .... Goldfish Society of America (EA)
GFSB .... GFS Bancorp [NASDAQ symbol] (SAG)
GFSB B .... GFSB Bancorp, Inc. [Associated Press] (SAG)
GFS Bcp ...... GFS Bancorp [Associated Press] (SAG)
GFSC .... Goddard Flight Space Center [NASA] (AAGC)
GFSE .... Government-Furnished Support Equipment (MCD)
GFsH........... United States Army, Fort Stewart/Hunter AAF Library, Fort Stewart, GA [Library symbol Library of Congress] (LCLS)
GFSL........... Gaffsail [Ship's rigging] (ROG)
GFSM .... Government-Furnished Surplus Material (MCD)
GFSP .... Government-Furnished Support Property (KSC)
GFSR .... General Function System Requirement
GFSR .... Generalized Feedback Shift Register [Mathematics]
GFSS .... Gunfire Support Ship
GFST........... Ground Fuel Start Tank (AAG)
GFSUSA....... Girls' Friendly Society of the USA (EA)
GFSY .... Government Finance Statistics [International Monetary Fund] [Information service or system] (CRD)
GFT............. Generalized Fast Transform (PDAA)
GFT............. Glass Fabric Tape
GFT............. Glass-Forming Tendency [Materials science]
GFT............. (Glucopyranosyl)fluorothymine [Biochemistry]
GFT............. Graphic Firing Table [Weaponry] (NATG)
GFT............. Green Forest Lumber Corp. [Toronto Stock Exchange symbol]
GFT............. Gruppo Finanziario Tessile [Commercial firm]
GFT............. Guided Flight Test (MCD)
GFT............. Gulfstream International Airlines, Inc. [ICAO designator] (FAAC)
G/FT²......... Grams per Square Foot
GFTA.......... Goldman-Fristoe Test of Articulation [Education]
GFTANSW..... Grain and Feed Trade Association of New South Wales [Australia]
GFTC-ER ..... General Freight Traffic Committee - Eastern Railroads
GFTO.......... Tongo [Sierra Leone] [ICAO location identifier] (ICLI)
GFTU .... General Federation of Trade Unions [Various countries]
GFTWR........ Giftwear
GFU............. Glazed Facing Units [Technical drawings]
GFUT .... Ground Fuel Ullage Tank (AAG)
GFV............. Fort Valley State College, Fort Valley, GA [OCLC symbol] (OCLC)
GFV............. Goldfever Resources Ltd. [Vancouver Stock Exchange symbol]
GfV............. Gueterfernverkehr [Carriage of Goods] [German Business term] (ILCA)
GFV............. Guided Flight Vehicle
GFW............. General Flight Work
GFW............. Gesellschaft fuer Weltraumforschung [Society for Space Research] [Germany]
GFW............. GFW Aviation [Australia] [FAA designator] (FAAC)
GFW............. Glass Filament Wound (IAA)
G-F-W......... Goldman-Fristoe-Woodcock Test of Auditory Discrimination [Education]
GFW............. Gram Formula Weight [Chemistry]
GFW............. Great French Writers [A publication]
GFW............. Ground-Fault Warning (IEEE)
GFWC .... General Federation of Women's Clubs (EA)
GFWI .... Greek Food and Wine Institute (NTPA)
GFWO .... Gulfwest Oil Co. [NASDAQ symbol] (SAG)
GFX............. Ghuraf [South Arabia] [Airport symbol] (AD)
GFX............. Grandfield, OK [Location identifier FAA] (FAAL)
GFX............. PLM Equipment Growth Fund I Ltd. [AMEX symbol] (SPSG)
GFY............. Government Fiscal Year (MCD)
GFY............. Grootfontein [South-West Africa] [Airport symbol] (OAG)
GFY............. PLM Equipment Growth Fund II Ltd. [AMEX symbol] (SPSG)
GFYE.......... Yengema [Sierra Leone] [ICAO location identifier] (ICLI)
GFZ............. Greenfield, IA [Location identifier FAA] (FAAL)
GFZ............. PLM Equipment Growth Fund III Ltd. [AMEX symbol] (SPSG)
GG .... Galloping Gourmet [TV program]
GG .... Gamma Globulin [Medicine]
GG .... Gas Generator (AAG)
GG .... Gatling Gun
GG .... Gem State Airlines [ICAO designator] (AD)
GG .... Gender Gap [Refers to women's tendency to vote for Democratic over Republican candidates, a phenomenon noticed by pollsters beginning with the 1980 election]
GG .... Generator Gas [System] [Nuclear energy] (NRCH)
GG .... Genito-Genital [Medicine]
GG .... Gewehrgranate [Rifle Grenade] [German military - World War II]
Gg.............. Gigagram
GG .... Girl Guides (BARN)
GG .... Glass Glover [Commercial firm British]
Gg.............. Glucagon [Endocrinology]
GG .... Glyceryl Guaiacolate [Expectorant] (AAMN)
GG .... Glycylglycine [Organic chemistry]
GG .... Goal Gradient [Psychology]
GG .... Going [Amateur radio shorthand] (WDAA)
GG .... Goldcorp [NYSE symbol] (SAG)
GG .... Golden Gloves Association of America [Later, GGA of A]
GG .... Government Girl
GG .... Government Grade [Followed by a number, 1-18; National Security Agency Employee Grade]
GG .... Government Guaranteed (EBF)
GG .... Governor General
GG .... Grand Guardian [Freemasonry]
GG .... Grant Greater Than [Dialog] [Searchable field] [Information service or system] (NITA)
GG .... Gravity Gradient (KSC)

GG .... Great Gatsby [Describes clothing style modeled after the type worn by characters in F. Scott Fitzgerald's novel, "The Great Gatsby"]
GG .... Great Gross [144 dozen] [Also, GGR]
GG .... Grenadier Guards [Military British]
GG .... Groove Gauge
GG .... Grounded Grid [Valve] (DEN)
GG .... Ground Guidance [Aerospace] (AAG)
GG .... Ground Gunner [Air Force British]
G-G............ Ground-to-Ground [Communications, weapons, etc.] (MSA)
GG .... Guaifenesin [An expectorant] [Pharmacology] (DAVI)
GG .... Guinea Gulf Line [Steamship] (MHDB)
GG .... Gutenberg Gesellschaft (EA)
GGA .... Gale Global Access [Also, GGAEA]
GGA .... General Gonadotropic Activity [Endocrinology] (MAE)
GGA .... Generalized Gradient Approximation [Mathematics]
GGA .... Girl Guides Association [British]
GGA .... Golden Glacier [Vancouver Stock Exchange symbol]
GGA .... Good Gardeners' Association [British]
GGA .... Grounded Grid Amplifier
GGA .... Group Gross Assets (ADA)
GGA .... Guanine Guanine Adenine [A triplet of bases coding for the amino acid, glycine] (EES)
GGA .... Guernsey Growers Association [British] (DBA)
GGA .... Gulf General Atomic [Commercial firm]
GGAA .... Girl Guides Association of Australia
GGAA .... Golden Gloves Association of America [Later, GGA of A] (EA)
GGaB .... Brenau College, Gainsville, GA [Library symbol Library of Congress] (LCLS)
GGAB .... Ghana Geographical Association. Bulletin [A publication]
GGaC .... Gainesville Junior College, Gainesville, GA [Library symbol] [Library of Congress] (LCLS)
GGaCL .... Chestatee Regional Library System, Gainsville, GA [Library symbol] [Library of Congress] (LCLS)
GGAEA .... Gale Global Access, Encyclopedia of Associations [Also, GGA]
GGA of A .... Golden Gloves Association of America (EA)
GGAR.......... Gas-Guided Aircraft Rocket
GGAWA........ Grape Growers' Association of Western Australia
GGBB .... Bambadinca [Guinea-Bissau] [ICAO location identifier] (ICLI)
GGBE .... Bedanda [Guinea-Bissau] [ICAO location identifier] (ICLI)
GGBF .... Bafata [Guinea-Bissau] [ICAO location identifier] (ICLI)
GGBG .... Governor-General's Bodyguard [British military] (DMA)
GGBI.......... Bissora [Guinea-Bissau] [ICAO location identifier] (ICLI)
GGBO .... Bolama [Guinea-Bissau] [ICAO location identifier] (ICLI)
GGBU .... Bubaque [Guinea-Bissau] [ICAO location identifier] (ICLI)
GGC .... Gamma-Glutamyl Carboxylase (DMAA)
GGC .... General Grand Chapter [Freemasonry]
GGC .... Georgia College, Milledgeville, GA [OCLC symbol] (OCLC)
GGC .... Georgia Gulf Corp. [NYSE symbol] (SPSG)
GGC .... Golden Gate College [California]
GGC .... Grey Goose Corp. Ltd. [Toronto Stock Exchange symbol]
GGC .... Ground Guidance Computer [Aerospace]
GGC .... Guanine Guanine Cytosine [A triplet of bases coding for the amino acid, glycine] (EES)
GGC .... Gun Group Commander [British military] (DMA)
GGCC.......... Cacine [Guinea-Bissau] [ICAO location identifier] (ICLI)
GGCC.......... Grand Gaming Corp. [NASDAQ symbol] (SAG)
GGCCW....... Grand Gaming Wrrt [NASDAQ symbol] (TTSB)
GGCF .... Cufar [Guinea-Bissau] [ICAO location identifier] (ICLI)
GGCG .... Cantchungo [Guinea-Bissau] [ICAO location identifier] (ICLI)
GGCST........ Gleb-Goldstein Color Sorting Test [Psychology]
GGCT .... Catio [Guinea-Bissau] [ICAO location identifier] (ICLI)
GGCV .... Caravela [Guinea-Bissau] [ICAO location identifier] (ICLI)
GGD .... General Government Division [GAO] (AAGC)
GGD .... Gold Bridge Development [Vancouver Stock Exchange symbol]
GGD .... Great Granddaughter
GGD .... Gregory Downs [Australia Airport symbol Obsolete] (OAG)
GGDA.......... Geocentric Datum of Australia [Geographic] (EERA)
GGDC.......... G. G. Drayton Club (EA)
GGDF.......... Gas Gathering Data File [Phillips Petroleum]
GGDPAC....... Government Geoscience Database Policy Advisory Committee [Commonwealth] (EERA)
GGE .... Gauge
GGE .... Generalized Glandular Enlargement [Medicine]
GGE .... Georgetown, SC [Location identifier FAA] (FAAL)
GGE .... Golden Group Explorations, Inc. [Vancouver Stock Exchange symbol]
GGE .... Gospelrama Gospel Expo [An association] (EA)
GGE .... Gradient Gel Electrophoresis
GGE .... Griffin Gaming & Entertainment [AMEX symbol] (SAG)
GGE .... Ground Guidance Equipment [Aerospace]
GGEN.......... GalaGen Inc. [NASDAQ symbol] (TTSB)
GGEP.......... Empada [Guinea-Bissau] [ICAO location identifier] (ICLI)
GGF .... Glass and Glazing Federation [British]
GGF .... Glial Growth Factor [Biochemistry]
GGF .... Global Government Plus Fund Ltd. [Toronto Stock Exchange symbol]
GGF .... Granges-Gontardes [France] [Seismograph station code, US Geological Survey Closed] (SEIS)
GGF .... Grant, NE [Location identifier FAA] (FAAL)
GGF .... Ground Gained Forward [Aerial photography]
GGFC .... Girl Groups Fan Club (EA)
GGFC .... Go Go's Fan Club [Defunct] (EA)
GGFO.......... Formosa [Guinea-Bissau] [ICAO location identifier] (ICLI)
GGFR.......... Farim [Guinea-Bissau] [ICAO location identifier] (ICLI)
G/G/FRIS.... Gal/Guy Fridays [Classified advertising]
GGFRJ .... Gas Generator Fueled Ramjet (MCD)
GGFU .... Fulacunda [Guinea-Bissau] [ICAO location identifier] (ICLI)

GGG .... Gadolinium, Gallium, Garnet [*Also, G3*] [*Substrate for magnetic film*]
GGG .... Gladewater-Kilgore-Longview [*Texas*] [*Airport symbol*] (AD)
GGG .... Glycine-Rich Gamma-Glycoprotein [*Immunology*]
GGG .... Goat Gamma-Globulin [*Immunology*]
GGG .... Graco, Inc. [*NYSE symbol*] (SPSG)
GGG .... Guanine Guanine Guanine [*A triplet of bases coding for teh amino acid, glycine*] (EES)
GGG .... Gummi Guttae Gambiae [*Gamboge*] [*Pharmacology*] (ROG)
GGG .... Gunnar Gold, Inc. [*Toronto Stock Exchange symbol*]
GGG .... Longview [*Texas*] [*Airport symbol*] (OAG)
GGGA .... Galinhas [*Guinea-Bissau*] [*ICAO location identifier*] (ICLI)
GGGB .... Gabu [*Guinea-Bissau*] [*ICAO location identifier*] (ICLI)
GGHP .... General Grand High Priest [*Freemasonry*]
GGI .... Greenhouse Gas Index
GGIA .... Granite Grit Institute of America (EA)
GGIT .... Geographics Inc. [*NASDAQ symbol*] (TTSB)
GGK .... Goldstein Golub Kessler [*Commercial firm*]
GGL .... Gain Guided LASER (IAA)
GGL .... Gerle Gold Ltd. [*Vancouver Stock Exchange symbol*]
GGL .... Gissing, Glen L., Evansville WI [*STAC*]
GGL .... Gravity-Gradient Libration [*Damper*]
GGL .... Ground Glass
GGL .... Guild of Guide Lecturers [*British*]
GGL .... Titusville, FL [*Location identifier FAA*] (FAAL)
GGIF .... Federal Law Enforcement Training Center, Glynco, GA [*Library symbol Library of Congress*] (LCLS)
GGM .... Geographici Graeci Minores [*A publication*] (OCD)
GGM .... Glitter Gold Mines [*Vancouver Stock Exchange symbol*]
GGM .... Glucose/Galactose Malabsorption [*Medicine*]
GGM .... Gravity Gradiometer Mission [*NASA*]
GGM .... Ground-to-Ground Missile
GGMA .... Glassine and Greaseproof Manufacturers Association [*Later, API*] (EA)
GGMA .... Government Gold Mining Areas
GGMK .... Great, Grand Master Key [*Locks*] (ADA)
GGMMA ...... Gabriel Garcia Moreno Memorial Association (EA)
GGMS .... Mansoa [*Guinea-Bissau*] [*ICAO location identifier*] (ICLI)
GGMWA ...... Grace of God Movement for the Women of America [*Later, GGMWW*] (EA)
GGMWW ...... Grace of God Movement for the Women of the World (EA)
GGN .... Air Georgian [*Canada*] [*FAA designator*] (FAAC)
GGN .... Gagnoa [*Ivory Coast*] [*Airport symbol*] (OAG)
GGNG .... Gelatin Glass Negative (VRA)
GGNI .... Governor-General of Northern Ireland (DAS)
GGNRA .... Golden Gate National Recreation Area Advisory Commission [*National Park Service*] [*San Francisco, CA*] (EGAO)
GGNRACAC... Golden Gate National Recreation Area Advisory Commission [*National Park Service*] [*San Francisco, CA*] (EGAO)
GGNS .... Genus, Inc. [*NASDAQ symbol*] (CTT)
GGNS .... Grand Gulf Nuclear Station (NRCH)
GGNS .... Grarid Guff Nuclear Station (COE)
GGO .... Getchell Gold Corp. [*AMEX symbol*] (SAG)
GGO .... Glavnaya Geofizicheskaya Observatory [*Main Geophysical Observatory*] [*Former USSR*]
GGO .... Governor-General's Order [*British military*] (DMA)
GGO .... Greater Greensboro [*North Carolina*] Open [*Golf tournament*]
GGO .... Guiglo [*Ivory Coast*] [*Airport symbol*] (OAG)
GG or S .... Glands, Goiter, or Stiffness [*Medicine*]
GGOV .... Bissau/Oswaldo Vieira International [*Guinea-Bissau*] [*ICAO location identifier*] (ICLI)
GGP .... Gas-Gathering Pipeline
GGP .... Gateway-to-Gateway Protocol [*Computer science*] (TNIG)
GGP .... General Growth Properties [*NYSE symbol*] (SPSG)
GGP .... Genl Growth Properties [*NYSE symbol*] (TTSB)
GGP .... George Resources Co. [*Vancouver Stock Exchange symbol*]
GGP .... Golden Gate Productions [*San Francisco, CA*] [*Telecommunications*] (TSSD)
GGP .... Good Gay Poets (EA)
GGP .... Good Guidance Practice [*Drug evaluation*]
GGP .... GPS [*Global Positioning System*] Guidance Package
GGP .... Gross Global Product
GGP .... Logansport, IN [*Location identifier FAA*] (FAAL)
GGPA .... Graduate Grade-Point Average [*Higher education*]
GGPC .... Pecixe [*Guinea-Bissau*] [*ICAO location identifier*] (ICLI)
GGPF .... Glial Growth Promoting Factor [*Neurology*]
GGPL .... Glycine, Glycine Phenylalanine, Leucine [*A synthetic peptide*]
GGPP .... Giant Gaseous Protoplanet [*Planetary science*]
GGPR .... Pirada [*Guinea-Bissau*] [*ICAO location identifier*] (ICLI)
GGQ .... Gagnoa [*Ivory Coast*] [*Airport symbol*] (AD)
GGR .... Gallagher Explorations Ltd. [*Vancouver Stock Exchange symbol*]
GGR .... Geschichte der Griechischen Religion [*A publication*] (OCD)
GGR .... Great Gross [*144 dozen*] [*Also, GG*]
GGR .... Ground Gunnery Range
GGRA .... Gelatine and Glue Research Association [*British*] (BI)
G Gracch ..... Gaius Gracchus [*of Plutarch*] [*Classical studies*] (OCD)
GGraG .... Gracewood State School and Hospital, Gracewood, GA [*Library symbol Library of Congress*] (LCLS)
GGriEx .... University of Georgia, Experiment Station, Griffin, GA [*Library symbol Library of Congress*] (LCLS)
GGS .... Gates-Gaudin-Schuhmann [*Particle size distribution*]
GGS .... Girls' Grammar School (ADA)
GGS .... Glands, Goiter, or Stiffness [*Of neck*] [*Medicine*] (STED)
GGS .... Global Geospace Science
GGS .... Global Geospace Study [*Proposed*] [*United States, Japan, and Europe*]

GGS .... Gobernador Gregores [*Argentina*] [*Airport symbol*] (OAG)
GGS .... Graphic Generator System
GGS .... Gravity-Gradient Satellite
GGS .... Gravity-Gradient Sensor
GGS .... Great Grandson
GGS .... Ground Gained Sideways [*Aerial photography*]
GGS .... Ground Guidance System [*Aerospace*] (AAG)
GGSA .... German Genealogical Society of America (EA)
GGSD .... Sao Domingos [*Guinea-Bissau*] [*ICAO location identifier*] (ICLI)
GGSE .... Gravity-Gradient Stabilization Experiment
GGSM .... Graduate Diploma of the Guildhall School of Music [*British*] (DBQ)
GGSP .... Giant-to-Giant Interneuron Synaptic Potential [*Neurochemistry*]
GGSPFWFH... Goose and Gander, Society for the Preservation of First Wives and First Husbands (EA)
GGT .... Gabelli Global Multimedia Tr [*NYSE symbol*] (TTSB)
GGT .... Gabelli Global Multimedia Trust, Inc. [*NYSE symbol*] (SAG)
GGT .... Gamma-Glutamyltransferase [*Also, GGTP, GT*] [*An enzyme*]
GGT .... Gamma-Glutamyl Transpeptidase [*Also, GGT, GT*] [*An enzyme*] (DAVI)
GGT .... George Town [*Bahamas*] [*Airport symbol*] (OAG)
GGT .... Georgetown, NY [*Location identifier FAA*] (FAAL)
GGT .... Gravity-Gradient Torque
GGT .... Greater Temagami [*Vancouver Stock Exchange symbol*]
GGTI .... GTI Corp. [*NASDAQ symbol*] (SAG)
GGTP .... Gamma-Glutamyl Transpeptidase [*Also, GGT, GT*] [*An enzyme*]
GGTS .... Gravity-Gradient Test Satellite [*NASA*]
GGTT .... Tite [*Guinea-Bissau*] [*ICAO location identifier*] (ICLI)
GGU .... Giant Gastric Ulcer [*Medicine*]
GGU .... Guanine Guanine Uracil [*A triplet of bases coding for the amino acid, glycine*] (EES)
GGUALE .... Golden Gate University Advanced Legal Education Program (DLA)
GGUN .... Uno [*Guinea-Bissau*] [*ICAO location identifier*] (ICLI)
GGUY .... [*The*] Good Guys, Inc. [*NASDAQ symbol*] (NQ)
GGV .... Gabriel Gonzalez Videla [*Antarctica*] [*Seismograph station code, US Geological Survey Closed*] (SEIS)
GGV .... Gas Generator Valve (KSC)
GGV .... Kwigillingok, AK [*Location identifier FAA*] (FAAL)
GGVB .... Gelatin, Glucose, and Veronal Buffer [*Medicine*] (DMAA)
GGVR .... Varela [*Guinea-Bissau*] [*ICAO location identifier*] (ICLI)
GGW .... Glasgow [*Montana*] [*Airport symbol*] (OAG)
GGX .... Golden Gate Explorations [*Vancouver Stock Exchange symbol*]
GGY .... Clanton, AL [*Location identifier FAA*] (FAAL)
GGY .... Greentree Energy [*Vancouver Stock Exchange symbol*]
GGZ .... Akron, OH [*Location identifier FAA*] (FAAL)
GH .... Gaseous Hydrogen (KSC)
GH .... Gate House (NRCH)
GH .... Gee-Herter [*Disease*] [*Medicine*] (DB)
GH .... Gemini Hatch [*NASA*]
GH .... General Headquarters [*Military*] (CDAI)
GH .... General Health (DMAA)
GH .... General Hospital [*Initialism also refers to a TV program*]
GH .... General Host Corp. [*NYSE symbol*] (SPSG)
GH .... Genetically Hypertensive [*Rat*] (STED)
GH .... Genetic Hypertension [*Medicine*] (DB)
GH .... Geniohyoid (STED)
GH .... Genl Host [*NYSE symbol*] (TTSB)
GH .... George Horne [*Refers to old news*] [*Slang*] (DSUE)
gh .... Ghana [*MARC country of publication code Library of Congress*] (LCCP)
GH .... Ghana [*ANSI two-letter standard code*] (CNC)
GH .... Ghana Airways [*ICAO designator*] (AD)
GH .... Gilford-Hutchinson [*Syndrome*] [*Medicine*] (STED)
GH .... Gilt Head [*Bookbinding*] (ROG)
GH .... Glenohumeral [*Joint*] [*Anatomy*] (DAVI)
GH .... Glenohumeral Joint [*Anatomy*] (DAVI)
G-H .... Goodenough-Harris Drawing Test [*Education*]
GH .... Good Health (STED)
GH .... Gougerot-Hailey [*Syndrome*] [*Medicine*] (DB)
GH .... Government House [*Canada*]
GH .... Gray Herbarium [*Harvard University*] [*Cambridge, MA*]
GH .... Grid Heading [*Navigation*]
GH .... Ground Handling [*Aerospace*]
GH .... Growth Hormone [*Somatotrophin*] [*Also, SH, STH Endocrinology*]
GH .... Guardhouse
GH .... Guest House
GH_2 .... Gaseous Hydrogen [*NASA*] (KSC)
GHA .... General Housekeeping Area [*NASA*] (NASA)
GHA .... Georgia Hospital Association [*Atlanta*] (TSSD)
GHA .... Georgia Southwestern College, Americus, GA [*OCLC symbol*] (OCLC)
GHA .... Gesneriad Hybridizers Association (EA)
GHA .... Ghana [*ANSI three-letter standard code*] (CNC)
GHA .... Ghana Airways Corp. [*ICAO designator*] (FAAC)
GHA .... Ghardaia [*Algeria*] [*Airport symbol*] (OAG)
GHA .... Glashutten [*Austria*] [*Seismograph station code, US Geological Survey*] (SEIS)
GHA .... Global Health Action (EA)
GHA .... Glucoheptanoic Acid [*Biochemistry*] (DAVI)
GHA .... Golden Hat Resources [*Vancouver Stock Exchange symbol*]
GHA .... Grassland Husbandry Adviser [*Ministry of Agriculture, Fisheries, and Food*] [*British*]
GHA .... Greenwich Hour Angle
GHA .... Ground Hazard Area (MUGU)
GHA .... Gyro Header Assembly
GHAA .... Group Health Association of America (EA)

GhAF .... Ghanaian Air Force
GHAF .... Grosvenor House Antiques Fair [*British*] (ITD)
GHAMS .... Greenwich Hour Angle of Mean Sun
GHANABATT... Ghana Battalion [*Military*]
GHAQ .... General High Altitude Questionnaire (PDAA)
GHARS .... Gyroscopic Heading and Altitude Reference System (SAA)
GHAT .... Ground Handling and Transportation [*Aerospace*] (KSC)
GHATS .... Greenwich Hour Angle of True Sun
GHB .... Gamma Hydroxy Butyrate [*Steroid*]
GHB .... Gamma-Hydroxybutyric Acid [*Organic chemistry*]
GHb .... Glycohemoglobin [*Biochemistry, medicine*]
GHB .... Glycosylated Hemoglobin [*Clinical chemistry*]
GHB .... Governor's Harbour [*Bahamas*] [*Airport symbol*] (OAG)
GHBA .... Galiceno Horse Breeders Association (EA)
GHBP .... Growth Hormone Binding Protein (DMAA)
GHC .... Gating Half-Cycle [*Computer science*]
GHC .... Generalized Hyperbolic Class
GHC .... Gold Hill [*California*] [*Seismograph station code, US Geological Survey*] (SEIS)
GHC .... Grays Harbor College [*Washington*]
GHC .... Great Harbour Cay [*Bahamas*] [*Airport symbol*] (OAG)
GHC .... Greyhound Computer of Canada Ltd. [*Toronto Stock Exchange symbol*]
GHC .... Ground Half Coupling (KSC)
GHC .... Group Health Cooperative (DMAA)
GHC .... Guidance Heater Control
GHC .... Halic Havacilik, AS [*Turkey*] [*FAA designator*] (FAAC)
GHCl .... Guanidine Hydrochloride [*Organic chemistry*]
GHCN .... Global Historical Climate Network [*Marine science*] (OSRA)
GHCP .... Georgia Hospital Computer Group
GHCR .... Gross Henle Chromoreaction [*Clinical chemistry*]
GHCS .... Good Housekeeping Check Sheet (AAG)
GHD .... Growth Hormone Deficiency [*Endocrinology*]
GHDT .... Goodenough-Harris Drawing Test [*Psychology*] (DAVI)
GHDV .... Gasoline-Engine Heavy-Duty Vehicle
GHE .... Gable House Estates Ltd. [*British*]
GHE .... Garachine [*Panama*] [*Airport symbol*] (OAG)
GHE .... Gaseous Helium (KSC)
GHe .... Gaseous Helium (NAKS)
GHE .... Gauss Hypergeometric Equation [*Mathematics*]
GHE .... Gibbs-Helmholtz Equation [*Physical chemistry*]
GHE .... Ginn, Herbert E., South Portland ME [*STAC*]
GHE .... Golden Hemlock [*Vancouver Stock Exchange symbol*]
GHE .... Ground Handling Equipment [*Aerospace*]
G Heb .... Gospel of the Hebrews [*Apocryphal work*]
GHEF .... Givat Haviva Educational Foundation (EA)
GHF .... Gauss Hypergeometric Function [*Mathematics*]
GHF .... Gradient Heating Facility
GHF .... Grassland Heritage Foundation (EA)
GHF .... Growth Hormone Transcription Factor [*Endocrinology*]
GHFC .... Gebhardt-Heriot Foundation for All Cats (EA)
GHFC .... Gunilla Hutton Fan Club (EA)
GHFF .... George Hamilton IV and Friends [*Defunct*] (EA)
GHG .... Galactic Hitchhiker's Guild (EA)
GHG .... [*The*] Good Hotel Guide [*A publication British*]
GHG .... Governor's Horse Guard
GHG .... Greenhouse Gas [*Climatology*]
GHG .... Greenhouse Gases (EERA)
GHG .... Grosshandelsgesellschaft [*Wholesale Business Establishment*] [*German*]
GHH .... Galveston, Houston & Henderson Railroad Co. [*AAR code*]
GHi .... Georgia Historical Society, Savannah, GA [*Library symbol Library of Congress*] (LCLS)
GHI .... German Historical Institute (EA)
GHI .... GHI Mortgage Investors [*Vancouver Stock Exchange symbol*]
GHI .... Gilbert Hill [*Idaho*] [*Seismograph station code, US Geological Survey Closed*] (SEIS)
GHI .... Global High Inc. Dollar Fd [*NYSE symbol*] (TTSB)
GHI .... Global High Income Dollar Fund [*NYSE symbol*] (SPSG)
GHI .... Group Health Insurance [*British*]
GHI .... Growth Hormone Insufficiency
GHIA .... Genealogical and Heraldic Institute of America (EA)
GHJ .... Gastonia, NC [*Location identifier FAA*] (FAAL)
GHK .... Greyhawk Resources Ltd. [*Vancouver Stock Exchange symbol*]
GHK .... Grosshandelskontor [*Wholesale Business Office*] [*German*]
GHK .... Handkommentar zum Alten Testament (Goettingen) [*A publication*] (BJA)
GHL .... Gatwick Handling Ltd. [*British ICAO designator*] (FAAC)
GHL .... George Henry Lewes [*Initials used as pseudonym*]
GHL .... [*A*] Grammar of the Hurrian Language [*A publication*] (BJA)
GHL .... Greyhound Lines of Canada Ltd. [*Toronto Stock Exchange symbol*]
GHL .... Guardhouse Lawyer [*Military slang*]
GH/LCD .... Guest-Host/Liquid Crystal Display [*Telecommunications*] (TEL)
GHLI .... Guilford-Holley L Inventory [*Psychology*]
GHM .... Aero Service Bolivia [*ICAO designator*] (FAAC)
GHM .... Centerville, TN [*Location identifier FAA*] (FAAL)
GHM .... Going-Home Money
GHM .... Graham Corp. [*AMEX symbol*] (SPSG)
GHM .... Guaranteed Hourly Minimum
GH-MATRIX... Generalized Hadamard Matrix
GHME .... Gott Hilf Mir Elenden [*God Help Miserable Me*] [*Motto of Eleonore, Electress of Brandenburg (1583-1607)*] [*German*]
GHMI .... Generalized Human-Machine Interface (MCD)
GHMS .... Home Mission Sisters of America (Glenmary) (TOCD)
GHN .... Generalized Hypertrophic Neuropathy

GHN .... Ghana Navy
GHN .... Goldhaven Resources Ltd. [*Vancouver Stock Exchange symbol*]
GHN .... Groupe Hygiene Naturelle [*European Natural Hygiene Society - ENHS*] (EAIO)
GHO .... Grahamstown [*South Africa*] [*Airport symbol*] (AD)
GHO .... Greater Hartford [*Connecticut*] Open [*Golf tournament*]
Ghose Mort... Ghose on Mortgages in India [*A publication*] (DLA)
GHOST......... Global Horizontal Sounding Technique [*Meteorology*]
GHOST......... Golf Head Optical Speed Trap [*Golf self-improvement program*]
GHP .... Gas High Pressure
GHP .... Grand High Priest [*Freemasonry*]
GHP .... Greater Hartford Process [*An association*] (EA)
GHP .... Great Hungarian Plain [*Geology*]
GHP .... Greenwich Hospital Pension [*British military*] (DMA)
GHP .... Gross Horsepower [*Engineering*]
GHP .... Guild of Hospital Pharmacists [*British*] (DBA)
GHPM .... General Health Policy Model
GHPP .... Genetically Handicapped Persons Program (MEDA)
GHPR .... Gliding Horse and Pony Registry (EA)
GHQ .... General Headquarters [*Military*]
GHQ .... General Health Questionnaire [*Personality development test*] [*Psychology*]
GHQAF......... General Headquarters Air Force
GHQC .... GH [*General Hospital*] Questionnaire Club [*Defunct*] (EA)
GHQF .... General Headquarters File [*Army*]
GHQS .... General Headquarters Exercise
GHR .... Golden Hope Resources, Inc. [*Vancouver Stock Exchange symbol*]
GHR .... Granulomatous Hypersensitivity [*Medicine*] (DMAA)
GHR .... Gross Heat Rate (DNAB)
GHR .... Growth Hormone Receptor [*Biochemistry*]
GHRC/USA ... Guatemala Human Rights Commission/United States of America (EA)
GH-RF .... Growth Hormone Releasing Factor [*Somatoliberin*] [*Also, GH-RH, GRF Endocrinology*]
GHRF .... Guardians of Hydrocephalus Research Foundation (EA)
GH-RH .... Growth Hormone Releasing Hormone [*Somatoliberin*] [*Also, GH-RF, GRF Endocrinology*]
GH-RIF .... Growth Hormone Release Inhibiting Factor [*Also, GH-RIH, GRIF, SRIF, SS*] [*Endocrinology*]
GH-RIH .... Growth Hormone Release Inhibiting Hormone [*Also, GH-RIF, GRIF, SRIF, SS*] [*Endocrinology*]
GHRP .... Growth Hormone Releasing Peptide [*Endocrinology*]
GHRS .... Goddard High-Resolution Spectrograph
GHRSP......... Guatemalan Health Rights Support Project (EA)
GHR/USA ..... Guatemalan Human Rights Commission/USA (EA)
GHS .... Garden History Society [*British*]
GHS .... Gatari Hutama Air Services PT [*Indonesia*] [*ICAO designator*] (FAAC)
GHS .... General Health Services, Inc. (EFIS)
GHS .... General Household Survey [*Office of Population Census and Surveys*] [*British*]
GHS .... Getchell Resources, Inc. [*Vancouver Stock Exchange symbol*]
GHS .... Gilroy Hot Springs [*California*] [*Seismograph station code, US Geological Survey*] (SEIS)
GHS .... Global Health Sciences Fd [*NYSE symbol*] (TTSB)
GHS .... Global Health Sciences Fund [*NYSE symbol*] (SPSG)
GHS .... Ground Handling System [*Aerospace*] (AAG)
GHS .... Group Health Service (GHCT)
GHS .... Growth Hormone Secretagogue [*Biochemistry*]
GHS .... Grunberg Hydrofoil System
GHSE .... Ground Handling and Servicing Equipment [*Aerospace*] (IAA)
GHSG .... Guest Housing [*Army*] (AABC)
GHSI .... GHS, Inc. [*Formerly, Global Health Systems, Inc.*] [*NASDAQ symbol*] (NQ)
GHS Inc .... GHS, Inc. [*Associated Press*] (SAG)
GHSV .... Gas Hour Space Velocity [*Chemical engineering*]
GHT .... Ghat [*Libya*] [*Airport symbol*] (OAG)
GHT .... Golden Hour Tango
GHT .... Goldhurst Resources [*Vancouver Stock Exchange symbol*]
GHT .... Ground Handling Test
GHU .... Gualeguaychu [*Argentina*] [*Airport symbol*] (OAG)
GHV .... Genesis Health Ventures [*NYSE symbol*] (SPSG)
GHV .... Genesis Hlth Ventures [*NYSE symbol*] (TTSB)
GHV .... Golden Hind Ventures Ltd. [*Vancouver Stock Exchange symbol*]
GHV .... Goose Hepatitis Virus [*Medicine*] (DMAA)
GHV .... Growth Hormone Variant [*Medicine*] (DMAA)
GHVL .... Groot Hertog von Luxemberg [*Grand Duke of Luxemburg*] [*Numismatics*] (ROG)
GHVM .... Global High-Visibility Mast
GHW .... Garrison Hill [*Washington*] [*Seismograph station code, US Geological Survey*] (SEIS)
GHW .... General Housewares Corp. [*NYSE symbol*] (SPSG)
GHW .... Genl Housewares [*NYSE symbol*] (TTSB)
GHW .... Guaranteed Hourly Wage
GHWP .... Greenhouse Warming Potential [*Environmental chemistry*]
GHWS .... Gas Hot Water Service [*Classified advertising*] (ADA)
GHX .... Graham, TX [*Location identifier FAA*] (FAAL)
GHX .... Ground Heat Exchanger
GHz .... Gigahertz [*1,000 megahertz*]
GHZ .... Golden Horizon [*Vancouver Stock Exchange symbol*]
GI .... Air Guinee [*ICAO designator*] (AD)
GI .... Galvanized Iron
GI .... Gastroenterology (DAVI)
GI .... Gastrointestinal [*Medicine*]
GI .... Gelatin Infusion [*Medium*] [*Biochemistry*] (DAVI)
GI .... Gelatin Infusion Medium [*Medicine*] (BABM)

GI................. Gelbray International (EA)
GI................. Gemeinschaft der Ikonenfreunde [*Society of Friends of Icons - SFI*] (EAIO)
GI................. Genealogical Institute (EA)
GI................. General Index
GI................. General Indulgence (ROG)
GI................. General Infantry [*Soldier*] [*Army*] (DAVI)
GI................. General Information (IAA)
GI................. General Input [*Computer science*] (IAA)
GI................. General Inspection [*Military*] (AABC)
GI................. General Instruments
GI................. General Issue
GI................. Generic Identifier [*Telecommunications*] (TEL)
GI................. Genesis Information (EA)
GI................. Genesis Institute [*An association*] (EA)
GI................. Genetics Institute, Inc.
GI................. Geodesic Isotensoid (IEEE)
GIAO............ Geographically Impossible (ADA)
GI................. Geometric Intelligence
GI................. Geon International Corp. (EFIS)
GI................. Geophysical Institute [*University of Alaska, Fairbanks*] [*Research center*]
GI................. Gerson Institute (EA)
GI................. Giant Industries [*NYSE symbol*] (SPSG)
GI................. Giant Interneurons [*Neurology*]
GI................. Gibraltar [*ANSI two-letter standard code*] (CNC)
gi................. Gibraltar [*MARC country of publication code Library of Congress*] (LCCP)
Gi................. Gideons International (EA)
Gi................. Gilbert [*A unit of magnetomotive force*]
GI................. Gill
GI................. Gingival Index [*Dentistry*]
GI................. Girls, Inc. (EA)
GI................. Glazed Interior [*Title*] (DICI)
GI................. Globin Insulin
GI................. Glomerular Index [*Medicine*] (AAMN)
GI................. Glomus intraradices [*A fungus*]
GI................. Glucose Isomerase (EDCT)
GI................. Goethe Institute (EA)
GI................. Gold Institute [*Also known as L'Institut de l'Or*] (EA)
GI................. Government and Industrial (IEEE)
GI................. Government Initiated (IEEE)
GI................. Government Issue [*Army*]
GI................. Government of India
GI................. Graded Index [*Optics*]
GI................. Grand Island [*Diocesan abbreviation*] [*Nebraska*] (TOCD)
GI................. Granuloma Inguinale [*Endocrinology*] (DAVI)
GI................. Grassroots International (EA)
GI................. Gravida I [*Gynecology and obstetrics*] (DAVI)
GI................. Gray Iron (MSA)
GI................. Gray's Inn [*London*] [*One of the Inns of Court*]
GI................. Great Indulgence
GI................. Green Island [*Plant pathology*]
GI................. Greenpeace International (EA)
GI................. Grid Interval (IAA)
GI................. Gross Impression [*Television ratings*] (NTCM)
GI................. Gross Income
GI................. Gross Inventory (MHDB)
GI................. Gross Investment
GI................. Ground Interception (IAA)
GI................. Group Insurance
GI................. Growth and Income [*Business term*]
GI................. Growth Index
GI................. Growth Inhibiting
GI................. Guardian Independent [*A publication*]
GI................. Guidance Inventory [*Psychology*]
GI................. Guided Imagery [*Psychology*]
GI................. Guido de Suzaria [*Deceased, 1293*] [*Authority cited in pre-1607 legal work*] (DSA)
GI................. Gunner Instructor [*Navy British*]
GI................. Gyro International (EA)
GI................. Royal Glasgow Institute of Fine Arts [*Scotland*]
GI................. Soldier [*Slang, probably from Government Issue*]
GIA............... Armed Islamic Group [*Anti-government faction*] [*Algeria*] [*Acronym is based on foreign phrase*] (ECON)
GIA............... Garden Industry of America [*Inactive*] (EA)
GIA............... Garuda Indonesian Airways Ltd.
GIA............... Garuda Indonesia PT [*ICAO designator*] (FAAC)
GIA............... Gastrointestinal Anastomosis [*Medicine*] (DAVI)
GIA............... Gemological Institute of America (EA)
GIA............... General Industry Applications (MCD)
GIA............... General International Agreement [*Legal term*] (DLA)
GIA............... Geographical Information Analysis
GIA............... Geophysical Institute, University of Alaska [*Alaska*] [*Seismograph station code, US Geological Survey Closed*] (SEIS)
GIA............... Glacial Isostatic Adjustment [*Geophysics*]
GIA............... Goodwill Industries of America (EA)
GIA............... Government Information and Advertising [*New South Wales, Australia*]
GIA............... GPC [*General Purpose Computer*] Interface Adapter (NASA)
GIA............... Grants-in-Aid
GIA............... Gross Internal Area
GIA............... Group Interaction Analysis
GIA............... Gummed Industries Association (EA)

GIABS.......... Gastrointestinal Absorption Database [*Environmental Protection Agency Information service or system*] (CRD)
GIAC............ General Industry Advisory Committee
GIAM.......... Global Impacts of Applied Microbiology [*International conferences*]
GIANT.......... Genealogical [*or Geological*] Information and Name Tabulating System [*Computer science*] (IEEE)
GIANT.......... General Information and Analysis Tool
GIANT.......... General Instrument Advanced Nitride Technology (IAA)
GIANT.......... General Integrated Analytical Triangulation Program [*National Oceanic and Atmospheric Administration*]
GIANT.......... Geographic Intelligence and Topographic System
GIANT.......... Giant Group Ltd. [*Associated Press*] (SAG)
GIANT.......... Graphic Interactive Analytic Network Technique (MCD)
GiantCmt...... Giant Cement Holding, Inc. [*Associated Press*] (SAG)
GiantFd....... Giant Foods [*Associated Press*] (SAG)
GiantIn....... Giant Industries [*Associated Press*] (SAG)
GIANTS........ Greater Independent Association of National Travel Services (EA)
GIAO............ Gauge-Invariant Atomic Orbital [*NASA*]
GIAR............ Grants-in-Aid of Research
GIAS............ Global Integration and Synthesis [*Climate change*] (EERA)
Giauq El ...... Giauque's Election Laws [*A publication*] (DLA)
GIAWA......... Gas Industry Association of Western Australia
GIB.............. Air Guinea [*Guinea*] [*ICAO designator*] (FAAC)
GIB.............. Gastric Ileal Bypass [*Medicine*] (DAVI)
GIB.............. Gastrointestinal Bleeding [*Medicine*] (DMAA)
GIB.............. General Information Booklet [*Navy*]
GIB.............. General Instruction Book
Gib.............. Gibbon's Reports, New York Surrogate Court [*A publication*] (DLA)
GIB.............. Gibilmanna [*Sicily*] [*Seismograph station code, US Geological Survey*] (SEIS)
GIB.............. Gibraltar [*ANSI three-letter standard code*] (CNC)
GIB.............. Gibraltar [*Airport symbol*] (OAG)
Gib.............. Gibraltar (ODBW)
GIB.............. Good in Bed (DSUE)
GIB.............. GPS [*Global Positioning System*] Integrity Broadcast [*Navigation systems*]
GIB.............. Gulf International Bank [*Bahrain*] (EY)
GIB.............. Guy in the Back [*Copilot*] [*Air Force slang*]
Gib Aids ..... Gibson's Aids to the Examinations [*A publication*] (DLA)
GIBAIR........ Gibraltar Airways Ltd.
Gib & Na Eq Jur... Gibbons and Nathans' Equitable Jurisdiction of County Courts [*A publication*] (DLA)
GIBAPA........ Guild of International Butler Administrators and Personal Assistants [*British*] (EAIO)
Gibbon......... Gibbon on Nuisances [*A publication*] (DLA)
Gibbon Rom Emp... Gibbon's History of the Decline and Fall of the Roman Empire [*A publication*] (DLA)
Gibbons....... Gibbon's Reports, New York Surrogate Court [*A publication*] (DLA)
Gibbons (NY)... Gibbon's Reports, New York Surrogate Court [*A publication*] (DLA)
Gibb Rom Emp... Gibbon's History of the Decline and Fall of the Roman Empire [*A publication*] (DLA)
Gibbs.......... Gibbs' Reports [*2-4 Michigan*] [*A publication*] (DLA)
GibbsC......... Gibbs Construction, Inc. [*Associated Press*] (SAG)
GibbsCn....... Gibbs Construction, Inc. [*Associated Press*] (SAG)
Gibbs F....... Gibbs' Practical Forms [*A publication*] (DLA)
Gibbs' Jud Chr... Gibbs' Judicial Chronicle [*A publication*] (DLA)
GIBBSSAR ... Gibbs & Hill, Inc., Standard Safety Analysis Report [*Nuclear energy*] (NRCH)
Gibb Sur...... Gibbon's Reports, New York Surrogate Court [*A publication*] (DLA)
Gibb Surr.... Gibbon's Reports, New York Surrogate Court [*A publication*] (DLA)
Gib Civ L .... Gibbons on the Civil Law [*A publication*] (DLA)
Gib Cod ...... Gibson's Codex Juris Ecclesiastia Anglicani [*A publication*] (DLA)
Gib Cont ..... Gibbons on Contracts [*A publication*] (DLA)
Gib Dec ...... Gibson's Scottish Decisions [*A publication*] (DLA)
Gib Dil......... Gibbon's Dilapidations and Nuisances [*2nd ed.*] [*1849*] [*A publication*] (DLA)
GIBF............ Gastrointestinal Bacterial Flora [*Medicine*] (MEDA)
Gib Fix........ Gibbon's Law of Fixtures [*1836*] [*A publication*] (DLA)
GIBG........... Gibson Greetings [*NASDAQ symbol*] (TTSB)
GIBG........... Gibson Greetings, Inc. [*NASDAQ symbol*] (NQ)
GI (Bill) .... Veterans Benefits Act, Public Law 345, 1944
GIBIS........... Graphical IBIS [*Issue-Based Information System*] [*Computer science*] (BYTE)
Gib Lim .... Gibbons' Lex Temporis, Limitations and Prescription [*A publication*] (DLA)
Gib LN .... Gibson's Law Notice [*1882-84*] [*A publication*] (DLA)
Gib Lynd .... Gibson's Memoir of Lord Lyndhurst [*A publication*] (DLA)
GIBMED....... Gibraltar Mediterranean Command [*NATO*] (NATG)
Gib Nui ...... Gibbon's Dilapidations and Nuisances [*2nd ed.*] [*1849*] [*A publication*] (DLA)
GibPack....... Gibraltar Packaging Group [*Associated Press*] (SAG)
Gibr............ Gibraltar
GibrStl .... Gibraltar Steel Corp. [*Associated Press*] (SAG)
GIBS........... Guy in the Backseat [*Copilot*] [*Air Force slang*]
Gibs Camd ... Gibson's Edition of Camden's Britannia [*A publication*] (DLA)
Gibs Code.... Gibson's Codex [*A publication*] (DLA)
Gibs LN ...... Gibson's Law Notes [*1882-84*] [*A publication*] (DLA)
GibsnG........ Gibson Greetings, Inc. [*Associated Press*] (SAG)
Gibson........ (Gibson of) Durie's Decisions, Scotch Court of Session [*1621-42*] [*A publication*] (DLA)
GIC............. Compagnie de Bauxites de Guinee [*Guinea*] [*ICAO designator*] (FAAC)
GIC............. Galit Resource Corp. [*Vancouver Stock Exchange symbol*]
GIC............. General Immunocompetence [*Immunology*] (DAVI)
GIC............. General Improvement Contractors Association (EA)

GIC .... General Input Channel (NITA)
GIC .... General Input/Output Channel
GIC .... General Instrument [NYSE symbol] [Formerly, Nextlevel Systems] (SG)
GIC .... General Instrument Corp. [NYSE symbol] (SPSG)
GIC .... Generalized Immittance [or Impedance] Converter (IEEE)
GIC .... Genl Instrument [NYSE symbol] (TTSB)
GIC .... Geomagnetically Induced Current
GIC .... German Information Center [Information service or system] (IID)
GIC .... Glass-Ionomer Cement [Dental material]
GIC .... Global Interdependence Center (EA)
GIC .... Goods in Custody (ADA)
GIC .... GPS [Global Positioning Systems] Integrity Channel [Navigation systems]
GIC .... Graduate Induction Campaign [Australia]
GIC .... Grains Industry Council [Australia]
GIC .... Graphite Intercalation Compound [Inorganic chemistry]
GIC .... Guaranteed Income Contract
GIC .... Guaranteed Investment Contract
GIC .... Gulf Intercoastal Conference
GICA .... Gastrointestinal Cancer Antigen [A tumor marker] (CDI)
GICA .... Goat Industry Council of Australia
GICC .... Glazing Industry Code Committee (NTPA)
GICC .... Government-Industry Coordinating Committee
GICCW ...... Government-Industry Conference against Chemical Weapons (EERA)
GICL .... Gila Cliff Dwellings National Monument
GICL .... Graphics Language [Computer science] (HGAA)
GICLDC ..... GI Civil Liberties Defense Committee
GICLE .... Institute of Continuing Legal Education in Georgia [University of Georgia School of Law] (DLA)
GICORP ..... Government-Industry Cooperative Oyster Research Program
GICR .... Goodwin Institute for Cancer Research [Nova University] [Research center] (RCD)
GICS .... Geographic Identification Code Scheme [Bureau of the Census] (GFGA)
GICS .... Global Instrumentation Control System (IAA)
GICS .... Grant Information and Control System [Environmental Protection Agency] (GFGA)
GICS .... Ground Instrumentation and Communications System (IAA)
GICWG .... Government Interface Control Working Group [Military]
GID .... Channel Aviation Ltd. [British ICAO designator] (FAAC)
GID .... Gastrointestinal Dialysis [Medicine]
GID .... Gender Identity Disorder [Medicine] (DMAA)
GID .... General Installation Dolly
GID .... Gesellschaft fuer Information und Dokumentation mbH [Society for Information and Documentation] [Information service or system] (IID)
GID .... Gitega [Burundi] [Airport symbol] (OAG)
GID .... Grupo Indl Durango ADS [NYSE symbol] (TTSB)
GID .... Grupo Industrial Durango SA de CV [NYSE symbol] (SAG)
GID .... Guilde International du Disque [Record label] [France]
GID .... Sud Air Transport SA [Guinea] [ICAO designator] (FAAC)
GIDAP .... Government Industry Data Exchange Program (CIST)
GIDAP .... Guidance Inertial Data Analysis Program
GIDAS .... Geoanomaly Interactive Data Analysis System (MCD)
GIDEON ..... Global Infectious Disease and Epidemiology Network
GIDEP .... Government-Industry Data Exchange Program [Formerly, IDEP] [Navy Information service or system]
GID-IZ .... Gesellschaft fuer Information und Dokumentation - Informationszentrum fuer Informationswissenschaft und -Praxis [Information Center for Information Science and Information Work] [Society for Information and Documentation] (IID)
GIDL .... Giddings & Lewis [NASDAQ symbol] (TTSB)
GIDL .... Giddings & Lewis, Inc. [NASDAQ symbol] (NQ)
GidLew ...... Giddings & Lewis, Inc. [Associated Press] (SAG)
GIDP .... Gale International Directory of Publications [A publication]
GIDP .... Grounded into Double Plays [Baseball]
GIE .... Galapagos Islands [Ecuador] [Seismograph station code, US Geological Survey] (SEIS)
GIE .... Glycerinisopropylidene Ether [Organic chemistry]
GIE .... Ground Instrumentation Equipment
GIE .... Grupo Interamericano de Editores [Interamerican publishers group] (NITA)
GIE .... Guinee Inter Air [Guinea] [ICAO designator] (FAAC)
GIEA .... German-American Information and Education Association (EA)
GIEE .... Graduate of the Institute of Electrical Engineers [British] (DAS)
GIER .... General Industrial Equipment Reserve
GIEUS .... Guide to International Education in the US [A publication]
GIE VI .... Groupe International Postal d'Echanges d'Information et d'Experience [International Group for the Exchange of Information and Experience Among Postal Savings Institutions] (EAIO)
GIEWS ...... Global Information and Early Warning System [FAO] [United Nations] (DUND)
GIF .... Gatan Imaging Filter (AAEL)
GIF .... General Image Format [Marine science] (OSRA)
GIF .... General Insurance Fund [Federal Housing Administration]
GIF .... German-Israeli Foundation [US and Israel]
GIF .... Gesellschaft fuer Informationsmarkt-Forschung [Society for Information-Market Research] [Database producer] (IID)
Gif .... Giffard's English Vice-Chancellors' Reports [65-66 English Reprint] [A publication] (DLA)
GIF .... Gifu [Japan] [Seismograph station code, US Geological Survey] (SEIS)
GIF .... Glucosylisoflavonoid (DB)
GIF .... Gonadotropin-Inhibitory Factor [Somatostatin] (STED)

gif .... Graphic Interchange Format [Computer science]
GIF .... Graphics Interchange Format [Computer technology]
GIF .... Gravito-Inertial Force
GIF .... Growth Hormone-Inhibiting Factor (STED)
GIF .... Growth-Hormone Release-Inhibiting Factor [Medicine] (DB)
GIF .... Growth Inhibiting Factor [Endocrinology] (MAE)
GIF .... Guardian International Income Fund Units [Toronto Stock Exchange symbol]
GIF .... Guinee Air Lines SA [Guinea] [ICAO designator] (FAAC)
GIF .... Gulf It to FORTRAN [Translator] [Computer science]
GIF .... Guy in the Front Seat [Pilot] [Slang] (DSUE)
GIF .... Winter Haven, FL [Location identifier FAA] (FAAL)
GIFA .... General Iron Fitters Association [A union] [British]
GIFA .... Geneva Infant Feeding Association
GIFA .... Governing International Fisheries Agreements
GIFA .... Governing International Fishing Agreement (MSC)
GIFAP .... Groupement International des Associations Nationales de Fabricants de Produits Agrochimiques [International Group of National Associations of Manufacturers of Agrochemical Products] (EAIO)
GIFC .... Gilligan's Island Fan Club (EA)
Giff .... Giffard's English Vice-Chancellors' Reports [65-66 English Reprint] [A publication] (DLA)
Giff & H .... Giffard and Hemming's English Chancery Reports [A publication] (DLA)
Giff (Eng) ... Giffard's English Vice-Chancellors' Reports [65-66 English Reprint] [A publication] (DLA)
GIFFI .... Group Inventory for Finding Interests [Educational test]
GIFH .... Golden Isles Financial Holdings, Inc. [NASDAQ symbol] (SAG)
GIFH .... Golden Isles Finl Hldg [NASDAQ symbol] (TTSB)
GIFHU .... Golden Isles Finl Hldg Unit [NASDAQ symbol] (TTSB)
GIFI .... General Information File Interrogation (PDAA)
GI for SS ... Goddard Institute for Space Studies [NASA]
GIFOV .... Ground Instantaneous Field-of-View (MCD)
GIFS .... Generalized Interrelated Flow Simulation (IEEE)
GIFS .... Gospel-in-Film Service [Australia]
GIFS .... Gray Iron Founders Society (EA)
GIFS .... Guggenheim Institute of Flight Structures (MUGU)
GIFT .... Gamete Intrafallopian Transfer [Fertilization technique]
GIFT .... Gas-Insulated Flow Tube (NRCH)
GIFT .... General Internal FORTRAN Translator [Computer science] (IEEE)
GIFT .... Geometric Information for Targets (MCD)
GIFT .... Glasgow International Freight Terminal [Scotland] (DS)
GIFT .... Granulocyte Immunofluorescence Test (STED)
GIFT .... Group Inventory for Finding Creative Talent [Educational test]
GIFTPOOL ... Datenbank ueber Gifte und Vergiftungen [Databank for Poisons and Poisoning] [German]
GIFTS .... Graphics-Oriented Interactive Finite Element Time-Sharing System (PDAA)
Gig .... De Gigantibus [Philo] (BJA)
GIG .... Genetics Interest Group [British]
GIG .... Gesellschaft fuer Internationale Geldgeschichte (EAIO)
GIG .... Gigi Resources Ltd. [Vancouver Stock Exchange symbol]
GIG .... Gluten Intolerance Group [Later, GIGNA] (EA)
GIG .... Glycidylisopropylideneglycerol [Organic chemistry]
GIG .... Rio De Janeiro [Brazil] [Airport symbol] (OAG)
GIG .... Scottsbluff, NE [Location identifier FAA] (FAAL)
GIGA .... Giga-Tronics, Inc. [NASDAQ symbol] (NQ)
giga .... One Billion (WDMC)
GigaInfo ..... Giga Information Group, Inc. [Associated Press] (SAG)
GigaTr .... Giga-Tronics, Inc. [Associated Press] (SAG)
GIGI .... Gamma Inspection of Grain Integrity
GIGI .... General Imaging Generator and Interpreter (IAA)
GIGL .... Gale Information Guide Library [Publication series]
GIGNA .... Gluten Intolerance Group of North America (EA)
GIGO .... Garbage In, Garbage Out [Computer science]
gigo .... Garbage In Garbage Out [Computer science] (ODBW)
GIGS .... Gemini Inertial Guidance System [NASA] (KSC)
GIGS .... Gravity-Gradient Test Satellite
GIGX .... Giga Information Group, Inc. [NASDAQ symbol] (SAG)
GIH .... Gastric Inhibitory Hormone [Medicine] (STED)
GIH .... Gastrointestinal Hemorrhage [Medicine] (DMAA)
GIH .... Gastrointestinal Hormone [Endocrinology]
GIH .... Groupe International Hachette [France]
GIH .... Growth Inhibiting Hormone [Endocrinology] (MAE)
GIH .... United States Geological Survey, Water Resources Division, Helena, MT [OCLC symbol] (OCLC)
GII .... Gastrointestinal Infection [Medicine]
GII .... General Industrial Insulation, Inc. (EFIS)
GII .... Global Information Infrastructure
GII .... Goodwill Industries International (EA)
GII .... Greiner Engineering, Inc. [NYSE symbol] (SPSG)
GII .... Guillevin International, Inc. [Toronto Stock Exchange symbol]
G-II .... Gulfstream II [Shuttle training aircraft] [NASA] (NASA)
GII .... Siguiri [Guinea] [Airport symbol] (AD)
GIIC .... Global Information Infrastructure Commission (DDC)
GIID .... GENSER Integration Information Display (MCD)
GIIGNL ...... Groupe Internationale des Importateur du Gaz Natural Liquefie
GIII .... G-III Apparel Group Ltd. [NASDAQ symbol] (NQ)
G-III .... GThree Apparel Group Ltd. [Associated Press] (SAG)
GIIP .... Groupement International de l'Industrie Pharmaceutique des Pays de la CEE [International Pharmaceutical Industry Group for the EEC Countries]
GIIR .... Government Idle Industrial Reserve (AAG)
GIIV .... Gated Image Intensifier Viewer
GIK .... Glucose, Insulin, and Potassium [Solution] [Medicine]

GIKA .... Gifts In Kind America (NFD)
GIL .... Gaseous Ion LASER
GIL .... General-Purpose Interactive Programming Language [*Computer science*] (MHDB)
Gil .... Gilbert [*A unit of magnetomotive force*]
Gil .... Gilbert's Cases in Law and Equity [*A publication*] (DLA)
Gil .... Gilbert's English Chancery Reports [*1705-27*] [*A publication*] (DLA)
Gil .... Gilfillan's Reports [*1-20 Minnesota*] [*A publication*] (DLA)
GIL .... Gilgit [*Pakistan*] [*Airport symbol*] (AD)
GIL .... Gill Aviation Ltd. [*British ICAO designator*] (FAAC)
Gil .... Gilman's Reports [*6-10 Illinois*] [*A publication*] (DLA)
Gil .... Gilmer's Virginia Reports [*21 Virginia*] [*A publication*] (DLA)
GIL .... Gilmore Creek [*Alaska*] [*Seismograph station code, US Geological Survey*] (SEIS)
GIL .... Grain Isolation Liner (MCD)
GIL .... Green Indicating Lamp
GIL .... Group Investment-Linked (ADA)
Gil .... Guillelmus Durandi [*Deceased, 1296*] [*Authority cited in pre-1607 legal work*] (DSA)
GIL .... United States Geological Survey, Metairie, LA [*OCLC symbol*] (OCLC)
Gil & Fal ..... Gilmour and Falconer's Cases, Scotch Court of Session [*A publication*] (DLA)
GilatSat .... Gilat Satellite Networks Ltd. [*Associated Press*] (SAG)
GILB .... Gilbert Associates, Inc. [*NASDAQ symbol*] (NQ)
Gilb .... Gilbert's Cases in Law and Equity [*A publication*] (DLA)
Gilb .... Gilbert's English Chancery Reports [*1705-27*] [*A publication*] (DLA)
GILBA .... Gilbert Assoc'A' [*NASDAQ symbol*] (TTSB)
Gilb Bank ..... Gilbert on Banking [*A publication*] (DLA)
Gilb Cas ...... Gilbert's Cases in Law and Equity [*A publication*] (DLA)
Gilb Cas L & Eq ... Gilbert's Cases in Law and Equity [*A publication*] (DLA)
Gilb Cas L & Eq (Eng) ... Gilbert's Common Pleas [*93 English Reprint*] [*A publication*] (DLA)
Gilb Ch .... Gilbert's English Chancery Reports [*1705-27*] [*A publication*] (DLA)
Gilb Com Pl ... Gilbert's Common Pleas [*93 English Reprint*] [*A publication*] (DLA)
Gilb CP .... Gilbert's Common Pleas [*93 English Reprint*] [*A publication*] (DLA)
Gilb Debt ..... Gilbert on the Action of Debt [*A publication*] (DLA)
Gilb Dev ...... Gilbert's Law of Devises [*A publication*] (DLA)
Gilb Dis ...... Gilbert on Distress and Replevin [*A publication*] (DLA)
Gilb Ej .... Gilbert on Ejectments [*A publication*] (DLA)
Gilb Eq .... Gilbert's English Equity Reports [*25 English Reprint*] [*1705-27*] [*A publication*] (DLA)
Gilb Eq (Eng) ... Gilbert's English Equity Reports [*25 English Reprint*] [*1705-27*] [*A publication*] (DLA)
Gilb Eq Rep ... Gilbert's English Equity Reports [*1705-27*] [*A publication*] (DLA)
Gilbert Ev .... Gilbert's Law of Evidence [*A publication*] (DLA)
Gilbert Uses by Sugd ... Gilbert's Uses and Trusts by Sugden [*A publication*] (DLA)
Gilb Ev .... Gilbert's Law of Evidence [*A publication*] (DLA)
Gilb Ex .... Gilbert's Executions [*A publication*] (DLA)
Gilb Exch ..... Gilbert's English Exchequer Reports [*A publication*] (DLA)
Gilb Exch Pr ... Gilbert's History and Practice of the Exchequer [*A publication*] (DLA)
Gilb For Rom ... Gilbert's Forum Romanum [*A publication*] (DLA)
Gilb Forum Rom ... Gilbert's Forum Romanum [*A publication*] (DLA)
Gilb Hist CP ... Gilbert's History of Common Pleas [*A publication*] (DLA)
Gilb KB .... Gilbert's Cases in Law and Equity [*A publication*] (DLA)
Gilb Lex Pr ... Gilbert's Lex Praetoria [*A publication*] (DLA)
Gilb PC .... Gilbert's Common Pleas [*93 English Reprint*] [*A publication*] (DLA)
Gilb Rem ...... Gilbert's Remainders [*A publication*] (DLA)
Gilb Rents ... Gilbert's Treatise on Rents [*A publication*] (DLA)
Gilb Rep ...... Gilbert's English Chancery Reports [*1705-27*] [*A publication*] (DLA)
Gilb Repl ..... Gilbert on Replevin [*A publication*] (DLA)
Gilb RR .... Gilbert's Railway Law of Illinois [*A publication*] (DLA)
GilbtA .... Gilbert Associates, Inc. [*Associated Press*] (SAG)
Gilb Ten ...... Gilbert on Tenures [*A publication*] (DLA)
Gilb Uses ..... Gilbert on Uses and Trusts [*A publication*] (DLA)
Gilchr .... Gilchrist's Local Government Cases [*A publication*] (DLA)
GILCU .... Gradual Increase in Length and Complexity of Utterance (STED)
GILD .... Gas Immersion LASER Doping (AAEL)
Gild .... Gildersleeve's Reports [*New Mexico*] [*A publication*] (DLA)
GILD .... Gilead Sciences [*NASDAQ symbol*] (TTSB)
GILD .... Gilead Sciences, Inc. [*NASDAQ symbol*] (SPSG)
Gildersleeve ... Gildersleeve's Reports [*New Mexico*] [*A publication*] (DLA)
Gildersleeve (N Mex) ... Gildersleeve's Reports [*New Mexico*] [*A publication*] (DLA)
Gildr .... Gildersleeve's Reports [*New Mexico*] [*A publication*] (DLA)
Gil Dur .... Guillelmus Durandi [*Deceased, 1296*] [*Authority cited in pre-1607 legal work*] (DSA)
Gilead .... Gilead Sciences, Inc. [*Associated Press*] (SAG)
Gilfillan .... Gilfillan's Reports [*1-20 Minnesota*] [*A publication*] (DLA)
Gilg .... Gilgames (BJA)
GILL .... Gillingham [*Municipal borough in England*]
Gill .... Gill's Maryland Court of Appeals Reports [*1843-51*] [*A publication*] (DLA)
Gill & J .... Gill and Johnson's Maryland Reports [*A publication*] (DLA)
Gill and J (Maryland) ... Gill and Johnson's Maryland Reports [*A publication*] (DLA)
Gill & J (MD) ... Gill and Johnson's Maryland Reports [*A publication*] (DLA)
Gill & Johns ... Gill and Johnson's Maryland Reports [*A publication*] (DLA)
Gillete .... Gillette Co. [*Associated Press*] (SAG)
Gillett Cr Law ... Gillett's Treatise on Criminal Law and Procedure in Criminal Cases [*A publication*] (DLA)
Gill (MD) ...... Gill's Maryland Reports [*A publication*] (DLA)
Gill Pol Rep ... Gill's Police Court Reports [*Boston, MA*] [*A publication*] (DLA)
Gilm .... Gilman's Reports [*6-10 Illinois*] [*A publication*] (DLA)
Gilm .... Gilmer's Virginia Reports [*21 Virginia*] [*A publication*] (DLA)
Gilm .... Gilmour's Reports, Scotch Court of Session [*A publication*] (DLA)
Gilman .... Gilman's Reports [*6-10 Illinois*] [*A publication*] (DLA)
Gilm & F ..... Gilmour and Falconer's Decisions, Scotch Court of Session [*1961-66*] [*A publication*] (DLA)
Gilm & Fal ... Gilmour and Falconer's Decisions, Scotch Court of Session [*1961-66*] [*A publication*] (DLA)
Gilm & Falc ... Gilmour and Falconer's Reports, Scotch Court of Session [*A publication*] (DLA)
GilmC .... Gilman & Ciocia, Inc. [*Associated Press*] (SAG)
Gilm Dig ...... Gilman's Illinois and Indiana Digest [*A publication*] (DLA)
Gilmer .... Gilmer's Virginia Reports [*21 Virginia*] [*1820-21*] [*A publication*] (DLA)
GILMER .... Guardian of Impressive Letters and Master of Excellent Replies
Gilmer (VA) .. Gilmer's Virginia Reports [*21 Virginia*] [*A publication*] (DLA)
Gilm (Ill) ..... Gilman's Reports [*6-10 Illinois*] [*A publication*] (DLA)
Gil (Minn) .... Gilfillan's Edition [*1-20 Minnesota*] [*A publication*] (DLA)
GilmnCio ..... Gilman & Ciocia, Inc. [*Associated Press*] (SAG)
GILN .... Glosa International Language Network (EAIO)
Gilp .... Gilpin's United States District Court Reports [*A publication*] (DLA)
Gilp Opin ..... Gilpin's Opinions of the United States Attorneys-General [*A publication*] (DLA)
GILS .... Global Information Locator Service
GILS .... Government Information Locator Service [*Internet*] (AAGC)
GILSP .... Good Industrial Large-Scale Practice
GILT .... General Internal Logic Test (PDAA)
GILT .... Gilat Satellite Networks Ltd. [*NASDAQ symbol*] (SAG)
GILTF .... Gilat Satellite Networks [*NASDAQ symbol*] (TTSB)
GIM .... Gaining Inventory Managers (AFM)
GIM .... Gas Injection Molding [*Plastic fabrications*]
GIM .... Geldermann Investment Management [*Finance British*]
GIM .... General Instrument Microelectronics [*British*] (NITA)
GIM .... Generalized Information Management [*Language*]
GIM .... Geneva Informal Meeting [*of International Non-Governmental Organizations*] [*British*]
GIM .... Glashow-Iliopoulos-Maiani [*Theory in particle physics*]
GIM .... Glass Insulation Material
GIM .... Gonadotropin-Inhibitory Material [*Endocrinology*] (MAE)
GIM .... Grace's Insect [*Growth*] Medium [*Microbiology*]
GIM .... Gruppe Internationale Marxisten [*International Marxist Group*] [*Germany Political party*] (PPW)
GIM .... Gulf International Minerals [*Vancouver Stock Exchange symbol*]
GIM .... Miele Mimbale [*Gabon*] [*Airport symbol*] (AD)
GIM .... Templeton Global Income [*NYSE symbol*] (SPSG)
GIMA .... Garden Industry Manufacturers Association [*British*] (DBA)
Gima .... Grupo Independente de Macau [*Independent Group of Macao*] [*Political party*] (PPW)
GIMADS ...... Generic Integrated Maintenance and Diagnostic System (MCD)
GIMB .... Gimbal (KSC)
GI Mech E ... Graduate of the Institution of Mechanical Engineers [*British*]
GIMI .... Graduate of the Institute of the Motor Industry [*British*] (DBQ)
GIMIC .... Guard Ring Isolated Monolithic Integrated Circuit
GIMMIS .... G-I Manpower Management Information System
GIMMS .... Geographic Information Mapping and Management System (EERA)
GIMMS .... Global Inventory Modeling and Monitoring Study (EERA)
GIMP .... Gimbal Positioning
GIMPS .... Great Internet Mersenne Prime Search
GIMPY .... Growing, Improving, Maturing - Puppy of the Year [*Canine award*]
GIMR .... Garvan Institute of Medical Research [*Australia*]
GIMRADA .... Geodesy, Intelligence, and Mapping Research and Development Agency [*Army*]
GIMS .... Geographic-Based Information Management System (PDAA)
GIMS .... Global Integrated Monitoring System (EERA)
GIMS .... Graduates of Italian Medical Schools (EA)
GIMS .... Ground Identification of Missions in Space
GIMT .... Gott Ist Mein Teil [*God Is My Portion*] [*Motto of Friedrich IV, Duke of Liegnitz (1552-96)*] [*German*]
GIMT .... Gott Ist Mein Trost [*God Is My Comfort*] [*Motto for a number of 16th and 17th century German and Bavarian rulers*]
GIMU .... Gimballess Inertial Measuring Unit
GIN .... Association de Recherche et d'Exploitation de Diamant et de l'Or [*Guinea*] [*ICAO designator*] (FAAC)
GIN .... Galilean Resources Corp. [*Vancouver Stock Exchange symbol*]
GIN .... Gimbaled Integral Nozzle
GIN .... Global Imaging Networks (DGA)
GIN .... Global Information Network (EA)
gin .... Glutamine [*Also, Q*] [*An amino acid*] (DOG)
GIN .... Glutamine (STED)
GIN .... Greenland-Iceland-Norway [*Gap*] (DOMA)
GIN .... Guinea [*ANSI three-letter standard code*] (CNC)
GIN .... Stromboli-Ginostra [*Italy*] [*Seismograph station code, US Geological Survey*] (SEIS)
GINA .... Gas Industries Network Analyzer (PDAA)
GINA .... Graphical Interactive NMR Analysis [*Computer science*]
G-in-C .... General Officer-in-Chief (WDAA)
GINETEX ..... Groupement International d'Etiquetage pour l'Entretien des Textiles [*International Association for Textile Care Labelling*] [*Barcelona, Spain*] (EA)
GING .... Gingiva [*Gum*] [*Latin*]
Ging .... Gingival (STED)
GINI .... Gazette International Networking Institute (EA)
GINLC .... Grosse Ile Nature and Land Conservancy
G in N .... Graduate in Nursing
GINNI .... Generic Interactive Neural Network Interpreter
GINNIE MAE ... Government National Mortgage Association [*See also GNMA*]
GINO .... Graphical Input/Output

GINO-F......... Graphical Input and Output in FORTRAN [*GST Computer Systems Ltd.*] [*Software package*] [*Computer science*] [*British*]

GInstM....... Graduate of the Institute of Marketing [*British*] (DBQ)

GINTRAP...... European Guide to Industrial Trading Regulations and Practice [*EC*] (ECED)

GIO .... Gas Identification Officer

GIO .... Generalist Intelligence Officer

GIO .... Generic Interface for Operations [*Telecommunications*] (ACRL)

GIO .... Giocossamente [*Humorously*] [*Music*] (ROG)

GIO .... Golden Trio Minerals [*Vancouver Stock Exchange symbol*]

GIO .... Government Information Organization [*Later, NAGC*]

GIO .... Group Intelligence Officer [*British military*] (DMA)

GIO .... Guaranteed Insurability Option

GIO .... Guild of Insurance Officials [*British*] (BI)

GIO .... Regionnair, Inc. [*Canada ICAO designator*] (FAAC)

GIOA .... Gregorian Institute of America [*Record label*]

GIOC .... Generalized Input/Output Controller [*Computer science*] (IEEE)

g-ion........... Gram-Ion [STED]

GIOP........... General-Purpose Input/Output Processor [*Computer science*]

GIOR........... GPETE Initial Outfitting Requirement [*Military*] (CAAL)

GIP.............. Galvanized Improved Plow [*Steel*]

GIP.............. Gastric Inhibitory Peptide [*Gastroenterology*] (DAVI)

GIP.............. Gastric [*or Gastrin*] Inhibitory Principle [*or Polypeptide*] [*Medicine*]

GIP.............. Gaussian Image Point [*Optics*]

GIP.............. General Implementation Plan

GIP.............. General Information Programme (NITA)

GIP.............. General Insertion Protein [*Genetics*]

GIP.............. General Internal Process [*Computer science*] (IAA)

GIP.............. Genetic Improvement Programs [*Queensland*] (EERA)

GIP.............. Giant Cell Interstitial Pneumonia [*Medicine*] (MAE)

GIP.............. Gileppe [*Belgium*] [*Seismograph station code, US Geological Survey*] (SEIS)

GIP.............. Glazed Imitation Parchment

GIP.............. Global Internet Project (TELE)

GIP.............. Global Inventory Project (TELE)

GIP.............. Gonorrheal Invasive Peritonitis [*Medicine*] (DMAA)

GIP.............. Good Import Practice (DB)

GIP.............. Great Indian Peninsular R. R.

GIP.............. Great Irish Painter [*Reference to Jack B. Yeats, ca. 1905*]

GIP.............. Gross Internal Product

GIP.............. Ground Instructor Pilot (DNAB)

GIP.............. Gunnery Improvement Program [*Military*] (CAAL)

GIPD .... B. F. Goodrich Institute for Personnel Development

GIPEC .... Groupe d'Etudes International pour l'Utilization de Profils Creux dans la Construction [*International Study Group on the Use of Hollow Sections in Construction*] [*Switzerland*] (PDAA)

GIPEIE .... Groupe International Postal d'Echanges d'Information et d'Experience [*International Group for the Exchange of Information and Experience among Postal Savings Institutions - IGEIEPSI*] (EAIO)

GIPGS......... Greenhouse Information Program Grants Scheme (EERA)

GI/PI .... General Inspection/Procurement Inspection (MCD)

GIPME .... Global Investigation of Pollution in the Marine Environment [*National Science Foundation*]

GIPS .... Gastrointestinal Pathology Society (NTPA)

GIPS .... Geographical Information Processing System (EERA)

GIPS .... Giga-Instructions per Second [*Computer science*] (NHD)

GIPS .... Government Imprinted Penalty Stationery Society (EA)

GIPS .... Ground Information Processing System

GIPSE .... Gravity Independent Photosynthetic Gas Exchanger

GIPSY .... Generalized Information Processing System

GIQ .... Giant Imperial Quart [*of beer*]

GIR .... Girder [*Technical drawings*]

GIR .... Global Improvement Rating (DMAA)

GIR .... Glucose Infusion Rate [*Physiology*]

GIR .... Golden Lion Resources Ltd. [*Vancouver Stock Exchange symbol*]

GIR .... Graduated Interest Rate [*Finance*] (BARN)

GIR .... Greens in Regulation Golf (BARN)

GIR .... Resource Appraisal Group Library, United States Geological Survey, Denver, CO [*OCLC symbol*] (OCLC)

GIRA .... Gallups Island Radio Association (EA)

GIRA .... Groupement Independant de Reflexion et d'Action [*Independent Grouping of Reflection and Action*] [*Central Africa*] (PD)

GIRA .... Group Individual Retirement Account

GIRAFFE ...... Graphic Interface for Finite Elements [*Graphics data processing*]

GIRAS.......... Geographic Information Retrieval and Analysis System [*Department of the Interior*]

GIRAST........ Groupe Interdisciplinaire de Recherche pour l'Amelioration des Situations de Travail [*University of Quebec at Rimouski*] [*Canada Research center*] (RCD)

GIRC .... Global Issues Resource Center (EA)

GIRD........... General Incentive for Research and Development [*Canada*]

GIRD........... Good Industrial Relations Directors [*Meetings sponsored by Master Printers of America*]

GIRD........... Grants for Industrial Research and Development (EERA)

GIRD........... Ground Integration Requirements Document (MCD)

GIREP......... International Group for the Advancement of Physics Teaching (AIE)

GIRGV......... Groupe International des Ressources Genetiques Vegetales [*International Board for Plant Genetic Resources - IBPGR*] (EA)

GIRL .... Generalized Information Retrieval Language [*US Defense Nuclear Agency*]

GIRL .... Graph Information Retrieval Language [*1970*] [*Computer science*] (CSR)

GIRLS......... General Indexing in Reciprocal Lattice Space (KSC)

GIRLS......... Generalized Information Retrieval and Listing System

GIRLS .... Global Interrogation Recording and Location System (MCD)

GIRM .... Generalized Internal Reference Method [*Statistical procedure*]

GIRMS........ Geographical Inter-University Resource Management Seminar

GIRO........... General Instructions for Routing and Reporting Officers

GIROQ .... Groupe Interuniversitaire des Recherches Oceanographiques du Quebec [*Interuniversity Group for Oceanographic Research of Quebec*] [*Laval University*] [*Canada*] [*Research center*] (RCD)

GIRPB......... Groupe International de Recherches sur la Preservation du Bois [*Sweden*] (EAIO)

GIRS .... Gallaudet Information Retrieval Service

GIRS .... Gimballess Inertial Reference System

GIRSO......... Groupement International pour la Recherche Scientifique en Stomatologie et Odontologie [*International Group for Scientific Research on Stomato-Odontology*] (EA)

GIRSS .... General Information Retrieval System Simulation

GIRSTERM... Groupe Interdisciplinaire de Recherche Scientifique et Appliquee en Terminologie [*INFOTERM*]

Gir WC........ Girard's Will Case Report [*A publication*] (DLA)

GIS............. Gamma Iota Sigma [*An association*] (NTPA)

GIS............. Gas in Stomach (MAE)

GIS............. Gas-Scintillation Imaging Spectrometer

GIS............. Gastrointestinal Series [*Radiology*]

GIS............. Gastrointestinal System [*Gastroenterology*] (DAVI)

GIS............. General Installation Subcontractor

GIS............. Generalized Information System [*IBM Corp.*]

GIS............. Generalized Inquiry System [*Computer science*]

GIS............. General Mills, Inc. [*NYSE symbol*] (SPSG)

GIS............. Genl Mills [*NYSE symbol*] (TTSB)

GIS............. Geographic Information System (EERA)

GIS............. Geographic Information Systems [*Fish and Wildlife Service*] (IID)

GIS............. Geological Information Systems [*University of Oklahoma*] [*Information service or system*] (IID)

GIS............. Geoscience Information Society (EA)

GIS............. Gisborne [*New Zealand*] [*Airport symbol*] (OAG)

GIS............. Gismondine [*A zeolite*]

GIS............. Gissar [*Former USSR Seismograph station code, US Geological Survey Closed*] (SEIS)

GIS............. Global Indexing System (GNE)

GIS............. Global Information Services, Inc. [*Flushing, NY*] [*Telecommunications*] (TSSD)

GIS............. Global Ionospheric Studies

GIS............. Global Issues [*Program*] [*Department of State*]

GIS............. Golden Iskut Resources [*Vancouver Stock Exchange symbol*]

GIS............. Government Information Service (WDAA)

GIS............. Government Information Services [*Republic of Ireland*]

GIS............. Government Information Subcommittee [*American Library Association*]

GIS............. Grain Inventory System [*Department of Agriculture*] (GFGA)

GIS............. Grand Inside Sentinel [*Freemasonry*] (ROG)

GIS............. Grant Information System [*Oryx Press*] (IID)

GIS............. Graphic Information System [*Computer databases*]

GIS............. Graphic Input System

GIS............. Grazing-Incidence Spectrometer (PDAA)

GIS............. Greatness Is Simplicity [*See also SIG*]

GIS............. Greenland Ice Sheet

GIs............. Gross Impressions [*Advertising*] (WDMC)

GIS............. Ground Instrumentation System (IAA)

GIS............. Guaranteed Income Stream [*UAW program included in the union's 1982 contract with General Motors Corp.*]

GIS............. Guaranteed Income Supplement [*Program*] [*Canada*]

GIS............. Guidance Information System [*Houghton Mifflin Co.*] [*Information service or system*] (IID)

GIS............. Guidelines Implementation Staff [*Environmental Protection Agency*] (GFGA)

GIS............. Guild for Infant Survival [*Later, ICIS*]

GIS............. Guild of the Infant Saviour [*Defunct*] (EA)

GIS............. Guinee Air Service [*Guinea*] [*ICAO designator*] (FAAC)

GIS............. United States Department of the Interior, United States Geological Survey, Reston, VA [*OCLC symbol*] (OCLC)

GISA .... Government in the Sunshine Act [*1976*]

GISAT .... Ground Identification of Satellites (MCD)

GISC .... Generic Intelligent Control System

GISC .... Government Information Services Committee [*Special Libraries Association*]

GISC .... Grail International Student Center [*Defunct*] (EA)

GISE........... Generalized Integrated Square Error [*Aeronautics*]

GI Sec .... General Inspectorate Section [*European Theater of Operations*] [*World War II*]

GISGE .... Good Intent Society of Galvanizers and Enamellers [*A union*] [*British*]

GISH .... Gish Biomedical [*NASDAQ symbol*] (TTSB)

GISH .... Gish Biomedical, Inc. [*NASDAQ symbol*] (NQ)

GishBi......... Gish Biomedical, Inc. [*Associated Press*] (SAG)

GISL........... Graphic Imaging Specification Language [*Printing technology*]

GISMO........ General Interpretative System for Matrix Operations [*Data processing system used in engineering*] [*Navy*]

GISOF......... Gas Industry Salaried Officers' Federation [*Australia*]

GISP .... General Information System for Planning (IAA)

GISP .... Grain Income Stabilization Plan

GISP .... Greenland Ice Sheet Project [*National Science Foundation*]

GISPA......... Guide to International Scientific Publications and Associations [*A publication*]

GISPRI........ Global Industrial and Social Progress Research Institute

GISS .... Goddard Institute for Space Studies [*NASA*]

GIST........... GARP International Sea Trial [*National Science Foundation*]

GIST........... Genome Informatics System of Transputers (HGEN)

GIST............ Girls into Science and Technology [British] (DI)
GIST............ Global Information System Technology, Inc. (PCM)
GIST............ Gochnour Idiom Screening Test
GISTA.......... Gruppo Italiano di Studio Tubercolosi e AIDS
GISTI .... Groupe d'Information et de Soutien des Travailleurs Immigres [Information and Support Group for Immigrant Workers] [France] (EAIO)
GISVS .... Generalized Information System Virtual Storage (IAA)
GIT............... Gastrointestinal Tract [Medicine]
GIT............... General Information Test
GIT............... Georgia Institute of Technology [Atlanta]
GIT............... Gilgit [Pakistan] [Geomagnetic observatory code]
Git................ Gittin (BJA)
GIT............... Glucose Infusion Test [Diabetes detection] (CPH)
GIT............... Glutathione-Insulin Transhydrogenase [An enzyme] (MAE)
GIT............... Graduate Institute of Technology [University of Arkansas at Little Rock] [Research center] (RCD)
GIT............... Graph Isomorphism Tester
GIT............... Grease Interceptor Trap
GIT............... [The] Great Ideas Today [A publication]
GIT............... Grit Resources, Inc. [Vancouver Stock Exchange symbol]
GIT............... Grooved for Iron Tongues
GIT............... Group Inclusive Tour [Airline fare]
GITC............ Government of Israel Trade Center (EA)
GITG............ Ground Interface Technical Group [NASA] (NASA)
GITI............. Global Information and Telecommunications Industries
GITI............. Government Issue Technical Inspection (INF)
GITIC .... Guangdong International Trust & Investment Corp. [China]
GITIS .... Georgia Institute of Technology School of Information Science [Report series code] (NITA)
GITL............ Government/Industry Technical Liaison Committee [Australia]
GITP............ Ground Integration Test Program (KSC)
GI tract .... Gastro-Intestinal Tract [Medicine] (WDAA)
GITS............ Gastrointestinal Therapeutic System [Medicine]
GITSG .... Gastrointestinal Tumor Study Group [Oncology] (DAVI)
GITT............ Glucose Insulin Tolerance Test [Medicine]
GITU............ Gastrointestinal Transcription Unit [Medicine]
GIU .... Gateway Interface Unit (DGA)
GIU .... General Intelligence Unit [US, London]
GIU .... Geoballistic Input Unit
GIU .... Guidance Integration Unit (MCD)
GIU .... Union Guineene de Transports [Guinea] [ICAO designator] (FAAC)
GIUK............ Greenland-Iceland-United Kingdom [NATO naval defense line]
GIuscII .... Grupo Iusacell SA de CV [Associated Press] (SAG)
GIuscI IL ..... Grupo Iusacell SA de CV [Associated Press] (SAG)
GIV.............. Given
GIV.............. Grivco International Ltd. [Romania] [FAA designator] (FAAC)
GIVE............ Government's Involvement in Volunteer Efforts Programs
GIVN .... Given (DAVI)
GIVS .... Goodwill Industries Volunteer Services (EA)
GIW .... Glass-Insulated Wire
GIW .... Greenwood, SC [Location identifier FAA] (FAAL)
GIW .... Gulf Intracoastal Waterway
GIWG .... Ground Interface Working Group
GIWW .... Gulf Intracoastal Waterway
GIX.............. Global Industrial Tech [NYSE symbol] (TTSB)
GIX.............. Global Industrial Technologies [NYSE symbol] (SAG)
GIX.............. Government Information Exchange [Internet] (AAGC)
GIXD............ Grazing-Incidence X-Ray Diffraction
GIXS............ Grazing-Incidence X-Ray Scattering [Imaging technique]
GIXU............ Grain Inspection X-Ray Unit (IAA)
GIY.............. Glamorgan Imperial Yeomanry [British military] (DMA)
GIZ.............. Gizan [Saudi Arabia] [Airport symbol] (OAG)
GIZ.............. Gizo [Solomon Islands] [Seismograph station code, US Geological Survey] (SEIS)
GIZ.............. Marshfield, WI [Location identifier FAA] (FAAL)
GIZH .... Gosudarstvennyi Institut Zhurnalistiki
GJ................ Ansett Airlines of South Australia [ICAO designator] (AD)
GJ................ British Guiana General Jurisdiction (Official Gazette) [1899-] [A publication] (ILCA)
GJ................ Gap Junction [Cytology]
GJ................ Gastric Juice [Medicine] (DMAA)
GJ................ Gastrojejunostomy [Surgery] (DAVI)
GJ................ General Journal [Accounting]
GJ................ Geographical Journal [A publication] (BRI)
GJ................ Germania Judaica (BJA)
GJ................ German Jewish (BJA)
GJ................ Gigajoule
GJ................ Gill and Johnson's Maryland Reports [A publication] (DLA)
GJ................ Goldreich-Julian [PULSAR theory]
GJ................ Graduate Jeweller
GJ................ Grand Jury
GJ................ Grapefruit Juice [Restaurant slang]
GJ................ Greenwich & Johnsonville Railway Co. [AAR code]
GJ................ Group Junction (MCD)
GJ................ Grown Junction (IEEE)
G+J.............. Gruner + Jahr [A publisher] [Hamburg, Germany] (WDMC)
GJB.............. Marie-Galante Island [Guadeloupe] [Airport symbol] (AD)
GJB.............. Trans-Air Link Corp. [ICAO designator] (FAAC)
GJC.............. Gainesville Junior College [Later, Cooke County Junior College] [Texas]
GJC.............. Grayson-Jockey Club Research Foundation (EA)
GJCAA......... Georgia Junior College Athletic Association (PSS)
GJCFC......... George Jones Country Fan Club (EA)
GJCO .... Gaylord Companies, Inc. [NASDAQ symbol] (SAG)

GJCO .... Gaylord Cos. [NASDAQ symbol] (TTSB)
GJCOW .... Gaylord Cos. Wrrt [NASDAQ symbol] (TTSB)
GJD.............. Channel Aviation Ltd. [British] [FAA designator] (FAAC)
GJD.............. Germanium Junction Diode (IDOE)
GJD.............. Global Jewish Database [Bar-Ilan University] [Information service or system] (CRD)
GJD.............. Grand Junior Deacon [Freemasonry]
GJE.............. Gauss-Jordan Elimination (IEEE)
GJF.............. Greensboro Justice Fund (EA)
GJFC............ George Jones Fan Club (EA)
GJG.............. Augusta College, Augusta, GA [OCLC symbol] (OCLC)
GJI.............. Ghetto Job Information [US Employment Service] [Department of Labor]
GJL.............. Geographical Journal (London) [A publication]
GJL.............. Jijel [Algeria] [Airport symbol] (OAG)
GJM............. Guajara Mirim [Brazil] [Airport symbol] (AD)
GJO.............. Grand Junction Office [Grand Junction, CO] [Department of Energy]
GJO.............. Greater Jacksonville [Florida] Open [Golf tournament]
GJOA .... G. J. Orphan & Associates [Telecommunications service] (TSSD)
GJP.............. Galactic Jupiter Probe [NASA]
GJP.............. Grand Jury Project (EA)
GJP.............. Graphic Job Processor (MCD)
GJPA .... Grammatik des Juedisch-Palaestinischen Aramaeisch [A publication] (BJA)
GJPO .... Grand Juction Projects Office [Department of Energy] [Grand Juction, CO] (GAAI)
GJPO .... Grand Junction Project Office [Department of Energy]
GJR.............. Gjogur [Iceland] [Airport symbol] (OAG)
GJRAP .... Grand Junction Remedial Action Project [Department of Energy] [Colorado] (GAAI)
GJS.............. Ghana Journal of Sociology [A publication]
GJT.............. Grand Junction [Colorado] [Airport symbol] (OAG)
GJTA .... Goldsmiths' and Jewellers' Trade Association [A union] [British]
GJV.............. Geschichte des Juedischen Volkes im Zeitalter Jesu Christi [A publication] (BJA)
GJW............. Grand Junior Warden [Freemasonry]
GJW............. Great Jurists of the World, by Sir John MacDonnel and Edward Manson [1913] [A publication] (DLA)
GK................ Gasser-Karrer [Syndrome] [Medicine] (DB)
GK................ Geographenkalender (BJA)
GK................ Ginze Kedem (BJA)
GK................ Glycerol Kinase [An enzyme] (MAE)
GK................ Goal Keeper [Netball]
GK................ Grand King [Freemasonry]
GK................ Granular Kidney [Medicine] (ROG)
GK................ Greek
GK................ Hebraeische Grammatik Voellig Umgearbeitet [Gesenius and E. Kautzsch] [A publication] (BJA)
GK................ Laker Airways [ICAO designator] (AD)
GK-101 .... N-Monochloroglycine [Dental caries treatment named for patent holders, Goldman and Kronman]
GKA .... Garter King of Arms
GKA .... Goroka [Papua New Guinea] [Airport symbol] (OAG)
GKA .... Goroka [Papua New Guinea] [Seismograph station code, US Geological Survey Closed] (SEIS)
GKA .... Grounded Kathode Amplifier
GKa .... Hebraeische Grammatik Voellig Umgearbeitet [Gesenius and E. Kautzsch] [A publication] (BJA)
GKA .... US Army Aeronautical Services [ICAO designator] (FAAC)
GKABL .... George Khoury Association of Baseball Leagues (EA)
GKB............. Garantie- und Kreditbank [Guaranty and Credit Bank] [Germany] (EG)
GKBZH .... Glowna Komisja Badania Zbrodni Hitlerowskich [A publication] (BJA)
GKC .... Gilbert Keith Chesterton [British journalist and author]
GKC .... Gold King Construction [Vancouver Stock Exchange symbol]
GKC .... Gold King River [Alaska] [Seismograph station code, US Geological Survey] (SEIS)
GKC .... Hebrew Grammar Gesenius, Kautzsch, Cowley [A publication] (BJA)
GKCS .... G. K. Chesterton Society (EA)
GKD............. Glycerol Kinase Deficiency [Medicine]
GKF............. Florence, SC [Location identifier FAA] (FAAL)
GKH............. G. K. Hall Co. [Publisher]
GKI.............. General Kinetics, Inc. [AMEX symbol] (SPSG)
GKI.............. Genl Kinetics [AMEX symbol] (TTSB)
GKI.............. Glon Kristy Resources [Vancouver Stock Exchange symbol]
GKJ.............. Kennesaw College, Marietta, GA [OCLC symbol] (OCLC)
GKJ.............. Meadville, PA [Location identifier FAA] (FAAL)
GKL............. Great Keppel Island [Australia Airport symbol] (OAG)
GKLC .... Law Companies Group, Inc., Kennesaw, GA [Library symbol] [Library of Congress] (LCLS)
GKLL............ Garage Keeper's Legal Liability [Insurance]
GKMDT .... Graham-Kendall Memory for Designs Test [Psychology] (DAVI)
GKN .... Guest, Kean & Nettlefolds [Steel-forging company] [British]
GKN .... Gulkana [Alaska] [Airport symbol] (OAG)
GKN .... Gulkana, AK [Location identifier FAA] (FAAL)
GKNHS .... Golden Key National Honor Society (EA)
GKNT .... Gosudarstvennyi Komitet po Nauki i Teknologii [State Committee for Science and Technology] [Former USSR] (LAIN)
GKO............. Gosudarstvennyi Komitet Oborony [State Defense Committee] [Former USSR World War II]
GKO............. Kongo Bumba [Gabon] [Airport symbol] (AD)
GKOd........... Greek Odeon [Record label]
GKQ............. Newark, NJ [Location identifier FAA] (FAAL)
GKR............. Goddard Kay Rogers Ltd. [British]

GKR .... Golden Knight Resources, Inc. [*Toronto Stock Exchange symbol Vancouver Stock Exchange symbol*]

GKR .... Government of the Khmer Republic [*Anticommunist government of Cambodia during the early seventies*] (VNW)

GKRV .... Golden Knight Resources, Inc. [*NASDAQ symbol*] (NQ)

GKRVE .... Golden Knight Res [*NASDAQ symbol*] (TTSB)

GKS .... Gesamtverzeichnis der Kongressschriften [*Union List of Conference Proceedings*] [*Deutsches Bibliotheksinstitut*] [*Germany*] [*Information service or system*] (CRD)

GKS .... Grand Keeper of the Seals [*Freemasonry*]

GKS .... Graphical Kernel System [*International Standards Organization*] [*Computer science*]

GKSRA .... G & K Services Cl'A' [*NASDAQ symbol*] (TTSB)

GKT .... Gasket [*Technical drawings*]

GKT .... General Knowledge Test

GKT .... Goldteck Mines Ltd. [*Toronto Stock Exchange symbol*]

GKTW .... Give Kids the World (EA)

GKW .... God Knows What

GKY .... Golden Key Resources Ltd. [*Vancouver Stock Exchange symbol*]

Gl .... Galatians [*New Testament book*] (BJA)

GL .... Galeries Lafayette [*Department store*] [*Paris, France*]

Gl .... Galleon [*Spanish vessel*] (DS)

GL .... Gallon (MCD)

Gl .... Galvanized [*Metallurgy*]

GL .... Gas LASER

GL .... Gate Leads (IEEE)

GL .... Gauge Length

GL .... Gear Lubricant [*Automotive engineering*]

GL .... General Laws [*A publication*] (DLA)

GL .... General Ledger (AABC)

GL .... General Letter

GL .... General Liability [*Insurance*]

GL .... General Linear [*Group theory, mathematics*]

Gl .... General List [*Navy British*] (DMA)

GL .... Generator Lorry [*British*]

GL .... Genius Loci [*Genius of the Place*] [*Latin*] (ROG)

GL .... Geographic Location (NITA)

GL .... Germanischer Lloyd [*German ship classification society*] (DS)

GL .... Gilbert Lereboullet [*Syndrome*] [*Medicine*] (DB)

gl .... Gill [*Oceanography*] (DAVI)

GL .... Gill [*Unit of weight*]

GL .... Gilt Leaves [*Bookbinding*] (ROG)

GL .... Gilt Lines [*Bookbinding*] (ROG)

GL .... Gimbal Limit Prearming Inhibiting Signal

GL .... Giustizia e Liberta [*Italy*] [*Political party*]

GL .... Glabella [*Anatomy*] (ROG)

GL .... Glacier (ROG)

GL .... Gladstonian Liberal [*British*] (ROG)

gl .... Gland

GL .... Glass

GL .... Glaucolacustrine Soil [*Agronomy*]

GL .... Glaze

Gl .... Gleaver's Reports [*Jamaica*] [*A publication*] (ILCA)

GL .... Glebe [*Ecclesiastical*] (ROG)

GL .... Global Learning (EA)

Gl .... Globigerina [*Quality of the bottom*] [*Nautical charts*]

Gl .... Globus (BJA)

GL .... Gloria [*Glory*] [*Latin*]

Gl .... Gloss (DSA)

GL .... Gloss (WDMC)

gl .... Gloss (WDMC)

GL .... Glossary (ROG)

gl .... Glossy (WDMC)

Gl .... Glucinium [*Also, G*] [*Old name for chemical element beryllium*]

GL .... Glycolipid (DB)

GL .... Glycosphingolipid [*Biochemistry*]

GL .... Gold Lease (ADA)

GL .... Go Long [*Investment term*]

GL .... Good Luck (MHDB)

GL .... Gothic Letter

GL .... Government Laboratory (BARN)

GL .... Grade Line

G/L .... Graduate in Law

G/L .... Grams per Liter

g/l .... Grams per Liter (MEC)

GL .... Grand Larceny

GL .... Grand Lodge [*Freemasonry*]

GL .... Grand Lot

GL .... Grant Less Than [*Dialog*] [*Searchable fields*] [*Information service or system*] (NITA)

GL .... Graphic Library

GL .... Greater London [*England*]

GL .... Greatest Length

GL .... Great Lakes [*Vessel load line mark*]

GL .... Great Lakes Forest Products Ltd. [*Toronto Stock Exchange symbol*]

gl .... Greenland [*MARC country of publication code Library of Congress*] (LCCP)

GL .... Greenland [*ANSI two-letter standard code*] (CNC)

GL .... Green Library [*See also BVM*] [*France*] (EAIO)

GL .... Green Light (MSA)

GL .... Grenade Launcher (AABC)

GL .... Grid Leak

GL .... Gronlandsfly [*ICAO designator*] (AD)

GL .... Gross Line [*Insurance*]

GL .... Ground Level

GL .... Guild Library [*Church of Scotland*] [*A publication*]

GL .... Gun Lay [*or Laying*] [*RADAR*]

GL .... Gun Licence [*British*] (DAS)

GL .... Gunnery Lieutenant [*British military*] (DMA)

GL .... Gustatory Lacrimation [*Medicine*] (DMAA)

GL .... Lanier Lake Regional and Gwinnett County Library, Lawrenceville, GA [*Library symbol Library of Congress*] (LCLS)

GL .... L-Glutamic [*acid*] and L-Lysine [*Copolymer*]

GLA .... Gamma-Linoleic Acid [*Organic chemistry*]

GLA .... Gamma-Linolenic Acid

GLA .... General Laboratory Associates

GLA .... General Learning Ability

GLA .... General Ledger Account (AFM)

GLA .... General Lighthouse Authority [*British*]

GLA .... Giant Left Atrium (DB)

GLA .... Gingivolinguoaxial [*Dentistry*]

GLA .... Glamis [*California*] [*Seismograph station code, US Geological Survey*] (SEIS)

GLA .... Glasgow [*Scotland*] [*Airport symbol*] (OAG)

GLA .... Glass [*Automotive engineering*]

GLA .... Gold Star Resources, Inc. [*Vancouver Stock Exchange symbol*]

GLA .... Grain Legume Association [*Australia*]

GLA .... Great Lakes Aviation Ltd. [*ICAO designator*] (FAAC)

GLA .... Gross Leasable Area

GLA .... Groupe de Liberation Armee [*Armed Liberation Group*] [*Guadeloupe*] (PD)

GLA .... Group Life Assurance [*British*]

GLA .... Guadeloupe Liberation Army

GLA .... Gulkana, AK [*Location identifier FAA*] (FAAL)

GLA .... Gust Load Alleviation [*Aviation*]

GLAAD .... Gay and Lesbian Alliance Against Defamation (EA)

GLAAD .... Global Learning at a Distance [*An association*]

GLAAD/NY .. Gay and Lesbian Alliance Against Defamation/New York (EA)

GLAADS ...... Gun Low-Altitude Air Defense System (NASA)

glab .... Glabrous [*Botany*] (BARN)

GLAC .... Gay and Lesbian Association of Choruses (EA)

GLAC .... General Ledger Account Code

glac .... Glacial [*Chemistry*] (DAVI)

GLAC .... Glacial

GLAC .... Glacier National Park

GLAC .... Grain Legume Advisory Committee [*Australia*]

GLACSEC .... Group of Latin American and Caribbean Sugar Exporting Countries [*See also GEPLACEA*] [*Mexico City, Mexico*] (EAIO)

GLAD .... Gay and Lesbian Advocates and Defenders (EA)

GLAD .... Gladiator Fighter Aircraft [*British*] (DSUE)

GLAD .... Gladiolus (DSUE)

GLAD .... Glancing Angle Deposition [*Coating technology*]

GLAD .... GLOTRAC [*Global Tracking*] Adjustment

GLAD .... Gold-labelled Antigen Detection [*Medicine*] (DMAA)

GLAD .... Government and Legal Affairs Division [*American Occupational Therapy Association*]

GLAD .... Grenade Launcher Attachment Development (MCD)

GLAD .... Group Learning about Drugs

GLADIS .... Ground-LASER Attack Designator/Identification System (MCD)

GLADS .... Great Falls Air Defense Sector [*Montana*] (SAA)

GLADS .... Gun Low-Altitude Air Defense System

GLAFLI .... Graded Levels of Achievement in Foreign Language Learning (AIE)

GLAG .... Ginzburg-Landau-Abrikosov-Gorkov [*Superconductivity theory*]

GLagC .... La Grange College, La Grange, GA [*Library symbol Library of Congress*] (LCLS)

GLagCM ...... Callaway Mills Co., Technical Library, LaGrange, GA [*Library symbol Library of Congress*] (LCLS)

GLagTAr ...... Troup County Archives, La Grange, GA [*Library symbol*] [*Library of Congress*] (LCLS)

GLAI .... Green Leaf Area Index (MCD)

GLAKES .... Great Lakes (MUGU)

GLAM .... Glamorganshire [*County in Wales*]

GLAM .... Greying, Leisured, Affluent, and Married [*Lifestyle classification British*]

Glamis .... Glamis Gold Ltd. [*Associated Press*] (SAG)

GLAMIS ...... Grant/Loan Accounting and Management Information System [*Department of Commerce*] (GFGA)

GLAMS .... Glamorganshire [*County in Wales*]

GLANCE ...... Global Lightweight Airborne Navigation Computer Equipment

gland .... Glandula [*Gland*] [*Endocrinology*] (DAVI)

gland .... Glandular (STED)

Gl & J .... Glyn and Jameson's English Bankruptcy Reports [*1821-28*] [*A publication*]

Glan El Cas .. Glanville's English Election Cases [*A publication*] (DLA)

Glanv El Cas ... Glanville's English Election Cases [*A publication*] (DLA)

GLAP .... Gay Legal Advice Project [*British*] (DI)

GLAPPAR .... General Ledger, Accounts Payable, and Accounts Receivable [*Accounting*]

GLAR .... Glas-Aire Indus Grp Ltd [*NASDAQ symbol*] (TTSB)

GLAR .... Glas-Aire Industries Group Ltd. [*NASDAQ symbol*] (SAG)

GLARE .... Glass Reinforced [*Organic chemistry*]

GLARE .... Ground-Level Attack, Reconnaissance, and Electronic Countermeasures (MCD)

GLaRGG ...... Great Lakes Regional Genetics Group (HGEN)

GLARP .... Grupo Latinoamericano de Rehabilitacion Profesional [*Latin American Vocational Rehabilitation Group*] [*Bogata, Colombia*] (EAIO)

Glas .... Glascock's Reports in All the Courts of Ireland [*A publication*] (DLA)

GLAS .... Glasgal Communications [*NASDAQ symbol*] (TTSB)

GLAS .... Glasgal Communities [*NASDAQ symbol*] (SAG)

GLAS .... Glasgow [*Scotland*]

GLAS .... Goddard Laboratory for Atmospheric Sciences (MCD)

GLAS .... Goddard Laboratory of Atmospheric Sciences [*Marine science*] [*Army*] (OSRA)
GlasAire ...... Glas-Aire Industries Group Ltd. [*Associated Press*] (SAG)
GLAS & SW... Glasgow & South-Western [*Railway*] [*Scotland*] (ROG)
Glasc .... Glascock's Reports in All the Courts of Ireland [*A publication*] (DLA)
Glascock...... Glascock's Reports in All the Courts of Ireland [*A publication*] (DLA)
GLASG .... Glasgow [*Scotland*] (ROG)
Glasgal .... Glasgal Communities [*Associated Press*] (SAG)
GLASLA ...... Great Lakes - St. Lawrence Association
GLASOD...... Global Assessment on Soil Degradation (EERA)
GLASS .... Geodetic LASER Survey System
GLASS .... Germanium-Lithium Argon Scanning System (NRCH)
GLASS .... Good Luck and Smooth Sailing [*Slang Military*] (DNAB)
Glassboro St C... Glassboro State College (GAGS)
GLASSEX ...... Glass Technology and Fabrication Exhibition (TSPED)
Glassf Ev .... Glassford on Evidence [*A publication*] (DLA)
Glassmst ...... Glassmaster Co. [*Associated Press*] (SAG)
GLAST .... Gamma Large Array Space Telescope [*A collaboration of physics groups*]
GLAST .... Gamma-Ray Large Area Space [*Proposed, 1996*]
GLASU .... Glasgal Communications Unit [*NASDAQ symbol*] (TTSB)
GLASW .... Glasgal Communications Wrrt [*NASDAQ symbol*] (TTSB)
GLAT............ Glutamic Acid, Lysine, Alanine, and Tyrosine (STED)
GLAT .... Government Lot Acceptance Test [*Military*] (CAAL)
Glatflt .... Glatfelter [*P.H.*] Co. [*Associated Press*] (SAG)
GLAU .... General Labourers' Amalgamated Union [*British*]
glau .... Glaucous [*Botany*] (BARN)
GLAVATOM... Chief Directorate to the Council of Ministries for the Utilisation of Atomic Energy [*British*] (NUCP)
GlaxcWeL .... Glaxo Wellcome PLC [*Associated Press*] (SAG)
GLB............. Galactosidase Beta (DMAA)
GLB............. Gas [*or Grease*] Lubricated Bearing
GLB............. Gilbues [*Brazil*] [*Airport symbol*] (AD)
GLB............. Girls' Life Brigade [*British*]
GLB............. Glass Block (AAG)
GLB............. Glass in Barrels [*Freight*]
GLB............. Glenborough Realty Trust [*NYSE symbol*] (TTSB)
GLB............. Glenborough Realty Trust, Inc. [*NYSE symbol*] (SAG)
GLB............. Global Air [*Bulgaria*] [*ICAO designator*] (FAAC)
GLB............. Great Lakes Freight Bureau Inc., Cleveland OH [*STAC*]
GLBA .... Glacier Bay National Monument
GLBA .... Great Lakes Booksellers Association (EA)
GLBBX .... Mgn. Stanley D. Witter Global Divd. Growth [*Mutual fund ticker symbol*] (SG)
GLBC .... Great Lakes Bancorp (EFIS)
GLBC .... Great Lakes Basin Commission [*Terminated, 1981*] (EGAO)
GlbCasn ...... Global Casinos [*Associated Press*] (SAG)
GlbDir .... Global Directmail Corp. [*Associated Press*] (SAG)
GLBE .... Globe Business Resources [*NASDAQ symbol*] (TTSB)
GLBE .... Globe Business Resources, Inc. [*NASDAQ symbol*] (SAG)
GlbeBus ...... Globe Business Resources, Inc. [*Associated Press*] (SAG)
GlbGvt .... Global Government Plus Fund, Inc. [*Associated Press*] (SAG)
GlbHlt .... Global Health Sciences Fund [*Associated Press*] (SAG)
GLBK .... Glendale Co-Operative Bank [*NASDAQ symbol*] (SAG)
GLBK .... Glendale Co. Operative Bk [*NASDAQ symbol*] (TTSB)
GLBL............ Global
GLBL............ Global Industries [*NASDAQ symbol*] (TTSB)
GLBL............ Global Industries Ltd. [*NASDAQ symbol*] (SAG)
GlblOcn ...... Global Ocean Carriers Ltd. [*Associated Press*] (SAG)
GlblOne ...... Global One Distribution & Merchandising, Inc. [*Associated Press*] (SAG)
GLBM............ Ground-Launched Ballistic Missile
GlbMktl........ Global Market Information, Inc. [*Associated Press*] (SAG)
GlbRsc .... Global Resources, Inc. [*Associated Press*] (SAG)
GLBS .... Globes [*Freight*]
GlbSpill .... Global Spill Management [*Associated Press*] (SAG)
GLBT .... Glastonbury Bank & Trust Co. [*NASDAQ symbol*] (SAG)
GlbTel.......... Global Telecommunications Solutions, Inc. [*Associated Press*] (SAG)
GLBU .... Buchanan [*Liberia*] [*ICAO location identifier*] (ICLI)
GlbVilag ...... Global Village Communications, Inc. [*Associated Press*] (SAG)
GLC............. Gas-Liquid Chromatography [*Analytical chemistry*]
GLC............. Gate Leakage Current
GLC............. Gay and Lesbian Caucus (EA)
GLC............. General Learning Corp. [*of Time, Inc.*]
GLC............. Generator Line Contractor (NASA)
GLC............. German Language Club (EA)
GLC............. Glace
glc .... Glaucoma (STED)
GLC............. Glaucoma
GLC............. Global LORAN Navigation Chart [*Air Force*]
Glc.............. Glucose [*Also, G, GLUC*] [*A sugar*]
GLC............. Greater London Council [*Information service or system*] (IID)
GLC............. Great Lakes Club (EA)
GLC............. Great Lakes Commission (EA)
GLC............. Great Little Car [*Mazda Motors of America*]
GLC............. Ground Level Concentration (EG)
GLC............. Philadelphia, PA [*Location identifier FAA*] (FAAL)
GLCA .... Gallery of Living Catholic Authors [*Defunct*] (EA)
GLCA .... Glen Canyon National Recreation Area
GlcA............ Gluconic Acid [*Biochemistry*]
GLCA .... Great Lakes Colleges Association (EA)
GLCBY .... Globo Cabo ADS [*Formerly, Multicanal Participacoes ADS*] [*NASDAQ symbol*]
GLCC .... Greater London County Council [*England*] (WDAA)
GLCCF .... Gaming Lottery [*NASDAQ symbol*] (TTSB)

GLCCF .... Gaming Lottery Corp. [*NASDAQ symbol*] (SAG)
GLCCF .... GLC Ltd. [*Formerly, Gaming Lottery*] [*NASDAQ symbol*]
GLCES .... Great Lakes Coastal Forecasting System [*Marine science*] (OSRA)
GLCFS .... Great Lakes Coastal Forecasting System (USDC)
GLCM.......... Graduate Diploma of the London College of Music [*British*] (DBQ)
GLCM.......... Ground-Launched Cruise Missile [*Pronounced "glick-em"*]
GLCM.......... Robertsport/Cape Mount [*Liberia*] [*ICAO location identifier*] (ICLI)
GLC/MS ...... Gas-Liquid Chromatography/Mass Spectrometry (STED)
GlcN............ Glucosamine [*Biochemistry*]
GLCNA .... German Lutheran Conference of North America (EA)
GlcNac........ N-Acetylglucosamine
GLCNSW...... Gem and Lapidary Council of New South Wales [*Australia*]
GLCP .... Harper/Cape Palmas [*Liberia*] [*ICAO location identifier*] (ICLI)
GlcrBc .... Glacier Bancorp, Inc. [*Associated Press*] (SAG)
GLC/SBS ..... Great Little Computer/Small Business System [*Business software*] [*Cumulus Computer Corp.*] (PCM)
GLCSNSW..... Gay and Lesbian Counselling Service of New South Wales [*Australia*]
GLCSSA ...... Gay and Lesbian Counselling Service of South Australia
GLCTS .... Global Land Cover Test Sites [*Remote sensing*] (EERA)
GlcUA .... Glucuronic Acid [*Also, GA*] [*Biochemistry*]
GlcWatr ...... Glacier Water Services, Inc. [*Associated Press*] (SAG)
GLD .... Cases in the Griqualand West Local Division of the Supreme Court [*1910-46*] [*South Africa*] [*A publication*] (DLA)
GLD .... Gas Leak Detector
GLD .... General Learning Disability
GLD .... Glad [*Amateur radio shorthand*] (WDAA)
GLD .... Glider
GLD .... Glide Slope [*Aviation*] (NASA)
GLD .... Globoid Leukodystrophy [*Medicine*] (DB)
GLD .... Glutamate Dehydrogenase (DMAA)
GLD .... Gold (MSA)
GLD .... Golden [*Colorado School of Mines*] [*Colorado*] [*Seismograph station code, US Geological Survey*] (SEIS)
GLD .... Golden Star Air Cargo Co. Ltd. [*Sudan*] [*ICAO designator*] (FAAC)
GLD .... Goodland [*Kansas*] [*Airport symbol*] (OAG)
GLD .... Gross Logical Design
GLD .... Ground-LASER Designators (RDA)
GLD .... Guild
Gld............. Guilder [*Modification of gulden*] [*Monetary unit*] [*Netherlands*]
GLD .... Santa Fe Pacific Gold Corp. [*NYSE symbol*] (SAG)
GLD .... Sante Fe Pacific Gold [*NYSE symbol*] (TTSB)
GLDA .... Gay and Lesbian Democrats of America [*Defunct*] (EA)
GLDB .... Gold Banc Corp., Inc. [*NASDAQ symbol*] (SAG)
GldBear .... Golden Bear Golf, Inc. [*Associated Press*] (SAG)
GLDC .... Golden Enterprises [*NASDAQ symbol*] (TTSB)
GLDC .... Golden Enterprises, Inc. [*NASDAQ symbol*] (NQ)
GldEagl........ Golden Eagle Group, Inc. [*Associated Press*] (SAG)
GldEg .... Golden Eagle Group, Inc. [*Associated Press*] (SAG)
GLDF .... Gold Fields of South Africa Ltd. [*NASDAQ symbol*] (NQ)
GldFld .... Goldfield Corp. [*Associated Press*] (SAG)
GLDFY .... Gold Fields S. Africa ADR [*NASDAQ symbol*] (TTSB)
GLDH .... Glutamate Dehydrogenase [*Organic chemistry*]
GldKngt........ Golden Knight Resources, Inc. [*Associated Press*] (SAG)
GLDMS .... Groupe de Liaison de Docimologues en Milieu Scolaire [*Canada*]
gldn .... Golden [*Philately*]
GLDN .... Golden
GLDN .... Golden Systems, Inc. [*NASDAQ symbol*] (SAG)
GldnSyst ...... Golden Systems, Inc. [*Associated Press*] (SAG)
GLDP .... Ginn Language Development Program (EDAC)
GLD PLTD... Gold Plated [*Freight*]
GldPoul........ Golden Poultry Co., Inc. [*Associated Press*] (SAG)
GldQual........ Golden Quail Resources Ltd. [*Associated Press*] (SAG)
GLDR .... Glider (FAAC)
GLDR .... Gold Reserve [*NASDAQ symbol*] (TTSB)
GLDR .... Gold Reserve Corp. [*NASDAQ symbol*] (NQ)
GLDR .... Groupe Liberal, Democratique, et Reformateur (EAIO)
GLDS .... Gemini Launch Data System [*NASA*] (MCD)
GLDS .... Ground LASER Designator Station (PDAA)
GldStarR ...... Golden Star Resources Ltd. [*Associated Press*] (SAG)
GldStd .... Gold Standard, Inc. [*Associated Press*] (SAG)
GLDT .... Gas LASER Discharge Tube
GLDTR .... Gladiator
GldWF .... Golden West Financial Corp. [*Associated Press*] (SAG)
GldwSam...... Goldwyn [*Samuel*] Co. [*Associated Press*] (SAG)
GLE............. Gainesville, TX [*Location identifier FAA*] (FAAL)
GLE............. Gemini LASER Experiment [*NASA*] (IAA)
GLE............. Gleason Corp. [*NYSE symbol*] (SPSG)
GLE............. Glenmuick [*New Zealand*] [*Seismograph station code, US Geological Survey Closed*] (SEIS)
GLE............. GLE Resources Ltd. [*Vancouver Stock Exchange symbol*]
GLE............. Gloss Low Emission [*Ink*] (DGA)
GLE............. Government-Loaned Equipment (MSA)
GLE............. Grade Level Equivalent [*Educational testing*]
GLE............. Grand Larousse Encyclopedique [*A publication*]
GLE............. Ground-Level Event [*Geophysics*]
GLE............. Ground Liaison Element (MCD)
GLE............. Gummed Long Edge [*Envelopes*] (DGA)
GLEAM........ Graphic Layout and Engineering Aid Method
GleasC .... Gleason Corp. [*Associated Press*] (SAG)
GLEDIC .... Great Lakes Environmental Information Center [*Ann Arbor, MI*]
GLEEP .... Graphite Low-Energy Experimental Pile [*Nuclear reactor*] [*British*]
GLEF .... Geothermal Loop Experimental Facility [*Department of Energy*]
GLEIS .... Great Lakes Environmental Information Sharing

GLEMEDS .... Great Lakes Embryo Mortality, Edema, and Deformities Syndrome [*Marine birds*]
GLEN .... Glen [*Commonly used*] (OPSA)
Glenayr....... Glenayre Techs, Inc. [*Associated Press*] (SAG)
Gl Ency .... Globe Encyclopaedia [*A publication*] (ROG)
GLENDAL..... Glendalough [*Valley in Ireland*] (ROG)
GlendCo....... Glendale Co-Operative Bank [*Associated Press*] (SAG)
GlenF........... Glendale Federal Bank Federal Savings Bank [*Associated Press*] (SAG)
GlenF........... Glendale Federal Bank FSB [*Associated Press*] (SAG)
GlenFed....... Glendale Federal Bank Federal Savings Bank [*Associated Press*] (SAG)
Glen High .... Glen's Highway Laws [*A publication*] (DLA)
Glenn.......... Glenn's Annual Reports [*16-18 Louisiana*] [*A publication*] (DLA)
Glen Pub H... Glen on the Public Health Laws [*A publication*] (DLA)
Glen Reg ..... Glen on Registration of Births and Deaths [*A publication*] (DLA)
GlenRT .... Glenborough Realty Trust, Inc. [*Associated Press*] (SAG)
GLENS .... Glens [*Commonly used*] (OPSA)
Glenway...... Glenway Financial Corp. [*Associated Press*] (SAG)
GLEP........... Group for Lunar Exploration and Planning (MCD)
GLERL .... Great Lakes Environmental Research Laboratory [*Ann Arbor, MI*] [*National Oceanic and Atmospheric Administration*] (GRD)
GLERR .... Great Lakes Ecosystem Restoration and Rehabilitation [*Canada*] (ASF)
GLES........... Great Lakes Forecasting System [*Marine science*] (OSRA)
GLET........... Government Logistics Evaluation and Testing (MCD)
GLF .... Gates Library Foundation
GLF .... Gaussian Lens Formula [*Optics*]
GLF .... Gay Liberation Front
GLF .... Generalized Lambda Family [*Statistics*]
GLF .... General Telephone Co. of Florida [*NYSE symbol*] (SPSG)
GLF .... Glass Fiber [*Technical drawings*]
GLF .... Golfito [*Costa Rica*] [*Airport symbol*] (OAG)
GLF .... Great Lakes Fisheries Laboratory, Ann Arbor, MI [*OCLC symbol*] (OCLC)
GLF .... GTE Florida, Inc. [*NYSE symbol*] (SAG)
GLF .... Gulfstream Aerospace Corp. [*ICAO designator*] (FAAC)
GLF .... McGill University, Law Library [*UTLAS symbol*]
GLFALSK .... Gulf of Alaska (FAAC)
GLFC........... Georganne LaPiere Fan Club (EA)
GLFC........... Ginger Lynn Fan Club [*Defunct*] (EA)
GLFC........... Gloria Loring Fan Club [*Defunct*] (EA)
GLFC........... Great Lakes Fishery Commission [*Canada and United States*] (NOAA)
GLFC........... Great Lakes Football Conference (PSS)
GLFC........... Guiding Light Fan Club (EA)
GLFCAL....... Gulf of California (FAAC)
GlfCda .... Gulf Canada Resources Ltd. [*Associated Press*] (SAG)
GLFD .... Guilford Pharmaceuticals [*NASDAQ symbol*] (TTSB)
GLFD .... Guilford Pharmaceuticals, Inc. [*NASDAQ symbol*] (SAG)
GLFDCC ...... Great Lakes Fish Disease Control Committee [*Canada*] (ASF)
GLFE........... Golf Enterprises [*NASDAQ symbol*] (TTSB)
GLFE........... Golf Enterprises, Inc. [*NASDAQ symbol*] (SAG)
GL/FICS ...... General Ledger / Financial Information and Control System
GLFL .... Great Lakes Fishery Laboratory [*Department of the Interior*] (GRD)
GLFMEX...... Gulf of Mexico (FAAC)
Glfmrk .... Gulfmark International [*Associated Press*] (SAG)
GLFPrA .... GTE Fla $1.25 Pfd [*NYSE symbol*] (TTSB)
GLFPrB .... GTE Fla $1.30cm B Pfd [*NYSE symbol*] (TTSB)
GLFPrC .... GTE Fla 8.16% Pfd [*NYSE symbol*] (TTSB)
GLFRB .... Great Lakes Fisheries Research Branch [*Canadian Department of Fisheries and Oceans*] [*Research center*] (RCD)
GLFRC .... Great Lakes Forest Research Centre [*Environment Canada*] [*Research center*] (RCD)
GlFRP .... Glass-Fiber-Reinforced Plastic [*Also, GFRP*]
GLFS........... Great Lakes Forecasting System (USDC)
GLFSTLAWR... Gulf of St. Lawrence (FAAC)
GlfSU .... Gulf States Utilities Co. [*Associated Press*] (SAG)
GLG .... Glamis Gold Ltd. [*Toronto Stock Exchange symbol NYSE symbol*]
GLG .... Glengyle [*Australia Airport symbol*]
GLG .... La Grange College, La Grange, GA [*OCLC symbol*] (OCLC)
GLGE .... Greenville/Sinoe [*Liberia*] [*ICAO location identifier*] (ICLI)
GLGL .... Gwinnett County Law Library, Lawrenceville, GA [*Library symbol*] [*Library of Congress*] (LCLS)
GLGS .... Gwinnett County Public Schools, Lawrenceville, GA [*Library symbol*] [*Library of Congress*] (LCLS)
GLGT .... Gwinnett Technical Institute, Lawrenceville, GA [*Library symbol*] [*Library of Congress*] (LCLS)
GLH .... Gentleman's Left Handed [*Golf club*]
GLH .... Giant Lymph Node Hyperplasia [*Medicine*] (DMAA)
GLH .... Glue Line Heating
GLH .... Go Like Hell [*In model name Omni GLH, proposed for Dodge car designed by Carroll Shelby*]
GLH .... Greenville [*Mississippi*] [*Airport symbol*] (OAG)
GLHA .... Great Lakes Harbor Association (EA)
GLH-S......... Goes Like Hell - Some More [*In model "GLH-S," Dodge car designed by Carroll Shelby*] [*Facetious translation: "Goes Like Hell - Squared"*]
GLHS .... Great Lakes Historical Society (EA)
GLHS .... Ground-Launched HELLFIRE System (MCD)
GLHSC .... Gay and Lesbian History on Stamps Club (EA)
GLI.............. Gale's Literary Index [*CD-ROM*]
GLI.............. Gallic Aviation [*France ICAO designator*] (FAAC)
GLI.............. Gamma LINAC Instrumentation
GLI.............. Glen Innes [*Australia Airport symbol*] (OAG)

GLI.............. Glicentin [*Biochemistry*]
GLI.............. Glider
GLI.............. Glucagon-Like Immunoreactivity [*or Immunoreactant*] [*Endocrinology*]
GLI.............. Grandma Lee's, Inc. [*Toronto Stock Exchange symbol*]
GLI.............. Greyhound Lines, Inc. (EFIS)
GLI.............. Gurkha Light Infantry [*British military*] (DMA)
GLIA............ Gliatech, Inc. [*NASDAQ symbol*] (SAG)
GLIAC .... Great Lakes Intercollegiate Athletic Conference
Gliatech....... Gliatech, Inc. [*Associated Press*] (SAG)
GLIB............ Gay and Lesbian Information Bureau (IID)
GliBad .... Glider Badge [*Military decoration*]
GLIC........... General Ledger Identification Code (AFM)
GLIFWC ...... Great Lakes Indian Fish and Wildlife Commission (EA)
GLIM........... Generalised Linear Interactive Modelling System [*Software*] (EERA)
GLIM........... General Light Inter-Reflection Model (PDAA)
GLIM........... General Linear Modeling Program [*Computer science*]
GlimchRt ..... Glimcher Realty Trust [*Associated Press*] (SAG)
GLIMPCE .... Great Lakes International Multidisciplinary Program on Crustal Evolution [*Geophysics*]
GLIMPSE .... Global Limb Photometric Scanning Experiment (MCD)
GLIN .... Georgia Library Information Network [*Library network*]
GLIN .... Great Lakes Information Network
GLINN .... Government Libraries Information Network in New South Wales [*Australia*]
GLINT .... Global Intelligence (IEEE)
GLINT .... Gospel Literature International (EA)
glio .... Glioma [*Neurology*] (DAVI)
GLIP .... Glide and Skip [*Bombing mission*]
GLIPAR........ Guide Line Identification Program for Antimissile Research [*ARPA*]
GLIPAR........ Guidelines for Investigation, Planning, and Research
GLIPS .... Giga Logical Inferences per Second (CIST)
GLIS .... Gleaner Life Insurance Society [*Adrian, MI*] (EA)
GLIS .... Glissando [*Gliding*] [*Music*] (ROG)
GLIS .... Global Land Information System (EERA)
GLISA .... Government Losses in Shipment Act [*1937*]
Gliss .... Glissando [*Gliding*] [*Music*]
glit .... Glitter (VRA)
GLITCH ...... Goblin Loose in the Computer Hut [*Computer science*]
GLJ .... Global Getra Ltd. [*Bulgaria*] [*ICAO designator*] (FAAC)
GLK .... Golden Lake Resources Ltd. [*Vancouver Stock Exchange symbol*]
GLK .... Great Lakes Chemical [*NYSE symbol*] (TTSB)
GLK .... Great Lakes Chemical Corp. [*NYSE symbol*] (SPSG)
GLL .... Galileo [*NASA*]
GLL .... Gay and Lesbian Literature
GLL .... General Leaseholds Ltd. [*Toronto Stock Exchange symbol*]
GLL .... Gilgames and the Land of the Living (BJA)
GLL .... Gill, CO [*Location identifier FAA*] (FAAL)
GLL .... Great Lakes Laboratory [*State University College at Buffalo*] [*Research center*] (RCD)
GLL .... McGill University Library [*UTLAS symbol*]
GLLB .... Buchanan [*Liberia*] [*ICAO location identifier*] (ICLI)
GLLD .... Ground-LASER Locator Designator (MCD)
GLLD-E .... Ground-LASER Locator Designator-Evaluator (MCD)
GLLD-TNS.... Ground-LASER Locator Designator-Thermal Night Sight (MCD)
GLLD/VLLD... Ground-LASER Locator Designator/Vehicular LASER Locator Designator (MCD)
GLLKA .... Great Lakes Lighthouse Keepers Association (EA)
GLLO .... Great Lakes Licensed Officers' Organization
GLLRY .... Gallery
GLM .... Generalized Lagrangian Multiplier [*Military*] (AFIT)
GLM .... Generalized Linear Model [*Statistics*]
GLM .... Generalized Linear Models [*Computer science*] (EERA)
GLM .... Gigabit Link Module [*Computer science*]
GLM .... Gilmore [*Alaska*] [*Also, GLN*] [*Seismograph station code, US Geological Survey*] (SEIS)
GLM .... Global Marine [*NYSE symbol*] (TTSB)
GLM .... Global Marine, Inc. [*NYSE symbol*] (SPSG)
GLM .... Gold Life-Saving Medal [*Military decoration*] (GFGA)
GLM .... Government-Loaned Material
GLM .... Graduated Length Method [*of learning to ski*] [*Later, Accelerated Length Method*]
GLM .... Grand Livre du Mois [*Best-selling book of the month*] [*French*]
GLM .... Graphics Lathe Module [*McDonnell-Douglas Automation Co.*]
GLM .... Great Lakes Megalopolis [*Proposed name for possible "super-city" formed by growth and mergers of other cities*]
GLM .... Growth-Limiting Medium [*For microorganisms*]
GLM .... McGill University, Medical Library [*UTLAS symbol*]
GLMA .... Glassmaster Co. [*NASDAQ symbol*] (SAG)
GLMA .... Great Lakes Mink Association (EA)
GLMC.......... Gay and Lesbian Media Coalition (EA)
GLMC.......... Monrovia City [*Liberia*] [*ICAO location identifier*] (ICLI)
GLMi .... Great Lakes Maritime Institute (EA)
GlMkt.......... Global Market Information, Inc. [*Associated Press*] (SAG)
GLMMM....... Grand Lodge of Mark Master Masons [*Freemasonry*]
GLMMS....... Groupement Latin et Mediterraneen de Medecine du Sport [*Latin and Mediterranean Group for Sport Medicine - LMGSM*] (EAIO)
GLMR .... Monrovia/Spriggs Payne [*Liberia*] [*ICAO location identifier*] (ICLI)
GlmRS......... Glutaminyl-RNA Synthetase [*An enzyme*]
GLMWC .... Great Lakes and Marine Waters Center [*University of Michigan*] [*Research center*] (RCD)
Glmy .... [*The*] Glenmary Home Missioners (TOCD)
glmy .... The Glenmary Home Missioners (TOCD)
GLN .... Gilmore [*Alaska*] [*Also, GLM*] [*Seismograph station code, US Geological Survey*] (SEIS)
GLN .... Glen

GLN .... Glenayre Electronics Ltd. [*Toronto Stock Exchange symbol*]
GLN .... Glendale Federal Bank [*NYSE symbol*] (SPSG)
Gln............. Glucagon [*Medicine*] (DMAA)
Gln............. Glutamine [*or Glu(NH₂)*] [*Also, Q An amino acid*]
GLN .... Lennox Airways, Gambia Ltd. [*ICAO designator*] (FAAC)
GLNA .... Nimba [*Liberia*] [*ICAO location identifier*] (ICLI)
GLNH .... Giant Lymph Node Hyperplasia [*Medicine*] (DMAA)
GLNPO ...... Great Lakes National Program Office [*Environmental Protection Agency*]
GLNPrE ...... Glendale Fed Bk Cv'E'Prd [*NYSE symbol*] (TTSB)
GlnRS .... Glutamine-Transfer Ribonucleic Acid Synthetase
GLNS .... Glens [*Postal Service standard*] (OPSA)
GLNSW ...... Gould League of New South Wales [*Australia*]
GLNTC .... Great Lakes Naval Training Center
GLO .... Cheltenham-Gloucester [*England*] [*Airport symbol*] (AD)
GLO .... Clovis, NM [*Location identifier FAA*] (FAAL)
GLO .... General Land Office [*Became part of Bureau of Land Management, 1946*]
GLO .... Get the Lead Out [*Of GLO week, sponsored by American Oil Co.*]
Glo............. Global
GLO .... Global Ocean Carriers [*AMEX symbol*] (TTSB)
GLO .... Global Ocean Carriers Ltd. [*AMEX symbol*] (CTT)
GLO .... Gloria [*Kyrgyzstan*] [*FAA designator*] (FAAC)
glo .... Gloss (VRA)
GLO .... Gloucester [*British depot code*]
GLO .... Gloucester [*Massachusetts*] [*Seismograph station code, US Geological Survey*] (SEIS)
GLO .... Glyoxalase [*An enzyme*]
Glo............. Glyoxalase (DB)
GLO .... Goddard Launch Operations [*NASA*]
GLO .... Gospel literature Outreach [*Australia*]
G LO .... Grand Lodge [*Freemasonry*] (ROG)
GLO .... Greens in Lowe [*Political party Australia*]
GLO .... Ground Liaison Officer [*Military*]
GLO .... Ground Logistics Operations [*NASA*] (KSC)
GLO .... Guaiacol-Linoleic Acid Hydroperoxide Oxidoreductase [*An enzyme*]
GLO .... Gunnery Liaison Officer [*Navy*]
GLO .... GVN [*Government of Vietnam*] Liaison Officer
GLO .... L-Gulanolactone Oxidase [*An enzyme*]
GLO .... Ultra Glow Cosmetics [*Vancouver Stock Exchange symbol*]
Gloag & Henderson... Gloag and Henderson's Introduction to the Law of Scotland [*7th ed.*] [*1968*] [*A publication*] (DLA)
GLOAS .... German Liaison Office for the Armament Sector [*Military*]
GLOB .... Globular
GLOB .... Globulin
GlobalPh..... Global Pharmaceutical Corp. [*Associated Press*] (SAG)
Globalstr...... Globalstar Telecommunications Ltd. [*Associated Press*] (SAG)
GLOBE .... Gay, Lesbian, or Bisexual Employees [*An association*]
GLOBE .... Global Backscatter Experiment [*NASA/MSFC*]
GLOBE .... Global Learning and Observations to Benefit the Environment [*NASA*]
GLOBE .... Global Legislators Organization for a Balanced Environment [*International coalition*]
GLOBE .... Global Lending and Overseas Banking Evaluator [*Chase Econometrics*] [*Database*]
GLOBE .... Global Observations to Benefit the Environment (EERA)
Globec........ Global Ocean Ecosystem Dynamics or Global Ocean-Ecosystem Coupling (USDC)
GLOBECOM... Global Communications System [*Air Force*]
GLOBEX ...... Global Electronic Exchange (NUMA)
GlobHi .... Global High Income Dollar Fund [*Associated Press*] (SAG)
GlobIndl...... Global Industrial Technologies [*Associated Press*] (SAG)
GLOBIXS ..... Global Information Exchange System (DOMA)
GlobInd....... Global Industries Ltd. [*Associated Press*] (SAG)
Globlink....... Globalink, Inc. [*Associated Press*] (SAG)
GlobInt........ Global Intellicom, Inc. [*Associated Press*] (SAG)
Globlstr....... Globalstar Telecommunictions Ltd. [*Associated Press*] (SAG)
GlobM......... Global Marine, Inc. [*Associated Press*] (SAG)
GlobNR........ Global Natural Resources, Inc. [*Associated Press*] (SAG)
GlobOut ...... Global Outdoors, Inc. [*Associated Press*] (SAG)
GlobPart...... Global Partners Income Fund [*Associated Press*] (SAG)
GlobSml ...... Global Small Cap Fund, Inc. [*Associated Press*] (SAG)
GlobTele...... Global Telecommunications Solutions, Inc. [*Associated Press*] (SAG)
GlobTR........ Global Total Return Fund [*Associated Press*] (SAG)
G-LOC......... Gravity-Induced Loss of Consciousness [*Aviation*]
GLOC .... Ground Line of Communications (AFM)
GLOCHANT.. Global Change and the Antarctica (EERA)
GLOCK........ Glockenspiel [*Music*]
GLOCOM...... Global Communications System [*Air Force*]
GLODIS........ General Language-Operated Decision Implementation System (PDAA)
GLOL .... Golay Logic Operating Language
GLOM .... Gross Lift-Off Mass [*NASA*] (KSC)
GLOMB .... Glide Bomb [*Air Force*]
GLOMEX ...... Global Oceanographic and Meteorological Experiment [*Marine science*] (MSC)
GLOMR........ Global Low-Orbiting Message Relay [*Satellite*]
GLONASS .... Global Navigation Satellite System [*Military*]
GLONASS .... Global Orbiting Navigational Satellite System [*FAA*] (TAG)
GLOP .... Gevic Logic Operation Program
GLOP .... Guidance and Launch Operation [*Aerospace*] (IAA)
GLOPAC....... Gyroscopic Low-Power Attitude Control
GLOPC......... Gyroscopic Lower Power Control (IAA)
Gl Ord......... Glossa Ordinaria [*A publication*] (DSA)
GLORIA........ Geological Long-Range Inclined ASDIC

GLOS .... Glossary
GLOS .... Gloucestershire [*County in England*]
Glos .... Gloucestershire [*County in England*] (ODBW)
GLOS .... Gun Line of Site [*Tank*] [*Army*]
GLOSS........ Global Ocean Surveillance System (IEEE)
GLOSS........ Global Sea Level Observing System [*Marine science*] (OSRA)
GLOSS........ Glossary
Gloss Lat .... Glossaria Latina [*A publication*] (OCD)
GLOSTER.... Gloucester [*City in England*] (ROG)
GLOTOS....... Graphical Representation of Language for Temporal Ordering Specification [*Telecommunications*] (OSI)
GLOTRAC.... Global Tracking [*RADAR*]
GLOUC........ Gloucester [*City in England*] (ROG)
GLOUC........ Gloucestershire [*County in England*] (ROG)
Gloucester .. Gloucestershire [*County in England*] (BARN)
GLOUC R .... Gloucestershire Regiment [*Military British*] (ROG)
GLOUCS....... Gloucestershire [*County in England*]
GLOV .... Gays and Lesbians Opposing Violence [*An association*]
Glov Mun Cor... Glover's Municipal Corporations [*A publication*] (DLA)
GLOW .... Giving and Learning Our Way [*An association*]
GLOW .... Global RADAR for Ocean Waves
GLOW .... Gross Lift-Off Weight [*NASA*]
GLOW .... Gross Lift-Off Weight [*Aerospace*] (NAKS)
GLOW .... Ground Lift-Off Weight [*Aerospace*] (NAKS)
GLOW .... Ground Lift-Off Weight [*NASA*] (NASA)
GLOWATS.... Global War Avoidance Telecommunications System (MCD)
GLP............ Gallup [*Diocesan abbreviation*] [*New Mexico*] (TOCD)
GLP............ Gelled Liquid Propellant
GLP............ Generalized Lattice-Point
GLP............ General Layout Plan (NATG)
GLP............ General Letter Package (PDAA)
GLP............ Glucagon-Like Peptide [*Biochemistry*]
GLP............ Glucose L-Phosphate (DB)
GLP............ Glycolipoprotein (DMAA)
GLP............ GOAL [*Ground Operations Aerospace Language*] Language Processor (MCD)
GLP............ Golden Princess [*Vancouver Stock Exchange symbol*]
GLP............ Golpazari [*Turkey*] [*Also, GPA*] [*Seismograph station code, US Geological Survey*] (SEIS)
GLP............ Good Laboratory Practice [*FDA*]
GLP............ Gospel Light Publications [*British*]
GLP............ Government-Lent Property (NG)
GLP............ Greek Literary Papyri [*A publication*] (OCD)
GLP............ Gross Lawyer Product [*Term for measurement of the income of attorneys*]
GLP............ Group-Living Program (DAVI)
GLP............ Guadeloupe [*ANSI three-letter standard code*] (CNC)
GLP............ Guide Line Paper [*of Washington Standardization Officers*] [*Military*]
GLP............ Guyana Labour Party [*Political party*] (EY)
GLPA .... Gay and Lesbian Press Association (EA)
GLPA .... Great Lakes Pilotage Administration [*Department of Transportation*]
GLP-AACR ... Gibraltar Labour Party - Association for the Advancement of Civil Rights [*Political party*] (PPW)
GLPC .... Gas-Liquid Partition Chromatography
GLPC .... Global Pharmaceutical Corp. [*NASDAQ symbol*] (SAG)
GLPCI .... Gay and Lesbian Parents Coalition International (EA)
GLPG .... Glow Plug
GLPIAC........ Great Lakes Physical Information Analysis Center
GLPP .... Glucose, Post Prandial [*Clinical chemistry*]
GLPR .... Goldstone Predict [*Orbit identification*] [*NASA*]
GL-PTC .... Gas Liquid Phase Transfer Catalysis [*Physical chemistry*]
GLQ............ Golden Adit Resources [*Vancouver Stock Exchange symbol*]
GLQ............ Greater-than-Lot Quantities
GLR............ Central Mountain Air Ltd. [*Canada ICAO designator*] (FAAC)
GLR............ G & L Realty Corp. [*NYSE symbol*] (SPSG)
GLR............ Gaylord, MI [*Location identifier FAA*] (FAAL)
GLR............ Gazette Law Reports [*New Zealand*] [*A publication*] (DLA)
GLR............ General Line Rate [*Advertising*]
GLR............ Gladiator Resources Ltd. [*Vancouver Stock Exchange symbol*]
GLR............ Glass LASER Rod
GLR............ Government Land Register [*of Western Australia*] [*State*] (EERA)
GLR............ Graphic Level Recorder
GLR............ Greater London Radio (WDAA)
GLR............ Great Lakes Rules [*Boating*] (DICI)
GLR............ Groom Lake Road [*Nevada*] [*Seismograph station code, US Geological Survey*] (SEIS)
GLR............ McGill University Rare Books [*UTLAS symbol*]
GLRA .... Gun-Launched/Rocket-Assisted (MCD)
GL RADAR ... Gun Laying RADAR
GLR-AV .... Grapevine Leafroll-Associated Virus [*Plant pathology*]
GLRB .... Monrovia/Roberts International [*Liberia*] [*ICAO location identifier*] (ICLI)
GLRC .... Gas-Liquid Radiochromatography [*Analytical chemistry*]
GLRC .... Grain Legume Research Council (EERA)
GLRC .... Grain Legumes Research Council [*Australia*]
GLRC .... Great Lakes Regional Conference
GLRE .... Geniki Laiki Rizospastiki Enosis [*General Union of Populists and Radicals*] [*Greek*] (PPE)
GLR (NZ) .... Gazette Law Reports [*New Zealand*] [*A publication*] (DLA)
GLRS .... Geodynamics LASER Ranging System [*NASA*]
GLRS .... Global Outdoors, Inc. [*NASDAQ symbol*] (SAG)
GLRS .... Global Res [*NASDAQ symbol*] (TTSB)
GLRS .... Global Resources, Inc. [*NASDAQ symbol*] (SAG)
GLRSHLD ... Glare Shield (MCD)
GLS............ Galveston [*Texas*] [*Airport symbol*] (OAG)

GLS.............. Gaylord Circulation Control System [*Information service or system*] (IID)
GLS.............. Generalized Least Squares [*Statistics*]
GLS.............. Generalized Lymphadenopathy Syndrome [*Medicine*] (DMAA)
GLS.............. General Ledger System [*Accounting*] (IAA)
GLS.............. General Lighting Service
GLS.............. General Lighting System [*Incadescent lighting*]
GLS.............. General Line School
GLS.............. Giles [*Australia Seismograph station code, US Geological Survey*] (SEIS)
GLS.............. Glass
gls.............. Glass (VRA)
GLS.............. Glide Slope [*Aviation*] (MSA)
GLS.............. Global International Ltd. [*Bulgaria*] [*ICAO designator*] (FAAC)
GLS.............. Golden Shield Resources Ltd. [*Toronto Stock Exchange symbol Vancouver Stock Exchange symbol*]
GLS.............. Government Launch Service (SSD)
GLS.............. Graduate Library School
GLS.............. Grand Lodge of Scotland [*Freemasonry*]
GLS.............. Great Lakes Screw
GLS.............. Green LASER System
GLS.............. Ground Launch Sequence [*or Sequencer*] (NASA)
GLS.............. Gypsy Lore Society, North American Chapter (EA)
GLS.............. Schuller Corp. [*NYSE symbol*] [*Formerly, Manville Corp.*] (SG)
GLSA .... General Ledger Subsidiary Account (AFM)
GLSA .... General Livestock Agent
GLSA .... Government Large Structures Assembly (SSD)
GLSA .... Gray Line Sightseeing Association [*Commercial firm*] (EA)
GLSA .... Great Lakes Seaplane Association [*Defunct*] (EA)
GLSBG .... Great Lakes Sugar Beet Growers (EA)
GLS(C)........ Government Launch Service (Cryogenic) (SSD)
GLSE .... Generalized Weighted Least Squares Estimates [*Statistics*]
GLSECT....... Ground Liaison Section [*Military British*]
GLSFC........ Great Lakes Sport Fishing Council (EA)
GLSGW .... Glasgow [*Scotland*]
GLSK .... Sanniquellie [*Liberia*] [*ICAO location identifier*] (ICLI)
GLSM.......... Gold Life Saving Medal [*Military decoration*]
glsn .... Glassine (VRA)
GLSOA........ Great Lakes Ship Owners Association (EA)
GLSP .... Good Large Scale Practice
GLSPI .... Great Lakes Spill Protection Institute
GLSS .... Ground-Launch Support System (MCD)
GLST.......... Sasstown [*Liberia*] [*ICAO location identifier*] (ICLI)
GLSTM........ Graduate of the London School of Tropical Medicine (DAS)
Glstnbry....... Glastonbury Bank & Trust Co. [*Associated Press*] (SAG)
GLT............. Gas LASER Tube
GLT............. General Corporation for Light Air Transport & Technical Sevices [*Libya*] [*ICAO designator*] (FAAC)
GLT............. General Labor and Trades
glt.............. Gilding (VRA)
glt.............. Gilt (VRA)
GLT............. Gilt [*Bookbinding*] (ROG)
GLT............. Gladstone [*Australia Airport symbol*] (OAG)
GLT............. Glass Lined Tubing
GLT............. Glatfelter [*P. H.*] Co. [*AMEX symbol*] (SPSG)
GLT............. Gloss Low Tack [*Ink*] (DGA)
GLT............. Golden Lion Tamarin [*South American monkey*]
GLT............. Greeting Letter Telegram (ADA)
GLT............. Gridded Line of Thrust (MCD)
GLT............. Ground-LASER Tracking
GLT............. Guide Light (AAG)
GL(T)......... Gun-Laying (Turret) (DEN)
GLTB.......... Goleta National Bank [*NASDAQ symbol*] (SAG)
GLTB.......... Greater London Training Board [*British*] (AIE)
GLTMC........ Golden Lion Tamarin Management Committee (EA)
GITN.......... Glomerulo-Tubulo-Nephritis [*Medicine*]
GLTN.......... Glomerulotubulonephritis (DB)
GLTN .... Guillotine (MSA)
GLTN .... Tchien [*Liberia*] [*ICAO location identifier*] (ICLI)
GLU .... Gambia Labour Union
GLU .... General Logic Unit [*Computer chip*]
GLU .... Global Land Use [*NASA*]
GLU .... Glucose [*Organic chemistry*] (DAVI)
GLU .... Glucuronidase (DB)
glu .... Glutamate [*An amino acid*] (DOG)
glu .... Glutamic Acid [*An amino acid*] (DOG)
Glu............. Glutamic Acid [*Also, E, GA*] [*An amino acid*]
Glu............. Glutamine [*An amino acid*] (DAVI)
GLU .... Great Lakes United (EA)
GLU .... Green Lake Resources Ltd. [*Vancouver Stock Exchange symbol*]
GLU .... Gruene Liste Umweltschutz [*Green List Ecology*] [*Germany*] (PPE)
GLU-5 .... Five-Hour Glucose Tolerance Test [*Medicine*] (DMAA)
GLUC .... Glucose [*Also, G, Glc*] [*A sugar*]
GLUC .... Glucosidase (DMAA)
GLUCEPTATE... Glucoheptonate [*USAN*] [*Organic chemistry*]
GLUC-S...... Urin Glucose Spot [*Test*] [*Endocrinology*] (DAVI)
Glucur......... Glucuronide [*Biochemistry*] (AAMN)
GLULAM ..... Glued Laminated Wood (PDAA)
GluN .... Glutamine [*An amino acid*] (BARN)
Glu(NH₂) ..... Glutamine [*or Gln*] [*Also, Q An amino acid*]
glu ox......... Glucose Oxidase [*Also, GO, GOD*] [*An enzyme*] (AAMN)
GluR .... Glutamate Receptor [*Biochemistry*]
GLUT .... Glucose Transporter [*Biochemistry*]
GLUTAM ..... Glutamine [*An amino acid*] (DAVI)
GLUX .... Great Lakes Aviation [*NASDAQ symbol*] (TTSB)

GLUX .... Great Lakes Aviation Ltd. [*NASDAQ symbol*] (SAG)
GLV .... Gemini Launch Vehicle [*NASA*]
GLV .... Gibbon Ape Leukemia Virus (DMAA)
GLV .... Globe Valve (AAG)
GLV .... Glove
GLV .... Golden Vale Explorations Corp. [*Vancouver Stock Exchange symbol*]
GLV .... Golovin [*Alaska*] [*Airport symbol*] (OAG)
GLV .... Gould League of Victoria [*Australia*]
GLV .... Gross Leukemia Virus
GLVA .... Voinjama [*Liberia*] [*ICAO location identifier*] (ICLI)
GLVC .... Great Lakes Valley Conference (PSS)
GLVNZNG .... Galvanizing
GLW........... Corning Delaware LP [*NYSE symbol*] (SAG)
GLW........... Corning, Inc. [*Wall Street slang name: "Glow Worm"*] [*NYSE symbol*] (SPSG)
GLW........... Glasgow, KY [*Location identifier FAA*] (FAAL)
GLW........... Gunnery Lieutenant's Writer [*British military*] (DMA)
GLWB .... Glazed Wallboard [*Technical drawings*]
GLWCAP...... Great Lakes Wetlands Conservation Action Plan [*Canada*]
GLWDA .... Great Lakes Waterways Development Association (EA)
GLWPrM....... Corning Del L.P. 6% 'MIPS' [*NYSE symbol*] (TTSB)
GLWQA....... Great Lakes Water Quality Agreement [*Environmental Protection Agency*]
GLWR .... Glassware
GLX .... Galela [*Indonesia*] [*Airport symbol*] (OAG)
GLX .... Glaxo Ltd. ADR [*Formerly, Glaxo Holdilngs Ltd. ADR*] [*NYSE symbol*] (SPSG)
GLX .... Glaxo Wellcome plc ADR [*NYSE symbol*] (TTSB)
Glx .... Glutamic Acid [*or Glutamine*] [*Also, Z An amino acid*]
GLX .... Goldex Mines Ltd. [*Toronto Stock Exchange symbol*]
GLX .... McGill University RECON [*UTLAS symbol*]
GlxyFd .... Galaxy Foods Co. [*Associated Press*] (SAG)
GLY .... Clinton, MO [*Location identifier FAA*] (FAAL)
GLY .... Galaxy Minerals, Inc. [*Toronto Stock Exchange symbol*]
GLY .... Glycerite (STED)
GLY .... Glycerol (STED)
Gly .... Glycerol [*Organic chemistry*] (DAVI)
gly .... Glycinate [*Organic chemistry*]
Gly .... Glycine [*Also, G*] [*An amino acid*]
gly .... Glycine [*An amino acid*] (DOG)
GLY .... Glycocoll (DB)
GLY .... Glycol (KSC)
GLY .... Glycyl (STED)
gly .... Glyph (VRA)
GLY .... Gully (ADA)
GLYC .... Glycerin
glyc........... Glyceritum [*Glycerite*] (MAE)
GLYCEROPH... Glycerophophas [*Pharmacy*] (ROG)
Glyc in W .... Glycerin in Water [*Medicine*] (DHSM)
GLYCN........ Glycerine
GLYCOS Hb.. Glycosylated Hemoglobin (STED)
GLYCYRRH... Glycyrrhiza [*Licorice*] [*Pharmacology*] (ROG)
Gly-IPC .... Glycinergic Interplexiform Cell [*Physiology*]
GLYME........ Ethylene Glycol Dimethyl Ether [*Also, DME, EGDE*] [*Organic chemistry*]
Glyn & J ...... Glyn and Jameson's English Bankruptcy Reports [*1821-28*] [*A publication*] (DLA)
Glyn & Jam... Glyn and Jameson's English Bankruptcy Reports [*1821-28*] [*A publication*] (DLA)
Glyn & J (Eng)... Glyn and Jameson's English Bankruptcy Reports [*1821-28*] [*A publication*] (DLA)
Glynn Wat Pow... Glynn on Water Powers [*A publication*] (DLA)
glypto .... Glypototheca (VRA)
GlyR .... Glycine Receptor [*Organic chemistry*]
GLYT........... Genlyte Group, Inc. [*NASDAQ symbol*] (NQ)
GLZ .... Glaze (MSA)
glz.............. Glaze (VRA)
glz.............. Glazed (VRA)
GLZ .... Great Lakes Group, Inc. [*Toronto Stock Exchange symbol*]
GLZD .... Glazed
GM............. Air America [*ICAO designator*] (AD)
GM............. Gabexate Mesilate [*A proteolytic enzyme inhibitor*]
GM............. Gainesville Midland Railroad Co. [*AAR code*]
G/M............ Gallons per Minute
gm .... Gambia [*MARC country of publication code Library of Congress*] (LCCP)
GM............. Gambia [*ANSI two-letter standard code*] (CNC)
GM............. Gamma [*Third letter of the Greek alphabet*] (DAVI)
Gm............. Gamma [*Subgroup of IgG*] [*Immunology*]
GM............. Gaseous Mixture (MSA)
GM............. Gas Meter
GM............. Gastric Mucosa [*Medicine*]
GM............. Gated Memory (IAA)
GM............. Gay Male [*Classified advertising*]
GM............. Geiger-MHller [*Counter*] (STED)
G-M............ Geiger-Mueller [*Radiation counter*]
GM............. Generalized Myotonia [*Medicine*]
GM............. General Maintenance [*Army*]
GM............. General Maintenance Aptitude Area [*Military*] (AFIT)
GM............. General Manager
GM............. General Medical (MAE)
GM............. General Medicine
GM............. General Meetings [*Quakers*]
GM............. General Merchandise
GM............. General Merit [*Military*]

GM............ General MIDI [*Musical Instrument Digital Interface*] (CDE)
GM............ General Mortgage [*Bond*]
GM............ General Motors Corp. [*NYSE symbol Toronto Stock Exchange symbol*] (SPSG)
GM............ Genetically Modified [*Medicine*] (WDAA)
GM............ Genetic Manipulation [*Medicine*] (DB)
GM............ Genl Motors [*NYSE symbol*] (TTSB)
GM............ Gentamicin [*Antibacterial compound*]
GM............ Gentil Membre [*Guest of Club Mediterranee, a vacation cooperative*]
GM............ Geometric Mean
GM............ George Medal [*British*]
GM............ Giant Melanoma [*Oncology*]
GM............ Giant Melanosome (STED)
gm............ Gigameter
GM............ Gilford-Hutchinson [*Disease*] [*Medicine*] (DB)
GM............ Gill-Morrell [*Valve oscillator*] (DEN)
GM............ Glass Metal (IAA)
GM............ Global Directmail Corp. [*NYSE symbol*] (SAG)
GM............ Global Marketplace
GM............ Gluteus Medius [*Anatomy*]
GM............ Gold Medal
GM............ Gold Medallist (DAS)
GM............ Golf Course Operations and Management Programs [*Association of Independent Colleges and Schools specialization code*]
GM............ Good Mason [*Freemasonry*] (ROG)
GM............ Good Morning [*Amateur radio*]
GM............ Gradient Mixer [*Chromatography*]
GM............ Grail Movement (EA)
GM............ Gram
gm............ Gram (IDOE)
g-m............ Gram-Meter (MAE)
GM............ Gramophone Motor (DEN)
Gm%............ Gram Percent [*Grams per deciliter*] [*Measurement*] (DAVI)
GM............ Grand Mal [*Epilepsy*]
GM............ Grand Marshal [*Freemasonry*] (ROG)
GM............ Grand Master [*Freemasonry*]
GM............ Grand Medal [*Ghana*]
GM............ Grand Minister [*Freemasonry*] (ROG)
GM............ Grandmother
GM............ Grand Multiparity [*Obstetrics*]
GM............ Grant Maintained (WDAA)
GM............ Granulocyte-Macrophage (STED)
G/M............ Granulocyte/Macrophage [*Ratio*] [*Hematology*]
GM............ Granulocyte Monocyte (STED)
GM............ Gravitational Mass
GM............ Greater Manchester [*County in England*]
GM............ Great Musicians [*A publication*]
GM............ Greenwich Meridian
GM............ Grid Modulation
G-M............ Grid-to-Magnetic Angle [*Navigation*] (INF)
GM............ Grog Money [*British military*] (DMA)
GM............ Gross Motor
GM............ Ground Malfunction
GM............ Ground Mode
GM............ Group Mark [*Computer science*]
GM............ Group Mobile (CINC)
GM............ Group MODEM (MCD)
GM............ Group per Message (IAA)
GM............ Growth Management (PA)
GM............ Growth Medium [*Medicine*] (STED)
GM............ Guam [*IYRU nationality code*] (IYR)
GM............ Guard Mail
GM............ Guessed Mean [*Psychology*] (BARN)
GM............ Guided Missile
GM............ Gun-Laying Mark I [*RADAR*]
GM............ Gunmetal
GM............ Gun Mount [*Military*] (CAAL)
GM............ Gunner's Mate [*Navy rating*]
GM............ Gypsy Moths [*An association*] (EA)
GM............ Metacentric Height [*Naval architecture*]
GM............ Monosialoganglioside [*Chemistry*]
Gm............ Mutual Conductance
GM............ Washington Memorial Library, Middle Georgia Regional Library, Macon, GA [*Library symbol Library of Congress*] (LCLS)
GM1............ Gunner's Mate, First Class [*Navy rating*]
GM²............ Grams per Square Meter (WDAA)
GM2............ Gunner's Mate, Second Class [*Navy rating*]
GM3............ Gunner's Mate, Third Class [*Navy rating*]
GM100........ Groupement Mobile 100 [*Elite French armed forces stationed in Vietnam*] (VNW)
GMA............ Gama Aviation Ltd. [*British ICAO designator*] (FAAC)
GMA............ Game Manufacturers Association (EA)
GMA............ Gardner, Mason, and Associates, Inc. (EFIS)
GMA............ Garment Manufacturers' Association [*Australia*]
GMA............ Gas Metal Arc
GMA............ Gated Mode Acquisition [*Telecommunications*] (LAIN)
GMA............ Gemena [*Zaire*] [*Airport symbol*] (OAG)
GMA............ General Maintenance Aptitude [*Military*] (MCD)
GMA............ General Marketing Application
GMA............ General Medical Assistance (TAD)
GMA............ General Mental Ability
GMA............ Geomechanics Abstracts [*Rock Mechanics Information Service*] [*Bibliographic database*] [*British*]
GMA............ Giant Molecular Association [*Galactic science*]

GMA............ Gilt Market Analysis [*MMS International*] [*Information service or system*] (CRD)
GMA............ Glyceryl Methacrylate [*Organic chemistry*] (DAVI)
GMA............ Glycidyl Methacrylate [*Organic chemistry*]
GMA............ Glycol Methacrylate [*Organic chemistry*]
GMA............ Good Morning America [*Television program*]
GMA............ Gospel Music Association (EA)
GMA............ Government Modification Authorization (AAG)
GMA............ Grail Movement of Australia
GMA............ Granite Mountain [*Alaska*] [*Seismograph station code, US Geological Survey*] (SEIS)
GMA............ Grizzle Methacrylate (EDCT)
GMA............ Grocery Manufacturers Association (COE)
GMA............ Grocery Manufacturers of America (EA)
GMA............ Grocery Manufacturers of Australia (EERA)
GMA............ Gross Motor Activities (HGAA)
GM/A............ Ground Meat/Analyzer [*USDA*]
GMA............ Growth and Maturation Activity [*Biochemistry*]
GMA............ Growth Management Act
GMA............ Guided Missile Ammunition (AABC)
GMA............ Whitefield, NH [*Location identifier FAA*] (FAAL)
GMAA............ Agadir/Inezgane [*Morocco*] [*ICAO location identifier*] (ICLI)
GMAA............ Gold Mining Association of America
GMAA............ Graduate Management Association of Australia
GMAB............ Guided Missile Assembly Building (SAA)
GMAC............ Gaining Motor Air Command (MCD)
GMAC............ Gas Metal Arc Cutting [*Welding*]
GMAC............ General Motors Acceptance Corp.
GMAC............ Genetic Manipulation Advisory Committee (EERA)
GMAC............ Graduate Management Admission Council [*Los Angeles, CA*] (EA)
GMAD............ General Motors Allison Division
GMAD............ General Motors Assembly Division
GMAG............ Genetic Manipulation Advisory Group [*British*]
GMagic........ General Magic, Inc. [*Associated Press*] (SAG)
GMAI............ Greg Manning Auctions [*NASDAQ symbol*] (TTSB)
GMAI............ Greg Manning Auctions, Inc. [*NASDAQ symbol*] (SAG)
GMAI............ Manning [*Greg*] Auctions, Inc. [*NASDAQ symbol*] (SAG)
GMAIC............ Guided Missile and Aerospace Intelligence Committee (AFM)
GMAIW........ Greg Manning Auctions Wrrt [*NASDAQ symbol*] (TTSB)
GMAJCOM... Gaining Major Command [*Military*] (AFM)
GMAL............ General Electric Macro Assembly Language (NASA)
GM & N...... Gulf Mobile & Northern Railroad
GM & O...... Gulf, Mobile & Ohio Railroad [*Later, Illinois Central Gulf Railroad*]
GM & S...... General Medicine and Surgery
GMann........ Greg Manning Auctions, Inc. [*Associated Press*] (SAG)
GMann........ Manning [*Greg*] Auctions, Inc. [*Associated Press*] (SAG)
GManning.... Greg Manning Auctions, Inc. [*Associated Press*] (SAG)
GMmanning... Manning [*Greg*] Auctions, Inc. [*Associated Press*] (SAG)
GMAP......... Generalized Macroprocessor
GMAP......... General Macroassembly Program [*Honeywell, Inc.*]
GMarC......... Cobb County-Marietta Public Library, Marietta, GA [*Library symbol Library of Congress*] (LCLS)
GMarK......... Kennesaw College, Marietta, GA [*Library symbol Library of Congress*] (LCLS)
GMarLC...... Life College, Marietta, GA [*Library symbol*] [*Library of Congress*] (LCLS)
GMarLG...... Lockheed-Georgia Co., Scientific and Technical Information Department, Marietta,GA [*Library symbol Library of Congress*] (LCLS)
GMarRR...... Reid-Rowell, Marietta, GA [*Library symbol*] [*Library of Congress*] (LCLS)
GMarS......... Southern Technical Institute, Marietta, GA [*Library symbol Library of Congress*] (LCLS)
GMAS......... Glovers' Mutual Aid Society [*A union*] [*British*]
GMAS......... Ground Munitions Analysis Study (AABC)
GMasec...... Grupo Industrial Maseca SA de CV [*Associated Press*] (SAG)
GMaseca.... Grupo Industrial Maseca SA de CV [*Associated Press*] (SAG)
GMASI........ Graduate Member of the Ambulance Service Institute [*British*] (DBQ)
GMason...... George Mason Bankshares [*Commercial firm Associated Press*] (SAG)
GMAT......... General Management Administration Test (WDAA)
GMAT......... General Mathematical Aptitude Test (BARN)
GMAT......... Graduate Management Admission Test
GMAT......... Greenwich Mean Astronomical Time
GMAT......... Tan-Tan/Plage Blanche [*Morocco*] [*ICAO location identifier*] (ICLI)
GMATS....... General Motors Air Transport System
GMAW....... Gas Metal Arc Welding
GMAWA...... Glass Merchants' Association of Western Australia
GMAW-P.... Gas Metal Arc Welding - Pulsed Arc
GMAW-S.... Gas Metal Arc Welding - Short Circuiting Arc
GMAX........ Graphics Multi-Axis Module [*McDonnell-Douglas Automation Co.*]
GMAZ........ Zagora [*Morocco*] [*ICAO location identifier*] (ICLI)
GMB............ Gambela [*Ethiopia*] [*Airport symbol*] (OAG)
GMB............ Gambia [*ANSI three-letter standard code*] (CNC)
GMB............ Gastric Mucosal Barrier (DB)
GMB............ General Mortgage Bond
GMB............ General, Municipal Boilermakers (WDAA)
GMB............ General Municipal Boilermakers and Allied Trades Union (WA)
GMB............ Glass Microballoon (MCD)
GMB............ Global Management Bureau
GMB............ Good Merchantable Brand [*Business term*]
GMB............ Good Morning Britain [*Early morning television program*] [*ITV*] [*British*]
GMB............ Grand Master of the Bath [*British*]
GMB............ Green Mountain Boy [*Pseudonym used by Henry Stevens*]

GMB............	Guided Missile Brigade [Army]
GMBATU......	General Municipal Boilermakers' and Allied Trades Union [British]
GMBE..........	Grand Master of the Order of the British Empire (EY)
GMBF..........	Gastric Mucosal Blood Flow [Medicine]
GmbH..........	Gesellschaft mit Beschraenkter Haftung [Limited Liability Company] [German]
GmbH & CoKG...	Gesellschaft mit Beschraenkter Haftung und Kommanditgesellschaft [Combined Limited Partnership and Limited Liability Company] [German]
GmbHG........	Gesetz Betreffend der Gesellschaft mit Beschraenkter Haftung [Law Governing Limited Liability Company] [German] (ILCA)
GMBIM	Genetics and Molecular Biology of Industrial Microorganisms [Conference]
GMBL..........	Gimbal (AAG)
GMBS	George Mason Bankshares [NASDAQ symbol] (SAG)
GMBS	Glenn Miller Birthplace Society (EA)
GMC...........	Ganglion Mother Cell [Cytology]
GMC...........	General Management Committee (WDAA)
GMC...........	General Medical Council [British]
GmC...........	General Microfilm Co., Cambridge, MA [Library symbol Library of Congress] (LCLS)
GMC...........	General Military Course (AFM)
GMC...........	General Monte Carlo Code [Computer science]
GMC...........	General Motors Corp. [ICAO designator] (FAAC)
GMC...........	Geological Museum of China [China]
GMC...........	Georgia Military College [Milledgeville]
GMC...........	Geostar Mining Corp. [Vancouver Stock Exchange symbol]
GMC...........	Germanic [Language, etc.]
GMC...........	Giant Molecular Cloud [Cosmology]
GMC...........	Gold Master Candidate [Compact-disc manufacturing]
GMC...........	Gordon Military College [Georgia]
GMC...........	Great Midwestern Conference [College reports]
GMC...........	Grivet Monkey Cell Line
GMC...........	Gross Maximum Capacity [Electronics] (IEEE)
GMC...........	Ground Mobile Cenetheodolite
GMC...........	Ground Movement Controller
GMC...........	Groundwater Management Caucus (EA)
GMC...........	Guaranteed Mortgage Certificate [Federal Home Loan Mortgage Corp.]
GMC...........	Guard-Cell Mother Cell [Botany]
GMC...........	Guided Missile Committee [Army]
GMC...........	Guided Missile Control (AAG)
GMC...........	Guild of Memorial Craftsmen [British] (BI)
GMC...........	Gun Motor Carriage
GMC...........	Gunner's Mate, Chief [Navy rating]
GMC...........	Middle Georgia College, Cochran, GA [OCLC symbol] (OCLC)
gm-cal........	Gram Calorie (IDOE)
GMCB.........	Gunner's Mate, Construction Battalion [Navy rating]
GMCBA.......	Gunner's Mate, Construction Battalion, Armorer [Navy rating]
GMCBP.......	Gunner's Mate, Construction Battalion, Powderman [Navy rating]
GMCC........	General Magnaplate Corp. [NASDAQ symbol] (NQ)
GMCC........	General NAS Maintenance Control Center [FAA] (TAG)
GMCC........	Genl Magnaplate [NASDAQ symbol] (TTSB)
GMCC........	Geophysical Monitoring for Climate Change (EERA)
GMCC........	Geophysical Monitoring for Climatic Change [National Oceanic and Atmospheric Administration]
GMCC........	Global Monitoring for Climatic Change [Environmental science] (COE)
GMCC........	Ground Mobile Command Center
GMCF........	Goddard Mission Control Facility [NASA] (KSC)
GMCF........	Guided Missile Control Facility (AAG)
GMCI.........	Giftware Manufacturers' Credit Interchange (EA)
GMCL........	Ground Measurements Command List (MCD)
gm-cm........	Gram-Centimeter (IDOE)
GMCM........	Guided Missile Countermeasure [NATO]
GMCM........	Gunner's Mate, Master Chief [Navy rating]
GMCO........	Guided Missile Control Officer (AAG)
GMCP.........	Guided Missile Control Party (IAA)
GMCR........	Globe Mackay Cable and Radio Corp. [Philippines] [Telecommunications]
GMCR........	Green Mountain Coffee [Commercial firm NASDAQ symbol] (SAG)
GMCRF.......	General Motors Cancer Research Foundation (HGEN)
GMCS........	Gunner's Mate, Senior Chief [Navy rating]
GM-CSA.....	Granulocyte-Macrophage Colony-Stimulating Activity [Hematology]
GM-CSF.....	Granulocyte-Macrophage Colony-Stimulating Factor [Biochemistry]
GMCT........	Giftware Manufacturers Credit Interchange (EA)
GMCY........	Grant-Makers for Children and Youth (EA)
GMD..........	Forschungszentrum Informationstechnik GmbH [National research center for informatics, communication, and media] [Germany] (DDC)
GMD	General Management Directive
GMD	General Marine Distress
GMD	General Material Designation
GMD	Genomic Map Design (HGEN)
GMD	Geometric Mean Distance
GMD	Geometrodynamics
GMD	Gesellschaft fuer Mathematik und Datenverarbeitung [Society for Mathematics and Data Processing] [Germany Information service or system] (IID)
GMD	Glycopeptide Moiety Modified Derivative (DB)
GMD	Government Maintenance Depot (MCD)
GMD	Ground Meteorological Detector [or Device]
GMD	Groupo Mexicano Desarrollo [NYSE symbol] (SPSG)
GMD	Grupo Mex de Desarrollo 'L'ADS [NYSE symbol] (TTSB)
GMD	Grupo Mexicano Desarrollo [NYSE symbol] (SAG)

GMDA.........	Golf Manufacturers and Distributors Association (EA)
GMDA.........	Groundwater Management Districts Association (EA)
GMDA.........	Group Method of Determining Arguments [Equation]
GMDC.........	General Merchandise Distributors Council [Colorado Springs, CO] (EA)
GMDD........	Guided Missile Development Division [NASA] (KSC)
GMDEP.......	Guided Missile Data Exchange Program [Navy]
GMDesB	Grupo Mexicano Desarrollo [Associated Press] (SAG)
GMDH........	Group Method of Data Handling [Mathematical technique]
GMDIL	General Motors Distribution Ireland Ltd. [Dublin, Ireland]
GMD-IZ	GMD-Informationszentrum fuer Informationswissenschaft und -Praxis [GMD Information Center for Information Science and Information Work] [Information service or system] (IID)
GMDP.........	Guaranteed Minimum Delivery Price (ADA)
GMDRL	General Motors Defense Research Laboratory (MCD)
GMDS	German Military Documents Section [of AGO, Army] [World War II]
GMDSS	Global Maritime Distress and Safety System (DA)
GM Dud	Dudley's Georgia Reports [A publication] (DLA)
GM Dudl	Dudley's Georgia Reports [A publication] (DLA)
GME..........	Gelatine Manufacturers of Europe (EAIO)
GME..........	General Microelectronics
GME..........	General Motors Corp. [NYSE symbol] (SAG)
GME..........	General Motors Europe
GME..........	Generic Macro Expander [Telecommunications] (TEL)
GME..........	Genl Motors CI'E' [NYSE symbol] (TTSB)
GME..........	German Minimum Economy [Allied German Occupation Forces]
GME..........	Gilt Marbled Edges [Bookbinding]
GME..........	Gimbal Mounted Electronics (KSC)
GME..........	Glimmer Resources, Inc. [Vancouver Stock Exchange symbol]
GME..........	Globe Microphone Evaluation
GME..........	Gmelinite [A zeolite]
GME..........	Graduate Medical Education [Program] [Army]
GME..........	Greater Middle East
GME..........	Great Meteor East [Nuclear energy] (NUCP)
GME..........	Green, M. E., Jefferson City MO [STAC]
GME..........	Group Modulation Equipment (IAA)
GME..........	Guided Missile Evaluator
GMED	GeneMedicine, Inc. [NASDAQ symbol] (SAG)
GM/EDS	General Motors Electronic Data Systems (NITA)
GMEFC.......	Golden Memories of Elvis Fan Club (EA)
GMEI.........	Gulf of Mexico Estuarine Inventory (PDAA)
GMEL.........	Groupement des Mathematiciens d'Expression Latine [Group of Mathematicians of Romance Languages - GMRL] (EAIO)
G-MEM.......	General Memory (NAKS)
GMEM........	GPC [General Purpose Computer] Memory (NASA)
GMENAC	Graduate Medical Education National Advisory Committee [Department of Health and Human Services]
GME-PC	General Motors Europe - Passenger Cars [Switzerland]
GMERD	Government Minimum Essential Requirements Document
GMET........	Graphical Munitions Effects Tables (MCD)
GMET........	Gun Metal
GMetO	Group Meteorological Officer [British military] (DMA)
GMEV........	General Motors Electric Vehicle [General Motors Corp]
GMEVALU ...	Guided Missile Evaluation Unit (MUGU)
GMexDes.....	Grupo Mexicano Desarrollo [Associated Press] (SAG)
GMF..........	Galactic Magnetic Field
GMF..........	Generalized Mainline Framework [Computer science]
GMF..........	General Motors Corp. and Fanuc Ltd. [In company name GMF Robotics Corp.]
GMF..........	Glass Manufacturers Federation
GMF..........	Glass Microfilter
GMF..........	Glial Maturation Factor [Biochemistry]
GMF..........	Global Matching Figures Test [Education] (EDAC)
GMF..........	Ground Mobile Forces [Military] (RDA)
GMF..........	Ground Monitor Facility (MCD)
GMF..........	Guided Missile Facilities (NG)
GMF..........	Milwaukee, WI [Location identifier FAA] (FAAL)
GMFA.........	Ouezzane [Morocco] [ICAO location identifier] (ICLI)
GMFC.........	Gary Morris Fan Club (EA)
GMFC.........	Guided Missile Fire Control
GMFCS	Guided Missile Fire Control System (NG)
GMFF.........	Fes/Saiss [Morocco] [ICAO location identifier] (ICLI)
GMFI.........	Ifrane [Morocco] [ICAO location identifier] (ICLI)
GMFJ.........	Ghana Movement of Freedom and Justice [Political party]
GMFK.........	Er-Rachidia [Morocco] [ICAO location identifier] (ICLI)
GMFM........	Meknes/Bassatine [Morocco] [ICAO location identifier] (ICLI)
GMFMC	Gulf of Mexico Fishery Management Council (MSC)
GMFN........	Nador/Taouima [Morocco] [ICAO location identifier] (ICLI)
GMFO........	Oujda/Angads [Morocco] [ICAO location identifier] (ICLI)
GMFP.........	Guided Missile Firing Panel
GMFS........	Ground Mobile Forces/Tactical Satellite Communications Program
GMFSC	Ground Mobile Forces Satellite Communications (MCD)
GMFT........	Touahar [Morocco] [ICAO location identifier] (ICLI)
GMF/TACSAT...	Ground Mobile Forces/Tactical Satellite Communications (MCD)
GMFU........	Fes/Sefrou [Morocco] [ICAO location identifier] (ICLI)
GMFZ........	Taza [Morocco] [ICAO location identifier] (ICLI)
GMG	Gott Mein Gut [God Is My Good] [Motto of Karl, Margrave of Baden-Durlach (1529-77); Ernst Friedrich, (1560-1604)] [German]
GMG	Grand Metropolitan and Guinness [Proposed company]
GMG	Grenade Machine Gun [Military]
GMG	Gross Maximum Generation [Electronics] (IEEE)
GMG	Gunner's Mate, Guns [Navy rating]
GMG1.........	Gunner's Mate, Guns, First Class [Navy rating] (DNAB)
GMG2.........	Gunner's Mate, Guns, Second Class [Navy rating] (DNAB)
GMG3.........	Gunner's Mate, Guns, Third Class [Navy rating] (DNAB)

GMGB .... Guards Machine Gun Battalion [*British military*] (DMA)
GMGC .... General Magic, Inc. [*NASDAQ symbol*] (SAG)
GMGC .... Gunner's Mate, Guns, Chief [*Navy rating*] (DNAB)
GMGR .... Guards Machine Gun Regiment [*British military*] (DMA)
GMGRU .... Guided Missile Group (MUGU)
GMGS .... Guided Missile General Support (MCD)
GMGSA .... Gunner's Mate, Guns, Seaman Apprentice [*Navy rating*] (DNAB)
GMGSN .... Gunner's Mate, Guns, Seaman [*Navy rating*] (DNAB)
GMH .... General Motors Corp. [*NYSE symbol*] (SAG)
GMH .... General Motors-Holden's Ltd. [*Australia*] (ADA)
GMH .... Georgia Mental Health Institute, Atlanta, GA [*OCLC symbol*] (OCLC)
gmh .... German, Middle High [*MARC language code Library of Congress*] (LCCP)
GMH .... Germinal Matrix Hemorrhage [*Medicine*] (DMAA)
GMH .... Greenville, KY [*Location identifier FAA*] (FAAL)
GMH .... Hughes Aircraft Co. (Aeronautical Operations) [*ICAO designator*] (FAAC)
GMHC .... Gay Men's Health Crisis (EA)
GMHC .... Grease Monkey Hldg [*NASDAQ symbol*] (TTSB)
GMHC .... Grease Monkey Holding Corp. [*NASDAQ symbol*] (NQ)
GMHE .... General Motors Hughes Electronics Corp.
GMI .... Galtaco, Inc. [*Toronto Stock Exchange symbol*]
GMI .... Garnes Mountain [*Idaho*] [*Seismograph station code, US Geological Survey*] (SEIS)
GMI .... Gasmata [*Papua New Guinea*] [*Airport symbol*] (OAG)
GMI .... Gelatin Manufacturers Institute of America (EA)
GMI .... Gemini Fund, Inc. [*NYSE symbol*] (SPSG)
GMI .... Gemini II [*NYSE symbol*] (TTSB)
GMI .... General Media International
GMI .... General Medical Intelligence (MCD)
GMI .... General Mills, Incorporated, Minneapolis, MN [*OCLC symbol*] (OCLC)
GMI .... General Motors Institute
GMI .... Genini II Fund [*NYSE symbol*] (SAG)
GMI .... Germania Fluggesellschaft Koln [*Germany ICAO designator*] (FAAC)
GMI .... Global Marine, Inc. (NOAA)
GMI .... Goddard Management Instruction [*NASA*]
g/mi .... Gram per Mile [*Automotive engineering*]
GMI .... Guaranteed Minimum Income (ADA)
GMI .... Guarantee Material Inspection (MCD)
GMIA .... Gelatin Manufacturers Institute of America (EA)
GMIC .... Graphic Memory Interface Controller [*Computer chip*]
GMIE .... Grand Master of the Order of the Indian Empire [*British*]
GMI-EMI ..... General Motors Institute - Engineering and Management Institute [*Flint, MI*]
GMIF .... Gandhi Memorial International Foundation (EA)
GMIFC .... George Michael International Fan Club (EA)
GMII .... Guaranteed Market Index Investment [*Canada*]
GMiM.......... Georgia Military College, Milledgeville, GA [*Library symbol Library of Congress*] (LCLS)
GMI Mech E... Graduate Member of the Institution of Mechanical Engineers [*British*]
GMIP .... General Motors Improvement Project [*Investigating team sponsored by consumer-advocate Ralph Nader*]
GMIPr .... Gemini II cm Income Shrs [*NYSE symbol*] (TTSB)
GMIS .... Generalized Management Information System
GMIS .... GMIS, Inc. [*NASDAQ symbol*] (SPSG)
GMIS .... Government Management Information Sciences (EA)
GMIS .... Grants Management Information System [*Department of Health and Human Services*] (GFGA)
GMISCA .... General Motors Information System and Communications Activity (HGAA)
GMiW .... Georgia College, Milledgeville, GA [*Library symbol Library of Congress*] (LCLS)
GMJ .... Macon Junior College, Macon, GA [*Library symbol Library of Congress*] (LCLS)
GMJC .... Green Mountain Junior College [*Vermont*]
GMJSU .... Gems, Minerals, and Jewelry Study Unit (EA)
GMK .... Gold Mark Minerals [*Vancouver Stock Exchange symbol*]
GMK.......... Grand Master Key [*Locks*] (ADA)
GMK.......... Green Monkey Kidney Cell
GMK.......... Gyromagnetic Kompass
GMKP .... Grand Master of the Knights of St. Patrick
GMKT......... Global Market Information, Inc. [*NASDAQ symbol*] (SAG)
GML .... Galvanometer-Mirror Lightbeam
GML .... Gemial [*Slovakia*] [*ICAO designator*] (FAAC)
GML .... Generalized Markup Language [*Computer science*]
GML .... General Measurement Loop (MCD)
GML .... Generic Markup Language (NITA)
GML .... Global DirectMail [*NYSE symbol*] (TTSB)
GML .... Glycerol Monolaurate [*Food-grade lipid*] [*Pharmacology*]
GML .... Gold Maple Leaf [*Canadian coin*]
GML .... Gold-Medal Resources Ltd. [*Vancouver Stock Exchange symbol*]
GML .... Gorgas Memorial Laboratory [*Panama*] [*Research center*] (RCD)
gm/l .... Grams per Liter (MAE)
GML .... Grand Master's Lodge [*Freemasonry*] (ROG)
GML .... Graphic Machine Language
GML .... Guided Missile Launcher (NG)
GML .... Mercer University, Law Library, Macon, GA [*OCLC symbol*] (OCLC)
GMLDG .... Garnish Molding [*Mechanical engineering*]
GMLR .... Guided Missile and Large Rocket
GMLS .... Guided Missile Launching System
GMLSC .... Guided Missile Launching System Control (DWSG)
GMM .... Galvanomagnetic Method (IAA)
GMM .... Gamboma [*Congo*] [*Airport symbol*] (AD)
GMM.......... General Matrix Manipulator (OA)

GMM .... General Methods of Moments [*Statistics*]
GMM .... Geometric Math Model (SSD)
GMM .... Glucose Monomycolate [*Biochemistry*]
GMM .... Goldberg-Maxwell-Morris [*Syndrome*] [*Medicine*] (DB)
GMM .... Goldberg-Maxwell-Morris [*Syndrome*] (STED)
GMM .... Goldsmith Minerals [*Vancouver Stock Exchange symbol*]
gm-m .... Gram Meter
GMM .... Graphical Multi-Meter
GMM .... Graphics Mill Module [*McDonnell-Douglas Corp.*]
GMM .... Gunner's Mate, Missile [*Navy rating*]
GMM .... Mercer University, Macon, GA [*Library symbol Library of Congress*] (LCLS)
GMM .... Mercer University, School of Medicine, Macon, GA [*OCLC symbol*] (OCLC)
GMM1 .... Gunner's Mate, Missile, First Class [*Navy rating*] (DNAB)
GMM2......... Gunner's Mate, Missile, Second Class [*Navy rating*] (DNAB)
GMM3......... Gunner's Mate, Missile, Third Class [*Navy rating*] (DNAB)
GMMA .... Gas Meter Makers' Association [*A union*] [*British*]
GMMA .... Gloucester Master Mariners Association (EA)
GMMA .... Golda Meir Memorial Association (EA)
GMMB .... Ben Slimane [*Morocco*] [*ICAO location identifier*] (ICLI)
GMMC......... Casablanca/ANFA [*Morocco*] [*ICAO location identifier*] (ICLI)
GMMC .... Gunner's Mate, Missile, Chief [*Navy rating*] (DNAB)
GMMD .... Beni-Mellal [*Morocco*] [*ICAO location identifier*] (ICLI)
GMME .... Rabat/Sale [*Morocco*] [*ICAO location identifier*] (ICLI)
GMMF......... Sidi Ifni [*Morocco*] [*ICAO location identifier*] (ICLI)
GMMG .... Grand Master of the Order of St. Michael and St. George [*British*]
GMMI .... Essaouira [*Morocco*] [*ICAO location identifier*] (ICLI)
GMMJ .... El Jadida [*Morocco*] [*ICAO location identifier*] (ICLI)
GMMK .... Khouribga [*Morocco*] [*ICAO location identifier*] (ICLI)
GMML .... Ground Master Measurements List
GMM-L .... Mercer University, School of Law, Macon, GA [*Library symbol Library of Congress*] (LCLS)
GMMM .... Casablanca [*Morocco*] [*ICAO location identifier*] (ICLI)
GMMN .... Casablanca/Mohamed V [*Morocco*] [*ICAO location identifier*] (ICLI)
GMMO .... Taroudant [*Morocco*] [*ICAO location identifier*] (ICLI)
GM MOL ...... Gram-Molecule (WDAA)
GMMR .... General Mobilization Material Readiness [*DoD*]
GMMRI .... Georgia Mining and Mineral Research Institute [*Georgia Institute of Technology*] [*Research center*] (RCD)
GMMS .... Safi [*Morocco*] [*ICAO location identifier*] (ICLI)
GMMSA .... Gunner's Mate, Missile, Seaman Apprentice [*Navy rating*] (DNAB)
GMMSN .... Gunner's Mate, Missile, Seaman [*Navy rating*] (DNAB)
GMMT......... Casablanca/Tit-Mellil [*Morocco*] [*ICAO location identifier*] (ICLI)
GMMX .... Marrakech/Menara [*Morocco*] [*ICAO location identifier*] (ICLI)
GMMY .... Kenitra/Tourisme [*Morocco*] [*ICAO location identifier*] (ICLI)
GMMZ .... Quarzazate [*Morocco*] [*ICAO location identifier*] (ICLI)
GMN .... Gorman [*TACAN station*] (MCD)
GMN .... Gorman, CA [*Location identifier FAA*] (FAAL)
GMN .... Greenman Brothers, Inc. [*AMEX symbol*] (SPSG)
GMN .... Greenwich Mean Noon (ROG)
GMNA .... Glutamyl(methoxy)naphthylamide [*Biochemistry*]
GmNE .... Graphic Microfilm of New England, Waltham, MA [*Library symbol Library of Congress*] (LCLS)
GmNY .... Graphic Microfilm Corp., Valley Stream, NY [*Library symbol Library of Congress*] (LCLS)
GMO .... Gadolinium Molybdate
GMO .... General Medical Officer [*Navy*] (DNAB)
GMO .... Genetically-Manipulated Organism [*Biochemistry*]
GMO .... Genetically Modified Organism [*Biochemistry*]
GMO .... Gill-Morrell Oscillator
GMO .... Glyceryl Monooleate [*Organic chemistry*]
GMO .... Groupe de Travail Charge de la Mise en Oeuvre de l'Information et de la Statistique Juridique [*Implementation Work Group on Justice Information and Statistics - IWG*] [*Canada*]
GMO .... Guided Missile Officer
GMO .... Gulf, Mobile & Ohio Railroad [*Later, Illinois Central Gulf Railroad*] [*AAR code*]
GMoC......... Colquitt-Thomas Regional Library, Moultrie, GA [*Library symbol Library of Congress*] (LCLS)
GMOC .... General Motors Corp. (EFIS)
GMOCU .... Guided Missile Operation and Control Unit
GMODC .... General Motors Overseas Distribution Corp.
GMOL .... Gram Molecule [*or Molecular*] [*Chemistry*] (IAA)
g-mol......... Gram-Molecule (STED)
GMOO .... Guided Missile Operations Officer (AAG)
GMorC .... Clayton Junior College, Morrow, GA [*Library symbol*] [*Library of Congress*] (LCLS)
GMorGE .... Genealogical Enterprises, Morrow, GA [*Library symbol Library of Congress*] (LCLS)
GMOS .... Generic Message Orientation System (SSD)
GMOs.......... Genetically Manipulated Organisms (EERA)
GMot.......... General Motors Corp. [*Associated Press*] (SAG)
GMOV .... Glycine Mottle Virus [*Plant pathology*]
GMP.......... Gap Media Project [*An association*] (EA)
GMP.......... Garrison Military Police [*British*]
GMP.......... Gay Men's Press [*GMP is now the name of the company*]
GMP.......... Gemini Management Panel [*NASA*] (KSC)
GMP.......... General Management Plan [*National Park Service*]
GMP.......... General Matrix Program
GMP.......... General Medical Practice (WDAA)
GMP.......... General Medical Problem
GMP.......... Geometric Modelling Project [*Software*] [*British*] (NITA)
GMP.......... Georgia Milk Producers (SRA)

GMP............ Glass, Molders, Pottery, Plastics, and Allied Workers International Union (NTPA)
GMP............ Glycomacropeptide [*Biochemistry*]
G-MP .... G-Myeloma Protein [*Biochemistry*] (MAH)
G-MP .... G-Myeloma Proteins [*Biochemistry*] (DAVI)
GMP............ Good Management Practice
GMP............ Good Manufacturing Practice
GMP............ Grand Master of the Order of St. Patrick
GMP............ Granule Membrane Protein
GMP............ Grass-Model Polygraph
GMP............ Green Mountain Power Corp. [*NYSE symbol*] (SPSG)
GMP............ Green Mountain Pwr [*NYSE symbol*] (TTSB)
GMP............ Ground Map Pencil (DNAB)
GMP............ Ground Movement Planner [*Aviation*] (OA)
GMP............ Groundwater Modeling Program [*US Army Engineer Waterways Experiment Station*] (RDA)
GMP............ Guanosine Monophosphate [*Biochemistry*]
GMP............ Guanylic Acid (STED)
GMP............ Guaranteed Minimum Pension [*British*]
GMP............ Guaranteed Minimum Price
GMP............ Guild of Metal Perforators [*British*] (DBA)
GMP............ Gurkha Military Police [*British military*] (DMA)
GMPA .... Game Meat Processors of Australia
GMPA .... General Material and Petroleum Activity [*NCAD*] [*Army*] (MCD)
GMPC .... Green Mountain Power Corp. (NRCH)
GMPCS .... Global Mobile Personal Communications System [*International Telecommunications Union*] [*Geneva, Switzerland*] (ECON)
GMPG .... General Motors Proving Grounds [*Automotive engineering*]
GMPI .... Guilford-Martin Personnel Inventory [*Psychology*]
GMPMA .... General Material and Petroleum Management Agency (MCD)
GMPPAW ..... Glass, Molders, Pottery, Plastics, and Allied Workers International Union (EA)
GMPR .... General Maximum Price Regulation [*World War II*]
GMPrD .... General Motors 7.92% Dep Pfd [*NYSE symbol*] (TTSB)
GMPrG .... General Motors 9.12% Dep Pfd [*NYSE symbol*] (TTSB)
GMPrQ .... General Motors 9.125% Dep Pfd [*NYSE symbol*] (TTSB)
GMPS .... Great Masters in Painting and Sculpture [*A publication*]
GMPT .... Gum Print [*Gum bichromates*] (VRA)
GMQ .... Geomaque Explorations Ltd. [*Toronto Stock Exchange symbol*]
GMQ .... Good Marketable Quality [*Business term*]
GMR .... Gallops, Murmurs, or Rubs [*Medicine*] (STED)
GMR .... Gambier Island [*French Polynesia*] [*Airport symbol*] (OAG)
GMR .... General Mobilization Reserves [*DoD*]
GMR .... General Modular Redundancy
GMR .... General Motors Research
GMR .... Geometric Mean Radii
GMR .... Giant Magnetoresistance [*Materials science*]
GMR .... Giant Magnetoresistive (CDE)
GMR .... Graduated Mobilization Response (DOMA)
GMR .... Grampian Helicopter Charter Ltd. [*British ICAO designator*] (FAAC)
GMR .... Graphics Metafile Resources [*Computer science*]
GMR .... Greater Manchester Radio [*England*] (WDAA)
GMR .... Ground Mapping RADAR
GMR .... Ground Mobile RADAR
GMR .... Ground Movement RADAR [*Military*]
GMR .... Group Medical Report
GMR .... Grupo Marxista Revolucionario [*Marxist Revolutionary Group*] [*Portuguese Political party*] (PPE)
GMRAO .... General Mobilization Reserve Acquisition Objective [*DoD*]
GMRC .... Green Mountain Railroad Corp. [*AAR code*]
GMRD .... Guards Motorized Rifle Division (MCD)
GMRD .... Guided Missile Range Division [*NASA*] (KSC)
GMRE .... General Motors Rotary Engine [*Automotive engineering*]
GMRK .... Gulfmark International [*NASDAQ symbol*] (SPSG)
GMRL .... General Motors Corp. Research Laboratories [*Warren, MI*]
GMRL .... Grain Marketing Research Laboratory [*Manhattan, KS*] [*Department of Agriculture*] (GRD)
GMRL .... Group of Mathematicians of Romance Languages [*See also GMEL*] [*Coimbra, Portugal*] (EAIO)
GMRMLN ..... Greater Midwest Regional Medical Library Network [*Illinois, Kentucky, Michigan, Ohio, S. Dakota*] (NITA)
GMRMO .... General Mobilization Reserve Materiel Objective [*DoD*]
GMRMR .... General Mobilization Reserve Materiel Requirement [*DoD*]
GMROI .... Gross Margin Return on Investment [*Air carrier designation symbol*]
GMRS .... General Mobile Radio Service [*Telecommunications*] (TSSD)
GMRS .... General Mobilization Reserve Stock [*DoD*]
GMRS .... Ground Marker Release System [*Army*] (INF)
GMRSO .... General Mobilization Reserve Stockage Objective [*DoD*]
GMRT .... Gates MacGinitie Reading Test [*Educational test*]
GMRT .... Giant Meterwave Radio Telescope [*India*]
GMRWG .... Guided Missile Relay Working Group [*Navy*]
GMS............ Gabriel Marcel Society (EA)
GMS............ Galvanized Mild Steel (EDCT)
GMS............ Gas Measurement System
GMCS .... Gelatin Matrix System
GMS............ Gemini Mission Simulator [*NASA*]
GMS............ General Maintenance System [*Computer science*] (BUR)
GMS............ General Material Services
GMS............ General Medical Service (STED)
GMS............ General Medical Services [*British*]
GMS............ General Micro Systems Ltd. (NITA)
GMS............ General Military Science
GMS............ General Milk Sales [*Inactive*] [*An association*] (EA)
GMS............ Generation Management Station
GMS............ Genomic Mismatch Scanning [*Genetic technique*]

GMS............ Geophysical Monitoring Satellite [*DoD, NOAA*]
GMS............ George MacDonald Society [*Lincoln, England*] (EAIO)
GMS............ Geostationary Meteorological Satellite [*Japan*]
GMS............ Geriatric Mental State [*Medicine*] (DMAA)
GMS............ Giant Motor Synapse [*Anatomy*]
GMS............ Gichner Mobile Shelters (MCD)
GMS............ Gilbert-Meulengracht Syndrome [*Medicine*] (DMAA)
GMS............ Gilbert M. Smith Herbarium [*Stanford University*] [*Pacific Grove, CA*]
GMS............ Glen Miller Society (EAIO)
GMS............ Glyceryl Monostearate [*Organic chemistry*]
GMS............ Gomori Methenamine Silver Stain [*Medicine*] (DMAA)
GMS............ Gomori's Methenamine Silver [*A biological stain*]
GMS............ Goniodysgenesis-Mental Retardation-Short Stature Syndrome [*Medicine*] (DMAA)
GMS............ Grant Maintained School (AIE)
GMS............ Grant Maintained Schools [*British*] (DET)
GMS............ Grant-Maintained Status (ODBW)
G/MS........... Graphics and/or Media Specialist
GMS............ Gravitational Mass Sensor
GMS............ Gravity Measuring System
GMS............ Greater Mekong Sub-Region [*East Asian development zone*]
GMS............ Ground Maintenance Support
GMS............ Ground Mapping [*or Marking*] System
GMS............ Groundwater Modeling System
GMS............ Group Membership Scores [*Psychometrics*]
GMS............ Guardian-Morton Shulman Precious Metals, Inc. [*Toronto Stock Exchange symbol Vancouver Stock Exchange symbol*]
GMS............ Guidance Monitor Set [*Aerospace*] (AAG)
GMS............ Guided Missile School [*Dam Neck, VA*]
GMSA .... Guided Missile Simulator [*Military*] (CAAL)
GMS............ Guided Missile System
GMS............ Master Construction Specification [*Canada*]
GMS............ Morehouse College, School of Medicine, Atlanta, GA [*OCLC symbol*] (OCLC)
GMSA .... General Motors South African
GMSA .... German Minesweeping Administration [*Allied German Occupation Forces*]
GMSA .... Seaman Apprentice, Gunner's Mate, Striker [*Navy rating*]
GMSC .... General Medical Services Council [*British*] (BI)
GMSER .... Guided Missile Service Report (NG)
GMSFC .... George Marshall Space Flight Center [*Huntsville, AL*] (IEEE)
GMSFN .... Global Manned Space Flight Network (SAA)
GMSI .... Grand Master of the Order of the Star of India [*British*]
GMSIA .... Guided Missile System, Intercept-Aerial (MCD)
GMSK .... Gaussian Filtered Minimum Shift Keying (MCD)
GMSK .... Gaussian Mean Shift Keying
G/MSL .... Guided Missile
GMSL .... Sidi Slimane [*Morocco*] [*ICAO location identifier*] (ICLI)
GMSN .... Seaman, Gunner's Mate, Striker [*Navy rating*]
GMSO .... German Mine Supplies Organization [*Allied German Occupation Forces*]
GMSQUAD ... Guided Missile Squadron (MUGU)
GMSR .... Guided Missile Service Record
GMSR .... Guided Missile Service Report (MCD)
GMSR .... Gunner's Mate, Ship Repair [*Navy rating Obsolete*]
GMSRON ..... Guided Missile Service Squadron (MUGU)
GMSRP .... Gunner's Mate, Ship Repair, Powderman [*Navy rating Obsolete*]
GMSS .... Graphical Modeling and Simulation System
GMST .... General Military Subjects Test
GMST .... Glossary of Merchant Ship Types (MCD)
GMST .... Greenwich Mean Sidereal Time (WGA)
GMSTE......... Gemstar Intl. [*NASDAQ symbol*] (TTSB)
GMSTF .... Gemstar International Group Ltd. [*NASDAQ symbol*] (SAG)
GMSTS .... Guided Missile System Test Set (NATG)
GMSU .... General Maritime Stevedores' Union [*Philippines*]
GMSU .... Guided Missile Service Unit [*Air Force*]
GMSW .... Gross Maximum Shipping Weight
GMT............ Garment
GMT............ Gas Missile Tube
GMT............ GATX Corp. [*Formerly, General American Transportation Corp.*] [*NYSE symbol*] (SPSG)
GMT............ Geiger-Mueller Tube
GMT............ Gemini Technology, Inc. [*Toronto Stock Exchange symbol Vancouver Stock Exchange symbol*]
GMT............ Generalized Multitasking
GMT............ General Machine Test [*Computer science*] (BUR)
GMT............ General Military Training (AFM)
GMT............ Generic Mapping Tools [*Marine science*] (OSRA)
GMT............ Geomarine Technology
GMT............ Geometric Mean [*Antibody titers*] (STED)
GMT............ Geometric Mean Titer [*Analytical chemistry*]
GMT............ Gingival Margin Trimmer [*Medicine*] (DMAA)
GMT............ Glass-Mat Reinforced Thermoplastic [*Automotive engineering*]
GMT............ Glass-Mat Thermoplastic
GMT............ Government Maturity Test (MCD)
GMT............ Governor Macquarie Tower [*Sydney, New South Wales, Australia*]
GMT............ Graphics Mouse Technology [*Computer science*] (CIST)
GMT............ Greenwich Mean [*or Meridian*] Time
GMT............ Grupoaereo Monterrey, SA de CV [*Mexico*] [*FAA designator*] (FAAC)
GMT............ Guided Missile Target (NG)
GMT............ Guided Missile Trainer
GMT............ Gunner's Mate, Technician [*Navy rating*]
GMT............ Gunnery Maintenance Trainer [*Army*]
GMT1........... Gunner's Mate, Technician, First Class [*Navy rating*] (DNAB)
GMT2........... Gunner's Mate, Technician, Second Class [*Navy rating*] (DNAB)

GMT3	Gunner's Mate, Technician, Third Class [*Navy rating*] (DNAB)
GMTA	Al Hoceima/Cote Du Rif [*Morocco*] [*ICAO location identifier*] (ICLI)
GMTA	Great Minds Think Alike [*Internet language*] (PCM)
GMtbC	Berry College, Mount Berry, GA [*Library symbol Library of Congress*] (LCLS)
GMTC	Chief Gunner's Mate, Technician [*Navy rating*]
GMTC	Glutamate Manufacturers Technical Committee (EA)
GMTCM	Master Chief Gunner's Mate, Technician [*Navy rating*]
GMTCS	Senior Chief Gunner's Mate, Technician [*Navy rating*]
GMTF	Gay Media Task Force (EA)
GMTF	Geometric Modulation Transfer Function (MCD)
GMTI	Greenman Technologies [*NASDAQ symbol*] (TTSB)
GMTI	Greenman Technologies, Inc. [*NASDAQ symbol*] (SAG)
GMTI	Ground Moving Target Indicator
GMTIW	Greenman Technologies Wrrt [*NASDAQ symbol*] (TTSB)
GMTN	Tetouan/Sania R'Mel [*Morocco*] [*ICAO location identifier*] (ICLI)
GMTO	General Military Training Office
GMTOA	Green Mountain Textile Overseers Association (EA)
GMTPr	GATX Corp. $2.50 Cv Pfd [*NYSE symbol*] (TTSB)
GMTPrA	GATX Corp. $3.875 cm Cv Pfd [*NYSE symbol*] (TTSB)
GMTR	Guided Missile Test Round [*Military*] (CAAL)
GMTRB	General Military Training Review Board (AFM)
GMTRY	Geometry (MSA)
GMTS	Guided Missile Test Set (AFM)
GMTSA	Gunner's Mate, Technician, Seaman Apprentice [*Navy rating*]
GMTSN	Gunner's Mate, Technician, Seaman [*Navy rating*]
GMTT	Tanger/Boukhalf [*Morocco*] [*ICAO location identifier*] (ICLI)
GMTTR	Geometric Mean Time to Repair [*Military*] (CAAL)
GMTU	Guided Missile Test Unit (IAA)
GMTU	Guided Missile Training Unit [*Navy*]
GMtvB	Brewton-Parker College, Mount Vernon, GA [*Library symbol Library of Congress*] (LCLS)
GMU	Gadjah Mada University [*Indonesia*]
GMU	George Mason University [*Virginia*]
GMU	Goose Management Unit
GMU	Gospel Missionary Union (EA)
GMU	Granite Mountain [*Utah*] [*Seismograph station code, US Geological Survey*] (SEIS)
GMU	Greenville, SC [*Location identifier FAA*] (FAAL)
GMU	Guided Missile Unit
GMU	Mercer University, Macon, GA [*OCLC symbol*] (OCLC)
GMUS	Guildhall Museum [*London*]
GMusRNCM(Hons)	Graduate in Music of the Royal Northern College of Music [*British*] (DBQ)
GMUTS	General Motors Uniform Test Standards [*Automotive engineering*]
GMV	Galinsoga Mosaic Virus
GMV	Generalized Minimum Variance [*Control technology*]
GMV	Glycine Mosaic Virus [*Plant pathology*]
GMV	Government Motor Vehicle (DNAB)
GMV	Gram Molecular Volume [*Chemistry*]
GMV	Grand Master of the Vails [*Freemasonry*]
GMV	Guaranteed Minimum Value
GMVDC	Gay Men's VD Clinic (EA)
GMVLS	Guided Missile Vertical Launch System [*Canadian Navy*]
GMW	General Microwave Corp. [*AMEX symbol*] (SPSG)
GMW	Generic Maintenance Workstation (SSD)
GMW	Genl Microwave [*AMEX symbol*] (TTSB)
GMW	Gold Mountain [*Washington*] [*Seismograph station code, US Geological Survey*] (SEIS)
GMW	Gram Molecular Weight [*Chemistry*]
GMW	Guevara-McInteer-Wageman
GMW	Wesleyan College, Macon, GA [*Library symbol Library of Congress*] (LCLS)
GMWA	Gospel Music Workshop of America (EA)
GMWC	Graphite Moderated, Water Cooled (PDAA)
GM/WM	Group Mark/Word Mark [*Computer science*] (OA)
GMWS	Guided Missile Weapon System [*Military*] (CAAL)
GMWU	General and Municipal Workers' Union [*British*]
GMX	Gasket Material Expert [*Automotive engineering*]
GMZ	Bowie, TX [*Location identifier FAA*] (FAAL)
GMZFO	Gouvernement Militaire de la Zone Francaise d'Occupation [*Military Government of the French Zone of Occupation*] [*of Germany*]
GN	Air Gabon [*ICAO designator*] (AD)
GN	Gain (NASA)
GN	Gandy-Nanta [*Disease*] [*Medicine*] (DB)
GN	Ganglion Nodosum [*Neurology*]
GN	Gathering of Nations (EA)
GN	Gaussian Noise (IAA)
GN	Gaylactic Network [*An association*] (EA)
GN	General (WGA)
GN	General Note (MSA)
GN	Generator (IAA)
Gn	Genesis [*Old Testament book*]
GN	[*The*] Georgia Northern Railway Co. (IIA)
GN	German
gn	Gilbert and Ellice Islands [*Tuvalu*] [*gb (Gilbert Islands) or tu (Tuvalu) used in records cataloged after October 1978*] [*MARC country of publication code*] [*Library of Congress*] (LCCP)
GN	Girls Nation (EA)
GN	Glomerular Nephritis [*Medicine*]
G:N	Glucose:Nitrogen [*Ratio*]
GN	Gnotobiote [*Medicine*] (DMAA)
GN	Godfrey-Nash [*Forerunner of British HRG and Frazer-Nash automobiles*]
GN	Golden Nematode [*A worm*]
GN	Golden Nugget, Inc. (EFIS)
GN	Golden Number [*Number used to fix the date of Easter*]
GN	Golden Titan Resources [*Vancouver Stock Exchange symbol*]
GN	Goldneck Summer Squash
Gn	Gonadotropin [*Endocrinology*]
GN	Gonococcus [*Medicine*] (MEDA)
GN	Good Night [*Amateur radio*]
Gn	Gradational, Non-Calcareous [*Soil*]
GN	Graduate Nurse
GN	Grain (MCD)
GN	Gram-Negative [*Also, GRN*] [*Microbiology*]
GN	Grand National [*Automobile racing*]
GN	Grand Nehemiah [*Freemasonry*] (ROG)
GN	Grandnephew (ADA)
GN	Grandniece (ADA)
GN	Grant Number (NITA)
GN	Great Northern Railway (MHDW)
GN	Green [*Maps and charts*]
GN	Grid North [*Army*] (ADDR)
GN	Ground Nester [*Ornithology*]
GN	Ground Network [*Remote sensing*] (EERA)
GN	Groundnut Meal (PDAA)
GN	Group Number [*Dialog*] [*Searchable fields*] [*Information service or system*] (NITA)
GN	Guanine Nucleotide [*Biochemistry*]
GN	Guide-Number [*Photography*]
GN	Guinea [*ANSI two-letter standard code*] (CNC)
GN	Gun [*s*] [*Freight*]
GN₂	Gaseous Nitrogen [*NASA*]
GNA	Gainsco, Inc. [*AMEX symbol*] (SPSG)
GNA	Galanthus Nivalis Agglutinin
GNA	Gay Nurses' Alliance (EA)
GNA	General Nursing Assistance (DMAA)
GNA	Georgia Nurses Association (SRA)
GNA	Ghana News Agency
GNA	Global Network Academy [*On-line education*] [*Information retrieval*]
GNA	Gnangara [*Australia Geomagnetic observatory code*]
GNA	Granada Exploration Corp. [*Vancouver Stock Exchange symbol*]
GNA	Grants Pass, OR [*Location identifier FAA*] (FAAL)
GNA	Graphics Network Architecture
GNA	Graysonia, Nashville & Ashdown Railroad Co. [*AAR code*]
GNA	Greek National Army
GNA	Servicios Aereos Gana SA de CV [*Mexico*] [*FAA designator*] (FAAC)
GNAACBJA	Greater North American Aviculturist and Color Bred Judges Association [*Formerly, GNACBJA*]
GNAB	Guide to New Australian Books [*A publication*]
GNAC	Great Northeast Athletic Conference (PSS)
GNAC	Guidance, Navigation and Control [*Military*] (IAA)
GNACBJA	Greater North American Color-Bred Judge Association [*Later, GNAACBJA*] (EA)
GnAcpt	General Acceptance Corp. [*Associated Press*] (SAG)
GNADS	Gimbaled Night and Day Sight
GNAGS	Ground Adjutant General Section [*World War II*]
GNAIW	Glacial North Atlantic Intermediate Water
GNAL	Georgia Nuclear Aircraft Laboratory (SAA)
GN & C	Guidance, Navigation, and Control (MCD)
GNAS	General NAS [*FAA*] (TAG)
GNAS	Grand National Archery Society [*British*]
G Nas	Guillelmus Naso [*Flourished, 1220-34*] [*Authority cited in pre-1607 legal work*] (DSA)
GNAT	General Numerical Analysis of Transport [*Computer program*]
GNAT	Global Network of Astronomical Telescopes [*Proposed network*]
GNATS	General Noise and Tonal System (NVT)
GNATS	General Nonlinear Analysis of Two-Dimensional Structures [*Computer program*]
GnAuto	General Automation, Inc. [*Associated Press*] (SAG)
GNavO	Group Navigation Officer [*British military*] (DMA)
GNB	Global Air Link [*Nigeria*] [*ICAO designator*] (FAAC)
GNB	Good News Bible [*Today's English Version*] [*A publication*] (BJA)
GNB	Gram-Negative Bacillus [*Microbiology*]
GNB	Granby, CO [*Location identifier FAA*] (FAAL)
GNB	Granby Resources Ltd. [*Vancouver Stock Exchange symbol*]
GNB	Grenoble [*France*] [*Airport symbol*] (OAG)
GNB	Guinea-Bissau [*ANSI three-letter standard code*] (CNC)
GNBM	Gram-Negative Bacillary Meningitis [*Medicine*]
GnBnd	General Binding Corp. [*Associated Press*] (SAG)
GNC	General Nautical Chart [*Navy*]
GNC	General Nursing Care [*Medicine*]
GNC	General Nursing Council
GNC	Geologic Names Committee [*US Geological Survey*]
GNC	Geriatric Nurse Clinician (DMAA)
GNC	Global Navigation Chart [*Military*]
GNC	Goddard Network Control [*NASA*] (MCD)
GNC	Grand National Championship [*Motorcycle racing*]
GNC	Graphic Numerical Control [*Deltacam Systems Ltd.*] [*Software package*] [*British*] (MCD)
GNC	Great National Coal (EFIS)
GNC	Great Northwest Conference (PSS)
GNC	Grid North Correction
GNC	Gross Neutron Counter (PDAA)
GNC	Guaranty National [*NYSE symbol*] (TTSB)
GNC	Guaranty National Corp. [*NYSE symbol*] (SPSG)
GNC	Guidance and Navigation Computer [*NASA*] (KSC)
GNC	Guidance, Navigation, and Control (NASA)
GNC	Seminole, TX [*Location identifier FAA*] (FAAL)

GnCable......	General Cable PLC [Associated Press] (SAG)
GNCAM......	Glia-Neuron Cell Adhesion Molecule [Cytology]
GNCCA........	Grand National Curling Club of America
GNCEW......	General Nursing Council for England and Wales
GNCFTS	GN & C [Guidance, Navigation, and Control] Flight Test Station (MCD)
GNCI	General Nutrition Co. [NASDAQ symbol] (SAG)
GNCI	Genl Nutrition [NASDAQ symbol] (TTSB)
GNCIS	Guidance, Navigation, and Control Integration Simulator (NASA)
GNCM	General Communication, Inc. [NASDAQ symbol] (NQ)
GNCMA........	Genl Communication'A' [NASDAQ symbol] (TTSB)
GNCN	Goran Capital, Inc. [NASDAQ symbol] (SAG)
GNCNF........	Goran Capital [NASDAQ symbol] (TTSB)
GnCom........	General Communications, Inc. [Associated Press] (SAG)
GNCS	Guidance, Navigation, and Control System (MCD)
GNCSA........	Good Neighbour Council of South Australia
GNCT	Good Neighbour Council of Tasmania [Australia]
GNCTS	GN & C [Guidance, Navigation, and Control] Test Station (MCD)
GND	Gram-Negative Diplococci [Medicine] (MEDA)
GND	Grand Airways, Inc. [FAA designator] (FAAC)
GND	Grand Casinos [NYSE symbol] (TTSB)
GND	Grand Casinos, Inc. [NYSE symbol] (SAG)
GND	Grandview Resources, Inc. [Toronto Stock Exchange symbol Vancouver Stock Exchange symbol]
GND	Grenada [Windward Islands] [Airport symbol] (OAG)
GND	Ground (AAG)
GND	Ground (IDOE)
gnd	Ground (IDOE)
GND	Ground-Detonated Flares [Military] (INF)
GND	Grounded [Electricity] [Electronics]
GND	North Georgia College, Stewart Library, Dahlonega, GA [OCLC symbol] (OCLC)
GnData	General DataComm Industries, Inc. [Associated Press] (SAG)
GNDCG	Ground Forces Commanding General [World War II]
GNDCK........	Ground Check [Aviation]
GND C/O	Ground Checkout [NASA] (NASA)
GNDCON......	Ground Control
GNDCP	Ground Command Post [Army]
GNDI	Gross National Disposable Income [Economics]
GNDR...........	Gander Mountain [NASDAQ symbol] (TTSB)
GNDR...........	Gander Mountain, Inc. [NASDAQ symbol] (NQ)
GnDyn........	General Dynamics Corp. [Associated Press] (SAG)
GNE	Gane Energy Corp. Ltd. [Toronto Stock Exchange symbol]
GNE	Genentech, Inc. [NYSE symbol] (SPSG)
GNE	Government Nomenclature Equipment (DNAB)
GNE	Gross National Effluent
GNE	Gross National Expenditure
GNE	Guidance and Navigation Electronics (KSC)
GNE	Guidance and Navigation Equipment
GNEC	General Nuclear Engineering Corp. (MCD)
GNEM	Global Network for Environmental Monitoring [Defunct] (EA)
GnEmp........	General Employment Enterprises, Inc. [Associated Press] (SAG)
GNESIT	Greater New England Society of Inhalation Therapists
GNF	Gannett Newspaper Foundation
GNFC	Graceland News Fan Club [Defunct] (EA)
GNFMS	Gaseous Nitrogen Flow Measuring System
GNG	Gaussian Noise Generator [Electronics]
GNG	Generation Gather Group [Computer science]
GNG	Gooding, ID [Location identifier FAA] (FAAL)
GNG	Granger Resources Corp. [Vancouver Stock Exchange symbol]
GNGCS.........	Ground Forces Chief of Staff [World War II]
GNGDC........	Ground Forces Deputy Chief of Staff [World War II]
GNGPS.........	Ground Forces Plans Section [World War II]
GNGRBRD....	Gingerbread
GnGrth	General Growth Properties [Associated Press] (SAG)
GNGS	Genoa Nuclear Generating Station (NRCH)
GNGSE........	Ground Forces Secretariat [World War II]
GNH	Grand National Hunt [British]
GNH	Gross Night Hour [Advertising] (WDMC)
GnHost........	General Host Corp. [Associated Press] (SAG)
GnHous........	General Housewares Corp. [Associated Press] (SAG)
GNI	Genco Industry, Inc. [Vancouver Stock Exchange symbol]
GNI	Generation of New Ideas (MHDB)
GNI	[The] GNI Group, Inc. [Associated Press] (SAG)
GNI	Grand Isle, LA [Location identifier FAA] (FAAL)
GNI	Great Northern Iron Ore Properties [NYSE symbol] (SPSG)
GNI	Grid Node Interface (PDAA)
GNI	Gross National Income [Economics]
GNI	Gross National Investment (EERA)
GNIB	Guatemala News and Information Bureau (EA)
GNIC	Gay News Information and Communication Network [Information service or system] (IID)
GNID	Gram-Negative Intracellular Diplococci [Microbiology]
GNIron	Great Northern Iron Ore Properties [Associated Press] (SAG)
GNIS	Geographic Names Information System [US Geological Survey] [Information service or system]
GNIS	Global Names Information System [Computer science]
GNJ	Lexington, KY [Location identifier FAA] (FAAL)
GNK	Globalink, Inc. [AMEX symbol] (SAG)
GNL	Galey & Lord, Inc. [NYSE symbol] (SAG)
GNL	General
GNL	Georgia Nuclear Laboratory [AEC]
GNL	Great National Land [Vancouver Stock Exchange symbol]
GNL	Greenwood [Mississippi] [Airport symbol] (AD)
GNLB	Genelabs Technologies [NASDAQ symbol] (SPSG)
GNLTD	Granulated (MSA)

GNM	Genetron Marine, Inc. [Vancouver Stock Exchange symbol]
GNM	Golden [New Mexico] [Seismograph station code, US Geological Survey] (SEIS)
GNM	Good News Mission (EA)
GNM	Guanambi [Brazil] [Airport symbol] (OAG)
GNMA	Government National Mortgage Administration (AAGC)
GNMA	Government National Mortgage Association [Nickname: Ginnie Mae]
GnMag.........	General Magnaplate Corp. [Associated Press] (SAG)
GnMicr........	General Microwave Corp. [Associated Press] (SAG)
GnMill	General Mills, Inc. [Associated Press] (SAG)
GnMotr........	General Motors Corp. [Associated Press] (SAG)
GNMP	Government Network Management Profile [National Institute of Standards and Technology]
GNMS	Gaseous Nitrogen Measuring System
GNMS	Ground Network Management System [Aviation] (DA)
GNN	Ghinnir [Ethiopia] [Airport symbol] (AD)
GNN	Giant North Resources Ltd. [Vancouver Stock Exchange symbol]
GNN	Global Network Navigator [An on-line publication and Internet reference guide] (ECON)
GNN	Gunnerudssatern [Sweden] [Seismograph station code, US Geological Survey] (SEIS)
GNO	Golden North Resource Corp. [Toronto Stock Exchange symbol Vancouver Stock Exchange symbol]
GNOC	Graphic Network Operator Console [Hughes Network Systems, Inc.]
GN of I	Great Northern of Ireland [Railway] (ROG)
Gnom...........	Gnomon [Munich] [A publication] (BJA)
GNOMAC......	Greater New Orleans Microform Cooperative [Library network]
G-NORM	Grounded - Not Operationally Ready Maintenance (MCD)
G-NORS	Grounded - Not Operationally Ready Supply (MCD)
GNOS	Gallium Nitride-on-Sapphire (AAEL)
GNOS	Goddard Network Operations Support [NASA] (KSC)
GNOZ	Grease Nozzle
GNP	Gas, Nonpersistent
GNP	Geriatric Nurse Practitioner (DMAA)
GNP	Gerontological Nurse Practitioner
GNP	Good Neighbour Program [Australia]
GNP	Graphics Nesting Processor (MCD)
GNP	Graphics Nesting Program (MCD)
GNP	Grenada National Party [Political party] (PPW)
GNP	Gross National Product [Economics]
GNP	Tulsa, OK [Location identifier FAA] (FAAL)
GNP & BR ...	Great Northern Piccadilly & Brompton Railway [British] (ROG)
GnPara	General Parametrics Corp. [Associated Press] (SAG)
GNPC	Global Navigation and Planning Chart [Military]
GnPhys	General Physics Corp. [Associated Press] (SAG)
GNpN	Norman Junior College, Norman Park, GA [Library symbol Library of Congress] (LCLS)
GNPP	Ginna Nuclear Power Plant (NRCH)
GNPP	Great Nigeria People's Party [Political party] (PPW)
GnPrcl	General Parcel Service, Inc. [Associated Press] (SAG)
GNPT	GP Financial Corp. [NASDAQ symbol] (SAG)
GNQ	Equatorial Guinea [ANSI three-letter standard code] (CNC)
GNR	Gaseous Nuclear Rocket
GNR	General Roca [Argentina] [Airport symbol] (OAG)
GNR	Geographical Names Register [New South Wales] [State] (EERA)
GNR	Global Natural Res [NYSE symbol] (TTSB)
GNR	Global Natural Resources, Inc. [NYSE symbol] (SPSG)
G/N R	Glucose to Nitrogen Ratio [Medicine] (AAMN)
GNR	Gram-Negative Rods (DMAA)
GNR	Great Northern Railway
GNR	Guest Name Record (IAA)
GNR	Gunner (AFM)
gnr	Gunner (WDAA)
G n R	Guns n' Roses [Rock recording group]
GNRA..........	Gateway National Recreation Area [New York] [Department of the Interior]
GNRA..........	Government National Railway Association [Proposed] [Nickname: Ginnie Rae]
GNRA..........	Grand National Racing Association (EA)
GnRad.........	GenRad, Inc. [Associated Press] (SAG)
GNRB	Grid Navigational Reference Beacon [Navy] (CAAL)
GNRE	Gross National Recreation Experience [Refers to cost of recreation in relation to gross national product]
GnRF	Gonadotropin-Releasing Factor [Also, GnRH, LH-RF, LH-RH, LH-RH/FSH-RH, LRF, LRH] [Endocrinology]
GnRH	Gonadotropin-Releasing Hormone [Also, GnRF, GnRF, LH-RF, LH-RH, LH-RH/FSH-RH, LRF, LRH] [Endocrinology]
GnRHA.........	Gonadotropin-Releasing Hormone Agonist [Endocrinology]
GNRP	General Neighborhood Renewal Plan
GNRP...........	Guanine Nucleotide Release Protein [Biochemistry]
GNRS	Great Northern Railway Society [British] (DBA)
GNRTN........	Generation
GNRTNG	Generating
GNRTR........	Generator
GNRY..........	Great Northern Railway
GNRY..........	Gunnery (AFM)
GNS	Eastern Executive Air Charter Ltd. [British] [FAA designator] (FAAC)
GNS	Gannett News Service
GNS	General Naval Staff [NATO] (NATG)
GN's	Global Negotiations
GNS	Global Network Service [British] (TELE)
G/NS	Glucose in Normal Saline [Medicine]
GNS	Glutamine Synthetase [Also, GS] [An enzyme]
GNS	Goose NORAD [North American Air Defense] Sector (IAA)
GNS	Grain Neutral Spirits [Alcohol]

GNS	Gram-Negative Sensitivity [to antibiotics]
GNS	Grand National Sportsman [Car racing division]
GNS	Great North of Scotland Railway (ROG)
GNS	Griffin's Nautical Series [A publication]
GNS	Group of Negotiations on Services [European Community]
GNS	Guidance and Navigation System
GNS	Guineas [Monetary unit] [Obsolete British]
GNSA	Gensia Inc. [NASDAQ symbol] (TTSB)
GNSA	Gensia Pharmaceuticals, Inc. [NASDAQ symbol] (SAG)
GNSAW	Gensia Pharmaceuticals Wrrt [NASDAQ symbol] (TTSB)
GNSH	Grey Nuns of the Sacred Heart [Roman Catholic religious order]
GNSI	Guild of Natural Science Illustrators (EA)
GNSM	Gensym Corp. [NASDAQ symbol] (TTSB)
GNSM	Graduate of the Northern School of Music [Obsolete British] (DBQ)
GNSMTH	Gunsmith
GNSO	Goddard Network Support Operations [King's College] [Wilkes-Barre, PA] [NASA] (KSC)
GNSP	Gross National Sports Product [Economics]
GNSR	Great North of Scotland Railway
GNSS	Genesis
GNSS	Global Navigation Satellite System
GNsS	Grammatik der Neusyrischen Sprache [A publication] (BJA)
GNST	Glossary of Naval Ship Types (MCD)
GNSW	Governor of New South Wales [Australia]
GNSWBR	Great New South Wales Bike Ride [Australia]
GNT	Business Air Ltd. [British ICAO designator] (FAAC)
GNT	General Naval Training [British military] (DMA)
GNT	Giant
GNT	Grant Exploration [Vancouver Stock Exchange symbol]
GNT	Grants, NM [Location identifier FAA] (FAAL)
GNT	Great Northern Telegraph Co. [Denmark] [Telecommunications] (TEL)
GNT	Green Tree Financial, Inc. [NYSE symbol] (SPSG)
GNT	Green Tree Finl [NYSE symbol] (TTSB)
GNT	Ground Test [NASA] (KSC)
GNTA	Genta, Inc. [NASDAQ symbol] (SPSG)
GNTC	Girls' Naval Training Corps [British]
GnthrInt	Gunther International Ltd. [Associated Press] (SAG)
GNTLMN	Gentlemen
GNTO	Greek National Tourist Organization (EA)
GNTP	Graduate Nurse Transition Program
GNTR	Generator (FAAC)
GNTX	Gentex Corp. [NASDAQ symbol] (NQ)
GNU	Golden Rule Resources Ltd. [Toronto Stock Exchange symbol]
GNU	Goodnews Bay [Alaska] [Airport symbol] (OAG)
GNUC	[The] GNI Group, Inc. [NASDAQ symbol] (NQ)
GNV	Gainesville [Florida] [Airport symbol]
GNV	Geneva Steel Co. [NYSE symbol] (SPSG)
GNV	Geneva Steel Co.'A' [NYSE symbol] (TTSB)
GNV	Genoveva Resources, Inc. [Vancouver Stock Exchange symbol]
GNV	Glycinenaphthol Violet [An indicator] [Chemistry]
GNV	Grand Airways, Inc. [ICAO designator] (FAAC)
GNVN	Government of North Vietnam
GNVQ	General National Vocational Qualification [British] (ODBW)
GnvStl	Geneva Steel [Associated Press] (SAG)
GNW	Greenwell Resources Corp. [Vancouver Stock Exchange symbol]
GNWP	Gross National Waste Product Forum [Defunct] (EA)
GNWR	Genessee & Wyoming Railroad Co. [AAR code]
GNX	Genex Resources [Vancouver Stock Exchange symbol]
GNY	Fort Jay, NY [Location identifier FAA] (FAAL)
GNY	German Navy [ICAO designator] (FAAC)
GNYADA	Greater New York Automobile Dealers Association (SRA)
GNYCFS	Greater New York Council for Foreign Students [Later, English in Action]
GNYO	Guild of New York Opera [Record label]
GNZ	Ghanzi [Botswana] [Airport symbol] (AD)
GNZ	Gisborne [New Zealand] [Seismograph station code, US Geological Survey] (SEIS)
GNZ	Government of New Zealand
GO	Canada - Transport Canada [Canada ICAO designator] (ICDA)
go	Gabon [MARC country of publication code Library of Congress] (LCCP)
GO	Galactose Oxidase [An enzyme]
GO	Gambia Air Shuttle [ICAO designator] (AD)
GO	Garrison Orders [British military] (DMA)
GO	Gasoffizier [Gas Officer] [German military - World War II]
GO	Gas Oil [Also, G] [Petroleum technology]
GO	Gas Operated (ADA)
GO	Gaussian Orbitals [Atomic physics]
GO	Gearhart-Owen Industries, Inc. (EFIS)
GO	Generale Occidentale [Commercial firm]
GO	Generalized Operations (MCD)
GO	Generaloberst [Full General] [German military - World War II]
GO	General Obligation [Bond] [Business term]
GO	General Office [or Officer] [Military]
GO	General Order
GO	General Organization [Identification card used at Madison Square Garden]
GO	Generated Output
GO	Genius Operator Advertising Data Bank [Gert Richter] [Germany Information service or system] (CRD)
GO	Gentil Organisateur [Genial Host] [Employee of Club Mediterranee, a vacation cooperative]
GO	Geometry-Optimized [Calculations]
GO	Global Options (EA)

GO	Global Outreach [An association] (EA)
GO	Glucose Oxidase [Also, glu ox, GOD] [An enzyme]
Go	Godecke AG [Germany] [Research code symbol]
Go	Goebel's Probate Court Cases [Ohio] [A publication] (DLA)
GO	Goethite [A mineral]
Go	Gofredus de Trano [Deceased, 1245] [Authority cited in pre-1607 legal work] (DSA)
go	Gold (VRA)
GO	Goniometer [JETDS nomenclature] [Military] (CET)
Go	Gonion (DMAA)
GO	Gordan-Overstreet [Syndrome] [Medicine] (DB)
GO	Gothic [Language, etc.] (ROG)
GO	Government Obligation [Economics]
GO	Government Obligation Bond (EBF)
GO	Government Operations Committee [US Senate]
GO	Government Owned
GO	Graduate Opportunities [British]
GO	Grand Orator [Freemasonry]
GO	Grand Organist [Freemasonry] (ROG)
GO	Grand Orient [Freemasonry] (ROG)
GO	Graphitic Oxide
GO	Grasp Objects [Psychometric test]
GO	Great Organ [Music]
GO	Ground Out [Baseball]
GO	Group Officer [British military] (DMA)
G-O	Grumman Olson [Grumman Corp.]
GO	Guest Option [Hotel plan, Hilton hotels]
GO	Gummed Only [Envelopes]
GO	Gunnery Officer [Navy British]
GO	Gunn Oscillator
GO	Gurkha Officer [British military] (DMA)
GO	Gym Officer (WDAA)
GO2	Gaseous Oxygen (MCD)
GO3OS	Global Ozone Observing System (USDC)
GOA	Alberta Government [Canada ICAO designator] (FAAC)
GOA	Generalized Osteoarthritis [Medicine]
GOA	General Operating Agency
GOA	Genoa [Italy] [Airport symbol] (OAG)
GOA	Georgia Oilmen's Association (SRA)
GOA	Georgia Optometric Association (SRA)
GOA	Glacier-Ocean-Atmosphere [Global system used for modelling]
GOA	Goa [Panjim] [India] [Seismograph station code, US Geological Survey] (SEIS)
GOA	Golden Seal Resources Ltd. [Vancouver Stock Exchange symbol]
GOA	Gone on Arrival [Police terminology] (IIA)
GOA	Government-Owned Aircraft
GOA	Group, Operations Analysis [Air Force] (MCD)
GOA	Gun Owners of America (EA)
GOA	Gyro Output Amplifier
GOAC	Geographic OPAREA [Operating Area] Coordinates (DNAB)
GOAC	Gun Owners Action Committee (EA)
GOAD	Good Order & Discipline (WDAA)
GOAD	Group of Ancient Drama
GOAL	Ascent Entertainment Group, Inc. [NASDAQ symbol] (SAG)
GOAL	Ascent Entertainment Grp [NASDAQ symbol] (TTSB)
GOAL	Game Oriented Activities for Learning (AIE)
GOAL	Gay Officers' Action League (EA)
GOAL	General Organization Analysis Language (IAA)
GOAL	Generator for Optimized Application Language (IAA)
GOAL	Ground Operations Aerospace Language [Computer science NASA]
GOAL	Ground Operations Assembly Language [Computer science]
GOALI	Grant Opportunities for Academic Liaison with Industry [National Science Foundation]
GOALS	Generalized Officer Assignment On-Line System [Navy] (NVT)
GOALS	General Operations and Logistics Simulation [Boeing]
GOALS	General Optronics Line of Sight Atmospheric Lightwave Communication System [General Optronics Corp.] [Edison, NJ] [Telecommunications service] (TSSD)
GOALS	Geometrical Optical Analysis of Lens Systems (PDAA)
GOALS	Global Ocean-Atmosphere-Land-Surface Interactions (EERA)
GOALS	Global Ocean-Atmosphere-Land System [Program] [Marine science] (OSRA)
GOALS	Goal-Oriented Approach to Life Cycle Software
GOALS	Greater Orlando Area Legal Services [Florida]
GOAM	Government-Owned and Maintained [Telecommunications] (TEL)
GOAR	Ground Observer Aircraft Recognition [Army]
GOAS	Guidance Optical Alignment Shelter (KSC)
GOase	Galactose Oxidase [An enzyme]
GOASEX	Gulf of Alaska SEASAT Experiment [National Oceanic and Atmospheric Administration]
GOAT	Galveston Orientation and Amnesia Test [Medicine] (DMAA)
GOAT	Gerber Oscillogram Amplitude Translator
GOAT	Goes Over All Terrain [Vehicle]
GOAT	Goings On About Town [The New Yorker magazine] (WDMC)
GOAT	Grouped Optimal Aggregation Technique (MCD)
GOATS	Group Operational Access Tester System [AT & T]
GOB	General Obligation Bonds [Finance]
GOB	General Officers Branch [Air Force]
GOB	General Order of Battle
GOB	Glass Oceanographic Buoy
GOB	Goba [Ehtiopia] [Airport symbol] (AD)
GOB	Gobble (DSUE)
GOB	Goldbrae Development Ltd. [Vancouver Stock Exchange symbol]
GOB	Good Ordinary Brand [Business term]
gob	Good Ordinary Brand [Business term] (ODBW)

GOB .... Government of Bangladesh
GOB .... Government of Burma (CINC)
GOB .... Grants Operations Balance [*Environmental Protection Agency*] (ERG)
GOB .... Ground Order of Battle (AFM)
GOBAB .... Gamma-Hydroxy-beta-aminobutyric Acid [*Pharmacology*]
GOBAC .... Gold-Plating Bath Analyzer and Controller (PDAA)
GOBEP .... Generalized One-Boson Exchange Potential
GOBI .... Growth Monitoring, Oral Rehydration, Breastfeeding, and Immunization [*Program*] [*UNICEF plan to reduce child mortality in Third World countries*]
GOBILS .... Government Bill of Lading System
GOBR .... Group of Officials on Biotechnology Regulation (EERA)
GOC .... Gas-Oil Contact
GOC .... Gas-Operated Core
GOC .... General Officer Commanding [*Navy*]
GOC .... General Operating Committee
GOC .... General Optical Council [*British*]
GOC .... Glas Owners Club (EA)
GOC .... Glycidoxycoumarin [*Biochemistry*]
GOC .... Gora [*Papua New Guinea*] [*Airport symbol*] (OAG)
GOC .... Government Operations Committee
GOC .... Graphic Option Controller (NITA)
GOC .... Greatest Overall Coefficient (TEL)
GOC .... Greek Orthodox Church (BARN)
GOC .... Griffith Observatory [*California*] [*Seismograph station code, US Geological Survey*] (SEIS)
GOC .... Ground Observer Corps
GOC .... Ground Operations Coordinator [*NASA*] (NASA)
GOC .... Group Operations Center (NATG)
GOC .... Guaranteed One Coat [*Brand of house paint*]
GOC .... Gunnery Officer's Console [*Army*] (AABC)
GOCA .... Graphics Object Content Architecture (CDE)
GOCA .... Ground Operations Control Area [*NASA*] (NASA)
GOCAP .... Graphic Output Circuit Analysis Program
GOCC .... GARP Operational Control Center [*Marine science*] (MSC)
GOCC .... GATE [*GARP Atlantic Tropical Experiment*] Operational Control Centre [*Marine science*] (MSC)
GOCC .... General Order of the Commander-in-Chief [*British military*] (DMA)
GOCC .... Geodetic Operations Control Center [*NASA*]
GOCESS .... Government-Operated Civil Engineering Supply Store
GOCHEM ...... Gulf Oil Chemicals Co.
GOCI .... General Operator-Computer Interaction (IEEE)
GOCI .... Graham Owners Club International (EA)
GOC-in-C ... General Officer Commanding-in-Chief [*British*]
GOCM .... Goals, Objectives, Commitments, and Measures [*Environmental science*] (COE)
GOCMV .... Greek Orthodox Community of Melbourne and Victoria [*Australia*]
GOCO .... Golden Oil Co. [*NASDAQ symbol*] (NQ)
GOCO .... Government-Owned/Commercial-Operated [*Facility*] (AFIT)
GO/CO .... Government-Owned/Contractor-Operated [*Facility*] (NG)
GOCOM .... General Officer Command [*US Army Reserve*] (AABC)
GOCR .... Gated-Off Controlled Rectifier
GOCRM .... General Officer Commanding Royal Marines [*British*]
GOD .... Generation of Diversity [*Immunology*]
GOD .... Glucose Oxidase [*Also, glu ox, GO*] [*An enzyme*]
God .... Gofredus de Trano [*Deceased, 1245*] [*Authority cited in pre-1607 legal work*] (DSA)
GOD .... Golden Sceptre Resources [*Toronto Stock Exchange symbol Vancouver Stock Exchange symbol*]
GOD .... Government-Owned Depot
GOD .... Grasped Objects Discrimination [*Psychometric test*]
GOD .... Guaranteed Overnight Delivery
GOD .... Guidance and Orbit Determination [*NASA*] (PDAA)
GODA .... Guild of Drama Adjudicators [*British*] (BI)
GODAS .... Graphically Oriented Design and Analysis System [*Computer science*]
GODB .... Gal Oya Development Board [*Sri Lanka*] (BUAC)
Godb (Eng)... Godbolt's English King's Bench Reports [*78 English Reprint*] [*A publication*] (DLA)
Goddard ...... Goddard on Easements [*A publication*] (DLA)
Goddard C ... Goddard College (GAGS)
Godd Ease ... Goddard on Easements [*A publication*] (DLA)
Godd Easem... Goddard on Easements [*A publication*] (DLA)
GODE .... Gulf Organization for Development in Egypt
Godef & Sh RC... Godefroi and Shortt on Railway Companies [*A publication*] (DLA)
Godefroi ...... Godefroi's Law of Trusts and Trustees [*A publication*] (DLA)
Godef Trust... Godefroi's Law of Trusts and Trustees [*A publication*] (DLA)
Godo .... Godolphin on Admiralty Jurisdiction [*A publication*] (DLA)
Godo .... Godolphin's Abridgment of Ecclesiastical Law [*A publication*] (DLA)
Godo .... Godolphin's Orphan's Legacy [*A publication*] (DLA)
Godo .... Godolphin's Repertorium Canonicum [*A publication*] (DLA)
Godol .... Godolphin's Orphan's Legacy [*A publication*] (DLA)
Godolph Adm Jur... Godolphin on Admiralty Jurisdiction [*2nd ed.*] [*1685*] [*A publication*] (DLA)
Godolph Ecc Law... Godolphin's Ecclesiastical Law [*A publication*] (DLA)
Godolph Leg... Godolphin's Orphan's Legacy [*A publication*] (DLA)
Godolph Orph Leg... Godolphin's Orphan's Legacy [*A publication*] (DLA)
Godolph Rep Can... Godolphin's Repertorium Canonicum [*A publication*] (DLA)
GODORT ...... Government Documents Round Table [*American Library Association*]
GODORT ETF... GODORT [*Government Documents Round Table*] Education Task Force
GODORT FDTF... GODORT [*Government Documents Round Table*] Federal Documents Task Force
GODORT IDTF... GODORT [*Government Documents Round Table*] International Documents Task Force

GODORT MRGITF... GODORT [*Government Documents Round Table*] Machine-Readable Government Information Task Force
GODORT SLDTF... GODORT [*Government Documents Round Table*] State and Local Documents Task Force
GOD/POD ..... Glucose Oxidase-Perioxidase Method (STED)
GOD-POD ..... Glucose Oxidase-Peroxidase [*Also, PGO*] [*Enzyme mixture*]
GODS .... Geniuses of Distinction Society [*Later, SGD*] (EA)
GODSEP .... Guidance and Orbit Determination for Solar Electric Propulsion [*NASA*]
Godson .... Godson's Mining Commissioner's Cases [*Ontario*] [*A publication*] (DLA)
Gods Pat..... Godson on Patents [*2nd ed.*] [*1840*] [*A publication*] (DLA)
GOE .... Gas, Oxygen, Ether [*Anesthesiology*]
GOE .... General Operating Expenses (MCD)
GOE .... General Ordination Examination
GOE .... Geodome Resources Ltd. [*Toronto Stock Exchange symbol Vancouver Stock Exchange symbol*]
GOE .... Gonalia [*Papua New Guinea*] [*Airport symbol*] (OAG)
GOE .... Gore [*New Zealand*] [*Airport symbol*] (AD)
GOE .... Government-Owned Equipment (MCD)
GOE .... Ground Operating Equipment [*Aerospace*] (NAKS)
GOE .... Ground Operational Equipment [*NASA*]
GOE .... Guide for Occupational Exploration [*A publication*] (DHP)
Goeb .... Goebel's Probate Court Cases [*Ohio*] [*A publication*] (DLA)
Goebel .... Goebel's Probate Reports [*Ohio*] [*A publication*] (DLA)
Goebel (Ohio)... Goebel's Probate Court Cases [*Ohio*] [*A publication*] (DLA)
Goebel's Rep... Goebel's Probate Reports [*Ohio*] [*A publication*] (DLA)
GOEDEB .... General Organisation for the Exploitation and Development of the Euphrates Basin [*Syria*] (BUAC)
GOE for OAO... Ground Operational Equipment for the Orbiting Astronomical Observatory [*NASA*] (MUGU)
GOE/RPIE..... Ground Operational Equipment/Real Property Installed Equipment [*NASA*] (AFM)
GOES .... Geostationary Operational Environmental Satellite [*National Oceanic and Atmospheric Administration*]
GOES .... Geostationary Orbital Earth Satellite (MCD)
GOES .... Geosynchronous Operational Environmental Satellite [*NASA*] (NASA)
GOES .... Geosynchronous Orbiting Earth Satellite
GOES .... Global Omnibus Environmental Survey (EERA)
GOES/DCP ... Geostationary Operational Environmental Satellite Data Collection Platform (MSC)
GOESECS ..... Geochemical Ocean Section Study [*International Decade of Ocean Exploration*] (USDC)
GOES-Next... Next-Generation GOES [*Geostationary Operational Environmental Satellite*] (USDC)
GOETO .... Grand Order of European Tour Operators (BUAC)
GOEZS .... Global Ocean Euphotic Zone Study [*Marine science*] (OSRA)
GOF .... Glass Optical Fiber [*Materials science*]
Gof .... Gofredus de Trano [*Deceased, 1245*] [*Authority cited in pre-1607 legal work*] (DSA)
GOF .... Goodness of Fit (MCD)
GOF .... Good Old Friday [*Slang*]
GOF .... Government-Owned Facility
GOF .... San Angelo, TX [*Location identifier FAA*] (FAAL)
GOFAR .... Global Ocean Floor Analysis and Research [*Navy*]
GOF E .... Goffered Edges [*Bookbinding*] (DGA)
GOFS .... Global Ocean Flux Study [*Federal government*]
GOFTA .... Golf Facilities Trades Association (BUAC)
GOG .... GEOSECS Operations Group [*Marine science*] (MSC)
GOG .... Gerrity Oil & Gas [*NYSE symbol*] (SPSG)
GOG .... Golden Tag Resources [*Vancouver Stock Exchange symbol*]
GOG .... Government of Ghana
GOG .... Gynecologic Oncology Group (EA)
GOGAT .... Glutamate Synthase (BARN)
GOGECA ...... Comite Generale de la Cooperation Agricole de la CEE [*General Committee of Agricultural Cooperation of the European Economic Community*] (PDAA)
GOGG .... Ziguinchor [*Senegal*] [*ICAO location identifier*] (ICLI)
GOGK .... Kolda [*Senegal*] [*ICAO location identifier*] (ICLI)
GOGO .... Global One Distribution & Merchandising, Inc. [*NASDAQ symbol*] (SAG)
GO/GO .... Government-Owned/Government-Operated [*Facility*]
Gog Or .... Goguet's Origin of Laws [*A publication*] (DLA)
GOGPr .... Gerrity O&G Cv Dep Pfd [*NYSE symbol*] (TTSB)
GOGS .... Cap Skirring [*Senegal*] [*ICAO location identifier*] (ICLI)
GOH .... Garments on Hangers [*Shipping*]
goh .... German, Old High [*MARC language code Library of Congress*] (LCCP)
GOH .... German Order of Harugari
GOH .... Geroderma Osteodysplastica Hereditaria [*Medicine*] (DMAA)
GOH .... Godthaab [*Denmark*] [*Airport symbol*]
GOH .... Goliath Gold Mines Ltd. [*Toronto Stock Exchange symbol Vancouver Stock Exchange symbol*]
GOH .... Goods on Hand (DS)
GOH .... Government of Honduras
GOH .... Nuuk [*Greenland*] [*Airport symbol*] (OAG)
GOHBPR ...... General Organization for Housing, Building, and Planning Research [*Egypt*] (BUAC)
GOI .... Fort Knox, KY [*Location identifier FAA*] (FAAL)
GOI .... Gallium Arsenide on Insulator (AAEL)
GOI .... Gate Oxide Integrity (AAEL)
GOI .... General Oriental Investments Ltd. [*Vancouver Stock Exchange symbol*]
GOI .... Goa [*India*] [*Airport symbol*] (OAG)
GOI .... Government of Indonesia

GOI	Government of Iran
GOI	Government of Israel (MCD)
GOI	Government of Italy
GOI	Government-Owned Installation
GOI	Group Operations Instruction [*British military*] (DMA)
GOI	Gun Owners, Inc. (EA)
GOIC	Gulf Organization for Industrial Consulting [*Doha, Qatar*] (EAIO)
GOIE	Government-Owned Industrial Equipment (SAA)
GOIFE	Government of Israel Furnished Equipment (MCD)
Goir Fr Co	Goirand's French Code of Commerce [*A publication*] (DLA)
GOIT	Goyer Organization of Ideas Test (EDAC)
GOJ	Blytheville, AR [*Location identifier FAA*] (FAAL)
GOJ	Eurojet Aviation Ltd. [*British ICAO designator*] (FAAC)
GOJ	Government of Japan (CINC)
GOK	God Only Knows [*Facetious diagnosis for a puzzling medical case*]
GOK	God Only Knows [*Medical slang used for a puzzling group of symptoms*]
GoK	Government of Kenya
GOK	Government of Korea
GOK	Guthrie, OK [*Location identifier FAA*] (FAAL)
GOL	General Operating Language [*Computer science*] (IEEE)
GOL	Glabello-Opisthion Line (STED)
GOL	Goal-Oriented Language
GOL	Gold Beach, OR [*Location identifier FAA*] (FAAL)
GOL	Golden [*Bergen Park*] [*Colorado*] [*Seismograph station code, US Geological Survey*] (SEIS)
GOL	Goldlund Mines Ltd. [*Toronto Stock Exchange symbol*]
GOL	Guinness Overseas Ltd. [*British*]
GOLD	Gate-Drain Overlapped Device (MCD)
GOLD	Generalized Organization of Large Databases (PDAA)
GOLD	Geometric On-Line Definition [*Computer science*] (PDAA)
Gold	Goldesborough's [*or Gouldsborough's*] English King's Bench Reports [*A publication*] (DLA)
GOLD	Gospel of Life Disciples [*An association*] (EA)
GOLD	Graphic Online Language [*Computer science*] (IEEE)
GOLD	Guild of Lady Drivers [*British*] (BI)
Gold & G	Goldsmith and Guthrie's Appeals Reports [*Missouri*] [*A publication*] (DLA)
GOLD BDE	Gold Bevelled Deckle Edges [*Printing*] (DGA)
GOLD BE	Gold Bevelled Edges [*Printing*] (DGA)
GOLDBERG	Generally Operational Linear Digit-Controlled Biphase Electrical Retardance Gate [*IBM Corp.*]
GoldBks	Golden Books Family Entertainment, Inc. [*Associated Press*] (SAG)
GoldBnc	Gold Banc Corp., Inc. [*Associated Press*] (SAG)
Gold Coast	Judgments of the Full Court, Privy Council, and Divisional Courts, Gold Coast [*A publication*] (DLA)
Goldcp	Goldcorp, Inc. [*Associated Press*] (SAG)
GoldcpA	Goldcorp [*Associated Press*] (SAG)
GoldcpB	Goldcorp [*Associated Press*] (SAG)
GOLD E	Gold Edges [*Printing*] (DGA)
GoldEn	Golden Enterprises, Inc. [*Associated Press*] (SAG)
Golden Gate U	Golden Gate University (GAGS)
Goldes	Goldesborough's [*or Gouldsborough's*] English King's Bench Reports [*A publication*] (DLA)
GOLDF	Silverado Mines [*NASDAQ symbol*] (TTSB)
GoldFd	Gold Fields of South Africa Ltd. [*Associated Press*] (SAG)
GoldIsl	Golden Isles Financial Holdings, Inc. [*Associated Press*] (SAG)
GoldnOil	Golden Oil Co. [*Associated Press*] (SAG)
GoldRs	Gold Reserve Corp. [*Associated Press*] (SAG)
Golds Eq	Goldsmith's Doctrine and Practice of Equity [*6th ed.*] [*1871*] [*A publication*] (DLA)
GOLD STAR	Generalized Organization of Large Databases / Set-Theoretic Approach to Relations
GoldTri	Golden Triangle Industries, Inc. [*Associated Press*] (SAG)
GoldTri	Golden Triangle Royalty & Oil, Inc. [*Associated Press*] (SAG)
GoletaN	Goleta National Bank [*Associated Press*] (SAG)
GOLF	Global Oscillations at Low Frequency [*Aerospace*]
go lf	Gold Leaf (VRA)
Golf	Olfactory G Protein [*Physiology*]
GOLF	S 2 Golf [*NASDAQ symbol*] (TTSB)
GOLF	STwo Golf, Inc. [*NASDAQ symbol*] (SAG)
Golf Ent	Golf Enterprises, Inc. [*Associated Press*] (SAG)
GolfTech	Golf Technology Holding, Inc. [*Associated Press*] (SAG)
GolfTS	Golf Training Systems, Inc. [*Associated Press*] (SAG)
GolfTSy	Golf Training Systems, Inc. [*Associated Press*] (SAG)
GOLIATH	Giant On-Line Instrument for the Acquisition and Total Handling of Data (MCD)
GOLKAR	Sekber Golongan Karya [*Joint Secretariat of Functional Groups*] [*Indonesia*] [*Political party*] (PPW)
GOLPH	Giannetti On-Line Psychosocial History [*Personality development test*] [*Psychology*]
GOLPS	Greek Orthodox Ladies Philoptochos Society (EA)
GOLS	General Online Stack System (IAA)
GOM	God's Own Medicine [*Also, God's Medicine*] [*Morphine*] [*Slang*]
GOM	Golden Eye Minerals [*Vancouver Stock Exchange symbol*]
GOM	Goma [*Zaire*] [*Airport symbol*] (OAG)
GOM	Government of Malaysia (CINC)
GOM	Government-Owned Material
GOM	Grand Old Man [*A venerated man, especially in a specific field*] [*Political slang See also HOM*]
GOM	Ground Operations Manager [*Aerospace*] (NAKS)
GOM	Group Occupancy Meter [*Telecommunications*] (NITA)
GOM	Gulf of Mexico [*Also, GLFMEX*]
GOM	Macon Junior College, Macon, GA [*OCLC symbol*] (OCLC)

GOM	or WSMR [*Hugh L. Dryden Flight Research Center*] [*White Sands Missile Range*] (NASA)
GOMA	General Officer Money Allowance [*Military*] (AABC)
GOMA	Good Outdoor Manners Association (EA)
GOMAC	Government Microcircuit Applications Conference
GOMAC	Groupement des Opticiens du Marche Commun [*Common Market Opticians' Group*] [*Paris, France*]
GOMALCO	Gobel O'Malley Co. [*Entertainer George Gobel's firm; O'Malley is business ma nager*]
GOME	Global Ozone Monitoring Experiment [*Marine science*] (OSRA)
GOMEET	Goals, Objectives, Means, Ends, Effects, and Timing [*Environmental science*] (COE)
GOMER	Get Out of My Emergency Room [*Used as a noun in reference to an elderly, chronically ill patient*]
Gomer	Get Out of My Emergency Room [*Medical slang describing a patient who cannot describe his/her symptoms*]
GOMMS	Ground Operations and Material Management System (MCD)
GOMOS	Global Ozone Monitoring by Occultation of Stars [*Marine science*] (OSRA)
GOMR	Global Ozone Monitoring Radiometer
GOMR & R	Government-Owned Material Repair and Reimbursement (MCD)
GOMS	Geostationary Operational Meteorological Satellite [*Marine science*] (OSRA)
GOMS	Ground Operations Management System [*NASA*] (NASA)
GON	Geon Co. [*NYSE symbol*] (SPSG)
gon	Gondi [*MARC language code Library of Congress*] (LCCP)
GON	Gonni Air Services Ltd. [*Suriname*] [*ICAO designator*] (FAAC)
GON	Gonococcal Ophthalmia Neonatorum [*Medicine*]
GON	New London [*Connecticut*] [*Airport symbol*] (OAG)
GOND	Glaucomatous Optic Nerve Damage [*Medicine*] (DMAA)
GOND	Gondola
GONG	Global Oscillations Network Group [*National Science Foundation*]
GONIO	Goniometer [*RADAR instrument*] (DSUE)
Gonio	Gonioscopy (STED)
GONT	Government on Taiwan
Gonzaga U	Gonzaga University (GAGS)
Gonz Pub Lab L Rep	Gonzaga Special Report. Public Sector Labor Law [*A publication*] (DLA)
GOO	Gastric Outlet Obstruction [*Gastroenterology*] (DAVI)
GOO	Generalized Overhauser Orbitals [*Atomic physics*]
GOO	Get Oil Out (EA)
GOO	Goldsil Resources Ltd. [*Toronto Stock Exchange symbol Vancouver Stock Exchange symbol*]
GOO	Goondiwindi [*Australia Airport symbol*] (OAG)
GOO	Goosecreekite [*A zeolite*]
GOO	Ground Observer Organization (NATG)
GOO	Ground Operation Order (NATG)
GOO	Group Operations Order [*British military*] (DMA)
GOOBS	Going Out of Business Sale
GOOD	Diourbel [*Senegal*] [*ICAO location identifier*] (ICLI)
Good & Wood	Full Bench Rulings, Edited by Goodeve and Woodman [*Bengal*] [*A publication*] (DLA)
GOOD-B'YE	God Be with You (ROG)
GOOD EGGS	Geriatric Order of Old Dolls Who Encourage the Generation Gap Singlemindedly [*Tongue-in-cheek teachers' organization*]
Good Ev	Goodeve's Law of Evidence [*India*] [*A publication*] (DLA)
Goodeve	Goodeve on Real Property [*1883-1906*] [*A publication*] (DLA)
Good Govt	Good Government [*A publication*]
GoodGy	[*The*] Good Guys, Inc. [*Associated Press*] (SAG)
Goodmrk	Goodmark Foods, Inc. [*Associated Press*] (SAG)
Good Pat	Goodeve's Abstract of Patent Cases [*1785-1883*] [*England*] [*A publication*] (DLA)
Good Pr	Goodwin's Probate Practice [*A publication*] (DLA)
Goodrch	Goodrich, BF, Co. [*Associated Press*] (SAG)
Goodrich-Amram	Goodrich-Amram Procedural Rules Service [*A publication*] (DLA)
GoodrP	Goodrich Petroleum [*Associated Press*] (SAG)
GoodrPet	Goodrich Petroleum [*Associated Press*] (SAG)
Good Ry C	Goodeve on Railway Companies and Passengers [*A publication*] (DLA)
GoodT	Good Times Restaurants, Inc. [*Associated Press*] (SAG)
GoodTm	Good Times Restaurants, Inc. [*Associated Press*] (SAG)
Goodyear	[*The*] Goodyear Tire & Rubber Co. [*Associated Press*] (SAG)
GOOFC	Grand Ole Opry Fan Club (EA)
GOOG	Linguere [*Senegal*] [*ICAO location identifier*] (ICLI)
GOOK	Kaolack [*Senegal*] [*ICAO location identifier*] (ICLI)
GOOMBY	Get Out of My Backyard [*Slang*]
GOONQ	Grand Officier de l'Ordre National du Quebec [*Canada*] (DD)
GOONS	Guild of One Name Studies [*Organization to link people with a common surname for the study of family history*] [*British*]
GOOO	Dakar [*Senegal*] [*ICAO location identifier*] (ICLI)
GOOS	Global Ocean Observation System (ECON)
GOOS	Global Ozone Observing System [*Marine science*] (OSRA)
GOOS	Gunnery Officers Ordnance School
GOOSE	Waysgoose [*Country fair*] (ROG)
GOOV	Dakar [*Senegal*] [*ICAO location identifier*] (ICLI)
GOOY	Dakar/Yoff [*Senegal*] [*ICAO location identifier*] (ICLI)
GOP	General Operational Plot
GOP	General Outpost [*Army*] (AABC)
GOP	Gold Point Resources [*Vancouver Stock Exchange symbol*]
GOP	Gorakhpur [*India*] [*Airport symbol*] (OAG)
GOP	Government of Pakistan (ECON)
GOP	Government of the Philippines (CINC)
GOP	Government-Owned Property
GOP	Grand Old Party [*The Republican Party*]

GOP .... Grille Opening Panel [*Automotive engineering*]
GOP .... Ground Observer Post
GOP .... Ground Operations Panel [*NASA*] (NASA)
GOP .... Group of Paths (SAA)
GOP .... Group of Pictures [*Computer science*]
GOPAC .... GOP Action Committee
GOPAL .... GOP [*Grand Old Party*] Women's Political Action League (EA)
GOPARS ...... Government-Operated Parts Store
GOPE .... Government-Owned Plant Equipment
GOPG .... Ground Operations Planning Group [*NASA*] (NASA)
GOPIRB .... General Officer Product Improvement Review Board
GOPITS .... Grand Offertory Procession in the Sky [*Corporate sobriquet used by novelist William X. Kienzle*]
GOPL .... General Outpost Line [*Army*]
GOPO .... Government-Owned/Privately-Operated (GFGA)
GOPR .... General Officers' Protocol Roster
GOPRINT ..... Government Printer [*Queensland, Australia*]
GOPS .... Giga Operations Per Second (NITA)
GOQ .... Genuine Occupational Qualification (DI)
GOQ .... Glucose Oxidation Quotient (STED)
GOQ .... Golmud [*China*] [*Airport symbol*] (OAG)
GOQS .... General On-Line Query System (MCD)
GOR .... Gained Output Ratio (IEEE)
GOR .... Gas-Oil Ratio (IEEE)
GOR .... Gastroesophageal Reflux [*Medicine*] (STED)
GOR .... General Ocean Research [*Navy ship symbol*]
GOR .... General Officer Review (MCD)
GOR .... General Operating Room
GOR .... General Operational Requirement
GOR .... General Overruling Regulation [*Office of Price Stabilization*] (DLA)
GOR .... Golden Range Resources, Inc. [*Toronto Stock Exchange symbol*]
GOR .... Goldstack Resources [*Vancouver Stock Exchange symbol*]
GOR .... Gore [*Ethiopia*] [*Airport symbol*] (OAG)
GOR .... Gori [*Former USSR Seismograph station code, US Geological Survey*] (SEIS)
GOR .... Gradual-Onset-Rate [*Air Force*] (DOMA)
GOR .... Grille Opening Reinforcement [*Automotive engineering*]
GOR .... Ground Operations Review (MCD)
GOR .... Gun Operations Room [*British military*] (DMA)
GOR .... Gurkha Other Rank [*Military British*]
GoranC .... Goran Capital, Inc. [*Associated Press*] (SAG)
GORD .... Gastro-Oesophageal Reflux Disease [*Medicine*] (WDAA)
Gord Dec .... Gordon on the Law of Decedents in Pennsylvania [*A publication*] (DLA)
Gord Dig ..... Gordon's Digest of United States Laws [*A publication*] (DLA)
GORD HIGHRS... Gordon Highlanders [*Military British*] (ROG)
Gordon .... Gordon's Reports [*24-26 Colorado and 10-13 Colorado Appeals*] [*A publication*] (DLA)
Gord Tr .... Gordon's Treason Trials [*A publication*] (DLA)
Gore-B Comp... Gore-Brown on Companies [*43rd ed.*] [*1977*] [*A publication*] (DLA)
GOREDCO .... Gulf Oil Real Estate Development Co.
GORF .... Goddard Optical Research Facility [*Goddard Space Flight Center*] [*NASA*]
GORG .... General Officers Review Group [*Air Force*]
Gorg .... Gorgias [*483-376BC*] [*Classical studies*] (OCD)
G Org .... Grand-Orgue [*Great Organ*] [*Music*]
G ORG .... Great Organ [*Music*]
GORID .... Ground Optical Recorder for Intercept Determination
GORJE .... Generic Ordnance Ramjet Engine (MCD)
GORK .... God Only Really Knows [*Facetious diagnosis for a puzzling medical case*]
GormRup ..... Gorman-Rupp Co. [*Associated Press*] (SAG)
GORP .... Ground Operational [*or Operations*] Requirements Plan [*NASA*]
GORP .... Ground Operations Review Panel [*NASA*] (NASA)
GORS .... Grant of Resident Status
GORS .... Ground Observation Reporting System
GORS .... Ground Observer RF [*Radio Frequency*] System [*NASA*] (NASA)
GORSP .... Government Officials Responsible for Standardization Policies [*Economic Commission for Europe*] [*United Nations*] (PDAA)
GORT .... Gilmore Oral Reading Test [*Psychology*] (DAVI)
GORT .... Gray Oral Reading Tests
GORT-R .... Gray Oral Reading Tests - Revised [*Educational test*]
GORX .... Graphite Oxidation from Reactor Excursion [*Engineering computer code*]
GOS .... Gate Operating System [*Aviation*] (DA)
GOS .... General Operating Specification [*Air Materiel Command*] (AAG)
GOS .... General Overhaul Specification
GOS .... Geodetic Optical System
GOS .... Glasgow Outcome Score [*Medicine*] (DMAA)
GOS .... Global Observing System (EERA)
GOS .... Global Observing Systems [*Weather*]
GOS .... Global Operating System (IAA)
GOS .... Golden State Resources [*Vancouver Stock Exchange symbol*]
GOS .... Goldfields Air Services [*Australia ICAO designator*] (FAAC)
GOS .... Gosford [*Australia Airport symbol Obsolete*] (OAG)
GOS .... Gossip (DSUE)
GOS .... Government of Singapore (CINC)
GOS .... Government of Spain
GOS .... Government of Sweden (MCD)
GOS .... Grade of Service
GOS .... Grand Outside Sentinel [*Freemasonry*] (ROG)
GOS .... Graphical Output Scheme (PDAA)
GOS .... Graphics Operating System [*Tektronix*]
GOS .... Gross Operating Surplus [*Economics*]
GOS .... Ground Operations System (MCD)

GOS .... Group Operating Services (NRCH)
GOS .... Guild of Surveyors (BUAC)
GOS .... Lakeview, OR [*Location identifier FAA*] (FAAL)
GOSC .... General Officer Steering Committee [*Military*] (MCD)
GOSEAC .... Group of Specialists on Environmental Affairs and Conservation (EERA)
Gosf .... Gosford's Manuscript Reports, Scotch Court of Session [*A publication*] (DLA)
GOSG .... General Officer Steering Group
GOSH .... Graphical Operating System Hack [*Computer science*]
GOSH .... Great Ormond Street Hospital (WDAA)
GOSH .... Grown Offspring, Still Home [*Lifestyle classification*]
GOSH .... Oshkosh B Gosh, Inc. [*NASDAQ symbol*] (SAG)
GOSHA .... Oshkosh B'Gosh Cl'A' [*NASDAQ symbol*] (TTSB)
GOSHB .... Oshkosh B'Gosh Cl'B' [*NASDAQ symbol*] (TTSB)
GOSIP .... Government Open Systems Implementation Protocol [*Telecommunications*]
GOSIP .... Government Open Systems Interconnection Profile [*National Institute of Standards and Technology*] (GFGA)
GOSIP .... Government Open Systems Interconnection Profiles Computer science (EERA)
GOSIP .... Government Open Systems Interconnect Protocol [*Computer science*] (CIST)
GOSL .... Government of Sri Lanka
GOSM .... Matam/Ouro Sogui [*Senegal*] [*ICAO location identifier*] (ICLI)
GOSP .... Gas-Oil Separation Plant
GOSP .... Golden Spike National Historic Site
GOSP .... Gospel (ROG)
GOSP .... Podor [*Senegal*] [*ICAO location identifier*] (ICLI)
GOSPLAN .... Gosudarstvennaja Planovaja Komissija [*Central Planning Commission*] [*Former USSR*]
GOSR .... Richard-Toll [*Senegal*] [*ICAO location identifier*] (ICLI)
GOSS .... Gossamer Hat [*Tall hat*] (ROG)
GOSS .... Ground Operational [*or Operations*] Support System [*NASA*]
GOSS .... Saint Louis [*Senegal*] [*ICAO location identifier*] (ICLI)
GOSSTCOMP... Global Sea Surface Temperature Computation
GOSSTRAKH... Gosudarstvennoe Strakhovanie [*State insurance*] [*Former USSR*]
GOST .... Committee of the Russian Federation for Standardisation, Metrology, and Certification (BUAC)
GOST .... Goddard Satellite Tracking [*NASA*] (MCD)
GOST .... Gosudarstvenny Obstschessojusny Standart [*All-Union State Standard*] [*Former USSR*]
GOST .... Guidance Optics and Sighting
GOT .... Air Express in Norrkoping AB [*Sweden ICAO designator*] (FAAC)
GOT .... Aspartate Aminotransferase [*An enzyme*] (DAVI)
GOT .... Glucose Oxidase Test [*Organic chemistry*] (DAVI)
GOT .... Glutamic-Oxaloacetic Transaminase [*Also, AAT, ASAT, AST*] [*An enzyme*]
GOT .... Goldbelt Mines [*Vancouver Stock Exchange symbol*]
GOT .... Goteborg [*Sweden*] [*Seismograph station code, US Geological Survey Closed*] (SEIS)
GOT .... Gothenburg [*Sweden*] [*Airport symbol*] (OAG)
got .... Gothic [*MARC language code Library of Congress*] (LCCP)
GOT .... Gottschalks, Inc. [*NYSE symbol*] (SPSG)
GOT .... Government of Tunisia
GOT .... Government-Owned Terminal
GOTA .... Green Olive Trade Association (EA)
GOTB .... Bakel [*Senegal*] [*ICAO location identifier*] (ICLI)
G/OTBSR...... Gas/Oil Tax Block Summary Record [*IRS*]
Gotchk .... Gottschalks, Inc. [*Associated Press*] (SAG)
GOTCO .... Gulf Oil Trading Co.
GOTG .... Government of the Gambia
Goth .... De Bello Gothico [*of Procopius*] [*Classical studies*] (OCD)
GOTH .... Gothic [*Language, etc.*]
Goth .... Gothic (VRA)
GOTH .... Gothic Energy [*NASDAQ symbol*] (TTSB)
GOTH .... Gothic Energy Corp. [*NASDAQ symbol*] (SAG)
GotHA .... Goteborgs Hogskolas Arsskrift [*Gothenburg*] [*A publication*] (BJA)
GothE .... Gothic Energy Corp. [*Associated Press*] (SAG)
Gothic .... Gothic Energy Corp. [*Associated Press*] (SAG)
GothicEn ..... Gothic Energy Corp. [*Associated Press*] (SAG)
GOTHW .... Gothic Energy Wrrt [*NASDAQ symbol*] (TTSB)
GOTHZ .... Gothic Energy Wrrt [*NASDAQ symbol*] (TTSB)
GOTK .... Geotek Communications, Inc. [*NASDAQ symbol*] (NQ)
GOTK .... Goetek Communications [*NASDAQ symbol*] (TTSB)
GOTK .... Kedougou [*Senegal*] [*ICAO location identifier*] (ICLI)
GOTLF .... Gotaas-Larsen Shipping Corp. (MHDW)
GOTN .... Niokolo Koba [*Senegal*] [*ICAO location identifier*] (ICLI)
GOTOH......... Go to Heaven [*Name of missionary, "Professor Gotoh," for Worldwide Church of God*]
G/OTPSR...... Gas/Oil Tax Program Summary Record [*IRS*]
GOTR .... Greek Orthodox Theological Review [*A publication*] (BJA)
GOTRAN ...... Load and Go FORTRAN [*Computer science*]
GOTS .... Government Off- The Shelf (DOMA)
GOTS .... Graphic-Oriented Timesharing System [*Computer science*] (IAA)
GOTS .... Gravity-Oriented Test Satellite [*NASA*]
GOTS .... Simenti [*Senegal*] [*ICAO location identifier*] (ICLI)
GOTT .... Tambacounda [*Senegal*] [*ICAO location identifier*] (ICLI)
Gott Anz ..... Goettingischer Gelehrte Anzeigen [*A publication*] (OCD)
GOTTEX .... Gottlieb Textiles
Gott Nachr.. Nachrichten von der Gesellschaft der Wissenschaften zu Goettingen [*A publication*] (OCD)
Gottschall ... Gottschall's Dayton Superior Court Reports [*Ohio*] [*A publication*] (DLA)
GOTU .... Glider Operational Training Unit [*British military*] (DMA)

GOTV .... Get Out the Vote (GNE)
GOU .... Garoua [*Cameroon*] [*Airport symbol*] (OAG)
gou .... Gouache (VRA)
GOU .... Government of Uganda (ECON)
GOU .... Grupo de Oficiales Unidos [*Group of United Officers*] [*Argentina*]
GOU .... Gulf Canada Resources [*NYSE symbol*] (TTSB)
GOU .... Gulf Canada Resources Ltd. [*AMEX symbol Toronto Stock Exchange symbol*]
GOU .... Oglethorpe University, Atlanta, GA [*OCLC symbol*] (OCLC)
Goucher C ... Goucher College (GAGS)
Goud Pand... Goudsmit's Pandects [*Roman law*] [*A publication*] (DLA)
Gould......... Gouldsborough's English King's Bench Reports [*A publication*] (DLA)
Gould & T... Gould and Tucker's Notes on Revised Statutes of United States [*A publication*] (DLA)
GouldP........ Goulds Pumps, Inc. [*Associated Press*] (SAG)
Gould Pl ...... Gould on the Principles of Pleading in Civil Actions [*A publication*] (DLA)
Gouldsb ...... Gouldsborough's English King's Bench Reports [*A publication*] (DLA)
Gouldsb (Eng)... Gouldsborough's English King's Bench Reports [*A publication*] (DLA)
Gould's Dig... Gould's Arkansas Digest of Laws [*A publication*] (DLA)
Gould Sten Rep... Gould's Stenographic Reporter [*Monographic Series*] [*Albany, NY*] [*A publication*] (DLA)
Gould Wat ... Gould on Waters [*A publication*] (DLA)
GOUPrA ...... Gulf Can ResAdjcm Ser 1 Pref [*NYSE symbol*] (TTSB)
Gour............ Gourick's Patent Digest [*1889-91*] [*A publication*] (DLA)
Gourl Gen Av... Gourlie on General Average [*A publication*] (DLA)
GOV .... Generator Output Voltage
GOV .... Global Government Plus Fund, Inc. [*NYSE symbol*] (SPSG)
GOV .... Golden Dividend Resources [*Vancouver Stock Exchange symbol*]
GOV .... Govalkot [*India*] [*Seismograph station code, US Geological Survey Closed*] (SEIS)
GOV .... Gove [*Australia Airport symbol*] (OAG)
GOV .... Govern (ROG)
Gov .... Governing (TBD)
GOV .... Government
gov............. Government (VRA)
GOV .... Government-Owned Vehicle [*GSA*] (TAG)
gov............. Governor (DD)
GOV .... Governor (AFM)
Gov .... Governor (TBD)
GOVAIR....... Government Aircraft (DNAB)
GOVAIRAUTHOUT... Travel via Government Aircraft Authorized Outside CONUS [*Military*]
GOVAIRAUTHVATL... Travel via Government Aircraft Authorized Outside CONUS Where Available [*Military*]
GOVAIRDIR... Travel via Government Aircraft Is Directed Where Necessary [*Military*]
GOVAIRDIROUT... Travel via Government Aircraft Is Directed Outside CONUS [*Military*]
GOVAIRDIRVAIL... Travel via Government Aircraft Is Directed Outside CONUS Where Available [*Military*]
GOVAIRPRI... Travel via Government Aircraft Outside CONUS Class _____ Priority Certified [*Military*]
GOVCOMLAIRAUTH... Travel via Government and/or Commercial Aircraft Authorized Where Necessary to Expedite Completion of Duty [*Military*]
GOVD........... Governed (ROG)
GoVd........... Go-Video, Inc. [*Associated Press*] (SAG)
Govett......... Govett & Co. Ltd. [*Associated Press*] (SAG)
GOVG.......... Governing (MSA)
GoVideo....... Go-Video, Inc. [*Associated Press*] (SAG)
GOV IS........ Governor's Island [*Massachusetts*] (WDAA)
GOVMAR...... Governor, Marshall Islands
GOVMERAIR... Government or Commercial Aircraft (DNAB)
GOVN.......... Govern (ROG)
Gov Ops....... Government Operations Committee [*House and Senate*] (AAGC)
Govr............ Governor
GOVS .... Governments Division [*Census*] (OICC)
GOV STD ..... Government Standards
Gov St U..... Governors State University (GAGS)
govt .... Government (DD)
GOVT .... Government (AFM)
Govt............ Government [*Business term*] (EBF)
GOVT .... Govett & Co. Ltd. [*NASDAQ symbol*] (SAG)
Gov't Cont Rep... Government Contracts Reporter [*Commerce Clearing House*] [*A publication*] (DLA)
GOVTEL .... Government Telegram (IAA)
GOVTHO ...... Government House [*Canada*] (DNAB)
GOVTL .... Governmental
GOVTLAIRNOREUR... Commander, Allied Air Forces, Northern Europe
GOVTRANSDIROUT... Travel via Government Transportation Directed Outside CONUS [*Military*]
GOVTRANSDIRVAIL... Travel via Government Transportation Directed Outside CONUS Where Available [*Military*]
GOW .... Gowganda Resources, Inc. [*Toronto Stock Exchange symbol Vancouver Stock Exchange symbol*]
Gow .... Gow's English Nisi Prius Cases [*171 English Reprint*] [*A publication*] (DLA)
GOW .... Grand Old Woman [*England's Queen Victoria*]
GOW .... Gunnery Officer's Writer [*Navy British*]
GOWEX........ Geometry of the Wake Experiment [*Military*] (MCD)
GOWG.......... Ground Operations Working Group (MCD)
GOWMA........ Gulf Oil Wholesale Marketers Association (EA)

Gow NP .... Gow's English Nisi Prius Cases [*171 English Reprint*] [*A publication*] (DLA)
Gow NP (Eng)... Gow's English Nisi Prius Cases [*171 English Reprint*] [*A publication*] (DLA)
GOWON ...... Gulf Offshore Weather Observing Network [*Marine science*] (OSRA)
Gow Part .... Gow on Partnerships [*A publication*] (DLA)
GOWR.......... Grand Order of Water Rats [*British*] (BI)
GOX .... Gaseous Oxygen
GOX .... Greenville, SC [*Location identifier FAA*] (FAAL)
GOY .... Gal Oya [*Ceylon*] [*Airport symbol*] (AD)
GOY .... Gorny [*Former USSR Seismograph station code, US Geological Survey Closed*] (SEIS)
GOY .... GWE [*Global Weather Experiment*] Operational Year [*Marine science*] (MSC)
GOYA .... Get Off Your After-End [*Slang Bowdlerized version*]
GOYA .... Greek Organisation of Young Australians
GOYA .... Greek Orthodox Youth of America [*Later, GOYAL*] (EA)
GOYAL......... Greek Orthodox Young Adult League (EA)
GOZ .... Gorna Orjachovica [*Bulgaria*] [*Airport symbol*] (OAG)
GP............... Albania [*License plate code assigned to foreign diplomats in the US*]
GP............... Ciba-Geigy AG [*Switzerland*] [*Research code symbol*]
GP............... Du Pont [*E. I.*] De Nemours & Co., Inc. [*Research code symbol*]
GP............... Galactic Plane [*Astronomy*]
GP............... Galactic Probe
GP............... Gallbladder Patient
GP............... Galley Proof (ADA)
GP............... Gallup Poll
GP............... Galvanized Pipe [*Technical drawings*]
GP............... Galvanized Plain [*Metal industry*]
GP............... Games Played [*Sports statistics*]
GP............... Gang Punch [*Computer science*]
GP............... Gas, Persistent
GP............... Gas-Plasma [*Computer display panel*]
GP............... Gas Pressure (MUGU)
GP............... Gas Projectile (MCD)
GP............... Gastric Pressure [*Physiology*]
GP............... Gastroplasty [*Medicine*]
GP............... Gauge Pressure (IAA)
GP............... Generalized Programming [*Computer science*]
GP............... General Paralysis [*or Paresis*] [*Medicine*]
GP............... General Paresis (DB)
GP............... General Pause [*Music*]
GP............... General Plant Telephone [*Nuclear energy*] (NRCH)
GP............... General Practice [*Medical specialty*] (DAVI)
GP............... General Practitioner [*of medicine*]
GP............... General Preferred Tariff [*Canada*]
GP............... General Principles [*FBI standardized term*]
GP............... General Processor
GP............... General Product (BUR)
GP............... General Protection [*Computer science*] (BYTE)
GP............... General Provision
GP............... General Public [*Merchandising slang*]
GP............... General Publication (KSC)
GP............... General Purpose
GP............... General with Parents' Consent [*Motion picture rating*] (BARN)
GP............... Genesis Project (EA)
GP............... Genetic Prediabetes [*Endocrinology*]
GP............... Geographical Pole
GP............... Geographical Position
GP............... Geographic Point
GP............... Geometric Phase [*Mathematics*]
GP............... Geometric Progression
GP............... Georgia-Pacific [*NYSE symbol*] (TTSB)
GP............... Georgia-Pacific Corp. [*NYSE symbol*] (SPSG)
GP............... German Patent (IAA)
GP............... Germinable Propagule [*Botany*]
GP............... Giant Pulse
GP............... Gimbal Package
GP............... Gimbal Platform (AAG)
GP............... Gimbal Point
GP............... Girard-Point [*Virus*]
GP............... Girls' PROUT [*Progressive Utilization Theory*] (EA)
GP............... Glia Precursor [*Biochemistry*]
GP............... Glide Path [*Aviation*]
GP............... Gliomatosis Peritonei [*Oncology*]
GP............... Globus Pallidus [*Brain anatomy*]
GP............... Gloria Patri [*Glory to the Father*] [*Latin*]
GP............... Glucose Phosphate [*Biochemistry*]
GP............... Glutathione Peroxidase [*An enzyme*] (MAE)
GP............... Glycerophosphate [*Biochemistry*]
GP............... Glycogen Phosphorylase [*An enzyme*]
GP............... Glycolyl Phthalate [*Organic chemistry*]
GP............... Glycopeptide (DB)
GP............... Glycoprotein
GP............... Goal Post
GP............... Goal Programming
GP............... Going Public [*Investment term*]
GP............... Gold Points [*Investment term*]
GP............... Goodpasture [*Syndrome*] [*Medicine*] (DAVI)
GP............... Good Practice
GP............... Government Property
GP............... Government Publications [*Northern Territory, Australia*]
GP............... Gozo Party [*Malta*] [*Political party*] (PPE)
GP............... Grace Period [*Business term*]
GP............... Graded Program

GP	Graduated Pension (WDAA)
GP	Graduate in Pharmacy [*British*] (ROG)
GP	Gram-Positive [*Also, GRP*] [*Microbiology*]
GP	Grandmothers for Peace (EA)
GP	Grand Passion
GP	Grand Patron [*Freemasonry*]
GP	Grand Prelate [*Freemasonry*]
GP	Grand Prix
GP	Grand Pursuivant [*Freemasonry*] (ROG)
GP	Graphic Panel (COE)
GP	Graphics Package [*Computer science*] (MHDI)
GP	Graphics Processor
G/P	Graphite Polyester
GP	Grass Pollen [*Immunology*]
GP	Gratitude Patient [*A nonpaying patient*] [*Medical slang*]
G/P	Gravida Para [*Gynecology and obstetrics*] (DAVI)
GP	Gravitational Redshift Space Probe [*Also, GRAVR*]
GP	Gray Panthers (EA)
GP	Great Peoples [*A publication*]
GP	Great Portland Street [*London*] (DSUE)
GP	Great Primer
GP	Greenhouse Perennial [*Horticulture*] (ROG)
GP	Green Party [*Germany*] (BUAC)
GP	Greenpeace
G/P	Green Phone [*NASA*] (KSC)
GP	Grid Pulse (IAA)
GP	Gross Premium [*Insurance*] (AIA)
GP	Gross Profit [*Business term*]
GP	Ground Pneumatic (AAG)
GP	Ground Post (IAA)
GP	Ground-Protective [*Relay*]
GP	Ground Rods [*JETDS nomenclature*] [*Military*] (CET)
GP	Group (AFM)
Gp	Group (DB)
gp	Group (VRA)
GP	Groupe de Paris [*France*] (EAIO)
GP	Growth in Total Profit (MHDB)
GP	Guadeloupe [*ANSI two-letter standard code*] (CNC)
gp	Guadeloupe [*MARC country of publication code Library of Congress*] (LCCP)
GP	Guidance Package
GP	Guided Projectile [*Military*] (CAAL)
GP	Guinea Pig
GP	Gun Pointer [*Naval gunnery*]
GP	Gun Program [*Military*] (MCD)
GP	Gutta-Percha [*Dentistry*] (MAE)
GP	Gutter Pair [*Philately*]
GP	GWEN [*Ground Wave Emergency Network*] Project (EA)
GP	Gyro Package
GP	Hadag Air Seebaederflug [*ICAO designator*] (AD)
GP	Parental Guidance Suggested [*Later, PG*] [*Movie rating*]
GPA	Ciba-Geigy Corp. [*Research code symbol*]
GPA	Garden Products Association (BUAC)
GPA	Garlic Processors Association (BUAC)
GPA	Gas Pressure Activator (MCD)
GPA	Gas Processors Association (EA)
GPA	Gate Pulse Amplifier [*Computer science*] (IAA)
GPA	Gay Press Association [*Later, GLPA*] (EA)
GPA	General Passenger Agent
GPA	General Public Assistance [*A form of public charity*]
GPA	General Purchasing Agency [*Allied German Occupation Forces*]
GPA	General-Purpose Amphibian [*Military vehicle*]
GPA	General-Purpose Amplifier
GPA	General-Purpose Analysis (IEEE)
GPA	General-Purpose Array
GPA	Georgians for Preservation Action [*An association*]
GPA	Geschichte der Perser und Araber zur Zeit der Sasaniden [*A publication*] (BJA)
GPa	Gigapascal [*SI unit of pressure*]
GPA	Global Program on AIDS [*Acquired Immune Deficiency Syndrome*] [*WHO*]
GPA	Glycerine Producers Association (EA)
GPA	Glycophorin A [*Biochemistry*]
GPA	Goat Producers Association [*British*] (DBA)
GPA	Gold Producers' Association [*Australia*]
GPA	Golpazari [*Turkey*] [*Also, GLP*] [*Seismograph station code, US Geological Survey*] (SEIS)
GPA	Government Procurement Agreement (WDAA)
GPA	Government Property Administration (MCD)
GPA	Grade-Point Average [*Education*]
GPA	Graduation Pledge Alliance [*An association*] (EA)
GPA	Grandparents Anonymous (EA)
GPA	Graphical PERT [*Program Evaluation and Review Technique*] Analog [*Computer science*] (IEEE)
GPA	Graphics Philately Association (EA)
GPA	Graphics Preparatory Association (EA)
GPA	Green Party of Australia [*Political party*]
GPA	Greenpeace Australia
GPA	Green Peach Aphid [*Entomology*]
GPA	Green Point Average [*Knowledge of the environment*] (WPI)
GPA	Grounded Plate Amplifier
GPA	Ground Plane Antenna
GPA	Group Practice Association [*Medicine*]
GPA	Guidance Platform Assembly [*Military*] (AABC)
GPA	Guidance Positioning Assembly
GPA	Guinea Pig Albumin
GPA	Guinness Peat Aviation [*Commercial firm British*]
GPA	Gulfcoast Pulpwood Association (EA)
GPA	Kingman Aviation, Inc. [*ICAO designator*] (FAAC)
GPA	United States Government Printing Office - Serials, Alexandria, VA [*OCLC symbol*] (OCLC)
GPAA	Gold Prospectors Association of America (EA)
g-p-ab	Gravida, Para, and Abortus [*Gynecology and obstetrics*] (DAVI)
GPABP	Guinea Pig Anti-Bovine Protection (OA)
GPAC	General-Purpose Analog Computer (DEN)
GPAC	Graphics Package [*Computer science*] (MHDI)
GPAC	Great Plains Agricultural Council (EA)
GPAC	Great Plains Asbestos Control, Inc. (EFIS)
GPACK	General Utility Package (MHDB)
GPAD	Gallons per Acre per Day [*Irrigation*]
GPAD	Graphics Program for Aircraft Design
GPADS	Guided Parafoil Aerial Delivery System
GPADS-L	Delivery System-Light [*Army*] (INF)
GPAFX	Guardian Park Ave. Cl.A [*Mutual fund ticker symbol*] (SG)
GPAIS	Guinea Pig Anti-Insulin Serum [*Immunochemistry*] (MAE)
GPALS	Global Protection against Limited Strike [*Military*]
GPAM	General-Purpose Armor Machine Gun
GPAM	Graduated-Payment Adjustable Mortgage
GPAP	General Purpose Associative Processor (PDAA)
GPAR	General Parametrics Corp. [*NASDAQ symbol*] (NQ)
GPARAFN	Green Party Anti-Racist and Anti-Fascist Network (BUAC)
GPARM	Graduated-Payment Adjustable-Rate Mortgage (WDAA)
GPARN	Graduated Payment Adjustable Rate Mortgage (EBF)
GPAS	General Performance Appraisals System
GPAS	General Product Acceptance Standard [*Automotive engineering*]
GPAS	General-Purpose Airborne Simulator
GPAT	General-Purpose Automatic Test [*Air Force*]
GPATE	General-Purpose Automatic Test Equipment [*Army*] (MSA)
GPATS	General-Purpose Automatic Test Set [*Air Force*] (IAA)
GPATS	General-Purpose Automatic Test Station
GPATS	General-Purpose Automatic Test System [*Air Force*]
GPAVTS	Great Planes Area Vocational Technical School [*Oklahoma*]
GPAX	General Purpose Automation Executive [*IBM*] (NITA)
GPAY	General Payments System
GPB	General Purchasing Board
GPB	General Purpose Basic [*Programming language*] (NITA)
GPB	General-Purpose Buffer
GPB	Geon Process Butadiene
GPB	Glossopharyngeal Breathing
GPB	Glucose Phosphorylase B [*An enzyme*]
GPB	Glycoprotein B [*Biochemistry*]
GPB	Government Patents Board [*Functions transferred to Secretary of Commerce, 1961*]
GP-B	Gravity Probe-B [*Experiment to test Einstein's Theory of General Relativity*]
GPB	Ground Power Breaker [*Electronics*] (OA)
GPB	Pittsburgh, PA [*Location identifier FAA*] (FAAL)
GPBA	General Produce Brokers Association (BUAC)
GPBIM	General-Purpose Buffer Interface Module [*Computer science*] (MCD)
GPBP	Guinea Pig Myelin Basic Protein [*Immunochemistry*]
GPBS	Gas Pressure Bending System
GPBTO	General-Purpose Barbed Tape Obstacle [*Army*] (RDA)
GPC	Gallons per Capita
GPC	Gandhi Peace Center (EA)
GPC	Gas-to-Particle Conversion [*Atmospheric science*]
GPC	Gastric Parietal Cell [*Cytology*] (AAMN)
GPC	Gastrointestinal Pathology Club [*Later, GPS*] (EA)
GPC	Gauge Pressure Control
GPC	Gay People at Columbia [*Later, CGLA*] (EA)
GPC	Gel Permeation Chromatography
GPC	General People's Congress [*Yemen*] [*Political party*] (EY)
GPC	General People's Congress [*or Committee*] [*Libya*] [*Political party*] (PPW)
GPC	General Peripheral Controller
GPC	General Petroleum Co. [*Egypt*] (BUAC)
GPC	General Physical Condition [*Medicine*]
GPC	General Precision Connector (IAA)
GPC	General-Purpose Carrier [*Military*]
GPC	General-Purpose Computer
GPC	General Purposes Committee [*British*] (DCTA)
GPC	Genuine Parts [*NYSE symbol*] (TTSB)
GPC	Genuine Parts Co. [*NYSE symbol*] (SPSG)
GPC	Geocentric Pendulum Control
GPC	Georgia Peanut Commission (EA)
gpc	Germanium Point-Contact (IDOE)
GPC	Ghana Publishing Co.
GPC	Giant Papillary Conjunctivitis [*Ophthalmology*]
GPC	Giant Piston Core [*Geology*]
GPC	Glass-Polymer Composite (PDAA)
GPC	Global Plotting Chart [*Air Force*]
GPC	Global Processing Center (EERA)
GPC	Glycerylphosphorylcholine [*Biochemistry*]
GPC	Golay Pneumatic Cell
GPC	Government Publications Center (SAA)
GPC	Government Purpose Classification
GPC	Gram-Positive Cocci [*Immunology*] (DAVI)
GPC	Grande Prairie Regional College Library [*UTLAS symbol*]
GPC	Granular Progenitor Cell [*Medicine*] (DMAA)
GPC	Graphical Picture Drawing Language [*Computer science*] (PDAA)
GPC	Grass Pollen Count [*Immunology*]

GPC .... Great Plains Coliseum [*Lawton, OK*]
GPC .... Greek Productivity Centre (BUAC)
GPC .... Gross Profit Contribution
GPC .... Ground Power Contactor
GPC .... Guinea Pig Complement [*Immunochemistry*]
GPC .... Gulf Publishing Co.
GPC .... Gypsum-Plaster Ceiling [*Technical drawings*]
GPCA .... General-Purpose Communications Adapter
GPCA .... Golf Products and Components Association [*Defunct*] (EA)
GPCA .... Great Pyrenees Club of America (EA)
Gp Capt ...... Group Captain [*British military*] (DMA)
GPCB .... General-Purpose Communications Base (MHDB)
GPCB .... GOAL [*Ground Operations Aerospace Language*] Program Control
          Block (MCD)
GPCC .... Global Precipitation Climatology Center [*Marine science*] (OSRA)
GPCC .... Global Precipitation Climatology Centre (EERA)
GPCC .... Grand Prix Contact Club [*British*] (DBA)
GPCD .... Gallons per Capita per Day
GPCE .... Groupement Pharmaceutique de la CE [*Pharmaceutical Group of the
          EC*] (ECED)
GPC-ERR ..... General Passenger Committee - Eastern Railroads [*Defunct*] (EA)
GPCF .... General-Purpose Computing Facility (MHDB)
GPCI .... Geographic Practice Cost Index [*Medicare*]
GPCL .... General-Purpose Closed Loop [*Nuclear energy*] (NRCH)
GP CMDR .... Group Commander [*Military*] (WDAA)
GPCO .... Global Perspective Country Outlooks [*Global Perspective, Inc.*]
          [*Information service or system*]
GPCOC .... General-Purpose Central Office Concentrator [*Telecommunications*]
GPCP .... Generalized Process Control Programming [*Computer science*]
          (IEEE)
GPCP .... General-Purpose Contouring Program
GPCP .... General-Purpose Controller Processor (IAA)
GPCP .... Global Precipitation Chemistry Project [*Study of rain properties*]
GPCP .... Global Precipitation Climatology Project [*Marine science*] (OSRA)
GPCP .... Great Plains Conservation Program
GPCR .... Gas-to-Particle Conversion Rate [*Physics*]
GPCR .... G-Protein-Coupled Receptor [*Biochemistry*]
GPCR .... Great Proletarian Cultural Revolution [*People's Republic of China*]
GPcRE .... Great Pacific Real Estate Investment Trust, Inc. [*Associated Press*]
          (SAG)
GPCS .... General-Purpose Control System (IAA)
GPCS .... Guinea Pig Control Serum (OA)
GPCSA .... General Practice Computer Suppliers Association (BUAC)
GPCT .... George Peabody College for Teachers [*Later, George Peabody
          College for Teachers of Vanderbilt University*] [*Tennessee*]
GPC/TP .... Glycerophosphorylcholine to Total Phosphate Ratio (STED)
GPD .... Gallons per Day
gpd .... Gallons per Day (COE)
GPD .... General Pair Decomposition (IAA)
GPD .... General Passenger Department
GPD .... General Police Duties [*British military*] (DMA)
GPD .... General Political Department [*China*] [*Military*]
GPD .... General Protocol Driver (NITA)
GPD .... General-Purpose Data
GPD .... General-Purpose Discipline [*IBM Corp.*]
GPD .... Generals for Peace and Disarmament [*Ittervoort, Netherlands*]
          (EAIO)
GPD .... Gimbal Position Display (KSC)
GPD .... Glass Plasma Display [*Electronics*] (BARN)
GPD .... Glucose-6-phosphate Dehydrogenase [*Also, G6PD, G6PDH*] [*An
          enzyme*]
GPD .... Glycerophosphate Dehydrogenase
GPD .... Graduate Performance Diploma (PGP)
GPD .... Grams per Denier
GPD .... Greenpond [*New Jersey*] [*Seismograph station code, US Geological
          Survey*] (SEIS)
GPD .... Guinea Pig Dander (STED)
GPDA .... Grand Prix Drivers' Association
GPDA .... Gypsum Plasterboard Development Association [*British*] (BI)
GPDA .... Gypsum Products Development Association [*British*] (DBA)
GPDC .... Generalized Pressure Drop Correlation [*Chemical engineering*]
GPDC .... General-Purpose Digital Computer
GPDF .... Gurage People's Democratic Front [*Ethiopia*]
GPDH .... Glycerolphosphate Dehydrogenase [*An enzyme*]
GPDM .... Geopotential Decameter [*Telecommunications*] (TEL)
GPDO .... General Permitted Development Order (WDAA)
GPDS .... General-Purpose Discrete Simulator (MHDI)
GPDS .... General-Purpose Display System
GPDSC .... Girl's Public Day School Co. [*British*] (ROG)
GPDST .... Girls' Public Day School Trust [*British*]
GPDU .... Groupe de Planification des Derives Urbaines [*Canada*]
GPDW .... Glacial Pacific Deep Water
GPDW .... Gypsum Dry Wall [*Technical drawings*]
GPE .... Gas Power Exchange
GPE .... General Precision Equipment (IAA)
GPE .... General-Purpose English (ADA)
GPE .... General-Purpose Equipment
GPE .... General-Purpose Evaporator [*Nuclear energy*] (NRCH)
GPE .... Geometric Position Error (MCD)
Gp E .... Geophysical Engineer
GPE .... Georgia Power Capital LP [*NYSE symbol*] (SAG)
GPE .... Georgia Power Capital Trust I [*NYSE symbol*] (SAG)
GPE .... Georgia Power Co. [*NYSE symbol*] (SPSG)
GPE .... Global Perspectives in Education (EA)
GPE .... Glycerylphosphorylethanolamine [*Biochemistry*] (MAE)

GPE .... Golden Pheasant [*Vancouver Stock Exchange symbol*]
GPE .... Government Preliminary Evaluation (MCD)
GPE .... GP Express Airlines, Inc. [*ICAO designator*] (FAAC)
GPE .... Grammaire du Palmyrenien Epigraphique [*A publication*] (BJA)
GPE .... Granulocyte Colony-Stimulating Factor Promoter Element (DMAA)
GPE .... Graphic Picture Enhancement
GPE .... Gravitational Potential Energy [*Geophysics*]
GPE .... Guided Projectile Establishment (BUAC)
GPE .... Guinea Pig Embryo [*Medicine*] (DMAA)
GPE .... Los Angeles, CA [*Location identifier FAA*] (FAAL)
Gp Engr ...... Geophysical Engineer
GPEP .... General Professional Education of the Physician [*Panel report*]
          [*Association of American Medical Colleges*]
GPEPr .... Georgia Pwr $7.72Pfd [*NYSE symbol*] (TTSB)
GPEPrB .... Georgia Pwr $7.80 Pfd [*NYSE symbol*] (TTSB)
GPEPrP .... Georgia Pwr $1.90'A'Pfd [*NYSE symbol*] (TTSB)
GPEPrQ .... Georgia Pwr $1.9875 'A' Pfd [*NYSE symbol*] (TTSB)
GPEPrR .... Georgia Pwr $1.9375'A'Pfd [*NYSE symbol*] (TTSB)
GPEPrS .... Georgia Pwr $1.925'A'Pfd [*NYSE symbol*] (TTSB)
GPER .... Gas Projectile, Extended Range (MCD)
GPER .... General Plant Equipment Requirements
GPERF .... Ground Passive Electronic Reconnaissance Facility
GPES .... Ground Proximity Extraction System
G Pet .... Gospel of Peter [*Apocryphal work*]
GPET .... Graphic Plan Evaluation Tool (DMAA)
GPETE .... General-Purpose Electronic Test Equipment (NVT)
GPEXS .... General Parts Explosion System (IAA)
GPF .... Gallons per Flush [*Plumbing*]
GPF .... Gandhi Peace Foundation [*India*] (EAIO)
GPF .... Gas Proof (AABC)
GPF .... Generalized Production Function [*Industrial economics*]
GPF .... General Protection Fault [*Computer programming*] (BYTE)
GPF .... General-Purpose Forces
GPF .... Glomerular Plasma Flow [*Medicine*] (DMAA)
GPF .... Grains per Foot
GPF .... Grande Puissance Filloux [*World War II*]
GPF .... Granulocytosis-Promoting Factor [*Hematology*]
GPF .... Groove between Parallel Folds
GPF .... Guardian Pacific Rim Corp. [*Toronto Stock Exchange symbol*]
GPF .... Guinea Pig Fibrinogen
GPF .... GUI [*Graphical User Interface*] Programming Facility [*Computer
          science*]
GPF black .... General Purpose Furnace Black (EDCT)
GPFC .... Galaxy Patrol Fan Club (EA)
GPFC .... Gene Pitney Fan Club (EA)
GPFC .... General Practice Finance Corp. (BUAC)
GPFC .... General-Purpose Function Code (NVT)
GPFI .... Grand Premier Financial, Inc. [*NASDAQ symbol*] (SAG)
GPFL .... Group Flashing [*Navigation signal lights*]
GPFLL .... Group Flashing Light [*Navigation*] (IAA)
GPFS .... General-Purpose Financial Statement (WDAA)
GPFS .... Greater Pacific Financial Services [*Australia*]
GPFU .... Gas Particulate Filter Unit (MCD)
GPG .... Gate Pulse Generator (IAA)
GPG .... General Planning Group
GPG .... Grains per Gallon [*Unit of measure for water hardness*]
GPG .... Grams per Gallon (GNE)
GPG .... Grande Portage [*Vancouver Stock Exchange symbol*]
GPG .... Ground Power Generator (DWSG)
GPG .... Growth-Promoting Genes [*Medicine*] (DB)
GPG .... Guinness Peat Group [*British*]
GPGA .... Georgia Pecan Growers Association (SRA)
GPGA .... Georgia Propane Gas Association (SRA)
GP (Gas)..... Persistent Chemical Agent Gas
GPGG .... Guinea Pig Gamma Globulin [*Immunochemistry*]
GPGL .... General-Purpose Graphic Language [*Computer science*] (IEEE)
GPGS .... Government Purchases of Goods and Services [*BTS*] (TAG)
GPGS .... Ground Power Generator System (DWSG)
GPH .... Gallons per Hour
GPH .... General Physics Corp. [*NYSE symbol*] (SPSG)
GPH .... Genl Physics [*NYSE symbol*] (TTSB)
G Ph .... Graduate in Pharmacy
GPH .... Graphite (MSA)
GPH .... Green Party of Hungary [*Political party*] (EAIO)
GPH .... Grenzpolizeihelfer [*Border Police Aide*] [*German*]
GPHA .... Great Plains Historical Association [*Later, IGP*] (EA)
GPHF .... General Pulaski Heritage Foundation (EA)
GPHLV .... Guinea Pig Herpes-Like Virus [*Medicine*] (DMAA)
GPHMG .... General-Purpose Heavy Machine Gun (MCD)
GPHMO .... Group Practice Health Maintenance Organization [*Insurance*]
          (WYGK)
GPHN .... Giant Pigmented Hairy Nevus (DMAA)
GPHP .... Give Peace Holiday Project (EA)
GPHS .... General-Purpose Heat Source [*Nuclear energy*]
GPHSC .... Group Project for Holocaust Survivors and Their Children (EA)
GPHV .... Guinea Pig Herpes Virus (DMAA)
GPHW .... Gay Public Health Workers Caucus [*Later, LGCPHW*] (EA)
GPI .... General Paralysis of the Insane [*Literal translation, but also medical
          slang for eccentricity*]
GPI .... General Paralysis/Paresis of Insane [*Medicine*] (STED)
GPI .... General Patents Index [*A publication*]
GPI .... General Periodicals Index [*Information Access Co.*] [*Information
          service or system*] (CRD)
GPI .... General, Precision, Inc.
GPI .... General Price Index (WDAA)

GPI............. General Printing Ink (DGA)
GPI............. General-Purpose Interface
GPI............. General-Purpose Inverter (KSC)
GPI............. Genetics and Public Issues Program (HGEN)
GPI............. Gimbal Position Indicator (KSC)
GPI............. Gingival-Periodontal Index [Dentistry]
GPI............. Glass Packaging Institute (EA)
GPI............. Glide Path Indicator [Aviation] (NATG)
GPI............. Glucophosphate Isomerase [An enzyme]
GPI............. Glycoprotein I (DMAA)
GPI............. Glycosyl-Phosphatidylinositol [Biochemistry]
GPI............. GOES [Geostationary Operational Environmental Satellite]
          Precipitation Index [Marine science] (OSRA)
GPI............. Gordon Personal Inventory [Psychology]
GPI............. Government Preliminary Inspection (MCD)
GPI............. Grain Products Irradiator [Nuclear energy]
GPI............. Grandmothers for Peace International [An association] (EA)
GPI............. Graphics Programming Interface [IBM Corp.] (PCM)
GPI............. Great Pacific Industries, Inc. [Toronto Stock Exchange symbol
          Vancouver Stock Exchange symbol]
GPI............. Greenpeace International [Netherlands] (EAIO)
GPI............. Grocery Prices Index [British]
GPI............. Ground Point of Impact
GPI............. Ground Point of Intercept (AFM)
GPI............. Ground Position Indicator [Dead-reckoning computer]
GPI............. Guapi [Colombia] [Airport symbol] (OAG)
GPI............. Guardsman Products, Inc. [NYSE symbol] (SPSG)
GPI............. Guinea Pig Ileum (DMAA)
GPIA .... General-Purpose Interface Adapter (IEEE)
GPIA .... General Purpose Interface Adaptor (NITA)
GPIA .... Generic Pharmaceutical Industry Association (NTPA)
GPIB .... General-Purpose Instrument Bus (IAA)
GPIB .... General-Purpose Interface Bus [Computer science]
GPIC .... General-Purpose Intelligent Cable (MHDB)
GPIC .... General-Purpose Intercomputer [Test] (NVT)
GPIC .... Gulf Petrochemical Industries Co. [Bahrain] (BUAC)
GPID .... Guidance Package Installation Dolly [Polaris missile]
GPIEM .... International Marine Environment Award [Marine science] (OSRA)
GPII .... Geist Picture Interest Inventory [Psychology] (AEBS)
GPIMH .... Guinea Pig Intestinal Mucosal Homogenate (MAE)
GPIO .... General-Purpose Input/Output [Computer science]
GPIP .... Glide Path Intercept Point [Aviation]
GPIPID .... Guinea Pig Intraperitoneal Infectious Dose [Clinical chemistry] (MAE)
GPIS .... Gemini Problem Investigation Status [NASA] (IEEE)
GPIS .... Groundwater Pumping Incentives Scheme [Victoria] (EERA)
GPJ............. Great Peace Journey [Sweden] (EAIO)
GPK............. Gentleman's Pocket Knife
GPK .... Goldpac Investments Ltd. [Vancouver Stock Exchange symbol]
GPK .... Guinea Pig Kidney Antigen [Immunochemistry] (MAE)
GPKA .... Guinea Pig Kidney Absorption (Test) [Clinical chemistry]
GPKD .... General-Purpose Keyboard and Display Control [Computer science]
          (MDG)
GPKT .... Grand Priory of the Knights of the Temple [Freemasonry]
GPL............. Gallahad Petroleum [Vancouver Stock Exchange symbol]
GPL............. Generalized Programming Language [Computer science]
GPL............. General Precision Laboratory
GPL............. General Price Level (ADA)
GPL............. General Public License (NHD)
GPL............. General-Purpose Laboratory (KSC)
GPL............. General-Purpose Language [Computer science] (CSR)
GPL............. General Purpose Loader (NITA)
GPL............. General-Purpose Loop [Nuclear energy] (NRCH)
GPL............. Geographic Position Locator [Navigation]
GPL............. Giant Pulse LASER
GPL............. Gimbal Pickoff Loop
GPL............. GOAL [Ground Operations Aerospace Language] Processing
          Language (MCD)
GPL............. Gravatom Projects Ltd. [British] (IRUK)
GPL............. Group Processing Logic (TEL)
GPL............. Guapiles [Costa Rica] [Airport symbol] (OAG)
GPL............. Guymon Public Library, Guymon, OK [OCLC symbol] (OCLC)
GPL............. Gypsum Lathe [Technical drawings]
GPLA .... General Price Level Accounting (ADA)
GPLA .... General Price-Level Adjusted [Finance] (PDAA)
GPLAN .... Generalized Database Planning System
GPLB .... Grand Prix Association of Long Beach [NASDAQ symbol] (SAG)
GPLC .... Guild of Professional Launderers and Cleaners [British] (BI)
GPLD .... Government Property Lost or Damaged [or Destroyed]
GPLE.......... Global Program Line Editor [Beagle Bros.]
GPLI........... Group-Page-Line-Inserts (MCD)
GPLP .... General-Purpose Linear Programming [Computer science] (IEEE)
GPLR .... Government-Purpose License Rights (AAGC)
GPLRG......... Gay Parents Legal and Research Group [Defunct] (EA)
GPLS .... Giant Pulse LASER System
GPLS .... Glide Path Landing System [Aviation] (IAA)
GPLY .... Gingivoplasty [Dentistry]
GPM............ Gallons per Mile
GPM............ Gallons per Minute
GPM............ Gas-Permeable Membrane
GPM............ Gas Plasma Monitor
GPM............ General Preventive Medicine
GPM............ General-Purpose Macrogenerator [Computer science] (IEEE)
GPM............ General-Purpose Maneuver
GPM............ General-Purpose Missile
GPM............ General-Purpose Module (MHDB)

GPM............ Geopotential Meter
GPM............ Georgia Southern College, Statesboro, GA [OCLC symbol] (OCLC)
GPM............ Gepanzerte Pioniermaschine [Armored Engineer Vehicle] [General
          Electric Co.] [German] (MCD)
GPM............ Giant Pigmented Melanosome [Medicine] (DMAA)
GPM............ Goettinger Predigt-Meditationen [A publication] (BJA)
GPM............ Government Payment Bond (EBF)
GPM............ Gradient Pump Module
GPM............ Graduated Payment Mortgage [Sometimes referred to as "Jeep"]
GPM............ Grams per Mile
GPM............ Grand Past Master [Freemasonry]
GPM............ Grand Prairie, TX [Location identifier FAA] (FAAL)
GPM............ Graphics Postprocessor Module [McDonnell-Douglas Corp.]
GPM............ Grey Power Movement [Australia]
GPM............ Gross Processing Margin (MHDB)
GPM............ Gross Profit Margin (WDAA)
GPM............ Ground Potential Model [Physics]
GPM............ Groups [of code transmitted] per Minute [or Message]
          [Telecommunications]
GPM............ Gunnery Prize Money [British military] (DMA)
GPMA .... Gasoline Pump Manufacturers Association (EA)
GPMA .... Grocery Products Manufacturers Association [Canada] (BUAC)
GPMAL .... Gravida, Para, Multiple Births, Abortions, Live Births [Obstetrics]
GPMC .... Grocery Products Manufacturers of Canada [See also FCPA]
GPMC .... Group and Pension Marketing Conference [LIMRA]
GPME......... Gas-Porous Membrane Electrode [Electrochemistry]
GPME......... General-Purpose Mission Equipment (NASA)
GPMF......... Gram Parsons Memorial Foundation (EA)
GPMFGND ... Great Peace March for Global Nuclear Disarmament [Defunct] (EA)
GPMG .... General-Purpose Machine Gun [Military]
GPMH .... Good Practices in Mental Health (PDAA)
GPMMA .... Grain Processing Machinery Manufacturers Association (EA)
GPMR .... Gallons Per Mile Ratio [DOE] (TAG)
GPMS .... Galileo Probe Mass Spectrometer
GPMS .... General-Purpose Microprogram Simulator [Computer science] (IEEE)
GPMS .... General-Purpose Multiplex System [Aviation]
GPMS .... Gross Performance Measuring System [Air Force]
GPMSP .... Good Postmarketing Surveillance Practice (DB)
GPMU .... Graphical, Paper and Media Union [British]
GPMU .... Graphical, Print & Media Union (WDAA)
GPN .... Garden Point [Australia Airport symbol] (OAG)
GPN .... General Performance Number
GPN .... Glass Plate Negative
GPN .... Gold-Pan Resources, Inc. [Vancouver Stock Exchange symbol]
GPN .... Government Packet Network [Canada]
GPN .... Graduated Payment Mortgage (EBF)
GPN .... Graduate Practical Nurse
GPN .... Grey Power News [Australia A publication]
GPNITL .... Great Plains National Instructional Television Library
GPO .... Gemini Program [or Project] Office [NASA] (KSC)
GPO .... General Periodicals Ondisc [Database]
GPO .... General Pico [Argentina] [Airport symbol] (OAG)
GPO .... General Post Office [British Defunct]
GPO .... General Practitioner Obstetrician
GPO .... General-Purpose Oscilloscope
GPO .... General-Purpose Outlet (ADA)
GPO .... General-Purpose Output [Space Flight Operations Facility, NASA]
GPO .... Genprobe Tech [Vancouver Stock Exchange symbol]
GPO .... GIANT Group [NYSE symbol] (TTSB)
GPO .... Giant Group Ltd. [NYSE symbol] (SPSG)
GPO .... Government Printing Office
GPO .... Granulopoietin [Hypothetical substance] [Hematology]
GPO .... Gross Product Originating [Department of Transportation]
GPO .... Group Purchasing Organization [Health insurance]
GPO .... Guaranteed Purchase Option [Insurance]
GPO .... Gunner's Primary Optics (MCD)
GPO .... Gun Position Officer (NATG)
GPO .... Library of Congress, Government Printing Office [Source file] [UTLAS
          symbol]
GPO .... Portland, OR [Location identifier FAA] (FAAL)
GPO .... United States Government Printing Office, Alexandria, VA [OCLC
          symbol] (OCLC)
GPOA .... Guild of Prescription Opticians of America [Later, OAA] (EA)
GPOA .... Gun Position Officer's Assistant [British military] (DMA)
GPOB .... Government Printing Office Bookstore (OICC)
GPOCC .... Group Occulting Lights [Navigation signal]
Gp Offr......... Group Officer [British military] (DMA)
GPOI .... General Public Organization for Industrialization [Libya] (BUAC)
GpoImsa ...... Groupo Imsa Sa de CV [Associated Press] (SAG)
GpoRadio ..... Grupo Radio Centro [Associated Press] (SAG)
GPOS .... General-Purpose Operating System
GPP .... Gambia People's Party [Political party] (EY)
GPP .... Generalized Post-Processor
GPP .... General Plant Project
GPP .... General Print and Punch (NITA)
GPP .... General Purchasing Power [Accounting]
GPP .... General Purpose Processor (MHDI)
GPP .... General-Purpose Programming [Computer science]
GPP .... Giant Pacific Petroleums, Inc. [Vancouver Stock Exchange symbol]
GPP .... Glycosylated Plasma Protein [Clinical chemistry]
GPP .... Goal Programming Problem
GPP .... Gordon Personal Profile [Psychology]
GPP .... Graphic Part Programmer (PDAA)
GPP .... Gross Primary Productivity
GPP .... Ground Power Panel

GPP .... Guarapuava [*Brazil*] [*Airport symbol*] (AD)
GPP .... Guild of Pastoral Psychology [*British*] (DBA)
GPP .... Guild of Public Pharmacists [*British*] (BI)
GPP .... Gyro Pitch Position
GPPA .... Gaelic Pre-School Playgroups Association (BUAC)
GPPA .... Georgia Peanut Producers Association (SRA)
GPPA .... Georgia Pork Producers Association (SRA)
GPPA .... Georgia Psychiatric Physicians Association (SRA)
GPPA .... Government Patent Policy Act [*1981*]
GPPAW .... Grenada Planned Parenthood Association (BUAC)
GPPAW .... Glass, Pottery, Plastics, and Allied Workers International Union (EA)
GPPB .... Gemini Program Planning Board [*NASA*] (KSC)
GPPB .... Government Procurement Practices Board [*Proposed*]
GPP-I .... Gordon Personal Profile and Inventory [*Personality development test*] [*Psychology*]
GPPIPCEE .... Groupement Professionel des Pharmaciens de l'Industrie Pharmaceutique de la CEE [*Professional Grouping of Pharmacists of the Pharmaceuticals Industry of the EEC*] (ECED)
GPPL .... Gypsum Plaster [*Technical drawings*]
gppm .... Graphics Pages per Minute [*Printer technology*] (PCM)
GPPQ .... General-Purpose Psychiatric Questionnaire
GPPS .... General Provisions Policy Statement (MCD)
GPPT .... Group Personality Projective Test [*Psychology*]
GPPV .... Graff Pay per View [*NASDAQ symbol*] (SAG)
GPQ .... Carrollton, GA [*Location identifier FAA*] (FAAL)
GPR .... General-Purpose RADAR (MCD)
GPR .... General-Purpose Radiometer
GPR .... General-Purpose Receiver
GPR .... General-Purpose Register [*Computer science*] (MDG)
GPR .... General-Purpose Relay
GPR .... General-Purpose Representative
GPR .... Genio Populi Romani [*To the Genius of the Roman People*] [*Latin*]
GPR .... Glider Pilot Regiment [*Military unit*] [*British*]
GPR .... Golden Pyramid Resources, Inc. [*Vancouver Stock Exchange symbol*]
GPR .... Government Plant Representative
GPR .... Government Property Register [*of New South Wales*] [*State*] (EERA)
GPR .... Government Purpose Rights (AAGC)
GPR .... Grade Point Ratio (DHP)
GPR .... Grain-Burning Pattern Regulation (MCD)
GPR .... Gran Premio Romeo [*Alfa Romeo race car*] [*Italian*]
GPR .... Great Pacific Real Estate Investment Trust, Inc. [*AMEX symbol*] (SAG)
GPR .... Ground-Penetrating RADAR
GPRA .... General Practice Reform Association [*Medicine*] (DAVI)
GPRA .... Gouvernement Provisoire de la Republique Algerienne [*Provisional Government of the Algerian Republic*]
GPRA .... Govenment Performance and Results Act [*1993*]
GPRA .... Government Performance and Results Act [*1993*] (RDA)
GPRA .... Government Public Relations Association [*Defunct*]
GPRBC .... Guinea-Pig Red Blood Cell (DB)
GPRC .... Geophysical and Polar Research Center [*University of Wisconsin*]
GPrcl .... General Parcel Service, Inc. [*Associated Press*] (SAG)
GPRE .... Government Program Review and Evaluation
GPRF-G .... General-Purpose Rocket Furnace - Gradient
GPRF-I .... General-Purpose Rocket Furnace - Isothermal
GPRG .... Gadsden Purchase Refund Group [*Formerly, PRI*] [*Defunct*] (EA)
GPRL .... Giant Pulse Ruby LASER (IAA)
GPRL .... Gulf Puerto Rico Lines [*Steamship*] (MHDB)
GPRMC .... Groupement des Plastiques Renforces et Materiaux Composites [*Organization of Reinforced Plastics and Composite Materials*] (EAIO)
GPRN .... GOAL [*Ground Operations Aerospace Language*] Test Procedure Release Notice [*NASA*] (NASA)
GPRP .... Government Production and Research Property (SSD)
GPRR .... General-Purpose Radio Receiver
GPRS .... General Parent Ring System [*Proposed chemical classification*]
GPRS .... General Plumbing & Roofing Services [*Commercial firm*] [*British*]
GPRSS .... General-Purpose Remote Sensor System (PDAA)
GPRT .... General-Purpose Radio Transmitter
GPRT .... Guanine Phosphoribosyltransferase [*An enzyme*]
GPS .... Galapagos Islands [*Ecuador*] [*Airport symbol*] (OAG)
GPS .... Gallons per Second
GPS .... Gap, Inc. [*Formerly, Gap Stores, Inc.*] [*NYSE symbol*] (SPSG)
GPS .... Gastrointestinal Pathology Society (EA)
GPS .... Gauge Pressure Switch
GPS .... Generality and Problem Solving
GPS .... Generalized Preference Scheme [*Tariff policy*]
GPS .... General Pavement Studies [*FHWA*] (TAG)
GPS .... General Problem Solver [*Computer science*]
GPS .... General Processing Subsystem (MCD)
GPS .... General Process Simulator
GPS .... General-Purpose Shelter
GPS .... General-Purpose Simulation [*Formerly, Systems Simulator*] [*IBM Corp.*] [*Computer science*] (IAA)
GPS .... Generic Processing System [*Computer science*] (TEL)
GPS .... German Pacific Society (BUAC)
GPS .... Germany Philatelic Society (EA)
GPS .... Gibraltar Philatelic Society (BUAC)
GPS .... GigaBIT [*Binary Digits*] per Second [*Transmission rate*] [*Computer science*]
GPS .... Global Positioning Satellite
GPS .... Global Positioning System [*Formerly, NAVSTAR*] [*Air Force*]
GPS .... Global Position System [*Instrument*] (EERA)
GPS .... Global Precision System

GPS .... Goodpasture's Syndrome [*Medicine*] (DAVI)
GPS .... Government Paper Specification Standards
GPS .... Government Procurement Service
GPS .... Graduated Pension Scheme [*British*] (BARN)
GPS .... Grams per Second
GPS .... Grand Past Sojourner [*Freemasonry*] (ROG)
GPS .... Grand Principal Sojourner [*Freemasonry*]
GPS .... Graphic Programming Services [*Computer science*] (IBMDP)
GPS .... Gray Platelet Syndrome [*Medicine*] (DMAA)
GPS .... Great Public Schools [*Australia*] (WDAA)
GPS .... Ground Plane Simulator
GPS .... Ground Power Supply [*NASA*] (NASA)
GPS .... Ground Processing Simulation (MCD)
GPS .... Ground Processing System [*Aviation*]
GPS .... Ground Proximity Sensor
GPS .... Ground Water Protection Strategy [*Environmental Protection Agency*] (GFGA)
GPS .... Groups of Pulses per Second (DEN)
GPS .... Guidance Power Supply
GPS .... Guinea Pig Serum
GPS .... Guinea Pig Spleen
GPS .... Gunner's Primary Sight (MCD)
GPS .... Gyroscope Parameter Shift
GPSA .... Gas Processors Suppliers Association (EA)
GPSA .... Global Positioning System-Active
GPSC .... Gas Proportional Scintillation Counters [*Spectroscopy*]
GPSC .... Guinea Pig Spinal Cord
GPSCO .... Global Position System Consortium (EERA)
GPSCS .... General-Purpose Satellite Communication System (MCD)
GPSDIC .... General-Purpose Scientific Document Image Code [*System*] [*National Institute of Standards and Technology*]
GPSDW .... General-Purpose Scientific Document Writer [*National Institute of Standards and Technology*]
GPSE .... General-Purpose Simulation Environment [*Computer science*]
GPSE .... Gunner's Primary Sight Extension
GPSG .... Generalized Phrase Structure Grammar [*Artificial intelligence*]
GPSIM .... Global Position System Integrity Monitoring [*System*] (EERA)
GPS/INS ...... Global Positioning System/Inertial Navigation System [*Air Force*]
GPSL .... General-Purpose Simulation Language [*Computer science*] (IAA)
GPSN .... General-Purpose Packet Satellite Network (MHDI)
GPS NCC ...... Global Positioning System Network Control Center [*Air Force*] (MCD)
GPSP .... General-Purpose Signal Processor
GPSP .... General-Purpose Software Program [*Computer science*]
GPSP .... General-Purpose String Processor (IAA)
GPSP .... Global Positioning System-Passive
GPS PC .... Global Positioning System Program Contractor [*Air Force*] (MCD)
GPSS .... General [*or Generic*] Problem Statement Simulator
GPSS .... General Process Simulation Studies
GPSS .... General-Purpose Simulation System [*formerly, Systems Simulator*] [*IBM Corp. 1961*] [*Computer science*]
GPSS .... General Purpose System Simulator (NITA)
GPSS .... Global Positioning Satellite System
GPSSM .... General-Purpose Surface-to-Surface Missile [*Army*]
GPSU .... Ground Power Supply Unit [*NASA*] (AAG)
GPSX .... General Parcel Service, Inc. [*NASDAQ symbol*] (NQ)
GPSX .... Genl Parcel Service [*NASDAQ symbol*] (TTSB)
GPSXW .... General Parcel Svc Wrrt [*NASDAQ symbol*] (TTSB)
GPT .... Gallons per Ton
GPT .... Gas Phase Titration
GPT .... Gas Power Transfer (IEEE)
GPT .... GEC Plessey Telecommunications [*British*] (ECON)
GPT .... Gemini Pad Test [*NASA*] (KSC)
GPT .... General Perturbation Theory [*Nuclear science*]
GPT .... General Plant Telephone [*Nuclear energy*] (GFGA)
GPT .... General Preferred Tariff [*Canada*]
GPT .... General-Purpose Terminal (IAA)
GPT .... General-Purpose Thermoplastic [*Insulation*]
GPT .... General-Purpose Tool
GPT .... General-Purpose Transport [*British military*] (DMA)
GPT .... Geometric and Positional Tolerance [*Drafting symbol*]
GPT .... Glass Precision Tubing
GPT .... Glass Probe Thermistor
GPT .... Glutamic-Pyruvic Transaminase [*Also, AAT, ALAT, ALT*] [*An enzyme*]
GPT .... Goldpost Resources, Inc. [*Toronto Stock Exchange symbol*]
GPT .... Governor Phillip Tower [*Sydney, New South Wales, Australia*]
GPT .... Grayson Perceptualization Test [*Psychology*]
GPT .... Greenpoint Financial Corp. [*NYSE symbol*] (SAG)
GPT .... Greenpoint Finl [*NYSE symbol*] (TTSB)
GPT .... Grid Pool Tank
GPT .... Group Projective Test [*Psychology*] (BARN)
GPT .... Guidance Position Tracking [*Aerospace*] (AAG)
GPT .... Gulfport/Biloxi [*Mississippi*] [*Airport symbol*] (OAG)
GPT .... Gypsum Tile [*Technical drawings*]
GPTA .... Gupta Corp. [*NASDAQ symbol*] (SAG)
GPTAE .... Gupta Corp. [*NASDAQ symbol*] (TTSB)
GPTC .... Gambia Public Transport Corp. (BUAC)
GPTC .... Gas Piping Technology Committee
GPT-C .... Glutamic-Pyruvic Transaminase-C [*An enzyme*] (OA)
GPTE .... General-Purpose Test Equipment (MCD)
GpTh .... Group Therapy
GPTI .... General-Purpose Terminal Interchanges [*Airline communication system*] [*Raytheon Co.*]
GPTI .... Guangdong Posts & Telecommunications Institute [*China*] (BUAC)
GPTR .... General-Purpose Tape Routine [*Computer science*] (PCM)

GPTR	Guidance Power Temperature Regulator
GPTS	Geomagnetic Polarity Timescale
GPTU	Glass Painters' Trade Union [*British*]
GPU	Gas Power Unit (MUGU)
GPU	Gas Pump Unit
GPU	General Postal Union [*Later, UPU*]
GPU	General Processor Unit
GPU	General Public Utilities Corp. [*NYSE symbol*] (SPSG)
GPU	Generating Power Unit
GPU	Genl Public Util [*NYSE symbol*] (TTSB)
GPU	Geopotential Unit (IAA)
GPU	Gosudarstvennoe Politicheskoe Upravlenie [*Government Political Administration*] [*Soviet secret service organization, also known as OGPU Later, KGB*]
GPU	GPU, Inc. [*NYSE symbol*] [*Formerly, General Public Utility*] (SG)
GPU	Graphics Processing Unit
GPU	Grapper Pick Up (COE)
GPU	Green Party of Ukraine (BUAC)
GPU	Ground Power Unit
GPU	Guinea Pig Unit [*Endocrinology*]
GPU	Gun Pod Unit [*Military*] (MUSM)
GPUN	General Public Utilities Nuclear Corp. (NRCH)
GPUR	GOAL [*Ground Operations Aerospace Language*] Test Procedure Update Request (MCD)
GPUSA	Greenpeace USA (EA)
GPUT	Galactose Phosphate Uridyl Transferase [*An enzyme*] (MAE)
GPV	General Public Virus [*Computer science*] (NHD)
GPV	General-Purpose Vehicle
GPV	General-Purpose Vessel
GPV	Gereformeerd Politiek Verbond [*Reformed Political League*] [*Netherlands Political party*] (PPE)
GPV	Gyroscope Pickoff Voltage
GPVB	General-Purpose Video Buffer
GPVEH	General-Purpose Vehicle
GPW	Geneva Convention Relative to Treatment of Prisoners of War, 12 August 1949 [*Army*] (AABC)
GPW	Global Point Warning [*Military*]
GPW	Gold Power Resources Corp. [*Vancouver Stock Exchange symbol*]
GPW	Great Plains Wheat, Inc. (EA)
GPW	Green Pulse Width [*Instrumentation*]
GPW	Gypsum-Plaster Wall [*Technical drawings*]
GPW 1929 ...	Geneva Convention Relative to Treatment of Prisoners of War, 27 July 1929 [*Army*]
GPWA	General Practitioners Writers Association (BUAC)
GPWA	Grain Pool of Western Australia
GPWC	Great Pines Water [*NASDAQ symbol*] (TTSB)
GPWC	Great Pines Water Co. [*NASDAQ symbol*] (SAG)
GPWD	General Political Warfare Department [*Military*]
GPWM	Guild for the Promotion of Welsh Music (EAIO)
GPWS	General-Purpose Workstation (SSD)
GPWS	Ground Proximity Warning System [*FAA*]
GPWU	Granite Polishers' and Workers' Union [*British*]
GPX	Generalized Programming Extended [*Livermore Atomic Research Computer*] [*Sperry UNIVAC*]
GPx	Glutathione Peroxidase [*An enzyme*]
GPX	GP Strategies [*NYSE symbol*] [*Formerly, National Patent Development*]
GPX	Greyhound Package Express
GPY	Government Property Yard
GPY	Gypsy Resources Ltd. [*Vancouver Stock Exchange symbol*]
GPYS	General-Purpose Yard Simulator (PDAA)
GPZ	Gazpromavia [*Former USSR*] [*FAA designator*] (FAAC)
GPZ	Gebbies Pass [*New Zealand*] [*Seismograph station code, US Geological Survey*] (SEIS)
GPZ	Grand Rapids [*Minnesota*] [*Airport symbol*] (OAG)
GPZOA	GPz Owners of America [*Defunct*] (EA)
GQ	Big Sky Airlines [*ICAO designator*] (AD)
GQ	Equatorial Guinea [*ANSI two-letter standard code*] (CNC)
GQ	General Quarters [*General Alert*] [*Navy*]
GQ	Gentlemen's Quarterly [*A publication*] (WDAA)
GQ	Golden West Airlines (MHDW)
GQ	Governor of Queensland [*Australia*]
GQ	Great Quotations [*A publication*]
GQ	North Korea [*License plate code assigned to foreign diplomats in the US*]
GQA	Get Quick Answer [*Communications*]
GQA	Give Quick Answer [*Communications*]
GQA	Government Quality Assurance (NATG)
GQ & A	General's Branch, Quarter Master's Branch, and Adjutant's Branch [*Main divisions of Staff Duties*] [*Military British*]
GQAP	General Question-Asking Program (STED)
GQE	Generalized Queue Entry [*Computer science*]
GQE	Gilmore, AR [*Location identifier FAA*] (FAAL)
GQG	Gallaudet College, Washington, DC [*OCLC symbol*] (OCLC)
GQG	Grand Quartier-General [*French GHQ*]
GQK	Gallaudet College, Kendall Demonstration School, Washington, DC [*OCLC symbol*] (OCLC)
GQM	Gallaudet College, Montessori School, Washington, DC [*OCLC symbol*] (OCLC)
GQM	Golden Queen Mining [*Vancouver Stock Exchange symbol*]
GQMS	Garrison Quartermaster-Sergeant [*British military*] (DMA)
GQN	U.S. Air Force Reserve (440th Airlift Wing) [*FAA designator*] (FAAC)
GQNA	Aioun El Atrouss [*Mauritania*] [*ICAO location identifier*] (ICLI)
GQNB	Boutilimit [*Mauritania*] [*ICAO location identifier*] (ICLI)
GQNC	Tichitt [*Mauritania*] [*ICAO location identifier*] (ICLI)

GQND	Tidjikja [*Mauritania*] [*ICAO location identifier*] (ICLI)
GQNE	Bogue [*Mauritania*] [*ICAO location identifier*] (ICLI)
GQNF	Kiffa [*Mauritania*] [*ICAO location identifier*] (ICLI)
GQNH	Timbedra [*Mauritania*] [*ICAO location identifier*] (ICLI)
GQNI	Nema [*Mauritania*] [*ICAO location identifier*] (ICLI)
GQNJ	Akjoujt [*Mauritania*] [*ICAO location identifier*] (ICLI)
GQNK	Kaedi [*Mauritania*] [*ICAO location identifier*] (ICLI)
GQNL	Moudjeria/Letfotar [*Mauritania*] [*ICAO location identifier*] (ICLI)
GQNM	Timbedra/Dahara [*Mauritania*] [*ICAO location identifier*] (ICLI)
GQNN	Nouakchott [*Mauritania*] [*ICAO location identifier*] (ICLI)
GQNR	Rosso [*Mauritania*] [*ICAO location identifier*] (ICLI)
GQNS	Selibabi [*Mauritania*] [*ICAO location identifier*] (ICLI)
GQNT	Tamchakett [*Mauritania*] [*ICAO location identifier*] (ICLI)
GQNU	M'Bout [*Mauritania*] [*ICAO location identifier*] (ICLI)
GQNV	Nouakchott [*Mauritania*] [*ICAO location identifier*] (ICLI)
GQP	Gas Quenching Process
GQPA	Atar [*Mauritania*] [*ICAO location identifier*] (ICLI)
GQPF	F'Derick [*Mauritania*] [*ICAO location identifier*] (ICLI)
GQPP	Nouadhibou [*Mauritania*] [*ICAO location identifier*] (ICLI)
GQPT	Bir Moghrein [*Mauritania*] [*ICAO location identifier*] (ICLI)
GQPZ	Zouerate [*Mauritania*] [*ICAO location identifier*] (ICLI)
GQQ	Galion [*Ohio*] [*Airport symbol*] (OAG)
GQR	Gauss Quadrature Rule
GQR	Golden Quail Resources Ltd. [*Vancouver Stock Exchange symbol*]
GQRV	Golden Quail Resources Ltd. [*NASDAQ symbol*] (NQ)
GQRVF	Golden Quail Res Ltd [*NASDAQ symbol*] (TTSB)
GQW	Denver, CO [*Location identifier FAA*] (FAAL)
GQX	Goldquest Exploration, Inc. [*Toronto Stock Exchange symbol*]
GR	Aurigny Air Services [*ICAO designator*] (AD)
GR	Carnegie Library, Rome, GA [*Library symbol Library of Congress*] (LCLS)
GR	Gambia Regiment [*British military*] (DMA)
GR	Game Reserve [*State*] (EERA)
GR	Gamma Ray [*or Roentgen*]
gr+	Gamma Roentgen (STED)
GR	Gamma Roentgen (STED)
GR	Gas Ratio
GR	Gastric Resection [*Medicine*]
GR	Gear (MSA)
GR	Geared Radial [*Aircraft engine*]
GR	Gear Ratio
GR	Generalized Rash [*Medicine*] (STED)
GR	General Purpose Register (NITA)
GR	General Radio
GR	General Reader
GR	General Reconnaissance [*Marine Corps*]
GR	General Register [*Computer science*]
GR	General Relativity [*Physics*]
GR	General Relief [*Medicine*] (STED)
GR	General Research
GR	General Reserve
GR	Generator Run (IAA)
GR	Genesis Rabbah (BJA)
GR	Gentleman Rider [*Horsemanship*]
GR	Georgist Registry [*An association*] (EA)
GR	Georgius Rex [*King George*]
GR	Germanium Rectifier
GR+	German Reports (MCD)
GR	German Roach [*Immunology*]
GR	Germ Ring [*Embryology*]
GR	Glass-Reinforced
GR	Glaxo Laboratories Ltd. [*Great Britain*] [*Research code symbol*]
GR	Gloucestershire Regiment [*Military unit*] [*British*]
GR	Glucocorticoid Receptor [*Endocrinology*]
GR	Glucose Response [*Medicine*] (STED)
GR	Glutathione Reductase [*An enzyme*]
G-R	Gnome-Rhone [*Aircraft engine*]
G-R	Goldbarg-Rutenberg [*Enzyme unit*]
GR	Golden Rule [*Freemasonry*] (ROG)
GR	Gold Reserve
GR	Good Recovery (STED)
GR	[*The*] Goodrich [*B. F.*] Co. [*NYSE symbol*] (SPSG)
GR	Gospel Recordings (EA)
GR	Government Regulation (AAG)
GR	Government Report (AAG)
GR	Government Reserve [*British*] (ADA)
GR	Government Responsibility (MCD)
gr	Government Revenue (MENA)
GR	Government Rubber [*Synthetic rubber*] (IIA)
GR	Grab Rod (AAG)
GR	Grade (KSC)
Gr	Grade (AL)
gr	Grade (WDMC)
GR	Gradual-Release [*Pharmacy*]
GR	Graduate
GR	Graduation Requirement (MCD)
GR	Grain (KSC)
gr	Grain (WDMC)
gr	Grains (ODBW)
GR	Gram (KSC)
GR	Grammar
gr-	Gram-Negative [*Bacteria*] (DAVI)
G-R	Gram-Negative Rods [*Biochemistry*] (DAVI)
gr+	Gram-Positive [*Bacteria*] (DAVI)
G+R	Gram-Positive Rods [*Biochemistry*] (DAVI)

GR	Grand [*Title*]
GR	Grand Rapids, Michigan
GR	Grand Recorder [*Freemasonry*]
GR	Grand Registrar [*Freemasonry*] (ROG)
GR	Grange [*or Manor, a religious residence*]
GR	Gran Rabinato (BJA)
GR	Grant
GR	Grant Recipient [*Job Training and Partnership Act*] (OICC)
Gr	Grant's Jamaica Reports [*A publication*] (DLA)
Gr	Grant's Pennsylvania Cases [*A publication*] (DLA)
Gr	Grant's Upper Canada Chancery Reports [*A publication*] (DLA)
GR	Granular Snow [*Skiing condition*]
GR	Granulocyte (STED)
Gr	Granum [*Grain*] [*Latin*]
GR	Graphic Reproduction [*A publication*] (DGA)
Gr	Graphite
Gr	Grashof Number [*IUPAC*]
Gr	Grasp
GR	Grass (ROG)
GR	Grasse River R. R. Corp. [*AAR code*]
GR	Grass Extract [*Immunology*]
GR	Grave Record [*Genealogy*]
GR	Graves Registration [*Military*]
gr	Gravid (STED)
GR	Gravid (STED)
Gr	Gravida [*Obstetrics*] (DAVI)
GR	Gravity
gr	Gravity (STED)
gr	Gray [*Unit*] [*Radiation therapy*] (DAVI)
GR	Gray [*Thoroughbred racing*]
GR	Gray
GR	Great (MCD)
GR	Great Roll [*of the Pipe*] [*British*]
GR	Grecian (ROG)
gr	Greece [*IYRU nationality code*] [*MARC country of publication code Library of Congress*] (LCCP)
GR	Greece [*ANSI two-letter standard code*] (CNC)
GR	Greek
Gr	Greenleaf's Reports [*1-9 Maine*] [*A publication*] (DLA)
GR	Green Realignment [*An association*] (BUAC)
Gr	Green's Reports [*A publication*] (DLA)
GR	Grid Resistor
GR	Grid Return
GR	Grind (ADA)
GR	Grooved Roofing [*Lumber*]
GR	Gross
gr	Gross (ODBW)
GR	Gross Rate [*Insurance*] (AIA)
GR	Gross Receipts [*Business term*]
GR	Gross Requirement (AABC)
GR	Gross Revenue [*Business term*]
Gr	Ground
GR	Ground Range
GR	Ground Rent (ROG)
GR	Ground Round, Inc. (EFIS)
GR	Ground Rule (MCD)
GR	Group
gr	Group (WDMC)
GR	Group Report
GR	Grove (ADA)
GR	Growth (SSD)
GR	Growth Rate [*Biology*]
GR	Guardrail
GR	Guard Ring (BARN)
GR	Gulf Rijad Bank [*Bahrain*]
GR	Gulielmus Rex [*King William*]
GR	Gun Control RADAR [*Military*] (CAAL)
GR	Gunner
GR	Gunnery Range
GR	Gurkha Rifles [*British military*] (DMA)
GR	Gypsum Requirement (OA)
GR	Hail [*ICAO*] (FAAC)
GRA	Fayetteville, NC [*Location identifier FAA*] (FAAL)
GRA	Gamma Ray Amplification
GRA	Garda Representative Association [*Ireland*] (BUAC)
GRA	Gated Radionuclide Angiography [*Medicine*] (DMAA)
GRA	German Research Association (EA)
GRA	Girls Rodeo Association [*Later, WPRA*] (EA)
GRA	Glucocorticoid-Remediable Aldosteronism [*Medicine*]
Gra	Glyceraldehyde [*Biochemistry*]
GRA	Glycyrrhizic Acid [*Biochemistry*] (DB)
GRA	Gombarts Reducing Agent [*Medicine*] (AAMN)
GRA	Gonadotropin-Releasing Agent [*Endocrinology*] (MAE)
GRA	Governmental Research Association (EA)
GRA	Government Reports Announcements [*Department of Commerce*] [*Database producer*]
GRA	Government Responsibility Action
GRA	Government Responsibility Authorized (MCD)
GR-A	Government Rubber-Acrylonitrile [*Synthetic rubber*]
GRA	Grace [*W. R.*] & Co. [*NYSE symbol*] (SPSG)
GRA	Grace (W.R.) [*NYSE symbol*] (TTSB)
GRA	Graduate Research Assistant
Gra	Graham's Reports [*98-107 Georgia*] [*A publication*] (DLA)
Gra	Grant [*Legal term*] (DLA)
GRA	Grant Aid [*Military*] (AABC)
GRA	Graphic Recording Ammeter (IAA)
gra	Graphics (VRA)
GRA	Grass Roots Association (EA)
Gra	Gratianus [*Flourished, 1151-59*] [*Authority cited in pre-1607 legal work*] (DSA)
GRA	Gray (MSA)
GRA	Graz [*Steiermark*] [*Austria*] [*Seismograph station code, US Geological Survey*] [*Closed*] (SEIS)
GRA	Great American Airways [*ICAO designator*] (FAAC)
GRA	Growth Rate Adjustment [*Business term*]
GRA	Guild for Religious Architecture [*Later, IFRAA*]
GRA	Gyro Reference Assembly
GRAAL	Graph Algorithmic Language [*Computer science*]
Gra & Wat NT	Graham and Waterman on New Trials [*A publication*] (DLA)
GRAB	Galactic Radiation and Background (MCD)
GRAB	Galatic Radiation and Background
GRAB	Group Room Availability Bank [*Sheraton Corp.*]
GRABS	Giant Reusable Air Blast Simulator [*Air Force*]
GRAC	Grand Royal Arch Captain [*Freemasonry*]
GRAC	Grand Royal Arch Chapter [*Freemasonry*] (ROG)
GRAC	Great Rivers Athletic Conference (PSS)
GRAC	Groupe de Recherche sur les Attitudes Envers la Criminalite [*Canada*]
Grace	Grace [*W.R.*] & Co. [*Associated Press*] (SAG)
GRACE	Graphic Arts Composing Equipment
GRACE	Grass Roots Art and Community Effort [*Vermont*]
GRACE	Gravity Recovery and Climate Experiment [*NASA proposed mission, 2001*]
GRACE	Group Routing and Charging Equipment [*British*]
GRACE	Mrs. Gould's Residential Advisory Centre for the Elderly [*British*] (CB)
Graco	Graco, Inc. [*Associated Press*] (SAG)
GRACO	Gray Co., Inc.
GRAD	Generalized Remote Access Database
GRAD	General Recursive Algebra and Differentiation (IEEE)
GRAD	Gradatim [*Gradually*] [*Pharmacy*]
GRAD	Gradient (AFM)
GRAD	Grading (WDAA)
GRAD	Gradual
grad	Gradual (WDAA)
grad	Graduate (WDAA)
Grad	Graduate (AL)
GRAD	Graduate
GRAD	Graduate Resume Accumulation and Distribution [*Computer science*]
GRADB	Generalized Remote Access Database (IEEE)
GradBHI	Graduate of the British Horological Institute (DBQ)
GradCert	Graduate Certificate
GradCertBus	Graduate Certificate in Business [*Australia*]
GradCertCommunic	Graduate Certificate in Communication [*Australia*]
GradCertFin	Graduate Certificate in Finance [*Australia*]
GradCertHelpSkills	Graduate Certificate in Helping Skills [*Australia*]
GradCertHRD	Graduate Certificate in Human Resource Development [*Australia*]
GradCertIndRels	Graduate Certificate in Industrial Relations [*Australia*]
GradCertLitEd	Graduate Certificate in Literacy Education [*Australia*]
GradCertMarkt	Graduate Certificate in Marketing [*Australia*]
GradCertMngt	Graduate Certificate in Management [*Australia*]
GradCertTESOL	Graduate Certificate in Teaching of English to Speakers of Other Languages [*Australia*]
Gradco	Gradco Systems, Inc. [*Associated Press*] (SAG)
GradDIndDes	Graduate Diploma in Industrial Design [*Australia*]
GradDipA	Graduate Diploma of Arts [*Australia*]
GradDipAbIsEd	Graduate Diploma in Aboriginal and Islander Education [*Australia*]
GradDipAcc	Graduate Diploma in Accounting [*Australia*]
GradDipAccom	Graduate Diploma in Accompaniment [*Australia*]
GradDipAcct	Graduate Diploma in Accounting
GradDipActng	Graduate Diploma in Accounting
GradDipAdmin	Graduate Diploma in Administration
GradDipAdultEd & Train	Graduate Diploma in Adult Education and Training [*Australia*]
GradDipAdvAcctg	Graduate Diploma in Advanced Accounting
GradDipAltDispRes	Graduate Diploma in Alternative Dispute Resolution [*Australia*]
GradDipAnalytChem	Graduate Diploma in Analytical Chemistry
GradDipAppCommunications	Graduate Diploma in Applied Communications
GradDipAppEc	Graduate Diploma in Applied Economics [*Australia*]
GradDipAppHist	Graduate Diploma in Applied History
GradDipAppLing	Graduate Diploma in Applied Linguistics
GradDipAppSc	Graduate Diploma in Applied Science [*Australia*]
GradDipAppScGenStud	Graduate Diploma in Applied Science, General Studies [*Australia*]
GradDipAppStats	Graduate Diploma in Applied Statistics
GradDipArts(ChLit)	Graduate Diploma in Arts (Children's Literature) [*Australia*]
GradDipArts(WelfAdmin)	Graduate Diploma in Arts (Welfare Administration) [*Australia*]
GradDipAsianLaw	Graduate Diploma in Asian Law [*Australia*]
GradDipAsianStudies	Graduate Diploma in Asian Studies
GradDipASOS	Graduate Diploma in Antarctic and Southern Ocean Studies [*Australia*]
GradDipAud	Graduate Diploma in Audiology [*Australia*]
GradDipAud	Graduate Diploma in Internal Auditing
GradDipBldgProjMgt	Graduate Diploma in Building Project Management
GradDipBus	Graduate Diploma in Business [*Australia*]
GradDipBusAdmin	Graduate Diploma in Business Administration
GradDipBusComp	Graduate Diploma in Business Computing

GradDipCCC... Graduate Diploma of Computer Control and Communications [*Australia*]
GradDipChildLit... Graduate Diploma in Children's Literature
GradDipClinBiochem... Graduate Diploma in Clinical Biochemistry
GradDipClinDent... Graduate Diploma in Clinical Dentistry [*Australia*]
GradDipCmlComptg... Graduate Diploma in Commercial Computing
GradDipComEd... Graduate Diploma in Commercial Education [*Australia*]
GradDipComLaw... Graduate Diploma of Commercial Law [*Australia*]
GradDipCommDataProc... Graduate Diploma in Commercial Data Processing
GradDipCommn... Graduate Diploma in Communication
GradDipCommunicationMgt... Graduate Diploma in Communication Management
GradDipComMus... Graduate Diploma of Community Music [*Australia*]
GradDipComMusMgmt... Graduate Diploma of Community Museum Management [*Australia*]
GradDipCompContSys... Graduate Diploma in Computer Controlled Systems
GradDipCompEd... Graduate Diploma in Computers in Education [*Australia*]
GradDipCompEng... Graduate Diploma in Digital Computer Engineering
GradDipCompSc... Graduate Diploma of Computer Science [*Australia*]
GradDipCompStud... Graduate Diploma in Computer Studies
GradDipComptgSc... Graduate Diploma in Computing Science
GradDipConfRes... Graduate Diploma in Conflict Resolution [*Australia*]
GradDipCouns... Graduate Diploma in Counselling
GradDipCPPhty... Graduate Diploma in Cardio Pulmonary Physiotherapy
GradDipCurric... Graduate Diploma in Curriculum [*Australia*]
GradDipDatAnal... Graduate Diploma in Data Analysis
GradDipDemog... Graduate Diploma in Demography
GradDipDesStud... Graduate Diploma in Design Studies
GradDipDiplSt... Graduate Diploma in Diplomatic Studies [*Australia*]
GradDipDP... Graduate Diploma in Data Processing
GradDipDramaEd... Graduate Diploma in Drama in Education [*Australia*]
GradDipE ..... Graduate Diploma in Engineering [*Australia*]
GradDipEarlyChildSt... Graduate Diploma in Early Childhood Studies [*Australia*]
GradDipEc ... Graduate Diploma in Economics
GradDipEcDev... Graduate Diploma in Economics of Development
GradDipEcHist... Graduate Diploma in Economic History
GradDipEcmetrics... Graduate Diploma in Econometrics
GradDipEconDev... Graduate Diploma in Economic Development [*Australia*]
GradDipEconGeol... Graduate Diploma in Economic Geology [*Australia*]
GradDipEconHist... Graduate Diploma in Economic History [*Australia*]
GradDipEconom... Graduate Diploma in Econometrics [*Australia*]
GradDipEd ... Graduate Diploma in Education
GradDipEdAdmin... Graduate Diploma in Educational Administration [*Australia*]
GradDipEdCouns... Graduate Diploma in Educational Counseling [*Australia*]
GradDipEdCouns... Graduate Diploma in Educational Counselling (ADA)
GradDipEd(IndArts)... Graduate Diploma in Education (Industrial Arts)
GradDipEdStSptTchg... Graduate Diploma in Educational Studies Support Teaching [*Australia*]
GradDipEdStudies... Graduate Diploma in Educational Studies
GradDipEd(TAFE)... Graduate Diploma in Education (Technical and Further Education)
GradDipEdTrain... Graduate Diploma in Education and Training [*Australia*]
GradDipEmpRels... Graduate Diploma in Employment Relations
GradDipEng... Graduate Diploma in Engineering [*Australia*]
GradDipEng-PlantMgnt... Graduate Diploma in Engineering - Plant Management
GradDipEnv & MunEng... Graduate Diploma in Environmental and Municipal Engineering
GradDipEnvSt... Graduate Diploma in Environmental Studies [*Australia*]
GradDipEpi... Graduate Diploma in Epidemiology [*Australia*]
GradDipExerSportSc... Graduate Diploma in Exercise and Sport Sciences
GradDipFA... Graduate Diploma of Fine Arts [*Australia*]
GradDipFamLaw... Graduate Diploma of Family Law [*Australia*]
GradDipFilm & Tele in Ed... Graduate Diploma in Film and Television in Education
GradDipFin... Graduate Diploma in Finance
GradDipFineArt... Graduate Diploma in Fine Art
GradDipForOdont... Graduate Diploma in Forensic Odontology [*Australia*]
GradDipGalSt... Graduate Diploma in Gallery Studies [*Australia*]
GradDipGeol... Graduate Diploma for Science Teachers (Geology)
GradDipGeront... Graduate Diploma in Gerontology
GradDipGraphCommEd... Graduate Diploma in Graphic Communication Education [*Australia*]
GradDipHealthServMgmt... Graduate Diploma in Health Services Management
GradDipHIM... Graduate Diploma in Health Information Management
GradDipHumanPhysiol & Pharmacol... Graduate Diploma in Human Physiology and Pharmacology [*Australia*]
GradDipImmunolMicrobiol... Graduate Diploma in Immunology and Microbiology [*Australia*]
GradDipIndDes... Graduate Diploma in Industrial Design
GradDipInfoMgt... Graduate Diploma in Information Management [*Australia*]
GradDipInfServ... Graduate Diploma in Information Services
GradDipInfStudies... Graduate Diploma in Information Studies
GradDipInfTech... Graduate Diploma in Information Technology [*Australia*]
GradDipIntComLaw... Graduate Diploma in International and Commercial Law [*Australia*]
GradDipIntLaw... Graduate Diploma in International Law
GradDipIntPropLaw... Graduate Diploma in Intellectual Property Law [*Australia*]
GradDipKnowlBasSys... Graduate Diploma in Knowledge Based Systems
GradDipLabRelLaw... Graduate Diploma in Labour Relations Law [*Australia*]
GradDipLandArch... Graduate Diploma in Landscape Architecture
GradDipLandDatMan... Graduate Diploma in Land Data Management
GradDipLangTchg... Graduate Diploma in Language Teaching [*Australia*]
GradDipLD... Graduate Diploma in Landscape Design
GradDipLegalPrac... Graduate Diploma in Legal Practice
GradDipLegSt... Graduate Diploma of Legal Studies [*Australia*]
GradDipLeisureStud... Graduate Diploma in Leisure Studies
GradDipLibInfStud... Graduate Diploma in Librarianship and Information Studies
GradDipLibSc... Graduate Diploma in Library Science (ADA)
GradDipLocalGovtEng... Graduate Diploma in Local Government Engineering
GradDipLoc & AppHist... Graduate Diploma in Local and Applied History
GradDipManipTh... Graduate Diploma in Manipulative Therapy
GradDipMatAnth... Graduate Diploma of Material Anthropology [*Australia*]
GradDipMatEng... Graduate Diploma in Materials Engineering [*Australia*]
GradDipMathMethods... Graduate Diploma in Mathematical Methods
GradDipMathSc... Graduate Diploma in Mathematics Science [*Australia*]
GradDipMathsEd... Graduate Diploma in Mathematics Education [*Australia*]
GradDipMediaComm & TechLaw... Graduate Diploma in Media Communications and Technology Law [*Australia*]
GradDipMelSt... Graduate Diploma of Melanesian Studies [*Australia*]
GradDipMentHlthSc... Graduate Diploma in Mental Health Science [*Australia*]
GradDipMgmt... Graduate Diploma in Management
GradDipMidwif... Graduate Diploma in Midwifery [*Australia*]
GradDipMinRes... Graduate Diploma in Mineral Resources
GradDipMktg... Graduate Diploma in Marketing
GradDipMolBiol... Graduate Diploma in Molecular Biology [*Australia*]
GradDipMovement & Dance... Graduate Diploma in Movement and Dance [*Australia*]
GradDipMultiStudies... Graduate Diploma in Multicultural Studies [*Australia*]
GradDipMunEng... Graduate Diploma in Municipal Engineering [*Australia*]
GradDipMus... Graduate Diploma in Music [*Australia*]
GradDipMusCur... Graduate Diploma of Museum Curatorship [*Australia*]
GradDipMusMgmt... Graduate Diploma in Museum Management [*Australia*]
GradDipMus(Op)... Graduate Diploma in Music (Opera) [*Australia*]
GradDipMus(Perf)... Graduate Diploma in Music (Performance) [*Australia*]
GradDipMus(Rep)... Graduate Diploma in Music (Repetiteur) [*Australia*]
GradDipNatResourcesLaw... Graduate Diploma in Natural Resources Law [*Australia*]
GradDipNurs... Graduate Diploma in Nursing
GradDipNursStudies... Graduate Diploma in Nursing Studies
GradDipNutr & Diet... Graduate Diploma in Nutrition and Dietetics
GradDipOffshEng... Graduate Diploma in Offshore Engineering [*Australia*]
GradDipOH & S... Graduate Diploma in Occupational Health and Safety
GradDipOR... Graduate Diploma in Operations Research
GradDipOrgDev... Graduate Diploma in Organisation Development
GradDipPaedPhty... Graduate Diploma in Paediatric Physiotherapy
GradDipPPT... Graduate Diploma in Pulp and Paper Technology [*Australia*]
GradDipProjMgt... Graduate Diploma in Project Management [*Australia*]
GradDipProp... Graduate Diploma in Property
GradDipPSM... Graduate Diploma in Public Sector Management
GradDipPsych... Graduate Diploma of Psychology [*Australia*]
GradDipPubEcPol... Graduate Diploma in Public Economic Policy
GradDipPubLaw... Graduate Diploma in Public Law
GradDipPubPol... Graduate Diploma in Public Policy
GradDipQlty... Graduate Diploma in Quality
GradDipQualTech... Graduate Diploma in Quality Technology
GradDipRc ... Graduate Diploma in Rehabilitation Counselling
GradDipSc ... Graduate Diploma in Science
GradDipScSoc... Graduate Diploma of Science and Society [*Australia*]
GradDipSEAsianStud... Graduate Diploma in Southeast Asian Studies
GradDipSecStud... Graduate Diploma in Secretarial Studies
GradDipSocAdmin... Graduate Diploma in Social Administration [*Australia*]
GradDipSocEcol... Graduate Diploma in Social Ecology [*Australia*]
GradDipSpecEd... Graduate Diploma in Special Education [*Australia*]
GradDipStats... Graduate Diploma in Statistics
GradDipStratSt... Graduate Diploma in Strategic Studies [*Australia*]
GradDipStrucEng... Graduate Diploma in Structural Engineering [*Australia*]
GradDipStudWel... Graduate Diploma in Student Welfare [*Australia*]
GradDipSurFin... Graduate Diploma in Metal Finishing and Surface Protection
GradDipSurvPrac... Graduate Diploma in Surveying Practice
GradDipT ..... Graduate Diploma in Teaching (ADA)
GradDipTax... Graduate Diploma in Taxation
GradDipTchrLib... Graduate Diploma in Teacher Librarianship (ADA)
GradDipTeach... Graduate Diploma in Teaching [*Australia*]
GradDipTeachLib... Graduate Diploma in Teacher Librarianship
GradDipTourism... Graduate Diploma of Tourism [*Australia*]
GradDipTrans & Dist... Graduate Diploma in Transport and Distribution
GradDipUEM... Graduate Diploma in Urban Estate Management
GradDipUltr... Graduate Diploma in Ultrasonography
GradDipUrb & RegPlan... Graduate Diploma in Urban and Regional Planning
GradDipURP... Graduate Diploma in Urban and Regional Planning
GradDip(VisArts)... Graduate Diploma in Visual Arts
GradDipWaterEng... Graduate Diploma in Water Engineering [*Australia*]
GradDipWeldTech... Graduate Diploma in Welding Technology
GradDipWelfAdmin... Graduate Diploma in Welfare Administration [*Australia*]
GradDipWomen'sStudies... Graduate Diploma in Women's Studies [*Australia*]
GradDipWomHlth... Graduate Diploma in Women's Health [*Australia*]
GRADE......... Gestalt Recognition by Asymptotic Differential Equations
GRADE......... Graphical Airspace Design Environment [*FAA*] (TAG)
Gradell .... Gradell Industries, Inc. [*Associated Press*] (SAG)
GRADEX......... Graded Exercise (NVT)
Grad Fix ...... Grady on Fixtures [*A publication*] (DLA)
Grad Hind Inh... Grady's Hindoo Law of Inheritance [*A publication*] (DLA)
Grad Hind L... Grady's Manual of Hindoo Law [*A publication*] (DLA)
GradIAE .... Graduate of the Institution of Automobile Engineers [*British*]
GradIElecIE... Graduate of the Institution of Electrical and Electronics Incorporated Engineers [*British*] (DBQ)
Grad IERE.... Graduate of the Institution of Electronic and Radio Engineers [*British*]
GradIISec .... Graduate of the Institute of Industrial Security [*British*] (DBQ)
Grad IM .... Graduate of the Institute of Metallurgists (BARN)
GradIMA .... Graduate Member of the Institute of Mathematics and Its Applications [*British*] (DBQ)
GradIManf ... Graduate Member of the Institute of Manufacturing [*British*] (DBQ)

Grad I Mech E... Graduate of the Institution of Mechanical Engineers [*British*]
GradIMF ...... Graduate of the Institute of Metal Finishing [*British*] (DBQ)
GradIMS ...... Graduate of the Institute of Management Specialists [*British*] (DBQ)
Grad Ind Co... Grady's Indian Codes [*A publication*] (DLA)
Grad Inst BE... Graduate Member of the Institute of British Engineers
GradInstBTM... Graduate of the Institute of Business and Technical Management [*British*] (DBQ)
GradInstNDT... Graduate of the British Institute of Non-Destructive Testing (DBQ)
Grad Inst P... Graduate Member of the Institute of Physics and the Physical Society [*British*]
GradInstPS... Graduate of the Institute of Purchasing and Supply [*British*] (DBQ)
GradIOP .... Graduate of the Institute of Printing [*British*] (DBQ)
GradIPM ...... Graduate of the Institute of Personnel Management [*British*] (DBQ)
GradIS .... Graduate Member of the Institute of Statisticians [*British*] (DBQ)
GradISM ...... Graduate of the Institute of Supervisory Management [*British*] (DBQ)
Grad MNDTS... Graduate Member of the Non-Destructive Testing Society of Great Britain
GradNIH....... Graduate of the National Institute of Hardware [*British*] (DBQ)
GradPRI........ Graduate of the Plastics and Rubber Institute [*British*] (DBQ)
Grad RIC...... Graduate Member of the Royal Institute of Chemistry [*British*]
GRADS......... Generalized Remote Access Database System (IEEE)
GRADS......... Ground RADAR Aerial Delivery System (MCD)
GRADSCOPE... Graduate Search by Computer after Personal Evaluation (AIE)
GradSCP...... Graduate of the Society of Certified Professionals [*British*] (DBQ)
GradSLAET... Graduate of the Society of Licensed Aircraft Engineers and Technologists [*British*] (DBQ)
GRADU .... Gradual
Graduate IElecIE... Graduate of the Institution of Electrical and Electronics Incorporated Engineers [*British*] (DBQ)
GradWeldI ... Graduate of the Welding Institute [*British*] (DBQ)
GRAE .... Generally Regarded [*or Recognized*] as Effective [*Medicine*]
GRAE .... Gouvernement de la Republique de l'Angola en Exile [*Government of the Republic of Angola in Exile*]
GRAE .... Governo Revolucionario de Angola no Exilio [*Revolutionary Angolan Government-in-Exile*] [*Portuguese*] (PD)
GR Aero S ... Graduate of the Royal Aeronautical Society [*British*]
GRAF .... Graffiti [*Slang*] [*British*]
GRAF .... Graphic Addition to FORTRAN [*Computer science*]
GRAF .... Ground Replay and Analysis Facility (GAVI)
GRAFCET ..... Graphe de Commande Etape-Transition [*State transition command graph*] [*Computer language*] (CDE)
GRAFEM ...... Graphic Finite Element Modeling [*Software*] [*Automotive engineering*]
GraffPay ...... Graff Pay per View [*Associated Press*] (SAG)
GRAFMA....... Grand Rapids Area Furniture Manufacturers Association (EA)
GRAFTABL... Load Graphics Table [*Computer science*]
Grafton .... Smith's New Hampshire Reports [*A publication*] (DLA)
Graham......... Graham Corp. [*Associated Press*] (SAG)
Grah & W New Trials... Graham and Waterman on New Trials [*A publication*] (DLA)
GRAI .... Government Reports Announcements and Index [*Department of Commerce A publication*]
GRAID.......... Graphical Aid [*Computer science*]
GRAIL .... Gene Recognition and Analysis Internet Link (HGEN)
GRAIL .... Graphic Input Language [*Computer science*] (PDAA)
GRAIN.......... Genetic Resources Action International [*Spain*]
GRAIN.......... Graphics-Oriented Relational Algebraic Interpreter
GRAINCORP... New South Wales Grain Corp. [*Australia Commercial firm*]
Graingr .... Grainger [*W.W.*], Inc. [*Associated Press*] (SAG)
GRAL .... General (ROG)
Gram .... De Grammaticis [*of Suetonius*] [*Classical studies*] (OCD)
GRAM .... Global Reference Atmosphere Model (SSD)
GRAM .... Grammar [*or Grammatical*]
gram .... Grammar [*Copyediting*] (WDMC)
Gram .... Gramophone [*Division of Record Corp. of America*] [*Record label*]
GRAM .... Granulocyte Activating Mediator [*Immunochemistry*]
GRAMA-COP... Grain Marketing Cooperative of the Philippines (BUAC)
Gramm Lat... Grammatici Latini [*A publication*] (OCD)
Gramm Rom Frag... Grammaticae Romana Fragmenta [*A publication*] (OCD)
gram-neg..... Gram-Negative [*Biochemistry*] (DAVI)
Gramo .... Gramola [*Record label*] [*Belgium*]
GRAMP........ Generalized Reliability and Maintainability Program [*Military*]
GRAMPA...... General Analytical Model for Process Analysis (IEEE)
GRAMPA...... Ground Resonance Automatic Multi-Point Apparatus (PDAA)
GRAMPIES... Growing Retired Active Monied Person in Excellent State [*Lifestyle classification*]
gram-pos..... Gram-Positive [*Biochemistry*] (DAVI)
GRAMPS...... Graphics for the Multipicture System [*Computer graphics*]
GRAMS........ Generalized Reliability and Maintainability Simulator (MCD)
GRAMS........ Gramophone Records [*Music or sound effects*]
GRAN........... Bank of Granite [*NASDAQ symbol*] (SAG)
GRAN........... Global Rescue Alarm Network [*Program*] [*Navy*]
GRAN........... Gombarts Reducing Agent - Negative [*Medicine*] (AAMN)
GRAN........... Grain
GRAN........... Grandmother (DSUE)
GRAN........... Granite (MSA)
gran .... Granite (VRA)
GRAN........... Granodize
GRAN........... Granular (WDAA)
GRAN........... Granulatus [*Granulated*] [*Pharmacy*]
GRANADA.... Grammatical Nonalgorithmic Data Description
GRANAS ...... Global Radio Navigation System [*Aviation*] (DA)
GRANAT....... Great Annihilator [*Commonwealth - French satellite*] (ECON)
GranBd .... Granite Broadcasting Corp. [*Associated Press*] (SAG)
GranCr .... GranCare, Inc. [*Associated Press*] (SAG)
Grand........... Grand Gaming Corp. [*Associated Press*] (SAG)
GRAND AM... Grand Marnier and Amaretto
GRANDE ...... Gamma Ray and Neutrino Detector Experiment [*Proposed*] [*University of California, Irvine*]
GrandG .... Grand Gaming Corp. [*Associated Press*] (SAG)
GRANDO ...... Grandioso [*Majestic*] [*Music*]
GR & P........ Grand Rapids & Petoskey Railway
GR & R........ Gauge Repeatability and Reproducibility [*Materials testing*]
GrandTel...... GrandeTel Technologies, Inc. [*Associated Press*] (SAG)
Grang........... Granges, Inc. [*Associated Press*] (SAG)
Granger .... Granger's State Reports [*22-23 Ohio*] [*A publication*] (DLA)
GRANIS........ Graphical Natural Inference System
GRANITE...... Gamma Ray Astrophysics New Imaging Telescope
GranitFn ...... Granite Financial, Inc. [*Associated Press*] (SAG)
GRANL......... Granulated
GRANO .... Granolithic
Grant .... Grant of Elchies' Scotch Session Cases [*A publication*] (DLA)
Grant .... Grant's Chancery Chamber Reports [*1850-65*] [*Upper Canada*] [*A publication*] (DLA)
Grant .... Grant's Jamaica Reports [*A publication*] (DLA)
Grant .... Grant's Pennsylvania Cases [*A publication*] (DLA)
Grant .... Grant's Upper Canada Chancery Reports [*A publication*] (DLA)
Grant Bank... Grant on Banking [*A publication*] (DLA)
Grant Cas .... Grant's Pennsylvania Cases [*A publication*] (DLA)
Grant Cas (PA)... Grant's Pennsylvania Cases [*A publication*] (DLA)
Grant Ch...... Grant's Upper Canada Chancery Reports [*A publication*] (DLA)
Grant Ch (Can)... Grant's Upper Canada Chancery Reports [*A publication*] (DLA)
Grant Corp... Grant on Corporations [*A publication*] (DLA)
Grant E & A... Grant's Error and Appeal Reports [*A publication*] (DLA)
Grant Err & App... Grant's Error and Appeal Reports [*A publication*] (DLA)
Grant Jamaica... Grant's Jamaica Reports [*A publication*] (DLA)
Grant PA...... Grant's Pennsylvania Cases [*A publication*] (DLA)
Gra N Tr...... Graham on New Trials [*A publication*] (DLA)
Grant's R..... Grant's Jamaica Reports [*A publication*] (DLA)
GrantSt .... Granite State Bankshares, Inc. [*Associated Press*] (SAG)
Grant UC...... Grant's Upper Canada Chancery Reports [*A publication*] (DLA)
granulo .... Granulocyte [*Hematology*] (DAVI)
GRAO........... Gamma Ray Astronomy Observatory
GRAP .... Greatest Response Amplitude Probability
GRAPD......... Greatest Response Amplitude Probability Data
GRAPD......... Guard Ring Avalanche Photodiode (IAA)
GRAPDEN .... Graphic Data Entry Unit [*Computer science*]
GRAPE .... Gamma Ray Attenuation Porosity Evaluator
GRAPE .... Graphical Analysis of Program Execution [*Computer science*]
GRAPE-4...... GRAvity PipE no. 4 [*Computer science*]
GRAPH......... Graphic
GRAPH......... Graphical Repair Discard Analysis Procedure Handbook
GRAPH......... Graphology (WDAA)
GRAPHDEN... Graphical Data Entry [*Computer science*] (MUGU)
GraphxZn..... Graphix Zone, Inc. [*Associated Press*] (SAG)
Grap Just..... Grapel's Translation of the Institutes of Justinian [*A publication*] (DLA)
GRAPO......... Grupos de Resistencia Anti-Fascista Primero de Octubre [*October First Antifascist Resistance Groups*] [*Spain Political party*] (PPE)
Gra Pr.......... Graham's Practice of the New York Supreme Court [*A publication*] (DLA)
Grap Rom Law... Grapel's Sources of the Roman Civil Law [*A publication*] (DLA)
GRAR........... Generally Recognized as Reasonable [*Medicine*] (DB)
GRAR........... Government Report Authorization and Record (AAG)
GRAR........... Grinding Arbor
GRARD .... Goddard Range and Range Data [*NASA*] (KSC)
GRARE......... Ground-Receiving and Analog Ranging Equipment [*AFSCF*] (MCD)
GRARR .... Goddard Range and Range Rate [*Tracking system*] [*NASA*]
GRAS........... Generally Recognized [*or Regarded*] as Safe [*FDA term*]
GRAS........... Ground Return Area Suppression (NATG)
GRASE......... Generally Recognized as Safe and Effective [*Medicine*] (DB)
GRASER....... Gamma Ray Amplification by Stimulated Emission of Radiation
GRASER....... Gamma Ray LASER (MCD)
GRASP......... Gamma Ray Astronomy with Spectroscopy and Positioning
GRASP......... GAO [*General Accounting Office*] Review and Approval of Accounting Systems Project (GFGA)
GRASP......... Generalized Read and Simulate Program
GRASP......... Generalized Reentry Application Simulation Program [*NASA*] (KSC)
GRASP......... Generalized Remote Acquisition and Sensor Processing
GRASP......... Generalized Retrieval and Storage Program [*Computer science*]
GRASP......... Generally Recognized as Safe Petition [*FDA*]
GRASP......... General Reduction and Analysis Support Package [*Military*] (CAAL)
GRASP......... General Resource Allocation and Selection Program [*NASA*] (KSC)
GRASP......... Generic RADAR Analysis and Synthesis Program
GRasp.......... Graphic Animation System for Professionals [*Software package*] [*Paul Mace Software*] (PCM)
GRASP......... Graphics-Augmented Structural Post-Processing [*Module*]
GRASP......... Graphic Service Program (IEEE)
GRASP Lab... General Robotics and Active Sensory Processing Laboratory [*University of Pennsylvania*] [*Research center*] (RCD)
GRASR......... General Railroad and Airline Stabilization Regulations [*A publication*] (DLA)
GRASS......... Gamma Ray Ablation Sensing System (SAA)
GRASS......... Gas Release and Swelling Subroutine (PDAA)
GRASS......... Generalized Reactor Analysis Subsystem
GRASS......... General Random Audit Sample Selection Technique [*Military*] (AFIT)
GRASS......... Geographical Resources Analysis Support System [*Software*] [*Computer science*] (EERA)
GRASS......... Geographic Resources Analysis Support System [*Army*] (RDA)
GRASS......... Germinating Ray Acoustics Simulation System (MCD)
GRASS......... Grassland Research and Serengeti Systems [*Model for simulation*]

GRASS........ Great Revolutionary American Standard System [*Book title*]
GRASS........ Ground-to-Air Scanner Surveillance
Grass R ...... Grass Roots [*A publication*]
GRAT .... Gratis [*Free*] [*Latin*] (ROG)
Grat .... Grattan's Virginia Reports [*A publication*] (DLA)
GRAT .... Gratuity (AABC)
Grat Act ...... Gratiarum Actio [*of Ausonius*] [*Classical studies*] (OCD)
GRATE .... Growth Rate [*Botany*]
GRATIS .... Generation, Reduction, and Training Input System (IEEE)
Gratt .... Grattan's Virginia Supreme Court Reports [*1844-80*] [*A publication*] (DLA)
Gratt (VA)... Grattan's Virginia Reports [*A publication*] (DLA)
GRAUL .... Grand Rapids Area Union List of Serials [*Library network*]
GRAV .... Gravid [*Pregnant*] [*Medicine*]
GRAV .... Gravitational
grav .... Gravity (CPH)
Grav De Jur Nat Gent... Gravina's De Jure Naturale Gentium, Etc. [*A publication*] (DLA)
Graves .... Proceedings in English King's Council [*1392-93*] [*A publication*] (DLA)
GRAVR........ Gravitational Redshift Space Probe [*Also, GP*]
Gray............ Gray's Massachusetts Supreme Judicial Court Reports [*67-82 Massachusetts*] [*1854-60*] [*A publication*] (DLA)
Gray............ Gray's Reports [*112-22 North Carolina*] [*A publication*] (DLA)
Gray Att Pr... Gray's Country Attorney's Practice [*9th ed.*] [*1869*] [*A publication*] (DLA)
GrayC......... Gray Communications Systems [*Associated Press*] (SAG)
GrayCom..... Gray Communications Systems [*Associated Press*] (SAG)
Gray Forms... Graydon's Forms of Conveyance [*A publication*] (DLA)
Gray (Mass)... Gray's Massachusetts Reports [*A publication*] (DLA)
Gray Perpetuities... Gray's Rule Against Perpetuities [*A publication*] (DLA)
GRAZ .... Grazioso [*Gracefully*] [*Music*]
GRAZO .... Grazioso [*Gracefully*] [*Music*]
GRB .... Gamma Ray Burst
GRB .... Garbo Industries [*Vancouver Stock Exchange symbol*]
GRB .... Gas Research Board (BUAC)
GRB .... Geophysics Research Board
GRB .... Gerber Scientific [*NYSE symbol*] (TTSB)
GRB .... Gerber Scientific, Inc. [*NYSE symbol*] (SPSG)
GRB .... Government Reservation Bureau
GRB .... Granatbuechse [*Antitank Grenade Rifle*] [*German*]
GRB .... Granolithic Base
GRB .... Green Bay [*Wisconsin*] [*Airport symbol*] (OAG)
GRBC.......... Goose Red Blood Cell
GRBDS......... Gyroscopes-Rate Bomb-Direction System (AAG)
GRBF.......... Generalized Radial Basis Function [*Mathematics*]
GRBL .... Garble (FAAC)
GRBM......... Global Range Ballistic Missile [*Air Force*]
GRBNKS ..... Grand Banks (FAAC)
Gr Br........... Great Britain (WGA)
Gr Brice....... Green's Edition of Brice's Ultra Vires [*A publication*] (DLA)
Gr Brit .... Great Britain
GRBS .... Gardeners' Royal Benevolent Society (BUAC)
GRBX .... Gearbox
GRC .... Gale Research Co. [*Later, GRI*]
GRC .... Garchy [*France*] [*Seismograph station code, US Geological Survey*] (SEIS)
GRC .... Gearcase (MSA)
GRC .... Gendarmerie Royale du Canada [*Royal Canadian Mounted Police - RCMP*]
GRC .... General Railway Classification [*British*]
GRC .... General Reinsurance Corp. (EFIS)
GRC .... General Research Corp. [*Information service or system*] (IID)
GRC .... Generation Review Committee [*Nuclear Regulatory Commission*] (NRCH)
GRC .... Geographic Resources Center [*University of Missouri - Columbia*] [*Research center*] (RCD)
GRC .... Geotechnical Research Centre [*McGill University*] [*Canada Research center*] (RCD)
GRC .... Geothermal Resources Council (EA)
GRC .... Gerontology Research Center [*Department of Health and Human Services*] [*Research center*]
GRC .... Glass-Fiber Reinforced Concrete
GRC .... Glass-Reinforced Composite
GRC .... Glenmary Research Center (EA)
GRC .... Global Reference Code [*Developed by Smithsonian Institution*]
GRC .... Gorman-Rupp [*AMEX symbol*] (TTSB)
GRC .... Gorman-Rupp Co. [*AMEX symbol*] (SPSG)
GRC .... Government of the Republic of China
GRC .... Government Research Centers Directory [*Later, GRD*] [*A publication*]
GRC .... Government Research Corp. [*Information service or system*] (IID)
GRC .... Grace
GRC .... Graduate Research Center of the Southwest [*Later, University of Texas at Dallas*]
GRC .... Grafted Rubber Concentrate [*Organic chemistry*]
GRC .... Grand Cess [*Liberia*] [*Airport symbol*] (OAG)
GRC .... Greece [*ANSI three-letter standard code*] (CNC)
grc .... Greek, Ancient [*MARC language code Library of Congress*] (LCCP)
GRC .... Greene County District Library, Xenia, OH [*OCLC symbol*] (OCLC)
GRC .... Greenlandair Charter AS [*Denmark ICAO designator*] (FAAC)
GRC .... Gross Replacement Cost (ADA)
GRC .... Guard Ring Capacitor
GRCA.......... Glassfibre Reinforced Cement Association [*British*]
GRCA.......... Golden Retriever Club of America (EA)
GRCA.......... Grand Canyon National Park

Gr Ca........... Grant's Cases [*A publication*] (DLA)
GRCA.......... Ground Reference Coverage Area (DOMA)
Gr Capt........ Group Captain [*British military*] (DMA)
GRCD.......... German Rhine Coordination Directorate [*Allied German Occupation Forces*]
GRCDA........ Governmental Refuse Collection and Disposal Association (EA)
GRCESD...... Guizhou Provincial Research Centre of Economic & Social Development [*China*] (BUAC)
GR CHAP ..... Grand Chapter [*Freemasonry*] (ROG)
GRCHRSCHR... Die Griechische Christliche Schriftsteller der Ersten Drei Jahrhunderten (BJA)
GR/CIDS ..... Genetic Resources/Communication, Information and Documentation System [*Databank*] (NITA)
GRC Int........ GRC International [*Associated Press*] (SAG)
GRCM......... Graduate of the Royal College of Music [*British*]
GRCO.......... Gradco Systems [*NASDAQ symbol*] (TTSB)
GRCO.......... Gradco Systems, Inc. [*NASDAQ symbol*] (NQ)
GR/CP......... Group Registration for Contributions to Periodicals [*US Copyright Office form*]
GrCr .... Grande Croix (EY)
GRCS .... Guard Rail Common Sensor [*Army*] (DOMA)
GR/CS .... Guardrail/Common Sensor System [*Military*]
GRCSCC...... Golden Ring Council of Senior Citizens Clubs [*Defunct*] (EA)
GRCSW....... Graduate Research Center of the Southwest [*Formerly, Southwest Center for AdvancedStudies; later, University of Texas at Dallas*]
GRCTS .... Ground Combat Training Squadron
GrCu .... University of Crete, Crete, Greece [*Library symbol*] [*Library of Congress*] (LCLS)
GRCV.......... Ground Cover [*Ecology*]
GRCV.......... Guard Receiver (MCD)
GRCWA....... Grain Research Committee of Western Australia
GRD .... Gastroesophageal Reflux Disease [*Gastroenterology*] (DAVI)
GRD .... General Radio Discriminator (IAA)
GRD .... Geophysics Research Directorate [*US*]
GRD .... Goldrich Resources, Inc. [*Vancouver Stock Exchange symbol*]
GRD .... Government Research Directory [*A publication*]
GRD .... Grading
GRD .... Gramicidin [*Antimicrobial compound*]
GR D .... Grand Duchess [*or Duke*] (ROG)
GRD .... Greatest Response Data
GRD .... Greenwood [*South Carolina*] [*Airport symbol*] (OAG)
GRD .... Grenada [*ANSI three-letter standard code*] (CNC)
GRD .... Grind (MSA)
GRD .... Ground
grd............. Ground (VRA)
GRD .... Ground Detector
GRD .... Ground Resolved Distance [*Satellite camera*]
GRD .... Ground Rule Double [*Baseball*]
Grd............. Ground Shells [*Quality of the bottom*] [*Nautical charts*]
GRD .... Guaranteed
GRD .... Guard
GRD .... National Grid Co. [*British ICAO designator*] (FAAC)
GRDA.......... Gin Rectifiers and Distillers Association [*British*] (DBA)
GRDAU........ Granddaughter (ROG)
GRDB.......... Geoscientific Resource Data Base [*Queensland*] [*State*] (EERA)
GRDC.......... Geological Research and Development Centre [*Indonesia*] (BUAC)
GRDC.......... Grains Research and Development Corporation [*Commonwealth*] [*State*] (EERA)
GrdCasn...... Grand Casinos, Inc. [*Associated Press*] (SAG)
GRDCUS...... Gulf Range Drone Control Upgrade System
GRDE.......... Grade
GrDelV........ Greater Delaware Valley Savings Bank [*Associated Press*] (SAG)
GRDEN........ Garden [*Commonly used*] (OPSA)
GRDF.......... Gypsum Roof Deck Foundation [*Later, NRDCA*] (EA)
GRDG.......... Garden Ridge [*NASDAQ symbol*] (TTSB)
GRDG.......... Garden Ridge Corp. [*NASDAQ symbol*] (SAG)
GRDL.......... Geodetic Research and Development Laboratory [*Rockville, MD*] [*Department of Commerce*] (MSC)
GRDL.......... Gradell Industries, Inc. [*NASDAQ symbol*] (SAG)
GRDL.......... Gradual [*NWS*] (FAAC)
GRDL.......... Griddle (MSA)
GRDN.......... Garden (ADA)
GRDN.......... Garden State Bancshares [*NASDAQ symbol*] (SAG)
GRDN.......... Guardian
GRDN.......... Guardian Technologies International, Inc. [*NASDAQ symbol*] (SAG)
GrdnB......... Guardian Bancorp [*Associated Press*] (SAG)
GRDNR........ Gardener
GRDNS........ Gardens [*Commonly used*] (OPSA)
GRDNU........ Guardian Tech Intl Unit [*NASDAQ symbol*] (TTSB)
GR/D/O .... Granddaughter Of [*Genealogy*]
GRDP.......... Graphic Data Processing (IAA)
GrdPrd........ Guardsman Products, Inc. [*Associated Press*] (SAG)
GRDPRO...... Grid Procedure (SAA)
GrdPrx........ Grand Prix Association of Long Beach [*Associated Press*] (SAG)
GRDQ.......... Groupe de Recherche sur la Demographie Quebecoise [*Research Group on Quebec Demography*] [*Canada*] (IRC)
GrdRnd....... Ground Round Restaurants, Inc. [*Associated Press*] (SAG)
GRDSR .... Geographically Referenced Data Storage and Retrieval System [*Canada*]
GrdTch........ Guardian Technologies International, Inc. [*Associated Press*] (SAG)
GRDTN........ Graduation (MSA)
Grdwtr........ Groundwater Technology, Inc. [*Associated Press*] (SAG)
GRE .... Gamma Ray Experiment
GRE .... Gamma Ray Explorer (NASA)
GRE .... Generated Repeatable Exams [*Education*]

GRE .... Generic Routing Encapsulation [*Computer science*]
GRE .... Glucocorticoid Responsive Element [*Endocrinology*]
GRE .... Gradient-Recalled Echo [*Physics*]
GRE .... Graduate Record Exam (GAGS)
GRE .... Graduate Record Examination [*Higher education*]
GRE .... Graduate Record Examinations Board (EA)
GRE .... Graduate Reliability Engineering
GRE .... Grant-Related Expenditure [*British*]
GRE .... Graphite-Reinforced Epoxy
GRE .... Gravitational Redshift Experiment (SSD)
GRE .... Greece (WDAA)
Gre............. Greece (VRA)
gre .... Greek, Modern [*MARC language code Library of Congress*] (LCCP)
GRE .... [*The*] Greens [*Australia Political party*]
GRE .... Greenstone Resources Ltd. [*Toronto Stock Exchange symbol*]
GRE .... Greenville, IL [*Location identifier FAA*] (FAAL)
GRE .... Grenada [*Seismograph station code, US Geological Survey*] (SEIS)
GRE .... Ground RADAR Equipment (IAA)
GRE .... Ground Reconnaissance Equipment
GRE .... Ground Reconstruction Electronics [*Used in photographing moon*] [*NASA*]
GRE .... Ground Reconstruction Equipment
GRE .... Ground Run-Up Enclosure [*Aviation*] (DA)
GRE .... Grove Real Estate Asset Trust [*AMEX symbol*] (SAG)
GRE .... Guardian Royal Exchange Assurance [*British*]
Gre............. National Library of Greenland [*Nunatta Atuagaategarfi*], Nuuk, Greenland [*Library symbol*] [*Library of Congress*] (LCLS)
GRE .... SEEA-Southeast European Airlines [*Greece*] [*ICAO designator*] (FAAC)
GREA .... Grant-Related Expenditure Assessments [*British*]
GREACAM... Guardian Royal Exchange Assurance Cameroun (BUAC)
GRE & E Div... Graves Registration and Effects Division [*Military*]
GREAT .... Geriatric Education and Training Act [*1985*]
GREAT .... Gifted Resources Education Action Team Project (EDAC)
GREAT .... Gorda Ridge Eruption Assessment Team [*Marine science*] (OSRA)
GREAT .... Grampian Region Early Anistreplase Trial [*Cardiology study*]
Greav Cr L... Greaves. Criminal Consolidation [*2nd ed.*] [*1862*] [*A publication*] (DLA)
Greaves....... Judgments of the Windward Islands Court of Appeal [*1866-1904*] [*A publication*] (DLA)
Greav Russ... Greaves' Edition of Russell on Crimes [*A publication*] (DLA)
GREB .... Galactic Radiation Experiment Background Satellite [*Navy transit satellite*]
GREB .... General Reciprocating Engine Bulletin [*A publication*] (DNAB)
GREB .... Graduate Records Examination Board (WDAA)
GRECC........ Geriatric Research, Education, and Clinical Center [*Veterans Administration*]
GRED .... Generalized Random Extract Device [*Computer science*]
GREDI .... Groupe d'Etudes en Developpement International [*International Development Studies Group*] [*Canada*]
GREE .... General Requests for Ground-Based Electronics Equipment [*NASA*]
GREEMAIN... Agreement to Remain on Active Duty Until Date Specified (DNAB)
GREEN .... Green [*Commonly used*] (OPSA)
Green.......... Green's Reports [*A publication*] (DLA)
GREEN .... Guild to Revive Exhausted Nurses
Green & H Conv... Greenwood and Horwood's Conveyancing [*A publication*] (DLA)
GreenAP...... Green [*A. P.*] Industries, Inc. [*Associated Press*] (SAG)
Green Bag.... Green Bag; A Legal Journal [*Boston*] [*A publication*] (DLA)
Green BL..... Green's Bankrupt Law [*A publication*] (DLA)
Greenbr .... [*The*] Greenbrier Companies, Inc. [*Associated Press*] (SAG)
Greenbri....... Greenbriar Corp. [*Associated Press*] (SAG)
Green Bri..... Green's Edition of Brice's Ultra Vires [*A publication*] (DLA)
Green Conv... Greenwood's Manual of Conveyancing [*9th ed.*] [*1897*] [*A publication*] (DLA)
Green Cr...... Green's Criminal Law [*England*] [*A publication*] (DLA)
Green Cr Cas... Green's Criminal Cases [*A publication*] (DLA)
Green Crim Reports... Criminal Law Reports, by Green [*United States*] [*A publication*] (DLA)
Green Cr Law R... Green's Criminal Law Reports [*A publication*] (DLA)
Green Cr L Rep... Green's Criminal Law Reports [*A publication*] (DLA)
Green Cr Rep... Criminal Law Reports, by Green [*United States*] [*A publication*] (DLA)
Green Cruise... Greenleaf's Edition of Cruise's Digest of Real Property [*A publication*] (DLA)
Green Cts .... Greenwood on Courts [*A publication*] (DLA)
Greene......... Greene's Reports [*7 New York Annotated Cases*] [*A publication*] (DLA)
Green Ev..... Greenleaf on Evidence [*A publication*] (DLA)
Green Forms... Greening's Forms of Declarations, Pleadings, Etc. [*A publication*] (DLA)
Greenh Pub Pol... Greenhood's Doctrine of Public Policy in the Law of Contracts [*A publication*] (DLA)
Greenh Sh ... Greenhow's Shipping Law Manual [*A publication*] (DLA)
Greenl .... Greenland (BARN)
Greenl .... Greenleaf's Reports [*1-9 Maine*] [*A publication*] (DLA)
Greenl Cr..... Greenleaf's Edition of Cruise's Digest of Real Property [*A publication*] (DLA)
Greenl Cruise... Greenleaf's Edition of Cruise's Digest of Real Property [*A publication*] (DLA)
Greenl Cruise Real Prop... Greenleaf's Edition of Cruise's Digest of Real Property [*A publication*] (DLA)
Greenl Ev..... Greenleaf on Evidence [*A publication*] (DLA)
Greenl Ov Cas... Greenleaf's Over-Ruled Cases [*A publication*] (DLA)
Greenl Test Ev... Greenleaf on the Testimony of the Evangelists [*A publication*] (DLA)

Greenman... Greenman Technologies, Inc. [*Associated Press*] (SAG)
Green (NJ)... Green's New Jersey Law or Equity [*A publication*] (DLA)
Green Ov Cas... Greenleaf's Over-Ruled Cases [*A publication*] (DLA)
Green (RI)... Green's Reports [*Rhode Island*] [*A publication*] (DLA)
Green Rom Law... Green's Outlines of Roman Law [*A publication*] (DLA)
GREENS....... Greens [*Commonly used*] (OPSA)
GreenS .... GreenStone Industries, Inc. [*Associated Press*] (SAG)
Green Sc Cr Cas... Green's Criminal Cases [*A publication*] (DLA)
Green Sc Tr... Green's Scottish Trials for Treason [*A publication*] (DLA)
Green Ship... Greenhow's Law of Shipowners [*A publication*] (DLA)
GreenSt....... Green Street Financial Corp. [*Associated Press*] (SAG)
GreenStn..... GreenStone Industries, Inc. [*Associated Press*] (SAG)
GreenTR ..... GreenTree Financial Corp. [*Associated Press*] (SAG)
Greenw & M Mag Pol... Greenwood and Martin's Magistrates' Police Guide [*A publication*] (DLA)
Greenw Conv... Greenwood's Manual of Conveyancing [*9th ed.*] [*1897*] [*A publication*] (DLA)
Greenw Cts... Greenwood on Courts [*A publication*] (DLA)
GreenwSt..... Greenwich Street Municipal Fund, Inc. [*Associated Press*] (SAG)
Greer .... Greer's Irish Land Acts, Leading Cases [*1872-1903*] [*A publication*] (DLA)
GREF .... General Reserve Engineer Force [*British military*] (DMA)
GREFICOR ... Groupe de Recherche sur l'Efficacite Organisationnelle [*University of Quebec at Hull*] [*Research center*] (RCD)
G/REG .... Generator-Regulator [*Automotive engineering*]
G REG .... Grand Registrar [*Freemasonry*] (ROG)
GREG .... Gregorian (ROG)
Greg........... Gregorowski's Reports of the High Court [*A publication*] (DLA)
GregLA .... Pontificiae Universitatis Gregorianae Liber Annuus [*Rome*] [*A publication*] (BJA)
GRegO .... Group Regiment Officer [*British military*] (DMA)
Gregorowski... High Court Reports, Orange Free State [*A publication*] (DLA)
GREI .... Groupe de Recherche en Enseignement Individualise [*Canada*]
GreifBrA...... Greif Brothers Corp. [*Associated Press*] (SAG)
GreifBrB...... Greif Brothers Corp. [*Associated Press*] (SAG)
Greiner .... Greiner Engineering, Inc. [*Associated Press*] (SAG)
Grein Pr....... Greiner's Louisiana Practice [*A publication*] (DLA)
GREM .... Geopotential Research Explorer Mission (MCD)
GREM .... Gremlin [*Refers to a person unskilled in skateboarding*] [*Slang British*] (DSUE)
GREMAS ..... Genealogische Recherche mit Magnetband-Speicherung [*Organic chemistry coding system*]
GREMAS ..... Generic Retrieval by Magnetic-Tape Storage [*Computer science*] (PDAA)
GREMEX ..... Goddard Research and Engineering Management Exercise [*NASA*]
GREMF .... Groupe de Recherche et d'Echange Multidisciplinaires Feministes [*Universite Laval, Quebec*] [*Canada*]
GREN .... Grenade (AABC)
Gren........... Grenier's Ceylon Reports [*A publication*] (DLA)
GRENAP...... Greenlease Kidnapping
GRENDR ...... Grenadier (AABC)
Grenfld .... Greenfield Industries, Inc. [*Associated Press*] (SAG)
Grenier .... Grenier's Ceylon Reports [*A publication*] (DLA)
Grenm .... Greenman Brothers, Inc. [*Associated Press*] (SAG)
grep .... Global Regular Expression and Print [*Computer science*] (CDE)
GREP .... Global Regular-Expression Purser [*Computer science*]
GREPAT ...... Greenland Patrol [*Navy*]
GrEq.......... Gresley's Equity Evidence [*A publication*] (DLA)
GRER .... Greenstone Resources Ltd. [*NASDAQ symbol*] (NQ)
GRERF .... Greenstone Res Ltd [*NASDAQ symbol*] (TTSB)
Gre Rom Law... Greene's Outlines of Roman Law [*A publication*] (DLA)
GRES .... Global Renewable Energy Services [*Swinden, England*] [*Commercial firm*]
GRES .... Greatest Amount of Resources
Gres EqEv... Gresley's Equity Evidence [*A publication*] (DLA)
GRESLET .... Groupe de Recherche en Semantique, Lexicologie, et Terminologie [*Universite de Montreal, Quebec*] [*Canada*]
GRETA .... Ground RADAR Emitter for Training Aviators [*Army*] (RDA)
GR et I......... Georgius Rex et Imperator [*George, King and Emperor*]
Gretton .... Oxford Quarter Sessions Records [*Oxford Record Society, No. 16*] [*A publication*] (DLA)
GrEv........... Greenleaf on Evidence [*A publication*] (DLA)
GREY .... Grey Advertising [*NASDAQ symbol*] (TTSB)
GreyAd....... Grey Advertising, inc. [*Associated Press*] (SAG)
Grey Deb .... Grey's House of Commons Debates [*A publication*] (DLA)
GreyhndL .... Greyhound Lines [*Associated Press*] (SAG)
GreyLne...... Greyhound Lines, Inc. [*Associated Press*] (SAG)
GRF .... Garbell Research Foundation (MCD)
GRF .... Gelatin, Resorcinol, and Formaldehyde
GRF .... Genetically-Related Factor [*Immunology*]
GRF .... Geographic Reference File [*Bureau of the Census*] (GFGA)
GRF .... Gerald Rudolf Ford [*US president, 1913-*]
GRF .... Gesneriad Research Foundation (EA)
GRF .... Golden Rule Foundation (EA)
GRF .... Gonadotropin-Releasing Factor [*Also, GnRF, GnRH, LH-RF, LH-RH/FSH-RH, LRF, LRH*] [*Endocrinology*]
GRF .... Graefenberg Array [*Erlangen*] [*Federal Republic of Germany*] [*Seismograph station code, US Geological Survey*] (SEIS)
GRF .... Grain Research Foundation [*Australia*]
GRF .... Grandfather
GRF .... Graphic Reproduction Federation (DGA)
GRF .... Grassland Research Foundation (EA)
GRF .... Gravity Research Foundation (EA)
GRF .... Greek Road Federation (BUAC)
GRF .... Ground Reaction Force [*Army*] (INF)

GRF	Group Repetition Frequency
GRF	Growth Hormone Releasing Factor [*Somatoliberin*] [*Also, GH-RF, GH-RH Endocrinology*]
GRF	Guaranty Reserve Fund
GRF	Guild Resource File [*Guild Products, Inc.*] [*Computer science*] (PCM)
GRF	Tacoma/Fort Lewis, WA [*Location identifier FAA*] (FAAL)
GRFC	Growth Financial Corp. [*NASDAQ symbol*] (SAG)
GR-FeSV	Gardner-Rasheed Feline Sarcoma Virus
GRFF	General Radio Frequency Fitting (IAA)
G/Rfg	Grooved Roofing [*Lumber*] (DAC)
GRFL	Gerald R. Ford Library
GRFL	Groundwater Remediation Field Laboratory [*Environmental science*] (BCP)
GRFM	General Radio Frequency Meter (IAA)
GRFMA	Grand Rapids Furniture Market Association [*Inactive*] (EA)
GRFO	Gun Range-Finder Operator
GrFRP	Graphite-Fiber-Reinforced Plastic [*Also, GFRP*]
GRFX	Grinding Fixture
GRG	Gastroenterology Research Group [*Defunct*] (EA)
GRG	Gearing (MSA)
GRG	Generalized Reduced Gradient
GRG	General Recurrent Grant
GRG	Georgetown [*Guyana*] [*Airport symbol*] (AD)
GRG	Glass-Fiber Reinforced Gypsum [*Substitute wood*]
GRG	Glycine-Rich Glycoprotein (DMAA)
GRG	Gordetsky [*G.R.*] Telecommunications and General Management Consulting [*San Diego, CA*] [*Telecommunications*] (TSSD)
Grg	Gorgias [*of Plato*] [*Classical studies*] (OCD)
GRG	Grandparents Raising Grandchildren (EA)
GRG	Graphical Rewriting Grammar
GRG	Gross Reserve Generation [*Electronics*] (IEEE)
GRGDB	Gryehound Racing Grounds Development Board [*Victoria, Australia*]
GRGE	Garage [*Classified Advertising*] (ADA)
GRGE	Gorge [*Board on Geographic Names*]
Gr Gesch	Griechische Geschichte [*A publication*] (OCD)
GRGI	Greenery Rehabilitation Group, Inc. (MHDW)
GRGL	Groundwater Residue Guidance Level [*Environmental Protection Agency*]
GRGS	Ground Roll Guidance System (MCD)
GRH	Garuahi [*Papua New Guinea*] [*Airport symbol*] (OAG)
GRH	Gas Recycle Hydrogenation [*Petroleum engineering*]
GRH	Gentlemen's Right Handed [*Golf club*]
GRH	Grahamstown [*South Africa*] [*Seismograph station code, US Geological Survey Closed*] (SEIS)
GRH	Gramm-Rudman-Hollings [*Law*]
GRH	Gramm-Rudman-Hollings Budget Deficit Control Act (AAGC)
GRH	GRC International [*NYSE symbol*] (SPSG)
GRH	Growth Hormone Releasing Hormone [*Somatoliberin*] [*Also, GH-RF, GRF Endocrinology*] (MAE)
GrhmFL	Graham-Field Health Products, Inc. [*Associated Press*] (SAG)
GRHQU	Gruppen-Hauptquartier [*Group Headquarters*] [*German military - World War II*]
GRHS	Germans-from-Russia Heritage Society (EA)
GRI	Gabriel Richard Institute (EA)
GRI	Gale Research, Inc.
GRI	Gallaudet Research Institute [*Gallaudet College*] [*Research center*] (RCD)
GRI	Gamma Ray Inspection
GRI	Gas Research Institute (EA)
GRI	Generic Run-Time [*Computer science*]
GRI	Geophysical Research Institute [*University of New England, Australia*]
GRI	Geoscience Research Institute
GRI	Gidley Research Institute [*Research center*] (RCD)
GRI	Ginseng Research Institute (EA)
GRI	Glider Developments, Inc. [*Vancouver Stock Exchange symbol*]
GRI	Global Readiness Index
Gri	Glyceric Acid [*Biochemistry*]
GRI	Gospel Recordings, Inc.
GRI	Government of the Ryukyu Islands
GRI	Government Reports Index [*Formerly, USGRDR-I*] [*Department of Commerce*]
GRI	Government Research Index (MCD)
GR-I	Government Rubber-Isobutylene [*Synthetic rubber*]
GRI	Grand Island [*Nebraska*] [*Airport symbol*] (OAG)
GRI	Grassland Research Institute [*Research center British*] (IRC)
GRI	Grassroots International (EA)
GRI	Gravure Research Institute [*Later, GAA*] (EA)
GRI	Gristede's Sloan's [*AMEX symbol*] [*Formerly, Sloan's Supermarkets*] (SG)
GRI	Groupe de Recherche et d'Intervention en Ideologie [*Universite du Quebec a Montreal*] [*Canada*]
GRI	Group Repetition Interval (IEEE)
GRI	Guaranteed Retirement Income
GRIB	Gridded Binary [*Data Format*] [*Marine science*] (OSRA)
GRIB	Gridded Binary Form [*Computer science*]
GRIBAT	Graphics Interface Basic Acceptance Test (MCD)
GRIC	Global Reach Internet Connection [*Computer science*]
GRIC	Global Roaming Internet Connection [*Computer science*]
GRIC	Graduate Member of the Royal Institute of Chemistry [*British*] (DBQ)
GRICAAS	Grassland Research Institute, Chinese Academy of Agricultural Sciences (BUAC)
GRID	Gas Research Institute Digest [*Acronym is used as title of publication*] [*A publication*]
GRID	Gay-Related Immune Disease [*Medicine*] (WDAA)
GRID	Gay-Related Immunodeficiency [*Also, AID, AIDS*] [*Medicine*]
GRID	GEC [*General Electric Company*] Rectangular Image Data Processor (NITA)
GRID	Global Resource Information Data Base [*UNEP*] [*Nairobi, Kenya*] [*Information service or system*] (IID)
GRID	Global Resource Information Database [*NASA*]
GRID	Graphic Interactive Display (IEEE)
GRID	Graphic Reproduction by Integrated Design
GRID	Graphic Retrieval and Information Display (NASA)
grid	Gridiron [*Typography*] [*Theater*] (WDMC)
GRIDEQ	Groupe de Recherche en Developpement de l'Est du Quebec [*Canada*]
GRIDS	Geographic Resources Information Data System [*Environmental Protection Agency*] (AEPA)
GRIDS	Geophysical Range Input Detection System
GRIDS	Guidelines for Review and Internal Development in Schools (AIE)
GRIF	Government Research Institute of Formosa
GRIF	Griffin Technology, Inc. [*NASDAQ symbol*] (NQ)
GRIF	Growth Hormone Release Inhibiting Factor [*Also, GH-RIF, GH-RIH, SRIF, SS*] [*Endocrinology*]
Grif Cr	Griffith on Arrangements with Creditors [*A publication*] (DLA)
Grif Ct Mar	Griffith on Military Law and Courts-Martial [*A publication*] (DLA)
Grif Eq	Griffith's Institutes of Equity [*A publication*] (DLA)
GRIFF	Groupe de Recherches Interdisciplinaires des Fertilisation des Forets [*Joint federal-provincial project*] [*Canada*]
Griffin Pat Cas	Griffin's Patent Cases [*1866-87*] [*A publication*] (DLA)
Griffin PC	Griffin's Abstract of Patent Cases [*England*] [*A publication*] (DLA)
Griffith	Griffith's Reports [*1-5 Indiana Appeals and 117-132 Indiana*] [*A publication*] (DLA)
Griffon	Griffon Corp. [*Associated Press*] (SAG)
Griff Pat Cas	Griffin's Patent Cases [*1866-87*] [*A publication*] (DLA)
GrifGam	Griffin Gaming & Entertainment [*Associated Press*] (SAG)
Grif Inst	Griffith's Institutes of Equity [*A publication*] (DLA)
Grif Jud Acts	Griffith on the Judicature Acts [*A publication*] (DLA)
Grif L Reg	Griffith's Law Register [*Burlington, NJ*] [*A publication*] (DLA)
Grif Mar Wom	Griffith's Married Women's Property Act [*A publication*] (DLA)
Grif Mil Law	Griffith on Military Law and Courts-Martial [*A publication*] (DLA)
Grif Pat C	Griffin's Patent Cases [*1866-87*] [*A publication*] (DLA)
Grif PC	Griffin's Patent Cases [*1866-87*] [*A publication*] (DLA)
Grif PLC	Griffith's London Poor Law Cases [*1821-31*] [*A publication*] (DLA)
Grif PL Cas	Griffith's London Poor Law Cases [*1821-31*] [*A publication*] (DLA)
Grif Pr	Griffith's Practice [*A publication*] (DLA)
Grif PRC	Griffith's Poor Rate Cases [*A publication*] (DLA)
Grif PR Cas	Griffith's English Poor Rate Cases [*A publication*] (DLA)
Grif St	Griffith's Stamp Duties [*A publication*] (DLA)
GrifTch	Griffin Technology, Inc. [*Associated Press*] (SAG)
GRIL	Gale Research International Ltd.
GRIL	Grill Concepts [*NASDAQ symbol*] (TTSB)
GRIL	Grill Concepts, Inc. [*NASDAQ symbol*] (SAG)
GrillCon	Grill Concepts, Inc. [*Associated Press*] (SAG)
Grim Bank	Grimsey's Proceedings in Bankruptcy [*A publication*] (DLA)
Grimke Ex	Grimke on Executors and Administrators [*A publication*] (DLA)
Grimke Jus	Grimke's Justice [*A publication*] (DLA)
Grimke PL	Grimke's Public Laws of South Carolina [*A publication*] (DLA)
GRIN	Germplasm Resources Information Network [*Department of Agriculture*] [*Beltsville, MD*]
GRIN	Graded-Index Fiber (ACRL)
GRIN	Graded Refractive-Index [*Optics*]
GRIN	Gradient of Refractive Index [*Optics*]
GRIN	Grands Toys Intl [*NASDAQ symbol*] (TTSB)
GRIN	Grand Toys International [*NASDAQ symbol*] (SAG)
GRIN	Graphical Input [*Language*] [*Computer science*]
GRIN	Great Plains [*AAR code*]
GRIN-2	Graphical Interaction [*Language*] [*Computer science*]
GRIND	Grinding
GRIND	Group Index (MCD)
GRINDER	Graphical Interactive Network Designer
GRINM	General Research Institute for Non-Ferrous Metals [*China*] (BUAC)
GRINS	General Retrieval Inquiry Negotiation Structure
GRINS	Graphical Input of SMILES [*Simplified Molecular Line Editor System*] Input
GRINSCH	Graded Index Separate Confinement Heterostructure (AAEL)
GRINW	Grand Toys Intl Wrrt [*NASDAQ symbol*] (TTSB)
GRIP	Gay Rights in Prison [*An association*] (BUAC)
GRIP	Gemini Reentry Integration Program [*NASA*]
GRIP	General Retrieval of Information Program [*Computer science*]
GRIP	General Retrieval of Information Program [*Hoechst Pharmaceutical Research Laboratories*] [*Personal indexing system*] [*British*] (NITA)
GRIP	Glucocorticoid Receptor-Interacting Protein [*Biology*]
GRIP	Glutamate Receptor Interacting Protein [*Neurochemistry*]
GRIP	Grandmet Information Processing [*British*]
GRIP	Graphics Interaction with Proteins [*Computer graphics*]
GRIP	Graphics Interactive Program (NITA)
GRIP	Graphics Interactive Programming
GRIP	Graphics Interactive Programming Language [*McDonnell-Douglas Corp.*]
GRIP	Greenland Icecore Project [*Europe*] [*Marine science*] (OSRA)
GRIP	Greenland Icesheet Program [*Europe*] [*Marine science*] (OSRA)
GRIP	Groupe de Recherche sur les Insectes Piqueurs [*University of Quebec at Trois-Rivieres*] [*Canada Research center*] (RCD)
GRIP	Guaranteed Recovery of Investment Principal [*Economics*]
GRIP	International Grouping of Pharmaceuticals Distributors in the EEC (ECED)
GRIP	Royal Grip [*NASDAQ symbol*] (TTSB)

GRIP	Royal Grip, Inc. [*NASDAQ symbol*] (SAG)
GRIPHOS	General Retrieval and Information Processor for Humanities Oriented Studies
GRIPS	Gaming, Random Interfacing, and Problem Structuring (PDAA)
GRIPS	General Relation Based Information Processing System (IAA)
GRIPS	Graphic Image Pagination System [*Penta Systems International*]
GRIPS	Ground Reconnaissance Information Processing System (DNAB)
GRIR	Groupe de Recherche et d'Intervention Regionales [*Universite du Quebec a Chicoutimi*] [*Canada*]
GRIS	Gamma-Ray Imaging Spectrometer
GRIS	Global Resources Information System
gris	Grisaille (VRA)
GRIS	Grisons [*Canton in Switzerland*] (ROG)
GRIS	Groupe de Recherche Interdisciplinaire en Sante [*Interdisciplinary Health Research Group - IHRG*] [*Universite de Montreal*] [*Canada*] [*Research center*]
GRISAH	Groupe de Recherche et d'Intervention sur les Systemes d'Activites Humaines [*University of Quebec at Rimouski*] [*Research center*] (RCD)
GRISS	Golombok Rust Inventory of Sexual Satisfaction [*Test*] [*Psychology*]
GRIST	Grazing-Incidence Solar Telescope
GristMil	Grist Mill Co. [*Associated Press*] (SAG)
GRISUR	Grupo de Informacion y Solidaridad Uruguay [*Switzerland*]
Grisw	Griswold's Reports [*14-19 Ohio*] [*A publication*] (DLA)
Griswold	Griswold's Reports [*14-19 Ohio*] [*A publication*] (DLA)
Grisw Und	Griswold's Fire Underwriter's Text-Book [*A publication*] (DLA)
GRIT	Graduated Reduction in Tensions [*Cold War term*]
GRIT	Grantor-Retained Income Trust [*Estate planning*]
GRITS	Gamma Ray Imaging Telescope System
GRITS	Geothermal Resource Interactive Temporal Simulation (PDAA)
GRITS	Goddard Range [*and Range Rate*] Instrumentation Tracking System [*NASA*] (AAG)
GRJ	George [*South Africa*] [*Airport symbol*] (OAG)
GRJ	Gorje [*Yugoslavia*] [*Seismograph station code, US Geological Survey Closed*] (SEIS)
GRJC	Grand Rapids Junior College [*Michigan*]
GRK	Gear Rack
GRK	Golden Rock Resources Ltd. [*Vancouver Stock Exchange symbol*]
GRK	Goroka [*Papua New Guinea*] [*Seismograph station code, US Geological Survey Closed*] (SEIS)
GRK	G Protein Receptor Kinase [*An enzyme*]
GRK	Greek [*Language, etc.*]
GRK	Killeen, TX [*Location identifier FAA*] (FAAL)
GRL	General
GRL	Geophysical Research Letters [*A publication*]
GRL	Gerontology Research Center, Baltimore, MD [*OCLC symbol*] (OCLC)
GRL	Goldenrod Resources & Technology, Inc. [*Vancouver Stock Exchange symbol*]
GRL	Grain Research Laboratory [*Canadian Grain Commission*] [*Research center*] (RCD)
GRL	Greenland [*ANSI three-letter standard code*] (CNC)
GRL	Grill
GRL	Grille
GRL	Gronlandsfly Ltd. [*Denmark ICAO designator*] (FAAC)
GRL	Gross Reference List (DNAB)
GRL	Grundrichtungslinie [*Base line, a gunnery term*] [*German military - World War II*]
Grld	Greenland (VRA)
GRLL	Roadhouse Grill, Inc. [*NASDAQ symbol*] (SAG)
GRLP	Ground Lamp (IAA)
GRLS	Great River Library System [*Library network*]
GRM	Generalized Reed-Muller [*Codes*] (IEEE)
GRM	Generalized Report Module Program [*Computer science*]
GRM	Geophysical Research Mission [*Marine science*] (OSRA)
GRM	Geopotential Research Mission [*NASA*]
GRM	Germ [*or Germination*] (WGA)
GRM	Global Range Missile [*Air Force*]
GRM	Grahamstown [*South Africa*] [*Seismograph station code, US Geological Survey*] (SEIS)
GRM	Gram (ADA)
GRM	Gramme [*Gram*] [*French*] (ROG)
GRM	Grand Marais, MN [*Location identifier FAA*] (FAAL)
GRM	Grand Metropolitan ADS [*NYSE symbol*] (SPSG)
GRM	Grandmother
GRM	Graziano, R. M., Washington DC [*STAC*]
GRM	Great Renunciation Movement (EA)
GRM	Gross Rent Multiplier [*Business term*] (EMRF)
GRM	Gruppe Revolutionaerer Marxisten [*Group of Revolutionary Marxists*] [*Austria Political party*] (PPE)
GRM	Guarded Relay Multiplexer
GRM	Guidance Rate Measurement
GRMBL	Grumble [*Computer hacker terminology*]
GRMN	Garment Graphics [*NASDAQ symbol*] (TTSB)
GRMN	Garment Graphics, Inc. [*NASDAQ symbol*] (SAG)
GRMNW	Garment Graphics Wrrt'A' [*NASDAQ symbol*] (TTSB)
GRMNZ	Garment Graphics Wrrt'B' [*NASDAQ symbol*] (TTSB)
GrMonk	Grease Monkey Holding Corp. [*Associated Press*] (SAG)
gr m p	Grosso Modo Pulverisatum [*Ground in a Coarse Way*] [*Latin*] (STED)
GRMPrA	Grand Met Del L.P. 9.42% Pfd [*NYSE symbol*] (TTSB)
GRMRA	Gift Retailers, Manufacturers, and Reps Association (EA)
GRMT	Garment
grmt	Garment (VRA)
GRMT	Grommet [*Automotive engineering*]
GRN	General Re Corp. [*NYSE symbol*] (SPSG)
Grn	Glycerone [*Biochemistry*]
GRN	Gordon, NE [*Location identifier FAA*] (FAAL)
Gr N	Graduate Nurse
GRN	Gram-Negative [*Also, GN*] [*Microbiology*]
GrN	Gram-Negative (STED)
GRN	Granite [*Technical drawings*]
GRN	Granule [*Medicine*]
GRN	Granulin (DMAA)
grn	Green (VRA)
Grn	Green (STED)
GRN	Green (KSC)
GRN	Greenair Hava Tasimaciligi AS [*Turkey*] [*ICAO designator*] (FAAC)
GRN	Greens [*Political party Australia*]
GRN	Greenville & Northern Railway Co. [*AAR code*]
GRN	Greenwich Library, Greenwich, CT [*OCLC symbol*] (OCLC)
GRN	Grenoble [*France*] [*Seismograph station code, US Geological Survey*] (SEIS)
GRN	Grenoble Energy [*Vancouver Stock Exchange symbol*]
gRNA	Guide Ribonucleic Acid [*Genetics*]
GRNC	Group Number No Count [*Military communication*]
GRNCM	Graduate of the Royal Northern College of Music [*British*] (DBQ)
GRND	Grand
GRND	Ground (ADA)
GrnDan	Green [*Daniel*] Co. [*Associated Press*] (SAG)
GrndM	Grand Metropolitan Delaware Ltd. [*Associated Press*] (SAG)
GRNDMA	Grandma
GrndMet	Grand Metropolitan Ltd. [*Associated Press*] (SAG)
GRNDPA	Grandpa
GrndPr	Grand Premier Financial, Inc. [*Associated Press*] (SAG)
GRNDR	Grinder [*s*] [*Freight*]
Grnds	Grounds (DD)
GrndToy	Grand Toys International [*Associated Press*] (SAG)
GrndUn	Grand Union Co. [*Associated Press*] (SAG)
GRNHS	Greenhouse
GRNL	Gay Rights National Lobby (EA)
grnln	Granulation (VRA)
Grnmn	Greenman Technologies, Inc. [*Associated Press*] (SAG)
GrnMtn	Green Mountain Coffee [*Associated Press*] (SAG)
GRNP	Grant Geophysical, Inc. [*NASDAQ symbol*] (SAG)
GrnPtFin	Greenpoint Financial Corp. [*Associated Press*] (SAG)
GRNR	[*The*] Grand River Railway Co. [*AAR code*]
GRNS	Greens [*Postal Service standard*] (OPSA)
grnsh	Greenish [*Philately*]
GrnStCA	Greenwich Street California Municipal Fund, Inc. [*Associated Press*] (SAG)
GrnstR	Greenstone Roberts Advertising, Inc. [*Associated Press*] (SAG)
GrnstRs	Greenstone Resources Ltd. [*Associated Press*] (SAG)
GRNT	Granite
GRNT	Grant Geophysical [*NASDAQ symbol*] (TTSB)
GRNT	Grant Geophysical, Inc. [*NASDAQ symbol*] (SPSG)
GRNTD	Guaranteed
GrnteC	Granite Construction, Inc. [*Associated Press*] (SAG)
GrntG	Grant Geophysical, Inc. [*Associated Press*] (SAG)
GrntGeo	Grant Geophysical, Inc. [*Associated Press*] (SAG)
GRNTP	Grant Geophysical $2.4375 Cv Pfd [*NASDAQ symbol*] (TTSB)
GrntrSft	Greentree Software, Inc. [*Associated Press*] (SAG)
GrntT	Grant Tensor Geophysical Corp. [*Associated Press*] (SAG)
GrnwAir	Greenwich Air Services, Inc. [*Associated Press*] (SAG)
GRO	Gamma Ray Observatory [*NASA*] (EGAO)
GRO	Gasoline Range Organic [*Chemistry*]
GRO	General Register Office [*British*]
GRO	General Register Office [*Scotland*] (BUAC)
GRO	General Routine Order
GRO	Gerona [*Spain*] [*Airport symbol*] (OAG)
Gro	Glycerol [*Biochemistry*]
GRO	Government Reform and Oversight Committee [*House of Representatives*] (AAGC)
GRO	Grandparents Rights Organization (EA)
GRO	Graphics Reporting Option [*Computer science*] (CIST)
GRO	Graves Registration Officer [*Military*]
GRO	Greenwich Royal Observatory [*British*] (BARN)
GRO	Gross (MSA)
Gro	Gross' Select Cases Concerning the Law Merchant [*Selden Society*] [*A publication*] (DLA)
Gro	Grotius' Rights of War and Peace [*Many eds.*] [*1625-1901*] [*A publication*] (DLA)
GRO	Ground Risks Only [*Insurance*] (AIA)
GRO	Group (WGA)
GRO	Grove
GRO	Growth Investment Corp. [*Toronto Stock Exchange symbol*]
GRO	Growth-Related Protein (DMAA)
GRO	Grozny [*Former USSR Seismograph station code, US Geological Survey*] (SEIS)
GRO	Lineas Aereas Allegro SA de CV [*Mexico ICAO designator*] (FAAC)
GRO	Rota Island, TT [*Location identifier FAA*] (FAAL)
GROBDM	General Register Office for Births, Deaths, and Marriages [*A publication*] (DLA)
GROC	Grocery (WDAA)
GROCAP	Gross Capability Estimator [*Air Force*]
GROFIS	Ground Forces Intelligence Study (MCD)
GROJ	Get Rid of Junk [*Garage sale sign*]
GROM	Graphic Read-Only Memory [*Computer science*] (IAA)
GROM	Grommet (KSC)
Gron	Gronningen. Siglum for Tablets [*Leiden*] [*A publication*] (BJA)
GROOM	Grooming

GROOVE ...... Generated Real-Time Output Operations on Voltage-Controlled Equipment [*Computer science*]
GROPAC ...... Group Pacific
GROS .... Grossman's, Inc. [*NASDAQ symbol*] (NQ)
gros .... Grossus [*Coarse*] [*Latin*] (MAE)
Grosmn .... Grossman's, Inc. [*Associated Press*] (SAG)
Gross St ...... Gross' Illinois Compiled Statutes [*A publication*] (DLA)
gro t .... Gross Tons (ODBW)
GROT .... Grote [*or Grotius*] [*Literature*] (ROG)
GROT .... Grotesque (ADA)
GROT .... Grotto (ROG)
Grot De JB.. Grotius. De Jure Belli et Pacis [*A publication*] (DLA)
Grot De JrB.. Grotius. De Jure Belli et Pacis [*A publication*] (DLA)
Grotius........ Grotius. Latin Law [*A publication*] (DLA)
Grotius De Jure Belli... Grotius. De Jure Belli et Pacis [*A publication*] (DLA)
Grot Soc'y ... Transactions. Grotius Society [*England*] [*A publication*] (DLA)
Ground Oper... Ground Operations Review Panel (NAKS)
Groupe........ Groupe AB SA [*Associated Press*] (SAG)
Group1 .... Group 1 Software, Inc. [*Associated Press*] (SAG)
Group Legal Rev... Group Legal Review [*A publication*] (DLA)
GROV........... Grove [*Commonly used*] (OPSA)
GROV........... Grove Bank for Savings [*NASDAQ symbol*] (NQ)
GROV........... Grove Bank (MA) [*NASDAQ symbol*] (TTSB)
GROVE........ Grove [*Commonly used*] (OPSA)
GroveB........ Grove Bank for Savings [*Associated Press*] (SAG)
GroveR .... Grove Real Estate Asset Trust [*Associated Press*] (SAG)
GROVES...... Groves [*Commonly used*] (OPSA)
GROW.......... Greater Opportunities through Work [*Proposed federal program*]
GROW.......... Group Relations Ongoing Workshops
Grow............ Growth [*A publication*]
GROW.......... US Global Investors, Inc. [*NASDAQ symbol*] (SAG)
GrowBiz .... Grow Biz International, Inc. [*Associated Press*] (SAG)
GROWBY ..... Green, Red, Orange, White, Blue, Yellow [*Military system of indicating what day of the week food products were made through colored packaging*]
GROWN .... Get-Rid-of-Westmoreland-Now [*Secret society whose members were junior Pentagon officers*] (VNW)
GROWTH ..... Get Rid of Waste through Team Harmony
GRP .... Gamma Ray Projector
GRP .... Gastrin-Releasing Peptide [*Endocrinology*]
GRP .... Gaussian Random Process [*Mathematics*]
GRP .... Gelatin Rigidized Panel
GRP .... General Receptor for Phosphoinositide [*Biochemistry*]
GRP .... Geographical Reference Points (GAVI)
GRP .... Giant Reef Petroleums [*Vancouver Stock Exchange symbol*]
GRP .... Glass-Reinforced Plastic [*or Polyester*]
GRP .... Glucocorticoid Receptor Protein [*Biochemistry*]
GRP .... Glucose Regulated Protein [*Biochemistry*]
GRP .... Gram-Positive [*Also, GP*] [*Microbiology*]
GrP .... Gram-Positive (STED)
GRP .... Granite Point, AK [*Location identifier FAA*] (FAAL)
GRP .... Grant-Related Poundage [*British*]
GRP .... Greater Romania Party [*Political party*] (BUAC)
GRP .... Greatest Response Probability
GrP .... Greenwood Publishing Corp., Westport, CT [*Library symbol Library of Congress*] (LCLS)
GRP .... Gross Rating Point [*Television*]
GRP .... Gross Regional Product
GRP .... Ground Relay Panel [*Aerospace*] (AAG)
GRP .... Group (KSC)
Grp. .... Group (TBD)
grp .... Group (DD)
GRP .... Group Reference Pilot [*Telecommunications*] (TEL)
GRP .... Grundrichtungspunkt [*Base point, a gunnery term*] [*German military - World War II*]
GRP .... Guardia Republicana [*Peru*]
GRP .... Guyana Republican Party [*Political party*] (EA)
GRPA.......... Genesee River Protection Act of 1989 (COE)
GRPA.......... Guyana Responsible Parenthood Association (BUAC)
GRPA.......... Guyana Rice Producers Association (BUAC)
GrPAB......... Gravida, Para, and Abortus [*Gynecology and obstetrics*] (DAVI)
GrPAB......... Pregnancy, Birth, Abortion [*Medicine*] (STED)
GRPC.......... Gulf Regional Planning Commission
Grp.Capt...... Group Captain [*British military*] (DMA)
GRPH.......... Graphic (MSA)
GRPH.......... Graphic Industries [*NASDAQ symbol*] (TTSB)
GRPH.......... Graphic Industries, Inc. [*NASDAQ symbol*] (NQ)
grph .... Graphite (VRA)
GRPHC........ Graphic
GrphIn .... Graphic Industries, Inc. [*Associated Press*] (SAG)
GRPJ .... Glass-Reinforced Plastic Joint
GRPL .... Grand Rapids Public Library [*Michigan*]
GRPP.......... Glass-Reinforced Polypropylene (PDAA)
GRPS.......... Glucose-Ringer-Phosphate Solution
GrpTech....... Group Technologies Corp. [*Associated Press*] (SAG)
GRQ .... Goldrite Mining [*Vancouver Stock Exchange symbol*]
GRQ .... Groningen [*Netherlands*] [*Airport symbol*] (OAG)
GRQU......... Gran Quivira National Monument
GRR .... Asia Tigers Fund [*NYSE symbol*] (SPSG)
GRR .... Gastric Reservoir Reduction [*Morbid obesity surgical treatment*]
GRR .... Gear Reduction Ratio [*Military*] (CAAL)
GRR .... Geneva Radio Regulations
GRR .... Genotypic Relative Risk [*Genetics*]
GRR .... Georgetown Railroad Co. [*AAR code*]
GRR .... Golden Rim Resources, Inc. [*Vancouver Stock Exchange symbol*]

GRR .... Gorron [*France*] [*Seismograph station code, US Geological Survey*] (SEIS)
GRR .... Government Research and Development Reports
GRR .... Grand Rapids [*Michigan*] [*Airport symbol*] (OAG)
GRR .... Greek Research Reactor
GRR .... Guidance Reference Release (KSC)
GRR .... Kent County International Airport [*FAA*] (TAG)
GRRA.......... Gramophone Record Retailers Association [*British*] (BI)
GRRC.......... Giant Resource Recovery Co. (EFIS)
GRRC.......... Gurkha Rifles Regimental Centre [*British military*] (DMA)
GRREG........ Graves Registration [*Military*]
GRRI........... Greenstone Roberts Adv [*NASDAQ symbol*] (TTSB)
GRRI........... Greenstone Roberts Advertising, Inc. [*NASDAQ symbol*] (SAG)
GRRRS .... Goddard Range and Range Rate System [*NASA*] (IAA)
GRS .... Beta-Glucuronidase [*Organic chemistry*] (DAVI)
GRS .... Gamma Radiation Source
GRS .... Gamma Radiation Spectrometer
GRS .... Gamma Ray Spectrometer
GRS .... Gamma Ray Spectrum
GRS .... Gaseous RADWASTE System [*Nuclear energy*] (NRCH)
GRS .... Generalized Retrieval System [*Computer science*]
GRS .... General Radio Service [*Canada*]
GRS .... General Reconnaissance School [*British military*] (DMA)
GRS .... General Records Schedules [*Military*] (AABC)
GRS .... General Register Set/Stack [*Computer science*]
GRS .... General Reporting System
GRS .... General Revenue Sharing [*Office of Revenue Sharing*]
GRS .... Geriatric Rating Scale [*Medicine*] (DB)
GRS .... German Dermatological Society (EAIO)
GRS .... German Research Satellite [*NASA*]
GRS .... Ghost Research Society (EA)
GRS .... Golabi-Rosen Syndrome [*Medicine*] (DMAA)
GRS .... Golden Rule Society (EA)
GRS .... Goris [*Former USSR Seismograph station code, US Geological Survey*] (SEIS)
GR-S .... Government Rubber-Styrene [*Also, SBR*] [*Synthetic rubber*]
GRS .... Graduate Rabbinical School (BJA)
GRS .... Grand Recording Scribe [*Freemasonry*] (ROG)
GRS .... Grandson (ROG)
GRS .... Grass [*Maps and charts*]
GRS .... Gratiam Resources [*Vancouver Stock Exchange symbol*]
GRS .... Graves Registration Service [*Military*]
GRS .... Gravity Reference Signal [*or System*]
GRS .... Grease (MSA)
GRS .... Great Red Spot [*on planet Jupiter*]
GRS .... Grid Reference Ship [*Navy*] (NVT)
GRS .... Grigori Rasputin Society (EA)
GRS .... Grosseto [*Italy*] [*Airport symbol*] (AD)
GRS .... Groupe Revolutionnaire Socialiste [*Socialist Revolution Group*] [*Martinique*] [*Political party*] (PPW)
GRS .... Groupe Revolutionnaire Socialiste [*Socialist Revolution Group*] [*France*] [*Political party*]
GRS .... Gyro Reference System (AAG)
GRS .... Shorter College, Rome, GA [*Library symbol Library of Congress*] (LCLS)
GRSA........... Germersheim Reserve Storage Activity (MCD)
GRSA........... Great Sand Dunes National Monument
GRS & MIC... Gross and Microscopic [*Medicine*] (MEDA)
GRSC.......... Graduate of the Royal Society of Chemistry [*British*] (DBQ)
GRSE.......... Gamma Ray Spectrometric Equipment
GRSE.......... Guild of Radio Service Engineers (BARN)
GRSHFT...... Gearshaft (MSA)
GrSimec ...... Grupo Simec [*Commercial firm Associated Press*] (SAG)
GRSL.......... Guam Reference Standards Laboratory (DNAB)
GRSLND ..... Grassland (RDA)
GRSM.......... Graduate of the Royal Schools of Music [*British*]
GRSM.......... Great Smoky Mountains National Park [*Also, GSMNP*]
GR/S/O........ Grandson Of [*Genealogy*]
GRSP.......... General Range Safety Plan [*NASA*]
GRSP.......... Glass-Reinforced Structural Plastic
GRSS .... IEEE Geoscience and Remote Sensing Society (EA)
GRST .... Grist Mill [*NASDAQ symbol*] (TTSB)
GRST .... Grist Mill Co. [*NASDAQ symbol*] (NQ)
GR ST .... Groom of the Stole [*British*]
Grs T .... Gross Ton (EBF)
GRST .... Gross Tons
GrStCA........ Greenwich Street California Municipal Fund, Inc. [*Associated Press*] (SAG)
GRSU.......... Geography Remote Sensing Unit [*University of California, Santa Barbara*]
GRT .... Gabon-Air-Transport [*ICAO designator*] (FAAC)
GRT .... Gamma Ray Telescope
GRT .... Gamma Ray Tube
GRT .... General Reactor Technology (NRCH)
GRT .... Geriatric Rehabilitation Team [*Australia*]
GRT .... Glimcher Realty Trust [*NYSE symbol*] (SPSG)
GRT .... Government Rate Tender
GRT .... Graduate Respiratory Therapist
Grt .... Grant's Pennsylvania Cases [*A publication*] (DLA)
grt .... Graphic Technician [*MARC relator code*] [*Library of Congress*] (LCCP)
GRT .... Gratio [*Tennessee*] [*Seismograph station code, US Geological Survey*] (SEIS)
GRT .... Great (ROG)
GRT .... Gross Registered Tonnes (EERA)

GRT	Gross Registered Tons [*Navigation*]
GRT	Ground-Received Times [*Solar wind measurements*]
GRT	Ground Resistance Tester
GRT	Group Rapid Transit [*TRB*] (TAG)
GRT	GTC Transcontinental Group Ltd. [*Toronto Stock Exchange symbol*]
GRT	Gujrat [*Pakistan*] [*Airport symbol*] (AD)
Gr(T)	Gunner (Torpedo) [*British military*] (DMA)
GRT	Tri-County Regional Library, Rome, GA [*Library symbol Library of Congress*] (LCLS)
GRTA	Government Reports and Topical Announcements [*Later, WGA*] [*National Technical Information Service*]
GRTA	Group Relations Training Association (AIE)
GrtBay	Great Bay Power Corp. [*Associated Press*] (SAG)
GrtBayPw	Great Bay Power Corp. [*Associated Press*] (SAG)
GRTC	Green River Test Complex
GRTC	Groupe de Recherches pour les Transports au Canada [*Canadian Transportation Research Forum*]
GrtCtrl	Great Central Mines [*Associated Press*] (SAG)
GRTE	Grand Teton National Park
GrteBayC	Greate Bay Casino [*Associated Press*] (SAG)
GrtFncl	Great Financial Corp. [*Associated Press*] (SAG)
GRTG	Granting
GRTG	Grating (MSA)
GRTG	Greeting
GRTH	Growth
GRTK	Group Technologies [*NASDAQ symbol*] (TTSB)
GRTK	Group Technologies Corp. [*NASDAQ symbol*] (SAG)
GRTLKS	Great Lakes (FAAC)
GRTLS	Glide Return to Landing Site (NASA)
GRTLS	Glide Return to Launch Site (MCD)
GRTM	Geared Roller Test Machine
GRTM	Gross Ton-Mile (ADA)
GRTN	Grid Return (MSA)
GrToy	Grand Toys International [*Associated Press*] (SAG)
GRTP	Glass-Fiber Reinforced Thermoplastics (PDAA)
GRTP	Glass Reinforced Thermoplastic
GrtPines	Great Pines Water Co. [*Associated Press*] (SAG)
GRTR	Grater (MSA)
GRTR	Greater [*Freight*]
GRTR	[*The*] Greater New York Savings Bank [*NASDAQ symbol*] (NQ)
GRTR	Greater N.Y. Svgs Bk [*NASDAQ symbol*] (TTSB)
GRTS	General Electric Remote Terminal Supervisor [*Honeywell*] (NITA)
GRTS	General Remote Terminal Supervisor
GRTS	Geomagnetic Reversal Time Scale
GRTS	Goddard Real Time System [*NASA*] (IAA)
GRTS	Ground Tracking System (MCD)
GRTSFC	Ginger Rogers: The Star Fan Club (EA)
GrtSoB	Great Southern Bancorp, Inc. [*Associated Press*] (SAG)
GrtSoBcp	Great Southern Bancorp, Inc. [*Associated Press*] (SAG)
GRTU	General Retailers and Traders Union [*Malta*] (BUAC)
Grtv ADR	Grootvlei Proprietary Mines Ltd. [*Associated Press*] (SAG)
GrtWall	Great Wall Electronic Internationl Ltd. [*Associated Press*] (SAG)
GRU	Genetic Resources Unit (GNE)
GRU	Glavnoe Razvedivatelnoe Upravlenie [*Chief Administration for Intelligence*] [*Division of the General Staff of the Soviet Army*] [*Former USSR*]
GRU	Gold Ridge Resources [*Vancouver Stock Exchange symbol*]
GRU	Grajau [*Brazil*] [*Airport symbol*] (AD)
GRU	Grid Reference Unit [*Military*] (CAAL)
GRU	Group
Gru	Grus [*Constellation*]
GRU	Guidance Regulator Unit
GRU	Gyroscope Reference Unit (MCD)
GRUB	Grocery Update and Billing
GrubbEL	Grubb & Ellis Co. [*Associated Press*] (SAG)
GRUCOM	Group Commander
Grudman	Gramm-Rudman-Hollings Bill [*Proposed deficit-reducing bill, 1985-1986*]
GrUff	Grand Ufficiale [*Grand Officer*] (EY)
GRUMB	Grumbalds [*England*]
Grumpie	Grim Ruthless Upwardly Mobile Professional [*Lifestyle classification*]
Grumpie	Grown-Up Mature Person [*Lifestyle classification*]
GRUNCH	Gross Universal Cash Heist [*Techno-economic term coined by Buckminster Fuller*]
GRUR	Gewerblicher Rechtsschutz und Urheberrecht [*A publication*] (ILCA)
GRUR Int	Gewerblicher Rechtsschutz und Urheberrecht, Internationaler Teil [*A publication*] (ILCA)
GRUSL	Group Sail [*Navy*] (NVT)
GRUSZAG	Georgian Telegraphic Agency, Tbilisi (BUAC)
GRV	Grantsville, MD [*Location identifier FAA*] (FAAL)
GRV	Granville Island Brewing Co. Ltd. [*Vancouver Stock Exchange symbol*]
GRV	Graphic Recording Voltmeter (IAA)
GRV	Graphite Rod Vaporization
grv	Gravure (VRA)
GRV	Greenville [*Lake Wappapelo*] [*Missouri*] [*Seismograph station code, US Geological Survey*] [*Closed*] (SEIS)
GRV	Groove (KSC)
GRV	Grosvenor Aviation Services [*British ICAO designator*] (FAAC)
GRV	Ground Reaction Vector (DMAA)
GRV	Grove
GRVA	Graphic Varmeter
GRVD	Grooved
GRVG	Grooving
GR VJ POND	Grana Sex Pondere [*Six Grains by Weight*] [*Pharmacy*] (ROG)
GRVL	Gravel
GRVR	Groover
GRVS	Groves [*Postal Service standard*] (OPSA)
GRW	Galactic Radio Wave
GRW	General Railway Warrants [*US Military Government, Germany*]
GRW	Giant Ragweed Test [*Medicine*] (DMAA)
GRW	Goodyear-Reston-Winthrop [*Publishing group*]
GRW	Graciosa Island [*Azores*] [*Airport symbol*] (OAG)
GRW	Graphic Recording Wattmeter (IAA)
GRW	Greenwich [*United Kingdom*] [*Later, HAD*] [*Geomagnetic observatory code*]
GRW	Greenwich Resources Ltd. [*Toronto Stock Exchange symbol Vancouver Stock Exchange symbol*]
GRW	Greenwood, MS [*Location identifier FAA*] (FAAL)
GRWS	Gimbaled Reaction Wheel Scanner
GRWT	Gross Weight
gr wt	Gross Weight (WDAA)
GRX	Granada [*Spain*] [*Airport symbol*] (OAG)
GRXR	Ground Round Rest [*NASDAQ symbol*] (TTSB)
GRXR	Ground Round Restaurants, Inc. [*NASDAQ symbol*] (SAG)
GRY	Gary [*Diocesan abbreviation*] [*Indiana*] (TOCD)
GRY	Gray (ADA)
GRY	Greyhound Racing
GRY	Greymouth [*New Zealand*] [*Seismograph station code, US Geological Survey Closed*] (SEIS)
GRY	Grey Power [*Political party Australia*]
GRY	Greystoke Exploration [*Vancouver Stock Exchange symbol*]
GRY	Grimsey [*Iceland*] [*Airport symbol*] (OAG)
gry	Gross Redemption Yield (BARN)
GryCm	Gray Communications Systems [*Associated Press*] (SAG)
GRYP	Gryphon Holdings [*NASDAQ symbol*] (SAG)
Gryphon	Gryphon Holdings [*Associated Press*] (SAG)
grysh	Grayish [*Philately*]
GRZ	Galapagos Rift Zone [*Marine science*] (MSC)
GRZ	Granophyric Roof Zone [*Geology*]
GRZ	Graz [*Austria*] [*Airport symbol*] (OAG)
GS	BAS Airlines [*ICAO designator*] (AD)
G-S	Gallard-Schlesinger [*Chemical manufacturing corporation*]
G/S	Gallons per Second
GS	Gallstone [*Medicine*] (DB)
GS	Galpin Society (EA)
GS	Galvanized Steel [*Telecommunications*]
GS	Games Started [*Baseball*]
GS	Gap Separation
GS	Gardner Syndrome [*Medicine*]
GS	Gasoline Supply
GS	Gas Servicer (MCD)
GS	Gas Sulfide [*Process for obtaining heavy water*]
GS	Gastric Shield [*Medicine*]
GS	Gaudium et Spes [*Pastoral Constitution on the Church in the Modern World*] [*Vatican II document*]
GS	Gauss [*Unit of magnetic flux density*] [*Preferred unit is T, Telsa*]
Gs	Gauss
GS	General Schedule [*Federal employee job classification GS-1 to GS-18*]
GS	General Search (IAA)
GS	General Secretariat
GS	General Secretary
GS	General Semantics
GS	General Service [*Literal translation, but used in sense of "excessively keen," or "overly acute"*] [*Army British*]
GS	General Sessions
GS	General Signal Corp. (EFIS)
GS	General Solution (OA)
GS	General Specials
GS	General Speed [*Military*]
GS	General Staff [*Military*]
GS	General Statistics
GS	General Storage (IAA)
GS	General Strike
GS	General Subjects (MCD)
GS	General Superintendent
GS	General Support [*Military*]
GS	General Surgery
GS	Genetical Society (BUAC)
GS	Geochemical Society (EA)
GS	Geological Society [*British*] (EAIO)
GS	Geological Survey [*Department of the Interior*]
GS	German Silver
GS	Gerontological Society [*Later, GSA*] (EA)
GS	Gesetzsammlung [*Collection of Statutes, Gazette*] [*German*] (ILCA)
GS	Giant Slalom
GS	Gilbert's Syndrome [*Medicine*]
GS	Girl Scouts of the USA (EA)
GS	Girls' School (ADA)
GS	Glamour Stock [*Investment term*]
GS	Gland Seal [*System*] [*Nuclear energy*] (NRCH)
GS	Glanzmann-Saland [*Syndrome*] [*Medicine*] (DB)
GS	Glazounov Society (EA)
GS	Glide Slope [*Aviation*]
GS	Glide Slope [*Aerospace*] (NAKS)
GS	Gliding School [*British military*] (DMA)
GS	Glomerular Sclerosis [*Medicine*]
GS	Glucose and Saline [*Medicine*]
GS	Glutamine Synthetase [*Also, GNS*] [*An enzyme*]

GS	Glycolytic Substrate
GS	Goal Shooter [Netball]
GS	Goat Serum (DB)
GS	Goldenhar Syndrome [Medicine] (DMAA)
GS	Golden Shamrock Resources Corp. [Vancouver Stock Exchange symbol]
GS	Gold Smoke [Dispersion of ultrafine metal particles]
GS	Gold Standards
GS	Goudy Society (EA)
GS	Gougerot-Sjoegren (DB)
GS	Government Security [Business term]
GS	Government Service
GS	Government Staffs [British]
GS	Grab Sample [Analytical technique]
GS	Grade System (AAG)
GS	Grain Size Metal (IAA)
GS	Grammar School
GS	Grand Scribe [Freemasonry]
GS	Grand Secretary [Freemasonry]
GS	Grand Sentinel [Freemasonry]
GS	Grand Sentry [Freemasonry]
GS	Grandson
GS	Grand Speed (BARN)
GS	Grand Steward [Freemasonry]
GS	Gran Sport [Automobile model designation]
GS	Graphics and Sound [in Apple IIGS] [Apple Computer, Inc.]
G/S	Gravity per Second (KSC)
GS	Great Seal [British]
GS	Greenhouse Shrub [Horticulture] (ROG)
GS	Grip Strength
GS	Grocery Store
GS	Groenblad-Strandberg [Syndrome] [Medicine] (DB)
GS	Gross Sales [Business term]
GS	Gross Spread [Business term]
GS	Ground Sensor
GS	Ground Speed [Aviation]
GS	Ground Stabilized (MUGU)
GS	Ground Station [Aerospace] (AAG)
GS	Ground Surface (IAA)
GS	Ground System (MCD)
G/S	Ground to Slant (MCD)
GS	Group Selector [Telecommunications] (TEL)
GS	Group Separator [Computer science]
gs	Group Specific [Antigen] [Immunology]
GS	Group Structured [Counseling group]
GS	Growth Stage
GS	Growth Stock [Investment term]
GS	Grupo Socialista [Socialist Group] [Portugal Political party] (PPE)
GS	Guardship
GS	Guard Society (EA)
GS	Guard Squadron
GS	Guerin-Stern [Syndrome] [Medicine] (DB)
GS	Guidance Simulator
GS	Guidance Station [Aerospace] (AAG)
GS	Guidance System [Aerospace] (AAG)
G/S	Guided Steering [Aerospace] (NAKS)
GS	Guide Slope (MUGU)
GS	Guild of Surveyors [Middlesex, England] (EAIO)
GS	Gulf Shelf [Marine science] (OSRA)
GS	Gum Skips [Philately]
GS	Gungywamp Society (EA)
GS	Gunnery and Searchlight [Control] [British World War II]
GS	Gunnery School [Air Force]
GS	Gunnery Sergeant
GS	Gunnery Support
GS	Gyroscope (IAA)
GS	Gyrostabilizer
GS	Pfizer Ltd. [Great Britain] [Research code symbol]
GS	Savannah Public and Chatham-Effingham-Liberty Regional Library, Savannah, GA [Library symbol Library of Congress] (LCLS)
GS	S. Georgia and S. Sandwich Island [Internet country code]
GS	Snow Pellets [ICAO] (FAAC)
GSA	Armstrong State College, Savannah, GA [Library symbol Library of Congress] (LCLS)
GSA	Gardenia Society of America (EA)
GSA	Garden Seed Association
GSA	Garden State Airlines, Inc. [ICAO designator] (FAAC)
GSA	Gastroenterological Society of Australia
GSA	Geinsheim Staging Activity
GSA	General Services Administration [Washington, DC]
GSA	General Services Administration, Washington, DC [OCLC symbol] (OCLC)
GSA	General Somatic Afferent [Nerve] [Anatomy]
GSA	General Studies Association [British]
GSA	General Support Announcement [Public television]
GSA	General Syntax Analyzer [Sperry UNIVAC]
GSA	Genetics Society of America (EA)
GSA	Geographic Systems Analysis [Information service or system] (IID)
GSA	Geological Society of Africa (BUAC)
GSA	Geological Society of America (EA)
GSA	Geological Society of Australia (EERA)
GSA	Geothermal Steam Act of 1970 (COE)
GSA	Germanistic Society of America (EA)
GSA	Gerontological Society of America (EA)
GSA	Girl Scouts of America
GSA	Girls' Schools Association [British]
GSA	Glasgow School of Art [Scotland]
GSA	Glass-Steagal Act [1933]
GSA	Glide Slope Antenna [Aviation]
GSA	Glutamatesemialdehyde [Organic chemistry]
GSA	Goldfish Society of America (EA)
GSA	Gourd Society of America [Superseded by AGS] (EA)
GSA	Government in the Sunshine Act (COE)
GSA	Governor of South Australia
GSA	Great Salinity Anomaly [Marine science] (OSRA)
GSA	Greenhouse Suppliers Association (EA)
GSA	[The] Green Party South Australia [Political party]
GSA	Gross Sarcoma Virus Antigen [Immunology] (MAE)
GSA	Gross Soluble Antigen
GSA	Ground-Based Surface-to-Air (MCD)
GSA	Ground Safety Approval (MUGU)
GSA	Groundstar Resources Ltd. [Vancouver Stock Exchange symbol]
GSA	Group-Specific Antigen [Immunology]
GSA	GS Financial Products [NYSE symbol] (SAG)
GSA	Guanidinosuccinic Acid (MAE)
GSA	Guidance System Analyst [Aerospace] (IAA)
GSA	Guild of Saint Alban
GSA	Gulf & South American Steamship Co. (MHDB)
GSA	Gusau [Nigeria] [Airport symbol] (AD)
GSA/ADTS	General Services Administration/Automated Data and Telecommunications Services (OICC)
GSA-AT	Glutamate Semialdehyde Aminotransferase [An enzyme]
GSAB	General Surveys and Analysis Branch [Department of Education] (GFGA)
GSA-BCA	General Services Administration - Board of Contract Appeals
GSAC	Genome Sequencing and Analysis Conference
GSAC	Golden State Athletic Conference (PSS)
GSA-CPO	General Services Administration - Civilian Personnel Office
GSA DPA	GSA Delegation of Procurement Authority (AAGC)
GSA/FPRS	General Services Administration/Federal Property Resources Services (OICC)
GSA/FSS	General Services Administration/Federal Supply Services (OICC)
GSAGR	General Short Arc Geodetic Reduction (PDAA)
GSAI	El Aaiun [Western Sahara] [ICAO location identifier] (ICLI)
GSAL	Grupo de Solidariedade com America Latina [Portugal]
GSAM	Generalized Sequential Access Method [Computer science]
GSAM	Generalized Standard Addition Method [Mathematics]
GSAM	Guangdong Society of Agri-Machinery [China] (BUAC)
GSA/NARS	General Services Administration/National Archives and Records Services [Franklin D. Roosevelt Library] [Hyde Park, NY] (OICC)
GS & F	Georgia Southern & Florida Railway Co.
GSA/OFR	General Services Administration/Office of the Federal Register (OICC)
GSA-OP	General Services Administration - Office of Preparedness
GSAP	General Supported Accommodation Program [New South Wales, Australia]
GSAP	Gun Sight Aiming Point
GSA-PBS	General Services Administration - Public Building Service
GSAR	General Services Acquisition Regulation
GSAR	General Services Administration Acquisition Regulations [A publication] (AAGC)
GSARRTS	Generator, Starter, Alternator, Regulator, and Rectifier Test Stand (MCD)
GSAT	General Satellite (NASA)
GSAT	Gesammelte Studien zum Alten Testament [A publication] (BJA)
GSAT	Global Satellite Data Acquisition Team [Marine science] (OSRA)
GS/ATE	General Support/Automatic Test Equipment (MCD)
GS/ATSS	General Support/Automatic Test Support System (MCD)
GSB	Gastric Stress Bleeding [Medicine]
GSB	General School Budget (AIE)
GSB	General Schools Budget [British] (DET)
GSB	General Services Building [Nuclear energy] (NRCH)
GSB	General Stud Book [Horses]
GSB	Ghana Standards Board (BUAC)
GSB	Goldsboro, NC [Location identifier FAA] (FAAL)
GSB	Gold Surface Barrier
GSB	Government Savings Bank [Australia]
GSB	Graduate School of Business [University of Chicago] (ECON)
GSB	Grand Standard Bearer [Freemasonry] (ROG)
GSB	Grand Sword-Bearer [Freemasonry]
GSB	Gypsum Sheathing Board [Technical drawings]
GSBC	Great Southern Bancorp [NASDAQ symbol] (TTSB)
GSBC	Great Southern Bancorp, Inc. [NASDAQ symbol] (NQ)
GSBCA	General Services Board of Contract Appeals
GSBG	Gonadal Steroid-Binding Globulin [Medicine]
GSBI	Gabungan Serikat Buruh Indonesia [Federation of Indonesian Trade Unions]
GSBI	Granite State Bancshares [NASDAQ symbol] (TTSB)
GSBI	Granite State Bankshares, Inc. [NASDAQ symbol] (NQ)
GSBP	Glycosylation Site Binding Protein [Biochemistry]
GSBPS	Global Space-Based Positioning and Navigation System
GSBR	Gravel-Surface Built-Up Roof [Technical drawings]
GSC	Galapagos Spreading Center [Oceanography]
GSC	Gascoyne Junction [Australia Airport symbol Obsolete] (OAG)
GSC	Gas-Solid Chromatography
GSC	Gelman Sciences [AMEX symbol] (TTSB)
GSC	Gelman Sciences, Inc. [AMEX symbol] (SPSG)
GSC	General Service Corps [Military unit] [British]
GSC	General Staff Corps [Military]
GSC	General Staff Council [Military] (AABC)

GSC	General Support Company [*Army*] (VNW)
GSC	Genetically Significant Concentration [*Mutagenesis*]
GSC	Genetics Society of China (BUAC)
GSC	Geodetic Spacecraft (AAG)
GSC	Geographical Society of China (BUAC)
GSC	Geological Society of China (BUAC)
GSC	Geological Survey of Canada [*Marine science*] (MSC)
GSC	Gerontological Society of China (BUAC)
GSC	Giant Serotonin-Containing [*Neuron*]
GSC	Girls' School Company Ltd. [*British*] (BI)
GSC	Gland Seal Condenser [*Nuclear energy*] (NRCH)
GSC	Gland Steam Condenser [*Nuclear energy*] (NRCH)
GSC	Glasgow [*Coma*] Scale [*Neurology*] (DAVI)
GSC	Glenville State College [*West Virginia*]
GSC	Golden Star Resources Ltd. [*Toronto Stock Exchange symbol*]
GSC	Goldstone [*California*] [*Seismograph station code, US Geological Survey*] (SEIS)
GSC	Good Samaritan Coalition [*Defunct*] (EA)
GSC	Gravity Settling Culture
GSC	Great Southwest Corp.
GSC	Grid Spot Converter (NVT)
GSC	Ground Services Cart
GSC	Ground-Speed Continuing [*Aviation*]
GSC	Ground Station Control (SSD)
GSC	Group Study Course
GSC	Group Switching Center [*British Telecommunications*] (TEL)
GSC	GSA [*General Services Administration*] Stock Catalog
GSC	Guardianship for Senior Citizens
GSC	Guiana Space Center (MCD)
GSC	Guidance Shipping Container
GSC	Guidance System Console [*Aerospace*] (AAG)
GSC	Gulf South Conference (PSS)
GSCA	Giant Schnauzer Club of America (EA)
GSCA	Gordon Setter Club of America (EA)
G/SCA	Gunite/Shotcrete Contractors Association (NTPA)
GSCARNGARP	General Staff Committees on Army National Guard and Army Reserve Policy (AABC)
GSCAX	Alliance Global: Small Cap.Cl.A [*Mutual fund ticker symbol*] (SG)
GSCC	General Steel Casting Corp.
GSCC	Global Simulation Control Center
GSCC	Greater Siamese Cat Club (EA)
GSCCMF	Gujarat State Co-Operative Cotton Marketing Federation [*India*] (BUAC)
GSCE	Gas Source Control Equipment [*Electronics*] (AAEL)
GSCF	Geriatric Sentence Completion Form [*Personality development test*] [*Psychology*]
GSCG	Ground Systems Coordination Group
GSCGX	Goldman Sachs Capital Growth Cl.A [*Mutual fund ticker symbol*] (SG)
GSCI	GeoScience Corp. [*NASDAQ symbol*] (TTSB)
GSCI	Goldman Sachs Commodity Index [*Finance*]
GSCI	Ground Sound Control, Inc.
GSCM	Gas Turbine Systems Technician, Master Chief [*Navy rating*] (DNAB)
GSCN	General Scannning, Inc. [*NASDAQ symbol*] (SAG)
GSCN	Genl Scanning [*NASDAQ symbol*] (TTSB)
GSCN	Giant Serotonin-Containing Neuron (BABM)
GSCNY	German Society of the City of New York (EA)
GSCO	Guidance Sustainer Cutoff [*Aerospace*] (AAG)
GSCS	Gas Turbine Systems Technician, Senior Chief [*Navy rating*] (DNAB)
GSCSCERS	Geographical Society of China Sub-Commission on Environmental Remote Sensing (BUAC)
GSCT	Goldstein-Scheerer Cube Test [*Psychology*]
GSCT	Guild of Sorting Clerks and Telegraphists [*A union*] [*British*]
GSCU	Ground Service [*or Support*] Cooling Unit (KSC)
GSCW	General Society of Colonial Wars (EA)
GSCW	Georgia State College for Women [*Later, Women's College of Georgia*] (AEBS)
GSCWPPC	Guam Stamp Club and Western Pacific Philatelic Collectors (EA)
GSD	Gate Stealer Display (MCD)
GSD	General Sewing Data
GSD	General Supply Depot
GSD	General Support Division [*Air Force*]
GSD	General System Description [*Military*] (AABC)
GSD	General System Development [*or Design*] (IAA)
GSD	General Systems Division [*IBM Corp.*]
GSD	Generating Significant Dose [*Nuclear energy*] (NRCH)
GSD	Generator Starter Drive
GSD	Generic Structure Diagram [*Telecommunications*] (TEL)
GSD	Genetically Significant Dosage [*X-Ray*]
GSD	Genetic Sex Determination [*Biology*]
GSD	Genotypic Sex Determination [*Embryology*]
GSD	Geographical Data of Sweden [*Sweden*] (EERA)
GSD	Geometric Standard Deviation [*Statistics*]
GSD	German Shepherd Dog (DI)
GSD	Gesco Industries, Inc. [*Toronto Stock Exchange symbol*]
GSD	Glycogen Storage Disease [*Medicine*]
GSD	Government Support Date (MCD)
GSD	Grand Senior Deacon [*Freemasonry*]
GSD	Grid Sphere Drag [*DoD satellite*]
GSD	Ground Station Data
GSD	Guild of Softward Distributors (BUAC)
GSDA	Great Southern Development Authority [*Western Australia*]
GSDA	Grounded Surface Distribution Apparatus (IAA)
GSDA	Ground-Speed Drift Angle [*Aviation*] (NG)
GSDB	Genome Sequence Data Base (HGEN)
GSDB	Genome Sequence Database (COE)
GSDB	Geophysics and Space Data Bulletin [*A publication Air Force*]
GSDC	Get Set Day Care Program [*Later, CDCP*] (EA)
GSDCA	German Shepherd Dog Club of America (EA)
GSDF	Global Sustainable Development Facility
GSDF	Ground Self-Defense Force [*Japan*]
GSDFJ	Ground Self-Defense Force Japan
GSDL	Ground Software Development Laboratory [*NASA*] (NASA)
GSDN	Garden Supply Dealers National (EA)
GSDO	General [*Aviation*] Safety District Office
GSDS	General Status Display System [*Graphics system*] (NITA)
GS/DS	General Support/Direct Support
GSDS	Goldstone Duplicate Standard [*Deep Space Instrumentation Facility*] [*NASA*]
GSDT	Generalized Syntax-Directed Translation (PDAA)
GSE	General Somatic Efferent [*Nerve*] [*Anatomy*]
GSE	General Support Equipment [*Military*] (MUGU)
GSE	Geocentric Solar Ecliptic [*System*] [*NASA*]
GSE	Geometric Standard Error (PDAA)
GSE	Glutagen Sensitive Enteropathy [*Medicine*]
GSE	Gluten-Sensitive Enteropathy [*Medicine*]
GSE	Government-Specified Equipment [*Military*] (DNAB)
GSE	Government Sponsored Enterprise [*FNMA*] (EMRF)
GSE	Graphics Screen Editor (NITA)
GSE	Grip Strong and Equal [*Neurology*] (DAVI)
GSE	Gross Subsidy Equivalent [*Tariffs*] [*Australia*]
GSE	Ground Service Equipment [*Air Force*]
GSE	Ground Servicing Equipment [*Aerospace*] (NAKS)
GSE	Ground Support Equipment [*Aerospace*] (NAKS)
GSE	Ground Support Equipment [*Aviation*]
GSE	Group of Scientific Experts
GSE	Group Support Equipment
GSE	Guias y Scouts de Europa [*Spain*] (EAIO)
GSE1	Gas Turbine Systems Technician, Electrical, First Class [*Navy rating*] (DNAB)
GSE2	Gas Turbine Systems Technician, Electrical, Second Class [*Navy rating*] (DNAB)
GSE3	Gas Turbine Systems Technician, Electrical, Third Class [*Navy rating*] (DNAB)
GSE-BI	Ground Support Equipment-Base Installation [*Aviation*] (SAA)
GSEC	Gas Turbine Systems Technician, Electrical, Chief [*Navy rating*] (DNAB)
G SEC	Grand Secretary [*Freemasonry*] (ROG)
GSECP	Ground Support Engineering Change Proposal [*Aerospace*] (AAG)
GSED	Ground Support Equipment Division [*Naval Air Engineering Center*]
GSEE	Geniki Synomospondia Ergaton Hellados [*General Confederation of Greek Labor*]
GSEEI	Ground Support Equipment End Item [*Military*]
GSEF	Ground Subsystem Evaluation Facility [*Army*] (RDA)
GSEFA	Gas Turbine Systems Technician, Electrical, Fireman Apprentice [*Navy rating*] (DNAB)
GSEFN	Gas Turbine Systems Technician, Electrical, Fireman [*Navy rating*] (DNAB)
GSEI	Ground Support Equipment Illustration [*Military*] (MCD)
GSEID	Ground Support Equipment Illustration Data [*Military*] (MCD)
GSEL	Government Specified Equipment List [*Military*] (CAAL)
GSEL	Ground Support Equipment List [*NASA*] (NASA)
GSEL	Guidance System Evaluation Laboratory [*Military*] (CAAL)
GSE-M	Ground Support Equipment-Mechanical [*Aviation*] (SAA)
GSE-ME	Ground Support Equipment-Maintenance Equipment [*Aviation*] (SAA)
GSE-MF	Ground Support Equipment-Maintenance Facility [*Aviation*] (SAA)
GSERD	Ground Support Equipment Recommendation Data [*Military*] (MCD)
GSES	Government-Sponsored Enterprises [*Federal National Mortgage Association, Student Loan Marketing Association, etc.*]
GSE-S	Ground Support Equipment-Structure [*Aviation*] (SAA)
GSES	GSE Systems [*NASDAQ symbol*] (TTSB)
GSES	GSE Systems, Inc. [*NASDAQ symbol*] (SAG)
GSESD	Ground Support Equipment Statistical Display (DNAB)
GSE-SE	Group Support Equipment-Support Equipment [*Aviation*] (SAA)
GSE-SS	Ground Support Equipment-Strategic System [*Aviation*] (SAA)
GSE-SS	Ground Support Equipment-System and Service [*Aviation*] (SAA)
GSE-SS	Ground Support Equipment-Systems Specification (IAA)
GSE Sy	GSE Systems, Inc. [*Associated Press*] (SAG)
GSE-T & H	Ground Support Equipment-Transportation and Handling [*Aviation*] (SAA)
GSETD	General Systems Engineering and Technical Direction
GSE-TS	Ground Support Equipment-Test Stand [*Aviation*] (SAA)
GSE-WSR	Ground Support Equipment-Weapon System Requirement [*Aviation*] (SAA)
GSF	ACM Government Securities [*NYSE symbol*] (SPSG)
GSF	ACM Gvt Securities [*NYSE symbol*] (TTSB)
GSF	Galactosemic Fibroblasts [*Medicine*]
GSF	General Semantics Foundation (EA)
GSF	General Supply Fund
GSF	General Support Force [*Air Force*]
GSF	Genital Skin Fibroblast [*Medicine*] (DMAA)
GSF	Georgia Southern & Florida Railway Co. [*AAR code*]
GSF	Global Strategy Fund [*British*]
GSF	Grenade Safety Fuze
GSF	Gross Square Feet
GSF	Ground Support Facilities [*Later, MGE*] [*Aerospace*] (AAG)
GSF	Ground Support Fighter (MCD)
GSF	Group of Soviet Forces
GSF	Group of Soviet Forces in Germany (MCD)
GSF	Gulf Sea Frontier

GSFA .... Genealogical Society of Flemish Americans (EA)
GSFC .... George Strait Fan Club (EA)
GSFC .... Goddard Space Flight Center [*Greenbelt, MD*] [*NASA*]
GSFC .... Green Street Financial [*NASDAQ symbol*] (TTSB)
GSFC .... Green Street Financial Corp. [*NASDAQ symbol*] (SAG)
GSFC .... Gujarat State Fertilizers Co. [*India*] (BUAC)
GSFC .... Gujarat State Financial Co. [*India*] (BUAC)
GSFG .... Group of Soviet Forces in Germany (NATG)
GS Fin .... GS Financial Products [*Associated Press*] (SAG)
GSFLT .... Graduate School Foreign Language Test
GSFR .... Granulocyte Colony-Stimulating Factor Receptor (DMAA)
GSFS .... General Specifications for Ships (DNAB)
GSFSR .... Ground Safety and Flight Safety Requirements (AAG)
GSFU .... Glazed Structural Facing Units [*Technical drawings*]
GSG .... Garment Salesmen's Guild of New York [*Later, AG*] (EA)
GSG .... Garn-St. Germain Depository Institutions Act (EBF)
GSG .... General Support Group [*Army*] (AABC)
GSG .... Glasgow, MT [*Location identifier FAA*] (FAAL)
GSG .... Glass-Silicone-Glass [*Electronics*] (DEN)
GSG .... Global Small Cap Fund [*AMEX symbol*] (TTSB)
GSG .... Global Small Capital Fund [*AMEX symbol*] (SPSG)
GSG .... Grammar School for Girls (ADA)
GSG .... Grenzschutzgruppe [*Border Protection Group*] [*German*]
GSG .... Ground Studies Group [*Military*] (VNW)
GSG .... Ground Systems Group [*Hughes Aircraft Co.*]
GSG .... Guild of St. Gabriel (BUAC)
GSGA .... Geode Specialty Growers Association (EA)
GSGB .... Golf Society [*British*] (DBA)
GSGB .... Golf Society of Great Britain (BUAC)
GSGG .... Gadolinium, Scandium, Gallium, Garnet (MCD)
GSGRX .... Goldman Sachs Growth & Income Cl.A [*Mutual fund ticker symbol*] (SG)
GSGS .... Geographical Section General Staff [*British*]
GSGT .... Gunnery Sergeant (DNAB)
GSH .... Gambia Air Shuttle Ltd. [*ICAO designator*] (FAAC)
GSH .... Gas Space Heater
GSH .... Gas Surge Header [*Nuclear energy*] (NRCH)
GSH .... Global Schoolhouse [*Computer science Telecommunications*]
GSH .... Glomerular-Stimulating Hormone [*Endocrinology*] (MAE)
GSH .... Glutathione [*Biochemistry*]
GSH .... Glutathione-SH [*Reduced glutathione*] [*Biochemistry*]
GSH .... Golden Syrian Hamster (DB)
GSH .... Goshen, IN [*Location identifier FAA*] (FAAL)
GSH .... Growth-Stimulating Hormone [*Endocrinology*] (DAVI)
GSH .... Guangshen Railway ADS [*NYSE symbol*] (TTSB)
GSH .... Reduced Gluthathione [*Biochemistry*] (DAVI)
GS-HG .... Geological Society-Hydrogeology Group (BUAC)
GSHP .... Reduced Glutathione Peroxidase (STED)
GSHR .... Gandhi Society for Human Rights (EA)
GSHR .... Grand Slam Home Runs [*Baseball*]
GSHV .... Ground Squirrel Hepatitis Virus
GSI .... General Safety Inspector [*Aviation*]
GSI .... General Service Infantry [*Army*]
GSI .... Generic Safety Issue (NRCH)
GSI .... Genetic Stock Identification [*Pisciculture*]
GSI .... Genuine Stress Incontinence [*Urology*] (DAVI)
GSI .... Geographical Society of Ireland (BUAC)
GSI .... Geographical Survey Institute (EERA)
GSI .... Geographic Systems, Inc. [*Information service or system*] (IID)
GSI .... Geological Society of Israel (BUAC)
GSI .... Geophysical Service, Inc.
GSI .... Gesneriad Society International (EA)
GSI .... Giant Scale Integration (IAA)
GSI .... Gigascale Integration [*Electronics*]
GSI .... Glide Slope Indicator [*Aviation*]
GSI .... Glide Slope Indicator [*Aerospace*] (NAKS)
GSI .... Glide Speed Indicator
GSI .... Global Severity Index [*Medicine*] (DMAA)
GSI .... Gonosomatic Indices
GSI .... Gordon Diagnostic System [*Attention deficit disorder test*]
GSI .... Government Source Inspection
GSI .... Grand Scale Integration (BUR)
GSI .... Graphic Structure Input
GSI .... Greenwich Street Municipal Fund, Inc. [*NYSE symbol*] (SAG)
GSI .... Greenwich Street Muni Fund [*NYSE symbol*] (TTSB)
GSI .... Ground-Speed Indicator [*Aviation*] (MCD)
GSI .... Guild of Saint Ives (EA)
GSIA .... Graduate School of Industrial Administration [*Carnegie Mellon University*]
GSIC .... Gujarat Small Industries Corp. [*India*] (BUAC)
GSICO .... Glaucoma Society of the International Congress of Ophthalmology (EA)
GSID .... Ground-Emplaced Seismic Intrusion Detector (NVT)
G/SIDBAD ..... General Staff Identification Badge [*Military decoration*] (GFGA)
GSIDC .... Arab Gulf States Information Documentation Center [*Information service or system*] (IID)
GSidekB ...... Grupo Sidek SA de CV [*Associated Press*] (SAG)
GSIdentBad... General Staff Identification Badge [*Military decoration*] (AABC)
GSIFC .... Gene Summers International Fan Club (EA)
GSIFC .... Georgia Satellites International Fan Club (EA)
GSIFX .... Goldman Sachs Intl. Equity Cl.A [*Mutual fund ticker symbol*] (SG)
GSigsO .... Group Signals Officer [*British military*] (DMA)
GSIHS .... Group for the Study of Irish Historic Settlement [*British*]
GSII .... General Surgical Innovations, Inc. [*NASDAQ symbol*] (SAG)
GSII .... Genl Surgical Innovations [*NASDAQ symbol*] (TTSB)

GSIL .... German Silver
GSIO .... General Staff Interpreter Officer [*Military British*]
GSIS .... Group for the Standardization of Information Services (NITA)
GSISEA .... Government Service Insurance System Employees' Association [*Philippines*]
GSIT .... Group Shorr Imagery Test [*Personality development test*] [*Psychology*]
GSIU .... Ground Standard Interface Unit (MCD)
GSJ .... Gold Spring Resources [*Vancouver Stock Exchange symbol*]
GSJBS .... Goldsmiths', Silversmiths', and Jewellers' Benevolent Society [*British*]
GSJV .... Green Street Joint Venture (EERA)
GSK .... General Storekeeper [*Navy*]
GSK .... George Simon Kaufman [*American playwright, 1889-1961*]
GSK .... Glycogen Synthase Kinase [*An enzyme*]
GSK .... Gold Seeker Resources Ltd. [*Vancouver Stock Exchange symbol*]
GSKT .... Gasket (KSC)
GSL .... Generalized Simulation Language [*Computer science*] (MDG)
GSL .... General Sales Licence (WDAA)
GSL .... General Sales List (DB)
GSL .... General Service Launch [*British military*] (DMA)
GSL .... Generation Strategy Language [*Computer science*] (IEEE)
GSL .... Geographic Air Surveys Ltd. [*Canada ICAO designator*] (FAAC)
GSL .... Geographic Sciences Laboratory [*Fort Belvoir, VA*] [*United States Army Engineer Topographic Laboratories*] (GRD)
GSL .... Geographic Systems Laboratory [*US Army Engineer Topographic Laboratories*]
GSL .... Geological Society of London (BARN)
GSL .... Geophysical Sciences Laboratory [*New York University*]
GSL .... Georgia Department of Education, Atlanta, GA [*OCLC symbol*] (OCLC)
GSL .... Girls' Service League [*Later, YCL*] (EA)
GSL .... Glycosphingolipid [*Biochemistry*]
GSL .... Gold Cup Resources [*Vancouver Stock Exchange symbol*]
GSL .... Gorilla Sign Language (BYTE)
GSL .... Graduate Student Loan
GSL .... Great Salt Lake [*Utah*]
GSL .... Great Somalia League
GSL .... Ground Systems Laboratory
GSL .... Guaranteed Student Loan [*later, Stafford Loan*] [*Department of Education*]
GSLABHF ..... Greater St. Louis Amateur Baseball Hall of Fame (EA)
GSLB .... Gold Star Lapel Button [*Military decoration*] (AABC)
GSLC .... Guaranty Financial [*NASDAQ symbol*] (TTSB)
GSLC .... Guaranty Financial Corp. [*NASDAQ symbol*] (SAG)
GSLC .... Guaranty Savings & Loan FA [*NASDAQ symbol*] (SAG)
GSLD .... Group Selector Long Distance [*Telecommunications*] (IAA)
GSLG .... German Studies Library Group (EAIO)
GSLO .... Gland Seal Leak Off [*Nuclear energy*] (NRCH)
GSLP .... Gibraltar Socialist Labour Party [*Political party*] (PPW)
GSLP .... Guaranteed Student Loan Program
GSLTA .... Girls' Schools Lawn Tennis Association [*British*] (BI)
GSLV .... Geostationary Launch Vehicle [*Indian Space Research Organization*]
GSLV .... Geostationary Satellite Launch Vehicle
GSM .... City of Savannah, Municipal Research Library, Savannah, GA [*Library symbol*] [*Library of Congress*] (LCLS)
GSM .... Garrison Sergeant-Major [*British*]
GSM .... Generalized Sequential Machine [*Computer science*]
GSM .... Generalized Sort/Merge [*Computer science*]
GSM .... General Sales Manager
GSM .... General Service Manager [*Automotive retailing*]
GSM .... General Service Medal [*British*]
GSM .... General Situation Map [*Military*] (NATG)
GSM .... General Stores Material [*Navy*]
GSM .... General Support Maintenance (MCD)
GSM .... General Synod Measures (ILCA)
GSM .... General System Mobile [*Telephone*]
GSM .... General System Model [*Computer science*] (EERA)
GSM .... Geocentric Solar Magnetospheric [*System*] [*NASA*]
GSM .... Geological Society of Malaysia (EAIO)
GSM .... Geological Survey of Great Britain and Museum of Practical Geology (BI)
GSM .... Gibson Spiral Maze [*Psychology*]
GSM .... Global System for Mobile Communication [*Computer science*]
GSM .... Global System for Mobiles [*European mobile-phone network*] (ECON)
GSM .... Gold Star Mothers
GSM .... Goldstream Resources Ltd. [*Vancouver Stock Exchange symbol*]
GSM .... Good Sound Merchantable
GSM .... Gradient Solidification Method [*Optics*]
GSM .... Grams per Square Meter
gsm .... Grams per Square Metre (WDAA)
GSM .... Graphics Schematics Module [*McDonnell-Douglas Corp.*]
GSM .... Graphics System Module
GSM .... Grass Mountain [*Washington*] [*Seismograph station code, US Geological Survey*] (SEIS)
GSM .... Greek Society for Microbiology (BUAC)
GSM .... Ground Signal Mixer
GSM .... Ground Station Modules [*Communications*] [*Army*]
GSM .... Ground Support Maintenance (MCD)
GSM .... Groupe Speciale Mobile [*European digital cellular radio standard*]
GSM .... Group Scout Master [*Scouting*]
GSM .... Guildhall School of Music [*London*]
GSM .... Guild of Saint Matthew
GSM1 .... Gas Turbine Systems Technician, Mechanical, First Class [*Navy rating*] (DNAB)

GSM2 .... Gas Turbine Systems Technician, Mechanical, Second Class [*Navy rating*] (DNAB)

GSM3 .... Gas Turbine Systems Technician, Mechanical, Third Class [*Navy rating*] (DNAB)

GSMA .... Goldstone-SFOF [*Space Flight Operations Facility*] Microwave Assembly [*NASA*]

GSMB .... Grain Sorghum Marketing Board [*New South Wales, Australia*]

GSMB .... Graphic Standards Management Board

GSMBE .... Gas-Source Molecular Beam Epitaxy [*Coating technology*]

GSMC .... Gas Turbine Systems Technician, Mechanical, Chief [*Navy rating*] (DNAB)

GSMD .... General Society of Mayflower Descendants (EA)

GSMD .... Guildhall School of Music and Drama [*London*] (DI)

GSME .... Ground Support Maintenance Equipment [*Aerospace*]

GSMFA .... Gas Turbine Systems Technician, Mechanical, Fireman Apprentice [*Navy rating*] (DNAB)

GSMFC .... Gulf States Marine Fisheries Commission

GSMFC .... Gulf States Marine Fisheries Compact (COE)

GSMFN .... Gas Turbine Systems Technician, Mechanical, Fireman [*Navy rating*] (DNAB)

GSMI .... Global Spill Management, Inc. [*NASDAQ symbol*] (SAG)

GSML .... Generalized Standard Markup Language [*Also, SGML*]

GSML .... General Stores Material List

GSMNP .... Great Smoky Mountains National Park [*Also, GRSM*]

GSMS .... Government Securities Management System [*The Bond Buyer, Inc.*] [*Information service or system*] (IID)

GSMS .... Growth of Strategic Materials in Space (MCD)

GSMS .... Gulf South Medical Supply [*NASDAQ symbol*] (TTSB)

GSMT .... General Society of Mechanics and Tradesmen (EA)

GSN .... Gesneriad Saintpaulia News [*A publication*]

GSN .... Giant Serotonin-Containing Neuron [*Medicine*] (DMAA)

GSN .... Green Student Network (BUAC)

GSN .... Greenwich Sidereal Noon (ROG)

GSN .... Mount Gunson [*Australia Airport symbol*] (OAG)

GSN .... Saipan International Airport [*FAA*] (TAG)

GSNA .... Goethe Society of North America (EA)

GSNC .... General Steam Navigation Co. [*British*]

GSNCO .... General Steam Navigation Co. [*Shipping*] [*British*]

GSNI .... Grandparent Strengths and Needs Inventory [*Test*] (TMMY)

GSNS .... Guidance Control and Navigation Subsystem

GSNSW .... Geographical Society of New South Wales [*Australia*]

GSNT .... Genealogical Society of the Northern Territory [*Australia*]

GSNX .... GaSonics International [*NASDAQ symbol*] (TTSB)

GSNX .... Gasonics International Corp. [*NASDAQ symbol*] (SAG)

GSO .... General Salary Order [*United States*] (DLA)

GSO .... General Services Officer

GSO .... General Spin Orbitals [*Atomic physics*]

GSO .... General Staff Officer [*Military*]

GSO .... General Stores Officer

GSO .... General Submarine Officer (DOMA)

GSO .... General Supply Office

GSO .... General Support Office

GSO .... Geo. S. Olive & Co. [*Telecommunications service*] (TSSD)

GSO .... Geostationary Orbit (MCD)

GSO .... Geosynchronous Orbit

GSO .... Government Services Organization (DOMA)

GSO .... Government Solicitor's Office [*Australian Capital Territory*]

GSO .... Government Statistician's Office [*Queensland, Australia*]

GSO .... Government Superannuation Office [*Queensland, Australia*]

GSO .... Graduate School of Oceanography [*University of Rhode Island*]

GSO .... Graduate Service Overseas of the National Union of Students [*British*] (AEBS)

GSO .... Greensboro/High Point/Winston Salem [*North Carolina*] [*Airport symbol*]

GSO .... Ground Safety Office [*or Officer*] [*Air Force*]

GSO .... Ground-Speed Oscillator [*Aviation*]

GSO .... Ground Support Office [*or Officer*] [*Military*] (AFIT)

GSO .... Ground Support Operations [*Aerospace*] (MCD)

GSO .... Ground Systems Operations (MCD)

GSO .... Growth Stock Outlook Trust, Inc. (MHDW)

GSO .... GSR Goldsearch Resources [*Vancouver Stock Exchange symbol*]

GSO .... Gun Safety Officer

GSO .... Gyro Storage Oven

GSO .... Olive [*Geo S.*] & Co. [*Indianapolis, IN*] (TSSD)

GSO .... Piedmont Triad International Airport [*FAA*] (TAG)

GSoA .... Gerontological Society of America (DAVI)

GSOC .... Gold Star Owners Club (EA)

GSOF .... Group 1 Software [*NASDAQ symbol*] (TTSB)

GSOF .... Group 1 Software, Inc. [*NASDAQ symbol*] (NQ)

GS of W ...... Grand Superintendent of Works [*Freemasonry*]

GSOIA .... General Security of Information Agreement

GSOP .... General Stock Ownership Plan

GSOP .... Guidance Systems Operation Plan [*NASA*] (KSC)

GSOR .... General Staff Operational Requirements [*Army*] (AABC)

GSOST .... Goldstein-Scheerer Object Sorting Test [*Psychology*]

GSOWM ...... Global Spectral Ocean Wave Model

GSP .... Galvanic Skin Potential [*Physiology*]

GSP .... Gel Supported Precipitation [*Method*] [*Chemistry*]

GSP .... Genealogical Society of Pennsylvania (EA)

GSP .... Generalised System of Preferences (ECON)

GSP .... Generalized System of Tariff Preferences [*US Customs Service*]

GSP .... General Sea Harvest [*Vancouver Stock Exchange symbol*]

GSP .... General Semantic Problem (AAG)

GSP .... General Simulation Program [*Programming language*] (IEEE)

GSP .... General Strike for Peace

GSP .... General Strike Plan (NATG)

GSP .... General Survey Panel (STED)

GSP .... General Syntactic Processor

GSP .... Geodetic Satellite Program

GSP .... Geographical Society of Philadelphia (BUAC)

GSP .... German Society of Pennsylvania (EA)

GSP .... Girl Scouts of the Philippines

GSP .... Gladstone Stream [*New Zealand*] [*Seismograph station code, US Geological Survey*] (SEIS)

GSP .... Glycogen Synthetase Phosphatase (STED)

GSP .... Glycosylated Serum Protein

GSP .... Good-Service Pension [*Navy British*]

GSP .... Government Selected Price

GSP .... Government Sponsored Promotion (ADA)

GSP .... Government Standard Parts

GSP .... Graphics System Processor [*Texas Instruments, Inc.*] [*Computer hardware*]

GSP .... Graphic Subroutine Package [*Computer science*]

GSP .... Greenville/Spartanburg [*South Carolina*] [*Airport symbol*]

GSP .... Greer, SC [*Location identifier FAA*] (FAAL)

GSP .... Gross Social Product [*Economics*]

GSP .... Gross State Product (OICC)

GSP .... Ground Safety Plan (MUGU)

GSP .... Group Select Panel (ECII)

GSP .... Growth Fund of Spain [*NYSE symbol*] (SPSG)

GSP .... Guidance Signal Processor (KSC)

GSP .... M & M Aviation, Inc. [*ICAO designator*] (FAAC)

GSP .... Royal Geographical Society. Proceedings [*A publication*]

GSPA .... Gold Star Parents for Amnesty [*Defunct*] (EA)

GSPA .... Grain Sorghum Producers Association (EA)

GSPC .... Gas Scintillation Proportional Counter [*Instrumentation*]

GSPC .... Graphic Standards Planning Committee (NITA)

GSPCA .... German Shorthaired Pointer Club of America (EA)

GSPE .... Georgia Society of Professional Engineers (EA)

GSPE .... Groupe Socialiste du Parlement Europeen [*Socialist Group in the European Parliament - SGEP*] (EAIO)

GSPHCT ...... Group Simplified Perturbed Hard Chain Theory [*Equation of state*]

GSPID .... Gain-Scheduled Proportional Integro-Differential (AAEL)

GSPL .... Gospel

GSPMR .... General Services Administration Property Management Regulation [*A publication*] (AAGC)

GSPN .... Greater Superficial Petrosal Neurectomy [*Neurosurgery*] (DAVI)

GSPO .... Gemini Spacecraft Project Office [*NASA*] (MCD)

G (Spot) ...... Graefenberg Spot [*Gynecology*]

GSPP .... Global Shared Productivity Program (WDAA)

GSPR .... General Session of Peace Roll [*British Legal term*] (ROG)

GSPR .... GSA [*General Services Administration*] Procurement Regulations

GSP-R .... Guidance Signal Processor-Repeater (KSC)

GSPRT .... Generalized Sequential Probability Ratio Test (PDAA)

GSPS .... Generating Station Protection System [*Nuclear energy*] (NRCH)

GSPS .... Guidance Spare Power Supply

GSPTEK ...... Graphics Support Processor/Tektronix

GSPWA .... Georgia Southern Peanut Warehousemen's Association (SRA)

GSQ .... Generalized Sinusoidal Quantity

GSQ .... Genus Equity Corp. [*Toronto Stock Exchange symbol*]

GSQ .... Geological Survey of Queensland [*Australia*]

GSQC .... Ground Surveillance Qualification Course [*Army*]

GSQT .... Gun Ship Qualification Trials (MCD)

GSR .... Galvanic Skin Resistance [*Physiology*] (DAVI)

GSR .... Galvanic Skin Response [*or Reflex*] [*Physiology*]

GSR .... Galvanic Stimulation Rate [*Physiology*]

GSR .... Gardo [*Somalia*] [*Airport symbol*] (OAG)

GSR .... Generalized Schartzman Reaction [*Medicine*]

GSR .... General Service Recruit [*Navy*]

GSR .... General Staff Requirement [*British*] (RDA)

GSR .... General Support Reinforcing [*Army*] (AABC)

GSR .... General Systems Research Ltd. [*Vancouver Stock Exchange symbol*]

GSR .... Geological Survey, Reston [*Virginia*] [*Seismograph station code, US Geological Survey*] (SEIS)

gsr .... Georgian Soviet Socialist Republic [*MARC country of publication code Library of Congress*] (LCCP)

GSR .... Germanium Stack Rectifier

GSR .... German Sanchez Ruiperez [*Founder and chairman of Anaya, a Spanish publishing enterprise*]

GSR .... Gland Steam Regulator [*Nuclear energy*] (NRCH)

GSR .... Glide Slope Receiver [*Aviation*]

GSR .... Global Shared Resources [*Computer science*] (IBMDP)

GSR .... Glutathione Reductase (STED)

GSR .... Golden Star Resources [*AMEX symbol*] (TTSB)

GSR .... Golden Star Resources Ltd. [*AMEX symbol*] (SPSG)

GSR .... Gongwer's State Reports [*Ohio*] [*A publication*] (DLA)

GSR .... Government Spares Release (MCD)

GSR .... Graphic Service Routines [*Computer science*] (MCD)

GSR .... Grid Space Relay

GSR .... Ground Sensor Relay (IAA)

GSR .... Ground Service Relay (MCD)

GSR .... Ground-Speed Returning [*Aviation*]

GSR .... Ground Surveillance RADAR

GSR .... Group Sales Representative [*Health insurance*] (GHCT)

GSR .... Group Selective Register

GSR .... Gunshot Residue [*Forensics*]

GSR .... Gun Sound Ranging [*An acoustic device*]

GSRB .... Glide Slope Reference Bar [*Aviation*]

GSRI .... Global Solar Radiation Index (PDAA)

GSRI .... Great Swamp Research Institute (EA)

GSRI .... Gulf South Research Institute
GSRP .... Gambian Socialist Revolutionary Party [*Political party*] (PD)
GSRS .... General Support Rocket System
GSRS .... Ground Support Rocket System (DWSG)
GSRS .... Ground Surveillance RADAR System
GSRT .... Gesell School Rediness Test (EDAC)
GSRVC .... Good Sam Recreational Vehicle Club (EA)
GSS .... Chieftain International Fund [*AMEX symbol*] (SPSG)
GSS .... Galvanized Steel Sheet [*Technical drawings*]
GSS .... Galvanized Steel Strand [*Telecommunications*] (TEL)
GSS .... Gamete Shedding Substance [*Endocrinology*]
GSS .... Gamma Scintillation System (MSA)
GSS .... Gamma Sigma Sigma (EA)
GSS .... General Service School [*Army*]
GSS .... General Simulation System [*Army*]
GSS .... General Social Survey [*National Opinion Research Center*]
GSS .... General Staff Support (IAA)
GSS .... General Supply Schedule
GSS .... General Support System
GSS .... Genesis Airways Ltd. [*British*] [*FAA designator*] (FAAC)
GSS .... Geodetic Stationary Satellite
GSS .... George Sand Studies (EA)
GSS .... Geostationary Satellite (PDAA)
GSS .... Gerontology Special Interest Section [*American Occupational Therapy Association*]
GSS .... Gerstmann-Staussler Syndrome [*Medicine*]
GSS .... Gerstmann-Straeussler-Scheinker [*Disease*]
GSS .... Gerstmann-StraHssler Syndrome [STED]
GSS .... Gerstmann-Straussler-Sheinker [*Disease*]
GSS .... Ghost Story Society [*British*] (DBA)
GSS .... Gilbert and Sullivan Society (EA)
GSS .... Global Space Station [*Proposed by NASA and ESA*]
GSS .... Global Subsurface System (DWSG)
GSS .... Global Surveillance Station (IAA)
GSS .... Global Surveillance System [*Air Force*]
GSS .... Gonad-Stimulating Substance [*Endocrinology*]
GSS .... Good Shepherd Sisters [*Australia*]
GSS .... Gossan Resources [*Vancouver Stock Exchange symbol*]
GSS .... Government Statistical Service [*British*]
GSS .... Graphic Software Systems Inc. (NITA)
GSS .... Graphic Support Software
GSS .... Gravity Sensors System [*Navigation*]
GSS .... Gray-Scale Sonography [*Medicine*]
GSS .... Ground Support Software [*NASA*] (NASA)
GSS .... Ground Support System [*Aerospace*] (AAG)
GSS .... Group Switching Subsystem (ACRL)
GSS .... Growth Space Station (KSC)
GSS .... Guidance System Simulator
GSS .... Gynecologic Surgery Society (NTPA)
GSS .... Rome, NY [*Location identifier FAA*] (FAAL)
GSSA .... General Support Service Area (MCD)
GSSA .... General Support Supply Activity (MCD)
GSSA .... Grassland Society of Southern Africa [*See also WVSA*] (EAIO)
GSSA .... Ground Support Systems Activation [*NASA*] (NASA)
GSSAPI ...... Generic Security Service Application Program Interface
GSSC .... Greater Super Six Club [*Defunct*] (EA)
GSSC .... Ground Support Simulation Computer [*Aerospace*] (KSC)
GSSC .... Ground Support Systems Contractor [*NASA*] (NASA)
GSSC .... Savannah State College, Savannah, GA [*Library symbol Library of Congress*] (LCLS)
GSSD .... Gerstmann-Straeussler-Scheinker Disease [*Medicine*] (DMAA)
GSSF .... General Supply Stock Fund [*Air Force*] (AFM)
GSSF .... Government Satellite Services Facility (SSD)
GSSF .... Ground Special Security Forces
GSSG .... Glutathione [*Oxidized*] [*Biochemistry*]
GSSG-R ...... Glutathione Reductase [*An enzyme*] (DAVI)
GSSI .... Ground Support System Integration (MCD)
GSsiHi .... Coastal Georgia Historical Society, St. Simons Island, GA [*Library symbol*] [*Library of Congress*] (LCLS)
GSsiM .... The Methodist Museum, St. Simons Island, GA [*Library symbol*] [*Library of Congress*] (LCLS)
GSSL .... General Staff Support Large (IAA)
GSSL .... Genoa, Savona, Spezia, or Leghorn [*Italian ports*] (DS)
GSSLD .... Group Selector of Secondary Long Distance [*Telecommunications*] (IAA)
GSSLNCV.... Genoa, Savona, Spezia, Leghorn, Naples, or Civita Vecchia [*Italian ports*] (DS)
GSSM .... General Staff Support Medium (IAA)
GSSO .... General Stores Supply Office
GSSP .... Global Stratotype Section and Point [*Paleontology*]
GSSPr .... Chieftain Intl Fd $1.8125 Cv Pfd [*AMEX symbol*] (TTSB)
GSSPS .... Gravitationally Stabilized Solar Power System
GSSq .... Geodetic Survey Squadron [*Air Force*] (AFM)
GSSQX........ Goldman Sachs Core U.S. Equity Cl.A [*Mutual fund ticker symbol*] (SG)
GSSR .... Generalized Sanarelli-Shwartzman Reaction [*Medicine*] (MAE)
GSSR .... General Salary Stabilization Regulations [*United States*] (DLA)
GSSR .... Ground Support System Review [*Aerospace*] (AAG)
GSSS .... Ground Support System Specification [*Aerospace*] (AAG)
GSSSP .... Graduate Science Student Support Postdoctorals Survey [*National Science Foundation*] (GFGA)
GSST .... Gatherer, Stitcher, Side Sewer, and Trimmer [*Publishing*]
GSST .... Goldstein-Scheerer Stick Test [*Psychology*]
GSSTFR ...... Gas-Solid-Solid Trickle Flow Reactor [*Chemical engineering*]
GSSW .... Gas-Shielded Stud Welding (PDAA)

GST .... Flying Boat [*Russian aircraft symbol*]
GST .... Garter Stitch [*Knitting*] (ADA)
GST .... Gas Surge Tank [*Nuclear energy*] (NRCH)
GST .... Gate Sensitive Thyristor (IAA)
GST .... Gemini System Trainer [*NASA*] (IAA)
GST .... Genealogical Society of Tasmania [*Australia*]
GST .... General Scholarship Test for High School Seniors [*Education*] (AEBS)
GST .... General Screening Test
GST .... General Service Test (NATG)
GST .... General Service Truck [*British*]
GST .... General Staff Target (NATG)
GST .... General Staff with Troops [*Army*]
GST .... General Systems Theory
GST .... Generation-Skipping Transfer Tax
GST .... Generic Scan Tool [*Automobile service*]
GST .... Geographical Specialist Team [*Army*] (AABC)
GST .... Gesammelte Studien zum Alten Testament [*A publication*] (BJA)
GST .... Glazed Structural Tile [*Technical drawings*]
GST .... Global Space Transport (IAA)
GST .... Global Symbol Table [*Computer science*] (CIST)
GST .... Glutathione S-Transferase [*An enzyme*]
GST .... Gold Salt Therapy [*Medicine*] (DMAA)
GST .... Gold Sodium Thiomalate [*Organic chemistry*] (DAVI)
GST .... Goods and Services Tax [*Canadian*] (ODBW)
GST .... Government Securities Trading [*Computer*]
GST .... Government Steam Train [*British*]
GST .... Graphic Stress Telethermometry [*Medicine*]
GST .... Greenwich Sidereal [*or Standard*] Time
GST .... Ground Sensor Terminal (AABC)
GST .... Ground Surface Temperature
GST .... Ground System Test [*NASA*] (NASA)
GST .... GST Telecommunications [*AMEX symbol*] (TTSB)
GST .... GST Telecommunications, Inc. [*AMEX symbol*] (SAG)
GST .... Gunner Skills Test [*Army*] (INF)
GST .... Gustavus [*Alaska*] [*Airport symbol*] (OAG)
GSTA .... Ground Surveillance and Target Acquisition [*Military*] (MCD)
GSTAMIDS... Ground Standoff Minefield Detection System [*Military*] (RDA)
GSTANSW... General Studies Teachers' Association of New South Wales [*Australia*]
G ST B .... Grand Standard Bearer [*Freemasonry*] (ROG)
GSTC .... Gorham State Teachers College [*Merged with University of Maine*]
GSTD .... Gold Standard [*NASDAQ symbol*] (TTSB)
GSTD .... Gold Standard, Inc. [*NASDAQ symbol*] (NQ)
G STD B ...... Grand Standard Bearer [*Freemasonry*]
GSTDN........ Ground Spacecraft Tracking and Data Network [*Computer science*] (MHDI)
GSTDN........ Ground Space Flight Tracking and Data Network (NAKS)
GSTE........... Guidance System Test Equipment
GSTF........... Ground Systems Test Flow [*NASA*] (NASA)
GStG .... Georgia Southern College, Statesboro, GA [*Library symbol Library of Congress*] (LCLS)
GSTK .... Good Stuff to Know
GSTM......... Gold Sodium Thiomalate [*Organic chemistry*] (DAVI)
GSTN .... General Switched Telephone Nertwork [*Telecommunications*] (OSI)
GSTP .... Generalized System of Tariff Preferences [*US Customs Service*] (MHDW)
GSTP .... Global System of Trade Preferences [*United Nations Conference on Trade and Development*] [*Proposed*]
GSTP .... Ground System Test Procedure (IAA)
GSTRF .... Globalstar Telecommunications Ltd. [*NASDAQ symbol*] (SAG)
GSTRF .... Golbalstar Telecommunications [*NASDAQ symbol*] (TTSB)
GSTS .... German Student Travel Service
GSTS .... Ground-Based Surveillance and Tracking System (MCD)
GSTS .... Guidance System Test Set
GSTS .... Gusts [*NWS*] (FAAC)
GSTT.......... Generation-Skipping Transfer Tax
GST Tele ..... GST Telecommunications, Inc. [*Associated Press*] (SAG)
GSTU .... Guidance System Test Unit
GSTV .... Digestive
GSTY .... Gusty [*NWS*] (FAAC)
GSU .... Entergy Gulf States [*NYSE symbol*] (SAG)
GSU .... Gas Servicer Unit (MCD)
GSU .... Gedaref [*Sudan*] [*Airport symbol*] (AD)
GSU .... General Service Unit [*Marine Corps*]
GSU .... General Support Unit [*Army*] (AABC)
GSU .... Generator Step-Up Transformer [*Nuclear energy*] (NRCH)
GSU .... Geographically Separated Units [*Military*] (AFM)
GSU .... Georgia State University, Atlanta, GA [*OCLC symbol*] (OCLC)
GSU .... Glazed Structural Unit [*Technical drawings*]
GSU .... Golden Seven Industry [*Vancouver Stock Exchange symbol*]
GSU .... Governors State University [*Illinois*]
GSU .... Grain Services Union
GSU .... Guaranteed Supply Unit [*Telecommunications*] (OA)
GSU .... Guidance Switching Unit [*Aviation*]
GSU .... Gulf States Utilities Co. [*NYSE symbol*] (SPSG)
GSUB .... Glazed Structural Unit Base [*Technical drawings*]
GSUC .... Ground Stub-Up Connection [*Aerospace*] (AAG)
GSUEG .... Governors State University Energy Group (EA)
GSUG .... Gross Seasonal Unavailable Generation [*Electronics*] (IEEE)
G (Suit) ...... Antigravity Suit [*Air Force clothing for supersonic flight*]
GSUPr......... Entergy Gulf States $1.75 Pref [*NYSE symbol*] (TTSB)
GSUPrB....... Entergy Gulf States $4.40 Pfd [*NYSE symbol*] (TTSB)
GSUPrD....... Entergy Gulf States Dep Adj B Pfd [*NYSE symbol*] (TTSB)
GSUPrE....... Entergy Gulf States $5.08 Pfd [*NYSE symbol*] (TTSB)

GSUPrG ...... Entergy Gulf States $4.52 Pfd [*NYSE symbol*] (TTSB)
GSUPrK .... Entergy Gulf States $8.80 Pfd [*NYSE symbol*] (TTSB)
G SUPT .... Grand Superintendent [*Freemasonry*]
GSUSA .... Gallipoli Society in the United States of America (EA)
GSUSA .... General Staff, United States Army
GSUSA .... Girl Scouts of the USA (EA)
GSV .... Gas Sampling Valve
GSV .... Genealogical Society of Victoria [*Australia*]
GSV .... Globe Stop Valve
GSV .... Golden Seville Resources Ltd. [*Vancouver Stock Exchange symbol*]
GSV .... Governor Steam Valve (IEEE)
GSV .... Ground-to-Surface Vessel [*RADAR*] (NATG)
GSV .... Grumman Submersible Vehicle
GSV .... Guided Space Vehicle [*Air Force*]
GSV .... Savannah Area Vocational/Technical School, Savannah, GA [*Library symbol*] [*Library of Congress*] (LCLS)
GSVAD .... General Service Volunteer Aid Detachment [*British military*] (DMA)
GSVC .... Generalized Supervisor Calls [*Computer science*] (IBMDP)
GSVO .... Villa Cisneros [*Western Sahara*] [*ICAO location identifier*] (ICLI)
GSVP .... Ground Support Verification Plan [*NASA*] (NASA)
GSVT .... Ground System Validation Test (MCD)
GSW .... Galvanized Steel Wire (IAA)
GSW .... General Service Wagon [*British military*] (DMA)
GSW .... Gold Star Wives of America (EA)
GSW .... Grand Senior Warden [*Freemasonry*] (ROG)
GSW .... Greater Southwest [*Ft. Worth and Dallas, Texas*] [*Airport symbol*] (AD)
GSW .... Great Southwest Railroad, Inc. [*AAR code*]
GSW .... Ground Saucer Watch (EA)
GSW .... GSW, Inc. [*Toronto Stock Exchange symbol*]
GSW .... Gunshot Wound [*Medicine*]
GSW 1812 ... General Society of the War of 1812 (EA)
GSWA .... Gold Star Wives of America [*Later, GSW*] (EA)
GSWA .... Gunshot Wound to the Abdomen
GSWA .... International PEN - Centre of German-Speaking Writers Abroad (EAIO)
G SWD B ..... Grand Sword Bearer [*Freemasonry*]
GSwE .... Emanuel County Junior College, Swainsboro, GA [*Library symbol Library of Congress*] (LCLS)
GSWR .... Galvanized Steel Wire Rope
GS-WRD ..... Geological Survey - Water Resources Division
GSWT .... General Staff with Troops [*Army*]
GSX .... General Signal Corp. [*NYSE symbol*] (SPSG)
GSX .... Genl Signal [*NYSE symbol*] (TTSB)
GSY .... Global Strategy Corp. [*Vancouver Stock Exchange symbol*]
GSY .... Gulf Science Year [*1970*]
GSYB .... [*The*] Girls' School Year Book [*A publication*] (ROG)
GSZ .... Golden Sitka Resources [*Vancouver Stock Exchange symbol*]
GSZ .... Guernsey, WY [*Location identifier FAA*] (FAAL)
GT .... Gabbart [*Ship's rigging*] (ROG)
GT .... Gait Training [*Orthopedics*] (DAVI)
GT .... Galactosyltransferase [*An enzyme*]
GT .... Game Theory
GT .... Gamma-Glutamyltransferase [*Also, GGT, GGTP*] [*An enzyme*]
GT .... Gamow-Teller [*Transition*] [*Nuclear physics*]
GT .... Garbage Truck
GT .... Gas Tight
GT .... Gastrin [*Biochemistry*]
GT .... Gastrostomy [*Gastroenterology*] (DAVI)
GT .... Gastrostomy Tube [*Gastroenterology*] (DAVI)
GT .... Gastrotomy Tube [*Gastroenterology*] (DAVI)
GT .... Gas Tube (IAA)
GT .... Gas Turbine
GT .... Gate Tube (IAA)
GT .... Gee-Thaysen [*Disease*] [*Medicine*] (DB)
GT .... Gelling Temperature [*Analytical biochemistry*]
GT .... Gel Tube [*Electrophoresis*]
GT .... Gemini-Titan [*NASA*]
GT .... General Tariff (ADA)
GT .... General Technical Aptitude Area
GT .... General/Technical Score [*Standardized test*] [*Military*] (INF)
GT .... General Test
GT .... General Tool
GT .... General Transport [*Military*]
GT .... Generation Time [*Microbiology*]
GT .... Genetic Therapy
GT .... Genomic Tested [*Genetics*]
GT .... Gentleman Traveller
GT .... German Title (NITA)
GT .... German Translation (MCD)
GT .... Gibraltar Airways Ltd. [*British ICAO designator*] (ICDA)
GT .... Gifted and Talented [*Education*]
GT .... Gift Tax (DLA)
GT .... Gigaton
Gt. .... gigatonne [*One billion tonnes*] (EERA)
GT .... Gilt
GT .... Gilt Top [*Bookbinding*]
gt .... Gilt Top [*Bookbinding*] (WDMC)
GT .... Gingiva Treatment [*Dentistry*] (MAE)
GT .... Glacial Till Soil [*Agronomy*]
GT .... Glanzmann Thrombasthenia [*Medicine*] (DMAA)
GT .... Glass Tube (DEN)
GT .... Globe Thermometer
GT .... Glow Tube (IAA)
GT .... Glucose Therapy [*Medicine*] (DMAA)

GT .... Glucose Tolerance [*Medicine*]
GT .... Glucose Transporter [*Biochemistry*]
GT .... Glucose Turnover [*Physiology*]
GT .... Glucuronosyltransferase [*An enzyme*]
GT .... Glumitocin [*Endocrinology*]
GT .... Glutamyl Transferase [*Liver-function test*] (CPH)
GT .... Glutamyl Transpeptidase [*An enzyme*]
GT .... Glycotyrosine [*Biochemistry*]
GT .... Gnomonic Tracking Chart [*Air Force*]
GT .... Good Templar
GT .... Good Tidings (EA)
GT .... Goodyear Canada, Inc. [*Toronto Stock Exchange symbol*]
GT .... Goodyear Tire & Rub [*NYSE symbol*] (TTSB)
GT .... [*The*] Goodyear Tire & Rubber Co. [*NYSE symbol*] (SPSG)
GT .... Gopher Tape Armor [*Telecommunications*] (TEL)
GT .... Governor of Tasmania [*Australia*]
g/t .... Grams per Ton
GT .... Grand Theft
GT .... Grand Tiler [*Freemasonry*]
GT .... Grand Totalizer
GT .... Grand Touring [*Automobile model designation*]
GT .... Grand Treasurer [*Freemasonry*]
GT .... Grant [*Legal shorthand*] (LWAP)
GT .... Gran Turismo [*Grand Touring*] [*Automotive term*]
G/T .... Granulation Time
G/T .... Granulation Tissue
GT .... Graphics Terminal
GT .... Grease Trap (AAG)
GT .... Great
GT .... Greater Than [*FORTRAN*]
GT .... Greater Trochanter [*Anatomy*]
Gt. .... Great Organ [*Music*]
GT .... Great Thoughts [*A publication*] (ROG)
GT .... Great Toe [*Medicine*] (DMAA)
GT .... Green Thumb (EA)
GT .... Green Thumbs [*National Weather Service and Department of Agriculture Extension Service telecommunication system*]
GT .... Greenwich Time
GT .... Greetings Telegram (IAA)
GT .... Gross Ton [*or Tonnage*]
GT .... Ground Team (MCD)
GT .... Ground Test [*NASA*] (NASA)
GT .... Ground Track
GT .... Ground Transmit (AFM)
GT .... Ground-Tree Foraging [*Ecology*]
GT .... Group Technology
GT .... Group Tensions [*Medicine*] (DMAA)
GT .... Group Therapy
GT .... Group Transformation
GT .... Grout [*Technical drawings*]
GT .... Guard of Tent [*Oddfellows*] (ROG)
GT .... Guatemala [*ANSI two-letter standard code*] (CNC)
gt .... Guatemala [*MARC country of publication code Library of Congress*] (LCCP)
GT .... Guidance Transmitter (NVT)
GT .... Gun Target (NVT)
GT .... Gun Tractor [*British*]
GT .... Gun Turret
GT .... Gutta [*Drop of Liquid*] [*Pharmacy*]
GT .... Gyro Torque (MCD)
GT .... Triganglioside [*Chemistry*]
GT1 .... Glycogenosis Type 1 [*Medicine*]
GTA .... Gas Toxicity Analysis
GTA .... Gas Tungsten Arc
GTA .... Gas Turbine Association (NTPA)
GTA .... Gay Theatre Alliance [*Defunct*] (EA)
GTA .... Gear Train Analyzer
GTA .... Gemini-Titan-Agena [*NASA*] (KSC)
GTA .... General Terms Agreement (MCD)
GTA .... General Training Assistance (ADA)
GTA .... Genetic Toxicology Association (EA)
GTA .... Gene Transfer Agent [*Genetics*]
GTA .... Gentra Inc. [*TS, exchange symbol*] (TTSB)
GTA .... German Teachers' Association [*British*]
GTA .... Gimbaled Telescope Assembly (MCD)
GTA .... Gitanair [*Italy ICAO designator*] (FAAC)
GTA .... Glass Tempering Association (EA)
GTA .... Glycerol Triacetate [*Known as Triacetin*] [*Organic chemistry*]
GTA .... Gospel Truth Association (EA)
GTA .... Government Telecommunications Agency [*Canada*]
GTA .... Graduate Teachers' Association [*A union*] [*British*]
GTA .... Graduate Teaching Assistant
GTA .... Grain Transportation Agency [*Winnipeg, MB*]
GTA .... Grand Theft Auto (WGA)
GTA .... Gran Turismo Americano [*In automobile name Pontiac Firebird GTA*]
GTA .... Gran Turismo Automatico [*Automobile model designation*]
GTA .... Graphic Training Aid
GTA .... Gravure Technical Association [*Later, GAA*] (EA)
GTA .... Ground Test Access (MCD)
GTA .... Ground Test Article [*NASA*] (NASA)
GTA .... Ground Torquing Assembly (MCD)
GTA .... Ground Training Aid [*Aerospace*] (AAG)
GTA .... Groupement Technique de Assureurs du Canada [*Government Telecommunications Agency*] [*Canada*]
GTA .... Group Training Association [*British*] (DCTA)

GTA.............	GT Aviation [*British*] [*FAA designator*] (FAAC)
GTA.............	Guide Tube Assembly (NRCH)
GTA.............	Gun Trade Association Ltd. [*British*] (BI)
GTA.............	Gutta [*Drop of Liquid*] [*Pharmacy*] (ROG)
GTAA	Groupe de Travail Inter Agences sur l'Afrique Australe [*Inter-Agency Working Group on Southern Africa - IAWGSA*] [*Canadian Council for International Cooperation*]
GTAC	Gas Tungsten Arc Cutting [*Welding*]
GTAC	General Technical Advisory Committee [*for fossil energy*] [*Energy Research and Development Administration*]
GTAC	Ground-to-Air Cycle
GTAM..........	Ground-to-Air Missile (RDA)
GtAMg	Great American Management & Investment, Inc. [*Associated Press*] (SAG)
GT & A	Ground Test and Acceptance [*NASA*] (NASA)
GT & C	General Terms and Conditions
GT & E.........	General Telephone & Electronics (NITA)
GT & E.........	General Telephone & Electronics Corp.
GT & TM.....	General Traffic and Transportation Manager
GTAO..........	Graphic Training Aids Officer [*Army*]
GTASA	Geography Teachers' Association of South Australia
GTASFA	Grand Traverse Area Sportfishing Association [*Michigan*]
GtAtPc	Great Atlantic & Pacific Tea Co., Inc. [*Associated Press*] (SAG)
GTAV..........	General Transport Administrative Vehicle
GTAW.........	Gas Tungsten Arc Weld [*or Welding*]
GTAW-P......	Gas Tungsten Arc Welding - Pulsed Arc
GTAX..........	Gilman & Ciocia, Inc. [*NASDAQ symbol*] (SAG)
GTAXW	Gilman & Ciocia Wrrt [*NASDAQ symbol*] (TTSB)
GTB.............	Fort Drum, NY [*Location identifier FAA*] (FAAL)
GTB.............	Gastrointestinal Tract Bleeding [*Medicine*] (DMAA)
GTB.............	General Tariff Bureau Inc. Lansing MI [*STAC*]
GTB.............	General Trade Books [*Publishing*]
GTB.............	Glycinethymol Blue [*An indicator*] [*Chemistry*]
GTB.............	Grand Traverse Bay, Michigan
GTB.............	Gran Turismo Berlinetta [*Automobile model designation*]
GTB.............	Guild of Traditional Butlers
GTBA	Gasoline-Grade Tertiary-Butyl Alcohol [*Organic chemistry*]
GTBA	Grade Tertiary Butyl Alcohol
GTBC	Guild of Teachers of Backward Children [*British*] (BI)
GTBicyc	GT Bicycles, Inc. [*Associated Press*] (SAG)
GT BR	Great Britain (ROG)
Gt Brit.........	Great Britain (WGA)
GTBWI	Grand Traverse Bay Watershed Initiative
GTBX	GT Bicycles [*NASDAQ symbol*] (TTSB)
GTBX	GT Bicycles, Inc. [*NASDAQ symbol*] (SAG)
GTC.............	Gain Time Constant (MCD)
GTC.............	Gain Time Control
GTC.............	Gas Turbine Compressor
GTC.............	Gateway to Care
GTC.............	Generalized Tonic-Clonic [*Seizure*] [*Medicine*] (DB)
GTC.............	General Teaching Council [*British*]
GTC.............	General Tool Contract (MCD)
GTC.............	General Transistor Corp. (AAG)
GTC.............	Georgia Teachers College [*Later, Georgia Southern College*] (AEBS)
GTC.............	Giant Cell Thyroiditis [*Medicine*] (DMAA)
GTC.............	Girls' Training Corps [*British*] (DAS)
GTC.............	Global Tomorrow Coalition (EA)
GTC.............	Glycol Trim Console (MCD)
GTC.............	Golder, Thoma & Cressey [*Chicago, IL*] [*Telecommunications service*] (TSSD)
GTC.............	Good Till Canceled [*as in a brokerage order*]
GTC.............	Government Telegraph Code [*British World War II*]
GTC.............	Government Training Centre [*British*]
GTC.............	Grand Touring Coupe [*In automobile name Lincoln Mark VII GTC*]
GTC.............	Grand Trunk Corp. (EFIS)
GTC.............	Gran Turismo Cabriolet [*Automobile model designation*]
GTC.............	Greater Toy Center (EA)
GTC.............	Ground Test Conductor (MCD)
GTC.............	Group for Technical Coordination [*Marine science*] (MSC)
GTC.............	Group Training Command [*Air Force British*]
GTC.............	Group Training Company
GTC.............	Guanidinium Thiocyanate [*Biochemistry*]
GTC.............	Guidance Transfer Container
GTC.............	Guild of Television Cameramen [*British*] (EA)
GTC.............	Gulf Transport [*AAR code*]
GTC.............	Man, WV [*Location identifier FAA*] (FAAL)
GTCC	Gas Turbine Combined Cycle [*Energy technology*]
GTCC	German Touring Car Championship
GTCC	Government's Total Contract Cost (AAGC)
GTCC	Greater-than-Class-C [*Radioactive waste level definition*]
GTCC	Group Technology Characterization Code (IAA)
GtChina.......	[*The*] Greater China Fund [*Associated Press*] (SAG)
GTCL	Graduate of Trinity College of Music, London
GTCM	Great Central Mines [*NASDAQ symbol*] (SAG)
GTCMY	Great Central Mines NL ADS [*NASDAQ symbol*] (TTSB)
GTCP	Gas Turbine Compressor and Power Unit (NG)
GTCP	General Telephone Call Processing
GTCP	Global Tropospheric Chemistry Program [*Federal government*]
GTCR	Gate-Turnoff Controlled Rectifier [*Electronics*] (IAA)
GTCS	General Teaching Council for School [*British*]
GTCU	Ground Thermal Conditioning Unit [*NASA*] (NASA)
GtD.............	Duarte Variant Allele [*Genetics*] (DAVI)
GTD	Gear Test Data
GTD	General Traffic Department
GTD	Geometrical Theory of Diffraction

GTD	Geometric and Technical Draughting [*British Olivetti Ltd.*] [*Software package*] (NCC)
GTD	Georgetown [*Delaware*] [*Seismograph station code, US Geological Survey*] (SEIS)
GTD	Gestational Trophoblastic Disease [*Medicine*] (MAE)
GTD	Graphic Tablet Display [*Computer science*] (IEEE)
GTD	Ground Target Detection
GTD	GT Global Developing Market Fund [*NYSE symbol*] (SPSG)
GTD	G.T. Global Dvlp Mkt Fund [*NYSE symbol*] (TTSB)
gtd	Guaranteed (WDAA)
GTD	Guaranteed
Gtd.............	Guaranteed (EBF)
GTD	Guaranteed Bond (EBF)
GTD	Guards Tank Division (MCD)
GTDB	Generic Transformed Database
GTDHD........	Give the Devil His Due [*Slang*]
GTDPL	Generalized Top-Down Parsing Language
GTDR	General Technical Data Restricted
GTDS	Goddard Trajectory Determination System [*NASA*]
GTDvMk	GT Global Developing Market Facts [*Associated Press*] (SAG)
GTE...........	Gas Turbine Engine
GTE...........	General-Purpose Thermoplastic Elastomer [*Insulation*]
GTE...........	General Telephone and Electronics [*Telecommunications company*] [*Stamford, CT*] (WDMC)
GTE...........	General Telephone Equipment (MCD)
GTE...........	Geothermal Energy
GTE...........	Gilt Top Edge [*Bookbinding*]
GTE...........	Global Tropospheric Experiment [*National Oceanic and Atmospheric Administration*]
GTE...........	Gothenburg, NE [*Location identifier FAA*] (FAAL)
GTE...........	Gran Turismo Europa [*Automobile model designation*]
GTE...........	Groote Island [*Australia Airport symbol*] (OAG)
GTE...........	Ground Telecommunication Equipment
GTE...........	Ground Test Equipment
GTE...........	Ground Training Engine [*Military*] (AFIT)
GTE...........	Ground Transport Equipment (KSC)
GTE...........	Group Translating Equipment
GTE...........	GTE Corp. [*Formerly, General Telephone & Electronics Corp.*] [*NYSE symbol*] (SPSG)
GTE...........	GTE Delaware LP [*NYSE symbol*] (SAG)
GTE...........	Guidance Test Equipment
GTE...........	Gunner Tracking Evaluator (PDAA)
GTEA..........	Group Test Equipment Assembly
GTEC..........	GTE California, Inc. [*Associated Press*] (SAG)
Gtech	GTECH Holdings Corp. [*Associated Press*] (SAG)
GTED	Gas Turbine Engine-Driven [*Generator*] (RDA)
GTEDE	GTE Delaware Ltd. [*Associated Press*] (SAG)
GTEE..........	Grantee [*Legal shorthand*] (LWAP)
GTEE..........	Guarantee
GTEF..........	GTE Florida, Inc. [*Associated Press*] (SAG)
GTEL..........	Groundwater Technology, Inc. (EFIS)
GTEL..........	GTE California, Inc. [*NASDAQ symbol*] (NQ)
GTelevsa	Grupo Televisa [*Associated Press*] (SAG)
GTELN	GTE Calif 5% cm Pfd [*NASDAQ symbol*] (TTSB)
GTELO	GTE Calif 4.50% cm Pfd [*NASDAQ symbol*] (TTSB)
GTELP	GTE Calif 4.50% cm Pfd [*NASDAQ symbol*] (TTSB)
GT-ENDOR...	General Triple-Electron Nuclear Double Resonance [*Spectroscopy*]
GTEP..........	General Telephone and Electronics Practice [*Telecommunications*] (TEL)
GTETDS	Gas Turbine and Engine Type Designation System
GTE TMD	Guillotine Trimmed [*Bookbinding*] (DGA)
GT Euro	GT Greater Europe Fund [*Associated Press*] (SAG)
GtewayD	Gateway Data Sciences Corp. [*Associated Press*] (SAG)
GTF.............	Generalized Trace Facility [*Computer science*] (MCD)
GTF.............	Generalized Transformation Function
GT/F...........	General Telephone Company of Florida (NITA)
GTF.............	General Transcription Factor [*Genetics*]
GTF.............	German Territorial Forces (MCD)
GTF.............	Glucose Tolerance Factor [*Medicine*] (DMAA)
GTF.............	Glucosyltransferase (DMAA)
GTF.............	Government Test Facility
GTF.............	Greater Than Flag (MHDB)
GTF.............	Great Falls [*Montana*] [*Airport symbol*] (OAG)
GTF.............	Grout Treatment Facility [*Environmental science*] (COE)
GTF.............	G.T. Greater Europe Fd [*NYSE symbol*] (TTSB)
GTF.............	GT Greater Europe Fund [*NYSE symbol*] (SPSG)
GTF.............	Guidance Test Fixture
GTF.............	Guilt Free Goodies [*Vancouver Stock Exchange symbol*]
GTFN	Great Financial [*NASDAQ symbol*] (TTSB)
GTFN	Great Financial Corp. [*NASDAQ symbol*] (SAG)
GTFT...........	Generous Tit for Tat [*Game strategy*]
GtG.............	Galactosemic Allele [*Genetics*] (DAVI)
GTG.............	Game-Tying Goals [*Hockey*]
GTG.............	Gas Turbine Generator
GTG.............	Golden Trend Energy [*Vancouver Stock Exchange symbol*]
GTG.............	Gold Thioglucose
GTG.............	Grantsburg, WI [*Location identifier FAA*] (FAAL)
GTG.............	Ground Timing Generator (IAA)
GTG.............	Ground-to-Ground [*Communications, weapons, etc.*]
GTGEEEPS ...	Groupe de Travail sur la Gestion de l'Energie dans les Etablissements d'Enseignement Post-Secondaire [*Postsecondary Education Task Force on Energy Management PETFEM*] [*Canada*]
GTGL	Give the Gift of Literacy Foundation [*Duxbury, MA*]
GTGS	Gas Turbine Generator Set (AABC)

GTGT	Gun Target (AABC)
GTH	Gas Tight High Pressure (IEEE)
GTH	Genomic Thymus [*Genetics*]
GTH	Gonadotropic Hormone [*Endocrinology*]
GTH	Groton Minerals Ltd. [*Vancouver Stock Exchange symbol*]
GTH	Guthrie, TX [*Location identifier FAA*] (FAAL)
GthEnvr	Growth Environmental, Inc. [*Associated Press*] (SAG)
GthFn	Growth Financial Corp. [*Associated Press*] (SAG)
G Thom	Gospel of Thomas [*Apocryphal work*]
GTHRNG	Gathering
GTHS	German-Texan Heritage Society (EA)
GthSpn	Growth Fund of Spain [*Associated Press*] (SAG)
GT-HTGR	Gas Turbine High-Temperature Gas-Cooled Reactor [*Nuclear energy*] (NRCH)
GTI	Atlas Air, Inc. [*ICAO designator*] (FAAC)
GTi	Coastal Plains Regional Library, Tifton, GA [*Library symbol Library of Congress*] (LCLS)
GTI	General Transportation Importance
GTI	Genital Tract Infection [*Medicine*] (CPH)
GTI	Glass Technical Institute [*Commercial firm*] (EA)
GTI	Glentech International Ltd. [*British*]
GTI	Grand Turk Island
GTI	Ground Test Instrumentation (MCD)
GTI	GTI Corp. [*Associated Press*] (SAG)
GTiA	Abraham Baldwin Agricultural College, Tifton, GA [*Library symbol Library of Congress*] (LCLS)
GTiE	Coastal Plains Experiment Station, Tifton, GA [*Library symbol Library of Congress*] (LCLS)
GTIG	Gamma Thermometer Interest Group [*Nuclear energy*] (NRCH)
GT II	Galactosyltransferase Isoenzyme II [*An enzyme*] (DAVI)
GTII	Golden Triangle Ind [*NASDAQ symbol*] (TTSB)
GTII	Golden Triangle Industries, Inc. [*NASDAQ symbol*] (SAG)
GTII	Golden Triangle Industry [*NASDAQ symbol*] [*Formerly, Golden Triangle Roy & Oil*] (SG)
GTIM	Good Times Restaurants [*NASDAQ symbol*] (TTSB)
GTIM	Good Times Restaurants, Inc. [*NASDAQ symbol*] (SAG)
GTIMW	Good Times Restaurants Wrrt [*NASDAQ symbol*] (TTSB)
GTIMZ	Good Times Restaurants Wrrt'B' [*NASDAQ symbol*] (TTSB)
GTIP	Ground Tilt Isolation Platform
GTIS	Gloucestershire Technical Information Service (NITA)
GTIS	Ground-Based Traffic Information System [*Aviation*] (DA)
GTIS	GT Interactive Software [*NASDAQ symbol*] (TTSB)
GTJ	Gold Torch Resources [*Vancouver Stock Exchange symbol*]
GTJ	Gran Turismo Junior [*Automobile model designation*]
GTK	Grand Turk [*British West Indies*]
GTK	Grosser Touren Kombiwagen [*Grand Touring Station Wagon*] [*German*]
GTK	Gross Tonne Kilometre (EERA)
GTK	GTECH Holdings [*NYSE symbol*] (TTSB)
GTK	GTECH Holdings Corp. [*NYSE symbol*] (SPSG)
GTL	Gaseous Tritium Light [*Device*] [*Nuclear energy*] (NRCH)
GTL	Gas Transport LASER
GTL	Gas Turbine Laboratory [*MIT*] (MCD)
GTL	Geomagnetic Tail Laboratory (MCD)
GTL	Geometric and Technical Language [*British Olivetti Ltd.*] [*Software package*] (NCC)
GTL	Georgia Tech Language [*Computer science*] (CSR)
GTL	Glass Training Ltd. (AIE)
GTL	Global Title Translation
GTL	Government Test Laboratory (MSA)
GTL	Great Lakes Nickel Ltd. [*Toronto Stock Exchange symbol*]
GTL	Gun/Target Line [*Navy*] (NVT)
gTLD	Generic Top-Level Domain [*Computer science*] (IGQR)
GT/LD	Gifted & Learning Disabled
gTLD-MoU	Generic Top Level Domain Memorandum of Understanding (TELE)
GtLkCh	Great Lakes Chemical Corp. [*Associated Press*] (SAG)
GtLkeAv	Great Lakes Aviation Ltd. [*Associated Press*] (SAG)
GTLS	Gaseous Tritium Light Source [*Nuclear energy*] (MCD)
GTM	Abraham Baldwin Agricultural College, Tifton, GA [*OCLC symbol*] (OCLC)
GTM	Gang Temperature Monitor [*Environmental science*] (COE)
GTM	Gas to Methanol [*Process developed by ICI*]
GTM	General Traffic Manager
GTM	Geometry Technology Module [*NASA*]
GTM	Getting the Message [*A reading program*]
GTM	Good This Month [*Business term*]
GTM	Ground Team Manager (MCD)
GTM	Ground Test Missile
GTM	Ground Test Motor (MCD)
GTM	Group Talk Microphone
GTM	Guatemala [*ANSI three-letter standard code*] (CNC)
GTM	Guild of Temple Musicians (EA)
GTMA	Galvanised Tank Manufacturers' Association [*British*] (BI)
GTMA	Gauge and Toolmakers Association [*British*] (DS)
GTMHR	Gas Turbine Modular Helium Reactor [*Nuclear reactor*]
GTMIE	Global Telemedia Intl [*NASDAQ symbol*] (TTSB)
GTMMM	Det Gamle Testament [*S. Michelet, S.Mowinckel, og N. Mersel*] [*Oslo*] [*A publication*] (BJA)
GTMO	Guantanamo Bay, Cuba
GTMS	Graphic Text Management System [*Computer science*] (DGA)
GTMS	Ground Target Marking System
GTMV	Gasoline-Tolerant Methanol Vehicle [*Chrysler Corp.*] [*Automotive engineering*]
GTN	Gestational Trophoblastic Neoplasia [*Medicine*] (STED)
GTN	Global Transportation Network (DOMA)
GTN	Global Trend Network (GNE)
GTN	Global Trends Network [*USA*] (EERA)
GTN	Glomerulotubulonephritis [*Medicine*] (STED)
GTN	Glomerulo-Tubulo-Nephritis [*Medicine*]
GTN	Glyceryl Trinitrate [*Also, NG, NTG*] [*Explosive, vasodilator*]
GTN	Gotenba [*Japan*] [*Seismograph station code, US Geological Survey Closed*] (SEIS)
GTN	Government Telecommunications Network [*British*] (EECA)
GTN	Great Eastern Line [*Vancouver Stock Exchange symbol*]
GTN	Washington, DC [*Location identifier FAA*] (FAAL)
GTNR	Gentner Communications [*NASDAQ symbol*] (TTSB)
GTNR	Gentner Communications Corp. [*NASDAQ symbol*] (NQ)
GTNRW	Gentner Communications Wrrt [*NASDAQ symbol*] (TTSB)
GTNW	General Telephone Co. of the Northwest
GtNYSv	[*The*] Greater New York Savings Bank [*Associated Press*] (SAG)
GTO	Gate Turn Off [*Computer science*]
GTO	Gaussian-Type Orbital (DB)
GTO	Gaussian-Type Orbitals [*Atomic physics*]
GTO	General Telecommunications Organization [*Oman*] [*Telecommunications service*]
GTO	Geostationary Transfer Orbit [*Space technology*]
GTO	Gigaton
GTO	Golgi Tendon Organ [*Anatomy*]
GTO	Gorontalo [*Indonesia*] [*Airport symbol*] (OAG)
GTO	Grand Touring Over 3.0 Liters [*Class of racing cars*]
GTO	Gran Turismo Omologato [*Grand Touring, Homologated*] [*Automotive engineering*] [*Italian*]
GTO	Graphics Text Organizer [*Computer science*]
GTO	Grenada Tourist Office (EA)
GTO	Guaranteed Time Observer [*For telescope viewing*]
GTOL	Graphic Take-Off Language [*Computer science*] (PDAA)
GTOL	Ground Takeoff and Landing (AAG)
GTOR	Grantor [*Legal shorthand*] (LWAP)
GT ORM H	Great Ormond Street Hospital for Children [*British*] (ROG)
GTOS	Gantos, Inc. [*NASDAQ symbol*] (SAG)
GTOS	Global Terrestrial Observing System [*Marine science*] (OSRA)
GTOS	Ground Terminal Operations Support (SSD)
GTOSCR	Gate Turnoff Silicon-Controlled Rectifier [*Electronics*] (IAA)
GTOSS	Generalized Tethered Object System Simulation (SSD)
GTOT	Gate Turn Off Thyristor (NITA)
GTOW	Gross Takeoff Weight [*of an aircraft*] [*Also, GTW*]
GTOWFC	George Takei's Official Worldwide Fan Club [*British*] (EAIO)
GTP	Gas Turbine Power Unit (NG)
GTP	General Telemetry Processor [*Telecommunications*] (ITD)
GTP	General Test Plan (AAG)
GTP	General Training Program
GTP	Generate Target Position [*Military*] (CAAL)
GTP	Global Technology Partners
GTP	Global Time and Position [*Navigation systems*]
GTP	Glutamyl Transpeptidase [*An enzyme*]
GTP	Golay Transform Processor (IAA)
GTP	Government Technology Productivity
GTP	Grand Touring Prototype [*Race car designation*]
GTP	Grand Trunk Pacific Railway
GTP	Graphic Transform Package (MHDI)
GTP	Great Northern Petroleums [*Vancouver Stock Exchange symbol*]
GTP	Great Trunk Pacific Railway [*British*] (ROG)
GTP	Green Tea Polyphenol [*Biochemistry*]
GTP	Ground Test Plan (MCD)
GTP	Ground Track Plotter
GTP	Group-Transfer Polymerization [*Du Pont process*] [*1983*]
GTP	Guanosine Triphosphate [*Biochemistry*]
GTPase	Guanosine Triphosphatase [*An enzyme*]
GTPI	Grupo de Trabajo para los Pueblos Indigenas [*Indigenous Peoples Working Group*] [*Netherlands*] (EAIO)
GTPR	Grand Trunk Pacific Railway
GTPS	Gas Turbine Power System
GTPS	Great American Bancorp [*NASDAQ symbol*] (TTSB)
GTPS	Great American Bancorp, Inc. [*NASDAQ symbol*] (SAG)
GTPSS	Ground Test Plan Summary Sheets (MCD)
GTPT	Geometrical and True Positioning Tolerance
GTPU	Gas Turbine Power Unit (MCD)
GTR	Columbus [*Mississippi*] [*Airport symbol*] (OAG)
GTR	Galvanic Tetanus Ratio [*Medicine*] (STED)
GTR	Gantry Test Rack [*Aerospace*] (AAG)
GTR	Garter (MSA)
GTR	Generalized Time Reflex (STED)
GTR	General Theory of Relativity
GTR	Geoid-to-Topography Ratio [*Planetary science*]
GTR	Golden Terrace Resource Corp. [*Toronto Stock Exchange symbol*]
GTR	[*The*] Goodyear Tire & Rubber Co.
GTR	Government Technical Report
GTR	Government Technical Representative
GTR	Government Transportation [*or Travel*] Request
GTR	Government Travel Request (MCD)
GTR	Grand Trunk Railway
GTR	Grantex Aviation [*British*] [*FAA designator*] (FAAC)
GTR	Granulocyte Turnover Rate [*Hematology*]
GTR	Great Barrier Island [*New Zealand*] [*Airport symbol*] (AD)
Gtr	Greater (BARN)
GTR	Ground Test Reactor [*Air Force*]
GTR	Grupo Tribasa S.A. ADS [*NYSE symbol*] (TTSB)
GTR	Grupo Tribasa SA de CV [*NYSE symbol*] (SPSG)
GT/R	Guard Transmit/Receive (MCD)

GTR .... Guitar [*Music*]
gtr............... Guitar (WDAA)
GTR .... Gurkha Transport Regiment [*Military unit*] [*British*]
GTRB .... Gas Turbine
GTRD .... Greatest Total Resource Demand
GTRE .... Global Tape Recording Exchange (EA)
G TREAS ..... Grand Treasurer [*Freemasonry*] (ROG)
GTRI .... Georgia Tech Research Institute [*Georgia Institute of Technology*] [*Research center*] (RCD)
GTribasa...... Grupo Tribasa SA de Cv [*Associated Press*] (SAG)
GTRN .... Great Train Store [*NASDAQ symbol*] (TTSB)
GTRN .... Great Train Stores Co. [*NASDAQ symbol*] (SAG)
GTRNW........ Great Train Store Wrrt [*NASDAQ symbol*] (TTSB)
GTRO .... Glyceryl Triricinoleate [*Organic chemistry*]
GTRO .... Golden Triangle Royalty & Oil, Inc. [*NASDAQ symbol*] (NQ)
GTRP .... General Transpose [*Computer science*]
GTRR .... Georgia Institute of Technology Research Reactor
GTRR .... Grand Trunk Railroad [*British*] (ROG)
GTRY .... Grand Trunk Railway
GTS .... Gas Turbine Ship (IIA)
GTS .... Gas Turbine Starter (MCD)
GTS .... Gated Transport Spectroscopy
GTS .... Generalized Transition State [*Physical chemistry*]
GTS .... General Tabulation System
GTS .... General Technical Services, Inc. (MCD)
GTS .... General Telephone System (IAA)
GTS .... General Test Support (MCD)
GTS .... General Theological Seminary [*New York, NY*]
GTS .... General Troubleshooting
GTS .... Generic Equipment Model Test System (AAEL)
GTS .... Geostationary Technology Satellite
GTS .... Gilles de la Tourette Syndrome [*Medicine*] (DMAA)
GTS .... Gimbal Trim System
GTS .... Girls' Technical School (ADA)
GTS .... Glider Training School [*British military*] (DMA)
GTS .... Global Telecommunication System [*World Meteorological Organization*] (IID)
GTS .... Global Tracking Systems
GTS .... Global Treasury Services [*Barclays Bank*] [*British*]
GT's .... Globetrotters' Club (EAIO)
GTS .... Glucose Transport System [*Medicine*] (STED)
GTS .... GN & C [*Guidance, Navigation and Control*] Test Station [*NASA*] (NASA)
GTS .... Golden Tech Resources Ltd. [*Vancouver Stock Exchange symbol*]
GTS .... Golden Treasury Series [*A publication*]
GTS .... Goldstone Tracking Station [*NASA*]
GTS .... Grand Touring Supreme [*Auto racing*]
GTS .... Gran Turismo Spider [*Automobile model designation*]
GTS .... Graphics Terminal Scheduler (MCD)
GTS .... Graphics Terminal Services
GTS .... Graphics Terminal System
GTS .... Green Tobacco Sickness [*Illness resulting from exposure to dissolved nicotine*]
GTS .... Greenwich Time Signal (DEN)
GTS .... Ground Telemetry Subsystem
GTS .... Ground Terminal System
GTS .... Ground Test Station
GTS .... Ground Tracking System (MCD)
GTS .... Ground Training System (MCD)
GTS .... Ground Transportation Services [*MTMC*] (TAG)
GTS .... Group Technology System (MCD)
GTS .... Group Teleconferencing System [*Telecommunications*]
GTS .... Guam Tracking Station [*NASA*] (MCD)
GTS .... Guidance Test Set (AAG)
GTS .... Guinean Trawling Survey [*United Nations*]
GTS .... Gunnery Training School [*British military*] (DMA)
gts .... Guttae [*Drops*] [*Pharmacy*] (DAVI)
GTS .... Gyro Tilt Signal
GTSC .... German Territorial Southern Command [*NATO*] (NATG)
GTS Drtk ..... GTS Duratek [*Associated Press*] (SAG)
GTSF........... Gifted and Talented Screening Form [*Educational test*]
GTSF........... Guidance Test and Simulation Facility
GTSI............ Government Technology Services [*NASDAQ symbol*] (SPSG)
GTSI............ Government Technology Svcs [*NASDAQ symbol*] (TTSB)
GTSPP .... Global Temperature and Salinity Pilot Project (EERA)
GTSS .... Gas Turbine Starting System (NG)
GTSS .... General Time Sharing System [*Computer science*]
GTST........... Global Telecomm Solutions [*NASDAQ symbol*] (TTSB)
GTST........... Global Telecommunications Solutions, Inc. [*NASDAQ symbol*] (SAG)
GTST........... Greatest (ABBR)
GTSTD .... Grid Test of Schizophrenic Thought Disorder [*Psychology*]
GTSTW .... Global Tele Solutions Wrrt [*NASDAQ symbol*] (TTSB)
GTSW .... Greentree Software, Inc. [*NASDAQ symbol*] (NQ)
GTSWC........ Greentree Software [*NASDAQ symbol*] (TTSB)
GTSX .... Golf Training Systems [*NASDAQ symbol*] (TTSB)
GTSX .... Golf Training Systems, Inc. [*NASDAQ symbol*] (SAG)
GTSXU .... Golf Training Systems Unit [*NASDAQ symbol*] (TTSB)
GTSXW .... Golf Training Sys Wrrt [*NASDAQ symbol*] (TTSB)
GTT............. Gelatin-Tellurite-Taurocholate [*Agar*] [*Medicine*] (MEDA)
GTT............. Gelatin-Tellurite-Taurocholate Agar [*Biochemistry*] (DAVI)
GTT............. Generated Target Tracking
GTT............. Geographical and Topographical Texts of the Old Testament [*A publication*] (BJA)
GTT............. Georgetown [*Australia Airport symbol*] (OAG)
GTT............. Glucose Tolerance Test [*Medicine*]

GTT.............. Goettingen [*Federal Republic of Germany*] [*Geomagnetic observatory code*]
GTT............. Gone to Texas [*Sign on doors of New Englanders who had gone West, nineteenth century*]
GTT............. Gottingen [*Federal Republic of Germany*] [*Seismograph station code, US Geological Survey*] (SEIS)
GTT............. Grand Teton Industries, Inc. [*Vancouver Stock Exchange symbol*]
GTT............. Group Timing Technique [*Industrial engineering*]
GTT............. Guttae [*Drops of Liquid*] [*Pharmacy*]
GTTC........... Goodfellow Technical Training Center [*Military*]
GTTC........... Gulf Transportation Terminal Command
GTTF........... Gas Turbine Test Facility
GTTIF.......... Grande Tel Technologies [*NASDAQ symbol*] (TTSB)
GTTIF.......... GrandeTel Technologies, Inc. [*NASDAQ symbol*] (SAG)
GTT QUIBUSD... Guttis Quibusdam [*With Some Drops*] [*Pharmacy*] (ROG)
GtTrain .... Great Train Stores Co. [*Associated Press*] (SAG)
GtTrn .... Great Train Stores Co. [*Associated Press*] (SAG)
GTTS............ Gyro Transfer Table System
GTU .... Gamma Theta Upsilon (EA)
GTU .... Gatelink Transceiver Unit [*Aviation*]
GTU .... Georgetown University, Medical Center Library, Washington, DC [*OCLC symbol*] (OCLC)
GTU .... Glycol Trim Unit (MCD)
GTU .... Graduate Theological Union, University of Saskatchewan [*UTLAS symbol*]
GTU .... Grand Touring Under 3.0 Liters [*Class of racing cars*]
GTU .... Ground Test Unit
GTU .... Guidance Test Unit
GTUC .... Ghana Trades Union Congress
GTUSIdentBad... Guard, Tomb of the Unknown Soldier Identification Badge [*Military decoration*] (AABC)
GTV .... Empresa de Aviacion Aerogaviota, SA [*Cuba*] [*FAA designator*] (FAAC)
GTV .... Galaxy Cablevision L.P. [*AMEX symbol*] (TTSB)
GTV .... Galaxy Cablevision Ltd. [*AMEX symbol*] (SPSG)
GTV .... Gas Toggle Valve
GTV .... Gate Valve (AAG)
GTV .... Gran Turismo Veloce [*Automobile model designation*]
GTV .... Ground Test Vehicle (KSC)
GTV .... Ground Transport Vehicle
GTV .... Growth Test Vehicle (MCD)
GTV .... Guidance [*or Guided*] Test Vehicle
GTV .... Guided Tactical Vehicle [*Army*]
GTW .... Gateway Aviation [*Zambia*] [*FAA designator*] (FAAC)
GTW .... Global Technology Watch [*Information service or system*] (IID)
GTW .... Good This Week [*Business term*]
GTW .... Gottwaldov [*Former Czechoslovakia*] [*Airport symbol*] (OAG)
GTW .... Grand Trunk Western Railroad Co. [*AAR code*]
GTW .... Gross Takeoff Weight [*of an aircraft*] [*Also, GTOW*]
GTW .... Gross Train Weight (DCTA)
GTW .... Guild of Travel Writers [*British*]
GTWAY .... Gateway [*Commonly used*] (OPSA)
GtWF .... Great Western Financial [*Associated Press*] (SAG)
GtWF .... Great Western Financial Corp. [*Associated Press*] (SAG)
GtWFn .... Great Western Financial Corp. [*Associated Press*] (SAG)
GTWR .... Gross Train Weight Rating
GTWT .... Gridded Traveling-Wave Tube (MCD)
GTWY .... Gateway (MCD)
gtwy........... Gateway (VRA)
GtwyKY........ Gateway Bancorp, Inc. (Kentucky) [*Associated Press*] (SAG)
GTX............. Alma, MI [*Location identifier FAA*] (FAAL)
GTX............. General Tool Experimental (MCD)
GTX............. Gold Texas Resources Ltd. [*Vancouver Stock Exchange symbol*]
GTX............. Gran Turismo Experimental [*Grand Touring, Experimental*] [*Automotive term*]
GTX............. Graphics within Texts (NITA)
GTX............. Grayanotoxin [*Toxicology*] (LDT)
GTX............. Ground Transport Express [*Airport baggage computer*]
GTXT........... Generate Character Text [*Computer science*] (IAA)
GTY............. Getty Petroleum [*NYSE symbol*] (TTSB)
GTY............. Getty Petroleum Corp. [*NYSE symbol*] (SPSG)
GTY............. Greatly (ABBR)
gty............. Gritty [*Quality of the bottom*] [*Nautical charts*]
Gty............. Guaranty (DLA)
GTY............. Guaranty Trustco Ltd. [*Toronto Stock Exchange symbol*]
GTY............. National Aviation Co. [*Egypt*] [*ICAO designator*] (FAAC)
GtyNtl .... Guaranty National Corp. [*Associated Press*] (SAG)
GTZ............. Gran Turismo Zagato [*Automobile model designation*]
GU .... Aviateca [*ICAO designator*] (AD)
GU .... Gasschutzunteroffizier [*Gas Noncommissioned Officer*] [*German military - World War II*]
GU .... Gastric Ulcer [*Medicine*]
GU .... Gear Up [*Aviation*]
GU .... Generations United (EA)
GU .... Generic Unit (TEL)
GU .... Genitourinary [*Medicine*]
GU .... Geographically Undesirable [*Slang*]
GU .... Georgetown University [*Washington, DC*]
GU .... Glycogenic Unit [*Medicine*]
GU .... Gonococcal Urethritis [*Medicine*]
GU .... Grafton & Upton Railroad Co. [*AAR code*]
GU .... Grand United Friendly Society [*Australia*]
GU .... Gravitational Ulcer [*Medicine*]
GU .... Greater Union Organisation [*Australia*]
GU .... Guam [*Postal code*] [*ANSI two-letter standard code*] (CNC)

gu .... Guam [*MARC country of publication code Library of Congress*] (LCCP)
GU .... Guanase [*An enzyme*]
GU .... Guarantee
GU .... Guatemala [*IYRU nationality code*] (IYR)
GU .... Guidance Unit
Gu .... Guillelmus de Tocco [*Authority cited in pre-1607 legal work*] (DSA)
GU .... Guinea
GU .... Gules [*Heraldry*]
GU .... Gunner (ADA)
GU .... University of Georgia, Athens, GA [*Library symbol Library of Congress*] (LCLS)
GUA .... Aerotaxis de Aguascalientes SA de CV [*Mexico ICAO designator*] (FAAC)
GUA .... Group of Units of Analysis [*Medicine*] (DMAA)
GUA .... Guam [*Mariana Islands*] [*Seismograph station code, US Geological Survey*]
Gua .... Guanine [*Also, G*] [*Biochemistry*]
GUA .... Guanine Uracil Adenine [*A triplet of bases coding for the amino acid, valine*] (EES)
gua .... Guarani [*MARC language code Library of Congress*] (LCCP)
GUA .... Guatemala City [*Guatemala*] [*Airport symbol*] (OAG)
GUA .... Guidance Unit Assembly
GUA .... Guinea [*Monetary unit*] [*Obsolete British*] (ROG)
GUA .... International Guards Union of America
GUA .... University of Georgia, Athens, GA [*OCLC symbol*] (OCLC)
GuaAF .... Nieves M. Flores Memorial Library, Agana, Guam [*Library symbol Library of Congress*] (LCLS)
GUAD .... Guadeloupe (ROG)
Gual .... Gualcosius [*Flourished, 11th-12th century*] [*Authority cited in pre-1607 legal work*] (DSA)
Gualc .... Gualcosius [*Flourished, 11th-12th century*] [*Authority cited in pre-1607 legal work*] (DSA)
GUALO .... General Union of Associations of Loom Overlookers [*British*] (DCTA)
Guam Admin R... Administrative Rules and Regulations of the Government of Guam [*A publication*] (DLA)
Guam Civ Code... Guam Civil Code [*A publication*] (DLA)
Guam Code Civ Pro... Guam Code of Civil Procedure [*A publication*] (DLA)
Guam Gov't Code... Guam Government Code [*A publication*] (DLA)
Guam Prob Code... Guam Probate Code [*A publication*] (DLA)
GUAR .... Guarantee (MSA)
Guar .... Guarantee [*Banking*] (TBD)
Guar. .... Guaranteed (EBF)
GUAR .... Guarantee Life Companies, Inc. [*NASDAQ symbol*] (SAG)
GUAR .... Guarantee Life Cos [*NASDAQ symbol*] (TTSB)
Guar. .... Guarnerius [*Irnerius*] [*Flourished, 1113-18*] [*Authority cited in pre-1607 legal work*] (DSA)
GUARD .... Government Employees United Against Discrimination [*An association*]
GUARD .... Guaranteed Assignment Retention Detailing [*Navy*] (NVT)
GUARD FIST... Guard Unit Armor Device Full-Crew Interaction Simulation Trainer
GUARDS ...... Generalized Unified Ammunition Reporting Data System (MCD)
GUARDSMAN... Guidelines and Rules for Data Systems Management (TEL)
GuardTc .... Guardian Technologies International, Inc. [*Associated Press*] (SAG)
GUAREE .... Guarantee (ROG)
GuarFin........ Guaranty Financial Corp. [*Associated Press*] (SAG)
GuarFS .... Guaranty Federal Savings Bank [*Associated Press*] (SAG)
GuarLife ...... Guarantee Life Companies, Inc. [*Associated Press*] (SAG)
GUAROR ..... Guarantor [*Legal term*] (ROG)
GuarSL .... Guaranty Savings & Loan FA [*Associated Press*] (SAG)
GUART........ Guaranty (ABBR)
GUARTE .... Guarantee (ABBR)
GUARTED ..... Guaranteed (ABBR)
GUARTEG .... Guaranteeing (ABBR)
GUARTR ...... Guarantor (ABBR)
GUASO......... Guatemalan Solidarity Committee (EA)
GUAT .... Guatemala
Guat............ Guatemala (VRA)
GuaU .... University of Guam, Agana, GU [*Library symbol Library of Congress*] (LCLS)
GUB .... Generalized Upper Bounding [*Computer science*]
GUB .... Government Union of Burma
GUB .... Greatest Upper Bound [*Computer science*]
GUB .... Guerrero Negro [*Mexico*] [*Airport symbol*]
GUB .... Law School Library, University of Georgia, Athens, GA [*OCLC symbol*] (OCLC)
GUBA .... Growing Up Born Again [*Pronounced "goobah"*] [*Book published by Fleming H. Revell Co.*]
GUBER........ Gubernatorial (ABBR)
GUBGF........ General Union of Bellhangers and Gas Fitters [*British*]
GUBI........... Gemeinschaft Unabhangiger Beratender Ingenieurbueros [*Association of German Consulting Engineers*]
GUBL .... Beyla [*Guinea*] [*ICAO location identifier*] (ICLI)
GUBR.......... Gentleman Usher of the Black Rod [*British*] (ROG)
GUBSMW..... General Union of Braziers and Sheet Metal Workers [*British*]
GUBTW .... General Union of Bedding Trade Workers [*British*]
GUBU.......... Grotesque, Unbelievable, Bizarre, Unprecedented [*Term coined by an Irish politician to describe certain incidents in Irish politics*]
GUC .... Good-until-Canceled Order [*Business term*]
GUC .... Groupe d'Union Camerounaise [*Group for Cameroonian Union*]
GUC .... Guanine Uracil Cytosine [*A triplet of bases coding for the amino acid, valine*] (EES)
GUC .... Gucci Group NV [*NYSE symbol*] (SAG)
GUC .... Gunnison [*Colorado*] [*Airport symbol*] (OAG)

GUC .... Union Catalog of the Atlanta-Athens Area, Atlanta, GA [*OCLC symbol*] (OCLC)
Gucci .... Gucci Group NV [*Associated Press*] (SAG)
GUCCIAAC ... General Union of Chamber of Commerce, Industry and Agriculture for Arab Countries [*Lebanon*] (EAIO)
GUCCO......... Guidance Computer Control Subsystem
GUCJ .... General Union of Carpenters and Joiners [*British*]
GUCL .... General-Use Consumable List [*Military*]
GUCO .... Grand Union [*NASDAQ symbol*] (TTSB)
GUCO .... Grand Union Co. [*NASDAQ symbol*] (SAG)
GUCO .... Guilford Courthouse National Military Park
GUCOTROIS... Great, Unopposable Commandant of the Realm of Inextinguishable Sagacity [*Rank in Junior Woodchucks organization mentioned in Donald Duck comic by Carl Barks*]
GUCOW........ Grand Un Wrrt Ser 1 [*NASDAQ symbol*] (TTSB)
GUCOZ........ Grand Un Wrrt Ser 2 [*NASDAQ symbol*] (TTSB)
GUCP .... Ground Umbilical Carrier Plate (MCD)
GUCY .... Conakry/Gbessia [*Guinea*] [*ICAO location identifier*] (ICLI)
GUD .... Good [*Amateur radio shorthand*] (WDAA)
GUD .... Goundam [*Mali*] [*Airport symbol*] (OAG)
GUD .... Guardian Resources Corp. [*Vancouver Stock Exchange symbol*]
GUD .... Guide (ABBR)
GUDBK .... Guidebook (ABBR)
GUDD.......... Didi [*Guinea*] [*ICAO location identifier*] (ICLI)
GUDD.......... Guided (ABBR)
GU-De .... University of Georgia, DeRenne Georgia Library, Athens, GA [*Library symbol Library of Congress*] (LCLS)
Gude Pr .... Gude. Practice of the Crown Side of the Court of King's Bench [*1828*] [*A publication*] (DLA)
GUDG.......... Guiding (ABBR)
GUDNC........ Guidance (ABBR)
GUDPST....... Guidepost (ABBR)
GUDSPA ...... General Union Democratic Students and Patriotic Afghan (EA)
GUE .... Graphical User Environment [*Computer science*]
GUE .... Group for the European Unitarian Left [*EC*] (ECED)
GUE .... University of Guelph [*UTLAS symbol*]
GUER .... Guerilla
GUERAP....... General Unwanted Energy Rejection Analysis Program [*Air Force*]
GUERL .... Guerilla (ABBR)
Guern Eq Jur... Guernsey's Key to Equity Jurisprudence [*A publication*] (DLA)
Guern Ins..... Guernsey on Questions of Insanity [*A publication*] (DLA)
Guern Mech L... Guernsey's Mechanics' Lien Laws of New York [*A publication*] (DLA)
GUESS .... General Purpose Expert System Shell [*Virginia Polytechnic Institute*] [*General framework for expert systems*] (NITA)
GuestS......... Guest Supply, Inc. [*Associated Press*] (SAG)
GUF .... French Guiana [*ANSI three-letter standard code*] (CNC)
GUF .... General University Funds (EERA)
GUF .... Global University Funding
GUF .... Grand Unified Force
GUFA .... Fria [*Guinea*] [*ICAO location identifier*] (ICLI)
GUFEX .... Gulf Underwater Flare Experiment [*Marine science*] (MSC)
GUFFAW ...... Government Undertaking for Finding Another Way [*Parliamentary slang*] [*British*] (DI)
GUFH .... Faranah/Badala [*Guinea*] [*ICAO location identifier*] (ICLI)
GUFMEX ...... Gulf of Mexico [*Project*] [*Marine science*] (OSRA)
GUFS .... Grand United Friendly Society [*Australia*]
GUFSA .... Griffith University Faculty Staff Association [*Australia*]
GUG .... Empresa Guatemalteca de Aviacion [*Guatemala*] [*ICAO designator*] (FAAC)
GUG .... Guanine Uracil Guanine [*A triplet of bases coding for the amino acid, valine*] (EES)
GUG .... Guari [*Papua New Guinea*] [*Airport symbol*] (OAG)
GUG .... N'Guigmi [*Niger*] [*Airport symbol*] (AD)
GUGA .... Grounded Unity Gain Amplifier (IAA)
GuGIC .... Instituto de Nutricion de Centro America y Panama, Guatemala City, Guatemala [*Library symbol Library of Congress*] (LCLS)
GuGIN .... Instituto Centro Americano de Investigacion y Tecnologia Industrial, Guatemala City, Guatemala [*Library symbol*] [*Library of Congress*] (LCLS)
GUGL .... Gaoual [*Guinea*] [*ICAO location identifier*] (ICLI)
GUGO......... Banankoro/Gbenko [*Guinea*] [*ICAO location identifier*] (ICLI)
GUGR.......... Gentleman Usher of the Green Rod [*British*] (ROG)
GuGS .... Universidad de San Carlos de Guatemala, Ciudad Universitaria, Guatemala City, Guatemala [*Library symbol Library of Congress*] (LCLS)
GUH .... Gunnedah [*Australia Airport symbol*] (OAG)
GUHA .... General Unary Hypothesis Automation (IEEE)
GUI .... Gay Union International [*Paris, France*] (EAIO)
GUI .... Genitourinary Infection [*Medicine*] (PDAA)
GUI .... Golfing Union of Ireland (EAIO)
GUI .... Graphical User Interface [*Computer science*] (EERA)
GUI .... Guiana (ROG)
Gui .... Guido de Cumis [*Flourished, 13th century*] [*Authority cited in pre-1607 legal work*] (DSA)
Gui.............. Guido de Suzaria [*Deceased, 1293*] [*Authority cited in pre-1607 legal work*] (DSA)
Gui.............. Guillelmus de Accursio [*Deceased, 1314*] [*Authority cited in pre-1607 legal work*] (DSA)
Gui.............. Guillelmus de Tocco [*Authority cited in pre-1607 legal work*] (DSA)
GUI .... Guiria [*Venezuela*] [*Airport symbol*] (OAG)
GUI .... Guitar [*Music*]
GUIAC......... Guaiacum [*Lignum Vitae*] [*Pharmacy*] (ROG)
GUIB .... Graphical User Interface for Blind People
GUID .... Globally Unique Identifier (PCM)

GUID............ Globally Unique Identifiers [*Microsoft Corp.*] [*Computer science*] (PCM)
GUID............ Guidance (AAG)
GUID............ Guide
GUID............ Kindia [*Guinea*] [*ICAO location identifier*] (ICLI)
Guidant........ Guidant Corp. [*Associated Press*] (SAG)
GUIDAR .... Guided Intrusion Detection and Ranging (PDAA)
GUIDE.......... General Usage Inventory Director (MCD)
GUIDE.......... Guidance for Users of Integrated Data Processing Equipment
Gui de Cu .... Guillelmus de Cuneo [*Deceased, 1335*] [*Authority cited in pre-1607 legal work*] (DSA)
Gui de Su .... Guido de Suzaria [*Deceased, 1293*] [*Authority cited in pre-1607 legal work*] (DSA)
Gui de Suz... Guido de Suzaria [*Deceased, 1293*] [*Authority cited in pre-1607 legal work*] (DSA)
Gui de Suza... Guido de Suzaria [*Deceased, 1293*] [*Authority cited in pre-1607 legal work*] (DSA)
GUIDN .... Guidance (AABC)
GUIDNC .... Guidance
GUIDO .... Guidance and Navigation Officer [*NASA*]
GUIDO .... Guidance Officer [*Aerospace*] (NAKS)
Guid Pancir... Guido Pancirolus [*Deceased, 1599*] [*Authority cited in pre-1607 legal work*] (DSA)
Guid Pancirol... Guido Pancirolus [*Deceased, 1599*] [*Authority cited in pre-1607 legal work*] (DSA)
Guid Pap ..... Guido Papa [*Deceased, 1487*] [*Authority cited in pre-1607 legal work*] (DSA)
GUIL .... Guilder (ABBR)
Guil Bene .... Guillelmus de Benedictis [*Flourished, 16th century*] [*Authority cited in pre-1607 legal work*] (DSA)
GUILD.......... Government, University, Industry, Laboratory Development [*Microelectronics*]
GUILDF........ Guildford [*City in England*] (ROG)
GUILDHL....... Guildhall (ABBR)
Guild Law.... Guild Lawyer [*National Lawyers' Guild*] [*New York Chapter*] [*A publication*] (DLA)
Guild Q .... National Lawyers Guild Quarterly [*A publication*] (DLA)
GUILFL......... Guileful (ABBR)
Guilford .... Guilford Mills, Inc. [*Associated Press*] (SAG)
GuilfrdP .... Guilford Pharmaceuticals, Inc. [*Associated Press*] (SAG)
GUILFY .... Guilefully (ABBR)
Guill........... Guillelmus Durandi [*Deceased, 1296*] [*Authority cited in pre-1607 legal work*] (DSA)
Guill de Montelaud... Guillelmus de Monte Lauduno [*Deceased, 1343*] [*Authority cited in pre-1607 legal work*] (DSA)
Guillel Bened... Guillelmus de Benedictis [*Flourished, 16th century*] [*Authority cited in pre-1607 legal work*] (DSA)
Guil Na........ Guillelmus Naso [*Flourished, 1220-34*] [*Authority cited in pre-1607 legal work*] (DSA)
GUILS .... Guileless (ABBR)
GUILSY .... Guilelessly (ABBR)
GUIMARC .... Guidelines Marketing Corp.
GUIN........... Guinea [*Monetary unit*] [*Obsolete British*] (ROG)
Guin........... Guinea (VRA)
GUIRR .... Government-University-Industry Research Roundtable [*Academy of Sciences*]
GUISE.......... Guidance System Evaluation [*Military*] (IAA)
Guit............ Guitar [*Music*]
Guiz........... Guizzardinus [*Deceased, 1222*] [*Authority cited in pre-1607 legal work*] (DSA)
Guizot Rep Govt... Guizot's History of Representative Government [*A publication*] (DLA)
GUJ............. Guaratingueta [*Brazil*] [*Airport symbol*] (OAG)
guj............. Gujarati [*MARC language code Library of Congress*] (LCCP)
Guj Ind........ Gujarat, India (ILCA)
Guj L Rep.... Gujarat Law Reporter [*A publication*] (ILCA)
GUK .... Guanylate Kinase [*An enzyme*]
GUKE.......... Kerouane [*Guinea*] [*ICAO location identifier*] (ICLI)
GUKR.......... Glavnoe Upravlenie Kontrrazvedkoi [*Chief Administration for Counter-intelligence*] [*of the Ministry of War*] [*Former USSR*] [*World War II*]
GUKR.......... Kamsar/Kawass [*Guinea*] [*ICAO location identifier*] (ICLI)
GUKU.......... Kissidougou [*Guinea*] [*ICAO location identifier*] (ICLI)
GUL .... Georgetown University, Law Library, Washington, DC [*OCLC symbol*] (OCLC)
GUL .... GSE [*Ground Support Equipment*] Utilization List [*NASA*] (NASA)
Gul............. Guillelmus de Cuneo [*Deceased, 1335*] [*Authority cited in pre-1607 legal work*] (DSA)
GUL .... Gull Air [*ICAO designator*] (FAAC)
GUL .... Gull Laboratories [*AMEX symbol*] (TTSB)
GUL .... Gull Laboratories, Inc. [*AMEX symbol*] (SPSG)
GUL .... Gully (ABBR)
GUL .... Gulmarg [*India*] [*Geomagnetic observatory code*]
GU-L .... University of Georgia, Law Library, Athens, GA [*Library symbol Library of Congress*] (LCLS)
GULAG........ Glavnoe Upravlenie Ispravitel'no-Trudovykh Lagerei [*Main Administration of Corrective Labor Camps*] [*Former USSR*]
GULB .... Gullible (ABBR)
GULB .... Labe/Tata [*Guinea*] [*ICAO location identifier*] (ICLI)
GULBLY .... Gullibly (ABBR)
GULBT .... Gullibility (ABBR)
GULC .... Georgetown University Law Center (AAGC)
GULC .... Glasgow University Language Centre [*University of Glasgow*] [*British*] (CB)
GULD .... Goulds Pumps [*NASDAQ symbol*] (TTSB)

GULD .... Goulds Pumps, Inc. [*NASDAQ symbol*] (NQ)
GULF .... Gulfwest Oil [*NASDAQ symbol*] (TTSB)
GULFCO....... Gulf United Corp. (EFIS)
GULFCOBASESERVUNIT... Gulf Coast Base Service Unit
GULFCON ..... Gulf Control
GULFNAVFACENGCOM... Gulf Division Naval Facilities Engineering Command
GULFSEAFRON... Gulf Sea Frontier
GulfSou........ Gulf South Medical Supply [*Associated Press*] (SAG)
GulfSou........ Sulf South Medical Supply [*Associated Press*] (SAG)
Gulfwest ..... Gulfwest Oil Co. [*Associated Press*] (SAG)
GULHEMP..... General Physique, Upper Extremity, Lower Extremity, Hearing, Eyesight, Mentality, and Personality [*Medicine*] (DMAA)
GULL .... Guillotine [*Bookbinding*] (DGA)
GullLb......... Gull Laboratories, Inc. [*Associated Press*] (SAG)
GULO .... General Union of Loom Overlookers (WDAA)
GULP .... General Upgrade LAN [*Limited Access Network*] Program [*Computer science*] (PCM)
GULP .... General Utility Library Program [*Computer science*]
GULP .... Grenada United Labour Party [*Political party*] (PPW)
GULP .... Group Universal Life Policy [*Insurance*] (DFIT)
GULP .... Group Universal Life Program
GULT .... Gullet (ABBR)
GULTN......... Guillotine (ABBR)
GULTND........ Guillotined (ABBR)
GULTNG........ Guillotining (ABBR)
GULYG......... Gullying (ABBR)
GUM .... General Utility Mechanic
GUM .... Glavnoe Upravleniye Militsii [*Main Administration of Militia*] [*Former USSR*] (LAIN)
GUM .... Glavny Universalny Magazin [*Department store in USSR*]
GUM .... Gosudarstvennyi Universal'nyi Magazin [*Government Department Store*] [*Moscow*]
GUM .... Grand Unified Monopoles [*Cosmology*]
GUM .... Guadalajara [*Mexico*] [*Seismograph station code, US Geological Survey*] (SEIS)
GUM .... Guam [*ANSI three-letter standard code*] (CNC)
GUM .... Guam [*Marianas*] [*Airport symbol*] (AD)
GUM .... Gulderand Mining [*Vancouver Stock Exchange symbol*]
GUMA .... Macenta [*Guinea*] [*ICAO location identifier*] (ICLI)
GUMM .... GumTech International, Inc. [*NASDAQ symbol*] (SAG)
GUMM .... GumTech Intl [*NASDAQ symbol*] (TTSB)
GUMMW........ GumTech Intl Wrrt [*NASDAQ symbol*] (TTSB)
GUMNS........ Gumminess (ABBR)
GUMO .... Guam [*Mariana Islands*] [*Seismograph station code, US Geological Survey*] (SEIS)
GUMP .... Gas, Undercarriage, Mixture, and Prop [*Checkout procedure*]
GumT.......... GumTech International, Inc. [*Associated Press*] (SAG)
GumTch .... GumTech International, Inc. [*Associated Press*] (SAG)
GUMZ .... Glavnoye Upravleniye Mestami Zaklyucheniya [*Main Administration of Places of Detention*] [*Former USSR*] (LAIN)
GUN .... Grantor Underwritten Note [*Banking*]
GUN .... Guaranteed Underwriting Facilities (TDOB)
GUN .... Guaranteed Underwritten Note (EBF)
GUN .... Guncotton (ABBR)
GUN .... Guncrete (ABBR)
GUN .... Gundle Environmental Systems, Inc. [*AMEX symbol*] (SPSG)
GUN .... Gundle/SLT Environmental [*AMEX symbol*] (TTSB)
GUN .... Gunnery (MSA)
GUN .... Gunny (ABBR)
GUN .... Gunpowder (ABBR)
GUN .... Gunsteel Resources, Inc. [*Vancouver Stock Exchange symbol*]
GUN .... Montgomery, AL [*Location identifier FAA*] (FAAL)
GUNBT........ Gunboat (ABBR)
Gunby .... Gunby's District Court Reports [*1885*] [*Louisiana*] [*A publication*] (DLA)
Gunby (LA)... Gunby's District Court Reports [*1885*] [*Louisiana*] [*A publication*] (DLA)
Gunby's Dec... Gunby's District Court Reports [*1805*] [*Louisiana*] [*A publication*] (DLA)
GUND .... Gunned (ABBR)
Gundle........ Gundle-SLT Environmental Systems, Inc. [*Associated Press*] (SAG)
Gundry........ Gundry. Manuscripts in Lincoln's Inn Library [*A publication*] (DLA)
GUNEX .... Gunnery Exercise [*Navy*] (NVT)
GUNFIT........ Gunfight (ABBR)
GUNFITR....... Gunfighter (ABBR)
GUNFR........ Gunfire (ABBR)
GUNG.......... Gunning (ABBR)
GUNMA........ Gunman (ABBR)
GUN MOLL... Gonif's Molly [*Thief's Girl*] [*Yiddish*]
Gunn Tolls... Gunning on Tolls [*A publication*] (DLA)
GUNPWDR..... Gunpowder (ABBR)
GUNR.......... Gunner (ABBR)
GUNRY .... Gunnery (ABBR)
GUNSGT .... Gunnery Sergeant
GUNSH........ Gunshot (ABBR)
GUNSM........ Gunsmith (ABBR)
GUNSS........ Gunnery Schoolship [*Navy*] (NVT)
GUNST........ Gunstock (ABBR)
GUNWHL ..... Gunwhale (ABBR)
GUNYBG ...... Gunnybag (ABBR)
GUNZ .... N,Zerekore/Konia [*Guinea*] [*ICAO location identifier*] (ICLI)
GUO .... Georgetown, TX [*Location identifier FAA*] (FAAL)
GUO .... Government Use Only (WDAA)
Guo .... Guanosine [*Also, G*] [*A nucleoside*]
GUOK .... Boke/Baralande [*Guinea*] [*ICAO location identifier*] (ICLI)

GUOO	Grand United Order of Oddfellows [*Australia*]
GUOOF	Grand United Order of Odd Fellows (EA)
GUP	Gallup [*New Mexico*] [*Airport symbol*] (OAG)
GUP	Gas Under Pressure
GUP	Glass-Fiber-Reinforced Unsaturated Polyester [*Organic chemistry*]
GU-P	Grifora Umbellata Polysaccharide [*Antineoplastic drug*]
GUP	Guppy (ABBR)
GU-P	University of Georgia, School of Pharmacy, Athens, GA [*Library symbol Library of Congress*] (LCLS)
GUPAC	Gulf Permanent Assistance Committee [*Persian Gulf*]
GUPB	GFS Bancorp [*NASDAQ symbol*] (TTSB)
GUPB	GFSB Bancorp, Inc. [*NASDAQ symbol*] (SAG)
GUPH	Group for the Use of Psychology in History (EA)
Guppie	Gay Urban Professional [*Lifestyle classification*]
GUPPY	Greater Underwater Propulsive Power [*Type of submarine*]
GUPS	Grand Unified Problem Solver
Gupta	Gupta Corp. [*Associated Press*] (SAG)
GUQ	Guanare [*Venezuela*] [*Airport symbol*] (OAG)
GUR	Alotau [*Papua New Guinea*] [*Airport symbol*] (OAG)
GUR	Ground under Repair
GUR	Gulfstream Resources Canada Ltd. [*Toronto Stock Exchange symbol*]
GUR	Gurgu (ABBR)
GURC	Gulf Universities Research Consortium (EA)
GURC	Gulf Universities Research Corp.
GURGLD	Gurgled (ABBR)
GURGLG	Gurgling (ABBR)
GURNT	Guarantee (ABBR)
GURNTD	Guaranteed (ABBR)
GURNTG	Guarantying (ABBR)
GURNTR	Guarantor (ABBR)
GURNTY	Guaranty (ABBR)
GURR	Gentleman Usher of the Red Rod [*British*] (ROG)
GURS	Kouroussa [*Guinea*] [*ICAO location identifier*] (ICLI)
GURTG	Guaranteeing (ABBR)
Gus	Conductance of Upstream Segment [*Physics*] (DAVI)
GUS	Generic Update System [*Computer science*]
GUS	Generic User System [*Computer science*]
GUS	Genitourinary System [*Medicine*]
GUS	Give Up Smoking [*Health Education Council campaign*] [*British*]
GUS	Glucuronidase [*An enzyme*]
GUS	Great Universal Stores [*Mail-order firm*] [*British*]
GUS	Group Unit Simulator (MCD)
GUS	Gunflint Resources Ltd. [*Vancouver Stock Exchange symbol*]
GUS	Gusset (MSA)
GUS	Peru, IN [*Location identifier FAA*] (FAAL)
GUSA	Sangaredi [*Guinea*] [*ICAO location identifier*] (ICLI)
GUSB	Guided Unified S-Band (MCD)
GUSB	Sambailo [*Guinea*] [*ICAO location identifier*] (ICLI)
GUSER	GCOS Security Module
GUSH	Fountain Oil [*NASDAQ symbol*] (TTSB)
GUSH	Fountain Oil, Inc. [*NASDAQ symbol*] (SAG)
GUSHD	CanArgo Energy [*NASDAQ symbol*] [*Formerly, Fountain Oil*]
GUSHG	Gushing (ABBR)
GUSHNS	Gushiness (ABBR)
GUSHR	Gushier (ABBR)
GUSHST	Gushiest (ABBR)
GUSI	Siguiri [*Guinea*] [*ICAO location identifier*] (ICLI)
GUSS	Guided Social Simulation
GUSSIES	Great Universal Stores [*Mail-order firm*] [*British*]
GUST	Gusset (ABBR)
GUSTNS	Gustiness (ABBR)
GUSTO	Global Utilization of Streptokinase and Tissue Plasminogen Activator for Occluded Coronary Arteries [*Cardiology study*]
GUSTO	Global Utilization of Streptokinase and TPA [*Tissue Plasminogen Activator*]for Occluded Arteries [*Comparative study*]
GUSTO	Guidance Using Stable Tuning Oscillations
GUSTR	Gustier (ABBR)
GUSTST	Gustiest (ABBR)
GUSTY	Gustily (ABBR)
GUT	Grand Unified Theory [*Cosmology*]
GUT	Gulf Titanium Ltd. [*Vancouver Stock Exchange symbol*]
GUT	Gutter (MSA)
GUT	Pittsburgh, PA [*Location identifier FAA*] (FAAL)
Gut Brac	Guterbock's Bracton [*A publication*] (DLA)
GUTD	Gutted (ABBR)
GUTG	Gutting (ABBR)
Guth L & T...	Guthrie's Landlord and Tenant [*A publication*] (DLA)
Guth Pr	Guthrie's Principles of the Laws of England [*1843*] [*A publication*] (DLA)
Guthrie	Guthrie's Reports [*33-83 Missouri Appeals*] [*A publication*] (DLA)
Guthrie	Guthrie's Sheriff Court Cases [*1861-92*] [*Scotland*] [*A publication*] (DLA)
Guth Sh Cas...	Guthrie's Sheriff Court Cases [*1861-92*] [*Scotland*] [*A publication*] (DLA)
Guth Sher Cas...	Guthrie's Sheriff Court Cases [*1861-92*] [*Scotland*] [*A publication*] (DLA)
Guth Tr Un...	Guthrie on Trade Unions [*A publication*] (DLA)
GUTR	Gutter (ABBR)
GUTRL	Gutteral (ABBR)
GUTRY	Gutterally (ABBR)
GUTS	Game on Urban Transport System [*Kins Developments Ltd.*] [*Software package*] (NCC)
GUTS	Georgians Unwilling to Surrender [*Organization founded by former governor, Lester Maddox*]
GUTS	Gothenburg University Terminal System [*IBM Corp.*] (EECA)
GUTS	Ground Up-to-Space (MCD)
GUTS	Guerilla Urban Traffic System [*Refers to driving in Boston*]
gutt	Goutte [*Drop*] [*Pharmacy*]
GUTT	Grand Unified Theory of the Tire
GUTT	Guttae [*Drops of Liquid*] [*Pharmacy*]
GUTT	Gutturi [*To the Throat*] [*Pharmacy*]
GUTTAT	Guttatim [*Drop by Drop*] [*Pharmacy*] (GPO)
GUTT QUIBUSD...	Guttis Quibusdam [*With a Few Drops*] [*Pharmacy*]
GUU	Grundarfjordur [*Iceland*] [*Airport symbol*] (OAG)
GUU	Guanine Uracil Uracil [*A triplet of bases coding for the amino acid, valine*] (EES)
GUU	Gulu [*Uganda*] [*Airport symbol*] (AD)
GUUAM	Georgia, Ukraine, Uzbekistan, Azerbaijan and Moldova
GUUG	Gross Unit Unavailable Generation [*Electronics*] (IEEE)
GUV	Gerecht und Volkommen [*Correct and Complete*] [*German*]
GUV	Guri [*Venezuela*] [*Seismograph station code, US Geological Survey*] (SEIS)
GUXD	Kankan/Diankana [*Guinea*] [*ICAO location identifier*] (ICLI)
GUY	Air Guyane [*France ICAO designator*] (FAAC)
GUY	French Guiana Space Center
GUY	Guyana [*ANSI three-letter standard code*] (CNC)
GUY	Guymon, OK [*Location identifier FAA*] (FAAL)
Guy For Med...	Guy's Forensic Medicine [*7th ed.*] [*1895*] [*A publication*] (DLA)
Guy Med Jur...	Guy's Medical Jurisprudence [*A publication*] (DLA)
Guyot Inst Feod...	Guyot's Instituts Feodales [*A publication*] (DLA)
Guy Rep	Guy's Repertoire de la Jurisprudence [*A publication*] (DLA)
GUZ	Guiratinga [*Brazil*] [*Airport symbol*] (AD)
GUZL	Guzzle (ABBR)
GUZLD	Guzzled (ABBR)
GUZLG	Guzzling (ABBR)
GUZLR	Guzzler (ABBR)
GV	Galvanized [*Technical drawings*]
GV	Gastric Volume [*Medicine*] (DMAA)
GV	Gas Ventilation [*Medicine*] (DMAA)
GV	Gate Valve (DAC)
GV	Genital Vein
GV	Gentian Violet [*Also, MRC*] [*A dye*]
GV	Germinal Vesicle (PDAA)
GV	Gigavolt
GV	Girls Volunteers [*Australia*]
GV	Give (ABBR)
GV	Goerz-Visier [*Bomb sight manufactured by Goerz Co.*] [*German military - World War II*]
GV	Goldfield Corp. [*AMEX symbol*] (SPSG)
GV	Gomphrena Virus [*Plant pathology*]
GV	Governor (DSUE)
GV	Governor of Victoria [*Australia*]
GV	Granulosis Virus
GV	Gravimetric Volume
G-V	Gravity-Velocity (MCD)
GV	Great Value [*In automobile name Yugo GV*]
GV	Green Valley [*Plant pathology*]
GV	Grid Variation [*Navigation*]
GV	Gross Virus [*Leukemogenesis*] [*Immunochemistry*]
GV	Ground Visibility
GV	Groundwater Vistas [*Computer science*]
GV	Group Velocity [*Physics*] (IAA)
GV	Growth Vessel
GV	Grow Victoria [*Mental health organisation*] [*Australia*]
GV	Guard Vessel [*Nuclear energy*] (NRCH)
gv	Guinea [*MARC country of publication code Library of Congress*] (LCCP)
G V	Gulfstream V
GV	Gulp Valve [*Automotive engineering*]
GV	Talair [*ICAO designator*] (AD)
GVA	Gamewardens of Vietnam Association (EA)
GVA	Gay Veterans Association (EA)
GVA	General Visceral Afferent [*Neurology*]
GVA	Geneva [*Switzerland*] [*Airport symbol*] (OAG)
GVA	Geschichte Vorderasien bis zum Hellenismus [*A publication*] (BJA)
GVA	Golden Nevada [*Vancouver Stock Exchange symbol*]
GVA	Golden Nevada Resources, Inc. [*Toronto Stock Exchange symbol*]
GVA	Goulburn Valley Airlines [*Australia*]
GVA	GOX [*Gaseous Oxygen*] Vent Arm (NASA)
GVA	Grapevine Virus A [*Plant pathology*]
GVA	Graphic Kilovolt-Ampere [*Meter*] (MSA)
GVA	Gyroscope Vibration Absorber
GVA	Henderson, KY [*Location identifier FAA*] (FAAL)
GVAC	Amilcar Cabral International/Sal Island [*Cape Verde*] [*ICAO location identifier*] (ICLI)
GVAC	Graphic Video Attributes Controller [*Computer chip*]
GVAL	Global Vaccine Awareness League (EA)
GVAO	Gross Value of Agricultural Output
GVaP	GEWEX [*Global Energy and Water Cycle Experiment*] Water Vapor Project [*Marine science*] (OSRA)
GVaS	Valdosta State College, Valdosta, GA [*Library symbol Library of Congress*] (LCLS)
GVAWY	Giveaway (ABBR)
GVB	Gelatine Veronal Buffer (PDAA)
GVB	Generalized Valence Bond [*Physics*]
GVB	Grapevine Virus B [*Plant pathology*]
GVB	Guaranteed Voltage Breakdown
GVBA	Boavista, Boavista Island [*Cape Verde*] [*ICAO location identifier*] (ICLI)

GVBD .... Germinal Vesicle Breakdown [*Cytology*]
GVC .... General Videotex Corp.
GVC .... Girls' Venture Corps [*British*] (BI)
GVC .... Glazed Vitrified Clay
GVC .... Grand View College [*Iowa*]
GVC .... Graphics Vendor Control
GVC .... Guild Vector Colorimeter
GVCAC .... Girls' Venture Corps Air Cadets [*British*] (DBA)
GVCO .... Grants to Voluntary Conservation Organisations (EERA)
GVD .... Gravdal [*Norway*] [*Airport symbol*] (AD)
GVD .... Group View Display (MCD)
GVDSN .... Gott Verlaeszt die Seinen Nicht [*God Forsakes Not His Own*] [*Motto of Dorothee, Duchess of Braunschweig-Wolfenbuttel (1607-34)*] [*German*]
GVE .... General Visceral Efferent [*Neurology*]
GVE .... Gordonsville, VA [*Location identifier FAA*] (FAAL)
GVE .... Group Value Engineering
GVE .... Grove (ADA)
GVF .... Garnisonsverwendungsfaehig Feld [*Fit for Garrison Duty in the Field*] [*German military - World War II*]
GVF .... Good Visual Field [*Ophthalmology*] (DAVI)
GVF .... Grazhdanskii Vozdushnyi Flot [*Civil Air Fleet*] [*Former USSR*]
GVFM .... Francisco Mendes, Santiago Island [*Cape Verde*] [*ICAO location identifier*] (ICLI)
GVG .... Flygaktiebolaget Gota Vingar [*Sweden*] [*FAA designator*] (FAAC)
GVG .... Gamma-Vinyl-GABA [*Biochemistry*]
GVG .... Giving (FAAC)
GVG .... Grundriss der Vergleichenden Grammatik der Semitischen Sprachen [*A publication*] (BJA)
GVGI .... General Visual Slope Indicator [*FAA*] (TAG)
GVGSS .... Grundriss der Vergleichenden Grammatik der Semitischen Sprachen [*A publication*] (BJA)
GVH .... Garnisonsverwendungsfaehig Heimat [*Fit for Garrison Duty in Zone of Interior*] [*German military - World War II*]
GVH .... Government Vehicle (FAAC)
GVH .... Graft Versus Host [*Immunology*]
GVHBCIFC.. Gene Vincent and His Blue Caps International Fan Club (EAIO)
GvHD .... Graft-Versus Host Disease [*Immunology*]
GvHR .... Graft-Versus-Host Reaction (STED)
GVHR .... Graft-Versus-Host Reaction [*Immunology*]
GVHRR .... Geosynchronous Very-High-Resolution Radiometer
GVI .... Gas Vent Institute [*Defunct*] (EA)
GVI .... Global Vegetation Index (MCD)
GVI .... Green River [*Papua New Guinea*] [*Airport symbol*] (OAG)
GVIAO .... Gross Value of Industrial and Agricultural Output
GVIdO .... Ohoopee Regional Library, Vidalia, GA [*Library symbol Library of Congress*] (LCLS)
GVIL .... Global Village Commun [*NASDAQ symbol*] (TTSB)
GVIL .... Global Village Communications, Inc. [*NASDAQ symbol*] (SAG)
GVIO .... Gross Value of Industrial Output
GVL .... Gainesville [*Georgia*] [*Airport symbol*] (AD)
GVL .... Gainesville, GA [*Location identifier FAA*] (FAAL)
GVL .... Gero Vita Laboratories
GVL .... Gold Vapor LASER [*Physics*]
GVL .... Gold Ventures Ltd. [*Vancouver Stock Exchange symbol*]
GvL .... Graft-Versus-Leukemia [*Medicine*]
GVL .... Gravel (KSC)
G/VLLD .... Ground/Vehicle Laser Locator Designation [*Homing device*] (NITA)
G/VLL-D .... Ground Vehicular LASER Locator Designator [*Military*]
GVM .... Generating Volt Meter (PDAA)
GVMA .... Maio, Maio Island [*Cape Verde*] [*ICAO location identifier*] (ICLI)
GVMDS .... Ground Vehicle Mine Dispensing System [*Military*]
GVMR .... Gross Vehicle Mass Rating [*Load that a vehicle can carry*]
GVMT .... Mosteiros, Fogo Island [*Cape Verde*] [*ICAO location identifier*] (ICLI)
GVN .... Given (ABBR)
GVN .... Goodyear Video Network [*Training and motivational program*]
GVN .... Government of Vietnam
GVO .... Gaviota, CA [*Location identifier FAA*] (FAAL)
GVO .... Graeber-Verwaltungsoffizier [*Graves Registration Officer*] [*German military - World War II*]
GVO .... Gross Value of Output (MHDW)
GVP .... Gasoline Vapor Pressure (GNE)
GVP .... General Vice President (WDAA)
GVP .... Gesamtdeutsche Volkspartei [*All-German People's Party*] [*Germany Political party*] (PPE)
GVP .... Government Vehicle Pool [*Victoria, Australia*]
GVP .... Gravis Computer Peripherals, Inc. [*Vancouver Stock Exchange symbol*]
GVP .... Greater Victoria Public Library [*UTLAS symbol*]
GVP .... Gross Value of Production
GVP .... Group Visionary Productions, Inc. [*Studio City, CA*] [*Telecommunications*] (TSSD)
GVPF .... Guinea Pig Vascular Permeability Factor [*Biochemistry*]
GVPM .... Grootvlei Proprietary Mines Ltd. [*NASDAQ symbol*] (SAG)
GVPN .... Global Virtual Private Network [*Computer science*] (CDE)
GVPR .... Praia/Praia, Santiago Island [*Cape Verde*] [*ICAO location identifier*] (ICLI)
GVQ .... Batavia, NY [*Location identifier FAA*] (FAAL)
GVR .... Gas Volume Ratio (COE)
GVR .... Glyn Valley Railway [*Formerly, E & GVR*] [*Wales*]
GVR .... Governador Valadares [*Brazil*] [*Airport symbol*] (OAG)
GVR .... Granville Resources, Inc. [*Vancouver Stock Exchange symbol*]
GVR .... Gray-Votaw-Rogers [*Psychology*] (AEBS)
GVR .... Green Valley Road [*California*] [*Seismograph station code, US Geological Survey*] (SEIS)

GVRNMTL.... Governmental
GVS .... Global Videophone Standard [*Telecommunications*] (CDE)
GVS .... Government Vehicle Service [*Postal Service*]
GVS .... Graniteville [*South Carolina*] [*Seismograph station code, US Geological Survey Closed*] (SEIS)
GVS .... Ground Vibration Survey [*Aerospace*]
GVSC .... Sal Oceanic Area Control Center [*Cape Verde*] [*ICAO location identifier*] (ICLI)
GVSF .... Sao Felipe, Fogo Island [*Cape Verde*] [*ICAO location identifier*] (ICLI)
GVSN .... Sao Nicolau, Sao Nicolau Island [*Cape Verde*] [*ICAO location identifier*] (ICLI)
GV-SOLAS ... Gesellschaft fuer Versuchstierkunde - Society of Labortory Animal Science [*Switzerland*] (EAIO)
G vs T .... Deceleration Units of Gravity versus Time (KSC)
GVSU .... Grand Valley State University [*Michigan*]
G vs V .... Deceleration Units of Gravity Versus Velocity (KSC)
GVSV .... Sao Vicente, Sao Vicente Island [*Cape Verde*] [*ICAO location identifier*] (ICLI)
GVT .... Dean Witter Government Income Trust SBI [*NYSE symbol*] (SPSG)
GVT .... Dean Witter Gvt Income SBI [*NYSE symbol*] (TTSB)
GVT .... Gated Video Tracker
GVT .... Glenvet Resources Ltd. [*Vancouver Stock Exchange symbol*]
GVT .... Government (WDAA)
GVT .... Gravity Vacuum Tube System [*High-speed ground transportation*]
GVT .... Greenville, TX [*Location identifier FAA*] (FAAL)
GVT .... Ground Vibration Test [*Aerospace*] (MCD)
GVTA .... Ground Vibration Test Article [*Aerospace*] (NASA)
GvtTch .... Government Technology Services [*Associated Press*] (SAG)
GVTW .... Gross Vehicle Test Weight [*Automotive engineering*]
GVTY .... Gingivectomy [*Dentistry*]
GVU .... Graphic, Visualization, and Usability Center [*Georgia Institute of Technology*]
GVUGA........ Grounded Voltage Unity-Gain Amplifier (PDAA)
GVV .... Grangeville, ID [*Location identifier FAA*] (FAAL)
GVVA .... Goulburn Valley Viticultural Association [*Australia*]
GVW .... Grandview, MO [*Location identifier FAA*] (FAAL)
GVW .... Gross Vehicle Weight (MCD)
GVW .... Gross Vehicular Weight (WPI)
GVWR .... Gross Vehicle Weight Rating
GVX .... Extra-Great Value [*In automobile name Yugo GVX*]
GVX .... Gavle [*Sweden*] [*Airport symbol*] (OAG)
GVX .... Geevax Ltd. [*British ICAO designator*] (FAAC)
GVX .... Grove Explorations Ltd. [*Vancouver Stock Exchange symbol*]
GVX .... Gruver, TX [*Location identifier FAA*] (FAAL)
GVY .... Green Valley Mine [*Vancouver Stock Exchange symbol*]
GW.............. Air Force Guide for Writing
GW.............. Cases in the Griqualand West Local Division of the Supreme Court [*1910-46*] [*South Africa*] [*A publication*] (DLA)
GW.............. Game Winning [*Baseball*]
GW.............. Gastric Wrap [*Morbid obesity surgical treatment*]
GW.............. General Warning
GW.............. General Will [*Collectivist theory of government*]
GW.............. George Washington [*US general and president, 1732-1799*]
GW.............. George Washington University [*Washington, DC*]
gw.............. Germany, West [*MARC country of publication code Library of Congress*] (LCCP)
GW.............. Germ Warfare
GW.............. Gigawatt
GW.............. Glauben und Wissen (BJA)
GW.............. Glazed Weatherproof [*Tile*] (DICI)
GW.............. Global Water (EA)
G/W............. Glucose in Water [*Medicine*]
GW.............. Glycerine in Water [*Medicine*]
GW.............. Golden West Airlines [*ICAO designator*] (AD)
GW.............. Good Words [*A publication*] (ROG)
GW.............. Gradual Withdrawal [*Medicine*] (DMAA)
GW.............. Grand Warder [*Freemasonry*]
GW.............. Gray-Wheelwright (STED)
GW.............. Great Writers [*A publication*]
GW.............. Green Weight (WDAA)
GW.............. Grenzwache [*Frontier Guard*] [*German military - World War II*]
GW.............. Grey Wolf [*AMEX symbol*] [*Formerly, DI Industries*] (SG)
GW.............. Gross Weight (NG)
GW.............. Groundwater (EPA)
GW.............. Ground Waves (NATG)
GW.............. Groundwork for a Just World (EA)
GW.............. Group Work (MAE)
GW.............. Growth [*Business term*]
GW.............. Guardian Weekly [*A publication*] (BRI)
GW.............. Guerrilla Warfare (AABC)
GW.............. Guided Weapon [*Air Force*]
GW.............. Guided Wire [*British military*] (DMA)
GW.............. Guinea-Bissau [*ANSI two-letter standard code*] (CNC)
GWA .... General Work Area [*NASA*] (NASA)
GWA .... Governor of Western Australia
GWA .... Grand Worthy Associate [*Freemasonry*] (ROG)
GWA .... Great Wall Airlines [*China*] [*ICAO designator*] (FAAC)
GWA .... Great Westrn Air, Inc. [*FAA designator*] (FAAC)
GWA .... [*The*] Greens (Western Australia) Inc.
GWA .... Gunshot Wound of the Abdomen [*Emergency medicine*] (DAVI)
GWA .... International PEN - Guatemalan Writers Abroad (EA)
GWAA .... Garden Writers Association of America (EA)
GWAA .... Golf Writers Association of America (EA)
GWAD .... Great Warbirds Air Display [*British*]

GWAH.......... Global Women of African Heritage (EA)

GWAI.......... German Workshop on Artificial Intelligence [A publication]

GWAL.......... Great Wall Electronic International Ltd. [NASDAQ symbol] (SAG)

GWALY........ Great Wall Electr Int. ADS [NASDAQ symbol] (TTSB)

GW & MRJS... Great Western & Midland Railway Joint Stock [British] (ROG)

GWasB........ Bartram Trail Regional Library, Washington, GA [Library symbol Library of Congress] (LCLS)

GWAY.......... Galway [County in Ireland] (ROG)

GWayC........ Waycross Junior College, Waycross, GA [Library symbol Library of Congress] (LCLS)

GWAZB........ Gott Wende Alles zum Besten [May God Turn Everything to the Best] [Motto of Amoene Amalie, Princess of Anhalt (d. 1626)] [German]

GWB.......... General Well-Being [Medicine] (DMAA)

GWB.......... Gesetz Gegen Wettbewerbsbeschrankungen [German Law Against Restraint of Competition] (DLA)

GWB.......... Glycosylated Whole Blood [Clinical chemistry]

GWB.......... Gypsum Wallboard [Technical drawings]

GW-BASIC ... Gee Whiz BASIC [Computer science]

GWBC.......... Gateway Bancorp, Inc. Kentucky [NASDAQ symbol] (SAG)

GWBC.......... Gateway Bancorp(Ky) [NASDAQ symbol] (TTSB)

GWBC.......... Governor William Bradford Compact [An association] (EA)

GWBOT........ Greater Washington Board of Trade (SRA)

GWBS.......... Global Ward Behavior Scale (DB)

GWC.......... Gardner-Webb College [Boiling Springs, NC]

GWC.......... George Williams College [Downer's Grove, IL]

GWC.......... Gippsland Waters Coalition (EERA)

GWC.......... Global Weather Central

GWC.......... Grand Worthy Chief [Templars] [Freemasonry] (ROG)

GWC.......... Great Whale River [Quebec] [Seismograph station code, US Geological Survey Closed] (SEIS)

GWC.......... Gross Weight Category (DNAB)

GWC.......... Ground Water Council [Defunct]

GWC.......... Guard Well Capacitor

GWC.......... Omaha, NE [Location identifier FAA] (FAAL)

GWC.......... West Georgia College, Carrollton, GA [OCLC symbol] (OCLC)

GWCA.......... George Washington Carver National Monument

GWCC.......... Georgia World Congress Center

GWCG.......... General Wiring Cables Group [British] (DBA)

GW CHAP .... Grand Worthy Chaplain [Templars] [Freemasonry] (ROG)

GWCI.......... Giftware Manufacturers' Credit Interchange [Buffalo, NY] (EA)

GWCS.......... General Wireless Communications Service [Telecommunications] (OTD)

GWCSA........ Greater World Christian Spiritualist Association (EA)

GWCSWBD... Gunnery Weapon Control Switchboard

GWCT.......... Grand Worthy Chief Templar [Templars] [Freemasonry] (ROG)

GWD.......... Gaseous Waste Disposal [System] [Nuclear energy] (NRCH)

GWd.......... Gigawatt-days

GWD.......... Grinding Wheel Dresser

GWD.......... Gwadar [Pakistan] [Airport symbol] (OAG)

GWD.......... South African Law Reports, Griqualand West Local Division [A publication] (DLA)

GWDB.......... Groundwater Database

GWDM.......... Grand Worthy Deputy Marshal [Templars] [Freemasonry] (ROG)

GWDRS........ Ground Winds Data Reduction System [NASA]

GWDS.......... Graphic Weather Display System [FAA] (TAG)

GWE.......... Gigawatt-Electric [DOE] (TAG)

GWe.......... Gigawatt Electrical

GWE.......... Global Weather Experiment [Marine science] (MSC)

GWE.......... Glycerin and Water Enema [Medicine]

GWE.......... Gwelo [Zimbabwe] [Airport symbol] (OAG)

GWEF.......... Guided Weapons Evaluation Facility (MCD)

GWEN.......... Ground Wave Emergency Network

GWeP.......... West Point-Pepperell, Inc., West Point, GA [Library symbol Library of Congress] (LCLS)

GWF.......... Galveston Wharves [AAR code]

GWF.......... Gating Waveform

GWF.......... Gay White Female [Classified advertising] (CDAI)

GWF.......... Global-Warming Factor [Meteorology]

GWF.......... Great Western Financial Corp. [NYSE symbol] (SPSG)

GWF.......... Great Westn Finl [NYSE symbol] (TTSB)

GWF.......... Lancaster, CA [Location identifier FAA] (FAAL)

GWFN.......... Global Weather Facsimile Network (MCD)

GWFPr.......... Great Westn Finl CvDep Pfd [NYSE symbol] (TTSB)

GWFPrA........ Great Westn Finl 8.30% Dep Pfd [NYSE symbol] (TTSB)

GWFPrT........ Great Westn Fin I 8.25% 'TOPrS' [NYSE symbol] (TTSB)

GWG.......... Game-Winning Goals [Hockey]

GWG.......... Gaussian Wave Group [Physics]

GWG.......... Generalized Wegener Granulomatosis [Medicine] (DMAA)

GWG.......... Gottes Wille Geschehe [God's Will Be Done] [Motto of Juliane Ursula, Margravine of Baden (d. 1614)] [German]

GWG.......... Groundwater Working Group [Australia]

GWG.......... Gullwing Group (EA)

GWGI.......... Gullwing Group International (EA)

GWh.......... Gigawatt-Hour

GWH.......... Gigawatt Hour [DOE] (TAG)

GWH.......... Great Water Holt (EA)

GWH.......... Guided Warheads

GWHF.......... George Williams Hooper Foundation [Research center] (RCD)

GWHIS........ Global-Wide Help and Information Systems [On-line help system for Mosaic developers]

GWI.......... Galvanized Wrought Iron (ADA)

GWI.......... General Wage Increase (MCD)

GWI.......... Global-Warming Index [Meteorology]

GWI.......... Government-Wide Index [Later, USGRDR]

GWI.......... Greenhouse Warming Index [Marine science] (OSRA)

GWI.......... Grinding Wheel Institute (EA)

GWI.......... Ground Water Institute [Defunct] (EA)

GWI.......... Gulf War Illness [Medicine]

GWIBIT........ Guild of Washington Incompetent Bureaucratic Idea Throatcutters [An organizati on rumored to have been active in World War II]

GWIC.......... Geothermal World Info Center [Later, REIC] (EA)

GWIC.......... Global Warming International Center [An association] (EA)

GWIG.......... Grand Worthy Inside Guard [Templars] [Freemasonry] (ROG)

GWIGWO...... Good Will In, Good Will Out [Computer science]

Gwil.......... Gwillim's Tithe Cases [England] [1224-1824] [A publication] (DLA)

Gwill.......... Gwillim's Tithe Cases [England] [A publication] (DLA)

Gwill Bac Abr... Gwillim's Tithe Cases [England] [A publication] (DLA)

Gwill T Cas... Gwillim's Tithe Cases [England] [A publication] (DLA)

Gwill Ti Cas... Gwillim's Tithe Cases [England] [A publication] (DLA)

Gwil Ti Cas... Gwillim's Tithe Cases [England] [A publication] (DLA)

GWIM.......... Global Warming Impact Model (AAEL)

GWIN.......... Goodwin Railroad, Inc. [AAR code]

GWIRD........ Government-Wide Index to Research and Development

GWJ.......... Chicopee Falls, MA [Location identifier FAA] (FAAL)

GWJ.......... Glue Weld Joint

GWJC.......... Gardner-Webb Junior College [Later, Gardner-Webb College] [North Carolina]

GWL.......... George Washington University, Law Library, Washington, DC [OCLC symbol] (OCLC)

GWL.......... Great-West Life Assurance Co. [Toronto Stock Exchange symbol]

GWL.......... Grosswetterlage [Meteorology]

GWL.......... Groundwater Level [Hydrology] (IAA)

GWL.......... Gwalior [India] [Airport symbol] (OAG)

GWL.......... Reports of Cases Decided in the Supreme Court of South Africa (Griqualand West Local Division), by Kitchin [A publication] (DLA)

GWLD.......... Gaming World International, Inc. [NASDAQ symbol] (SAG)

GWLD.......... Gaming World Intl. [NASDAQ symbol] (TTSB)

GWLD.......... South Africa Law Reports, Griqualand West Local Division [A publication] (DLA)

GWLDW...... Gaming World Intl. Wrrt'A'. [NASDAQ symbol] (TTSB)

GWLL.......... Great Western Lacrosse League (PSS)

GWM.......... Gay White Male [Classified advertising]

GWM.......... George Washington University, Medical Library, Washington, DC [OCLC symbol] (OCLC)

GWM.......... Grand Worthy Marshal [Templars] [Freemasonry] (ROG)

GWM.......... Ground Water Monitor [A publication]

GWM.......... Ground Water Monitoring

GWM.......... Guam Tracking Station [NASA] (KSC)

GWM.......... Guaranteed Weekly Minimum

GWMC.......... Galvanized Ware Manufacturers Council (EA)

GWMD.......... Ground Water Management District

GWMR.......... Ground Water Monitoring Review [A publication]

GWMS.......... Gaseous Waste Management System [Nuclear energy] (NRCH)

GWMS.......... Gas-Water Module Storage [Nuclear energy] (NRCH)

GWMU.......... Government Workforce Management Unit [Victoria, Australia]

GWN.......... Golden West Network [Australia]

GWN.......... Goldwinn Resources Ltd. [Vancouver Stock Exchange symbol]

GWND.......... Gowned (ABBR)

GWO.......... General Watch Officer [Army] (AABC)

GWO.......... Great-West Lifeco, Inc. [Toronto Stock Exchange symbol]

GWO.......... Greenwood [Mississippi] [Airport symbol] (OAG)

GWOA.......... Guerrilla Warfare Operational Area [Army]

GWO & HP.... Gas Wall Oven and Hot Plate [Classified advertising] (ADA)

GWOG.......... Grand Worthy Outside Guard [Templars] [Freemasonry] (ROG)

GWOTH........ Ground Wave Over-the-Horizon RADAR (DNAB)

GW OU .... Groundwater OU [Operable Unit] [Environemental science] (BCP)

GWP.......... Gesellschaft fuer Wirtschaftspublizistik GmbH [Society for Public Economics] [Germany] (IID)

GWP.......... Gift with Purchase

g-w-p.......... Gift With Purchase [Retail] (WDMC)

GWP.......... Global-Warming Potential [Meteorology]

GWP.......... Government White Paper

GWP.......... Grand Worthy Patriarch [Freemasonry] (ROG)

GWP.......... Great Western Petroleum Corp. [Vancouver Stock Exchange symbol]

GWP.......... Greenhouse Warming Potential (EERA)

GWP.......... Gross World Product

GWP.......... Guided Writing Procedure [Reading improvement method]

GWPAS........ General Work Force Performance Appraisal System [Marine science] (OSRA)

GWPC.......... Ground Water Protection Council (NTPA)

GWPCA........ German Wirehaired Pointer Club of America (EA)

GWPM.......... Gross Words per Minute [Computer science] (IAA)

GWPMS....... Ground Water Policy and Management Staff [Environmental Protection Agency] (GFGA)

GWPS.......... Gaseous Waste Processing System [Nuclear energy] (NRCH)

GWPS.......... Ground Water Protection Standard [Environmental Protection Agency] (GFGA)

GWpSO........ Group Weapons Staff Officer [British military] (DMA)

GWPU.......... General Workers Professional Unions [Bulgaria]

GWQ.......... GWR Resources [Vancouver Stock Exchange symbol]

GWQ.......... San Francisco, CA [Location identifier FAA] (FAAL)

GWQAP........ Government-Wide Quality Assurance Program

GWQE.......... General Water-Quality Engineering [Survey] [Army] (RDA)

GWR.......... General War Reserves [Army] (AABC)

GWR.......... Gill Withdrawal Reflex

GWR.......... [The] Great Western Railway Co. [Prior to nationalization] [AAR code]

GWR.......... Great World Resources [Vancouver Stock Exchange symbol]

GWR.......... Griqualand High Court Reports [A publication] (DLA)

GWR .... Gwinner, ND [*Location identifier FAA*] (FAAL)
GW-RBI .... Game-Winning Run Batted In [*Baseball*]
GWRDC .... Grape and Wine Research and Development Corporation (EERA)
GWRDC .... Grape and Wine Research and Development Council [*Australia*]
GWRI .... Ground Water Resources Institute [*Later, Ground Water Council*]
GWRRA .... Gold Wing Road Riders Association (EA)
GWRX .... Geoworks [*NASDAQ symbol*] (TTSB)
GWS .... Gar Wood Society (EA)
GWS .... Gaseous Waste System [*Nuclear energy*] (NRCH)
GWS .... GEEIA [*Ground Electronics Engineering Installation Agency*] Workload Schedule (AFM)
GWS .... General War Subsystem (MCD)
GWS .... Geneva Convention for the Amelioration of the Condition of the Wounded and Sick in Armed Forces in the Field, 12 August 1949 [*Army*] (AABC)
GWS .... German Wine Society [*Canada*] (EAIO)
GWS .... Glashow-Weinberg-Salam Theories [*Physics*]
GWS .... Glenwood Springs, CO [*Location identifier FAA*] (FAAL)
GWS .... Grand Worthy Scribe [*Templars*] [*Freemasonry*] (ROG)
GWS .... Great Western Society (EA)
GWS .... Great West Steel Industries Ltd. [*Toronto Stock Exchange symbol Vancouver Stock Exchange symbol*]
GWS .... Great White Spot [*Planetary science*]
GWS .... Guided Weapon Station (IAA)
GWS .... Gulf War Syndrome [*Medicine*]
GWS .... Gun Weapon System [*Military*] (CAAL)
GWS .... Gwil Industries, Inc. [*Toronto Stock Exchange symbol Vancouver Stock Exchange symbol*]
GWS 1929 ... Geneva Convention for the Amelioration of the Condition of the Wounded and Sick in Armed Forces in the Field, 27 July 1929 [*Army*]
GWS-A & L... Girl Watchers Society - Ankle and Leg Division
GWSAE .... Greater Washington Society of Association Executives (SRA)
GWSC .... Ghana Water and Sewerage Corp.
GWSC .... Greater World Spiritual Centre [*British*] (EAIO)
GWSD .... Guild of Weavers, Spinner & Dyers (WDAA)
GWSF .... Georgia Warm Springs Foundation [*Later, RWSF*] (EA)
Gw Sh .... Gwynne on Sheriffs [*A publication*] (DLA)
GWSIP .... Gun Weapon System Improvement Program [*Military*] (CAAL)
GWSR .... General Wage Stabilization Regulations [*United States*] (DLA)
GWSRP .... Gun Weapon System Replacement Program (NVT)
GWSS .... Groundwater Supply Survey (GNE)
GWS Sea .... Geneva Convention for the Amelioration of the Condition of the Wounded, Sick, and Shipwrecked Members of the Armed Forces at Sea, 12 August 1949 [*Army*] (AABC)
GWSTN .... Ground Wireless Station (IAA)
GWSTV .... Golden West Subscription Television [*Cable TV programming service*]
GWT .... Chicopee Falls, MA [*Location identifier FAA*] (FAAL)
GWt .... Gigawatt Thermal
GWT .... Glazed Wall Tile [*Technical drawings*]
GWT .... Grand Worthy Templar [*Templars*] [*Freemasonry*] (ROG)
GWT .... Gross Weight
GWT .... Ground Winds Tower [*NASA*] (NASA)
GWT .... Gunshot Wound of the Throat [*Emergency medicine*] (DAVI)
GWT .... Westerland [*Germany Airport symbol*] (OAG)
GWTA .... Gift Wrappings and Tyings Association [*Defunct*] (EA)
GWTB .... Glazed Wall Tile Base [*Technical drawings*]
GWTF .... Ground Water Task Force [*Office of Solid Waste and Emergency Response*] (COE)
GWTI .... Groundwater Technology, Inc. [*NASDAQ symbol*] (NQ)
GWTP .... Groundwater Treatment Plant [*Environmental science*] (BCP)
GW TREAS... Grand Worthy Treasurer [*Templars*] [*Freemasonry*] (ROG)
GWTUF .... Government Workers' Trade Union Federation [*Ceylon*]
GWTW .... Gone with the Wind [*A novel by Margaret Mitchell; also, a motion picture*]
GWU .... George Washington University [*Washington, DC*]
GWU .... Granite Workers' Union [*British*]
GWU .... International Glove Workers' Union of America [*Later, ACTWU*]
GWV .... Glendale, WV [*Location identifier FAA*] (FAAL)
GWVA .... Great War Veterans' Association [*Canada*]
GWVSS .... Ground Wind Vortex Sensing System [*Aviation*] (DA)
GWVT .... Grand Worthy Vice Templar [*Templars*] [*Freemasonry*] (ROG)
GWW .... Goldsboro, NC [*Location identifier FAA*] (FAAL)
GWW .... Grainger, [*W. W.*] Inc. [*NYSE symbol*] (SPSG)
GWW .... Grainger (W.W.) [*NYSE symbol*] (TTSB)
GWW .... Ground Water for Windows [*Computer program*]
GWW .... Guaranteed Weekly Wage
GWWS .... Gott Wirds Wohl Schaffen [*God Will Arrange*] [*Motto of Dorothee Auguste, Duchess of Braunschweig (1577-1625)*] [*German*]
GWY .... Galway [*Ireland*] [*Airport symbol*]
GWY .... Goldways Resources [*Vancouver Stock Exchange symbol*]
GWY .... Gwynedd-Mercy College, Gwynedd, PA [*OCLC symbol*] (OCLC)
GWYN .... Gwynedd [*County in Wales*] (WGA)
GX .... Gencor Indus [*AMEX symbol*] (TTSB)
GX .... Gencor Industries [*AMEX symbol*] (SAG)
GX .... Glycinxylidide [*Biochemistry*]
Gx .... Graded Exercise
GX .... Great Lakes Airlines [*ICAO designator*] (AD)
GXA .... CountryBaskets [*NYSE symbol*] (SAG)
GXA .... Countrybkts Australia Index Fd [*NYSE symbol*] (TTSB)
GXA .... Gunn-Diode X-Band Amplifier
GXD .... General X-Ray Diagnosis [*Medicine*]
GXD .... Graded [*Medicine*] (DAVI)
GXD EKG ..... Graded Exercixe Electrocardiogram [*Cardiology*] (DAVI)

GXF .... CountryBaskets [*NYSE symbol*] (SAG)
GXF .... Countrybkts France Index Fd [*NYSE symbol*] (TTSB)
GXG .... CountryBaskets [*NYSE symbol*] (SAG)
GXG .... Countrybkts Germany Index Fd [*NYSE symbol*] (TTSB)
GXG .... Negage [*Angola*] [*Airport symbol*] (OAG)
GXH .... CountryBaskets [*NYSE symbol*] (SAG)
GXH .... Countrybkts Hong Kong Index Fd [*NYSE symbol*] (TTSB)
GXI .... CountryBaskets [*NYSE symbol*] (SAG)
GXI .... Countrybkts Italy Index Fd [*NYSE symbol*] (TTSB)
GXI .... Glenex Industries, Inc. [*Vancouver Stock Exchange symbol*]
GXI .... Global Exchange, Inc.
GXJ .... CountryBaskets [*NYSE symbol*] (SAG)
GXJ .... Countrybkts Japan Index Fd [*NYSE symbol*] (TTSB)
GXK .... CountryBaskets [*NYSE symbol*] (SAG)
GXK .... Countrybkts UK Index Fd [*NYSE symbol*] (TTSB)
GXL .... General-Purpose Crosslinked Polyethylene [*Insulation*]
GXL .... Granges, Inc. [*AMEX symbol Toronto Stock Exchange symbol*] (SPSG)
GXL .... Grinnell, IA [*Location identifier FAA*] (FAAL)
GXM .... Gordex Minerals Ltd. [*Toronto Stock Exchange symbol*]
GXM .... Medical College of Georgia, Augusta, GA [*OCLC symbol*] (OCLC)
G/XMTR .... Guidance Transmitter (AAG)
GXO .... Butler, PA [*Location identifier FAA*] (FAAL)
GXQ .... Coyhaique [*Chile*] [*Airport symbol*] (AD)
GXR .... CountryBaskets [*NYSE symbol*] (SAG)
GXR .... Countrybkts S.Africa Index Fd [*NYSE symbol*] (TTSB)
GXS .... Goldex Resources [*Vancouver Stock Exchange symbol*]
GXSP .... Guierrezia Xylem Sap Potential [*Botany*]
GXT .... Graded Exercise Testing
GXU .... CountryBaskets [*NYSE symbol*] (SAG)
GXU .... Countrybkts US Index Fd [*NYSE symbol*] (TTSB)
GXU .... Wrightstown, NJ [*Location identifier FAA*] (FAAL)
GXV .... Golden Exodus [*Vancouver Stock Exchange symbol*]
GXY .... Galaxy Airways Ltd. [*Nigeria*] [*ICAO designator*] (FAAC)
GXY .... Galaxy Industry Ltd. [*Vancouver Stock Exchange symbol*]
GXY .... Greeley, CO [*Location identifier FAA*] (FAAL)
GY .... Gaily (ABBR)
GY .... Galley
GY .... Galley-Yarn [*Crooked*] [*Slang British*] (DSUE)
GY .... Gardan [*France ICAO aircraft manufacturer identifier*] (ICAO)
GY .... GenCorp [*NYSE symbol*] (TTSB)
GY .... GenCorp, Inc. [*NYSE symbol*] (SPSG)
GY .... Germany
Gy .... Gray [*Symbol*] [*SI unit for absorbed dose acceleration*]
GY .... Gray
GY .... Greenish Yellow
GY .... Grey [*Unit of inpingent energy*]
GY .... Guaranty Trust Co. of Canada [*Toronto Stock Exchange symbol*]
GY .... Guidance Year [*DoD*]
GY .... Gunnery (ABBR)
gy .... Guyana [*MARC country of publication code Library of Congress*] (LCCP)
GY .... Guyana [*ANSI two-letter standard code*] (CNC)
GY .... Guyana Airways [*ICAO designator*] (AD)
GY .... Gyro (ABBR)
GY .... Gyrocar (ABBR)
GY .... Gyrocompass (ABBR)
GY .... Gyrodyne (ABBR)
GY .... Gyroscope
Gy .... Gyrus [*Brain anatomy*]
GYA .... Got Ya Again [*Initialism used as name of second successful phony event staged by Washington, DC, law enforcement agents posing as fences*] [*See PFF Inc*]
GYA .... Guayaramerin [*Bolivia*] [*Airport symbol*] (OAG)
GYA .... Guyana Airways Corp. [*ICAO designator*] (FAAC)
GyAR .... Rhein-Westfalische Technische Hochschule, Aachen, Germany [*Library symbol*] [*Library of Congress*] (LCLS)
GyAsH .... Hofbibliothek, Aschaffenburg, Germany [*Library symbol*] [*Library of Congress*] (LCLS)
GYB .... Giddings, TX [*Location identifier FAA*] (FAAL)
GyBaA .... Archiv des Kreises Asch, Fernleihe, Bayern, Federal Republic of Germany [*Library symbol Library of Congress*] (LCLS)
GyBFU .... Freie Universitaet (Berlin), Garystrasse, Berlin, Germany [*Library symbol Library of Congress*] (LCLS)
GyBFU-P ...... Freie Universitaet (Berlin), Fachbereich Politische Wissenschaft, Bibliothek, Berlin, Germany [*Library symbol Library of Congress*] (LCLS)
GyBIAI .... Ibero-Amerikanisches Institu Preussicher Kulturbesitz, Berlin, Germany [*Library symbol*] [*Library of Congress*] (LCLS)
GyBiU .... Universitat Bielfeld, Kurt Schumacher, Bielfeld, Germany [*Library symbol Library of Congress*] (LCLS)
GyBochU ...... Ruhr-Universitat Bochum, Bochum, Germany [*Library symbol Library of Congress*] (LCLS)
GyBoDB .... Deutscher Bundestag, Abteilung Wissenschaftliche Dokumentation, Bonn, Germany [*Library symbol Library of Congress*] (LCLS)
GyBoFE .... Friedrich-Ebert-Stiftung, Archiv der Sozialen Demokratie, Bonn, Germany [*Library symbol Library of Congress*] (LCLS)
GyBoFN .... Friedrich-Naumann-Stiftung, Bonn, Germany [*Library symbol Library of Congress*] (LCLS)
GyBoGI .... Gesamtdeutsches Institut, Bonn, Germany [*Library symbol Library of Congress*] (LCLS)
GyBraTU ..... Technische Universitat Carolo Wilhelmina zu Braunschweig, Braunschweig, Federal Republic of Germany [*Library symbol Library of Congress*] (LCLS)

GyBrSU .... Staatsbibliothek und Universitatsbibliothek, Breitenweg, Bremen, Germany [*Library symbol Library of Congress*] (LCLS)
GyBrU .... Universitaet Bremen, Bremen, Germany [*Library symbol Library of Congress*] (LCLS)
GyBTU .... Technische Universitat Berlin, Berlin, Germany [*Library symbol Library of Congress*] (LCLS)
GYC .... Glasgow Yeomanry Cavalry [*British military*] (DMA)
GYC .... Global Energy Ltd. [*Vancouver Stock Exchange symbol*]
GYC .... Greater Yellowstone Coalition (EA)
GYC .... Young Harris College, Young Harris, GA [*Library symbol Library of Congress*] (LCLS)
GyDaD .... Deutsches Kunststoff-Institut, Darmstadt, Germany [*Library symbol Library of Congress*] (LCLS)
GyDaH .... Hessische Landes- und Hochschulbibliothek, Darmstadt (Schloss), Germany [*Library symbol Library of Congress*] (LCLS)
GyDaM .... E. Merck AG, Darmstadt, Germany [*Library symbol Library of Congress*] (LCLS)
GyDIZ .... Institut fur Zeitungsforschung, Dortmund, Germany [*Library symbol Library of Congress*] (LCLS)
GyDMA .... Mikrofilmarchiv der Deutschsparchigen Presse e.V., Dortmund, Germany [*Library symbol Library of Congress*] (LCLS)
GyDuiH .... Gesamthochschulbibliothek Duisburg, Duisburg, Germany [*Library symbol Library of Congress*] (LCLS)
GyDuU .... Universitat Dusseldorf, Grabbeplatz, Dusseldorf, Germany [*Library symbol Library of Congress*] (LCLS)
GYE .... Glory Explorations [*Vancouver Stock Exchange symbol*]
GYE .... Guayaquil [*Ecuador*] [*Airport symbol*] (OAG)
GyEU .... Friedrich-Alexander-Universitat zu Erlangen-Nurnberg, Erlangen, Germany [*Library symbol Library of Congress*] (LCLS)
GYFM .... General Yielding Fracture Mechanics (OA)
GyFmB .... Beilstein-Institut, Frankfurt/Main, Germany [*Library symbol Library of Congress*] (LCLS)
GyFmDB ..... Deutsche Bibliothek, Zeppelinallee, Frankfurt am Main, Germany [*Library symbol Library of Congress*] (LCLS)
GyFmSU ..... Stadt u Universitatsbibliothek, Senckenbergische Bibliothek Fernleihe, Frankfurt/Main, Federal Republic of Germany [*Library symbol Library of Congress*] (LCLS)
GYG .... Grayling, MI [*Location identifier FAA*] (FAAL)
GYG .... Valdosta State College, Valdosta, GA [*OCLC symbol*] (OCLC)
GyGiU .... Justus Liebig Universitatsbibliothek Giessen, Giessen/Lahn, Federal Republic of Germany [*Library symbol Library of Congress*] (LCLS)
GyGoN .... Niedersachsische Staats- und Universitatsbibliothek, Gottingen, Germany [*Library symbol Library of Congress*] (LCLS)
GYH .... Greenville, SC [*Location identifier FAA*] (FAAL)
GyHanM ...... Medizinische Hochschule, Karl Wiechert, Hannover-Kleefeld, Germany [*Library symbol Library of Congress*] (LCLS)
GyHaS .... Staats- und Universitatsbibliothek Hamburg, Hamburg, Germany [*Library symbol Library of Congress*] (LCLS)
GyHeM .... Max-Planck-Institut fuer Medizinisch Forschung, Heidelberg, Germany [*Library symbol Library of Congress*] (LCLS)
GyHeU-SS .... Universitat Heidelberg Sinologisches Seminar de Universitat Heidelberg, Heidelberg, Germany [*Library symbol*] [*Library of Congress*] (LCLS)
GyHGU .... University of Gottingen, Hannover, Germany [*Library symbol Library of Congress*] (LCLS)
GyHoU .... Universitat Hohenheim (Landwirtschaftliche Hochschule), Stuttgart-Hohenheim, Germany [*Library symbol Library of Congress*] (LCLS)
GyHTIB .... Universitaetsbibliothek der Technischen Universitaet Hannover und Technische Informationsbibliothek, Hannover, Federal Republic of Germany [*Library symbol Library of Congress*] (LCLS)
GYIL .... German Yearbook of International Law [*A publication*] (DLA)
GyJuK .... Kernforschungsanlage Julich, Julich, Germany [*Library symbol Library of Congress*] (LCLS)
GyKaU .... Universitat Trier-Kaiserslautern, Kaiserslautern, Germany [*Library symbol Library of Congress*] (LCLS)
GyKG .... Gesellschaft fuer Kernforschung mbH, Karlsruhe, Germany [*Library symbol Library of Congress*] (LCLS)
GyKiU .... Christian-Albrechts-Universitat Kiel, Kiel, Germany [*Library symbol Library of Congress*] (LCLS)
GyKoB .... Bundesanzeiger Verlagsgesellschaft, mbH, Koln, Germany [*Library symbol*] [*Library of Congress*] (LCLS)
GYM .... General Yardmaster [*Railroading*]
GYM .... Guaymas [*Mexico*] [*Seismograph station code, US Geological Survey*] (SEIS)
GYM .... Guaymas [*Mexico*] [*Airport symbol*] (OAG)
GYM .... Guaymas, Mexico [*Remote site*] [*NASA*] (NASA)
GYM .... Gymnasium
gym .... Gymnasium (VRA)
GYM .... Gymnastic
GYM .... Gymnastics (ADA)
GYM .... Sport Supply Group [*AMEX symbol*] (SAG)
GYM .... Sport Supply Group [*NYSE symbol*] (SPSG)
GyMB .... Boehringer Mannheim GmbH, Mannheim, Germany [*Library symbol Library of Congress*] (LCLS)
GYMB .... [The] Gymboree Corp. [*NASDAQ symbol*] (SAG)
Gymbree ...... [The] Gymboree Corp. [*Associated Press*] (SAG)
GyMIZ .... Institut fur Zeitgeschichte [*Institute of Modern History*], Munchen, Federal Republic of Germany [*Library symbol Library of Congress*] (LCLS)
GyMLM .... Ludwig Maxmilians Universitatsbibliothek Munchen, Munich, Federal Republic of Germany [*Library symbol Library of Congress*] (LCLS)
GYMM .... HealthTech Intl [*NASDAQ symbol*] (TTSB)

GYMMW ..... HealthTech Intl Wrrt'A' [*NASDAQ symbol*] (TTSB)
GYMN .... Gymnasium (ABBR)
GYMNST ..... Gymnast (ABBR)
GYMST .... Gymnast (ABBR)
GYMSTC ..... Gymnastic (ABBR)
GYMSTCY ... Gymnastically (ABBR)
GYMSTIC .... Gymnastic [*Freight*]
GyMuW .... Westfalische Wilhelms-Universitat Munster, Munster, Germany [*Library symbol Library of Congress*] (LCLS)
GYM.WS ..... Sport Supply Grp Wrrt [*AMEX symbol*] (TTSB)
GYN .... Goiania [*Brazil*] [*Airport symbol*] (OAG)
GYN .... Gynecologist
GYN .... Gynecology
GYNAE .... Gynaecology [*British*]
GYNAEC ...... Gynaecologist [*or Gynaecology*] [*British*] (ADA)
GYNAECOL .. Gynaecology [*British*]
GYNC .... Gynecologic (ABBR)
GYNCL .... Gynecological (ABBR)
GYNCLGY .... Gynecology
GYNE .... Gynecare [*NASDAQ symbol*] (SAG)
GYNE .... Gynecare Inc. [*NASDAQ symbol*] (TTSB)
gyne .... Gynecology [*Medicine*] (DAVI)
GyNeA .... Augustana Hochschule Bibliothek, Neuendettelsau, Federal Republic of Germany [*Library symbol Library of Congress*] (LCLS)
Gynecol ...... Gynecology
Gynecre ...... Gynecare, Inc. [*Associated Press*] (SAG)
GYNST .... Gynecologist (ABBR)
GyNU .... Friedrich-Alexander-Universitat zu Erlangen-Nurnberg, Abteilung fur Wirtschafts-und Socialwissenschaften, Nurnberg, Germany [*Library symbol Library of Congress*] (LCLS)
GYP .... CGC, Inc. [*Toronto Stock Exchange symbol*]
GYP .... Eagle Aviation [*British*] [*FAA designator*] (FAAC)
GYP .... Guild of Young Printers (DGA)
GYP .... Gympie [*Australia Airport symbol*]
GYP .... Gypsum (KSC)
GYP .... Gypsy (ABBR)
GYP .... Gyro Yaw Position
GYPD .... Gypped (ABBR)
GYPG .... Gypping (ABBR)
GYPS .... Gypsum
GYPSIOL ..... Gypsiologic (ABBR)
GYPSY .... General Image Processing System
GYR .... Gigayear [*A billion years*]
GYR .... Goodyear, AZ [*Location identifier FAA*] (FAAL)
GYR .... Gyrafrance [*France ICAO designator*] (FAAC)
GYR .... Gyration (ABBR)
GYR .... Gyrus (ABBR)
GYRA .... Gyrate (ABBR)
GYRAD .... Gyrated (ABBR)
GYRAG .... Gyrating (ABBR)
GYRAN .... Gyration (ABBR)
GYRAR .... Gyrator (ABBR)
GYRARY ...... Gyratory (ABBR)
GYRCMPS ... Gyrocompass (ABBR)
GYRMTR ..... Gyrometer (ABBR)
GYRO .... Gyrocompass (ABBR)
GYRO .... Gyrodyne [*NASDAQ symbol*] (SAG)
GYRO .... Gyrodyne Co. Amer [*NASDAQ symbol*] (TTSB)
GYRO .... Gyroplane (ABBR)
GYRO .... Gyroscope (AAG)
GYROA .... Gyro A (NAKS)
GYROCOMP .. Gyrocompassing (NAKS)
GYROCOMP .. Gyroscope Compassing
GYROCOP .... Gyrocopter (ABBR)
Gyrody .... Gyrodyne Company of America, Inc. [*Associated Press*] (SAG)
GYRODYN ... Gyrodynamic (ABBR)
GYRPLN ...... Gyroplane (ABBR)
GYRSCP ...... Gyroscope (ABBR)
GYRSTBR .... Gyrostabilizer (ABBR)
GYRTD .... Gyrated (ABBR)
GyRU .... Universitat Regensburg, Regensburg, Germany [*Library symbol Library of Congress*] (LCLS)
GySalS .... Stadtbucherei Salzgitter, Joachim Campe, Salzgitter, Germany [*Library symbol Library of Congress*] (LCLS)
GySaU .... Universitat des Saarlandes, Saarbrucken, Germany [*Library symbol Library of Congress*] (LCLS)
GYSCO .... Great Yarmouth Shipping Co. (MHDW)
GYSGT .... Gunnery Sergeant
GySIA .... Institut fuer Auslandsbeziehungen, Stuttgart, Germany [*Library symbol Library of Congress*] (LCLS)
GYSR .... Geyser (ABBR)
GySU .... Universitat Stuttgart, Stuttgart, Germany [*Library symbol Library of Congress*] (LCLS)
GySW .... Wuerttembergische Landesbibliothek, Konrad Adenauer, Stuttgart, Germany [*Library symbol Library of Congress*] (LCLS)
GyTrU .... Universitat Trier-Kaiserslautern, Schneidershof, Trier, Germany [*Library symbol Library of Congress*] (LCLS)
GYW .... International Finance Corp. [*AMEX symbol*] (SAG)
GyWitS .... Stadtbucherei Witten, Witten, Germany [*Library symbol Library of Congress*] (LCLS)
GyWK .... Kalle Aktiengesellschaft, Litteraturabteilung, Wiesbaden-Biebrich, Germany [*Library symbol Library of Congress*] (LCLS)
GyWoS .... Niedersachsische Staatsarchiv, Wolfenbuttel, Germany [*Library symbol Library of Congress*] (LCLS)
GYY .... Gary, IN [*Location identifier FAA*] (FAAL)

GZ .... Air Rarotonga [*ICAO designator*] (AD)
GZ .... Ganzfeld [*Whole Field*] [*ESP test*] [*German*]
gz .... Gaza Strip [*MARC country of publication code Library of Congress*] (LCCP)
GZ .... Gigahertz [*1,000 megahertz*] [*Preferred form is GHz*] (MCD)
Gz .... Graetz Number [*Physics*]
GZ .... Ground Zero [*Atomic detonation*]
GZ .... Ground Zero [*An association*] (EA)
GZ .... Guilford-Zimmerman Personality Test [*Psychology*] (MAE)
Gz .... Guizzardinus [*Deceased, 1222*] [*Authority cited in pre-1607 legal work*] (DSA)
GZA .... Alverno College, Milwaukee, WI [*OCLC symbol*] (OCLC)
GZA .... GZA GeoEnvironmental Technologies, Inc. [*Associated Press*] (SAG)
GZAS ...... Guilford-Zimmerman Aptitude Survey [*Test*]
GZAS:GR ..... Guilford-Zimmerman Aptitude Survey: General Reasoning [*Test*]
GZAS:NO ..... Guilford-Zimmerman Aptitude Survey: Numerical Operations [*Test*]
GZAS:PS ..... Guilford-Zimmerman Aptitude Survey: Perceptual Speed [*Test*]
GZAS:SO ..... Guilford-Zimmerman Aptitude Survey: Spatial Orientation [*Test*]
GZAS:SV ..... Guilford-Zimmerman Aptitude Survey: Spatial Visualization [*Test*]
GZAS:VC ..... Guilford-Zimmerman Aptitude Survey: Verbal Comprehension [*Test*]
GZB .... Carroll College, Waukesha, WI [*OCLC symbol*] (OCLC)
GZC .... Carthage College, Kenosha, WI [*OCLC symbol*] (OCLC)
GZD .... Glazed (DGA)
GZD .... Milwaukee Public Library, Milwaukee, WI [*OCLC symbol*] (OCLC)
GZE .... University of Wisconsin-Eau Claire, Eau Claire, WI [*OCLC symbol*] (OCLC)
GZEA .... GZA GeoEnvironmental Tech [*NASDAQ symbol*] (TTSB)
GZEA .... GZA GeoEnvironmental Technologies [*NASDAQ symbol*] (SAG)
GZEA .... GZA GeoEnvironmental Technologies, Inc. (NQ)
GZF .... Eau Claire Public Library, Eau Claire, WI [*OCLC symbol*] (OCLC)
GZG .... Blackford, VA [*Location identifier FAA*] (FAAL)
GZG .... Brown County Library, Green Bay, WI [*OCLC symbol*] (OCLC)
GZG .... Gonzales Gold Mines Ltd. [*Vancouver Stock Exchange symbol*]
GZH .... University of Wisconsin-Madison, Health Sciences, Madison, WI [*OCLC symbol*] (OCLC)
GZI .... University of Wisconsin-Madison, Instructional Materials Center, Madison, WI [*OCLC symbol*] (OCLC)
GZII .... Guilford-Zimmerman Interest Inventory [*Vocational guidance test*]
GZJ .... University of Wisconsin-Milwaukee, School of Library Science, Milwaukee, WI [*OCLC symbol*] (OCLC)
GZK .... Oshkosh Public Library, Oshkosh, WI [*OCLC symbol*] (OCLC)
GZL .... Gazelle Resources Ltd. [*Vancouver Stock Exchange symbol*]
GZL .... Guzzle (ABBR)
GZL .... University of Wisconsin-Madison, Law Library, Madison, WI [*OCLC symbol*] (OCLC)
GZLD .... Guzzled (ABBR)
GZLG .... Guzzling (ABBR)

GZLR .... Guzzler (ABBR)
GZM .... Gaz Metropolitain, Inc. [*Toronto Stock Exchange symbol*]
GZM .... University of Wisconsin-Madison, Madison, WI [*OCLC symbol*] (OCLC)
GZMG .... Gradient Zone Melting (IAA)
GZN .... Ground Zero [*Nevada*] [*Seismograph station code, US Geological Survey Closed*] (SEIS)
GZN .... University of Wisconsin-Milwaukee, Milwaukee, WI [*OCLC symbol*] (OCLC)
GZO .... Gizo [*Solomon Islands*] [*Airport symbol*] (OAG)
GZO .... University of Wisconsin-Oshkosh, Oshkosh, WI [*OCLC symbol*] (OCLC)
GZOB .... Glowna Zydowska Organizacja Bojowa [*A publication*] (BJA)
GZON .... Graphix Zone [*NASDAQ symbol*] (TTSB)
GZON .... Graphix Zone, Inc. [*NASDAQ symbol*] (SAG)
GZP .... University of Wisconsin-Parkside, Kenosha, WI [*OCLC symbol*] (OCLC)
GZPP .... Ground Zero Pairing Project (EA)
GZQ .... Marquette University, Milwaukee, WI [*OCLC symbol*] (OCLC)
GZR .... Golden Zone Resources [*Vancouver Stock Exchange symbol*]
GZR .... Wisconsin Department of Public Instruction, Reference and Loan Library, Madison, WI [*OCLC symbol*] (OCLC)
GZRC .... Ground Zero Resource Center [*Defunct*] (EA)
GZS .... Gesellschaft fuer Zahlungssysteme [*International banking*] [*Germany*]
GZS .... Gozaisho [*Japan*] [*Seismograph station code, US Geological Survey Closed*] (SEIS)
GZS .... Pulaski, TN [*Location identifier FAA*] (FAAL)
GZS .... University of Wisconsin-Stout, Menomonie, WI [*OCLC symbol*] (OCLC)
GZT .... Gaziantep [*Turkey*] [*Airport symbol*] (OAG)
GZT .... Greenwich Zone Time
GZT .... University of Wisconsin-Whitewater, Whitewater, WI [*OCLC symbol*] (OCLC)
GZTC .... Genzyme Transgenics [*NASDAQ symbol*] (TTSB)
GZTC .... Genzyme Transgenics Corp. [*NASDAQ symbol*] (SAG)
GZTPRD ...... Ground Zero Tape Read (IAA)
GZTS .... Guilford-Zimmerman Temperament Survey [*Psychology*]
GZU .... University of Wisconsin-La Crosse, La Crosse, WI [*OCLC symbol*] (OCLC)
GZV .... University of Wisconsin-Platteville, Platteville, WI [*OCLC symbol*] (OCLC)
GZW .... University of Wisconsin-Green Bay, Green Bay, WI [*OCLC symbol*] (OCLC)
GZX .... La Crosse Public Library, La Crosse, WI [*OCLC symbol*] (OCLC)
GZX .... Peoria, IL [*Location identifier FAA*] (FAAL)
GZY .... Wisconsin Interlibrary Loan Service, Madison, WI [*OCLC symbol*] (OCLC)

H

By Acronym

H.............	Air Force Training Category
H.............	Altitude
H.............	Altitude Rate [*Symbol*] (NASA)
H.............	Atmospheric Head (AAG)
H.............	Boltzmann Function [*Physics*] (BARN)
H.............	Bracco Industria Chimica [*Italy*] [*Research code symbol*]
h.............	Coefficient of Heat Transfer [*Symbol*] [*Thermodynamics*]
H.............	Declared or Paid after Stock Dividend or Split-Up [*Investment term*] (DFIT)
h.............	Dihydro [*As substituent on nucleoside*] [*Biochemistry*]
H.............	Enthalpy [*Symbol*] [*IUPAC*] (DEN)
H.............	Exposure [*Symbol*] [*IUPAC*]
h-----.........	French Union [*MARC geographic area code Library of Congress*] (LCCP)
h.............	Hacia [*Around*] [*Spanish*]
H.............	Haemaphysalis [*A genus of tick*] [*Entomology*] (DAVI)
H.............	Haftarah (BJA)
H.............	Hagelkorn [*Hailstone*] [*Bomb*] [*German military - World War II*]
H.............	Haggai [*Freemasonry*]
H.............	Hail [*Meteorology*]
H.............	Haler [*Monetary unit*] [*Former Czechoslovakia*]
H.............	Half
H.............	Half-Word Designator [*Computer science*]
H.............	Hall
H.............	HALON [*Halogenated Hydrocarbon*] (NFPA)
H.............	Halothane [*Also, HAL*] [*An anesthetic*]
H.............	Halt [*Computer science*] (MDG)
H.............	Hamiltonian Function [*Mathematics*]
H.............	Hamlet
H.............	Hamlyn Publishing [*British*]
H.............	Hand [*Music*]
H.............	Handbook (SAA)
H.............	Handily [*Horse racing*]
h.............	Hand-Rearing [*of experimental animals*] (DMAA)
H.............	Handy's Ohio Reports [*12 Ohio Decisions*] [*A publication*] (DLA)
H.............	Harbor [*Maps and charts*]
H.............	Harcourt General [*NYSE symbol*] (TTSB)
H.............	Harcourt General, Inc. [*Formerly, General Cinema Corp.*] [*NYSE symbol*] (SPSG)
H.............	Hard [*or Hardness*] [*Pencil leads*]
H.............	Hardness [*Of precious stones*]
H.............	Hardware [*Computer science*] (MDG)
H.............	Hardy [*Horticulture*]
H.............	Hare's English Chancery Reports [*A publication*] (DLA)
H.............	Harmonic (IDOE)
H.............	Harmonic Mean [*Psychology*]
h.............	Harmonized [*Apparent inconsistency explained and shown not to exist*] [*Used in Shepard's Citations*] [*Legal term*] (DLA)
H.............	Harrier (ROG)
H.............	Harry [*Phonetic alphabet*] [*Royal Navy World War I Pre-World War II*] (DSUE)
H.............	Has
H.............	Hassle [*Sweden*] [*Research code symbol*]
H.............	Hatch [*Technical drawings*]
H.............	Hauch [*Antigen*] [*Immunology*]
H.............	Haustus [*A Drink*] [*Pharmacy*]
H.............	Have (ROG)
H.............	Haven (ADA)
H.............	Hawaii Reports [*A publication*] (DLA)
(H).............	Hazardous [*Task classification*] [*NASA*] (NASA)
H.............	Hazardous Cargo [*Shipping*]
H.............	Haze [*Weather reports*]
H.............	Hazor (BJA)
H.............	Hazy (ABBR)
H.............	H-Beam [*Architecture*]
H.............	Head [*Linguistics*]
H.............	Head [*Anatomy*] (DAVI)
H.............	Head [*Horse racing*]
H.............	Header (NFPA)
H.............	Head, Hand, and Chest Sets [*JETDS nomenclature*] [*Military*] (CET)
H.............	Headlines (ABBR)
H.............	Headquarters (ABBR)
H.............	Healthy
H.............	Hearing Power (ROG)
H.............	Heart [*Freemasonry*] (ROG)
H.............	Hearts (ADA)
H.............	Heart Trouble [*Classification system used by doctors on Ellis Island to detain, re-examine, and possibly deny entry to certain immigrants*]
H.............	Heartwood [*Forestry*]
H.............	Heat [*or Heater*]
H.............	Heater (ABBR)
H.............	Heaton Mint [*British*]
H.............	Heavy [*Chain*] [*Biochemistry, immunochemistry*]
H.............	Heavy (AAG)
H.............	Heavy Lift Cargo Airlines Ltd. [*British*]
H.............	Heavy Sea [*Navigation*]
H.............	Hebrew (BJA)
h.............	Hecto [*A prefix meaning multiplied by 10^2*] [*SI symbol*]
H.............	Heel [*Music*]
H.............	Heelstick [*Medicine*] (DAVI)
H.............	Heft [*Part*] [*German*]
H.............	Height
h.............	Height [*Symbol*] [*IUPAC*]
H.............	Heir
H.............	Helicopter [*When the second letter or only letter*] [*Designation for all US military aircraft*]
H.............	Helicopteros do Brasil SA [*Brazil ICAO aircraft manufacturer identifier*] (ICAO)
H.............	Helium [*Chemical symbol is He*] (AAG)
H.............	Helix
H.............	Hemagglutinating [*Virology*]
H.............	Hematite [*A mineral*]
H.............	Hemic Subgroup [*Magnetite, chromite, hematite*] [*CIPW classification Geology*]
H.............	Hemin [*Hematology*]
H.............	Hemisphere [*Anatomy*] (DAVI)
H.............	Hemophilus [*Microbiology*] (MAE)
H.............	Hence
H.............	Henry [*Symbol*] [*SI unit of inductance*]
H.............	Henry (King of England) (DLA)
H.............	Henry's Law Constant
H.............	Heparin [*Pharmacology*] (DAVI)
h.............	Heplode [*Electronics*] (OA)
H.............	Herb [*Botany*]
H.............	Herbivore
H.............	Heres [*Heir*] [*Legal term Latin*]
H.............	Hermit
H.............	Hernia [*Gastroenterology*] (DAVI)
H.............	Heroin [*Slang*]
H.............	Hertzog's High Court Reports [*South Africa*] [*A publication*] (DLA)
H.............	Heterophyes [*A genus of trematode worms*] [*Gastroenterology*] (DAVI)
H.............	Heterozygosity [*Cytology*]
H.............	Hettangian [*Geology*]
H.............	Hexadecimal (BUR)
H.............	Hexapole (OA)
H.............	Hexode [*Electronics*] (OA)
H.............	Hic [*Here*] [*Latin*]
H.............	Hieroglyphics [*Freemasonry*] (ROG)
H.............	High [*Engineering*]
H.............	Highest [*Price Quoted of a Stock*] [*Finance*] (BARN)
H.............	High Season [*Airline fare code*]
H.............	High-Viscosity Fuel
H.............	Hilary Term [*England*] [*Legal term*] (DLA)
H.............	Hilkoth (BJA)
H.............	Hill (ROG)
H.............	Hill's New York Reports [*A publication*] (DLA)
H.............	Hindu (ABBR)
H.............	Hinged [*Philately*]
H.............	Hippelates [*A genus of insects*] [*Entomology*] (DAVI)
H.............	Hispanic
H.............	Histamine [*Anesthesiology*]
H.............	Histidine [*One-letter symbol*]
H.............	Histoplasma [*Biochemistry*] (DAVI)
H.............	Historiae [*of Sallust*] [*Classical studies*] (OCD)
H.............	Historical Re-Issue [*Record cataloging*]
H.............	History [*Secondary school course*] [*British*]
H.............	Hits [*Baseball*]
H.............	Hoffmann [*Reflex*] [*Neurology*]
H.............	Holding [*Electronics*]
H.............	Holiness (BJA)

H................. Holland [*IYRU nationality code*] (IYR)
H................. Holy
H................. Holzknecht [*Unit*]
H................. Home
H................. Homobonus de Cremona [*Deceased, 1272*] [*Authority cited in pre-1607 legal work*] (DSA)
H................. Homosexual
H................. Honor
H................. Honorary [*Academic degree*]
H................. Hooker
H................. Hope [*Freemasonry*] (ROG)
H................. Hopper-Tainer [*A form of container*] [*British*] (DCTA)
h................. Hora [*Hour*] [*Latin*]
H................. Horizon (ABBR)
H................. Horizontal
h................. Horizontal (WDMC)
H................. Horizontal Force of the Earth's Magnetism [*Amplitude of a tide*]
H................. Hormone [*Endocrinology*]
H................. Horn
H................. Horrific [*Film certificate*] [*British*]
H3................ Horror [*Literary genre*] (WDAA)
H................. Horse [*Thoroughbred racing*]
H................. Hose (NFPA)
H................. Hospital [*Traffic sign*] [*British*]
H................. Hospital Plane [*When suffixed to Navy plane designation*]
H................. Host [*Freemasonry*] (ROG)
H................. Hostiensis [*Deceased, 1271*] [*Authority cited in pre-1607 legal work*] (DSA)
H................. Hostile [*Military*]
H................. Hot
H................. Hotel
H................. Hounsfield Unit [*Medicine*] (MAE)
H................. Hour [*Also, h*]
H................. House
H................. House Bill [*Legal term*] (DLA)
H................. House of Representatives
H................. How [*Phonetic alphabet*] [*World War II*] (DSUE)
H................. Howard's United States Supreme Court Reports [*42-65 United States*] [*A publication*] (DLA)
H................. Hoy [*Ship's rigging*] (ROG)
H................. Hoyre [*Conservative Party*] [*Norway Political party*] (PPE)
h................. HTML [*Hypertext Markup Language*] [*Computer science*] [*Telecommunications*]
H................. Hugolinus de Presbyteris [*Flourished, 1197-1238*] [*Authority cited in pre-1607 legal work*] (DSA)
H................. Huguccio [*Deceased, 1210*] [*Authority cited in pre-1607 legal work*] (DSA)
H................. Hull (ADA)
H................. Human
h................. Human (DB)
H................. Human Being [*Rorschach*] [*Psychology*]
H................. [*The*] Humanitarian [*A publication*] (ROG)
H................. Humidity
H................. Hundred
h................. Hundred (WDMC)
H................. Hungary
H................. Hun-Stoffe [*Mustard gas*] [*Formerly, HS Also, HD, HT, M*]
H................. Husband
H................. Hussars [*Military unit*] [*British*]
H................. Hydrant
H................. Hydraulics (ADA)
H................. Hydrodynamic Head
H................. Hydrogen [*Chemical*] (EERA)
H................. Hydrographic Survey [*Navy British*]
H................. Hydrolysis
H................. Hydroxydaunomycin [*See also ADR, Adriamycin*] [*Antineoplastic drug*]
H................. Hygiene [*Preventive and Industrial Medicine*] [*Medical Officer designation*] [*British*]
H................. Hymenolepis [*A genus of tapeworm*] [*Gastroenterology*] (DAVI)
H................. Hyoscine [*Organic chemistry*]
H................. Hypermetropia [*Ophthalmology*]
H................. Hyperopia [*Ophthalmology*] (ROG)
H................. Hyperphoria [*Ophthalmology*] (DAVI)
H................. Hyperplasia [*Medicine*]
H................. Hypodermic
h................. Hypodermic (DMAA)
H................. Hypothalamus [*Medicine*] (DB)
H................. Hypothesis
H................. Instructor [*Army skill qualification identifier*] (INF)
H................. Magnetic Field Strength [*Symbol*]
H................. Magnetizing Force [*Symbol*] (DEN)
H................. Momentum [*Measurement*]
H................. Mustard Gas [*Also, HD, HS, HT, M*] [*Poison Gas US Chemical Corps symbol*]
H................. Nondirectional Radio Homing Beacon [*Navigation charts*]
H................. Oersted [*Unit of magnetizing force*] [*Physics*] (DMAA)
h................. Planck Constant [*Symbol*] [*IUPAC*]
H................. Regarding [*JETDS nomenclature*]
H................. Restaurants, Cafes, and Hotel Lounges [*Public-performance tariff class*] [*British*]
H................. Search/Rescue [*When the first letter of a pair*] [*Designation for all US military aircraft*]
H................. Silo Stored [*Missile launch environment symbol*]

H................. St Louis [*Branch in the Federal Reserve regional banking system*] (BARN)
H................. Total Energy (ROG)
H................. Turkiye Halk Bankasi [*Bank*] [*Turkey*]
H................. Vectorcardiogram Electrode [*Cardiology*] (DAVI)
H_0............... Hubble's Constant [*Astronomy*]
H_1............... Alternative Hypothesis (DAVI)
H1................ Haploid Cell Line 1
H^1............... Protium [*or Light hydrogen*] [*Chemical element*] (DAVI)
H^2............... Deuterium [*Also, D*] [*Radioisotope of hydrogen*]
H^2............... Hawaii (Kauai) [*Spaceflight Tracking and Data Network*] [*NASA*]
H^2............... Hot and Heavy [*In reference to a romance*]
H2................ Hydrogen
H_2BT........... Hydrogen Breath Test
H20............... Water [*Compound*] (RDA)
H_2O.............. Water (GNE)
H_2O_2............. Hydrogen Peroxide [*Pharmacology*] (DAVI)
H_2S.............. Hydrogen Sulfide (GNE)
H_2SO_4.......... Sulfuric Acid [*Chemistry*] (DAVI)
H_2Urd.......... Dihydrouridine [*Also, D, hU*] [*A nucleoside*]
H_3............... Tritium [*Also, T*] [*Radioisotope of hydrogen*]
H_3BO_3........... Boric Acid [*Pharmacology*] (DAVI)
H4................ Solomon Islands [*Aircraft nationality and registration mark*] (FAAC)
H_4............... Tetrahydro [*Biochemistry*]
$H_4folate$........ Tetrahydrofolate [*Biochemistry*]
H_4furan......... Tetrahydrofuran [*Organic chemistry*]
H_4pyran......... Tetrahydropyranyl [*Organic chemistry*]
H5................ Henry V [*Shakespearean work*]
H8................ Henry VIII [*Shakespearean work*]
H24............... Twenty-Four Hour [*Continuous*] Operation [*Aviation*]
HA................ Apogee Altitude (NASA)
HA................ CASA [*Construcciones Aeronauticas Sociedad Anonima*] [*Spain ICAO aircraft manufacturer identifier*] (ICAO)
HA................ Chem. Werke Albert [*Germany*] [*Research code symbol*]
HA................ Habitual Abortion [*Medicine*]
Ha................ Hahnium [*Proposed name for chemical element 105*]
HA................ Haiti [*or Haitian*] (WDAA)
HA................ Half Adder [*Circuitry*] (MSA)
Ha................ Hallah (BJA)
HA................ Hallux Abductus [*Orthopedics*] (DAVI)
HA................ Hand Actuated (IAA)
H/A............... Hand/Automatic [*Nuclear energy*] (NRCH)
HA................ H Antigen (DB)
HA................ Hardness Assurance (MSA)
HA................ Hardware [*Computer science*] (IAA)
HA................ Hardy Annual [*Horticulture*] (ROG)
Ha................ Hare's English Vice-Chancellors' Reports [*66-68 English Reprint*] [*1841-53*] [*A publication*] (DLA)
HA................ Harmonie Associates (EA)
HA................ Harness Assembly
Ha................ Hartmann Number [*IUPAC*]
HA................ Hatch Act [*1887*]
HA................ Hatchway (DS)
HA................ Hawaii [*or Hawaiian*] (WDAA)
HA................ Hawaiian Airlines 'A' [*AMEX symbol*] (TTSB)
HA................ Hawaiian Airlines, Inc. [*AMEX symbol*] (SAG)
HA................ Hawaiian Airlines, Inc. [*ICAO designator*] (ICDA)
HA................ Hazard Analysis (NASA)
HA................ Hazard Assessment [*Environmental science*] (COE)
HA................ Hazardous Area
HA................ Headache
HA................ Headmasters [*or Headmistresses*] Association (EA)
HA................ Headquarters Administration Division [*Coast Guard*]
H/A............... Head to Abdomen (DMAA)
HA................ Health Academy [*An association*] (EA)
HA................ Health Act (OICC)
HA................ Health Advisory (GNE)
HA................ Health Affairs [*Army*] (DOMA)
HA................ Health Alliance [*Consumer representation*] (ECON)
HA................ Health Assessment (BCP)
HA................ Healthy America [*An association Defunct*] (EA)
HA................ Hearing Aid
HA................ Heavy Artillery
HA................ Heavy Atoms
HA................ Hectare (AAG)
ha S.............. Hectare (DMAA)
HA................ Hectocotylized Arm
HA................ Heeres-Atmer [*Service Oxygen Breathing Apparatus*] [*German military - World War II*]
HA................ Hefte von Auschwitz (BJA)
HA................ Height Age (MAE)
HA................ Height of Apogee
HA................ Heir Apparent
HA................ Hellenic Army (MCD)
HA................ Hemadsorption [*Hematology*]
HA................ Hemagglutinating Activity [*Hematology*] (DAVI)
HA................ Hemagglutinating Antibody [*Hematology*] (DAVI)
HA................ Hemagglutinating Antigen [*Hematology*] (DAVI)
HA................ Hemagglutination [*Hematology*]
HA................ Hemolytic Anemia [*Hematology*]
HA................ Henry Adams, Inc. [*Baltimore, MD*] (TSSD)
HA................ Henson Associates [*Television production company*]
HA................ Hepatic Artery [*Anatomy*] (MAE)
HA................ Hepatitis Associated [*Virus*]
HA................ Heptaldehyde-Aniline (EDCT)

HA...............	Heptaldehyde-Aniline Condensate (EDCT)
HA...............	Herpes Association [British] (DBA)
HA...............	Heterophile Antibody [Immunochemistry]
HA...............	Heyden Antibiotic [Pharmacology]
HA...............	High Altitude
HA...............	High Amplitude (IAA)
HA...............	High Angle
HA...............	High Anxiety (MAE)
HA...............	High Authority of the ECSC [European Coal and Steel Community] (ILCA)
HA...............	Higher Authority
HA...............	Highways Act [British] (ILCA)
HA...............	Hiram Abiff [Freemasonry] (ROG)
HA...............	Histamine [Medicine] (DB)
HA...............	Histocompatibility Antigen (DB)
HA...............	Historia Animalium [of Aristotle] [Classical studies] (OCD)
HA...............	Historical Association [British] (EAIO)
HA...............	History Abstracts [Database] (NITA)
HA...............	Hoc Anno [This Year] [Latin]
HA...............	Hockey Association [British]
H/A.............	Holding Activity
HA...............	Holiness Army (ROG)
HA...............	Home Address
HA...............	Homesteaders Association [Defunct] (EA)
HA...............	Horse Artillery
HA...............	Horticultural Abstracts
HA...............	Hosanna Army (ROG)
HA...............	Hospice Association (EA)
HA...............	Hospital Academy (EA)
HA...............	Hospital Admission
HA...............	Hospital Apprentice [Navy rating]
HA...............	Hostile Aeroplane [British military] (DMA)
HA...............	Hot Air
HA...............	Hounsfield Unit [On computerized tomography] [Radiology] (DAVI)
HA...............	Hour Angle [Navigation]
HA...............	House Account [Business term]
HA...............	House Administration (DLA)
HA...............	Housewives Association [Australia]
HA...............	Housing Allowance [Military]
HA...............	Housing Assistance [HUD]
HA...............	Housing Authority
HA...............	Hoverclub of America (EA)
H-A.............	Howson-Algraphy (DGA)
HA...............	Huius Anni [This Year's] [Latin]
HA...............	Human Adaptability
HA...............	Human Argininosuccinate Lyase [An enzyme]
HA...............	Humanitarian Assistance [Environmental science] (COE)
HA...............	Humic Acid [Organic chemistry]
HA...............	Humor Association (EA)
HA...............	Humorolics Anonymous (EA)
HA...............	Hungarian Association [Australia]
HA...............	Hyaluronic Acid [Biochemistry]
HA...............	Hydraulic Association of Great Britain (BI)
HA...............	Hydrocephalus Association (EA)
HA...............	Hydrophone Allowance [British military] (DMA)
HA...............	Hydroxyapatite [Also, HAP] [A mineral]
HA...............	Hydroxylapatite [Inorganic chemistry]
HA...............	Hyperalimentation [Intravenous feeding] (DAVI)
HA...............	Hypermetropia, Absolute [Ophthalmology]
HA...............	Hypersensitivity Alveolitis [Medicine] (DB)
HA...............	Hypoglycemic Association [Australia]
HA...............	Hypothalmic Amenorrhea [Medicine] (DAVI)
HA...............	Netherlands [IYRU nationality code] (IYR)
HA1.............	Hemadsorption [Virus], Type 1 [Hematology] (DAVI)
HA2.............	Hemadsorption Type 2 [Virus] [Medicine] (DB)
HAA.............	Haflinger Association of America (EA)
HAA.............	Haitian-American Association [Defunct]
HAA.............	Haloacetic Acids [Environmental chemistry]
HAA.............	Handbooks of Archaeology and Antiquities [A publication]
HAA.............	Handicapped Artists of America (EA)
HAA.............	Hands Across America [Defunct] (EA)
HAA.............	Harrison Air [Canada ICAO designator] (FAAC)
HAA.............	Hasvik [Norway] [Airport symbol] (OAG)
HAA.............	Head Access Area [Nuclear energy] (NRCH)
HAA.............	Hearing Aid Amplifier
HAA.............	Heater Amplifier Assembly
HAA.............	Heavy Antiaircraft Artillery
HAA.............	Height above Airport (AFM)
HAA.............	Helicopter Airline Association (EA)
HAA.............	Helicopter Association of America [Later, HAI] (EA)
HAA.............	Helicopter Association of Australia
HAA.............	Hemolytic Anemia Antigen [Immunochemistry]
HAA.............	Hepatitis Associated Antigen [Clinical chemistry]
HAA.............	Heptaminol Adenosinemonophosphate Amidate [Biochemistry]
HAA.............	High-Altitude Abort [NASA] (KSC)
HAA.............	High-Altitude Application
HAA.............	Hispanic American Almanac [A publication]
HAA.............	Historic Aircraft Association [British]
HAA.............	Home Automation Association (EA)
HAA.............	Honduran-American Association (EA)
HAA.............	Horticulture Awareness Association (EA)
HAA.............	Hospice Association of America (NTPA)
HAA.............	Hospital Activity Analysis [British]
HAA.............	Hotel Accountants Association of New York City (EA)
HAA.............	Houseboat Association of America (EA)

HAA	Housing Assistance Administration [HUD]
HAA	Human Asset Accounting (ADA)
HAAA	Addis Ababa [Ethiopia] [ICAO location identifier] (ICLI)
HAAB	Addis Ababa/Bole International [Ethiopia] [ICAO location identifier] (ICLI)
HAAC	Heart of America Athletic Conference (PSS)
HAAC	Heavy Attack Aircraft Commander (DNAB)
HAAC	Housing Aid & Advice Centre [England]
HAAC	Hydraulic Actuator Assembly Container
HAACT	Heavy Attack Aircraft Commander Training (DNAB)
HAAD	Adaba [Ethiopia] [ICAO location identifier] (ICLI)
HAAD	High-Altitude Aircraft Detection
HAADA	Horatio Alger Association of Distinguished Americans (EA)
HAADF	High-Angle Annular Dark-Field [Microscopy]
HAAFCE	Headquarters, Allied Air Force, Central Europe [NATO]
HAAFE	Hawaiian Army and Air Force Exchange [Military]
HAAG	Agordat [Ethiopia] [ICAO location identifier] (ICLI)
HAAg	Hepatitis A Antigen [Immunology] (DAVI)
HAAL	Addis Ababa/Liddetta [Ethiopia] [ICAO location identifier] (ICLI)
HAALS	High-Accuracy Airborne Location System (MCD)
HAAM	Arba Minch [Ethiopia] [ICAO location identifier] (ICLI)
Ha & Tw	Hall and Twell's English Chancery Reports [1849-50] [A publication] (DLA)
HAAO	High-Altitude Airborne Observation
HAAP	Hawthorne Army Ammunition Plant (MCD)
HAAP	High Air Pollution Potential
HAAP	High-Altitude Air Pollution Program [FAA] (MCD)
HAAP	Holston Army Ammunition Plant
HAAP	Home-Based Advanced Assignment Program [Military]
hAAP	Human Amyloid-Precursor Protein [Neurobiology]
Ha App	Appendix to Volume 10 of Hare's Vice-Chancellor's Reports [England] [A publication] (DLA)
HAARP........	High-Altitude Auroral Research Project [Jointly operated by the Department of Defense and the Geophysical Institute at the University of Alaska]
HAARS........	High-Altitude Airdrop Resupply System
HAARS........	Hourly Attendance and Absence Reporting System [Military] (MCD)
HAART	Highly Active Antiretroviral Therapy [Medicine]
HAAS	Asmara App [Ethiopia] [ICAO location identifier] (ICLI)
HAAS	Honeywell Automotive Accounting System (IAA)
HAAT	Height above Average Terrain
HAAT	Height of Antenna Above Average Terrain [Broadcasting] (WDMC)
HAATC	High-Altitude Air Traffic Control
HAAW	Awash [Ethiopia] [ICAO location identifier] (ICLI)
HAAW	Heavy Antitank/Assault Weapon [Army]
HAAX	Axum [Ethiopia] [ICAO location identifier] (ICLI)
HAAY	Asmara/Yohannes IV [Ethiopia] [ICAO location identifier] (ICLI)
HAB	Habacuc [Old Testament book] [Douay version]
Hab.............	Habakkuk [Old Testament book]
HAB	Habitat [Dwelling] (ROG)
HAB	Habitation
HAB	Habitual [FBI standardized term]
HAB	Haboro [Japan] [Seismograph station code, US Geological Survey Closed] (SEIS)
HAB	Hamilton, AL [Location identifier FAA] (FAAL)
HAB	Hazards Analysis Board [Air Force]
HAB	Hearing Aid Battery
HAb	Heart Antibody [Medicine] (CPH)
HAB	Heavy Assault Bridge
HAB	Hepatitis B [Virus] [Infectious diseases] (DAVI)
HAB	High-Altitude Bombing [Military]
HAB	High-Alumina Basalt [Geology]
HAB	Hiram Abiff [Freemasonry] (ROG)
HAB	Historic American Buildings [Survey] [Library of Congress]
HAB	Home Address Block
HAB	Horizontal Assembly Building [NASA] (KSC)
HAB	Horizontal Axis Bearing
HAB	Hot Air Balloon
HAB	Hybrid Antibody [Immunology]
HABA	Health and Beauty Aids [Retailing] (AABC)
haba	Health and Beauty Aids [Advertising] (WDMC)
HABA	(Hydroxyazobenzene)benzoic Acid [Also, HBABA] [Organic chemistry]
HaBaD	Hokhmah, Bimah, Daat [Germinal, Developmental, and Conclusive Knowledge] [Hebrew]
HABB	Bunno Bedele [Ethiopia] [ICAO location identifier] (ICLI)
HABBA	(Hydroxyazobenzene)benzoic Acid [Organic chemistry]
HABC	Baco [Ethiopia] [ICAO location identifier] (ICLI)
HABC	Habersham Bancorp [NASDAQ symbol] (SAG)
HAB CORP...	Habeas Corpus [You Have the Body] [Legal] [Latin] (ROG)
HABD	Bahar Dar [Ethiopia] [ICAO location identifier] (ICLI)
HABD	Hydrazobenzene Derivative [Organic chemistry]
HABE	Beica [Ethiopia] [ICAO location identifier] (ICLI)
Habersh.......	Habersham Bancorp [Associated Press] (SAG)
HABF	Hepatic Artery Blood Flow
HAB FAC POSS...	Habere Facias Possessionem [A writ to put the plaintiff in possession] [Latin Legal term] (ROG)
Hab Fa Poss...	Habere Facias Possessionem [A writ to put the plaintiff in possession] [Legal term Latin]
HAB FA SEIS...	Habere Facias Seisenam [A writ to put the plaintiff in actual possession] [Latin Legal term] (ROG)
HAB FA SEIS...	Habere Facias Seisinam [That You Cause to Have Seisin] [Latin Legal term] (DLA)
HABGT........	Hutt Adaptation of the Bender-Gestalt Test
habit............	Habitat (BARN)

HABP .... Hypersonic Arbitrary Body Program [*NASA*]
HABS .... High-Altitude Bombsight (NATG)
HABS .... Historic American Buildings Survey [*Library of Congress*]
HABT .... Habeat [*Let Him Have*] [*Pharmacy*]
HABT .... Habitability Technology (SSD)
HABTA .... Habituate (ABBR)
HABTAD ...... Habituated (ABBR)
HABTAG ...... Habituating (ABBR)
HABTAN ...... Habitation (ABBR)
HABTAN ...... Habituation (ABBR)
HABTB .... Habitable (ABBR)
HABTL .... Habitual (ABBR)
HABTLNS ..... Habitualness (ABBR)
HABTU .... Habitue (ABBR)
HABTY .... Habitually (ABBR)
HABU .... Bulchi [*Ethiopia*] [*ICAO location identifier*] (ICLI)
HABY .... Haberdashery (DSUE)
HAC .... Hachijojima Island [*Japan*] [*Airport symbol*] (OAG)
HAC .... Hachinohe [*Japan*] [*Seismograph station code, US Geological Survey*] (SEIS)
HAC .... Haitian Air Corps
HAC .... Handicapped Action Committee
HAC .... Hazards Assessment Center [*Environmental science*] (COE)
HAC .... Heading Alignment Circle [*NASA*] (NASA)
HAC .... Heading Alignment Cone [*NASA*] (NASA)
HAC .... Heading Alignment Cylinder (MCD)
HAC .... Headquarters Area Command [*Military*]
HAC .... Health Advisory Council [*New South Wales, Australia*]
HAC .... Health Advisory Council [*Generic term*] (DHSM)
HAC .... Hearing Aid with Compression
HAC .... Heavy-Aggregate Concrete (DEN)
HAC .... Heavy Antitank Convoy
HAC .... Heavy Attack Aircraft Commander
HAC .... Helicopter Air Control [*Military*] (CAAL)
HAC .... Helicopter Aircraft Commander (NVT)
HAC .... Hellenic Advancement Council [*Australia*]
HAC .... Henebury Aviation Co. [*Australia ICAO designator*] (FAAC)
HAC .... Herbicide Assessment Commission
HAC .... Hexamethylmelamine [*Altretamine*], Adriamycin, Cyclophosphamide [*Antineoplastic drug regimen*]
HAC .... Hierarchical Abstract Computer (MHDI)
HAC .... High-Acceleration Cockpit [*Air Force*]
HAC .... High-Altitude Compensation [*Automotive engineering*]
HAC .... High-Aluminous Concrete
HAC .... Highway Action Coalition
HAC .... Hines Administrative Center [*Veterans Administration*]
HAC .... Historians of American Communism (EA)
HAC .... Historical Artillery Corps [*British*] [*An association*] (DBA)
HAC .... Historical Atlas of Canada [*Project*]
HAC .... Holland America Cruises [*Formerly, Holland-America Line*]
HAC .... Holland Australia Club [*Australia*]
HAC .... Honourable Artillery Co. [*Military unit*] [*British*]
HAC .... Horticultural Advisory Council for England and Wales (BI)
HAC .... Hospitals Accreditation Committee [*Australia*]
HAC .... Hot and Cold (IAA)
HAC .... House Appropriations Committee [*US Congress*] (AAG)
HAC .... Housing Advisory Council [*South Australia*]
HAC .... Housing Assistance Council (EA)
HAC .... Hover and Approach Coupler (MCD)
HAC .... Hughes Aircraft Co.
HAC .... Human Artificial Chromosome [*Genetics*]
HAC .... Humanities Association of Canada [*See also ACH*]
HAC .... Hydrogenated Amorphous Carbon [*Inorganic chemistry*]
HACC .... Hellenic-American Chamber of Commerce (NTPA)
HACC .... Help and Action Coordinating Committee [*Defunct France*] (EAIO)
HACCP .... Hazard Analysis Critical Control Point [*Quality control*]
HACCP .... Hazard Analysis Critical Control Points
HACE .... High-Altitude Cerebral Edema [*Medicine*]
HACEK .... Hemophilus, Actinobacillus, Cardiobacterium, Eikenella, and Kingella [*Gram-negative bacilli*]
HACH .... Hach Co. [*NASDAQ symbol*] (NQ)
HACHD .... Hatched (ABBR)
HACHG .... Hatching (ABBR)
HAChT .... High-Affinity Choline Transport
HACHWY ..... Hatchway (ABBR)
HACHY .... Hatchery (ABBR)
HACI .... Hughes Aircraft Co., International Division
HACK .... Hackney [*Borough of London*]
Hack Gen Aw... Hackett on the Geneva Award Acts [*A publication*] (DLA)
HACL .... Harvard Air Cleaning Laboratory (NRCH)
HACL .... Hostility Adjective Check List [*Psychology*]
HACLA .... Housing Authority of the City of Los Angeles
HACLCS ...... Harpoon Aircraft Command and Launch Control Set [*Missiles*] (NVT)
HACLS .... Harpoon Aircraft Command and Launch Subsystem [*Missiles*] (MCD)
HACN .... Hacienda (ABBR)
HAC NOCT ... Hac Nocte [*Tonight*] [*Pharmacy*]
HACOM .... Headquarters Area Command [*Military*]
HACR .... Hereditary Adenomatosis of the Colon and Rectum [*Medicine*] (DMAA)
HACS .... Hazard Assessment Computer System [*Coast Guard*]
HACS .... High-Angle Control System [*British military*] (DMA)
HACS .... Homeostatic Adaptive Control System
HACS .... Hyperactive Child Syndrome
HACSG .... Hyper Active Children's Support Group [*British*]
HACT .... High-Affinity Choline Transport

HACTU .... Human Action Counselling and Training Unit [*British*] (DI)
HACU .... Hispanic Association of Colleges and Universities
HAD .... Casper, WY [*Location identifier FAA*] (FAAL)
HAD .... Hadassah (BJA)
Had .... Haddington's Manuscript Reports, Scotch Court of Session [*A publication*] (DLA)
Had .... Hadley's Reports [*45-48 New Hampshire*] [*A publication*] (DLA)
HAD .... Half Amplitude Duration [*Telecommunications*] (TEL)
HAD .... Halmstad [*Sweden*] [*Airport symbol*] (OAG)
HAD .... Handicappers for Accountable Democracy (EA)
HAD .... Hardness Assurance Document
HAD .... Hartland [*United Kingdom*] [*Geomagnetic observatory code*]
HAD .... Hassan Addakhil Dam [*Morocco*] [*Seismograph station code, US Geological Survey*] (SEIS)
HAD .... Hawaii Air Defense
HAD .... Head Acceleration Device (PDAA)
HAD .... Health Assessment Document [*Environmental Protection Agency*] (GFGA)
HAD .... Health Care Alternatives Development (HCT)
HAD .... Hearing Aid Dispenser [*Otorhinolaryngology*] (DAVI)
HAD .... Heat-Activated Device (NRCH)
HAD .... Helicopter Approach/Departure [*Military*] (CAAL)
HAD .... Helicopteros Andes [*Chile*] [*ICAO designator*] (FAAC)
HAD .... Helium Abundance Detector [*Instrumentation*]
HAD .... Hemadsorption [*Hematology*]
HAD .... Herein After Described [*Legal*] [*British*] (MHDI)
HAD .... Hexamethylmelamine, Adriamycin, Diamminedichloroplatinum [*Cisplatin*] [*Antineoplastic drug regimen*]
HAD .... High-Accuracy Data [*System*] (MUGU)
HAD .... High Alcohol Drinking [*Rat strain*]
HAD .... High-Altitude Density [*Sounding rocket*]
HAD .... High-Altitude Diagnostic [*Unit*] [*Rocket launcher*]
HAD .... Hole-Accumulated Diode [*Sony Corp.*]
HAD .... Horizontal Array of Dipoles
HAD .... Hospital Administration [*or Administrator*]
HAD .... Hypersonic Aerothermal Dynamics (SAA)
HADA .... Hawaiian Defense Area
HADAPS....... Hydrographic Automated Data Acquisitioning and Processing System (MCD)
HADAS........ Helmet Airborne Display and Sight (MCD)
HADB .... Dagabour [*Ethiopia*] [*ICAO location identifier*] (ICLI)
HADB .... Hazardous Substances Data Bank [*National Library of Medicine*] [*Information service or system*]
HADB .... High-Altitude Dive Bomb [*Military*]
HADC .... Dessie/Combolcha [*Ethiopia*] [*ICAO location identifier*] (ICLI)
HADC .... HIV [*Human Immunodeficiency Virus*] -Associated Dementia Complex [*Medicine*]
HADC .... Holloman Air Development Center [*Air Force*]
Had Chy Jur... Haddan's Administrative Jurisdiction of the Court of Chancery [*A publication*] (DLA)
Hadco .... Hadco Corp. [*Associated Press*] (SAG)
HADD .... Dembidollo [*Ethiopia*] [*ICAO location identifier*] (ICLI)
Hadd .... Haddington's Manuscript Reports, Scotch Court of Session [*A publication*] (DLA)
HADD .... Hawaiian Air Defense Division
HADD .... Hydroxyapatite Deposition Disease [*Medicine*] (DAVI)
Haddington... Haddington's Manuscript Reports, Scotch Court of Session [*A publication*] (DLA)
HA-DEC........ Hour Angle-Declination [*Type of antenna mounting*]
HADES......... Hypersonic Air Data Entry System
HAd-I.......... Hemadsorption Inhibition (STED)
HADIOS........ Honeywell Analog-Digital Input-Output Subsystem (IAA)
HADIS......... Hadamard Imaging Spectrometer (PDAA)
HADIS......... Huddersfield and District Information Service [*British*] (NITA)
HADIZ......... Hawaiian Air Defense Identification Zone
HADL.......... Dallol [*Ethiopia*] [*ICAO location identifier*] (ICLI)
Hadl.......... Hadley's Reports [*45-48 New Hampshire*] [*A publication*] (DLA)
Hadley......... Hadley's Reports [*45-48 New Hampshire*] [*A publication*] (DLA)
Hadl Rom Law... Hadley's Introduction to the Roman Law [*A publication*] (DLA)
HADM.......... Debre Marcos [*Ethiopia*] [*ICAO location identifier*] (ICLI)
HADM.......... Heavy Atomic Demolition Munition [*Military*] (AABC)
HADN.......... Danguilla [*Ethiopia*] [*ICAO location identifier*] (ICLI)
HAD(N)....... Head of Aircraft Department (Naval) [*British*]
Hadng.......... Hardinge, Inc. [*Associated Press*] (SAG)
HADO.......... Dodola [*Ethiopia*] [*ICAO location identifier*] (ICLI)
HADOPAD ... High-Altitude Delayed Opening Parachute Actuation Device (MCD)
HADOSS ...... HWWA-Dossiers [*Society for Business Information*] [*Information service or system*] (IID)
HADR.......... Dire Dawa/Aba Tenna Dejazmatch Yilma [*Ethiopia*] [*ICAO location identifier*] (ICLI)
Hadr.......... Hadrian [*of Scriptores Historiae Augustae*] [*Classical studies*] (OCD)
HADR.......... Hughes Air Defense RADAR [*Military*]
HADS.......... Hawaii Air Defense System
HADS.......... Hospital Anxiety and Depression Scale [*Medicine*] (DMAA)
HADS.......... Hypersonic Air Data Sensor (IEEE)
HADT.......... Debre Tabor [*Ethiopia*] [*ICAO location identifier*] (ICLI)
HADTS......... High-Accuracy Data Transmission System (MUGU)
HAE............ Haemonetics Corp. [*NYSE symbol*] (SPSG)
HAE............ Hannibal, MO [*Location identifier FAA*] (FAAL)
HAE............ Hatia [*Bangladesh*] [*Airport symbol*] (AD)
HAE............ Havasupai [*Arizona*] [*Airport symbol*] (OAG)
HAE............ Health Appraisal Examination (DMAA)
HAE............ Hearing Aid Evaluation [*Otorhinolayrngology*] (DAVI)
HAE............ Hepatic Artery Embolization [*Medicine*] (DAVI)
HAE............ Hereditary Angioedema [*Medicine*] (STED)

HAE............	Hereditary Angioneurotic Edema [*Medicine*]
HAEC..........	High Altitude Economic Carrier (PDAA)
HAEC..........	Human Aortic Endothelial Cell
HAEC..........	Human Artificial Episomal Chromosome (HGEN)
HAEE..........	Harwell Atomic Energy Establishment
HAEH..........	Horizontal Axis Electrical Hairspring
HAEM..........	Haemolysis [*British*]
HAEMAT	Haematocrit [*British*]
HAEMATOL...	Haematology [*British*]
Haemon.....	Haemonetics Corp. [*Associated Press*] (SAG)
HAEMORRH...	Haemorrhage [*British*]
HAEMP	High-Altitude Electromagnetic Pulse
HAER	Historic American Engineering Record [*Department of the Interior*]
HAES	Hawaii Agricultural Experiment Station [*Honolulu*]
HAES	High-Altitude Effects Simulation [*Defense Nuclear Agency*]
HaF.............	Hageman Factor (STED)
HAF.............	Haifa [*Israel*] [*Seismograph station code, US Geological Survey Closed*] (SEIS)
HAF.............	Half Moon Bay, CA [*Location identifier FAA*] (FAAL)
HAF.............	Hallmark Financial Services [*AMEX symbol*] (SAG)
HAF.............	Headquarters, Air Force (AFM)
HAF.............	Headquarters, Allied Forces
HAF.............	Heavy Aircraft Fuel (MSA)
HAF.............	Hebrew Arts Foundation (EA)
HAF.............	Helicopter Assault Force (NVT)
HAF.............	Hellenic Air Force [*Greece*] [*ICAO designator*] (FAAC)
HAF.............	Hellenic Armed Forces (NATG)
HAF.............	Helms Athletic Foundation [*Later, Citizens Savings Athletic Foundation*] (EA)
HAF.............	Hepatic Arterial Flow [*Medicine*] (STED)
HAF.............	High-Abrasion Furnace (IEEE)
HAF.............	High-Altitude Fluorescence (IEEE)
HAF.............	High-Altitude Fuze [*To activate weapons*]
HAF.............	Human Antitumor Factor [*Biochemistry*]
HAF.............	Hypersonic Aerothermaldynamic Facility
HAFB	Heavy Assault Floating Bridge [*British military*] (DMA)
HAFB	Hill Air Force Base (SAA)
HAFB	Holloman Air Force Base [*New Mexico*]
HAFBLCK.....	High-Abrasion Furnace Black (IAA)
HAFC	High-Altitude Forecast Center
HAFC	Hoyt Axton Fan Club (EA)
HAFE	Harpers Ferry National Historical Park
HAFID	Hydrogen Atmosphere Flame Ionization Detector
HAFMED	Headquarters, Allied Forces, Mediterranean
HAFN	Fincha [*Ethiopia*] [*ICAO location identifier*] (ICLI)
HAFO	Home Accounting and Finance Office
HAFOE	High Air Flow with Oxygen Enrichment (PDAA)
HAFP	Hawaii Academy of Family Physicians (SRA)
HAFRA	Hat and Allied Feltmakers' Research Association [*British*] (BI)
HAFS	Homosexuals Anonymous Fellowship Services (EA)
HAFSE	Headquarters, Allied Forces, Southern Europe (NATG)
HafsInd.......	Hafslund Nycomed AS [*Associated Press*] (SAG)
HafsInd.......	Hafslund Nycomed AS [*Associated Press*] (SAG)
HAFTB	Holloman Air Force Test Base [*New Mexico*] (AAG)
Hag.............	Hagan's Reports [*West Virginia*] [*A publication*] (DLA)
Hag.............	Hagan's Reports [*Utah*] [*A publication*] (DLA)
Hag.............	Haggai [*Old Testament book*]
Hag.............	Haggard's English Admiralty Reports [*A publication*] (DLA)
Hag.............	Hagigah (BJA)
HAG	[*The*] Hague [*Netherlands*] [*Airport symbol*] (AD)
HAG	Harvest Aviation Ltd. [*British ICAO designator*] (FAAC)
HAG	Heat-Aggregated Globulin (DB)
HAG	Helicopter Action Group (NVT)
HAG	High-Explosive Antiarmor Grenade [*Weaponry*] (MCD)
HAG	Hold for Arrival of Goods
HAG	Home Address Gap [*Computer science*] (MHDB)
HAG	Housing Association Grant [*British*]
HAG	Humanitarian Assistance Group [*Iraq*]
HAG	Hydrothermally-Altered Granite [*Geology*]
HAG	Hydroxyaminoguanidine [*Biochemistry*]
Hag Adm	Haggard's English Admiralty Reports [*A publication*] (DLA)
Hagan........	Hagan's Reports [*Utah*] [*A publication*] (DLA)
HAGB..........	Goba [*Ethiopia*] [*ICAO location identifier*] (ICLI)
HAG COM	Haga Comitum [*The Hague*] [*Imprint*] (ROG)
Hag Con	Haggard's English Consistory Reports [*161 English Reprint*] [*A publication*] (DLA)
Hag Ecc	Haggard's English Ecclesiastical Reports [*162 English Reprint*] [*A publication*] (DLA)
HAGG..........	Heat-Aggregated Gamma Globulin [*Clinical chemistry*]
HAGG..........	Hyperimmune Antivariola Gamma Globulin
Hagg Adm ...	Haggard's English Admiralty Reports [*A publication*] (DLA)
Hagg Adm (Eng)...	Haggard's English Admiralty Reports [*161 English Reprint*] [*A publication*] (DLA)
Haggar........	Haggar Corp. [*Associated Press*] (SAG)
Hagg Con.....	Haggard's English Consistory Reports [*161 English Reprint*] [*A publication*] (DLA)
Hagg Cons...	Haggard's English Consistory Reports [*161 English Reprint*] [*A publication*] (DLA)
Hagg Consist...	Haggard's English Consistory Reports [*161 English Reprint*] [*A publication*] (DLA)
Hagg Consist (Eng)...	Haggard's English Consistory Reports [*161 English Reprint*] [*A publication*] (DLA)
Hagg Ecc	Haggard's English Ecclesiastical Reports [*162 English Reprint*] [*A publication*] (DLA)

Hagg Eccl	Haggard's English Ecclesiastical Reports [*162 English Reprint*] [*1827-33*] [*A publication*] (DLA)
Hagg Eccl (Eng)...	Haggard's English Ecclesiastical Reports [*162 English Reprint*] [*A publication*] (DLA)
HAGH..........	Ghinnir [*Ethiopia*] [*ICAO location identifier*] (ICLI)
HAGH..........	Hydroxyacyl-Glutathione Hydrolase (DMAA)
HAGIOL.......	Hagiology (ABBR)
HAGL	Galadi [*Ethiopia*] [*ICAO location identifier*] (ICLI)
HAGL	Haggle (ABBR)
HAGL	Handheld Grenade-Launcher
HAGLD........	Haggled (ABBR)
HAGLG........	Haggling (ABBR)
HAGLR........	Haggler (ABBR)
HAGLST.......	Hagiologist (ABBR)
HAGM.........	Gambella [*Ethiopia*] [*ICAO location identifier*] (ICLI)
HAGN.........	Gondar [*Ethiopia*] [*ICAO location identifier*] (ICLI)
Hagn & M...	Hagner and Miller's Reports [*2 Maryland Chancery*] [*A publication*] (DLA)
Hagn & Mill...	Hagner and Miller's Reports [*2 Maryland Chancery*] [*A publication*] (DLA)
HAGO.........	Gode [*Ethiopia*] [*ICAO location identifier*] (ICLI)
HAGO.........	Heavy Atmospheric Gas Oil [*Petroleum product*]
HAGR.........	Gore [*Ethiopia*] [*ICAO location identifier*] (ICLI)
HAGR.........	Hamilton Grange National Memorial
HAGS	Hispanic American Geriatrics Society (EA)
HAGTNS......	Haughtiness (ABBR)
HAGTR	Haughtier (ABBR)
HAGTST	Haughtiest (ABBR)
HAGTY	Haughtily (ABBR)
HAGU.........	Gura [*Ethiopia*] [*ICAO location identifier*] (ICLI)
Hague Ct Rep...	Hague Court Reports [*A publication*] (DLA)
HAH	Healthcare Association of Hawaii (SRA)
HAH	Jacksonville, NC [*Location identifier FAA*] (FAAL)
HAH	Moroni [*Comoro Islands*] Hahaia Airport [*Airport symbol*] (OAG)
HA-HA-SO...	Help, Assert, Humor, Avoid, Self-Talk, and Own It [*Assertive strategy*]
HAHI	Help At Home [*NASDAQ symbol*] (TTSB)
HAHI	Help At Home, Inc. [*NASDAQ symbol*] (SAG)
HAHIW........	Help At Home Wrrt [*NASDAQ symbol*] (TTSB)
HAHM.........	Debre Zeit/Harar Meda [*Ethiopia*] [*ICAO location identifier*] (ICLI)
HAHN.........	Hahn Automotive Warehouse [*NASDAQ symbol*] (TTSB)
HAHN.........	Hahn Automotive Warehouse, Inc. [*NASDAQ symbol*] (SAG)
HahnAut......	Hahn Automotive Warehouse, Inc. [*Associated Press*] (SAG)
Hahnemann U...	Hahnemann University (GAGS)
HAHO.........	Harmony Holdings [*NASDAQ symbol*] (TTSB)
HAHO.........	Harmony Holdings, Inc. [*NASDAQ symbol*] (SAG)
HAHO.........	High Altitude/High Opening [*Army*] (ADDR)
HAHR.........	Hispanic American Historical Review [*A publication*] (BRI)
HAHS	Hooved Animal Humane Society (EA)
HA(HS)........	Hospital Apprentice, High School
HAHS	Hossana [*Ethiopia*] [*ICAO location identifier*] (ICLI)
HAHST	High-Altitude High-Speed Target [*Formerly, HAST*] (MCD)
HAHT..........	Hypersonic Arc-Heated Tunnel [*Langley Research Center*] [*NASA*]
HAHTG	Horse Anti-Human Thymus Globulin [*Immunology*] (MAE)
HAHU.........	Humera [*Ethiopia*] [*ICAO location identifier*] (ICLI)
HAI.............	Century Aviation International Ltd. [*Canada*] [*FAA designator*] (FAAC)
hai.............	Haida [*MARC language code Library of Congress*] (LCCP)
HAI.............	Haiti (ABBR)
HAI.............	Haiwee [*California*] [*Seismograph station code, US Geological Survey Closed*] (SEIS)
HAI.............	Hampton Indus [*AMEX symbol*] (TTSB)
HAI.............	Hampton Industries, Inc. [*AMEX symbol*] (SPSG)
HAI.............	Handwriting Analysts, International (EA)
HAI.............	Hawaiian Airlines, Inc. (EFIS)
HAI.............	Health Action International (EA)
HAI.............	Helicopter Association International (EA)
HAI.............	Helicopter Attitude Indicator
HAI.............	Hellenic Aerospace Industry [*Greek*]
HAI.............	Hellenic Arms Industry [*Greek*]
HAI.............	Hemagglutination Inhibition [*Immunochemistry*]
HAI.............	Hemagglutinin Inhibition (STED)
HAI.............	Hepatic Arterial Infusion (STED)
HAI.............	Hepatic Artery Infusion [*Chemotherapy*]
HAI.............	Holland Automation International [*Software retailer*] (NITA)
HAI.............	Hospital-Acquired Infection [*Medicine*]
HAI.............	Hospital Audiences (EA)
HAI.............	Hot Air Intake [*Automotive engineering*]
HAI.............	Three Rivers, MI [*Location identifier FAA*] (FAAL)
HAIA	Hearing Aid Industry Association [*British*] (DBA)
HAIA	Honorary Member, American Institute of Architects (DAC)
HAIC	Hearing Aid Industry Conference [*Later, HIA*] (EA)
HAIC	Hetero-Atom-in-Context
HAID	Hand-Emplaced Acoustic Intrusion Detector (NVT)
HAID	Hispanic Americans Information Directory [*A publication*]
HAIDE.........	Hostile Aircraft Identification Equipment (DWSG)
HAIDEX.......	Hughes Artificial Intelligence Diagnostic Expert [*Hughes Aircraft Co.*] [*Army*]
HAIIS	Headquarters Administrative Issuance Index System [*Military*] (DNAB)
HAIL...........	Holographic Array for Ionospheric Lightning [*Astrophysics*]
Hailes.........	Dalrymple (Lord Hailes). Decisions of the Scotch Court of Session [*1776-91*] [*A publication*] (DLA)
Hailes Ann...	Hailes' Annals of Scotland [*A publication*] (DLA)
Hailes Dec...	Hailes' Decisions, Scotch Court of Sessions [*A publication*] (DLA)
HainFood.....	Hain Food Group, Inc. [*Associated Press*] (SAG)

Hain JP....... Haine's Illinois Justice of the Peace [*A publication*] (DLA)

HAINS.......... High-Accuracy Inertial Navigation System [*Aerospace*] (NAKS)

HAIR .... Help Alopecia International Research [*Defunct*] (EA)

HAIR .... High-Accuracy Instrumentation RADAR (DNAB)

HAIR-AN ...... Hyperandrogenism, Insulin Resistance, and Acanthosis Nigricans Syndrome [*Medicine*] (DMAA)

HAIRCTTNG... Haircutting

HAIRDS......... High-Altitude Infrared Detecting Set (MCD)

HAIRS.......... High-Altitude Test and Evaluation of Infrared Sources (MCD)

HAISAM .... Hashed Index Sequential Access Method (PDAA)

HAISS .... High-Altitude Infrared Sensor System

HAIT............ Haiti

HAIT............ Hash Algorithm Information Table

HAJ.............. Hajvairy Airlines [*Pakistan*] [*ICAO designator*] (FAAC)

HAJ.............. Hanover [*Germany Airport symbol*] (OAG)

HAJC............ Hawaiian Area Joint Committee [*Military*] (CINC)

HAJJ............ Jijiga [*Ethiopia*] [*ICAO location identifier*] (ICLI)

HAJM .... Jimma [*Ethiopia*] [*ICAO location identifier*] (ICLI)

HAK .... Adelanto, CA [*Location identifier FAA*] (FAAL)

HAK .... Haikou [*China*] [*Airport symbol*] (OAG)

HAK .... Hakodate [*Japan*] [*Seismograph station code, US Geological Survey*] (SEIS)

HAK .... Harka Air Services [*Nigeria*] [*FAA designator*] (FAAC)

HAK .... Hawkish (ABBR)

HAK .... Horizontal Access Kit (NASA)

HAKASH........ Hayl Kashish [*Elderly Army*] [*Israel*]

HAKD .... Kabre Dare [*Ethiopia*] [*ICAO location identifier*] (ICLI)

HAKL .... Kelafo [*Ethiopia*] [*ICAO location identifier*] (ICLI)

Hal .... Halakha (BJA)

Hal .... Halieuticon Liber [*of Ovid*] [*Classical studies*] (OCD)

HAL.............. Halifax [*Nova Scotia*] [*Seismograph station code, US Geological Survey*] (SEIS)

Hal .... Hallah (BJA)

HAL.............. Halliburton Co. [*NYSE symbol Toronto Stock Exchange symbol*] (SPSG)

HAL.............. Halogen (WDAA)

hal .... Halogen (IDOE)

HAL.............. Haloperidol [*A tranquilizer*]

HAL.............. Halothane [*Also, H*] [*An anesthetic*]

HAL.............. Hamburg-Amerika Linie [*Hamburg-America Steamship Co.*]

HAL.............. Handicapped Assistance Loan

HAL.............. Hardware Abstraction Layer [*Computer science*] (PCM)

HAL.............. Harwell Automated Loans [*Library circulation system*]

HAL.............. Hash Algorithm Library

HAL.............. Hawaiian Airlines, Inc. [*ICAO designator*] (FAAC)

HAL.............. Hazards Assessment Laboratory [*Colorado State University*] [*Research center*] (RCD)

H-A-L .... Head-Arm-Leg [*Medicine*]

HAL.............. Heads-Up Audio-Vision Logistics [*NASA*]

HAL.............. Height above Landing [*Area*]

HA(L)........... Helicopter Attack Squadron (Light) (CINC)

HAL.............. Hemispheric Activation Level [*Computer science*] (BYTE)

HAL.............. Hepatic Artery Ligation [*Medicine*]

HAL.............. Heuristically-Programmed Algorithmic [*Name of computer in film, "2001: A Space Odyssey." Acronym is also considered to have been formed by combining the letters before IBM in the alphabet*]

HAL.............. Highly Active Liquid [*Nuclear energy*] (NUCP)

HAL.............. Highly Automated Logic [*Computer science*]

HAL.............. High-Order Algorithmic Language (SSD)

HAL.............. High-Order Articulated Language [*Computer science*] (MCD)

HAL.............. High-Order Assembly Language [*Computer science*] (NASA)

HAL.............. Hindustan Aeronautics Ltd.

HAL.............. Hoechst Australia Ltd. [*Commercial firm*]

HAL.............. Holding and Approach-to-Land [*Procedure*] [*Aviation*]

HAL.............. Holland-America Line [*Later, Holland America Cruises*]

HAL.............. Home Automated Living

HAL.............. Houston Aerospace Language [*NASA*] (NASA)

HAL.............. Human Access Language [*Computer science*]

HAL.............. Hyperalimentation [*Intravenous feeding*] (DAVI)

HAL.............. Hypogastric Artery Ligation [*Medicine*]

HALA .... Awash [*Ethiopia*] [*ICAO location identifier*] (ICLI)

Hal Anal ...... Hale's Analysis of the Law [*A publication*] (DLA)

Hal & Tw..... Hall and Twell's English Chancery Reports [*47 English Reprint*] [*A publication*] (DLA)

HALAT .... Hebraeisches und Aramaeisches Lexikon zum Alten Testament [*Leiden*] (BJA)

HALB .... Halberton [*England*]

Halbtn.......... Halliburton Co. [*Associated Press*] (SAG)

Halc .... Halcomb's Mining Cases [*England*] [*A publication*] (DLA)

HALC .... High Affinity-Low Capacity (DMAA)

HALCA .... Highly Advanced Laboratory for Communications and Astronomy [*Japanese satellite*]

Hal Civ Law... Hallifax's Analysis of the Civil Law [*A publication*] (DLA)

Halc Min Cas... Halcomb's Mining Cases [*England*] [*A publication*] (DLA)

HALCON........ High-Altitude Long-Focus Convergent Mapping System

Hal Const Hist... Hallam's Constitutional History of England [*A publication*] (DLA)

HALDIS........ Halifax and District Information Service [*British*] (NITA)

HALE .... Haleakala National Park

Hale .... Hale's English Common Law [*A publication*] (DLA)

Hale .... Hale's Reports [*33-37 California*] (DLA)

HALE .... High-Altitude, Long-Endurance [*Proposed unmanned reconnaissance drone*] [*Military*]

HALE........... Hilevel Assembly Language Environment [*Hilever Technology Inc.*] [*Operating systems assembler*] (NITA)

Hale Anal .... Hale's Analysis of the Law [*A publication*] (DLA)

Hale C L .... Hale's History of the Common Law [*A publication*] (DLA)

Hale Com Law... Hale's History of the Common Law [*A publication*] (DLA)

Hale Cr Prec... Hale's Precedents in (Ecclesiastical) Criminal Cases [*1475-1640*] [*A publication*] (DLA)

Hale De Jure Mar... Hale's De Jure Maris, Appendix to Hall on the Sea Shore [*A publication*] (DLA)

Hale De Port Mar... Hale's De Portibus Maris [*A publication*] (DLA)

Hale Ecc ...... Hale's English Ecclesiastical Reports [*1583-1736*] [*A publication*] (DLA)

Hale Hist Eng Law... Hale's History of the English Law [*A publication*] (DLA)

Hale Jur HL... Hale's Jurisdiction of the House of Lords [*1796*] [*A publication*] (DLA)

HalEP.......... Hallwood Energy Partners Ltd. [*Associated Press*] (SAG)

Hale Parl..... Hale's History of Parliament [*2nd ed.*] [*1745*] [*A publication*] (DLA)

Hale PC .... Hale's Pleas of the Crown [*England*] [*A publication*] (DLA)

Hale PC (Eng)... Hale's Pleas of the Crown [*England*] [*A publication*] (DLA)

Hale Prec .... Hale's Precedents in (Ecclesiastical) Criminal Cases [*1475-1640*] [*A publication*] (DLA)

Hale's.......... Hale's Precedents in (Ecclesiastical) Criminal Cases [*1475-1640*] [*A publication*] (DLA)

Hale Sug CM... Hale's Suggestion on Courts-Martial [*A publication*] (DLA)

Hale Sum .... Hale's Summary of the Pleas of the Crown [*England*] [*A publication*] (DLA)

Hal Ev.......... Halsted's Digest of the Law of Evidence [*A publication*] (DLA)

HALF........... Half-plate (VRA)

HALFSEE...... Headquarters, Allied Land Forces, Southeastern Europe

halftmb........ Half-timber (VRA)

Halh Gent L... Halhed's Code of Gentoo Laws [*A publication*] (DLA)

Halifax........ Halifax Corp. [*Associated Press*] (SAG)

Halifax Anal... Halifax' Analysis of the Roman Civil Law [*A publication*] (DLA)

Hal Int Law... Halleck's International Law [*A publication*] (DLA)

Halk .... Halkerston's Compendium of Scotch Faculty Decisions [*A publication*] (DLA)

Halk .... Halkerston's Digest of the Scotch Marriage Law [*A publication*] (DLA)

Halk .... Halkerston's Latin Maxims [*A publication*] (DLA)

Halk Comp... Halkerston's Compendium of Scotch Faculty Decisions [*A publication*] (DLA)

Halk Dig ...... Halkerston's Digest of the Scotch Marriage Law [*A publication*] (DLA)

Halk Lat Max... Halkerston's Latin Maxims [*A publication*] (DLA)

Halk Max .... Halkerston's Latin Maxims [*A publication*] (DLA)

Halk Tech Terms... Halkerston's Technical Terms of the Law [*A publication*] (DLA)

Hall .... Decisions of the Water Courts [*1913-36*] [*South Africa*] [*A publication*] (DLA)

Hall .... Hallett's Reports [*1, 2 Colorado*] [*A publication*] (DLA)

Hall .... Hallmark [*Record label*] [*Canada*]

HALL............ Hallmark Capital [*NASDAQ symbol*] (TTSB)

HALL............ Hallmark Capital Corp. [*NASDAQ symbol*] (SAG)

HALL............ Hall Occupational Orientation Inventory [*Hall and Tarrier*] (TES)

Hall .... Hall's New York Superior Court Reports [*A publication*] (DLA)

Hall .... Hall's Reports [*56, 57 New Hampshire*] [*A publication*] (DLA)

HALL............ Lalibela [*Ethiopia*] [*ICAO location identifier*] (ICLI)

Hall Adm ..... Hall's Admiralty Practice and Jurisdiction [*A publication*] (DLA)

Hall ALJ ...... Hall's American Law Journal [*A publication*] (DLA)

Hallam......... Hallam's Constitutional History of England [*A publication*] (DLA)

Hall Am LJ... Hall's American Law Journal [*A publication*] (DLA)

Hall & T ...... Hall and Twell's English Chancery Reports [*47 English Reprint*] [*A publication*] (DLA)

Hall & Tw.... Hall and Twell's English Chancery Reports [*47 English Reprint*] [*A publication*] (DLA)

Hall & Tw (Eng)... Hall and Twell's English Chancery Reports [*47 English Reprint*] [*A publication*] (DLA)

Hal Law....... Halsted's New Jersey Law Reports [*6-12 New Jersey*] [*A publication*] (DLA)

Hall Ch Pr ... Halliday's Elementary View of Chancery Proceedings [*A publication*] (DLA)

Hall Civ Law... Hallifax's Analysis of the Civil Law [*A publication*] (DLA)

Hall (Col)..... Hallett's Reports [*1, 2 Colorado*] [*A publication*] (DLA)

Hall Const Hist... Hallam's Constitutional History of England [*A publication*] (DLA)

Hall Const L... Hall's Tracts on Constitutional Law [*A publication*] (DLA)

Halleck Int Law... Halleck's International Law [*A publication*] (DLA)

Hall Emerig Mar Loans... Hall's Essay on Maritime Loans from the French of Emerigon [*A publication*] (DLA)

Hallett .... Hallett's Reports [*1, 2 Colorado*] [*A publication*] (DLA)

Hall Hist...... Hallam's Constitutional History of England [*A publication*] (DLA)

Hallifax Anal (of Civil Law)... Hallifax's Analysis of the Civil Law [*A publication*] (DLA)

Hallif CL ..... Hallifax's Analysis of the Civil Law [*A publication*] (DLA)

Hall Int Law... Halleck's International Law [*A publication*] (DLA)

Hall Int Law... Hall on International Law [*A publication*] (DLA)

Hall Jour Jur... Journal of Jurisprudence (Hall's) [*A publication*] (DLA)

Hall Law of W... Halleck's Law of War [*A publication*] (DLA)

Hall LJ........ Hall's American Law Journal [*A publication*] (DLA)

Hall Marit Loans... Hall's Essay on Maritime Loans from the French of Emerigon [*A publication*] (DLA)

Hall Mex Law... Hall's Laws of Mexico Relating to Real Property, Etc. [*A publication*] (DLA)

HallmF......... Halmark Financial Services [*Associated Press*] (SAG)

HallmkCa..... Hallmark Capital Corp. [*Associated Press*] (SAG)

Hall Neut..... Hall's Rights and Duties of Neutrals [*1874*] [*A publication*] (DLA)

Hall NH....... Hall's Reports [*56, 57 New Hampshire*] [*A publication*] (DLA)

Hall (NY) ..... Hall's New York Superior Court Reports [*A publication*] (DLA)

HALLO .... Hang Alle Laffe Landverraders Op [*Hang All Cowardly Traitors to Their Country*] [*Greeting for Dutch Nazis allegedly coined by the Netherlands people during World War II*]

HALLO	Hang Alle Landverraders Op [*Hang all traitors*] [*Dutch*] [*WWII phrase*]
Hall Profits a Prendre...	Hall's Treatise on the Law Relating to Profits a Prendre, Etc. [*A publication*] (DLA)
HallRlty	Hallwood Realty Partners [*Associated Press*] (SAG)
HallRty	Hallwood Realty Partners Ltd. [*Associated Press*] (SAG)
Hall's Am LJ..	Hall's American Law Journal [*A publication*] (DLA)
Hall Shores...	Hall's Rights in the Sea Shores [*A publication*] (DLA)
Hall's J Jur..	Journal of Jurisprudence (Hall's) [*A publication*] (DLA)
HALLUC	Hallucination
Hallwd	Hallwood Group, Inc. [*Associated Press*] (SAG)
HallwdCon..	Hallwood Consolidated Resources [*Associated Press*] (SAG)
Hal Min Law..	Halleck's Mining Laws of Spain and Mexico [*A publication*] (DLA)
HALO	HA-LO [*NASDAQ symbol*] (SAG)
HALO	HA-LO Industries [*NASDAQ symbol*] (TTSB)
HA-LO	HA-LO Industries, Inc. [*Associated Press*] (SAG)
HALO	Handling of Alarms with Logic [*Nuclear reactors*]
HALO	High-Altitude Large Optics [*Air Force*] (MCD)
HALO	High Altitude Long Operation [*Airplane*]
HALO	High-Altitude, Low-Opening Parachute Jump
HALO	High Arcal Learning Objectives (AIE)
HALO	Hughes Automated Lunar Observer [*NASA*]
HALOE	Halogen Occulation Experiment (MCD)
HALON	Halogenated Hydrocarbon
HALP	HAWK [*Homing All the Way Killer*] Equipment Logistics Program [*Army*]
HALP	Husbands of Airline Pilots
HAL-PC	Houston Area League of PC [*Personal Computer*] Users
HALPRO	Halverson Project [*World War II plan to bomb Japan from China*]
Hals	Halsted's New Jersey Law Reports [*6-12 New Jersey*] [*A publication*] (DLA)
HAL/S	High-Order Assembly Language for Shuttle Flight Computer (MCD)
HAL/S	High-Order Assembly Language for Spacelab Usage [*NASA*] (NASA)
HAL/S	High-Order Assembly Language/ Shuttle (NAKS)
HAL/S	High Order Programming Language for Spacelab Usage (NAKS)
HALS	Hindered Amine Light Stabilizers [*for plastics*]
HALS	Houston Area Library System [*Library network*]
HALS	Hydrographic Airborne LASER Sounder (PDAA)
Halsbury	Halsbury's Statutes of England [*A publication*] (DLA)
Halsbury's S Is..	Halsbury's Statutory Instruments [*A publication*] (DLA)
Halsbury's Statutes...	Halsbury's Statutes of England [*A publication*] (DLA)
Hals Ch	Halsted's New Jersey Equity Reports [*A publication*] (DLA)
Hals Eq	Halsted's New Jersey Equity Reports [*A publication*] (DLA)
Halsey	Halsey Drug Co. [*Associated Press*] (SAG)
HALSIM	Hardware Logic Simulator [*Computer science*] (IEEE)
HALSOL	High-Altitude Solar Energy (PS)
HALST	Halstead [*Urban district in England*]
Halst	Halsted's New Jersey Equity Reports [*A publication*] (DLA)
Halst	Halsted's New Jersey Law Reports [*6-12 New Jersey*] [*A publication*] (DLA)
Halst Ch	Halsted's New Jersey Chancery Reports [*A publication*] (DLA)
HalstdE	Halstead Energy Corp. [*Associated Press*] (SAG)
HalstdEn	Halstead Energy Corp. [*Associated Press*] (SAG)
Halsted (NJ)...	Halsted's New Jersey Chancery Reports [*A publication*] (DLA)
Halst Ev	Halsted's Digest of the Law of Evidence [*A publication*] (DLA)
HALT	Help Abolish Legal Tyranny [*In organization name HALT-ALR*] (EA)
HALT	High-Altitude LASER Transmittance (MCD)
HALT	Holdup Alert - Local Transmission [*Bank robbery alarm system*]
HALT	Hungry Angry Lonely Tired [*Slogan used by Alcoholics Anonymous members to determine whether their emotions are so out of control that they may be tempted to take a drink*]
HALT-ALR...	HALT - An Organization of Americans for Legal Reform (EA)
HalterM	Halter Marine Group, Inc. [*Associated Press*] (SAG)
HaLV	Hamster Leukemia Virus
HalwdCn	Hallwood Consolidated Resources Corp. [*Associated Press*] (SAG)
HAM	Hairy Anatomy Marine [*See also BAM*] [*Slang term for male marines*] [*Bowdlerized version*]
HAM	Hamarfly, AS [*Norway*] [*FAA designator*] (FAAC)
HAM	Hamburg [*Germany*] [*Seismograph station code, US Geological Survey*] (SEIS)
HAM	Hamburg [*Germany Airport symbol*] (OAG)
Ham	(Hamilton of) Haddington's Manuscript Cases, Scotch Court of Session [*A publication*] (DLA)
Ham	Hamlet [*Shakespearean work*]
ham	Hammered (VRA)
Ham	Hammond's India and Burma Election Cases [*A publication*] (DLA)
Ham	Hammond's Reports [*1-9 Ohio*] [*A publication*] (DLA)
HAM	Hampshire College, Amherst, MA [*OCLC symbol*] (OCLC)
HAM	Hardware Associative Memory [*Computer science*] (DIT)
HAM	Harry Armenius Miller [*Automotive engineer*]
HAM	Hearing Aide of Minnesota (SRA)
HAM	Hearing Aid Microphone
HAM	Heavy Atom Method
HAM	Heavy Automotive Maintenance
HAM	Height Adjustment Maneuver (MCD)
HAM	Hexamethylmelamine, Adriamycin, L-Phenylalanine Mustard [*Antineoplastic drug regimen*] (DAVI)
HAM	Hexamethylmelamine, Adriamycin, Melphalan [*Antineoplastic drug regimen*]
HAM	Hexamethylmelamine, Adriamycin, Methotrexate [*Antineoplastic drug regimen*]
HAM	Hierarchical Access Method
HAM	High-Activity Mode (IAA)
HAM	High-Altitude Missile (MCD)
HAM	High-Availability Manager (IAA)
HAM	High-Speed Automatic Monitor
HAM	Histocompatibility Antigen Modifier [*Genetics*]
HAM	Hold and Modify [*Computer display mode*]
HAM	Home Access Mortgage
HAM	Home Amateur [*Radio*]
HAM	Honda of America Manufacturing
HAM	HTLV-1-Associated Myelopathy [*Medicine*]
HAM	Human Albumin Microsphere [*Clinical anesthesiology*]
HAM	Human Alveolar Macrophage [*Immunology*]
HAm	Human Amnion (DMAA)
HAM	Human Associative Memory
HAM	Hymns Ancient and Modern
HAM	Hypoparathyroidism, Addison's Disease, and Musculocutaneous Candidiasis [*Medicine*]
HAMA	Hamilton Anxiety Scale [*Psychiatry*] (DMAA)
HAMA	Human Anti-Mouse Antibody [*Medicine*]
HAMA	Human Anti-Murine Antibody [*Medicine*] (DMAA)
Ham A & O...	Hamerton, Allen, and Otter's English Magistrates' Cases [*3 New Sessions Cases*] [*A publication*] (DLA)
Ham & J..	Hammond and Jackson's Reports [*45 Georgia*] [*A publication*] (DLA)
HAMB	Hambledon [*England*]
HAMB	Hamburg [*West Germany*] (ROG)
HAMB	Hamburger Hamlet Restaurants [*NASDAQ symbol*] (SPSG)
HAMBGR	Hamburger
HAMCHAM...	Haitian-American Chamber of Commerce and Industry (EA)
HAMCHAM...	Honduran-American Chamber of Commerce [*See also CCHA*] (EA)
HAMCO	HAWK [*Homing All the Way Killer*] Assembly and Missile Checkout (AAG)
Ham Cont	Hammon on Contracts [*A publication*] (DLA)
Ham Cust....	Hamel's Laws of the Customs [*A publication*] (DLA)
HAMD	Hamilton Depression [*Scale*] [*Psychology*] (DB)
HAM-D	Hamilton Psychiatric Rating Scale for Depression
HAMD	Helicopter Ambulance Medical Detachment
HAME	Mieso [*Ethiopia*] [*ICAO location identifier*] (ICLI)
Hamel Cust...	Hamel's Laws of the Customs [*A publication*] (DLA)
Ham Fed.....	Hamilton's Federalist [*A publication*] (DLA)
Hamilton	(Hamilton of) Haddington's Manuscript Cases, Scotch Court of Session [*A publication*] (DLA)
Hamilton	Hamilton on Company Law [*3 eds.*] [*1891-1910*] [*A publication*] (DLA)
Hamilton	Hamilton's American Negligence Cases [*A publication*] (DLA)
HAMIM	Hizbul Muslimin [*Islamic Front*] [*Malaysia*] [*Political party*] (FEA)
Ham Ins.....	Hammond on Fire Insurance [*A publication*] (DLA)
Ham Ins.....	Hammond on Insanity [*A publication*] (DLA)
Ham Int	Hamel's International Law [*A publication*] (DLA)
HAMJ	Maji [*Ethiopia*] [*ICAO location identifier*] (ICLI)
HAMK	Makale [*Ethiopia*] [*ICAO location identifier*] (ICLI)
Haml	Hamlet [*Shakespearean work*] (BARN)
HAML	Masslo [*Ethiopia*] [*ICAO location identifier*] (ICLI)
HamlFn	Hamilton Financial Services Corp. [*Associated Press*] (SAG)
Hamlin	Hamlin's Reports [*81-93 Maine*] [*A publication*] (DLA)
Hamline U ...	Hamline University (GAGS)
HAMM	Metema [*Ethiopia*] [*ICAO location identifier*] (ICLI)
Ham Mar Laws...	Hammick's Marriage Laws [*2nd ed.*] [*1887*] [*A publication*] (DLA)
HAMMARR...	Hazardous Materials Management and Resource Recovery [*University of Alabama*] [*Research center*] (RCD)
Hammond	Hammond's Reports [*1-9 Ohio*] [*A publication*] (DLA)
Hammond....	Hammond's Reports [*36-45 Georgia*] [*A publication*] (DLA)
Hammond & Jackson...	Hammond and Jackson's Reports [*45 Georgia*] [*A publication*] (DLA)
HAMN	Mendi [*Ethiopia*] [*ICAO location identifier*] (ICLI)
Ham NP......	Hammond's Nisi Prius [*A publication*] (DLA)
HAMO	Motta [*Ethiopia*] [*ICAO location identifier*] (ICLI)
HAMOS	High-Altitude Synoptic Meteorological Observation (SAA)
HAMOTS	High-Altitude Multiple Object Tracking System [*Air Force*]
HAMP	Hampshire Group Ltd [*NASDAQ symbol*] (TTSB)
HAMP	Hampstead [*Region of London*]
HAMP	Hampton National Historic Site
HAMP	Hexamethylmelamine, Adriamycin, Methotrexate, Cisplatin [*Antineoplastic drug regimen*] (DAVI)
HAMP	High-Altitude Measurement Probe
HAMP	Hop and Stamp [*Dance terminology*]
Ham Part	Hammond on Parties to Action [*A publication*] (DLA)
Ham Parties..	Hammond on Parties to Action [*A publication*] (DLA)
HampGp	Hampshire Group Ltd. [*Associated Press*] (SAG)
Ham Pl	Hammond's Principles of Pleading [*1819*] [*A publication*] (DLA)
HAMPS	Hampshire [*County in England*]
HAMPS	Heavy Airborne Multipurpose System (MCD)
Hamps Co Cas...	Hampshire County Court Reports [*England*] [*A publication*] (DLA)
HAMPS R......	Hampshire Regiment [*Military unit*] [*British*] (ROG)
Hamptl	Hampton Industries, Inc. [*Associated Press*] (SAG)
Hampton U...	[*The*] Hampton University (GAGS)
Hamp Tr	Hampson. Trustees [*2nd ed.*] [*1830*] [*A publication*] (DLA)
HAMR	Mui River [*Ethiopia*] [*ICAO location identifier*] (ICLI)
HAMRC	Hammers Plastic Recycling [*NASDAQ symbol*] (TTSB)
HAMS	Hardness Assurance Monitoring System (MCD)
HAMS	Headquarters and Maintenance Squad
HAMS	Hour Angle of the Mean Sun [*Navigation*]
HAMS	Massawa [*Ethiopia*] [*ICAO location identifier*] (ICLI)
HAMS	Smithfield Companies [*NASDAQ symbol*] (SAG)
HAMS	Smithfield Cos. [*NASDAQ symbol*] (TTSB)
HAMSA	Hearing Aid Manufacturers' and Suppliers' Association [*British*] (BI)
HAMSDET	Headquarters and Maintenance Squadron Detachment [*Marine Corps*] (DNAB)
HaMSV	Harvey Murine Sarcoma Virus [*Medicine*] (MEDA)

HAMT.........	Human-Aided Machine Translation
HAMT.........	Mizan Teferi [Ethiopia] [ICAO location identifier] (ICLI)
HAMTC......	Hanford [Washington] Atomic Metal Trades Council
HAMTF........	Hispanic American Ministries Task Force of JSAC [Joint Strategy and Action Committee] [Defunct] (EA)
HaMuSV	Harvey Murine Sarcoma Virus
HAN	Chandler, AZ [Location identifier FAA] (FAAL)
HAN	Hambro Resources, Inc. [Vancouver Stock Exchange symbol]
Han............	Handy's Ohio Reports [12 Ohio Decisions] [A publication] (DLA)
HAN	Hanford [Washington] [Seismograph station code, US Geological Survey] (SEIS)
Han............	Hannay's New Brunswick Reports [12, 13 New Brunswick] [A publication] (DLA)
HAN	Hanoi [Vietnam] [Airport symbol] (OAG)
HAN	Hanover [Former state in Germany]
Han............	Hansard's Book of Entries [1685] [A publication] (DLA)
HAN	Hanson Ltd. [AMEX symbol] (SAG)
Han............	Hanson PLC [Associated Press] (SAG)
Han............	Hanson plc ADR [NYSE symbol] (TTSB)
Han............	Hanson's Bankruptcy Reports [1915-17] [A publication] (DLA)
HAN	Hanson Trust Ltd. [NYSE symbol] (SPSG)
HAN	Hawaii Association of Nurserymen (SRA)
HAN	Health Activation Network [Later, WHAN] (EA)
HAN	Heroin-Associated Nephropathy [Medicine] (DAVI)
HAN	Hex Aluminum Nut
HAN	Hydroxylamine Nitrate [Organic chemistry] (NUCP)
HAN	Hydroxylammonium Nitrate [Component of liquid propellants] [Inorganic chemistry]
HAN	Hyperplastic Alveolar Nodules [Precancerous lesions in mice]
HANA.........	Halibut Association of North America (EA)
HANA.........	Helvetia Association of North America [Defunct] (EA)
HANBA.......	Hollow Anistropic Beam Analysis (PDAA)
Hanb Pat	Hanbury's Judicial Error in the Law of Patents [A publication] (DLA)
Hanb Us	Hanbury-Jones on Uses [A publication] (DLA)
HancBT.......	Hancock [John] Bank & Thrift Opportunity Fund [Associated Press] (SAG)
Hanc Conv ...	Hancock's System of Conveyancing [Canada] [A publication] (DLA)
HancFab.....	Hancock Fabrics, Inc. [Associated Press] (SAG)
HancHd.......	Hancock Holding Co. [Associated Press] (SAG)
HAND.........	Handex Corp. [NASDAQ symbol]
HAND.........	Handex Environmental Recovery, Inc. [NASDAQ symbol] (NQ)
Hand...........	Hand's Reports [40-45 New York] [A publication] (DLA)
Hand...........	Handy's Ohio Reports [12 Ohio Decisions] [A publication] (DLA)
HAND.........	Have a Nice Day
H & A	Health and Accident [Insurance]
H&A............	Honours and Awards (ACII)
H & A Ins ...	Health and Accident Insurance (DAVI)
HandAms.....	Handes Amsorya [Vienna] (BJA)
H & ASHD ...	Hypertension and Arteriosclerotic Heart Disease [Medicine]
HANDB.......	Handbook
H & B	Holland & Barrett [Grocery and health food shop chain] [British]
H & B	Hudson and Brooke's Irish King's Bench Reports [1827-31] [A publication] (DLA)
Handb Gk Myth...	Handbook of Greek Mythology [A publication] (OCD)
Handb Mag...	Handbook for Magistrates [1853-55] [A publication] (DLA)
H & BR.......	Hull & Barnsley Railway [British] (ROG)
H & BT	Huntingdon & Broad Top Railroad
H & BTM	Huntingdon & Broad Top Mountain Railroad & Coal Co. (IIA)
H & BTM	Huntington & Broad Top Mountain Railroad & Coal Co. (MHDB)
H & C	Head and Cover (MSA)
H and C	Heroin and Cocaine (DSUE)
H&C............	Heroin & Cocaine (WDAA)
H & C	Hoffmann & Campe [Publisher] [Germany]
H&C............	Hot and Cold (DMAA)
H & C	Hurlstone and Coltman's English Exchequer Reports [A publication] (DLA)
Hand Ch P ...	Hand's Chancery Practice [A publication] (DLA)
H & Cie	Hentsch & Compagnie [Bank] [Switzerland]
H&CP..........	Hospital and Community Psychiatry (DMAA)
H & CR	Handling and Checkout Requirements
Hand Cr Pr...	Hand's Crown Practice [A publication] (DLA)
H & D	Hardened and Dispersed (AFM)
H&D............	Hunter and Driffield [Curve] (STED)
H & D	Hurter and Driffield [Chemists for whom H & D Curve and H & D Speed System are named] (DEN)
H & D	Lalor's Supplement to Hill and Denio's New York Reports [A publication] (DLA)
H & D Pr	Holmes and Disbrow's Practice [A publication] (DLA)
H & E.........	Hematoxylin and Eosin [Biological stain]
H & E.........	Hemorrhage and Exudate [Medicine]
H & E.........	Heredity and Environment
H & E.........	History and Examination
HANDE.......	Hydrofoil Analysis and Design [Computer science]
Han Deb	Hansard's Parliamentary Debates [A publication] (DLA)
Handex	Handex Environmental Recovery, Inc. [Associated Press] (SAG)
Hand Fines...	Hand on Fines and Recoveries [A publication] (DLA)
H & G.........	Harden and Grind [Technical drawings]
H & G.........	Harris and Gill's Maryland Court of Appeals Reports [1826-29] [A publication] (DLA)
H & G.........	Headed and Gutted [Fish processing]
H & G.........	Hicks & Greist [Advertising agency]
H & G.........	Home and Garden Bulletins [A publication]
H & G.........	Hurlstone and Gordon's English Exchequer Reports [A publication] (DLA)
HandH........	Handy & Harman [Associated Press] (SAG)
H & H	Harrison and Hodgin's Upper Canada Municipal Reports [1845-51] [A publication] (DLA)
H & H	Hemoglobin and Hematocrit [Clinical chemistry]
H & H	Holland & Holland [Custom gun maker]
H&H............	Horn & Hardart Co. (EFIS)
H & H	Horn and Hurlstone's English Exchequer Reports [1838-39] [A publication] (DLA)
H & HQ	Headquarters and Headquarters Company [Army]
H & HS	Headquarters and Headquarters Squadron [Marine Corps]
H & I	Harassing and Interdiction
H and I	Harassment and Interdiction Fires [Military]
HANDICP	Handicap
HANDITAL...	Association of Italian Families and Friends of Handicapped Children [Australia]
H & J	Harris and Johnson's Maryland Court of Appeals Reports [1800-26] [A publication] (DLA)
H & J	Hayes and Jones' Irish Exchequer Reports [1832-34] [A publication] (DLA)
H & J	Hyphenation and Justification [Typography]
H & J Forms...	Hayes and Jarman's Concise Forms of Wills [18th ed.] [1952] [A publication] (DLA)
H & J Ir	Hayes and Jones' Irish Exchequer Reports [1832-34] [A publication] (DLA)
H & John.....	Harris and Johnson's Maryland Reports [A publication] (DLA)
H & K	Hill & Knowlton, Inc. [Public relations firm]
H & K	Holbrook & Kellogg [Publisher] (AAGC)
H & L	Heart and Lungs [Medicine]
HandIm.......	Handleman Co. [Associated Press] (SAG)
H & M	Hay and Marriott's English Admiralty Reports [A publication] (DLA)
H & M	Hemming and Miller's English Vice-Chancellors' Reports [A publication] (DLA)
H & M	Hening and Munford's Reports [11-14 Virginia] [A publication] (DLA)
H & M	Hit and Miss (WDAA)
H & McH......	Harris and McHenry's Maryland Court of Appeals Reports [1785-99] [A publication] (DLA)
H & M Ch	Hemming and Miller's English Vice-Chancellors' Reports [A publication] (DLA)
H & McHenry...	Harris and McHenry's Maryland Reports [A publication] (DLA)
handmd.......	Handmade (VRA)
H & MS	Headquarters and Maintenance Squadron [Marine Corps]
H & M (VA)...	Hening and Munford's Reports [11-14 Virginia] [A publication] (DLA)
H & N	Head and Neck [Medicine]
H & N	Holmes and Narver, Inc. (NRCH)
H & N	Hum and Noise (DEN)
H & N	Hurlstone and Norman's English Exchequer Reports [156, 158 English Reprint] [A publication] (DLA)
H & NH.......	Hartford & New Haven Railroad
H&N mot	Head and Neck Motion (STED)
H & P	History and Physical [Examination] [Medicine]
H&P............	Hodgen and Pearson [Suspension traction] (STED)
H & P	Hopwood and Philbrick's English Election Cases [1863-67] [A publication] (DLA)
Hand Pat	Hand on Patents [A publication] (DLA)
H & Q	Hambrecht & Quist [Investment banking firm]
H & Q Hlt	H & Q Healthcare Fund [Associated Press] (SAG)
H & Q Lfe....	H & Q Life Sciences Investors [Associated Press] (SAG)
H & R	Harper & Row Publishers, Inc.
H & R	Harrison and Rutherfurd's English Common Pleas Reports [1865-66] [A publication] (DLA)
H & R	Holding and Reconsignment [Military]
H & R	Hysterectomy and Radiation [Medicine]
H & R Bank...	Hazlitt and Roche's Bankruptcy Reports [A publication] (DLA)
H & RPO......	Holding and Reconsignment Point [Military]
H & S	Harris and Simrall's Reports [49-52 Mississippi] [A publication] (DLA)
H & S	Head and Shoulders [Photography]
H & S	Headquarters and Service [Battery] [Army]
H & S	Headquarters and Supply Company [Marine Corps] (VNW)
H&S............	Hemorrhage and Shock [Medicine] (STED)
HANDS........	High-Altitude Nuclear Detection Studies [National Institute of Standards and Technology]
H & S	Hysterotomy and Sterilization [Medicine]
handscr.......	Handscroll (VRA)
H & SCTB	Heavy & Specialized Carriers Tariff Bureau
H&SE..........	Health & Safety Executive (WDAA)
H&SM..........	Health and Safety Manual [A publication] [Department of Energy] (COE)
H & STR	Headquarters and Service Troop [Army]
H & T..........	Hall and Twell's English Chancery Reports [1849-50] [A publication] (DLA)
H & T..........	Handling and Transportation (KSC)
H & T..........	Hardened and Tempered [Steel]
H & T..........	Hospitalization and Treatment
H & T Self-Def...	Harrigan and Thompson's Cases on the Law of Self-Defense [A publication] (DLA)
H & Tw	Hall and Twell's English Chancery Reports [1849-50] [A publication] (DLA)
H and V	Heating and Ventilation (NATG)
H & V	Hemigastrectomy and Vagotomy [Medicine]
H&V............	Horizontal and Vertical (WDMC)
H & W	Harrison and Wollaston's English King's Bench Reports [A publication] (DLA)
H & W	Hazzard and Warburton's Prince Edward Island Reports [A publication] (DLA)
H & W	Holm & Wonsild [Steamship] (MHDB)

H & W .... Hurlstone and Walmsley's English Exchequer Reports [1840-41] [*A publication*] (DLA)
Handy .... Handy's Ohio Reports [*12 Ohio Decisions*] [*A publication*] (DLA)
Handy (Ohio) ... Handy's Ohio Reports [*12 Ohio Decisions*] [*A publication*] (DLA)
Handy R ...... Handy's Cincinnati Superior Court Reports [*Ohio*] [*A publication*] (DLA)
HANE .... Hereditary Angioneurotic Edema [*Medicine*]
HANE .... High-Altitude Nuclear Effects [*Study*]
HANE .... High-Altitude Nuclear Explosion
Hane Cr Dig ... Hanes' United States Digest of Criminal Cases [*A publication*] (DLA)
Han Ent ...... Hansard's Book of Entries [*1685*] [*A publication*] (DLA)
Hanes .... Hanes' English Chancery [*A publication*] (DLA)
HANES .... Health and Nutrition Examination Survey [*Public Health Service*]
Hanf .... Hanford's Entries [*1685*] [*A publication*] (DLA)
HANFORD ... Hanford Site [*Department of Energy*] [*Richland, WA*] (GAAI)
Hanfrd .... Hannaford Brothers, Inc. [*Associated Press*] (SAG)
HANG .... Hawaiian Air National Guard (FAAC)
HANG .... Neghelle [*Ethiopia*] [*ICAO location identifier*] (ICLI)
HANGB .... Headquarters Air National Guard Bureau (MUSM)
HangOr .... Hanger Orthopedic Group, Inc. [*Associated Press*] (SAG)
Hanh Mar Wom ... Hanhart on the Laws Relating to Married Women [*A publication*] (DLA)
Han Hor ...... Hanover on the Law of Horses [*A publication*] (DLA)
HANJ .... Nejjo [*Ethiopia*] [*ICAO location identifier*] (ICLI)
HanJI .... Hancock, John, Investors Trust [*Associated Press*] (SAG)
HanJI .... John Hancock Investors Trust [*Associated Press*] (SAG)
HanJS .... Hancock, John, Income Securities Trust [*Associated Press*] (SAG)
HanJS .... John Hancock Income Securities Trust [*Associated Press*] (SAG)
HANK .... Nekemte [*Ethiopia*] [*ICAO location identifier*] (ICLI)
HAN/LCD ...... Hybrid Assigned Nematic/Liquid Crystal Display (TEL)
Hanm .... Lord Kenyon's English King's Bench Reports, Notes, Edited by Hanmer [*A publication*] (ILCA)
Han Mar Wom ... Hanhart on the Laws Relating to Married Women [*A publication*] (DLA)
Hanmer .... Lord Kenyon's English King's Bench Reports, Notes, Edited by Hanmer [*A publication*] (DLA)
Hann .... Hannay's New Brunswick Reports [*12, 13 New Brunswick*] [*A publication*] (DLA)
Hanna .... Hanna [*M. A.*] Co. [*Associated Press*] (SAG)
Han (NB) ...... Hannay's New Brunswick Reports [*12, 13 New Brunswick*] [*A publication*] (DLA)
HanovGld ..... Hanover Gold Company, Inc. [*Associated Press*] (SAG)
hANP .... Human Atrial Natriuretic Peptide [*Biochemistry*]
HANP .... Human Atrium Natriuretic Peptide (DB)
Han Prob ...... Hanson on the Probate and Legacy Acts [*A publication*] (DLA)
HanPtDiv ...... Hancock [*John*] Patriot Premium Dividend Fund I [*Associated Press*] (SAG)
HanPtDv2 .... Hancock [*John*] Patriot Premium Dividend Fund II [*Associated Press*] (SAG)
HanPtGlb ...... Hancock [*John*] Patriot Global Dividend Fund [*Associated Press*] (SAG)
HanPtPfd ..... Hancock, John, Patriot Preferred Dividend Fund [*Associated Press*] (SAG)
HanPtPfd ..... Hancock [*John*] Patriot Prferred Dividend Fund [*Associated Press*] (SAG)
HanPtSel .... Hancock [*John*] Patriot Select Dividend Trust [*Associated Press*] (SAG)
HANS .... Hansen Nat [*NASDAQ symbol*] (TTSB)
Hans .... Hansen Natural Corp. [*Associated Press*] (SAG)
HANS .... Hansen Natural Corp. [*NASDAQ symbol*] (SAG)
HANS .... High-Altitude Navigation System
Hans Al ...... Hansard on Aliens [*A publication*] (DLA)
Hansb .... Hansbrough's Reports [*76-90 Virginia*] [*A publication*] (DLA)
Hans Deb ..... Hansard's Parliamentary Debates [*A publication*] (DLA)
Hansen .... Hansen Natural Corp. [*Associated Press*] (SAG)
Hans Ent ...... Hansard's Book of Entries [*1685*] [*A publication*] (DLA)
Hanson .... Hanson Trust Ltd. [*Associated Press*] (SAG)
Hans Parl Deb ... Hansard's Parliamentary Debates [*A publication*] (DLA)
Hans Pr ...... Hanson on Probate Acts [*A publication*] (DLA)
HANTS .... Hampshire [*County in England*]
HanvDir ...... Hanover Direct, Inc. [*Associated Press*] (SAG)
HANYS .... Healthcare Association of New York State (SRA)
HAO .... Hamilton, OH [*Location identifier FAA*] (FAAL)
HAO .... Hardware Action Officer [*Military*] (AABC)
HAO .... Hearing Aid Follow-Up and Orientation [*Otorhinolaryngology*] (DAVI)
HAO .... High-Altitude Observatory [*Boulder, CO*] [*National Center for Atmospheric Research*]
HAO .... Hospitals, Administration, and Organizations [*British*]
HAOA .... High Angle of Attack [*Combat aircraft*] [*Navy*]
HAOC .... Haynes-Apperson Owners Club (EA)
HAOC .... Hexaazaoctadecahydrocoronene [*Organic chemistry*]
HAOG .... Handbuch der Altorientalischen Geisteskultur [*A publication*] (BJA)
HA or D ...... Havre, Antwerp, or Dunkirk [*Business term*]
HAOS .... Houston Area Oxidant Study [*Environmental Protection Agency*] (GFGA)
HAOS .... Hydroxylamine-ortho-sulfonic Acid [*Organic chemistry*]
HAOSS .... High-Altitude Orbital Space Station (IEEE)
HAP .... Hafnium Column Product [*Nuclear energy*] (NRCH)
HAP .... Hampshire Aircraft Parks [*British military*] (DMA)
HAP .... Handicapped Aid Program (DAVI)
HAP .... Happy
HAP .... Happy Bay [*Australia Airport symbol*] (OAG)
HAP .... Hardware Allocation Panel
HAP .... Harwood Academic Publishers [*British*]

HAP .... Hazardous Air Pollutant
HAP .... Heading Axis Perturbation
HAP .... Health Alliance Plan
HAP .... Heat Shock Activator Protein [*Biochemistry*]
HAP .... Height Above Plate [*Roofing*]
HAP .... Held After Positioning (STED)
HAP .... Heredopathia Atactica Polyneuritiformis [*Medicine*]
HAP .... High-Acid Column Product (NRCH)
HAP .... High-Altitude Platform
HAP .... High-Altitude Probe (AAG)
HAP .... High-Amplitude Peristalsis (STED)
HAP .... Hilson Adolescent Profile [*Psychology*] (DHP)
HAP .... Histamine Acid Phosphate (STED)
HAP .... Histamine Phosphate Acid [*Biochemistry*] (DAVI)
HAP .... Home Owners Assistance Program [*Military*] (AABC)
HAP .... Honeycomb Aluminum Panel
HAP .... Hook-Associated Protein [*Genetics*]
HAP .... Horizontal Axis Pivot
HAP .... Hospital Acquired Pneumonia [*Medicine*] (STED)
HAP .... Host-Associated Population [*Ecology*]
HAP .... Housing Assistance Program
HAP .... Humoral Antibody Production [*Medicine*] (DMAA)
HAP .... Huntingtin-Associated Protein [*Biochemistry*]
HAP .... Hutch Apparel Ltd. [*Vancouver Stock Exchange symbol*]
HAP .... Hydrated Antimony Pentaoxide [*Inorganic chemistry*]
HAP .... Hydrolyzed Animal Protein [*Food technology*]
HAP .... Hydroxyacetophenone [*Organic chemistry*]
HAP .... Hydroxyapatite [*Also, HA*] [*A mineral*]
HAP .... Hydroxyapatite [*Fractionation procedure*] (STED)
HAP .... Hydroxylamine Perchlorate [*Organic chemistry*]
HAP .... Hyperboloid Approximation Procedure
HAP .... Hyperpolarizing Afterpotential [*Electrophysiology*]
HAP .... Whitsunday Resort (Long Island) [*Australia Airport symbol*]
HAPA .... Handicapped Adventure Playground Association [*British*] (DBA)
HAPA .... Hemagglutinating Anti-Penicillin Antibody [*Virology*] (MAE)
HAPAB .... Health Aspects of Pesticides Abstract Bulletin [*Environmental Protection Agency*]
HAPC .... Hospital-Acquired Penetration Contact [*Medicine*] (MAE)
HAPCWS ..... Holt-Atherton Pacific Center for Western Studies [*University of the Pacific*] [*Research center*] (RCD)
HAPDAR ..... Hard Point Demonstration Array RADAR
HAPDEC ...... Hard Point Decoys (MCD)
HAPE .... High-Altitude Pulmonary Edema
HAPEMS ...... Hazardous Air Pollutants Enforcement Management System [*Environmental Protection Agency*] (GFGA)
HAPEX .... Hydrological Atmospheric Pilot Experiment [*Marine science*] (OSRA)
HAPEX .... Hydrological Atmospheric Pilot Experiments (EERA)
HAPFF-EUR ... HAWK [*Homing All the Way Killer*] Project Field Facility - Europe (MCD)
HAPI .... Harris API [*Application Programming Interface*] [*Computer science*]
HAPI .... Helicopter Approach Path Indicator (MCD)
HAPI .... Holding as Previously Instructed [*Aviation*] (FAAC)
HAPI .... Host Application Programming Interface
HAPLR .... Hennen's American Public Library Rating [*Index*]
HAP-NICA .... Humanitarian Assistance Project for Independent Agricultural Development in Nicaragua [*Defunct*] (EA)
HAPO .... Hanford Atomic Products Operations [*General Electric Co.*]
HAPO .... High-Altitude Pulmonary Oedema [*Medicine*] (DMAA)
HAPORTH ... Halfpennyworth [*British*] (ROG)
H App .... Heir Apparent (DAS)
HAPP .... High Air Pollution Potential
HAPP .... High-Altitude Pollution Project [*FAA*]
HAPP .... High-Altitude Powered Platforms (MCD)
HAPPE .... High-Altitude Particle Program Experiment [*NASA*]
HAPPE .... Honeywell Associative Parallel Processing Ensemble
HAPPI .... Height and Plan Position Indicator (PDAA)
HAPPI .... Household and Personal Products Industry [*A publication*]
Happiness ... Happiness Express, Inc. [*Associated Press*] (SAG)
HAPPS .... Hazardous Air Pollutant Prioritization System [*Environmental Protection Agency*] (GFGA)
HAPS .... Hazardous Air Pollutants
HAPS .... Health Aspects of Pesticides
HAPS .... Hepatic Arterial Perfusion Scintigraphy [*Cardiology*] (DAVI)
HAPS .... Historic Aircraft Preservation Society Ltd. [*British*] (BI)
HAPS .... Houston Automatic Priority Spooling [*Computer science*] (NRCH)
HAPS .... Hydroxyalkylpropyl Sephadex [*Analytical biochemistry*]
HAPT .... Haptoglobin [*Hematology*] (DAVI)
HAPTO .... Haptoglobin (STED)
HAPTONG ... Haptong Tongsin [*Press agency*] [*South Korea*]
HAPUB .... High-Speed Arithmetic Processing Unit Board
HAP-USA .... Handicapped Aid Program - USA [*Defunct*] (EA)
HAPY .... Happiness Express [*NASDAQ symbol*] (TTSB)
HAPY .... Happiness Express, Inc. [*NASDAQ symbol*] (SAG)
HAQ .... Headache Assessment Questionnaire [*Neurology*] (DAVI)
HAQ .... Health Assessment Questionnaire (DMAA)
HAQO .... Hydroxyaminoquinoline Oxide [*Organic chemistry*]
Har .... Harari (BJA)
HAR .... Harbor (AFM)
HAR .... Harbor Advisory RADAR
HAR .... Harbor Airlines, Inc. [*ICAO designator*] (FAAC)
HAR .... Hardness Assessment Report
HAR .... Hardware Affiliated Representatives [*Defunct*] (EA)
HAR .... Harford Community College, Bel Air, MD [*OCLC symbol*] (OCLC)
HAR .... Harman International [*NYSE symbol*] (TTSB)
HAR .... Harman International Industries, Inc. [*NYSE symbol*] (SPSG)

HAR .... Harmonic
Har .... Harradine Group [*Australia Political party*]
Har .... Harrington's Delaware Reports [*A publication*] (DLA)
Har .... Harrington's Michigan Chancery Reports [*A publication*] (DLA)
HAR .... Harrisburg-New Cumberland [*Pennsylvania*] [*Airport symbol*] (AD)
HAR .... Harrisburg, PA [*Location identifier FAA*] (FAAL)
Har .... Harrison's Condensed Louisiana Reports [*A publication*] (DLA)
Har .... Harrison's Michigan Chancery Reports [*A publication*] (DLA)
Har .... Harrison's Reports [*15-17, 23-29 Indiana*] [*A publication*] (DLA)
HAR .... Hartford [*Connecticut*] [*Seismograph station code, US Geological Survey Closed*] (SEIS)
HAR .... Harum [*Of These*] [*Pharmacy*] (ROG)
HAR .... Hazard Action Report (MCD)
HAR .... Heinemann, A. R., East Saint Louis IL [*STAC*]
HAR .... High-Altitude Recombination Energy (IAA)
HAR .... High-Altitude Retinopathy [*Medicine*] (STED)
HAR .... Highway Advisory Radio [*Vehicle communications*]
HAR .... Highway Advisory Radio [*Federal program*]
HAR .... Home Address Register
HAR .... Homogeneous Aqueous Reactor [*Nuclear energy*] (NUCP)
HAR .... Honorary Air Reserve [*Air Force*]
HAR .... Horse of the Americas Registry (EA)
HAR .... Hover Agility Rotor (RDA)
HAR .... Hyperacute Rejection [*Medicine*]
H-Ar .... Public Archives, Honolulu, HI [*Library symbol Library of Congress*] (LCLS)
HARA .... High-Altitude RADAR Altimeter [*NASA*]
HARA .... High-Assault Risk Area [*DoD*]
HARAC .... High-Altitude Resonance Absorption Calculation (IEEE)
Har & G .... Harris and Gill's Maryland Reports [*A publication*] (DLA)
Har & Gil .... Harris and Gill's Maryland Reports [*A publication*] (DLA)
Har & Gill ... Harris and Gill's Maryland Reports [*A publication*] (DLA)
Har & G Rep... Harris and Gill's Maryland Reports [*A publication*] (DLA)
Har & J .... Harris and Johnson's Maryland Reports [*A publication*] (DLA)
Har & J (MD)... Harris and Johnson's Maryland Reports [*A publication*] (DLA)
Har & John... Harris and Johnson's Maryland Court of Appeals Reports [*1800-26*] [*A publication*] (DLA)
Har & Johns MD Rep... Harris and Johnson's Maryland Reports [*A publication*] (DLA)
Har & McH... Harris and McHenry's Maryland Reports [*A publication*] (DLA)
Har and M'Hen... Harris and McHenry's Maryland Reports [*A publication*] (DLA)
Har & Ruth... Harrison and Rutherford's English Common Pleas Reports [*1865-66*] [*A publication*] (DLA)
Har & W ...... Harrison and Wollaston's English King's Bench Reports [*A publication*] (DLA)
Har & Woll... Harrison and Wollaston's English King's Bench Reports [*A publication*] (DLA)
Har App .... Hare's English Chancery Reports, Appendix to Vol. X [*A publication*] (DLA)
HARAS .... Hughes Active RADAR Augmentation System
HARB .... Harbor [*Maps and charts*] (ROG)
HARB .... Harbor Federal Savings Bank [*NASDAQ symbol*] (SAG)
HARB .... Harbor Federal Svgs Bk [*NASDAQ symbol*] (TTSB)
Harb & Nav C... Harbors and Navigation Code [*A publication*] (DLA)
HarbFed .... Harbor Federal Bancorp [*Associated Press*] (SAG)
Harbngr .... Harbinger Corp. [*Associated Press*] (SAG)
HARBOR ...... Harbor [*Commonly used*] (OPSA)
HarborH ...... Harborside Healthcare Corp. [*Associated Press*] (SAG)
HARBORS ..... Harbors [*Commonly used*] (OPSA)
HarbourF ..... Harbourton Financial Services LP [*Associated Press*] (SAG)
HARBR .... Harbor [*Commonly used*] (OPSA)
HarbrFd .... Harbor Federal Savings Bank [*Associated Press*] (SAG)
Harbrgr .... Harbinger Corp. [*Associated Press*] (SAG)
Har Bus R .... Harvard Business Review [*A publication*] (BRI)
HARC .... Halon Alternatives Research Corporation (NTPA)
Harc .... Harcarse's Decisions, Scotch Court of Session [*1681-91*] [*A publication*] (DLA)
HARC .... Harcor Energy [*NASDAQ symbol*] (TTSB)
HARC .... HarCor Energy Co. [*NASDAQ symbol*] (NQ)
HARC .... Helical Axial Rate Control (MCD)
HARC .... Heritage Arms Rescue Committee (WDAA)
HARC .... Hester Adrian Research Centre [*University of Manchester*] [*British*] (CB)
HARC .... High-Altitude RADAR Controller
HARC .... Houston Advanced Research Center
HARCFT .... Harbor Craft
HarcG .... Harcourt General, Inc. [*Associated Press*] (SAG)
HarcGn .... Harcourt General, Inc. [*Associated Press*] (SAG)
Har Ch .... Harrington's Michigan Chancery Reports [*A publication*] (DLA)
Har Ch Pr ... Harrison's Chancery Practice [*A publication*] (DLA)
Har Chy ...... Harrington's Michigan Chancery Reports [*A publication*] (DLA)
HARCO .... Hyperbolic Area Control (IAA)
HARCO .... Hyperbolic Area Coverage [*Navigation*]
Har Col Jur ... Hargrave's Collectanea Juridica [*1791-92*] [*A publication*] (DLA)
Har Com ...... Harrison's Compilation of the Laws of New Jersey [*A publication*] (DLA)
Har Com Proc... Harrison's Common Law Procedure Act [*Canada A publication*] (DLA)
HarcorE .... HarCor Energy Co. [*Associated Press*] (SAG)
Har Ct Mar... Harwood's Practice of United States Naval Courts-Martial [*A publication*] (DLA)
HARCVS ...... Honorary Associate of the Royal College of Veterinary Surgeons [*British*]
Hard .... Hardin's Kentucky Reports [*A publication*] (DLA)

Hard............ Hardres' English Exchequer Reports [*145 English Reprint*] [*A publication*] (DLA)
HARD .... Hardware (WDAA)
HARD .... Horizontal Acoustic Range Depiction (NVT)
hardbd .... Hardboard (VRA)
Hard Eccl L.. Harding on Ecclesiastical Law [*A publication*] (DLA)
Har Del .... Harrington's Delaware Reports [*1-5 Delaware*] [*A publication*] (DLA)
Hard El Pet... Hardcastle on Election Petitions [*A publication*] (DLA)
Hardes .... Hardesty's Delaware Term Reports [*A publication*] (DLA)
HARDEX....... Harbor Defense Exercise [*Navy*] (NG)
Har Dig .... Harris' Georgia Digest [*A publication*] (DLA)
Har Dig .... Harrison's Digest of English Common Law Reports [*A publication*] (DLA)
Hardin .... Hardin Bancorp, Inc. [*Associated Press*] (SAG)
Hardin .... Hardin's Kentucky Reports [*A publication*] (DLA)
Harding U .... Harding University (GAGS)
Hardin (KY).. Hardin's Kentucky Reports [*A publication*] (DLA)
Hardin-Simmons U... Hardin-Simmons University (GAGS)
HARDIS........ Hotel and Restaurant Design and Interiors Exhibition [*British*] (ITD)
HARDMAN ... Hardware-Manpower Program [*Navy*]
HARDMON ... Hardware Monitor [*Computer science*] (MHDI)
Hardr .... Hardres' English Exchequer Reports [*145 English Reprint*] [*1655-69*] [*A publication*] (DLA)
Hardr (Eng)... Hardres' English Exchequer Reports [*145 English Reprint*] [*A publication*] (DLA)
Hardres........ Hardres' English Exchequer Reports [*145 English Reprint*] [*A publication*] (DLA)
HARDS........ High-Altitude Radiation Detection System (MCD)
Hard St L..... Hardcastle on Statutory Law [*A publication*] (DLA)
Hard Tr M.... Hardingham on Trade Marks [*A publication*] (DLA)
HARDTS........ High-Accuracy RADAR Data Transmission System (MUGU)
Hardw .... Cases Tempore Hardwicke, by Lee [*England*] [*A publication*] (DLA)
Hardw .... Cases Tempore Hardwicke, by Ridgeway [*England*] [*A publication*] (DLA)
Hardw Cas Temp... Cases Tempore Hardwicke, by Lee and Hardwicke [*A publication*] (DLA)
Hardw (Eng)... Cases Tempore Hardwicke, by Lee [*England*] [*A publication*] (DLA)
Hardw (Eng)... Cases Tempore Hardwicke, by Ridgeway [*England*] [*A publication*] (DLA)
Hardw NB .... Hardwicke's Note Books [*A publication*] (DLA)
HARDWR ..... Hardware [*Computer science*]
Hare........... Hare's English Vice-Chancellors' Reports [*66-68 English Reprint*] [*1841-53*] [*A publication*] (DLA)
HARE .... High-Altitude Ramjet Engine
HARE .... High-Altitude Recombination-Energy Propulsion (AAG)
HARE .... Humans Against Rabbit Exploitation (EA)
HARE .... Hydrazine Auxiliary Rocket Engine
Hare & W .... Hare and Wallace's American Leading Cases [*A publication*] (DLA)
Hare & Wallace Amer Leading Cases... American Leading Cases, Edited by Hare and Wallace [*A publication*] (DLA)
Hare & Wallace Lead Cases (Am)... American Leading Cases, Edited by Hare and Wallace [*A publication*] (DLA)
Hare & Wal LC... American Leading Cases, Edited by Hare and Wallace [*A publication*] (DLA)
Hare App ..... Hare's English Chancery Reports, Appendix to Vol. X [*A publication*] (DLA)
Hare Const Law... Hare's American Constitutional Law [*A publication*] (DLA)
Hare Disc .... Hare on Discovery of Evidence [*A publication*] (DLA)
Hare Elec.... Hare on Elections [*A publication*] (DLA)
Hare (Eng)... Hare's English Vice-Chancellors' Reports [*66-68 English Reprint*] [*1841-53*] [*A publication*] (DLA)
Hare Ev....... Hare on Discovery of Evidence [*A publication*] (DLA)
HAREM .... Heparin Assay Rapid Easy Method [*Medicine*] (DMAA)
HARES .... High Altitude Radiation Environment Study [*FAA*] (PDAA)
HARF .... Holland Australia Retirement Foundation of Victoria [*Australia*]
Harg........... Hargrave's State Trials [*A publication*] (DLA)
Harg........... Hargrove's Reports [*68-75 North Carolina*] [*A publication*] (DLA)
HARG.......... Harper Group [*NASDAQ symbol*] (TTSB)
HARG.......... Harper Group, Inc. [*NASDAQ symbol*] (NQ)
HARG.......... High-Speed Autoradiography
Harg & B Co Litt... Hargrave and Butler's Edition on Coke upon Littleton [*A publication*] (DLA)
Harg Co Litt... Hargrave's Notes to Coke on Littleton [*A publication*] (DLA)
Harg Coll Jur... Hargrave's Collectanea Juridica [*1791-92*] [*A publication*] (DLA)
Harg Exer.... Hargrave's Juriconsult Exercitations [*A publication*] (DLA)
Harg Jur Arg... Hargrave's Juridical Arguments and Collections [*A publication*] (DLA)
Harg Law Tracts... Hargrave's Law Tracts [*A publication*] (DLA)
Harg LT .... Hargrave's Law Tracts [*A publication*] (DLA)
Hargrave & Butlers Notes on Co Litt... Hargrave and Butler's Notes on Coke upon Littleton [*A publication*] (DLA)
Hargr Co Litt... Hargrave's Notes to Coke on Littleton [*A publication*] (DLA)
Hargrove....... Hargrove's Reports [*68-75 North Carolina*] [*A publication*] (DLA)
Harg State Tr... Hargrave's State Trials [*A publication*] (DLA)
Harg St Tr ... Hargrave's State Trials [*A publication*] (DLA)
Harg Th .... Hargrave on the Thellusson Act [*A publication*] (DLA)
HARH .... High-Altitude Retinal Hemorrhage [*Medicine*]
Hari Rao...... Indian Income Tax Decisions [*A publication*] (DLA)
HARIS .... High-Altitude Radiological Instrumentation System
HarisHa .... Harris & Harris Group [*Associated Press*] (SAG)
HarisSvg ...... Harris Savings Bank [*Associated Press*] (SAG)
Haristn .... Hariston Corp. [*Associated Press*] (SAG)
Har Just....... Harris' Justinian [*A publication*] (DLA)
HARK .... Hardened Reentry Kill [*Air Force*]
Harken .... Harken Energy Corp. [*Associated Press*] (SAG)

HARL .... Harleysville Savings Association [*NASDAQ symbol*] (NQ)
HARL .... Harleysville Savings Bank [*NASDAQ symbol*] (TTSB)
Harland.......... Manchester Court Leet Records [*A publication*] (DLA)
HARL CBM... Harleian Collection, British Museum (DLA)
HarleyD .... Harley Davidson, Inc. [*Associated Press*] (SAG)
Harleys....... Harleysville Group, Inc. [*Associated Press*] (SAG)
HARL MISC... Harleian Miscellany [*British*] (ROG)
HARL MSS... Harleian Manuscripts [*British*] (ROG)
HarInd .... Harland [*John H.*] Co. [*Associated Press*] (SAG)
HARLOT....... Height [*Depth*] of Burst, Altitude of Targets, Resources, Location, Objectives, and Time [*Nuclear war games*]
HARLS........ Horse Antiserum to Rabbit Lymphocytes [*Immunology*]
Harlyn........ Harlyn Products, Inc. [*Associated Press*] (SAG)
HarlyNat...... Harleysville National Corp. [*Associated Press*] (SAG)
HarlySV....... Harleysville Savings Association [*Associated Press*] (SAG)
HARM .... Harmonic (WDAA)
Harm .... Harmonica [*of Ptolemy*] [*Classical studies*] (OCD)
Harm .... Harmon's Reports [*13-15 California*] [*A publication*] (DLA)
Harm .... Harmon's Upper Canada Common Pleas Reports [*A publication*] (DLA)
HARM .... Harmony
HARM .... Hazardous Atmospheric Release Model [*Marine science*] (OSRA)
HARM .... Heparin Assay Rapid Method (DMAA)
HARM .... High-Acceleration Rocket-Missile
HARM .... High-Speed Anti-RADAR Missile
HARM .... High-Speed Anti-Radiation Missile (COE)
HARM .... Hypervelocity Antiradiation Missile
Harma .... Harmannus [*Authority cited in pre-1607 legal work*] (DSA)
Harman....... Harman International Industries, Inc. [*Associated Press*] (SAG)
HarmBrk...... Harmony Brook, Inc. [*Associated Press*] (SAG)
HarmLgt...... Harmonic Lightwaves, Inc. [*Associated Press*] (SAG)
HarmLt .... Harmonic Lghtwaves, Inc. [*Associated Press*] (SAG)
Harmon....... Harmon Industries, Inc. [*Associated Press*] (SAG)
Harmon....... Harmon's Upper Canada Common Pleas Reports [*A publication*] (DLA)
HARMONICA... Harmonised Access and Retrieval for Music-Oriented Networked Information-Concerted Action (TELE)
HarmPd .... Harmony Products, Inc. [*Associated Press*] (SAG)
Harm Pens... Harmon's Manual of United States Pension Laws [*A publication*] (DLA)
HARN.......... Harness (MSA)
HARN.......... High Accuracy Reference Network [*Mathematics*]
HARNET....... [*The*] Hong Kong Academic and Research Network [*Computer science*] (TNIG)
HARNG .... Hawaii Army National Guard (CINC)
Harnish....... Harnischfeger Industries, Inc. [*Associated Press*] (SAG)
Harold........ Harold's Stores, Inc. [*Associated Press*] (SAG)
HAROTS....... High-Accuracy RADAR Data Transmission System
HARP .... Halpern's AntiRADAR Point
Harp........... Harper's South Carolina Equity Reports [*A publication*] (DLA)
Harp........... Harper's South Carolina Law Reports [*1823-30*] [*A publication*] (DLA)
Harp........... Harpocration [*Classical studies*] (OCD)
HARP .... Harpoon (WDAA)
HARP .... Harpsichord (WDAA)
HARP .... Hazard Assessment of Rocket Propellants
HARP .... Heater above Reheat Point (DNAB)
HARP .... Heating, Air Conditioning, Refrigeration, Plumbing (ADA)
HARP .... Heimlich-Armstrong-Rieveschl-Patrick [*Heart pump for aerospace use*]
HARP .... High-Altitude Reconnaissance Platform
HARP .... High-Altitude Relay Point
HARP .... High-Altitude Research Probe (IAA)
HARP .... High-Altitude Research Program [*or Project*] [*Military*]
HARP .... High-Altitude Rocket Probe [*Army*]
HARP .... Hitachi Arithmetic Processor [*Computer science*] (IEEE)
HARP .... Holding and Reconsignment Point (IAA)
HARP .... Homeless and At-Risk Population (DMAA)
HARP .... Hybrid Automated Reliability Predictor
Harp Con Cas... Harper's Conspiracy Cases [*Maryland*] [*A publication*] (DLA)
Har Pen Man... Harmon's Manual of United States Pension Laws [*A publication*] (DLA)
Harp Eq .... Harper's South Carolina Equity Reports [*A publication*] (DLA)
Harp Eq (SC)... Harper's South Carolina Equity Reports [*A publication*] (DLA)
Harper .... Harper's Conspiracy Cases [*Maryland*] [*A publication*] (DLA)
Harper .... Harper's South Carolina Equity Reports [*A publication*] (DLA)
Harper .... Harper's South Carolina Law Reports [*1823-30*] [*A publication*] (DLA)
HarpGp .... Harper Group, Inc. [*Associated Press*] (SAG)
HARPI......... Hardpoint Interceptor
Harp L .... Harper's South Carolina Law Reports [*1823-30*] [*A publication*] (DLA)
Harp L (SC)... Harper's South Carolina Law Reports [*1823-30*] [*A publication*] (DLA)
HARPPS....... Heat, Absence of Use, Redness, Pain, Pus, Swelling [*Medicine*] (MEDA)
Har Prob...... Harrison on Probate and Divorce [*A publication*] (DLA)
HARPS........ Hybrid AUTODIN Red Patch System (MCD)
HARPY........ Hydrofoil Advanced Research Study Program [*Navy*]
Harr .... Harrington's Delaware Reports [*1-5 Delaware*] [*A publication*] (DLA)
Harr .... Harrington's Michigan Chancery Reports [*A publication*] (DLA)
Harr .... Harrison's Law Reports [*16-19 New Jersey*] [*A publication*] (DLA)
Harr .... Harrison's Reports [*15-17, 23-29 Indiana*] [*A publication*] (DLA)
Harr .... Harris' Reports [*A publication*] (DLA)
Harr Adv ..... Harris' Hints on Advocacy [*18th ed.*] [*1943*] [*A publication*] (DLA)
HarrahE ...... Harrahs Entertainment, Inc. [*Associated Press*] (SAG)
Harr & Cl Conv... Harris and Clarkson on Conveyancing, Etc. [*A publication*] (DLA)
Harr & G...... Harris and Gill's Maryland Reports [*A publication*] (DLA)

Harr & H...... Harrison and Hodgin's Upper Canada Municipal Reports [*1845-51*] [*A publication*] (DLA)
Harr & Hodg... Harrison and Hodgin's Upper Canada Municipal Reports [*1845-51*] [*A publication*] (DLA)
Harr & J...... Harris and Johnson's Maryland Reports [*A publication*] (DLA)
Harr & J (MD)... Harris and Johnson's Maryland Reports [*A publication*] (DLA)
Harr & M...... Harris and McHenry's Maryland Reports [*A publication*] (DLA)
Harr & McH... Harris and McHenry's Maryland Reports [*A publication*] (DLA)
Harr & McHen... Harris and McHenry's Maryland Reports [*A publication*] (DLA)
Harr & McH (MD)... Harris and McHenry's Maryland Reports [*A publication*] (DLA)
Harr & M'H... Harris and McHenry's Maryland Reports [*A publication*] (DLA)
Harr & R...... Harrison and Rutherford's English Common Pleas Reports [*1865-66*] [*A publication*] (DLA)
Harr & Ruth... Harrison and Rutherford's English Common Pleas Reports [*1865-66*] [*A publication*] (DLA)
Harr & Sim... Harris and Simrall's Reports [*49-52 Mississippi*] [*A publication*] (DLA)
Harr & W..... Harrison and Wollaston's English King's Bench Reports [*A publication*] (DLA)
Harr & W (Eng)... Harrison and Wollaston's English King's Bench Reports [*A publication*] (DLA)
Harr & Woll... Harrison and Wollaston's English King's Bench Reports [*A publication*] (DLA)
Harr Ch....... Harrington's Michigan Chancery Reports [*A publication*] (DLA)
Harr Ch (Mich)... Harrington's Michigan Chancery Reports [*A publication*] (DLA)
Harr Ch R.... Harrington's Michigan Chancery Reports [*A publication*] (DLA)
Harr Con LA R... Harrison's Condensed Louisiana Reports [*A publication*] (DLA)
Harr Cr L.... Harris' Principles of the Criminal Law [*22nd ed.*] [*1973*] [*A publication*] (DLA)
Harr (Del)... Harrington's Delaware Reports [*1-5 Delaware*] [*A publication*] (DLA)
Harr Dig...... Harrison's Digest of English Common Law Reports [*A publication*] (DLA)
Har Resp ..... De Haruspicum Responso [*of Cicero*] [*Classical studies*] (OCD)
Harr (GA).... Harris' Georgia Digest [*A publication*] (DLA)
Harr Hints... Harris' Hints on Advocacy [*18th ed.*] [*1943*] [*A publication*] (DLA)
Harring .... Harrington's Delaware Reports [*1-5 Delaware*] [*A publication*] (DLA)
Harring .... Harrington's Michigan Chancery Reports [*A publication*] (DLA)
Harring Ch (Mich)... Harrington's Michigan Chancery Reports [*A publication*] (DLA)
Harrington ... Harrington's Delaware Supreme Court Reports [*1832-55*] [*A publication*] (DLA)
Harrington ... Harrington's Michigan Chancery Reports [*A publication*] (DLA)
Harris .... Harris Corp. [*Associated Press*] (SAG)
Harris .... Harris' Reports [*A publication*] (DLA)
Harris & G.... Harris and Gill's Maryland Reports [*A publication*] (DLA)
Harris & Gill's MD R... Harris and Gill's Maryland Reports [*A publication*] (DLA)
Harris & J.... Harris and Johnson's Maryland Reports [*A publication*] (DLA)
Harris & S.... Harris and Simrall's Reports [*49-52 Mississippi*] [*A publication*] (DLA)
Harris & Sim... Harris and Simrall's Reports [*49-52 Mississippi*] [*A publication*] (DLA)
Harris & Simrall... Harris and Simrall's Reports [*49-52 Mississippi*] [*A publication*] (DLA)
HarrisCS...... Harris Computer Systems Corp. [*Associated Press*] (SAG)
Harris Dig.... Harris' Georgia Digest [*A publication*] (DLA)
Harrison ...... Harrison's Law Reports [*16-19 New Jersey*] [*A publication*] (DLA)
Harrison ...... Harrison's Reports [*15-17, 23-29 Indiana*] [*A publication*] (DLA)
Harrison Ch... Harrison's Chancery Practice [*A publication*] (DLA)
Harrison Dig... Harrison's Digest of English Common Law Reports [*A publication*] (DLA)
Harr Just ..... Harris' Translation of the Institute of Justinian [*A publication*] (DLA)
Harr (Mich)... Harrington's Michigan Chancery Reports [*A publication*] (DLA)
Harr Min ..... Harris on Titles to Mines [*A publication*] (DLA)
Harr Mun Law... Harrison's Municipal Law of Ontario [*A publication*] (DLA)
Harr NJ....... Harrison's Law Reports [*16-19 New Jersey*] [*A publication*] (DLA)
Harrod .... Harrodsburg First Financial Bancorp, Inc. [*Associated Press*] (SAG)
Harr Prin ..... Harris' Principiae Primae Legum [*A publication*] (DLA)
Harr Proc.... Harrison's Common Law Procedure Act [*Canada*] [*A publication*] (DLA)
Harr Rom Law... Harris' Elements of Roman Law [*A publication*] (DLA)
HARRS........ High-Altitude Radio Relay System (DNAB)
HARS .... Harris Savings Bank [*NASDAQ symbol*] (SAG)
HARS .... Hazardous Area Reporting Service [*Aviation*] (FAAC)
HARS .... Heading Attitude Reference System (MCD)
HARS .... Heavy Assault Rocket System (MCD)
HARS .... Helicopter Attitude Reference System (MCD)
HARS .... High Altitude Route System [*FAA*] (TAG)
HARS .... Historic Aircraft Restoration Society [*Australia*]
HARSAP....... Harbor Survey Assistance Program [*Naval Oceanographic Office*]
Harsco .... Harsco Corp. [*Associated Press*] (SAG)
Hars Pr....... Harston's California Practice and Pleading [*A publication*] (DLA)
Har St Tr ..... Hargrave's State Trials [*A publication*] (DLA)
HART .... Halt All Racist Tours [*British*] (DI)
HART .... Hardened Amplifier for Radiation Transients
Hart .... Hartley's Digest of Texas Laws [*A publication*] (DLA)
Hart .... Hartley's Reports [*4-10 Texas*] [*A publication*] (DLA)
HART .... Hayden Analysis and Reporting Tool [*Computer science*]
HART .... Heartland Wireless Commun [*NASDAQ symbol*] (TTSB)
HART .... Heartland Wireless Communications, Inc. [*NASDAQ symbol*] (SAG)
HART .... Heparin-Aspirin Reinfarction Trial [*Medicine*] (DMAA)
HART .... Heparin-Aspirin Reperfusion Trial [*Cardiology*]
HART .... High-Acceleration Rocket, Tactical (DNAB)
HART .... Highway Aid by Radio Truck (IAA)
HARTE .... Hospital Access and Response Terminal [*Health insurance*] (GHCT)
HART .... Hypervelocity Aircraft Rocket, Tactical
Hart & H...... Hartley and Hartley's Reports [*11-21 Texas*] [*A publication*] (DLA)
Hart Bank .... Hart's Bankrupt Law and Practice [*A publication*] (DLA)

HartC .... Hartford Capital I [*Associated Press*] (SAG)
HartC .... Hartford Capital II [*Associated Press*] (SAG)
Hart Dig...... Hartley's Digest of Texas Laws [*A publication*] (DLA)
Hart Hartm... Hartmannus Hartmanni [*Deceased, 1586*] [*Authority cited in pre-1607 legal work*] (DSA)
HartHnk ...... Harte Hanks Communications [*Associated Press*] (SAG)
Hartley........ Hartley's Reports [*4-10 Texas*] [*A publication*] (DLA)
Hartley & Hartley... Hartley and Hartley's Reports [*11-21 Texas*] [*A publication*] (DLA)
Hartley & Hartley Rep... Hartley and Hartley's Reports [*11-21 Texas*] [*A publication*] (DLA)
Hartman Pist... Hartmannus Pistoris [*Deceased, 1601*] [*Authority cited in pre-1607 legal work*] (DSA)
Hartm Pistor... Hartmannus Pistoris [*Deceased, 1601*] [*Authority cited in pre-1607 legal work*] (DSA)
Hartmx........ Hartmarx Corp. [*Associated Press*] (SAG)
Hart Pist ...... Hartmannus Pistoris [*Deceased, 1601*] [*Authority cited in pre-1607 legal work*] (DSA)
HARTRAN .... Hardwell FORTRAN [*Computer science*] (IEEE)
HARTS .... Hardening Technology Studies Program (MCD)
HARU.......... Handbuch fuer Rundfunk und Fernsehen [*Handbook for Radio and Television*] [*NOMOS Datapool Database*]
HARV .... Harassment Vehicle (MCD)
HARV .... Harvard University [*Massachusetts*]
Harv .... Harvard Vocarium [*Record label*]
HARV .... Harvest
HARV .... Harvey Universal, Inc. [*NASDAQ symbol*] (SAG)
HARVAN ...... Harriman and Vance [*Code name for 1968 Paris peace talks on Vietnam, derived from the surnames of US negotiators W. Averell Harriman and Cyrus R. Vance*]
HARV and MARV... Harvey Ratner and Marvin Wolfenson [*Proprietors of Target Centre basketball arena*] (ECON)
Harvard U.... Harvard University (GAGS)
Harv Bus World... Harvard Business World (DLA)
HarvCas ...... Harveys Casinos Resorts [*Associated Press*] (SAG)
Harv CR CL Law Rev... Harvard Civil Rights - Civil Liberties Law Review [*A publication*] (ILCA)
Harv Ed Rev... Harvard Educational Review [*A publication*] (DLA)
Harv Env L Rev... Harvard Environmental Law Review [*A publication*] (DLA)
HARVEST..... Highly Active Residues Vitrification and Engineered Storage [*Nuclear energy British*] (NUCP)
HARVEST..... Highly Active Residues Vitrification Engineering Studies [*Nuclear energy British*] (NUCP)
HarvestH...... Harvest Home Financial Corp. [*Associated Press*] (SAG)
HarveyE ...... Harvey Entertainment Co. [*Associated Press*] (SAG)
HarveyU....... Harvey Universal, Inc. [*Associated Press*] (SAG)
HarvI............ Harvard Industries, Inc. [*Associated Press*] (SAG)
HarvInd .... Harvard Industries, Inc. [*Associated Press*] (SAG)
Harv Int'l L Club Bull... Harvard International Law Club. Bulletin [*A publication*] (DLA)
Harv Int'l L Club J... Harvard International Law Club. Journal [*A publication*] (DLA)
Harv L Lib Inf Bull... Harvard Law Library. Information Bulletin [*A publication*] (DLA)
Harv LS Rec... Harvard Law School. Record [*A publication*] (DLA)
HarvstFn ...... Harvest Financial Corp. [*Associated Press*] (SAG)
Harv Stud .... Harvard Studies in Classical Philology [*A publication*] (OCD)
Harv Women's LJ... Harvard Women's Law Journal [*A publication*] (DLA)
Harv W Tax Ser... Harvard World Tax Series [*A publication*] (DLA)
HARVY........ Harvard Securities Group PLC (MHDW)
HARW......... Harwich [*Municipal borough in England*]
HARWAS...... Horizontal-Axis Rotating-Wing Aeronautical System (PDAA)
HARY .... Harry's Farmers Market [*NASDAQ symbol*] (TTSB)
HARY .... Harry's Farmers Markets [*NASDAQ symbol*] (SAG)
HaryFar........ Harry's Farmers Markets [*Associated Press*] (SAG)
HARYOU-ACT... Harlem Youth Opportunities Unlimited - Associated Community Teams [*A kind of Peace Corps for Harlem area of New York City*]
HAS .... Hail [*Saudi Arabia*] [*Airport symbol*] (OAG)
HAS .... Hamburg Airlines, GmbH [*Germany ICAO designator*] (FAAC)
HAS .... Hamilton Anxiety Scale [*Psychology*] (DB)
HAS .... Harassment Vehicle [*Military*]
HAS .... Hardened Aircraft Shelter [*British military*] (DMA)
HAS .... Hasbro, Inc. [*AMEX symbol*] (SPSG)
HAS .... Hastings [*New Zealand*] [*Seismograph station code, US Geological Survey Closed*] (SEIS)
HAS .... Heading Altitude Sensor (IAA)
HAS .... Heading Altitude System
HAS .... Health Advocacy Services [*AARP*]
HAS .... Helical Antenna System
HAS .... Helicopter Anti-Submarine
HAS .... Helicopter Avionics System [*Air Force*]
HAS .... Helium Atom-Beam Scattering [*Materials science*]
HAS .... Hellenic Affiliation Scale [*Psychology*]
HAS .... High-Altitude Sampler
HAS .... High-Angle Strafe
HAS .... Highest Asymptomatic [*Dose*] [*Medicine*]
HAS .... Highest Average Salary
HAS .... Holddown Alignment Support (NASA)
HAS .... Holograph Assessment System
HAS .... Horatio Alger Society (EA)
HAS .... Hospital Adjustment Scale [*Psychology*]
HAS .... Hospital Administrative Services
HAS .... Hospital Advisory Service [*British*]
HAS .... Hover Augmentation System
HAS .... Human Albumin Solution [*Clinical chemistry*]

HAS .... Hyaluronic Acid Synthase [*An enzyme*]
HAS .... Hydraulic Actuation System (MCD)
HAS .... Hydraulic Adjustable Speed
HAS .... Hydrogen Actuation System (NASA)
HAS .... Hydroxy-Aluminosilicate [*Inorganic chemistry*]
HAS .... Hydroxylamine Acid Sulfate [*Inorganic chemistry*]
HAS .... Hydroxylammonium Sulfate [*Inorganic chemistry*]
HAS .... Hyperalimentation Solution [*Pharmacology*] (DAVI)
HAS .... Hypertensive Arteriosclerotic [*Cardiology*]
HAS .... Hypoxanthine and Azaserine [*Medium*]
HASAWA ...... Health and Safety at Work Act [*1974*] [*British*] (NUCP)
HASB .... Assab [*Ethiopia*] [*ICAO location identifier*] (ICLI)
Hasb .... Hasbrouck's Reports [*Idaho*] [*A publication*] (DLA)
Hasbro......... Hasbro, Inc. [*Associated Press*] (SAG)
HASC .... Headquarters, Air Service Command [*Air Force*]
HASC .... Historical Automobile Society of Canada
HASC .... Hospitality Association of South Carolina (SRA)
HASC .... House Armed Services Committee [*US Congress*] (AABC)
HASC .... Hyderabad Army Service Corps [*British military*] (DMA)
HASCI......... Human Applications Standard Computer Interface [*Keyboard*] (MCD)
HASCO........ Haitian-American Sugar Co.
HASCO........ HAWK [*Homing All the Way Killer*] Assembly System Checkout (SAA)
HASCVD...... Hypertensive Arteriosclerotic Cardiovascular Disease [*Cardiology*] (MAE)
HASD .... Sodo [*Ethiopia*] [*ICAO location identifier*] (ICLI)
HASE .... Head Angulation Sighting Equipment [*British military*] (DMA)
HASE .... Hydrophobic Alkali Soluble Emulsion [*Paint technology*]
haSH........... Human Achaete-Scute Homologue [*Genetics*]
HASH.......... Sheik Hussein [*Ethiopia*] [*ICAO location identifier*] (ICLI)
HASINS....... High Accuracy Submersible Inertial Navigation System (PDAA)
HASIS .... House Armed Services Investigation Subcommittee [*US Congress*]
HASJPL....... H. Allen Smith Jet Propulsion Laboratory [*Former name, JPL, continues to be used as official name*] [*Name adopted in 1973 to honor retiring congressman*]
Hask .... Haskell's Reports for United States Courts in Maine (Fox's Decisions) [*A publication*] (DLA)
Haskel .... Haskel International, Inc. [*Associated Press*] (SAG)
HASL .... Health and Safety Laboratory [*ERDA*]
HASL .... Hertfordshire Association of Special Libraries [*British*] (NITA)
HASL .... Hot-Air Solder Leveling [*Materials science*]
Hasl Med Jur... Haslam's Medical Jurisprudence [*A publication*] (DLA)
HASO .... Assosa [*Ethiopia*] [*ICAO location identifier*] (ICLI)
HAsP........... Health Aspects of Pesticides [*Medicine*] (DMAA)
HASP .... High Altitude Sampling Plane
HASP .... High-Altitude Sampling Program [*Air Force*]
HASP .... High-Altitude Sounding Program (IAA)
HASP .... High-Altitude Sounding Projectile
HASP .... High-Altitude Space Platform
HASP .... High-Altitude Space Probe (IAA)
HASP .... High-Level Automatic Scheduling Program (BUR)
HASP .... Hospital Admission and Surveillance Program (MEDA)
HASP .... Houston Automatic Spooling Priority System [*Computer science*]
HASP .... Houston Automatic Spooling Processor [*IBM equipment operating system*] (NITA)
HASPA .... High-Altitude Superpressure Powered Aerostat [*Navy*]
HASPID....... House Armed Services Permanent Investigations Subcommittee [*US Congress*] (AAG)
HASPS .... Hardened Array Solar Power System [*Military*]
HASQ .... Hardware-Assisted Software Queue
HASR .... High-Altitude Sounding Rocket
HASRD........ Health and Safety Research Division [*Oak Ridge National Laboratory*]
HASSS .... High-Accuracy Spacecraft Separation System (IAA)
Hast............ Hastings' Reports [*69, 70 Maine*] [*A publication*] (DLA)
HAST .... Hausa Speaking Test [*Center for Applied Linguistics*] (TES)
HAST .... High-Altitude Selection Test [*British military*] (DMA)
HAST .... High-Altitude Supersonic Target [*Later, HAHST*] (MCD)
HAST .... Highly Accelerated Stress Testing (AAEL)
HAST .... Humanitarian Assistance Survey Team
HASTAM ...... Health and Safety Technology Management (AIE)
Hast Cen R... Hastings Center Report [*A publication*] (BRI)
HASTE .... Hazard Assessment System for Toxic Emissions [*Computer-based emergency management system*] [*Environmental Research & Technology*]
HASTE .... Helicopter Assault Survivability in a Threat Environment (MCD)
HASTI .... High-Altitude Strike Indicator
Hasting........ Hastings Manufacturing Co. [*Associated Press*] (SAG)
Hastings C Law... University of California Hastings College of Law (GAGS)
Hast Int & Comp L Rev... Hastings' International and Comparative Law Review [*A publication*] (DLA)
Hast Tr .... Trial of Warren Hastings [*A publication*] (DLA)
HASVR........ High-Altitude Space Velocity RADAR (AAG)
HASWA .... Health and Safety at Work Act [*British*]
HAT............ Handbuch zum Alten Testament [*A publication*] (BJA)
HAT............ Handover Transmitter (IAA)
HAT............ Harbour Acceptance Trials [*Missile*] [*British*]
HAT............ Hardened and Tempered (IAA)
HAT............ Hardness Assurance Test
HAT............ Harmonic Attenuation Table [*or Test*] (DAVI)
Hat............ Hatran (BJA)
HAT............ Hatteras Income Sec [*NYSE symbol*] (TTSB)
HAT............ Hatteras Income Securities, Inc. [*NYSE symbol*] (SPSG)
HAT............ Hatteras, NC [*Location identifier FAA*] (FAAL)
HAT............ Hawaiian Archives for Tsunamis

HAT	Head, Arms, and Trunk [*Anatomy*] (DAVI)
HAT	Heathlands [*Australia Airport symbol Obsolete*] (OAG)
HAT	Heavy Artillery Tractor [*British military*] (DMA)
HAT	Height above Runway Touchdown Zone Elevation [*Aviation*]
HAT	Height above Terrain
HAT	Height Above Touchdown (PDAA)
HAT	Helicopter Acquisition Test (MCD)
HAT	Heterophil Antibody Titer (DB)
HAT	High-Altitude Target
HAT	High Altitude Temperature (PDAA)
HAT	High-Altitude Temperature Rocket
HAT	High-Altitude Testing [*Sounding rocket*]
HAT	High-Altitude Transmitter
HAT	High-Angle Threat
HAT	Highest Astronomical Tide
HAT	Highly Aphid Transmissible [*Plant pathology*]
HAT	Histone Acetyltransferase [*An enzyme*]
HAT	History Advertising Trust [*British*] (DBA)
HAT	Home Area Toll [*Telecommunications*] (TEL)
HAT	Horizontal Alidade Tie
HAT	Hospital Alliance of Tennessee (SRA)
HAT	Housing Action Trust [*British*] (ECON)
HAT	Hug-a-Tree and Survive (EA)
HAT	Hypoxanthine-Aminopterin-Thymidine [*Medium*] [*Biochemistry*]
HATACS	Helicopter Air-to-Air Combat Simulation (MCD)
HATCDS	High-Altitude Terrain Contour Data Sensor (MSA)
Hatcher's Kan Dig	Hatcher's Kansas Digest [*A publication*] (DLA)
HATF	Hydraulic Actuator Test Fixture
HATFPEV	Hatfield Peverel [*England*]
HATG	Horse Anti-Human Thymocyte Globulin [*Immunology*] (AAMN)
HATH	Hathaway Corp. [*NASDAQ symbol*] (NQ)
HATH	Heterosexual Attitudes toward Homosexuality [*Scale*]
Hathwy	Hathaway Corp. [*Associated Press*] (SAG)
HAT/LANT	Habitability Assistance Team/Atlantic (DNAB)
HATLS	Hostile Artillery Positions (RDA)
HATO	Handling Tool (AAG)
HATO	Tendaho [*Ethiopia*] [*ICAO location identifier*] (ICLI)
HATOFF	Highest Astronomical Tide of the Foreseeable Future (PDAA)
HATOL	Horizontal Altitude Take-Off and Landing (PDAA)
HATOM	Highest Astronomical Tide of the Month (PDAA)
HATOY	Highest Astronomical Tide of the Year (PDAA)
HATP	Tippi [*Ethiopia*] [*ICAO location identifier*] (ICLI)
HAT/PAC	Habitability Assistance Team/Pacific (DNAB)
HATR	Hazardous Air Traffic Report
HATR	Horizontal Attenuated Total Reflection [*Spectroscopy*]
HATRA	Hosiery and Allied Trades Research Association [*British*] (BI)
HATRAC	Handover Transfer and Receiver Accept Change [*SAGE*]
HATREMS	Hazardous and Trace Emissions Monitoring System [*Environmental science*] (COE)
HATREMS	Hazardous and Trace Emissions System [*Environmental Protection Agency*]
HATRICS	Hampshire Technical Research Industrial and Commercial Service [*British*] (NITA)
HATRON	Heavy Attack Squadron (MUGU)
HATS	Hardened Tactical Shelters
Hats	Hatsell's Parliamentary Precedents [*1290-1818*] [*A publication*] (DLA)
HATS	Hazard Abatement Tracking System [*Environmental science*] (COE)
HATS	Head and Torso Simulator [*A dummy developed by British Telecommunications Ltd.*]
HATS	Heading, Altitude, True Airspeed [*Aviation*] (CAAL)
HATS	Helicopter Advanced Tactical System (MCD)
HATS	Helicopter Attack System
HATS	Helmut Attitude Tracking System (MCD)
HATS	Heuristic Automated Transportation System (MCD)
HATS	High-Accuracy Targeting Subsystem
HATS	High-Altitude Terrain Contour Data Sensor
HATS	High-Altitude Test Stand
HATS	Holden's Air Transport Services [*Australia*]
HATS	Hour Angle of the True Sun [*Navigation*]
HATS	Huntsville Association of Technical Societies
HATS	Tessenei [*Ethiopia*] [*ICAO location identifier*] (ICLI)
Hats Pr	Hatsell's Parliamentary Precedents [*1290-1818*] [*A publication*] (DLA)
Hats Prec	Hatsell's Parliamentary Precedents [*1290-1818*] [*A publication*] (DLA)
Hatt	Hattusilis (BJA)
HATT	Heparin-Associated Thrombocytopenia and Thrombosis [*Medicine*] (DMAA)
HATTS	Hemagglutination Treponemal Test for Syphilis [*Medicine*] (DMAA)
HattSe	Hatteras Income Securities, Inc. [*Associated Press*] (SAG)
HATU	Heavy Air Training Unit
HATU	Heavy Attack Training Unit
HATV	High-Altitude Test Vehicle
HATWING	Heavy Attack Wing
HATWINGLANT	Heavy Attack Wing, Atlantic Fleet
HATWINGPAC	Heavy Attack Wing, Pacific Fleet
HAU	Haudompre [*France*] [*Seismograph station code, US Geological Survey*] (SEIS)
HAU	Haugesund [*Norway*] [*Airport symbol*] (OAG)
HAU	Haultain Resources Ltd. [*Vancouver Stock Exchange symbol*]
hau	Hausa [*MARC language code Library of Congress*] (LCCP)
HAU	Hebrew Actors Union (EA)
HAU	Helena, MT [*Location identifier FAA*] (FAAL)
HAU	Hemagglutination Unit [*Hematology*]
HAU	Horizontal Arithmetic Unit
HAU	Hybrid Arithmetic Unit
HAUL	Allied Holdings [*NASDAQ symbol*] (TTSB)

HAUL	Allied Holdings, Inc. [*NASDAQ symbol*] (SAG)
HAUP	Hauppauge Digital [*NASDAQ symbol*] (TTSB)
HAUP	Hauppauge Digital, Inc. [*NASDAQ symbol*] (SAG)
HaupD	Hauppauge Digital, Inc. [*Associated Press*] (SAG)
HaupgD	Hauppauge Digital, Inc. [*Associated Press*] (SAG)
HAUPTW	Hauptwerk [*Masterpiece*] [*German*]
HAUPW	Hauppague Digital Wrrt'A' [*NASDAQ symbol*] (TTSB)
HAURIEND	Hauriendus [*To Be Drunk*] [*Pharmacy*] (ROG)
HAUS	Hauser Chemical Research [*NASDAQ symbol*] (TTSB)
HAUS	Hauser Chemical Research, Inc. [*NASDAQ symbol*] (SAG)
HAUS	Hauser, Inc. [*NASDAQ symbol*] (SAG)
HausCh	Hauser Chemical Research, Inc. [*Associated Press*] (SAG)
Hauser	Hauser, Inc. [*Associated Press*] (SAG)
haust	Haustus [*Drink*] [*Latin*] (STED)
HAUST	Haustus [*A Drink*] [*Pharmacy*]
HAUST PURG	Haustus Purgans [*Purging Draught*] [*Pharmacy*] (ROG)
HAUT	Hautboy [*Oboe*]
Haut	Heautontimorumenos [*of Terence*] [*Classical studies*] (OCD)
HAV	Hallux Abducto Valgus [*Orthopedics*] (DAVI)
HAV	Havana [*Cuba*] [*Airport symbol*] (OAG)
HAV	Havering [*Borough in England*]
HAV	Haversine [*Mathematics*]
HAV	Havilah [*California*] [*Seismograph station code, US Geological Survey Closed*] (SEIS)
Hav	Haviland's Prince Edward Island Chancery Reports, by Peters [*1850-72*] [*Canada*] [*A publication*] (DLA)
Hav	Havildar [*British military*] (DMA)
HAV	Heavily Armed Vessels
HAV	Hemadsorption Virus [*Medicine*] (DB)
HAV	Hepatitis A Virus
HAV	High-Accuracy Voltmeter
HAV	High-Activity Variant [*Cells*] (DB)
HAV	Hilprecht Anniversary Volume. Studies in Assyriology and Archaeology Dedicated to Hermann V. Hilprecht [*Leipzig*] [*A publication*] (BJA)
HAV	Hot Air Vulcanization
HAV	Hypovirulence-Associated Virus
HAVA	Harvard Industries [*NASDAQ symbol*] (TTSB)
HAVA	Harvard Industries, Inc. [*NASDAQ symbol*] (NQ)
HAVAB	Hepatitis A Virus Antibody [*Medicine*] (STED)
HAVAg	Hepatitis A Virus Antigen [*Immunochemistry*]
HAVC	Health Audiovisual On-Line Catalog [*Northeastern Ohio Universities*] [*Information service or system Defunct*]
Hav Ch Rep	Haviland's Prince Edward Island Chancery Reports [*1850-72*] [*A publication*] (DLA)
HAVCO	Have Complied
HAVE	Heating and Ventilation Estimating [*Tipdata Ltd.*] [*Software package*] (NCC)
HAVE	Height Average (IAA)
HAVE	Homemaking and Volunteer Experience (DICI)
HAVEN	Haven [*Commonly used*] (OPSA)
HAVENB	Help Addicts Voluntarily End Narcotics
HavenB	Haven Bancorp [*Associated Press*] (SAG)
Haverty	Haverty Furniture Companies, Inc. [*Associated Press*] (SAG)
Havil	Haviland's Prince Edward Island Reports [*A publication*] (DLA)
Hav-Maj	Havildar-Major [*British military*] (DMA)
HAVN	Haven [*Commonly used*] (OPSA)
HAVN	Haven Bancorp [*NASDAQ symbol*] (SAG)
HAVO	Hawaii Volcanoes National Park
HAVOC	Histogram Average Ogive Calculator
Hav PEI	Haviland's Prince Edward Island Reports [*A publication*] (DLA)
HAVREP	Abridged Arrival Report [*Navy*] (NVT)
HAVREP	Have Report [*Navy*] (ANA)
Havrfld	Haverfield Corp. [*Associated Press*] (SAG)
Havrty	Haverty Furniture Companies, Inc. [*Associated Press*] (SAG)
HAVS	Harpoon Asset Visibility System (MCD)
HAVT	Hardness Assurance Verification Testing (MCD)
HAVT	Haverty Furniture [*NASDAQ symbol*] (TTSB)
HAVT	Haverty Furniture Companies, Inc. [*NASDAQ symbol*] (NQ)
HAVTA	Haverty Furniture'A' [*NASDAQ symbol*] (TTSB)
HAW	Fargo, ND [*Location identifier FAA*] (FAAL)
HAW	Hafnium Column Waste [*Nuclear energy*] (NRCH)
HAW	Hawaii (KSC)
haw	Hawaiian [*MARC language code Library of Congress*] (LCCP)
Haw	Hawaii Supreme Court Reports [*A publication*] (DLA)
Haw	Hawarde's Star Chamber Cases [*A publication*] (DLA)
Haw	Hawkins' Annual Reports [*19-24 Louisiana*] [*A publication*] (DLA)
Haw	Hawkins' Pleas of the Crown [*England*] [*A publication*] (DLA)
HAW	Hawksbill Resources, Inc. [*Vancouver Stock Exchange symbol*]
Haw	Hawley's Reports [*10-20 Nevada*] [*A publication*] (DLA)
HAW	Heavy Antiarmor Weapon
HAW	Heavy Antitank Weapon (INF)
HAW	Heavy Assault Weapon
HAW	Helicopter Assault Wave
HAW	High-Acid Waste [*Nuclear energy*] (NRCH)
HAW	High Active Waste [*Nuclear energy*]
HAW	Highly Active Waste
HAW	Holidays and Anniversaries of the World [*A publication*]
HAW	Home All the Way [*Military*] (CAAL)
HAW	Hypersonic Aerodynamic Weapon (DOMA)
HAWA	Hawaii
Hawaii	Hawaii Reports [*A publication*] (DLA)
Hawaii Rep	Hawaii Reports [*A publication*] (DLA)
Hawaii BN	Hawaii Bar News [*A publication*] (DLA)
Hawaii Dist	United States District Court, District of Hawaii (DLA)

Hawaii PUC Dec...   Hawaii Public Utilities Commission Decisions [*A publication*] (DLA)
Hawaii Rep...   Hawaii Reports [*A publication*] (DLA)
Hawaii Rev Stat...   Hawaii Revised Statutes [*A publication*] (DLA)
Hawaii Rules & Reg...   Hawaii Rules and Regulations [*A publication*] (DLA)
Hawaii Sess Laws...   Session Laws of Hawaii [*A publication*] (DLA)
HawAir........   Hawaiian Airlines, Inc. [*Associated Press*] (SAG)
Hawarde........   Hawarde's Star Chamber Cases [*A publication*] (DLA)
Hawarde St Ch...   Hawarde's Star Chamber Cases [*A publication*] (DLA)
Haw Ass......   Hawes on Assignments [*A publication*] (DLA)
HAWB..........   House Air Waybill [*Shipping*] (DS)
HAWC..........   Homing and Warning Computer (MCD)
HAWC..........   Wacca [*Ethiopia*] [*ICAO location identifier*] (ICLI)
Haw Cr Rep...   Hawley's American Criminal Reports [*A publication*] (DLA)
HAWDC.........   Hotel Association of Washington, D.C. (SRA)
HAWE..........   Hamburg-Wechsler Intelligence Test [*Psychology*]
HawEl........   Hawaiian Electric Industries, Inc. [*Associated Press*] (SAG)
Hawes Jur...   Hawes on Jurisdiction of Courts [*A publication*] (DLA)
Haw Fed......   Hawaii Federal [*Legal term*] (DLA)
HAWHA........   Heart of America Walking Horse Association (EA)
HAWIC.......   Hamburg-Wechsler Intelligence Test for Children (STED)
HAWIK.......   Hamburg-Wechsler-Intelligenztest fuer Kinder [*Hamburg-Wechsler Intelligence Test for Children*] [*Psychology*]
HAWK..........   Have Alimony, Will Keep
HAWK..........   Hawkesbury [*England*]
Hawk..........   Hawkins' Pleas of the Crown [*England*] [*A publication*] (DLA)
HAWK..........   Hawks Industries [*NASDAQ symbol*] (TTSB)
HAWK..........   Hawks Industries, Inc. [*NASDAQ symbol*] (NQ)
HAWK..........   Homing All the Way Killer [*Small missile*]
HAWK..........   Hunting and Angling With Kids
Hawk Abr...   Hawkins' Abridgment of Coke upon Littleton [*A publication*] (DLA)
HawkB........   Hawkeye Bancorp [*Associated Press*] (SAG)
HawkC.........   Hawkins Chemical, Inc. [*Associated Press*] (SAG)
Hawk Coke Abr...   Hawkins' Abridgment of Coke upon Littleton [*A publication*] (DLA)
Hawk Co Litt...   Hawkins' Coke upon Littleton [*A publication*] (DLA)
Hawkins....   Hawkins' Annual Reports [*19-24 Louisiana*] [*A publication*] (DLA)
Hawk PC......   Hawkins' Pleas of the Crown [*England*] [*A publication*] (DLA)
Hawk Pl Cr...   Hawkins' Pleas of the Crown [*England*] [*A publication*] (DLA)
Hawks.......   Hawks Industries, Inc. [*Associated Press*] (SAG)
Hawks.......   Hawks' North Carolina Reports [*A publication*] (DLA)
Hawks (NC)...   Hawks' North Carolina Reports [*A publication*] (DLA)
Hawk Wills...   Hawkins' Construction of Wills [*A publication*] (DLA)
Hawl..........   Hawley's Reports [*10-20 Nevada*] [*A publication*] (DLA)
Hawl Cr R...   Hawley's American Criminal Reports [*A publication*] (DLA)
Hawley.......   Hawley's American Criminal Reports [*A publication*] (DLA)
Hawley.......   Hawley's Reports [*10-20 Nevada*] [*A publication*] (DLA)
Hawley's Crim Rep...   Hawley's American Criminal Reports [*A publication*] (DLA)
Hawn.........   Hawaii Reports [*A publication*] (DLA)
HAWP.........   Homing and Warning Programmer (MCD)
HAWR.........   Helicopter Attack Warning RADAR (NVT)
Haw Rep......   Hawaii Reports [*A publication*] (DLA)
Haw Rev Stat...   Hawaii Revised Statutes [*A publication*] (DLA)
Haw Rev Stat Ann...   Hawaii Revised Statutes Annotated [*A publication*] (AAGC)
HAWSEAFRON...   Hawaiian Sea Frontier
Haw Sess Laws...   Session Laws of Hawaii [*A publication*] (DLA)
HAWT.........   Horizontal Axis Wind Turbine [*Generator*] [*Also, HAWTG*] (MCD)
HAWTADS....   Helicopter All-Weather Target Acquisition and Designation System
HAWTADS....   HELLFIRE [*Heliborne LASER Fire and Forget*] All-Weather Target Acquisition and Destruction System (MCD)
HawtFn.......   Hawthorne Financial Corp. [*Associated Press*] (SAG)
HAWTG........   Horizontal Axis Wind Turbine Generator [*Also, HAWT*]
Haw WC .....   Hawes' Will Case [*A publication*] (DLA)
HAX ....   Hafnium Column Extractant [*Nuclear energy*] (NRCH)
HAX ....   Hangar 5 Air Services Norway [*FAA designator*] (FAAC)
HAX ....   Helicopter Armored Experiment
HAX ....   Muskogee, OK [*Location identifier FAA*] (FAAL)
HAY ....   Haycock, AK [*Location identifier FAA*] (FAAL)
HAY ....   Hayes-Dana, Inc. [*Toronto Stock Exchange symbol*]
Hay ....   Hayes' Irish Exchequer Reports [*1830-32*] [*A publication*] (DLA)
Hay ....   Hayes' Reports [*Calcutta*] [*A publication*] (DLA)
HAY ....   Hayes Wheels International [*NYSE symbol*] (SPSG)
HAY ....   Hayfield [*California*] [*Seismograph station code, US Geological Survey*] (SEIS)
Hay ....   Hay's High Court Appeals Reports [*1862-63*] [*Bengal, India*] [*A publication*] (DLA)
Hay ....   Hay's Poor Law Decisions [*1711-1859*] [*Scotland*] [*A publication*] (DLA)
Hay ....   Hay's Scotch Decisions [*A publication*] (DLA)
Hay ....   Haywood's North Carolina Reports [*A publication*] (DLA)
Hay ....   Haywood's Tennessee Reports [*A publication*] (DLA)
Hay Acc......   Hay's Decisions on Accidents and Negligence [*1860*] [*Scotland*] [*A publication*] (DLA)
Hay & H ......   Hayward and Hazelton's United States Circuit Court Reports [*District of Columbia*] [*A publication*] (DLA)
Hay & Haz...   Hayward and Hazelton's United States Circuit Court Reports [*District of Columbia*] [*A publication*] (DLA)
Hay & J ......   Hayes and Jones' Irish Exchequer Reports [*A publication*] (DLA)
Hay & Jo .....   Hayes and Jones' Irish Exchequer Reports [*1832-34*] [*A publication*] (DLA)
Hay & M .....   Hay and Marriott's English Admiralty Reports [*A publication*] (DLA)
Hay & Mar...   Hay and Marriott's English Admiralty Reports [*A publication*] (DLA)
Hay & Marr...   Hay and Marriott's English Admiralty Reports [*A publication*] (DLA)
Hay & M (Eng)...   Hay and Marriott's English Admiralty Reports [*A publication*] (DLA)

Hay (Calc) ...   Hay's Reports [*Calcutta*] [*A publication*] (DLA)
Hay Dec.......   Hay's Decisions on Accidents and Negligence [*1860*] [*Scotland*] [*A publication*] (DLA)
Hay Eq.........   Haynes' Outlines of Equity [*5th ed.*] [*1880*] [*A publication*] (DLA)
Hayes ....   Hayes' Irish Exchequer Reports [*1830-32*] [*A publication*] (DLA)
Hayes ....   Hayes Wheels International [*Associated Press*] (SAG)
Hayes & J ...   Hayes and Jones' Irish Exchequer Reports [*1832-34*] [*A publication*] (DLA)
Hayes & J (Ir)...   Hayes and Jones' Irish Exchequer Reports [*1832-34*] [*A publication*] (DLA)
Hayes & Jo...   Hayes and Jones' Irish Exchequer Reports [*1832-34*] [*A publication*] (DLA)
Hayes & Jon...   Hayes and Jones' Irish Exchequer Reports [*1832-34*] [*A publication*] (DLA)
Hayes & J Wills...   Hayes and Jarman's Concise Forms of Wills [*18th ed.*] [*1952*] [*A publication*] (DLA)
Hayes Con Conv...   Hayes' Concise Conveyancer [*A publication*] (DLA)
Hayes Conv...   Hayes on Conveyancing [*A publication*] (DLA)
Hayes Cr & P...   Hayes on Crimes and Punishments [*A publication*] (DLA)
Hayes Exch...   Hayes' Irish Exchequer Reports [*1830-32*] [*A publication*] (DLA)
Hayes Exch (Ir)...   Hayes' Irish Exchequer Reports [*1830-32*] [*A publication*] (DLA)
Hayes Heirs...   Hayes' Dispositions to Heirs in Tail, Etc. [*A publication*] (DLA)
Hayes Intr....   Hayes' Introduction to Conveyancing [*A publication*] (DLA)
Hayes Lim ...   Hayes on Limitations as to Heirs of the Body, Etc. [*A publication*] (DLA)
Hayes R Est...   Hayes' Real Estate [*A publication*] (DLA)
Hayes UD & T...   Hayes' Law of Uses, Devises, and Trust [*A publication*] (DLA)
Hay Exch....   Hayes' Irish Exchequer Reports [*1830-32*] [*A publication*] (DLA)
Hay Exp ......   Hay on Expatriation [*A publication*] (DLA)
Hayford.......   Gold Coast Native Institutions [*A publication*] (DLA)
Hayn Ch Pr...   Haynes' Chancery Practice [*1879*] [*A publication*] (DLA)
Hayn Eq ......   Haynes' Outlines of Equity [*5th ed.*] [*1880*] [*A publication*] (DLA)
Haynes Eq ...   Haynes' Outlines of Equity [*5th ed.*] [*1880*] [*A publication*] (DLA)
Hayn Lead Cas...   Haynes' Students' Leading Cases [*A publication*] (DLA)
Hay PL.........   Hay's Poor Law Decisions [*1711-1859*] [*Scotland*] [*A publication*] (DLA)
HAYR..........   Hayridge [*England*]
HAYSTAQ.....   Have You Stored Answers to Questions [*Computer science*]
Hayw ....   Haywood's North Carolina Reports [*A publication*] (DLA)
Hayw ....   Haywood's Tennessee Reports [*A publication*] (DLA)
Hayw & H ....   Hayward and Hazelton's United States Circuit Court Reports [*District of Columbia*] [*A publication*] (DLA)
Hayw & HDC...   Hayward and Hazelton's United States Circuit Court Reports [*District of Columbia*] [*A publication*] (DLA)
HaywdB ......   Haywood Bancshares, Inc. [*Associated Press*] (SAG)
Hayw LR......   Hayward's Law Register [*Boston*] [*A publication*] (DLA)
Hayw Man ...   Haywood's Manual of the Statute Laws of North Carolina [*A publication*] (DLA)
Hayw NC......   Haywood's North Carolina Reports [*A publication*] (DLA)
Haywood Tenn Rep...   Haywood's Tennessee Reports [*A publication*] (DLA)
Hayw Tenn...   Haywood's Tennessee Reports [*A publication*] (DLA)
HAZ............   Hayes Lemmerz International [*NYSE symbol*] [*Formerly, Hayes Wheels International*] (SG)
HAZ............   Hazard [*or Hazardous*] (KSC)
HAZ............   Hazardous Cargo [*Environmental science*] (COE)
HAZ............   Heat-Affected Zone
HAZ............   Heat-Annealed Zone [*Metallurgy*]
HAZAL.........   Hahameinu Zikhronam Livrakha [*Our Sages of Blessed Memory*] [*Hebrew*]
HAZAN ....   Hazard Analysis
Haz & R M War...   Hazlitt and Roche on Maritime Warfare [*A publication*] (DLA)
HAZCHEM ....   Hazardous Chemical
HAZCOM......   Hazardous Communication Standards [*Occupational Safety and Health Administration*] (RDA)
HAZCON......   Hazardous Condition (NVT)
HAZEL........   Homogeneous Assembly Zero Energy Level [*AERE*]
HAZFILE......   Hazards File [*National Chemical Emergency Centre*] [*British*] (NITA)
HAZINF.......   Hazardous Chemicals Information and Disposal [*University of Alberta*] [*Canada Information service or system*] (CRD)
HAZMACON...   West Coast Hazardous Materials Management Conference (TSPED)
HAZMAT......   Hazardous Material
HazMat ....   Hazardous Material [*Environmental science*] (COE)
HAZMAT ......   Hazardous Material Response and Assessment Division [*Marine science*] (OSRA)
HAZMAT ......   Hazardous Materials Response and Assessment Division [*National Oceanic and Atmospheric Administration*] (USDC)
HAZMIN.......   Hazardous Waste Minimization
HAZOP........   Hazard and Operability [*Chemical engineering*]
Haz PA Reg...   Hazard's Pennsylvania Register [*A publication*] (DLA)
Haz PA Reg (PA)...   Hazard's Pennsylvania Register [*A publication*] (DLA)
Haz P Reg ...   Hazard's Pennsylvania Register [*A publication*] (ILCA)
HAZRAP.......   Hazardous Waste Remedial Actions Program [*Environmental science*] (COE)
Haz Reg.......   Hazard's Pennsylvania Register [*A publication*] (DLA)
Haz US Reg...   Hazard's United States Register [*A publication*] (DLA)
HAZWOPER...   Hazardous Waste Operations and Emergency Response Regulation
HAZWRAP....   Hazardous Waste Remedial Action Program [*Oak Ridge National Laboratory*]
HB..............   Air Melanesiae [*ICAO designator*] (AD)
HB..............   Bell Helicopter Co., Brantly Helicopter Corp., Brditschka [*Heinrich Brditschka Flugzeugbau*] [*ICAO aircraft manufacturer identifier*] (ICAO)
HB..............   Brinell Hardness Number [*Also, BH, BHN, BHNo*]
H$_B$..............   Deuterium [*Radioisotope of hydrogen*] (DAVI)
HB..............   Farbwerke Hoechst AG [*Germany*] [*Research code symbol*]

Hb	Habakkuk [Old Testament book]
Hb	Haemoglobin [Medicine] (WDAA)
HB	Halfback [Football]
HB	Half Bound [Bibliography]
HB	Half Bow [Music] (ROG)
HB	Half Breadth (AAG)
HB	Halk Bankasi [Peoples Bank of Turkey] [See also THB]
HB	Hallelujah Band
HB	Halogen Bulb
HB	Hampton & Branchville Railroad Co. [AAR code]
HB	Handbook (NASA)
HB	Handlebar (ROG)
HB	Hard Black [Pencil leads]
HB	Hardboard (ADA)
HB	Hard-Boiled [Egg]
HB	Hardy Biennial [Horticulture] (ROG)
HB	Hatchback [Automotive advertising]
HB	Head Backward (STED)
HB	Headband (IAA)
HB	Health Benefit
HB	Health Board [Ireland]
HB	Heart Block [Medicine]
HB	Heat to Boiling Point [Calorimetry]
HB	Heavy Barrel [Rifles]
HB	Heavy Bombardment [or Bomber]
Hb	Hebrew (BJA)
HB	Heel to Buttock (DMAA)
HB	Held Back (DMAA)
HB	Held Backward (STED)
HB	Hemoglobin [Medicine] (DMAA)
Hb	Hemoglobin [Biochemistry, medicine]
HB	Hemolysis Blocking [Medicine] (STED)
HB	Henricus Boich [Flourished, 1320-30] [Authority cited in pre-1607 legal work] (DSA)
HB	Hepatitis B [Medicine]
HB	Herba [Herb] [Pharmacology] (ROG)
HB	Herders Bibelkommentar [A publication] (BJA)
HB	Herri Batazuna [Union of the People] [Spain Political party] (PPE)
H-B	Hexadecimal-to-Binary [Computer science] (IEEE)
HB	High Band (AAG)
HB	High Bay (KSC)
HB	High Boilers
HB	Highways and Byways [A publication]
HB	Hill-Burton [Federal grant and loan program for construction and modernization of medical facilities]
HB	Hillenbrand Indus [NYSE symbol] (TTSB)
HB	Hillenbrand Industries, Inc. [NYSE symbol] (SPSG)
HB	Hinged Block [British military] (DMA)
HB	His Beatitude [or His Blessedness]
HB	His Bundle [Cardiology]
HB	Historical Branch [Army]
HB	Hit by Ball [or Hit Batsman] [Baseball]
HB	Hold Breakfast [Medicine]
HB	Holiness Band
HB	Hollowback (DAC)
HB	Homing Beacon [Aviation]
HB	Honey Bee
HB	Honeywell-Bull
HB	Horizontal Baffle (NRCH)
HB	Horizontal Bands [Navigation markers]
HB	Horizontal Bomber
HB	Horizontal-Branch [Astronomy]
HB	Horizontal Bridgman [Crystal growing technique]
HB	Hormone Binding [Endocrinology]
HB	Horn Book Magazine [A publication] (BRI)
HB	Hose Bib (AAG)
HB	Hospital Bed (DAVI)
HB	Hot Boning [Meat processing]
HB	House Bill [In state legislatures]
HB	Housebound (MAE)
HB	Housebreaking
HB	Household Battalion [British military] (DMA)
HB	Household Goods/Baggage
HB	Housing Benefit [British]
HB	Human Behavior [National Science Foundation project]
HB	Human Being [Slang]
HB	Huntington Beach [California]
HB	Hutchinson-Boeck [Disease] [Medicine] (DB)
HB	Hybridoma [Cytology]
HB	Hybridoma Bank (DMAA)
HB	Hyoid Body (DMAA)
HB-8	Hexagonal Bipyramidal (DB)
HB-9	Heptagonal Bipyramidal (DB)
HBA	Bible Atlas [Hurlbut] [A publication] (BJA)
HBA	General Hotel, Boarding House, and Apartments [British]
HBA	Halley Bay [Antarctica] [Seismograph station code, US Geological Survey Closed] (SEIS)
HBA	Handbook Art
HBA	Handicapped Boaters Association [Defunct] (EA)
HBA	Harrison Bay, AK [Location identifier FAA] (FAAL)
HBA	Health and Beauty Aid [Retailing]
HBA	Health Benefit Advisor [CHAMPUS]
HbA	Hemoglobin, Adult [Medicine]
HBA	Herring Buyers Association [British] (DBA)
HBA	Hispanic Bar Association (EA)
HBA	Hobart [Tasmania] [Airport symbol] (OAG)
HBA	Home Baking Association (EA)
HBA	Home Base [Military] (NVT)
HBA	Honest Ballot Association (EA)
HBA	Honours Bachelor of Arts in Business Administration (DD)
HBA	Horizontal Baffle Assembly [Nuclear energy] (NRCH)
HBA	Host Bus Adapter [Computer science]
HBA	Human Biology Association (NTPA)
HBA	Hydraulic and Boatyard Association [A union] [British]
HBA	Hydrazinobenzoic Acid [Organic chemistry]
HBA	Hydrobenzoate [Organic chemistry]
HBA	Hydrogen-Bond Acceptor [Chemistry]
HBA	Trail Lake Flying Service, Inc. [ICAO designator] (FAAC)
HBAb	Hepatitis B Antibody [Immunology]
HBABA	(Hydroxybenzeneazo)benzoic Acid [Also, HABA] [Organic chemistry]
HBAG	Handbag
HBAg	Hepatitis B Antigen [Immunology]
HBAH	Hydroxybenzoic Acid Hydrazide [Reagent]
HBAM	Historic Buildings and Ancient Monuments Act [Town planning] [British]
HBAM	Home Builders Association of Maryland (SRA)
HBAM	Home Builders Association of Massachusetts (SRA)
HBAN	Huntington Bancshares [NASDAQ symbol] (TTSB)
HBAN	Huntington Bancshares, Inc. [NASDAQ symbol] (NQ)
HB & T	Houston Belt & Terminal Railway Co.
HBAR	Head Bar Address Register [Computer science] (MHDB)
H-BAR	Heavy Barrel [Rifles]
HBARO	Barometric Altitude (GAVI)
HbAS	Hemoglobin A and Hemoglobin S [Medicine] (MEDA)
HBAT	Having Been Assigned to This Organization [or Headquarters]
HBAVS	Human Betterment Association for Voluntary Sterilization [Later, AVS] (EA)
HbB	Hemoglobin in the Blood [Medicine] (DB)
HBB	Historic Buildings Bureau [British]
HBB	Hobbs, NM [Location identifier FAA] (FAAL)
HBB	Hook-Basal Body [Genetics]
HBB	Hospital Blood Bank
HBB	Human Beta-Globin [Genetics]
HBB	Hydroxybenzyl Benzimidazole [Clinical chemistry] (MAE)
HBBA	Bujumbura [Burundi] [ICAO location identifier] (ICLI)
HbBC	Hemoglobin-Binding Capacity [Medicine] (DB)
HBBD	Hydroxybenzylbutanediol [Clinical chemistry]
HBBE	Gitega [Burundi] [ICAO location identifier] (ICLI)
HBBI	Home Building Bancorp [NASDAQ symbol] (SAG)
HBBK	Kiofi-Mosso [Burundi] [ICAO location identifier] (ICLI)
HBBL	Hydroxybenzylbutyrolactone [Clinical chemistry]
HBBL	Nyanza-Lac [Burundi] [ICAO location identifier] (ICLI)
HBBM	Mugera [Burundi] [ICAO location identifier] (ICLI)
HBBN	Nyakagunda [Burundi] [ICAO location identifier] (ICLI)
HBBW	Hold Breakfast for Blood Work [Medicine]
HBC	Haitian Aviation Line SA [ICAO designator] (FAAC)
HBC	Hajji Baba Club (EA)
HBC	Handbooks for Bible Classes [A publication]
HBC	Handlebar Control [Early automobiles] (ROG)
HBC	Health Benefit Card (ADA)
Hb C	Hemoglobin C [An abnormal hemoglobin] [Hematology] (DAVI)
HBc	Hepatitis B Core [Immunology] (MAE)
HBC	Highamerica Balloon Club (EA)
HBC	High Blood Cholesterol
HBC	High Breaking Capacity (IAA)
HBC	Historic Buildings Council [British]
HBC	[The] History Book Club
HBC	Hobart Brothers Co. (EFIS)
HBC	Homogeneous Boundary Condition
HBC	Honeywell Business Computer [or Compiler]
HBC	Hong Kong Bank of Canada (ECON)
HBC	Horseshoe Bay [British Columbia] [Seismograph station code, US Geological Survey Closed] (SEIS)
HBC	Hostage Bracelet Committee (EA)
HBC	House Budget Committee
HBC	Hudson's Bay Co. [TS, exchange symbol] (TTSB)
HBC	Hudson's Bay Company [Facetious translations include "Here before Christ," "Here before Columbus," and "Hungry Belly Co.."]
HBC	Human Biology Council (EA)
HBC	Human Body Counter (IAA)
HBC	Hydrogen Bubble Chamber
HBC	Hyperbaric Chamber (SSD)
HBcAb	Hepatitis B Core Antibody [Immunology] (MAE)
HBCAg	Hepatitis B Core Antigen [Immunology]
HBCAG	Hepatitis B Core Antigen [Medicine] (DB)
HBCC	Hosted Bus Controller Chip [Electronics]
HBCC	Hosted Bus Controller Circuit [Electronics]
HBCCA	Heftel Broadcasting'A' [NASDAQ symbol] (TTSB)
HBCCA	Heftel Broadcasting Corp. [NASDAQ symbol] (SAG)
HBCD	Hexabromocyclododecane [Flame retardant] [Organic chemistry]
HBCF	Hydrobromofluorocarbons [Organic chemistry]
HBCI	Heritage Bancorp [NASDAQ symbol] (TTSB)
HBCI	Heritage Bancorp, Inc. [NASDAQ symbol] (SAG)
HBCN	Hazard Beacon (MSA)
HbCO	Hemoglobin, Carboxy [Biochemistry, medicine]
HBCO	Hungarian Broadcasting [NASDAQ symbol] (TTSB)
HBCO	Hungarian Broadcasting Corp. [NASDAQ symbol] (SAG)
HBCOW	Hungarian Broadcasting Wrrt [NASDAQ symbol] (TTSB)
Hb CS	Hemoglobin Constant Spring [An abnormal hemoglobin] [Hematology] (DAVI)

HBCU	Historically Black Colleges and Universities
HBCU/MI	Historically Black Colleges, Universities, and Minority Institutions (RDA)
HBD	Hardboard [*Technical drawings*]
HBD	Has Been Drinking [*Medical notation*]
Hb D	Hemoglobin D [*An abnormal hemoglobin*] [*Hematology*] (DAVI)
HbD	Hemoglobin D [*Medicine*] (STED)
HBD	Hepatobiliary Dysfunction [*Medicine*]
HBD	Hormone Binding Domain [*Endocrinology*]
HBD	Hubbard, OH [*Location identifier FAA*] (FAAL)
HBD	Hydrogen Bond Donor [*Solvent*]
HBD	Hydroxybutyrate Dehydrogenase [*Also, HBDH*] [*An enzyme*]
HBDC	Home Base Development Committee [*Navy*]
HBDE	Huntington Beach Development Engineering [*McDonnell Douglas Aircraft Corp.*]
HBDH	Hydroxybutyrate Dehydrogenase [*Also, HBD*] [*An enzyme*]
HBDIX	SMBS Investment Grade Bond Cl.B [*Mutual fund ticker symbol*] (SG)
HBDMA	Hat Block and Die Makers Association (EA)
HBDMI	Historical Biographical Dictionaries Master Index [*A publication*]
HBDR	Helicopter Battle Damage Repair (RDA)
HBDS	Hypergraph-Based Data Structures
HBDT	High BIT [*Binary Digit*] Density Tape [*Skylab*] [*NASA*]
HBDT	Human Basophil Degranulation Test [*Medicine*] (DMAA)
HBE	Hamilton Board of Education Schools [*UTLAS symbol*]
HbE	Hemoglobin E [*Medicine*] (STED)
HBe	Hepatitis B Early [*Antibody or antigen*] [*Immunology*] (DAVI)
HBE	His Bundle Electrogram [*Cardiology*]
HBEA	Hawaii Business Education Association (EDAC)
HBₑAb	Hepatitis B Early Anitibody [*Immunology*] (DAVI)
HBeAb	Hepatitis B Early Antibody [*Medicine*] (STED)
HBEAG	Hepatitis B Early Antigen [*Medicine*] (STED)
HBeAg	Hepatitis B, Early Antigen [*or Antibody*] [*Immunology*]
HBED	Bis(hydroxybenzyl)ethylenediaminediacetic Acid [*Organic chemistry*]
HBEF	Health and Beauty Employers Federation [*British*] (DBA)
HBEF	Hubbard Brook Experimental Forest
HBEI	Home Bancorp of Elgin, Inc. [*NASDAQ symbol*] (SAG)
HBEN	High Byte Enable
HBEN	Home Beneficial Corp. [*NASDAQ symbol*] (NQ)
HBENB	Home BeneficialCl'B' [*NASDAQ symbol*] (TTSB)
HBEP	Hispanic and Black Employment Programs (COE)
HBES	Human Behavior and Evolution Society [*An association*]
HBF	Fetal Hemoglobin [*Medicine*] (STED)
HBF	Hamilton Board of Education [*UTLAS symbol*]
HBF	Hand Blood Flow [*Cardiology*] (DAVI)
HBF	Harts Bluff [*South Carolina*] [*Seismograph station code, US Geological Survey*] (SEIS)
HBF	Hauptbahnhof [*Main Railroad Station*] [*German*]
HBF	Hemispheric Blood Flow [*Medicine*] (DMAA)
HbF	Hemoglobin F [*Medicine*] (STED)
HbF	Hemoglobin, Fetal [*Also, HgF*] [*Medicine*]
HBF	Hemoglobinuric Bilious Fever [*Medicine*] (DB)
HBF	Hepatic Blood Flow
HBF	High Bleeding Frequency [*Medicine*]
HBF	House-Builders Federation [*British*] (DBA)
HBF	Hypothalamic Blood FLow [*Medicine*] (DMAA)
HBFW	Home Bancorp [*NASDAQ symbol*] (SAG)
HBG	Harrisburg [*Diocesan abbreviation*] [*Pennsylvania*] (TOCD)
HBG	Hattiesburg [*Mississippi*] [*Airport symbol*] (AD)
HBG	Hattiesburg, MS [*Location identifier FAA*] (FAAL)
HBG	Hope Brook Gold, Inc. [*Toronto Stock Exchange symbol*]
HBG	Hydroxybenzoylglycine [*Biochemistry*]
HBG	(Hydroxybutyl)guanine [*Biochemistry*]
HBGF	Heparin-Binding Growth Factor [*Biochemistry*]
HBGI	Holson Burnes Group, Inc. [*NASDAQ symbol*] (SAG)
HBGM	Home Blood Glucose Monitoring [*Medicine*]
HBGM	Hypersonic Boost-Glide Missile
HBGMA	Hughes Basic Gross Motor Assessment [*Jeanne E. Hughes*] (TES)
HBGS	Human Blood Group Substance [*Medicine*] (DB)
HB Guide	Horn Book Guide [*A publication*] (BRI)
Hb H	Hemoglobin H [*An abnormal hemoglobin*] [*Hematology*] (DAVI)
HBH	History Behind the Headlines [*A publication*]
HBH	Hobart Bay [*Alaska*] [*Airport symbol*] (OAG)
HBH	Hydraulic Brake Hose [*Automotive engineering*]
HBHC	Hancock Holding [*NASDAQ symbol*] (TTSB)
HBHC	Hancock Holding Co. [*NASDAQ symbol*] (SAG)
HBHC	Hospital-Based Home Care
HBI	Hemibody Irradiation [*Oncology*]
HbI	Hemoglobin I [*Biochemistry, medicine*]
HBI	High Serum-Bound Iron [*Biochemistry*] (MAE)
HBI	Hindustan Bible Institute (EA)
HBI	Horizontal Blanking Interval (DOM)
HBI	Hospital Bureau, Inc. [*Formerly, HBSS*] (EA)
HBI	Hot Biquetted Iron
HBI	House-Breaking Implements [*British police term*]
HBI	Houston Biotechnology [*AMEX symbol*] (TTSB)
HBI	Houston Biotechnology, Inc. [*AMEX symbol*] (SPSG)
HBIA	Hairdressing and Beauty Industry Association [*Australia*]
HBIG	Hepatitis B Immune Globulin [*Immunology*]
HBJ	Harcourt Brace & Jovanovich (EFIS)
HBJ	Harcourt Brace Jovanovich, Inc. (EFIS)
HBJ	High-Band Jammer (MCD)
HBK	Habekacin [*Antibacterial*]
HBK	Handbook
HBK	Hardback [*Book cover*] (NTCM)
HBK	Hardwood Bleached Kraft [*Pulp and paper technology*]

HBK	Hartebeesthoek [*South Africa*] [*Geomagnetic observatory code*]
HBk	Herders Bibelkommentar [*A publication*] (BJA)
HBK	Hinchinbrook, AK [*Location identifier FAA*] (FAAL)
HBK	Hollow Back [*Of lumber*] (BARN)
HBL	Harbor Belt Line Railroad
HBL	Heeresbetriebsstofflager [*Army Gasoline-Supply Depot*] [*German military - World War II*]
HBL	Hepatoblastoma (DB)
HBL	Huntington Beach Public Library, Huntington Beach, CA [*OCLC symbol*] (OCLC)
HBLA	Human B-Lymphocyte Antigen (DB)
HBLB	Horserace Betting Levy Board [*British*]
HBLC	Host Based Library Catalogue [*Computer science*]
HBLLSB	Heard Best at Left Lower Sternal Border [*Cardiology*] (DAVI)
HBLO	Home Base, Ledger Office [*British military*] (DMA)
HBLR	Hidden Broad-Line Region [*Spectra*]
HBLRR	Harbor Belt Line Railroad (MHDB)
HBLUSB	Heard Best at Left Upper Sternal Border [*Cardiology*] (DAVI)
HBLV	Human B-Lymphotropic Virus
HBM	Half Bridge Monorail [*Mobot Corp.*] [*Gantry robot*] (NITA)
HBM	Health Belief Model (DMAA)
HBM	Heavy Ballistic Missile
HBM	Held by Manufacturer
HbM	Hemoglobin M [*Biochemistry*] (MAH)
HBM	High-Beta Model (MCD)
HBM	His [*or Her*] Britannic Majesty
HBM	Hobart Mills [*California*] [*Seismograph station code, US Geological Survey*] (SEIS)
HBM	Horizontal Boring Mill
HBM	Hudson Bay Mining & Smelting Co. Ltd. [*Toronto Stock Exchange symbol*]
HBM	Hydraulic Bore-Hole Mining [*Coal*]
HBM	Hypertonic Buffered Medium (DMAA)
HBM	Mali-Tinbouctou Air Service [*ICAO designator*] (FAAC)
HBMA	Home-Based Maintenance Allowance
HBMC	Homebush Bay Ministerial Council [*New South Wales, Australia*]
HBMS	His [*or Her*] Britannic Majesty's Service
HBMS	His [*or Her*] Britannic Majesty's Ship (ROG)
HBN	Hazard Beacon
HBN	Health-Based Number [*Environmental science*]
HB(N)	Heavy Bomber (Night) [*British military*] (DMA)
HBNK	Highland Federal Bank [*NASDAQ symbol*] (SAG)
HBNR	Hydrogen-Bond Network Rearrangement [*Physical chemistry*]
HBO	HBO & Co. [*Associated Press*] (SAG)
HBO	Health Benefits Organization [*Insurance*]
H Bo	Henricus Boich [*Flourished, 1320-30*] [*Authority cited in pre-1607 legal work*] (DSA)
HBO	Home Box Office [*Cable-television system*]
HBO	Horizontal-Branch Oscillation [*Astronomy*]
HBO	Humboldt, NE [*Location identifier FAA*] (FAAL)
HBO	Hyperbaric Oxygen [*Also, HPO, OHP*] [*Medicine*]
HBO₂	Hyperbaric Oxygenation (DMAA)
HbO₂	Hemoglobin, Oxy [*Biochemistry, medicine*]
HBOC	HBO & Co. [*NASDAQ symbol*] (NQ)
HBOI	Harbor Branch Oceanographic Institution [*Fort Pierce, FL*]
H-bomb	Hydrogen Bomb (WDAA)
HbOr	Handbuch der Orientalistik [*Leiden*] [*A publication*] (BJA)
HBOT	Hyperbaric Oxygen Therapy [*Medicine*] (DAVI)
HBP	Dauphin County Library System, Harrisburg, PA [*OCLC symbol*] (OCLC)
HBP	Hamilton Board of Education, Education Centre Library [*UTLAS symbol*]
HBP	Handbook Production
HBP	Heartbeat Period [*Medicine*] (DMAA)
HBP	Held for Blueprint (MCD)
HBP	Hepatic Binding Protein [*Biochemistry*]
HBP	High Blood Pressure [*Medicine*]
HBP	Highway Bridge Parapet (PDAA)
HbP	Hilfsbuch des Pehlevi [*A publication*] (BJA)
HBP	Hit by Pitcher [*Baseball*]
HBP	Hospital-Based Practice (DMAA)
HBP	Hospital Benefits Payment
HBP	Hydraulic Bench Press
HBP	Hydrocortisone(butyrate)propionate [*Endocrinology*]
HbP	Primitive [*Fetal*] Hemoglobin
HBPA	Horsemen's Benevolent and Protective Association (EA)
HBPA	Hydrogenated Bisphenol A [*Organic chemistry*]
HBPE	Health Based Physical Education
H-BPH	Hawaii Regional Library for the Blind and Physically Handicapped, Honolulu, HI [*Library symbol Library of Congress*] (LCLS)
HBPIC	High Blood Pressure Information Center [*Public Health Service*] (IID)
HBPM	Home Blood Pressure Monitoring [*Medicine*]
HBPP	Humboldt Bay Power Plant (NRCH)
HBPSA	Hydroxybutylidene-p-aminobenzenesulfonic [*Organic chemistry*]
HBR	Haibara [*Japan*] [*Seismograph station code, US Geological Survey*] (SEIS)
HBR	Ham Band Receiver (IAA)
HBR	Hansell's Bankruptcy Reports [*1915-17*] [*A publication*] (DLA)
HBR	Harbor [*Maps and charts*]
HBR	Harborside Healthcare Corp. [*NYSE symbol*] (SAG)
HBR	Has Been Reviewed (AAG)
HBR	High BIT [*Binary Digit*] Rate (KSC)
HBR	High Burst Rate (PDAA)
HBR	Hobart, OK [*Location identifier FAA*] (FAAL)
HBr	Hydrobromic Acid (MAE)

HBr	Hydrogen Bromide (LDT)
HbR	Methemoglobin Reductase (STED)
HBRACW	Has Been Reviewed and Concurred With (AAG)
HBRDC	Honey Bee Research and Development Council [*Australia*]
HBRF	Hercules-Baachus Resin Formulation
HBRI	Hospital Bureau Research Institute [*Defunct*] (EA)
H/BRK	Hand Brake [*Automotive engineering*]
HBRK	Harmony Brook [*NASDAQ symbol*] (TTSB)
HBRK	Harmony Brook, Inc. [*NASDAQ symbol*] (SAG)
Hbr Mr	Harbor Master
HBR-online	Harvard Business Review-Online [*John Wiley & Son*] (NITA)
HBRRP	Highway Bridge Replacement and Rehabilitation Program [*Department of Transportation*]
HBRS	Harbors [*Postal Service standard*] (OPSA)
HBS	Half Bar Symbology
HBS	Hanks Balanced Salt [*Solution*] [*Cell incubation medium*]
HBS	Harbor Boat Service [*Military*]
HBS	Harvard Business School
HBS	Harvard Business School, Boston, MA [*OCLC symbol*] (OCLC)
HBS	Havergal Brian Society (EAIO)
HBS	Haywood Bancshares, Inc. [*AMEX symbol*] (SAG)
HBS	Health Behavior Scale [*Psychiatry*] (DAVI)
HBS	Heavy Bomber Support
HBS	Helicopter Blade Slap
HbS	Hemoglobin, Sickle [*Medicine*]
HBS	Henry Bradshaw Society [*British*]
HB$_s$	Hepatitis B Surface [*Antibody or antigen*] [*Immunology*] (DAVI)
HBS	Hepatitis B Surface [*Medicine*] (STED)
HBS	Hermanas Contemplativas del Buen Pastor (TOCD)
HBS	Herringbone Strutting [*Construction*]
HBS	High-Beta Stellarator (PDAA)
HBS	High Byte Strobe [*Computer science*] (MHDI)
HBS	Hoboken Shore Railroad [*AAR code*]
HBS	Hole-Burning Spectroscopy
HBS	Honey Bee Spiroplasma [*Bacteriology*]
HBS	Horizontal Bracing Systems [*Environmental science*] (COE)
HBS	Hot Blade Stripper
HBS	Hyperkinetic Behavior Syndrome [*Medicine*]
HbS	Sickle-Cell Hemoglobin [*Medicine*] (STED)
HbS	Sulfhemoglobin [*Medicine*] (STED)
HBSA	Historical Breechloading Smallarms Association [*British*] (DBA)
HBSA	Hungarian Boy Scout Association (EA)
HBSAB	Hepatitis B Surface Antibody [*Immunology*] (PDAA)
HBsAB	Hepatitis B Surface Antibody [*Medicine*] (STED)
HBSAG	Hepatitis B Surface Antigen [*Medicine*] (DB)
HB$_s$Ag	Hepatitis B Surface Antigen [*Immunology*] (DAVI)
HBsAg/adr	Hepatitis B Surface Antigen Manifesting Group-Specific Determinant A and Subtype-Specific Determinants D and R [*Medicine*] (STED)
HBSANSW	Health and Building Surveyors' Association of New South Wales [*Australia*]
HBSC	Hematopoietic Blood Stem Cell [*Medicine*] (DMAA)
HbSC	Hemoglobin C Sickle Cell Disease [*Medicine*]
HBSG	Home Birth Support Group [*Australia*]
HBSMA	Hack and Band Saw Manufacturers Association of America
HBSMAA	Hack and Band Saw Manufacturers Association of America (EA)
HBSS	Hanks Balanced Salt Solution [*Cell incubation medium*]
HBSS	Hospital Bureau of Standards and Supplies [*Later, HBI*]
HBT	Habeat [*Let Him Have*] [*Pharmacy*] (ROG)
HBT	Harbor Bay Telecommunications [*Alameda, CA*] (TSSD)
HBT	Harbourton Financial Services LP [*NYSE symbol*] (SAG)
HBT	Harbourton Finl Svcs L.P. [*NYSE symbol*] (TTSB)
HBT	Heflex Bioengineering Test [*NASA*]
HBT	Herringbone Twill
HBT	Heterojunction Bipolar Transistor [*Electronics*]
HBT	Heterostructure Bipolar Transistor (MED)
HBT	Hetrojunction Bipolar Mobility Transistor (NITA)
HBT	Hobart Mills [*California*] [*Seismograph station code, US Geological Survey*] (SEIS)
HBT	Houston Belt & Terminal Railway Co. [*AAR code*]
HBT	Human Brain Thromboplastin [*Clinical chemistry*]
HBT	Human Breast Tumor [*Type of cell line*]
HBT	Hydroxybenzotriazole [*Organic chemistry*]
HBT	Sand Point, AK [*Location identifier FAA*] (FAAL)
HBTA	HB [*Homeward Bound Ministries*] Tract Association (EA)
HBTA	Hutchinson Board of Trade Association (EA)
HBTX	High Beta Toroidal Experiment (PDAA)
HBU	Aurora, OR [*Location identifier FAA*] (FAAL)
HBU	Hollandsche Bank-Unie [*Netherlands*]
HBU	Houston Baptist University [*Texas*]
HBUA	Hungarian Baptist Union of America (EA)
HBV	Harrisonburg [*Virginia*] [*Seismograph station code, US Geological Survey*] (SEIS)
HBV	Hebbronville, TX [*Location identifier FAA*] (FAAL)
HBV	Hepatitis B Vaccine
HBV	Hepatitis B Virus
HBV	Honey Bee Venom [*Immunology*]
HBVP	Hepatitis B Virus Polymerase [*An enzyme*]
HBVS	Hepatitis B Virus Integration Site [*Medicine*] (DMAA)
HBW	Half Bandwidth [*Electronics*]
HBW	High Birth Weight [*Medicine*] (MAE)
HBW	High-Speed Black and White [*Photography*]
HBW	Hillsboro, WI [*Location identifier FAA*] (FAAL)
HBw	Historische Burowelt [*A publication*]
HBW	Hot Bridgewire (KSC)
HBW	Wolf [*Howard B.*], Inc. [*AMEX symbol*] (SPSG)
HBWA	High-Band Warning Antenna (MCD)
HBWMA	Home Brewing and Winemaking Manufacturers Association [*British*] (DBA)
HBWR	Halden Boiling Water Reactor [*Norway Nuclear energy*]
HBWR	High-Band Warning Receiver (MCD)
HBWTA	Home Brewing and Winemaking Trade Association [*British*] (DBA)
HBY	Hereby (ROG)
HBZ	Heber Springs, AR [*Location identifier FAA*] (FAAL)
HbZ	Hemoglobin Zuerich (DB)
HC	Command Chaplain [*AFSC*]
HC	Critical Height [*Aviation*] (DA)
HC	Cross of Honour [*British military*] (DMA)
HC	Crystal Holder [*JETDS nomenclature*] [*Military*] (CET)
HC	Ecuador [*International civil aircraft marking*] (ODBW)
HC	Habeas Corpus [*You Have the Body*] [*Legal term Latin*] (DLA)
HC	Habitual Criminal
HC	Hague Convention
HC	Hair Cell [*Otology*]
HC	Hairdressing Council (BUAC)
HC	Haiti Air International [*ICAO designator*] (AD)
HC	Half Calf
HC	Half-Caste (ADA)
HC	Half-Changes [*Statistics*]
HC	Half Chest
HC	Half Covered [*Marine insurance*] (ROG)
HC	Handbooks for the Clergy [*A publication*]
HC	Hand Carry
HC	Hand-Colored [*Photography*]
HC	Hand Control [*Technical drawings*]
HC	Hand Controller [*Aerospace*] (NAKS)
HC	Hand Crank
HC	Hand Cut [*Envelopes*]
HC	Hand-Held Unit Chromatography
HC	Handicapped [*Medicine*]
HC	Handling Capacity (DEN)
HC	Hanging Ceiling (OA)
HC	Hannibal Connecting R. R. [*AAR code*]
HC	Hard Copy [*Computer science*]
HC	Hardcore
HC	Hardware Capability (NITA)
HC	Hastings Center (EA)
HC	Hatz Club (EA)
HC	Hauling Class
HC	Hauling Code
HC	Haute-Contre [*Alto*] [*Music*]
HC	Hazardous Constitutients (GNE)
HC	Head Circumference [*Medicine*]
HC	Head Compression (AAMN)
HC	Headcount
HC	Headmaster Commander [*Navy British*]
HC	Headmasters Conference (BUAC)
HC	Headquarters City [*Dialog*] [*Searchable field*] [*Information service or system*] (NITA)
HC	Headquarters Command [*Military*]
HC	Health Certificate [*British*] (ADA)
HC	Heal the Children (EA)
HC	Healthy Control [*Medicine*] (DMAA)
HC	Heart Cycle [*Cardiology*] (MAE)
HC	Heat Capacity [*Electronics*] (EECA)
HC	Heat Control (IAA)
HC	Heated Coil (NITA)
HC	Heater Cord
HC	Heating Cabinet (AAG)
HC	Heating Coil (AAG)
HC	Heat of Combustion (ROG)
HC	Heavy Chain [*Immunoglobulin*]
HC	Heavy Current [*Electronics*] (IAA)
HC	Held Covered [*Insurance*]
HC	Helene Curtis Industries, Inc. [*NYSE symbol*] (SPSG)
H/C	Helicopter (NATG)
HC	Helicopter Combat (NVT)
HC	Helicopter Combat Support Squadron [*Navy*] (DNAB)
HC	Helicopter Command (NVT)
HC	Helicopter Coordinator [*Military*] (CAAL)
HC	Helicopter Council
HC	Helium Circulation [*System*]
HC	Helminthosporium carbonum [*A toxin-producing fungus*]
HC	Helper Component [*Biology*]
HC	Hematopoietic Cell [*Hematology*]
HC	Hemoglobin Concentration [*Medicine*] (HGAA)
HC	Hepatic Catalase [*An enzyme*] (MAE)
HC	Hepatic Coma [*Medicine*]
HC	Heralds' College [*British*]
HC	Herding Certified [*Purebred canine award*]
HC	Hereditary Coproporphyria (DB)
HC	Heritage Committee [*Australian Capital Territory*]
HC	Herzberg Continuum [*Spectral region*]
HC	Heuristic Concepts (IEEE)
HC	Hexachloroethane [*Organic chemistry*]
HC	Hickman Catheter [*Medicine*] (DAVI)
HC	High Calorie (AAMN)
HC	High-Capacity
HC	High Carbon [*Steel*]
HC	High Church
HC	High Churchman [*British*] (ROG)

HC	High Color (CDE)
HC	High Commissioner
HC	High Compression
HC	High Conditioners [Psychology]
HC	High Conductivity [Copper]
HC	High Cost of Living
HC	High Court
HC	High Current
HC	Higher Certificate [Academic degree] (AIE)
HC	Highland Cyclists [British military] (DMA)
HC	Highway Code [A publication] (DLA)
HC	Highway Contract (TBD)
HC	Hippocampal
HC	Hire Car (ADA)
HC	Histamine Club [Later, HRSNA] (EA)
HC	Historical Commission
HC	Historical Cost (ADA)
HC	Hockey Club
HC	Holding Coil (MSA)
HC	Holding Company [Business term]
HC	Holiday Camps [Public-performance tariff class] [British]
HC	Hollow Core [Technical drawings]
HC	Holy Communion
HC	Holy Cross
HC	Home Care
HC	Home Computer (IAA)
HC	Honor Contracts [Insurance]
HC	Honoris Causa [For the Sake of Honor, Honorary] [Latin]
HC	Horizontal Cell [Eye anatomy]
HC	Horizontal Check (IAA)
Hc	Hornyhead Chub [Ichthyology]
HC	Hors Concours [Not Competing] [French]
HC	Hose Cabinet [or Connection] [NFPA pre-fire planning symbol] (NFPA)
HC	Hose Cart [Early fire engines] (ROG)
HC	Hose Clamp (MSA)
HC	Hospital Corps [or Corpsman] [Navy]
HC	Hospital Course (DAVI)
HC	Host Cell [Parasitology]
HC	Host Computer
HC	Host Country (NATG)
HC	Hostel Care
HC	Hot and Cold
HC	Hour Circle
HC	House Cable [Telecommunications] (TEL)
HC	House Call [Medicine]
HCS	Household Cavalry [British]
HC	House of Commons [British]
HC	House of Correction
HC	Housing Census
HC	Housing Commission [Australia]
HC	Housing Corp. [British] (BI)
HC	Hroswitha Club (EA)
HC	Hug Club (EA)
HC	Humid Crepidations [Medicine] (ROG)
HC	Humidity Control
HC	Hungarian Congress (EA)
HC	Huntington's Chorea [Medicine]
HC	Hupmobile Club (EA)
HC	Hyaline Casts [Clinical chemistry]
HC	Hybrid Circuit [Electronics] (IAA)
HC	Hybrid Computer [for processing both analog and digital data] (NASA)
HC	Hyderabad Contingent [British military] (DMA)
HC	Hydranencephaly [Medicine] (AAMN)
HC	Hydraulic Clean (MSA)
HC	Hydraulic Concussion (DB)
HC	Hydraulic Coupling (DCTA)
HC	Hydraulic Cylinder
HC	Hydrocarbon [Organic chemistry]
HC	Hydrocarbons [Chemical] (EERA)
HC	Hydrocodone [Medicine] (MEDA)
Hc	Hydrocolloid (DMAA)
HC	Hydrocortisone [Endocrinology]
HC	Hydrocracking
HC	Hydrogen Chloride (AABC)
H/C	Hydrogen to Carbon Atomic Ratio (EG)
HC	Hydrographic Center [Defense Mapping Agency]
HC	Hydrophobic Cellulose (DB)
HC	Hypatia Cluster [Defunct] (EA)
HC	Hysteresis Comparator
HC	Pechiney-Progil [France] [Research code symbol]
HC	Reports of the High Court of Griqualand West [South Africa] [A publication] (DLA)
HC	Screening Smoke [Mixture]
HC-3	Hemicholinium-3 (LDT)
HC4	Helicopterborne Command and Control Communications Central
HCA	Absent by Reason of Being Held by Civil Authorities [Military]
HCA	Big Spring [Texas] [Airport symbol] (AD)
HCA	Habitat Conservation Area
HCA	Haitian Coalition on AIDS (EA)
HCA	Harness and Cable Assembly
HCA	Hazardous Communications Act (COE)
HCA	Head of Contracting Activity [Military] (AABC)
HCA	Head of Contracting Agency (DOMA)
HCA	Headquarters Commitment Authorization [Military] (DNAB)
HCA	Health Care Administration
HCA	Health Care Aide (DAVI)
HCA	Health Care Assistant (MEDA)
HCA	Heart Cell Aggregate [Cytology]
HCA	Heisey Collectors of America (EA)
HCA	Held by Civil Authorities
HCA	Helicopter Club of America (EA)
HC(A)	Helicopter Coordinator (Airborne) (NVT)
HCA	Hepatocellular Adenoma [Medicine]
HCA	Heterocyclic Antidepressant [Psychopharmaceutical]
HCA	Hexachloroacetone [Organic chemistry]
HCA	High Courts of Admiralty [British]
HCA	Hispanic Computing Association (EA)
HCA	Historic Cost Accounts [London Stock Exchange]
HCA	Hobby Clubs of America (EA)
HCA	Hobie Class Association (EA)
HCA	Hollow Cylinder Apparatus [Nuclear energy] (NUCP)
HCA	Holy Childhood Association (EA)
HCA	Home Care Aide [Medicine] (DMAA)
HCA	Homocysteate [Biochemistry]
HCA	Horizon Crossing Ascending
HCA	Hospital Caterers Association [British]
HCA	Hospital Corp. of America (EFIS)
HCA	Hot Cranking Amperes [Battery] [Automotive engineering]
HCA	Human Component Analysis
HCA	Humanitarian and Civic Assistance (DOMA)
HCA	Humanitarian Civic Action
HCA	Hunter Club of America (EA)
HCA	Hunting-Clan Air Transport Ltd.
HCA	Hyderabad Contingent Artillery [British military] (DMA)
HCA	Hydrocortisone Acetate [Pharmacology]
HCA	Hypertrophic Cardiomyopathy Association (BUAC)
HCA	Lake Havasu Air Service [ICAO designator] (FAAC)
HCAA	Hebrew Christian Alliance of America [Later, MJAA]
HCAAO	Hawaii Council of Associations of Apartment Owners (SRA)
HCAC	Hazardous Chemicals Advisory Committee [New South Wales, Australia]
HCAM	Health Care Association of Michigan (SRA)
HC & C	Harvard Capital & Consulting [An investment fund] [Czechoslovakia] (ECON)
HCAP	Handicapped
H-CAP	Hexamethylmelamine, Cyclophosphamide, Adriamycin, Platinol [Cisplatin] [Antineoplastic drug regimen]
HCAR	Higher Committee for Agrarian Reform [Egypt] (BUAC)
HCAR	Historic Commands of the American Revolution (EA)
HCAS	Highway Cost Allocation Study [Also, FHCAS]
HCAV	Hunt Clubs Association of Victoria [Australia]
HCAV	Hyperactive Children's Association of Victoria [Australia]
HCAW	Home Care Association of Washington (SRA)
HCB	Hard Convex Body [Equation of state]
HCB	Hard-Covered Book (WDAA)
HCB	Heaviside-Campbell Bridge [Electronics]
HCB	Hemisphere Cylinder Body
HCB	Hexachlorobenzene [Organic chemistry]
HCB	High Capability Buoy [Marine science] (MSC)
HCB	High-Capacity Bomb
HCB	Highland Cyclist Battalion [British military] (DMA)
HCB	Hollow Concrete Block
HCB	Hoopes Conductivity Bridge [Electronics]
HCB	House of Commons Bill [British]
HCB	Hungarian Credit Bank
HCB	Hydrocortisone Butyrate [Glucocorticoid]
HCBD	Hexachlorobutadiene [Organic chemistry]
HCBI	Health Conference for Business and Industry [Defunct]
HCBK	Hudson Chartered Bancorp [NASDAQ symbol] (TTSB)
HCBK	Hudson Chartered Bancorp, Inc. [NASDAQ symbol] (SAG)
HCBP	Hexachlorobiphenyl [Organic chemistry]
HCBS	Home and Community-Based Services [Department of Health and Human Services] (GFGA)
HCBS	Host Computer Basic Software (IAA)
HCBWAG	Home and Community-Based Waiver for Aged [Department of Health and Human Services] (GFGA)
HCBWAGD	Home and Community-Based Waiver for Aged and Physically and Developmentally Disabled [Department of Health and Human Services] (GFGA)
HCBWAGPD	Home and Community-Based Waiver for Aged and Physically Disabled [Department of Health and Human Services] (GFGA)
HCBWMI	Home and Community-Based Waiver for Mentally Ill [Department of Health and Human Services] (GFGA)
HCBWMRDD	Home and Community-Based Waiver for Mentally Retarded and Developmentally Disabled [Department of Health and Human Services] (GFGA)
HCBWPDS	Home and Community-Based Waiver for Physically Disabled [Department of Health and Human Services] (GFGA)
HCC	Hand Control Clutch (DNAB)
HCC	Hardware Capability Code [Dialog] [Searchable field] [Information service or system] (NITA)
HCC	Harlem Cultural Council (EA)
HCC	Hawaii Control Center [Missiles] (MUGU)
HCC	HCC Insurance Hldgs [NYSE symbol] (TTSB)
HCC	HCC Insurance Holdings [NYSE symbol] (SAG)
HCC	Health Care Card (ADA)
HCC	Health Care Center (WDAA)
HCC	Health Care Corp. [Proposed] (DHSM)

HCC	Health Coordinating Council
HCC	Heat Conservation Center (STED)
HCC	Heliax Coaxial Cable
HCC	Helicopter Control Center (NVT)
HCC	Helicopter Coordination Center
HCC	Helicopter Crash Crane (DNAB)
HCC	Hepatitis Contagiosa Canis [*Virus*]
HCC	Hepatocellular Carcinoma [*Oncology*]
HCC	Hepatoma Carcinoma Cell [*Medicine*] (DB)
HCC	Hereditary Colon Cancer
HCC	Hermetic Chip Carrier
HCC	Hexachlorocyclohexane (STED)
HCC	Hibbing Community College, Hibbing, MN [*OCLC symbol*] (OCLC)
HCC	History of Chief Complaint [*Medicine*]
HCC	Hobart Chamber of Commerce [*Australia*]
HCC	Hollow Copper Conductor
HCC	Hollywood Comedy Club (EA)
HCC	Holy Cross [*California*] [*Seismograph station code, US Geological Survey*] (SEIS)
HCC	Holyoke Community College [*Massachusetts*]
HCC	Home Care Coordinator [*Medicine*]
HCC	Honda Car Club [*Defunct*] (EA)
HCC	Honda Civic Club [*Later, H-I*] (EA)
HCC	Honeycomb Corrugated Construction
HCC	Hospital Chaplaincies Council (BUAC)
HCC	Hospital Conveyance Corps [*British military*] (DMA)
HCC	Host Country Contributions [*Peace Corps*]
HCC	Housing Consultative Council for England (BUAC)
HCC	Hovermail Collectors' Club (BUAC)
HCC	Hubcap Collector's Club (EA)
HCC	Hull Construction Certificate
HCC	Hummel Collectors Club (EA)
HCC	Humor Correspondence Club (EA)
HCC	Hyderabad Commercial Corp [*India*] (BUAC)
HCC	Hyderabad Contingent Cavalry [*British military*] (DMA)
HCC	Hydraulic Cement Concrete
HCC	Hydrocarbon Concentration [*Automotive engineering*]
HCC	Hydroxycholecalciferol [*Biochemistry*]
HCCA	Heavy Construction Contractors Association
HCCA	Hellenic Chamber of Commerce in Australia
HCCA	Horseless Carriage Club of America (EA)
HCCAACT	Health Care Consumers' Association of the Australian Capital Territory
HCCAPS	Helmet Compatible Communications/Aural Protection System
HCCBE	Hungarian Central Committee for Books and Education (EA)
HCCC	Computer Center [*Haverford College*] [*Research center*] (RCD)
HCCC	HealthCare COMPARE [*NASDAQ symbol*] (TTSB)
HCCC	HealthCare COMPARE Corp. [*NASDAQ symbol*] (NQ)
HCCC	Health Care Complaints Commission [*Australia*]
HCCC	Helix Countercurrent Chromatography
HCCC	Hyderabad Co-Operative Commercial Corp. [*India*] (BUAC)
HCCG	Discharge [*from Military Service*] under Honorable Conditions, Convenience of Government
HCCH	Hexachlorocyclohexane [*Organic chemistry*]
HCC Ins	HCC Insurance Holdings [*Associated Press*] (SAG)
HCCM	Discharge [*from Military Service*] under Honorable Conditions, Convenience of Man
HCCM	Hadley Centre Climate Model
HCCM	High-Performance Common Channel Module [*Telecommunications*]
HCCO	Hector Communications [*NASDAQ symbol*] (TTSB)
HCCO	Hector Communications Corp. [*NASDAQ symbol*] (SAG)
HCCP	Hexachlorocyclopentadiene [*Also, HCP, HEX*] [*Organic chemistry*]
HCCP	Honorary Certified Claims Professional
HCCPD	Hexachlorocyclopentadiene (COE)
HC/CPP	Historical Cost/Current Purchasing Power
HCD	College of the Holy Cross, Worcester, MA [*OCLC symbol*] (OCLC)
HCd	Hair Cadmium Level [*Medicine*]
HCD	Handcarried (AABC)
HCD	Hard-Copy Device [*Computer science*] (ECII)
HCD	Heavy Chain Disease [*Protein*]
HCD	Helath Care Delivery (STED)
HCD	High Caloric Density (STED)
HCD	High Carbohydrate Diet [*Medicine*] (DMAA)
HCD	High-Current Density
HCD	High-Current Diode
HCD	Highest Common Denominator
HCD	Hoffman Core Driver
HCD	Hollow Cathode Discharge [*Spectrometry*]
HCD	Homologous Canine Distemper [*Antiserum*]
HCD	Horizon Crossing Descending
HCD	Horizontal Correlation Distance
HCD	Hot-Carrier Diode (IEEE)
HCD	Hughes Communications Division (SAA)
HCD	Hutchinson, MN [*Location identifier FAA*] (FAAL)
HCD	Hydrocolloid Dressing [*Dermatology*]
HCD	Hyundai California Design [*Concept car*]
HCDA	Housing and Community Development Act (GFGA)
HCDA	Hydrodynamic Core Disruptive Accident [*Nuclear energy*] (NRCH)
HCDA	Hypothetical Core Disruptive Accident [*Nuclear energy*]
HCDB	Historical Cost Database
HCDD	Hexachlorodibenzodioxin [*Organic chemistry*]
HCDE	Homothetic-Constant Differences of Elasticities of Substitution [*Statistics*]
HCDM	Hungarian Christian Democratic Movement [*Slovakia*] (BUAC)

HCDP	Discharge [*from Military Service*] under Honorable Conditions, Dependency Existing Prior to Enlistment
HCDR	Hardware Critical Design Review (MCD)
HCDR	Hours and Cost Detail Report
HCDV	Hilcoast Development [*NASDAQ symbol*] (TTSB)
HCDV	Hilcoast Development Corp. [*NASDAQ symbol*] (SAG)
hce	Hard-Coal Equivalents (BARN)
HCE	Haveth Childer Everywhere [*Key phrase in "Finnegan's Wake"*]
HCE	Health Care Education
HCE	Here Comes Everybody [*Key phrase in "Finnegan's Wake"*]
HCE	Hic Conditus Est [*Here Lies Buried*] [*Latin*]
HCE	Highly Compensated Employee [*Human resources*] (WYGK)
HCE	Hollow-Cathode Effect (IEEE)
HCE	Human-Caused Error
HCE	Humphrey Chimpden Earwicker [*Hero of "Finnegan's Wake"*]
HCEA	Hairdressers and Cosmetologists Employers' Association [*Australia*]
HCEA	Healthcare Convention & Exhibitors Association (NTPA)
HCEA	Health Care Exhibitors Association (EA)
HCEA	Holland Cheese Exporters Association [*Later, DDB*] (EA)
HCEBT	Houston Cotton Exchange and Board of Trade [*Defunct*] (EA)
HCEC	Hospital Care Evaluation Committee (MEDA)
HCEC	Hospital Committee of the European Community (BUAC)
HCED	Hand Controller Engage Driver (NASA)
HCEE	Discharge [*from Military Service*] under Honorable Conditions, Expiration of Enlistment
HCEEP	Handicapped Children's Early Education Programs
HCEI	Hydrocarbon Emission Index [*Automotive engineering*]
HCEX	High-Speed Color Exterior
HCF	Fluorocarbon without Chlorine (ECON)
HCF	Hagerstown CATI [*Computer-Assisted Telephone Interviewing*] Facility [*Bureau of the Census*] (GFGA)
HCF	Halt and Catch Fire [*Computer hacker terminology*] (NHD)
HCF	Hardened Compact Fiber
HCF	Health Care Finder
HCF	[*The*] Healthcare Forum (EA)
HCF	Heat Control Filter
HCF	Hebrew Christian Fellowship (EA)
HCF	Hebrew Culture Foundation (EA)
HCF	Height Correction Factor
HCF	Hereditary Capillary Fragility [*Medicine*] (DMAA)
HCF	High Carbohydrate, High Fiber [*Nutrition*]
HCF	High-Carbon Ferrochrome [*Metallurgy*]
HCF	High Circle Fatique
HCF	High Coefficient of Friction [*Engineering*]
HCF	High-Cycle Fatigue [*Rocket engine*]
HCF	Highest Common Factor [*Mathematics*]
HIM	[*Hardware Interface Module*] Configuration File [*NASA*] (NASA)
HCF	Honeycomb Foundation (IIA)
HCF	Honorary Chaplain to the Forces [*British*]
HCF	Hood College, Frederick, MD [*OCLC symbol*] (OCLC)
HCF	Host Command Facility
HCF	Hot Channel Factor [*Environmental science*] (COE)
HCF	Hungarian Cultural Foundation (EA)
HCF	Hypocaloric Carbohydrate Feeding (DB)
HCFA	Health Care Financing Administration [*HHS*]
HCFAR	Health Care Financing Administration Rulings [*A publication*] (DLA)
HCFC	Helen Cornelius Fan Club (EA)
HCFC	Hydrochlorofluorocarbon [*Organic chemistry*]
HCFC	Hydrochlorofluorocarbons (EERA)
HCFD	Hydrochemical Form Die [*Tool*] (AAG)
HCFF	High-Capacity Fog Foam [*Navy*] (NVT)
HCFF/AFFF	High-Capacity Fog Foam/Aqueous Film-Forming Foam (DNAB)
HCFMS	Holy Cross Foreign Mission Society (EA)
HCFP	HealthCare Financial Partners, Inc. [*NASDAQ symbol*] (SAG)
HCFR	Health Care Financing Review [*A publication*] (DLA)
HCF Rev	Health Care Financing Review [*A publication*] (DLA)
HCFSG	Health Care Financing Study Group (EA)
HCFTA	Home and Contract Furnishing Textiles Association [*British*] (DBA)
hCFTR	Human Cystic Fibrosis Transmembrane Conductance Regulator [*Genetics*]
hCFU	Human Colony-Forming Unit [*Genetics*]
HCG	Griqualand High Court Reports [*A publication*] (DLA)
HCG	Hardware Character Generator
HCG	Hermanas Catequistas Guadalupanas [*Sister Catechists of Guadeloupe*] [*Roman Catholic women's religious order*]
HCG	Home Capital Group, Inc. [*Toronto Stock Exchange symbol*]
HCG	Horizontal Location of Center of Gravity
HCG	Human Chorionic Gonadotrophin [*Endocrinology*]
hCG	Human Chorionic Gonadotropin [*A hormone*] (PAZ)
HCGB	Helicopter Club of Great Britain (BUAC)
HCGB	Hover Club [*British*] (DBA)
HCGF	Haematopoietic Cell Growth Factor [*Biochemistry*]
HCGN	Hypocomplementemic Glomerulonephritis [*Nephrology*] (DAVI)
HCGO	Heavy Coker Gas Oil [*Petroleum technology*]
HCGPF	Hematopoietic Cell Growth Potentiating Factor (DB)
hCGRP	Human Calcitonin Gene-Related Peptide [*Biochemistry*]
HCGS	Hope Creek Generating Station (NRCH)
HCH	Crossville, TN [*Location identifier FAA*] (FAAL)
H-CH	Handy-Cap Horizons [*Defunct*] (EA)
HCH	Health Care for the Homeless (DMAA)
HCH	Health-Chem [*AMEX symbol*] (TTSB)
HCH	Health-Chem Corp. [*AMEX symbol*] (SPSS)
HCH	Herbert Clark Hoover [*US president, 1874-1964*]
HCH	Herding Champion [*Prefix*]
HCH	Hexachlorocyclohexane [*Also, BHC, GBH*] [*Insecticide*]

HCHASC...... House of Commons Home Affairs Select Committee [British] (WDAA)
HCHBK........ Hatchback [Automotive advertising]
HCHC.......... High Carbon, High Chrome
HChD .... Diploma in Higher Chiropodial Theory of the Institute of Chiropodists [British] (DBQ)
HCHF.......... High Carbohydrate, High Fiber [Nutrition]
Hchg.......... Hechinger Co. [Associated Press] (SAG)
HCHGC........ Hollingworth Center for Highly Gifted Children (EA)
HCHO.......... Aldehydes [Organic chemistry]
HCHO.......... Formaldehyde [Organic chemistry] (DAVI)
HCHP.......... Harvard Community Health Plan (DMAA)
HCHP.......... Health Care for the Homeless Program [Defunct] (EA)
HCHP.......... High-Capacity Heat Pipe (SSD)
HCHS.......... Handicapped Children's Home Service [Later, Easter Seal Home Service] (EA)
HCHWA-D .... Hereditary Cerebral Hemorrhage with Amyloidosis of the Dutch Type [Medicine]
HCI.............. Handgun Control, Inc. (EA)
HCI.............. Hardness-Critical Item (MSA)
HCI.............. Hawthorne Communications, Inc.
HCI.............. HCI Holdings Ltd. [Toronto Stock Exchange symbol]
HCI.............. Health Care International [British]
HCI.............. Health Commons Institute
HCI.............. Hierarchically Classified Index
HCI.............. High-Current Inductor
HCI.............. Home Center Institute (EA)
HCI.............. Host Computer Interface
HCI.............. Hot Carrier Injection (AAEL)
HCI.............. Hotel and Catering Institute [South Africa] (BUAC)
HCI.............. Hotel and Catering Institute [British] (BI)
HCI.............. Hughes Communications, Inc. [Hughes Aircraft Co.] [Los Angeles, CA]
HCI.............. Human-Computer Interaction [Computer science]
HCI.............. Human-Computer Interface (RDA)
HCI.............. Hybrid Computer Interface (MHDB)
HCI.............. Hyderabad Contingent Infantry [India] [Army]
HCI.............. Hydrochloride (CPH)
HCIA .... HCIA, Inc. [NASDAQ symbol] (SAG)
HCIA .... Highlander Class International Association (EA)
HCIH.......... Hubei Cancer Institute and Hospital [China] (BUAC)
HCIL.......... Human-Computer Interaction Laboratory [University of Maryland] (PCM)
HCIm .... HealthCare Imaging Services, Inc. [Associated Press] (SAG)
HCIMA .... Hotel, Catering, and Institutional Management Association [British] (DBA)
HcIMP.......... Hydrocolloid Impression [Dentistry]
HCIS .... Health Care Information System (DMAA)
HCIS .... Hospital Communication and Information System [McDonnell Douglas Automation Co.]
HCIS .... House Committee on Internal Security [Formerly, HUAC] [Dissolved, 1975 US Congress]
HCITB .... Hotel and Catering Industry Training Board [British] (BI)
HCITE.......... Horizontal Cargo Integration Test Equipment (MCD)
HCJ.............. High Court of Justice
HCJA.......... High Court Journalists' Association (BUAC)
HCJB.......... High Court Junior Beadle [Ancient Order of Foresters]
HCJC.......... Henderson County Junior College [Texas]
HCJC.......... Howard County Junior College [Texas]
HCJFC......... Harry Connick, Jr., Fan Club (EA)
HC Jour ...... House of Commons Journals [England] [A publication] (DLA)
HCJW.......... High Court Junior Woodward [Ancient Order of Foresters]
HCK .... Hematopoietic Cell Kinase (DMAA)
HCK .... Holtzer-Cabot Corp. (EFIS)
HCK .... Human Cervical Keratinocyte [Cytology]
HCKRY .... Hickory
HCL.............. Central Hispano Capital Ltd. [NYSE symbol] (SAG)
HCL.............. Hairy Cell Leukemia [Medicine]
HCL.............. Hamburg-Chicago Line [Steamship] (MHDB)
HCL.............. Hard Contact Lens [Ophthalmology]
HCL.............. Hardware Compatibility List [Microsoft Corp.]
HCL.............. Harold Cohen Library [University of Liverpool] [British] (NITA)
HCL.............. Harpoon Check List [Missiles] (MCD)
HCL.............. Helenair Corp [Saint Lucia] [FAA designator] (FAAC)
HCL.............. Helium Cadmium LASER
HCL.............. High, Common, Low [Relay] (IEEE)
HCL.............. High Cost of Living
HCL.............. Hollow Cathode Lamp
HCL.............. Horizontal Center Line
HCL.............. Human Cultured Lymphoblastoid [Cells]
HCL.............. Human Cultured Lymphoblasts [Medicine] (DMAA)
HCL.............. Huron College [UTLAS symbol]
HCL.............. Husson College, Bangor, ME [OCLC symbol] (OCLC)
HCL.............. Hyderabad Contingent Lancers [British military] (DMA)
HCl.............. Hydrochloric Acid
HCl.............. Hydrogen Chloride (LDT)
HCL.............. International Hod Carriers', Building and Common Laborers' Union of America [Later, Laborers' International Union of North America]
HCLA .... Hungarian Catholic League of America (EA)
HCLD .... Housing Construction and Land Development
HCLE .... Humanities Center for Liberal Education
HCLF .... Health Care Libraries Forum [Association of Specialized and Cooperative Library Agencies]
HCLF.......... High Carbohydrate, Low Fiber [Nutrition]
HCLF.......... Horizontal Cask Lifting Fixture [Nuclear energy] (NRCH)
HCLIP .... Harvard Computer-Aided Legal Instruction Project (DLA)

HcllMed....... Housecall Medical Resources, Inc. [Associated Press] (SAG)
HCLM.......... Health Care Labor Manual [A publication] (DLA)
HC-LN .... High Control/Low Nurturance [Psychology]
HCLP.......... Home Conversion Loan Program [Canada]
HCLPr........ Centl Hispano Cap 10.50% Pref [NYSE symbol] (TTSB)
HCLPrB .... Central Hispano Cap 9.43% Pref [NYSE symbol] (TTSB)
HCM........... Haitian Campaign Medal
HCM........... Half-Cycle Magnetizer (IDOE)
HCM........... Halifax Conservatory of Music
HCM........... Harcum, VA [Location identifier FAA] (FAAL)
HCM........... Hard Copy Module (NASA)
HCM........... Hard Core Monitor [Computer science] (IAA)
HCM........... HARDMAN [Hardware-Manpower Program] Comparability Methodology [Army]
HCM........... Health Care Maintenance (DAVI)
HCM........... High Capacity Multiplexing [Telecommunications] (ACRL)
HCM........... Highway Capacity Manual [FHWA] (TAG)
HCM........... His [or Her] Catholic Majesty
HCM........... Hundred Club of Massachusetts (EA)
HCM........... Hydraulic Core Mock-Up [Nuclear energy] (NRCH)
HCM........... Hydrocarbon Mass [Automotive engineering]
HCM........... Hypercalcemia of Malignancy [Medicine]
HCM........... Hypertrophic Cardiomyopathy [Cardiology]
HCMA.......... Alula [Somalia] [ICAO location identifier] (ICLI)
HCMA.......... Hotel Credit Managers Association [Defunct] (EA)
HCMB.......... Baidoa [Somalia] [ICAO location identifier] (ICLI)
HCMC.......... Candala [Somalia] [ICAO location identifier] (ICLI)
HCMC.......... Ho Chi Minh City [Vietnam]
HCMD.......... Bardera [Somalia] [ICAO location identifier] (ICLI)
HCME.......... Eil [Somalia] [ICAO location identifier] (ICLI)
HCME.......... United Hatters, Cap, and Millinery (BUAC)
HCMF.......... Bosaso [Somalia] [ICAO location identifier] (ICLI)
HCMF.......... Henry Clay Memorial Foundation (EA)
HCMG.......... Gardo [Somalia] [ICAO location identifier] (ICLI)
HCMH.......... Hargeisa [Somalia] [ICAO location identifier] (ICLI)
HCMI.......... Berbera [Somalia] [ICAO location identifier] (ICLI)
HCMI.......... Homeless Chronically Mentally Ill [Medicine]
HCMJ.......... Lugh Ferrandi [Somalia] [ICAO location identifier] (ICLI)
HCMK.......... Kisimayu [Somalia] [ICAO location identifier] (ICLI)
HCML.......... El Bur [Somalia] [ICAO location identifier] (ICLI)
HCMM.......... Heat Capacity Map Mission [NASA]
HCMM.......... Heat Capacity Mapping Mission [Satellite] (EERA)
HCMM.......... Heavy Capability Mapping Mission [Satellite]
HCMM.......... Hereditary Cutaneous Malignant Melanoma [Medicine] (DMAA)
HCMM.......... Mogadishu [Somalia] [ICAO location identifier] (ICLI)
HCMMS ...... Health Care Material Management Society (EA)
HCMN.......... Belet Uen [Somalia] [ICAO location identifier] (ICLI)
HCMO.......... Obbia [Somalia] [ICAO location identifier] (ICLI)
HCMOS........ High-Density Complementary Metal-Oxide Semiconductor (AAEL)
HCMOS........ High-Speed Complementary Metal-Oxide Semiconductor (MCD)
HCMP.......... Las Anod [Somalia] [ICAO location identifier] (ICLI)
HCMPA........ Home Counties Master Printers' Alliance [British] (DGA)
HCMR.......... Galcaio [Somalia] [ICAO location identifier] (ICLI)
HCMR.......... Heat Capacity Mapping Radiometer [NASA]
HCMS.......... Discharge [from Military Service] under Honorable Conditions, Medical Survey
HCMS.......... Scusciuban [Somalia] [ICAO location identifier] (ICLI)
HCMTS........ High-Capacity Mobile Telecommunications System (TEL)
HCMU.......... Discharge [from Military Service] under Honorable Conditions, under Age of Authorized Enlistment
HCMU.......... Erigavo [Somalia] [ICAO location identifier] (ICLI)
HCMU.......... Hebrew Cabinet Makers' Union [British]
HCMV.......... Burao [Somalia] [ICAO location identifier] (ICLI)
HCMV.......... Human Cytomegalovirus
HCMW.......... Discharge [from Military Service] under Honorable Conditions, Minor Enlisted Without Consent, under Eighteen at Time of Discharge
HCMW.......... United Hatters, Cap, and Millinery Workers International Union (EA)
HCN........... Health Care REIT [NYSE symbol] (SAG)
HCN........... Health Communications Network [Medical University of South Carolina] [Charleston] [Telecommunications] (TSSD)
HCN........... Hilton Communications Network [Hilton Hotels Corp.] [Beverly Hills, CA] [Telecommunications service] (TSSD)
HCN........... Historical Climate Network
HCN........... Home Counties Newspapers [British] (DGA)
HCN........... Hydrocyanic Acid [Inorganic chemistry]
HCN........... Hydrogen Cyanide [Also, AC] [Inorganic chemistry]
HCN........... Hygienic Community Network ()
HCN........... Nereditary Chronic Nephritis [Medicine] (DMAA)
HCNM.......... High Commissioner on National Minorities (BUAC)
HCNSW........ Heritage Council of New South Wales [Australia]
HCO........... Hackney Carriage Office [British] (WDAA)
HCO........... Hangar Control Officer [Navy]
HCO........... Harco Air Services [Nigeria] [ICAO designator] (FAAC)
HCO........... Harvard College Observatory
HCO........... Head of Contracting Office [Marine science] (OSRA)
HCO........... Headquarters Catalog Office
HCO........... Health Care Officer (WDAA)
HCO........... Health Care Organization (HCT)
HCO........... Hearing Carry-Over [Hearing-impaired technology]
HCO........... Heavy Cycle Oil [Petroleum technology]
HCO........... Helicopter Control Officer [British military] (DMA)
HCO........... Higher Clerical Officer [Civil Service] [British]
HCO........... Highly-Chlorinated Oil (IAA)
HCO........... Horizontal Control Operator [Military]
HCO........... Huntco, Inc. [NYSE symbol] (SAG)

HCO	Huntco Inc'A' [*NYSE symbol*] (TTSB)
HCO	Hydrogenated Coconut Oil (PDAA)
HCO₃	Bicarbonate [*Pharmacology*] (DAVI)
HCOC	Honorary Colonel of the Corps [*Army*]
H Conf Rept...	House of Representatives Conference Report (BARN)
HCONN	Hose Connector
HConRes...	House Concurrent Resolution (WPI)
H Con Res...	House of Representatives Concurrent Resolution (DLA)
HCOP	Health Care Opportunities Program [*Department of Health and Human Services*]
HCOPIL	Hague Conference on Private International Law (BUAC)
HCOR	HealthCor Holdings, Inc. [*NASDAQ symbol*] (SAG)
HCOR	Honorary Colonel of the Regiment
HCP	Habitat Conservation Plan [*Ecology*]
HCP	Hamiltonian Cycle Problem [*Computer science*]
HCP	Handicap
HCP	Handicap Race [*Horse racing*]
HCP	Hangar Control Position [*Navy*]
HCP	Harbor Control Post
HCP	Hard Copy Printer [*Computer science*]
HCP	Hardness-Critical Process (MSA)
HCP	Health Care Products, Inc. [*Toronto Stock Exchange symbol*]
HCP	Health Care Property Investors, Inc. [*NYSE symbol*] (SPSG)
HCP	Health Care Prop Inv [*NYSE symbol*] (TTSB)
HCP	Healthy Cities Project (BUAC)
HCp	Heat of Combustion (of an Element under Constant Pressure) (ROG)
HCP	Hemispherical Candlepower [*Optics*] (IAA)
HCP	Hepatocatalase Peroxidase [*An enzyme*] (MAE)
HCP	Hereditary Coproporphyria [*Medicine*] (MAE)
HCP	Hexachlorocyclopentadiene [*Also, HCCP, HEX*] [*Organic chemistry*]
HCP	Hexachlorophene [*Germicide*]
HCP	Hexagonal Close-Packed [*Crystallography*]
HCP	High-Calcium Pyroxene [*Mineralogy*]
HCP	High Cell Passage (DB)
HCP	Holiday Caravan Parks [*Public-performance tariff class*] [*British*]
HCP	Home Consumption Price
HCP	Horizontal Candlepower
HCP	Host Communications Processor
HCP	Hungarian Civic Party [*Slovakia*] (BUAC)
HCP	Hybrid Combustion Process (RDA)
HCP	Hydorthermal Coal Process [*Environmental science*] (COE)
HCP	Hydrazine Catalytic Plenum
HCP	Hydroxycalcium Phenoxide [*Organic chemistry*]
HCP	Hydroxycyclopentenone
HCP	Hydroxyproline-Containing Protein
HCP	Hypervelocity Countermeasures Program
HCP	Hypothermal Coal Process (GNE)
HCPAA	Hungarian Catholic Priests' Association in America (EA)
HCPC	Health Care Compliance Packaging Council (EA)
HCPCS	HCFA [*Health Care Financing Administration*] Common Procedures Coding System [*Department of Health and Human Services*] (GFGA)
HCPDG	Health Care Professionals Discussion Group [*American Occupational Therapy Association*]
HCPNY	Harbor Carriers of the Port of New York (EA)
HCPOTP	Health Care Practitioner Other Than Physician (MEDA)
HCPOTP	Health Care Professionals other than Physicians (HCT)
HCPP	Health Care Prepayment Plan
HCPRU	Hot Climate Physiological Research Unit [*Nigeria*] (BUAC)
HCPS	Hemispherical Candlepower Second [*Optics*] (IAA)
HCPS	Horizontal Candlepower Seconds
HCP-SAD	High Cell Passage Street-Alabama-Dufferin [*Strain*] [*Medicine*] (DB)
HCPT	Handicapped Childrens Pilgrimage Trust (BUAC)
HCPT	Historic Churches Preservation Trust [*British*] (BI)
HCPT	Hydroxycamptothecin [*Antineoplastic drug*]
HCPTR	Helicopter (CINC)
HCPV	Hydrocarbon Pore Volume [*Petroleum technology*]
HCPWT	House Committee on Public Works and Transportation (COE)
H/CQ	Habitability/Crew Quarters (KSC)
HCQ	Halls Creek [*Australia Airport symbol Obsolete*] (OAG)
HCQ	Harbours Corp. of Queensland [*Australia*]
HCQ	Hot Carrier Quad
HCQ	Hydroxychloroquine [*Disease modifying antirheumatic drug*]
HCQIA	Health Care Quality Improvement Act [*1986*] (HCT)
HCR	Hard Copy Response (SAA)
HCR	Hardware Check Routine
HCR	Hardware Correction Report
HCR	Haut Commissariat des Nations Unies pour les Refugies [*United Nations High Commission for Refugees - UNHCR*] [*Switzerland*]
HCR	Health Care & Retirement [*NYSE symbol*] (TTSB)
HCR	Health Care & Retirement Corp. [*NYSE symbol*] (SPSG)
HCR	HealthCare and Retirement Corp. [*Associated Press*] (SAG)
HCR	Height Cross Range (MCD)
HCR	Heme-Controlled Repressor (DB)
HCR	Hemin Controlled Repressor [*Biochemistry*]
HCR	High Charge Retention (PDAA)
HCR	High Chief Ranger [*Ancient Order of Foresters*]
HCR	High Court Reports, India [*A publication*] (DLA)
HCR	High Cross Range
HCR	Highway Contract Route
HCR	Holy Cross [*Alaska*] [*Airport symbol*] (OAG)
HCR	Host-Cell Reactivation (STED)
HCR	House Concurrent Resolution [*US Congress*]
HCR	Household Cavalry Regiment [*British military*] (DMA)
HCr	Houston's Delaware Criminal Cases [*A publication*] (DLA)

HCR	Human-Controlled Repressor [*Genetics*] (DAVI)
HCR	Hurricane Rescue Craft, Inc. [*Vancouver Stock Exchange symbol*]
HCR	Hydrochloric Acid [*Organic chemistry*] (DAVI)
HCR	Hysterical Conversion Reaction [*Psychiatry*] (DAVI)
HCRC	Hallwood Consolidated Res. [*NASDAQ symbol*] (TTSB)
HCRC	Hallwood Consolidated Resources Corp. [*NASDAQ symbol*] (SAG)
HCRC	Hillsdale County Railroad Co., Inc. [*AAR code*]
HCRC	Hotel and Catering Research Centre [*British*] (IRUK)
HCRC	Human Communication Research Centre (BUAC)
HCRD	Health Care Research Division [*Brooke Army Medical Center*]
HCRE	Homeopathic Council for Research and Education (EA)
HCREF	Health Care Research and Educational Foundation [*Later, AAMAREF*] (EA)
HC Res	House of Representatives Concurrent Resolution [*Legal term*] (DLA)
HCRF	Health Care Research Foundation [*Australia*]
HCRI	Health Care Research Institution [*Australia*]
HCRIS	Hospital Cost Report Information System (MEDA)
H'CRIT	Hematocrit [*Medicine*]
H'crit	Hematocrit (STED)
HCRM	Holocaust Curriculum Resources Material (BJA)
HCRNWF	High Court Reports, North West Frontier [*A publication*] (DLA)
HCRNWP	High Court Reports, Northwest Provinces [*India*] [*A publication*] (DLA)
HCRO	High Cross-Range Orbiter (KSC)
HCRON	Helicopter Combat Support Squadron [*Navy*] (DNAB)
HCRP	Hominid Corridor Research Project [*Palaeontology*]
HCRR	Home Counties Reserve Regiment [*British military*] (DMA)
HCRS	Heritage Conservation Recreation Service [*Abolished, 1981, functions transferred to National Park Service*] [*Department of the Interior*]
HCRST	Hardware Clipping, Rotation, Scaling, and Translation (MHDI)
HCRSV	Hibiscus Chlorotic Ringspot Virus [*Plant pathology*]
HCRW	Hot and Cold Running Water
HCS	Hajdu-Cheney Syndrome [*Medicine*] (DMAA)
HCS	Hammered Chainmakers' Society [*A union*] [*British*]
HCS	Handicapped Children's Services
HCS	Hard-Clad Silica [*Materials science*]
HCS	Hard Copy System [*Computer science*] (MHDI)
HCS	Harris Consultive Services, Inc. [*Information service or system*] (IID)
HCS	Harry C. Stutz [*Designer of early automobile*]
HCS	Harvey Lushing Society [*Later, AANS*] (EA)
HCS	Hazard Communication Standard [*OSHA*]
HCS	Hazardous Chemicals Secretariat [*Victoria, Australia*]
HCS	Header Check Sequence [*Computer science*]
HCS	Health Care Support [*System*] [*IBM Corp.*]
HCS	Health Computing Services [*Australia*]
HCS	Healthy Cities Secretariat [*Australia*]
HCS	Hebei Crop Society (BUAC)
HCS	Helicopter Control Ship [*Navy*] (NVT)
HCS	Helicopter Coordination Section (COE)
HCS	Helium Circulator Seal (IEEE)
HCS	Hellenic Chamber of Shipping (BUAC)
HCS	High-Carbon Steel
HCS	High Clad Silica (PDAA)
HCS	High-Compression Swirl [*Automotive engineering*]
HCS	High Court Secretary [*Ancient Order of Foresters*]
HCS	Histochemical Society (EA)
HCS	Holy Crown Society [*Hungary*] (BUAC)
HCS	Home Civil Servant [*British*]
HCS	Home Civil Service [*British*]
HCS	Home Run Control System [*Computer science*]
HCS	Homogeneous Computer System
HCS	Hospital Car Service
HCS	Host Composition System [*Infograph Ltd.*] (NITA)
HCS	Hot-Carrier Suppressed (AAEL)
HCS	Hourglass Contraction of Stomach [*Gastroenterology*] (DAVI)
HCS	House Committee Substitute [*US Congress*]
HCS	Hover Coupler System (DWSG)
HCS	HUD [*Housing and Urban Development*] Clearinghouse Service
HCS	Human Chorionic Somatomammotrophin [*Also, CGP, hcs, HPL*] [*Endocrinology*]
hCS	Human Chorionic Somatomammotropin [*Human Placental Lactogen*] [*Medicine*] (STED)
HCS	Human Chorionic Somatotropin (STED)
hCS	Human Choriosomatotropin (EDCT)
HCS	Human Cord Serum
HCS	Hummocky Cross-Stratification [*Sedimentology*]
HCS	Hundred Call Seconds [*Telecommunications*]
HCS	Hybrid Computation and Simulation (SSD)
HCS	Hydrogen Control System (NRCH)
HCS	Hydromechanical Control System (KSC)
HCS	Hydroxycorticosteroids [*Pharmacology*] (DAVI)
HCS	Membership Section for Health Care Systems [*An association*] (EA)
HCSA	Halogenated Cleaning Solvent Association (EA)
HCSA	Hate Crimes Statistics Act
HCSA	Hexylcarbonate of Salicylic Acid [*Analgesic*]
HCSA	Hospital Consultants' and Specialists' Association [*British*] (DCTA)
HCSA	House Committee on Space and Astronautics [*US Congress*] (AAG)
HCSB	High Court Senior Beadle [*Ancient Order of Foresters*]
HCSBC	Historical Commission, Southern Baptist Convention (EA)
HCSCIA	Health Care Studies and Clinical Investigation Activity [*Fort Sam Houston, TX*] [*Army*]
HCSD	Health Care Studies Division [*Academy of Health Sciences*] [*Army*]
HCSDS	High-Capacity Satellite Digital Service [*AT & T*] (TSSD)
HCSF	Histamine-Producing Cell-Stimulating Factor [*Biochemistry*]
HCSG	Healthcare Services Group (EFIS)

HCSG	Health Care Services Group [*NASDAQ symbol*] (SAG)
HCSG	Healthcare Services Group, Inc. [*NASDAQ symbol*] (NQ)
HCSG	Healthcare Svcs Group [*NASDAQ symbol*] (TTSB)
HCSG	Hyperactive Children's Support Group [*England*]
HCSHT	High-Carbon Steel, Heat-Treated
HCSI	Hughes Communications Services, Inc. (NASA)
HCSL	Hybrid Computational Science Laboratory
HCSL	Hybrid Computation and Simulation Laboratory
HCSLP	Hungarian Committee of Socialist Labor Party [*Defunct*] (EA)
HCSM	Human Chorionic Somatomammotropin [*Endocrinology*]
HCSM	Mogadishu [*Somalia*] [*ICAO location identifier*] (ICLI)
HCSNSW	Home Care Service of New South Wales [*Australia*]
HCSP	Health Care Service for Prisoners (WDAA)
HCSP	High-Capacity Signal Processor
HCSPR	Hundred Call Seconds Per Hour [*Telecommunications*] (ACRL)
HCSR	E. O. Hulburt Center for Space Research (MCD)
HCSRDG	Health and Community Services Research and Development Grants [*Australia*]
HCSS	Head Compartment Support Structure [*Nuclear energy*] (NRCH)
HCSS	High-Capacity Storage System [*Novell, Inc.*] [*Computer science*] (PCM)
HCSS	Home and Colonial School Society [*British*]
HCSS	Hospital Computer Sharing System (IEEE)
HCSTR	Homogeneous Continuous Stirred Tank Reactor [*Chemical engineering*]
HCSW	High Court Senior Woodward [*Ancient Order of Foresters*]
HCT	Hardware Compatibility Test [*Microsoft Corp.*] (PCM)
HCT	Hayes Center, NE [*Location identifier FAA*] (FAAL)
HCT	Health Check Test (DMAA)
HCT	Heart-Circulation-Training [*Physical fitness*]
HCT	Heater Center Tap [*Electronics*] (ECII)
HCT	Heater Center Top
HCT	Hematocrit [*Medicine*]
HCT	Herpetological Conservation Trust (BUAC)
HCT	High Commission Territories Corps [*Military unit*] [*British*]
H Ct	High Court
HCT	High Court Treasurer [*Ancient Order of Foresters*]
HCT	High-Speed Complementary Metal-Oxide Semiconductor Transistor-Transistor Logic Compatible (AAEL)
HCT	Histamine Challenge Test [*Biochemistry*] (DAVI)
HCT	Historic Control Trial [*Medicine*] (DMAA)
HCT	Hollow Cathode Tube
HCT	Homocytotropic [*Medicine*] (MAE)
HCT	Hot Cathode Tube
HCT	Howitzer Crew Trainer [*Military*]
HCT	Hull Collector Tank
hCt	Human Calcitonin [*Endocrinology*]
HCT	Human Chorionic Thyrotrophin [*Endocrinology*]
HCT	Hydraulic Components Test
HCT	Hydrochlorothiazide [*Drug*] [*Also, HCTZ, HCZ*] [*Organic chemistry*]
HCT	Hydrocortisone [*Endocrinology*]
HCTA	Health Careers Tutors' Association (BUAC)
HCTB	Hotel and Catering Training Board [*British*]
HCTBA	Hotel and Catering Trades Benevolent Association [*British*] (BI)
HCTC	Hotel and Catering Training Co. (AIE)
HCTDS	High-Capacity Terrestrial Digital Service [*AT & T*] (TSSD)
HCTF	Helium Component Test Facility [*Nuclear energy*] (NUCP)
HCTL	Healthcare Technologies Ltd. [*NASDAQ symbol*] (NQ)
HCTLF	Healthcare Technologies Ltd [*NASDAQ symbol*] (TTSB)
HCTLR	High Commission Territories Reports [*Basutoland, Bechuanaland, and Swaziland*] [*A publication*] (DLA)
HCTS	House Call Tax Service
HCTSS	Health Care Technology Study Section [*HEW*] (EGAO)
HCTU	Home Cervical Traction Unit [*Medicine*] (DAVI)
HCTZ	Hydrochlorothiazide [*Drug*] [*Also, HCT, HCZ*] [*Organic chemistry*]
HCU	Handheld Computer Unit
HCU	Harbor Clearance Unit [*Navy*] (NVT)
HCU	Harbor Control Unit
HCU	Hard Copy Unit
HCU	Health Care Unit [*DoD*] (GFGA)
HCU	Heavy Conversion Unit [*British military*] (DMA)
HCU	Helicopter Control Unit (NVT)
HCU	Helium Charging Unit (AAG)
HCU	Homing Comparator Unit (AAG)
HCU	Homocystinuria [*Medicine*]
HCU	Horse Canyon [*Utah*] [*Seismograph station code, US Geological Survey*] (SEIS)
HCU	Hydraulic Charging Unit (NASA)
HCU	Hydraulic Control Unit [*Nuclear energy*] (NRCH)
HCU	Hydraulic Coupling Unit [*Automotive engineering*]
HCU	Hydraulic Cycling Unit (AFM)
HCU	Hyperplasia Cystica Uteri [*Medicine*] (DMAA)
HCUA	Honeywell Computer Users Association (HGAA)
HCUDET	Harbor Clearance Unit Detachment [*Navy*] (DNAB)
HCUND	Hospitality Committee for United Nations Delegations (EA)
HCUP	Hospital Cost and Utilization Project [*Department of Health and Human Services*] (GFGA)
HCUS	Discharge [*from Military Service*] under Honorable Conditions, Unsuitable
HCUT	Homfray Carpets Unit Trust [*Commercial firm*] [*British*]
HCV	Hand Control Valve (NRCH)
HCv	Heat of Combustion (of an Element under Constant Volume) (ROG)
HCV	Hepatitis C Virus
HCV	Hercules Ventures [*Vancouver Stock Exchange symbol*]
HCV	High Calorific Value [*of a fuel*]

HCV	High Capacity Voice (ACRL)
HCV	Hog Cholera Virus (DMAA)
HCV	Hull Check Valve
HCV	Human Coronavirus
HCV	Hutchinson Cablevision [*British*]
HCV	Hydraulic Check Valve (GFGA)
HCV	Hydraulic Control Valve
HCVC	Historic Commercial Vehicle Club [*British*] (DCTA)
HCVC	Historic Commercial Vehicle Society (BUAC)
HCVCS	Historic Commercial Vehicle Cooperative Society [*Australia*]
HCVD	Hypertensive Cardiovascular Disease [*Medicine*]
HCVIS	High Clouds Visible [*NWS*] (FAAC)
HCVRCS	Hill Counselor Verbal Response Category System (EDAC)
HCW	Health Care Worker (TAD)
HCW	Home Computing Weekly [*British*] (NITA)
HCW	Hoosier Conference for Women (PSS)
HCW	Paine Webber Group [*AMEX symbol*] (SAG)
HCWI	High-Chromium White Iron
HC Wkly Inf Bull	House of Commons Weekly Information Bulletin [*A publication*] (DLA)
HCWU	Hotel and Catering Workers Union (BUAC)
HCY	Cowley/Lovell/Byron, WY [*Location identifier FAA*] (FAAL)
Hcy	Homocysteine [*An amino acid*]
HCZ	Hydrochlorothiazide [*Drug*] [*Also, HCT, HCTZ*] [*Organic chemistry*]
HCZ	Hydrogen Convection Zone
HD	Air-Conditioning Apparatus [*JETDS nomenclature*] [*Military*] (CET)
HD	Air-Cushion Vehicle built by Hovercraft Development [*England*] [*Usually used in combination with numerals*]
HD	Haab-Dimmer [*Syndrome*] [*Medicine*] (DB)
HD	Hajna-Damon Broth [*Medicine*] (DMAA)
HD	Half Duplex Transmission [*Data communication*] (CET)
HD	Hand (ROG)
HD	Hand-Drawn
HD	Hansen's Disease [*Leprosy*] [*Medicine*]
HD	Harbor Defense [*Military*]
HD	Hard (MSA)
HD	Hard Disk [*Computer science*]
HD	Hard-Drawn [*Metallurgy*]
HD	Hardware Design
H-D	Harley-Davidson
HD	Harmonic Distortion
HD	Hawaiian Department [*Army World War II*]
HD	Head (AAG)
Hd	Head (TBD)
hd	Head (WDMC)
HD	Head Diameter
HD	Head Driver (IAA)
HD	Heading
Hd	Headland [*Maps and charts*]
HD	Heard (ROG)
HD	Hearing Distance [*Medicine*]
HD	Heart Disease [*Medicine*]
HD	Heat Detector [*NFPA pre-fire planning symbol*] (NFPA)
HD	Heat Dissipation (DNAB)
HD	Heavy Distillate [*Fuel technology*]
HD	Heavy-Duty
HD	Helicopter Delivered
HD	Helicopter Direction (DNAB)
HD	Helicopter Director [*Military*] (CAAL)
HD	Heloma Durum [*A hard corn*] [*Orthopedics*] (DAVI)
HD	Hemidesmosome [*Cytology*]
HD	Hemodialysis [*Nephrology*]
HD	Hemodilution
HD	Hemolyzing Dose [*Medicine*]
HD	Henry Draper Catalogue [*Astronomy*]
HD	Hepatosis Diaetetica [*Veterinary science*] (OA)
HD	Herniated Disc [*Medicine*]
HD	Hexadecimal Code [*Computer science*] (IAA)
H-D	Hexadecimal-to-Decimal [*Computer science*] (IEEE)
HD	Hexagonal Domain Structure
HD	Hexanedione [*Organic chemistry*]
HD	Hierarchical Direct
HD	High Density
HD	High Detergent (WGA)
HD	High Dose [*Medicine*]
HD	High Drag [*Navy*] (NVT)
HD	High Dust
HD	High Dynamic
HD	Highland Division [*British military*] (DMA)
HD	Highly Desirable (KSC)
HD	Hilda Doolittle [*Initials used as pen name of American poet, 1886-1961*]
HD	Hip Disarticulation [*Medicine*]
HD	Hirschsprung's Disease [*Medicine*] (DMAA)
HD	Histone Deacetylase [*An enzyme*]
HD	Historical Development
HD	Historical Division [*Air Force*]
HD	Historic Deerfield (EA)
HD	Hodgkin's Disease [*Medicine*]
HD	Hogshead
HD	Holddown
HD	Home Defence [*British World War II*]
HD	Home Depot [*NYSE symbol*] (TTSB)
HD	[*The*] Home Depot, Inc. [*NYSE symbol*] (SPSG)
HD	Homoeodomain [*Genetics*]

HD .... Homoserine Dehydrogenase [*An enzyme*]
HD .... Honorable Discharge [*Military*]
HD .... Honorary Degree [*Freemasonry*] (ROG)
HD .... Hora Decubitus [*At Bedtime*] [*Pharmacy*]
hd .... Hora Decubitus [*At Bedtime*] [*Latin*] (STED)
HD .... Horizontal Distance [*Photography*] (OA)
HD .... Horizontal Drain
HD .... Horizontal Drive
HD .... Hormone-Dependent [*Medicine*] (DB)
HD .... Horse-Drawn
HD .... Hospital Day (DAVI)
HD .... Hourly Difference [*Navigation*]
HD .... House Document
HD .... House Dust (DMAA)
HD .... Housing Debtline [*Telephone service*] [*British*]
HD .... Housing Density
HD .... Huddersfield [*Postcode*] (ODBW)
HD .... Human Development
HD .... Humanitarian Deferment [*Military*]
HD .... Humanitarian Demining [*Military*]
HD .... Humper Dears (EA)
HD .... Hundred
HD .... Hunter and Driffield [*System to indicate film emulsion speed*] (BARN)
HD .... Huntington's Disease [*Medicine*]
HD .... Hurel Dubois [*Societe de Construction des Avions Hurel Dubois*] [*France ICAO aircraft manufacturer identifier*] (ICAO)
HD .... Hurricane Deck
HD .... Hydatid Disease [*Medicine*] (MAE)
HD .... Hydralazine [*Antihypertensive drug*]
HD .... Hydrogen Drain (MCD)
HD .... Hydroxydopamine (DB)
H-D .... Hypothetico-Deductive
HD .... Hypotonic Duodenogram [*Medicine*]
HD .... Mustard Gas [*Also, H, HS, HT, M*] [*Poison gas US Chemical Corps symbol*]
HD .... New York Helicopter [*ICAO designator*] (AD)
HDA .... Hail Detection Algorithm [*Marine science*] (OSRA)
HDA .... Halopredone Diacetate [*Endocrinology*]
HdA .... Handwoerterbuch des Deutschen Aberglaubens [*A publication*] (BJA)
HDA .... Harding Lake [*Alaska*] [*Seismograph station code, US Geological Survey*] (SEIS)
HDA .... Hardwood Distributors Association (EA)
HDA .... Harris Daishowa Australia Ltd. [*Commercial*] (EERA)
HDA .... Head Disk Assembly
HDA .... Headquarters, Department of the Army
HDA .... Heaviest Duty Available [*Motor vehicle specifications*]
HDA .... Heavy-Duty Amplifier
HDA .... Held for Detail Available (MCD)
HDA .... Heteroduplex Analysis (DMAA)
HDA .... Hexadecenyl Acetate [*Pheromone*] [*Organic chemistry*]
HDA .... Hexanediamine [*or Hexamethylenediamine*] [*Organic chemistry*]
HDA .... High-Density Acid
HDA .... High-Density Amorph [*Materials science*]
HDA .... High Duty Alloys Ltd.
HDA .... Higher Duties Allowance (ADA)
HDA .... Hispanic Dental Association (NTPA)
HDA .... Hodgkin's Disease Association [*British*] (DBA)
HDA .... Holddown Arm (KSC)
HDA .... Holistic Dental Association (EA)
HDA .... Honda [*Colombia*] [*Airport symbol*] (AD)
HDA .... Hong Kong Dragon Airlines Ltd. [*ICAO designator*] (FAAC)
HDA .... Horizontal Danger Angle [*Navigation*]
HDA .... Horticultural Dealers Association (EA)
HDA .... Hospital Doctors Association [*British*] (DBA)
HDA .... Housekeeping Data Acquisition (MCD)
HDA .... Housing and Development Administration [*New York City*]
HDA .... Housing Developers Association Ltd. [*British*] (BI)
HDA .... Huldra Silver [*Vancouver Stock Exchange symbol*]
HDA .... Huntington's Disease Association [*Australia*]
HDA .... Hydrodealkylation (EDCT)
HDA .... Hydrogen Diffusion Anode [*Electrochemistry*]
HDA .... Hydroxydopamine [*Also, HDM, OHDA*] [*Biochemistry*]
HDAC .... Dictionary of the Apostolic Church [*James Hasting*] [*A publication*] (BJA)
HDAC .... Headache (KSC)
HDAC .... Heavy-Duty Air Cylinder
HDAC .... High-Dose Cytarabine (STED)
HDAC .... Histone Deacetylase [*An enzyme*]
HDAg .... Hepatitis Delta Antigen [*Immunology*]
HDAI .... Huntington's Disease Association of Ireland (BUAC)
HDAL .... Hexadecenal [*Pheromone*] [*Organic chemistry*]
HDAM .... Hierarchical Direct Access Method [*Computer science*] (MCD)
HDAP .... Heavy-Duty Automatic Press
HDARAC ...... High Dose Cytarabine [*Medicine*] (DMAA)
HDAS .... Hardened Digital Data Acquisition System [*US Army Waterways Experiment Station*] (RDA)
HDAS .... Historical Dictionary of American Slang [*Random House*]
HDAS .... Home Deposit Assistance Scheme [*Australia*]
HDAS .... House Defense Appropriations Subcommittee [*US Congress*] (AAG)
HDAS .... Hybrid Data Acquisition System
HDAS .... Hydrographic Data Acquisition System
HDASHY ..... Haberdashery
HDATA .... Hydrogene Data [*National College of Chemistry of Paris*] [*France*] [*Information service or system*] (IID)
HDATZ .... High-Density Air Traffic Zone

HdAW .... Handbuch der Altertumswissenschaft [*A publication*] (BJA)
HDB .... [*A*] Dictionary of the Bible [*James Hasting*] [*A publication*] (BJA)
HDB .... Hamper, Deritend, Birmingham [*Pseudonym used by William Hamper*]
HDB .... Health Database Plus [*Information Access Co.*] [*Information service or system*] (PCM)
HDB .... Herpes-Dissociated Buffer [*Medicine*]
HDB .... High-Density Binary (TEL)
HDB .... High Density Bipolar (NITA)
HDB .... High-Density Bipolar Code [*Telecommunications*] (TEL)
HDB .... Horizontal Dynamic Balancing
HDB .... Hunter Development Board [*Australia*]
HDB3 .... High-Density Binary Three Level Signal (TEL)
HDB-3 .... High-Density Bipolar-3 (IDOE)
HDBA .... Horizontal Dynamic Balancing Adjustment
HDBD .... Hydroxybutyric Dehydrogenase [*An enzyme*] (DAVI)
HDBF .... Heavy Duty Business Forum (EA)
HDBH .... Hydroxybutyric Dehydrogenase [*Clinical chemistry*] (CPH)
HDBK .... Handbook (AFM)
hdbk .... Handbook (WDMC)
HDBMS .... Hierarchical Database Management System
HDC .... Claremont Men's College, Claremont, CA [*OCLC symbol*] (OCLC)
HDC .... Half Double Crochet
HDC .... Harbor Defense Command [*Army*]
HDC .... Harry Diamond Center [*Army*]
HDC .... Hasselblad Data Camera (MCD)
HDC .... Hawaiian Defense Command
HDC .... Heavy-Duty Contractor (MCD)
HDC .... Helicopter Direction Center
HDC .... Hierarchical Distributed Control [*Computer science*]
HDC .... High Dirt Capacity [*A type of filter*] [*Pall Trinity Micro Corp.*]
HDC .... High Duty Cycle (IAA)
HDC .... Histidine Decarboxylase [*An enzyme*]
HDC .... Holder in Due Course [*Owner or holder of a negotiable instrument at some future time*]
HDC .... Holston Defense Corp. (MCD)
HDC .... Hospital Data Center [*American Hospital Association*] [*Information service or system*] (IID)
HDC .... Hough Development Corp. [*Cleveland*]
HDC .... Housing Development Corp. (EA)
HDC .... Human Diploid Cell [*Cytology*] (DAVI)
HDC .... Hungarian Data Center [*Defunct*] (EA)
HDC .... Hybrid Device Controller (NASA)
HDC .... Hydrodynamic Chromatography
HDC .... Hydrogen Depolarized Carbon Dioxide Concentrator (OA)
HDC .... Hypodermoclysis (STED)
HDCCAMS.... High-Dose Cyclophosphamide and Adriamycin [*Antineoplastic drug regimen*] (DAVI)
HDCD........... High Definition Compatible Digital [*Compact-disc technology*] (PS)
HDCES......... Hot/Dry Clothing and Equipment System [*Army*] (INF)
HDCG........... Dictionary of Christ and the Gospels [*James Hasting*] [*A publication*] (BJA)
HDCG........... Honorable Discharge, Convenience of Government [*Military*]
HDCH........... Headache
HDCM.......... Honorable Discharge, Convenience of Man [*Military*]
HDCO........... Hadco Corp. [*NASDAQ symbol*] (NQ)
HDCOL......... Hand Colored (VRA)
HDCR........... Hard Chromium
HDCR(R) or (T)... Higher Award in Radiodiagnosis or Radiotherapy, College of Radiographers [*British*] (DBQ)
HDCS .... Human Diploid Cell Strains [*Immunology*]
HDCS .... Human Diploid Cell System (STED)
HDCSV......... Human Diploid Cell Strain Vaccine [*Medicine*] (DB)
HDCV .... Human Diploid Cell Vaccine [*For rabies*]
HDD .... Halogenated Dibenzodioxin [*Organic chemistry*]
HDD .... Hard Disk Drive [*Computer science*]
HDD .... Head-Down Display [*Aviation*]
HDD .... Headsdown Display
HDD .... Heating Degree Days [*Agriculture*]
HDD .... Heavy-Duty Detergent
HDD .... Heavy-Duty Diesel [*Vehicle*]
HDD .... Heavy Duty Distribution [*A publication*]
HDD .... High-Density Data (KSC)
HDD .... High-Dosage Depth [*Medicine*] (DMAA)
HDD .... Higher Dental Diploma [*British*]
HDD .... Homopolar Disk Dynamo
HDD .... Human Disorientation Device
HDD .... Hyderabad [*Pakistan*] [*Airport symbol*] (OAG)
HDD .... Hydrogen Donor Diluents [*Petroleum chemistry*]
HDDA .... Hexadecadienyl Acetate [*Pheromone*] [*Organic chemistry*]
HDDA .... Hexanediol Diacrylate [*Also, HDODA*] [*Organic chemistry*]
HDDE........... Heavy-Duty Diesel Engine [*Motor vehicle specifications*]
HD-DI........... Heavy-Duty Direct Injection [*Diesel engines*]
HDDP........... Honorable Discharge, Dependency Existing Prior to Enlistment [*Military*]
HDDP........... Hospital Discharge Demonstration Project (EDAC)
HDDR........... High-Density Digital Recording
HDDS .... High-Density Data System [*Computer science*]
HDDS .... Honorable Discharge, Dependency Arising Since Enlistment [*Military*]
HDDT........... High-Density Digital Tape
HDDV........... Heavy-Duty Diesel Vehicle
HDE .... Heavy Duty Engine [*Automotive engineering*]
HDE .... High-Dose Epinephrine [*Medicine*]
HDE .... Holdrege, NE [*Location identifier FAA*] (FAAL)
HDE .... Homogeneous Differential Equation

HDEC .... Holocaust Documentation and Education Center (EA)
HDED .... Heavy-Duty Enzyme Detergent
HDEE .... Honorable Discharge, Expiration of Enlistment [*Military*]
HDEG .... Union List of Higher Degree Theses in Australian Libraries [*University of Tasmania Library*] [*Australia Information service or system*] (CRD)
HDeH .... Hawker De Havilland [*Australia*]
HDEP .... High Definition Electronic Production (NTCM)
HDEP .... High-Density Electronic Packaging
HDES .... Hydrodynamic Equilibrium System [*For chromatography*]
HDEU .... Heating and Domestic Engineers' Union [*British*]
HDF .... Haitian Development Fund [*Later, MH*] (EA)
HDF .... Halogenated Dibenzofuran [*Organic chemistry*]
HDF .... Handle Door Fastener
HDF .... Hartmann Dispersion Formula
HDF .... Hereditary Disease Foundation (EA)
HDF .... Hierarchical Data Format [*Computer science*]
HDF .... High-Density Flexible
HDF .... High-Frequency Direction Finding [*Electronics*]
HDF .... Horizontal Distributing Frame
HDF .... Host Defensive Factor [*Immunology*] (AAMN)
HDF .... Hubble Deep Field [*Astronomy*]
HDF .... Human Diploid Fibroblasts [*Cytology*]
H/DF .... Human/Dolphin Foundation (EA)
HDF .... Hungarian Democratic Forum [*Political party*] (EY)
HDFP .... Hypertension Detection and Follow-Up Program [*NHLBI*]
HDFRZ .... Hard Freeze [*NWS*] (FAAC)
HDG .... Halsey Drug [*AMEX symbol*] (TTSB)
HDG .... Halsey Drug Co. [*AMEX symbol*] (CTT)
HDG .... Heading (AFM)
HDG .... Heavy-Duty Gasoline [*Vehicle*]
HDG .... High-Dose Group [*Medicine*] (DMAA)
HDG .... Hot Dip Galvanization
HDGA .... Hot Dip Galvanizers Association [*British*] (BI)
HDGAF .... Hot Dip Galvanizing After Fabrication [*Metallurgy*]
HDGCP .... Human Dimensions of Global Change Programme [*Canada*] (EAIO)
HDGEC .... Human Dimensions of Global Environmental Change (EERA)
HDGECP .... Human Dimensions of Global Environmental Change Program [*Marine science*] (OSRA)
HDGP .... High-Drag General-Purpose [*Navy*] (DNAB)
HDGS .... High Dollar Group Sort (EBF)
HDG SEL ...... Heading Select (GAVI)
HDGV .... Heavy Duty Gasoline-Powered Vehicle (COE)
HDH .... Hauptverband der Deutschen Holz und Kunststoffe Verarbeitenden Industrie und Verwandter Industriezweige eV [*Germany*] (EY)
HDH .... Heart Disease History [*Medicine*] (MAE)
HDH .... Hemihydrate-Dihydrate [*Chemical technology*]
HDH .... Histidinol Dehydrogenase [*An enzyme*]
HDH .... Howden [*D. H.*] & Co. Ltd. [*Toronto Stock Exchange symbol*]
HDH .... Hydrocracking-Distillation-Hydrotreatment (ECON)
HDH .... Hydrogen Dehydrogenase [*An enzyme*]
HDH .... Mokuleia, HI [*Location identifier FAA*] (FAAL)
HDHD .... Hilf Du Heilige Dreifaltigkeit [*Help Thou Holy Trinity*] [*Motto of Johann Georg I, Prince of Anhalt-Dessau (1567-1618)*] [*German*]
HD/HE .... Hospital Design/Hospital Equipment [*British*]
HDHL .... High-Density Helicopter Landing [*Army*]
HDHQ .... Hostility and Direction of Hostility Questionnaire [*Psychology*]
HDHS .... Haul Down and Handling System [*Canadian Navy*]
HD-HT .... Hemodilution Combined with Hypotension
HDHVPS .... High-Density/High-Voltage Power Supply (DNAB)
HDI .... Cleveland, TN [*Location identifier FAA*] (FAAL)
HDI .... Hamilton Depression Inventory [*Test*] (TMMY)
HDI .... Hard Drives International (PCM)
HDI .... Harley-Davidson [*NYSE symbol*] (TTSB)
HDI .... Harley-Davidson, Inc. [*NYSE symbol*] (SPSG)
HDI .... Hawaiian Development Irradiator [*AEC*]
HDI .... Head-Disc Interference [*Head crash*] (NITA)
HDI .... Headquarters Operating Instruction
HDI .... Heavy-Duty Industrial [*Internal combustion engines*]
HDI .... Heidi Device Interface
HDI .... Helicopter Direction Inbound [*Military*] (CAAL)
HDI .... Hemorrhagic Disease of Infants [*Medicine*] (DMAA)
HDI .... Henry Dunant Institute [*Switzerland*] (BUAC)
HDI .... Hexamethylene Diisocyanate [*Organic chemistry*]
HDI .... High Definition Imaging
HDI .... High-Density Interconnect
HDI .... Horizontal Display Indicator (NG)
HDI .... Hoteles Dinamicos SA de CV [*Mexico ICAO designator*] (FAAC)
HDI .... House Dress Institute (EA)
HDI .... Household Disposable Income
HDI .... Human Development Index [*Human Development Report*] [*United Nations Development Program*]
HDI .... Human Development Institute
HDIE .... Healthdyne Info Enterprises [*NASDAQ symbol*] (TTSB)
HDIF .... Heavy-Duty Industrial Filter
HDIL .... Health and Drug Information Library
HDIP .... Hazardous Duty Incentive Pay [*Air Force*] (AFM)
HDIP .... High Density Integrated Processor
HDIP .... High-Dose Immunological Paralysis [*Medicine*]
H Dip E .... Higher Diploma in Education [*British*]
HDipEd .... Higher Diploma in Education [*Academic degree*] (AIE)
HDipT .... Higher Diploma of Teaching
HDIR .... Heavy-Duty Industrial Relay
H Dist Ct ..... United States District Court, District of Hawaii (DLA)
HDIT .... Hereditament [*Legal shorthand*] (LWAP)

HDIT .... Home Drug Infusion Therapy [*Medicine*]
HDIV .... Hughes Dynamic Imagery Viewer
HDK .... Hidaka [*Japan*] [*Seismograph station code, US Geological Survey*] (SEIS)
HDK .... Husband Doesn't Know (IIA)
HDKF .... Handkerchief
HDL .... Handel Society [*Record label*]
HDL .... Handle (KSC)
HDL .... Handleman Co. [*NYSE symbol*] (SPSG)
HDL .... Hardware Description Language [*Computer science*]
HDL .... Harry Diamond Laboratories [*Formerly, DOFL*] [*Adelphi, MD*] [*Army*]
HDL .... Headline (WGA)
HDL .... Hidalgo County Library System, McAllen, TX [*OCLC symbol*] (OCLC)
HDL .... High-Density Lipoprotein [*Biochemistry*]
HDL .... Holdenville, OK [*Location identifier FAA*] (FAAL)
HDL .... Hydrologic Data Laboratory [*Agricultural Research Service*] (PDAA)
HDLA .... High-Level Data Link Control Adapter [*Data communication*] (MHDI)
HDLC .... Hierarchical Data Link [*Computer science*] (CIST)
HDL-C .... High-Density Lipoprotein - Cell Surface Receptor [*Biochemistry*]
HDLC .... High-Density Lipoprotein Cholesterol [*Physiology*]
HDL-C .... High Density Lipoprotein Fraction [*Biochemistry*] (DAVI)
HDLC .... High-Level Data Link Control [*International Standards Organization*] [*Data communication*]
HDLD .... Heavy-Duty Liquid Detergent
HDLE .... Hurdle
HDLG .... Handling (AABC)
HDLM .... High-Level Data Linkage Module [*Data communication*] (MHDB)
HDLNR .... Headliner
HDLP .... High-Density Lipoprotein [*Biochemistry*] (AAMN)
HDLP .... Holdup [*FBI standardized term*]
HDLR .... Handler (AABC)
HDLR .... Hexadecimal Symbolic Loader [*Computer science*] (MHDI)
HDLS .... Hardware Description Language System (IAA)
HDLS .... Headless (KSC)
HDLW .... Distance at Which a Watch Is Heard with Left Ear [*Medicine*]
HDM .... Haddam [*Connecticut*] [*Seismograph station code, US Geological Survey*] (SEIS)
HDM .... Hamadan [*Iran*] [*Airport symbol*] (AD)
HDM .... Hand-Deboned Meat
HDM .... Harmonic Distortion Meter (DEN)
HDM .... Hexadimethrine (STED)
HDM .... Hierarchical Development Method [*Computer science*]
HDM .... High-Density Microsome [*Cytology*]
HDM .... Hizbia Dighill e Mirifle [*Somali political party*]
HDM .... Hot Dark Matter [*Astronomy*]
HDM .... House Dust Mite
HDM .... Hudson & Manhattan [*AAR code*]
HDM .... Humic Degradation Matter (DICI)
HDM .... Hydrodemetalation [*Petroleum refining*]
HDM .... Hydrodynamic Machining [*Manufacturing term*]
HDM .... Hydrodynamic Modulation
HDM .... Hydroxydopamine [*Also, HDA, OHDA*] [*Biochemistry*]
HDMA .... Hardwood Dimension Manufacturers Association [*Later, NDMA*] (EA)
HDMA .... Heavy Duty Manufacturers' Association
HDMC .... Helicopter Depot Maintenance Center (MCD)
HDMCC .... Howdy Doody Memorabilia Collectors Club (EA)
HDMI .... High-Density Multichip Interconnect [*Semiconductor packaging*]
HDML .... Handheld Device Markup Language [*Computer science*] (PCM)
HDML .... Harbor Defense Motor Launch [*NATO*] (NATG)
HDMP .... High-Dose Methylprednisolone (STED)
HDMP .... Horizon Definition Measurement Program (DNAB)
HDMR .... High-Density Moderated Reactor (IEEE)
HDMR .... High-Density Multitrack Recording (MCD)
HDMS .... High-Density Memory System
HDMS .... High-Density MODEM System [*Microcom*] [*Norwood, MA*] [*Computer science*]
HDMS .... Hizb Dastur Mustaghil Somalia [*Somali Independent Constitution Party*]
HDMS .... Honeywell Distributed Manufacturing System (NITA)
HDMS .... Honorable Discharge, Medical Survey [*Military*]
HDMSW .... High-Density Mach Shock Wave
HDMT .... High-Density Multi-Track
HDMTX .... High Dose Methotrexate [*Antineoplastic drug regimen*]
HDMTX-CF ... High-Dose Methotrexate-Citrovorum Factor [*Antineoplastic drug regimen*]
HDMTX-LV ... High-Dose Methotrexate, Leucovorin [*Antineoplastic drug regimen*]
HDMU .... Honorable Discharge, under Age of Authorized Consent [*Military*]
HDMW .... Honorable Discharge, Minors Enlisted without Consent, under Eighteen at Discharge [*Military*]
HDN .... Harden (KSC)
HDN .... Hayden, CO [*Location identifier FAA*] (FAAL)
HDN .... Hemolytic Disease of the Newborn [*Medicine*]
Hdn .... Herodianus [*Greek scholar, c. 200AD*] [*Classical studies*] (OCD)
HDN .... High-Density Nebulizer [*Medicine*] (MAE)
HDN .... Hildon Mining [*Vancouver Stock Exchange symbol*]
HDN .... Hydrodenitrogenation [*of chemical compounds*]
HDN .... Steamboat Springs [*Colorado*] [*Airport symbol Obsolete*] (OAG)
hDNA .... Deoxyribonucleic Acid, heteroduplex [*Biochemistry, genetics*]
hDNA .... Deoxyribonucleic Acid, Histone [*Biochemistry, genetics*]
HDNA .... Habonim Dror North America (EA)
HDNA .... Hinged Deoxyribonucleic Acid [*Biochemistry, genetics*]
HDNG .... Hardinge, Inc. [*NASDAQ symbol*] (SAG)
HDNPRSGR ... Headquarters Squadron Personnel Group
HDNS .... Hardness (MSA)
HDNSW .... High-Density Nuclear Shock Wave

HDNT	Headnote
HdO	Handbuch der Orientalistik [*Leiden*] [*A publication*] (BJA)
HDO	Harbor Defence Only [*Military*] (WDAA)
HDO	Helicopter Direction Outbound [*Military*] (CAAL)
HDO	Hondo, TX [*Location identifier FAA*] (FAAL)
HDOC	Handy Dandy Orbital Computer (IEEE)
HDOC	House Document
HDOCP	Heavy-Duty Oil Classification Panel [*Automotive engineering*]
HDODA	Hexanediol Diacrylate [*Also, HDDA*] [*Organic chemistry*]
HDOL	Hexadecenol [*Pheromone*] [*Organic chemistry*]
HDOP	Horizontal Dilution of Precision
HDOS	Hard Disk Operating System
HDOT	Inertial Vertical Speed (GAVI)
HDOV	Hardover
HDP	Hankyore Democratic Party [*South Korea Political party*] (EY)
HDP	Harpoon Data Processor [*Missiles*] (MCD)
HDP	Hearing Dog Project [*Later, HDRC*] (EA)
HDP	Hexose Diphosphate [*Biochemistry*]
HDP	Hiburd Properties [*Vancouver Stock Exchange symbol*]
HDP	High Delta Pressure (COE)
HDP	High-Density Plasma (SAA)
HDP	High-Density Polyethylene (STED)
HDP	High Detonation Pressure
HDP	High-Discharge Pressure (IEEE)
HDP	Holddown Post (NASA)
HDP	Horizontal Data Processing
HDP	Housing Development Program
HDP	Huer Demokrat Parti [*Free Democrat Party*] [*Turkish Cyprus*] [*Political party*] (EY)
HDP	Human Dimension of Global Environmental Change Programme [*The International Social Science Council*] (ECON)
HDP	Huntington's Disease Protein [*Biochemistry*]
HDP	Hydrostatic Deformation Potent (AAEL)
HDP	Hydroxydimethylpyrimidine [*Organic chemistry*]
HDPAA	Heparin-Dependent Platelet-Associated Antibody [*Medicine*] (DMAA)
HDPC	Health Data Policy Committee [*Department of Health and Human Services*] (GFGA)
HDPE	High-Density Polyethylene [*Plastics*]
HDPPA	Housing Development and Public Participation Administration [*Turkey*] (ECON)
HDPS	High-Density Power Supply
HDQ	Headquarters [*Colorado*] [*Seismograph station code, US Geological Survey Closed*] (SEIS)
HDQR	Headquarters
HDQRS	Headquarters
HDQTRS	Headquarters (NASA)
HDR	Hair's Daily Requirement [*Brand of shampoo*]
HDR	Hand Rail
HDR	Hardening Design Responses
HDR	Header [*Automotive engineering*]
HDR	[*File*] Header Label [*Computer science*] (ECII)
HDR	Health Data Recorder [*Computer science*] (PDAA)
HDR	High Data Rate
HDR	High Data Register
HDR	High Definition RADAR
HDR	High-Density Recorder [*Deep Space Instrumentation Facility, NASA*]
HDR	High Density Recording (NITA)
HDR	High Dose Rate [*Medicine*] (DMAA)
HDR	Holddown and Release (AAG)
HDR	Home Dockyard Regulations [*Navy*] (MCD)
H-Dr	Horse-Drawn [*Obsolete Army*]
HDR	Hot Dry Rock [*Geothermal science*]
HDR	Humanitarian Daily Ration [*Army*] (INF)
HDRA	Heavy Duty Representatives Association (EA)
HDRA	Henry Doubleday Research Association [*Coventry, England*] (EAIO)
HDRA	High-Data-Rate Assembly (MCD)
HDRA	High Desert Racing Association
HDRAA	Henry Doubleday Research Association of Australia
HDRANCE	Hindrance (ROG)
HDRC	Hearing Dog Resource Center (EA)
HDRF	Heart Disease Research Foundation (EA)
HDRI	Hannah Dairy Research Institute [*British*] (BI)
HDRL	High-Data-Rate LASER (MCD)
HDRM	High-Data-Rate Multiplexer (MCD)
HDRO	House Democratic Research Organization [*Defunct*] (EA)
HD-ROM	High Density-Read-Only Memory [*Computer science*]
HDRR	High-Data Rate Recorder
HDRR	Holloman Development Research Report [*Air Force*] (MCD)
HDRS	Hamilton Depression Rate Scale [*Psychiatry*] (DAVI)
HDRS	High-Data Rate Switch (MCD)
HDRSS	High-Data-Rate Storage System [*or Subsystem*] [*NASA*] (MCD)
HDRV	Human Diploid-Cell Rabies Vaccine
HDRW	Distance at Which a Watch Is Heard with Right Ear [*Medicine*]
HDRW	Hearing Distance, Right, Watch [*Distance from which watch ticking is heard by right ear*] (STED)
HDS	Handicapped Driving Systems [*Burnsville, MN*]
HDS	Hardware Description Sheet (NASA)
HDS	HDS Network Systems, Inc. [*Associated Press*] (SAG)
HDS	Head of Defence Sales [*British*] (RDA)
HDS	Heads [*Automotive engineering*]
HDS	Head Set [*Telecommunications*] (TEL)
HDS	Health and Diet Survey [*Department of Health and Human Services*] (GFGA)
HDS	Help Desk Services

HDS	Herbicide Delivery Systems [*Aquatic Plant Control Research Program*] [*Army Corps of Engineers*]
HDS	Herdis International Canada, Inc. [*Vancouver Stock Exchange symbol*]
HDS	Hermes Data System [*Hermes Precisa International*] (NITA)
HDS	Herniated Disc Syndrome [*Medicine*]
HDS	Hills Department Stores, Inc. [*NYSE symbol*] (SPSG)
HDS	Hills Stores [*NYSE symbol*] (TTSB)
HDS	Hills Stores Co. [*NYSE symbol*] (SAG)
HDS	Historical Data System [*Air Force*] (MCD)
HDS	Historical Diving Society (BUAC)
HDS	History of Dermatology Society (EA)
HDS	Holographic Diffractive Structure [*Advanced Environmental Research Group*]
HDS	Holy Days of Obligation [*Roman Catholicism*] (ROG)
HDS	Hospital Discharge Survey [*Public Health Service*]
HDS	Household Delivery Service [*British Post Office facility*] (DCTA)
HDS	Hrvatski Demokratski Stranka [*Croatian Democratic Party*] [*Political party*] (EY)
HDS	Humungous Development Syndrome (EERA)
HDS	Hybrid Development System
HDS	Hydrodesulfurization
HDS	Hydrogen Detection System
HDS	Office of Human Development Services [*Department of Health and Human Services*]
HDSA	Huntington's Disease Society of America (EA)
HDSB	Heavy Dry Support Bridge [*Army*] (RDA)
HDSC	Harpoon Data System Cabinet [*Missiles*] (MCD)
HdSchm	Head Schoolmaster [*Navy British*]
HDSCS	Hospital Disaster Support Communications System
HDSD	Hydrogen Defect Shallow Donors (AAEL)
HD(S)E	Home Defence Security Executive [*British World War II*]
HDSHK	Handshake [*Computers*] (MSA)
HDSL	High Bit Rate Digital Subscriber Line [*Computer science*] (CDE)
HDSL	High-Data-Rate Digital Subscriber Line [*Telecommunications*] (DOM)
HDSL	High-Speed Digital Subscriber Loop [*Computer science*]
HDSN	Hudson Technologies Inc. [*NASDAQ symbol*] (TTSB)
HDSN	Hudson Technology, Inc. [*NASDAQ symbol*] (SAG)
HDS-NA	High Definition System for North America
HDS Nt	HDS Network Systems, Inc. [*Associated Press*] (SAG)
HDSP	Hardship (AABC)
HDSPr	Hills Stores Sr'A' Cv Pfd [*NYSE symbol*] (TTSB)
HDSR	Historical Data Storage and Retrieval
HDSS	Holographic Data Storage System
HDST	Headset (MCD)
HDST	Headstart [*Education*] (OICC)
HDST	High-Density Shock Tube (IEEE)
HDSVLY	Hudson Valley (FAAC)
HDSW	Handwoerterbuch der Sozialwissenschaft [*Dictionary of the Social Sciences*] [*A publication*]
HDSX	HDS Network Systems [*NASDAQ symbol*] (TTSB)
HDSX	HDS Network Systems, Inc. [*NASDAQ symbol*] (SAG)
HDSXW	HDS Network Sys Wrrt [*NASDAQ symbol*] (TTSB)
HDT	Half Duplex Teletype (KSC)
HDT	Hard Disk ToolKIT [*Computer science*]
HDT	Heat Deflection Temperature [*of plastics*]
HDT	Heat Distortion Temperature
HDT	Heavy-Duty Thermoplastic Insulation [*Automotive engineering*]
HDT	Heavy Duty Truck [*Environmental Protection Agency*]
Hdt	Herodotus [*Greek historian, c. 484BC*] [*Classical studies*] (OCD)
HDT	Hexadecanethiol [*Organic chemistry*]
HDT	Hexamethylene Diisocyanate (EDCT)
HDT	Hi-Pot Dwell Time
HDT	Host Digital Terminal [*Telecommunications*] (ACRL)
HDT	Humboldt, TN [*Location identifier FAA*] (FAAL)
HDT	Hydrotreating [*or Hydrotreated*] [*Petroleum technology*]
HDTA	High-Density Traffic Airport
HDTC	Healthdyne Technologies [*NASDAQ symbol*] (SAG)
HDTC	Heavy Duty Transient Cycle
HDTCS	Hexadecyltrichlorosilane [*Organic chemistry*]
HDTM	Half-Duplex Transmission Module [*Telecommunications*] (ACRL)
HDTMA	Heavy-Duty Truck Manufacturers Association (EA)
HDTMA	Hexadecyltrimethylammonium
HDTV	High-Definition Television [*Offers wider-screen pictures with high resolution that improves their depth, clarity, and detail*]
HDU	Hard Disc Unit (NITA)
HDU	Heads-Up Display Unit [*Aviation*] (RDA)
HDU	Hemodialysis Unit [*Medicine*]
HDU	High Dependency Unit [*Medicine*] (DMAA)
HDU	Home Defence Unit [*British military*] (DMA)
HDU	Hose Down Unit (DOMA)
HDU	Hyde Park [*Utah*] [*Seismograph station code, US Geological Survey*] (SEIS)
HDUE	High Dynamic User Equipment
HDUR	Hungarian Democratic Union of Romania [*Political party*] (BUAC)
HDV	Halt Device (IAA)
HDV	Heavy Duty Vehicle [*Environmental Protection Agency*]
HDV	Hepatitis Delta Virus
HDV	Hepatitis D Virus [*Medicine*] (DMAA)
HDV	Hepatocyte-Directed Vesicle (DB)
HDV	High-Definition Video
HDV	High-Dollar Value
HDV	Horse-Drawn Vehicle
HDV	Hydrodevanadization [*Petroleum technology*]
HDV	Hydrodynamic Voltammogram [*Electrochemistry*]

HDV	Hydrodynamic Volume [*Physical chemistry*]
HD Vest	H. D. Vest, Inc. [*Associated Press*] (SAG)
HDVIP	Heavy-Duty Vehicle Inspection Program
HDVS	H.D.Vest [*NASDAQ symbol*] (TTSB)
HDVS	High Definition Video System
HDVS	Vest [*H.D.*], Inc. [*NASDAQ symbol*] (SPSG)
HDW	Hard-Drawn Wire [*Metallurgy*] (IAA)
HDW	Hardware [*Computer science*] (KSC)
HDW	Hearing Distance with Watch [*Medicine*]
HDW	High-Pressure Demineralized Water (NRCH)
HDW	Hydrodynamic Welding
HDWA	Hardware [*Computer science*] (IAA)
HDWA	Health Department of Western Australia
HDWC	Hardware Cloth
HDWD	Hardwood
HDWE	Hardware
hdwe	Hardware (VRA)
HDWND	Headwind (FAAC)
HDWR	Hardware
HDWRE	Hardware (WGA)
HDWS	How Do We Stand
Hdwt	Hundredweight
HDWY	Headway Corporate Resources
HDWY	Headway Corporate Resources, Inc. [*NASDAQ symbol*] (SAG)
HDWY	Hideaway
HDX	Half Duplex [*Telecommunications*] (NITA)
HDX	Half Duplex Transmission [*Data communication*]
HDX	Hand-Held Dental X-Ray (RDA)
HDY	Haadyai [*Thailand*] [*Airport symbol*] (OAG)
HDY	Heavy-Duty
HDYN	Healthdyne, Inc. [*NASDAQ symbol*] (NQ)
HDZ	Croatian Democratic Union [*Political party*] (BUAC)
HDZ	Hrvatska Demokratska Zajednica [*Croatian Democratic Union*] [*Political party*] (EY)
HDZNV	De Handschriften van de Dode Zee in Nederlandse Vertaling [*Amsterdam*] [*A publication*] (BJA)
HE	Altitude Error (GAVI)
HE	Green Bay Aviation [*ICAO designator*] (AD)
HE	Hall Effect [*Electromagnetism*] (OA)
HE	Handling Equipment
HE	Hard Exudate [*Ophthalmology*] (DAVI)
HE	Hardware Evaluator [*NASA*]
HE	Hardware Executive
HE	Hawaiian Elec Indus [*NYSE symbol*] (TTSB)
HE	Hawaiian Electric Industries, Inc. [*NYSE symbol*] (SPSG)
he	Head [*Anatomy*] (DAVI)
HE	Head End
HE	Header Extension [*Telecommunications*] (ACRL)
HE	Hearing Examiner [*Also, ALJ*]
HE	Hearsay Evidence [*Legal shorthand*] (LWAP)
He	Heart (DMAA)
HE	Heat Engine
HE	Heat Exchange [*or Exchanger*]
HE	Heavy Enamel (AAG)
HE	Heavy Equipment (AFM)
HE	[*The*] Hebrew [*A publication*] (BJA)
HE	Hebrews [*Old Testament book*]
He	Hedstrom Number [*Chemistry*] (DAVI)
HE	Height of Eye [*Navigation*]
HE	Heinkel [*German aircraft type*] [*World War II*]
HE	Hektoen Enteric Agar [*Medicine*] (DMAA)
HE	Helio Aircraft Co. [*ICAO aircraft manufacturer identifier*] (ICAO)
He	Helium [*Chemical element*]
HE	Hemagglutinating Encephalomyelitis [*Neurology*] (DAVI)
HE	Hematoxylin and Eosin [*Biological stain*]
HE	Hemicylindrical [*Leaf characteristic*] [*Botany*]
HE	Hemoglobin Electrophoresis [*Medicine*] (AAMN)
HE	Hepatic Encephalography [*Medicine*]
HE	Hepatic Encephalopathy [*Medicine*]
HE	Hepatic Extraction [*Endocrinology*]
HE	Hepatoma (DB)
HE	Hereditary Elliptocytosis [*Medicine*]
HE	Hexane-Extractable Compound
HE	Hic Est [*Here Is, That is, or This is*] [*Latin*]
HE	High Efficiency
HE	High Energy (MCD)
HE	High-Energy Astrophysics (NASA)
HE	Higher Education [*Educational Resources Information Center (ERIC) Clearinghouse*] [*George Washington University*] (PAZ)
HE	Higher Elongation (MCD)
HE	Highest Electroendosmosis [*Analytical biochemistry*]
HE	High Explosive (AAG)
HE	His Eminence
HE	His [*or Her*] Excellency
HE	Historia Ecclesiastica [*of Eusebius*] [*Classical studies*]
HE	Historical Period Ending Date [*Dialog*] [*Searchable field*] [*Information service or system*] (NITA)
HE	Hoc Est [*That Is or This Is*] [*Latin*]
HE	Hollis & Eastern Railroad Co. [*AAR code*]
HE	Hollow Enzyme [*Medicine*] (DMAA)
HE	Holy Empire [*Freemasonry*]
HE	Holy Eucharist
HE	Home Economics [*Secondary school course*] [*British*]
HE	Honda Engineering
HE	Horizontal Equivalent

HE	Horticultural Enterprise [*A publication*]
HE	House Error [*Publishing*] (WDMC)
HE	Housekeeping Element (TEL)
HE	Hub End (BARN)
HE	Human Engineering
HE	Human Enolase [*An enzyme*]
HE	Human Enteric [*Virology*]
HE	Human Error [*Environmental science*] (COE)
HE	Human Events [*A publication*] (BRI)
HE	Human Exposure Dose [*Medicine*]
HE	Hydraulics Engineer
HE	Hydroelectric (IAA)
HE	Hydrogen Embrittlement
HE	Hydromagnetic Emission (IAA)
HE	Hydrophone Effect [*Navy*] (NVT)
HE	Hydroxyecdysone [*Endocrinology*]
HE	Hygienic Effect
HE	Hygienic Electrician [*British*] (ROG)
HE	Hypo Eliminator [*Photography*] (DGA)
HE	Hypogonadotrophic Eunuchoidism [*Medicine*]
HE	Hypophysectomy [*Medicine*] (DAVI)
HEA	Centre des Hautes Etudes Americaines [*Paris*]
HEA	Hairdressing Employers Association (BUAC)
HEA	Health Education Authority [*British*]
HEA	Health Effects Assessment [*Environmental Protection Agency*] (AEPA)
HEA	Heating Engineering Association (BUAC)
HEA	Heliavia-Transporte Aereo Lda. [*Portugal ICAO designator*] (FAAC)
HEA	Hemorrhagic Arteries [*Veterinary medicine*]
HEA	Herat [*Afghanistan*] [*Airport symbol Obsolete*] (OAG)
HEA	Hexone-Extracted Acetone [*Chemistry*] (DAVI)
HEA	High-Efficiency Antireflection [*Optics*]
HEA	Higher Education Act [*1965*]
HEA	Higher Education Authority [*Ireland*] (AIE)
HEA	Higher Education Awards (ACII)
HEA	Hockey East Association (PSS)
HEA	Horticultural Education Association [*British*]
HEA	Horticulture Exhibitors Association [*British*] (DBA)
HEA	Hot Electron Amplifier
HEA	Human Erythrocyte Antigen [*Hematology*] (DAVI)
HEA	Hunter Education Association (EA)
HEA	Hydroxyethyl Acrylate [*Organic chemistry*]
HEAA	Higher Education Act Amendment [*1992*]
HEAA	High-Explosive, Antiaircraft [*Weaponry*]
HEAA	High-Explosive, Antiarmor [*Weaponry*] (MCD)
HEAA	Home Economics Association for Australia (BUAC)
HEAA	Home Economics Association of Africa (BUAC)
HEAC	Higher Education Accommodation Consortium [*British*] (DBA)
HEAD	Hand-Held Encryption and Authentication Device (RDA)
Head	Head's Tennessee Supreme Court Reports [*1858-59*] [*A publication*] (DLA)
HEAD	Helium-Atom Diffraction (PDAA)
HEADCOM	Headquarters Command [*Military*]
HEADE	High Erucic Acid Development Effort
HEADSS	Helicopter Escort, Air Defense Suppression System
Head (Tenn)	Head's Tennessee Reports [*38-40 Tennessee*] [*A publication*] (DLA)
Headway	Headway Corporate Resources, Inc. [*Associated Press*] (SAG)
HEAE	Hyperacute Experimental Autoimmune Encephalomyelitis [*Medicine*] (PDAA)
HEAF	Heavy End Aviation Fuel
HEAF	Higher Education Assistance Foundation
HEAF	High Explosives Application Facility
HEAFS	High-Explosive Anti-Tank Fin-Stabilized [*Military*] (PDAA)
HEAL	Health Education Assistance Loan [*Bureau of Health Professions*]
HEAL	Healthwatch, Inc. [*NASDAQ symbol*] (NQ)
HEAL	Human Ecology Action League (EA)
HEAL	Human Exposure Assessment Location [*Environmental Protection Agency*] (GFGA)
HEALD	Healthwatch Inc. [*NASDAQ symbol*] (TTSB)
Heal JS Comp	Healy on Joint Stock Companies [*A publication*] (DLA)
Heal Pews	Heale's Law of Church Pews [*A publication*] (DLA)
HEALS	Honeywell Error Analysis and Logging System
HealSB	Health Standards Board
HEALT	Helicopter Employment and Assault Landing Table (NVT)
HEALTH	Happiness, Energy, and Longevity through Health [*Title of 1979 film directed by Robert Altman*]
Health & SC	Health and Safety Code [*A publication*] (DLA)
HEALTHLINE	Health Planning and Administration [*National Library of Medicine*] [*Database*]
HEAMF	Hydroxyethylated Acid Modified Flour (OA)
HEANET	Higher Education Authority Network [*Irish*] [*Computer science*] (TNIG)
HEAO	High-Energy Astronomy Observatory [*Pronounced "hee-oh"*] [*NASA*]
HEAP	Helicopter Extended Area Platform
HEAP	High-Energy Aim Point [*Weaponry*] (MCD)
HEAP	High-Explosive, Antipersonnel [*Weaponry*]
HEAP	High-Explosive Armor-Piercing [*Weaponry*]
HEAP	Hydrogen Electric Arc Pyrolysis (EDCT)
HEAPS	Hawaiian Environmental Analysis and Prediction System (MUGU)
HEAPS	High Energy Alpha-Proton Spectrometer (PDAA)
HEAR	El Arish/El Arish [*Egypt*] [*ICAO location identifier*] (ICLI)
HEAR	Health Associated Representatives [*Later, HIRA*] (EA)
HEAR	Hear Center (EA)
HEAR	Hearing

HEAR	Hearing Education and Awareness for Rockers [*An association*]
HEAR	Hearing Education through Auditory Research [*In association name, HEAR Center*] (EA)
HEAR	Hereafter (ROG)
HEAR	High Erucic Acid Rapeseed [*Agricultural chemistry*]
HEAR	Hospital Emergency Ambulance Radio (LAIN)
HEAR	Human Error Action Report [*NASA*] (KSC)
Heard Civ Pl	Heard's Civil Pleading [*A publication*] (DLA)
Heard Cr Pl	Heard's Criminal Pleading [*A publication*] (DLA)
Heard Cur Rep	Heard's Curiosities of the Law Reporters [*A publication*] (DLA)
Heard Eq Pl	Heard's Equity Pleading [*A publication*] (DLA)
Heard Lib & Sl	Heard on Libel and Slander [*A publication*] (DLA)
Heard's Shortt Extr Rem	Heard's Edition of Shortt on Extraordinary Legal Remedies [*A publication*] (DLA)
Hear Exam	Hearing Examiner [*Legal term*] (DLA)
HEAR-FOUND	Hearing, Educational Aid and Research Foundation [*Defunct*] (EA)
Hearnshaw	Southampton Court Leet Records [*A publication*] (DLA)
HEARS	Higher Education Administration Referral Service [*Defunct*] (EA)
HEART	Hardened Electronic and Radiation Technology
HEART	Hardened Electronics and Radiation Technology (MCD)
HEART	Health Equity and Access Reform Today [*Plan*]
HEART	Health Evaluation and Risk Tabulation (MCD)
HEART	Higher Education Action Research Team (AIE)
HEART	Household Employment Association for Reevaluation and Training [*Later, Personnel Resources*]
HEART	Hydrometer Erosion and Recession Test (MCD)
HEARTHFIRE	High-Energy Accelerator and Reactor for Thermonuclear Fusion with Ion Beams of Relativistic Energies
HeartInd	Heartland Partners Ltd. [*Associated Press*] (SAG)
Heartprt	Heartport, Inc. [*Associated Press*] (SAG)
Heartsong R	Heartsong Review [*A publication*] (BRI)
Heartst	Heartstream, Inc. [*Associated Press*] (SAG)
HeartTc	Heart Technology, Inc. [*Associated Press*] (SAG)
Hearx	Hearx Ltd. [*Associated Press*] (SAG)
HEAS	Home Energy Advisory Service [*Victoria, Australia*]
HEASDA	Home Economics Association of Seventh-Day Adventists (EA)
HEAST	Health Effects Assessment Summary Tables
HEAT	Asyut [*Egypt*] [*ICAO location identifier*] (ICLI)
HEAT	Helicopter External Air Transport (MCD)
HEAT	Helpdesk Expert Automation Tool [*Bendata Management Systems, Inc.*]
HEAT	High Energy Antimatter Telescope
HEAT	High-Enthalpy Ablation Test
HEAT	High Enthalpy Arc Tunnel [*NASA*]
HEAT	High-Explosive, Antitank [*Weaponry*]
HEAT	Human Erythrocyte Agglutination Test [*Hematology*]
HEAT	Petroleum Heat & Pwr'A' [*NASDAQ symbol*] (TTSB)
Heath	Heath's Reports [*36-40 Maine*] [*A publication*] (DLA)
HEATH	Higher Education and the Handicapped [*An association*] (EA)
Heath Max	Heath's Maxims [*A publication*] (DLA)
HEAT-MP	High-Explosive Antitank, Multipurpose [*Weaponry*] (MCD)
HEAT-MP-T	High-Explosive Antitank, Multipurpose, Tracer [*Weaponry*] (MCD)
HEAT-T	High-Explosive Antitank-Tracer [*Weaponry*] (AABC)
HEAT-TP	High-Explosive Antitank, Training Projectile [*Weaponry*] (MCD)
HEAT-TP-T	High-Explosive Antitank, Target Practice, Tracer [*Weaponry*] (MCD)
Heaven B	Heaven Bone
HEAVYPHOTORON	Heavy Photographic Squadron
HEAX	Alexandria [*Egypt*] [*ICAO location identifier*] (ICLI)
HEB	Handheld Electronic Book (TELE)
HEB	Hebraic [*Language, etc.*] (ROG)
heb	Hebrew [*MARC language code Library of Congress*] (LCCP)
HEB	Hebrew
Heb	Hebrews [*New Testament book*]
HEB	Heinemann Educational Books [*London, England*]
HEB	Hematoencephalic Barrier [*or Blood brain barrier*] [*Medicine*] (DAVI)
HEB	Hepar Embryonis Bovis [*Embryonic bovine liver cells used in tissue culture studies of viruses*] [*Medicine*]
HEB	Hollow Electron Beam
HEBA	Home Extension Building Association (BUAC)
HEBAH	Heat Engine/Battery Hybrid (PDAA)
HEBBLE	High-Energy Benthic Boundary Layer Experiment [*Oceanography*]
HEBC	Heavy Enamel Bonded Cotton [*Wire insulation*]
HEBD	Hebdomada [*A Week*] [*Pharmacy*] (ROG)
HEBDC	Heavy Enamel Bonded Double Cotton [*Wire insulation*] (AAG)
HEBDOM	Hebdomada [*A Week*] [*Pharmacy*]
hebdom	Hebdomada [*First Week of Life*] [*Latin*] (STED)
HEBDP	Heavy Enamel Bonded Double Paper [*Wire insulation*] (AAG)
HEBDS	Heavy Enamel Bonded Double Silk [*Wire insulation*] (AAG)
HEBE	Higher Education Business Enterprises Ltd. (AIE)
HEBL	Abu Simbel [*Egypt*] [*ICAO location identifier*] (ICLI)
HEBP	Heavy Enamel Bonded Paper [*Wire insulation*]
Hebr	Hebraic (BJA)
HEBR	Hebrew
Hebrew C	Hebrew College (GAGS)
HEBS	Health Education Board for Scotland (BUAC)
HEBS	Heavy Enamel Bonded Silk [*Wire insulation*]
HEBS	High-Energy Battery System
HEBT	High-Energy Beam Transport [*For protons*]
HEC	Ecole des Hautes Etudes Commerciales, Bibliotheque [*UTLAS symbol*]
HEC	Hamster Embryo Cell (STED)
HEC	Hamster Embryonic Cell
HEC	Hardened Electronic Component
HEC	Harken Energy [*AMEX symbol*] (TTSB)
HEC	Harken Energy Co. [*AMEX symbol*] (SPSG)

HEC	Hasselblad Electric Camera
HEC	Hastings Environment Council (EERA)
HEC	Hautes Etudes Commerciales (DD)
HEC	Hazeltine Electronics Corp. (MCD)
HEC	Header Error Control [*Telecommunications*] (ACRL)
HEC	Health Education Council [*British*] (DAVI)
HEC	Health Evaluation Center
HEC	Heavy Enamel Single Cellophane [*Wire insulation*] (IAA)
HEC	Heavy Enamel Single Cotton [*Wire insulation*] (AAG)
Hec	Hecate [*A publication*]
HEC	Hector, CA [*Location identifier FAA*] (FAAL)
HEC	Hector Resources, Inc. [*Vancouver Stock Exchange symbol*]
Hec	Hecuba [*of Euripides*] [*Classical studies*] (OCD)
HEC	Helicopter Element Coordinator [*Navy*] (ANA)
HEC	Heliservicio Campeche SA de CV [*Mexico ICAO designator*] (FAAC)
HEC	Hella Electronics Corp. [*Automotive industry supplier*]
HEC	Hepatoma Cells [*Oncology*]
HEC	High Emission Cathode
HEC	High-Energy Chemistry
HEC	Higher Education (ECON)
HEC	Hodgin's Election Cases [*Ontario*] [*A publication*] (DLA)
HEC	Hollerith Electronic Computer
HEC	Home Equity Conversion
HEC	Human Economy Center (EA)
HEC	Human Endometrial Cancer [*Oncology*]
HEC	Human Endothelial Cell [*Cytology*]
HEC	Human Enteric Coronavirus
HEC	Human Environment Center (EA)
HEC	Human Epithelial Cell [*Cytology*]
HEC	Hydro Electricity Commission [*of Tasmania*] [*State*] (EERA)
HEC	Hydrogen Embrittlement Cracking (PDAA)
HEC	Hydrologic Engineering Center [*Davis, CA*] [*Army*] (GRD)
HEC	Hydroxyergocalciferol [*Organic chemistry*] (MAE)
HEC	(Hydroxyethyl)cellulose [*Organic chemistry*]
HEC	Hydroxyethylcysteine [*Organic chemistry*]
HEC	United States Department of Health and Human Services, Health Care Financial Administration, Baltimore, MD [*OCLC symbol*] (OCLC)
HECA	Cairo/International [*Egypt*] [*ICAO location identifier*] (ICLI)
HECA	Harpoon Environmental Correction Aid [*Navy*] (ANA)
HECAD	Human Engineering Computer-Aided Design [*Air Force*]
HECATE	Heat Exchanger Computerized Aid for Technical Engineering (IAA)
HECC	Cairo [*Egypt*] [*ICAO location identifier*] (ICLI)
HECC	Higher Education Coordinating Council of Metropolitan St. Louis [*Library network*]
HECC	Hooker Electro-Chemical Co.
HECC	House Energy and Commerce Committee (GFGA)
HECD	Hall Electrolytic Conductivity Detector [*Analytical instrumentation*]
HECD	Helium Cadmium [*LASER*] (DGA)
HECH	Hechinger Co. [*NASDAQ symbol*] (NQ)
HECHA	Hechinger Co. Cl'A' [*NASDAQ symbol*] (TTSB)
HECHB	Hechinger Co. Cl'B' Cv [*NASDAQ symbol*] (TTSB)
HECI	Hawkins Energy [*NASDAQ symbol*] (TTSB)
HECI	Hawkins Energy Corp. [*NASDAQ symbol*] (SAG)
HECI	Human-Interface Equipment Catalog Item (TEL)
Heck Cas	Hecker's Cases on Warranty [*A publication*] (DLA)
HeclaM	Hecla Mining Co. [*Associated Press*] (SAG)
HECLINET	Health Care Literature Information Network [*Institut fuer Krankenhausbau*] [*Germany Information service or system*] (IID)
HeclM	Hecla Mining Co. [*Associated Press*] (SAG)
HE Cls B	Heating Coils in Bunkers [*on a ship*] (DS)
HE Cls C	Heating Coils in Cargo Tanks [*on a ship*] (DS)
HECM	Home Equity Conversion Mortgage [*Federal Housing Authority*]
HECMAR	Human Engineering Criteria for Maintenance and Repair [*GE, NASA*]
HECP	Harbor Entrance Control Post [*Nautical charts*]
HECRE	High-Energy Cosmic Ray Experiment [*Balloon flight*] [*NASA*]
HECSA	Humphreys Engineering Center Support Activity (AAGC)
HECSAGON	Horowitz-Eastman-Crane Symbol Array Governed by Orthodox Notation (NITA)
HECSE	Higher Education Consortium on Special Education (EDAC)
HECSU	Higher Education Careers Service Unit (AIE)
HECT	Head Equivalent Computed Tomography (DB)
HECT	Hectare (WDAA)
HectCm	Hector Communications Corp. [*Associated Press*] (SAG)
HECTO	Hectograph
HECTOG	Hectogram
HECTOL	Hectoliter
HECTOM	Hectometer [*100 meters*]
HECTOR	Heated Experimental Carbon Thermal Oscillator Reactor [*British*]
HECUA	Higher Education Consortium for Urban Affairs (EA)
HECV	Heavy Enamel Cotton Varnish [*Wire insulation*]
HECV	Helium Check Valve (MCD)
HECV	Human Enteric Coronavirus
HECVES	Harbor Entrance Control Vessel
HED	Hall Effect Device
HED	Haut-Einheits-Dosis [*Unit Skin Dose*] [*Radiation therapy*]
HED	Haut-Erythem-Dosis [*Skin erythema dose*] [*Radiation therapy*] (DAVI)
HED	Hazard Evaluation Division [*Environmental Protection Agency*]
HED	Headline [*Advertising*] (DOAD)
hed	Headline (WDMC)
HED	Headquarters (CINC)
HED	Hedley Pacific Mining [*Vancouver Stock Exchange symbol*]
HeD	Helper Determinant (STED)
HED	Herendeen Bay, AK [*Location identifier FAA*] (FAAL)
HED	Hidrotic Ectodermal Dysplasia [*Dermatology*]

HED .... High-Energy Detector [NASA]
HED .... High-Explosive Delay [Weaponry] (MCD)
HED .... Historical Earthquake Data (NRCH)
HED .... Historical English Dictionary [A publication]
HED .... Horizontal Electrical Dipole (IEEE)
HED .... Howardite, Eucrite, Diogenite [Meteorite composition]
HED .... Human Engineering Data
HED .... Human Engineering Discrepancy [Nuclear energy] (NRCH)
HED .... Hydraulically Extendable Dipperstick [for tractors]
HED .... Hydrotropic Electron-Donor [Medicine] (DMAA)
HED .... Hymnal-Epic Dialect (BJA)
HED .... Hypohidrotic Ectodermal Dysplasia [Medicine]
HEDC .... Hasselblad Electric Data Camera
HEDC .... Heavy Enamel Double Cotton [Wire insulation]
HEDCC .... Human Error Data Control Center [NASA] (KSC)
HEDCO........ Higher Education for Development Cooperation [Eire] (BUAC)
HEDCOM...... Headquarters Command [Military]
HEDCV .... Heavy Enamel Double Cotton Varnish [Wire insulation] (AAG)
HEDDS .... Hawaii Educational Dissemination Diffusion System [Hawaii State Department of Education] [Honolulu] [Information service or system] (IID)
HEDF .... High Energy Density Facility [Proposed site for testing nuclear bombs]
HEDF .... High-Speed Electro-Drive Fan [Automotive engineering]
HEDGE .... Human Factor Evaluation Data for General Equipment
HEDGE .... Human Factors Engineering Data Guide for Evaluation
Hedges .... Hedges' Reports [2-6 Montana] [A publication] (DLA)
HEDH .... Hypohidrotic Ectodermal Dysplasia-Hypothyroidism [Syndrome] [Medicine] (DMAA)
HEDI .... High Endoatmospheric Defense Interceptor [Military] (RDA)
HEDING....... Hedingham [England]
HEDIS .... Health Plan Employer Data and Information Set
HEDL .... Hanford Engineering and Development Laboratory [Richland, WA] [Department of Energy]
HEDP .... Hearing Ear Dog Program (EA)
HEDP .... High-Explosive Dual-Purpose [Cartridge] (RDA)
HEDP .... (Hydroxyethylidene)diphosphonic Acid [Also, EHDP] [Organic chemistry]
HEDR .... Hanford Environmental Dose Reconstruction [Radiobiology]
HEDRON ...... Headquarters Squadron [Obsolete]
HEDRONFAIRWING... Headquarters Squadron Fleet Air Wing
HEDS .... Heavy Enamel Double Silk [Wire insulation]
HEDS .... Herpetic Eye Disease Study
HEDS .... High Endoatmospheric Defense System
HEDS .... Higher Education Data Sharing (EDAC)
HEDS .... High-Explosive, Discarding Sabot [Weaponry] (AAG)
HEDS .... Hydraulic End Design System [Computer-aided design]
HEDSUPPACT... Headquarters Support Activity
HEDSV .... Heavy Enamel Double Silk Varnish [Wire insulation] (AAG)
HEDTA .... Hydroxyethylenediaminetriacetic Acid [Organic chemistry]
HEE............. Heerlen [Netherlands] [Seismograph station code, US Geological Survey] (SEIS)
HEE............. Helena/West Helena, AR [Location identifier FAA] (FAAL)
HEE............. Heli Europe [Belgium ICAO designator] (FAAC)
HEE............. Hemiconvulsion, Hemiplegia, and Epilepsy Syndrome [Neurology] (DAVI)
HEE............. Household Earnings and Expenditure
HEEA .... Home Economics Education Association (EA)
HEEB.......... High-Energy Electrolyte Battery
HEED .... Health and Environmental Effects Document [Environmental Protection Agency] (AEPA)
HEED .... High-Energy Electron Diffraction
HEEDTA ...... (Hydroxyethyl)ethylenediaminetetracetate [or -tetracetic] Acid [Organic chemistry]
HEEEL .... High-Energy Electronically Excited LASER
HEEI........... (Hydroxyethyl)ethyleneimine [Organic chemistry]
HEEM........ Embaba [Egypt] [ICAO location identifier] (ICLI)
HEEM......... Hardsite Engagement Effectiveness Model (PDAA)
HEENT .... Head, Ears, Eyes, Nose, Throat
HEEO .... High Electroendosmosis [Analytical biochemistry]
HEEP........... Health and Environmental Effects Profile [Environmental Protection Agency] (AEPA)
HEEP........... Health Effects of Environmental Pollutants [A publication]
HEEP........... Health Effects of Environmental Pollution [Database] (NITA)
HEEP........... Highway Engineering Exchange Program (EA)
HEERA .... Higher Education External Relations Association (AIE)
HEF............. Haemagglutintin-Esterase-Fusion [Protein]
HEF............. Hamster Embryo Fibroblast [Medicine] (DMAA)
HEF............. Health Education Foundation (EA)
HEF............. Hearth Electric Furnace
HEF............. Heat-Curing Epoxy Film
HEF............. Heated Effluents [Cornell University] [Database] (NITA)
HEF............. Heavy Element Facility [Nuclear energy] (NUCP)
HEF............. High Energy Forming
HEF............. High-Energy Fuel [Air Force]
HEF............. High-Expansion Foam
HEF............. Hispanic Energy Forum [Defunct] (EA)
HEF............. Human Ecology Fund (EA)
HEF............. Human Embryo Fibroblast [A cell line]
HEF............. Hydroxyethylflurazepam [Sedative]
HEF............. Manassas, VA [Location identifier FAA] (FAAL)
HEFA.......... Higher Education Facilities Act of 1963
HEFA.......... Higher Education Funding Act [Australia]
HEFA.......... Hospital Employees' Federation of Australia (BUAC)
HEFA.......... Human Embryo and Fertilisation Authority (BUAC)

HEFC........... Higher Education Facilities Commission
HEFC........... Higher Education Funding Council (WDAA)
HEFCE......... Higher Education Funding Council for England
HEFG.......... Hall Effect Function Generator
HEFOE......... Hydraulic Electrical Fuel Oxygen Engine (COE)
HEFOE......... Hydraulic, Engine, Fuel, Oxygen, Electrical (DNAB)
HEFRAG........ High-Explosive, Fragmentation [Artillery] (INF)
HEFT........... Heavy-Element Fission Tracer
Heftel.......... Heftel Broadcasting Corp. [Associated Press] (SAG)
HEFTH......... Henceforth (ROG)
HEFU.......... High-Energy Firing Unit [Army] (AABC)
HEG........... Haftentschaedigungsgesetz [A publication] (BJA)
HEG........... Hall Effect Generator
HEG........... Heavy Enamel Single Glass [Wire insulation] (AAG)
HEG........... Helium Gauge (MCD)
HEG........... Hemgold Resources Ltd. [Vancouver Stock Exchange symbol]
HEG........... Hemorrhagic Erosive Gastritis [Gastroenterology] (DAVI)
HEG........... Hexaethylene Glycol [Organic chemistry]
HEG........... Histioeosinophilic Granuloma [Medicine]
HEG........... Homogeneous Exposure Group [Concept for acessing cancer risk]
HEG........... Jacksonville, FL [Location identifier FAA] (FAAL)
HEGF.......... High-Energy Gas Fracturing [For freeing natural gas from rock]
HEGF.......... Human Epidermal Growth Factor [Biochemistry]
HEGIS......... Higher Education General Information Survey [Office of Education]
HEGN.......... Hurghada [Egypt] [ICAO location identifier] (ICLI)
HEGO.......... Heated Exhaust Gas Oxygen [Automotive engineering]
HEGOG........ Heated Exhaust Gas Oxygen Ground [Automotive engineering]
HEGR.......... El-Gora [Egypt] [ICAO location identifier] (ICLI)
HEGR.......... High-Energy Gamma Ray
HEGRA........ High-Energy Gamma Ray Array [Canary Islands]
HEGRA........ High Energy Gamma Ray Astronomy
HEGS.......... Helicopter External Gondola System
HEGV.......... Helium Gauge Valve (MCD)
HEH........... Heho [Myanmar] [Airport symbol] (OAG)
HEH........... His [or Her] Exalted Highness [Term applied only to personages of British India]
HEH........... (Hydroxyethyl)hydrazine [Organic chemistry]
HEH........... Newark, OH [Location identifier FAA] (FAAL)
HEHC.......... Hydroxyethylhomocysteine [Organic chemistry]
HEHF.......... Hanford Environmental Health Foundation [Nuclear energy]
HEHO.......... Herbert Hoover National Historic Site
HEHP.......... Heavy Equipment Handling Package
HEHR.......... Highest Equivalent Heart Rate [Cardiology] (DAVI)
HEHS.......... Health, Education, and Human Services Division [GAO] (AAGC)
HEI............. Hall-Effect Imaging [Medical imaging]
HEI............. Hangar Engineering Item
HEI............. Health and Energy Institute (EA)
HEI............. Health Effects Institute [Research center] (RCD)
HEI............. Heat Exchange Institute (EA)
HEI............. Heico Corp. [AMEX symbol] (SPSG)
HEI............. Heidelberg [Konigstuhl] [Federal Republic of Germany] [Seismograph station code, US Geological Survey] (SEIS)
HEI............. Heidelberg College, Tiffin, OH [OCLC symbol] (OCLC)
HEI............. Hettinger, ND [Location identifier FAA] (FAAL)
HEI............. High-Energy Ignition (KSC)
HEI............. High-Energy Intermediate [Medicine] (DAVI)
HEI............. Higher Education Institute [Australia]
HEI............. Higher Education Institution
HEI............. Higher Education International (BUAC)
HEI............. High-Explosive, Incendiary [Weaponry]
HEI............. Holographic Exposure Index (PDAA)
HEI............. Homogeneous Enzyme Immunoassay [Biochemistry] (DAVI)
HEI............. Hospice Education Institute (EA)
HEI............. Hourly Earnings Index (OICC)
HEI............. House Ear Institute (EA)
HEI............. Human Embryonic Intestine Cells [Medicine] (DMAA)
HEI............. Human Engineering Institute
HEI............. Humidity-Electronic Indicator
HEIA.......... Hydrogen Energy Industry Association (BUAC)
HEIAC......... Hydraulic Engineering Information Analysis Center [Army Corps of Engineers] (IID)
HEI-AR........ Health Effects Institute-Asbestos Research
HEIAS .... Human Engineering Information and Analysis Service [Tufts University]
HEIB.......... Home Economists in Business (EA)
HEIC.......... Honourable East India Co. [British]
HE-ICM .... High Explosive - Improved Conventional Ammunition
HEICN......... Honourable East India Co. Navy [British military] (DMA)
Heico.......... Heico Corp. [Associated Press] (SAG)
HEICS......... Honourable East India Company's Service [British]
HEID.......... Heidemij NV [NASDAQ symbol] (SAG)
HEIDA......... (Hydroxyethyl)iminodiacetic Acid [Organic chemistry]
HEIDELB ...... Heidelberg [City in Germany] (ROG)
Heidemj....... Heidemij NV [Associated Press] (SAG)
HEIDF......... Heidemij N.V. [NASDAQ symbol] (TTSB)
HEIDI.......... Higher Education Data Base [Information service or system] (IID)
HEIE.......... High-Energy Isotope Experiment (SSD)
HEIFER........ High Frequency Relay (NVT)
HEIGHT....... Heights [Commonly used] (OPSA)
HEIGHTS..... Heights [Commonly used] (OPSA)
HEII.......... HEI, Inc. [NASDAQ symbol] (NQ)
Heilig.......... Heilig-Meyers Co. [Associated Press] (SAG)
HEI Mn .... HEI, Inc. [Associated Press] (SAG)
Hein........... William S. Hein and Co., Inc. [Publisher] (DLA)
HE inj .... Hyperextension Injury [Orthopedics] (DAVI)

HeinWr.........	Hein-Werner Corp. [*Associated Press*] (SAG)
Heinz...........	Heinz [*H.J.*] Co. [*Associated Press*] (SAG)
HEIP.............	High-Explosive, Incendiary Plug [*Weaponry*] (NATG)
HEIR.............	Health Effects of Ionizing Radiation [*Medicine*] (DAVI)
HEIR.............	High-Energy Ionizing Radiation [*Radiation therapy*] (DAVI)
HEIS.............	High-Energy Ion Scattering Spectroscopy
HEIS.............	Higher Education Information Service (AIE)
HEISD...........	High-Explosive, Incendiary Self-Destroying [*Weaponry*] (NATG)
Heisk...........	Heiskell's Tennessee Supreme Court Reports [*1870-74*] [*A publication*] (DLA)
Heisk (Tenn)...	Heiskell's Tennessee Reports [*48-59 Tennessee*] [*A publication*] (DLA)
HEIST..........	High-Energy Isotope Spectrometer Telescope (MCD)
HEIST..........	Higher Education Information Services Trust (BUAC)
HeistC..........	Heist [*C. H.*] Corp. [*Associated Press*] (SAG)
HEIT.............	High-Explosive, Incendiary [*Shell*] Traced [*i.e., fitted with tracer*] [*Weaponry*]
HEITDISD.....	High-Explosive, Incendiary Tracer, Dark Ignition, Self-Destroying [*Weaponry*] (NATG)
HEITSD	High-Explosive, Incendiary Tracer, Self-Destroying [*Weaponry*] (NATG)
HEITV...........	Higher Education Instructional Television [*West Virginia*] (EDAC)
HEIX.............	Home Economics Information Exchange (BUAC)
HEK.............	Heavy Enamel Single Cellophane [*Wire insulation*] (AAG)
HEK.............	Hemingway, SC [*Location identifier FAA*] (FAAL)
HEK.............	Human Embryo Kinase [*Medicine*] (DMAA)
HEK.............	Human Embryonic Kidney [*Type of cell line*]
HEKB...........	El Nakab/El Nakab [*Egypt*] [*ICAO location identifier*] (ICLI)
HEL.............	Handbooks of English Literature [*A publication*]
HEL.............	Hardware Emulation [*Computer science*]
HEL.............	Hardware Emulation Layer [*Computer science*]
HEL.............	Header Extension Length [*Telecommunications*] (ACRL)
HEL.............	Helena [*Diocesan abbreviation*] [*Montana*] (TOCD)
HEL.............	Helicol Helicopteros Nacionales de Colombia [*ICAO designator*] (FAAC)
HEL.............	Helicopter (AABC)
Hel.............	Heliodor [*Record label*] [*Great Britain*]
hel.............	Heliotrope [*Philately*]
HEL.............	Hellenic Resources [*Vancouver Stock Exchange symbol*]
Hel.............	Hellenistic [*Period*]
HEL.............	Helsingfors [*Helsinki*] [*Finland*] [*Seismograph station code, US Geological Survey*] (SEIS)
HEL.............	Helsinki [*Finland*] [*Airport symbol*] (OAG)
HEL.............	Helvetia [*Switzerland*] (ROG)
HEL.............	Hen-Egg White Lysozyme [*Also, HEWL*] [*An enzyme*]
HEL.............	High-Energy LASER
HEL.............	History of English Law, Edited by W. Holdsworth [*A publication*] (DLA)
HEL.............	Home Equity Loan
HEL.............	Hugoniot Elastic Limit [*Thermodynamics*]
HEL.............	Human Embryonic Lung [*Type of cell line*]
HEL.............	Human Engineering Laboratory [*Aberdeen Proving Ground, MD*] [*Army*]
HEL.............	Human Erythroleukemia [*Type of cell line*]
HEL.............	Hunting Engineering Ltd.
HEL.............	Hydraulic Engineering Laboratory [*University of California at Berkeley*]
HeLa...........	Helen Lake [*Tumour cells*] [*Medicine*] (BABM)
HeLa...........	Henrietta Lacks [*Pseudonym, Helen Lake*] [*Line of tumor cells*]
HELAB.........	High-Energy LASER Assessment Board (MCD)
HELAC.........	Helix Linear Accelerator (PDAA)
HELAIRDET...	Helicopter Air Detachment [*Canadian Navy*]
HELANTISUBRON...	Helicopter Antisubmarine Squadron [*Navy*]
HELANTISUBRONDET...	Helicopter Antisubmarine Squadron Detachment [*Navy*] (DNAB)
HELAPS	High Efficiency Linear Amplification by Parametic Synthesis (PDAA)
HELASRON...	Helicopter Antisubmarine Squadron [*Navy*]
HELAST.......	Human Engineering Laboratory Armor Systems Test [*Army*] (RDA)
HELATKRON...	Helicopter Attack Squadron [*Navy*] (DNAB)
HELB...........	High-Energy LASER Beam
HELB...........	High-Energy Line Break [*Nuclear energy*] (NRCH)
HELBAT.......	Human Engineering Laboratories Battalion Artillery Test [*Army*]
HELCAP	Human Engineering Laboratory Counterair Program [*Army*] (RDA)
HELCAR	Helicopter Collision Avoidance RADAR (NG)
HELCIS	Helicopter Command Instrumentation System (MCD)
HELCM	High-Energy LASER Countermeasures (MCD)
HELCO........	Hartford Electric Light Co.
HELCOM	Baltic Marine Environment Protection Commission - Helsinki Commission (EAIO)
HELCOMBSUPPRON...	Helicopter Combat Support Squadron [*Navy*] (DNAB)
HELCOS	High-Energy LASER Component Servicing (MCD)
HELDREF	Helen Dwight Reid Educational Foundation
HELE...........	Helen of Troy Corp. [*NASDAQ symbol*] (NQ)
HELE...........	Helen of Troy Ltd [*NASDAQ symbol*] (TTSB)
HELEN	Hydrogenous Exponential Liquid Experiment [*British*]
HeleneC.......	Helene Curtis Industries, Inc. [*Associated Press*] (SAG)
HelenTr.......	Helen of Troy Corp. [*Associated Press*] (SAG)
HELEX.........	Helium Extraction
HELF...........	Human Embryonic Lung Fibroblasts [*Biochemistry*]
HELFAST......	Human Engineering Laboratory Forward Area Supply and Transfer [*Army*] (RDA)
HEL-FI	Human Engineering Laboratory Field Office [*Charlottesville, VA*] [*Military*]
HEL-FIO	Human Engineering Laboratory Field Office [*Charlottesville, VA*] [*Military*]

HELHAT......	Human Engineering Laboratory Helicopter Armament Test [*Army*] (RDA)
HELI............	Helicopter (AFM)
HELI............	Heliport [*ICAO designator*] (FAAC)
HELI............	Helisys Inc. [*NASDAQ symbol*] (TTSB)
Helian........	Helian Health Group, Inc. [*Associated Press*] (SAG)
HELILEX......	Helicopter Landing Exercise [*Amphibious*] [*Navy*] (NVT)
HELIOD.......	Heliodorus [*Greek writer, c. 200AD*] (OCD)
Heliogab......	Heliogabalus [*of Scriptores Historiae Augustae*] [*Classical studies*] (OCD)
Heliont.......	Helionetics, Inc. [*Associated Press*] (SAG)
HELIOS	Handicapped People in Europe Living Independently in Open Society (BUAC)
Helios........	Helios - Joies de la Musique [*Record label*] [*France*]
HELIOS	Heteropowered Earth-Launched Inter-Orbital Spacecraft (KSC)
HELIP.........	HAWK [*Homing All the Way Killer*] European Limited Improvement Program [*NATO*]
HELIPATH ...	Helicopter Position and Terrain Height
HELIST........	Human Engineering Laboratory Infantry System Test [*Army*] (RDA)
Helisys.......	Helisys, Inc. [*Associated Press*] (SAG)
HELITEAM....	Helicopter Team
HELITECH....	International Helicopter Technology and Operations Conference and Exhibition [*British*] (ITD)
HELIVALS	Helicopter In-flight Validation System (PDAA)
HELIX.........	Harwell Electrochemical Ion Exchange Process [*British*] (NUCP)
HelixTch	Helix Technologies [*Associated Press*] (SAG)
Hell...........	Hellenica [*of Xenophon*] [*Classical studies*] (OCD)
HELL..........	Higher Education Learning Laboratory (EA)
Hell Dicht	Hellenistische Dichtung in der Zeit des Kallimachos [*A publication*] (OCD)
Hellen.........	Hellenic [*Classical studies*] (BARN)
HELLFIRE	Heliborne LASER Fire and Forget [*Missile system*] [*Army*] (RDA)
HELLFIRE/GLD...	HELLFIRE [*Heliborne LASER Fire and Forget*]/Ground LASER Designator [*Army*] (RDA)
HelloD........	Hello Direct, Inc. [*Associated Press*] (SAG)
HELLOG........	Human Engineering Laboratory Logistics [*Systems concept study*] (MCD)
Hell Oxy	Hellenica Oxyrhynchia [*Classical studies*] (OCD)
HELLP.........	Hemolysis, Elevated Liver Enzymes, and Low Platelet Count [*Clinical chemistry*]
HELM..........	Helmet Cells [*Cytology*] (DAVI)
Helm..........	Helm's Reports [*2-9 Nevada*] [*A publication*] (DLA)
HELMEPA ...	Hellenic Marine Environmental Protection Association (EERA)
HELMEPA ...	Hellenic Marine Environment Protection Association
HELMINERON...	Helicopter Mine Countermeasures Squadron [*Military*] (MUSM)
HelmP........	Helmerich & Payne, Inc. [*Associated Press*] (SAG)
HelmRes.....	Helm Resources, Inc. [*Associated Press*] (SAG)
HELMS........	Helicopter Lift Margin System (MCD)
HELMS........	Helicopter Multifunction System
Helmstr......	Helmstar Group [*Associated Press*] (SAG)
HELNAVS	Helicopter Navigation System (RDA)
HELO..........	Heavy Lift Operability (PDAA)
HELO..........	Helicopter (NG)
HELO..........	Hello Direct [*NASDAQ symbol*] (TTSB)
HELO..........	Hello Direct, Inc. [*NASDAQ symbol*] (SAG)
HELO..........	High-Energy Liquid Oxidizer
HELO..........	Hispanic Elected Local Officials (EA)
HELOA........	Higher Education Liaison Officers Association (BUAC)
HELOC	Home Equity Line of Credit (EBF)
HELOPS.......	Helicopter Operations (DNAB)
HELOPSUPPFAC...	Helicopter Operational Support Facility (DNAB)
HELOQUALS...	Helicopter Qualifications [*Navy*] (NVT)
HELORADE..	Helicopter Operations in Selected RADAR Environment (MCD)
HELORS.......	Hellenic Operational Research Society [*Greece*] (BUAC)
HELOS	Harwell Electro Osmosis Process [*British*] (NUCP)
HELOS	Highly Eccentric Lunar Occultation Satellite
HELOSID......	Helicopter-Delivered Seismic Intrusion Detector (NVT)
HELOTNG....	Helicopter Training (NVT)
HELP..........	Harlem Eastside Lifesaving Program [*Television program*]
HELP..........	Harris Enhanced Language for Programmable Logic (NITA)
HELP..........	Hawaii Early Learning Profile [*Child development test*] [*Psychology*]
HELP..........	HAWK [*Homing All-the-Way Killer*] Equipment Logistics Program [*Military*] (GFGA)
HELP..........	Health and Energy Learning Project (EA)
HELP..........	Health Education Library Program [*Library network*]
HELP..........	Health Emergency Loan Program [*Planned parenthood*] (DAVI)
HELP..........	Health Evaluation and Learning Program
HELP..........	Health Evaluation through Logical Processing [*Computer science*] (DAVI)
HELP..........	Heat Escape Lessening Posture [*First aid technique*]
HELP..........	Heavy Vehicle Electronic License Plate
HELP..........	Helicopter Electronic Landing Path [*Army*]
HELP..........	Helium Liquid Program [*NASA*]
HELP..........	Help End Lead in Petrol [*An association*] (BUAC)
HELP..........	Help Establish Lasting Peace
HELP..........	Help-Institute for Body Chemistry (EA)
HELP..........	HELP, International [*Defunct*] (EA)
HELP..........	Helpmate Robotics [*NASDAQ symbol*] (TTSB)
HELP..........	Helpmate Robotics, Inc. [*NASDAQ symbol*] (SAG)
HELP..........	Heroin Emergency Life Project
HELP..........	Herpetics Engaged in Living Productively [*Later, Herpes Research Center*] (EA)
HELP..........	High-Energy Lightweight Propellant
HELP..........	Highly Extendable Language Processor [*Computer science*]
HELP..........	Highway Emergency Locating Plan

HELP............	Holiday Endeavour for Lone Patients [*An association*] (BUAC)
HELP............	Home Education Livelihood Program [*New Mexico*]
HELP............	Home Emergency Ladies' Pal [*Book title*]
HELP............	Homophile Effort for Legal Protection [*An association Defunct*] (EA)
HELP............	Honeywell Equipment Lease Plan
HELP............	Hospital Equipment Loan Project
HELP............	Housewives Elect Lower Prices [*New York women's lobby group*]
HELP............	Howitzer Extended Life Program
HELP............	Hughes Emergency Locator Pack
HELP............	Hydrologic Evaluation of Landfill Performance [*Environmental Protection Agency*]
HELPIS	Higher Education Learning Programmes Information Service [*British Universities Film & Video Council*] [*Database*]
Helpmte.......	Helpmate Robotics, Inc. [*Associated Press*] (SAG)
HELPR	Handbook of Electronic Parts Reliability
HELPS	Handicapped Education Learner's Planning System [*Battelle Memorial Institute*] [*Information service or system*] (IID)
HELPS	Health Environment Long-Range Planning Support [*A computer model*]
HELPS	Heavy Equipment Lift Pre-Positioning Ship (MUSM)
HELPS	Helmet-Position Sensing System
HELPS	Highway Emergency Locating Paging Service [*For motorist assistance*]
HELPU	Helpmate Robotics Unit [*NASDAQ symbol*] (TTSB)
HELPW	Helpmate Robotics Wrrt [*NASDAQ symbol*] (TTSB)
HELRAS	Helicopter Long-Range Acoustic Sensor [*Military*] (CAAL)
HELRATS	High-Energy LASER RADAR Acquisition and Tracking System (MCD)
HELREC	Health Record
HelrFn	Heller Financial [*Associated Press*] (SAG)
HELRG	High-Energy LASER Review Group [*Terminated, 1977*] [*DoD*]
HELS	High-Energy LASER System
HELSRD	Health Effects and Life Science Research Division (HGEN)
HELST	Helston [*Municipal borough in England*]
HELSTF	High-Energy LASER System Test Facility [*Army*] (DOMA)
HELSUPPRON...	Helicopter Combat Support Squadron [*Navy*]
HELSUPPRONDET...	Helicopter Combat Support Squadron Detachment [*Navy*] (DNAB)
HELT	Hedonism Limitation Talks [*British*] (DI)
HELTAD	Helicopter Tank Destroyer [*Military*]
HELTADS	High-Energy LASER Tactical Air Defense System
HELTAS	High-Energy LASER Technology Applications Study (MCD)
HELTRARON..	Helicopter Training Squadron [*Navy*]
Helv	Ad Helviam [*of Seneca the Younger*] [*Classical studies*] (OCD)
HELV	Helvetica [*Typography*] (WDAA)
Helv Chim Acta...	Helvetica Chimica Acta (MEC)
HELWEPS	High-Energy LASER Weapon System [*Navy*] (MED)
HELWS	High-Energy LASER Weapon System (MCD)
HELX...........	Helix Technology [*NASDAQ symbol*] (TTSB)
HELX...........	Helix Technology Corp. [*NASDAQ symbol*] (NQ)
HELX...........	Luxor [*Egypt*] [*ICAO location identifier*] (ICLI)
HEM	Hall Effect Multiplier
HEM	Handbook on Emergency Measures (NATG)
HEM	Harmonisation of Environmental Measurement (EERA)
HEM	Hatchlike Experiment Module [*NASA*] (NASA)
HEM	Heat Exchanger Method (RDA)
HEM	Heavy Equipment Maintenance
HEM	Hematite [*A mineral*]
HEM	Hematology [*Medicine*] (DHSM)
hem	Hematuria [*Urology*] (DAVI)
HEM	Hemisphere
HEM	Hemlo Gold Mines [*AMEX symbol*] (TTSB)
HEM	Hemlo Gold Mines, Inc. [*Toronto Stock Exchange symbol AMEX symbol*]
HEM	Hemmeter Aviation, Inc. [*ICAO designator*] (FAAC)
HEM	Hemoglobin [*Medicine*] (WDAA)
HEM	Hemolysis [*Medicine*]
Hem	Hemolytic [*Hematology*] (DAVI)
HEM	Hemorrhage [*Medicine*] (WDAA)
hem	Hemorrhoid [*Gastroenterology*] (DAVI)
HEM	HEPES-Buffered EMEM
HEM	Hitchhike Experiment Module (MCD)
HEM	Homogeneous Equilibrium Model (NRCH)
HEM	Human Exposure Model [*Environmental science*] (COE)
HEM	Human Exposure Modeling (GFGA)
HEM	Hybrid Electromagnetic [*Wave*]
HEM	Hydrogenic Effective Mass (AAEL)
HEM	Hydroxyethylmorpholine [*Organic chemistry*]
HEM	Sparta, TN [*Location identifier FAA*] (FAAL)
HEMA...........	Health Education Media Association [*Defunct*] (EA)
HEMA...........	HemaCare Corp. [*NASDAQ symbol*] (NQ)
HEMA...........	Hematology Profile [*Medicine*] (DAVI)
HEMA...........	Hot Melt Equipment Manufacturers Association (EA)
HEMA...........	Hydroxyethyl Methacrylate [*Organic chemistry*]
HemaC........	HemaCare Corp. [*Associated Press*] (SAG)
HEMAC........	Hybrid Electromagnetic Antenna Coupler
Hemagn.......	Hemagen Diagnostics [*Associated Press*] (SAG)
Hem & M....	Hemming and Miller's English Vice-Chancellors' Reports [*A publication*] (DLA)
Hem & M (Eng)...	Hemming and Miller's English Vice-Chancellors' Reports [*A publication*] (DLA)
Hem & Mill...	Hemming and Miller's English Vice-Chancellors' Reports [*A publication*] (DLA)
HEMAR	Human Engineering Criteria for Maintenance and Repair [*GE, NASA*]
Hemasure....	Hemasure, Inc. [*Associated Press*] (SAG)
HEMAT........	Heavy Expanded Mobility Ammunition Trailer [*Military*]

hemat	Hematocrit [*Medicine*] (DAVI)
HEMAT........	Hematology [*Medicine*]
hemat ab	Hematologic Abnormality [*Medicine*]
hematem	Hematemesis [*Gastroenterology*] (DAVI)
HEMATL.......	Hematologist
HEMATLGY...	Hematology
Hematol.......	Hematology [*or Hematologist*] [*Medicine*]
HEMDE	Hemdale Communications [*NASDAQ symbol*] (TTSB)
HEME...........	Hostile Electromagnetic Emission (MCD)
HEME...........	Hydroxyethyl Methyl (Cellulose) [*Organic chemistry*]
HEMF...........	Handling Equipment Maintenance Facility [*Charleston Naval Shipyard*]
HEMF...........	Hydroxy (Ethyl) Methyl Furanone [*Organic chemistry*]
Hemgn........	Hemagen Diagnostics [*Associated Press*] (SAG)
HEMI...........	Hemiparalysis [*Medicine*]
HEMI...........	Hemiplegia [*Medicine*]
Hemi...........	Hemisphere [*Neurology*] (DAVI)
HEMI...........	Hemispherical [*Automotive engineering*]
HEMI...........	Hemispherical [*S-band antenna*]
Heming........	Hemingway's Mississippi Reports [*A publication*] (DLA)
Heming (Miss)...	Hemingway's Mississippi Reports [*A publication*] (DLA)
HEMIS	Hemisphere (AFM)
Hemis..........	Hemispherx BioPharma, Inc. [*Associated Press*] (SAG)
HEMISEARCH...	Hemispherical Search [*First frequency-scanning RADAR*] (MCD)
Hemispx......	Hemispherx BioPharma, Inc. [*Associated Press*] (SAG)
HEML.........	High-Energy Microwave Laboratory [*Kirtland AFB*] [*Air Force*] (DOMA)
HEMLAW	Helicopter Mounted LASER Weapon (MCD)
Hemlo	Hemlo Gold Mines, Inc. [*Associated Press*] (SAG)
HEMLOC	Heliborne Emitter Location/Countermeasures
HEMM..........	Mersa-Matruh [*Egypt*] [*ICAO location identifier*] (ICLI)
Hemmant....	Hemmant's Select Cases in Exchequer Chamber [*Selden Society Publications, Vol. 51*] [*1377-1460*] [*A publication*] (DLA)
HEMMS.......	Hand-Emplaced Minefield Marking System (MCD)
hemo	Hemoglobin [*Medicine*] (DAVI)
HEMO	Hemolysis [*or Hemolyze*] [*Medicine*] (DAVI)
hemo	Hemophilia [*Medicine*] (DAVI)
hemocyt......	Hemocytometer (MAE)
HEMOR	Hemorrhage [*Medicine*]
hemorr........	Hemorrhage [*Medicine*] (DAVI)
HEMOSID......	Hemosiderin (STED)
HEMP..........	Help End Marijuana Prohibition [*An association*]
Hemp..........	Hempstead's Arkansas Reports [*A publication*] (DLA)
Hemp..........	Hempstead's United States Circuit Court Reports [*A publication*] (DLA)
HEMP..........	High-Altitude Electromagnetic Pulse (MCD)
HEMPA	Hexamethylphosphoric Triamide [*Also, HMP, HMPA, HMPT, HPT*] [*Organic chemistry*] (MCD)
HEMPAS	Hereditary Erythroblastic Multinuclearity Associated with a Positive Acidified-Serum Test [*Hematology*]
HEMPAS	Hereditary Erythrocytic Multinuclearity with a Positive Acidified-Serum [*Test*] [*Hematology*]
HEMPE........	Henry, Edward, Mary, Philip, Elizabeth [*Bacon's prophecy*]
Hempst........	Hempstead's Arkansas Reports [*A publication*] (DLA)
Hempst........	Hempstead's United States Circuit Court Reports [*A publication*] (DLA)
HEMRI	Hereditary Multifocal Relapsing Inflammation [*Medicine*] (DMAA)
HEMS..........	Helicopter Emergency Medical Services (STED)
HEMSiD	Hemosiderin [*Hematology*] (DAVI)
HEMT..........	HF Bancorp [*NASDAQ symbol*] (TTSB)
HEMT..........	HF Bancorp, Inc. [*NASDAQ symbol*] (SAG)
HEMT..........	High Electron Mobility Transistor [*Computer science*]
HEMT..........	Hydrodynamic Elastic Magnets Plastic
HEMT FET....	High Electron Mobility Transistor FET [*Field Effect Transistor*] [*Honeywell*] (NITA)
HEMTT........	Heavy Expanded Mobility Tactical Truck [*Army*] (RDA)
HEMT/UMHE...	Higher Education Ministries Team/United Ministries in Higher Education (EA)
HEMV..........	Helium Manual Valve (MCD)
HEMW..........	Hybrid Electromagnetic Wave (MSA)
HEMX..........	Hemispherx BioPharma, Inc. [*NASDAQ symbol*] (SAG)
HEMXU........	Hemispherx BioPharma Unit [*NASDAQ symbol*] (TTSB)
HEN	Cape Henry (GAAI)
HEN	Harris Electronic News [*Service suspended*] [*Information service or system*] (IID)
HEN	Heat-Exchanger Network [*Chemical engineering*]
HEN	Hemorrhages, Exudates, and/or Nicking [*Ophthalmology*] (DAVI)
HEN	Hengchun [*Republic of China*] [*Seismograph station code, US Geological Survey*] (SEIS)
HEN	Henley International, Inc. [*Later, MAXXIM Medical*] [*AMEX symbol*] (SPSG)
Hen............	Henricus Boich [*Flourished, 1320-30*] [*Authority cited in pre-1607 legal work*] (DSA)
Hen............	Henry (King of England) (DLA)
HEN	Holistic Education Network (EDAC)
HEN	Home Enteral Nutrition [*Medicine*] (DMAA)
HEN	Home Entertainment Network [*Cable-television system*]
HEN	Hotel, Echo, November [*Russian submarine*]
HENA..........	Hemeroteca Nacional [*Database*] [*Ministerio de Cultura*] [*Spanish*] [*Information service or system*] (CRD)
Hen Am Pl...	Hening's American Pleader [*A publication*] (DLA)
Hen & M.....	Hening and Munford's Virginia Supreme Court Reports [*1806-10*] [*A publication*] (DLA)
Hen & Mun...	Hening and Munford's Reports [*11-14 Virginia*] [*A publication*] (DLA)

Hen Bo	Henricus Boich [*Flourished, 1320-30*] [*Authority cited in pre-1607 legal work*] (DSA)
HENDEL	Helium Engineering Demonstration Loop [*Nuclear energy*] (NUCP)
Henderson St U	Henderson State University (GAGS)
HENE	Helium Neon [*LASER*] (DGA)
Hen For L	Henry on Foreign Law [*A publication*] (DLA)
Hen Forms	Hennell's Forms [*A publication*] (DLA)
HENILAS	Helicopter Night-Landing System
Hen JP	Hening's Virginia Justice of the Peace [*A publication*] (DLA)
Hen LA Dig	Hennen's Louisiana Digest [*A publication*] (DLA)
Hen Law	Hennepin Lawyer [*A publication*] (DLA)
Hen Man Cas	Henry's Manumission Cases [*A publication*] (DLA)
Hen Max	Hening's Maxims [*A publication*] (DLA)
HENNA	Home Executives National Networking Association
HENP	High Energy and Nuclear Physics Program [*Department of Energy*]
HENRE	High-Energy Neutron Reactions Experiment [*Nuclear energy*]
Henric	Henricus Boich [*Flourished, 1320-30*] [*Authority cited in pre-1607 legal work*] (DSA)
HenryJk	Henry [*Jack*] & Associates, Inc. [*Associated Press*] (SAG)
Henry Judg	Henry's Judgment in Ordwin V. Forbes [*A publication*] (DLA)
Hen St	Hening's Statutes [*Virginia*] [*A publication*] (DLA)
HENT	Head, Eyes, Ears, Nose, and Throat [*Medicine*] (HGAA)
Hent Forms	Hent's Forms and Use of Blanks in California [*A publication*] (DLA)
HENV	New Valley [*Egypt*] [*ICAO location identifier*] (ICLI)
HEO	High Earth Orbit (IEEE)
HEO	High Elliptical Orbit Satellite
HEO	High-Energy Orbit [*NASA*] (NASA)
HEO	Higher Executive Officer [*Civil service*] [*British*]
HEO	Higher Executive Order
HEO(A)	Higher Executive Officer (Administration) [*Civil service*] [*British*]
HEOB	High-Energy Organic Battery
HEOC	Higher Education Opportunities Committee (EA)
HEOD	Harbor Explosive Ordnance Disposal Team [*Navy*] (VNW)
HEOD	Hexachloroepoxyoctahydro-exo-endo-dimethanonaphthalene [*Dieldrin*] [*Insecticide*]
HEOEBS	High-Energy Organic Electrolyte Battery System
HEOI	Higher Education Orientation Inventory (DHP)
HEOP	Higher Equal Opportunity Program [*Education*]
HEOS	Highly Eccentric [*or Elliptical*] Orbit Satellite
HEOY	Handicapped Employee of the Year [*Award given to federal employees*] (RDA)
HEP	Habitat Evaluation Procedure [*Fishery science*]
HEP	Halkin Emek Partisi [*People's Labor Party*] [*Turkey Political party*] (EY)
HEP	Hall Effect Probe
HEP	Hallwood Energy Partners Ltd. [*AMEX symbol*] (SPSG)
HEP	Hallwood Energy Ptnrs L.P. [*AMEX symbol*] (TTSB)
HEP	Hardsite Engagement Program
HEP	Hemolysis End Point [*Medicine*] (STED)
HEP	Heparin [*Medicine*] (STED)
HEP	Hepatic [*Pertaining to the liver*] [*Pharmacy*] (ROG)
hep	Hepatitis [*Gastroenterology*] (DAVI)
HEP	Hepatoerythropoietic Porphyria [*Medicine*]
HEP	Hepatology [*Gastroenterology*] (DAVI)
HEP	Heterogeneous Element Processor [*Computer science*] (RDA)
HEP	High Egg Passage [*Rabies vaccine*]
HEP	High-Energy Particle
HEP	High-Energy Phosphate [*Biochemistry*]
HEP	High-Energy Physics
HEP	High-Energy Pulse
HEP	Higher Education Panel (EA)
HEP	High-Explosive Plastic [*Weaponry*]
HEP	High-Explosive Plugged [*Weaponry*]
HEP	High School Equivalency Program
HEP	Hi-Peg Resources Ltd. [*Vancouver Stock Exchange symbol*]
HEP	Hispanic Employment Program [*DoD*] (MCD)
HEP	Histamine Equivalent Prick Unit [*Immunology*]
HEP	Hole-Electron Pair
HEP	Homogenous Element Processor (NITA)
hEP	Human Endorphin [*Medicine*] (STED)
HEP	Human Engineering Plan
HEp	Human Epithelial [*Cells*]
HEP	Human Error Probability (IEEE)
HEP	Hydrazine Electrolysis Plenum
HEP	Hydroelectric Plant
HEP	Hydroelectric Power
HEP	Hydrogen Embrittlement Proof
HEp-1	Human Cervical Carcinoma Cells [*Medicine*] (STED)
HEp-2	Human Laryngeal Tumor Cells [*Medicine*] (STED)
HEPA	High-Efficiency Particle Accumulator (NASA)
HEPA	High-Efficiency Particle Air Filters (EDCT)
HEPA	High-Efficiency Particulate Air [*Filter*]
HEPA	Hydroxyethyl Phosphonic Acid [*Organic chemistry*]
HEP-AC	Hepatitis Battery-Acute [*Gastroenterology*] (DAVI)
HEPAD	High-Energy Proton and Alpha Detector
HEPAF	High-Efficiency Particle Air Filter
HEPALIS	Higher Education Policy and Administration Library and Information Service
HEPAP	High-Energy Physics Advisory Panel [*Department of Energy Washington, DC*] (EGAO)
HEPAT	High-Explosive Plastic Antitank [*Weaponry*] (NATG)
Hepb	Hepburn's Reports [*California*] [*A publication*] (DLA)
Hepb	Hepburn's Reports [*Pennsylvania*] [*A publication*] (DLA)
HEPB	High-Energy Pipe Break [*Nuclear energy*] (NRCH)
HEP.C	Hallwood Energy Ptnrs L.P.'C' [*AMEX symbol*] (TTSB)
HEPC	Handloom Export Promotion Council [*India*] (BUAC)
Hep-C	Hepatitis C Virus
HEPC	Hydro-Electric Power Commission [*Canada*] (PDAA)
HEPCA	House Employees Position Classification Act [*1964*]
HEPCAT	Helicopter Pilot Control and Training
HEPCC	Heavy Electrical Plant Consultative Council (BUAC)
HE-PD	High-Explosive - Point Detonating [*Weaponry*] (MCD)
HEPDEX	High-Energy Proton Detection Experiment
HEPDNP	High-Explosive, Point Detonating Nose Plug [*Weaponry*] (NATG)
HEPES	Hydroxyethylpiperazineethanesulfonic Acid [*A buffer*]
HEPI	Haute Ecole Populaire Internationale [*Denmark*] (BUAC)
HEPI	HEP [*High Energy Physics*] Index (NITA)
HEPI	Higher Education Price Index (EDAC)
HEPL	High-Energy Physics Laboratory [*Stanford University*] (MCD)
HEPL	High-Energy-Pulse LASER (PDAA)
HEPM	Hispanic Employment Program Manager [*DoD*]
HEPM	Human Embryonic Palatal Mesenchymal [*Type of cell line*]
HEPnet	High Energy Physics Network [*Computer science*] (TNIG)
HEPOD	Hereditary Expansile Polyostotic Dysplasia [*Medicine*] (DMAA)
HEPP	High-Energy Particle Physics Group [*Florida State University*] [*Research center*] (RCD)
HEPP	Hoffmann Evaluation Program and Procedure (IAA)
HEPP	Human Engineering Program Plan
HEPP	Northwest Association of Horticulturists, Entomologists, and Plant Pathologists [*Defunct*] (EA)
HEPPS	Hydroxyethylpiperazinepropanesulfonic Acid [*A buffer*]
HEPRA	Hellenic Public Relations Association (BUAC)
HEPS	Helicopter Personnel Escape, Protection, and Survival (DNAB)
HEPS	High-Energy Particle Spectrometer (MCD)
HEPS	High Energy Prespark [*Analytical chemistry*]
HEPS	High-Energy Propellant Safety (MCD)
HEPS	Port Said [*Egypt*] [*ICAO location identifier*] (ICLI)
HEPSS	Helicopter Escape and Personnel Survival System (MCD)
HEP-T	High-Explosive Plastic Tracer [*Weaponry*] (AABC)
HEP-UP	High School Education Program at University of Pennsylvania
HE-PX	High-Explosive Proximity Fuse [*Weaponry*] (MCD)
HEQ	Holyoke, CO [*Location identifier FAA*] (FAAL)
HEQC	Higher Education Quality Control [*British*] (DET)
HEQC	Higher Education Quality Council (BUAC)
HER	Harvard Educational Review [*A publication*] (BRI)
HER	Health and Education Resources (EA)
HER	Hearsay Evidence Rule [*Legal shorthand*] (LWAP)
HER	Hemorrhagic Encephalopathy of Rats (DMAA)
HER	Heraklion [*Greece*] [*Airport symbol*] (OAG)
Her	Herald [*Record label*] [*Great Britain*]
HER	Heraldry
her	Heraldry (VRA)
Her	Hercules [*Constellation*]
her	Herero [*MARC language code Library of Congress*] (LCCP)
HER	Heres [*Heir*] [*Legal term Latin*]
HER	Heritage Petroleum [*Vancouver Stock Exchange symbol*]
Her	Hermannus [*Authority cited in pre-1607 legal work*] (DSA)
HER	Hermanus [*South Africa*] [*Seismograph station code, US Geological Survey*] (SEIS)
Her	Herne's Law of Charitable Uses [*A publication*] (DLA)
Her	Herodian [*Period*]
Her	Heroides [*of Ovid*] [*Classical studies*] (OCD)
HER	Hershey Foods Corp., Hershey, PA [*OCLC symbol*] (OCLC)
HER	Hex'air [*France ICAO designator*] (FAAC)
HER	High-Efficiency Radiator [*General Motors Corp.*] [*Automotive engineering*]
HER	High-Energy Ray
HER	High-Energy Rotor [*Helicopter*] [*Army*]
HER	HIM [*Hardware Interface Module*] Equipment Rack [*NASA*] (NASA)
HER	Horizontal Earth Rate
HER	Human EGF [*Epidermal Growth Factor*] Receptor [*Biochemistry*]
HER	Human Embryonic Retinoblast
HER	Human Error Rate
HER	Human Estrogen Receptor [*Endocrinology*]
HER	Hydrogen Evolution Reaction [*Metallurgy*]
HER	Hyperenvironmental RADAR
Her	Quis Rerum Divinarum Heres [*Philo*] (BJA)
HER2	Human Epidermal Growth Factor Receptor2 [*Medicine*]
HERA	Hadron-Elektron-Ring Anlage [*Hadron-Electron Ring Accelerator*] [*Germany*]
HERA	Heritage Australia Information System [*Computer science*] (EERA)
HERA	High Energy Reaction Analysis Group [*Switzerland*] (BUAC)
HERA	High-Explosive Rocket Assisted [*Weaponry*]
HERA	Homemakers Equal Rights Association [*Defunct*] (EA)
HERAC	Health and Environmental Research Advisory Committee [*Department of Energy*] [*Washington, DC*] (EGAO)
Heracl	Heraclidae [*of Euripides*] [*Classical studies*] (OCD)
Heraclid Pont	Heraclides Ponticus [*Fourth century BC*] [*Classical studies*] (OCD)
Her Aconza	Henricus Acconzaiooco [*Flourished, 1374-82*] [*Authority cited in pre-1607 legal work*] (DSA)
HERALD	Harbor Echo Ranging and Listening Device
HERALD	Highly Enriched Reactor, Aldermaston [*British*] (DEN)
HERAP	Health and Environmental Risk Analysis Program [*Department of Energy*]
HERAP	Human Error Research and Analysis Program (MCD)
HERATES	Hourly Earnings Rate
HERB	Herbaceous (WDAA)
HERB	Herbalife International, Inc. [*NASDAQ symbol*] (NQ)
HERB	Herbalife Intl. [*NASDAQ symbol*] (TTSB)
HERB	Herbalist (ROG)

HERB .... Herbarium (WDAA)
Herb Ant ..... Herbert's Antiquities of the Inns of Court, Etc. [*A publication*] (DLA)
HERBB .... Hanscom Electronic Request [*for Proposals*] Bulletin Board [*Air Force*]
HERBIC .... Herbicide
Herblfe .... Herbalife International, Inc. [*Associated Press*] (SAG)
HERB RECENT... Herbarium Recentium [*Of Fresh Herbs*] [*Pharmacy*]
HERBRECS... Queensland Herbarium Plant Specimen Data Base [*State*] [*Computer science*] (EERA)
HERC .... Hadson Energy Resources (EFIS)
HERC .... Health Economics Research Center [*University of Wisconsin - Madison*] [*Research center*] (RCD)
HERC .... HERC Products [*NASDAQ symbol*] (SAG)
Herc............ Hercules [*Constellation*]
HERC .... Home Education Resource Center [*Defunct*] (EA)
Her Char U... Herne's Law of Charitable Uses [*A publication*] (DLA)
Her Chat ..... Herman on Chattel Mortgages [*A publication*] (DLA)
HERCULE ..... Heritage and Culture through Libraries in Europe (TELE)
HERCULES.... Helicopter Remote Classification and Localization System (PDAA)
HERCULES.... High-Energy Radiation Camera Using Light-Emitting Showers
Herculs........ Hercules, Inc. [*Formerly, Hercules Power Co.*] [*Associated Press*] (SAG)
HERD .... Health and Environmental Review Division [*Environmental Protection Agency*] (GFGA)
HERD .... High-Explosives Research and Development (MCD)
HerdCor....... Herder Correspondence [*London/New York*] [*A publication*] (BJA)
HERDESNAVAV... Hereby Designated as a Student Naval Aviator (DNAB)
HERDET .... Hereby Detached from Duty Assigned [*Military*]
HerdKor....... Herder-Korrespondenz [*Freiburg Im Breisgau*] [*A publication*] (BJA)
HERDUFLY... Hereby Detailed to Duty Involving Flying (DNAB)
HERE .... Hastings' Encyclopaedia of Religion and Ethics [*A publication*] (BJA)
HERE .... Herefordshire [*County in England*]
HERE .... Home Economics Resources in Education [*British*] (DBA)
HERE .... Hotel Employees and Restaurant Employees International Union (EA)
hered........... Hereditary (DMAA)
HERED .... Heredity
HEREDET ..... Hereby Detached from Duty Assigned [*Military*] (DNAB)
HEREDITS... Hereditaments (ROG)
HEREF .... Herefordshire [*County in England*]
Hereford ...... Herefordshire [*County in England*] (BARN)
HEREFORDS... Herefordshire [*County in England*]
HEREFS .... Herefordshire [*County in England*]
Heref/Worcs... Hereford and Worcester [*County in Wales*] (WGA)
HEREIU .... Hotel Employees and Restaurant Employees International Union (NTPA)
Herenn Modest... Herennius Modestinus [*Flourished, 3rd century*] [*Authority cited in pre-1607 legal work*] (DSA)
Her Est .... Herman's Law of Estoppel [*A publication*] (DLA)
Her Ex .... Herman's Law of Executors [*A publication*] (DLA)
HERF .... Hazards of Electromagnetic Radiation to Fuel (TEL)
HERF .... High Energy Radiation to Fuel
HERF .... High-Energy Rate Forging [*Metalworking*]
HERF .... High-Energy Rate Forming
HERI .... Heavy Oil/Enhanced Recovery Index [*Alberta Oil Sands Technology and Research Authority*] [*Information service or system*]
HERI .... Henan Energy Research Institute (BUAC)
HERI .... Higher Education Research Institute [*University of California, Los Angeles*] [*Research center*]
HERI .... Home Economics Research Institute [*Iowa State University*] [*Research center*] (RCD)
HeritPpn ...... Heritage Propane Partners LP [*Associated Press*] (SAG)
HeritUS........ Heritage US Government [*Associated Press*] (SAG)
HERJ............ High-Explosive Ramjet [*Weaponry*]
Her Jur .... Heron's Jurisprudence [*1860*] [*A publication*] (DLA)
HERL .... Health Effects Research Laboratory [*Research Triangle Park, NC*] [*Environmental Protection Agency*] (GRD)
Herley......... Herley Industries, Inc. [*Associated Press*] (SAG)
Herm .... Hermand's Consistorial Decisions [*Scotland*] [*A publication*] (DLA)
Herm .... Hermogenianus [*Flourished, 4th century*] [*Authority cited in pre-1607 legal work*] (DSA)
HERMAN..... Hierarchical Environmental Retrieval for Management Access and Networking [*Biological Information Service*] [*Database on biology*] (NITA)
HERMAN..... Hierarchical Environmental Retrieval for Management and Networking [*Biological Information Service*] [*Riverside, CA*]
Hermand...... Hermand's Consistorial Decisions [*Scotland*] [*A publication*] (DLA)
Herm Chat Mortg... Herman on Chattel Mortgages [*A publication*] (DLA)
Her (Mel)..... Herald (Melbourne) [*A publication*]
HERMES ..... Heavy Element and Radioactive Material Electromagnetic Separator [*British*]
Herm Estop... Herman's Law of Estoppel [*A publication*] (DLA)
Herm Ex'ns... Herman's Law of Executions [*A publication*] (DLA)
HERMIES ..... Hostile Environment Robotic Machine Intelligence Experiment Series [*Oak Ridge National Laboratory*]
Hermo .... Hermogenianus [*Flourished, 4th century*] [*Authority cited in pre-1607 legal work*] (DSA)
Her Mort ..... Herman on Mortgages of Real Estate [*A publication*] (DLA)
Hermot .... Hermotimus [*of Lucian*] [*Classical studies*] (OCD)
Herm Schil... Hermannus Schildis [*Deceased, 1357*] [*Authority cited in pre-1607 legal work*] (DSA)
HERN .... Hernia [*or Herniated*] [*Medicine*]
HERN .... High Explosive, Rocket-Assisted
HERN .... Ras-Nasrani [*Egypt*] [*ICAO location identifier*] (ICLI)
HERO .... Hazards of Electromagnetic Radiation to Ordnance

HERO .... Health Education Resource Organization (EA)
HERO .... Heath Educational Robot [*Heath Co.*]
HERO .... Heritage Education and Review Organization [*Defunct*] (EA)
He-Ro .... He-Ro Group [*Associated Press*] (SAG)
HERO .... High-Energy Radiation to Ordnance [*Army*]
HERO .... Historical Evaluation and Research Organization (AEBS)
HERO .... Home Economics Related Occupations
HERO .... Hot Experimental Reaction of O Power [*Nuclear energy*]
HERO .... Hydrothermal Environment Research Observatory [*US-French Marine collaboration*]
Herod.......... Herodas [*Third century BC*] [*Classical studies*] (OCD)
HEROD......... Herodotus [*Greek historian, c. 484BC*] [*Classical studies*] (ROG)
HERODIAN ... Herodianus [*Greek scholar, c. 200AD*] [*Classical studies*] (ROG)
HERP .... Hazards of Electromagnetic Radiation to Personnel (TEL)
HERP .... Herpetology [*or Herpetologist*]
HERP .... High-Energy Radiation to Personnel
HERP .... Human Exposure Dose/Rodent Potency Dose [*Toxicology*]
HERPES ...... High-Energy Recovery Pressure and Enthalpy Sensor (IAA)
HERPET ...... Herpetology (ADA)
Her Prec ..... Herne's Precedents [*A publication*] (DLA)
HERR .... Home Economics Research Reports
HERS .... Hardware Error Recovery System [*Sperry UNIVAC*]
HERS .... Health Education Research Service [*Department of Health and Human Services*]
HERS .... Health Evaluation and Referral Service
HERS .... Heart and Estrogen/Progestin Replacement Study [*Medicine*]
HERS .... Heritage Financial Services, Inc. [*NASDAQ symbol*] (NQ)
HERS .... Heritage Finl Svcs [*NASDAQ symbol*] (TTSB)
HERS .... Herself
HERS .... High-Energy-Range Spectrometer [*Instrumentation*]
HERS .... Higher Education Resource Services (EA)
HERS .... Highway Economic Requirements System [*FHWA*] (TAG)
HERS .... Home Economics Reading Service [*Recipe clipping service*]
HERS .... Home Emergency Response System
HERS .... Home Energy Rating System [*Thermal technology*] (PS)
HERS .... Hyperion Energy Recovery System (GNE)
HERS .... Hysterectomy Educational Resources and Services Foundation (EA)
HERS .... National Heart Education Research Society (EA)
HERSCP....... Hazardous Exposure Reduction and Safety Criteria Plan [*NASA*] (NASA)
HERTF .... Hertford [*City in England*] (ROG)
HERTF .... High-Energy Radiation Test Facility [*Military*]
HertgBc........ Heritage Bancorp, Inc. [*Associated Press*] (SAG)
HertgFS ...... Heritage Financial Services [*Associated Press*] (SAG)
HERTIS .... Hertfordshire Technical Library and Information Service [*British*] (NITA)
HERTIS .... High-Energy Real-Time Inspections System (PDAA)
Hert M & Serv... Hertslet on Master and Servant [*A publication*] (DLA)
Hert Map Eur... Hertslet's Map of Europe [*A publication*] (DLA)
HERTS .... Hertfordshire [*County in England*] (EY)
Herts........... Hertfordshire [*County in England*] (ODBW)
Hert Treat.... Hertslet's Treaties [*A publication*] (DLA)
Hertzog....... Hertzog's Reports of Transvaal High Court [*A publication*] (DLA)
HertzT........ Hrtz Technology Group [*Associated Press*] (SAG)
HertzTc....... Hertz Technology Group [*Associated Press*] (SAG)
HERU .... Health Economics Research Unit [*University of Aberdeen*] [*Scotland*] (IRC)
HERV .... Hostile Environment Recovery Vehicle
HERV .... Human Endogenous Retrovirus
HervTS........ Hervormde Teologiese Studies [*Pretoria, South Africa*] [*A publication*] (BJA)
HervTST...... Hervormde Teologiese Studies [*Pretoria, South Africa*] [*A publication*] (BJA)
HERZ .... Hertz Technology Group [*NASDAQ symbol*] (SAG)
HerzfldC....... Herzfeld Caribbean Basin Fund [*Associated Press*] (SAG)
HES............. Hamlet Evaluation Survey [*South Vietnam*]
HES............. Hanford Engineering Service [*Nuclear energy*] (NRCH)
HES............. Harvard Expedition to Samaria (BJA)
HES............. Hawaiian Entomological Society (BUAC)
HES............. Head End Steering
HES............. Healthcare Evaluation System [*National Planning Data Corp.*] [*Information service or system*] (CRD)
HES............. Health Examination Survey [*NCHS*]
HES............. Heavy Enamel Single Silk [*Wire insulation*] (AAG)
HES............. Heli Services [*France ICAO designator*] (FAAC)
HES............. Helium Emergency Supply
HES............. Hesiod [*Greek poet, c. 800BC*] [*Classical studies*] (ROG)
HES............. Hess Environmental Services, Inc. (EFIS)
HES............. Hetastarch [*Biochemistry*]
HES............. Hic Est Sepultus [*Here Is Buried*] [*Latin*] (ROG)
HES............. High Early Strength Cement [*Technical drawings*]
HES............. Higher Elementary School (ADA)
HES............. High-Explosive Spotting [*Weaponry*]
HES............. History of Economics Society (EA)
HES............. History of Education Society (EA)
HES............. Home Entertainment Service [*Cable-television system*] (IAA)
HES............. Home Entertainment System
HES............. Homeowners Emergency Services, Inc.
HES............. House Exchange System [*Telecommunications*] (NITA)
HES............. Hughes Earth Station [*Aerospace*]
HES............. Human Embryonic Skin [*or Spleen*] [*Medicine*] (DMAA)
HES............. Hydroxyethyl Starch [*Plasma volume expander*]
HES............. Hypereosinophilic Syndrome [*Medicine*]
HES............. Hypertext Editing System [*Computer science*]
HES............. Lonely, AK [*Location identifier FAA*] (FAAL)

HESB .... Hahnemann Elementary School Behavior Rating Scale [*Test*]

HESB .... Hessische Bibliographie [*Database*] [*Arbeitsgemeinschaft Hessische Bibliographie*] [*German*] [*Information service or system*] (CRD)

HESC .... International Congress of Scientists on the Human Environment (BUAC)

HESC .... St. Catherine/St. Catherine [*Egypt*] [*ICAO location identifier*] (ICLI)

HESCA .... Health Sciences Communications Association (EA)

HESD .... High-Explosive, Self-Destroying [*Weaponry*] (NATG)

HESD .... Hospital Equipment and Supplies Directory [*A publication*]

HESDC .... Higher Education Student Data Collection [*Australia*]

HESDEP .... Helicopter Sensor Development Program

HESE .... Helium Selenium [*LASER*] (DGA)

HESES .... Higher Education Students Early Statistics (AIE)

HESF .... High-Energy Symmetric Fission

HESH .... High-Explosive, Squash Head [*Weaponry*] (NATG)

HESI-M .... Hudson Education Skills Inventory-Mathematics (TES)

HESI-W .... Hudson Education Skills Inventory-Writing (TES)

HESN .... Aswan [*Egypt*] [*ICAO location identifier*] (ICLI)

HESO .... High-Energy Solid Oxidizer

HESO .... Hospital Educational Services Officer [*Navy*]

HESODAC .... Helicopter SONAR Data Collection

HESP .... Health and Environmental Studies Program [*Department of Energy*] (IID)

HESP .... High-Efficiency Solar Panel

HESRE .... Hamlet Evaluation System Monthly Report (MCD)

HESS .... High-Energy Squib Simulator [*NASA*] (NASA)

HESS .... History of Earth Sciences Society (EA)

HESS .... Human Engineering Systems Simulator [*Air Force*]

HESSAD .... Household Expenditure Survey - Small Area Data [*Australian Bureau of Statistics*]

HESSES .... High-Energy Squib Simulators [*NASA*] (KSC)

HEST .... HEAF Emergency Service Tanks

HEST .... Herbrew Speaking Test [*Center for Applied Linguistics*] (TES)

HEST .... High Energy Shock Tunnel (IAA)

HEST .... High Explosives Simulation Technique

HESV .... Heavy Enamel Single Silk Varnish [*Wire insulation*] (AAG)

HET .... Haldane Educational Trust (BUAC)

HET .... Hall Effect Thruster [*Electric thruster type*]

HET .... Hall Effect Transducer

HET .... Harrah's Entertainment [*NYSE symbol*] (TTSB)

HET .... Harrahs Entertainment, Inc. [*NYSE symbol*] (SAG)

HET .... Harris Environmental Technologies, Inc. (EFIS)

HET .... Health Education Technologies [*New York, NY*] (TSSD)

HET .... Health-Education Telecommunications [*HEW*]

HET .... Heavy Equipment Transporter

HET .... Helium Equilibration Time (MAE)

HET .... Henryetta, OK [*Location identifier FAA*] (FAAL)

HET .... Heritage Education Trust (BUAC)

HET .... Heterodyne (DEN)

HET .... Heterozygosity [*Cytology*]

Het .... Hetley's English Common Pleas Reports [*124 English Reprint*] [*A publication*] (DLA)

HET .... High-Energy Telescope [*Geophysics*]

HET .... Higher Educational Test [*British military*] (DMA)

HET .... High-Explosive [*Shell*] Traced [*i.e., fitted with tracer*] [*Weaponry*]

HET .... HITIL [*Hardware in-the-Loop*] Encapsulation Methodology

HET .... Hobby Eberly Telescope [*Texas*]

HET .... Hohhot [*China*] [*Airport symbol*] (OAG)

HET .... Horizontal Electrical Tunnel (NRCH)

HET .... Houston - ET [*Texas*] [*Seismograph station code, US Geological Survey Closed*] (SEIS)

HET .... Hydroxyethyl Terephthalate [*Organic chemistry*]

HET .... TAF Helicopters SA [*Spain ICAO designator*] (FAAC)

HETA .... Hazard Evaluation and Technical Assistance [*National Institute for Occupational Safety and Health*]

HETAC .... Heavy Transport Aircraft [*Military*]

HETB .... Heart of England Tourist Board (DCTA)

HET-BE .... Heterophile Beef [*Immunology*] (DAVI)

HETC .... Heavy Equipment Test Chamber (MCD)

Het CP .... Hetley's English Common Pleas Reports [*124 English Reprint*] [*A publication*] (DLA)

HETDI .... High-Explosive, Tracer, Dark Ignition [*Weaponry*] (NATG)

HETE .... High Energy Transient Experiment [*NASA*]

HETE .... High Energy Transient Explorer

HETE .... Higher Education Teachers of English (AIE)

HETE .... Hydroxyeicosatetraenoic Acid [*Biochemistry*]

Het (Eng).... Hetley's English Common Pleas Reports [*124 English Reprint*] [*A publication*] (DLA)

HETERO ...... Heterosexual (DSUE)

HETEROG.... Heterogeneous (ROG)

HETF .... Hill Engineering Test Facility [*Air Force*]

HET-GP........ Heterophile Guinea Pig [*Immunology*] (DAVI)

Hetl.......... Hetley's English Common Pleas Reports [*124 English Reprint*] [*A publication*] (DLA)

HETM .... Hybrid Engineering Test Model (NASA)

HETMA........ Heavy Edge Tool Manufacturers' Association [*British*] (BI)

HETMAC ..... (Hydroxyethyl)trimethylammonium Chloride [*Organic chemistry*]

HETOC .... Hudson-Essex-Terraplane Owners Club (EA)

HETP .... Head End Treatment Plant [*Nuclear energy British*]

HETP .... Height Equivalent to a Theoretical Plate [*Chemical engineering*]

HETP .... Hexaethyl Tetraphosphate [*Organic chemistry*]

HETP .... Human Engineering Test Plan

HET-PR........ Heterophile Presumptive [*Immunology*] (DAVI)

HETR .... El-Tor [*Egypt*] [*ICAO location identifier*] (ICLI)

HETS .... Heavy Equipment Transporter System [*Army*] (RDA)

HETS .... Height Equivalent to a Theoretical Stage [*Chemical engineering*] (NRCH)

HETS .... High-Efficiency Transfer Solution [*CINNA/BIOTECX International, Inc.*] [*Analytical biochemistry*]

HETS .... High-Energy Telescope System [*Geophysics*]

HETS .... High-Energy Transfer Stage

HETS .... Hyperenvironmental Test Station [*or System*] [*Air Force*]

HETSD .... High Explosive, Tracer, Self-Destroying [*Weaponry*] (SAA)

HEU .... Heulandite [*A zeolite*]

HEU .... High Estimate Unconstrained

HEU .... Highly Enriched Uranium [*Nuclear reactor technology*]

HEU .... Hull Electronics Unit [*Military*] (RDA)

HEU .... Hydroelectric Unit

HEU .... Schenectady, NY [*Location identifier FAA*] (FAAL)

HEU EIS...... Disposition of Surplus Highly Enriched Uranium Environmental Impact Statement

HEUI .... Hydraulic Electronic Unit Injector [*Fuel system*] [*Automotive engineering*]

HEUNI .... Helsinki Institute for Crime Prevention and Control Affiliated with the United Nations (BUAC)

HEUR .... Hydrophobic Ethoxylated Urethane Resin [*Paint technology*]

HEURAS...... Secretariat of the European Associations in Higher Education (BUAC)

HEUS .... High-Energy Upper Stage [*NASA*]

HEV .... Health and Environment (AABC)

HEV .... Hemagglutinating Encephalomyelitis Virus [*Medicine*] (DMAA)

HEV .... Hepatoencephalomyelitis Virus [*Medicine*] (DB)

HEV .... High Endothelial Venule [*Cytology*]

HEV .... High-Walled Endothelial Venule [*Anatomy*]

HEV .... Human Enteric Virus

HEV .... Hybrid-Electric Vehicle

Hev .... Nahal Hever Caves (BJA)

HEVA .... Hydrolyzed Ethylene-Vinyl Acetate [*Plastics technology*]

HEVAC .... Heating, Ventilating, and Air-Conditioning Association [*Federation of Environmental Trade Associations*] [*British*]

HEVAC .... Heating, Ventilating, and Air Conditioning Manufacturers Association Ltd. [*British*] (BI)

HEVR .... Heavier (WDAA)

HEVS .... Helenium Virus S [*Plant pathology*]

HEW .... Department of Health, Education, and Welfare [*Sometimes facetiously translated "Halls of Eternal Warfare"*] [*Later, HHS*]

HEW .... Department of Health, Education, and Welfare, Washington, DC [*OCLC symbol*] (OCLC)

HEW .... Hanford Engineering Works [*Nuclear energy*]

HEW .... Health Education and Welfare [*Marine science*] (OSRA)

HEW .... Houston, TX [*Location identifier FAA*] (FAAL)

HEWC .... Highly Enriched Waste Concentrate (PDAA)

HEWGAR...... Department of Health, Education and Welfare Grant Appeals Board (AAGC)

HEWH .... High-Explosive Warhead [*Weaponry*]

HEWL .... Hen Egg White Lysozyme [*Also, HEL*] [*An enzyme*]

HewlPk .... Hewlett-Packard Co. [*Associated Press*] (SAG)

HEWPR .... Department of Health, Education, and Welfare [*Later, HHS*] Procurement Regulations

HEX .... Handicapped Education Exchange [*Amateur Radio Research and Development Corp.*] [*Information service or system*] (IID)

HEx .... Hard Exudate (STED)

HEX .... Hatfield Executive Aviation Ltd. [*British ICAO designator*] (FAAC)

HEX .... Heat Exchanger (KSC)

HEX .... Hemlo Explorations [*Vancouver Stock Exchange symbol*]

HEX .... Hexachlorocyclopentadiene [*Also, HCCP, HCP*] [*Organic chemistry*]

HEX .... Hexachord [*Music*] (ADA)

HEX .... Hexadecimal [*System*]

HEX .... Hexagon [*or Hexagonal*]

HEX .... Hexamethylmelamine [*Altretamine*] [*Also, HMM, HXM*] [*Antineoplastic drug*]

Hex .... Hexamethylmelamine (STED)

HEX .... Hexateuch (ROG)

hex. .... Hexatic (MEC)

HEX .... Hexosaminidase (DB)

HEX .... High Explosive (DNAB)

HEX .... Hydraulics, External (DNAB)

HEX .... Santo Domingo [*Dominican Republic*] [*Airport symbol*] (OAG)

HEXA .... Hexamethylene Tetramine [*Organic chemistry*] (WDAA)

HEX-A .... Hexosaminidase-A

HEX A .... Hexosaminidase A (STED)

Hexa-CAF .... Hexamethylmelamine, Cyclophosphamide, Amethopterin [*Methotrexate*], Fluorouracil [*Antineoplastic drug regimen*]

HEX B .... Hesosaminidase B (STED)

HEX-B .... Hexosaminidase-B

HEX-BCH...... Hexachloronorbornadiene [*Organic chemistry*] (EPA)

HEXCALC .... Hexadecimal Calculator [*Computer science*] (MHDI)

Hexcel .... Hexcel Corp. [*Associated Press*] (SAG)

HEXE .... High Energy X-Ray Experiment

HEXFET........ Hexagonal Field Effect Transistor (NITA)

HEXHD........ Hexagonal Head

HEXIT .... Hexadecimal Digit [*Computer science*] (NHD)

HEXL .... Methohexital [*A barbiturate*] [*Pharmacology*] (DAVI)

HEY .... Ozark/Fort Rucker, AL [*Location identifier FAA*] (FAAL)

Heyl Imp D... Heyl's United States Import Duties [*A publication*] (DLA)

HEYM .... Herrold's Egg Yolk Medium [*For growing microorganisms*]

Heyw Ca ...... Heywood's Table of Cases [*Georgia*] [*A publication*] (DLA)

Heyw Co Ct.. Heywood's County Courts Practice [*4th ed.*] [*1876*] [*A publication*] (DLA)

Heyw Elec ... Heywood on Elections [*A publication*] (DLA)

Heywood & Massey... Heywood and Massey's Court of Protection Practice [*9th ed.*] [*1971*] [*A publication*] (DLA)
HEZ............. Natchez [*Mississippi*] [*Airport symbol*] (OAG)
HEZOBOLLAH... Hezb Allah [*Party of God*] [*Arabic*] [*An Irananian terrorist organization*]
Hez-PBAN .... Heliothis Zea Pheromone Biosynthesis Activating Neuropeptide
HF............. Dorsey Laboratories [*Research code symbol*]
HF............. First Air [*ICAO designator*] (AD)
Hf............. Hafnium [*Chemical element*]
HF............. Hageman Factor [*Factor XII*] [*Hematology*]
HF............. Hagen Factor (DB)
HF............. Hale Foundation (EA)
HF............. Half (AAG)
hf............. Half (WDMC)
HF............. Half Forward (ADA)
HF............. Hammer Form (MCD)
H/F............. Handling Fee [*Coupon redemption*]
HF............. Handling Fixture (MCD)
HF............. Handwriting Foundation
HF............. Hankes Foundation (EA)
HF............. Hanuman Foundation (EA)
HF............. Haplotype Frequency (STED)
HF............. Harassing Fire [*Military*] (AABC)
HF............. Hard Failure
HF............. Hard Feces (STED)
HF............. Hard Filled [*Capsules*] [*Pharmacy*]
HF............. Hard Firm [*Pencil leads*]
HF............. Harry Franco [*Pseudonym used by Charles F. Briggs*]
HF............. Hartree-Fock [*Orbitals*] [*Atomic structure*]
HF............. Harvest Fluid (DB)
HF............. Hay Fever [*Medicine*]
HF............. Hazard Function
HF............. Haze Filter [*Photography*]
HF............. Hazelden Foundation (EA)
HF............. Head Forward (STED)
HF............. Head of Fetus (STED)
HF............. Heart Failure [*Medicine*]
HF............. Heat Flow [*Physiology*]
Hf............. Heat of Combustion of Fuel [*Aviation*] (DA)
HF............. Heavy Fuel [*Engine technology*]
HF............. Heeresfahrzeug [*Army Vehicle*] [*German military - World War II*]
HF............. Height Finder [*or Finding*] [*RADAR*]
H/F............. HeLa [*Helen Lake*]/Fibroblast [*Hybrid*] [*Cytology*] (DAVI)
H/F............. Held For [*Investment term*] (DFIT)
HF............. Helper Factor [*Immunology*]
HF............. Hemochromatosis Foundation (EA)
HF............. Hemofiltration (STED)
HF............. Hemorrhagic Factor [*Medicine*]
HF............. Hemorrhagic Fever [*Medicine*] (DAVI)
HF............. Hepatic Fat
HF............. Hepatocyte Function (STED)
HF............. Hercules Furens [*of Euripides*] [*Classical studies*] (OCD)
H/F............. Heritage Foundation [*Washington, DC*] (EA)
HF............. Hertz Frequency (STED)
HF............. Hesperian Foundation (EA)
HF............. High Fat [*Type of diet*]
HF............. High Field (IAA)
HF............. High Flow (MAE)
HF............. High Flux (IAA)
HF............. High Foliage Forager [*Ecology*]
HF............. High Food Density [*Ecology*]
HF............. High Frequency [*Electronics*]
hf............. High Frequency (WDMC)
HF............. High Frontier (EA)
HF............. High Rate Forward
HF............. Hippocampal Fissure [*Neuroanatomy*]
HF............. Hold Fire [*Military*]
HF............. Holding Fixture (MSA)
HF............. Hollow Fiber
HF............. Hollow Filter [*Dialyzer*] (STED)
H-F............. Holstein-Friesian [*Cattle breed*]
HF............. Holyearth Foundation (EA)
HF............. Holy Father (ROG)
HF............. Home Fleet [*Obsolete British*]
HF............. Home Forces [*Military British*]
HF............. Home Front
HF............. Homeopathic Foundation [*Later, FHR*] (EA)
HF............. Horizontal Flight (NASA)
HF............. Hot Finished [*Drawing*] (DAC)
HF............. Hot Firing (MCD)
HF............. Hot Fomentation (STED)
HF............. House File (OICC)
HF............. House Formula [*An in-house formula found in a particular hospital or clinic*] (DAVI)
HF............. House of Fabrics, Inc. [*NYSE symbol*] (SPSG)
HF............. Hull Filter
HF............. Human Factors
HF............. Human Fibroblast [*Medicine*] (DMAA)
HF............. Human Foreskin [*Anatomy*]
HF............. Huna Forschunggesellschaft [*Huna Research Association - HRA*] [*Switzerland*] (EAIO)
HF............. Hundred Feet
HF............. Hydrofluoric Acid (LDT)
HF............. Hydrogen Fill (MCD)
HF............. Hydrogen Fluoride [*Inorganic chemistry*] (AFM)

HF............. Hyperfiltration (NASA)
HF............. Messerschmitt-Boelkow-Blohm [*Germany ICAO aircraft manufacturer identifier*] (ICAO)
HF............. Wander AG [*Switzerland*] [*Research code symbol*]
HFA............. Haemophilia Foundation of Australia
HFA............. Haifa [*Israel*] [*Airport symbol*] (OAG)
HFA............. Hardened Flexible Array
HFA............. Hard Fibres Association (EA)
HFA............. Hardware Federation of Australia
HFA............. Harmelink Family Association (EA)
HFA............. [*The*] Harry Fox Agency
HFA............. Hartshorn Family Association (EA)
HFA............. Hawaii Flooring Association (SRA)
HFA............. Headquarters Field Army (NATG)
HFA............. Heat and Flame Resistant, Armored (IAA)
HFA............. Heavy Field Artillery
HFA............. Hexafluoroacetone [*Organic chemistry*]
HFA............. Hexafluoroaceytlacetone [*Organic chemistry*]
HFA............. Higdon Family Association (EA)
HFA............. High Flow Alarm (IEEE)
HFA............. High Force Actuator [*Engineering*]
HFA............. High-Frequency Accelerometer (NASA)
HFA............. High-Frequency Amplifier [*Electronics*] (IAA)
HFA............. High-Frequency Antenna (KSC)
HFA............. High Functioning Autism
HFA............. Hinman Family Association (EA)
HFA............. Hired Fishermen's Association [*A union*] [*British*]
HFA............. Historical Farm Association (EA)
HFA............. Hitchhikers for America (EA)
HFA............. Homofolic Acid [*Biochemistry*]
HFA............. Hospital Finance Authority (GHCT)
HFA............. Housing Finance Agency [*Eire*] (BUAC)
HFA............. Humane Farming Association (EA)
HFA............. Hydrofluoroalkane [*Organic chemistry*]
HFA............. Hydrogen-Fueled Aircraft
HFAA............. Hardanger Fiddle Association of America (EA)
HFAA............. High-Frequency Airborne Antenna
HFAA............. Holstein-Friesian Association of America (EA)
HFAB............. House of Fabrics, Inc. [*NASDAQ symbol*] (SAG)
HFAC............. Human Factors Association of Canada
HFAF............. Hawaii Foundation for American Freedoms (EA)
HFAJ............. High-Frequency Antijam (DWSG)
HFAK............. Hollow Fiber Artificial Kidney [*Medicine*] (AAMN)
HFAM............. Helicopter Familiarization (MCD)
HF & OR...... Human Factors and Operations Research [*Army*] (MCD)
HFARA............. Honorary Foreign Associate of Royal Academy [*British*]
HFAS............. High-Frequency Antenna System (KSC)
HFAS............. Honeywell File Access System
HFB............. Hand Form Block (MSA)
HFB............. Helium Filled Bubble [*For study of air flow*]
HFB............. Heptafluorobutyrate [*or Heptafluorobutyric*] [*Organic chemistry*]
HFB............. Horizontal Flow Barrier [*Computer science*]
HFBA............. Hebrew Free Burial Association (EA)
HFBA............. Heptafluorobutyric Acid [*Organic chemistry*]
HFBC............. High Frequency Broadcasting Schedule [*Databank*] (NITA)
HFBcp............. HF Bancorp, Inc. [*Associated Press*] (SAG)
HF BD............. Half-Bound [*or Binding*] (WDAA)
Hf-Bd............. High-Frequency Band [*Electricity*]
HFBI............. Heptafluorobutyrylimidazole [*Organic chemistry*]
HFBR............. High-Flux Beam Reactor (GAAI)
HFBR............. High Flux Beam Research Reactor [*Nuclear energy*]
HFBR............. Hollow-Fiber Bioreactor [*Chemical engineering*]
HFBUP............. High-Frequency Backup Program [*Military*] (CAAL)
HFC............. Hand-Filled Capsules [*Pharmacy*] (DAVI)
HFC............. Hard-Filled Capsules [*Pharmacy*] (DAVI)
HFC............. Harpers Ferry Center [*National Park Service*] (GRD)
HFC............. Heart Fan Club (EA)
HFC............. Heat Flow and Convection (NASA)
HFC............. Hierarchical File System [*Computer science*] (DDC)
HFC............. High-Energy LASER Fire Control
HFC............. Higher Fire Control [*British military*] (DMA)
HFC............. High-Frequency Choke
HFC............. High-Frequency Correction
HFC............. High-Frequency Current
HFC............. Histamine-Forming Capacity (DB)
HFC............. Historians Film Committee (NTPA)
HFC............. Holy Family College [*California, Pennsylvania, Wisconsin*]
HFC............. Holy Family College, Philadelphia, PA [*OCLC symbol*] (OCLC)
HFC............. Home Finance Contract
HFC............. Hope Foundation Communicators [*Australia*]
HFC............. Hospital Financial Control [*McDonnell Douglas Automation Co.*]
HFC............. Household Financing Corp. (CDAI)
HFC............. Household Food Consumption
HFC............. Human Factors Checklists [*Navy*]
HFC............. Hybrid Fiber and Coax [*Cable technology*] (PCM)
HFC............. Hybrid Fiber-Coax [*Telecommunications*]
HFC............. Hydraulic Flight Control (NASA)
HFC............. Hydrofluorocarbon [*Organic chemistry*]
HFC............. Hyperfine Coupling [*Spectroscopy*]
HFCA............. Holy Family Christian Association [*In 1983 movie "Zelig"*]
HFCAA............. Hatters' Fur Cutters Association of America [*Formerly, HFCAUS*] (EA)
HFCAUS...... Hatters' Fur Cutters Association of the United States [*Later, HFCAA*]
HFCC............. Henry Ford Community College [*Dearborn, MI*]
HFCD............. Hino Fuel Economy Clean Air High-Durability [*Hino diesel engines*]

HFCE	HFIR [*High-Flux Isotope Reactor*] Critical Experiment [*Nuclear energy*] (NRCH)
HF-CF	Half-Calf [*Bookbinding*] (DGA)
HF-CL	Half-Cloth [*Bookbinding*] (DGA)
HF-COL	Half Column [*Advertisement*] (DGA)
HFCRSP	High-Frequency Communications Replacement System Program (LAIN)
HFCS	Harpoon Fire Control System [*Missiles*] (MCD)
HFCS	High-Fructose Corn Sweetener [*or Syrup*]
HFCS	Honeywell Financial and Corporate Planning System (HGAA)
HFCT	Hydraulic Flight Control Test (NASA)
HFCUR	High-Frequency Current
HFCV	Helium Flow Control Valve (KSC)
HFCVD	Hot Filament Chemical Vapor Deposition [*Coating technology*]
HFCVSTP	Hydrogen Fuel Cell Vehicle Study and Test Program [*Environmental science*] (COE)
HFD	Halifax Developments Ltd. [*Toronto Stock Exchange symbol*]
HFD	Hartford, CT [*Location identifier FAA*] (FAAL)
HFD	Hatfield BAE [*British ICAO designator*] (FAAC)
HFD	Held for Detail
HFD	Helium Fill to Distribution Unit [*Aerospace*] (AAG)
HFD	Hemorrhagic Fever of Deer [*Medicine*] (DMAA)
HFD	Hereford [*British depot code*]
HFD	Herefordshire [*County in England*] (ROG)
HFD	High-Fiber Diet (DMAA)
HFD	High Forceps Delivery [*Obstetrics*] (DAVI)
HFD	HomeFed Corp. (EFIS)
HFD	Home Furnishings Daily [*A publication*] [*Formerly HFD-Weekly Home Furnishings*] (WDMC)
HFD	Horizon Flight Director [*Aircraft*]
HFD	Hospital Field Director [*Red Cross*]
HFD	Host Funding 'A' [*AMEX symbol*] (TTSB)
HFD	Host Funding, Inc. [*AMEX symbol*] (SAG)
HFD	Hot Form Die
HFD	Human Factor Division [*Air Research and Development Command*] [*Air Force*] (AAG)
HFD	Human Factors Design (DMAA)
HFD	Human Figures Drawing Test [*Education*] (EDAC)
HFD	Hydro-Form Die
HFDA	High Fidelity Dealers Association (BUAC)
HFDA	High Film Density Area (DMAA)
HFDA	Hospital Food Directors Association
HFdeSJ	Franciscan Sisters of St. Joseph (Mexico City) (TOCD)
HFDF	High-Frequency Direction Finding [*Pronounced "huff duff"*] [*Electronics*]
HFDF	High-Frequency Distribution Frame (IEEE)
HF/DF	Hydrogen Fluoride/Deuterium Fluoride (MCD)
HFDK	Human Fetal Diploid Kidney [*Type of cell line*]
HFDL	Host Forms Description Language [*Xerox software*] (NITA)
HFDL	Human Fetal Diploid Lung [*Type of cell line*]
HFDM	High-Frequency Digital MODEM (LAIN)
HFDS	Hydrogen Fluid Distribution System (MCD)
HFdSvF	Home Federal Financial Corp. [*Associated Press*] (SAG)
HFDT	Human Figures Drawing Test [*Psychology*] (DHP)
HFE	Health Facility for the Elderly
HFE	Heat-Flow Electronics
HFE	Heat-Flow Experiment
HFE	Hefei [*China*] [*Airport symbol*] (OAG)
HFE	Helmholtz Free Energy
HFE	Hexafluorodiethyl Ether [*Convulsant*]
HFE	High Frequency Executive (NASA)
HFE	Hillside Energy [*Vancouver Stock Exchange symbol*]
HFE	Human Factors Engineering (AABC)
HFE	Human Factors Evaluation (MCD)
HFE	Human Factors in Electronics (MCD)
HFE	Hydrofluorether
HFE	Pittsburgh, PA [*Location identifier FAA*] (FAAL)
HFEA	Human Factors Engineering Analysis [*or Assessment*] [*Army*] (RDA)
HFEA	Human Fertilization and Embryology Authority [*British*]
HFEAA	Historic Fire Engine Association of Australia
HFEC	Human Foreskin Epithelial Cell [*Medicine*] (DMAA)
HFEF	High Flux Experimental Facility [*Nuclear energy*]
HFEF	Hot Fuel Examination Facility [*Nuclear energy*]
HFES	Human Factors and Ergonomics Society (NTPA)
HFET	Hellmann-Feynmann Electrostatic Theorem [*Physics*]
HFET	Heterojunction Field Effect Transistor (AAEL)
HFET	Highway Fuel Economy Test [*Environmental Protection Agency*]
HFET	Human Factors Engineering Testing (MCD)
HFeU	Hepatic Iron (Ferrum) Uptake [*Physiology*]
HFF	Heavy Freight Flight [*British military*] (DMA)
HFF	High Flight Foundation (EA)
HFF	High-Frequency Furnace
HFF	Hoffman, NC [*Location identifier FAA*] (FAAL)
HFF	Horizontal Falling Film (PDAA)
hFF	Human Follicular Fluid [*Physiology*]
HFF	Human Foreskin Fibroblast [*A cell line*]
HFF	Hydraulic Fluid Filter
HFF	Hypervelocity Flow Field
HFFB	Harrodsburg First Financial Bancorp, Inc. [*NASDAQ symbol*] (SAG)
HFFB	Harrodsburg First Finl Bancorp [*NASDAQ symbol*] (TTSB)
HFFC	Hart Family Fan Club (EA)
HFFC	Helen Forrest Fan Club (EA)
HFFC	HF Financial [*NASDAQ symbol*] (TTSB)
HFFC	HF Financial Corp. [*NASDAQ symbol*] (SAG)
HFFF	Djibouti/Ambouli [*Djibouti*] [*ICAO location identifier*] (ICLI)
HFFF	Hungarian Freedom Fighters Federation USA (EA)
HFFF	Hypervelocity Free Flight Facility
HF Fnc	HF Financial Corp. [*Associated Press*] (SAG)
HFFS	HELLFIRE Fire and Forget Seeker [*Missile*]
HFG	Harmonic Frequency Generator
HFG	Heavy Free Gas (IEEE)
HFG	High Frequency Gas (WDAA)
HFG	Human Factors Group
HFGA	Hall of Fame for Great Americans (EA)
HFGI	Harrington Financial Group, Inc. [*NASDAQ symbol*] (SAG)
HFGI	Harrington Fin'l Grp [*NASDAQ symbol*] (TTSB)
HFH	Harnischfeger Industries [*NYSE symbol*] (SAG)
HFH	Home from Hospital (BUAC)
HFHI	Habitat for Humanity International (EA)
HFHL	High-Frequency Hearing Loss [*Otorhinolaryngology*] (DAVI)
HFHT	Handling Fixture - Hoist Tool (MCD)
HFI	Health Facilities Information File [*Australia*]
HFI	Health First International (EA)
HFI	Helicopter Foundation International (EA)
HFI	Hepatitis Foundation International
HFI	Hereditary Fructose Intolerance [*Medicine*]
HFI	High Fidelity Institute
HFI	High-Frequency Input (IAA)
HFI	Hjukrunarfelag Islands (BUAC)
HFI	Hocker Federation International (EA)
HFI	Home for Incurables [*Australia*]
HFI	Hubei Fisheries Science Research Institute [*China*] (BUAC)
HFI	Hudson Foods Cl'A' [*NYSE symbol*] (TTSB)
HFI	Hudson Foods, Inc., Class A [*NYSE symbol*] (SPSG)
HFI	Human Fibroblast Interferon [*Medicine*] (DMAA)
HFI	Hydraulic Fluid Index (PDAA)
HFI	Hyperfine Interaction
HFIA	Heat and Frost Insulators and Asbestos Workers (MHDB)
HFIA	Home Furnishings International Association (EA)
HFIAW	International Association of Heat and Frost Insulators and Asbestos Workers (EA)
HFIB	Hexafluoroisobutylene [*Organic chemistry*]
HFIC	Harpoon Firing Interlock Closed [*Missiles*] (MCD)
HFIC	High-Frequency Intra-Task Force Communications (LAIN)
HFIC	Home Furnishings Industry Committee [*Defunct*] (EA)
HFIC	Human Factors Information Center (SAA)
HFID	Heated Flame Ionization Detection [*Analytical chemistry*]
HFIF	Human Fibroblast Interferon [*Cytology*]
HFIH	High-Frequency Induction Heating (PDAA)
HFIM	High-Frequency Instruments and Measurements (IEEE)
HFIP	Hexafluoroisopropanol [*or Hexafluoroisopropyl*] [*Organic chemistry*]
HFIP	High-Frequency Improvement Program (LAIN)
HFIR	High Flux Isotope Reactor
HFITR	High-Field Ignition Test Reactor [*Nuclear energy*] (MCD)
HFIW	High-Frequency Induction Welding [*Manufacturing term*]
HFJ	High-Frequency Jammer
HFJV	High-Frequency Jet Ventilation [*Pulmonary ventilation*]
HFK	Human Foreskin Keratinocyte [*Cytology*]
HFL	Heliflyg AG [*Sweden ICAO designator*] (FAAC)
HFL	Helium Fill Line
HFL	Hesperia Fine Sandy Loam [*A soil type*]
HFL	Homestead Financial (EFIS)
HFL	Human Factors Laboratory [*University of South Dakota*] [*National Institute of Standards and Technology Research center*]
HFL	Human Fetal Lung
HFLA	Handling Fixture - Line Accessory (MCD)
HFLD	Handling Fixture - Line Dolly (MCD)
H flu	Hemophilus Influenzae [*Bacteriology*] (DAVI)
HFM	Hachette Filipacchi Magazines [*A publication*]
HFM	Hand, Foot, and Mouth [*Disease*]
HFM	Heavy Force Modernization [*Army*]
HFM	Held for Manufacturing
HFM	Held for Material
HFM	Hemifacial Microsomia [*Medicine*] (DMAA)
HFM	High-Field Magnetometer [*Instrumentation*]
HFM	High-Frequency Mode (IAA)
HFM	Hold for Money [*Business term*]
HFM	Hollow Fiber Membrane (NASA)
HFM	Horizonatal Flexible Mandrel (PDAA)
HFM	National Society for Healthcare Foodservice Management (NTPA)
HFMA	Hardwood Flooring Manufacturers' Association (BUAC)
HFMA	Healthcare Financial Management Association (EA)
HFMA	Health Food Manufacturers Association [*British*] (DBA)
HFMA	Hospital Financial Management Association [*Later, Healthcare Financial Management Association*] (EA)
HFMB	Hollow-Fiber Membrane Bioreactor (DB)
HFMD	Hand-Foot-and-Mouth Disease (PDAA)
HFMD	Home Federal Corp. [*NASDAQ symbol*] (NQ)
HFMD	Home Federal (MD) [*NASDAQ symbol*] (TTSB)
HFMF	Hone-Finish Monolithic Floor [*Technical drawings*]
HFMI	Highly Filled Materials Institute [*Stevens Institute of Technology*]
HF-MOR	Half-Morocco [*Bookbinding*] (DGA)
HFMR	HF [*High Frequency*] Modem Replacement (DOMA)
HFMRA	Honorary Foreign Member of the Royal Academy
HFMS	Highway Fleet Management System (MCD)
HFMS	Human Factors Measurement System
HFMSS	Heavy Force Modernization Survivability System
HFMSSP	Heavy Force Modernization System Safety Plan [*Army*]
HFMU	High-Fidelity Mock-Up [*NASA*] (NASA)
HFN	Hofn [*Iceland*] [*Airport symbol*] (OAG)

HFN	Human Fibronectin [*Cytochemistry*]
HFNC	HFNC Financial [*NASDAQ symbol*] (TTSB)
HFNC	HFNC Financial Corp. [*NASDAQ symbol*] (SAG)
HFNCFn	HFNC Financial Corp. [*Associated Press*] (SAG)
HFO	Heavy Fuel Oil
HFO	Heavy Fuel Oils [*Database*] [*Department of Energy*]
HFO	Height Finder Operator (MUGU)
HFO	High-Frequency Oscillator
HFO	Honolulu, HI [*Location identifier FAA*] (FAAL)
HFORL	Human Factors Operation Research Laboratory [*Air Force*]
HFOSL	Human Factors and Organizational Systems Laboratory [*Navy Personnel Research and Development Center*] [*San Diego, CA*]
HFOV	High-Frequency Oscillatory Ventilation [*Medicine*] (DAVI)
HFP	Hamdard Foundation Pakistan (EAIO)
HFP	Held for Planning (MCD)
HFP	Helical Flight Path
HFP	Helium Fuel-Tank Pressurization (AAG)
HFP	Hexafluoropropylene [*Organic chemistry*]
HFP	Highfield Property Investments Ltd. [*Toronto Stock Exchange symbol*]
HFP	Hostile Fire Pay [*Special pay for hazardous duty*] [*Military*] (AABC)
HFP	Hot Full Power [*Nuclear energy*] (NRCH)
HFP	Huron Forest Products Joint Venture [*Commercial*] (EERA)
HFP	Hybrid Fabrication Procedure (MCD)
HFP	Hypofibrinogenic Plasma
HFPA	Hollywood Foreign Press Association (EA)
HFPA	Home Fashions Products Association (EA)
HFPA	Hydroxyfarnesylphosphonic Acid [*Organic chemistry*]
HFPAC	High Frequency Powder Air Conveyor (PDAA)
HFPCS	Health Facilities Planning and Construction Service
HFPO	Hexafluoropropylene Epoxide (EDCT)
HFPO	Hexafluoropropylene Oxide [*Organic chemistry*]
HFPPV	High-Frequency Positive Pressure Ventilation [*Medicine*]
HFPR	Handling Fixture - Production (MCD)
HFPR	Human Factors and Personnel Resources (DNAB)
HFPS	Hay Fever Prevention Society
HFPS	High-Frequency Phase Shifter [*Telecommunications*]
HFPS	Home Fallout Protection Survey [*Formerly, EFPH*] [*Civil Defense*]
HFPSI	Human Factors Personnel Selection Inventory [*Interpersonal skills and attitudes test*]
HFPT	Health Fitness Physical Therapy [*NASDAQ symbol*] (SAG)
HFPT	Held for Perishable Tools
HFPT	Hlth Fitness Physl Therapy [*NASDAQ symbol*] (TTSB)
HFR	Height Finder RADAR (CET)
HFR	Heli France [*ICAO designator*] (FAAC)
HFR	High Fill Rate [*Valve*] [*Automotive engineering*]
HFR	High Flux Reactor [*Netherlands*] [*Nuclear energy*]
Hfr	High Frequency (STED)
HFR	High Frequency of Recombination [*Medicine*]
HFR	High-Frequency Resistor
HFR	Hold for Release [*Advertising*] (BARN)
HFR	Human Factors Research
HFRA	High-Frequency Recovery Antenna (KSC)
HFRA	Honorary Fellow of the Royal Academy [*British*]
HFRDF	High-Frequency Radio Direction Finding (IAA)
HFRDF	High-Frequency Repeater Distribution Frame (DEN)
HFRE	Hydraulic Fluid Replenishment Equipment
HFRG	High-Frequency Radio Group [*Military*] (CAAL)
Hfr mutant	High-Frequency Recombination Mutant (STED)
HFRO	Hill Farming Research Organisation [*British*]
HFRR	Hydrofluoric Acid Reprocessor Return [*System*] (AAEL)
HFRS	Hemorrhagic Fever with Renal Syndrome [*Medicine*]
HFRT	High-Frequency Radio Transmitter
HFRW	High-Frequency Resistance Welding [*Manufacturing term*]
HFRZ	Halbfranzband [*Half-Calf Binding*] [*Publishing*] [*German*]
HFS	French Frigate Shoals, HI [*Location identifier FAA*] (FAAL)
HFS	Hagfors [*Sweden*] [*Seismograph station code, US Geological Survey*] (SEIS)
HFS	Harrison Fisher Society (EA)
HFS	Heat Flux Sensor
HFS	Heavy Flushing Spray
HFS	Hemifacial Spasm [*Medicine*]
HFS	HFS, Inc. [*Associated Press*] (SAG)
HFS	Hierarchical File Storage (ACRL)
HFS	Hierarchical File System [*Computer science*]
HFS	High-Frequency Stimulation [*Physiology*]
HFS	High-Fructose Syrup (EDCT)
HFS	Holstein Friesian Society of Great Britain and Ireland (DBA)
HFS	Holy Family Seminary [*Connecticut*]
HFS	Horizontal Flight Simulator (MCD)
HFS	Hospital Financial Support (DMAA)
HFS	Hospitality Franchise Systems [*NYSE symbol*] (SPSG)
HFS	Hostile Fire Simulator [*Military*] (MCD)
HFS	Household Financial Services [*Australia*]
HFS	Human Factors Society (EA)
HFS	Human Factors Study
HFS	HyperFine Shift (AAEL)
HFS	Hyperfine Structure
hfs	Hyperfine Structure (STED)
HFS	Hypothetical Future Samples [*Statistics*]
HFSA	Hardin Bancorp [*NASDAQ symbol*] (TTSB)
HFSA	Hardin Bancorp, Inc. [*NASDAQ symbol*] (SAG)
HFSA	Hydrofluorsilicic Acid [*Inorganic chemistry*]
HFSC	Hamilton Financial Services Corp. [*NASDAQ symbol*] (SAG)
HFSC	Human Fetal Spinal Cord
HFSC	Hyperfine Splitting Constant [*Spectroscopy*]
HF-SCF	Hartee-Fock Self-Consistent Field (MEC)
HFSE	High-Field-Strength Elements [*Geochemistry*]
HFSE	Human Factors and Safety Engineering (DNAB)
HFSF	Home Federal Financial Corp. [*NASDAQ symbol*] (SAG)
HFSG	Healthcare Financing Study Group (EA)
HFSH	Human Follicle Stimulating Hormone [*Endocrinology*]
hFSH	Human Follicle-Stimulating Hormone [*Medicine*] (STED)
HFSIW	Hospitality Franchise Sys Wrrt [*NASDAQ symbol*] (TTSB)
HFSP	Hanukah Factor Serine Protease (DMAA)
HFSP	Human Frontier Science Program [*An international effort, proposed by Japan in 1987*]
HFSS	High-Frequency Sounder System (SSD)
HFSSB	High-Frequency Single Sideband [*Telecommunications*]
HFSSC	High-Frequency Swept Spectrum Communications
HFST	Hearing-for-Speech Test
HFST	High-Flux Scram Trip [*Nuclear energy*] (IEEE)
HFSU	Heat Flux Sensing Unit
HFSV	High Flow Shutoff Valve
HFT	Hachette-Filipacchi Telematique [*Information service or system*] (IID)
HFT	Hammerfest [*Norway*] [*Airport symbol*] (OAG)
HFT	Heavy Fire Team [*Military*]
HFT	Heft (ROG)
HFT	Heiney Family Tree (EA)
HFT	Held for Tooling
HFT	Hidden Frames Test [*Education*] (EDAC)
HFT	High-Flux Telescope
HFT	High-Frequency of Transduction [*Virology*]
HFT	High-Frequency Transduction (STED)
HFT	High-Frequency Transfer (DB)
HFT	Hollyfordair Travel Ltd. [*New Zealand*] [*ICAO designator*] (FAAC)
HFT	Home Farm Trust (BUAC)
HFT	Horizontal Flight Test (NAKS)
HFT	Horizontal Flight Testing [*NASA*] (KSC)
HFT	Hot Functional Testing [*Nuclear energy*] (NRCH)
HFT	International Symposium on Human Factors in Telecommunications (BUAC)
HFTA	Hexafluorothioacetone [*Organic chemistry*]
HFTB	Handling Fixture - Tow Bar (MCD)
HFTE	Human Factors Test and Evaluation [*Military*] (MCD)
HFTF	Horizontal Flight Test Facility [*NASA*] (NASA)
HFTL	Held for Tool Liaison
HFTS	Horizontal Flight Test Simulator [*NASA*] (NASA)
HFTS	Human Factors Trade Studies [*Navy*]
HFU	Hand-Foot-Uterus Syndrome [*Medicine*] (DMAA)
HFU	Heat-Flow [*or Flux*] Unit [*Nuclear energy*]
HFU	Heeres-Funkstelle [*Army Radio Station*] [*German military - World War II*]
HFUPR	Hourly Fetal Urine Production Rate [*Medicine*] (AAMN)
HFUS	Historic Festivals of the United States [*A publication*]
HFV	High-Frequency Ventilation [*Medicine*]
HFV	Horizontal Flight Vector
HFV	Human Foamy Virus
HF-VEL	Half-Vellum [*Bookbinding*] (DGA)
HFVOA	Hull Fishing Vessel Owners' Association (BUAC)
HFW	Haverfordwest [*Wales*] [*Airport symbol*] (AD)
HFW	Hole Full of Water [*Drilling*] (DICI)
HFW	Housing for Women (BUAC)
HFWA	High-Frequency Wave Analyzer
HFWB	High Freqency Wire Broadcasting (PDAA)
HFWE	Having Fun with Elvis [*Fan club*] (EA)
HFWF	Hired Farm Working Force
HFX	Halifax City Regional Library [*UTLAS symbol*]
HFX	High-Frequency Transceiver [*or Transducer*]
HG	Centreline Air Services Ltd. [*British ICAO designator*] (ICDA)
HG	Die Hethitischen Gesetze. Documenta et Monumenta Orientis Antiqui 7 [*Leiden*] [*A publication*] (BJA)
Hg	Haggai [*Old Testament book*]
HG	Half Gross (DNAB)
HG	Hammurabi's Gesetz (BJA)
HG	Hand Generator
HG	Hand Grip (DMAA)
HG	Handgrip Exercise (DB)
HG	Harbor Airlines [*ICAO designator*] (AD)
HG	Hard Gelatin [*Pharmacy*]
HG	Harmonic Generator
HG	Harrogate [*Postcode*] (ODBW)
HG	Having (ROG)
HG	Head Gasket [*Automotive engineering*]
HG	Headgear [*Mining engineering*] (IAA)
HG	Hectogram
HG	Heliogram
HG	Hemoglobin [*Biochemistry, medicine*]
HG	Heptadecapeptide Gastrin [*Endocrinology*]
HG	Herpes Genitalis [*Infectious disease*] (DAVI)
HG	Herpes Gestationis [*Medicine*]
HG	Herter-Gee [*Syndrome*] [*Medicine*] (DB)
HG	Herter-Gee [*Syndrome*] (STED)
HG	Heschl's Gyrus [*Brain anatomy*]
Hg	Heterodera glycenes [*A nematode*]
HG	Hexylene Glycol [*Organic chemistry*]
HG	Higher Grade
HG	High German [*Language, etc.*]
HG	High Glucose [*Clinical chemistry*]
HG	High Grain (NASA)
HG	His [*or Her*] Grace

HG .... Holy Ghost
HG .... Home Guard [*British*]
HG .... Homing Guidance (AAG)
HG .... Horizon Grow [*Astronomy*] (OA)
HG .... Horse Guards [*British*]
HG .... Hotchkiss Gunner [*British military*] (DMA)
HG .... Housing Guaranty
HG .... Hull Gauge
HG .... Human Gonadotrophin [*Endocrinology*]
HG .... Human Growth [*Factor*] [*Endocrinology*] (DAVI)
HG .... Hutchinson-Gilford [*Syndrome*] (STED)
HG .... Hutchinson-Gilford [*Disease*] [*Medicine*] (DB)
Hg .... Hydrargyrum [*Mercury*] [*Chemical element*]
HG .... Hydrogen Gas [*System*] [*Nuclear energy*] (NRCH)
HG .... Hydrogen Generator
HG .... Hydrophilic Group [*Surfactant technology*]
HG .... Hyperglycemic-Glycogenolytic [*Factor*] [*Endocrinology*]
HG .... Hypertensive Group [*Cardiology*]
HG .... Hypobranchial Gland
HG .... Hypoglycemia [*Medicine*] (DMAA)
Hg .... Mercury [*Chemical*] (EERA)
HG .... Workout Handily from Gate [*Horse racing*]
HGA .... Hammel Green and Abrahamson, Inc. [*A national leader in innovative design*]
HGA .... Handweavers Guild of America (EA)
HGA .... Hang Glider Association (EA)
HGA .... Hardware Graphics Accelerator [*Computer science*]
HGA .... Hargeisa [*Somalia*] [*Airport symbol*] (OAG)
HGA .... Harvey Gray & Associates
HGA .... Heat Generator Assembly (KSC)
HGA .... Heptagonal Games Association (EA)
HGA .... Hercules Graphics Adapter (PCM)
HGA .... Hereditary Grand Almoner [*Freemasonry*]
HGA .... Heritage U.S. Government Income Fund [*NYSE symbol*] (SPSG)
HGA .... Heritage U.S. Govt Income Fd [*NYSE symbol*] (TTSB)
HGA .... High Gain Antenna
HGA .... Hobby Greenhouse Association (EA)
HGA .... Hobby Greenhouse Owners Association of America [*Defunct*] (EA)
HGA .... Hobby Guild of America (EA)
HGA .... Hogan Air [*ICAO designator*] (FAAC)
HGA .... Homogentisate [*Biochemistry*]
HGA .... Homogentisic Acid [*Biochemistry*] (MAE)
HGA .... Hop Growers of America (EA)
HGA .... Hotel Greeters of America [*Later, HMGI*]
HGAA .... Hydride Generation Atomic Absorption [*Analytical chemistry*]
HGAC .... High Gain Antenna Controller
HGAC .... Human Genetics Advisory Commission [*British*]
HGAC .... Human Genetics Advisory Committee (WDAA)
H G & L Rev... Harvard Gay & Lesbian Review [*A publication*] (BRI)
HGAS .... High Gain Antenna System (IEEE)
HGB .... Handelsgesetzbuch [*Commercial Code*] [*German Legal term*] (DLA)
HGB .... Hanford Gable Butte [*Washington*] [*Seismograph station code, US Geological Survey*] (SEIS)
HGB .... Hemoglobin [*Biochemistry, medicine*]
Hgb .... Hemoglobin [*Medicine*] (DB)
HGB .... Hot Gas Bonder
HGB .... Household Goods Carriers' Bureau Agent, Arlington VA [*STAC*]
Hgb & Hct ... Hemoglobin and Hematocrit [*Hematology*] (DAVI)
HGB EL .... Hemoglobin Electrophoresis [*Hematology*] (DAVI)
HGB Elect .... Hemoglobin Electrophoresis [*Hematology*] (DAVI)
Hgb F .... Hemoglobin Fetal [*Also, HbF, HgF*] [*Medicine*] (DAVI)
HGBN .... Herringbone [*Electronics, engineering*]
HGB-PL .... Hemoglobin Plasma [*Hematology*] (DAVI)
HGBS .... Methemoglobin-Sulfhemoglobin [*Hematology*] (DAVI)
HGC .... Hercules Graphics [*Computer science*] (CDE)
HGC .... Hudson General [*AMEX symbol*] (TTSB)
HGC .... Hudson General Corp. [*AMEX symbol*] (SPSG)
HGC .... Hypergolic Clean
HGCA .... Home Grown Cereals Authority (PDAA)
HGCB .... Household Goods Carriers' Bureau (EA)
HGCC .... Human Genome Coordinating Committee (HGEN)
HG-CSF .... Human Granulocyte, Colony Stimulation Factor [*Hematology*]
HGCU .... Heavy Glider Conversion Unit [*British military*] (DMA)
HGD .... Hangard Aviation Ltd. [*Mongolia*] [*ICAO designator*] (FAAC)
HGD .... Hawthorne Gold [*Vancouver Stock Exchange symbol*]
HGD .... High Grade Dysplasia [*Medicine*]
HGD .... Hogshead
HGD .... Hourglass Device [*Military decoration*] (AFM)
HGD .... Hughenden [*Australia Airport symbol*] (OAG)
hg den .... Hearing Denied [*Legal term*] (HGAA)
HGDFS .... High Gain Direction Finding System (PDAA)
HGDH .... His [*or Her*] Grand Ducal Highness
HGDP .... Human Genome Diversity Project [*Genetics*]
HGDS .... Hazardous Gas Detection Systems (KSC)
HGE .... Handling Ground Equipment
HGE .... Hemorrhage [*Medicine*] (ROG)
HGE .... Het Gilgamesj-Epos [*A publication*] (BJA)
HGE .... Hinge [*Automotive engineering*]
HGE .... Human Granulocytic Ehrlichiosis [*Medicine*]
HGE .... Hybrid Geotempered Envelope [*Architecture*]
HGE .... Hydraulic Grade Elevations (NRCH)
HGED .... High-Gain Emissive Display [*Technology*]
HGF .... Heliglobe Industries [*France*] [*FAA designator*] (FAAC)
HGF .... Helmholtz-Gemeinschaft Deutscher Forschungs-zentren [*Helmholtz association of German research centres*]

HGF .... Hematopoietic Growth Factor [*Biochemistry Medicine*]
HgF .... Hemoglobin, Fetal [*Also, HbF*] [*Medicine*]
HGF .... Hemopoietic Growth Factor [*Hematology*]
HGF .... Hepatocyte Growth Factor [*Biochemistry*]
HGF .... Horizontal Gradient Freeze (AAEL)
HGF .... Household Goods Forwarders Tariff Bureau, Washington DC [*STAC*]
HGF .... Human Growth Foundation (EA)
HGF .... Hyperglycemic-Glycogenolytic Factor [*Later, Glucagon*] [*Endocrinology*]
HGFA .... Henry George Foundation of America (EA)
HGFA .... Household Goods Forwarders Association of America [*Washington, DC*]
HGFN .... HomeGold Financial [*NASDAQ symbol*] [*Formerly, Emergent Group*]
HGG .... Herpetic Geniculate Ganglionitis [*Medicine*] (DB)
HGG .... Hot Gas Generator
HGG .... Human Gamma-Globulin [*Endocrinology*]
HGGR .... Haggar Corp. [*NASDAQ symbol*] (SAG)
HGH .... Hangchow [*China*] [*Airport symbol*] (AD)
HGH .... Hangzhou [*China*] [*Airport symbol*] (OAG)
HGH .... Historische Grammatik der Hebraeischen Sprache [*H. Bauer and P. Leander*] [*A publication*] (BJA)
HGH .... Human Growth Hormone [*Also, hGH*] [*Endocrinology*]
hGH .... Human Growth Hormone (DOG)
HGHGHG...... Hilf Gott, Hilf Gott, Hilf Gott [*God Help, God Help, God Help*] [*Motto of Sophie Elisabeth, Countess of Schwarzenburg (1565-1621)*]
Hghland....... Highland Federal Bank [*Associated Press*] (SAG)
Hghlds......... Highlands (DD)
HGHR .... Higher
hGHR .... Human Growth Hormone Receptor [*Genetics*] (DOG)
HGHSC .... Home Grown Herbage Seeds Committee (BUAC)
HghwyH....... Highway Holdings Ltd. [*Associated Press*] (SAG)
HGI .... Henry George Institute (EA)
HGI .... HGI Realty [*NYSE symbol*] (TTSB)
HGI .... Horizon Group [*NYSE symbol*] [*Formerly, HGI Realty*] (SG)
HGI .... Horizon Group, Inc. [*NYSE symbol*] (SAG)
HGI .... Horizon Outlet Centers [*NYSE symbol*] (SPSG)
HGI .... Hostility-Guilt Inventory (DB)
HGIC .... Harleysville Group [*NASDAQ symbol*] (TTSB)
HGIC .... Harleysville Group, Inc. [*NASDAQ symbol*] (NQ)
HGI Rlty ...... HGI Realty, Inc. [*Associated Press*] (SAG)
HGJ .... Hongo [*Japan*] [*Seismograph station code, US Geological Survey*] (SEIS)
HGL .... Hamilton Group Ltd. [*Toronto Stock Exchange symbol*]
HGL .... Helgoland [*Germany Airport symbol*] (OAG)
HGL .... Heregulin (DMAA)
HGL .... Hewlett-Packard Graphics Language [*Image Format*] (AAEL)
HGL .... High Gain Link
HGL .... High Go Low Test
HGL .... Homach Gap Lathe
HGL .... Hyperbolic Type Gas Lens (IAA)
HGLDS .... Highlands (MCD)
HGLF .... High-Grain/Low-Fiber [*Cereal*] (OA)
HGLND........ Highland
HGM .... Hectogram (ROG)
HGM .... Hereditary Grand Master [*Freemasonry*] (ROG)
HGM .... Hot Gas Manifold (NASA)
HGM .... Human Gene-Mapping
HGM .... Human Genome Meeting (HGEN)
HGMAA........ Hang Glider Manufacturers Association of America [*Defunct*] (EA)
HGMC .... Harmony Gold Mining Co. Ltd. [*NASDAQ symbol*] (SAG)
HGMCR .... Human Genetic Mutant Cell Repository
HGMF .... High-Gradient Magnetic Filtration
HGMGR........ Household Goods Military and Government Rate Tariff
HGMIS .... Human Genome Management Information System (HGEN)
HGML .... Human Gene-Mapping Library [*Database*]
HGMM .... Hereditary Grand Master Mason [*Freemasonry*]
HGMN .... Herb Growing and Marketing Network (EA)
HGMS .... Helicopter Gravity-Measuring System [*Naval Oceanographic Office*]
HGMS .... High-Gradient Magnetic Separation (EDCT)
HGMS .... High-Gradient Magnetic Separator (NRCH)
HGMU .... Heavy Glider Maintenance Unit [*British military*] (DMA)
HGMUS........ Horizontal Generator Mock-Up System [*NASA*]
HGN .... Horizontal Gaze Nystagmus Test
HGN .... Human Genome News [*A publication*] (HGEN)
HGN .... Hypogastric Nerve [*Anatomy*]
HGN .... Mae Hong Son [*Thailand*] [*Airport symbol*] (OAG)
HG/NG .... Hydrogen Gas/Nitrogen Gas (NRCH)
HGO .... Halsgerichtsordnung [*German*]
HGO .... Heavy Gas Oils [*Petroleum product*]
HGO .... Hepatic Glucose Output [*Physiology*]
HGO .... Hermes Global Orbiter [*NASA, proposed*]
HGO .... Hugo, CO [*Location identifier FAA*] (FAAL)
HGO .... Human Glucose Output [*Hematology*] (DMAA)
HGO .... Korhogo [*Ivory Coast*] [*Airport symbol*] (OAG)
HGP .... Hard Gas-Permeable [*Contact lenses*]
HGP .... Hepatic Glucose Production [*Hematology*] (DMAA)
HGP .... Horizontal Ground Plane [*Automotive engineering*]
HGP .... Hormonal Growth Promotant
HGP .... Human Genome Program [*Genetics*]
HGP .... Human Genome Project (HGEN)
HGP .... Hungarian Green Party [*Political party*] (BUAC)
HGP .... Hungarian Gypsy Party [*Political party*] (BUAC)
HGP .... Hyperglobulinemic Purpura [*Medicine*] (DMAA)
HGP-OIMLA... Hindustani Ghadar Party-Organization of Indian Marxist-Leninists Abroad

HGPRT......... Hypoxanthine-Guanine Phosphoribosyltransferase [AO HPRT] [An enzyme]
HG-PRTase... Hypoxanthine-Guanine Phosphoribosyltransferase [Also, HGPRT, HPRT] [An enzyme] (DAVI)
HGPRT LOCUS... Hypoxanthine Guanine Phosphoribosyl Transferase Locus (LDT)
HGPS .... High-Grade Plow Steel
HGPS .... Hutchinson-Gilford Progeria Syndrome [Medicine] (DMAA)
HGR .... Hagerstown [Maryland] [Airport symbol] (OAG)
HGR .... Hangar (KSC)
HGR .... Hanger
HGR .... Hanger Orthopedic Group, Inc. [AMEX symbol] (SPSG)
HGR .... Hanger Orthopedic Grp [NASDAQ symbol] (TTSB)
HGR .... Haubitzgranate [Howitzer Shell] [German military - World War II]
HGR .... Headgear Receiver [Mining engineering] (IAA)
HGR .... High Group Receiving
HGR .... High River Resources Ltd. [Vancouver Stock Exchange symbol]
HGR .... Histoire Generale des Religions [A publication] (BJA)
HGR .... Hot Gas Reinjection (PDAA)
HGR .... Human Glucocorticoid Receptor [Endocrinology]
HGR & SPTFAC... Hangar and Support Facility [NASA] (NASA)
HGRF .... Hot Gas Radiating Facility
HGRF .... Human Growth-Hormone Releasing Factor [Biochemistry]
HGRM .... Hemogram [Hematology] (DAVI)
HGS .... Congregation de Hermanas Guadalupanas de la Salle (TOCD)
HGS .... Freetown [Sierra Leone] Hastings Airport [Airport symbol] (OAG)
HGS .... Hagensborg Resources Ltd. [Vancouver Stock Exchange symbol]
HGS .... Harness Goat Society (BUAC)
HGS .... Head-Up Guidance System [Aviation]
HGS .... Hot Gas System
HGS .... Human Genome Sciences [Commercial firm]
H-GS .... Hurdy-Gurdy Society [British] (DBA)
HGS .... Hydrogen Gas Saver (MCD)
HGSC .... Hyperbolic Grid System
HGSC .... Hoare Govett Small Companies Index [British]
HGSD .... Heavy Gauge Solid Drawn [Conduit]
HGSDP .... Hungarian Gypsy Social Democratic Party [Political party] (BUAC)
HGSE .... Harvard Graduate School of Education
HGSE .... Hot Gas Soldering Equipment
HGSEI .... Home and Garden Show Executives International [Defunct] (EA)
HGSHS .... Harvard Group Scale of Hypnotic Susceptibility [Psychology]
HGSI .... Human Genome Sciences [NASDAQ symbol] (TTSB)
HGSI .... Human Genome Sciences, Inc. [NASDAQ symbol] (SAG)
HGSITVC...... Hot Gas Secondary Injection Thrust Vector Control (PDAA)
HGSW .... Heavy Gauge Screwed Welded [Conduit]
HGSW .... Horn Gap Switch
HGT .... Fort Hunter-Liggett (Jolon), CA [Location identifier FAA] (FAAL)
HGT .... Height (KSC)
HGT .... High Gelling Temperature [Analytical biochemistry]
HGT .... High Group Transmitting
HGT .... Household Goods Transportation Association, Washington DC [STAC]
HGT .... Hydrostatic-Gauging Technology [Engineering]
HGT .... Hypergeometric Group Testing [Computer science] (OA)
HGTA .... Honours Graduate Teachers' Association [British]
HGTAC......... Home Grown Timber Advisory Committee (BUAC)
HGTMC........ Home Grown Timber Marketing Corp. Ltd. [British] (BI)
HGTS .... Heights [Commonly used] (OPSA)
HGTV .... Home & Garden Television
HGTV .... Home and Garden Television Network
HGTVC......... Hot Gas Thrust Vector Control
HGU .... Horizon Gyroscope Unit [Aviation] (AIA)
HGU .... Mount Hagen [Papua New Guinea] [Airport symbol] (OAG)
HGUC........... Helsinki Guarantees for Ukraine Committee [Defunct] (EA)
HGV .... Heavy Goods Vehicles
HGV .... Hepatitis G Virus
HGV .... Highgrade Ventures [Vancouver Stock Exchange symbol]
HGV .... Hydrogen Gas Valve (MCD)
HGVSX .... SMBS Govt. Securities Cl.B [Mutual fund ticker symbol] (SG)
HGVT .... Horizontal Ground Vibration Test [NASA] (NASA)
HGW .... Heat-Generative Radioactive Wastes [Nuclear energy]
HGW .... Hyper-Quenched Glassy Water [Material science]
HGWP .... Halocarbon Global-Warming Potential [Meteorology]
HGWS.......... H. G. Wells Society (EA)
HGWY .... Highway (WGA)
HgwyH......... Highway Holdings Ltd. [Associated Press] (SAG)
HGX .... Lawrence, MA [Location identifier FAA] (FAAL)
HGZG .... Hilf Gott zu Glueck [May God Help Us to Fortune] [Motto of Magdalene, Princess of Anhalt (1585-1657)] [German]
HH .... Double Hard [Pencil leads]
HH .... Extra Hard [Pencil leads]
HH .... Fairchild/Republic [ICAO aircraft manufacturer identifier] (ICAO)
HH .... Habitat for Humanity (EA)
HH .... Half Hard [Metallurgy]
HH .... Half Hardy [Horticulture]
H/H .... Half Height [of an International Standards Organization container] (DCTA)
HH .... Halothane Hepatitis [Medicine] (DMAA)
HH .... Halothane Hypoxia [Medicine]
HH .... Hamish Hamilton [Publisher] [British]
HH .... Hamizrah Hehadash [Jerusalem] [A publication] (BJA)
HH .... Hampshire Hunt [British]
HH .... Handhole (AAG)
HH .... Hands [Units of measure, especially for the height of horses]
HH .... Hanging Handset [Telecommunications] (TEL)
HH .... Happy Humpers (EA)

HH .... Hard of Hearing
HH .... Harvest Help [An association British] (EAIO)
HH .... Hashomer Hatzair (EA)
HH .... Haunt Hunters (EA)
H/H .... Havre to Hamburg [Shipping]
HH .... Hawaii State Library System, Honolulu, HI [Library symbol Library of Congress] (LCLS)
HH .... Hayward and Hazelton's United States Circuit Court Reports [District of Columbia] [A publication] (DLA)
HH .... Head, Head [Coin-tossing possibility]
HH .... Head-Holmes [Syndrome] [Medicine] (DB)
HH .... Headlamp Housing [Automotive engineering]
HH .... Head-to-Head [Polymer structure]
HH .... Healthy Hemophiliac [Medicine] (DMAA)
HH .... Heavy Helicopter [Military] (VNW)
HH .... Heavy Hinged [Philately]
HH .... Heavy Hydrogen
HH .... Heil Hitler [Political organization] [British]
HH .... Helen Hunt Jackson [American novelist, 1830-1885] [Initials used as pseudonym]
H-H .... Heli-Home [Recreational vehicle]
HH .... Hemmets Haerold [Record label] [Sweden]
H/H .... Hemoglobin and Hematocrit [Medicine] (STED)
Hh. .... Hemopoietic Histocompatibility (STED)
HH .... Henderson and Haggard [Inhaler] [Medicine] (DAVI)
HH .... Herbig-Haro [Astronomy]
HH .... Hereditary Haemochromatosis [Medicine]
HH .... Here's Health [Exhibition] [British]
HH .... Herfindahl-Hirschman [Economic indicator]
HH .... Herman Hospital [Houston, TX]
HH .... Hertfordshire Hunt [British] (ROG)
HH .... Hetch Hetchy [Railroad] (MHDW)
HH .... Hetch Hetchy Railroad (IIA)
HH .... Hiatal Hernia [Medicine]
HH .... High-Powered, Nondirectional Radio Homing Beacon [Navigation]
HH .... His [or Her] Highness
HH .... His Holiness
HH .... His Honour [British] (ADA)
HH .... Historical Handbook
HH .... Hodgson's Horse [British military] (DMA)
HH .... Hogarth [H.] and Sons [Steamship line] (MHDW)
HH .... Hogshead (DNAB)
HH .... Hold Harmless (OICC)
HH .... Holidays for Humanity [An association] (EA)
HH .... Holistic Health [Medicine] (DAVI)
HH .... Home Health [Medicine] (DAVI)
HH .... Home Help [Medicine]
HH .... Hommel AG [Switzerland] [Research code symbol]
HH .... Homonymous Hemianopsia [Ophthalmology]
HH .... Hooper Holmes [AMEX symbol] (TTSB)
HH .... Hooper Holmes, Inc. [AMEX symbol] (SPSG)
HH .... Hour Hand [Clocks] (ROG)
HH .... Household
H/H .... House to House (ADA)
HH .... Hughes Helicopters (MCD)
HH .... Human Hair [Doll collecting]
HH .... Humbert Humbert [Character in Vladimir Nabokov's "Lolita"]
HH .... Hunter-Hurler [Syndrome] [Medicine] (DB)
HH .... Hydroxyhexamide [Organic chemistry] (MAE)
HH .... Hydroxyhexenal [Organic chemistry]
HH .... Hyperactive Help [Australia]
HH .... Hypergastrinemic Hyperchlorhydria [Medicine] (DB)
HH .... Hypogonadism [Endocrinology] (DAVI)
HH .... Hypogonadotrophic [Endocrinology] (DAVI)
HH .... Hyporeninemic Hypoaldosteronism [Endocrinology]
HH .... Les Hieroglyphes Hittites [A publication] (BJA)
HH .... Rotary-Wing Air-Sea-Rescue Aircraft [Navy symbol] (MUGU)
HH .... Somali Airlines [ICAO designator] (AD)
HHA .... Anderson [H. H.] Line [Steamship] (MHDB)
HHA .... Half-Hardy Annual [Horticulture] (ROG)
H(Ha)........... Hare Tempore Wigram, Etc. [1841-53] [A publication] (DLA)
HHA .... Hatton Heritage Association (EA)
HHA .... Health Hazard Appraisal (STED)
HHA .... Health Hazard Assessment [Army]
HHA .... Hereditary Hemolytic Anemia [Medicine]
HHA .... Hickory Handle Association (EA)
HHA .... High High Alarm (ECII)
HHA .... Historic House Association [British]
HHA .... Home Health Agency
HHA .... Home Health Aid (DAVI)
HHA .... Hungarian Horse Association (EA)
HHA .... Hydro Home Appliances Ltd. [Formerly, Hemgold Resources Ltd.] [Vancouver Stock Exchange symbol]
HHA .... Hypothalamo-Hypophyseal-Adrenal [Endocrinology]
HHAA .... Historic House Association of America (EA)
HHAA .... Hypothalamo-Hypophyseal-Adrenal Axis (STED)
HHAG .... Human Health Assessment Group [Environmental Protection Agency]
HHALSA....... Heritage Hills Area Library Services Authority [Library network]
HHANES....... Hispanic Health and Nutrition Examination Survey [Department of Health and Human Services] (GFGA)
HHAR .... Health Hazard Assessment Report [Army]
HHB .... Bernice Pauahi Bishop Museum, Honolulu, HI [Library symbol Library of Congress] (LCLS)
HHB .... Half-Hardy Biennial [Horticulture] (ROG)
HHB .... Happy Hours Brotherhood (EA)

HHB	Hattiesburg, MS [*Location identifier FAA*] (FAAL)
HHB	Headquarters and Headquarters Battery [*Army*]
HHb	Hemoglobin, Reduced [*Biochemistry, medicine*]
HHb	Hemoglobin Un-Ionized [*Hematology*] (DAVI)
HHB	Hypochemoglobinemia [*Medicine*] (STED)
HHBC	Honourable Hudson's Bay Co. [*Canada*]
HHBLG	Hobby Horse Brigade of the Legion of Guardsmen (EA)
HHC	Chatham College, Pittsburgh, PA [*OCLC symbol*] (OCLC)
HHC	Hammer Head Crane (NASA)
HHC	Handheld Computer
HHC	Harley Hummer Club (EA)
HHC	Harte-Hanks Communications, Inc. (EFIS)
HHC	Headquarters and Headquarters Company [*Army*]
HHC	Heavy Helicopter Company [*Military*] (VNW)
HHC	Hemoglobin-Haptoglobin Complex (DB)
HHC	Higher Harmonic Control (MCD)
HHC	Highland Crow Resources Ltd. [*Toronto Stock Exchange symbol Vancouver Stock Exchange symbol*]
HHC	Home Health Care [*Medicine*] (DAVI)
HHC	Honolulu Community College, Honolulu, HI [*Library symbol Library of Congress*] (LCLS)
HHC	Hoover Historical Center (EA)
HHC	Horizon/CMS Healthcare [*NYSE symbol*] (TTSB)
HHC	Horizon CMS Healthcare Corp. [*NYSE symbol*] (SAG)
HHC	Horizon Healthcare Corp. [*NYSE symbol*] (SPSG)
HHC	Houdini Historical Center (EA)
HHC	Hovercraft-Helicopter Carrier
HHC	Hughes Helicopter Co.
HHC	New York City Health and Hospitals Corp. (EA)
HHCA	Home Health Corp. of Amer [*NASDAQ symbol*] (TTSB)
HHCA	Home Health Corp. of America, Inc. [*NASDAQ symbol*] (SAG)
HHCC	Higher Harmonic Circulation Control [*Rotor*] [*Navy*]
hHCF	Human Humoral Hypercalcemic Factor [*Oncology*]
HHCL	Hale's History of the Common Law [*A publication*] (DLA)
HHCL	H-Hour Coordinating Line [*Army*] (AABC)
HHCL	Howell Henry Chaldecott Lury [*Advertising agency*] [*British*]
HHCS	High-Altitude Hypertrophic Cardiomyopathy Syndrome [*Medicine*] (STED)
HHD	Doctor of Honorary Humanities
HHD	Doctor of Humanities
HHD	Headquarters and Headquarters Detachment [*Army*] (AABC)
HHD	High Heparin Dose [*Medicine*] (DMAA)
HHD	High Heparin Doses [*Medicine*] (DB)
HHD	High Holy Days (BJA)
HHD	Hogshead
HHD	Home Dialysis [*Medicine*] (DMAA)
HHD	Home Hemodialysis [*Medicine*] (STED)
HHD	Hypertensive Heart Disease [*Medicine*]
HHDDE	Heavy Heavy-Duty Diesel Engine [*Motor vehicle specifications*]
HHDN	Hexachlorohexahydrodimethanonaphthalene [*Insecticide, commonly called Aldrin*]
HHDW	Heavy Handy Deadweight [*Scrap*] [*Shipping*]
HHDWS	Heavy Handy Deadweight Scrap Iron [*Shipping*] (DS)
HHE	Hand-Held Equipment (DWSG)
HHE	Heli-Holland BV [*Netherlands ICAO designator*] (FAAC)
HHE	Helium to Heat Exchanger (AAG)
HHE	Hemiconvulsions, Hemiplegia, Epilepsy [*Medicine*]
HHE	Herringer-Hulster Effect
HHE	Household Economics Research Division [*of ARS, Department of Agriculture*]
HHE	Household Effects [*Insurance*]
HHE	Human Health and the Environment (GNE)
HHEC	Hispanic Higher Education Coalition [*Defunct*] (EA)
HHEFG	Hughes Hall Effect Function Generator
HHEG	Hughes Hall Effect Generator
HHE-P	East-West Center, Population Institute, Honolulu, HI [*Library symbol Library of Congress*] (LCLS)
HHES	Hex Head Electrical Squib
HHES	Housing and Household Economic Statistics [*US Census Bureau*]
HHESD	Population Division and Housing and Household Economics Statistics Division [*Bureau of the Census*] [*Also, an information service or system*] (IID)
HHF	Canadian, TX [*Location identifier FAA*] (FAAL)
HHF	Friends of the Library of Hawaii, Honolulu, HI [*Library symbol Library of Congress*] (LCLS)
HHF	Health for Haiti Foundation (EA)
HHF	Household Furniture [*Insurance*]
HHF	Hyper-High-Frequency (DEN)
HHFA	Housing and Home Finance Agency [*Terminated 1965, functions taken over by HUD*]
HHFC	Harvest Home Financial Corp. [*NASDAQ symbol*] (SAG)
HHFC	Harvest Home Finl [*NASDAQ symbol*] (TTSB)
HHFC	H. H. Franklin Club (EA)
HHFM	High-Humidity Face Mask [*Medicine*] (MEDA)
HHFS	Hilar High-Frequency Stimulation [*Neurophysiology*]
HHFT	Heavy Helicopter Fire Team (DNAB)
HHFT	Heavy Helo Fire Team [*Military*] (VNW)
HHFTH	National Foundation for Happy Horsemanship for the Handicapped (EA)
HHG	High-Harmonic Generation [*Physics*]
HH-G	Hitchhiker (Goddard Space Flight Center) [*NASA*]
HHG	Household Goods [*Insurance*]
HHG	Hypertrophic Hypersecretory Gastropathy [*Medicine*] (DMAA)
HHG	Hypogonadotropic Hypogonadism [*Medicine*]
HHGCB	Household Goods Carriers Bureau
HHGFAA	Household Goods Forwarders Association of America (EA)
HHGP	Harris & Harris Group [*NASDAQ symbol*] (TTSB)
HHGP	Harris & Harris Group, Inc. [*NASDAQ symbol*] (NQ)
HHGR	Helian Health Group, Inc. [*NASDAQ symbol*] (NQ)
HHH	Devine, TX [*Location identifier FAA*] (FAAL)
HHH	Harrison Horncastle Holdings [*Investment firm*] [*British*]
HHH	Hash House Harriers International (BUAC)
HHH	Hawaii Medical Library, Inc., Honolulu, HI [*Library symbol Library of Congress*] (LCLS)
HHH	Helicsa [*Spain*] [*FAA designator*] (FAAC)
HHH	Helm Capital [*AMEX symbol*] [*Formerly, Helm Resources*] (SG)
HHH	Helm Resources [*AMEX symbol*] (TTSB)
HHH	Helm Resources, Inc [*AMEX symbol*] (SAG)
HHH	Hilton Head Island [*South Carolina*] [*Airport symbol*] (OAG)
HHH	Hincherton Hayfever Helmet [*Clear plastic head-enclosing device that allegedly relieves hayfever symptoms*]
HHH	Holistic Health Havens (EA)
HHH	Hubert Horatio Humphrey [*American politician, 1911-1978*]
HHH	Hyperornithinemia, Hyperammonemia, Homocitrillinuria Syndrome [*Medicine*] (DMAA)
HHH	Triple Hard [*Pencil leads*]
HHHA	Homemaker Home Health Aide (OICC)
HHH-CRC	Hubert H. Humphrey Cancer Research Center [*Boston University*] [*Research center*] (RCD)
HHHH	FourHealth, Inc. [*NASDAQ symbol*] (SAG)
HHHH	Head, Heart, Hands, and Health [*As in 4H organizations*]
HHHHH	Hilf, Himmlischer Herr, Hoechster Hort [*Help, Heavenly Father, Highest Treasure*] [*Motto of Elisabeth, Duchess of Saxony-Coburg (1540-94)*] [*German*]
HHHMU	Hydrazine Hand-Held Maneuvering Unit (MCD)
HHHO	Hypotonia-Hypomentia-Hypogonadism-Obesity [*Medicine*]
HHI	Ha-Hevra ha-Historit ha-Israelit [*Historical Society of Israel*] (EAIO)
HHI	Harmony Heights [*Idaho*] [*Seismograph station code, US Geological Survey Closed*] (SEIS)
HHI	Harness Horsemen International (EA)
HHi	Hawaiian Historical Society, Honolulu, HI [*Library symbol Library of Congress*] (LCLS)
HHI	Hawaii County Library, Hilo, HI [*Library symbol Library of Congress*] (LCLS)
HHI	Head-of-Household Income (WDMC)
HHI	Histologic HCM [*Hypertrophic Cardiomyopathy*] Index
HHI	Home Holdings [*NYSE symbol*] (SPSG)
HHI	Homer Hoyt Institute
HHI	Horton Hydrocarbons, Inc. [*Vancouver Stock Exchange symbol*]
HHI	Hughes Helicopter, Inc.
HHI	Wahiawa, HI [*Location identifier FAA*] (FAAL)
HHIA	Headway Head Injuries Association (BUAC)
HHIC	Hilo College, Hilo, HI [*Library symbol Library of Congress*] (LCLS)
HHIP	Hand-Held Information Processor
HHIRF	Holifield Heavy Ion Research Facility [*Department of Energy*]
HHJ	Hunt, Harold, Jr., Bala-Cynwyd PA [*STAC*]
HHK	Kapiolani Community College, Honolulu, HI [*Library symbol Library of Congress*] (LCLS)
HHL	Court of Session Cases, House of Lords [*Scotland*] [*A publication*] (DLA)
HHL	Haddon Hall Library [*A publication*]
HHL	Helicopter Hire Ltd. [*British ICAO designator*] (FAAC)
HHL	Hollywood Hotline [*Information service or system*] (IID)
HHLA	Handkerchief and Household Linens Association (BUAC)
HHLD	Household [*Marketing*]
HHLGCS	[*Department of*] Health, Housing, Local Government and Community Services (EERA)
HHLH	Heaviest Heavy Lift Helicopter (MCD)
HHLR	Hand-Held LASER Range-Finder [*Military*] (RDA)
HHLR	Horace Hardy Lestor Reactor
HHLRF	Hand-Held LASER Range-Finder [*Military British*] (INF)
HHIU-W	University of Hawaii at Hilo, West Hawaii Library, Kealakekua, HI [*Library symbol*] [*Library of Congress*] (LCLS)
H + Hm	Compound Hypermetropic Astigmatism [*Ophthalmology*]
HHM	Hawkes Hospital of Mount Carmel, Mount Carmel Medical Center Library, Columbus, OH [*OCLC symbol*] (OCLC)
HHM	Health and Healing Ministries (EA)
HH-M	Hitchhiker (Marshall Space Flight Center) [*NASA*]
HHM	Humoral Hypercalcemia of Malignancy [*Medicine*]
HHM	Hungry Horse [*Montana*] [*Seismograph station code, US Geological Survey*] (SEIS)
HHM	Kotzebue, AK [*Location identifier FAA*] (FAAL)
HHM	Sisters of the Holy Humility of Mary [*Roman Catholic religious order*]
HHMC	Hawaiian Mission Children's Society, Honolulu, HI [*Library symbol Library of Congress*] (LCLS)
HHMHDB	Hispanic Health and Mental Health Data Base [*National Institute of Mental Health*] [*Information service or system*] (CRD)
HHMI	Howard Hughes Medical Institute
hh/mm	Hours/Minutes (HGAA)
HHMS	His Hellenic Majesty's Ship
HHMT	Helene Harris Memorial Trust (BUAC)
HHMU	Handheld Maneuvering Unit [*NASA*]
HHN	Hahnemann Medical College and Hospital, Philadelphia, PA [*OCLC symbol*] (OCLC)
HHN	Hand-Held Nebulizer [*Pharmacology*] (DAVI)
HHN	Hot Hydrogen Nozzle
HHNA	Home Healthcare Nurses Association (NTPA)
HHNC	His Highness the Nizam's Cavalry [*British military*] (DMA)
HHNC	Hyperglycemic Hyperosmolar Nonketotic Coma [*Endocrinology*] (CPH)

HHNK	Hyperosmolar Hyperglycemic Nonketotic (Coma) [Also, NKHHC] [Medicine]
HHO	Houston Helicopters, Inc. [ICAO designator] (FAAC)
HHOC	Holistic Health Organizing Committee (EA)
HHOCC	Holiday Happenings Ornament Collectors Club (EA)
HHOJ	Ha Ha Only Joking [Computer hacker terminology] (NHD)
HHOK	Ha Ha Only Kidding
HHOS	Ha Ha Only Serious
HHP	Half-Hardy Perennial [Horticulture] (ROG)
HHP	Handheld Processor
HHP	Head of Household Program [IRS]
HHP	Hospital Health Plan
HHP	Household Pet (WGA)
HHP	Hydraulic Hand Pump
HHP	Hydraulic Horse Power
HHP	Pineapple Research Institute, Honolulu, HI [Library symbol Library of Congress] (LCLS)
HHPA	Hexahydrophthalic Anhydride [Organic chemistry]
HHPC	Hale's History of the Pleas of the Crown [A publication] (DLA)
HHPC	Hand-Held Programmable Calculator (MCD)
HHPC	High Harmonic Pitch Control (PDAA)
HHPLA	Herbert Hoover Presidential Library Association (EA)
HHPP	Hydro-Hydrogen Pilot Project
HHPRT	Human Hypoxanthine Phosphoribosyltransferase [An enzyme]
HHPS	Hot High Pressure Separator [Chemical engineering]
HHR	Handheld RADAR (AABC)
HHR	Hawthorne, CA [Location identifier FAA] (FAAL)
HHR	High Reserve Resources [Vancouver Stock Exchange symbol]
HHR	Hydralazine, Hydrochlorothiazide, and Reserpine (DMAA)
HHRD	Horsehead Resource Dvlp [NASDAQ symbol] (TTSB)
HHREA	Health and Human Relations Education Association [Australia]
HHRH	Hereditary Hypophosphatemic Rickets with Hypercalciuria [Medicine] (DMAA)
HHRH	Hypothalamic Hypophysiotropic Releasing Hormone (DB)
HHRSD	Helicopter Hauldown and Rapid Securing Device [Military] (CAAL)
HHS	Department of Health and Human Services [Formerly, HEW]
HHS	Hand-Held Scanner (CIST)
HHS	Harte-Hanks Communications [NYSE symbol] (TTSB)
HHS	Harte-Hanks Communications, Inc. [NYSE symbol] (SPSG)
HHS	Harte-Hanks, Inc. [NYSE symbol] [Formerly, Harte-Hanks Communications]
HHS	Hawaiian Historical Society (BUAC)
HHS	Hawaiian Sugar Planters' Association, Experiment Station, Honolulu, HI [Library symbol Library of Congress] (LCLS)
HHS	Health and Human Services (DICI)
HHS	Helpers of the Holy Souls [France] (BUAC)
HHS	Hex Head Squib
HHS	Hex Head Steel (IAA)
HHS	High Strength Steel (EDCT)
HHS	Historical Harp Society (BUAC)
HHS	Horse Hemolyzate Supernatant
HHS	Huguenot Historical Society (EA)
HHS	Hungarian Historical Society [Australia]
HHS	Hypothenar Hammer Syndrome [Medicine]
HHS	Society of Helpers (TOCD)
HHS	Society of Helpers of the Holy Souls [Roman Catholic women's religious order]
HHS	US Department of Health and Human Services (GNE)
HHSA	Home Health Services Association [Later, HHSSA] (EA)
HHSA	Honolulu Star-Bulletin and Advertiser, Honolulu, HI [Library symbol Library of Congress] (LCLS)
HHSAR	Department of Health and Human Services Acquisition Regulations (GFGA)
HHSAR	Health and Human Services Acquisition Regulation (AAGC)
HHSB	Hahnemann High School Behavior Rating Scale [Psychology]
HHSD	Holographic Horizontal Situation Display
HHSF	Habitat and Human Settlements Foundation [United Nations] (EY)
HHSG	Herpes Help Support Group [Australia]
HHSGAB	Department of Health and Human Services Grant Appeals Board (AAGC)
HHSI	High-Head Safety Injection [Nuclear energy] (NRCH)
HHSMU	Hand-Held Self-Maneuvering Unit (SAA)
HHSPR	Health and Human Services Procurement Regulations (AAGC)
HHSSA	Home Health Services and Staffing Association (EA)
HHSZYM	Hashomer Hatzair Socialist Zionist Youth Movement (EA)
HHT	Headquarters and Headquarters Troop [Army] (AABC)
HHT	Hereditary Hemorrhagic Telangiectasia [Medicine]
HHT	High-Temperature Helium Turbine (PDAA)
HHT	Holland Historical Trust (EA)
HHT	Homoharringtonine [Antineoplastic drug]
HHT	Horn-Hellersberg Test [Psychology]
HHT	Hurricane Hollow [Tennessee] [Seismograph station code, US Geological Survey Closed] (SEIS)
HHT	Hush House Tiedown
HHT	Hydroxyheptadecatrienoic Acid [Organic chemistry]
HHTA	Hypothalamohypophyseothyroidal Axis (STED)
HHTG	House Heating [Freight]
HHTI	Hand-Held Thermal Imager [Navy British]
HHTM	United States Army, Tripler Army Medical Center, Honolulu, HI [Library symbol Library of Congress] (LCLS)
HHTNSW	Historic Houses Trust of New South Wales [Australia]
HHTR	Hand-Held Tactical RADAR (DNAB)
HHTT	Hexahexylthiotriphenylene [Organic chemistry]
HHTTFS	Huddersfield Healders and Twisters Trade and Friendly Society [A union] [British] (DCTA)
HHTV	Handheld Thermal Viewer (RDA)
HHTx	Head Halter Traction (STED)
HHV	Handheld Viewer
HHV	Heavy-High-mobility [Multipurpose Wheeled] Vehicle [See also HMMWV] (DOMA)
HHV	Help Hospitalized Veterans (EA)
HHV	High Heating Value Hydrocyclone (EDCT)
HHV	High Heat [or Heating] Value
HHV	Human Herpes Virus
HHV-6	Human Herpes Virus-6 [Medicine] (TAD)
HHW	Higher High Water [Tides and currents]
HHW	High-Heat Waste (NRCH)
HHW	Household Hazardous Waste
HHWI	Higher High-Water Interval
HHWP	Household Hazardous Waste Project (EA)
HHX	Heavy-Lift Helicopter, Experimental (SAA)
HHY	Savannah, TN [Location identifier FAA] (FAAL)
HHYF	Harness Horse Youth Foundation (EA)
HHZYM	Hashomer Hatzair Zionist Youth Movement (EA)
HI	Habitability Improvement [Navy] (NVT)
HI	Hair International (NTPA)
HI	Handicap International [Belgium] (BUAC)
HI	Handicap Introductions (EA)
HI	Handling Instructions (MCD)
HI	Harcost Industries
HI	Hardware Interrupt
HI	Harold Institute [Defunct] (EA)
HI	Harvest Index [Agronomy]
HI	Hat Institute (EA)
HI	Hawaii [Postal code]
HI	Hawaiian Islands
HI	Hawaii Reports [A publication] (DLA)
HI	Hazard Index (GNE)
HI	Head Injury [Neurology] (DAVI)
HI	Health Inspector [British military] (DMA)
HI	Health Insurance
HI	Heard Island [Region] (EERA)
HI	Hearing Impaired (OICC)
HI	Heart Infusion (STED)
HI	Heartland Institute [Research center] (RCD)
HI	Heat Inactivated (STED)
HI	Heat Index
HI	Heat Input (STED)
HI	Heavily Included [Colored gemstone grade]
HI	Height Indicator (NVT)
HI	Hemagglutination Inhibition [Immunochemistry]
HI	Hepatic Insufficiency (STED)
HI	Hepatobiliary Imaging [Medicine] (BABM)
Hi	Hiburnium [Supposed chemical element, discovered 1922]
HI	Hic Iacet [Here Lies] [Latin]
HI	Hideaways International [Commercial firm] (EA)
HI	High [Computer science] (AAG)
HI	High Impact
HI	High Impulsiveness (MAE)
HI	High Intensity
HI	Hindi (WDAA)
HI	Hirth KG [Germany ICAO aircraft manufacturer identifier] (ICAO)
HI	Hispanic Institute (EA)
HI	Histadruth Ivrith of America
Hi	Histidine [An amino acid] (MAE)
HI	Histidine (STED)
HI	Hofmann Industries, Inc. (EFIS)
HI	Holiday Inns, Inc. (EFIS)
HI	Holton Inter-Urban Railway Co. [AAR code]
HI	Homicidal Ideation [Psychiatry] (DAVI)
HI	Homoridal Ideation (STED)
H-I	Hondacar International (EA)
HI	Honeywell, Inc. (NASA)
HI	Horizontal Interval
HI	Hormone Dependent [Medicine] (STED)
HI	Hormone-Independent [Medicine] (DB)
HI	Hormone Insensitive [Medicine] (STED)
HI	Hospital Induced (STED)
HI	Hospital Insurance
HI	Hot Issue [Investment term]
HI	Hotline International (BUAC)
HI	Household Capital Trust [NYSE symbol] (SAG)
HI	Household Capital Trust II [NYSE symbol] (SAG)
HI	Household International, Inc. [NYSE symbol] (SPSG)
HI	Household Intl [NYSE symbol] (TTSB)
HI	Housing Improvement
HI	Hudson Institute (EA)
HI	Human Interaction
HI	Human Interest
HI	Human Interface [Computer science] (EERA)
HI	Humanity International [An association] (EA)
HI	Humidity Index
HI	Humoral Immunity (DB)
HI	Hybrid Index [Botany]
HI	Hydraulic Institute (EA)
HI	Hydriodic Acid [Inorganic chemistry]
HI	Hydrodynamic Interaction [Chemistry]
HI	Hydrogen Iodide [Inorganic chemistry]
HI	Hydronics Institute (EA)
HI	Hydroxyindole [Biochemistry] (DAVI)

HI	Hyperglycemic Index [*Medicine*] (STED)	HIBOR	Hong Kong Interbank Offered Rate (DFIT)
HI	Hypomelanosis of Ito [*Medicine*] (DMAA)	HIBR	Huxley Institute for Biosocial Research (EA)
HI	Hypothermic Ischemia (DB)	HIBREL	High-Brightness Relay [*Military*] (SDI)
HI	Methemoglobin [*Symbol*] [*Medicine*]	HibrnFd	Hibernia Foods Ltd. [*Associated Press*] (SAG)
HI	Papillon Airways [*ICAO designator*] (AD)	HIBS	Heavy Ion Backscattering Spectrometry (AAEL)
HI-12	High Twelve International (EA)	HIBT	High-Interest Books for Teens [*A publication*]
HIA	Canadian Eagle Aviation Ltd. [*ICAO designator*] (FAAC)	HIBT	Howard Ink Blot Test [*Psychology*]
HIA	Handkerchief Industry Association [*Defunct*] (EA)	HIBU	Hydrological Institute of Belgrade University [*Marine science*] [*Yugoslavia*] (OSRA)
HIA	Harrisburg International Airport (MCD)	HIBUF	Hibernia Foods PLC [*NASDAQ symbol*] (SAG)
HIA	Hawaiian Irrigation Authority (BUAC)	HIBUF	Hibernia Foods Unit [*NASDAQ symbol*] (TTSB)
HIA	Headwear Institute of America (EA)	HIBW	Hibernia Foods PLC [*NASDAQ symbol*] (SAG)
HIA	Health Industries Association [*Later, HIMA*]	HIBWF	Hibernia Foods Wrrt'C' [*NASDAQ symbol*] (TTSB)
HIA	Hearing Industries Association (EA)	HIBZ	Hibernia Foods PLC [*NASDAQ symbol*] (SAG)
HIA	Heart Infusion Agar [*Medicine*]	HIBZF	Hibernia Foods Wrrt'D' [*NASDAQ symbol*] (TTSB)
HIA	Heat Infusion Agar [*Microbiology*] (DAVI)	HIC	Habitat International Coalition (BUAC)
HIA	Held [*or Hold*] in Abeyance [*Military*] (AFM)	HIC	Habitat International Council [*The Hague, Netherlands*] (EAIO)
HIA	Hemagglutination Inhibition Antibody [*Immunochemistry*]	HIC	Hand Indicator Controller (NRCH)
HIA	Histadruth Ivrith of America (EA)	HIC	Happy Irish Celebration
HIA	Hobby Industry Association of America	HIC	Hardware Indenture Code (KSC)
HIA	Hold in Abeyance [*Military*]	HIC	Hayes International Corp.
HIA	Homopolar Inductor Alternator (PDAA)	HIC	Head Injury Criteria [*Medicine*]
HIA	Horological Institute of America [*Later, AWI*]	HIC	Health Information Council [*An association*] (EA)
HIA	Housing Industry Association	HIC	Health Insurance Claim Number [*Medicare*] (DHSM)
HIA	Whitehall, MT [*Location identifier FAA*] (FAAL)	HIC	Health Insurance Council [*Later, Consumer and Professional Relations Division of HIAA*] (EA)
HIAA	Health Insurance Association of America [*Washington, DC*] (EA)	HIC	Heart Information Center
HIAA	Hobby Industry Association of America (EA)	HIC	Heavy Ion Cloud [*Astrophysics*]
HIAA	Hydroxyindoleacetic Acid [*Organic chemistry*]	HIC	Hemispheric Insurance Conference
HIAC	Health Industry Advisory Committee [*Terminated, 1974*] (EGAO)	HIC	Hickam Air Force Base, Hawaii [*NASA*] (NASA)
HIAC	Health Insurance Advisory Committee [*Australia*]	HI-C	High-Conversion Critical Experiment (IEEE)
HIAC	High Accuracy [*RADAR*]	HIC	High Dielectric Constant (IAA)
HIAD	Handbook of Instructions for Aircraft Designers	HIC	Highest Incoming Channel [*Telecommunications*] (CIST)
HIADS	Hawaiian Integrated Air Defense System	HIC	High-Integrity Containers (GAAI)
HIAFSB	Handbook of Instructions for Air Force Subsystem Designers	HIC	High-Intensity Conflict [*Military*]
HIAG	Healthcare International Audit Group (EA)	HIC	Highlands Insurance Group [*NYSE symbol*] (TTSB)
HIAGSE	Handbook of Instructions for Aircraft Ground Support Equipment Designers	HIC	Highly Indebted Country
HIAGSED	Handbook of Instructions for Aircraft Ground Support Equipment Designers	HIC	Highly Ionized Cloud [*Galactic science*]
HIAK	Harpoon Interface Adapter Kit (DWSG)	HIC	Historical Intelligence Collection [*CIA*]
HIAL	Hawaii Intercollegiate Athletic League (PSS)	HIC	Hole-in-Corner [*Paper*] (DSUE)
HIALS	High-Intensity Approach Lighting System [*Airport runways*]	HIC	Homosexual Information Center (EA)
HIALT	High Altitude (MCD)	HIC	Honduras Information Center (EA)
HI/AMBBA	Hair International/Associated Master Barbers and Beauticians of America (EA)	HIC	Hot Idle Compensation [*Automotive engineering*]
HI and RH	His [*or Her*] Imperial and Royal Highness	HIC	Hot Isostatic Compaction
HIANG	Hawaii Air National Guard (MUSM)	HIC	Household and Industrial Chemical
HIAP	Human Intracisternal A-Type Particle [*Cytology*]	HIC	Humidity Indicator Controller [*Aerospace*]
HIAPSD	Handbook of Instructions for Aerospace Personnel Subsystem Designers	HIC	Hybrid Integrated Circuit
HIARA	Hail Insurance Adjustment and Research Association [*Later, NCIA*] (EA)	HIC	Hydrogen-Induced Cracking [*Metallurgy*]
HIAS	Hebrew Immigrant Aid Society	HIC	Hydrographic Information Committee [*NATO*] (NATG)
HIAS	High Incidence Auto-Stabilizer (PDAA)	HIC	Hydrologist in Charge (NOAA)
HIASD	Handbook of Instructions for Aerospace Systems Design	HIC	Hydrophobic Interaction Chromatography
HIAVED	Handbook of Instructions for Aerospace Vehicle Equipment Design	HIC	White Cloud, MI [*Location identifier FAA*] (FAAL)
HI-AYH	Hostelling International-American Youth Hostels [*An association*] (EA)	HICA	Honey Industry Council of America [*Defunct*] (EA)
HIB	Haemophilus Influenzae, Type B	HICA	Hydroxyisocaproic Acid (DMAA)
Hib	Haemophilus Influenzae Type B (PAZ)	hi-cal	High Calorie [*or Caloric*] [*Type of diet*] (DAVI)
HIB	Hawaiian Freight Tariff Bureau Inc., Maywood CA [*STAC*]	HICA/MYDP	Hazard Identification Capability Assessment and Multi-Year Development Plan [*Federal Emergency Management Agency*] (GFGA)
HIB	Heart Infusion Broth [*Medicine*] (DMAA)	HICAP	High-Capacity (IAA)
HIB	Hemolytic Immune Body (DB)	Hicap	High-Capacity Digital Transport Service [*Pacific Bell*]
HIB	Hemophilus Influenzae Type B [*Medicine*]	HICAP	High-Capacity Firefighting Foam Station [*Environmental science*] (COE)
HIB	Herring Industries Board [*British*]	HICAP	High-Capacity Projectile (NVT)
HIB	Hibbing [*Minnesota*] [*Airport symbol*] (OAG)	HICAP	High [*Altitude*] Combat Air Patrol (NVT)
HIB	Hibernia [*Ancient name for Ireland*] (ROG)	HICAPCOM	High-Capacity Communication System
HIB	Hibernia Corp. CI'A' [*NYSE symbol*] (TTSB)	HICAS	High-Capacity Active Control Suspension [*Automotive engineering*]
HIB	Hibernia Corp. Class A [*NYSE symbol*] (SPSG)	HICAT	High-Altitude Clear Air Turbulence [*Aviation*]
HIB	Hibiscus Air Services Ltd. [*New Zealand*] [*ICAO designator*] (FAAC)	HI-CC	High-Conversion Critical Experiment [*Nuclear energy*] (GFGA)
HIB	High-Impedance Bridge	HICCUP	Hearing Impaired Consultants Creating Unique Partnerships [*An association*]
HIB	High Iron Briquetting (DICI)	H-ICDA	International Classification of Diseases - Adopted Code for Hospitals
HIB	Hoop-Iron Bond [*Construction*]	HICF	Health Insurance Claim Form
HIBA	Hawaiian International Billfish Association (EA)	HICHS	Helicopter Internal Cargo Handling System
Hi-B.A.	High School Evangelism Fellowship (EA)	HICK	Hickok Electrical Instrument Co. [*NASDAQ symbol*] (SAG)
HIBA	Hydroxyisobutyric Acid [*Organic chemistry*]	HICK	Hickok, Inc. [*NASDAQ symbol*] (SAG)
HIBAC	Health Insurance Benefits Advisory Council [*Department of Health and Human Services Inactive*]	hick	Hickory (VRA)
HIBAL	High-Altitude Balloon	HICKA	Hickok Inc. 'A' [*NASDAQ symbol*] (TTSB)
Hibb	Hibbard's Reports [*New Hampshire*] [*A publication*] (DLA)	Hick Ct Mar.	Hickman on Naval Courts-Martial [*A publication*] (DLA)
Hibb	Hibbard's Reports [*Opinions Attorneys-General*] [*A publication*] (DLA)	Hickok	Hickok, Inc. [*Associated Press*] (SAG)
HIBB	Hibbett Sporting Goods, Inc. [*NASDAQ symbol*] (SAG)	Hickory	Hickory Tech Corp. [*Associated Press*] (SAG)
Hibbett	Hibbett Sporting Goods, Inc. [*Associated Press*] (SAG)	Hicks Ethics	Hicks' Organization and Ethics of Bench and Bar [*A publication*] (DLA)
HIBC	Hydrogen-Induced Blister Cracking [*Metallurgy*]	Hicks Leg Research	Hicks on Materials and Methods of Legal Research [*A publication*] (DLA)
HIBCC	Health Industry Business Communications Council (EA)	Hicks Men & Books	Hicks on Men and Books Famous in the Law [*A publication*] (DLA)
Hibern	Hibernia Corp. [*Associated Press*] (SAG)	HICLASS	Hierarchical Classification [*Indexing*]
Hibern	Hibernia Corp, Class A [*Associated Press*] (SAG)	HI CLASS	Hughes Integrated Classification System [*Hughes Aircraft Co.*] (NITA)
HiberSv	Hibernia Savings Bank [*Associated Press*] (SAG)	HiCN	Cyanmethemoglobin [*Immunology*] (DAVI)
HIBEX	High-Impulse Booster Experiments [*DARPA/Army*]	HICOA	Head Injury Council of Australia
HIBEX/HAPDAR	High Impulse Booster Experiment / Hardpoint Demonstration Array RADAR (SAA)	HICOG	High Commissioner for Germany
HiBiCMOS	Hitachi Bipolar CMOS [*Complementary Metal Oxide Semiconductor*] (NITA)	HICOM	Heavy Industries Corp. of Malaysia (ECON)
Hibid	Hong Kong Interbank Bid Rate (NUMA)	HICOM	High Command
HIBN	Hibernia Foods Ltd. [*NASDAQ symbol*] (SAG)	HICOM	High Commission [*or Commissioner*]
HIBNY	Hibernia Foods plc ADS [*NASDAQ symbol*] (TTSB)	HICOMRY	High Commissioner of Ryukyu Islands

HICOMSEVONET... High Command Secure Voice Network [*Navy*] (NVT)
HICOMTERPACIS... High Commissioner Trust Territory, Pacific Islands
hi-con .... High Contrast [*Cinematography*]
HICRV.......... Human Intracisternal Retrovirus [*Medicine*]
HICS .... Hardened Intersite Cable System (CET)
HICS .... Hierarchical Information Control System [*Japanese*]
HICS .... Holt International Children's Services (EA)
HICSS .... Hawaii International Conference on System Sciences (BUAC)
HID .... Hamer Butte [*Idaho*] [*Seismograph station code, US Geological Survey*] (SEIS)
HID .... Hardware Installation Data (CAAL)
HID .... Hardware Interface Device (NASA)
HID .... Headache, Insomnia, Depression [*Syndrome*]
HID .... Helium Ionization Detector [*Instrumentation*]
HID .... Herniated Intervertebral Disc [*Medicine*] (DMAA)
HID .... Hierarchical Identification
HID .... High Density (IAA)
HID .... High-Impact Design (NRCH)
HID .... High-Intensity Discharge [*Vapor lamp*]
HID .... High-Iron Diamine
HID .... HIM [*Hardware Interface Module*] Interface Distributor (NASA)
HID .... Housing Industry Dynamics [*Originator and databank*] (NITA)
HID .... Human Immune Deficiency [*Immunology*]
HID .... Human Infectious Dose [*Medicine*] (DMAA)
HID .... Hyperkinetic Impulse Disorder [*Medicine*]
HIDA .... Health Industry Distributors Association (EA)
HIDA .... Hepatoiminodiacetic Acid [*Scan*] [*Radiology*] (DAVI)
HIDA .... Home Improvement Dealers Association of America (EA)
HID-AB .... High-Iron Diamine-Alcian Blue [*A biological stain*]
HIDACZ .... High-Density Airspace Control Zone (MCD)
HIDAD .... Helicopter Insecticide Dispersal Apparatus, Dry (NG)
HIDAF .... Helicopter Insecticide Dispersal Apparatus, Fog (NG)
HIDAL .... Helicopter Insecticide Dispersal Apparatus, Liquid (NG)
HIDAM .... Hierarchical Indexed Direct Access Method [*Computer science*] (BUR)
HIDAN.......... High-Density Air Navigation
HIDB .... Highlands and Islands Development Board [*Scotland*] (ECON)
HIDC .... Housing Industry Development Council [*Australia*]
HIDE .... Helicopter Integrated Direction Equipment
HIDE .... High-Absorption Integrated Defense Electromagnetic Warfare System
HIDE .... Human Insulin-Degrading Enzyme [*An enzyme*]
HIDEC .... Highly Integrated Digital Engine Control (MCD)
HIDF .... Horizontal Side of an Intermediate Distribution Frame [*Telecommunications*] (TEL)
HIDI .... Health-Care Instruments and Devices Institute [*State University of New York at Buffalo*] [*Research center*] (RCD)
HiD/LoD ...... High-Density/Low-Density Tariff
HIDM .... High Information Delta Modulation [*Computer science*] (BUR)
HIDTA .... High Intensity Drug Trafficking Area
HIDTC .... Hangar and Industrial Door Technical Council [*Defunct*] (MSA)
HIE .... Heat Input Equivalent (PDAA)
HIE .... Height Integration Equipment
HIE .... Help in Emergency (ADA)
HIE .... Hibernation Information Exchange [*Later, IHS*]
HIE .... Homelessness Information Exchange (EA)
HIE .... Human Intestinal Epithelium [*Medicine*] (DMAA)
HIE .... Hypoxi-Ischemic Encephalopathy [*Neurology*] (DAVI)
HIE .... Whitefield, NH [*Location identifier FAA*] (FAAL)
HIEAT.......... Highest Temperature Equaled for All Time [*NWS*] (FAAC)
HIEFM.......... Highest Temperature Equaled for the Month [*NWS*] (FAAC)
HIEFSS .... Hospital, Institution, and Educational Food Service Society [*Later, Dietary Managers Association - DMA*] (EA)
HIER .... Hieroglyphics (WDAA)
Hier .... Hieronymus [*Jerome*] [*348-420AD*] (BJA)
HIER .... Hierusolymo [*Jerusalem*] (ROG)
HIER .... Hungarian Institute for Educational Research (BUAC)
Hier Gabr..... Hieronymus Gabrielius [*Deceased, 1587*] [*Authority cited in pre-1607 legal work*] (DSA)
hiergl .... Hieroglyph (VRA)
Hiero .... Hieroglyphics
Hiero Cag .... Hieronymus Cagnolus [*Deceased, 1551*] [*Authority cited in pre-1607 legal work*] (DSA)
Hiero Cagno... Hieronymus Cagnolus [*Deceased, 1551*] [*Authority cited in pre-1607 legal work*] (DSA)
Hieron .... Hieronymus [*Jerome*] [*348-420AD*] (OCD)
Hieron Cagno... Hieronymus Cagnolus [*Deceased, 1551*] [*Authority cited in pre-1607 legal work*] (DSA)
Hieron Gabriel... Hieronymus Gabrielius [*Deceased, 1587*] [*Authority cited in pre-1607 legal work*] (DSA)
Hieron Grat... Hieronymus Gratus [*Deceased, 1544*] [*Authority cited in pre-1607 legal work*] (DSA)
Hier Schurf... Hieronymus Schurff [*Deceased, 1554*] [*Authority cited in pre-1607 legal work*] (DSA)
Hier Torniel... Hieronymus Torniellus [*Deceased, 1575*] [*Authority cited in pre-1607 legal work*] (DSA)
HIES............ Hadassah Israel Education Services [*Jerusalem*]
HIES............ Health Insurance/Employer Survey [*Department of Health and Human Services*] (GFGA)
HIESE.......... Highest Temperature Equaled so Early [*NWS*] (FAAC)
HIESL.......... Highest Temperature Equaled so Late [*NWS*] (FAAC)
HIF .... Health Information Foundation
HIF .... Heavy Ion Fusion (PDAA)
HIF .... Higher Integrative Functions [*Neurology*]
HIF .... High-Impedance Follower

HIF .... Horizontal Integral Float [*Automotive engineering*]
HIF .... Housing Insurance Fund [*New Deal*]
HIF .... Human-Initiated Failure
HIF .... Hypoxia-Inducible Factor [*Physiology*]
HIF .... International Helsinki Federation for Human Rights [*Austria*] (EAIO)
HIF .... Ogden, UT [*Location identifier FAA*] (FAAL)
HIF .... Salomon Bros High Income Fd [*NYSE symbol*] (TTSB)
HIF .... Salomon Brothers High Income Fund [*NYSE symbol*] (SPSG)
HIFA............ Home Insurance Federation of America
HIFAM .... High-Fidelity Amplitude Modulation (DEN)
HIFAR .... High-Frequency Fixed Array RADAR
HIFBS .... Heat-Inactivated Fetal Bovine Serum [*Immunology*]
HIFC............ Hog Intrinsic Factor Concentrate
HIFCS .... Heat-Inactivated Fetal Calf Serum (DB)
HIFI............. Cambridge SoundWorks [*NASDAQ symbol*] (TTSB)
HIFI............. Cambridge Soundworks, Inc. [*NASDAQ symbol*] (SAG)
HIFI............. Hawaii Imaging Fabry-Perot Interferometer
HIFI............. HFIR [*High-Flux Isotope Reactor*] Irradiation Facility Improvement [*Nuclear energy*]
HIFI............. High Fibre Biscuits [*British*]
HI-FI .... High-Fidelity [*Usually, in reference to home sound-reproducing equipment*]
hi-fi .... High-Fidelity [*Printing*] (WDMC)
HIFI............. High Fidelity Records [*Record label*]
HIFI............. High-Intensity Food Irradiator
HIFN .... Human Interferon (DB)
hIFNa .... Human Interferon Type Alpha (DB)
HIFO .... Highest In, First Out [*Accounting*]
HIFO .... High Input, First Output [*Computer science*] (ECII)
HIFOR .... High-Level Forecast [*Meteorology*]
HIFPA .... Hispanic Institute for the Performing Arts [*Defunct*] (EA)
HIFR .... Helicopter In-Flight Refueling (NVT)
HIFRAG........ High Fragmentation (MCD)
HIFRENSA.... Sociedad Hispano-Francesa de Energia Nuclear SA [*Nuclear energy Spanish*] (NRCH)
HIFS............ Hingham Institution for Savings [*NASDAQ symbol*] (CTT)
HIFT .... Hardware Implemented Fault Tolerance
HIFT .... Heard Island Feasibility Test [*Marine science*] (OSRA)
HIFTO .... How I Feel Toward Others [*Psychology*] (EDAC)
HIG .... Hartford Capital I [*NYSE symbol*] (SAG)
HIG .... Hartford Capital II [*NYSE symbol*] (SAG)
HIG .... Hawaii Institute of Geophysics [*Marine science*] (OSRA)
HIG .... Hawaii Institute of Geophysics [*University of Hawaii*] [*Seismograph station code, US Geological Survey Research center*] (SEIS)
HIG .... Heli-Inter Guyane [*France*] [*FAA designator*] (FAAC)
HIG .... Hermetically Sealed, Integrating Gyroscope
HIG .... Higginsville, MO [*Location identifier FAA*] (FAAL)
HIG .... High Input Grant [*Real estate*] [*Canada*]
HIG .... High-Integrating Gyroscope (KSC)
HIG .... Honeywell Integrating Gyro
HIg .... Human Immunoglobulin [*Biochemistry*] (MAE)
HIG .... Hypervelocity Intercept Guidance
HIG .... ITT Hartford Group [*NYSE symbol*] (TTSB)
HIGAD.......... High-Impulse Gun Airborne Demonstrator (MCD)
HIGE .... Hovering in Ground Effect [*Army*]
HIGED.......... Handbook of Instructions for Ground Equipment Designers (MCD)
HIGFET .... Heterostructure Insulated Gate Field Effect Transistor (NITA)
Higgins........ Higgins' Tennessee Court of Civil Appeals Reports [*A publication*] (DLA)
HIGH............ Highland Railway [*British*] (ROG)
HIGHB.......... Highbury College of Divinity [*British*] (ROG)
High Bail ..... Highmore on Bail [*A publication*] (DLA)
High Ct........ High Court Reports, Northwest Provinces [*India*] [*A publication*] (DLA)
High Ex Rem... High on Extraordinary Legal Remedies [*A publication*] (DLA)
High Extr Leg Rem... High on Extraordinary Legal Remedies [*A publication*] (DLA)
HIGH GASSER... High Geographic Aerospace Search RADAR
High Inj .... High on Injunctions [*A publication*] (DLA)
HighIdInc...... Highlander Income Fund, Inc. [*Associated Press*] (SAG)
HIGH LI....... Highland Light Infantry [*Military British*] (ROG)
High Lun...... Highmore on Lunacy [*A publication*] (DLA)
High Mort .... Highmore on Mortmain [*A publication*] (DLA)
High Pressu... High Pressure (NAKS)
High Rec ..... High on the Law of Receivers [*A publication*] (DLA)
HIGHRS ...... Highlanders [*British*]
Hight............ Hight's Reports [*57-58 Iowa*] [*A publication*] (DLA)
Highvld........ Highveld Steel & Vanadium Corporation Ltd. [*Associated Press*] (SAG)
HIGHWAY .... Highway [*Commonly used*] (OPSA)
Highwd .... Highwood Resources Ltd. [*Associated Press*] (SAG)
Highwd .... Highwoods Properties, Inc. [*Associated Press*] (SAG)
HIGHWY .... Highway [*Commonly used*] (OPSA)
Highwy .... HighwayMaster Communications, Inc. [*Associated Press*] (SAG)
Highwym...... HighwayMaster Communications, Inc. [*Associated Press*] (SAG)
HIGNFY....... Have I Got News for You (WDAA)
Hig Pat Dig... Higgins' Digest of Patent Cases [*1890*] [*A publication*] (DLA)
HIGPrQ .... Hartford Cap I 7.70% 'QUIPS' [*NYSE symbol*] (TTSB)
HIGS .... Hypervelocity Interceptor Guidance Simulation
HIGSED........ Handbook of Instructions for Aircraft Ground Support Equipment Designers
HIGSS.......... Hypervelocity Intercept Guidance Simulator Study
Hig Waterc... Higgins' Pollution and Obstruction of Watercourses [*1877*] [*A publication*] (DLA)
HIH .... Greensboro, NC [*Location identifier FAA*] (FAAL)
HIH .... His [*or Her*] Imperial Highness

HIH .... Hypertensive Intracerebral Hemorrhage [*Medicine*] (DMAA)
HIHA .... High Impulsiveness, High Anxiety [*Psychology*] (DAVI)
HIHAT .... High-Resolution Hemispherical Reflector Antenna Technique
HIHE .... Hunter Institute of Higher Education [*Australia*]
HI-HICAT ...... High High-Altitude Clear Air Turbulence [*Aviation*]
HIHO .... Highway Holdings Ltd. [*NASDAQ symbol*] (SAG)
HIHOE .... Hydrogen, Ions, Helium, Oxygen in the Exosphere (MUGU)
HIHRC .... Humanitas International Human Rights Committee (EA)
HIHW .... Highway Holdings Ltd. [*NASDAQ symbol*] (SAG)
HII .... Health Images [*NYSE symbol*] (TTSB)
HII .... Health Images, Inc. [*NYSE symbol*] (SPSG)
HII .... Health Industries Institute (EA)
HII .... Health Insurance Institute (EA)
HII .... Heard Island [*Seismograph station code, US Geological Survey Closed*] (SEIS)
HII .... Hemagglutination-Inhibition Immunoassay [*Immunochemistry*] (DAVI)
HII .... Heritage Interpretation International
HII .... High Input Impedance
HII .... Housing Institute of Ireland (BUAC)
HIID .... Harvard Institute for International Development [*Harvard University*] [*Research center*] (RCD)
HIID .... Heavy Ion-Induced Desorption [*Analytical chemistry*]
HiInco .... High Income Advantage Trust [*Associated Press*] (SAG)
HiIncoOp ...... High Income Opportunity Fund [*Associated Press*] (SAG)
HiInIII .... High Income Advantage Trust III [*Associated Press*] (SAG)
HIIP .... High Impact Incarceration Program [*60-day paramilitary regimen for prisoners*]
HIIPS .... HUD [*Department of Housing and Urban Development*] Integrated Information Processing Service (GFGA)
HIIS .... Honeywell Institute for Information Science (IEEE)
HIIS .... Schistocytes [*Hematology*] (DAVI)
HIJ .... Hiroshima [*Japan*] [*Airport symbol*] (OAG)
HIJ .... Sisters of the Holy Infant Jesus [*Roman Catholic religious order*]
HIJMS .... His Imperial Japanese Majesty's Ship
HIK .... High Permittivity (DEN)
HIK .... Hikone [*Japan*] [*Seismograph station code, US Geological Survey*] (SEIS)
HIK .... Hikurangi Airlines [*New Zealand*] [*FAA designator*] (FAAC)
HIK .... Honolulu, HI [*Location identifier FAA*] (FAAL)
HIL .... Great Bend, KS [*Location identifier FAA*] (FAAL)
HIL .... Hardware-in-the-Loop
HIL .... Hees International Bancorp, Inc. [*Toronto Stock Exchange symbol*]
HIL .... Helium Impurities Loop [*Nuclear energy*] (NRCH)
HIL .... High-Intensity Light
HIL .... Hilary Term [*England*] [*Legal term*] (DLA)
HIL .... Hilo [*Hawaii*] [*Seismograph station code, US Geological Survey*] (SEIS)
HIL .... Hypoxic-Ischemic Lesion [*Medicine*] (DAVI)
HILA .... High Impulsiveness, Low Anxiety (MAE)
HILAB .... Heavy Ion Laboratory (PDAA)
Hil Abr .... Hilliard's American Law [*A publication*] (DLA)
HILAC .... Heavy-Ion Linear Accelerator [*Nuclear energy*]
HILAP .... High Latitude Particle (PDAA)
HILASD .... Hard Link Arm Safe Device (MCD)
HILAST .... High-Altitude Large Area Surveillance Tactic [*Military*] (CAAL)
HILAT .... High-Latitude Research Satellite [*Defense Nuclear Agency*]
HilbRog .... Hilb, Rogal & Hamilton Co. [*Associated Press*] (SAG)
HILC .... Hampshire Inter-Library Center [*Library network*]
HILC .... High-Intermediate Level Cell [*Nuclear energy*] (NRCH)
HilcstDv ...... Hilcoast Development Corp. [*Associated Press*] (SAG)
HILDCAA .... High-Intensity, Long-Duration, Continuous Aurora Event, Activity [*Astrophysics*]
Hild Ins ...... Hildyard on Insurance [*A publication*] (DLA)
Hild Mar Ins .. Hildyard's Marine Insurance [*A publication*] (DLA)
Hil Elem Law .. Hilliard's Elements of Law [*A publication*] (DLA)
HILEX .... High-Level Exercise [*NATO*] (MUSM)
HILI .... Heavy Ion, Light Ion
HILI .... Higher Layers and Internetworking [*Computer science*] (ACRL)
HILI .... Hilite Industries [*NASDAQ symbol*] (TTSB)
HILI .... Hilite Industries, Inc. [*NASDAQ symbol*] (SAG)
HILIS .... High Light Intensity System (PDAA)
Hilite .... Hilite Industries, Inc. [*Associated Press*] (SAG)
HILL .... Hill [*Commonly used*] (OPSA)
Hill .... Hill's New York Supreme Court Reports [*1841-44*] [*A publication*] (DLA)
Hill .... Hill's South Carolina Law Reports [*A publication*] (DLA)
Hill Abr ...... Hilliard's Abridgment of Real Property Law [*A publication*] (DLA)
Hill Am Jur ... Hilliard's American Jurisprudence [*A publication*] (DLA)
Hill Am Law ... Hilliard's American Law [*A publication*] (DLA)
Hill & D ...... Lalor's Supplement to Hill and Denio's New York Reports [*A publication*] (DLA)
Hill & Den .... Lalor's Supplement to Hill and Denio's New York Reports [*A publication*] (DLA)
Hill & Den Supp ... Lalor's Supplement to Hill and Denio's New York Reports [*A publication*] (DLA)
Hill & D Supp ... Hill and Denio's Lalor's Supplement [*New York*] [*A publication*] (DLA)
Hill & Redman ... Hill and Redman's Law of Landlord and Tenant [*16th ed.*] [*1976*] [*A publication*] (DLA)
Hill B & I .... Hilliard on Bankruptcy and Insolvency [*A publication*] (DLA)
Hill Bank ..... Hilliard on Bankruptcy and Insolvency [*A publication*] (DLA)
HillBd .... Hillside Bedding Corp. [*Associated Press*] (SAG)
Hill Ch .... Hill's Equity South Carolina Reports [*1833-37*] [*A publication*] (DLA)
Hill Ch Pr .... Hill's Chancery Practice [*A publication*] (DLA)
Hill Cont ..... Hilliard on Contracts [*A publication*] (DLA)

Hill Elem Law ... Hilliard's Elements of Law [*A publication*] (DLA)
Hillenbd ...... Hillenbrand Industries, Inc. [*Associated Press*] (SAG)
Hill Eq .... Hill's Equity South Carolina Reports [*1833-37*] [*A publication*] (DLA)
Hill Eq (SC) .. Hill's Equity South Carolina Reports [*1833-37*] [*A publication*] (DLA)
Hill Fixt ..... Hill's Law of Fixtures [*A publication*] (DLA)
Hilliard RP ... Hilliard on Real Property [*A publication*] (DLA)
Hill Ill Chy .. Hill's Illinois Chancery Practice [*A publication*] (DLA)
Hill Ill Com Law ... Hill's Illinois Common Law Jurisdiction and Practice [*A publication*] (DLA)
Hill Inj ...... Hilliard on the Law of Injunctions [*A publication*] (DLA)
Hill Lib & Law ... Hill's Liberty and Law [*A publication*] (DLA)
Hill Mor ...... Hilliard's Law of Mortgages [*A publication*] (DLA)
Hill Mortg .... Hilliard's Law of Mortgages [*A publication*] (DLA)
Hill New Trials ... Hilliard on New Trials [*A publication*] (DLA)
Hill N Tr ..... Hilliard on New Trials [*A publication*] (DLA)
Hill NY .... Hill's New York Reports [*A publication*] (DLA)
Hill NYR ...... Hill's New York Reports [*A publication*] (DLA)
Hill Prob ..... Hill's Illinois Probate Jurisdiction and Practice [*A publication*] (DLA)
Hill Real Prop ... Hilliard on Real Property [*A publication*] (DLA)
Hill Rem ...... Hilliard on Remedies for Torts [*A publication*] (DLA)
HILLS .... Hills [*Commonly used*] (OPSA)
Hill Sales .... Hilliard on Sales of Personal Property [*A publication*] (DLA)
Hill's Ann Codes & Laws ... Hill's Annotated Codes and General Laws [*Oregon*] [*A publication*] (DLA)
Hill's Ann St & Codes ... Hill's Annotated General Statutes and Codes [*Washington*] [*A publication*] (DLA)
HillsBd .... Hillside Bedding Corp. [*Associated Press*] (SAG)
Hill SC .... Hill's Equity South Carolina Reports [*1833-37*] [*A publication*] (DLA)
Hill SC .... Hill's South Carolina Law Reports [*A publication*] (DLA)
Hill's Code ... Hill's Annotated Codes and General Laws [*Oregon*] [*A publication*] (DLA)
Hill's Code ... Hill's Annotated General Statutes and Codes [*Washington*] [*A publication*] (DLA)
HillsStrs ..... Hills Stores Co. [*Associated Press*] (SAG)
HillStr .... Hills Stores Co. [*Associated Press*] (SAG)
Hill Tax ...... Hilliard on the Law of Taxation [*A publication*] (DLA)
Hill Torts .... Hilliard on the Law of Torts [*A publication*] (DLA)
Hill Tr .... Hill on Trustees [*A publication*] (DLA)
Hill Vend ..... Hilliard on the Law of Vendors [*A publication*] (DLA)
Hillyer .... Hillyer's Reports [*20-22 California*] [*A publication*] (DLA)
HILNNEP .... Health Information Library Network of Northeastern Pennsylvania [*Library network*]
HiLo .... Hi-Lo Automotive, Inc. [*Associated Press*] (SAG)
HILOW .... Health Information Libraries of Westchester [*Library network*]
HILP .... Health Information Library Program [*Library network*]
HILS .... Halogen Interchangeable Light Source
HILS .... High-Intensity Learning Systems
HILS .... High Intensity Lightweight Searchlight (PDAA)
HILT .... High Impetus, Low Flame Temperature (MCD)
HILT .... High-Intensity Language Training (AEBS)
Hil T .... Hilary Term [*England*] [*Legal term*] (DLA)
Hilt .... Hilton's New York Common Pleas Reports [*A publication*] (DLA)
Hil Term 4 Will IV ... Hilary Term 4, William IV [*A publication*] (DLA)
Hilt (NY) ..... Hilton's New York Common Pleas Reports [*A publication*] (DLA)
Hilton .... Hilton Hotels Corp. [*Associated Press*] (SAG)
Hil Torts ..... Hilliard on the Law of Torts [*A publication*] (DLA)
HIL VAC .... Hilary Vacation [*British Legal term*] (DLA)
HILY SITTGS ... Hilary Sittings [*British Legal term*] (ROG)
HIM .... Hardware Interface Module [*NASA*] (NASA)
HIM .... Hardware Interface Module Hierarchy of Interpretive Modules (MHDI)
HIM .... Health Insurance Manual
HIM .... Heavy Interdiction Missile
HIM .... Helps International Ministries (EA)
HIM .... Hemopoietic Inductive Microenvironment (STED)
HIM .... Hepatitis-Infectious Mononucleosis [*Medicine*] (DB)
HIM .... Herald International Mailings Ltd. [*British*]
HIM .... Hexosephosphate Isomerase (STED)
HIM .... High Impact
HIM .... High-Intensity Microphone
HIM .... Hill Interaction Matrix [*Psychology*]
him .... Himachali [*MARC language code Library of Congress*] (LCCP)
HIM .... Himac Resources Ltd. [*Vancouver Stock Exchange symbol*]
HIM .... Himeji [*Japan*] [*Seismograph station code, US Geological Survey*] (SEIS)
HIM .... His [*or Her*] Imperial Majesty
HIM .... Horizontal Impulse
HIM .... Host Interface Manager (NITA)
HIM .... Hotel Institute Montreux [*Switzerland*] (ECON)
HIM .... Hot Ionized Medium [*Astrophysics*]
HIM .... Human Individual Metamorphosis [*Flying saucer cult*]
HIM .... Human Integrated Manufacturing
HIM .... Hyperimmunoglobulin M Syndrome [*Medicine*]
HIM .... Hyper Immunoglobulin Syndrome [*Medicine*]
HIMA .... Health Industry Manufacturers Association (EA)
HIM-A .... Hill Interaction Matrix-A [*Personality development test*] [*Psychology*]
HIMAC .... Heavy-Ion Medical Accelerator in Chiba [*Japan*]
HIMAD .... High-to-Medium-Altitude Air Defense (AABC)
HIMAG .... High-Mobility-Agility [*Test for combat vehicles*] (RDA)
HIMARS .... High Mobility Artillery Rocket System [*Army*] (DOMA)
HIMAT .... Highly Maneuverable Aircraft Technology Testbed [*Rockwell International Corp.*] (MCD)
HIMB .... Hawaii Institute of Marine Biology [*University of Hawaii*] [*Research center*] (RCD)
HIMC .... Hepatic Intramitochondrial Crystalloid [*Medicine*] (DMAA)
HIMD .... Handbook of Instructions for Missile Designers

HIMI............ Heilongjiang Institute of Medical Information [*China*] (BUAC)
HI MI .... High Mileage (WDAA)
HIMIC.......... Highly-Indebted Middle-Income Country
HIMO .... High Mobility [*Vehicle analysis*] (MCD)
HIMOS .... High-Injection Metal-Oxide Semiconductor (CIST)
HIMOWC..... High-Mobility Weapons Carrier [*Army*] (MCD)
HIMP .... High-Dose Intravenous Methylprednisolone [*Medicine*] (DMAA)
HIMP .... High Impact
Him Pra....... All India Reporter, Himachal Pradesh [*A publication*] (DLA)
HIMR.......... Handbook of Inspection Maintenance Requirements [*Navy*] (MCD)
HIMR.......... Hearing-Impaired Mentally Retarded
HIMS .... Heavy Interdiction Missile System (MCD)
HIMS .... Helicopter In-Flight Monitoring System [*Army*] (RDA)
HIMS .... Himself
HIMS .... HMMWV [*High-Mobility Multipurpose Wheeled Vehicle*] Interchange
     Mount System [*Military*] (INF)
HIMS .... Housing Information Management System
HIMS .... HUMINT [*Human Intelligence*] Information Management System
HIMSEUR.... HAWK [*Homing All the Way Killer*] Intensified Management System
     Europe Program [*Military*]
HIMSS .... Healthcare Information and Management Systems Society (EA)
HIMT........... Hemagglutination Inhibition Morphine Test [*Immunochemistry*]
     (DMAA)
HIMV .... Hippeastrum Mosaic Virus [*Plant pathology*]
HIN .... Chadron, NE [*Location identifier FAA*] (FAAL)
HIN .... Health Identification Number
HIN .... Heli Inter [*France ICAO designator*] (FAAC)
HIN .... Heterotrophic Intestinal Nitrification [*Metabolism*]
HIN .... Hidden Lake Gold Mines [*Vancouver Stock Exchange symbol*]
HIN .... High Intensity
HIN .... High-Intensity Noise
HIN .... Hinchinbrook Island [*Alaska*] [*Seismograph station code, US
     Geological Survey*] (SEIS)
hin .... Hindi [*MARC language code Library of Congress*] (LCCP)
HIN .... Holocaust Information Network (EA)
HIN .... Hull Identification Number [*USCG*] (TAG)
HIN .... Hybrid Integrated Network [*Bell System*] [*Telecommunications*]
HIN .... Hydrocarbon-Induced Nephropathy [*Medicine*]
HINAS .... Historic Naval Ships Association of North America (EA)
HINASW...... Historic Naval Ships of the World [*Later, HINAS*] (EA)
HIncII .... High Income Advantage Trust II [*Associated Press*] (SAG)
Hincmar Epist... Hincmari Epistolae [*A publication*] (DLA)
HINCS......... Heat-Inactivated Newborn Calf Serum (DB)
HIND.......... Health Care Item Name Directory [*A publication*]
HIND........... Hindi (WDAA)
HIND........... Hindu (WDAA)
Hind............ Hindustan
HIND........... Hindustani [*Language, etc.*]
HinD............ Housewives in Dialogue [*An association*] (BUAC)
HINDALCO ... Hindustan Aluminium Corp. [*India*] (BUAC)
H in DC....... Holder in Due Course [*Owner or holder of a negotiable instrument at
     some future time*]
Hinde Ch Pr... Hinde's Modern Practice of the High Court of Chancery
     [*A publication*] (DLA)
HINDEX....... HANES [*Health and Nutrition Examination Survey*] Data Index
     [*Department of Health and Human Services*] (GFGA)
Hind LJ........ Hindu Law Journal [*A publication*] (DLA)
Hind LQ....... Hindu Law Quarterly [*A publication*] (DLA)
Hind Pat...... Hindmarch on Patents [*A publication*] (DLA)
Hind Pr....... Hind's Practice [*A publication*] (DLA)
Hine & N Ass... Hine and Nicholas on Assignment of Life Policies [*A publication*]
     (DLA)
Hine & N Dig... Hine and Nicholas. Insurance Digest [*A publication*] (DLA)
HINEKF....... Hinekford [*England*]
Hines.......... Hines' Reports [*83-96 Kentucky*] [*A publication*] (DLA)
HINF .... Hypodermoclysis Infusion [*Medicine*]
H Inf .... Hypodermoclysis Infusion (STED)
HING .... High-Intensity Noise Generator
HingmS........ Hingham Institution for Savings [*Associated Press*] (SAG)
HINIL.......... High-Noise-Immunity Logic (MCD)
HINS .... Hanover Insurance (EFIS)
HINS .... Health Information Network Services [*Database search service*]
     (OLDSS)
HINS .... Helicopter Integrated Navigation System [*Canadian Navy*]
Hinsdle .... Hinsdale Financial Corp. [*Associated Press*] (SAG)
HINT .... Happy Idiot News Talk
HINT .... Happy Idiot News Team [*Also, Happy Idiot News Talk*]
     [*Broadcasting*] (WDMC)
HINT .... High Intensity
HINT .... Hinton [*Test*] [*Medicine*]
Hint............. Hinton [*Flocculation test for syphilis*] [*Medicine*] (STED)
HINT .... Housewares Industry News and Topics [*A publication*] (EAAP)
HIO .... Health Insuring Organization (DMAA)
HIO .... High Income Opp Fd [*NYSE symbol*] (TTSB)
HIO .... High Income Opportunity Fund [*NYSE symbol*] (SAG)
HIO .... Hillsboro, OR [*Location identifier FAA*] (FAAL)
HIO .... Hypoiodism [*Medicine*]
HIO .... Hypoiodite [*Salt of hypoiodous acid*] (STED)
HIO .... Smith Barney High Income Opportunity Fund [*NYSE symbol*] (SPSG)
HIOMT .... Hydroxyindole O-Methyltransferase [*Also, HOMT*] [*An enzyme*]
HIOS .... Headquarters Integrated Office System [*Military*] (GFGA)
HIOS .... High Index of Suspicion [*Medicine*] (DMAA)
HIP............. Habitability Improvement Plan [*Navy*]
HIP............. Hanford Isotopes Plant [*Nuclear energy*]
HIP............. Hardware Interface Program (NASA)

HIP............. Harpoon Indicator Panel [*Missiles*] (MCD)
HIP............. HAWK [*Homing All the Way Killer*] Improvement Program
HIP............. Hazard Input Program (SAA)
HIP............. Health Illness Profile (DMAA)
HIP............. Health Insurance Plan
HIP............. Hearing Impaired Peer
HIP............. Help for Incontinent People (EA)
HIP............. Hierachical Information Processor (PDAA)
HIP............. High-Impact Pressure
HIP............. High-Intent Priority [*In the record business, a heavily promoted disk*]
HIP............. High Internal Phase [*Emulsion chemistry*]
HIP............. Highly Ionized Plasma
HIP............. High-Potential Iron Protein
Hip............. Hippocampus (DB)
HIP............. Homeless Information Project (BUAC)
HIP............. Homograft Incus Prosthesis [*Medicine*] (DMAA)
HIP............. Hoover Institution Press (DGA)
HIP............. Horizontal Injection Press
HIP............. Hospital Improvement Project
HIP............. Hospital Insurance Program
HIP............. Host Information Processor (NITA)
HIP............. Host Interface Port [*Computer science*]
HIP............. Host Interface Processor [*Computer science*] (PDAA)
HIP............. Hot Isostatically Pressed [*Materials processing*]
HIP............. Housing Improvement Program [*Federal government*]
HIP............. Howitzer Improvement Program
HIP............. Hydrostatic Indifference Point
HIP............. Hyperbolic Integer Programming [*Computer science*] (PDAA)
HIP............. Hypnotic Induction Profile
HIPA .... Health Insurance Persistency Award [*Later, HIQA*] [*LIMRA*]
HIPA .... Heparin-Induced Platelet Activation [*Medicine*] (DMAA)
HIPA .... Home Improvement Products Association [*Defunct*] (EA)
HIPA .... Honey Importers and Packers Association (BUAC)
HIPAAS ...... High-Performance Advanced Attack Systems (MCD)
HIPAAS ...... High-Performance Attack Aircraft System (MCD)
HIPAC .... Heavy-Ion Plasma Accelerator (IAA)
HIPAC .... High-Performance Aircraft Cannon (MCD)
HIPAC .... Hitachi Parametron Automatic Computer
HIPAR .... High-Performance Precision Approach Control RADAR (MCD)
HIPAR .... High-Power Acquisition RADAR (AAG)
HIP/ATBM ... HAWK [*Homing All the Way Killer*] Improvement Program / Anti-
     Tactical Ballistic Missile (SAA)
HIPC .... Health Information Policy Council [*Department of Health and Human
     Services*] (GFGA)
HIPC .... Health Insurance Plan of California
HIPC .... Health Insurance Purchasing Collective (DMAA)
HIPC .... Health Insurance Purchasing Cooperative (ECON)
HIPC .... Heavily Indebted Poor Country
HIPC .... High Chamber Pressure (NAKS)
HIPC .... High Plains Corp. [*NASDAQ symbol*] (NQ)
HIPC .... High Pressure Chamber
HIPE.......... Hospital In-Patient Enquiry [*British*]
HIPEG .... High-Performance External Gun
HIPEHT ...... High-Performance Electrothermal Hydrazine Thruster (MCD)
HIPERARC ... High-Performance Archiheater (MCD)
HI-PERF...... High Performance [*Automotive engineering*]
HIPERFLIR ... High-Performance Forward-Looking Infrared (PDAA)
HIPERNAS ... High-Performance Navigation System
HIPERTHINO... High-Performance Throttleable Injector (KSC)
HIPEX .... Harmonic Identification Pitch Extraction (PDAA)
HIPG .... Human Information Processing Group [*Princeton University*]
HIPH .... High Institute of Public Health Alexandria University [*Egypt*] (BUAC)
HI-PI........... High-Performance Intercept
HIPIC .... High-Pressure Impregnation Carbonization (MCD)
HIPIP .... High Potential Iron Protein [*Biochemistry*]
HIPIR .... High-Power Illuminator RADAR [*Army*] (AABC)
HiPlains...... High Plains Corp. [*Associated Press*] (SAG)
HIPO .... Hemihypertrophy, Intestinal Web, Preauricular Skin Tag, and
     Congenital Corneal Opacity Syndrome [*Medicine*] (DMAA)
HIPO .... Hierarchical Input/Process Output (NAKS)
HIPO .... Hierarchical Input Process Output [*Diagram used in software
     assessment*] (NITA)
HIPO .... Hierarchy Plus InPut/Process/Output (NAKS)
HIPO .... Hierarchy plus Input-Process-Output [*Computer science*]
Hipo........... High-Potential Employee
HIPO .... High Potential Incident [*Environmental science*] (COE)
HIPO .... Highway Post Office [*Bus or truck equipped with mail distribution
     facilities*]
HIPO .... Hilfspolizei [*Auxiliary Police*] [*German*]
Hipo........... Hippolytus Marsilius [*Deceased, 1529*] [*Authority cited in pre-1607
     legal work*] (DSA)
HIPO .... Hospital Indicator for Physicians' Orders
HIPOT .... High Potential (KSC)
hipot.......... High Potential (IDOE)
HIPOTT ...... High-Potential Test (IEEE)
HIPOW........ Hot Isostatic Pressing of Waste [*Nuclear energy*] (NUCP)
HIPOX .... High-Pressure Oxygen (AAEL)
HIPP .... High-Energy Impulse Pumpable Propellant (MCD)
HIPP .... Hippocrates [*Greek physician, 460 -377 BC*]
Hipp........... Hippolytus [*of Euripides*] [*Classical studies*] (OCD)
Hipparch...... Hipparchus [*of Plato*] [*Classical studies*] (OCD)
Hipparcos.... High-Precision Parallax Collecting Satellite [*European Space Agency*]
Hipp Bonacoss... Hippolytus Bonacossa [*Deceased, 1591*] [*Authority cited in pre-
     1607 legal work*] (DSA)
HIPPI .... High Performance Parallel Interface [*Computer science*]

HIPPO .... Habitat Destruction, Introduced Species, Pollution, Population Growth, Overexploitation
HIPPO .... High Internal Pressure Producing Orifice (MCD)
HIPPO .... Hippodrome [*London*] (DSUE)
HIPPO .... Hippopotamus (DSUE)
Hippoc ...... Hippocrates [*Greek physician, 460 -377 BC*] [*Classical studies*] (OCD)
HIPPY .... Home Instruction Program for Preschool Youngsters [*Israel*]
HIPR .... High Internal Phase Ratio
HIPR .... High Pressure (KSC)
HIPRES .... High Pressure
HIPRI .... High Priority (NG)
Hip Riminal... Hippolytus Riminaldus [*Deceased, 1589*] [*Authority cited in pre-1607 legal work*] (DSA)
HIPrJ .... Houshld 7.35% cm Dep Pfd [*NYSE symbol*] (TTSB)
HiPro .... High-Protein (MEDA)
HIPrT .... Househld Cap Tr 8.25% 'TOPrS' [*NYSE symbol*] (TTSB)
HIPrX .... Househld 9.50%'91 cm Dep Pfd [*NYSE symbol*] (TTSB)
HIPrZ .... Household 8.25% cm Dep Pfd [*NYSE symbol*] (TTSB)
HIPS .... Health Insurance Plans Survey [*Department of Health and Human Services*] (GFGA)
HIPS .... Helmet Initiated Pointing System (MCD)
HIPS .... High-Impact Polystyrene [*Plastics technology*]
HIPS .... Hyperintense Proximal Scanning
HIPSA .... Hallicrafters Incremental Power Spectrum Analyzer
HIPSF .... High-Performance Space Feed
HIQ .... High Quality [*Home video system*] (IAA)
HIQ .... Housing Intelligence Quotient
HIQ .... New York, NY [*Location identifier FAA*] (FAAL)
HIQA .... Health Insurance Quality Award [*Formerly, HIPA*] (LIMRA)
HIR .... Hammersley Iron Proprietary Ltd. Railway [*Australia*] (DCTA)
HIR Rep ...... Handbook of Inspection Requirements [*Navy*] (MCD)
HIR .... Harvard International Review [*A publication*]
HIR .... Hazardous Incident Report (MCD)
HIR .... Head Injury Routine [*Medicine*] (DMAA)
HIR .... Health Insurance Regulation
HIR .... Helicopter Instrument Rules
HIR .... HELWS-Integrated RADAR
HIR .... Hierarchy [*Computer science*]
HIR .... Hilton Resource Corp. [*Vancouver Stock Exchange symbol*]
HIR .... Hiram College, Hiram, OH [*OCLC symbol*] (OCLC)
HIR .... Hiring (ROG)
HIR .... Hiroshima [*Japan*] [*Seismograph station code, US Geological Survey*] (SEIS)
HIR .... Honiara [*Guadalcanal*] [*Airport symbol*] (OAG)
HIR .... Horizontal Impulse Reaction (MSA)
HIR .... Household Issuance Record [*Food Stamp Program*] (GFGA)
HIR .... Human Insulin Receptor [*Biochemistry*]
HIR .... Hydrospace Information Report (MCD)
HIR .... Hydrostatic Impact Rocket (NATG)
HIRA .... Handheld Infrared Alarm (PDAA)
HIRA .... Health Industry Representatives Association (EA)
HIRAC .... High Random Access
HIRAN .... High-Precision SHORAN (AAG)
HiRAP .... High-Resolution Accelerometer Package (MCD)
HiRAP .... High-Resolution Accelerometer Package (NAKS)
HIRC .... Head Injuries Rehabilitation Centre [*British*] (CB)
HIRC .... Health Information Resource Center (EA)
HIRC .... Holy Innocents Reparation Committee (EA)
HIRCIS .... High-Resolution Capacitive Imaging Sensor [*Instrumentation*]
HIRD .... High-Intensity Radiation Device
HIRDL .... High-Intensity Radiation Development Laboratory [*Brookhaven National Laboratory*] [*Department of Energy*]
HIRE .... Help through Industry Retraining and Employment [*Program*] [*Department of Labor*]
HIREL .... High Reliability (IAA)
HirelHld ...... Hirel Holdings, Inc. [*Associated Press*] (SAG)
HI Rep .... Hawaiian Islands Reports [*A publication*] (DLA)
HI-RES .... High Resolution [*Computer science*]
HIRES .... High-Resolution Echelle Spectrograph
HIRES .... Hypersonic In-Flight Refueling System
HIREWIMP... High-Resolution Wind Measurement Program (MUGU)
HIRF .... High-Intensity Radiated Field [*Aviation*]
HIRF .... High-Intensity Reciprocity Failure
HIRI .... Hi-Rise Recycling Sys [*NASDAQ symbol*] (TTSB)
HIRI .... Hi Rise Recycling Systems [*NASDAQ symbol*] (SAG)
HIRI .... Home Improvement Research Institute (EA)
HIRIS .... High-Resolution Imaging Spectrometer
HiRise .... Hi Rise Recycling Systems [*Associated Press*] (SAG)
HIRIV .... How Will Arrival Report Be Filed Concerning [*Aviation*] (FAAC)
HIRL .... High-Intensity Runway Lights [*Aviation*]
HIRL .... Hirel Holdings, Inc. [*NASDAQ symbol*] (SAG)
HIRM .... High-Incidence Research Model (MCD)
HIRO .... Health Insurance Regional Office
HIROP .... Hand-Held Infrared Controller Overpopulation [*Computer science*]
HIRS .... Harker's Information Retrieval Systems [*Harker's Specialist Book Importers*] [*Information service or system*] (IID)
HIRS .... High-Impulse Retrorocket System
HIRS .... High-Resolution Infrared Sounder [*Marine science*] (OSRA)
HIRS .... High-Resolution Infrared Radiation Sounder
Hirsch .... Hirsch International Corp. [*Associated Press*] (SAG)
HIRSO .... High-Resolution Solar Optical Telescope
HIRSS .... Hover Infrared Suppressor Subsystem
HIRT .... High Reynolds Number Tunnel
HIRTA .... High Intensity Radio Transmission Area [*Army*] (DOMA)

HIRUD .... Hirudo [*A Leech*] [*Pharmacy*] (ROG)
HIS .... CIGNA High Income Shares [*NYSE symbol*] (SPSG)
HIS .... CIGNA High Income Shs [*NYSE symbol*] (TTSB)
HIS .... Haptic Intelligence Scale [*Psychology*] (AEBS)
HIS .... Hardware Information System (MCD)
HIS .... Hardware Interrupt System (IAA)
HIS .... Hayman Island [*Australia Airport symbol*] (OAG)
HIS .... Health Information Series [*Federal government*]
HIS .... Health Information Services [*Australia*]
HIS .... Health Information Services [*Department of Health and Human Services*]
HIS .... Health Information System (DMAA)
HIS .... Health Interview Survey [*National Institutes of Health*]
HIS .... Heavy-Ion Source
HIS .... Heiss Island [*Former USSR Geomagnetic observatory code*]
HIS .... Heliborne Illumination System (CINC)
HIS .... Hic Iacet Sepultus [*Here Lies Buried*] [*Latin*]
HIS .... Hierarchical Intensive Search [*of the literature*]
HIS .... High Integrity Systems [*Computer company*] [*British*] (NITA)
HIS .... High-Intensity Spectrometer
HIS .... High-Interest Shipping (MCD)
HIS .... High-Resolution Interferometer Spectrometer
HIS .... Hispaniola Airways [*Dominican Republic*] [*ICAO designator*] (FAAC)
HIS .... Histatin (DMAA)
his .... Histidine [*An amino acid*] (DOG)
HIS .... Histidine (DB)
His .... Histidine [*An amino acid*]
HIS .... Histogram Scanning
HIS .... Historian [*or History*] (EY)
HIS .... Hit Indicator System
HIS .... Homogeneous Information Sets
HIS .... Honeywell Information Systems, Inc. (IEEE)
HIS .... Hood Inflation System (DNAB)
HIS .... Horwitz Information Services [*Information service or system*] (IID)
HIS .... Hospital Infection Society [*British*] (DBA)
HIS .... Hospital Information System [*Computer science*]
HIS .... Hospitality and Information Service (EA)
HIS .... House Information Systems [*House of Representatives*] [*Washington, DC*]
HIS .... Hunters' Improvement and National Light Horse Breeding Society (BUAC)
HIS .... Hunters' Improvement Society [*British*] (BI)
HIS .... Hybrid Infrared Source
HIS .... Hyperimmune Serum [*Medicine*] (DMAA)
HISA .... Hawaii International Services Agency
HISA .... Headquarters and Installation Support Activity [*Army*] (AABC)
HISAC .... High-Speed Airdrop Container [*Military*] (RDA)
HISAM .... Hardware Initiated Standalone Memory (NASA)
HISAM .... Hierarchical Indexed Sequential Access Method [*Computer science*] (BUR)
HISAR .... Hughes Integrated Synthetic Aperture Radar [*Hughes Electronics*]
HISARS .... Hydrologic Information Storage and Retrieval System [*North Carolina State University*] [*Raleigh, NC*]
HISB .... Health Insurance Standards Board
HISC .... House Internal Security Committee
HI-SCALE ..... Heliospheric Instrument for Spectra, Composition, and Anisotropy at Low Energies [*Astronomy*]
HISDAM .... Hierarchical Indexed Sequential Direct Access Method [*Computer science*]
HISE .... High Interference Signaling Environment
HISEACOTS... High Sea State Container Transfer System [*Army*] (RDA)
HISG .... Human Immune Serum Globulin [*Immunochemistry*]
HISGS .... Human Insulin Solicitors Group Scotland (BUAC)
HISHA .... Highlands and Islands Sheep Health Association (BUAC)
HiShear ...... Hi-Shear Industries, Inc. [*Associated Press*] (SAG)
HiShearT .... Hi Shear Technology Corp. [*Associated Press*] (SAG)
HiShearTc... Hi Shear Technology Corp. [*Associated Press*] (SAG)
HISI .... Honeywell Information Systems, Inc.
HISKEW .... Health Insurance Skeleton Eligibility Write-off File [*Department of Health and Human Services*] (GFGA)
HISM .... How I See Myself Scale [*Psychology*] (EDAC)
HISP .... Heat-Inactivated Serum Pool [*Clinical chemistry*]
Hisp .... Hispania [*A publication*] (BRI)
HISP .... Historic Independent Smallholders' Party [*Hungary*] [*Political party*] (BUAC)
Hispa .... Hispavox [*Record label*] [*Spain*]
HISPA .... International Association for the History of Physical Education and Sport [*Belgium*]
HISPID .... Herbarium Information Standards and Protocols for Interchange of Data [*Australia*]
HISPOT .... High-Altitude Surveillance Platform for Over-the-Horizon Targeting (MCD)
HISRAN .... High-Precision SHORAN [*Short-Range Navigation*]
HISS .... Healthcare Imaging Services [*NASDAQ symbol*] (TTSB)
HISS .... HealthCare Imaging Services, Inc. [*NASDAQ symbol*] (SAG)
HISS .... Helicopter Icing Spray System (RDA)
HISS .... Helicopter Inflight Spray System (MCD)
HISS .... Herpetological Information Search Systems
HISS .... High-Intensity Sound Simulator
HISS .... High-Intensity Sound System
HISS .... Holographic Ice Surveying System (PDAA)
HISS .... Hospital Information Support System (WDAA)
HISSG .... Healthcare Information Systems Sharing Group (EA)
HiSSS .... High Speed Strike System [*Military*]
HISSZ .... Healthcare Imaging Sv Wrrt'B' [*NASDAQ symbol*] (TTSB)

HIST............. Gallery of History [*NASDAQ symbol*] (TTSB)
HIST............. Gallery of History, Inc. [*NASDAQ symbol*] (SAG)
HIST............. High Input Shock Test
Hist.............. Histamine [*Medicine*] (DB)
Hist.............. Histidinemia [*Medicine*] (AAMN)
HIST............. Histoire [*History*] [*French*] (ROG)
HIST............. Histology (ADA)
Hist.............. Historia [*A publication*] (OCD)
Hist.............. Historiae [*of Tacitus*] [*Classical studies*] (OCD)
HIST............. Historian [*or History*] (AFM)
HIST............. Historical [*Linguistics*]
Hist.............. Historical (AL)
Hist.............. History (AL)
hist.............. History (VRA)
HIST............. Hospital In-Service Training
HIST............. Hyderabad Imperial Service Troops [*British military*] (DMA)
Hist An .... Historia Animalium [*of Aristotle*] [*Classical studies*] (OCD)
Hist Anc Geog... [*A*] History of Ancient Geography [*A publication*] (OCD)
Hist&PolSc... History & Political Science (DD)
Hist & T...... History and Theory [*A publication*] (BRI)
Hist Athen Const... [*A*] History of the Athenian Constitution [*A publication*] (OCD)
Hist Aug ..... Historia Augusta [*A publication*] (OCD)
Hist Conscr... Quomodo Historia Conscribenda Sit [*of Lucian*] [*Classical studies*] (OCD)
Hist Eccl ..... Historia Ecclesiastica [*of Eusebius*] [*Classical studies*] (OCD)
Hist Ed R .... History of Education Review [*A publication*]
HISTEP .... High-Speed Integrated Space Transportation Evaluation Program (IAA)
Hist G .... History of Greece [*A publication*] (OCD)
Hist Gk Phil... History of Greek Philosophy [*A publication*] (OCD)
Hist J.......... Historisches Jahrbuch [*A publication*] (ODCC)
HISTL......... Historical
HISTLINE ..... History of Medicine On-Line [*National Library of Medicine*] [*Bibliographic database*] (IID)
HISTN .... Historian (AABC)
Hist Num ..... Historia Numorum [*A publication*] (OCD)
histo .... Histology [*Medicine*] (DAVI)
histo .... Histoplasma [*Medicine*] (DAVI)
histo .... Histoplasmin [*Skin test*] [*Medicine*] (DAVI)
histo .... Histoplasmosis [*Medicine*] (DAVI)
Hist of Greek Maths... History of Greek Mathematics [*A publication*] (OCD)
HISTOL .... Histology
HISTORIA .... Heraldic Images Storing Applications (TELE)
Hist Pl .... Historia Plantarum [*of Theophrastus*] [*Classical studies*] (OCD)
HISTRAP ..... Heavy Ion Storage Ring for Atomic Physics
HISTRCL ...... Historical
Hist Rom Rel... Roemische Religions-Geschichte [*A publication*] (OCD)
HISTRU........ Hydraulic System Test and Repair Unit [*Army*] (MCD)
HISWA......... Herd Improvement Service of Western Australia [*Animal husbandry*]
HISXE .... Heavy Ion-Induced Satellite X-Ray Emission [*Analytical chemistry*]
HIT............. Hawthorn Institute of Technology [*Australia*]
HIT............. Hazard Information Transmission [*Chemical Manufacturers Association*] (FFDE)
HIT............. Headline International Talent [*Commercial firm*]
HIT............. Health Indication Test [*Engine system*]
HIT............. Health Insurance Tax [*Social Security Administration*] (GFGA)
HIT............. Heavy Industrial Turbines (EFIS)
HIT............. HELWS-Integrated Tracker
HIT............. Hemagglutination Inhibition Test [*for pregnancy*] [*Medicine*]
HIT............. Heparin Induced Thrombocytopenia [*Hematology*] (DAVI)
HIT............. Heuristic Ideation Technique [*A procedure for generating ideas or solutions to a problem by analyzing a series of generalizations*] (WDMC)
HIT............. Hibernation Induction Trigger [*Biochemistry*]
HIT............. High Incidence Target [*Crime computer*]
HIT............. High Intensity Tutoring (EDAC)
HIT............. High-Interest Tracker (MCD)
HIT............. High Interest Tracks
HIT............. High-Isolation Transformer (IEEE)
HIT............. High Italian Technology [*Automotive engineering*]
HIT............. High-Level Interprocessor Transfer (DGA)
HIT............. High Torque [*Engineering*] (IAA)
HIT............. Histamine Inhalation Test [*Immunology*]
HIT............. Histamine Ion Transfer (STED)
HIT............. Histidine Triad [*Biochemistry*]
HIT............. Hitachi Ltd. [*NYSE symbol*] (SPSG)
HIT............. Hitachi,Ltd ADR [*NYSE symbol*] (TTSB)
Hit.............. Hittite (BJA)
HIT............. Holtzman Inkblot Technique (STED)
HIT............. Holtzman Inkblot Test [*Psychology*]
HIT............. Homing Interceptor Technology [*Navigation*] (IEEE)
HIT............. Housing Investment Trust [*AFL-CIO*]
HIT............. Houston International Teleport [*Houston, TX*] [*Telecommunications*] (TSSD)
HIT............. Hughes Improved Terminal [*Aviation*] (MCD)
HIT............. Hughes, Induced Turbulence
HIT............. Hunter Institute of Technology [*Australia*]
HIT............. Hypersonic Interference Technique
HIT............. Hypertrophic Infiltrative Tendinitis [*Medicine*] (MAE)
HIT............. Hypertrophied Inferior Turbinate (STED)
HIT............. Hypervelocity Impulse Tunnel (MCD)
HITA............ Hamper Industry Trade Association [*British*] (DBA)
HITAB .... High-Altitude Target and Background [*Program*] (MUGU)
HITAC .... Hitachi Computer (DIT)
HITAC .... Hitachi Computer Services (NITA)

Hitachi........ Hitachi Ltd. [*Associated Press*] (SAG)
HITADS....... Helmet Integrated Tracking and Display System (MCD)
HITAHR........ Hawaii Institute of Tropical Agriculture and Human Resources [*University of Hawaii*] [*Research center*] (RCD)
HIT and MISS... Hitler and Mussolini [*Slang*] (DSUE)
HITB........... Haemophilus Influenzae Type B [*Meningitis*] [*Medicine*] (STED)
HI/TC.......... Half Inch Tape Cartridge [*Pressure group*] (NITA)
Hitch Pr & Proc... Hitch's Practice and Procedure in the Probate Court of Massachusetts [*A publication*] (DLA)
HiTcPhr........ Hi Tech Pharmacal Co. [*Associated Press*] (SAG)
HITEC.......... Health Information Technologies and Education Center [*University of Texas Health Science Center*] [*Houston, TX*] [*Computer science*]
HITEC.......... Highway Innovation Technology
HITECC........ Higher Introductory Technology and Engineering Conversion Courses [*Education*] [*British*]
HI TECH....... High Technology (WDAA)
HI-TEMP ...... High Temperature (WDAA)
Hi Ten .... High Tensile
HITES.......... Hydrocortisone, Insulin, Transferrin, Estradiol, and Selenium (STED)
HITF........... Health Insurance Trust Fund
HitFd........... Hibernia Foods PLC [*Associated Press*] (SAG)
HITHA......... Historic Irish Tourist Houses and Gardens Association (BUAC)
HITI........... High Integrity Trip Initiator (PDAA)
HITK.......... Hi-Tech Pharmacal [*NASDAQ symbol*] (TTSB)
HITK.......... Hi Tech Pharmacal Co. [*NASDAQ symbol*] (SAG)
HITL........... Hardware-in-the-Loop
HITLS......... Hardware in the Loop Simulation [*Computer science*] (MCD)
HITMORE...... Helicopter Installed Television Monitor and Recorder (MCD)
HITMP .... Highest Temperature [*NWS*] (FAAC)
Hitox.......... Hitox Corporation of America [*Associated Press*] (SAG)
HITP........... High-Ignition-Temperature Propellant
HITPRO....... Hit Probability [*Military*] (MCD)
HITP-SEAP... High-Ignition-Temperature Propellants Self-Extinguishing at Atmospheric Pressure [*Cartridge*] (RDA)
HITS........... Handbook of Information Technology Standards [*A publication*]
HITS........... HAWK [*Homing All the Way Killer*] Institutional Training System [*Military*] (RDA)
HITS........... Hercules Integrated Telecommunications System [*Telecommunications*]
HITS........... High Income Trust Securities [*Drexel Burnham Lambert, Inc.*]
HITS........... High-Rate Multiplexer Input/Output Test System (NASA)
HITS........... High-Speed Integrated Test System
HITS........... Hobbyist's Interchange Tape Standard [*Data recording*]
HITS........... Holloman Infrared Target Simulator (OA)
HITS........... Home Information Technology Study [*Department of Education*] (GFGA)
HITT........... Hittite
Hitt Cod ..... Hittell's California Codes [*A publication*] (DLA)
Hittell's Laws... Hittell's California General Laws [*A publication*] (DLA)
HITTS.......... Heparin-Induced Thrombosis-Thrombocytopenia Syndrome [*Medicine*] (DMAA)
HITWG .... Hole In The Wall Gang [*A sleep-away camp for kids with life-threatening illnesses*] (PCM)
hiu .... Hawaii [*MARC country of publication code Library of Congress*] (LCCP)
HIU .... Head Injury Unit (STED)
HIU .... Headseat Interface Unit (MCD)
HIU .... Headset Interface Unit (NAKS)
HIU .... High Interest Unit [*Navy*] (ANA)
Hi-U .... High-Usage [*Telecommunications*]
HIU .... Higuerote [*Venezuela*] [*Airport symbol*] (AD)
HIU .... Homing Instrumentation Unit (MCD)
HIU .... Host Interface Unit
HIU .... Hyperplasia Interstitialis Uteri [*Medicine*] (DMAA)
HIUS .... Hispanic Institute in the United States [*Later, HI*] (EA)
HIV .... Helium Isolation Valve [*NASA*] (NASA)
HIV .... History Institute Victoria [*Australia*]
HIV .... Human Immunodeficiency Virus
HIV-1 PR ..... Human Immunodeficiency Virus-1 Protease [*An enzyme*]
HIV-Ab .... Human Immunodeficiency Virus Antibody [*Medicine*] (TAD)
HIVAC .... High-Value Accounting Control
HIVAC .... High-Value Asset Control
HIVAC .... Human Immunodeficiency Virus Vaccine [*Medicine*]
HI-VALU ...... High-Priority Air Force Contract [*Generally in missile field*] (AAGC)
HIVAN .... Human Immunodeficiency Virus-Associated Nephropathy [*Medicine*] (DMAA)
HIVAP .... High Velocity Armor-Piercing Projectile (SAA)
HIVD .... Herniated Intervertebral Disc [*Medicine*] (DAVI)
HIVE.......... High Integrity Voting Equipment (PDAA)
HIVES .... High-Volume Electrostatic Sampler (MCD)
HIVIES .... Human Immunodeficiency Virus Information Exchange and Support Group (EA)
HIVIG .... Human Immunodeficiency Virus Immunoglobulin [*Medicine*]
HiVit .... High Vitamin [*Pharmacology*] (DAVI)
hi-vol .... High-Volume Air Sampler [*Environmental science*] (FFDE)
HI-VOL........ High-Volume Sampler (COE)
HIVOS .... High-Vacuum Orbital Simulator
HIVOS .... Humanistisch Institut voor Ontwikkelings Samenwerking [*Humanistic Institute for Co-Operation with Developing Countries*] [*Hague, Netherlands*] (EAIO)
HIVR .... Host Interactive Voice Response [*Telecommunications*] (ITD)
HIV-SF .... HIV-Suppressive Factors [*Medicine*]
HIW .... Highwoods Properties [*NYSE symbol*] (TTSB)
HIW .... Highwoods Properties, Inc. [*NYSE symbol*] (SAG)
HIWAS .... Hazardous Inflight Weather Advisory Service [*Aviation*] (FAAC)

HIWAY	Highway [*Commonly used*] (OPSA)
HIWD	Highwood Resources Ltd. [*NASDAQ symbol*] (NQ)
HIWDF	Highwood Res Ltd [*NASDAQ symbol*] (TTSB)
HIWRP	Hoover Institution on War, Revolution, and Peace (EA)
HIWS	High-Level Waste and Standards [*Environmental science*] (COE)
HIWSC	Health Industry Wage and Salary Committee [*Terminated, 1974*] (EGAO)
HIWSD	Handbook of Instructions for Weapon Systems Designers
HIWY	Highway [*Commonly used*] (OPSA)
HIX	Heat-Inactivated Muscle Extract
HIX	Helix Systems Ltd. [*Vancouver Stock Exchange symbol*]
HIX	Hopkinsville, KY [*Location identifier FAA*] (FAAL)
HIXAT	Highest Temperature Exceeded for All Time [*NWS*] (FAAC)
HIXFM	Highest Temperature Exceeded for the Month [*NWS*] (FAAC)
HIXSE	Highest Temperature Exceeded so Early [*NWS*] (FAAC)
HIXSL	Highest Temperature Exceeded so Late [*NWS*] (FAAC)
HIY	Hampshire Imperial Yeomanry [*British military*] (DMA)
HIY	Hertfordshire Imperial Yeomanry [*British military*] (DMA)
HIY	Holiday Institute of Yonkers (EA)
HiYdPl	High Yield Plus Fund [*Associated Press*] (SAG)
HiYld	High Yield Income Fund [*Associated Press*] (SAG)
HIZA	Informationsdienst-AUSTAUSCH [*Information Service-EXCHANGE*] [*NOMOS Datapool Database*] (IID)
HJ	Air-Cushion Vehicle built by Hoverjak [*England*] [*Usually used in combination with numerals*]
HJ	Air-Cushion Vehicle built by Hoverjet [*Usually used in combination with n umerals*] [*Canada*]
HJ	Halt and Jump [*Computer science*] (BUR)
HJ	Hebra-Jadassohn [*Disease*] [*Medicine*] (DB)
HJ	Heilige Johannes [*Saint John*] [*Freemasonry*] [*German*]
HJ	Hepatojugular [*Reflex*] [*Medicine*]
HJ	Hermanas Josefinas (TOCD)
HJ	Heterojunction [*Electronics*]
HJ	Hic Jacet [*Here Lies*] [*Latin*]
HJ	High Jump
HJ	Hinge Jaw (MSA)
HJ	Holt-Jackson [*Commercial firm British*]
HJ	Honest John [*A type of short range, unguided Army rocket*]
HJ	Hose Jacket (KSC)
HJ	Howell-Jolly [*Bodies*] [*Hematology*]
HJ	Station Open from Sunrise to Sunset [*ITU designation*] (CET)
HJ	Sunrise to Sunset [*ICAO*] (FAAC)
HJA	Air Haiti [*ICAO designator*] (FAAC)
HJAS	Harry James Appreciation Society (EAIO)
HJAS	Harvard Journal of Asiatic Studies [*A publication*] (BRI)
HJB	Howell-Jolly Bodies [*Hematology*] (DAVI)
HJB	Hydrodynamic Journal Bearing
HJBT	Heterojunction Bipolar Transistor (MCD)
HJC	Hagerstown Junior College [*Maryland*]
HJC	Hansoms of John Clayton [*An association*] (EA)
HJC	Harcum Junior College [*Pennsylvania*]
HJC	Heathrow Jet Charter Ltd. [*British ICAO designator*] (FAAC)
HJC	Hibbing Junior College [*Later, Hibbing Community College*] [*Minnesota*]
HJC	Highland Junior College [*Kansas*]
HJC	Hinds Junior College [*Raymond, MS*]
HJC	Holmes Junior College [*Goodman, MS*]
HJC	Holyoke Junior College [*Later, Holyoke Community College*] [*Massachusetts*]
HJC	Hutchinson Junior College [*Kansas*]
HJCC	Honolulu Japanese Chamber of Commerce (EA)
HJCF	Hungarian Jewish Cultural Federation (BUAC)
HJD	Heliocentric Julian Day [*Astronomy*]
HJD	Heterojunction Device
HJD	Las Hermanas de Juan Diego (TOCD)
HJD	Los Hermanos de Juan Diego (TOCD)
HJE	Hot Jet Exhaust
HJH	Hebron, NE [*Location identifier FAA*] (FAAL)
HJI	Hachtmann, J. I., Newark NJ [*STAC*]
HJJ	Hachijojima [*Japan*] [*Seismograph station code, US Geological Survey*] (SEIS)
HJL	Hamlin Jet Ltd. [*British ICAO designator*] (FAAC)
HJL	Honest John Launcher [*See also HJ*] [*Army*]
HJLP	Hungarian Justice and Life Party [*Political party*] (BUAC)
HJM	Akron-Canton, OH [*Location identifier FAA*] (FAAL)
HJM	H. J. Mulliner [*British coachbuilder*]
HJM	Hot Jet Model
H Joint Res	House Joint Resolution (AAGC)
HJP	Hand Jewel Pusher
HJP	Heat Jacketed Pump
HJPP	Heat Jacketed Proportioning Pump
HJR	Hepatojugular Reflex [*Medicine*]
HJR	Honest John Rocket [*See also HJ*] [*Army*]
HJR	House Joint Resolution
HJR	Khajuraho [*India*] [*Airport symbol*] (OAG)
HJ Res	House Joint Resolution
HJRes	House Joint Resolution (WPI)
HJS	Hebrew Jewellers' Society [*A union*] [*British*]
HJS	Helijet [*Spain ICAO designator*] (FAAC)
HJS	Helsingen Juutalainen Seurakunta [*Finland*] [*A publication*] (BJA)
HJS	Hic Jacet Sepultus [*Here Lies Buried*] [*Latin*]
HJSA	Hamburger Jute und Sisal Association (BUAC)
HJSC	Hospital Junior Staff Committee [*British*] (DI)
HJT	Head Joint [*Technical drawings*]
HK	Handelskammer [*Chamber of Commerce*] [*German*]

HK	Handkommentar zum Alten Testament [*Goettingen*] [*A publication*] (BJA)
H-K	Hands to Knee [*Medicine*]
HK	Hank [*Cotton*] (ROG)
HK	Hauptwerk [*Masterpiece*] [*German*]
HK	Hawker De Havilland Australia Pty. Ltd., Kaman Aircraft Corp. [*ICAO aircraft manufacturer identifier*] (ICAO)
HK	Heater Kit
HK	Heat Killed [*Medicine*] (MAE)
HK	Heckler and Koch [*Machine gun*] (MCD)
HK	Heel-to-Knee (DMAA)
HK	Hevra Kaddisha (BJA)
HK	Hexokinase [*An enzyme*]
HK	High-Priority Key [*IRS*]
HK	Hoeheres Kommando [*Higher Command*] [*German military - World War II*]
HK	Hoffa-Kastert [*Syndrome*] [*Medicine*] (DB)
HK	Homoserine Kinase [*An enzyme*]
hk	Hong Kong [*MARC country of publication code Library of Congress*] (LCCP)
HK	Hong Kong [*ANSI two-letter standard code*] (CNC)
HK	Hook
HK	Hotkey [*Computer science*] (PCM)
HK	Housekeeping
HK	House of Keys [*Isle Of Man*]
Hk	Hulk [*Nautical charts*]
HK	Human Kidney
H-K	Hunter-Killer [*Missile*] (MUGU)
H-K	Hypoascorbemia-Kwashiorkor [*Orthomolecular medicine*]
HK	Knoop Hardness Number
HK	People's Liberation [*Revolutionary group*] [*Turkey*]
HK	South Pacific Island Airways [*ICAO designator*] (AD)
HKA	Blytheville, AR [*Location identifier FAA*] (FAAL)
HKA	Hand Knitting Association (EA)
HKA	Hong Kong Airways Ltd.
HKA	Superior Aviation, Inc. [*ICAO designator*] (FAAC)
HKAB	Hong Kong Association of Banks (ECON)
HKAFO	Hip-Knee-Ankle-Foot Orthosis [*Medicine*]
HKAM	Amboseli [*Kenya*] [*ICAO location identifier*] (ICLI)
HKamCF	Canada-France-Hawaii Telescope Corp. Kamuela, HI [*Library symbol*] [*Library of Congress*] (LCLS)
HKAO	Hip-Knee-Ankle Orthosis [*Medicine*]
HkAT	Handkommentar zum Alten Testament [*Goettingen*] [*A publication*] (BJA)
HKB	Hard Kernel Bunch (IAA)
HKB	Hepatitis Knowledge Base (NITA)
HKBA	Busia [*Kenya*] [*ICAO location identifier*] (ICLI)
HKBA	Hong Kong Bank Australia
HKBC	Hong Kong Bank of Canada
HKBR	Bura [*Kenya*] [*ICAO location identifier*] (ICLI)
HKBU	Bungoma [*Kenya*] [*ICAO location identifier*] (ICLI)
HKC	Henkel Corp., Minneapolis, MN [*OCLC symbol*] (OCLC)
HKC	Hong Kong [*Seismograph station code, US Geological Survey*] (SEIS)
HKC	Human Kidney Cell [*Medicine*] (DMAA)
HKC	Shirley, NY [*Location identifier FAA*] (FAAL)
HKCC	Hong Kong Cable Communications
HKCE	Hong Kong Commodities Exchange
HKCEC	Hong Kong Catholic Education Council (BUAC)
HKCS	Hong Kong Chemical Society
HKCS	Hong Kong Computer Society (DDC)
HKCW	Hong Kong Council of Women (BUAC)
HKD	Hakodate [*Japan*] [*Airport symbol*] (OAG)
HKDS	Croatian Christian Democratic Party [*Political party*]
HKEL	Eldoret [*Kenya*] [*ICAO location identifier*] (ICLI)
HKEM	Embu [*Kenya*] [*ICAO location identifier*] (ICLI)
HKES	Eliye Springs [*Kenya*] [*ICAO location identifier*] (ICLI)
HKF	Halbkettenfahrzeug [*Half-Track Vehicle*] [*German military - World War II*]
HKF	Hancock Fabrics [*NYSE symbol*] (TTSB)
HKF	Hancock Fabrics, Inc. [*NYSE symbol*] (SPSG)
HKF	Handkerchief
HKF	Middletown, OH [*Location identifier FAA*] (FAAL)
HKFE	Hong Kong Futures Exchange
HKFG	Kalokol [*Kenya*] [*ICAO location identifier*] (ICLI)
HKG	Hong Kong [*ANSI three-letter standard code*] (CNC)
HKG	Hong Kong [*British Crown Colony*] [*Airport symbol*] (AD)
HKG	Housekeeping (SSD)
HKGA	Garissa [*Kenya*] [*ICAO location identifier*] (ICLI)
HKGS	Church of Jesus Christ of Latter-Day Saints, Genealogical Society Library, Kaneohe Stake Branch, Kaneohe, HI [*Library symbol Library of Congress*] (LCLS)
HKGT	Garba Tula [*Kenya*] [*ICAO location identifier*] (ICLI)
HKH	Chicago, IL [*Location identifier FAA*] (FAAL)
HKHB	Homa Bay [*Kenya*] [*ICAO location identifier*] (ICLI)
HKHO	Hola [*Kenya*] [*ICAO location identifier*] (ICLI)
HKI	Helen Keller International (EA)
HKI	Husiki [*Japan*] [*Seismograph station code, US Geological Survey*] (SEIS)
HKIA	Hong Kong Institute of Architects (BUAC)
HKIBOR	Hong Kong Inter-Bank Offered Rate (MHDW)
HKIS	Isiolo [*Kenya*] [*ICAO location identifier*] (ICLI)
HKJ	Hashemite Kingdom of Jordan (BARN)
HKJSMA	Hong Kong Jade and Stone Manufacturers Association (BUAC)
HKK	Hokitika [*New Zealand*] [*Airport symbol*] (OAG)

HKKA	Kabarak [*Kenya*] [*ICAO location identifier*] (ICLI)
HKKE	Keekorok [*Kenya*] [*ICAO location identifier*] (ICLI)
HKKG	Kakamega [*Kenya*] [*ICAO location identifier*] (ICLI)
HKKI	Kisumu [*Kenya*] [*ICAO location identifier*] (ICLI)
HKKK	Helsingin Kauppakorkeakoulun Kirjasto [*Helsinki School of Economics Library*] [*Finland*] [*Information service or system*] (IID)
HKKL	Kilaguni [*Kenya*] [*ICAO location identifier*] (ICLI)
HKKR	Kericho [*Kenya*] [*ICAO location identifier*] (ICLI)
HKKS	Kisii [*Kenya*] [*ICAO location identifier*] (ICLI)
HKKT	Kitale [*Kenya*] [*ICAO location identifier*] (ICLI)
HKL	Haleakala [*Hawaii*] [*Seismograph station code, US Geological Survey*] (SEIS)
HKL	Hoyrekvinners Landsforbund [*Women's Organization of the Conservative Party*] [*Norway Political party*] (EAIO)
HKLA	Hong Kong Library Association (BUAC)
HKLG	Lokitaung [*Kenya*] [*ICAO location identifier*] (ICLI)
HKLJ	Hong Kong Law Journal [*A publication*] (DLA)
HKLK	Lokichoggio [*Kenya*] [*ICAO location identifier*] (ICLI)
HKLM	Heat-Killed Listeria Monocytogene [*Medicine*] (MAE)
HKLO	Lodwar [*Kenya*] [*ICAO location identifier*] (ICLI)
HKLR	Hong Kong Law Reports [*A publication*] (DLA)
HKLT	Loitokitok [*Kenya*] [*ICAO location identifier*] (ICLI)
HKLU	Lamu [*Kenya*] [*ICAO location identifier*] (ICLI)
HKLY	Loyengalani [*Kenya*] [*ICAO location identifier*] (ICLI)
HKM	Hypermetropic Keratomileusis [*Ophthalmology*]
HKM	Hypervelocity Kill Mechanism [*Air Force*]
HKM	Morgan Stanley Group, Inc. [*AMEX symbol*] (SAG)
HKMA	Hawick Knitwear Manufacturers Association [*British*] (DBA)
HKMA	Hong Kong Management Association (BUAC)
HKMA	Hong Kong Monetary Authority [*Banking*]
HKMA	Mandera [*Kenya*] [*ICAO location identifier*] (ICLI)
HKMB	Marsabit [*Kenya*] [*ICAO location identifier*] (ICLI)
HKMG	Magadi [*Kenya*] [*ICAO location identifier*] (ICLI)
HKMI	Maralal [*Kenya*] [*ICAO location identifier*] (ICLI)
HKMK	Mulika [*Kenya*] [*ICAO location identifier*] (ICLI)
HKML	Malindi [*Kenya*] [*ICAO location identifier*] (ICLI)
HKMO	Mombasa/Moi International [*Kenya*] [*ICAO location identifier*] (ICLI)
HKMR	Mackinnon Road [*Kenya*] [*ICAO location identifier*] (ICLI)
HKMS	Hong Kong Mathematical Society (BUAC)
HKMSC	Hong Kong Military Service Corps [*British military*] (DMA)
HKMU	Makindu [*Kenya*] [*ICAO location identifier*] (ICLI)
HKMY	Moyale [*Kenya*] [*ICAO location identifier*] (ICLI)
HKN	Harken Technologies, Inc. [*Vancouver Stock Exchange symbol*]
HKN	Hoskins [*Papua New Guinea*] [*Airport symbol*] (OAG)
HKN	Jim Hankins Air Service, Inc. [*FAA designator*] (FAAC)
HKNA	Nairobi/Jomo Kenyatta International [*Kenya*] [*ICAO location identifier*] (ICLI)
HKNC	Helen Keller National Center for Deaf-Blind Youths and Adults (EA)
HKNC	Nairobi [*Kenya*] [*ICAO location identifier*] (ICLI)
HKNCDBYA	Helen Keller National Center for Deaf-Blind Youths and Adults (EA)
HKNI	Nyeri [*Kenya*] [*ICAO location identifier*] (ICLI)
HKNK	Nakuru [*Kenya*] [*ICAO location identifier*] (ICLI)
HKNMA	Hong Kong National Musicology Association (BUAC)
HKNMRS	Hong Kong National Music Research Society (BUAC)
HKNO	Narok [*Kenya*] [*ICAO location identifier*] (ICLI)
HKNT	Handkommentar zum Neuen Testament [*A publication*] (BJA)
HKNV	Naivasha [*Kenya*] [*ICAO location identifier*] (ICLI)
HKNW	Nairobi/Wilson [*Kenya*] [*ICAO location identifier*] (ICLI)
HKNY	Nanyuki [*Kenya*] [*ICAO location identifier*] (ICLI)
HKO	Hip-Knee Orthosis [*Medicine*]
HKP	Hidden Lake [*Pennsylvania*] [*Seismograph station code, US Geological Survey Closed*] (SEIS)
HKP	Hong Kong Polytechnic (BUAC)
HKP	Hookup (MSA)
HKP	Kaanapali [*Hawaii*] [*Airport symbol*] (OAG)
HKPC	Hong Kong Productivity Council and Centre (BUAC)
HKR	Hallmark Resources [*Vancouver Stock Exchange symbol*]
HKR	Hong Kong Regiment [*British military*] (DMA)
HKR	Hooker [*Ship's rigging*] (ROG)
HKR	Hydrolytic Kinetic Resolution
HKRE	Nairobi/Eastleigh [*Kenya*] [*ICAO location identifier*] (ICLI)
HKS	Heel-Knee-Shin [*Test*] [*Neurology*] (DAVI)
HKS	Helikopter Service AS [*Norway ICAO designator*] (FAAC)
HKS	Hyperkinesis Syndrome [*Medicine*] (DMAA)
HKS	Jackson, MS [*Location identifier FAA*] (FAAL)
HKSA	East African School of Aviation [*Kenya*] [*ICAO location identifier*] (ICLI)
HKSB	Samburu [*Kenya*] [*ICAO location identifier*] (ICLI)
HKSC	Hong Kong Study Circle (EA)
HKSRA	Hong Kong and Singapore Royal Artillery [*British military*] (DMA)
HKSRGA	Hong Kong and Singapore Royal Garrison Artillery [*British military*] (DMA)
HKSU	Hong Kong Seamen's Union
HKT	Hiram, King of Tyre [*Freemasonry*]
HKT	Hockley [*Texas*] [*Seismograph station code, US Geological Survey*] (SEIS)
HKT	Hollow Kathode Tube
HKT	Hong Kong Telecom ADR [*NYSE symbol*] (TTSB)
HKT	Hong Kong Telecommunications Ltd. [*NYSE symbol*] (CTT)
HKT	Hot Kathode Tube
HKT	Phuket [*Thailand*] [*Airport symbol*] (OAG)
HKTAG	Hong Kong Trade Advisory Group [*British Overseas Trade Board*] (DS)
HKTDC	Hong Kong Trade Development Council (BUAC)

HK Tel	Hong Kong Telecommunications Ltd. [*Associated Press*] (SAG)
HKU	Hong Kong University
HkU	University of Hong Kong, Hong Kong, Hong Kong [*UK*] [*Library symbol Library of Congress*] (LCLS)
HKUST	Hong Kong University of Science and Technology (ECON)
HKVC	Hong Kong Volunteer Corps [*British military*] (DMA)
HKVO	Voi [*Kenya*] [*ICAO location identifier*] (ICLI)
HKWJ	Wajir [*Kenya*] [*ICAO location identifier*] (ICLI)
HKX	Ellington Air Force Base, TX [*Location identifier FAA*] (FAAL)
HKY	Canstar Sports, Inc. [*Toronto Stock Exchange symbol*]
HKY	Hickory [*North Carolina*] [*Airport symbol*] (OAG)
HKYNA	Hydroxykynurenic Acid [*Organic chemistry*]
HKZ	Minneapolis, MN [*Location identifier FAA*] (FAAL)
HL	Das Heilige Land (BJA)
HL	Hairline (DAVI)
HL	Half Length [*Photography*] (DGA)
HL	Half-Life [*of radioactive elements*]
HL	Half Line [*Illustration*] (DGA)
hl	Halite [*CIPW classification*] [*Geology*]
HL	Hallux Limitus [*Podiatry*] (DAVI)
HL	HALON [*Halogenated Hydrocarbon*] System [*NFPA pre-fire planning symbol*] (NFPA)
HL	Haloperidol (DAVI)
HL	Hand Lantern (AAG)
HL	Hard Labor
HL	Hardline (MCD)
HL	Harelip
HL	Hariana Lancers [*British military*] (DMA)
HL	Haul (MSA)
HL	Hawser Laid
HL	Header Label [*Computer science*] (IAA)
HL	Headlamp [*Automotive engineering*]
HL	Head Linesman [*Football*]
HL	Headmaster-Lieutenant [*Navy British*]
HL	Hearing Level
HL	Hearing Loss
HL	Heavy Lift
HL	Heavy Loading (IAA)
HL	Hebrew Leader (BJA)
HL	Hebrew Letters (BJA)
HL	Hebrew Literature (BJA)
HL	Hecla Mining [*NYSE symbol*] (TTSB)
HL	Hecla Mining Co. [*NYSE symbol*] (SPSG)
HL	Hectoliter (GPO)
hL	Hectoliter (STED)
HL	Heel Line (MSA)
HL	Height-Length
HL	Height Loss [*Aviation*] (DA)
HL	Heilig [*Holy, Saint*] [*German*]
HL	Heir-at-Law
HL	Helium Level
HL	Heparin Lock [*Pharmacology*] (DAVI)
HL	Heptagonal League (PSS)
HL	Herpetologists' League (EA)
HL	Hickman Line [*Cardiology*] (DAVI)
HL	High Level
H/L	Highlight (DGA)
HL	Highline (MSA)
H/L	High or Low
HL	Hill
HL	Hinge Line [*Technical drawings*]
HL	Histiocytic Lymphoma [*Oncology*]
HL	Histocompatibility Locus [*Immunology*]
HL	Hittite Laws (BJA)
HL	Hoc Loco [*In This Place*] [*Latin*]
HL	Hodges-Lehmann Estimator [*Statistics*]
HL	Hodgkin's Lymphoma [*Medicine*]
HL	Holiday Airlines (MHDW)
HL	Home Lines [*Steamship*] (MHDW)
HL	Honors List (ADA)
HL	Horizontal Landing (KSC)
HL	Horizontal Line
HL	Hose-Layer (WDAA)
HL	Host Language
HL	Hot Line [*Alert system*] (AAG)
HL	House of Lords [*British*]
HL	House of Lords Cases (Clark) [*England*] [*A publication*] (DLA)
HL	Howard League [*An association*] (EAIO)
HL	Huius Loci [*Of This Place*] [*Latin*]
HL	Human Lymphoid [*Immunology*]
HL	Hyborean Legion (EA)
HL	Hydraulics Laboratory [*Army*]
HL	Hydrodynamics Laboratory [*MIT*] (MCD)
HL	Hydrogen Line (MCD)
HL	Hydrology Laboratory [*Department of Agriculture*] [*Information service or system*] (IID)
H/L	Hydrophile/Lipophile [*Followed by a number*]
HL	Hygienic Laboratory [*US*]
HL	Hypermetropia, Latent [*Ophthalmology*]
HL	Hypermetropia, Latent [*Medicine*] (DMAA)
Hl	Hyperopia Latent [*Ophthalmology*] (DAVI)
HL	Hypertrichosis Lanuginosa [*Medicine*]
HL	Law Reports, House of Lords, English and Irish Appeals [*1866-75*] [*A publication*] (DLA)
HL	Mustard/Lewisite Mix [*Poisonous gas*] [*Army*]

HL............. VEB Deutsche Hydrierwerk, Rodleben [*East Germany*] [*Research code symbol*]

HLA............. Hall's Lagoon [*Australia Seismograph station code, US Geological Survey Closed*] (SEIS)

HLA............. Hat Leather Association (EA)

HLA............. Hawaii Library Association (BUAC)

HLA............. Heavy-Lift Airship (MCD)

HLA............. Heavylift Cargo Airlines Ltd. [*British ICAO designator*] (FAAC)

HLA............. Helicopter Loggers Association (EA)

HLA............. Highlander Income Fund [*AMEX symbol*] (TTSB)

HLA............. Highlander Income Fund, Inc. [*AMEX symbol*] (SAG)

HLA............. High-Level Analog (MCD)

HLA............. High Level Architecture [*Department of Defense*]

HLA............. High Low Alarm [*Electronics*] (ECII)

HLA............. High-Speed Line Adapter (MHDI)

HLA............. Histocompatibility Leukocyte Antigen (DB)

HLA............. Histocompatibility Locus Antigens [*System*] [*Immunology*]

HLA............. Historical Labor Applications [*Military*] (AFIT)

HLA............. Homologous Leucocytic Antibodies

HLA............. Homologous Leukocyte Antibody (STED)

HLA............. Horizontal Line Array (MCD)

HLA............. Human Leucocyte Antigen [*Immunology*]

HLA............. Human Leucocyte Antigen System [*Medicine*] (WDAA)

HL-A............ Human Leukocyte- [*or Lymphocyte-*] Antigen [*System for recognizing foreign tissue*] [*Immunology*]

HLA............. Human Life Amendment

HLA............. Human Lymphocyte Antibody (STED)

HLA............. Human Lymphocyte Antigen (STED)

HLA............. Hungarian Logistics Association (BUAC)

HLA............. Hydraulic Lash Adjuster [*Automotive engine design*]

HLA............. Hypoplastic Left Atrium [*Cardiology*] (DAVI)

HLaB............ Brigham Young University, Hawaii Campus, Laie, HI [*Library symbol Library of Congress*] (LCLS)

HLAC............ Host Link Adapter Card [*Ideacomm Gateway*]

HLAD............ Hearing-Lookout Assist Device [*Navigation*] (OA)

HLAD............ High-Level Air Defence [*Military British*]

HLAD............ Horse-Liver Alcohol Dehydrogenase [*Also, HLADH, HLALD*] [*An enzyme*]

HLADH......... Horse-Liver Alcohol Dehydrogenase [*Also, HLAD, HLALD*] [*An enzyme*]

HLA/DZ......... Helicopter Landing Area/Drop Zone [*Military*] (MCD)

HLA/DZS....... Helicopter Landing Area/Drop Zone Study [*Military*] (MCD)

HLAF............ High-Level Arithmetic Function

HLaGS......... Church of Jesus Christ of Latter-Day Saints, Genealogical Society Library, Laie Branch, Laie, HI [*Library symbol Library of Congress*] (LCLS)

HLAHWG...... High Level Ad Hoc Working Group [*NATO*] (NATG)

HLAIS.......... High-Level Analog Input Subsystem [*Computer science*] (MHDI)

HLAIS.......... High Level Analog Input System (NITA)

HLAL........... High Level Assembler Language (NAKS)

HLAL........... High-Level Assembly Language (MCD)

HLALD......... Horse-Liver Alcohol Dehydrogenase [*Also, HLAD, HLADH*] [*An enzyme*]

HL-A LD....... Human Lymphocyte-Antigen Lymphocyte Defined [*Immunology*]

HLA-LD........ Human Lymphocyte Antigen-Lymphocyte Defined (STED)

H-LAND........ Headland (ADA)

HL & T......... Hunter's Landlord and Tenant [*Scotland*] [*A publication*] (DLA)

HLA negative... Heart, Lungs, and Abdomen Negative [*Medicine*] (STED)

HLAS.......... Handbook of Latin American Studies

HLAS.......... Hot Line Alert System

HLASD......... Hand-Link Arm Safe Device

HL-A SD....... Human Lymphocyte-Antigen Serologically Defined [*Immunology*]

HLA-SD........ Human Lymphocyte Antigen-Serologically Defined (STED)

HLAV.......... Horseradish Latent Virus [*Plant pathology*]

HLB............. Batesville, IN [*Location identifier FAA*] (FAAL)

HLB............. Federal Home Loan Bank Board, Accounts Payable, Washington, DC [*OCLC symbol*] (OCLC)

HLB............. High-Line Airways, Inc. [*Canada ICAO designator*] (FAAC)

HLB............. Hydrophile-Lipophile Balance [*Surfactant technology*]

HLB............. Hypotonic Lysis Buffer [*Analytical biochemistry*]

HLBB.......... Home Loan Bank Board [*Federal agency*] (GPO)

HLBI........... Human Lymphoblastoid Interferon [*Antineoplastic drug*]

HLBR.......... Heel Breaster

HLBRD........ Halberd

HLC............ HAWK [*Homing All the Way Killer*] Logistics Complex (MCD)

HLC............ Headmaster Lieutenant-Commander [*Navy British*]

HLC............ Heat Loss Center (DMAA)

HLC............ Heavy/Light Corps (MCD)

HLC............ Helicap [*France ICAO designator*] (FAAC)

HLC............ High Level Caves (COE)

HLC............ High-Level Cell [*Nuclear energy*] (NRCH)

HLC............ High-Level Center (IAA)

HLC............ High-Level Compiler (IAA)

HLC............ Hill City, KS [*Location identifier FAA*] (FAAL)

HLC............ Hispanic Literature Criticism [*A publication*]

HLC............ Homeowner's Land Corp. [*Federal agency formed in 1932*] [*Investment term*]

HLC............ Homogenized Leaf Curing [*Tobacco industry*]

HLC............ House of Lords Cases (Clark) [*England*] [*A publication*] (DLA)

HLC............ Human Lactation Center (EA)

HLC............ Human Life Center (EA)

HLCA.......... Hill Livestock Compensatory Allowances [*British*] (WDAA)

HLCADS....... High-Level Container Airdrop System [*Army*] (RDA)

HL Cas........ House of Lords Cases (Clark) [*England*] [*A publication*] (DLA)

HL Cas (Eng)... House of Lords Cases [*A publication*] (DLA)

HLC-ATC...... Heavy-Lift Helicopter Advanced Technology Component [*Program*] [*Army*] (RDA)

HLCC.......... Home-Laundering Care Code [*British*] (DI)

HLCC.......... Home-Laundering Consultative Council [*British*] (DI)

HLCF.......... Hardened Launch Control Facility (MUGU)

HLCF.......... Heat-Labile Citrororum Factor [*Biochemistry*]

HLCF.......... Holy Land Conservation Fund (EA)

HLCL.......... Helical

HLCL.......... Human Lymphoblastoid Cell Line (DB)

HLCM.......... Holy Land Christian Mission (EA)

HLCMI......... Holy Land Christian Mission International [*Later, HLCM*] (EA)

HLCPS........ Helical Compression

HLCPTR....... Helicopter (MSA)

HLCS.......... Heat Limiter Control Switch

HLCS.......... High-Level Compaction Station [*Nuclear energy*] (NRCH)

HLCS.......... High-Level Control Station [*Hazardous materials control*]

HLCV.......... Hot Leg Check Valve [*Nuclear energy*] (NRCH)

HLD............ Doctor of Humane Letters

HLD............ Hailar [*China*] [*Airport symbol*] (OAG)

HL-D........... Haloperidol Decanoate [*Pharmacology*] (DAVI)

HLD............ Harold's Stores [*AMEX symbol*] (TTSB)

HLD............ Harold's Stores, Inc. [*AMEX symbol*] (SPSG)

HLD............ Helium Leak Detector

HLD............ Herniated Lumbar Disc [*Medicine*]

HLD............ Hold

hld............ Hold (WDMC)

HLD............ Holdings [*Online database field identifier*]

HLD............ Holiday Airlines Havacilik Ve Turizm Sanayi Ve Ticaret, AG [*Turkey*] [*FAA designator*] (FAAC)

HLD............ Hollywood Investments [*Vancouver Stock Exchange symbol*]

HLD............ Home Laundry Detergent

HLD............ Hypersensitivity Lung Disease [*Medicine*]

HLDA.......... Hold Acknowledge [*Computer science*]

HLDC.......... High-Level Data Link Control (MCD)

HLDDN........ Holddown

HLDG.......... Holding (MSA)

HLDH.......... Heat-Stable Lactic Dehydrogenase [*Clinical chemistry*]

HLDI........... Highway Loss Data Institute (EA)

HLDLC......... High-Level Data Link Control [*Computer science*] (DOM)

HLDN.......... Holddown (MSA)

HLDNG........ Holding

HLDR.......... Holder

Hldr of Proc... Holder of Procuration [*Banking*] (TBD)

HLDS.......... Hydrogen Leak Detection System (NASA)

HLDS.......... Vermont-New Hampshire-New York Hospital Libraries [*Library network*]

HLDTL......... High Level Data Transistor Logic (NITA)

HLDTL......... High-Level Diode Transistor Logic [*Computer science*] (MHDI)

HLDY.......... Holiday

HldyRV........ Holiday RV Superstores, Inc. [*Associated Press*] (SAG)

HLE............ First Air [*British ICAO designator*] (FAAC)

HLE............ Hailey, ID [*Location identifier FAA*] (FAAL)

HLE............ Hale Resources Ltd. [*Toronto Stock Exchange symbol*]

HLE............ Halle [*German Democratic Republic*] [*Seismograph station code, US Geological Survey*] (SEIS)

HLE............ Hazleton Laboratories Europe Ltd. [*British*] (IRUK)

HLE............ High-Low-Junction Emitter (PDAA)

HLE............ Human Leucocyte Elastase [*An enzyme*]

HLE............ Hydrogen Line Emission

HLED.......... Home Leave Eligibility Date (WDAA)

HLEG.......... Hydrolysate Lactalbumin Earle's Glucose [*Medicine*] (DMAA)

HLEXT......... Helical Extension

HLF............ Hall's Legal Forms [*A publication*] (DLA)

HLF............ Hapag Lloyd Fluggesellschaft GmbH [*Germany ICAO designator*] (FAAC)

HLF............ Heart and Lung Foundation [*Defunct*] (EA)

HLF............ Heat-Labile Factor

HLF............ Heller Financial [*NYSE symbol*] (SPSG)

HLF............ Hepatic Leukaemia Factor [*Medicine*]

HLF............ Hidden Lake Formation [*Geology*]

HLF............ High Loss Ferrite

HLF............ Holistic Life Foundation [*Later, Feathered Pipe Foundation*] (EA)

HLF............ Horizontal Laminar Flow (AAEL)

HLF............ Horizontal Line Frequency

HLF............ House Leadership Fund (EA)

HLF............ Hultsfred [*Sweden*] [*Airport symbol*] (OAG)

HLF............ Human Lactoferrin [*Biochemistry*]

HLF............ Human Life Foundation (EA)

HLF............ Human Lung Fluid [*Medicine*]

HLF............ Hyperbolic LOFAR Fix [*Military*] (CAAL)

HLFL.......... Buattifel [*Libya*] [*ICAO location identifier*] (ICLI)

HLFM.......... Half-Moon

HLFM.......... High-Level Flux Monitor

HLFPrA........ Heller Finl 8.125% Sr'A' Pfd [*NYSE symbol*] (TTSB)

HLFT.......... Holographic Lensless Fourier Transform (PDAA)

HLFTN........ Halftone (VRA)

HLG............ Dr. John W. Tintera Memorial Hypoglycemia Lay Group (EA)

HLG............ Hauling

HLG............ HAWK [*Homing All the Way Killer*] Logistics Group (AABC)

HLG............ Heligoland [*Federal Republic of Germany*] [*Seismograph station code, US Geological Survey*] (SEIS)

HLG............ High-Level Group [*NATO*]

HLG............ Historic Landscapes Group [*British*] (DBA)

HLG............ Hollinger, Inc. [*Toronto Stock Exchange symbol Vancouver Stock Exchange symbol*]

HLG	Homing Level Gauge
HLG	Hot Leg [*Nuclear energy*]
HLG	Housing and Local Government [*A publication*] (DLA)
HLG	Hybrid Lens Guide (PDAA)
HLG	Wheeling [*West Virginia*] [*Airport symbol*] (AD)
HLG	Wheeling, WV [*Location identifier FAA*] (FAAL)
HLGC	Hannibal-La Grange College [*Missouri*]
HLGL	Giallo/Warehouse 59 E [*Libya*] [*ICAO location identifier*] (ICLI)
HLGRF	Hollinger Inc. [*NASDAQ symbol*] (TTSB)
HLGS	Hot Line Gunsight System
HLGT	Ghat [*Libya*] [*ICAO location identifier*] (ICLI)
HLH	Heavy-Lift Helicopter
HLH	Helix-Loop-Helix [*Genetics*]
HLH	Hertfordshire Light Horse [*British military*] (DMA)
HLH	High-Level Heating [*Nuclear science*] (OA)
HLH	Human Luteinizing Hormone [*Endocrinology*]
HLH	Hypoplastic Left Heart [*Cardiology*]
HLH	Ulanhot [*China*] [*Airport symbol*] (OAG)
HLHS	Heavy-Lift Helicopter System
HLHS	Hypoplastic Left-Heart Syndrome [*Medicine*]
HLI	Hemolysis Inhibition [*Medicine*] (AAMN)
HLI	Highland Light Infantry [*Military unit*] [*British*]
HLI	Holly Springs, MS [*Location identifier FAA*] (FAAL)
HLI	Holmium LASER Illuminator
HLI	Host Language Interface
HLI	Human Leukocyte Interferon [*Medicine*] (DMAA)
HLI	Human Life International (EA)
HLIA	Historic Landmarks of Irish America [*A publication*]
HLIC	Highland Light Infantry of Canada [*Military unit*]
H/LIN	Head Lining [*Automotive engineering*]
HLISRDI	Hubei Light Industrial Scientific Research Design Institute [*China*] (BUAC)
HLIT	Harmonic Lightwaves [*NASDAQ symbol*] (TTSB)
HLIT	Harmonic Lightwaves, Inc. [*NASDAQ symbol*] (SAG)
HLIV	High-Level Input Voltage
HLIV	Hot Leg Isolation Valve [*Nuclear energy*] (NRCH)
HLJ	Hindu Law Journal [*A publication*] (DLA)
HL Jour	House of Lords Journals [*England*] [*A publication*] (DLA)
HLK	Haleakala [*Hawaii*] [*Seismograph station code, US Geological Survey*] (SEIS)
HLK	Heart, Liver, Kidney [*Medicine*] (MAE)
HLK	Heli-Link [*Switzerland ICAO designator*] (FAAC)
HLK	Kauai Public Library Association, Linhue, HI [*Library symbol Library of Congress*] (LCLS)
HLK	Salomon, Inc. [*AMEX symbol*] (SAG)
HLK	Salomon Inc. 5.25% HP'ELKS' [*AMEX symbol*] (TTSB)
HLKF	Kufra [*Libya*] [*ICAO location identifier*] (ICLI)
HLL	Hallett [*Antarctica*] [*Seismograph station code, US Geological Survey Closed*] (SEIS)
HLL	Halley Resources Ltd. [*Vancouver Stock Exchange symbol*]
HLL	Hard Lunar Landing [*Aerospace engineering*] (IAA)
HLL	Havelet Leasing Ltd. [*British ICAO designator*] (FAAC)
HLL	Hebrew Language and Literature (BJA)
HLL	High-Level Language [*Computer science*]
HLL	High-Level Logic (IAA)
HLL	High Liquid Level [*Engineering*]
HLL	Hill [*Board on Geographic Names*]
HLL	Hypoplastic Left Lung [*Medicine*] (DMAA)
HLLAPI	High-Level Application Program Interface [*Computer science*] (PCM)
HLLAPI	High Level Language Application Program Interface (NITA)
HLLB	Benghazi/Benina [*Libya*] [*ICAO location identifier*] (ICLI)
HLLL	Tripoli [*Libya*] [*ICAO location identifier*] (ICLI)
HLLMRK	Hallmark
HLLO	Metega [*Libya*] [*ICAO location identifier*] (ICLI)
HLLQ	El Beida/Labraq [*Libya*] [*ICAO location identifier*] (ICLI)
HLLS	Sebha [*Libya*] [*ICAO location identifier*] (ICLI)
HLLT	Tripoli/International [*Libya*] [*ICAO location identifier*] (ICLI)
HLLV	Heavy-Lift Launch Vehicle [*Rocketry*] (MCD)
HLLW	High-Level Liquid Waste [*Nuclear energy*]
HLLW	Hollow [*Commonly used*] (OPSA)
HLLWT	High-Level Liquid Waste Tank [*Nuclear energy*] (NRCH)
HllywP	Hollywood Productions, Inc. [*Associated Press*] (SAG)
HLM	Hampshire Local Militia [*British military*] (DMA)
HLM	Harpoon Logic Module [*Missiles*] (MCD)
HLM	Helmstar Group [*AMEX symbol*] (SPSG)
HLM	Helmville [*Montana*] [*Seismograph station code, US Geological Survey Closed*] (SEIS)
HLM	Henry Louis Mencken [*American author/critic*]
HLM	Heterogeneous LAN [*Local Area Network*] Manager (ACRL)
HLM	Hierarchical Linear Modeling
HLM	High-Latitude Mode
HLM	High-Level Meeting (DCTA)
HLM	High-Level Mixer
HLM	Holland, MI [*Location identifier FAA*] (FAAL)
HLMB	Marsa Brega [*Libya*] [*ICAO location identifier*] (ICLI)
HLMI	High-Load Melt Index [*Plastics*] [*Automotive engineering*]
HLML	High-Level Microprogramming Language
HLMR	Hunter-Leggitt Military Reservation (AABC)
HLMS	High Latitude Monitoring Station [*Marine science*] (OSRA)
HLMS	Holmes Protection Group [*NASDAQ symbol*] (TTSB)
HLMS	Holmes Protection Group, Inc. [*NASDAQ symbol*] (SAG)
HLMT	Helmet (NASA)
HLN	Halton Reinsurance Co. Ltd. [*Toronto Stock Exchange symbol*]
HLN	Helena [*Montana*] [*Airport symbol*] (OAG)
HLN	Hellenic Air SA [*Greece*] [*ICAO designator*] (FAAC)

HLN	Hualilan [*Argentina*] [*Seismograph station code, US Geological Survey*] (SEIS)
HLN	Human Lesch-Nyhan [*Cell*] (DB)
HLN	Hyperplastic Liver Nodules [*Medicine*]
HLNCC	High-Level Neutron Coincidence Counter [*Nuclear energy*] (NRCH)
HLND	Highlands [*Board on Geographic Names*]
HLND	Homeland Bankshares [*NASDAQ symbol*] (TTSB)
HLND	Homeland Bankshares Corp. [*NASDAQ symbol*] (SAG)
HLNE	Hillsboro & North Eastern Railway Co. [*AAR code*]
HLNF	Ras Lanouf V 40 [*Libya*] [*ICAO location identifier*] (ICLI)
HLNFPF	Human Life and Natural Family Planning Foundation [*Defunct*] (EA)
HLNG	Headlining
HLNL	Hydroxylysinonorleucine [*Biochemistry*]
HLNR	Health Lawyers News Report [*A publication*] (DLA)
HLNSS	Holiness
HLNW	High-Level Nuclear Waste (BARN)
HLO	High-Latitude Operation
HLO	High-Level Override [*Nuclear energy*] (NRCH)
HLO	Hi-Lo Automotive [*NYSE symbol*] (SPSG)
HLO	Horizontal Lockout
HLO	Samaritan Air Service Ltd. [*Canada ICAO designator*] (FAAC)
HLOA	Heart Labs of America, Inc. [*NASDAQ symbol*] (SAG)
HLOAE	Heart Labs Amer [*NASDAQ symbol*] (TTSB)
HLON	Hon [*Libya*] [*ICAO location identifier*] (ICLI)
HLOV	High-Level Output Voltage
HLOWE	Heart Labs Amer Wrrt [*NASDAQ symbol*] (TTSB)
H/LP	Headlamp [*Automotive engineering*]
HLP	Heavy-Lift Pontoon
HLP	Heavy-Lift Preposition [*Ship*] (DOMA)
HLP	Hel [*Poland*] [*Geomagnetic observatory code*]
HLP	Helper
HLP	Help File [*Computer science*]
HLP	Hepatic Lipoperoxidation (DB)
HLP	Hilina Pali [*Hawaii*] [*Seismograph station code, US Geological Survey*] (SEIS)
HLP	Hind-Leg Paralysis [*Veterinary Science*] (DB)
HLP	Holophane Corp. [*NYSE symbol*]
HLP	Home and Law Publishers [*British*]
HLP	Hyperlipoproteinemia [*Medicine*]
HLP	Hypersonic Local Pressure
HLP	Jakarta [*Indonesia*] [*Airport symbol*] (OAG)
HLPH	Holophane Corp. [*NASDAQ symbol*] (SAG)
HlpHm	Help At Home, Inc. [*Associated Press*] (SAG)
HlpHme	Help At Home, Inc. [*Associated Press*] (SAG)
HLPI	Higher Layer Protocol Identifier [*Telecommunications*] (ACRL)
HLPI	High-Level Programming Interface
HLPL	Howard League for Penal Reform [*An association British*] (EAIO)
Hlpmte	Helpmate Robotics, Inc. [*Associated Press*] (SAG)
HLPR	Helper
Hlpr	Helper (BARN)
HLPrB	Hecla Mining Sr'B'Cv Pfd [*NYSE symbol*] (TTSB)
HLPS	Heavy Lift Prepositioning Ship [*Navy*]
HLPS	Human Life Protection Society [*Australia*]
HLPSA	Hazardous Liquid Pipeline Safety Act (GFGA)
HLQ	High-Level Question (DMAA)
HLQ	Highly Luminous QUASAR [*Astronomy*]
HLQC	Hora Locoque Consuetis [*At the Usual Time and Place*] [*Latin*]
HLQL	High-Level Query Language
HLQN	Harlequin (WGA)
HLQS	Hora Locoque Solitis [*At the Usual Time and Place*] [*Latin*]
HLR	Hand-Held LASER Range-Finder
HLR	Harvard Law Review [*A publication*] (BRI)
HLR	Heart-Lung Resuscitation [*or Resuscitator*] [*Medicine*]
HLR	Heli Air Services [*Bulgaria*] [*ICAO designator*] (FAAC)
HLR	Helicopter LASER Range-Finder
HLR	Highland Ranch [*Colorado*] [*Seismograph station code, US Geological Survey Closed*] (SEIS)
HLR	High-Level Representation
HLR	High Level Resources Ltd. [*Vancouver Stock Exchange symbol*]
HLR	Holder (KSC)
HLR	Hollinger International, Inc. [*NYSE symbol*] (SAG)
HLR	Home Location Register (ACRL)
HLR	Houston Law Review [*A publication*]
HLR	Killeen, TX [*Location identifier FAA*] (FAAL)
HLRA	Dahra/Warehouse 32 [*Libya*] [*ICAO location identifier*] (ICLI)
HLRA	Handbag Liners and Repairers Association (BUAC)
HLRA	Health Labour Relations Association [*Canada*]
HLRC	High Latitude Rocket Campaign [*A cooperative study by 7 laboratories in the UK*] (PDAA)
HL Rep	English House of Lords Reports [*A publication*] (DLA)
HLRF	Jaref/Sirte [*ICAO location identifier*] (ICLI)
HLRM	High-Level Radio Modulator
HLRO	House of Lords Record Office [*British*] (DLA)
HLRS	Homosexual Law Reform Society [*British*] (BI)
HLRSC	Holland Lop Rabbit Specialty Club (EA)
HLRT	HealthRite, Inc. [*NASDAQ symbol*] (SAG)
HLRV	Heavy Lift Research Vehicle [*Military*]
HLRV	Hibiscus Latent Ringspot Virus [*Plant pathology*]
HLRW	High-Level Radioactive Waste (GNE)
HLS	Haiti Air Freight [*ICAO designator*] (FAAC)
HLS	Harmonic Light Scattering [*Physics*]
HLS	Harvard Law School [*Massachusetts*]
HLS	Harvard University, Cambridge, MA [*OCLC symbol*] (OCLC)
HLS	Health Learning Systems
HLS	Heavy-Lift System

HLS	Heavy Logistics System
HLS	Helicopter Landing Site [*Military*] (INF)
HLS	High Level Scheduler (NITA)
HLS	High-Level Service [*Computer science*]
HLS	Hills (MCD)
HLS	Hippel-Lindau Syndrome [*Medicine*] (DMAA)
HLS	Hoc Loco Situs [*Laid in This Place*] [*Latin*]
HLS	Holes (ADA)
HLS	Holograph Letter Signed
HLS	Horizontal Liquid Spring
HLS	Hue, Lightness, and Saturation [*Color model*] (BYTE)
HLS	Hurricane Statement [*Telecommunications*] (OTD)
HLS	St. Helens [*Tasmania*] [*Airport symbol*] (AD)
HLSC	Helicopter Logistic Support Center (NVT)
HL Sc App Cas	English Law Reports, House of Lords, Scotch and Divorce Appeal Cases [*1866-75*] [*A publication*] (DLA)
HLSD	Essider [*Libya*] [*ICAO location identifier*] (ICLI)
HLSD	Heel Sanding
HLSE	High-Level, Single-Ended
HLSI	Hybrid Large Scale Integrated (PDAA)
HLSP	Heitler-London-Slater-Pauling [*Method*] [*Physics*]
HLSTO	Hailstones [*NWS*] (FAAC)
HLSUA	Honeywell Large Systems Users Association (EA)
HLSV	Helium Latching Solenoid Valve
HLSW	High-Level Solidified Waste [*Nuclear energy*] (NRCH)
HLT	Halt [*Computer science*] (MDG)
HLT	Hamilton [*Australia Airport symbol*] (OAG)
HLT	Heart-Lung Transplantation [*Medicine*] (DMAA)
HLT	Heli Transport [*France ICAO designator*] (FAAC)
HLT	Heterodyne Look-Thru [*Telecommunications*] (TEL)
HLT	Hierarchial Lapped Transform [*Telecommunications*]
HLT	High-Level Tactical
HLT	High-Level Terminal (CAAL)
HLT	Highly Leveraged Transaction [*Banking*]
HLT	Hilton Hotels [*NYSE symbol*] (TTSB)
HLT	Hilton Hotels Corp. [*NYSE symbol*] (SPSG)
HLT	Human Lipotropin [*Medicine*] (DMAA)
hLT	Human Lymphocyte Transformation [*Immunology*] (MAE)
HLTA	Halt Acknowledge [*Computer science*]
HltCmp	HealthCare COMPARE Corp. [*Associated Press*] (SAG)
HltCrlm	HealthCare Imaging Services, Inc. [*Associated Press*] (SAG)
HltcrRty	Healthcare Realty Trust [*Associated Press*] (SAG)
HltcrTc	Healthcare Technologies Ltd. [*Associated Press*] (SAG)
HLTD	Ghadames [*Libya*] [*ICAO location identifier*] (ICLI)
HLTF	High-Level Task Force (DOMA)
hlth	Health (STED)
HLTH	Health
HlthCFP	HealthCare Financial Partners, Inc. [*Associated Press*] (SAG)
HlthCh	Health-Chem Corp. [*Associated Press*] (SAG)
HlthCor	HealthCor Holdings, Inc. [*Associated Press*] (SAG)
HlthCP	Health Care Property Investors, Inc. [*Associated Press*] (SAG)
HlthCr	Health Care REIT [*Associated Press*] (SAG)
HlthCSv	Health Care Services Group [*Associated Press*] (SAG)
Hlthdyn	Healthdyne, Inc. [*Associated Press*] (SAG)
HlthdynT	Healthdyne Technologies [*Associated Press*] (SAG)
HlthdyT	Healthdyne Technologies [*Associated Press*] (SAG)
HlthFit	Health Fitness Physical Therapy [*Associated Press*] (SAG)
HlthMSys	Health Management Systems, Inc. [*Associated Press*] (SAG)
Hlthpln	Healthplan Services Corp. [*Associated Press*] (SAG)
HlthplnSv	Healthplan Services Corp. [*Associated Press*] (SAG)
HlthPro	Health Professionals [*Associated Press*] (SAG)
HlthPwr	Health Power [*Associated Press*] (SAG)
HlthRite	HealthRite, Inc. [*Associated Press*] (SAG)
HlthRsk	Health Risk Management, Inc. [*Associated Press*] (SAG)
Hlthsrc	Healthsource, Inc. [*Associated Press*] (SAG)
Hlthsrce	Healthsource, Inc. [*Associated Press*] (SAG)
Hlthsth	Healthsouth Corp. [*Associated Press*] (SAG)
HlthSys	Health Systems Design Corp. [*Associated Press*] (SAG)
HlthSys	Health Systems International [*Associated Press*] (SAG)
HlthTc	HealthTech International, Inc. [*Associated Press*] (SAG)
HlthTch	HealthTech International, Inc. [*Associated Press*] (SAG)
HlthTech	HealthTech International, Inc. [*Associated Press*] (SAG)
Hlthwtch	Healthwatch, Inc. [*Associated Press*] (SAG)
Hltlmg	Health Images, Inc. [*Associated Press*] (SAG)
HLTL	High-Level Test Language
HLTL	High-Level Transistor Logic
HltMetr	Health O Meter Products [*Associated Press*] (SAG)
HltMgt	Health Management Associates, Inc. [*Associated Press*] (SAG)
HltMInc	Health Management, Inc. [*Associated Press*] (SAG)
HltMSys	Health Management Systems, Inc. [*Associated Press*] (SAG)
HLTP	Hilltop
HltPlanet	Healthy Planet Products, Inc. [*Associated Press*] (SAG)
Hltplx	Healthplex, Inc. [*Associated Press*] (SAG)
HltRet	Health & Retirement Property Trust [*Associated Press*] (SAG)
HLTRF	Hospitality Lodging and Travel Research Foundation [*Also known as Research Foundation*] (EA)
HLTTL	High-Level Transistor Translator Logic
HLTV	High-Loan-to-Value [*Business term*]
HltwAm	Healthwise of America, Inc. [*Associated Press*] (SAG)
HLU	Heli Union Heli Prestations [*France ICAO designator*] (FAAC)
HLU	Houailou [*New Caledonia*] [*Airport symbol*] (OAG)
HLU	House Logic Unit
HLV	Hallsville, MO [*Location identifier FAA*] (FAAL)
HLV	Heavy-Lift Vehicle
HLV	Heliserv SA de CV [*Mexico ICAO designator*] (FAAC)
HLV	Heracleum Latent Virus [*Plant pathology*]
HLV	Herpes-Like Virus
HLV	Hypoplastic Left Ventricle [*Cardiology*] (DAVI)
HLVG	Das Heilige Land in Vergangenheit und Gegenwart [*A publication*] (BJA)
HLW	Halbleinwand [*Half-Bound Cloth*] [*Bookbinding, publishing*] [*German*]
HLW	Handbuch der Literaturwissenschaft [*Potsdam*] [*A publication*] (BJA)
HLW	Hattiesburg, Camp Shelby, MS [*Location identifier FAA*] (FAAL)
HLW	Helwan [*Egypt*] [*Seismograph station code, US Geological Survey*] (SEIS)
HLW	Higher Low Water
HLW	High-Level Radioactive Waste (LDT)
HLW	High-Level Waste [*Nuclear energy*]
HLWC	High-Level Waste Calcination [*Nuclear energy*] (NRCH)
HLWC	High-Level Waste Concentrate [*Nuclear energy*] (NRCH)
HLWD	High-Level Waste Concentrator Distillate [*Nuclear energy*] (NRCH)
HlwdE	Hallwood Energy Corp. [*Associated Press*] (SAG)
HlwdP	Hollywood Park, Inc. [*Associated Press*] (SAG)
HlwdPk	Hollywood Park, Inc. [*Associated Press*] (SAG)
HLWF	High-Level Waste Concentrator Feed [*Nuclear energy*] (NRCH)
HLWI	Higher Low-Water Interval
HLWIP	High Level Waste Immobilisation Program [*Nuclear energy*] (NUCP)
HL Wkly Inf Bull	House of Lords Weekly Information Bulletin [*A publication*] (DLA)
HLWN	Highest Low-Water Neap Tide (WDAA)
HLW/OC	Hard Labor without Confinement
HLWOG	High-Level Liquid Waste Off-Gas [*Nuclear energy*] (NRCH)
HLWS	High-Level Waste Surge [*Nuclear energy*] (NRCH)
HLX	Galax/Hillsville, VA [*Location identifier FAA*] (FAAL)
HLX	Halter Marine Group, Inc. [*AMEX symbol*] (SAG)
HLX	Helix
HLX	Helix Circuits, Inc. [*Toronto Stock Exchange symbol*]
HLXA	Helix Angle
HLY	Haley Industries Ltd. [*Toronto Stock Exchange symbol*]
HLY	Halley Bay [*United Kingdom*] [*Geomagnetic observatory code*]
HLY	Valparaiso, FL [*Location identifier FAA*] (FAAL)
HlyPd	Holly Products [*Associated Press*] (SAG)
HLYW	Hollywood Entertainment [*NASDAQ symbol*] (TTSB)
HLYW	Hollywood Entertainment Corp. [*NASDAQ symbol*] (SAG)
HlywdCa	Hollywood Casino Corp. [*Associated Press*] (SAG)
HlywdE	Hollywood Entertainment Corp. [*Associated Press*] (SAG)
HLZ	Hamilton [*New Zealand*] [*Airport symbol*] (OAG)
HLZ	Helicopter Landing Zone
HLZA	Zella 74 [*Libya*] [*ICAO location identifier*] (ICLI)
HLZBL	Holzblaeser [*Woodwind Instrument*] [*Music*]
HLZL	Helicopter Landing Zone Locator
HM	Air-Cushion Vehicle Built by Hovermarine [*Usually used in combination with numerals*]
HM	Air Mahe [*ICAO designator*] (AD)
HM	Habitation Module (SSD)
HM	Half Morocco
HM	Hallmark
HM	Hamarein Air [*United Arab Emirates*] [*ICAO designator*] (ICDA)
HM	Handmade
HM	Hand Motion [*Vision*] [*Neurology*] (DAVI)
HM	Hand Movement
HM	Hands of Mercy [*An association*] (EA)
HM	Harbor Master
HM	Hardness Maintenance (MSA)
HM	Hardware Multiple
HM	Harmonic Mean [*Music*]
HM	Harper's Magazine [*A publication*] (BRI)
HM	Hazardous Material (DNAB)
HM	Headmaster [*or Headmistress*]
HM	Head Motion [*Gravity*]
HM	Health Maintenance (DB)
HM	Health Ministries (EA)
HM	Health Monitoring [*Environmental science*] (COE)
HM	Healthy Male (ROG)
hm	Heard and McDonald Islands [*MARC country of publication code Library of Congress*] (LCCP)
HM	Heard and McDonald Islands [*ANSI two-letter standard code*] (CNC)
HM	Heart Murmur [*Cardiology*] (MAE)
HM	Heater Middle (IAA)
HM	Heavily Muscled (STED)
HM	Heavy Maintenance [*Ordnance*]
HM	Heavy Metal [*Inorganic chemistry*]
HM	Heavy Metal [*Rock music type*]
HM	Heavy Mobile
HM	Hectometer [*100 meters*]
HM	Heine-Medin [*Disease*] [*Medicine*] (DB)
HM	Heloma Molle [*Soft corn*] (STED)
hm	Hematite [*CIPW classification*] [*Geology*]
HM	Hemifacial Microsomia (STED)
H/m	Henry per Meter
HM	Hepatic Metabolism (STED)
HM	Hepatic Microcirculation [*Physiology*]
HM	Heritage Manor (BJA)
HM	Hermeter Master [*Freemasonry*] (ROG)
hM	Herrschende Meinung [*Prevailing Opinion*] [*German*] (ILCA)
HM	Hexamethylmelamine (STED)
HM	High-Meaningfulness [*Psychology*]
HM	High Melting (OA)
HM	High Molecular [*Weight*] [*Also, HMW*] [*Organic chemistry*]
HM	Hinge Mount (MCD)

HM............... His [*or Her*] Majesty
HM............... Hoc Mense [*In This Month*] [*Latin*]
HM............... Hollow Metal [*Technical drawings*]
HM............... Holter Monitor   (STED)
HM............... Holter Monitoring [*Medicine*]   (DMAA)
HM............... Home   (ROG)
HM............... Home Mission
HM............... Homestake Mining [*NYSE symbol*]   (TTSB)
HM............... Homestake Mining Co. [*NYSE symbol*]   (SPSG)
HM............... Homogenization Medium
HM............... Honorary Member [*Freemasonry*]   (ROG)
HM............... Horizontal Marriage
HM............... Horizontal Meridian [*Optics, eye anatomy*]
HM............... Horniman Museum [*London*]
HM............... Hoshen Mishpat, Shulhan 'Arukh   (BJA)
HM............... Hospital Corpsman [*Navy rating*]
HM............... Hospital Management   (STED)
HM............... Houghton Mifflin Co. [*Publisher*]
HM............... Hours, Minutes   (ROG)
HM............... House Magazine [*Australia A publication*]
HM............... Housing Management [*HUD*]
HM............... Huius Mensis [*This Month's*] [*Latin*]
HM............... Human Milk [*Biochemistry*]   (MAE)
HM............... Huntingdon Militia [*British military*]   (DMA)
HM............... Hydatidiform Mole [*Gynecology*]
HM............... Hydra Medium [*Culture medium*]
HM............... Hydrogen MASER
HM............... Hydrometeorological
hm............... Hydroxymethyl [*As substituent on nucleoside*] [*Biochemistry*]
HM............... Hyperimmune Mice
HM............... Hyperimmune Mouse   (STED)
Hm............... Hyperopia Manifest [*Ophthalmology*]   (DAVI)
HM............... Hypothetical Machine   (MHDB)
HM............... Hypoxic-Metabolic   (STED)
HM............... Hysteresis Motor [*Electronics*]   (IAA)
Hm............... Manifest Hypermetropia [*Medicine*]
HM............... Marine Helicopter Squadron
HM............... Master of Humanities
HM............... Sandoz [*Italy*] [*Research code symbol*]
HM............... Sisters of the Humility of Mary [*Roman Catholic religious order*]
HM1............. Hospital Corpsman, First Class [*Navy rating*]
HM2............. Hospital Corpsman, Second Class [*Navy rating*]
HM² .... Square Hectometer
HM³ .... Cubic Hectometer   (WDAA)
HM3............. Hospital Corpsman, Third Class [*Navy rating*]
HMA............. Hapten-Modified Agent   (DB)
HMA............. Hardware Manufacturers' Association [*British*]   (BI)
HMA............. Hardwood Manufacturers Association   (EA)
Hma............. Harmona [*Record label*] [*Austria*]
HMA............. Hawaii Medical Association   (BUAC)
HMA............. Headmasters Association   (NTPA)
HMA............. Health Management Associates, Inc. [*NYSE symbol*]   (SPSG)
HMA............. Health Mgt Associates'A' [*NYSE symbol*]   (TTSB)
HMA............. Hellenic Marketing Association   (BUAC)
HMA............. Heteroduplex Mobility Analysis [*Genetics*]
HMA............. High Memory Area [*Computer science*]   (PCM)
HMA............. His [*or Her*] Majesty's Airship
HMA............. Hoist Manufacturers Association [*Later, HMI*]   (EA)
HMA............. Home Manufacturers Association [*Later, HMC*]   (EA)
HMA............. Home Medical Advisor [*Schueler Corp.*]
HMA............. Home Mission Association [*Episcopalian*]
HMA............. Hondo, TX [*Location identifier FAA*]   (FAAL)
HMA............. Hop Merchants Association [*British*]   (BI)
HMA............. Hot Melt Adhesive
HMA............. Hot Melt Applicator
HMA............. Hydroxymethyladenine [*Biochemistry*]
HMA............. Hypergol Maintenance Area   (MCD)
HMA............. Hyundai Motor America, Inc.
HMA............. Marine Attack Helicopter Squadron   (VNW)
HMA............. Marine Helicopter Squadron Attack   (NVT)
HMAA .... Haitian Medical Association Abroad [*Later, AMHE*]   (EA)
HMAC .... Hazardous Materials Advisory Council   (EA)
HMAC .... Health Manpower Advisory Council
HMAC .... High-Performance Memory Array Controller   (CIST)
HMAC .... His [*or Her*] Majesty's Aircraft Carrier
HMAC .... Horticultural Market Access Committee [*Australia*]
HMACI .... His [*or Her*] Majesty's Alkali and Clean Air Inspectorate [*British*]   (DCTA)
HMAF.......... His [*or Her*] Majesty's Armed Forces
H MAJ:T ...... Hans Majestaet [*His Majesty*] [*Swedish*]
HMANA........ Hawk Migration Association of North America   (EA)
HM & LP ...... Hand Motion and Light Perception [*Medicine*]   (DAVI)
HM & M .... Home Maintenance and Modification Program [*Australia*]
HM & SG .... Hirshhorn Museum and Sculpture Garden [*Smithsonian Institution*]
HMAR.......... Hvide Marine Inc. [*NASDAQ symbol*]   (SAG)
HMAS .... Her/His Majesty's Australian Ship   (WDAA)
HMAS .... Her Majesty's Australian Ship   (DOMA)
HMAS .... Hyperimmune Mouse Ascite [*Medicine*]   (DMAA)
HmaScn....... HumaScan, Inc. [*Associated Press*]   (SAG)
HMAV.......... His [*or Her*] Majesty's Army Vessel [*British military*]   (DMA)
HMB............. Garden City, KS [*Location identifier FAA*]   (FAAL)
HMB............. Haemophilus Maintenance Broth [*Microbiology*]
HMB............. Hamburg [*New York*] [*Seismograph station code, US Geological Survey Closed*]   (SEIS)
HMB............. Hazara Mountain Battery [*British military*]   (DMA)

HMB............. Hexamethylbenzene [*Organic chemistry*]
HMB............. Holderbank Management und Beratung AG [*Switzerland*]
HMB............. Homatropine Methylbromide [*Anticholinergic*]
HMB............. Hops Marketing Board [*British*]
HMB............. Horton-Magath-Brown [*Syndrome*] [*Medicine*]   (DB)
HMB............. Hughes Mining Barge [*Support vessel for Glomar Explorer*]
HMB............. Hukbong Mapagpalaya ng Batan [*People's Liberation Army*] [*Philippines*]
HMB............. Hydroxy(methoxy)benzaldehyde [*Organic chemistry*]
HMB............. Hydroxymethoxybenzophenone [*Organic chemistry*]
HMBA......... Hebrew Master Bakers Association [*Defunct*]   (EA)
HMBA......... Hexamethylene Bis(Acetamide) [*Organic chemistry*]
HMBA......... Hotel and Motel Brokers of America   (EA)
HMBA......... Hydroxymethyl(methyl)benzanthracene [*Organic chemistry*]
HmBBc........ Home Building Bancorp [*Associated Press*]   (SAG)
HMBC .... Heteronuclear Multiple-Bond Correlation [*Physics*]
HMBCEE ..... Horace Mann Bond Center for Equal Education [*Defunct*]   (EA)
HMBDV...... His [*or Her*] Majesty's Boom Defence Vessel
HmBElg........ Home Bancorp of Elgin, Inc. [*Associated Press*]   (SAG)
HmbHm ...... Hamburger Hamlet Restaurants, Inc. [*Associated Press*]   (SAG)
H-MBP-H .... Human-Mannose Binding Protein-H
HMBS......... His [*or Her*] Majesty's British Ship
HMBT......... Hydrazino(methyl)Benzothiazole [*Organic chemistry*]
HMC............. Halley Multicolor Camera [*Instrumentation*]
HMC............. Hammerson Canada, Inc. [*Toronto Stock Exchange symbol*]
HMC............. Hand-Mirror Cell [*Oncology*]
HMC............. Hastings Manufacturing Co.   (EFIS)
HMC............. Heading Marker Correction   (SAA)
HMC............. Head Masters' Conference [*British*]
HMC............. Healing Ministry Centre [*Australia*]
HMC............. Health Ministers Council   (EERA)
HMC............. Her Majesty's Customs and Excise [*British*]   (BI)
HMC............. Hermits of Mount Carmel   (TOCD)
HMC............. Heroin, Morphine, and Cocaine [*Mixture*] [*Slang*]
HMC............. High Moisture Shelled Corn   (OA)
HMC............. High-Strength Sheet Molding Compound
HMC............. His [*or Her*] Majesty's Council   (ROG)
HMC............. His [*or Her*] Majesty's Customs
HmC............. Historian's Microfilm Co., Cazenovia, NY [*Library symbol Library of Congress*]   (LCLS)
HMC............. Historical Manuscripts Commission [*British*]
HMC............. Holland Mills [*Quebec*] [*Seismograph station code, US Geological Survey Closed*]   (SEIS)
HMC............. Home Manufacturers Councils of NAHB [*National Association of Home Builders of the US*]   (EA)
HMC............. Honda Motor ADR [*NYSE symbol*]   (TTSB)
HMC............. Honda Motor Co. Ltd. [*NYSE symbol*]   (SPSG)
HMC............. Horizontal Motion Carriage [*Engineering*]   (OA)
HMC............. Horticultural Marketing Council [*British*]   (BI)
HMC............. Hospital Corpsman, Chief [*Navy rating*]
HMC............. Houghton Mifflin Co., Boston, MA [*OCLC symbol*]   (OCLC)
HMC............. Household Mortgage Corp.   (ODBW)
HMC............. Howard Mold Count [*Food quality measure*]
HMC............. Howitzer Motor Carriage
HMC............. Hundred Million Club   (EA)
HMC............. Hybrid Microcircuit   (NASA)
HMC............. (Hydroxymethyl)carboline [*Biochemistry*]
HMC............. Hydroxymethylcystosine [*Organic chemistry*]
HMC............. Hydroxymethyl Cytosine [*Biochemistry*]   (DAVI)
HMC............. Hydroxypropyl(methyl)cellulose [*Synthetic food gum*] [*Organic chemistry*]
HMC............. Hyoscine, Morphine, and Cactine [*Tablets*] [*Medicine*]
HMC............. Hypergolic Maintenance and Checkout   (NASA)
HMCA......... Hospital and Medial Care Association [*British*]   (DBA)
HMC & E .... His [*or Her*] Majesty's Customs and Excise [*British*]   (DCTA)
HMCC .... Hazardous Materials Control Committee [*General Motors Corp.*]
HMCC .... Housewife/Mother Career Concept   (EDAC)
HMCC .... Houston Mission Control Center [*NASA*]   (KSC)
HMCC .... Hypergolic Maintenance and Checkout Cell   (NASA)
HMCCMP ..... Human Mammary Carcinoma Cell Membrane Proteinase [*Medicine*]   (DMAA)
HMC Council... Healthcare Marketing & Communications Council   (NTPA)
HMCF......... Hypergolic Maintenance and Checkout Facility [*NASA*]   (NASA)
HMCI .... Her Majesty's Chief Inspector of Schools [*British*]   (BUAC)
HMCI .... Homecorp, Inc. [*NASDAQ symbol*]   (SAG)
HMCII .... Higher Military Command, Interior and Islands   (MCD)
HMCIP .... His/Her Majesty's Chief Inspector of Prisons [*British*]   (WDAA)
HMCL......... Hand-Mirror Cell Leukemia [*Oncology*]
HMCM .... Hospital Corpsman, Master Chief [*Navy rating*]
HMCN .... His [*or Her*] Majesty's Canadian Navy
HMCRI .... Hazardous Materials Control Research Institute   (EA)
HMCS .... His [*or Her*] Majesty's Canadian Ship
HMCS .... His [*or Her*] Majesty's Civil Service
HMCS .... His [*or Her*] Majesty's Colonial Steamer [*In use in 19th century*]
HMCS .... Hoffman Modulation Contrast System
HMCS .... Hospital Corpsman, Senior Chief [*Navy rating*]
HMCV......... Human Cytomegalovirus
HMD .... Charlie Hammonds Flying Service, Inc. [*FAA designator*]   (FAAC)
HMD .... Hamada [*Japan*] [*Seismograph station code, US Geological Survey*]   (SEIS)
HMD .... Head-Mounted Display [*Virtual reality technology*]   (PS)
HMD .... Heard Island and McDonald Islands [*ANSI three-letter standard code*]   (CNC)
HMD .... Helmet-Mounted Display
HMD .... Heterodyne Matrix Detector

HMD .... His [or Her] Majesty's Destroyer [British military] (DMA)
HMD .... His [or Her] Majesty's Dockyard [Navy British]
HMD .... His [or Her] Majesty's Drifter
HMD .... Hollow-Metal Door (DAC)
HMD .... Homeopathic Medical Doctor [Medicine]
HMD .... Hot Metal Detector [Electronics] (IAA)
HMD .... Humid (MSA)
HMD .... Hyaline Membrane Disease [Later, RDS] [Medicine]
HMD .... Hydraulic Mean Depth
HMD .... HydrazinomethylDOPA [Biochemistry]
HMD .... Hydrostatic Motor-Driven
HMDA .... Hexamethylenediamine [Organic chemistry]
HMDA .... Home Mortgage Disclosure Act
HMDAA .... Hydroxymethyl Diacetone Acrylamide [Organic chemistry]
HMDBA .... Hollow Metal Door and Buck Association (EA)
HMDD .... Helmet-Mounted Display Device [Military]
HMDE .... Hanging Mercury Drop Electrode [Electrochemistry]
HMDF .... Hollow Metal Door and Frame [Technical drawings]
HMDF .... Horizontal Side of Main Distribution Frame (TEL)
hMDH .... Halophilic Malate Dehydrogenase [An enzyme]
HMDI .... Hexamethylene Diisocyanate [Organic chemistry]
HMDP .... Homology Database (HGEN)
HMDP .... Hydroxymethylenediphosphonate [Organic chemistry]
HMDS .... Her Majesty's Diplomatic Service [British] (BUAC)
HMDS .... Hexamethyldisilazane [Organic chemistry]
HMDS .... Hexamethyldisiloxane [Organic chemistry]
HMDS .... Hospital Morbidity Data System
HMDSO .... Hexamethyldisiloxane [Organic chemistry]
HMDZ .... Hexamethyldisilazane [Organic chemistry]
HME .... Hassi Messaoud [Algeria] [Airport symbol] (OAG)
HME .... Health Media Education (EA)
HME .... Heat and Moisture Exchanger (MAE)
HME .... Heat, Massage, Exercise [Medicine]
HME .... High Vinyl-Modified Epoxy (MCD)
HME .... Home Medical Equipment
HME .... Home Properties of New York [NYSE symbol] (SAG)
HME .... Hull, Mechanical, Electrical [Ship equipment] [Navy]
HMEA .... Hatters Machinery and Equipment Association [Defunct] (EA)
HmeBc .... Home Bancorp [Associated Press] (SAG)
HMEC .... Human Mammary Epithelial Cell [Cytology]
Hmecrp .... Homecorp, Inc. [Associated Press] (SAG)
HMED .... Heavy Military Electronics Department (SAA)
HmeDep ...... [The] Home Depot, Inc. [Associated Press] (SAG)
HMEED .... Heavy Military Electronic Equipment Division [General Electric Co.] (AAG)
HmeHlth ...... Home Health Corporation of America, Inc. [Associated Press] (SAG)
HMEIA .... Health Manpower Education Initiative Award
HmeOil .... Home Oil Co. Ltd. [Associated Press] (SAG)
Hmeplx .... Homeplex Mortgage Investments [Associated Press] (SAG)
HmePrp .... Home Properties of New York [Associated Press] (SAG)
HMES .... Heavy Military Electronic System [General Electric Co.] (IAA)
HmeStat ...... Home State Holdings, Inc. [Associated Press] (SAG)
HMF 5-Hydroxymethylfurfural
HMF .... Handbook of Military Forces (MCD)
HMF .... Harbor Maintenance Fee [Import/Export fee]
HMF .... Hastings Manufacturing Co. [AMEX symbol] (SPSG)
HMF .... Hastings Mfg [AMEX symbol] (TTSB)
HMF .... Health Maintenance Facility (MCD)
HMF .... Heliospheric Magnetic Field [Solar physics]
HMF .... High Mach Flow
HMF .... High Magnetic Field
HMF .... His [or Her] Majesty's Forces
HMF .... Horizontal Mating Facility [NASA] (KSC)
HMF .... Hum Modulation Factor (DEN)
HMF .... Hydroxymethylfuraldehyde [Organic chemistry]
HMF .... Hydroxymethylfurfural [Organic chemistry] (DAVI)
HMF .... Hypergol Maintenance Facility [NASA] (NASA)
HMFblack ... High Modulus Furnace Black (EDCT)
HmFedIN ..... Home Federal Bancorp [Associated Press] (SAG)
HMFF .... Hoc Monumentum Fieri Fecit [Caused This Monument to Be Made] [Latin]
HMFG .... Heavy Metal Fluoride Glass
HMFI .... His [or Her] Majesty's Factory Inspectorate [Department of Employment] [British]
HMFIC .... Head Military Figure in Charge
HMFIHQ ...... His [or Her] Majesty's Factory Inspectorate Headquarters [Department of Employment] [British]
HmFnFL ...... Home Financial Corp. Florida [Associated Press] (SAG)
HMfW .... Help Model for Windows
HMG .... Hardware Message Generator [Telecommunications] (TEL)
HMG .... Harvard University, Gutman Library, Cambridge, MA [OCLC symbol] (OCLC)
HMG .... Heavy Machine Gun
HMG .... High Mobility Group [of nonhistone proteins] [Biochemistry]
HMG .... High Modulus Graphite [Epoxy composite] (MCD)
HMG .... His [or Her] Majesty's Government
HMG .... HMG/Courtland Prop [AMEX symbol] (TTSB)
HMG .... HMG Property Investors, Inc. [Formerly, Hospital Mortgage Group] [AMEX symbol] (SPSG)
HMG .... Human Menopausal Gonadotrophin [Endocrinology]
hMG .... Human Menopausal Gonadotropin [Medicine] (DMAA)
HMG .... Hydroxymethylglutaryl [Biochemistry]
HMGB .... His [or Her] Majesty's Gunboat
HMGC .... HMG Worldwide [NASDAQ symbol] (TTSB)
HMGC .... HMG Worldwide Corp. [NASDAQ symbol] (SAG)

HMGCC....... Her Majesty's Government Communications Centre [British] (PDAA)
HMGCO....... Hydroxymethylglutarylcoenzyme [Organic chemistry]
HMG CoA.... Hepatic Hydroxymethylglutaryl Coenzyme A [Organic chemistry] (DAVI)
HMG-CoA.... Hydroxy-Methylglutaryl-Coenzyme A Reductase [Medicine] (MEDA)
HMGF .... High Modulus Glass Fiber
HMGI .... Hotel-Motel Greeters International (EA)
HMGN .... Hemagen Diagnostics [NASDAQ symbol] (SAG)
HMGT .... Homegate Hospitality, Inc. [NASDAQ symbol] (SAG)
HMG Wd .... HMG Worldwide Corp. [Associated Press] (SAG)
HMH .... Heintz, M. H., Chicago IL [STAC]
HMH .... His [or Her] Majesty's Household
HMH .... Hispanic Marketing Handbook [A publication]
HMH .... Home Hill [Australia Airport symbol]
HMH .... Horizon Mental Health Management [AMEX symbol] (SAG)
HMH .... Marine Helicopter Squadron Heavy
HMHB .... Healthy Mothers, Healthy Babies (EA)
HMHB .... Healthy Mothers, Healthy Babies National Coalition (PAZ)
HMHCY .... Hexamethyl Hexacyclen [Organic chemistry]
HMHD .... High Molecular Weight, High Density
HMHEC .... Hydrophobically-Modified Hydroxyethylcellulose [Organic chemistry]
HMHF .... Hydrophobic Microporous Hollow Fiber [Membranes for chemical reactions]
HMHM .... Horizon Mental Health Management [NASDAQ symbol] (SAG)
HMHM .... Horizon Mental Health Mgmt [NASDAQ symbol] (TTSB)
HMHP .... Hospital Management, Hospital Problems [British]
HMHS .... His [or Her] Majesty's Hospital Ship
HMI .... Hahn-Meitner Institute [Germany]
HMI .... Handbook of Maintenance Instructions
HMI .... Hardware Monitor Interface
HMI .... Hazardous Material Incident [Nuclear energy]
HMI .... Healed Myocardial Infarction [Cardiology] (AAMN)
HMI .... Her Majesty's Inspectorate of Schools [British] (BUAC)
HMI .... Hexamethyleneimine [Trademark] [Celanese Corp.]
HMI .... His [or Her] Majesty's Inspector
HMI .... Hoist Manufacturers Institute (EA)
HMI .... Horizontal Motion Index [Printer technology]
HMI .... Horticultural Marketing Inspectorate [Ministry of Agriculture, Fisheries, and Food] [British]
HMI .... Host Micro Interface [CompuServe, Inc.] [Computer science] (PCM)
HMI .... House Magazine Institute [Later, NY/IABC]
HMI .... Hub Management Interface [Novell, Inc.] (PCM)
HMI .... Human Machine Interface
HMI .... Hydragyrum Mercury Medium Arc Length and Iodide [An arc lamp] (WDMC)
HMI .... Hypomelanosis of Ito [Medicine] (DMAA)
HMIC .... Heinkel-Messerschmitt-Isetta Club [Defunct] (EA)
HMIF .... His [or Her] Majesty's Inspector of Factories (ROG)
HMII .... Health Mor, Inc. [NASDAQ symbol] (SAG)
HMII .... HMI Industries [NASDAQ symbol] (SAG)
HMI Ind ...... HMI Industries [Associated Press] (SAG)
HMIMF .... His [or Her] Majesty's Indian Military Forces
HMIN .... His [or Her] Majesty's Indian Navy
HMIO .... Haitian Migrant Interdiction Operation [Haitian-US agreement, allowing US Coast Guard to board Haitian vessels on high seas]
HMIP .... His [or Her] Majesty's Inspectorate of Pollution [British]
hMIP .... Human Macrophage Inflammatory Protein [Immunochemistry]
HMIPI .... His [or Her] Majesty's Industrial Pollution Inspectorate for Scotland (DCTA)
HMIS .... Hazardous Materials Identification System [National Paint and Coating Association]
HMIS .... Hazardous Materials Information System (MCD)
HMIS .... Hazardous Materials Inventory Statement (AAEL)
HMIS .... Health Management [NASDAQ symbol] (TTSB)
HMIS .... Health Management, Inc. [NASDAQ symbol] (SAG)
HMIS .... His [or Her] Majesty's Indian Ship [British military] (DMA)
HMIS .... His [or Her] Majesty's Inspector of Schools (ROG)
HMIS .... Hospital Management Information System
HMIS .... Hospital Medical Information System [Medicine] (DMAA)
Hmisph .... Hemispherx BioPharma, Inc. [Associated Press] (SAG)
HMIT .... Her [or His] Majesty's Inspector of Taxes [British] (ODBW)
HMJ .... Homer, IL [Location identifier FAA] (FAAL)
HMK .... Heart Muscle Kinase [An enzyme]
HMK .... Highmark Resources [Vancouver Stock Exchange symbol]
HML .... Hamilton [Ontario] [Seismograph station code, US Geological Survey Closed] (SEIS)
HML .... Hammond Metallurgical Laboratory [Yale] (MCD)
HML .... Harbor Motor Launch
HML .... Hard Mobile Launcher [Boeing Aerospace-Loral Defense Systems]
HML .... Hardware Modelling Library [Mentor Graphics] (NITA)
HML .... Hawaii Medical Library, Inc., Honolulu, HI [OCLC symbol] (OCLC)
HML .... Heeresmunitionslager [Army Ammunition Depot] [German military - World War II]
HML .... His [or Her] Majesty's Lieutenant
HML .... Horace Mann League of the USA (EA)
HML .... Houston Metals Corp. [Vancouver Stock Exchange symbol]
HML .... Human Milk Lysozyme [An enzyme]
HML .... Huntsman Marine Laboratory [Canada] (MSC)
HMLC .... Marine Helicopter Squadron Light
HMLC .... High-Mobility Load Carrier [British military] (DMA)
HMLD .... Handmade Loft-Dried Paper (DGA)
HMLI .... Horace Mann-Lincoln Institute of School Experimentation [Columbia University] (AEBS)
HmlnBk....... Homeland Bankshares Corp. [Associated Press] (SAG)
HMLR .... His [or Her] Majesty's Land Registry

HMLT............	Hamlet
HMM............	Hamamatsu [*Japan*] [*Seismograph station code, US Geological Survey*] (SEIS)
HMM............	Hamilton, MT [*Location identifier FAA*] (FAAL)
HMM............	Hammond Manufacturing Co. Ltd. [*Toronto Stock Exchange symbol*]
HMM............	Hardware Multiply Module
HMM............	Heavy Meromyosin [*Biochemistry*]
HMM............	Hexamethoxy(methyl)melamine
HMM............	Hexamethylmelamine [*Altretamine*] [*Also, HEX, HXM*] [*Antineoplastic drug*]
HMM............	Hidden Markov Modeling [*Computer science*]
HMM............	Marine Helicopter Squadron Medium
HMMA.........	4-Hydroxy-3-Methoxymandelic Acid (STED)
HMMA.........	Hexamethoxymethyl Melamine
HMMA.........	Hydroxymethoxymandelic Acid [*Also, VMA*] [*Biochemistry*]
HMMFC.......	House Merchant Marine and Fisheries Committee
HMMHE......	High-Mobility Materiel Handling Equipment [*Army*]
HMML..........	Hill Monastic Manuscript Library [*Saint John's University, Collegeville, MN*]
HMML..........	His [*or Her*] Majesty's Motor Launch
HMMMS......	His [*or Her*] Majesty's Motor Mine Sweeper
HMMP........	Hazardous Materials Management Plan (AAEL)
HMMP........	HyperMedia Management Protocol [*Computer science*]
HMMR........	High-Resolution Multifrequency Microwave Radiometer (MCD)
HMMS........	HELLFIRE Modular Missile System
HMMS........	Hino Micro Mixing System [*Diesel engines*]
HMMS........	Hyper-Media Management Schema [*Computer science*]
HMMWV......	High-Mobility Multipurpose Wheeled Vehicle [*Nicknamed "hummer"*] [*Army*] (RDA)
HMMWV-L..	High-Mobility Multipurpose Wheeled Vehicle - Lightweight
HMN............	Alamogordo, NM [*Location identifier FAA*] (FAAL)
HMN............	Hemmings Motor News [*A publication*]
HMN............	Heptamethylnonane [*Fuel*]
HMN............	Horace Mann Educators [*NYSE symbol*] (TTSB)
HMN............	Horace Mann Educators Corp. [*NYSE symbol*] (SPSG)
HMN............	Human
Hmn............	Human (TBD)
HMNAO........	Her Majesty's Nautical Almanac Office [*British*] (PDAA)
HMNC.........	Harmonic (MSA)
HMNF.........	HMN Financial [*NASDAQ symbol*] (TTSB)
HMNF.........	HMN Financial, Inc. [*NASDAQ symbol*] (SAG)
HMNFE.......	Her Majesty's Norfolk Flax Establishment [*British*] (BUAC)
HMN Fn......	HMN Financial, Inc. [*Associated Press*] (SAG)
HMNIP........	Hydrophobically-Modified Nonionic Polymers [*Organic chemistry*]
Hmn Res	Human Resources (TBD)
HMNZS........	His [*or Her*] Majesty's New Zealand Ship
HMO............	Habitability Module Outfitting (SSD)
HMO............	Hardware Microcode Optimizer
HMO............	Health Maintenance Organization
HMO............	Heart Minute Output [*Cardiology*]
HMO............	Hermosillo [*Mexico*] [*Airport symbol*] (OAG)
HMO............	H. Mason [*Oregon*] [*Seismograph station code, US Geological Survey*] (SEIS)
HMO............	Honolulu Magnetic Observatory (CINC)
HMO............	Hueckel Molecular Orbital [*Atomic physics*]
HMOA..........	Health Maintenance Organization Acts of 1973 and 1988 (WYGK)
HMOC..........	Hybrid Method of Characteristics [*Environmental Protection Agency*] (AEPA)
HMOCS........	His [*or Her*] Majesty's Overseas Civil Service
HMOM.........	HyperMedia Object Manager [*Computer science*]
HMOS..........	Habitability Module Outfitting System (SSD)
HMOS..........	Health Maintenance Organization Service [*Public Health Service*]
HMOS..........	High-Density Metal-Oxide Semiconductor (AAEL)
HMOS..........	High-Performance Metal-Oxide Semiconductor (AAEL)
HMOS..........	High-Speed Metal-Oxide Semiconductor [*ROM*]
HMOS-E.......	HMOS [*High Speed Metal Oxide Semiconductor*] Erasable (NITA)
HMOW.........	His [*or Her*] Majesty's Office of Works (ROG)
HmowG........	Homeowners Group, Inc. [*Associated Press*] (SAG)
HMOX..........	Heme Oxygenase (DMAA)
HMP............	Habitat Management Plan
HMP............	Handmade Paper
HMP............	Harper's Magazine Press
HMP............	Heavy Machine-Gun Pod [*Military*] (MUSM)
HMP............	Helmet-Mounted Pick-Offs (MCD)
HMP............	Her [*or His*] Majesty's Prison [*British*] (BARN)
HMP............	Hexamethylphosphoramide [*or Hexamethylphosphoric Triamide*] [*Also, HEMPA, HMPA, HMPT, HPT*] [*Organic chemistry*]
HMP............	Hexasodium Metaphosphate [*Inorganic chemistry*]
HMP............	Hexose Monophosphate [*Biochemistry*]
HMP............	Hexose Monophosphate Pathway [*Biochemistry*] (DAVI)
HMP............	High Melting Point
HMP............	High-Methoxy Pectin [*Food technology*]
HMP............	His/Her Majesty's Prison [*British*] (WDAA)
HMP............	Hoc Monumentum Posuit [*He, or She, Erected This Monument*] [*Latin*]
HMP............	Honda-Mrkos-Pajdusakova [*Comet*]
HMP............	Hot Moist Packs [*Medicine*]
HMP............	Human Menopausal [*Medicine*] (STED)
HMP............	Humidity Monitoring Panel
HMP............	Hydraulic Maintenance Panel (AAG)
HMP............	Hydromotive Pressure (STED)
HMP............	Hydroxymethyl Hydroperoxide [*Organic chemistry*]
HMP............	Hydroxymethyl(methyl)propanediol [*Organic chemistry*]
HMP............	Hydrozene Monopropellant (MCD)
HMP............	Papair Terminal SA [*Haiti*] [*ICAO designator*] (FAAC)

HMPA	Hawaii Macadamia Producers Association (BUAC)
HMPA	Hexamethylphosphoramide [*or Hexamethylphosphoric Triamide*] [*Also, HEMPA, HMP, HMPT, HPT*] [*Organic chemistry*]
HMPA	Hydroxymethyl Phosphonic Acid [*Organic chemistry*]
HMPAA	Hydrophobically-Modified Polyacrylamide [*Organic chemistry*]
HMPAO	Hexamethylpropylenamine Oxime [*Organic chemistry*]
HMPD	Hoffman Military Products Division
HMPDH	2-Hydroxy-4-Methylpentanoic Acid Dehydrogenase (DB)
HMPG	Hydroxy(methoxy)phenylglycol [*Biochemistry*] (AAMN)
HMPGTS	His [*or Her*] Majesty's Procurator General and Treasury Solicitor
HMPI	His [*or Her*] Majesty's Pollution Inspectorate [*British*] (DCTA)
HMPIPI	Her Majesty's Industrial Pollution Inspectorate (EERA)
HMPMA	Historical Motion Picture Milestones Association
HMPP	Hexose Monophosphate Pathway [*Biochemistry*]
HmPrt	Home Port Bancorp, Inc. [*Associated Press*] (SAG)
HMPS	Hexose Monophosphate Shunt [*Biochemistry*]
HMPSA	Hot Melt Pressure Sensitive Adhesive
HMPT	Hexamethylphosphoric Triamide [*Also, HEMPA, HMP, HMPA, HPT*] [*Organic chemistry*]
HMPT..........	Human Factors, Manpower, Personnel, and Training [*Military*] (RDA)
HmpU	Hampton Utilities Trust [*Associated Press*] (SAG)
HMQ	Homer, LA [*Location identifier FAA*] (FAAL)
HMQC	Heteronuclear Multiple-Quantum Coherence [*Physics*]
HMR	Hamilton Ranch [*California*] [*Seismograph station code, US Geological Survey*] (SEIS)
HMR	Hammer (MSA)
HMR	Hazardous Materials Regulation [*Department of Transportation*]
HMR	Headquarters Modification Request [*Military*] (CAAL)
HMR	Health Management Resources [*Diet program*]
HMR	High Moisture Resistant
HMR	Histocytic Medullary Reticulosis [*Oncology*]
HMR	HMR World Enterprise [*Vancouver Stock Exchange symbol*]
HMR	Hoboken Manufacturers [*AAR code*]
HMR	Hoechst Marion Roussel
HMR	Home Meal Replacement
Hmr	Homer (DA)
HMR	Hotel, Motel, Resort Database [*American Database Corp.*] [*Santa Barbara, CA*] [*Information service or system*] (IID)
HMR	Human Milk Ribonuclease [*An enzyme*]
hMR	Human Mineralocorticoid Receptor [*Endocrinology*]
HMR	Hungry Mind Review [*A publication*] (BRI)
HMR	Hybrid Modular Redundancy
HMRA	Hadassah Medical Relief Association (EA)
HMRB	Hazardous Materials Regulation Board
HMRI	Hubei Mechanical Research Institute [*China*] (BUAC)
HMRI	Huntington Medical Research Institutes [*Huntington Memorial Hospital*] [*Research center*] (RCD)
HMRL	His [*or Her*] Majesty's Royal Licence (ROG)
HMRN	Hull Moulding Release Note
H-mRNA	Ribonucleic Acid, H-Chain Messenger [*Biochemistry, genetics*]
HMRP	Hurricane Microseismic Research Problem [*Aerology*]
HMRR	His [*or Her*] Majesty's Reserve Regiment [*British military*] (DMA)
HMRRP.......	Hazardous Materials Release Response Policy [*Stanford University*]
HMRS	Historical Model Railway Society [*British*] (BI)
HMRTE	Human Milk Reverse Transcriptase Enzyme [*Medicine*] (DMAA)
HMS...........	Hammer Makers' Society [*A union*] [*British*]
HMS...........	Hanford Meteorology Surveys [*Nuclear energy*] (NRCH)
HMS...........	Hardened Memory System
HMS...........	Harmonic Multiplier Source
HMS...........	Harvard University Medical School, Countway Library of Medicine, Boston, MA [*OCLC symbol*] (OCLC)
HMS...........	Hazardous Materials Safety [*RSPA*] (TAG)
HMS...........	Hazardous Materials Systems [*A publication*] (EAAP)
HMS...........	Hazards Monitoring System [*NASA*] (KSC)
HMS...........	Health Mobilization Series
HMS...........	Heavy Materiel Supply Units [*Military*]
HMS...........	Heavy-Media Separation [*Mining engineering*] (IAA)
HMS...........	Helmet-Mounted Sight [*Aviation*]
HMS...........	Hemin Storage
HMS...........	Hemus Air [*Bulgaria*] [*ICAO designator*] (FAAC)
HMS...........	Hexagonal Mesoporous Silica [*Inorganic chemistry*]
HMS...........	Hexose Monophospate Shunt (PDAA)
HMS...........	Hierarchical Memory Storage [*Computer science*]
HMS...........	High Melt Strength [*Plastic moldings*]
HMS...........	Highway Mobile Source [*Environmental Protection Agency*] (GFGA)
HMS...........	His [*or Her*] Majesty's Service
HMS...........	His [*or Her*] Majesty's Ship
HMS...........	His [*or Her*] Majesty's Steamer
HMS...........	Historical Metallurgy Society [*British*] (EAIO)
HMS...........	History Memory System (MCD)
HMS...........	Honeywell's Manufacturing System [*Honeywell Information Systems Ltd.*] [*Software package*] (NCC)
HMS...........	Hospital Marketing Services, Inc. [*Commercial firm*] (DAVI)
HMS...........	Host Marriott Services [*NYSE symbol*] (TTSB)
HMS...........	Host Marriott Services Corp. [*NYSE symbol*] (SAG)
HMS...........	Hours, Minutes, Seconds
HMS...........	Hull Monitoring System (PDAA)
HMS...........	Humility of Mary Service (EA)
HMSA	Hardware Manufacturers Statistical Association [*Later, BHMA*]
HMSA	Hawk Mountain Sanctuary Association (EA)
HMSA	Health Manpower Shortage Area
HMSA	Historic Motor Sports Association (EA)
HMSA	Hydroxymethanesulfonate [*Organic chemistry*]
HMSAS	His [*or Her*] Majesty's South African Ship (DAS)
HMSAS	Hypertrophic Muscular Subaortic Stenosis [*Cardiology*] (MAE)

HMS(BOE) ...	Hazardous Materials Systems (Bureau of Explosives) (EA)
HMSC	Hatfield Marine Science Center [*Marine science*] (OSRA)
HMSC	HumaScan, Inc. [*NASDAQ symbol*] (SAG)
HMSI	Hebei Machinery Science Institute [*China*] (BUAC)
HMSM	Heavy Mortar, Smart Munition
HMS/M	His [*or Her*] Majesty's Submarine
HMSO	His [*or Her*] Majesty's Stationery Office
HMSO	Honolulu Magnetic and Seismological Observatory
HMSR	HemaSure Inc. [*NASDAQ symbol*] (TTSB)
HMSRR	Harpoon Missile Select Relay Rack [*Missiles*] (MCD)
HMSS	Helmet-Mounted Sight Set
HMSS	Hospital Management Systems Society [*Later, HIMSS*] (EA)
HMSS	Religious Sisters of the Apostolate of the Blessed Sacrament (TOCD)
HMSS	Sisters of Mercy of the Blessed Sacrament (TOCD)
HMSTD	Homestead
Hmstke	Homestake Mining Co. [*Associated Press*] (SAG)
HMSY	Health Management Systems [*NASDAQ symbol*] (TTSB)
HMSY	Health Management Systems, Inc. [*NASDAQ symbol*] (SAG)
HMT	Air Nova [*British ICAO designator*] (FAAC)
HMT	Hand Microtelephone (IAA)
HMT	Hazardous Materials Table [*Environmental science*] (COE)
HmT	Helminthosporium maydis race T [*A toxin-producing fungus*]
HMT	Hemet, CA [*Location identifier FAA*] (FAAL)
HMT	Her Majesty's Treasury [*British*] (BUAC)
HMT	Hexamethoxytriphenylene [*Organic chemistry*]
HMT	Hexamethylenetetramine [*Also, HMTA*] [*Organic chemistry*]
HMT	High Mobility Trailer
HMT	His [*or Her*] Majesty's Transport
HMT	His [*or Her*] Majesty's Trawler
HMT	His [*or Her*] Majesty's Troopship [*British military*] (DMA)
HMT	His [*or Her*] Majesty's Tug [*British military*] (DMA)
HMT	Histamine Methyltransferase [*An enzyme*]
HMT	Host Marriot [*Formerly, Marriott Corp.*] [*NYSE symbol*] (SPSG)
HMT	Human Metallothioneine [*Biochemistry*]
hMT	Human Molar Thyrotropin (MAE)
HMT	Hydrazine Monopropellant Thruster
hMT	Hydroxymethyl Uracil [*Organic chemistry*] (DAVI)
HMTA	Hazardous Materials Transportation Act [*1975*]
HMTA	Hexamethylenetetramine [*Also, HMT*] [*Organic chemistry*]
HMTA	Hexamethylenetriamine [*Organic chemistry*]
HMTC	Hazardous Materials Technical Center [*Rockville, MD*] [*DoD*] (GRD)
HMTPSD	HAWK [*Homing All the Way Killer*] Missile Test Program System Device (DWSG)
HMTR	Hazardous Materials Transportation Regulations [*Environmental science*] (COE)
HMTS	Health Message Testing Services [*Department of Health and Human Services*] (GFGA)
HMTS	His [*or Her*] Majesty's Telegraph Ship
HMTSF	Hexamethylenetetraselenafulvalenium [*Organic chemistry*]
HMTT	Hexamethyltrithiane [*Organic chemistry*]
HMTT	High-Mobility Tactical Trucks (MCD)
HMTT	HMT Technology [*NASDAQ symbol*] (TTSB)
HMTT	HMT Technology Corp. [*NASDAQ symbol*] (SAG)
HMTTch	HMT Technology Corp. [*Associated Press*] (SAG)
HMTUSA	Hazardous Materials Transportation and Uniform Safety Act
HmtwBc	Hometown Bancorp, Inc. [*Associated Press*] (SAG)
HMU	Hammond, LA [*Location identifier FAA*] (FAAL)
HMU	Hardware Mockup (NASA)
HMU	Hydraulic Management Unit
HMU	Hydraulic Mock-Up
HMU	Hydromechanical Unit
HMU	Hydroxymethyluracil [*Organic chemistry*]
HMUX	Hybrid Multiplexer [*Telecommunications*]
HMV	Henbane Mosaic Virus [*Plant pathology*]
HMV	High Magnification Viewer
HMV	High Mass Vehicle
HMV	His Master's Voice [*Phonograph records*]
HMV	Holston Mountain, TN [*Location identifier FAA*] (FAAL)
HMV	Hydrodynamically Modulated Voltammetry [*Analytical chemistry*]
HMV	Hydrogen Manual Valve (MCD)
HMVEC	Human Dermal Microvascular Endothelial Cell [*Biochemistry*]
HMW	Health, Morale, and Welfare (COE)
HMW	High Molecular Weight [*Also, HM*] [*Organic chemistry*]
HMW	How to Market to Women [*A publication*]
HMWA	Hairdressing Manufacturers' and Wholesalers' Association [*British*] (BI)
HMWC	Health of Munition Workers Committee [*World War I*] [*British*]
HMWC	High-Mobility Weapons Carrier [*Army*]
HMWC/CSV...	High-Mobility Weapons Carrier/Combat Support Vehicle [*Army*] (MCD)
HMWG	Huma Multipurpose Women's Group [*Kenya*] (BUAC)
HMWGP	High Molecular Weight Glycoprotein [*Medicine*] (DMAA)
HMWK	Advanced Voice Technologies [*NASDAQ symbol*] (TTSB)
HMWK	Advanced Voice Technologies, Inc. [*NASDAQ symbol*] (SAG)
HMWK	High Molecular Weight Kininogen [*Biochemistry*]
HMWKa	High Molecular Weight Kallikrein [*Biochemistry*]
HMWKU	Advanced Voice Tehcnol's 'Unit' [*NASDAQ symbol*] (TTSB)
HMWKW	Advanced Voice Technol Wrrt [*NASDAQ symbol*] (TTSB)
HMWP	High-Molecular-Weight Protein [*or Polypeptide*] [*Biochemistry*]
HMWPE	High-Molecular-Weight Polyethylene [*MCD*]
HMWRK	Homework
HMX	Denver, CO [*Location identifier FAA*] (FAAL)
HMX	Hartmarx Corp. [*NYSE symbol*] (SPSG)
HMX	Heat, Massage, Exercise [*Medicine*]
HMX	High-Melting Explosive [*Proprietary name for cyclotetramethylene tetramintriamine*]
HMX	Marine Helicopter Experimental Squadron
HMX-1	Marine Helicopter Experimental Squadron One [*Organized in 1947 for the development and study of helicopter tactics*]
HMXB	High-Mass X-Ray Binary [*Star system*]
HMY	Heilig-Meyers [*NYSE symbol*] (TTSB)
HMY	Heilig-Meyers Co. [*NYSE symbol*] (SPSG)
HMY	High Modulus Yarn
HMY	His [*or Her*] Majesty's Yacht [*Navy British*]
HMY	Lexington, OK [*Location identifier FAA*] (FAAL)
HMZ	Nigerian International Air Services Ltd. [*ICAO designator*] (FAAC)
hn	Hac Nocte [*This Night*] [*Latin*] (WDAA)
HN	Haematemesis Neonatorum (DB)
HN	Hafslund Nycomed ADS [*NYSE symbol*] (SPSG)
HN	Hardware Capability Name (NITA)
Hn	Haven [*Maps and charts*]
HN	Head and Neck (DMAA)
HN	Headline News [*Cable television channel*]
HN	Head Nurse
HN	Headquarters Name [*Dialog*] [*Searchable field*] [*Information service or system*] (NITA)
HN	Hear Now [*An association*] (EA)
HN	Helium Neon [*LASER*] (DGA)
HN	Heller-Nelson [*Syndrome*] [*Medicine*] (DB)
HN	Hemagglutinin-Neuraminidase [*An enzyme*]
HN	Hematemesis Neonatorum [*Medicine*] (DMAA)
HN	Hemorrhage of Newborn [*Medicine*] (DMAA)
hn	Henna [*Philately*]
Hn	Henricus de Baila [*Flourished, 1169-70*] [*Authority cited in pre-1607 legal work*] (DSA)
HN	Hereditary Nephritis [*Medicine*] (MAE)
HN	Heroes of the Nations [*A publication*]
HN	Herpes Network [*Defunct*] (EA)
hn	Heterogeneous Nuclear [*Biochemistry*]
HN	Hexagonal Nut
HN	High Foliage Nester [*Ecology*]
HN	High Necrosis [*Medicine*] (DMAA)
HN	High Nitrogen [*Clinical chemistry*]
HN	High Nutrition
HN	Hilar Node [*Medicine*] (MAE)
HN	Hindustan-Aeronautics Ltd. [*India*] [*ICAO aircraft manufacturer identifier*] (ICAO)
HN	Histamine-Containing Neuron (DB)
HN	Hoc Nocte [*Tonight*] [*Pharmacy*]
HN	Home Nursing
HN	Honduras [*ANSI two-letter standard code*] (CNC)
HN	Horn
hn	Horn (WDAA)
HN	Hospitalman [*Nonrated enlisted man*] [*Navy*]
HN	Host Nation (AABC)
HN	Host to Network [*Computer science*]
HN	House Nigger [*Derogatory nickname for an obsequious black person*]
HN	Human Nutrition [*Dietetics*] (DAVI)
HN	Human Nutrition Research Division [*of ARS, Department of Agriculture*]
HN	[*The*] Hutchinson & Northern Railway Co. [*AAR code*]
HN	Hypertrophic Neuropathy [*Medicine*] (DMAA)
HN	Naturalis Historia [*of Pliny the Elder*] [*Classical studies*] (OCD)
HN	Nitrogen Mustard [*Also, M, MBA, NM*] [*Antineoplastic drug, war-gas base Army symbol used with numerals, as HN1*]
HN	NLM-Dutch Airlines [*ICAO designator*] (AD)
HN	Sunset to Sunrise [*ICAO*] (FAAC)
HN₂	Mechlorethamine [*Nitrogen mustard*] (MEDA)
HN₂	Nitrogen Mustard [*Antineoplastic drug*] (DAVI)
HNA	Chicago, IL [*Location identifier FAA*] (FAAL)
HNA	Hanamaki [*Japan*] [*Airport symbol Obsolete*] (OAG)
HNA	Harrison Narcotic Act
HNA	Heparin Neutralizing Activity [*Medicine*]
HNA	Hierarchical Network Architecture
HNA	High Nickel Alloy
HNA	Hitachi Network Architecture
HNA	Hockey North America (EA)
HNA	Hospice Nurses Association (EA)
HNA	Hungarian National Alliance (BUAC)
HNAA	Holistic Nurses Association of Australia
HNAB	Hexanitroazobenzene [*Organic chemistry*]
HNADC........	Honorary Naval Aide-de-Camp [*British*]
HNARMENTD...	Hereinafter Mentioned [*Legal*] [*British*] (ROG)
HNB	Hrvatska Narodna Banka [*Croatian National Bank*]
HNB	Human Neuroblastoma (DB)
HNB	Huntingburg, IN [*Location identifier FAA*] (FAAL)
HNB	Hydroxynitrobenzyl [*Organic chemistry*]
HNB	Hydroxynitrobenzylbromide [*Organic chemistry*] (MAE)
HNB	New Britain General Hospital, Health Sciences Library, New Britain, CT [*OCLC symbol*] (OCLC)
HNBA	Hispanic National Bar Association (EA)
HNBC	Harleysville National Corp. [*NASDAQ symbol*] (SAG)
HNBC	Harleysville Natl [*NASDAQ symbol*] (TTSB)
HNBEFMENTD...	Hereinbefore Mentioned [*Legal*] [*British*] (ROG)
HNBK	Handbook (WDAA)
HNC	Center for Disease Control, Atlanta, GA [*OCLC symbol*] (OCLC)
HNC	Hand Numerical Control (IAA)
HNC	Hartford National Corp. (EFIS)
HNC	Higher National Certificate [*British*]

HNC .... High National Council
HNC .... Human Nutrition Center [*Oklahoma State University*] [*Research center*] (RCD)
HNC .... Hypernephroma Cell (DB)
HNC .... Hypothalamo-Neurohypophyseal Complex [*Endocrinology*]
HNC/D .... Higher National Certificate/Diploma (ACII)
HNCMT .... Hawkesbury Nepean Catchment Management Trust [*Resource management*] [*Australia*]
HNCS .... HNC Software [*NASDAQ symbol*] (TTSB)
HNCS .... HNC Software, Inc. [*NASDAQ symbol*] (SAG)
HNC Sft .... HNC Software, Inc. [*Associated Press*] (SAG)
HND .... Hand (WGA)
HND .... Higher National Diploma [*British*]
HND .... Highways for National Defense [*MTMC*] (TAG)
HND .... Honduras [*ANSI three-letter standard code*] (CNC)
HND .... Huntsville Nuclear Division [*Army Corps of Engineers*] (RDA)
HND .... State Historical Society of North Dakota, Bismarck, ND [*OCLC symbol*] (OCLC)
HND .... Tokyo [*Japan*] Haneda Airport [*Airport symbol*] (OAG)
HNDBK .... Handbook
HNDCPD ...... Handicapped
HNDCRFT ..... Handicraft
HNDLER .... Handler (NASA)
HNDLR .... Handler
HNDP .... Handicap
HNDPRNT .... Handprint
HNDR .... Heteronuclear Double Resonance (IAA)
HNDRL .... Hand Rail
HNDST .... Handset
HNDT .... Holographic Nondestructive Testing
HNDWL .... Handwheel
HNDY .... Handy
HNDYMN ..... Handyman
HNE .... Harriman & Northeastern R. R. [*AAR code*]
HNE .... HN Engineering, Inc. [*Burnaby, BC*] [*Telecommunications*] (TSSD)
HNE .... Human Neutrophil Elastase [*An enzyme*]
HNE .... Hydronuclear Experiment
HNE .... Hydronuclear Experiments [*Nuclear physics*]
HNE .... Hydroxynonenal [*Biochemistry*]
HNE .... National Institute of Environmental Health Sciences, Research Triangle Park, NC [*OCLC symbol*] (OCLC)
HNE .... Tahneta Pass Lodge, AK [*Location identifier FAA*] (FAAL)
HNED .... Horizontal Null External Distance (OA)
HNEI .... Hawaii Natural Energy Institute [*University of Hawaii at Manoa*] [*Research center*] (RCD)
HNEPI .... Hunan Environmental Protection Institute [*China*] (BUAC)
HNET .... Houston Network Controller [*NASA*] (KSC)
HNF .... Hepatocyte Nuclear Factor [*Biochemistry*]
HNF1 .... Hungarian National Front [*Political party*] (BUAC)
HNF1 .... Hepatocyte Nuclear Factor 1 [*Genetics*]
HNFBR .... Horn Fiber
HNFC .... Hinsdale Financial [*NASDAQ symbol*] (TTSB)
HNFC .... Hinsdale Financial Corp. [*NASDAQ symbol*] (SAG)
HNG .... Hanging (MSA)
hng .... Hanging (VRA)
HNG .... Heavy Narrow Gap [*Nuclear energy*] (NUCP)
HNG .... Hienghene [*New Caledonia*] [*Airport symbol Obsolete*] (OAG)
HNG .... Hilfsfonds fuer die Opfer der Nuernberger Gesetze [*A publication*] (BJA)
HNG .... Hinge (MSA)
HNG .... Hongo [*Japan*] [*Seismograph station code, US Geological Survey Closed*] (SEIS)
HNGL .... Helium Neon Gas LASER
HNGNA .... Hellenic National Graduate Nurses Association [*Greece*] (BUAC)
HNGR .... Hangar (KSC)
HNGRY .... Hungry
HNGS .... Hamilton National Genealogical Society (EA)
hngscr .... Hanging Scroll (VRA)
HNH .... Handy & Harman [*NYSE symbol*] (SPSG)
HNH .... Hanover [*New Hampshire*] [*Seismograph station code, US Geological Survey*] (SEIS)
HNH .... Hoonah [*Alaska*] [*Airport symbol*] (OAG)
HNHIA .... Headway National Head Injuries Association (BUAC)
HNHIC .... Hepatic Nonheme Iron Content [*Physiology*]
HNI .... Health News Institute [*Defunct*]
HNI .... Holmes & Narver, Inc. (MCD)
HNI .... HON Industries [*NYSE symbol*]
HNI .... National Institutes of Health, Bethesda, MD [*OCLC symbol*] (OCLC)
HNIC .... Head Nigger in Charge [*Slang*]
HNIC .... Hockey Night in Canada [*Television program*]
HNickJS .... Hicksville Junior High School, Hicksville, NY [*Library symbol*] [*Library of Congress*] (LCLS)
HNIG .... Human Normal Immunoglobulin [*Medicine*] (PDAA)
HNIL .... High-Noise-Immunity Logic
HNIS .... Human Nutrition Information Service [*Hyattsville, MD*] [*Department of Agriculture*]
HNIW .... Hexanitrohexazaisowurtzitane [*An explosive*]
HN(JC) .... Hospitalman (Junior College) [*Navy*] (DNAB)
HNK .... Hancock, NY [*Location identifier FAA*] (FAAL)
HNK .... Hinchinbrook Island [*Australia Airport symbol*]
HNKDC .... Hyperosmolar Nonketotic Diabetic Coma [*Medicine*] (STED)
HNKDS .... Hyperosmolar Nonketotic Diabetic State [*Medicine*] (STED)
HNL .... Helium Neon LASER
HNL .... Holifield National Laboratory [*Later, Oak Ridge National Laboratory*]
HNL .... Honolulu [*Hawaii*] [*Airport symbol*] (OAG)

HNL .... Honolulu [*Hawaii*] [*Seismograph station code, US Geological Survey Closed*] (SEIS)
HNL .... Hourly Noise Level
HNLC .... High Nutrient, Low Chlorophyll [*Biological oceanography*]
HNLG .... Handling
HNLM .... High Noise-Level Margin
HNLN .... Hospitalization No Longer Necessary (STED)
HNM .... Hana [*Hawaii*] [*Airport symbol*] (OAG)
HNM .... Helicopter Noise Model [*OST*] (TAG)
HNM .... Hertzberg-New Method [*Standard periodical binding*]
HNM .... Hexanitromannite [*Organic chemistry*]
HNML .... Hindu Meal [*Airline notation*]
HNMR .... High-Resolution Nuclear Magnetic Resonance
HNMS .... Her Netherlands Majesty's Ship
HNMS .... High NATO Military Structure (NATG)
HNN .... Henderson, WV [*Location identifier FAA*] (FAAL)
HNO .... Henderson, TX [*Location identifier FAA*] (FAAL)
HNO .... Hercegnovi [*Yugoslavia*] [*Airport symbol*] (AD)
HNO .... Honcho Gold Mines, Inc. [*Vancouver Stock Exchange symbol*]
HNO .... Hrvatski Narodni Odbor [*Croatian National Resistance*] [*Former Yugoslavia*] (PD)
HNO$_3$ .... Nitric Acid [*Chemistry*] (DAVI)
HNP .... Haddam Neck Plant [*Nuclear energy*] (NRCH)
HNP .... Hartsville Nuclear Plant (NRCH)
HNP .... Harvard Negotiation Project
HNP .... Hereditary Nephritic Protein (STED)
HNP .... Herniated Nucleus Pulposus [*Medicine*]
HNP .... Herstigte Nasionale Party [*Reconstituted National Party*] [*South Africa*] [*Political party*] (PPW)
HNP .... High Needle Position [*on dial*]
HNP .... Huaneng Power International, Inc. [*NYSE symbol*] (SAG)
HNP .... Huaneng Power Intl ADS [*NYSE symbol*] (TTSB)
HNP .... Human Neurophysin (STED)
HNP .... Hungarian National Party [*Political party*] (BUAC)
HNP .... Minneapolis, MN [*Location identifier FAA*] (FAAL)
HNP .... Parklawn Health Library, Rockville, MD [*OCLC symbol*] (OCLC)
HNPA .... Home Numbering Plan Area [*AT & T*]
HNPCC .... Hereditary Nonpolyposis Colon Cancer [*Medicine*]
HNPCC .... Hereditary Nonpolyposis Colorectal Cancer [*Medicine*] (HGEN)
HNPF .... Hallam Nuclear Power Facility [*Decommissioned*] [*AEC*]
HNPL .... High-Level Network Processing Language [*Computer science*] (MHDI)
HNPP .... Hereditary Neuropathy with Liability to Pressure Palsies
HNPSA .... Homeland Non-Party Serbian Association (BUAC)
HNQ .... Hydroxynaphthoquinone [*Organic chemistry*]
HNPI .... Haiti National Airlines [*ICAO designator*] (FAAC)
HNR .... Handwritten Numeral Recognition (IAA)
HNR .... Harlan, IA [*Location identifier FAA*] (FAAL)
HNR .... Heaston Resources Ltd. [*Vancouver Stock Exchange symbol*]
HNR .... Honiara [*Solomon Islands*] [*Seismograph station code, US Geological Survey*] (SEIS)
hnr .... Honoree [*MARC relator code*] [*Library of Congress*] (LCCP)
HNR .... Nordic Council of Organisations for the Disabled (BUAC)
HNRC .... USDA [*United States Department of Agriculture*] Human Nutrition Research Center on Aging at Tufts [*Tufts University*] [*Research center*] (RCD)
HNRIM .... Human Nutrition Research and Information Management System [*National Institute of Health*]
hnRNA .... Ribonucleic Acid, Heterogeneous Nuclear [*Biochemistry, genetics*]
hnRNP .... Ribonucleoprotein, Heterogeneous [*Biochemistry*]
HNRS .... Honors (ADA)
HNS .... Haines [*Alaska*] [*Airport symbol*] (OAG)
HNS .... Hamilton Normal School
HNS .... Haveeru News Service [*Maldives*] (EY)
HNS .... Hazardous and Noxious Substance
HNS .... Head and Neck Surgery [*Medical specialty*] (DHSM)
HNS .... Head, Neck, and Shaft [*of a bone*] [*Osteology*]
HNS .... Hexanitrostilbene [*High explosive*]
HNS .... Holy Name Society [*Defunct*] (EA)
HNS .... Home Nursing Supervisor [*Red Cross*]
HNS .... Host Nation Support [*Military*]
HNS .... Hrvatska Narodna Stranka [*Croatian People's Party*] [*Political party*]
HNS .... Hughes Network Systems
HNSA .... Host Nation Support Agreement [*Navy*] (ANA)
HNSD .... Hansard (DCTA)
HNSF .... Hungarian National Sports Federation (EA)
HNSHA .... Hereditary Nonspherocytic Hemolytic Anemia [*Medicine*]
HNSHA .... Hereditary Nonspherocytic Hemolytic Leukemia [*Medicine*] (STED)
HNSI .... Home Nutritional Services (EFIS)
HNST .... Hexanitrostilbene [*High explosive*] (MCD)
HNSX .... Honeywell-NEC Supercomputers, Inc.
HNT .... Handbuch zum Neuen Testament [*A publication*] (BJA)
HNT .... Helicopteros Internacionales, SA de CV [*Mexico*] [*FAA designator*] (FAAC)
HNT .... Hostage Negotiating Team (LAIN)
HNT .... National Center for Toxicological Research, Jefferson, AR [*OCLC symbol*] (OCLC)
HNTB .... Halstead Neuropsychological Test Battery (EDAC)
HNTD .... Highest Non-Toxic Dose (OA)
HNTG .... Hunting (MSA)
HntgIn .... Huntingdon International Holdings Ltd. [*Associated Press*] (SAG)
H-NTLA .... Hiskey-Nebraska Test of Learning Aptitude (EDAC)
HNTR .... Hunter
HNU .... Hainan University (BUAC)
HNU .... Henan University (BUAC)

HNV	Hanover Direct [*Formerly, Horn & Hardart Co.*] [*AMEX symbol*] (SPSG)
HNV	Has Not Voided [*Urology*]
HNVS	Helicopter Night Vision System (PDAA)
HNVS	Hughes Night Vision System [*Aviation*]
HNW	Head, Nut, and Washer [*Construction*]
HNW	Heeresnachrichtenwesen [*Army Communications System*] [*German military - World War II*]
HNW	Hein-Werner [*AMEX symbol*] (TTSB)
HNW	Hein-Werner Corp. [*AMEX symbol*] (SPSG)
HNW	Placerville, CA [*Location identifier FAA*] (FAAL)
HNY	Hamilton [*New York*] [*Seismograph station code, US Geological Survey*] (SEIS)
HNY	Happy New Year
HNY	Hennessy Resource Corp. [*Vancouver Stock Exchange symbol*]
HNY	Honey (WGA)
HNYB	Honeybee
HNYCMB	Honeycomb
HNZ	Havelock North [*New Zealand*] [*Seismograph station code, US Geological Survey Closed*] (SEIS)
HNZ	Heinz [*H. J.*] Co. [*NYSE symbol*] (SPSG)
HNZ	Heinz (H.J.) [*NYSE symbol*] (TTSB)
HNZPr	Heinz $1.70 cm Cv Pfd [*NYSE symbol*] (TTSB)
HO	Airways International [*ICAO designator*] (AD)
HO	Charterair [*ICAO designator*] (AD)
HO	Haem Oxygenase [*An enzyme*]
HO	Hale Observatories [*Formerly, Mount Palomar and Mount Wilson Observatories*]
H-O	Half of 'O' Gauge [*Model railroading*]
HO	Halogenated Organic Carbons (GNE)
HO	Hand Orthosis [*Medicine*]
HO	Hand Over (MCD)
H/O	Handover (NAKS)
H/O	Hard Over (KSC)
HO	Harmonic Oscillator
HO	Hazardous Organics [*Environmental science*]
HO	Head Office
HO	Heel Off Ground [*Medicine*]
H/O	Hematology and Oncology (DAVI)
HO	Heterotopic Ossification [*Osteology*]
HO	High Oblique [*Aerospace*]
HO	High Order [*Computer science*] (OA)
HO	High Output [*Automotive engineering*]
HO	High Oxygen (MAE)
HO	Hip Orthosis [*Medicine*]
H/O	History Of [*Medicine*]
HO	History Office (MCD)
HO	Hoist
HO	Hold [*Shipping*] (DS)
HO	Holding Out [*Cashier fraud*]
HO	Holdover [*Theater*]
Ho	Holmium [*Chemical element*]
HO	Holt-Oram [*Syndrome*] [*Medicine*] (DB)
HO	Holy Day of Obligation [*Roman Catholicism*]
HO	Holy Orders (ROG)
HO	Home Office [*British*]
HO	Home Only [*British military*] (DMA)
HO	Homeowners' [*Insurance*]
Ho	Homobonus de Cremona [*Deceased, 1272*] [*Authority cited in pre-1607 legal work*] (DSA)
ho	Honduras [*MARC country of publication code Library of Congress*] (LCCP)
HO	Horizontally Opposed [*Automotive engineering*]
HO	Horizontal Output (IAA)
Ho	Horse (DMAA)
Ho	Hosea [*Old Testament book*] (BJA)
Ho	Hostiensis [*Deceased, 1271*] [*Authority cited in pre-1607 legal work*] (DSA)
HO	Hostilities Only [*Applied to men who joined for duration of war only*] [*Navy British World War II*]
HO	Hotel (ROG)
HO	Hours of Operation
HO	House
HO	House Officer
HO	Human Operator (IAA)
HO	Hunting Oscillator (IAA)
HO	Hydraulic Operator (NRCH)
HO	Hydrogen-Oxygen [*NASA*] (NASA)
HO	Hydrographic Office [*Terminated, 1963; later, NOO*] [*Navy*]
ho	Hydroxy [*As substituent on nucleoside*] [*Also, oh*] [*Biochemistry*]
HO	Hyperbaric Oxygen [*Medicine*]
HO	Observation Helicopter
Ho	Observed Altitude
HO	Service Available to Meet Operational Requirements [*ICAO*] (FAAC)
HOA	Hands Off - Automatic (AAG)
HOA	Heavy Observation Aircraft
HOA	Hechalutz Organization of America [*Defunct*] (EA)
HOA	Hip Osteoarthritis [*Medicine*] (DMAA)
HOA	Home Owner Association
HOA	Homeowners Assistance Fund, Defense [*DoD*]
HOA	Homeowner's Association [*Computer science*]
HOA	House of Assembly [*South Australia*]
HOA	(Hydroxyethyl)oxamic Acid [*Organic chemistry*]
HOA	Hypertrophic Osteoarthropathy [*Medicine*] (DMAA)
HOAA	Home Office Association of America (NTPA)

HOAB	Heptyloxyazoxybenzene [*Organic chemistry*]
HOACGA	Heart of America Carnival Glass Association (EA)
HOAI	Home Office Addicts' Index (WDAA)
HOAI	Human Outreach and Advancement Institute
HOAL	Homes on Aboriginal Land [*Australia*]
HOALM	Holographic Optic Addressed Light Modulation (IAA)
HOAM	Healthwise of America, Inc. [*NASDAQ symbol*] (SAG)
HO & RC	Humble Oil & Refining Co. (MHDW)
HOANSW	Hospital Officers' Association of New South Wales [*Australia*]
HOAP	Home Ownership Assistance Program [*Farmers Home Administration*]
HOAP	Housing Opportunity Assistance Program [*Federal Home Loan Bank Board*]
HOAP	Hydroxydaunomycin [*Adriamycin*], Cytosine Arabinoside, Vincristine, Prednisone [*Antineoplastic drug regimen*] (DAVI)
HOAP-BLEO	, ara-C , Prednisone, Bleomycin [*Vincristine*] [*Cytarabine*] [*Antineoplastic drug regimen*]
HoaRhLG	Horse Anti-Rhesus Lymphocyte Globulin [*Immunology*]
HOARS	Hands-On Annotated Recorded Search (NITA)
HOATS	Human Ovarian Antitumor Serum [*Antineoplastic compound*]
HoaTTG	Horse Anti-Tetanus Toxoid Globulin [*Immunology*]
HOB	Half-Octave Bandwidth
HOB	Head of Bed [*Medicine*]
HOB	Head of Bus (ACRL)
HOB	Height [*Depth*] of Burst
Hob	Hobart's English King's Bench Reports [*80 English Reprint*] [*A publication*] (DLA)
HOB	Hobbs [*New Mexico*] [*Airport symbol*] (OAG)
HOB	Hobbs Public Library, Hobbs, NM [*OCLC symbol*] (OCLC)
HOB	Hobby
HOB	Home-on-Burn
HOB	Homing on Offset Beacon
HOB	Horizontal Oscillating Barrel (PDAA)
HOB	Hot Ore Briquetting (DICI)
HOB	House Office Building [*US Congress*]
HOBA	[*A*] History of the Book in Australia [*Project*]
Hobart	Hobart's English King's Bench Reports [*80 English Reprint*] [*A publication*] (DLA)
Hobart (Eng)	Hobart's English King's Bench Reports [*80 English Reprint*] [*A publication*] (DLA)
HOBDH	Hydroxybutyrate Dehydrogenase (DB)
HOBE	Horseshoe Bend National Military Park
HOBGI	Honorable Order of the Blue Goose, International [*West Bend, WI*] (EA)
HOBIS	Home Ownership Building Industry Scheme [*Australia*]
HOBIS	Hotel Billing Information System [*Telecommunications*] (TEL)
HOBITS	Haifa On-line Bibliographic Text System [*University of Haifa Library*] [*Information service or system*] (IID)
HOBN	Home Office Business Network [*Information service or system*] (IID)
HOBO	Homing Optical Bomb (MCD)
Hobonus	Homobonus de Cremona [*Deceased, 1272*] [*Authority cited in pre-1607 legal work*] (DSA)
HOBOS	Homing Bomb System [*Air Force*]
HOBP	Hydroxy(octylidene)bis(phosphonic Acid) [*Organic chemistry*]
Hob R	Hobart's English Common Pleas Reports [*80 English Reprint*] [*1613-25*] [*A publication*] (DLA)
Hob R	Hobart's English King's Bench Reports [*80 English Reprint*] [*A publication*] (DLA)
HOBS	High-Orbital Bombardment System (KSC)
HOBS	Home and Office Banking Service [*Bank of Scotland*] (ECON)
HOBS	Homing Bomb System [*Air Force*]
HOBT	Hydroxybenzotriazole
HOBUPSOB	Head of Bed Up for Shortness of Breath [*Medicine*] (DAVI)
HOBY	Hugh O'Brian Youth Foundation (EA)
HOBYAA	Hugh O'Brian Youth Foundation Alumni Association (EA)
HOC	Halogenated Organic Compound [*Organic chemistry*] (FFDE)
HOC	Halogenated Organic Compounds
HOC	Handover Coordinator (SAA)
HOC	Hands-On Component
HOC	Health Officer Certificate (DAVI)
HOC	Heat of Combustion
HOC	Heavy Oil Cracking [*Process*] [*Petroleum industry*]
HOC	Height Overlap Coverage [*RADAR*]
HOC	Heterodyne Optical Correlation (IAA)
HOC	Highest Outgoing Channel [*Telecommunications*] (CIST)
HOC	High Output Current
HOC	Hillman Owners Club [*Lancing, Sussex, England*] (EAIO)
HOC	Hillsboro, OH [*Location identifier FAA*] (FAAL)
HOC	History of Coverage (MCD)
HOC	Holly Corp. [*AMEX symbol*] (SPSG)
HOC	Hollywood Overseas Committee (IIA)
HOC	House of Commons [*British*]
HoC	Hoven & Co., Bakersfield, CA [*Library symbol Library of Congress*] (LCLS)
HOC	Human Ovarian Cancer [*Cytology*]
HOC	Hurricane Operations Center (AFM)
HOC	Hydraulic Overspeed Control [*Mechanical power transmission*]
HOC	Hydrofoil Ocean Combatant
HOC	Hydrophobic Organic Chemical [*Physical chemistry*]
HOC	Hydrophobic Organic Compound [*Marine science*] (OSRA)
HOC	Hydrophobic Organic Contaminant [*Environmental science*]
HOC	Hydroxycorticosteroid [*Endocrinology*]
HOCA	High Osmolar Contrast Agent [*Medicine*]
HOCA	Hurst/Olds Club of America (EA)
HOCarm	Hermits of Our Lady of Mt. Carmel (TOCD)

HOCCU.........	Heavy Oil Catalytic Cracking Unit [*Petroleum refining*]
HOCM	High Osmolar Contrast Medium (DB)
HOCM	Hypertrophic Obstructive Cardiomyopathy [*Cardiology*]
HOCOLEA.....	Heads of Commonwealth Operational Law Enforcement Agencies [*Australia*]
HOCRE.........	Home Office Central Research Establishment (BUAC)
HoCT	Household Capital Trust [*Associated Press*] (SAG)
HoCT	Household Capital Trust II [*Associated Press*] (SAG)
HOCUS.........	Hand or Computer Universal Simulation [*PE Computer Services Ltd.*] [*Software package*] [*British*]
HOC VESP ...	Hoc Vespere [*Tonight*] [*Pharmacy*]
HOD	Head of Department
HoD	Head of Department [*British*] (DET)
HOD	Heat of Detonation
HOD	Hebrew Order of David
HOD	Highway Overlay District (PA)
HOD	Historic Overlay District (PA)
HOD	Hodeidah [*Yemen Arab Republic*] [*Airport symbol*] (OAG)
Hod	Hodges' English Common Pleas Reports [*1835-37*] [*A publication*] (DLA)
HoD	Hodgkin's Disease [*Oncology*] (DAVI)
HOD	Hoffer-Osmond Diagnostic Test [*Psychology*]
HOD	Home on Decoy [*Military*] (CAAL)
HOD	Hurt on Duty
HOD	Hyperbaric Oxygen Drenching
HODA	Hawkfarm One Design Association (EA)
HODAG	Housing Development Action Grant [*HUD*]
HODCRA	Hampton One-Design Class Racing Association (EA)
Hodg	Hodges' English Common Pleas Reports [*1835-37*] [*A publication*] (DLA)
Hodg	Hodgin's Election Cases [*Ontario*] [*A publication*] (DLA)
Hodg Can Elec Cas...	Hodgin's Canada Election Cases [*A publication*] (DLA)
Hodg El........	Hodgins' Upper Canada Election Cases [*A publication*] (DLA)
Hodg El Cas...	Hodgin's Election Cases [*Ontario*] [*A publication*] (DLA)
Hodg El Cas (Ont)...	Hodgin's Election Cases [*Ontario*] [*A publication*] (DLA)
Hodge Presb Law...	Hodge on Presbyterian Law [*A publication*] (DLA)
Hodges	Hodges' English Common Pleas Reports [*1835-37*] [*A publication*] (DLA)
Hodges (Eng)...	Hodges' English Common Pleas Reports [*1835-37*] [*A publication*] (DLA)
Hodg Ont Elect...	Hodgin's Election Cases [*Ontario*] [*A publication*] (DLA)
Hodg Ry	Hodges' Law of Railways [*A publication*] (DLA)
HODI	Homozygous Diabetes Insipidus [*A genetic variety of rat*]
HODS	Hydrographic Oceanographic Data Sheets (NG)
HOE	Height of Eye [*Navigation*]
HOE	Hoechst-Roussel Pharmaceuticals, Inc. [*Research code symbol*]
HOE	Holographic Optical Element
HOE	Homerville, GA [*Location identifier FAA*] (FAAL)
HOE	Homing Overlay Equipment (MCD)
HOE	Homing Overlay Experiment [*Ballistic missile defense*] (RDA)
HOE	Human and Organizational Errors [*Engineering*]
HOE	Hydraulically Operated Equipment
HOEI	Hover-One-Engine-Inoperative (PDAA)
HOEN	Hoenig Group [*NASDAQ symbol*] (TTSB)
HOEN	Hoenig Group, Inc. [*NASDAQ symbol*] (SPSG)
Hoenig..........	Hoenig Group, Inc. [*Associated Press*] (SAG)
HOET	Heavy Oil Engine Tractor [*British*]
HOF	Hafuf [*Saudi Arabia*] [*Airport symbol*] (OAG)
HOF	Hall of Fame
HoF	Head of Faculty [*British*] (DET)
HOF	Head of Faculty [*Education*] (AIE)
HOF	Head of Form (IAA)
HOF	Heat of Formation
HoF	Height of Fundus [*Obstetrics*]
HOF	Hepatic Outflow [*Medicine*] (DMAA)
HOF	Hof [*Federal Republic of Germany*] [*Seismograph station code, US Geological Survey*] (SEIS)
HOF	Home Office Facility
HOF	Homing Fixture (MCD)
HOF	Horizons of Friendship [*Canada*] (BUAC)
HOF	House of Fraser [*Department store conglomerate*] [*British*]
HOF	St. Paul, MN [*Location identifier FAA*] (FAAL)
HOFC	Hall and Oates Fan Club (EA)
H of C..........	House of Commons [*British*]
HofC............	House of Commons [*British*] (WDAA)
HOFCO	Horizontal Function Checkout (KSC)
HOFD	Heterogeneous Opposed Flow Diffusion
H of F..........	Hall of Fame (WDAA)
H of F	Height of Fundus [*Obstetrics*]
HofF............	Height of Fundus [*Obstetrics*] (DAVI)
HOFF	Hoffmann [*Reflex*] [*Medicine*]
Hoff.............	Hoffman's Land Cases, United States District Court [*A publication*] (DLA)
Hoff.............	Hoffman's New York Chancery Reports [*A publication*] (DLA)
Hoff Ch	Hoffman's New York Chancery Reports [*A publication*] (DLA)
Hoff CR........	Hoffman's New York Chancery Reports [*A publication*] (DLA)
Hoff Dec	Hoffman's Decisions [*A publication*] (DLA)
Hoff Ecc L....	Hoffman's Ecclesiastical Law [*A publication*] (DLA)
Hoff Land.....	Hoffman's Land Cases, United States District Court [*A publication*] (DLA)
Hoff Land Cas..	Hoffman's Land Cases, United States District Court [*A publication*] (DLA)
Hoff LC	Hoffman's Land Cases, United States District Court [*A publication*] (DLA)

Hoff L Cas ...	Hoffman's Land Cases, United States District Court [*A publication*] (DLA)
Hoff Lead Cas...	Hoffman's Leading Cases [*A publication*] (DLA)
Hoff Leg St...	Hoffman's Course of Legal Study [*A publication*] (DLA)
HOFFM	Hereditary Order of the First Families of Massachusetts (EA)
Hoffm...........	Hoffman's Land Cases, United States District Court [*A publication*] (DLA)
Hoffm...........	Hoffman's New York Chancery Reports [*A publication*] (DLA)
Hoffman Ch R...	Hoffman's New York Chancery Reports [*A publication*] (DLA)
Hoffman's Ch R...	Hoffman's New York Chancery Reports [*A publication*] (DLA)
Hoff Mast.....	Hoffman's Master in Chancery [*A publication*] (DLA)
Hoff Mast Ch...	Hoffman's Master in Chancery [*A publication*] (DLA)
Hoffm Ch	Hoffman's Land Cases, United States District Court [*A publication*] (DLA)
Hoffm Ch	Hoffman's New York Chancery Reports [*A publication*] (DLA)
Hoffm Ch (NY)...	Hoffman's New York Chancery Reports [*A publication*] (DLA)
Hoffm Dec (F)...	Hoffman's Decisions, United States District Court [*A publication*] (DLA)
Hoffm Land Cas (F)...	Hoffman's Land Cases, United States District Court [*A publication*] (DLA)
Hoffm Ops (F)...	Hoffman's Opinions, United States District Court [*A publication*] (DLA)
Hoffm Rep Land Cases...	Hoffman's Land Cases, United States District Court [*A publication*] (DLA)
Hoff NY........	Hoffman's New York Chancery Reports [*A publication*] (DLA)
Hoff Op........	Hoffman's Opinions [*A publication*] (DLA)
Hoff Out........	Hoffman's Legal Outlines [*A publication*] (DLA)
Hoff Pr Rem...	Hoffman's Provisional Remainders [*A publication*] (DLA)
Hoff Pub P...	Hoffman's Public Papers [*New York*] [*A publication*] (DLA)
Hoff Ref........	Hoffman on Referees [*A publication*] (DLA)
H of H..........	Holy of Holies [*Freemasonry*] (ROG)
H of IF.........	House of Ill Fame
H of J..........	Hospitallers of Jerusalem [*Freemasonry*] (ROG)
HOFL	Home Financial [*NASDAQ symbol*] (TTSB)
HOFL	Home Financial Corporation of Florida [*NASDAQ symbol*] (SAG)
H of N..........	Hydrographer of the Navy [*British*]
HOFR	Home of Franklin D. Roosevelt and Vanderbilt Mansion National Historic Sites
H of S..........	House of Solomon [*Freemasonry*] (ROG)
HOFS	Hydrogen-Oxygen Fuel System [*NASA*]
HOFSL	Home Office Forensic Science Laboratory [*British*]
Hofstra Lab LF...	Hofstra Labor Law Forum [*A publication*] (DLA)
Hofstra Lab LJ...	Hofstra Labor Law Journal [*A publication*] (DLA)
Hofstra U	Hofstra University (GAGS)
HOFTU	Hunter Operational Fighter Training Unit [*India*] [*Air Force*]
HOG	Halothane, Oxygen, and Gas [*Nitrous oxide*] [*Anesthesiology*] (DAVI)
HOG	Harley-Davidson Owners Group (BUAC)
HOG	Harley Owners' Group (EA)
HOG	Head End Off-Gas [*Nuclear energy*] (NRCH)
HOG	Head of Government (ADA)
HOG	Heavy Ordnance Gunship (NVT)
HOG	High Old Genius [*Slang British*]
Hog	(Hogan of) Harcarse's Scotch Session Cases [*A publication*] (DLA)
Hog	Hogan's Irish Rolls Court Reports [*A publication*] (DLA)
HOG	Holguin [*Cuba*] [*Airport symbol*] (OAG)
HOG	Homing Optical Guidance
HOG	Hondo Oil & Gas [*AMEX symbol*] (TTSB)
HOG	Hondo Oil & Gas Co. [*AMEX symbol*] (SPSG)
HOGA	Hyperornithinemia with Gyrate Atrophy [*Medicine*] (DMAA)
Hogan..........	(Hogan of) Harcarse's Scotch Session Cases [*A publication*] (DLA)
Hogan..........	Hogan's Irish Rolls Court Reports [*A publication*] (DLA)
Hogan..........	Hogan Systems, Inc. [*Associated Press*] (SAG)
Hogan (Ir)...	Hogan's Irish Rolls Court Reports [*A publication*] (DLA)
HOGC	Handbook of Occupational Groups and Series of Classes
HOGE	Hover out of Ground Effect
HOGE	Hover-Out-of-Ground Environment
HOGEN.........	Hold Off Generator (MSA)
HOGN..........	Hogan Systems, Inc. [*NASDAQ symbol*] (NQ)
HOGS	Homing Optical Guidance System
Hog St Tr....	Hogan's Pennsylvania State Trials [*A publication*] (DLA)
Hogue..........	Hogue's Reports [*1-4 Florida*] [*A publication*] (DLA)
HOH.............	Hard of Hearing (MAE)
HOH.............	Head of Household [*IRS*]
HOH.............	Heard on the Hill [*US Congress*]
HOH.............	Help Our Headaches Group [*Australia*]
HOH.............	Hereford Otter Hounds
HOH.............	High-Degree Helioseismometer
HOH.............	Hohenheim [*Federal Republic of Germany*] [*Seismograph station code, US Geological Survey Closed*] (SEIS)
HOH.............	Hydrogen-Oxygen-Hydrogen [*Water*] (HGAA)
HOHI	Handbook of Overhaul Instructions [*Navy*]
HOH of J......	Holy Order of the Hospital of Jerusalem [*Freemasonry*] (ROG)
HOHP...........	Holocaust Oral History Project [*An association*] (EA)
HOI	Handbook of Operating Instructions [*Navy*]
HOI	Handbook of Overhaul Instructions [*Navy*] (MCD)
HOI	Hao Island [*French Polynesia*] [*Airport symbol*] (OAG)
HOI	Headquarters Office Instruction
HOI	Headquarters Operating Instructions [*Air Force*] (AFM)
HOI	Health Optimizing Institute (EA)
HOI	Hear O Israel
HOI	Hospital Onset of Infection [*Medicine*] (DMAA)
HOI	House of Issue [*Banking*]
HOI	Hypoiodous Acid (STED)
Holg.............	Horse Immunoglobulin [*Immunology*]
HoInt...........	Household International, Inc. [*Associated Press*] (SAG)

HOIS .... Hostile Intelligence Service [*Military*] (MCD)
HOJ .... Home on Jamming
HOJ .... Hope [*Jamaica*] [*Seismograph station code, US Geological Survey*] (SEIS)
HOJO .... Howard Johnson [*Restaurant chain*] [*Slang*]
HOK .... Hellmuth, Obata & Kassabaum [*Architectural firm*]
HOK .... Hohkeppel [*Federal Republic of Germany*] [*Seismograph station code, US Geological Survey*] (SEIS)
HOK .... Hoko Exploration [*Vancouver Stock Exchange symbol*]
HOK .... Hooker Creek [*Airport symbol*]
HOK .... House of Keys [*Isle Of Man*]
HOKEYS ...... Home Owners' Loan Corporation Bonds (MHDB)
HOL .... Higher Order Logic [*Computer science*]
HOL .... High- [*or Higher-*] Order Language [*Computer science*]
HOL .... Holco Mortgage Acceptance Corp. [*AMEX symbol*] (SPSG)
HOL .... Holiday (AFM)
HOL .... Holiday Airlines, Inc. [*ICAO designator*] (FAAC)
HOL .... Holiday and Leave [*Military*] (NVT)
HOL .... Hollinger Argus Ltd. [*Toronto Stock Exchange symbol*]
HOL .... Hollow (MSA)
HOL .... House of Lords [*British*]
HOL .... Humanization of Labor (IID)
HOLA .... Hispanic Organization of Latin Actors (EA)
HOLA .... Home Owners' Loan Act of 1933
HOLC .... High-Order Language Computer (NASA)
HOLC .... Home Owners' Loan Corp. [*Terminated, 1942*]
Ho L Cas ..... Clark's House of Lords Cases [*1847-66*] [*England*] [*A publication*] (DLA)
Holc Debt & Cr... Holcombe's Law of Debtor and Creditor [*A publication*] (DLA)
Holc Eq Jur... Holcombe's Equity Jurisdiction [*A publication*] (DLA)
Holc L Cas... Holcombe's Leading Cases of Commercial Law [*A publication*] (DLA)
Holco .... Holco Mortgage Acceptance Corp. [*Associated Press*] (SAG)
HOLD .... American Holdings, Inc. [*NASDAQ symbol*] (SAG)
HOLD .... Call Hold [*Telecommunications*] (DOM)
HOLD .... Hemostatic Occlusive Leverage Device [*Cardiology*] (DAVI)
HOLDET .... Higher Order Language Development and Evaluation Tool [*Computer science*] (MHDB)
HOLF .... Helicopter Outlying Field
Holg .... Horse Immunoglobulin [*Immunology*] (DAVI)
holgr............ Hologram (VRA)
HOLI .... Hollinger International, Inc. [*NASDAQ symbol*] (SAG)
Holinger ...... Hollinger, Inc. [*Associated Press*] (SAG)
HOLL .... Holland
Holl .... Holland (VRA)
Holl .... Hollinshead's Reports [*1 Minnesota*] [*A publication*] (DLA)
HOLLAND ... Here Our Love Lives and Never Dies [*Correspondence*] (DSUE)
Holl Comp Deeds... Holland on Composition Deeds [*A publication*] (DLA)
Holl El Jur... Holland's Elements of Jurisprudence [*A publication*] (DLA)
Hollinger ..... Hollinger International, Inc. [*Associated Press*] (SAG)
Hollins C ..... Hollins College (GAGS)
Hollinshead... Hollinshead's Reports [*1 Minnesota*] [*A publication*] (DLA)
Holl Jur .... Holland's Elements of Jurisprudence [*A publication*] (DLA)
Holl Just....... Holland's Institutes of Justinian [*A publication*] (DLA)
Hollng.......... Hollinger International, Inc. [*Associated Press*] (SAG)
HOLLOW..... Hollow [*Commonly used*] (OPSA)
HOLLOWS.... Hollow [*Commonly used*] (OPSA)
HollyCp .... Holly Corp. [*Associated Press*] (SAG)
HollyH .... Holly Holdings, Inc. [*Associated Press*] (SAG)
HollyHld ..... Holly Holdings, Inc. [*Associated Press*] (SAG)
HollyP .... Holly Holdings, Inc. [*Associated Press*] (SAG)
HollyPd .... Holly Products [*Associated Press*] (SAG)
HOLM .... Higher-Order Language Machine [*Computer science*] (KSC)
Holm............ Holmes' Reports [*15-17 Oregon*] [*A publication*] (DLA)
Holm............ Holmes' United States Circuit Court Reports [*A publication*] (DLA)
Holm Com Law... Holmes on the Common Law [*A publication*] (DLA)
Holmes .... Holmes' United States Circuit Court Reports [*A publication*] (DLA)
HOLMES ...... Home Office Large Major Enquiry System [*Computer system*] [*British*]
HolmPr .... Holmes Protection Group, Inc. [*Associated Press*] (SAG)
Holm Statesman... Holmes' Statesman [*A publication*] (DLA)
HOLO .... Holograph (WDAA)
HOLO .... HoloPak Technologies [*NASDAQ symbol*] (SPSG)
HOLO .... Holotype
Hologic .... Hologic, Inc. [*Associated Press*] (SAG)
HoLoPak...... HoloPak Technologies [*Associated Press*] (SAG)
Holophne..... Holophane Corp. [*Associated Press*] (SAG)
Ho Lords C... Clark's House of Lords Cases [*1847-66*] [*England*] [*A publication*] (DLA)
Ho Lords Cas... Clark's House of Lords Cases [*1847-66*] [*England*] [*A publication*] (DLA)
HOLS .... Home Opportunity Loans Scheme [*Australia*]
HOLSA........ Health-Oriented Libraries of San Antonio [*Library network*]
HolsnB........ Holson Burnes Group, Inc. [*Associated Press*] (SAG)
HOLSW .... Holsworthy [*England*]
Holt.............. Holt's English Equity Reports [*1845*] [*A publication*] (DLA)
Holt.............. Holt's English King's Bench Reports [*A publication*] (DLA)
Holt.............. Holt's English Nisi Prius Reports [*A publication*] (DLA)
Holt Adm ..... Holt's English Admiralty Cases (Rule of the Road) [*1863-67*] [*A publication*] (DLA)
Holt Adm Ca... Holt's English Admiralty Cases (Rule of the Road) [*1863-67*] [*A publication*] (DLA)
Holt Adm Cas... Holt's English Admiralty Cases (Rule of the Road) [*1863-67*] [*A publication*] (DLA)
Holt Eq .... Holt's English Equity Reports [*1845*] [*A publication*] (DLA)
Holthouse .... Holthouse's Law Dictionary [*A publication*] (DLA)

Holt KB........ Holt's English King's Bench Reports [*A publication*] (DLA)
Holt L Dic... Holthouse's Law Dictionary [*A publication*] (DLA)
Holt Lib ...... Holt on Libels [*A publication*] (DLA)
Holt Nav ...... Holt on Navigation [*A publication*] (DLA)
Holt NP........ Holt's English Nisi Prius Reports [*A publication*] (DLA)
Holt Reg...... Holt on Registration of Title [*A publication*] (DLA)
Holt R of R... Holt's English Admiralty Cases (Rule of the Road) [*A publication*] (DLA)
Holt Sh .... Holt on Shipping [*A publication*] (DLA)
Holt Shipp ... Holt on Shipping [*A publication*] (DLA)
HOLUA........ Home Office Life Underwriters Association [*St. Louis, MO*] (EA)
HOLUG........ Houston On Line Users Group (NITA)
HOLUPK...... Holiday, Upkeep [*Military*] (NVT)
HOLV .... Hop Latent Virus [*Plant pathology*]
HOLW .... Hollow
HOLWG....... High- [*or Higher-*] Order Language Working Group [*Computer science*] (RDA)
HOLWS .... Hollow [*Commonly used*] (OPSA)
HOLX .... Holiday Airlines, Inc. [*Air carrier designation symbol*]
HOLX .... Hologic Inc. [*NASDAQ symbol*] (TTSB)
Holy Names C... Holy Names College (GAGS)
HOLZ .... Higher Order Laue Zone [*Crystal diffraction lines*]
HOM .... Heartless Old Man [*Alternative sobriquet for William Gladstone, 1809-98, British statesman and prime minister, who was known to admirers as GOM, which see*]
HOM .... Hectometric Emissions [*Radio astronomy*]
HOM .... Hexamethylmelamine, Oncovin [*Vincristine*], Methotrexate [*Antineoplastic drug regimen*] (DAVI)
HOM .... High-Order Multiplier (IAA)
HOM .... High Osmolar Medium (STED)
HOM .... Homer [*Greek poet, c. 800BC*] [*Classical studies*] (ROG)
HOM .... Homer [*Alaska*] [*Airport symbol*] (OAG)
HOM .... Homer [*Alaska*] [*Seismograph station code, US Geological Survey*] (SEIS)
HOM .... Homily (ROG)
HOM .... Homing
Hom............. Homobonus de Cremona [*Deceased, 1272*] [*Authority cited in pre-1607 legal work*] (DSA)
Hom............. Homoptera [*Entomology*]
HoM............. Howell Microfilms Co., College, MD [*Library symbol Library of Congress*] (LCLS)
HOMA .... Heads of Marine Agencies [*Commonwealth*] [*State*] (EERA)
HOMAC........ Home Mortgage Access Corp. (EMRF)
HomBen....... Home Beneficial Corp. [*Associated Press*] (SAG)
HomBib........ Homiletica en Biblica [*The Hague*] [*A publication*] (BJA)
HOME .... Home Centers (DIY) Ltd. [*NASDAQ symbol*] (SAG)
HOME .... Home Observation for Measurement of the Environment [*Child development test*] [*Psychology*]
HOME .... Home Oncology Medical Extension [*A home treatment program*]
HOME .... Home Oriented Maternity Experience [*Defunct*] (EA)
HOME .... Home Ownership Made Easy Association [*Defunct*] (EA)
Home............ Home's Manuscript Decisions, Scotch Court of Session [*A publication*] (DLA)
HOME .... Homestead National Monument
HOME .... Homeworkers Organized for More Employment (EA)
HOMECp ...... Horned Order's Magickal Existence [*An association*] (EA)
Home (CI)... Clerk Home's Decisions, Scotch Court of Session [*1735-44*] [*A publication*] (DLA)
Home (Clk)... Home's Manuscript Decisions, Scotch Court of Session [*A publication*] (DLA)
HomeCnt...... Home Centers (DIY) Ltd. [*Associated Press*] (SAG)
Home Ct of Sess... Home's Manuscript Decisions, Scotch Court of Session [*A publication*] (DLA)
HOMEF .... Home Centers [*NASDAQ symbol*] (TTSB)
Homegte....... Homegate Hospitality, Inc. [*Associated Press*] (SAG)
Home H Dec... Home's Manuscript Decisions, Scotch Court of Session [*A publication*] (DLA)
HomeHld ..... Home Holdings [*Associated Press*] (SAG)
HOMEO .... Homeopathy (ADA)
Homeo......... Homeopathy (STED)
HOMEOP...... Homeopathy [*Medicine*]
HomePNA..... Home Phoneline Networking Alliance [*Telecommunications*]
HomePNA..... Home Phone Networking Alliance
HOMER........ Hazardous Organic Mass Emission Rate (AAEL)
HOMER........ High-Altitude Ozone Measuring and Educational Rocket [*NASA*]
HOMES .... Homeowner-Mortgage Eurosecurities [*Salomon Brothers*] [*Real estate*]
HOMES .... Housing Operations Management System [*DoD*]
HOMES .... Huron, Ontario, Michigan, Erie, Superior [*Great Lakes*]
HomeSh........ Home Shopping Network, Inc. [*Associated Press*] (SAG)
HOMESWEST... Western Australian State Housing Commission
HomeTB....... Hometown Buffet, Inc. [*Associated Press*] (SAG)
HomeV .... Homestead Village, Inc. [*Associated Press*] (SAG)
HomeVil ...... Homestead Village, Inc. [*Associated Press*] (SAG)
HOMF .... Home Fed Bancorp [*NASDAQ symbol*] (TTSB)
HOMG .... Homeowners Group [*NASDAQ symbol*] (TTSB)
HOMG .... Homeowners Group, Inc. [*NASDAQ symbol*] (NQ)
HOMI .... Homicide (DLA)
HOMIC .... Homicide [*Legal shorthand*] (LWAP)
HOMO .... Highest Occupied Molecular Orbital [*Atomic physics*]
HOMO .... Homeopath [*or Homeopathic*] (WDAA)
HOMO .... Homogenous
HOMO .... Homosexual
homo........... Homosexual (STED)

Homob.........	Homobonus de Cremona [*Deceased, 1272*] [*Authority cited in pre-1607 legal work*] (DSA)
HOMOCO	Homemakers & Mothers Cooperatives, Inc.
HomoD	Homo Dei. Przeglad Ascetyczno-Duszpasterski [*Warsaw/Wroclaw*] [*A publication*] (BJA)
HOMOEO......	Homoeopathy [*Medicine*]
HOMOLAT...	Homolateral [*Medicine*]
homolat......	Homolateral (STED)
HOMP	Halifax Ocean Meeting Point
HOMS	Harbor Operations and Maintenance Support [*Navy*] (VNW)
HOMS	Hellfire Optimized Missile System [*Army*] (DOMA)
HOMS	Home State Holdings [*NASDAQ symbol*] (TTSB)
HOMS	Home State Holdings, Inc. [*NASDAQ symbol*] (SAG)
HOMS	Hydrological Operational Multipurpose Subprogramme [*World Meteorological Organization*] [*Information service or system*] (IID)
hom sap	Homo Sapiens (BARN)
HOMSTD......	Homestead (DLA)
HOMT	Hydroxyindole O-Methyltransferase [*Also, HIOMT*] [*An enzyme*]
HOMV	Hop Mosaic Virus [*Plant pathology*]
HON	Handbook of the Nations [*A publication*]
HON	Hazardous Organic NESHAP [*National Emission Standards for Hazardous Air Polluta nts*] (GNE)
HON	Hazardous Organic NESHAP (National Emission Standards for Hazardous Air Pollutants) [*Environmental Protection Agency*]
HON	Hold Off Normal
HON	Honduras
HON	Honey (DSUE)
HON	Honeywell Electro-Optics Center Library, Lexington, MA [*OCLC symbol*] (OCLC)
HON	Honeywell, Inc. [*Formerly, MH, M-H*] [*NYSE symbol*] (SPSG)
HON	Honington FTU [*British ICAO designator*] (FAAC)
HON	Honiton [*Municipal borough in England*]
HON	Honolulu [*Hawaii*] [*Seismograph station code, US Geological Survey*] (SEIS)
HON	Honorable
Hon	Honorable (TBD)
HON	Honorary (MSA)
Hon	Honorary (WDAA)
Hon	Honorius de Kent [*Flourished, 1185-1208*] [*Authority cited in pre-1607 legal work*] (DSA)
Hon.............	Honourable (WDAA)
HON	Huron [*South Dakota*] [*Airport symbol*] (OAG)
HON	Hydroxyoxo-L-norvaline [*Antibiotic*]
HONA	Health of Naval Aviation (DOMA)
HON AF........	Honorary Admiral of the Fleet [*Navy British*] (ROG)
Hon ARAM...	Honorary Associate of the Royal Academy of Music [*British*]
HonARCM...	Honorary Associate of the Royal College of Music [*British*] (DI)
HonASTA	Honorary Associate of the Swimming Teachers' Association [*British*] (DBQ)
HONBLE.......	Honorable
HONCAUS...	Honoris Causa [*For the Sake of Honor, Honorary*] [*Latin*] (ADA)
HOND..........	Honduras
Hond..........	Honduras (VRA)
HOND..........	Honoured (ROG)
Honda.........	Honda Motors Co. Ltd. [*Associated Press*] (SAG)
HonDLitt	Honorary Doctor of Letters
Hondo.........	Hondo Oil & Gas Co. [*Associated Press*] (SAG)
HonDrRCA ..	Honorary Doctorate of the Royal College of Art [*British*] (DBQ)
HonDSc.......	Honorary Doctor of Science
HONEST.......	Helicopter Operations in a Night Environment Against a Simulated Target [*Military*] (MCD)
HonFBID	Honorary Fellow of the British Institute of Interior Design (DBQ)
Hon FEIS	Honorary Fellow of the Educational Institute of Scotland
HonFHCIMA..	Honorary Fellow of the Hotel, Catering, and Institutional Management Association [*British*] (DBQ)
HonFIGasE...	Honorary Fellow of the Institution of Gas Engineers [*British*] (DBQ)
HonFIIM.......	Honorary Fellow of the Institution of Industrial Managers [*British*] (DBQ)
HonFIMarE...	Honorary Fellow of the Institute of Marine Engineers [*British*] (DBQ)
HonFIMechE...	Honorary Fellow of the Institution of Mechanical Engineers [*British*] (DBQ)
HonFIMM.....	Honorary Fellow of the Institution of Mining and Metallurgy [*British*] (DBQ)
HonFInstE...	Honorary Fellow of the Institute of Energy [*British*] (DBQ)
HonFInstMC...	Honorary Fellow of the Institute of Measurement [*British*] (DBQ)
HonFInstNDT...	Honorary Fellow of the British Institute of Non-Destructive Testing (DBQ)
HonFIOP	Honorary Fellow of the Institute of Printing [*British*] (DI)
HonFIQA	Honorary Fellow of the Institute of Quality Assurance [*British*] (DBQ)
HonFIRSE ...	Honorary Fellow of the Institution of Railway Signal Engineers [*British*] (DBQ)
HonFITD	Honorary Fellow of the Institute of Training and Development [*British*] (DI)
HonFIWHTE..	Honorary Fellow of the Institution of Works and Highways Technician Engineers [*British*] (DBQ)
Hon FNDTS...	Honorary Fellow of the Non-Destructive Testing Society of Great Britain
HonFPRI	Honorary Life Member of the Plastics and Rubber Institute [*British*] (DBQ)
Hon FRAM ...	Honorary Fellow of the Royal Academy of Music [*British*]
Hon FRCM ...	Honorary Fellow of the Royal College of Music [*British*] (WDAA)
Hon FRPS ...	Honorary Fellow of the Royal Photographic Society [*British*]
HonFSCP	Honorary Fellow of the Society of Certified Professionals [*British*] (DBQ)
HonFSE........	Honorary Fellow of the Society of Engineers, Inc. [*British*] (DBQ)
HonFSGT	Honorary Fellow of the Society of Glass Technology [*British*] (DBQ)
HonFSLAET...	Honorary Fellow of the Society of Licensed Aircraft Engineers and Technologists [*British*] (DBQ)
Hon FTCL	Honorary Fellow of Trinity College of Music, London [*British*] (WDAA)
Hon FTSC	Honorary Fellow of the Tonic Sol-fa College (WDAA)
HonFWeldI...	Honorary Fellow of the Welding Institute [*British*] (DBQ)
Hong Kong LJ...	Hong Kong Law Journal [*A publication*] (DLA)
Hong Kong LR...	Hong Kong Law Reports [*A publication*] (DLA)
Hong Kong UL Jo...	Hong Kong University. Law Journal [*A publication*] (DLA)
HonGSM	Honorary Member of the Guildhall School of Music and Drama [*British*] (DBQ)
HONI............	HON Indus [*NASDAQ symbol*] (TTSB)
HONI............	Hon Industries, Inc. [*NASDAQ symbol*] (NQ)
HonInd.........	Hon Industries, Inc. [*Associated Press*] (SAG)
HON L..........	Honorary Lieutenant [*Navy British*] (ROG)
HON M.........	Honorary Member (ROG)
HonMInst NDT...	Honorary Member of the British Institute of Non-Destructive Testing (DBQ)
Hon MNDTS...	Honorary Member of the Non-Destructive Testing Society of Great Britain
HonMRIN.....	Honorary Member of the Royal Institute of Navigation [*British*] (DBQ)
HonMWES...	Honorary Member of the Women's Engineering Society [*British*] (DBQ)
HONO..........	Honolulu [*Hawaii*] (CINC)
Hon RAM	Honorary Member of the Royal Academy of Music [*British*]
HonRCM	Honorary Member of the Royal College of Music [*British*] (DBQ)
HonRNCM....	Honorary Member of the Royal Northern College of Music [*British*] (DBQ)
Hon RSCM ...	Honorary Member of the Royal School of Church Music [*British*]
honry	Honorary (DD)
Hons	Honors (DD)
HONS..........	Honors
HON SCH MOD LANG...	Honour School of Modern Languages [*British*] (ROG)
HON SEC	Honorary Secretary (ROG)
HON SURG LIEUT COL...	Honorary Surgeon Lieutenant-Colonel [*Military British*] (ROG)
Hon TCL	Honorary Member of Trinity College of Music, London [*British*] (WDAA)
HON VA	Honorary Vice-Admiral [*Navy British*] (ROG)
HONY..........	Honorary (WGA)
Honywel	Honeywell, Inc. [*Associated Press*] (SAG)
HOO	Avila College, Kansas City, MO [*OCLC symbol*] (OCLC)
HOO	Glacier Water Services [*AMEX symbol*] (TTSB)
HOO	Glacier Water Services, Inc. [*AMEX symbol*] (SAG)
HOO	Hanford Operations Office [*Nuclear energy*] (MCD)
HOO	Hiroo [*Japan*] [*Seismograph station code, US Geological Survey*] (SEIS)
HOO	Quang Duc [*South Vietnam*] [*Airport symbol*] (AD)
HOOD..........	Hereditary Osteo-Onychodysplasia [*Medicine*]
HOOD..........	Hierarchical Object-Oriented Design [*Computer science*] (ODBW)
Hood	Neighborhood [*Slang*]
Hood C	Hood College (GAGS)
Hood Ex......	Hood on Executors [*A publication*] (DLA)
HOODS........	Hereditary Onycho-Osteodysplasia Syndrome [*Medicine*] (STED)
HOOI...........	Hall Occupational Orientation Inventory (STED)
HOOK..........	Handbook of Occupational Keywords [*For use in employment services*] [*Department of Labor*]
Hook	Hooker's Reports [*25-62 Connecticut*] [*A publication*] (DLA)
HOOK..........	Redhook Ale Brewery [*NASDAQ symbol*] (TTSB)
HOOK..........	Redhook Ale Brewery, Inc. [*NASDAQ symbol*] (SAG)
Hooker	Hooker's Reports [*25-62 Connecticut*] [*A publication*] (DLA)
Hoon	Hoonahan's Sind Reports [*India*] [*A publication*] (DLA)
Hoonahan	Hoonahan's Sind Reports [*India*] [*A publication*] (DLA)
HOOP..........	Handbook of Operating Procedures
HOOP..........	Sure Shot International, Inc. [*NASDAQ symbol*] (SAG)
HOOP..........	Sure Shot Intl Inc. [*NASDAQ symbol*] (TTSB)
HoopHI	Hooper Holmes, Inc. [*Associated Press*] (SAG)
HOOPS........	Hierarchical Object-Oriented Picture System [*Computer science*]
HOOPW........	Sure Shot Intl Wrrt [*NASDAQ symbol*] (TTSB)
HOP	Handoff Point [*Aviation*] (FAAC)
HOP	HEDL [*Hanford Engineering Development Laboratory*] Overpower [*Nuclear energy*] (NRCH)
HOP	Helicopter Operations (FAAC)
HOP	Helium Oxidizer-Tank Pressure (AAG)
HOP	Help Other People [*Scout motto*]
HOP	Heritage of Pride [*An association*] (EA)
HOP	High-Order Position (AFIT)
HOP	High Oxygen Pressure
HOP	Holding Procedures (SAA)
HOP	Holidays One-Parents [*An association*] (BUAC)
HOP	Hope [*Jamaica*] [*Seismograph station code, US Geological Survey Closed*] (SEIS)
HOP	Hopkinsville, KY [*Location identifier FAA*] (FAAL)
HOP	House Operating Tape [*Telecommunications*] (TEL)
HOP	Hybrid Operating Program [*Computer science*] (IEEE)
HOP	Hydrographic Office Publications [*Obsolete Navy*]
HOP	Hydroxydaunomycin [*Adriamycin*], Oncovin , Prednisone [*Vincristine*] [*Antineoplastic drug regimen*]
HOPA	Hopantenate Calcium [*Cerebral activator*]
Hop & C	Hopwood and Coltman's English Registration Appeal Cases [*A publication*]
Hop & Colt...	Hopwood and Coltman's English Registration Appeal Cases [*A publication*] (DLA)
Hop & Ph.....	Hopwood and Philbrick's English Registration Appeal Cases [*A publication*] (DLA)

Hop & Phil... Hopwood and Philbrick's English Registration Appeal Cases [*A publication*] (DLA)
HOPD.......... Hospital Out-Patient Department (MEDA)
HOPE.......... Hackers on Planet Earth [*An association*]
HOPE.......... Halley Optical Probe Experiment
HOPE.......... Healthcare Opposed to Euthanasia [*An association*] (BUAC)
HOPE.......... Health Opportunity for People Everywhere [*Philanthropic project operating hospital ship*]
HOPE.......... Health Organization to Preserve the Environment
HOPE.......... Health-Oriented Physician Education
HOPE.......... Hellenic Organisation for the Promotion of Exports (BUAC)
HOPE.......... Help Obese People Everywhere
HOPE.......... Help Organise Peaceful Energy [*An association*] (BUAC)
HOPE.......... Highlights of Personal Experience in Agriculture Department
HOPE.......... Highly Instrumented Orbiting Primate Experiment
HOPE.......... Hispanic Organization of Professionals and Executives [*Silver Spring, MD*] (EA)
HOPE.......... Holistic Orthogonal Parameter Estimation [*Medicine*] (DMAA)
HOPE.......... Home Ownership and Opportunity for People Everywhere [*Program*] [*HUD*]
HOPE.......... Homes of Private Enterprise (EA)
Hope.......... Hope (of Kerse). Manuscript Decisions, Scotch Court of Session [*A publication*] (DLA)
HOPE.......... Hospital-Oriented Programmed Environment
HOPE.......... Housing Our People Economically
HOPE.......... Humanistic Organization for Personal Expansion
HOPE.......... Hydrogen-Oxygen Primary Extraterrestrial [*Fuel cell*] [*NASA*]
HOPE.......... People-to-People Health Foundation (EA)
HOPEC........ Hand-Operated Positive Energy Control
HOPEC........ Hydrogen Organization for Progress, Education, and Cooperation [*Defunct*] (EA)
HOPECO....... Hormoz Petroleum Co. [*Iran*] (BUAC)
Hope Com Law... Hope's Compendium of the Commercial Law of the Pacific [*A publication*] (DLA)
Hope Dec..... Hope (of Kerse). Manuscript Decisions, Scotch Court of Session [*A publication*] (DLA)
Hope Maj Pr... Hope's Major Practicks [*Scotland*] [*A publication*] (DLA)
Hope Min Pr... Hope's Minor Practicks [*Scotland*] [*A publication*] (DLA)
HOPES......... High Oxygen-Pulping Enclosed System (PDAA)
HOPG.......... Highly Oriented Pyrolytic Graphite [*Engineering*]
HOPH.......... Home of Peace Hospitals [*Australia*]
HOPI.......... Handbook of Operating Instructions [*Navy*] (MCD)
HOPI.......... History of Present Illness [*Medicine*] (HGAA)
HOPING....... Helping Other Parents in Normal Grieving (EA)
Hopk.......... Hopkins' New York Chancery Reports [*A publication*] (DLA)
Hopk Adm.... Hopkinson's Pennsylvania Admiralty Judgments [*A publication*] (DLA)
Hopk Adm Dec... Admiralty Decisions of Hopkinson in Gilpin's Reports [*A publication*] (DLA)
Hopk Av...... Hopkins' Average [*4th ed.*] [*1884*] [*A publication*] (DLA)
Hopk CC...... Hopkins' New York Chancery Reports [*A publication*] (DLA)
Hopk Ch...... Hopkins' New York Chancery Reports [*A publication*] (DLA)
Hopk Chanc Rep... Hopkins' New York Chancery Reports [*A publication*] (DLA)
Hopk Judg... Hopkinson's Pennsylvania Admiralty Judgments [*A publication*] (DLA)
Hopk Mar Ins... Hopkins on Marine Insurance [*A publication*] (DLA)
Hopk Rep.... Hopkins' New York Chancery Reports [*A publication*] (DLA)
Hopk W...... Hopkinson's Works [*Pennsylvania*] [*A publication*] (DLA)
Hopk Wks.... Hopkinson's Works [*Pennsylvania*] [*A publication*] (DLA)
Hopk Works (PA)... Hopkinson's Works [*Pennsylvania*] [*A publication*] (DLA)
HOPL.......... History of Programming Languages
HOPM......... Hydraulic Oil Power Module (DNAB)
Hop Min...... Hope's Minor Practicks [*Scotland*] [*A publication*] (DLA)
HOPO......... Holders of Public Office
HOPR......... Holly Holdings, Inc. [*NASDAQ symbol*] (SAG)
HOPR......... Holly Products [*NASDAQ symbol*] (SAG)
HOPRD....... Holly Products 10% Cv'D'Pfd [*NASDAQ symbol*] (TTSB)
HOPRW....... Holly Products Wrrt [*NASDAQ symbol*] (TTSB)
HOPS......... Hart Brewing [*NASDAQ symbol*] (TTSB)
HOPS......... Heineken Operations Planning System [*Heineken USA*]
HOPS......... Helmet-Mounted Optical Projection System
HOPS......... Heterodyne Optical Optimization Communication System with Stops [*NASA*]
HOPS......... HOst Proximity Service [*Computer science*]
HOPT......... Hypoparathyroidism [*Endocrinology*]
Hopw & C.... Hopwood and Coltman's English Registration Appeal Cases [*A publication*] (DLA)
Hopw & Colt... Hopwood and Coltman's English Registration Appeal Cases [*A publication*] (DLA)
Hopw & P.... Hopwood and Philbrick's English Registration Appeal Cases [*A publication*] (DLA)
Hopw & Phil... Hopwood and Philbrick's English Registration Appeal Cases [*A publication*] (DLA)
HOQ.......... Hansard Oral Questions [*Database*] [*House of Commons*] [*Canada*] [*Information service or system*] (CRD)
HOQ.......... Hof [*Germany Airport symbol*] (OAG)
HOQ.......... Home Office Quote (NITA)
HOQ.......... Hysteroid-Obsessoid Questionnaire [*Psychology*]
HOQNO....... Heptyl(hydroxy)quinoline N-Oxide [*Organic chemistry*]
HOR.......... Heliocentric Orbit Rendezvous (MCD)
HOR.......... Hoger Onderwijs Reactor
HOR.......... Holder of Record [*Investment term*]
HOR.......... Home of Record
HOR.......... Hoover-Owens-Rentschler [*Engines*]
HOR.......... Horace [*Roman poet, 65-8BC*] [*Classical studies*] (ROG)
Hor.......... Horayoth (BJA)
HOR.......... Horizon (KSC)

HOR.......... Horizon Air-Taxi Ltd. [*Switzerland ICAO designator*] (FAAC)
HOR.......... Horizontal
hor.......... Horizontal (WDMC)
Hor.......... Horizontal Lights [*Navigation signal*]
HOR.......... Horn & Hardart Co. [*Later, Hanover Direct*] [*AMEX symbol*] (SPSG)
Hor.......... Horologium [*Constellation*]
HOR.......... Horology
HOR.......... Horta [*Azores*] [*Seismograph station code, US Geological Survey*] (SEIS)
HOR.......... Horta [*Azores*] [*Airport symbol*] (OAG)
HOR.......... Hot Resources Ltd. [*Vancouver Stock Exchange symbol*]
HOR.......... Hydrogen-Oxygen Reaction (SAA)
HOR.......... University of Minnesota, the Hormel Institute, Austin, MN [*OCLC symbol*] (OCLC)
HORA......... High Out of Range Alarm [*Electronics*] (ECII)
HORAD....... Horizontal RADAR Display
Hor & Th Cas... Horrigan and Thompson's Cases on Self-Defense [*A publication*] (DLA)
HORA SOM... Hora Somni [*At Bedtime*] [*Latin*] (WDAA)
HORATIO..... Human Operator Response Analyser and Timer for Infrequent Occurrences (PDAA)
Horat Mand... Horatius Mandosius [*Deceased, 1594*] [*Authority cited in pre-1607 legal work*] (DSA)
HOR CL....... Horizontal Clearance [*Nautical charts*]
HORD......... Hordeum [*Barley*] [*Pharmacy*] (ROG)
HOR DECU.. Hora Decubitus [*At Bedtime*] [*Pharmacy*]
HOR DECUB.. Hora Decubitus [*At Bedtime*] [*Pharmacy*] (ROG)
hor decub.... Hora Decubitus [*At Bedtime*] [*Latin*] (WDAA)
HO-RE-CA... Federation Internationale des Organisations d'Hoteliers, Restaurateurs, et Cafetiers [*International Organization of Hotel and Restaurant Associations*] (EAIO)
HORECOM ... International Exhibition for the Hotel and Restaurant Trades Communities
HOREN........ Horizontal Enlarger [*Photography*]
HOREP........ Hot Photographic Report
HOREP........ Hot Report
HOR INTERM... Horis Intermediis [*In the Intermediate Hours*] [*Pharmacy*]
Horitz........ Horizontal (NITA)
HORIZ........ Horizon (MSA)
HORIZ........ Horizontal (AABC)
horiz........ Horizontal (IDOE)
HORIZ........ Horizontal Polarization
HorizFS....... Horizon Financial Services Corp. [*Associated Press*] (SAG)
HorizMH...... Horizon Mental Health Management [*Associated Press*] (SAG)
HoriznGp...... Horizon Group, Inc. [*Associated Press*] (SAG)
HORM......... Hybrid Orbital Rehybridization Method [*Atomic physics*]
Hormel........ Hormel [*George*] & Co. [*Associated Press*] (SAG)
HorMn........ Horace Mann Educators Corp. [*Associated Press*] (SAG)
HORMV....... Hordeum Mosaic Virus [*Plant pathology*]
Horn & H.... Horn and Hurlstone's English Exchequer Reports [*1838-39*] [*A publication*]
Hornbk........ Hornbeck Offshore Services, Inc. [*Associated Press*] (SAG)
Horne Dip.... Horne on Diplomacy [*A publication*] (DLA)
Horne Mir.... Horne's Mirror of Justice [*A publication*] (DLA)
Horne MJ.... Horne's Mirror of Justice [*A publication*] (DLA)
Horner........ Horner's Reports [*11-23 South Dakota*] [*A publication*] (DLA)
Horner's Ann St... Horner's Annotated Revised Statutes [*Indiana*] [*A publication*] (DLA)
Horner's Rev St... Horner's Annotated Revised Statutes [*Indiana*] [*A publication*] (DLA)
HORN GN..... Hornblende Gneisses [*Geology*]
Horo.......... Horologium [*Constellation*]
HOROL....... Horology
Horr & B Mun Ord... Horr and Bemis' Treatise on Municipal Police Ordinances [*A publication*] (DLA)
Horr & T Cas Self-Def... Horrigan and Thompson's Cases on Self-Defense [*A publication*] (DLA)
Horr & Th.... Horrigan and Thompson's Cases on Self-Defense [*A publication*] (DLA)
HORSCERA... House of Representatives Standing Committee on the Environment (EERA)
HORSC-ERA... House of Representatives Standing Committee on the Environment Recreation, and the Arts [*Australia*] (BUAC)
HORSE........ Heavy Operational Repair Squadron Engineer [*Air Force*] (AFM)
HORSE........ Hydrofoil-Operated Rocket Submarine (NATG)
HORSEC....... House of Representatives Standing Committee on Environment and Conservation [*Australia*] (BUAC)
Horsh.......... Horsham Corp. [*Associated Press*] (SAG)
Horshd......... Horsehead Resource Development Company, Inc. [*Associated Press*] (SAG)
HOR SOM.... Hora Somni [*At Bedtime*] [*Pharmacy*]
hort.......... Hortensis [*Of a Garden*] [*Latin*]
HORT......... Horticulture
Hort.......... Horticulture [*A publication*] (BRI)
HORTI........ Horticulture [*Freight*]
HORTIC....... Horticulture
HORTL........ Horticultural
HORU......... Home Office Research Unit (BUAC)
HOR UN SPAT... Horae Unius Spatio [*At the End of an Hour*] [*Pharmacy*]
HOR UN SPATIO... Horae Unius Spatio [*At the End of an Hour*] [*Pharmacy*] (ROG)
HORV......... Hydraulic and Optical Repair Vehicle (PDAA)
Horw YB..... Horwood's Year Books of Edward I [*A publication*] (DLA)
HorzBcTx.... Horizon Bancorp, Inc. (TX) [*Associated Press*] (SAG)
HorznFin...... Horizon Financial Corp. [*Associated Press*] (SAG)
HOS.......... Croatian Defense Association [*Political party*]

HOS .... Hardwire Operating System (IAA)
HOS .... Health Online Service [*Computer science*] [*Medicine*]
HOS .... Heated Oxygen Sensor [*Automotive engineering*]
HOS .... Heat of Solution
HOS .... Heckscher-Ohlin-Samuelson [*Theorem*]
HOS .... Higher Order Software, Inc.
HOS .... High-Order Software [*Computer science*] (NASA)
HOS .... Home Orchard Society (EA)
HOS .... Horizontal Obstacle SONAR (IAA)
HoS .... Horse Serum [*Immunology*]
HOS .... Hosana [*Ethiopia*] [*Airport symbol*] (AD)
Hos .... Hosea [*Old Testament book*]
HOS .... Hosebe, SIC [*Ukraine*] [*FAA designator*] (FAAC)
Hos .... Hostiensis [*Deceased, 1271*] [*Authority cited in pre-1607 legal work*] (DSA)
HOS .... Human Operator Simulator (MCD)
HOS .... Human Osteosarcoma [*Medicine*]
HOS .... Hydrographic Office Scale [*Obsolete*]
HOSA .... Health Occupations Students of America (EA)
HOSA .... Hearing Office Systems Administrator [*Computer science*]
HOSC .... Hardened Operational Site Concept (AAG)
HOSC .... History of Science Cases
HOSC .... Huntsville Operations Support Center [*NASA*] (KSC)
HOSCORP ... New York City Health and Hospitals Corp. (EA)
Hosea .... Hosea's Reports [*Ohio*] [*A publication*] (DLA)
Hosea's Rep.. Cincinnati Superior Court Decisions [*Ohio*] [*A publication*] (DLA)
HOSI .... Handbook of Service Instructions
HOSJ .... Sovereign Hospitaller Order of Saint John (EA)
Hoskins ...... Hoskins' Reports [*2 North Dakota*] [*A publication*] (DLA)
HOSP .... Hospital
hosp .... Hospital (VRA)
Hosp .... Hospital (AL)
HOSP .... Hospital Aircraft [*ICAO designator*] (FAAC)
HOSP .... Hosposable Products [*NASDAQ symbol*] (TTSB)
HOSP .... Hosposable Products, Inc. [*NASDAQ symbol*] (NQ)
HOSP .... Hot Springs National Park
HOSPACT .... Hospital Patient Accounting (PDAA)
Hosp Admin... Hospital Administration [*A publication*]
HOSPCO ...... Hospital Co. [*Marine Corps*]
Hosp Hlth Care... Hospital and Health Care [*A publication*]
Hosp Ins ...... Hospital Insurance (DAVI)
Hosp J .... Hospital Journal [*A publication*]
Hosp J Aust... Hospital Journal of Australia [*A publication*]
Hospos .... Hosposable Products, Inc. [*Associated Press*] (SAG)
HospPT .... Hospitality Properties Trust [*Associated Press*] (SAG)
HOSPRATS... Hospital Rations [*Navy*]
Hosp Sgt...... Hospital Sergeant (GFGA)
HospSt......... Hospital Staffing Services, Inc. [*Associated Press*] (SAG)
HOSPTY....... Hospitality
HospWwde.. Hospitality Worldwide Services, Inc. [*Associated Press*] (SAG)
HOSS .... Halo Orbit Space Station [*NASA*]
HOSS .... Hand Order Transmeter
HOSS .... Homing Optical System Study
HOSS .... Homing System Survey (MCD)
HOSS .... Hornbeck Offshore Services, Inc. [*NASDAQ symbol*] (NQ)
HOSS .... Hydrogen/Oxygen Second Stage (MCD)
HOS-STPL... Hospital Operating System - Structured Programming Language [*Computer science*] (CSR)
HOST .... Amerihost Properties [*NASDAQ symbol*] (TTSB)
HOST .... Amerihost Properties, Inc. [*NASDAQ symbol*] (NQ)
HOST .... Harmonic Optimized Stabilization Technique (IAA)
HOST .... Hawaii Ocean Science and Technology Park [*Research center*] (RCD)
Host............. Hostiensis [*Deceased, 1271*] [*Authority cited in pre-1607 legal work*] (DSA)
HOST .... Hostile
HOST .... Hosting for Overseas Students [*An association*] (BUAC)
HOST .... Hot Spot Tracking (DNAB)
HOST .... Hypo-Osmotic Shock Treatment [*Analytical biochemistry*]
HOSTAC ...... Helicopter Operations from Ships other than Aircraft Carriers [*Supplement*] (DOMA)
HOSTEX ...... Home Study Exchange (EA)
HostFdg ...... Host Funding, Inc. [*Associated Press*] (SAG)
Hosti .... Hostiensis [*Deceased, 1271*] [*Authority cited in pre-1607 legal work*] (DSA)
HOSTID....... Host Identifier (ACRL)
HostM......... Host Marriott Corp. [*Associated Press*] (SAG)
HostMar....... Host Marriott Corp. [*Associated Press*] (SAG)
HostMS....... Host Marriott Services Corp. [*Associated Press*] (SAG)
HOSTS .... Hostess (ROG)
HOSTWOY ... Home of Selection and Completion of Travel within One Year Is Authorized [*Military*]
HOT .... Baltic Airlines Ltd. [*ICAO designator*] (FAAC)
HOT .... Birmingham Aerocentre, Ltd. [*British*] [*FAA designator*] (FAAC)
HOT .... Hand Over Transmitter
HOT .... Hands-on-Training
HOT .... HAT [*Hypoxanthine-Aminopterin-Thymidine*] with Ouabain [*Growth medium*] [*Biochemistry*]
HOT .... Hawaiian Ocean Time Series (USDC)
HOT .... Hawk and Owl Trust (BUAC)
HOT .... High-Subsonic Optically Teleguided [*Antitank system*] (INF)
HOT .... Holographic One-Tube [*Goggles*] (MCD)
HOT .... Holographic-One-Two (PDAA)
HOT .... Home on Target [*Military*] (CAAL)
HOT .... Horizontal Output Transformer

HOT .... Horizontal Output Tube
HOT .... Hot Springs [*Arkansas*] [*Airport symbol*] (OAG)
HOT .... Human Old Tuberculin
HOT .... Hyperbaric Oxygen Therapy [*Medicine*] (DAVI)
HOT .... Hypertension Optimal Treatment [*Antihypertensive medicine*]
HOT .... Starwood Hotels & Resorts [*NYSE symbol*] [*Formerly, HSN, Inc.*] (SG)
HOT .... Starwood Lodging Tr [*NYSE symbol*] (TTSB)
HOT .... Starwood Lodging Trust [*NYSE symbol*] (SAG)
HOT .... Starwood Lodging Trust [*AMEX symbol*] (SAG)
HOTAC .... Helicopter Optical Tracking and Control
HOTAC .... Hotel Accommodation Service [*British*]
HOTAS .... Hands on Throttle and Stick [*Aviation*] (MCD)
HOTBUN ...... Have Not Yet Begun to Fight [*Simulated war game*]
HOTC .... Heart of Texas Conference (PSS)
HOTCE .... Hot Critical Experiments [*Nuclear energy*]
HOTCOG ...... Heart of Texas Council of Governments
HOTEF .... Helicopter Operational Test and Evaluation Flight [*Canadian Navy*]
HOTLIPS ..... Honorary Order of Trumpeters Living in Possible Sin
HOTO .... Health of the Oceans [*Marine science*] (OSRA)
HOTOL .... Horizontal Takeoff and Landing [*Name of proposed aircraft under development by the British government*]
HOTPHOTOREP... Hot Photographic Report (MCD)
HOTRAN ...... Hover and Transition [*Simulator*]
HOTREC ...... Confederation of the National Hotel and Restaurant Associations in the EC (ECED)
HOTS .... Hands-On Training Simulator [*Vehicle*]
HOTS .... Hearing Office Tracking System [*Computer science*]
HOTS .... Higher Order Thinking Skills [*Education*]
HOT-SHOT ... Hydrogen-Oxygen Turbine: Super-High Operating Temperatures [*Hydrogen utilization technology*]
HOTSIT .... Hot Situation (MCD)
HOTT .... Hands-on Turret Trainer [*Military*]
HOTT .... Hot Topic, Inc. [*NASDAQ symbol*] (SAG)
HotTopic ..... Hot Topic, Inc. [*Associated Press*] (SAG)
HOTX .... Hands-On Training Exercise [*Military*] (ADDR)
HOU .... [*William P.*] Hobby Airport [*FAA*] (TAG)
HOU .... Houston [*Texas*] [*Seismograph station code, US Geological Survey*] (SEIS)
HOU .... Houston [*Texas*] [*Airport symbol*]
HOU .... Houston Indus [*NYSE symbol*] (TTSB)
HOU .... Houston Industries, Inc. [*NYSE symbol*] (SPSG)
Hou .... Houston's Delaware Reports [*A publication*] (DLA)
HOU .... United States Department of Housing and Urban Development, Washington, DC [*OCLC symbol*] (OCLC)
Hou Ang Sax Law... Houard's Anglo-Saxon Laws, Etc. [*A publication*] (DLA)
Houard Ang Sax Laws... Houard's Anglo-Saxon Laws [*A publication*] (DLA)
HouB........... Houston Biotechnology, Inc. [*Associated Press*] (SAG)
Houck Mech Lien... Houck on Mechanics' Lien Law [*A publication*] (DLA)
Houck Riv..... Houck on the Law of Navigable Rivers [*A publication*] (DLA)
Hou Dict ...... Houard's Dictionary of the Customs of Normandy [*A publication*] (DLA)
Hough Am Cons... Hough's American Constitutions [*A publication*] (DLA)
Hough CM ... Hough's Military Law and Courts-Martial [*A publication*] (DLA)
Hough C-M Cas... Hough's Court-Martial Case Book [*1821*] [*London*] [*A publication*] (DLA)
Houghtn...... Houghton Pharmaceuticals, Inc. [*Associated Press*] (SAG)
Houghton..... Houghton's Reports [*97 Alabama*] [*A publication*] (DLA)
Hough V-Adm... Reports of Cases in Vice-Admiralty of Province of New York [*1715-88*] [*1925 Reprint*] [*A publication*] (DLA)
HougM........ Houghton Mifflin Co. [*Associated Press*] (SAG)
HouInd........ Houston Industries, Inc. [*Associated Press*] (SAG)
HOUS........... Housing
HOUS........... Housing Division [*Census*] (OICC)
Hous .... Houston's Delaware Reports [*A publication*] (DLA)
Hous & Dev Rep... Housing and Development Reporter [*Bureau of National Affairs*] [*A publication*] (DLA)
HousBio...... Houston Biotechnology, Inc. [*Associated Press*] (SAG)
HOUSE-INFO... Homeowners Using Savings and Energy Information to Negotiate Fair Offers [*Student legal action organization*] (EA)
House Mag.... House Magazine [*A publication*]
House of L... House of Lords Cases [*A publication*] (DLA)
HOUSG .... Housing
HOUSHD...... Household [*Marketing*] (ROG)
HoushInt...... Household International, Inc. [*Associated Press*] (SAG)
Housing & Devel Rep... Housing and Development Reporter [*Bureau of National Affairs*] [*A publication*] (DLA)
Housing Aust... Housing Australia [*A publication*]
Housing Vic... Housing Victoria [*A publication*]
Housing W Aust... Housing Western Australia [*A publication*]
Hous Law ... Houston Lawyer [*A publication*] (DLA)
Hous Life Ass... Houseman's Life Assurance [*9th ed.*] [*1977*] [*A publication*] (DLA)
Hous Pr ...... Housman's Precedents in Conveyancing [*1861*] [*A publication*] (DLA)
Houst........... Houston's Delaware Reports [*A publication*] (DLA)
Houst Cr ...... Houston's Delaware Criminal Cases [*A publication*] (DLA)
Houst Cr Cas.. Houston's Delaware Criminal Cases [*A publication*] (DLA)
Houst Crim Cas... Delaware Criminal Cases [*A publication*] (DLA)
Houst Crim Cases... Delaware Criminal Cases [*A publication*] (DLA)
Houst Crim (Del)... Houston's Delaware Criminal Cases [*A publication*] (DLA)
Houst Crim Rep... Delaware Criminal Cases [*A publication*] (DLA)
Houst Cr Rep... Delaware Criminal Cases [*A publication*] (DLA)
HoustEx...... Houston Exploration Co. (The) [*Associated Press*] (SAG)
HoustInd...... Houston Industries, Inc. [*Associated Press*] (SAG)
Houston ...... Houston's Delaware Supreme Court Reports [*1855-93*] [*A publication*] (DLA)

Houston Law...	Houston Lawyer [*A publication*] (DLA)
Houst St Tr...	Houston's Law of Stoppage in Transitu [*A publication*] (DLA)
HOV	Heat of Vaporization
HOV	High Occupancy Vehicle [*Commuter routes*] [*Acronym usually followed by a number indicating the minimum number of people per vehicle*]
HOV	Homogeneity of Variance [*Statistics*]
Hov	Hovenden on Frauds [*A publication*] (DLA)
Hov	Hovenden's Supplement to Vesey, Jr.'s, English Chancery Reports [*1789-1817*] [*A publication*] (DLA)
HOV	Hovercraft [*Military British*]
HOV	Hovnanian Enterpr CI'A' [*AMEX symbol*] (TTSB)
HOV	Hovnanian Enterprises, Inc. [*AMEX symbol*] (SPSG)
HOV	Orsta/Volda [*Norway*] [*Airport symbol*] (OAG)
HOV	United States Department of Housing and Urban Development, Region I, Boston, MA [*OCLC symbol*] (OCLC)
HOV	Wichita, KS [*Location identifier FAA*] (FAAL)
Hov Ann	Hoveden's Annals [*A publication*] (DLA)
HOVE	Hovenweep National Monument
Hoved	Hoveden's Chronica [*A publication*] (DLA)
Hov Fr	Hovenden on Frauds [*A publication*] (DLA)
HOVI	Handbook of Overhaul Instructions [*Navy*]
HOVI	Hopewell Village National Historic Site
Hovis	Hominis Vis [*The Strength of Man*] [*Latin*]
HovnEn	Hovnanian Enterprises, Inc. [*Associated Press*] (SAG)
Hov Sup	Hovenden's Supplement to Vesey, Jr.'s, English Chancery Reports [*1789-1817*] [*A publication*] (DLA)
Hov Supp	Hovenden's Supplement to Vesey, Jr.'s, English Chancery Reports [*1789-1817*] [*A publication*] (DLA)
HOVVAC	Hovering Vehicle Versatile Automatic Control
HOW	Handicapped Organized Women [*In association name, HOW, Inc.*] (EA)
HOW	Hand over Word
HOW	Hands Off Our Water [*An association*] (BUAC)
HOW	Happiness of Womanhood [*Also known as LOH*] [*Defunct*]
HOW	Healing Our World [*An association*]
HOW	Help Our World
HOW	Hercules on Water [*Aircraft*] (MCD)
HOW	High-Order Word (SSD)
HOW	Home Owners Warranty [*National Association of Home Builders*]
How	Howard's New York Practice Reports [*A publication*] (DLA)
How	Howard's Reports [*2-8 Mississippi*] [*A publication*] (DLA)
How	Howard's United States Supreme Court Reports [*42-65 United States*] [*A publication*] (DLA)
HOW	Howell Indus [*AMEX symbol*] (TTSB)
HOW	Howell Industries, Inc. [*AMEX symbol*] (SPSG)
How	Howell's Reports [*22-26 Nevada*] [*A publication*] (DLA)
HOW	Howitzer (KSC)
HOW	Howrah [*India*] [*Seismograph station code, US Geological Survey*] (SEIS)
HO-W	Hydrographic Office-Washington, DC [*Terminated, 1963; later, NOO*] [*Navy*] (MCD)
How A Cas...	Howard's New York Appeal Cases [*A publication*] (DLA)
How & Beat...	Howell and Beatty's Reports [*22 Nevada*] [*A publication*] (DLA)
How & H St..	Howard and Hutchinson's Mississippi Statutes [*A publication*] (DLA)
How & N......	Howell and Norcross' Reports [*23, 24 Nevada*] [*A publication*] (DLA)
How & Nor...	Howell and Norcross' Reports [*23, 24 Nevada*] [*A publication*] (DLA)
How Ann St..	Howell's Annotated Statutes [*Michigan*] [*A publication*] (DLA)
How App......	Howard's New York Appeal Cases [*A publication*] (DLA)
How App Cas...	Howard's New York Court of Appeals Cases [*A publication*] (DLA)
How App Cases...	Howard's New York Court of Appeals Cases [*A publication*] (DLA)
Howard........	Howard's Mississippi Supreme Court Reports [*1834-43*] [*A publication*] (DLA)
Howard Pr...	Howard's New York Practice Reports [*A publication*] (DLA)
Howard Pr Rep...	Howard's New York Practice Reports [*A publication*] (DLA)
Howard Rep...	Howard's United States Supreme Court Reports [*A publication*] (DLA)
Howard SC...	United States Reports [*Vols. 42-65*] [*A publication*] (DLA)
Howard's Prac Reports...	Howard's New York Practice Reports [*A publication*] (DLA)
Howard's Practice...	Howard's New York Practice Reports [*A publication*] (DLA)
Howard's Spec Term Rep...	Howard's New York Practice Reports [*A publication*] (DLA)
Howard U	Howard University (GAGS)
HOWBTRY ...	Howitzer Battery (DNAB)
How C.........	Howard's Irish Chancery Practice [*A publication*] (DLA)
How Cas......	Howard's New York Court of Appeals Cases [*A publication*] (DLA)
How Cas......	Howard's Property Cases [*A publication*] (DLA)
How Ch.......	Howard's Irish Chancery Practice [*A publication*] (DLA)
How Ch P...	Howard's Irish Chancery Practice [*A publication*] (DLA)
How Ch Pr...	Howard's Irish Chancery Practice [*A publication*] (DLA)
How Cr Tr...	Howison's Virginia Criminal Trials [*A publication*] (DLA)
How Ct App Cas...	Howard's New York Court of Appeals Cases [*A publication*] (DLA)
How EE.......	Howard's Irish Equity Exchequer Reports [*A publication*] (DLA)
Howell NP ...	Howell's Nisi Prius Reports [*Michigan*] [*A publication*] (DLA)
Howell St Tr...	Howell's English State Trials [*1163-1820*] [*A publication*] (DLA)
Howe Pr	Howe's Practice [*Massachusetts*] [*A publication*] (DLA)
How Eq Exch...	Howard's Irish Equity Exchequer Reports [*A publication*] (DLA)
How J........	Howard Journal [*A publication*] (DLA)
HOWL	Hands Off Wildlife [*British*] (DI)
HOWL	Help Our Wolves Live
HowlC........	Howell Corp. [*Associated Press*] (SAG)
HowlCp.......	Howell Corp. [*Associated Press*] (SAG)
Howl In........	Howell Industries, Inc. [*Associated Press*] (SAG)
How L Rev...	Howard Law Review [*A publication*] (DLA)
HOWLS.......	Hostile Weapons Locator Study [*DARPA/Army*] (MCD)
How NP (Mich)...	Howell's Nisi Prius Reports [*Michigan*] [*A publication*] (DLA)
How NS	Howard's New York Practice Reports, New Series [*A publication*] (DLA)
How (NY)....	Howard's New York Practice Reports [*A publication*] (DLA)
How Pat......	Howson on Patents [*A publication*] (DLA)
How Po Ca...	Howard's Property Cases [*A publication*] (DLA)
How Po Cas..	Howard's Irish Property Cases [*1720-73*] [*A publication*] (DLA)
How Pr	Howard's New York Practice Reports [*A publication*] (DLA)
How Prac.....	Howard's New York Practice Reports [*A publication*] (DLA)
How Prac NS...	Howard's New York Practice Reports, New Series [*A publication*] (DLA)
How Prac (NY)...	Howard's New York Practice Reports [*A publication*] (DLA)
How Prac Rep...	Howard's New York Practice Reports [*A publication*] (DLA)
How Pr NS...	Howard's New York Practice Reports, New Series [*A publication*] (DLA)
How Prob Pr...	Howell's Probate Practice [*Ontario, Canada*] [*A publication*] (DLA)
How Pr Rep...	Howard's New York Practice Reports [*A publication*] (DLA)
How Pr Sup C...	Howard's New York Practice Reports [*A publication*] (DLA)
HOWR.......	However
Howr..........	Howitzer [*British military*] (DMA)
How SC.......	Howard's United States Supreme Court Reports [*A publication*] (DLA)
Hows Pat.....	Howson on Patents [*A publication*] (DLA)
HOWSR.......	Howsoever (ROG)
Hows Reis Pat...	Howson on Reissued Patents [*A publication*] (DLA)
How St.......	Howell's Annotated Statutes [*Michigan*] [*A publication*] (DLA)
How State Tr...	Howell's English State Trials [*1163-1820*] [*A publication*] (DLA)
How St Tr	Howell's English State Trials [*1163-1820*] [*A publication*] (DLA)
HOWT	Howard Terminal [*Later, HT*] [*AAR code*]
HOWT	Howtek Inc. [*NASDAQ symbol*] (TTSB)
Howtek.......	Howtek, Inc. [*Associated Press*] (SAG)
HOW-TO	Housing Operation with Training Opportunity [*Office of Economic Opportunity*]
How US	Howard's United States Supreme Court Reports [*A publication*] (DLA)
HOX	Homeobox [*Genetics*]
HOX	New Orleans, LA [*Location identifier FAA*] (FAAL)
HOY	Hoy Island [*Scotland*] [*Airport symbol Obsolete*] (OAG)
Hoyt Comp L..	Hoyt's Compiled Laws of Arizona [*A publication*] (DLA)
HOZ	Horizontal
HP	Air Hawaii [*ICAO designator*] (AD)
HP	ALAS, SA [*Uruguay*] [*ICAO designator*] (ICDA)
HP	All India Reporter, Himachal Pradesh [*A publication*] (DLA)
HP	America West Airlines [*ICAO designator*] (AD)
HP	Haemophilus Pleuropneumoniae (DB)
HP	Half Pay
HP	Half Plate [*Photography*]
HP	Half Price (ROG)
HP	Handicapped Person
H-P	Handley-Page Ltd.
HP	Handling and Propulsion (AAG)
HP	Handling Procedure (MCD)
HP	Handmade Paper
HP	Handpainted (WGA)
Hp	Haptoglobin [*Hematology*]
HP	Hard Plastic [*Doll collecting*]
HP	Hard Point
HP	Hardy Perennial [*Horticulture*] (ROG)
HP	Harmonic Progression
Hp	Harp [*Music*]
HP	Hauptpunkte [*Crystallography*]
HP	Haustus Purgans [*Purging Draught*] [*Pharmacy*] (ROG)
HP	Haut Parleur [*Loudspeaker*] [*French*]
HP	Hawker Siddeley Aviation Ltd. [*British ICAO aircraft manufacturer identifier*] (ICAO)
HP	Hay-Pasturage [*Agriculture*]
HP	Hazard Prevention [*A publication*] (EAAP)
HP	Head Postmaster [*British*] (DCTA)
HP	Headquarters Pamphlet [*Military*] (MCD)
HP	Healthcare Product
HP	Health Physics [*Nuclear energy*] (NRCH)
hp	Heaping (STED)
HP	Heating Plant (NATG)
HP	Heenan Petroleum Ltd. [*Toronto Stock Exchange symbol*]
HP	Height of Perigee
HP	Heir Presumptive
HP	Helicopter (NATG)
HP	Heliodor [*Record label*] [*Great Britain*]
HP	Hellas Planitia [*A filamentary mark on Mars*]
HP	Helmerich & Payne [*NYSE symbol*] (TTSB)
HP	Helmerich & Payne, Inc. [*NYSE symbol*] (SPSG)
Hp	Hematoporphyrin (STED)
HP	Hemel Hempstead [*Postcode*] (ODBW)
H/P	Hemipelvectomy [*Medicine*]
Hp	Hemiplegia [*Medicine*]
HP	Henderson & Pollard Ltd. [*New Zealand*]
HP	Heptode [*Electronics*] (IAA)
Hp	Heptyl [*Biochemistry*]
HP	Hesperian Foundation (EA)
HP	Hewlett-Packard Co.
HP	Hexamethylmelamine and Cisplatin [*Cisplatinum*] [*Antineoplastic drug*] (DAVI)

HP............ Hiding Power [*Paint technology*]
HP............ Highest Possible (ROG)
HP............ Highly Purified
HP............ High Pass [*Electronics*]
HP............ High Performance
H/P............ High Position (MDG)
HP............ High-Positive (MDG)
HP............ High-Potency [*Pharmacy*]
HP............ High Power
HP............ High Pressure
h-p............ High-Pressure (IDOE)
HP............ High-Pressure Cylinder [*Especially, a locomotive cylinder*]
HP............ High Priest
HP............ High Priority
HP............ High Protein [*Nutrition*]
H-P............ High Purity
HP............ High Purity (AAEL)
HP............ Hippocampal Pyramidal Cell [*Neuroanatomy*]
HP............ Hire Purchase
HP............ Historical Period [*Dialog*] [*Searchable field*] [*Information service or system*] (NITA)
HP............ Hit by Pitcher [*Baseball*]
HP............ Holding Pattern [*Aviation*]
HP............ Holding Pipette
HP............ Holding Potential [*Neurophysiology*]
HP............ Holiday Pay [*Army*] (AABC)
HP............ Holiday Project (EA)
HP............ Hollow Point Bullet
HP............ Homeland Party [*Afghanistan*] [*Political party*] (BUAC)
HP............ Homeopathic Pharmacopoeia
HP............ Horizontal Parallax [*Navigation*]
HP............ Horizontal Polarization
HP............ Horsepower
hp............ Horsepower (IDOE)
HP............ Hospital Participation [*Blood program*] [*Red Cross*]
HP............ Host Processor
HP............ Hot Pack [*or Pad*] [*Physical therapy*]
HP............ Hot Pilot [*An egotistic flying cadet*] [*Slang Air Force*]
HP............ Hot-Pressed [*Paper*]
HP............ House Painter (ROG)
HP............ House Physician
HP............ Houses of Parliament [*British*]
HP............ Humanist Party [*Australia Political party*]
HP............ Human Pituitary [*Endocrinology*] (MAE)
HP............ Human Plasma [*Hematology*]
HP............ Human Potential (DHP)
HP............ Humeral Plate [*Entomology*]
HP............ Hundred Pounds
HP............ Hunger Project (EA)
HP............ Hydraulic Platform (WDAA)
HP............ Hydrocollator Pack [*Physical therapy*] (DAVI)
HP............ Hydrogen Purge (MCD)
HP............ Hydrophilic Petrolatum [*Pharmacology*] (DAVI)
HP............ Hydrostatic Pressure
HP............ Hydroxyproline [*An amino acid*]
HP............ Hygroscopicity Potential (PDAA)
HP............ Hyperparathyroidism [*or Hyperthyroidism*] [*Endocrinology*]
HP............ Hyperphoria
HP............ Hyperpolarization
HP............ Hypersensitivity Pneumonitis [*Medicine*]
HP............ Hypertension and Proteinuria [*Medicine*]
HP............ Hypertransfused Polycythemic [*Medicine*]
HP............ Hypophsrynx [*Qtorhinolaryngology*] (DAVI)
HP............ Hysterical Personality
HP............ Perigee Altitude (NASA)
HP............ Smith & Nephew Pharmaceuticals Ltd. [*Great Britain*] [*Research code symbol*]
HPA............ Handley Page Association [*British*] (DBA)
HPA............ Head of a Procuring Activity [*Army*] (AABC)
HPA............ Head Post Assembly
HPA............ Head Postmen's Association [*A union*] [*British*]
HPA............ Heads of Procuring Activities (MCD)
HPA............ Health Policy Agenda for the American People (HCT)
HPA............ Health Projects Abroad [*An association*] (BUAC)
HPA............ Hearth Products Association (NTPA)
HPA............ Hectopascal [*ICAO designator*] (FAAC)
HPA............ Hemagglutinating Penicillin Antibody [*Medicine*] (DB)
HPA............ Hen Packers Association [*British*] (DBA)
HPA............ Heritage Preservation Association (WDAA)
HPA............ Heteropoly Acid [*Inorganic chemistry*]
HPA............ Heteropolyanion (DB)
HPA............ Heuristic Path Algorithm
HPA............ High-Power Amplifier
HPA............ High-Pressure Air
HPA............ Historical Preservation of America [*Publisher*] (EA)
HPA............ Holding and Positioning Aid (IEEE)
HPA............ Horizontal Planar Array (CAAL)
HPA............ Hospital Physicians Association [*British*]
HPA............ Hospital Presidents Association (NTPA)
HPA............ Host Processor Adapter (IAA)
HPA............ House Plants Australia
HPA............ Human Papillomavirus [*or Parvovirus*] (MAE)
HPA............ Hurlingham Polo Association [*Midhurst, Sussex, England*] (EAIO)
HPA............ Hybridization Protection Assay [*Analytical biochemistry*]
HPA............ Hydraulic Pneumatic Area (AAG)

HPA............ Hydroxyphenylacetic Acid [*Biochemistry*] (DB)
HPA............ Hydroxypropyl Acrylate [*Organic chemistry*]
HPA............ Hypothalamic-Pituitary-Adrenal [*Axis*] [*Endocrinology*] (DAVI)
HPA............ Hypothalamic-Pituitary-Adrenocortical [*Endocrinology*]
HPA............ Lifuka [*Tonga Islands*] [*Airport symbol*] (OAG)
HPA............ Pearl Airways Compagne Haitienne [*Haiti*] [*ICAO designator*] (FAAC)
HPAA............ High-Performance Antenna Assembly (MHDI)
HPAA............ High-Pressure Air Accumulator
HPAA............ Hispanic Public Affairs Association (EA)
HPAA............ Housing Pressure Altitude Advance [*Automotive engineering*]
HPAA............ Hydroperoxyarachidonic Acid (STED)
HPAA............ Hydroxyphenylacetic Acid [*Biochemistry*] (MAE)
HPAA............ Hyoothalamo-Pituitary-Adrenal Axis (STED)
HPAAS............ High-Performance Aerial Attack System (MCD)
HPAC............ Health Policy Advisory Center (EA)
HPAC............ High-Performance Affinity Chromatography
HPAC............ High-Pressure Air Compressor (NVT)
HP/A/C............ Home Port/Area/City [*Code*] [*Navy*] (DNAB)
H-PAC............ Human-Piloted Alien Craft [*Flying saucer*]
HPAC............ Hydropress Accessory [*Tool*] (AAG)
HPAC............ Hypothalamo-Pituitary-Adreno-Cortical [*Medicine*] (DMAA)
HPAD............ Host Packet Assembler/Disassembler (ACRL)
HPAE............ High-pH Anion-Exchange [*Analytical chemistry*]
HPAEC............ High pH Anion Exchange Chromatography
HPAF............ Hydraulic Performance Analysis Facility (MCD)
HPAG............ High-Performance Air-to-Ground
HPAH............ Hydroxy Polycyclic Aromatic Hydrocarbon [*Environmental chemistry*]
HPAL............ High Plains Agriculture Laboratory [*University of Nebraska - Lincoln*] [*Research center*] (RCD)
HP & A............ Hull Propulsion and Auxiliaries [*Navy*] (DNAB)
HP&R............ Highway Planning and Research [*MTMC*] (TAG)
HPANH............ Hydroxy Polycyclic Aromatic Nitrogen Heterocycle [*Environmental chemistry*]
HPAP............ Human Placental Alkaline Phosphatase [*An enzyme*]
HPAR............ Air-Resistance Horsepower [*Automotive engineering*]
HPAS............ High-Performance Adhesive System
HPASH............ Hydroxy Polycyclic Aromatic Sulfur Heterocycle [*Environmental chemistry*]
HPB............ Handmaids of the Precious Blood [*Roman Catholic religious order*]
HPB............ Hand-Printed Books
HPB............ Harbor Patrol Boat
HPB............ Helena Petrovna Blavatsky [*Famous 19th-century occultist*]
HPB............ Hepatobiliary [*Medicine*] (DMAA)
HPB............ High-Probability Behavior
HPB............ Hinged Plotting Board
HPB............ Hooper Bay [*Alaska*] [*Airport symbol*] (OAG)
HPBC............ Home Port Bancorp [*NASDAQ symbol*] (TTSB)
HPBC............ Home Port Bancorp, Inc. [*NASDAQ symbol*] (CTT)
HPBC............ Hyperpolarizing Bipolar Cell [*In the retina*]
HPBF............ Hepatotrophic Portal Blood Factor [*Medicine*] (DMAA)
HPBL............ Human Peripheral Blood Leukocyte
HPBN............ Hot-Pressed Boron Nitride [*Materials science and technology*]
HPBVWA............ High-Power Broadband Vehicular Whip Antenna [*Army*]
HPBW............ Half-Power Beamwidth [*or Bandwidth*] (IEEE)
HPC............ Hale's Pleas of the Crown [*England*] [*A publication*] (DLA)
HPC............ Handheld PC [*Personal Computer*]
HPC............ Hard Processing Channel (IAA)
HPC............ Hawkins' Pleas of the Crown [*England*] [*A publication*] (DLA)
HPC............ Health Physics Center [*Nuclear energy*] (NRCH)
HPC............ Health Policy Council [*Defunct*] (EA)
HPC............ Helicopter Performance Computer (NG)
HPC............ Helicopter Plane Commander
HPC............ Hemangiopericytoma (STED)
HPC............ Hematopoietic Progenitor Cell [*Hematology*]
HPC............ Hemipalmitoylcarnitinium [*Biochemistry*]
HPC............ Hemisphere Publishing Co.
HPC............ Hercules, Inc. [*Formerly, Hercules Powder Co.*] [*NYSE symbol*] (SPSG)
HPC............ Hereditary Prostate Cancer [*Medicine*]
HPC............ High Performance Computing (EGAO)
HPC............ High Point College [*North Carolina*]
HPC............ High-Pressure Compressor (MCD)
HPC............ High-Pressure Constant (DNAB)
HPC............ Hindustan Paper Corp. [*India*] (BUAC)
HPC............ Hippocampal Pyramidal Cell [*Neuroanatomy*]
HP/C............ Hippocampus [*Brain anatomy*]
HPC............ History of Present Complaint [*Medicine*] (STED)
HPC............ Hobart Peace Centre [*Australia*]
HPC............ Home Policy Committee of War Cabinet [*British World War II*]
HPC............ Hope, AR [*Location identifier FAA*] (FAAL)
HPC............ Horticultural Policy Council (EERA)
HPC............ Hot Pipe Chase [*Nuclear energy*] (NRCH)
HPC............ Howard Payne College [*Texas*]
HPC............ Hydraulic Package Container
HPC............ Hydraulic Piston Corer
HPC............ Hydroxyphenylcinchoninic Acid [*Pharmacology*]
HPC............ Hydroxypropylcellulose [*Organic chemistry*]
HPCA............ High-Performance Communications Adapter
HPCA............ High Performance Computing Act (TNIG)
HPCA............ Hiroshima Peace Center Associates [*Defunct*] (EA)
HPCA............ Housing Pressure Cold Advance [*Automotive engineering*]
HPCblack............ Hard Processing Channel Black (EDCT)
HPCBR............ High-Pressure Chamber
HPCC............ High Performance Computing and Communication [*Computer science*]

HPCC .... High-Performance Computing and Communications [*Computer science*] (EERA)
HPCC .... High-Performance Computing and Communications Program [*Department of Energy*]
HPCC .... High Performance Computing and Communications Program and Information Technology (USDC)
HPCC .... High-Performance Control Center [*Aerospace*] (AAG)
HPCE .... High-Performance Capillary Electrophoresis [*Analytical biochemistry*]
HPCF .... High-Performance Carbon Fiber [*Materials science*]
HPCHD .... Harpsichord [*Music*]
HPCI .... High-Pressure Coolant Injection [*Nuclear energy*] (NRCH)
HPCIS .... High-Pressure Coolant Injection System [*Nuclear energy*] (NRCH)
HPCL .... Hewlett-Packard Control Language [*Computer science*] (DDC)
HPCL .... Hindustan Petroleum Corp. Ltd. [*India*] (BUAC)
HPcL .... Leeward Community College, Pearl City, HI [*Library symbol Library of Congress*] (LCLS)
HPCM .... Human Placenta Conditioned Medium
HPCM .... Hybrid Pulse Code Modulation (PDAA)
HPCO .... High-Pressure Cut-Off [*Air conditioning systems*] [*Automotive engineering*]
HPCPC .... High-Performance Centrifugal Partition Chromatography
HPCRB .... Hydraulic Power Control Relay Box
HPCRC .... High-Performance Computer and Research Center [*Department of Energy*]
HPCS .... High-Pressure Core Spray [*Nuclear energy*] (NRCH)
HPCUS .... Homeopathic Pharmacopoeia Convention of the United States
HP CYL .... High-Pressure Cylinder (WDAA)
HPD .... Dialysate of Hydropenic Plasma [*Hematology*] (DAVI)
HPD .... Haloperidol [*Tranquilizer*]
HPD .... Hammerson Properties Investment & Development Corp. Ltd. [*Toronto Stock Exchange symbol*]
HPD .... Hand-Point Defense [*Military*] (IIA)
HPD .... Hard Point Defense
hpd .... Harpsichord (WDAA)
HPD .... Hearing Protection Device
HPD .... Hematoporphyrin Derivative [*Antineoplastic compound*]
HPD .... Highly Probably Drink [*Chemical depedency*] (DAVI)
HPD .... High-Performance Drone
HPD .... High-Power Density
HPD .... High-Pressure Drain (DNAB)
HPD .... High-Protein Diet
HPD .... Home Peritoneal Dialysis [*Nephrology*] (DAVI)
HPD .... Horizontal Polar Diagram
H-PD .... Hough-Powell Digitizer
HPD .... Hourly Precipitation Data [*A publication*]
HPD .... Hydraulic Pump Discharge (AAG)
HPD .... Hydraulic Pump Drive [*Mechanical engineering*]
HPDC .... High Pressure Data Center [*National Institute of Standards and Technology Information service or system*] (IID)
HPDF .... High-Performance Demonstration Facility
HPDF .... Horizontal Payloads Processing Facility
HPDGF .... Human Platelet-Derived Growth Factor [*Biochemistry*]
HP-DHA .... High-Purity Dual Hardness Armor (KSC)
HPDI .... Hard Point Defense Interceptor
HPDIM .... Hard Point Defense Intercept Missile (MCD)
HPDLRL .... High-Power Diffraction Limited Raman LASER
HPDM .... High-Performance Demonstration Motor (MCD)
HPDO .... Hadia People's Democratic Organisation [*Ethiopia*]
HPDO .... High Performance Diesel Oil (PDAA)
HPDP .... Hispanic Policy Development Project (EA)
HPDPI .... Health Promotion and Disease Prevention Initiative [*Pronounced "hippy dippy"*] [*Department of Health and Human Services*]
HpD-PT .... Hepatoporphyrin Derivative-Phototherapy [*Medicine*]
HPDS .... Hard Point Defense System
HPE .... Harbor Patrol Element [*Navy*] (VNW)
HPE .... Heat-Producing Element
HPE .... Heptasaccharide Phytoalexin Elicitor [*Organic chemistry*]
HPE .... High-Performance Estate Wagon [*Automobile model designation*]
HPE .... High-Power Effects [*Radio interference*]
HPE .... History and Physical Examination [*Medicine*]
HPE .... Holoprosencephaly [*Medicine*]
HPE .... Hope [*Amateur radio shorthand*] (WDAA)
HPcL .... Human Proenkephalin [*Biochemistry*]
HPE .... Hydrogenous Polyethylene
HPE .... Inomeni Parataksis Ethnikofronon [*United Front of Nationalists*] [*Political party*] (PPE)
HPEC .... Handicraft Promotion and Export Centre [*Afghanistan*] (BUAC)
HPEC .... High-Productivity Energy Crop
HPEC .... Hydroxpropylethylcellulose (DB)
HP EGS .... Hewlett Packard Engineering Graphics System (NITA)
HPEK .... Paul B. Elder Co. [*Research code symbol*]
HPEL .... Horn Point Environmental Laboratories [*University of Maryland*] (PDAA)
HPEM .... Hybrid Plasma Equipment Model (AAEL)
HPEO .... Protonous Poly(ethylene oxide) [*Organic chemistry*]
HPER .... Hastings and Prince Edward Regiment [*British military*] (DMA)
HPER .... Health, Physical Education, and Recreation
HPERD .... Health, Physical Education, Recreation, and Dance (AEE)
HPES .... Human Performance Enhancement System [*Engineering*]
HPETE .... Hydroxyperoxyeicosatetraenoic Acid [*Biochemistry*]
HPEW .... High-Powered Early Warning
HPF .... Hammond, LA [*Location identifier FAA*] (FAAL)
HPF .... Harbor Patrol Fleet
HPF .... Hazardous Processing Facility (SSD)
HPF .... Heat Pipe Furnace

HPF .... Heparin-Precipitable Fraction (MAE)
HPF .... Hepatic Plasma Flow [*Medicine*] (DMAA)
HPF .... Highest Possible [*or Probable*] Frequency [*Electronics*]
hpf .... Highest Possible Frequency (WDMC)
HPF .... High Pass Filter
HPF .... High Performance FORTRAN [*Computer language*]
HPF .... High-Power Field [*Microscopy*]
HPF .... High-Protein Fraction [*Food technology*]
HPF .... Historic Preservation Fund [*National Trust for Historic Preservation*]
HPF .... Historic Pullman Foundation (EA)
HPF .... Horace Plunkett Foundation for Cooperative Studies (BUAC)
HPF .... Horizontal Position Finder (IAA)
HPF .... Horizontal Processing Facility [*Operation and Checkout*] [*NASA*] (NASA)
HPF .... Host Preparation Facility (MHDI)
HPF .... Hot-Pressed Ferrite (IAA)
HPF .... Human Powered Flight (DICI)
HPF .... Hypocaloric Protein Feeding (DB)
HPFC .... High-Performance Fuel Cell
HPFF .... High Pressure Fluid-Filled
HPFH .... Hereditary Persistence of Fetal Hemoglobin [*Hematology*]
HPFL .... Highpass Filter (MSA)
HPFL .... High-Performance Fuels Laboratory
HPFL .... Holly Park Field Laboratory [*University of Nevada - Reno*] [*Research center*] (RCD)
HPFM .... Hydropress Form [*Tool*] (AAG)
HPFP .... High-Pressure Fire Protection (NRCH)
HPFP .... High-Pressure Fuel Pump (KSC)
HPFS .... High-Performance File System [*Computer science*]
hPFSH .... Human Pituitary Follicle-Stimulating Hormone [*Endocrinology*] (MAE)
HPFSH .... Human Pituitary Follicle-Stimulating Hormone [*Medicine*] (STED)
HPFSH .... Human Pituitary Gonadotropin (DB)
HPFT .... High-Pressure Fuel Turbopump [*Aerospace*] (NAKS)
HPFTP .... High-Pressure Fuel Turbopump (NASA)
HPG .... Harvard Presentation Graphics [*Software Publishing Corp.*] [*Computer software*]
HPG .... Heritage Propane Partners LP [*NYSE symbol*] (SAG)
HPG .... High-Power Generator
HPG .... High-Power Ground (IAA)
HPG .... High-Power Group
HPG .... High-Pressure Gas (KSC)
HPG .... High-Pressure Gelatine (IAA)
HPG .... Homopolar Generator [*To power high-technology experiments*]
HPG .... Horticultural Postharvest Group [*Queensland, Australia*]
HPG .... Human Pituitary Gonadotrophin [*Endocrinology*]
hPG .... Human Pituitary Gonadotropin [*Medicine*] (STED)
HPG .... Hydroxypropyl Guar [*Organic chemistry*]
HPG .... Hyperpure Germanium [*Also, HpGe*] [*Chemistry*]
HPG .... Hypothalamic, Pituitary, Gonadal [*Endocrinology*]
HPG .... p-Hydroxyphenylglycine (DB)
HPGC .... Heading per Gyro Compass [*Navigation*]
HPGC .... Hypopressure Gas Chromatography
HPGe .... High Purity Germanium (STED)
HpGe .... Hyperpure Germanium [*Also, HPG*] [*Chemistry*]
HPGF .... Hybridoma/Plasmacytome Growth Factor [*Biochemistry*]
HPGL .... Gross Load Horsepower [*Automotive engineering*]
HPGL .... Hewlett-Packard Graphics Language
HPGMI .... Hunter Postgraduate Medical Institute [*Australia*]
HPGPM .... Hits per Gun per Minute (NVT)
hpGRF .... Human Pancreas Growth Hormone-Releasing Factor [*Immunochemistry*]
HPGS .... High-Performance Graphics System [*Computer science*] (MHDB)
HPGS .... High-Pressure Gas System (NASA)
HPH .... Halothane-Percent-Hour (STED)
HPH .... Harnischfeger Indus [*NYSE symbol*] (TTSB)
HPH .... Harnischfeger Industries [*NYSE symbol*] (SAG)
HPH .... High-Performance Hoist (MCD)
HPH .... High-Pressure Hose
HPH .... Horsepower-Hour
HPHC .... Harvard Pilgrim Health Care
HPHD .... High-Pressure High-Density
HPHF .... Hereditary Persistence of Hemoglobin F [*Genetics*] (DOG)
HPHP .... Hydroxypivalyl Hydroxypivalate [*Organic chemistry*]
HP-HR .... Horsepower-Hour
HPHT .... High Pressure High Temperature [*Engineering*]
HPI .... Cleveland, OH [*Location identifier FAA*] (FAAL)
HPI .... Handicap Problems Inventory [*Psychology*]
HPI .... Hardwood Plywood Institute [*Later, HPMA*] (EA)
HPI .... Health Practices Inventory (EDAC)
HPI .... Health Professionals [*AMEX symbol*] (TTSB)
HPI .... Health Professionals, Inc. [*AMEX symbol*] (SPSG)
HPI .... Health Promotion Institute (EA)
HPI .... Heavy Positive Ion
HPI .... Heifer Project International (EA)
HPI .... Height-Position Indicator (DEN)
HPI .... Hellenic Purchasing Institute (BUAC)
HPI .... Helpful Programs, Inc. [*Computer science*]
HPI .... Hepatic Perfusion Index [*Medicine*] (DMAA)
HPI .... Heston Personality Inventory [*Test*] (STED)
HPI .... High-Performance Insulation (MCD)
HPI .... High Performance Isolation (AAEL)
HPI .... High-Power Illuminator (NATG)
HPI .... High-Pressure Injection [*Nuclear energy*] (NRCH)
HPI .... History of Present Illness
HPI .... Hogan Personality Inventory [*Test*] (TMMY)

HPI.............. Homing Position Indicator (NATG)

HPI.............. Hours Post Inoculation

HPI.............. Howe Peak [*Idaho*] [*Seismograph station code, US Geological Survey*] (SEIS)

HPI.............. Hull Product Improvement [*Navy*] (CAAL)

HPI.............. Human Productivity Institute (EA)

HPI.............. Human Proinsulin (DB)

HPI.............. Human Protein Index (DB)

HPI.............. Hydraulic Pressure Indicator

HPI.............. Hydrocarbon Processing Industry

HPIA.............. (Hydroxyphenylisopropyl)adenosine

HP-IB.............. Hewlett-Packard Interface Bus [*Instrumentation*]

HPIC.............. Health Promotion Information Centre (BUAC)

HPIC.............. Hearing Performance Inventory for Children

HPIC.............. High-Performance Immunoaffinity Chromatography

HPIEC.......... High-Performance Ion Exchange Chromatography

HPIEC.......... High-Pressure Ion Exchange Chromatography

HP IL.............. Hewlett Packard Interface Loop (NITA)

HPIM.............. High-Pressure Injection Molding (EDCT)

HPI-MSRG ... Human Performance International, Motor Sport Research Group [*Research center*] (RCD)

HPIP .... High-Pressure Intensifier Pump

HPIP .... Houghton Pharmaceuticals [*NASDAQ symbol*] (TTSB)

HPIP .... Houghton Pharmaceuticals, Inc. [*NASDAQ symbol*] (SAG)

HPIR .... High-Power Illuminator RADAR [*Army*] (AABC)

HPIR .... High-Probability-of-Intercept Receiver [*Telecommunications*] (IEEE)

HPIS .... High-Performance Insulation System

HPIS .... High-Pressure Injection System [*Nuclear energy*] (NRCH)

HPISS .... High-Power Illuminator Signal Source (MCD)

HPIT............ High-Performance Infiltrating Technique [*Materials science*]

HPJ.............. Help Project [*Computer science*] (PCM)

HPJ.............. High-Power Jammer

HPJ.............. High-Pressure Jet

HPJC.......... Highland Park Junior College [*Later, Highland Park College*] [*Michigan*]

HPK.............. High-Power Klystron

HPK .... Histidine Protein Kinase [*An enzyme*]

HPK .... Honorary Physician to the King [*British*]

HPKA.......... High-Power Klystron Amplifier

HPKMB .... Hieratische Papyrus aus den Koeniglichen Museen zu Berlin [*A publication*] (BJA)

HPL.............. Hamilton Public Library [*UTLAS symbol*]

HPL.............. Hartford Public Library, Hartford, CT [*OCLC symbol*] (OCLC)

HPL.............. Heliportugal-Trabalhos e Transporte Aereo, Representacoes, Importacao e Exportacao Lda. [*Portugal ICAO designator*] (FAAC)

HPL.............. High Performance Logic (AAEL)

HPL.............. High Polar Latitude [*Geophysics*]

HPL.............. High-Power LASER

HPL.............. Hotel Properties Ltd. [*Singapore*] (ECON)

HPL.............. Human Pancreatic Lipase [*An enzyme*]

HPL.............. Human Parotid Lysozyme [*An enzyme*]

HPL.............. Human Performance Laboratory [*Ball State University*] [*Research center*] (RCD)

HPL.............. Human Peripheral Lymphocyte

HPL.............. Human Placental Lactogen [*Also, CGP, HCS*] [*Endocrinology*]

hPL.............. Human Placental Lactogen (STED)

HPL.............. Hybrid Programming Language [*Computer science*]

HPL.............. Hyperplexia (STED)

HPL.............. Nucla, CO [*Location identifier FAA*] (FAAL)

HPLA .... Hydroxyphenyllactic Acid [*Pharmacology*] (MAE)

HPLAC.......... High-Performance Liquid Affinity Chromatography

HPLAC.......... High-Pressure Liquid-Affinity Chromatography (DMAA)

HPLAP .... Human Placental Alkaline Phosphatase [*An enzyme*]

HPLC.......... High-Performance [*or High-Pressure*] Liquid Chromatography

HPLC.......... High-Pressure Liquid Chromatography (STED)

HPLF.......... High-Pressure Low-Flow

HPLF............ Hydrolyzed Polar Lipid Fraction [*Biochemistry*]

HPLJ............ High-Pressure Liquid Jet

HPLL............ High Pressure Life Laboratory (PDAA)

HPLL............ Hybrid Phase-Locked Loop (PDAA)

HPLO............ High-Performance, Low-Observable

HP/LP............ High-Power/Low-Power

HPLPC .... High-Performance Low-Pressure Chromatography

HPLR............ Hinge Pillar [*Technical drawings*]

HPLRP .... Health Professionals Loan Repayment Program [*Military*]

HPLV............ High-Pressure Low-Volume [*Automotive painting*]

HPLX .... Healthplex, Inc. [*NASDAQ symbol*] (NQ)

HPM.............. Harding-Passey Melanoma [*Oncology*] (AAMN)

HPM.............. Hazardous Production Material [*Forest industry*] (WPI)

HPM.............. Head Positioning Mechanism

HPM.............. Head Position Monitor

HPM.............. Head Postmaster's Manual [*British*] (DCTA)

HPM.............. Hemiplegic Migraine [*Neurology*] (DAVI)

HPM.............. High-Performance Membrane [*Medicine*] (DMAA)

HPM.............. High-Polymer Molecular [*Film*]

HPM.............. High-Power Microwave

HPM.............. High-Power Multiplier (DNAB)

HPM.............. High-Priority Mail (TSSD)

HPM.............. High Purity Metal (AAEL)

HPM.............. Honeycomb Propellant Matrix (SAA)

HPM.............. Horizontal Panel Mount

HPM.............. Hot Press Molding

HPM.............. How Products are Made [*A publication*]

HPM............ Human Performance Model [*Human Engineering Laboratory*] [*Aberdeen Proving Ground, MD*] (RDA)

HPM............ Human Peritoneal Macrophage [*Immunology*]

HPM............ Human Potential Movement [*Psychotherapy*]

HPM............ Hydraulic Punching Machine

HPM............ Hyper-Page-Mode [*Computer science*] (PCM)

HPMA.......... Hardwood Plywood Manufacturers Association [*Reston, VA*] (EA)

HPMA.......... Heat Pump Manufacturers' Association [*British*]

HPMA.......... High-Power Microwave Assembly (AAG)

HPMA.......... Hydroxypropyl Methacrylate [*Organic chemistry*]

HPMAA.......... Honey Packers and Marketers' Association of Australia

HPMC.......... High-Performance Membrane Chromatography

HPMC.......... Housing Production and Management Credit [*HUD*]

HPMC.......... Hydroxypropyl(methyl)cellulose [*Synthetic food gum*] [*Organic chemistry*]

HPMCF.......... High Purity Milled Carbon Fiber

Hp Mi .... Hippias Minor [*of Plato*] [*Classical studies*] (OCD)

HPMIDC.......... Himachul Pradesh Mineral and Industrial Development Corp. [*India*] (BUAC)

HPMM .... Horizontal Planar Motion Mechanism (PDAA)

HPMNJ .... High-Power Microelectronic Noise Jammer

HPMS .... High-Performance Main Storage (IAA)

HPMS .... Highway Performance-Monitoring System [*Department of Transportation*] (GFGA)

HPMSK .... High-Priority Mission Support Kit [*Military*] (AFIT)

HPMV .... High-Pressure Mercury Vapor

HPN .... Central Hispano International, Inc. [*NYSE symbol*] (SAG)

HPN .... Harrison, Purchase, and North Castle [*Airport*]

HPN .... Haustus Purgans Noster [*Purging Draught from the Doctor's Own Prescription*] [*Pharmacy*] (ROG)

HPN .... Health Physics Network [*Nuclear energy*] (NRCH)

HPN .... Heavy Primary Nuclei

HPN .... Hepsin (DMAA)

HPN .... High Pass Network

HPN .... High Pass Notch (IAA)

HPN .... Home Parenteral Nutrition

HPN .... Horsepower Nominal

HPN .... Hydrogenation of Pyrolysis Naphtha [*Petroleum refining*]

HPN .... Hydroxypropyl Nitrate [*Organic chemistry*]

HPN .... Hypertension [*Medicine*]

HPN .... White Plains [*New York*] [*Airport symbol*] (OAG)

HPND .... Human Pronatriodilatin [*Endocrinology*]

HPNJ .... High-Power Noise Jammer

HPnP .... Home Plug and Play [*Technology*]

HPNPr.......... Centl Hispano Intl9.875% 'MIPS' [*NYSE symbol*] (TTSB)

HPNS .... High-Pressure Nervous Syndrome [*Deep-sea diving*]

HPNS .... Hunters Point Naval Shipyard

HPO .... Head Post Office

HPO .... Health Care Purchasing Organization [*Insurance*] (WYGK)

HPO .... High-Performance Option (MCD)

HPO .... High-Pressure Oxygen [*Also, HBO, OHP*]

HPO .... Highway Post Office [*Bus or truck equipped with mail distribution facilities*]

HPO .... Hippo Valley [*Zimbabwe*] [*Airport symbol*] (AD)

HPO .... Home Port [*Navy*] (NVT)

HPO .... Hourly Postflight (MCD)

HPO .... Hydrogenated Palm Oil

HPO .... Hydroperoxide (DMAA)

HPO .... Hydrophilic Ointment [*Pharmacy*] (DAVI)

HPO .... Hydroxylamine Phosphate Oxime [*Organic chemistry*]

HPO .... Hypertrophic Pulmonary Osteoarthropathy [*Medicine*] (DAVI)

HPOD .... Hydroperoxyoctadecadienoic Acid [*Organic chemistry*]

HPOF .... High-Pressure Oil-Filled [*Cable*]

HPOL .... Health Manpower Shortage Area Placement Opportunity List [*Department of Health and Human Services*] (GFGA)

HPOP .... High-Pressure Oxidizer Pump (NASA)

HPOT .... Helipotentiometer

HPOT .... High Potential (IAA)

HPOT .... High-Pressure Oxidizer Turbopump [*Aerospace*] (NAKS)

HPOT .... Hydroperoxyoctadecatrienoic Acid [*Organic chemistry*]

HPOTP .... High-Pressure Oxidizer Turbopump

HPOX .... High-Pressure Oxygen (AFM)

HPP .... Half Page Printer

HPP .... Half Power Point [*LASER technology*]

HPP .... Hamiltonian Path Problem [*Mathematics*]

HPP .... Harvard Project Physics

HPP .... Health Physics Program (NRCH)

HPP .... Health Promotion Pilot

HPP .... Healthy Planet Prod [*AMEX symbol*] (TTSB)

HPP .... Healthy Planet Products, Inc. [*AMEX symbol*] (SAG)

HPP .... Hepp [*Alaska*] [*Seismograph station code, US Geological Survey*] (SEIS)

HPP .... Hereditary Pyropoikilocytosis [*Medicine*]

HPP .... Hernieuwde Progressieve Partij [*Renewed Progressive Party*] [*Surinam*] [*Political party*] (PPW)

HPP .... High-Performance Plastic

HPP .... Holding under Promise of Payment

HPP .... Hot Processing Plant [*Nuclear energy*]

HPP .... Human Pancreatic Polypeptide [*Endocrinology*]

HPP .... Hungarian People's Party [*Croatia*] [*Political party*] (BUAC)

HPP .... Hydraulic Pneumatic Panel (AAG)

HPP .... Hydroxyphenyl Pyruvate [*Organic chemistry*]

HPPA .... High Performance Pipe Association (BUAC)

HPPA .... Horses' and Ponies' Protection Association [*British*] (DI)

HPPA .... Hydroxyphenylpyruvic Acid [*Organic chemistry*]

HPPC	Health Plan Purchasing Cooperatives
HPPC	High Performance Computing and Communications (TNIG)
HP PCIB	Hewlett Packard Personal Computer Instruments Bus (NITA)
HPPCL	Hewlett-Packard Printer Control Language
HPPD	Hours per Patient Day [Medicine] (DMAA)
HPPF	Horizontal Payloads Processing Facility (MCD)
HPPH	(Hydroxyphenyl)phenylhydantoin [Biochemistry] (AAMN)
HPPI	High-Performance Parallel Interface [Computer science]
HPPLC	High-Performance Preparative Liquid Chromatography
HPPM	High-Performance Propulsion Module (MCD)
HPPO	High Pressure Partial Oxidation (PDAA)
HPPP	High-Pressure Pump Pad (COE)
HPPP	High-Priority Production Program [NATO] (NATG)
HPPR	Hydroxypyrazolopyrimidine Ribonucleoside [Biochemistry]
HPPS	Hewlett-Packard Printer Submodule (IAA)
HPPS	Hughes Post Processor, Surveyor
HPPT	Hypertext Text Transfer Protocol [Computer science] (TNIG)
HPPTS	Hydraulic Package Pressure Test Set
HPQ	Highly Polarized Quasar [Galactic science]
HPQY	High Purity Quartz Yarn [Materials science]
HPR	Halden Reactor Project [Norway]
HPR	Halt and Proceed [Computer science] (SAA)
HPR	Hardware Problem Report (MCD)
HPR	Heart Profile Recorder [Medicine]
HPR	Heat Pipe Reactor
HPR	Hic Pace Requiescat [May He Here Rest in Peace] [Latin] (ROG)
HPR	Highly Protected Risk [Insurance]
HPR	High Penetration Resistant (PDAA)
HPR	High-Performance Routing [Computer science] (CDE)
HPR	High-Polymer Rheology
HPR	High-Powered RADAR (NATG)
HPR	Holding Period Return (PDAA)
HPR	Hopper [Freight]
HPR	Horsepower
HPR	Hosptial Peer Review (MEDA)
HPR	Host-Plant Resistance [Entomology, phytochemistry]
HPR	Hot Particle Rolling (PDAA)
HPR	Housing and Planning References [A publication]
HPR	Howard's New York Practice Reports [A publication] (DLA)
HPr	Howard's New York Practice Reports, New Series [A publication] (DLA)
HPR	HPR, Inc. [Associated Press] (SAG)
HPR	Hughes Photoelectric Reader
HPR	Human Performance Reliability
HPR	Human Progesterone Receptor [Endocrinology]
HPR	Human Prolactin [Endocrinology]
HPR	Hydrogen Pressure Regulator (MCD)
HPR	Hydroxyphenylretinamide [Biochemistry]
HPR	Hyperion Resources [Vancouver Stock Exchange symbol]
HPR	Rick Lucus Helicopters Ltd. [New Zealand] [FAA designator] (FAAC)
HPrA	Harcourt Genl'A'cm CvStk [NYSE symbol] (TTSB)
HPRA	Hungarian Public Relations Association (BUAC)
HPRC	Hereditary Papillary Renal Cancer [Medicine]
HPRCC	High Plains Regional Climate Center [NCPO]
HPRES	Pressure Altitude (GAVI)
HPRF	High Pulse Recurrence Frequency (MCD)
HPRF	Hypersonic Propulsion Research Facility
HPRI	HPR Inc. [NASDAQ symbol] (SAG)
HPRILIM	Hangzhou Project and Research Institute of Light Industry Machinery [China] (BUAC)
HPRK	Hollywood Park [NASDAQ symbol] (TTSB)
HPRK	Hollywood Park, Inc. [NASDAQ symbol] (SAG)
HPRKZ	Hollywood Park $0.70 Dep Cv Pfd [NASDAQ symbol] (TTSB)
HPRL	Human Performance Research Laboratory [University of Utah] [Research center] (RCD)
HPRL	Human Prolactin [Endocrinology]
HPRP	High-Performance Reporting Post (NATG)
HPRP	High-Powered RADAR Post (NATG)
HPRP	Homes Per Rating Point [Advertising] (DOAD)
HPRP	Human Platelet-Rich Plasma [Medicine] (DMAA)
HPRP	Human Potential Research Project [University of Surrey] [British] (AIE)
HPRPC	High-Performance Reversed Phase Chromatography
HPRR	Health Physics Research Reactor [Oak Ridge, TN] [Oak Ridge National Laboratory] [Department of Energy]
HPRS	Hellenic Public Relations Society [Greece] (BUAC)
HPRS	High-Pressure Recirculation System [Nuclear energy] (NRCH)
HPRS	Hopkins Psychiatric Rating Scale [Personality development test] [Psychology]
HPRS	Houghton Poultry Research Station [British] (ARC)
HPRT	Heartport Inc. [NASDAQ symbol] (TTSB)
HPRT	Hypoxanthine-Guanine-Phosphoribosyl Transferase (DOG)
HPRT	Hypoxanthine Phosphoribosyltransferase [Also, HGPRT] [An enzyme]
HPRU	Handicapped Persons Research Unit (NITA)
HPRV	High-Pressure Relief Valve (KSC)
HPS	Antisubmarine Helicopter (NATG)
HPS	Haitian Philatelic Society (EA)
HPS	Hanford Plant Standard [Formerly, HWS] [Nuclear energy] (NRCH)
HPS	Hanna Pacific [Vancouver Stock Exchange symbol]
HPS	Hantavirus Pulmonary Syndrome [Medicine]
HPS	Hardened Power System
HPS	Hardy Plant Society (EAIO)
HPS	Harpsicord [Music] (WGA)
HPS	Hazardous Polluting Substances [Shipping] (DCTA)

HPS	Health Physics Society (EA)
HPS	Health Physics Society Standards Committee
HPS	Health Physics Station [Nuclear energy] (NRCH)
HPS	HealthPlan Services [NYSE symbol] (TTSB)
HPS	Healthplan Services Corp. [NYSE symbol] (SAG)
HPS	Heat Protection System
HPS	Helium Pressure Switch (MCD)
HPS	Hellenic Philatelic Society (BUAC)
HPS	Hellenic Physical Society (BUAC)
HPS	Hematoxylin-Phloxine-Saffron [Biochemistry] (MAE)
HPS	Hermansky-Pudlak Syndrome [Medicine]
HPS	Hermetic Pivoting Seal
HPS	Hidden Predictive Saccades [Ophthalmology]
HPS	Highest Points Scored (ROG)
HPS	Highland Pony Society (BUAC)
HPS	High-Pressure Separator [Chemical engineering]
HPS	High-Pressure Sintering [Ceramic technology]
HPS	High-Pressure Sodium
HPS	High-Pressure Steam [Technical drawings]
HPS	High Primary Sequence (IAA)
HPS	High-Protein Supplement [Nutrition]
HPS	His-Purkinje System (DB)
HPS	Hospitalization Proneness Scale [Psychometrics]
HPS	Hull Pressure Switch
HPS	Human Placental Somatomammotropin (DB)
HPS	Hybrid Propulsion System
HPS	Hydraulic Power Section [Later, HPU] (AAG)
HPS	Hydraulic Power Supply
HPS	Hydraulic Power System (KSC)
HPS	Hydroxypropyl Starch [Organic chemistry]
HPS	Hypertrophic Pyloric Stenosis [Medicine]
HPSA	Health Professional Shortage Area (DMAA)
HPSA	Hellenic Philatelic Society of America (EA)
HPSA	Honors Program Student Association of the American Sociological Association (EA)
HPSA	Hydraulic Package Servovalve Actuator
HPSC	Heading per Standard Compass [Navigation]
HPSC	Health Programs Systems Center
HPSC	HPSC, Inc. [NASDAQ symbol] (NQ)
HPSC	Hydraulic Package Storage Container
HPSCI	House Permanent Select Committee on Intelligence (MCD)
HPSD	High-Power Switching Device
HPSEB	Himachal Pradash State Electricity Board [India] (BUAC)
HPSEC	High-Performance Size Exclusion Chromatography
HPSEC	High-Pressure Size Exclusion Chromatography
HPSF	High-Pressure Stopped Flow [Spectrometry]
HPSG	Head Driven Phrase Structure Grammar [Artificial intelligence]
HPSI	Harpsichord [Music]
HPSI	Health Professions Stress Inventory [Medicine]
HPSI	High-Pressure Safety Injection (NRCH)
HPSI	High-Pressure Spray Post-Accident Injection [Environmental science] (COE)
HPSIP	High-Pressure Safety Injection Pump (NRCH)
HPSIS	High-Pressure Safety Injection System (IEEE)
HPSK	Hydraulic Power Supply Kit
HPSL	Health Professions Student Loans
HPSN	Hot-Pressed Silicon Nitride (RDA)
HPSOM	High-Performance Stand-Off Motor (MCD)
HPSP	Health Professions Scholarship Program [Army]
HPSR	High-Pressure Spray Post-Accident Recirculation [Environmental science] (COE)
HPSS	Hogan Personnel Selection Series (DHP)
HPSS	Hrvatska Pucka Seljacka Stranka [Croatian People's Peasant Party] [Former Yugoslavia] [Political party] (PPE)
HPSSNJ	High-Power Self-Screening Noise Jammer [Military] (CAAL)
HPSTGC	Heading per Steering Compass [Navigation]
HPSTI	Human Pancreatic Secretory Trypsin Inhibitor (DB)
HPSV	High-Pressure Solenoid Valve
HPSW	High-Pressure Service Water [Nuclear energy] (NRCH)
HPSW	Horizontally Polarized Shear Wave [Physics]
HPSWS	High-Pressure Service Water System [Nuclear energy] (NRCH)
HPT	Hampton, IA [Location identifier FAA] (FAAL)
Hpt.	Haptoglobin (STED)
HPT	Head per Track (BUR)
HPT	Hexamethylphosphoric Triamide [Also, HEMPA, HMP, HMPA, HMPT] [Organic chemistry]
HPT	High-Payoff Target [Military] (INF)
HPT	High-Performance Train (ADA)
HPT	High Point
HPT	High-Potential Test [or Tester]
HPT	High-Power Transmitter Memory (DWSG)
HPT	High-Pressure Tap
HPT	High-Pressure Test
HPT	High-Pressure Turbine (NRCH)
HPT	High Profile Terminal (IAA)
HPT	Histamine Provocation Test (STED)
HPT	Home Port [Navy] (NVT)
HPT	Homonuclear Polarization Transfer [Physics]
HPT	Horizontal Plot Table
HPT	Hormone Pregnancy Test
HPT	Horsepower Tonnage (DOMA)
HPT	Hospitality Properties Trust [NYSE symbol] (SAG)
HPT	Hot Plate Test (STED)
hPT	Human Placental Thyrotropin (STED)
HPT	Human Placenta Thyrotropin [Endocrinology]

HPT............. Hydrocylic Pressure Testing
HPT............. Hydropneumatic Trailer (MCD)
HPT............. Hygromycin Phosphotransferase
HPT............. Hyperparathyroidism [or Hyperthyroidism] [Endocrinology]
HPT............. Hypothalmic-Pituitary-Thyroid (STED)
HPTA .... High Pressure Technology Association [British]
HPTA .... Hinckley Pilot 35 Association (EA)
HPTA .... Hire Purchase Trade Association [British] (BI)
HPTB .... High-Pressure Turbine [on a ship] (DS)
HPTD .... High Point, Thomasville & Denton Railroad Co. [AAR code]
HPTDC .... Himachal Pradesh Tourist Development Corp. [India]
HPTE .... Bis(hydroxyphenyl)trichloroethane [Organic chemistry]
HPTE .... Heptachlor Epoxide
HPTE .... High-Performance Turbine Engine [Air Force]
HPTF .... Hydraulic Power Transmission Fluid (MCD)
HPTH .... Hyperparathyroid Hormone (DB)
HPTH .... Hyperparathyroidism [Medicine] (MEDA)
HPTIN .... Human Pancreatic Trypsin Inhibitor [Medicine] (STED)
HPTL .... High-Payoff Target List [Military] (INF)
HPTLC .... High-Performance Thin-Layer Chromatography
HPTM .... Home Prothrombin Time Monitoring (STED)
HPTP .... Hydraulic Power Transfer Panel
HPTS .... High-Performance Third Stage [Rocket] [Army] (AABC)
HPTS .... High-Powered Transmit Set (DWSG)
HPTS .... Hydroxypyrenetrisulfonic Acid [Organic chemistry]
HPTW .... Hauptwerk [Masterpiece] [German]
HPU .... Hale Pohaku [Hawaii] [Seismograph station code, US Geological
               Survey] (SEIS)
HPU .... Hansard's Publishing Union (ROG)
HPU .... Heater Probe Unit (DMAA)
HPU .... High-Pressure Unit
HPU .... Hydraulic Power Unit (MCD)
HPU .... Hydraulic Pumping Unit (AABC)
HP(UK) .... Hunter Personnel (United Kingdom) Ltd.
HPUS .... Homeopathic Pharmacopoeia of the United States
HPV .... Haemophilus Pertussis Vaccine [Medicine] (STED)
HPV .... Helium Pressure Vessel
HPV .... Hemophilus Pertussis Vaccine [Medicine] (MAE)
HPV .... Hepatic Portal Vein [Medicine] (DB)
HPV .... High-Passage Virus
HPV .... High-Powered Vehicle
HPV .... High-Power Veractor
HPV .... High-Pressure Valve
HPV .... High-Pressure Vent (AAEL)
HPV .... High-Priority Violator (GNE)
HPV .... High Production Volume [Manufacturing]
HPV .... Human Papillomavirus [or Parvovirus]
HPV .... Human Parvovirus [Medicine] (DB)
HPV .... Human-Powered Vehicle
HPV .... Hypoxic Pulmonary Vasoconstriction [Medicine]
HPV .... Princeville [Hawaii] [Airport symbol] (OAG)
HPVA .... Hardwood, Plywood, and Veneer Association (NTPA)
HPVD .... Hypertensive Pulmonary Vascular Disease [Medicine]
HPV-DE .... High-Passage Virus [Grown in] Duck Embryo [Cells]
HPV-DK .... High-Passage Virus [Grown in] Dog Kidney [Cells]
HPVG .... Hepatic Portal Venous Gas (MAE)
HPVR .... Hypoxic Pulmonary Vascular Response [Anesthesiology]
HPVS .... Hydropneumatic Vehicle Suspension [Automotive engineering]
HP VUE .... Hewlett-Packard Visual User Environment [Computer science]
HP/W .... Health Promotion/Wellness Program [Medicine] (DMAA)
HPW .... High-Purity Water
HPW .... Hopewell, VA [Location identifier FAA] (FAAL)
HPW .... Hot Pressure Welding
HPW .... Hours per Week
HPW .... Paine Webber Group [AMEX symbol] (SAG)
HPWO .... High Performance Work Organization
HPWR .... Health Power [NASDAQ symbol] (SAG)
HPWSol .... High-Protein Wash Solution [Clinical chemistry]
HPX .... Homeplex Mortgage Investments [NYSE symbol] (SPSG)
HPX .... Homeplex Mtge Invmts [NYSE symbol] (TTSB)
HPX .... (Hydroxypropyl)xylan [Organic chemistry]
HPX .... Partial Hepatectomy (DB)
HPY .... Baytown, TX [Location identifier FAA] (FAAL)
HPY .... HPY Industry Ltd. [Vancouver Stock Exchange symbol]
HPZ .... Helicopter Protected Zone [Military] (DA)
HPZ............. High-Pressure Zone
HPZE .... High-Performance Zone Electrophoresis
HQ .... Business Express [ICAO designator] (AD)
H-Q .... Hamstring-Quadriceps [Anatomy]
HQ .... Hawker Siddeley Aviation Ltd. [British ICAO designator] (ICDA)
HQ .... Hazard Quotient [Toxicology]
HQ .... Headquarters
Hq .... Headquarters (AL)
HQ .... Headquarters Companies [San Francisco, CA] (TSSD)
HQ .... Health Systems International [NYSE symbol] (SAG)
HQ .... Health Systems Intl'A' [NYSE symbol] (TTSB)
HQ .... Heussler Air Service [ICAO designator] (AD)
HQ .... Highly Qualified (AFM)
HQ .... High Quality [Home video systems]
HQ .... Historical Quotes [Information retrieval]
HQ .... Hoc Quaere [Look For This or See This] [Latin]
HQ .... Home Quarters Warehouse, Inc.
HQ .... Hong Qi [Red Flag] [China]
HQ .... Hoop Quotient [Basketball]
HQ .... HQ Minerals Ltd. [Vancouver Stock Exchange symbol]

HQ .... Hydro-Quebec [Institut de Recherche d'Hydro-Quebec] [Canada]
HQ .... Hydroquinone [Organic chemistry]
HQ .... Hydroxyquinoline [Organic chemistry]
HQ .... New York Helicopter [ICAO designator] (AD)
HQ(A) .... Headquarters Administration Office [British police]
HQA .... Middletown, PA [Location identifier FAA] (FAAL)
HQ & SERV... Headquarters and Service [Marine Corps]
HQASC........ Headquarters, Air Support Command [NATO] (NATG)
HQB .... Los Angeles, CA [Location identifier FAA] (FAAL)
HQBA .... Headquarters Base Area
HQBC .... Headquarters, Bomber Command [Later, HQSTC] [British] (NATG)
HQBN .... Headquarters Battalion (DNAB)
HQBP .... High Quality Bonus Point [Advancement system] [Navy] (NVT)
HQBTRY...... Headquarters Battery [Military] (DNAB)
HQC .... Handling Quality Criteria
HQC .... Headquarters Command [Air Force]
HQC .... High ™Q∫ Circuit [or Coil]
HQC .... Hydraulic Quick Coupler
HQC .... Hydroquinone Cream [Pharmacy] (DAVI)
HQC .... Hydroxyquinoline Citrate [Antiseptic]
HQC .... Hyperquasicenter
HQ-CAP ...... Headquarters, Civil Air Patrol
HQCC .... Headquarters, Coastal Command [British] (NATG)
HQCDO .... Headquarters Case Development Officer [Environmental Protection
               Agency] (GFGA)
HQCMD....... Headquarters Command [Military]
HQCO.......... Headquarters Company [Military] (DNAB)
HQCOM....... Headquarters Command [Military] (KSC)
HQCOMD .... Headquarters Command [Air Force]
HQCOMDT ... Headquarters Commandant (NATG)
HQCOMDUSAF... Headquarters Command, United States Air Force
HQCS .... Heraldic Quality Control System (AABC)
HQDA.......... Headquarters, Department of the Army
HQDM .... Headquarters Data Manager (KSC)
HQDP .... Headquarters, Department of the Pacific [Marine Corps]
HQ DSA ...... Headquarters, Defense Supply Agency
HQDTMS..... Headquarters, Defense Traffic Management Service
HQE .... Hansard Questions Ecrites [Hansard Written Question - HWQ]
               [Database House of Commons] [French] [Information service or
               system] (CRD)
HQE .... Hardware Quality Engineer (MCD)
HQEARC...... Headquarters, Equipment Authorization Review Center [Army]
HQES .... High-Quality Epitaxial Silicon
HQF .... High Quality Facsimile (DGA)
HQFC .... Headquarters, Fighter Command [NATO] (NATG)
HQG .... Hugoton, KS [Location identifier FAA] (FAAL)
HQH .... H&Q Healthcare Inv [NYSE symbol] (TTSB)
HQH .... H & Q Healthcare Investors [NYSE symbol] (SPSG)
HQHRA .... Half-Quarter Horse Registry of America (EA)
HQIADS....... Headquarters, Integrated Air Defense System [Air Force]
HQJTF......... Headquarters, Joint Task Force (MCD)
HQK .... Gulf of Mexico, LA [Location identifier FAA] (FAAL)
HQL .... Cullowhee, NC [Location identifier FAA] (FAAL)
HQL .... H&Q Life Sciences Investors [NYSE symbol] (TTSB)
HQL .... High-Quality Life
HQM .... Highland Queen Mines Ltd. [Vancouver Stock Exchange symbol]
HQM .... High-Quality Matrix [Electronics]
HQM .... Hoquiam, WA [Location identifier FAA] (FAAL)
HQM .... Hydro-Quebec, Bibliotheque [UTLAS symbol]
HQMC .... Headquarters, Marine Corps
HQMD .... Headquarters Management Directive [NASA]
HQMME ...... Hydroquinone Monomethyl Ether [Organic chemistry]
HQMTMTS ... Headquarters, Military Traffic Management Terminal Service (DNAB)
HQN .... Haplequin Lake [Alaska] [Seismograph station code, US Geological
               Survey] (SEIS)
HQNAVMARCORMARSTA... Headquarters, Navy-Marine Corps Military Affiliate
               Radio System Station (DNAB)
HQNAVMATCOM... Headquarters, Naval Material Command
HQNMC .... Headquarters, Naval Material Command (AFIT)
HQNO.......... Heptyl(hydroxy)quinoline N-Oxide [Organic chemistry]
HQO .... Hansard Questions Orale [Hansard Oral Questions - HOQ]
               [Database House of Commons] [French] [Information service or
               system] (CRD)
HQOC.......... Headquarters Operational Command [Australia]
HQR .... Handling Qualities Rating [Cooper-Harper]
HQRS.......... Handling Qualities Rating Scale (MCD)
HQS .... Headquarters
HQS .... Headquarters Staff [British military] (DMA)
HQS .... High-Quality Silicon
HQS .... High-Quality Sound [Home video system] (IAA)
HQSA.......... Hydroxyquinolinesulfonic Acid [Organic chemistry]
HQSC.......... Headquarters, Signals Command [British] (NATG)
HQSQ.......... Headquarters Squadron
HQSQDN ..... Headquarters, Support Squadron [Military] (DNAB)
HQSQN .... Headquarters Squadron [Marine Corps]
HQSRN .... Headquarters Staff of the Royal Navy [British]
HQSTC........ Headquarters, Strike Command [Formerly, HQBC] [British] (NATG)
HQSVCBN ... Headquarters, Service Battalion [Military] (DNAB)
HQSVCCO ... Headquarters, Service Company [Military] (DNAB)
HQT .... Coats, NC [Location identifier FAA] (FAAL)
HQT .... Halogen Quenched Tube
HQTC .... Headquarters, Transport Command [British] (NATG)
HQTC .... High ™Q∫ Tuned Circuit
HQTR.......... Headquarters (KSC)
HQTV.......... High-Quality Television [Home video system] (IAA)

HQUSACE	Headquarters, U.S. Army Corps of Engineers
HQ USAF	Headquarters, United States Air Force (AFM)
HR	Air Bremen [*ICAO designator*] (AD)
HR	Croatia [*Internet country code*]
HR	Hague Resolutions
HR	Hail and Rain [*Meteorology*] (BARN)
hr	Hair (VRA)
hr	Hairless Mouse [*Endocrinology*] (DMAA)
hr	Hairspace [*Printing*] (WDMC)
HR	Hair Space between Letters [*Proofreader's mark*]
HR	Half-Reversal [*Psychometrics*]
HR	Half-Yearly Review
HR	Hallux Rigidus [*Orthopedics*] (DAVI)
HR	Hall Wardrobes [*Classified advertising*] (ADA)
HR	Halorhodopsin [*Biochemistry*]
HR	Halstead-Reitan [*Neuropsychological battery*] (DAVI)
HR	Halton Rifles [*British military*] (DMA)
HR	Hamman-Rich [*Syndrome*] [*Medicine*] (DB)
HR	Handling Room
HR	Hand RADAR (IAA)
HR	Hand Reach [*Automotive engineering*]
HR	Hand Receipt (AABC)
HR	Hand Reset
HR	Hard Rolled
HR	Hardware Reliability (MCD)
HR	Harrington Rod [*Orthopedics*] (DAVI)
HR	Hazard Report (MCD)
HR	Healthcare Realty Tr [*NYSE symbol*] (TTSB)
HR	Healthcare Realty Trust [*NYSE symbol*] (SPSG)
HR	Hear [*Amateur radio shorthand*] (WDAA)
HR	Heart Rate [*Medicine*]
HR	Heart Rhythm [*Cardiology*]
HR	Heater (IAA)
HR	Heat Reflector
HR	Heat Resisting [*Technical drawings*]
HR	Heavy-Duty Relay (IAA)
HR	Height Range [*RADAR*]
HR	Heir (ROG)
HR	Helicopter Request [*Military*] (NVT)
HR	Helium Rebottled [*System*]
HR	Helium, Refrigerated (AAG)
HR	Hellenic Register [*Greek ship classification society*] (DS)
HR	Hemirectococcygeus (DB)
HR	Hemophilia Research [*An association Defunct*] (EA)
HR	Hemorrhagic Retinopathy [*Ophthalmology*]
Hr	Henricus de Baila [*Flourished, 1169-70*] [*Authority cited in pre-1607 legal work*] (DSA)
HR	Henry Russell [*Astronomy*]
HR	Here [*Amateur radio shorthand*] (WDAA)
HR	Hermetic Rite [*Freemasonry*] (ROG)
HR	Heroes of the Reformation [*A publication*]
HR	Herr [*Sir, Mr.*] [*German*]
H-R	Hertzsprung-Russell [*Diagram*] [*Astronomy*]
HR	Hessischer Rundfunk [*Hessian Radio Network*] [*Germany*]
HR	Heterosexual Relations [*Scale*]
HR	Higher (ROG)
HR	Higher Rate
HR	Highhams Railway [*Wales*]
HR	Highland Railway [*Scotland*]
HR	Highland Regiment [*British military*] (DMA)
HR	High-Range [*RADAR*] (DEN)
HR	High-Rate Reverse [*Ecology*]
HR	High Reduction [*Microforms*] (NITA)
HR	High Reflector (IAA)
HR	High Resilience [*Plastics*]
HR	High Resistance
HR	High Resolution (MCD)
HR	High Risk
HR	High Run
HR	High-Speed Radial [*Automotive tires*]
hr	Hinge Remnant [*Philately*]
HR	Histamine Release [*Immunology*]
HR	Historical Record (NASA)
HR	History Report (MCD)
HR	Hit Rate (MUGU)
HR	Hit Ratio
HR	Hoechst-Roussel Pharmaceuticals, Inc. [*Research code symbol*]
HR	Hoerner [*Horns*] [*Music*]
HR	Hoge Raad [*Dutch Supreme Court*] (DLA)
HR	Hojesteret [*Supreme Court*] [*Netherlands*] (ILCA)
HR	Holding Register
HR	Holiday Route (CDAI)
HR	Homeostatic Regulators [*British*]
HR	Home Rule
HR	Home Run [*Baseball*]
HR	Homoreactant [*Medicine*]
HR	Hook Rail (MSA)
HR	Horizontal Resistance [*Plant pathology*]
HR	Horizontal Retort
HR	Hormonal Response [*Medicine*] (DMAA)
HR	Hormone Receptor Complex [*Endocrinology*]
HR	Hormone-Responsive (DB)
HR	Horology Program [*Association of Independent Colleges and Schools specialization code*]
HR	Hose Rack (AAG)

HR	Hospitalman Recruit
HR	Hospital Record
HR	Hospital Recruit
HR	Hospital Report (MAE)
HR	Hot Rolled (MSA)
HR	Hour (AAG)
hr	Hour
HR	Hourly Report (DNAB)
HR	House of Representatives
HR	House of Representatives Bill [*with Number*]
HR	House of Ruth (EA)
HR	House Recedes
HR	House Report
HR	House Resolution
HR	House Roll [*Legal term*] (DLA)
HR	Howship-Romberg [*Syndrome*] [*Medicine*] (DB)
HR	Hudson Review [*A publication*] (BRI)
HR	Humanitarian Reassignment [*Military*] (AFM)
HR	Human Reliability
HR	Human Resources
HR	Human Rights Convention [*Council of Europe*] (DLA)
HR	Humber Register [*St. Albans, Hertfordshire, England*] (EAIO)
HR	Humidity, Relative
Hr	Hussar [*British military*] (DMA)
HR	Hydraulics Research Ltd. [*British*] (IRUK)
HR	Hydrogen Recombiner (NRCH)
HR	Hydrogen Relief (NASA)
HR	Hypersensitive Response [*Biology*]
HR	Hypophosphatemic Rickets [*Medicine*] (DMAA)
HR	Robin Avions [*Pierre Robin*] [*France ICAO aircraft manufacturer identifier*] (ICAO)
HR	Shore
HR2D	High-Resolution, Two-Dimensional [*Electrophoresis*]
HR 10	Keogh Plan (EBF)
HRA	Harbin Railway Administration [*China*] (BUAC)
HRA	Hard Replacement Assembly (MCD)
HRA	Harness Release Actuator (DNAB)
HRA	Haura [*South Arabia (Yemen)*] [*Airport symbol*] (AD)
HRA	Health Resources Administration [*Abolished, 1982, functions transferred to Health Resources and Services Administration*] [*HEW*]
HRA	Health Risk Appraisal [*or Assessment*] [*Medicine*]
HRA	Heart Rate Acceleration
HRA	Heart Rate Audiometry
HRA	Heavy Replaceable [*or Replacement*] Assembly
HRA	Heli-Iberica [*Spain ICAO designator*] (FAAC)
HRA	Hemispherical Reflective Antenna
HRA	HF [*High-Frequency*] Recovery Antenna
HRA	High-Radiation Area (DNAB)
HRA	High Right Atrium [*Anatomy*]
HRA	High-Speed Research Aircraft (PDAA)
HRA	Histamine Releasing Activity [*Medicine*] (DAVI)
HRA	Honorary Royal Academician [*British*]
HRA	Horse Rangers' Association (BUAC)
HRA	Horticultural Research Association (BUAC)
HRA	Hour of Revival Association [*British*]
HRA	Housing Revenue Account [*British*]
HRA	Humanitarian and Refugee Affairs [*Department of Defense*]
HRA	Human Reliability Analysis [*Engineering*]
HRA	Human Resource Accounting (ADA)
HRA	Human Rights Advocates (EA)
HRA	Huna Research Association [*See also HF*] [*Switzerland*] (EAIO)
HRA	Hydraulic Rotary Actuator
HRA	Hypersonic Research Airplane [*NASA*]
HRAA	High-Rate Acquisition Assembly (MCD)
HRAA	Hire and Rental Association of Australia
HRAD	Hunger Relief and Development [*An association*] (EA)
HRA EIS	Hanford Remedial Action Environmental Impact Statement
HRAF	Human Relations Area Files (EA)
HRAF	Human Relations Areas Files [*Yale University*]
HRAG	International Human Rights Advisory Group [*Switzerland*]
HRAI	Heating, Refrigerating, and Air Conditioning Institute of Canada
HRAI	Human Rights Advocates International (EA)
HRAM	Hazard Ranking and Allocation Methodology (MCD)
HRAM	Hierarchical Random Access Memory [*Computer science*]
HR & IH	His [*or Her*] Royal and Imperial Highness (ROG)
HRANSW	Harness Racing Authority of New South Wales [*Australia*]
HRAP	Housing Relocation Assistance Program [*US Army Corps of Engineers*]
HRAR	Hereafter
HRART	Hampton Roads Army Terminal
HRAS	High-Rate Activated Sludge [*Waste treatment*]
HRAT	Hampton Roads Army Terminal
HRAT	Hereat [*Legal*] [*British*] (ROG)
HRAV	Human Resources Availability (NVT)
HRB	Block (H&R) [*NYSE symbol*] (TTSB)
HRB	Block [*H. & R.*], Inc. [*NYSE symbol*] (SPSG)
HRB	Croatian Revolutionary Brotherhood [*Former Yugoslavia*] (PD)
HRB	H & R Block (EFIS)
HRB	Harbin [*Manchuria*] [*Airport symbol*] (OAG)
HRB	Hardship Relief Board [*Victoria, Australia*]
HRB	Hazard Review Board
HRB	High Rate Bioreactor [*Chemical Engineering*]
HRB	High-Resolution Bathymetry [*Instrumentation*]
HRB	Highway Research Board [*Later, TRB*] (EA)

HRB	Hinged Rotor Blade
HRB	Hockey Rules Board [*Walton-On-Thames, Surrey, England*] (EAIO)
HRB	House of Representatives Bill
HRB	Hurbanovo [*Czechoslovakia*] [*Seismograph station code, US Geological Survey*] (SEIS)
HRBA	Havana Rabbit Breeders Association (EA)
HRBA	Hoist Rotation Beam Assembly [*Military*] (CAAL)
HRBC	Harbinger Corp. [*NASDAQ symbol*] (SAG)
HRBC	Horse Red Blood Cells [*Also, HRC*]
HRBF	Harbor Federal Bancorp [*NASDAQ symbol*] (SAG)
HRBI	Hotot Rabbit Breeders International (EA)
HRBOR	Harbor [*Commonly used*] (OPSA)
HRC	Hairdressers' Registration Council [*British*] (BI)
HRC	Haitian Refugee Center (EA)
HRC	Hardness Rockwell C [*Materials testing*]
HRC	Hardwood Research Council (EA)
HRC	Harris Ranch [*California*] [*Seismograph station code, US Geological Survey Closed*] (SEIS)
HRC	Hasselblad Reflex Camera (MCD)
HRC	HEALTHSOUTH Corp. [*NYSE symbol*] (TTSB)
HRC	HEALTHSOUTH Rehabilitation Corp. [*NYSE symbol*] (SPSG)
HRC	HEATH [*Higher Education and the Handicapped*] Resource Center (EA)
HRC	Helium Research Center
HRC	Herpes Resource Center (EA)
HRC	Herpes Resource Center American Social Health Association (EA)
HRC	Highland Regional Council [*Scotland*]
HRC	High-Resolution Chromatography (DB)
HRC	High-Rupturing Capacity
HRC	Holiday Rambler Corp.
HRC	Hollycroft Resource Corp. [*Vancouver Stock Exchange symbol*]
HRC	Holocaust Resource Center (EA)
HRC	Holy Roman Church (WDAA)
HRC	Honda Racing Corp.
HRC	Honey Research Council [*Australia*]
HRC	Horizontal Redundancy Check (IEEE)
HRC	Horse Red Blood Cells [*Also, HRBC*]
HRC	Horticultural Research Center [*Southern Illinois University at Carbondale*] (RCD)
HRC	Horticultural Research Center [*University of Massachusetts*] (RCD)
HRC	Howard Research Corp.
HRC	Human Relations Committee [*Military*] (VNW)
HRC	Human Renal Carcinoma [*Medicine*] (DB)
HRC	Human Resources Center (EA)
HRC	Human Resources Committee
HRC	Human Resources Council (GNE)
HRC	Human Rights Campaign (EA)
HRC	Human Rights Commission
HRC	Human Rights Committee
HRC	Huntingdon Research Centre Ltd. [*British*] (IRUK)
HRC	Hunting Retriever Club (EA)
HRC	Hybrid Receiver Circuit
HRC	Hybrid Ring Control [*Computer science*] (TNIG)
HRC	Hydraulics-Resonance Changer (DNAB)
HRC	Hypertension Research Center [*Indiana University*] [*Research center*] (RCD)
HRC	Hypothetical Reference Circuit [*Telecommunications*] (TEL)
HRC	Rockwell Hardness (C Scale)
HRCA	Honorary Royal Cambrian Academician [*British*]
HRCC	High-Ratio Compact Chamber [*Automotive engineering*]
HRCC	Humanities Research Council of Canada [*See also CCRH*] [*Later, SSHRCC*]
HRC/CCPR	Human Rights Committee (EA)
HRCF	Human Rights Campaign Fund (EA)
HRCFFD	Human Rights Campaign Fund's Field Division (EA)
HR Con Res	House of Representatives Concurrent Resolution [*Legal term*] (DLA)
HRCPX	Heritage Capital Apprec. Trust Cl.A [*Mutual fund ticker symbol*] (SG)
HRCQ	Highway-Route-Controlled Quantities [*Environmental Protection Agency*]
HRCT	High-Resolution Computed Tomography (STED)
HRCVX	Heritage Income-Growth Trust Cl.A [*Mutual fund ticker symbol*] (SG)
HRD	Hannaford Bros [*NYSE symbol*] (TTSB)
HRD	Hannaford Brothers, Inc. [*NYSE symbol*] (SPSG)
hrd	Hard [*Quality of the bottom*] [*Nautical charts*]
HRD	Harding Carpets Ltd. [*Toronto Stock Exchange symbol*]
HRD	Hard Top [*Automotive advertising*]
HRD	Harstad [*Norway*] [*Airport symbol*] (AD)
HRD	Heard [*Amateur radio shorthand*] (WDAA)
HRD	Heroin-Related Death [*Epidemiology*]
HRD	Hertzsprung-Russell Diagram [*Astronomy*]
HRD	High-Rate Demultiplexer (SSD)
HRD	High-Rate Discharge (MCD)
HRD	High-Rate Dosimeter (MCD)
HRD	High-Resolution Display
HRD	High Roughage Diet (PDAA)
HRD	Holocaust Remembrance Day (BJA)
HRD	Human Related Deaths
HRD	Human Resource Development (EERA)
HRD	Human Resources Data
HRD	Human Resources Development
HRD	Human Resources Division [*GAO*] (AAGC)
HRD	Hurricane Research Division [*Miami, FL*] [*National Oceanic and Atmospheric Administration*] (GRD)
HRD	Hydraulic Rate Damper
HRD	Kountze/Silsbee, TX [*Location identifier FAA*] (FAAL)

HRDA	High-Rate Data Assembly (MCD)
HRDA	High-Rate Deposit Account (WDAA)
HRDB	Human Resources Development Branch [*Environmental Protection Agency*] (EPA)
HRDC	Honeybee Research and Development Committee [*Australia*]
HRDC	Human Resources Development Command [*Military*] (DNAB)
HRDG	Harding Lawson Assoc Grp [*NASDAQ symbol*] (TTSB)
HRDG	Harding Lawson Associates Group, Inc. [*NASDAQ symbol*] (SAG)
HRDG	Human Resources Development Group [*British*]
HrdgLaw	Harding Lawson Associates Group, Inc. [*Associated Press*] (SAG)
HRDI	High-Rate Demultiplexer Instrument (SSD)
HRDI	High-Resolution Doppler Imager (MCD)
HRDI	High-Resolution Dynamic Imaging [*Electrophoresis*]
HRDI	Human Resources Development Institute (EA)
HRDITS	Hereditaments [*Legal*] [*British*] (ROG)
HRDL	Hudson River Day Line [*AAR code*]
HRDM	High-Rate Demultiplexer (MCD)
HR Doc	House of Representatives Document (DLA)
HRDP	Human Resources [*Research*] and Development Program
HRDP	Hypothetical Reference Digital Path [*Meteorology*]
HRDPO	Human Resources Development Project Office [*Military*] (DNAB)
HRDR	High-Rate Digital Recorder (MCD)
HRDRSSR	Hairdresser
HRDS	High-Rate Data Section (NASA)
HRDS	Human Resource Development Staff
HRDTY	Heredity
hrdwd	Hardwood (REAL)
hrdwd flrs	Hardwood Floors (REAL)
HRDWRE	Hardware (WGA)
HRE	Aerosucre SA [*Colombia*] [*ICAO designator*] (FAAC)
HRE	Harare [*Zimbabwe*] [*Airport symbol*] (OAG)
HRE	High-Resolution Electrocardiography
HRE	High-Resolution Electrophoresis [*Analytical biochemistry*]
HRE	Highridge Exploration Ltd. [*Toronto Stock Exchange symbol*]
HRE	Holy Roman Emperor [*or Empire*]
HRE	Homogeneous Reactor Experiments (NRCH)
HRE	Hormone Receptor Enzyme [*Endocrinology*] (DMAA)
HRE	Hormone Regulatory Element [*Endocrinology*]
HRE	Hormone-Responsive Element [*Endocrinology*]
HRE	Hovering Rocket Engine (MCD)
HRE	HRE Properties [*Formerly, Hubbard Real Estate Investments*] [*Associated Press*] (SAG)
HRE	HRE Properties [*Formerly, Hubbard Real Estate Investments*] [*NYSE symbol*] (SPSG)
HRE	Human Relations Education (MCD)
HRE	Human Research and Engineering Directorate [*Army*] (RDA)
HRE	Human Response Element of DNA [*Endocrinology*]
HRE	Hydrazine Rocket Engine
HRE	Hydro Reconnaissance Experimental [*British military*] (DMA)
HRE	Hypersonic Ramjet Engine
HRE	Hypersonic Research Engine [*NASA*]
HRE	Hypoxia-Responsive Element [*Molecular medicine*]
HREAA	Health and Research Employees' Association of Australia
HREBIU	Hotel and Restaurant Employees and Bartenders International Union [*Later, HERE*] (EA)
HREC	Health Record
HREC	Hepatic Reticuloendothelial Cell (STED)
H Rec A Sc	Historical Records of Australian Science [*A publication*]
HREELS	High-Resolution Electron Energy Loss Spectroscopy
HREF	Hypertext Reference [*Computer science*] (CDE)
HREH	High Renin Essential Hypertension [*Medicine*] (DB)
HRELES	High-Resolution Energy-Loss Electron Spectroscopy
HRELS	High-Resolution Energy-Loss Spectroscopy (MCD)
HREM	High-Resolution Electron Microscopy
HREOC	Human Rights and Equal Opportunity Commission (EERA)
H Rep	House of Representatives Report (AAGC)
HRept	House of Representatives Reports [*A publication*] (DLA)
HRES	High-Resolution Electronic System
HRes	House Resolution (WPI)
H Res	House Resolution, United States House of Representatives
HRET	Health Related Fitness Test (EDAC)
HRET	Hospital Research and Educational Trust (EA)
HREU	Hotel and Restaurant Employees and Bartenders International Union [*Later, HERE*]
HRF	Harris Return Flow (STED)
HRF	Height-Ranger Finder
HRF	Hemochromatosis Research Foundation (EA)
HRF	Herb Research Foundation (EA)
HRF	High Rate of Fire (NATG)
HRF	High-Resolution Facsimile [*Telecommunications*]
HRF	Histamine Releasing Factor [*Immunology*]
HRF	History Record Folder (MCD)
HRF	Human Research Facility (SSD)
HRF	Hypersonic Rarefied Flow
HRF	Sisters of the Holy Rosary of Fatima (Mexico) (TOCD)
HRFA	High-Resolution Frequency Analysis [*of periodic phenomena*]
HRFA	Hungarian Reformed Federation of America (EA)
HRFA	Huron River Fishing Association [*Michigan*]
HRFAX	High-Resolution Facsimile [*Telecommunications*] (TEL)
HRFBS	Hill Radnor Flock Book Society [*British*] (DBA)
HRG	Halford-Robins-Godfrey [*British sports car maker*]
HRG	Harrington Public Library, Harrington, DE [*OCLC symbol*] (OCLC)
HRG	Health Research Group
HRG	Hearing (ROG)
HRG	Hemispherical Resonating Gyro (PDAA)

HRG	Heritage Roses Group (EA)
HRG	He-Ro Group [*NYSE symbol*] (SPSG)
HRG	High River Gold [*Vancouver Stock Exchange symbol*]
HRG	High River Gold Mines Ltd. [*Toronto Stock Exchange symbol*]
HRG	Histidine-Rich Glycoprotein [*Biochemistry*]
HRG	Human Rights Group [*Edinburgh, Scotland*] [*Defunct*] (EAIO)
HRG	Hurghada [*Egypt*] [*Airport symbol*] (OAG)
HRGC	High-Resolution Gas Chromatography
HRGM	High-Resolution Ground Map
HRGM	Hogg Robinson & Gardner Mountain [*Insurance broker*] [*British*]
HRGP	Hydroxyproline-Rich Glycoprotein [*Biochemistry*]
HRH	Hand Receipt Holder (MCD)
HRH	High-Rate Heat
HRH	Hilb, Rogal & Hamilton [*NYSE symbol*] (TTSB)
HRH	His [*or Her*] Royal Highness
HRH	Howard Robard Hughes [*1905-1976*] [*American businessman*]
HRH	Hypoplastic Right Heart [*Cardiology*]
HRH	Hypothalamic-Releasing Hormone (DB)
HRH	Royal Tongan Airlines [*Tonga*] [*ICAO designator*] (FAAC)
HRHA	Honorary Member of the Royal Hibernian Academy [*British*]
HRHA	Hydronic Radiant Heating Association (EA)
HRHR	High-Risk Hearing Register
HR(HS)	Hospital Recruit (High School) [*Navy*] (DNAB)
HRI	Hannah Research Institute [*British*]
HRI	Hard Rock International [*Restaurant chain*]
HRI	Harrington Rod Instrumentation [*Orthopedics*] (DAVI)
HRI	Hayes Resources, Inc. [*Toronto Stock Exchange symbol*]
HRI	Health Research, Inc. [*New York State Department of Health*] [*Research center*] (RCD)
HRI	Heart Research Institute [*Australia*]
HRI	Height-Range Indicator [*Electronics*]
HRI	Hierarchical Richness Index [*Biodiversity*] (EERA)
HRI	High-Resolution Image [*or Imager*] [*Astronomy*]
Hrl	Holbrook Research Institute, Oxford, MA [*Library symbol*] [*Library of Congress*] (LCLS)
HRI	Holcomb Research Institute [*Butler University*]
HRI	Honorary Member of the Royal Institute of Painters in Water Colours [*British*]
HRI	Horizon Reference Indicator [*Aerospace*] (AAG)
HRI	Horticultural Research Institute (EA)
HRI	Hotel, Restaurant, and Institutional [*Business*]
HRI	Human Relations Inventory [*Psychology*]
HRI	Human Resources Institute [*State University of New York at Buffalo*] [*Research center*] (RCD)
HRI	Human Rights International (EA)
HRI	Human Rights Internet (EA)
HRI	Internet: International Human Rights Documentation Network (EA)
HRIF	Histamine-Release Inhibitory Factor [*Antiinflammatory*]
HRIG	Human Rabies Immune Globulin [*Immunology*]
HRIG	Human Rabies Immunoglobulin [*Medicine*] (STED)
HRIN	Herein [*Legal*] [*British*] (ROG)
HRIN	Human Resource Information Network [*Executive Telecom System, Inc.*] [*Information service or system*] (IID)
HRINAR	Hereinafter [*Legal*] [*British*] (ROG)
HRINBEFE	Hereinbefore [*Legal*] [*British*] (ROG)
HRINBFR	Hereinbefore [*Legal*] [*British*] (ROG)
HRIO	Height-Range Indicator Operator [*Electronics*]
HRIO	Horticultural Research Institute of Ontario [*Canada Research center*] (RCD)
HRIP	Hic Requiescit in Pace [*Here Rests in Peace*] [*Latin*]
HRIP	Highway Research in Progress [*British*]
HRIR	High-Resolution Infrared Radiometer
HRIR	High Resolution Infrared Receiver (IAA)
HRIRS	High-Resolution Infrared Radiation Sounder
HRIRS	High Resolution Infra-Red Spectroscopy
HRIS	High-Repetition Illuminator System
HRIS	High Resolution Imaging Spectrometer [*Instrument*] (EERA)
HRIS	Highway Research Information Service [*National Academy of Sciences*] [*Washington, DC*]
HRIS	House of Representatives Information System
HRIS	Human Resources Information System (WYGK)
HRISM	Human Resources for Information Systems Management
HRJ	High-Range Juno [*Survey meter for radiation*]
HRJ Res	House of Representatives Joint Resolution [*Legal term*] (DLA)
HRK	Hardrock Extension, Inc. [*Toronto Stock Exchange symbol*]
HRK	Kharkov [*Former USSR Airport symbol*] (OAG)
HRK	Racine, WI [*Location identifier FAA*] (FAAL)
HR-KMAG	Historical Report - Korea Military Advisory Group
HRL	Hardware Requirements List
HRL	Harlingen [*Texas*] [*Airport symbol*] (OAG)
HRL	Harlin Resources [*Vancouver Stock Exchange symbol*]
HRL	Head Rotated Left [*Medicine*]
HRL	Heat Rejection Loop
HRL	High Refraction Layer
HRL	High-Repetition LASER
HRL	High-Resolution LOFAR [*Military*] (CAAL)
HRL	Historical Record Log (SAA)
HRL	Horizontal Reference Line [*Technical drawings*]
HRL	Hormel [*Geo. A.*] & Co. [*NYSE symbol*] (SPSG)
HRL	Hormel Foods [*NYSE symbol*] (TTSB)
HRL	Hughes Research Laboratories [*Hughes Aircraft Co.*]
HRL	Human Resources Laboratory [*Air Force*] (MCD)
HRL	Hydraulics Research Laboratory [*British*]
HRL	Hydrological Research Laboratory [*Silver Spring, MD*] [*National Weather Service*] (GRD)
HRLA	Human Reovirus-Like Agent [*Medicine*] (DMAA)
HRLC	High-Resolution Liquid Chromatography
HRLDD	Human Resources, Learning and Development Director
HRLI	High-Repetition LASER Illuminator
HRLIS	High-Repetition LASER Illuminating System
HRLM	High-Resolution Light Microscopy
HRLS	High-Repetition LASER System
HRLSD	Health and Rehabilitative Library Services Division [*Later, ASCLA*] [*American Library Association*]
HRLY	Herley Industries [*NASDAQ symbol*] (TTSB)
HRLY	Herley Industries, Inc. [*NASDAQ symbol*] (NQ)
HRM	Hardware Read-In Mode
HRM	Hermes Ventures [*Vancouver Stock Exchange symbol*]
HRM	High-Rate Multiplexer (MCD)
HRM	High-Ratio Multiplier (NASA)
HRM	High-Reliability Module (IAA)
HRM	High-Resolution Monitor (MCD)
HRM	His [*or Her*] Royal Majesty [*British*]
HRM	Hoisting and Rigging Manual (COE)
HRM	Holistic Resource Management (ECON)
HRM	Human Resources Management
HRM	Human Rights Monitor [*A publication*]
HRM	University of Hartford, West Hartford, CT [*OCLC symbol*] (OCLC)
HRMA	[*British Columbia*] Human Resources Management Association (AC)
Hrm ADR	Harmony Gold Mining Co. Ltd. [*Associated Press*] (SAG)
HR Mag	HR Magazine [*A publication*] (BRI)
HRMC	Harts Range Meta-igneous Complex [*Geology*]
HRMC	Human Resources Management Center
HRMC/D	Human Resources Management Center/Detachment [*Navy*] (DNAB)
HRMD	Human Resources Management Detachment [*Navy*] (DNAB)
HRMDDHG	Herr, Regiere Mich durch Deinen Heiligen Geist [*Lord, Rule Me through Thy Holy Spirit*] [*Motto for a number of 16th and 17th century German and Bavarian rulers*]
HrmHld	Harmony Holdings, Inc. [*Associated Press*] (SAG)
HRMI	Health Risk Management [*NASDAQ symbol*] (TTSB)
HRMI	Health Risk Management, Inc. [*NASDAQ symbol*] (SAG)
HRMI	Human Resources Management Instructor [*Navy*] (DNAB)
HRMN	Harmon Indus [*NASDAQ symbol*] (TTSB)
HRMN	Harmon Industries, Inc. [*NASDAQ symbol*] (NQ)
HRMOB	Association of Human Resources Management and Organizational Behavior [*Later, AM*] (EA)
HRMP	Harvard Radio Meteor Project
HRMR	Human Read/Machine Read [*Microfilm memory system*]
HRMS	Health Risk Management Service [*Australian Capital Territory*]
HRMS	Height Root Mean Square (IAA)
HRMS	High-Resolution Mass Spectrometry
HRMS	High Resolution Microwave Survey [*Astronomy*]
HRMS	Human Resource Management Services, Inc. [*Database producer*] (IID)
HRMS	Human Resource Management System
HRMS	Human Resources Management School [*Navy*] (DNAB)
HRMSS	Human Resources Management Specialist [*Navy*] (NVT)
HRMSS	Human Resources Management Support System [*Navy*] (NVT)
HRMST	Human Resources Management Support Team [*Navy*] (DNAB)
HRMTG	Hermitage
HR/MTI	High-Resolution/Moving Target Indicator (DNAB)
HRMY	Harmony Products, Inc. [*NASDAQ symbol*] (SAG)
HRN	Airwork Ltd. [*British ICAO designator*] (FAAC)
HRN	Harlyn Products [*AMEX symbol*] (TTSB)
HRN	Harlyn Products, Inc. [*AMEX symbol*] (SPSG)
HRN	Harness
HRN	Harwin Exploration & Development, Inc. [*Vancouver Stock Exchange symbol*]
HRN	Herrn [*Sirs, Gentlemen*] [*German*] (ROG)
HRN	Hoerner [*Horns*] [*Music*]
HRN	Human Research Need (RDA)
HRN	Human Resources Need (MCD)
HRN	Human Resources Network [*Information service or system*] (EA)
HRN	Human Rights Network [*British*]
HRNA	Haflinger Registry of North America (EA)
hRNA	Ribonucleic Acid, Heterogeneous [*Biochemistry, genetics*]
HRNAR	Hereinafter
HRNB	History: Reviews of New Books [*A publication*] (BRI)
HRNES	Host Remote Node Entry System
HRNG	Hearing
HRNTWT	High Reynolds Number Transonic Wind Tunnel
HRO	Harrison [*Arkansas*] [*Airport symbol*] (OAG)
HRO	Hermiston [*Oregon*] [*Seismograph station code, US Geological Survey*] (SEIS)
HRO	HERO Industries Ltd. [*Toronto Stock Exchange symbol Vancouver Stock Exchange symbol*]
HRO	Homes Registration Office
HRO	Housing Referral Office [*Military*]
HROI	Honorary Member of the Royal Institute of Oil Painters [*British*]
HRON	Hereon [*Legal*] [*British*] (ROG)
HRP	Haitian Refugee Project [*Defunct*] (EA)
HRP	Health & Retirement Properties Trust [*Formerly, Health/Rehabilitation Property*] [*NYSE symbol*] (SPSG)
HRP	Health & Retirement Prop Tr [*NYSE symbol*] (TTSB)
HRP	Heat-Resistant Phenolic
HRP	Heat-Resisting Plastic
HRP	High-Risk Patient [*Medicine*] (DMAA)
HRP	Highway Regulating Point (AABC)
HRP	Histidine-Rich Protein [*Biochemistry, immunochemistry*]
HRP	Historical Review Press [*British*]

HRP	Holding and Reconsignment Point [*Military*] (AABC)
HRP	Horizontal Radiation Pattern [*Electronics*] (DEN)
HRP	Horseradish Peroxidase [*An enzyme*]
HRP	HRPT Properties Tr. [*NYSE symbol*] [*Formerly, Health & Retirement Properties Tr.*]
HRP	Human Reliability Program (AFM)
HRP	Human Rights Party [*Ann Arbor, MI*]
HRP	Human Rights Program [*Harvard University*] [*Research center*] (RCD)
HRP	Hypergroup Reference Pilot [*Telecommunications*] (NITA)
HRPA	Hebrew Religious Protection Association of Greater New York (EA)
HRPAC	Human Rights Political Action Committee (EA)
HRPC	High-Range Pressure Control
HRPD	Hamburg Rating Scale for Psychiatric Disorders [*Medicine*] (DMAA)
HRPD	High-Resolution Powder Diffractometer [*Crystallographic instrument*]
HRPI	High-Resolution Pointable Imager
HRPM	High-Resolution Permanent Magnet (MHDI)
HRPO	Horseradish Peroxidase [*Also, HRP*] [*An enzyme*]
HRPO	Hot Rolled, Pickled, and Oiled (MSA)
hr pp	Hours Postprandial [*Usually preceded by a numeral*] [*Pharmacology*] (DAVI)
HRPP	Human Rights Protection Party [*Western Samoa*] [*Political party*] (PPW)
HRPRAS	High-Risk, People-Related Accident Syndrome (DICI)
HRPS	Hazard Reduction Precedence Sequence (NASA)
HRPS	High Risk Point Sources [*Environmental science*] (COE)
HRPS	Human Resource Planning Society [*New York, NY*] (EA)
HRPS	Hydrogen Recombination and Purge System [*Nuclear energy*] (NRCH)
HRPT	High-Resolution Picture Transmission [*Service*]
HRPT	Highway Regulating Point Team [*MTMC*] (TAG)
HRPT	Hyperparathyroidism [*Medicine*] (DMAA)
HRPVD	High-Rate Physical Vapor Deposition [*Metal*]
HRQ	Hold Request (IAA)
HRQL	Health-Related Quality-of-Life [*Medicine*]
HRQOL	Health Related Quality of Life
HRR	Hardy-Rand Rittler [*Test for color vision*]
HRR	Head Rotated Right [*Medicine*]
HRR	Healy, AK [*Location identifier FAA*] (FAAL)
HRR	Heart Rate Range [*Medicine*]
HRR	Heat Rejection Radiator
HRR	Heat Release Rate [*Engineering*]
HRR	Heat Release Rate [*Flammability testing*] [*Fire safety*]
HRR	Heiliges Roemisches Reich [*Holy Roman Empire*] [*German*] (ROG)
HRR	Heron Resources Ltd. [*Vancouver Stock Exchange symbol*]
HRR	High-Reliability Relay
HRR	High-Resolution RADAR
HRRC	Hearing Rehabilitation Research Center [*Walt Disney*] (BABM)
HRRC	Home Recording Rights Coalition (EA)
HRRC	Human Resources Research Center
HRRC	Human Rights Resource Center (EAIO)
HRRC	Walt Disney Hearing Rehabilitation Research Center [*Ear Research Institute*]
HRRD	Human Resources Research Development Program
HR Rel	Historicorum Romanorum Reliquiae [*A publication*] (OCD)
HR Rep	House of Representatives Reports [*A publication*] (DLA)
HR Rept	House of Representatives Reports [*A publication*] (DLA)
HRRI	Heart Rate Retardation Index [*Medicine*] (DMAA)
HRRI	Human Resources Research Institute
Hrringtn	Harrington Financial Group, Inc. [*Associated Press*] (SAG)
HRRL	Human Resources Research Laboratory [*Air Force*] (MCD)
HRRM	High Range-Resolution Monopulse (PDAA)
hrRNA	Ribonucleic Acid, Heavy Ribosomal [*Biochemistry, genetics*]
HRRO	Human Resources Research Office [*NASA*] (AAG)
HRRVC	Holiday Rambler Recreational Vehicle Club (EA)
HRRWC	Hudson River Region Wine Council (EA)
HRS	Hair Replacement System
HRS	Hal Roach Studios, Inc.
HRS	Hamilton Rating Scale (MAE)
HRS	Hard Red Spring [*Wheat*]
HRS	Harp Renaissance Society [*Defunct*] (EA)
HRS	Harris Corp. [*NYSE symbol*] (SPSG)
HRS	Harris, GA [*Location identifier FAA*] (FAAL)
HRS	Hawaii Revised Statutes [*A publication*]
HRS	Hazard Ranking System [*Environmental Protection Agency*]
HRS	Heading Reference System (AAG)
HRS	Heat Rejection System
HRS	Hepatorenal Syndrome [*Medicine*]
HRS	High-Rate Station
HRS	High-Resolution Spectrograph [*Hubble Space Telescope*] [*NASA*]
HRS	High Resolution Spectrometer [*Marine science*] (OSRA)
HRS	High-Resolution System
HRS	Historic Record Society [*Record label*]
HRS	Holographic Readout System (AAEL)
HRS	Home Reunion Society [*British*]
HRS	Honorary Reserve Section
HRS	Horizon Reference Set (MCD)
HRS	Horizontal Recovery System
HRS	Hormone Receptor Site [*Endocrinology*]
HRS	Hospital Reading Society [*Defunct*] (EA)
HRS	Host Resident Software
HRS	Hot Rolled Steel
HRS	Hours (NATG)
hrs	Hours (ODBW)
HRS	Housing Referral Service [*Military*] (AABC)

HRS	Hovering Rocket System [*Army*]
HRS	Human Resources System (MHDB)
HRS	Hunza Research Society [*Defunct*] (EA)
HRS	Hurricane Research Service [*Information service or system*] (IID)
HRS	Hussars [*Military unit*] [*British*]
HRS	Hydrant Refuelling System (IAA)
HRS	Hydraulics Research Station [*Research center British*]
HRS	Hyper-Rayleigh Scattering [*Physics*]
HRS	Missionary Sisters of Our Lady of the Holy Rosary [*Roman Catholic religious order*]
HRSA	Health Resources and Services Administration [*Department of Health and Human Services*]
HRSA	Historical Radio Society of Australia
HRSA	Honorary Member of the Royal Scottish Academy
HRSA	Hotel & Restaurant Suppliers Association Inc. (AC)
HRSC	Hudson River Sloop Clearwater (EA)
HRSCMR	High-Resolution Surface-Composition Mapping Radiometer (PDAA)
HRSCX	Heritage Small Cap Stock Cl.A [*Mutual fund ticker symbol*] (SG)
HRS-D	Hamilton Rating Scale for Deafness
HRS-D	Hamilton Rating Scale for Depression [*Medicine*] (DMAA)
HRSD	Hard Rock Silo Development
HRSD	Hazardous Response Support Division [*Environmental Protection Agency*]
HRSEM	High-Resolution Scanning Electron Microscopy (OA)
HRSG	Heat Recovery Steam Generator [*Industrial engineering*]
hrsg	Herausgegeben [*Edited, Published*] [*German*]
HRSH	Hirsch International Corp. [*NASDAQ symbol*] (SAG)
HRSH	Hirsch Intl. Corp'A' [*NASDAQ symbol*] (TTSB)
Hrshey	Hershey Foods Corp. [*Associated Press*] (SAG)
HRSI	High-Temperature Reusable Surface Insulation [*Space shuttle*] [*NASA*]
HRSN	Hariston Corp. [*NASDAQ symbol*] (SAG)
HRSNA	Histamine Research Society of North America (EA)
HRSNF	Hariston Corp. [*NASDAQ symbol*] (TTSB)
HRSP	Association of Human Resource Systems Professionals (EA)
HRSR	Heat Recovery/Seed Recovery [*System*]
HRSR	High Resolution Scanning Radiometer [*Instrument*] (EERA)
HRSS	Host Resident Software System
HRSS	Hrvatska Republikanska Seljacka Stranka [*Croatian Republican Peasant Party*] [*Former Yugoslavia*] [*Political party*] (PPE)
HRSSCC	High-Resolution Spin Scan Cloud Camera (NOAA)
HRSTYLNG	Hairstyling
HRSTYLST	Hairstylist
HRSV	Hydrangea Ringspot Virus [*Plant pathology*]
HRSW	Honorary Member of the Royal Scottish Water Colour Society
HRT	Arrhythmia Research Tech [*AMEX symbol*] (TTSB)
HRT	Arrhythmia Research Technology [*AMEX symbol*] (SPSG)
HRT	Hartford [*Diocesan abbreviation*] [*Connecticut*] (TOCD)
HRT	Hartwell Railway Co. [*AAR code*]
HRT	Heart
Hrt	Heart (WPI)
HRT	Heart Rate [*Cardiology*] (DAVI)
HRT	Heat Rejection and Transport (SSD)
HRT	Heavy Rail Transit (PDAA)
HRT	Helmholtz Reciprocal Theorem [*Physics*]
Hrt	Hertfordshire [*County in England*] (WGA)
HRT	High-Rate Telemetry [*NASA*]
HRT	High-Resolution Tracker
HRT	Hillcrest Resources Ltd. [*Toronto Stock Exchange symbol*]
HRT	Hiring, Retention, and Tenure [*of college professors*]
HRT	Homogeneous Reactor Test
HRT	Horizontal Return Tubular Burner (EDCT)
HRT	Hormone Replacement Therapy [*Medicine*]
HRT	Hospitals Remuneration Tribunal [*Australia*]
HRT	Hostage Rescue Team [*Pronounced "hurt"*] [*FBI standardized term*]
HRT	Human Resources Training
HRT	Hydraulic Retention Time
HRT	Mary Esther, FL [*Location identifier FAA*] (FAAL)
HRTC	Transporte Aereo Rioplatense [*Argentina ICAO designator*] (FAAC)
HRTC	Historic Rehabilitation Tax Credit
HrtCC	Heart Cubic Content (DAC)
HRTD	High-Rising Terminal Declarative [*Linguistics*]
HRTE	Human Reverse-Transcriptase Enzyme (DB)
HRTEM	High-Resolution Transmission Electron Microscope [*or Microscopy*]
HRTF	High-Resolution Tangential Flow Filtration
HrtFa	Heart Facial Area (DAC)
HrtfdSt	Hartford Steam Boiler & Inspection [*Associated Press*] (SAG)
HrtG	Heart Girth (DAC)
HRTG	Heritage
HrtgMd	Heritage Media Corp. [*Associated Press*] (SAG)
HrtgMda	Heritage Media [*Associated Press*] (SAG)
HrtLabs	Heart Labs of America [*Associated Press*] (SAG)
HrtLb	Heart Labs of America [*Associated Press*] (SAG)
HrtlndE	Heartland Express, Inc. [*Associated Press*] (SAG)
HRTS	High-Rate Telemetry System [*NASA*]
HRTS	High-Resolution Telescope and Spectrograph
HRTS	High-Risk Test Site [*Later, Research Test Site*]
HRTS	Hollywood Radio and Television Society (EA)
HRTT	Heart Technology, Inc. [*NASDAQ symbol*] (SAG)
HRTVX	Heartland Value Fund [*Mutual fund ticker symbol*] (SG)
HRTWD	Heartwood [*Forestry*] (WGA)
Hrtwd	Heartwood (WPI)
HrtWire	Heartland Wireless Communications, Inc. [*Associated Press*] (SAG)
HRTWN	Hawaii Regional Tsunami Warning Network [*Marine science*] (OSRA)
HRU	Harrisburg-Dayton [*Vancouver Stock Exchange symbol*]

HRU	Heading Reference Unit
HRU	Herrington, KS [*Location identifier FAA*] (FAAL)
HRU	Hostage Rescue Unit (LAIN)
HRUP	High-Risk Urban Problem [*Environmental Protection Agency*] (GFGA)
HRV	Harvard - Oak Ridge [*Massachusetts*] [*Seismograph station code, US Geological Survey*] (SEIS)
HRV	Heat Rate Variability
HRV	Heat Recovery Ventilator
HRV	Heavy Recovery Vehicle [*Marine Corps*] (VNW)
HRV	High Resolution Visible [*Imager*]
HRV	Historical Records of Victoria [*A publication*]
HRV	Human Reovirus [*Medicine*] (DMAA)
HRV	Human Rhinovirus [*Medicine*]
HRV	Human Rotaviruses
HRV	Hydraulic Relief Valve
HRV	Hypersonic Research Vehicle
HRV	New Orleans, LA [*Location identifier FAA*] (FAAL)
HRVL	Human Resources, Veterans, and Labor [*Office of Management and Budget*]
HRVLA	Human Reovirus-Like Agent (CPH)
HRVY	Harvey Entertainment [*NASDAQ symbol*] (TTSB)
HRVY	Harvey Entertainment Co. [*NASDAQ symbol*] (SAG)
HRW	Hard Red Winter [*Wheat*]
HRW	Heated Rear Window [*Automotive accessory*]
HRW	Human Rights for Women (EA)
HRW	Human Rights Watch (EA)
HRWA	Human Rights Watch/Africa [*New York*] (EA)
HRWH	Human Rights Watch - Helsinki [*An association*] (EA)
HRWMC	House of Representatives Ways and Means Committee (WDAA)
HRWS	Helicopter Remote Wind Sensor
HRX	Hereford, TX [*Location identifier FAA*] (FAAL)
HRX	Hypothetical Reference Connection [*Meteorology*]
HRXRS	High-Resolution X-Ray Spectroscopy
HRY	Hallwood Realty Partners Ltd. [*AMEX symbol*] (SPSG)
HRY	Hallwood Rlty Ptnrs L.P. (New) [*AMEX symbol*] (TTSB)
HRY	Head Rice Yield
HRYG	Gisenyi [*Rwanda*] [*ICAO location identifier*] (ICLI)
HRYI	Butare [*Rwanda*] [*ICAO location identifier*] (ICLI)
HRYO	Gabiro [*Rwanda*] [*ICAO location identifier*] (ICLI)
HRYR	Kigali [*Rwanda*] [*ICAO location identifier*] (ICLI)
HRYU	Ruhengeri [*Rwanda*] [*ICAO location identifier*] (ICLI)
HRZ	High Rainfall Zone
HRZA	Kamembe [*Rwanda*] [*ICAO location identifier*] (ICLI)
HRZB	Horizon Bank [*NASDAQ symbol*] (NQ)
HRZB	Horizon Financial [*NASDAQ symbol*] (TTSB)
HRZB	Horizon Financial Corp. [*NASDAQ symbol*] (SAG)
HrzBcWV	Horizon Bancorp (West Virginia) [*Associated Press*] (SAG)
HrzBTX	Horizon Bancorp, Inc. (Texas) [*Associated Press*] (SAG)
HrzHlt	Horizon CMS Healthcare Corp. [*Associated Press*] (SAG)
HrzHlt	Horizon Healthcare Corp. [*Associated Press*] (SAG)
HrzMH	Horizon Mental Health Management [*Associated Press*] (SAG)
HRZN	Horizon (MSA)
HS	Aeronoleggi e Lavoro Aereo (AERAL) [*Italy ICAO designator*] (ICDA)
HS	Air-Cushion Vehicle built by Hoversport [*US*] [*Usually used in combination with numerals*]
HS	CHS Electronics [*NYSE symbol*]
HS	Die Heilige Schrift des Alten Testaments [*Bonn*] [*A publication*] (BJA)
HS	Habitability System [*NASA*] (KSC)
HS	Habituation Stimulus [*to light*]
HS	Hair Space [*Publishing*] (DGA)
HS	Hakluyt Society (EA)
HS	Halfsheet [*Publishing*] (DGA)
HS	Half Strength
HS	Half Subtractor [*Circuitry*]
HS	Halleworden-Spatz [*Syndrome*] [*Medicine*] (DB)
H-S	Hamilton Standard (SAA)
HS	Handset
HS	Hand-Starter
HS	Hand Surgery [*Medical specialty*] (DHSM)
HS	Hand Switch [*Nuclear energy*] (NRCH)
HS	Hansard Society [*British*] (ILCA)
HS	Hardened Site
HS	Hardness Surveillance (MSA)
HS	Hard Sized Paper (DGA)
H/S	Hard/Soft [*Two tops for convertible automobile*]
HS	Hardstand
HS	Hard Stripping [*Agriculture*] (OA)
HS	Harmonised System [*Customs commodity coding and description*] [*British*]
HS	Harness or Saddlery
HS	Hartford & Slocomb Railroad Co. [*AAR code*]
HS	Hartman's Solution [*Dentistry*]
HS	Harvey Society (EA)
Hs	Hassium [*Proposed name and symbol for recently-discovered element*]
HS	Hauptsatz [*Leading Theme*] [*Music*]
HS	Hawker Siddeley Aviation Ltd. [*British ICAO aircraft manufacturer identifier*] (ICAO)
HS	Haydn Society [*Record label*]
HS	Headquarters State (NITA)
HS	Head Set [*Telecommunications*] (IAA)
HS	Head Sling
HS	Headspace [*Above liquids*]
HS	Headspace Sampler [*Instrumentation*]
HS	Head Suppression (AAG)

HS	Healthsource, Inc. [*NYSE symbol*] (SPSG)
HS	Heart Sounds [*Medicine*]
HS	Heather Society (EA)
HS	Heating Surface
HS	Heating System
HS	Heat Shield [*Aerospace*] (AAG)
HS	Heat Stable
HS	Heaviside [*Ionosphere*] (AAG)
HS	Heel Spur [*Orthopedics*] (DAVI)
HS	Heel Stick [*For blood samples*] [*Medicine*] (DAVI)
HS	Heel Strike [*Medicine*]
H-S	Heel-to-Shin [*Test*] [*Neurology*] (DAVI)
HS	Height above Spherical Earth
HS	Helicopter Squadron
HS	Helicopter Squadron, Antisubmarine (MCD)
HS	Helicopter System
HS	Helios Semiconductor (IAA)
HS	Helmet Shield
HS	Helminthosporium sacchari [*A toxin-producing fungus*]
H/S	Helper/Suppressor [*Cell ratio*]
HS	Heme Synthetase [*An enzyme*] (AAMN)
HS	Hemingway Society (EA)
HS	Hemlock Society (EA)
HS	Hemorrhagic Shock [*Medicine*]
HS	Hemstitched
HS	Henoch-Schoenlein Syndrome [*Medicine*]
HS	Heparin Sulfate [*Biochemistry*]
HS	Hepatic Scintigraphy [*Medicine*]
HS	Hepatosplenic Schistosomiasis [*Medicine*]
HS	Heraldisk Selskab [*Denmark*] [*An association*] (EAIO)
HS	Heraldry Society (EA)
HS	Hereditary Spherocytosis [*Medicine*]
HS	Hermetically Sealed (IAA)
HS	Herpes Simplex
HS	Hic Sepultus [*Here Is Buried*] [*Latin*]
HS	Hic Situs [*Here Lies*] [*Latin*] (GPO)
HS	Hidradenitis Suppurative [*Medicine*]
HSI	Hierarchically Structured [*Indexing language*] (NITA)
HS	Highest Score (ADA)
HS	Highly Sensitive System (MCD)
HS	High School
HS	High Sensitivity
HS	High Shock Resistant (IAA)
HS	High-Similarity [*Psychology*]
HS	High Speed
HS	High-Speed Adapter (IAA)
HS	High-Speed Arithmetic (IAA)
HS	High Spin (EDCT)
HS	High Spontaneous Activity
HS	High Stage (MCD)
HS	High Strength [*Steel*] [*Automotive engineering*]
HS	Hindenberg Society (EA)
HS	Hinged Seat (AAG)
HS	Hinge Side
HS	Histamine Sensitive [*Immunology*]
HS	Historical Period Starting Date [*Dialog*] [*Searchable field*] [*Information service or system*] (NITA)
HS	Historical Survey
hs	History [*Medicine*] (DMAA)
HS	History Section [*Reference and Adult Services Division*] [*American Library Association*]
HS	Hoc Sensu [*In This Sense*] [*Latin*] (GPO)
HS	Hohenzollern Society (EA)
HS	Hollaender-Simons [*Disease*] [*Medicine*] (DB)
HS	Holographic Stereogram (OA)
HS	[*The*] Holy See
HS	Home Secretary [*British*]
HS	Home Station [*DoD*]
HS	Homestead (ADA)
HS	Home Surgeon [*Medicine British*]
HS	Homing Sequence (IAA)
HS	Homologous Serum
HS	Honorary Secretary
HS	Horae Soederblomianae (BJA)
HS	Hora Somni [*At Bedtime*] [*Pharmacy*]
hs	Hora Somni [*Hour of Sleep*] [*Latin*] (STED)
HS	Horizon Scanner
HS	Horizon Sensor
HS	Horizontally Selective [*Medicine*] (DMAA)
HS	Horizontal Shear
HS	Horizontal Stripes [*On buoys, beacons*]
HS	Horizontal Synchronous [*Computer science*]
HS	Horizontal System [*Government arrangement*] (OICC)
HS	Horner Syndrome [*Medicine*] (DMAA)
HS	Horse Serum [*Immunology*]
HS	Hospital Ship
HS	Hospital Staff
HS	Hospital Surgeon [*British military*] (DMA)
HS	Hot Shop [*Nuclear energy*] (NRCH)
HS	Hot Soak [*Automotive engineering*]
HS	Hot Spraying
HS	Hot Stuff [*Slang Bowdlerized version*]
HS	Hours of Sleep [*Medicine*]
hs	House (VRA)
HS	House Supervisor

HS................	House Surgeon
HS................	Housing Scheme [*British*]
HS................	Housing Statistics
HS................	Housman Society (EA)
HS................	Humane Society (ROG)
HS................	Humanite Society (EA)
HS................	Hume Society (EA)
HS................	Humic Substances [*Biology*]
HS................	Hundred Square Feet (DNAB)
HS................	Hun-Stoffe [*US Chemical Corp. symbol for mustard gas*] [*Also, HD, HT, M Later, H*]
HS................	Hurler's Syndrome [*Medicine*]
HS................	Hybrid Switching [*Telecommunications*]
HS................	Hydraulic Supply
HS................	Hydraulic System
HS................	Hydrazine Sulfate [*Toxic substance*] [*Inorganic chemistry*]
HS................	Hydrofoil Ship
HS................	Hydrogen Sulfide (GNE)
HS................	Hydrogen Swelling [*Chemistry*]
HS................	Hydroxylamine Sulfate (EDCT)
HS................	Hypersonic
Hs................	Hypochondriasis [*Psychology*]
HS................	Hypothetical Syllogism [*Rule of inference*] [*Logic*]
HS................	Marshall's Air [*ICAO designator*] (AD)
HS................	Sandoz Pharmaceuticals [*Research code symbol*]
HS................	Service Available During Scheduled Operations [*ICAO*] (FAAC)
HS................	Siglum for Tablets in the Frau Professor Hilprecht Collection of Babylonian Antiquities [*Jena*] (BJA)
HS................	Thailand [*International civil aircraft marking*] (ODBW)
HSA	CHS Aviation Ltd. [*Kenya*] [*ICAO designator*] (FAAC)
HSA	Haiku Society of America (EA)
HSA	Handicapped SCUBA Association (EA)
HSA	Harvard Student Agencies [*Inc.*]
HSA	Hawaii Surfing Association (EA)
HSA	Hawker Siddeley Aviation Ltd. [*British*]
HSA	Hawley-Smoot Act [*1930*]
HSA	Hazardous Substances Act (DMAA)
HSA	Headquarters Support Activity
HSA	Health Service Academy [*Pakistan*]
HSA	Health Service Action [*Later, CNHS*] [*An association*] (EA)
HSA	Health Service Agreement
HSA	Health Service Area [*Military*] (AABC)
HSA	Health Services Administration [*Abolished, 1982, functions transferred to Health Resources and Services Administration*]
HSA	Health Systems Agency [*New York, NY*]
HSA	Heat Shield Abort [*Aerospace*] (IAA)
HSA	Heat-Stable Antigen [*Immunochemistry*]
HSA	Hegel Society of America (EA)
HSA	Hepatic Stimulating Activity [*Physiology*]
HSA	Heraldry Society of Australia
HSA	Herb Society of America (EA)
HSA	Hereditary Sideroblastic Anemia [*Medicine*] (DMAA)
HSA	High Specific Activity [*Radioisotope*]
HSA	High-Strength Adhesive
HSA	Highway Safety Act [*1970*]
HSA	Hill Start Assist [*Transmission and braking systems*] [*Automotive engineering*]
HSA	Hispanic Society of America (EA)
HSA	Hispanic Surname American
HSA	Historic Sites Act of 1935 (COE)
HSA	Hollandse Signaalapparaten [*Dutch*]
HSA	Holly Society of America (EA)
HSA	Holocaust Survivors of Auschwitz (EA)
HSA	Homo Sapiens [*Human species*]
HSA	Horizon Sensor Assembly
HSA	Horsemanship Safety Association (EA)
HSA	Horse Serum Albumin [*Immunology*]
HSA	Hospital Saving Association [*British*] (BI)
HSA	Hospital Savings Association (DAVI)
HSA	Humane Society of Australia
HSA	Human Serum Albumin
HSA	Hungarian Scouts Association (EA)
HSA	Hunt Saboteurs Association (EAIO)
HSA	Hydroponic Society of America (EA)
HSA	Hymn Society of America [*Later, HSUSC*] (EA)
HSA	Hypersomnia-Sleep Apnea Syndrome [*Medicine*] (MAE)
HSA	New Hampshire State Library, Processing Center, Concord, NH [*OCLC symbol*] (OCLC)
HSAA	Health Sciences Advancement Award [*National Institutes of Health*]
HSAAP	Holston Army Ammunition Plant (AABC)
HSAB	Hard and Soft Acids and Bases [*Chemistry*]
HSAB	Hydroxy(succinimidyl)azidobenzoate [*Organic chemistry*]
HSAC	Health Security Action Council (EA)
HSAC	Helicopter Safety Advisory Conference (EA)
HSAC	High-Speed Analog Computer (DEN)
HSAC	Historic Shipwrecks Advisory Committee [*Victoria, Australia*]
HSAC	House Science and Astronautics Committee [*US Congress*] (AAG)
HSAFOKF......	Help Save America for Our Kids' Future (EA)
HSAG	HEPES-Saline-Albumin-Gelatin [*Medium*] [*Microbiology*]
HSAK	Akobo [*Sudan*] [*ICAO location identifier*] (ICLI)
HSALU	High-Speed Arithmetic and Logic Unit (IAA)
HSAM	Helicopter Survivability Assessment Model (MCD)
HSAM	Hierarchical Sequential Access Method [*Computer science*]
HSAM	High-Speed Accounting Machine (IAA)
HS&F	Huntin', Shootin' & Fishin' [*Antiquarian book category*] (WDAA)

HS & O	Heads of Services and Offices [*Red Cross*]
HS & SS	Headquarters and Service Squadron
HSANSW.......	Health Services Association of New South Wales [*Australia*]
HSAP	Heat-Stable Alkaline Phosphatase [*An enzyme*]
HSAP	Honeycomb Sandwich Aluminum Panel
HSAPrA........	HSBC AmericasAdj Rt cm A Pfd [*NYSE symbol*] (TTSB)
HSARG.........	High-Speed Scintillation Autoradiography
HSAS	Hard Stability Augmentation System
HSAS	Headquarters Support Activity - Saigon [*Obsolete Military*] (CINC)
HSAS	Hypertrophic Subaortic Stenosis [*Cardiology*]
HSAT	Atbara [*Sudan*] [*ICAO location identifier*] (ICLI)
HSAT	Die Heilige Schrift des Alten Testaments [*Bonner Bibel*] [*A publication*] (BJA)
H-SAT	Heavy Satellite (PDAA)
HSATes........	Die Heilige Schrift des Alten Testaments [*Bonner Bibel*] [*A publication*] (BJA)
HSA-UWC	Holy Spirit Association for the Unification of World Christianity
HSAW	Aweil [*Sudan*] [*ICAO location identifier*] (ICLI)
HSB	Harrisburg, IL [*Location identifier FAA*] (FAAL)
HSB	Hartford Steam Boiler Inspection & Insurance Co. [*NYSE symbol*] (SPSG)
HSB	Hartford Stm Boiler Ins [*NYSE symbol*] (TTSB)
HSB	Heat-Shield Boost [*Aerospace*]
HSB	Helmet Stowage Bag [*NASA*] (KSC)
HSB	Hermetically Sealed Bushing
HSB	High School and Beyond Survey [*Department of Education*] (GFGA)
HSB	High Speed Boat (DOMA)
HSB	High-Speed Buffer
HSB	High-Speed Bus [*Computer science*]
HSB	Hobbyists Sourcebook [*A publication*]
HSB	Horizontal Sounding Balloon (IAA)
HSB	Hospitals Superannuation Board [*Victoria, Australia*]
HSB	Hue/Saturation/Brightness [*Color model*] [*Printer technology*] (PCM)
HSB	Hunter-Schreger Bands [*Tooth structure*]
HSB	Hutterian Brethren [*Hutterian Society of Brothers*] [*Acronym is based on former name,*] (EA)
HSBA	Herdwick Sheep Breeders Association [*British*] (DBA)
HSBA	High Speed Bus Adaptor (NITA)
HSBA	Historic Statistics of Black America [*A publication*]
HSBA	Horizontal Static Balancing Adjustment
HSBC	Hongkong and Shanghai Banking Corp.
HSBG	Heel Stick Blood Gas [*Medicine*] (DAVI)
HSBI	Hyde Stud Bloodstock Investments Ltd. [*British*]
HSBK	Hibernia Savings Bank [*NASDAQ symbol*] (NQ)
HSBK	Hibernia Savings Bk [*NASDAQ symbol*] (TTSB)
HSBP	High-Speed Bench Press
HSBR	Bor [*Sudan*] [*ICAO location identifier*] (ICLI)
HSBR	High-Speed Bombing RADAR
HSBT	Bentu [*Sudan*] [*ICAO location identifier*] (ICLI)
HS + C	Half-Sample plus Complement [*Statistics*]
HS-C	Hamilton Standard Carbon Dioxide Absorbent Material (NASA)
HSC	Hampden-Sydney College [*Virginia*]
HSC	Hand-Schueller-Christian [*Disease*] [*Medicine*]
HSC	Hardware-Software Configuration [*Computer science*]
HSC	Hardware/Software Coordination (NASA)
HSC	Harmonized System Code [*File indexing*]
HSC	Harsco Corp. [*NYSE symbol*] (SPSG)
HSC	Hawker Siddeley Canada, Inc. [*Toronto Stock Exchange symbol Vancouver Stock Exchange symbol*]
HSC	Hawker Siddeley Cda [*TS, exchange symbol*] (TTSB)
HSC	Hazardous Materials Spill Center [*Department of Energy*]
HSC	Health and Safety Commission [*Department of Employment*] [*British*]
HSC	Health Sciences Consortium (EA)
HSC	Health Services Centre [*Institute of Organisation and Social Studies, Brunel University*] [*British*] (CB)
HSC	Health Services Command [*Army*]
HSC	Heat-Shock Cognate [*Biochemistry*]
HSC	Heat Sterilization Compound
HSC	Heavy & Specialized Carriers Tariff Bureau, Washington DC [*STAC*]
HSC	Hematopoietic Stem Cell [*Hematology*]
HSC	Henderson State College [*Later, Henderson State University*] [*Arkansas*]
HSC	Heraldry Society of Canada (EAIO)
HSC	Hermetic-Sealed Container (MSA)
HSC	Hierarchical Storage Controller (ACRL)
HSC	Higher School Certificate [*British*]
HSC	High School Completion (OICC)
HSC	High-Speed Carry
HSC	High-Speed Channel [*Computer science*]
HSC	High-Speed Concentrator
HSC	High Sulphur Content (PDAA)
HSC	High-Swirl Combustion [*Engine*]
HSC	Holly Sugar Corp. (EFIS)
HSC	Home Products Safety Council (EA)
HSC	Home Shopping Club [*of the Home Shopping Network*]
HSC	Horizon Scanner (MSA)
HSC	Hospital for Sick Children [*Toronto, ON*] [*Canada*]
HSC	Hot Stove Club (EA)
HSC	House Space Committee [*US Congress*] (AAG)
HS/C	House Spacecraft (KSC)
HSC	Human SERVE [*Service Employees Registration and Voter Education*] Campaign (EA)
HSC	Human Skin Collagen
HSC	Humboldt State College [*Later, Humboldt State University*] [*California*]

HSC .... Humor Stamp Club (EA)
HSC .... Hunting Surveys & Consultants [*Commercial firm*] [*British*]
HSC .... Huntington Society of Canada
HSC .... Hydrogen Stress Cracking (PDAA)
HSCA .... Health Sciences Communications Association (DAVI)
HSCA .... Horizontal Sweep Circuit Analyzer
HSCC .... Heavy Specialized Carriers Conference [*Later, SC & RA*]
HSCC .... Hollywood Studio Collectors Club (EA)
HSCD .... Hand-Schueller-Christian Disease (MEDA)
HSCD .... Hazardous Site Control Division [*Environmental Protection Agency*] (GFGA)
HSCE .... Higher School Certificate Examination (ADA)
HSCF .... Health Sciences Computing Facility [*UCLA*]
HSCG .... Erkowit/Carthago [*Sudan*] [*ICAO location identifier*] (ICLI)
HSchein ..... Henry Schein, Inc. [*Associated Press*] (SAG)
H Sch M ..... High School Magazine [*A publication*] (BRI)
HSCI .... High School Characteristics Index [*Research test*] [*Psychology*]
HSCL .... High-Speed Command Link
HSCL .... Hopkins Symptom Checklist [*Psychology*] (DHP)
HSCL .... Housecall Medical Resources [*NASDAQ symbol*] (TTSB)
HSCL .... Housecall Medical Resources, Inc. [*NASDAQ symbol*] (SAG)
HSCLCS ...... Harpoon Shipboard Command and Launch Control Set [*Missiles*] (NVT)
HSCLS .... Harpoon Shipboard Command and Launch Subsystem [*Missiles*] (MCD)
HS-CoA .... Reduced Coenzyme A [*Biochemistry*] (DAVI)
HSCOCS ...... House Select Committee on the Outer Continental Shelf [*US Congress*] [*Marine science*] (MSC)
HSCOR .... House Staff Check on Rounds [*Medicine*]
HSCP .... Health Science Cluster Program [*University of Connecticut*] [*Research center*] (RCD)
HSCP .... Heat-Shock Cognate Protein [*Biochemistry*]
HSCP .... High-Speed Card Punch [*Computer science*] (AABC)
HSCP .... Historical Sources Collection Program
HSCR .... High-Speed Card Reader [*Computer science*] (AABC)
HSCR .... High-Strength Cold-Rolled (PDAA)
HSCR .... High Sub-Chief Ranger [*Ancient Order of Foresters*]
HSCRG .... Historic Stock Car Racing Group
HSCS .... Helicopter Subcontrol Ship [*Navy*] (NVT)
HSCSC .... Hodgkin Self-Concept Scale for Children [*Psychology*] (DHP)
HSCT .... High-Speed Civil Transport [*Supersonic plane*]
HSCT .... High Speed Commercial Transport [*MTMC*] (TAG)
HSCT .... High-Speed Compound Terminal [*Computer science*] (MCD)
HSCT .... Hughes Satellite Communications Terminal
HSCT .... Hypersonic Commercial Transport [*Airplane*]
HSCTT .... High-Speed Card Teletypewriter Terminal [*Computer science*] (CET)
HSCU .... Helicopter Subcontrol Unit (NVT)
HSCU .... Hydraulic Supply and Checkout Unit (NASA)
HS/CV .... Home Shopper/Cable Value [*Cable television channel*]
HSCW .... Helicopter Sea Control Wing (NVT)
HSD .... Doctor of Health and Safety (PGP)
HSD .... Hamilton Standard Division (NASA)
HSD .... Hardsite Defense [*Army*] (AABC)
HSD .... Hard/Soft Display (NITA)
HSD .... Harnosand [*Sweden*] [*Airport symbol*] (AD)
HSD .... Hawker-Siddeley Dynamics
HSD .... Heat-Sensing Device (DNAB)
HSD .... Height Sensing Device
HSD .... Hemisphere Development Corp. [*Vancouver Stock Exchange symbol*]
HSD .... Hierarchical Structured Data Set (IAA)
HSD .... Higher Anti-Submarine Detector [*British military*] (DMA)
HSD .... High-Speed Data
HSD .... High-Speed Displacement (IEEE)
HSD .... High-Speed Draft [*Print quality*]
HSD .... High-Sulfur Diesel Fuel [*Petroleum marketing*]
HSD .... Hit Scoring Device
H(SD) .... Holtzman Sprague-Dawley Rat [*Medicine*] (DMAA)
HSD .... Homer Semana Dia (BJA)
HSD .... Home Satellite Dish (NTCM)
HSD .... Homestead Village, Inc. [*AMEX symbol*] (SAG)
HSD .... Honestly Significant Difference
HSD .... Horizontal Situation Display
HSD .... Hot Shutdown (IEEE)
HSD .... Hot Side
HSD .... Human Services Division [*Air Force*]
HSD .... Human Systems Division [*Brooks Air Force Base, TX*] [*United States Air Force Systems Command*] (GRD)
HSD .... Hydraulic Steering and Diving [*System*] (DNAB)
HSD .... Hydropneumatic Suspension Device
HSD .... Hydroxysteroid Dehydrogenase [*An enzyme*]
HSD .... Hypertonic Saline Dextran [*Medicine*]
HSDA .... Heat Strain Decision [*Army*] (RDA)
HSDA .... High-Speed Data Acquisition [*Computer science*]
HSDA .... High-Speed Data Assembly [*Ground Communications Facility, NASA*]
HS-DARS ..... High-Speed Data Acquisition and Reduction System
HSDB .... Debba [*Sudan*] [*ICAO location identifier*] (ICLI)
HSDB .... Hastings' Shorter Dictionary of the Bible [*A publication*] (BJA)
HSDB .... Hazardous Substances Data Bank [*National Library of Medicine*] [*Information service or system*] (IID)
HSDB .... High-Speed Data Buffer
HSDB .... High Speed Data Bus [*Computer science*] (DOMA)
HSDC .... Hawaii State Data Center [*Hawaii State Department of Planning and Economic Development*] [*Information service or system*] (IID)
HSDC .... Health Systems Design [*NASDAQ symbol*] (TTSB)
HSDC .... Health Systems Design Corp. [*NASDAQ symbol*] (SAG)

HSDC .... High-Speed Data Channel (IAA)
HSDE .... High School Driver Education [*Department of Transportation*]
HSDF .... High-Speed Digital Filter
HSDG .... Hamburg-Sudamerikanische Dampschiffarts-Gesellschaft [*Hamburg-South American Steamship Co.*] [*Shipping*] (ROG)
HSDG .... High School Diploma Graduate [*Military*]
HSDI .... Health Self Determination Index (MEDA)
HSDI .... High-Speed Data Interface
HSDI .... High-Speed Direct Injection [*Diesel engines*]
HS Dir .... Director of Health and Safety (PGP)
HSDL .... Dilling [*Sudan*] [*ICAO location identifier*] (ICLI)
HSDL .... High-Speed Data Line [*or Link*]
HSDL .... High-Speed Digital Subscriber Line [*Telecommunications*] (ITD)
HSDLA .... Home School Legal Defense Association (PAZ)
HSDM .... Dueim [*Sudan*] [*ICAO location identifier*] (ICLI)
HSDM .... High-Speed Die Mounter
HSDMS .... Highly Secure Database Management System [*Computer science*] (MHDI)
HSDN .... Dongola [*Sudan*] [*ICAO location identifier*] (ICLI)
HSDP .... Hardsite Data Processor [*Army*] (AABC)
HSDP .... Hungarian Social Democratic Party [*Political party*] (EY)
HSDS .... Horizontal Situation Display System
HSDT .... High-Speed Distributor Transmitter
HSDT .... Hopper Side Tanks [*on a ship*] (DS)
HSDZ .... Damazin [*Sudan*] [*ICAO location identifier*] (ICLI)
HSE .... Compania Helicopteros del Sureste SA [*Spain ICAO designator*] (FAAC)
HsE .... Hawker-Siddeley Electronics Ltd., Microform Division, Fairfield, V, Australia [*Library symbol Library of Congress*] (LCLS)
HSE .... Health and Safety Executive [*Department of Employment*] [*Sheffield, England*]
HSE .... Heat Shield Entry [*Aerospace*] (IAA)
HSE .... Heat-Shock Element [*Genetics*]
HSE .... Heat-Stable Esterase (PDAA)
HSE .... Helsinki Stock Exchange [*Finland*]
HSE .... Hemorrhagic Shock and Encephalopathy [*Medicine*] (DMAA)
HSE .... Herpes Simplex Encephalitis [*Medicine*]
HSE .... Hic Sepultus Est [*Here Lies Buried*] [*Latin*]
HSE .... Highly Siderophile Element [*Biology*]
HSE .... High School Equivalency (OICC)
HSE .... High-Speed Encoder (IAA)
HSE .... High-Speed Signal Control Equipment [*Data communication*] (MHDI)
HSE .... Historically Socialist Economy (ECON)
HSE .... Home Sports Entertainment [*Cable-television system*]
HSE .... Honolulu Stock Exchange [*Hawaii*]
HSE .... House
HSE .... HS Resources [*NYSE symbol*] (TTSB)
HSE .... HS Resources, Inc. [*NYSE symbol*] (SAG)
HSEAD .... Historical Society of Early American Decoration [*Defunct*] (EA)
HSEC .... Historical Society of the Episcopal Church (EA)
HSED .... Hazardous Site Evaluation Division [*Office of Solid Waste and Emergency Response*] (COE)
HSEF .... High School Evangelism Fellowship (EA)
HseFbr .... House of Fabrics, Inc. [*Associated Press*] (SAG)
HseFbrc ...... House of Fabrics, Inc. [*Associated Press*] (SAG)
HSEHLD ...... Household
HSEHOLD .... Household
HSEKPR .... Housekeeper (ROG)
HSEL .... High-Speed Selector Channel
HSELINE ..... Health and Safety Executive Online [*Health and Safety Executive*] [*Bibliographic database*] [*British*]
HSEN .... Home Sports Entertainment Network [*Cable TV programming service*]
HSEP .... Heart Synchronized Evoked Potential [*Medicine*] (DMAA)
HSEP .... High-Speed Electrostatic Printer
HSEP .... Hospital Surgical Expansion Package [*Air Force*] (DOMA)
HSERC .... Historical Society of the Evangelical and Reformed Church [*Later, ERHS-UCC*] (EA)
H/serf .... High-Scope Educational Research Foundation (EA)
HSES .... Helper Self-Exploration Scale [*Psychology*] (DHP)
HSES .... Hemorrhagic Shock-Encephalopathy Syndrome [*Medicine*] (DMAA)
HSES .... Hughes Satellite Earth Station
HSES .... Hydrostatic Equilibrium System [*For chromatography*]
HSET .... Hino Super Flow Turbine [*Diesel engine*]
HSETC .... Health Sciences Education and Training Command [*Navy*] (DNAB)
HSEUBC ...... Historical Society of the Evangelical United Brethren Church [*Later, General Commission on Archives and History of the United Methodist Church*] (EA)
HSF .... Hartford Seminary Foundation [*Connecticut*]
HSF .... Hawaiian Sea Frontier
HSF .... Heat-Shock Transcription Factor [*Genetics*]
HSF .... Heat-Stable Fraction
HSF .... Heat Stimulated Flow (PDAA)
HSF .... Hepatocyte Stimulating Factor [*Endocrinology*]
HSF .... High Seas Fleet [*British military*] (DMA)
HSF .... High-Starch Fraction [*Food technology*]
HSF .... Histamine-Induced Suppressor Factor [*Immunology*]
HSF .... Histamine-Sensitizing Factor [*Immunology*]
HSF .... Home Service Force [*British*] (BARN)
HSF .... Hotel Sundry Fund [*Air Force*]
HSF .... Human Services Forum [*Defunct*] (EA)
HSF .... Hyderabad State Force [*British military*] (DMA)
HSF .... Hypergol Servicing Facility [*NASA*] (NASA)
HSF .... Hypersonic Flow
HSF .... Hypothalamic Secretory Factor [*Endocrinology*]

HSF-ACTH.... Hypothalmic Secretory Factor for Adreno-Corticotropic Hormone (PDAA)
HSFAE .... High-Speed Fuel Air Explosive
HSFB .... High Speed Fleet Broadcast (DOMA)
HSFC .... Hank Snow Fan Club [Defunct] (EA)
HSFF .... High-Speed Force Feed
HSFG .... High Strength Friction Grip (PDAA)
HSFMCV ...... Huguenot Society of the Founders of Manakin in the Colony of Virginia (EA)
HSFO .... High Sulphur Fuel Oil
HSFPJ .... Holocaust Survivors and Friends in Pursuit of Justice (EA)
HSFS .... El Fasher [Sudan] [ICAO location identifier] (ICLI)
HSFS .... High-Speed Flight Station [NASA]
HSFV .... High Speed Freight Vehicle (PDAA)
HSG .... Harris Steel Group, Inc. [Toronto Stock Exchange symbol]
HSG .... Headquarters, Support Group [Military]
HSG .... Health and Safety Guide [Toxicology]
HSG .... Herpes Simplex Genitalis
HSG .... High School for Girls (ADA)
HSG .... High School Graduate [Classified advertising]
HSG .... High Sierra Group [Nevada-based group proposing CD-ROM standards]
HSG .... High Speed Generation [Hybrid vehicles] [Automotive engineering]
HSG .... High-Speed Grinding (PDAA)
HSG .... High Sustained G2 Acceleration [NASA] (NASA)
HSG .... Holy Shroud Guild (EA)
HSG .... Home-Station Gunnery [Military] (INF)
HSG .... Horizontal Sweep Generator [Telecommunications] (OA)
HSG .... Housing (AABC)
HSG .... Human Standard Globulin [Medicine]
HSG .... Hydroshift Gun
HSG .... Hysterectomy Support Group [British] (DBA)
HSG .... Hysterosalpingogram [Gynecology]
HSG .... Hysterosalpingography [Medicine] (DMAA)
HSGB .... Haflinger Society [British] (DBA)
HSGB .... Hysterosalpingography [Gynecology] (DAVI)
HSGBI .... Huguenot Society of Great Britain and Ireland (EAIO)
HS-GC .... Headspace Sampling-Gas Chromatography
HSGF .... Gedaref/Azaza [Sudan] [ICAO location identifier] (ICLI)
HSGF .... Hematopoietic Stem-Cell Growth Factor (DB)
HSGF .... Human Skeletal Growth Factor
HSGG .... Dinder/Galegu [Sudan] [ICAO location identifier] (ICLI)
HSGM .... Honorary Sergeant Major of the Regiment
HSGMOC..... Honorary Sergeant Major of the Corps [Marine Corps]
HSGMOR ..... Honorary Sergeant Major of the Regiment [Army]
HSGN .... Geneina [Sudan] [ICAO location identifier] (ICLI)
HSGO .... Gogerial [Sudan] [ICAO location identifier] (ICLI)
HSGP .... High School Geography Project [Defunct]
HSGP .... Human Sialoglycoprotein [Biochemistry] (DB)
HSGPA........ High School Grade Point Average (DHP)
HSGPC .... High-Speed Gel Permeation Chromatography
HSGREFSVCSYS... Housing Referral Service Record System [Military] (DNAB)
HSGT .... High-Speed Ground Transportation
HSGTC .... High-Speed Ground Test Center [Later, TTC] [Pueblo, CO]
HSH .... Handmaids of the Sacred Heart of Pohang (TOCD)
HSH .... Hebrew School Headache (BJA)
HSH .... Heinemann's Scientific Handbooks [A publication]
HSH .... Helix-Span-Helix [Protein structure]
HSH .... His [or Her] Serene Highness [Used for certain Continental European princes or princesses]
HSH .... Horseshoe (ROG)
HSHC .... Hemisuccinate of Hydrocortisone (STED)
HSHH .... Hill Staffers for the Hungry and Homeless (EA)
H/SHLD .... Heat Shield [Automotive engineering]
HSHLD .... Household (MSA)
HSHP .... High School for Health Professions
HSHRSSS .... High-Speed/High-Resolution Side Scan Sonar System [National Oceanic and Atmospheric Administration]
HS/HT .... Harmonised System/Harmonised Tariff [British] (WDAA)
HSI .... Handbook of Service Instructions (MCD)
HSI........... Hang Seng Index [Hong Kong Futures Exchange Index]
HSI........... Hardware/Software Interface (IAA)
HSI........... Harpoon Standard Initiator (MCD)
HSI........... Hastings [Nebraska] [Airport symbol] (OAG)
HSI........... Headquarters Staff Instruction
HSI........... Headquarters Staff Instructor (AAGC)
HSI........... Health Development Services, Inc. [Toronto Stock Exchange symbol]
HSI........... Heat Stress Index
HSI........... Heraldry Society of Ireland (EA)
HSI........... Herpes Simplex I [Titer and virus] [Medicine] (DAVI)
HSI........... HERTIS [Hertfordshire Technical Library and Information Service] Subj ect Index (NITA)
HSI........... High School Equivalency Index
HSI........... High Solar Intensity
HSI........... High Speed Impact (SAA)
HSI........... High-Speed Interferometer [Measures chemical components of smog] (KSC)
HSI........... High Strand Intensity
HSI........... Hi-Shear Indus [NYSE symbol] (TTSB)
HSI........... Hi-Shear Industries, Inc. [NYSE symbol] (SPSG)
HSI........... Hispanic Serving Institution
HSI........... Home and School Institute (EA)
HSI........... Horizontal Situation Indicator [Aviation]
HSI........... Horizontal Situation Indicator [Aerospace] (NAKS)
HSI........... Hoya Society International (EA)

HSI.............. Hsinkong [Republic of China] [Also, SGK] [Seismograph station code, US Geological Survey] (SEIS)
HSI.............. Hue-Saturation-Intensity [Video monitor] (BYTE)
HSI.............. Human Seminal Plasma Inhibitor [Medicine] (DMAA)
HSI.............. Human Systems Integration
HSIA............ Halogenated Solvents Industry Alliance (EA)
HSIC............ Henry Schein, Inc. [NASDAQ symbol] (SAG)
HSIC............ Schein (Henry) [NASDAQ symbol] (TTSB)
HSIC............ Schein [Henry], Inc. [NASDAQ symbol] (SAG)
HSI/CDI........ Horizontal Situation Indicator / Course Deviation Indicator [Aviation] (PDAA)
HSICNI......... Honourable Society of the Inns of Court of Northern Ireland
HSIF............ Hardware/Software Integration Facility (SSD)
HSIIL........... High-Speed Integrated Injection Logic (IAA)
HSIL............ High-Grade Squamous Intraepithelial Lesions [OCLC symbol]
HSIM........... Hill Samuel Investment Management [British]
HSIMP......... High-Speed Interface Message Processor (IAA)
HSIP............ Hsinchu Science-Based Industrial Park [Taiwan] (ECON)
HSIQ............ High School Interest Questionnaire [Vocational guidance test]
H/SIR........... Hardware/Software Integration Review (MCD)
HSIRMC....... Hazardous Substance Incident Response Management Course [Navy]
HSIS........... Highway Safety Information Service [National Highway Safety Administration] (IID)
HSJ............. Heat Shield Jettison [Aerospace] (IAA)
HSJ............. Honeycombed Sandwich Joint
HSJ............. Hoshina [Japan] [Seismograph station code, US Geological Survey] (SEIS)
HSK............ Hackensack, MN [Location identifier FAA] (FAAL)
HSK............ Heat Sink Kit
HSK............ Herpes Simplex Keratitis [Medicine] (DMAA)
HSK............ Herpes Stromal Keratitis [Medicine]
HSK............ Honeysuckle Creek Tracking Station [NASA] (KSC)
HSK............ Honorary Surgeon of the King [British]
HSK............ Horizontal Sling Kit [NASA] (NASA)
HSK............ Hsinking [Sirkyo, Chang Chun] [Republic of China] [Seismograph station code, US Geological Survey] (SEIS)
HSK............ HSK Minerals Ltd. [Toronto Stock Exchange symbol]
HSKA........... Kassala [Sudan] [ICAO location identifier] (ICLI)
HSKG........... Khashm El Girba [Sudan] [ICAO location identifier] (ICLI)
HSKI........... Kosti/Rabak [Sudan] [ICAO location identifier] (ICLI)
HSKJ........... Kago Kaju [Sudan] [ICAO location identifier] (ICLI)
HSKL........... Haskel International, Inc. [NASDAQ symbol] (SAG)
HSKL........... Haskel Intl 'A' [NASDAQ symbol] (TTSB)
HSKP........... Kapoeta [Sudan] [ICAO location identifier] (ICLI)
HSKPG......... Housekeeping (AFM)
hskpr.......... Housekeeper (BARN)
HSL............ Hardware Simulation Laboratory (NASA)
HSL............ Hazardous Substance List [Code of Federal Regulations] (FFDE)
HSL............ Health Service Laboratory [Army] (AABC)
HSL............ Heenan Senlac Resources Ltd. [Toronto Stock Exchange symbol]
HSL............ Helicopter Antisubmarine Squadron Light (NVT)
HSL............ Herpes Simplex Labialis
HSL............ High-Speed Launch [Navy]
HSL............ High-Speed Logic
HSL............ Highway Safety Literature [Database] (NITA)
HSL............ Highway Safety Literature Service [National Academy of Science] [Washington, DC]
HSL............ Hispania Lineas Aereas SL [Spain ICAO designator] (FAAC)
HSL............ Home-School Liaison (AIE)
Hsl............. Homoserine Lactone [An amino acid]
HSL............ Hormone-Sensitive Lipase [An enzyme]
HSL............ Hue, Saturation, Lightness [Color model] (PCM)
HSL............ Huslia [Alaska] [Airport symbol] (OAG)
HSL............ Hytran Simulation Language [Computer science] (PDAA)
HSLA.......... High Speed Line Adaptor (NITA)
HSLA.......... High-Strength Low-Alloy [or Light-Alloy] [Steel]
HSLAN........ High Speed Local Area Network [Telecommunications] (ACRL)
HSLC.......... High-Speed Liquid Chromatography
HSLC.......... High-Speed Single Line Controller (MHDB)
HSLCG........ Health Science Libraries of Central Georgia [Library network]
HSLDA........ Home School Legal Defense Association (EA)
HSLI.......... Kadugli [Sudan] [ICAO location identifier] (ICLI)
HSLIC......... Health Science Libraries Information Cooperative [Library network]
HSLLADS.... High-Speed, Low-Level Airdrop System [Military] (INF)
HSLLC........ High-Speed Liquid-Liquid Chromatography
HSLN.......... High-Speed Local Network [Telecommunications] (OSI)
HSLP.......... Haydn Society [Record label]
HSLR.......... Lirangu [Sudan] [ICAO location identifier] (ICLI)
HSL'S .... Hlinkova Slovenska l'Udova Strana [Hlinka's Slovak People's Party] [Also, SL'S] [Political party] (PPE)
HSLWI......... Helical Spring Lock Washer Institute
HSM........... Hand and Shoe Monitor [Radiation detection]
HSM........... Hardened Silo Missile
HSM........... Hard Structure Module
HSM........... Hard Structure Munition
HSM........... Harmonic Subcarrier Method (MCD)
HSM........... Harvard Semitic Museum (BJA)
HSM........... Health Services and Mental Health Administration [Later, ADAMHA] [Abolished, 1973] [HEW]
HSM........... Hepatosplenomegaly [Gastroenterology] (DAVI)
HSM........... Hermit Sisters of Mary (TOCD)
HSM........... Hierarchical Storage Manager [or Management]
HSM........... High-Speed Machining (MCD)
HSM........... High-Speed Measurement (IAA)

HSM............ High-Speed Memory [Computer science]
HSM............ High-Speed Motor [Electrical engineering]
HSM............ His [or Her] Serene Majesty
HSM............ Holosystolic Murmur [Cardiology] (DAVI)
HSM............ Horsham [Australia Airport symbol Obsolete] (OAG)
HSM............ Horsham Corp. [Toronto Stock Exchange symbol NYSE symbol]
HSM............ Hospital - Surgical - Medical
HSM............ Humanitarian Service Medal (MCD)
HSM............ Hydraulic System Module (MCD)
HSMA .... Hotel Sales Management Association [Later, HSMAI] (EA)
HSMAI........ Hospitality Sales and Marketing Association International (NTPA)
HSMAI........ Hotel Sales and Marketing Association International (EA)
HSMAI-EO.... Hotel Sales and Marketing Association International - European Office [Utrecht, Netherlands] (EAIO)
HSMB .... Hybrid Superconducting Magnetic Bearing
HSMCDR...... High-Speed Multichannel Data Recorder [Instrumentation]
HSMD.......... Maridi [Sudan] [ICAO location identifier] (ICLI)
HSMF.......... Holocaust Survivors Memorial Foundation (EA)
HSMGC....... Heavy Section Machine Gun Corps [British military] (DMA)
HSMHA....... Health Services and Mental Health Administration [Later, ADAMHA] [Abolished, 1973] [HEW]
HSMIMP ..... High-Speed Modular Interface Message Processor
HSMK .... Rumbek [Sudan] [ICAO location identifier] (ICLI)
HSMO .... High-Speed Membrane Osmometry (MCD)
HSMO .... Hospital Senior Medical Officer [Australia]
HSMO .... Hydraulic System Mineral Oil [Mechanical engineering]
HSMR .... Merowe [Sudan] [ICAO location identifier] (ICLI)
HSMS .... Hazardous Substance Management System (BCP)
HSMS .... High Speed Message Services (AAEL)
HSMS .... High-Speed Microwave Switch
HSMSR .... Hardsite Missile Site RADAR [Army] (AABC)
HSM-WA..... Hard Structure Munition Weaponization Analysis (MCD)
HSN............ Haglund Industry International [Vancouver Stock Exchange symbol]
HSN............ Hanson-Street Nail (MEDA)
HSN............ Hereditary Sensory Neuropathy [Neurology]
HSN............ Hermaphrodite-Specific Neuron [Cytology]
HSN............ Herpes Simplex Neonatorum (STED)
HSN............ High Speed Network
HSN............ Home Shopping Network [Cable-television system]
HSN............ Home Shopping Network, Inc. [NYSE symbol] (SPSG)
HSN............ Hospital Satellite Network [Los Angeles, CA] [Cable-television system]
HSN............ Hsinchu [Republic of China] [Seismograph station code, US Geological Survey] (SEIS)
HSN............ Hughes Sports Network [Formerly, SNI]
HSNA .... Southern Air Ltd. [British ICAO designator] (FAAC)
HSNA .... Nasir [Sudan] [ICAO location identifier] (ICLI)
HSND.......... Shendi [Sudan] [ICAO location identifier] (ICLI)
HSNG.......... Housing
HSNH.......... Nahud [Sudan] [ICAO location identifier] (ICLI)
H/SNK........ Heat Sink [Automotive engineering]
HSNL.......... Nyala [Sudan] [ICAO location identifier] (ICLI)
HSNM.......... Nimule/Nimule [Sudan] [ICAO location identifier] (ICLI)
HSNP.......... Hawker-Siddeley Nuclear Power Co. Ltd. [British]
HSNP.......... High-Speed Nonimpact Printer [Acronym pronounced "hisnip"] [Computer science]
HSNPP........ Hlinka Slovak National People's Party [Political party]
HSNR.......... Halstead Energy [NASDAQ symbol] (TTSB)
HSNR.......... Halstead Energy Corp. [NASDAQ symbol] (SAG)
HSNR.......... Sennar [Sudan] [ICAO location identifier] (ICLI)
HSNS .... High School News Service [Fleet Hometown News Center] (DNAB)
HSNSW....... Haemophilia Society of New South Wales [Australia]
HSNT .... Historical Society of the Northern Territory [Australia]
HSNTA........ New Testament Apocrypha [E. Henneke and W. Schneemelcher] [A publication] (BJA)
HSNW......... New Halfa [Sudan] [ICAO location identifier] (ICLI)
HSNY......... Holland Society of New York (EA)
HSO .... Compania Helicopteros de Transporte SA [Spain ICAO designator] (FAAC)
HSO .... Habitation/Station Operations (SSD)
HSO .... Haifa Symphony Orchestra (BJA)
HSO .... Headquarters Signal Officer (NATG)
HSO .... Higher Scientific Officer [British]
HSO .... High Specific Output [Automotive engineering]
HSO .... High Speed Optimized [General Tire Co.] [Automobile tires]
HSOB .... Hydrogen Seal Oil [System] (NRCH)
HSOB .... El Obeid [Sudan] [ICAO location identifier] (ICLI)
HSOD .... Human Superoxide Dismutase [An enzyme]
HSOM .... Habitation/Station Operations Module (SSD)
H SOM........ Hora Somni [At Bedtime] [Pharmacy]
h som........ Hora Somni [Hour of Sleep] [Latin] (STED)
HSORS........ High Seas Oil Recovery System
HSOT .... Howitzer Strap-On Trainer [Military] (RDA)
HSP .... Half-Shade Plate
HSP .... Hardwire Safing Panel
HSP .... Haute Societe Protestante [Protestant High Society] (IIA)
HSP .... Head Start Program [Education]
HSP .... Health and Safety Plan (BCP)
HSP .... Health and Safety Practices (COE)
HSP .... Health Service Plan
HSP .... Health Stabilization Program [NASA] (NASA)
HSP .... Health Systems Plan [HEW]
HSP .... Heat Shock Protein [Physiology]
hsp............. Heat Shock Protein [Gene] (DMAA)
HSP .... Heavy, Stressed Platform

HSP .... Hemostatic Screening Profile [Medicine] (DMAA)
HSP .... Henoch-Schoenlein Purpura [Medicine] (AAMN)
HSP .... Heparin Sulfate Proteoglycan [Biochemistry]
HSP .... Hereditary Spastic Paraplegia [Medicine]
HSP .... High-Speed Printer [Computer science]
HSP .... High-Speed Pulse
HSP .... High-Speed Punch (IAA)
HSP .... Historical Society of Pennsylvania
HSP .... Hollow Soft Point [Bullet] (DICI)
HSP .... Home Services Program [Australia]
HSP .... Hospital Service Plan [British]
HSP .... Hot Springs [Virginia] [Airport symbol] (AD)
HSP .... Hot Springs, VA [Location identifier FAA] (FAAL)
HSP .... Hot Stamping Press
HSP .... Hrvatska Stranka Prava [Croatian Party of Rights] [Former Yugoslavia] [Political party] (PPE)
HSP .... Human Sciences Project [National Science Foundation]
HSP .... Human Serum Prealbumin
HSP .... Human Serum Protein (DB)
HSP .... Hungarian Socialist Party [Political party] (EY)
HSP .... Hydrocarbon Solids Process [Tosco Corp.] [Oil shale pyrolysis]
HSP .... Hysterosalpingography (STED)
HSPA .... Hawaiian Sugar Planters' Association (EA)
HSPA .... High-Speed Parallel Adder
HSPA .... Human Service Personnel Association [Defunct] (EA)
HSPA .... Pachella [Sudan] [ICAO location identifier] (ICLI)
HSPC .... Heat Sterilizable Potting Compound
HSPC .... Hospice
HSPDP .... Hill State People's Democratic Party [India] [Political party] (PPW)
HSPE .... High Strength Polyethylene [Organic chemistry]
HSPEX........ SMBS Special Equities Cl.B [Mutual fund ticker symbol] (SG)
HSPF .... Heating Seasonal Performance Factor
HSPF .... Hydrologic Simulation Program Fortran
HSPG .... Heparan Sulfate Proteoglycan [Biochemistry]
HSPI .... High-Speed Printer Interface (MCD)
HSPI .... Pibor [Sudan] [ICAO location identifier] (ICLI)
HSPLS .... Hawaii State Public Library System [Hawaii State Department of Education] [Information service or system] (IID)
HSPQ .... High School Personality Questionnaire [Psychology]
HSPR .... High School Percentile Rank
HSpS .... Daughters of the Holy Spirit Nazareth of the Good Shepherd (TOCD)
HSPS .... Heat Shock Protein Synthesis
HSPS .... Henoch-Schoelein Purpura Syndrome [Medicine] (WDAA)
HSPS .... Highway Safety Program Standard [Department of Transportation]
HSPS .... Hydrographic Survey Platform System (MCD)
HSPSD .... High-Speed Packet Switched Data [Computer science] (ACRL)
HSPT .... High School Placement Test
HSPTAL ...... High-Speed Paper Tape Absolute Loader [Computer science] (MDG)
HSPTP .... High-Speed Paper Tape Punch [Computer science] (AABC)
HSPTR .... High-Speed Paper Tape Reader [Computer science] (CET)
HSPU .... Householders for Safe Pesticide Use [Australia]
HSQ .... Heat-Shield Qualification [NASA] (KSC)
HSQ .... Helping Smokers Quit [American Cancer Society] (EA)
HSQ .... Home Screening Questionnaire [Test] [Psychology]
HSQ .... Houston, TX [Location identifier FAA] (FAAL)
HSQB .... Health Standards and Quality Bureau [HEW]
HSQC .... Heteronuclear Single Quantum Coherence [Spectrum]
HSQC .... Heteronuclear Single Quantum Correlation [Spectrum]
HSQR .... High-Strength Quick Release (MCD)
HSR .... Hampshire Swine Registry (EA)
HSR .... Handbook of Structural Repair (MCD)
HSR .... Harbor Surveillance RADAR [Navigation] (IAA)
HSR .... Hardware Status Register (MCD)
HSR .... Harleco Synthetic Resin (MAE)
HSR .... Hart-Scott-Rodino Antitrust Improvements Act [1976]
HSR .... Health Service Region [Army] (AABC)
HSR .... Heated Serum Reagin [Immunochemistry] (DAVI)
HSR .... Heat Shield Recovery [Aerospace] (IAA)
HSR .... High School Percentile Rank
HSR .... High-Speed RADAR (MCD)
HSR .... High-Speed Rail
HSR .... High-Speed Reader [Computer science]
HSR .... High-Speed Relay
HSR .... High Stocking Rate [Agriculture] (OA)
HSR .... Hi-Shear Technology [AMEX symbol] (TTSB)
HSR .... Hi Shear Technology Corp. [AMEX symbol] (SAG)
HSR .... Homestead Resources, Inc. [Vancouver Stock Exchange symbol]
HSR .... Homogeneously Staining Region [Cytology]
HSR .... Horizontal Size Ratio [Ophthalmology]
HSR .... Hot Springs [South Dakota] [Airport symbol] (AD)
HSR .... Hot Springs, SD [Location identifier FAA] (FAAL)
HSR .... Human Science Research [Concept car] [Automotive engineering]
HSRA .... Half Saddlebred Registry of America (EA)
HSRA .... Harvard-Smithsonian Reference Atmosphere
HSRA .... Health Services and Resources Administration (DAVI)
HSRA .... High-Speed Data Regeneration Assembly [Ground Communications Facility, NASA]
HSRA .... High Speed Rail Association (EA)
HSRA .... Hollow Shaft Rotary Actuator
HSR & D...... Health Services Research and Development Service [Washington, DC Veterans Administration] (GRD)
HSRC.......... Health Services Research Center [Georgia Institute of Technology] [Research center] (RCD)
HSRC.......... High School Red Cross

HSRC .... Highway Safety Research Center [*University of North Carolina, Chapel Hill*] [*Research center*]   (RCD)
HSRC .... Human Sciences Research Council [*South Africa*]
HSRC .... Human-Subjects Review Committee [*Medicine*]   (BABM)
HSRD .... Health Services Research and Development [*Series*] [*A publication*]
HSRD .... Hypertension Secondary to Renal Disease [*Medicine*]
HSrep .... Health & Safety Representative   (WDAA)
HSRFO .... High-Sulfur Residual Fuel Oil [*Petroleum technology*]
HSRI .... Health Systems Research Institute
HSRI .... Highly Sensitive Refractive Index
HSRI .... Highway Safety Research Institute [*University of Michigan*]
HSRIOP .... High Speed RAD [*Rapid Access Data Dram*] Input/Output Processor [*Xerox*]   (NITA)
HSRJ .... Raga [*Sudan*] [*ICAO location identifier*]   (ICLI)
HSR/MLA ...... High Speed Rail/Maglev Association
HSRN .... Heavy Straight Run Naphtha [*Petroleum chemistry*]
HSRN .... Renk [*Sudan*] [*ICAO location identifier*]   (ICLI)
HSRO .... High-Speed Repetitive Operation
HSRP .... Headquarters Systems Replacement Program [*Military*]   (GFGA)
HSRP .... High Speed Research Program [*NASA*] [*Marine science*]   (OSRA)
HSRP .... High-Speed Rotary Prism
HSRRB .... Human Subjects Research Review Board [*Army*]   (RDA)
HSRS .... Health-Sickness Rating Scale   (DMAA)
HSRS .... Hurricane Supersonic Research Site
HS Rsc .... HS Resources, Inc. [*Associated Press*]   (SAG)
HSRTC .... Health and Safety Research and Test Center [*Bureau of Mines*]
HSRTM .... High-Speed Resin Transfer Molding [*Automotive engineering*]
HSRTP .... Health Services Research and Training Program [*Purdue University*] [*Research center*]   (RCD)
HSRV .... Human Spumaretrovirus
HSS .... British Library Catalog: Humanities and Social Sciences [*Information service or system*]   (CRD)
HSS .... Habitability Support System   (MCD)
HSS .... Hallervorden-Spatz Syndrome [*Medicine*]   (AAMN)
HSS .... Hardware Specification Sheet   (IAA)
HSS .... Hars Systems, Inc. [*Vancouver Stock Exchange symbol*]
HSS .... Health Service Support [*Army*]   (DOMA)
HSS .... Health Surveillance System [*Shell Oil Co.*]
HSS .... Heeres-Sauerstoffschutzgeraet [*Service Oxygen Breathing Apparatus*] [*German military - World War II*]
HSS .... Helmet Sight Subsystem   (RDA)
HSS .... Hepatic Stimulator Substance
HSS .... Heraldry Society of Scotland [*Edinburgh*]   (EAIO)
HSS .... Hermanas del Servico Social   (TOCD)
HSS .... Hierarchy Service System [*Toshiba Corp.*]
HSS .... High School Size
HSS .... High Speed Reader   (NAKS)
HSS .... High-Speed Simultaneous [*Electric trip mechanism*]
HSS .... High-Speed Storage [*Computer science*]   (IEEE)
HSS .... High-Speed Supernatant [*Medicine*]   (DAVI)
HSS .... High-Speed System [*Ground Communications Facility, NASA*]
HSS .... High Spread Shears
HSS .... High-Strength Stainless Steel   (PDAA)
HSS .... High-Strength, Steel
HSS .... High-Stress Strain   (MCD)
HSS .... Hispano-Suiza Society   (EA)
HSS .... Historiae Societatis Socius [*Fellow of the Historical Society*] [*Latin*]
HSS .... History of Science Society   (EA)
HSS .... Hokkaido University [*Japan*] [*Seismograph station code, US Geological Survey*]   (SEIS)
HSS .... Honeycomb-Supported Screen
HSS .... Hospital and Specialist Services [*British*]
HSS .... Hospital Staffing Services, Inc. [*NYSE symbol*]   (SPSG)
HSS .... Hospital Staffing Svcs [*NYSE symbol*]   (TTSB)
HSS .... Hot Springs, NC [*Location identifier FAA*]   (FAAL)
HSS .... Hrvatska Seljacka Stranka [*Croatian Peasant Party*] [*Former Yugoslavia*] [*Political party*]   (PPE)
HSS .... Hull Seal Section
HSS .... Hunter Sensor Suite [*Military*]
HSS .... Hybrid Simulation System
HSS .... Hydraulic Subsystem Simulator   (NASA)
HSS .... Hydraulic System Simulator   (MCD)
HSS .... Hydrologic Sensing Satellite   (DNAB)
HSS .... Hydropneumatic Suspension System   (MCD)
HSS .... HyperSonic Sound
HSS .... Hypertonic Saline Solution
HSS .... Hypertrophic Subaortic Stenosis [*Cardiology*]
HSSA .... Handbag Supply Salesmen's Association   (EA)
HSSA .... Health and Safety Science Abstracts [*Cambridge Scientific Abstracts*] [*Information service or system*]   (CRD)
HSSA .... High Speed Steel Association [*British*]   (BI)
HSSALB .... Health Service Support Air Land Battle
HSSC .... Heavy SEAL [*Sea-Air-Land*] Support Craft   (NVT)
HSSD .... High-Speed Serial Data [*Automotive electronics*]
HSSD .... Hospital Sterile Supply Department   (DMAA)
HSSDB .... High-Speed Serial Data Buffer   (MCD)
HSSDS .... High-Speed Switched Digital Service [*AT & T*]   (TSSD)
HSSE .... High Soap Suds Enema [*Gastroenterology*]   (DAVI)
HSSG .... Heeres-Sauerstoffschutzgeraet [*Service Oxygen Breathing Apparatus*] [*German military - World War II*]
HSSG .... High-Speed Symbol Generator
HSSG .... Holograph Stress Strain Gauge
HSSGT .... High-Speed Guided Ground Transportation [*TXDOT*]   (TAG)
HSSI .... High-Speed Serial Interface [*Telecommunications*]
HSSI .... High-Speed Synchronous Interface [*Computer science*]

HSSI .... Highway Safety Statistical Indicator
HSSJ .... Juba [*Sudan*] [*ICAO location identifier*]   (ICLI)
HSSM .... Malakal [*Sudan*] [*ICAO location identifier*]   (ICLI)
HSSP .... Port Sudan [*Sudan*] [*ICAO location identifier*]   (ICLI)
HSSPF .... Hoehere SS und Polizeifuehrer   (BJA)
HSSR .... Hermit Sisters of Romuald   (TOCD)
HSSR .... Hydrogeochemical and Stream Sediment Reconnaissance   (PDAA)
HSSS .... Khartoum [*Sudan*] [*ICAO location identifier*]   (ICLI)
HSSSM .... Highly Sensitive Ship Synthesis Model   (DNAB)
HSSSR .... High School Students for Social Responsibility   (EA)
HSST .... Heavy Section Steel Technology [*Nuclear Regulatory Commission*]
HSST .... High-Speed Surface Transport   (MCD)
HSSTD .... Historical Sea Surface Temperature Data Project [*WMO*]   (MSC)
HSSTD .... Historical Sea Surface Temperature Dataset [*Marine science*]   (OSRA)
HSSU .... Hospital Sterile Supply Unit   (DMAA)
HSSW .... High Salinity Shelf Water [*Oceanography*]
HSSW .... Wadi Halfa/Nuba Lake [*Sudan*] [*ICAO location identifier*]   (ICLI)
HST .... Harmonic and Spurious Totalizer
HST .... Harry S Truman [*US president, 1884-1972*]
HST .... Harvard Step Test [*Physical tolerance test*]
HST .... Hawaiian-Aleutian Standard Time
HST .... Hawaiian Standard Time
H ST .... Head Steward [*Navy British*]   (ROG)
HST .... Health Screening Test   (DAVI)
HST .... Heat Shrinkable Tubing
HST .... Hebrew Speaking Test   (TMMY)
HST .... Heist [*C.H.*] Corp. [*AMEX symbol*]   (SPSG)
HST .... Helicopter Support Team [*Navy*]   (NVT)
HST .... Hemoccult Slide Test   (DB)
HST .... Hexobarbital Sleeping Time [*In experimental animals*]
HST .... High Speed Taxi-Way Turn Off [*Aviation*]   (DA)
HST .... High-Speed Technology [*Computer science*]   (BYTE)
HST .... High-Speed Telemetry
HST .... High-Speed Train [*British*]
HST .... High-Speed Tunnel [*NASA*]
HST .... Hoist   (MSA)
HST .... Homestead [*Florida*] [*Airport symbol*]   (OAG)
HST .... Homestead, FL [*Location identifier FAA*]   (FAAL)
HST .... Homogenate Survival Time
HST .... Horizontal Seismic Trigger   (IEEE)
HST .... Hot Shot Tunnel
HST .... Housing Study Tours [*British*]
HST .... Hoyer-Schlesinger-Turner, Inc.   (EFIS)
HST .... Hubble Space Telescope [*Great Observatory Program*] [*NASA*]
HST .... Hunter Stockton Thompson
HST .... Hydrostatic Transmission [*Automotive engineering*]
HST .... Hypersonic Transport [*Aircraft*]
HST .... Hypervelocity Shock Tunnel   (OA)
HSTA .... Honda Sport Touring Association   (EA)
HSTAMIDS .... Handheld Standoff Minefield Detection System [*Military*]   (RDA)
HSTAR .... Helicopter Surveillance and Target Acquisition RADAR
HSTAT .... Health Services/Technology Assessment Text [*National Library of Medicine*] [*Information service or system*]
HSTC .... Henderson State Teachers College [*Later, HSC*] [*Arkansas*]
HSTCO .... High-Stability Temperature-Compensated Crystal Oscillator [*Electronics*]   (OA)
HSTCXO .... High-Stability Temperature-Compensated Crystal Oscillator
H STEPH ...... Henricus Stephanus [*Imprint*] [*Latin*]   (ROG)
HSTF........... Heat-Shock Transcription Factor [*Genetics*]
HSTF........... Human Serum Thymus Factor [*Immunochemistry*]   (DAVI)
HSTH .... Hose Thread
HSTK .... Herpes Simplex Thymidine Kinase [*An enzyme*]
HSTL .... Harry S Truman Library
HSTL .... High-Speed Telemetry Link
HSTO .... Tong [*Sudan*] [*ICAO location identifier*]   (ICLI)
HSTP .... Hard Stop   (MCD)
HSTP .... Heat Sterilization Test Program
HSTR .... Amer Homestar [*NASDAQ symbol*]   (TTSB)
HSTR .... American Homestar Corp. [*NASDAQ symbol*]   (SAG)
HSTR .... Torit [*Sudan*] [*ICAO location identifier*]   (ICLI)
HSTRA .... High-Strength Thermal-Resistant Alloy
HSTRU .... Hydraulic System Test and Repair Unit [*Army*]   (RDA)
HSTS .... High-Pressure Side Temperature Sensor [*Air conditioning systems*] [*Automotive engineering*]
HSTS .... Horizontal Stabilizer Trim Setting
HSTS .... Host Software Testing Section [*Social Security Administration*]
HSTS .... Hydraulic Subsystems Test Station   (MCD)
HSTSF .... Harry S Truman Scholarship Foundation   (EA)
HSTT........... High-Speed Test Track
HSTTL .... High-Speed Transistor-Transistor Logic
HSTU .... Tumbura [*Sudan*] [*ICAO location identifier*]   (ICLI)
HSTV .... High-Survivability Test Vehicle   (MCD)
HSTVL .... High Survivability Test Vehicle, Lightweight [*Military*]
HSTVX .... Heritage Value Equity Cl.A [*Mutual fund ticker symbol*]   (SG)
HSTW .... Humane Society of Tinplate Workers [*A union*] [*British*]
HSU .... Hardin-Simmons University [*Texas*]
HSU .... Hartridge Smoke Unit [*Automotive engineering*]
HSU .... Helium Service Unit   (MCD)
HSU .... Helium Speech Unscrambler [*Deep sea diving*]
HSU .... Henderson State University [*Arkadelphia, AR*]
HSU .... Hero of the Soviet Union [*Award*]   (DOMA)
HSU .... Highway Speed Uniformity [*Automotive tire testing*]
HSU .... Humboldt State University [*Los Angeles, CA*]
HSU .... Hydraulic Supply Unit

HSUA	Health Services Union of Australia
HSUG	Housing Statistics Users Group (EA)
HS/UMC	Historical Society of the United Methodist Church (EA)
HSUNA	Humanist Student Union of North America
HSUR	Half Symmetric Unstable Resonator (PDAA)
HSURIA	Half Symmetric Unstable Resonator with Intracavity Axicon (PDAA)
HSUS	Humane Society of the United States (EA)
HSUSA	Hemlock Society U.S.A. (EA)
HSUSA	Heraldry Society of the United States of America (EA)
HSUSC	Hymn Society in the United States and Canada (EA)
HSV	Haemophilia society of Victoria [*Australia*]
HSV	Head Small Veins [*Anatomy*]
HSV	Head Suppression Valve (AAG)
HSV	Heliservico-Sociedade Portuguesa de Exploracao de Meios Aeros Lda. [*Portugal ICAO designator*] (FAAC)
HSV	Herpes Simplex Virus
HSV	Highly Selective Vagotomy [*Medicine*]
HSV	High-Speed Video [*Instrumentation*]
HSV	High-Stage Valve (MCD)
HSV	Hop Stunt Viroid [*Medicine*] (DMAA)
HSV	Hue, Saturation, and Value [*Color model*] (BYTE)
HSV	Hull Solenoid Valve
HSV	Huntsville [*Alabama*] [*Airport symbol*]
HSV	Hydraulic Selector Valve
HSV	Hydrogen Saturated Vacancy [*Photovoltaic energy systems*]
HSV	Hydroxyinterlayered Smectite or Vermiculite
HSV	Hyperviscosity Syndrome [*Medicine*] (DB)
HSV-1	Herpes Simplex [*Medicine*] (TAD)
HSV-2	Herpes Simplex II [*Medicine*] (TAD)
HSVA	Health Systems Vendors Association [*San Francisco, CA*] (EA)
HSVE	Herpes Simplex Virus Encephalitis [*Medicine*]
HSVgD	Herpes Simplex Virus Glycoprotein D [*Biochemistry*]
HSVL	Highveld Steel & Vanadium Corp. Ltd. [*NASDAQ symbol*] (NQ)
HSVLY	Highveld Steel & VanadiumADR [*NASDAQ symbol*] (TTSB)
HSVtk	Herpes Simplex Virus Thymidine Kinase [*Medicine*] (DMAA)
HSW	Aerocombi SA [*Spain ICAO designator*] (FAAC)
HSW	Heat Sink Welding [*Nuclear energy*]
HSW	Helena Southwestern Railroad Co. [*AAR code*]
HSW	Hot Spot [*Washington*] [*Seismograph station code, US Geological Survey Closed*] (SEIS)
HSWA	Hazardous and Solid Waste Amendments [*1984 amendments to RCRA*]
HSWDC	Historical Society of Washington, DC (EA)
HSWG	High-Speed Wire Guidance
HSWH	High-Solid Waste Header [*Nuclear energy*] (NRCH)
HSWP	Hungarian Socialist Workers' Party [*Political party*] (PPW)
HSWRS	Housewares
HSWW	Wau [*Sudan*] [*ICAO location identifier*] (ICLI)
HSX	Hollywood Stock Exchange
HSY	Hershey Foods Corp. [*NYSE symbol*] (SPSG)
HSY	Hosiery
HSYA	Yambio [*Sudan*] [*ICAO location identifier*] (ICLI)
HSYE	Yei [*Sudan*] [*ICAO location identifier*] (ICLI)
HSYL	Yirol [*Sudan*] [*ICAO location identifier*] (ICLI)
HSyn	Heme Synthase (DB)
HSYNC	Horizontal Synchronous [*Computer science*]
HSZA	Zalingei [*Sudan*] [*ICAO location identifier*] (ICLI)
HSZD	Hermetically Sealed Zener Diode
HT	Air Tchad [*ICAO designator*] (AD)
HT	Haavara-Transfer (BJA)
HT	Hadamard-Transform [*Mathematics*]
ht	Haiti [*MARC country of publication code Library of Congress*] (LCCP)
HT	Haiti [*ANSI two-letter standard code*] (CNC)
HT	Half-Tilt Containers (DCTA)
HT	Half-Time [*Survey*] [*Shipping*]
HT	Half-Title [*Publishing*]
ht	Halftone [*Photography*] [*Art*] (WDMC)
HT	Half Tone [*Printing*] (NITA)
HT	Half-Tracked [*Vehicle*] (NATG)
H-T	Half-Truck [*British*]
HT	Halt and Transfer
HT	Hammer Toe [*Orthopedics*] (DAVI)
HT	Hand-Held Terminal [*Computer science*] (MHDB)
HT	Handling Time
HT	Handmaids of the Most Holy Trinity (TOCD)
HT	Hand Test [*Psychology*]
HT	Hand Transceiver
HT	Hand Translation (MCD)
HT	Handy Talky [*Radio*]
HT	Hard Top [*Automobile advertising*]
HT	Hashimoto's Thyroiditis [*Medicine*] (DMAA)
HT	Haustus [*A Drink*] [*Pharmacy*]
HT	Hawaiian Territory [*Prior to statehood*]
HT	Hawaiian Theater [*Military*]
HT	Hawaiian Time
HT	Headed Type
H/T	Head per Track
HT	Head, Tail [*Coin-tossing probability*]
HT	Head-to-Tail [*Polymer structure*]
HT	Head Turn [*Industrial engineering*]
HT	Hearing Test (CPH)
HT	Heart
HT	Heart Tones [*Medicine*]
HT	Heart Transplantation
HT	Heat (AAG)

HT	Heat Transfer (NASA)
HT	Heat Treat
HT	Heavy Tank
HT	Heavy Terminal [*AFSCF*] (MCD)
HT	Heavy Thermoplastic (IAA)
HT	Hebrew Text (BJA)
HT	Height (AAG)
ht	Height [*Also, h*] (WDMC)
Ht	Height of Heart (STED)
HT	Height of Target
HT	Heights [*Commonly used*] (OPSA)
HT	Height Technician [*Air Force*]
HT	Height Telling [*RADAR*]
HT	Helen Thomas [*British author*]
HT	Helicopter Training Squadron [*Navy symbol*] (NVT)
HT	Hemagglutination Titer [*Medicine*] (MAE)
HT	Herd Test
Ht.	Heterozygote [*Medicine*] (DMAA)
HT	Hibernation Trigger (BARN)
HT	High Technology (MCD)
HT	High Temperature
HT	High Tension
Ht.	High Tension (STED)
HT	High Tide
HT	High Torque [*Engineering*] (IAA)
HT	High Transform [*Computer science*]
HT	High Treason
HT	Histologic Technician [*or Technologist*] (MAE)
HT	Histologic Transformation [*Medicine*]
HT	Historic Towns [*A publication*]
HT	History Today [*A publication*] (BRI)
HT	Hittite Texts in the Cuneiform Character from Tablets in the British Museum [*London*] (BJA)
HT	Hoc Tempore [*At This Time*] [*Latin*]
HT	Hoc Titulo [*In, or Under, This Title*] [*Latin*]
HT	Hoisting Tool (MCD)
HT	Holding Time [*Telecommunications*] (TEL)
HT	Hollow Tile [*Technical drawings*]
HT	Holy Trinity
HT	Home Treatment [*Medicine*]
HT	Homing Terrier [*Missile*]
HT	Homing Transponders
HT	Homing Type (NATG)
HT	Horizontal Tab [*Computer science*] (DOM)
HT	Horizontal Tabulate (NITA)
HT	Horizontal Tabulation [*Computer science*]
HT	Horological Times [*A publication*] (EAAP)
HT	Horsed Transport [*Military*]
HT	Horserace Totalisator [*Set up in 1926 to provide alternative form of betting and to generate income from improvement of racing*] [*British*]
HT	Hospital Train
HT	Hot Report (NATG)
HT	Hot Tin (MSA)
HT	Hot Topics
HT	Hot Transient Exhaust Emissions [*Automotive engineering*]
HT	Houma-Thibodaux [*Diocesan abbreviation*] [*Louisiana*] (TOCD)
HT	House Trailer (AFM)
HT	Howard Terminal [*AAR code*]
HT	Hubbard Tank [*Medicine*]
HT	Huhner Test [*Gynecology*]
HT	Hull Technician [*Navy*]
HT	Human Teratocarcinoma [*A cell line*]
HT	Human Thrombin [*Cytochemistry*]
HT	Human Tumor [*Oncology*]
HT	Hunter Transport [*Commercial firm British*]
HT	Hybrid Tea [*Roses*] (ROG)
HT	Hydrocortisone Test [*Medicine*] (DB)
HT	Hydrolyzable Tannin Level
HT	Hydrophobic Tail [*Surfactant technology*]
HT	Hydrotalcite [*Mineralogy*]
HT	Hydrotherapy [*Medicine*]
HT	Hydrothermally Treated [*Environmental science*] (COE)
HT	Hydrotreating [*Also, HDT*] [*Petroleum technology*]
HT	Hydroxyl Terminated (MCD)
HT	Hydroxytryptamine [*Biochemistry*]
Ht.	Hypermetropia, Total [*Ophthalmology*]
Ht.	Hyperopia, Total [*Ophthalmology*] (AAMN)
HT	Hypertension [*Cardiology*] (DAVI)
HT	Hyperthyroidism [*Endocrinology*] (MAE)
HT	Hypertransfusion (DB)
HT	Hypertriglyceridemia [*Medicine*]
HT	Hypertropia [*Medicine*]
HT	Hypodermic Tablet [*Medicine*]
HT	Hypotension [*Medicine*]
HT	Hypothalamus [*Neurology*]
Ht.	Hypothalamus (STED)
HT	Hypothermally Treated (GNE)
H(T)	Intermittent Hypertropia (STED)
HT	Mustard Gas [*Also, H, HD, HS, M*] [*Poison gas US Chemical Corps symbol*]
HT1	Hull Maintenance Technician, First Class [*Navy*] (DNAB)
HT2	Hull Maintenance Technician, Second Class [*Navy*] (DNAB)
HT3	Hull Maintenance Technician, Third Class [*Navy*] (DNAB)
HTA	Handbooks of Theology [*A publication*]

HTA	Harness Tracks of America (EA)
HTA	Harris Tweed Association [*British*] (DBA)
HTA	Heavier than Air
HTA	Hedge-to-Arrive [*Business term*]
HTA	Help the Aged [*AAIA*] [*Superseded by*] (EA)
HTA	Herb Trade Association (EA)
HTA	Heteroduplex Tracking Analysis [*Genetics*]
HTA	Heterophil Transplantation Antigen [*Medicine*] (DMAA)
HTA	High-Temperature Adhesive
HTA	High Temperature Alarm [*Environmental science*] (COE)
HTA	High-Temperature Alloy
HTA	High-Temperature Ashing [*Analytical chemistry*]
HTA	Highway Traffic Act
HTA	Hohenfels Training Area [*NATO*]
HTA	Horticultural Trades Association [*British*] (BI)
HTA	Household Textiles Association [*British*] (BI)
HTA	Humanist Teachers' Association [*British*]
HTA	Human Thymocyte Antigen (STED)
HTA	Hydroxytryptamine [*Biochemistry*] (MAE)
HTA	Hyperion 1997 Term Trust [*NYSE symbol*] (SPSG)
HTA	Hypophysiotropic Area [*of hypothalamus*] [*Endocrinology*]
HTAB	Hexadecytrimethylammonium Bromide [*Organic chemistry*]
HTAC	Hexadecyltrimethylammonium Chloride [*Organic chemistry*]
HTAC	High-Tension Alternating Current (IAA)
HTACS	Human Thyroid Adenyl Cyclase Stimulator [*Endocrinology*]
HTAD	High Temperature Aerosol Decomposition [*Chemistry*]
ht aer	Heated Aerosol [*Pharmacology*] (DAVI)
HTAH	High-Temperature Air Heat [*for magnetohydrodynamic power plants*] (MCD)
HT & C	Heat Transfer and Cryogenics
HTANSW	History Teachers' Association of New South Wales [*Australia*]
HTAR	Arusha [*Tanzania*] [*ICAO location identifier*] (ICLI)
HTAS	Hug-a-Tree and Survive (EA)
HT(ASCP)	Histologic Technician (American Society of Clinical Pathologists) (DMAA)
HTAT	Human Tetanus Antitoxin [*Medicine*] (CPH)
HTB	Hairdressing Training Board (AIE)
HTB	Hair Tuning Bar
HTB	Heat Treat Block (MCD)
HTB	Hexadecimal-to-Binary [*Computer science*]
H-TB	High-Tension Battery
HTB	High-Tension Braided Sheath [*Automotive engineering*]
HTB	Highway Tariff Bureau [*Later, AMCTB*]
HTB	Hot Tub Bath [*Medicine*]
HTB	Howitzer Test Bed (RDA)
HTB	Human Tumor Bank [*Medicine*] (DMAA)
HTB	Hungarian Tourist Board (EAIO)
HTB	Hypergolic Test Building (KSC)
HTB	Hyperion 2002 Term Trust [*NYSE symbol*] (SPSG)
HTBA	Hood's Texas Brigade Association (EA)
HTBB	HomeTown Buffet [*NASDAQ symbol*] (TTSB)
HTBB	Hometown Buffet, Inc. [*NASDAQ symbol*] (SAG)
HTBDR	High-Temperature Burner-Duct Recuperator System
Htbk	Hatchback (BARN)
HTBU	Bukoba [*Tanzania*] [*ICAO location identifier*] (ICLI)
HTC	Haiti Trans Air SA [*ICAO designator*] (FAAC)
HTC	Handicapped Travel Club (EA)
HTC	Hand Tool Carrier [*NASA*] (KSC)
HTC	Harris Teachers College [*Missouri*]
HTC	Harris Transducer Corp. (MCD)
HTC	Hartco Enterprises, Inc. [*Toronto Stock Exchange symbol*]
HTC	Head to Come [*Publishing*]
HTC	Healing the Children [*An association*] (EA)
HTC	Health Care Telecommunications Corp. [*Camp Hill, PA*] (TSSD)
HTC	Heavy Teflon Coating
HTC	Heavy Terminal Complex (MCD)
HTC	Hebrew Teachers College [*Massachusetts*]
HTC	Hebrew Theological College [*Skokie, IL*] (BJA)
HTC	Height-to-Time Converter
HTC	Height Tracking Console (MCD)
HTC	Helicopter Transit Controller (MCD)
HTC	Hepatoma Cells [*Cytology*] (DAVI)
HTC	Hepatoma Tissue Culture [*Medicine*]
HTC	High-Tar Content [*of cigarettes*]
HTC	High-Temperature Carbonization
HTC	High-Temperature Catalyst
HTC	High-Temperature Coil
HTC	High-Temperature Conditioning
HTC	Highway Traffic Control
HTC	Homozygous Typing Cells [*Immunochemistry*]
HTC	Hughes Tool Co.
HTC	Hull Maintenance Technician, Chief [*Navy*] (DNAB)
HTC	Hungarian Tel & Cable [*AMEX symbol*] (TTSB)
HTC	Hungarian Telephone and Cable Corp. [*AMEX symbol*] (SAG)
HTC	Huston-Tillotson College [*Austin, TX*]
HTC	Huston-Tillotson College, Austin, TX [*OCLC symbol*] (OCLC)
HTC	Hybrid Technology Computer
HTC	Hydraulic Temperature Control (AAG)
HTC	Hydraulic Test Chamber (AAG)
HTC	Hydrofoil Test Craft
HTC	Hydrogen Transfer Catalysis [*Chemistry*]
HTC	Hypertensive Crisis [*Cardiology*] (DAVI)
HTCA	Human Tumor Clonogenic Assay [*In-vitro testing system*]
HTCC	Hungarian Telephone & Cable Corp. [*NASDAQ symbol*] (SAG)
HTCD	High-Temperature Catalytic Oxidation [*Chemistry*]
HTCH	Chunya [*Tanzania*] [*ICAO location identifier*] (ICLI)
HTCH	Hutchinson Technology [*NASDAQ symbol*] (TTSB)
HTCH	Hutchinson Technology, Inc. [*NASDAQ symbol*] (NQ)
HTCHNG	Hitching
HTCHY	Hatchery
HTCI	High-Tensile Cast Iron
HTCM	Master Chief Hull Maintenance Technician [*Formerly, SFCM*] [*Navy rating*]
HTCO	Hickory Tech [*NASDAQ symbol*] (TTSB)
HTCO	Hickory Tech Corp. [*NASDAQ symbol*] (SAG)
HTCO	High-Temperature Catalytic Oxidation [*Chemistry*]
HTCS	High Critical Temperature Superconductor (AAEL)
HTCS	Senior Chief Hull Maintenance Technician [*Formerly, SFCS*] [*Navy rating*]
HTCV	Hop Trefoil Cryptic Virus [*Plant pathology*]
HTD	Hand Target Designator
HTD	Hand-Tool Dexterity [*Motor performance test*]
HTD	Heated (MSA)
HTD	Higher Telegraphist Detector [*British military*] (DMA)
HTD	High-Temperature Distillation
HTD	High-Torque Drive [*Engineering*]
HTD	Horizontal Tactical Display (NG)
HTD	Human Therapeutic Dose
HTD	Huntingdon International Holdings Ltd. [*NYSE symbol*] (CTT)
HTD	Huntingdon Intl ADR [*NYSE symbol*] (TTSB)
HTDA	Dar Es-Salaam/Dar Es-Salaam [*Tanzania*] [*ICAO location identifier*] (ICLI)
HTDC	Dar Es-Salaam [*Tanzania*] [*ICAO location identifier*] (ICLI)
HTDC	High-Tension Direct Current (IAA)
HTDE	High-Technology Demonstrator Engine (MCD)
HTDL	High-Temperature Detection Lens
HTDM	Helicopter Team Defense Missile
HTDO	Dodoma [*Tanzania*] [*ICAO location identifier*] (ICLI)
HTDQ	Dar Es-Salaam [*Tanzania*] [*ICAO location identifier*] (ICLI)
HTDS	Hydrofoil Tactical Data System
HTDT	Heavy Truck Driver Trainer [*Army*]
HTDU	Horizontal Tactical Display Unit
HTE	England AFB (Alexandria), LA [*Location identifier FAA*] (FAAL)
HTE	Heavy-Duty Thermoplastic Elastomer Insulation [*Automotive engineering*]
HTE	High-Temperature Electrolysis (MCD)
HTE	High Temperature Electronics (AAEL)
HTE	Hydraulic Test Equipment
HTE	Hypergroup Translating Equipment (NITA)
HTE	Hypertensive Encephalopathy [*Medicine*] (CPH)
HTEC	High Technology
HTEC	Hydrogen Technology Evaluation Center [*Upton, NY*] [*Brookhaven National Laboratory*] [*Department of Energy*] (GRD)
HTEC	Hydron Technologies [*NASDAQ symbol*] (TTSB)
HTEC	Hydron Technologies, Inc. [*NASDAQ symbol*] (SPSG)
HTEF	Heat Transfer Efficiency Factor [*Engineering*]
HTEL	Hungarian Teleconstruct [*NASDAQ symbol*] (SAG)
HTEM	Human Thymic Epithelial Medium [*Endocrinology*]
HTES	High-Technology Ejection Seat
HTES	High-Technology Escape System (MCD)
HTESP	High-Temperature Electrostatic Precipitator [*Anti-smoke pollution device*]
HTEXCH	Heat Exchanger (MCD)
HTF	Heat Transfer Fluid
HTF	Heat Treat Fixture (MCD)
HTF	Height Finding (MSA)
HTF	Heritage Trails Fund (EA)
HTF	Heterothyrotropic Factor [*Medicine*] (MAE)
HTF	Highway Trust Fund
HTF	House Tube Feeding [*Medicine*] (DMAA)
HTF	Housing Trust Fund (PA)
HTF	How-to-Fight [*Manuals*] [*Military*]
HTF	Hypersonic Tunnel Facility [*NASA*]
HTF	Societe Helitrans France [*ICAO designator*] (FAAC)
HTFA	Hull Maintenance Technician, Fireman Apprentice [*Navy*] (DNAB)
HTFC	High-Temperature Fuel Cell
HTFFR	High-Temperature Fast-Flow Reactor [*See also HTFS*]
HTFFS	Heat Transfer and Fluid Flow Service [*British*]
HTFFT	Heat Transfer Fluid Flow Thermodynamics (NRCH)
HTFI	Fort Ikoma [*Tanzania*] [*ICAO location identifier*] (ICLI)
HTFM	How to Fight Manual [*Military*] (MCD)
HTFMI	Heat Transfer and Fluid Mechanics Institute (MCD)
HTFN	Hull Maintenance Technician, Fireman [*Navy*] (DNAB)
HTFORE	Heretofore (ROG)
HTFS	Heat Transfer and Fluid Flow Service [*Also, HTFFS*] [*British*]
HTF/S	How to Fight/How to Support [*Military*] (MCD)
HTFW	High-Temperature Fluid-Wall [*Incineration process*]
HTFX	Heat Treat Fixture
HTG	Handbuch Theologischer Grundbegriffe [*Munich*] [*A publication*] (BJA)
HTG	Heating (KSC)
HTG	Heritage Media'A' [*AMEX symbol*] (TTSB)
HTG	Heritage Media Corp. [*AMEX symbol*] (CTT)
HTG	High-Temperature Gas [*Reactor*]
HTG	Hobart Town Gazette [*A publication*]
HTG	Honest-to-God Cash Flow Yields [*Finance*] (EMRF)
HTG	Hypertriglyceridemia [*Medicine*]
HTGC	High-Temperature Gas-Cooled Reactor (BARN)
HTGCR	High-Temperature Gas-Cooled Reactor
HTGF	Human Transforming Growth Factor [*Biochemistry*]

HTGL .... Hepatic Triglyceride Lipase [*An enzyme*]
HTGL .... High Temperature Gasdynamics Laboratory [*Stanford University*] [*Research center*] (RCD)
HTGPF .... High-Temperature General-Purpose Furnace
HTGR .... High-Temperature Gas-Cooled Reactor
HTGR .... High Temperature Gas Reactor (EERA)
HTGR-CX ..... High-Temperature Gas-Cooled-Reactor Critical Experiment
HTGRE .... High-Temperature Gas-Cooled-Reactor Experiment
HTH .... Hawthorne [*Nevada*] [*Airport symbol Obsolete*] (OAG)
HTH .... Head-to-Head (AAEL)
HTH .... Heart to Heart Foundation (EA)
HTH .... Helix-Turn-Helix [*Protein structure*]
HTH .... Hexagon Tungsten Honeycomb
HTH .... High-Temperature Heater
HTH .... High-Test Hypochlorite (WGA)
HTH .... Homeostatic Thymus Hormone [*Immunology*]
HTH .... Home Town Honey [*Slang*]
HTH .... Hypothalamus [*Medicine*] (DMAA)
HTHA .... Hearing and Tinnitus Help Association [*Later, AEAR*] (EA)
HtHaN .... Northern Montana College, Havre, MT [*Library symbol Library of Congress*] (LCLS)
HTHD .... Hypertensive Heart Disease [*Medicine*] (MAE)
HTHM .... High Toxic Hazard Material
HTHR .... Hawthorne Financial Corp. [*NASDAQ symbol*] (NQ)
HTHR .... Hawthorne Finl [*NASDAQ symbol*] (TTSB)
HTHR .... High-Tension/High-Resistance [*Automotive engineering*]
HT-HS .... High-Temperature, High-Shear Viscometer
HTHSR .... High-Temperature, High-Shear-Rate [*Viscosity measurement*]
HTI .... Haiti [*ANSI three-letter standard code*] (CNC)
HTI .... Haiti International Air SA [*ICAO designator*] (FAAC)
HTI .... Hamilton Island [*Australia Airport symbol*] (OAG)
HTI .... Hamilton Technology, Inc.
HTI .... Hand Tools Institute (EA)
HTI .... Heat Transfer Instrument System [*Nuclear energy*] (NUCP)
HTI .... Hemispheric Thrombotic Infarction [*Medicine*] (DMAA)
HTI .... Hemorrhagic Toxin Inhibitor [*Hematology*]
HTI .... High-Temperature Incinerator
HTI .... High-Temperature Isotropic
HTI .... Home Testing Institute, Inc. (NTCM)
HTI .... Horizons Technology, Inc.
HTI .... Horizontal Tactics Indicator
HTI .... Horizontal Technology Insertion
HTI .... Horizontal Technology Integration [*Business term*] (INF)
HTIG .... Homologous Tetanus Immune Globulin [*Medicine*] (DMAA)
hTIg .... Human Tetanus Immunoglobulin [*Medicine*] (STED)
HTIR .... Iringa [*Tanzania*] [*ICAO location identifier*] (ICLI)
HTIS .... Heat Transfer Instrument System (NRCH)
HT/IT .... Homing Terrier/Improved Tartar [*Missile*] (MCD)
HTJ .... H-Plane Tee Junction
HTK .... Hard-Target Kill [*Military*] (GFGA)
HTK .... Head to Come [*A notation on copy that the headline will be written and set later*] (WDMC)
HTK .... Head to Kum [*Come*] [*Publishing*]
HTK .... Heel to Knee (DMAA)
HTKA .... Kigoma [*Tanzania*] [*ICAO location identifier*] (ICLI)
HTKI .... Kilwa Masoko [*Tanzania*] [*ICAO location identifier*] (ICLI)
HTKJ .... Kilimanjaro [*Tanzania*] [*ICAO location identifier*] (ICLI)
HTKNT .... Herders Theologischer Kommentar zum Neuen Testament [*Freiburg*] [*A publication*] (BJA)
HTKO .... Kongwa [*Tanzania*] [*ICAO location identifier*] (ICLI)
HTKP .... Hard-Target Kill Potential [*Military*] (MCD)
HTKT .... Kilimatinde [*Tanzania*] [*ICAO location identifier*] (ICLI)
HTL .... Hamster Tumor Line (DB)
HTL .... Hearing Threshold Level
HTL .... Heartland Partners L.P.'A' [*AMEX symbol*] (TTSB)
HTL .... Heartland Partners Ltd. Class A [*AMEX symbol*] (SPSG)
HTL .... Heat Transfer Laboratory [*MIT*] (MCD)
HTL .... Heat Transfer Loop (NRCH)
HTL .... Helicopter Transportable Launcher (MUGU)
HTL .... Helper T-Lymphocyte [*Immunology*]
HTL .... High-Temperature Lacquer
HTL .... High Threshold Logic
HTL .... High Turbulence Level
HTL .... Histologic Technologist [*Medicine*] (MEDA)
HTL .... Histotechnologist [*Medicine*] (STED)
HTL .... Hotel (WDAA)
HTL .... Hotel Call, Time, and Charges Mandatory [*Telecommunications*] (TEL)
HTL .... Houghton Lake, MI [*Location identifier FAA*] (FAAL)
HTL .... Human T-Cell Leukemia [*Medicine*] (STED)
HTL .... Human T-Cell Lymphoma [*Medicine*] (STED)
HTL .... Human Thymic Leukemia [*Medicine*] (STED)
HTLA .... High-Titer, Low-Acidity [*Hematology*]
HTLA .... Human T-Lymphocyte Antigen (DMAA)
HTL(ASCP) ... Histotechnologist (American Society of Clinical Pathologists) (DMAA)
HTLB .... High-Technology Light Brigade [*Army*] (INF)
HTLD .... Heartland Express [*NASDAQ symbol*] (TTSB)
HTLD .... Heartland Express, Inc. [*NASDAQ symbol*] (NQ)
HTLD .... High-Technology Light Division [*DoD*]
HTLD .... Houston Test for Language Development [*Education*]
HTLI .... Lindi [*Tanzania*] [*ICAO location identifier*] (ICLI)
HTLL .... High Test Level Language (NASA)
HTLM .... Lake Manyara [*Tanzania*] [*ICAO location identifier*] (ICLI)
HTLO .... Lobo Wildlife Lodge [*Tanzania*] [*ICAO location identifier*] (ICLI)
HTLR .... High-Tension/Low-Resistance [*Automotive engineering*]
HTLR .... High Torque, Low Rev
HTLS .... Higher Torque/Low-Speed (DNAB)
HTLT .... HTL Telemanagement Ltd. [*Burtonsville, MD*] (TSSD)
HTLT .... Hughes Transportable Link Terminal
HTLTR .... High-Temperature Lattice Test Reactor
HTLV .... Human T-Cell Lymphotropic [*formerly, Leukemia*] Virus
HTLV-1 .... Human T-Cell Lymphotropic Virus 1 [*medicine*] (MEC)
HTLV-I .... Human T Cell Lymphotropic Virus I [*Medicine*] (TAD)
HTLV-II .... Human T Cell Lymphotropic Virus II [*Medicine*] (TAD)
HTLV-III .... Human T-Cell Lymphotrophic Virus-Type Three
HTLV-III/LAV ... Human T-Cell Lymphotropic Virus Type Three/Lymphadenopathy-Associated Virus
HTLV-MA ...... Human T-Cell Leukemia Virus-Associated Membrane Antigen [*Medicine*] (STED)
HTLVR .... Human T-Cell Leukemia Virus Receptor [*Medicine*] (DMAA)
HTM .... Hard Tube Modulator [*Electronics*]
HTM .... Hard Tube Monitor [*Electronics*] (IAA)
HTM .... Harpoon Trainer Module [*Missiles*] (MCD)
HTM .... Heat Transfer Medium [*Engineering*]
HTM .... Heat Transfer Meter
HTM .... Heat Transfer Module [*Furnace*]
HTM .... High Temperature (IEEE)
HTM .... High-Temperature Materials
HTM .... High-Temperature Metallography
HTM .... High Throughput Mission (SSD)
HTM .... High-Trajectory Missiles (NRCH)
HTM .... Hole-Transport Material [*Materials science*]
HTM .... Hypothesis Testing Model (IEEE)
HTM .... Whitman, MA [*Location identifier FAA*] (FAAL)
HTMA .... Hydraulic Tool Manufacturers Association [*Milwaukee, WI*] (EA)
HTMA .... Mafia [*Tanzania*] [*ICAO location identifier*] (ICLI)
HTMAEW ...... Home Timber Merchants' Association of England and Wales (BI)
HTMB .... Mbeya [*Tanzania*] [*ICAO location identifier*] (ICLI)
HTMD .... High-Technology Motorized Division
HTMD .... Hold Time Management Display [*NASA*]
HTMD .... Mwadui [*Tanzania*] [*ICAO location identifier*] (ICLI)
HTM-DB .... High Temperature Materials Data Bank [*Commission of the European Communities*] [*Information service or system*] (IID)
HTMG .... Morgororo [*Tanzania*] [*ICAO location identifier*] (ICLI)
HTMI .... Masasi [*Tanzania*] [*ICAO location identifier*] (ICLI)
HTMIAC .... High Temperature Materials Information Analysis Center Information Analysis Center [*Formerly, TEPIAC*] [*West Lafayette, IN*] [*DoD*] (GRD)
HTMK .... Mikumi [*Tanzania*] [*ICAO location identifier*] (ICLI)
HTML .... High Temperature Materials Laboratory [*Oak Ridge, TN*] [*Oak Ridge National Laboratory*] [*Department of Energy*] (GRD)
html .... Hypertext Markup Language [*Computer science*]
HTML .... Hypertext Markup Language [*Telecommunication*]
HTMMP .... Helo Transportable Mulit-Mission Platform [*Experimental military vehicle*]
HTMO .... Mombo [*Tanzania*] [*ICAO location identifier*] (ICLI)
HTMP .... High-Temperature Thermomechanical Processing [*Alloy heat resistance*]
HTMP .... High-Temperature Thermomechanical Pulp [*Pulp and paper technology*]
HTMP .... Hydroxy(tetramethyl)piperidineoxyl [*Organic chemistry*]
HTMP .... Mpanda [*Tanzania*] [*ICAO location identifier*] (ICLI)
HTMR .... High Temperature Metals Recovery [*For hazardous waste treatment*]
HTMR .... High Threshold Mechanoreceptor [*Neurophysiology*]
HTMR .... Msembe-Ruaha National Park [*Tanzania*] [*ICAO location identifier*] (ICLI)
HTMS .... High-Temperature Mass Spectrometry
HTMS .... Moshi [*Tanzania*] [*ICAO location identifier*] (ICLI)
HTMT .... Mtwara [*Tanzania*] [*ICAO location identifier*] (ICLI)
HTMU .... Musoma [*Tanzania*] [*ICAO location identifier*] (ICLI)
HTMW .... Mwanza [*Tanzania*] [*ICAO location identifier*] (ICLI)
HTMX .... Mpwapwa [*Tanzania*] [*ICAO location identifier*] (ICLI)
HTN .... Haiti North Airline [*ICAO designator*] (FAAC)
HTN .... Hantaan [*Virus*]
HTN .... HazTECH News [*A publication*]
HTN .... Heterodyne (FAAC)
HTN .... Hocking Technical College, Nelsonville, OH [*OCLC symbol*] (OCLC)
HTN .... Home Theatre Network [*In network name "HTN Plus"*] [*Cable-television system*]
HTN .... Hotan [*China*] [*Airport symbol*] (OAG)
HTN .... Houghton Mifflin [*NYSE symbol*] (TTSB)
HTN .... Houghton Mifflin Co. [*NYSE symbol*] (SPSG)
HTN .... HUD [*Department of Housing and Urban Development*] Teleprocessing Network
HTN .... Hughes Television Network [*New York, NY*] [*Cable-television system*]
HTN .... Hypertension [*Medicine*]
HTN .... Hypertensive Nephropathy [*Medicine*] (STED)
HTN .... Hypertensive Nephropathy [*Medicine*] (DB)
HTN .... Miles City, MT [*Location identifier FAA*] (FAAL)
HTNA .... Nachingwea [*Tanzania*] [*ICAO location identifier*] (ICLI)
htnd .... Heightened (VRA)
HTNG .... Ngerengere [*Tanzania*] [*ICAO location identifier*] (ICLI)
HTNJ .... Njombe [*Tanzania*] [*ICAO location identifier*] (ICLI)
HTNR .... High-Temperature Nitric Oxide Reduction [*Combustion technology*]
HTNSL .... High Tensile [*Mechanics*]
HTNT .... High Technology National Training (AIE)
HTO .... East Hampton [*New York*] [*Airport symbol*] (OAG)
HTO .... Hazardous Tritium Oxides [*Environmental science*] (COE)
HTO .... Hereto (ROG)
HTO .... Heterotopic Ossification [*Orthopedics*] (DAVI)

HTO	High-Temperature Oxidation (IEEE)
HTO	High Throughput Screening [*Chemistry*]
HTO	High Tibial Osteotomy [*Orthopedics*] (DAVI)
HTO	Highway Transportation Officer [*Army*]
HTO	Horizontal Takeoff
HTO	Hospital Transfer Order
HTO	Hydrous Titanium Oxide (PDAA)
HTO	Hyperion 2005 Investment Grade Opportunity Term Trust [*NYSE symbol*] (SPSG)
HTO	Hyperion 2005 Inv Grd Oppt Tr [*NYSE symbol*] (TTSB)
HTOFORE	Heretofore
H to H	Heel to Heel
HTOH	Hydroxytryptophol [*Laboratory*] (DAVI)
HTOHL	Horizontal Takeoff, Horizontal Landing (KSC)
HTOL	Horizontal Takeoff and Landing [*Proposed aircraft under development by the British government*] (IAA)
HTOS	High Throughput Organic Synthesis [*Chemistry*]
HTOT	High-Temperature Operating Test (MCD)
HTOVL	Horizontal Take-Off Vertical Landing [*Aviation*] (PDAA)
HTP	Hardness Test Plan [*Army*] (AABC)
HTP	Heat Transfer Printing [*Textile technology*]
HTP	High Temperature and Pressure (GNE)
HTP	High-Temperature Photochemistry [*Aerochem Research Laboratories, Inc.*] [*Analytical chemistry*]
HTP	High-Temperature Photolysis [*Physics*]
HTP	High-Test Hydrogen-Peroxide
HTP	Highway Traffic Point [*MTMC*] (TAG)
H-T-P	[*A*] House, a Tree, a Person [*Psychological drawing test*]
HTP	Humidity Test Procedure
HTP	Humor Test of Personality [*Psychology*]
HTP	Hydroxytryptophan [*Biochemistry*]
HTP	Hypothromboplastinemia [*Medicine*] (DB)
HTPB	Hydroxyl-Terminated Polybutadiene [*Organic chemistry*]
HTPB	Hydroxyl-Terminated Polybutylene [*Organic chemistry*] (NASA)
HTPB	Hydroxy-Terminated Polybutadiene [*Organic chemistry*]
H-T-P/D-A-P	House-Tree-Person and Draw-a-Person as Measures of Abuse in Children: A Quantitative Scoring System [*Test*] (TMMY)
HTPE	Pemba [*Tanzania*] [*ICAO location identifier*] (ICLI)
HTPFP	High Technology Professionals for Peace [*Defunct*] (EA)
HTPHA	Huguenot-Thomas Paine Historical Association (EA)
HTPM	Harvard Total Project Manager [*Computer software*]
HTPN	Home Total Parenteral Nutrition [*Medicine*]
HTPO	Human Thyroid Peroxidase [*An enzyme*]
HTPP	Hardness Test Program Plan
HTPS	Hull-Turret Position Sensor [*Military*] (RDA)
HTPV	High-Temperature Power and Voltage (IAA)
HTR	Halt and Transfer
HTR	Hanford Test Reactor (NRCH)
HTR	Hard Tissue Replacement [*Dentistry*]
HTR	Harvard Theological Review [*A publication*] (ODCC)
HTR	Hateruma [*Japan*] [*Airport symbol*] (OAG)
HTR	Heated-Tube Reactor [*Chemical engineering*]
HTR	Heater (AAG)
HTR	Hemolytic Transfusion Reaction [*Medicine*]
HTR	High-Temperature Reactor
HTR	High-Temperature Resistor
HTR	Highway Traffic Regulation (AABC)
HTR	Hitachi Training Reactor [*Japan*]
HTR	Holstenair Lubeck, Luftverkehrsservice GmbH [*Germany ICAO designator*] (FAAC)
HTR	Homing Terrier Retrofit [*Missile*] (MCD)
HTR	Homogeneous Thorium Reactor
HTR	Hours to Run (ADA)
HTR	Household Tracking Report [*Television ratings*] (NTCM)
HTR	HTR Industries, Inc. [*Vancouver Stock Exchange symbol*]
HTR	Human Transferrin Receptor [*Biochemistry*]
HTR	Hydroxyl Terminated Polybutyiene (NAKS)
HTR	Hyperion Total Return Fd [*NYSE symbol*] (TTSB)
HTR	Hyperion Total Return Fund [*NYSE symbol*] (SPSG)
HTR	Hypermetropia, Right [*Ophthalmology*] (DAVI)
HTRAC	Half-Track [*A type of military vehicle*] (AABC)
HTRAP	Height Reply Analysis Processor (SAA)
HTRB	High-Temperature Reverse Bias [*Electronics*] (IAA)
HTRD	Heat Transfer Rotating Disc [*Engineering*]
HTRDA	High-Temperature Reactor Development Associates
HTRE	Heat Transfer Reactor Experiment
HTRE	High-Temperature Reactor Experiment [*Department of Energy*] (GAAI)
HTRF	Homogeneous Time Resolved Fluorescence [*Analytical Chemistry*]
HTRF	Human Telomeric Repeat-Binding Factor [*Genetics*]
HTRI	Heat Transfer Research Institute (NRCH)
HTRI	High Technology Recruitment Index [*A publication*]
HTRIN	Holy Trinity
HTRK	Half-Track [*A type of military vehicle*]
HTROL	Help To Run Our-Lines [*Military*]
H TRON	Home TRON [*The Real-Time Operating System Nucleus*] (NITA)
HTRR	Harpoon Transfer Relay Rack [*Missiles*] (MCD)
HTRS	High-Temperature Reflectance Spectroscopy (DB)
HTRW	Hazardous, Toxic, and Radiological Waste [*US Army Corps of Engineers*]
HTS	Half-Time Survey [*Shipping*]
HTS	Hamden Testing Services, Inc.
HTS	Harness Tracks Security [*Defunct*] (EA)
HTS	Harvard Theological Studies [*A publication*] (ODCC)
HTS	Hawaiian Tracking Station

HTS	Head, Track, and Selector
HTS	Head Traumatic Syndrome [*Medicine*] (DMAA)
HTS	Heal-¡0-Shin [*Test*] [*Neurology*] (DAVI)
HTS	Heat Transfer Section
HTS	Heat Transfer System
HTS	Heat Transport Section [*Apollo*] [*NASA*]
HTS	Heat Transport System [*NASA*] (NASA)
HTS	Heat-Treated Steel
HTS	Heavy-Duty Thermoset Elastomer Insulation [*Automotive engineering*]
HTS	Heights (MCD)
Hts	Heights (TBD)
HTS	Height-Telling Surveillance
HTS	HeLa Tumor Suppression [*Medicine*] (DMAA)
HTS	Helitrans Air Service, Inc. [*ICAO designator*] (FAAC)
HTS	Hemangioma-Thrombocytopenia Syndrome [*Medicine*] (MEDA)
HTS	High Technology Solution (DGA)
HTS	High-Temperature Steam
HTS	High-Temperature Superconductivity (ECON)
HTS	High-Temperature Superconductor [*Materials science*]
HTS	High-Tensile Steel
HTS	High Tensile Strength [*Mechanics*]
HTS	High-Tension Separation (IAA)
HTS	High-Tension Supply (IAA)
HTS	High-Tension Synthetic Insulation [*Automotive engineering*]
HTS	High Throughput Screening [*For drug screening*]
HTS	Home Team Sports [*Cable-television system*]
HTS	Host-to-Satellite
HTS	How to Support [*Manuals*] [*Military*] (MCD)
HTS	Human Thyroid Stimulator [*Endocrinology*]
HTS	Huntington [*West Virginia*] [*Airport symbol*] (OAG)
HTS	Hybrid Test Set
HTS	Hydraulic Test Set [*or Station*]
HTS	Hydrodynamic Test System
HTSA	Highway Traffic Safety Administration (COE)
HTSA	History Trust of South Australia
HTSA	Host-Tenant Support Agreement [*Military*]
HTSC	High-Temperature Semiconductor [*Electronics*]
HTSC	High-Temperature Superconductivity [*Materials science*]
HTSC	High-Temperature Superconductor [*Materials science*]
HTSC	Highway Traffic Safety Center [*Michigan State University*]
HTSC	Hughes Technical Services Co.
HTSCA	Human Tumor Stem Cell Assay [*Oncology*]
HTSD	Singida [*Tanzania*] [*ICAO location identifier*] (ICLI)
HTSE	Same [*Tanzania*] [*ICAO location identifier*] (ICLI)
HTSEC	High-Temperature Size-Exclusion Chromatography
HTSF	High-Temperature Sodium Facility [*Nuclear energy*] (NRCH)
HTSF	Hydrated Textured Soy Flour
HTSH	Human Thyroid Stimulating Hormone [*Also, htsh*] [*Endocrinology*]
HTSH	Mafinga [*Tanzania*] [*ICAO location identifier*] (ICLI)
HTSHLD	Heat Shield
HTSI	Human Thyroid-Stimulating Immunoglobulin (PDAA)
HTSIM	Height Stimulator (IAA)
HTSK	Heat Sink (MSA)
HTSL	Heat Transfer Simulation Loop (IEEE)
HTSL	High Temperature Sodium Loop (PDAA)
HTSM	High-Temperature Skim Milk (OA)
HTSN	Seronera [*Tanzania*] [*ICAO location identifier*] (ICLI)
HTSO	Songea [*Tanzania*] [*ICAO location identifier*] (ICLI)
HTSR	High-Temperature Strain Gauge
HTSS	Honeywell Time-Sharing System [*Computer science*] (IEEE)
HTSSE	High-Temperature-Superconductivity Space Experiment [*Navy*]
HTST	Heartstream Inc. [*NASDAQ symbol*] (TTSB)
HTSt	Hervormde Teologiese Studies [*Pretoria, South Africa*] [*A publication*] (BJA)
HTST	High-Temperature Short-Time [*Pasteurization*] [*Food processing*]
HTSU	Sumbawanga [*Tanzania*] [*ICAO location identifier*] (ICLI)
HTSUP	Height Supervisor [*RADAR*]
HTSUS	Harmonized Tariff Schedule of the United States [*Formerly, TSUS*]
HTSY	Shinyanga [*Tanzania*] [*ICAO location identifier*] (ICLI)
HT/SZ	Height/Size (DNAB)
HTT	Air Tchad, Societe de Transport Aeriens [*Chad*] [*ICAO designator*] (FAAC)
HTT	Hallett [*Australia Seismograph station code, US Geological Survey*] (SEIS)
HTT	Heat-Treatment Temperature
HTT	Heavy Tactical Transport
HTT	High Technology Transfer Co. [*Czechoslovakia*] (ECON)
HTT	High-Temperature Tetragonal [*Physics*]
HTT	High-Temperature Thermomechanical Treatment [*Steel forging*]
HTT	High Temperature Treatment [*Materials science*]
HTT	High-Temperature Tunnel [*NASA*]
HTT	High-Tension Thermoplastic Insulation [*Automotive engineering*]
HTT	Hook Tongue Terminal
HTT	Hydraulics, Turbine Throttle (DNAB)
HTT	Hyperion 1999 Term Trust [*NYSE symbol*] (SPSG)
HTTA	Highway and Traffic Technicians Association [*British*] (EAIO)
HTTB	High-Technology Test Bed [*Army*]
HTTB	Tabora [*Tanzania*] [*ICAO location identifier*] (ICLI)
HTTG	Tanga [*Tanzania*] [*ICAO location identifier*] (ICLI)
HTTL	High-Power Transistor-Transistor Logic (IEEE)
HTTL	High-Speed Transistor-Transistor Logic (IAA)
HTTMT	High-Temperature Thermomechanical Treatment [*Steel forging*]
http	Hypertext Transfer Protocol (AAEL)
HTTP	Hypertext Transfer Protocol [*Telecommunication*]

HTTP	HyperText Transport Protocol [*Computer science*] (IGQR)
HTTPD	Hypertext Transfer Protocol Daemon [*Computer science*]
HTTPS	HyperText Transport Protocol Secure [*Computer science*] (IGQR)
HTTPS	HyperText Transport Protocol Server [*Computer science*] (DDC)
HTTR	Heat Treat
HTTS	Hybrid Thermal Treatment System [*Incinerator*] [*IT Corp.*] (RDA)
HTTS	Hydroquench Thrust Termination System [*NASA*] (KSC)
HTTT	High-Temperature Turbine Technology [*Power generation*]
HTTU	Tunduru [*Tanzania*] [*ICAO location identifier*] (ICLI)
HTU	Handheld Terminal Unit
HTU	Handheld Thermal Unit
HTU	Heat Transfer Unit
HTU	Height of a Transfer Unit [*Distillation*]
HTU	Horizontal Trail Unit (MCD)
HTU	Hoyt Peak [*Utah*] [*Seismograph station code, US Geological Survey*] (SEIS)
HTUR	Urambo [*Tanzania*] [*ICAO location identifier*] (ICLI)
HTV	Half Thickness Value (NRCH)
HTV	Harlech Television [*Wales*]
HTV	Hearst-Argyle Television [*NYSE symbol*]
HTV	Herpes-Type Virus
HTV	High-Altitude Test Vehicle (MUGU)
HTV	Hi Tech Ventures, Inc. [*Vancouver Stock Exchange symbol*]
HTV	Home Video Tutorial
HTV	Homing Test Vehicle (NG)
HTV	Hospital Patient Transport Vehicle
HTV	Hull Test Vehicle [*for submarines*] (MCD)
HTV	Hybrid Test Vehicle [*Gasoline and electric motor*]
HTV	Hydrothermal Vent [*Geology*]
HTV	Hypersonic Test Vehicle [*Air Force*]
HTVD	Hypertensive Vascular Disease [*Cardiology*] (DAVI)
HTW	Chesapeake, OH/Huntington, WV [*Location identifier FAA*] (FAAL)
HTW	Haystack [*Washington*] [*Seismograph station code, US Geological Survey*] (SEIS)
HTW	Hazardous and Toxic Waste
HTW	Helicopter Trap Weapon (SAA)
HTW	High-Temperature Water
HTW	High-Temperature Wire
HTW	Hoosac Tunnel & Wilmington R. R. [*AAR code*]
HTWH	Wazo Hill [*Tanzania*] [*ICAO location identifier*] (ICLI)
HTWK	Ngare Nairobi [*Tanzania*] [*ICAO location identifier*] (ICLI)
ht wkt	Hit Wicket [*Cricket*] (BARN)
HTWN	Hometown Bancorp [*NASDAQ symbol*] (TTSB)
HTWN	Hometown Bancorp, Inc. [*NASDAQ symbol*] (NQ)
HTWS	Hawaii Tsunami Warning System [*Marine science*] (OSRA)
HTX	Histrionicotoxin (DB)
HTXA	Hitox Corp. [*NASDAQ symbol*] (TTSB)
HTXA	Hitox Corp. of America [*NASDAQ symbol*] (CTT)
HTXGR	Heat Exchanger (KSC)
HTXR	High Temperature X-Ray Powder Diffraction (EDCT)
HTXRD	High-Temperature X-Ray Diffraction
HTY	Hatizyo [*Japan*] [*Geomagnetic observatory code*]
HTYP	Heliotype [*Modified collotype*] (VRA)
HTZ	Hato Corozal [*Colombia*] [*Airport symbol*] (OAG)
HTZA	Zanzibar [*Tanzania*] [*ICAO location identifier*] (ICLI)
HU	Central Airlines Ltd. [*Nigeria*] [*ICAO designator*] (ICDA)
hU	Dihydrouridine [*Two-letter symbol; see* H₂Urd]
HU	Haifa University (BJA)
HU	Hamburger University [*McDonald's Corp.*]
HU	Hangup [*Telecommunications*] (TEL)
HU	Harvard University [*Cambridge, MA*]
HU	Heat Unit (MAE)
H/U	Heatup [*Nuclear energy*] (NRCH)
HU	Hebrew University [*Jerusalem*] (BJA)
HU	Hemagglutinating Unit [*Immunochemistry*]
HU	Hemoglobin Unit [*Of hydrolytic enzyme activity*]
HU	Hemolytic Unit [*Hematology*]
HU	High-Usage [*Telecommunications*] (TEL)
HU	Horizontal Arithmetic Unit [*Computer science*] (MHDI)
HU	Hospital Unit (DOMA)
HU	Housing Unit [*Bureau of the Census*] (GFGA)
HU	Hubbert Unit [*Petroleum technology*]
Hu	Hughes' Kentucky Reports [*A publication*] (DLA)
HU	Hughes Tool Co. [*Aircraft Division*] [*ICAO aircraft manufacturer identifier*] (ICAO)
Hu	Hughes' United States Circuit Court Reports [*A publication*] (DLA)
Hu	Hugo de Alberico [*Flourished, 1168-71*] [*Authority cited in pre-1607 legal work*] (DSA)
Hu	Hugolinus de Presbyteris [*Flourished, 1197-1238*] [*Authority cited in pre-1607 legal work*] (DSA)
Hu	Huguccio [*Deceased, 1210*] [*Authority cited in pre-1607 legal work*] (DSA)
HU	Hull (DNAB)
Hu	Human (DB)
HU	Human Urine [*Medicine*] (DMAA)
HU	Hungary [*ANSI two-letter standard code*] (CNC)
hu	Hungary [*MARC country of publication code Library of Congress*] (LCCP)
HU	Hydroxyurea [*Also, HYD, HYDREA*] [*Antineoplastic drug*]
HU	Hyperemia Unit
HU	Trinidad and Tobago Air Services [*ICAO designator*] (AD)
HU	University of Hawaii, Honolulu, HI [*Library symbol Library of Congress*] (LCLS)
HUA	Hockey Umpires' Association [*British*]

HUA	Huancayo [*Peru*] [*Seismograph station code, US Geological Survey*] (SEIS)
HUA	Human Urinary Albumin [*Clinical chemistry*]
HUA	Humber Aviation Ltd. [*British ICAO designator*] (FAAC)
HUA	Huntsville, AL [*Location identifier FAA*] (FAAL)
HUA	Hurricane Watch [*Telecommunications*] (OTD)
HUAA	Home Uterine Activity Assessment [*Medicine*] (DMAA)
HUAC	House Un-American Activities Committee [*Later, HCIS*] [*US Congress*]
HUAM	Home Uterine Activity Monitoring
HuanPw	Huaneng Power International, Inc. [*Associated Press*] (SAG)
HUAR	Arua [*Uganda*] [*ICAO location identifier*] (ICLI)
Hu-Ar	Magyar Orszagos Leveltar, Budapest, Hungary [*Library symbol Library of Congress*] (LCLS)
HUB	Handicapped United in Brotherhood
HUB	Houston, TX [*Location identifier FAA*] (FAAL)
HUB	Hub Airlines, Inc. [*FAA designator*] (FAAC)
HUB	Hubbell [*Harvey*] [*NYSE symbol*] (SAG)
HUBA	Hudson Bay [*AAR code*]
Hubb	Hubbard's Reports [*45-51 Maine*] [*A publication*] (DLA)
Hubbard	Hubbard's Reports [*45-51 Maine*] [*A publication*] (DLA)
HubelB	Hubbell, Harvey [*Associated Press*] (SAG)
Hubb Succ	Hubback's Evidence of Succession [*A publication*] (DLA)
HUBC	HUBCO, Inc. [*NASDAQ symbol*] (SAG)
HUBCO	HUBCO, Inc. [*Associated Press*] (SAG)
HubelA	Hubbell [*Harvey*], Inc. [*Associated Press*] (SAG)
HubelB	Hubbel [*Harvey*], Inc. [*Associated Press*] (SAG)
Hub Ev	Hubback's Evidence of Succession [*A publication*] (DLA)
HUBF	Human Upstream Binding Factor [*Genetics*]
HuBG	Allamin Gorkij Konyvtar, Budapest, Hungary [*Library symbol Library of Congress*] (LCLS)
HUBG	Hub Group 'A' [*NASDAQ symbol*] (TTSB)
HUBG	Hub Group, Inc. [*NASDAQ symbol*] (SAG)
HubGrp	Hub Group, Inc. [*Associated Press*] (SAG)
HuBKPV	Human BK Polyomavirus
Hub Leg Direc	Hubbell's Legal Directory [*A publication*] (DLA)
HuBM	Orszagos Muszaki Konyvtar es Dokumentacios Kozpont, Budapest, Hungary [*Library symbol Library of Congress*] (LCLS)
Hub Prael JC	Huber's Praelectiones Juris Civilis [*A publication*] (DLA)
Hub Suc	Hubback's Evidence of Succession [*A publication*] (DLA)
HUBZone	Historically Underutilized Business Zone (AAGC)
HUC	Hebrew Union College [*Later, HUC-JIR*]
HUC	Hebrew Union College, Jewish Institute of Religion, Cincinnati, OH [*OCLC symbol*] (OCLC)
HUC	Hook Up and Commissioning Conference [*Offshore Conference and Exhibitions Ltd.*] [*British*]
HUC	Humacao [*Puerto Rico*] [*Airport symbol*] (OAG)
HUC	Hypouricemia [*Medicine*]
HUCI	Haitian Unity Council, Inc. [*Defunct*] (EA)
HUC-JIR	Hebrew Union College - Jewish Institute of Religion [*Formerly, HUC*] [*Cincinnati, OH*]
HUCO	Hughes NADGE [*NATO Air Defense Ground Environment*] Consortium
HUCR	Harvard University Character Recognizer [*Computer science*]
HUCR	Highest Useful Compression Ratio [*Aerospace*]
HUD	Department of Housing and Urban Development
HUD	Handicapped Users' Database [*CompuServe Information Service*] [*Information service or system*] (CRD)
HUD	Headsup Display
HUD	Head-Up Display
HUD	Horizons Unlimited [*FAA designator*] (FAAC)
HUD	Horizontal Unit Displacement [*Military*] (INF)
HUD	Hudson Resources Ltd. [*Vancouver Stock Exchange symbol*]
HUDA	Housing and Urban Development Act
HUDAC	Housing and Urban Development Association of Canada
Hud & B	Hudson and Brooke's Irish King's Bench Reports [*1827-31*] [*A publication*] (DLA)
Hud & Br	Hudson and Brooke's Irish King's Bench Reports [*1827-31*] [*A publication*] (DLA)
Hud & Bro	Hudson and Brooke's Irish King's Bench Reports [*1827-31*] [*A publication*] (DLA)
HUDAR	Housing and Urban Development Acquisition Regulations [*A publication*] (AAGC)
HUD BCA	Department of Housing and Urban Development Board of Contract Appeals (AAGC)
HudCB	Hudson Chartered Bancorp, Inc. [*Associated Press*] (SAG)
HUDD	Housing and Urban Development Department [*More commonly, HUD*] (KSC)
HUDDLE	Hull Urban Design Development Laboratory Enterprises, Inc.
HUDE	Head-Up Display Electronics (NASA)
HuDeAgE	Debreceni Agrartudomanyi Egyetem, Debrecen, Hungary [*Library symbol Library of Congress*] (LCLS)
HU/DEAP	Harvard University Division of Engineering and Applied Physics [*Cambridge, MA*]
HuDeK	Debreceni Reformatus Kollegium Nagykonyvtara, Debrecen, Hungary [*Library symbol Library of Congress*] (LCLS)
HuDeOE	Debreceni Orvostudomanyi Egyetem, Debrecen, Hungary [*Library symbol Library of Congress*] (LCLS)
Hud Exec	Hudson's Executor's Guide [*A publication*] (DLA)
HudGn	Hudson General Corp. [*Associated Press*] (SAG)
HUDMAP	HUD [*Department of Housing and Urban Development*] Mortgage Accounting Project
HUDPR	Housing and Urban Development [*Department*] Procurement Regulations
HUDS	Hudson Hotels Corp. [*NASDAQ symbol*] (SAG)

HudsFd	Hudson Foods, Inc. [Associated Press] (SAG)
HudsHotl	Hudson Hotels Corp. [Associated Press] (SAG)
HudsnCB	Hudson Chartered Bancorp, Inc. [Associated Press] (SAG)
Hudson	Hudson on Building Contracts [A publication] (DLA)
HudsonTc	Hudson Technology, Inc. [Associated Press] (SAG)
HUDU	Heads-Up Display Unit [Aviation]
HUDWAC	Heads-Up Display Weapons Aiming Computer (IEEE)
HUDWAS	Heads-Up Display Weapons Aiming System [Air Force] (MCD)
Hud Wills	Hudson on Wills [A publication] (DLA)
HUE	Humera [Ethiopia] [Airport symbol] (OAG)
HUEC	Entebbe Area Control Center [Uganda] [ICAO location identifier] (ICLI)
HUEN	Entebbe/International [Uganda] [ICAO location identifier] (ICLI)
huEPO	Human Erythropoietin [Biochemistry]
HUF	Highway Users Federation for Safety and Mobility [Later, ASF] (EA)
HUF	Huffy Corp. [NYSE symbol] (SPSG)
HUF	Terre Haute [Indiana] [Airport symbol] (OAG)
Huffy	Huffy Corp. [Associated Press] (SAG)
HUFP	Fort Portal [Uganda] [ICAO location identifier] (ICLI)
HUFSAM	Highway Users Federation for Safety and Mobility [FHWA] (TAG)
HU-FSH	Human Urinary Follicle-Stimulating Hormone [Medicine] (DMAA)
HUFSM	Highway Users Federation for Safety and Mobility
HUG	Hastech Users Group (EA)
HUG	Head of Units Group [American Library Association]
HUG	Hiram Ulysses Grant [US general and president, 1822-1885]
HUG	Honeywell Users Group
HUG	Hopitaux Universitaires de Geneve [Switzerland]
HUG	Hughes Supply [NYSE symbol] (TTSB)
HUG	Hughes Supply, Inc. [NYSE symbol] (SPSG)
HUG	Hug-Laf-Luv (EA)
Hug	Hugo de Alberico [Flourished, 12th century] [Authority cited in pre-1607 legal work] (DSA)
Hug	Hugolinus de Presbyteris [Flourished, 1197-1238] [Authority cited in pre-1607 legal work] (DSA)
Hug	Huguccio [Deceased, 1210] [Authority cited in pre-1607 legal work] (DSA)
HUG	Lonely, AK [Location identifier FAA] (FAAL)
HUGA	Human Genome Analyzer [System for analysis of DNA] [Institute of Physical and Chemical Research, Japan Genetics]
HUGE	High-Field, Ultrathin Gel Electrophoresis [Analytical biochemistry]
Hugh	Hughes' Circuit Court Reports [A publication] (DLA)
Hugh	Hughes' Kentucky Reports [A publication] (DLA)
Hugh Abr	Hughes' Abridgment [1663-65] [England] [A publication] (DLA)
Hugh Con	Hughes' Precedents in Conveyancing [2nd ed.] [1855-57] [A publication] (DLA)
Hugh Conv	Hughes' Precedents in Conveyancing [2nd ed.] [1855-57] [A publication] (DLA)
Hugh Ent	Hughes' Entries [1659] [A publication] (DLA)
Hugh Eq D	Hughes' Edition of Van Heythuysen's Equity Draftsman [A publication] (DLA)
Hughes	Hughes Air West [ICAO designator] (AD)
Hughes	Hughes' Kentucky Supreme Court Reports [1785-1801] [A publication] (DLA)
Hughes	Hughes Resources, Inc. [Associated Press] (SAG)
Hughes	Hughes' United States Circuit Court Reports [A publication] (DLA)
Hughes Fed Prac	Hughes' Federal Practice [A publication] (DLA)
Hughes (US)	Hughes' Circuit Court Reports [United States] [A publication] (DLA)
Hugh Ins	Hughes on Insurance [A publication] (DLA)
Hugh Prec	Hughes' Precedents in Conveyancing [2nd ed.] [1855-57] [A publication] (DLA)
HughSp	Hughes Supply, Inc. [Associated Press] (SAG)
Hugh Wills	Hughes on Wills [A publication] (DLA)
Hugh Wr	Hughes on Writs [A publication] (DLA)
HUGO	Highly Unusual Geophysical Operation [A meteorological research vehicle]
Hugo	Hugolinus [Authority cited in pre-1607 legal work] (DSA)
HUGO	Hugoton Energy [NASDAQ symbol] (TTSB)
HUGO	Hugoton Energy Corp. [NASDAQ symbol] (SAG)
HUGO	Human Genome Organization [Genetics]
Hugo Hist Dr Rom	Hugo's Histoire du Droit Romain [A publication] (DLA)
Hugo Hist du Droit Rom	Hugo's Histoire du Droit Romain [A publication] (DLA)
Hugol	Hugolinus de Presbyteris [Flourished, 1197-1238] [Authority cited in pre-1607 legal work] (DSA)
HugotEn	Hugoton Energy Corp. [Associated Press] (SAG)
HUG's	Home User Groups [Computer science]
HUG-SMS	Honeywell Users Group - Small and Medium Systems [Later, NAHU]
HUGU	Gulu [Uganda] [ICAO location identifier] (ICLI)
Hugu	Huguccio [Deceased, 1210] [Authority cited in pre-1607 legal work] (DSA)
HUH	Huahine [French Polynesia] [Airport symbol] (OAG)
HUH	Hualalai [Hawaii] [Seismograph station code, US Geological Survey] (SEIS)
HUH	University of Hawaii, Hamilton Library, Honolulu, HI [OCLC symbol] (OCLC)
HUI	Headache Unit Index [Medicine] (DMAA)
HUI	Hue [South Vietnam] [Airport symbol] (AD)
HUIFM	Human Leukocyte Interferon Milieu [Biochemistry] (DAVI)
HuIFN	Human Interferon [Biochemistry]
HUIS	High-Dose Urea in Invert Sugar (AAMN)
HUJ	Hebrew University [Jerusalem] (BJA)
HuJCPV	Human JC Polyomavirus
HUJI	Jinja [Uganda] [ICAO location identifier] (ICLI)
HUK	Human Urinary Kallikrein [Medicine] (DMAA)
HUK	Hungarian-Ukrainan Heavy Lift Ltd. [Hungary ICAO designator] (FAAC)

HUK	Hunter-Killer [Operations against submarines] [Navy]
HUKASWEX	Hunter-Killer Antisubmarine Warfare Exercise [Navy] (NVT)
HUKB	Hostile, Unknown, Faker, and Big Photo [Used in Semi-Automatic Ground Environment to designate certain tracks and raids] (SAA)
HUKB	Kabale [Uganda] [ICAO location identifier] (ICLI)
HuKeAgE	Agrartudomanyi Egyetem, Keszthely, Hungary [Library symbol Library of Congress] (LCLS)
HUKF	Kabalega Falls [Uganda] [ICAO location identifier] (ICLI)
HUKFOR	Hunter-Killer Forces [Navy]
HUKFORLANT	Hunter-Killer Forces, Atlantic [Navy]
HUKFORPAC	Hunter-Killer Forces, Pacific [Navy]
HUKP	Hostile, Unknown, Faker, and Pending [Used in SAGE to designate certain tracks and raids]
HUKP	Hostile, Unknown, Faker, Pending Track Identities [Used in Semi-Automatic Ground Environment to designate certain tracks and raids] (SAA)
HUKS	Hostile, Unknown, Faker, Special Track Identities [Used in SAGE to designate certain tracks and raids] (SAA)
HUKS	Hukbong Mapagpalaya ng Bayan [People's Liberation Army, Philippines] (CINC)
HUKS	Hunter-Killer Submarine [Navy]
HUKS	Kasese [Uganda] [ICAO location identifier] (ICLI)
HUL	Hardware Utilization List (NASA)
HUL	Harvard University, Cambridge, MA [OCLC symbol] (OCLC)
HUL	Home University Library [A publication]
HUL	Houlton [Maine] [Airport symbol] (OAG)
HUL	Houlton, ME [Location identifier FAA] (FAAL)
Hul	Hullin (BJA)
HULA	Lake George [Uganda] [ICAO location identifier] (ICLI)
HULAX	Hawaiian Tax Free Trust [Mutual fund ticker symbol] (SG)
HULI	Lira [Uganda] [ICAO location identifier] (ICLI)
HULL	High-Usage Load List (DNAB)
Hull Costs	Hullock on Costs [A publication] (DLA)
Hult Conv	Hulton's Convictions [1835] [A publication] (DLA)
HULTEC	Hull-to-Emitter Correlation [Navy] (CAAL)
HULTIS	Hull Technical Interloan Scheme [British] (NITA)
HUM	Health and Usage Monitoring (DA)
HUM	Heat or Hot Packs, Ultrasound, and Massage [Medicine] (STED)
HUM	Hematourimetry (STED)
HUM	Highly Unusual Methods (ECON)
HUM	Houma [Louisiana] [Airport symbol] (OAG)
HUM	Human (ROG)
HUM	Humana, Inc. [NYSE symbol] (SPSG)
Hum	Humanist [A publication] (BRI)
HUM	Humanitarian (ROG)
HUM	Humanities
Hum	Humanities (AL)
HUM	Humble (ROG)
hum	Humerus (STED)
HUM	Humidity (NASA)
HUM	Hummingbird Helicopters Maldives (Pvt) Ltd. [ICAO designator] (FAAC)
HUM	Humorous (ADA)
Hum	Humphrey's Tennessee Supreme Court Reports [1839-51] [A publication] (DLA)
HU-M	University of Hawaii, Leahi Hospital, Hastings H. Walker Medical Library, Honolulu, HI [Library symbol Library of Congress] (LCLS)
HUMA	Mbarara/Obote [Uganda] [ICAO location identifier] (ICLI)
HUMAN	Help Us Make a Nation (EA)
Humana	Humana, Inc. [Associated Press] (SAG)
Human Rts J	Human Rights Journal [A publication] (DLA)
Human Rts Rev	Human Rights Review [A publication] (DLA)
HUMARIS	Human Materials Resources Information System (DIT)
Humb	Humble
Humber	Humberside [County in England] (WGA)
Humber de Bou	Humbertus de Bouen [Authority cited in pre-1607 legal work] (DSA)
Humbird	Hummingbird Communication Industries [Associated Press] (SAG)
HUMCAT	Humanoid Catalog [Mutual Unidentified Flying Object Network]
HUMCF	Hummingbird Communication Industries [NASDAQ symbol] (SAG)
HUMCF	Hummingbird Communications [NASDAQ symbol] (TTSB)
Hume	Hume's Court of Session Decisions [1781-1822] [Scotland] [A publication] (DLA)
Hume Com	Hume's Commentaries on Crimes [Scotland] [A publication] (DLA)
Hume Hist Eng	Hume's History of England [A publication] (DLA)
HUMEVAC	Humanitarian Emergency Evacuation [Military] (NVT)
HumGen	Human Genome Sciences, Inc. [Associated Press] (SAG)
HUMI	Masindi [Uganda] [ICAO location identifier] (ICLI)
HUMID	Hughes Unit Malfunction Isolation Detector
HUMINT	Human Intelligence [Spies, double agents, etc.] [CIA] (AFM)
HUMO	Highest Unoccupied Molecular Orbital (DB)
HUMO	Moroto [Uganda] [ICAO location identifier] (ICLI)
HUMP	Humphrey Hospitality Tr Inc. [NASDAQ symbol] (TTSB)
HUMP	Humphrey Hospitality Trust, Inc. [NASDAQ symbol] (SAG)
Humph	Humphrey's Tennessee Reports [20-30 Tennessee] [A publication] (DLA)
Humph Dist Reg	Humphreys. District Registry Practice and Procedure [1977] [A publication] (ILCA)
Humph Prec	Humphry's Common Precedents in Conveyancing [2nd ed.] [1882] [A publication] (DLA)
Humphry	Humphrey Hospitality Trust, Inc. [Associated Press] (SAG)
HUMRESMANDET	Human Resources Management Detachment [Navy] (DNAB)
HUMRESMANSCOL	Human Resources Management School [Navy] (DNAB)
HUMRESMANSCOLDET	Human Resources Management School Detachment [Navy] (DNAB)

HumRRO......	Human Resources Research Office [*George Washington University*]
HumRRO......	Human Resources Research Organization (EA)
Hum Rts LJ...	Human Rights Law Journal [*A publication*] (DLA)
Hum Rts Q...	Human Rights Quarterly [*A publication*] (DLA)
Hum Rts USSR...	Human Rights in the Union of Soviet Socialist Republics [*A publication*] (DLA)
HUMS..........	Humanitarian Reasons
HUN............	Hualien [*Taiwan*] [*Airport symbol*] (OAG)
HUN............	Hundersingen [*Federal Republic of Germany*] [*Seismograph station code, US Geological Survey*] (SEIS)
HUN............	Hundred (MUGU)
hun............	Hungarian [*MARC language code Library of Congress*] (LCCP)
HUN............	Hungary [*ANSI three-letter standard code*] (CNC)
Hun............	Hun's New York Appellate Division Supreme Court Reports [*A publication*] (DLA)
HUN............	Hunt Corp. [*NYSE symbol*] [*Formerly, Hunt Manufacturing*] (SG)
HUN............	Hunting Business Aviation [*British ICAO designator*] (FAAC)
HUN............	Huntington Resources, Inc. [*Vancouver Stock Exchange symbol*]
HUN............	Hunt Manufacturing Co. [*NYSE symbol*] (SPSG)
HUN............	Hunt Mfg. [*NYSE symbol*] (TTSB)
Hun............	New York Supreme Court Reports [*A publication*] (DLA)
HUNA..........	Huna Research [*An association*] (EA)
HUNA..........	Namulonge Agrometeorology Station [*Uganda*] [*ICAO location identifier*] (ICLI)
HUND..........	Hundred
HUNDREDSB...	Hundredsbarrow [*England*]
HUNG..........	Hungary
Hung..........	Hungary (VRA)
HUNGARNET...	Hungarian Academic and Research Network (TELE)
HungB.........	Hungarian Broadcasting Corp. [*Associated Press*] (SAG)
HungBd.......	Hungarian Broadcasting Corp. [*Associated Press*] (SAG)
HungBrd	Hungarian Broadcasting Corp. [*Associated Press*] (SAG)
HUNGF........	Hungerford [*England*]
HUNGN........	Hungarian
HungTel.......	Hungarian Telephone and Cable Corp. [*Associated Press*] (SAG)
HungTelc	Hungarian Teleconstruction & Cable Corp. [*Associated Press*] (SAG)
Hunt...........	Hunter's Torrens Cases [*Canada*] [*A publication*] (DLA)
Hunt...........	Hunt's Annuity Cases [*England*] [*A publication*] (DLA)
Hunt Ann Cas...	Hunt's Annuity Cases [*England*] [*A publication*] (DLA)
HuntBnk.......	Huntington Bankshares [*Associated Press*] (SAG)
Hunt Bound...	Hunt's Law of Boundaries and Fences [*A publication*] (DLA)
Hunt Cas......	Hunt's Annuity Cases [*England*] [*A publication*] (DLA)
Huntco	Huntco, Inc. [*Associated Press*] (SAG)
Hunt Eq.......	Hunt's Suit in Equity [*A publication*] (DLA)
Hunter C (CUNY)...	Hunter College of The City University of New York (GAGS)
Hunter Rom Law...	Hunter on Roman Law [*A publication*] (DLA)
Hunter Suit Eq...	Hunter's Proceeding in a Suit in Equity [*A publication*] (DLA)
HUNTEST.....	Hunting and Testing [*Apollo*] [*NASA*]
Hunt Fr Conv...	Hunt's Fraudulent Conveyances [*2nd ed.*] [*1897*] [*A publication*] (DLA)
hunth	Hundred Thousand (BARN)
HuntJB........	Hunt [*J.B.*] Transport Services, Inc. [*Associated Press*] (SAG)
Hunt L & T...	Hunter's Landlord and Tenant [*Scotland*] [*A publication*] (DLA)
Hunt Mer Mag...	Hunt's Merchants' Magazine [*A publication*] (DLA)
HuntMf........	Hunt Manufacturing Co. [*Associated Press*] (SAG)
Hunt Rom L...	Hunter on Roman Law [*A publication*] (DLA)
HUNTS........	Huntingdonshire [*County in England*]
Hunt's AC ...	Hunt's Annuity Cases [*England*] [*A publication*] (DLA)
Hunt Suit	Hunter's Proceeding in a Suit in Equity [*A publication*] (DLA)
Hunt Torrens...	Hunter's Torrens Cases [*Canada A publication*] (DLA)
Hunt Tr	Huntington's Trial [*A publication*] (DLA)
Huntwy........	Huntway Partners Ltd. [*Associated Press*] (SAG)
HUO............	Huguenot, NY [*Location identifier FAA*] (FAAL)
HuOSzK........	Orszagos Szechenyi Konyvtar [*National Szechenyi Library*], Budapest, Hungary [*Library symbol Library of Congress*] (LCLS)
HUP	Hangup
HUP	Harvard University Press (DGA)
HUP	Helicopter Utility (Piasecki)
HUP	Homogenous Uniparental Embryo [*Embryology*]
HUP	Hospital of the University of Pennsylvania
HUP	Hospital Utilization Project [*Western Pennsylvania*]
HUP	Hudspeth, TX [*Location identifier FAA*] (FAAL)
hup	Hupa [*MARC language code Library of Congress*] (LCCP)
HUP	Hydrogen Uranyl Phosphate [*Inorganic chemistry*]
HuPaB	Pannonhalmi Szent Benedek Rend Kozponti Konyvtara, Pannonhalma, Hungary [*Library symbol Library of Congress*] (LCLS)
HUPATS.......	Heuristic Paper Trimming System (BUR)
HUPCM........	Hybrid Unidigit Pulse Code Modulation (IAA)
HuPE...........	Pecsi Tudomanyegyetem, Pecs, Hungary [*Library symbol Library of Congress*] (LCLS)
HUPPIE........	Hispanic Urban Professional [*Lifestyle classification*]
HUPW..........	Hot Ultrapure Water (AAEL)
HUQ............	Houn [*Libya*] [*Airport symbol*] (OAG)
HUR............	Hardware Usage Report (MCD)
HUR............	Heat Up Rate (IEEE)
HUR............	Homes Using Radio [*Ratings*] (NTCM)
HUR............	Hurn [*England*] [*Airport symbol*] (AD)
HUR............	Hurricane [*Alaska*] [*Seismograph station code, US Geological Survey*] (SEIS)
HUR............	Hydroxyurea [*Antineoplastic drug*] (DAVI)
HUR............	Miami Air Charter [*ICAO designator*] (FAAC)
HURA..........	Health Underserved Rural Areas
HURC..........	Hurco Companies [*NASDAQ symbol*] (TTSB)
HURC..........	Hurco Companies, Inc. [*NASDAQ symbol*] (NQ)

HURCN	Hurricane
Hurco...........	Hurco Companies, Inc. [*Associated Press*] (SAG)
Hurd F & B...	Hurd on the Laws of Freedom and Bondage in the United States [*A publication*] (DLA)
Hurd Hab Cor...	Hurd on the Writ of Habeas Corpus [*A publication*] (DLA)
Hurd Pers Lib...	Hurd on Personal Liberty [*A publication*] (DLA)
Hurd's Rev St...	Hurd's Illinois Revised Statutes [*A publication*] (DLA)
Hurd St	Hurd's Illinois Statutes [*A publication*] (DLA)
HUREP........	Hurricane Report
HUREVAC	Hurricane Evacuation (NVT)
HURI............	Harvard Ukrainian Research Institute
HURI............	Hughes Resources, Inc. [*NASDAQ symbol*] (SAG)
HURIDOCS...	Human Rights Information and Documentation System (EA)
HURIDOCS...	Human Rights International Documentation System (EA)
HURL	Hawaii Undersea Research Laboratory [*University of Hawaii*] [*Research center*] (RCD)
Hurl & C	Hurlstone and Coltman's English Exchequer Reports [*A publication*] (DLA)
Hurl & Colt..	Hurlstone and Coltman's English Exchequer Reports [*A publication*] (DLA)
Hurl & G	Hurlstone and Gordon's English Exchequer Reports [*A publication*] (DLA)
Hurl & Gord...	Hurlstone and Gordon's English Exchequer Reports [*A publication*] (DLA)
Hurl & N	Hurlstone and Norman's English Exchequer Reports [*156, 158 English Reprint*] [*A publication*] (DLA)
Hurl & Nor...	Hurlstone and Norman's English Exchequer Reports [*156, 158 English Reprint*] [*A publication*] (DLA)
Hurl & W	Hurlstone and Walmsley's English Exchequer Reports [*1840-41*] [*A publication*] (DLA)
Hurl & Walm...	Hurlstone and Walmsley's English Exchequer Reports [*1840-41*] [*A publication*] (DLA)
Hurl Bonds...	Hurlstone on Bonds [*A publication*] (DLA)
Hurl Colt......	Hurlstone and Coltman's English Exchequer Reports [*A publication*] (DLA)
Hurls & W (Eng)...	Hurlstone and Walmsley's English Exchequer Reports [*1840-41*] [*A publication*] (DLA)
Hurlst & C ...	Hurlstone and Coltman's English Exchequer Reports [*A publication*] (DLA)
Hurlst & C (Eng)...	Hurlstone and Coltman's English Exchequer Reports [*A publication*] (DLA)
Hurlst & G ...	Hurlstone and Gordon's English Exchequer Reports [*A publication*] (DLA)
Hurlst & N (Eng)...	Hurlstone and Norman's English Exchequer Reports [*156, 158 English Reprint*] [*A publication*] (DLA)
Hurlst & W...	Hurlstone and Walmsley's English Exchequer Reports [*1840-41*] [*A publication*] (DLA)
Hurr	Hurrian (BJA)
HURRA	Housing and Urban-Rural Recovery Act of 1983
HURRAH......	Help Us Reach and Rehabilitate America's Handicapped [*State-Federal rehabilitation program*]
HURRAN......	Hurricane Analog
HURRAO......	Human Use Review and Regulatory Affairs Office [*Army*] (RDA)
HURR-EVAC...	Hurricane Evacuation (DNAB)
HURT..........	HealthRite, Inc. [*NASDAQ symbol*] (SAG)
HURT..........	Hospital Utilization Review Team (STED)
HUS............	Hardened Unique Storage [*Environmental science*] (COE)
HUS............	Helicopter Utility Squadron
HUS............	Hemolytic-Uremic Syndrome [*Nephrology*]
HUS............	Heussler Air Service Corp. [*ICAO designator*] (FAAC)
HUS............	Hughes [*Alaska*] [*Airport symbol*] (OAG)
HUS............	Husband [*Legal shorthand*] (LWAP)
HUS............	Hyaluronidase Unit for Semen (MAE)
HuSA..........	Human Serum Albumin (DB)
HUSAFICPA...	Headquarters, United States Army Forces, Central Pacific Area
HUSAFMIDPAC...	Headquarters, United States Army Forces, Middle Pacific [*World War II*]
HUSAT	Human Sciences Advanced Technology Unit [*Longborough University*] [*British*]
HUSAT	Human Sciences and Advanced Technology Research Centre [*University of Technology*] [*British*] (CB)
husb............	Husband
HUSB	Husbandry
HUSB & W...	Husband and Wife (DLA)
HUSBC	Hungarian-United States Business Council (NTPA)
HUSBD........	Husband (ROG)
Husb For Med...	Husband's Forensic Medicine [*A publication*] (DLA)
Husb Mar Wom...	Husband on Married Women [*A publication*] (DLA)
HUSBN........	Husbandman
HUSICON	Humanities, Science, and Conservation [*Environment*]
HUSLONET...	Hungarian-Slovak Network (TELE)
HUSO..........	Soroti [*Uganda*] [*ICAO location identifier*] (ICLI)
HuSpK	Sarospataki Reformatus Kollegium Nagykonyvtara, Sarospatak, Hungary [*Library symbol Library of Congress*] (LCLS)
HUSS	Hussars [*Military unit*] [*British*] (ROG)
Hust............	Hustings Court [*As in Virginia*] [*Legal term*] (DLA)
HUSTLE	Helium Underwater Speech Translating Equipment
Hust L Tit	Huston on Land Titles in Pennsylvania [*A publication*] (DLA)
HuSzOE.......	Szegedi Orvostudomanyi Egyetem, Szeged, Hungary [*Library symbol Library of Congress*] (LCLS)
HUT	Hard Upper Torso (MCD)
HUT	HEDL [*Hanford Engineering Development Laboratory*] Up Transient [*Nuclear energy*] (NRCH)
HUT	Held-Up Transient (IAA)
HUT	Helsinki University of Technology

HUT	High-Usage Intertoll Trunk [Data communication] (MHDI)
HUT	Hold Up Tank (IEEE)
HUT	Homes Using Television [Television ratings]
HUT	Hopkins Ultraviolet Telescope
HUT	Households Using Television [Television ratings]
HUT	Humboldt Energy [Vancouver Stock Exchange symbol]
HUT	Hutchinson [Kansas] [Airport symbol] (OAG)
Hut	Hutton's English Common Pleas Reports [1612-39] [A publication] (DLA)
HUTCH	Humidity-Temperature Chart (PDAA)
Hutch	Hutcheson's Reports [81-84 Alabama] [A publication] (DLA)
Hutch Car ...	Hutchinson on Carriers [A publication] (DLA)
Hutch Carr ...	Hutchinson on Carriers [A publication] (DLA)
Hutch Code...	Hutchinson's Code [Mississippi] [A publication] (DLA)
Hutch JP	Hutcheson's Justice of the Peace [A publication] (DLA)
HutchT	Hutchinson Technology, Inc. [Associated Press] (SAG)
Hut Ct Req...	Hutton's Courts of Requests [A publication] (DLA)
HUTHAS	Human Thymus Anti-Serum [Medicine] (MAE)
HUTI	Human Urinary Trypsin Inhibitor (DB)
HUTO	Tororo [Uganda] [ICAO location identifier] (ICLI)
HUTR	Hubbell Trading Post National Historic Site
HUTRON	Helicopter Utility Squadron
HUTSAT	Helsinki University of Technology Satellite
Hutt	Hutton's English Common Pleas Reports [1612-39] [A publication] (DLA)
Hutt Ct Req...	Hutton's Courts of Requests [A publication] (DLA)
Hutton	Hutton's English Common Pleas Reports [1612-39] [A publication] (DLA)
Hutton (Eng)...	Hutton's English Common Pleas Reports [1612-39] [A publication] (DLA)
HUU	Detroit, MI [Location identifier FAA] (FAAL)
HUU	Huanuco [Peru] [Airport symbol] (OAG)
HUV	Hudiksvall [Sweden] [Airport symbol] (OAG)
HUV	Human Umbilical Vein [Medicine] (DMAA)
HUVE	Human Umbilical Vein Endothelial
HUVEC	Human Umbilical Vein Endothelial Cell [Cytology]
HUW	Hurricane Warning [Telecommunications] (OTD)
HUX	Harvard University [Cambridge, MA]
HUX	Sacramento, CA [Location identifier FAA] (FAAL)
Hux Judg	Huxley's Second Book of Judgments [1675] [England] [A publication] (DLA)
HUY	Hull [England] [Airport symbol] (AD)
HUY	Humberside [England] [Airport symbol] (OAG)
HUZ	Huaraz [Peru] [Seismograph station code, US Geological Survey] (SEIS)
HUZ	Mesquite, TX [Location identifier FAA] (FAAL)
HUzT	Hermeneutische Untersuchungen zur Theologie [Tuebingen] [A publication] (BJA)
HV	Air Central [ICAO designator] (AD)
HV..............	Air-Cushion Vehicle built by Hover Vehicles [New Zealand] [Usually used in combination with numerals]
HV	Boeing-Vertol Division [The Boeing Co.] [ICAO aircraft manufacturer identifier] (ICAO)
HV..............	Hallux Valgus [Orthopedics] (DAVI)
HV..............	Hand Valve [Nuclear energy] (NRCH)
HV..............	Hard Valve (DEN)
HV..............	Hardware Virtualizer [Computer science] (IEEE)
HV..............	Haricots Verts [Green Beans] [French]
HV..............	Has Voided [Medicine] (DAVI)
HV..............	Have [Amateur radio shorthand] (WDAA)
HV..............	Health Visitor
HV..............	Heater Voltage
HV..............	Heating and Ventilation (AAG)
HV..............	Heat of Vaporization (ROG)
HV..............	Heavy (AABC)
hv	Heavy (VRA)
H-V	Height-Velocity
HV..............	Helminthosporium victoriae [A toxin-producing fungus]
HV..............	Hepatic Vein [Anatomy]
HV..............	Herpesvirus
HV..............	Hic Verbis [In These Words] [Latin]
HV..............	High in Volatiles [Commercial grading]
HV..............	Highly Variegated Maize
HV..............	High Vacuum (ADA)
HV..............	High Velocity
HV..............	High Visibility (DS)
HV..............	High Voltage
hv	High Voltage (WDAA)
HV..............	High Volume
HV..............	Hoc Verbum [This Word] [Latin]
HV..............	Home Video [Television]
HV..............	Horizontal-Vertical Intersection [Lighting] [Automotive engineering]
HV..............	Hospital Visit (AAMN)
HV..............	Hyaline-Vascular [Oncology]
HV..............	Hydrogen Vent (MCD)
HV..............	Hydroxyl Value [Analytical chemistry]
HV..............	Hypervariable
HV..............	Hypervelocity (AABC)
HV..............	Hyperventilation
HV..............	Vatican [International civil aircraft marking] (ODBW)
HV..............	Vickers Hardness Number [Also, VH, VHN]
HV6.............	Heracleum Virus 6 [Plant pathology]
HVA	Analalava [Madagascar] [Airport symbol] (OAG)
HVA	Health Visitors' Association [A union] [British] (DCTA)

HVA	Heeresverwaltungsamt [Army Administration Office] [German military - World War II]
HVA	Herpesvirus Ateles
HVA	High-Voltage Anomaly [Seismology]
HVA	High-Voltage-Activated [Neurochemistry]
HVA	Homovanillic Acid [Biochemistry]
HVA	Methoxy-Hydroxyphenylacetic Acid [Chemistry] (DAVI)
HVA	Newair, Inc. [ICAO designator] (FAAC)
HVAA	High-Value Airborne Assets (DOMA)
HVAC	Heating, Ventilating, and Air Conditioning
HVAC	Heating, Ventilation, Air Conditioning [Marine science] (OSRA)
HVAC	High Vacuum (IEEE)
HVAC	High-Voltage Actuator [Electronics] (IEEE)
HVAC	High-Voltage Alternating Current
HVAC	House Veterans' Affairs Committee [House of Representatives]
HVACC	High-Voltage Apparatus Coordinating Committee [ANSI]
HVAF	High-Velocity Air Filter (EG)
H vag	Hemophilus Vaginalis [Gynecology] (DAVI)
HV & C	Heating, Ventilating, and Cooling (AAG)
HVAO	Hybrid-Valence Atomic Orbital (MEC)
HVAP	High-Velocity, Armor-Piercing [Projectile]
HVAPDS	High-Velocity, Armor-Piercing, Discarding Sabot [Projectile]
HVAPDS	Hypervelocity, Armor-Piercing, Discarding Sabot Projectile [Army] (SAA)
HVAPDSFS...	High-Velocity, Armor-Piercing, Discarding Sabot, Fin Stabilized [Projectile] (MCD)
HVAPDSFS...	Hypervelocity, Armor-Piercing, Discarding Sabot, Fin Stabilized Projectile [Army] (SAA)
HVAPFSDS...	High-Velocity, Armor-Piercing, Fin Stabilized, Discarding Sabot [Projectile] (MCD)
HVAP-T	Hypervelocity, Armor-Piercing - Tracer [Projectile] (AABC)
HVAR	High-Velocity Aircraft Rocket
HVAR(HE)....	High-Velocity Aircraft Rocket (High Explosive) (DNAB)
HVAS	Hydraulic Valve Adjuster System [Automotive engineering]
HVAT	High-Velocity Antitank [Projectile]
HVATKRON...	Heavy Attack Squadron (DNAB)
HVB	Hauptverbandplatz [Clearing Station] [German military - World War II]
HVB	Hervey Bay [Australia Airport symbol] (OAG)
HVB	High-Voltage Bias
HVC	Hardened Voice Channel [NASA] (KSC)
HVC	Hardened Voice Circuit (CET)
HVC	Haverford College, Haverford, PA [OCLC symbol] (OCLC)
HVC	Hav-Info Computers, Inc. [Vancouver Stock Exchange symbol]
HVC	Hayden's Viburnum Compound [Medicine]
HVC	Health Visitor's Certificate [British]
HVC	Hernandez Valley [California] [Seismograph station code, US Geological Survey] (SEIS)
HVC	High-Velocity Cloud [Astronomy] (OA)
HVC	High Vocal Center [Songbird anatomy]
HVC	High-Voltage Connector
HVC	High-Voltage Control
HVC	Hopkinsville, KY [Location identifier FAA] (FAAL)
HVC	Hudson Valley Conference (PSS)
HVC	Hydrogen Check Valve (NAKS)
HVc	Hyperstriatum Ventralis Pars Caudalis [Bird brain anatomy]
HVc	Ventral Hyperstriatum Caudal Nucleus [Neuroanatomy]
HVCA	Heating and Ventilating Contractors' Association [British]
HVCC	Hairy Vetch as a Cover Crop [Agriculture]
HVCE	High-Voltage Capillary Electrophoresis
HVCH	Hardened Voice Channel (MSA)
HVCMOS......	High Voltage CMOS [Complementary Metal Oxide Semiconductor] (NITA)
HVCS	High-Vacuum Calibration System (PDAA)
HVD	Half-Value Depth (IAA)
HVD	Heaters, Vents, and Drains [System] [Nuclear energy] (NRCH)
HVD	Height-Velocity Diagram
HVD	Hendrik Verwoerd Dam [South Africa] [Seismograph station code, US Geological Survey] (SEIS)
HVD	High-Velocity Detonation
HVD	High-Viscosity Dispenser [Packaging]
HVD	Hydroviscous Drive (DNAB)
HVD	Hypertensive Vascular Disease [Medicine]
HVDC	High-Voltage Direct Current
HVDCT	High-Voltage Direct-Current Transmission [Electronics]
HVDF	High- and Very-High-Frequency Direction Finding
HVDP	Heavy Drop [Military] (AABC)
HVDRR	Hypocalcemic Vitamin D-Resistant Rickets [Medicine]
HVDS	Hypergolic Vapor Detection System [NASA] (NASA)
HVE	Hanksville, UT [Location identifier FAA] (FAAL)
HVE	Hepatic Vascular Exclusion [Medicine] (MEDA)
HVE	High-Vacuum Environment
HVE	High-Vacuum Evaporator
HVE	High-Voltage Electrophoresis (AAMN)
HVE	Horizontal Vertex Error (OA)
HVEC	High Voltage Engineering Corp.
HVEC	Human Vascular Endothelial Cells
HVEF	Harvest Financial Corp. [NASDAQ symbol] (SAG)
HVEL	Hypervelocity
HVEM	High-Voltage Electron Microscopy
HVES	High-Vacuum Evaporation System
HVES	High-Voltage Electrical Stimulation [Meat treatment]
HVF	Harmonically Varying Field
HVF	Haverford College, Haverford, PA [OCLC symbol] (OCLC)
HVF	High-Viscosity Fuel Oil (DCTA)

HVFB	High-Velocity Fluidized Bed [Chemical engineering]
HVFD	Haverfield Corp. [NASDAQ symbol] (NQ)
HVFS	High-Vacuum Flame Sterilization [Food technology]
HVG	High-Voltage Generator
HVG	High-Voltage Gradient
HVG	Honningsvag [Norway] [Airport symbol] (OAG)
HVG	Host Versus Graft [Medicine]
HVG	Hypervelocity Gun [Military] (SDI)
HVGL	High Velocity Grenade Launcher [Projectile] (PDAA)
HVGLS	High-Velocity Grenade Launcher System [Projectile] (MCD)
HVGO	Hanover Gold [NASDAQ symbol] (TTSB)
HVGO	Hanover Gold Company, Inc. [NASDAQ symbol] (SAG)
HVGO	Heavy Vacuum Gas Oil [Petroleum product]
HVH	Herpesvirus Hominis
HVH	Hydrogen Vent Header [Nuclear energy] (NRCH)
HVHA	High-Velocity Hot-Air [Oven]
HVHAI	High-Velocity Hot-Air Impingement [Organic chemistry]
HVHD	High-Voltage-Hold-Down (PDAA)
HVHF	High and Very-High Frequency (IAA)
HVHMA	Herpesvirus Hominis Membrane Antigen [Medicine] (MEDA)
HVHMD	Holographic Visor Helmet-Mounted Display [Air Force]
HVI	Hartman Value Inventory [Psychology]
HVI	Hepatic Volumetric Index
HVI	High-Value Item (NATG)
HVI	High Viscosity Index [Lubricants]
HVI	High-Volume Instrument [Agricultural research]
HVI	Home Ventilating Institute [Later, HVIDAMCA] (EA)
HVI	Horizon Village [Vancouver Stock Exchange symbol]
HVIC	High-Voltage Integrated Circuit [Computer science]
HVIDAMCA	Home Ventilating Institute Division of the Air Movement Control Association (EA)
HVideM	Hvide Marine, Inc. [Associated Press] (SAG)
HVIO	High-Volume Industrial Organics [Environmental science] (GFGA)
HVIRS	Hull Vibration Information Retrieval System (PDAA)
HVIT	High-Volume Information Transfer
HVJ	Hemagglutinating Virus of Japan [Medicine]
HVK	Holmavik [Iceland] [Airport symbol] (OAG)
HVK	Hovik Medical [Vancouver Stock Exchange symbol]
HVL	Half-Value Layer [Radiology]
HVL	Heeresverpflegungslager [Army Ration Depot] [German military - World War II]
HVL	Highly Volatile Liquid (TAG)
HVL	High Voltage Laboratory [MIT] (MCD)
HVL	Hypervelocity Launcher [Military] (SDI)
HVLL	Hudson Valley Lacrosse League (PSS)
HVLP	High-Velocity, Low Penetration Paint
HVLP	High-Volume Low-Pressure [Spray-painting process]
HVLS	Huron Valley Library System [Library network]
HVM	Heterodyne Vegetation Meter (IAA)
HVM	High Velocity Metalworking (PDAA)
HVM	High-Velocity Missile [Military] (DAVI)
HVM	High-Voltage Mode
HVM	Hydraulic Valve Motor
HVM	Hypervelocity Missile
HVM	Hypervelocity Munition
HVM	Sisters, Home Visitors of Mary [Roman Catholic religious order]
HVMAC	Hudson Valley Men's Athletic Conference (PSS)
HVMC	High-Variation Medical Condition
HVMS	Hypervelocity, Medium Support
HVMVI	High-Voltage Mercury-Vapor Isolator
HVN	Hang Khong Viet Nam [ICAO designator] (FAAC)
HVN	Havana [Cuba] [Geomagnetic observatory code]
HVN	Haven (MCD)
HVN	Home View Network [Cable-television system]
HVN	New Haven [Connecticut] [Airport symbol] (OAG)
HVO	Hawaiian Volcano Observatory [Kilauea] [Hawaii] [Seismograph station code, US Geological Survey] (SEIS)
HVO	Health Volunteers Overseas (EA)
HVOC	Halogenated Volatile Organic Compound
HVOF	High-Velocity Oxygen/Fuel [Coating technology]
HVOSM	Highway Vehicle Object Simulation Model [Computer-aided design] [Automotive engineering]
HVOT	Hooper Visual Organization Test [Psychology]
HVP	Half-Value Period
HVP	Hardware Verification Program (CAAL)
HVP	Hartman Value Profile [Personality development test] [Psychology]
HVP	Hayes Verification Protocol [Computer science]
HVP	Heart Valve Prostheses [Medicine]
HVP	Herpes Virus Papio [Medicine] (DB)
HVP	High-Vacuum Pump
HVP	High-Value Product
HVP	High Video Pass (NVT)
HVP	High-Voltage Potential (IAA)
HVP	High-Voltage Pump
HVP	Host Vehicle Pallet
HVP	Hydrolyzed Vegetable Protein [Food additive]
HVP	Hypervelocity Projectile [Military] (MUSM)
HVPE	High-Voltage Paper Electrophoresis
HVPE	Hydride Vapor Phase Epitaxy [Crystallography]
HVPF	Human Vascular Permeability Factor [Biochemistry]
HVPG	Hepatic Venous Pressure Gradient [Medicine]
HVPHOTORON	Heavy Photographic Squadron (DNAB)
HVPI	High-Voltage Plasma Interaction (SSD)
HVPI	Holland Vocational Preference Inventory [Psychology]
HVPR	High-Voltage Phase Retard

HVPS	High-Voltage Power Supply
HVPS	High-Volume Printing System [Computer science]
HVPVE	High-Voltage Photovoltaic Effect [Physics]
HVR	Hardware Vector to Raster
HVR	Havre [Montana] [Airport symbol] (OAG)
HVR	Helicopter Visual Rules
HVR	Highland Valley Resources Ltd. [Vancouver Stock Exchange symbol]
HVR	Highly Variable Regions [Of chromosomes] [Genetics]
HVR	High-Resolution Visible Range
HVR	High-Vacuum Rectifier
HVR	High-Voltage Rectifier
HVR	High-Voltage Regulator (MSA)
HVR	High-Voltage Relay
HVR	High-Voltage Resistor
HVR	Home Video Recorder (NTCM)
HVR	Hover (MCD)
HVR	Hyderabad Volunteer Rifles [British military] (DMA)
HVR	Hypervariable Region [Genetics]
HVR	Hypoxic Ventilatory Response [Medicine]
HVRA	Heating and Ventilating Research Association [British]
HVRAP	Hyper-Velocity Rocket-Assisted Projectile (PDAA)
HVRL	High Voltage Research Laboratory [MIT] (MCD)
HVRNG	Hovering
HVS	Hartsville, SC [Location identifier FAA] (FAAL)
HVS	Herpesvirus of Saimiri
HVS	High-Voltage Switch
HVS	Hue, Value, Saturation [Graphic arts] (WDMC)
HVS	Human Vaginal Swab [Medicine]
HVS	Human Visual System
HVSA	Hypersonic Vehicle Shield
HVSA	High-Voltage Solar Array
H vs A	Home Versus Advice [Medicine] (STED)
HVSCR	High-Voltage Selenium Cartridge Rectifier
HVSD	Hydrogen-Detected Ventricular Septal Defect [Medicine] (MAE)
HVSE	High-Voltage Solar Experiment
HVSF	High Velocity Sheet Forming (PDAA)
HVSF	Honeywell Verification Simulation Facility (NASA)
HVSL	Holidays, Vacation, and Sick Leave (NASA)
hVSMC	Human Vascular Smooth Muscle Cell [Biology]
HVSP	High-Voltage Solar Panel
HVSS	Horizontal Volute Spring Suspension [Projectile]
HVST	High-Voltage Switching Transistor
HVSU	Heating Ventilating Supply Unit (NRCH)
HVT	Half-Value Thickness
HVT	Haverty Furniture [NYSE symbol]
HVT	Herpesvirus of Turkeys (STED)
HVT	Hidden Variable Theory [Physics]
HVT	High-Value Target (NVT)
HVT	High-Voltage Termination
HVT	High-Voltage Tester
HVT	High-Voltage Threshold (IAA)
HVT	High-Voltage Transformer
HVTB	Hydraulic Variable-Valve Train [Automotive engine design]
HVTB	High-Voltage Thermal Battery (DNAB)
HVTEM	High-Voltage Transmission Electron Microscopy (DB)
HVTP	High-Velocity, Target-Practice [Projectile]
HVTP	Hypervelocity, Target-Practice [Projectile]
HVTPDS	High-Velocity, Target-Practice, Discarding Sabot [Projectile]
HVTP-T	Hypervelocity, Target-Practice - Tracer [Projectile] (AABC)
HVTR	Home Videotape Recorder (IAA)
HVTS	High-Volume Time Sharing [Computer science]
HVU	Altus, OK [Location identifier FAA] (FAAL)
HVU	Hansel Valley [Utah] [Seismograph station code, US Geological Survey] (SEIS)
HVU	Heating Ventilation Unit (MCD)
HVU	High-Value Unit [Torpedo defense system] (MCD)
HVUCAP	High-Value Unit Combat Air Patrol [Navy] (DOMA)
HVUS	Hypocomplementemic Vasculitis Urticaria Syndrome [Medicine] (STED)
HVV	Helium Vent Valve (MCD)
HVW	High-Voltage Waveform
HVW	High-Voltage Wire
HVWAC	Hudson Valley Women's Athletic Conference (PSS)
HVWP	Hospitalized Veterans Writing Project (EA)
HVWS	Hebrew Veterans of the War with Spain (EA)
HVY	Happy Valley, AK [Location identifier FAA] (FAAL)
HVY	Harveys Casinos Resorts [NYSE symbol] (SAG)
HVY	Heavy (AFM)
HW	Hairy Woodpecker [Ornithology]
HW	Half Wave
HW	Half Word (CET)
HW	Handset, Wall Model (TEL)
HW	Handwritten (BJA)
HW	Hardware [Computer science] (NASA)
H/w	Hardware (NAKS)
HW	Hard Wired (NITA)
HW	Hardwood
HW	Hardy-Weinberg Equilibrium [of genes] [Also, HWE]
HW	Hauptwachtmeister [First Sergeant] [German military - World War II]
HW	Hauptwerk [Masterpiece] [German]
HW	Havasu Airlines [ICAO designator] (AD)
HW	Hayem-Widal [Syndrome] [Medicine] (DB)
HW	Hayrem-Widal [Syndrome] (STED)
HW	Hazardous Waste (GFGA)
HW	Headwaiter

HW.............. Head Wardmaster [*Navy British*] (ROG)
HW.............. Head Width
HW.............. Head Wind [*Navigation*]
HW.............. Healing Well (DMAA)
HW.............. Heart Weight (STED)
HW.............. Heavy Wall
HW.............. Heavy Water
HW.............. Heavy Weapons [*British military*] (DMA)
HW.............. Hemisphere Width (STED)
HW.............. Heparin Well [*Pharmacology*] (DAVI)
HW.............. Herewith [*Enclosures*] [*Navy*]
HW.............. Hertwig-Weyers [*Syndrome*] [*Medicine*] (DB)
HW.............. Hethitisches Woerterbuch [*Heidelberg*] [*A publication*] (BJA)
HW.............. High Water [*Tides and currents*]
H/W............. Highway
HW.............. High Wing [*Aviation*] (AIA)
HW.............. Hispanic Writers [*A publication*]
HW.............. His-Werner [*Disease*] [*Medicine*] (DB)
HW.............. Hit Wicket
HW.............. Homing Weapons (NVT)
HW.............. Hot Water
HW.............. Hotwell [*Nuclear energy*] (NRCH)
HW.............. Hot Wire (KSC)
HW.............. Housewife
HW.............. How (WGA)
HW.............. Howard Aero Manufacturing [*ICAO aircraft manufacturer identifier*] (ICAO)
HW.............. Howler [*Communications; electronics*]
HW.............. Hunter-Wheel
HW.............. North-Wright Air Ltd. [*ICAO designator*] (AD)
HWA .... Hallman, W. A., St. Paul MN [*STAC*]
HWA .... Handwritten by Amanuensis (BJA)
HWA .... Hawa-Air [*Belgium ICAO designator*] (FAAC)
HWA .... High Wind Watch [*Telecommunications*] (OTD)
HWA .... Holloway White Allom [*Building contractor*] [*British*]
HWA .... Home Workers Association (NTPA)
HWA .... Hops Warehousing Association [*British*] (BI)
HWA .... Horror Writers of America [*An association*]
HWA .... Hot Wire Anemometer
HWA .... Hwalien [*Karenko*] [*Republic of China*] [*Seismograph station code, US Geological Survey*] (SEIS)
HWAA .... Heereswaffenamt [*Army Ordnance Office*] [*German military - World War II*]
HWAAP .... Hawthorne Army Ammunition Plant (AABC)
HWADM ...... Hypersonic Wide-Area Defense Missile (MCD)
HWAI .... Horseback Writers and Artists, International (EA)
HWAIFC ...... Hank Williams Appreciation International Fan Club (EA)
HWAL .... Holland West-Afrika Line [*Steamship*] (MHDB)
HWAY .... Highway [*Commonly used*] (OPSA)
HWB .... Handwoerterbuch [*Pocket Dictionary*] [*German*]
HWB .... Hot Water Boiler [*on a ship*] (DS)
hwb .... Hot Water Bottle
HWB .... Hot Water Bottle (STED)
HWB .... Hot Weather Boot [*Military*] (INF)
HWBC .... Hartford Whalers Booster Club (EA)
HWBDU .... Hot Weather Battle Dress Uniform [*Army*] (INF)
HWBF .... High-Water-Based Fluid [*Hydraulic and cutting fluids*]
HWBI .... Handwoerterbuch des Islam [*Leiden*] [*A publication*] (BJA)
HWBR .... Half-Wave Bridge Rectifier
HWBTA .... Home Wine and Beer Trade Association (EA)
HWC .... Health and Welfare Canada
HWC .... Hein-Werner Corp. (EFIS)
HWC .... Hot Water Circulating [*Technical drawings*]
HWC .... Hurricane Warning Center [*Marine science*] (OSRA)
HWCA .... Housing of Working Classes Act [*British*] (ROG)
HWCC .... Harpoon Weapon Control Console [*Missiles*] (MCD)
HWCC .... Hollywood Casino'A' [*NASDAQ symbol*] (TTSB)
HWCC .... Hollywood Casino Corp. [*NASDAQ symbol*] (SAG)
HWCF .... High-Water-Content Fluid [*Nonpetroleum lubricant*]
HWCF .... High Water Content Fluid [*Hydraulics*]
HWCI .... Hardware Configuration Item
HWCR .... Higher Worth Control Rod [*Nuclear energy*] (NUCP)
HWCS .... Helicopter Wire Cutter System (MCD)
HWCTR .... Heavy-Water Components Test Reactor [*Nuclear energy*]
HWCU .... Heated Window Control Unit
HWD .... Hardwood [*Technical drawings*]
HWD .... Hayward, CA [*Location identifier FAA*] (FAAL)
HWD .... Hazardous Waste Disposal
HWD .... Heartworm Disease (DMAA)
HWD .... Highwood Resources Ltd. [*Toronto Stock Exchange symbol*]
HWD .... Hill/Wendover/Dugway [*Ranges*] [*Military*] (MCD)
HWD .... Horizontal Weather Depiction
HWD .... Hot Wire Detector [*Analytical instrumentation*]
HWDMS ...... Hazardous Waste Data [*or Disposal*] Management System [*Environmental Protection Agency*]
HWDYKY ...... How Well Do You Know Yourself [*Psychological testing*]
HWE .... East West Center, Honolulu, HI [*OCLC symbol*] (OCLC)
HWE .... Hardy-Weinberg Equilibrium [*of genes*] [*Also, HW*]
HWE .... Hardy-Weinberg Expectation [*Genetics*]
HWE .... Healthy Worker Effect (DMAA)
HWE .... Hot Water Extract (DMAA)
HWEC .... Hallwood Energy Corp. [*NASDAQ symbol*] (NQ)
HWED .... Hazardous Waste Enforcement Division [*Environmental Protection Agency*] (EPA)
HWEP .... Hot Wire Emissive Probe

HWERL .... Hazardous Waste Engineering Research Laboratory [*Cincinnati, OH*] [*Environmental Protection Agency*] (GRD)
HWF............ Aberdeen/Amory, MS [*Location identifier FAA*] (FAAL)
HWF............ Hazardous Waste Federation (EA)
HWF & C ..... High-Water Full and Change [*Tides and currents*]
HWFET........ Highway Fuel Economy Test [*Environmental Protection Agency*]
HW-FW .... Half Wave - Full Wave (EPA)
HWG .... Hallwood Group [*NYSE symbol*] (TTSB)
HWG .... Hallwood Group, Inc. [*NYSE symbol*] (SPSG)
HWG .... House Wednesday Group (EA)
HWGCR....... Heavy-Water Moderated Gas-Cooled Reactor [*Nuclear energy*]
HWGTF .... Hazardous Waste Groundwater Task Force [*Environmental Protection Agency*] (GFGA)
HWGW .... Hiram Walker - Gooderham & Worts [*Canada*]
HWH.......... Hot Water Heater (MSA)
HWHH......... Half-Width at Half-Height (PDAA)
HWHM........ Half Width at Half Maximum (AAEL)
HWI .... Hardware Interpreter
HWI .... Hardware Wholesalers, Inc.
HWI .... Hawk Inlet, AK [*Location identifier FAA*] (FAAL)
HWI .... Hawkwatch International (EA)
HWI .... Head Width Index
HWI .... Helical Washer Institute [*Defunct*] (EA)
HWI .... High-Water Interval
HWIL.......... Hardware-in-the-Loop
HWIM .... Hear What I Mean [*Speech recognition system*]
HWIN .... Hot Water-Insoluble Nitrogen [*Analytical chemistry*]
HWIR .... Hazardous Waste Indentification Rule [*Environmental Protection Agency*]
HWJFC........ Hank Williams Jr. Fan Club (EA)
HWK .... Hawker [*Australia Airport symbol*] (OAG)
HWK .... Hawk Resources, Inc. [*Vancouver Stock Exchange symbol*]
HWK .... Kaufman [*H. W.*] Financial Group, Inc. [*AMEX symbol*] (SPSG)
HWK .... Swazi Air Charter (Pty) Ltd. [*Swaziland*] [*ICAO designator*] (FAAC)
HWKB .... Hawkeye Bancorp [*NASDAQ symbol*] (NQ)
HwkEn .... Hawkins Energy Corp. [*Associated Press*] (SAG)
HWKN .... Hawkins Chemical [*NASDAQ symbol*] (TTSB)
HWKN .... Hawkins Chemical, Inc. [*NASDAQ symbol*] (NQ)
HWL .... Harvey Woods Ltd. [*Toronto Stock Exchange symbol*]
HWL .... Hauptwiderstandslinie [*Main line of resistance in a delaying action*] [*German military - World War II*]
HWL .... Henry Wadsworth Longfellow [*Initials used as pseudonym*]
HWL .... High-Water Line [*Technical drawings*]
HWL .... Historic World Leaders [*A publication*]
HWL .... Hot Water Line (AAG)
HWL .... Hotwell
HWL .... Howell Corp. [*NYSE symbol*] (SPSG)
HWLC .... Harold Washington Library Center [*Chicago Public Library*]
HWLC .... Hotwell Level Control [*System*] [*Nuclear energy*] (NRCH)
HWLI .... High-Water Lunitidal Interval
HWLL .... Howell Corp. [*NASDAQ symbol*] (SAG)
HWLLP .... Howell Corp.$3.50 Cv'A'Pfd [*NASDAQ symbol*] (TTSB)
HWLS .... Hostile Weapons Locating System (MCD)
HWLT .... Hazardous Waste Land Treatment (GNE)
HWLWR ...... Heavy-Water-Moderated, Boiling Light-Water-Cooled Reactor [*Nuclear energy*] (NRCH)
HWM .... Hazardous Waste Management
HWM .... Hersham & Walton Motors [*British specialty car maker*]
HWM .... High Molecular Weight
HWM .... High-Water Mark [*Maps and charts*]
HWM .... High Wet Modulus [*Test for rayon*]
HWM .... Hot-Water-Cure Mortar (PDAA)
HWM .... Maui County Free Library, Wailuku, HI [*Library symbol Library of Congress*] (LCLS)
HWMA .... Hazardous Waste Management Association
HWMC .... House Ways and Means Committee
HWMD .... Hazardous Waste Management Division [*Environmental Protection Agency*] (GFGA)
HWMF .... Hazardous Waste Management Facility
HWMP .... Hazardous Waste Management Plan
HWMR .... Heavy Water Moderated Reactor [*Nuclear energy*] (NUCP)
HWN .... Haldwani [*India*] [*Airport symbol*] (AD)
HWN .... Hazard Warning Network
HWN .... High-Water Neaps
HWN .... Honolulu, HI [*Location identifier FAA*] (FAAL)
HWNA .... Hosiery Wholesalers National Association (EA)
HWO .... Hollywood, FL [*Location identifier FAA*] (FAAL)
HWO .... Homosexual World Organization
HWO .... Hot Water Oxidizer (PDAA)
HWO .... Hurricane Warning Office [*National Weather Service*]
HWOCR....... Heavy-Water Moderated Organic-Cooled Reactor [*Nuclear energy*]
HWOK .... Heel Walking Normal (STED)
HWOST....... High-Water Ordinary Spring Tides [*Maps and charts*]
HWP .... Half-Wave Plate
HWP .... Hardware Work Package (MCD)
HWP .... Harmonic Wire Projector (IAA)
HWP .... Heavy-Water Plant [*Nuclear energy*]
HWP .... Hepatic Wedge Pressure (STED)
HWP .... Hewlett-Packard [*NYSE symbol*] (TTSB)
HWP .... Hewlett-Packard Co. [*NYSE symbol*] (SPSG)
HWP .... Hot Wet Pack (MCD)
HWP .... Hours Waiting Parts (MCD)
HWP .... Hungarian Workers' Party [*Political party*] (PPW)
HWP .... Hutchinson-Weber-Pentz [*Syndrome*] (STED)
HWPB .... Heavy Weather Patrol Boats (CINC)

HWPC	Hollywood Women's Political Committee (EA)
HWQ	Hansard Written Questions [Database] [House of Commons] [Canada] [Information service or system] (CRD)
HWQ	Harlowton, MT [Location identifier FAA] (FAAL)
HWQ	High-Water Quadrature
HWR	Half-Wave Rectifier
HWR	Heavy-Water Reactor [Nuclear energy]
HWR	Hot Water Return
HWR	Walker [Hiram] Resources Ltd. [Toronto Stock Exchange symbol Vancouver Stock Exchange symbol] (SPSG)
HWRC	Hazardous Waste Research Center [Louisiana State University] [Research center] (RCD)
HWRC	Hot-Water Recirculation (DAC)
HWRTF	Hazardous Waste Restrictions Task Force (GNE)
HWS	Hanford Works Standard [or Specification] [Later, HPS] [Nuclear energy] (NRCH)
HWS	Harassment Weapon System (MCD)
HWS	Harpoon Weapons System (NVT)
HWS	Helicopter Weapons System
HWS	High Water of Spring Tide
HWS	Hot Water Soluble
HWS	Hurricane Warning System (WDAA)
HWSA	Hazardous Waste Services Association [Defunct] (EA)
HWSFC	Hazardous Waste Superfund Collection [Environmental Protection Agency] (AEPA)
HWSFD	Hazardous Waste Superfund Database [Environmental Protection Agency] (AEPA)
HWSS	Hazardous Waste and Superfund Staff [Environmental Protection Agency] (GFGA)
HWSSG	Heavy Weapons Special Study Group [Military] (MCD)
HWSTD	High Water Speed Technology Demonstrator [Marine Corps] (DOMA)
HW/SW	Hardware/Software (MCD)
HWT	Heavy-Weight Torpedo (DOMA)
hwt	Hot Water Tank (REAL)
HWT	Hot Water Temperature
HWT	Hypersonic Wind Tunnel
HWTC	Hazardous Waste Treatment Council (EA)
HWTC	Highway Traffic Control
HWTH	Herewith (ROG)
HWTR	Heavy Weapons Testing Range [Military] (MCD)
HWTS	Humm-Wadsworth Temperament Scale [Psychology]
HWVE	Hot-Wall Vacuum Evaporation [Photovoltaic energy systems]
HWVP	Hanford Waste Vitrification Plant [Department of Energy] (GAAI)
HWVP	Hanford Waste Vitrification Program (COE)
HWVR	However (FAAC)
HWW	High Wind Warning [Telecommunications] (OTD)
HWW	Horan, Wall & Walker [Publisher] (ADA)
HWW	H. W. Wilson Co. [Publisher]
HWWB	Hardwood Weather Board (ADA)
HWWS	Hyperfiltration Wash Water Recovery System [NASA] (NASA)
HWY	Highway
Hwy	Highway (ASC)
HWY	Hundred Woman Years [of exposure] [Radiation]
HWY	Huntway Partners LP [NYSE symbol]
HWY	Huntway Refining [NYSE symbol] [Formerly, Huntway Partners LP]
HWYM	HighwayMaster Communic [NASDAQ symbol] (TTSB)
HWYM	HighwayMaster Communications, Inc. [NASDAQ symbol] (SAG)
HWZOA	Hadassah, The Women's Zionist Organization of America (EA)
HX	Half Duplex (IAA)
HX	Halifax Corp. [AMEX symbol] (SPSG)
HX	Hamburg Airlines [ICAO designator] (AD)
HX	Heat Exchanger (MCD)
HX	Hereodox [Commercial firm British]
HX	Hexagonal [Technical drawings]
Hx	Hexode (DEN)
Hx	Hexyl [Biochemistry]
HX	High Expansion Foam (WDAA)
HX	Histiocytosis X [or Histocytosis X] [Hematology]
Hx	History [Medicine]
Hx	Hospitalization (DAVI)
HX	Hydrogen Exchange (PDAA)
Hx	Hypophysectomized [Medicine]
Hx	Hypoxanthine [Also, Hyp, HYPX] [Biochemistry]
HX	No Specific Working Hours [ICAO] (FAAC)
HXB	Helix Biotech [Vancouver Stock Exchange symbol]
hXBP	Human X Box Binding Protein [Genetics]
HXBT	Helicopter Expendable Bathythermograph [Naval Oceanographic Office]
HXC	Bear Stearns Companies, Inc. [AMEX symbol] (SAG)
HxCDD	Hexachlorodibenzo-para-dioxin [Organic chemistry]
HXCL	Hexcel
HXF	Hartford, WI [Location identifier FAA] (FAAL)
HXIS	Hard X-Ray Imaging Spectrometer
HXK	Berlin, NH [Location identifier FAA] (FAAL)
HXL	Hexcel Corp. [NYSE symbol] (SPSG)
HXM	Hazleton, PA [Location identifier FAA] (FAAL)
HXM	Helicopter Experimental, Medium (MCD)
HXM	Hexamethylmelamine [Altretamine] [Also, HEX, HMM] [Antineoplastic drug]
HXO	Oxford, NC [Location identifier FAA] (FAAL)
HXP	Bear Stearns Companies, Inc. [AMEX symbol] (SAG)
HXQ	Hard X-Ray Quanta
HXRBS	Hard X-Ray Burst Spectrometer
HXT	Hard X-Ray Telescope
HXV	Herpes Simplex Virus [Infectious disease] (DAVI)
HXW	Hopkinsville, KY [Location identifier FAA] (FAAL)
HXWXL	Height by Width by Length (IEEE)
HXX	Hay [Australia Airport symbol] (OAG)
HX-XO	Hypoxanthine-Xanthine Oxidase (DB)
Hy	All India Reporter, Hyderabad [A publication] (DLA)
H-Y	Harvard-Yale (WDAA)
HY	Heavy [Track condition] [Thoroughbred racing]
HY	Hebrew Year [Freemasonry] (ROG)
hy	Henry [Variation of the preferred H] (IDOE)
HY	Hertfordshire Yeomanry [British military] (DMA)
Hy	Highway
HY	High Yield [Material Strength] (DOMA)
H-Y	Histocompatibility Y [Immunology]
Hy	History [Medicine]
HY	Hundred Yards
HY	Hybrid (AAEL)
HY	Hydrant (ADA)
HY	Hydrocollator [Hot] Pack [Medicine]
HY	Hydrography
Hy	Hypermetropia [Ophthalmology]
Hy	Hyperopia [Ophthalmology] (MAE)
hy	Hypersthene [CIPW classification] [Geology]
HY	Hypobranchial [Gland]
Hy	Hypothenar [Anatomy]
hy	Hysteria [Psychiatry] (DAVI)
HY	Metro Airlines [ICAO designator] (AD)
HYA	Hyack Air Ltd. [Canada ICAO designator] (FAAC)
HYA	Hyannis [Massachusetts] [Airport symbol] (OAG)
Hya	Hydra [Constellation] (WDAA)
Hya	Hydrus [Constellation]
HYACS	Hybrid Analog-Switching Attitude Control System for Space Vehicles
Hyacs	Hydrofoil Air Cushlon Ship
HYAI	Hear You Are, Inc. [An association] (PAZ)
HYAL	Hyal Pharmaceutical Corp. [NASDAQ symbol] (SAG)
HYALF	Hyal Pharmaceutical [NASDAQ symbol] (TTSB)
HyalPhr	Hyal Pharmaceutical Corp. [Associated Press] (SAG)
HY & T	Hooppole, Yorktown & Tampico Railroad (IIA)
HYAPP	Hays Army Ammunition Plant
HYAS	Hydrogasification [Gas from coal fuel]
HYB	Hybrid (MSA)
HYB	Hybrid Systems [Telecommunications] (NITA)
HYB	Hyderabad [India] [Seismograph station code, US Geological Survey] (SEIS)
HYB	New Amer Hi Income Fd [NYSE symbol] (TTSB)
HYB	New American High Income Fund [NYSE symbol] (SPSG)
HYBALL	Hybrid Analog Logic Language (MCD)
HYBD	Hycor Biomedical [NASDAQ symbol] (TTSB)
HYBD	Hycor Biomedical, Inc. [NASDAQ symbol] (NQ)
HYBDW	Hycor Biomedical Wrrt [NASDAQ symbol] (TTSB)
HYBLOC	Hybrid Computer Block Oriented Compiler (IAA)
HYBMED	Hybrid Microelectronic Device (MSA)
HYBN	Hybridon Inc. [NASDAQ symbol] (TTSB)
Hybridon	Hybridon, Inc. [Associated Press] (SAG)
HYC	Hampshire Yeomanry Cavalry [British military] (DMA)
HYC	Haney [British Columbia] [Seismograph station code, US Geological Survey] (SEIS)
HYC	Hertfordshire Yeomanry Cavalry [British military] (DMA)
HYC	Hydraulic Coupling [of a ship] (DS)
HYCATS	Hydrofoil Collision Avoidance and Tracking System [Developed by Sperry]
HYCOL	Hybrid Computer Link
HY-COM	Highway Communications
Hycor	Hycor Biomedical, Inc. [Associated Press] (SAG)
HYCOTRAN	Hybrid Computer Translator
HYCOTRANS	Hybrid Composit Structures for Crashworthy Body Shells and Safe Transportation Structures
HYCPP	High Yield Catalyst Polypropylene (PDAA)
Hyd	All India Reporter, Hyderabad [A publication] (DLA)
HYD	Coeur D'Alene, ID [Location identifier FAA] (FAAL)
HYD	Hyderabad [India] [Airport symbol] (OAG)
HYD	Hydrant (MSA)
HYD	Hydrargyrum [Mercury] [Pharmacy]
HYD	Hydrated
HYD	Hydraulic (AAG)
HYD	Hydraulics (NAKS)
HYD	Hydraulic Subsystem (NAKS)
HYD	Hydroelectric Power [Type of water project]
HYD	Hydrogenation [Chemistry]
HYD	Hydrographic
HYD	Hydrostatics
HYD	Hydrous
HYD	Hydroxyurea [Also, HU, HYDREA] [Antineoplastic drug]
Hyd	Hydrus [Constellation] (WDAA)
HYDAC	Hybrid Digital-Analog Computing [System] [Satellite]
HYDAP	Hybrid Digital-Analog Pulse Time (MCD)
HYDAPT	Hybrid Digital-Analog Pulse Time
HYDAS	Hydrographic Data Acquisition System (PDAA)
HYDAT	Hydrodynamic Analysis Tool (DNAB)
HYDATA	Hydrological Database & Analysis
HYDE	Hyde Athletic Industries, Inc. [NASDAQ symbol] (NQ)
Hyde	Hyde's Bengal Reports [India] [A publication] (DLA)
HYDEA	Hyde Athletic Indus'A' [NASDAQ symbol] (TTSB)
HydeAt	Hyde Athletic Industries, Inc. [Associated Press] (SAG)
HydeAth	Hyde Athletic Industries, Inc. [Associated Press] (SAG)
HYDEB	Hyde Athletic Indus'B' [NASDAQ symbol] (TTSB)

Hyderabad...	Indian Law Reports, Hyderabad Series [*A publication*] (DLA)
Hydi	Hydrus [*Constellation*]
HYDICE	Hyper-spectral Digital Imagery Collection Experiment [*National Oceanic and Atmospheric Administration*]
HYDLAPS	Hydrographic Data Logging and Plotting System (EERA)
HYDM	Hydrometer
HYDO	Hydraulic Oil
HYD'PR	Hydroxyproline [*An amino acid*] (DAVI)
HYD PRO UN...	Hydraulic Propulsion Units [*on a ship*] (DS)
HYDR	Hydragogue [*Cathartic*] [*Pharmacy*] (ROG)
HYDR	Hydraulic (MSA)
Hydr	Hydrographer [*British military*] (DMA)
HYDR	Hydrostatics (ROG)
HYDRA	Hydramatic [*Automotive engineering*]
HYDRA	Hydraulic [*or Hydrologic*] Analysis
HYDRA	Hydrographic Digital Positioning and Depth Recording [*System*] [*NOO*]
HYDRARG	Hydrargyrum [*Mercury*] [*Pharmacy*]
HYDRAT	Chloral Hydrate [*Pharmacology*] (DAVI)
HYDRAUL ...	Hydraulics (ROG)
HYDREA	Hydroxyurea [*Also, HU, HYD*] [*Antineoplastic drug*]
HYDRELC	Hydroelectric (MSA)
HYDRLC	Hydraulic
HYDRO	Hydrographic Office [*Terminated, 1963; later, NOO*] [*Navy*]
HYDRO	Hydrography
HYDRO	Hydropathic (ADA)
HYDRO	Hydrostatic (KSC)
HYDRO	Hydrotherapy [*Medicine*]
HYDRODYN...	Hydrodynamics
HYDROELEC...	Hydroelectric
Hydrog	Hydrogeography
Hydrog	Hydrographer of the Navy [*British*]
HYDROG	Hydrographic
Hydrogen Re...	Hydrogen Relief (NAKS)
HYDROL	Hydrologic
HYDROLANT...	Hydrographic Information for the Atlantic [*Navy*] (DNAB)
HYDROPAC...	Hydrographic Information for the Pacific [*Navy*] (DNAB)
HYDROPNEU...	Hydropneumatic [*Freight*]
hydros	Hydrostatics (BARN)
HYDROX	Hydrogen-Oxygen [*Fuel system*] (DNAB)
HYDRST	Hydrostatic (MSA)
HydrTch	Hydron Technologies, Inc. [*Associated Press*] (SAG)
HYDT	Hydrant (ADA)
HYDTD	Hydrated (MSA)
HYDX	Hydroxide (IAA)
HYE	Healthy Years Equivalent (DMAA)
HYE	Hyeres Aero Service [*France ICAO designator*] (FAAC)
HYF	Hayfields [*Papua New Guinea*] [*Airport symbol*] (OAG)
HYF	Humbligny [*France*] [*Seismograph station code, US Geological Survey*] (SEIS)
HyF	Hytone Film Lab, Inc., Des Moines, IA [*Library symbol Library of Congress*] (LCLS)
HYFAC	Hypersonic Research Facilities [*NASA*]
HYFES	Hypersonic Flight Environmental Simulator
HYFIX	Hyperbolic Fix
HYFT	High-Yield Fallout Trajectory (DNAB)
HYG	Hydaburg [*Alaska*] [*Airport symbol*] (OAG)
HYG	Hygiene
HYG	Hygroscopic
HYGAS	Hydrogen Gasification
HYGL	Hypergolic (KSC)
HYGN	Hygiene
HYGNST	Hygienist
HYGST	Hygienist (AABC)
HY/HS	High Yield/High Stereospecificity Technology [*for polypropylene*] [*Himont Corp.*]
HYI	High Yield Income Fd [*NYSE symbol*] (TTSB)
HYI	High Yield Income Fund [*NYSE symbol*] (SPSG)
HYL	Hollis, AK [*Location identifier FAA*] (FAAL)
HYL	Hoyle Resources Ltd. [*Vancouver Stock Exchange symbol*]
Hyl	Hydroxylysine [*Also, Hylys*] [*An amino acid*]
HYLA	Hybrid Language Assembler
HYLIFE	High-Yield Lithium Injection Fusion Energy (MCD)
HYLO	Hyaline [*Cytology*] (DAVI)
HYLO	Hybrid LORAN
Hylys	Hydroxylysine [*or (OH)Lys*] [*Also, Hyl An amino acid*]
HYM	Hyman, TX [*Location identifier FAA*] (FAAL)
Hym	Hymenoptera [*Entomology*]
HYMA	Hebrew Young Men's Association
HYMATIC	Hydraulic Multiplate Active Traction Intelligent Control [*Automotive engineering*]
Hymn Hom Ap...	Hymnus Homericus ad Apollinem [*Classical studies*] (OCD)
Hymn Hom Bacch...	Hymnus Homericus ad Bacchum [*Classical studies*] (OCD)
Hymn Hom Cer...	Hymnus Homericus ad Cererem [*Classical studies*] (OCD)
Hymn Hom Mart...	Hymnus Homericus ad Martem [*Classical studies*] (OCD)
Hymn Hom Merc...	Hymnus Homericus ad Mercurium [*Classical studies*] (OCD)
Hymn Hom Pan...	Hymnus Homericus ad Panem [*Classical studies*] (OCD)
Hymn Hom Ven...	Hymnus Homericus ad Venerem [*Classical studies*] (OCD)
HYMNS	Hydrogen MASER for Navigation Satellite (MCD)
HYMOSS	Hybrid Mosaic on Stacked Silicon [*Materials science*]
HYMV	Hypochoeris Mosaic Virus [*Plant pathology*]
HYN	Halcyon Resources Ltd. [*Vancouver Stock Exchange symbol*]
HYOSCYAM...	Hyoscyamus [*Henbane*] [*Pharmacology*] (ROG)
HYP	Harvard, Yale, and Princeton Universities
HYP	High Yield Plus Fund [*NYSE symbol*] (SPSG)

HYP	Hydroxybenzylpindolol [*Neuropharmacology*]
Hyp	Hydroxyproline [*Also, Hypro*] [*An amino acid*]
hyp.	Hypalgesia (STED)
HYP	Hypergolic
HYP	Hyperresonance
HYP	Hypertrophy
HYP	Hyphen Character [*Computer science*]
HYP	Hypnosis
HYP	Hypodermic (ROG)
hyp.	Hypophysis (STED)
HYP	Hypotenuse [*Mathematics*]
HYP	Hypothalamus [*Neuroanatomy*]
HYP	Hypothesis
HYP	Hypothetical (WDAA)
Hyp	Hypoxanthine [*Also, Hx, HYPX*] [*Biochemistry*]
Hyp2005	Hyperion 2005 Investment Grade Opportunity Term Trust [*Associated Press*] (SAG)
HYPACE	Hybrid Programmable Attitude Control Electronics [*NASA*]
HYPAR	Hysterectomy Produced and Artificially Reared (PDAA)
HYPARS	Hyperbolic Paraboloid Surface (MCD)
HYPER	Hydrographic Personnel [*Navy*]
HYPER	Hyperhydrated, Hyperventilating with Hyperpyrexia, Hyperexcitability, and Hyperrigidity [*Characteristics of drowning*]
hyper A	Hyperactive (STED)
hyperal	Hyperalimentation [*Intravenous feeding*] [*Medicine*] (DAVI)
HYPERB	Hyperbola [*Mathematics*]
HYPERDOP...	Hyperbolic Doppler
hyper-IgE	Hyperimmunoglobulinemia E [*Medicine*] (STED)
HYPERIGN	Hypergolic Ignition (KSC)
HYPERLIB	Hypertext Interfaces to Library Information Systems (TELE)
hyperpara	Hyperparathyroidism [*Endocrinology*] (DAVI)
hyper T & A...	Hypertrophy of Tonsils and Adenoids [*Medicine*] (MAE)
hyper T & A...	Hypertropy of Tonsils and Adenoids [*Otorhinolaryngology*] (DAVI)
hypes	Hypesthesia (STED)
HYPH	Hydrophone
HypmdCm	Hypermedia Communications, Inc. [*Associated Press*] (SAG)
HYPN	Hypertension
hypn.	Hypertension (DMAA)
hypno	Hypnosis (STED)
HYPNO	Hypnosis
HYPNOT	Hypnotism
HYPNS	Hypnosis
HYPO	High Power [*Water boiler atomic reactor*] [*Dismantled*]
HYPO	Hypochondria (DSUE)
hypo	Hypochromaria (STED)
hypo	Hypochromasia [*Hematology*]
HYPO	Hypodermic
hypo	Hypodermic (STED)
Hypo	Hypodermic (DMAA)
hypo	Hyposulfate [*Solium Thiosulphate*] [*A compound used in photography*] (WDMC)
HYPO	Hyposulfite of Sodium [*Photography*] (ROG)
HYPOC	Hypochromasia [*Hematology*] (DAVI)
HYPOCON	Hypochondria (DSUE)
HYPOT	Hypotenuse [*Mathematics*] (ROG)
HYPOTH	Hypothesis (ADA)
HYPOTH	Hypothetical (MSA)
HYPOX	Hypophysectomy [*Medicine*]
HYPP	Hyperkalemic Periodic Paralysis [*Medicine*]
HYPP	Hypersegmented Neutrophil [*Hematology*] (DAVI)
HYPR	Hypermedia Communications [*NASDAQ symbol*] (SAG)
HYPREM	Hyperresponse Electric Motor
HypRF	Hypothalamic Releasing Factor (DB)
HyprnSft	Hyperion Software, Inc. [*Associated Press*] (SAG)
HyprnTR	Hyperion Total Return & Income Fund [*Associated Press*] (SAG)
Hypro	Hydroxyproline [*or (OH)Pro*] [*Also, Hyp An amino acid*]
HyprSf	Hyperion Software, Inc. [*Associated Press*] (SAG)
Hyps	Hypsipyle [*of Euripides*] [*Classical studies*] (OCD)
HYPSES	Hydrographic Precision Scanning Echo Sounder
hypst	Hypostyle (VRA)
HypT02	Hyperion 2002 Term Trust [*Associated Press*] (SAG)
HypT97	Hyperion 1997 Term Trust [*Associated Press*] (SAG)
HypT99	Hyperion 1999 Term Trust [*Associated Press*] (SAG)
HYPUB	Hypanthium Pubescence [*Botany*]
HYPX	Hypoxanthine [*Also, Hx, Hyp*] [*Biochemistry*]
HYR	Hayward [*Wisconsin*] [*Airport symbol*] (OAG)
HYR	Hycroft Resources & Development Corp. [*Vancouver Stock Exchange symbol*]
HYRROM	Hydrological Rainfall Runoff Model
HYS	Hays [*Kansas*] [*Airport symbol*] (OAG)
HYS	Hysterectomy [*Medicine*] (AAMN)
HYS	Hysteria
HYSAM	Hypersonic Surface-to-Air Missile (MCD)
HYSAS	Hydrofluidic Stability Augmentation System
HYSIM	Highway Driving Simulator [*MM*] (TAG)
HYSL	Hyperion Solutions [*Formerly, Arbor Software*] [*NASDAQ symbol*]
HY-SPLIT	Hybrid Single Particle Lagrangian Integrated Trajectories [*Model*] [*Marine science*] (OSRA)
hyst	Hysterectomy [*Medicine*]
HYSTAD	Hydrofoil Stabilization Device
HYSTCK	Haystack
hyster	Hysterectomy [*Gynecology*] (DAVI)
HYSTERO	Hysterosalpingogram [*Gynecology*] (DHSM)
HYSTRU	Hydraulic System Test and Repair Unit [*Army*] (MCD)
HYSURCH	Hydrographic Surveying and Charting [*System*] [*NOO*]

HYSW .... Hyperion Software [*NASDAQ symbol*] (TTSB)
HYSW .... Hyperion Software, Inc. [*NASDAQ symbol*] (SAG)
Hyswas .... Hydrofoil Small Waterplane Area Ship
HYT .... High Year of Tenure
HYT .... High-Yield Tax-Exempt [*Finance*] (BARN)
HYT .... Humaita [*Brazil*] [*Airport symbol*] (AD)
HYTAC .... Hydraulic Tachometer
HYTAM .... Hypersonic Tactical Missile (MCD)
HYTEC .... Hydrogen Thermal Electrochemical Converter
HYTIWYG..... How You Test is What You Get [*Education*] (AIE)
HYTRAN........ Hybrid Translator (IAA)
HYTREC .... Hydrospace Target Recognition, Evaluation, and Control
HYTRESS ..... High-Test Recorder and Simulator System (IEEE)
HYTROSS .... High-Test Recorder and Simulator System
HYU .... Chesterfield, VA [*Location identifier FAA*] (FAAL)
HYU .... Lilly Contingent Payment Units [*AMEX symbol*] (SPSG)
HYU .... Lilly CtgntPymt Units [*AMEX symbol*] (TTSB)
HYV .... High Yielding Variety [*Agriculture*]
HYVE .... Hydrogen Ventilated Enclosure (PDAA)
HYVIA .... Hypervelocity Interceptor Armament
HYW .... Conway, SC [*Location identifier FAA*] (FAAL)
HYWAYS...... Hybrid with Advanced Yield for Surveillance [*Strategic Defense Initiative*]
HYWN .... Hypersonic Wedge Nozzle (MCD)
HYWV .... High-Yielding Wheat Variety (GNE)
HYX .... Hydra Explorations Ltd. [*Toronto Stock Exchange symbol*]
HYZ .... Thief River Falls, MN [*Location identifier FAA*] (FAAL)
HZ .... Dust Haze [*Aviation*]
HZ .... Habitable Zone [*Beyond the solar system*]
HZ .... Haze (WDAA)
Hz .... Headquarters Zip Code [*Dialog*] [*Searchable field*] [*Information service or system*] (NITA)
HZ .... Henebery Aviation [*ICAO designator*] (AD)
HZ .... Herpes Zoster [*Medicine*]
Hz .... Hertz [*Symbol*] [*SI unit of frequency*] (AABC)

HZ .... Historische Zeitschrift [*A publication*] (ODCC)
HZ .... Hydralazine [*Antihypertensive agent*]
HZ .... Saudi Arabia [*International civil aircraft marking*] (ODBW)
HZA .... Hauptzollamt [*Chief Customs Office*] [*German*] (DLA)
HZA .... Herut Zionists of America (EA)
HZBL .... Holzblaeser [*Woodwind Instrument*] [*Music*]
HZE .... High Z and E [*Particles in outer space*]
Hzea .... Heliothis Zea [*Corn ear worm*]
HZFO .... Hamster Zona-Free Ovum [*Test*] [*Medicine*] (MEDA)
HZFS .... Horizon Financial Services Corp. [*NASDAQ symbol*] (SAG)
HZFS .... Horizon Financial Svcs [*NASDAQ symbol*] (TTSB)
HZG .... Hanzhong [*China*] [*Airport symbol*] (OAG)
HZI .... Hy & Zel's, Inc. [*Toronto Stock Exchange symbol*]
HZK .... Atlanta, GA [*Location identifier FAA*] (FAAL)
HZK .... Husavik [*Iceland*] [*Airport symbol*] (OAG)
HZL .... Hazelton Airlines [*Australia ICAO designator*] (FAAC)
HZL .... Hazleton [*Pennsylvania*] [*Airport symbol Obsolete*] (OAG)
HZMP .... Horizontal Impulse (IEEE)
HZN .... Hazen, NV [*Location identifier FAA*] (FAAL)
HZN .... Horizon Airlines Ltd. [*Nigeria*] [*FAA designator*] (FAAC)
HzNPV .... Heliothis Zea Nuclear Polyhedrosis Virus
HZNT .... Handbuch zum Neuen Testament [*Lietzmann*] [*A publication*] (BJA)
HZO .... Herpes Zoster Ophthalmicus [*Ophthalmology*]
HZP .... Hot Zero Power [*Nuclear energy*] (NRCH)
HZP .... Hyperbolic Zone Plate (PDAA)
HZP .... Zionsville, IN [*Location identifier FAA*] (FAAL)
HZR .... New Roads, LA [*Location identifier FAA*] (FAAL)
HZRN .... Horizontal Reaction
HZV .... Herpes Zoster Virus
HZW .... Wichita, KS [*Location identifier FAA*] (FAAL)
HZWV .... Horizon Bancorp West Virginia [*NASDAQ symbol*] (SAG)
HZWV .... Horizon Bancorp (WV) [*NASDAQ symbol*] (SAG)
HZY .... Hazy (WGA)
HZYC .... Hadassah Zionist Youth Commission (EA)
HZYO .... Hashomer Hatzair Zionist Youth Organization [*Later, HHSZYM*] (EA)

I

By Acronym

I	Air Force Training Category [*No training*]
I	Angle of Incidence
I	Carlo Erba [*Italy*] [*Research code symbol*]
i	Class Interval [*Statistics*]
I	Electric Current [*Symbol*] [*IUPAC*]
I	Fighter [*Russian aircraft symbol*]
I	First Interstate Bancorp. [*NYSE symbol*] (SPSG)
I	I-Beam [*Structural metal shape*]
I	Ibuprofen [*A drug*]
I	Iconoscope (IAA)
I	Id [*That*] [*Latin*] (GPO)
I	Idaho
I	Identification
I	Idus [*The Ides*] [*Latin*]
I	Ihr [*Your*] [*German*]
I	Illinois State Library, Springfield, IL [*Library symbol Library of Congress*] (LCLS)
I	Illite [*A mineral*]
I	Illuminated (WDMC)
I	Illumination (IAA)
I	Image [*File*] [*Computer science*] [*Telecommunications*]
I	Imaginary (IAA)
i	Imaginary Unit (WGA)
I	Immortalis [*Immortal*] [*Latin*] (GPO)
I	Imperator [*or Imperatrix*] [*Emperor or Empress*] [*Latin*]
I	Imperial
I	Imperial Paper (DGA)
I	Implantation (STED)
I	Implicit
I	Impression (DAVI)
i	Improbatur [*Latin*]
I	Inactive [*Chemistry*]
I	Inactive (STED)
I	Inboard (DS)
I	Incendiary [*Bomb*]
I	Incident Ray (IDOE)
I	Incisal [*Dentistry*] (DAVI)
I	Incisor (Deciduous) [*Dentistry*]
I	Incisor (Permanent) [*Dentistry*]
I	Inclination
I	Income
I	Incompatible
I	Incomplete
I	Incontinent [*Medicine*]
I	Increased (STED)
I	Incumbent (ROG)
I	Independent
I	Independent Pump [*Liquid gas carriers*]
I	Independent School [*British*]
I	Index
I	India [*Phonetic alphabet*] [*International*] (DSUE)
I	Indian (WGA)
I-----	Indian Ocean [*MARC geographic area code Library of Congress*] (LCCP)
I	Indicated [*or Indicative*]
I	Indicated Horsepower
I	Indicated Main Engine
I	Indicator
I	Induction
I	Industrial
I	Industrial Premises [*Public-performance tariff*] [*British*]
I	Industrial Training School [*British*] (ROG)
I	Inertia (AAG)
I	Infantry
I	Infield
I	Informal [*FCC special temporary authorization*] (NTCM)
I	Information [*Computer science*]
I	Infra (IAA)
I	Inhalation (DMAA)
I	Inhibition (STED)
I	Inhibitor (DMAA)
I	Inhibitory
I	Initial
I	Ink [*Phonetic alphabet*] [*Royal Navy World War I Pre-World War II*] (DSUE)
i	Ink (VRA)
I	Inlet [*Rotary piston meter*]
I	Inner
I	Inosine [*One-letter symbol; see Ino*]
I	Input
I	Inside
I	Inside Edge [*Skating*]
I	Insoluble
I	Inspector
I	Inspiration (STED)
I	Inspired [*Medicine*] (DAVI)
I	Instantaneous
I	Instantaneous Current (IDOE)
I	Instantaneous Value (IDOE)
I	Institute [*or Institution*]
I	Institutional (WDMC)
I	Instruction
I	Instructional Program (NTCM)
I	Instructor (WDAA)
I	Instrumental [*or Instrumentation*]
I	Instrument Correction
I	Insulated (DS)
I	Insulated Tank [*Liquid gas carriers*]
I	Insulin (STED)
I	Intact (DAVI)
I	Intake (AAMN)
I	Integer (IAA)
I	Integral (IAA)
I	Intelligence
I	Intensity
I	Intensity of Magnetism (STED)
I	Interbank [*Credit cards*]
I	Intercalary (STED)
I	Intercept-Aerial [*Missile mission symbol*]
I	Interceptor
I	Interchangeability (AAG)
I	Intercooled [*Automotive engineering*]
I	Interest [*Economics*]
I	Interference [*Broadcasting*]
I	Interim [*FCC*] (NTCM)
I	Interlocked Metallic Armor [*Technical drawings*]
I	Intermediate [*Vessel load line mark*]
I	Intermediate Slope [*Skiing*]
I	Intermittent (DMAA)
I	Intermittent Operation during the Time Indicated [*Broadcasting*]
I	Intern
I	Internal
I	Internal Medicine (AAMN)
I	International
I	Internist [*Medicine*]
I	Interphone (IAA)
I	Interpole (IAA)
I	Interpreter
I	Interrupt [*Computer science Telecommunications*]
I	Interstate [*Highways*]
I	Intestine
I	Intransitive
I	Intrapictures [*Electronics*] (ACRL)
I	Intrinsic Semiconductor (IDOE)
I	Intrinsic-Type, Semiconductor Material
I	Introduced [*Ecology*]
I	Invasive
I	Inventory
I	Inverted Sentence [*Used in correcting manuscripts, etc.*]
I	Inverter
I	Investment
I	Iodine [*Chemical element*]
I	Ionic Strength
i	I-Orbital (MEC)
I	Iota [*Ninth letter of the Greek alphabet*] (DAVI)
I	Iraqi
I	Ireland
I	Irnerius [*Flourished, 1113-18*] [*Authority cited in pre-1607 legal work*] (DSA)
I	Iron [*Symbol is Fe*] [*Chemical element*] (ROG)
I	Irradiated (NASA)
I	Irregular (ROG)

I	Irrigation [*Medicine*]
I	Island [*Maps and charts*]
I	Isle
i	Isochromosome (MAE)
I	Isoflurane [*An anesthetic*]
I	Isoleucine [*One-letter symbol; see Ile*] [*An amino acid*]
I	Isometric [*Botany*]
i	Isopentenyl [*As substituent on nucleoside*] [*Biochemistry*]
I	Isopin (WDAA)
I	Isoproterenol [*An adrenergic*]
I	Isotope (DMAA)
I	Israeli
I	Issue (ROG)
I	Italy [*YRU nationality code*]
I	Item [*Phonetic alphabet*] [*World War II*] (DSUE)
I	Luminous Intensity [*Symbol*] [*IUPAC*]
I	Minneapolis [*Branch in the Federal Reserve regional banking system*] (BARN)
I	Moment of Inertia [*Symbol*] [*IUPAC*]
I	One [*Roman numeral*]
I	Paid This Year, Dividend Omitted, Deferred, or No Action Taken at Last Dividend Meeting [*Investment term*] (DFIT)
I	Radiant Intensity [*Symbol*] [*IUPAC*]
I	Registro Italiano [*Shipping*] (ROG)
I	Requires a Doctor [*Search and rescue symbol that can be stamped in sand or snow*]
i	Tourist Information [*Traffic sign*] [*British*]
I⁰	Primary (DAVI)
I2	Image Intensification
I2	International Interchangeability
I₂	Iodine [*Chemical element*] (DAVI)
I²C	Inter-Integrated Circuit [*Philips*] (NITA)
I²L	Integrated Injection Logic [*Microprocessing*]
I2L	Integrated Injector Logic (AAEL)
I²L2AS	Infantry Issues and Lessons Learned Analysis System [*Software*] (INF)
I²R	Imaging Infrared [*Pronounced "eye-squared ar"*]
I2S	Integrated Information System [*Marine Corps*]
I2S2	Intelligence Information Subsystem [*Military*]
I2S(FIN)	Integrated Information System (Financial) [*Marine Corps*]
I2S(LOG)	Integrated Information System (Logistics) [*Marine Corps*]
I2S(MPR)	Integrated Information System (Manpower) [*Marine Corps*]
I2S(MPR/MMS)	Integrated Information System (Manpower and Functional Area Manpower Management System) [*Marine Corps*]
I2S(OPS)	Integrated Information System (Operational) [*Marine Corps*]
I2T2	Intelligence Interactive Test Terminal
I³L	Isoplanar Integrated Injection Logic
I5/W	Invert Sugar [*5%*] in Water [*Medicine*]
I-10/S	Invert Sugar [*10%*] in Saline [*Medicine*]
I14Y	Interoperability [*The 14 replaces the fourteen letters between I and Y*] [*Computer hacker terminology*] (NHD)
I18N	Internationalization [*The 18 replaces the eighteen letters between I and N*] [*Computer hacker terminology*] (NHD)
I-129	Iodine-129
I300I	International 300mm Initiative (AAEL)
IA	Comando de Material - Fabrica Militar de Aviones [*Argentina ICAO aircraft manufacturer identifier*] (ICAO)
IA	IATA [*International Air Transport Association*] Containers [*Shipping*] (DCTA)
IA	Ibotenic Acid [*Organic acid*] (DMAA)
IA	Ice Age
IA	Ileostomy Association of Great Britain and Ireland
IA	Image Acquisition [*Computer graphics*]
IA	Image Amplification [*Radiology*] (DAVI)
IA	Imagery Analyst (MCD)
IA	Im Auftrage [*By Order Of*] [*German*]
IA	Imitation Art Paper (DGA)
IA	Immediate Access (IAA)
IA	Immediate Action [*Military*]
IA	Immediate Annuity
IA	Immediately Available
IA	Immune Adherence [*Immunology*]
Ia	Immune Region Associated Antigen [*Immunology*]
Ia	Immune Response Gene-Associated Antigen [*Immunology*] (DAVI)
IA	Immunobiologic Activity [*Immunology*] (AAMN)
IA	Impedance Angle
IA	Imperial Airways Ltd. [*British*] (ADA)
IA	Implementing Agency (KSC)
IA	Import Annual Data [*Department of Commerce*] (GFGA)
IA	Impotents Anonymous (EA)
IA	In Absentia [*In Absence*] [*Latin*]
IA	Inactive Account [*Banking*]
IA	Inactive Aerospace Vehicle [*or Aircraft*]
IA	Incentive Award [*Military*]
IA	Incident Actions [*Environmental science*] (COE)
IA	Incidental Appendectomy [*Medicine*]
IA	Income Averaging (MHDB)
IA	Incorporated Accountant
IA	Incremental Analysis [*Statistics*]
IA	Incurred Accidentally [*Medicine*] (MEDA)
IA	Independent Action (EA)
IA	Independent Americans (EA)
IA	Index Array (IAA)
IA	India Alert [*An association*] (EA)
IA	Indiana [*Obsolete*] (ROG)
IA	Indian Affairs (DLA)
IA	Indian Airlines (PDAA)
IA	Indian Army
IA	Indian Artillery [*British military*] (DMA)
IA	Indicated Altitude [*Navigation*]
IA	Indicator of Authoritativeness [*Library symbol*]
IA	Indirect Address (NITA)
IA	Indirect Addressing
IA	Indo-Aryan [*Linguistics*]
IA	Indolaminergic-Accumulating [*Cytology*] (DAVI)
IA	Indulin Agar [*Microbiology*]
IA	Industrial Arts (OICC)
IA	Industry Application (IAA)
IA	Infected Area
IA	Inferior Angle [*Anatomy*]
IA	Information Agency
IA	Information America [*Information service or system*] (IID)
IA	Information Association (COE)
IA	Infra-Audible [*Sound*]
IA	Initial Appearance [*RADAR*]
IA	Initial Assessment [*Environmental science*] (COE)
IA	Initial Authorization
IA	Initiative America (EA)
I/A	Innovative/Alternative [*Recycling technologies*]
IA	Input Acknowledge (MCD)
IA	Input Axis (KSC)
IA	Insertion Approval (NRCH)
IA	Inspection Administration [*Navy*]
IA	Inspection Authorization (GAVI)
I/A	Installment Agreement
IA	Institut de l'Amiante [*Asbestos Institute - AI*] (EA)
IA	Institute of Actuaries [*British*]
IA	Institute of Architects [*Australia*]
IA	Instruction Address [*Computer science*]
IA	Instructional Allowance [*British military*] (DMA)
IA	Instrument Abstracts
IA	Instrument Air [*System*] [*Nuclear energy*] (NRCH)
IA	Instrumentation Amplifier (IEEE)
IA	Insulin Antibody [*Immunology*]
IA	Insurance Adjustment
I/A	Insurance Auditor
IA	Intangible Asset [*i.e., Patented rights*]
IA	Integrated Adapter
IA	Intelligence Analysis
IA	Intelligence Assessment (DOMA)
IA	Intelligent Actuatot (ACII)
IA	Intelligent Agent
IA	Intelligent Assistant [*Computer science*]
IA	Intelligenzalter [*Mental Age*] [*Psychology*]
IA	Intemperate to Alcohol [*An alcoholic*] [*Slang*]
IA	Inter-Action (MCD)
IA	Interagency Agreement (GNE)
IA	Inter Aide [*France*] (BUAC)
IA	Inter Alia [*Among Other Things*] [*Latin*]
IA	Intercept Arm (MUGU)
IA	Intercessors for America (EA)
IA	Interchangeable Alternate
IA	Interchange Address (NITA)
IA	Interciencia Association [*Caracas, Venezuela*] (EAIO)
IA	Intercity Airways [*Australia*]
IA	Intercoiffure America (EA)
IA	Intercultural Awareness
I/A	Interface Adapter (NASA)
IA	Interface Amplifier
IA	Interflora Australia
IA	Intermediate Air [*Combustion*]
IA	Intermediate Amplifier
IA	Internal Audit
IA	Internal Auditory (Ear)
IA	International Affiliation of Independent Accounting Firms [*Later, Independent Accountants International*] (EA)
IA	International Alert (EA)
IA	International Alliance of Theatrical Stage Employees (NTCM)
IA	International Alliance of Theatrical Stage Employees and Moving Picture Machine Operators of the United States and Canada
IA	International Alphabet
IA	International Angstrom
IA	Interval Availability
IA	Intra-Amniotic [*Medicine*] (AAMN)
IA	Intra Aortic [*Cardiology*] (MAE)
IA	Intra-Arterial [*Cardiology*]
ia	Intraarterial [*Medicine*] (DB)
IA	Intra-Articular [*Medicine*]
IA	Intra-Atrial [*Cardiology*]
IA	Intra-Auricular [*Cardiology*] (DAVI)
IA	Inverter Assembly
IA	Iowa [*Postal code*]
IA	Iowa Reports [*A publication*] (DLA)
Ia	Iowa State Library Commission, Des Moines, IA [*Library symbol Library of Congress*] (LCLS)
IA	Iphigenia Aulidensis [*of Euripides*] [*Classical studies*] (OCD)
IA	Iraqi Airways [*ICAO designator*]
IA	Iron Age
IA	Irrigation Area (ADA)
IA	Irrigation Association (EA)

I/A .... Isle Of Angelsey [*Wales*] (ROG)
IA .... Isle Of Aran
IA .... Isolation Amplifier
IA .... Isophthalic Acid [*Organic chemistry*]
IA .... Issuing Agency (AFM)
IA .... Italian Army (NATG)
I/A .... Item Accounting (MCD)
IA .... Law Reports, Privy Council, Indian Appeals [*India*] [*A publication*] (DLA)
IA .... Millenia, Inc. [*AMEX symbol*] (SAG)
IA .... Telegraph and Public Address [*JETDS nomenclature*]
IA-1 .... Image Array Processor (NITA)
IA-2 .... International Alphabet-2 [*Standard telegraphy code*] (NITA)
IA-5 .... International Alphabet 5 (NITA)
IaA .... Ames, Public Library, Ames IA [*Library symbol Library of Congress*] (LCLS)
IAA .... Chicago State University, Chicago, IL [*OCLC symbol*] (OCLC)
IAA .... Ibero-Armorican Arc [*A geological area of western Europe*]
IAA .... Illinois Agricultural Association (SRA)
IAA .... Imidazoleacetic Acid [*Also, I-AC, IMAA*] [*Biochemistry*]
IAA .... Immediate Action Authority (AAG)
IAA .... Inactive Aerospace Vehicle [*or Aircraft*] Authorization
IAA .... In Amguel [*Issek Toufreg*] [*Algeria*] [*Seismograph station code, US Geological Survey*] [*Closed*] (SEIS)
IAA .... Incorporated Accountants and Auditors [*British*] (DAS)
IAA .... Independent Administrators Association of California (SRA)
IAA .... Independent Airlines Association (EA)
IAA .... Indian Army Act [*British military*] (DMA)
IAA .... Indian Association of America (EA)
IAA .... Indoleacetic Acid [*Plant growth promoter*]
IAA .... Inex Adria Aviopromet [*Yugoslavia*] [*ICAO designator*] (FAAC)
IAA .... Infectious Agent Arthritis [*Medicine*] (DB)
IAA .... Inpatient Ambulatory Activity Questionnaire [*Medicine*]
IAA .... Institute for Alternative Agriculture (EA)
IAA .... Institute for Arthritis and Autoimmunity [*Nile Research Center*] [*West Haven, CT*]
IAA .... Institute of Administrative Accountants [*Sevenoaks, Kent, England*] (EAIO)
IAA .... Institute of Administrative Accounting and Data Processing Limited [*British*] (NITA)
IAA .... Institute of African Alternatives (BUAC)
IAA .... Institute of Arbitrators Australia
IAA .... Institute of Archeology and Anthropology [*University of South Carolina at Columbia*] [*Research center*] (RCD)
IAA .... Institute of Automobile Assessors [*British*] (BI)
IAA .... Instrumental Activation Analysis
IAA .... Insulin Autoantibody [*Immunology*]
IAA .... Insurance Accountants Association [*Later, SIA*]
IAA .... Intelligence Analysts Associates [*Air Force*]
IAA .... Interamerican Accounting Association [*Mexico City, Mexico*] (EA)
IAA .... Interim Access Authorization
IAA .... Interment Association of America [*Later, PIAA*] (EA)
IAA .... International Academy of Architecture (BUAC)
IAA .... International Academy of Astronautics [*Paris, France*] (EA)
IAA .... International Acetylene Association [*Later, CGA*]
IAA .... International Actuarial Association (BUAC)
IAA .... International Advertising Association [*Later, AAF*] (EA)
IAA .... International Aerosol Association [*Zurich, Switzerland*] (EAIO)
IAA .... International Aerospace Abstracts [*American Institute of Aeronautics and Astronautics*] [*A publication*] (AEBS)
IAA .... International Antituberculosis Association (DAVI)
IAA .... International Apple Association [*Later, IAI*] (EA)
IAA .... International Arthroscopy Association (EA)
IAA .... International Association for Aerobiology (BUAC)
IAA .... International Association of Agriculturists (BUAC)
IAA .... International Association of Allergology [*Later, IAACI*]
IAA .... International Association of Art [*See also IAIAP*] (EA)
IAA .... International Association of Astacology (EA)
IAA .... International Astrological Association
IAA .... International Astronautical Academy (BUAC)
IAA .... International Aviation Affairs [*FAA*] (MCD)
IAA .... Interruption of the Aortic Arch [*Medicine*] (DMAA)
IAA .... Intimate Apparel Associates [*Defunct*] (EA)
IAA .... Inventors Association of America (EA)
IAA .... Investment Advisers Act [*1940*]
IAA .... Iodoacetamide [*Organic chemistry*]
IAA .... Iododacetic Acid [*Organic chemistry*]
IAA .... Iowa Auctioneers Association (SRA)
IAA .... Ireland-Australia Association (BUAC)
IAA .... Irish Aquaculture Association (BUAC)
IAA .... Irish Architectural Archive (BUAC)
IAA .... Irish Astronomical Association (EAIO)
IAA .... Israel Antiquities Authority
IAA .... Israel Archives Association (BUAC)
IAAA .... Illinois Agricultural Aviation Association (SRA)
IAAA .... Inflammatory Abdominal Aortic Aneurysm [*Medicine*] (DMAA)
IAAA .... Institute of Afro-American Affairs [*New York University*] [*Research center*] (RCD)
IAAA .... Integrated Advance Avionics for Aircraft
IAAA .... Inter-American Accounting Association
IAAA .... Intermarket Association of Advertising Agencies [*Dayton, OH*] (EA)
IAAA .... International Academy of Aquatic Art (EA)
IAAA .... International Airforwarders and Agents Association (EA)
IAAA .... International American Albino Association (NTPA)
IAAA .... Irish Amateur Athletic Association (BUAC)

IAAA .... Irish Association of Advertising Agencies (BUAC)
IAAAA .... Intercollegiate Association of Amateur Athletes of America (EA)
IAAABBP ..... International Association of African and American Black Business People [*Detroit, MI*] (EA)
IAAALD .... Inter-American Association of Agricultural Librarians and Documentalists [*Cost Rica*] (BUAC)
IAAAM .... International Association for Aquatic Animal Medicine (EA)
IaAAR .... United States Department of Agriculture, Agricultural Research Service, National Animal Disease Laboratory, Ames, IA [*Library symbol Library of Congress*] (LCLS)
IAAATDC ..... International Association for Advancement of Appropriate Technology for Developing Countries (EA)
IAAB .... Inter-American Association of Broadcasters [*Later, IAB-AIR*]
IAAB .... Interim Aviation Airframe Bulletin (DNAB)
IAABB .... International Association of Amateur Boat Builders (EA)
IAABO .... International Association of Approved Basketball Officials (EA)
IaAc .... Ackley Public Library, Ackley, IA [*Library symbol Library of Congress*] (LCLS)
IAAC .... Interagency Assessment Advisory Committee (GNE)
IAAC .... International Agricultural Aviation Centre [*Defunct*] (EA)
IAAC .... International Antarctic Analysis Centre (BUAC)
IAAC .... International Assets Holding Corp. [*NASDAQ symbol*] (SAG)
IAAC .... International Association of Art Critics [*Australia*]
IAAC .... Intl Asset Holding [*NASDAQ symbol*] (TTSB)
IAACC .... Ibero-American Association of Chambers of Commerce [*See also AICO*] [*Bogota, Colombia*] (EAIO)
IAACC .... Inter-Allied Aeronautical Commission of Control
IAACI .... International Association of Allergology and Clinical Immunology (EA)
IAACN .... International and American Associations of Clinical Nutritionists (NTPA)
IAACW .... International Assets Hldg Wrrt [*NASDAQ symbol*] (TTSB)
IaAcW .... World Journal, Ackley, IA [*Library symbol Library of Congress*] (LCLS)
IaAdeCoC .... Dallas County Courthouse, Adel, IA [*Library symbol Library of Congress*] (LCLS)
IaAdeN .... Dallas County News, Adel, IA [*Library symbol Library of Congress*] (LCLS)
IAADFS .... International Association of Airport Duty Free Stores (EA)
IaAdN .... Adair News, Adair, IA [*Library symbol Library of Congress*] (LCLS)
IAADS .... Integrated Antiairborne Defense System
IAAE .... Institute for Application of Atomic Energy [*China*] (BUAC)
IAAE .... Institute of Automotive and Aeronautical Engineers (WDAA)
IAAE .... International Association Autism-Europe (BUAC)
IAAE .... International Association of Agricultural Economists (EA)
IAAE .... Israel Association of Agricultural Engineering (BUAC)
IAAEE .... International Association for the Advancement of Ethnology and Eugenics (BUAC)
IAAEES .... International Association for the Advancement of Earth and Environmental Sciences (EA)
IAAEM .... International Association of Aquaculture Economics and Management
IAAER .... International Association for the Advancement of Educational Research
IAAF .... International Agricultural Aviation Foundation (EA)
IAAF .... International Amateur Athletic Federation [*See also FIAA*] [*British*] (EAIO)
IAAF .... International Association of Art for the Future [*Indonesia*] (EAIO)
IAAFA .... Inter-American Air Force Academy [*Operated by US Air Force to provide training for Latin American countries*]
IAAFF .... Iona Appliances, Inc. [*NASDAQ symbol*] (SAG)
IaAfSE .... Afton Star-Enterprise, Afton, IA [*Library symbol Library of Congress*] (LCLS)
IAAG .... Inter-American Association of Gastroenterology (EA)
IAAH .... International Action Against Hunger (EAIO)
IAAH .... International Association for Adolescent Health (BUAC)
IAAHU .... International Association of Accident and Health Underwriters [*Later, NAHU*]
IAAI .... Insurance Auto Auctions [*NASDAQ symbol*] (SPSG)
IAAI .... International Airports Authority of India (BUAC)
IAAI .... International Association of Arson Investigators (EA)
IAAI .... Italian Association for Artificial Intelligence (BUAC)
IaAIBI .... IBIA News, Ames, IA [*Library symbol Library of Congress*] (LCLS)
IAAIP .... Inter-American Association of Industrial Property [*See also ASIPA*] [*Buenos Aires, Argentina*] (EAIO)
IaAIS .... Iowa Starter, Iowa State University, Ames, IA [*Library symbol Library of Congress*] (LCLS)
IAAJ .... International Association of Agricultural Journalists (BUAC)
IaAkRT .... Akron Register-Tribune, Akron, IA [*Library symbol Library of Congress*] (LCLS)
IAAL .... International Association of Applied Linguistics (EA)
IaAlb .... Albia Public Library, Albia, IA [*Library symbol Library of Congress*] (LCLS)
IaAlbMHi ..... Monroe County Historical Society, Albia, IA [*Library symbol Library of Congress*] (LCLS)
IaAlbN .... Monroe County News, Albia, IA [*Library symbol Library of Congress*] (LCLS)
IaAlbUR .... Albia Union-Republican, Albia, IA [*Library symbol Library of Congress*] (LCLS)
IaAlcAM .... Appeal and Marathon Republic, Albert City, IA [*Library symbol Library of Congress*] (LCLS)
IaAld .... Alden Public Library, Alden, IA [*Library symbol Library of Congress*] (LCLS)
IAALD .... International Association of Agricultural Librarians and Documentalists (EA)
IaAlg .... Algona Public Library, Algona, IA [*Library symbol Library of Congress*] (LCLS)

IaAlgKA...... Kossuth County Advance, Algona, IA [*Library symbol Library of Congress*] (LCLS)
IaAlgUD....... Upper Des Moines, Algona, IA [*Library symbol Library of Congress*] (LCLS)
IaAll............. Allerton Public Library, Allerton, IA [*Library symbol Library of Congress*] (LCLS)
IaAlnBCo...... Butler County Courthouse, Allison, IA [*Library symbol Library of Congress*] (LCLS)
IaAlnTJ........ Butler County Tribune-Journal, Allison, IA [*Library symbol Library of Congress*] (LCLS)
IaAlta........... Alta Public Library, Alta, IA [*Library symbol Library of Congress*] (LCLS)
IaAltaA........ Alta Advertiser, Alta, IA [*Library symbol Library of Congress*] (LCLS)
IaAltn........... Alton Public Library, Alton, IA [*Library symbol Library of Congress*] (LCLS)
IaAlto........... Altoona Public Library, Altoona, IA [*Library symbol Library of Congress*] (LCLS)
IaAltoH........ Herald-Mitchellville Index, Altoona, IA [*Library symbol Library of Congress*] (LCLS)
IAAM............. Incorporated Association of Assistant Masters [*British*]
IAAM............. Independent Accountants Association of Michigan (SRA)
IAAM............. International Association of Assembly Managers (NTPA)
IAAM............. International Association of Auditorium Managers (EA)
IAAM............. International Association of Automotive Modelers [*Defunct*] (EA)
IAAM............. Irish Anti-Apartheid Movement (EAIO)
IAAMC......... International Association of Association Management Companies (NTPA)
IAAMRH....... International Association of Agricultural Medicine and Rural Health (EA)
IaAna........... Anamosa Public Library, Anamosa, IA [*Library symbol Library of Congress*] (LCLS)
IaAnaE........ Anamosa Eureka, Anamosa, IA [*Library symbol Library of Congress*] (LCLS)
IaAnaJ........ Anamosa Journal, Anamosa, IA [*Library symbol Library of Congress*] (LCLS)
IA & T.......... Integration, Assembly, and Test
IAANG.......... Iowa Air National Guard (MUSM)
IaAniF.......... Fontanelle Observer, Anita, IA [*Library symbol Library of Congress*] (LCLS)
IaAniT.......... Anita Tribune, Anita, IA [*Library symbol Library of Congress*] (LCLS)
IaAnk........... Kirkendall Public Library, Ankeny, IA [*Library symbol Library of Congress*] (LCLS)
IaAnkD......... Des Moines Area Community College, Ankeny, IA [*Library symbol Library of Congress*] (LCLS)
IaAnkFB....... Faith Baptist Bible College, Ankeny, IA [*Library symbol Library of Congress*] (LCLS)
IaAnkP......... Ankeny Press-Citizen, Ankeny, IA [*Library symbol Library of Congress*] (LCLS)
IaAnt........... Anthon Public Library, Anthon, IA [*Library symbol Library of Congress*] (LCLS)
IaAntH......... Anthon Herald, Anthon, IA [*Library symbol Library of Congress*] (LCLS)
IAAO............ International Association of Assessing Officers (EA)
IAAOC......... International Association of Addictions and Offender Counseling (EA)
IAAOPA........ International Association of Aircraft Owners and Pilots Association (BARN)
IaAp............. Aplington Legion Memorial Library, Aplington, IA [*Library symbol Library of Congress*] (LCLS)
IAAP............ International Association for Analytical Psychology (EA)
IAAP............ International Association of Amusement Parks [*Later, IAAPA*]
IAAP............ International Association of Applied Psychology [*Nijmegen, Netherlands*] (EA)
IAAP............ Iowa Army Ammunition Plant (AABC)
IAAPA......... International Association of Amusement Parks and Attractions (EA)
IAAPEA........ International Association Against Painful Experiments on Animals (EA)
IAAPF.......... Iona Appliances [*NASDAQ symbol*] (TTSB)
IAAPO......... International Association of Amusement and Park Owners
IAAR............ Imidazoleacetic Acid Ribonucleotide (DMAA)
IAAR............ Independent Associaton of Accredited Registrars [*For quality control*]
IAAR............ United States Information Agency Acquisition Regulation [*A publication*] (AAGC)
IAARC......... International Administrative Aeronautical Radio Conference [*Also known as WARC*]
IaArl............ Arlington Public Library, Arlington, IA [*Library symbol Library of Congress*] (LCLS)
IaArmJ........ Armstrong Journal, Armstrong, IA [*Library symbol Library of Congress*] (LCLS)
IAAS............ Immigrants Appeals Advisory Service (BUAC)
IAAS............ Incorporated Association of Architects and Surveyors [*British*] (DBA)
IAAS............ Institute of Acoustics, Academia Sinica (BUAC)
IAAS............ Institute of African Asian Studies (BUAC)
IAAS............ Institute of Auctioneers and Appraisers in Scotland (EAIO)
IAAS............ Institute of Auctioneers and Apprentices in Scotland (BUAC)
IAAS............ International Association for Atmospheric Science (BUAC)
IAAS............ International Association of Agricultural Students [*See also AIEA*] [*Uppsala, Sweden*] (EAIO)
IaAS............ Iowa State University of Science and Technology, Ames, IA [*Library symbol Library of Congress*] (LCLS)
IAASA......... Indian Australian Association of South Australia
IAASE.......... Independent Appeals Authority for School Examinations (AIE)
IAASE.......... Inter-American Association of Sanitary Engineering [*Later, Inter-American Association of Sanitary and Environmental Engineering*] (EA)

IAASEES...... Inter-American Association of Sanitary Engineering and Environmental Sciences (EAIO)
IAASM......... International Academy of Aviation and Space Medicine (EAIO)
IAASP.......... International Association of Airport and Seaport Police [*Canada*] (EAIO)
IAASS......... International Association of Applied Social Scientists [*Later, CCI*]
IaAS-V......... Iowa State University of Science and Technology, School of Veterinary Medicine, Ames, IA [*Library symbol Library of Congress*] (LCLS)
IaAT............ Ames Daily Tribune, Ames, IA [*Library symbol Library of Congress*] (LCLS)
IaAt............. Atlantic Public Library, Atlantic, IA [*Library symbol Library of Congress*] (LCLS)
IAAT............ International Association Against Torture (EAIO)
IAATI........... International Association Auto Theft Investigators (EA)
IaAtL........... Atlantic Public Library, Atlantic, IA [*Library symbol*] [*Library of Congress*] (LCLS)
IAATM......... International Association for Accident and Traffic Medicine (EA)
IaAtNT........ Atlantic News-Telegraph, Atlantic, IA [*Library symbol Library of Congress*] (LCLS)
IaAu............ Audubon Public Library, Audubon, IA [*Library symbol Library of Congress*] (LCLS)
IaAub.......... Auburn Public Library, Auburn, IA [*Library symbol Library of Congress*] (LCLS)
IaAubE........ Auburn Enterprise, Auburn, IA [*Library symbol Library of Congress*] (LCLS)
IaAuCoC...... Audubon County Courthouse, Audubon, IA [*Library symbol Library of Congress*] (LCLS)
IaAuNA........ Audubon News-Advocate, Audubon, IA [*Library symbol Library of Congress*] (LCLS)
IaAur........... Aurelia Public Library, Aurelia, IA [*Library symbol Library of Congress*] (LCLS)
IaAurS........ Aurelia Sentinel, Aurelia, IA [*Library symbol Library of Congress*] (LCLS)
IAAV............ Alliance of Atomic Veterans [*International Alliance of Atomic Vetrans*] [*Acronym is based on former name,*] (EA)
IaAv............ Avoca Public Library, Avoca, IA [*Library symbol Library of Congress*] (LCLS)
IAAV............ International Association of Airborne Veterans (EA)
IaAvJH......... Avoca Journal-Herald, Avoca, IA [*Library symbol Library of Congress*] (LCLS)
IAAW.......... Internatinal Association of African Writers (BUAC)
IaAWD......... Wildlife Disease Association, Ames, IA [*Library symbol Library of Congress*] (LCLS)
IAAWS......... Infantry Antiarmor Weapon Systems [*Military*] (INF)
IaB.............. Burlington Free Public Library, Burlington, IA [*Library symbol Library of Congress*] (LCLS)
IAB.............. Identa-Band (DAVI)
IAB.............. Idle Air Bleed [*Fuel system*] [*Automotive engineering*]
IAB.............. Immigration Appeal Board [*Canada*]
IAB.............. Indirect Address Buffer
IAB.............. Industrial Accident Board
IAB.............. Industrial Advisers to the Blind Ltd. [*British*] (BI)
IAB.............. Industrial Advisory Board [*World War II*]
IAB.............. Industrial Arbitration Board [*British*]
IAB.............. Institute of Animal Behavior [*Rutgers University*] [*Research center*] (RCD)
IAB.............. Institute of Arctic Biology [*Research center*] (RCD)
IAB.............. Institut fuer Arbeitsmarkt- und Berufsforschung [*Institute for Employment Research*] [*Federal Employment Institute*] [*Germany*] (IID)
IAB.............. Instrumentation Analysis Branch (SAA)
IAB.............. Interagency Board of Examiners [*Civil Service Commission*]
IAB.............. Inter-America Bank (WDAA)
IAB.............. Interim Airframe Bulletin (MCD)
IAB.............. Interim Armament Bulletin (MCD)
IAB.............. International Abstracting Board [*Also, ICSU AB*] [*International Council of Scientific Unions*]
IAB.............. International Aquatic Board (BUAC)
IAB.............. International Association of Bibliophiles [*See also AIB*] [*Paris, France*] (EAIO)
IAB.............. International Association of Boards of Examiners in Optometry (EA)
IAB.............. International Association of Bookkeepers [*British*] (EAIO)
IAB.............. International Association of Broadcasting (NTCM)
IAB.............. International Association of Business (EA)
IAB.............. Internationale Akademie fuer Bader-, Sport-, und Freizeitheitbau [*International Board for Aquatic, Sports, and Recreation Facilities*] [*Bad Neustadt/Saale, Federal Republic of Germany*] (EAIO)
IAB.............. Internet Architecture Board
IAB.............. Interrupt Address to Bus [*Computer science*]
IAB.............. Intra-Abdominal [*Artery*]
IAB.............. Intra-Aortic Balloon [*Cardiology*]
IAB.............. Iowa Administrative Bulletin [*A publication*] (AAGC)
IAB.............. Irish Association for the Blind (BI)
IAB.............. Island Arc Basalt [*Geology*]
IAB.............. Italian American Business [*American Chamber of Commerce in Italy*] [*A publication*]
IAB.............. IUS [*Interior Upper Stage*] Assembly Building [*NASA*] (MCD)
IAB.............. John Crerar Library, Chicago, IL [*OCLC symbol*] (OCLC)
IAB.............. Wichita, KS [*Location identifier FAA*] (FAAL)
IABA............ Inter-American Bar Association (EA)
IABA............ International Amateur Boxing Association
IABA............ International Association of Aircraft Brokers and Agents [*Norway*] (EAIO)
IABA............ Intra-Aortic Balloon Assist [*Cardiology*]

IABA............ Irish Amateur Boxing Association (BI)

IaBag........... Bagley Public Library, Bagley, IA [*Library symbol Library of Congress*] (LCLS)

IaBagG......... Bagley Gazette, Bagley, IA [*Library symbol Library of Congress*] (LCLS)

IAB-AIR........ International Association of Broadcasting - Asociacion Internacional de Radiodifusion [*Formerly, Inter-American Association of Broadcasters*] (EA)

IaBanR......... Bancroft Register, Bancroft, IA [*Library symbol Library of Congress*] (LCLS)

IA Bar Rev... Iowa Bar Review [*A publication*] (DLA)

IaBatB.......... Batavia Beacon, Batavia, IA [*Library symbol Library of Congress*] (LCLS)

IaBaxNE...... Baxter New Era, Baxter, IA [*Library symbol Library of Congress*] (LCLS)

IaBaxWC...... Baxter Women's Club, Baxter, IA [*Library symbol Library of Congress*] (LCLS)

IaBay........... Bayard Public Library, Bayard, IA [*Library symbol Library of Congress*] (LCLS)

IaBayN......... Bayard News, Bayard, IA [*Library symbol Library of Congress*] (LCLS)

IABB............ Inter-American Bank Bond (MHDW)

IABBE.......... International Association for Better Basic Education (EA)

IABBE.......... International Association of Black Business Educators [*Defunct*] (EA)

IABBS.......... International Amateur Boat Building Society [*Defunct*]

IABC............ Idle Air Bypass Control [*Fuel system*] [*Automotive engineering*]

IABC............ International Association of Building Companions [*See also IBO*] [*Marche-En-Famenne, Belgium*] (EAIO)

IABC............ International Association of Business Communicators (EA)

IABC............ Intra-Aortic Balloon Catheter [*Cardiology*] (DAVI)

IABC............ Intra-Aortic Balloon Counterpulsation [*Cardiology*]

IaBclHi......... Ida County Historical Society, Battle Creek, IA [*Library symbol Library of Congress*] (LCLS)

IaBcT .... Battle Creek Times, Battle Creek, IA [*Library symbol Library of Congress*] (LCLS)

IaBDHi......... Des Moines County Historical Society, Burlington, IA [*Library symbol Library of Congress*] (LCLS)

IABE............ Ibero-American Bureau of Education [*See also OEI*] [*Madrid, Spain*] (EAIO)

IaBedTP....... Bedford Times-Press, Bedford, IA [*Library symbol Library of Congress*] (LCLS)

IaBelm......... Belmond Public Library, Belmond, IA [*Library symbol Library of Congress*] (LCLS)

IaBelmI........ Belmond Independent, Belmond, IA [*Library symbol Library of Congress*] (LCLS)

IABEM.......... International Association for Boundary Element Methods (BUAC)

IaBepU......... Belle Plaine Union, Belle Plaine, IA [*Library symbol Library of Congress*] (LCLS)

IaBetN .... Bettendorf News, Bettendorf, IA [*Library symbol Library of Congress*] (LCLS)

IaBev .... Bellevue Public Library, Bellevue, IA [*Library symbol Library of Congress*] (LCLS)

IaBevHL....... Bellevue Herald-Leader, Bellevue, IA [*Library symbol Library of Congress*] (LCLS)

IABF............ Inter-American Bar Foundation (EA)

IABF............ International Association of Business Forecasting (EA)

IABG .... International Association of Botanic Gardens [*Australia*] (EA)

IABG .... International Association of Buying Groups [*See also IVE*] (EAIO)

IABG .... International Association on Biomedical Gerontology (BUAC)

IABK............ International Association of Book-Keepers [*Sevenoaks, Kent, England*] (EA)

IaBl............. Bloomfield Public Library, Bloomfield, IA [*Library symbol Library of Congress*] (LCLS)

IABL............ Independent Association of Builders' Labourers [*A union*] [*British*]

IABLA........... Inter-American Bank for Latin America (WDAA)

IaBlak.......... Blakesburg Public Library, Blakesburg, IA [*Library symbol Library of Congress*] (LCLS)

IaBlaSP....... South Benton Star Press, Blairstown, IA [*Library symbol Library of Congress*] (LCLS)

IaBID .... Bloomfield Democrat, Bloomfield, IA [*Library symbol Library of Congress*] (LCLS)

IaBIDR .... Davis County Republican, Bloomfield, IA [*Library symbol Library of Congress*] (LCLS)

IaBlGen........ Davis County Genealogical Society, Bloomfield, IA [*Library symbol Library of Congress*] (LCLS)

IABM........... International Academy of Biological Medicine [*Defunct*] (EA)

IABM........... International Association of Broadcasting Manufacturers [*Hayes, Middlesex, England*] (EAIO)

IABM........... International Association of Broadcast Monitors (EA)

IABMCP .... International Academy of Behavioral Medicine, Counseling and Psychotherapy (EA)

IABMCP .... International Academy of Behavioral Medicine, Counseling, and Psychotherapy (NTPA)

IABMS .... International Association of Botanical and Mycological Societies (BUAC)

IaBo .... Ericson Public Library, Boone, IA [*Library symbol Library of Congress*] (LCLS)

IABO .... Internacia Asocio de Bibliistoj kaj Orientalistoj [*International Association of Biblicists and Orientalists - IABO*] (EA)

IABO .... International Association for Biological Oceanography [*Aberdeen, Scotland*] (EAIO)

IABO .... International Association of Biblicists and Initialists (BUAC)

IaBoCoC....... Boone County Courthouse, Boone, IA [*Library symbol Library of Congress*] (LCLS)

IaBonR......... Bonaparte Record-Republican, Bonaparte, IA [*Library symbol Library of Congress*] (LCLS)

IaBoNR........ Boone News-Republican, Boone, IA [*Library symbol Library of Congress*] (LCLS)

IaBonRR ...... Bonaparte Record-Republican, Bonaparte, IA [*Library symbol*] [*Library of Congress*] (LCLS)

IABP............ International Arctic Buoy Program [*Marine science*] (OSRA)

IABP............ International Association of Businessmen and Professionals (EA)

IABP............ Intra-Aortic Balloon Pump [*Cardiology*]

IABPA .... Intra-Aortic Balloon Pumping Assistance [*Cardiology*] (AAMN)

IABPAI .... International Association of Blue Print and Allied Industries [*Later, IRGBA, IRA*] (EA)

IABPBD .... International Alliance of Bill Posters, Billers, and Distributors of US and Canada [*Defunct*]

IABPC .... International Association of Book Publishing Consultants [*Inactive*] (EA)

IABPC .... Intraaortic Balloon Counterpulsation [*Medicine*] (DB)

IABPFF .... International Association of Black Professional Fire Fighters (EA)

IABR .... Index to Australian Book Reviews [*A publication*]

IaBrBEN ...... Brighton Enterprise-News, Brighton, IA [*Library symbol*] [*Library of Congress*] (LCLS)

IaBreN .... Breda News, Breda, IA [*Library symbol Library of Congress*] (LCLS)

IaBrEN .... Brighton Enterprise-News, Brighton, IA [*Library symbol Library of Congress*] (LCLS)

IA B Rev ...... Iowa Bar Review [*A publication*] (DLA)

IaBriNT .... Britt News-Tribune, Britt, IA [*Library symbol Library of Congress*] (LCLS)

IABRM .... International Association for Bear Research and Management (EA)

IaBroC .... Brooklyn Chronicle, Brooklyn, IA [*Library symbol Library of Congress*] (LCLS)

IABS............ Installation Automated Budget System [*Army*]

IABS............ International Absorbents [*NASDAQ symbol*] (SAG)

IABS............ International Alban Berg Society (EA)

IABS............ International Association for Biological Standardization (BUAC)

IABS............ International Association for Business and Society (BUAC)

IABS............ International Association for Byzantine Studies [*See also AIEB*] [*Thessaloniki, Greece*] (EAIO)

IABS............ International Association of Biological Standardization [*See also AISB*] [*ICSU Geneva, Switzerland*] (EAIO)

IABS............ International Association of Buddhist Studies (EA)

IABS............ International Association of Byznatine Studies (BUAC)

IABSE........... International Association for Bridge and Structural Engineering [*ICSU*] [*Zurich, Switzerland*] [*Research center*] (EA)

IABSF........... Internatoinal Amateur Boat Surfing Federation (BUAC)

IABSF........... Intl Absorbents [*NASDAQ symbol*] (TTSB)

IABSIW .... International Association of Bridge, Structural, and Ornamental Iron Workers (BARN)

IABSOIW...... International Association of Bridge, Structural, and Ornamental Iron Workers (EA)

IABT............ Illinois Association of Biology Teachers (EDAC)

IABTI........... International Association of Bomb Technicians and Investigators (EA)

IaBucCT .... Buffalo Center Tribune, Buffalo Center, IA [*Library symbol Library of Congress*] (LCLS)

IABWMT ...... International Association of Black and White Men Together [*Later, NABWMT*] (EA)

IAC.............. Chicago, IL [*Location identifier FAA*] (FAAL)

IAC.............. De Paul University, Chicago, IL [*OCLC symbol*] (OCLC)

IAC.............. Iceberg Athletic Club (EA)

IAC.............. Identification Accuracy [*Rate*] (MCD)

IAC.............. Idle Air Control [*Automotive engineering*]

I-Ac............. Imidazoleacetic Acid [*Biochemistry*] (AAMN)

IAC.............. Immigration Appeal Cases [*Canada*] [*A publication*] (DLA)

IAC.............. Immunization Action Coalition (EA)

IAC.............. Improved Anode Catalyst

IAC.............. In Any Case [*Computer hacker terminology*]

IAC.............. Indiana Administrative Code [*A publication*] (AAGC)

IAC.............. Indian Airlines Corp. [*ICAO designator*] (FAAC)

IAC.............. Indian Army Circular [*British military*] (DMA)

IAC.............. Industrial Accident Commission Decisions [*A publication*] (DLA)

IAC.............. Industries Assistance Commission (EERA)

IAC.............. Industry Advisory Committee [*World War II*]

IAC.............. Industry Advisory Committee on Survey and Mapping [*Queensland*] [*State*] (EERA)

IAC.............. Industry Advisory Conference [*Underwriters Laboratories*] [*Telecommunications*]

IAC.............. Industry Advisory Council [*Formerly, DIAC*]

IAC.............. Ineffective Airway Clearance [*Medicine*] (DMAA)

IAC.............. Information Access Co. [*Information service or system*] (IID)

IAC.............. Information Analysis Center [*DoD*]

IAC.............. Information and Communication

IAC.............. Inheritance of Acquired Characteristics

IAC.............. Initial Approach Course [*Aviation*]

IAC.............. Inner Approach Channel

IAC.............. Installation and Checkout (IAA)

IAC.............. Instantaneous Airborne Count (MCD)

IAC.............. Institute for Advanced Concepts [*In 1980 film "Simon"*]

IAC.............. Institute for Antiquity and Christianity [*Claremont University*] [*Research center*] (RCD)

IAC.............. Institute of Administration and Commerce of South Africa (BUAC)

IAC.............. Institute of Amateur Cinematographers [*British*] (BI)

IAC.............. Institute of Applied Clicheology

IAC.............. Institute of Astrophysics of the Canaries

IAC.............. Instrument Approach Chart (AAG)

IAC.............. Instrument Array Cable

IAC.............. Instrumentation and Control (IAA)

IAC.............. Insurance Advertising Conference [*Later, IMCA*] (EA)
IAC.............. Integrating Assembly Contractor
IAC.............. Integrating Associate Contractor
IAC.............. Integration, Assembly, and Checkout
IAC.............. Intelligence Advisory Committee
IAC.............. Intelligence Analysis Center [*Marine Corps*] (MCD)
IAC.............. Intelligent Asynchronous Controller [*Computer terminal connector*] (NITA)
IAC.............. Interactive Array Computer
IAC.............. Inter-African Committee on Traditional Practices Affecting the Health of Women and Children in Africa (BUAC)
IAC.............. Inter Afrique Charters (BUAC)
IAC.............. Interagency Committee for Outdoor Recreation [*Department of the Interior*]
IAC.............. Interagency Conference (MCD)
IAC.............. Inter-American Council
IAC.............. Interapplication Communication [*Apple Computer, Inc.*]
IAC.............. InterApplication Communications [*Computer science*] (CDE)
IAC.............. Inter-Applications Communication [*Computer science*] (EERA)
IAC.............. Interarray Communications (NVT)
IAC.............. Interdepartmental Advisory Committee [*World War II*]
IAC.............. Interface Assurance Contractor
IAC.............. Intergrated Avionics Computer (DA)
IAC.............. Interim Acceptance Criteria (NRCH)
IAC.............. Interim Action Committee [*British*]
IAC.............. Intermediate Air Command [*Air Force*] (AFM)
IAC.............. Intermittent Abdominal Compression
IAC.............. Internal Auditory Canal [*Anatomy*]
IAC.............. International Academy of Ceramics [*See also AIC*] [*Geneva, Switzerland*] (EAIO)
IAC.............. International Academy of Cytology [*Quebec, PQ*] (EA)
IAC.............. International Activities Committee [*American Chemical Society*]
IAC.............. International Advisory Committee [*ANSI*]
IAC.............. International Advisory Council for Homosexual Men and Women in Alcoholics Anonymous (EA)
IAC.............. International Aerobatic Club (EA)
IAC.............. International Agricultural Club (EA)
IAC.............. International Air Convention
IAC.............. International Algebraic Compiler
IAC.............. International Alpine Conference (BUAC)
IAC.............. International Analysis Code [*Meteorology*]
IAC.............. International Anti-Counterfeiting Coalition (EA)
IAC.............. International Artists' Cooperation (EAIO)
IAC.............. International Association for Cybernetics [*See also AIC*] [*Namur, Belgium*] (EAIO)
IAC.............. International Association of Charities [*See also AIC*] (EAIO)
IAC.............. International Astronautical Congress
IAC.............. International Athletes Club (BUAC)
IAC.............. Interposed Abdominal Compression [*Medicine*] (STED)
IAC.............. Interposed Abdominal Counterpulsation [*Medicine*]
IAC.............. Inter-Regional Athletic Conference (PSS)
IAC.............. Interview-after-Combat
IAC.............. Intra-Arterial Chemotherapy [*Medicine*]
IAC.............. Inventory of Anger Communication [*Personality development test*] [*Psychology*]
IAC.............. Iowa Administrative Code [*A publication*] (AAGC)
IAC.............. Ipsilateral Associational-Commissural [*Anatomy*]
IAC.............. Irvine Apartment Communities [*NYSE symbol*] (SAG)
IAC.............. Isolated Adrenal Cell [*Endocrinology*] (DAVI)
IAC.............. Israel Aliyah Center (EA)
IAC.............. Italian Aircraft Corp.
IaCa.............. Duncan Memorial Library, Casey, IA [*Library symbol Library of Congress*] (LCLS)
IACA............. Independent Air Carriers Association [*Defunct*] (EA)
IACA............. Indian Arts and Crafts Association (EA)
IACA............. Inter-American College Association (EA)
IACA............. Inter-American Cultural Association (EA)
IACA............. International Air Carrier Association [*Zaventhem, Belgium*] (EAIO)
IACA............. International Air Charter Association [*Switzerland*] (BUAC)
IACA............. International Arts and Culture Association
IACA............. International Association for Classical Archaeology [*See also AIAC*] [*Rome, Italy*] (EAIO)
IACA............. International Association of Consulting Actuaries (MHDB)
IACA............. Intra-Application Communication Area [*Computer science*] (PCM)
IACA............. Irish American Cultural Association (EA)
IACAAC......... International Artists' Cooperation Audio Art Center [*Defunct*] (EA)
IACAAN........ International Committee on Avian Anatomical Nomenclature (BUAC)
IACAC.......... Inter-American Commercial Arbitration Commission (BUAC)
IACAC.......... International Association on Civil Aviation Chaplains (EA)
IAC/ADP........ Interagency Committee on Automatic Data Processing [*Office of Management and Budget*]
IACAHP........ Inter-African Advisory Committee for Animal Health and Production (BUAC)
IACAPAP...... International Association for Child and Adolescent Psychiatry and Allied Professions [*Copenhagen, Denmark*] (EA)
IaCar........... Carroll Public Library, Carroll, IA [*Library symbol Library of Congress*] (LCLS)
IaCarCH....... Carroll County Historical Society Museum, Carroll, IA [*Library symbol Library of Congress*] (LCLS)
IaCarl......... Carlisle Public Library, Carlisle, IA [*Library symbol Library of Congress*] (LCLS)
IaCarlC....... Carlisle Citizen, Carlisle, IA [*Library symbol Library of Congress*] (LCLS)
IaCarsT....... Carson Times, Carson, IA [*Library symbol Library of Congress*] (LCLS)

IaCarTH........ Daily Times-Herald, Carroll, IA [*Library symbol Library of Congress*] (LCLS)
IaCasPA....... Cascade Pioneer-Advertiser, Cascade, IA [*Library symbol Library of Congress*] (LCLS)
IaCb........... Council Bluffs Free Public Library, Council Bluffs, IA [*Library symbol Library of Congress*] (LCLS)
IACB.......... Indian Arts and Crafts Board [*Department of the Interior*]
IACB.......... Inter-Agency Consultative Board (EY)
IACB.......... International Advisory Committee on Bibliography [*UNESCO*] (WDAA)
IACB.......... International Association of Convention Bureaus [*Later, IACVB*] (EA)
IACB.......... Intra-Aortic Counterpulsation Balloon [*Cardiology*] (DAVI)
IACBC......... International Advisory Committee on Biological Control (BUAC)
IACBD......... International Academy for Child Brain Development (EA)
IACBDT....... International Advisory Committee on Bibliogaphy, Documentation and Terminology (NITA)
IaCbN......... Nonpareil, Council Bluffs, IA [*Library symbol Library of Congress*] (LCLS)
IACC.......... Icelandic American Chamber of Commerce (NTPA)
IACC.......... India-America Chamber of Commerce (EA)
IACC.......... Indo-American Chamber of Commerce (PDAA)
IACC.......... Industrial Analysis and Control Council
IACC.......... Integrating Assembly and Checkout Contractor
IACC.......... Inter-Agency Air Cartographic Committee
IACC.......... Interamerican Confederation of Cattlemen (EA)
IACC.......... Inter-American Cultural Council (EA)
IACC.......... International Agricultural Coordination Commission (BUAC)
IACC.......... International Air Cargo Corp. [*Egypt*] [*ICAO designator*] (FAAC)
IACC.......... International Alliance of Catholic Churches
IACC.......... International Americas Cup Class [*Yachting*]
IACC.......... International Anticounterfeiting Coalition (EA)
IACC.......... International Art Cinemas Confederation (EAIO)
IACC.......... International Association for Cell Culture (BUAC)
IACC.......... International Association of Commercial Collectors (NTPA)
IACC.......... International Association of Conference Centers (EA)
IACC.......... International Association of Congress Centres (BUAC)
IACC.......... Iran American Chamber of Commerce (EA)
IACC.......... Island Arts and Crafts Club, Victoria [*1910, IACS from 1922*] (NGC)
IACC.......... Israel-America Chamber of Commerce and Industry (EAIO)
IACC.......... Italian-American Chamber of Commerce (EA)
IACC.......... Italy-America Chamber of Commerce (EA)
IaCc........... John E. Clegg Library, Central City, IA [*Library symbol Library of Congress*] (LCLS)
IACCA......... Irish Association of Company and Commercial Accountants (BUAC)
IACCB......... Illinois Association of Community College Biologists (EDAC)
IACCC......... International Association for Cross-Cultural Communication (BUAC)
IACCE......... Inter-American Confederation for Catholic Education [*Bogota, Colombia*] (EAIO)
IACCHE....... Inter-American Confederation of Chemical Engineering (BUAC)
IACCI......... International Association of Computer Crime Investigators [*Defunct*] (EA)
IACCI......... International Association of Credit Card Investigators (EA)
IACCI......... International Association of Financial Crimes Investigators (NTPA)
IaCcL......... Linn News-Letter, Central City, IA [*Library symbol Library of Congress*] (LCLS)
IACCN......... Inventory Accounting Cost Control Number System (MCD)
IACCP......... Inter-American Council of Commerce and Production
IACCP......... International Association for Cross-Cultural Psychology [*Canada*] (EA)
IAC-CPR...... Interposed Abdominal Compression - Cardiopulmonary Resuscitation
IACD.......... Implantable Automatic Cardioverter-Defibrillator [*Medicine*] (STED)
IACD.......... International Association for Community Development (BUAC)
IACD.......... International Association of Clothing Designers (EA)
IACD.......... Intra-Atrial Conduction Defect (STED)
IACD.......... Irish Association for Curriculum Development (AIE)
IACDB......... International Action Committee for Democracy in Burma (BUAC)
IACDE......... International Association of Clothing Designers and Executives (NTPA)
IAC Dec ...... Decisions of the Industrial Accident Commission of California [*A publication*] (DLA)
IACDLA........ International Advisory Committee on Documentation, Libraries, and Archives [*UNESCO*] (DIT)
IACDT......... International Advisory Committee for Documentation and Terminology (BUAC)
IACDT......... International Association of Certified Duncan Teachers (EA)
IACE........... Intergovernmental Advisory Council on Education (AEE)
IACE........... International Air Cadet Exchange
IACE........... International Association for Computing in Education [*Also, an information service or system*] (EA)
IACED......... Inter-African Advisory Committee on Epizootic Diseases
IACED......... Interagency Committee on Environment and Development (EERA)
IACEE......... International Association for Continuing Engineering Education (BUAC)
IaCenv .... Drake Public Library, Centerville, IA [*Library symbol Library of Congress*] (LCLS)
IaCenvl....... Iowegian & Citizen, Centerville, IA [*Library symbol Library of Congress*] (LCLS)
IACES.......... International Air Cushion Engineering Society (BUAC)
IACESC .... Inter-American Council for Education, Science, and Culture
IACESR....... Irish Association for Cultural, Economic, and Social Relations (BUAC)
IACET.......... International Association for Continuing Education and Training (EA)
IaCf........... Cedar Falls Public Library, Cedar Falls, IA [*Library symbol Library of Congress*] (LCLS)
IACF.......... Inter-American Cement Federation [*Colombia*] (EAIO)
IACF.......... International Amateur Cycling Federation (EA)
IACF.......... International Association for Cultural Freedom [*Defunct*] (EA)

IACFA........... International Adult Cystic Fibrosis Association [*Netherlands*] (BUAC)

IaCfE............. Eastern Area Library Cooperative, Cedar Falls, IA [*Library symbol Library of Congress*] (LCLS)

IACFHG........ Inter Action Council of Former Heads of Government (EA)

IaCfHi.......... Cedar Falls Historical Society, Cedar Falls, IA [*Library symbol Library of Congress*] (LCLS)

IACFM........... International Association of Concert and Festival Managers [*Later, ISPAA*] (EA)

IaCfNI.......... Northern Iowan, Cedar Falls, IA [*Library symbol Library of Congress*] (LCLS)

IaCfR........... Cedar Falls Record, Cedar Falls, IA [*Library symbol Library of Congress*] (LCLS)

IaCfT............ University of Northern Iowa, Cedar Falls, IA [*Library symbol Library of Congress*] (LCLS)

IACG............ Institute for American Church Growth (EA)

IaCh............. Free Public Library, Chariton, IA [*Library symbol Library of Congress*] (LCLS)

IACH............ Inter-Association Committee on Health

IACH............ International Association of Colour Healers (BUAC)

IACHA.......... Iowa Automated Clearing House Association

IaChc........... Charles City Public Library, Charles City, IA [*Library symbol Library of Congress*] (LCLS)

IaChcP.......... Charles City Press, Charles City, IA [*Library symbol Library of Congress*] (LCLS)

IaChe........... Cherokee Public Library, Cherokee, IA [*Library symbol Library of Congress*] (LCLS)

IACHE.......... International Association of Cylindrical Hydraulic Engineers (EA)

IaCheCHi..... Cherokee County Historical Society, Cherokee, IA [*Library symbol Library of Congress*] (LCLS)

IaCheCoC..... Cherokee County Courthouse, Cherokee, IA [*Library symbol Library of Congress*] (LCLS)

IACHEI......... International Association of Consultants in Higher Education Institutions (BUAC)

IaChHP........ Chariton Herald-Patriot, Chariton, IA [*Library symbol Library of Congress*] (LCLS)

IaChL........... Chariton Leader, Chariton, IA [*Library symbol Library of Congress*] (LCLS)

IaChoT......... Charter Oak Times, Charter Oak, IA [*Library symbol Library of Congress*] (LCLS)

IACHR.......... Inter-American Commission on Human Rights (EA)

IACHT.......... International Association Colon Hydro Therapy (NTPA)

IaChu........... Churdan City Library, Churdan, IA [*Library symbol Library of Congress*] (LCLS)

IACI.............. Idiopathic Arterial Calcification of Infancy [*Medicine*] (DMAA)

IACI.............. Industrial Acoustics Co., Inc. [*NASDAQ symbol*] (NQ)

IACI.............. Inter-American Children's Institute [*Uruguay*] [*Research center*] (IRC)

IACI.............. Inter-American Copyright Institute (BUAC)

IACI.............. International Association of Conference Interpreters (BUAC)

IACI.............. Iran Aircraft Industries (MCD)

IACI.............. Irish American Cultural Institute (EA)

IACIA........... Interagency Committee for International Athletics [*Defunct*]

IACID........... Inter-American Center for Integral Development [*OAS*]

IACIS........... International Association for Computer Information Systems (NTPA)

IACIS........... International Association of Colloid and Interface Scientists (BUAC)

IACITC......... International Advisory Committee of the International Teletraffic Congress (EAIO)

IACJ............. Inter-American Council of Jurists [*Organization of American States*] [*Washington, DC*]

IaCjGS......... Columbus Gazette & Columbus Safeguard, Columbus Junction, IA [*Library symbol Library of Congress*] (LCLS)

IACKL........... Interrupt Acknowledgment Latency [*Computer science*]

IaCkvS......... Clarksville Star, Clarksville, IA [*Library symbol Library of Congress*] (LCLS)

IACL............. Internal Association of Criminal Law (BUAC)

IACL............. International Academy of Comparative Law (BUAC)

IACL............. International Aeradio Caribbean Ltd.

IACL............. International Association of Constitutional Law [*See also AIDC*] [*Belgrade, Yugoslavia*] (EAIO)

IaCla............ Clarion Public Library, Clarion, IA [*Library symbol Library of Congress*] (LCLS)

IACLA.......... International Association of Clinical Laser Acupuncturists (EA)

IaClad.......... Clarinda Public Library, Clarinda, IA [*Library symbol Library of Congress*] (LCLS)

IaCladHJ...... Clarinda Herald-Journal, Clarinda, IA [*Library symbol Library of Congress*] (LCLS)

IaClaM......... Wright County Monitor, Clarion, IA [*Library symbol Library of Congress*] (LCLS)

IaClar........... Edna Zybell Memorial Library, Clarence, IA [*Library symbol Library of Congress*] (LCLS)

IaClarCHi..... Cedar County Historical Society, Clarence, IA [*Library symbol Library of Congress*] (LCLS)

IACLE.......... International Association of Contact Lens Educators

IACLEA........ International Association of Campus Law Enforcement Administrators (EA)

IaClfC.......... Clearfield Chronicle, Clearfield, IA [*Library symbol Library of Congress*] (LCLS)

IaCli............. Clinton Public Library, Clinton, IA [*Library symbol Library of Congress*] (LCLS)

IaCliC........... Clinton Corn Processing Co., Clinton, IA [*Library symbol Library of Congress*] (LCLS)

IaCliCC........ Clinton Community College, Clinton, IA [*Library symbol Library of Congress*] (LCLS)

IaCliCHi....... Clinton County Historical Society, Clinton, IA [*Library symbol Library of Congress*] (LCLS)

IaCliH.......... Clinton Herald, Clinton, IA [*Library symbol Library of Congress*] (LCLS)

IaCliM.......... Mount Saint Clare College, Clinton, IA [*Library symbol Library of Congress*] (LCLS)

IaCll............. Clear Lake Public Library, Clear Lake, IA [*Library symbol Library of Congress*] (LCLS)

IaClvS.......... Clarksville Star, Clarksville, IA [*Library symbol Library of Congress*] (LCLS)

IACM............ Institute of Applied and Computational Mathematics [*Greece*] (BUAC)

IACM............ International Association for Computational Mechanics [*International Council of Scientific Unions*]

IACM............ International Association of Circulation Managers

IACM............ International Association of Color Manufacturers (NTPA)

IACM............ International Association of Concert Managers [*Later, ISPAA*] (EA)

IACMAG....... International Association for Computer Methods and Advances in Geomechanics (BUAC)

IACME.......... Inter-American Committee of Mathematical Education (BUAC)

IACME.......... International Association of Coroners and Medical Examiners (EA)

IACME.......... International Association of Crafts and Small- and Medium-Sized Enterprises [*Switzerland*] (EY)

IACMHA....... Illinois Association of Community Mental Health Agencies (SRA)

IACMP......... International Association of Career Management Professionals (NTPA)

IACNET........ Inter-American Citrus Network [*Chile*] (BUAC)

IACNRE........ International Association for Conservation of Natural Resources and Energy

IACO............ Conservative Orthopedics International Association (EA)

IACO............ Illinois Association of County Officials (SRA)

IACO............ Integrated Assembly and Checkout (SSD)

IACO............ Inter-African Coffee Organization (EAIO)

IACO............ Inter-American Coffee Organisation (BUAC)

IACO............ International Association of Correctional Officers (EA)

IACOA.......... Independent Armored Car Operators Association (EA)

IACOCCA..... I Am Chairman of Chrysler Corp. of America [*Acronym formed from name of Chrysler chairman Lee Iacocca*]

IACODLA..... International Advisory Committee on Documentation, Libraries, and Archives [*UNESCO*] (BUAC)

IAC of Cal.... Decisions of the Industrial Accident Commission of California [*A publication*] (DLA)

IaCogM........ Coggan Monitor, Coggan, IA [*Library symbol Library of Congress*] (LCLS)

IaCol............ Colfax Free Public Library, Colfax, IA [*Library symbol Library of Congress*] (LCLS)

IaColJ.......... Jasper County Tribune, Colfax, IA [*Library symbol Library of Congress*] (LCLS)

IaColn.......... Collins Public Library, Collins, IA [*Library symbol Library of Congress*] (LCLS)

IACOMS....... International Advisory Committee on Marine Sciences [*UNESCO*] (ASF)

IaCon........... Conrad Public Library, Conrad, IA [*Library symbol*] [*Library of Congress*] (LCLS)

IaConR........ Conrad Record, Conrad, IA [*Library symbol Library of Congress*] (LCLS)

IaCoon......... Coon Rapids Enterprise, Coon Rapids, IA [*Library symbol Library of Congress*] (LCLS)

IACOP......... International Armaments Cooperative Opportunities Plan

IaCorn.......... Corning Free Public Library, Corning, IA [*Library symbol Library of Congress*] (LCLS)

IaCornFP...... Adams County Free Press, Corning, IA [*Library symbol Library of Congress*] (LCLS)

IaCorrN........ Correctionville News, Correctionville, IA [*Library symbol Library of Congress*] (LCLS)

IaCorv.......... Coralville Public Library, Coralville, IA [*Library symbol Library of Congress*] (LCLS)

IaCorvC........ Coralville Courier, Coralville, IA [*Library symbol Library of Congress*] (LCLS)

IaCorwH....... Corwith Herald, Corwith, IA [*Library symbol Library of Congress*] (LCLS)

IaCoryTR...... Corydon Times-Republican, Corydon, IA [*Library symbol Library of Congress*] (LCLS)

IaCoryWC.... Wayne County Courthouse, Corydon, IA [*Library symbol*] [*Library of Congress*] (LCLS)

IaCoryWCoC... Wayne County Courthouse, Corydon, IA [*Library symbol Library of Congress*] (LCLS)

IACP............ Industrial Arts Curriculum Project [*Education*] (AEE)

IACP............ Integrated Air Cancer Project [*Environmental Protection Agency*]

IACP............ Inter-African Council for Philosophy (BUAC)

IACP............ International Association for Child Psychiatry and Allied Professions [*Later, IACAPAP*]

IACP............ International Association of Chiefs of Police (EA)

IACP............ International Association of Cities and Ports (BUAC)

IACP............ International Association of Computer Programmers

IACP............ International Association of Cooking Professionals (EA)

IACP............ International Association of Culinary Professionals (NTPA)

IACP............ Intra-Aortic Counterpulsation [*Cardiology*] (DAVI)

IACP............ Investment Advisory Centre of Pakistan (BUAC)

IACPA.......... Inter-American Council of Psychiatric Associations (DAVI)

IACPAP........ International Association for Child Psychiatry and Allied Professions [*Later, IACAPAP*]

IACPP.......... International Association for Cross-Cultural Psychology (BUAC)

IACPP.......... International Association of Crime Prevention Practitioners (EA)

IACPR.......... Inter-American Committee of Presidential Representatives

IACPR.......... International Association of Corporate and Professional Recruitment (NTPA)

IACPR .... International Association of Corporate and Professional Resources (NTPA)

IACPS .... Inter-American Committee on Peaceful Settlement [*Defunct Defunct*] (EA)

IACPS .... International Academy of Chest Physicians and Surgeons (EA)

IACPWR ...... Inter-Allied Committee on Post-War Requirements [*World War II*]

IaCr .... Cedar Rapids Public Library, Cedar Rapids, IA [*Library symbol Library of Congress*] (LCLS)

IACR .... Institue of Arable Crop Research [*British*]

IACR .... Inter-American Congress of Radiology

IACR .... International Agreement Competitive Restrictions (AAGC)

IACR .... International Association for Cryptologic Research (EA)

IACR .... International Association of Cancer Registries [*Lyon, France*] (EAIO)

IACRAO .... Illinois Association of Collegiate Registrars and Admissions Officers (SRA)

IaCrC .... Coe College, Cedar Rapids, IA [*Library symbol Library of Congress*] (LCLS)

IACRD .... Inter-American Center for Regional Development (EAIO)

IACRDP .... International Association of Cross-Reference Directory Publishers (EA)

IACRDVT ...... Inter-American Centre for Research and Documentation on Vocational Training [*See also CINTERFOR*] [*Montevideo, Uruguay*] (EAIO)

IaCre .... Cresco Public Library, Cresco, IA [*Library symbol*] [*Library of Congress*] (LCLS)

IACREE .... International Association of Corporate Real Estate Executives (EA)

IaCreHC .... Howard County Courthouse, Cresco, IA [*Library symbol*] [*Library of Congress*] (LCLS)

IACREOT ...... International Association of Clerks, Recorders, Election Officials, and Treasurers (EA)

IaCres .... Matilda J. Gibson Memorial Library, Creston, IA [*Library symbol Library of Congress*] (LCLS)

IaCresco ...... Cresco Public Library, Cresco, IA [*Library symbol Library of Congress*] (LCLS)

IaCrescoCoC... Howard County Courthouse, Cresco, IA [*Library symbol Library of Congress*] (LCLS)

IaCrescoTP... Cresco Times-Plain Dealer, Cresco, IA [*Library symbol Library of Congress*] (LCLS)

IaCresNA ..... Creston News-Advertiser, Creston, IA [*Library symbol Library of Congress*] (LCLS)

IaCreTP .... Cresco Times-Plain Dealer, Cresco, IA [*Library symbol*] [*Library of Congress*] (LCLS)

IaCrG .... Cedar Rapids Gazette, Cedar Rapids, IA [*Library symbol Library of Congress*] (LCLS)

IaCrK .... Kirkwood Community College, Cedar Rapids, IA [*Library symbol Library of Congress*] (LCLS)

IACRL .... Italian-American Civil Rights League

IaCrL .... Linn County Heritage Society, Cedar Rapids, IA [*Library symbol Library of Congress*] (LCLS)

IACRLRD ...... International Association for Comparative Research on Leukemia and Related Diseases (EA)

IaCrM .... Iowa Masonic Library, Cedar Rapids, IA [*Library symbol Library of Congress*] (LCLS)

IaCrMM .... Mount Mercy College, Cedar Rapids, IA [*Library symbol Library of Congress*] (LCLS)

IaCrMT .... Micro-Technology, Inc., Cedar Rapids, IA [*Library symbol Library of Congress*] (LCLS)

IaCroyHi ...... Wayne County Historical Society, Croydon, IA [*Library symbol*] [*Library of Congress*] (LCLS)

IACRP .... International Association for the Child's Right to Play (EAIO)

IACRS .... International Association of Concrete Repair Specialists (EA)

IACS .... IAL Consultancy Services [*Southall, England*] [*Telecommunications*] (TSSD)

IACS .... Indian Association for the Cultivation of Science (BUAC)

IACS .... Inertial Attitude Control System [*Aerospace*]

IACS .... Integrated Access and Crossconnect System (ACRL)

IACS .... Integrated Acoustic Communication System [*Military*] (NVT)

IACS .... Integrated Armament Control System (MCD)

IACS .... Integrated Avionics Control System (RDA)

IACS .... Interactive Computer System [*Information science*]

IACS .... Intermediate Altitude Communication Satellite (IAA)

IACS .... International Academy of Christian Sociologists (BUAC)

IACS .... International Academy of Cosmetic Surgery [*Rome, Italy*] (EA)

IACS .... International Annealed Copper Standard

IACS .... International Arms-Control Symposium

IACS .... International Association of Classification Societies (EAIO)

IACS .... International Association of Cooking Schools (EA)

IACS .... International Association of Counseling Services (EA)

IACS .... Island Arts and Crafts Society, Victoria [*1922, founded 1910 as IACC*] (NGC)

IACS .... Italian-American Cultural Society (EA)

IACSC .... International Association of Cold Storage Contractors (NTPA)

IACSE .... Interagency Advisory Committee on Security Equipment

IACS-LDR .... Integrated Acoustic Communication System - Low Data Rate (MCD)

IACSM .... International Association of Computer Service Managers

IACSP .... International Association of Counterterrorism and Security Professionals

IACSS .... Inter-American Conference on Social Security [*See also CISS*] [*Mexico City, Mexico*] (EAIO)

IACSS .... International Association for Computer Systems Security (EA)

IACST .... Inter-American Committee for Science and Technology

IACST .... International Association for Commodity Science and Technology (EAIO)

IACSW .... Interstate Association of Commissions on the Status of Women

IACT .... Inter-Association Commission on Tsunami [*Brussels, Belgium*] (EAIO)

IACT .... International Association for Clear Thinking (EA)

IACT .... International Association of Colon Therapy (EA)

IACT .... International Association of Counselors and Therapists (EA)

IACT .... International Association to Combat Terrorism [*Defunct*] (EA)

IACTP .... International Association of Correctional Training Personnel (NTPA)

IACUC .... Institutional Animal Care and Use Committee [*Department of Agriculture*]

IACUG .... International Association of Computer Users Groups (EA)

IACV .... Idle Air Control Valve [*Fuel system*] [*Automotive engineering*]

IACVB .... International Association of Convention and Visitor Bureaus (EA)

IACVF .... International Association of Cancer Victors and Friends (EA)

I/ACVIA .... Interaction/American Council for Voluntary International Action (EA)

IACW .... Inter-American Commission of Women [*Organization of American States*] [*Washington, DC*]

IACW .... International Association of Crime Writers (EAIO)

IAD .... Eastern Illinois University, Charleston, IL [*OCLC symbol*] (OCLC)

IAD .... Immediate Action Directive

IAD .... Immediate Action Drill [*Military*] (LAIN)

IAD .... Inactivating Dose [*Medicine*] (DMAA)

IAD .... Index of Axis Deficiency [*Embryology*]

IAD .... Information and Documentation [*British Film Institute*]

IAD .... Inhibiting Antibiotic Dose [*Medicine*] (STED)

IAD .... Initial Address Designator [*Computer science*] (CIST)

IAD .... Initiation Area Discriminator [*RADAR*]

IAD .... Inland Steel Indus [*NYSE symbol*] (TTSB)

IAD .... Inland Steel Industries, Inc. [*NYSE symbol*] (SPSG)

IAD .... Installation, Assembly or Detail (AAG)

IAD .... Institute for American Democracy (EA)

IAD .... Instructional Advance Directive

IAD .... Integrated Access Device [*BBN Communications Corp.*]

IAD .... Integrated Airbase Defense

IAD .... Integrated Automatic Documentation [*System*]

IAD .... Interactive Debugging [*Computer science*] (CIST)

IAD .... Interface Agreement Document (KSC)

IAD .... Interface Analysis Document (KSC)

IAD .... Internal Absorbed Dose

IAD .... Internal Audit Division [*Environmental Protection Agency*] (GFGA)

IAD .... International Association of Documentalists and Information Officers [*France*] (EY)

IAD .... International Astrophysical Decade

IAD .... International Automotive Design

IAD .... Internationale Arbeitsgemeinschaft Donauforschung [*International Working Association for Danube Research*] (EAIO)

IAD .... Inventory Adjustment Document

IAD .... Inventory Available Date (TEL)

IAD .... Ion-Assisted Deposition [*Coating technology*]

IAD .... Ion Beam Activated Deposition [*Coating technology*]

IAD .... Washington [*District of Columbia*] Dulles Airport [*Airport symbol*]

IaDa .... Davenport Public Library, Davenport, IA [*Library symbol Library of Congress*] (LCLS)

IADA .... Idaho Automobile Dealers Association (SRA)

IADA .... Illinois Automobile Dealer Association (SRA)

IADA .... Independent Aeronautical Dealers Association [*Defunct*] (EA)

IADA .... Independent Automotive Damage Appraisers Association [*Milwaukee, WI*] (EA)

IADA .... Inland Auto Dismantlers Association (SRA)

IADA .... International Atomic-Development Authority [*Proposed by Bernard M. Baruch, 1946, but never created*]

IADA .... Internationale Arbeitsgemeinschaft der Archiv-, Bibliotheks-, und Graphikrestauratoren [*International Association for Conservation of Books, Paper, and Archival Material*] (EAIO)

IADA .... Interstate Agreement on Detainers Act [*1970*]

IADA .... Iowa Automobile Dealers Association (SRA)

IaDaCM .... Catholic Messenger, Davenport, IA [*Library symbol Library of Congress*] (LCLS)

IaDaCoC ..... Scott County Courthouse, Davenport, IA [*Library symbol Library of Congress*] (LCLS)

IaDaGL .... Grant Law Library, Davenport, IA [*Library symbol Library of Congress*] (LCLS)

IaDaM .... Davenport Public Museum, Davenport, IA [*Library symbol Library of Congress*] (LCLS)

IaDaMC .... Marycrest College, Davenport, IA [*Library symbol Library of Congress*] (LCLS)

IaDaP .... Palmer College of Chiropractic, Davenport, IA [*Library symbol Library of Congress*] (LCLS)

IaDaPM .... Putnam Museum, Davenport, IA [*Library symbol Library of Congress*] (LCLS)

IaDaQT .... Quad City Times, Davenport, IA [*Library symbol*] [*Library of Congress*] (LCLS)

IaDaSA .... Saint Ambrose College, Davenport, IA [*Library symbol Library of Congress*] (LCLS)

IADA-UT .... Independent Auto Dealers Association - Utah (SRA)

IaDayR .... Dayton Review, Dayton, IA [*Library symbol Library of Congress*] (LCLS)

IADB .... Inter-American Defense Board (EA)

IADB .... Inter-American Development Bank [*Also, IDB*]

IADB-MED... Inter-American Defense Board Medal [*Military decoration*]

IADBWA ...... Inter-American Development Bank's Wives Association (EA)

IaDc .... Dallas Center Public Library, Dallas Center, IA [*Library symbol Library of Congress*] (LCLS)

IADC .... Inter-American Defense College [*Washington, DC*]

IADC .... Inter-American Development Commission

IADC .... Interdepartmental Advisory and Development Committee (EERA)

IADC .... International Alliance for Distribution by Cable [*Formerly, International Alliancefor Distribution by Wire*] (EA)
IADC .... International Association of Defense Counsel (EA)
IADC .... International Association of Dentistry for Children [*British*] (EAIO)
IADC .... International Association of Dredging Companies [*The Hague, Netherlands*] (EA)
IADC .... International Association of Drilling Contractors
IaDCC .... College Chips, Luther College, Decorah, IA [*Library symbol Library of Congress*] (LCLS)
I/ADCSP ...... Initial/Advanced Defense Communications Satellite Program (SAA)
I/ADCSP ...... Interim/Advanced Defense Communications Satellite Program (DNAB)
IADD .... International Association of Diecutting and Diemaking (NTPA)
IADE .... Integral of Absolute Delay Error (IAA)
IAdEM .... Internacia Asocio de Esperantistaj Matematikistoj [*International Association of Esperantist Mathematicians*] (EAIO)
IaDen .... Denison Carnegie Library, Denison, IA [*Library symbol Library of Congress*] (LCLS)
IaDenB .... Denison Bulletin, Denison, IA [*Library symbol Library of Congress*] (LCLS)
IaDenR .... Denison Review, Denison, IA [*Library symbol Library of Congress*] (LCLS)
IaDewO .... Observer, De Witt, IA [*Library symbol Library of Congress*] (LCLS)
IaDexM .... Dexter Museum, Dexter, IA [*Library symbol Library of Congress*] (LCLS)
IADF .... Icelandic Air Defense Force (MUGU)
IADF .... Inter-American Association for Democracy and Freedom (EA)
IADF .... Irish American Defense Fund [*Defunct*] (EA)
IADH .... Inappropriate Antidiuretic Hormone [*Endocrinology*] (MAE)
IADH .... International Association of Dentistry for the Handicapped [*Toronto, ON*] (EAIO)
IADHS .... Inappropriate Antidiuretic Hormone Syndrome [*Endocrinology*]
IaDiaR .... Diagonal Reporter, Diagonal, IA [*Library symbol Library of Congress*] (LCLS)
IADIC .... Integration Analog-to-Digital Converter (IEEE)
IADIS .... Irish Association for Documentation and Information Services (NITA)
IADIWU .... International Association for the Development of International and World Universities [*See also AIDUIM*] [*Aulnay-Sous-Bois, France*] (EAIO)
IaDJ .... Decorah Journal, Decorah, IA [*Library symbol Library of Congress*] (LCLS)
IADL .... Instrumental Activities of Daily Living Survey [*Department of Health and Human Services*] (GFGA)
IADL .... International Association of Democratic Lawyers [*Brussels, Belgium*] (EA)
IaDL .... Luther College, Decorah, IA [*Library symbol Library of Congress*] (LCLS)
IaDm .... Des Moines Public Library, Des Moines, IA [*Library symbol Library of Congress*] (LCLS)
IaDmB .... Iowa Commission for the Blind, Des Moines, IA [*Library symbol Library of Congress*] (LCLS)
IaDmBR .... Business Record, Des Moines, IA [*Library symbol*] [*Library of Congress*] (LCLS)
IaDmC .... Iowa State Commerce Commission, Records and Information Center, Des Moines, IA [*Library symbol Library of Congress*] (LCLS)
IaDmCI .... Central Iowa Regional Library System, Des Moines, IA [*Library symbol*] [*Library of Congress*] (LCLS)
IaDmD .... Drake University, Des Moines, IA [*Library symbol Library of Congress*] (LCLS)
IaDmDC .... Dowling College, Des Moines, IA [*Library symbol Library of Congress*] (LCLS)
IaDmD-L ...... Drake University, Law School, Des Moines, IA [*Library symbol Library of Congress*] (LCLS)
IaDmE .... Iowa State Education Association, Des Moines, IA [*Library symbol Library of Congress*] (LCLS)
IAD-MEMA ... International Aftermarket Division - Motor and Equipment Manufacturers Association (NTPA)
IADMFR .... International Association of Dento-Maxillo-Facial Radiology (EAIO)
IaDmG .... Grand View College, Des Moines, IA [*Library symbol Library of Congress*] (LCLS)
IaDmHN .... Highland Park News, Des Moines, IA [*Library symbol Library of Congress*] (LCLS)
IaDmL .... Iowa Legionnaire, Des Moines, IA [*Library symbol Library of Congress*] (LCLS)
IaDmLN .... Lee Town News, Des Moines, IA [*Library symbol Library of Congress*] (LCLS)
IaDmMet ...... Des Moines Metropolitan Service Area Library Cooperative, Des Moines, IA [*Library symbol Library of Congress*] (LCLS)
IaDmOF .... Odd Fellows Temple, Des Moines, IA [*Library symbol Library of Congress*] (LCLS)
IaDmPH .... Pioneer Hi-Bred International, Inc., Des Moines, IA [*Library symbol Library of Congress*] (LCLS)
IaDmR .... Daily Record, Des Moines, IA [*Library symbol Library of Congress*] (LCLS)
IaDmRT .... Des Moines Register-Tribune, Des Moines, IA [*Library symbol Library of Congress*] (LCLS)
IaDmS .... College of Osteopathic Medicine and Surgery, Des Moines, IA [*Library symbol Library of Congress*] (LCLS)
IADMS .... International Association for Dance Medicine and Science
IaDmV .... United States Veterans Administration Hospital, Des Moines, IA [*Library symbol Library of Congress*] (LCLS)
IaDN .... Norwegian-American Historical Museum and Library, Decorah, IA [*Library symbol Library of Congress*] (LCLS)
IaDo .... Dows Community Library, Dows, IA [*Library symbol Library of Congress*] (LCLS)

IADO .... Instituto Argentine de Oceanografia [*Marine science*] (OSRA)
IaDon .... Donnellson Public Library, Donnellson, IA [*Library symbol Library of Congress*] (LCLS)
IaDonS .... Donnellson Star, Donnellson, IA [*Library symbol Library of Congress*] (LCLS)
IaDooP .... Press, Doon, IA [*Library symbol Library of Congress*] (LCLS)
IADP .... INTELSAT Assistance and Development Program
IADP .... Inter-American Driving Permit
IADP .... International Association of Dollbaby Parents [*Defunct*] (EA)
IADPC .... Interagency Data Processing Committee
IADPG .... Intelligence Automatic Data Processing Group (CINC)
IaDPO .... Decorah Public Opinion, Decorah, IA [*Library symbol Library of Congress*] (LCLS)
IaDQT .... Quad City Times, Davenport, IA [*Library symbol Library of Congress*] (LCLS)
IADR .... Institute for Animal Disease Research [*Research center British*] (IRC)
IADR .... International Association for Dental Research (EA)
IADRS .... International Association of Dive Rescue Specialists (EA)
IADS .... Immunoadsorbent (DB)
IADS .... Integrated Air Defense System (MCD)
IADS .... International Agricultural Development Service [*Later, WIIAD*] [*Department of Agriculture*]
IADS .... International Association of Dental Students [*British*]
IADS .... International Association of Department Stores [*See also AIGM*] (EAIO)
IA DSA .... Intra-Arterial Digital Subtraction Arteriography [*Cardiology*] (DAVI)
IADSA .... Intraaterial Digital Subtraction Angiography [*Medicine*]
IADT .... Initial Active Duty for Training [*Military*] (AABC)
IADT .... Integrated Automatic Detection and Tracking [*Military*] (CAAL)
IaDu .... Carnegie-Stout Free Public Library, Dubuque, IA [*Library symbol Library of Congress*] (LCLS)
IaDuA .... Aquinas Institute, Dubuque, IA [*Library symbol Library of Congress*] (LCLS)
IaDuAn .... Antique Trade Weekly, Dubuque, IA [*Library symbol Library of Congress*] (LCLS)
IaDuCl .... Clarke College, Dubuque, IA [*Library symbol Library of Congress*] (LCLS)
IaDuCo .... Clarke Courier, Dubuque, IA [*Library symbol Library of Congress*] (LCLS)
IaDuL .... Loras College, Dubuque, IA [*Library symbol Library of Congress*] (LCLS)
IaDuLe .... Dubuque Leader, Dubuque, IA [*Library symbol Library of Congress*] (LCLS)
IaDuN .... New Melleray Abbey, Dubuque, IA [*Library symbol Library of Congress*] (LCLS)
IaDunR .... Dunlap Reporter, Dunlap, IA [*Library symbol Library of Congress*] (LCLS)
IaDuT .... Schools of Theology in Dubuque, Dubuque, IA [*Library symbol Library of Congress*] (LCLS)
IaDuU .... University of Dubuque, Dubuque, IA [*Library symbol Library of Congress*] (LCLS)
IaDuU-S ...... University of Dubuque, Theological Seminary, Dubuque, IA [*Library symbol Library of Congress*] (LCLS)
IaDuW .... Wartburg Theological Seminary, Dubuque, IA [*Library symbol Library of Congress*] (LCLS)
IaDuWi .... Dubuque Witness, Dubuque, IA [*Library symbol Library of Congress*] (LCLS)
IaDv .... Denver Public Library, Denver, IA [*Library symbol Library of Congress*] (LCLS)
IaDvF .... Forum, Denver, IA [*Library symbol Library of Congress*] (LCLS)
IADWS .... Interim Air Defense Weapon System [*Army*]
IaDy .... Matthias M. Hoffman Public Library, Dyersville, IA [*Library symbol Library of Congress*] (LCLS)
IaDyC .... Dyersville Commercial, Dyersville, IA [*Library symbol Library of Congress*] (LCLS)
IaDysR .... Dysart Reporter, Dysart, IA [*Library symbol Library of Congress*] (LCLS)
IaE .... Eagle Grove Public Library, Eagle Grove, IA [*Library symbol Library of Congress*] (LCLS)
IAE .... Felician College, Chicago, IL [*OCLC symbol*] (OCLC)
IAE .... In Any Event [*Internet language*] [*Computer science*]
IAE .... Information and Education (IAA)
IAE .... Infrared Auroral Emission
IAE ...., Institut d'Administration des Entreprises [*Institute of Company Management*] [*Information service or system*] (IID)
IAE .... Institute for the Advancement of Engineering (EA)
IAE .... Institute of Atomic Energy [*Academy of Sciences, USSR*]
IAE .... Institute of Automobile Engineers
IAE .... Integral of Absolute Error
IAE .... Inter-Asia Equities [*Vancouver Stock Exchange symbol*]
IAE .... International Association of Ethicists (EA)
IAE .... Interstate Airlines Ltd. [*Nigeria*] [*ICAO designator*] (FAAC)
IAE .... Intra-Atrial Electrocardiogram [*Cardiology*] (MAE)
IAE .... Iscrizioni Antico-Ebraici Palestinesi (BJA)
IAE .... Iskra Associated Enterprise [*Yugoslavia*] [*Telecommunications*]
IAEA .... Institute of Automotive Engineer Assessors [*British*] (EAIO)
IAEA .... Inter-American Education Association (EA)
IAEA .... International Advertising Executives' Association (NTCM)
IAEA .... International Agricultural Exchange Association [*British*] (EA)
IAEA .... International Association for Educational Assessment (EA)
IAEA .... International Association of Empirical Aesthetics [*Paris, France*] (EAIO)
IAEA .... International Atomic Energy Accord (DOMA)
IAEA .... International Atomic Energy Agency [*Database originator and operator*] [*United Nations*] [*Austria*]

IAEAC............ International Association of Environmental Analytical Chemistry [*Therwil, Switzerland*] (EAIO)
IAEACPD...... Inter-American Emergency Advisory Committee for Political Defense
IAEA-MEL .... International Atomic Energy Agency Marine Environmental Laboratory [*Marine science*] (OSRA)
IaEarE.......... Earlham Echo, Earlham, IA [*Library symbol Library of Congress*] (LCLS)
IaEarv .... Ruth Suckhow Memorial Library, Earlville, IA [*Library symbol Library of Congress*] (LCLS)
IaEaryN........ Early News, Early, IA [*Library symbol Library of Congress*] (LCLS)
IAEC.............. International Association of Electrical Contractors [*See also AIE*] (EAIO)
IAEC.............. International Association of Environmental Coordinators [*Belgium*] (DCTA)
IAEC.............. International Atomic Energy Committee
IAECOSOC.... Inter-American Economic and Social Council [*United Nations*]
IAED.............. International Association of Exchange Dealers [*British*] (EA)
IaEdd .... Eddyville Public Library, Eddyville, IA [*Library symbol Library of Congress*] (LCLS)
IaEddT .... Eddyville Tribune, Eddyville, IA [*Library symbol Library of Congress*] (LCLS)
IaEdgR......... Edgewood Reminder, Edgewood, IA [*Library symbol Library of Congress*] (LCLS)
IAEDP .... International Association of Eating Disorders Professionals (EA)
IAEDT........... International Association of Equine Dental Technicians (EA)
IaEE .... Eagle, Eagle Grove, IA [*Library symbol Library of Congress*] (LCLS)
IAeE .... Institute of Aeronautical Engineers
IAEE .... International Association for Earthquake Engineering [*ICSU*] [*Tokyo, Japan*] (EAIO)
IAEE .... International Association for Energy Economics (EERA)
IAEE .... International Association of Energy Economists (EA)
IAEG............. International Association of Engineering Geology [*International Union of Geological Sciences*] [*ICSU Paris, France*] (EA)
IAEI .... International Association of Electrical Inspectors (EA)
IAEJ .... Interfaith Action for Economic Justice (EA)
IAEKM.......... International Association of Electronic Keyboard Manufacturers (NTPA)
IAEL .... Initial Allowance Equipage List [*Military*] (CAAL)
IAEL.............. International Association for Esperanto in Libraries [*See also TEBA*] (EAIO)
IAEL .... International Association of Electrical Leagues [*Later, ILEA*] (EA)
IAEL .... International Association of Entertainment Lawyers [*Amsterdam, Netherlands*] (EAIO)
IaElbTHi....... Tama County Historical Society, Elberon, IA [*Library symbol Library of Congress*] (LCLS)
IaEld .... Eldon Carnegie Library, Eldon, IA [*Library symbol Library of Congress*] (LCLS)
IaEldF.......... Eldon Forum, Eldon, IA [*Library symbol Library of Congress*] (LCLS)
IaEldoHHi .... Hardin County Historical Society, Eldora, IA [*Library symbol Library of Congress*] (LCLS)
IaEldoHi....... Hardin County Historical Society, Eldora, IA [*Library symbol*] [*Library of Congress*] (LCLS)
IaEldoHL...... Herald-Ledger, Eldora, IA [*Library symbol Library of Congress*] (LCLS)
IaEldoI......... Hardin County Index, Eldora, IA [*Library symbol Library of Congress*] (LCLS)
IaEldr........... Scott County Library, Eldridge, IA [*Library symbol Library of Congress*] (LCLS)
IaEldrN......... North Scott Press, Eldridge, IA [*Library symbol Library of Congress*] (LCLS)
IaElgE.......... Elgin Echo, Elgin, IA [*Library symbol Library of Congress*] (LCLS)
IaElk .... Elkader Public Library, Elkader, IA [*Library symbol Library of Congress*] (LCLS)
IaElkCR........ Clayton County Register, Elkader, IA [*Library symbol Library of Congress*] (LCLS)
IaElkHi.......... Elkader Historical Society, Elkader, IA [*Library symbol Library of Congress*] (LCLS)
IaElkhR........ Elk Horn-Kimballton Review, Elk Horn, IA [*Library symbol Library of Congress*] (LCLS)
IaEll.............. Elliott Public Library, Elliott, IA [*Library symbol Library of Congress*] (LCLS)
IaElmR......... Elma Reminder, Elma, IA [*Library symbol Library of Congress*] (LCLS)
IaEls .... Ellsworth Public Library, Ellsworth, IA [*Library symbol Library of Congress*] (LCLS)
IaEm .... Emmetsburg Public Library, Emmetsburg, IA [*Library symbol Library of Congress*] (LCLS)
IAEM............ International Association for Exposition Management (NTPA)
IAEM............ International Atomic Energy Agency (USDC)
IaEmD.......... Emmetsburg Democrat, Emmetsburg, IA [*Library symbol*] [*Library of Congress*] (LCLS)
IaEmR.......... Emmetsburg Reporter, Emmetsburg, IA [*Library symbol*] [*Library of Congress*] (LCLS)
IAEMS.......... International Association of Environmental Mutagen Societies [*Helsinki, Finland*] (EAIO)
IAEP............. International Academy of Eclectic Psychotherapists [*St. Ives, NSW, Australia*] (EAIO)
IaEpD........... Divine Word College, Epworth, IA [*Library symbol Library of Congress*] (LCLS)
IAEPO .... International Association of Educational Peace Officers (EA)
IAER............. Institute of Applied Economic Research [*Concordia University*] [*Canada Research center*] (RCD)
IaEs .... Estherville Public Library, Estherville, IA [*Library symbol Library of Congress*] (LCLS)
IAES............. Institute of Aerospace [*formerly, Aeronautical*] Sciences

IAES............. Interim Aquanaut Equipment System (PDAA)
IAES............. International Academy for Environmental Safety
IAES............. International Association of Electrotypers and Stereotypers [*Later, Printing Platemakers Association*]
IAESC.......... Inter-American Economic and Social Council [*United Nations*]
IAESC.......... International Association of Evening Student Councils [*Later, USAES*] (EA)
IaEsN .... Estherville Daily News, Estherville, IA [*Library symbol Library of Congress*] (LCLS)
IAESR.......... Institute of Applied Economic and Social Research (EERA)
IAESTE......... International Association for the Exchange of Students for Technical Experience [*Lisbon, Portugal*] (EAIO)
IAESTE/US.... International Association for the Exchange of Students for Technical Experience - United States [*Later, AIPT*]
IaEsxFN .... First National Bank, Essex, IA [*Library symbol Library of Congress*] (LCLS)
IaEsxI .... Essex Independent, Essex, IA [*Library symbol Library of Congress*] (LCLS)
IAET............. In-Flight Aeromedical Evacuation Team
IAET............. International Association for Enterostomal Therapy (EA)
IAETF........... International Anti-Euthanasia Task Force (EA)
IAETL........... International Association of Environmental Testing Laboratories (EA)
IaEveN .... Everly News, Everly, IA [*Library symbol Library of Congress*] (LCLS)
IAEVG .... International Association for Educational and Vocational Guidance [*See also AIOSP*] [*Belfast, Northern Ireland*] (EAIO)
IAEVI............ International Association for Educational and Vocational Information [*See also AIISUP*] [*Paris, France*] (EAIO)
IaEvS .... Black Hawk County Sun, Evansdale, IA [*Library symbol Library of Congress*] (LCLS)
IAEWP .... International Association of Educators for World Peace (EA)
IaExJ............ Audubon County Journal, Exira, IA [*Library symbol Library of Congress*] (LCLS)
IAF............... EPAG - Group Air France [*ICAO designator*] (FAAC)
IAF............... First Australia Fund [*AMEX symbol*] (TTSB)
IAF............... First Australia Fund, Inc. [*AMEX symbol*] (SPSG)
IAF............... Governors State University, Park Forest South, IL [*OCLC symbol*] (OCLC)
IAF............... Idiopathic Alveolar Fibrosis [*Medicine*] (DMAA)
IAF............... Image Analysis Facility [*Computer science*] (PDAA)
IAF............... Immobilizing Accelerating Factor (PDAA)
IAF............... Independent Air Force [*British military*] (DMA)
IAF............... Indian Air Force
IAF............... Indian Army Form [*British military*] (DMA)
IAF............... Indian Auxiliary Force [*British*]
IAF............... Indium Arsenide Filter
IAF............... Indonesian Air Force
IAF............... Induced-Air Flotation [*Chemical engineering*]
IAF............... Industrial Air Filtration
IAF............... Industrial Areas Foundation (EA)
IAF............... Information and Forwarding (MUGU)
IAF............... Initial Approach Fix [*Aviation*] (AFM)
IAF............... Initiative America Foundation (EA)
IAF............... Institut Armand-Frappier [*University of Quebec*] [*Formerly, Institute of Microbiology and Hygiene of Montreal*] [*Research center*] (RCD)
IAF............... Institute for Alternative Futures [*Defunct*] (EA)
IAF............... Institute on American Freedoms [*Defunct*]
IAF............... Instrument Air Filter
IAF............... Instrument Approach Fix
IAF............... Interactive Facility [*Control Data Corp.*]
IAF............... Interallied Force [*NATO*] (NATG)
IAF............... Inter-American Foundation (MCD)
IAF............... International Abolitionist Federation [*India*]
IAF............... International Accreditation Forum [*For quality control*]
IAF............... International Activities Fund [*Canadian Labour Congress*] [*See also FAI*]
IAF............... International Aeronautical Federation
IAF............... International Aikido Federation [*Tokyo, Japan*] (EAIO)
IAF............... International Apparel Federation [*Berlin, Federal Republic of Germany*] (EAIO)
IAF............... International Aquaculture Foundation (EA)
IAF............... International Arab Federation
IAF............... International Archery Federation (EA)
IAF............... International Association for Falconry and Conservation of Birds of Prey (EAIO)
IAF............... International Astronautical Federation [*ICSU*] [*Research center France*]
IAF............... International Athletic Footwear and Apparel Manufacturers Association [*Zurich, Switzerland Defunct*] (EAIO)
IAF............... International Autumn Fair [*British*] (ITD)
IAF............... Internet Address Finder [*Computer science*]
IAF............... Intra-Alaska Facsimile [*National Weather Service*]
IAF............... (Iodoacetamido)fluorescein [*Biochemical label*]
IAF............... Islamic Action Front [*Political party*] [*Jordan*]
IAF............... Israel Air Force (BJA)
IAF............... Israeli Air-Force [*ICAO designator*] (FAAC)
IAF............... Italian Air Force (NATG)
IAF............... Italian American Forum [*Defunct*] (EA)
IAF............... Office of Information for the Armed Forces (AABC)
IAFA............. Inter-American Foundation for the Arts [*Defunct*]
IAFA............. International Association for the Fantastic in the Arts (EA)
IAFA............. International Aviation Facilities Act [*1948*]
IAFAE........... Inter-American Federation for Adult Education
IaFair........... Fairfield Public Library, Fairfield, IA [*Library symbol Library of Congress*] (LCLS)

IaFairL......... Fairfield Daily Ledger, Fairfield, IA [*Library symbol Library of Congress*] (LCLS)

IaFairM........ Maharishi International University, Fairfield, IA [*Library symbol Library of Congress*] (LCLS)

IaFarmL....... Van Buren County Leader, Farmington, IA [*Library symbol Library of Congress*] (LCLS)

IAFAW .... International Association of Friends of Angkor Wat (EAIO)

IaFay .... Fayette Community Library, Fayette, IA [*Library symbol Library of Congress*] (LCLS)

IaFayHHi...... Fayette County Helpers Club and Historical Society, Fayette, IA [*Library symbol Library of Congress*] (LCLS)

IaFayL .... Fayette Leader, Fayette, IA [*Library symbol Library of Congress*] (LCLS)

IaFayU......... Upper Iowa University, Fayette, IA [*Library symbol Library of Congress*] (LCLS)

IAFB............ Interim Airframe Bulletin

IAFC............ Instantaneous Automatic Frequency Control

IAFC............ Inter-American Freight Conference - Section C (EA)

IAFC............ Interim Airframe Change (NG)

IAFC............ International Association of Financial Consultants (BARN)

IAFC............ International Association of Fire Chiefs (EA)

IAFC............ Irwin Allen Fan Club [*Defunct*] (EA)

IAFCF........... International Association of Fire Chiefs Foundation (EA)

IAFCI........... Inter-American Federation of the Construction Industry [*See also FIIC*] [*Mexico City, Mexico*] (EAIO)

IaFcS .... Forest City Summit, Forest City, IA [*Library symbol Library of Congress*] (LCLS)

IAFCT.......... International Association of French-Speaking Congress Towns [*See also AIVFC*] [*France*] (EAIO)

IaFcW .... Waldorf College, Forest City, IA [*Library symbol Library of Congress*] (LCLS)

IaFd .... Fort Dodge Public Library, Fort Dodge, IA [*Library symbol Library of Congress*] (LCLS)

IAFD............ International Association on Food Distribution

IaFdIC.......... Iowa Central Community College, Fort Dodge, IA [*Library symbol Library of Congress*] (LCLS)

IaFdM .... Fort Dodge Messenger, Fort Dodge, IA [*Library symbol Library of Congress*] (LCLS)

IAFE............ International Association of Fairs and Expositions (EA)

IAFE............ International Association of Fish Ethologists [*Normal, IL*] (ASF)

IAFEC........... International Association of Family Entertainment Center (NTPA)

IAFES........... International Association for the Economics of Self-Management [*Belgrade, Yugoslavia*] (EAIO)

IAFF............ International Air Freight Forwarder (AABC)

IAFF............ International Association of Fire Fighters (EA)

IAFI............. Infantile Amaurotic Family Idiocy [*Medicine*]

IAFIS........... Integrated Automated Fingerprint Identification System [*FBI standardized term*]

IAFLUP .... International Association of French-Language University Presses [*Defunct*] (EA)

IaFm............ Cattermole Memorial Library, Fort Madison, IA [*Library symbol Library of Congress*] (LCLS)

IAFM............ Integrated Air-Fuel Module

IaFmD.......... Fort Madison Democrat, Fort Madison, IA [*Library symbol Library of Congress*] (LCLS)

IaFmLHi....... North Lee County Historical Society, Fort Madison, IA [*Library symbol Library of Congress*] (LCLS)

IAFMM......... International Association of Fish Meal Manufacturers [*Potters Bar, Hertfordshire, England*] (EAIO)

IAFN............ International Association of Forensic Nurses (NTPA)

IAFN............ International Association of Forensic Nursing (EA)

IaFon .... Fonda Public Library, Fonda, IA [*Library symbol Library of Congress*] (LCLS)

IaFonT .... Fonda Times, Fonda, IA [*Library symbol Library of Congress*] (LCLS)

IaFontO........ Fontanelle Observer, Fontanelle, IA [*Library symbol Library of Congress*] (LCLS)

IAFP............ Intergovernmental Affairs Fellowship Program (RDA)

IAFP............ International Alliance of Film Producers [*Later, IAIP*] (EA)

IAFP............ International Association for Financial Planning (EA)

IAFP............ International Association of Filipino Patriots (EA)

IAFPE........... Indian American Forum for Political Education (EA)

IaFre............ Upham Memorial Library, Fredericksburg, IA [*Library symbol Library of Congress*] (LCLS)

IaFremG....... Fremont Gazette, Fremont, IA [*Library symbol Library of Congress*] (LCLS)

IaFreN .... Fredericksburg News, Fredericksburg, IA [*Library symbol Library of Congress*] (LCLS)

IaFreR .... Fredericksburg Review, Fredericksburg, IA [*Library symbol*] [*Library of Congress*] (LCLS)

IAFS............ Integrated Air-Fuel System [*Automotive engineering*]

IAFS............ International Animated Film Society (EA)

IAFS............ International Association for Food Self-Sufficiency (EA)

IAFS............ International Association of Family Sociology (EA)

IAFS............ International Association of Forensic Sciences [*Defunct*] (EA)

IAFSA.......... International Association of French-Speaking Aircrews (EAIO)

IAFSDEI....... International Association of French-Speaking Directors of Educational Institutions (EAIO)

IAFSS.......... International Association for Fire Safety Science (NTPA)

IAFTA.......... Integrated Avionics Fault Tree Analyzer (MCD)

IAFU............ Improved Assault Fire Units [*Military*] (MCD)

IAFV............ Infantry Armored Fighting Vehicle (NATG)

IAFVH .... Indian Advanced Field Veterinary Hospital [*British military*] (DMA)

IAFWA.......... International Association of Fish and Wildlife Agencies (EA)

IAFWNO....... Inter-American Federation of Working Newspapermen's Organizations

IAG.............. Epag-Group Air France [*FAA designator*] (FAAC)

IAG.............. Greenville College, Greenville, IL [*OCLC symbol*] (OCLC)

IAG.............. Industry Advisory Group [*Underwriters Laboratories*] [*Telecommunications*]

IAG.............. Institute for Australasian Geodynamics [*Flinders University*] [*Australia*]

IAG.............. Instruction Address Generation [*Computer science*]

IAG.............. Intelligence Analysis Group [*Military*]

IAG.............. Interactive Application Generator (HGAA)

IAG.............. Interagency Advisory Group [*Civil Service Commission*]

IAG.............. Interagency Agreement

IAG.............. Inter-Association Group

IAG.............. Intergovernmental Agreement on the Environment [*Commonwealth*] [*State*] (EERA)

IAG.............. International Academy of Gnathology - American Section (EA)

IAG.............. International Applications Group [*IFIP*]

IAG.............. International Art Guild (EA)

IAG.............. International Association of Geodesy [*ICSU*] [*Paris, France*] (EAIO)

IAG.............. International Association of Gerontology (EA)

IAG.............. International Auditing Guideline

IAG.............. Niagara Falls, NY [*Location identifier FAA*] (FAAL)

IaG.............. Stewart Public Library, Grinnell, IA [*Library symbol Library of Congress*] (LCLS)

IAGA........... International Association of Geomagnetism and Aeronomy [*ICSU*] [*Scotland*] (ASF)

IAGA........... International Association of Golf Administrators (EA)

IAGA........... Irish Amateur Gymnastics Association (EA)

IAGAE.......... International Association for Gerda Alexander Eutony [*See also AIEGA*] [*Switzerland*] (EAIO)

IAGAL.......... Industry Advisory Group for Air Logistics

IaGar........... Garner Public Library, Garner, IA [*Library symbol Library of Congress*] (LCLS)

IaGarL.......... Garner Leader and Signal and Herald, Garner, IA [*Library symbol Library of Congress*] (LCLS)

IaGavoHi...... Garnavillo Historical Society, Garnavillo, IA [*Library symbol Library of Congress*] (LCLS)

IaGavoT .... Granavillo Tribune, Granavillo, IA [*Library symbol Library of Congress*] (LCLS)

IaGc............. Gilmore City Public Library, Gilmore City, IA [*Library symbol Library of Congress*] (LCLS)

IAGC............ Instantaneous Automatic Gain Control [*or Circuit*] [*RADAR*]

IAGC .... International Association of Geochemistry and Cosmochemistry [*Edmonton, AB*] (EA)

IAGC .... International Association of Geophysical Contractors (EA)

IAGCW......... International Association of Greeting Card Workers

IAGD........... Iowa Academy of General Dentistry (SRA)

IaGen........... Iowa State Genealogical Society, Genealogical Library, Des Moines, IA [*Library symbol Library of Congress*] (LCLS)

IaGeoN......... Lyon County News, George, IA [*Library symbol Library of Congress*] (LCLS)

IaGeoR......... Lyon county Register, George, IA [*Library symbol*] [*Library of Congress*] (LCLS)

IAGFA.......... International Association of Governmental Fair Agencies (EA)

IAGFCC .... International Association of Game, Fish, and Conservation Commissioners [*Later, IAFWA*] (EA)

IaGG .... Grinnell College, Grinnell, IA [*Library symbol Library of Congress*] (LCLS)

IaGHR .... Herald-Register, Grinnell, IA [*Library symbol Library of Congress*] (LCLS)

IaGjG .... Globe Free Press, Grand Junction, IA [*Library symbol Library of Congress*] (LCLS)

IAGL............ Interactive Applicon Graphics Language [*Automotive engineering*]

IaGle............ Glenwood Public Library, Glenwood, IA [*Library symbol*] [*Library of Congress*] (LCLS)

IaGleOT .... Opinion-Tribune, Glenwood, IA [*Library symbol Library of Congress*] (LCLS)

IaGliG .... Glidden Graphic, Glidden, IA [*Library symbol Library of Congress*] (LCLS)

IAGLL........... International Association of Germanic Languages and Literatures [*See also IVG*] (EAIO)

IAGLO .... International Association of Governmental Labor Officials [*Later, NAGLO*] (EA)

IAGLP........... International Association of Great Lakes Ports (EA)

IAGLR........... International Association for Great Lakes Research (EA)

IAGM .... International Association of Garment Manufacturers [*Absorbed by NOSA*] (EA)

IAGMA.......... Illuminating and Allied Glassware Manufacturers Association [*Defunct*] (EA)

IAGMA.......... International Assembly of Grocery Manufacturers Associations (EAIO)

IAGOD.......... International Association of the Genesis of Ore Deposits [*ICSU*] [*Prague, Czechoslovakia*] (EAIO)

IaGow........... Gowrie News, Gowrie, IA [*Library symbol Library of Congress*] (LCLS)

IAGP............ Illinois Association of Groundwater Professionals (SRA)

IAGP .... International Antarctic Glaciological Project [*Defunct*] (EA)

IAGP .... International Association of Geographic Pathology (DAVI)

IAGP .... International Association of Group Psychotherapy (EA)

IaGra .... Graettinger Public Library, Graettinger, IA [*Library symbol Library of Congress*] (LCLS)

IaGraT .... Graettinger Times, Graettinger, IA [*Library symbol Library of Congress*] (LCLS)

IaGrc........... Grundy Center Public Library, Grundy Center, IA [*Library symbol Library of Congress*] (LCLS)

IaGrcI........... Iowa Farm Bureau Spokesman, Grundy Center, IA [*Library symbol Library of Congress*] (LCLS)

IaGrcR .... Grundy Center Register, Grundy Center, IA [*Library symbol Library of Congress*] (LCLS)

IaGre .... Greene Public Library, Greene, IA [*Library symbol Library of Congress*] (LCLS)

IAgrE .... Institution of Agricultural Engineers [*British*] (DBA)

IaGrefFP ...... Adair County Free Press, Greenfield, IA [*Library symbol Library of Congress*] (LCLS)

IaGreR .... Greene Recorder, Greene, IA [*Library symbol Library of Congress*] (LCLS)

IaGrisA .... Griswold American, Griswold, IA [*Library symbol Library of Congress*] (LCLS)

IAgS .... Institute of Agricultural Secretaries (DBA)

IAGS .... Inter-American Geodetic Survey

IAGS .... International Association for Germanic Studies (EAIO)

IAGS .... Irish Assessment & Guidance Service (ACII)

IaGucG .... Guthrian, Guthrie Center, IA [*Library symbol Library of Congress*] (LCLS)

IaGucT .... Guthrie Center Times, Guthrie Center, IA [*Library symbol Library of Congress*] (LCLS)

IAGUS .... International Association of Genito-Urinary Surgeons (DAVI)

IaGut .... Guttenberg Public Library, Guttenberg, IA [*Library symbol Library of Congress*] (LCLS)

IaGutP .... Guttenberg Press, Guttenberg, IA [*Library symbol Library of Congress*] (LCLS)

IAH .... Houston [*Texas*] Intercontinental [*Airport symbol*] (OAG)

IAH .... Idiopathic Adrenal Hyperplasia [*Medicine*]

IAH .... Illinois Institute of Technology, Chicago, IL [*OCLC symbol*] (OCLC)

IAH .... Immune Adherence Haemagglutination [*Immunochemistry*] (PDAA)

IAH .... Implantable Artificial Heart

IAH .... Institute for Animal Health [*Agricultural and Food Research Council*] [*British*] (IRC)

IAH .... Institute for the Advancement of Health [*Defunct*] (EA)

IAH .... International Association of Hydrogeologists [*Arnhem, Netherlands*] (EA)

IAH .... International Association of Hydrology

IAH .... Internationales Arbeiter-Hilfswerk [*International Workers Aid*] [*Bonn, Federal Republic of Germany*] (EAIO)

IAHA .... Immune Adherence Hemagglutination [*Immunochemistry*]

IAHA .... Indiana Association of Homes for the Aging (SRA)

IAHA .... Institute for the Advancement of Hawaiian Affairs

IAHA .... Inter-American Hospital Association [*Defunct*]

IAHA .... Inter-American Hotel Association

IAHA .... International Arabian Horse Association (EA)

IAHA .... International Association of Historians of Asia [*Quezon City, Philippines*] (EA)

IAHA .... International Association of Hospitality Accountants [*Austin, TX*] (EA)

IAHA .... Iowa Association of Homes for the Aging (SRA)

Ia-HA .... Iowa State Department of History and Archives, Des Moines, IA [*Library symbol Library of Congress*] (LCLS)

IAHAIO .... International Association of Human-Animal Interaction Organizations (EA)

IaHamb .... Hamburg Public Library, Hamburg, IA [*Library symbol Library of Congress*] (LCLS)

IaHambR ..... Hamburg Reporter, Hamburg, IA [*Library symbol Library of Congress*] (LCLS)

IaHampC ...... Hampton Chronicle, Hampton, IA [*Library symbol Library of Congress*] (LCLS)

IaHampCoC .. Franklin County Courthouse, Hampton, IA [*Library symbol Library of Congress*] (LCLS)

IaHampFC .... Franklin County Courthouse, Hampton, IA [*Library symbol*] [*Library of Congress*] (LCLS)

IaHampFN ... US Farm News, Hampton, IA [*Library symbol Library of Congress*] (LCLS)

IaHampHi .... Franklin County Historical Society, Hampton, IA [*Library symbol Library of Congress*] (LCLS)

IaHampJ ...... Dumont Journal, Hampton, IA [*Library symbol Library of Congress*] (LCLS)

IaHampT ...... Hampton Times, Hampton, IA [*Library symbol Library of Congress*] (LCLS)

IaHar .... Harlan Public Library, Harlan, IA [*Library symbol Library of Congress*] (LCLS)

IaHarNA ...... Harlan News-Advertiser, Harlan, IA [*Library symbol Library of Congress*] (LCLS)

IaHarS .... Shelby County Museum, Harlan, IA [*Library symbol Library of Congress*] (LCLS)

IaHarT .... Harlan Tribune, Harlan, IA [*Library symbol Library of Congress*] (LCLS)

IaHart .... Hartley Public Library, Hartley, IA [*Library symbol Library of Congress*] (LCLS)

IaHartP .... Hartley Public Library, Hartley, IA [*Library symbol*] [*Library of Congress*] (LCLS)

IaHartS .... Hartley Sentinel, Hartley, IA [*Library symbol Library of Congress*] (LCLS)

IaHaw .... Hawarden Public Library, Hawarden, IA [*Library symbol Library of Congress*] (LCLS)

IAHB .... Institute for the Advancement of Human Behavior (EA)

IAHB .... International Association of Human Biologists [*ICSU*] [*Newcastle-Upon-Tyne, England*] (EAIO)

IAHC .... International Ad Hoc Committee (PCM)

IAHC .... Internet Ad Hoc Coalition [*Computer science*]

IAHC .... Internet Ad Hoc Committee

IAHCP .... International Academy of Health Care Professionals (EA)

IAHCSM .... International Association of Healthcare Central Service Materials Management (EA)

IAHCSMM .... International Association of Healthcare Central Service Material Management (NTPA)

IAHD .... Idiopathic Acquired Hemolytic Disease [*Medicine*] (MAE)

IAHD .... International Association of Hillel Directors (EA)

IAHE .... International Association for Hydrogen Energy (EA)

IAHEES .... Iowa Agriculture and Home Economics Experiment Station [*Iowa State University*] [*Research center*] (RCD)

IaHeJ .... Hedrick Journal, Hedrick, IA [*Library symbol Library of Congress*] (LCLS)

IAHES .... Implantable Artificial Heart Energy System

IAHFIAW ...... International Association of Heat and Frost Insulators and Asbestos Workers

IAHHP .... International Association of Holistic Health Practitioners (EA)

IAHI .... International Association of Hail Insurers (EA)

IAHI .... International Association of Holiday Inns (EA)

IaHi .... State Historical Society of Iowa, Iowa City, IA [*Library symbol Library of Congress*] (LCLS)

IAHIC .... International Association of Home Improvement Councils [*Defunct*] (EA)

IAHM .... Incorporated Association of Head Masters [*British*]

IAHM .... International Academy of the History of Medicine [*Defunct*] (EA)

IAHMS .... International Association of Hotel Management Schools (EA)

IaHoDHi ...... Delaware County Historical Society, Hopkinton, IA [*Library symbol Library of Congress*] (LCLS)

IaHoDL .... Delaware County Leader, Hopkinton, IA [*Library symbol Library of Congress*] (LCLS)

IaHoL .... Lenox College, Hopkinton, IA [*Library symbol Library of Congress*] (LCLS)

IaHol .... Stubbs Public Library, Holstein, IA [*Library symbol Library of Congress*] (LCLS)

IaHolA .... Holstein Advance, Holstein, IA [*Library symbol Library of Congress*] (LCLS)

IAHP .... Institutes for the Achievement of Human Potential (EA)

IAHP .... International Association of Heart Patients [*Formerly, IAPP*] (EA)

IAHP .... International Association of Horticultural Producers

IAHP .... International Association of Hygienic Physicians (NTPA)

IAHR .... International Association for Hydraulic Research [*ICSU*] [*Delft, Netherlands*] (EA)

IAHR .... International Association for the History of Religions [*Marburg, Federal Republic of Germany*] (EAIO)

IAHRC .... Inter-American Human Rights Commission

IAHRONA .... International Arabian Horse Registry of North America (EA)

IAHS .... International Academy of the History of Science [*Paris, France*] (EA)

IAHS .... International Association for Hospital Security [*Later, IAHSS*] (EA)

IAHS .... International Association for Housing Science (EA)

IAHS .... International Association of Hydrological Sciences

IAHS .... International Automotive Hall of Shame (EA)

IAHSS .... International Association for Healthcare Security and Safety (EA)

IAHSSP .... International Association of Home Safety and Security Professionals (EA)

IAHU .... International Association of Health Underwriters [*Later, NAHU*] (EA)

IaHubS .... South Hardin Signal-Review, Hubbard, IA [*Library symbol Library of Congress*] (LCLS)

IaHud .... Hudson Public Library, Hudson, IA [*Library symbol Library of Congress*] (LCLS)

IaHudH .... Hudson Herald, Hudson, IA [*Library symbol Library of Congress*] (LCLS)

IaHul .... Sioux County Index, Hull, IA [*Library symbol Library of Congress*] (LCLS)

IaHulR .... Sioux County Index-Reporter, Hull, IA [*Library symbol Library of Congress*] (LCLS)

IaHum .... Humbolt Public LIbrary, Humbolt, IA [*Library symbol Library of Congress*] (LCLS)

IaHume .... Humeston Public Library, Humeston, IA [*Library symbol Library of Congress*] (LCLS)

IaHumeN .... Humeston New Era, Humeston, IA [*Library symbol Library of Congress*] (LCLS)

IaHumHi ...... Humbolt County Historical Association, Humbolt, IA [*Library symbol Library of Congress*] (LCLS)

IaHumI .... Humbolt Independent, Humbolt, IA [*Library symbol Library of Congress*] (LCLS)

IaHumR .... Humbolt Republican, Humbolt, IA [*Library symbol Library of Congress*] (LCLS)

IaHweye ...... Hawkeye Public Library, Hawkeye, IA [*Library symbol Library of Congress*] (LCLS)

IAI .... Hayner Public Library, Alton, IL [*Library symbol Library of Congress*] (LCLS)

IAI .... Illinois State University, Normal, IL [*OCLC symbol*] (OCLC)

IAI .... Inactive Aerospace Vehicle [*or Aircraft*] Inventory

IAI .... Independent Accountants International (EAIO)

IAI .... Indo-Africa, Inc. (ECON)

IAI .... Infertility Associates International [*Commercial firm*] (EA)

IAI .... Informational Acquisition and Interpretation

IAI .... Information Associates of Ithaca [*Information service or system*] (IID)

IAI .... Initial Address Information [*Telecommunications*] (TEL)

IAI .... Integrated Aircraft Instrumentation

IAI .... Inter-American Institute (USDC)

IAI .... Inter-American Institute for Global Change Research [*Marine science*] (OSRA)

IAI .... International Affiliation of Independent Accounting Firms (NTPA)

IAI .... International African Institute [*British*]

IAI .... International Apple Institute (EA)

IAI .... International Association for Identification (EA)

IAI .... International Association of Incubators (EA)

IAI .... Intra-Abdominal Infection [*Gastroenterology*] (DAVI)

IAI	Ion Acoustic Instability Enterprises (PDAA)
IAI	Ion Atom Interaction
IAI	Isethionyl Acetimidate [*Biochemistry*]
IAI	Israel Aircraft Industries Ltd. [*ICAO designator*] (FAAC)
IAI	Istituto Affairi Internazionali [*Institute for International Affairs*] [*Italy*]
IAIA	Institute of American Indian and Alaska Native Culture and Arts Development (EA)
IAIA	International Association for Impact Assessment (EA)
IaIa	Iowa City Public Library, Iowa City, IA [*Library symbol Library of Congress*] (LCLS)
IAIAA	International Association for Iranian Art and Archaeology (EA)
IAIABC	International Association of Industrial Accident Boards and Commissions (EA)
IAIAD	International Acronyms, Initialisms, and Abbreviations Dictionary [*A publication*]
IAIAF	International Affiliation of Independent Accounting Firms (EA)
IaIaI	Daily Iowan, Iowa City, IA [*Library symbol Library of Congress*] (LCLS)
IAIALAR	Ibero-American Institute of Agrarian Law and Agrarian Reform [*See also IIDARA*] [*Mexida, Venezuela*] (EAIO)
IaIaP	Iowa City Press-Citizen, Iowa City, IA [*Library symbol Library of Congress*] (LCLS)
IAIAS	Inter-American Institute of Agricultural Sciences [*Later, IICA*] [*OAS*]
IaIaS	Seven Rivers Library Cooperative, Iowa City, IA [*Library symbol Library of Congress*] (LCLS)
IAIB	International Association of Islamic Banks
IAIC	International Academy of Indian Culture (EAIO)
IAIC	International Association of Insurance Counsel [*Later, IADC*] (EA)
IAICM	International Association of Ice Cream Manufacturers [*Later, IICA*] (EA)
IAICU	International Association of Independent Colleges and Universities (EA)
IAICV	International Association of Ice Cream Vendors (NTPA)
IAID	Indium Arsenide Infrared Detector
IaIdgIHi	Ida County Historical Society, Ida Grove, IA [*Library symbol Library of Congress*] (LCLS)
IaIdgPR	Ida County Pioneer-Record, Ida Grove, IA [*Library symbol Library of Congress*] (LCLS)
IAIDPA	International Association for Information and Documentation in Public Administration (EAIO)
IAIE	Integral of Absolute Ideal Error (IAA)
IAIE	Inter-American Institute of Ecology [*Ecological Society of America*]
IAIE	International Association for Integrative Education [*Versoix, Switzerland*] (EAIO)
IAIES	Institute for Advanced Interdisciplinary Engineering Studies [*Purdue University*] (MCD)
IAIES	International Association of Intermodal Equipment Surveyors [*Defunct*] (EA)
IaIf	Carnegie Ellsworth Public Library, Iowa Falls, IA [*Library symbol Library of Congress*] (LCLS)
IaIfC	Iowa Falls Citizen, Iowa Falls, Iowa [*Library symbol Library of Congress*] (LCLS)
IaIfE	Ellsworth Community College, Iowa Falls, IA [*Library symbol Library of Congress*] (LCLS)
IaIfT	Hardin County Times, Iowa Falls, IA [*Library symbol Library of Congress*] (LCLS)
IAIG	Industrial Analytical Instrumentation Group (ACII)
IAII	Inter-American Indian Institute [*OAS*] [*Mexico City, Mexico*] (EA)
IAIM	International Association of Infant Massage (EA)
IAIMS	Integrated Academic Information Management System [*Georgetown University Medical Center*]
IAIN	International Association of Institutes of Navigation [*British*] (EAIO)
IaInd	Indianola Public Library, Indianola, IA [*Library symbol*] [*Library of Congress*] (LCLS)
IaIndianR	Record-Herald and Tribune, Indianola, IA [*Library symbol Library of Congress*] (LCLS)
IaIndianS	Simpson College, Indianola, IA [*Library symbol Library of Congress*] (LCLS)
IaIndpB	Independence Bulletin-Journal, Independence, IA [*Library symbol*] [*Library of Congress*] (LCLS)
IaIndpBC	Buchanan County Courthouse, Independence, IA [*Library symbol*] [*Library of Congress*] (LCLS)
IaIndpC	Independence Conservative, Independence, IA [*Library symbol Library of Congress*] (LCLS)
IaIndpCoC	Buchanan County Courthouse, Independence, IA [*Library symbol Library of Congress*] (LCLS)
IaIndR	Record-Herald and Tribune, Indianola, IA [*Library symbol*] [*Library of Congress*] (LCLS)
IaIndS	Simpson College, Indianola, IA [*Library symbol*] [*Library of Congress*] (LCLS)
IA International	Independent Accountants International (BUAC)
IaInwH	West Lyon Herald, Inwood, IA [*Library symbol Library of Congress*] (LCLS)
IaIonCHi	Chickasaw County Historical Society, Ionia, IA [*Library symbol Library of Congress*] (LCLS)
IAIP	Inorganic Ablative Insulative Plastic
IAIP	International Association of Independent Producers (EA)
IAIP	International Association of Individual Psychology (EA)
IAIPS	Integrated Automated Intelligence Processing System (MCD)
IAIR	International Association of Industrial Radiation [*France*] (PDAA)
IAIR	International Association of Insurance Receivers (NTPA)
IAIRI	International Association of Insurance and Reinsurance Intermediaries [*See also BIPAR*] [*Paris, France*] (EAIO)
IAIRS	Installation Aircraft Inventory Reporting System [*Army*]
IAIS	Industrial Aerodynamics Information Service [*British*] (IID)
IAIS	Insulin Autoimmune Syndrome [*Medicine*] (DMAA)
IAIS	International Association of Independent Scholars (EA)
IAITO	International Association of Independent Tanker Owners
IAIU	Insurance Agents International Union
IAJ	Idle Air Jet [*Fuel system*] [*Automotive engineering*]
IAJ	Institute for Administrative Justice [*University of the Pacific*] [*Research center*] (RCD)
IAJ	International Association of Judges [*Rome, Italy*] (EAIO)
IaJ	Jefferson Public Library, Jefferson, IA [*Library symbol Library of Congress*] (LCLS)
IAJA	International Association of Jazz Appreciation (EA)
IAJAM	Industrial Association of Juvenile Apparel Manufacturers (EA)
IAJAP	International Association of Jai Alai Players (EA)
IaJB	Jefferson Bee, Jefferson, IA [*Library symbol Library of Congress*] (LCLS)
IAJBBSC	International Association of Jim Beam Bottle and Specialties Clubs (EA)
IAJC	Inter-American Juridical Committee
IAJE	Internacia Socio de Juristoj-Esperantistoj [*International Association of Esperantist Lawyers*]
IAJE	International Association of Jazz Educators (EA)
IaJesC	Jesup Citizen Herald, Jesup, IA [*Library symbol Library of Congress*] (LCLS)
IaJew	Montgomery Memorial Library, Jewell, IA [*Library symbol Library of Congress*] (LCLS)
IaJewR	South Hamilton Record-News, Jewell, IA [*Library symbol Library of Congress*] (LCLS)
IAJFCM	International Association of Juvenile and Family Court Magistrates [*Paris, France*] (EA)
IaJGCoC	Greene County Courthouse, Jefferson IA [*Library symbol Library of Congress*] (LCLS)
IaJH	Jefferson Herald, Jefferson, IA [*Library symbol Library of Congress*] (LCLS)
IaJoN	Northern Polk County News, Johnston, IA [*Library symbol Library of Congress*] (LCLS)
IAJP	Interamerican Journal of Psychology [*A publication*] (DHP)
IAJRC	International Association of Jazz Record Collectors (EA)
IAJS	International Al Jolson Society (EA)
IAJV	International Association of Justice Volunteerism (EA)
IAJVS	International Association of Jewish Vocational Services (NTPA)
IAK	International Air Cargo Corp. [*Egypt*] [*ICAO designator*] (FAAC)
IAK	Internationales Auschwitz-Komitee [*International Auschwitz Committee*] [*Warsaw, Poland*] (EAIO)
IaK	Keokuk Public Library, Keokuk, IA [*Library symbol Library of Congress*] (LCLS)
IAK	Lake Forest College, Lake Forest, IL [*OCLC symbol*] (OCLC)
IaKaIN	Kalona News, Kalona, IA [*Library symbol Library of Congress*] (LCLS)
IaKan	Kanawha Public Library, Kanawha, IA [*Library symbol Library of Congress*] (LCLS)
IaKanR	Kanawha Reporter, Kanawha, IA [*Library symbol Library of Congress*] (LCLS)
IaKanRL	Rural Life, Kanawha, IA [*Library symbol Library of Congress*] (LCLS)
IAKE	International Association of Knowledge Engineers (EA)
IaKe	Keosauqua Public Library, Keosauqua, IA [*Library symbol Library of Congress*] (LCLS)
IaKen	Kensett Public Library, Kensett, IA [*Library symbol Library of Congress*] (LCLS)
IaKeoE	Keota Eagle, Keota, IA [*Library symbol Library of Congress*] (LCLS)
IaKeVR	Van Buren County Register, Keosauqua, IA [*Library symbol Library of Congress*] (LCLS)
IaKey	Keystone Public Library, Keystone, IA [*Library symbol Library of Congress*] (LCLS)
IAKF	International Amateur Karate Federation (EA)
IaKG	Keokuk Gate City, Keokuk, IA [*Library symbol Library of Congress*] (LCLS)
IaKiN	Kingsley News-Tribune, Kingsley, IA [*Library symbol Library of Congress*] (LCLS)
IaKK	Keosippi Library Cooperative, Keokuk, IA [*Library symbol Library of Congress*] (LCLS)
IaKn	Knoxville Public Library, Knoxville, IA [*Library symbol Library of Congress*] (LCLS)
IaKnE	Knoxville Express, Knoxville, IA [*Library symbol Library of Congress*] (LCLS)
IaKnJ	Knoxville Journal, Knoxville, IA [*Library symbol Library of Congress*] (LCLS)
IaKnV	United States Veterans Administration Hospital, Knoxville, IA [*Library symbol Library of Congress*] (LCLS)
IAKS	Internationaler Arbeitskreis Sport- und Freizeiteninrichtungen [*International Working Group for the Construction of Sports and Leisure Facilities*] (EAIO)
IaKS	Keokuk Savings Bank and Trust Co., Keokuk, IA [*Library symbol*] [*Library of Congress*] (LCLS)
IAL	Immediate Action Letter (NASA)
IAL	Imperial Airways Ltd. [*British*]
IAL	Imperial Art League [*British*] (BI)
IAL	Indian Airlines (PDAA)
IAL	Infrared Aiming Light [*Military*] (INF)
IAL	Inland Airlines
IAL	Installation and Logistics (IAA)
IAL	Instrument Approach and Landing Chart [*Aviation*]
IAL	Interlaminar Adhesive Layer
IAL	International Aeradio Ltd. [*British*]
IAL	International Aeradio PLC [*British ICAO designator*] (FAAC)
IAL	International Affairs (London) [*A publication*]

IAL .... International Algebraic Language [*Programming language*] [*Replaced by ALGOL*]

IAL .... International Algorithmic Language [*Computer science*] (BUR)

IAL .... International Aluminum Corp. [*NYSE symbol*] (SPSG)

IAL .... International Association of Laryngectomees (EA)

IAL .... International Association of Limnology (PDAA)

IAL .... International Association of Linguistics (DIT)

IAL .... International Association of Theoretical and Applied Limnology [*ICSU*] (EA)

IAL .... Intl Aluminum [*NYSE symbol*] (TTSB)

IAL .... Investment Analysis Language [*Computer science*] (BUR)

Ia-L .... Iowa State Law Library, Des Moines, IA [*Library symbol Library of Congress*] (LCLS)

IAL .... Irish Academy of Letters (BI)

IaL .... Lamoni Public Library, Lamoni, IA [*Library symbol Library of Congress*] (LCLS)

IAL .... Loyola University, Chicago, IL [*OCLC symbol*] (OCLC)

IALA .... International African Law Association

IALA .... International Association of Lighthouse Authorities [*Paris, France*] (EA)

IALA .... International Auxiliary Language Association [*Later, UMI*]

IALA .... Islamic Alliance for the Liberation of Afghanistan (PD)

IALACS .... International Association of Latin American and Caribbean Studies (EAIO)

IaLamtL .... Lamont Leader, Lamont, IA [*Library symbol Library of Congress*] (LCLS)

IaLanJ .... Allamakee Journal, Lansing, IA [*Library symbol Library of Congress*] (LCLS)

IaLau .... Laurens Public Library, Laurens, IA [*Library symbol Library of Congress*] (LCLS)

IaLauS .... Laurens Sun, Laurens, IA [*Library symbol Library of Congress*] (LCLS)

IAlb .... Albion Public Library, Albion, IL [*Library symbol Library of Congress*] (LCLS)

IA L Bull ...... Iowa Law Bulletin [*A publication*] (DLA)

IALC .... Instantaneous Automatic Level Control (IDOE)

IALC .... Institute of Allegheny Life and Culture (EA)

IALC .... Instrument Approach and Landing Chart [*Aviation*]

IALC .... International Arid Lands Consortium (EERA)

IALC .... International Association of Lions Clubs

IALC .... International Association of Lyceum Clubs

IALC .... Irish-American Labor Coalition [*Later, ALCHRNI*] (EA)

IALC .... Italian American Librarians Caucus (EA)

IaLC .... Lamoni Chronicle, Lamoni, IA [*Library symbol Library of Congress*] (LCLS)

IaLcG .... Lake City Graphic, Lake City, IA [*Library symbol Library of Congress*] (LCLS)

IALCO .... International Aircraft Leasing Co.

IAlCU .... Alton Community Unit 11, Alton, IL [*Library symbol Library of Congress*] (LCLS)

IALD .... International Association of Lighting Designers (EA)

IAIE .... East Alton Elementary 13, Alton, IL [*Library symbol Library of Congress*] (LCLS)

IALE .... Instrumented Architectural Level Emulation

IALE .... Integral of Absolute Linear Error (IAA)

IALEFI .... International Association of Law Enforcement Firearms Instructors (EA)

IALEIA .... International Association of Law Enforcement Intelligence Analysts (EA)

IaLelS .... Daily Sentinel, Lellars, IA [*Library symbol*] [*Library of Congress*] (LCLS)

IaLem .... Le Mars Public Library, Le Mars, IA [*Library symbol Library of Congress*] (LCLS)

IaLemS .... Daily Sentinel, Le Mars, IA [*Library symbol Library of Congress*] (LCLS)

IaLemW .... Westmar College, Le Mars, IA [*Library symbol Library of Congress*] (LCLS)

IaLeo .... Leon Public Library, Leon, IA [*Library symbol Library of Congress*] (LCLS)

IaLeoJR .... Leon Journal-Reporter, Leon, IA [*Library symbol Library of Congress*] (LCLS)

IaLew .... Lewis Public Library, Lewis, IA [*Library symbol Library of Congress*] (LCLS)

IALF .... Inter-American Literacy Foundation (EA)

IALF .... International Association of Law Firms [*Defunct*] (EA)

IaLG .... Graceland College, Lamoni, IA [*Library symbol Library of Congress*] (LCLS)

IALGPC .... International Association of Lesbian/Gay Pride Coordinators (EA)

IAIH .... Alton Memorial Hospital, Alton, IL [*Library symbol Library of Congress*] (LCLS)

IALHI .... International Association of Labour History Institutions [*Zurich, Switzerland*] (EAIO)

IALL .... International Association for Learning Laboratories (EA)

IALL .... International Association of Law Libraries (EAIO)

IaLL .... Lamoni Public Library, Lamoni, IA [*Library symbol*] [*Library of Congress*] (LCLS)

IALL Bull ..... Bulletin. International Association of Law Libraries [*A publication*] (DLA)

IALM .... Integrated Anchor Leg Mooring [*Naval engineering*]

IALMC .... International Association of Lighting Maintenance Contractors [*Later, NALMCO*] (EA)

IaLmG .... Lake Mills Graphic, Lake Mills, IA [*Library symbol Library of Congress*] (LCLS)

IAIMH .... Alton Mental Health Center, Development and Training Center, Staff Library, Alton, IL [*Library symbol Library of Congress*] (LCLS)

IALMH .... International Academy of Law & Mental Health (AC)

IaLnP .... Lost Nation Press, Lost Nation, IA [*Library symbol Library of Congress*] (LCLS)

IaLoH .... Logan Herald-Observer, Logan, IA [*Library symbol Library of Congress*] (LCLS)

IaLoHi .... Harrison County Historical Society, Logan, IA [*Library symbol Library of Congress*] (LCLS)

IaLohr .... J. J. Hands Library, Lohrville, IA [*Library symbol Library of Congress*] (LCLS)

IaLowS .... Sun News, Lowden, IA [*Library symbol Library of Congress*] (LCLS)

IALP .... International Association of Logopedics and Phoniatrics [*Dublin, Republic of Ireland*] (EA)

IaLpcPR ...... La Porte City Progress-Review, La Porte City, IA [*Library symbol Library of Congress*] (LCLS)

IaLpN .... Lake Park News, Lake Park, IA [*Library symbol Library of Congress*] (LCLS)

IALRW .... International Association of Liberal Religious Women (EA)

IALS .... Institute of Applied Language Studies [*Edith Cowan University*] [*Australia*]

IALS .... International Association of Legal Science [*See also AISJ*] [*Paris, France*] (EAIO)

IAlsA .... Alsip-Merrionette Park Library District, Alsip, IL [*Library symbol Library of Congress*] (LCLS)

IaLsH .... Lime Springs Herald, Lime Springs, IA [*Library symbol Library of Congress*] (LCLS)

IALSSA .... International Air Line Stewards and Stewardesses Association

IAlStA .... Saint Anthony's Hospital, Medical Library, Alton, IL [*Library symbol Library of Congress*] (LCLS)

IAlStJ .... Saint Joseph's Hospital, Medical Information Services, Alton, IL [*Library symbol Library of Congress*] (LCLS)

IAlta .... Altamont Public Library, Altamont, IL [*Library symbol Library of Congress*] (LCLS)

IaLtR .... Lone Tree Reporter, Lone Tree, IA [*Library symbol Library of Congress*] (LCLS)

IaLuHi .... Lucas County Historical Society, Lucas, IA [*Library symbol Library of Congress*] (LCLS)

IaLv .... Lake View Public Library, Lake View, IA [*Library symbol Library of Congress*] (LCLS)

IaLvR .... Lake View Resort, Lake View, IA [*Library symbol Library of Congress*] (LCLS)

IAM .... Altos Hornos de Mexico SA de CV [*NYSE symbol*] (SAG)

IAM .... Anderson Public Library, Anderson, IN [*OCLC symbol*] (OCLC)

IAM .... Ignition Ackowledge Module [*Diesel engine controls*] [*Automotive engineering*]

IAM .... ILA [*Instruction Look Ahead*] Associative Memory [*Computer science*]

IAM .... Image Analyzing Microscope (PDAA)

IAM .... Imagery Analysis Memorandum (MCD)

IAM .... Immobilized Artificial Membranes [*Chemistry*]

IAM .... Impulse Amplitude Modulation (IAA)

IAM .... In Amenas [*Algeria*] [*Airport symbol*] (OAG)

IAM .... Incidental Amplitude Modulation

IAM .... Indefinite Admittance Matrix [*Network analysis*] (IEEE)

IAM .... Information Asset Management (SSD)

IAM .... Initial Address Message (TEL)

IAM .... Innovation Access Method [*Computer science*] (MHDI)

IAM .... Inscriptions Antiques du Maroc (BJA)

IAM .... Institute of Administrative Management [*British*] (DCTA)

IAM .... Institute of Advanced Motorists [*British*]

IAM .... Institute of Appliance Manufacturers [*Later, GAMA*] (EA)

IAM .... Institute of Applied Mathematics [*University of British Columbia*] [*Canada Research center*] (RCD)

IAM .... Institute of Aviation Medicine [*Royal Canadian Air Force*]

IAM .... Institute of the American Musical (EA)

IAM .... Intelligent Actuation & Measurement (ACII)

IAM .... Interactive Algebraic Manipulation [*Computer science*]

IAM .... Interaural Amplitude Modulation [*Audiology*]

IAM .... Intermediate Access Memory (NITA)

IAM .... Internal Acoustic Meatus [*Medicine*] (MAE)

IAM .... Internal Auditory Meatus [*Anatomy*]

IAM .... International Academy of Management [*Knoxville, TN*] (EA)

IAM .... International Academy of Metabology (EA)

IAM .... International Academy of Myodontics (EA)

IAM .... International Academy of Myodontics, Oceanic Chapter [*Sydney, NSW, Australia*] (EAIO)

IAM .... International Afro-American Museum [*Later, AAM*] (EA)

IAM .... International Amco Corp. [*Toronto Stock Exchange symbol*]

IAM .... International Association of Machinists and Aerospace Workers (EA)

IAM .... International Association of Metaphysicians

Ia-M .... Iowa State Medical Library, Des Moines, IA [*Library symbol Library of Congress*] (LCLS)

IAMA .... Incorporated Advertising Managers' Association [*British*] (BI)

IAMA .... Independent Agricultural Merchants' Association [*Australia*]

IAMA .... Informed Americans Monitor (EA)

IAMA .... International Abstaining Motorists' Association [*Hagersten, Sweden*] (EAIO)

IAMA .... International Academy of Myodontics, Asian Chapter [*Tokyo, Japan*] (EAIO)

IAMA .... International Arts Medicine Association [*Philadelphia, PA*]

IAMA .... Intimate Apparel Manufacturers Association (EA)

IaMa .... Marshalltown Public Library, Marshalltown, IA [*Library symbol Library of Congress*] (LCLS)

IAMACS .... International Association for Mathematics and Computers in Simulation

IaMall .... Mallard Public Library, Mallard, IA [*Library symbol Library of Congress*] (LCLS)

IaMalv .... Malvern Public Library, Malvern, IA [*Library symbol Library of Congress*] (LCLS)

IaMalvL .... Malvern Leader, Malvern, IA [*Library symbol Library of Congress*] (LCLS)

IAMAM .... International Association of Museums of Arms and Military History [*Ingolstadt, Federal Republic of Germany*] (EA)

IaMancP ...... Manchester Press, Manchester, IA [*Library symbol Library of Congress*] (LCLS)

Iam & fus .... Laminectomy and Fusion [*Medicine*] (STED)

IAMANEH ..... International Association for Maternal and Neonatal Health [*Zurich, Switzerland*] (EAIO)

IaMannM ...... Manning Monitor, Manning, IA [*Library symbol Library of Congress*] (LCLS)

IaManS .... Marion Sentinel, Marion, IA [*Library symbol Library of Congress*] (LCLS)

IaMansJ .... Manson Journal, Manson, IA [*Library symbol Library of Congress*] (LCLS)

IaManT .... Manilla Times, Manilla, IA [*Library symbol Library of Congress*] (LCLS)

IaManyS ...... Manly Signal, Manly, IA [*Library symbol Library of Congress*] (LCLS)

IAMAP .... International Association of Meteorology and Atmospheric Physics (EA)

IaMap .... Mapleton Public Library, Mapleton, IA [*Library symbol Library of Congress*] (LCLS)

IaMapP .... Mapleton Press, Mapleton, IA [*Library symbol Library of Congress*] (LCLS)

IaMaq .... Maquoketa Free Public Library, Maquoketa, IA [*Library symbol Library of Congress*] (LCLS)

IaMaqHi .... Jackson County Historical Society, Maquoketa, IA [*Library symbol Library of Congress*] (LCLS)

IaMaqP .... Maquoketa Community Press, Maquoketa, IA [*Library symbol Library of Congress*] (LCLS)

IaMaqS .... Jackson Sentinel, Maquoketa, IA [*Library symbol Library of Congress*] (LCLS)

IaMara .... Marathon Public Library, Marathon, IA [*Library symbol Library of Congress*] (LCLS)

IaMarc .... Marcus Public Library, Marcus, IA [*Library symbol Library of Congress*] (LCLS)

IaMare .... Marengo Public Library, Marengo, IA [*Library symbol Library of Congress*] (LCLS)

IaMarePR .... Marengo Pioneer-Republican, Marengo, IA [*Library symbol Library of Congress*] (LCLS)

IaMari .... Marion Carnegie Library, Marion, IA [*Library symbol Library of Congress*] (LCLS)

IAMAS .... International Association of Meteorology and Atmospheric Sciences (EERA)

IAMAT .... International Association for Medical Assistance to Travellers (EA)

IaMaTR .... Marshalltown Times-Republican, Marshalltown, IA [*Library symbol Library of Congress*] (LCLS)

IAMAW .... International Association of Machinists and Aerospace Workers (MCD)

IaMaxHi .... Community Historical Society, Maxwell, IA [*Library symbol Library of Congress*] (LCLS)

IaMay .... Maynard Community Library, Maynard, IA [*Library symbol Library of Congress*] (LCLS)

IaMayr .... Mount Ayr Public Library, Mount Ayr, IA [*Library symbol Library of Congress*] (LCLS)

IaMayrHi ...... Ringgold County Historical Society, Mount Ayr, IA [*Library symbol Library of Congress*] (LCLS)

IaMayrR .... Record-News, Mount Ayr, IA [*Library symbol Library of Congress*] (LCLS)

IAMB .... International Association for the Protection of Monuments and Restoration of Buildings (EAIO)

IAMB .... Irish Association of Master Bakers (BI)

IAMBE .... International Association of Medicine and Biology of Environment [*See also AIMBE*] [*Paris, France*] (EAIO)

IAMBI .... Iambic Verse (DSUE)

IaMbr .... Marble Rock Public Library, Marble Rock, IA [*Library symbol Library of Congress*] (LCLS)

IAMC .... Indian Army Medical Corps

IAMC .... Institute for Advancement of Medical Communication [*Defunct*] (EA)

IAMC .... Institute of Association Management Companies (EA)

IAMC .... Inter-American Markets Corp. [*Latin America*]

IAMC .... Inter-American Music Council (EAIO)

IAMC .... International Association for Mobilization of Creativity

IaMc .... Mason City Public Library, Mason City, IA [*Library symbol Library of Congress*] (LCLS)

IAMCA .... International Association of Milk Control Agencies (EA)

IaMcG .... Mason City Globe-Gazette, Mason City, IA [*Library symbol Library of Congress*] (LCLS)

IaMcg .... McGregor Public Library, McGregor, IA [*Library symbol Library of Congress*] (LCLS)

IaMcGG .... Mason City Globe-Gazette, Mason City, IA [*Library symbol*] [*Library of Congress*] (LCLS)

IaMcgHi .... McGregor Historical Society, McGregor, IA [*Library symbol Library of Congress*] (LCLS)

IaMcgN .... North Iowa Times, McGregor, IA [*Library symbol Library of Congress*] (LCLS)

IaMcN .... North Iowa Cooperative Library Extension, Mason City, IA [*Library symbol Library of Congress*] (LCLS)

IaMcNC .... North Iowa Area Community College, Mason City, IA [*Library symbol Library of Congress*] (LCLS)

IAMCR .... International Association for Mass Communication Research [*British*]

IAMCS .... International Alliance of Messianic Congregations and Synagogues (EA)

IAME .... International Association for Modular Exhibitry (EA)

IAME .... International Association of Medical Esperantists (EA)

IaMedi .... Mediapolis Public Library, Mediapolis, IA [*Library symbol Library of Congress*] (LCLS)

IaMediN .... New Era, Mediapolis, IA [*Library symbol Library of Congress*] (LCLS)

IaMel .... Melvin Public Library, Melvin, IA [*Library symbol Library of Congress*] (LCLS)

IaMelbR .... Melbourne Record, Melbourne, IA [*Library symbol Library of Congress*] (LCLS)

IaMer .... Merrill Public Library, Merrill, IA [*Library symbol Library of Congress*] (LCLS)

IAMFC .... International Association for Marriage and Family Counselors (EA)

IAMFE .... International Association on Mechanization of Field Experiments [*Aas, Norway*] (EA)

IAMFES .... International Association of Milk, Food, and Environmental Sanitarians (EA)

IAMFPA .... International Association of Mouth and Foot Painting Artists (EA)

IAMFS .... International Association for Maxillo-Facial Surgery (EA)

IAMG .... International Association for Mathematical Geology (EA)

IAMHIST ...... International Association of Audio-Visual Media in Historical Research and Education [*Bologna, Italy*] (EAIO)

IAMIC .... International Association of Music Information Centres (TELE)

IAMIC .... International Association of Mutual Insurance Companies [*See also AISAM*] (EAIO)

IaMidaHA .... Amana Heritage Society, Middle Amana, IA [*Library symbol*] [*Library of Congress*] (LCLS)

IaMil .... Milo Public Library, Milo, IA [*Library symbol Library of Congress*] (LCLS)

IaMilf .... Milford Memorial Library, Milford, IA [*Library symbol Library of Congress*] (LCLS)

IaMilfM .... Milford Mail, Milford, IA [*Library symbol Library of Congress*] (LCLS)

IaMilfN .... Milford News, Milford, IA [*Library symbol Library of Congress*] (LCLS)

IaMisv .... Missouri Valley Public Library, Missouri Valley, IA [*Library symbol Library of Congress*] (LCLS)

IaMisvTN ..... Missouri Valley Times-News, Missouri Valley, IA [*Library symbol Library of Congress*] (LCLS)

IAML .... International Association of Music Libraries (NITA)

IAML .... International Association of Music Libraries, Archives, and Documentation Centers (EA)

IAMLADP .... Inter-Agency Meeting on Language Arrangements, Documentation, and Publications [*United Nations*]

IAMLO .... International African Migratory Locust Organization [*See also OICMA*] (EA)

IAMLT .... International Association of Medical Laboratory Technologists [*Bootle, Merseyside, England*] (EA)

IAML-US ...... International Association of Music Libraries, United States Branch (NTPA)

IAMM .... International Association of Medical Museums [*Later, IAP*]

IAMMA .... Institute of Agricultural Market Management & Administration [*India*]

IAMM & D ... Institute for Advanced Materials, Mechanics, and Design [*Army Materiel Command*]

IAMMM .... International Association of Margaret Morris Method [*Glasgow, Scotland*] (EAIO)

IAMN .... Istanbul Asariatica Muzeleri Nesriyati (BJA)

i amniot .... Intra-Amniotic [*Medicine*] (AAMN)

IaMonM .... Monroe Mirror, Monroe, IA [*Library symbol Library of Congress*] (LCLS)

IaMono .... Murphy Memorial Library, Monona, IA [*Library symbol Library of Congress*] (LCLS)

IaMonoB ...... Monona Billboard, Monona, IA [*Library symbol Library of Congress*] (LCLS)

IaMonoHi ..... Monona Historical Society, Monona, IA [*Library symbol Library of Congress*] (LCLS)

IaMont .... Monticello Public Library, Monticello, IA [*Library symbol Library of Congress*] (LCLS)

IaMontE .... Monticello Express, Monticello, IA [*Library symbol Library of Congress*] (LCLS)

IaMonteR ..... Montezuma Republican, Montezuma, IA [*Library symbol Library of Congress*] (LCLS)

IaMontHi ...... Jones County Historical Society, Monticello, IA [*Library symbol*] [*Library of Congress*] (LCLS)

IaMontJHi .... Jones County Historical Society, Monticello, IA [*Library symbol Library of Congress*] (LCLS)

IaMoraU ...... Moravia Union, Moravia, IA [*Library symbol Library of Congress*] (LCLS)

IaMorn .... Mellinger Memorial Library, Morning Sun, IA [*Library symbol Library of Congress*] (LCLS)

IaMornN ...... Morning Sun News-Herald, Morning Sun, IA [*Library symbol Library of Congress*] (LCLS)

IaMou .... Garrett Memorial Library, Moulton, IA [*Library symbol Library of Congress*] (LCLS)

IaMouT .... Moulton Weekly Tribune, Moulton, IA [*Library symbol Library of Congress*] (LCLS)

IAMP .... Imagery Acquisition and Management Plan

IAMP .... Inter-Agency Motor Pool (WDAA)

IAMP .... International Academy of Medicine and Psychology [*Australia*] (EA)

IAMP .... International Association of Mathematical Physics (EA)

IAMP .... International Association of Meat Processors (EA)

IAMP .... International Association of Mercury Producers [*Spain, Italy, Turkey, Yugoslavia, Peru, Algeria*]

IaMp .... Mount Pleasant Public Library, Mount Pleasant, IA [*Library symbol Library of Congress*] (LCLS)

IaMpl........... Iowa Wesleyan College, Mount Pleasant, IA [*Library symbol Library of Congress*] (LCLS)

IaMpN.......... Mount Pleasant News, Mount Pleasant, IA [*Library symbol Library of Congress*] (LCLS)

IAMPTH .... International Association of Master Penmen and Teachers of Handwriting (EA)

IAMR .... Institute of Arctic Mineral Resources [*University of Alaska*]

IAMR .... International Association for Medical Research and Cultural Exchange

IAMRC .... International Antarctic Meteorological Research Center (PDAA)

IAMRC .... International Antarctic Meteorological Research Centre (PDAA)

IAMS........... Individual Aerial Mobility System [*Military*] (MCD)

IAMS........... Initial Attack Management System [*Weather system*]

IAMS........... Instantaneous Audience Measurement System

IAMS........... Institute for Archaeo-Metallurgical Studies [*British*] (IRUK)

IAMS........... Institute of Advanced Manufacturing Sciences [*University of Cincinnati*]

IAMS........... Institute of Advanced Marketing Studies - American Marketing Association (EA)

IAMS........... Institute of Applied Mathematics and Statistics [*University of British Columbia*] [*Research center*] (RCD)

IAMS........... International Advanced Microlithography Society [*Defunct*] (EA)

IAMS........... International Association for Mission Studies [*Hamburg, Federal Republic of Germany*] (EAIO)

IAMS........... International Association of Microbiological Societies [*ICSU*] [*Later, IUMS*]

IAMS........... International Association of Municipal Statisticians [*Later, IARUS*]

IAMSLIC ...... International Association of Aquatic and Marine Science Libraries & Information Centers [*Marine science*] (OSRA)

IAMSLIC ...... International Association of Marine Science Libraries and Information Centers (EA)

IAMSO .... Inter-African and Malagasy States Organization (NATG)

IAMT........... International Association for Machine Translation

IAMTACT...... Institute of Advanced Machine Tool and Control Technology [*British*]

IAMTCT....... Institute of Advanced Machine Tool and Control Technology (MCD)

IAM/TMD ..... Institute of Administrative Management / Telecommunications Managers Division (HGAA)

IAMTS .... International Association of Model and Talent Scouts (EAIO)

IaMu .... P. M. Musser Public Library, Muscatine, IA [*Library symbol Library of Congress*] (LCLS)

IaMuJ .... Muscatine Journal, Muscatine, IA [*Library symbol Library of Congress*] (LCLS)

IAMUS .... Installation Automated Manpower Utilization System [*Army*]

IaMvC .... Cornell College, Mount Vernon, IA [*Library symbol Library of Congress*] (LCLS)

IaMvCor....... Cornellian, Mount Vernon, IA [*Library symbol Library of Congress*] (LCLS)

IaMvH .... Hawkeye and Libson Herald, Mount Vernon, IA [*Library symbol Library of Congress*] (LCLS)

IaMvS .... Sun Hawkeye Record, Mount Vernon, IA [*Library symbol Library of Congress*] (LCLS)

IAMW........... Improved Antimateriel Warhead

IAMWH .... Improved Antimateriel Warhead

IAMWMW .... International Association of Ministers' Wives and Ministers' Widows (EAIO)

IAN............... Compania Internadia de Aviacion [*Colombia*] [*ICAO designator*] (FAAC)

IAN............... Idiopathic Aseptic Necrosis [*Medicine*] (DMAA)

IAN............... Illustrated Australian News [*A publication*]

IAN............... Imagery Analysis Notice (MCD)

IAN............... Indoleacetonitrile (LDT)

IAN............... Informatsionnoye Agentstvo Novosti [*Novosti Press Agency*] [*Russian Federation*]

IAN............... Interim Admission Note [*Medical records*] (DAVI)

IAN............... Intern Admission Note [*Medical records*] (DAVI)

IAN............... International Artist Network (EA)

IAN............... Internationale des Amis de la Nature [*International Federation of Friends of Nature*]

IAN............... Kennedy-King College of the City College of Chicago, Chicago, IL [*OCLC symbol*] (OCLC)

IAN............... Kiana [*Alaska*] [*Airport symbol*] (OAG)

IANA .... Intermodal Association of North America

IANA .... International Alliance of Nutrimedical Associations (EA)

IANA .... Internet Address Naming Authority [*Computer science*] (ACRL)

IANA .... Internet Assigned Numbers Authority

IANAD.......... I Am Not a Doctor [*Internet*]

IANAL .... I Am Not a Lawyer [*Internet*]

IANAP.......... Interagency Noise Abatement Program

IaNas........... Nashua Public Library, Nashua, IA [*Library symbol Library of Congress*] (LCLS)

IaNasCHi ..... Chickasaw County Historical Society, Nashua, IA [*Library symbol*] [*Library of Congress*] (LCLS)

IaNasPN ..... Plainfield News, Nashua, IA [*Library symbol Library of Congress*] (LCLS)

IaNasR......... Nashua Reporter, Nashua, IA [*Library symbol Library of Congress*] (LCLS)

IANC .... International Academy of Nutritional Consultants [*AANC*] [*Absorbed by*] (EA)

IANC .... International Airline Navigators Council [*Defunct*]

IANC .... International Air Navigation Convention

IANC .... International Anatomical Nomenclature Committee [*British*] (EAIO)

IANC .... Invest-in-America National Council [*Later, RA*] (EA)

IANCA......... Interamerican Naval Coordinating Authority (CINC)

IAND .... International Association of Nitrox Divers

I & A........... Indexing and Abstracting (NITA)

I & A........... Information and Action (MUGU)

I & A........... Inspection and Acceptance

I & A........... Irrigation and Aspiration [*Ophthalmology*] (DAVI)

I & B........... Improvement and Betterments [*Real estate*]

I & C........... Impact and Capabilities [*Study*] [*DoD*]

I & C........... Incision and Curettage [*Medicine*] (CPH)

I & C........... Information and Coordination (ADA)

I & C........... Inspected and Condemned [*Military*] (AAG)

I & C........... Installation and Calibration (SAA)

I & C........... Installation and Checkout [*Military*] (AFM)

I & C........... Installation and Construction [*Military*]

I & C........... Instrument and Controls

I and C .... Instrumentation and Communication

I & C........... Instrumentation and Communications [*Cable system*] (KSC)

I & C........... Instrumentation and Control [*Aerospace*] (AAG)

I & C........... Integration and Checkout (KSC)

I & C........... Issues and Criteria

I & C in Scot... Instrumentation and Control in Scotland [*A publication*]

I & C/O ...... Installation and Checkout (NASA)

I & CRB ...... Investigation and Censure Review Branch [*BUPERS*]

I & C(S)...... Instrumentation and Communication (System)

I & D .... Incision and Drainage [*Medicine*]

I and D .... Information and Documentation (NITA)

I & D .... Initiation and Development

I & D .... Install and Dismantle [*Expositions and exhibitions*]

I & D .... Integrate and Dump Detection [*Telecommunications*] (TEL)

I & D .... Irrigation and Debridement [*Surgery*] (DAVI)

I & D .... Irrigation and Drainage [*Surgery*] (DAVI)

i&e............... Identification and Exposition [*Also, ident-and-expo*] (WDMC)

I & E .... Industrial and Entertainment Funds [*Correctional institutions*]

I & E .... Information and Editorial [*Career program*]

I & E .... Information and Education [*Military*]

I & E .... Innovation and Entrepreneurship

I & E .... Intake and Exhaust [*Automotive engineering*]

I & E .... Internally and Externally (NRCH)

I & H .... Information and Historical [*Military*]

I&I............... Illness and Injuries (DMAA)

I & I........... Industrial and Institutional [*Business term*]

I & I........... Infiltration and Inflow [*Environmental science*] (FFDE)

I & I........... Insolence and Insubordination [*Military*] (MUSM)

I&I............... Insolence and Insubordination [*Military*] (MUSM)

I & I........... Inspector and Instructor [*For reserve units*] [*Marine Corps*] (DOMA)

I & I........... Intelligence and Interdiction [*Military*] (VNW)

I & I........... Intoxication and Intercourse

I & IA........... Interior and Insular Affairs

I & KP .... Initial and Key Personnel

I & L........... Installations and Logistics

I & M........... Improvement and Modernization (AABC)

I & M........... Inspection and Maintenance

I&M............. Inspection and Maintenance [*Environmental science*] (COE)

I & M........... Installation and Maintenance

I & MA........ Inventory and Management Analysis (AFM)

I & N .... Immigration and Nationality Laws Administrative Decisions [*Department of Justice*] [*A publication*] (DLA)

I & N .... Immigration and Naturalization [*Service*] [*Department of Justice*]

I & N Dec .... Immigration and Nationality Laws Administrative Decisions [*A publication*] (DLA)

I & O .... In and Out (MAE)

I & O .... Inlet and Outlet (MSA)

I & O .... Intake and Output [*Medicine*]

I & O .... Issues & Observations [*A publication*] (EAAP)

I & OH .... Inlet and Outlet Head (MSA)

I & OM .... Intermediate and Organizational Maintenance (MCD)

I & OP .... In and Out Processing [*Computer science*] (AFM)

I & P........... Indexed and Paged

I & P........... Inerting and Preheating [*Nuclear energy*] (NRCH)

I & R .... Information and Referral [*Services*] [*Used to assist the handicapped*]

I & R .... Initiative and Referendum

I&R............. Insertion and Removal [*Medicine*] (STED)

I & R .... Instruction and Research [*Individually-guided education*] (AEE)

I & R .... Integrity and Reliability [*Military*] (AFIT)

I & R .... Intelligence and Reconnaissance

I & R .... Interchangeability and Replaceability [*or Replacement*] (AAG)

I & RS .... Instrumentation and Range Safety [*NASA*] (KSC)

I&S .... Industries & Science Department (ACII)

I & S .... Inspection and Security

I & S .... Installation and Services

I & S........... Interchangeability and Substitutability (AFM)

IANDS......... International Association for Near-Death Studies [*See also AEEPM*] (EA)

I & S .... Investigation and Suspension

I & S........... Iron and Steel

I & SE .... Installation and Service Engineering (IEEE)

I & SM........ Iron & Steelmaker [*A publication*] (EAAP)

I & SSFR ..... Investigation and Security Service Field Representative [*Veterans Administration*]

I & T........... Inspection and Test (NRCH)

I & T........... Installation and Test [*Army*] (AABC)

I & T........... Integration and Test

I&T............. Internal Thoracic Artery [*Medicine*] (DMAA)

I&T............. Intolerance and Toxicity [*Medicine*] (DMAA)

I & T(P) ...... Inspection and Test (Planning) (MCD)

I & TT........ Ike and Tina Turner [*Singers*]

I&V............. Infection and Vaccinology

I&W .... Indication and Warning [*Environmental science*] (COE)

I&W .... Indications and Warning [*Military*] (MUSM)

IANEC .... Inter-American Nuclear Energy Commission [*Organization of American States*] (NRCH)

IaNeoG .... Gazette Reporter and Minden-Shelby News, Neloa, IA [*Library symbol Library of Congress*] (LCLS)

IANET .... Integrated Access Network [*Computer science*] (MHDB)

IaNev .... Nevada Public Library, Nevada, IA [*Library symbol Library of Congress*] (LCLS)

IaNevJ .... Nevada Evening Journal, Nevada, IA [*Library symbol Library of Congress*] (LCLS)

IaNewM .... Newell Mirror, Newell, IA [*Library symbol Library of Congress*] (LCLS)

IaNewt .... Newton Public Library, Newton, IA [*Library symbol Library of Congress*] (LCLS)

IaNewtCoC... Jasper County Courthouse, Newton, IA [*Library symbol Library of Congress*] (LCLS)

IaNewtHi...... Newton Historical Society, Newton, IA [*Library symbol Library of Congress*] (LCLS)

IaNewtJC .... Jasper County Courthouse, Newton, IA [*Library symbol*] [*Library of Congress*] (LCLS)

IaNewtN .... Newton Daily News, Newton, IA [*Library symbol Library of Congress*] (LCLS)

IANF............. Individual Account Number File [*IRS*]

IANF............. Inter-Allied Nuclear Force (AABC)

IaNhE........... New Hampton Economist, New Hampton, IA [*Library symbol Library of Congress*] (LCLS)

IaNhT........... New Hampton Tribune, New Hampton, IA [*Library symbol*] [*Library of Congress*] (LCLS)

IANI .... Intelligent Access to Nordic Information (TELE)

IaNl.............. H. J. Nugen Public Library, New London, IA [*Library symbol Library of Congress*] (LCLS)

IaNlJ .... New London Journal, New London, IA [*Library symbol Library of Congress*] (LCLS)

IA/NLP .... International Association for Neuro-Linguistic Programming (EAIO)

IANLP .... International Association of Neuro-Linguistic Programming (EA)

IANLS .... International Association for Neo-Latin Studies [*St. Andrews, Scotland*] (EAIO)

IaNm .... New Market Public Library, New Market, IA [*Library symbol Library of Congress*] (LCLS)

IaNmM......... New Market Monitor, New Market, IA [*Library symbol Library of Congress*] (LCLS)

IaNoengR .... North English Record, North English, IA [*Library symbol Library of Congress*] (LCLS)

IaNosA......... Nora Springs Advertiser, Nora Springs, IA [*Library symbol Library of Congress*] (LCLS)

IaNowdA ...... Northwood Anchor, Northwood, IA [*Library symbol Library of Congress*] (LCLS)

IaNowdCoC.. Worth County Courthouse, Northwood, IA [*Library symbol Library of Congress*] (LCLS)

IaNowdWC... Worth County Courthouse, Northwood, IA [*Library symbol*] [*Library of Congress*] (LCLS)

IaNowkN ...... North Warren Town and County News, Norwalk, IA [*Library symbol Library of Congress*] (LCLS)

IANPE .... Institute for the Advancement of Notary Public Education (EA)

IANPM .... International Academy of Nutrition and Preventive Medicine (EA)

IANRP.......... International Association of Natural Resource Pilots (EA)

IANS .... Institute of Applied Natural Science (EA)

IaNsS........... New Sharon Star, New Sharon, IA [*Library symbol*] [*Library of Congress*] (LCLS)

IANSW......... Ileostomy Association of New South Wales [*Australia*]

IANTD .... International Association of Nitrox and Technical Divers

IANTN .... Inter-American Naval Telecommunications Network (MCD)

IANU .... Italo American National Union (EA)

IaNv............. New Virginia Public Library, New Virginia, IA [*Library symbol Library of Congress*] (LCLS)

IaNvN .... New Virginian, New Virginia, IA [*Library symbol Library of Congress*] (LCLS)

IANVOCC...... International Association of Non-Vessel Operating Common Carriers (NTPA)

IANVS .... International Association for Non-Violent Sport [*See also AICVS*] [*Monte Carlo, Monaco*] (EAIO)

IAO............... Immediately after Onset [*Medicine*]

IAO............... In and Out of Clouds [*ICAO*] (FAAC)

IAO............... Incorporated Association of Organists [*British*]

IAO............... Independent Aviation Operators

IAO............... Information Activities Office [*or Officer*]

IAO............... Institute of Ambulance Officers [*Australia*]

IAO............... Institute of Apostolic Oblates (EA)

IAO............... Insurers' Advisory Organization of Canada

IAO............... Intermittent Aortic Occlusion [*Cardiology*]

IAO............... Internal Automation Operation

IAO............... International Association of Orthodontics (EA)

IAO............... Northeastern Illinois University, Chicago, IL [*OCLC symbol*] (OCLC)

IAOA .... Indicated Angle-of-Attack (GAVI)

IAOAD.......... International Association of Original Art Diffusors (EAIO)

IaOak.......... Eckels Memorial Library, Oakland, IA [*Library symbol Library of Congress*] (LCLS)

IaOakA......... Oakland Acorn, Oakland, IA [*Library symbol Library of Congress*] (LCLS)

IAOC .... Indian Army Ordnance Control [*British*]

IAOC .... Irish Amateur Open Championship [*Golf*] (ROG)

IaOcD.......... Democrat, Orange City, IA [*Library symbol Library of Congress*] (LCLS)

IaOch.......... Ocheyedan Public Library, Ocheyedan, IA [*Library symbol Library of Congress*] (LCLS)

IaOchMH..... Melvin News, Ocheyedan, IA [*Library symbol Library of Congress*] (LCLS)

IaOchMN..... Melvin News, Ocheyedan, IA [*Library symbol*] [*Library of Congress*] (LCLS)

IaOchP......... Ocheyedan Press, Ocheyedan, IA [*Library symbol Library of Congress*] (LCLS)

IaOcM .... Mid-America Reformed Seminary, Orange City, IA [*Library symbol*] [*Library of Congress*] (LCLS)

IaOcN.......... Northwestern College, Orange City, IA [*Library symbol Library of Congress*] (LCLS)

IaOcSC........ Sioux County Capital, Orange City, IA [*Library symbol Library of Congress*] (LCLS)

IAOD .... In Addition to Other Duties [*Military*]

IAOD .... International Academy of Optimum Dentistry [*Defunct*] (EA)

IAOD .... International Association of Opera Directors (EAIO)

IaOdC.......... Odebolt Chronicle, Odebolt, IA [*Library symbol Library of Congress*] (LCLS)

IAOE............ International Association of Optometric Executives (EA)

IaOe............ Oelwein Public Library, Oelwein, IA [*Library symbol Library of Congress*] (LCLS)

IaOeR .... Daily Register, Oelwein, IA [*Library symbol Library of Congress*] (LCLS)

IaOgd .... Ogden Public Library, Ogden, IA [*Library symbol Library of Congress*] (LCLS)

IaOgdR .... Ogden Reporter, Ogden, IA [*Library symbol Library of Congress*] (LCLS)

IAOH .... In Appreciation of the Hollies (EA)

IAOHRA....... International Association of Official Human Rights Agencies (EA)

IAOL............ International Association of Orientalist Librarians (EA)

IAOM .... International Association of Oral Myology (DMAA)

IAOMO .... International Association of Olympic Medical Officers [*Rugby, Warwickshire, England*] (EAIO)

IAOMS .... International Association of Oral and Maxillofacial Surgeons (EA)

IAOMT .... International Academy of Oral Medicine and Toxicology

IaOn .... Onawa Public Library, Onawa, IA [*Library symbol Library of Congress*] (LCLS)

IaOnCoC ..... Monona County Courthouse, Onawa, IA [*Library symbol Library of Congress*] (LCLS)

IaOnD .... Onawa Democrat, Onawa, IA [*Library symbol Library of Congress*] (LCLS)

IaOnS........... Onawa Sentinel, Onawa IA [*Library symbol Library of Congress*] (LCLS)

IAOO .... Irish Agricultural Officers Organisation (BI)

IAOP .... International Association of Oral Pathologists (EA)

IAOPA .... International Council of Aircraft Owner and Pilot Associations (EA)

IAOPS .... Indiana Association of Osteopathic Physicians and Surgeons (SRA)

IaOrM .... Mid-American Reformed Seminary, Orange City, IA [*Library symbol Library of Congress*] (LCLS)

IAOS .... International Association for Official Statistics [*International Statistical Institute*] [*Voorburg, Netherlands*] (EAIO)

IAOS .... International Association of Ocular Surgeons (EA)

IAOS .... International Association of Oral Surgeons (EAIO)

IAOS .... Irish Agricultural Organisation Society Ltd. (BI)

IaOsa .... Sage Library, Osage, IA [*Library symbol Library of Congress*] (LCLS)

IaOsaCoC.... Mitchell County Courthouse, Osage, IA [*Library symbol Library of Congress*] (LCLS)

IaOsaP......... Mitchell County Press-News, Osage, IA [*Library symbol Library of Congress*] (LCLS)

IaOsc .... Osceola Public Library, Osceola, IA [*Library symbol Library of Congress*] (LCLS)

IaOscCoC.... Clarke County Courthouse, Osceola, IA [*Library symbol*] [*Library of Congress*] (LCLS)

IaOscS .... Osceola Sentinel, Osceola, IA [*Library symbol Library of Congress*] (LCLS)

IaOsk .... Oskaloosa Public Library, Oskaloosa, IA [*Library symbol Library of Congress*] (LCLS)

IaOskH........ Oskaloosa Daily Herald, Oskaloosa, IA [*Library symbol Library of Congress*] (LCLS)

IaOskMHi.... Mahaska County Historical Society, Oskaloosa, IA [*Library symbol Library of Congress*] (LCLS)

IaOskW........ William Penn College, Oskaloosa, IA [*Library symbol Library of Congress*] (LCLS)

IaOss ....,. Ossian Public Library, Ossian, IA [*Library symbol Library of Congress*] (LCLS)

IaOssB......... Ossian Bee, Ossian, IA [*Library symbol Library of Congress*] (LCLS)

IAOT............ International Association for Oxygen Therapy

IAOT............ International Association of Organ Teachers USA [*Later, KTA*] (EA)

IaOt............. Ottumwa Public Library, Ottumwa, IA [*Library symbol Library of Congress*] (LCLS)

IaOtC .... Ottumwa Heights College, Ottumwa, IA [*Library symbol Library of Congress*] (LCLS)

IaOtCo .... Ottumwa Courier, Ottumwa, IA [*Library symbol Library of Congress*] (LCLS)

IaOtS .... Southern Iowa Library Cooperative, Ottumwa, IA [*Library symbol Library of Congress*] (LCLS)

IaOxj............ Wreigie Memorial Library, Oxford Junction, IA [*Library symbol Library of Congress*] (LCLS)

IAP............... Image Array Processor

IAP............... Imaging Atom Probe (AAEL)

IAP............... Imitation Art Paper (DGA)

IAP............... Immunosuppressive Acidic Protein [*Immunochemistry*] (DMAA)

IAP............... Improved Accuracy Program (MCD)

IAP............... Incentive Awards Program [*of the federal government, administered by CSC*]

IAP............... Indoor Air Pollution

IAP.............. Industry Applications Programs [*Computer science*] (IBMDP)
IAP.............. Inerting and Preheating (IAA)
IAP.............. Inhibitor of Apoptosis Protein [*Cytology*]
IAP.............. Initial Aiming Point [*Gunnery*]
IAP.............. Initial Approach [*Aviation*]
IAP.............. Initial Approved Program
IAP.............. Inlet Absolute Pressure
IAP.............. Inorganic Ablative Plastic
IAP.............. Inosinic Acid Pyrophosphorylase (DB)
IAP.............. Institute of Animal Physiology [*British*]
IAP.............. Institute of Arthropodology and Parasitology [*Georgia Southern University*] [*Research center*] (RCD)
IAP.............. Institute of Atmospheric Physics [*University of Arizona*] [*Research center*]
IAP.............. Institution of Analysis and Programmers (WDAA)
IAP.............. Instrument Approach Procedure [*Aviation*] (AFM)
IAP.............. Insurance Accounting Principles
IAP.............. Integrated Action Plan
IAP.............. Integrated Aeronautic Program [*Military*] (AFIT)
IAP.............. Interactive Programming [*Computer science*]
IAP.............. Interarray Processor (NVT)
IAP.............. Interceptor Aim Points
IAP.............. Intermittent Acute Porphyria [*Medicine*]
IAP.............. Internal Air Portability
IAP.............. Internal Array Processor [*Data General Corp.*]
IAP.............. International Academy of Pathology (EA)
IAP.............. International Academy of Proctology [*Defunct*] (EA)
IAP.............. International Activities Program [*US Army Western Command*]
IAP.............. International Aero Press
IAP.............. International Airport
IAP.............. International Association of Parapsychologists (EA)
IAP.............. International Association of Photoplatemakers (EA)
IAP.............. International Association of Planetology [*Brussels, Belgium*] (EA)
IAP.............. International Association of Pteridologists (EERA)
IAP.............. Intra-Abdominal Pressure
IAP.............. Intra-Arterial Pressure
IAP.............. Intracisternal A-Particle [*Biochemistry*]
IAP.............. Iodoantipyrine [*Biochemistry*]
IAP.............. Iona Appliances, Inc. [*Toronto Stock Exchange symbol*]
IAP.............. Iranian Aircraft Program [*Military*] (MCD)
IAP.............. Islet-Activating Protein [*Biochemistry*]
IAP.............. Isopropylantipyrine [*Biochemistry*]
IAP.............. Oakton Community College, Morton Grove, IL [*OCLC symbol*] (OCLC)
IAP.............. Portland, OR [*Location identifier FAA*] (FAAL)
IAPA............ Idaho Association of Public Accountants (SRA)
IAPA............ Illinois Academy of Physician Assistants (SRA)
IAPA............ Illinois Asphalt Pavement Association (SRA)
IAPA............ Industrial Accident Prevention Association [*Canada*] (HGAA)
IAPA............ Instrument Approach Procedures Automation [*FAA*] (TAG)
IAPA............ Inter-American Police Academy (AABC)
IAPA............ Inter-American Press Association (EA)
IAPA............ International Airline Passengers Association (EA)
IAPA............ International Association of Physicians in Audiology (EAIO)
IAPAC.......... Injection Assistee par Air Comprise [*Pneumatic Direct Fuel Injection*] [*French*]
IAPAC.......... International Association of Physicians in AIDS Care (EA)
IaPal........... Palmer Public Library, Palmer, IA [*Library symbol Library of Congress*] (LCLS)
IaPanV........ Guthrie County Vedette, Panora, IA [*Library symbol Library of Congress*] (LCLS)
IaParE......... Eclipse-News-Review, Parkersburg, IA [*Library symbol Library of Congress*] (LCLS)
IaParnHi...... Iowa County Historical Society, Parnell, IA [*Library symbol Library of Congress*] (LCLS)
IAPA/SIP..... Inter American Press Association (NTPA)
IaPau.......... Paullina Free Public Library, Paullina, IA [*Library symbol Library of Congress*] (LCLS)
IaPauT........ Paullina Times, Paullina, IA [*Library symbol Library of Congress*] (LCLS)
IAPB........... Inter-Allied Personnel Board [*World War II*]
IAPB........... International Agency for the Prevention of Blindness (EA)
IAPB........... International Association for the Prevention of Blindness [*Later, InternationalAgency for the Prevention of Blindness*] (EA)
IAPBPPV..... International Association of Plant Breeders for the Protection of Plant Varieties (EAIO)
IAPBT......... International Association of Piano Builders and Technicians (EA)
IAPC........... Institute for the Advancement of Philosophy for Children (EA)
IAPC........... Instrument Approach Procedure Chart [*Aviation*] (NOAA)
IAPC........... Inter-American Peace Committee [*Later, Inter-American Committee on Peacef ul Settlement*] [*OAS*]
IAPC........... International Association for Pollution Control [*Defunct*] (EA)
IAPC........... International Association of Pet Cemeteries (EA)
IAPC........... International Association of Political Consultants (EA)
IAPC........... International Auditing Practices Committee
IaPcN......... Prairie City News, Prairie City, IA [*Library symbol Library of Congress*] (LCLS)
IAPCO........ International Association of Professional Congress Organizers [*Brussels, Belgium*] (EAIO)
IAPD .... International Association of Paediatric Dentistry [*British*] (EAIO)
IAPD .... International Association of Parents of the Deaf [*Later, ASDC*] (EA)
IAPD .... International Association of Plastics Distributors (NTPA)
IAPE .... Independent Association of Publishers' Employees (EA)
IaPe .... Pella Public Library, Pella, IA [*Library symbol Library of Congress*] (LCLS)

IaPeC........... Central College, Pella, IA [*Library symbol Library of Congress*] (LCLS)
IaPeCh......... Pella Chronicle, Pella, IA [*Library symbol Library of Congress*] (LCLS)
IaPeCR .... Central Ray, Pella, IA [*Library symbol Library of Congress*] (LCLS)
IaPerC .... Chief, Perry, IA [*Library symbol Library of Congress*] (LCLS)
IaPersHi ..... Harrison County Historical Society, Persia, IA [*Library symbol Library of Congress*] (LCLS)
IAPES.......... International Association of Personnel in Employment Security (EA)
IAPESGW .... International Association of Physical Education and Sport for Girls and Women (EA)
IaPet........... Kirchner-French Memorial Library, Peterson, IA [*Library symbol Library of Congress*] (LCLS)
IaPetP......... Peterson Patriot, Peterson, IA [*Library symbol Library of Congress*] (LCLS)
IAPF............ Inter-American Peacekeeping Force
IAPG........... Iberian Atlantic Planning Guidance (NATG)
IAPG........... Interagency Advanced Power Group
IAPG........... Interagency Arctic Policy Group [*Marine science*] (OSRA)
IAPG........... Inter-American Parliamentary Group on Population and Development [*An association*] (EA)
IAPG........... International Association of Physical Geography (BARN)
IAPG........... International Association of Psychoanalytic Gerontology [*Paris, France*] (EAIO)
IAPG........... Item Analysis Program, General (PDAA)
IAPGPD....... Inter-American Parliamentary Group on Population and Development (EA)
IAPGR........ Institute of Animal Physiology and Genetics Research [*Research center British*] (IRC)
IAPH .... International Association of Paper Historians (DGA)
IAPH .... International Association of Ports and Harbors [*Japan*]
IAPHC......... International Association of Printing House Craftsmen (EA)
IAPI............ Industrial Air Pollution Inspectorate (PDAA)
IAPI............ Institute of Advertising Practitioners in Ireland (BI)
IAPI............ Institute of American Poultry Industries [*Later, PEIA*] (EA)
IaPierP........ Pierson Press, Pierson, IA [*Library symbol Library of Congress*] (LCLS)
IAPIP.......... International Association for the Protection of Industrial Property
IAPL........... Initial Allowance Parts List [*Military*] (CAAL)
IAPL........... International Association for Philosophy and Literature (EA)
IAPL........... International Association of Penal Law [*Freiburg, Federal Republic of Germany*] (EAIO)
IaPlaBHi...... Bremer County Historical Society, Plainsfield, IA [*Library symbol Library of Congress*] (LCLS)
IaPleN........ Marion County News, Pleasantville, IA [*Library symbol Library of Congress*] (LCLS)
IAPLLT........ Interamerican Program for Linguistics and Language Teaching (EA)
IAPLSP .... International Association for Philosophy of Law and Social Philosophy [*See also AIPDPS*]
IAPM........... Institute of Applied Physiology and Medicine [*Formerly, Institute of Environmenta l Medicine and Physiology*] [*Research center*] (RCD)
IAPM........... International Academy of Preventive Medicine (EA)
IAPM........... International Association of Photoplate Makers (DGA)
IAPMA........ International Association of Hand Papermakers and Paper Artists (EAIO)
IAPMO .... International Association of Plumbing and Mechanical Officials (EA)
IAPN........... International Association of Professional Numismatists [*See also AINP*] [*Zurich, Switzerland*] (EAIO)
IAPNH......... International Association of Professional Natural Hygienists (EA)
IAPO .... Industrial Accountable Property Officer [*Air Force*]
IAPO .... Interchangeable at Attachment Point Only (AAG)
IAPO .... International Association of Physical Oceanography [*Later, IAPSO*]
IAPO .... International Association of Printers' Overseers (DGA)
IaPocR........ Pocahontas Record Democrat, Pocahontas, IA [*Library symbol Library of Congress*] (LCLS)
IaPolc......... Polk City Community Library, Polk City, IA [*Library symbol Library of Congress*] (LCLS)
IaPolcN........ Big Creek News, Polk City, IA [*Library symbol Library of Congress*] (LCLS)
IaPom......... Pomeroy Public Library, Pomeroy, IA [*Library symbol Library of Congress*] (LCLS)
IaPomH....... Pomeroy Herald, Pomeroy, IA [*Library symbol Library of Congress*] (LCLS)
IaPos.......... Postville Public Library, Postville, IA [*Library symbol Library of Congress*] (LCLS)
IaPosH........ Postville Herald, Postville, IA [*Library symbol Library of Congress*] (LCLS)
IAPP........... Insulinoma Amyloid Polypeptide (DB)
IAPP........... International Association for Plant Physiology [*Australia*] (EAIO)
IAPP........... International Association for Preventive Pediatrics (DAVI)
IAPP........... International Association of Pacemaker Patients [*Later, IAHP*] (EA)
IAPP........... International Association of Police Professors [*Later, ACJS*]
IAPP........... Ion Acoustic Plasma Pulse
IAPP........... Islet Amyloid Polypeptide [*Biochemistry*]
IAPPHAP...... International Association for Past and Present History of the Art of Printing (EA)
IAPPI .... International Association of Public Pawnbroking Institutions [*Milan, Italy*] (EA)
IAPPP .... International Amateur-Professional Photoelectric Photometry [*An association*]
IAPPW .... International Association of Pupil Personnel Workers (EA)
IAPR .... Institute of Advanced Philosophic Research (EA)
IAPR .... International Association for Pattern Recognition [*British*] (EA)

IAPR .... International Association for Psychotronic Research [*Prague, Czechoslovakia*] (EA)

IaPrcWHi ..... Wayne County Historical Society, Promise City, IA [*Library symbol*] [*Library of Congress*] (LCLS)

IaPreT......... Preston Times, Preston, IA [*Library symbol Library of Congress*] (LCLS)

IaPreWHi ..... Wayne County Historical Society, Promise City, IA [*Library symbol Library of Congress*] (LCLS)

IAPRI .... International Association of Packaging Research Institutes [*British*] (EAIO)

IaPri .... Primghar Public Library, Primghar, IA [*Library symbol Library of Congress*] (LCLS)

IaPriB .... O'Brien County Bell, Primghar, IA [*Library symbol Library of Congress*] (LCLS)

IAPS........... Incorporated Association of Preparatory Schools [*British*] (DCTA)

IAPS........... Independent Association of Preparatory Schools

IAPS........... Inductosyn Angle Position Simulator

IAPS........... Institute for Advanced Pastoral Studies (EA)

IAPS........... Interim Antenna Pointing Subsystem [*Deep Space Instrumentation Facility, NASA*]

IAPS........... International Association for the Properties of Steam [*Later, IAPWS*] (EA)

IAPS........... Ion Auxiliary Propulsion System [*for satellites*]

IAPSAC .... International Association of Parents and Professionals for Safe Alternatives in Childbirth (EA)

IAPSC .... Inter-African Phytosanitary Commission

IAPSC .... International Association of Pipe Smokers Clubs (EA)

IAPSC .... International Association of Professional Security Consultants (EA)

IAPSO .... International Association for the Physical Sciences of the Ocean (EA)

IAPSP .... Inter-American Program for Social Progress [*AID*]

IAPSRS .... International Association of Psycho-Social Rehabilitation Services (EA)

IAPT........... International Association for Plant Taxonomy [*Utrecht, Netherlands*] (EA)

IAPT........... International Association of Plant Taxonomists (EERA)

IA/PT.......... Item Acquisition/Production Trade-Off Model

IAPTA .... International Allied Printing Trades Association (EA)

IAPTE .... International Academy of Pediatric Transdisciplinary Education [*British*] (EAIO)

IAPUP .... International Association on the Political Use of Psychiatry [*Amsterdam, Netherlands*] (EAIO)

IAPV .... Institute Against Prejudice and Violence (EA)

IAPV........... Intermittent Abdominal Pressure Ventilation [*Medicine*] (DMAA)

IAPW .... International Association for Personnel Women (EA)

IaPwdC .... Packwood Clarion, Packwood, IA [*Library symbol Library of Congress*] (LCLS)

IAPWS .... International Association for the Properties of Water and Steam (EA)

IAQ............. Independent Activities Questionnaire [*Psychology*]

IAQ............. Indoor Air Quality

IAQ............. International Academy for Quality [*Grobenzell, Federal Republic of Germany*] (EAIO)

IAQ............. Parkland College, Champaign, IL [*OCLC symbol*] (OCLC)

IAQA/C .... Interstate Air Quality Agencies /Commissions [*Environmental Protection Agency*]

IAQC .... International Association of Quality Circles (EA)

IAQDE .... Independent Association of Questioned Document Examiners (EA)

IAQ INFO ..... Indoor Air Quality Information Clearinghouse [*Environmental Protection Agency*] (AEPA)

IAR............. Iliamna Air Taxi, Inc. [*ICAO designator*] (FAAC)

I-Ar .... Illinois State Library, Archives Division, Springfield, IL [*Library symbol Library of Congress*] (LCLS)

IAR............. Imagery Analysis Report (MCD)

IAR............. Inactive Air Reserve

IAR............. Indirect Address Register

IAR............. Individual Action Report

IAR............. Information Analysis and Retrieval [*Computer science*] (ECII)

IAR............. Initial Address Register [*Computer science*] (HGAA)

IAR............. Inspection Acceptance Record (SAA)

IAR............. Institute for Aerobics Research (EA)

IAR............. Institute for Air Research (WDAA)

IAR............. Institute of American Relations [*Defunct*] (EA)

IAR............. Institute of Andean Research (EA)

IAR............. Institute of Asian Research [*Canada*] (IRC)

IAR............. Instruction Address Register [*Computer science*] (MDG)

IAR............. Instrument Air Receiver (AAG)

IAR............. Integrated Alternator Regulator [*Automotive engineering*]

IAR............. Integrity and Reliability [*Military*] (AFIT)

IAR............. Intelligence and Reconnaissance (IAA)

IAR............. Interagency Rate (AFM)

IAR............. Interavia Aerospace Review [*Interavia Publications*] [*Information service or system*] (CRD)

IAR............. Interment Is Authorized for the Remains Of [*Military*]

IAR............. International Art Register

IAR............. International Association of Radiopharmacology (EA)

IAR............. Interrupt Address Register

IAR............. Intersection of Air Routes [*Aviation*]

IAR............. Inventory Adjustment Rate

IAR............. Inventory Adjustment Report [*Military*]

IAR............. Iodine-Azide Reaction (DB)

IAR............. Isobaric Analog Resonance [*Nuclear structure*]

IAR............. Roosevelt University, Chicago, IL [*OCLC symbol*] (OCLC)

IARA .... Industrial Arbitration Registrars' Association [*Australia*]

IARA .... Inter-Allied Reparations Agency [*Brussels*]

IARA .... International Animal Rights Alliance [*Defunct*] (EA)

IARA .... International Association of Rebekah Assemblies, IOOF [*Independent Order of Odd Fellows*] (EA)

IaRa............ Rake Public Library, Rake, IA [*Library symbol Library of Congress*] (LCLS)

IA RAN .... Institute of Archaeology, Russian Academy of Sciences (BUAC)

IARASM .... Institute for Advanced Research in Asian Science and Medicine (EA)

IARB .... Inspection Analysis Review Board (MCD)

IArb .... Institute of Arbitrators [*British*] (DI)

IArc............. Arcola Public Library, Arcola, IL [*Library symbol Library of Congress*] (LCLS)

IARC .... Independent Assessment and Research Centre [*British*] (CB)

IARC .... International Action for the Rights of the Child [*See also AIDE*] [*Paris, France*] (EAIO)

IARC .... International Agency for Research on Cancer [*World Health Organization*] [*Lyon, France*] [*Research center*] (EAIO)

IARC .... International Agricultural Research Center

IARC .... International Agricultural Research Centre (EERA)

IAR/C .... Interviewing, Assessment, and Referral or Counseling (ADA)

IARCA .... International Association Residential and Community Alternatives (EAIO)

IARCA .... International Community Corrections Association (NTPA)

IaRcA.......... Rockwell City Advocate, Rockwell City, IA [*Library symbol Library of Congress*] (LCLS)

IARCC .... Interagency Arctic Research Coordinating Committee [*Terminated, 1978*] [*National Science Foundation*]

IaRcCHi .... Calhoun County Historical Society, Rockwell City, IA [*Library symbol Library of Congress*] (LCLS)

IaRcfR .... Rockford Register, Rockford, IA [*Library symbol Library of Congress*] (LCLS)

IArcSD .... Arcola Community Unit School District, Arcola, IL [*Library symbol*] [*Library of Congress*] (LCLS)

IARD .... Information Analysis and Retrieval Division [*American Institute of Physics*] (PDAA)

IARD .... International Association for Rural Development (AIE)

IARE........... Improved Amphibious Reconnaissance Equipment [*Military*] (MCD)

IARE........... Institute of Animal Resource Ecology [*University of British Columbia*] [*Research center*] (RCD)

IARE........... International Association of Railway Employees (EA)

IAREC .... Irrigated Agriculture Research and Extension Center [*Washington State University*] [*Research center*] (RCD)

IaRedf .... Redfield Public Library, Redfield, IA [*Library symbol Library of Congress*] (LCLS)

IaRedfRS ..... Dexfield Review Sentinel, Redfield, IA [*Library symbol Library of Congress*] (LCLS)

IaRedo......... Red Oak Public Library, Red Oak, IA [*Library symbol Library of Congress*] (LCLS)

IaRedoE....... Red Oak Express, Red Oak, IA [*Library symbol Library of Congress*] (LCLS)

IaReiC .... Reinbeck Courier, Reinbeck, IA [*Library symbol Library of Congress*] (LCLS)

IaRemBE...... Remsen Bell-Enterprise, Remsen, IA [*Library symbol Library of Congress*] (LCLS)

IaRen.......... Renwick Public Library, Renwick, IA [*Library symbol Library of Congress*] (LCLS)

IARF........... International Amateur Racquetball Federation (EA)

IARF........... International Association for Religious Freedom [*Germany*] (EY)

IARF........... International Association for Religious Freedom, United States Chapter (EA)

IARF........... Ischemic Acute Renal Failure [*Medicine*] (DB)

IARFA .... Independent Aluminum Residential Fabricators Association (EA)

IARFP .... International Association of Registered Financial Planners (EA)

IArg............ Argonne National Laboratory, Argonne, IL [*Library symbol Library of Congress*] (LCLS)

IArgoC .... CPC International, Inc., Argo, IL [*Library symbol Library of Congress*] (LCLS)

IARI .... Indian Agricultural Research Institute

IARI .... Industrial Advertising Research Institute [*Later, CMC*] (EA)

IaRicP .... Richland Plainsman, Richland, IA [*Library symbol Library of Congress*] (LCLS)

IARIGAI....... International Association of Research Institutes for the Graphic Arts Industry [*St. Gallen, Switzerland*]

IARIL .... International Association of Rural and Isolated Libraries [*Australia*]

IaRinD .... Ringsted Dispatch, Ringsted, IA [*Library symbol Library of Congress*] (LCLS)

IaRiR .... Riceville Record, Riceville, IA [*Library symbol Library of Congress*] (LCLS)

IARIW .... International Association for Research in Income and Wealth (EA)

IARIW .... International Association for Research on Income and Wealth (EERA)

IARLD .... International Association for Research in Learning Disabilities

IArlh........... Arlington Heights Public Library, Arlington Heights, IL [*Library symbol Library of Congress*] (LCLS)

IARM .... Inspectorate of Armaments (PDAA)

IARM .... Interim Antiradiation Missile (MCD)

IARMCLRS... International Agreement Regarding the Maintenance of Certain Lights in the Red Sea (EA)

IARMI .... International Association of Rattan Manufacturers and Importers [*Defunct*] (EA)

IARN .... International Amateur Radio Network

IARO .... Indian Army Reserve of Officers

IaRol.......... Rolfe Public Library, Rolfe, IA [*Library symbol Library of Congress*] (LCLS)

IaRolA .... Rolfe Arrow, Rolfe, IA [*Library symbol Library of Congress*] (LCLS)

IAROO........ International Association of Railway Operating Officers (EA)

IARP .... International Association for Religion and Parapsychology [*Tokyo, Japan*] (EA)

IARP	International Association of Retired Persons [*Superseded by IFA*] (EA)
IARQ	Intellectual Achievement Responsibility Questionnaire [*Psychology*] (EDAC)
IARR	International Association for Radiation Research [*Rijswijk, Netherlands*] (EAIO)
IaRrLCoC	Lyon County Courthouse, Rock Rapids, IA [*Library symbol Library of Congress*] (LCLS)
IaRrLR	Lyon County Reporter, Rock Rapids, IA [*Library symbol Library of Congress*] (LCLS)
IARS	Improved Aerial Refueling System Program
IARS	Independent Air Revitalization System (NASA)
IARS	Institute for Advanced Russian Studies [*Smithsonian Institution*]
IARS	International Anesthesia Research Society (EA)
IARSA	Idiopathic Acquired Refractory Sideroblastic Anemia [*Medicine*] (DMAA)
IARSB	International Association of Rolling Stock Builders [*See also AICMR*] (EAIO)
IARSC	International Association of Religious Science Churches [*Later, RSI*] (EA)
IARSL	Institute of Agriculture Remote Sensing Laboratory [*University of Minnesota*]
IArt	Arthur Public Library, Arthur, IL [*Library symbol Library of Congress*] (LCLS)
IART	Integra Life Sciences [*NASDAQ symbol*] (TTSB)
IART	Integra LifeSciences Corp. [*NASDAQ symbol*] (SAG)
i arter	Intra-Arterial [*Cardiology*] (AAMN)
IArtSD	Arthur Community School District, Arthur, IL [*Library symbol*] [*Library of Congress*] (LCLS)
IARU	International Amateur Radio Union (EA)
IARU	Irish Amateur Rowing Union [*British*] (EAIO)
IaRu	Ruthven Public Library, Ruthven, IA [*Library symbol Library of Congress*] (LCLS)
IARUS	International Association for Regional and Urban Statistics [*Voorburg, Netherlands*] (EA)
IaRuZ	Ruthven Zipcode, Ruthven, IA [*Library symbol Library of Congress*] (LCLS)
IaRvB	Rock Valley Bee, Rock Valley, IA [*Library symbol Library of Congress*] (LCLS)
IARW	International Association of Refrigerated Warehouses (EA)
IAS	Iasi [*Romania*] [*Airport symbol*] (OAG)
IAS	Iasi [*Romania*] [*Seismograph station code, US Geological Survey*] (SEIS)
IAS	Ideal Adsorbed Solution [*Physical chemistry*]
IAS	IEEE Industry Applications Society (EA)
IAS	Illness Adaptation Scale (EDAC)
IAS	Immediate Access Storage (AFM)
IAS	Immunosuppressive Acidic Substance [*Biochemistry*] (DB)
IAS	Impact Assessment Sheet (NASA)
IAS	Impact Assessment Study
IAS	India-America Society
IAS	Indian Administrative Service [*British*]
IAS	Indian Astronautical Society
IAS	Indicated Air Speed
IAS	Individual Article Supply (TELE)
IAS	Inelastic Atom Scattering (PDAA)
IAS	Information Acquisition System (MCD)
IAS	Initial Assessment Study (BCP)
IAS	Inspector of Army Schools [*British military*] (DMA)
IAS	Institute for Advanced Studies [*Army*]
IAS	Institute for American Strategy [*Later, ASCF*]
IAS	Institute for Atmospheric Sciences [*South Dakota School of Mines*] [*Research center Environmental Science Services Administration*]
IAS	Institute for the Advancement of Sailing [*Commercial firm*] (EA)
IAS	Institute of Advanced Studies [*Australian National University*]
IAS	Institute of Aerospace [*formerly, Aeronautical*] Sciences [*Later, AIAA*]
IAS	Institute of Alcohol Studies [*British*] (DBA)
IAS	Institute of Andean Studies (EA)
IAS	Institute of Animal Sciences (ASF)
IAS	Institute of Applied Physics [*Russia*]
IAS	Institute of Asian Studies (EA)
IAS	Institute of Aviation Studies [*University of Newcastle*] [*Australia*]
IAS	Instructor Aid System (MCD)
IAS	Instrument Air System [*Nuclear energy*] (NRCH)
IAS	Instrument Approach System
IAS	Integrated Analytical System (IAA)
IAS	Integrated Assessment System [*Test*] (TMMY)
IAS	Integrated AUTODIN [*Automatic Digital Information Network*] System [*DoD*]
IAS	Integrated Automation Systems
IAS	Integrated Avionics System (MCD)
IAS	Intelligence Analysis Squadron
IAS	Intelligent Array Subsystem Core
IAS	Intelligent Authoring Systems (EDAC)
IAS	Intellisoft Accounting Series [*Computer science*] (PCM)
IAS	Interactive Analysis System [*Computer science*] (PCM)
IAS	Interactive Applications Supervisor
IAS	Interactive Application System (IAA)
IAS	Inter-American System
IAS	Interatrial Septum [*Cardiology*] (MAE)
IAS	Interatrial Shunting [*Medicine*] (DMAA)
IAS	Interest Assessment Scales
IAS	Internal Alignment Sensor (MCD)
IAS	International Academy of Sciences (EAIO)
IAS	International Accountants Society
IAS	International Accounting Standards
IAS	International AIDS Society (EAIO)
IAS	International Air Service Co. [*ICAO designator*] (FAAC)
IAS	International Applied Systems (NITA)
IAS	International Army Staff (MCD)
IAS	International Aroid Society (EA)
IAS	International Association of Sedimentologists [*Liege, Belgium*] (EA)
IAS	International Association of Siderographers (EA)
IAS	International Atherosclerosis Society (EA)
IAS	International Audiovisual Society (EA)
IAS	International Aviation Service [*FAA*]
IAS	International Aviation Services [*Belgium*]
IAS	Intra-Amniotic Saline [*Infusion*] [*Medicine*]
IAS	Intra-Articular Steroid [*Physiology*]
IAS	Intrusion Alarm System
IAS	Invariant-Azimuth States (PDAA)
IAS	Inventory of American Sculpture
IAS	Isobaric Analog State
IAS	Israeli Air Services (MCD)
IAS	Los Angeles, CA [*Location identifier FAA*] (FAAL)
IAS	Sangamon State University, Springfield, IL [*OCLC symbol*] (OCLC)
IASA	Idaho Association of School Administrators (SRA)
IASA	Ileostomy Association of South Australia
IASA	Illinois Association of School Administrators (SRA)
IASA	Importers' Association of South Australia
IASA	Independent Automotive Service Association (EA)
IASA	Indo-American Sports Association [*Later, FIA-USC*]
IASA	INSCOM [*Intelligence and Security Command*] Automated Systems Support Activity [*Army*] (MCD)
IASA	Institute for Atomic Sciences in Agriculture
IASA	Institute of Agricultural Secretaries of Australasia
IASA	Insurance Accounting and Statistical Association [*Later, Insurance Accounting and Systems Association*] (EA)
IASA	Insurance Accounting and Systems Association [*Durham, NC*] (EA)
IASA	Integrated Assessment of Security Assistance [*Military*]
IASA	Integrated AUTODIN [*Automatic Digital Information Network*] System Architecture (MCD)
IASA	Interatrial Septal Aneurysm [*Medicine*] (DMAA)
IASA	International Air Safety Association (EA)
IASA	International Alliance for Sustainable Agriculture
IASA	International Association of Schools in Advertising
IASA	International Association of Sound Archives [*Milton, Keynes, England*] (EAIO)
IASA	Irish Amateur Swimming Association (EAIO)
IASAA	International Agricultural Students Association of the Americas (EA)
IaSab	Sabula Public Library, Sabula, IA [*Library symbol Library of Congress*] (LCLS)
IASAC	International Association of Silver Art Collectors (EA)
IaSacLS	Lytton Star, Sac City, IA [*Library symbol Library of Congress*] (LCLS)
IaSacS	Sac Sun, Sac City, IA [*Library symbol Library of Congress*] (LCLS)
IASAIL	International Association for the Study of Anglo-Irish Literature [*Maynooth, Republic of Ireland*] (EAIO)
IASAJ	International Association of Supreme Administration Jurisdictions GG2 [*See also AIHJA*] (EAIO)
IaSal	Crew Public Library, Salem, IA [*Library symbol Library of Congress*] (LCLS)
IaSan	Sanborn Public Library, Sanborn, IA [*Library symbol Library of Congress*] (LCLS)
IaSanP	Sanborn Pioneer, Sanborn, IA [*Library symbol Library of Congress*] (LCLS)
IASAP	Intercollegiate Association for Study of the Alcohol Problem (EA)
IASAP	International Arctic Seas Assessment Project [*Marine science*] (OSRA)
IASB	Illinois Association of School Boards (EDAC)
IASB	Installation Aviation Standardization Board (MCD)
IASB	International Academy at Santa Barbara (EA)
IASB	Iowa Association of School Boards (SRA)
IASBFLC	Institute for the Advanced Study of Black Family Life and Culture (EA)
IASC	Indexing and Abstracting Society of Canada [*Toronto, ON*]
IASC	Indian Army Service Corps [*British military*] (DMA)
IASC	Inter-American Safety Council (EA)
IASC	Inter-American Scout Committee [*See also CIE*] [*San Jose, Costa Rica*] (EAIO)
IASC	Inter-American Statistical Teaching Center
IASC	International Accounting Standards Committee [*of the International Federation of Accountants*] [*British*] (EAIO)
IASC	International Afroid Science Conference (MCD)
IASC	International Aloe Science Council (EA)
IASC	International Arctic Science Committee
IASC	International Association for Statistical Computing (EA)
IASC	International Association of Seed Crushers [*British*] (EAIO)
IASC	International Association of Skal Clubs [*Spain*] (EAIO)
IASc	Intimate Apparel Square Club (EA)
IASc	Italian American Stamp Club (EA)
IaSc	Sioux City Public Library, Sioux City, IA [*Library symbol Library of Congress*] (LCLS)
IASCA	International Auto Sound Challenge Association (EA)
IaScB	Briar Cliff College, Sioux City, IA [*Library symbol Library of Congress*] (LCLS)
IASCB	Ibero-American Society for Cell Biology [*See also SIABC*] (EAIO)
IASCB	International Association of Sand Castle Builders (EA)
IASCD	Idaho Association of Soil Conservation Districts (SRA)
IASCD	Illinois Association for Supervision and Curriculum Development (SRA)

IASCE............ International Association for the Study of Cooperation in Education (EA)

IaSce .... Sioux Center Public Library, Sioux Center, IA [*Library symbol Library of Congress*] (LCLS)

IaSceD......... Dordt College, Sioux Center, IA [*Library symbol Library of Congress*] (LCLS)

IaSchH......... Schaller Herald, Schaller, IA [*Library symbol Library of Congress*] (LCLS)

IaSchIL........ Schleswig Leader, Schleswig, IA [*Library symbol Library of Congress*] (LCLS)

IaScM.......... Morningside College, Sioux City, IA [*Library symbol Library of Congress*] (LCLS)

IaScNR .... Northwest Regional Library System, Sioux City, IA [*Library symbol Library of Congress*] (LCLS)

IASCO .... International Association of Service Companies [*NACSA*] [*Absorbed by*] (EA)

IASCP .... Institute for Advanced Study of the Communication Processes [*University of Florida*] [*Research center*] (RCD)

IASCP .... International Association for the Study of Common Property (EA)

IASCS .... International Association for Shopping Center Security (EA)

IaScS .... Siouxland Libraries Cooperative, Sioux City, IA [*Library symbol Library of Congress*] (LCLS)

IaScT .... Trinity College, Sioux City, IA [*Library symbol Library of Congress Obsolete*]

IaScWI......... West Iowa Technical Community College, Sioux City, IA [*Library symbol Library of Congress*] (LCLS)

IASD .... Interatrial Septal Defect [*Cardiology*]

IASD .... Interauricular Septal Defect [*Medicine*] (DB)

IASDI .... Inter-American Social Development Institute [*Later, IAF*]

IASEES......... International Association of South-East European Studies [*See also AIESEE*] [*Bucharest, Romania*] (EAIO)

IaSeyH......... Seymour Herald, Seymour, IA [*Library symbol Library of Congress*] (LCLS)

IASF............ Instrumentation in Aerospace Simulation Facilities

IASF............ International Amateur Surfing Federation (EA)

IASF............ International Amateur Swimming Federation (EA)

IASF............ International Atlantic Salmon Foundation [*Canada*] (EA)

IASF............ Irish American Sports Foundation (EA)

IASG .... Inflation Accounting Steering Group (MHDB)

IASG .... International Airline Support Group (EFIS)

IASH .... International Association of Scientific Hydrology [*Later, International Association of Hydrological Sciences*] [*of International Union of Geodesy and Geophysics*]

IASH .... Isolated Asymmetric Septal Hypertrophy [*Medicine*] (DMAA)

IASH .... Israeli Academy of Sciences and Humanities

IaSh............ Shenandoah Public Library, Shenandoah, IA [*Library symbol Library of Congress*] (LCLS)

IaShe........... Sheldon Public Library, Sheldon, IA [*Library symbol Library of Congress*] (LCLS)

IaShefP........ Sheffield Press, Sheffield, IA [*Library symbol Library of Congress*] (LCLS)

IaSheHi........ Sheldon County Historical Society, Sheldon, IA [*Library symbol Library of Congress*] (LCLS)

IaSheM........ Sheldon Mail, Sheldon, IA [*Library symbol Library of Congress*] (LCLS)

IaSheS......... Sheldon Sun, Sheldon, IA [*Library symbol Library of Congress*] (LCLS)

IaShr........... Shell Rock Public Library, Shell Rock, IA [*Library symbol Library of Congress*] (LCLS)

IaShrN .... Shell Rock News, Shell Rock, IA [*Library symbol*] [*Library of Congress*] (LCLS)

IASHS .... Institute for Advanced Study in Human Sexuality (DAVI)

IASI............. Inter-American Statistical Institute (EA)

IASI............. International Alliance Services, Inc. [*NASDAQ symbol*] (SAG)

IASI............. International Association for Sports Information [*The Hague, Netherlands*] (EA)

IASIA .... International Association of Schools and Institutes Administration (BUAC)

IASIA .... International Association of Schools and Institutes of Administration (BUAC)

IaSibCoC...... Osceola County Courthouse, Sibley, IA [*Library symbol*] [*Library of Congress*] (LCLS)

IaSibG .... Sibley Gazette and Tribune, Sibley, IA [*Library symbol*] [*Library of Congress*] (LCLS)

IaSidAH .... Sidney Argus-Herald, Sidney, IA [*Library symbol*] [*Library of Congress*] (LCLS)

IaSidCoC...... Fremont County Courthouse, Sidney, IA [*Library symbol*] [*Library of Congress*] (LCLS)

IaSigCoC...... Keokuk County Courthouse, Sigourney, IA [*Library symbol*] [*Library of Congress*] (LCLS)

IaSigNR .... Sigourney News-Review, Sigourney, IA [*Library symbol*] [*Library of Congress*] (LCLS)

IASILL.......... International Association for the Study of the Italian Language and Literature [*See also AISLLI*] [*Padua, Italy*] (EAIO)

IASL............ Inter-American School of Librarianship [*Colombia*] (BUAC)

IASL............ International Association for the Study of the Liver [*Gottingen, Federal Republic of Germany*]

IASL............ International Association of School Librarianship (PDAA)

IASL............ International Association of State Lotteries (BUAC)

IaSl............. Storm Lake Public Library, Storm Lake, IA [*Library symbol Library of Congress*] (LCLS)

IaSla .... Slater Public Library, Slater, IA [*Library symbol Library of Congress*] (LCLS)

IaSlaT.......... Tri County Times, Slater, IA [*Library symbol*] [*Library of Congress*] (LCLS)

IaSIB............ Buena Vista College, Storm Lake, IA [*Library symbol Library of Congress*] (LCLS)

IASLC.......... International Association for the Study of Lung Cancer (EA)

IASLIC .... Indian Association for Special Libraries and Information Centres (NITA)

IaSIPT.......... Storm Lake Pilot-Tribune, Storm Lake, IA [*Library symbol*] [*Library of Congress*] (LCLS)

IASM........... Independent Association of Stocking Manufacturers [*Defunct*]

IASM........... Institute of Aerospace Safety and Management [*University of Southern California*]

IASM........... International Association for Seminar Management (EA)

IASM........... International Association of Structural Movers (EA)

IASM........... Istituto per l'Assistenza allo Sviluppo del Mezzogiorno [*Italy*] (EY)

IASMAL....... International Academy of Social and Moral Sciences, Arts, and Letters (BUAC)

IASMHF .... International Association of Sports Museums and Halls of Fame (EA)

IASMIRT ..... International Association for Structural Mechanics in Reactor Technology (EAIO)

IASMW .... International Association of Sheet Metal Workers (BARN)

IAS/NAB....... International Arthurian Society/North American Branch [*Canada*] (EAIO)

IASnet.......... [*The*] Institute for Automated Systems Network (TNIG)

IASOC .... International Association for the Study of Organized Crime (EA)

IaSolE .... Solon Economist, Solon, IA [*Library symbol*] [*Library of Congress*] (LCLS)

IASOR.......... Ice and Snow on Runway [*Aviation*]

IASOS .... Institute of Antarctic and Southern Ocean Studies (EERA)

IASP............ Integrated Attack Sensor Package

IASP............ Inter-American Society of Psychology (BUAC)

IASP............ International Arts and Sciences Press

IASP............ International Association for Social Progress

IASP............ International Association for Suicide Prevention (EA)

IASP............ International Association for the Study of Pain (EA)

IASP............ International Association in Support of Perestroika (BUAC)

IASP............ International Association of Scholarly Publishers [*Norway*]

IASP............ International Association of Science Parks [*France*] (BUAC)

IASP............ International Association of Space Philatelists (EA)

IASP............ International Association of Sports Physicians [*Defunct*] (EA)

IASP............ International Association of Sublimation Printers (EA)

IASPA .... International Auto Show Producers Association (EA)

IASPC .... International Association of Strategic Planning Consultants [*Defunct*] (EA)

IaSpeHi........ Parker Historical Society of Clay County, Spencer, IA [*Library symbol*] [*Library of Congress*] (LCLS)

IASPEI .... International Association of Seismology and Physics of the Earth's Interior [*ICSU*] [*Newbury, Berkshire, England*] (EAIO)

IASPHA .... International American Saddlebred Pleasure Horse Association (EA)

IaSpIB .... Spirit Lake Beacon, Spirit Lake, IA [*Library symbol*] [*Library of Congress*] (LCLS)

IaSpICoC...... Dickinson County Courthouse, Spirit Lake, IA [*Library symbol*] [*Library of Congress*] (LCLS)

IASPM .... International Association for the Study of Popular Music [*Berlin, German Democratic Republic*] (EAIO)

IASPPV .... International Association of Former Soviet Political Prisoners and Victims of Communist Regime

IaSpr........... Springville Public Library, Springville, IA [*Library symbol Library of Congress*] (LCLS)

IASPS .... International Association for Statistics in Physical Sciences

IASR .... Intermediate Altitude Sounding Rocket (MUGU)

IASR .... Interruption Address Storage Register (NITA)

IASRA .... International Arthur Schnitzler Research Association (EA)

IaSrBP .... Bulletin-Press, Sioux Rapids, IA [*Library symbol*] [*Library of Congress*] (LCLS)

IASRI .... Indian Agricultural Statistics Research Institute (BUAC)

IASRR.......... Institute of African Studies. Research Review [*A publication*]

IASS........... Institute of Advanced Architectural Studies (BUAC)

IASS........... Insurance Accounting and Statistical Society

IASS........... International Air Safety Seminar

IASS........... International Association for Scandinavian Studies [*Norwich, England*] (EAIO)

IASS........... International Association for Semiotic Studies (BUAC)

IASS........... International Association for Shell and Spatial Structures [*Madrid, Spain*] (EA)

IASS........... International Association of Sanskrit Studies (EA)

IASS........... International Association of Security Service (EA)

IASS........... International Association of Semiotic Studies [*Palermo, Italy*] (EA)

IASS........... International Association of Soil Science

IASS........... International Association of Survey Statisticians [*See also AISE*] [*France*] (EA)

IASS........... Inverter/ATCS [*Active Thermal Control Subsystem*] Support Structure (MCD)

IASSD .... International Association of School Security Directors [*Later, NASSD*] (EA)

IASSIST .... International Association for Social Science Information Service and Technology (EA)

IASSIST .... International Association for Social Science Information Services and Technology (NITA)

IASSMD .... International Association for the Scientific Study of Mental Deficiency [*Dublin, Republic of Ireland*] (EA)

IASSRF .... International Amateur Snowshoe Racing Federation (EA)

IASSW .... International Association of Schools of Social Work [*Austria*]

IAST............ Instrument for the Analysis of Science Teaching (EDAC)

IAST............ Integrated Avionic System Trainer [*Military*] (CAAL)

IAST............ International Association of Scuba Technicians

IAST............ International Association to Save Tyre (BUAC)

IAST	Irish Association for Sail Training (BUAC)
IASTA	Institute for Advanced Studies in the Theatre Arts (EA)
IaStacM	Monitor-Review, Stacyville, IA [Library symbol] [Library of Congress] (LCLS)
IaStaE	Saint Ansgar Enterprise, St. Ansgar, IA [Library symbol Library of Congress] (LCLS)
IaStan	Stanton Community Library, Stanton, IA [Library symbol Library of Congress] (LCLS)
IaStanV	Stanton Viking, Stanton, IA [Library symbol] [Library of Congress] (LCLS)
IaStaw	Stanwood Public Library, Stanwood, IA [Library symbol] [Library of Congress] (LCLS)
IaStc	Gutenkunst Public Library, State Center, IA [Library symbol Library of Congress] (LCLS)
IaStcE	State Center Enterprise, State Center, IA [Library symbol] [Library of Congress] (LCLS)
IASTE	International Association for the Study of Traditional Environments (BUAC)
IASTED	International Association of Science and Technology for Development [Calgary, AB] (EAIO)
IASTG	International Association of Structural/Tectonic Geologists (BUAC)
IaStoc	Story City Public Library, Story City, IA [Library symbol Library of Congress] (LCLS)
IaStocH	Story City Herald, Story City, IA [Library symbol] [Library of Congress] (LCLS)
IaStrp	Strawberry Point Public Library, Strawberry Point, IA [Library symbol Library of Congress] (LCLS)
IaStrpP	Strawberry Point Press-Journal, Strawberry Point, IA [Library symbol Library of Congress] (LCLS)
IaStuH	Stuart Herald, Stuart, IA [Library symbol] [Library of Congress] (LCLS)
IASTWL	International Association for Social Tourism and Workers' Leisure (EAIO)
IaSu	General N. B. Baker Library, Sutherland, IA [Library symbol Library of Congress] (LCLS)
IASU	International Association of Satellite Users [Later, IASUS] (EA)
IA Sup Vol	English Law Reports, Indian Appeals, Supplementary Volume [A publication] (DLA)
IASUS	International Association of Satellite Users and Suppliers (EA)
IASV	Internationale Arbeitsgemeinschaft von Sortimentsbuchhaendler Vereinigungen [International Community of Booksellers' Associations]
IASW	Irish Association of Social Workers [Ireland] (BUAC)
IaSwc	Swea City Public Library, Swea City, IA [Library symbol Library of Congress] (LCLS)
IASWG	Inter-Country Adoption Social Workers Group (BUAC)
IASWG	Inter-Country Adoption Social Workers Group (BUAC)
IASWR	Institute for Advanced Studies of World Religions (EA)
IASWS	International Association for Sediment Water Science [Switzerland] (BUAC)
IASWS	International Association of Severe Weather Specialists (NTPA)
IAsy	Ashley Public Library, Ashley, IL [Library symbol Library of Congress] (LCLS)
IASY	International Active Sun Years
IAsyCD	Ashley Community Consolidated District 15, Ashley, IL [Library symbol Library of Congress] (LCLS)
IAT	Image Auto Tracker
IAT	Immunoaugmentative Therapy [Oncology]
IAT	Indexible Address Tag (SAA)
IAT	Indicated Air Temperature (AFM)
IAT	Indirect Antiglobulin Test [Clinical chemistry]
IAT	Individual Acceptance Tests
IAT	Individual Aircraft Tracking Program (MCD)
IAT	Information Assessment Team (NRCH)
IAT	Inside Air Temperature
IAT	Inspection Apply Template (MCD)
IAT	Installation Abortion Time [Medicine] (STED)
IAT	Institute for Academic Technology
IAT	Institute for Advanced Technology [Control Data Corp.] [Bloomington, MN] [Telecommunications]
IAT	Institute for Applied Technology [Superseded by NEL] [National Institute of Standards and Technology]
IAT	Institute of Agricultural Technology [Vietnam] (BUAC)
IAT	Institute of Air Transport (BUAC)
IAT	Institute of Animal Technology [London]
IAT	Institute of Asphalt Technology [British]
IAT	Intake Air Temperature [Automotive engineering]
IAT	Integrated Avionics Test (MCD)
IAT	Integration Acceptance Test [Military] (CAAL)
IAT	Intelligent Actuators & Transmitters (ACII)
IAT	Interactive Audio Teletraining System [Valencia Community College] [Orlando, FL] (TSSD)
IAT	Interionic Attraction Theory
IAT	Internal Air Transportability (MCD)
IAT	International Air Transport Association [ICAO designator] (FAAC)
IAT	International Association for Time-Keeping (BUAC)
IAT	International Association of Trichologists (EA)
IAT	International Atomic Time
IAT	International Automatic Time
IAT	Intraoperative Autologous Transfusion [Medicine]
IAT	Invasive Activity Test [Oncology]
IAT	Inventory of Affective Tolerance [Psychology]
IAT	Iodine Azide Test [Medicine]
IAT	Iowa Achievement Test [Psychology] (DAVI)
IAT	Iowa Terminal Railroad Co. [AAR code]

IAT	Southern Illinois University, Edwardsville Campus, Edwardsville, IL [OCLC symbol] (OCLC)
IATA	International Air Transport [formerly, Traffic] Association [Canada]
IATA	International Air Transport Authority (BUAC)
IATA	International Amateur Theatre Association [Denmark]
IATA	International Appropriate Technology Association [Defunct] (EA)
IATA	Is Amended to Add
IATACS	Improved Army Tactical Communications System (DOMA)
IATADS	Initial Airborne Target Acquisition Designation System (MCD)
IATAE	International Accounting and Traffic Analysis Equipment [Telecommunications] (NITA)
IATAFI	International Association for Technology Assessment and Forecasting Institutions (BUAC)
IATAL	International Association of Theoretical and Applied Limnology [See also SILTA] (EA)
IATB	International Aviation Theft Bureau [ACPI] [Superseded by] (EA)
IATC	India America Trade Council
IATC	Inter-American Telecommunications Commission
IATC	Inter-American Travel Congresses
IATC	International Air Traffic Communications
IATC	International Association of Theatre Critics (BUAC)
IATC	International Association of Tool Craftsmen (EA)
IATC	International Association of Torch Clubs (EA)
IATC	International Association of Trauma Counseling (NTPA)
IATC	International Association of Triathlon Clubs (EA)
IATCA	International Air Transportation Competition Act of 1979
IATCB	Interdepartmental Air Traffic Control Board
IATCL	International Association for Textile Care Labelling (EA)
IATCR	International Air Traffic Communications Receiver Station
IATCS	International Air Traffic Communications Station
IATCS	International Air Traffic Communications System (MCD)
IATCT	International Air Traffic Communications Transmitter Station
IATD	Is Amended to Delete
IATDB	Interim Air Toxics Data Base (GNE)
IATDP	International Association of Textile Dyers and Printers [See also AITIT] (EAIO)
IATE	Intermediate Automatic Test Equipment
IATE	Intermediate-Level Automatic Test Equipment (PDAA)
IATE	International Accounting and Traffic Analysis Equipment [Telecommunications] (TEL)
IATE	International Association for Television Editors
IATE	International Association for Temperance Education [Later, IVES] (EA)
IATE	International Association of Trade Exchanges [Later, IRTA] (EA)
IATE	International Association of Travel Exhibitors (EA)
IATEFL	International Association of Teachers of English as a Foreign Language [Whitstable, Kent, England] (EAIO)
IATF	Interagency Task Force [for Indochina] [South Vietnam refugee relief]
IATF	Inter-Association Task Force on Campus Alcohol and Other Substance Abuse Issues [An association] (EA)
IATF	International Airline Training Fund (BUAC)
IATFAI	Inter-Association Task Force on Alcohol Issues (EA)
IATG	International Association of Teachers of German [See also IDV] [Copenhagen, Denmark] (EAIO)
IATH	Institute for Advanced Technology in the Humanities (BUAC)
IATI	Inter-Alpha-Trypsin Inhibitor (DMAA)
IATI	International Association of Teachers of Italian [Belgium] (EAIO)
IaTip	Tipron Public Library, Tipron, IA [Library symbol Library of Congress] (LCLS)
IaTipCoC	Cedar County Courthouse, Tipton, IA [Library symbol] [Library of Congress] (LCLS)
IaTit	Titonka Public Library, Titonka, IA [Library symbol Library of Congress] (LCLS)
IATJ	International Association of Travel Journalists (EA)
IATL	International Academy of Trial Lawyers (EA)
IATL	International Association of Theological Libraries
IATM	International Association for Testing Materials (IEEE)
IATM	International Association of Tour Managers (DI)
IATM	International Association of Transport Museums [See also AIMT] [Berne, Switzerland] (EAIO)
IATM-NAR	International Association of Tour Managers - North American Region (EA)
IATMO	International Academy of Tumor Marker Oncology (BUAC)
IATN	International Association of Telecomputer Networks (EA)
IATO	International Air Transport Organization (BUAC)
IaTo	Toledo Public Library, Toledo, IA [Library symbol Library of Congress] (LCLS)
IaToC	Toledo Chronicle, Toledo, IA [Library symbol] [Library of Congress] (LCLS)
IATOD	In Addition to Other Duties [Military]
IATP	Individual Aircraft Tracking Program (MCD)
IATP	Institute for Agriculture and Trade Policy (EA)
IATP	International Agricultural Training Programme (BUAC)
IATP	International Airlines Technical Pool (PDAA)
IATP	International Association of Tungsten Producers
IATR	International Association for Tamil Research [Malaysia] (BUAC)
IATR	International Association of Teachers of Russian (BUAC)
IATR	Is Amended to Read
IATRA	International Academy of Toxicological Risk Assessment (EA)
IaTraS	Traer Star-Clipper, Traer, IA [Library symbol] [Library of Congress] (LCLS)
IaTriL	Tripoli Leader, Tripoli, IA [Library symbol] [Library of Congress] (LCLS)

IATROS........ Organisation Mondiale des Medicins Independants [*International Organization of Private and Independent Doctors*] (EAIO)

IatrosHlt ...... Iatros Health Network, Inc. [*Associated Press*] (SAG)

IATS............ Individual Accession and Training System (MCD)

IATS............ Institute for Advanced Talmudic Studies [*Beth Medrash Govoha*] [*Canada*] (IRC)

IATS............ Intake Air Temperature Sensor [*Automotive engineering*]

IATS............ International Association for Tibetan Studies (BUAC)

IATSC.......... International Aeronautical Telecommunications Switching Center

IATSE.......... International Alliance of Theatrical Stage Employees and Moving Picture Machine Operators of the US and Canada (EA)

IATSE.......... International Alliance of Theatrical Stage Employes [*An AFL-CIO union*] [*New York, NY*] (WDMC)

IATSIS .... Institute of Aboriginal and Torres Strait Islander Studies [*Australia*]

IATSS.......... International Association of Traffic and Safety Sciences [*Tokyo, Japan*] (EAIO)

IATSW .... Indian Association of Trained Social Workers (BUAC)

IATT............ International Academy of Twirling Teachers (EA)

IATTC.......... Inter-American Tropical Tuna Commission (EA)

IATU............ Inter-American Telecommunications Union [*US*]

IATUL.......... International Association of Technical University Libraries (BUAC)

IATUL.......... International Association of Technological University Libraries [*Goteborg, Sweden*]

IATV............ ACTV, Inc. [*NASDAQ symbol*] (SAG)

IATV............ Income Approach to Value (MHDB)

IATV............ Interactive Alphanumeric Television

IATVPM........ International Association of Teachers of Veterinary Preventive Medicine (BUAC)

IAU............ Austin College, Sherman, TX [*OCLC symbol*] (OCLC)

IAU............ Infrastructure Account Unit (NATG)

IAU............ Initial Alignment Unit

IAU............ Institute for American Universities (EA)

IAU............ Interface Adapter Unit [*Computer science*] (MCD)

IAU............ International Academic Union (EA)

IAU............ International Association of Universities [*France*]

IAU............ International Astronomical Union [*ICSU*] [*Paris, France*] [*Research center*] (IRC)

IAU............ Internationale Armbrustschutzen Union [*International Crossbow Shooting Union*] (EAIO)

iau .... Iowa [*MARC country of publication code Library of Congress*] (LCCP)

IAU............ Italian Actors Union (EA)

IaU............ University of Iowa, Iowa City, IA [*Library symbol Library of Congress*] (LCLS)

IAub............ Auburn Public Library, Auburn, IL [*Library symbol Library of Congress*] (LCLS)

IaU-B .... University of Iowa, Botany-Chemistry Library, Iowa City, IA [*Library symbol Library of Congress*] (LCLS)

IAUC .... Irish American Unity Conference (EA)

IAUD .... International Association for a Union of Democracies [*Defunct*] (EA)

IAUEC .... International Association of Underwater Engineering Contractors (BUAC)

IAUF............ Interamerican Underwater Festival

IAug .... Tri-County Public Library District, Augusta, IL [*Library symbol Library of Congress*] (LCLS)

IAUL............ Inter-African Union of Lawyers (BUAC)

IaU-L .... University of Iowa, College of Law, Iowa City, IA [*Library symbol Library of Congress*] (LCLS)

IaU-M .... University of Iowa, Health Sciences Library, Iowa City, IA [*Library symbol Library of Congress*] (LCLS)

IAUMS .... Installation, Administrative Use, and Command Design Motor Vehicle Management System [*Army*]

IAUP .... International Association of University Presidents

IAUPE .... International Association of University Professors of English [*British*]

IAUPL .... International Association of University Professors and Lecturers (EAIO)

IaUpV .... Vennard College, University Park, IA [*Library symbol Library of Congress*] (LCLS)

IAur............ Aurora Public Library, Aurora, IL [*Library symbol*] [*Library of Congress*] (LCLS)

IAUR .... Institute for Art and Urban Resources (EA)

IaUr .... Urbandale Public Library, Urbandale, IA [*Library symbol Library of Congress*] (LCLS)

IAurC .... Aurora College, Aurora, IL [*Library symbol*] [*Library of Congress*] (LCLS)

IAURIF .... Institut d'Amenagement et d'Urbanisme de la Region de l'Ile de France (NITA)

IaUrN .... Urbandale News, Urbandale, IA [*Library symbol*] [*Library of Congress*] (LCLS)

IaUrP .... Urbandale Public Library, Urbandale, IA [*Library symbol*] [*Library of Congress*] (LCLS)

IaUte .... Ute Public Library, Ute, IA [*Library symbol Library of Congress*] (LCLS)

IAV............ Airavia [*France ICAO designator*] (FAAC)

IAV............ Identified Aerial Vehicle

IA(V).......... Ileostomy Association (Victoria) [*Australia*]

IAV............ Index of Adjustment and Values (AEBS)

IAV............ Indium Antimode Varactor

IAV............ Infantry Armored Vehicle [*Army*] (MUSM)

IAV............ Innotech Aviation Enterprises Ltd. [*Toronto Stock Exchange symbol*]

IAV............ Institute for American Values (EA)

IAV............ Intermittent Assisted Ventilation [*Medicine*] (MEDA)

IAV............ Intra-Arterial Vasopressin [*Cardiology*]

IAV............ Intransit Asset Visibility (MCD)

IAV............ Inventory Adjustment Voucher [*Military*] (AFM)

IAV............ Island-Arc Volcanic [*Geology*]

IAV............ Issue Authority Voucher

IAV............ Southern Illinois University, School of Medicine, Springfield, IL [*OCLC symbol*] (OCLC)

IAV............ VIDION/International Association of Video (EA)

IAVA............ Industrial Audio-Visual Association [*Later, AVMA*] (EA)

IaVaO.......... Vail Observer, Vail, IA [*Library symbol*] [*Library of Congress*] (LCLS)

IAVC............ Indian Army Veterinary Corps [*British military*] (DMA)

IAVC............ Instantaneous Automatic Video Control (IEEE)

IAVC............ Instantaneous Automatic Volume Control [*Electronics*]

IAVCEI .... International Association of Volcanology and Chemistry of the Earth's Interior [*Germany*]

IAVCM .... International Association of Visual Communications Management [*Formerly, SRE*]

IAVD .... Interactive Videodisc [*Army*] (INF)

IAVE............ Industrial Arts and Vocational Education (AEBS)

IAVE............ International Association for Volunteer Education (EA)

IAVE............ International Association of Volunteer Effort (EA)

IAVFH .... International Association of Veterinary Food Hygienists

IAVG .... International Association for Vocational Guidance

IAVI............ International AIDS Vaccine Initiative

IAVI............ International Association of Voice Identification [*Later, IAI*] (EA)

IaVilR .... Villisca Review, Villisca, IA [*Library symbol*] [*Library of Congress*] (LCLS)

IaVin........... Vinton Public Library, Vinton, IA [*Library symbol Library of Congress*] (LCLS)

IaVinT .... Cedar Valley Times, Vinton, IA [*Library symbol*] [*Library of Congress*] (LCLS)

IAVM........... Intramedullary Arteriovenous Malformation [*Medicine*] (STED)

IaVol........... Volga Public Library, Volga, IA [*Library symbol Library of Congress*] (LCLS)

IAVRT .... Independent Association of Victorian Registered Teachers [*Australia*]

IAVS........... International Association for Vegetation Science [*See also IVV*] [*Gottingen, Federal Republic of Germany*] (EAIO)

IAVSD .... International Association for Vehicle Systems Dynamics [*ICSU*] [*Delft, Netherlands*] (EAIO)

IAVTC.......... International Audio-Visual Technical Centre [*Netherlands*]

IAW............ Improved Antimateriel Warhead

IAW............ In Accordance With

IAW............ Institute of the American West [*Later, INAW*] (EA)

IAW............ International Alliance of Women [*See also AIF*] [*Valetta, Malta*] (EAIO)

IAW............ International Association of Wholesalers [*Defunct*]

IAW............ Iraqi Airways [*ICAO designator*] (FAAC)

IAW............ Isotopic Atomic Weight

IAW............ Triton College, River Grove, IL [*OCLC symbol*] (OCLC)

IaW............ Waterloo Public Library, Waterloo, IA [*Library symbol Library of Congress*] (LCLS)

IAWA .... Independent American Whiskey Association [*Later, ABAA*] (EA)

IAWA .... International Association of Wood Anatomists [*Utrecht, Netherlands*] (EA)

IAWA .... International Aviation Women Association (NTPA)

IAWA .... Irish Amateur Weightlifting Association (EAIO)

IAWA .... Irish Amateur Wrestling Association (EAIO)

IaWa........... Washington Public Library, Washington, IA [*Library symbol Library of Congress*] (LCLS)

IaWaJ.......... Washington Evening Journal, Washington, IA [*Library symbol Library of Congress*] (LCLS)

IaWal.......... Walnut Public Library, Walnut, IA [*Library symbol Library of Congress*] (LCLS)

IaWall......... Wall Lake Public Library, Wall Lake, IA [*Library symbol Library of Congress*] (LCLS)

IaWap......... Wapello Public Library (Keck Memorial Library), Wapello, IA [*Library symbol Library of Congress*] (LCLS)

IaWapCoC.... Louisa County Courthouse, Wapello, IA [*Library symbol*] [*Library of Congress*] (LCLS)

IaWapR........ Wapello Republican, Wapello, IA [*Library symbol*] [*Library of Congress*] (LCLS)

IaWas......... Washta Library, Washta, IA [*Library symbol Library of Congress*] (LCLS)

IaWauE........ Jerico Community Echo, Waucoma, IA [*Library symbol Library of Congress*] (LCLS)

IaWaukAC.... Allamakee County Courthouse, Waukon, IA [*Library symbol*] [*Library of Congress*] (LCLS)

IaWaukCoC.. Allamakee County Courthouse, Waukon, IA [*Library symbol Library of Congress*] (LCLS)

IaWaukD...... Waukon Democrat, Waukon, IA [*Library symbol Library of Congress*] (LCLS)

IaWauke....... Waukee Public Library, Waukee, IA [*Library symbol Library of Congress*] (LCLS)

IaWaukR...... Waukon Republican-Standard, Waukon, IA [*Library symbol Library of Congress*] (LCLS)

IaWavBHi ..... Bremer County Historical Society, Waverly, IA [*Library symbol Library of Congress*] (LCLS)

IaWavCoC.... Bremer County Courthouse, Waverly, IA [*Library symbol Library of Congress*] (LCLS)

IaWavD........ Waverly Democrat, Waverly, IA [*Library symbol Library of Congress*] (LCLS)

IaWavH........ Waverly House, Waverly, IA [*Library symbol Library of Congress*] (LCLS)

IaWavI......... Bremer County Independent, Waverly, IA [*Library symbol Library of Congress*] (LCLS)

IaWavW....... Wartburg College, Waverly, IA [*Library symbol Library of Congress*] (LCLS)

IaWayN........ Wayland News, Wayland, IA [*Library symbol Library of Congress*] (LCLS)

IaWb............ Enlow Public Library, West Branch, IA [*Library symbol Library of Congress*] (LCLS)

IaWbe.......... West Bend Public Library, West Bend, IA [*Library symbol Library of Congress*] (LCLS)

IaWbeJ .... West Bend Journal, West Bend, IA [*Library symbol Library of Congress*] (LCLS)

IaWbH .... Herbert Hoover Presidential Library, West Branch, IA [*Library symbol Library of Congress*] (LCLS)

IaWbT.......... West Branch Times, West Branch, IA [*Library symbol Library of Congress*] (LCLS)

IaWbuN........ Des Moines County News, West Burlington, IA [*Library symbol Library of Congress*] (LCLS)

IaWC............ Daily Courier, Waterloo, IA [*Library symbol Library of Congress*] (LCLS)

IAWC .... In Accordance with Contract

IAWCC .... International Association of Wall and Ceiling Contractors [*Later, AWCI*] (EA)

IAWCC/GD ... International Association of Wall and Ceiling Contractors - Gypsum Drywall Contractors International [*Later, AWCI*] (EA)

IAWCM .... International Association of Wiping Cloth Manufacturers (EA)

IAWCR .... International Association of Women Chefs and Restaurateurs (NTPA)

IaWdmB .... New Iowa Bystander, West Des Moines, IA [*Library symbol Library of Congress*] (LCLS)

IaWdmGS .... Church of Jesus Christ of Latter-Day Saints, Genealogical Society Library, Des Moines Branch, West Des Moines, IA [*Library symbol Library of Congress*] (LCLS)

IaWdmNB .... New Iowa Bystander, West Des Moines, IA [*Library symbol Library of Congress*] (LCLS)

IAWE............ International Association for Wind Engineering [*Aachen, Federal Republic of Germany*] (EAIO)

IaWec .... Kendall Young Library, Webster City, IA [*Library symbol Library of Congress*] (LCLS)

IaWecAJ ...... Aberdeen-Angus Journal, Webster City, IA [*Library symbol Library of Congress*] (LCLS)

IaWecF .... Freeman-Journal, Webster City, IA [*Library symbol Library of Congress*] (LCLS)

IaWelmA...... Wellman Advance, Wellman, IA [*Library symbol Library of Congress*] (LCLS)

IaWels .... Wellsburg Public Library, Wellsburg, IA [*Library symbol Library of Congress*] (LCLS)

IAWF............ International Association of Wildland Fire (NTPA)

IaWG .... Henry W. Grout Museum of History and Science, Waterlook, IA [*Library symbol Library of Congress*] (LCLS)

IAWG .... Interagency Working Group (MCD)

IAWG .... Inter-American War Game (MCD)

IAWGSA....... Inter-Agency Working Group on Southern Africa [*Canadian Council for International Cooperation*]

IaWH .... Hawkeye Institute of Technology, Area VII, Waterloo, IA [*Library symbol Library of Congress*] (LCLS)

IAWH .... Improved Antimateriel Warhead

IaWhaP........ What Cheer Patriot-Chronicle, What Cheer, IA [*Library symbol Library of Congress*] (LCLS)

IaWhHi .... Loess Hills Historical Society of Monona County, Whiting, IA [*Library symbol*] [*Library of Congress*] (LCLS)

IaWhitC........ Whittmore Champion, Whittmore, IA [*Library symbol Library of Congress*] (LCLS)

IAWHPJ .... International Association of Women and Home Page Journalists (EA)

IaWij............ Wilton Public Library, Wilton Junction, IA [*Library symbol Library of Congress*] (LCLS)

IaWijS .... S-R Advocate News, Wilton Junction, IA [*Library symbol Library of Congress*] (LCLS)

IaWinfB........ Beacon and Wayland News, Winfield, IA [*Library symbol Library of Congress*] (LCLS)

IaWinN .... Winthrop News, Winthrop, IA [*Library symbol Library of Congress*] (LCLS)

IaWint.......... Winterset Public Library, Winterset, IA [*Library symbol Library of Congress*] (LCLS)

IaWintM....... Winterset Madisonian, Winterset, IA [*Library symbol Library of Congress*] (LCLS)

IAWISP .... International Accidental War Information Sharing Project [*Nuclear Age Peace Foundation*] (EA)

IaWl............. Free Public Library, West Liberty, IA [*Library symbol Library of Congress*] (LCLS)

IAWL............ International Association for Water Law [*See also AIDA*] [*Rome, Italy*] (EAIO)

IaWlI............ West Liberty Index, West Liberty, IA [*Library symbol Library of Congress*] (LCLS)

IAWM........... International Alliance for Women in Music (NTPA)

IAWM........... International Association of Women Ministers (EA)

IaWmbgI...... Iowa County Farmer, Williamsburg, IA [*Library symbol Library of Congress*] (LCLS)

IaWmbgJT ... Williamsburg Jounal-Tribune, Williamsburg, IA [*Library symbol Library of Congress*] (LCLS)

IAWMC .... International Association of Workers for Troubled Children and Youth [*See also AIEJI*] (EAIO)

IaWob.......... Woodbine Public Library, Woodbine, IA [*Library symbol Library of Congress*] (LCLS)

IaWobT .... Woodbine Twiner, Woodbine, IA [*Library symbol Library of Congress*] (LCLS)

IaWow .... Woodward Public Library, Woodward, IA [*Library symbol Library of Congress*] (LCLS)

IaWowN .... Northeast Dallas County Record, Woodward, IA [*Library symbol Library of Congress*] (LCLS)

IAWP .... Inter-National Association for Widowed People (EA)

IAWP .... International Association of Women Philosophers [*Zurich, Switzerland*] (EAIO)

IAWP .... International Association of Women Police (EA)

IaWp .... West Point Public Library, West Point, IA [*Library symbol Library of Congress*] (LCLS)

IaWpB.......... West Point Bee, West Point, IA [*Library symbol Library of Congress*] (LCLS)

IAWPR .... International Association of Water Polo Referees (EA)

IAWPR .... International Association on Water Pollution Research [*Later, IAWPRC*]

IAWPRC...... International Association on Water Pollution Research and Control [*British*] (EA)

IAWR .... Institute of Air Weapons Research [*Air Force*]

IAWR .... Internationale Arbeitsgemeinschaft der Wasserwerke im Rheineinzugsgebiet [*International Association of Waterworks in the Rhine Basin Area - IAWRBA*] (EAIO)

IAWRBA....... International Association of Waterworks in the Rhine Basin Area (EAIO)

IAWRT .... International Association of Women in Radio and Television (NTCM)

IAWS .... Intercollegiate Association of Women Students (AEBS)

IAWS .... Irish Agricultural Wholesale Society Ltd. (BI)

IAWTC .... Integrated Air Warfare Training Complex [*Military*] (CAAL)

IaWu .... Heiseman Memorial Library, West Union, IA [*Library symbol Library of Congress*] (LCLS)

IaWuCoC..... Fayette County Courthouse, West Union, IA [*Library symbol Library of Congress*] (LCLS)

IaWuU .... Fayette County Union, West Union, IA [*Library symbol Library of Congress*] (LCLS)

IAWWE .... International Association of Workshop Way Educators (EA)

IaWyo .... Roche Memorial Library, Wyoming, IA [*Library symbol Library of Congress*] (LCLS)

IAX.............. University of Illinois at the Medical Center, Chicago, IL [*OCLC symbol*] (OCLC)

IAY.............. Island Canyon Mines, Inc. [*Vancouver Stock Exchange symbol*]

IAY.............. University of Illinois at Chicago Circle, Chicago, IL [*OCLC symbol*] (OCLC)

IAYB............ Interim Accessory Bulletin (DNAB)

IAYC............ Interim Accessory Change (MCD)

IAYF............ Information at Your Fingertips

IAYM........... International Association of Youth Magistrates [*Later, IAJFCM*]

IAYMC .... International Association of Y's Men's Clubs [*Geneva, Switzerland*] (EA)

IAZ.............. Industrie Air Charter [*France ICAO designator*] (FAAC)

IAZ.............. Inner Artillery Zone

IAZ.............. Western Illinois University, Macomb, IL [*OCLC symbol*] (OCLC)

IaZN............ Tri-County News, Zearing, IA [*Library symbol Library of Congress*] (LCLS)

IB................ I-Beam [*Lumber*] (DAC)

IB................ Iberia Air Lines of Spain [*ICAO designator*] (AD)

ib................ Ibidem [*Latin*] [*In the same place*] (WDMC)

IB................ Ibidem [*In the Same Place*] [*Latin*]

Ib................ Ibis [*of Ovid*] [*Classical studies*] (OCD)

IB................ Ibrahim-Beck [*Disease*] [*Medicine*] (DB)

IB................ Identification Beacon [*Aviation*] (IAA)

IB................ Identifier Block

IB................ Imbibition Printing [*Cinematography*] (WDMC)

IB................ Immune Body

IB................ Impact Bag (SAA)

IB................ Inboard (NASA)

IB................ In Bond [*Wines and Spirits*]

IB................ Inbound

IB................ In Bulk (IAA)

IB................ Incendiary Bomb

IB................ Incentive-Based Policy [*for environmental improvement*]

IB................ Inclusion Body [*Cytology*]

ib................ Indent Both (WDMC)

IB................ Index of Body Build [*Anatomy*]

IB................ India-Burma [*World War II*]

IB................ Individual Bias

IB................ Induction Balance (ADA)

IB................ Induction Brazing

IB................ Industrial Business [*Insurance term*] [*British*]

IB................ Industrialized Building (PDAA)

IB................ Inert Building [*NASA*] (KSC)

IB................ Infantry Battalion [*Army*]

IB................ Infantry Brigade [*British military*] (DMA)

IB................ Infectious Bronchitis [*Medicine*]

IB................ Information Bulletin

IB................ Information Bureau [*Telecommunications*] (TEL)

IB................ Information Bus (IAA)

IB................ Inner Bottom [*Technical drawings*]

IB................ Input Buffer [*Telecommunications*] (TEL)

IB................ Input Bus [*Computer science*]

IB................ Inspection Bulletin

IB................ Institute of Bankers [*Later, CIB*] [*British*] (DI)

IB................ Institute of Biology [*British*]

IB................ Institute of Brewing [*Also, IOB*] [*British*]

IB................ Institute of Building [*British*]

IB................ Instruction Bank [*Computer science*]

IB................ Instruction Book

IB................ Instruction Bus [*Computer science*]

IB................ Intelligence Branch

IB................ Interbank (EBF)

IB................ Interface Bus [*Computer science*]

IB................ Internal Bond [*Pulp and paper technology*]

IB .... Internal Browning [of Fruits and Vegetables] (BARN)
IB .... Internal Bus [Computer science]
IB .... International Baccalaureate
IB .... International Bank (EFIS)
IB .... International Bank for Reconstruction and Development [Also known as World Bank]
IB .... International Broadcasting
IB .... International Butec Industry [Vancouver Stock Exchange symbol]
IB .... Interpreter's Bible
IB .... Introducing Broker (MHDB)
IB .... Investigation Branch [British Australia] (DCTA)
IB .... Invoice Book [Business term]
IB .... Irish Baron (ROG)
IB .... Iron Bolts
IB .... Ironing Board (MSA)
IB .... Is Between (MHDB)
IB .... Isolation Bed [Infectious disease] (DAVI)
IB .... Issue Book [DoD]
IB .... Lineas Aereas du Espanalos [Iberia] [Spain ICAO designator]
IB .... RAB [Radio Advertising Bureau] Instant Background [A publication]
IBa .... Barrington Area Library District, Barrington, IL [Library symbol] [Library of Congress] (LCLS)
IBA .... Bradley University, Peoria, IL [OCLC symbol] (OCLC)
IBA .... Ibadan [Nigeria] [Airport symbol] (OAG)
IBA .... Igniter Booster Assembly [Aerospace]
IBA .... Ignorant Bloody Aircrafthand [British Royal Air Force slang]
IBA .... Independent Bakers Association (EA)
IBA .... Independent Bar Association (EA)
IBA .... Independent Board Authority [Board granting franchises to new companies] [British]
IBA .... Independent Broadcasting Authority [Formerly, ITA] [British]
IBA .... Indian Banks Association (PDAA)
IBA .... Indolebutyric Acid [Plant growth regulator]
IBA .... Indonesian-British Association (DS)
IBA .... Industrial Bankers' Association [British] (BI)
IBA .... Industrial Biotechnology Association (EA)
IBA .... Inflatable Boat Association (EA)
IBA .... Inhomogeneously Broadened Absorber [Optics]
IBA .... Inner Blanket Assembly [Nuclear energy] (NRCH)
IBA .... Inspection by Attribute
IBA .... Institute for Bioenergetic Analysis [Later, IIBA] (EA)
IBA .... Institute for Briquetting and Agglomeration (EA)
IBA .... Institute of British Architects
IBA .... Institute of Business Appraisers (EA)
IBA .... Institution of Business Agents [British]
IBA .... International Backgammon Association (EA)
IBA .... International Backpackers Association [Later, AHS] (EA)
IBA .... International Balloon Association (EA)
IBA .... International Banana Association (EA)
IBA .... International Banker Association (EA)
IBA .... International Banking Act [1978]
IBA .... International Bar Association [British] (EA)
IBA .... International Bartenders Association [Paris, France] (EAIO)
IBA .... International Baseball Association (EA)
IBA .... International Basketball Association [Defunct] (EA)
IBA .... International Bauxite Association [Kingston, Jamaica]
IBA .... International Biliary Association [Later, IHBPA] (EAIO)
IBA .... International Biometric Association (EA)
IBA .... International Board of Auditors (NATG)
IBA .... International Bocce Association (EA)
IBA .... International Bodyguard Association (EA)
IBA .... International Border Area
IBA .... International Braford Association (EA)
IBA .... International Bridge Academy [The Hague, Netherlands] (EA)
IBA .... International Bryozoology Association [See also AIB] [Paris, France] (EAIO)
IBA .... Investing Builders Association
IBA .... Investment Bankers Association of America [Later, SIA] (EA)
IBA .... Iodosobenzoic Acid [Organic chemistry] (RDA)
IBA .... Ion-Backscattering Analysis (IAA)
IBA .... Ion Beam Analysis
IBA .... Isobutylamine [Organic chemistry]
IBA .... Lineas Aereas Iberoamericanas [Chile] [FAA designator] (FAAC)
IBAA .... Independent Bankers Association of America (EA)
IBAA .... International Business Aircraft Association (DA)
IBAA .... International Business Analysts Association (NTPA)
IBAA .... Italian Baptist Association of America [Later, AEIM] (EA)
IBAC .... Caligula [the Poisoner] [the Hun the Emperor Initials that form the name of the villain in "Captain Marvel" comic strip and indicate the sources of his power]
IBAC .... Information Bulletin of Australian Criminology [A publication]
IBAC .... Instantaneous Broadcast Audience Counting (IAA)
IBAC .... International Business Aviation Council (EA)
IBACOS .... Integrated Building and Construction Solutions
IBAD .... Ion-Beam-Assisted Deposition [Organic chemistry]
IBAE .... Ion Beam Assisted Etching (AAEL)
IBAF .... Interim Brigade Afloat Force [Prepositioning force] [Army] (DOMA)
IBAG .... Ich Bau auf Gott [I Build on God] [Motto of Heinrich Posthumus, Count Reuss (1572-1635)] [German]
IBAH .... IBAH, Inc. [NASDAQ symbol] (SAG)
IBAHP .... Inter-African Bureau for Animal Health and Protection
IBAHRS .... Inflatable Body and Head Restraint System [Aviation] (RDA)
IBALS .... Interactive Balancing through Simulation (PDAA)
IBAN .... Imperial Bancorp [NASDAQ symbol] (NQ)
I (Bank) .... Instruction Bank [Computer science]

IBAP .... Intervention Board for Agricultural Products [Government body] [British]
I Bar .... I Baruch [Apocrypha] (BJA)
IBAR .... Inter-African Bureau of Animal Resources [Kenya]
IBarA .... American Can Co., Barrington, IL [Library symbol Library of Congress] (LCLS)
IBarAS .... Allstate Insurance Co., Barrington, IL [Library symbol] [Library of Congress] (LCLS)
IBarQ .... Quaker Oats Co., Research Library, Barrington, IL [Library symbol Library of Congress] (LCLS)
IBart .... Alpha Park Public Library, Bartonville, IL [Library symbol Library of Congress] (LCLS)
IBartL .... Limestone Community High School, Bartonville, IL [Library symbol Library of Congress] (LCLS)
IBAS .... Improved Bradley Acquisition Subsystem [Army] (RDA)
IBAS .... Improved Bradley Acquisition System [Army] (INF)
IBAS .... Informationssystem Beliebiger Andwendungssystem [Germany] (NITA)
IBAS .... Instructional-Based Appraisal System [Education]
IBAS .... Intelligent Body Assembly System [Robotics] [Nissan Motor Co. Ltd.]
IBASF .... Intervals Between Aircraft in Stream Type Formation [Aviation] (FAAC)
IBAT .... Improved Brilliant Anti-Armor [Army] (RDA)
IBAT .... Independent Bankers Association of Texas (SRA)
IBAT .... Intravascular Bronchoalveolar Tumor [Medicine] (DMAA)
IBatF .... FERMILAB, Batavia, IL [Library symbol Library of Congress] (LCLS)
IBAW .... Independent Community Bankers Association of Wisconsin (TBD)
IBA West .... Insurance Brokers and Agents of the West
IBB .... Binter Canarias [Spain ICAO designator] (FAAC)
IBB .... Chicago Transit Authority, Chicago, IL [OCLC symbol] (OCLC)
IBB .... Institute of British Bakers (BI)
IBB .... Intentional Bases on Balls [Baseball]
IBB .... International Bank Bond (MHDB)
IBB .... International Book Bank (EA)
IBB .... International Bortherhood of Boilermakers, Iron Ship Builders, Blacksmiths, Forgers, and Helpers (NTPA)
IBB .... International Bowling Board (EA)
IBB .... International Brotherhood of Bookbinders [Later, Graphic Arts International Union]
IBB .... Intestinal Brush Border [Medicine] (MAE)
IBB .... Invest in Britain Bureau
IBB .... Isobutylbenzene [Organic chemistry]
IBBA .... Inland Bird Banding Association (EA)
IBBA .... International Brangus Breeders Association (EA)
IBBA .... International Business Brokers Association [Defunct] (EA)
IBBA .... Irish Basketball Association (DBA)
IBBBA .... International Bundle Branch Block Association (EA)
IBBC .... International Business Communications Council [Japan] (ECON)
IBBCA .... International Bathymetric Chart of the Caribbean Sea and Gulf of Mexico [Marine science] (OSRA)
IBBFIC .... International B & B [Bed and Breakfast] Fly-Inn Club (EA)
IBBH .... Internationaler Bund der Bau-Haolzarbeiter [International Federation of Building and Woodworkers]
IBBIT .... Internal Bean Bacterial Infusion Test [Plant pathology]
IBBL .... Islamic Bank of Bangladesh [Commercial bank] (EY)
IBBM .... Ion-Binding/Ion-Bouncing Model [Physical chemistry]
IBBM .... Iron Body Bronze-Mounted
IBBN .... Inhomogeneous Big Bang Nucleosynthesis [Cosmology]
IBBR .... International Beefalo Breeders' Registry (EA)
IBBRIS .... International Biodeterioration Bulletin. Reference Index [A publication]
IBBTPS .... Ivory and Bone Brushmakers' Trade Protection Society [A union] [British]
IBBY .... International Board on Books for Young People [Basel, Switzerland] (EA)
IBC .... De Paul University, Law Library, Chicago, IL [OCLC symbol] (OCLC)
IBC .... Iceland Base Command [Army World War II]
IBC .... Idaho Bean Commission (SRA)
IBC .... Illini-Badger Conference (PSS)
IBC .... Imperial Bushmen Contingent [British military] (DMA)
IBC .... Independent Bakers' Cooperative [W. E. Long Co.] (EA)
IBC .... Independent Bankers of Colorado (TBD)
IBC .... Informatica Bulgarien Corp. [Bulgaria] [ICAO designator] (FAAC)
IBC .... Information-Based Complexity [Mathematics]
IBC .... Input Bias Current
IBC .... Insect Biotech Canada [Queen's University] [Research center] (RCD)
IBC .... Inside Back Cover
ibc .... Inside Back Cover [Publishing] (WDAA)
IBC .... Institute for Biomedical Communication [South African Medical Research Council] [Information service or system] (IID)
IBC .... Institute of Building Control [British] (DBA)
IBC .... Institutional Biosafety Committee [National Institutes of Health]
IBC .... Instrument Bus Computer
IBC .... Insurance Bureau of Canada
IBC .... Integrated Block Channel (MHDB)
IBC .... Integrated Block Controller (NITA)
IBC .... Integrated Broadband Communications (MHDB)
IBC .... Integrated Business Communications [British] (NITA)
IBC .... Integrated Business Computers [Manufacturer] (NITA)
IBC .... Intelligent Broadband Controller (NITA)
IBC .... Intelligent Buildings Corp. [Broomfield, CO] [Telecommunications service] (TSSD)
IBC .... Interboard Committee for Christian Work in Japan [Later, JNAC] (EA)
IBC .... Interconnect Backplane Capability
IBC .... Intermediate Bulk Containers [Shipping]

IBC..............	International Ballet Competition
IBC..............	International Ballet Council
IBC..............	International Banana Club (EA)
IBC..............	International Banking Centre [*British*]
IBC..............	International Bathymetric Chart [*Marine science*] (OSRA)
IBC..............	International Betta Congress (EA)
IBC..............	International Biographical Centre [*British*] (CB)
IBC..............	International Biophysical Center
IBC..............	International Biotoxicological Center [*World Life Research Institute*] [*US*] (ASF)
IBC..............	International Board of Cytopathology [*International Academy of Cytology*] [*Quebec, PQ*] (EAIO)
IBC..............	International Borzoi Council (EA)
IBC..............	International BRCA [*Breast Cancer*] Consortium
IBC..............	International Brightness Coefficient
IBC..............	International Broadcasting Convention [*Legal term*] (DLA)
IBC..............	International Broadcasting Corp. [*Vancouver Stock Exchange symbol*]
IBC..............	International Bulk Chemical
IBC..............	International Bus Collectors Club (EA)
IBC..............	International Business Communications [*Commercial firm British*]
IBC..............	International Business Consultants [*Commercial firm*]
IBC..............	International Business Contacts
IBC..............	International Business Corp.
IBC..............	International Business Council (EA)
IBC..............	International Federation of the Blue Cross [*Formerly, International Federation of the Temperance Blue Cross Societies*] (EA)
IBC..............	Internet Business Center [*Information service or system*] (IID)
IBC..............	Interstate Bakeries [*NYSE symbol*] (TTSB)
IBC..............	Interstate Bakeries Corp. [*NYSE symbol*] (SPSG)
IBC..............	Inverted Bowl Centrifuge
IBC..............	Iodine Binding Capacity [*of starch*]
IBC..............	Iowa Business Council (SRA)
IBC..............	Iron-Binding Capacity [*Clinical chemistry*]
IBC..............	Isobaric Cooling [*Geology*]
IBC..............	World Institute of Buddhist Culture
IBCA..............	Department of the Interior Board of Contract Appeals
IBCA..............	Idaho Building Contractors Association (SRA)
IBCA..............	Illinois Bulk Carriers Association (SRA)
IBCA..............	Indiana Beef Cattle Association (SRA)
IBCA..............	Industry Bar Code Alliance (EA)
IBCA..............	Institute of Burial and Cremation Administration [*British*]
IBCA..............	Interior Board of Contract Appeals (in United States Interior Decisions) [*A publication*] (DLA)
IBCA..............	International Braille Chess Association [*Abcoude, Netherlands*] (EA)
IBCA..............	International Brick Collectors' Association (EA)
IBCA..............	Isobutyl Cyanoacrylate [*Organic chemistry*]
IBCAM..........	Institute of British Carriage and Automobile Manufacturers (BI)
IBCASA	International Banking Campaign Against South Africa [*Later, ICABA*] (EAIO)
IBCC..............	International Building Classification Committee [*Netherlands*]
IBCC..............	International Business Communications Council (ECON)
IBCC..............	International Business Contact Club
IBCC..............	Intra-Bureau Change Committee
IBCE..............	Indo-British Cultural Exchange
IBCE..............	International Binding Center at Elat [*Israel*]
IBCEA..........	International Bathymetric Chart of the Central Eastern Atlantic [*Marine science*] (OSRA)
IBCFA..........	Injected Beam Cross Field Amplifier (IAA)
IBCFP..........	International Board of Standards and Practices for Certified Financial Planners (EA)
IBCL..............	Instrument Bus Control Language [*National Instruments Corp.*] [*Austin, TX*]
IBCL..............	Interface Bus Control Language [*Computer science*]
IBCM..........	Integrated Battlefield Casualty Manikin [*Medical training*] [*Navy*]
IBCM..........	International Business Council Midamerica (EA)
IBCN..........	Integrated Broadband Communication Network [*Telecommunications*]
IBCP..........	Imperial British Conservative Party [*Political party*] (ADA)
IBCP..........	Independent Bank [*NASDAQ symbol*] (TTSB)
IBCP..........	Independent Bank Corp. [*NASDAQ symbol*] (NQ)
IBCRSGA......	International Bathymetric Chart of the Red Sea and Gulf of Aden [*Proposed*] [*Marine science*] (OSRA)
IBCS..........	Inflight Blood Collection System [*On space flights*]
IBCS..........	Integrated Battlefield Control System [*Army*]
IBCS..........	Interlink Business and Communications Services [*British telecommunications service company*] (NITA)
IBCS/TRICAP...	Integrated Battlefield Communications Systems / Triple Capability-Armoured, Infantry and Air Cavalry [*Military*] (PDAA)
IBCSVP	International Breeding Consortium for St. Vincent Parrot (EAIO)
IBCWIO	International Bathymetric Chart of the Western Indian Ocean [*Marine science*] (OSRA)
IBCWP	International Bathymetric Chart of the Western Pacific [*Marine science*] (OSRA)
IBD..............	Baylor College of Dentistry, Dallas, TX [*OCLC symbol*] (OCLC)
IBD..............	Ibadan [*Nigeria*] [*Geomagnetic observatory code*]
IBD..............	Identical-By-Descent [*Genetics*]
IBD..............	Incomplete Block Design (MCD)
IBD..............	Incorporated Institute of British Decorators and Interior Designers (BI)
IBD..............	Infectious Bursal Disease [*Avian pathology*]
IBD..............	Inflammatory Bowel Disease [*Medicine*]
IBD..............	Inhabited Building Distance [*Army*] (AABC)
IBD..............	Institute of Business Designers (EA)
IBD..............	Interest Bearing Deposit [*Banking*] (ADA)
IBD..............	Interior Ballistic Division [*Ballistic Research Laboratory*] [*Army*] (RDA)

IBD..............	Intermediate Block Diagram (IAA)
IBD..............	International Business Database [*Information service or system*] (IID)
IBD..............	International Business Development Program [*Northwestern University*] [*Research center*] (RCD)
IBD..............	Internationale Bildungs- und Informations- Datenbank [*International Education and Information Data Bank*] [*Thiede & Thiede Mittelstandische Systemberatung GmbH*] [*Information service or system*] (IID)
IBD..............	Investor's Business Daily [*A publication*]
IBD..............	Ion Beam Deposition [*Coating technology*]
IBD..............	Irritable Bowel Disease [*Medicine*] (DMAA)
IBD..............	Ischemic Bowel Disease [*Medicine*] (DAVI)
IBD..............	Sandoz Pharmaceuticals [*Research code symbol*]
IBDA	Indirect Bomb-Damage Assessment
IBDA	International Balance Disorder Association [*Defunct*] (EA)
IBD-APM...	Identity-By-Descent Affected-Pedigree-Member [*Genetics*]
IBDB	Internationaal Belasting Documentatie Bureau [*International Bureau of Fiscal Documentation*] (EAIO)
IBDB	International Battery Data Base [*Robert Morey Associates*] [*Information service or system*] (IID)
IBDCC	International Barbie Doll Collectors Club (EA)
IBDEA	Inernational Beverage Dispensing Equipment Association (NTPA)
IBDI	International Bureau of Documentation and Information on Sport (NITA)
IBDM	Interim Bomber Defense Missile
IBDN	Insulated Building Distribution Network [*Northern Telecom*]
IBDPW	International Brotherhood of Du Pont Workers (EA)
IBDS	Improved Biological Detection System [*Military*] (MCD)
IBDT	Insulation Breakdown Tester
IBDU	Isobutylidenediurea [*Organic chemistry*]
IBDV	Infectious Bursal Disease Virus
IBDVS	Indian Base Depot Veterinary Stores [*British military*] (DMA)
IBE	Ibague [*Colombia*] [*Airport symbol*] (OAG)
IBE	Iberia-Lineas Aereas de Espana SA [*Spain ICAO designator*] (FAAC)
IBE	Inert-Ion Beam Etching
IBE	Inner Back End (MSA)
IBE	Institute for Biological Engineering
IBE	Institute of British Engineers (DAS)
IBE	Institute of Broadcast Engineers [*Later, SBE*] (NTCM)
IBE	Institute of Building Estimators Ltd. [*British*] (BI)
IBE	Institution of Body Engineers [*British*] (BI)
IBE	International Beverage Co. [*Vancouver Stock Exchange symbol*]
IBE	International Bureau for Epilepsy [*Alderley Edge, Cheshire, England*] (EAIO)
IBE	International Bureau of Education [*See also BIE*] [*UNESCO*] (EAIO)
IBE	Interval Between Eruptions [*of Geyser*]
IBE	Inventory by Exception (MHDB)
IBE	Ion Beam Etching (AAEL)
IBE	Isoelectronic Bound Exciton [*Electronics*] (AAEL)
IBE	Rosary College, River Forest, IL [*OCLC symbol*] (OCLC)
IBea	Beardstown Public Library, Beardstown, IL [*Library symbol Library of Congress*] (LCLS)
IBEA	Industrial Base Engineering Activity (RDA)
IBE(A)	Institution of Biomedical Engineering (Australia)
IBEAR	International Business Education and Research Program [*University of Southern California*] [*Research center*] (RCD)
IBEC	International Bank for Economic Cooperation [*Moscow, USSR*] (EY)
IBEC	International Basic Economic Cooperation [*Investment term*] (DS)
IBECO	Inboard Booster Engine Cutoff (MCD)
IBED	Inter-African Bureau for Epizootic Diseases [*Later, IBAR*]
IBEDOC	International Bureau of Education Documentation and Information System (NITA)
IBEE	International Builders Exchange Executives (EA)
IBEF	International Bio-Environmental Foundation (EA)
IBEG	International Book Export Group
IBel	Belleville Public Library, Belleville, IL [*Library symbol Library of Congress*] (LCLS)
IBEL	Interest-Bearing Eligible Liabilities
IBelC	Belleville Area College, Belleville, IL [*Library symbol Library of Congress*] (LCLS)
IBelHS	Altoff High School, Belleville, IL [*Library symbol Library of Congress*] (LCLS)
IBelHSD	Harmony-Emge-Ellis School District 175, Belleville, IL [*Library symbol Library of Congress*] (LCLS)
IBelS	Saint Henry's Seminary, Belleville, IL [*Library symbol Library of Congress*] (LCLS)
IBelSCM	Saint Clair County Mental Health Board, Belleville, IL [*Library symbol Library of Congress*] (LCLS)
IBelSD	Belleville Public Schools District 118, Belleville, IL [*Library symbol Library of Congress*] (LCLS)
IBelSH	Saint Elizabeth's Hospital, Belleville, IL [*Library symbol Library of Congress*] (LCLS)
IBelTSD	Belleville Township High School District 201, Belleville, IL [*Library symbol Library of Congress*] (LCLS)
IBelv	Ida Public Library, Belvidere, IL [*Library symbol Library of Congress*] (LCLS)
IBelVS	Belle Valley School, Belleville, IL [*Library symbol Library of Congress*] (LCLS)
IBelw	Bellwood Public Library, Bellwood, IL [*Library symbol Library of Congress*] (LCLS)
IBem	Bement Township Library, Bement, IL [*Library symbol Library of Congress*] (LCLS)
IBEM	International Board of Environmental Medicine (EA)
IBemSD	Bement Community Unit School District, Bement, IL [*Library symbol*] [*Library of Congress*] (LCLS)

IBEN............ Incendiary Bomb with Explosive Nose

IB-EP .... Immunoreactive Beta-Endomorphin [*Immunochemistry*] (DMAA)

IBEP............. Integrated Border Environment Plan [*Mexico/US border policy*] (CROSS)

IBer............. Berwyn Public Library, Berwyn, IL [*Library symbol Library of Congress*] (LCLS)

IBER............ Institute for Biomedical Engineering Research [*University of Akron*] [*Research center*] (RCD)

IBerk........... Berkeley Public Library, Berkeley, IL [*Library symbol Library of Congress*] (LCLS)

IBERLANT ... Iberian Atlantic Area [*NATO*] (NATG)

IBerMH .... MacNeal Memorial Hospital, Berwyn, IL [*Library symbol Library of Congress*] (LCLS)

IBerO .... Olympic Savings & Loan Association, Berwyn, IL [*Library symbol Library of Congress*] (LCLS)

IBERT........... Institute for Better Education through Resource Technology

IBES............. Institutional Brokers Estimate System [*Lynch, Jones & Ryan*] [*Database*] [*New York, NY Information service or system*] (IID)

IBES............. Integration Building and Equipment Scheduling (PDAA)

IBES............. International Bronchoesophagological Society (EA)

IBES............. International Business Earth Stations [*Communications Satellite Corp.*]

IBET............. Trans World Gaming [*NASDAQ symbol*] (TTSB)

IBET............. Trans World Gaming Corp. [*NASDAQ symbol*] (SAG)

IBETA........... Irish Business Equipment Trade Association (DBA)

IBeth........... Bethalto Public Library, Bethalto, IL [*Library symbol Library of Congress*] (LCLS)

IBethCU .... Bethalto Community Unit 8, Bethalto, IL [*Library symbol Library of Congress*] (LCLS)

IBETW.......... Trans World Gaming Wrrt [*NASDAQ symbol*] (TTSB)

IBEU............. Independent Bakery Employees Union (EA)

IBEW............ International Brotherhood of Electrical Workers (EA)

IBEX............. International Biotechnology Expo (HGEN)

IBEX............. International Building Exposition

IBF............... Chicago Municipal Reference Library, Chicago, IL [*OCLC symbol*] (OCLC)

IBF............... First Iberian Fund [*AMEX symbol*] (TTSB)

IBF............... First Iberian Fund, Inc. [*AMEX symbol*] (SPSG)

IBF............... Imaginary Basketball Federation (EA)

IBF............... Immature Brown-Fat [*Cells*]

IBF............... Immunoglobulin-Binding Factor [*Immunology*] (MAE)

IBF............... Input Buffer Full [*Computer science*] (MHDB)

IBF............... Institute of British Foundrymen (EAIO)

IBF............... Internally Blown Flap [*Aviation*]

IBF............... International Badminton Federation [*Cheltenham, Gloustershire, England*] (EAIO)

IBF............... International Balint Federation [*Brussels, Belgium*] (EAIO)

IBF............... International Balut Federation [*Bangkok, Thailand*] (EAIO)

IBF............... International Bandy Federation [*Lulea, Sweden*] (EAIO)

IBF............... International Banking Facility

IBF............... International Bar Fly [*Sign in Harry's New York Bar, Paris*]

IBF............... International Bicycle Fund (EA)

IBF............... International Bobsled Federation

IBF............... International Booksellers Federation [*Formerly, ICBA*] [*Austria*] (EA)

IBF............... International Boxing Federation (EA)

IBF............... Internationales Begegnungszentrum Friedenshaus [*Germany*] (EAIO)

IBFAN........... International Baby Food Action Network (EA)

IBFC............. Iron Butterfly Fan Club [*Later, IBIN*] (EA)

IBFCC........... International Border Fancy Canary Club (EA)

IBFD............. International Bureau of Fiscal Documentation (EAIO)

IBFEG........... Internationaler Bund Freier Evangelischer Gemeinden [*International Federation of Free Evangelical Churches - IFFEC*] (EA)

IBFF............. Impulse Base Flow Facility [*NASA*]

IBFG............. Internationaler Bund Freier Gewerkschaften [*International Confederation of Free Trade Unions*]

IBFI.............. International Business Forms Industries (EA)

IBFM............ Institute of Broadcasting Financial Management [*Later, BCFMA*]

IBFMP.......... International Bureau of the Federations of Master Printers

IBFN............. Integrated Broadband Fiber Optic Network [*Telecommunications*]

IBFO............. International Brotherhood of Firemen and Oilers (EA)

IBFRBTWB .. International Book Fair of Radical Black and Third World Books

IBFS............. Interim Billing and Follow-Up System [*Social Security Administration*] (GFGA)

IBFS............. International Benjamin Franklin Society [*Defunct*] (EA)

IBG............... CNA Financial Corp., Library, Chicago, IL [*Inactive*] [*OCLC symbol*] (OCLC)

IBG............... Incorporated Brewers' Guild [*British*] (EAIO)

IBG............... Insoluble Bone Gelatin [*Cardiology*] (DMAA)

IBG............... Institute for Behavioral Genetics [*University of Colorado - Boulder*] [*Research center*] (RCD)

IBG............... Institute of British Geographers (BI)

IBG............... Inter Block Gap

IBG............... Intermediate BTU [*British Thermal Unit*] Gas

IBG............... International Boxing Guild

IBG............... Internationale Begegnung in Gemeinschaftsdiensten [*Germany*] (EAIO)

IBG............... Internationale Brecht Gesellschaft [*International Brecht Society*] (EAIO)

IBG............... Internationale Bruckner Gesellschaft [*Vienna, Austria*] (EAIO)

IBG............... Internationales Buro fuer Gebirgsmechanik [*International Bureau of Strato-Mechanics - IBSM*] (EAIO)

IBGS .... Intravascular Blood Gas System [*Medicine*] (DB)

IBH............... Initial Beachhead [*Military*]

IBHA .... Insulation, Building, and Hard Board Association [*British*] (BI)

IBHA .... International Buckskin Horse Association (EA)

IBHD .... Initial Beachhead [*Military*]

IBHF............ International Boxing Hall of Fame (EA)

IBHFC .... Illini-Badger-Hawkeye Football Conference (PSS)

IBHR .... International Bibliography of the History of Religions [*A publication*] (BJA)

IBi............... Blue Island Public Library, Blue Island, IL [*Library symbol Library of Congress*] (LCLS)

i-bi-- .... British Indian Ocean Territory [*MARC geographic area code Library of Congress*] (LCCP)

IBI............... College of Du Page, Glen Ellyn, IL [*OCLC symbol*] (OCLC)

IBI............... Independent Black Institution

IBI............... Independent Broadcast Institute [*British*]

IBI............... Individualized Bilingual Instruction (EDAC)

IBI............... Information Builders, Inc. [*New York*] [*Commercial firm*] (CDE)

IBI............... Institute for Biotechnology Information (HGEN)

IBI............... Insulation Board Institute [*Later, ABPA*] (EA)

IBI............... Intelligent Buildings Institute (EA)

IBI............... Interburst Interval [*Electrophysiology*]

IBI............... Intergovernmental Bureau for Informatics [*Telecommunications*] (EA)

IBI............... Interim Ballistic Instrumentation

IBI............... Intermittent Bladder Irrigation [*Medicine*]

IBI............... International Bankers, Inc.

IBI............... International Biomass Institute (EA)

IBI............... International Biotechnologies, Inc.

IBI............... International Brace Resources [*Vancouver Stock Exchange symbol*]

IBI............... International Broadcast Institute [*Later, IIC*]

IBI............... International Bureau for Informatics (CSR)

IBi............... International Business Intelligence [*A publication*]

IBI............... Internationales Burgen-Institut [*International Castles Institute*] [*Rozendaal, Netherlands*] (EA)

IBI............... Interpersonal Behavior Inventory [*Veterans Administration*]

IBI............... Interview-Oriented Background Investigation (MCD)

IBI............... Intimate Brands 'A' [*NYSE symbol*] (TTSB)

IBI............... Intimate Brands, Inc. [*NYSE symbol*] (SAG)

IBI............... Invoice Book Inward [*Business term*]

IBI............... Ischemic Brain Infarction [*Medicine*] (DMAA)

IBI............... Islamic Bank International

IBIA............. Institute of British Industrial Art

IBIA............. Interior Board of Indian Affairs (in United States Interior Decisions) [*A publication*] (DLA)

IB (I and II)... Information Bank (I and II) (NITA)

IBIB............. Isobutyl Isobutyrate [*Organic chemistry*]

IBIC............. Interface Bus Interactive Control [*Computer science*]

IBICC........... Incorporated British Institute of Certified Carpenters (BI)

IBICT........... Instituto Brasileiro de Informacao em Ciencia e Tecnologia [*Brazilian Institute for Information in Science and Technology*] [*National Council of Scientific and Technological Development*] [*Information service or system*] (IID)

IBID .... Ibidem [*In the Same Place*] [*Latin*]

IBID .... International Bibliographical Description

IBI-ICC......... IBI [*Intergovernmental Bureau for Informatics*] International Computation Centre (NITA)

IBI-ICC......... Intergovernmental Bureau for Informatics - International Computation Center (CSR)

IBIN .... Integrated Brands [*NASDAQ symbol*] (SAG)

IBIN .... Integrated Brands 'A' [*NASDAQ symbol*] (TTSB)

IBIN .... Iron Butterfly Information Network (EA)

IBiol............ Institute of Biology [*British*] (DI)

IBIP............. International Books in Print [*A publication*]

IBIS............. Ibis Technology [*NASDAQ symbol*] (TTSB)

IBIS............. Ibis Technology Corp. [*NASDAQ symbol*] (SAG)

IBIS............. ICAO [*International Civil Aviation Organization*] Bird Strike Information System [*Information service or system*] (IID)

IBIS............. Industrialk Base Information System (AAGC)

IBIS............. Infrared Background Imaging Seeker (MCD)

IBiS............. Initiative in Biomolecular Structures [*University of New South Wales*] [*Australia*]

IBIS............. Inspectors Based in Schools [*British*] (AIE)

IBIS............. Integrated Botanical Information System [*Computer database*]

IBIS............. Integrated Building Industry System (PDAA)

IBIS............. Intelligent Business Information System (NITA)

IBIS............. Intense Bunched Ion Source (IEEE)

IBIS............. Intensive Biometric Intertidal Survey [*Botany*]

IBIS............. International Bank Information System

IBIS............. International Book Information Service

IBIS............. International Breast Cancer Intervention Study

IBIS............. Intranet Business Information System (PDAA)

IBIS............. Inventaire Bibliographique des Isiaca (BJA)

IBiS............. Issue-Based Information System [*Computer science*]

IBiS............. Saint Francis Hospital, Blue Island, IL [*Library symbol Library of Congress*] (LCLS)

IBisSD .... Bismarck-Henning Community Unit School District, Bismarck, IL [*Library symbol*] [*Library of Congress*] (LCLS)

IbisTc.......... Ibis Technology Corp. [*Associated Press*] (SAG)

IbisTech....... Ibis Technology Corp. [*Associated Press*] (SAG)

IBISW .... Ibis Technology Wrrt [*NASDAQ symbol*] (TTSB)

IBIT............. ICBM [*Intercontinental Ballistic Missile*] Blast Interference Test (MCD)

IBIT............. Initiated BIT (MCD)

IBIT............. Issue by Issue Tally

IBJ............... Industrial Bank of Japan

IBJ............... Instrument Bearing Jewel

IBJ............... Loop College, Chicago, IL [*OCLC symbol*] (OCLC)

IBJCA.......... International Blue Jay Class Association (EA)

IBJ Data ...... Industrial Bank of Japan Database [*Originator and databank on trade and economics*] [*Japan*] (NITA)

IBJI	Industrial Bank of Japan International Ltd. (ECON)
IBJM	International Board of Jewish Missions (EA)
IBK	Independent Bankshares [*AMEX symbol*] (TTSB)
IBK	Independent Bankshares, Inc. [*AMEX symbol*] (SAG)
IBK	[*The*] Industrial Bank of Kuwait
IBK	Infectious Bovine Keratoconjunctivitis [*Veterinary medicine*]
IBK	Innsbruck [*Austria*] [*Seismograph station code, US Geological Survey*] (SEIS)
IBK	Institute of Bookkeepers [*British*] (DAS)
IBK	Knox College, Galesburg, IL [*OCLC symbol*] (OCLC)
IBKA	Ikatan Buruh Kereta Api [*Railroad Workers' Union*] [*Indonesia*]
IBKB	Ikatan Buruh Kendaaran Bermotor [*Motor Transport Workers' Union*] [*Indonesia*]
IBKC	Infectious Bovine Keratoconjunctivitis (PDAA)
I BKR	Ice Breaker [*Freight*]
IBL	Boehringer Mannheim Corp., Indianapolis, IN [*OCLC symbol*] (OCLC)
IBL	Immunoblastic Lymphadenopathy [*Medicine*] (CPH)
IBL	Inside of the Battery Limits [*Engineering Economics*]
IBL	Interest-Bearing Liability
IBL	Interior Ballistics Laboratory [*Aberdeen, MD*] [*Army*]
IBL	Intermediate Behavioral Language (SAA)
IBL	International Brotherhood of Longshoremen
IBLA	Inter-American Bibliographical and Library Association (EA)
IBLA	Interior Board of Land Appeals [*Department of the Interior*]
IBLC	International B-24 Liberator Club (EA)
IBLE	International Brotherhood of Locomotive Engineers (EA)
IBLM	International Bureau of Legal Metrology
IBlo	Withers Public Library, Bloomington, IL [*Library symbol Library of Congress*] (LCLS)
IBloA	Illinois Agricultural Association, Bloomington, IL [*Library symbol Library of Congress*] (LCLS)
IBloC	Corn Belt Library System, Bloomington, IL [*Library symbol Library of Congress*] (LCLS)
IBloHi	McLean County Historical Society, Bloomington, IL [*Library symbol Library of Congress*] (LCLS)
IBloMH	Mennonite Hospital Association, Medical-Nursing Library, Bloomington, IL [*Library symbol Library of Congress*] (LCLS)
IBloSF	State Farm Insurance Co., Bloomington, IL [*Library symbol*] [*Library of Congress*] (LCLS)
IBloStJ	Saint Joseph's Hospital, Bloomington, IL [*Library symbol Library of Congress*] (LCLS)
IBloW	Illinois Wesleyan University, Bloomington, IL [*Library symbol Library of Congress*] (LCLS)
IBLP	Institute of Basic Life Principals (EA)
IBLS	International Brotherhood of Live Steamers (EA)
IBM	Ice-Binding Motif [*Biochemistry*]
IBM	Inclusion Body Myositis
IBM	Independent Community Bankers of Maine (TBD)
IBM	Individual-Based Model [*Marine science*] (OSRA)
IBM	Instant Big Mouth [*Martini*] [*Slang*]
IBM	Institute of Baths Management [*British*] (BI)
IBM	Institute of Builders Merchants [*British*] (DBA)
IBM	Instituto de Biologia Marina, San Antonia [*Argentina*] [*Marine science*] (OSRA)
IBM	Interacting Boson Model [*Of nuclear structure*]
IBM	Intercontinental Ballistic Missile
IBM	International Brotherhood of Magicians (EA)
IBM	International Business Machines [*Associated Press*] (SAG)
IBM	International Business Machines Corp. [*Facetious translations: I Buil t a Macintosh; I Buy Money; Inferior But Marketable; Insidious Black Magic; It'sBeen Malfunctioning; Incontinent Bowel Movement*] [*NYSE symbol Toronto Stock Exchange symbol*] (SPSG)
IBM	Intl Bus. Machines [*NYSE symbol*] (TTSB)
IBM	Kimball, NE [*Location identifier FAA*] (FAAL)
IBM	Kirkland & Ellis, Chicago, IL [*OCLC symbol*] (OCLC)
IBMA	Independent Battery Manufacturers Association (EA)
IBMA	Interior Board of Mine Operations Appeals (in United States Interior Decisions) [*A publication*] (DLA)
IBMA	International Bluegrass Music Association (EA)
IBMA	International Business Music Association (NTPA)
IBMA	Isobutoxymethyl Acrylamide [*Organic chemistry*]
IBMC	International Brotherhood of Motorcycle Campers (EA)
IBMC	International Buddhist Meditation Center (EA)
IBMCUA	IBM Computer Users' Association (NITA)
IBME	Institute of Biomedical Engineering [*University of Toronto*] [*Research center*] (RCD)
IBMK	Isobutyl Methyl Ketone [*Organic chemistry*]
IBMM	Integrated Book Manufacturing Machine
IBMNSW	Independent Bread Manufacturers of New South Wales [*Australia*]
IBMOC	Intercontinental Ballistic Missile Operational Capability (AAG)
IBMP	International Board of Medicine and Psychology [*Later, IAMP*] (EA)
IBMP	Isobutyl(methoxy)pyrazine [*Organic chemistry*]
IBMPrA	Intl Bus. Mach 7 1/2% Dep Pfd [*NYSE symbol*] (TTSB)
IBMS	Ion Beam Mass Spectrometer
IBMTR	International Bone Marrow Transplant Registry
IBM TSS	International Business Machine's Timesharing System (TEL)
IBM WU	IBM Workers United (EA)
IBMX	Isobutylmethylxanthine [*Also, MIX*] [*Biochemistry*]
IBN	Blackburn College, Carlinville, IL [*OCLC symbol*] (OCLC)
IBN	Identification Beacon
IBN	Indexed by Name (IAA)
IBN	Institut Belge de Normalisation [*Belgian Institute for Standardization*] [*Information service or system*] (IID)
IBN	International Biosciences Network
IBND	Independent Community Banks of North Dakota (TBD)
IBNJ	Independence Bancorp, Inc. [*NASDAQ symbol*] (SAG)
IBNJ	Independence Bancorp NJ [*NASDAQ symbol*] (TTSB)
IBNJP	Independence Banc 9% Cv Pfd [*NASDAQ symbol*] (TTSB)
IBNM	Independent Community Bankers of New Mexico (TBD)
IBNR	Incurred but Not Reported [*Insurance*]
IBNS	Inter-Borough Nomination Scheme [*British*] (DI)
IBNS	International Bank Note Society (EA)
IBNY	Independent Bankers Association of New York State (TBD)
IBO	Ibotenic Acid [*Organic acid*]
IBO	Idabel, OK [*Location identifier FAA*] (FAAL)
IBO	Instruction by Objective
IBO	International Baccalaureate Office [*See also OBI*] [*Later, International Baccalaureate Organization Grand-Saconnex, Switzerland*] (EAIO)
IBO	International Bowhunting Organization
IBO	International Broadcasting Organization
IBO	Internationale Bouworde [*International Association of Building Companions - IABC*] [*Marche-En-Famenne, Belgium*] (EAIO)
IBO	Invoice Book Outbound [*Business term*]
IBO	Lutheran General Hospital, Park Ridge, IL [*OCLC symbol*] (OCLC)
IBOA	Irish Bank Officials' Association [*Northern Ireland*]
IBOB	International Brotherhood of Old Bastards (EA)
IBOC	Iso and Bizzarrini Owners Club (EA)
IBOC	Isobutoxycarbonylation [*Organic chemistry*]
IB of TCWHA	International Brotherhood of Teamsters, Chauffeurs, Warehousemen, and Helpers ofAmerica
IBOL	Interactive Business-Oriented Language
IBOLS	Integrated Business-Oriented Language Support (IAA)
IBOND	IGOSS [*Integrated Global Ocean Station System*] Basic Observation Network Design [*Marine science*] (MSC)
IBOP	Institute of British Oil Paintings
IBOP	International Balance of Payments (AAGC)
IBOP	International Balance of Payments Reporting System
IBOP	International Brotherhood of Operative Potters [*Later, IBPAW*] (EA)
IBOS	International Business Opportunities Service [*World Bank*] [*United Nations*] (DUND)
IBOT	In-Branch Operator Training [*British*] (DCTA)
IBOT	Introduction to the Books of the Old Testament [*A publication*] (BJA)
IBoT	Istanbul Arkeoloji Muzelerinde Bulunan Bogazkoy Tableteri I and II [*Istanbul*] [*A publication*] (BJA)
IBOW	Intact Bag of Waters [*Medicine*] (STED)
IBP	IBP, Inc. [*NYSE symbol*] (SPSG)
IBP	Indicated Boiling Point [*Physics*]
IBP	Industrial Base Program
IBP	Informed Birth and Parenting [*Later, IH/IBP*] (EA)
IBP	Initial Boiling Point (MCD)
IBP	Inner [*Edge of*] Basal Piece
IBP	Institute for Better Packaging [*Later, PPC*] (EA)
IBP	Institute for Business Planning
IBP	Institute of British Photographers (DGA)
IBP	Insulated Binding Post
IBP	Integrated Basic Research [*of ASRA*] [*National Science Foundation*]
IBP	International Balance of Payments (AFM)
IBP	International Biological Program [*Concluded, 1974*] [*National Academy of Sciences*]
IBP	International Book Project (EA)
IBP	Intra-Aortic Ballon Pumping [*Cardiology*] (DMAA)
IBP	Intraspecific Brood Parasitism [*Biology*]
IBP	Ion Beam Projector
IBP	Iron-Binding Protein
IBP	Principia College, Elsah, IL [*OCLC symbol*] (OCLC)
IBPA	Illinois State Bowling Proprietors Association (SRA)
IBPA	Iminobispropylamine [*Organic chemistry*]
IBPA	Indiana Bowling Proprietors Association (SRA)
IBPA	International Book Printers Association [*Later, NABM*] (EA)
IBPA	International Bridge Press Association (EA)
IBPA	International Business Press Associates (PDAA)
IBPAT	International Brotherhood of Painters and Allied Trades (EA)
IBPAW	International Brotherhood of Pottery and Allied Workers [*Formerly, IBOP*] (EA)
IBpB	Bedford Park Public Library District, Bedford Park, IL [*Library symbol Library of Congress*] (LCLS)
IBPCA	International Bureau of the Permanent Court of Arbitration (EAIO)
IBP/CT	International Biological Programme/Conservation of Terrestrial Biological Communities [*London, England*]
IBPCT	International Customs Tariffs Bureau [*International Bureau for the Publi cation of Customs Tariffs*] [*Acronym is based on former name,*] (EA)
IBPDMS	Improved Point Defense Missile System [*Sea Sparrow*] (DOMA)
IBPDSMS	Improved Basic Point Defense Surface Missile System (DNAB)
IBPF	International Black Peoples' Foundation [*Defunct*] (EA)
IBPFM	Independent Board for Presbyterian Foreign Missions (EA)
IBPG	Icon-Based Program Generators [*Software*] [*Computer science*]
IBPGR	International Board for Plant Genetic Resources [*FAO*] [*Italy*]
IBPM	International Brotherhood of Papermakers [*Later, United Paperworkers International Union*]
IBPMS	Indirect Blood Pressure Measuring System
IBPO	International Brotherhood of Police Officers (EA)
IBPOEW	Improved Benevolent Protective Order of Elks of the World (EA)
IBPSA	International Bowling Pro Shop and Instructors Association (NTPA)
IBQ	Illness Behavior Questionnaire (STED)
IBQ	Institutional Bond Quote Service [*Database*] [*Chase Econometrics Interactive Data*] [*Information service or system*] (CRD)
IBQ	International Baron Resources [*Vancouver Stock Exchange symbol*]

IBQ	Quincy College, Quincy, IL [*OCLC symbol*] (OCLC)
IBQA	Institute of Building Quality Australia
IBR	Iberia Air Lines of Spain (MCD)
IBR	Incorporation by Reference (COE)
IBR	Infectious Bovine Rhinotracheitis [*Also, IBRV*] [*Virus*]
IBR	Information Bearing Radiation
IBR	Infrablack Region
IBR	Institute for Basic Research [*National Institute of Standards and Technology*]
IBR	Institute for Behavioral Research [*York University*] [*Canada Research center*] (IID)
IBR	Institute for Biblical Research (EA)
IBR	Institute for Biotechnology Research [*University of Waterloo*] [*Research center*] (RCD)
IBR	Institute of Boiler and Radiator Manufacturers [*Later, Hydronics Institute*] (EA)
IBR	Institutes for Behavior Resources (EA)
IBR	Integral Boiling Reactor
IBR	Integrated Bridge Rectifier (IEEE)
IBR	International Business Reply [*Post Office*] [*British*]
IBR	Irish Broadcasting Revenue
IBR	Issues in Bank Regulation [*Bank Administration Institute*] [*A publication*]
IBR	Rockford College, Rockford, IL [*OCLC symbol*] (OCLC)
IBra	Bradford Public Library, Bradford, IL [*Library symbol Library of Congress*] (LCLS)
IBRA	International Bee Research Association [*Cardiff, Wales*] (EA)
IBRA	International Bible Reading Association [*Redhill, Surrey, England*] (EAIO)
IBRAPE	Industria Brasileira de Produtos Eletronicos e Electricos, SA
IBRC	Indiana Business Research Center [*Indiana University*] [*Bloomington, IN*] [*Information service or system*] (IID)
IBRD	International Bank for Reconstruction and Development [*Also known as World Bank*]
IBre	Breese Public Library, Breese, IL [*Library symbol Library of Congress*] (LCLS)
IBreD	Breese Elementary District 12, Breese, IL [*Library symbol Library of Congress*] (LCLS)
IBreMHS	Mater Dei High School, Breese, IL [*Library symbol Library of Congress*] (LCLS)
IBreSJH	Saint Joseph's Hospital, Breese, IL [*Library symbol Library of Congress*] (LCLS)
IBRG	International Biodeterioration Research Group (EA)
IBri	Brighton Memorial Library, Brighton, IL [*Library symbol Library of Congress*] (LCLS)
IBRI	Interdisciplinary Biblical Research Institute (EA)
IBRIC	Institute for Behavioral Research in Creativity [*Research center*] (RCD)
IBritishE	Institute of British Engineers
IBRL	Initial Bomb Release Line
IBRM	Institute of Baths and Recreation Management [*British*]
IBRM	Institute of Boiler and Radiator Manufacturers [*Later, Hydronics Institute*]
IBRM	International Basic Res [*NASDAQ symbol*] (TTSB)
IBRM	International Basic Resources, Inc. [*NASDAQ symbol*] (NQ)
IBRMA	Institute for Biophysical Research and Macromolecular Assemblies [*Johns Hopkins University*]
IBRMR	Institute for Basic Research on Mental Retardation
IBro	Brookfield Free Public Library, Brookfield, IL [*Library symbol Library of Congress*] (LCLS)
IBRO	International Brain Research Organization [*Paris, France*] (EA)
IBrov	Broadview Public Library, Broadview, IL [*Library symbol Library of Congress*] (LCLS)
IBrowSD	Brownstown Community School District No. 201, Brownstown, IL [*Library symbol Library of Congress*] (LCLS)
IBRRC	International Bird Rescue Research Center (EA)
IBRS	Index to Book Reviews in the Sciences [*A publication*]
IBRS	Inpatient Behavioral Rating Scale [*Medicine*] (DB)
IBRS	Inpatient Behavior Rating Scale (STED)
IBrS	Suburban Library System, Burr Ridge, IL [*Library symbol Library of Congress*] (LCLS)
IBrus	South County Public Library District of Calhoun County, Brussels, IL [*Library symbol Library of Congress*] (LCLS)
IBrusRSD	Brussels-Richwood Community Consolidated School District 41, Brussels, IL [*Library symbol Library of Congress*] (LCLS)
IBrusSD	Brussels Community High School District 37, Brussels, IL [*Library symbol Library of Congress*] (LCLS)
IBrv	Bridgeview Public Library, Bridgeview, IL [*Library symbol Library of Congress*] (LCLS)
IBRV	Infectious Bovine Rhinotracheitis Virus [*Also, IBR*]
IBS	Ball State University, Muncie, IN [*OCLC symbol*] (OCLC)
IBS	Ibis [*Belgium ICAO designator*] (FAAC)
IBS	Ichthyosis Bullosa of Siemens [*Medicine*]
IBS	Identical by State [*Genetics*]
IBS	Imidazole Buffered Saline [*Clinical chemistry*]
IBS	Immediate Business Systems [*Commercial firm British*]
IBS	Immunoblastic Sarcoma [*Medicine*] (DMAA)
IBS	Impulse Balance System
IBS	Incentive Bonus Scheme [*British*]
IBS	Incorporated Bronte Society [*Keighley, West Yorkshire, England*] (EAIO)
IBS	Inflatable Boat, Small (NVT)
IBS	Inside Bathing Solution [*Medicine*] (STED)
IBS	Institute for Basic Standards [*Later, NSL*] [*National Institute of Standards and Technology*]
IBS	Institute for Biotechnological Studies [*University of Kent*] [*British*] (IRUK)
IBS	Institute for Brew Studies (NTPA)
IBS	Institute of Behavioral Science [*University of Colorado - Boulder*] [*Research center*] (RCD)
IBS	Institute of Behavioural Studies [*University of Newcastle*] [*Australia*]
IBS	Institute of Black Studies [*Defunct*] (EA)
IBS	Integrated Booking System [*Army*] (RDA)
IBS	Integrated Bridge System (MCD)
IBS	Integrated Business Systems [*Trifid Software*] (NITA)
IBS	INTELSAT Business Service [*MCI Communications Corp.*]
IBS	Interbed-Storage Package [*Geological program*]
IBS	Interbomb Spacing (DNAB)
IBS	Inter-Byte Separation [*Automotive engineering Electronics*]
IBS	Inter-Byte Spacing [*Computer science*]
IBS	Intercollegiate Broadcasting System (EA)
IBS	Interference Blanker Set
IBS	International Bach Society [*Defunct*] (EA)
IBS	International Bank for Settlements (MHDW)
IBS	International Benchrest Shooters (EA)
IBS	International Benevolent Society (EA)
IBS	International Bentham Society (EAIO)
IBS	International Bible Society (EA)
IBS	International Bibliography of the Social Sciences, Economics, and Sociology [*International Committee for Social Science Information and Documentation*] [*Information service or system*] (CRD)
IBS	International Biometric Society (NTPA)
IBS	International Bookbinders Secretariat (DGA)
IBS	International Book Service, Inc.
IBS	International Boundary Study [*A publication*]
IBS	International Brancusi Society (EA)
IBS	International Brecht Society [*See also IBG*] (EA)
IBS	International Bronchoesophagological Society (EA)
IBS	International Bulb Society (EAIO)
IBS	International Business Services [*Switzerland*] (ECON)
IBS	International Business Services [*Telecommunications*] (TSSD)
IBS	Interpersonal Behavior Survey [*Psychology*]
IBS	Intron Binding Site [*Genetics*]
IBS	Ion Beam Scanning
IBS	Ion Beam Sputtering
IBS	Ionospheric Beacon Satellite (PDAA)
IBS	Iota Beta Sigma [*An association*] (WDMC)
IBS	Irritable Bowel Syndrome [*Medicine*]
IBS	Island Base Section [*Navy*]
IBS	Isobaric Solution (DMAA)
IBSA	Immunoreactive Bovine Serum Albumin [*Immunochemistry*]
IBSA	Immunoreactive Bovine Serum Albumin (STED)
IBSA	International Barber Schools Association (EA)
IBSA	International Bible Students Association (EA)
IBSA	International Blind Sports Association [*See also AISA*] [*Farsta, Sweden*] (EAIO)
IBSA	Iodinated Bovine Serum Albumin (DMAA)
IBSAC	Industrialized Building Systems and Components (IEEE)
IBSAT	Indexing by Statistical Analysis Techniques (PDAA)
IBSC	Independent Banks of South Carolina (SRA)
IBSCA	Ion Beam Spectrochemical Analysis (PDAA)
IB(Scot)	Institute of Bankers in Scotland (ODBW)
IBSD	Independent Community Bankers of South Dakota (TBD)
IBSD	Information-Based School Development
IBSDF	International Business Schools [*NASDAQ symbol*] (SAG)
IBSDF	Intl Business Schs [*NASDAQ symbol*] (TTSB)
IBSEDEX	International Building Services Index [*Database*] [*BSRIA*] [*Information service or system*] (CRD)
IBSF	IBS Financial [*NASDAQ symbol*] (TTSB)
IBSF	IBS Financial Corp. [*NASDAQ symbol*] (SAG)
ibsf	Little Brothers of Saint Francis (TOCD)
IBSFC	International Baltic Sea Fishery Commission [*Warsaw, Poland*] (ASF)
IBS Fncl	IBS Financial Corp. [*Associated Press*] (SAG)
IBSH	Institute of the Brothers of the Sacred Heart [*See also IFSC*] [*Rome, Italy*] (EAIO)
IBSHR	Integral Boiling and Superheat Reactor
IBSM	Institute of Building Site Management [*British*] (BI)
IBSM	International Bureau of Strata Mechanics [*See also IBG*] (EAIO)
IBSMA	Interior Board of Surface Mine Appeals (in United States Interior Decisions) [*A publication*] (DLA)
IBSN	Infantile Bilateral Striatal Necrosis [*Ophthalmology*]
IBSP	Integrin-Binding Sialoprotein (DMAA)
IBSP	Individual Battle Shooting Range (PDAA)
IBSR	Interactive Bibliographic Search and Retrieval (NITA)
IBSR	Inverse Boresight Ranging (MCD)
IBSRAM	International Board for Soil Research and Management [*Thailand*]
IBSS	Infrared Background Signature Survey [*Military*] (SDI)
IBSS	Insect Balanced Salt Solution [*Cytology*]
IBS/SPS	Inflatable Boat, Small/Silent Propulsion System (MCD)
IBSSU	Internal Bearing Stabilized Sighting Unit (MCD)
IBST	Institute of British Surgical Technicians (BI)
IBST	International Bureau of Social Tourism [*See also BITS*] [*Brussels, Belgium*] (EAIO)
IBSTP	International Bureau of Software Test
IBSTP	International Bureau for the Suppression of Traffic in Persons (DI)
IBSWU	International Boot and Shoe Workers' Union
IBSYS	International Business Machines System
IBT	Field Museum of Natural History, Chicago, IL [*OCLC symbol*] (OCLC)
IBT	Ibertrans Aerea SL [*Spain*] [*FAA designator*] (FAAC)
IBT	IBS Technologies Ltd. [*Vancouver Stock Exchange symbol*]

IBT	Immunobead Binding Test [*Biochemistry*]
IBT	Immunoblastic T-Cell [*Lymphadenopathy*]
IBT	Implantable Beacon Transmitter [*Oceanography*]
IBT	Inclined Bottom Tank [*Fermenter*]
IBT	Income Before Taxes (AAGC)
IBT	Incompatible Blood Transfusion (PDAA)
IBT	Independent Bankers Division of Tennessee Bankers Association (TBD)
I-BT	India-Burma Theater [*World War II*]
IBT	Indianapolis Ballet Theatre
IBT	Industrial Bio-Test Laboratories, Inc.
IBT	Initial Boiling-Point Temperature
IBT	Initial Brake Temperature [*Automotive engineering*]
IBT	Ink Blot Test [*Rorschach test*] [*Psychology*] (DAVI)
IBT	Instrumented Bend Test
IBT	Insulation Breakdown Tester
IBT	Integrated Business Terminal [*Computer science*] (PDAA)
IBT	[*The*] International Bridge & Terminal Co. [*AAR code*]
IBT	International Broadcasting Trust [*British*]
IBT	International Brotherhood of Teamsters [*Union*]
IBT	International Brotherhood of Teamsters, Chauffeurs, Warehousemen, and Helpers ofAmerica (EA)
IBT	Ion Beam Technology
IBT	Ion-Implanted Base Transistor
IBT	Irrational Beliefs Test [*Psychology*]
IBT	Isatin-beta-thiosemicarbazone [*Organic chemistry*]
IBTA	Interest-Bearing Transaction Account (DICI)
IBTA	International Baton Twirling Association of America and Abroad [*Defunct*] (EA)
IBTC	International Brands and Their Companies [*Formerly, ITND*] [*A publication*]
IBTF	Investment Bank for Trade and Finance [*United Arab Emirates*]
IBTMA	International Black Toy Manufacturers Association (EA)
IBTO	International Broadcasting and Television Organization (NTCM)
IBTOM	Iranian B'nei Torah Movement (EA)
IBTR	Ipsilateral Breast Tumor Recurrence [*Medicine*] (STED)
IBTS	Insert Bit String [*Computer science*] (PCM)
IBTS	International Beer Tasting Society (EA)
IBTS	International Bicycle Touring Society (EA)
IBTTA	International Bridge, Tunnel, and Turnpike Association (EA)
IBTU	Instructors Basic Training Unit
IBU	Eureka College, Eureka, IL [*OCLC symbol*] (OCLC)
IBU	Ibukiyama [*Ibukisan*] [*Japan*] [*Seismograph station code, US Geological Survey*] [*Closed*] (SEIS)
IBU	Ibuprofen [*Medicine*] (STED)
IBU	Ikatan Buruh Umum [*General Workers' Union*] [*Indonesia*]
IBU	Imperial Bushel (WDAA)
IBU	Independent Business Unit
IBU	Instruction Buffer Unit [*Computer science*] (IAA)
IBU	Interference Blanking Unit
IBU	International Benzoate Unit [*Pharmacology*]
IBU	International Broadcasting Union [*Defunct*] (NTCM)
IBU	International Burgers Now Ltd. [*Vancouver Stock Exchange symbol*]
IBU	International Business Unit [*British Information service or system*] (IID)
IBU	Itambacuri [*Brazil*] [*Airport symbol*] (AD)
IBucSD	Buckley-Loda Community Unit School District, Buckley, IL [*Library symbol*] [*Library of Congress*] (LCLS)
IBud	Mason Memorial Public Library, Buda, IL [*Library symbol Library of Congress*] (LCLS)
IBun	Bunker Hill Public Library, Bunker Hill, IL [*Library symbol Library of Congress*] (LCLS)
IBunMCD	Macoupin Community District 8, Bunker Hill, IL [*Library symbol Library of Congress*] (LCLS)
IBur	South Stickney District Library, Burbank, IL [*Library symbol Library of Congress*] (LCLS)
IBure	Leepertown Township Library, Bureau, IL [*Library symbol Library of Congress*] (LCLS)
IBureLSD	Leepertown Consolidated Community School District 175, Bureau, IL [*Library symbol Library of Congress*] (LCLS)
IBV	Infectious Bronchitis Vaccine [*Pharmacology*] (DAVI)
IBV	Infectious Bronchitis Virus [*Avian*]
IBV	Inspection by Variables
IBV	International Bellevue Ventures Ltd. [*Vancouver Stock Exchange symbol*]
IBV	Internationale Buchhandler-Vereinigung [*International Booksellers Federation - IBF*] (EAIO)
IBV	Newberry Library, Chicago, IL [*OCLC symbol*] (OCLC)
IBVA	Interactive Brain Wave Analyzer [*IBVA Technology*] [*Computer science*] (PCM)
IBVE	Isobutyl Vinyl Ether [*Organic chemistry*]
IBVM	Institute of the Blessed Virgin Mary [*Sisters of Loretto*] [*Roman Catholic religious order*]
IBW	Borg-Warner Corp., Des Plaines, IL [*OCLC symbol*] (OCLC)
IBW	Ideal Body Weight [*Medicine*]
IBW	Impulse Bandwidth (MCD)
IBW	In Black and White [*A publication*]
IBW	Institute of the Black World [*Defunct*] (EA)
IBW	Intelligence Bandwidth
IBW	Internal Bore Weld [*Nuclear energy*] (NUCP)
IBW	International Black Writers (EA)
IBW	International Business Week
IBW	Ion Beam Weapon
IBW	Irrotationally Bound Water [*Biophysics*]

IBW	Israel Book World [*A publication*]
IBWA	International Bank for West Africa Ltd.
IBWA	International Black Writers and Artists (EA)
IBWA	International Bottled Water Association (EA)
IBWA	International Boxing Writers Association (EA)
IBWC	International Black Women's Congress (EA)
IBWC	International Black Writers Conference [*Later, IBW*] (EA)
IBWC	International Boundary and Water Commission
IBWCA	International Barbed Wire Collectors Association (EA)
IBWDA	Idaho Beer and Wine Distributors Association (SRA)
IBWM	International Bureau of Weights and Measures
IBWN	International Bureau of Weights and Measures (ECII)
IBX	Iberiotoxin [*Biochemistry*]
IBX	Integrated Business Exchange (MCD)
IBX	Schiff, Hardin & Waite, Chicago, IL [*OCLC symbol*] (OCLC)
IBY	International Bank of Yemen
IBY	International Biological Year
IBY	International Book Year [*1972*] [*UNESCO*]
IBY	International Business Aircraft, Inc. [*FAA designator*] (FAAC)
Ibyc	Ibycus [*Sixth century BC*] [*Classical studies*] (OCD)
IBYC	Institute in Basic Youth Conflicts (EA)
IBZ	Columbia College, Chicago, IL [*Inactive*] [*OCLC symbol*] (OCLC)
IBZ	Ibiza [*Spain*] [*Airport symbol*] (OAG)
IBZ	Inner Border Zone
IBZ	International Business Air [*Sweden ICAO designator*] (FAAC)
IC	Chicago Public Library, Chicago, IL [*Library symbol Library of Congress*] (LCLS)
IC	Ice Chest
IC	Ice Crystals
ic	Iceland [*MARC country of publication code Library of Congress*] (LCCP)
IC	Iceland [*NATO*]
IC	Icing [*Aviation*] (FAAC)
IC	Icon [*Plate engraving*]
IC	Icteric [*Medicine*] (DAVI)
IC	Identification Code
IC	Identity Card (BARN)
IC	Iesus Christus [*Jesus Christ*] [*Latin*]
IC	Ileocecal [*Gastroenterology*] (DAVI)
IC	Iliac Chamber [*Anatomy*] (IAA)
IC	Iliococcygeal [*Muscle*] [*Anatomy*] (DAVI)
IC	Iliocostal [*Muscle*] [*Anatomy*] (DAVI)
IC	Illinois Central [*Illinois Central Gulf Railroad Co.*] [*AAR code*]
IC	Illinois Central Corp. [*NYSE symbol*] (SPSG)
IC	Image Chamber (IAA)
IC	Image Check (IAA)
IC	Image Communications [*Computer graphics*]
IC	Immediate Constituent
IC	Immune Complex [*Immunology*]
IC	Immune Cytotoxicity [*Immunochemistry*] (DAVI)
IC	Immunocytochemistry [*Immunochemstry*] (DAVI)
IC	Imperial College [*London*] (WDAA)
IC	Implementation and Conversion (MCD)
IC	Implementation of Change
IC	Imported Content
IC	Impoverished Conditions
IC	Impression Cylinder [*Typography*] (DGA)
IC	Improved Capability [*for aircraft*] (MCD)
IC	Impulse Conductor (MSA)
IC	Incarnational Consecration (TOCD)
ic	In Casu [*In This Case*] [*Latin*]
IC	Incense Cedar [*Botany*]
IC	Incentive Compensation (MCD)
i/c	In Charge (WDAA)
IC	In Charge Of
IC	Incident Commander [*Environmental science*] (COE)
IC	Incident Control [*Environmental science*] (COE)
I/C	Incoming [*Telecommunications*] (TEL)
IC	In Command (ADA)
IC	In-Commission (MCD)
IC	Incomplete (DAVI)
IC	In Compliance [*FDA*]
IC	Increase (IAA)
IC	Incremental Cost (KSC)
IC	Incue [*News broadcasting*] (NTCM)
IC	Incurved Cactus [*Horticulture*]
IC	Independent Contractor
IC	Independent Telephone Co. [*Telecommunications*]
IC	Index Catalogue
IC	Index Chemicus [*See also ICRS*]
I/C	Index Concordance [*International Serials Catalogue*] [*A publication*]
IC	Index Correction [*on a sextant*] [*Navigation*]
IC	Index Correlation (WDAA)
IC	Index of Coincidence (MHDB)
IC	Indian Airlines [*ICAO designator*] (AD)
IC	Indian Cases [*India*] [*A publication*] (DLA)
IC	Indicating Controller (NRCH)
IC	Indication Cycle (IAA)
IC	Indicator and Control
IC	Indifference Curve [*Economics*]
IC	Indirect Calorimetry [*Physiology*] (DAVI)
IC	Individual/Collective (MCD)
IC	Individual Counsel (DNAB)
IC	Individual Counseling [*Psychology*] (DAVI)
IC	Indochina

IC	Inductance-Capacitance
IC	Inductive Coupling
I/C	Industrial/Commercial
IC	Industrial Concentration (MHDB)
IC	Industrial Court (DLA)
IC	Industry Competitive (AFIT)
IC	Inertial Component
IC	Infection Control (HCT)
IC	Inferior Colliculus [*Also, ICC*] [*Brain anatomy*]
IC	Infinite Capitalism [*Book title*]
IC	Informal Communication
IC	Information Center
IC	Information Circular
IC	Information Codes (NITA)
IC	Information Content (DEN)
IC	Infrastructure Committee of the North Atlantic Council [*NATO*]
IC	Ingenieur Constructeur [*Academic degree*]
IC	Inhibition Concentration [*Biochemistry*]
IC	Inhibitory Concentration [*Toxicology*]
IC	Iniciativia per Catalunya [*Spain Political party*] (EY)
IC	Initial Calibration
IC	Initial Conditions
IC	Initial Course [*Navigation*]
IC	Initiation of Contraction
IC	Inland Container [*Shipping*] (DCTA)
IC	Inlet Contact
IC	Inner Cabin
IC	Inner Canthal Distance [*Medicine*] (DMAA)
IC	Inner Circle [*An association*] (EA)
IC	Inner Circle [*Numismatics*]
IC	Inner Core [*Geology*]
IC	Innocent Civilian [*Military*]
IC	Inorganic Carbon
IC	Input Circuit
IC	Input Code (IAA)
I/C	Input Controller (MCD)
IC	Input Current
IC	Inscribed Circle (IAA)
IC	Inside Cloud Lightning [*Meteorology*]
IC	Inspected and Condemned [*Military*]
IC	Inspecting Commander [*Military British*] (ROG)
IC	Inspection Card
IC	Inspection Chamber
IC	Inspection Committee
IC	Inspiratory Capacity [*Physiology*]
IC	Inspiratory Center [*Physiology*]
IC	Installed Capacity [*Electronics*] (IEEE)
IC	Institute for Congress
IC	Institute of Ceramics [*Stoke-On-Trent, Staffordshire, England*] (EAIO)
IC	Institute of Charity [*Rosminians*] [*Roman Catholic religious order*]
ic	Institute of Charity (TOCD)
IC	Institute of Chemistry [*British*]
IC	Institutional Care [*British*]
IC	Institutional Characteristics [*of the Integrated Postsecondary Education Data System*] [*Department of Education*] (GFGA)
IC	Instruction Card (MSA)
IC	Instruction Cell
IC	Instruction Code (AAG)
IC	Instruction Counter [*Computer science*]
IC	Instruction Cycle [*Computer science*] (IAA)
IC	Instructor in Cookery [*Navy British*] (ROG)
IC	Instrumentation Controller (KSC)
IC	Instrument Correction
IC	Instrument Correlation (WDAA)
IC	Insulated Conductors (MCD)
IC	Insulating Compound (IAA)
IC	Intake Closes [*Valve position*]
IC	Integrated Chromatography
IC	Integrated Circuit [*Electronics*]
IC	Integrated Communications (MCD)
IC	Integrating Center
IC	Integrating Contractor (AAG)
IC	Integration Control (MCD)
IC	Integrator Card (IAA)
IC	Intelligence Center (CAAL)
IC	Intelligence Collator [*British police term*]
IC	Intelligence Collection [*Military*] (MCD)
IC	Intelligence Committee [*NATO*] (NATG)
IC	Intelligence Community [*Military*] (MCD)
IC	Intelligence Corps [*Military unit*] [*British*]
IC	Intelligence Cycle (LAIN)
IC	Intelligent Copier [*Electrophotography*] (DGA)
IC	Intensive Care [*Medicine*]
IC	Intercept Controller
IC	Interceptor Command
IC	Interceptor Computer (IAA)
I/C	Interchange
IC	Interchange Center
IC	Inter Cibos [*Between Meals*] [*Pharmacy*]
I/C	Intercom (KSC)
IC	Intercommunications
I/C	Intercommunicator
IC	Intercomputer (MCD)
IC	Intercomputer Channel (KSC)
IC	Intercomputer Communication (NAKS)
IC	Interconnect Carrier [*Telecommunications*]
IC	Interconnection (IAA)
IC	Intercostal [*Between the ribs*] [*Medicine*]
IC	Intercrystalline Corrosion [*Metallurgy*]
IC	Interexchange Carrier [*Telecommunications*]
IC	Interface Control [*or Controller*]
IC	Interface Coordinator (MCD)
IC	Interfacial Communications (MCD)
IC	Interference Control (IAA)
IC	Interim Change (AFM)
IC	Interim Commission
IC	Interim Committee
IC	Interior Communication
IC	Interior Communications Electrician [*Navy rating*]
IC	Intermediate Care [*Medicine*]
IC	Intermediate Chain [*Biochemistry*]
IC	Intermediate Circuit (IAA)
IC	Intermediate Command
IC	Intermittent Catheterization [*Urology*] (DAVI)
IC	Intermittent Claudication [*Medicine*] (MAE)
IC	Internal Capsule [*Neuroanatomy*]
IC	Internal Carotid [*Artery*] [*Cardiology*] (DAVI)
IC	Internal Cerebral [*Neurology*] (DAVI)
IC	Internal Cholecystectomy [*Gastroenterology*] (DAVI)
IC	Internal Combustion
IC	Internal Communications (CAAL)
IC	Internal Conjugate [*Diameter*] [*Gynecology*] (DAVI)
IC	Internal Connection [*Electronics*]
IC	Internal Control [*Business term*] (EBF)
IC	Internal Conversion [*Nuclear science*] (OA)
IC	International Classification (DAVI)
IC	International Conference
IC	International Control
IC	International Cooperation
IC	International Corp. [*Generic term*]
IC	International Curator Resources [*Vancouver Stock Exchange symbol*]
IC	Internet Commerce
IC	Internment Camp
IC	Internuclear Company
IC	Interpretation Canada [*Federal agency*]
IC	Interrupting Capacity (IAA)
IC	Interruption Code (IAA)
IC	Interspecies Communication [*An association*] (EA)
IC	Interstate Club (EA)
IC	Interstate Commerce Reports [*A publication*] (DLA)
IC	Interstitial Cells [*Histology*]
IC	Interstitial Cyst [*Pulmonary medicine*]
IC	Interstitial Cystitis [*Nephrology*]
IC	Intervalve Coupling (DEN)
IC	Intracapsular (CPH)
IC	Intracardiac [*Medicine*]
IC	Intracarotid [*Medicine*] (MAE)
IC	Intracavitary [*Medicine*]
IC	Intracellular
IC	Intracerebral [*Medicine*]
ic	Intracerebroventricular [*Also, ICTV, ICV*] [*Brain anatomy*]
IC	Intracisternal [*Nerulogy*] (DAVI)
IC	Intracloud [*Climatology*]
IC	Intracoronary [*Cardiology*]
IC	Intracranial
IC	Intracutaneous [*Medicine*]
IC	Intraductal Carcinoma [*Medicine*] (MEDA)
IC	Intrapleural Catheter [*Medicine*] (DAVI)
IC	Inverse Check
IC	Investement Council (AAEL)
IC	Investment Company
IC	Investment Counselor (MHDB)
IC	Investment Tax Credit
IC	Invited Contractor
IC	Ion Chamber [*Nucleonics*]
IC	Ion Chromatography
IC	Ionization Chamber
IC	Iowa Conference (PSS)
IC	Irish Constitution (ADA)
IC	Iron City [*Pittsburgh, PA*]
IC	Irregular Cavalry [*British military*] (DMA)
IC	Irritable Colon [*Medicine*]
IC	Ischemic Cardiomyopathy [*Cardiology*]
IC	Ischemic Contracture [*Hematology*]
IC	I See [*Computer hacker terminology*]
IC	Islamic Congress
IC	Island of Calleja [*Neuroanatomy*]
IC	Islet Cells [*of the pancreas*] [*Endocrinology*]
IC	Isolation Condenser (NRCH)
IC	Isovolumic Contraction [*Medicine*] (DMAA)
IC	Izquierda Cristiana [*Christian Left*] [*Chile*] [*Political party*] (EY)
IC	Jesus [*First and third letters of His name in Greek*]
IC	Vietnamese Sisters Incarnational Consecration (TOCD)
IC1	Interior Communications Electrician, First Class [*Navy rating*]
IC2	Interior Communications Electrician, Second Class [*Navy rating*]
IC3	Interior Communications Electrician, Third Class [*Navy rating*]
IC4A	Intercollegiate Association of Amateur Athletes of America [*Also, IAAAA, ICAAAA*]
IC50	Inhibition of Protein Content, 50% [*Biochemistry*]

ICA.............. Art Institute of Chicago, Chicago, IL [*Library symbol Library of Congress*] (LCLS)
ICA.............. Aurora College, Aurora, IL [*OCLC symbol*] (OCLC)
ICa.............. Cairo Public Library, Cairo, IL [*Library symbol Library of Congress*] (LCLS)
ICA.............. Empresas ICA Socledad ADS [*NYSE symbol*] (SPSG)
ICA.............. Ica [*Peru*] [*Seismograph station code, US Geological Survey*] (SEIS)
ICA.............. Icabaru [*Venezuela*] [*Airport symbol*] (AD)
ICA.............. Icaro [*Italy*] [*FAA designator*] (FAAC)
ICA.............. Ice Cream Alliance Ltd. [*British*] (BI)
ICA.............. Idaho Cattle Association (SRA)
ICA.............. Ignition Control Additive (IAA)
ICA.............. Illinois Coal Association (SRA)
ICA.............. Illinois Cosmetology Association (SRA)
ICA.............. Immediate Constituent Analyzer [*Computer science*] (DIT)
ICA.............. Immunocytochemical Analysis
ICA.............. Immunological Chromatographic Analysis
ICA.............. Imperial Corp. of America (EFIS)
ICA.............. Independent Cattlemen's Association of Texas (SRA)
ICA.............. Independent Colleges of Arkansas (SRA)
ICA.............. Independent Cost Analysis (AAGC)
ICA.............. Independent Cost Assessment (MCD)
ICA.............. Index of Competitive Ability (PDAA)
ICA.............. Indian Community Action
ICA.............. Indigenous Communications Association (EA)
ICA.............. Individual Combat Actions [*Army*]
ICA.............. Industrial Catering Association [*British*]
ICA.............. Industrial Communications Association (HGAA)
ICA.............. Industrial Cooperative Association (EA)
ICA.............. Industry and Commerce Association of South Dakota (SRA)
ICA.............. Initial Cruise Altitude
ICA.............. Inner Circle of Advocates [*Tucson, AZ*] (EA)
ICA.............. Institut Canadien d'Acupuncture [*Canadian Acupuncture Institute*]
ICA.............. Institut Canadien des Actuaires [*Canadian Institute of Actuaries*]
ICA.............. Institut Culturel Africain [*African Cultural Institute*] (EAIO)
ICA.............. Institute for Cell Analysis [*University of Miami*] [*Research center*] (RCD)
ICA.............. Institute of Chartered Accountants in England and Wales (BI)
ICA.............. Institute of Clinical Analysis
ICA.............. Institute of Company Accountants [*British*] (DAS)
ICA.............. Institute of Consumer Advisers [*British*] (DBA)
ICA.............. Institute of Contemporary Arts [*British*]
ICA.............. Institute of Cost Analysis [*Later, SCEA*] (EA)
ICA.............. Institute of Cultural Affairs (EA)
ICA.............. Instrumentation Control and Automation [*Water industry*] [*British*]
ICA.............. Instrument Compressed Air (AAG)
ICA.............. Instrument Control and Automation
ICA.............. Integrated Circuit Array
ICA.............. Integrated Communications Adapter (MCD)
ICA.............. Integrated Communications Architecture [*Navy*] (DOMA)
ICA.............. Integrated Conformal Array
ICA.............. Integrated Cost Accounting
ICA.............. Integration Change Allowance (MCD)
ICA.............. Intelligence Collection Area [*Military*] (NATG)
ICA.............. Intelligent Communications Adapter [*Computer hardware*] (PCM)
ICA.............. Intelligent Console Architecture (PCM)
ICA.............. Interapplication Communication Architecture [*Computer science*] (BTTJ)
ICA.............. Interbank Card Association [*Mastercard International*] (EA)
ICA.............. Inter City Airlines [*British*]
ICA.............. Intercompany Agreement (IAA)
ICA.............. Intercomputer Adapter
ICA.............. Intercountry Adoption (STED)
ICA.............. Interface Control Agreement
ICA.............. Intergovernmental Council for ADP [*Automatic Data Processing*]
ICA.............. Interlochen Center for the Arts (EA)
ICA.............. Intermediate Care Area (STED)
ICA.............. Intermountain College Association (AEBS)
ICA.............. Intermuseum Conservation Association (EA)
ICA.............. Internal Carotid Artery [*Anatomy*]
ICA.............. International Cartographic Association [*Australia*] (EA)
ICA.............. International Carwash Association (EA)
ICA.............. International Caterers Association [*Defunct*] (EA)
ICA.............. International Catholic Auxiliaries (EA)
ICA.............. International Center for Aquaculture [*Auburn University*] [*Research center*] (RCD)
ICA.............. International Ceramic Association (EA)
ICA.............. International Chefs' Association (EA)
ICA.............. International Chianina Association (EAIO)
ICA.............. International Chiropractors Association (EA)
ICA.............. International Claim Association [*Rock Island, IL*] (EA)
ICA.............. International Clarinet Association (NTPA)
ICA.............. International Coffee Agreement [*Signed September, 1962*]
ICA.............. International College of Angiology (EA)
ICA.............. International Commercial Arbitration (BARN)
ICA.............. International Commission on Acoustics [*Aachen, Federal Republic of Germany*] (EAIO)
ICA.............. International Commodity Agreement
ICA.............. International Communication Agency [*Also, USICA*] [*Formerly called BECA and USIA, it later became known again as USIA*]
ICA.............. International Communication Association (EA)
ICA.............. International Communications Association (EA)
ICA.............. International Computer Association
ICA.............. International Confederation of Accordionists [*Vienna, Austria*] (EA)

ICA.............. International Conference of Administrators of Residential Centers for Youth [*Defunct*] (EA)
ICA.............. International Congress of Acarology
ICA.............. International Congress of Accountants
ICA.............. International Congress of Africanists [*Lagos, Nigeria*] (EAIO)
ICA.............. International Congress of African Studies (EAIO)
ICA.............. International Congress of Americanists [*Manchester, England*] (EA)
ICA.............. International Cooperation Administration [*Later, Agency for International Development*]
ICA.............. International Co-Operative Alliance [*Grand-Saconnex, Switzerland*] (EA)
ICA.............. International Copper Association [*British*] (IRC)
ICA.............. International Council on Archives [*UNESCO*] (EA)
ICA.............. International Credit Association [*St. Louis, MO*] (EA)
ICA.............. Interstate Commerce Act [*1887*]
ICA.............. Interstitial Cystitis Association (EA)
ICA.............. Intracranial Anatomy [*Medicine*] (STED)
ICA.............. Intracranial Aneurysm [*Medicine*]
ICA.............. Invalid Care Allowance [*British*]
ICA.............. Inventors Clubs of America (EA)
ICA.............. Investigative and Corrective Action (KSC)
ICA.............. Investment Canada Act
ICA.............. Investment Company Act [*1940*]
iCa.............. Ionized Calcium (STED)
ICA.............. Ionized Calcium Analyzer
ICA.............. Iowa Cattlemen's Association (SRA)
ICA.............. Iowa Code, Annotated [*A publication*] (DLA)
ICA.............. Irish Countrywomen's Association (BI)
ICA.............. Iron Caulkers' Association [*A union*] [*British*]
ICA.............. Islet Cell Antibody [*Immunology*]
ICA.............. Isotropically Conductive Adhesive [*Electronics*] (AAEL)
ICA.............. Italian Charities of America (EA)
ICA.............. Item Change Analysis (KSC)
ICA.............. Item Control Area (NRCH)
ICAA.............. Indian Church Aid [*British*] (BI)
ICAA.............. Institut Canadien des Affaires Africaines [*Canadian Institute of African Affairs*]
ICAA.............. Insulation Contractors Association of America (EA)
ICAA.............. Integrated Cost Accounting Application
ICAA.............. International Christian Accrediting Association (EA)
ICAA.............. International Civil Airports Association [*Orly, France*] (EAIO)
ICAA.............. International Civil Aviation Authority [*Database originator*] [*Canada*] (NITA)
ICAA.............. International Committee on Arctic Arboviruses
ICAA.............. International Council of Accrediting Agencies [*Australia*] (EAIO)
ICAA.............. International Council on Alcohol and Addictions [*Switzerland*]
ICAA.............. Invalid Children's Aid Association [*London*]
ICAA.............. Investment Counsel Association of America (EA)
ICAAAA ...... Intercollegiate Association of Amateur Athletes of America [*Also, IAAAA, IC4A*] (EA)
ICAAC ...... Interscience Conference on Antimicrobial Agents and Chemotherapy
ICAAS ...... Integrated Control and Avionics for Air Superiority (MCD)
ICAB.............. International Cargo Advisory Bureau
ICAB.............. International Council Against Bullfighting (EA)
ICAb.............. Islet Cell Antibody (STED)
ICABA ...... International Campaign Against Banking on Apartheid (EAIO)
ICABF.......... American Bar Foundation, Chicago, IL [*Library symbol Library of Congress*] (LCLS)
ICAC.............. American College of Surgeons, Chicago, IL [*Library symbol Library of Congress*] (LCLS)
ICAC.............. Independent College Assistance Center (EA)
ICAC.............. Independent Commission Against Corruption
ICAC.............. Indiana Collegiate Athletic Conference (PSS)
ICAC.............. Institute of Clean Air Companies (NTPA)
ICAC.............. Instrumentation Calibration and Checkout (IAA)
ICAC.............. International Committee for Accounting Co-Operation
ICAC.............. International Cotton Advisory Committee (EA)
ICACCP........ International Commission Against Concentration Camp Practices [*Brussels, Belgium*] [*Defunct*] (EAIO)
ICACGP........ International Commission on Atmospheric Chemistry and Global Pollution (USDC)
ICACGP........ International Commission on Atmospheric Chemistry Global Pollution [*Marine science*] (OSRA)
ICACM .... Associated Colleges of the Midwest, Periodical Bank, Chicago, IL [*Library symbol Library of Congress*] (LCLS)
ICACMu........ American Conservatory of Music, Chicago, IL [*Library symbol Library of Congress*] (LCLS)
ICAD .... Individual Concern and Deficiency [*Environmental science*] (COE)
ICAD .... Inhibitor of Caspase-Activated Deoxyribonuclease [*Biochemistry*]
ICAD .... Integrated Control and Display
ICAD .... Intelligent Computer-Aided Design
ICAD .... International Committee for Automobile Documentation
ICADA .... American Dental Association, Chicago, IL [*Library symbol Library of Congress*] (LCLS)
ICADE .... Interactive Computer-Aided Design Evaluation
ICADI .... Inter-American Center for Agricultural Documentation and Information (NITA)
ICADIS .... Instituto Centroamericano de Documentacion y Investigacion Social (EA)
ICADS .... Integrated Correlation and Display System [*Air Force*] (DOMA)
ICADS .... Integrated Cover and Deception Systems [*Military*] (MCD)
ICADTS .... International Committee on Alcohol, Drugs, and Traffic Safety [*Linkoping, Sweden*] (EA)
ICAE.............. Insurance Consumer Affairs Exchange (NTPA)
ICAE.............. Integrated Communications Adapter Extended (BUR)

ICAE............ International Centre for Art Education (EAIO)
ICAE............ International Commission of Agricultural Engineering
ICAE............ International Commission on Atmospheric Electricity (EA)
ICAE............ International Conference of Agricultural Economists [Later, IAAE]
ICAE............ International Council for Adult Education [Toronto, ON] (EAIO)
ICAE............ United States Army, Corps of Engineers, Chicago, IL [Library symbol Library of Congress] (LCLS)
ICAEC.......... International Confederation of Associations of Experts and Consultants [Paris, France] (EA)
ICAEO .... International Center for Athletic and Educational Opportunities (EA)
ICAEW......... Institute of Chartered Accountants in England and Wales
ICAF............ [The] Industrial College of the Armed Forces [Later, UND]
ICAF............ Internal Carotid Artery Flow [Medicine] (STED)
ICAF............ International Committee on Aeronautical Fatigue [Delft University of Technology] [Netherlands] (EAIO)
ICAF............ International Contemporary Art Fair [London, England]
ICAFFH .... International Committee for the Anthropology of Food and Food Habits [Defunct] (EA)
ICAG .... Altheimer & Gray, Chicago, IL [Library symbol] [Library of Congress] (LCLS)
ICAH .... American Hospital Association, Chicago, IL [Library symbol Library of Congress] (LCLS)
ICah............ Cahokia Public Library, Cahokia, IL [Library symbol Library of Congress] (LCLS)
ICahP.......... Parks College of Saint Louis University, Cahokia, IL [Library symbol] [Library of Congress] (LCLS)
ICahSD .... Cahokia Community Unit School District 187, Cahokia, IL [Library symbol Library of Congress] (LCLS)
ICAI............ American Institute of Baking, Chicago, IL [Library symbol Library of Congress] (LCLS)
ICAI............ Institut Canadien des Affaires Internationales [Canadian Institute of International Affairs]
ICAI............ Institute of Chartered Accountants in Ireland (EAIO)
ICAI............ Institute of Cultural Affairs International (EA)
ICAI............ Intelligent Computer-Assisted Instruction
ICAI............ International Commission for Agricultural Industries
ICAIE.......... International Committee Against Involuntary Exile (EA)
ICAIF.......... International Computer-Assisted Instruction Facility (AEBS)
ICAITI.......... Instituto Centroamericano de Investigacion y Tecnologia Industrial [Central American Institute of Research and Industrial Technology] [Guatemala] [Research center] (IRC)
ICAJ............ Institut Canadien d'Administration de la Justice (AC)
ICAK........... International College of Applied Kinesiology (EA)
ICaL............ Cairo Public Library, Cairo, IL [Library symbol] [Library of Congress] (LCLS)
ICAL........... Initiative on Communication Arts for Children (AIE)
ICALA.......... American Library Association, Chicago, IL [Library symbol Library of Congress] (LCLS)
ICALEO .... International Congress on Applications of Lasers and Electro-Optics [Laser Institute of America]
ICALU .... International Confederation of Arab Labour Unions
ICAM........... American Medical Association, Chicago, IL [Library symbol Library of Congress] (LCLS)
ICAM........... Improved Cobra Agility and Maneuverability [Military] (MCD)
ICAM........... Institute of Corn and Agricultural Merchants Ltd. [British] (BI)
ICAM........... Integrated Communications Access Method [Computer science]
ICAM........... Integrated Computer-Aided Manufacturing (IEEE)
ICAM........... Intercellular Adhesion Molecule [Biochemistry]
ICAM........... International Confederation of Architectural Museums [Montreal, PQ] (EAIO)
ICAMA .... Interstate Compact on Adoption and Medical Assistance [Public human service program] (PHSD)
ICAMAS .... International Center for Advanced Mediterranean Agronomic Studies [FAO]
ICAMC .... International Conference on Automatic Control of Mines and Collieries
ICAME .... International Center for the Advancement of Management Education [Stanford University]
ICAME .... International Conference on the Applications of the Mossbauer Effect
ICAMI.......... International Committee Against Mental Illness (EA)
ICAMP .... Integrated Conventional Ammunition Maintenance Plan [DoD] (RDA)
ICAMQ .... International Committee of Automation of Mines and Quarries [Budapest, Hungary] (EAIO)
ICAMR .... Interagency [or Interdepartmental] Committee for Applied Meteorological Research
ICAMR .... Interdepartmental Committee for Applied Meteorological Research (USDC)
ICAMRS .... International Civil Aviation Message Routing System
ICAMS .... Industrial Central Atmosphere Monitoring System [Perkin Elmer Corp.] [Computer controlled chemical detection system] (NITA)
ICAMT......... International Centre of Ancient and Modern Tapestry
ICAN .... Individual Circuit Analysis [Telecommunications] (TEL)
ICAN .... Iniciativa Canaria [Spain Political party] (EY)
ICAN .... Integrated Circuit Analysis [Computer science]
ICAN .... Interlibrary Cooperation & Networking [Association of Specialized and Cooperative Library Agencies] [American Library Association]
ICAN .... Interlibrary Cooperation and Networking Section [ASCLA] (AL)
ICAN .... International Cesarean Awareness Network [Formerly Cesarean Prevention Movement (CPM)] (PAZ)
ICAN .... International College of Applied Nutrition (EA)
ICAN .... International Commission for Air Navigation
ICAN .... Invalid Children's Aid Nationwide [British] (EAIO)
ICAN .... Iowa Computer-Assisted Network [Iowa State Library] [Des Moines] [Information service or system] (IID)

ICan .... Parlin-Ingersoll Public Library, Canton, IL [Library symbol Library of Congress] (LCLS)
ICA/NCC ...... International Carwash Association/National Carwash Council [Later, ICA] (EA)
IC & C .... Installation Calibration and Checkout (KSC)
IC & C .... Instrumentation Calibration and Checkout (SAA)
IC & C .... Invoice Cost and Charges [Business term]
IC & CY .... Inns of Court and City Yeomanry [Military unit] [British]
IC & FCD ...... Interior Communication and Fire Control Distribution (MSA)
IC & RFS ..... Indoor Citrus and Rare Fruit Society [Defunct] (EA)
IC & RR ...... Inventory Control and Requirements Review Board [CNO]
ICANN .... Internet Corporation for Assigned Names & Numbers
ICanS.......... Spoon River College, Canton, IL [Library symbol Library of Congress] (LCLS)
ICAO .... American Osteopathic Association, Chicago, IL [Library symbol Library of Congress] (LCLS)
ICAO .... Internal Carotid Artery Occlusion [Medicine] (MAE)
ICAO .... International Civil Aviation Organization [Montreal, PQ] [United Nations]
ICAOPA .... International Council of Aircraft Owner and Pilot Associations (DI)
ICAP........... Improved Capability [for aircraft] (MCD)
ICAP........... Improved Cobra Armament Program [Military] (MCD)
ICAP........... Independent Cinema Artists and Producers (EA)
ICAP........... Indian Community Action Program (OICC)
ICAP........... Inductively Coupled Argon Plasma [Spectrometry]
ICAP........... Institute of Certified Ambulance Personnel [British] (BI)
ICAP........... Instituto Centroamericano de Administracion Publica [Central American Institute of Public Administration] [Costa Rica]
ICAP........... Integrated Correction Action Plan [Military] (MCD)
ICAP........... Integrated Criminal Apprehension Program
ICAP........... Inter-American Committee for the Alliance for Progress [Superseded by Permanent Executive Committee of the Inter-American Economic and Social Council]
ICAP........... Intermediate Communication Associative Processor [Computer science]
ICAP........... International Centre for the Application of Pesticides [British] (IRUK)
ICAP........... International Code of Advertising Practice (DI)
ICAP........... International College Art Program [Red Cross Youth]
ICAP........... International Committee of Architectural Photogrammetry
ICAP........... International Congress of Applied Psychology (PDAA)
ICAP........... Intracisternal A Particle (DB)
ICAP........... Inventory for Client and Agency Planning (TES)
ICAPES .... Inductively Coupled Argon Plasma Emission Spectroscopy (MEC)
ICAPP .... Integrated Conventional Ammunition Procurement Plan
ICAPR .... Interdepartmental Committee on Air Pollution Research [British]
ICAPR .... International Communications Agency Procurement Regulation [A publication] (AAGC)
ICAPS .... Integral Carrier ASW [Antisubmarine Warfare] Prediction System [Marine science] (MSC)
ICAPS .... Integrated Carrier Acoustic Prediction System [Navy] (NVT)
ICAPS .... Integrated Command ASW [Antisubmarine Warfare] Prediction System [Navy] (CAAL)
ICAPS .... Intelligence Civic Actions Program [Army] (VNW)
ICAPS .... Internal Control Audit Planning Summary (AAGC)
ICAQUO....... Inventory of Contaminants in Aquatic Organisms [Databank] (NITA)
ICAR........... ICAR [Interstate Cinderellans and Revenuers] Educational Club (EA)
ICAR........... Indian Council for Agricultural Research
ICAR........... Inner Circle of American Revenuers
ICAR........... Institute for Conflict Analysis and Resolution [George Mason University] [Research center] (RCD)
ICAR........... Integrated Command Accounting and Reporting
ICAR........... Intercargo Corp. [NASDAQ symbol] (NQ)
ICAR........... Interface Control Action Request (NRCH)
I-CAR.......... Inter-Industry Conference on Auto Collision Repair (EA)
ICAR........... International Cannabis Alliance Reform (DI)
ICAR........... Inventory of Canadian Agri-Food Research [Canandian Agricultural Research Council] [Information service or system]
ICAR........... Investigation and Corrective Action Report (KSC)
ICARA .... International Child Abduction Remedies Act [1988]
ICARA .... International Conference on Assistance for Refugees in Africa [See also CIARA] [United Nations Geneva, Switzerland] (EA)
IC Arb Q ...... Indian Council of Arbitration. Quarterly [A publication] (DLA)
ICarbS .... Southern Illinois University, Carbondale, IL [Library symbol Library of Congress] (LCLS)
ICARDA........ International Center for Agricultural Research in Dry Areas [Syria]
ICARDS........ Integrated Carrier [or Command] ASW Prediction System
ICARE .... International Christian Aid Relief Enterprises [Australia]
ICARES .... Institut International Catholique de Recherches Socio-Ecclesiales [International Catholic Institute for Socio-Religious Research] [Later, FERES]
ICarl............ Carlinville Public Library, Carlinville, IL [Library symbol Library of Congress] (LCLS)
ICarlB .... Blackburn College, Carlinville, IL [Library symbol Library of Congress] (LCLS)
ICarlMCD..... Macoupin Community District 1, Carlinville, IL [Library symbol Library of Congress] (LCLS)
ICarly.......... Case-Halstead Library, Carlyle, IL [Library symbol Library of Congress] (LCLS)
ICarlyS......... Carlyle School, Carlyle, IL [Library symbol Library of Congress] (LCLS)
ICARMO........ International Council of the Architects of Historical Monuments
ICArmour ..... Armour & Co., Chicago, IL [Library symbol Library of Congress Obsolete] (LCLS)
ICarr........... Carrollton Public Library, Carrollton, IL [Library symbol Library of Congress] (LCLS)

ICarrCD........ Carrollton Community Unit, District 1, Carrollton, IL [*Library symbol Library of Congress*] (LCLS)

ICarSD .... Charleston Community Unit School District, Charleston, IL [*Library symbol*] [*Library of Congress*] (LCLS)

ICart............. Carthage Public Library, Carthage, IL [*Library symbol Library of Congress*] (LCLS)

ICARUS........ Index of Conservation and Analytical Records: Unified System [*Computer science*]

ICARUS........ Inter-Continental Aerospacecraft-Range Unlimited System

ICARVS........ Interplanetary Craft for Advanced Research in Vicinity of Sun

ICAS............. Acme Steel Co., Chicago, IL [*Library symbol Library of Congress*] (LCLS)

ICas .... Casey Township Library, Casey, IL [*Library symbol Library of Congress*] (LCLS)

ICAS............. Improved Cobra Armament System [*Military*] (MCD)

ICAS............. Independent Collision Avoidance System

ICAS............. Instant Computer Arbitration Search [*Database*] [*Labor Relations Press*] [*Information service or system*] (CRD)

ICAS............. Institute of Chartered Accountants of Scotland (AIE)

ICAS............. Institute of Combined Arms and Support [*Fort Leavenworth, KS*] [*Army*]

ICAS............. Institute of Contemporary Asian Studies [*Monash University*] [*Australia*]

ICAS............. Intel Communications Amplifications Specification [*Interface*]

ICAS............. Interdepartmental Committee for Atmospheric Sciences [*Terminated, 1976*]

ICAS............. Interdepartment Council on Radio Propagation and Standards (NTCM)

ICAS............. Interface Control Action Sheet (DNAB)

ICAS............. Intermittent Commercial and Amateur Service [*Radio*]

ICAS............. International Council of Air Shows (EA)

ICAS............. International Council of Associations of Surfing (EA)

ICAS............. International Council of the Aeronautical Sciences

ICAS............. Isolated Children's Assistance Scheme

ICA-S .... School of the Art Institute of Chicago, Chicago, IL [*Library symbol Library of Congress*] (LCLS)

ICASALS ...... International Center for Arid and Semi-Arid Land Studies [*Texas Technological University*]

ICASC .... Acme Steel Co., Chicago, IL [*Library symbol*] [*Library of Congress*] (LCLS)

ICASC .... International Contraception, Abortion, and Sterilization Campaign [*Later, WGNRR*] (EAIO)

ICASE........... Injection-Coupled Acoustic Stability Evaluation (MCD)

ICASE........... Institute for Computer Applications in Science and Engineering [*Universities Space Research Association*] [*Research center*] (RCD)

I-CASE .... Integrated Computer-Aided Software Engineering

ICASE........... International Council of Associations for Science Education [*See also FIAPS*] (EAIO)

ICASIS .... International Conference of African States on Insurance Supervision [*See also CICA*] [*Gabon*] (EAIO)

ICASO .... International Committee of Acquired Immunodeficiency Syndrome Service Organisations (DMAA)

ICasSD........ Casey Community Unit School District, Casey, IL [*Library symbol*] [*Library of Congress*] (LCLS)

ICASSP .... International Conference on Acoustics, Speech, and Signal Processing (MCD)

ICasv .... Caseyville Public Library, Caseyville, IL [*Library symbol Library of Congress*] (LCLS)

ICat.............. Catlin Public Library, Catlin, IL [*Library symbol Library of Congress*] (LCLS)

ICAT............. In Commission, Active [*Vessel status*] [*Navy*] (DNAB)

I-CAT .... Intelligent Computer-Aided Troubleshooting

ICAT............. International Committee for the Coordination of Clinical Application and Teaching of Autogenic Therapy [*North Vancouver, BC*] (EAIO)

ICATL........... International Council of Associations of Theological Libraries (EA)

ICATS........... Intermediate Capacity Automated Telecommunications System [*Air Force*] (CET)

ICATU .... International Confederation of Arab Trade Unions

ICATVT........ International Centre for Advanced Technical and Vocational Training [*British*]

ICAV............. American Veterinary Medical Association, Chicago, IL [*Library symbol Library of Congress*] (LCLS)

ICAV............. Intracavity [*or Intracavitary*] [*Medicine*]

ICAVE........... International Coalition Against Violent Entertainment (EA)

ICAVS .... United States Army, Medical Department, Veterinary School, Chicago, IL [*Library symbol Library of Congress*] (LCLS)

ICAWA .... Indo-Chinese Australian Women's Association [*Australia*]

ICB............... Barat College of the Sacred Heart, Lake Forest, IL [*OCLC symbol*] (OCLC)

ICB............... Icebird Airline Ltd. [*Iceland*] [*ICAO designator*] (FAAC)

ICB............... Image Capture Board [*Video monitor*] [*AT & T*] (BYTE)

ICB............... Incoming Call Barred [*Telecommunications*] (TEL)

ICB............... Individual Case Basis (TEL)

ICB............... Industrial and Commercial Bank [*China*]

ICB............... Inertia Compensated Balance

ICB............... Information Collection Budget [*Office of Management and Budget*] (GFGA)

ICB............... Inner-Core Boundary [*Geology*]

ICB............... Institute of Collective Bargaining and Group Relations (EA)

ICB............... Institute of Comparative Biology (BARN)

ICB............... Integrated Circuit Breadboard [*Electronics*] (IAA)

ICB............... Integration Change Board [*NASA*]

ICB............... InterCapital Income Securities, Inc. [*NYSE symbol*] (SPSG)

ICB............... InterCapital Inc. Sec [*NYSE symbol*] (TTSB)

ICB............... Interface Control Board (NRCH)

ICB............... Interim Change Bulletin (NASA)

ICB............... Interior Control Board

ICB............... Internal Common Bus [*Computer science*]

ICB............... International Christian Broadcasters [*Defunct*] (EA)

ICB............... International City Bank & Trust Co. (EFIS)

ICB............... International Competitive Bid (NATG)

ICB............... International Computer Bibliography [*A publication of National Computing Center*]

ICB............... International Container Bureau [*Paris*]

ICB............... International Co-operative Bulletin [*A publication*]

ICB............... Interrupt Control Block (NASA)

ICB............... Intracranial Bleeding [*Medicine*] (STED)

ICB............... Ivory Coast Basin [*Geology*]

ICBA............. Independent Community Bankers of Alabama (TBD)

ICBA............. International Community of Booksellers' Associations [*Later, IBF*]

ICBAH .... Booz, Allen & Hamilton, Inc., Chicago, IL [*Library symbol Library of Congress*] (LCLS)

ICBAM .... Interpersonal Communication Behavior Analysis Method (PDAA)

ICBB............. Ind Coope Burton Brewery [*British*]

ICBB............. International Commission for Bee Botany [*Later, ICPBR*] (EA)

ICBBA .... International Cornish Bantam Breeders' Association (EA)

ICBC............. Blue Cross Association, Chicago, IL [*Library symbol Library of Congress*] (LCLS)

ICBC............. Inclined Cleated Belt Conveyor

ICBC............. Institute of Certified Business Counselors (EA)

ICBC............. Interagency Committee on Back Contamination [*Aerospace*]

ICBC............. International Cataloguing and Bibliographic Control [*Library science*] (TELE)

ICBC............. International Center for Biological Control [*University of California, Berkeley and Riverside*]

ICBC............. International Commercial Bank of China [*Taiwan*]

ICBCG .... Boston Consulting Group, Chicago, IL [*Library symbol Library of Congress*] (LCLS)

ICBCL........... Brook College, Chicago, IL [*Library symbol*] [*Library of Congress*] (LCLS)

ICBD .... International Children's Book Day [*Australia*]

ICBD .... International Council of Ballroom Dancing [*British*] (EAIO)

ICBD .... Ionized Cluster Beam Deposition [*Coating technology*]

ICBE............. International Commission on Biological Effects (COE)

ICBF............. Beatrice Foods Co., Chicago, IL [*Library symbol Library of Congress*] (LCLS)

ICBF............. Inner Cortical Blood Flow [*Medicine*] (DMAA)

ICBG............. Idiopathic Calcification of Basal Ganglia [*Medicine*] (DMAA)

ICBIF............ Inner City Business Improvement Forum

ICBK............. Intercontinental Bank [*NASDAQ symbol*] (SAG)

ICBK............. International Centrum voor Beurzen en Kongressen [*Belgium*] (EAIO)

ICBLB .... International Committee for Breaking the Language Barrier

ICBM............. Bank Marketing Association, Chicago, IL [*Library symbol Library of Congress*] (LCLS)

ICBM............. Independent Community Bankers of Minnesota (TBD)

ICBM............. Intercontinental Ballistic Missile

ICBMS .... Intercontinental Ballistic Missile System

ICBMTMS .... Intercontinental Ballistic Missile Test Maintenance Squadron

ICBN............. International Code of Botanical Nomenclature

ICBN............. International Commission on the Biological Effects of Noise (GNE)

ICBo............. Bozzel & Jacobs Corp., Information Center, Chicago, IL [*Library symbol*] [*Library of Congress*] (LCLS)

ICBO............. International Conference of Building Officials (EA)

ICBO............. Interracial Council for Business Opportunity [*New York, NY*] (EA)

ICBOSS .... Interactive Computer-Based Office Support System [*Military*] (MCD)

ICBP............. International Council for Bird Preservation [*Cambridge, England*] (EAIO)

ICBP............. Intracellular-Binding Proteins [*Medicine*]

ICBPA .... Insurance Company and Bank Purchasing Agents Association

ICBP(AS) ..... International Council for Bird Protection (Australian Section)

IC-BPH........ Illinois Regional Library for the Blind and Physically Handicapped, Chicago Public Library, Chicago, IL [*Library symbol Library of Congress*] (LCLS)

ICBR .... Ice-Cuber

ICBR .... Increased Chromosomal Breakage Rate [*Medicine*] (DMAA)

ICBR .... Input Channel Buffer Register [*Computer science*] (IAA)

ICBR .... Institute for Child Behavior Research (IID)

ICBRSD........ International Council for Building Research, Studies, and Documentation (DIT)

ICBS............. Impulsive Classroom Behavior Scale (EDAC)

ICBS............. Incorporated Church Building Society [*British*]

ICBS............. Interconnected Business System

ICBS............. International Cigar Band Society [*Defunct*] (EA)

ICBS............. National Association of Blue Shield Plans [*Later, BSA*], Chicago, IL [*Library symbol Library of Congress*] (LCLS)

ICBT............. Intercontinental Ballistic Transport

ICBT............. Intercostobronchial Trunk [*Medicine*] (DAVI)

ICBWR .... Improved-Cycle Boiling-Water Reactor [*Nuclear energy*]

ICC............... Article 19 - International Centre on Censorship (EAIO)

ICC............... Association Internationale de Chimie Cerealiere [*International Association for Cereal Chemistry*] [*Also, AICC*]

ICc............... Calumet City Public Library, Calumet City, IL [*Library symbol Library of Congress*] (LCLS)

ICC............... Calumet College, Whiting, IN [*OCLC symbol*] (OCLC)

ICC............... Cook County Clerk's Office, Chicago, IL [*Library symbol*] [*Library of Congress*] (LCLS)

ICC............... Ice Crystal Cloud

ICC............... Ignition Control Compound (EDCT)

ICC.............. Illinois Cancer Council Comprehensive Cancer Center [*Research center*] (RCD)
ICC.............. Image Converter Camera
ICC.............. Immunocompetent Cell [*Medicine*] (MAE)
ICC.............. Immunocytochemistry [*Immunology*]
ICC.............. Imperial Camel Corps [*British military*] (DMA)
ICC.............. Imperial Communications [*World War II*]
ICC.............. Inadequate Core Cooling [*Nuclear energy*] (NRCH)
ICC.............. Income Capital Certificate
ICC.............. Independent Community Consultants (EA)
ICC.............. Index of Cranial Capacity [*Cladistics*]
ICC.............. Indian Childhood Cirrhosis [*Medicine*] (MAE)
ICC.............. Indian Claims Commission [*Terminated, 1976*]
ICC.............. Indian Cultural Center [*Defunct*] (EA)
ICC.............. Individual Concealment Cover
ICC.............. Industrial and Commercial Company
ICC.............. Industrial Capacity Committee of the Production Council [*British World War II*]
ICC.............. Industrial Communication Council
ICC.............. Industrial Control Center (NITA)
ICC.............. Inferior Colliculus [*Also, IC*] [*Brain anatomy*]
ICC.............. Infinity Color-Corrected System [*Optics*]
ICC.............. Information and Coordination Central
ICC.............. Information Center Complex [*ORNL*] (GRD)
ICC.............. Information Control Center [*Military*] (IAA)
ICC.............. Information Control Console (DNAB)
ICC.............. Information Coordination Control [*Computer*] (MCD)
ICC.............. Initial Communications Connectivity [*DoD*]
ICC.............. Initial Contingency Capability (MCD)
ICC.............. Injury Control Center [*An association*] (EA)
ICC.............. Installation Calibration and Checkout (KSC)
ICC.............. Institut Canadien de Conservation [*Canadian Conservation Institute - CCI*]
ICC.............. Institute Circumpolaire Canadien [*Canadian Circumpolar Institute, University of Alberta*] (IRC)
ICC.............. Institute of Chinese Culture (EA)
ICC.............. [*Myasnikov*] Institute of Clinical Cardiology [*Russian*]
ICC.............. Instituto Cartografico de Cataluna [*Spain ICAO designator*] (FAAC)
ICC.............. Instrumentation Checkout Complex (MCD)
ICC.............. Instrumentation Control Center (AAG)
ICC.............. Instrument Control Center (KSC)
ICC.............. Instrument Control Computer
ICC.............. Integrated Chip Circuit
ICC.............. Integrated Cluster Controller
ICC.............. Integrated Communications Center (MCD)
ICC.............. Integrated Communications Control (MCD)
ICC.............. Intelligent Cruise Control [*Automotive engineering*]
ICC.............. Intensive Care Certificate [*Medicine*]
ICC.............. Intensive Coronary Care [*Medicine*]
ICC.............. Inter-American Cultural Council
ICC.............. Interchangeable Cycle Check (MCD)
ICC.............. Interchannel Communicator (MCD)
ICC.............. Inter-Company Correspondence
ICC.............. Intercomputer Channel (NASA)
ICC.............. Intercomputer Communication (MCD)
ICC.............. Intercomputer Coupler (IAA)
ICC.............. Interface Control Chart (NASA)
ICC.............. Interior Communications Electrician, Chief [*Navy rating*]
ICC.............. Intermarket Clearing Corp. (NUMA)
ICC.............. Intermediate Cryptanalysis Course [*Military*] (DNAB)
ICC.............. Internal Conversion Coefficient [*Radiology*]
ICC.............. International Association for Cereal Science and Technology [*Formerly, International Association of Cereal Chemists*] [*Acronym represents association's former name*] [*Austria*]
ICC.............. International Cablecasting Technologies [*Vancouver Stock Exchange symbol*]
ICC.............. International Camaro Club (EA)
ICC.............. International Cello Centre [*Duns, Scotland*] (EAIO)
ICC.............. International Chamber of Commerce [*See also CCI*] [*Paris, France*] (EAIO)
ICC.............. International Chessology Club (EA)
ICC.............. International Children's Centre [*Paris, France*]
ICC.............. International Clergy Council (EA)
ICC.............. International College in Copenhagen [*Denmark*]
ICC.............. International College of Chiropractors (EA)
ICC.............. International Color Consortium
ICC.............. International Committee of ICOM [*International Council of Museums*] for Conservation [*Later, ICOM-CC*] (EAIO)
ICC.............. International Communications Corp. [*Miami, FL*] (CSR)
ICC.............. International Computaprint Corp. [*Fort Washington, PA*]
ICC.............. International Computation Center [*Sponsored by UNESCO*] [*Rome, Italy*]
ICC.............. International Computer Casting [*Information service or system*] (IID)
ICC.............. International Computer Center (HGAA)
ICC.............. International Computing Centre [*United Nations*] (ECON)
ICC.............. International Conference on Communications [*IEEE*]
ICC.............. International Congregational Council
ICC.............. International Control Centre [*Telecommunications*] (NITA)
ICC.............. International Control Commission [*Representatives of Canada, India, and Poland charged with supervising the cease-fire in Laos established at Geneva Conference of 1962*]
ICC.............. International Controls Corp.
ICC.............. International Convention Center [*British*] (ECON)
ICC.............. International Cooperation Council [*Later, UDC*]

ICC.............. International Coordinating Committee for the Presentation of Science and the Development of Out-of-School Scientific Activities [*See also CIC*] (EAIO)
ICC.............. International Corrosion Council [*Orsay, France*] (EAIO)
ICC.............. International Counseling Center (EA)
ICC.............. International Cricket Conference (EA)
ICC.............. [*The*] International Critical Commentary on the Holy Scriptures of the Old and New Testament [*Edinburgh*] [*A publication*] (BJA)
ICC.............. Internet Content Coalition [*Computer science*]
ICC.............. Interprocessor Communication and Control Routine (MCD)
ICC.............. Interstate Carriers Conference (EA)
ICC.............. Interstate Commerce Commission [*Independent government agency*]
ICC.............. Interventional Cardiac Catheterization [*Medicine*]
ICC.............. Intra-Class Correlation
ICC.............. Intra-Class Correlation Coefficient
ICC.............. Intracompany Correspondence (AAG)
ICC.............. Inuit Circumpolar Conference [*Godthaab, Greenland, Denmark*] (EAIO)
ICC.............. Invasive Cancer of the Cervix [*Oncology*]
ICC.............. Inventory Control Center [*of Field Army Support Command*]
ICC.............. Inventory Control Company
ICC.............. Invitational Computer Conference
ICC.............. Irish Council of Churches
ICC.............. Issue Category Code (NITA)
ICC.............. Italian Chamber of Commerce (EA)
ICC.............. Italian Culture Council (EA)
ICC.............. Item Category Code
ICC.............. Item Characteristic Curve [*Statistics*]
ICCA............ Independent Computer Consultants Association (EA)
ICCA............ Infants' and Children's Coat Association [*Later, ICGSCA*] (EA)
ICCA............ Initial Cash Clothing Allowance [*Military*]
ICCA............ Institut Canadien de la Construction en Acier [*Canadian Institute of Steel Construction*]
ICCA............ Institut Canadien des Comptables Agrees [*Canadian Institute of Chartered Accountants*]
ICCA............ Interagency Coordinating Committee for Astronomy [*Federal Council for Science and Technology*] [*Terminated, 1976*]
ICCA............ InterAmericas Communications Corp. [*NASDAQ symbol*] (SAG)
ICCA............ International Commission on Commercial Activities (EAIO)
ICCA............ International Community Corrections Association (EA)
ICCA............ International Computer Chess Association
ICCA............ International Conference on Computer Applications [*in developing countries*] [*1977*]
ICCA............ International Congress and Convention Association [*Amsterdam, Netherlands*] (EA)
ICCA............ International Consumer Credit Association [*Later, ICA*] (EA)
ICCA............ International Conventions and Congresses Association [*Australia*]
ICCA............ International Correspondence of Corkscrew Addicts (EA)
ICCA............ International Corrugated Case Association [*Paris, France*] (EAIO)
ICCA............ International Council for Commercial Arbitration [*Vienna, Austria*] (EAIO)
ICCA............ International Council of Chemical Associations
ICCaC.......... Carnow, Coninleas & Associates, Ltd., Chicago, IL [*Library symbol*] [*Library of Congress*] (LCLS)
ICCAC .... Interagency Clean Car Advisory Committee [*HEW Terminated*] (EGAO)
ICCAD .... International Center for Computer-Aided Design (MHDB)
ICCAD .... International Centre for Computer Aided Design (PDAA)
ICCAIA .... International Coordinating Council of Aerospace Industries Associations (EA)
ICCAM .... International Committee of Children's and Adolescents' Movements
ICCAP .... International Coordination Committee for the Accounting Profession
ICCARD........ International Commission for Central American Recovery and Development
ICCAS .... Chicago Academy of Sciences, Matthew Laflin Memorial Library, Chicago, IL [*Library symbol Library of Congress*] (LCLS)
ICCAS .... International Center for Communication Arts and Sciences
ICCAT........... International Commission for the Conservation of Atlantic Tunas [*Spain*]
ICCATCI .... International Committee to Coordinate Activities of Technical Groups in CoatingsIndustry [*Paris, France*] (EAIO)
ICCB............ Insulated Case Circuit Breaker (DWSG)
ICCB............ Integrated Change Control Board [*NASA*] (NASA)
ICCB............ Intermediate Change Control Board
ICCB............ Intermediate Configuration Control Board [*Western Electric*] (AABC)
ICCB............ International Catholic Child Bureau [*Geneva, Switzerland*]
ICCB............ International Center for Cooperation in BioInformatics [*UNESCO*]
ICCB............ Internet Control and Configuration Board [*Computer science*] (ACRL)
IC-CBPH....... Chicago Library Services for the Blind and Physically Handicapped (Subregional),Chicago Public Library, Chicago, IL [*Library symbol Library of Congress*] (LCLS)
ICCC............ Columbia College, Chicago, IL [*Library symbol Library of Congress*] (LCLS)
ICCC............ Ice Cream Connoisseurs Club [*Defunct*] (EA)
ICCC............ ImmuCell Corp. [*NASDAQ symbol*] (NQ)
ICCC............ Imperial College Computing Center (PDAA)
ICCC............ Infantry Captains Career Course [*Military*]
ICCC............ Information Center on Children's Cultures [*Defunct*] (EA)
ICCC............ International Center for Comparative Criminology (EA)
ICCC............ International Color Computer Club (EA)
ICCC............ International Concentration Camp Committee [*Vienna, Austria*] (EAIO)
ICCC............ International Concerns Committee for Children (EA)
ICCC............ International Concerns for Children [*An association*] (EA)
ICCC............ International Conference of Catholic Charities

ICCC............ International Conference of Coordination Chemistry
ICCC............ International Conference on Circuits and Computers (MCD)
ICCC............ International Council for Computer Communication (EA)
ICCC............ International Council of Christian Churches (EA)
ICCC............ International Council of Community Churches (EA)
ICCCA......... International C Class Catamaran Association of America (EA)
ICCCS .... Integrated Continuous Controlled Color System (DGA)
ICCD .... Improved Computer-Controlled Dwell [*Automotive engineering*]
ICCD .... Information Center on Crime and Delinquency [*National Council on Crime and Delinquency*] (IID)
ICCD .... Institute of Chocolate and Confectionery Distributors [*British*] (BI)
ICCD .... Intensified Charge-Coupled Device [*Electronics*]
ICCD .... Intergovernmental Commission for Chagas Disease (ECON)
ICCD .... Internal Coordination Control Drawing
ICCDP......... Integrated Circuit Communications Data Processor (MHDI)
ICCE............ Iceland Communications and Control Enhancement
ICCE............ International Congress on Combustion Engines
ICCE............ International Council for Computers in Education (EA)
ICCE............ International Council for Correspondence Education [*Later, ICDE*]
ICCE............ International Council of Commerce Employers
ICCE............ Intracapsular Cataract Extraction [*Ophthalmology*]
ICCEA......... International Committee for the Study and Conservation of Earthen Architecture (EAIO)
ICCEC......... India Chemists and Chemical Engineers Club (EA)
ICCEcPI....... Intracapsular Cataract Extraction with Peripheral Iridectomy [*Ophthalmology*]
ICCERSP..... Interagency Coordinating Committee for Earth Resource Survey Programs [*National Aeronautics and Space Council*]
ICCET.......... Imperial College of Science and Technology Centre for Environmental Technology [*British*] (IRUK)
ICCF............ Interaction Computing and Control Facility (NITA)
ICCF............ Interactive Computing and Control Facility [*IBM Corp. program product*]
ICCF............ Interexchange Carrier and Carrier Forum [*Exchange Carriers Standards Association*] [*Telecommunications*]
ICCF............ International Correspondence Chess Federation
ICCFM........ International Confederation of Christian Family Movements (EAIO)
ICCFS......... Imperial College of Science and Technology Centre for Fusion Studies [*British*] (IRUK)
ICCFTI......... International Center for Companies of the Food Trade and Industry (EA)
ICCG .... Incomplete Conjugate Gradient (AAEL)
ICCG .... Intercommunication-Communication Control Group [*Navy*] (NVT)
ICCG .... International Catholic Conference of Guiding (EAIO)
ICCG .... International Conference on Crystal Growth (PDAA)
ICCGB .... Indian Chamber of Commerce in Great Britain (DS)
ICCGB .... Italian Chamber of Commerce in Great Britain (DS)
ICCGR......... Intergranular Cyclic Crack Growth Rate [*Nuclear energy*] (NUCP)
ICCH .... Cook County Hospital, Dr. Frederick Tice Memorial Library, Chicago, IL [*Library symbol Library of Congress*] (LCLS)
ICch .... Country Club Hills Public Library District, Country Club Hills, IL [*Library symbol Library of Congress*] (LCLS)
ICCH .... International Catholic Confederation of Hospitals [*Later, IHF*] (EA)
ICCH .... International Commodities Clearing House [*British Business term*]
ICCH .... International Conference on Computers and the Humanities
ICChC......... Chapman & Cutter, Law Library, Chicago, IL [*Library symbol*] [*Library of Congress*] (LCLS)
ICChH .... Children's Memorial Hospital, Joseph Brennemann Medical Library, Chicago, IL [*Library symbol Library of Congress*] (LCLS)
ICchP.......... Country Club Hills Public Library District, Country Club Hills, IL [*Library symbol*] [*Library of Congress*] (LCLS)
ICCHRLA...... Inter-Church Committee on Human Rights in Latin America [*Canada*] (EAIO)
ICCHS......... Intercampus Committee for Handicapped Students (EA)
ICCIA .... Italian Chamber of Commerce and Industry in Australia
ICCICA........ Interim Co-ordinating Committee for International Commodity Arrangements
ICCICE........ Islamic Chamber of Commerce, Industry and Commodity Exchange [*See also CICIEM*] [*Karachi, Pakistan*] (EAIO)
ICCILMB...... Interim Committee for Coordination of Investigations of the Lower Mekong Basin (EA)
ICCIR.......... International Coordination Committee for Immunology of Reproduction [*Bulg aria*] [*Research center*] (IRC)
ICCJ............ International Committee for the Cooperation of Journalists (NATG)
ICCJ............ International Council of Christians and Jews [*Heppenheim, Federal Republic of Germany*] (EAIO)
ICCK............ Chadwell, Kayser, Ruggles, McGee & Hasting, Chicago, IL [*Library symbol Library of Congress*] (LCLS)
ICCL............ Cook County Law Library, Chicago, IL [*Library symbol Library of Congress*] (LCLS)
ICCL............ Interface Control Configuration List
ICCL............ International Committee for the Centennial of Light
ICCL............ International Council of Cruise Lines (NTPA)
ICCL............ Irish Council for Civil Liberties (EAIO)
ICCLA......... International Center for Coordination of Legal Assistance [*Switzerland*] (PDAA)
ICCLY......... International Council to Combat Lethal Yellowing
ICCM........... Idiopathic Congestive Cardiomyopathy [*Medicine*]
ICCM........... Inadequate Core Cooling Monitor [*Nuclear energy*] (NUCP)
ICCM........... Institute for Computer Capacity Management (NTPA)
ICCM........... Institute of Critical Care Medicine [*University of Southern California*] [*Research center*] (RCD)
ICCM........... Intercontinental Cruise Missile (IAA)
ICCM........... International Christian Classic Motorcyclists (EA)

ICCM........... International Committee for the Conservation of Mosaics [*Hungerford, Berkshire, England*] (EAIO)
ICCM........... International Council of Catholic Men [*See also FIHC*] [*Vatican City, Vatican City State*] (EAIO)
ICCM........... Interstitial Cell-Conditioned Medium [*Clinical chemistry*]
ICCM........... Master Chief Interior Communications Electrician [*Navy rating*]
ICCM........... University of Health Sciences - Chicago Medical School, Chicago, IL [*Library symbol Library of Congress*] (LCLS)
ICCMB .... International Committee for the Conservation of Mud-Brick (EAIO)
ICCMG .... Clausen, Miller, Gorman, Caffrey & Witous, Chicago, IL [*Library symbol Library of Congress*] (LCLS)
ICCMHC ...... Idiana Council of Community Mental Health Centers (SRA)
ICCMO .... International College of Cranio-Mandibular Orthopedics (NTPA)
ICCN .... Cook County School of Nursing, Chicago, IL [*Library symbol Library of Congress*] (LCLS)
ICCN .... International Committee of Catholic Nurses [*See also CICIAMS*] [*Vatican City, Vatican City State*] (EAIO)
ICCNA .... CNA Financial Corp., Chicago, IL [*Library symbol Library of Congress*] (LCLS)
ICCNA .... International Center for Control of Nutritional Anemia [*University of Kansas*] [*Research center*] (RCD)
ICCNL .... International Committee of Chairmen of National Libraries (WDAA)
ICCO .... Chicago College of Osteopathic Medicine, Chicago, IL [*Library symbol Library of Congress*] (LCLS)
ICCO .... International Carpet Classification Organization [*Brussels, Belgium*] (EAIO)
ICCO .... International Cocoa Organization [*London, England*] (EAIO)
ICCO .... International Council of Containership Operators [*British*] (DCTA)
ICC of H & HH... International Club for Collectors of Hatpins and Hatpin Holders (EA)
ICCComE...... Commonwealth Edison Co., Chicago, IL [*Library symbol Library of Congress*] (LCLS)
ICCon......... Continental Group Co., Inc., Chicago, IL [*Library symbol Library of Congress*] (LCLS)
ICConB........ Continental Illinois National Bank and Trust Co., Research and Information Services, Chicago, IL [*Library symbol*] [*Library of Congress*] (LCLS)
ICcP .... Calumet City Public Library, Calumet City, IL [*Library symbol*] [*Library of Congress*] (LCLS)
ICCP .... Impressed Current Corrosion Protection
ICCP .... Information, Computer and Communications Policy (MHDI)
ICCP .... Institute for Certification of Computer Professionals (EA)
ICCP .... Integrated Communication Control Panel (MCD)
ICCP .... Intelligence Civilian Career Program [*Army*] (AABC)
ICCP .... Interface Coordination and Control Procedure (NASA)
ICCP .... International Camp Counselor Program (EA)
ICCP .... International Committee for Coal Petrology [*Liege, Belgium*] (EAIO)
ICCP .... International Conference on Cataloging Principles
ICCP .... International Council for Children's Play [*Groningen, Netherlands*] (EAIO)
ICCPBS .... International Chemical Congress of Pacific Basin Societies (EA)
ICCPC......... International Computing Center's Preparatory Committee
ICCR .... Interactive Cash and Credit Register [*Datacap Systems, Inc.*]
ICCR .... Interfaith Center on Corporate Responsibility (EA)
ICCR .... International Committee for Coal Research [*Brussels, Belgium*] (EAIO)
ICCR .... International Committee for Contraceptive Research
ICCR .... Interstate Commerce Commission Reports [*A publication*] (DLA)
ICCra .... Crane Co., Chicago, IL [*Library symbol Library of Congress*] (LCLS)
ICC Rep ...... Interstate Commerce Commission Reports [*A publication*] (DLA)
ICCROM...... International Centre for the Study of the Preservation and the Restoration of Cultural Property [*Rome, Italy*] (EAIO)
ICCS .... Integrated Carrier Cataput Station (MCD)
ICCS .... Integrated Carrier Cataput System (DNAB)
ICCS .... Integrated Catapult Control Station (MCD)
ICCS .... Integrated Chassis Control System [*Automotive*]
ICCS .... Integrated Communications Collection System [*Military*] (MCD)
ICCS .... Intercomputer Communication System
ICCS .... Interdisciplinary Center for Creative Studies [*State University College at Buffalo*] [*Research center*] (RCD)
ICCS .... Interface Configuration Control System (DNAB)
ICCS .... Interim Command and Control System (MCD)
ICCS .... International Center for Criminological Studies (BARN)
ICCS .... International Centre for Chemical Studies [*See also CIEC*] (EAIO)
ICCS .... International Classification of Clinical Services (HCT)
ICCS .... International Commission of Control and Supervision [*Composed of representatives of Canada, Hungary, Indonesia, and Poland, and charged with supervising the ceasefire in Vietnam, 1973*]
ICCS .... International Commission on Civil Status [*See also CIEC*] [*Strasbourg, France*] (EAIO)
ICCS .... International Committee of Creole Studies [*Aix-En-Provence, France*] (EAIO)
ICCS .... International Committee on Clinical Sociology [*See also CISC*] [*Later, International Group on Clinical Sociology*] (EAIO)
ICCS .... International Conference on Composite Structures [*Paisley, Scotland*] (EAIO)
ICCS .... International Convention on the Continental Shelf (NOAA)
ICCS .... International Cork Cutters' Society [*A union*]
ICCS .... International Council for Canadian Studies [*See also CIEC*]
ICCS .... International Group on Clinical Sociology [*Formerly, International Committee on Clinical Sociology*] (EA)
ICCS .... Senior Chief Interior Communications Electrician [*Navy rating*]
ICCSASW .... International Commission for the Co-ordination of Solidarity among Sugar Workers [*Canada*]

ICCSHE .... Interagency Committee for Computer Support of Handicapped Employees [*General Services Administration*] (EGAO)
ICCSP .... Chicago School of Professional Psychology, Chicago, IL [*Library symbol Library of Congress*] (LCLS)
ICCSR .... Interagency Committee on Climate Services and Research
ICCSSSAR.... International Coordinating Committee on Solid State Sensors and Actuators Research (EA)
ICCSTR .... International Coordinating Committee on Solid State Transducers Research (EA)
ICCT............. Consoer, Townsend & Associates, Chicago, IL [*Library symbol Library of Congress*] (LCLS)
ICCT............. Initial Contact Control Time [*Aerospace*] (AAG)
ICCT............. Iowa Community College Telenetwork [*Marshalltown*] (TSSD)
ICCTA........... International Consultative Council of Travel Agents
ICC Tch........ ICC Technologies, Inc. [*Associated Press*] (SAG)
ICC-TM .... Interstate Commerce Commission Transport Mobilization [*Federal emergency order*]
ICCTR........... Intelligence Case Control and Time Reporting System [*IRS*]
ICCU .... Intensive Coronary Care Unit [*of a hospital*]
ICCU .... Inter-Channel Comparison Unit [*Nuclear energy*] (NRCH)
ICCU .... Intercomputer Communication Unit (IAA)
ICCU .... Intercomputer Compatibility Unit [*Computer science*]
ICCU .... Intermediate Coronary Care Unit [*Medicine*]
ICCU .... International Cross-Country Union (EA)
ICCUS .... International Claims Commission of the United States [*Abolished, 1954*] [*Department of State*]
ICCUSA .... Interagency Coordinating Committee on US-Soviet Affairs [*Department of State*]
ICCUSA .... International Child Care (USA) (EA)
ICCUSA .... Ireland Chamber of Commerce in the United States (NTPA)
ICC Valuation Rep... Interstate Commerce Commission Valuation Reports [*A publication*] (DLA)
ICCVAM .... Interagency Coordinating Committee on the Validation of Alternative Methods [*To amend for biological testing*]
ICCW .... In-Containment Chilled Water [*Nuclear energy*] (NRCH)
ICCY............. International Cultural Centers for Youth (EA)
ICCYM .... Central YMCA Community College, Chicago, IL [*Library symbol Library of Congress*] (LCLS)
ICD............... College of Saint Francis, Joliet, IL [*OCLC symbol*] (OCLC)
ICD............... De Paul University, Chicago, IL [*Library symbol Library of Congress*] (LCLS)
ICD............... Idiopathic Cerebral Dysfunction [*Medicine*] (CPH)
ICD............... Iesu Christo Duce [*With Jesus Christ as Leader*] [*Latin*]
ICD............... Imitative Communication Deception [*Military*]
ICD............... Immune Complex Disease
ICD............... Implantable Cardioverter-Defibrillator [*Medical device for heart patients*]
ICD............... Induced Circular Dichroism [*Physics*]
ICD............... Industrial Cooperation Division [*Navy*]
ICD............... Informal Clearance Document [*Customs*]
ICD............... Inguinal Compressive Device (DB)
ICD............... Initial Case Design (MCD)
ICD............... Initial Claudication Distance (DB)
ICD............... Initiative Communications Deception (PDAA)
ICD............... Inland Clearance Depot [*Shipping*]
ICD............... Installation Completion Date (CET)
ICD............... Installation Control Drawing [*DoD*]
ICD............... Instantaneous Cardiac Death [*Cardiology*] (DAVI)
ICD............... Institute for Crippled and Disabled (DAVI)
ICD............... Institute of Civil Defence [*British*] (EAIO)
ICD............... Institute of Community Development [*British*] (DBA)
ICD............... Institute of Cooperative Directors (ODBW)
ICD............... Instrumentation Control Document (KSC)
ICD............... Inter Canadian Development [*Vancouver Stock Exchange symbol*]
ICD............... Intercanthal Distance [*Anatomy*]
ICD............... Interface Connecting Device [*Air Force*] (DOMA)
ICD............... Interface Control Diagram (NRCH)
ICD............... Interface Control Dimension (IAA)
ICD............... Interface Control Document [*Apollo*] [*NASA*]
ICD............... Interface Control Drawings (NRCH)
ICD............... Interim Checkout Device
ICD............... International Candle
ICD............... International Center for the Disabled (EA)
ICD............... International Circulation Distributors, Inc.
ICD............... International Classification of Diseases [*A publication*]
ICD............... International Climatic Decades
ICD............... International Code Designator [*Telecommunications*] (OSI)
ICD............... International College of Dentists (EA)
ICD............... International Congress for Data Processing
ICD............... International Cooperation for Development [*Commercial firm British*] (ECON)
ICD............... Intracervical Device [*Medicine*] (DB)
ICD............... Intracommunity Directive [*Meat-shipping plants*] [*European Community*]
ICD............... Intrauterine Contraceptive Device [*Medicine*]
ICD............... Investment Company Data, Inc. [*Database producer*] (IID)
ICD............... Ion-Controlled Diode [*Electronics*] (IAA)
ICD............... Ischemic Coronary Disease [*Medicine*]
ICD............... Isocitrate Dehydrogenase [*Also, ICDH, IDH*] [*An enzyme*]
ICD-9 .... International Classification of Diseases. 9th Revision [*A publication*] (DHSM)
ICD-9-CM.... International Classification of Diseases. 9th Revision. Clinical Modification [*A publication*] (DHSM)
ICDA .... Industrial Civil Defence Association [*British*] (BI)
ICDA .... Industrial Compressor Distributors Association (EA)

ICDA .... Infantry Combat Developments Agency [*Pronounced "ick-da"*] [*Army*]
ICDA .... Institute for Community Design Analysis (EA)
ICdA............ International Cadmium Association (NTPA)
ICDA .... International Catholic Deaf Association (EA)
ICDA .... International Cheese and Deli Association [*Later, IDDA*] (EA)
ICDA .... International Classification of Diseases, Adopted for Use in the United States
ICDA .... International Coalition for Development Action [*See also CIAD*] (EAIO)
ICDA .... International Congress of Dealers Associations (EA)
ICDA .... International Cooperative Development Association [*Later, ACDI*]
ICDA-8 .... International Classification of Diseases, Adopted for Use in the United States. 8th Revision [*A publication*] (DHSM)
ICDB .... Integrated Corporate Database
ICDBL .... International Committee for the Defense of the Breton Language [*See also CISLB*] [*Brussels, Belgium*] (EAIO)
ICDC .... Industrial and Commercial Development Corp. [*Kenya*]
ICDC .... National Dairy Council, Chicago, IL [*Library symbol Library of Congress*] (LCLS)
ICDCP .... Interface Control Drawings Change Proposal (IAA)
ICDD .... International Center for Dynamics of Development (EA)
ICDDB .... DDB Needham Worldwide, Inc. Information Center, Chicago, IL [*Library symbol*] [*Library of Congress*] (LCLS)
ICDDB .... Internal Control Description Database
ICDDR .... International Center for Diarrhoeal Diseases Research (PDAA)
ICDDR .... International Centre for Diarrhoeal Disease Research [*Bangladesh*]
ICDDRB .... International Centre for Diarrhoeal Disease Research, Bangladesh (ECON)
ICDDS .... Institute of Civil Defence and Disaster Studies [*British*] (EAIO)
ICDE .... International Council for Distance Education [*Australia*] (EAIO)
ICDF .... International Christian Dance Fellowship (EAIO)
ICDFS .... Increased Capacity Drum Feed System (MCD)
ICDH .... Isocitrate Dehydrogenase [*Also, ICD, IDH*] [*An enzyme*]
ICDI .... Imperial Court, Daughters of Isis (EA)
ICDIA .... International Compact Disc Interactive Association (NTPA)
ICD-L .... De Paul University, Law Library, Chicago, IL [*Library symbol Library of Congress*] (LCLS)
ICDL .... Integrated Circuit Description Language
ICDL .... Inter-Center Data Link (MCD)
ICDL .... Interface Control Documentation Log (KSC)
ICDL .... Internal Control Description Language
ICDL .... International Centre for Distance Learning [*United Nations University*] (DUND)
ICDLA .... Internal Control Description Language Analyzer [*Computer science*] (MHDI)
ICDM .... Industrial Civil Defense Management
ICDM .... Institut Canadien pour la Deficience Mentale [*Canadian Institute on Mental Retardation*] [*Canada*]
ICDMA .... Independent Carbon-Dioxide Manufacturers Association (EA)
ICDNA .... Imidazole (Carbonic Acid) Dinitroanilide [*Organic chemistry*]
ICDO .... International Civil Defence Organization [*Switzerland*]
ICDP .... Integrated Circuits Demonstration Plant [*Taiwan*] (NITA)
ICDP .... Intelligence Career Development Program (AFM)
ICDP .... International Center for Development Policy (EA)
ICDP .... International Confederation for Disarmament and Peace [*British*]
ICDP .... International Continental Scientific Drilling Program [*Originated by the US, China, and Germany*]
ICDR .... Incremental Critical Design Review (NASA)
ICDR .... International Council for Dispute Resolution (EA)
ICDR .... Inward Call Detail Recording [*Telecommunications*] (TEL)
ICDR .... Ion Cyclotron Double Resonance
IC DRUM ..... Intercommunication Drum (MSA)
ICDS .... Improved Conventional Dive System (DOMA)
ICDS .... Integrated Child Development Scheme (DMAA)
ICDS .... Integrated Circuit Design System (CIST)
ICDS .... Integrated Control and Display System (MCD)
ICDS .... Interim Contractor Depot Support [*DoD*]
ICDS .... International Cardiac Doppler Society (DMAA)
ICDSP .... Interim Contractor Depot Support Plan [*DoD*]
ICDSRHP ..... International Committee for the Defense of Salman Rushdie and His Publishers (EAIO)
ICDT............. Chicago Daily Tribune, Chicago, IL [*Library symbol Library of Congress*] (LCLS)
ICDT............. Incident (AABC)
ICDT............. Inverse Discrete Cosine Transform [*Mathematics*]
ICDT............. Islamic Centre for Development of Trade [*See also CIDC*] [*Casablanca, Morocco*] (EAIO)
ICDU .... Inertial Coupling Data Unit (NASA)
ICDU .... Inertial Coupling Display Unit (KSC)
ICD-USA ...... International College of Dentists, United States of America Section (NTPA)
ICDV .... Import Certificate Delivery Verification [*Military*]
ICE.............. Concordia Teachers College, River Forest, IL [*OCLC symbol*] (OCLC)
ICE.............. Economist Newspapers, Chicago, IL [*Library symbol Library of Congress*] (LCLS)
ICE.............. Ice, Compression, Elevation (CPH)
ICE.............. Iceland
ICE.............. Icelandair [*ICAO designator*] (FAAC)
ice .... Icelandic [*MARC language code Library of Congress*] (LCCP)
ICE.............. Ice Station Resources [*Vancouver Stock Exchange symbol*]
ICE.............. Illness-Correctional Environments
ICE.............. Immediate Cable Equalizer (IAA)
ICE.............. Implicit Continuous-Fluid Eulerian
ICE.............. Improved Cost Estimate (RDA)

ICE .... Improving Career Education (OICC)
ICE .... In-Car Entertainment [*Automotive audio system*]
ICE .... Incidental Campaign Expense [*Ticket scalping*]
ICE .... In-Circuit Emulator [*A trademark*]
ICE .... Increased Combat Effectiveness (AFM)
ICE .... Independent Cost Estimate
ICE .... Index of Combat Effectiveness (CINC)
ICE .... Indiana Computer Educators (EDAC)
ICE .... Individual Career Exploration [*Vocational guidance test*]
ICE .... Individual Commitment to Excellence [*DoD*]
ICE .... Individual Compass Error (IAA)
ICE .... Induction Certificate Examination [*British Institute of Innkeeping*]
ICE .... Industrial Combustion Emissions Model [*Environmental Protection Agency*] (GFGA)
ICE .... Industrial Computer Enclosure (IAA)
ICE .... Industrial Cost Exclusion [*Amendment to Federal Clean Water Act which limits use of federal money*]
ICE .... Information and Content Exchange
ICE .... Information Center on Education [*New York State Education Department*] [*Albany*] [*Information service or system*] (IID)
ICE .... Information Centre Exchange [*Canada*] (EAIO)
ICE .... Information Collection and Exchange [*Peace Corps*]
ICE .... Infrared Countermeasures Equipment [*Military Electronics*] (CAAL)
ICE .... Initial Combat Employment [*of new munitions*]
ICE .... Initial Cooling Experiment [*Nuclear physics research*]
ICE .... Inner City Enterprises [*British*]
ICE .... Input-Checking Equipment
ICE .... Input Control Element (MCD)
ICE .... Institute for Chemical Education (EA)
ICE .... Institute for Christian Education [*Australia*]
ICE .... Institute for Community Economics (EA)
ICE .... Institute for Consumer Ergonomics [*British*] (IRUK)
ICE .... Institute for Continuing Education (AIE)
ICE .... Institute of Ceramic Engineers (NUCP)
ICE .... Institution of Chemical Engineers [*British*] (EAIO)
ICE .... Institution of Civil Engineers [*British*]
ICE .... Instrumentation Communication Equipment (NASA)
ICE .... Instrument Checkout Equipment [*NASA*] (KSC)
ICE .... Instrument Communication
ICE .... Integrated Circuits Engineering Corp.
ICE .... Integrated Clinical Encounters
ICE .... Integrated Coil Electronic [*Automotive engineering*]
ICE .... Integrated Communications Environment [*Computer architecture*] (NITA)
ICE .... Integrated Conceptual Environment [*Computer science*]
ICE .... Integrated Cooling for Electronics
ICE .... Integrated Curriculum Environment [*Army*]
ICE .... Integration with Controlled Error (MCD)
ICE .... Intelligence and Counterespionage [*Fictitious organization in the Matt Helm series of books and movies*]
ICE .... Intelligent Concept Extraction [*Technology*] [*Computer science*]
ICE .... Interactive Concurrent Engineering [*Software*]
ICE .... Inter City Express [*Electric train*] [*Germany*]
ICE .... Intercomputer Electronics (IAA)
ICE .... Interface Cancellation Equipment [*Telecommunications*] (EECA)
ICE .... Interfaith Coalition on Energy (EA)
ICE .... Interference Cancellation Equipment [*Telecommunications*]
ICE .... Interleukin-Converting Enzyme [*Biochemistry*]
ICE .... Intermediate Cable Equalizers (IEEE)
ICE .... Internal Combustion Engine
ICE .... International Center for the Environment
ICE .... International Centre for Economics [*British*]
ICE .... International Cirrus Experiment [*Funded by West Germany, Britain, France, Sweden, and the European Communities Commission*] [*Climatology*]
ICE .... International Cometary Explorer [*Formerly, International Sun-Ea rth Explorer*] [*NASA*]
ICE .... International Commercial Exchange [*Defunct*] (EA)
ICE .... International Computer Component Exchange
ICE .... International Congress of Entomology [*Later, CICE*] (EA)
ICE .... International Construction Equipment Exhibition (ITD)
ICE .... International Council on Electrocardiology [*Glasgow, Scotland*] (EAIO)
ICE .... International Cultural Exchange [*An association*] (EA)
ICE .... Internet Commerce Exchange
ICE .... Internet Connections for Engineering
ICE .... Interstate Cost Estimate [*Federal Highway Administration*]
ICE .... Inventory Control Effectiveness
ICE .... Ion Chromatography Exclusion
ICE .... Ion Convection Electrodynamics (MCD)
ICE .... Irridescent Color Exchange [*Heat-sensitive clothing*]
ICE .... Islamic Council of Europe
ICE .... Isothermal Controlled Electrophoresis
ICE .... Italian Cultural Exchange in the United States (EA)
ICE .... It's Close Enough
ICEA .... Institut Canadien d'Education des Adultes [*Canadian Institute of Adult Education*]
ICEA .... Institution of Chemical Engineers in Australia
ICEA .... Instrument Contracting and Engineering Association (EA)
ICEA .... Insulated Cable Engineers Association (EA)
ICEA .... International Childbirth Education Association (EA)
ICEA .... International Christian Education Association (EA)
ICEA .... International Christian Esperanto Association (EA)
ICEA .... International Commission for Environmental Assessment (GNE)
ICEA .... International Consulting Economists Association [*British*] (DBA)
ICEAM .... Institute of Computer Aided Engineering and Management [*University of Dundee*] [*British*] (IRUK)
ICEAM .... International Committee on Economic and Applied Microbiology [*ICSU*] (EAIO)
ICEATT .... Index of Continuing Education Attitudes
ICEB .... Indonesian Commodity Exchange Board [*Badan Pelaksana Bursa Komoditi*] [*Indonesia*] (FEA)
ICEBAC .... International Council of Employers of Bricklayers and Allied Craftsmen (EA)
ICE/BAC .... International Council of Employers of Bricklayers and Allied Craftworkers (NTPA)
ICEC .... Interagency Career Education Committee (OICC)
ICEC .... International Committee of Enamelling Creators (EAIO)
ICEC .... International Conference on Education in Chemistry
ICEC .... International Cost Engineering Council (EA)
ICEC .... International Council for Exceptional Children [*Later, CEC*]
ICEC .... International Cryogenic Engineering Committee (EAIO)
ICEC .... Interuniversity Consortium for Educational Computing [*Database*]
ICECA .... Indochina Ethnic Chinese Association of Victoria [*Australia*]
ICECAN .... Iceland-Canada Cable (NITA)
ICECAN .... Iceland-Canada Submarine Cable System [*Telecommunications*] (TEL)
ICECAP .... Infrared Chemistry Experiments Coordinated Auroral Program [*Defense Nuclear Agency*] (PDAA)
ICECON .... Control of Sea Ice Information (NATG)
ICECS .... Integrated Closed-Loop Environmental Control System (PDAA)
ICED .... Industrial and Construction Equipment Division (EA)
ICED .... Institute for Community Education Development [*Ball State University*] [*Research center*] (RCD)
ICED .... Interface Control Envelope Drawings (KSC)
ICED .... Interface Control Environment Drawing (IAA)
ICED .... International Coalition on Energy for Development
ICED .... International Congress on the Education of the Deaf
ICED .... International Council for Educational Development (EA)
ICED .... Interprofessional Council on Environmental Design (EA)
ICEDEFOR .... Iceland Defense Force
ICEdit .... EDITEC, Chicago, IL [*Library symbol Library of Congress*] (LCLS)
ICEDS .... Insurance Company Education Directors Society (EA)
ICEEC .... International Congress of Electrical and Electronic Communications
ICEED .... International Center for Energy and Economic Development
ICEED .... International Research Center for Energy and Economic Development [*University of Colorado*] [*Research center*]
ICEF .... Institute for the Community as Extended Family (EA)
ICEF .... Interactive Composition and Editing Facility [*IBM Corp.*]
ICEF .... International Chemical and Energy Workers Federation
ICEF .... International Children's Emergency Fund [*United Nations*] (DLA)
ICEF .... International Committee for Research and Study on Environmental Factors
ICEF .... International Council for Educational Films [*Later, ICEM*]
ICEI .... Independent Cold Extruders Institute
ICEI .... Institution of Civil Engineers of Ireland (BI)
ICEI .... Internal Combustion Engine Institute [*Later, EMA*] (EA)
Icel .... Iceland (VRA)
ICEL .... Icelandic
ICEL .... Intercel, Inc. [*NASDAQ symbol*] (SAG)
ICEL .... International Committee for Ethnic Liberty [*See also IKEL*] (EAIO)
ICEL .... International Committee on English in the Liturgy (EA)
ICEL .... International Council of Environmental Law [*Bonn, Federal Republic of Germany*] (EA)
ICEM .... Incremental Cost Effectiveness Model
ICEM .... Independent Cluster Emission Model [*Atomic physics*]
ICEM .... Induced Contamination Experimental Monitor (MCD)
ICEM .... Intergovernmental Committee for European Migration [*Later, ICM*]
ICEM .... International Confederation for Electroacoustic Music (EA)
ICEM .... International Council for Educational Media [*Formerly, ICEF*]
ICEM .... Inverted Coaxial Magnetron (MCD)
ICEM .... Irish Council European Movement
ICen .... Centralia Public Library, Centralia, IL [*Library symbol Library of Congress*] (LCLS)
ICEN .... [*The*] Israel Commercial Economic Newsletter [*A publication Also, an information service or system*] (IID)
ICEnB .... Encyclopaedia Britannica, Inc., Chicago, IL [*Library symbol*] [*Library of Congress*] (LCLS)
ICenC .... Centralia Correctional Center, Centralia, IL [*Library symbol Library of Congress*] (LCLS)
ICenHS .... Centralia District High School, District 200, Centralia, IL [*Library symbol Library of Congress*] (LCLS)
ICEOB .... Sea Ice Observation Code [*Marine science*] (MSC)
ICEP .... Iberoamerican Cultural Exchange Program [*An association*] (EA)
ICEP .... Institut Canadien d'Enseignement Personnalise Inc. (AC)
ICEP .... Institute for Cultural Exchange thru Photography (EA)
ICEP .... Instituto do Comercio Externo (Lisbon, Portugal) [*Institute of Commercial Exports*] (EY)
ICEPART .... Index of Continuing Education Participation
ICEPAT .... Iceland Patrol [*Navy*]
ICEPF .... International Commission for the Eriksson Prize Fund (EAIO)
ICEPM .... Internal Combustion Engine Powered Material (MCD)
ICEQ .... Individualized Classroom Environment Questionnaire (EDAC)
ICER .... Information Centre of the European Railways
ICER .... Infrared Cell, Electronically Refrigerated
ICER .... Institute for Central European Research (EA)
ICER .... Interdepartmental Committee of External Relations [*Canada*]
ICERA-VIC .... Indo-Chinese Elderly Refugee Association of Victoria [*Australia*]
ICEROCC .... Iceland Regional Operational Control Center [*Aircraft surveillance*]
ICERP .... Internal Combustion Engine Repair Shop

ICERR	Interstate Congress for Equal Rights and Responsibilities (EA)
ICES	Ice, Compression, Elevation, Support [Medicine] (MEDA)
ICES	Import Cargo Electronic System
ICES	Information Collection and Evaluation System (DMAA)
ICES	Institution of Civil Engineering Surveyors [British] (DBA)
ICES	Institution of Surveyors in Civil Engineering [British]
ICES	Instructor and Course Evaluation System (EDAC)
ICES	Integrated Civil Engineering Software System (CIST)
ICES	Integrated Civil Engineering System [Programming language] [Computer science]
IC/ES	Intercommunications/Emergency Station (MCD)
ICES	International Centre for Ethnic Studies (EA)
ICES	International Commission on Erosion Sedimentation (NUCP)
ICES	International Council for the Exploration of the Sea [Denmark]
ICES	International Council of Electrophoresis Societies (HGEN)
ICES	International Cultural Exchange Service
ICES	Interuniversity Centre for European Studies [Canada] (IRC)
ICES	National Easter Seal Society for Crippled Children and Adults, Chicago, IL [Library symbol Library of Congress] (LCLS)
ICESA	International Conference on Environmental Sensing and Assessment
ICESA	Interstate Conference of Employment Security Agencies (EA)
ICESC	Industry Crew Escape Systems Committee
ICESC	International Committee for European Security and Co-Operation [See also CISCE] (EAIO)
ICESSP	International Council for Elementary and Secondary School Philosophy (EA)
ICET	Forty-Eight Item Counseling Evaluation Test [Psychology]
ICET	Institute for Comparative and Environmental Toxicology [Cornell University] [Research center] (RCD)
ICET	Institute for the Certification of Engineering Technicians [Later, National Institute for Certification in Engineering Technologies]
ICET	Interagency Committee on Excavation Technology [Federal Council for Science and Technology] [Terminated, 1976]
ICET	International Centre for Earth Tides [See also CIMT] [Belgium] (EAIO)
ICET	International Council on Education for Teaching (EA)
ICETK	International Committee of Electrochemical Thermodynamics and Kinetics (IEEE)
ICETT	Industrial Council for Educational Training Technology [British] (DS)
ICEUM	International Conference on Energy Use Management
ICEV	Initial Condition Evaluation [Orbit identification]
ICEV	Internal Combustion Engine Vehicle
ICEVH	International Council for Education of the Visually Handicapped [Bensheim, Federal Republic of Germany] (EAIO)
ICEX	Integrated Civil Engineering Executive (MHDI)
ICEX	Intelligence Coordination and Exploitation [Joint CIA-MACV program]
ICF	Field Museum of Natural History, Chicago, IL [Library symbol Library of Congress] (LCLS)
ICF	George Williams College, Downers Grove, IL [OCLC symbol] (OCLC)
ICF	Ice Cream Federation Ltd. [British] (BI)
ICF	ICF Kaiser International [NYSE symbol] (SPSG)
ICF	Indirect Centrifugal Flotation
ICF	Industrial Christian Fellowship [British] (DBA)
ICF	Inertial Confinement Fusion [Nuclear physics]
ICF	Inspection Check Fixture (MSA)
ICF	Installation Confinement Facility [Army] (AABC)
ICF	Institut Canadien du Film [Canadian Film Institute - CFI]
ICF	Institute for Canadian Futures
ICF	Institute of Chart Foresters [British] (DBA)
ICF	Integrated Catalog Facility (HGAA)
ICF	Integrated Control Facility [Sperry UNIVAC]
ICF	Integrated Crystal Filter (IAA)
ICF	Intelligence Contingency Funds (CINC)
ICF	Intensive Care Facility [Medicine]
ICF	Interacting Correlated Fragment [Physical chemistry]
ICF	Interactive Communications Feature [IBM Corp.]
ICF	Interactive Computer Facility (NITA)
ICF	Inter-Bureau Citation of Funds [Navy]
ICF	Intercellular Fluorescence (DB)
ICF	Interciliary Fluid (STED)
ICF	Intercommunication Flip-Flop [Computer science]
ICF	Interconnect Facility
ICF	Interface Control Function (MCD)
ICF	Intermediate Care Facility [Medicine]
ICF	International Canoe Federation [See also FIC] [Florence, Italy] (EAIO)
ICF	International Cardiology Foundation (EA)
ICF	International Carpet Fair
ICF	International Casting Federation (EAIO)
ICF	International Cheerleading Foundation (EA)
ICF	International Congregational Fellowship (EA)
ICF	International Congress on Fracture [ICSU] [Sendai, Japan] (EAIO)
ICF	International Consultants Foundation (EA)
ICF	International Crane Foundation (EA)
ICF	International Craniofacial Foundations (EA)
ICF	International Cremation Federation (EAIO)
ICF	International Curling Federation (EAIO)
ICF	International Federation of Chemical and General Workers Union
ICF	Intracellular Fluid [Physiology]
ICF	Intravascular Coagulation and Fibrinolysis Syndrome [Medicine]
ICF	Intrinsic Coercive Force
ICF	Iota-Cam Fiberscope [Also, ICFS]
ICF	Italian Catholic Federation Central Council (EA)
ICF-A	Field Museum of Natural History, Edward E. Ayer Ornithological Library, Chicago, IL [Library symbol Library of Congress] (LCLS)

ICFA	Fireman Apprentice, Interior Communications Electrician, Striker [Navy rating]
ICFA	Incomplete Freund Adjuvant (STED)
ICFA	Independent College Funds of America [Later, FIHE] (EA)
ICFA	Induced Complement-Fixing Antigen (STED)
ICFA	Inland Commercial Fisheries Association (EA)
ICFA	Institute of Chartered Financial Analysts [Later, AIMR] (EA)
ICFA	International Cemetery and Funeral Association (NTPA)
ICFA	International Committee on Future Accelerators [International Union of Pure and Applied Physics]
ICFA	International Computer Facsimile Association (PS)
ICFAC	Inertial Confinement Fusion Advisory Committee [Department of Energy]
ICFAD	International Council of Fine Arts Deans (EA)
ICFAR	Federal Archives and Records Center, General Services Administration, Chicago, IL [Library symbol Library of Congress] (LCLS)
ICFAR	Indianapolis Center for Advanced Research [Indiana University - Purdue University at Indianapolis] [Research center] (RCD)
ICFATCM	Individual Cleared for Access to Classified Material (AAG)
ICFATCMUTAI...	Individual Cleared for Access to Classified Material Up to and Including
ICFAX	Integrated Circuit Failure Analysis Expert System
ICFC	Felician College, Chicago, IL [Library symbol Library of Congress] (LCLS)
ICFC	Industrial and Commercial Finance Corp. [British]
ICFC	International Centre of Films for Children
ICFC	International Council of Fan Clubs [Defunct] (EA)
ICFCB	Foote, Cone & Belding Advertising, Inc., Corporate Inforamtion Center, Chicago, IL [Library symbol] [Library of Congress] (LCLS)
ICFCM	International Convention of Faith, Churches, and Ministers (EA)
ICFCYP	International Centre of Films for Children and Young People [France] (EY)
ICFE	Independent Colleges of Further Education [British]
ICFE	Institute for Consumer Financial Education (EA)
ICFE	International Contract Flooring Exhibition [British] (ITD)
ICFE	Intra-Collisional Field Effect (IAA)
ICFET	Inhomogeneous Channel Field-Effect Transistor (PDAA)
ICFF	International Contemporary Furniture Fair (ITD)
ICFFO	International Council of Folklore Festival Organizations and Folk Art (EA)
ICFG	International Commission on Fungal Genetics [International Council of Scientific Unions]
ICFI	International Cooperative Fracture Institute
ICFI	Iota-Cam Fiberscope Instrument
ICF Int	ICF Kaiser International [Associated Press] (SAG)
ICFK	Friedman and Koven, Library, Chicago, IL [Library symbol Library of Congress] (LCLS)
ICFL	International Council of the French Language [See also CILF] [Paris, France] (EAIO)
ICFLC	International Curling Federation - Ladies Committee [Defunct] (EA)
ICFLPRMFS...	Items Not Available through Cannibalization, Fabrication, or Local Procurement or Replacement from Maintenance Float Stock
ICFM	In-Core Fuel Management (PDAA)
ICFM	Inlet Cubic Feet per Minute (PDAA)
ICFM	Institute of Charity Fundraising Managers [British] (DBA)
ICFM	International Company for Finance and Investment [Russian bank]
ICFM	International Convention of Faith Ministries (EA)
ICFMA	International Cystic Fibrosis Mucoviscidosis Association (EA)
ICFMC	FMC Corp., Chicago, IL [Library symbol Library of Congress] (LCLS)
ICFMH	International Committee on Food Microbiology and Hygiene [ICSU] [Frederiksberg, Denmark] (EAIO)
ICF-MR	Intermediate-Care Facility for Mentally Retarded (STED)
ICFMR	Intermediate Care Facility for the Mentally Retarded
ICF-MR/DD...	Intermediate Care Facility for the Mentally Retarded/Developmentally Disabled
ICFN	Fireman, Interior Communications Electrician, Striker [Navy rating]
ICFNB	First National Bank of Chicago, Chicago, IL [Library symbol Library of Congress] (LCLS)
ICFP	Institute of Certified Financial Planners (EA)
ICFPW	International Confederation of Former Prisoners of War
ICFR	Intercollegiate Conference of Faculty Representatives (EA)
ICFRB	Federal Reserve Bank of Chicago, Chicago, IL [Library symbol Library of Congress] (LCLS)
ICFRU	Idaho Cooperative Fishery Research Unit [University of Idaho] [Research center] (RCD)
ICFS	Industry Coalition for Fire Safety [Defunct] (EA)
ICFS	Installation CONUS FORSTAT System [Military]
ICFS	Iota-Cam Fiberscope [Also, ICF]
ICFSHG	International Committee of French-Speaking Historians and Geographers (EAIO)
ICFSRT	International Council of French-Speaking Radio and Television (EAIO)
ICFTU	International Confederation of Free Trade Unions [Belgium]
ICFTU	International Council of Free Trade Unions
ICFTU-ARO...	International Confederation of Free Trade Unions-Asian Regional Organisation [India]
ICFTUE	International Center of Free Trade Unionists in Exile [France Defunct]
ICFU	International Council on the Future of the University [Defunct]
IC fx	Intracapsular Fracture [Medicine] (STED)
ICG	Icelandic Coast Guard [ICAO designator] (FAAC)
ICG	ICG Communications [AMEX symbol] [Formerly, IntelCom Group] (SG)

ICG............. ICG Communications, Inc. [AMEX symbol] (SAG)
ICG............. Icing [Meteorology] (BARN)
ICG............. Illinois Benedictine College, Lisle, IL [OCLC symbol] (OCLC)
ICG............. Illinois Central Gulf Railroad Co. [AAR code]
ICG............. Illinois Council for the Gifted (EDAC)
ICG............. Impedance Cardiogram [Medicine] (DMAA)
ICG............. Indochina Curriculum Group [Defunct] (EA)
ICG............. Indocyanine Green [Liver function test] [Medicine]
ICG............. In-Flight Coverall Garment [Apollo] [NASA]
ICG............. Institute of Cytology and Genetics [Akademgorodek, Russia]
ICG............. Integrated Combat Group [Air Force]
ICG............. Interactive Computer Graphics
ICG............. International Commission on Glass [See also CIV] [Prague,
               Czechoslovakia] (EAIO)
ICG............. International Conference Group [Commercial firm] (EA)
ICG............. International Congress of Genetics
ICG............. International Coordination Group (USDC)
ICG............. Interviewer's Classification Guide
ICG............. IntlCom Group [AMEX symbol] (TTSB)
ICG............. Isotope Cisternography (DMAA)
ICGA .... Directory of International and Corporate Giving in America and
               Abroad [A publication]
ICGA .... Illinois Corn Growers Association (SRA)
ICGA .... International Carnival Glass Association (EA)
ICGA .... International Conference on Genetic Algorithms
ICGA .... Iowa Corn Growers Association (SRA)
ICGB .... International Cargo Gear Bureau (EA)
ICGCD.......... Gardner, Carton, and Douglas, Chicago, IL [Library symbol Library of
               Congress] (LCLS)
ICG Com...... ICG Communications, Inc. [Associated Press] (SAG)
ICGE............ International Center of Genetic Epistemology [Geneva, Switzerland]
ICGEB .... International Centre for Genetic Engineering and Biotechnology
               [United Nations Development Organization] (EAIO)
ICGEBNET .... International Centre for Genetic Engineering and Biotechnology
               Network [United Nations Development Organization] (DUND)
ICGEC .... Interagency Collaborative Group on Environmental Carcinogenesis
               [Bethesda , MD] [National Institutes of Health] (EGAO)
ICGGI .... Internationale Coronelli-Gesellschaft fuer Globen- und
               Instrumentkunde [International Coronelli Society - ICS] (EAIO)
ICGH .... Greeley & Hansen Engineering Library, Chicago, IL [Library symbol
               Library of Congress] (LCLS)
ICGH .... International Confederation of Genealogy and Heraldry [See also
               CIGH] [Paris, France] (EAIO)
ICGI .... International Council of Goodwill Industries (EA)
ICGIC .... Icing in Clouds [NWS] (FAAC)
ICGICIP........ Icing in Clouds and Precipitation [NWS] (FAAC)
ICGIP .... Icing in Precipitation [NWS] (FAAC)
ICG-ITSU..... International Coordination Group for the Tsunami Warning System in
               the Pacific [Marine science] (OSRA)
ICG/ITSU...... Intrnational Coordination Group for the Tsunami Warning System in
               the Pacific (USDC)
ICGM .... Intercontinental Glide [or Guided] Missile (KSC)
ICGM .... International Colloquium about Gas Marketing (EA)
ICGN .... ICC Technologies [NASDAQ symbol] (TTSB)
ICGN .... ICC Technologies, Inc. [NASDAQ symbol] (SAG)
ICGN .... Immune Complex-Mediated Glomerulonephritis (STED)
ICGR .... Gas Research Institute, Chicago, IL [Library symbol] [Library of
               Congress] (LCLS)
ICGR .... Ivory Coast - Ghana Ridge [Geology]
ICGRC .... International Connoisseurs of Green and Red Chile (EA)
ICGS .... Interactive Careers Guidance System (AIE)
ICGS .... International Catholic Girls' Society
ICGS .... Interreligious Committee of General Secretaries (EA)
ICGSCA........ Infants', Children's, and Girls' Sportswear and Coat Association (EA)
ICh .... Chicago Heights Free Public Library, Chicago Heights, IL [Library
               symbol Library of Congress] (LCLS)
ICH............. ICH Corp. [Later, Southwestern Life] [AMEX symbol] (SPSG)
ICH............. Ichthyology
ICH............. Idiopathic Cortical Hyperostosis [Medicine] (DMAA)
ICH............. Illinois College, Jacksonville, IL [OCLC symbol] (OCLC)
ICH............. IMPAC Commercial Holdings [AMEX symbol] [Formerly, IMH
               Commercial Holdings] (SG)
ICH............. Incumbent Come Home [Political humor] [Pronounced "itch"]
ICH............. Induction-Conduction Heating
ICH............. Infectious Canine Hepatitis [Veterinary medicine]
ICH............. Information Clearing House, Inc.
ICH............. Inhalation Cycle Histogram [Biometrics]
ICH............. Instituto Cubao de Higrafia [Cuba] [Marine science] (OSRA)
ICH............. Instructor Contact Hours (MCD)
ICH............. Interchange
ICH............. Interchanger (NASA)
ICH............. Intermediate Chain Home (IAA)
ICH............. International Conference Harmonization
ICH............. Intracerebral Hemorrhage [Medicine]
ICH............. Intracranial Hemorrhage [Medicine]
ICH............. Israel Chemical Ltd. [NYSE symbol] (SAG)
IChaAF........ United States Air Force, Chanute Air Force Base Library, Chanute Air
               Force Base, IL [Library symbol] [Library of Congress] (LCLS)
ICham.......... Champaign Public Library, Champaign, IL [Library symbol Library of
               Congress] (LCLS)
IChamBH ..... Burnham City Hospital, Champaign, IL [Library symbol Library of
               Congress] (LCLS)
IChamCE...... United States Army Construction Engineering Research Laboratory,
               Champaign, IL [Library symbol Library of Congress] (LCLS)

IChamGS ..... Church of Jesus Christ of Latter-Day Saints, Genealogical Society
               Library, Champaign Stake Branch, Champaign, IL [Library symbol
               Library of Congress] (LCLS)
IChamIG ...... Illinois State Geological Survey, Champaign,IL [Library symbol]
               [Library of Congress] (LCLS)
IChamL........ Lincoln Trail Libraries, Champaign, IL [Library symbol Library of
               Congress] (LCLS)
IChamMH .... Illinois Department of Mental Health and Developmental Disabilities,
               Herman M. Adler Center Library, Champaign, IL [Library symbol
               Library of Congress] (LCLS)
IChamNG ..... News-Gazette, Champaign, IL [Library symbol] [Library of
               Congress] (LCLS)
IChamP........ Parkland College, Champaign, IL [Library symbol Library of
               Congress] (LCLS)
ICHAP .... Improved Chaparral [Military] (MCD)
IChar........... Charleston Carnegie Public Library, Charleston, IL [Library symbol
               Library of Congress] (LCLS)
ICharE......... Eastern Illinois University, Charleston, IL [Library symbol Library of
               Congress] (LCLS)
ICharF......... Charleston Area Cooperative Film Library, Charleston, IL [Library
               symbol] [Library of Congress] (LCLS)
ICharH .... Charleston Community Memorial Hospital, Charleston, IL [Library
               symbol Library of Congress] (LCLS)
ICharSD ...... Charleston Community Unit School District, Charleston, IL [Library
               symbol] [Library of Congress] (LCLS)
ICHC .... International Committee for Horticultural Congresses
ICHC .... International Congress of Heterocyclic Chemistry
ICHCA .... International Cargo Handling Coordination Association [London,
               England] (EA)
ICHD .... Inter-Society Commission for Heart Disease Resources (EA)
ICHDA .... International Cooperative Housing Development Association
ICHDR .... Intersociety Commission for Heart Disease Resources [American
               Heart Assoc iation - AHA] [Absorbed by]
I Ch E .... Institution of Chemical Engineers [British]
ICHE........... International Commission on Human Ecology (EA)
ICHE........... International Councils on Higher Education [Defunct]
I Chem E ..... Institution of Chemical Engineers [British]
ICHEO .... Interuniversity Council for Higher Education Overseas [British] (DI)
ICherSD ...... Cherry School District 92, Cherry, IL [Library symbol Library of
               Congress] (LCLS)
IChevE .... Cherry Valley Elementary School, Cherry Valley, IL [Library symbol]
               [Library of Congress] (LCLS)
ICHF........... Child Health Foundation [Formerly, International Child Health
               Foundation] (EA)
ICHF........... International Child Health Foundation (EA)
ICHFC .... Household Finance Corp., Chicago, IL [Library symbol Library of
               Congress] (LCLS)
ICHFST .... International Council of Health Fitness and Sports Therapists [British]
ICHG .... International Conference on the Holocaust and Genocide (EAIO)
ICHG .... International Congress of Human Genetics (HGEN)
IChGS .... Church of Jesus Christ of Latter-Day Saints, Genealogical Society
               Library, Chicago Heights Branch, Chicago Heights, IL [Library
               symbol Library of Congress] (LCLS)
ICHi............ Chicago Historical Society, Chicago, IL [Library symbol Library of
               Congress] (LCLS)
ICHID .... Harrington Institute of Interior Design, Chicago, IL [Library symbol
               Library of Congress] (LCLS)
IChil........... Chillicothe Township Free Public Library, Chillicothe, IL [Library
               symbol Library of Congress] (LCLS)
IChL........... Chicago Heights Free Public Library, Chicgo Heights, IL [Library
               symbol] [Library of Congress] (LCLS)
ICHLM .... International Conference of Historians of the Labour Movement
               [Vienna, Austria] (EAIO)
ICHM .... Institute of Care-Home Managers [British] (DBA)
ICHM .... International College of Hotel Management
ICHMH .... Interstate Clearing House on Mental Health [Defunct]
ICHMT .... International Centre for Heat and Mass Transfer (EAIO)
IChO........... International Chemistry Olympiad [For high school students]
ICHOHYP ..... International Committee of Hard of Hearing Young People
               [Frederiksberg, Denmark] (EAIO)
ICHOR.......... ICHOR Corp. [Associated Press] (SAG)
ICHP........... Illinois Council on Health System Pharmacists (SRA)
ICHP........... International Commission of Health Professionals for Health and
               Human Rights (EA)
ICHP........... Investors Chronicle/Hillier Parker [British A publication]
IChP........... Prairie State College, Learning Center, Chicago Heights, IL [Library
               symbol Library of Congress] (LCLS)
ICHPER........ International Council for Health, Physical Education, and Recreation
               (EA)
IChr............ Chrisman Public Library, Chrisman, IL [Library symbol Library of
               Congress] (LCLS)
ICHR .... ICHOR Corp. [NASDAQ symbol] (SAG)
ICHR .... Indian Council of Historical Research
ICHR .... Inter-American Commission on Human Rights [OAS] (PD)
ICHR .... Interfaith Council for Human Rights (EA)
I Ch R .... Irish Chancery Reports [A publication] (DLA)
ICHRI .... Islamic Committee for Human Rights in Iraq [Later, IODHRI] (EA)
ICHRPI........ International Commission for the History of Representative and
               Parliamentary Institutions [Rome, Italy] (EAIO)
ICHRT .... International Committee for Human Rights in Taiwan (EA)
ICHS .... Inter-African Committee for Hydraulic Studies [See also CIEH]
               [Ouagadougou, Burkina Faso] (EAIO)
ICHS .... International Center for Holocaust Studies (EA)
ICHS .... International Committee for Historical Sciences [Paris, France] (EA)

ICHS .... International Council of Homehelp Services [*See also CISAF*] [*Driebergen-Rijsenburg, Netherlands*] (EAIO)

ICHSMSS..... International Commission for the History of Social Movements and Social Structures [*Paris, France*] (EAIO)

ICHSPP........ International Congress on High-Speed Photography and Photonics (EA)

ICHSWW...... International Committee for the History of the Second World War (EAIO)

ICHT............. Harris Trust and Savings Bank, Chicago, IL [*Library symbol Library of Congress*] (LCLS)

ICHT............. International Council of Holistic Therapists [*British*]

ICHTH .... Ichthyology

ichthyol........ Ichthyology (BARN)

ICHTHYS..... Jesous Christos, Theou Uios Soter [*Jesus Christ, Son of God, Savior*]

ICHTSP .... International Conference on the Hydraulic Transport of Solids in Pipes (PDAA)

ICHY .... International Council of Hindoo Youth (EAIO)

ICI .... Cicia [*Fiji*] [*Airport symbol*] (OAG)

ICI................ Ice Condenser Instrumentation [*Nuclear energy*] (NRCH)

ICI................ ICI Pharmaceuticals [*Great Britain*] [*Research code symbol*]

ICI................ Illinois Institute of Technology, Chicago, IL [*Library symbol Library of Congress*] (LCLS)

ICI................ Imperial Chemical Industries Ltd. [*NYSE symbol*] (SPSG)

ICI................ Imprial Chem Ind ADR [*NYSE symbol*] (TTSB)

ICI................ Incoming Call Identification [*Telecommunications*]

ICI................ Independent Commercial Importer [*Automotive retailing*]

ICI................ Independent Curators, Inc. (EA)

ICI................ Individual/Collective Integration

ICI................ Information & Communications, Inc.

ICI................ Information Centre International [*Telecommunications service*] (TSSD)

ICI................ Information Concepts, Inc.

ICI................ Information Consultants, Inc. [*Information service or system*] (IID)

ICI................ Initial Capabilities Inspection [*Military*] (AFM)

ICI................ Institut Canadien des Ingenieurs [*Engineering Institute of Canada*]

ICI................ Institute of Chemistry of Ireland (BI)

ICI................ Intelligent Communications Interface (IEEE)

ICI................ Interagency Committee on Intelligence

ICI................ Interagency Cooperative Issuances (OICC)

ICI................ Inter-American Children's Institute [*OAS*]

ICI................ Inter-American Cooperative Institute

ICI................ Intercarrier Interface (ACRL)

ICI................ Interclick Interval [*Entomology*]

ICI................ Interexchange Carrier Interface [*Telecommunications*] (ACRL)

ICI................ Interim Cargo Integrator (MCD)

ICI................ Internal Change Identifier (MCD)

ICI................ International Castles Institute (EA)

ICI................ International Commission on Illumination [*Since 1951, has been known exclusively as CIE, which see*]

ICI................ Interpersonal Communication Inventory [*Interpersonal skills and attitudes test*]

ICI................ Intracardiac Infection [*Medicine*] (DMAA)

ICI................ Intracisternal (DMAA)

ICI................ Inuit Cultural Institute [*Canada*]

ICI................ Investment Casting Institute (EA)

ICI................ Investment Company Institute (EA)

ICI................ Ion Composition Instrument [*Cometary physics*]

ICI................ Istituto Chemioterapico Italiano [*Italy*] [*Research code symbol*]

ICI................ Italian Cultural Institute (EA)

ICI................ MacMurray College, Jacksonville, IL [*OCLC symbol*] (OCLC)

ICI-A .... Illinois Institute of Technology, Armour Research Foundation, Chicago, IL [*Library symbol Library of Congress*] (LCLS)

ICIA............. Industrial, Commercial, and Institutional Accountant (DD)

ICIA............. Institute of Cultural Affairs International [*Information service or system*] (IID)

ICIA............. International Center of Information on Antibiotics (EAIO)

ICIA............. International Communications Industries Association (EA)

ICIA............. International Conference Industry Association [*Defunct*] (EA)

ICIA............. International Credit Insurance Association [*Zurich, Switzerland*] (EAIO)

ICIA............. International Crop Improvement Association [*Later, AOSCA*] (EA)

ICIAO .... International Association of Assessing Officers, Chicago, IL [*Library symbol*] [*Library of Congress*] (LCLS)

ICIAP .... Interagency Committee on International Aviation Policy [*Department of State*] (AFM)

ICIASF .... International Congress on Instrumentation in Aerospace Simulation Facilities

ICIc .... Cicero Public Library, Cicero, IL [*Library symbol Library of Congress*] (LCLS)

ICIC............. Interagency Committee on Intermodal Cargo

ICIC............. Interdisciplinary Committee on Institutes and Conferences

ICIC............. International Cancer Information Center [*Public Health Service*] [*Information service or system*] (IID)

ICIC............. International Copyright Information Centre [*UNESCO*] (PDAA)

ICIC............. International Copyrights Information Center (WDAA)

ICICI............ Industrial Credit & Investment Corp. of India Ltd.

ICICLE......... Integrated Cryogenic Isotope Cooling Equipment

ICIcM.......... Morton College, Cicero, IL [*Library symbol Library of Congress*] (LCLS)

ICICO .... Illinois College of Optometry, Chicago, IL [*Library symbol Library of Congress*] (LCLS)

ICICS .... International College of Surgeons, Chicago, IL [*Library symbol Library of Congress*] (LCLS)

ICI-D .... Illinois Institute of Technology, Institute of Design, Chicago, IL [*Library symbol Library of Congress*] (LCLS)

ICID .... Information Center for Individuals with Disabilities (EA)

ICID .... Intensified Charge Injection Device [*For television camera used in astronomy*]

ICID .... International Commission on Irrigation and Drainage [*See also CIID*] [*ICSU New Delhi, India*] (EAIO)

ICIDH .... International Classification of Impairments, Disabilities, and Handicaps [*Occupational therapy*]

ICIDI .... Independent Commission on International Development Issues [*Also known as the Brandt Commission*] [*Studies problems arising from the inequity between more developed Northern nations and less developed Southern countries*]

ICIDR .... International Collaboration in Infectious Diseases Research [*Tulane University*] [*Research center*] (RCD)

ICIDS .... Integrated Commercial Intrusion Detection System [*Army*]

ICIE............. Infogrow Communications Information Exchange [*Database directory*] (NITA)

ICIE............. Information Center for Internal Exposure [*Department of Energy*] [*Defunct*] (IID)

ICIE............. International Center for Industry and the Environment (DCTA)

ICIE............. International Council of Industrial Editors [*Later, IABC*]

ICIE............. International Council of Industrial Engineers

ICIEQ .... Illinois Institute for Environmental Quality, Chicago, IL [*Library symbol Library of Congress*] (LCLS)

ICIF............. Independent Colleges of Indiana Foundation (SRA)

ICIF............. International Cooperative Insurance Federation [*Manchester, England*] (EAIO)

ICIFI .... International Council of Infant Food Industries

ICI-G .... Illinois Institute of Technology, Institute of Gas Technology, Chicago, IL [*Library symbol Library of Congress*] (LCLS)

ICIg............. Intracytoplasmic Immunoglobulin

ICIHSOP....... International Convention Relating to Intervention on the High Seas in Cases of Oil Pollution Casualties of 1969 (COE)

ICII.............. Imperial Credit [*NASDAQ symbol*] (TTSB)

ICII.............. Imperial Credit Industries, Inc. [*NASDAQ symbol*] (SAG)

ICII.............. International Culture Institute [*Japan*] (EAIO)

ICIJ.............. Institute for Juvenile Research, Chicago, IL [*Library symbol Library of Congress*] (LCLS)

ICI-K .... Illinois Institute of Technology, Chicago-Kent College of Law, Chicago, IL [*Library symbol Library of Congress*] (LCLS)

ICIL............. IFIP [*International Federation for Information Processing*] Committee for International Liaison

ICILB............ Isham-Lincoln-Beale, Chicago, IL [*Library symbol*] [*Library of Congress*] (LCLS)

ICIM............ Institute for Computer Integrated Manufacturing [*Strathclyde University*] [*British*]

ICIMOD .... International Centre for Integrated Mountain Development [*Kathmandu*] (ECON)

ICINR .... Institute of Natural Resources, Chicago, IL [*Library symbol Library of Congress*] (LCLS)

ICIntR .... Library of International Relations, Chicago, IL [*Library symbol Library of Congress*] (LCLS)

ICIO .... Interim Cargo Integration Operations (MCD)

icio .... Interim Cargo Integration Operations [*NASA*] (NAKS)

ICIP............. Indirect Component Improvement Program

ICIP............. Institute for Psychoanalysis, Chicago, IL [*Library symbol Library of Congress*] (LCLS)

ICIP............. International Conference on Information Processing [*Paris, 1959*]

ICIP............. Vespasian Warner Public Library, Clinton, IL [*Library symbol*] [*Library of Congress*] (LCLS)

ICIPE........... International Centre of Insect Physiology and Ecology [*ICSU*] [*Nairobi, Kenya*] (EAIO)

ICipSD .... Cissna Park Community Unit School District, Cissna Park, IL [*Library symbol*] [*Library of Congress*] (LCLS)

ICIR .... In Commission, In Reserve [*Vessel status*] [*Navy*]

ICIREPAT .... International Cooperation in Information Retrieval among Examining Patent Offices

ICIRO .... Interim Commission of the International Refugee Organization

ICIS............. ICIS Management Group, Inc. [*NASDAQ symbol*] (SAG)

ICIS............. ICIS Mgmt Group [*NASDAQ symbol*] (TTSB)

ICIS............. Independent Chemical Information Services Ltd. [*Information service or system*] (IID)

ICIS............. Integrated Chemical Information System [*Information Consultants, Inc.*] [*Information service or system*] (IID)

ICIS............. Intelligent Configuration Identification System [*NASA*]

ICIS............. Interactive Construction Industry System [*NCR Ltd.*] [*Software package*] (NCC)

ICIS............. Interdepartmental Committee on Internal Security [*Washington, DC*]

ICIS............. International Centre for Industrial Studies [*United Nations*]

ICIS............. International Council for Infant Survival [*Later, NCGIS*] (EA)

ICIS............. IUD Claims Information Source (EA)

ICis............. Willow Branch Library, Cisco, IL [*Library symbol Library of Congress*] (LCLS)

ICISI............ International Center for Interdisciplinary Studies of Immunology at Georgetown [*Georgetown University*] [*Research center*] (RCD)

ICIS Mgt ...... ICIS Management Group, Inc. [*Associated Press*] (SAG)

ICISS .... Impact-Collision Ion Scattering Spectroscopy

ICIST........... Institut Canadien de l'Information Scientifique et Technique [*Canadian Institute for Scientific and Technical Information - CISTI*]

ICIT .... Information Center on Instructional Technology

ICIT............. Intensified Conventional Insulin Therapy [*Medicine*]

ICITA........... International Chain of Industrial and Technical Advertising Agencies (EA)

ICITA............ International Cooperative Investigations of the Tropical Atlantic [*Navy*]

ICITAP .... International Criminal Investigative Training Assistance Program [*Department of Justice*]

ICITO .... Interim Commission for the International Trade Organization

ICIU .... University of Illinois at Chicago Circle, Chicago, IL [*Library symbol Library of Congress*] (LCLS)

ICIU-PM....... University of Illinois at Chicago Circle, Peoria School of Medicine, Peoria, IL [*Library symbol Library of Congress*] (LCLS)

ICIU-RM....... University of Illinois at Chicago Circle, Rockford School of Medicine, Rockford, IL [*Library symbol Library of Congress*] (LCLS)

ICIU-S .... University of Illinois at Chicago Circle, Science Library, Chicago, IL [*Library symbol Library of Congress*] (LCLS)

ICIWWW...... International Congress of Industrial Waste Water and Wastes

ICIX............. Intermedia Communications [*NASDAQ symbol*] (TTSB)

ICIX............. Intermedia Communications, Inc. [*NASDAQ symbol*] (SAG)

ICJ.............. Ileocecal Junction [*Anatomy*] (DAVI)

ICJ.............. Ileocolonic Junction [*Anatomy*]

ICJ.............. Incoming Junction [*Telecommunications*] (TEL)

ICJ.............. International Commission of Jurists [*Switzerland*]

ICJ.............. International Court of Justice [*United Nations*]

ICJ.............. Interstate Compact on Juveniles [*Public human service program*] (PHSD)

ICJ.............. John Crerar Library, Chicago, IL [*Library symbol Library of Congress*] (LCLS)

ICJ.............. McKendree College, Lebanon, IL [*OCLC symbol*] (OCLC)

ICJA............ Intelligence and Criminal Justice Academy [*Defunct*] (EA)

ICJA............ International Criminal Justice Association (EA)

ICJAS........... International Commission of Jurists Australian Section

ICJB............ Jenner and Block, Chicago, IL [*Library symbol Library of Congress*] (LCLS)

ICJC............ Immaculate Conception Junior College [*New Jersey*]

ICJC............ International Council of Jews from Czechoslovakia [*British Defunct*] (EAIO)

ICJC............ International Criminal Justice Clearinghouse [*Law Enforcement Assistance Administration*] [*Information service or system*]

ICJCM.......... John T. and Catherine McArthur Foundation, Chicago, IL [*Library symbol*] [*Library of Congress*] (LCLS)

ICJCS........... International Conference of Jewish Communal Service [*Later, WCJCS*] (EA)

ICJKM.......... Jesuit-Krauss-McCormick Library, Chicago, IL [*Library symbol Library of Congress*] (LCLS)

ICJL............. Institute for Computers in Jewish Life (EA)

ICJM............ John Marshall Law School, Chicago, IL [*Library symbol Library of Congress*] (LCLS)

ICJP............. Irish Commission for Justice and Peace [*An association*] (EAIO)

ICJR............. Institute for Criminal Justice, University of Richmond (DLA)

ICJS............. Independent Carpenters' and Joiners' Society [*A union*] [*British*]

ICJS............. Spertus College of Judaica, Chicago, IL [*Library symbol Library of Congress*] (LCLS)

ICJSh........... John G. Shedd Aquarium, Chicago, IL [*Library symbol Library of Congress*] (LCLS)

ICJST........... Jesuit School of Theology in Chicago, Chicago, IL [*Library symbol Library of Congress*] (LCLS)

ICJUB.......... Intercontinental Jet Unmanned Bomber

ICJV............. Jewish Vocational Service Library, Chicago, IL [*Library symbol Library of Congress*] (LCLS)

ICJW........... International Council of Jewish Women (EA)

ICK............. Inscriptions Cuneiformes du Kultepe (BJA)

ICK............. Interdepartmental Committee on Nuclear Energy [*Netherlands*] (EY)

ICK............. International Cherokee [*Vancouver Stock Exchange symbol*]

ICK............. Metlakatla, AK [*Location identifier FAA*] (FAAL)

ICK............. Millikin University, Decatur, IL [*OCLC symbol*] (OCLC)

ICK............. Nieuw Nickerie [*Surinam*] [*Airport symbol*] (OAG)

ICKCMX....... Integrated Circuit Keyset Central Multiplexer (CAAL)

ICKE............ Kirkland & Ellis, Chicago, IL [*Library symbol Library of Congress*] (LCLS)

ICKK........... Kennedy-King College of the City College of Chicago, Chicago, IL [*Library symbol Library of Congress*] (LCLS)

ICKL........... International Council of Kinetography Laban (EA)

ICKMC .... Keck, Mahin, and Cate, Chicago, IL [*Library symbol Library of Congress*] (LCLS)

ICKMZ......... Katten, Munchin & Zavis, Pearl, Greenburger & Galler, Chicago, IL [*Library symbol*] [*Library of Congress*] (LCLS)

ICL.............. Cavei Avir Lemitanim [*Israel*] [*ICAO designator*] (FAAC)

ICL.............. Clarinda, IA [*Location identifier FAA*] (FAAL)

ICL.............. Income Contingent Loan

ICL.............. Incoming Correspondence Log (AAG)

ICL.............. Incoming Line

ICL.............. Indal Ltd. [*Toronto Stock Exchange symbol*]

ICL.............. Inflight Calibration Lamp [*Instrumentation*]

ICL.............. Inserted Connection Loss [*Telecommunications*]

ICL.............. Instructional Center Library

ICL.............. Instrumentation Configuration Log (IAA)

ICL.............. Instrument Calibration Laboratory

ICL.............. Instrument Control Language [*Computer science*]

ICL.............. Instrument-Controlled Landing [*Aviation*] (IAA)

ICL.............. Integrated Circuit Logic

ICL.............. Integrated Configuration List (NG)

ICL.............. Intellicall, Inc. [*NYSE symbol*] (SPSG)

ICL.............. Interactive Computer Learning

ICL.............. Interagency Checklist [*United States Employment Service*] (OICC)

ICL.............. Intercommunication Logic

ICL.............. Intercomputer Communication Logic (NITA)

ICL.............. Interdepartmental Committee on Land [*Canada*]

ICL.............. Interest Checklist [*US Employment Service*] [*Department of Labor*]

ICL.............. Internal Control Loop [*Chemical engineering*]

ICL.............. International Cancer League [*Defunct*] (EA)

ICL.............. International Catholic Library [*A publication*]

ICL.............. International Christian Leadership (EA)

ICL.............. International Clinical Laboratories, Inc.

ICL.............. International Communications Ltd. [*Fayville, MA*] [*Telecommunications service*] (TSSD)

ICL.............. International Computers Ltd. [*Great Britain*] [*Computer manufacturer*]

ICL.............. International Cooperative Logistics (AFIT)

ICL.............. International Council for Christian Leadership (EA)

ICL.............. Interpersonal Check List [*Psychology*]

ICL.............. Interpretive Coding Language

ICL.............. Inter-Union Commission on the Lithosphere [*NASA*]

ICL.............. Iris-Clip Lens (DMAA)

ICL.............. Irish Central Library for Students (BI)

ICL.............. Isocitrate Lyase [*An enzyme*]

ICL.............. Loyola University, Chicago, IL [*Library symbol Library of Congress*] (LCLS)

ICL.............. Monmouth College, Monmouth, IL [*OCLC symbol*] (OCLC)

ICl.............. Vespasian Warner Public Library, Clinton, IL [*Library symbol Library of Congress*] (LCLS)

ICLA............ International Committee on Laboratory Animals

ICLA............ International Comparative Literature Association (EA)

ICLAE.......... International Council of Library Association Executives (EA)

ICLAM.......... International Committee for Life Assurance Medicine [*Zurich, Switzerland*] (EAIO)

ICLARM........ International Center for Living Aquatic Resources Management [*Makati, Metro Manila, Philippines*] (EAIO)

ICLAS........... Intracavity LASER Absorption Spectroscopy

ICLaw .... Chicago Law Institute, Chicago, IL [*Library symbol Library of Congress*] (LCLS)

ICL-B .... Loyola University, Julia Deal Lewis Library, Chicago, IL [*Library symbol Library of Congress*] (LCLS)

IcLc............ Identity Correct, Location Correct [*Psychology*]

ICLC............ International Centre for Local Credit [*The Hague, Netherlands*] (EAIO)

ICLC............ International Congress on Lightweight Concrete (PDAA)

ICLC............ International Criminal Law Commission (EA)

ICLCP.......... International Conference on Large Chemical Plants [*Antwerp, Belgium*] (EA)

ICLD............ International Center for Law in Development (EA)

ICL-D .... Loyola University, Dental School, Chicago, IL [*Library symbol Library of Congress*] (LCLS)

ICLE............ Institute of Continuing Legal Education [*Research center*] (RCD)

ICLE............ Intacapsular Lens Extraction [*Ophthalmology*] (DAVI)

ICLEI............ International Council for Local Environmental Initiatives [*Marine science*] (OSRA)

ICLEP.......... Individualized Computer Literacy Education Plan (EDAC)

ICLES.......... International Common Law Exchange Society (EA)

ICLES.......... International Conference on Large Electrical Systems

IClh............ Clarendon Hills Public Library, Clarendon Hills, IL [*Library symbol Library of Congress*] (LCLS)

ICLH............ Imperial College - London Hospital [*British*] (DI)

ICIH............ John Warner Hospital, Clinton, IL [*Library symbol Library of Congress*] (LCLS)

ICIhP........... Clarendon Hills Public Library, Clarendon Hills, IL [*Library symbol*] [*Library of Congress*] (LCLS)

IcLi............. Identity Correct, Location Incorrect [*Psychology*]

ICLID .... Incoming Caller Identification [*Telecommunications*]

ICL-L........... Loyola University, Law Library, Chicago, IL [*Library symbol*] [*Library of Congress*] (LCLS)

ICLM........... Induced Course Load Matrix (PDAA)

ICLM........... Inter-California Line in Mexico R. R. [*AAR code*]

ICLM........... International Christian Leprosy Mission (EA)

ICL-M........... Loyola University, School of Medicine, Maywood, IL [*Library symbol Library of Congress*] (LCLS)

ICLMC.......... Intersociety Council on Laboratory Medicine of Canada

ICLoop......... Loop College, Chicago, IL [*Library symbol Library of Congress*] (LCLS)

ICLP............ Internal Connectionless Protocol [*Telecommunications*]

ICLR............ Interdepartmental Committee on Labour Requirements [*British World War II*]

ICLR............ International Committee for Lift Regulations [*See also CIRA*] [*Saint-Yvelines, France*] (EAIO)

ICLR............ Irish Common Law Reports [*A publication*] (DLA)

ICLR Can ..... Index to Current Legal Research in Canada [*A publication*] (DLA)

ICLREW .... Incorporated Council of Law Reporting for England and Wales [*Established in 1866*]

ICLRN .... Interagency Council on Library Resources for Nursing (EA)

ICLRSQ........ Incorporated Council of Law Reporting for the State of Queensland [*Australia*]

ICLS............ Inequality Constrained Least-Squares [*Statistics*]

ICLS............ Instrument Carrier Landing System [*Navy*] (DOMA)

ICLS............ Integrated Carrier Landing System [*Military*] (MCD)

ICLS............ International Courtly Literature Society (EA)

ICLS............ Irish Central Library for Students (TELE)

ICLSA........... United States League of Savings Associations, Chicago, IL [*Library symbol Library of Congress*] (LCLS)

ICLT............ International Committee of Lawyers for Tibet

ICLT............ Lutheran School of Theology, Chicago, IL [*Library symbol Library of Congress*] (LCLS)

ICLTC.......... Illinois Council on Long Term Care (SRA)

ICLW........... Latham & Watkins, Chicago, IL [*Library symbol*] [*Library of Congress*] (LCLS)

ICM.............	Immune Combination Molecules (DB)
ICM.............	Improved Capability Minuteman (SAA)
ICM.............	Improved Capability Missile [Air Force]
ICM.............	Improved Conventional Munitions
ICM.............	In-Can Melter [Nuclear energy] (NUCP)
ICM.............	Incoming Message [Telecommunications]
ICM.............	Independent Citizens' Movement [US Virgin Islands] (PPW)
ICM.............	Independent Color Matching [Computer science]
ICM.............	Indian Campaign Medal
ICM.............	Individual Case Management (WYGK)
ICM.............	Individual Clutch Modulation [Automotive engineering]
ICM.............	Infracostal Margin [Anatomy] (DAVI)
ICM.............	Initiator Command Module
ICM.............	Inner Cell Mass [Embryology]
ICM.............	Installable Compression, Manager [Computer science]
ICM.............	Instantaneous Center of Motion
ICM.............	Institut Canadien de la Mediterranee [Canadian Mediterranean Institute]
ICM.............	Institut Canadien des Mines et de la Metallurgie [Canadian Institute of Mining and Metallurgy] (EAIO)
ICM.............	Institute for Complementary Medicine [An association] (EAIO)
ICM.............	Institute for Composite Materials [Defunct] (EA)
ICM.............	Institute for Court Management of the National Center for State Courts (EA)
ICM.............	Institute of Caster Manufacturers (EA)
ICM.............	Institute of Construction Management [British]
ICM.............	Institute of Credit Management [British]
ICM.............	Instituto de Ciencias del Mar [Barcelona, Spain] [Marine science] (OSRA)
ICM.............	Instruction Control Memory
ICM.............	Instrumentation and Communications Monitor
ICM.............	Integral Charge-Control Model [Electronics] (OA)
ICM.............	Integrated Catchment Management [Water resources]
ICM.............	Integrated Circuit Mask
ICM.............	Integrated Compact Mill [Steel manufacture]
ICM.............	Integrated Controller Module [Automotive engineering]
ICM.............	Integrated Coverage Measurement [Statistical technique]
ICM.............	Integrated Crop Management [Agriculture]
ICM.............	Interchangeable Control Media (MCD)
ICM.............	Intercommunication (MSA)
ICM.............	Intercomp (EFIS)
ICM.............	Intercontinental Missile (IAA)
ICM.............	Intercostal Margin [Anatomy]
ICM.............	Interface Coordination Memorandum (MCD)
ICM.............	Interference Control Monitor (AAG)
ICM.............	Intergovernmental Committee for Migration (EBF)
ICM.............	Interim Catalog Module [MEDLARS]
ICM.............	Internacional De Ceramica ADS [NYSE symbol] (TTSB)
ICM.............	Internacional de Ceramica SA de CV [NYSE symbol] (SAG)
ICM.............	International Chaplain's Ministry (EA)
ICM.............	International Colour Management [Commercial firm British]
ICM.............	International Confederation of Midwives [British] (EAIO)
ICM.............	International Congress of Mathematicians
ICM.............	International Congress on Mechanical Behaviour of Materials (EAIO)
ICM.............	International Control Mechanism
ICM.............	International Creative Management [Commercial firm]
ICM.............	Interoperability Configuration Manager
ICM.............	Intracluster Medium [Galactic science]
ICM.............	Intracompany Memorandum
ICM.............	Inventory Control Manager (MCD)
ICM.............	Investment Casting Mold (MCD)
ICM.............	Ion Chromatography Module
ICM.............	Ion Conductance Modulator [Cytochemistry]
ICM.............	Irish Church Missions
ICM.............	Ischemic Cardiomyopathy [Also, IC] [Cardiology]
ICM.............	Isolation, Control, and Monitoring [Pollution control]
ICM.............	Missionary Sisters of the Immaculate Heart of Mary (TOCD)
ICM.............	Mundelein College, Chicago, IL [OCLC symbol] (OCLC)
ICM.............	Soeurs Missionnaires du Coeur Immacule de Marie [Missionary Sisters of the Immaculate Heart of Mary] [Italy] (EAIO)
ICMA.............	Imino(cyanomorpholinyl)deaminoadriamycin [Antineoplastic drug]
ICMA.............	Independent Cabinet Makers' Association [A union] [British]
ICMA.............	Independent Cable Makers' Association [British] (BI)
ICMA.............	Initial Clothing Monetary Allowance [Military]
ICMA.............	Institute for Computational Mathematics and Applications [University of Pittsburgh] [Research center] (RCD)
ICMA.............	Institute of Certified Management Accountants [Montvale, NJ] (EA)
ICMA.............	Institute of Cost and Management Accountants [British]
ICMA.............	International Card Manufacturers Association (NTPA)
ICMA.............	International Center of Medieval Art (EA)
ICMA.............	International Christian Maritime Association [Felixstone, Suffolk, England] (EAIO)
ICMA.............	International Cigarette Makers' Association [A union]
ICMA.............	International Circulation Managers Association (EA)
ICMA.............	International City Management Association [Later, ICMA-The Professional Local Government Management Association] (EA)
ICMA.............	International County Managers Association (PA)
ICMAD.........	Independent Cosmetic Manufacturers and Distributors (EA)
ICMARD.......	International Center for Marine Resources Development (ASF)
ICMAREP.....	Interagency Committee on Marine Environmental Prediction [Marine science] (OSRA)
ICMASA.......	Intersociety Committee on Methods for Air Sampling and Analysis (EA)
ICMay..........	Mayfair College, Chicago, IL [Library symbol Library of Congress] (LCLS)
ICMB.............	International Center for Monetary and Banking Studies [Switzerland] (ECON)
ICMB.............	Moody Bible Institute, Chicago, IL [Library symbol Library of Congress] (LCLS)
ICMBP	Mayer, Brown & Platt Law Library, Chicago, IL [Library symbol Library of Congress] (LCLS)
ICMC.............	International Catholic Migration Commission [See also CICM] [Geneva, Switzerland] (EAIO)
ICMC.............	International Christian Media Commission (EA)
ICMC.............	International Cryogenic Materials Conference (EA)
ICMCA	Museum of Contemporary Art, Chicago, IL [Library symbol] [Library of Congress] (LCLS)
ICMcC.........	McCormick Theological Seminary, Chicago, IL [Library symbol Library of Congress] (LCLS)
ICMcDW	McDermott, Will & Emory, Chicago, IL [Library symbol] [Library of Congress] (LCLS)
ICME.............	International Clearinghouse on the Military and the Environment (EA)
ICME.............	International Code of Medical Ethics
ICME.............	International Conference on Medical Electronics
ICME.............	International Congress on Mathematical Education [International Council of Scientific Unions]
ICME.............	International Contemporary Music Exchange (EA)
ICME.............	International Council on Metals and the Environment
ICMe.............	Meadville Theological School, Chicago, IL [Library symbol Library of Congress] (LCLS)
ICMEDC	International Council of Masonry Engineering for Developing Countries [Formerly, International Symposium on Reinforced and Prestressed Masonry] (EA)
ICMen.........	Chicago Mercantile Exchange, Chicago, IL [Library symbol Library of Congress] (LCLS)
ICMer...........	Charles E. Merriam Center for Public Administration, Merriam Center Library, Chicago, IL [Library symbol Library of Congress] (LCLS)
ICMG	International Commission for Microbial Genetics [International Council of Scientific Unions]
ICMH	Institut Canadien de Microreproductions Historiques [Canadian Institute for Historical Microreproductions - CIHM]
ICMH	International Commission of Military History
ICMH	Interstate Compact on Mental Health [Public human service program] (PHSD)
ICMH	Mercy Hospital and Medical Center, Chicago, IL [Library symbol Library of Congress] (LCLS)
ICMI	Index of Childhood Memory and Imagination
ICMI	Indonesian Muslim Intellectuals Association [Political party] (EY)
ICMI	International Commission on Mathematical Instruction [British]
ICMICA	Pax Romana, International Catholic Movement for Intellectual and Cultural Affairs [See also MIIC] [Geneva, Switzerland] (EAIO)
ICMID	International Committee for Microbiological and Immunological Documentation [International Council of Scientific Unions]
ICMIS..........	Integrated Computerized Management Information System (PDAA)
ICMJE.........	International Committee of Medical Journal Editors [An association]
ICML..........	International Center for Medicine and Law (EA)
ICMLT.........	International Congress of Medical Laboratory Technologists
ICMM..........	Illinois Masonic Medical Center, Chicago, IL [Library symbol Library of Congress] (LCLS)
ICMM..........	Incomplete Correlation Matrix Memory (PDAA)
ICMM..........	International Committee of Military Medicine [Belgium] (EAIO)
ICMM..........	International Congress of Maritime Museums (EA)
ICMMA........	Industrial Cleaning Machine Manufacturers Association [British] (DBA)
ICMMB........	International Conference on Mechanics in Medicine and Biology (EA)
ICM/MIRV	Intercontinental Missile / Multiple Independently-Fuided Reentry Vehicle (PDAA)
ICMMP........	Integrated CONUS [Continental United States] Medical Mobilization Pla n (DOMA)
ICMMP........	International Committee of Military Medicine and Pharmacy [Belgium]
ICMO..........	Indirect Cost Monitoring Office (AAGC)
ICMO..........	Integrated Configuration Management Office [NASA] (NASA)
ICMP..........	Interchannel Master Pulse
ICMP..........	International Confederation of Music Publishers [British] (EAIO)
ICMP..........	International Conference on Marine Pollution (ILCA)
ICMP..........	Internet Control and Message Protocol [Telecommunications]
ICMPD	International Centre for Migration Policy Development [Austria] (ECON)
ICMPH	International Center of Medical and Psychological Hypnosis [Milan, Italy] (EA)
ICMPS	Induction Compass
ICMR	Chicago Municipal Reference Library, Chicago, IL [Library symbol Library of Congress] (LCLS)
ICMR	Indian Council of Medical Research
ICMR	Instrument Calibration and Maintenance Record (MCD)
ICMR	Interagency Committee on Medical Records (AAGC)
ICMRD	International Center for Marine Resources Development [University of Rhode Island]
ICMREF.......	Interagency Committee on Marine Science, Research, Engineering, and Facilities
ICMS..........	Indirect Cost Management System (NASA)
icms..........	Indirect Cost Management System (NAKS)
ICMS..........	Information Center Management System [Cullinet] (NITA)
ICMS..........	Institute of Club Managers and Secretaries [Australia]
ICMS..........	Instrument Calibration and Maintenance Schedule
ICMS..........	Integrated Circuit and Message Switch
ICMS..........	Integrated Circuit Measurement System (AAEL)
ICMS..........	Interdepartmental Committee for Meteorological Services [National Weather Service]

ICMS............ International Centre for Mathematical Sciences [*Heriot-Watt University*] (ECON)
ICMS............ International Commission on Mushroom Science [*Later, ISMS*] (EA)
ICMS............ Intracortical Microstimulation [*For study of brain function*]
ICMSA........ Institute of Corporate Managers, Secretaries and Administrators [*Australia*]
ICMSA........ Irish Creamery Milk Suppliers' Association (BI)
ICMSE.......... Interagency Committee on Marine Science and Engineering [*Federal Council for Science and Technology*]
ICMSF.......... International Commission on Microbiological Specifications for Foods (EA)
ICMST......... International Conference on Machine Searching and Translation
ICMT........... Intercontract Material Transfer
ICMT........... International Commission on Mycotoxicology [*International Council of Scientific Unions*]
ICMTO........ Independent Carrier Military Traffic Office [*MTMC*] (TAG)
ICMU.......... Isolation Configuration and Monitor Unit (MCD)
ICMUA........ International Commission on the Meteorology of the Upper Atmosphere
ICMund........ Mundelein College, Chicago, IL [*Library symbol Library of Congress*] (LCLS)
ICMUP........ Instruction Control Memory Update Processor (MHDB)
ICMW.......... Inherent Corrective Maintenance Workload
ICMX.......... Malcolm X College of the City College of Chicago, Chicago, IL [*Library symbol Library of Congress*] (LCLS)
ICN............. ICN Pharmaceuticals [*NYSE symbol*] (TTSB)
ICN............. ICN Pharmaceuticals, Inc. [*Formerly, SPI Pharmaceuticals*] [*NYSE symbol*] (SPSG)
icn .... Icon (VRA)
ICN............. Idle Channel Noise (IAA)
ICN............. In Christi Nomine [*In the Name of Christ*] [*Latin*]
ICN............. Inclusion Conjunctivitis Neonate [*Ophthalmology*]
ICN............. Index of Community Noise
ICN............. Indicator Coupling Network (IAA)
ICN............. Inocan Technologies Ltd. [*Vancouver Stock Exchange symbol*]
ICN............. Instrumentation and Calibration Network (AAG)
ICN............. Integrated Computer Network
ICN............. Intensive Care Nursery [*Medicine*]
ICN............. Inter-Canadian [*ICAO designator*] (FAAC)
ICN............. Interface Change Notice (MCD)
ICN............. Interim Change Notice (AFM)
ICN............. International Communes Network (EAIO)
ICN............. International Conference on Nutrition [*United Nations*]
ICN............. International Council of Nurses [*Switzerland*] (EY)
ICN............. Intromogenous Computer Network
ICN............. Newberry Library, Chicago, IL [*Library symbol Library of Congress*] (LCLS)
ICN............. North Central College, Naperville, IL [*OCLC symbol*] (OCLC)
ICNA........... Infants' and Children's Novelties Association (EA)
ICNAF .... International Commission for the Northwest Atlantic Fisheries [*Superseded by NAFO*]
ICNAF .... International Committee of North American Federation
ICNAF .... International Convention of the Northwest Atlantic Fisheries (USDC)
IC/NATAS .... International Council - National Academy of Television Arts and Sciences (EA)
IC/NATVAS ... International Council of the National Academy of Television Arts and Sciences (EA)
ICNB .... International Committee on Nomenclature of Bacteria
ICNCP .... International Commission for the Nomenclature of Cultivated Plants [*Wageningen, Netherlands*] (EA)
ICND .... Irish Campaign for Nuclear Disarmament (EAIO)
ICNDT .... International Committee on NDT [*Nondestructive Testing*] [*Brazil*] (EAIO)
ICNDT .... International Conference on Non-Destructive Testing (PDAA)
ICNE .... Income Collected, Not Earned (EBF)
ICNE .... Northeastern Illinois University, Chicago, IL [*Library symbol Library of Congress*] (LCLS)
ICNEM .... Internacia Centro de la Neutrala Esperanto-Movado [*International Center of the Neutral Esperanto Movement*] [*Defunct*] (EAIO)
ICNEP .... Initiative Committee for National Economic Planning
ICNF........... Irredundant Conjunctive Normal Formula
ICNI .... Integrated Communication, Navigation, Identification [*System*]
ICNI .... Integrated Communications Network, Inc. [*NASDAQ symbol*] (SAG)
ICNI .... Integrated Commun Ntwk [*NASDAQ symbol*] (TTSB)
ICNIA .... Integrated Communication, Navigation, and Identification Avionics [*Air Force*]
ICNICP .... Integrated Communication/Navigation/Identification Control Panel (MCD)
ICNICS .... Integrated Communication/Navigation/Identification Control Set (MCD)
ICNND.......... Interdepartmental Committee on Nutrition for National Defense
ICNP .... International Classification of Nursing Practice (DMAA)
ICNP .... International Commission on National Parks [*Later, CNPAA*] (EA)
ICN Ph .... ICN Pharmaceuticals, Inc. [*Formerly, International Chemical & Nuclear Corp.*] [*Associated Press*] (SAG)
ICNPT .... North Park College and Theological Seminary, Chicago, IL [*Library symbol Library of Congress*] (LCLS)
ICNS .... Information Center on Nuclear Standards [*American Nuclear Society*] [*Information service or system*]
ICNS .... Integrated Communications and Navigation System
ICNS .... National Safety Council, Chicago, IL [*Library symbol Library of Congress*] (LCLS)
ICNT.......... INCOMNET, Inc. [*Formerly, Intelligent Commercial Net*] [*NASDAQ symbol*] (NQ)

ICNT.......... Informal Composite Negotiating Text [*United Nations Conference on the Law of the Sea*]
ICNT.......... Northern Trust Co., Chicago, IL [*Library symbol Library of Congress*] (LCLS)
ICNTG .... Intracoronary Nitroglycerine [*Pharmacology*]
ICNU .... National College of Education, Urban Campus, Chicago, IL [*Library symbol Library of Congress*] (LCLS)
ICNV .... International Committee on Nomenclature of Viruses [*Later, ICTV*]
ICNY .... International Center in New York (EA)
ICNY .... Islamic Center of New York (EA)
ICO............. ICO, Inc. [*Associated Press*] (SAG)
ICO............. Identified Camouflaged Objects [*Hunting*]
ICO............. Idiopathic Cyclic Oedema [*Medicine*] (DMAA)
ICO............. Illinois College of Optometry [*Chicago*]
ICO............. Illinois Wesleyan University, Bloomington, IL [*OCLC symbol*] (OCLC)
ICO............. Immediate Commanding Officer
ICO............. Impedance Cardiac Output [*Medicine*] (DMAA)
ICO............. In Case Of
ICO............. Incident Command Organization [*Environmental science*] (COE)
ICO............. Independent Conducting Officer
ICO............. Indian Commissioned Officer [*British military*] (DMA)
ICO............. Information for the Contracting Officer (MCD)
ICO............. Input Current Offset [*Computer science*]
ICO............. Inspecting Chief Officer [*Military British*] (ROG)
ICO............. Institut Canadien des Oceans [*Oceans Institute of Canada*] (IRC)
ICO............. Institute of Careers Officers [*British*]
ICO............. Institute of Chemists-Opticians [*British*] (DAS)
ICO............. Instrumentation Control Officer (AAG)
ICO............. Integrated Checkout (NASA)
ico............. Integrated Checkout (NAKS)
ICO............. Integrator Cutoff
ICO............. Interagency Committee on Oceanography [*Later, ICMSE*]
ICO............. Intercristo [*An association*] (EA)
ICO............. Intergovernmental Commission on Oceanography (NUCP)
ICO............. Interim Care Order (WDAA)
ICO............. Interim Conservation Order
ICO............. International Carbohydrate Organization [*Aberdeen, Scotland*] (EAIO)
ICO............. International Cardero Resources [*Vancouver Stock Exchange symbol*]
ICO............. International Catholic Organizations
ICO............. International Civil Aviation Organization [*ICAO designator*] (FAAC)
ICO............. International Coffee Organization (EAIO)
ICO............. International College of Officers [*Salvation Army*]
ICO............. International Commission for Optics [*See also CIO*] [*ICSU Delft, Netherlands*] (EAIO)
ICO............. International Computer Orphanage (EA)
ICO............. International Council of Ophthalmology (EA)
ICO............. Internet Connectivity Option [*Galacticomm, Inc.*] [*Telecommunications*]
ICO............. Inventory Control Officer
ICO............. Le Iscrizioni Fenicie e Puniche delle Colonie in Occidente (BJA)
ICOA .... International Castor Oil Association (EA)
ICOA .... International CBX Owners Association (EA)
ICOBA .... International Confederation of Book Actors (EA)
ICOC .... ICO, Inc. [*NASDAQ symbol*] (NQ)
ICOC .... Instructions for Commodores of Convoys [*Navy Obsolete*]
ICOC .... International Commission for Orders of Chivalry (EA)
ICOCS .... Interim Circuit Order Control System [*Bell System*]
ICOCZ .... ICO Inc. 6.75% Cv Dep Pfd [*NASDAQ symbol*] (TTSB)
ICOD .... Intelligence Cutoff Date [*Military*] (MCD)
ICOD .... International Centre for Ocean Development [*See also CIEO*] [*Canada*]
ICOD .... International Council on Disability (EA)
ICODS .... Interagency Committee on Dam Safety [*Federal Emergency Management Agency*] [*Washington, DC*] (EGAO)
ICOE .... International Center for Orthopaedic Education
ICOEES .... Interagency Committee on Ocean Exploration and Environmental Services [*Terminated, 1971*] (NOAA)
ICOEES .... International Committee on Ocean Exploration and Environmental Services [*Defunct*] (USDC)
ICOEI .... Integral Components of End Items (MCD)
ICOF........... Industrial Common Ownership Finance [*An association British*]
I-COFT .... Institutional Conduct of Fire Trainer [*Army*]
ICOGRADA... International Council of Graphic Design Associations [*British*] (EA)
ICOH .... International Commission of Occupational Health (EA)
ICOH .... Olive-Harvey College Library, City Colleges of Chicago, Chicago, IL [*Library symbol*] [*Library of Congress*] (LCLS)
ICOHEPANS... International Conference on High Energy Physics and Nuclear Structure
ICOHH.......... International Concatenated Order of Hoo-Hoo [*Later, International Order of Hoo-Hoo*] (EA)
ICOHTEC ...... International Committee for the History of Technology (EA)
ICOI .... International Congress of Oral Implantologists (EA)
ICO Inc .... ICO, Inc. [*Associated Press*] (SAG)
ICol............. Collinsville Public Library, Collinsville, IL [*Library symbol Library of Congress*] (LCLS)
ICOLC .... International Coalition of Library Consortia
IColCU .... Collinsville Community Unit 10, Collinsville, IL [*Library symbol Library of Congress*] (LCLS)
ICOLD .... International Commission on Large Dams [*See also CIGB*] [*ICSU Paris, France*] (EAIO)
ICOLP .... Industry Cooperative for Ozone Layer Protection
IColu........... Columbia Public Library, Columbia, IL [*Library symbol Library of Congress*] (LCLS)

IColuD .... Columbia Unit District 4, Columbia, IL [*Library symbol Library of Congress*] (LCLS)
ICOM .... Challenger International [*NASDAQ symbol*] (SAG)
ICOM .... Improved Conventional Mine System [*Military*] (MCD)
ICOM .... Industrial Common Ownership Movement [*British*]
ICOM .... Institute of Computational Mechanics [*University of Cincinnati*] [*Research center*] (RCD)
ICOM .... Intelect Communications Systems Ltd. [*NASDAQ symbol*] (SAG)
ICOM .... Intercommunications (NASA)
ICOM .... Interfaith Church of Metaphysics (EA)
ICOM .... International Church of Metaphysics (EA)
ICOM .... International Council of Museums [*France*]
IComA .... Institute of Company Accountants [*British*] (EAIO)
ICOMC .... International Conference on Organometallic Chemistry
ICOM-CC ...... ICOM [*International Council of Museums*] Committee for Conservation (EAIO)
ICOME .... International Committee on Microbial Ecology [*ICSU*] (EAIO)
ICOMF .... Intelect Communications [*NASDAQ symbol*] (TTSB)
ICOMIA .... International Council of Marine Industry Associations [*Weybridge, Surrey, England*] (EA)
ICOMOS .... International Council of Monuments and Sites [*France*] (EA)
ICOMP .... Iceland Ocean Meeting Point [*Navy*]
iCOMP .... Intel Comparative Microprocessor Performance Index (PCM)
ICOMP .... International Council on Management of Population Programmes [*Kuala Lumpur, Malaysia*] (EAIO)
ICON .... Iconoclasm (ADA)
ICON .... Iconography
ICON .... Imagery Communications and Operations Node (DOMA)
ICON .... Indexed Currency Option Note [*Student Loan Marketing Association*]
ICON .... Indexed Currency Option Notes (EBF)
ICON .... Integrated COMSEC [*Communications Security*] [*Army*] (DOMA)
ICON .... Integrated Control
ICON .... Inter-Institutional Committee on Nutrition
ICON .... International Communication of Orthodox Nations
ICONCLASS... Iconography Classification [*Netherlands*] (NITA)
ICONDA .... International Construction Database [*Information Centre for Regional Planning and Building Construction of the Fraunhofer-Society*] [*Database*]
ICONMIG ...... International Conference on Numerical Methods in Geomechanics
ICONS .... Information Center on Nuclear Standards [*American Nuclear Society*] [*La Grange Park, IL*] [*Information service or system*]
ICONS .... Inner Continental Shelf Sediments and Structure Program [*Army Corps of Engineers*] (GFGA)
ICONS .... International Communication and Negotiation Simulation
ICONS .... Isotopes of Carbon, Oxygen, Nitrogen, and Sulfur [*AEC project*]
iconst .... Iconostasis (VRA)
ICOP .... Imported Crude Oil Processing
ICOP .... Intelligence Collect Program
ICOP .... Interagency Contingency Options Plan [*Military*]
ICOP .... Inventory Control Point
ICOPAMP ..... Integrated Circuit Operational Amplifier [*Electronics*] (IAA)
ICOPS .... Institute for the Comparative Study of Political Systems
ICOR .... In Charge of Room [*Military*] (DNAB)
ICOR .... Incremental Capital Output Ratio
ICOR .... Intergovernmental Conference on Oceanic Research
ICORRST ...... Institution of Corrosion Science and Technology (PDAA)
ICORRT .... Institution of Corrosion Technology (PDAA)
ICORS .... International Conference of Raman Spectroscopy
ICOS .... ICOS Corp. [*NASDAQ symbol*] (SPSG)
ICOS .... Improved Crew Optical Sight (NASA)
icos .... Improved Crew Optical Sight [*NASA*] (NAKS)
ICOS .... Integrated Checkout System (KSC)
ICOS .... Integrated Cost Operation System (IAA)
ICOS .... Interactive COBOL Operating System
ICOS .... International Committee of Onomastic Sciences [*Belgium*]
ICOS .... Interpretation Canada. Ontario Section [*A publication*]
ICOS .... Irish Council for Overseas Students
ICOSA .... International Council of Seamen's Agencies (EA)
ICOSI .... International Committee on Smoking Issues [*Brussels, Belgium*] (EAIO)
ICOSO .... International Committee for Outer Space Onomastics
ICOSS .... Inertial-Command Off-Set System (MCD)
ICOT .... ICOT Corp. [*NASDAQ symbol*] (NQ)
Icot .... ICOT Corp. [*Associated Press*] (SAG)
ICOT .... Institute of Coastal Oceanography and Tides [*British*]
ICOT .... Institute of New Generation Computer Technology [*Japan*]
ICOTAS .... International Committee on the Organisation of Traffic at Sea [*British*] (DS)
ICOTS .... Interagency Committee on Transportation Security [*Department of Transportation*]
ICOTS .... International Conference on Teaching Statistics
ICOTT .... Industry Coalition on Technology Transfer (EA)
ICOTY .... Import Car of the Year [*Automotive promotion*]
icou .... Inertial Coupling Data Unit (NAKS)
ICOU .... International Consommateurs Organization des Unions [*International Organization of Consumers Unions*]
ICP .... ICS [*Interpretive Computer Simulator*] Control Program [*Army*]
ICP .... Ignition Control Programmer (MCD)
ICP .... Impact Copolymer Polypropylene [*Plastics*] [*Automotive engineering*]
ICP .... Incentive Compensation Plan (MCD)
ICP .... Incident Command Post [*Environmental science*] (COE)
ICP .... Incident Control Point [*Environmental science*] (COE)
ICP .... INCOLSA [*Indiana Cooperative Library Services Authority*] Processing Center, Indianapolis, IN [*OCLC symbol*] (OCLC)
ICP .... Incoming [*Message*] Process [*Telecommunications*] (TEL)
ICP .... Incubation Period [*Medicine*] (DB)
ICP .... Indian Communications Project
ICP .... Indicator Control Panel
ICP .... Indo-Chinese Communist Party [*Vietnam*] [*Political party*] (VNW)
ICP .... Induction Coupled Plasma (EDCT)
ICP .... Inductively Coupled Plasma [*Spectrometry*]
ICP .... Inductively Coupled Plasma [*Chemical analysis*]
ICP .... Industrial Control Products (MCD)
ICP .... Industrial Coupling Program [*Refers to university-industry interaction*]
ICP .... Industry Cooperative Program [*United Nations*]
ICP .... Infection-Control Practitioner [*Medicine*]
ICP .... Infectious Cell Protein [*Genetics*]
ICP .... Initial Connection Protocol [*Computer science Telecommunications*]
ICP .... Inner City Partnership [*EEC and British program to regenerate blighted areas*]
ICP .... Insecticidal Crystal Protein [*Agrochemistry*]
ICP .... Installation Input Change Package (MCD)
ICP .... Instant Control Point [*British police*]
ICP .... Institute for Circadian Physiology [*Boston, MA*]
ICP .... Institute for Comprehensive Planning [*Defunct*] (EA)
ICP .... Institutional Conservation Program (GNE)
ICP .... Instructor Control Panel
ICP .... Instrument Calibration Procedure
ICP .... Insurance Conference Planners (EA)
ICP .... Integral Circuit Package
ICP .... Integrated Chemists of the Philippines
ICP .... Intelligence Collection Plan [*Military*] (AFM)
ICP .... Intelligent Communications Processor
IC-P .... Intelligent Copier-Printer [*Electrophotography*]
ICP .... Interdisciplinary Care Plan [*Information service or system*] (HCT)
ICP .... Interdisciplinary Communications Program
ICP .... Interface Change Proposal
ICP .... Interface Control Panel (MCD)
ICP .... Internal Combustion Powered (ADA)
ICP .... Internal Connection Protocol [*Telecommunications*]
ICP .... International Center of Photography (EA)
ICP .... International Classification of Patents [*Council of Europe*] (PDAA)
ICP .... International Comfort Products
ICP .... International Computer Programs, Inc. [*Indianapolis, IN*] [*Information service or system*]
ICP .... International Congress of Publishers (DIT)
ICP .... International Control Plan (MCD)
ICP .... International Council of Psychologists (EA)
ICP .... International Institute of Cellular and Molecular Pathology [*Belgium*] (IRC)
ICP .... Internet Content Provider [*Computer science*]
ICP .... Internet Control Protocol [*Telecommunications*] (PCM)
ICP .... Interoceanic Canal Project [*National Oceanic and Atmospheric Administration*] (NOAA)
ICP .... Inter-University Case Program
ICP .... Inter-University Cooperation Program [*EC*] (ECED)
ICP .... Intracarcass Pressure [*Tire technology*]
ICP .... Intracranial Pressure [*Medicine*]
ICP .... Intracuff Pressure [*In mechanical ventilation*] [*Medicine*]
ICP .... Intracytoplasmic [*Medicine*] (DB)
ICP .... Intrinsically Conductive Plastic [*Organic chemistry*]
ICP .... Inventory Control Point
ICP .... Ion Coupled Plasma [*Oil analysis*]
ICP .... Iraqi Communist Party [*Political party*] (PPW)
ICP .... Irish Company Profiles [*Institute of Industrial Research and Standards - IIRS*] [*Dublin, Ireland*] [*Information service or system*] (IID)
ICP .... Ischemic Cardiac Pain [*Cardiology*]
ICP .... Islands of Cartilage Pattern [*Anatomy*]
ICP .... Italian Communist Party
ICP .... Item Control Point (AFM)
ICPA .... Information Centre for Polish Affairs (EAIO)
ICPA .... Insurance Conference Planners Association (NTPA)
ICPA .... International Cast Polymer Association (NTPA)
ICPA .... International Commission for the Prevention of Alcoholism [*Later, InternationalCommission for the Prevention of Alcoholism and Drug Dependency*]
ICPA .... International Conference of Police Associations [*Defunct*]
ICPA .... International Cooperative Petroleum Association (EA)
ICPA .... International Cruise Passengers Association (EA)
ICPA .... Public Administration Service, Joint Reference Library, Chicago, IL [*Library symbol Library of Congress*] (LCLS)
ICPAC .... Instantaneous Compressor Performance Analysis Computer
ICPADD .... International Commission for the Prevention of Alcoholism and Drug Dependency (EA)
ICP-AES .... Inductively Coupled Plasma - Atomic Emission Spectrometry [*See also ICPES*]
ICPAM .... International Centre for Pure and Applied Mathematics [*United Nations*] (EA)
ICPAN .... Interfaith Council for the Protection of Animals and Nature (EA)
ICPAS .... Illinois Certified Public Accountants Society (SRA)
ICPAS .... Indiana Certified Public Accountants Society (SRA)
ICPas .... Passionist Academic Institute, Chicago, IL [*Library symbol Library of Congress*] (LCLS)
ICPB .... Inert Components Parts Building
ICPBC .... Institute of Certified Professional Business Consultants [*Chicago, IL*] (EA)
ICPBR .... International Commission for Plant-Bee Relationships (EAIO)
ICPC .... International Cable Protection Committee [*British*] (EAIO)
ICPC .... International Commission of Catholic Prison Chaplains (EA)

ICPC............. International Confederation of Popular Credit [*See also CICP*] [*Paris, France*] (EAIO)

ICPC............. International Conference of Police Chaplains (EA)

ICPC............. International Criminal Police Commission [*Later, INTERPOL*]

ICPC............. Interrange Communications Planning Committee

ICPC............. Interstate Compact on the Placement of Children [*Public human service program*] (PHSD)

ICPC............. Intracranial Pressure Catheter [*Neurology*] (DAVI)

ICPCC.......... International Council for Pastoral Care and Counselling (EAIO)

ICPCI........... International Conference on the Performance of Computer Installations (PDAA)

ICPDATA...... Commodity Production Statistics [*United Nations Statistical Office*] [*Information service or system*] (CRD)

ICPDATA...... International Commodity Production Data [*United Nations Statistical Office*] (NITA)

ICPDES........ International Cancer Patient Data Exchange System

ICPDS.......... Interactive Continuous Process Dynamic Simulation (PDAA)

ICPE............. Internal Combustion Piston Engine (PDAA)

ICPE............. International Center for Public Enterprises in Developing Countries [*Ljubljana, Yugoslavia*] (EAIO)

ICPE............. International Commission on Physics Education [*See also CIEP*] (EA)

ICPE............. International Conference on Public Education [*International Bureau of Education*] [*Switzerland*]

ICPE............. Inventory Control Point Europe

ICPEAC........ International Conference on the Physics of Electronic and Atomic Collisions

ICPEM.......... Independent Computer Peripheral Equipment Manufacturers

ICPEMC........ International Commission for Protection Against Environmental Mutagens and Carcinogens [*Rijswljk, Netherlands*] (EAIO)

ICPERS........ Instant Computer Public Employment Relations Search [*Database*] [*Labor Relations Press*] [*Information service or system*] (CRD)

ICPES.......... Inductively Coupled Plasma Emission Spectrometry [*See also ICP-AES*]

ICPES.......... Intergovernmental Committee for Physical Education and Sport [*United Nations France*] (EY)

ICPF............. International Corrugated Packaging Foundation (NTPA)

ICPFF........... Incentive Cost plus Fixed Fee [*Contracts*]

ICPFR .... International Council for Physical Fitness Research [*Research center Canada*] (IRC)

ICPG .... People Gas Light Co., Chicago, IL [*Library symbol Library of Congress*] (LCLS)

ICPHS .... International Council for Philosophy and Humanistic Studies [*Paris, France*]

ICPI.............. Insurance Crime Prevention Institute [*Westport, CT*] (EA)

ICPI.............. Interagency Committee on Product Information (EA)

ICPI.............. Interlocking Concrete Pavement Institute

ICPI.............. Intersociety Committee on Pathology Information (EA)

ICPIC .... International Cleaner Production Information Clearinghouse (GNE)

ICPIC .... International Conference on Phenomena in Ionised Gases (PDAA)

ICPIC .... International Council for Philosophical Inquiry with Children [*Iceland*] (EAIO)

ICPICH .... International Commission for the Preservation of Islamic Cultural Heritage (EA)

ICPIG .... International Conference on Phenomena in Ionised Gases (PDAA)

ICPIGP .... Internationale Chretienne Professionelle pour les Industries Graphiques et Papetieres [*International Federation of Christian Trade Unions of Graphical and Paper Industries*]

ICPIWC .... International Council for Philosophical Inquiry with Children (EA)

ICpKSD .... J. F. Kennedy Consolidated Community School District 129, Cedar Point, IL [*Library symbol Library of Congress*] (LCLS)

ICPL............. Initial Control Program Load [*Computer science*] (IAA)

ICPL............. International Committee of Passenger Lines (PDAA)

ICPL............. Iowa City Public Library [*Iowa*]

ICPLS........... International College of Podiatric Laser Surgery (EA)

ICPM............ Illinois College of Podiatric Medicine, Chicago, IL [*Library symbol Library of Congress*] (LCLS)

ICPM............ Institute of Certified Professional Managers [*Harrisonburg, VA*] (EA)

ICPM............ International Congress of Physical Medicine (PDAA)

ICPME.......... International Center for Peace in the Middle East (EA)

ICPMM......... Incisors, Canines, Premolars, Molars [*Dentistry*]

ICPMM......... Peat, Marwick, and Mitchell, Chicago, IL [*Library symbol Library of Congress*] (LCLS)

ICPMP .... International Commission for the Protection of the Moselle Against Pollution (EA)

ICP-MS .... Inductively Coupled Plasma - Mass Spectrometry

ICPMS .... International Council of Prison Medical Services [*Vancouver, BC*] (EAIO)

ICPN .... International Committee of Plant Nutrition (EA)

ICPO .... Institute for Certified Park Operators (EA)

ICPO .... International CLIVAR [*Climate Variability and Prediction*] Project Office [*Marine science*] (OSRA)

ICPO .... International Criminal Police Organization [*France*]

ICPO .... Investment Co-Operative Programme Office [*UNIDO*]

ICPOA.......... Intelligence Center, Pacific Ocean Areas [*Obsolete*]

ICP-OES....... Inductively Coupled Plasma - Optical Emission Spectrometry

ICPP............. Idaho Chemical Processing Plant [*AEC*]

ICPP............. Institutional Child Protection Project [*Ohio State University*] (EDAC)

ICPP............. Interactive Computer Presentation Panel [*To display computer-generated information for military use*]

ICPP............. International Comparative Political Parties Project [*Northwestern University*] [*Inactive*] (IID)

ICPP............. Intubated Continuous Positive Pressure [*Medicine*] (DAVI)

ICPP............. Isochromic Color Perception Plates [*Ophthalmology*] (DAVI)

ICPR .... Incoming Capital Property Record

ICPR .... Industrial Cost and Performance Report (NG)

ICPR .... Integrated Circuit Parameter Retrieval [*Information Handling Services*] [*Database*]

ICPR .... Inter-University Consortium for Political Research [*Later, ICPSR*] (EA)

ICPRAP........ International Commission for the Protection of the Rhine Against Pollution [*See also ICPRP, IKSR*] [*Germany*] (EAIO)

ICPRB .... Interstate Commission on the Potomac River Basin

ICPRCPCO ... Intergovernmental Committee for Promoting the Return of Cultural Property to ItsCountries of Origin or Its Restitution in Case of Illicit Appropriation (EA)

ICPRCU........ Polish Roman Catholic Union of America, Chicago, IL [*Library symbol Library of Congress*] (LCLS)

ICPrM .... Provident Medical Center, Chicago, IL [*Library symbol*] [*Library of Congress*] (LCLS)

ICPRS .... Petersen, Ross, Schloerb & Seidel, Library, Chicago, IL [*Library symbol Library of Congress*] (LCLS)

ICPS............. ICBM [*Intercontinental Ballistic Missile*] Code Processing System (DWSG)

ICPS............. Inductively Coupled Plasma Spectroscopy (MEC)

ICPS............. Industrial and Commercial Power Systems (MCD)

ICPS............. Institute for Cultural Policy Studies [*Griffith University*] [*Australia*]

ICPS............. Interamerican College of Physicians and Surgeons (EA)

ICPS............. International Carnivorous Plant Society (EA)

ICPS............. International Cerebral Palsy Society [*British*] (EAIO)

ICPS............. International Conference on the Properties of Steam

ICPS............. International Congress of Photographic Science

ICPS............. International Council of Perfusion Societies [*Defunct*] (EA)

ICPS............. Interpersonal Cognitive Problem Solving (STED)

ICPS............. Interpersonal Cognitive Problem-Solving Program (EDAC)

ICPSR .... Inter-University Consortium for Political and Social Research (EA)

ICPTO .... International China Painting Teachers Organization [*Later, International Porcelain Artist Teachers*]

ICPTUR........ International Conference for Promoting Technical Uniformity on Railways [*Berne, Switzerland*] (EAIO)

ICPU .... International Catholic Press Union [*Later, UCIP*]

ICPUAE .... International Conference on the Peaceful Uses of Atomic Energy

ICPV .... International Committee on Polar Viruses

ICPVT........... International Council for Pressure Vessel Technology (EA)

ICPYY .... Institute of Clinical Pharmacology PLC (MHDW)

i-cq-- .... Comoro Islands [*MARC geographic area code Library of Congress*] (LCCP)

ICQ.............. Internal Control Questionnaire (ADA)

ICQ.............. International Capri Resources [*Vancouver Stock Exchange symbol*]

ICQ.............. I Seek You [*Internet dialog*]

ICQA .... International Columbian Quincentenary Alliance (EA)

ICQC .... International Conference on Quality Control (PDAA)

ICr................ Chicago Ridge Public Library, Chicago Ridge, IL [*Library symbol Library of Congress*] (LCLS)

ICR.............. Eagle Aero, Inc. [*ICAO designator*] (FAAC)

ICR.............. Identification and Compliance Record (MCD)

ICR.............. Iliac Crest [*Anatomy*]

ICR.............. Illinois Central Railroad

ICR.............. Illustration Change Request

ICR.............. Immunodeficiency Cancer Registry

ICR.............. In-Commission Rate

ICR.............. Independent Component Release [*Computer science*] (IBMDP)

ICR.............. Indirect Control Register [*Computer science*]

ICR.............. Individual Census Report (GFGA)

ICR.............. Individually Carried Records [*Military*]

ICR.............. Inductance-Capacitance-Resistance

ICR.............. Industrial Cases Reports [*Law reports*] [*British*] (DCTA)

ICR.............. Industrial Cost Recovery [*Environmental Protection Agency*]

ICR.............. Industrial Court Reports [*England*] [*A publication*] (DLA)

ICR.............. Inertial Confinement Fusion Reactor [*Nuclear energy*] (MCD)

ICR.............. Information Collection Request [*Paperwork Reduction Act*] (GFGA)

ICR.............. Information Collection Rule [*Environmental Protection Agency*]

ICR.............. Input and Compare Register

ICR.............. Input Control Register [*Computer science*]

ICR.............. Instantaneous Center of Rotation

ICR.............. Institute for Cancer Research (EA)

ICR.............. Institute for Communications Research [*Texas Tech University*] [*Research center*] (RCD)

ICR.............. Institute for Computer Research [*University of Waterloo*] [*Canada Research center*] (RCD)

ICR.............. Institute for Constitutional Research (EA)

ICR.............. Institute for Cooperative Research

ICR.............. Institute for Creation Research (EA)

ICR.............. Institute for Cultural Research [*Research center British*] (IRC)

ICR.............. Institute of Coal Research [*University of Newcastle*] [*Australia*]

ICR.............. Instruction Change Request (NASA)

ICR.............. Instrumentation Control Racks (AAG)

ICR.............. Insulated Core Reactor

ICR.............. Integral Cesium Reservoir

ICR.............. Integrated Color Removal [*Printing technology*]

ICR.............. Integration of Cellular Responses [*Research initiative*] [*bbswrc - Biotechnology and Biological Sciences Research Council*] [*British*]

ICR.............. Intelligence Collection Requirement [*Army*] (RDA)

ICR.............. Intelligent Character Recognition [*Computer science*]

ICR.............. Intensive Care Room [*Medicine*] (DAVI)

ICR.............. Interactive Conflict Resolution (PDAA)

ICR.............. Intercity Relay [*Broadcasting*] (NTCM)

ICR.............. Intercolonial Railway [*1858-1923*] [*Canada*]

ICR.............. Intercooled Recuperative [*Engine*] (DOMA)

ICR	Intercultural Relations (DNAB)
ICR	Interest Coverage Ratio
ICR	Interface Compatibility Record (NASA)
ICR	Interface Control Register (IAA)
ICR	Intermediate Circulating Reflux [Chemical engineering]
ICR	Intermittent Catheter Routine [Medicine] (DMAA)
ICR	Internal Control Region [Genetics]
ICR	Internal Control Review [DoD]
ICR	International Calibrated Ratio (STED)
ICR	International Celebrity Register (EFIS)
ICR	International Committee on Refugees [World War II]
ICR	International Computer Resources, Inc. [Information service or system] (IID)
ICR	International Congress of Radiology
ICR	International Consumer Reports [Consumers' Association] [British Information service or system] (IID)
ICR	International Corona Resources Ltd. [Vancouver Stock Exchange symbol]
ICR	International Council for Reprography
IC/R	International Cruiser/Race Class [Yachting]
ICR	Interrupt Control Register [Computer science]
ICR	Intracardiac Catheter Recording [Medicine] (DMAA)
ICR	Intracranial Reinforcement
ICR	Inventory Change Report
ICR	Ion Cyclotron Radiation
ICR	Ion Cyclotron Resonance [Spectrometry]
ICR	Irish Chancery Reports [A publication] (DLA)
ICR	Irish Circuit Reports [1841-43] [A publication] (DLA)
ICR	Iron-Core Reactor (MSA)
ICR	Item Change Request (AFIT)
ICR	Nicaro [Cuba] [Airport symbol Obsolete] (OAG)
ICRA	Indian Civil Rights Act [1968]
ICRA	Industrial Chemical Research Association (EA)
ICRA	Industrial Copyright Reform Association [British] (DBA)
ICRA	Interagency Committee on Radiological Assistance
ICRA	International Cartridge Recycling Association (EA)
ICRA	International Catholic Rural Association
ICRA	International Centre for Research in Accounting [University of Lancaster] [British] (CB)
ICRA	International Compressor Remanufacturers Association (NTPA)
ICRA	Iowa Court Reporters Association (SRA)
ICRA	Islamic Correctional Reunion Association (EA)
ICRAEE	International Commission on Rules for the Approval of Electrical Equipment [Later, CEE]
ICRAF	Institut Canadien de Recherches pour l'Avancement de la Femme [Canadian Research Institute for the Advancement of Women]
ICRAF	International Council for Research in Agroforestry [See also ICRAF] [Kenya] (EAIO)
ICRaH	Ravenswood Hospital Medical Center, Chicago, IL [Library symbol Library of Congress] (LCLS)
ICRand	Rand McNally & Co., Chicago, IL [Library symbol Library of Congress] (LCLS)
ICRAR	Interfaith Center to Reverse the Arms Race (EA)
ICRAS	International Committee for the Release of Anatoly Scharansky [Defunct] (EA)
ICRA(V)	Indo-Chinese Refugee Association (Victoria) [Australia]
ICRB	International Center for Research on Bilingualism [Universite Laval] [Canada]
ICRB	International Co-Operative Reinsurance Bureau [Manchester, England] (EAIO)
ICRC	Imperial College Reactor Centre [Imperial College of Science and Technology] [British] (WND)
ICRC	Infant Care Review Committee [Medicine] (DMAA)
ICRC	Interagency Classification Review Committee [Abolished, 1978] [DoD]
ICRC	International Committee to the Red Cross [Geneva, Switzerland] (EAIO)
ICRC	Roosevelt University, Chicago, IL [Library symbol Library of Congress] (LCLS)
ICRC-N	Roosevelt University, North Campus, Arlington Heights, IL [Library symbol Library of Congress] (LCLS)
ICRD	Index of Codes for Research Drugs [A publication]
ICRD	Input Collection Reports Data [IRS]
ICRD	Interior Committee on Research and Development
ICRD	Richard J. Daley College, Chicago, IL [Library symbol] [Library of Congress] (LCLS)
ICRDA	Independent Cash Register Dealers Association (EA)
ICRDB	International Cancer Research Data Bank [National Cancer Institute] [Database producer] (IID)
ICRDD	Institute for Community Resource Development [Australia]
ICre	Crete Public Library, Crete, IL [Library symbol Library of Congress] (LCLS)
ICRE	Ignitability Corrosivity, Reactivity, Extraction (GNE)
ICRE	Ignitable, Corrosive, Reactive, and/or Effluent [Environmental science] (COE)
ICRE	International Commission on Radiological Education (DMAA)
ICREB	International Champlain-Richelieu Engineering Board [Canada]
ICREF	Institut Canadien de Recherches sur les Femmes (AC)
IC Rep	Interstate Commerce Commission Reports [A publication] (DLA)
ICRETT	International Cancer Research Technology Transfer [Program]
ICREW	International Cancer Research Workshop
I-CRF	Immunoreactive Corticotropin-Releasing Factor [Medicine] (STED)
ICRF	Imperial Cancer Research Fund [British]
ICRF	Ion Cyclotron Radio Frequency
ICRF	Ion Cyclotron Resonance Frequency [Nuclear energy]
ICRF 159	Imperial Cancer Research Fund 159 [Razoxane] [Antineoplastic drug]
ICRFSDD	Independent Citizens Research Foundation for the Study of Degenerative Diseases (EA)
ICRGR	International Consultative Research Group on Rape [See also GCIRC] (EAIO)
ICRH	Information Center - Recreation for the Handicapped
ICRH	Institute for Computer Research in the Humanities [New York University]
ICRH	Ion Cyclotron Resonance Heating (MCD)
ICRH	Michael Reese Hospital and Medical Center, Lillian W. Florsheim Memorial Library, Chicago, IL [Library symbol Library of Congress] (LCLS)
ICRHO	Ross, Hardies, O'Keefe, Babcock, and Parsons, Chicago, IL [Library symbol Library of Congress] (LCLS)
ICRHS	Illinois Central Railroad Historical Society (EA)
ICRI	International Child Resource Institute (EA)
ICRI	International Coma Recovery Institute (EA)
ICRI	International Concrete Repair Institute (NTPA)
ICRI	Iron Casting Research Institute (EA)
ICRI	Rehabilitation Institute of Chicago, Chicago, IL [Library symbol] [Library of Congress] (LCLS)
ICRICE	International Centre of Research and Information on Collective Economy
ICRIP	International Circle for Research in Philosophy [Research center] (RCD)
ICRISAT	International Crops Research Institute for the Semi-Arid Tropics [India]
ICRL	Center for Research Libraries, Chicago, IL [Library symbol Library of Congress] (LCLS)
ICRL	Individual Component Repair List [DoD]
ICRL	Injury Control Research Laboratory [HEW]
ICRL(ARL)	Foreign Newspaper Microfilm Project, Association of Research Libraries, Center for Research Libraries, Chicago, IL [Library symbol Library of Congress] (LCLS)
ICRL(CAMP)	Cooperative Africana Microform Project, Archives-Libraries Committee, African Studies Association, Center for Research Libraries, Chicago, IL [Library symbol Library of Congress] (LCLS)
ICrIF	Follett Library Book Co., Crystal Lake, IL [Library symbol] [Library of Congress] (LCLS)
ICRL-LA	Latin America Microform Project, Center for Research Libraries, Chicago, IL [Library symbol] [Library of Congress] (LCLS)
ICRLP	International Center for Research on Language Planning [Laval University] (IRC)
ICRL-RR	Injury Control Research Laboratory Research Report [HEW]
ICRL(SAMP)	South Asian Microform Project, South Asian Microform and Library Committee, Association for Asian Studies, Center for Research Libraries, Chicago, IL [Library symbol Library of Congress] (LCLS)
ICRL-SEA	South East Asia Microform Project, Center for Research Libraries, Chicago, IL [Library symbol] [Library of Congress] (LCLS)
I CRM	Ice Cream [Freight]
ICRM	Institute of Certified Records Managers (NTPA)
ICRM	Intercontinental Reconnaissance Missile (DNAB)
ICRM(V)	International Carpet and Rug Market (ITD)
ICRM	International Cliff Richard Movement (EAIO)
ICRM	Rush Medical College, Chicago, IL [Library symbol Library of Congress] (LCLS)
ICRMS	Integrated Computer-Reactor Monitoring System (PDAA)
ICRO	Interallied Confederation of Reserve Officers [See also CIOR] (EAIO)
ICRO	International Cell Research Organization [ICSU] [Paris, France] (EAIO)
ICROSS	International Community for the Relief of Starvation and Suffering (EA)
ICRP	Internal Control Review Program [Air Force] (DOMA)
ICRP	International Climatic Research Program
ICRP	International Commission on Radiological Protection [International Society of Radiology] [British]
ICRPDS	Ion Cyclotron Resonance Photodissociation [Spectrometry]
ICRPG	Interagency Chemical Rocket Propulsion Group
ICRPMA	International Committee for Recording the Productivity of Milk Animals [See also CICPLB] [Rome, Italy] (EAIO)
ICRS	Imagery Collection Requirements Subcommittee [Military]
ICRS	Index Chemicals Registry System [Databank] (NITA)
ICRS	Index Chemicus Registry System [Information service or system A publication]
ICRS	Institute of Contemporary Russian Studies [Fordham University]
ICRS	Instrument Calibration and Recall System [Nuclear energy] (NRCH)
ICRS	Integrated Chemical Retrieval System [Pergamon InfoLine] [Computer science]
ICRS	Intelligence Collection Reporting System [Military] (MCD)
ICRSC	International Council for Research in the Sociology of Co-operation
ICRSDT	International Committee on Remote Sensing and Data Transmission [Marine science] (OSRA)
ICRT	Individual Criterion-Referenced Test [Education]
ICRT	Intelligent Content Recognition Technology [Computer science]
ICRT-MATH	Individualized Criterion Referenced Testing Mathematics [Strotman and Steen] (TES)
ICRT-READING	Individualized Criterion Referenced Testing-Reading (TES)
ICRU	International Commission on Radiation Units and Measurements (EA)
ICRU	International Commission on Radiological Units (STED)
IcRU	University of Icelands (Haskoli Islands), Reykjavik, Iceland [Library symbol Library of Congress] (LCLS)

ICRUM	International Commission on Radiation Units and Measurements
ICRV	Inns of Court Rifle Volunteers [*Military British*] (ROG)
ICRW	International Center for Research on Women (EA)
ICRW	International Convention for the Regulation of Whaling (ASF)
ICRW	Rednik & Wolfe, Chicago, IL [*Library symbol*] [*Library of Congress*] (LCLS)
ICS	Identifying Criteria for Success [*Software package*] [*Development Dimensions Inc.*]
ICS	Ileocecal Sphincter [*Medicine*] (DMAA)
ICS	Illinois Chiropractic Society (SRA)
ICS	Immotile Cilia Syndrome [*Medicine*] (DMAA)
ICS	Immunochemistry System [*Medicine*]
ICS	Imperial College of Science [*British*]
ICS	Impulse Conducting System [*Physiology*]
ICS	In-Can System [*Device that improves quality of beer and ale*] [*British*]
ICS	Incident Command System [*Regional emergency response system*] (DHSM)
ICS	Indian Civil Service [*British*]
ICS	Induction Communications System
ICS	Industrial Computing Society (DDC)
ICS	Industrial Control System
ICS	Infinity Color-Corrected System [*Optics*]
ICS	Information Calling Services [*Telecommunications*]
ICS	Information Centers Service [*United States Information Agency*] (IID)
ICS	Information Collection System (MHDI)
ICS	Information Computer System (IAA)
ICS	Information Control System [*Military*]
ICS	Infrared Calibration System
ICS	Infrared Camera System
ICS	Infrared Communications System
ICS	Infrared Countermeasures System [*Military Electronics*]
ICS	Injection Compression System
ICS	Inland Computer Service (IEEE)
ICS	Innes Clan Society (EA)
ICS	Input Contactor Switch
ICS	Input Control Subsystem
ICS	Insert Card Section
ICS	Institute for Chemical Studies (GNE)
ICS	Institute for Christian Studies
ICS	Institute for Cognitive Science [*University of California, San Diego*] [*Research center*] (RCD)
ICS	Institute for Computer Sciences (HGAA)
ICS	Institute for Contemporary Studies (EA)
ICS	Institute for Cultural Studies [*Defunct*] (EA)
ICS	Institute for the Comparative Study of History, Philosophy, and the Sciences Ltd. [*British*] (BI)
ICS	Institute of Caribbean Studies (EA)
ICS	Institute of Chartered Shipbrokers [*British*]
ICS	Institute of Child Study [*University of Toronto*] [*Research center*] (RCD)
ICS	Institute of Cognitive Science [*University of Colorado, Boulder*] [*Research center*] (RCD)
ICS	Institute of Commonwealth Studies [*British*]
ICS	Institute of Complementary Sciences [*Defunct*] (EA)
ICS	Institute of Cornish Studies [*British*]
ICS	Institution of Computer Sciences [*British*] (DIT)
ICS	Instructional Communications Systems [*University of Wisconsin*] [*Telecommunications service*] (TSSD)
ICS	Instrumentation and Communication Subsystem [*NASA*] (KSC)
ICS	Instrumentation and Control Subsystem
ICS	Instrumentation Checkout Station (AAG)
ICS	Insurance Communication Service [*IBM Information Network*] [*Tampa, FL*] [*Telecommunications*] (TSSD)
ICS	Integrated Case Study [*Medicine*] (DMAA)
ICS	Integrated Checkout System (KSC)
ICS	Integrated Circuit System (IMH)
ICS	Integrated Collection System [*IRS*]
ICS	Integrated Combat Ship
ICS	Integrated Combat System
ICS	Integrated Command System
ICS	Integrated Communication Systems, Inc. [*Roswell, GA*] [*Telecommunications*] (IEEE)
ICS	Integrated Composite Spinning (PDAA)
ICS	Integrated Computer Solutions
ICS	Integrated Computer Systems [*Culver City, CA*] [*Telecommunications service*] (TSSD)
ICS	Integrated Configuration Summary (AAG)
ICS	Integrated Conning System (PDAA)
ICS	Integrated Control Storage [*Computer science*]
ICS	Integrated Control System (NRCH)
ICS	Intelligence Center and School [*Army*] (RDA)
ICS	Intelligence Community Staff [*Military*] (MCD)
ICS	Intensive Care Society [*British*] (EAIO)
ICS	Intensive Care, Surgical [*Medicine*]
ICS	Interactive Communications Software
ICS	Interactive Compatibility Software [*Gateway Communications, Inc.*] [*Computer science*] (PCM)
ICS	Interactive Counting System (IAA)
ICS	Interagency Communications System [*Military*]
ICS	InterCapital Ins Cal Muni Sec [*NYSE symbol*] (TTSB)
ICS	InterCapital Insured California Municipal Securities [*NYSE symbol*] (SAG)
ICS	Intercarrier Sound (IAA)
ICS	Intercellular Space (DMAA)
ICS	Inter-Celtic Society (EAIO)
ICS	Intercistronic Spacer [*Genetics*]
ICS	Intercockpit Communications System [*Navy*] (DOMA)
ICS	Intercommunication Control Station (KSC)
ICS	Intercommunications System
ICS	Intercontinental Church Society [*British*] (EAIO)
ICS	Intercostal Space [*Medicine*]
ICS	Interface Control Specification (MCD)
ICS	Interference Check Sample [*Spectroscopy*]
ICS	Interim Contractor Support (MCD)
ICS	Interior Contractor Support
ICS	Interlinked Computerized Storage and Processing System of Food and Agricultural Data [*Databank*] [*United Nations Information service or system*]
ICS	Intermittent Control Strategy [*Environmental Protection Agency*] (GFGA)
ICS	Intermittent Control System [*Environmental Protection Agency*]
ICS	Internal Chemical Shift
ICS	Internal Communication System [*Space Flight Operations Facility, NASA*]
ICS	Internal Countermeasures Set (MCD)
ICS	International Camellia Society [*Worcester, England*] (EAIO)
ICS	International Cardiovascular Society
ICS	International Catacomb Society (EA)
ICS	International Chamber of Shipping [*British*] (EAIO)
ICS	International Chemical Society [*Proposed*]
ICS	International Chemometrics Society [*Brussels, Belgium*] (EAIO)
ICS	International Chili Society (EA)
ICS	International Churchill Society (EA)
ICS	International Clarinet Society [*Later, ICS/CI*] (EA)
ICS	International Code of Signals (IAA)
ICS	International Cogeneration Society (EA)
ICS	International Cold Storage
ICS	International College of Scientists [*See also ISK*] [*International Academy of Sciences*] [*Paderborn, Federal Republic of Germany*] (EAIO)
ICS	International College of Surgeons (EA)
ICS	International Committee of Slavists [*Sofia, Bulgaria*] (EAIO)
ICS	International Committee on Sarcoidosis [*British*] (EAIO)
ICS	International Communications Sciences
ICS	International Communications System
ICS	International Computer System (IAA)
ICS	International Connecting Set (IAA)
ICS	International Conrad Society (EA)
ICS	International Controlled Industry [*Vancouver Stock Exchange symbol*]
ICS	International Coronelli Society [*See also ICGGI*] (EAIO)
ICS	International Correspondence School
ICS	International Craniopathic Society [*SORSI*] [*Absorbed by*] (EA)
ICS	International Crocodilian Society [*Defunct*] (EA)
ICS	Internet Connection Sharing
ICS	Interphone Control Station
ICS	Interphone Control System
ICS	Interpretive Computer Simulator
ICS	Interpretive Computer System
ICS	Interviewer Card Scheme [*Business term*]
ICS	Intracapillary Space [*In bioreactor*]
ICS	Intracellular-Like Solution [*Cardioplegic solution*] [*Pharmacology*] (DAVI)
ICS	Intracommunication System
ICS	Intracranial Self-Stimulation [*Also, ICSS*] [*Neurophysiology*]
ICS	Intracranial Stimulation [*Neurophysiology*]
ICS	Inventory Control System [*Computer science*]
ICS	Inverse Conical Scan (DNAB)
ICS	Ion-Channel Switch [*Biochemistry*]
ICS	Ionization Current Source (PDAA)
ICS	Iowa Chiropractic Society (SRA)
ICS	Irish Computer Society
ICS	Iron Castings Society (EA)
ICS	Irritable Colon Syndrome [*Medicine*] (DMAA)
ICS	Isolation Containment Spray [*Nuclear energy*] (IEEE)
ICS	Issued Capital Stock
ICS	Saint Xavier College, Chicago, IL [*OCLC symbol*] (OCLC)
ICS	Society of Inter-Celtic Arts and Culture (EA)
ICS2	Intelligent Communication Subsystem Two Board [*Controls input from computer terminals to mainframe*] [*Prime Computer, Inc.*]
ICSA	In-Core Shim Assembly [*Nuclear energy*] (NRCH)
ICSA	Indian Council of South America [*See also CISA*] [*Lima, Peru*] (EAIO)
ICSA	Information and Computing Services Association (ACII)
ICSA	Institute of Chartered Secretaries and Administrators (AIE)
ICSA	International Cemetery Supply Association (EA)
ICSA	International Chain Salon Association (EA)
ICSA	International Christian Studies Association (EA)
ICSA	International Claims Settlement Act of 1949
ICSA	International Committee Against Apartheid, Racism, and Colonialism in Southern Africa [*British Defunct*] (EAIO)
ICSA	International Computer Security Association
ICSA	International Correspondence Society of Allergists (EA)
ICSA	International Correspondence Society of Allergists and Clinical Immunologists [*Formerly, International Correspondence Society of Allergists*] (EA)
ICSA	International Customer Service Association [*Chicago, IL*] (EA)
ICSA	Intracranial Self-Administration [*Neurophysiology*]
ICSA	Islet Cell Surface Antibody [*Immunology*]

ICSA............ Sidley and Austin Library, Chicago, IL [*Library symbol Library of Congress*] (LCLS)

ICSAB .... International Civil Service Advisory Board

ICSAC .... International Confederation of Societies of Authors and Composers

ICSAC .... International Council of Regional School Accrediting Commissions (NTPA)

ICSac .... Sachnoff Weaver & Rubenstein, Chicago, Il [*Library symbol*] [*Library of Congress*] (LCLS)

ICSAF.......... International Commission for the Southeast Atlantic Fisheries [*See also CIPASE*] (EAIO)

ICSAL.......... Integrated Communications System, Alaska [*Air Force, FAA*]

ICSAPI .... Internet Connection Services [*Computer science*] (PCM)

ICSAR .... Interagency Committee on Search and Rescue (COE)

ICSB............ Interim Command Switchboard [*Navy*] (NVT)

ICSB............ International Committee on Systematic Bacteriology [*London, ON*] (EA)

ICSB............ International Council for Small Business (EA)

ICSBC .... Interstate Council of State Boards of Cosmetology [*Later, NIC*]

ICSBS .... International Chinese Snuff Bottle Society (EA)

ICSC............ Institute for Cardiovascular Studies [*University of Houston*] [*Research center*] (RCD)

ICSC............ Integrated Command Support Center [*Military*] (MCD)

ICSC............ Interim Commission on Satellite Communication (NITA)

ICSC............ Interim Communications Satellite Committee

ICSC............ Interior Communication Switching Center (DNAB)

ICSC............ International Chemical Safety Card

ICSC............ International Civil Service Commission (EA)

ICSC............ International Commission for Supervision and Control [*Composed of delegates from Canada, India and Poland established by the 1954 Geneva Accords*] (VNW)

ICSC............ International Communications Satellite Consortium (MCD)

ICSC............ International Communications Systems Consultants [*British*] (NITA)

ICSC............ International Council of Shopping Centers (EA)

ICSC............ International Council of Shopping Centres [*Australia*]

ICSC............ Inter-Ocean Canal Study Commission (PDAA)

ICSC............ Irish Christian Study Centre [*New University of Ulster*] [*British*] (CB)

ICSC............ Irvine Computer Sciences Corporation (NITA)

ICSC............ Italy and Colonies Study Circle (EA)

ICSC............ Swift & Company, Research Laboratory Library, Chicago, IL [*Library symbol Library of Congress*] (LCLS)

ICSCA .... Institute for Computing Science and Computer Applications [*University of Texas at Austin*] [*Research center*] (RCD)

ICSch .... Schiff, Harden & Waite, Chicago, IL [*Library symbol*] [*Library of Congress*] (LCLS)

ICS/CI .... International Clarinet Society/Clarinetwork International (EA)

ICSCN .... Sonnenschein, Carlin, Nath & Rosenthal, Chicago, IL [*Library symbol*] [*Library of Congress*] (LCLS)

ICSD .... Inorganic Crystal Structure Database [*University of Bonn*] [*Germany*]

ICSD .... Ionization Chamber Smoke Detector [*Nuclear energy*] (NRCH)

ICSD .... Metropolitan Sanitary District of Greater Chicago, Chicago, IL [*Library symbol Library of Congress*] (LCLS)

ICS/DMC ...... Institute for Continuing Studies in Design, Management and Communication [*University of Cincinnati*] [*Research center*] (RCD)

ICSDV .... Ice-Cutter Semi-Submersible Drilling Vessel (PDAA)

ICSDW .... International Council of Social Democratic Women [*Later, SIW*] (EA)

ICSE............ Interdepartmental Committee on Software Engineering [*British*]

ICSE............ Intermediate Current Stability Experiment (DEN)

ICSEAF........ International Commission for the Southeast Atlantic Fisheries

ICSears........ Sears, Roebuck & Co., Chicago, IL [*Library symbol Library of Congress*] (LCLS)

ICSEES......... International Committee for Soviet and East European Studies (EAIO)

ICSEM.......... International Center of Studies on Early Music

ICSEM.......... International Commission for the Scientific Exploration of the Mediterranean Sea (EAIO)

ICSEMS........ International Commission for the Scientific Exploration of the Mediterranean Sea (NOAA)

ICSEP.......... International Center for the Solution of Environmental Problems (EA)

ICSEP.......... International Council of Sex Education and Parenthood (EA)

ICSey .... Seyfarth, Shaw, Fairweather & Geraldson, Chicago, IL [*Library symbol Library of Congress*] (LCLS)

ICSF............ International Collegiate Sports Foundation (EA)

ICSG .... International Center for Social Gerontology [*Later, TCSG*] [*Defunct*] (EA)

ICSH .... International Committee for Standardization in Haematology [*Louvain, Belgium*] [*Research center*] (EAIO)

ICSH .... Interstitial Cell Stimulating Hormone [*Also, LH, LSH*] [*Endocrinology*]

ICSHB .... International Committee for Standardization in Human Biology

ICSI............ Institut Canadien de la Sante Infantile [*Canadian Institute of Child Health*]

ICSI............ Institute for Clinical Systems Integration (DMAA)

ICSI............ International Commission on Snow and Ice

ICSI............ International Conference on Scientific Information

ICSI............ International Container System (EFIS)

ICSI............ Intracytoplasmic Sperm Injection [*In vitro fertilization*]

ICSID .... International Centre for Settlement of Investment Disputes (EA)

ICSID .... International Council of Societies of Industrial Design [*Helsinki, Finland*] (EA)

ICSISP .... International Center for Science Information Services in Phytovirology

ICSK............ International Cultural Society of Korea [*Seoul, Republic of Korea*] (EAIO)

ICSK............ Intracoronary Streptokinase [*An enzyme*]

ICSL............ Inner-City Simulation Laboratory [*Teacher training game*]

ICSL............ Inns of Court School of Law [*British*] (DI)

ICSL............ Interactive Computer Systems Ltd. (NITA)

ICSL............ Interactive Continuous Simulation Language [*Computer science*] (PDAA)

ICSL............ Intercollegiate Swimming League (PSS)

ICSL............ Presbyterian Saint Luke's Hospital, Chicago, IL [*Library symbol Library of Congress*] (LCLS)

ICSLS .... International Convention for Safety of Life at Sea (BARN)

ICSM............ Instant Corn-Soya-Milk

ICSM............ International Confederation of Societies of Music (EA)

ICSMM......... International Conference on Superlattices, Microstructures, and Microdevices

ICSMP .... Integrated Command System Management Plan [*Military*] (DNAB)

ICSMP .... Interactive Continuous Systems Modeling Program

ICSMS .... Integrated Conventional Stores Management System [*DoD*] (DWSG)

ICSN............ Chicago Sun-Times and Chicago Daily News, Chicago, IL [*Library symbol Library of Congress*] (LCLS)

ICSOBA........ International Congress on Bauxite-Alumina-Aluminium (PDAA)

ICSOG .... International Correspondence Society of Obstetricians and Gynecologists (EA)

ICSOM .... International Conference of Symphony and Opera Musicians (EA)

ICSon........... Sonicraft, Inc., Chicago, IL [*Library symbol Library of Congress*] (LCLS)

ICSP............ Illinois State Psychiatric Institute, Chicago, IL [*Library symbol Library of Congress*] (LCLS)

ICSP............ In Commission, Special [*Vessel status*] [*Navy*] (DNAB)

ICSP............ Interim Contractor Support Plan

ICSP............ International Council of Societies of Pathology (EA)

ICSPE.......... International Council of Sport and Physical Education

ICSPFT........ International Committee on the Standardization of Physical Fitness Tests

ICSPM .... Dr. William M. Scholl College of Podiatric Medicine, Chicago, IL [*Library symbol*] [*Library of Congress*] (LCLS)

ICSPP .... Interstate Compact for Supervision of Parolees and Probationers [*Public human service program*] (PHSD)

ICSPRDC...... International Committee on Social Psychological Research in Developing Countries (EA)

ICSPRO......... Inter-Secretariat Committee on Scientific Problems Relating to Oceanography [*United Nations*]

ICS/R .... Individual Soldier's Computer/Radio [*Military*]

ICSR .... Interuniversity Centre for the Study of Religion [*Canada*]

ICSR .... Scottish Rite of Freemasonry Library, Chicago, IL [*Library symbol Library of Congress*] (LCLS)

ICSRE .... International Centre for Studies in Religious Education [*Brussels, Belgium*] (EA)

ICSRI .... Intelligent Computer Systems Research Institute [*University of Miami*] [*Research center*] (RCD)

ICSRI .... Interfaith Committee on Social Responsibility in Investments [*Later, ICCR*] (EA)

ICSS............ International Commission on Signs and Symbols

ICSS............ International Committee for the Sociology of Sport

ICSS............ International Conference on Solid Surfaces

ICSS............ International Council for the Social Studies (DIT)

ICSS............ Inter-University Committee on the Superior Student [*Defunct*] (EA)

ICSS............ Intracranial Self-Stimulation [*Also, ICS*] [*Neurophysiology*]

ICSSD .... International Committee for Social Science Information and Documentation [*Information service or system*] (IID)

ICSSD .... International Committee for Social Sciences Documentation and Information (NITA)

ICSSEA .... Integrated Communications System South-East Asia [*Australia*]

ICSSID .... International Committee for Social Science Information and Documentation [*Paris, France Information service or system*] (IID)

ICSSPE .... International Council of Sport Science and Physical Education (EA)

ICSST.......... Institute of Child Study Security Test [*Psychology*]

ICSST.......... International Conference on Solid State Transducers (EA)

ICSSVM ...... International Commission for Small Scale Vegetation Maps [*Pondicherry, India*] (EAIO)

ICST............ Imperial College of Science and Technology (PDAA)

ICST............ Institute for Chemical Science and Technology [*Canada*]

ICST............ Institute [*formerly, Center*] for Computer Sciences and Technology [*Gaithersburg, MD*] [*NIST*]

ICST............ Institution of Corrosion Science and Technology (PDAA)

ICST............ Integrated Circuit Sys [*NASDAQ symbol*] (TTSB)

ICST............ Integrated Circuit Systems [*NASDAQ symbol*] (SPSG)

ICST............ Integrated Combined System Test

ICST............ International Concept Study Team [*for bridges*] [*US, Great Britain, Germany*] (RDA)

ICSTF .... Integrated Combat Systems Test Facility (NVT)

ICSTI .... International Center for Scientific and Technical Information [*Moscow, USSR*] (EAIO)

ICSTI .... International Council for Scientific and Technical Information [*Information service or system*] (IID)

ICStJ.......... St. Joseph Hospital, Chicago, IL [*Library symbol*] [*Library of Congress*] (LCLS)

ICSTK .... Intracoronary Streptokinase [*An enzyme*]

ICSTND........ Information Center of Science and Technology for National Defense [*Chinese library*]

ICSTO .... International Civil Service Training Organization

ICSU .... Chicago State University, Chicago, IL [*Library symbol Library of Congress*] (LCLS)

ICSU .... Independent Canadian Steelworkers' Union

ICSU .... Intelligent Channel Service Unit (CIST)

ICSU .... International Council of Scientific Unions [*Research center France*]

ICSU AB....... International Council of Scientific Unions Abstracting Board [*Also, IAB*] [*Later, ICSTI*] (EA)

ICSU-CTS ..... Committee on the Teaching of Science of the International Council of Scientific Unions [*York, England*] (EAIO)
ICSW .... Interdepartmental Committee on the Status of Women [*Terminated, 1978*]
ICSW .... International Committee on Seafarer's Welfare Office (EAIO)
ICSW .... International Conference of Social Work
ICSW .... International Council on Social Welfare (EA)
ICSW .... Sherwin Williams Chemicals, Chicago, IL [*Library symbol Library of Congress*] (LCLS)
ICSWBD ...... Interior Communications Switchboard
ICSWSA .... International Chain Saw Wood Sculptors Association (EA)
ICSX .... Saint Xavier College, Chicago, IL [*Library symbol Library of Congress*] (LCLS)
ICT .... Chicago Theological Seminary, Chicago, IL [*Library symbol Library of Congress*] (LCLS)
ICT .... Icterus [*Jaundice*] [*Medicine*]
ICT .... Ideal Cycle Time (AAEL)
ICT .... Iesu Christo Tutore [*With Jesus Christ as Protector*] [*Latin*]
ICT .... Igniter Circuit Test (IAA)
IC/T .... Image Compression/Transmission
ICT .... Image Converter Tube
ICT .... Image Creation Terminal (NITA)
ICT .... Immunoreactive Calcitonin [*Endocrinology*]
ICT .... In Circuit Test [*Electronics*] (EECA)
ICT .... Incoming Trunk [*Telecommunications*] (BUR)
ICT .... Indirect Coombs' Test [*Immunochemistry*]
ICT .... Indirect Coulometric Titration [*Analytical chemistry*]
ICT .... Individual Collective Training [*Army*]
ICT .... Inflammation of Connective Tissue [*Medicine*]
ICT .... Influence Coefficient Tests (MCD)
ICT .... Information and Communication Technology
ICT .... Insect Carrier Toxicant
ICT .... Inspection Check Template (MSA)
ICT .... Inspection Control Test (SAA)
ICT .... Institut Canadien des Textiles [*Canadian Textiles Institute*] (EAIO)
ICT .... Institute of Circuit Technology [*Oxford, England*] [*Defunct*] (EAIO)
ICT .... Institute of Circuit Technology Ltd. (NITA)
ICT .... Institute of Clay Technology [*British*]
ICT .... Institute of Computer Technology
ICT .... Institute of Concrete Technology [*British*]
ICT .... Institution of Corrosion Technology (PDAA)
ICT .... Insulated [*or Insulating*] Core Transformer
ICT .... Insulin Coma Therapy [*Medicine*]
ICT .... Insulin Convulsive Therapy [*Medicine*] (MAH)
ICT .... Integrated Circuit Tester
ICT .... Integrated Computer Telemetry
ICT .... Integrated Concept Team [*Army*] (INF)
ICT .... Intelligence Cycle Time (MCD)
ICT .... Intensive Conventional Therapy [*Medicine*] (DAVI)
ICT .... Interaction Control Table [*Computer science*] (OA)
ICT .... Interactive Command Test [*Computer science*]
ICT .... Inter Cable Communications, Inc. [*Toronto Stock Exchange symbol*]
ICT .... Interchangeability Control Tool (MCD)
ICT .... Interchangeability Test (MCD)
ICT .... Intercontinental de Aviacion Ltd. [*Colombia*] [*ICAO designator*] (FAAC)
ICT .... Interface Control Tooling (NASA)
ICT .... Interference Compliance Test (SAA)
ICT .... Intermittent Cervical Traction [*Orthopedics*] (DAVI)
ICT .... Internal COMPOOL [*Communications Pool*] Table (SAA)
ICT .... International Call for Tenders (NATG)
ICT .... International Campaign for Tibet (EA)
ICT .... International Circuit Technology [*Electronics*] (IAA)
ICT .... International CMOS Technology [*Computer science*]
ICT .... International Commission on Trichinellosis (EA)
ICT .... International Computers and Tabulators Ltd. [*Later, ICL*]
ICT .... International Council of Tanners [*See also CIT*] [*Lewes, East Sussex, England*] (EAIO)
ICT .... International Critical Tables
ICT .... Intracardiac Thrombus [*Medicine*] (DB)
ICT .... Intradermal Cancer Test [*Oncology*]
ICT .... Intramolecular Charge Transfer [*Physical chemistry*]
ICT .... Irrigated, Conventionally Tilled [*Agriculture*]
ICT .... Isometric Contraction Time [*Medicine*] (DAVI)
ICT .... Isovolumic Contraction Time [*Cardiology*]
ICT .... Trinity College, Deerfield, IL [*OCLC symbol*] (OCLC)
ICT .... Wichita [*Kansas*] [*Airport symbol*] (OAG)
ICTA .... Chicago Transit Authority, Chicago, IL [*Library symbol Library of Congress*] (LCLS)
ICTA .... Industry Council for Tangible Assets [*Washington, DC*] (EA)
ICTA .... Institute of Certified Travel Agents (EA)
ICTA .... International Center for the Typographic Arts
ICTA .... International Centre for Technology Assessment
ICTA .... International Computer Training Association (PCM)
ICTA .... International Confederation for Thermal Analysis [*Jerusalem, Israel*] (EA)
ICTAA .... Imperial College of Tropical Agriculture Association [*British*] (BI)
ICTAB .... Institut Canadien de Tole d'Acier en Batiment [*Canadian Sheet Steel Building Institute*]
ICTAM .... International Congress of Theoretical and Applied Mechanics (PDAA)
ICTASD .... International Convention on Transistors and Semiconductor Devices
ICTB .... International Companies and Their Brands [*A publication*]
ICTB .... International Customs Tariffs Bureau (DLA)
ICTBA .... Infants', Children's, and Teens' Wear Buyers Association (EA)
ICTC .... Inertial Components Temperature Controller (KSC)
ICTC .... International Cooperative Training Center
ICTCD .... Insecticide (MSA)
ICTD .... Individual and Collective Training Development (MCD)
ICTD .... Inter-Channel Time Displacement
ICTE .... Inertial Component Test Equipment
ICTED .... International Cooperation in the Field of Transport Economics Documentation [*European Conference of Ministers of Transport*] [*Information service or system*] (IID)
ICTF .... Interagency Crisis Task Force
ICTF .... International Cocoa Trades Federation [*British*]
ICTF .... International Commission on the Taxonomy of Fungi
ICTF .... International Conference on Thin Films (PDAA)
ICTG .... ICT Group, Inc. [*NASDAQ symbol*] (SAG)
ICT Grp .... ICT Group, Inc. [*Associated Press*] (SAG)
ICTH .... International Commission for the Teaching of History [*Brussels, Belgium*] (EA)
ICTH .... International Committee on Thrombosis and Hemostasis
ICTI .... International Committee of Toy Industries (EA)
ict ind .... Icterus Index [*Liver function test*] [*Medicine*] (AAMN)
ICTL .... Image Control Table (MCD)
ICTL .... Industrial Control (IAA)
ICTL .... International Cabletel, Inc. [*NASDAQ symbol*] (SAG)
ICTL .... Intl Cabletel [*NASDAQ symbol*] (TTSB)
ICTM .... International Coal Trade Model [*Department of Energy*] (GFGA)
ICTM .... International Council for Traditional Music (EA)
ICTME .... International Conference on Tribo-Terotechnology and Maintenance Engineering (PDAA)
ICTMM .... International Congresses on Tropical Medicine and Malaria
ICTN .... Industry Center for Trade Negotiations [*Defunct*]
ICTOC .... Independent Corps Tactical Operations Center
ICTP .... Individual/Collective Training Plan [*Army*]
ICTP .... Institute for Certification of Tax Professionals (EA)
ICTP .... Intensified Combat Training Program
ICTP .... International Center for Theoretical Physics [*Trieste, Italy*] (EA)
ICTPDC .... Imperial College Thermophysical Properties Data Centre [*British*] (CB)
ICTR .... Institut Canadien de Recherches en Telecommunications (AC)
ICTR .... Institute of Commercial and Technical Representatives Ltd. [*British*] (BI)
ICTR .... International Center of Theatre Research (EA)
ICTr .... Truman College, Chicago, IL [*Library symbol Library of Congress*] (LCLS)
ICTRM .... Interagency Committee on the Transportation of Radioactive Materials
ICTRTQM ..... Institute for Control Theory, Reality Therapy and Quality Management (EA)
ICTS .... Idiopathic Carpal Tunnel Syndrome [*Medicine*] (DMAA)
ICTS .... In-Car Temperature Sensor [*Automotive engineering*]
ICTS .... Integrated Circuit Test Set
ICTS .... Integrated Computerized Test Set
ICTS .... Intermediate Capacity Transit System
ICTS .... International Catholic Truth Society (EA)
ICTS .... International Congress of the Transplantation Society
ICTSI .... International Container Terminal Services, Inc. [*Philippines*] [*Commercial firm*]
ICTT .... Intensified Confirmatory Troop Test (AABC)
ICTU .... Catholic Theological Union, Chicago, IL [*Library symbol Library of Congress*] (LCLS)
ICTU .... Independent Canadian Transit Union
ICTU .... Iraqi Confederation of Trade Unions
ICTU .... Irish Congress of Trade Unions
ICTV .... Interactive Cable Television
ICTV .... International Committee on Taxonomy of Viruses [*ICSU*] [*Rennes, France*] (EAIO)
ICTV .... Intracerebroventricular [*Also, ic, ICV*] [*Brain anatomy*]
ICtvS .... Shawnee Library System, Carterville, IL [*Library symbol Library of Congress*] (LCLS)
ICTX .... Intermittent Cervical Traction [*Medicine*] (DMAA)
ICTY .... International Criminal Tribunal for the Former Yugoslavia
ICTZ .... I Corps Tactical Zone [*Vietnamese designation for both a military zone and a political region*]
ICU .... ICG Utility Investments Ltd. [*Toronto Stock Exchange symbol*]
ICU .... Immunologic Contact Urticaria [*Medicine*] (DMAA)
ICU .... Indicator Control Unit
ICU .... Industrial Control Unit (IAA)
ICU .... Industry Capacity Utilization [*Engineering economics*]
ICU .... Infant Care Unit [*Medicine*] (DMAA)
ICU .... InfoColor Conversion Unit (DGA)
ICU .... Informatie en Communicatie Unie [*Information and Communication United*] [*Dutch publishing house*]
ICU .... Infrared Command Unit
ICU .... Institut d'Urbanisme du Canada [*Town Planning Institute of Canada*]
ICU .... Instruction Cache Unit [*Computer science*]
ICU .... Instruction Control Unit
ICU .... Intelligent Connector Unit [*Telecommunications*] (TSSD)
ICU .... Intensive-Care Unit [*of a hospital*]
ICU .... Intensive Caring Unlimited [*An association*] (EA)
ICU .... Interactive Chart Utility [*IBM Corp.*]
ICU .... Interconnection Unit [*Computer science*]
ICU .... Interface Control Unit [*Army*]
ICU .... Intermediate Care Unit [*of a hospital*]
ICU .... International Chick Unit (DB)
ICU .... International Christian University [*Tokyo*]
ICU .... International Christian University Library [*UTLAS symbol*]
ICU .... International Code Use (BARN)

ICU............ International [*or Internal*] Communication Unit [*Telecommunications*] (TEL)
ICU............ International Cycling Union (EA)
ICU............ Interrupt Control Unit [*Computer science*] (IAA)
ICU............ Texas Christian University, Fort Worth, TX [*OCLC symbol*] (OCLC)
ICU............ University of Chicago, Chicago, IL [*Library symbol Library of Congress*] (LCLS)
ICUA .... Institute for College and University Administrators [*Later, CPAA*] (EA)
ICUA .... Interdenominational Church Ushers Association
ICUAE .... International Congress of University Adult Education [*Fredericton, NB*] (EAIO)
ICUAER .... International Committee on Urgent Anthropological and Ethnological Research [*Vienna, Austria*] (EAIO)
ICUC .... Union Carbide Corp., Film-Packaging Division, Chicago, IL [*Library symbol Library of Congress*] (LCLS)
ICUD .... Index to Current Urban Documents [*Information service or system*] (IID)
ICU-D.......... University of Chicago, Divinity School, Chicago, IL [*Library symbol Library of Congress*] (LCLS)
ICUE........... International Committee on the University Emergency (EA)
ICUEPR .... International Conference on University Education for Public Relations
ICU-FE .... University of Chicago, Far Eastern Library, Chicago, IL [*Library symbol Library of Congress*] (LCLS)
ICUFON....... Intercontinental UFO Galactic Spacecraft Research and Analytic Network (EA)
ICUFR .... International Council on United Fund Raising (EA)
ICUG .... United States Gypsum Co., Chicago, IL [*Library symbol*] [*Library of Congress*] (LCLS)
ICUGA......... International Computer Users Groups Association [*Defunct*] (EA)
ICU-H.......... University of Chicago, Center for Health Administration Studies, Chicago, IL [*Library symbol Library of Congress*] (LCLS)
ICUI .... ICU Medical [*NASDAQ symbol*] (TTSB)
ICUI .... ICU Medical, Inc. [*NASDAQ symbol*] (SAG)
ICUIS .... Institute on the Church in Urban-Industrial Society [*Defunct*]
ICU-L .... University of Chicago, Law Library, Chicago, IL [*Library symbol Library of Congress*] (LCLS)
ICU-LS .... University of Chicago, Graduate Library School, Chicago, IL [*Library symbol Library of Congress*] (LCLS)
ICU-M .... University of Chicago, Bio-Medical Libraries, Chicago, IL [*Library symbol Library of Congress*] (LCLS)
ICU Med ..... ICU Medical, Inc. [*Associated Press*] (SAG)
ICUMSA .... International Commission for Uniform Methods of Sugar Analysis [*Mackay, QLD, Australia*] (EAIO)
ICUnC .... University Club of Chicago, Chicago, IL [*Library symbol Library of Congress*] (LCLS)
ICUnW .... United Way of Metropolitan Chicago, Chicago, IL [*Library symbol Library of Congress*] (LCLS)
ICUP .... Individual Circuit Usage and Peg Count [*Telecommunications*] (TEL)
ICUP .... International Catholic Union of the Press (EA)
ICUPLANT.... Instructor's Computer Utility Programming Language for Interactive Teaching (IAA)
ICURR......... Intergovernmental Committee on Urban and Regional Research [*Canada*]
ICUS .... Inside Continental United States [*Military*]
ICUS .... International Committee on Urgent Surgery [*Milan, Italy*] (EAIO)
ICUS .... International Conference on the Unity of the Sciences
ICUSA .... International Christians for Unity in Social Action (EA)
ICUSQ .... United States Quartermaster Corps, Food and Container Institute [*for the Armed Forces*], Chicago, IL [*Library symbol Library of Congress*] (LCLS)
ICUT........... Independent Colleges and Universities of Texas (SRA)
ICUT........... Initial COHORT [*Cohesion, Operational Readiness Training*] Unit Training [*Military*] (GFGA)
ICUT........... International Cutlery Ltd. [*NASDAQ symbol*] (SAG)
ICUT........... Intl Cutlery [*NASDAQ symbol*] (TTSB)
ICUTO .... International Conference of University Teacher Organizations
ICUTW........ Intl Cutlery Wrrt'A' [*NASDAQ symbol*] (TTSB)
ICUTZ......... Intl Cutlery Wrrt'B' [*NASDAQ symbol*] (TTSB)
ICU-Y .... University of Chicago, Yerkes Observatory, Williams Bay, WI [*Library symbol Library of Congress*] (LCLS)
ICUZ........... Integrated Compatible Use Zone [*Army*] (RDA)
ICV............. Elmhurst College, Elmhurst, IL [*OCLC symbol*] (OCLC)
ICV............. Ice-Cream Van [*Slang British*]
ICV............. Improved Capital Value [*Business term*] (ADA)
ICV............. Individual Cell Voltmeter (DNAB)
ICV............. Individually Controlled Ventilation
ICV............. Indoor Cricket Victoria [*Australia An association*]
ICV............. Infantry Combat Vehicle (MCD)
ICV............. Initial Calibration Verification
ICV............. Initial Chaining Value [*Computer science*]
ICV............. Inter-Center Vector (MCD)
ICV............. Interdecadal Climate Variability [*Marine science*] (OSRA)
ICV............. Internal Correction Voltage
ICV............. Interphase Chromosome Volume
ICV............. Intracellular Virus [*Medicine*] (PDAA)
ICV............. Intracerebroventricular [*Also, ic, ICTV*] [*Brain anatomy*]
ICV............. United States Veterans Administration, West Side Hospital, Chicago, IL [*Library symbol Library of Congress*] (LCLS)
ICVA........... International Council of Voluntary Agencies (GNE)
ICVAN......... International Committee on Veterinary Anatomical Nomenclature [*See also CINAV*] [*Zurich, Switzerland*] (EAIO)
ICVC........... VanderCook College of Music, Chicago, IL [*Library symbol Library of Congress*] (LCLS)
ICVD .... Inns of Court Volunteer Decoration [*Military British*] (ROG)
ICVD .... Isotopic Chemical Vapor Deposition (PDAA)

ICVF........... Inner-City Ventures Fund [*National Trust for Historical Preservation*]
ICVGAN....... International Committee on Veterinary Gross Anatomical Nomenclature [*Cornell University*] [*Ithaca, NY*] (EY)
ICVH .... Ischemic Cerebrovascular Headache [*Medicine*] (DAVI)
ICVI........... Isothermal Chemical Vapor Infiltration [*Materials science*]
ICVNA .... Visiting Nurses Association, Chicago, IL [*Library symbol Library of Congress*] (LCLS)
ICvR........... River Bend Library System, Coal Valley, IL [*Library symbol Library of Congress*] (LCLS)
ICVS........... International Cardiovascular Society (EA)
ICVS........... International Society for Cardiovascular Surgery (EA)
ICVT........... Intracerebroventricular [*Medicine*] (DB)
ICw............ Crestwood Library District, Crestwood, IL [*Library symbol Library of Congress*] (LCLS)
ICW............ In Compliance With (MUGU)
ICW............ In Conjunction With (AAGC)
ICW............ In Connection With
ICW............ India-China Wing [*World War II*]
ICW............ Initial Condition Word [*Computer science*]
ICW............ Input Command Word
ICW............ Input Control Word [*Computer science*] (MCD)
ICW............ Institute of Clay Workers [*British*] (BI)
ICW............ Institute of Clerks of Work (PDAA)
ICW............ Intake Cooling Water (IEEE)
ICW............ Interactive Courseware [*Air Force*]
ICW............ Inter-American Commission of Women [*OAS*]
ICW............ Interblock Communication Word (IAA)
ICW............ Intercoastal Waterway
ICW............ Interface Control Word [*Computer science*]
ICW............ International Chemical Workers Union
ICW............ International Council of Women [*France*]
ICW............ Internet Connection Wizard [*Computer science*]
ICW............ Interrupted Continuous Wave [*Electronics*]
icw............ Interrupted Continuous Wave (NAKS)
ICW............ Intracellular Water [*Physiology*]
ICW............ Intracoastal Waterway
ICW............ Western Society of Engineers, Chicago, IL [*Library symbol Library of Congress*] (LCLS)
ICW............ Wheaton College, Wheaton, IL [*OCLC symbol*] (OCLC)
ICWA .... Indian Child Welfare Act [*1978*]
ICWA .... Institute of Cost and Works Accountants [*British*] (BI)
ICWA .... Institute of Current World Affairs (EA)
ICWA .... International Carwash Association
ICWA .... International Coil Winding Association (EA)
ICWAR .... Improved Continuous-Wave Acquisition RADAR [*Army*] (AABC)
ICWB .... Intermediate Cold-Wet Boot [*Military*] (INF)
ICWB .... World Book-Childcraft International, Inc., Chicago, IL [*Library symbol Library of Congress*] (LCLS)
ICWC .... Wilbur Wright Community College, Chicago, IL [*Library symbol Library of Congress*] (LCLS)
ICWD .... Interface Control/Weapon Delivery
ICWDP........ International Committee for World Day of Prayer (EA)
ICWeH .... Louis A. Weiss Memorial Hospital, Chicago, IL [*Library symbol Library of Congress*] (LCLS)
ICWES .... International Conference of Women Engineers and Scientists
ICWF........... Interactive Computer Worded Forecast [*Marine science*] (OSRA)
ICWF........... International Christian Women's Fellowship (EA)
ICWG .... Interface Control Working Group [*NASA*] (KSC)
ICWG .... International Clubroot Working Group (EAIO)
ICWG .... International Co-operative Women's Guild
ICWG .... International Coordination Working Group [*Marine science*] (OSRA)
ICWGA........ Interface Control Working Group Action [*NASA*] (KSC)
ICWHA .... Wildman, Harrold, Allen & Dixon, Chicago, IL [*Library symbol*] [*Library of Congress*] (LCLS)
ICWI .... International Car Wash Institute (EA)
ICwL .... Crestwood Library District, Crestwood, IL [*Library symbol*] [*Library of Congress*] (LCLS)
ICWL .... International Creative Writers League (EA)
ICWM.......... Institute for Chemical Waste Management (GNE)
ICWM.......... Interdepartmental Committee on Weather Modification [*Military*]
ICWM.......... International Committee on Weights and Measures
ICWM.......... International Congress on Women in Music [*Defunct*] (EA)
ICWMA .... International Country and Western Music Association (EA)
ICWO .... Indications Center Watch Officer [*Military*] (MCD)
ICWO .... Intercomponent Work Order
ICWORR ...... International Conference on Waste Oil Recovery and Reuse
ICWP .... International Council of Women Psychologists [*Later, ICP*]
ICWP .... Interstate Conference on Water Policy (EA)
ICWR .... Interagency Committee on Water Resources
ICWS .... Improved Commander's Weapon Station
ICWS .... Institute of Civil War Studies (EA)
ICWS .... Winston & Strawn, Chicago, IL [*Library symbol Library of Congress*] (LCLS)
ICWSG .... Infants' and Children's Wear Salesmen's Guild (EA)
ICWT.......... Inter-Component Work Transmitted (MCD)
ICWT.......... Interrupted Continuous Wave Telegraphy (IAA)
ICWU .... International Chemical Workers Union (EA)
ICWWP .... Interagency Committee for World Weather Programs [*Department of Commerce*] (NOAA)
ICX............. Immune Complex (STED)
ICX............. Inferior Colliculus
ICX............. International Charter Xpress Limited Liability Co. [*ICAO designator*] (FAAC)
ICX............. International Computer Exchange (IAA)
ICX............. International Cultural Exchange

ICX............	Internet College Exchange [*Database*] [*Computer science*]
ICX............	Lewis University, Lockport, IL [*OCLC symbol*] (OCLC)
ICY............	Augustana College, Rock Island, IL [*OCLC symbol*] (OCLC)
ICY............	Instruction Cycle [*Computer science*] (IAA)
ICY............	International Christian Youth (EA)
ICY............	International Commission on Yeasts and Yeast-Like Microorganisms [*ICSU*] [*France*] (EAIO)
ICY............	International Cooperation Year [*1965*] [*20th anniversary of UN*]
I-cycle........	Instruction Cycle (NITA)
ICYE..........	International Christian Youth Exchange (EA)
ICYF..........	Institute for Children, Youth, and Families [*Michigan State University*] [*Research center*] (RCD)
ICYF..........	International Catholic Youth Federation [*Later, WFCY*]
ICYO..........	International Committee of Youth Organizations (EAIO)
ICYP..........	Iodocyanopindolol [*Biochemistry*]
ICYRA.........	Inter-Collegiate Yacht Racing Association [*of North America*] [*Later, ICYRA/NA*]
ICYRA/NA	Inter-Collegiate Yacht Racing Association of North America (EA)
ICYT..........	Instituto de Informacion y Documentacion en Ciencia y Tecnologia [*Institute for Information and Documentation in Science and Technology*] [*Database originator and host*] [*Information service or system*] [*Spain*] (IID)
ICZ............	International Climate Zone
ICZ............	Intertropical Convergence Zone [*Trade winds*] [*Meteorology*]
ICZ............	Isthmian Canal Zone
ICZ............	North Park College and Theological Seminary, Chicago, IL [*OCLC symbol*] (OCLC)
ICZM..........	Integrated Coastal Zone Management [*Marine science*] (OSRA)
ICZN..........	International Commission on Zoological Nomenclature [*British*] (EAIO)
ID.............	Apollo Airlines [*ICAO designator*] (AD)
ID.............	[*Official Decisions of the*] Department of Interior (AAGC)
ID.............	Idaho [*Postal code*]
ID.............	Idaho Operations Office [*Energy Research and Development Administration*]
ID.............	Idaho Reports [*A publication*] (DLA)
Id.............	Idaho State Library, Boise, ID [*Library symbol Library of Congress*] (LCLS)
ID.............	Iddin-Dagan (BJA)
ID.............	Idea [*Slang*]
ID.............	Idem [*The Same*] [*Latin*]
ID.............	Identification [*Computer science*]
ID.............	Identification Data
ID.............	Identification Date
ID.............	Identification Dissector (MCD)
ID.............	Identifier [*Dialog*] [*Searchable field*] (NITA)
ID.............	Identify [*or Identification*] (DAVI)
ID.............	Identity
ID.............	[*The*] Ides
ID.............	Iditol Dehydrogenase (MAE)
Id.............	Idylls [*of Theocritus*] [*Classical studies*] (OCD)
ID.............	Ifostamide, Doxorubicin [*Antineoplastic drug*] (CDI)
ID.............	Ill-Defined (STED)
ID.............	Image Digitizer [*Computer science*]
ID.............	Image Dissector (KSC)
ID.............	Immediate Delivery [*Shipping*]
ID.............	Immunodeficiency [*Immunology*]
ID.............	Immunodiffusion [*Immunology*]
ID.............	Immunoglobulin Deficiency [*Immunology*] (AAMN)
ID.............	Immunological Distance [*in primate phylogeny*]
ID.............	Import Duty [*Customs*] (DS)
ID.............	Inanna's Descent (BJA)
ID.............	Inappropriate Disability (STED)
ID.............	Inaugural Dissertation (BJA)
ID.............	Inclusion Disease [*Medicine*]
ID.............	Inclusive Depth [*Typography*] (DGA)
ID.............	Income Debenture [*Type of bond*] [*Investment term*]
ID.............	Increased Deployability [*Posture*] (DOMA)
ID.............	Indefinite Delivery [*Shipping*]
ID.............	Independence Dogs [*An association*] (EA)
ID.............	Independent Dealer [*Automobile sales*]
ID.............	Independent Distributor
ID.............	Index of Discrimination
ID.............	Index of Dissimilarity
ID.............	Indicating Device
ID.............	Indicator Driver (MSA)
ID.............	Indirect Damage [*Insurance*]
ID.............	Indirect Departmental (DGA)
I/D............	Indirect Labor (AAG)
ID.............	Individual Development
ID.............	Individual Dose [*Radioactivity calculations*]
ID.............	Indonesia [*ANSI two-letter standard code*] (CNC)
ID.............	Induced Draft
ID.............	Inductance [*Electromagnetism*] (IAA)
ID.............	Induction Delivery (STED)
ID.............	Industrial Democracy
ID.............	Industrial Design (WGA)
ID.............	Industrial Development
ID.............	Industrial Dynamics [*Management analysis*]
ID.............	Inelastic Demand (MHDB)
ID.............	Infant Death (MAE)
ID.............	Infantry Division
ID.............	Infectious Disease [*Medicine*]
ID.............	Infective Dose
ID.............	Inferior Division [*Medicine*] (DAVI)

ID.............	Informal Decorative [*Horticulture*]
ID.............	Information and Documentation [*Royal Tropical Institute*] [*Information service or system*] (IID)
ID.............	Information Distributor
ID.............	Inhibitory Dose [*Medicine*]
ID.............	Inhomogeneous Deposition (STED)
ID.............	Initial Denial Authority (AAGC)
ID.............	Initial Diagnosis [*Medicine*] (CPH)
ID.............	Initial Distribution
ID.............	Initial Dose [*Medicine*] (CPH)
ID.............	Initial dyskinesia [*Medicine*] (DMAA)
ID.............	Injected Dose
ID.............	Inner Diameter
ID.............	Inniskilling Dragoons [*Military British*]
ID.............	Innovator's Digest [*The Infoteam, Inc.*] [*Information service or system*] (IID)
ID.............	Inoculum Density
ID.............	Input Display [*Computer science*] (IAA)
ID.............	Insertion Device [*Series of magnets*] [*Physics*]
ID.............	Inside Diameter
ID.............	Inside Dimensions
ID.............	Installation Data
ID.............	Institute of Distribution [*Defunct*] (EA)
ID.............	Instructional Developer (MCD)
I/D............	Instruction/Data (IEEE)
ID.............	Instrumentation Directorate [*White Sands Missile Range*] [*Army*]
ID.............	Insufficient Data (STED)
ID.............	Insulation Displacement
ID.............	Integral Derivative (IAA)
ID.............	Integrated Diagnostics (AAGC)
ID.............	Intellectual Digest [*A publication*]
ID.............	Intelligence Department [*Army*] (MCD)
ID.............	Intelligence Division [*NATO*] (NATG)
ID.............	Intelligence Duties
ID.............	Intelligent Device [*Computer science*] (CIST)
ID.............	Intelligent Digitizer
ID.............	Intelligent Documentation [*Computer science*]
I-D............	Intensity Duration (Curve)
ID.............	Interactive Debugging (IEEE)
ID.............	Intercept Direction (SAA)
ID.............	Intercommunication Devices (MCD)
ID.............	Interconnection Device (MCD)
ID.............	Interconnection Diagram (IAA)
ID.............	Interdigital [*Telecommunications*] (IEEE)
ID.............	Interdigitating Cells (STED)
ID.............	Interdisciplinary
ID.............	Interest Deductible [*Banking*] (ADA)
ID.............	Interface Device (MCD)
ID.............	Interface Document (NASA)
ID.............	Interferometer and Doppler
ID.............	Interim Dividend [*Investment term*]
ID.............	Interior Department
ID.............	Interior Department Decisions [*United States*] [*A publication*] (DLA)
ID.............	Interlocking Directorate [*Business term*]
ID.............	Intermediate Description (IEEE)
ID.............	Intermittent Duty (IAA)
ID.............	Intermodulation Distortion
ID.............	Internal Diameter (MSA)
ID.............	International Daleco Technology [*Vancouver Stock Exchange symbol*]
ID.............	International Division [*Army Service Forces*] [*World War II*]
ID.............	Interrectal Spike Discharge [*Neurophysiology*]
ID.............	Interstitial Disease (STED)
ID.............	Intestinal Distress
ID.............	Intradermal [*Medicine*]
id.............	Intradermal [*Medicine*] (WDAA)
ID.............	Intraductal [*Anatomy*]
ID.............	Intraduodenal [*Medicine*] (MAE)
ID.............	Intrinsicoid Deflection [*Cardiology*]
ID.............	Introduction (WDMC)
ID.............	Inventory Difference [*Formerly, MUF*] [*NRC/ERDA*]
ID.............	Invoice Distribution
ID.............	Iraqi Dinar [*Monetary unit*] (BJA)
ID.............	Iris Diaphragm [*Photography*]
ID.............	Irish Duke (ROG)
ID.............	Islamic Dinar [*Monetary unit*] (EY)
ID.............	Island (ADA)
ID.............	Isosorbide Dinitrate (STED)
ID.............	Isotope Dilution
ID.............	Issue Date
ID.............	Item Description
ID.............	Item Descriptor [*Computer science*] (CIST)
ID.............	Item Documentation (IEEE)
ID.............	Izquierda Democratica [*Democratic Left*] [*Ecuador*] [*Political party*] (PPW)
ID.............	Noncathode Ray Tube Indicators [*JETDS nomenclature*] [*Military*] (CET)
ID.............	Sumitomo Chemical Co. [*Japan*] [*Research code symbol*]
ID$_{50}$............	Infective Dose, Median
ID-86.........	Infantry Division - 1986
IDA............	Dallas Baptist College, Dallas, TX [*OCLC symbol*] (OCLC)
IDA............	Idaho
IDA............	Idaho Array [*Idaho*] [*Seismograph station code, US Geological Survey Closed*] (SEIS)
IDA............	Idaho Falls [*Idaho*] [*Airport symbol*] (OAG)

IDA............	Idaho Power [*NYSE symbol*] (TTSB)
IDA............	Idaho Power Co. [*NYSE symbol*] (SPSG)
Ida............	Idaho Reports [*A publication*] (DLA)
IDA............	Identification Data Accessory (NTCM)
IDA............	Image Display and Analysis (MAE)
IDA............	Iminodiacetic Acid [*Organic chemistry*]
IDA............	Immediate Damage Assessment
IDA............	Immortalis Dei Auspicio [*With the Help of God*] [*Latin*]
IDA............	Import Duty Act [*British*] (DS)
IDA............	In Defense of Animals (EA)
IDA............	Independent Distributors Association (NTPA)
IDA............	Indicator Digest Average [*Stock exchange term*] (SPSG)
IDA............	Indonesia Air Transport PT [*ICAO designator*] (FAAC)
IDA............	Industrial Design Award
IDA............	Industrial Development Abstracts [*Database*] [*UNIDO*] (CRD)
IDA............	Industrial Development Authority [*Ireland*]
IDA............	Industrial Diamond Association of America (EA)
IDA............	Industrial Distribution Association (NTPA)
IDA............	Industry Development Arrangement
IDA............	Infant-Toddler Developmental Assessment [*Test*] (TMMY)
IDA............	Information, Decision, Action
IDA............	Infrared Detection Array
IDA............	Initial Denial Authority (AABC)
IDA............	Inpatient Data Administration (PDAA)
IDA............	Input Data Assembler
IDA............	Inspekteur der Artillerie [*Inspector of Artillery*] [*German military - World War II*]
IDA............	Institute for Defense Analyses (EA)
IDA............	Institute for Development Anthropology (EA)
IDA............	Institute of Domestic Arts (WDAA)
IDA............	Integrated Data Access (NITA)
IDA............	Integrated Debugging Aid (IAA)
IDA............	Integrated Digital Access [*Telecommunications*]
IDA............	Integrated Digital Avionics (MCD)
IDA............	Integrated Disbursing and Accounting (MCD)
IDA............	Integrated Disk Adapter [*Sperry UNIVAC*]
IDA............	Integro-Differential Analyzer
IDA............	Intelligent Data Access
IDA............	Intelligent Database Assistant
IDA............	Intelligent Drive Array [*COMPAQ Computer Corp.*] [*Computer science*]
IDA............	Interactive Data on Accidents [*Engineering*]
IDA............	Interactive Debugging Aid
IDA............	Interactive Differential Analyzer
IDA............	Intercept Distance Aid (SAA)
IDA............	Intercollegiate Dramatic Association [*Defunct*] (EA)
IDA............	Interconnect Device Arrangement (HGAA)
IDA............	Interdigitated Array [*Electronics*]
IDA............	Inter-Divisional Agreement
IDA............	Interface Display Assembly [*NASA*] (NASA)
IDA............	International Dance Alliance (EA)
IDA............	International Data and Analysis [*Bureau of Mines*]
IDA............	International Database Association [*Defunct*] (EA)
IDA............	International Defenders of Animals (EA)
IDA............	International Deployment of Accelerometers [*Project*] [*Seismography*]
IDA............	International Desalination Association (EA)
IDA............	International Development Agency [*United Nations*] (NUCP)
IDA............	International Development Association (EA)
IDA............	International Discotheque Association [*Defunct*] (EA)
IDA............	International Dispensary Association [*Acronym is used as association name*] (EAIO)
IDA............	International Documentary Association (EA)
IDA............	International Doll Association [*Defunct*] (EA)
IDA............	International Downtown Association (EA)
IDA............	International Drapery Association (EA)
IDA............	International Dredging Association
IDA............	Intrusion Detection Alarm (CINC)
IDA............	Investment Dealers Association of Canada
IDA............	Ionospheric Dispersion Analysis [*Air Force*]
IDA............	Irish Dental Association (BI)
IDA............	Irish Drug Association (BI)
IDA............	Iron Deficiency Anemia [*Medicine*]
IDA............	Islamic Democratic Alliance [*Pakistan*] [*Political party*]
IDA............	Isotope Dilution Analysis
IDA............	Isotopic Dilution Analysis
IDA............	Iterative Differential Analyzer (IAA)
IDAA	Industrial Diamond Association of America
IDAA	International Diabetic Athletes Association (EA)
IDAA	International Dictionary of Architects and Architecture [*A publication*]
IDAA	International Doctors in Alcoholics Anonymous (EA)
IDAAS	International Directory of Astronomical Associations and Societies [*A publication*]
IdAb	Aberdeen Public Library, Aberdeen, ID [*Library symbol*] [*Library of Congress*] (LCLS)
IDAB	Industrial Development Advisory Board [*British*]
IDABEE	Institute of Defense Analysis Compiler (SAA)
ID AC	Idem Ac [*The Same As*] [*Latin*]
IDAC	Industrial Data Acquisition Control (IAA)
IDAC	Instant Data Access Control [*National Design Center, Inc.*] [*Information service or system*] (IID)
IDAC	Integrated Data Acquisition and Control [*Jet Propulsion Laboratory, NASA*]
IDAC	Integrated Digital-Analog Converter (MCD)
IDAC	Interconnecting Digital-Analog Converter (NG)
IDAC	Interim Digital-Analog Converter
IDAC	International Decorative Accessories Center (EA)
IDAC	International Disaster Advisory Committee
IDACE	Association des Industries des Aliments Dietetiques de la CEE [*Association of Dietetic Foods Industries of the European Economic Community*]
ID-ACK	Identification-Acknowledge (MCD)
IDACON	Iterative Differential Analyzer Control
IDA-CRD	Institute for Defense Analysis-Communications Research Division
IDACS	Integrated Detection and Classification Station
IDAD	Internal Defense and Development [*Army*] (AABC)
IDADS	Interactive Drafting and Digitizing System (MCD)
IDAF...........	International Defence and Aid Fund for Southern Africa [*British*] (EAIO)
IDAF...........	International Defense and Aid Fund for Southern Africa, US Committee [*Defunct*] (EA)
IDAFIPS	Integrated Disbursing and Accounting Financial Information Processing System [*DoD*]
IDAFMS	Integrated Disbursing and Accounting Financial Management System (DNAB)
IDAGAM.......	Institute for Defense Analysis Gaming Model (MCD)
IDA-HEAL-NET...	Idaho Health Libraries Network [*Library network*]
Idaho	Idaho Supreme Court Reports [*A publication*] (DLA)
Idaho Adm Code...	Idaho Administrative Code [*A publication*] (AAGC)
Idaho LJ	Idaho Law Journal [*A publication*] (DLA)
Idaho NS	Idaho Reports, New Series [*A publication*] (DLA)
IdahoP........	Idaho Power Co. [*Associated Press*] (SAG)
Idaho Sess Laws...	Session Laws of Idaho [*A publication*] (DLA)
Idaho St U..	Idaho State University (GAGS)
Ida IAB	Idaho Industrial Accident Board Reports [*A publication*] (DLA)
IdAI............	Albion Community Library, Albion, ID [*Library symbol*] [*Library of Congress*] (LCLS)
IDAL...........	Indirect Data Address List [*Computer science*] (ECII)
IdAIN	Albion State Normal School, Albion, ID [*Library symbol Library of Congress*] (LCLS)
IdAIS..........	Southern Idaho College of Education, Albion, ID [*Library symbol Library of Congress Obsolete*] (LCLS)
IdAm	American Falls District Library, American Falls, ID [*Library symbol*] [*Library of Congress*] (LCLS)
IDAM	Indexed Direct Access Method
IdAmHS	American Falls High School, American Falls, ID [*Library symbol*] [*Library of Congress*] (LCLS)
IDAMIS	Integrated Drug Abuse Management Information Systems
IDAMS	Image Display and Manipulation System [*NASA*]
IDAMS	Isotope Dilution Analysis Mass Spectrometry
IDAMST	Integrated Digital Avionics for Medium STOL Transport (MCD)
IDAN	Idan Software Industries ISI Ltd. [*NASDAQ symbol*] (NQ)
I/D & C	Instrumentation/Displays and Controls [*Subsystem*] (MCD)
ID & CA	Inverter Distribution and Control Assembly (MCD)
ID & PD......	Industrial Democracy and Personnel Development
IDANF.........	Idan Software Ind ISI [*NASDAQ symbol*] (TTSB)
IdanSft.......	Idan Software Industries ISI Ltd. [*Associated Press*] (SAG)
IDanvi.........	Danville Public Library, Danville, IL [*Library symbol Library of Congress*] (LCLS)
IDanviC........	Danville Junior College, Danville, IL [*Library symbol Library of Congress*] (LCLS)
IDanviCS......	Central Vermillion County Schools Cooperative, Danville, IL [*Library symbol*] [*Library of Congress*] (LCLS)
IDanviHS	Schlarman High School, Danville, IL [*Library symbol*] [*Library of Congress*] (LCLS)
IDanviL........	Lake View Memorial Hospital, Doctor's Library, Danville, IL [*Library symbol Library of Congress*] (LCLS)
IDanviSD	Danville Community Unit School District, Danville, IL [*Library symbol*] [*Library of Congress*] (LCLS)
IDanviSE......	Saint Elizabeth Hospital, Danville, IL [*Library symbol*] [*Library of Congress*] (LCLS)
IDanviStE.....	Saint Elizabeth Hospital, Danville, IL [*Library symbol Library of Congress*] (LCLS)
IDanviVA......	United States Veterans Administration Hospital, Danville, IL [*Library symbol Library of Congress*] (LCLS)
IDAP	Industrial Design Assistance Program [*National Design Council, Canada*]
IDAP	Integrated Defensive Avionics Program [*Navy*] (DOMA)
IDAP	Internal Development and Assistance Program (AFM)
IDAP	International Development and Assistance Program (KSC)
IDAP	Isomorphously Doped Ammonium Perchlorate
IDAP	Iterative Differential Analyzer Pinboard
IDAPA	Idaho Administrative Code [*A publication*] (AAGC)
IDAPI	Independent Database Application Program Interface (PCM)
IDAPR.........	Individual DSS [*Direct Support System*] Activity Performance Report
IDAPS	Image Data Processing System
IdAr...........	Lost River District Library, Arco, ID [*Library symbol*] [*Library of Congress*] (LCLS)
IDARP.........	Integrated Drug Abuse Reporting Process [*National Institutes of Health*]
IDART	Individual Drill Attendance and Retirement Transaction [*Military*] (DNAB)
IdAs	Ashton Public Library, Ashton, ID [*Library symbol*] [*Library of Congress*] (LCLS)
IDAS	Industrial Data Acquisition System (IAA)
IDAS	Information Displays Automatic Drafting System (IEEE)
IDAS	Instrument Data Acquisition System
IDAS	Integrated Data Acquisition System (MCD)
IDAS	Integrated Defense Avionics System [*Air Force*] (DOMA)
IDAS	Integrated Design Automation System (MCD)
IDAS	Intelligent Data Acquisition System

IDAS	International Database Access Service [*Bahrain Telecommunications Co.*] [*Information service or system*] (IID)
IDAS	Intrusion Detection Alarm System
IDAS	Isotope Dilution Alpha Spectrometry
IDAS	Iterative Differential Analyzer Slave
IDASA	Institute for Democracy in South Africa
IDAST	Interpolated Data and Speech Transmission [*Computer science*]
Ida Supp	Idaho Supplement [*A publication*] (DLA)
IDAT	Interfacility Data (FAAC)
IDATU	Irish Distributive and Administrative Trade Union (EAIO)
IDA (USA)	Indian Dental Association (USA) (EA)
IDAV	Immune Deficiency Associated Virus
IdB	Boise Public Library, Boise, ID [*Library symbol Library of Congress*] (LCLS)
IDB	Illicit Diamond Buyer [*or Buying*]
IDB	Illinois Central College, East Peoria, IL [*OCLC symbol*] (OCLC)
IDB	Incomplete Data Base [*Statistics*] (DAVI)
IDB	Inductance Decade Box
IDB	Industrial Data Bank Department [*Gulf Organization for Industrial Consulting*] [*Qatar*] [*Information service or system*] (IID)
IDB	Industrial Development Bank [*Kenya*] (IMH)
IDB	Industrial Development Bank [*Jordan*]
IDB	Industrial Development Board [*Northern Ireland*] (GEA)
IDB	Industrial Development Bond
IDB	Inertial Data Box (KSC)
IDB	Infared Diving Binoculors (MCD)
IDB	INPADOC [*International Patent Documentation Center*] Data Base [*Information service or system*] (CRD)
IDB	Input Data Buffer
IDB	Inspection Data Bulletin
IDB	In-Suit Drink Bag [*Aerospace*] (MCD)
IDB	Insurance Development Bureau [*Guelph, ON*] (EAIO)
IDB	Integrated Data Base [*Computer science*]
IDB	Interaction Database
IDB	Inter-American Defense Board (EA)
IDB	Inter-American Development Bank [*Also, IADB*]
IDB	Intercept During Boost [*Aerospace*]
IDB	Inter-Dealer Broker [*British*]
IDB	Inter-Dynamic Balance
IDB	Intermediary Dealer Broker [*Investment term*] (NUMA)
IDB	International Data Base [*Bureau of Census*] [*Database*]
IDB	Interpreter's Dictionary of the Bible
IDB	Interpretive Debugger [*Computer science*] (ECII)
IDB	Inverni & Della Beffa [*Italy*] [*Research code symbol*]
IDB	Islamic Development Bank [*Saudi Arabia*]
IDB	Israel Discount Bank
IDBA	International Deli-Bakery Association [*Defunct*] (EA)
IdBB	Boise State College, Boise, ID [*Library symbol Library of Congress*] (LCLS)
IdBBC	Boise Bible College, Boise, ID [*Library symbol*] [*Library of Congress*] (LCLS)
IdBBC	Boise Cascade Corp. Library, Boise, ID [*Library symbol*] [*Library of Congress*] (LCLS)
IdBC	Ada County District Library, Boise, ID [*Library symbol*] [*Library of Congress*] (LCLS)
IdBCH	CH2M Hill Library, Boise, ID [*Library symbol*] [*Library of Congress*] (LCLS)
IdBDB	Diocese of Boise, Resource Center, Boise, ID [*Library symbol*] [*Library of Congress*] (LCLS)
IdBe	Bellevue Public Library, Bellevue, ID [*Library symbol*] [*Library of Congress*] (LCLS)
IDBE	ID Biomedical Corp. [*NASDAQ symbol*] (SAG)
IDBEF	ID Biomedical [*NASDAQ symbol*] (TTSB)
IdBEH	Idaho Elks Rehabilitation Hospital, Medical Library, Boise, ID [*Library symbol*] [*Library of Congress*] (LCLS)
IdBf	Blackfoot Public Library, Blackfoot, ID [*Library symbol*] [*Library of Congress*] (LCLS)
IdBfBH	Bingham Memorial Hospital, Medical Library, Blackfoot, ID [*Library symbol*] [*Library of Congress*] (LCLS)
IdBFG	Fish & Game Library, Boise, ID [*Library symbol*] [*Library of Congress*] (LCLS)
IdBfGS	Church of Jesus Christ of Latter-Day Saints, Genealogical Society Library, Blackfoot West Branch, Stake Center, Blackfoot, ID [*Library symbol Library of Congress*] (LCLS)
IdBfH	State Hospital South, Medical Library, Blackfoot, ID [*Library symbol*] [*Library of Congress*] (LCLS)
IdBfS	Snake River School and Community Library, Blackfoot, ID [*Library symbol*] [*Library of Congress*] (LCLS)
IdBG	Genealogical Library, Boise, ID [*Library symbol*] [*Library of Congress*] (LCLS)
IdBHP	Hewett-Packard, Boise Site Library, Boise, ID [*Library symbol*] [*Library of Congress*] (LCLS)
IDBI	Industrial Development Bank of India (ECON)
IDBI	Industrial Development Bank of Israel (IMH)
IdBI	Information and Referral Service, Boise, ID [*Library symbol*] [*Library of Congress*] (LCLS)
ID Bio	ID Biomedical Corp. [*Associated Press*] (SAG)
ID Biom	ID Biomedical Corp. [*Associated Press*] (SAG)
IdBL	Idaho Legislative Council, Legislative Library, Boise, ID [*Library symbol*] [*Library of Congress*] (LCLS)
IdBLM-B	Bureau of Land Management, Boise, ID [*Library symbol Library of Congress*] (LCLS)
IDBMA	International Data Base Management Association (EA)
IdBMK	Morrison-Krudsen Co., Inc., Records and Micrographics Center, Boise, ID [*Library symbol Library of Congress*] (LCLS)
IDBMS	Integrated Database Management System
IDBN	Integrated Digital Backbone Network [*Telecommunications*]
IdBnf	Boundary County Library District, Bonners Ferry, ID [*Library symbol*] [*Library of Congress*] (LCLS)
IDBPF	Interdigital Band-Pass Filter [*Electronics*] (IAA)
Id-BPH	Idaho State Library, Blind and Physically Handicapped Services, Boise, ID [*Library symbol Library of Congress*] (LCLS)
IdBr	Bruneau District Library, Bruneau, ID [*Library symbol*] [*Library of Congress*] (LCLS)
IDBR	Indirect Bilirubin [*Biochemistry*] (DAVI)
IDBR	Input Data Buffer Register [*Computer science*] (MHDB)
IDBRA	International Drivers' Behaviour Research Association [*Paris, France*] (EAIO)
IdBRC	Roman Catholic Diocese of Boise, Boise, ID [*Library symbol*] [*Library of Congress*] (LCLS)
IdBRE	Real Estate Comm. Library, Boise, ID [*Library symbol*] [*Library of Congress*] (LCLS)
IdBS	Idaho Statesman Library, Boise, ID [*Library symbol*] [*Library of Congress*] (LCLS)
IDBS	Infantile Diffuse Brain Sclerosis [*Medicine*] (DB)
IdBSA	Saint Alphonsus Regional Medical Center, Medical Library, Boise, ID [*Library symbol*] [*Library of Congress*] (LCLS)
IdBSH	Boise Senior High School, Boise, ID [*Library symbol*] [*Library of Congress*] (LCLS)
IdBSL	Saint Luke's Regional Center Medical Library, Boise, ID [*Library symbol*] [*Library of Congress*] (LCLS)
IDBT	Industrial Development Bank of Turkey (PDAA)
IdBTI	Mountain State Tumor Institute Medical Library, Boise, ID [*Library symbol*] [*Library of Congress*] (LCLS)
IdBuh	Buhl Public Library, Buhl, ID [*Library symbol*] [*Library of Congress*] (LCLS)
IdBur	Burley Public Library, Burley, ID [*Library symbol*] [*Library of Congress*] (LCLS)
IdBurGS	Church of Jesus Christ of Latter-Day Saints, Genealogical Society Library, Burley Branch, Burley, ID [*Library symbol Library of Congress*] (LCLS)
IdBV	United States Veterans Administration Medical Center, Medical Library, Boise, ID [*Library symbol*] [*Library of Congress*] (LCLS)
IdC	Coeur D'Alene Public Library, Coeur D'Alene, ID [*Library symbol Library of Congress*] (LCLS)
IDC	Idiopathic Dilated Cardiomyopathy [*Cardiology*]
IDC	Image Dissector Camera
IDC	IMBLMS [*Integrated Medical Behavioral Measurement System*] Digital Computer (MCD)
IDC	Imperial Defence College [*British*]
IDC	Indirect Costs
IDC	Individual Defense Counsel
IDC	Industrial Design Certificate [*British*]
IDC	Industrial Development Certificate [*Department of Industry*] [*British*]
IDC	Industrial Development Corp.
IDC	Industries Development Committee
IDC	Information and Direction Center
IDC	Information and Documentation Center [*Royal Institute of Technology Library*] [*Information service or system*] (IID)
IDC	Information Design Change (NG)
IDC	Information Dynamics Corp.
IDC	Infrared Detector Cryostat
IDC	Inner Dead-Center (DNAB)
IDC	Input Display Console [*Computer science*]
IDC	Inspection Data Card (MCD)
IDC	Insulation Displacement Connector [*Electronics*]
IDC	Intangible Drilling Costs [*Petroleum industry*]
IDC	Integrated Device Controller
IDC	Integrated Disk Control [*NCR Corp.*]
IDC	Integrated Displays and Controls (MCD)
IDC	Interactive Data Class [*Telecommunications*]
IDC	Interactive Data Corporation (NITA)
IDC	Interagency Defector Committee
IDC	Interceptor Distance Computer
IDC	Interdepartmental Committee
IDC	Interdepartmental Communication
IDC	Interdigital Communications [*AMEX symbol*] (SPSG)
IDC	Interdigitating Cell [*Medicine*] (DMAA)
IDC	Inter Documentation Co. AG, Zug, Switzerland [*Library symbol Library of Congress*] (LCLS)
IDC	Interest During Construction
IDC	Interface Document Control (MCD)
IDC	Interior Designers of Canada [*See also DIC*]
IDC	Internal Data Channel
IDC	Internal Document Control
IDC	International Dairy Committee
IDC	International Dance Council [*See also CIDD*] (EAIO)
IDC	International Data Connector
IDC	International Data Consultants [*Market research organization*] (NITA)
IDC	International Data Corp. [*Information service or system*] (IID)
IDC	International Development Conference (EA)
IDC	International Development Corp. [*Proposed corporation to combine Alliance for Progress and Agency for International Development*]
IDC	International Diamond Council [*Antwerp, Belgium*] (EAIO)
IDC	International Diastema Club (EA)
IDC	International Display Corp. [*Vancouver Stock Exchange symbol*]
IDC	International Documentation Center
IDC	International Documentation in Chemistry (DIT)
IDC	International Drycleaners Congress (EA)

IDC.............. Internationale Democrate Chretienne [*Christian Democrat International*] [*Belgium*] (EAIO)

IDC.............. Internationale Dokumentationsgesellschaft fuer Chemie [*International Company for Documentation in Chemistry*] [*Frankfurt, West Germany*]

IDC.............. Internet Database Connector [*Computer science*] (PCM)

IDC.............. Intraductal Carcinoma [*Oncology*]

IDC.............. Intransit Data Card (AFM)

IDC.............. Inventor's Desktop Companion [*A publication*]

IDC.............. Iodine Dextrin Color

IDC.............. Iranian Democratic Committee (EA)

IDC.............. Irrigated, Double Cropped [*Agriculture*]

IDC.............. Item Design Change

IDC.............. Item Detail Card [*Military*] (AABC)

IDC.............. Iterated Deferred Correction (PDAA)

IDC.............. Peoples Gas, Light & Coke Co., Chicago, IL [*OCLC symbol*] (OCLC)

IdCa.............. Caldwell Public Library, Caldwell, ID [*Library symbol Library of Congress*] (LCLS)

ID(C)A.......... Indecent Displays (Control) Act [*British*]

IDCA .... Indian Diamond and Colorstone Association (EA)

IDCA .... International Design Conference in Aspen (EA)

IDCA .... International Development Cooperation Act of 1979

IDCA .... [*United States*] International Development Cooperation Agency (USGC)

IDCA .... International Dolphin Conservation Act [*1993*]

IDCA .... International Dragon Class Association (EAIO)

IDCA .... Inverter Distribution and Control Assembly (NAKS)

IdCaC.......... College of Idaho, Caldwell, ID [*Library symbol Library of Congress*] (LCLS)

IdCaH.......... West Valley Medical Center, Medical Library, Caldwell, ID [*Library symbol*] [*Library of Congress*] (LCLS)

IdCar.......... Little Wood River District Library, Carey, ID [*Library symbol*] [*Library of Congress*] (LCLS)

IDCAS .... Industrial Development Center for Arab States [*Later, AIDO*]

IdCC.......... Consolidated Free Library District, Coeur d'Alene, ID [*Library symbol*] [*Library of Congress*] (LCLS)

IDCC .... Integrated Data Communications Controller

IDCC .... Integrated Dual-Use Commercial Companies

IDCC .... INTEK Diversified [*NASDAQ symbol*] (TTSB)

IDCC .... INTEK Diversified Corp. [*NASDAQ symbol*] (NQ)

IDCC .... Interactive Display and Control Component (MCD)

IDCC .... Inter-Departmental Consultative Committee

IdCC-A .... Consolidated Free Library District, Athol Branch, Athol, ID [*Library symbol*] [*Library of Congress*] (LCLS)

IDCCC .... Interim Data Communications Collection Center

IDCCC .... International Dredging Conference Coordinating Committee (EAIO)

IdCCIN .... Cooperative Information Network, Coeur d'Alene, ID [*Library symbol*] [*Library of Congress*] (LCLS)

IdCC-R .... Consolidated Free Library District, Rathdrum Branch, Rathdrum, ID [*Library symbol*] [*Library of Congress*] (LCLS)

IdCC-SC .... Consolidated Free Library District, Service Center, Couer d'Alene, ID [*Library symbol*] [*Library of Congress*] (LCLS)

IdCC-SL .... Consolidated Free Library District, Spirit Lake Branch, Spirit Lake, ID [*Library symbol*] [*Library of Congress*] (LCLS)

IDCDA.......... Independent Dealer Committee Dedicated to Action (EA)

IDCF.......... Immunodiffusion Complement Fix [*Immunochemistry*] (DAVI)

IDCF.......... Indirect Command File [*Computer science*] (WDAA)

IDCFC .... International David Cassidy Fan Club (EAIO)

IDCH .... International Directory of Company Histories [*A publication*]

IdCH.......... Kootenai Medical Center, Medical Library, Couer d'Alene, ID [*Library symbol*] [*Library of Congress*] (LCLS)

IdCha.......... Challis Public Library, Challis, ID [*Library symbol*] [*Library of Congress*] (LCLS)

IdCHM .... Hecla Mining Co. Library, Couer d'Alene, ID [*Library symbol*] [*Library of Congress*] (LCLS)

IdChP.......... Portneuf Library District, Chubbuck, ID [*Library symbol*] [*Library of Congress*] (LCLS)

IdCHS .... Couer d'Alene High School, Couer d'Alene, ID [*Library symbol*] [*Library of Congress*] (LCLS)

IDCI .... Intradiplochromatid Interchange (PDAA)

IdCl.......... Clarkia District Library, Clarkia, ID [*Library symbol*] [*Library of Congress*] (LCLS)

IdCL.......... Coeur d'Alene Public Library, Coeur d'Alene, ID [*Library symbol*] [*Library of Congress*] (LCLS)

IDCL.......... Information Design Change List (MCD)

IdCm.......... Cambridge District Library, Cambridge, ID [*Library symbol*] [*Library of Congress*] (LCLS)

IDCMA .... Independent Data Communications Manufacturers Association (EA)

IDCN .... Interchangeability Document Change Notice (KSC)

IdCN.......... North Idaho College, Coeur d'Alene, ID [*Library symbol Library of Congress*] (LCLS)

IDCNA.......... Insulation Distributor Contractors National Association [*Later, NICA*] (EA)

IdCnL.......... Council District Library, Council, ID [*Library symbol*] [*Library of Congress*] (LCLS)

IDCNY.......... International Design Center, New York

IDCOP.......... Integral Driver Coil on Plug

IDCOR.......... Industry Degraded Core Rulemaking Program [*Nuclear industry sponsored group*]

IdCoStG .... College of Saint Gertrude, Library, Cottonwood, ID [*Library symbol*] [*Library of Congress*] (LCLS)

IDCP .... International Data Collecting Platform (TEL)

IDCR .... Interchangeability Document Change Request (MCD)

IDCR .... International Decade of Cetacean Research

IdCs .... Cascade Public Library, Cascade, ID [*Library symbol*] [*Library of Congress*] (LCLS)

IDCS .... Image Dissector Camera System

IDCS .... Initial Defense Communications Satellite (MCD)

IDCS .... Instrumentation/Data Collection System

IDCS .... Integrated Data Coding System (NG)

IDCS .... Interdepartment Courier Service

IDCS .... International Digital Channel Service [*Federal Trade Commission*]

IDCSP .... Initial Defense Communications Satellite Program [*or Project*]

IDCSP .... Interim Defense Communications Satellite Program [*DoD*]

IDCSP-A .... Initial Defense Communications Satellite Program-Augmented (CET)

IDCSP/ADCSP... Initial Defense Communications Satellite Program / Advanced Defense Communications Satellite Program (SAA)

IDCSS .... Initial Defense Communications Satellite System (NATG)

IDCSS .... Intermediate Defense Communications Satellite System (IAA)

IDCT.......... Integrated Daily Cycle Test (MCD)

IDCT.......... Inverse Discrete Cosine Transform [*Electronics*] (ACRL)

IDCTR .... Inductor (MSA)

IDD .... Detroit Diesel Allison Division, General Motors Corp., Indianapolis, IN [*OCLC symbol*] (OCLC)

IDD .... Illicit Diamond Dealing (ROG)

IDD .... Image Definition Device

IDD .... Indirect by Direct (MCD)

IDD .... Industrial Development Division [*Vietnam*]

IDD .... Infant Development Distress Syndrome [*Medicine*] (ADA)

IDD .... Institute for Drafting and Design [*Australia*]

IDD .... Insulin-Dependent Diabetes

IDD .... Integrated Data Dictionary

IDD .... Intelligence Data Handling Division [*United States European Command*]

IDD .... Inter-Director Designation (NG)

IDD .... Interface Definition Document (MCD)

IDD .... Interface Designation Drawing

IDD .... Interface Design Document (DOMA)

IDD .... Interim Drydocking [*Navy*] (NVT)

IDD .... International Defense Directory [*A publication*]

IDD .... International Direct Dialing [*Telecommunications*]

IDD .... International Dorado Resources [*Vancouver Stock Exchange symbol*]

IDD .... Inventory to Diagnose Depression [*Psychology*]

IDD .... Iodine Deficiency Disorders [*Medicine*]

IdD.......... South Bannock District Library, Downey Branch, Downey, ID [*Library symbol*] [*Library of Congress*] (LCLS)

IDDA .... Interior Decorators and Designers Association [*British*] (EAIO)

IDDA .... International Dairy-Deli Association (EA)

IDDAS .... Intelligent Dummy Data Acquisition System [*Crash testing*] [*Automotive engineering*]

IDDC .... International Demographic Data Center [*Bureau of the Census*] [*Database*] [*Information service or system*] (IID)

IDDC .... International Development Data Center [*Georgia Institute of Technology*]

IDDD .... International Demographic Data Directory [*Agency for International Development*] (IID)

IDDD .... International Direct Distance Dialing [*AT & T*]

IDDE .... Integrated Development and Debugging Environment [*Symantec Corp.*] [*Computer science*] (PCM)

IDDE .... Interactive Development and Debugging Environment (PCM)

IDDF .... Intermediate Data Distribution Facility (COE)

IDDF .... Intermediate Digital Distribution Frame [*Telecommunications*] (TEL)

Iddings DRB... Iddings' Dayton Term Reports [*Ohio*] [*A publication*] (DLA)

Iddings TRD... Iddings' Dayton Term Reports [*Ohio*] [*A publication*] (DLA)

IDDIS .... IDD Information Services, Inc. (IID)

IDDJ.......... Interim Decisions of the Department of Justice

IDDL .... Interactive Database Laboratory [*Computer science*] (MHDB)

IdD-L .... South Bannock District Library, Lava Hot Springs Branch, Lava Hot Springs, ID [*Library symbol*] [*Library of Congress*] (LCLS)

IDDM .... Insulin-Dependent Diabetes Mellitus

IDDP .... Interface Design Definition Paper [*Military*] (CAAL)

IDDP .... International Dairy Development Programme [*FAO/DANIDA Dairy Development P rogramme and International Scheme for the Coordination of Dairy Development*] [*Formed by a merger of United Nations*] (EAIO)

IDDP .... Isodecyl Diphenyl Phosphate [*Organic chemistry*]

IDDRG .... International Deep Drawing Research Group [*British*]

IdDrGS .... Church of Jesus Christ of Latter-Day Saints, Genealogical Society Library, Driggs Branch, Driggs, ID [*Library symbol Library of Congress*] (LCLS)

IDDS .... Implantable Drug Delivery System [*Pharmacology*] (DAVI)

IDDS .... Improved Data Display System

IDDS .... Institute for Defense and Disarmament Studies (EA)

IDDS .... Instrumentation Data Distribution System (MUGU)

IDDS .... Integrated Data Display System

IDDS .... Integrated Display Development Station (MCD)

IDDS .... International Dairy Development Scheme

IDDS .... International Digital Data Service [*Western Union Corp.*] [*Data transmission service*]

IDD TR........ Iddings' Dayton Term Reports [*Ohio*] [*A publication*] (DLA)

IDE.............. Imbedded Drive Electronics [*Computer science*]

IDE.............. Independent Development Environment [*Computer science*] (PCM)

IDE.............. Industry-Developed Equipment (AAG)

IDE.............. Infrared Decoy Evaluator

IDE.............. Initial Design Evaluation (MCD)

IDE.............. Inner Dental Epithelium (DB)

IDE.............. Institute for Democratic Education [*Absorbed by Anti-Defamation League of B'nai B'rith*] (EA)

IDE.............. Institute of Developing Economics, Tokyo [*UTLAS symbol*]

IDE............... Insulin-Degrading Enzyme [*Biochemistry*]
IDE............... Integrated Development Environment
IDE............... Integrated Device Electronics
IDE............... Integrated Drive Electronics [*Hard disk interface*] [*Computer science*] (PCM)
IDE............... Intelligent Distributed Editor (HGAA)
IDE............... Intelligent Drive Electronics
IDE............... Interactive Data Entry
IDE............... Interchange Data Element [*Telecommunications*] (OSI)
IDE............... Interdisciplinary Enquiry [*Education*] (AIE)
IDE............... Interim Data Element [*Army*] (AABC)
IDE............... Intrusion Detection Equipment
IDE............... Investigational Device Exemption [*Food and Drug Administration*]
IDE............... Isla Desecheo [*Puerto Rico*] [*Seismograph station code, US Geological Survey*] (SEIS)
IdEa .... Eagle Public Library, Eagle, ID [*Library symbol*] [*Library of Congress*] (LCLS)
IDEA............. IDEAssociates, Inc. [*Telecommunications*] (TSSD)
IDEA............. Identification, Distribution, and Exchange for Action [*Project*]
IDEA............. Improved Data Effectiveness and Availability
IDEA............. Index for Design Engineering Applications [*Data retrieval service*] [*Product engineering*]
IDEA............. Individuals with Disabilities Education Act [*Formerly, The Education for All Handicapped Children Act*] (PAZ)
IDEA............. Inductive Data Exploration and Analysis [*Computer science*]
IDEA............. Industrial Design Excellence Award
IDEA............. Innovasive Devices, Inc. [*NASDAQ symbol*] (SAG)
I/D/E/A .... Institute for Development of Educational Activities (EA)
IDEA............. Integrated Data for Enforcement Analysis System [*Environmental science*]
IDEA............. Integrated Design Engineering Aid [*Computer science*] (RDA)
IDEA............. Integrated Digital Electric Aircraft (PDAA)
IDEA............. Integrated Digital Electronic Automatic (PDAA)
IDEA............. Integrated Dose Environment Analysis
IDEA............. Interactive Data Entry Access [*Data General Corp.*]
IDEA............. Interactive Digital Electronic Appliance [*Computer science*]
IDEA............. Interactive Digital Electronic Appliances
IDEA............. Interface and Display Electronics Assembly
IDEA............. International Association of Fitness Professionals (EA)
IDEA............. International Dalkon Shield Victims Education Association (EA)
IDEA............. International Dance-Exercise Association (EA)
IDEA............. International Data Encryption Algorithm [*Telecommunications*]
IDEA............. International Desalination and Environmental Association [*Later, IDA*] (EA)
IDEA............. International District Energy Association (NTPA)
IDEA............. International Diving Educators Association
IDEA............. International Downtown Executives Association [*Later, IDA*] (EA)
IDEA............. Isolation of Dimensions and Elimination of Alternatives
Idea .... Patent, Trademark, and Copyright Journal of Research and Education [*A publication*] (DLA)
IDEAL........... Integrated Design Engineering and Logistics (PDAA)
IDEAL........... Interdisciplinary Drug Engineering and Assessment Laboratory [*Medicine*] (DB)
IDEAL........... International Digital Electronic Access Library
IDEALS .... Ideal Design of Effective and Logical Systems
IDEALS .... Information Directory of European Automated Library Services (TELE)
IDEALS .... Institute for the Development of Emotional and Life Skills (EA)
IDEAS .... Innovations Deserving Exploratory Analysis Program [*FHWA*] (TAG)
IDEAS .... Inquiry Data Entry Access System (IAA)
IDEAS .... Institutional Development and Economic Affairs Service [*Defunct*] (EA)
IDEAS .... Integrated Design Analysis System [*Space shuttle*] [*NASA*]
IDEAS .... Integrated Design and Engineering Automated System (IEEE)
IDEAS .... Intelligence Data Element Authorization Standards [*Military*] (MCD)
IDEAS .... Interest Determination and Assessment System [*Vocational guidance test*]
IDEAS .... Interest Determination, Exploration, and Assessment System [*Test*] [*Charles B. Johansson*] (TES)
IDEAS .... International Data Exchange for Aviation Safety [*ICAO*] (DA)
IDEAS .... International Decade of Exploration and Assessment of the Seas [*Inactive*] [*Marine science*] (OSRA)
IDEAS .... International Development - Economics Awareness System
IDEB .... Intermittent Dual-Fluid Exhaust Burner
IDec .... Decatur Public Library, Decatur, IL [*Library symbol Library of Congress*] (LCLS)
IDEC............. IDEC Pharmaceuticals Corp. [*Associated Press*] (SAG)
IDEC............. Indirect Evaporative Cooler
IDEC............. Interior Design Educators Council (EA)
IDEC............. International Drug Enforcement Conference
IDECC .... Interstate Distributive Education Curriculum Consortium (EDAC)
IDecH........... Decatur Memorial Hospital, Medical Staff and Nursing School Library, Decatur, IL [*Library symbol Library of Congress*] (LCLS)
IDecJ .... James Millikin University, Decatur, IL [*Library symbol Library of Congress*] (LCLS)
IdEcL .... Elk City School/Community Library, Elk City, ID [*Library symbol*] [*Library of Congress*] (LCLS)
IDecM........... Adolph Meyer Mental Health Center, Decatur, IL [*Library symbol Library of Congress*] (LCLS)
IDecR........... Rolling Prairie Libraries, Decatur, IL [*Library symbol Library of Congress*] (LCLS)
IDecS........... A.E. Staley Manufacturing Co., Decatur, IL [*Library symbol*] [*Library of Congress*] (LCLS)
IDECS .... Image Discrimination, Enhancement, and Combination System [*Electronic optical system*]

IDecStM........ Saint Mary's Hospital, Medical Staff and Nursing Library, Decatur, IL [*Library symbol Library of Congress*] (LCLS)
ID/ED .... Internal Diameter to External Diameter [*Ratio for cardiac valve replacement*] [*Cardiology*] (DAVI)
IDEDS .... International Development Education Documentation Service [*University of Pittsburgh*] (IID)
IdEdS .... Silver & Gold Senior Citizens Library, Eden, ID [*Library symbol*] [*Library of Congress*] (LCLS)
IDEE............. Institute for Democracy in Eastern Europe (EA)
IDEEA .... Information and Data Exchange Experimental Activities
IDEEA .... Instantaneous Drilling Evaluation Log (PDAA)
IDEEA .... International Defense Equipment Exhibitors Association (EA)
IDEF............. ICAM Definition (MCD)
IDEF............. Institut International de Droit d'Expression Francaise [*International Institute of Law of the French Speaking Countries - IILFSC*] [*Paris, France*] (EAIO)
IDEF............. Integrated System Definition Language [*Computer science*] (IEEE)
IDeKN .... Northern Illinois University, De Kalb, IL [*Library symbol Library of Congress*] (LCLS)
IDeKN-L........ Northern Illinois University, College of Law, De Kalb, IL [*Library symbol*] [*Library of Congress*] (LCLS)
IDeKN-LS...... Northern Illinois University, Department of Library Sciences, De Kalb, IL [*Library symbol Library of Congress*] (LCLS)
IDelan.......... Goose Creek Township Carnegie Library, De Land, IL [*Library symbol Library of Congress*] (LCLS)
IDelanSD ...... Bond County Community Unit, School District 2, De Land, IL [*Library symbol Library of Congress*] (LCLS)
IDelav.......... Ayer Public Library, Delavan, IL [*Library symbol Library of Congress*] (LCLS)
IdEm .... Emmett Public Library, Emmett, ID [*Library symbol*] [*Library of Congress*] (LCLS)
Idem .... Italian Derivatives Market (NUMA)
IDEMA .... International Disk Drive Equipment and Materials Association (NTPA)
iDEN .... Integrated Digital Enhanced Network [*Telecommunications*]
IDEN .... Interactive Data Entry Network [*Computer science*] (MHDB)
IDENT .... Identical (MSA)
IDENT .... Identification (AFM)
Ident .... Identification [*Business term*] (EBF)
IDENT .... Identify (ECII)
IDENTIFD ..... Identified (ROG)
Identificat ..... Identification Data [*Aerospace*] (NAKS)
Identix .... Identix, Inc. [*Associated Press*] (SAG)
Ideo .... Ideological
Ideon .... Ideon Group, Inc. [*Associated Press*] (SAG)
IDep .... DePue Public Library, DePue, IL [*Library symbol Library of Congress*] (LCLS)
IDEP .... Industry Data Exchange Program
IDEP .... Institut Africain de Developpement Economique et de Planification [*African Institute for Economic Development and Planning*] [*Dakar, Senegal*] (AF)
IDEP............. Interagency Data Exchange Program [*Later, GIDEP*] (RDA)
IDEP............. Inter-Department Data Exchange Program [*Air Force*] (AFM)
IDEP............. International Data Exchange Program (NITA)
IDEP............. Interservice Data Exchange Program (AFIT)
IDEP............. Ion Density Electronics Package
IDepSD .... DePue Unit, School District 103, DePue, IL [*Library symbol Library of Congress*] (LCLS)
IDEPT.......... Image Document Entry Processing Terminal [*Computer science*] (CIST)
IdEr............. Elk River School/Community Library, Elk River, ID [*Library symbol*] [*Library of Congress*] (LCLS)
IDERA .... International Development Education Resources Association
i derm .... Intradermal [*Medicine*] (AAMN)
IDES............. Image Dissector Echelle Spectrograph [*Instrumentation*]
IDES............. Incoterm Data Entry Software [*Incoterm*] (NITA)
IDES............. Information and Data Exchange System (IAA)
IDES............. Institute for Demographic and Economic Studies [*Research center*] (RCD)
IDES............. Integrated Defense System
IDES............. Interactive Data Entry System [*Computer science*] (MHDI)
IDES............. Interactive Drawing Editing Station (MCD)
IDesA .... American Foundrymen's Society, Des Plaines, IL [*Library symbol Library of Congress*] (LCLS)
IDesB .... Borg-Warner Corp., Ingersoll Research Center, Des Plaines, IL [*Library symbol Library of Congress*] (LCLS)
IDesD .... De Soto, Inc., Des Plaines, IL [*Library symbol Library of Congress*] (LCLS)
IDesN .... National Association of Independent Insurers, Des Plaines, IL [*Library symbol Library of Congress*] (LCLS)
IDesS .... Signal Research Center, Inc., Des Plaines, IL [*Library symbol*] [*Library of Congress*] (LCLS)
IDesSC......... Sandoz Crop Protection Corp., Des Plaines, IL [*Library symbol*] [*Library of Congress*] (LCLS)
IDesU .... Universal Oil Products Co., Des Plaines, IL [*Library symbol Library of Congress*] (LCLS)
IDETX .... IDEX II: Growth Ptfl. Cl.A [*Mutual fund ticker symbol*] (SG)
Idex .... IDEX Corp. [*Associated Press*] (SAG)
IDEX............ Initial Defense Experiment (IEEE)
IdexxLb........ IDEXX Laboratories, Inc. [*Associated Press*] (SAG)
IDF............... Belleville Area College, Belleville, IL [*OCLC symbol*] (OCLC)
IDf............... Deerfield Public Library, Deerfield, IL [*Library symbol Library of Congress*] (LCLS)
IDF............... Identifier (IAA)
IDF............... Image Description File
IDF............... Immune Deficiency Foundation (EA)

IDF...............	Indicating Direction Finder (IAA)
IDF...............	Indigenous Defense Fighter [*Military*]
IDF...............	Industrial Diesel Fuel
IDF...............	Infantile Digital Fibromatosis [*Medicine*] (DB)
IDF...............	In-Flight Diverted Force (CINC)
IDF...............	Ink Donor Film (EDCT)
IDF...............	Innovative Design Fund, Inc. (EA)
IDF...............	Instantaneous Direction Finding (MCD)
IDF...............	Instructional Dialogue Facility (IAA)
IDF...............	Integrated Data File
IDF...............	Interactive Dialogue Facility [*Programming language*] (CSR)
IDF...............	Interceptor Day Fighter (NATG)
IDF...............	Intermediate Distributing Frame [*Telecommunications*]
IDF...............	Intermediate Distribution Frame (ACRL)
IDF...............	Internal Delay Factor [*Computer science*]
IDF...............	Internal Distribution Frame [*Television*] (IAA)
IDF...............	International Dairy Federation [*See also FIL*] [*Brussels, Belgium*] (EAIO)
IDF...............	International Democratic Fellowship
IDF...............	International Dental Federation [*British*]
IDF...............	International Development Foundation (EA)
IDF...............	International Diabetes Federation [*See also FID*] (EAIO)
IDF...............	International Distress Frequency (MUGU)
IDF...............	International Domesticated Furs Ltd. [*Vancouver Stock Exchange symbol*]
IDF...............	International Drilling Federation (EA)
IDF...............	International Drilling Fluids [*Singapore*]
IDF...............	Inverse Document Frequency (NITA)
IDF...............	Iron Dragon-Fly Ltd. [*Russian Federation*] [*ICAO designator*] (FAAC)
IDF...............	Isotropic Distribution Function
IDF...............	Israeli Defense Forces
IDF...............	Item Data File (MCD)
IdFa	Camas County District Library, Fairfield, ID [*Library symbol*] [*Library of Congress*] (LCLS)
IDFA.............	Infant and Dietetic Foods Association [*British*] (DBA)
IDFA.............	International Dairy Foods Association (EA)
IDFB.............	Internationales Daunen- und Federn-Bureau [*International Down and Feather Bure au*] (EAIO)
IDFC.............	Immature Dead Female Child [*Neonatology*] (DAVI)
IdFe	Tri-Community Library, Fernwood, ID [*Library symbol*] [*Library of Congress*] (LCLS)
IDFF.............	Internationale Demokratische Frauenfoederation [*Women's International Democratic Federation*]
IdFh	Shoshone-Bannock Library, Fort Hall, ID [*Library symbol*] [*Library of Congress*] (LCLS)
IdFi	Filer Public Library, Filer, ID [*Library symbol*] [*Library of Congress*] (LCLS)
IDFM.............	Induced Directional FM
IDFN	In Domino Fiducia Nostra [*In the Lord Is Our Trust*] [*Motto of August, Prince of Anhalt-Plotzkau (1575-1653)*] [*Latin*]
IDFOR	Idle Waiting Convoy Forward [*Vessel status*] [*Navy*]
IdFr...............	Franklin County District Library, Franklin, ID [*Library symbol*] [*Library of Congress*] (LCLS)
IDFR	Identified Friendly [*Military*]
IDFS.............	Interferometer Direction Finding System [*Military*] (CAAL)
IDFSS	Infantry Direct-Fire Simulation System (MCD)
IDFT.............	Inverse Discrete Fourier Transform [*Electronics*] (IEEE)
IDfT..............	Trinity Evangelical Divinity School, Deerfield, IL [*Library symbol Library of Congress*] (LCLS)
IDFTA............	International Dwarf Fruit Trees Association (EA)
IDfTD	Trinity Evangelical Divinity School, Deerfield, IL [*Library symbol Library of Congress*] (LCLS)
IDFUN	International Dull Folks Unlimited [*Defunct*] (EA)
IDFV.............	In Deo Faciemus Virtutem [*Through God We Shall Do Valiantly*] [*(Ps., IX. 12) Motto of August, Prince of Anhalt-Plotzkau (1575-1653)*] [*Latin*]
IDFW	Institute for a Drug-Free Workplace (EA)
IDG	Chicago Theological Seminary, Chicago, IL [*OCLC symbol*] (OCLC)
IDG	Ida Grove, IA [*Location identifier FAA*] (FAAL)
IDG	Immunodiffusion in Gel (PDAA)
IDG	Indigo Technologies, Inc. [*Vancouver Stock Exchange symbol*]
IDG	Individual Drop Glider
IDG	Industrial Development Group (MCD)
IDG	Inniskilling Dragoon Guards [*British military*] (DMA)
IDG	Inspector of Degaussing [*Navy*]
IDG	Integrated Drive Generator (MCD)
IDG	Interdisciplinary Group (STED)
IDG	Intermediate-Dose Group [*Medicine*] (STED)
IDG	Internal Drive Generator
IDG	International Data Group [*Publisher of computer magazines*] [*Framingham, MA*]
IdGa..............	Garden Valley District Library, Garden Valley, ID [*Library symbol*] [*Library of Congress*] (LCLS)
IdGc	Garden City Public Library, Garden City, ID [*Library symbol*] [*Library of Congress*] (LCLS)
IDG/CMG......	IDG Conference Management Group [*Framingham, MA*] (TSSD)
IdGf..............	Glenns Ferry Public Library, Glenns Ferry, ID [*Library symbol*] [*Library of Congress*] (LCLS)
IdGg..............	Grangeville Public Library, Grangeville, ID [*Library symbol*] [*Library of Congress*] (LCLS)
IdGi..............	Gibbonsville Community Library, Gibbonsville, ID [*Library symbol*] [*Library of Congress*] (LCLS)
IDGIT	Integrated Data Generation Implementation Technique
IdGo..............	Gooding Public Library, Gooding, ID [*Library symbol*] [*Library of Congress*] (LCLS)
IdGoPS	Gooding Public School District, Gooding, ID [*Library symbol*] [*Library of Congress*] (LCLS)
IdGoS............	Idaho State School for the Deaf and Blind, Gooding, ID [*Library symbol*] [*Library of Congress*] (LCLS)
IdGr	Grace District Library, Grace, ID [*Library symbol*] [*Library of Congress*] (LCLS)
IdGv	Eastern Owyhee County District Library, Grand View, ID [*Library symbol*] [*Library of Congress*] (LCLS)
IDH	Isocitrate Dehydrogenase [*Also, ICD, ICDH*] [*An enzyme*]
IDH	Isocitric Acid Dehydrogenase (STED)
IDH	Meadville Theological School, Chicago, IL [*OCLC symbol*] (OCLC)
IDH1	Isocitrate Dehydrogenase, Soluble (STED)
IDH2	Isocitrate Dehydrogenase Mitochondrial (STED)
IDHA	International District Heating Association [*Later, IDHCA*] (EA)
IdHamSD	Hamer Elementary School, Hamer, ID [*Library symbol*] [*Library of Congress*] (LCLS)
IdHb.............	Horseshoe Bend District Library, Horseshoe Bend, ID [*Library symbol*] [*Library of Congress*] (LCLS)
IDHCA..........	International District Heating and Cooling Association (EA)
IDHEC	Institut des Hautes Etudes Cinematographiques [*French institute for the study of the motion picture*]
IDHF	International Dental Health Foundation (EA)
IdHg.............	Hagerman Public Library, Hagerman, ID [*Library symbol*] [*Library of Congress*] (LCLS)
IDHHB	Institute for the Development of the Harmonious Human Being (EA)
IdHi.............	Idaho State Historical Society, Boise, ID [*Library symbol Library of Congress*] (LCLS)
IDHIDH	In dem Herrn Ist das Heil [*In the Lord Is Salvation*] [*Motto of Dorothee, Princess of Anhalt (1580-1618)*] [*German*]
IdHi-G...........	Idaho Genealogical Society, Boise, ID [*Library symbol Library of Congress*] (LCLS)
IdHl.............	Hailey Public Library, Hailey, ID [*Library symbol*] [*Library of Congress*] (LCLS)
IdHlH	Blaine County Medical Center, Medical Library, Hailey, ID [*Library symbol*] [*Library of Congress*] (LCLS)
IdHm.............	Homedale Public Library, Homedale, ID [*Library symbol*] [*Library of Congress*] (LCLS)
IdHn.............	Hansen Public Library, Hansen, ID [*Library symbol*] [*Library of Congress*] (LCLS)
IdHr	Harrison Public Library, Harrison, ID [*Library symbol*] [*Library of Congress*] (LCLS)
IDHS	Information Data Handling System
IDHS	Integrated Data Handling System
IDHS	Intelligence Data Handling System (AFM)
IDH-S	Isocitrate Dehydrogenase, Soluble (STED)
IDHSC..........	Intelligence Data Handling System Communications (MCD)
IdHyl.............	Hayden Lake Library, Hayden Lake, ID [*Library symbol*] [*Library of Congress*] (LCLS)
IDI	Bethany and Northern Baptist Theological Seminaries Library, Oak Brook, IL [*OCLC symbol*] (OCLC)
IDI.................	Immunologically Detectable Insulin [*Medicine*] (DMAA)
IDI.................	Improved Data Interchange
IDI.................	Indiana, PA [*Location identifier FAA*] (FAAL)
IDI.................	Indirect Injection Engine [*Engineering*]
IDI.................	Induction-Delivery Interval [*Medicine*]
IDI.................	Industrial Designers' Institute [*Later, IDSA*] (EA)
IDI.................	Industrial Development Institute [*France*]
IDI.................	Information Dimensions, Inc. [*Information service or system*] (IID)
IDI.................	Initial Domain Identifier [*Computer science*] (TNIG)
IDI.................	Initial Domain Part [*Telecommunications*] (OSI)
IDI.................	Inspection Departmental Instruction (AAG)
IDI.................	Instant Drug Index [*A publication*] (DAVI)
IDI.................	Institut de Droit International [*Institute of International Law*]
IDI.................	Instructional Dynamics, Inc. (AEBS)
IDI.................	Instrumentation Data Items (NASA)
IDI.................	Integrated Design Inspection (NRCH)
IDI.................	Integrated Direct Ignition [*Automotive engineering*]
IDI.................	Intelligent Dual Interface
IDI.................	Intercomp Design, Inc. [*Neshanic Station, NJ*] [*Telecommunications*] (TSSD)
IDI.................	Inter-Dentale Inferius [*Medicine*] (DMAA)
IDI.................	Interdivision Invoice (AAG)
IDI.................	International Development Institute [*Agency for International Development program*]
IDI.................	International Diabetes Institute [*Australia*] (IRC)
IDI.................	International Dialect Institute
IDI.................	International Disaster Institute [*British*]
IDI.................	Intractable Diarrhea of Infancy [*Pediatrics*]
IDI.................	Ion Dipole Interaction
IDI.................	Iron Disorders Institute
IDIA	Industrial Disputes Investigation Act [*Canada*]
IDIA	Internal Defense Identification Area (SAA)
IDIA	International Digital Imaging Association (NTPA)
IDIB	Industrial Diamond Information Bureau [*British*] (BI)
IdIc	Boise Basin District Library, Idaho City, ID [*Library symbol*] [*Library of Congress*] (LCLS)
IDIC	Institut de Developpement International et de Cooperation [*Institute for International Development and Cooperation IIDC*] [*University of Ottawa*] [*Canada*]
IDIC	Intelligence Division Indications Center [*Military*] (MCD)
IDIC	Internal Dose Information Center [*ORNL*]
IDIC	International Drought Information Center
IDID	Comparator Sys [*NASDAQ symbol*] (TTSB)
IDID	Comparator Systems Corp. [*NASDAQ symbol*] (SAG)

IDID .... Industrial Documentation and Information Department [*Industrial Development Center for Arab States*] [*Information service or system*] (IID)

IDIDAS......... Interactive Digital Image Display and Analysis System [*Marine science*] (OSRA)

IdIf .... Idaho Falls Public Library, Idaho Falls, ID [*Library symbol Library of Congress*] (LCLS)

IdIfA............. Aerojet Nuclear Co., Idaho Falls, ID [*Library symbol Library of Congress*] (LCLS)

IdIfAL........... Argonne National Laboratory, Argonne-West Technical Library, Idaho Falls, ID [*Library symbol*] [*Library of Congress*] (LCLS)

IdIfC............. Bonneville County District Library, Idaho Falls, ID [*Library symbol*] [*Library of Congress*] (LCLS)

IdIfE............. Energy Incorp., Idaho Falls, ID [*Library symbol*] [*Library of Congress*] (LCLS)

IdIfEG........... EG & G Idaho, Inc., INEL Technical Library, Idaho Falls, ID [*Library symbol*] [*Library of Congress*] (LCLS)

IdIfGS .... Church of Jesus Christ of Latter-Day Saints, Genealogical Society Library, IdahoFalls Branch, Idaho Falls, ID [*Library symbol Library of Congress*] (LCLS)

IdIfH............. Eastern Idaho Regional Medical Center, Medical Library, Idaho Falls, ID [*Library symbol*] [*Library of Congress*] (LCLS)

IDIIOM......... Information Displays, Incorporated, Input-Output Machine

IDIL............. Institute for the Development of Indian Law (EA)

IDIM............. Integrated Departmental Instructions Manual

IDIMS........... Interactive Digital Image Manipulation System [*Minicomputer*]

Idings TRD... Iddings' Dayton Term Reports [*Ohio*] [*A publication*] (DLA)

IDIOT .... Instrumentation Digital On-Line Transcriber [*Computer science*]

IDIP .... Intelligence Data Input Package (MCD)

IDIP .... Intensified Drug Inspection Program [*FDA*]

IDIP .... International Directories in Print [*A publication*]

IDIQ .... Indefinite Delivery, Indefinite Quantity [*Type of contract*] (AAGC)

IDIS .... Idaho Drug Information Service [*Information service or system*] (IID)

IDIS .... Institut fuer Dokumentation, Information, und Statistik [*Institute for Documentation, Information, and Statistics*] [*Information service or system*] (IID)

IDIS .... Institut fuer Dokumentation und Information ueber Sozialmedizin und Oeffentliches Gesundheitswesen [*Institute for Documentation and Information in Social Medicine and Public Health*] [*Information retrieval Germany*]

IDIS .... Intrusion Detection and Identification System (PDAA)

IDIS .... Iowa Drug Information Service [*University of Iowa*] [*Information service or system*] (IID)

IDIU .... Interdivisional Information Unit [*Department of Justice intelligence unit*]

IDJ .... Catholic Theological Union, Chicago, IL [*OCLC symbol*] (OCLC)

IDJ .... I Dance Jazz [*Jazz music group*] (ECON)

IDJ .... Information Design Journal [*A publication*] (DGA)

IdJ .... Jerome Public Library, Jerome, ID [*Library symbol*] [*Library of Congress*] (LCLS)

IDJC .... India Docks Joint Committee (ROG)

IdJH............. Saint Benedict's Family Medical Center, Medical Library, Jerome, ID [*Library symbol*] [*Library of Congress*] (LCLS)

IdK .... Community Library Association, Inc., Ketchem, ID [*Library symbol*] [*Library of Congress*] (LCLS)

IDK.............. Internal Derangement of Knee [*Medicine*] (DMAA)

IDK.............. Internal Derangement of Knee Joint

IDK.............. Jesuit-Krauss-McCormick Library, Chicago, IL [*OCLC symbol*] (OCLC)

IdKe............. Kellogg Public Library, Kellogg, ID [*Library symbol*] [*Library of Congress*] (LCLS)

IdKi............. Kimberly Public Library, Kimberly, ID [*Library symbol*] [*Library of Congress*] (LCLS)

IdKo............. Kooskia Public Library, Kooskia, ID [*Library symbol*] [*Library of Congress*] (LCLS)

IdKu............. Kuna School/Comm Library, Kuna, ID [*Library symbol*] [*Library of Congress*] (LCLS)

Id-L.............. Idaho Supreme Court, Idaho State Law Library, Boise, ID [*Library symbol Library of Congress*] (LCLS)

IDL.............. Ideal

IDL.............. Ideal Group of Companies, Inc. [*Toronto Stock Exchange symbol*]

IDL.............. Idler

IDL.............. Indentured Drawing List

IDL.............. Index to Dental Literature (STED)

IDL.............. Indianola, MS [*Location identifier FAA*] (FAAL)

ID(L)........... Infantry Division (Light) [*Army*] (INF)

IDL.............. Information Description Language

IDL.............. Insertion-Deletion Loop-Type [*Genetics*]

IDL.............. Instructional Development Laboratory [*University of Minnesota of Minneapolis Saint Paul*] [*Research center*] (RCD)

IDL.............. Instruction Definition Language

IDL.............. Instrument Detection Level [*Analytical chemistry*]

IDL.............. Instrument Development Laboratories

IDL.............. Intensity Difference Limen (STED)

IDL.............. Interactive Data Language [*Marine science*] (OSRA)

IDL.............. Interdisciplinary Materials Laboratory [*Various universities*]

IDL.............. Interface Definition Language [*Computer science*]

IDL.............. Interfacility Data Link [*FAA*] (TAG)

IDL.............. Intermediate Density Lipoprotein [*Biochemistry*]

IDL.............. International Date Line (MCD)

IDL.............. Isotope Development Ltd.

IdL .... Lewiston City Library, Lewiston, ID [*Library symbol*] [*Library of Congress*] (LCLS)

IDL.............. Rush University, Chicago, IL [*OCLC symbol*] (OCLC)

IDL & RS ..... International Data Library and Reference Service

IDLC............ Integrated Digital Logic Circuit

IDLC............ Integrated Digital Loop Carrier [*Telecommunications*] (ACRL)

IdLe .... Leadore Community Library, Leadore, ID [*Library symbol*] [*Library of Congress*] (LCLS)

IdLES .... Lewiston Elementary Schools, Lewiston, ID [*Library symbol*] [*Library of Congress*] (LCLS)

IdLES-CM .... Lewiston Elementary Schools, Camelot Elementary School, Lewiston, ID [*Library symbol*] [*Library of Congress*] (LCLS)

IdLES-CN .... Lewiston Elementary Schools, Centennial Elementary School, Lewiston, ID [*Library symbol*] [*Library of Congress*] (LCLS)

IdLES-MG .... Lewiston Elementary Schools, McGhee Elementary School, Lewiston, ID [*Library symbol*] [*Library of Congress*] (LCLS)

IdLES-MS .... Lewiston Elementary Schools, McSorley Elementary School, Lewiston, ID [*Library symbol*] [*Library of Congress*] (LCLS)

IdLES-OR .... Lewiston Elementary Schools, Orchards Elementary School, Lewiston, ID [*Library symbol*] [*Library of Congress*] (LCLS)

IdLES-WB .... Lewiston Elementary Schools, Webster Elementary School, Lewiston, ID [*Library symbol*] [*Library of Congress*] (LCLS)

IdLES-WH .... Lewiston Elementary Schools, Whitman Elementary School, Lewiston, ID [*Library symbol*] [*Library of Congress*] (LCLS)

IdLGS .... Church of Jesus Christ of Latter-Day Saints, Genealogical Society Library, Lewiston Branch, Stake Center, Lewiston, ID [*Library symbol Library of Congress*] (LCLS)

IDLH .... Immediately Dangerous to Life and Health

IDLHC .... Immediately Dangerous to Life or Health Concentration [*Toxicology*]

IdLHS .... Lewiston High School, Lewiston, ID [*Library symbol*] [*Library of Congress*] (LCLS)

IdLI .... Independent School District No. 1, Lewiston, ID [*Library symbol*] [*Library of Congress*] (LCLS)

IdLI-C .... Independent School District No. 1, Curriculum Resource Center, Lewiston, ID [*Library symbol*] [*Library of Congress*] (LCLS)

IDLIS .... International Desert Locust Information Service

ID LJ .... Idaho Law Journal [*A publication*] (DLA)

IdLN............. Lewis-Clark State College, Lewiston, ID [*Library symbol Library of Congress*] (LCLS)

IdLNP.......... Nez Perce County Free Library District, Lewiston, ID [*Library symbol Library of Congress*] (LCLS)

IdLNP-Cu ..... Nez Perce County District Library, Culdesac Branch, Culdesac, ID [*Library symbol*] [*Library of Congress*] (LCLS)

IdLNP-L .... Nez Perce County District Library, Lapwai Branch, Lapwai, ID [*Library symbol*] [*Library of Congress*] (LCLS)

IdLNP-N....... Nez Perce County District Library, Nez Perce Branch, Nez Perce, ID [*Library symbol*] [*Library of Congress*] (LCLS)

IdLNP-P....... Nez Perce County District Library, Peck Branch, Peck, ID [*Library symbol*] [*Library of Congress*] (LCLS)

IdLNP-W...... Nez Perce County District Library, Winchester Branch, Winchester, ID [*Library symbol*] [*Library of Congress*] (LCLS)

IDLOD......... Idle Waiting to Load [*Shipping*]

IDLR............ Instrumentation Development Laboratory Report (MCD)

IDLS............ Integrated Decoy Launching System [*Navy*] (CAAL)

IdLSJH........ Saint Joseph's Hospital, Medical Library, Lewiston, ID [*Library symbol*] [*Library of Congress*] (LCLS)

IDLT............ Identification Light

IDLT............ Increment-Decrement Life Table [*Statistics*]

IDM............. Idiopathic Disease of the Myocardium [*Cardiology*] (MAE)

IDM............. IDM Environmental Corp. [*Associated Press*] (SAG)

IDM............. Ignition Diagnostic Monitor [*Automotive engineering*]

IDM............. Illinois Valley Library System, Pekin, IL [*OCLC symbol*] (OCLC)

IDM............. Immune Defense Mechanism [*Medicine*] (DMAA)

IDM............. Improved Data Modem [*Air Force*] (DOMA)

IDM............. Indirect Method

IDM............. Induced Dipole Moment

IDM............. Infant of Diabetic Mother [*Medicine*]

IDM............. Information and Data Management (SSD)

IDM............. Information Document Matching Program [*IRS*]

IDM............. Instant Dimmer Memory (IAA)

IDM............. Integral and Differential Monitoring [*Telecommunications*] (OA)

IDM............. Integrated Delta Modulation (IAA)

IDM............. Integrated Design Methodology [*Electrical engineering*]

IDM............. Integrative Decision Making (MCD)

IDM............. Intelligent Database Machine [*Computer science*]

IDM............. Intelligent Document Management [*Computer science*]

IDM............. Interactive Data Machines [*British*] (NITA)

IDM............. Interdiction Mission [*Air Force*]

IDM............. Intermediate-Dose Methotrexate [*Medicine*] (DMAA)

IDM............. International Direct Mail [*British*]

IDM............. Interpolating Delta Modulator

IDM............. Ion Drift Meter [*Instrumentation*]

IDM............. Issue Definition Memorandum [*Jimmy Carter Administration*]

IDMA........... Insurance Data Management Association

IDMA........... International Dancing Masters Association (BARN)

IDMA........... International Destination Management Association (EAIO)

IDMA........... International Doll Makers Association (EA)

IdMa .... Oneida County District Library, Malad City, ID [*Library symbol*] [*Library of Congress*] (LCLS)

IdMac .... Mackay District Library, Mackay, ID [*Library symbol*] [*Library of Congress*] (LCLS)

IdMaGS....... Church of Jesus Christ of Latter-Day Saints, Genealogical Society Library, MaladStake Branch, Malad City, ID [*Library symbol Library of Congress*] (LCLS)

IdMar.......... Lizard Butte District Library, Marsing, ID [*Library symbol*] [*Library of Congress*] (LCLS)

IDMAS......... Interactive Database Manipulator and Summarizer

IDMB........... International Dictionary of Medicine and Biology [*A publication*]

IDMC .... IDM Environmental [*NASDAQ symbol*] (TTSB)

IDMC .... IDM Environmental Corp. [*NASDAQ symbol*] (SAG)
IDMC .... Immature Dead Male Child [*Neonatology*] (DAVI)
IDMC .... Interdigestive Motility Complex [*Gastroenterology*]
IDMC .... International Dull Men's Club (EA)
IdMC .... Moscow-Latah County Library System, Moscow, ID [*Library symbol*] [*Library of Congress*] (LCLS)
IdMC-D .... Moscow-Latah County District Library, Deary Branch, Deary, ID [*Library symbol*] [*Library of Congress*] (LCLS)
IdMC-G .... Moscow-Latah County District Library, Genesee Branch, Genesee, ID [*Library symbol*] [*Library of Congress*] (LCLS)
IdMC-J .... Moscow-Latah County District Library, Juliaetta Branch, Juliaetta, ID [*Library symbol*] [*Library of Congress*] (LCLS)
IdMcP .... McCall Public Library, McCall, ID [*Library symbol*] [*Library of Congress*] (LCLS)
IdMC-P .... Moscow-Latah County District Library, Potlatch Branch, Potlatch, ID [*Library symbol*] [*Library of Congress*] (LCLS)
IdMC-T .... Moscow-Latah County District Library, Troy Branch, Troy, ID [*Library symbol*] [*Library of Congress*] (LCLS)
IDMCW .... IDM Environmental Wrrt'A' [*NASDAQ symbol*] (TTSB)
IdMe .... Meridian Library District, Meridian, ID [*Library symbol*] [*Library of Congress*] (LCLS)
IdMen .... Jefferson County District Library, Menan Branch, Menan, ID [*Library symbol*] [*Library of Congress*] (LCLS)
IdMen-H ...... Jefferson County District Library, Hamer Branch, Hamer, ID [*Library symbol*] [*Library of Congress*] (LCLS)
IdMen-HV .... Jefferson County District Library, Heart of the Valley Branch, Terreton, ID [*Library symbol*] [*Library of Congress*] (LCLS)
IdMenSD ...... School District No. 251, Menan, ID [*Library symbol*] [*Library of Congress*] (LCLS)
IDM Env....... IDM Environmental Corp. [*Associated Press*] (SAG)
IdMGH .... Gritman Memorial Hospital, Medical Library, Moscow, ID [*Library symbol*] [*Library of Congress*] (LCLS)
IDMH .... Input Destination Message Handler
IdMh .... Mountain Home Public Library, Mountain Home, ID [*Library symbol*] [*Library of Congress*] (LCLS)
IdMhAF........ United States Air Force, Mountain Home Air Force Base Library, Mountain Home, ID [*Library symbol*] [*Library of Congress*] (LCLS)
IdMhH......... Elmore Memorial Hospital, Medical Library, Mountain Home, ID [*Library symbol*] [*Library of Congress*] (LCLS)
IdMhP .... Prairie District Library, Mountain Home, ID [*Library symbol*] [*Library of Congress*] (LCLS)
IdMHS .... Moscow High School, Moscow, ID [*Library symbol*] [*Library of Congress*] (LCLS)
IDMI........... Interface Document Master Index (DNAB)
IDMI........... International Dun's Market Identifiers [*Dun & Bradstreet International*] [*Information service or system*] (IID)
IdMi .... Middleton Public Library, Middleton, ID [*Library symbol*] [*Library of Congress*] (LCLS)
IdMid .... Midvale District Library, Midvale, ID [*Library symbol*] [*Library of Congress*] (LCLS)
IdMin .... Minidoka-Acequia District Library, Minidoka, ID [*Library symbol*] [*Library of Congress*] (LCLS)
IdMJH .... Moscow Junior High School, Moscow, ID [*Library symbol*] [*Library of Congress*] (LCLS)
IDML.......... Internal Data Manipulation Language [*Computer science*] (PDAA)
IDMM.......... Intermediate and Depot Maintenance Manual (NASA)
IdMoGS........ Church of Jesus Christ of Latter-Day Saints, Genealogical Society Library, MooreBranch, Lost River Stake Center, Moore, ID [*Library symbol Library of Congress*] (LCLS)
IdMonB........ Bear Lake County District Library, Montpelier, ID [*Library symbol*] [*Library of Congress*] (LCLS)
IdMonB-P ..... Bear Lake County District Paris Branch, Paris, ID [*Library symbol*] [*Library of Congress*] (LCLS)
IdMonGS...... Church of Jesus Christ of Latter-Day Saints, Genealogical Society Library, Bear Lake Branch, Montpelier, ID [*Library symbol Library of Congress*] (LCLS)
IDMP .... Intraductal Mammary Pressure
IDMS .... Image and Document Management System [*Aquidneck Data Corp.*] (NITA)
IDMS .... Improved Deep Moored Sweep [*Military*] (MCD)
IDMS .... Information and Data Management System (SSD)
IDMS .... Information for Decision-Makers System (MCD)
IDMS .... Integrated Database Management System
IDMS .... Integrated Disposal Management System [*DoD*]
IDMS .... International Directory of Marine Scientists [*Marine science*] (OSRA)
IDMS .... Isotope Dilution Mass Spectrometry
IdMu .... Mullan Public Library, Mullan, ID [*Library symbol*] [*Library of Congress*] (LCLS)
I-DMV .... Internet Department of Motor Vehicles
IDN .... Chicago, IL [*Location identifier FAA*] (FAAL)
IDN .... Inanna's Descent to the Netherworld (BJA)
IDN .... Indagen [*Papua New Guinea*] [*Airport symbol*] (OAG)
IDN .... In Dei Nomine [*In God's Name*] [*Latin*]
IDN .... Indonesia [*ANSI three-letter standard code*] (CNC)
IDN .... Inspection Due Notice [*Military*]
IDN .... Integrated Digital Network [*Telecommunications*]
IDN .... Integrated Healthcare Network [*Health care provider*]
IDN .... Intelligent Data Network
IDN .... International Destron Technologies, Inc. [*Vancouver Stock Exchange symbol*]
IDN .... International Directory Network (USDC)
IdN .... Nampa Public Library, Nampa, ID [*Library symbol*] [*Library of Congress*] (LCLS)

IDN .... United Way of Metropolitan Chicago, Chicago, IL [*OCLC symbol*] (OCLC)
IDNB .... Association of Registered Interior Designers of New Brunswick [*Association des Designers d'Interieur Immatricules du Nouveau-Brunswick*] (AC)
IDNC .... Integrated Direct Numerical Control [*Burroughs Machines Ltd.*] [*Software package*] (NCC)
IDNDR .... International Decade for Natural Disaster Reduction [*1990's*] [*United Nations*]
IDNE .... Indictione [*In the Indiction*] [*Latin*] (ROG)
IDNE .... Inertial Doppler Navigation Equipment (DNAB)
IDNF .... Irredundant Disjunctive Normal Formula
IdNI .... Idaho State School & Hospital, Medical Library, Nampa, ID [*Library symbol*] [*Library of Congress*] (LCLS)
IDNIYRA ...... International DN [*Detroit News*] Ice Yacht Racing Association (EA)
IdNm.......... Meadows Valley Community Library, New Meadows, ID [*Library symbol*] [*Library of Congress*] (LCLS)
IdNMH .... Mercy Medical Center, Medical Library, Nampa, ID [*Library symbol*] [*Library of Congress*] (LCLS)
IdNN .... Northwest Nazarene College, Nampa, ID [*Library symbol Library of Congress*] (LCLS)
ID NO......... Identification Number (DNAB)
IdNo.......... Notus Public Library, Notus, ID [*Library symbol*] [*Library of Congress*] (LCLS)
IdNP.......... Lewis County Free District Library, Nez Perce, ID [*Library symbol*] [*Library of Congress*] (LCLS)
IdNp-K .... Lewis County District Library, Kamiah Branch, Kamiah, ID [*Library symbol*] [*Library of Congress*] (LCLS)
IdNpm........ Armoral Tutle Public Library, New Plymouth, ID [*Library symbol*] [*Library of Congress*] (LCLS)
IDNS .... Illinois Department of Nuclear Safety
IDNSS........ International Directory of Non-Official Statistical Sources [*A publication*]
IdNTS........ National Reactor Testing Station, Technical Library, Phillips Petroleum Co., Idaho Falls, ID [*Library symbol Library of Congress*] (LCLS)
IDNX .... Integrated Digital Network Exchange [*Telecommunications*] (ACRL)
IDO .... Idaho Operations Office [*Energy Research and Development Administration*] (MCD)
IDO .... Identification Officer [*Military*]
IDO .... Indoleamine-Dioxygenase [*An enzyme*]
IDO .... Industrial Development Organization [*United Nations*]
IDO .... Industrial Diesel Oil (ADA)
IDO .... Infrared Drying Oven
IDO .... Inspekteur der Ordnungspolizei [*Inspector of Uniformed Police*] [*German military - World War II*]
IDO .... Intelligence Duty Officer
IDO .... Interdivisional Operations [*NASA*] (NASA)
IDO .... Interdivisional Order
IDO .... Interface Definition Object [*Computer science*]
IDO .... Interim Development Order (ADA)
IDO .... Interim Development Ordinance (PA)
IDO .... Internal Distribution Only (SAA)
IDO .... International Disarmament Organization
IDO .... International District Office
IdO .... Osburn Public Library, Osburn, ID [*Library symbol Library of Congress*] (LCLS)
IDO .... Santa Isabel Do Morro [*Brazil*] [*Airport symbol*] (OAG)
IdOa.......... Oakley District Library, Oakley, ID [*Library symbol*] [*Library of Congress*] (LCLS)
IDOC .... Inside Diameter of Outer Conductor
IDOC .... International Documentation and Communication Center [*Formerly, Council for Development of Religious Information and Documentation - IDOC International*] [*Rome, Italy*] (SLS)
IDOC .... International Documentation on the Contemporary Church [*Later, International Documentation and Communication Center*] (EA)
IDOCS......... Intrusion Detection Optical Communications System [*Computer system security*]
ID/OD......... Inside Diameter/Outside Diameter
IDOD .... International Directory of Directories [*A publication*]
IDOE .... International Decade of Ocean Exploration [*1970's*]
IDOFOR....... Improving the Definition of the Objective Force [*Military*]
IDol.......... Dolton Public Library District, Dolton, IL [*Library symbol Library of Congress*] (LCLS)
IdOl.......... Ola District Library, Ola, ID [*Library symbol*] [*Library of Congress*] (LCLS)
IDON .... Idongus [*Proper*] [*Pharmacy*] (ROG)
IDON VEHIC... Idoneo-Vehiculo [*In a Suitable Vehicle*] [*Pharmacy*]
IdOr .... Clearwater Memorial Public Library, Orofino, ID [*Library symbol*] [*Library of Congress*] (LCLS)
IdOrHS........ Orofino High School Library, Orofino, ID [*Library symbol*] [*Library of Congress*] (LCLS)
IDOS .... Interactive Disk Operating System [*Computer Associates, Inc.*]
IDOS .... Interrupt Disk Operating System
IDOT .... Instrumentation Online Transcriber (IDOE)
IDoV.......... United States Veterans Administration Hospital, Downey, IL [*Library symbol Library of Congress*] (LCLS)
IDow .... Downers Grove Public Library, Downers Grove, IL [*Library symbol Library of Congress*] (LCLS)
IDowG........ George Williams College, Downers Grove, IL [*Library symbol Library of Congress*] (LCLS)
IDP........... Image Data Processor
IDP........... Immunodiffusion Procedure [*Immunochemistry*]
IDP........... Improvement Data Plan (MCD)
IDP........... Incremental Dividend Preferred [*Share*] [*Investment term*]

IDP.............. Indenture Part List (KSC)
IDP.............. Independence [Kansas] [Airport symbol] (AD)
IDP.............. Independence, KS [Location identifier FAA] (FAAL)
IDP.............. Independence Petroleums [Vancouver Stock Exchange symbol]
IDP.............. Independent Democratic Party [Liberia] [Political party] (EY)
IDP.............. Independent Democratic Party [Gibraltar] [Political party]
IDP.............. Individual Development Plan (RDA)
IDP.............. Individual Development Program [Civil Service Commission]
IDP.............. Industrial Data Processing
IDP.............. Information and Data Base Publishing Report [A publication]
IDP.............. Information Data Processing
IDP.............. Initial Delay Position [Military] (AABC)
IDP.............. Initial Domain Part [Telecommunications] (OSI)
IDP.............. Initial Dose Period [Medicine] (MAE)
IDP.............. Inosine Diphosphate [Biochemistry]
IDP.............. Input Data Processor (CET)
IDP.............. Instantaneous Diastolic Pressure (MAE)
IDP.............. Institute of Data Processing [Later, IDPM]
IDP.............. Instructor Display Panel
IDP.............. Instrumentation Development Plan (MCD)
IDP.............. Integrated Data Presentation (MCD)
IDP.............. Integrated Data Processing
IDP.............. Integrated Data Processor (NAKS)
IDP.............. Intelligence Data Processing (MCD)
IDP.............. Interactive Database Processor [Xerox Corp.] (MCD)
IDP.............. Interactive Display Panel (MCD)
IDP.............. Intercept Deployment Plan [National Security Agency]
IDP.............. Interdigit Pause [Telecommunications] (TEL)
IDP.............. Interface Design Plan [Air Force]
IDP.............. Intermodulation Distortion Percentage
IDP.............. Internal Data Processing (IAA)
IDP.............. Internal Defense Plans (CINC)
IDP.............. Internal Design Pressure (PDAA)
IDP.............. Internal Development and Production Program
IDP.............. Internal Distribution Publication [Navy] (MCD)
IDP.............. Intern-Architect Development Program (DICI)
IDP.............. International Driving Permit
IDP.............. Internet Datagram Protocol [Computer science] (ACRL)
IDP.............. Interpersonal Diagnosis of Personality [Psychology]
IDP.............. Interplanetary Dust Particle
IDP.............. Investment Dollar Premium (ADA)
IDP.............. Isotope Development Program [AEC] (MCD)
IdP.............. Pocatello Public Library, Pocatello, ID [Library symbol] [Library of Congress] (LCLS)
IDPA............ Inland Daily Press Association
IDPAI.......... International Directory of Professional Astronomical Institutions [A publication]
IDPAR......... Institute of Donations and Public Affairs Research [Former name of Canadian Centre for Business in the Community] (NFD)
IdPar........... Parma Public Library, Parma, ID [Library symbol] [Library of Congress] (LCLS)
IdPay.......... Payette Public Library, Payette, ID [Library symbol] [Library of Congress] (LCLS)
IdPBH........ Bannock Regional Medical Center, Medical Library [Library symbol] [Library of Congress] (LCLS)
IDPC.......... Integrated Data Processing Center
IDPF........... Integrated Digital Photogrammetric Facility [National Oceanic and Atmospheric Administration]
IdPf........... Post Falls Public Library, Post Falls, ID [Library symbol Library of Congress] (LCLS)
IDPG.......... Impact Data Pulse Generator (IAA)
IdPGS........ Church of Jesus Christ of Latter-Day Saints, Genealogical Society Library, Pocatello Branch, Pocatello, ID [Library symbol Library of Congress] (LCLS)
IDPH.......... IDEC Pharmaceuticals [NASDAQ symbol] (TTSB)
IDPH.......... IDEC Pharmaceuticals Corp. [NASDAQ symbol] (SPSG)
IDPH.......... Idiopathic Pulmonary Hemosiderosis [Medicine]
IdPH.......... Pocatello Regional Medical Center, Medical Library, Pocatello, ID [Library symbol] [Library of Congress] (LCLS)
IdPI........... Idaho State University, Pocatello, ID [Library symbol Library of Congress] (LCLS)
IDPI........... International Data Processing Institute (MCD)
IdPi........... Pierce District Library, Pierce, ID [Library symbol] [Library of Congress] (LCLS)
IdPiES........ Pierce Elementary School, Pierce, ID [Library symbol] [Library of Congress] (LCLS)
IdPin......... Pinehurst-Kingston Library, Pinehurst, ID [Library symbol] [Library of Congress] (LCLS)
IdPlu......... Plummer Public Library, Plummer, ID [Library symbol] [Library of Congress] (LCLS)
IDPM......... Industry Direct Purchase Manufacturer (AFIT)
IDPM......... Initial Draft Presidential Memorandum
IDPM......... Institute for Development Policy and Management [University of Manchester] [British] (ECON)
IDPM......... Institute of Data Processing Management [DPMA and Institute of Data Proce ssing - IDP] [Formed by a merger of] (EAIO)
IdPM......... Pocatello Regional Medical Center, Pocatello, ID [Library symbol] [Library of Congress] (LCLS)
IDPN......... Iminodipropionitrile [Biochemistry]
IDPR......... Inmate Development Pre-release (WDAA)
IdPr........... Priest River Library, Priest River, ID [Library symbol] [Library of Congress] (LCLS)
IdPre......... Preston Carnegie Library, Preston, ID [Library symbol] [Library of Congress] (LCLS)

IdPrP......... Priest Lake Community Library, Priest River, ID [Library symbol] [Library of Congress] (LCLS)
IDPS.......... Improvement Data Plan Sheet (MCD)
IDPS.......... Incremental Differential Pressure System (AAG)
IDPS.......... Instrument Data Processing System
IDPS.......... Integrated Data Processing System
IDPS.......... Interactive Direct Processing System [NCR Corp.]
IDPS.......... Interface Digital Processor (MCD)
IDPS/LF...... IDPS/Large File (NITA)
IDPSS........ IGOSS [Integrated Global Ocean Station System] Data Processing and Services System (MSC)
IDPT.......... Image Dissector Photomultiplier Tube
IDPT.......... International Donkey Protection Trust (EAIO)
IDPTF........ Indirect Productive Time Factors (MCD)
IdQ........... Identification Qualification
IDQ........... Individualized Dementia Questionnaire [Medicine] (DMAA)
IDQ........... Industrial Development Quotient
IDQ........... International Dairy Queen, Inc. (EFIS)
IDQ........... International Delta Resources [Vancouver Stock Exchange symbol]
IDQ........... Quincy Public Library, Quincy, IL [OCLC symbol] (OCLC)
IDQA......... Individual Documented Quality Assurance
IDR........... Greeley & Hansen, Chicago, IL [OCLC symbol] (OCLC)
IDR........... Identification Record [Computer science] (MCD)
IDR........... Im Deutschen Reich. Zeitschrift des Central-Vereins Deutscher Staatsbuerger Juedischen Glaubens [Berlin] [A publication] (BJA)
IDR........... Iminodaunorubicin [Antineoplastic drug]
IDR........... Implementation Delay Report [Social Security Administration]
IDR........... Incremental Digital Recorder
IDR........... Independent Design Review (NRCH)
IDR........... Indian Defense Rules
IDR........... Indicator Co. [Hungary] [FAA designator] (FAAC)
IDR........... Individual Data Record
IDR........... Indore [India] [Airport symbol] (AD)
IDR........... Industrial Damage Reports [Formerly, ITR] [British World War II]
IDR........... Industrial Data Reduction (MUGU)
IDR........... Industrial Development Revenue Bond [Investment term]
IDR........... Infantry Drill Regulations
IDR........... Infinite-Duration Impulse (IAA)
IDR........... Information Descriptor Record (MHDB)
IDR........... Information Dissemination and Retrieval [System] [Reuters Ltd.]
IDR........... Initial Design Review
IDR........... Input Data Request
IDR........... Inspection Discrepancy Report (MCD)
IDR........... Installation Data Record
IDR........... Institute for Delphinid Research (EA)
IDR........... Instrumentation Development Request (MCD)
IDR........... Integral Dryway Route [Nuclear energy] (NUCP)
IDR........... Integrated Dry Route (PDAA)
IDR........... Intelligent Disaster Recovery [Computer science]
IDR........... Intercept During Reentry [Aerospace] (IAA)
IDR........... Interface Data Report (NRCH)
IDR........... Interim Depot Repair
IDR........... Interim Design Review (MCD)
IDR........... Interim Development Report
IDR........... Interim Discrepancy Report
IDR........... Intermediate Design Review (NASA)
IDR........... Intermittent-Duty Rating
IDR........... Internal Development Report
IDR........... International Damascus Resources [Vancouver Stock Exchange symbol]
IDR........... International Defense Review [Interavia Publications] [Information service or system A publication] (CRD)
IDR........... International Depositary Receipt [Investment term]
IDR........... International Drawing Rights
IDR........... Internet Domain Registrars
IDR........... Intradermal Reaction [Medicine] (MAE)
IDR........... Invoice Discrepancy Report [Business term]
IdR........... Madison County Library District, Rexburg, ID [Library symbol] [Library of Congress] (LCLS)
IDR........... Winder, GA [Location identifier FAA] (FAAL)
IDRA......... Insanity Defense Reform Act of 1984
IDRA......... Intercultural Development Research Association (EA)
IDRA......... International Desert Racing Association [Automobile racing]
IDRA......... International Disaster Recovery Association (EA)
IDRA......... Irish Dinghy Racing Association (BI)
IDR & DS.... International Directory of Research and Development Scientists [A publication]
IDRB......... Industrial-Development Revenue Bond [Issued by a state or local government to finance construction by a private company, which then becomes responsible for repaying the debt] [Investment term]
IDRC......... Industrial Development Research Council (EA)
IDRC......... International Development Research Centre [ICSU] [Research center Canada]
IDRD......... Information Definition Requirements Document (NASA)
IDRD......... Internal Data Requirement Description (MCD)
IDREA....... Idle Other Reasons [Vessel status] [Navy]
IDRF......... International Development and Refugee Foundation
IdRg......... Salmon River Public Library, Riggins, ID [Library symbol] [Library of Congress] (LCLS)
IDRH......... Madison Memorial Hospital, Medical Library, Rexburg, ID [Library symbol] [Library of Congress] (LCLS)
IdRi......... Richfield District Library, Richfield, ID [Library symbol] [Library of Congress] (LCLS)

IdRig............ Rigby Public Library, Rigby, ID [*Library symbol*] [*Library of Congress*] (LCLS)

IdRir .... Ririe Public Library, Ririe, ID [*Library symbol*] [*Library of Congress*] (LCLS)

IDRL .... Intercompany Data Requirements List (MCD)

IdRMH .... Madison Memorial Hospital, Rexburg, ID [*Library symbol*] [*Library of Congress*] (LCLS)

IdRo............. Roberts Public Library, Roberts, ID [*Library symbol*] [*Library of Congress*] (LCLS)

IdRoc .... Rockland School/Community Library, Rockland, ID [*Library symbol*] [*Library of Congress*] (LCLS)

IDRP .... Intellectual Disability Review Panel

IDRP .... Interdomain Routing Protocol [*Computer science*] (TNIG)

IdRR .... Ricks College, Rexburg, ID [*Library symbol Library of Congress*] (LCLS)

IDRS .... Integrated Data Retrieval System [*Department of the Treasury*]

IDRS .... Intellectual Disability Rights Service

IDRS .... International Double Reed Society (EA)

IDRTY .... Indirectly

IdRu .... DeMary Memorial Public Library, Rupert, ID [*Library symbol*] [*Library of Congress*] (LCLS)

IdRuH .... Minidoka Memorial Hospital, Medical Library, Rupert, ID [*Library symbol*] [*Library of Congress*] (LCLS)

IDRV .... Ionic Drive

IDS............... Identification Section

IDS............... Identification Supervisor [*Military*]

IDS............... IDS Aircraft Lt. [*British*] [*FAA designator*] (FAAC)

IDS............... Iduronate Sulfatase [*An enzyme*]

IDS............... Image Display System

IDS............... Image Dissector Scanner [*Instrumentation*]

IDS............... Immune Deficiency State

IDS............... Improvement Data System (MCD)

IDS............... Impulse Duplexer Study

IDS............... Inadvertent Destruct [*Aerospace*] (AAG)

IDS............... Inclined Drive Shaft (DA)

IDS............... Income Data Service [*Research firm*] [*British*]

IDS............... Income Distribution Survey

IDS............... Incremented Dynamic Scanning (DAVI)

IDS............... India Development Service (EA)

IDS............... Indicator Drive Screw

IDS............... Industries Development Strategy

IDS............... Industry Data Sources [*Information Access Co.*] [*Information service or system*] (CRD)

IDS............... Inertial Data System

IDS............... Inertial Doppler System

IDS............... Infectious Disease Service (DAVI)

IDS............... Information Data Search, Inc. [*Information service or system*] (IID)

IDS............... Information Delivery Service [*Telecommunications*]

IDS............... Information Display System

IDS............... Information Dissemination System (OICC)

IDS............... Infrared Detection Set

IDS............... Infrared Discrimination System

IDS............... Inhibitor of DNA Synthesis [*Immunochemistry*]

IDS............... Input Data Strobe

IDS............... Institute for Democratic Socialism (EA)

IDS............... Institute of Development Studies [*University of Sussex*] [*British*]

IDS............... Institut fuer Deutsche Sprache [*Institute for German Language*] [*Information service or system*] (IID)

IDS............... Instruction Set Process (ECII)

IDS............... Instrument Data System

IDS............... Instrument Development Section

IDS............... Instrument Development Set

IDS............... Integral Direct Station Selection (PDAA)

IDS............... Integrated Database (COE)

IDS............... Integrated Data Storage (NITA)

IDS............... Integrated Data Store [*or System*] [*Honeywell, Inc.*] [*Computer science*]

IDS............... Integrated Defensive System

IDS............... Integrated Display Set

IDS............... Integrated Display Situation

IDS............... Intellectual Disability Services [*Australian Capital Territory, Queensland*]

IDS............... Intelligence Data System

IDS............... Intelligent Disk Subsystem [*Northgate Computer Systems*] [*Computer science*] (PCM)

IDS............... Intelligent Display System [*Computer science*]

IDS............... Interactive Data System [*Computer science*]

IDS............... Interactive Design Software (NITA)

IDS............... Interactive Diagnostic System (AAEL)

IDS............... Interactive Display System

IDS............... Interagency Dialing System [*Telephones*]

IDS............... Interdepartmental Dial Service [*or System*] [*Telephones*]

IDS............... Interdictor Strike

IDS............... Inter-Disciplinary Studies [*Education*] (AIE)

IDS............... Interface Data Sheet (NASA)

IDS............... Interface Design Specification (CAAL)

IDS............... Interface Design Standards (COE)

IDS............... Interim Decay Storage [*Nuclear energy*] (NRCH)

IDS............... Interior Design Society (EA)

IDS............... Interlibrary Delivery Service of Pennsylvania [*Library network*]

IDS............... Intermediate Decay Storage [*Nuclear energy*] (NRCH)

IDS............... Intermediate Direct Support [*DoD*]

IDS............... Intermediate Drum Storage (CET)

IDS............... Internal Distribution System [*Television*]

IDS............... International Data Services Corp. [*Vancouver Stock Exchange symbol*]

IDS............... International Development Services

IDS............... International Development Strategy [*United Nations*]

IDS............... International Doctor's Society (EA)

IDS............... International Documents Service [*Defunct*] (EA)

IDS............... International Dostoevsky Society (EA)

IDS............... International Dove Society [*Defunct*] (EA)

IDS............... Interstate Dept. Stores, Inc. (EFIS)

IDS............... Intrusion Detection System (MCD)

IDS............... Inventory of Drinking Situations [*Test*] (TMMY)

IDS............... Investigative Dermatological Society (DAVI)

IDS............... Investors Diversified Services, Inc. [*Mutual funds*]

IDS............... Ion Dip Spectroscopy

IDS............... Ion Drift Semiconductor

IDS............... Isotope Detection System [*Nuclear energy*] (NRCH)

IDS............... Item Description Sheet (NASA)

Id-S............. Office of the Secretary of State, Boise, ID [*Library symbol Library of Congress*] (LCLS)

IdS............... Shelley Public Library, Shelley, ID [*Library symbol*] [*Library of Congress*] (LCLS)

IDS............... Spoon River College, Canton, IL [*OCLC symbol*] (OCLC)

IDSA .... Industrial Designers' Society of America (EA)

IDSA .... Industrial Services of America, Inc. [*NASDAQ symbol*] (SAG)

IDSA .... Infectious Diseases Society of America (EA)

IDSA .... Interactive Digital Software Association (NTPA)

IDSA .... International Dark-Sky Association (EA)

IDSA .... International Diving Schools Association (EA)

IdSa .... St. Anthony Public Library, St. Anthony, ID [*Library symbol*] [*Library of Congress*] (LCLS)

IdSaF .... Fremont County District Library, St. Anthony, ID [*Library symbol*] [*Library of Congress*] (LCLS)

IdSal .... Salmon Public Library, Salmon, ID [*Library symbol*] [*Library of Congress*] (LCLS)

IdSalH .... Steel Memorial Hospital, Salmon, ID [*Library symbol*] [*Library of Congress*] (LCLS)

IdSan .... East Bonner County Free Public Library District, Sandpoint, ID [*Library symbol*] [*Library of Congress*] (LCLS)

IdSan-C....... East Bonner County District Library, Clark Fork Branch, Clark Fork, ID [*Library symbol*] [*Library of Congress*] (LCLS)

IdSanH........ Bonner General Hospital, Medical Library, Sandpoint, ID [*Library symbol*] [*Library of Congress*] (LCLS)

IDSB .... Independent Double Sideband

IDSC .... International Die Sinkers' Conference (EA)

IdSc .... Sugar Salem School/Community Library, Sugar City, ID [*Library symbol*] [*Library of Congress*] (LCLS)

IDSCM .... Initial Defense Satellite Communication (KSC)

IDSCP .... Initial Defense Satellite Communications Project [*Telecommunications*] (TEL)

IDSCS .... Initial Defense Satellite Communication System (KSC)

IDSD .... Institutional Data System Division [*Johnson Space Center*] [*NASA*] (NASA)

IDSEG .... International Development Studies Group

IDSF .... Intelligence Defector Source File [*Military*] (MCD)

IDSF............ Inter-Agency Data Systems Facility [*General Services Administration*] (MCD)

IDSF .... Interim Data Switching Facility (ADA)

IdSh .... Shoshone Public Library, Shoshone, ID [*Library symbol*] [*Library of Congress*] (LCLS)

IDSI .... Interactive Data Services, Inc. [*Database producer*] [*Information service or system*] (IID)

IDSIA .... Immune Deficiency Syndrome ™Innocently ∫Acquired (ADA)

IDS/IGS....... Intermediate Direct Support/Intermediate General Support [*Army*]

IDSL............ Intrusion Detection and Sensor Laboratory [*Army*] (RDA)

IDSM .... Indian Distinguished Service Medal [*British*]

IDSM .... Inertial Dampened Servomotor

IDSM .... Integrated Direct Support Maintenance (MCD)

IDSM .... Intermediate Direct Support Maintenance (MCD)

IdSm .... St. Maries Public Library, St. Maries, ID [*Library symbol*] [*Library of Congress*] (LCLS)

IdSmB......... Benewah County Library District, St. Maries, ID [*Library symbol*] [*Library of Congress*] (LCLS)

IDSO .... Interdivisional Sales Order [*NASA*] (NASA)

IDSO .... International Diamond Security Organization (BARN)

IDSOT .... Interim Daily System Operational Test [*Navy*] (NG)

IDSRS .... Ionization-Detected Stimulated Raman Spectroscopy

IDSS .... ICAM [*Integrated Computer-Aided Manufacturing*] Decision Support System (IEEE)

IDSS .... Image Data System Simulation [*NASA*]

IDSS .... Information Decision Support System (MCD)

IDSS .... International Development Support Services Pty. Ltd. [*Australia*] (ECON)

IDSS .... Interoperability Decision Support System (COE)

IdSs .... Soda Springs Public Library, Soda Springs, ID [*Library symbol*] [*Library of Congress*] (LCLS)

IDST............ Information and Documentation on Science and Technology (NITA)

IdSt............. Stanley City Library, Stanley, ID [*Library symbol*] [*Library of Congress*] (LCLS)

IDSTO .... Idle Used for Storage [*Shipping*]

IdSuIGS .... Church of Jesus Christ of Latter-Day Saints, Genealogical Society Library, Salmon Branch, Salmon River Stake Center, Salmon, ID [*Library symbol Library of Congress*] (LCLS)

IdSvH.......... Moritz Community Hospital, Medical Library, Sun Valley, ID [*Library symbol*] [*Library of Congress*] (LCLS)

IDT............... I-Load Data Tape (NASA)

IDT............. Image Dissector Tube
IDT............. Immune Diffusion Test [*Medicine*] (DMAA)
IDT............. Immunodiffusion Test [*Medicine*] (DB)
IDT............. Implantation Doping Technique
IDT............. Improved Definition Television (NTCM)
IDT............. Inactive Duty Training [*Military*] (AABC)
IDT............. Industrial Data Terminal
IDT............. Industrial Data Terminals Corporation (NITA)
IDT............. Industrial Disputers Tribunal [*British*]
IDT............. Information Display Technology (EFIS)
IDT............. Inspection Discrepancy Tag (KSC)
IDT............. Instillation Delivery Time [*Medicine*] (DMAA)
IDT............. Instrument Definition Team
IDT............. Integrated Device Technology, Inc. (PS)
IDT............. Integrated Dynamic Tester
IDT............. Intelligent Data Terminal
IDT............. Interactive Display Terminal (MCD)
IDT............. Interdigital Transducer [*Physics*]
IDT............. Interdisciplinary Team [*Education*]
IDT............. Interdivision Time [*Cytology*]
IDT............. Interdivision Transfer (AAG)
IDT............. International Diagnostic Technology [*Medicine*]
IDT............. International Discount Telecommunications (ECON)
IDT............. Interrupt-Descriptor Table [*Computer science*]
IDT............. Intradermal Typhoid [*Medicine*] (DMAA)
IDT............. Ion Doping Technique
IDT............. Isodensitracer
IDT............. Peoria Heights Public Library, Peoria Heights, IL [*OCLC symbol*] (OCLC)
IDTA........... Institute of Drug Technology Australia
IDTA........... Interdivisional Technical Agreement [*NASA*] (NASA)
IDTA........... International Differential Treatment Association
IDTC........... IDT Corp. [*NASDAQ symbol*] (TTSB)
IDTC........... Indefinite Delivery Type Contract [*DoD*]
IDTCorp .... IDT Corp. [*Associated Press*] (SAG)
IDTE........... ID Table Entry [*Galaxy*] [*Computer science*]
ID TER......... Idaho Territory
IdTerSD .... West Jefferson School District No. 253, Terreton, ID [*Library symbol*] [*Library of Congress*] (LCLS)
IDTF........... International Documents Task Force [*Government Documents Round Table*] [*American Library Association*]
IdTf........... Twin Falls Public Library, Twin Falls, ID [*Library symbol Library of Congress*] (LCLS)
IdTfGS .... Church of Jesus Christ of Latter-Day Saints, Genealogical Society Library, Twin Falls Branch, Twin Falls, ID [*Library symbol Library of Congress*] (LCLS)
IdTfH.......... Magic Valley Regional Medical Center, Medical Library, Twin Falls, ID [*Library symbol*] [*Library of Congress*] (LCLS)
IdTfSI......... College of Southern Idaho, Twin Falls, ID [*Library symbol*] [*Library of Congress*] (LCLS)
IDTI........... Integrated Device Tech [*NASDAQ symbol*] (TTSB)
IDTI........... Integrated Device Technology [*NASDAQ symbol*] (SAG)
IDTI........... Integrated Device Technology, Inc. (NQ)
IDTIMS .... Isotope Dilution Thermal Ionization Mass Spectrometry
IDTM........... Integrated Development Test Matrix [*Army*]
IDTOC......... Independent Division Tactical Operations Center [*Army*] (AABC)
IDTP........... Integrated Data Transmittal Package
IDTR........... Interdivisional Transfer Register
IDTS........... Improved Doppler Tracking System
IDTS........... Instrumentation Data Test Station
IDTS........... Instrumentation Data Transmission System
IDTS........... Integrated Development Test Schedule
IDTS........... Iron Dressers Trade Society [*A union*] [*British*]
IDTSC .... Instrumentation Data Transmission System Controller
IDTU .... Intoxicated Driver Testing Unit [*Criminology*] (LAIN)
IDTV .... Improved Definition Television
IDTV .... Interactive Digital Television
IDTW .... International Union of Doll and Toy Workers of the US and Canada [*Later, IUANPW*] (EA)
IDTY .... Intermittent Duty (MSA)
IDU .... De Pauw University, Greencastle, IN [*OCLC symbol*] (OCLC)
idu .... Idaho [*MARC country of publication code Library of Congress*] (LCCP)
IDU .... Idle Signal Unit [*Electronics*] (EECA)
IDU .... Idoxuridine [*or Iododeoxyuridine*] [*Also, IDUR, IdUrd, IUDR*] [*Pharmacology*]
IDU .... Immunological Distance Unit [*Genetics*]
IDU .... Indicator Drive Unit (IAA)
IDU .... Industrial Development Unit (IEEE)
IDU .... Industry, TX [*Location identifier FAA*] (FAAL)
IDU .... Infrared Detection Unit
IDU .... Injecting Drug User
IDU .... Interface Demonstration Unit (NASA)
IDU .... Intermittent Drive Unit
IDU .... International Democrat Union (EA)
IDU .... International Dendrology Union
IDU .... Iododeoxyuridine (DB)
IdU .... University of Idaho, Moscow, ID [*Library symbol Library of Congress*] (LCLS)
IdUA .... Iduronic Acid
IDUD........... Independent Deployable Unit Detachment (MCD)
IDUF .... Interactive Display and Update Facility (SSD)
IdU-L .... University of Idaho, Law Library, Moscow, ID [*Library symbol Library of Congress*] (LCLS)

IDun........... Dunlap Public Library District, Dunlap, IL [*Library symbol Library of Congress*] (LCLS)
IDup........... A. C. Dougherty Memorial Township Library, Dupo, IL [*Library symbol Library of Congress*] (LCLS)
IDupHS .... Dupo Junior-Senior High School, Dupo, IL [*Library symbol Library of Congress*] (LCLS)
IDUR .... Idoxuridine [*or Iododeoxyuridine*] [*Also, IDU, IdUrd, IUDR*]
IDUR .... Intercept During Unpowered Rise [*Aerospace*] (IAA)
IdUrd .... Iododeoxyuridine [*Also, IDU, IDUR, IUDR*] [*Pharmacology*]
IDV............ Dunlap Public Library District, Dunlap, IL [*OCLC symbol*] (OCLC)
IDV............ Indinavir [*An antiviral drug*]
idv .... Individuals
IDV............ Initial Development Ltd. [*Vancouver Stock Exchange symbol*]
IDV............ Integrating Digital Voltmeter
IDV............ Intermittent Demand Ventilation [*Medicine*]
IDV............ International Distillers & Vintners [*British*]
IDV............ Internationaler Deutschlehrerverband [*International Association of Teachers of German - IATG*] [*Copenhagen, Denmark*] (EAIO)
IdV............ Valley of Tetons District Library, Victor, ID [*Library symbol*] [*Library of Congress*] (LCLS)
IDVC .... Indwelling Venous Catheter [*Medicine*]
IDVID .... Immersed Deflection Vidicon Device (IAA)
IDVM .... Integrating Digital Voltmeter
IDVP .... Independent Design Verification Program (NRCH)
IDW........... Input Data Word
IDW........... Institut fuer Dokumentationswesen [*Germany*]
IDW........... Investigation-Derived Waste (BCP)
IdW........... Wallace Public Library, Wallace, ID [*Library symbol*] [*Library of Congress*] (LCLS)
IDW........... Washington Township Library, Washington, IL [*OCLC symbol*] (OCLC)
IDWA .... Interdivisional Work Authorization
IDWD .... Input Data Word (MCD)
IdWe .... Weippe Public Library, Weippe, ID [*Library symbol*] [*Library of Congress*] (LCLS)
IdWeES........ Weippe Elementary School, Weippe, ID [*Library symbol*] [*Library of Congress*] (LCLS)
IdWei .... Weiser Public Library, Weiser, ID [*Library symbol*] [*Library of Congress*] (LCLS)
IdWen .... Wendell Public Library, Wendell, ID [*Library symbol*] [*Library of Congress*] (LCLS)
IdWenSD .... Wendell School District, Wendell, ID [*Library symbol*] [*Library of Congress*] (LCLS)
IDWF .... Individual Drinking Water Flavors [*Developed by Natick Research and Development Center to encourage soldiers to drink more fluids to prevent dehydration*] (INF)
IDWI .... Imperial Direct West India Mail Service Co. (ROG)
IdWi .... Wilder District Library, Wilder, ID [*Library symbol*] [*Library of Congress*] (LCLS)
IDWO .... Inter-Division Work Order
IDWR .... Interim Design and Workmanship Rules (PDAA)
IDX............ Caterpillar Tractor Co., Peoria, IL [*OCLC symbol*] (OCLC)
IDX............ Identix, Inc. [*AMEX symbol*] (SPSG)
IDX............ Index (MSA)
IDX............ Individual Index File [*Computer science*] (PCM)
IDX............ Intelligent Digital Exchange (NITA)
IDXC .... IDX Systems Corp. [*NASDAQ symbol*] (SAG)
IDXC .... IDX Systmes [*NASDAQ symbol*] (TTSB)
IDXSys......... IDX Systems Corp. [*Associated Press*] (SAG)
IDXX .... IDEXX Laboratories [*NASDAQ symbol*] (SPSG)
IDY............ Fondulac Public Library District, East Peoria, IL [*OCLC symbol*] (OCLC)
IDYN .... Innerdyne, Inc. [*NASDAQ symbol*] (SAG)
IDZ............ Bank Marketing Association, Chicago, IL [*OCLC symbol*] (OCLC)
IDZ............ Inner Defense Zone
IE............. Evanston Public Library, Evanston, IL [*Library symbol Library of Congress*] (LCLS)
IE............. Idees pour l'Europe [*Paris, France*] (EAIO)
IE............. Id Est [*That Is*] [*Latin*]
IE............. Imbedded Error [*Factor analysis*]
IE............. Immediate-Early [*Genetics*]
IE............. Immobilized Enzyme [*Physiology*]
IE............. Immunitaetseinheit [*Immunizing Unit*] [*Medicine*]
IE............. Immunoelectrophoresis [*Analytical biochemistry*]
IE............. Import Executive [*British*]
IE............. Independent Estimate [*Army*]
IE............. Independent Evaluation (MCD)
IE............. Independent Expenditure [*Campaign-finance law provision*]
IE............. Index Error [*Navigation*]
IE............. Index of Enrichment
IE............. Indicator Equipment (IAA)
IE............. Indo-European
IE............. Industrial Electronics (MCD)
IE............. Industrial Energy (EFIS)
IE............. Industrial Engineer [*or Engineering*]
IE............. In Excess
IE............. Infection Efficiency [*Pathology*]
IE............. Infective Endocarditis [*Cardiology*]
IE............. Information and Education (AAGC)
IE............. Information Element (ACRL)
IE............. Information Engineering (CDE)
IE............. Information Enterprises [*Chesterfield, MO*] [*Telecommunications service*] (TSSD)
IE............. Information Environment
IE............. Infrared Emission

I/E	Ingress/Egress
IE	Initial Equipment [*Navy aircraft*]
IE	Initial Establishment [*British military*] (DMA)
IE	Initiating Event (NRCH)
IE	Insert Exon [*Genetics*]
IE	Insert Extract (IAA)
IE	Inside Edge
IE	Inspection and Enforcement (NRCH)
I/E	Inspection and Evaluation [*Environmental science*] (COE)
IE	Inspection Equipment
IE	Inspection Error (KSC)
I/E	Inspiratory-Expiratory (Ratio) [*Physiology*]
IE	Installation Equipment [*Army*] (AABC)
IE	Institute of Energy [*An association*] (EAIO)
IE	Institute of Engineers and Technicians [*British*]
IE	Institute of Expertology (EA)
IE	Institute of Export [*British*]
IE	Instruction Execution (IAA)
IE	Instrument Engineering
IE	Intake (of a Unit of Food) Energy [*Nutrition*]
IE	Interconnection Equipment
IE	Intermediate Early [*Genetics*]
IE	Intermediate Erection
IE	Internal Elastica [*Artery anatomy*]
IE	Internal Environment
IE	International Exhibition (IMH)
IE	Internet Explorer [*Microsoft Corp.*]
IE	Interrogation Entry Register (IAA)
IE	Interrupt Enable [*Computer science*]
I/E	Introversion/Extroversion [*Psychology*] (AEE)
IE	Ion Exchange (WDAA)
IE	Ionization Energy [*Chemistry*]
IE	Ionospheric Explorer [*NASA/National Bureau of Standards*]
ie	Ireland [*MARC country of publication code Library of Congress*] (LCCP)
IE	Ireland [*ANSI two-letter standard code*] (CNC)
IE	Ireland [*Internet country code*]
IE	Irish Earl (ROG)
IE	Irradiation Effects (NRCH)
IE	Isoetharine [*Medicine*]
IE	Solomon Islands Airways [*ICAO designator*] (AD)
ie	That Is [*Id est*] [*Latin*] (WDMC)
IEA	American Hospital Supply Corp., Evanston, IL [*Library symbol Library of Congress*] (LCLS)
IEa	East Alton Public Library, East Alton, IL [*Library symbol Library of Congress*] (LCLS)
IEA	East Texas State University, Commerce, TX [*OCLC symbol*] (OCLC)
IEA	Idaho Education Association (SRA)
IEA	Illinois Education Association (SRA)
IEA	Immediate Early Antigen (DB)
IEA	Immuno-Electroadsorption [*Medicine*] (DMAA)
IEA	Immunoelectrophoretic Analysis (STED)
IEA	Immunoenzyme Assay [*Biochemistry*] (DAVI)
IEA	Import Entitlement Agreement [*United Arab Republic*]
IEA	Index of Economic Activity (ADA)
IEA	Indian-Eskimo Association of Canada [*Later, CASNP*] (EA)
IEA	Indian Evidence Act (ROG)
IEA	Indoleethanol [*Organic chemistry*]
IEA	Industrial Editors Association
IEA	Industrial Engineering Activity [*Army*] (AAGC)
IEA	Infectious Equine Anemia [*Veterinary medicine*] (DMAA)
IEA	Institute for Economic Analysis (EA)
IEA	Institute for Educational Affairs (EA)
IEA	Institute for Environmental Awareness (EA)
IEA	Institute for Expressive Analysis (EA)
IEA	Institute of Applied Economics [*University of Montreal*] [*Canada*] (IRC)
IEA	Institute of Economic Affairs [*British*]
IEA	Institute of Environmental Action (EA)
IEA	Instruments, Electronics, and Automation [*Exhibit*]
IEA	Insurance Educational Association
IEA	Integral Error Squared (PDAA)
IEA	Integrated Electronic Assembly [*NASA*]
IEA	Integrated Electronic Assembly (NAKS)
IEA	Intereuropean Airways Ltd. [*British ICAO designator*] (FAAC)
IEA	Interface Electronics Assembly
IEA	Interment Exchange of America
IEA	Intermountain Electrical Association (SRA)
IEA	International Association for the Evaluation of Educational Achievement [*See also AIERS*] [*University of Stockholm*] [*Sweden*] (EAIO)
IEA	International Economic Association [*See also AISE*] [*Paris, France*] (EAIO)
IEA	International Education Act
IEA	International Education Assembly [*World War II*]
IEA	International Education Association
IEA	International Emergency Action [*See also AUI*] [*Paris, France*] (EAIO)
IEA	International Energy Agency [*OECD*] [*Research center France*] (IRC)
IEA	International Entrepreneurs Association [*Later, AEA*] (EA)
IEA	International Epidemiological Association (EA)
IEA	International Ergonomics Association (EA)
IEA	International Exchange Association (EA)
IEA	International Executives Association (EA)
IEA	International Exhibitors Association (EA)

IEA	Intravascular Erythrocyte Aggregation [*Hematology*]
IEA	Ion Energy Analysis (AAEL)
IEA	Irish Exporters Association (EAIO)
IEAB	Internacia Esperanto-Asocio de Bibliotekistoj [*International Association of Esperanto-Speaking Librarians*] [*Later, IAEL*] (EA)
IEAC	IEEE [*Institute of Electrical and Electronics Engineers*] Automatic Control (IAA)
IEACS	Institut Europeen des Armes de Chasse et de Sport [*European Institute of Hunting and Sporting Weapons - EIHSW*] (EAIO)
IEAEMM	International Energy Agency Emergency Management Manual [*A publication*] (COE)
IEAF	Imperial Ethiopian Air Force
IEAH	American Hospital Supply Corp., Evanston, IL [*Library symbol*] [*Library of Congress*] (LCLS)
IEAHC	Institute of Early American History and Culture (EA)
IEAJ	Internacia Esperanto - Asocio de Juristoj [*International Esperanto - Association of Jurists*] [*Graz, Austria*] (EAIO)
IEAK	Internet Explorer Administration Kit
IE & ID	Interiors Engineering and Industrial Design (MCD)
IEAP	Institut Europeen d'Administration Publique [*European Institute of Public Administration - EIPA*] (EAIO)
IEar	Earl Township Public Library, Earlville, IL [*Library symbol Library of Congress*] (LCLS)
IEAR	Internacia Esperanto-Amikaro de Rotarianoj [*International Esperanto Fellowship of Rotarians*] [*British*] (EAIO)
IEarFSD	Freedom Community Unit, School District 245, Earlville, IL [*Library symbol Library of Congress*] (LCLS)
IEARN	International Education and Resource Network [*Information service or system*] (IID)
IEarSD	Earlville Community Unit, School District 9, Earlville, IL [*Library symbol Library of Congress*] (LCLS)
IEAS	Institute of East Asian Studies [*University of California, Berkeley*] [*Research center*] (RCD)
IEAS	International Economic Appraisal Service [*The Economist Publications Ltd.*] [*British Information service or system*]
IEASMA	International Electronic Article Surveillance Manufacturers Association (NTPA)
IEATP	Information Engineering Advanced Technology Programme [*British*]
IEB	Elkhart Public Library, Elkhart, IN [*OCLC symbol*] (OCLC)
IEB	Industrial Evaluation Board [*BDSA*]
IEB	Infanterie-Ersatzbataillon [*Infantry Replacement Training Battalion*] [*German military - World War II*]
IEB	Institute of Economic Botany [*New York Botanical Garden*]
IEB	Interdiction Executive Board (MCD)
IEB	International Energy Bank Ltd. [*British*]
IEB	International Environmental Bureau for the Non-Ferrous Metals Industry
IEB	International Executive Board [*UAW*]
IEB	International Exhibitions Bureau
IEB	Irish Evangelistic Band
IEB	Irish Export Board
IEB	Office of Inspection and Enforcement. Bulletin [*A publication*] (NRCH)
IEBL	Inter-Entity Boundary Line [*Military*] (INF)
IEBM	Institute of Epidemiology and Behavioral Medicine [*Medical Research Institute of San Francisco*] [*Research center*] (RCD)
IEBR	Institute for Economic and Business Research [*University of Kansas*] [*Research center*] (RCD)
IEC	Earlham College, Richmond, IN [*OCLC symbol*] (OCLC)
IEC	Experimental Cardiology [*Russian*]
IEC	Illinois Environmental Council (SRA)
IEC	Imaginative Educational Cooperation Project (EDAC)
IEC	Independent Electrical Contractors (EA)
IEC	Industrial Electrification Council [*Later, TEC*] (EA)
IEC	Industrial Energy Conservation (ODBW)
IEC	Inflatable Exit Cone (MCD)
IEC	Information Exchange Center
IEC	Infused Emitter Coupling
IEC	Inherent Explosion Clause [*Insurance*]
IEC	Injection Electrode Catheter
IEC	Inpatient Exercise Center [*Rehabilitation*] (DAVI)
IEC	Institut d'Etudes Congolaises [*Congolese Institute of Studies*]
IEC	Institute of Early Childhood [*Macquarie University*] [*Australia*]
IEC	Institute of Educational Cinematography [*British*]
IEC	Institute of Employment Consultants Ltd. [*British*]
IEC	Institute of Engineers of Chile
IEC	Institut Europeen de la Communication [*European Institute for the Media - EIM*] (EAIO)
IEC	Integrated Electronic Components (BUR)
IEC	Integrated Electronic Control
IEC	Integrated Engine Control
IEC	Integrated Environmental Control (AAG)
IEC	Integrated Equipment Component
IEC	Intelligence Evaluation Committee [*Department of Justice*]
IEC	Interexchange Carrier [*Telecommunications*]
IEC	Interface Efficiency Council [*Computer science*]
IEC	Intermittent Electrical Contact (IAA)
IEC	International Edsel Club (EA)
IEC	International Educational and Cultural Exchange
IEC	International Egg Commission [*British*] (EAIO)
IEC	International Electronics Corp. (MUGU)
IEC	International Electrotechnical Commission [*See also CEI*] [*Standards body Geneva, Switzerland*] (EAIO)
IEC	International Energy Commission (WDAA)
IEC	International Engineering Consortium (NTPA)
IEC	Interstate Electronics Corp. (MCD)

IEC .... Intraepithelial Carcinoma [*Medicine*]
IEC .... Intrinsic Electron Conduction (IAA)
IEC .... Inverse Electrode Current
IEC .... Ion Exchange Chromatography
IEC .... Iowa Egg Council (SRA)
IEC .... Iris Epithelium Cell [*Cytology*]
IEC .... Iso-Echo Contour
IEC .... Israel Economic Conference
IEC .... Item Entry Control (AFM)
IEC .... Office of Inspection and Enforcement. Circular [*A publication*] (NRCH)
IEC .... PEC Israel Economic [*NYSE symbol*]
IEC .... PEC Israel Economic Corp. Ltd. [*NYSE symbol*] (SAG)
IECA .... Independent Educational Consultants Association (EA)
IECA .... Independent Election Corp. of America (WDMC)
IECA .... Industry, Education Councils of America (OICC)
IECA .... International Erosion Control Association (EA)
IE Ca cx ...... Intraepithelial Carcinoma of Cervix [*Medicine*] (STED)
IECC .... International Economic Conversion Campaign [*Defunct*] (EA)
IECD .... Ignition Energetics Characterization Device (MCD)
IECE .... IEC Electronics [*NASDAQ symbol*] (TTSB)
IECE .... IEC Electronics Corp. [*NASDAQ symbol*] (NQ)
IECE .... Institute on East Central Europe [*Columbia University*] [*Research center*] (RCD)
IECEC .... Intersociety Energy Conversion Engineering Conference
IECEE .... International Electrotechnical Commission System for Conformity Testing to Standards for Safety of Electrical Equipment [*Switzerland*] (EA)
IECEJ .... Institute of Electronic Communications Engineers of Japan
IECEJ .... Interreligious Emergency Campaign for Economic Justice (EA)
IEC Elc .... IEC Electronics Corp. [*Associated Press*] (SAG)
IECG .... Independent Energy Consultants Group [*British*]
IECG .... Interagency Emergency Coordinating Group [*Federal disaster planning*]
IECI .... Industrial Electronics and Control Instrumentation (MCD)
IECI .... Institute for Esperanto in Commerce and Industry (EA)
IECIC .... International Engineering and Construction Industries Council (PDAA)
IECL .... Instrumentation Equipment Configuration Log (SAA)
IECL .... International Esperantist Chess League [*See also ESLI*] (EAIO)
IECM .... Induced Environmental Contamination Monitor (MCD)
IECM .... Internal Electronic Countermeasure
IECMS .... Inflight Engine Condition Monitoring System [*Military*] (CAAL)
IECO .... Inboard Engine Cutoff
IECOK .... International Economic Consultative Organization for Korea [*Ten-nation consortium*]
IECP .... Injected Electric Current Perturbation
IECP .... Interface Engineering Change Procedure
IECPS .... International Electronic Packaging Symposium (MCD)
IECQU .... International Electrotechnical Commission Quality Assessment (PDAA)
IECS .... Igloo Environment Control Subsystem (MCD)
IECS .... Intelligence Evaluation Center [*Saigon*] [*Obsolete*] (CINC)
IECS .... Internal-External Control Scale [*Psychology*] (DHP)
IECT .... IEEE [*Institute of Electrical and Electronics Engineers*] Circuit Theory (IAA)
IECT .... Impulsive Ergodic Collision Theory [*Mathematics*]
IEd .... Edwardsville Free Public Library, Edwardsville, IL [*Library symbol Library of Congress*] (LCLS)
IED .... Impact Energy Density
IED .... Improved Explosive Device
IED .... Improvised Explosive Device
IED .... Improvised Explosive Device Disposal (PDAA)
IED .... Incident Energy Density
IED .... Income Eligibility Determination [*Food and Nutrition Service*] [*Department of Agriculture*] (GFGA)
IED .... Income Equalization Deposit (ADA)
IED .... Independent Exploratory Development [*Navy*] (NG)
IED .... Individual Effective Dose (IEEE)
IED .... Inherited Epidermal Dysplasia [*Medicine*] (DMAA)
IED .... Initial Effective Data (IAA)
IED .... Initial Engine Development [*Air Force*]
IED .... Initiative Electronic Deception (ADDR)
IED .... Insertion/Extraction Device [*Aviation*]
IED .... Inspection Equipment Drawing
IED .... Institute for Educational Development [*Defunct*]
IED .... Institution of Engineering Designers [*British*] (BI)
IED .... Instrumental Engineering Division [*National Weather Service*]
IED .... Integrated Electric Drive [*Navy*] (DOMA)
IED .... Integrated Engineering Design Service (PDAA)
IED .... Integrated Environmental Design (PDAA)
IED .... Interacting Equipment Documents (MCD)
IED .... Intermittent Explosive Disorder
IED .... International Electron Devices Meeting (PDAA)
IED .... International Electronic Devices [*Conference*] (MCD)
IED .... Ion Exchange Desalination
IED .... Ionospheric Electron Density
IED .... Suburban Library System, Burr Ridge, IL [*OCLC symbol*] (OCLC)
IEDF .... Ion Energy Distribution Function (AAEL)
IeDL .... Lembaga Ilmu Pengetahuan Indonesia, Pusat Dokumentasi Ilmiah Nasional, Jakarta, Indonesia [*Library symbol Library of Congress*] (LCLS)
IEdL .... Lewis and Clark Library System, Edwardsville, IL [*Library symbol Library of Congress*] (LCLS)
IEdL-A .... Lewis and Clark Library System, Alhambra, Alhambra, IL [*Library symbol Library of Congress*] (LCLS)

IEdL-C .... Lewis and Clark Library System, Chesterfield, Chesterfield, IL [*Library symbol Library of Congress*] (LCLS)
IEdL-H .... Lewis and Clark Library System, Hamel, Hamel, IL [*Library symbol Library of Congress*] (LCLS)
IEdL-HP .... Lewis and Clark Library System, Hillsboro Prison, Edwardsville, IL [*Library symbol Library of Congress*] (LCLS)
IeDLIP .... Lembaga Ilmu Pengetahuan Indonesia, Pusat Dokumentasi Ilmiah Nasional, Jakarta, Indonesia [*Library symbol*] [*Library of Congress*] (LCLS)
IEdL-L .... Lewis and Clark Library System, Livingston, Livingston, IL [*Library symbol Library of Congress*] (LCLS)
IEdL-M .... Lewis and Clark Library System, Marine, Marine, IL [*Library symbol Library of Congress*] (LCLS)
IEdL-Mg .... Lewis and Clark Library System, Mulberry Grove, Mulberry Grove, IL [*Library symbol Library of Congress*] (LCLS)
IEdL-P .... Lewis and Clark Library System, Palmyra, Palmyra, IL [*Library symbol Library of Congress*] (LCLS)
IEdL-Sh .... Lewis and Clark Library System, Shipman, Shipman, IL [*Library symbol Library of Congress*] (LCLS)
IEdL-StJ ...... Lewis and Clark Library System, St. Jacob, St. Jacob, IL [*Library symbol Library of Congress*] (LCLS)
IEdMC .... Pere Marquette Youth Center, Edwardsville, IL [*Library symbol*] [*Library of Congress*] (LCLS)
IEDO .... Institution of Economic Development Officers [*British*] (DBA)
IeDP .... Perpustakaan Museum Pusat, Jakarta, Indonesia [*Library symbol Library of Congress*] (LCLS)
IEDS .... Income Equalization Deposits Scheme
IEDS .... International Environmental Data Service [*European Commodities Exchange*] [*United Nations*] (DUND)
IEDS .... international Environment and Development Service (GNE)
IEdS .... Southern Illinois University, Edwardsville Campus, Edwardsville, IL [*Library symbol Library of Congress*] (LCLS)
IEdSD .... Edwardsville Community Unit, School District 7, Edwardsville, IL [*Library symbol Library of Congress*] (LCLS)
IEdS-D .... Southern Illinois University, School of Dental Medicine, Biomedical Library, Edwardsville, IL [*Library symbol Library of Congress*] (LCLS)
IEDSS .... Institute of European Defence and Strategic Studies [*British*] (DBA)
IEE .... Induced Electrical Effect
IEE .... Induced Electron Emission
IEE .... Industrial Electronic Engineer (IAA)
IEE .... Information Expert Environment [*Software*] [*Market research organization*] (NITA)
IEE .... Inner Enamel Epithelium [*Dentistry*]
IEE .... Institute for Earth Education (EA)
IEE .... Institute for Environmental Education (EA)
IEE .... Institute of Electrical Engineering [*Hitchin, Herts., England*] (NATG)
IEE .... Institute of Electrology Educators (EA)
IEE .... Institute of Environmental Engineers [*Later, IES*]
IEE .... Institution of Electrical Engineers [*London, England*] [*Database producer*]
IEE .... Intelligent Electronics Europa (NITA)
IEE .... Interim Expendable Emitter (NVT)
IEE .... International Electrology Educators (NTPA)
IEE .... International Institute for Hydraulic and Environmental Engineering [*Netherlands*] (IRC)
IEE .... National College of Education, Evanston, IL [*Library symbol Library of Congress*] (LCLS)
IEE .... North Suburban Library System, Wheeling, IL [*OCLC symbol*] (OCLC)
IEEC .... IEEE [*Institute of Electrical and Electronics Engineers*] Electronic Computer (IAA)
IEEC .... Integrated Electronics Engineering Center [*State University of New York, Binghamton*] [*Research center*] (RCD)
IEEE .... Institute of Electrical and Electronics Engineering (NITA)
IEEE .... Institute of Electrical and Electronics Engineers (IGQR)
IEEE-CS .... Institute of Electrical and Electronics Engineers - Computer Society
IEEE Exp ...... IEEE Expert: Intelligent Systems and Their Applications [*A publication*] (BRI)
IEEE/PES ...... Power Engineering Society of the Institute of Electrical and Electronic Engineers (ITD)
IEEF .... Ion Exchange Evaporation Filter (PDAA)
IEEI .... IEEE [*Institute of Electrical and Electronics Engineers*] Electrical Insulation (IAA)
IEEI .... International Electronics Engineering, Inc. (AAG)
IEEI .... University of Illinois Hospital Eye and Ear Infirmary [*University of Illinois at Chicago*] [*Research center*] (RCD)
IEEIE .... Institution of Electrical and Electronics Inc. Engineers (DS)
IEELG .... International Education Exchange Liaison Group (EA)
IEENSW .... Institution of Electrical Engineers New South Wales [*Australia*]
IEEP .... Incapacitated Emergency Egress Practice [*NASA*] (KSC)
IEEP .... Institute for European Environmental Policy [*Germany*] (EAIO)
IEEP .... Interagency Energy/Environment Program [*Environmental Protection Agency*]
IEEPA .... International Emergency Economic Powers Act [*1977*]
IEER .... Institute for Energy & Environmental Research
IEES .... International Education Exchange Service [*Department of State*]
IEETE .... Institution of Electrical and Electronics Technician Engineers (MCD)
IEEU .... Instituto de Estudios de Estados Unidos [*Studies Mexico/US relations, US domestic politics, US economy, and US foreign policy*] [*Mexico*] (CROSS)
IEEV .... Institution of Electrical Engineers Victoria [*Australia*]
IE-Ex .... Evanston Public Library, Extension (Bookmobile), Evanston, IL [*Library symbol Library of Congress*] (LCLS)
IEF .... Imaging Energy Filter (AAEL)

IEF .... Indian Educators Federation (NTPA)
IEF .... Indian Expeditionary Force [*British military*] (DMA)
IEF .... Information Engineering Facility (CDE)
IEF .... Instruction Execution Function (NITA)
IEF .... INTACT [*Infants Need to Avoid Circumcision Trauma*] Educational Foundation [*Later, NO-CIRC*] (EA)
IEF .... Integral Equation Formulation (PDAA)
IEF .... International Equestrian Federation (EAIO)
IEF .... International Exhibitions Foundation (EA)
IEF .... International Eye Foundation (EA)
IEF .... Isoelectric Focusing [*Analytical chemistry*]
IEF .... Israel Education Fund
IEF .... Italian Expeditionary Force
IEF .... Starved Rock Library System, Ottawa, IL [*OCLC symbol*] (OCLC)
IEFC .... International Emergency Food Council [*Post-World War II*]
IEFP .... International Exposition for Food Processors (ITD)
IEFR .... International Esperanto Fellowship of Rotarians [*See also IEAR*] (EAIO)
IEFS .... Integrated Electronic Filing System [*Computer science*] (DGA)
IEFUA .... International Electronic Facsimile Users Association (EA)
IEG .... Garrett-Evangelical Theological Seminary, Evanston, IL [*Library symbol Library of Congress*] (LCLS)
IEG .... Harry S Truman College, Chicago, IL [*OCLC symbol*] (OCLC)
IEG .... Imagery Exploitation Group
IEG .... Immediately Early Gene [*Genetics*]
IEG .... Imperial Ethiopian Government (CINC)
IEG .... Independent Evaluation Group (SDI)
IEG .... Industrial Electronics Group [*of General Motors Corp.*]
IEG .... Information Exchange Group [*National Institutes of Health*]
IEG .... Internal Engine Generator (PDAA)
IEG .... Internet Entertainment Group, Inc.
IEG .... Zielona Gora [*Poland*] [*Airport symbol*] (OAG)
IEGE .... IEEE [*Institute of Electrical and Electronics Engineers*] Geoscience Electronics (IAA)
IEGP .... Interagency Economic Growth Project [*Department of Transportation*]
IEH .... American Library Association, Chicago, IL [*OCLC symbol*] (OCLC)
IEHA .... International Economic History Association [*Paris, France*] (EA)
IEHA .... International Executive Housekeepers Association (NTPA)
IEHD .... Institute for the Editing of Historical Documents
IEHIURM ..... Institute for Encyclopedia of Human Ideas on Ultimate Reality and Meaning (EA)
IEHMO .... Iterative Extended Hueckel Molecular Orbital (DB)
IEHO .... Institute of Environmental Health Officers [*British*]
IEHS .... Evanston Township High School, Evanston, IL [*Library symbol*] [*Library of Congress*] (LCLS)
IEI .... Immunocytochemistry, ELISA [*Enzyme-Linked Immunosorbent Assay*], and Immunoblotting
IEI .... Indeterminate Engineering Items
IEI .... Indiana Energy [*NYSE symbol*] (TTSB)
IEI .... Indiana Energy, Inc. [*NYSE symbol*] (SPSG)
IEI .... Industrial Education Institute
IEI .... Industrial Engineering Institute
IEI .... Institute for Educational Innovation [*Later, Education Development Center*]
IEI .... Institution of Engineering Inspection [*British*] (BI)
IEI .... Institution of Engineers of Ireland (ACII)
IEI .... International Educator's Institute (EA)
IEI .... International Enamellers Institute [*Derby, England*] (EAIO)
IEI .... International Epitek, Inc. [*Toronto Stock Exchange symbol*]
IEI .... International Evaluations, Inc.
IEI .... Investment Education Institute (EA)
IEI .... Iran Electronics Industries
IEI .... Isoelectric Interval (DMAA)
IEIA .... Installation Environmental Impact Assessment (PDAA)
IEIA .... Insurance Employers' Industrial Association [*Australia*]
IEIA .... Integrated Educational Information System (PDAA)
IEIAS .... Institut Europeen Interuniversitaire de l'Action Sociale [*Inter-University European Institute on Social Welfare - IEISW*] (EAIO)
IEIB .... International Electronics, Inc. [*NASDAQ symbol*] (NQ)
IEIC .... Institution of Engineers-in-Charge [*British*] (BI)
IEIDATA ...... International Economic Indicators Database [*Columbia Business School*] [*Information service or system*] (CRD)
IEIE .... International Electrs [*NASDAQ symbol*] (TTSB)
IEIM .... IEEE [*Institute of Electrical and Electronics Engineers*] Instrumentation and Measurement Society (IAA)
IEIP .... Institut Europeen des Industries de la Pectine [*European Institute of the Pectin Industries*]
IEIP .... International Education Information Program
IEIS .... Integrated Engine Instrument System (MCD)
IEISW .... Inter-University European Institute on Social Welfare (EA)
IEIT .... IEEE [*Institute of Electrical and Electronics Engineers*] Information Theory Society (IAA)
IEJ .... Deere & Co., Moline, IL [*OCLC symbol*] (OCLC)
IEJ .... Infite Ltd. [*British ICAO designator*] (FAAC)
IEJ .... Institut Europeen du Jouet [*European Toy Institute - ETI*] (EAIO)
IEJE .... Institut d'Etudes Juridiques Europeennes [*Benelux*]
IEK .... Kendall College, Evanston, IL [*Library symbol*] [*Library of Congress*] (LCLS)
IEKA .... Internacia Esperanto Klubo Automobilista [*International Automobile Esperanto Club*] (EAIO)
IEKKK .... Invisible Empire Knights of the Ku Klux Klan (EA)
IEKV .... Internationale Eisenbahn-Kongress-Vereinigung [*International Railway Congress Association*]
IEL .... IE Industries, Inc. (MHDW)
IEL .... Illustrative Evaluation Scenario [*Environmental science*] (COE)

IEL .... Improved Efficiency of Learning [*Project*] (AIE)
IEL .... Improved Erector-Launcher (SAA)
IEL .... Information Exchange List [*Military*] (AABC)
IEL .... Institute for Educational Leadership (EA)
IEL .... Internal Elastic Lamina [*Medicine*] (DMAA)
IEL .... International Electrochemical Commission
IEL .... Intimal Elastic Lamina [*Medicine*] (STED)
IEL .... Intraepithelial Lymphocyte [*Hematology*]
IEL .... Iota Exploration Ltd. [*Vancouver Stock Exchange symbol*]
IEL .... Parlin Public Library, Canton, IL [*OCLC symbol*] (OCLC)
IELA .... International Exhibition Logistics Associates [*Geneva, Switzerland*] (EAIO)
IElg .... Gail Borden Public Library, Elgin, IL [*Library symbol Library of Congress*] (LCLS)
IELG .... International Esperantist League for Go (EA)
IElgB .... Brethren Historical Library and Archives, Elgin, IL [*Library symbol Library of Congress*] (LCLS)
IElgC .... Elgin Community College, Elgin, IL [*Library symbol Library of Congress*] (LCLS)
IElm .... Elmhurst Public Library, Elmhurst, IL [*Library symbol Library of Congress*] (LCLS)
IElmC .... Elmhurst College, Elmhurst, IL [*Library symbol Library of Congress*] (LCLS)
IELS .... Isotope Exciter Light Source
IElsP .... Principia College, Elsah, IL [*Library symbol Library of Congress*] (LCLS)
IElw .... Morrison and Mary Wiley Public Library, Elmwood, IL [*Library symbol Library of Congress*] (LCLS)
IElwp .... Elmwood Park Public Library, Elmwood Park, IL [*Library symbol Library of Congress*] (LCLS)
IEM .... East Texas State University, Metroplex Center, Commerce, TX [*OCLC symbol*] (OCLC)
IEM .... Ideal Effort Multiplier
IEM .... Immune Electron Microscopy
IEM .... Inactive Equipment Maintenance (DNAB)
IEM .... Inborn Error of Metabolism [*Medicine*]
IEM .... Individual Engagement Model (MCD)
IEM .... Industrial Engineer for Management
IEM .... Infrared Projector Energy Monitor (MCD)
IEM .... Installation Equipment Management System (MCD)
IEM .... Institute of Experimental Meteorology [*Former USSR*]
IEM .... Interim Examination and Maintenance [*Nuclear energy*] (NRCH)
IEM .... Internal Environment Monitoring
IEM .... Intromission and Ejaculatory Mechanism [*Physiology*]
IEM .... Ion Exchange Membrane
IEMA .... Immunoenzymometric Assay [*Clinical chemistry*]
IEMA .... Independent Electrical Manufacturers Association (EA)
IEMAE .... Institute of Evolutionary Morphology and Animal Ecology [*Commonwealth of Independent States*]
IEMATS .... Improved Emergency Message Automatic Transmission System (MCD)
IEMBA .... International Executive Masters of Business Administration (PGP)
IEMC .... IEEE [*Institute of Electrical and Electronics Engineers*] Electromagnetic Compatibility Society (IAA)
IEMC .... Independent Electronic Music Center [*Defunct*]
IEMC .... Industrial Equipment Manufacturers Council [*Later, ICED*] (EA)
IEMC .... International Electronics Manufacturing Co. (AAG)
IEMCAP .... Intrasystem Electromagnetic Compatibility Analysis Program [*Computer science Air Force*]
IEMD .... Integrated Environmental Management Division [*Environmental Protection Agency*] (EPA)
IEME .... Corps of Indian Electrical and Mechanical Engineers [*British military*] (DMA)
IEME .... Inspectorate of Electrical and Mechanical Engineering [*Military*] (IAA)
IEMG .... Integrated Electromyogram [*Medicine*]
IEMIS .... Integrated Emergency Management Information System [*Federal Emergency Management Agency*] (GFGA)
IEMO .... Installation Equipment Management Office [*Military*] (AFIT)
IEMP .... Induced Electromagnetic Pulse (RDA)
IEMP .... Institute of Environmental Medicine and Physiology
IEMP .... Integrated Environmental Management Project [*Environmental Protection Agency*] (GFGA)
IEMP .... Interior Electromagnetic Pulse (MCD)
IEMP .... Internal Electromagnetic Pulse
IEMP .... International Executive Masters Programme [*London Business School*]
IEMS .... Installation Equipment Management System
I/EMS .... Intergraph Corp./Engineering Modeling System
IEMS .... Interim Electronic Maintenance Support (AFIT)
IEMSA .... Iowa Emergency Medical Services Association (SRA)
IEMT .... Intermediate Emergency Medical Technician [*Also, EMT-I*] (DHSM)
IEMTF .... Interim Examination and Maintenance Training Facility [*Nuclear energy*] (NRCH)
IEMU .... Integrated Extravehicular Mobility Unit (SSD)
IEMVT .... Institut d'Elevage et de Medecine Veterinaire des Pays Tropicaux [*Institute of Stockraising and Veterinary Medicine in Tropical Countries*] [*France*]
IEN .... Die Israelitischen Eigennamen [*A publication*] (BJA)
IE-N .... Evanston Public Library, North Branch, Evanston, IL [*Library symbol Library of Congress*] (LCLS)
IEN .... Interpenetrating Elastomeric Networks [*Organic chemistry*]
IEN .... Northwestern University, Evanston, IL [*Library symbol Library of Congress*] (LCLS)
IENC .... Income Earned, Not Collected (EBF)

IEN-C .... Northwestern University, Joseph Schaffner Library of Commerce, Chicago, IL [*Library symbol Library of Congress*] (LCLS)
IEN-D .... Northwestern University, Dental School, Chicago, IL [*Library symbol Library of Congress*] (LCLS)
IEng .... Incorporate Engineer (ACII)
IEN-L .... Northwestern University, Law Library, Chicago, IL [*Library symbol Library of Congress*] (LCLS)
IEN-M .... Northwestern University, Medical School, Chicago, IL [*Library symbol Library of Congress*] (LCLS)
IEN-Mu .... Northwestern University, Music Library, Evanston, IL [*Library symbol*] [*Library of Congress*] (LCLS)
IEN-T .... Northwestern University, Technological Institute, Evanston, IL [*Library symbol Library of Congress*] (LCLS)
IEN-Tr .... Northwestern University, Transportation Library, Evanston, IL [*Library symbol Library of Congress*] (LCLS)
IEnvSc .... Institution of Environmental Sciences [*British*] (DBA)
IEO .... Incoherent Electronic Oscillator
IEO .... Industry and Environment Office (GNE)
IEO .... Installation Engineers Office (SAA)
I/EO .... Instructor/Equipment Operator
IEO .... Integrated Electronic Office (NITA)
IEO .... Interim Engineering Order (AAG)
IEO .... Intermediate Earth Orbit (SSD)
IEO .... International Education Office [*World War II*]
IEO .... International Exchange Office (AFM)
IEOCS .... Interim Equipment Order Control System [*Bell System*]
IEON .... International Esperantist Organization of Naturists [*See also INOE*] [*Frankfurt, Federal Republic of Germany*] (EAIO)
IEOP .... Immunoelectroosmophoresis [*Analytical biochemistry*]
IEOS .... Integrated Electronic Office System (IAA)
IEOTSG .... Integral Economizer Once-Through Steam Generator (NRCH)
IEP .... Evansville Public Library and Vanderburgh County Public Library, Evansville, IN [*OCLC symbol*] (OCLC)
IEp .... Fondulac District Library, East Peoria, IL [*Library symbol Library of Congress*] (LCLS)
IEP .... Image Edge Profile [*Photography*] (OA)
IEP .... Immunoelectrophoresis [*Analytical biochemistry*]
IEP .... Independent Evaluation Plan
IEP .... Independent Exchange Plan
IEP .... Indicateur Electronique de Pilotage [*Electronic Pilotage Indicator*] [*Aviation*]
IEP .... Individual Education Plan
IEP .... Individual Evaluation Plan [*Army*]
IEP .... Individualized Education Plan [*Special education*] (PAZ)
IEP .... Individualized Education Program [*For the education of a handicapped person*]
IEP .... Information Exchange Program [*or Project*] [*Military*]
IEP .... Ingestion Exposure Pathway [*Nuclear emergency planning*]
IEP .... Initial Enrollment Period [*Insurance*]
IEP .... Instantaneous Effective Photo
IEP .... Instantaneous Effective Photo Cathodes (NAKS)
IEP .... Institute for Ecological Policies [*Defunct*] (EA)
IEP .... Institute for Experimental Psychiatry
IEP .... Institut Europeen pour la Promotion des Entreprises
IEP .... Institut fuer Europaeische Politik [*Institute of European Politics*] (EAIO)
IEP .... Instrument for Evaluation of Photographs
IEP .... Integrated Engineering Program
IEP-C .... Intelligence Estimate for Planning
IEP .... Internal Economic Problems [*British*]
IEP .... International Economic Policy
IEP .... International Education Project [*American Council on Education*] (PDAA)
IEP .... International Energy Program
IEP .... International Potential [*Vancouver Stock Exchange symbol*]
IEP .... Intext Educational Publishers
IEP .... Inverted Energy Population
IEP .... Isoelectric Point [*Also, IP, PH₁, pI*] [*Chemistry*]
IEPA .... Illinois Environmental Protection Agency (DOGT)
IEPA .... Independent Electron Pair Approximation [*Physics*]
IEPA .... International Economic Policy Act of 1972
IEPA .... International Economic Policy Association (EA)
IEPA .... International Environment Protection Act of 1983
IEPA .... Intra-European Payments Agreement
IEPALA .... Instituto de Estudios Politicos para America Latina y Africa [*Spain*]
IEPB .... Interagency Emergency Planning Board [*Federal disaster planning*]
IEPC .... Instantaneous Effective Photocathodes (MCD)
IEPC .... Interagency Emergency Planning Committee
IEPD .... Industrial and Extractive Processes Division [*Environmental Protection Agency*] (EPA)
IEpE .... East Peoria Elementary School District, East Peoria, IL [*Library symbol Library of Congress*] (LCLS)
IEPFCHK ..... International Elvis Presley Fan Club, Hong Kong (EAIO)
IEPG .... Independent European Program Group [*NATO*]
IEPG .... Internet Engineering Planning Group
IEpI .... Illinois Central College, East Peoria, IL [*Library symbol Library of Congress*] (LCLS)
IEPP .... Institute of Earth and Planetary Physics [*University of Alberta*] [*Research center*] (RCD)
IEPPA .... International Encyclopedia of Public Policy and Administration [*A publication*]
IEPPL .... Integrated Engineering Planning Parts List
IEPR .... Integrated Engine Pressure Ratio (GAVI)
IEPRC .... International Electronic Publishing Research Centre [*British*] (IRC)
IEPS .... Incentives and Earned Privileges Scheme (WDAA)

IEPS .... International Electronics Packaging Society (EA)
IEQ .... Illinois Prairie District Public Library, Metamora, IL [*OCLC symbol*] (OCLC)
IEQ .... Index of Environmental Quality (WDAA)
IEQE .... IEEE [*Institute of Electrical and Electronics Engineers*] Quantum Electronics (IAA)
I Eq R .... Irish Equity Reports [*A publication*] (DLA)
IER .... Independent Evaluation Report
IER .... Individual Education Record
IER .... Individual Evaluation Report
IER .... Industrial Equipment Reserve
IER .... Infanterie-Ersatzregiment [*Infantry Replacement Training Regiment*] [*German military - World War II*]
IER .... Inherent Equipment Reliability
IER .... Initial Engagement Range (MCD)
IER .... Installation Enhancement Release [*Computer science*]
IER .... Institute for Econometric Research (EA)
IER .... Institute for Education by Radio [*Defunct*] (NTCM)
IER .... Institute for Environmental Research [*Environmental Science Services Administration*]
IER .... Institute of Educational Research [*Defunct*] (EA)
IER .... Institute of Engineering Research [*Research center British*] (IRC)
IER .... Institute of Engineering Research [*University of California*] [*Research center*] (MCD)
IER .... Institute of Exploratory Research [*Army*]
IER .... Interface Evaluation Report (KSC)
IER .... Interim Engineering Report
IER .... Internal Economic Rate of Return
IER .... Inventory Equipment Requirement
IER .... Ion Exchange Resin
IER .... Irish Equity Reports [*A publication*] (DLA)
IER .... Mackinaw Township Library, Mackinaw, IL [*OCLC symbol*] (OCLC)
IER .... Natchitoches, LA [*Location identifier FAA*] (FAAL)
IER .... Organization for International Economic Relations [*Vienna, Austria*] (EAIO)
IERC .... Industrial Equipment Reserve Committee (SAA)
IERC .... International Electronic Research Corp. (MCD)
IERD .... Industry Energy Research and Development Program [*Canada*]
IERE .... Institute of Electronics and Radio Engineers [*British*]
IERESM .... Institut Europeen de Recherches et d'Etudes Superieures en Management [*European Institute for Advanced Studies in Management - EIASM*] [*Brussels, Belgium*] (EA)
IERF .... International Education Research Foundation (EA)
IERI .... Illuminating Engineering Research Institute (EA)
IERL .... Industrial Environmental Research Laboratory [*Environmental Protection Agency*]
IERM .... Individual Employment Rights Manual [*A publication*]
IERN .... Internal-External Recurrent Neural Network (AAEL)
IERO .... Institute for Engineering Research in the Oceans [*Marine science*] (MSC)
IERS .... International Earth Rotation Services
IERS .... International Educational Reporting Service [*International Bureau of Education*] [*United Nations*] (EY)
IERS .... Inventory Equipment Requirement Specification
IERT .... Institute for Education by Radio-Television (NTCM)
IERTM .... Institute for Environmental Research Technical Memorandum
IERW .... Initial Entry Rotary Wing [*Student*] (MCD)
IEs .... East St. Louis Public Library, East St. Louis, IL [*Library symbol Library of Congress*] (LCLS)
IES .... Eli Lilly & Co., Indianapolis, IN [*OCLC symbol*] (OCLC)
IE-S .... Evanston Public Library, South Branch, Evanston, IL [*Library symbol Library of Congress*] (LCLS)
IES .... Id, Ego, Superego [*Test*] [*Psychology*]
IES .... IEEE Industrial Electronics Society (EA)
IES .... IES Industries [*NYSE symbol*] (SPSG)
IES .... Illuminating Engineering Society
IES .... Illustrative Evaluation Scenario (DOMA)
IES .... Imagery Exploitation System (DOMA)
IES .... Income and Expense Statement (MHDW)
IES .... Incoming Echo Suppressor [*Telecommunications*] (TEL)
IES .... Independent Educational Services
IES .... Indian Educational Service [*British*]
IES .... Inductive Energy Storage
IES .... Industrial Electronic System
IES .... Industrial Engineering Services
IES .... Industrial Engineering Standard (MCD)
IES .... Information Exchange Systems [*British*]
IES .... Institute for Earth Sciences [*Environmental Science Services Administration*]
IES .... Institute for Environmental Studies [*University of Wisconsin, Madison*] [*Research center*] (RCD)
IES .... Institute for Environmental Studies [*University of Toronto*] [*Research center*] (RCD)
IES .... Institute for Environmental Studies [*University of Washington*] [*Research center*] (RCD)
IES .... Institute of Ecosystem Studies
IES .... Institute of English Studies (DBA)
IES .... Institute of Environmental Sciences (EA)
IES .... Institute of European Studies (EA)
IES .... Institution of Engineers and Shipbuilders [*Scotland*] (DI)
IES .... Institution of Environmental Sciences (EAIO)
IES .... Integral Error Squared (IEEE)
IES .... Integrated Electronic System
IES .... Intelligence Evaluation Staff
IES .... Intelligence Exploitation Squadron [*Air Force*]

IES .... Intensive Employability Services [*Work Incentive Program*]
IES .... Inter-Island Air Services Ltd. [*Grenada*] [*ICAO designator*] (FAAC)
IES .... Internal Environment Simulator
IES .... International Ecology Society (EA)
IES .... International Education Exchange Service [*Department of State*]
IES .... International Education Series [*A publication*]
IES .... International Exchange Service [*For publications*] [*Smithsonian Institution*]
IES .... International Explorers Society
IES .... Intrinsic Electric Strength (IEEE)
IES .... Invariant-Ellipticity States (PDAA)
IES .... Inventory Equipment Sheet
IES .... Inverness Petroleum Ltd. [*Toronto Stock Exchange symbol*]
IES .... Inverted Echo Sounder
IES .... Ion Energy Selector
IES .... Ion Engine Simulator
IES .... Ion Engine System
IES .... Irish Emigrant Society (EA)
IES .... Irradiation Effects Simulation (NRCH)
IESA .... Instituto de Estudios Superiores de Administracion [*Institute of Higher Studies of Administration*] [*Venezuela*]
IESA .... Insurance Economics Society of America [*Defunct*] (EA)
IEsAHS .... Assumption High School, East St. Louis, IL [*Library symbol Library of Congress*] (LCLS)
IESC .... International Executive Service Corps [*Stamford, CT*] (EA)
IEsCH .... Christian Welfare Hospital, East St. Louis, IL [*Library symbol Library of Congress*] (LCLS)
IEsCTH .... Centreville Township Hospital, East St. Louis, IL [*Library symbol Library of Congress*] (LCLS)
IESD .... Instrumentation and Electronic Systems Division [*NASA*] (MCD)
IES-DC .... IES [*Information Exchange System*] Data Collections [*Commission of the European Communities*] [*Information service or system*] (CRD)
IESG .... Internet Engineering Steering Group [*Computer science*] (ACRL)
IESM .... Inductive Energy Storage Modulator
IESNA .... Illuminating Engineering Society of North America (EA)
IESP .... Integrated Electronic Signal Processor
IEsP .... Parks College of Aeronautical Technology, East St. Louis, IL [*Library symbol Library of Congress*] (LCLS)
IEsPC .... Project Choice, East St. Louis, IL [*Library symbol Library of Congress*] (LCLS)
IESq .... Intelligence Exploitation Squadron [*Air Force*]
IESR .... International English Shepherd Registry (EA)
IESRA .... Interim Employment Services Regulatory Authority
IESS .... Intergroup Ewing Sarcoma Study [*Medicine*] (DMAA)
IESS .... International Encyclopedia of the Social Sciences [*A publication*]
IESS .... Ion Engine System Section
IESSC .... Irish El Salvador Support Committee (EAIO)
IEsSC .... State Community College of East St. Louis, Learning Resources Center, East St. Louis, IL [*Library symbol Library of Congress*] (LCLS)
IEsSD .... East Saint Louis Public School District 189, East St. Louis, IL [*Library symbol Library of Congress*] (LCLS)
IEsSMH .... Saint Mary's Hospital, East St. Louis, IL [*Library symbol Library of Congress*] (LCLS)
IEST .... Impulses, Ego, and Superego Test [*Psychology*] (AEBS)
IEST .... Taiwan Provincial Institute for Elementary School Teachers In-Service Education
IESU .... IEEE [*Institute of Electrical and Electronics Engineers*] Sonics and Ultrasonics (IAA)
IES Ut25 ...... IES Utilities [*Associated Press*] (SAG)
IESV .... Institute for Epidemiologic Studies of Violence (EA)
IET .... East Texas State University, Texarkana, Texarkana, TX [*OCLC symbol*] (OCLC)
IET .... Impact Excited Transmitter
IET .... Implanted Electrode Technique
IET .... Independent Evaluation Teams [*Army Systems Acquisitions Review Council*] (MCD)
IET .... Initial Engine Test
IET .... Initial Entry Training
IET .... Institute of Educational Technology [*British*]
IET .... Institute of Engineers and Technicians [*British*] (EAIO)
IET .... Instrument and Electrical Technician (MCD)
IET .... Integrated Equipment Test [*Nuclear energy*]
IET .... Interest Equalization Tax
IET .... Intermolecular Energy Transfer [*Chemistry*]
IET .... Interval Embossed Tube
IETA .... International Electrical Testing Association (EAIO)
IETAS .... Interim Escort Towed Array System (MCD)
IETC .... Initial Education and Training Committee (ACII)
IETC .... Interagency Emergency Transportation Committee
IETC .... International Environmental Technology Centre [*United Nations*] (ECON)
IETCA .... International E-22 Class Association (EA)
IETE .... Institution of Electronics and Telecommunications Engineers [*Information service or system*] (TSSD)
IETEJ .... Institute of Electronics & Telecommunications Engineers of Japan (NITA)
IETF .... Initial Engine Test Facility
IETF .... Initial Engine Test Firing (IAA)
IETF .... Integrated Equipment Test Facility [*Department of Energy*]
IETF .... International Engineering Task Force [*Computer science*]
IETF .... Internet Engineering Task Force
IETM .... Interactive Electronic Technical Manual [*Military*] (RDA)
IETO .... Interagency Environmental Technologies Office (BCP)

IETP .... Individualized Education and Training Plan (OICC)
IETS .... Inelastic Electron Tunneling Spectroscopy
I-ETS .... Interim European Telecommunication Standard (OSI)
IETS .... Intermediate Examiner Training School [*Federal Home Loan Bank Board*]
IETS .... International Embryo Transfer Society (EA)
IETTAB .... International Environmental Technology Transfer Advisory Board [*Environmental Protection Agency*] (EGAO)
IEU .... Forum International: International Ecosystems University (EA)
IEU .... IES Util 7.875%JrSubDebs [*NYSE symbol*] (TTSB)
IEU .... IES Utilities [*NYSE symbol*] (SAG)
IEU .... Independent Education Union [*Australia*]
IEU .... Input Expansion Unit
IEU .... Instruction Execution Unit [*Computer science*] (IAA)
IEU .... Integrated Electronics Unit (MCD)
IEU .... Interface Electronics Unit [*NASA*]
IEU .... Intermediate Education Unit
IEU .... Ion Exchange Unit
IEU .... Lewis and Clark Library System, Edwardsville, IL [*OCLC symbol*] (OCLC)
IEuC .... Eureka College, Eureka, IL [*Library symbol Library of Congress*] (LCLS)
IEUP .... Institut fuer Europaeische Umweltpolitik [*Institute for European Environmental Policy - IEEP*] (EA)
IEV .... International Electrotechnical Vocabulary (IEEE)
IEV .... Intracellular Enveloped Virus
IEV .... Kewanee Public Library, Kewanee, IL [*OCLC symbol*] (OCLC)
IEV .... Kiev [*Former USSR Airport symbol*] (OAG)
IEVD .... Integrated Electronic Vertical Display
IEvp .... Evergreen Park Public Library, Evergreen Park, IL [*Library symbol Library of Congress*] (LCLS)
IEVS .... Income Eligibility Verification Systems (BARN)
IE-W .... Evanston Public Library, West Branch, Evanston, IL [*Library symbol Library of Congress*] (LCLS)
IEW .... Information Engineering Workbench (CDE)
IEW .... Intelligence and Electronic Warfare [*System*] [*Military*] (RDA)
IEW .... Pekin Public Library, Pekin, IL [*OCLC symbol*] (OCLC)
IEW .... Winters, TX [*Location identifier FAA*] (FAAL)
IEWCS .... Intelligent Electronic Warfare Common Sensor (DWSG)
I/EW FOSS... Intelligence/Electronic Warfare Family of Systems Study [*Military*] (MCD)
IEWI .... Indirect Environmental Warming Impact
IEWNI .... Washington National Insurance Co., Evanston, IL [*Library symbol Library of Congress*] (LCLS)
IEWS .... Integrated Electronic Warfare System
IEWSE .... Intelligence Electronic Warfare Support Element (ADDR)
IEWT .... National Woman's Christian Temperance Union, Evanston, IL [*Library symbol Library of Congress*] (LCLS)
IEW-UAV ..... Intelligence/Electronic Warfare Unmanned Aerial Vehicle [*Army*]
IEX .... Harrington Institute of Interior Design, Design Library, Chicago, IL [*OCLC symbol*] (OCLC)
IEX .... IDEX Corp. [*NYSE symbol*] (SPSG)
IEX .... Instruction Execution [*Computer science*] (IAA)
IEX .... Ion Exchanger
IEX .... Issue Exception Code [*Air Force*] (AFIT)
IEXPE .... Institute of Explosive Engineers (PDAA)
IEXS .... Integrated Expert System [*Computer science*]
IEY .... Barrow, AK [*Location identifier FAA*] (FAAL)
IEY .... Chicago Board of Trade, Chicago, IL [*OCLC symbol*] (OCLC)
IEY .... International Education Year [*UN designation*]
IEZ .... Cumberland Trail Library System, Flora, IL [*OCLC symbol*] (OCLC)
IEZ .... Institut Europeen du Zinc [*European Zinc Institute - EZI*] (EA)
IF .... Ice Fog
IF .... Ideational Fluency [*Research test*]
IF .... Idiopathic Fibroplasia [*Medicine*] (DMAA)
IF .... Idiopathic Flushing [*Medicine*] (DMAA)
IF .... Idirect Fluorescence [*Medicine*] (DMAA)
IF .... Image Frequency (IAA)
I/F .... Image-to-Frame Ratio (MUGU)
IF .... Immersion Fixation [*Microbiology*]
IF .... Immersion Foot [*Medicine*] (DMAA)
IF .... Immunofluorescence [*Immunochemistry*]
IF .... Imperial Father [*of the Chapel*] [*Unions*] [*British*] (DGA)
IF .... Importance Factor [*Statistics*]
IF .... Imprest Fund (MCD)
IF .... Independent Force [*British military*] (DMA)
IF .... Independent Foundation
IF .... Indian Financial Questions [*British*]
IF .... Indirect Fluorescent
IF .... Indonesia Fund [*NYSE symbol*] (SPSG)
IF .... Industrial Appointment Full Time [*Chiropody*] [*British*]
IF .... Industrial Fund (AFM)
IF .... Infielder [*Position in baseball*]
IF .... In-Flight (AAG)
IF .... Information Collector (SAA)
IF .... Information Feedback
IF .... Infrared (MCD)
IF .... Infrared Filter
IF .... In Full
IF .... Inhibiting Factor
IF .... Initiation Factor [*Protein biosynthesis*]
IF .... Inner Forme [*Imposition*] (DGA)
IF .... Inside Face (DAC)
IF .... Inside Frosted
IF .... Installation Fixtures (MCD)

IF	Instantaneous Flow [*Medicine*] (DMAA)
IF	Institute of Fuel [*British*]
IF	Instructional Television, Fixed [*FCC*] (NTCM)
IF	Instruction Field
IF	Instruction Folder (MSA)
IF	Instrument Flight (IAA)
IF	Instrument Flying [*Aviation*]
IF	Insufficient Funds
IF	Insular Force
IF	Integration Facility (MCD)
IF	Intellectual Framework
IF	Intellectual Freedom
IF	Intelligence Fusion [*Army*] (RDA)
IF	Intensity Factor
I/F	Interface [*Computer science*] (KSC)
IF	Interference Filter
IF	Interferon [*Also, IFN*] [*Biochemistry*]
IF	Interferon Foundation [*Defunct*] (EA)
IF	Interflug [*ICAO designator*] (AD)
IF	Interfuture (EA)
IF	Interior Facet [*Medicine*] (DMAA)
IF	Intermediate Filament [*Anatomy*]
IF	Intermediate Fix [*FAA*] (TAG)
IF	Intermediate Forward [*Army*]
IF	Intermediate Frequency [*Electronics*]
IF	Internal Fixation [*Orthopedics*] (DAVI)
IF	Internal Function [*Electronics*] (ECII)
IF	Internally Flawless [*Diamond clarity grade*]
IF	International Federation of American Homing Pigeon Fanciers (EA)
IF	International Forum (EA)
IF	International Foundation (EAIO)
IF	International Foundation fo Employee Benefit Plans (NTPA)
IF	Interrupt Flag [*Computer science*]
IF	Interstitial Fluid [*Physiology*]
IF	Interstitial-Free [*Metallurgical engineering*]
IF	Interventional Fluoroscopy [*Medicine*] (DMAA)
IF	Intrinsic Factor [*Biochemistry*]
IF	Inventrepreneurs' Forum (EA)
IF	Inverted File (NITA)
IF	Involved Field [*Medicine*]
IF	Ipse Fecit [*He Did It Himself*] [*Latin*]
IF	Ipso Facto [*By the Fact Itself*] [*Latin*]
IF	Ireland Fund (EA)
IF	Irish Fusiliers [*British military*] (DMA)
IF	Irregular Force [*Military*] (CINC)
IF	Isotta-Fraschini [*Italian luxury auto maker*]
IFA	Association Internationale de l'Industrie des Engrais [*International Fertilizer Industry Association - IFA*] (EAIO)
IFA	FAI Airservice, Nurnberg [*Germany*] [*FAA designator*] (FAAC)
IFA	Fort Worth Public Library, Fort Worth, TX [*OCLC symbol*] (OCLC)
IFA	Idiopathic Fibrosing Alveolitis [*Medicine*] (DMAA)
IFA	Igniter-Fuel Assembly
IFA	Imero Fiorentino Associates, Inc. [*New York, NY*] [*Telecommunications*] (TSSD)
IFA	Immunofluorescence [*or Immunofluorometric*] Assay [*Also, IFMA*] [*Analytical biochemistry*]
IFA	Immunofluorescent Antibody [*Immunochemistry*]
IFA	Incomplete Freund's Adjuvant
IFA	Independent Fee Appraiser, Member [*National Association of Independent Fe e Appraisers, Inc.*] [*Designation awarded by*]
IFA	Independent Financial Adviser [*British*] (ECON)
IFA	Independent Financial Analysis (ADA)
IFA	Indirect Fluorescence Assay (DB)
IFA	Indirect Fluorescent Antibody [*Immunochemistry*]
IFA	Individualized Functional Assessment [*Social Security Administration*]
IFA	Industrial Forestry Association [*Later, NFA*] (EA)
IFA	In-Flight Abort (MCD)
IFA	In-Flight Alignment (PDAA)
IFA	In-Flight Analysis
IFA	Information Flow Analysis (MHDB)
IFA	Inslee Family Association (EA)
IFA	Institute of Field Archaeologists [*British*] (DBA)
IFA	Institute of Financial Accountants (EAIO)
IFA	Instrumented Fuel Assembly (PDAA)
IFA	Insulation Fabricators Association [*Defunct*] (EA)
IFA	Integrated Feed Antenna
IFA	Integrated File Adapter [*Computer science*] (BUR)
IFA	Intensive Flux Array [*Marine science*] (OSRA)
IFA	Intercessors for America (EA)
IFA	Intercollegiate Fencing Association (EA)
IFA	Interface Functional Analysis (NASA)
IFA	Inter-Financial Association (EA)
IFA	Interim Functional Alternate
IFA	Intermediate Frequency Amplifier [*or Attenuator*]
IFA	International Federation of Accountants (ADA)
IFA	International Federation of Actors
IFA	International Federation of Airworthiness [*Middlesex, England*] (EAIO)
IFA	International Federation on Ageing (EA)
IFA	International Ferret Association (EA)
IFA	International Fertility Association [*Defunct*]
IFA	International Fertilizer Industry Association [*Paris, France*] (EAIO)
IFA	International Festivals Association (EA)
IFA	International Fiction Association (EAIO)
IFA	International Fighter Aircraft
IFA	International Filariasis Association (EA)

IFA	International Finance Alert [*Financial Times Business Information*] [*British Information service or system*] (CRD)
IFA	International Finn Association [*Madrid, Spain*] (EAIO)
IFA	International Fiscal Association [*Rotterdam, Netherlands*] (EAIO)
IFA	International Florists Association [*Later, National Florists Association*] (EA)
IFA	International Footprint Association (EA)
IFA	International Footwear Association (EA)
IFA	International Formalwear Association (NTPA)
IFA	International Franchise Association (EA)
IFA	International Freight Apron
IFA	International Frisbee Association [*Later, IFDA*]
IFA	Interracial Family Alliance (EA)
IFA	Ionization Front Accelerator [*Physics*]
IFA	Iowa Falls, IA [*Location identifier FAA*] (FAAL)
IFA	Irish Features Agency [*News agency*]
IFA	Irish Football Association (BI)
IFA	Israel Folktale Archive (BJA)
IFA	Istituto di Fisica dell'Atmosfera [*Institute of Atmospheric Physics*] [*Italy*]
IFA	Majma'a al-Fiqh al-Islami [*Islamic Jurisprudence Academy - IJA*] (EAIO)
IFAA	International Federation of Advertising Agencies [*Sarasota, FL*] (EA)
IFAA	Internationale Federation of Associations of Anatomists (EA)
IFAA	International Flight Attendants Association (EA)
IFAA	International Flow Aids Association (EA)
IFAA	International Furniture and Accessory Association (EA)
IFAAB	International Fiscal Association, Australian Branch
IFAB	Integrated Fire Direction System for the Artillery Battery [*German*]
IFABC	International Federation of Audit Bureaux of Circulations (EAIO)
IFAC	Independent Fee Appraiser/Counselor [*National Association of Independent Fee Appraisers, Inc.*] [*Designation awarded by*]
IFAC	Interfirm Accounting Project (IAA)
IFAC	International Federation of Accountants [*New York, NY*] (EA)
IFAC	International Federation of Automatic Control [*Laxenburg, Austria*]
IFAC	International Food Additives Council (EA)
IFACE	Interface Element (NITA)
IFAD	Interactive Finite Element Analysis and Design [*Software*] [*Automotive engineering*]
IFAD	International Foundation for Agricultural Development [*Defunct*] (EA)
IFAD	International Fund for Agricultural Development [*United Nations*]
IF-ADD ICMA	Insular Force - Additional Initial Clothing Monetary Allowance [*Military*] (DNAB)
IFAE	International Farmers Association for Education [*Defunct*] (EA)
IFaf	Fairfield Public Library, Fairfield, IL [*Library symbol Library of Congress*] (LCLS)
IFAFA	Italian Folk Art Federation of America (EA)
IFAHPF	International Federation of American Homing Pigeon Fanciers (EA)
IFAI	Industrial Fabrics Association International (EA)
IFAI	International Fire Administration Institute
IFai	Vance Township Library, Fairmount, IL [*Library symbol*] [*Library of Congress*] (LCLS)
IFALPA	International Federation of Air Line Pilots Associations [*Egham, England*] (EAIO)
IFAM	Initial-Final Address Message [*Telecommunications*] (TEL)
IFAM	Inverted File Access Method
IFAMP	If Approach Missed Proceed [*Aviation*] (FAAC)
IFAMS	Integrated Force Administration System [*Bell System*]
IFAN	Institut Francais d'Afrique Noire [*French Institute of Black Africa*]
IFAN	Internationale Foderation der Ausschusse Normenpraxis [*International Federation for the Application of Standards*] (EAIO)
IFANC	International Free Academy of New Cosmology (EA)
IF & F	Intermediate Flush and Fill (AAG)
IFAO Bibl d'Et	Institut Francais d'Archeologie Orientale du Caire. Bibliotheque d'Etude [*A publication*] (BJA)
IFAP	International Federation of Agricultural Producers (BARN)
IFAP	International Foundation for Airline Passengers (EAIO)
IFAPA	International Foundation of Airline Passengers Associations (EAIO)
IFAPAO	International Federation of Asian and Pacific Associations of Optometrists [*Australia*] (EAIO)
IFAPP	International Federation of Associations of Pharmaceutical Physicians [*Italy*] (EAIO)
IFAPWE	Institute of Ferro-Alloy Producers in Western Europe [*Defunct*] (EA)
IFAR	Injector Face Acoustic Resonator (MCD)
IFAR	International Forum for AIDS Research [*Institute of Medicine*]
IFAR	International Foundation for Art Research (EA)
IFARD	International Federation of Agricultural Research Systems for Development [*Netherlands*]
IFarE	Farmington East Unit District No. 324, Farmington, IL [*Library symbol Library of Congress*] (LCLS)
IFARS	Individual Flight Activity Reporting System [*Navy*]
IFAS	Independent Fee Appraiser, Senior [*National Association of Independent Fe e Appraisers, Inc.*] [*Designation awarded by*]
IFAS	Institute for First Amendment Studies
IFAS	International Federation for the Application of Standards (PDAA)
IFAS	International Federation of Aquarium Societies
IFASC	Integrated Functions Assessment Steering Committee [*NASA*] (NASA)
IFaSD	Farina-LaGrove Community Unit, School District 206, Farina, IL [*Library symbol Library of Congress*] (LCLS)
IFAST	Integrated Facility for Avionics System Test [*Air Force*]
IFAT	Indirect Fluorescent Antibody Test [*Immunology*]
IFAT	Indirect Immunofluorescent Antibody Test [*Clinical chemistry*]
IFATCA	International Federation of Air Traffic Controllers' Associations [*Dublin, Republic of Ireland*] (EAIO)

IFATE .... International Federation of Airworthiness Technology and Engineering [*Later, IFA*]
IFATSEA ...... International Federation of Air Traffic Safety Electronic Associations [*British*] (EAIO)
IFAVWU .... International Federation of Audio-Visual Workers Unions [*See also FISTA*] (EAIO)
IFAW .... International Fund for Animal Welfare (EA)
IFAWPCA ..... International Federation of Asian and Western Pacific Contractors' Associations [*Pasig, Metro Manila, Philippines*] (EAIO)
IFAX .... International Facsimile Service [*Telecommunications*] (TEL)
IFAXA .... International Facsimile Association (EA)
IFB .... Fort Wayne Bible College, Fort Wayne, IN [*OCLC symbol*] (OCLC)
IFB .... Incendiary Fragmentation Bomb
IFB .... Independent Forward Bloc [*Mauritian political party*]
IFB .... Initiation for Bid
IFB .... Institute of Foreign Bankers [*New York, NY*] (EA)
IFB .... Internationales Federn-Bureau [*International Feather Bureau - IFB*] (EAIO)
IFB .... International Federation of the Blind [*Later, WBU*]
IFB .... Interrupted Feedback [*Wireless earphone*] (NTCM)
IFB .... Interrupt Feedback Line [*Computer science*] (IAA)
IFB .... Investment Finance Bank Ltd. [*Malta*]
IFB .... Invitation for Bid [*Marine science*] (OSRA)
IFBA .... International Fire Buff Associates (EA)
IFBA .... International Foodservice Brokers Association (NTPA)
IFBB .... International Federation of Bodybuilders [*Montreal, PQ*] (EA)
IFBC .... International Federation of the Blue Cross (EA)
IFBDO .... International Federation of Blood Donor Organizations [*See also FIODS*] [*Dole, France*] (EAIO)
IFBE .... International Federation for Business Education (NTPA)
IFBH .... Intermediate Force Beachhead [*Military*] (DNAB)
IFBM .... Improved Fleet Ballistic Missile
IFBPW .... International Federation of Business and Professional Women (EA)
IFBS .... International Fashion and Boutique Show (ITD)
IFBSO .... International Federation of Boat Show Organisers (EA)
IFBSS .... Individual Flexible Barrier Shelter Systems (MCD)
IFBWW .... International Federation of Building and Wood Workers [*Sweden*]
IFC .... Cefi Aviation SRL [*Italy ICAO designator*] (FAAC)
IFC .... Franklin College of Indiana, Franklin, IN [*OCLC symbol*] (OCLC)
IFC .... Idiots Fools and Clowns (MUSM)
IFC .... Imasco Financial Corp. [*Vancouver Stock Exchange symbol Toronto Stock Exchange symbol*]
IFC .... Improved Flotation Chamber
IFC .... Incremental Frequency Control
IFC .... Independent Film Channel
IFC .... Independent Fire Control [*Area*] (NATG)
IFC .... Indicated Final Cost (SAA)
IFC .... Industrial Frequency Changer
IFC .... Infant Formula Council (EA)
IFC .... In-Flight Calibration (KSC)
IFC .... Infrared Fire Control
IFC .... Initial Floristic Composition [*Theory of plant succession*]
IFC .... Inside Front Cover [*Publishing*] (NTCM)
ifc .... Inside Front Cover [*Publishing*] (WDAA)
IFC .... Inspiratory Flow Cartridge (STED)
IFC .... Installed First Cost (ACRL)
IFC .... Instantaneous Frequency Correlation
IFC .... Institut Forestier du Canada [*Formerly, Canadian Society of Forest Engineers*] (AC)
IFC .... Instrument Flight Center [*Air Force*]
IFC .... Insulated Food Container [*Military*] (INF)
IFC .... Integrated Fire Control [*RADAR*]
IFC .... Integrated Forcing Contribution [*Environmental science*]
IFC .... Intellectual Freedom Committee [*American Library Association*]
IFC .... Interface Clear (IAA)
IFC .... Inter-Faith Compassionists (EA)
IFC .... Interfirm Comparison (ADA)
IFC .... Interfruitlet Corking [*of pineapple*]
IFC .... Intermittent Flow Centrifugation (STED)
IFC .... Internal Fission Counter [*Environmental science*] (COE)
IFC .... International Facilitating Committee [*World Resources Institute*]
IFC .... International Federation of Master-Craftsmen [*See also IFH*] (EAIO)
IFC .... International Film Completion Corp.
IFC .... International Finance Corp. [*Affiliate of International Bank for Reconstruction and Development*]
IFC .... International Financial Corporation (EBF)
IFC .... International Firestop Council (NTPA)
IFC .... International Fisheries Commission [*Later, IPHC*] [*US and Canada*]
IFC .... International Fuel Cells
IFC .... Internet Foundation Classes [*Netscape*] (IGQR)
IFC .... Interracial Family Circle [*An association*]
IFC .... Interstate and Foreign Commerce (DLA)
IFC .... Intrinsic Factor Concentrate [*Biochemistry*]
IFC .... Istituto di Fisica Cosmica [*Italy*]
IFCA .... Independent Fundamental Churches of America (EA)
IFCA .... Instrumentation to Follow the Course of an Accident [*Nuclear energy*] (NRCH)
IFCA .... International Fan Club Association [*Formerly, FCA*] (EA)
IFCA .... International Federation of Catholic Alumnae (EA)
IFCAA .... International Fire Chiefs' Association of Asia (EAIO)
IFCAM .... Industrial Fuel Choice Analysis Model [*Environmental Protection Agency*] (GFGA)
IFCAS .... Indirect Fire Casualty Assessment/Suppression System [*Military*] (MCD)

IFCATI .... International Federation of Cotton and Allied Textile Industries [*Later, ITMF*]
IFCB .... International Federation of Cell Biology [*Toronto, ON*] (EAIO)
IFCB .... International Friendly Circle of the Blind (EAIO)
IFCbl .... Intrinsic Factor Cobalamin (Complex) [*Biochemistry*]
IFCC .... Iconized Flowchart Compilers [*Software*] [*Computer science*]
IFCC .... Initial Fleet Command Center [*Navy*] (CAAL)
IFCC .... Interim Fleet Command Center [*Navy*] (MCD)
IFCC .... International Federation of Camping and Caravanning
IFCC .... International Federation of Children's Communities [*Later, FICE*]
IFCC .... International Federation of Clinical Chemistry [*Vienna, Austria*] (EA)
IFCCA .... International Federation of Community Centre Associations
IFCCTE .... International Federation of Commercial, Clerical, and Technical Employees
IFCDG .... Injection of Fuel Containing Dissolved Gas [*Diesel engines*]
IFCE .... Integral Fire Control Equipment (AAG)
IFCE .... International Federation of Consulting Engineers (NUCP)
IFCF .... Integrated Fuel Cycle Facilities [*Nuclear energy*] (NRCH)
IFCF .... Intermediate Frequency Crystal Filter
IFCF .... International Frederic Chopin Foundation [*Poland*] (EAIO)
IFCGWU .... International Federation of Chemical and General Workers Union
IFCI .... International Fibercom, Inc. [*NASDAQ symbol*] (SAG)
IFCI .... Intl Fibercom Inc. [*NASDAQ symbol*] (TTSB)
IFCIW .... International Fibercom Wrrt [*NASDAQ symbol*] (TTSB)
IFCJ .... International Federation of Catholic Journalists
IFCL .... Intermittent Flow Centrifugation Leukapheresis (STED)
IFCM .... International Federation for Choral Music (EA)
IFCM .... International Federation of Christian Metalworkers Unions
IFCMI .... International Federation of Children of Mary Immaculate [*Paris, France*] (EAIO)
IFCMU .... International Federation of Christian Miners' Unions
IFCN .... Interfacility Communication Network
IFCN .... Inter-Facility Flow Control Network [*FAA*] (TAG)
IFCN .... International Federation of Clinical Neurophysiology (EAIO)
IFCO .... International Fan Club Organization (EA)
IFCO .... International Fisheries Cooperative Organization (BARN)
IFCO .... Interreligious Foundation for Community Organization (EA)
IFCP .... Institute for Financial Crime Prevention [*Later, NACFE*] (EA)
IFCP .... International Federation of Catholic Pharmacists
IFCP .... International Federation of the Cinematographic Press [*See also FIPRESCI*] (EAIO)
IFCP .... International Fund for Concerned Photography [*Later, ICP*]
IFCPC .... International Federation of Cervical Pathology and Colposcopy [*Dundee, Scotland*] (EAIO)
IFCR .... Interface Control Register (IAA)
IFCRA .... International Foundation for Cancer Research (EA)
IFCRA .... International Floor Covering Representatives Association (NTPA)
IFCRM .... International Federation of Catholic Rural Movements (EAIO)
IFCS .... Improved Fire Control System [*Military*] (MCD)
IFCS .... Inactivated Fetal Calf Serum [*Medicine*] (DMAA)
IFCS .... In-Flight Checkout System (IEEE)
IFCS .... Infrared Fire Control System
IFCS .... Institute for Family and Child Study [*Michigan State University*] [*Research center*] (RCD)
IFCS .... Integrated Flight Control System
IFCS .... Intergovernmental Forum on Chemical Safety
IFCS .... International Federation of Computer Sciences
IFCSC .... Intercollegiate Fencing Conference of Southern California (PSS)
IFCSS .... Independent Federation of Chinese Students and Scholars (EA)
IFCTIO .... International Federation of Commercial Travelers Insurance Organizations [*Later, CTIF*] (EA)
IFCTU .... International Federation of Christian Trade Unions [*Often uses initialism CISC, based on name in French, to avoid confusion with ICFTU*]
IFCTUBWW... International Federation of Christian Trade Unions of Building and Wood Workers
IFCTUGP...... International Federation of Christian Trade Unions of Graphical and Paper Industries
IFCU .... Interface Control Unit [*Army*] (IAA)
IFCU .... International Federation of Catholic Universities [*See also FIUC*] [*Paris, France*] (EAIO)
IFCUAW .... International Federation of Christian Unions of Agricultural Workers
IFCWU .... International Federation of Chemical Workers' Unions
IFD .... Idealization to Frustration to Demoralization
IFD .... Image File Directory [*Computer science*]
IFD .... Incipient Fire Detection
IFD .... Indentation Force Deflection [*Automotive seat testing*]
IFD .... In Flagrante Delicto [*Caught in the Act*] [*Latin*]
IFD .... In-Flight Deployment
IFD .... Infrared Detector
IFD .... Initial Fill Date [*Army*] (AABC)
IFD .... In-Line Filter Degasser
IFD .... Instantaneous Frequency Discriminator (IEEE)
IFD .... Integrated Flight Director [*Aviation*]
IFD .... Intelligent Field Device (ACII)
IFD .... Interfiber Distance
IFD .... Inter-Fighter Director
IFD .... Internal Friction Damping (PDAA)
IFD .... Internationale Federation des Dachdeckerhandwerks [*International Federation of Roofing Contractors*] (EAIO)
IFD .... International Federation for Documentation [*Also, FID*] [*Later, IFID*]
IFD .... International Foundation Directory [*A publication*]
IFDA .... Independent Film Distributors' Association [*British*]
IFDA .... Institutional Food Distributors of America [*Later, NAWGA*] (EA)
IFDA .... International Foodservice Distributors Association (EA)

IFDA............. International Foundation for Development Alternatives [*See also FIPAD*] [*Nyon, Switzerland*] (EAIO)
IFDA............. International Franchised Dealers Association [*Later, SFDA*] (EA)
IFDA............. International Frisbee Disc Association [*Formerly, IFA*] (EA)
IFDA............. International Furnishings and Design Association (EA)
IFDAPS........ Integrated Flight Data Processing System [*Air Force*]
IFDAS......... International Federation of Dental Anesthesiology Societies [*British*] (EAIO)
IFDC............. Industrial Funding Corp. [*NASDAQ symbol*] (NQ)
IFDC............. Integrated Facilities Design Criteria (SAA)
IFDC............. International Fertilizer Development Center (EA)
IFDC............. Intraductal and Infiltrating Duct Carcinoma [*Oncology*]
IFDCAUS...... International Flying Dutchman Class Association of the US (EA)
IFDCO.......... International Flying Dutchmen Class Organization [*Berlin, Federal Republic of Germany*] (EAIO)
IFDFA.......... International Freeze-Dry Floral Association (EA)
IFDI............. International Fibre Drum Institute (NTPA)
IFDI............. Israel Folk Dance Institute (EA)
IFDM............ International Foundation of Doll Makers (EA)
IFDO .... International Federation of Dalit Organizations (EA)
IFDO .... International Federation of Data Organizations for the Social Sciences [*Amsterdam, Netherlands*] (EAIO)
IFDP............. Institute for Food and Development Policy (EA)
IFDR............ Interface Data Register (IAA)
IFDS............ Inertial Flight Data System (KSC)
IFDS............ Integrated Flagship Data System [*Navy*] (NG)
IFDS............ Isolated Follicle-Deficiency Syndrome [*Medicine*] (STED)
IFDVS .... Indian Field Depot Veterinary Stores [*British military*] (DMA)
IFE............... Federal Electoral Institute [*Mexico City, Mexico*]
IFE............... Image Feature Extraction [*Air Force*]
IFE............... Immunofixation Electrophoresis [*Clinical chemistry*]
IFE............... Incipient Failure Everywhere [*Hypothesis descending forces in a sand-pile*]
IFE............... In-Flight Emergency (MCD)
IFE............... In-Flight Entertainment
IFE............... Inner Front End (MSA)
IFE............... Institute for Fluitronics Education (EA)
IFE............... Institute of Federal Elections [*Mexico City, Mexico*]
IFE............... Institute of Financial Education [*Chicago, IL*] (EA)
IFE............... Institute of Fire Engineers
IFE............... Institut Francais de l'Energie [*French Institute of Energy*] [*Paris*] [*Information service or system*] (IID)
IFE............... Intelligent Front End (NITA)
IFE............... Interfollicular Epidermis (DB)
IFE............... Interfollicular Epidermis [*Medicine*] (STED)
IFE............... Internal Field Emission
IFE............... International Family Entertainment
IFE............... International Fasteners Exposition (ITD)
IFE............... International Food and Drink Exhibition [*British*] (ITD)
IFE............... Intl Flavors/Fragr [*NYSE symbol*] (TTSB)
IFEA............. In-Flight Emergency Assistance [*FAA*] (TAG)
IFEA............. Institute of Fire Engineers in Australia
IFEAT........... International Federation of Essential Oils and Aroma Trades [*British*] (EAIO)
IFEBP........... International Foundation of Employee Benefit Plans (EA)
IFEBS.......... Integrated Foreign Exchange and Banking System (PDAA)
IFEC............ International Foodservice Editorial Council (EA)
IFED............ Integrated Fuel/Engine Display (MCD)
IFEEX........... International Fishing Equipment Exposition [*Canada*] (ITD)
IFEF............ Internacia Fervojista Esperanto Federacio [*International Federation of Esperantist Railwaymen*] (EAIO)
IFEH............. International Federation of Europe Houses [*See also FIME*] (EAIO)
IFEI............. Integrated Fuel/Engine Instrument (MCD)
IFEL............. Inverse Free Electron LASER [*Plasma physics*]
IFEM............ In-Flight Engine Monitor (MCD)
IFEM .... Institute of Fireplace Equipment Manufacturers (EA)
IFEMA.......... Industrial Finishing Equipment Manufacturers Association (EA)
IFEMS.......... International Federation of Electron Microscope Societies
IFEN............. Institut Francais de l'Environnement [*Marine science*] [*France*] (OSRA)
IFEN............. Intercompany File Exchange Network (TELE)
IFenE........... Institute of Fence Engineers [*British*] (DBA)
IFEP............. Inflation from an Energy Perspective [*Economic theory*]
IFEP............. In-Flight Experiments Panel
IFEP............. Integrated Front End Processor (NITA)
IFEPFC........ International Federation of Elvis Presley Fan Clubs [*Defunct*] (EA)
IFEPT........... International Federation for Enteric Phage Typing [*International Council of Scientific Unions*]
IFER............. Internationale Foederation der Eisenbahn-Reklame-Gesellschaften [*International Federation of Railway Advertising Companies*] [*British*] (EA)
IFER............. International Federation of Engine Reconditioners [*See also FIRM*] [*Paris, France*] (EAIO)
IFER............. International Foundation for Ethical Research (EA)
IFERS........... International Flat Earth Research Society (EA)
IFES............. Image Feature Extraction System [*Air Force*]
IFES............. International Fellowship of Evangelical Students (EA)
IFES............. International Foundation for Electoral Systems (EA)
IFESLG........ International Fellowship of Evangelical Students Link Group (EA)
IFeT............ Intestinal Iron (Ferrum) Transport [*Physiology*]
IFEW........... Inter-American Federation of Entertainment Workers
IFf............... Frankfort Public Library District, Frankfort, IL [*Library symbol Library of Congress*] (LCLS)
IFF............... Identification, Friend or Foe [*Military*]
IFF .... If and Only If (IEEE)

IFF............... Iffley [*Australia Airport symbol Obsolete*] (OAG)
IFF............... Individual Freedom Federation (EA)
IFF............... Induced Fluid Flow
IFF............... Industrial Funding Fee (AAGC)
IFF............... Inert Fluid Fill (AAG)
IFF............... Inner Fracture Face [*Medicine*] (DB)
IFF............... Institute for the Future
IFF............... Institute of Freight Forwarders [*British*]
IFF............... Institute of Natural Resources, Springfield, IL [*OCLC symbol*] (OCLC)
IFF............... Intensity Fluctuation Factor [*Telecommunications*] (TEL)
IFF............... Interchange File Format [*Computer science*]
IFF............... Interfreight Forwarding Ltd. [*Sudan*] [*ICAO designator*] (FAAC)
IFF............... International Federal Film [*Fictitious organization of agents in TV series "Scarecrow and Mrs. King"*]
IFF............... International Federation of Falerists (EA)
IFF............... International Fencing Federation [*Paris, France*] (EA)
IFF............... International Film Foundation
IFF............... International Flavors & Fragrances, Inc. [*NYSE symbol*] (SPSG)
IFF............... International Flying Farmers (EA)
IFF............... International Forum Foundation
IFF............... International Freedom Foundation (EA)
IFF............... Ionized Flow Field
IFF............... Iran Freedom Foundation (EA)
IFF............... Isoelectric Focusing Facility
IFF............... Item Intelligence File [*DoD*]
IFFA............. Independent Federation of Flight Attendants (EA)
IFFA............. Interactive Flash Flood Analyzer
IFFA............. International Federation of Film Archives
IFFA............. International Fly Fishing Association (EAIO)
IFFA............. International Frozen Food Association (EA)
IFFAA.......... Inland Fish Farming Association of Australia
IFF/ATCRBS... Identification Friend or Foe/Air-Traffic Control RADAR Beacon System [*Military*]
IFFC............ Integrated Flight and Fire Control
IFFCS.......... International Fancy Food and Confection Show (ITD)
IFFEC.......... International Federation of Free Evangelical Churches (EA)
IFFEX.......... International Frozen Food Exhibition and Congress
IFFF............ Internationale Frauenliga fuer Frieden und Freiheit [*Women's International League for Peace and Freedom*]
IFFH............ International Federation for Family Health [*Bandung, Indonesia*] (EA)
IFFIT .... International Facility for Food Irradiation Technology [*Netherlands*] (WND)
IFFJ............ International Federation of Free Journalists [*British*]
IFFJP........... International Federation of Fruit Juice Producers [*See also FIJU*] [*Paris, France*] (EAIO)
IFFLP.......... International Federation for Family Life Promotion (EA)
IFFN............ Identification, Friend or Foe or Neutral (MCD)
IFFPA.......... International Federation of Film Producers' Associations
IFFS............ Identification, Friend or Foe, Switching Circuit [*Military*] (MSA)
IFFS............ Intermediate Future Forecasting System [*Department of Energy*] (GFGA)
IFFS............ International Federation of Fertility Societies (EAIO)
IFFS............ International Federation of Film Societies
IFFSA.......... Inflight Food Service Association (EA)
IFFSH.......... Instrument Formation Flight System for Helicopters
IFF/SIF......... Identification, Friend or Foe/Selective Identification Feature [*Military*]
IFFT............ International Federation of Forensic Toxicologists [*Medicine*] (WDAA)
IFFT............ Inverse Fast Fourier Transform (IAA)
IFFTU.......... International Federation of Free Teachers' Unions [*See also SPIE*] [*Amsterdam, Netherlands*] (EAIO)
IFFU............ Identification, Friend or Foe Unit (MCD)
IFF-UK .... International Freedom Foundation - United Kingdom Branch (EAIO)
IFG.............. Inferior Frontal Gyrus [*Brain anatomy*]
IFG.............. Inland Fisher Guide [*General Motors Corp.*]
IFG.............. Institute for Research on Educational Finance and Governance [*Department of Education*] (GRD)
IFG.............. Instream Flow Service Group [*United States Fish and Wildlife Service*]
IFG.............. International Fashion Group [*Later, Fashion Group International*] (EA)
IFG.............. Inter-Regional Financial Group, Inc. [*NYSE symbol*] (SPSG)
IFG.............. Inter-Regional Fin. Gr. [*NYSE symbol*] (TTSB)
IFG.............. Kaskaskia Library System, Smithton, IL [*OCLC symbol*] (OCLC)
IFGA............ International Fancy Guppy Association (EA)
IFGA............ International Federation of Grocers' Associations [*See also IVLD*] [*Bern, Switzerland*] (EAIO)
IFGAE.......... International Federation for Gerda Alexander Eutony [*Belgium*] (EAIO)
IFGB............ Institute of Chartered Foresters [*British*]
IFGE............ International Foundation for Gender Education (EA)
IFGL............ Initial File Generation Language
IFGMA......... International Federation of Grocery Manufacturers Associations (EA)
IFGO .... International Federation of Gynecology and Obstetrics
IFGS............ International Fantasy Gaming Society (EA)
IFGS............ Interstitial Fluids and Ground Substance (STED)
IFGVP.......... International Federation of Gastronomical and Vinicultural Press
IFH.............. Industrial Facilities Handbook [*A publication*] (AAGC)
IFH.............. In-Flight Helium
IFH.............. Internationale Foderation des Handwerks [*International Federation of Master-Craftsmen - IFMC*] [*Vienna, Austria*] (EAIO)
IFH.............. International Foundation for Homeopathy (EA)
IFH.............. Judson College Library, Elgin, IL [*OCLC symbol*] (OCLC)
IFHBT.......... International Federation of Health and Beauty Therapists
IFHE............ International Federation for Home Economics [*See also FIEF*] [*Paris, France*] (EAIO)

IFHE	International Federation of Hospital Engineering (PDAA)
IFHG	Institute of Family History and Genealogy (EA)
IFhGS	Grant-Illini School 110, Fairview Heights, IL [*Library symbol Library of Congress*] (LCLS)
IFhGSD	Grant Community Consolidated School District 110, Fairview Heights, IL [*Library symbol Library of Congress*] (LCLS)
IFHOH	International Federation of the Hard of Hearing [*Kampen, Netherlands*] (EAIO)
IFHOL	If Holding [*Aviation*] (FAAC)
IFHP	International Federation for Housing and Planning [*Netherlands*]
IFHP	International Federation of Health Professionals (EA)
IFHPM	International Federation of Hydraulic Platform Manufacturers [*Later, IPAF*] (EAIO)
IFHPMSM	International Foundation for Hygiene, Preventative Medicine, Social Medicine (BABM)
IFhPSD	Pontiac-William Holliday School District 105, Fairview Heights, IL [*Library symbol Library of Congress*] (LCLS)
IFHPSM	International Federation for Hygiene, Preventive, and Social Medicine [*France*] (EAIO)
IFHRO	International Federation of Health Records Organizations [*Munich, Federal Republic of Germany*] (EAIO)
IFHS	Irish Family History Society (EA)
IFHTM	International Federation for the Heat Treatment of Materials (PDAA)
IFHTP	International Federation for Housing and Town Planning
IFI	Immune Interferon (DMAA)
IFI	Imperial Forestry Institute [*British*] (BI)
IFI	Industrial Fasteners Institute (EA)
IFI	Infisy Systems, Inc. [*Vancouver Stock Exchange symbol*]
IFI	In-Flight Insertion (NG)
IFI	Information for Industry Inc. (NITA)
IFI	Inspector Followup Items [*Environmental science*] (COE)
IFI	Institutional Functioning Inventory [*Psychologic test*] (STED)
IFI	Institutional Functioning Inventory [*Psychology*] (DHP)
IFI	Inter-Freight International [*Steamship*] (MHDB)
IFI	International Fabricare Institute (EA)
IFI	International Federation of Interior Architects/Interior Designers [*Amsterdam, Netherlands*] (EAIO)
IFI	International Feedstuffs Institute [*Utah State University*] [*Research center Defunct*] (RCD)
IFI	International Film Institute
IFI	International Financial Institution
IFI	International Foundation for Independence (EA)
IFI	International Fund for Ireland [*United States, Canada, and New Zealand*]
IFI	Italian for Idiots [*Facetious travel terminology*]
IFI	Kingfisher, OK [*Location identifier FAA*] (FAAL)
IFI	Sidley & Austin, Chicago, IL [*OCLC symbol*] (OCLC)
IFIA	Intermountain Forest Industry Association (EA)
IFIA	International Federation of Inventors' Associations [*Stockholm, Sweden*] (EAIO)
IFIA	International Federation of Ironmongers and Iron Merchants Associations [*See also FIDAQ*] [*Zurich, Switzerland*] (EAIO)
IFIA	International Fence Industry Association (EA)
IFIA	International Financial Institutions Act [*1977*]
IFIA NAC	International Federation of Inspection Agencies - North American Committee (NTPA)
IFIAS	International Federation of Institutes for Advanced Study [*ICSU*] [*Toronto, ON*] (EAIO)
IFIAT	International Federation of Independent Air Transport
IFIC	International Ferrocement Information Center [*Asian Institute of Technology*] (IID)
IFIC	International Food Information Council (EA)
IFICB	International Finance Investment and Commerce Bank Ltd. [*Bangladesh*] (EY)
IFICO	Industrial Finance and Investment Corp. [*British*]
IFICS	In-Flight Interceptor Communications System [*Military*]
IFID	International Federation for Information and Documentation [*See also FIID*] (EAIO)
IFIDA	Independent Film Importers and Distributors of America [*Defunct*] (EA)
IFIEC	International Federation of Industrial Energy Consumers [*Geneva, Switzerland*] (EA)
I (field)	Information Field (NITA)
IFIF	International Federation for Internal Freedom [*Later, Castalia Foundation*] (EA)
IFIF	International Federation of Industrial Organizations and General Workers' Unions
IFIF	International Forum for Internal Freedom (WDAA)
IFIFR	International Federation of International Furniture Removers [*See also FIDI*] [*Brussels, Belgium*] (EA)
IFIJG	International Federation of Infantile and Juvenile Gynecology [*See also FIGIJ*] [*Sierre, Switzerland*] (EAIO)
IFILE	Interface File (NITA)
IFIM	International Flight Information Manual
IFIN	Investors Financial Services Corp. [*NASDAQ symbol*] (SAG)
IFIN	Investors Finl Svcs [*NASDAQ symbol*] (TTSB)
IFINS	If Instrument Conditions Encountered [*Aviation*] (FAAC)
IFIO	Information for Industry Office [*Air Force*] (MCD)
IFIP	International Federation for Information Processing [*Formerly, IFIPS*] (EA)
IFIP	International Food Irradiation Project [*Food and Agricultural Organization*] (PDAA)
IFIPS	International Federation of Information Processing Societies [*Later, IFIP*]
IFIRA	Information Facility for Indigenous Resources for Australia
IFIS	Industry File Index System [*Chemical Information Systems, Inc.*] [*Information service or system*] (CRD)
IFIS	Infrared Flight Inspection System (IAA)
IFIS	Instrument Flight Instructors School [*Navy*]
IFIS	Integrated Flight Instrument System
IFIS	International Financial Intelligence Service (NITA)
IFIS	International Food Information Service [*Database producer*] [*Germany*]
IFISRR	International Federation of Institutes for Socio-Religious Research [*Louvain, Belgium*] (EA)
IFIWA	International Federation of Importers and Wholesale Grocers Associations [*The Hague, Netherlands*] (EAIO)
IFIX	Immunofixation (STED)
IFJ	Franklin-Johnson County Public Library, Franklin, IN [*OCLC symbol*] (OCLC)
IFJ	International Federation of Journalists [*See also FIJ*] [*Brussels, Belgium*] (EA)
IFJ	Isafjordur [*Iceland*] [*Airport symbol*] (OAG)
IFJ	Winnfield, LA [*Location identifier FAA*] (FAAL)
IFK	Installations Fragenkommission [*Later, International Commission on Rules for the Approval of Electrical Equipment*] [*CEE*]
IFK	Interfunk & Co. [*Yugoslavia*] [*ICAO designator*] (FAAC)
IFK	River Bend Library System, Coal Valley, IL [*OCLC symbol*] (OCLC)
IFKC	International Federation of Kennel Clubs (EA)
IFKM	Internationale Foederation fuer Kurzschrift und Maschinenschreiben [*International Federation of Shorthand and Typewriting*]
IFKT	International Federation of Knitting Technologists [*See also FITB*] [*Frauenfeld, Switzerland*] (EAIO)
IFL	Flora Carnegie Library, Flora, IL [*Library symbol Library of Congress*] (LCLS)
IFL	Icelandic Federation of Labor
IFL	Immunofluorescence (DB)
IFL	Imperial Fascist League [*British*]
IFL	Induction Field Locator (IAA)
IFL	Inflatable (MSA)
IFL	Initial Flight Level
IFL	Innisfail [*Australia Airport symbol*]
IFL	Integer Function Language [*Computer science*] (PDAA)
IFL	Integrated Fuse Logic (NITA)
IFL	Intelligent Fault Locator [*McDonnell Douglas Helicopter Co.*] [*Army*]
IFL	Intelligent Forms Language [*Delrina Corp.*] [*Computer science*] (PCM)
IFL	Interfacility Link (LAIN)
IFL	International Frequency List (NATG)
IFL	International Friendship League [*Defunct*] (EA)
IFLA	International Federation of Landscape Architects [*Versailles, France*] (EAIO)
IFLA	International Federation of Library Associations (NITA)
IFLA	International Federation of Library Associations and Institutions
IFLA	International Finance and Leasing Association (MHDB)
IFLASC	International Federation of Latin American Study Centers [*Mexico City, Mexico*] (EAIO)
IFLB	Islamic Front for the Liberation of Bahrain [*Political party*] (PD)
IFLBP	International Federation of the Little Brothers of the Poor [*See also FIPFP*] (EAIO)
IFLC	International Frequency List Committee
IFICL	Cumberland Trail Library System, Flora, IL [*Library symbol Library of Congress*] (LCLS)
IFL-DFL	Inflating-Deflating
IFLG	International Federation of Leather Guilds (EA)
IFLIPS	Integrated Flight Prediction System [*Aviation*] (DA)
IFLN	Interstate Freeze Lobbying Network (EA)
IFlo	Flossmoor Public Library, Flossmoor, IL [*Library symbol Library of Congress*] (LCLS)
IFLO	IFlow Corp. [*NASDAQ symbol*] (SAG)
IFLO	Islamic Front for Liberation of Oromo [*Ethiopia*] [*Political party*] (EY)
IFLOT	Intermediate Focal Length Optical Tracker
I-Flow	IFlow Corp. [*Associated Press*] (SAG)
IFLOWS	Integrated Flood Observing and Warning System [*National Oceanic and Atmospheric Administration*]
IFLrA	Recombinant Human Leukocyte Interferon A [*Pharmacology*] (DAVI)
IFL Rev	International Financial Law Review [*A publication*] (DLA)
IFLRY	International Federation of Liberal and Radical Youth (EAIO)
IFLS	International Federation of Law Students (DLA)
IFLS	International Federation of Little Singers (EAIO)
IFLTT	Intermediate Focal Length Tracking Telescope (MUGU)
IFLWU	International Fur and Leather Workers Union (MHDB)
IFM	Improved Frequency Modulation (MCD)
IFM	In-Flight Maintenance
IFM	Instantaneous Frequency Measurement
IFM	Institute of Fisheries Management [*British*]
IFM	Instrument Flag Motor
IFM	Integrating Fluctuation Meter
IFM	Interactive File Manager [*Computer science*]
IFM	Interfacial-Force Microscope
IFM	Intermediate Frame Memory [*Computer science*]
IFM	Internal Fetal Monitor [*Medicine*] (DMAA)
IFM	International Falcon Movement
IFM	International Finance Managers Study [*Database*] [*Research Services Ltd.*] [*Information service or system*] (CRD)
IFM	International Financial Markets Trading Ltd.
IFM	International Fund for Monuments
IFM	Intrafusal Muscle [*Anatomy*]
IFM	Iowa Farm-to-Market Carriers Tariff Bureau, Ottumwa IA [*STAC*]
IFM	Tifton, GA [*Location identifier FAA*] (FAAL)

IFMA............ Immunofluorescence [*or Immunofluorometric*] Assay [*Also, IFA*] [*Analytical biochemistry*]
IFMA............ Immunofluorometric Assay [*Analytical biochemistry*]
IFMA............ Independent Furniture Manufacturers' Associaiton [*British*] (DBA)
IFMA............ Interdenominational Foreign Mission Association of North America (EA)
IFMA............ International Facility Management Association (EA)
IFMA............ International Farm Management Association [*Reading, Berkshire, England*] (EAIO)
IFMA............ International Federation of Margarine Associations [*Brussels, Belgium*] (EAIO)
IFMA............ International Foodservice Manufacturers Association (EA)
IFMA............ Irish Flour Millers Association (BI)
IFMBE........ International Federation for Medical and Biological Engineering [*ICSU*] [*Ottawa, ON*] (EA)
IFMC............ International Federation of Master-Craftsmen (EA)
IFMC............ International Federation of Motorhome Clubs [*Belgium*] (EAIO)
IFMC............ International Folk Music Council [*Later, ICTM*]
IFME............ International Federation for Medical Electronics
IFME............ International Federation of Municipal Engineers [*See also FIIM*] [*British*] (EAIO)
IF/MF.......... Intermediate Frequency/Medium Frequency (NATG)
IFMIF.......... International Fusion Materials Irradiation Facility (COE)
IFMIS.......... Implementation Field Microfilm/Micrographics Information System
IFMIS.......... Industrial Facilities and Material Information System
IFMIS.......... Integrated Facilities Management Information System
IFML............ International Film Management Ltd. [*Australia*]
IFMM.......... International Federation of Manual Medicine (EA)
IFMO.......... Imperial and Foreign Money Orders
IFMOD........ Interactive Forecasting Model (GFGA)
IFMP............ International Federation for Medical Psychotherapy [*See also IGAP*] [*Oslo, Norway*] (EAIO)
IFMP............ International Federation of Maritime Philately [*Livorno, Italy*] (EAIO)
IFMP............ International Federation of Married Priests (EAIO)
IFMPO........ Integrated Farm Management Program Option [*Department of Agriculture*]
IFMS............ Impact Force Measuring System
IFMS............ In-Flight Management System
IFMS............ Integrated Farm Management System
IFMS............ Integrated Financial Management System (AABC)
IFMS............ Interagency Fleet Management System [*GSA*] (TAG)
IFMS............ International Federation of Magical Societies [*See also FISM*] (EAIO)
IFMSA.......... International Federation of Medical Students Associations [*See also FIAEM*] [*Vienna, Austria*] (EAIO)
IFM-SEI....... International Falcon Movement - Socialist Educational International
IFMSS.......... International Federation of Multiple Sclerosis Societies [*British*] (EAIO)
IFMX............ Informix Corp. [*NASDAQ symbol*] (NQ)
IFN............... India Fund [*NYSE symbol*] (TTSB)
IFN............... India Fund, Inc. [*NYSE symbol*] (SAG)
IFN............... Information [*Computer science*] (MDG)
IFN............... Interferon [*Also, IF*] [*Biochemistry*]
IFN............... International Feminist Network
IFN............... International Friends of Nature [*See also NFI*] [*Zurich, Switzerland*] (EAIO)
IFN............... Isfahan [*Iran*] [*Airport symbol*] (OAG)
IFN............... Items for Negotiation
IFN-A........... Alpha-Interferon [*Medicine*] (TAD)
IFNA............ International Federation of Netball Associations [*Glasgow, Scotland*] (EAIO)
IFNA............ International FidoNet Association [*Defunct*] (EA)
IFNA............ International Flying Nurses Association (EA)
IFNC............ Integrated Flight Control/Navigation Computer (MCD)
IFNE............ International Federation for Narcotic Education
IFNG........... Interferon Gamma [*Medicine*] (DMAA)
IFNP........... International Federation of Newspaper Publishers (NTCM)
IFNs............ Interferons [*Biology*] (DOG)
IFNS............ Irish Family Names Society (EA)
IFNY............ Infinity, Inc. [*NASDAQ symbol*] (SAG)
IFO............... Identified Flying Object [*Air Force*]
IFO............... Improved Fiber Optics
IFO............... Information Systems Office [*NASA*] (NASA)
IFO............... Info-Stop Communications [*Vancouver Stock Exchange symbol*]
IFO............... In Front Of (WDAA)
IFO............... International Fortran Organization (NITA)
IFOA............ Isotta Fraschini Owner's Association [*Defunct*] (EA)
IFOAD......... International Federation of Original Art Diffusors [*France*] (EAIO)
IFOAM........ International Federation of Organic Agriculture Movements [*Witzenhausen, Federal Republic of Germany*] (EA)
IFOB............ Improved Fiber Optics Bundle
IFOBRL........ In-Flight Operable Bomb Rack Lock (MCD)
IFOBS........ International Federation for Open Bibliographic Systems (TELE)
IFOC............ Intermountain Field Operations Center [*Bureau of Mines*] [*Denver, CO*] (GRD)
IFOCUS....... Interprofessional Fostering of Ophthalmic Care for Underserved Sectors [*An association*] (EA)
IFOFSAG...... International Fellowship of Former Scouts and Guides [*Brussels, Belgium*]
IFOG........... Interferometric Fiber Optic Gyroscope
IFOMA........ Independent Fuel Oil Marketers of America [*Defunct*] (EA)
IFOMA........ Instructions for Mailers [*A publication*]
IFop............ Forest Park Public Library, Forest Park, IL [*Library symbol Library of Congress*] (LCLS)
IFOP............ Institut Francais d'Opinion Publique [*French Institute of Public Opinion*]

IFOPA......... International Fibrodysplasia Ossificans Progressiva Association (EA)
Ifor............... Implementation Force [*Bosnia*] (WDAA)
IFOR............ Intelligent Forces [*Army*] (RDA)
IFOR............ Interactive FORTRAN [*Formula Translating System*] [*Computer science*] (IAA)
IFOR............ Internal Format Object Report (MCD)
IFOR............ International Federation of Operation Research Societies (BARN)
IFOR............ International Fellowship of Reconciliation [*Alkmaar, Netherlands*] (EA)
IFORD......... Institut de Formation et de Recherche Demographiques [*Institute for Training and Demographic Research - ITDR*] (EAIO)
IFORO......... Interphone (Service F) Resumed Operation [*Aviation*] (FAAC)
IFORS......... International Federation of Operational Research Societies [*ICSU*] [*Lyngby, Denmark*] (EAIO)
IFORVU....... International Federation of Recreational Vehicle Users [*Later, FOR*] (EA)
IFOS............ International Federation of Ophthalmological Societies [*Nijmegen, Netherlands*] (EA)
IFOS............ International Federation of Oto-Rhino-Laryngological Societies [*Berchem, Belgium*] (EAIO)
IFOS............ Ion Formation from Organic Solids [*International conference*]
IFOSA......... International Federation of Scoliosis Associations (EA)
IFOSS......... Intelligence Family of Systems Study [*Military*] (MCD)
IFOT............ In-Flight Operations and Training (MCD)
IFOTES........ International Federation of Telephonic Emergency Services [*Jorn, Sweden*] (EA)
IFOV............ Individual Field of View
IFOV............ Instantaneous Field of View
IFOV............ Instrument Field of View
IFOX............ Irish Futures and Options Exchange (NUMA)
IFP............... Illinois Functional Programming Language [*Computer science*]
IFP............... Imperial and Foreign Post (IAA)
IFP............... Independent Feature Project (EA)
IFP............... Indexes of Firepower Potential
IFP............... Inflammatory Fibroid Polyp [*Gastroenterology*]
IFP............... In-Flight Performance
IFP............... In Forma Pauperis [*As a Pauper*] [*Latin*]
IFP............... Inkatha Freedom Party [*Afrikaans Political party*] (ECON)
IFP............... Institute of Fluid Power
IFP............... Institute of Physical Problems [*Former USSR*] (MCD)
IFP............... Institut Francais du Petroles [*French Institute of Petroleum*] [*Paris*]
IFP............... Instruction Fetch Pipeline [*Computer science*]
IFP............... Integrated File Processor
IFP............... Intermediate Filament Protein [*Biochemistry*] (DB)
IFP............... International Federation of Pedestrians (EA)
IFP............... International Federation of Purchasing
IFP............... International Fixed Public
IFP............... International Forest Products Ltd. [*Toronto Stock Exchange symbol Vancouver Stock Exchange symbol*]
IFP............... Interns for Peace (EA)
IFP............... Intrapatellar Fat Pad (DMAA)
IFP............... Invitation for Proposal (NOAA)
IFPA............ Independent Film Producers of America (NTCM)
IFPA............ Independent Fluorspar Producers Association (EA)
IFPA............ Independent Forest Products Association (NTPA)
IFPA............ Independent Free Papers of America (EA)
IFPA............ Industrial Fire Protection Association of Great Britain
IFPA............ Information Film Producers of America [*Later, Association of Visual Communicators*] (EA)
IFPA............ Institute for Foreign Policy Analysis, Inc. [*Tufts University*] [*Research center*] (RCD)
IFPA............ International Federation of Photographic Art
IFPA............ International Federation of Psoriasis Associations [*Stockholm, Sweden*] (EAIO)
IFPA............ International Fighter Pilots Academy [*Slovak Air Force*]
IFPA............ International Fire Photographers Association (EA)
IFPA............ International Fresh-Cut Produce Association (NTPA)
IFPA............ Isoelectric Focusing in Polyacrylamide [*Gel*] [*Analytical chemistry*]
IFPAAW....... International Federation of Plantation, Agricultural, and Allied Workers [*Switzerland*]
IFPC............ Integrated Flight and Propulsion Control (MCD)
IFPCA.......... International Federation of Press Cutting Agencies (EA)
IFPCS.......... International Federation of Unions of Employees in Public and Civil Services
IFPCW........ International Federation of Petroleum and Chemical Workers (EA)
IFPD............ International Federation of Postcard Dealers (EA)
IFPDA.......... International Fine Print Dealers Association
IFPE............ Institute of Fiscal and Political Education [*Defunct*] (EA)
IFPE............ International Federation for Parent Education [*See also FIEP*] [*Sevres, France*] (EAIO)
IFPEC.......... Independent Film Producers Export Corp. [*Defunct*]
IFPFP.......... Individual Flight Plans from This Point [*Aviation*] (FAAC)
IFPI............ International Federation of the Phonographic Industry (EAIO)
IFPI............ International Federation of the Photographic Industry
IFPL............ In-Flight Power Loss (MCD)
IFPL/SD....... In-Flight Power Loss/Shutdown (MCD)
IFPM............ In-Flight Performance Monitor
IFPM............ International Federation of Physical Medicine
IFPMA.......... International Federation of Pharmaceutical Manufacturers Associations [*See also FIIM*] [*Geneva, Switzerland*] (EAIO)
IFPMM.......... International Federation of Purchasing and Materials Management [*Aarau, Switzerland*] (EAIO)
IFPMO........ International Federation of Psychological-Medical Organizations [*See also FIOPM*] [*Lausanne, Switzerland*] (EAIO)
IFPMR......... International Federation of Physical Medicine and Rehabilitation (EA)

IFPNT	International Federation of Practitioners of Natural Therapeutics [*British*]
IFPO	Institute of Fire Prevention Officers [*British*] (DBA)
IFPO	International Foundation for Protection Officers (EA)
IFPO	International Freelance Photographers Organization
IFPP	Imperial and Foreign Parcel Post (IAA)
IFPP	Industrial Facilities Protection Program [*DoD*]
IFPP	Industrial Fugitive Process Particulate (GNE)
IFPP	Irradiated Fuel Processing Plant (DEN)
IFPRA	Interamerican Federation of Public Relations Associations
IFPRA	International Family Planning Research Association [*Later, ISRM*] (EA)
IFPRA	International Federation of Park and Recreation Administration [*Reading, England*] (EAIO)
IFPRI	International Fine Particle Research Institute
IFPRI	International Food Policy Research Institute (EA)
IFPS	In-Flight Performance Signal [*Aviation*] (IAA)
IFPS	Integrated Initial Flight Plan Processing System [*Aviation*] (DA)
IFPS	Interactive Financial Planning System [*Harris Systems Ltd.*] [*Software package*] (NCC)
IFPS	International Federation of Palynological Societies (EAIO)
IFPS	International Federation of Philosophical Societies [*See also FISP*] [*Fribourg, Switzerland*] (EAIO)
IFPS	International Federation of Popular Sports [*See also IVV*] (EAIO)
IFPS	International Federation of Psychoanalytic Societies (EA)
IFPSM	International Federation for Preventive and Social Medicine (EAIO)
IFPTE	International Federation of Professional and Technical Engineers (EA)
IFPTO	International Federation of Popular Travel Organisations [*Paris, France*] (EAIO)
IFPTS	Intertype Fototronic Photographic System (DIT)
IFPUG	International Function Point Users Group (NTPA)
IFPV	International Federation of Pelota Vasca (EA)
IFPVP	International Federation of Phonogram and Videogram Producers (EA)
IFPW	International Federation of Petroleum Workers
IFPW	International Federation of Pharmaceutical Wholesalers (NTPA)
IFPWA	International Federation of Protestant Workers' Associations
IFPWA	International Federation of Public Warehousing Associations [*Formerly, IFPWKA*] (EAIO)
IFPWKA	International Federation of Public Warehouse Keepers Associations [*Later, IFPWA*] (EAIO)
IFQ	Invitation for Quote (MCD)
IFR	Ifrane [*Morocco*] [*Seismograph station code, US Geological Survey*] (SEIS)
IFR	IFR Systems, Inc. [*Associated Press*] (SAG)
IFR	Image-to-Frame Ratio
IFR	Immediate Free Recall (PDAA)
IFR	Imported Food Regulations [*British*]
IFR	Impulse Fast Reactor [*Former USSR*]
IFR	Increasing Failure Rate
IFR	Incremental Financial Rate of Return
IFR	Indian Foodgrain Requirements [*British*]
IFR	Industrial Fuels & Resources, Inc. (EFIS)
IFR	In-Flight Refueling
IFR	In-Frame Response [*Automotive engineering Electronics*]
IFR	Infrared
IFR	Infrared Filter Radiometer
IFR	Inspiratory Flow Rate [*Physiology*]
IFR	Instantaneous Frequency [*Indicating*] Receivers (IEEE)
IFR	Institute of Fisheries Research [*University of North Carolina*]
IFR	Institute of Food Research [*British*]
IFR	Institut Federatif de Recherche [*Federal Research Institute*] [*France*]
IFR	Instituts Federatifs de Recherche [*France*]
IFR	Instrument Flight Recovery [*NASA*]
IFR	Instrument Flight Rules [*Aviation*]
IFR	Insufficient Data For Reporting (WDMC)
IFR	Integral Fast Reactor [*Nuclear energy*]
IFR	Interface Register
IFR	Interim Final Rule [*RSPA*] (TAG)
IFR	Intermediate Frequency Range (MCD)
IFR	Internal Function Register
IFR	Internationaler Frauenrat [*International Council of Women*]
IFR	International Fighter RADAR
IFR	International Film Representatives [*Division of International Film Completion Corp.*]
IFR	International Financing Review [*A publication*]
IFR	International Flyer Resources Ltd. [*Vancouver Stock Exchange symbol*]
IFR	Interrupt Flag Register [*Computer science*] (IAA)
IFR	Isolated Flow Responder [*Physiology*]
IFRA	INCA [*International Newspaper Color Association*]-FIEJ Research Association [*Federation Internationale des Editeurs de Journaux*] [*Research center Germany*] (IRC)
IFRA	Increasing Failure Rate Average [*Statistics*]
IFRA	Independent Fabric Retailers Association [*Defunct*] (EA)
IFRA	Independent Footwear Retailers Association [*British*] (DBA)
IFRA	Indirect Fluorescent Rabies Antibody Test [*Immunology*] (MAE)
IFRA	Infrasonics, Inc. [*NASDAQ symbol*] (NQ)
IFRA	International Family Recreation Association (EA)
IFRA	International Foundation for Research in the Field of Advertising
IFRA	International Fragrance Association [*Geneva, Switzerland*] (EAIO)
IFRA	International Fund-Raising Association (EA)
IFRAA	Interfaith Forum on Religion, Art, and Architecture (EA)
IFRAC	Imported Food Risks Advisory Committee [*Australia*]
IFRAC	International Federation of Railway Advertising Companies [*British*] (EA)
IFRB	International Frequency Registration Board [*ITU*] [*United Nations*]
IFRC	Inland Forest Resource Council (EA)
IFRC	Instantaneous Frequency Correlation (NG)
IFRC	International Federation of Roofing Contractors [*See also IFD*] (EAIO)
IFRC	International Ford Retractable Club (EA)
IFRC	International Futures Research Conference (PDAA)
IFRCC	International Fight'n Rooster Cutlery Club (EA)
IFRD	International Federation of Retail Distributors (EAIO)
IFRE	Institute for Family Research and Education [*Defunct*] (EA)
IFREMER	Institut Francais de Recherche pour l'Exploitation de la Mer [*French Research Institute for Ocean Utilization*] [*Research center*] (IID)
IFREQ	Industrial Forecast Requirements (DNAB)
IFRF	International Federation of Resistance Fighters (BJA)
IFRG	International Genealogy and Heraldry Fellowship of Rotarians (EA)
IFrHS	Freeburg Community High School 77, Freeburg, IL [*Library symbol Library of Congress*] (LCLS)
IFRI	International Fund-Raising Institute [*Later, IFRA*]
IFRIP	Institut Francais de Recherche et de Technologie Polaires [*Public interest group*] [*French Southern and Antarctic Territories*] (EY)
IFRIS	Intelligence Finished Reports Information Subsystem [*Computer science*]
IFRM	International Federation of Resistance Movements [*Vienna, Austria*] (EA)
IFRM	International Federation of the Rights of Man (EA)
IFRO	Internal Feed Rate Override
IFRP	International Fertility Research Program [*Later, FHI*]
IFRRO	International Federation of Reproductive Rights Organisations (AIE)
IFRS	IFR Systems [*NASDAQ symbol*] (TTSB)
IFRS	IFR Systems, Inc. [*NASDAQ symbol*] (NQ)
IFRS	Individuals for a Rational Society [*Defunct*] (EA)
IFRT	Intellectual Freedom Round Table [*American Library Association*]
IFRT	Internal Floating Roof Tank [*Engineering*]
IFRT	Involved Field Radiotherapy [*Medicine*] (DMAA)
IFRTA	International Federation of Railwaymen's Travel Associations (EA)
IFRU	In-Flight Replaceable Unit (KSC)
IFRU	Interference Frequency Rejection Unit [*Military*]
i-fs--	French Southern and Antarctic Lands [*MARC geographic area code Library of Congress*] (LCCP)
IFS	Identification, Friend or Foe, Switching Circuit [*Military*]
IFS	Inactivated Fetal-Calf Serum [*Immunology*]
IFS	In-Band Framing System [*Simulation Laboratories, Inc.*]
IFS	Increased Forward Stocking [*Military*] (DNAB)
IFS	Independent Front Suspension [*Automotive engineering*]
IFS	Indian Forest Service [*British*]
IFS	In-Flight Safety
IFS	Inflight Survey [*USTTA*] (TAG)
IFS	Information Fatigue Symdrome (WDAA)
IFS	Information Flow Standards (KSC)
IFS	Infrared Frequency Synthesis
IFS	Inshore Fire Support Ship [*Later, LFR*]
IFS	Insignia Financial Group [*NYSE symbol*] (SAG)
IFS	Insignia Financial Grp'A' [*NYSE symbol*] (TTSB)
IFS	Installable File System [*Computer science*]
IFS	Institute for Fiscal Studies [*British*]
IFS	Institute of Financial Services [*Australia*]
IFS	Institute of Flight Structures [*Columbia University*]
IFS	Instructions for Service
IFS	Instrument Flight Simulator (MCD)
IFS	Integrated Facilities System [*Army*]
IFS	Integrated Flight System
IFS	Intelligent File Store [*British*]
IFS	Interactive File Sharing
IFS	Interactive Flow Simulator (TEL)
IFS	Interchange File Separator [*Computer science*] (BUR)
IFS	Interface Specification
IFS	Intermediate Frequency Strip
IFS	Internal Focus Sensor (PDAA)
IFS	International Federation of Settlements and Neighbourhood Centers (EAIO)
IFS	International Federation of Surveyors [*See also FIG*] (EAIO)
IFS	International Film Seminars (EA)
IFS	International Flying Services SRL [*Italy ICAO designator*] (FAAC)
IFS	International Focus Resources, Inc. [*Vancouver Stock Exchange symbol*]
IFS	International Foodservice Systems, Inc. (EFIS)
IFS	International Foundation for Science [*See also FIS*] [*ICSU Stockholm, Sweden*] (EAIO)
IFS	International Foundation for Stutterers (EA)
IFS	International Frankenstein Society (EA)
IFS	Internationella Forsurningssekretariatet [*International Secretariat on Acid Rain*] [*Sweden*] (EAIO)
IFS	Interrelated Flow Simulation
IFS	Interstitial Fluid Space [*Medicine*] (DMAA)
IFS	Investment Feasibility Studies (TEL)
IFS	Ionospheric Forward Scatter (TEL)
IFS	Irish Free State [*Later, Republic of Ireland*]
IFS	Iron Fortified Common Salt [*Nutrition*]
IFS	Iterated Function System [*Computer science*] (BYTE)
IFSA	Instock Footwear Suppliers Association [*British*] (DBA)
IFSA	International Federation of Scoliosis Associations (EA)
IFSA	International Federation of Sports Acrobatics [*Sofia, Bulgaria*] (EAIO)
IFSA	International Fuzzy Systems Association (EA)

IFSA............ International Inflight Food Service Association (NTPA)
IFSA............ Intumescent Fire Seals Association [*British*] (DBA)
IFSAL........... Integral Frequency Scan Approach and Landing
IFSAR.......... Interferometric Synthetic Aperture RADAR (RDA)
IFSAS.......... Interim Fire Support Automation System [*Army*] (DOMA)
IFSAT.......... International Financial Services and Technology Exhibition [*British*]
IFSB............ Independence Federal Savings Bank [*NASDAQ symbol*] (NQ)
IFSB............ Independence Fed Svgs Bk [*NASDAQ symbol*] (TTSB)
IFSB............ International Flying Saucer Bureau [*Defunct*]
IFSBAC........ Institute for Folklore Studies in Britain and Canada
IFSC............ Interferon Sciences [*NASDAQ symbol*] (TTSB)
IFSC............ Interferon Sciences, Inc. [*NASDAQ symbol*] (NQ)
IFSC............ International Federation of Surgical Colleges [*Dublin, Republic of Ireland*] (EAIO)
IFSC............ Introduction to the Federal Supply Catalog System
IFSCC.......... International Federation of Societies of Cosmetic Chemists [*Luton, England*] (EAIO)
IFSCS.......... International Federation of the Societies of Classical Studies (EA)
IFSD............ Inflight Shutdown (MCD)
IFSDA .... International Federation of Stamp Dealers' Associations (EA)
IFSDP.......... International Federation of the Socialist and Democratic Press [*Milan, Italy*] (EAIO)
IFSEA.......... International Federation of Scientific Editors' Associations (EA)
IFSEA.......... International Food Service Executive's Association (EA)
IFSEC.......... International Fire and Security Exhibition and Conference [*British*] (ITD)
IFSECN .... International Federation of Societies for Electroencephalography and Clinical Neurophysiology [*Amsterdam, Netherlands*] (EA)
IFSED.......... Initial Full-Scale Engineering Development
IFSEM.......... International Federation of Societies for Electron Microscopy (EA)
IFSF............ Investment Feasibility Study Facility [*United Nations Development Programme*] [*Ghana*]
IFSF............ Irradiated Fuels Storage Facility [*National Reactor Testing Station*]
IFSH............ International Federation of Sound Hunters (EA)
IFSHC .... International Federation of Societies for Histochemistry and Cytochemistry (EAIO)
IFSHJ.......... International Federation for Secular Humanistic Judaism (EA)
IFSHJ.......... International Federation of Secular Humanistic Jews (EA)
IFSI............ Interface, Inc. [*NASDAQ symbol*] (NQ)
IFSIA.......... Interface Inc.'A' [*NASDAQ symbol*] (TTSB)
IF-SICMA ..... Insular Force - Special Initial Clothing Monetary Allowance [*Military*] (DNAB)
IFSIS........... Iterated Function System-Image Synthesizer [*Computer science*] (BYTE)
IFSIT........... In-Flight Safety Inhibit Test
IFSL............ Indiana Federal [*NASDAQ symbol*] (TTSB)
IFSL............ Indiana Federal Corp. [*NASDAQ symbol*] (NQ)
IFSL............ Industrial Fire Safety Library [*National Fire Protection Association*]
IFSM........... International Federation of Sports Medicine (EA)
IFSMA.......... International Federation of Shipmasters Associations [*See also FIAPN*] (EAIO)
IFSMTF .... International Fusion Superconducting Magnet Test Facility [*Oak Ridge National Laboratory*]
IFSNC .... International Federation of Settlements and Neighbourhood Centres [*Defunct*]
IFSO............ International Federation of Sanitarians Organizations [*Defunct*] (EA)
IFSOT.......... Irradiated Fused Silica Open Tubular [*Column for chromatography*]
IFSP............ Individualized Family Service Plan [*Required under the Individuals with Disabilities Education Act (IDEA)*] (PAZ)
IFSP............ International Federation of Societies of Philosophy
IFSPO .... International Federation of Senior Police Officers (EA)
IFSPS.......... International Federation of Students in Political Sciences
IFSR............ International Federation for Systems Research (EAIO)
IFSRC.......... Independent Family Schools Resource Center (EA)
IFSRC.......... International Financial Services Research Center [*Massachusetts Institute of Technology*] [*Research center*] (RCD)
IFSS............ If Signal Source (MCD)
IFSS............ Index of Federal Specifications and Standards
IFSS............ Inertia Fuel Shutoff Switch [*Automotive engineering*]
IFSS............ Instrument Flight Safety System (MUGU)
IFSS............ International Federation of Sleddog Sports (EA)
IFSS............ International Fertilizer Supply Scheme [*FAO*] [*United Nations*]
IFSS............ International Flight Service Station [*FAA*]
IFSSEC.......... International Fire, Security and Safety Exhibition and Conference (PDAA)
IFSSH .... International Federation of Societies for Surgery of the Hand (EA)
IFSSO .... International Federation of Social Science Organizations [*See also FIOSS*] [*Copenhagen, Denmark*] (EAIO)
IFSSPC .... International Fatigue Syndromes Share and Prayer Chain (EA)
IFST............ Institute of Food Science and Technology of the United Kingdom
IFST............ International Federation of Shorthand and Typewriting
IFSTA.......... International Fire Service Training Association (EA)
IFSTAD .... Islamic Foundation for Science, Technology, and Development (BARN)
IFSTD.......... Interim Fund for Science and Technology for Development [*International Council of Scientific Unions*]
IFSTD.......... Islamic Foundation for Science, Technology and Development [*Saudi Arabia*] (PDAA)
IFSTM.......... International Federation of Sewing Thread Manufacturers (EA)
IFSW........... International Federation of Social Workers [*Switzerland*]
IFSWA.......... International Figure Skating Writers Association [*Defunct*]
IFT............ Immunofluorescence Test [*Immunology*]
IFT............ Income Opportunities Fd 2000 [*NYSE symbol*] (TTSB)
IFT............ Income Opportunities Fund 2000 [*NYSE symbol*] (SPSG)
IFT............ Indexed, Folioed, and Titled [*Publishing*] (DGA)

IFT .... Industrial Field Trip (DOMA)
IFT .... In-Flight Test [*Air Force*]
IFT .... Inland Fisheries Trust, Inc. [*Republic of Ireland*] (BI)
IFT .... Innovative Feasibility Test
IFT .... Input Frequency Tolerance [*Computer science*]
IFT .... Instantaneous Field Tube [*Astrophysics*]
IFT .... Instantaneous Fourier Transform [*Computer science*]
IFT .... Institute of Family Therapy [*British*] (DBA)
IFT .... Institute of Food Technologists (EA)
IFT .... Instructor-Flown Advisory Target
IFT .... Instrument Flight Trainer (MCD)
IFT .... Interface Tool (MCD)
IFT .... Interfacial Tension [*Physical chemistry*]
IFT .... Interfacial Test
IFT .... Interflight [*British ICAO designator*] (FAAC)
IFT .... Intermediate Frequency Transformer
IFT .... International Federation of Translators [*See also FIT*] [*Ghent, Belgium*] (EAIO)
IFT .... International Foundation for Telemetering (EA)
IFT .... International Foundation for Timesharing (EA)
IFT .... International Frequency Tables
IFT .... Io Flux Tube [*Cosmology*]
IFT .... Ion Focusing Technique
IFT .... Isolation Functional Testing (PDAA)
IFTA .... In-Flight Thrust Augmentation
IFTA .... In-Flight Training Aid
IFTA .... International Federation of Teachers' Associations [*Later, WCOTP*] (EAIO)
IFTA .... International Federation of Television Archives [*See also FIAT*] [*Madrid, Spain*] (EAIO)
IFTA .... International Federation of Thanatologists Associations [*Saint-Ouen, France*] (EA)
IFTA .... International Free Trade Area
IFTA .... International Fuel Tax Agreement [*FHWA*] (TAG)
IFTAC .... Inter-American Federation of Touring and Automobile Clubs [*See also FITAC*] (EAIO)
IF TACCA ..... Intermediate Frequency Time Averaged Clutter Coherent Airborne [*RADAR*] (DNAB)
IF TACCAR... Intermediate Frequency Time Averaged Clutter Coherent Airborne RADAR (NG)
IFTAD.......... Initial and Final Terminal Arrival Date [*Army*] (AABC)
IFTBCS......... International Federation of the Temperance Blue Cross Societies [*Later, IBC*] (EA)
IFTC............ International Federation of Thermalism and Climatism [*Bad Ragaz, Switzerland*] (EA)
IFTC............ International Film and Television Council [*Rome, Italy*]
IFTC............ International Fox-Tango Club [*Defunct*] (EA)
IFTDO........... International Federation of Training and Development Organizations (EA)
IFTE............ Integrated Family of Test Equipment [*Army*] (RDA)
IFTE............ Intermediate Forward Test Equipment
IFTEX .... International Flower Trades Exhibition [*British*] (ITD)
IFTF............ Institute for the Future [*Research center Telecommunications*] (RCD)
IFTF............ Inter-Faith Task Force (EA)
IFTF............ International Federation of Teachers of French [*See also FIPF*] [*Sevres, France*] (EAIO)
IFTF............ International Fur Trade Federation [*British*] (EAIO)
IFTI............ Ionic Fuel Technology [*NASDAQ symbol*] (TTSB)
IFTI............ Ionic Fuel Technology, Inc. [*NASDAQ symbol*] (SAG)
IFTIW.......... Ionic Fuel Technology Wrrt'A' [*NASDAQ symbol*] (TTSB)
IFTIZ.......... Ionic Fuel Technology Wrrt'B' [*NASDAQ symbol*] (TTSB)
IFTL............ Institute for Friendship through Learning (EA)
IFTM........... In-Flight Test and Maintenance (KSC)
IFTM........... Inverse Fourier Transform Module [*An enzyme*] (MCD)
IFTO............ International Federation of Tour Operators [*Lewes, East Sussex, England*] (EAIO)
IFTOA.......... Independent Fuel Terminal Operators' Association
IFToMM ...... International Federation for the Theory of Machines and Mechanisms [*Warsaw, Poland*] (EAIO)
IFTPNDC...... Institute on the Federal Theatre Project and New Deal Culture [*George Mason University*] [*Research center*] (RCD)
IFTPP.......... International Federation of the Technical and Periodical Press (DIT)
IFTR............ International Federation for Theatre Research [*British*] (EAIO)
IFTR............ International Federation of Teachers of Rhythmics (EA)
IFTR............ International Foundation for Theatrical Research (EA)
IFTRS.......... Individual Flying Time Report System [*Military*] (DNAB)
IFTS............ In-Flight Test System
IFTS............ International Federation of Teratology Societies (EA)
IFTS............ Irradiated Fuel Transfer System [*Nuclear energy*] (NRCH)
IFTSSS......... In-Flight Test System Scan Select (IAA)
IFTU............ International Federation of Teachers' Unions
IFTU............ International Federation of Trade Unions
IFTU............ Iraq Federation of Trade Unions
IFTUTW........ International Federation of Trade Unions of Transport Workers [*See also FIOST*] [*Brussels, Belgium*] (EAIO)
IFTW........... International Federation of Tobacco Workers
IFTWA.......... International Federation of Textile Workers' Associations
IFTwA.......... International Federation of Tiddlywinks Associations (EA)
IFU............ Inflatable Ward Unit (SAA)
IFU............ Infusion-Forming Units [*Medicine*]
IFU............ Instruction Fetch Unit [*Computer science*]
IFU............ Integrated Fluorescence Unit [*Image formation*]
IFU............ Intelligence Field Unit [*Navy*]
I/FU............ Interface Unit [*Computer science*] (NASA)
IFU............ Interferon Unit [*Medicine*] (DMAA)

IFUN	If Unable [*Aviation*] (FAAC)
IF/USA	Interfurnishings USA (TSPED)
IFUW	International Federation of University Women (EA)
IFV	Igniter-Fuel Valve (KSC)
IFV	Infantry Fighting Vehicle
IFV	Instantaneous Field of View (DNAB)
IFV	Internationaler Faustball-Verband (EAIO)
IFV	Intracellular Fluid Volume [*Physiology*]
IFVA	Independent Film and Video Makers' Association [*British*]
IFVC	International Federation for Victory over Communism
IF-VCA	Immunofluorescence-Viral Capsid Antigen [*Clinical chemistry*]
IFVH	Indian Field Veterinary Hospital [*British military*] (DMA)
IFVHSF	Federation of Health Funds - International [*International Federation of Voluntary Health Service Funds*] [*Later, FHF*] [*Acronym is based on former name,*] (EAIO)
IFVLS	If Flight Visibility Becomes Less Than [*Aviation*] (FAAC)
IFVM	Intermediate Frequency Video Microwave (MCD)
IFVME	Inspectorate of Fighting Vehicles and Mechanical Equipment [*Military*]
IFVPA	Independent Film, Video, and Photographers Association [*British*] (DBA)
IFVR	If Visibility Remains [*Aviation*] (FAAC)
IFVTCC	Internationale Foderation der Vereine der Textilchemiker und Coloristen [*International Federation of Associations of Textile Chemists and Colorists*] (EAIO)
IFW	International Federation of Wargaming [*Defunct*] (EA)
IFWA	International Federation for Weeks of Art
IFWC	Integrated Flight/Weapons Controls (MCD)
IFWEA	International Federation of Workers' Educational Associations [*See also IVB*] [*Tel Aviv, Israel*] (EAIO)
IFWG	Interface Working Group [*NASA*] (SSD)
IFWHA	International Federation of Women's Hockey Associations
IFWJ	Indian Federation of Working Journalists
IFWL	International Federation of Women Lawyers (EA)
IFWRI	Institute of the Furniture Warehousing and Removing Industry (EAIO)
IFWS	International Federation of Wines and Spirits [*See also FIVS*] (EAIO)
IFWSTI	International Federation of Wines and Spirits, Trade, and Industry (EA)
IFWTO	International Federation of Women's Travel Organizations (EA)
IFWTWA	International Food, Wine, and Travel Writers Association (EAIO)
IFX	Immunofixation [*Clinical chemistry*]
IFY	Independent Fission Yield
IFYC	International Federation of Young Cooperators
IFYE	International Farm Youth Exchange
IFYGL	International Field Year for the Great Lakes
IG	Alisarda [*ICAO designator*] (AD)
IG	ALISARDA SpA [*Italy ICAO designator*] (ICDA)
IG	Galesburg Public Library, Galesburg, IL [*Library symbol Library of Congress*] (LCLS)
IG	IGI, Inc. [*AMEX symbol*] (SPSG)
IG	Igloo [*Spacelab Pallet Missions*]
IG	Ignitor [*Electron device*] (MSA)
IG	Illawarra Greens [*Political party Australia*]
IG	Illustrators Guild [*Later, GA*] (EA)
IG	Image Generator (MCD)
IG	Immature Granule (DMAA)
IG	Immune Globulin
Ig	Immunoglobulin [*Immunology*]
IG	Immunology [*Medical specialty*] (DHSM)
IG	Immunoreactive Gastrin [*Medicine*] (MEDA)
IG	Imperial Gallon
IG	Impulse Generator (IAA)
IG	Index of Gravity [*Engineering*]
IG	Indicator Group (MCD)
I/G	Individual/Group (ACRL)
IG	Indo-Germanic [*Language, etc.*]
IG	Industrial Grade
IG	Industriegewerkschaft [*Industrial Trade Union*] [*Germany*]
IG	Inertial Guidance
IG	Inertial Gyroscope
IG	Ingot (DNAB)
IG	In-Ground (ADA)
IG	Inner Gimbal
IG	Inner Guard [*Freemasonry*]
IG	Inscriptiones Graecae [*Epigraphic notation*]
IG	Inside Guardian [*Freemasonry*] (ROG)
IG	Inspection Gauge (MCD)
IG	Inspector General [*Air Force, Army, Marine Corps*]
IG	Instantaneous Grid (IAA)
IG	Institute of Geophysics [*Later, IGPP*] [*University of California*] (MCD)
IG	Institute of Groundsmanship (EA)
IG	Institution of Geologists (EAIO)
IG	Instruction [*or Instructor*] Guide
IG	Instructor in Gunnery [*Military British*]
IG	Instrumentation Group
IG	Instrument Ground (NASA)
IG	Insulated Gate (DEN)
IG	Insulin and Glucose [*Medicine*] (DMAA)
IG	Integrated Genetics
IG	Intelligence Generator
IG	IntelliGenetics (HGEN)
IG	Intendant-General
IG	Interagency Group [*Federal government*]
IG	Interconnect Group (CAAL)
IG	Interdepartmental Group [*DoD*]

IG	Interest Group
IG	Inter-Gas System
IG	Intergranular [*Metallurgy*]
IG	Internal Guidance (NASA)
IG	Internationale Kunstgilde [*International Art Guild - IAG*] (EAIO)
IG	International General (EA)
IG	International Graphics [*Formerly, IGI*] (EA)
IG	International Guides' Club (EAIO)
IG	Intestinal Groove
IG	Intragastric
ig	Intragastrically [*Medicine*] (DB)
IG	Inverse Gain (NVT)
IG	Inverse Gaussian [*Statistics*]
IG	Investment Grant [*British*]
IG	Iris Guide (PDAA)
IG	Irish Guards [*Military unit*]
IG	Irritable Gut [*Medicine*] (DMAA)
IG	Irvine Group [*An association*] (EA)
IG	Izmenyaemaya Geometriya [*Variable Geometry*] [*Suffix letters on Soviet combat aircraft*]
IGA	Dallas Public Library, Dallas, TX [*OCLC symbol*] (OCLC)
IGA	Great Inagua Island [*Bahamas*] [*Airport symbol*] (AD)
IgA	Human Immunoglobulin A (DOG)
IgA	Immunoglobulin A [*Immunology*]
IGA	Inagua [*Bahamas*] [*Airport symbol*] (OAG)
IGA	Independent Grocers Alliance Distributing Co. [*Facetious translation: "I Get Attention"*] (EA)
IGA	Industry and General Applications (MCD)
IGA	Infantile Genetic Agranulocytosis [*Medicine*] (DMAA)
IGA	Inhaled Gas Analyzer
IGA	Inner Gimbal Angle (NASA)
IGA	Inner Gimbal Assembly
IGA	Inner Gimbal Axis
IGA	Inscriptiones Graecae Antiquissimae (BJA)
IGA	Integrated Grant Administration
IGA	Integrating Gyro Accelerometer
IGA	Intergovernmental Agreement (COE)
IGA	Intergranular Attack [*Nuclear energy*] (NRCH)
IGA	International Galdos Association (EA)
IGA	International Gamers Association (EA)
IGA	International Gay Association - International Association of Lesbians/Gay Women and Gay Men (EAIO)
IGA	International General Aviation
IGA	International Geneva Association (EA)
IGA	International Geographical Association [*Esperantist*]
IGA	International Glaucoma Association (EAIO)
IGA	International Golf Association (EA)
IGA	International Graduate Achievement [*Defunct*] (EA)
IGA	International Grains Arrangement
IGA	International Green Alliance (EA)
IGA	Interstate Gambling Activities
IGA	Ion Gun Assembly
IGA	Irish Gas Association (BI)
IGAA	Intermountain Graphic Arts Association (DGA)
IGAAS	Integrated Ground/Airborne Avionics System (MCD)
IGAB	International Group of Agents and Bureaus (EA)
IGAC	International Global Atmospheric Chemistry [*Project*] (USDC)
IGAC	International Global Atmospheric Chemistry Program [*Marine science*] (OSRA)
IGACS	Integrated Guidance and Control System [*Aerospace*]
IGaDC	Illinois State Department of Conservation, Division of Parks and Memorials, Galena, IL [*Library symbol Library of Congress*] (LCLS)
IGADD	Intergovernmental Authority on Drought and Development [*Djibouti*] (EY)
IGAE	Intergovernmental Agreement on the Environment [*Australia*]
IGAEA	International Graphic Arts Education Association (EA)
IGAeM	Internationale Gesellschaft fuer Aerosole in der Medizin [*International Society for Aerosols in Medicine - ISAeM*] (EAIO)
IGAF	Intergovernmental Affairs Fellowship Program [*Military*] (MCD)
IgAIC	Immunoglobulin A Immune Complex [*Immunochemistry*]
IGal	Galva Township Library, Galva, IL [*Library symbol Library of Congress*] (LCLS)
IGAM	Internationale Gesellschaft fuer Allgemeinmedizin [*International Society of General Medicine*]
IGAM	International Game Technology (MHDW)
IgAN	Immunoglobulin A Nephropathy [*Nephrology*]
IG & GA	International Grooving and Grinding Association (EA)
IGAP	Institute for Grassland and Animal Production [*Research center British*] (IRC)
IGAP	Internationale Gesellschaft fuer Arztliche Psychotherapie [*International Federation for Medical Psychotherapy - IFMP*] [*Oslo, Norway*] (EAIO)
IGARSS	International Geoscience and Remote Sensing Symposium (MCD)
IGAS	Inspection Generale des Affaires Sociales [*General Inspection of Social Affairs*] [*France*]
IGAS	Interactive General Accounting System (MHDB)
IGAS	International General Assembly of Spiritualists [*Later, LDTF*] (EA)
IGAS	International Graphic Arts Society (EA)
IGAS	International Graphoanalysis Society (EA)
IGAUP	Interceptor Generation and Umpiring Program (SAA)
IGAX	Inner Gimbal Axis (NASA)
IGB	Columbus, MS [*Location identifier FAA*] (FAAL)
IGB	Illicit Gold Buyer [*or Buying*]
IGB	Inlet Gear Box (MCD)

IGB.............. Intercontinental Glide Bomber [Unmanned]
IGB.............. Interference Guard Bands
IGB.............. Inter-German Border (MCD)
IGB.............. Intermediate Gearbox (DA)
IGB.............. Internationaler Genossenschaftsbund [International Cooperative Alliance]
IGB.............. Internationales Gewerkschafts Buro [International Trades Union Office]
IGB.............. International Gravimetric Bureau [Toulouse, France] (EAIO)
IGB.............. Israelitisches Gemeindeblatt [Muelheim/Koeln] [A publication] (BJA)
IGB.............. National College of Education, Evanston, IL [OCLC symbol] (OCLC)
IGBC............ Interagency Grizzly Bear Committee [Forest Service] [Missoula, MT] (EGAO)
IGBD............ Impotent Grain Boundary Dislocation
IGBE............ International Gold Bullion Exchange [Bankrupt investment firm]
IGBM............ International Group on Breastfeeding Monitoring (WDAA)
IGBP............ Immunoglobulin-Binding Protein
IGBP............ International Geosphere-Biosphere Program [ICSU] [Proposed for 1992]
IGBP............ International Geosphere-Biosphere Programme [Australia]
IGBP-DIS..... Data and Information System [Marine science] (OSRA)
IGBS............ International Gas Bearings Symposium (PDAA)
IGBST.......... Interagency Grizzly Bear Study Team [Montana State University] [Bozeman, MT] (EGAO)
IGBT............ Insulated Gate Bipolar Transistor [Electronics] (AAEL)
IGBT............ Isolated Gate Bipolar Transistor [Electronics]
IGC.............. Goshen College, Goshen, IN [OCLC symbol] (OCLC)
IGC.............. Inspector-General of Communications [British military] (DMA)
IGC.............. Institute for Global Communications [Internet]
IGC.............. Institute for Graphic Communication [Defunct] (EA)
IGC.............. Intellectually Gifted Children
IGC.............. Intelligence Graphics Controller [Computer science]
IGC.............. Interactive Gaming & Communications Corp.
IGC.............. Intergovernmental Committee on Refugees [Post-World War II] (DLA)
IGC.............. Inter-Governmental Conference [European Union] (ECON)
IGC.............. Inter-Governmental Conferences [European Community]
IGC.............. Intergovernmental Copyright Committee [See also CIDA] [Paris, France] (EAIO)
IGC.............. Intergranular Corrosion (PDAA)
IGC.............. Intermagnetics General Corp.
IGC.............. Internal Gain Control (IAA)
IGC.............. International Garden Club (EA)
IGC.............. International Geological Congress
IGC.............. International Geophysical Committee [Also, CIG]
IGC.............. International Geophysical Cooperation [World Meteorological Organization]
IGC.............. International Glaucoma Congress (EA)
IGC.............. International Grassland Congress
IGC.............. International Guides' Club (EAIO)
IGC.............. Interstate General Ltd. [AMEX symbol] (SPSG)
IGC.............. Interstate Genl L.P. [AMEX symbol] (TTSB)
IGC.............. Inter-Union Geodynamics Commission [Also, ICG] (MSC)
IGC.............. Intragastric Cannula (STED)
IGC.............. Inverse Gas Chromatography
IGC.............. Ion Gun Collector
IGC.............. Irish Goods Council (ACII)
IGC.............. Isothermal Gas Chromatography
IGCA .... Innovative Gaming Corp. [NASDAQ symbol] (SAG)
IGCA .... Innovative Gaming Corp. Amer [NASDAQ symbol] (TTSB)
IGCA .... International Guild of Candle Artisans (EA)
IGCA .... Italian Greyhound Club of America (EA)
IGCBT .... Interagency Group for Computer-Based Training [Later, IGITT] (EA)
IGCC .... Institute on Global Conflict and Cooperation [University of California, Berkeley]
IGCC .... Insulating Glass Certification Council (EA)
IGCC .... Integrated Gasification-Combined Cycle [Chemical engineering]
IGCC .... Interagency Geothermal Coordinating Council
IGCC .... Intergovernmental Copyright Committee [See also CIDA]
IGCC .... Intergovernmental Panel on Climate Change [World Meteorological Organization]
IGCE .... Independent Government Cost Estimate [Army]
IGCG .... Inertial Guidance and Calibration Group [Air Force]
IGCI .... Industrial Gas Cleaning Institute (EA)
IGCJAP .... International Guild of Craft Journalists, Authors, and Photographers [Inactive] (EA)
IGCO .... International Genealogy Consumer Organization (EA)
IGCP .... Intelligence Guidance for COMINT [Communications Intelligence] Programming (MCD)
IGCP .... International Geological Correlation Programme [See also PICG] [ICSU Paris, France] (EAIO)
IGCPK .... Industrie Gewerkschaft Chemie, Papier, und Keramik [West German union]
IGCR .... Intergovernmental Committee on Refugees [Post-World War II]
IGCS .... Imperial Glass Collectors Society (EA)
IGCS .... Integrated Guidance and Control System [Aerospace] (AAG)
IGCSE .... International General Certificate of Secondary Education (AIE)
IG-CUFMG ... Instituto de Geociencias Universidade Federal de Minas Gerais
IGD .... Illicit Gold Dealer
IgD .... Immunoglobulin D [Immunology]
IGD .... Indian Gold Resources Ltd. [Vancouver Stock Exchange symbol]
IGD .... Inspector General Division [Environmental Protection Agency] (GFGA)
IGD .... Inspector General's Department
IGD .... Institute of Grocery Distribution Ltd. [British]
IGD .... Interaction Graphics Display

IGD .... Interactive Grafics Digitizer [Computer science]
IGD .... Interglobal Distance (STED)
IGD .... Irma Graphics for DOS [Digital Operation System] [DCA, Inc.]
IGD .... Isolated Gonadotropin Deficiency (STED)
IGDE .... Idiopathic Gait Disorders of Elderly [Medicine] (STED)
IGDM .... Infant of Gestational Diabetic Mother [Obstetrics]
IGDM .... Infant of Mother With Gestational Diabetes Mellitus [Medicine] (STED)
IGDMR .... Initial Gross Depot Maintenance Requirement [Military]
IGDO .... International Guild of Opticians [International Guild of Dispensing Optic ians] [Acronym is based on former name,] (EAIO)
IGDOD .... Inspector General, Department of Defense (USGC)
IGDR .... Interim Geophysical Data Record [From spacecraft data]
IGDS .... Integrated Graduate Development Scheme [British]
IGDS .... Interactive Graphics Design System (MCD)
IGDS .... Interactive Graphics Display Systems [Computer monitor] [Military]
IGDS .... Iodine Generating and Dispensing System (NASA)
IGE .... Iguela [Gabon] [Airport symbol Obsolete] (OAG)
IgE .... Immunoglobulin E [Immunology]
IGE .... Impaired Gas Exchange (DMAA)
IGE .... Independent Government Estimate (MCD)
IGE .... Individually Guided Education [for upgrading students' skills]
IGE .... In-Ground Effect [Aviation] (NG)
IGE .... Institution of Gas Engineers [British] (DAS)
IGE .... Instrumentation Ground Equipment (MCD)
IGE .... International Geographics [Vancouver Stock Exchange symbol]
IGE .... International Geophysical Extension
IGE .... International Greenland Expedition
IGE .... International Guiding Eyes (EA)
IGEB .... Intergency Global Positioning System Executive Board
IGEIEPSI ..... International Group for the Exchange of Information and Experience Among Postal Savings Institutions [Geneva, Switzerland] (EAIO)
IGEMS .... Interactive Generalized Modeling System (PDAA)
IGEN .... Current Source (MSA)
IGEN .... IGEN, Inc. [NASDAQ symbol] (SAG)
IGenD .... DuPage Library System, Geneva, IL [Library symbol Library of Congress] (LCLS)
IGeo .... Georgetown Public Library, Georgetown, IL [Library symbol Library of Congress] (LCLS)
IGeoSD .... Georgetown Community Unit School District, Georgetown, IL [Library symbol] [Library of Congress] (LCLS)
IGER .... Institute of Grassland and Environmental Research [British]
IGERT .... Integrating Graduate Education and Research Training [National Science Foundation]
IGES .... Initial Graphics Exchange Specification [or System] [National Standards Institute]
IGES .... Integrated Graphics Exchange System (AAEL)
IGES .... International Genetics Epidemiology Societies (HGEN)
IGES .... International Graphics Exchange Specification [Computer science]
IGES .... International Graphics Exchange Standard (NITA)
IGES/PDES ... Initial Graphics Exchange Specification/Product Definition Exchange Specification
IGESUCO ..... International Ground Environment Subcommittee [NATO]
IG-EV .... Interagency Group on Energy Vulnerability (COE)
IGF.............. Fondation Internationale pour la Sauvegarde du Gibier [International Foundation for the Conservation of Game] (EAIO)
IGF.............. IGF Metals, Inc. [Vancouver Stock Exchange symbol]
IGF.............. Image Generation Facility (MCD)
IGF.............. India Growth Fund [NYSE symbol] (TTSB)
IGF.............. India Growth Fund, Inc. [NYSE symbol] (CTT)
IGF.............. Inspector-General of Fortifications [British]
IGF.............. Insulin Gene Family
IGF.............. Insulin-Like Growth Factor
IGF.............. International Genetics Federation [See also FIG] [England] (EA)
IGF.............. International Graphical Federation [See also FGI] [Berne, Switzerland] (EAIO)
IGF.............. International Gymnastic Federation [See also FIG] (EAIO)
IGF.............. Irish Genealogical Foundation (EA)
IGF.............. Island Games Foundation [Canada] (EAIO)
IGF-1 .... Insulin-Like Growth Factor-1
IGFA............ Inspector General, Foreign Assistance [Department of State]
IGFA............ Interessen Gemeinschaft der Farbenindustrie Aktiengesellschaft [A dye trust] [Germany]
IGFA............ International Game Fish Association (EA)
IGFA............ Isaac Garrison Family Association (EA)
IGFBP .... Insulin-Like Growth Factor Binding Protein [Biochemistry]
IGFES.......... Interactive Graphics Finite Element System (RDA)
IGFET.......... Insulated-Gate Field-Effect Transistor [Electronics]
IGFET.......... Isolated-Gate Field-Effect Transistor [Electronics]
IGFL............ Integral Green Fluorescence (DMAA)
IGFM........... Internal Gamma Flux Monitor
IGFM........... Internationale Gesellschaft fuer Menschenrechte [International Society for Human Rights - ISHR] (EA)
IGFO .... Inspector General Field Office [Military]
IGFOV.......... Instantaneous Geometric Field of View
IGFPIL......... International Grotius Foundation for the Propagation of International Law
IGFR .... Insulin-Like Growth Factor Receptor (DMAA)
IGFR .... International Genealogical Fellowship of Rotarians (EA)
IGFS .... International Gem Finders Society
IGFVP .... Interservice Group for Flight Vehicle Power [Military]
IGG .... Igiugig [Alaska] [Airport symbol] (OAG)
IgG .... Immunoglobulin G [Immunology]
IGG .... Inert Gas Generator

IGG .... Internationale Gesellschaft fuer Geschichtsdidaktik [*International Society for History Didactics*] (EAIO)
IGGA .... International Grooving and Grinding Association (NTPA)
IG-GCI .... International Geological-Geophysical Cruise Inventory [*Marine science*] (OSRA)
IGGDA .... International G. G. Drayton Association (EA)
IGGI .... Inter-Governmental Group for Indonesia [*Defunct*]
IgGIC .... Immunoglobulin G Immune Complex [*Immunochemistry*]
IGGT .... Institute for Guided Ground Transport [*Canada*] (PDAA)
IGH .... Icy Grain Halo [*Model of comet structure*]
IGH .... Idiopathic Growth Hormone [*Medicine*] (MAE)
IgH .... Immunoglobulin Heavy Chain [*Biochemistry*]
IGH .... Immunoreactive Growth Hormone [*Immunology*] (MAE)
IGH .... Ingham [*Australia Airport symbol*]
IGH .... International Guild of Hypnotists (EA)
IGHAT .... Integrated Gasification Humid Air Turbine [*Chemical engineering*]
IGHD .... Isolated Growth Hormone Deficiency [*Medicine*]
IGHIA .... International Garden Horticultural Industry Association (EA)
IGHMHS .... Inventory of General Hospital Mental Health Services [*Department of Health and Human Services*] (GFGA)
IGI .... IGI, Inc. [*Associated Press*] (SAG)
IGI .... Industrial Graphics International [*Later, IG*] [*An association*] (EA)
IGI .... Industrial Guest Investigator [*NASA*]
IGI .... Information Gatekeepers, Inc. [*Telecommunications Information service or system*] (IID)
IGI .... Information General, Inc. [*Information service or system*] (IID)
IGI .... Inner Grid Injection
IGI .... Institutional Goals Inventory [*Test*]
IGI .... Interlocked Grain Index [*Botany*]
IGI .... Intermountain Gas Industries, Inc. (EFIS)
IGI .... International Gallery Invitational (ITD)
IGI .... International Genealogical Index [*A publication Australia*]
IGI .... International Graphics, Inc. [*Defunct*] (EA)
IGI .... International Wallcovering Manufacturers Association [*Belgium*] (EAIO)
IGI .... Investigative Group International
IGI .... Investors Group, Inc. [*Toronto Stock Exchange symbol*]
IGIA .... Interagency Group on International Aviation
IGib .... Moyer Library, Gibson City, IL [*Library symbol Library of Congress*] (LCLS)
IGibH .... Gibson Community Hospital, Gibson City, IL [*Library symbol Library of Congress*] (LCLS)
IGibSD .... Gibson City Community Unit School District, Gibson City, IL [*Library symbol*] [*Library of Congress*] (LCLS)
IGIC .... International Gay Information Center [*Defunct*] (EA)
IGIcB .... Chicago Botanic Gardens, Glencoe, IL [*Library symbol*] [*Library of Congress*] (LCLS)
IGIER .... Innocenzo Gasparini Institute for Economic Research
IGIF .... Interferon Gamma-Inducing Factor [*Biochemistry*]
IGIF .... International Geographic Information Foundation
IGil .... Douglas Township Library, Gilman, IL [*Library symbol Library of Congress*] (LCLS)
IGill .... Gillespie Public Library, Gillespie, IL [*Library symbol Library of Congress*] (LCLS)
IGillMCD ...... Macoupin Community District 7, Gillespie, IL [*Library symbol Library of Congress*] (LCLS)
IGinseng ...... Imprial Ginseng Products Ltd. [*Associated Press*] (SAG)
IGIP .... Internationale Gesellschaft fuer Ingenieurpaedagogik [*International Society for Engineering Education*] (EAIO)
IGIPAS .... Interagency Group on International Programs in Atmospheric Science
IGir .... Girard Township Library, Girard, IL [*Library symbol Library of Congress*] (LCLS)
IGirMCD ...... Macoupin Community District 3, Girard, IL [*Library symbol Library of Congress*] (LCLS)
IGIS .... Intelligent Geographic System [*Computer science*]
IGITT .... Interagency Group for Interactive Training Technologies (EA)
IGIV .... Immune Globulin, Intravenous (CPH)
IGIW .... Indices of General Industrial Worth
IGK .... Infanteriegeschuetz - Kompanie [*Infantry Howitzer Co.*] [*German military - World War II*]
IGK .... Knox College, Galesburg, IL [*Library symbol Library of Congress*] (LCLS)
IGKB .... Internationale Gewasserschutz Kommission fur den Bodensee [*International Commission for the Protection of Lake Constance*] (EA)
IGKG .... Internationale Gesellschaft fuer Kiefer- und Gesichtschirurgie [*International Association for Maxillo-Facial Surgery*] (EAIO)
IGL .... Ideal Gas Law
IGL .... Igloolik [*Northwest Territories*] [*Seismograph station code, US Geological Survey*] (SEIS)
IGL .... IMC Global [*NYSE symbol*] (TTSB)
IGL .... IMC Global, Inc. [*Formerly, IMC Fertilizer Group*] [*NYSE symbol*] (SAG)
IGL .... Index Guided LASER (IAA)
IGL .... Information Grouping Logic [*Computer science*]
IGL .... Infrared Gunfire Locator
IGL .... Interactive Graphics Language
IGL .... Intergeniculate Leaflet [*Anatomy*]
IGL .... Internal Granule Layer [*Cytology*]
IGL .... Internationale Gesellschaft fuer Lymphologie [*International Society of Lymphology*] (EAIO)
IGL .... Ionized Gas LASER
IGL .... Izmir [*Turkey*] Cigli Airport [*Airport symbol*] (OAG)
IGlc .... Glencoe Public Library, Glencoe, IL [*Library symbol Library of Congress*] (LCLS)

IGlca .... Glen Carbon Library, Glen Carbon, IL [*Library symbol Library of Congress*] (LCLS)
IGLD .... International Great Lakes Datum
IGle .... Glen Ellyn Public Library, Glen Ellyn, IL [*Library symbol Library of Congress*] (LCLS)
IGleD .... College of Du Page, Glen Ellyn, IL [*Library symbol Library of Congress*] (LCLS)
IGleM .... Maryknoll Seminary, Glen Ellyn, IL [*Library symbol Library of Congress*] (LCLS)
IGLF .... Issa Gurgura Liberation Front [*Ethiopia*]
IGLFA .... International Gay and Lesbian Franchise Association (NTPA)
IGLHRC .... International Gay and Lesbian Human Rights Commission (EA)
IGLM .... Limnos [*Greece*] [*ICAO location identifier*] (ICLI)
IGlN .... United States Naval Training Center, Great Lakes, IL [*Library symbol Library of Congress*] (LCLS)
IGLOSS .... Integrated Global Ocean Station System [*Surrey, England*] [*See also IGOSS UNESCO*]
IGlvK .... Kraftco Corp., Research and Development Library, Glenview, IL [*Library symbol Library of Congress*] (LCLS)
IGlvK-L .... Kraft, Inc., Law Library, Glenview, IL [*Library symbol*] [*Library of Congress*] (LCLS)
IGlw .... Glenwood Public Library District, Glenwood, IL [*Library symbol Library of Congress*] (LCLS)
IGM .... I Got Mine [*Slang describing attitude of some nouveaux riches*]
IgM .... Immunoglobulin M [*Immunology*]
IgM .... Immunoglobulin Macro [*Also known as RF*] [*Immunology*]
IGM .... Inertial Guidance Mode
IGM .... Interactive Guidance Mode (NASA)
IGM .... Intergalactic Medium
IGM .... Internationale Gesellschaft fuer Menschenrechte [*International Society for Human Rights - ISHR*] (EAIO)
IGM .... International Grail Movement
IGM .... Interplanetary Global Model [*Marine science*] (OSRA)
IGM .... Irma Graphics for Macintosh [*DCA, Inc.*]
IGM .... ISDN [*Integrated Services Digital Network*] Gateway Module [*Telecommunications*]
IGM .... Iterative Guidance Mode [*NASA*]
IGM .... Kingman [*Arizona*] [*Airport symbol*] (OAG)
IGMA .... International Guild of Miniature Artisans (EA)
IGMC .... Independent Gasoline Marketers Council [*Defunct*] (EA)
IGMCA .... Imperial German Military Collector's Association (EA)
IGMF .... Inertial Guidance Maintenance Facility (IAA)
IGMF .... Intergalactic Magnetic Fields
IGMG .... Institute of Geriatric Medicine and Gerontology [*British*]
IGMG .... Internationale Gustav Mahler Gesellschaft [*International Gustav Mahler Society*] (EA)
IgMIC .... Immunoglobulin M Immune Complex [*Immunochemistry*]
IGMP .... Internet Group Management Protocol [*Computer science*]
IgM-RF .... Immunoglobulin M - Rheumatoid Factor [*Medicine*]
IGMT .... Impingement [*Engineering*]
IGN .... Ignition (KSC)
IGN .... Ignitron [*Electronics*]
IGN .... Ignorant
IGN .... Ignotus [*Unknown*] [*Latin*]
IGN .... Iligan [*Philippines*] [*Airport symbol*] (OAG)
IGN .... International-Great Northern [*AAR code*]
IGN .... Kingston, NY [*Location identifier FAA*] (FAAL)
IGNC .... International Good Neighbor Council [*See also CIBV*] [*Monterrey, Mexico*] (EAIO)
IgND .... Immunoglobulin ND [*Immunology, provisional class*]
IGNDET .... Ignition Detector
IGNET .... Inspector General Network [*Military*] (GFGA)
IGNR .... Igniter
IGNS .... Interactive Graphics Network System (MCD)
IGNTR .... Igniter (MSA)
IGO .... Chigorodo [*Colombia*] [*Airport symbol*] (OAG)
IGO .... Inspector General's Office [*Air Force*]
IGO .... Intergovernmental Organization [*Generic term*]
IGO .... Investment Grant Office [*British*]
IGOA .... Independent Garage Owners of America [*Later, Automotive Service Councils*] (EA)
IGoL .... Lewis and Clark Community College, Godfrey, IL [*Library symbol Library of Congress*] (LCLS)
IGOM .... Integrated Global Ocean Monitoring [*Marine science*] (OSRA)
IGoM .... Monticello College, Godfrey, IL [*Library symbol Library of Congress*] (LCLS)
IGOR .... Instrument Ground Optical Recording
IGOR .... Interactive Guidance on Routes [*FHWA*] (TAG)
IGOR .... Intercept Ground Optical Recorder [*NASA*]
IGORTT .... Intercept Ground Optical Recorder Tracking Telescope [*NASA*]
IGOS .... Inward Grade of Service (DNAB)
IGOSS .... Industry/Government Open Systems Specification (ACRL)
IGOSS .... Integrated Global Ocean Services System [*Marine science*] (OSRA)
IGOSS .... Integrated Global Ocean Station System [*See also IGLOSS*] [*UNESCO*] [*British*]
IGOSS .... International Group on Soil Sampling
IGP .... Gary Public Library, Gary, IN [*OCLC symbol*] (OCLC)
IGP .... Igap [*Former USSR*] [*FAA designator*] (FAAC)
IGP .... Igneous & Geothermal Processes [*Marine science*] (OSRA)
IGP .... Imidazole Glycerol Phosphate [*Biochemistry*]
IGP .... Imitation Greaseproof Parchment (DGA)
IGP .... Inertial Guidance Package
IGP .... Inertial Guidance Platform
IGP .... Inspection Gauges Production (MCD)
IGP .... Institute of the Great Plains (EA)

IGP...............	Instituto Geofisico del Peru [*Marine science*] (OSRA)
IGP...............	Intelligent Gateway Processor [*Computer science*]
IGP...............	Intelligent Graphics Processor [*Computer science*] (PCM)
IGP...............	Interior Gateway Protocol [*Computer science*] (TNIG)
IGP...............	International Garment Processors
IGP...............	International Geodynamics Project
IGP...............	International Green Party (EA)
IGP...............	International Green Party - Ecologism USA (EA)
IGP...............	International Guild of Prestidigitators [*Defunct*] (EA)
IGP...............	Intestinal Glycoprotein [*Biochemistry*] (MAE)
IGP...............	Inverted Groundplane (PDAA)
IGP...............	Investment Guaranty Program [*AID*]
IGP...............	Ion-Getter-Pumping [*Electron microscopy*]
IGPA	Igor-Patrick Air Force Base (KSC)
IGPAC	Intergovernmental Policy Advisory Committee on Trade
IGPC	Inter-Governmental Philatelic Corp. (EA)
IGPD	Imidazoleglycerol-phosphate Dehydratase [*An enzyme*]
IGPE	International Guild of Professional Electrologists (EA)
IGPF...........	Canadian Imperial Ginseng Products Ltd. [*NASDAQ symbol*] (SAG)
IGPF...........	Imperial Ginseng Products Ltd. [*NASDAQ symbol*] (SAG)
IGPFF.........	Imperial Ginseng Prod [*NASDAQ symbol*] (TTSB)
IGPM	Imperial Gallons per Minute
IGPP	Institute of Geophysics and Planetary Physics [*Livermore, CA*] [*Department of Energy*] (MCD)
IGPP	Interactive Graphics Packaging Program [*Computer science*]
IGR	Grace College, Winona Lake, IN [*OCLC symbol*] (OCLC)
IGR	Igitur [*Therefore*] [*Latin*] (ADA)
IGR	Iguazu [*Argentina*] [*Airport symbol*] (OAG)
IGR	Immediate Generalized Reaction (DB)
IGR	Improved Ground Rents (ROG)
IGR	Increased Growth Response [*Botany*]
IGR	Infanteriegranate [*Infantry Howitzer Shell*] [*German military - World War II*]
IGR	Inscriptiones Graecae ad Res Romanas Pertinentes [*A publication*] (BJA)
IGR	Insect Growth Regulator
IGR	Institute of Geomantic Research (EAIO)
IGR	Integra, Inc. [*AMEX symbol*] [*Formerly, A pogee, Inc.*]
IGR	Inter-Globe Resources Ltd. [*Vancouver Stock Exchange symbol*]
IGR	Intergovernmental Review System (OICC)
IGR	Intrauterine Growth Retardation [*Neonatology*] (DAVI)
IGRA	Indian Gaming Regulatory Act
IGrac...........	Granite City Public Library, Granite City, IL [*Library symbol Library of Congress*] (LCLS)
IGracCU	Granite City Community Unit 12, Granite City, IL [*Library symbol Library of Congress*] (LCLS)
IGRAF	Inspector-General of the Royal Air Force [*British*]
IGrafPM	Pere Marquette Residential Center, Grafton, IL [*Library symbol Library of Congress*] (LCLS)
IGralC	College of Lake County, Grayslake, IL [*Library symbol Library of Congress*] (LCLS)
IGR & P	Inert Gas Receiving and Processing (NRCH)
IGranHS.......	Hopkins Elementary School, Granville, IL [*Library symbol Library of Congress*] (LCLS)
IGranPSD.....	Putnam County Community Unit, School District 535, Granville, IL [*Library symbol Library of Congress*] (LCLS)
IGRAP	Inert Gas Receiving and Processing (IAA)
IGRDC.........	Institute for Genome Research for Developing Countries [*Tunisia*] [*Proposed for 1996*]
IGRE	Improved Ground Reconnaissance Equipment [*Military*] (MCD)
IGref	Greenfield Public Library, Greenfield, IL [*Library symbol Library of Congress*] (LCLS)
IGrefCU........	Greenfield Community Unit, District 10, Greenfield, IL [*Library symbol Library of Congress*] (LCLS)
IGrevi..........	Greenville Public Library, Greenville, IL [*Library symbol Library of Congress*] (LCLS)
IGreviC........	Greenville College, Greenville, IL [*Library symbol Library of Congress*] (LCLS)
IGRF	International Geomagnetic Reference Field
IG Rom	Inscriptiones Graecae ad Res Romanas Pertinentes [*A publication*] (OCD)
IGRP	Indus Group [*NASDAQ symbol*] (TTSB)
IGRP	Indus Group, Inc. (The) [*NASDAQ symbol*] (SAG)
IGRP	Interior Gateway Routing Protocol [*Cisco Systems, Inc.*]
IGRP	International Genetic Resources Programme [*Later, RAFI-USA*] (EA)
IGRP	Internet Gateway Resolution Protocol (CIST)
IGRP	Isophthalic Glass Reinforced Plastic [*Materials science*]
IGRPS	Inert Gas Receiving and Processing System (NRCH)
IGRS	Irish Genealogical Research Society (EAIO)
IGrSD.........	Grand Ridge Consolidated Community School District 95, Grand Ridge, IL [*Library symbol Library of Congress*] (LCLS)
IGRV	Improved Guard Rail V [*Army*] (DOMA)
IGRV	Integrated GUARDRAIL V
IGS.............	Carl Sandburg Birthplace Association, Galesburg, IL [*Library symbol Library of Congress*] (LCLS)
IGS.............	Gary Community School Corp., Gary, IN [*OCLC symbol*] (OCLC)
IGS.............	Image Guided Surgery
IGS.............	Immigrant Genealogical Society (EA)
Igs.............	Immunoglobulins [*Chemistry*] (MEC)
IGS.............	Immunogold Stain [*Cytochemistry*]
IGS.............	Imperial General Staff
IGS.............	Improved Gray Scale
IGS.............	Inappropriate Gonadotrophin Secretion [*Endocrinology*]
IGS.............	Indicator Group Speed
IGS.............	Inert Gas Storage

IGS.............	Inert Gas System [*Engineering*]
IGS.............	Inertial Guidance System [*NASA*]
IGS.............	Information Group Separator
IGS.............	Inner Glide Slope [*Aviation*] (NASA)
IGS.............	Inner Gulf Shelf [*Marine science*] (OSRA)
IGS.............	Institute of General Semantics (EA)
IGS.............	Institute of Geological Sciences [*British*] [*Marine science*] (OSRA)
IGS.............	Institute of Government Studies [*University of California at Berkeley*]
IGS.............	Instrumentation Ground System
IGS.............	Instrument Guidance System [*Aviation*] (DA)
IGS.............	Integrated Graphics System [*Computer science*] (BUR)
IGS.............	Interactive Graphics System [*Computer science*]
IGS.............	Intercapillary Glomerulosclerosis (PDAA)
IGS.............	Interchange Group Separator [*Computer science*] (BUR)
IGS.............	Interchromatin Granular Cluster [*Cytology*]
IGS.............	Intergenic Spacer [*Genetics*]
IGS.............	Intermediate General Support [*Army*]
IGS.............	Internal Guide Sequence [*Genetics*]
IGS.............	International Geranium Society (EA)
IGS.............	International Glaciological Society [*Cambridge, England*]
IGS.............	International Graphological Society (EA)
IGS.............	Irish Genealogical Society (EA)
IGS.............	Irish Georgian Society (EA)
IGS.............	Irish Graphical Society (BI)
IGS.............	Isla Grande Flying School [*Puerto Rico*] [*ICAO designator*] (FAAC)
IGS.............	Morgan StanGp 6.50% IGT'PERQS' [*AMEX symbol*] (TTSB)
IGS.............	Morgan Stanley Group, Inc. [*AMEX symbol*] (SAG)
IGSA	Indoor Gardening Society of America (EA)
IGSA	International Golf Sponsors' Association [*Later, AGS*]
IGSC	Carl Sandburg College, Galesburg, IL [*Library symbol Library of Congress*] (LCLS)
IgSC	Immunoglobulin-Secreting Cell (DB)
IGSC	Inspector General, Supply Corps
IGSCC.........	Intergranular Stress-Corrosion Cracking [*Plant engineering*]
IGSE	In-Space Ground Support Equipment [*NASA*] (NASA)
IGSE	Instrument Ground Support Equipment (MCD)
IgSF	Immunoglobulin Superfamily [*Immunology*]
IGSHPA.......	International Ground Source Heat Pump Association (EA)
IGSM	Indian General Service Medal [*British*]
IGSM	Interim Ground Station Module [*Joint Surveillance/Target Attack RADAR Syste m*] (DOMA)
IGSM	International Graduate School of Management
IGSMA	Inertial Guidance System Maintenance Area [*Aerospace*] (AAG)
IGSN	International Gravity Standardization Net (PDAA)
IGSOBM......	International Guild of Symphony, Opera, and Ballet Musicians (EA)
IGSP	Institute for Gravitational Strain Pathology (EA)
IGSP	Internationale Gesellschaft der Schriftpsychologie [*International Society for the Psychology of Writing*]
IGSP	International Greenland Sea Project (USDC)
IGSP	Interntional Greenland Sea Project [*Marine science*] (OSRA)
IGSPS	International Gold and Silver Plate Society (EA)
IGSS	Immunogold Silver Staining [*Cytochemistry*]
IGSS	Inertial Guidance System Simulator [*NASA*] (IAA)
IGST...........	Intergovernmental Committee on Science and Technology (BARN)
IGSU	Improved Gunner's Sight Unit [*Military*] (MCD)
IGT.............	Impaired Glucose Tolerance [*Physiology*]
IGT.............	Improved Gas Turbine (MCD)
IGT.............	Ingot (MSA)
IGT.............	Ingot Resources Ltd. [*Vancouver Stock Exchange symbol*]
IGT.............	Inspector-General of Transportation [*British military*] (DMA)
IGT.............	Inspector-General to the Forces for Training [*British military*]
IGT.............	Institute of Gas Technology (EA)
IGT.............	Instrument Guide Tube [*Nuclear energy*] (NRCH)
IGT.............	Insulated-Gate Tetrode (IAA)
IGT.............	Integrated Ground Test
IGT.............	Intelligent Graphics Terminal [*Tektronix*] (NITA)
IGT.............	Interactive Graphics Terminal [*Computer science*]
IGT.............	International Game Technology [*NYSE symbol*] (SPSG)
IGT.............	Intl Game Technology [*NYSE symbol*] (TTSB)
IGT.............	Intragastric Titration [*Gastroenterology*]
IGT.............	Ionization Gauge Tube
IGT.............	Nightmute, AK [*Location identifier FAA*] (FAAL)
IGTA	International Gay Travel Association (EA)
IGTC	Inertial Guidance Test Center [*Aerospace*] (IAA)
IGTC	International Glutamate Technical Committee (EA)
IGTDS	Interactive Graphic Transit Design System (PDAA)
IGTEX.........	IDEX II: Tax Exempt Ptfl. Cl.A [*Mutual fund ticker symbol*] (SG)
IGTI...........	Image Guided Technologies, Inc. [*NASDAQ symbol*] (SAG)
IGTI...........	International Gas Turbine Institute [*Later, ASMEIGTI*] (EA)
IGTS	Interactive Graphic Transit Simulator (PDAA)
IGTT...........	Intravenous Glucose Tolerance Test [*Clinical medicine*]
IGTYF.........	International Good Templar Youth Federation [*Oslo, Norway*] (EAIO)
IGU.............	Iguassu Falls [*Brazil*] [*Airport symbol*] (OAG)
IGU.............	Infantile Gastroenteritis Virus [*Medicine*] (PDAA)
IGU.............	Internationale Gewerbeunion [*International Association of Crafts and Small and Medium Sized Enterprises - IACME*] [*Berne, Switzerland*] (EAIO)
IGU.............	International Gas Union [*See also UIIG*] (EAIO)
IGU.............	International Geographical Union [*ICSU*] [*Edmonton, AB*] (EA)
IGU.............	International Geophysical Union
IGUA	International Guards Union of America (EA)
IGUC	Information Gained per Unit Cost [*Computer science*]
IGUCC........	International Geographical Union Commission on Climatology [*Switzerland*] (EAIO)
IGV.............	Incremental Growth Vehicle (MCD)

IGV.............	Inlet Guide Valve (MCD)
IGV.............	Inlet Guide Vane
IGV.............	International Gravis Computer Technology, Inc. [Formerly, Gravis Computer Peripherals, Inc.] [Vancouver Stock Exchange symbol]
IGV.............	Intrathoracic Gas Volume [Medicine] (MAE)
IGVP	International Guild of Vatican Philatelists [Defunct] (EA)
IGW	Image West Entertainment Corp. [Vancouver Stock Exchange symbol]
IGW	Information Group West Corp., Calgary, Alberta [National Library of Canad a] [Library symbol] (IID)
IGW	Internal Gravity Wave [in the atmosphere]
IGW	Irma Graphics for Windows [DCA, Inc.]
IGWAP	CPA [Canadian Psychological Association] Interest Group on Women and Psychology
IGWES	Inert Gas Wire Enamel Stripper (PDAA)
IGWF	International Garment Workers' Federation
IGWIS	Integrated Ground Water Information System
IGWMC	International Ground Water Modeling Center [Butler University]
IGWP	International Group of Women Pilots (EA)
IGWT	Internationale Gesellschaft fuer Warenkunde und Technologie [International Association for Commodity Science and Technology] (EA)
IGWU	International Glove Workers' Union of America [Later, ACTWU]
IGWUA	International Glove Workers Union of America (MHDB)
IGY.............	International Geophysical Year [1958-1959] [ICSU]
IGYN	Imagyn Medical [NASDAQ symbol] (TTSB)
IGYN	Imagyn Medical, Inc. [NASDAQ symbol] (SAG)
IGY-WDC	International Geophysical Year, World Data Center
IGZ.............	Iguatu [Brazil] [Airport symbol] (AD)
IH.................	Channel Flying [ICAO designator] (AD)
IH.................	Hinsdale Public Library, Hinsdale, IL [Library symbol Library of Congress] (LCLS)
IH.................	Iacet Hic [Here Lies] [Latin]
IH.................	Ice Haulage
IH.................	Idiopathic Hemachromatosis [Medicine]
IH.................	Idiopathic Hypercalciuria [Medicine]
IH.................	Immediate Hypersensitivity [Immunology]
IH.................	Immobilized Histamine [Biochemistry]
IH.................	Impact on Hunger (EA)
IH.................	Incipient Heavies [Slang for rising young bureaucrats in the foreign policy field]
IH.................	Indent Hanging [Graphic arts] (DGA)
IH.................	Index of Homogeneity [Botany]
IH.................	Indirect Hemagglutination [Hematology] (DAVI)
IH.................	Indirectly Heated (DEN)
IH.................	Indo-Hittite (BJA)
I/H...............	Industria del Hierro [Part of a large Mexican industrial complex]
IH.................	Industrial House (ROG)
IH.................	Industrial Hygiene (COE)
IH.................	Industrial Hygienist [Occupational Safety and Health Administration]
IH.................	Infectious Hepatitis [Medicine]
IH.................	Informed Homebirth [Later, IH/IBP] (EA)
IH.................	Inguinal Hernia [Gastroenterology] (DAVI)
IH.................	Inhibit
IH.................	Inhibiting Hormone
IH.................	In Home [Men's lacrosse position]
IH.................	In-House
IH.................	Initial Heading
IH.................	Innateness Hypothesis [Linguistics]
IH.................	Inner Half (MAE)
IH.................	Inner Housing (COE)
IH.................	Inpatient, Hospital
IH.................	Inside Height
IH.................	Inside Home [Baseball]
IH.................	Inspector-General of Hospitals and Fleets [Navy British] (ROG)
IH.................	Inspired Humidity [Anesthesiology]
IH.................	Installation Handbook
IH.................	Institute of Housing [British]
IH.................	Institute of Hydrology [Research center British]
IH.................	Instrument Head
IH.................	Interaction Handler [Computer science] (OA)
IH.................	Internationale Horngesellschaft [International Horn Society] (EAIO)
IH.................	International Harvester Co.
IH.................	Interrupt Handler [Computer science] (IAA)
IH.................	Irish Horse [British military] (DMA)
IH.................	Iron Hematoxylin [A dye]
IH.................	Isme-Dagan Hymn (BJA)
IH.................	Israel's Herald [A publication] (BJA)
IH.................	Itavia [ICAO designator] (AD)
IH3PA	International Home and Private Poker Players Association (EA)
IHa...............	Harvey Public Library, Harvey, IL [Library symbol Library of Congress] (LCLS)
IHA.............	Idaho Hospital Association (SRA)
IHA.............	Idiopathic Hyperaldosteronism [Medicine] (DMAA)
IHA.............	Idiopathic Hyperplastic Aldosteronism [Endocrinology]
IHA.............	Illinois Hospital and Health Systems Association (SRA)
IHA.............	Immune Hemolytic Anemia [Medicine]
IHA.............	Independent Hospitals Association [British] (DBA)
IHA.............	Indian Housing Authorities (USGC)
IHA.............	Indian Housing Authority [Department of Housing and Urban Development] (GFGA)
IHA.............	Indirect Hemagglutination [Clinical chemistry]
IHA.............	Indirect Hemagglutination Antibody [Medicine] (DMAA)
IHA.............	Individual Housing Account
IHA.............	Infusion Hepatic Angiography [Medicine]
IHA.............	Institute of Hospital Administrators [British] (BI)
IHA.............	Integrated Hazards Assessments [Environmental science] (COE)
IHA.............	Interfaith Hunger Appeal (EA)
IHA.............	Interim Housing Allowance [Military] (AFM)
IHA.............	International Hahnemannian Association [Defunct]
IHA.............	International Herb Association (NTPA)
IHA.............	International Hopkins Association
IHA.............	International Hotel Association [Paris, France] (EA)
IHA.............	International House Association [Defunct]
IHA.............	Iowa Hospitality Association (SRA)
IHA.............	Issuing Houses Association [British Defunct] (DI)
IHA.............	Reese Hospital and Medical Center, Chicago, IL [OCLC symbol] (OCLC)
IHAA	International Hard Anodizing Association (NTPA)
IHAB	International Horticultural Advisory Board
IHAC	Industrial Health Advisory Council [British]
IHAD	I Have a Dream Foundation (EA)
IHADSS	Integrated Helmet and Display Sight System
IHAF	Institut d'Histoire de l'Amerique Francaise [Institute of French America History] [Canada]
IHAH	Illustrated Handbooks of Art History [A publication]
IHaI	Ingalls Memorial Hospital, Harvey, IL [Library symbol Library of Congress] (LCLS)
IHAI	Institute of Heating and Air-Conditioning Industries
IH & HU	Industrial Health and Hazards Update [Merton Allen Associates] [Information service or system] (CRD)
IH & MEE.....	International Hotel and Motel Educational Exposition [Later, IHM & RS] (EA)
IH&S............	Industrial Hygiene and Safety (COE)
IH-ANES.......	Inhalation Anesthesia
IHAP	International Human Assistance Programs (EA)
IHar............	Mitchell Carnegie Public Library, Harrisburg, IL [Library symbol] [Library of Congress] (LCLS)
IHardCSD......	Calhoun Community Unit, School District 40, Hardin, IL [Library symbol Library of Congress] (LCLS)
IHardR	Hardin Reading Center, Hardin, IL [Library symbol Library of Congress] (LCLS)
IHart	Hartford Public Library, Hartford, IL [Library symbol Library of Congress] (LCLS)
IHAS	Icelandic Horse Adventure Society (EA)
IHAS	Idiopathic Hypertrophic Aortic Stenosis [Cardiology] (DAVI)
IHAS	Illinois Hearing Aid Society (SRA)
IHAS	Integrated Helicopter Avionics System [Navy] (NG)
IHAS	Iowa Hearing Aid Society (SRA)
IHASFC	International Hearts Air Supply Fan Club [Defunct] (EA)
IHAS/ILAAS...	Integrated Helicopter Avionics System / Integrated Light Attack Avionics System [Navy] (SAA)
IHATIS	International Hide and Allied Trades Improvement Society
IHAWK	Improved Homing All the Way Killer [Missile]
IHB.............	Barnes, Hickam, Pantzer & Boyd, Indianapolis, IN [OCLC symbol] (OCLC)
IHB.............	Incomplete Heart Block [Cardiology] (DAVI)
IHB.............	Indiana Harbor Belt Railroad Co. [AAR code]
IHB.............	Inhibin [Biochemistry]
IHB.............	Internationale Hoptrenbaubuero [International Hop Growers Convention]
IHB.............	International Hydrographic Bureau [Later, IHO] [Monaco]
IHBC	International Health and Beauty Council [British]
IHBCA	International H Boat Class Association (EA)
IHBPA	International Hepato-Biliary-Pancreatic Association (EA)
IHBS	International Hajji Baba Society (EA)
IHBT............	Incompatible Hemolytic Blood Transfusion
IHBTD	Incompatible Hemolytic Blood Transfusion Disease (MAE)
IHC.............	Hanover College, Hanover, IN [OCLC symbol] (OCLC)
IHC.............	Identified Hair Cell (DB)
IHC.............	Idiopathic Hemochromatosis [Medicine] (CPH)
IHC.............	Idiopathic Hypercalcemia [Medicine]
IHC.............	Idiopathic Hypercalciuria (STED)
IHC.............	Immaculate Heart College [California]
IHC.............	Immobilization Hypercalcemia [Medicine] (DAVI)
IHC.............	Immunohistochemical
IHC.............	Immunohistochemistry
IHC.............	Indian Heritage Council (EA)
IHC.............	Indian Hospital Corps [British military] (DMA)
IHC.............	Indirectly Heated Cathode
IHC.............	Infant Hypercalcemia [Medicine]
IHC.............	Inner Hair Cells [of cochlea] [Anatomy]
IHC.............	Institute of Hospital Catering [Australia]
IHC.............	Intelligence Handling Committee [Military]
IHC.............	International Harvester Co.
IHC.............	International Health Center
IHC.............	International Health Consultants (EA)
IHC.............	International Health Council (EA)
IHC.............	International Help for Children
IHC.............	International Hug Center [Defunct] (EA)
IHC.............	Intrahepatic Cholestasis (STED)
IHC.............	Ionic Heated Cathode
IHCA	Individual Health Care Account (HCT)
IHCA	In Hands of Civil Authorities [Military]
IHCA	International Hebrew Christian Alliance [Ramsgate, Kent, England] (EA)
IHCA	International Hobie Class Association (EA)
IHCA	Isocapnic Hyperventilation with Cold Air [Medicine] (DMAA)
IHCC	Illinois Home Care Council (SRA)
IHCC	Intensiva HealthCare Corp. [NASDAQ symbol] (SAG)

IHCC .... International Harvester Credit Corp. (ADA)
IHCM .... Idiopathic Hypertrophic Cardiomyopathy [Cardiology]
IHCNE .... Institute for Hospital Clinical Nursing Education (EA)
IHCOS .... Isotope-Heated Catalytic Oxidizer System (KSC)
IHCP .... Institute on Hospital and Community Psychiatry (EA)
IHCPV .... Initial Hydrocarbon Pore Volume [Petroleum technology]
IHCSERS ...... International Health Centre of Socio-Economics Researches and
          Studies [See also CIERSES] [Lailly En Val, France] (EAIO)
IHD .... American Hospital Association Library, Chicago, IL [OCLC symbol]
          (OCLC)
IHD .... In-Center Hemodialysis [Medicine] (DMAA)
IHD .... Indian Head, PA [Location identifier FAA] (FAAL)
IHD .... Institute of Human Development [University of California, Berkeley]
          [Research center] (RCD)
IHD .... Institut Henry-Dunant [Henry Dunant Institute] [Geneva,
          Switzerland] (EAIO)
IHD .... International Hard Suits [Vancouver Stock Exchange symbol]
IHD .... International Hydrological Decade [UNESCO] [Later, IHP]
IHD .... Intrahepatic Duct [or Ductule] [Gastroenterology] (DAVI)
IHD .... Ischemic Heart Disease
IHDA .... International Hardware Distributors Association (NTPA)
IHDI .... International Hearing Dog, Inc. (EA)
IHDP .... Independent Hungarian Democratic Party [Political party Hungary]
          (EAIO)
IHDP .... Infant Health and Development Program
IHDP .... International Human Dimensions of Global Change Programme
IHDRT .... Interim High-Data Rate Terminal (CAAL)
IHDS .... Institute for Higher Defense Studies [National Defense University]
IHDS .... Integrated Helmet Display System
IHE .... Evanston Public Library, Evanston, IL [OCLC symbol] (OCLC)
IHE .... Insensitive High Explosive (MCD)
IHE .... Institute for the Human Environment (EA)
IHE .... Institute of Health Education [British]
IHE .... Institute of Higher Education
IHE .... Institute of Highway Engineers [British]
IHE .... Institute of Home Economics [of ARS, Department of Agriculture]
IHE .... Institute of Hospital Engineering (EAIO)
IHE .... Intergranular Hydrogen Embrittlement [Metallurgy]
IHE .... Intermediate Heat Exchanger [Nuclear energy]
IHE .... International Historic Enterprises
IHE .... International Institute for Hydraulic and Environmental Engineering
          [Netherlands Universities Foundation for International
          Cooperation] [Research center]
IHE .... Interservice Home Exchange [Commercial firm] (EA)
IHEA .... Industrial Heating Equipment Association (EA)
IHEA .... International Health Evaluation Association (EA)
IHEc .... Institute of Home Economics [British] (DBA)
IHEEM .... Institute of Healthcare Engineering & Estate Management (WDAA)
IHEMI .... International Health Economics and Management Institute (EA)
IHen .... Henry Public Library, Henry, IL [Library symbol Library of
          Congress] (LCLS)
IHenn .... Putnam County Library, Hennepin, IL [Library symbol Library of
          Congress] (LCLS)
IHennC .... Hennepin Attendance Center, Hennepin, IL [Library symbol Library of
          Congress] (LCLS)
IHenn-G .... Putnam County Library, Granville Branch, Granville, IL [Library
          symbol Library of Congress] (LCLS)
IHenn-H .... Putnam County Library, Hennepin Branch, Hennepin, IL [Library
          symbol Library of Congress] (LCLS)
IHenn-M ...... Putnam County Library, Magnolia Branch, Magnolia, IL [Library
          symbol Library of Congress] (LCLS)
IHenn-Mc .... Putnam County Library, McNabb Branch, McNabb, IL [Library symbol
          Library of Congress] (LCLS)
IHenn-P .... Putnam County Library, Condit Branch, Putnam, IL [Library symbol
          Library of Congress] (LCLS)
IHenn-S .... Putnam County Library, Standard Branch, Standard, IL [Library
          symbol Library of Congress] (LCLS)
IHEP .... Insensitive High Explosives and Propellants [DoD/DOE program]
          (RDA)
IHEP .... Institute for High-Energy Physics [China]
IHEP .... Institute of High Energy Physics [Former USSR]
IHERC .... Inter-Hemispheric Education Resource Center (EA)
IHERC .... Inter-Hemispheric Resource Center (EA)
IHERS .... Institute of Higher Education Research and Services [University of
          Alabama] [Research center] (RCD)
IHES .... Idiopathic Hypereosinophilic Syndrome [Medicine] (DMAA)
IHETS .... Indiana Higher Education Telecommunication System [Indianapolis]
          [Telecommunications] (TSSD)
IHEU .... International Humanist and Ethical Union [Utrecht, Netherlands] (EA)
IHF .... Improved High Explosive [Military] (MUSM)
IHF .... Independent High Frequency (IAA)
IHF .... Industrial Health Foundation (EA)
IHF .... Industrial Hygiene Foundation of America
IHF .... Inhibit Halt Flip-Flop [Computer science]
IHF .... Inspection Holding Fixture (MCD)
IHF .... Institute of Gas Technology, Chicago, IL [OCLC symbol] (OCLC)
IHF .... Institute of High Fidelity [Formerly, IHFM] [Later, EIA] (EA)
IHF .... Integrated Hazard Function
IHF .... Integration Host Factor [Genetics]
IHF .... Intermediate High Frequency (IIA)
IHF .... International Handball Federation [Basel, Switzerland] (EA)
IHF .... International Health Foundation [Brussels, Belgium] (EAIO)
IHF .... International Helicopter Foundation [Later, HFI] (EA)
IHF .... International Helsinki Federation for Human Rights (ECON)
IHF .... International Hockey Federation (BARN)

IHF .... International Hospital Federation (EA)
IHF .... International Lawn Hockey Federation
IHF .... Inverse Hyperbolic Function
IHF .... Irish Heritage Foundation (EA)
IHF .... Irish Hotels Federation (EAIO)
IHF .... Isothermal Heating Furnace
IHF .... Israel Histadrut Foundation (EA)
IHFAS .... Integrated High-Frequency Antenna System
IHFF .... Inhibit Halt Flip-Flop [Computer science] (MSA)
IHFHR .... International Helsinki Federation for Human Rights (EA)
IHFM .... Institute of High Fidelity Manufacturers [Later, IHF]
IHFMA .... International Home Furnishings Marketing Association (EA)
IHFR .... Improved High-Frequency Radio (INF)
IHFR .... Institute of Health Food Retailing [British] (DBA)
IHFRA .... International Home Furnishings Representatives Association (EA)
IHG .... Ichthyosis Hystrix Gravior (STED)
IHG .... Internationale Hegel Gesellschaft (EA)
IHG .... Skokie Public Library, Skokie, IL [OCLC symbol] (OCLC)
IHGC .... International Hop Growers Convention [See also CICH] [Zalec,
          Yugoslavia] (EAIO)
IHGD .... Isolateral Human Growth Deficiency [Medicine] (DMAA)
IHGMA .... International Herb Growers and Marketers Association [Defunct] (EA)
IHGS .... Institute of Heraldic and Genealogical Studies [British]
IHh .... Eisenhower Public Library District, Harwood Heights, IL [Library
          symbol Library of Congress] (LCLS)
IHH .... Huntington College, Huntington, IN [OCLC symbol] (OCLC)
IHH .... Idiopathic Hypogonadotropic Hypogonadism [Endocrinology]
IHH .... Infectious Human Hepatitis [Medicine] (DMAA)
IHHA .... Indiana Hospital and Health Association (SRA)
IHHA .... International Halfway House Association (EA)
IHHI .... In Home Health, Inc. [NASDAQ symbol] (NQ)
IHHNV .... Infectious Hypodermal and Hematopoietic Necrosis Virus
          [Aquaculture]
IHHO .... Institute of Home Help Organisers [British]
IHHS .... Idiopathic Hyperkinetic Heart Syndrome [Medicine] (DMAA)
IHi .... Illinois State Historical Library, Springfield, IL [Library symbol Library
          of Congress] (LCLS)
IHI .... Impact of Hypertension Information Study [Department of Health and
          Human Services] (GFGA)
IHI .... Improved Holographic Image
IHI .... Institute for Healthcare Improvement (DMAA)
IHI .... Integrated Hit Indicator
IHI .... Ishikawajima-Harima Heavy Industries [Japan] (ECON)
IHI .... Ishikawajima-Harima Heavy Industries Co. Ltd. [Japan]
IHI .... Lincoln Trail Libraries System, Champaign, IL [OCLC symbol]
          (OCLC)
IHIA .... Include This Headquarters Information Addressee [Army] (AABC)
IHIA .... International Health Industries Association (EA)
IH/IBP .... Informed Homebirth/Informed Birth and Parenting (EA)
IHIE .... Institute of Highway Incorporated Engineers [British] (EAIO)
IHig .... Louis Latzer Memorial Library, Highland, IL [Library symbol Library of
          Congress] (LCLS)
IHigp .... Highland Park Public Library, Highland Park, IL [Library symbol
          Library of Congress] (LCLS)
IHigSD .... Highland Community Unit, School District 5, Highland, IL [Library
          symbol Library of Congress] (LCLS)
IHII .... Independent Health Insurance Institute [Inactive] (EA)
IHII .... Industrial Holdings [NASDAQ symbol] (TTSB)
IHII .... Industrial Holdings, Inc. [NASDAQ symbol] (SAG)
IHIIW .... Industrial Holdgs Wrrt'A' [NASDAQ symbol] (TTSB)
IHIIZ .... Industrial Hldgs Wrrt'B' [NASDAQ symbol] (TTSB)
IHil .... Hillside Public Library, Hillside, IL [Library symbol Library of
          Congress] (LCLS)
IHilb .... Hillsboro Public Library, Hillsboro, IL [Library symbol Library of
          Congress] (LCLS)
IHilbGC .... John A. Graham Correctional Center, Hillsboro, IL [Library symbol]
          [Library of Congress] (LCLS)
IHilbSD .... Hillsboro Community Unit, School District 3, Hillsboro, IL [Library
          symbol Library of Congress] (LCLS)
IHineJ .... John J. Madden Mental Health Center, Training Staff Development
          Library, Hines, IL [Library symbol Library of Congress] (LCLS)
IHineV .... United States Veterans Administration Hospital, Hines, IL [Library
          symbol Library of Congress] (LCLS)
IHIPIR .... Improved High-Power Illuminator RADAR [IHAWK Missile] (MCD)
IHIS .... Integrated Hit Indicator System
IHIS .... Integrated Hospital Information System (DMAA)
IHIYX .... IDEX II: Income Plus Cl.A [Mutual fund ticker symbol] (SG)
IHJ .... International Heroines of Jericho [Later, General Conference of
          Grand Courts Heroines of Jericho, Prince Hall Affiliation, USA]
          (EA)
IHK .... Imperial Holly Corp. [AMEX symbol] (SPSG)
IHK .... International Homestock Resources Ltd. [Vancouver Stock Exchange
          symbol]
IHK .... Ionic Heated Kathode
IHL .... Illinois Health Libraries Consortium [Library network]
IHL .... Imperial Light Horse [Military British] (ROG)
IHL .... International Hockey League (EA)
IHL .... International Homeopathic League
IHL .... Internet Header Length [Computer science] (ACRL)
IHLCADS ...... Interim High-Level Container Airdrop System
IHLS .... International Herring Larvae Survey
IHLZY .... Ichud Habonim Labor Zionist Youth (EA)
IHM .... Brothers of the Immaculate Heart of Mary (TOCD)
ihm .... Brothers of the Immaculate Heart of Mary (TOCD)

IHM............. *[The]* California Institute of the Sisters of the Most Holy and Immaculate Heart of the Blessed Virgin Mary (TOCD)

IHM............. Daughters of the Immaculate Heart of Mary *[Roman Catholic religious order]*

i-hm--........ Heard and McDonald Islands *[MARC geographic area code Library of Congress]* (LCCP)

IHM............. Imitation Handmade Paper (DGA)

IHM............. Institute of Housing Managers *[British]* (BI)

IHM............. Mansfield, MA *[Location identifier FAA]* (FAAL)

IHM............. Sisters of the Immaculate Heart of Mary *[California Institute of the Most Holy and Immaculate Heart of the BVM]* *[Roman Catholic religious order]*

IHM............. Sisters of the Most Holy and Immaculate Heart of Blessed Virgin Mary (Wichita Foundation) (TOCD)

IHM............. Sisters, Servants of the Immaculate Heart of Mary *[Roman Catholic religious order]*

IHMA .... Indiana Hotel and Motel Association (SRA)

IHMA .... Industrialized Housing Manufacturer's Association (EA)

IHMA .... International Hazardous Materials Association (NTPA)

IHM & RS.... International Hotel/Motel and Restaurant Show (EA)

IHMDE........ Imitation Handmade Deckle Edges Paper (DGA)

IHMI............ Institute for Housing Management Innovations (EA)

IHMM.......... Institute of Hazardous Materials Management (NTPA)

IHMSA........ International Handgun Metallic Silhouette Association (EA)

IHM-SBF...... Insan Haklari Merkezi, Siyasal Bilgiler Fakueltesi *[Turkey]*

IHN............. Infectious Hematopoietic Necrosis *[Fish pathology]*

IHN............. In His Name

IHN............. Integrated Delivery Networks *[Health care provider]*

IHN............. International Handicappers' Net (EA)

IHN............. Iron Horse Resources, Inc. *[Vancouver Stock Exchange symbol]*

IHNI........... Iatros Health Network *[NASDAQ symbol]* (TTSB)

IHNI........... Iatros Health Network, Inc. *[NASDAQ symbol]* (SAG)

IHNIW........ Iatros Health Network Wrrt *[NASDAQ symbol]* (TTSB)

IHo............. Hoopestown Public Library, Hoopestown, IL *[Library symbol Library of Congress]* (LCLS)

IHO............. Idiopathic Hypertrophic Osteoarthropathy *[Medicine]*

IHO............. Impartial Hearing Officer

IHO............. Impeded Harmonic Operation

IHO............. In Honor Of

IHO............. Inorganic Halogen Oxidizer

IHO............. Institute of Human Origins (EA)

IHO............. International Hydrographic Organization *[See also BHI]* *[Monaco]*

IHod............ Hodgkins Public Library District, Hodgkins, IL *[Library symbol Library of Congress]* (LCLS)

IHoF........... Vermilion County Elementary Film Library, Hoopeston, IL *[Library symbol]* *[Library of Congress]* (LCLS)

IHoH .... Hoopestown Community Memorial Hospital, Hoopestown, IL *[Library symbol Library of Congress]* (LCLS)

IHom........... Homer Community Library, Homer, IL *[Library symbol Library of Congress]* (LCLS)

IHOP .... IHOP Corp. *[NASDAQ symbol]* (SAG)

IHOP .... International House of Pancakes *[Restaurant chain]* *[Pronounced "eye-hop"]*

IHOP .... Isophosphamide, Hydroxydaunomycin *[Adriamycn]*, Oncovin , Prednisone *[Vincristine]* *[Antineoplastic drug regimen]* (DAVI)

IHOPCp....... IHOP Corp. *[Associated Press]* (SAG)

IHOSPE....... Institute of Hospital Engineering (PDAA)

IHot........... Hometown Public Library, Hometown, IL *[Library symbol Library of Congress]* (LCLS)

IHOU .... Institute of Home Office Underwriters *[Louisville, KY]* (EA)

IHow .... Homewood Public Library, Homewood, IL *[Library symbol Library of Congress]* (LCLS)

IHP.............. Hammond Public Library, Hammond, IN *[OCLC symbol]* (OCLC)

IHP.............. Idiopathic Hypoparathyroidism *[Medicine]*

IHP.............. Idiopathic Hypopituitarism *[Medicine]* (AAMN)

IHP.............. Indicated Horsepower

IHP.............. Individualized Habilitation Plan

IHP.............. Information Handling Project (DIT)

IHP.............. Inner Helmholtz Plane (IAA)

IHP.............. Inositol Hexaphosphate *[Biochemistry]*

IHP.............. Institute for Human Progress *[Defunct]*

IHP.............. Instrumentation Habitability Power (MCD)

IHP.............. Intergovernmental Council for the International Hydrological Programme (EA)

IHP.............. International Hydrographic Program

IHP.............. International Hydrological Program *[UNESCO]* *[France]*

IHP.............. Inverted Hand Position *[Neuropsychology]*

IHP.............. Isostatic Hot Pressing (PDAA)

IHPA........... International Hand Protection Association (NTPA)

IHPA........... International Hardwood Products Association (EA)

IHPBA......... International Hepato-Pancreato-Biliary Association (EA)

IHPC........... International Hydrolyzed Protein Council (EA)

IHPC .... Intrahepatic Cholestasis *[Medicine]* (DMAA)

IHPD .... International Health Physics Data Base *[Creative Information Systems, Inc.]* *[Information service or system]* (CRD)

IHPH .... Indicated Horsepower-Hour

IHPH .... Intrahepatic Portal Hypertension *[Medicine]* (MAE)

IHP-HR .... Indicated Horsepower-Hour

IHPI .... IHS *[Information Handling Services]* Product/Subject Index *[Information service or system]* (CRD)

IHPI .... Improved High-Power Illuminator (CAAL)

IHPMI .... International Health Policy and Management Institute (EAIO)

IHPO .... International Health Program Office *[Atlanta, GA]* *[Department of Health and Human Services]* (GRD)

IHPP .... Intergovernmental Health Policy Project (EA)

IHPRPT....... Integrated High Payoff Rocket Propulsion Technology

IHPRS .... International Husserl and Phenomenological Research Society (EA)

IHPST .... Institute for the History and Philosophy of Science and Technology *[University of Toronto]* *[Canada]* (IRC)

IHPTET........ Integrated High-Performance Turbine Engine Technology Initiative *[NASA and DOD]*

IHPVA .... International Human Powered Vehicle Association (EA)

IHQ .... International Headquarters (DNAB)

IHQ .... Rolling Prairie Libraries, Decatur, IL *[OCLC symbol]* (OCLC)

IH/QAS....... Indian Head *[Maryland]* - Quality Assurance Department *[Naval ordnance station]*

IHR .... Carl Sandburg College, LRC, Galesburg, IL *[OCLC symbol]* (OCLC)

IHR .... Cocoa, FL *[Location identifier FAA]* (FAAL)

IHR .... Increased Hazard Rate

IHR .... Infrared Heterodyne Radiometer

IHR .... Institute for Historical Review (EA)

IHR .... Institute of Horticultural Research *[Research center British]* (IRC)

IHR .... Intrahepatic Resistance *[Medicine]* (MAE)

IHR .... Intrinsic Heart Rate *[Cardiology]*

IHR .... Ishihara *[Japan]* *[Seismograph station code, US Geological Survey Closed]* (SEIS)

IHRA .... Increasing Hazard Rate Average

IHRA .... International Hot Rod Association (EA)

IHRB .... Industrial Health Research Board *[British]*

IHRBLR....... International Human Resources, Business, and Legal Research Association (EA)

IHRC :......... Immigration History Research Center *[University of Minnesota]* *[Research center]* (RCD)

IHRC .... In-Home Respite Care

IH/RE .... Indian Head Research and Development Department *[Naval Ordnance Station]* *[Maryland]*

IHRG .... Interdisciplinary Health Research Group *[See also GRIS]* *[Universite de Montreal]* *[Canada]* *[Research center]*

IHRIM .... International Association for Human Resource Information Management (NTPA)

IHRLG......... International Human Rights Law Group (EA)

IHRMA........ Irish Hotel and Restaurant Managers' Association (BI)

IHRR .... Institute for Human Rights (EA)

IHRR .... Institute for Human Rights Research (EA)

IHRSA......... International Health Racquet, and Sportsclub Association (NTPA)

IHRWG....... Iranian Human Rights Working Group (EA)

IHS............. Fort Carson, CO *[Location identifier FAA]* (FAAL)

IHS............. Idiopathic Headache Score *[Neurology]* (DAVI)

IHS............. Iesous Hemeteros Soter *[Jesus, Our Savior]* *[Greek]*

IHS............. Iesus Heiland Seligmacher *[Jesus, Savior, Sanctifier]* *[German]*

IHS............. Iesus Hominum Salvator *[Jesus, Savior of Mankind]* *[Latin]* (ADA)

IHS............. Immigration History Society (EA)

IHS............. Improved HAWK Simulator *[Military]*

IHS............. Inactivated Horse Serum *[Immunology]*

IHS............. Inclined Heterolithic Stratification *[Geology]*

IHS............. Indescor Hydrodynamics, Inc. *[Vancouver Stock Exchange symbol]*

IHS............. Indian Health Service

IHS............. Information Handling Services *[Englewood, CO]*

IHS............. Infrared Homing System (AAG)

IHS............. Infrared Horizon Sensor

IHS............. In Hoc Signo (Vinces) *[In This Sign (You Will Conquer)]* *[Latin]*

IHS............. Institute for Housing Urban Development Studies *[Netherlands]*

IHS............. Institute for Humane Studies, Inc. *[Research center]* (RCD)

IHS............. Institute for Hydrogen Systems *[UTLAS symbol]*

IHS............. Institute of Home Safety *[British]* (DBA)

IHS............. Institute of Hypertension Studies - Institute of Hypertension School of Research *[Later, NIHS]* (EA)

IHS............. Integrated Headgear Subsystem *[Army]* (RDA)

IHS............. Integrated Health Services, Inc. *[NYSE symbol]* (SPSG)

IHS............. Integrated Health Svcs *[NYSE symbol]* (TTSB)

IHS............. Integrated Heat Sink (PDAA)

IHS............. Interactive Home System (PDAA)

IHS............. International Health Society (EA)

IHS............. International Hearing Society (PAZ)

IHS............. International Heritage Site *[UNESCO]*

IHS............. International Hibernation Society (EA)

IHS............. International Horn Society (EA)

IHS............. International Hurling Society

IHS............. International Hydrofoil Society (EAIO)

IHS............. Intrahepatic Arteriovenous Shunt *[Medicine]*

IHs............. Iris Hamartoma *[Oncology]* (DAVI)

IHS............. Isotope Heat Source

IHS............. Italian Historical Society of America (EA)

IHS............. Suburban Library System, Hinsdale, IL *[Library symbol Library of Congress]* (LCLS)

IHS............. University of Texas, Health Science Center at Dallas, Dallas, TX *[OCLC symbol]* (OCLC)

IHSA .... Intercollegiate Horse Show Association (EA)

IHSA .... International Headquarters of the Salvation Army (EA)

IHSA .... Intervention on the High Seas Act (COE)

IHSA .... Iodinated Human Serum Albumin

IHSB .... In-Flight Helmet Stowage Bag (KSC)

IHSBR......... Improved High-Speed Bombing RADAR

IHSC .... Immunoreactive Human Skin Collagenase *[Medicine]* (DB)

IHSC .... InSight Health Services Corp. *[NASDAQ symbol]* (SAG)

IHSD .... Inertial Height Sensing Device

IHSD .... In-House Systems Developer *[Personal computer]* (PCM)

IHSDC......... Irish Health Services Development Corp.

IHSG .... Internationale Heinrich Schutz-Gesellschaft *[International Heinrich Schutz Society]* (EAIO)

IHSGB .... Icelandic Horse Society [*British*] (DBA)
IHSI .... Induction Heating Stress Improvement [*Nuclear energy*] (NUCP)
IHSM .... Institute of Health Services Management (DBA)
IHSPCB .... International Healthcare Safety Professional Certification Board (EA)
IHSR .... Improved High Speed Rail (PDAA)
IHSR .... Institute for Health Services Research [*Tulane University*] [*Research center*] (RCD)
IH/SR .... Integration Hardware and Software Review (MCD)
IHSRC .... International Heat Stress Research Center [*Sudan*] (IRC)
IHSS .... Idiopathic Hypertrophic Subaortic Stenosis [*Medicine*]
IHSS .... In-Home Support Services [*Medicine*] (MEDA)
IHSS .... Institute of Human Science and Services [*University of Rhode Island*] [*Research center*] (RCD)
IHSS .... Integrated Hydrographic Survey System (PDAA)
IHSS .... International Heinrich Schutz Society [*See also IHSG*] [*Germany*] (EA)
IHSS .... International Humic Substances Society
IHT .... Icelandic Horse Trekkers (EA)
IHT .... Ideal Handler Time (AAEL)
IHT .... Impact Hand Tool
IHT .... Inheritance Tax [*British*]
IHT .... Innsuites Hospitality SBI [*Formerly, Realty Refund SBI*] [*NYSE symbol*]
IHT .... Inspection Hold Tag
IHT .... Institute of Heat Technology
IHT .... Institution of Highways and Transportation [*British*] (DBA)
IHT .... Insulin Hypoglycemia Test [*Endocrinology*] (DAVI)
IHT .... International Association of Health and Therapy Instruments [*Japan*] (EAIO)
IHT .... International Herald Tribune [*A publication*]
IHT .... Intravenous Histamine Test [*Clinical Medicine*] (MAE)
IHT .... Trinity Evangelical Divinity School, Rolfing Memorial Library, Deerfield, IL [*OCLC symbol*] (OCLC)
IHTA .... International Health and Temperance Association (EA)
IH-TAS .... Improved HAWK-Tracking Adjunct System [*Military*] (MCD)
IHTD .... Improved HAWK Training Detachment
IHTS .... Integrated Hybrid Transistor Switch (PDAA)
IHTS .... Intermediate Heat Transport System [*Nuclear energy*] (NRCH)
IHTTA .... International High-Technology Training Association (EA)
IHTU .... Interservice Hovercraft Trials Unit [*Military*]
IHTV .... Interim Hypersonics Test Vehicle [*NASA*] (NASA)
IHU .... Chicago Mercantile Exchange, Chicago, IL [*OCLC symbol*] (OCLC)
IHU .... Ihu [*Papua New Guinea*] [*Airport symbol*] (OAG)
IHU .... Instantaneous Unit Hydrograph (PDAA)
IHU .... Interservice Hovercraft Unit [*Military*]
IHumSD .... Shiloh Community Unit School District, Hume, IL [*Library symbol*] [*Library of Congress*] (LCLS)
IHuSD .... Hutsonville Community Unit, School District 1, Hutsonville, IL [*Library symbol Library of Congress*] (LCLS)
IHV .... Highland Park Public Library, Highland Park, IL [*OCLC symbol*] (OCLC)
IHV .... Independent Hardware Vendor [*Computer science*] (CDE)
IHV .... Institute of Human Values [*See also IMH*] [*Canada*]
IHV .... Institute of Human Virology [*University of Maryland*]
IHV .... Internationale Hegel-Vereinigung [*Munich, Federal Republic of Germany*] (EAIO)
IHVE .... Institution of Heating and Ventilating Engineers [*Later, CIBSE*]
IHVS .... Intelligent Vehicle Highway Systems
IHW .... Inner Heel Wedge [*Orthopedics*] (DAVI)
IHW .... International Halley Watch [*Defunct*] (EA)
IHW .... John G. Shedd Aquarium, Chicago, IL [*OCLC symbol*] (OCLC)
IHWG .... Internationale Hugo Wolf Gesellschaft [*Vienna, Austria*] (EAIO)
IHWU .... Independent Hospital Workers Union (EA)
I-Hwy .... Interstate Highway (TBD)
IHX .... Interim Hypersonics Test Vehicle
IHX .... Interloop Heat Exchanger [*NASA*] (NASA)
IHX .... Intermediate Heat Exchanger [*Nuclear energy*]
IHX .... Western Illinois Library System, Monmouth, IL [*OCLC symbol*] (OCLC)
IHXGV .... Intermediate Heat Exchanger Guard Vessel [*Nuclear energy*] (NRCH)
IHY .... Ela Area Public Library District, Lake Zurich, IL [*OCLC symbol*] (OCLC)
IHY .... I Heard You (MHDI)
IHYP .... Iodohydroxybenzylpindolol [*Organic chemistry*]
IHZ .... Warren-Newport Public Library District, Gurnee, IL [*OCLC symbol*] (OCLC)
II .... Aer Arann Teoranta [*Ireland*] [*ICAO designator*] (ICDA)
ii .... Bid in Die [*Twice a Day*] [*Symbol*] [*Pharmacology*] (DAVI)
I/I .... Current to Current [*Converter*] (NRCH)
II .... Igniter Initiator
II .... Ikebana International [*Japan*]
II .... Illegal Immigrant
II .... Illinium [*or Promethium*] [*Cardiology*] (DAVI)
II .... Image Intensifier
II .... Imagery Interpretation
II .... Immigrant Inspector [*Immigration and Naturalization Service*]
II .... Imperial Airlines [*ICAO designator*] (AD)
II .... Imperial Institute [*British*] (DAS)
II .... Implementation Instructions (MCD)
II .... Incarcerated Innocent
II .... Independent Inspector (AIE)
ii .... India [*MARC country of publication code Library of Congress*] (LCCP)
II .... Individualized Instruction
II .... Indochina Institute (EA)
I/I .... Indorsement Irregular [*Banking*]
I/I .... Industrial and Institutional [*Waste*] (GAAI)
II .... Information Index [*LIMRA*]
II .... Information Indicator (ACRL)
II .... Ingot Iron
II .... Initial Issue
II .... Innovators International [*Defunct*] (EA)
II .... Input Impedance
II .... Insol International (EA)
I-I .... Inspector-Instructor [*Marine Corps*]
II .... Installation Instruction
II .... Institute of Inventors [*British*] (BI)
II .... Institutional Investor [*Business term*]
II .... Instituto Interamericano (EA)
II .... Instruction and Inspection (IAA)
I/I .... Interfaith Impact for Justice and Peace [*An association*] (EA)
II .... Interlingua Institute (EA)
II .... Interrupt Inhibit
II .... Intersystems, Inc. [*Formerly, Bamberger Polymers, Inc.*] [*AMEX symbol*] (SPSG)
II .... Interval International (EA)
II .... Intransit Inventory (AFM)
II .... Inventions and Inventors [*A publication*]
II .... Inventory and Inspection Report [*Army*]
II .... Ion Implant (AAEL)
II .... Irish Institute (EA)
II .... Item Identification (MSA)
II .... London City Airways [*ICAO designator*] (AD)
II .... Requires Medical Supplies [*Search and rescue symbol that can be stamped in sand or snow*]
IIA .... Carnegie Public Library, Angola, IN [*OCLC symbol*] (OCLC)
IIA .... If Incorrect Advise [*Aviation*]
IIA .... ILA [*Instruction Look Ahead*] Interrupt Address [*Computer science*]
IIA .... Image Intensifier Assembly
IIA .... Impotence Institute of America (EA)
IIA .... Incinerator Institute of America [*Later, NSWMA*] (EA)
IIA .... Independent Innkeepers Association (EA)
IIA .... Independent Inspection Agency [*RSPA*] (TAG)
IIA .... Indirect Immunofluorescence Assay [*AIDS confirmation test*] (CPH)
IIA .... Inertial Instrument Assembly
IIA .... Information Industry Association (EA)
IIA .... Information Interchange Architecture [*Computer science*] (IGQR)
IIA .... Information Interchange Architecture [*IBM Corp.*]
IIA .... Institute of Inter-American Affairs [*Washington, DC*]
IIA .... Institute of Internal Affairs
IIA .... Institute of Internal Auditors [*Altamonte Springs, FL*] (EA)
IIA .... Institute of International Affairs
IIA .... Institut International d'Anthropologie [*International Institute of Anthropology*] (EAIO)
IIA .... Insurance Institute of America (EA)
IIA .... Intelligence Industries Association (EA)
IIA .... Interamericana de Aviacion Ltda. [*Colombia*] [*ICAO designator*] (FAAC)
IIA .... International Internet Association
IIA .... International Illawarra Association [*Defunct*] (EA)
IIA .... International Imagery Association (EA)
IIA .... International Information Administration [*Transferred to U SIS, 1953*] [*Department of State*]
IIA .... International Institute of Agriculture
IIA .... International Institute of Andragogy [*See also INSTIA*] (EAIO)
IIA .... International Inventor's Association [*Defunct*] (EA)
IIA .... International Investors Association (EA)
IIA .... Invention Industry Association of America
IIA .... Invert Indicator from Accumulator (SAA)
IIAA .... Independent Insurance Agents of America [*New York, NY*] (EA)
IIAA .... Institute of Inter-American Affairs [*United Nations*]
IIAANY .... Independent Insurance Agents Association of New York (SRA)
IIAAR .... International Institute for Arab-American Relations [*Defunct*] (EA)
IIABC .... Independent Insurance Agents and Brokers of California
IIAC .... Impulse International Auto Club [*Defunct*] (EA)
IIAC .... Independent Insurance Agents of Connecticut (SRA)
IIAC .... Industrial Injuries Advisory Council [*British*] (DCTA)
IIAC .... Infrared Information and Analysis Center [*University of Michigan*] (MCD)
IIAC .... Inter-Image Amplifying Chemistry [*Color film technology*]
IIAC .... International Insurance Advisory Council [*Later, IIC*] (EA)
IIAC .... Iowa Intercollegiate Athletic Conference (PSS)
IIAD .... Independent Insurance Agents of Delaware (SRA)
IIAF .... Imperial Iranian Air Force
IIAFC .... International Irwin Allen Fan Club (EA)
IIAG .... Interbureau Insurance Advisory Group
IIAI .... International Institute of American Ideals (EA)
IIAILS .... Interim Integrated Aircraft Instrumentation and Letdown System
IIAL .... International Institute of African Languages and Culture (BARN)
IIAL .... International Institute of Arts and Letters
IIALM .... International Institute for Adult Literacy Methods [*Tehran, Iran*] (EAIO)
IIANC .... Independent Insurance Agents of North Carolina (SRA)
II & W .... Intelligence Interface and Warning [*Military*] (MCD)
IIANH .... Independent Insurance Agents of New Hampshire (SRA)
IIANJ .... Independent Insurance Agents of New Jersey (SRA)
IIANM .... Independent Insurance Agents of New Mexico (SRA)
IIAO .... Independent Insurance Agents of Oregon (SRA)
IIAP .... Independent Insurance Agents of Pennsylvania (SRA)
IIAP .... Institut International d'Aluminium Primaire [*International Primary Aluminum Institute*] (EAIO)

IIAP..............	Insurance Institute for Asia and the Pacific (DS)
IIAR	Incurably Ill for Animal Research (EA)
IIAR	International Institute of Ammonia Refrigeration (EA)
IIARI	Independent Insurance Agents of Rhode Island (SRA)
IIAS..............	Institute of Interamerican Studies [*University of Miami*] [*Research center*] (RCD)
IIAS..............	International Institute for Advanced Studies (EA)
IIASA	Institute of Islamic and Arabic Sciences in America (EA)
IIASA	International Institute for Applied Systems Analysis
IIASC	Independent Insurance Agents of South Carolina (SRA)
IIAU	Independent Insurance Agents of Utah (SRA)
IIAV..............	Independent Insurance Agents of Vermont (SRA)
IIB..............	Butler University, Indianapolis, IN [*OCLC symbol*] (OCLC)
IIB..............	Illinois Intrastate Motor Carrier Rate & Tariff Bureau, Springfield IL [*STAC*]
IIB..............	Independence, IA [*Location identifier FAA*] (FAAL)
IIB..............	Independent Infantry Battalion
IIB..............	Industrial Information Bulletin [*A publication*]
IIB..............	Information Industry Bulletin [*Digital Information Group*] [*Information service or system*] (IID)
IIB..............	Institute for Independent Business (EA)
IIB..............	Institut International de Bibliographie
IIB..............	Institut International des Brevets [*International Patent Institute*]
IIB..............	Intense Ion Beam
IIB..............	International Institute of Biotechnology [*University of Kent at Canterbury*] [*British*] (IRC)
IIB..............	International Investment Bank [*Moscow, USSR*]
IIB..............	Internordic Investment Bank [*Scandinavia*]
IIB..............	Iowa Independent Bankers (TBD)
IIB..............	Irish Intercontinental Bank Ltd.
IIB..............	Italian International Bank
IIBA..............	International Institute for Bioenergetic Analysis (EA)
IIBA..............	International Intelligent Buildings Association [*Washington, DC*] (EA)
II Bar	II Baruch [*Pseudepigrapha*] (BJA)
IIBC..............	International Institute of Biological Control [*CAB International*] [*British*] (IRC)
IIBD	Incorporated Institute of British Decorators (DAS)
IIBDID	Incorporated Institute of British Decorators and Interior Designers (BI)
IIBH	International Institute of Biological Husbandry [*Ipswich, Suffolk, England*] [*Defunct*] (EAIO)
IIBS..............	Interactive International Banking System [*NCR Corp.*]
IIBTT	Ion-Implanted Base Transistor Technology (IAA)
IIC..............	AMIGOS [*Access Method for Indexed Data Generalized for Operating System*] Bibliographic Council, Dallas, TX [*OCLC symbol*] (OCLC)
IIC..............	Igniter Initiator Cartridge [*or Container*]
IIC..............	Image Interpretation Cell
IIC..............	Imagery Interpretation Center
IIC..............	Impact Isolation Class [*Noise rating of insulation*]
IIC..............	Independent Insurance Conference
IIC..............	Independent Investment Co. [*British*]
IIC..............	Industrial Intelligence Centre [*British World War II*]
IIC..............	Inflation-Indexed Charge [*Medicare*] (GFGA)
IIC..............	Information Industries Committee [*Information service or system*] (IID)
IIC..............	Innovation Information Center [*George Washington University*] (PDAA)
IIC..............	Insearch Institute of Commerce [*University of Technology, Sydney, Australia*]
IIC..............	Institute of Insurance Consultants [*British*] (DBA)
IIC..............	Institut International des Communications [*International Institute of Communications*] (EA)
IIC..............	Instructional Improvement Committee [*Individually-guided education*] (AEE)
IIC..............	Insurance Institute of Canada
IIC..............	Integrated Interface Circuit (IAA)
IIC..............	Intelligence Information Center [*Military*] (MCD)
IIC..............	InterCapital California Insurance Municipal Income Fund [*NYSE symbol*] (SPSG)
IIC..............	InterCapital Cal Ins Muni Inc. [*NYSE symbol*] (TTSB)
IIC..............	Interceptor Identification Capability
IIC..............	Intercraft Industries Corp. (EFIS)
IIC..............	Interdepartmental Intelligence Conference [*Interagency conference of the National Security Council*] (EGAO)
IIC..............	International Ice Patrol [*Coast Guard*]
IIC..............	International Institute for Conservation of Historic and Artistic Works [*British*] (EAIO)
IIC..............	International Institute for Cotton [*Belgium*] (FEA)
IIC..............	International Institute for the Conservation of Museum Objects
IIC..............	International Institute of Communications [*Formerly, IBI*] (EA)
IIC..............	International Insurance Council (EA)
IIC..............	International Ionarc, Inc. [*Vancouver Stock Exchange symbol*]
IIC..............	Ion-Ion Collision
IIC..............	Iron Information Center [*Battelle Memorial Institute*] [*Information service or system*] (IID)
IIC..............	Isotopes Information Center [*ORNL*]
IIC..............	Item Identification Code
IIC..............	Rita Coyotepec [*Mexico*] [*Seismograph station code, US Geological Survey*] (SEIS)
IICA..............	Indians into Communications Association (EA)
IICA..............	Instituto Internacional de Ciencias Administrativas [*International Institute of Administrative Sciences*]
IICA..............	Interamerican Institute for Cooperation on Agriculture [*Formerly, IAIAS*] (EA)

IICA..............	International Ice Cream Association (EA)
IICA..............	Islamic Information Center of America (EA)
IICBM..............	Intermediate Intercontinental Ballistic Missile
IICC..............	Institut International d'Etude et de Documentation en Matiere de Concurrence Commerciale [*International Institute for Commercial Competition*] [*Belgium*] (EA)
IICC..............	International Institute for Study and Research in the Field of Commercial Competition
IICE..............	Institute for Internal Combustion Engines (MCD)
IICE..............	Institut International des Caisses d'Epargne [*International Savings Banks Institute - ISBI*] [*Geneva, Switzerland*] (EAIO)
IICF..............	Insurance Industry Charitable Foundation
IICG	ICSU [*International Council of Scientific Unions*] Inter-Union Commission for Geodynamics [*Marine science*] (MSC)
IICHAW	International Institute for Conservation of Historic and Artistic Works
IICI..............	Image Industry Council International (NTPA)
IIC Ind	IIC Industries, Inc. [*Associated Press*] (SAG)
IICIT..............	International Institute of Connector and Interconnection Technology (NTPA)
IICL..............	Institute of International Container Lessors (EA)
IICLRR	International Institute for Children's Literature and Reading Research [*Vienna, Austria*] (EA)
IICM..............	International Institute of Convention Management (NTPA)
IICMFA..........	Integrated Information Centre of the Ministry of Foreign Affairs [*Saudi Arabia*] (NITA)
IICMSD	International Institute for Comparative Music Studies and Documentation [*Berlin, Federal Republic of Germany*] (EA)
IiCN	National Library of India, Calcutta, India [*Library symbol Library of Congress*] (LCLS)
IICNTR..........	International Institute of Children's Nature and Their Rights (EA)
IICP..............	Increased Intracranial Pressure (CPH)
IICP..............	International Intersociety Committee on Pathology
IICR..............	IIC Industries [*NASDAQ symbol*] (TTSB)
IICR..............	IIC Industries, Inc. [*NASDAQ symbol*] (SAG)
IICR..............	Inspection Item Change Request (MCD)
IICS..............	Intelligent Image Caching Software [*Courtland Group, Inc.*] (PCM)
IICS..............	International Interactive Communications Society [*San Francisco, CA*] [*Telecommunications service*] (TSSD)
IICU..............	Infant Intensive Care Unit [*of a hospital*]
IICU..............	Intermediate Intensive Care Unit [*Medicine*]
IICUC..............	Institute of Inspection Cleaning and Restoration (NTPA)
IICUC..............	International Institute of Carpet and Upholstery Certification (EA)
IICY..............	International Independent Christian Youth [*See also JICI*] [*Paris, France*] (EAIO)
IID..............	Iida [*Japan*] [*Seismograph station code, US Geological Survey*] (SEIS)
IID..............	Image Intensifier Device
IID..............	Impact Ionization Diode
IID..............	Independent Identically Distributed [*Statistics*] (IEEE)
IID..............	Information Industry Directory [*A publication*]
IID..............	Infrared Intrusion Detection (NVT)
IID..............	Institute for Integral Development (EA)
IID..............	Insulin-Dependent Diabetes [*Mellitus*] [*Endocrinology*] (DAVI)
IID..............	Insulin-Independent Diabetes Mellitus (MAE)
IID..............	Insurgent Incident Data
IID..............	Integrated Information Display (MCD)
IID..............	Integrated Instrument Development
IID..............	Interaural Intensity Disparity [*Audiology*]
IID..............	Intermittent-Integrated Doppler (OA)
IID..............	Intrinsic Infrared Detector
IID..............	Investment in Default [*Business term*]
IID..............	Ion Implantation Doping
IID..............	Ionospheric Ion Density
IIDA..............	Indivisualized Instruction for Data Access [*Drexel University and Franklin Institute*] [*Education package*] (NITA)
IIDA..............	Instituto Interamericano de Direito de Autor [*Interamerican Copyright Institute*] (EAIO)
IIDA..............	International Interior Design Association (NTPA)
IIDARA..........	Instituto Iberoamericano de Derecho Agrario y Reforma Agraria [*Ibero-American Institute of Agrarian Law and Agrarian Reform - IAIALAR*] (EAIO)
IiDaU	University of North Bengal, Darjeeling District, West Bengal, India [*Library symbol Library of Congress*] (LCLS)
IIDC..............	Institute for International Development and Cooperation [*University of Ottawa*] [*See also IDIC*] [*Canada*]
IIDD..............	Interface Identification Data Document (DNAB)
IIDET..............	International Institute of Dental Ergonomics and Technology [*Germany*] (EAIO)
IIDH..............	Institut International de Droit Humanitaire [*International Institute of Humanitarian Law - IIHL*] (EAIO)
IIDH..............	Instituto Interamericano de Derechos Humanos [*Inter-American Institute of Human Rights - IIHR*] (EA)
IIDLC	Institut International de Droit Linguistique Compare [*International Institute of Comparative Linguistic Law*] (EAIO)
IIDP	Integrated Instrument Development Program
IIDP	Integrated Intelligence Development Plan (MCD)
IIDS	Integrated Information Display System (MCD)
IIDS	Integrated Instrumentation Display System
IIDT	Ion Implantation Doping Technique
IIE..............	Idiopathic Ineffective Erythropoiesis [*Hematology*] (AAMN)
IIE..............	Imperial Institute of Entomology [*British*]
IIE..............	Initial Ion Event
IIE..............	Installation Identification Element (MCD)
IIE..............	Institute for Independent Education (EA)
IIE..............	Institute for International Economics

IIE	Institute of Industrial Economics [*University of Newcastle*] [*Australia*]
IIE	Institute of Industrial Engineers (EA)
IIE	Institute of International Education (EA)
IIE	Institut International de l'Epargne
IIE	Instituto Interamericano de Estadistica [*Inter-American Statistical Institute - IASI*] [*Washington, DC*]
IIE	Inter-American Institute of Ecology [*Ecological Society of America*]
IIE	International Institute of Embryology [*Later, ISDB*]
IIEA	Immediate Identifiable Emergency Action [*Red Cross*]
IIEA	International Institute for Environmental Affairs [*Later, IIED*]
IIEC	Inter-Industry Emission Control [*Program*] (EA)
IIEC	International Institute for Energy Conservation (EA)
IIED	International Institute for Environment and Development [*Research center British*] (IRC)
iied	International Institute for Environment and Development [*British*]
IIEE	Institut International d'Etudes sur l'Education [*International Institute for Education Studies*]
IIEG	Interest Inventory for Elementary Grades [*Psychology*]
IIEL	Institut International d'Etudes Ligures [*International Institute for Ligurian Studies - IILS*] (EAIO)
IIEP	Illionois Inventory of Educational Progress (EDAC)
IIEP	International Institute for Educational Planning [*Paris, France*] [*United Nations*] (EA)
IIEQ	Illinois Institute for Environmental Quality (PDAA)
IIER	International Institute for Economic Research (ASF)
IIES	International Institute for Environmental Studies (ASF)
IIETF	Information Industries Education and Training Foundation [*Australia*]
IIExE	Institution of Incorporated Executive Engineers [*British*] (DBA)
IIF	IBM [*International Business Machines Corp.*] IGES Format [*Initial Graphics Exchange Specification*]
IIF	Immune Interferon [*Cell biology*]
IIF	Imprint Immuno-Fixation [*Immunochemistry*]
IIF	Independent Investors Forum [*Information service or system*] (IID)
IIF	Indirect Immunofluorescence [*Immunochemistry*]
IIF	Institute of International Finance [*Washington, DC*] (EA)
IIF	Institut International du Froid [*International Institute of Refrigeration*]
IIF	Intense Irregular Field
IIF	Internals Indexing Fixture (NRCH)
IIF	International Institute of Forecasters [*See also IIM*] (EA)
IIF	Morgan Stanley India Investment Fund [*NYSE symbol*] (SAG)
IIF	Morgan Stanley India Inv Fd [*NYSE symbol*] (TTSB)
IIFA	International Institute of Films on Art
IIFAR	Incurably Ill for Animal Research (EA)
IIFAS	Integration of Intelligence from All Sources (MCD)
IIFET	International Institute of Fisheries Economics and Trade (EA)
IIFFL	International Institute of Foods and Family Living (EA)
IIFP	Institut International de Finances Publiques [*International Institute of Public Finance*] (EAIO)
IIFS	Integrated Individual Fighting System [*US Army Natick Research, Development, and Engineering Center*] (INF)
IIFSO	International Islamic Federation of Student Organizations [*Salimiyan, Kuwait*] (EAIO)
IIFSP	Integrated Individual Fighting System Program [*Army*] (INF)
IIFT	Indirect Immunofluorescence Technique [*Immunochemistry*]
IIFV	Interim Infantry Fighting Vehicle [*Military*] (MCD)
IIG	Illuminated Internal Graticule
IIG	Imagery Intelligence Group [*Military*] (MCD)
IIG	Investors Ins Group [*AMEX symbol*] (TTSB)
IIG	Investors Insurance Group [*Formerly, Gemco National, Inc.*] [*AMEX symbol*] (SPSG)
IIG	Item Identification Guide
IIGA	IEEE [*Institute of Electrical and Electronics Engineers*] Industry and General Applications (IAA)
IIGB	International Institute of Genetics and Biophysics [*Italy*]
IIGF	Imperial Iranian Ground Forces
IIGR	Ipsilateral Instinctive Grasp Reaction [*Medicine*] (DMAA)
IIGS	Initial Image Generating Subsystem [*ERTS*] (MCD)
IIH	Isoimmune Hydrops [*Medicine*]
IIHA	Intercollegiate Ice Hockey Association [*Later, ECHA*] (EA)
IIHD	Institute for International Health and Development (EA)
IIHF	International Ice Hockey Federation
IIHHT	International Institute of Health and Holistic Therapies [*British*]
IIHL	International Institute for Home Literature [*See also MIKK*] [*Belgrade, Yugoslavia*] (EAIO)
IIHL	International Institute of Humanitarian Law [*See also IIDH*] [*San Remo, Italy*] (EAIO)
IIHR	Institute for International Human Resources (NTPA)
IIHR	Inter-American Institute of Human Rights [*See also IIDS*] [*San Jose, Costa Rica*] (EAIO)
IIHR	International Institute of Human Rights (EA)
IIHR	Iowa Institute of Hydraulic Research [*University of Iowa*] [*Research center*] (MCD)
IIHS	Insurance Institute for Highway Safety (EA)
IIHSC	Inter-Industry Highway Safety Committee [*Later, DSMC*] (EA)
III	Idealist International, Inc. (EA)
III	Illinois, Indiana, Iowa (IIA)
III	Illumination Industries, Inc.
III	Incapacity, Illness, or Injury [*Environmental science*] (COE)
III	Indiana Central University, Indianapolis, IN [*OCLC symbol*] (OCLC)
III	Information Intelligence, Inc. [*Information service or system*] (IID)
III	Information International, Inc. [*Phoenix, AZ*] [*Information broker*] (MCD)
III	Innovative Interfaces, Inc. [*Information service or system*] (IID)
III	Insteel Industries [*NYSE symbol*] (SAG)
III	Insteel Industries Inc. [*NYSE symbol*] (TTSB)
III	Institute for Information Industry [*Information service or system*] (IID)
III	Institute of the Ironworking Industry (EA)
III	Insurance Information Institute [*New York, NY*] (EA)
III	Inter-American Indian Institute [*OAS*]
III	International Industrial Information Ltd. [*Information service or system*] (IID)
III	International Institute of Interpreters [*United Nations*] (BARN)
III	International Insurance Intelligence
III	International Intertrade Index [*No longer available online*] [*Information service or system*] (IID)
III	Interstate Identification Index [*NCIC*]
III	Investors in Industry [*British*]
III	Sturgeon Bay, WI [*Location identifier FAA*] (FAAL)
iii	Ter in Die [*Three Times a Day*] [*Symbol*] [*Pharmacology*] (DAVI)
IIIA	International Investment Insurance Agency [*Of IBRID*] (EBF)
III Bar	III Baruch [*Pseudepigrapha*] (BJA)
IIIC	International Irrigation Information Center (IID)
IIIC (LN)	International Institute of Intellectual Cooperation of the League of Nations [*Obsolete*]
IIIHS	International Institute of Integral Human Sciences [*See also IISHI*] (EAIO)
IIII	Innotech Inc. [*NASDAQ symbol*] (TTSB)
IIIL	International Institute of Iberoamerican Literature (EA)
IIIL	Isoplanar Integrated Injection Logic (MCD)
IIIMB	International Institute of Investment and Merchant Banking [*Washington, DC*] (EA)
IIIP	Institute for International Information Programs [*University of Maryland*] (NITA)
IIIR	Integrated Instructional Information Resource [*Educational Products Information Exchange Institute*] [*Information service or system*] (CRD)
IIIS	Interim International Information Service [*World War II*]
IIIT	International Institute of Instructional Technology [*British*]
IIIT	International Institute of Islamic Thought (EA)
IIIVC	Infrahepatic Interruption of the Inferior Vena Cava [*Medicine*] (AAMN)
IIJ	Internet Initiative Japan
IIJM	Institut International Jacques Maritain [*International Jacques Maritain Institute - IJMI*] (EAIO)
IIK	Imagery Interpretation Key
IIK	Kipnuk, AK [*Location identifier FAA*] (FAAL)
IIL	India International Airways (P) Ltd. [*ICAO designator*] (FAAC)
IIL	Indianapolis Law Catalog Consortium, Indiana University School of Law Library, Indianapolis, IN [*OCLC symbol*] (OCLC)
IIL	Induction Ion LASER
IIL	Institute of Industrial Launderers (EA)
IIL	Institute of International Law [*Geneva, Switzerland*] (EA)
IIL	Integrated Injection Logic [*Microprocessing*] (BUR)
IIL	Invert Indicator of the Left Half (IAA)
IILA	Institute for the Integration of Latin America
IILA	Instituto Italo Latino Americano [*Italo-Latin American Institute*] (EAIO)
IILA	Istituto Italo-Latino-Americano [*Italian-Latin American Institute*] [*Rome, Italy*]
IiLc	Identity Incorrect, Location Correct [*Psychology*]
IILE	Ion-Induced Light Emission (MCD)
IILFSC	International Institute of Law of the French Speaking Countries [*See also IDEF*] [*Paris, France*] (EAIO)
IiLi	Identity Incorrect, Location Incorrect [*Psychology*]
IILI	Instituto Internacional de Literatura Iberoamericana [*International Institute of Iberoamerican Literature*]
IILP	Index to Indian Legal Periodicals [*A publication*] (DLA)
IILP	Institute of International Licensing Practitioners (EAIO)
IILP	International Institute for Lath and Plaster (EA)
IILR	Institute of International Labor Research (EA)
IILS	International Institute for Labor Studies [*Switzerland*]
IILS	International Institute for Ligurian Studies (EA)
IIM	Children's Museum of Indianapolis, Indianapolis, IN [*OCLC symbol*] (OCLC)
IIM	Individual Indian Money
IIM	Institute for Information Management (EA)
IIM	Institut International des Meteorologists [*International Institute of Forecasters*] (EAIO)
IIM	Institut International du Manganese [*International Insitute of Manganese*] [*France*] (EAIO)
IIM	Institution of Industrial Managers [*British*]
IIM	Interagency Intelligence Memorandum (MCD)
IIM	InterCapital Ins Muni Income [*NYSE symbol*] (TTSB)
IIM	InterCapital Insurance Municipal Income Fund [*NYSE symbol*] (SPSG)
IIM	International Investment Monitor [*Global Analysis Systems*] [*Information service or system*] (CRD)
IIM	Inventory in Motion
IIM	Item Intelligence Maintenance [*DoD*]
IIMA	Insurance Industry Meetings Association [*St. Louis, MO*] (EA)
IIMC	International Industrial Marketing Club [*Formerly, MMEC*] [*Defunct*] (EA)
IIMC	International Institute of Maritime Culture (EA)
IIMC	International Institute of Municipal Clerks (EA)
IIME	Institute of International Medical Education
IIMI	International Irrigation Management Institute [*Sri Lanka*] [*Research center*] (IRC)
I-IMP	I-Labeled Iodoamphetamine
IIMS	Intensive Item Management System (AABC)
IIMS	Ion Implantation Manufacturing System
IIMT	International Institute for the Management of Technology [*Defunct*] (EA)

IIN.............. IBM [*International Business Machines Corp.*] Information Network (HGAA)

IIN.............. Instituto Interamericano del Nino [*Inter-American Children's Institute*] [*Uruguay*] (EA)

IIN.............. INX Insearch Group of Companies Ltd. [*Vancouver Stock Exchange symbol*]

IIN.............. Item Identification Number (AFM)

IIN.............. ITT Industries [*NYSE symbol*] (TTSB)

IIN.............. ITT Industries, Inc. Indiana [*NYSE symbol*] (SAG)

IINA........... International Islamic News Agency [*Jeddah, Saudi Arabia*] (EAIO)

IiNaU......... University of Nagpur, Nagpur, India [*Library symbol Library of Congress*] (LCLS)

IINC .... International Institute of Novel Computing [*Japan*]

I Inf Sc ...... Institute of Information Scientists [*British*] (DLA)

IiNI............. Indian National Scientific Documentation Center, Hillside Road, New Delhi, India [*Library symbol*] [*Library of Congress*] (LCLS)

IiNI............. Indian National Scientific Documentation Centre, New Delhi, India [*Library symbol Library of Congress*]

IiNN .... Nehru Memorial Museum and Library, New Delhi, India [*Library symbol Library of Congress*] (LCLS)

IINREN........ Interagency Interim National Research and Education Network (TNIG)

IINS .... Image Intensifier Night Sight

I/Ins .... Inactive Insurance (DLA)

IINS .... Incoherent Inelastic Neutron Scattering [*Physics*]

IINS .... Inelastic Incoherent Neutron Scattering [*Spectrometry*]

IINS .... Integrated Inertial Navigation System (MCD)

IINSE .... International Institute of Nuclear Science and Engineering

IINT .... Information International, Inc. [*NASDAQ symbol*] (NQ)

IINTE.......... Instytut Informacji Naukowej, Technicznej, i Ekonomicznej [*Institute of Scientific, Technical, and Economic Information*] [*Information service or system*] (IID)

IIO............. Image Intensifier Orthicon

IIO............. Information Item Only

IIO............. Institute for International Order [*Later, IWO*]

IIO............. Inter-Allied Insurance Organization [*NATO*] (NATG)

IIOC .... Intelligent Input Output Channel (NITA)

IIODRFES.... International Information Office of the Democratic Revolutionary Front of El Salvador [*See also OIIFDRES*] [*San Jose, Costa Rica*] (EAIO)

IIOE........... International Indian Ocean Expedition [*Navy*]

IIOIC .... International Intra-Ocular Implant Club (EAIO)

IIOP .... Integrated Input/Output Processor

IIOP .... Intelligent Input/Output Processor [*Disk Controller*]

IIOP .... Internet Interface Operating Procedures (TELE)

IIOP .... Internet Inter-Object Request Broker Protocol [*Computer science*] (IGQR)

IIOP .... Internet Inter-ORG [*Object Request Broker*] Protocol [*Computer science*]

IIP.............. El Pinto [*Mexico*] [*Seismograph station code, US Geological Survey*] (SEIS)

IIP.............. Idiopathic Interstitial Pneumonia [*Medicine*] (STED)

IIP.............. Idiopathic Intestinal Pseudo-Obstruction [*Medicine*] (STED)

IIP.............. Immediate Impact Point (SAA)

IIP.............. Implantable Insulin Pump

IIP.............. Implementation/Installation Plan [*Telecommunications*] (TEL)

IIP.............. Inadvertent Ignition Panel

IIP.............. Increasing Intracranial Pressure [*Medicine*]

IIP.............. Index of Industrial Production

IIP.............. Individual Implementation Plan [*For the education of a handicapped person*]

IIP.............. Industrial Incentive Plan [*NAVFAC*] (DNAB)

IIP.............. Initial Issue Provisioning [*Marine Corps*] (DOMA)

IIP.............. Inorganic Insulative Plastic

IIP.............. Instantaneous Impact Points (KSC)

IIP.............. Instantaneous Impact Predictor

IIP.............. Institute of Incorporated Photographers [*British*]

IIP.............. Institut International de la Potasse [*International Potash Institute*] (EAIO)

IIP.............. Institut International de la Presse [*International Press Institute*]

IIP.............. Institut International de Philosophie [*International Institute of Philosophy*] (EAIO)

IIP.............. Interceptor Improvement Program

IIP.............. Intergovernmental Informatics Programme [*UNESCO*]

IIP.............. Interim Impact Predictor (AAG)

IIP.............. International Ice Patrol [*Coast Guard*]

IIP.............. International Institute for Peace [*Vienna, Austria*] (EA)

IIP.............. International Institute of Philosophy (AEBS)

IIP.............. International Inter-Visitation Program in Educational Administration [*UniverstiyCouncil for Educational Administration*] (AEE)

IIP.............. Irish Independence Party [*Political party*] (PPW)

IIPA............ Institute of Incorporated Practitioners in Advertising [*British*] (BI)

IIPA............ International Icelandic Pony Association (EA)

IIPA............ International Index to the Performing Arts [*Website*]

IIPA............ International Intellectual Property Association (EA)

IIPACS .... Integrated Information Presentation and Control System [*Aviation*]

IIPC............ Image Intensifier Plumbicon Camera

IIPE............ Institut International de Planification de l'Education [*International Institute for Educational Planning*]

IIPEC.......... Institute for Interconnecting and Packaging Electronic Circuits (EA)

IIPER .... International Institute for Production Engineering Research (EAIO)

IIPF............ International Institute of Public Finance [*Saarbrucken, Federal Republic of Germany*] (EAIO)

IIPG .... International Institute of Practical Geomancy [*Formerly, Society for Symbolic Studies*] (EA)

IIPL............ Independent Investor Protective League (EA)

IIPM........... Irish International Peace Movement (EAIO)

IIPO .... Illinois Inventory of Parent Opinion

IIPP .... International Institute for Promotion and Prestige [*Geneva, Switzerland*] (EAIO)

IIPR .... Installation Inspection Procedure Report

IIPR .... Istituto Internazionale di Psicologia della Reliosita' [*International Institute for the Psychology of Religion*] [*Italy*] (IRC)

IIPS .... Instantaneous Impact Prediction System (DNAB)

IIPS .... Interactive Instructional Presentation System [*IBM*] (NITA)

IIQ............. Initial Issue Quantities [*Military*]

IIR............. Image Interpreter Response

IIR............. Imaging Infrared [*Air Force*] (MCD)

IIR............. Infinite-Duration Impulse-Response (IEEE)

IIR............. Infinite Impulse Response [*Electronics*]

IIR............. Institute of Industrial Relations [*Loyola University of Chicago*] [*Research center*] (RCD)

IIR............. Institute of Intermodal Repairers (EA)

IIR............. Institut International du Froid [*International Institute of Refrigeration*] [*France*] (EA)

IIR............. Integrated Instrumentation RADAR

IIR............. Intelligence Information Report (NVT)

IIR............. Intercom Information Resources, Inc. [*Information service or system*] (IID)

IIR............. Intermediate Infrared

IIR............. International Impala Resources [*Vancouver Stock Exchange symbol*]

IIR............. International Institute for Robotics (EA)

IIR............. International Institute of Rehabilitation [*Defunct*] (EA)

IIR............. International Inventors Registry (NITA)

IIR............. Inventory and Inspection Report [*Army*] (MUGU)

IIR............. Invert Indicator of the Right Half (SAA)

IIR............. Isobutene-Isoprene Rubber

IIRA .... Integrated Inertial Reference Assembly (PDAA)

IIRA .... International Ice Racing Association

IIRA .... International Industrial Relations Association [*Geneva, Switzerland*] (EA)

IIRB .... Institut International de Recherches Betteravieres [*International Institute for Sugar Beet Research*] [*Brussels, Belgium*] (EA)

IIRC .... Inactive Item Review Card [*Military*] (AFIT)

IIRC .... Incident Investigation Review Committee [*Nuclear Regulatory Commission*] (NRCH)

IIRC .... Indiana Interstate Railroad Co., Inc. [*AAR code*]

IIRC .... Interrogation and Information Reception Circuit [*Telecommunications*] (OA)

IIRD .... International Interdependent Research and Development (AABC)

IIRE .... International Institute for Resource Economics [*Defunct*] (EA)

IIRF............ Intergalactic Infrared Radiation Field

IIRG .... Institut International de Recherches Graphologiques

IIRM........... Improved Infrared Missile

IIRM........... Irish Immigration Reform Movement (EA)

IIRMP .... Interim Indoor Radon Measurement Protocol [*Environmental science*] (COE)

IIRMS .... Industrial Information's Record Management System [*Computer science*]

IIRP .... Integrated Installation Requirement Plan (MCD)

IIRR .... Institute of Industrial Race Relations

IIRR .... International Institute of Rural Reconstruction (EA)

IIRS .... Institute of Industrial Research and Standards [*Ireland*] [*Research center Database producer*] (IID)

IIRS .... Instrumentation Inertial Reference Set [*Aviation*]

IIRV .... Improved Inter-Range Vector (MCD)

IIS.............. IBM [*International Business Machines Corp.*] Information Services (HGAA)

IIS.............. IIS Intelligent Information Systems [*Associated Press*] (SAG)

IIS.............. Image Intensified System

IIS.............. Imagery Interpretation System (MCD)

IIS.............. Improved Infrared Source

IIS.............. INA Investment Sec [*NYSE symbol*] (TTSB)

IIS.............. INA Investment Securities, Inc. [*NYSE symbol*] (SPSG)

IIS.............. Indexation Information Statement [*Accounting*]

IIS.............. Index to International Statistics [*A publication*]

IIS.............. Indirect Identification System [*Military*] (MCD)

IIS.............. Industrial Information Services [*Southern Methodist University*] [*Dallas, TX*]

IIS.............. Inflationary Impact Statement [*Economics*]

IIS.............. Infrared Imaging System

IIS.............. Infrared Instrumentation System

IIS.............. Inmate Information System [*Bureau of Prisons*] (GFGA)

IIS.............. Inspection Instruction Sheet

IIS.............. Inspection Item Sheet (MCD)

iis.............. Inspection Item Sheet (NAKS)

IIS.............. Inspections and Investigations Staff [*Vietnam*]

IIS.............. Institute for Information Studies [*Inactive*] [*Research center*] (RCD)

IIS.............. Institute for Intercultural Studies (EA)

IIS.............. Institute of Informatics Systems [*Russia*] (DDC)

IIS.............. Institute of Information Scientists [*British*] (EAIO)

IIS.............. Institute of International Studies (EA)

IIS.............. Institut International de la Soudure [*International Institute of Welding - IIW*] (EAIO)

IIS.............. Institut International de Statistique [*International Statistical Institute*]

IIS.............. Integrated Information System

IIS.............. Integrated Instrument Sheet (MCD)

IIS.............. Integrated Instruments System

IIS.............. Integrated Insulation System

IIS.............. Intelligence Information System [*Military*] (DNAB)

IIS............... Intensive Immunosuppression [*Medicine*] (DMAA)
IIS............... Interactive Instructional System [*IBM Corp.*]
IIS............... Intermittent Infusion Sets (STED)
IIS............... Internationales Institut der Sparkassen [*International Savings Banks Institute*]
IIS............... International Information Service Ltd. [*Information service or system*] (IID)
IIS............... International Institute of Seismology and Earthquake Engineering [*Japan*] [*Seismograph station code, US Geological Survey*] (SEIS)
IIS............... International Institute of Sociology
IIS............... International Institute of Stress (EA)
IIS............... International Institutional Services (EA)
IIS............... International Insurance Seminars [*University, AL*] (EA)
IIS............... International Insurance Society (EAIO)
IIS............... International Isotope Society (EA)
IIS............... International Medical Imagery [*Vancouver Stock Exchange symbol*]
IIS............... Internet Information Server [*Computer science*] (PCM)
IIS............... Invert Indicator From Storage (SAA)
IIS............... Investment Income Surcharge [*Finance*] (MHDW)
IIS............... Ion Implantation Study
IIS............... Irish Institute of Secretaries Ltd. (BI)
IIS............... Nissan Island [*Papua New Guinea*] [*Airport symbol*] (OAG)
IISA............. Institut International des Sciences Administratives [*International Institute for Administrative Sciences*]
IISA............. Integrated Inertial Sensor Assembly (MCD)
IISA............. Interservice/Interagency Support Agreement (MCD)
IISBR........... International Institute for Sugar Beet Research (EA)
IISD............ If Incorrect Service Direct (FAAC)
IISD............ International Institute for the Study of Death (EA)
IISDI........... International Institute for the Study of Death and Immortality [*Later, IISD*] (EA)
IISE............ International Institute of Social Economics [*Hull, England*] (EAIO)
IISG............ Internationaal Instituut voor Sociale Geschiedenis [*International Institute for Social History*] (EA)
IISHI........... Institut International des Sciences Humaines Integrales [*International Institute of Integral Human Sciences - IIIHS*] (EAIO)
IISI............. International Iron and Steel Institute [*Brussels, Belgium*] [*Research center*] (EA)
IISJ............. Institute for Independent Social Journalism (EA)
IISL............ IIS [*Intelligent Information Systems*] Ltd. [*NASDAQ symbol*]
IISL............ International Institute of Space Law [*Baarn, Netherlands*] (EAIO)
IISL............ Istituto Internazionale di Studi Liguri [*International Institute for Ligurian Studies*]
IISLF.......... I.I.S. Intellig't Info [*NASDAQ symbol*] (TTSB)
IISP............ Improved Industrial Standard Process (MCD)
IISP............ Information Infrastructure Standards Panel (ITD)
IISP............ Interim Interswitch Signaling Protocol [*Telecommunications*] (ACRL)
IISP............ International Institute of Site Planning (EA)
IISPA.......... Interactive Instructional Systems-Presentation and Authoring Special Interest Group [*Association for the Development of Computer-Based Instructional Systems*] (EDAC)
IISRP.......... International Institute of Synthetic Rubber Producers (EA)
IISS............ Integrated Information Support System [*Computer science*]
IISS............ Intelligence Information Subsystem [*Military*] (MCD)
IISS............ International Institute for Strategic Studies (EA)
IISS............ International Institute for the Science of Sintering [*Belgrade, Yugoslavia*] (EAIO)
IISSM.......... Istituto Internazionale Suore di Santa Marcellina [*Milan, Italy*] (EAIO)
IIST............ Institute for Information Storage Technology [*University of Santa Clara*] [*Research center*] (RCD)
IIST............ Intense Islet Stimulation Test [*Endocrinology*]
IIST............ International Institute for Safety in Transportation [*Formerly, IST*] (EA)
IIST............ International Institute of Sports Therapy [*British*]
IISWM......... Institute of Iron and Steel Wire Manufacturers (MHDB)
IIT............... Illinois Institute of Technology (IID)
IIT............... Image Intensifier Tube
IIT............... Inclinable Indexing Table
IIT............... Indian Institute of Technology
IIT............... Individual Inclusive Tour [*Air fare plan*]
IIT............... Indonesian Satellite Corp. [*NYSE symbol*] (SAG)
IIT............... Industrial Information Transfer (NITA)
IIT............... Ineffective Iron Turnover (DMAA)
IIT............... Institut des Ingenieurs des Transports [*Institute of Transportation Engineers*] [*Canada*]
IIT............... Institut Interafricain du Travail
IIT............... Institut International du Theatre [*International Theatre Institute - ITI*] (EAIO)
IIT............... Integrated Information Transport (ACRL)
IIT............... Integrated Isometric Tension (STED)
IIT............... International Investment Trust
IIT............... Intra-Industry Trade
IIT............... Islet-Infiltrating T
IIT............... Israel Institute of Technology (KSC)
IIT............... Perusahaan PT IndoSatADS [*NYSE symbol*] (TTSB)
IITA............. Information Infrastructure Technology Applications [*Marine science*] (OSRA)
IITA............. Inland International Trade Association [*Sacramento, CA*] (EA)
IITA............. International Institute of Tropical Agriculture [*Ibadan, Nigeria*] [*Research center*] (EA)
IITC............. IITC Holdings Ltd. [*NASDAQ symbol*] (SAG)
IITC............. Insurance Industry Training Council (PDAA)
IITC............. Intera Information Technologies Corp. [*NASDAQ symbol*] (SAG)
IITC............. International Indian Treaty Council (EA)

IITCF........... IITC Holdings [*NASDAQ symbol*] (TTSB)
IITCHId........ IITC Holdings Ltd. [*Associated Press*] (SAG)
IITCS........... Igloo Internal Thermal Control Section [*Aerospace*] (MCD)
IITD............. Institute of International Trade and Development (EA)
IITE............. Information Infrastructure Task Force [*Marine science*] (OSRA)
I/ITEC......... Interservice/Industry Training Equipment Conference [*Military*]
IITF............. In-Core Instrument Test Facility [*Nuclear energy*] (IAA)
IITF............. Information Infrastructure Task Force (USDC)
IITI............. International Information Technology Institute (CIST)
IITM............ International Institute for Traditional Music [*Germany*] (EAIO)
IITPW.......... Inertial Interchange True Polar Wander [*Geophysics*]
IIT RES IN ... Illinois Institute of Technology Research Institute (MCD)
IITRI........... Illinois Institute of Technology Research Institute [*Information service or system*] (IID)
IITS............ Igniter Initiator Test Set
IITS............ Intratheater Imagery Transmission System [*Air Force*]
I/ITSC......... Interservice/Industry Training Systems Conference [*Military*]
IITT-IITW ... Institut International du Travail Temporaire - International Institute for Temporary Work (EAIO)
IITV............. Image-Intensified Television (MCD)
IITYWYBMAD... If I Tell You, Will You Buy Me a Drink [*Tavern sign*]
IIU............... Input Interface Unit [*Computer science*]
IIU............... Instruction Input Unit
IIV............... Image Intensifier Viewer
IIV............... International Institute of Valuers (EA)
IIVD............ Image Intensifier Viewing Device
IIVI............. II-VI, Inc. [*NASDAQ symbol*] (NQ)
IIVI 0-7 .... International Institute for Visually Impaired, Zero-7 (EA)
IIVS............ Intransit Item Visibility System (MCD)
IIVT............. Intensive Intravenous Treatment [*Medicine*]
IIVW........... Internationales Institut fuer Verwaltungswissenschaften [*International Institute of Administrative Sciences*]
IIW............. International Institute of Welding [*See also IIS*] [*British*] (EAIO)
IIWG........... International Industry Working Group [*of the Air Transport Association of America*] (EA)
IIWI............ Interior Insulating Window Institute [*Defunct*] (EA)
IIWP............ Institute for Individual and World Peace (EA)
IIWPA........... International Information/Word Processing Association [*Formerly, IWPA*] [*Later, IWP*] (EA)
IIWPL.......... International Institute for Women's Political Leadership [*Defunct*] (EA)
IIWS............ Intersystems Inc. Wrrt [*AMEX symbol*] (TTSB)
IIYA............ Institute for International Youth Affairs
IJ................ Ilejejunal [*Gastroenterology*] (DAVI)
IJ................ Ileojejunal (STED)
IJ................ Im Jahre [*In the Year*] [*German*]
IJ................ Indian Jurist, Old Series [*A publication*] (DLA)
IJ................ Indirect to Job Costs (DGA)
IJ................ Institute of Journalists [*British*] (NTCM)
IJ................ Instructor's Journal [*Air Force*]
IJ................ Internal Jugular [*Anatomy*]
IJ................ Internal Junctor [*Electronics*] (IAA)
IJ................ Intrajejunal (STED)
IJ................ Jacksonville Public Library, Jacksonville, IL [*Library symbol Library of Congress*] (LCLS)
IJ................ Sisters of the Holy Infant Jesus [*Roman Catholic religious order*]
IJ................ Sisters of the Infant Jesus (TOCD)
IJ................ Touraine Air Transport [*ICAO designator*] (AD)
IJA............. Imperial Japanese Army [*World War II*]
IJA............. Institute of Jewish Affairs (EA)
IJA............. Institute of Judicial Administration (EA)
IJA............. International Jugglers Association (EA)
IJA............. Inventory of Job Attitudes [*LIMRA*]
IJA............. Irving Independent School District, Irving, TX [*OCLC symbol*] (OCLC)
IJA............. Islamic Jurisprudence Academy [*See also IFA*] (EAIO)
IJAB .... Internationaler Jugendaustausch und Besucherdienst der Bundesrepublik Deutschland [*International Youth Exchange and Visitor Service of the Federal Republic of Germany*]
IJAHS.......... International Journal of African Historical Studies [*A publication*]
IJAJ............ Intentional Jitter Antijam [*Military*]
IJB............. Internationale Jugendbibliothek [*International Youth Library - IYL*] [*Munich, Federal Republic of Germany*] (EAIO)
IJB............. Interstate Job Bank
IJBBA.......... International Junior Brangus Breeders Association (EA)
IJBF............ International Jacques Brel Foundation (EA)
IJBS............ Integrated Joint Broadband System [*Army*] (AABC)
IJC............. Interjob Communications (MHDB)
IJC............. International Joint Commission (EA)
IJC............. Irvine's Justiciary Cases [*England*] [*A publication*] (DLA)
IJC............. Irving Public Library System, Irving, TX [*OCLC symbol*] (OCLC)
IJC............. Itasca Junior College [*Later, Itasca Community College*] [*Minnesota*]
IJC............. Itawamba Junior College [*Fulton, MS*]
IJCAA.......... Iowa Junior College Athletic Association (PSS)
IJCAI.......... International Joint Conference on Artificial Intelligence
IJ Cas .... Irvine's Justiciary Cases [*England*] [*A publication*] (DLA)
IJCIC.......... International Jewish Committee on Interreligious Consultations (EA)
IJCNN .... International Joint Conference on Neural Networks
IJCR........... Institute for Jewish-Christian Relations (EA)
IJCS........... Integrated Joint Communication System [*Military*] (AABC)
IJCS-PAC .... Integrated Joint Communication System - Pacific [*Military*] (AABC)
IJD............. Inflammatory Joint Disease [*Medicine*] (DMAA)
IJD............. Institutum Judaicum Delitzschianum (BJA)
IJDA........... International Joseph Diseases Association (EA)
IJDF........... International Joseph Diseases Foundation (EA)
IJDW.......... Im Jahre der Welt [*In the Year of the World*] [*German*]

IJE	Avijet SA de CV [*Mexico ICAO designator*] (FAAC)
IJE	Institute of Jewish Education [*British*] (DBA)
IJE	Inverse Joule Effect
IJe	Jerseyville Free Library, Jerseyville, IL [*Library symbol Library of Congress*] (LCLS)
IJeH	Jersey Community Hospital, Jerseyville, IL [*Library symbol Library of Congress*] (LCLS)
IJeSD	Jersey Community Unit, School District 100, Jerseyville, IL [*Library symbol Library of Congress*] (LCLS)
IJF	Internationale Judo Foederation [*International Judo Federation*] [*Germany*] (EA)
IJF	International Jazz Federation (EA)
IJF	Robinson Crusoe Island [*Juan Fernandez Archipelago*] [*Seismograph station code, US Geological Survey*] (SEIS)
IJFRS	Irish Joint Fiction Reserve Scheme (AIE)
IJI	Illegal Jewish Immigrant [*British occupation of Palestine, 1945-48*] (DI)
IJI	Illinois College, Jacksonville, IL [*Library symbol Library of Congress*] (LCLS)
IJI	Internationaal Juridisch Instituut [*International Juridical Institute*] [*BENELUX*]
IJI	Islamic Jamhoori Ittedad [*Islamic Democratic Alliance*] [*Pakistan*] [*Political party*]
IJIN	International Jensen, Inc. [*NASDAQ symbol*] (SAG)
IJIN	IntlJensen [*NASDAQ symbol*] (TTSB)
IJIR	International Journal of Impotence Research [*A publication*]
IJIR	International Journal of Intercultural Relations [*A publication*] (DHP)
IJJU	Intentional Jitter Jamming Unit [*Military*]
IJK	Internationale Juristen-Kommission [*International Commission of Jurists*]
IJL	Institute of Jewish Life Media Project [*Later, JMS*]
IJL	International Journal of Leprosy [*A publication*]
IJL	Interstate/Johnson Lane [*NYSE symbol*] (TTSB)
IJL	Interstate Johnson Lane, Inc. [*NYSE symbol*] (SAG)
IJLB	International Jewish Labor Bund (EA)
IJMA	Infant and Juvenile Manufacturers Association (EA)
IJMA	International Jewish Media Association (NTPA)
IJMac	MacMurray College, Jacksonville, IL [*Library symbol Library of Congress*] (LCLS)
IJMI	International Jacques Maritain Institute [*See also IIJM*] (EAIO)
IJMS	Interim JTIDS [*Joint Tactical Information Distribution System*] Message Standard
IJMVT	International Journal of Micrographics and Video Technology [*A publication*]
IJN	Imperial Japanese Navy [*World War II*]
IJN	International Justice Network [*Defunct*] (EA)
IJO	Independent Jewelers Organization (EA)
IJO	Individual Job Order
IJO	International Journal of Osteoarchaeology [*A publication*]
IJO	International Juridical Organization [*Later, IJOED*] (EAIO)
IJO	Inventory of Job Openings [*State Employee Security Agency*] (OICC)
IJOA	International Juvenile Officers' Association (EA)
IJOED	International Juridical Organization for Environment and Development (EAIO)
IJol	Joliet Public Library, Joliet, IL [*Library symbol Library of Congress*] (LCLS)
IJolStF	College of Saint Francis, Joliet, IL [*Library symbol Library of Congress*] (LCLS)
IJP	Idiopathic Juvenile Periodontitis [*Dentistry*] (PDAA)
IJP	Inhibitory Junction Potential [*Neurophysiology*]
IJP	Ink Jet Printing
IJP	Internal Job Processing (IAA)
IJP	Internal Jugular Pressure [*Medicine*] (MAE)
IJP	International Juvenile Publications
IJP	Israel Jewish Press (BJA)
IJPA	International Jelly and Preserve Association (EA)
IJPPR	Institute for Jewish Policy Planning and Research [*Defunct*] (EA)
IJPSMHI	Industrial Jacks Product Section of the Material Handling Institute [*Defunct*] (EA)
IJR	Institute for Justice Research [*American University*] [*Research center*] (RCD)
IJR	Institute for Juvenile Research [*Illinois Department of Mental Health-University of Illinois at Chicago*] [*Research center*] (RCD)
IJRCS	International Joint Rules Committee on Softball [*Later, ASA*] (EA)
IJS	Institute of Jazz Studies [*Rutgers University, University of New Jersey*] [*Research center*] (EA)
IJS	Interactive Job Submission [*Computer science*]
IJS	Interrupt Jet Sensor
IJS	Rutgers-[*The*] State University, Institute of Jazz Studies, Newark, NJ [*OCLC symbol*] (OCLC)
IJS	Silvair, Inc. [*ICAO designator*] (FAAC)
IJSB	International Journal of Systematic Bacteriology [*A publication*] (EES)
IJSBA	International Jet Ski Boating Association (EA)
IJSHOF	International Jewish Sports Hall of Fame
IJSS	International John Steinbeck Society (EA)
IJT	Interflight (Learjet) Ltd. [*British ICAO designator*] (FAAC)
IJU	Ijui [*Brazil*] [*Airport symbol*] (OAG)
IJV	Internal Jugular Vein [*Medicine*] (DMAA)
IJV	Jeffersonville Township Public Library, Jeffersonville, IN [*OCLC symbol*] (OCLC)
IJWU	International Jewelry Workers Union [*Later, Service Employees International Union*] (EA)
IJX	Jacksonville, IL [*Location identifier FAA*] (FAAL)
IJZ	Summersville, WV [*Location identifier FAA*] (FAAL)
IK	Eureka Aero Industries [*ICAO designator*] (AD)

IK	Ihud ha-Kibbutsim (BJA)
IK	Imitation Kraft [*Paper*] (DGA)
IK	Immobilized Knee [*Orthopedics*]
IK	Immunekoerper [*Immune Bodies*] [*Medicine*]
IK	Immunoconglutinin (MAE)
IK	Indicator Kit
IK	Infanteriekolonne [*Infantry Supply Column*] [*German military - World War II*]
IK	Infusoria Killing [*Unit*] [*Medicine*]
IK	Inner Keel
I/K	Inspector/Killer
IK	Interbank (ADA)
IK	Intercollegiate Knights [*An association*] (EA)
IK	Interkinase Domain [*Genetics*]
IK	Interlake Corp. [*NYSE symbol*] (TTSB)
IK	Interstitial Keratitis [*Ophthalmology*]
IK	Inverse Kinematics [*Computer science*]
IKA	International Kitefliers Association [*Defunct*] (EA)
IKampR	Kampsville Reading Center, Kampsville, IL [*Library symbol Library of Congress*] (LCLS)
IKan	Kansas Community Memorial Library, Kansas, IL [*Library symbol Library of Congress*] (LCLS)
IKanSD	Kansas Community Unit School District, Kansas, IL [*Library symbol*] [*Library of Congress*] (LCLS)
IKAR	Internationale Kommission fuer Alpines Rettungswesen [*International Commission for Alpine Rescue*] [*Birchwil, Switzerland*] (EAIO)
IKAT	Interactive Keyboard and Terminal [*Computer science*] (MCD)
IKB	Internationale Kommunistenbond [*International Communist League*] [*Netherlands*] (PPW)
IKB	International Klein Blue [*Color named after French painter Yves Klein*]
IKB	Wilkesboro, NC [*Location identifier FAA*] (FAAL)
IKBD	Intelligent Keyboard Device
IKBM	Integrated Knowledge Based Modelling (NITA)
IKBS	Intelligent Knowledge-Based System [*Artificial intelligence*]
IKC	In-Kind Contribution (COE)
IKC	Interkernal Communication (NITA)
IKC	International Kennel Club of Chicago (EA)
IKC	Kankakee Community College, Kankakee, IL [*Library symbol Library of Congress*] (LCLS)
ike	Iconoscope [*A television camera tube*] (WDMC)
IKE	Ion Kinetic Energy
IKe	Kewanee Public Library, Kewanee, IL [*Library symbol Library of Congress*] (LCLS)
IKEA	Ingvar Kamprad, Elmtaryd, Agunnaryd [*Initialism is company name derived from the names of its founder, the farm on which he grew up, and a Swedish village*]
IKeB	Black Hawk College, East Campus, Kewanee, IL [*Library symbol Library of Congress*] (LCLS)
IKEC	InterAction Media Corp. [*NASDAQ symbol*] (SAG)
IKECA	International Kitchen Exhaust Cleaning Association (NTPA)
IKEL	Internacia Komitato por Etnaj Liberecoj [*International Committee for Ethnic Liberty - ICEL*] [*Eschweiler, Federal Republic of Germany*] (EAIO)
IKES	Ion Kinetic Energy Spectrometry
IKET	Individual Knowledge Evaluation Test (AFM)
IKF	International Kart Federation (EA)
IKF	International Korfball Federation (EA)
IKF	International Kraft Federation (EA)
IKFC	International Knife and Fork Clubs (EA)
IKFS	International Kids Fashion Show (ITD)
IKG	Champaign Public Library, Champaign, IL [*OCLC symbol*] (OCLC)
IKG	Internationale Kommission fuer Glas [*International Commission on Glass*]
IKG	Israelitische Kultusgemeinde [*Vienna*] [*A publication*] (BJA)
IKH	Ihre Koenigliche Hoheit [*His (or Her) Royal Highness*] [*German*]
IKHS	International Kodak Historical Society (EA)
IKI	Iki [*Japan*] [*Airport symbol*] (OAG)
IKI	Institute of Space Research [*Former USSR Acronym is based on foreign phrase*]
IKIF	Individual Name and Address Key Index File [*IRS*]
IKIHS	I-Know-It's-Here-Somewhere [*Keyboarding technique*]
IKIM	Institute of Islamic Understanding [*Think-tank*] [*Malaysia*] (ECON)
IKJ	Ikusaka [*Japan*] [*Seismograph station code, US Geological Survey*] (SEIS)
IKJ	Internationales Kuratorium fuer das Jugendbuch [*International Board on Books for Young People*]
IKK	Kankakee, IL [*Location identifier FAA*] (FAAL)
IKL	Ikela [*Zaire*] [*Airport symbol*] (AD)
IKL	Isaenmaallinen Kansanliike [*Patriotic People's Movement*] [*Finland Political party*] (PPE)
IKM	In Kind Matching (OICC)
IKM	Institut Kimia Malaysia
IKM	Texas State Library and Historical Commission, Austin, TX [*OCLC symbol*] (OCLC)
IKMB	Internationale Katholische Mittelstandsbewegung [*International Catholic Union of the Middle Class*]
IKN	Delco Electronics Division, General Motors Corp., Technical Library, Kokomo, IN [*OCLC symbol*] (OCLC)
IKN	Internationale Kommission fuer Numismatik [*International Numismatic Commission*]
IKO	Nikolski [*Alaska*] [*Airport symbol*] (OAG)
IKON	Olivet Nazarene College, Kankakee, IL [*Library symbol Library of Congress*] (LCLS)
IKOR	Immediate Knowledge of Results

IKOS	IKOS Systems [*NASDAQ symbol*] (TTSB)
IKOS	Ikos Systems, Inc. [*NASDAQ symbol*] (SAG)
IKP	Indiai Kommunista Part [*Communist Party of India*] [*Political party*]
IKP	Indian Communist Party [*Political party*]
IKP	Indonesian Communist Party [*Political party*]
IKP	Inkopah [*California*] [*Seismograph station code, US Geological Survey*] (SEIS)
IKP	Instructor and Key Personnel
IKP	Irakskaia Kommunisticheskaia Partiia [*Iraqi Communist Party*] [*Political party*]
IKP	Iranian Communist Party [*Political party*]
IKP	Iraqi Communist Party [*Political party*]
IKP	Irish Communist Party [*Political party*]
IKP	Israeli Communist Party [*Political party*]
IKP	Italian Communist Party [*Political party*]
IKP	Kokomo Public Library, Kokomo, IN [*OCLC symbol*] (OCLC)
IKPO	Internationale Kriminalpolizeiliche Organisation [*International Criminal Police Organization*]
IKPT	Instructor and Key Personnel Training
IKR	Ikaros DK [*Denmark ICAO designator*] (FAAC)
IKRA	International Kirlian Research Association (EA)
IKRD	Inverse Kinetics Rod Drop [*Nuclear energy*] (NRCH)
IKRK	Internationales Komitee vom Roten Kreuz [*International Committee of the Red Cross*]
IKS	Imaging Kernel System [*Computer science*] (BTTJ)
IKS	Integrated Key Set [*Computer science*]
IKS	International Kodaly Society (EAIO)
IKS	International Kolping Society [*See also IKW*] [*Cologne, Federal Republic of Germany*] (EAIO)
IKS	Inverse Kinetics Simulator
IKSR	Internationale Kommission zum Schutze des Rheins Gegen Verunreinigung [*International Commission for the Protection of the Rhine Against Pollution - ICPRAP*] (EAIO)
IKT	Iakutaviatrans [*Russian Federation*] [*ICAO designator*] (FAAC)
IKT	Irkutsk [*Former USSR Airport symbol*] (OAG)
IKTS	International Klaus Tennstedt Society [*Defunct*] (EA)
IKU	Infusoria-Killing Unit (DB)
IKU	Interface Keying Unit [*Computer science*] (KSC)
IKUE	Internacia Katolika Unuigo Esperantista [*International Catholic Esperanto Association*] (EA)
IKV	Internationaler Krankenhausverbund [*International Hospital Federation*]
IKVSA	Internationale Katholische Vereinigung fuer Soziale Arbeit [*Catholic International Union for Social Service*]
IKW	Indicated Kilowatts per Hour [*Engine emissions testing*]
IKW	Internationales Kolpingwerk [*International Kolping Society - IKS*] [*Cologne, Federal Republic of Germany*] (EAIO)
IKX	Windsor Locks, CT [*Location identifier FAA*] (FAAL)
IL	Bomber [*Russian aircraft symbol*]
IL	Iceland [*IYRU nationality code*]
IL	Identification List
IL	Idle (BUR)
IL	Ileum (DB)
Il	Iliad [*of Homer*] [*Classical studies*] (OCD)
IL	Illinium (MAE)
IL	Illinois [*Postal code*]
IL	Illinois Supreme Court Reports [*A publication*] (DLA)
IL	Illite [*A mineral*]
IL	Illium [*Anatomy*] (IAA)
il	Illustrated [*or Illustrator*]
IL	Illustration
il	Ilmenite [*Also, ILM*] [*CIPW classification Geology*]
IL	Ilyushin [*Former USSR ICAO aircraft manufacturer identifier*] (ICAO)
IL	I'm Leavin' Elvis Photos, Exclusive (EA)
IL	Imperial Life Assurance Co. of Canada [*Toronto Stock Exchange symbol*]
I/L	Import License
IL	Incisolingual [*Dentistry*]
IL	Inclined Ladder (AAG)
IL	Including Loading
IL	Incoming Letter
IL	Indent Left [*Typography*] (DGA)
il	Indent Left (WDMC)
IL	Independent Living [*An association Defunct*] (EA)
IL	Index Linked [*Government bonds*] [*British*]
IL	Index Lists [*DoD*]
IL	Indicating Light
IL	Individualized Learning (OICC)
IL	Individual Line (IAA)
IL	Inertial Laboratory [*NASA*] (KSC)
IL	Information Labeling
IL	Injection Long Wheelbase [*Automotive engineering*]
IL	In Ladestreifen [*Loaded in Clips*] [*German military - World War II*]
I-L	In-Law
IL	In-Lock
IL	Insensible Weight Loss (MEDA)
IL	Insertion Loss
IL	Inside Layer [*Technical drawings*]
IL	Inside Left [*Soccer position*]
IL	Inside Leg (ADA)
IL	Inside Length [*Technical drawings*]
IL	Institute of Linguists [*British*] (BI)
IL	Instruction Leaflet (MSA)
IL	Instruction List
IL	Instructor-Lieutenant [*Navy British*]

IL	Instrumentation Laboratory (MCD)
IL	Instrument Landing (IAA)
IL	Insulation Level (IAA)
IL	Insulators [*JETDS nomenclature*] [*Military*] (CET)
IL	Intelligence Liaison [*Program*] [*Department of State*]
IL	Intensity Level [*Physics*] (IAA)
IL	Intereact Ltd. [*British*]
IL	Interior Length
IL	Interleukin [*Biochemistry*]
IL	Interline
IL	Intermediary Letter
IL	Intermediate Land (DNAB)
IL	Intermediate Language [*Computer science*] (BUR)
IL	Intermediate Level (MCD)
IL	Intermediate Loop
IL	International League [*Baseball*]
IL	International Library [*A publication*]
IL	International List
IL	International Logistics (AABC)
IL	Interpolated Learning [*Psychology*]
IL	Interpretive Language (PDAA)
il	Intralesional (DB)
IL	Intralipid [*Pharmacology*] (DAVI)
IL	Intraocular Lens [*Ophthalmology*] (DAVI)
IL	Irish Land Reports (Fitzgibbon) [*A publication*] (DLA)
IL	Island Air [*ICAO designator*] (AD)
IL	Israel [*ANSI two-letter standard code*] (CNC)
IL	Israel Lira (BJA)
IL	Italiana Luce (EFIS)
IL	Italian Lira [*Monetary unit*]
IL	Item List (AFIT)
IL	Ives Laboratories [*Research code symbol*]
IL	Ivy League (EA)
IL	L'Internationale Liberale
IL	Lisle Library District, Lisle, IL [*Library symbol Library of Congress*] (LCLS)
IL1	Interleukin I (LDT)
IL2	Interleukin II (LDT)
IL 2d	Illinois Supreme Court Reports, Second Series [*A publication*] (DLA)
ILA	Ilan [*Giran*] [*Republic of China*] [*Seismograph station code, US Geological Survey*] (SEIS)
ILA	Illaga [*Indonesia*] [*Airport symbol*] (OAG)
IL A	Illinois Appellate Court Reports [*A publication*] (DLA)
ILa	Incisolabial [*Dentistry*]
ILA	Independent Label Association (EA)
ILA	Indian Limitation Act [*British*] (ROG)
ILA	Informationsstelle Lateinamerika [*Germany*]
ILA	Injection Locked Amplifier (PDAA)
ILA	Institute of Landscape Architects [*British*]
ILA	Instruction Look-Ahead [*Unit*] [*Computer science*]
ILA	Instrument Landing Aid
ILA	Instrument Landing Approach
ILA	Instrument Low Approach [*Aircraft landing method*]
ILA	Insulin-Like Activity
ILA	Insurance Logistics Automated (PDAA)
ILA	Integrated Laboratory Automation
ILA	Intelligent Line Adapter
ILA	Intermediate Level Amplifier (MHDB)
ILA	International Language for Aviation
ILA	International Laundry Association
ILA	International Law Association [*British*] (EA)
ILA	International Leprosy Association [*India*]
ILA	International Listening Association (EA)
ILA	International Llama Association (EA)
ILA	International Longshoremen's Association (EA)
ILA	Internet Library Association (TELE)
ILA	Iterative Logic Array (MCD)
ILA	Lafayette School Corp., Lafayette, IN [*OCLC symbol*] (OCLC)
ILa	Lansing Public Library, Lansing, IL [*Library symbol Library of Congress*] (LCLS)
ILA	Williams, CA [*Location identifier FAA*] (FAAL)
IL A 2d	Illinois Appellate Court Reports, Second Series [*A publication*] (DLA)
IL A 3d	Illinois Appellate Court Reports, Third Series [*A publication*] (DLA)
ILAA	Independent Literary Agents Association (EA)
ILAA	International Lawyers in Alcoholics Anonymous (EA)
ILAA	International Legal Aid Association [*Defunct*]
ILAADS	Interim Low-Altitude Air Defense System
ILAAS	Integrated Light Attack Aircraft [*or Attack Avionics*] System
ILAAT	Interlaboratory Air-to-Air Missile Technology (MCD)
ILAB	Bureau of International Labor Affairs [*Department of Labor*]
ILAB	Instrumental Laboratory SpA [*NASDAQ symbol*] (SAG)
ILAB	International League of Antiquarian Booksellers [*See also LILA*] [*Bonn, Federal Republic of Germany*] (EAIO)
ILAB	Irish Laboratory Accreditation Board [*Now the Irish National Accreditation Board*] (ACII)
ILABC	Inter-Laboratory Committee (SAA)
I-Lac	Imidazolelactic Acid [*Medicine*] (MEDA)
ILAC	International Laboratory Accreditation Conference [*Gaithersburg, MD*] [*National Institute of Standards and Technology*] (EGAO)
ILACD	Ibero Latin American College of Dermatology (EA)
ILACDE	Instituto Latinoamericano de Cooperacion y Desarrollo [*Latin American Institute for Cooperation and Development*] (EAIO)
ILACO	International Land Development Consultants Ltd.
ILACS	Integrated Library Administration and Cataloguing System (PDAA)

ILad .... Ladd Public Library, Ladd, IL [*Library symbol Library of Congress*] (LCLS)
ILADES .... Instituto Latinoamericano de Doctrina y Estudios Sociales [*Latin American Institute of Social Doctrine and Social Studies*] [*Chile*] (EAIO)
ILadSD........ Ladd Consolidated Community School District 94, Ladd, IL [*Library symbol Library of Congress*] (LCLS)
ILADT.......... Instituto Latinoamericano de Derecho Tributario [*Latin American Tax Law Institute*] (EAIO)
ILAE............ International League Against Epilepsy (EA)
ILAEDS........ Illinois Association for Educational Data Systems (EDAC)
ILAF............ Identical Location of Accelerometer and Force [*NASA*]
ILAFA.......... Instituto Latinoamericano del Fierro y el Acero [*Latin American Iron and Steel Institute*] (EAIO)
ILAG............ INLOGOV [*Institute of Local Government*] Local Authority Game
ILag .... La Grange Public Library, La Grange, IL [*Library symbol Library of Congress*] (LCLS)
ILagp .... La Grange Park Library District, La Grange Park, IL [*Library symbol Library of Congress*] (LCLS)
ILagpS .... Suburban Audio-Visual Service, La Grange Park, IL (LCLS)
ILAI............ Italo-Latin American Institute (EA)
ILAIS.......... Institute for Latin American and Iberian Studies [*Columbia University*] [*Research center*] (RCD)
ILAM.......... Institute of Leisure and Amenity Management (EAIO)
ILam .... LaMoille-Clarion District Library, LaMoille, IL [*Library symbol Library of Congress*] (LCLS)
ILAMA.......... International Life-Saving Appliance Manufacturers Association (PDAA)
ILAMS.......... Infrared LASER Atmospheric Monitoring System
ILamSD........ LaMoille Community Unit, School District 303, LaMoille, IL [*Library symbol Library of Congress*] (LCLS)
ILAN............ Industrial Local Area Network [*Telecommunications*] (OSI)
ILAN............ [*The*] Israeli Academic Network [*Computer science*] (TNIG)
IL & FM .... Assistant Secretary of the Army for Installations, Logistics, and Financial Management (MCD)
IL&FM .... Installation, Logistics and Financial Management (AAGC)
IL & M .... Ichthyological Laboratory and Museum [*University of Miami*]
ILANG.......... Illinois Air National Guard (MUSM)
ILAP............ Integrated Local Area Planning
ILAR............ Institute of Laboratory Animal Resources (EA)
ILAR............ International League Against Rheumatism (EA)
ILAR............ International League for Animal Rights (EA)
ILARTS .... Integrated Launch and Recovery Television System (MCD)
ILAS............ Improved Limb Atmospheric Spectrometer [*Matsushita Electronics*]
ILAS............ Institute of Latin American Studies [*China*] (IRC)
ILAS............ Instrument Landing Approach System [*Aviation*] (IAA)
ILAS............ Instrument Low-Approach System [*Aircraft landing method*]
ILAS............ International Laser Acupuncture Society (EA)
ILAS............ Interrelated Logic Accumulating Scanner
ILas .... LaSalle Public Library, LaSalle, IL [*Library symbol Library of Congress*] (LCLS)
ILasC .... Carus Chemical Co., Inc., LaSalle, IL [*Library symbol Library of Congress*] (LCLS)
ILASE .... Internacia Ligo de Agrikulturaj Specialistoj-Esperantistoj [*International League of Agricultural Specialists-Esperantists - ILASE*] (EAIO)
ILasH .... Hygiene Institute, Medical Library, LaSalle, IL [*Library symbol Library of Congress*] (LCLS)
ILasJ .... Jefferson Elementary School, LaSalle, IL [*Library symbol Library of Congress*] (LCLS)
ILasL .... Lincoln Junior High School, LaSalle, IL [*Library symbol Library of Congress*] (LCLS)
ILasN .... Northwest Elementary School, LaSalle, IL [*Library symbol Library of Congress*] (LCLS)
ILASS.......... Integrated Light Attack Avionics System [*Navy*] (NVT)
ILASS.......... Intermediate Level Avionics Support System (MCD)
ILasSD........ LaSalle-Peru Township High School, LaSalle, IL [*Library symbol Library of Congress*] (LCLS)
I-LAW .... Improved Light Antiarmor [*or Antitank*] Weapon (RDA)
ILaw............ Lawrence Township Library, Lawrenceville, IL [*Library symbol Library of Congress*] (LCLS)
ILB .... Eli Lilly & Co., Business Library, Indianapolis, IN [*OCLC symbol*] (OCLC)
ILB .... Independent Lateral Band (IAA)
ILB .... Infant, Low Birth Weight [*Medicine*] (DMAA)
ILB .... Initial Load Block
ILB .... Initial Lung Burden [*Medicine*] (DMAA)
ILB .... Inner Lead Bond [*Integrated circuit technology*]
ILB .... Inshore Life Boat (PDAA)
ILB .... Insurance Law Bulletin [*Australia A publication*]
ILB .... Involvement Limited to Bone [*Oncology*]
ILBA............ International League for Bolivarian Action (EA)
ILBB............ Improved Life Blower Bearing
ILBC............ Independent Living Behavior Checklist (TES)
ILBC............ International Livestock Brand Conference (EA)
ILBE............ International League of Blind Esperantists [*See also LIBE*] [*Belgrade, Yugoslavia*] (EAIO)
ILBFRLP ...... International Lelio Basso Foundation for the Rights and Liberation of Peoples (EA)
ILBTC.......... International Livestock Brand and Theft Conference (EA)
ILBW............ Infant, Low Birth Weight
ILC .... Ichthyosis Linearis Circumflex [*Medicine*] (DMAA)
ILC .... Idiopathic CD4-Lymphocytopenia [*Medicine*]
ILC .... Idle Load Compensator [*Automotive engineering*]
ILC .... Improved Line Charge (DOMA)
ILC .... Incipient Lethal Concentration

ILC .... Independent Labor Congress [*Nigeria*]
ILC .... Industrial Liaison Centre [*British*]
ILC .... Industry-Labor Council (EA)
ILC .... Infantry Leader Course [*Army*] (INF)
ILC .... Initial Launch Capability [*Aerospace*]
ILC .... Input Language Converter [*Computer science*] (IAA)
ILC .... Institute for Liberty and Community (EA)
ILC .... Institute of Land Combat [*Army*]
ILC .... Instruction Length Code [*Computer science*] (BUR)
ILC .... Instruction Length Counter [*Computer science*] (IAA)
ILC .... Instruction Location Counter
ILC .... Instructor Lieutenant-Commander [*Navy British*]
ILC .... Integrated Launch Complex (MCD)
ILC .... Integrated Logic Circuit
ILC .... Intermediate-Level Cell [*Nuclear energy*] (NRCH)
ILC .... Internal Locus of Control [*Psychology*]
ILC .... International Labelling Centre [*Defunct*] (EA)
ILC .... International Labor Conference [*A section of the International Labor Organization*] [*United Nations*]
ILC .... International Latex Corp.
ILC .... International Law Commission [*United Nations*]
ILC .... International Leadership Center [*Defunct*] (EA)
ILC .... International Legal Center [*Formerly, SAILER*] [*Later, International Center for Law and Development*] (EA)
ILC .... International Licensed Carrier [*Telecommunications*]
ILC .... International Lines of Communication (MCD)
ILC .... International Logistics Center [*Army*]
ILC .... Irrevocable Letter of Credit [*Business term*]
ILC .... ISDN [*Integrated Services Digital Network*] Link Controller [*Telecommunications*]
ILC .... Lake County Public Library, Merrillville, IN [*OCLC symbol*] (OCLC)
ILC .... Wilson Creek, NV [*Location identifier FAA*] (FAAL)
ILCA............ Belgique Judiciaire [*A publication*] (ILCA)
ILCA............ Indian Land Consolidation Act [*1983*]
ILCA............ Insurance Loss Control Association [*Indianapolis, IN*] (EA)
ILCA............ International Labor Communications Association (EA)
ILCA............ International Lactation Consultant Association (EA)
ILCA............ International Lightning Class Association (EA)
ILCA............ International Livestock Centre for Africa [*Addis Ababa, Ethiopia*]
ILCA............ Inverter Light Control Assembly (MCD)
ILCC............ Initial Launch Capability Complex [*Aerospace*]
ILCC............ Integrated Launch Control and Checkout (KSC)
ILCC............ Integrated Living Communities, Inc. [*NASDAQ symbol*] (SAG)
ILCC............ Italian Language and Culture Center [*Australia*]
ILCCG .... International Laity and Christian Community Group [*See also LAEEC*] [*Sion, Switzerland*] [*Defunct*] (EAIO)
IIC CI .... Illinois Court of Claims Reports [*A publication*] (DLA)
ILCCS.......... Integrated Launch Control and Checkout System
ILCCTC........ International Liaison Committee on Co-Operative Thrift and Credit [*Paris, France*] (EA)
ILCEP.......... Inter-Laboratory Committee on Editing and Publishing [*Navy*] (MCD)
ILCF............ Inter-Laboratory Committee on Facilities [*Navy*] (MCD)
ILCK............ Inductosyn Linearity Checkout Kit
ILCM............ Individual Level Cost Method [*Insurance*]
ILC Newl...... International Legal Center. Newsletter [*A publication*] (DLA)
ILCO............ Infrastructural, Logistics, Council Operations [*NATO*]
ILCO............ Instantaneous Launch Control Officer [*Aerospace*] (AAG)
ILCO............ Intercontinental Life Corp. [*NASDAQ symbol*] (NQ)
ILCO............ Intercontl Life [*NASDAQ symbol*] (TTSB)
ILCO............ International Logistics Control Office (AAGC)
ILCOP.......... International Liaison Committee of Organizations for Peace
ILCORK........ International Liaison Committee for Research on Korea
ILCOS .... Instantaneous Lead Computing Optical Sight [*Gunsight*] [*Navy*] (DOMA)
ILCRPK........ International Liaison Committee for Reunification and Peace in Korea (EAIO)
ILCS............ Induction Loop Communications System
ILCT............ ILC Technology [*NASDAQ symbol*] (TTSB)
ILCT............ ILC Technology, Inc. [*NASDAQ symbol*] (NQ)
ILCTA.......... International League of Commercial Travelers and Agents (EA)
ILC Tc .... ILC Technology, Inc. [*Associated Press*] (SAG)
ILC (UN) ...... International Law Commission of the United Nations
ILCV............ Inscriptiones Latinae Christianae Veteres
ILD .... Eli Lilly & Co., Agricultural Library, Greenfield, IN [*OCLC symbol*] (OCLC)
ILD .... I Love Dance [*Competition in US and Canada*]
ILD .... Indent Load Deflection [*Measure of hardness*]
ILD .... Inductive Loop Detector
ILD .... Information Lead Distance
ILD .... Initial Lung Deposit (PDAA)
ILD .... Injection LASER Diode (TEL)
ILD .... Injection Luminescence Device
ILD .... Inland Recovery Group [*Vancouver Stock Exchange symbol*]
ILD .... In-Lock Detector
ILD .... Instructional Logic Diagram (IAA)
ILD .... Instrument Loop Diagram (ACII)
ILD .... Integrating Light Detector (PDAA)
ILD .... Interlayer Dielectric (AAEL)
ILD .... Interlevel Dielectric (AAEL)
ILD .... Intermediate-Level Diagram (IAA)
ILD .... Internal Load Deflection [*Automotive seating*]
ILD .... International Labor Defense [*An association*]
ILD .... Intersection Loop Detection (MHDI)
ILD .... Interstitial Lung Disease
ILD .... Intraoperative Localization Device [*Medicine*] (DMAA)

ILD.............. Ischemic Leg Disease [*Medicine*]
ILD.............. Ischemic Limb Disease [*Medicine*]
ILD.............. Isolated Lactase Deficiency [*Medicine*] (DMAA)
ILDA............ Independent Laboratory Distributors Association (NTPA)
ILDA............ Industrial Lands Development Authority [*Australia*]
ILDA............ Industrial Lighting Distributors of America (EA)
ILDA............ Inter Laboratory Data Acceptance (PDAA)
ILDA............ International LASER Display Association (EA)
ILDA............ International Lutheran Deaf Association (EA)
ILDC............ International Legal Defense Counsel (EA)
ILDC............ Israel Land & Development Co. [*NASDAQ symbol*] (SAG)
ILDCSI........ Individual Learning Disabilities Classroom Screening Instruments
ILDCY .... Israel Ld Dev Ltd [*NASDAQ symbol*] (TTSB)
I L de Gaule... Inscriptions Latines des Trois Gaules [*A publication*] (OCD)
ILDIS .... International Legume Database and Information Service
ILDM........... Institute of Logistics and Distribution Management [*British*] (DBA)
ILDP............ Interlook Dormant Period (NVT)
ILDR............ Index of Limited Distribution Reports [*A publication*]
ILDS............ Integrated Logistics Data System
ILDS............ International League of Dermatological Societies [*Vancouver, BC*] (EAIO)
ILDSC .... Industrial Land Development Subcommittee [*New South Wales, Australia*]
ILDT............ Item Logistics Data Transmittal
ILDTF .... Item Logistics Data Transmittal Form (NATG)
ILE.............. Ileum [*Anatomy*]
ILE.............. Indiana Law Encyclopedia [*A publication*] (DLA)
ILE.............. Inel Resources Ltd. [*Vancouver Stock Exchange symbol*]
ILE.............. Institute of Legal Executives [*Australia*]
ILE.............. Institution of Lighting Engineers (EAIO)
ILE.............. Integral Linear Error (IAA)
ILE.............. Intelligent Life Elsewhere
ILE.............. Interface Latching Element
Ile.............. Isoleucine [*or iLeu, Ileu*] [*Also, I An amino acid*]
ile.............. Isoleucine [*An amino acid*] (DOG)
ILE.............. Killeen [*Texas*] [*Airport symbol*] (OAG)
ILE.............. Killeen, TX [*Location identifier FAA*] (FAAL)
ILE.............. Lincolnwood Public Library District, Lincolnwood, IL [*OCLC symbol*] (OCLC)
ILEA............ Inner London Education Authority [*British*]
ILEA............ International League of Electrical Associations (EA)
ILeb............ Lebanon Public Library, Lebanon, IL [*Library symbol Library of Congress*] (LCLS)
ILebHS........ Lebanon High School, Lebanon, IL [*Library symbol Library of Congress*] (LCLS)
ILebM .... McKendree College, Lebanon, IL [*Library symbol Library of Congress*] (LCLS)
ILeD............ De Andreis Seminary, Lemont, IL [*Library symbol Library of Congress*] (LCLS)
ILEED.......... Inelastic Low-Energy Electron Diffraction (IAA)
ILEF............ Internacia Ligo de Esperantistaj Foto-Kino-Magnetofon-Amatoroj [*International League of Esperantist Amateur Photographers, Cinephotographers, and Tape-Recording*] (EAIO)
ILEI............ Internacia Ligo de Esperantistaj Instruistoj [*International League of Esperantist Teachers*] (EAIO)
ILEJ............ Internet Library of Early Journals (TELE)
ILelSD .... Leland Community Unit, School District 1, Leland, IL [*Library symbol Library of Congress*] (LCLS)
ILEM .... Inter-Library Electronic Mail (NITA)
ILEMP......... Immigration Law Enforcement Monitoring Project [*American Friends Service Committee*] (CROSS)
ILEOA.......... International Law Enforcement Officers Association (EA)
ILEP............ Federation Internationale des Associations Contre la Lepre [*International Federation of Anti-Leprosy Associations - ILEP*] (EAIO)
ILERA.......... International League of Esperantist Radio Amateurs (EA)
ILERT.......... Independent Librarians Exchange Round Table [*American Library Association*]
ILESA.......... International Law Enforcement Stress Association (EA)
i-lesion .... Intralesional [*Medicine*] (MEDA)
ILET............ Instituto Latinoamericano de Estudios Transnacionales [*Latin American Institute for Transnational Studies - LAITS*] (EAIO)
Ileu............ Isoleucine [*or iLeu, Ile*] [*Also, I An amino acid*]
ILEV............ Inherently Low-Emissions Vehicle
ILE(V)......... Institute of Legal Executives (Victoria) [*Australia*]
ILEX........... ILX, Inc. [*NASDAQ symbol*] (SAG)
ILEX............ Institute of Legal Executives [*British*] (DBA)
ILF.............. Idaho Laboratory Facility [*Later, IRC*] [*Idaho Falls, ID*] [*Department of Energy*] (GRD)
ILF.............. Immigrants in the Labour Force [*British*]
ILF.............. Indian Local Forces [*Military British*]
ILF.............. Inductive Loss Factor (IEEE)
ILF.............. Industrial Leathers Federation [*British*] (BI)
ILF.............. Infra Low-Frequency [*Telecommunications*] (TEL)
ILF.............. Integral Lift Fan [*Aviation*]
ILF.............. Integrity Loss Factor
ILF.............. International Falcon Resources Ltd. [*Vancouver Stock Exchange symbol*]
ILF.............. International Lacrosse Federation (EA)
ILF.............. International Landworkers' Federation [*Later, IFPAAW*]
ILF.............. International Liaison Forum of Peace Forces [*See also FILFP*] [*Moscow, USSR*] (EAIO)
ILF.............. International Lifeboat Federation [*England*] (EAIO)
ILF.............. International Lotto Fund
ILF.............. International Luge Federation [*Austria*]

ILf.............. Lake Forest Library, Lake Forest, IL [*Library symbol Library of Congress*] (LCLS)
ILF.............. Milford Haven [*Wales*] [*Airport symbol*] (AD)
ILfB............ Barat College of the Sacred Heart, Lake Forest, IL [*Library symbol Library of Congress*] (LCLS)
ILFC.......... Immature Living Female Child [*Neonatology*] (DAVI)
ILfC........... Lake Forest College, Lake Forest, IL [*Library symbol Library of Congress*] (LCLS)
ILFCG......... International Logistics Functional Coordinating Group (MCD)
ILFI............ International Labour Film Institute [*Defunct*]
ILFO........... International Logistics Field Office [*Army*] (AABC)
ILFP............ Forum International de Liaison des Forces de la Paix [*International Liaison Forum of Peace Forces - ILF*] (EA)
ILFZ........... Ivanhoe Lake Fault Zone [*Geology*] [*Canada*]
ILG............ Consolidated Inland Recovery [*Vancouver Stock Exchange symbol*]
ILG............ Inge Lehmann [*Greenland*] [*Seismograph station code, US Geological Survey Closed*] (SEIS)
ILG............ Instrument Landing Guidance
ILG............ International Leisure Group [*Commercial firm British*]
ILG............ Irish Linen Guild [*Defunct*] (EA)
ILG............ University of Illinois, Graduate School of Library Science, Urbana, IL [*OCLC symbol*] (OCLC)
ILG............ Wilmington [*Delaware*] [*Airport symbol*] (OAG)
ILGA.......... Immiscible Lattice-Gas Automata [*Fluid mechanics*]
ILGA.......... Institute of Local Government Administration [*British*]
ILGA.......... International Lesbian and Gay Association [*Formerly, International Gay Association*] (EA)
ILGB.......... International Laboratory of Genetics and Biophysics
ILGF.......... Insulin-Like Growth Factor
ILGPNWU ... International Leather Goods, Plastic, and Novelty Workers' Union (EA)
ILGSA .... Indoor Light Gardening Society of America (EA)
ILGWU .... International Ladies' Garment Workers' Union (EA)
ILH............ Del Rio, TX [*Location identifier FAA*] (FAAL)
ILH............ Immunoreactive Luteinizing Hormone (DMAA)
ILH............ Imperial Light Horse [*Military British*] (ROG)
ILH............ Jus Liberorum Habens [*Possessing the Right of Children*] [*Latin*]
ILH............ Northern Illinois University, Department of Library Science, De Kalb, IL [*OCLC symbol*] (OCLC)
ILHA.......... International Labor History Association
ILHL.......... International Leisure Hosts Ltd. [*NASDAQ symbol*] (NQ)
ILHL.......... Intl Leisure Hosts [*NASDAQ symbol*] (TTSB)
ILHR.......... International League for Human Rights (EA)
ILI............ Ili [*Former USSR Seismograph station code, US Geological Survey Closed*] (SEIS)
ILI............ Iliamna [*Alaska*] [*Airport symbol*] (OAG)
ILI............ Iliamna, AK [*Location identifier FAA*] (FAAL)
ILI............ Indiana Limestone Institute of America (EA)
ILI............ Indiana University, School of Law Library, Indianapolis, IN [*OCLC symbol*] (OCLC)
ILI............ Influenza-Like Illness [*Medicine*]
ILI............ Injection LASER Illuminator
ILI............ Instant Lunar Ionosphere
ILI............ Institute for Land Information [*Research center Information service or system*] (RCD)
ILI............ Institute of Life Insurance [*Later, ACLI*] (EA)
ILI............ Inter-African Labour Institute
ILI............ Interamerican Labour Institute
ILI............ Intercan Leasing, Inc. [*Toronto Stock Exchange symbol*]
ILI............ Interlott Technologies [*AMEX symbol*] [*Formerly, International Lottery*] (SG)
ILI............ International Law Institute (EA)
ILI............ International Lottery, Inc. [*AMEX symbol*] (SAG)
ILIA.......... Indiana Limestone Institute of America
ILIA.......... International Livestock Investigators Association (EA)
ILib.......... Cook Memorial Public Library District, Libertyville, IL [*Library symbol Library of Congress*] (LCLS)
ILIC.......... In-Line Integrated Circuit
ILIC.......... International Library Information Center (EA)
IL-IC-IM... It's Life, I Can't, I Must [*Element of psychotherapist Joseph Bird's self-help theory*]
I-LIDS .... Indian Legal Information Development Service (EA)
ILIERS .... Integrated Library Information Education and Retrieval System (TELE)
ILIF............ International Logistics Information File (MCD)
ILIMA......... International Licensing Industry and Merchandisers' Association (EA)
ILINC .... Interactive Learning International Corp.
i-line.......... Identification Line [*Photojournalism*] (WDMC)
ILinL.......... Lincoln Christian College, Lincoln, IL [*Library symbol Library of Congress*] (LCLS)
ILinw.......... Lincolnwood Public Library, Lincolnwood, IL [*Library symbol Library of Congress*] (LCLS)
ILIOS.......... In-Line Infinity Optical System
ILIP............ In-Line Instrument Package [*Nuclear energy*] (NRCH)
ILIR........... In-House Laboratories Independent Research Program [*Army*] (RDA)
ILIR........... Institute of Labor and Industrial Relations [*University of Illinois*] [*Research center*] (RCD)
ILIR........... Institute of Labor and Industrial Relations [*University of Michigan*] [*Research center*] (RCD)
ILit............ Litchfield Carnegie Public Library, Litchfield, IL [*Library symbol Library of Congress*] (LCLS)
I-LITE.......... Iowa Library Information Teletype Exchange [*Des Moines, IA*] [*Telecommunications Library network*]
ILitSD .... Litchfield Community Unit, School District 12, Litchfield, IL [*Library symbol Library of Congress*] (LCLS)

ILivSD Livingston Community Consolidated School District, Livingston, IL [*Library symbol Library of Congress*] (LCLS)

ILJ Springfield, MO [*Location identifier FAA*] (FAAL)

ILK IIT Chicago-Kent College of Law, Chicago, IL [*OCLC symbol*] (OCLC)

ILK Integrin-Linked Kinase [*An enzyme*]

ILK Interlock [*Technical drawings*]

ILKE Internacia Libro-Klubo Esperantista (EA)

ILL Illinois (AFM)

Ill Illinois Reports [*A publication*] (AAGC)

ill Illuminated (WDMC)

ILL Illuminated (NTCM)

ILL Illuminating [*Ammunition*] (NATG)

ILL Illusion

ill Illustrated (BJA)

ILL Illustration

ill Illustration (WDMC)

ill Illustrator [*MARC relator code*] [*Library of Congress*] (LCCP)

ILL Illustrissimus [*Most Illustrious*] [*Latin*]

ILL Impact Limit Lines (MUGU)

ILL Individual Learning Laboratory (OICC)

ILL Input Logic Level

ILL Institute of Languages and Linguistics (DIT)

ILL Institute of Lifetime Learning (EA)

ILL Institut Laue-Langevin [*Grenoble, France*] (ECON)

ILL Interlibrary Loan

ILL Intermediate Lymphocytic Lymphoma [*Medicine*]

ILL International Larder Minerals, Inc. [*Toronto Stock Exchange symbol*]

ILL Interstate Loan Library [*Council of State Governments*] (IID)

ILL Intl Lottery [*AMEX symbol*] (TTSB)

ILL Irving Langmuir Laboratory [*New Mexico Institute of Mining and Technology*] [*Research center*] (RCD)

ILL Ontario Library Service - Escarpment, Hamilton [*UTLAS symbol*]

ILL Willmar, MN [*Location identifier FAA*] (FAAL)

Ill 2d Illinois Reports, Second Series [*A publication*] (DLA)

Ill A Illinois Appellate Court Reports [*A publication*] (DLA)

Ill Adm Code Illinois Administrative Code [*A publication*] (AAGC)

Ill Admin Code Illinois Administrative Code [*A publication*] (AAGC)

Ill Admin Reg Illinois Register [*A publication*] (DLA)

Ill Ann Stat Smith-Hurd Illinois Annotated Statutes [*A publication*] (AAGC)

Ill Ann Stat Smith-Hurd's Illinois Annotated Statutes [*A publication*] (DLA)

Ill Ap Illinois Appellate Court Reports [*A publication*] (DLA)

Ill App Illinois Appellate Court Reports [*A publication*] (DLA)

Ill App 2d Illinois Appellate Court Reports, Second Series [*A publication*] (DLA)

Ill App 3d Illinois Appellate Court Reports, Third Series [*A publication*] (DLA)

Ill App Ct Rep Illinois Appellate Court Reports [*A publication*] (DLA)

Ill App Illinois Appellate Court Reports [*A publication*] (AAGC)

Ill Apps Illinois Appellate Court Reports [*A publication*] (DLA)

ILLB Insurance and Liability Law Bulletin [*A publication*]

Ill BA Bull Illinois State Bar Association. Quarterly Bulletin [*A publication*] (DLA)

Ill CC Illinois Commerce Commission Opinions and Orders [*A publication*] (DLA)

Ill CC Matthew and Bangs' Illinois Circuit Court Reports [*A publication*] (DLA)

Ill Cir Illinois Circuit Court (DLA)

Ill Cir Ct Illinois Circuit Court Reports [*A publication*] (DLA)

Ill Cont L Ed Illinois Continuing Legal Education [*A publication*] (DLA)

ILLCS Intralaunch Facility and Launch Control Facility Cabling Subsystem (IAA)

Ill Ct Cl Illinois Court of Claims (AAGC)

ILLD Illustrated (ROG)

Ill Dec Illinois Decisions [*A publication*] (DLA)

ILLEGIT Illegitimate (WDAA)

IL LF Illinois Law Forum (DLA)

ILLIAC Illinois Algorithmic Decoder [*Southern Illinois University*] (SAA)

ILLIAC Illinois Institute for Advanced Computing

ILLIAC Illinois Integrator and Automatic Computer [*University of Illinois*] (BUR)

ILLIC LAG OBTURAT Illico Lagena Obturatur [*Stopper the Bottle at Once*] [*Pharmacy*]

illic lag obturat Illico Lagena Obturatur [*Let the Bottle be Closed at Once*] [*Latin*] (STED)

IlliCtr Illinois Central Corp. [*Associated Press*] (SAG)

ILLIN Illinantur [*Anoint*] [*Pharmacy*] (ROG)

ILLINEND Illinendus [*To Be Smeared*] [*Pharmacy*]

ILLINET Illinois Library and Information Network [*Library network*]

IlliniSup Illinois Superconductor Corp. [*Associated Press*] (SAG)

Illinois Rep Illinois Reports [*A publication*] (DLA)

Illinova Illinova Corp Holding Co. [*Formerly, Illinois Power*] [*Associated Press*] (SAG)

Ill Inst Tech Illinois Institute of Technology (GAGS)

ILLIT Illiterate

ILLL International Lutheran Laymen's League (EA)

Ill Laws Laws of Illinois [*A publication*] (DLA)

Ill LB Illinois Law Bulletin [*A publication*] (DLA)

Ill Legis Serv Illinois Legislative Service (West) [*A publication*] (DLA)

Ill Leg N Illustrated Legal News [*India*] [*A publication*] (DLA)

Ill LQ Illinois Law Quarterly [*A publication*] (DLA)

Ill L Rec Illinois Law Record [*A publication*] (DLA)

ILLLTV Integrated Low-Light-Level Television

ILLMO Illustrissimo [*Most Illustrious*] [*Latin*]

ILLODIE-AIF Illinois University Logical Design by Implicit Enumeration Using the All-Interconnection Inequality Formulation (PDAA)

illog Antilog [*Mathematics*] (BARN)

Ill Op Att'y Gen Illinois Attorney General's Opinion [*A publication*] (DLA)

IllP Illinois Power Co. [*Associated Press*] (SAG)

ILLPC Illinois Power Capital Ltd. [*Associated Press*] (SAG)

IllPF Illinois Power Financing I [*Associated Press*] (SAG)

Ill PUC Ops Illinois Public Utilities Commission Opinions and Orders [*A publication*] (DLA)

Ill R Illinois Reports [*A publication*] (DLA)

Ill R & WC Illinois Railroad and Warehouse Commission Reports [*A publication*] (DLA)

Ill R & WCD Illinois Railroad and Warehouse Commission Decisions [*A publication*] (DLA)

ILL rate Illiteracy Rate

Ill Reg Illinois Register [*A publication*] (AAGC)

Ill Rep Illinois Reports [*A publication*] (DLA)

Ill Rev Stat Illinois Revised Statutes [*A publication*] (AAGC)

ILLRI Industrial Lift and Loading Ramp Institute [*Defunct*] (EA)

ILLRP Inscriptiones Latinae Liberae Rei Publicae [*A publication*] (OCD)

ILLS Illinois (ROG)

Ills Illinois Reports [*A publication*] (DLA)

Ills App Illinois Appellate Court Reports [*A publication*] (DLA)

Ill SBA Illinois State Bar Association. Reports [*A publication*] (DLA)

Ill SBAQB Illinois State Bar Association. Quarterly Bulletin [*A publication*] (DLA)

Ills R Illinois Reports [*A publication*] (DLA)

Ills Rep Illinois Reports [*A publication*] (DLA)

ILLSTN Illustration

Ill St U Illinois State University (GAGS)

ILLT Illinois Terminal Railroad Co.

ILLUM Illuminate (KSC)

illum Illuminated (VRA)

ILLUS Illustrate [*or Illustration*] (AABC)

illus Illustrated (WDMC)

illus Illustration (WDMC)

illus Illustrator (WDMC)

illus mat Illustrative Material (VRA)

ILLUSTN Illustration

ILLUSTR Illustrator (ROG)

Ill WCC Illinois Workmen's Compensation Cases [*A publication*] (DLA)

ILM Iliamna [*Alaska*] [*Seismograph station code, US Geological Survey*] (SEIS)

ILM Ilmenite [*Also, il*] [*Geology*]

ILM Immobilized-Liquid Membrane [*Chemical engineering*]

ILM Independent Landing Monitor [*RADAR-TV landing guidance*] [*NASA*]

ILM Independent Learning Modules (ACII)

ILM Industrial Learning Modules (ACII)

ILM Industrial Light & Magic [*Special effects company owned by George Lucas*]

ILM Industrial Light Magic [*Electronics Commercial firm*]

ILM Information Logic Machine (IEEE)

ILM Institute of Labour Management

ILM Insulin-Like Material

ILM Integrated LASER Modulator (AAEL)

ILM Integrated Logistic Management (DNAB)

ILM Intelligent Library Manager [*Computer science*] (CIST)

ILM Interceptor Launch Module [*Military*]

ILM Intermediate Language Machine [*Computer science*]

ILM Internal Limiting Membrane [*Medicine*] (DMAA)

ILM Lincoln Library, Springfield, IL [*OCLC symbol*] (OCLC)

ILM Wilmington [*North Carolina*] [*Airport symbol*] (OAG)

ILM Wilmington, NC [*Location identifier FAA*] (FAAL)

ILMA Immunochemiluminometric Assay [*Analytical biochemistry*]

ILMA Incandescent Lamp Manufacturers Association [*Defunct*] (EA)

ILMA Independent Lubricant Manufacturers Association (EA)

ILMA International Licensing and Merchandisers' Association [*Later, ILIMA*] (EA)

ILMA Intraocular Lens Manufacturers Association [*Defunct*] (EA)

ILMA Morton Arboretum, Lisle, IL [*Library symbol Library of Congress*] (LCLS)

ILMC Immature Living Male Child [*Neonatology*] (DAVI)

ILMD Item Logistics Management Data [*DoD*]

ILMH Institute for Labor and Mental Health (EA)

ILMI Index-Linked Mortgage and Investment (DI)

ILMI Inferolateral Myocardial Infarct [*or Infarction*] [*Cardiology*] (DAVI)

ILMN Incomplete Lower Motor Neuron [*Lesion*] [*Neurology*] (DAVI)

ILMO Illustrissimo [*Most Illustrious*] [*Latin*] (WGA)

ILMP Integrated Logistic Management Program (NG)

ILMP International Literary Market Place [*A publication*]

ILMS Improved Launcher Mechanical System [*Military*]

ILMT Integrated Logistics Management Team

ILMT Intermediate-Level Maintenance Training

ILMWSC International Lifesaving Museum and Water Safety Center [*Defunct*] (EA)

ILN East Peoria Elementary Schools, East Peoria, IL [*OCLC symbol*] (OCLC)

ILN Idle Line Network

ILN Illinois League for Nursing (SRA)

ILN Illinova Corp. [*NYSE symbol*] (TTSB)

ILN Illinova Corp. Holding Co. [*Formerly, Illinois Power*] [*NYSE symbol*] (SAG)

ILN Illustrated London News [*A publication*] (BRI)

ILN International Law News [*A publication*]

ILN International Logistics Negotiations [*Military export sales*]

ILN Island Lagoon [*Australia Seismograph station code, US Geological Survey Closed*] (SEIS)

ILN Wilmington, OH [*Location identifier FAA*] (FAAL)

ILNY International League of New York

ILo	Helen M. Plum Memorial Library, Lombard, IL [*Library symbol*] [*Library of Congress*] (LCLS)
ilo	Ilocano [*MARC language code Library of Congress*] (LCCP)
ILO	Iloilo [*Philippines*] [*Airport symbol*] (OAG)
ILO	Iloilo [*Philippines*] [*Seismograph station code, US Geological Survey Closed*] (SEIS)
ILO	Individual Load Operation
ILO	Industrial Liaison Organization [*MIT*]
ILO	Injection-Locked Oscillator (IEEE)
ILO	In Lieu Of
ILO	Internally Linked Operation
ILO	International Labor Office [*A section of the International Labor Organization*] [*United Nations*]
ILO	International Labour Organisation [*Geneva, Switzerland*] [*United Nations*] (EA)
ILO	Interservice Liaison Office [*Military*] (CAAL)
ILo	Iodine Lotion [*Medicine*]
ILO	Islamic Liberation Organization
ILO	School of the Art Institute of Chicago Library, Chicago, IL [*OCLC symbol*] (OCLC)
ILOA	Industrial Life Offices Association [*British*] (BI)
ILOAD	Initialization Load (MCD)
I-load	Initial-Load (NAKS)
ILOC	Irrevocable Letter of Credit [*Business term*] (DS)
ILoc	Lockport Township Public Library, Lockport, IL [*Library symbol Library of Congress*] (LCLS)
ILoC	National College of Chiropractic, Lombard, IL [*Library symbol Library of Congress*] (LCLS)
ILoCC	National College of Chiropractic, Lombard, IL [*Library symbol*] [*Library of Congress*] (LCLS)
ILocL	Lewis University, Lockport, IL [*Library symbol Library of Congress*] (LCLS)
ILocL-L	Lewis University, College of Law, Glen Ellyn, IL [*Library symbol Library of Congress*] (LCLS)
ILod	Loda Public Library, Loda, IL [*Library symbol Library of Congress*] (LCLS)
ILoE	National College of Education, Lombard, IL [*Library symbol Library of Congress*] (LCLS)
ILOGS	Integrated Logistics System [*Army*] (RDA)
ILoM	MidCon Corp., Lombard, IL [*Library symbol*] [*Library of Congress*]
ILOP	Initial Light Off Procedure (MCD)
ILos	Lostant Community Library, Lostant, IL [*Library symbol Library of Congress*] (LCLS)
ILosHSD	Lostant Consolidated High School District 400, Lostant, IL [*Library symbol Library of Congress*] (LCLS)
ILOSS	Integrated LASER Optical Sight Set
ILosSD	Lostant Consolidated Community School District 25, Lostant, IL [*Library symbol Library of Congress*] (LCLS)
ILOST	International Liaison Center of Schools of Cinema and Television
ILOSU	International Labor Organization Staff Union [*Geneva, Switzerland*] (EAIO)
ILOUE	In Lieu of Until Exhausted [*Military*]
ILovjD	Lovejoy Unit, District 188, Lovejoy, IL [*Library symbol Library of Congress*] (LCLS)
ILP	Clausen, Miller, Gorman, Caffrey & Witous, Chicago, IL [*OCLC symbol*] (OCLC)
ILP	Ile Des Pins [*New Caledonia*] [*Airport symbol*] (OAG)
ILP	Illinois Law and Practice [*A publication*] (DLA)
ILP	Ilpo Aruba Cargo NV [*ICAO designator*] (FAAC)
ILP	Inadequate Luteal Phase (STED)
ILP	Independent Labour Party [*British*]
ILP	Independent Liberal Party [*Israel*] [*Political party*] (BJA)
ILP	Individual Learning Package (OICC)
ILP	Individual Learning Programme (AIE)
ILP	Industrial Liaison Program [*Refers to university-industry interaction*]
ILP	In-Line Printer
ILP	Instruction-Level Parallelism [*Computer science*]
ILP	Integer Linear Programming Model [*Statistics*]
ILP	Integrated Logistics Panel (NASA)
ILP	Intermediate Language Processor [*Computer science*] (BUR)
ILP	Intermediate Language Program [*Computer science*]
ILP	International Links Program [*Overseas aid*] [*Australia*]
ILP	International Logistics Program
ILP	Interstitial Lymphocytic Pneumonia [*Medicine*] (STED)
ILP	Inventory of Learning Processes [*Psychology*] (DHP)
ILP	Irish Labour Party [*Political party*] (ROG)
ILP	Islamic Liberation Party [*Tunisia*] [*Political party*] (MENA)
ILP	Isle des Pins [*New Caledonia*] [*Airport symbol*] (AD)
ILP	Israel Labor Party [*Political party*]
ILPA	International Labor Press Association (EA)
ILPA	Iowa Limestone Producers Association (SRA)
ILpB	Barber Colman Co., Technical Library, Loves Park, IL [*Library symbol*] [*Library of Congress*] (LCLS)
ILPBC	International League of Professional Baseball Clubs (EA)
ILPC	International Linen Promotion Commission (EA)
ILPES	Instituto Latinoamericano de Planificacion Economica y Social [*Latin American Institute for Economic and Social Planning*] [*Santiago, Chile*] [*United Nations*]
ILPF	Ideal Low Pass Filter
ILPH	International League for the Protection of Horses (DI)
ILPL	Index to Legal Periodical Literature [*1887-1937*] [*A publication*] (DLA)
IlPow	Illinois Power Co. [*Associated Press*] (SAG)
ILPPSM	International Library of Philosophy, Psychology, and Scientific Method [*Book publishing*] [*British*]
ILPS	Industrial Location Planning System [*Department of Commerce*] (GFGA)
ILPS	International Lecithin and Phospholipid Society
ILQ	Chadwell, Kayser, Ruggles, McGee & Hastings, Chicago, IL [*OCLC symbol*] (OCLC)
ILQ	Indian Law Quarterly [*A publication*] (DLA)
ILQ	International Law Quarterly [*A publication*] (AAGC)
ILQR	Indian Law Quarterly Review [*A publication*] (DLA)
ILR	Air Iliria [*Yugoslovia*] [*ICAO designator*] (FAAC)
ILR	Burns, OR [*Location identifier FAA*] (FAAL)
ILR	Ilorin [*Nigeria*] [*Airport symbol*] (OAG)
ILR	Incurred Loss Ratio [*Insurance*]
ILR	Independent Local Radio [*British*]
ILR	Indian Law Reports [*A publication*] (DLA)
ILR	Indicating Light Relay
ILR	Industrial and Labor Relations
ILR	Industrial Law Review [*A publication*] (ILCA)
ILR	Infanterie-Lehrregiment [*Infantry Demonstration Regiment*] [*German military - World War II*]
ILR	In-Line Reciprocator
ILR	Inner Lindblad Resonance [*Galactic science*]
ILR	Institute of Library Research [*University of California*] (DIT)
ILR	Institute of Logistics Research [*Army*] (RDA)
ILR	Instruction Location Register (NITA)
ILR	Insurance Law Reporter [*A publication*] (DLA)
ILR	Interleukin Receptor [*Medicine*] (DMAA)
ILR	International Labour Review [*A publication*] (BRI)
ILR	International Laco Resources [*Vancouver Stock Exchange symbol*]
ILR	International Law Reports [*A publication*]
ILR	International Luggage Registry [*Computer system for recovery of airline luggage*]
ILR	Irish Law Reports [*A publication*] (DLA)
ILR	Irreversible Loss Rate (DB)
ILRA	Inbred Livestock Registry Association (EA)
ILRA	International Log Rolling Association
ILRAD	International Laboratory for Research on Animal Diseases [*Nairobi, Kenya*]
ILR All	Indian Law Reports, Allahabad Series [*A publication*] (DLA)
ILR And	Indian Law Reports, Andhra Series [*A publication*] (DLA)
ILR Assam	Indian Law Reports, Assam Series [*A publication*] (DLA)
ILR Bom	Indian Law Reports, Bombay Series [*A publication*] (DLA)
ILRC	Indian Law Reports, Calcutta Series [*A publication*] (DLA)
ILRC	Indian Law Resource Center (EA)
ILRC	International LASER RADAR Conference (PDAA)
ILR Cal	Indian Law Reports, Calcutta Series [*A publication*] (DLA)
ILR Calc	Indian Law Reports, Calcutta Series [*A publication*] (DLA)
ILR Cut	Indian Law Reports, Orissa Series [*A publication*] (DLA)
ILRERF	International Labor Rights Education and Research Fund (EA)
ILRF	International Labor Rights Fund (EA)
ILR Hyderabad	Indian Law Reports, Hyderabad Series [*A publication*] (DLA)
ILRIS	Intermediate Long-Range Interceptor System
ILR Kar	Indian Law Reports, Karachi Series [*A publication*] (DLA)
ILR Ker	Indian Law Reports, Kerala Series [*A publication*] (DLA)
ILR Lah	Indian Law Reports, Lahore Series [*A publication*] (DLA)
ILRLP	International League for the Rights and Liberation of Peoples [*Rome, Italy*] (EAIO)
ILR Luck	Indian Law Reports, Lucknow Series [*A publication*] (DLA)
ILRM	International League for the Rights of Man [*Later, ILHR*]
ILR Mad	Indian Law Reports, Madras Series [*A publication*] (DLA)
ILR Madhya Bharat	Indian Law Reports, Madhya Bharat Series [*A publication*] (DLA)
ILR Mysore	Indian Law Reports, Mysore Series [*A publication*] (DLA)
ILRN	International Livedo Reticularis Network (EA)
ILR Nag	Indian Law Reports, Nagpur Series [*A publication*] (DLA)
ILRO	Industrial Labor Relations Office [*DoD*]
ILR Or	Indian Law Reports, Orissa Series [*A publication*] (DLA)
ILRP	Indian Law Reports, Patna Series [*A publication*] (DLA)
ILR Pat	Indian Law Reports, Patna Series [*A publication*] (DLA)
ILR Patiala	Indian Law Reports, Patiala Series [*A publication*] (DLA)
ILR Pun	Indian Law Reports, Punjab Series [*A publication*] (DLA)
ILRR	Industrial and Labor Relations Review [*A publication*] (BRI)
ILR Rajasthan	Indian Law Reports, Rajasthan Series [*A publication*] (DLA)
ILR Ran	Indian Law Reports, Rangoon Series [*A publication*] (DLA)
ILR Rev	Industrial and Labor Relations Review [*A publication*] (DLA)
ILRRJ	International League for the Repatriation of Russian Jews (EA)
ILRRP	International Long-Range Reconnaissance Patrol
ILRS	International League of Religious Socialists [*Aerdenhout, Netherlands*] (EAIO)
ILRT	Integrated Leak Rate Test [*Nuclear energy*] (NRCH)
ILRT	Intermediate Level Reactor Test (IEEE)
ILR Trav-Cochin	Indian Law Reports, Kerala Series [*A publication*] (DLA)
ILRU	Independent Living Research Utilization Program (PAZ)
ILRV	In-Line Relief Valve
ILRV	Integral [*or Integrated*] Launch and Recovery Vehicle [*or Reentry*] [*NASA*]
ILRVS	Integral [*or Integrated*] Launch and Recovery Vehicle System [*or Reentry*] [*NASA*]
ILRWG	International Labor Rights Working Group (EA)
ILS	Ideal Liquidus Structures (IEEE)
ILS	Identification List
ILS	Idiopathic Leucine Sensitivity (STED)
ILS	Idiopathic Lymphadenopathy Syndrome (STED)
ILS	Illinois Benedictine College, Lisle, IL [*Library symbol Library of Congress*] (LCLS)
ILS	Incorporated Law Society [*British*]

ILS .... Increase in Life-Span
ILS .... Incremental Life Support (DB)
ILS .... Independent Living Skills [*Needed by the handicapped*]
ILS .... Indiana Union List of Serials, Indianapolis, IN [*OCLC symbol*] (OCLC)
ILS .... Industrial Locomotive Society [*British*]
ILS .... Information & Library Services [*Information service or system*] (IID)
ILS .... Infrared Liver Scanner (STED)
ILS .... Infrared Live Scanner [*Medicine*] (DMAA)
ILS .... Inland Library System [*Library network*]
ILS .... Inscriptiones Latinae Selectae [*A publication*] (ODCC)
ILS .... Inspection Lot Size
ILS .... Institute of Life Sciences [*British*] (DBA)
ILS .... Institute of Lithuanian Studies (EA)
ILS .... Instrument Landing System [*Aviation*]
ILS .... Integrated Laboratory Sequence [*A system of teaching chemistry devised by Mary L. Good at Louisiana State University in New Orleans*]
ILS .... Integrated LASER System [*Salford Engineering*]
ILS .... Integrated LASER Systems [*Software*] [*British*]
ILS .... Integrated Learning System (AIE)
ILS .... Integrated Library System [*National Library of Medicine*] [*Information service or system*] (IID)
ILS .... Integrated Logistics Support [*DoD*]
ILS .... Integrated Logistics System
ILS .... Interactive Laboratory System (NITA)
ILS .... Interferometric LASER Source
ILS .... Intergovernmental Liaison Staff [*Environmental Protection Agency*] (GFGA)
ILS .... International Latitude Service
ILS .... International Laughter Society [*Commercial firm*] (EA)
ILS .... International Learning Systems
ILS .... International Lilac Society (EA)
ILS .... International Limnological Society [*See also SIL*] (ASF)
ILS .... International Line Selector
ILS .... International Lunar Society [*Spain*]
ILS .... Interrupt Level Subroutine (CMD)
ILS .... Interstate Land Sales [*HUD*]
ILS .... Intracavity LASER Spectroscopy (AAEL)
ILS .... Intralobar Sequestration (DB)
ILS .... Intralobular Sequestration (STED)
ILS .... Inventory Locator Service [*Database*] [*Inventory Locator Service, Inc.*] [*Information service or system*] (CRD)
ILS .... Irish Literary Supplement [*A publication*] (BRI)
ILSA .... Industry Large Structures Assembly (SSD)
ILSA .... Insured Locksmiths and Safemen of America [*Defunct*] (EA)
ILSA .... Integrated Logistic Support Analysis Paper (MCD)
ILSA .... Inter-American Legal Services Association (EA)
ILSA .... International Law Students Association (EAIO)
ILSA .... International Lending Supervision Act of 1983
ILSA .... International Lung Sounds Association (EA)
ILSA .... Interstate Land Sales Full Disclosure Act (COE)
ILSA .... Italian Longitudinal Study of Aging
ILSAA .... Improved Lighting System for Army Aircraft (RDA)
ILSAC .... International Legal Services Advisory Committee
ILSAC .... International Lubricant Standardization and Approval Committee [*Automotive engine oils*]
ILSAM .... International Language for Servicing and Maintenance (PDAA)
ILSAP .... Instrument Landing System Approach [*Aviation*]
ILS(C) .... Industry Launch Service (Cryogenic) (SSD)
ILSC .... Integrated Logistics Support Cadre (AFIT)
ILSCM .... Integrated Logistics Support Control Manual (MCD)
ILSCM .... Integrated Logistics Support Coordination Meeting (MCD)
ILSDF .... Integrated Logistics Support Data File
ILSDP .... International Logistics Supply Delivery Plan (MCD)
ILS-DS .... Integrated Logistic Support - Detail Specification
ILSE .... Interagency Life Sciences Supporting Space Research and Technology Exchange
ILSE .... Intermediate-Level Support Equipment (MCD)
ILSES .... Integrated Library and Survey-Data Extraction Service (TELE)
ILSF .... Incandescent Liquid Spheroidal Formation [*Combustion technology*]
ILSF .... Intermediate Level Sample Flow (IEEE)
ILSF .... Iterative Least-Squares Fitting [*Mathematics*]
ILSG .... Integrated Logistics Subgroup [*Military*] (MCD)
ILSG .... Interim Logistics Support Guide (NVT)
ILSGB .... International Language Society of Great Britain
ILSI .... International Life Sciences Institute [*Later, ILSI-NF*] (EA)
ILSI .... International Life Services, Inc. (EA)
ILSINA .... International Life Sciences Institute-North America (EA)
ILSI-NF .... International Life Sciences Institute - Nutrition Foundation (EA)
ILS/IS/D .... Integrated Logistics Support/Information System/Dictionary
ILS/LAR .... Integrated Logistics System and Logistics Assessment Review (MCD)
ILSM .... Integrated Logistics Support Manager [*Military*] (MCD)
ILSM .... Integrated Logistics Support Model [*Military*] (MCD)
ILSMH .... International League of Societies for Persons with Mental Handicap [*Brussels, Belgium*] (EA)
ILSMP .... Integrated Logistic Support Maintenance [*or Management*] Plan (MCD)
ILSMRS .... Integrated Logistics Support Milestone Reporting System [*Military*] (MCD)
ILSMRT .... Integrated Logistic Support Management Review Team
ILSMT .... Integrated Logistic Support Management Team
ILSNI .... Incorporated Land Society of Northern Ireland
ILSO .... Incremental Life Support Operations
ILSO .... Integrated Logistic Support Office [*DoD*]
ILSOM .... Improved Light-Scattering Dust Monitor (PDAA)
ILSP .... Integrated Logistics Support Plan
ILSP .... Integrated Logistic Support Plan [*or Program*]
ILSP .... International Library of Sports and Pastimes [*A publication*]
ILSPER .... Integrated Logistics Support Performance Evaluation Report [*Military*] (MCD)
ILSPIP .... International Logistics Supply Performance Improvement Program (NG)
ILSR .... Institute for Local Self-Reliance (EA)
ILSR .... Integrated Logistics Support Review [*Military*] (MCD)
ILSRO .... Interstate Land Sales Registration Office [*HUD*] (IAA)
ILSS .... Industry Launch Services - Storable (SSD)
ILSS .... Integrated Life Support System [*NASA*]
ILSS .... Integrated Logistics Support System (SSD)
ILSS .... Interlaminar Shear Strength (MCD)
ILSSE .... Integrated Life Science Shuttle Experiments (MCD)
ILSTAC .... Instrument Landing System and TACAN
ILSUS .... Integrated Library System Users Society [*Defunct*] (EA)
ILS/VOR .... Instrument Landing System / VHF [*Very-High-Frequency*] Omnidirectional Range [*Aviation*] (SAA)
ILSW .... Interrupt Level Status Word
ILSWG .... Integrated Logistics Support Working Group (SSD)
ILT .... Albuquerque, NM [*Location identifier FAA*] (FAAL)
ILT .... Iliotibial Tract [*Medicine*] (DMAA)
ILT .... Infantry Liaison Team (INF)
ILT .... Infectious Laryngo-Tracheitis [*Medicine*] (ADA)
ILT .... Inferolateral Trunk [*Neuroanatomy*]
ILT .... In Lieu Thereof [*Military*]
ILT .... Installation Lead Time
ILT .... Interferometric Landmark Tracker (PDAA)
ILT .... Interlayer Tunneling [*Model for superconductivity*]
ILT .... Intermediate Lay-Up Tool [*Plastics technology*]
ILT .... International Logistics Training
ILT .... Ion Laser Technology [*AMEX symbol*] (TTSB)
ILT .... Ion Laser Technology, Inc. [*AMEX symbol*] (SAG)
ILT .... Iultin [*Former USSR Seismograph station code, US Geological Survey*] (SEIS)
ILT .... Keck, Mahin & Cate, Chicago, IL [*OCLC symbol*] (OCLC)
ILTA .... Independent Liquid Terminals Association (EA)
ILTC .... International Leadership Training Conference
ILTCP .... Inventory of Long-Term Care Places [*Department of Health and Human Services*] (GFGA)
ILTEB .... Inner London Tertiary Education Board [*British*] (AIE)
ILTF .... International Lawn Tennis Federation [*Later, ITF*]
ILTIA .... International Livestock Theft Investigators Association (NTPA)
ILT Jo .... Irish Law Times Journal [*A publication*] (DLA)
ILTMS .... International Leased Telegraph Message Switching Service [*British Telecom*] [*Telecommunications*] (TEL)
ILTO .... Industrial Liaison Technical Officer [*British*] (DI)
ILTR .... Irish Law Times Reports [*A publication*] (DLA)
ILTS .... Industrial Language Training Service [*British*]
ILTS .... Integration Level Test Series [*Psychology*]
ILTS .... Intermediate Level Test Station (MCD)
ILTS .... International Liver Transplantation Society (NTPA)
ILTTA .... International Light Tackle Tournament Association (EA)
ILTV .... Association of Local Television Stations (NTPA)
ilu .... Illinois [*MARC country of publication code Library of Congress*] (LCCP)
ILU .... Illinois University (IEEE)
ilu .... Illuminator [*MARC relator code*] [*Library of Congress*] (LCCP)
ILU .... Institute of London Underwriters (ECON)
ILU .... Inventory of Land Use (BARN)
ILU .... Texas Tech University, Lubbock, TX [*OCLC symbol*] (OCLC)
ILUMS .... Innovations in Land Use Management Symposium
ILUVM .... I Love You Very Much [*Correspondence*] (DSUE)
ILV .... Impatiens Latent Virus [*Plant pathology*]
ILV .... Industrial Launch Vehicle
ILV .... International Laser Tech, Inc. [*Vancouver Stock Exchange symbol*]
ILv .... Lake Villa District Library, Lake Villa, IL [*Library symbol Library of Congress*] (LCLS)
ILV .... Sonnenschein, Carlin, Nath & Rosenthal, Chicago, IL [*OCLC symbol*] (OCLC)
ILVBIDT .... In Liebe Vereint bis in dem Tod [*United in Love until Death*] [*German*]
ILVSI .... Instant Lead Vertical Speed Indicator (MCD)
ILW .... Institute of Land Warfare [*Association of the US Army*] (DOMA)
ILW .... Intermediate-Level Wastes (IEEE)
ILW .... International Association of Assessing Officers, Chicago, IL [*OCLC symbol*] (OCLC)
ILW .... International Low Water
ILW .... Investment Laws of the World [*A publication*] (DLA)
ILWAS .... Integrated Lake-Watershed Acidification Study
ILWC .... Intermediate-Level Waste Concentrate [*Nuclear energy*] (NRCH)
ILWC .... International League of Women Composers (EA)
ILWCHSG .... International Labor and Working Class History Study Group (EA)
ILWD .... Intermediate-Level Waste Distillate [*Nuclear energy*] (NRCH)
ILWF .... Intermediate-Level Waste Feed [*Nuclear energy*] (NRCH)
ILWML .... International Lutheran Women's Missionary League (EA)
ILWS .... Intermediate-Level Waste Storage [*Nuclear energy*] (GFGA)
ILWU .... International Longshoremen's and Warehousemen's Union (EA)
ILX .... Visiting Nurse Association of Chicago, Chicago, IL [*OCLC symbol*] (OCLC)
ILX Inc .... ILX, Inc. [*Associated Press*] (SAG)
ILY .... International Literacy Year
ILY .... Islay [*Scotland*] [*Airport symbol*] (OAG)
ILY .... Italian Liberal Youth [*Political party*] (EAIO)

ILy .... Lyons Public Library, Lyons, IL [*Library symbol Library of Congress*] (LCLS)
ILY .... Northern Illinois University, Law Library, Glen Ellyn, IL [*OCLC symbol*] (OCLC)
ILYA .... Inland Lake Yachting Association (EA)
I-LYA .... Inter-Lake Yachting Association (EA)
ILz .... Ela Area Public Library, Lake Zurich, IL [*Library symbol Library of Congress*] (LCLS)
ILZ .... Isham, Lincoln & Beale, Chicago, IL [*OCLC symbol*] (OCLC)
ILZ .... Newport, RI [*Location identifier FAA*] (FAAL)
ILZRO .... International Lead Zinc Research Organization (EA)
ILZSG .... International Lead and Zinc Study Group [*British*] (EA)
IM .... Ideal Modulation (IAA)
IM .... Idle Money [*Business term*] (MHDB)
Im .... Imaginary [*Mathematics*]
IM .... Immature
IM .... Im Mittel [*On an Average*] [*German*]
IM .... Immunoassay [*Marine science*] (OSRA)
IM .... Immuno-Suppression Method [*For increasing fertility*]
IM .... Impact Memorandum (MCD)
IM .... Imperial Measure
IM .... Implementation Monitoring (HCT)
IM .... Import Monthly Data [*Department of Commerce*] (GFGA)
IM .... Impulse Modulation
IM .... Income Maintenance (OICC)
IM .... Index Marker (MHDB)
IM .... Individual Medley [*Swimming*]
IM .... Indomethacin [*An analgesic*]
IM .... Induced Magnetization
IM .... Industrial Manager
IM .... Industrial Medicine (DAVI)
IM .... Industry Motion Picture [*FCC*] (MCD)
IM .... Infantile Myofibromatosus [*Medicine*]
IM .... Infant Mortality (ROG)
IM .... Infectious Mononucleosis [*Medicine*]
IM .... Informal Memorandum (MCD)
IM .... Information Management (AAGC)
IM .... Information Manager [*A publication*]
IM .... Information Market [*Commission of the European Communities*] [*Information service or system*] (IID)
IM .... Information Memory (MCD)
IM .... Ingot Metallurgy
IM .... Ingram Micro, Inc. [*NYSE symbol*] (SAG)
IM .... Initial Mass [*Agronomy*]
IM .... Injection Mold (MCD)
IM .... Inland Marine [*Insurance*]
IM .... In Maintenance
im .... In Margine [*On the Margin*] [*Latin*]
IM .... Inner Marker [*Part of an instrument landing system*] [*Aviation*]
IM .... Inner Membrane (DB)
IM .... Inoffizielle Mitarbeiter [*Unofficial Collaborators*] [*German*]
IM .... Insensitive Munitions (MCD)
I/M .... Inside of Metal (MSA)
I/M .... Inspection and Maintenance (ERG)
IM .... Inspection Manual (MCD)
IM .... Inspection Memorandum
IM .... Inspector of Machinery
IM .... Installation Material (AAGC)
IM .... Installment Mortgage (WDAA)
IM .... Instant Message [*Computer science*]
IM .... Instant Messaging [*Computer science*]
IM .... Institute of Marketing (EAIO)
IM .... Institute of Medicine [*National Academy of Sciences*]
IM .... Institution of Metallurgists [*British*]
IM .... Instruction Manual
IM .... Instruction Memory
IM .... Instrumentation (MDG)
IM .... Instrumentation and Measurement (MCD)
IM .... Instrumentation Manager [*NASA*] (KSC)
IM .... Instrumentman [*Navy rating*]
IM .... Instrument Myopia (PDAA)
IM .... Integrated Master (NRCH)
IM .... Integrated Model (AAEL)
IM .... Integrated MODEM
IM .... Integration Modified
IM .... Intelligence Memorandum
IM .... Intelligent Measurement [*Function*] (ACII)
IM .... Intensity Measuring Devices [*JETDS nomenclature*] [*Military*] (CET)
IM .... Intensity Modulation
IM .... Interactive Mode (IAA)
IM .... Interact Ministries [*An association*] (EA)
IM .... Interceptor Missile
IM .... Interdepartmental Memorandum (AAG)
IM .... Interface Module (MCD)
IM .... Interfaith Movement [*Defunct*] (EA)
IM .... Interim Measures
IM .... Interim Memorandum
IM .... Intermediate Maintenance (MCD)
IM .... Intermediate Megaloblast (DB)
IM .... Intermediate Missile (MSA)
IM .... Intermediate Modeling [*Marine science*] (OSRA)
IM .... Intermediate Modulation
IM .... Intermediate Moisture (KSC)
IM .... Intermetatarsal [*Anatomy*] (DAVI)

IM .... Inter Mirifica [*Decree on the Instruments of Social Communication*] [*Vatican II document*]
IM .... Intermodulation
IM .... Intermodulation Distortion (NTCM)
IM .... Intermuscular [*Anatomy*] (DAVI)
IM .... Internal Medicine
IM .... Internal Memorandum
IM .... International Missions [*An association*] (EA)
IM .... Interrupt Mask
IM .... Intestinal Metaplasia [*Medicine*]
IM .... Intramedullary [*Medicine*]
IM .... Intramural
IM .... Intramuscular [*Injection*] [*Medicine*]
IM .... In-Use Maintenance Test
IM .... Invasive Mole
I/M .... Inventory Management [*Business term*]
IM .... Inventory Manager [*Military*]
IM .... Inverted Microscope [*Instrumentation*]
IM .... Invisible Ministry (EA)
IM .... Iowa Mountaineers (EA)
IM .... Irish Marquis (ROG)
IM .... Isle of Man [*England*]
IM .... Istanbuler Mitteilungen [*A publication*] (BJA)
IM .... Item Management
IM .... Item Manager (AAGC)
IM .... Item Mark (BUR)
IM .... Jamaire [*ICAO designator*] (AD)
IM .... Sisters of Charity of the Infant Mary (TOCD)
IM1 .... Instrumentman, First Class [*Navy rating*]
IM2 .... Instrumentman, Second Class [*Navy rating*]
IM2 .... Integrated Materiel Management [*Military*]
IM3 .... Instrumentman, Third Class [*Navy rating*]
IMA .... Iamalele [*Papua New Guinea*] [*Airport symbol*] (OAG)
IMA .... Idaho Medical Association (SRA)
IMA .... Idaho Mining Association (SRA)
IMA .... Illinois Manufacturers Association (SRA)
IMA .... Immobilized Metal Affinity [*Protein chromatography*]
IMA .... Impedance Matching Attenuator
IMA .... Independent Manufacturing Assessment (MCD)
IMA .... Independent Midwives Association [*British*] (DBA)
IMA .... Independent Music Association (EA)
IMA .... Indiana Manufacturers Association (SRA)
IMA .... Indian Military Academy
IMA .... Indian Mountain [*Alaska*] [*Seismograph station code, US Geological Survey*] (SEIS)
IMA .... Individual Mobilization Augmentation [*or Augmentees*] [*DoD*]
IMA .... Individual Mobilization Augmentee (AAGC)
IMA .... Industrial Marketing Associates (EA)
IMA .... Industrial Medical Association [*Later, AOMA*] (EA)
IMA .... Inferior Mesenteric Artery [*Anatomy*]
IMA .... Information Medicale Automatisee [*Automated Medical Information*] [*INSERM*] [*Information service or system*] (IID)
IMA .... Information Mission Area
IMA .... Inherent Mobile Availability [*Military*]
IMA .... Initial Military Assistance (CINC)
IMA .... Input Message Acknowledgment [*Computer science*]
IMA .... Installation Maintenance Activity (MCD)
IMA .... Institute for Mathematics and Its Applications [*University of Minnesota*] [*Research center*] (RCD)
IMA .... Institute for Media Analysis (EA)
IMA .... Institute for Mediterranean Affairs (EA)
IMA .... Institute for Military Assistance [*Army*]
IMA .... Institute of Management Accountants (EBF)
IMA .... Institute of Management Accounting (EA)
IMA .... Institute of Mathematics and Its Applications [*South-End-On-Sea, England*] (CSR)
IMA .... Instituto Magdalena Aulina [*Magdalena Aulina Institute*] [*Barcelona, Spain*] (EAIO)
IMA .... Integrated Modular Avionics [*Honeywell, Inc.*]
IMA .... Interactive Multimedia Association [*Database producer*] (IID)
IMA .... Interbank Merchants Association [*Pigeon Forge, TN*] (EA)
IMA .... Interchurch Medical Assistance (EA)
IMA .... Interdisciplinary Master of Arts (PGP)
IMA .... Interface Management Agent (MCD)
IMA .... Intermediate Maintenance Activity
IMA .... Inter-Mountain Airways [*ICAO designator*] (FAAC)
IMA .... Internal Mammary Artery (Implant) [*Medicine*]
IMA .... International Magnesium Association (EA)
IMA .... International Maintenance Agency
IMA .... International Management Association [*Later, AMA/I*] (EA)
IMA .... International Massage Association (EA)
IMA .... International Medical Assistance [*Society*]
IMA .... International Message Centre [*Vancouver Stock Exchange symbol*]
IMA .... International Messaging Associates [*Commercial firm*]
IMA .... International Metaphysical Association [*Defunct*] (EA)
IMA .... International MIDI [*Musical Instrument Digital Interface*] Association (EA)
IMA .... International Military Archives (EA)
IMA .... International Milling Association [*See also AIM*] [*Brussels, Belgium*] (EAIO)
IMA .... International Mineralogical Association [*ICSU*] [*Marburg, Federal Republic of Germany*] (EA)
IMA .... International Minilab Association (EA)
IMA .... International Mobjack Association (EA)
IMA .... International Mohair Association (EAIO)

IMA International Music Association
IMA International Mycological Association [*See also AIM*] [*England*] (EAIO)
IMA International Mycophagist Association (EA)
IMA Invalid Memory Address [*Computer science*]
IMA Inventory Management Activity
IMA Ion Microprobe Analyzer
IMA Irish Medical Association
IMA Iron Mining Association of Minnesota (SRA)
IMA Islamic Medical Association (EA)
IMA Islamic Mission of America (EA)
IMA Issues Management Association (EA)
IMA Item Manager [*DoD*]
IMAA Imidazoleacetic Acid [*Biochemistry*]
IMAA Industrial Medical Administrators' Association [*Later, OMAA*] (EA)
IMAA Institute for Mediterranean Art and Archaeology [*Defunct*] (EA)
IMAA Intelligence Mission Area Analysis [*Military*] (MCD)
IMAA International Marketing Audit Association (EA)
IMAA Iodinated Macroaggregated Albumin [*Medicine*] (MAE)
IMAAWS Infantry Manportable Antiarmor Weapon System
IMAB Internal Mammary Artery Bypass [*Medicine*] (DMAA)
IMAC Ifosfamide, Mesna, Adriamycin, Cisplatin [*Antineoplastic drug*] (CDI)
IMAC Illinois Microfilm Automated Cataloging [*Illinois State Library*] (NITA)
IMAC Illinois State Library Microfilm Automated Catalog (PDAA)
IMAC Immobilized Metal Affinity Chromatography
IMAC Information Management, Archiving, and Communication (DMAA)
IMAC Integrated Microwave Amplifier Converter
IMAC International Metals Acquisition Corp. [*NASDAQ symbol*] (SAG)
IMAC International Movement of Apostolate of Children [*Paris, France*] (EA)
IMAC 90 Immigration Act of 1990 (WYGK)
IMACA International Mobile Air Conditioning Association (EA)
IMACE Association des Industries Margarinieres des Pays de la CEE [*Association of Margarine Industries of the EEC Countries*] [*Belgium*]
IMACHA Intermountain Automated Clearing House Association (MHDW)
IMacoW Western Illinois University, Macomb, IL [*Library symbol Library of Congress*] (LCLS)
IMACS International Association for Mathematics and Computers in Simulation (EA)
IMAD Integrated Multisensor Airborne Display
IMad Madison Public Library, Madison, IL [*Library symbol Library of Congress*] (LCLS)
IMadCU Madison Community, Unit 12, Madison, IL [*Library symbol Library of Congress*] (LCLS)
IMADE International Military and Defense Encyclopedia [*A publication*]
IMAF International Martial Arts Federation (EAIO)
IMAG IEEE [*Institute of Electrical and Electronics Engineers*] Magnetics (IAA)
IMAG Image Industries [*NASDAQ symbol*] (SAG)
IMAG Imagine [*or Imaginary*] (MSA)
Imag Imagines [*of Philostratus*] [*Classical studies*] (OCD)
IMAG Instituut voor Mechanistie Arbeid en Gebouwen [*Netherlands*] (NITA)
IMAG Internal Mammary Artery Graft [*Cardiology*] (DAVI)
IMAGE Information Management by Application Generation (IAA)
IMAGE Institute for Molecular and Agricultural Genetic Engineering [*University of Idaho*] [*Research center*]
IMAGE Instruction in Motivation Achievement and General Education [*YMCA program*]
IMAGE Integrated Molecular Analysis of Gene Expression (HGEN)
IMAGE International Monitor for Auroral Geomagnetic Effects
IMAGE International Multicenter Angina Exercise (DMAA)
IMAGE Intruder Monitoring and Guidance Equipment (MCD)
ImageInd Image Industries [*Associated Press*] (SAG)
ImagEn Image Entertainment, Inc. [*Associated Press*] (SAG)
ImageS Image Sensing Systems, Inc. [*Associated Press*] (SAG)
IMAGES Instructional Material Adequacy Guide and Evaluation Standard (RDA)
IMAGES Instrumental Manual Adequacy Guide and Evaluation Standard
IMAGES Interactive Modal Analysis and Gain Estimation for Eigensystem [*NASA digital computer program*]
IMAGES International Marine Global Change Study [*Research programs*]
ImageSft Image Software, Inc. [*Associated Press*] (SAG)
Imagyn Imagyn Medical, Inc. [*Associated Press*] (SAG)
IMah Mahomet Township Public Library, Mahomet, IL [*Library symbol Library of Congress*] (LCLS)
IMAI Imaging Management Associates [*NASDAQ symbol*] (SAG)
IMAI Imaging Mgmt Assoc [*NASDAQ symbol*] (TTSB)
IMAI Internal Mammary Artery Implant [*Medicine*] (DMAA)
IMAJ Initiative d'Un Mouvement d'Animation Jeunesse pour l'Annee Internationale de laJeunesse en 1985 [*Canada*]
IMAK International Imaging Materials, Inc. [*NASDAQ symbol*] (SAG)
IMAK Intl Imaging Materials [*NASDAQ symbol*] (TTSB)
IMA MOD Information Mission Area Modernization [*Army*] (RDA)
IMan Blue Ridge Township Public Library, Mansfield, IL [*Library symbol Library of Congress*] (LCLS)
IMAN International Mail Art Network (EA)
IMANCO Image Analysing Computers, Inc.
IM & AWU International Molders' and Allied Workers' Union [*AFL-CIO*] (EA)
IM & D Image Mapping and Display (NOAA)
IM & TPR Information Management and Telecommunications Pentagon Renovation (RDA)
IMANF Institute of Manufacturing [*Royal Leamington Spa, Warwickshire, England*] (EAIO)
IMAO In My Arrogant Opinion [*Computer hacker terminology*] (NHD)
IMAO International Military Assistance Office
IMAP Immediately After Passing [*Aviation*] (FAAC)
IMAP Institute of Materials and Advanced Processes [*University of Idaho*] [*Research center*] (RCD)
IMAP Interactive Manpower Alternatives Processor (DNAB)
IMAP International Merger and Acquisition Professionals (NTPA)
IMAP Internet Mail Access Protocol [*Computer science*]
IMAP Internet Message Access Protocol [*Computer science*]
IMAP Internet Messaging Access Protcol [*Computer science*]
IMAP Internet Messaging Access Protocol [*Computer science*] (IGQR)
IMAP4 Internet Message Access Protocol [*Computer science*]
IMAP4 Internet Message Access Protocol 4 [*Electronic mail*]
IMAPPA International Martial Arts Pen Pal Association [*Defunct*] (EA)
IMAPS Intake Manifold Absolute Pressure Sensor [*Automotive engineering*]
IMAPS International Microelectronics and Packaging Society (NTPA)
IMar Markham Public Library, Markham, IL [*Library symbol Library of Congress*] (LCLS)
IMarE Institute of Marine Engineers [*British Database producer*]
Imari Marion Carnegie Library, Marion, IL [*Library symbol*] [*Library of Congress*] (LCLS)
IMARPE Instituto del Mar de Peru [*Marine science*] (OSRA)
IMars Marshall Public Library, Marshall, IL [*Library symbol Library of Congress*] (LCLS)
IMarse Marseilles Public Library, Marseilles, IL [*Library symbol Library of Congress*] (LCLS)
IMarseHS Marseilles High School, Marseilles, IL [*Library symbol Library of Congress*] (LCLS)
IMarseMSD Miller Township Consolidated Community, School District 210, Marseilles, IL [*Library symbol Library of Congress*] (LCLS)
IMART International Medical Association for Radio and Television [*Brussels, Belgium*] (EAIO)
IMart Martinsville Township Library, Martinsville, IL [*Library symbol Library of Congress*] (LCLS)
IMartSD Martinsville Community Unit Schools District, Martinsville, IL [*Library symbol*] [*Library of Congress*] (LCLS)
IMaryR Maryville Reading Center, Maryville, IL [*Library symbol Library of Congress*] (LCLS)
IMAS Impurity Monitoring and Analysis System [*Nuclear energy*] (NRCH)
IMAS Industrial Management Assistance Survey [*Air Force*]
IMAS International Marine and Shipping Conference (NOAA)
IMas Mascoutah Public Library, Mascoutah, IL [*Library symbol Library of Congress*] (LCLS)
IMasHS Mascoutah High School, Mascoutah, IL [*Library symbol Library of Congress*] (LCLS)
IMAT Imatron, Inc. [*NASDAQ symbol*] (NQ)
IMAT Integrated, Modification and Trial
IMAT Interactive Multimedia Arts and Technologies Association [*Canada*] (DDC)
IMAT Interim Maintenance Assistance Team (MCD)
IMAT Intermodal Automated Transfer (PDAA)
IMAT International Mechanism for Appropriate Technology
IMat Mattoon Public Library, Mattoon, IL [*Library symbol*] [*Library of Congress*] (LCLS)
IMATA Independent Military Air Transport Association [*Later, Independent Airlines Association*]
IMATCE Information Mission Area Training Center of Excellence [*Army*] (RDA)
IMATDFW International Movement ATD Fourth World [*France*] (EAIO)
Imatec Imatec Ltd. [*Associated Press*] (SAG)
IMatH Memorial Hospital District Library, Mattoon, IL [*Library symbol Library of Congress*] (LCLS)
IMatL Sara Bush Lincoln Health Center, Mattoon, IL [*Library symbol Library of Congress*] (LCLS)
ImatLC Lake Land College, Mattoon, IL [*Library symbol Library of Congress*] (LCLS)
Imatrn Imatron, Inc. [*Associated Press*] (SAG)
IMatt Matteson Public Library, Matteson, IL [*Library symbol Library of Congress*] (LCLS)
IMAU International Movement for Atlantic Union (EA)
IMAV Intermediate Maintenance Availability
IMAW International Molders' and Allied Workers' Union [*AFL-CIO*]
IMAX Image-Maximum [*Photography*]
IMAX Isotope Matter Antimatter Experiment
Imax Cp Imax Corp. [*Associated Press*] (SAG)
IMAXF Imax Corp. [*NASDAQ symbol*] (SAG)
IMay Maywood Public Library, Maywood, IL [*Library symbol Library of Congress*] (LCLS)
IMB Imbaimadai [*Guyana*] [*Airport symbol*] (OAG)
IMB Independent Mixed Brigade [*Military*]
IMB Independent Mortar Battery [*British military*] (DMA)
IMB Indian Mountain Battery [*British military*] (DMA)
IMB Input Memory Buffer [*Computer science*]
IMB Institute for Marine Biochemistry [*British*]
IMB Institute of Microbiology
IMB Institute of Molecular Biophysics [*Florida State University*] [*Research center*] (RCD)
IMB Institute of Molecular Biotechnology [*Germany*]
IMB Instrument Material Bulletin (MCD)
IMB InterCapital Ins Muni Bd Fd [*NYSE symbol*] (TTSB)
IMB InterCapital Insurance Municipal Bond Fund [*NYSE symbol*] (SPSG)
IMB Intercontinental Medical Book Corp.
IMB Intermenstrual Bleeding [*Medicine*]
IMB Inter-Module Bus (NITA)
IMB Intermountain Tariff Bureau, Inc., Salt Lake City UT [*STAC*]
IMB Internationaler Metalarbeiterbund [*International Metalworkers' Federation*]

IMB............. International Maritime Bureau [*Research center British*] (IRC)
IMB............. International Mission Board (EA)
IMB............. Irvine/Michigan/Brookhaven [*Experiment on proton decay*]
IMB............. Kimberly, OR [*Location identifier FAA*] (FAAL)
IMBA........... Integrative Master of Business Administration (PGP)
IMBA........... International Master of Busness Administration [*University of South Carolina*]
IMBA........... International Media Buyers Association [*Defunct*] (EA)
IMBA........... International Morab Breeders Association (EA)
IMBA........... International Mountain Bicycling Association (EA)
IMBB........... Institute of Molecular Biology and Biochemistry [*Simon Fraser University*] [*Canada*]
IMBB........... Institute of Molecular Biology and Biotechnology [*Greece*]
IMBC........... Indirect Maximum Breathing Capacity [*Medicine*]
IMBC........... International Marine Biotechnology Conference
IMBE........... Improved Multi-Band Encoding [*Telecommunications*] (ACRL)
IMBE........... Institute for Minority Business Education [*Defunct*] (EA)
IMBEX......... International Men's and Boys' Wear Exhibition
IMBI............ Institute of Medical and Biological Illustration [*British*]
IMBL........... Independent Meat Buyers Ltd. [*British*] (BI)
IMBLM........ Integrated Medical and Behavioral Laboratory Management (DNAB)
IMBLMS...... Integrated Medical and Behavioral Laboratory Measurement System
IMBM......... Institute of Maintenance and Building Management [*British*] (DBA)
IMBM......... Institute of Municipal Building Management [*British*]
IMBN.......... International Molecular Biology Network
IMBO .... Indian and Metis Brotherhood Organization
IMBR .... Institute of Marine Biomedical Research [*University of North Carolina at Wilmington*] [*Research center*] (RCD)
IMBS........... Individual Motor Behavior Survey [*Test*]
IMBT........... Iron Masters Board of Trade
IMC............. Chief Instrumentman [*Navy rating*]
IMC............. Consolata Missionaries (TOCD)
imc............. Consolata Missionaries (TOCD)
IMC............. Image Motion Compensation [*or Compensator*]
IMC............. Image Motion Configuration
IMC............. Imco Resources Ltd. [*Vancouver Stock Exchange symbol*]
IMC............. Improved Meteorological Conditions (MCD)
IMC............. Incident Management Center [*Nuclear Regulatory Commission*] (NRCH)
IMC............. Indigent Medical Care (HCT)
IMC............. Industrial Metal Containers Section of the Material Handling Institute (EA)
IMC............. Industrial Microcomputer
ImC............. Industrial Microfilm Co., Detroit, MI [*Library symbol Library of Congress*] (LCLS)
IMC............. Information Management Consultants [*Database producer*] (IID)
IMC............. Information-Memory-Concentration (DMAA)
IMC............. Initial Marks [*Held*] Constant [*Psychology*]
IMC............. Initial Moisture Content (IAA)
IMC............. In-Mold Coating [*Organic chemistry*]
IMC............. In-Mold Compounding
IMC............. Inspection Method Control
IMC............. Institute of Management Consultants [*New York, NY*] (EA)
IMC............. Institute of Measurement and Control [*British*]
IMC............. Institute of Motorcycling [*British*] (DBA)
IMC............. Instructional Materials Center
IMC............. Instrument [*Flight*] Meteorological Conditions [*Aviation*]
IMC............. Integrated Maintenance Chart [*or Concept*]
IMC............. Integrated Marketing Communications [*Advertising*] [*Public relations*] (WDMC)
IMC............. Integrated Microcircuits, Inc. (EFIS)
IMC............. Integrated Microelectronic Circuitry (AAG)
IMC............. Integrated Microwave Circuit
IMC............. Integrated Monolithic Circuit
IMC............. Integrated Multiplexer Channel
IMC............. Intelligent Matrix Control [*T-Bar, Inc.*]
IMC............. Intensity Millicurie [*Nucleonics*] (IAA)
IMC............. Interactive Module Controller
IMC............. Interceptor Monitor and Controller
IMC............. Intercollegiate Men's Chorus, a National Association of Male Choruses (EA)
IMC............. Interdigestive Migrating Contractions [*Medicine*] (DMAA)
IMC............. Interdigestive Myoelectric Complex [*Gastroenterology*]
IMC............. Interim Message Change
IMC............. INTERMARC [*International Machine-Readable Cataloging*] [*French National Library Source file*] [*UTLAS symbol*]
IMC............. Intermediate Maintenance Costs (MCD)
IMC............. Intermediate Message Change (AAGC)
IMC............. Intermediate Metal Conduit
IMC............. Intermetallic Compound [*Materials science*]
IMC............. Intermetallic Matrix Composite [*Materials science*]
IMC............. Intermodal Marketing Company [*A third-party shipping broker*] (ECON)
IMC............. Intermodule Connector (SSD)
IMC............. Internal Mammary Chain [*Medicine*] (DAVI)
IMC............. Internal Management Control (DOMA)
IMC............. Internal Model Control [*Chemical engineering*] [*Computer science*]
IMC............. International Conference Management, Inc. [*Telecommunications service*] (TSSD)
IMC............. International Information Management Congress (EA)
IMC............. International Magazine Collection [*JA Micropublishing, Inc.*] [*Eastchester, NY*] [*Information service or system*] (IID)
IMC............. International Mailbag Club (EA)
IMC............. International Maintenance Control [*Telecommunications*]
IMC............. International Management Center [*Hungary*] (ECON)

IMC............. International Management Communications, Inc. [*Database producer*]
IMC............. International Management Consultants, Ltd.
IMC............. International Management Council (EA)
IMC............. International Maritime Committee
IMC............. International Marketing Commission [*See also CIM*] [*Brixham, Devonshire, England*] (EAIO)
IMC............. International Materials Conference (DCTA)
IMC............. International Medical Centers
IMC............. International Medical Commission for Health and Human Rights [*Switzerland*]
IMC............. International Medical Corps (EA)
IMC............. International Meeting Center [*Germany*] (EAIO)
IMC............. International Meteorological Committee
IMC............. International Micrographic Congress (EA)
IMC............. International Minerals & Chemical Corp.
IMC............. International Missionary Council [*Later, CWME*]
IMC............. International Monetary Conference (ECON)
IMC............. International Morse Code (ADDR)
IMC............. International Multifoods Corp. [*NYSE symbol*] (SPSG)
IMC............. International Music Conference (AEBS)
IMC............. International Music Council [*Paris, France*] (EA)
IMC............. Internet Message Center
IMC............. Intestinal Mast Cells [*Anatomy*]
IMC............. Intl Multifoods [*NYSE symbol*] (TTSB)
IMC............. Inventory Management Center (MCD)
IMC............. Inventory of Marital Conflicts [*Psychology*] (DHP)
IMC............. Isochronous Maintenance Channel [*Electronics*]
IMC............. Item Management Coding [*Military*] (AABC)
IMC............. Item Management Concept
IMC............. Item Master Card [*Military*] (AABC)
IMC............. Marion College, Marion, IN [*OCLC symbol*] (OCLC)
IMC............. Preparatory Committee for the International Medical Commission for Health and Human Rights (EAIO)
IMCA.......... Indian Major Crimes Act [*1909*]
IMCA.......... Indian Motorcycle Club of America (EA)
IMCA.......... Information Management and Consulting Association [*Information service or system*] (IID)
IMCA.......... Insurance Marketing Communications Association (EA)
IMCA.......... International Motor Contest Association (EA)
IMCA.......... Investment Management Consultants Association (EA)
IMCAB........ Internal Mammary Coronary Artery Bypass [*Cardiology*]
IMCAC........ Intermountain Collegiate Athletic Conference (PSS)
IMCAR .... International Movement of Catholic Agricultural and Rural Youth G2 [*See also MIJARC*]
IMCARY ..... International Movement of Catholic Agricultural and Rural Youth [*See also MIJARC*] [*Louvain, Belgium*] (EAIO)
IMCAS........ Interactive Man/Computer Augmentation System
IMCAST....... Instructor Model Characteristics for Automated Speech Technology (MCD)
IMCA-US..... International Moth Class Association - US (EA)
IMCB.......... Institute of Molecular & Cell Biology [*Singapore*]
IMCC.......... Image Motion Compensation and Calibration
IMCC.......... IMC Mortgage Co. [*NASDAQ symbol*] (SAG)
IMCC.......... Integrated Mission Control Center [*NASA*]
IMCC.......... Interstate Mining Compact Commission (EA)
IMCC.......... Item Management Control Code (AABC)
IMcc.......... McCook Public Library District, McCook, IL [*Library symbol Library of Congress*] (LCLS)
IMccA .... Armak Co., McCook, IL [*Library symbol Library of Congress*] (LCLS)
IMCCSRA.... International MC Class Sailboat Racing Association (EA)
IMCD .... Information Management and Compliance Division [*Department of Education*] (GFGA)
IMCD .... Inner Medullary Collecting Ducts [*Kidney anatomy*]
IMCD .... Input Marginal Checking and Distribution
IMCE .... Institute for Molecular and Cellular Evolution [*University of Miami*] [*Research center*] (RCD)
IMCE .... International Meeting of Cataloging Experts
IMCEA........ International Military Club Executives Association (EA)
IMCEA........ International Military Community Executives Association (NTPA)
IMC Glob .... IMC Global, Inc. [*Formerly, IMC Fertilizer Group*] [*Associated Press*] (SAG)
IMchF .... Follett Software Co., McHenry, IL [*Library symbol*] [*Library of Congress*] (LCLS)
IMCI............ Individual and Marriage Counseling Inventory [*Psychology*]
IMCI............ Infinite Machines [*NASDAQ symbol*] (TTSB)
IMCI............ Infinite Machines Corp. [*NASDAQ symbol*] (SAG)
IMC-IFR ...... Instrument [*Flight*] Meteorological Conditions - Instrument Flight Rules [*Aviation*] (DNAB)
IMCIW .... Infinite Machines Wrrt [*NASDAQ symbol*] (TTSB)
IMCJ .... International Movement of Catholic Jurists (EAIO)
IMCL............ ImClone Systems [*NASDAQ symbol*] (TTSB)
IMCL............ ImClone Systems, Inc. [*NASDAQ symbol*] (SPSG)
IMCL............ International Movement of Catholic Lawyers [*France*]
Imclne .... ImClone Systems, Inc. [*Associated Press*] (SAG)
IMCM .... In Medio Currere Metuo [*I Fear to Go in the Middle*] [*Motto of Julius, Duke of Braunschweig-Wolfenbuttel (1529-89)*] [*Latin*]
IMCM .... Master Chief Instrumentman [*Navy rating*]
IMC Mt .... IMC Mortgage Co. [*Associated Press*] (SAG)
IMCO .... IMCO Recycling, Inc. [*Associated Press*] (SAG)
IMCO .... IMPCO Technologies [*NASDAQ symbol*] [*Formerly, AirSensors, Inc.*] (SG)
IMCO .... Improved Combustion
IMCO .... Intergovernmental Maritime Consultative Organization
IMCO .... International Maritime Consultive Organization
IMCO .... International Metered Communications

IMCOA .... Insulation Materials Corp. of America
IMCoS .... International Map Collectors' Society (EAIO)
IMCP .... Integrated Monitor and Control Panel (MCD)
IMCP .... Item Management Coding Program [Military] (AFM)
IMCPM .... Improved Capability Missile [Air Force] (IAA)
IMCR .... Institute for Mediation and Conflict Resolution (EA)
IMC/RMC ..... Instructional Materials Centers/Regional Media Centers
IMCS .... Individual Microclimate Cooling System [Army] (INF)
IMCS .... Intelligent Motion Control System (PDAA)
IMCS .... Interactive Manufacturing Control System [NCR Ltd.] [Software package] (NCC)
IMCS .... Interactive Multimedia Computing Systems (TELE)
IMCS .... International Meeting in Community Service [Germany] (EAIO)
IMCS .... International Movement of Catholic Students [France]
IMCS .... Pax Romana, International Movement of Catholic Students [See also MIEC] [Fribourg, Switzerland Paris, France] (EAIO)
IMCS .... Senior Chief Instrumentman [Navy rating]
IMCSAC .... International Movement of Catholic Students - African Secretariat [An association] (EAIO)
IMcSC .... John Swaney Attendance Center, McNabb, IL [Library symbol Library of Congress] (LCLS)
IMCSMHI ..... Industrial Metal Containers Section of the Material Handling Institute (EA)
IMCSRS .... Installation Materiel Condition Status Reporting System [Army]
IMCTS .... Intake Manifold Charge Temperature Sensor [Automotive engineering]
IMCU .... Intensity Millicurie [Nucleonics] (IAA)
IMCWR .... International Movement of Conscientious War Resisters [Tel Aviv, Israel] (EAIO)
IMCX .... ImageMatrix Corp. [NASDAQ symbol] (SAG)
IMD .... Immunologically Mediated Disease [Medicine]
IMD .... Imo Industries [NYSE symbol] (TTSB)
IMD .... Imo Industries, Inc. [NYSE symbol] (SPSG)
IMD .... Imonda [Papua New Guinea] [Airport symbol] (OAG)
IMD .... Incremental Multiple Development (PDAA)
IMD .... Independent Module Development (PDAA)
IMD .... Indianapolis-Marion County Public Library, Indianapolis, IN [OCLC symbol] (OCLC)
IMD .... Indian Medical Department [British military] (DMA)
IMD .... Inertia-Measuring Device [Mechanical engineering]
IMD .... Information Management Division [Environmental Protection Agency] (GFGA)
IMD .... Inhibit Momentum Dump
IMD .... Institute for Marine Dynamics [Canada] (PDAA)
IMD .... Institute for Muscle Disease [Defunct] (EA)
IMD .... Institut fur Maschinelle Dokumentation (NITA)
IMD .... Institutions for Mental Diseases [Department of Health and Human Services] (GFGA)
IMD .... Interactive Map Definition (IAA)
IMD .... Intercept Monitoring Display
IMD .... Intermediate (NASA)
IMD .... Intermetal Dielectric (AAEL)
IMD .... Intermittent Motion Driver
IMD .... Intermodulation Distortion (MSA)
IMD .... International Institute for Management Development
IMD .... International Market Development Program [Department of Energy]
IMD .... International MTM [Methods-Time-Measurement] Directorate (EA)
IMD .... Invasive Meningococcal Disease
IMD .... Ion Mobility Detector [Instrumentation]
IMD .... Isove's Modified Dulbrecco's Medium [Oncology]
IMDA .... Independent Medical Distributors Association (EA)
IMDA .... Indian Mineral Development Act of 1982
IMDA .... International Magic Dealers Association (EA)
IMDA .... International Mail Dealers Association (EA)
IMDA .... International Map Dealers Association (EA)
IMDB .... Integrated Maintenance Database (MCD)
IMDC .... Inamed Corp. [NASDAQ symbol] (NQ)
IMDC .... Instructional Media Distribution Center [University of Wisconsin - Madison] [Research center] (RCD)
IMDC .... Interceptor Missile Direction Center
IMDC .... Internal Message Distribution Center (NATG)
IMDC .... Intramedullary Metatarsal Decompression [Medicine] (DMAA)
IMDD .... Idiopathic Midline Destructive Disease [Dentistry]
IMDEG .... Insurance Management Decision Game
IMDES .... Item Management Data Element Standardization [or System] [Military]
IMDFNA .... Inhibited Maximum Density Fuming Nitric Acid (MCD)
IMDG .... International Maritime Dangerous Goods
IMDGC .... International Maritime Dangerous Goods Code (MCD)
IMDI .... International Management and Development Institute
IMDL .... Inter-Laboratory Method Detection Limit [Environmental Protection Agency]
IM/DM .... Information Management / Data Management (HGAA)
IMDM .... Iscove's Modified Dulbecco's Medium [For nematode culture]
IMDO .... Installation and Materiel District Office [FAA]
IMDO .... Intelligence Material Development Office [Military] (MCD)
IMDP .... Integrated Management Development Program [Australia]
IMDQ .... Injected Minimum Detectable Quantity [Analytical chemistry]
IMDR .... Intelligent Mark Document Reader (MHDI)
IMDR .... Item Management Data Reply (MCD)
IMDS .... International Meat Development Scheme [United Nations Defunct] (EAIO)
IMDS .... International Microform Distribution Service (NITA)
IMDSO .... Intelligence Materiel Development and Support Office [Army] (RDA)
imdt .... Immediately (BARN)

IMDT .... International Institute for Music, Dance, and Theatre in the Audio-Visual Media [Later, Mediacult International Institute for Audio-Visual Communication and Cultural Development]
IMDTLY .... Immediately (WGA)
IMDur .... Inscriptiones Mithriacae Duranae (BJA)
IME .... Immobilized Enzyme
IME .... Incendiary Munitions Evaluation
IME .... Independent Medical Evaluation
IME .... Independent Medical Examination [British]
IME .... Independent Medical Examiner (HGAA)
IME .... Indiana & Michigan Power [NYSE symbol] (SAG)
IME .... Indirect Manufacturing Expense
IME .... Indirect Medical Education [Department of Health and Human Services] (GFGA)
IME .... Industria Machine Electroniche [Computer manufacturer] [Italy] (NITA)
IME .... Information Management & Engineering Ltd. [Information service or system] (IID)
IME .... Institute for Municipal Engineering
IME .... Institute of Makers of Explosives (EA)
IME .... Institute of Marine Engineers [British]
IME .... Institute of Mathematics Education [La Trobe University] [Australia]
IME .... Institute of Mechanical Engineers [British]
IME .... Institute of Mining Engineers [British]
IME .... Institute on the Military and the Economy (EA)
IME .... International Magnetospheric Explorer [NASA/ESRO]
IME .... International Materiel Evaluation Program [Army] (RDA)
IME .... International Medical Exchange [Defunct] (EA)
IME .... International Microcomputer Exhibition (NITA)
IME .... International Microcomputer Exposition
IME .... International Mirtone, Inc. [Toronto Stock Exchange symbol]
IME .... Interplanetary Meteoroid Experiment [NASA]
IME .... Mennonite Biblical Seminary Library, Elkhart, IN [OCLC symbol] (OCLC)
IMEA .... Indirect Medical Education Adjustment
IMEA .... International Middle East Association (EA)
IME(AB) .... Institution of Mechanical Engineers (Australian Branch)
IMEAC .... Northeast Interagency Motor Equipment Advisory Committee [Terminated, 1981] [General Services Administration] (EGAO)
IMEASY .... Integrated Management and Economic Analysis Model [Federal Emergency Management Agency] (GFGA)
IMEB .... International Movement of Esperantist Bicyclists [See also BEMI] [The Hague, Netherlands] (EAIO)
IMEC .... Imatec Ltd. [NASDAQ symbol] (SAG)
IMEC .... Institut Mondial d'Ecologie et de Cancerologie [World Institute of Ecology and Cancer - WIEC] (EAIO)
IMEC .... Interstate Migrant Education Council (EA)
IMEC .... Item Mission Essentially Code (MCD)
I Mech E ..... Institution of Mechanical Engineers [British]
IMECHIE ...... Institution of Mechanical Incorporated Engineers [British] (EAIO)
IMED .... Informedics, Inc. [NASDAQ symbol] (SAG)
IMEG .... Innovations in Medical Education Grant (DMAA)
IMEG .... International Management and Engineering Group [British]
IMEKO .... Internationale Messtechnische Konfoderation [International Measurement Confederation] [ICSU Budapest, Hungary] (EAIO)
IMEL .... IAEA [International Atomic Energy Agency] Marine Environment Laboratory [Marine science] (OSRA)
IMel .... Melvin Public Library, Melvin, IL [Library symbol Library of Congress] (LCLS)
IMelF .... Ford County Film Cooperative, Melvin, IL [Library symbol] [Library of Congress] (LCLS)
IMelp .... Melrose Park Public Library, Melrose Park, IL [Library symbol Library of Congress] (LCLS)
IMelpA .... Alberto-Culver Co., Melrose Park, IL [Library symbol Library of Congress] (LCLS)
IMelSD .... Melvin-Sibley Community Unit School District, Melvin, IL [Library symbol] [Library of Congress] (LCLS)
IMEM .... Improved Minimum Essential Medium [Microbiology]
IMEM .... International Mass Education Movement (EA)
IMEM-HS ..... Improved Minimal Essential Medium, Hormone Supplemented (DB)
IMEMME ...... Institution of Mining Electrical and Mining Mechanical Engineers (EAIO)
IMEMO .... Institute of World Economics and International Affairs [Russian] (BARN)
IMen .... Graves Public Library, Mendota, IL [Library symbol Library of Congress] (LCLS)
IMenHS .... Mendota High School, Mendota, IL [Library symbol Library of Congress] (LCLS)
IMenN .... Northbrook Elementary School, Mendota, IL [Library symbol Library of Congress] (LCLS)
IMEO .... Initial Mass in Earth Orbit [NASA]
IMEO .... Interim Maintenance Engineering Order (AAG)
IMEP .... Indicated Mean Effective Pressure [Aerospace]
IMEP .... International Materiel Evaluation Program [Army] (RDA)
IMER .... Immobilized-Enzyme Reactor
IMER .... Institute for Marine Environmental Research [British] (ARC)
IMerD .... Meredosia-Chambersburg River Valley Public Library District, Meredosia, IL [Library symbol Library of Congress] (LCLS)
IMES .... Integrated Missile Electronics Set
IMET .... International Military Education and Training [Program of grant military training in the United States for foreign military and civilian personnel]
IMET .... Isometric Endurance Time (STED)
I METH .... Independent Methodist (WDAA)
IMETP .... International Military Education and Training Program [DoD]

IMETS........... Integrated Meteorological System [*Army*] (RDA)
IMEX............ Imex Medical Systems [*NASDAQ symbol*] (TTSB)
IMEX............ Imex Medical Systems, Inc. [*NASDAQ symbol*] (NQ)
IMEX............ Integrated Manufacturing Exposition [*Penton/IPC*] (TSPED)
IMF............. Allen County Public Library, Fort Wayne, IN [*OCLC symbol*] (OCLC)
IMF............. Idiopathic Myelofibrosis (STED)
IMF............. Ifosfamide, Mesna Uroprotection, Methotrexate, and Fluorouracil (STED)
IMF............. Ifosfamide, Methotrexate, Fluorouracil (CDI)
IMF............. Image-Matched Filter (IAA)
IMF............. Immunofixation [*Analytical biochemistry*]
IMF............. Immunofluorescent [*Immunology*]
IMF............. Impact Mechanical Fuse (MCD)
IMF............. Imphal [*India*] [*Airport symbol*] (OAG)
IMF............. Impossible Mission Force [*Fictitious group of undercover agents in TV series, "Mission: Impossible"*]
IMF............. Individual Master File
IMF............. [*The*] Inefficient-Market Fund [*AMEX symbol*] (SPSG)
IMF............. Initial Mass Function [*Galactic science*]
IMF............. Installation Master File (MCD)
IMF............. Institut de Mecanique des Fluides [*Originator and database on fluid mechanics*] [*France*] (NITA)
IMF............. Institute for Metal Forming [*Lehigh University*] [*Research center*] (RCD)
IMF............. Institute for Monetary Freedom (EA)
IMF............. [*The*] Institute of Metal Finishing [*British*]
IMF............. Integrated Maintenance Facility
IMF............. Intelligent Minefield [*Army*] (MUSM)
IMF............. Intense Magnetic Field
IMF............. Interactive Mainframe Facility (HGAA)
IMF............. Interim Minesweeping Force [*Military*]
IMF............. Intermaxillary Fixation (MAE)
IMF............. Intermediate Filament (STED)
IMF............. Intermediate Maintenance Facility
IMF............. Intermediate Moisture Food
IMF............. Internal Magnetic Focus
IMF............. International Marketing Federation [*Paris, France*] (EAIO)
IMF............. International Metalworkers Federation [*See also FIOM*] [*Geneva, Switzerland*] (EAIO)
IMF............. International Ministerial Federation [*Defunct*] (EA)
IMF............. International Monetary Fund [*United Nations*] (EA)
IMF............. International Myomassethics Federation (EA)
IMF............. Interplanetary Magnetic Field
IMF............. Inventory Master File (NASA)
IMF............. Iowa Medical Foundation
IMF............. Israel Music Foundation (EA)
IMF............. Item Master File (MCD)
IMF............. Iuliu Maniu American Romanian Relief Foundation (EA)
i-mf--.......... Mauritius [*MARC geographic area code Library of Congress*] (LCCP)
IMFA............ Immigration Marriage Fraud Amendments Act of 1986
IMFC............ Immaculate Mary Fan Club (EA)
IMFC............ Iron Maiden Fan Club [*British*] (EAIO)
IMFET.......... Internally Matched FETs [*Field Effect Transistor*] [*Avantek*] (NITA)
IMFHS......... Isle of Man Family History Society [*British*] (EAIO)
IMF/IBRD ..... International Monetary Fund and International Bank for Reconstruction and Development
IMFK........... Integrated Multifunction Keyboard (MCD)
IMFL........... Inventory of Marriage and Family Literature [*Sage Publications, Inc.*] (IID)
IM/FM .... Intensity Modulated / Frequency Modulated (WDAA)
IMFP............ Inelastic Mean Free [*or Face*] Path [*Surface analysis*]
IMFP............ Interaction Mean Free Path [*Astrophysics*]
IMFR........... Institute of Marriage and Family Relations (EA)
IMFRAD....... Integrated Multifrequency RADAR (MCD)
IMFSS......... Integrated Missile Flight Safety System
IMFU.......... Imperial Military Foul-Up [*Bowdlerized version*] (DSUE)
IMFWUNA.... International Molders' and Foundry Workers' Union of North America [*Later, IM &AWU*]
IMG............. Image
IMG............. Immigration
ImG............. Immunogenetics
IMG............. Imperial Cargo Airlines Ltd. [*Ghana*] [*ICAO designator*] (FAAC)
IMG............. Inertial Measurement Group (KSC)
IMG............. Inferior Mesenteric Ganglia [*Anatomy*]
IMG............. Inferior Mesenteric Ganglion [*Medicine*] (STED)
IMG............. Informational Media Guaranty
IMG............. Installation and Maintenance Guide
IMG............. Interactive Media Group
IMG............. Intermagnetics General Corp. [*AMEX symbol*] (SPSG)
IMG............. Internal Medicine Group [*Group practice*] (DAVI)
IMG............. International Mail Gram (MHDB)
IMG............. International Maintenance Group [*FAA*] (TAG)
IMG............. International Management Group
IMG............. International Marxist Group [*British*] (PPW)
IMG............. International Music Guide [*A publication*]
IMG............. Mead Johnson & Co., Research Library, Evansville, IN [*OCLC symbol*] (OCLC)
IMg............. Morton Grove Public Library, Morton Grove, IL [*Library symbol Library of Congress*] (LCLS)
IMGCN........ Integrated Missile Ground Control Network
IMGCSA...... Islamic Missionaries Guild of the Caribbean and South America (EAIO)
ImgeGud...... Image Guided Technologies, Inc. [*Associated Press*] (SAG)
ImgeM......... ImageMatrix Corp. [*Associated Press*] (SAG)
ImgeMat...... ImageMatrix Corp. [*Associated Press*] (SAG)

IMGG .... Institute of Marine Geology and Geophysics [*Russian Federation*] [*Marine science*] (OSRA)
IMGG .... Intramuscular Gammaglobulin [*Medicine*] (DMAA)
IMGI .... Improved Maintenance Guidance Information
ImgMgt .... Imaging Management Associates [*Associated Press*] (SAG)
IMGN .... Immuncogen, Inc. [*NASDAQ symbol*] (SAG)
IMGN .... ImmunoGen, Inc. [*NASDAQ symbol*] (NQ)
IMGNG........ Imaging
IMGNTN...... Imagination
IMgO .... Oakton Community College, Morton Grove, IL [*Library symbol Library of Congress*] (LCLS)
IMgO-Dp ...... Oakton Community Colleges, Learning Resources Center, Des Plaines, IL [*Library symbol Library of Congress*] (LCLS)
IMGS .... International Mammalian Genome Society (HGEN)
IMGT .... Interim Missile Guidance Test (MCD)
IMgT .... Travenol Laboratories, Morton Grove, IL [*Library symbol Library of Congress*] (LCLS)
IMGTechE .... Institution of Mechanical General Technician Engineers [*British*]
IMGX .... Network Imaging Corp. [*NASDAQ symbol*] (SAG)
IMGXP .... Network Imaging $2.00 Cv Pfd [*NASDAQ symbol*] (TTSB)
IMGXW .... Network Imaging Wrrt [*NASDAQ symbol*] (TTSB)
IMH .... Idiopathic Myocardial Hypertrophy [*Cardiology*]
IMH .... IMPAC Mortgage Holdings [*AMEX symbol*] [*Formerly, Imperial Credit Mortgage Holdings*] (SG)
IMH .... Imperial Credit Mortagage Holdings, Inc. [*AMEX symbol*] (SAG)
IMH .... Imperial Credit Mtge Hldgs [*AMEX symbol*] (TTSB)
IMH .... Indirect Microhemagglutination Test [*Medicine*] (DMAA)
IMH .... Inlet Manhole [*Technical drawings*]
IMH .... Institut des Moeurs Humaines [*Institute of Human Values - IHV*] [*Canada*]
IMH .... Institute of Materials Handling [*British*] (BI)
IMH .... International Majestic Holdings Ltd. [*Formerly, Majestic Resources Corp.*] [*Vancouver Stock Exchange symbol*]
IMH .... International Marketing Handbook [*A publication*]
IMH .... Mennonite Historical Library, Goshen College, Goshen, IN [*OCLC symbol*] (OCLC)
IMHA .... Interamerican Medical and Health Association (EA)
IMHE .... Industrial Materials Handling Equipment
IMHE .... Institutional Management in Higher Education (AIE)
IMHEP .... Ideal Man Helicopter Engineering Project
IMHEPFC .... Idol of My Heart Elvis Presley Fan Club (EA)
IMHI........... Infomed Holdings, Inc. [*NASDAQ symbol*] (SAG)
IMHI........... Institute for Mental Health Initiatives (EA)
IMHO .... In My Honest Opinion
IMHO .... In My Humble Opinion [*Internet language*] [*Computer science*]
IMHO .... Inventory of Mental Health Organizations [*Department of Health and Human Services*] (GFGA)
IMHOF .... International Motor Sports Hall of Fame [*Automotive racing history*]
IMHO/GHMHS... Inventory of Mental Health Organizations and General Hospital Mental Health Services [*Department of Health and Human Services*] (GFGA)
IMHP .... Iodomercuri-Hydroxypropane [*Chemistry*] (DAVI)
IMHP .... Isopropyl Methyl Pyrimidinone [*Organic chemistry*]
IMHQ .... International Military Headquarters (CINC)
IMHR .... International Miniature Horse Registry (EA)
IMHSSACE... Inventory of Mental Health Services in State Adult Correctional Facilites [*Department of Health and Human Services*] (GFGA)
IMHV .... Intermediate and Medial Part of the Hyperstriatum Ventrale [*Bird brain anatomy*]
IMI .... ICAN Minerals Ltd. [*Toronto Stock Exchange symbol*]
IMI .... Ignition Manufacturers Institute [*Later, TMI*] (EA)
ImI .... IMI of Philadelphia, Camp Hill, PA [*Library symbol Library of Congress*] (LCLS)
IMI .... Imipramine [*Antidepressant*]
IMI .... Immunologically Measurable Insulin [*Medicine*] (AAMN)
IMI .... Impact Message Inventory (EDAC)
IMI .... Imperial Metal Industries Ltd. [*British*]
IMI .... Implantable Micro-Identification Device [*for laboratory animals*]
IMI .... Improved Manned Interceptor [*Proposed plane*] [*Air Force*]
IMI .... Improved Massed Intercept (MCD)
IMI .... Incentives Management Index [*Test*]
IMI .... Ine [*Marshall Islands*] [*Airport symbol*] (OAG)
IMI .... Inferior Myocardial Infarction [*Cardiology*]
IMI .... Information Marketing International [*Information service or system*] (IID)
IMI .... Infrared Measurement Instrument
IMI .... Installation and Maintenance Instruction
IMI .... Institute for Marine Information [*Defunct*] (EA)
IMI .... Institute of the Motor Industry, Inc. [*British*] (BI)
IMI .... Institute on Money and Inflation (EA)
IMI .... Institut Metapsychique International [*International Metaphysics Institute*] [*France*] (EAIO)
IMI .... Integrally Molded Insulation
IMI .... Intensive Management Items (MCD)
IMI .... Interim Manned Interceptor (PDAA)
IMI .... Intermediate Machine Instruction
IMI .... Intermediate Manned Interceptor (MUGU)
IMI .... International Maintenance Institute (EA)
IMI .... International Management Institute [*Switzerland*]
IMI .... International Manganese Institute [*France*] (EAIO)
IMI .... International Maple Institute
IMI .... International Marina Institute (NTPA)
IMI .... International Market Index (NUMA)
IMI .... International Marketing Institute (EA)

IMI.............. International Market Intelligence [Databank originator] [Norway] (NITA)
IMI.............. International Masonry Institute (EA)
IMI.............. International Meteorological Institute [Marine science] (OSRA)
IMI.............. International Ministries to Israel (EA)
IMI.............. International Missions (EA)
IMI.............. Intramuscular Injection [Medicine] (MAE)
IMI.............. Intraoperative Myocardial Ischemia [Cardiology]
IMI.............. Invention Marketing, Inc. [Information service or system] (IID)
IMI.............. Invention Marketing Institute (EA)
IMI.............. Investment Management Institute [Information service or system] (IID)
IMI.............. Ion Microwelding Instrument
IMI.............. Irish Management Institute (EAIO)
IMI.............. Istituto Mobiliare Italiano [NYSE symbol] (SAG)
IMI.............. Istituto Mobiliare Ital ADS [NYSE symbol] (TTSB)
IMI.............. Istituto Mobiliare Italiana [Italian state-owned bank] (ECON)
IMI.............. Marian College, Indianapolis, IN [OCLC symbol] (OCLC)
IMIA.......... Institute of Mathematics and Its Applications [South-End-On-Sea, England]
IMIA.......... International Machinery Insurers Association [Munich, Federal Republic of Germany] (EAIO)
IMIA.......... International Medical Informatics Association [IFIP special interest group] [Richmond Hill, ON] (EAIO)
IMIAT........ International Masonry Institute Apprenticeship and Training (EA)
IMIB.......... Inland Marine Insurance Bureau [Later, ISO] (EA)
IMIC.......... Independent Medical Insurance Consultants Ltd. [British]
IMIC.......... Industir-Matematik International Corp. [NASDAQ symbol] (SAG)
IMIC.......... Inhibitor of Mevalonate Incorporation to Cholesterol [Food science]
IMIC.......... International Medical Information Center, Inc. [Tokyo, Japan]
IMIC.......... International Music Industry Conference
IMIC.......... Interval Modulation Information Coding (PDAA)
IMID.......... Inadvertent Missile Ignition Detection
IMID.......... Infrared Miniaturized Intrusion Detector (PDAA)
IMid.......... Midlothian Public Library, Midlothian, IL [Library symbol Library of Congress] (LCLS)
IMIDCA........ Interim Motorized Infantry Division Capability Analysis [Military]
IMIE.......... Institution of Mining Engineers [British]
IMIF.......... International Maritime Industries Forum [British] (EAIO)
IMIG.......... Intramuscular Immunoglobulin [Immunology] (DAVI)
IMII.......... Intelligent Medical Imaging, Inc. [NASDAQ symbol] (SAG)
IMII.......... Intelligent Med'l Imaging [NASDAQ symbol] (TTSB)
IMil.......... Milford Township Public Library, Milford, IL [Library symbol Library of Congress] (LCLS)
IMIlsSD........ Millstadt Community Consolidated School District 160, Millstadt, IL [Library symbol Library of Congress] (LCLS)
IMiM.......... Inner Mitochondrial Membrane [Cytology]
IMIMI.......... Industrial Mineral Insulation Manufacturers Institute [Later, TIMA]
IMinE.......... Institution of Mining Engineers [British]
IMINICO........ Iranian Marine International Oil Co.
IMINT.......... Imaginary Intelligence (COE)
IMINT.......... Imaging Intelligence [RADAR, photos, etc.]
IMIP.......... Industrial Management Improvement Program (NG)
IMIP.......... Industrial Modernization Improvement Plan [DoD] (RDA)
IMIP.......... Industrial Modernization Incentive Program [DoD]
IM/IPF.......... Information Management / Information Processing Family (HGAA)
IMIR.......... Interceptor Missile Interrogation RADAR
IMIS.......... Installation Management Information System [Army]
IMIS.......... Instructional Materials Information System [Database]
IMIS.......... Integrated Management Information System [Air Force]
IMIS.......... Integrated Manufacturing Information System
IMIS.......... Integrated Motorists' Information System [Computerized guidance system to speed traffic and avoid tie-ups]
IMIS.......... Integrated Municipal Information System (IAA)
IMIS.......... Intelligence Management Information System [Military] (MCD)
IMIS.......... Interim Maneuver Identification System (IAA)
IMIT.......... Imitate [or Imitative] (WDAA)
IMIT.......... Imitation (MSA)
IMIT.......... Institute of Musical Instrument Technology [British] (BI)
IM-IT.......... Insured Municipals-Income Trust [Investment term]
IMITAC.......... Image Input to Automatic Computers
IMITS.......... Interim Mobile Independent Target System [Military] (INF)
IMIX.......... Imaging Workstation in X-Ray Microanalysis
IMJ.......... Indiana & Michigan Power [NYSE symbol] (SAG)
IMJ.......... Indiana Mich Pwr 8%JrSubDebs [NYSE symbol] (TTSB)
IMJ.......... Infrared Miniaturized Jammer
IMJ.......... RCA [Radio Corp. of America] Consumer Electronics Library, Indianapolis, IN [OCLC symbol] (OCLC)
IMJHCA.......... International Messianic Jewish Hebrew Christian Alliance [British] (EAIO)
IMK.......... Identification Mark (IAA)
IMK.......... Income Monitoring Kit
IMK.......... Increased Maneuverability Kit
IMK.......... Injection Molding Kit
IMK.......... Instrument Marking Kit
IMK.......... International Makaoo [Vancouver Stock Exchange symbol]
IMK.......... Simikot [Nepal] [Airport symbol] (OAG)
IMK.......... Union Carbide Corp., Library, Indianapolis, IN [OCLC symbol] (OCLC)
IMKE.......... Inmark Enterprises, Inc. [NASDAQ symbol] (SAG)
IMKR.......... Inner Marker [Part of an instrument landing system] [Aviation]
IMKT.......... Ingles Markets, Inc. [NASDAQ symbol] (NQ)
IMKTA.......... Ingles Markets'A' [NASDAQ symbol] (TTSB)
IML.......... Imperial, NE [Location identifier FAA] (FAAL)
IML.......... Incoming Matching Loss [Telecommunications] (TEL)

IML.............. Indusmin Ltd. [Toronto Stock Exchange symbol]
IML.............. Information Manipulation Language
IML.............. Initial Machine Load [Computer science] (IBMDP)
IML.............. Initial Measurement List (KSC)
IML.............. Initial Microprogram Load [Also, IMPL] [Computer science] (IBMDP)
IML.............. Inside Mold Line [Technical drawings]
IML.............. Institute of Modern Languages
IML.............. Instructional Media Laboratory
IML.............. Interactive Maintenance Language [Denelcor] (NITA)
IML.............. Intermediary Musical Language (PDAA)
IML.............. Intermediary Music Language (NITA)
IML.............. Intermediate Language [Computer science] (TEL)
IML.............. Intermediate Maintenance Level
IML.............. Internal Medullary Lamina [Neuroanatomy]
IML.............. International Microgravity Laboratory
ImL.............. Irish Microforms Ltd., Dublin, Ireland [Library symbol Library of Congress] (LCLS)
IML.............. Irradiated Materials Laboratory
IML.............. Island Air Ltd. [Fiji] [ICAO designator] (FAAC)
IML.............. Merrill Lynch & Co. [NYSE symbol] (SAG)
IML.............. Miles Laboratories, Inc., Library Resources and Services, Elkhart, IN [OCLC symbol] (OCLC)
IMLA.......... Intramural Left Anterior Artery [Medicine] (DMAA)
IMLC.......... Infantry Mortar Leader's Course [Army] (INF)
IMLS.......... Institute of Medical Laboratory Sciences [British]
IMLSG.......... Interim Mobile Logistic Support Group [Military] (CAAL)
IMLSS.......... Integrated Maneuvering and Life Support System [NASA]
IMLT.......... Institute of Medical Laboratory Technology [British] (DI)
ImLy.......... Immune Lysis [Medicine] (DMAA)
IMM.......... Immaculata College, Immaculata, PA [OCLC symbol] (OCLC)
IMM.......... Immediate
IMM.......... Immersion (ECII)
IMM.......... Immokalee, FL [Location identifier FAA] (FAAL)
IMM.......... Immune [or Immunization] (AFM)
IMM.......... Impairing the Morals of a Minor [Police terminology] (IIA)
IMM.......... Independent Manned Manipulator [NASA] (KSC)
IMM.......... Inhibitor-Containing Minimal Medium [Microbiology]
IMM.......... Inner Mitochondrial Membrane [Cytology]
IMM.......... Institute for Manpower Management (EA)
IMM.......... Institute for Molecular Manufacturing
IMM.......... Institute of Clinical Molecular Biology [British] (DBA)
IMM.......... Institute of Male Masseurs [British] (DBA)
IMM.......... Institute of Materials Management [British] (DBA)
IMM.......... Institution of Mining and Metallurgy [London, England]
IMM.......... Integrated Magnetic Memory (IAA)
IMM.......... Integrated Maintenance Management
IMM.......... Integrated Maintenance Manual
IMM.......... Integrated Materiel Management [or Manager]
IMM.......... Intelligent Memory Manager [Computer science]
IMM.......... Intel Mobile Module [Computer science]
IMM.......... Interactive Multimedia
IMM.......... Intermediate Maintenance Manual [Military] (CAAL)
IMM.......... Internal Medial Malleolus [Medicine] (DMAA)
IMM.......... International Maggie Mines Ltd. [Vancouver Stock Exchange symbol]
IMM.......... International Maritime Mobile [Telecommunications]
IMM.......... International Monetary Market [Chicago Mercantile Exchange]
IMM.......... International Money Management [Business term]
IMM.......... Intersection Midblock Model [Environmental Protection Agency] (GFGA)
IMMA.......... Institute of Muslim Minority Affairs (EAIO)
IMMA.......... International Model Managers Association (EA)
IMMA.......... International Motorcycle Manufacturers Association (EAIO)
IMMA.......... Ion Microprobe Mass Analyzer
IMMAC.......... Immaculate
IMMAC.......... Inventory Management and Material Control (IAA)
Imm AR.......... Immigration Appeal Reports [A publication] (DLA)
Immarsat.......... International Maritime Satellite Organization (WA)
IMMAT.......... Immaterial (AABC)
IMMAT.......... Immature
IMMC.......... Integrated Materiel Management Center [Army]
IMMC.......... Interdigestive Migrating Motor Complex [Medicine] (DMAA)
IMMCLT.......... Immaculate
IMMD.......... Intensity-Maximizing Multidither (PDAA)
IMMDELREQ.......... Immediate Delivery Required (DNAB)
IMMDT.......... Immediate
IMME.......... Institute of Municipal Maintenance Engineers [British] (BI)
IMME.......... Isobaric Multiplet Mass Equation
IMMED.......... Immediate (AFM)
IMMED.......... Immediate [Classified advertising]
IMMEX.......... Interactive Multi-Media Exercises [A Windows-based program]
IMMGRTN.......... Immigration
IMMH.......... Indirect Maintenance Man-Hour
IMMI.......... Inphynet Medical Management [NASDAQ symbol] (SAG)
IMMI.......... International Irrigation Management Institute (GNE)
IMMI.......... International Mass Media Institute (EA)
IMMIG.......... Immigration
Immig & Naturalization Serv Mo Rev... United States Immigration and Naturalization Service, Monthly Review [A publication] (DLA)
Immig B Bull... Immigration Bar Bulletin [A publication] (DLA)
Immig Newsl... Immigration Newsletter [A publication] (DLA)
IMMIRS.......... Integrated Maintenance Management Information Retrieval System [DoD]
IMMITTANCE.......... Impedance and Admittance (IAA)
IMMLEP.......... Immunization Against Leprosy Program [World Health Organization]
IMMLS.......... Interim Military Microwave Landing System (RDA)

IMMOB	Immobilize [Medicine]
IMMOBIL	Immobilize (BABM)
IMMP	Information Management Master Plan [DoD]
IMMP	Information Mission Management Plan
IMMP	Integrated Maintenance Management Plan
IMMR	Installation, Modification, Maintenance, and Repair (AAG)
IMMR	Institute for Mining and Mineral Research [University of Kentucky] [Research center] (RCD)
IMMRL	Individual Maintenance Material Readiness List (MCD)
IMMRRI	Idaho Mining and Minerals Resources Research Institute [University of Idaho] [Research center] (RCD)
IMMS	Indore Mill Mazdoor Sangh [Indore Textile Labour Association] [India]
IMMS	Installation Maintenance Management System (MCD)
IMMS	Integrated Maintenance Management System [Army]
IMMS	Interactive Multimedia System (MCD)
IMMS	Interim Manpower Maintenance System
IMMS	International Material Management Society (EA)
IMMT	Integrated Maintenance Management Team
IMMTS	Indian Mercantile Marine Training Ship [British]
ImmU	Immunizing Unit [Medicine] (MEDA)
IMMU	Immunomedics, Inc. [NASDAQ symbol] (NQ)
IMMU	Independent Munitions Maintenance Unit
IMMU	InPhyNet Medical Mgmt [NASDAQ symbol] (TTSB)
ImmuCell	ImmuCell Corp. [Associated Press] (SAG)
IMMUN	Immunity
IMMUN	Immunization (WDAA)
IMMUN	Immunology (ADA)
IMMUNHMTLGY	Immunohematology
IMMUNO	Immunoglobulin [Immunology] (DAVI)
IMMUNOL	Immunology
Immut	Quod Deus Sit Immutabilis [Philo] (BJA)
IMMV	Iris Mild Mosaic Virus
IMMY	Immediately
IMMY	Information Marketing Achievement Award [Information Industry Association]
IMN	Idiopathic Membranous Nephropathy [Nephrology]
IMN	Indicated Mach Number (AFM)
IMN	Internal Mammary [Lymph] Node [Medicine] (DAVI)
IMN	Internal-Mix Nozzle
IMN	Manchester College, North Manchester, IN [OCLC symbol] (OCLC)
IMNB	Isopropyl(methyl)nitrobenzene [Organic chemistry]
Imnet	Imnet Systems, Inc. [Associated Press] (SAG)
IMNET	International MarketNet [System of broker work stations created by IBM Corp. and Merrill Lynch & Co.] [New York, NY]
IMNH	Idaho Museum of Natural History [Idaho State University] [Research center] (RCD)
IMNR	Immune Response Corp. [NASDAQ symbol] (SAG)
IMNS	Imperial Military Nursing Service [British]
IMNSHO	In My Not-So-Humble Opinion [Computer hacker terminology] (NHD)
IMNT	IMNET Systems [NASDAQ symbol] (TTSB)
IMNT	Imnet Systems, Inc. [NASDAQ symbol] (SAG)
IMNX	Immunex Corp. [NASDAQ symbol] (NQ)
IMO	Asheville, NC [Location identifier FAA] (FAAL)
IMO	Immobilized (NVT)
IMO	Imperial Oil Ltd. [AMEX symbol Toronto Stock Exchange symbol Vancouver Stock Exchange symbol] (SPSG)
IMO	Improper Order
IMO	Indianapolis Museum of Art, Indianapolis, IN [OCLC symbol] (OCLC)
IMO	Information Market Observatory (TELE)
IMO	In My Opinion [Internet language] [Computer science]
IMO	Installation Maintenance Officer [Military] (AABC)
IMO	Institute of Market Officers [British]
IMO	Integrated Multiple Option
IMO	Inter-American Municipal Organization
IMO	Interband Magneto-Optic [Effect] (DEN)
IMO	Interface Management Office
IMO	International Maritime Organization [See also OMI] [ICSU London, England] (EAIO)
IMO	International Materials Organization (NATG)
IMO	International Mathematical Olympiad (RDA)
IMO	International Messianic Outreach (EA)
IMO	International Meteorological Organization [Later, World Meteorological Organization]
IMO	International Money Order [Business term] (DS)
IMO	Isla Mona [Puerto Rico] [Seismograph station code, US Geological Survey] (SEIS)
IMOA	International Mercury Owners Association (EA)
IMOG	Interagency Mechanical Operations Group [Lawrence Livermore Laboratory]
IMoH	John and Mary Kirby Hospital, Monticello, IL [Library symbol Library of Congress] (LCLS)
ImoInd	Imo Industries, Inc. [Associated Press] (SAG)
IMol	Moline Public Library, Moline, IL [Library symbol Library of Congress] (LCLS)
IMolB	Black Hawk College, Moline, IL [Library symbol Library of Congress] (LCLS)
IMolD	Deere & Co., Moline, IL [Library symbol Library of Congress] (LCLS)
IMOM	Improved Many-on-Many [Computer science]
IMonC	Monmouth College, Monmouth, IL [Library symbol Library of Congress] (LCLS)
IMont	Allerton Public Library, Monticello, IL [Library symbol Library of Congress] (LCLS)
IMontF	Piatt County Schools Film Library, Monticello, IL [Library symbol] [Library of Congress] (LCLS)

IMontSD	Monticello Community Unit School District, Monticello, IL [Library symbol] [Library of Congress] (LCLS)
IMonW	Western Illinois Library System, Monmouth, IL [Library symbol Library of Congress] (LCLS)
IMOP	Infantry Mortar Program (MCD)
IMORL	Infrared Mobile Optical Radiation Laboratory [Navy] (PDAA)
IMort	Morton Public Library, Morton, IL [Library symbol Library of Congress] (LCLS)
IMOS	Inadvertent Modification of the Stratosphere [Interagency government task force]
IMOS	Interactive Multiprogramming Operating System [NCR Corp.]
IMOS	Ion-Implanted Metal-Oxide Semiconductor
IMOT	Installed Maximum Operating Time
IMOT	Interim Maximum Operating Time
IMOX-S	Ion Implantation, Oxide Isolation with Scaling (NITA)
IMP	Cargo Information Message Procedures [IATA] (DS)
IMP	Idiopathic Myeloid Proliferation (DMAA)
IMP	Illustrated Melbourne Post [A publication]
IMP	Image Processing Program [Computer program]
IMP	Imager for Mars Pathfinder [Instrumentation]
IMP	Immunoperoxidase [An enzyme]
IMP	Impact (KSC)
IMP	Impaction [or Impacted] [Medicine] (DAVI)
imp	Impaction [Medicine] (DMAA)
IMP	Impact Predictor [NASA] (MUGU)
IMP	Impaired
imp	Impasse (DD)
IMP	Impedance (KSC)
IMP	Impeller
IMP	Imperative
imp	Imperative (WDMC)
IMP	Imperator [or Imperatrix] [Emperor or Empress] [Latin]
IMP	Imperatriz [Brazil] [Airport symbol] (OAG)
IMP	Imperfect
imp	Imperfect (WDMC)
Imp	Imperial [Record label]
IMP	Imperial (AFM)
IMP	Imperial Air [Peru] [ICAO designator] (FAAC)
IMP	Imperious [Grammar] (ROG)
IMP	Imperium [Empire] [Latin]
IMP	Impersonal
IMP	Impersonating [FBI standardized term]
Imp	Impetus [A publication]
IMP	IMP, Inc. [Associated Press] (SAG)
IMP	Implement (AFM)
IMP	Implementation (COE)
IMP	Implementation Language [Edinburgh multiaccess system] (CSR)
Imp	Import (EBF)
imp	Import (WDMC)
IMP	Important (WDMC)
IMP	Important
IMP	Imported
IMP	Importer (WDAA)
imp	Importer (WDAA)
IMP	Impracticable (FAAC)
IMP	Impression
imp	Impression (WDAA)
IMP	Imprimatur [Let It Be Printed] [Latin]
imp	Imprimatur [Latin for let it be printed] (WDMC)
Imp	Imprime [Printed] [French] (ILCA)
Imp	Imprimeur [Printer] [French] (ILCA)
IMP	Imprimis [In the First Place] [Latin] (WGA)
IMP	Imprint
IMP	Impropriator (ROG)
IMP	Improved
IMP	Improved Maintenance Program [Air Force] (AFM)
IMP	Improved Manufacturing Procedure [Computer science] (PDAA)
IMP	Improved Mobility Package [Wheelchair system]
IMP	Improvement [Real estate]
Imp	Improvement [Business term] (EBF)
IMP	Improvement Maintenance Program (MCD)
IMP	Impulse (KSC)
IMP	Impulse Generator
IMP	Incomplete Male Pseudohermaphroditism [Medicine] (AAMN)
IMP	Independent Motion Picture Co.
IMP	Indeterminate Mass Particle
IMP	Index to Maritime Publications [A publication]
IMP	Individual Merit Promotion
IMP	Industrial Management Program
IMP	Industrial Membrane Processing [Chemical engineering]
IMP	Industrial Mobilization Planning
IMP	Industrial Models and Patterns [A publication] (EAAP)
IMP	Industry Market Potential [Business term] (MHDW)
IMP	Infantry Mortar Plan (MCD)
IMP	Inflatable Micrometeoroid Paraglide
IMP	Information Management Plan [DoD]
IMP	Information Management Processor (NITA)
IMP	Information Management Program [Army]
IMP	Initial Memory Protection (MCD)
IMP	Initial Military Program (NATG)
IMP	Injection Microwave Plasma [Oak Ridge National Laboratory]
IMP	Inosine Monophosphate [Biochemistry]
IMP	Inosinic Acid [Biochemistry] (DAVI)
IMP	Inpatient Multidimensional Psychiatric Scale
IMP	Input Message Processor

IMP.............	Insoluble Metaphosphate [*Inorganic chemistry*]
IMP.............	Installation Master Planning [*Military*]
IMP.............	Institute of Modern Procedures [*Defunct*] (EA)
IMP.............	Institute of Molecular Pathology [*Austria*]
IMP.............	Instrumented Monkey Pod
IMP.............	Instrument Maintenance Procedure [*Nuclear energy*] (NRCH)
IMP.............	Integral Membrane Protein [*Cytology*]
IMP.............	Integrated Maintenance Plan [*or Procedure*]
IMP.............	Integrated Manufacturing Plan (IAA)
IMP.............	Integrated Master Plan [*Business term*] (RDA)
IMP.............	Integrated Mathematics Project (AIE)
IMP.............	Integrated Memory Processor
IMP.............	Integrated Message Processor (NITA)
IMP.............	Integrated Microprocessor [*National Semiconductor*]
IMP.............	Integrated Micro Products [*British*] (NITA)
IMP.............	Integrated Microwave Package (IAA)
IMP.............	Integrated Microwave Products (IEEE)
IMP.............	Integrated MIDI [*Musical Instrument Digital Interface*] Processor
IMP.............	Integrated Modular Personnel Software [*Percom*] (NITA)
IMP.............	Integrated Monitoring Panel
IMP.............	Integrating Motor Pneumotachograph
IMP.............	Intelligent Message Processor [*Delta Data Systems*] (NITA)
IMP.............	Intelligent Multiport Cards [*Computer hardware*] (PCM)
IMP.............	Interactive Mathematics Program [*High school curriculum*]
IMP.............	Interactive Microprogrammable Control (MCD)
IMP.............	Interagency Integrated Pest Management Coordinating Committee [*Terminated, 1980*] [*Council on Environmental Quality*] (EGAO)
IMP.............	Interface Management Plan [*Air Force*]
IMP.............	Interface Message Processor [*Computer science*]
IMP.............	Interim Monitoring Program
IMP.............	Inter-Industry Management Program (IAA)
IMP.............	Intermeccanica-Puch [*Italian-Austrian specialty car maker*]
IMP.............	Intermessage Processor (IAA)
IMP.............	Intermodulation Product
IMP.............	International Maple Leaf Resource Corp. [*Vancouver Stock Exchange symbol*]
IMP.............	International Match Point [*Game of bridge*]
IMP.............	International Microelectronic Products, Inc. [*Associated Press*] (SAG)
IMP.............	International Micro-Print Preservation, Inc.
IMP.............	International Mimes and Pantomimists [*Defunct*]
IMP.............	Interplanetary Magnetometer Probe
IMP.............	Interplanetary Measurement Probe
IMP.............	Interplanetary Monitoring Platform [*A spacecraft*]
IMP.............	Interplanetary Monitoring Probe [*A spacecraft*]
IMP.............	Intra-Industry Management Program [*Small Business Administration*]
IMP.............	Intramembranous Particle [*Cytology*]
IMP.............	Intramuscular Compartment Pressure [*Medicine*] (DMAA)
IMP.............	Intrinsic Multiprocessing (IEEE)
IMP.............	Inventory Management Plan [*Military*] (AFIT)
IMP.............	Ion Microprobe [*Surface analysis*]
IMP.............	Ion Moderated Partition [*Chromatography*]
IMP.............	Item Management Plan (AAGC)
IMP.............	Marathon, TX [*Location identifier FAA*] (FAAL)
IMP.............	Mishawaka Public Library, Mishawaka, IN [*OCLC symbol*] (OCLC)
IMPA.........	Incisal Mandibular Plane Angle [*Dentistry*]
IMPA.........	Independent Media Producers Association [*Later, IMPC*] (EA)
IMPA.........	Information Management and Processing Association [*Defunct*] (EA)
IMPA.........	Initialized Moore Probabilistic Automation (IAA)
IMPA.........	International Maritime Pilots Association (EAIO)
IMPA.........	International Master Printers Association [*Brussels, Belgium*]
IMPA.........	International Meat Processors Association (EA)
IMPA.........	International Motor Press Association (EA)
IMPA.........	International Museum Photographers Association (EA)
IMPA.........	International Myopia Prevention Association (EA)
IMPA.........	Ion Microprobe Analysis
IMPAC.......	Immediate Psychiatric Aid and Referral Center
IMPAC.......	Industrial Multilevel Process Analysis and Control (IAA)
IMPAC.......	Information for Management Planning Analysis and Coordination (PDAA)
IMPAC.......	Interagency Map and Publications Acquisitions Committee [*Department of State*] [*Washington, DC*]
IMPAC.......	International Merchant Purchases Authorization Care [*Visa*] (RDA)
IMPAC.......	International Microfiche Parts Access Catalogue [*Auto parts*] [*A publication*]
IMPACS......	International Packet-Switching Service [*MCI International, Inc.*] [*Rye Brook, NY*] [*Telecommunications*] (TSSD)
IMPACT.......	Illinois Microarchitecture Project Utilizing Advanced Compiler Technology
IMPACT.......	Image Processing and Color Transmission [*Time, Inc. photograph transmission center*]
IMPACT.......	Implanted Advanced Composed Technology [*Texas Instruments, Inc.*]
IMPACT.......	Implementation Planning and Control Technique [*Computer science*]
IMPACT.......	Improved Management Procurement and Contracting Technique (AABC)
IMPACT.......	Improved Manpower Production and Controller Technique [*Navy*]
IMPACT.......	Improved Modern Pricing and Costing Techniques [*Air Force*] (MCD)
IMPACT.......	Information Market Action Program (TELE)
IMPACT.......	Integrated Management Planning and Control Technique [*British*]
IMPACT.......	Integrated Managerial Programming Analysis Control Technique [*Air Force*]
IMPACT.......	Integrated Materials Handling Production and Control Technology
IMPACT.......	Integrated Microform Parts Cataloging (PDAA)
IMPACT.......	Integrated Model of Plumes and Atmosphere in Complex Terrain [*Environmental Protection Agency*] (GFGA)

IMPACT.......	Intensive Matched Probation and After-Care Treatment (PDAA)
IMPACT.......	Interdisciplinary Model Programs in the Arts for Children and Teachers
IMPACT.......	International Marketing Program for Agricultural Commodities and Trade Center [*Washington State University*] [*Research center*] (RCD)
IMPACT.......	Intervention Moves Parents and Children Together [*Drug abuse treatment program sponsored by Phoenix House Foundation*]
IMPACT.......	Inventory Management Program and Control Technique [*IBM Corp.*] [*Computer science*]
Impacts Aust Econ...	Impacts on the Australian Economy [*A publication*]
IMPALA......	International Motion Picture and Lecturers Association (EA)
IMPAS-WG...	Improved Military Parts Availability and Selection Working Group [*Army*] (RDA)
IMP-ATACMS...	Improved Army Tactical Missile System (RDA)
Impath.........	Impath, Inc. [*Associated Press*] (SAG)
IMPATT.......	Impact Ionization Avalanche Transit Time [*Solid state diodes*] [*Transistor technology*]
IMPAV	Inter-Urban Microwave-Powered Air-Cushion Vehicle (PDAA)
IMPBA	International Model Power Boat Association (EA)
IMPC.........	Independent Media Producers Council (EA)
IMPC.........	Infantry Mortar Platoon Course (INF)
IMPC.........	Institutional and Municipal Parking Congress (EA)
IMPC.........	International Myopia Prevention Centre (DAVI)
IMPCA	International Methanol Producers and Consumers Association [*British*]
IMPCE.......	Importance
ImpCM.......	Imperial Credit Mortgage Holdings, Inc. [*Associated Press*] (SAG)
IMPCM.......	Improved Capability Missile [*Air Force*] (MCD)
ImpCMtg....	Imperial Credit Mortgage Holdings, Inc. [*Associated Press*] (SAG)
IMPCON......	Inventory Management and Production Control [*ISTEL*] [*Software package*] (NCC)
ImpCrd.......	Imperial Credit Industries, Inc. [*Associated Press*] (SAG)
ImpctSy.....	Impact Systems, Inc. [*Associated Press*] (SAG)
IMP CYL	Impression Cylinder [*Publishing*] (DGA)
IMPD	Impedance [*Electricity*]
IMPD	Improved [*Real estate*] (ROG)
IMPDAA......	Independent Motion Picture Distributors Association of America
IMPDH.......	Inosine Monophosphate Dehydrogenase [*An enzyme*]
IMP DICT	Imperial Dictionary [*A publication*] (ROG)
IMPDMNT....	Impediment
IMPE.........	Impregnate (IAA)
IMPEL.......	Insurance Management Performance Evaluation Life (MHDB)
IMPEND......	Improved Effectiveness Nuclear Depth Bomb
IMPER	Imperative
IMPER	Imperfect
IMPER	Impersonal (ROG)
IMPERF.......	Imperfect
Imperf.........	Imperfect (STED)
imperf.........	Imperforate (STED)
IMPERF.......	Imperforate [*Philately*]
IMPERS	Impersonal
IMPES.........	Implicit Pressure, Explicit Saturation [*Petroleum reservoir simulation*]
IMPEX.......	Immediate Postexercise (STED)
IMPF.........	Imperfect (MSA)
IMPFT.......	Imperfect (ADA)
IMPG	Imperial Group Ltd.
IMPG	Impregnate (KSC)
IMPGAC	Improved Guidance and Control (MCD)
IMPGEN......	Impulse Generator (IAA)
IMPH	Impath Inc. [*NASDAQ symbol*] (TTSB)
ImpHly........	Imperial Holly Corp. [*Associated Press*] (SAG)
IMPI.........	International Microwave Power Institute (EA)
IMPICS	Integrated Manufacturing Program Information and Control System (PDAA)
IMPIS.........	Indirect Material Purchasing Information Standards
IMPIS.........	Integrated Management Planning Information Systems [*Computer science*]
IMPL.........	Illustrated Maintenance Parts List
Impl...........	Imperial [*British military*] (DMA)
IMPL.........	Implement (AABC)
IMPL.........	Implementation Language (NITA)
IMPL.........	Impulse (FAAC)
IMPL.........	Initial Microprogram Load [*Also, IML*] [*Computer science*]
IMPL.........	International Microwave Power Institute (PDAA)
IMPLNTN	Implementation
IMPLR	Impeller [*Mechanical engineering*]
IMPLS.........	Impulse (MSA)
Imp Man......	Impey's Law and Practice of Mandamus [*1826*] [*A publication*] (DLA)
IMPN	Importation
IMPO.........	Imposition (DSUE)
ImpOil........	Imperial Oil Ltd. [*Associated Press*] (SAG)
IMPOP.......	Integrated Maintenance Program Operation (MCD)
IMPOS.......	Interactive Multi-Programming Operating System (PDAA)
IMPOSN......	Imposition (ROG)
IMPOSS......	Impossible (ADA)
IMPOT.......	Imposition (DSUE)
IMPP.........	Industrial Mobilization Production Planning [*DoD*]
IMPPA	Independent Motion Picture Producers Association [*Defunct*] (EA)
Imp Pl	Impey's Modern Pleader [*2nd ed.*] [*1814*] [*A publication*] (DLA)
Imp Pr CP....	Impey's Practice, Common Pleas [*A publication*] (DLA)
Imp Pr KB...	Impey's Practice, King's Bench [*A publication*] (DLA)
IMPR	Impedor
IMPR	Impractical (AABC)
IMPR	Impression (ROG)

Impr............	Impressionism (VRA)
IMPR	Imprint [Online database field identifier]
IMPR	Imprint Records, Inc. [NASDAQ symbol] (SAG)
IMPR	Improved
IMPRAC.......	Impracticable (DSUE)
ImprAr........	Imperial Aramaic (BJA)
ImprBc........	Imperial Bancorp [Associated Press] (SAG)
IMPRD	Impaired
IMPREG.......	Impregnable (ADA)
IMPREG.......	Impregnated (TEL)
IMPRESS	Impression
IMPRESS	Interdisciplinary Machine Processing for Research and Education in Social Sciences [Dartmouth College, Hanover, NH] [Data processing system]
IMPRG.........	Impregnate (AABC)
IMPRIGA......	Imprimerie Centrale d'Afrique [Publisher] [Gabon] (EY)
IMPRINT......	Imbricated Program for Information Transfer [Computer science]
Imprint.......	Imprint Records, Inc. [Associated Press] (SAG)
IMPRINT......	Improved Medical Programs and Readiness Immediately, Not Tomorrow [TROA]
ImprintR	Imprint Records, Inc. [Associated Press] (SAG)
IMPRL.........	Imperial (MSA)
imprm.........	Imprimatura (VRA)
IMPROP.......	Improper (ADA)
IMPROV.......	Improvement (MSA)
IMPROVE....	Interagency Monitoring of Protected Visual Emissions (COE)
IMPROVE....	Interagency Monitoring of Protected Visual Environments [Marine science] (OSRA)
IMPROVE.....	Inventory Management, Product Replenishment and Order Validity Evaluation (MHDB)
IMPRS	Information Management Process Reporting System (HGAA)
IMPRSN.......	Impression (MSA)
IMPRT	Import
IMPRTD	Imported
IMPRTNG......	Importing
IMPRTR	Importer
IMPRV	Improvement (AABC)
IMPRVMNT...	Improvement
IMPRVMT	Improvement
IMPS...........	Imperial Tobacco Co. Shares [Stock exchange term British] (DSUE)
IMPS...........	Impose (MSA)
IMPS...........	Individual Multipurpose Shelter [Army] (INF)
IMPS...........	Industry Media Publishing System [Omni Industry Corp.] [Information service or system] (IID)
IMPS...........	Inpatient Multidimensional Psychiatric Scale
IMPS...........	Institutional Meat Purchase Specification [Department of Agriculture]
IMPS...........	Intact Months of Patient Survival [Medicine] (DMAA)
IMPS...........	Integrated Mail Preparation System
IMPS...........	Integrated Master Programming and Scheduling
IMPS...........	Integrated Microcomputer Processing System [Bureau of the Census] (GFGA)
IMPS...........	Integrated Modular Panel System
IMPS...........	Interface Message Processors [Computer science] (NITA)
IMPS...........	Intermediate Minimum Property Standards [Department of Housing and Urban Development] (GFGA)
IMPS...........	International Microprogrammers' Society
IMPS...........	International M [formerly, Mensa] Philatelists Society (EA)
Imp Sh.......	Impey's Office of Sheriff [6th ed.] [1835] [A publication] (DLA)
impst..........	Impasto (VRA)
impt............	Important (BARN)
Impt...........	Imprisonment [British military] (DMA)
IMPT...........	Improvement [Real estate] (ROG)
IMPT...........	Integrated Micro Products [NASDAQ symbol] (SAG)
ImpThft.......	Imperial Thrift & Loan Association [Associated Press] (SAG)
IMPTN	Imputation
IMPTR	Importer (ADA)
IMPTS	Improved Programmer Test Station (IEEE)
IMPUTN	Imputation
IMPV...........	Imperative
IMPVD.........	Improved [Real estate] (ROG)
IMPVE.........	Improve [Real estate] (ROG)
Impvt	Improvement (STED)
Impx	Impacted [Medicine] (DMAA)
IMPX...........	Impaction [Dentistry]
IMPX...........	Imperatrix [Empress] [Latin]
IMPX...........	IMP, Inc. [NASDAQ symbol] (SAG)
IMQ..............	Industrial Management Qualification
IMQ..............	La Porte County Library, La Porte, IN [OCLC symbol] (OCLC)
IMR..............	IMCO Recycling [NYSE symbol] (TTSB)
IMR..............	IMCO Recycling [NYSE symbol] (NQ)
IMR..............	Impala Resources [Vancouver Stock Exchange symbol]
IMR..............	Imperial Military Railways [British military] (DMA)
IMR..............	Improved Military Rifle (PDAA)
IMR..............	Impulse-Aero [Russian Federation] [ICAO designator] (FAAC)
IMR..............	Independent Modification Review [Military] (AFIT)
IMR..............	Individual Medical Record
IMR..............	Infant Mortality Rate
IMR..............	Infant Mortality Risk [Medicine] (DMAA)
IMR..............	Infectious Mononucleosis Receptor [Biochemistry] (AAMN)
IMR..............	Informal Memorandum Report
IMR..............	Information Management Review [A publication] (NITA)
IMR..............	Initial Missile Report (CINC)
IMR..............	Initial Mortality Rate
IMR..............	Inmate Medical Record (WDAA)
IMR..............	Inner Metropolitan Region (ADA)
IMR.............	Institute for Materials Research [Later, NSL] [National Institute of Standards and Technology]
IMR.............	Institute for Medical Research [Camden, New Jersey]
IMR.............	Institute of Man and Resources
IMR.............	Institute of Marine Resources [University of California] [Research center] (RCD)
IMR.............	Institute of Masonry Research [Defunct] (EA)
IMR.............	Institute of Metal Repair (EA)
IMR.............	Institution for Mentally Retarded [Generic term] (DHSM)
IMR.............	Integrated Model Respository (AAEL)
IMR.............	Integrated Multiport Repeater [Computer science] (PCM)
IMR.............	Intelligent Machine Research (NITA)
IMR.............	Internal Mold Release [Plastics technology]
IMR.............	International Medical Research
IMR.............	Interrupt-Mask Register [Computer science]
IMR.............	Inventory Management Record [Military] (AFM)
IMR.............	Inventory Management Review
IMR.............	Inventory Modified Round
IMR.............	Isla Mona [Puerto Rico] [Seismograph station code, US Geological Survey Closed] (SEIS)
IMR.............	Isolation Mode Rejection (IAA)
IMR.............	Monroe County Public Library, Bloomington, IN [OCLC symbol] (OCLC)
IMRA	Incentive Manufacturers Representatives Association [Naperville, IL] (EA)
IMRA	Independent Motorcycle Retailers of America [Defunct] (EA)
IMRA	Independent Music Retailers Association (NTPA)
IMRA	Industrial Marketing Research Association [British]
IMRA	Infrared Monochromatic Radiation
IMRA	Insurance Market Risk Assessment
IMRA	International Manufacturers Representatives Association [Tulsa, OK] (EA)
IMRA	International Mass Retail Association (NTPA)
IMRA	International Military Recreation Association [Defunct] (EA)
IMRA	International Mission Radio Association (EA)
IMRAD	Introduction, Methodology, Results, and Discussion (WDMC)
IMRAD	Introduction, Methods, Results, and Discussion [Scientific writing]
IMRADS	Information Management, Retrieval, and Dissemination System (DIT)
IMRAN	International Marine Radio Aids to Navigation
IMRB	Improved Main Rotor Blade (RDA)
IMRC	Indian Muslim Relief Committee (EA)
IMRC	Indigenous Minorities Research Council [British]
IMRC	Instructional Materials Reference Center [American Printing House for the Blind - APH] [Absorbed by] (EA)
IMRC	Inventory [or Item] Management Responsibility Code
IMRE	IMRE Corp. [NASDAQ symbol] (NQ)
IMRE	Institute for Medical Record Economics (EA)
IMREC	Interior Ministerial Real Estate Committee [Vietnam]
IMREP	Immediately Report
IMRETES.......	Immunization Readiness Training Exercises [Army]
IMRF	Independent Manufacturers Representatives Forum (EA)
IMRF	International Medical and Research Foundation [Later, AMREF] (EA)
IMRF/SMRF...	International Medical Relief Fund/Salvadoran Medical Relief Fund (EA)
IMRHS	Inactive Materiel Request History and Status File [Army]
IMRI	Integrated Medical Resources, Inc. [NASDAQ symbol] (SAG)
IMRI	International Marian Research Institute [University of Dayton] [Research center] (RCD)
IMRL	Immediate Material Requirement List
IMRL	Individual Maintenance Readiness List
IMRL	Individual Material Readiness List [DoD]
IMRL	Integrated Materials Research Laboratory [Sandia National Laboratories]
IMRL	Intermediate Maintenance Repair Level (MCD)
IMRL	Intermediate Maintenance Requirements List
IMRO	Internal Macedonian Revolutionary Organization [Bulgaria] [Political party] (PPE)
IMRO	Interplant Material Requisition Order
IMRO	Investment Managers' Regulatory Authority [British] (NUMA)
IMRO	Investment Managers Regulatory Organisation [British] (ECON)
IMRO-DPMNU...	Internal Macedonian Revolutionary Organization - Democratic Party for Macedonian[Bulgaria] National Unity [Political party] (EY)
IMRP	International Meeting on Radiation Processing (EA)
IMRR	Isolation Mode Rejection Ratio (IAA)
IMRRS	Installation Materiel Readiness Reporting System [Army]
IMRRS	Institute of Market and Reward Regional Surveys [British]
IMRS	Immersion (MSA)
IMRS	IMRglobal Corp. [Formerly, Information Management Resources] [NASDAQ symbol]
IMRS	Information Management Resources, Inc. [NASDAQ symbol] (SAG)
IM-RSI	International Military Rationalization, Standardization, and Interoperability (RDA)
IMRT	Infant Mortality Review Team [Department of Health and Human Services] (GFGA)
IMRU	Institute of Microbiology, Rutgers University [New Jersey]
IMS.............	Air Images [British] [FAA designator] (FAAC)
IMS.............	Idle Matrix Search [Computer science]
IMS.............	IEEE Instrumentation and Measurement Society (EA)
IMS.............	Ignition Module Signal [Automotive engineering]
IMS.............	Image Management System [Filenet] (NITA)
IMS.............	Image Motion Simulator
IMS.............	Imasco Ltd. [Toronto Stock Exchange symbol Vancouver Stock Exchange symbol]
ImS.............	Immune Serum [Also, IS]

IMS..............	Income Matching System
IMS..............	In-Core Monitoring System [*Nuclear energy*] (NRCH)
IMS..............	Incurred in Military Service [*Medicine*] (MAE)
IMS..............	Index Management System (PDAA)
IMS..............	Indianapolis Motor Speedway [*Auto racing venue*]
IMS..............	Indian Medical Service [*British*]
IMS..............	Indirect Measuring System
IMS..............	Individualized Mathematics System [*Education*]
IMS..............	Industrial Management Society (EA)
IMS..............	Industrial Mathematics Society (EA)
IMS..............	Industrial Measurement Systems/ Institute of Manpower Studies [*British*]
IMS..............	Industrial Methylated Spirit
IMS..............	Inertial Measuring Set [*or System*] (NVT)
IMS..............	In-Flight Management System
IMS..............	Information Management Specialists, Inc. [*Denver, CO*] [*Information service or system*] (IID)
IMS..............	Information Management Staff [*Environmental Protection Agency*] (GFGA)
IMS..............	Information Management System [*IBM Corp.*] [*Computer science*]
IMS..............	Infrared Measuring System
IMS..............	Initial Measurement System [*Nuclear missiles*]
IMS..............	In-Mold Surfacing [*Plastics technology*]
IMS..............	Inshore Minesweeper [*Navy British*]
IMS..............	Institute for Mesoamerican Studies [*State University of New York, Albany*] [*Research center*] (RCD)
IMS..............	[*The*] Institute of Management Sciences
IMS..............	Institute of Management Services [*British*]
IMS..............	Institute of Management Specialists [*Royal Leamington Spa, Warwickshire, England*] (EAIO)
IMS..............	Institute of Manpower Studies [*Department of Employment*] [*British*]
IMS..............	Institute of Marine Science [*University of Alaska*] [*Research center*]
IMS..............	Institute of Materials Science (KSC)
IMS..............	Institute of Mathematical Statistics (EA)
IMS..............	Institute of Mental Subnormality [*British*]
IMS..............	Institute of Museum Services [*National Foundation of the Arts and the Humanities*] (GRD)
IMS..............	Institute on Man and Science [*Formerly, Council on World Tensions*]
IMS..............	Instructional Management System (IEEE)
IMS..............	Instrumented Measuring System
IMS..............	Integrated Maintenance Schedule
IMS..............	Integrated Maintenance System
IMS..............	Integrated Manufacturing System (MHDI)
IMS..............	Integrated Mapping System
IMS..............	Integrated Master Schedule [*Business term*] (RDA)
IMS..............	Integrated Medical Services
IMS..............	Integrated Meteorological System [*Army*] (IEEE)
IMS..............	Integrated Microcomputer Systems, Inc.
IMS..............	Intelligent Manufacturing Systems [*Japan*] [*Agreement for conducting cooperative global research*]
IMS..............	Intensive Manpower Services (OICC)
IMS..............	Interactive Market Systems [*New York, NY Information service or system*] (IID)
IMS..............	Interactive Media Systems [*Information service or system*] (IID)
IMS..............	InterCapital Ins Muni Sec [*NYSE symbol*] (TTSB)
IMS..............	InterCapital Insured Municipal Securities [*NYSE symbol*] (SAG)
IMS..............	Interceptor Missile (IAA)
IMS..............	Interceptor Mission Sheet (SAA)
IMS..............	Interim Meteorological Satellite
IMS..............	Intermediate Maintenance Squadron (MCD)
IMS..............	Intermembrane Space [*Biochemistry*]
IMS..............	Inter-Message Separation [*Communications*]
IMS..............	Intermodal Management System [*VDOT*] (TAG)
IMS..............	Internal Management System [*Military*] (AFIT)
IMS..............	Internal Measurement System
IMS..............	International Magnetospheric Study [*1976-78*] [*National Science Foundation*]
IMS..............	International Maledicta Society (EA)
IMS..............	International Management Services, Inc. [*Framingham, MA*] [*Information service or system*] (IID)
IMS..............	International Marketing Services
IMS..............	International Measurement System [*Sailing*]
IMS..............	International Medication Systems [*Pharmacology*] (DAVI)
IMS..............	International Meditation Society
IMS..............	International Metallographic Society (EA)
IMS..............	International Metric System
IMS..............	International Micro Systems (EFIS)
IMS..............	International Military Services Ltd. [*Ministry of Defence*] [*British*]
IMS..............	International Military Staff [*NATO*]
IMS..............	International Monitoring System [*For nuclear tests*]
IMS..............	International Montessori Society
IMS..............	International Mountain Society (EA)
IMS..............	International Multihull Society [*Formerly, International Hydrofoil and Multihull Society*] [*Defunct*] (EA)
IMS..............	International Musicological Society [*Basel, Switzerland*] (EA)
IMS..............	Internet Multicasting Service [*Non-profit information service*]
IMS..............	Interplanetary Measurement Satellite (IAA)
IMS..............	Interplanetary Mission Support
IMS..............	Interplanetary Monitor Satellite (IAA)
IMS..............	Intrinsic Monomer Stress [*Physical chemistry*]
IMS..............	Inventory Management and Simulator
IMS..............	Inventory Management System (NASA)
IMS..............	Inviscid Melt Spinning (EDCT)
IMS..............	Ionization and Momentum Sensor
IMS..............	Ion Mass Spectrometer

IMS..............	Ion Mobility Spectrometry
IMS..............	Irish Mathematics Society
IMS..............	Irradiance Measuring System
IMS..............	Island Missionary Society (EA)
IMS..............	Madison, IN [*Location identifier FAA*] (FAAL)
IMS..............	St. Mary-Of-The-Woods College, Library, St. Mary-Of-The-Woods, IN [*OCLC symbol*] (OCLC)
IMSA..........	Illinois Mathematics and Science Academy
IMSA..........	International Management Systems Association [*Later, Internet-International Management Systems Association*] (EA)
IMSA..........	International Memorialization Supply Association (NTPA)
IMSA..........	International Metallic Silhouette Association (DICI)
IMSA..........	International Motor Sports Association (EA)
IMSA..........	International Municipal Signal Association (EA)
IMSA..........	Seaman Apprentice, Instrumentman, Striker [*Navy rating*]
IMSAM........	Interceptor Missile, Surface-to-Air-Missile (MCD)
IMSAP........	International Marine Sciences Affairs Panel [*Defunct*] (USDC)
IMSC..........	Industry Missile and Space Conference
IMSC..........	Integrated Measurement Sys [*NASDAQ symbol*] (TTSB)
IMSC..........	Integrated Measurement Systems [*NASDAQ symbol*] (SAG)
IMSC & D	Inventory Manager Stock Control and Distribution [*Military*] (AFM)
IMSC & DS...	Inventory Manager Stock Control and Distribution System [*Military*]
IMSCO	Initial Maritime Satellite Consortium [*Six United States and two British oil companies and tanker operators*] (PDAA)
IMSCOM	International Military Staff Communication [*NATO*] (NATG)
IMSD	Information Management and Services Division [*Environmental Protection Agency*] (GFGA)
IMS-DB	IMS-Database (NITA)
IMS-DC........	IMS-Data Communications (NITA)
IMSDP	Innovator Multiple Source Drug Product
IMSE..........	Integrated Mean Square Error [*Statistics*]
IMSE..........	Interagency Materials Sciences Exchange
IMSE..........	Intermediate Maintenance Support Equipment [*Army*]
IMSG..........	Imperial Merchant Service Guild [*A union*] [*British*]
IMSI..........	Information Management System Interface
IMSI..........	International Maple Syrup Institute (EA)
IMSI..........	International Microcomputer Software, Inc. [*NASDAQ symbol*] (SAG)
IMSI..........	Intl Microcomputer Software [*NASDAQ symbol*] (TTSB)
IMSIM........	Information Management Simulation (KSC)
IMS INC	International Management Services, Inc. [*Franklyn, MA*] (TSSD)
IMS/INQ......	Information Management System Inquiry
IMSL..........	International Mathematical and Statistical Libraries, Inc.
IMSL..........	International Mathematics and Statistics Library [*Marine science*] (OSRA)
IMSM..........	Institute of Marketing and Sales Management [*British*] (BI)
IMSM..........	International Military Staff Memorandum [*NATO*] (NATG)
IMSN	Internal-Mix Spray Nozzle
IMSN	Seaman, Instrumentman, Striker [*Navy rating*]
IMSO	Initial Materiel Support Office [*Army*] (AABC)
IMSOC	Interceptor Missile Squadron Operations Center [*Air Force*]
IMSP	Integrated Mass Storage Processor
IMSR	Interplanetary Mission Support Requirements
IMSS..........	In-Flight Medical Support System [*Skylab*] [*NASA*]
IMSS..........	Item Management Statistical Series
IMSSCE........	Interceptor Missile Squadron and Supervisory Control Equipment
IMSSS	Institute for Mathematical Studies in the Social Sciences [*Stanford University*] [*Research center*] (RCD)
IMSSS	Interceptor Missile Squadron Supervisory Station
IMS/SSC	International Magnetospheric Study / Satellite Situation Committee [*NASA*] (PDAA)
IMST..........	Institute of Marine Sciences and Technology
IMST..........	International Mushroom Society for the Tropics (EAIO)
IMSTI.........	Institute of Marine Scientific and Technological Information [*China*] [*Marine science*] (OSRA)
IMSU	International Muslim Students Union (EA)
IMSUM........	International Military Staff Summary [*NATO*] (NATG)
IMS/VS	Information Management System/Virtual Storage (MCD)
IMSW..........	Institute of Medical Social Workers [*British*] (BI)
IMSWE........	Investigations of Marine Shallow Water Ecosystems (NOAA)
IMSWEP	Investigations of Marine Shallow-Water Ecosystems Program [*Smithsonian Institution*] (GFGA)
IMSWM........	International Military Staff Working Memorandum [*NATO*] (NATG)
IMT..............	Idaho Motor Tariff Bureau, Boise ID [*STAC*]
IMT..............	Immediate
IMT..............	Immediate Money Transfer (DCTA)
IMT..............	Impulse-Modulated Telemetry (IAA)
IMT..............	Independent Model Triangulation (PDAA)
IMT..............	Individual Movement Technique [*Military*] (INF)
IMT..............	Induced Muscular Tension [*Physiology*]
IMT..............	Industrial & Materials Technologies (ACII)
IMT..............	Information and Manufacturing Technologies Division [*British*]
IMT..............	Inspiratory Muscle Training [*Medicine*] (DMAA)
IMT..............	Institute of Municipal Transport [*British*] (DBA)
IMT..............	Integrated Microimage Terminal [*Kodak*] (NITA)
IMT..............	Intelligent Microimage Terminal [*Kodak*]
IMT..............	InterCapital Ins Muni Tr [*NYSE symbol*] (TTSB)
IMT..............	InterCapital Insured Municipal Trust [*NYSE symbol*] (SAG)
IMT..............	Intermachine Trunk [*Telecommunications*] (TEL)
IMT..............	Intermediate Maintenance Trainer [*Army*]
IMT..............	Intermediate Tape [*Telecommunications*] (TEL)
IMT..............	International Markatech [*Vancouver Stock Exchange symbol*]
IMT..............	International Military Tribunal [*Post-World War II*]
IMT..............	Intestinal Mutagenicity Test [*Clinical chemistry*]
IMT..............	Ion Microtomography [*High-resolution imaging technique*]
IMT..............	Iron Mountain [*Michigan*] [*Airport symbol*] (OAG)

IMT	Iron Mountain/Kingsford, MI [*Location identifier FAA*] (FAAL)
IMT	Morton Grove Public Library, Morton Grove, IL [*OCLC symbol*] (OCLC)
IMT-2000	International Mobile Telecommunications for the Year 2000
IMTA	Institut de la Medecine du Travail et des Ambiances [*Institute of Occupational and Environmental Health*] [*Canada*]
IMTA	Institute of Municipal Treasurers and Accountants [*Later, CIPFA*] [*British*]
IMTA	Intensive Military Training Area (DA)
IMTA	International Map Trade Association (NTPA)
IMTA	International Marine Transit Association (EA)
IMTA	International Mass Transit Association (EA)
IMTAC	Information Management Technology [*NASDAQ symbol*] (SAG)
IMTAL	International Museum Theater Alliance (NTPA)
IMTB	Isle Of Man Tourist Board (DCTA)
IMTC	Imtec, Inc. [*NASDAQ symbol*] (NQ)
IMTC	Infantry Moving Target Carrier [*Army*]
IMTC	International Multimedia Teleconferencing Consortium
IMtca	Mount Carmel Public Library, Mt. Carmel, IL [*Library symbol Library of Congress*] (LCLS)
IMtcaSD	Mount Carmel Community Unit School District No. 348, Mt. Carmel, IL [*Library symbol Library of Congress*] (LCLS)
IMTD	Institute of Master Tutors of Driving [*British*] (BI)
IMTE	Institut de la Medecine du Travail et de l'Environnement [*Institute of Occupational and Environmental Health*] [*Canada*]
IMTE	International Military Tribunal for Europe [*Post-World War II*]
Imtec	Imtec, Inc. [*Associated Press*] (SAG)
IMTEC	Information Management and Technology (CIST)
IMTEC	Institute of Marine and Terrestrial Ecology [*Research center*] (RCD)
IMTEC	International Marine Trades Exhibit and Convention [*National Marine Manufacturers Association*]
IMTEC	International Movements toward Educational Change [*Later, IMTEC-The International Learning Cooperative*] (EAIO)
IMTED	Information Management and Technology Division (AAGC)
IMTFC	International Movement for Therapeutic Free Choice [*France*] (EAIO)
IMTFJ	International Military Tribunal for Japan [*Post-World War II*]
IMTG	Internationale Moor und Torf-Gesellschaft [*International Peat Society - IPS*] (EAIO)
IMTK	Information Management Technology [*NASDAQ symbol*] (SAG)
IMTKA	Information Mgmt Tech'A' [*NASDAQ symbol*] (TTSB)
IMTKW	Information Mgmt Tech Wrrt'A' [*NASDAQ symbol*] (TTSB)
IMTLYM	Immature Lymphocytes [*Hematology*] (DAVI)
IMTN	Iron Mountain [*NASDAQ symbol*] (TTSB)
IMTN	Iron Mountain, Inc. [*NASDAQ symbol*] (SAG)
IMTNE	International Meteorological Teletype Network Europe (NATG)
IMto	Mount Olive Public Library, Mount Olive, IL [*Library symbol Library of Congress*] (LCLS)
IMtoMCD	Macoupin Community, District 5, Mount Olive, IL [*Library symbol Library of Congress*] (LCLS)
IMTP	Industrial Mobilization Training Program
IMTP	Injection-Molded Thermoplastic [*Materials science*]
IMTP	Integrated Maintenance Test Plan
IMTP	International Musa Testing Program [*United Nations*] (ECON)
IMTP	Itim Mizrah News Agency. Teleprinter Service (BJA)
IMTRAN	Implicit Transport (PDAA)
IMTRO	Integrated Maintenance Test Requirement Outline
IMTS	Improved Mobile Telephone Service [*Telecommunications*]
IMTS	Individualized Manpower Training System (OICC)
IMTS	International Machine Tool Show (ITD)
IMtv	Mount Vernon Public Library, Mt. Vernon, IL [*Library symbol Library of Congress*] (LCLS)
IMtvSD	Summersville School District 79, Mount Vernon, IL [*Library symbol Library of Congress*] (LCLS)
IMTWC	Information Management Technology [*NASDAQ symbol*] (SAG)
IMTX	Interactive Media Technologies, Inc. (NQ)
IMU	Immudyne, Inc. [*Vancouver Stock Exchange symbol*]
IMU	Impedance Matching Unit (MCD)
IMU	Income Maintenance Unit [*Work Incentive Program*] [*Department of Labor*]
IMU	Increment Memory Unit
IMU	Index of Medical Underservice (DMAA)
IMU	Inertial Measurement Unit
IMU	Information Management Unit (NITA)
IMU	Instruction Memory Unit
IMU	Interference Mockup (IAA)
IMU	Internal Measurement Unit (NASA)
imu	Internal Measurement Unit (NAKS)
IMU	Internationale Metall Union [*International Metal Union*] (EA)
IMU	International Mailers Union [*Later, International Typographical Union*] (EA)
IMU	International Mathematical Union [*See also UMI*] [*ICSU Helsinki, Finland*] (EAIO)
IMU	International Milliunit
IMU	Irish Missionary Union (EAIO)
IMU	Muncie Public Library, Muncie, IN [*OCLC symbol*] (OCLC)
IMUA	Inland Marine Underwriters Association [*New York, NY*] (EA)
IMUA	Interservice Materiel Utilization Agency [*Military*] (AABC)
Imucor	Immucor, Inc. [*Associated Press*] (SAG)
IMUDS	Illustration Makeup Data Sheet
IMUGSE	Inertial Measurement Unit Ground Support Equipment (SAA)
IMUL	ImmuLogic Pharmaceutical [*NASDAQ symbol*] (TTSB)
IMUL	ImmuLogic Pharmaceutical Corp. [*NASDAQ symbol*] (SPSG)
IMUL	Integer Multiply [*Computer science*]
IMulgSD	Mulberry Grove Community Unit, School District 1, Mulberry Grove, IL [*Library symbol Library of Congress*] (LCLS)
ImuLog	ImmuLogic Pharmaceutical Corp. [*Associated Press*] (SAG)
IMunE	Institution of Municipal Engineers [*British*]
Imunex	Immunex Corp. [*Associated Press*] (SAG)
Imungn	Immuncogen, Inc. [*Associated Press*] (SAG)
Imunmd	Immunomedics, Inc. [*Associated Press*] (SAG)
ImunRsp	Immune Response Corp. [*Associated Press*] (SAG)
IMunS	Saint Mary of the Lake Seminary, Mundelein, IL [*Library symbol Library of Congress*] (LCLS)
IMUR	Interactive Multiple Regression System (MCD)
IMUS	Internal Measuring Unit System (MCD)
IMUS	Inventario Musical [*Database*] [*Ministerio de Cultura*] [*Spanish*] [*Information service or system*] (CRD)
IMUT	Imutec Corp. [*NASDAQ symbol*] (SAG)
Imutec	Imutec Corp. [*Associated Press*] (SAG)
IMUTF	IMUTEC Corp. [*NASDAQ symbol*] (TTSB)
IMUX	Intelligent Multiplexer [*Telecommunications*] (ACRL)
IMV	Cornell College, Mount Vernon, IA [*OCLC symbol*] (OCLC)
IMV	Industrija Motornih Vozil [*Yugoslav automaker*]
IMV	Inferior Mesenteric Vein [*Anatomy*]
IMV	Intermittent Mandatory Ventilation [*Respiratory therapy*] [*Medicine*]
IMV	Intermittent Mechanical Ventilation [*Respiratory therapy*] [*Medicine*] (DAVI)
IMV	Internal Motor Vehicle [*Type of tugboat*] (DS)
IMV	Internationaler Metzgermeisterverband [*International Federation of Meat Traders' Associations*] (EAIO)
IMV	Internationaler Milchwirtschaftverband [*International Dairy Federation*]
IMV	International Movie Group, Inc. [*Vancouver Stock Exchange symbol*]
IMV	Intracellular Mature Virus
IMV	Isophosphamide, Methotrexate, and Vincristine [*Medicine*] (DMAA)
IMVCi	Indole, Methyl-Red, Voges-Proskauer, Citrate Test [*Bacteriology*]
IM/VE	Information Management / Virtual Environment (HGAA)
IMVH	Indian Military Veterinary Hospital [*British military*] (DMA)
IMVHO	In My Very Humble Opinion [*Computer hacker terminology*]
IMViC	Indole, Methyl Red, Voges-Proskauer, Citrate [*Reaction and test*] [*Biochemistry*] (DAVI)
IMViC	Indol, Methyl Red, Voges-Proskauer, Citrate Reactions [*Bacteriology*] [*Medicine*] (BABM)
IMVIC	International Motor Vehicle Inspection Committee [*Belgium*] (EAIO)
IMVP	Ifostamide, Methotrexate, VePesid (CDI)
IMVP	International Motor Vehicle Program [*MIT*]
IMVP-16	Isophosphamide, Methotrexate, Vesposide [*Antineoplastic drug regimen*] (DAVI)
IMVS	Indian Mobile Veterinary Stores [*British military*] (DMA)
IMVTS	Industrial Model Vocational Training Systems (EDAC)
IMW	Institute of Masters of Wine (BARN)
IMW	International Map of the World
IMW	Knox County Public Library, Vincennes, IN [*OCLC symbol*] (OCLC)
IMWA	International Mine Water Association [*Madrid, Spain*] (EAIO)
IMWA	International Ministers' and Widows' Association (EA)
IMWoodT	Institute of Machine Woodworking Technology [*British*] (BI)
IMX	Indiana Institute of Technology, McMillen Library, Fort Wayne, IN [*OCLC symbol*] (OCLC)
IMX	Inquiry Message Exchange
IMX	Island Mining [*Vancouver Stock Exchange symbol*]
IMX	Zimex Aviation Ltd. [*Switzerland ICAO designator*] (FAAC)
IMY	Groupo Imsa Sa de CV [*NYSE symbol*] (SAG)
IMY	Ida-May Resources Ltd. [*Vancouver Stock Exchange symbol*]
IMY	International Mahogany Corp. [*Toronto Stock Exchange symbol Vancouver Stock Exchange symbol*]
IMY	Michigan City Public Library, Michigan City, IN [*OCLC symbol*] (OCLC)
IMZ	Binghamton, NY [*Location identifier FAA*] (FAAL)
IMZ	Internationales Musikzentrum [*International Music Center*] [*Vienna, Austria*] (EAIO)
IM/ZEUS	Information Management / Zero Effort User System (HGAA)
IN	East Hampton Air [*ICAO designator*] (AD)
IN	Ice (Deposition) Nuclei [*Atmospheric science*]
IN	Icterus Neonatorum [*Medicine*]
IN	Idaho Nuclear (MCD)
IN	Ilioinguinal Nerve [*Anatomy*]
IN	Illinois Northern Railway [*AAR code*]
IN	Impetigo Neonatorum [*Medicine*] (DMAA)
in	Inch
IN	Inch (EY)
in	Inches (VRA)
In	Income
IN	India [*ANSI two-letter standard code*] (CNC)
IN	Indian (WDAA)
IN	Indiana [*Postal code*]
In	Indiana State Library, Indianapolis, IN [*Library symbol Library of Congress*] (LCLS)
IN	Indian Navy
In	Indian Reports [*A publication*] (DLA)
In	Indium [*Chemical element*]
IN	Inertial (MCD)
IN	Inertial Navigation (IAA)
IN	Infantry [*Army*]
IN	Information Systems Directorate [*Kennedy Space Center*] [*NASA*] (NASA)
IN	Infundibular Nucleus (DB)
IN	Ingress Node (ACRL)
IN	Initial Dose [*Medicine*]
IN	Inlet [*Maps and charts*]
IN	Input (MDG)
in	Input (IDOE)

IN...............	INS Insurance [*Vancouver Stock Exchange symbol*]
IN...............	Institute of Navigation [*US and British*]
IN...............	Institution [*Online database field identifier*]
In...............	Instructor [*Navy British*]
IN...............	Instructor Navigator (AFM)
IN...............	Instrumentation Notice (AAG)
IN...............	Instrument Note
IN...............	Insulated [*Shipping*] (DCTA)
In...............	Insulin
IN...............	Insurance
IN...............	Intake
IN...............	Integon Corp. [*NYSE symbol*] (SAG)
IN...............	Intelligence
IN...............	Intelligence Corps [*Army*] (RDA)
IN...............	Intelligent Network [*Telecommunications*]
IN...............	Intensity
IN...............	Interactive Network
IN...............	Interception [*Football*]
IN...............	Interconnecting Network (MHDI)
IN...............	Interest [*Finance, Law*] (ADA)
IN...............	Interference-to-Noise Ratio (IEEE)
IN...............	Intermittent Noise
IN...............	Internal Note
IN...............	International House - World Trade Center [*Later, WTC*] (EA)
IN...............	Internegative [*Photography*] (WDMC)
IN...............	Interneuron [*Neurology*] (DAVI)
IN...............	Interstitial Nephritis [*Medicine*] (DMAA)
IN...............	Intertechnique
IN...............	Intraductal [*Medicine*]
IN...............	Intranasal
In...............	Inulin [*Biochemistry*] (DAVI)
IN...............	Inventors [*Pergamon-Infoline*] (NITA)
IN...............	Inventory Nonrecurring (MCD)
IN...............	Investigator
IN...............	Investigator Name [*Dialog*] [*Searchable field*] (NITA)
IN...............	Irish Nationalist (ROG)
IN...............	Irritation of Nociceptors [*Medicine*] (DMAA)
IN...............	Italian Navy (NATG)
IN...............	Item Name [*Military*]
IN...............	Item Number (IAA)
IN...............	Neisler Laboratories, Inc. [*Research code symbol*]
IN...............	Office of Inspection and Enforcement Information Notice [*Nuclear energy*] (NRCH)
IN²	Square Inch
IN³	Cubic Inch
INA.............	Anderson College, Anderson, IN [*OCLC symbol*] (OCLC)
INA.............	Department of Indian and Northern Affairs Library [*UTLAS symbol*]
INA.............	Icana [*Brazil*] [*Airport symbol*] (AD)
INA.............	Ice Nucleating Activity [*Biology*] [*Physics*]
INA.............	Iinan [*Japan*] [*Seismograph station code, US Geological Survey*] (SEIS)
INA.............	Immigration and Nationality Act (GFGA)
INA.............	Immunonephelometric Assay [*Clinical chemistry*]
INA.............	Inactivator Accelerator [*Immunology*]
INA.............	Independent Newsletter Association
InA.............	Indiana Appellate Court Reports [*A publication*] (DLA)
INA.............	Indian and Northern Affairs Department [*Canada*]
INA.............	Indian National Airways
INA.............	Indian National Army [*World War II*]
INA.............	Individual Nonrecurrence Action (KSC)
INA.............	Industrija Nafta [*State-owned company*] [*Yugoslavia*]
INA.............	Infectious Nucleic Acid (DMAA)
INA.............	Inferior Nasal Artery [*Medicine*] (DMAA)
INA.............	Information Networking Alliance [*British*] (TELE)
INA.............	Information Not Available (OICC)
INA.............	Innopac, Inc. [*Toronto Stock Exchange symbol*]
INA.............	Inspector of Naval Aircraft
INA.............	Institute for Anthropology [*State University of New York at Albany*] [*Research center*] (RCD)
INA.............	Institute for New Antibiotics [*Former USSR*]
INA.............	Institute of Nautical Archaeology (EA)
INA.............	Institution of Naval Architects [*British*]
INA.............	Institut National de la Communication Audiovisuelle [*France*] (NITA)
INA.............	Insurance Co. of North America
INA.............	Integrated Network Architecture
INA.............	Interair Aviation Ltd. [*British ICAO designator*] (FAAC)
INA.............	International Nanny Association (EA)
INA.............	International Naturopathic Association [*Later, IAHHP*] (EA)
INA.............	International Neurological Association (DAVI)
INA.............	International Neurotoxicology Association
INA.............	International Newsreel and News Film Association [*Later, INANEWS*] (EAIO)
INA.............	International Normal Atmosphere
INA.............	International Nurses Anonymous (EA)
INA.............	Iodonaphthyl Azide [*Organic chemistry*]
INA.............	Iraqi News Agency
INA.............	Irish Northern Aid
INA.............	Iron Nickel Alloy
INA.............	Isonicotinic Acid [*Organic chemistry*]
INA.............	Israel News Agency
INA.............	Jena Nomina Anatomic a [*Also, INA*] [*Anatomy*] (DAVI)
INAA............	Instrumental Neutron Activation Analysis
INAA............	Irish National Association of Australasia
INAAP	Indiana Army Ammunition Plant (AABC)
INAB	[*The*] Irish National Accreditation Board (ACII)
INABU	Imprimerie Nationale du Burundi [*Government publishing house*] [*Burundi*] (EY)
INAC	Inacom Corp. [*NASDAQ symbol*] (SAG)
inac	Inactive
InAcdC-T.......	Anderson College, Graduate School of Theology, Anderson, IN [*Library symbol Library of Congress*] (LCLS)
INACDUTRA...	Inactive Duty Training [*Air Force*] (AFM)
Inacom	Inacom Corp. [*Associated Press*] (SAG)
InAcous.......	Industrial Acoustics Co., Inc. [*Associated Press*] (SAG)
INACS	Interstate Airways Communications Station (IAA)
INACT	Inactive (AABC)
INACTFLTLANT...	Inactive Fleet, Atlantic Fleet (DNAB)
INACTFLTPAC...	Inactive Fleet, Pacific Fleet
INACTLANT...	Inactive Fleet, Atlantic Fleet
INACTPAC....	Inactive Fleet, Pacific Fleet
INACTSERVCRAFAC...	Inactive Service Craft Facility [*Military*] (DNAB)
INACTSHIPFAC...	Inactive Ship Maintenance Facility [*Navy*]
INACTV	Inactivate [*or Inactive*] (MSA) (MSA)
INAD	Inadequate (AFM)
INAD	Inadvertent
INAD	Infantile Neuroaxonal Dystrophy [*Medicine*] (DMAA)
INAD	Investigational New Animal Drug [*Food and Drug Administration*]
INADQT	Inadequate (FAAC)
INAE..........	International Newspaper Advertising Executives [*Later, INAME*] (EA)
INAETP	Indian and Native American Employment and Training Program [*Department of Labor*]
InAF...........	Indian Air Force
INAF..........	Individual Name and Address File [*IRS*]
INAFBO	International Association for Business Organizations [*Baltimore, MD*] (EA)
INAH	Interstitial Nuclei of the Anterior Hypothalamus [*Brain anatomy*]
INAH	Isonicotinic Acid Hydrazide [*See also INH, ISONIAZID*] [*Antituberculous agent*]
INAI	IntelliCorp, Inc. [*NASDAQ symbol*] (NQ)
INAI	Iowa Natural Areas Inventory [*Iowa State Conservation Commission*] [*Des Moines*] [*Information service or system*] (IID)
INA/IC	Inactive - In Commission, In Reserve [*Vessel status*] [*Navy*]
INAIn	INA Investment Securities, Inc. [*Associated Press*] (SAG)
INA/IS	Inactive - In Service, In Reserve [*Vessel status*] [*Navy*]
InAk	Akron Carnegie Public Library, Akron, IN [*Library symbol Library of Congress*] (LCLS)
IN AL	Inter Alia [*Among Other Things*] [*Latin*] (WDAA)
InAlb	Noble County Public Library, Albion, IN [*Library symbol Library of Congress*] (LCLS)
InAle	Alexandria Public Library, Alexandria, IN [*Library symbol Library of Congress*] (LCLS)
InAleN	Alexandria News, Alexandria, IN [*Library symbol Library of Congress*] (LCLS)
InAleTT	Alexandria Times-Tribune, Alexandria, IN [*Library symbol Library of Congress*] (LCLS)
InAlGaP	Indium Aluminum Gallium Phophide [*Organic chemistry*]
INAME	International Newspaper Advertising and Marketing Executives (EA)
Inamed	Inamed Corp. [*Associated Press*] (SAG)
InAnd	Anderson Carnegie Public Library, Anderson, IN [*Library symbol Library of Congress*] (LCLS)
InAndB	Anderson Daily Bulletin, Anderson, IN [*Library symbol Library of Congress*] (LCLS)
InAndC........	Anderson College, Anderson, IN [*Library symbol Library of Congress*] (LCLS)
InAndC-T.......	Anderson College, Graduate School of Theology, Anderson, IN [*Library symbol*] [*Library of Congress*] (LCLS)
IN & EA	International Nuclear and Energy Association [*Defunct*] (EA)
InAndH.........	Anderson Herald, Anderson, IN [*Library symbol Library of Congress*] (LCLS)
INANEWS....	International Newsreel Association (EAIO)
InAng	Carnegie Public Library, Angola, IN [*Library symbol Library of Congress*] (LCLS)
InAngT	Tri-State University, Angola, IN [*Library symbol Library of Congress*] (LCLS)
InAnw	Andrews-Dallas Township Public Library, Andrews, IN [*Library symbol Library of Congress*] (LCLS)
INAO	Institut National des Appellations d'Origine [*Semigovernmental organization that fixes the appellations on all French wines*]
INA/OC	Inactive - Out of Commission, In Reserve [*Vessel status*] [*Navy*]
INA/OS........	Inactive - Out of Service, In Reserve [*Vessel status*] [*Navy*]
INAP	Integrated Neutron Activation Prediction [*Code system*]
INap	Nichols Library, Naperville, IL [*Library symbol Library of Congress*] (LCLS)
INapC.........	College & Seminary Library, Inc., Naperville, IL [*Library symbol Library of Congress Obsolete*] (LCLS)
INAPEN	International AIDS Prospective Epidemiology Network (EA)
INapGS	Church of Jesus Christ of Latter-Day Saints, Genealogical Society Library, Naperville Branch, Naperville, IL [*Library symbol Library of Congress*] (LCLS)
INapN	North Central College, Naperville, IL [*Library symbol Library of Congress*] (LCLS)
INapS.........	Standard Oil Research Center, Naperville, IL [*Library symbol Library of Congress*] (LCLS)
InAr..........	Argos Public Library, Argos, IN [*Library symbol Library of Congress*] (LCLS)
IN ARCH	Inland Architect [*A publication*] (ROG)
INARCO........	International Artware Corp. (EFIS)
InArcT........	Tri Town Topics, Arcadia, IN [*Library symbol Library of Congress*] (LCLS)
InARP	Inverse Address Resolution Protocol [*Telecommunications*] (ACRL)

InArT	Argos Tribune, Argos, IN [*Library symbol Library of Congress*] (LCLS)
INAS	Indexing and Abstracting Services
InAs	Indium Arsenide (MED)
INAS	Industrial Naval Air Stations (NG)
INAS	Inertial Navigation and Attack System (MCD)
INAS	Inpatient Non-Availability Statement [*DoD*]
INAS	Interbank National Authorization System
INas	Nashville Public Library, Nashville, IL [*Library symbol Library of Congress*] (LCLS)
INasHS	Nashville High School, Nashville, IL [*Library symbol Library of Congress*] (LCLS)
INAsicrz	Istituto Nazionale Delle Assicoraziono SPA [*Associated Press*] (SAG)
INasSD	Nashville Community High School District 99, Nashville, IL [*Library symbol Library of Congress*] (LCLS)
INat	New Athens Public Library, New Athens, IL [*Library symbol Library of Congress*] (LCLS)
INATAPROBU	International Association of Professional Bureaucrats (EA)
INatCD	New Athens Community Consolidated District 60, New Athens, IL [*Library symbol Library of Congress*] (LCLS)
INATS	International New Age Trade Show
INATS	Interruption of Air Traffic Services (FAAC)
InAtt	Attica Public Library, Attica, IN [*Library symbol Library of Congress*] (LCLS)
InAttCF	Covington Friend, Attica, IN [*Library symbol Library of Congress*] (LCLS)
InAttFO	Attica Friendly Oracle, Attica, IN [*Library symbol Library of Congress*] (LCLS)
InAttLT	Attica Daily Ledger Tribune, Attica, IN [*Library symbol Library of Congress*] (LCLS)
InAub	Eckhart Public Library, Auburn, IN [*Library symbol Library of Congress*] (LCLS)
InAubS	Auburn Evening Star, Auburn, IN [*Library symbol Library of Congress*] (LCLS)
INAUG	Inaugurated (ADA)
InAur	Aurora Public Library, Aurora, IN [*Library symbol Library of Congress*] (LCLS)
IN AUR	In Auri [*To the Ear*] [*Pharmacy*]
InAurHi	Hillforest Historical Foundation, Inc., Aurora, IN [*Library symbol Library of Congress*] (LCLS)
InAusN	Austin-Crothersville News, Austin, IN [*Library symbol Library of Congress*] (LCLS)
INAW	Institute of the Northamerican West (EA)
INAZ	Interference Accommodation Zone [*Geology*]
INB	Bartholomew County Library, Columbus, IN [*OCLC symbol*] (OCLC)
InB	Bedford Public Library, Bedford, IN [*Library symbol Library of Congress*] (LCLS)
IN B	In Bonis [*In the Goods Of*] [*Latin*] (ADA)
INB	In Bono [*In Good Order*]
INB	Independence [*Belize*] [*Airport symbol*] (OAG)
INB	Indiana Motor Rate and Tariff Bureau Inc., Indianapolis IN [*STAC*]
INB	Instalbud [*Poland ICAO designator*] (FAAC)
INB	Interbev Packaging Corp. [*Vancouver Stock Exchange symbol*]
INB	Internuclear Bridging (DMAA)
INB	Intl Thunderbird Gaming [*Exchange symbol*] (TTSB)
INb	Northbrook Public Library, Northbrook, IL [*Library symbol Library of Congress*] (LCLS)
INB	Oakland, CA [*Location identifier FAA*] (FAAL)
INBA	International Nubian Breeders Association (EA)
INBACS	Infantry Battalion as a Combat System [*Study*] (MCD)
InBaHT	Batesville Herald Tribune, Batesville, IN [*Library symbol Library of Congress*] (LCLS)
INbAS	Allstate Insurance, Inc., Corporate Library, Northbrook, IL [*Library symbol*] [*Library of Congress*] (LCLS)
INBC	InnoPet Brands Corp. [*NASDAQ symbol*] (SAG)
INBC	Interlibrary Network of Baltimore County [*Library network*]
InBCR	Lawrence County Recorder's Office, Bedford, IN [*Library symbol Library of Congress*] (LCLS)
INbD	Dart & Kraft, Inc., Northbrook, IL [*Library symbol*] [*Library of Congress*] (LCLS)
INBD	Inboard (KSC)
INBD	Inbound
InBer	Berne Public Library, Berne, IN [*Library symbol Library of Congress*] (LCLS)
INBH	Brokaw Hospital Medical Center, Normal, IL [*Library symbol Library of Congress*] (LCLS)
INBI	Industrial Bancorp [*NASDAQ symbol*] (TTSB)
INBI	Industrial Bancorp, Inc. [*NASDAQ symbol*] (SAG)
InBiKN	Knox County Daily News, Bicknell, IN [*Library symbol Library of Congress*] (LCLS)
INBio	Biodiversity Institute [*Center established to inventory wildlife*] (PS)
INBIT	Input BIT [*Binary Digit*] [*Computer science*] (NASA)
InBl	Bloomfield Public Library, Bloomfield, IN [*Library symbol Library of Congress*] (LCLS)
InBlCR	Greene County Recorder's Office, Bloomfield, IN [*Library symbol Library of Congress*] (LCLS)
InBLHi	Lawrence County Historical Society, Bedford, IN [*Library symbol Library of Congress*] (LCLS)
InBlo	Monroe County Public Library, Bloomington, IN [*Library symbol Library of Congress*] (LCLS)
InBloHT	Bloomington Herald-Telephone, Bloomington, IN [*Library symbol Library of Congress*] (LCLS)
InBloKi	Alfred C. Kinsey Institute for Sex Research, Bloomington, IN [*Library symbol Library of Congress*] (LCLS)
InBlu	Bluffton-Wells County Public Library, Bluffton, IN [*Library symbol Library of Congress*] (LCLS)
InBlWN	Bloomfield Evening World and News, Bloomfield, IN [*Library symbol Library of Congress*] (LCLS)
INBNX	IDS Bond Cl.A [*Mutual fund ticker symbol*] (SG)
InBoM	Borden Museum, Borden, IN [*Library symbol Library of Congress Obsolete*] (LCLS)
InBoo	Boonville Warrick County Public Library, Boonville, IN [*Library symbol Library of Congress*] (LCLS)
InBooE	Warrick Enquirer, Boonville, IN [*Library symbol Library of Congress*] (LCLS)
InBooS	Boonville Standard, Boonville, IN [*Library symbol Library of Congress*] (LCLS)
InBosE	Boswell Enterprise, Boswell, IN [*Library symbol Library of Congress*] (LCLS)
InBou	Bourbon Public Library, Bourbon, IN [*Library symbol Library of Congress*] (LCLS)
In-BPH	Indiana State Library, Blind and Physically Handicapped Division, Indianapolis, IN [*Library symbol Library of Congress*] (LCLS)
INBR	Inbrand Corp. [*NASDAQ symbol*] (SAG)
InBra	Brazil Public Library, Brazil, IN [*Library symbol Library of Congress*] (LCLS)
InBraCHi	Clay County Historical Society, Brazil, IN [*Library symbol Library of Congress*] (LCLS)
Inbrand	Inbrand Corp. [*Associated Press*] (SAG)
InBraT	Brazil Times, Brazil, IN [*Library symbol Library of Congress*] (LCLS)
InBrb	Brownsburg Public Library, Brownsburg, IN [*Library symbol Library of Congress*] (LCLS)
InBrbG	Brownsburg Guide, Brownsburg, IN [*Library symbol Library of Congress*] (LCLS)
INBRD	Inboard (ADA)
InBre	W. E. Walter Memorial Library (Bremen Public Library), Bremen, IN [*Library symbol Library of Congress*] (LCLS)
InBreE	Bremen Enquirer, Bremen, IN [*Library symbol Library of Congress*] (LCLS)
InBri	Bristol-Washington Township Public Library (Bristol Public Library), Bristol, IN [*Library symbol Library of Congress*] (LCLS)
InBriEHi	Elkhart County Historical Society, Bristol, IN [*Library symbol Library of Congress*] (LCLS)
InBrkvA	Brookville American, Brookville, IN [*Library symbol Library of Congress*] (LCLS)
InBrkvCR	Franklin County Recorder's Office, Brookville, IN [*Library symbol Library of Congress*] (LCLS)
InBrkvD	Brookville Democrat, Brookville, IN [*Library symbol Library of Congress*] (LCLS)
InBro	Brook-Iroquois Public Library, Brook, IN [*Library symbol Library of Congress*] (LCLS)
InBroA	George Ade Hazeldon Home, Brook, IN [*Library symbol Library of Congress*] (LCLS)
InBrt	Brownstown Public Library, Brownstown, IN [*Library symbol Library of Congress*] (LCLS)
InBrtB	Brownstown Banner, Brownstown, IN [*Library symbol Library of Congress*] (LCLS)
InBrtHi	Jackson County Historical Society, Brownstown, IN [*Library symbol Library of Congress*] (LCLS)
INBSV	Interim Narrow-Band Secure Voice (NVT)
InBTM	Bedford Times-Mail, Bedford, IN [*Library symbol Library of Congress*] (LCLS)
InBu	Butler Carnegie Library, Butler, IN [*Library symbol Library of Congress*] (LCLS)
InBuB	Butler Bulletin, Butler, IN [*Library symbol Library of Congress*] (LCLS)
INbW	Wiss, Janney, Elstner, & Associates, Northbrook, IL [*Library symbol Library of Congress*] (LCLS)
InC	Crawfordsville District Public Library, Crawfordsville, IN [*Library symbol Library of Congress*] (LCLS)
INC	Ice Navigation Center [*Marine science*] (MSC)
INC	Idaho Nuclear Corp.
INC	Iglesia Ni Cristo [*Religious organization*]
INC	Igniter Nozzle Closure
INC	Incendiary
INC	Inchon [*Tyosen, Zinsen*] [*South Korea*] [*Seismograph station code, US Geological Survey*] [*Closed*] (SEIS)
INC	Incidit [*Engraved*] [*Latin*] (ROG)
INC	Incinerator
INC	Incisal (STED)
inc	Incised (VRA)
INC	Incision (STED)
inc	Incision
Inc	Incisional (STED)
INC	Incisus [*Being Cut*] [*Pharmacy*] (ROG)
INC	Inclosure
INC	In Clouds [*ICAO*] (FAAC)
INC	Including
Inc	Including (STED)
INC	Inclusive
INC	Income (ROG)
Inc	Income (EBF)
inc	Income (WDMC)
INC	Incoming [*Telecommunications*] (KSC)
INC	Incoming Trunk [*Telecommunications*] (TEL)
Inc	Incompatibility (STED)
INC	Incomplete
inc	Incomplete (WDMC)
INC	Inconclusive
Inc	Inconclusive (STED)

Inc	Incontinent (STED)
INC	Incontinent [*Medicine*]
INC	Incorporated (EY)
Inc	Incorporated (EBF)
Inc	Incorporated (STED)
inc	Incorporated (WDMC)
inc	Increase (WDMC)
INC	Increase (AABC)
INC	Increment
Inc	Increment (STED)
INC	Incumbent (ROG)
inc	Incurred
INC	Indiana Cooperative Library Services Authority, Indianapolis, IN [*OCLC symbol*] (OCLC)
INC	Indian National Congress
inc	Indic [*MARC language code Library of Congress*] (LCCP)
INC	Inertial Navigation Computer (MCD)
INC	Information and Censorship [*Allied Forces*] [*World War II*]
INC	In Nomine Christi [*In the Name of Christ*] [*Latin*]
INC	Input Control System [*Military*]
INC	Insectivorous Cyprinids [*Pisciculture*]
INC	Insertable Nuclear Components (MCD)
INC	Inside-the-Needle Catheter [*Cardiology*] (DAVI)
INC	Installation Notice Card (KSC)
INC	Installation Notification Certification (MCD)
INC	Integrated Network Corp. (PCM)
INC	Intelligence Coordination [*Program*] [*Department of State*]
INC	International Negotiating Committee [*World Resources Institute*]
INC	International Numismatic Commission
INC	International Nut Council (EAIO)
INC	Interstitial Nucleus of Cajal [*Brain anatomy*]
INC	Invermay Resources [*Vancouver Stock Exchange symbol*]
INC	Iraqi National Congress [*Political party*] (ECON)
INC	Irish National Caucus (EA)
INC	Ironfounders' National Confederation [*British*] (BI)
INC	Item Name Code [*Military*] (AFM)
INC	Jet Air Internacional Charters CA [*Venezuela*] [*ICAO designator*] (FAAC)
INC.	Nutrition Education Association (EA)
INC.	Yinchuan [*China*] [*Airport symbol*] (OAG)
INcA	Abbott Laboratories, North Chicago, IL [*Library symbol Library of Congress*] (LCLS)
InCa	Carlisle Public Library, Carlisle, IN [*Library symbol Library of Congress*] (LCLS)
INCA	Idaho Nuclear Code Automation [*AEC*]
INCA	Implementation of New Carrier Arrangements [*Telecommunications*]
INCA	In-Core Analysis [*Nuclear energy*] (NRCH)
INCA	Information Council of the Americas (EA)
INCA	Innovation through Creative Analysis (PDAA)
INCA	Institute for Numerical Computation and Analysis (MCD)
INCA	Integrated Catalog Algorithm (MCD)
INCA	Integrated Communications Agency [*Air Force*]
INCA	Integrated Navigation and Communications, Automatic
INCA	Integrated Network Communication Architecture (OSI)
INCA	Integrated Nuclear and Chemical Analysis
INCA	Integrated Nuclear Communications Assessment
INCA	Integrated Numerical Control Approach
INCA	Intelligence Communications Architecture
INCA	Interactive Controls Analysis [*NASA*] (CIST)
INCA	International Narcotics Control Act
INCA	International Newspaper and Colour Association [*Later, IFRA*] (EA)
INCA	Inventory Control and Analysis (MHDB)
Inc Ab	Incomplete Abortion [*Obstetrics*] (DAVI)
INCAD	Incapacitated Passengers' Handling Advice [*British*]
INCAE	Instituto Centroamericano de Administracion de Empresas [*Central American Institute of Business Administration*] [*Nicaragua*]
INCAIR	Including Air
InCaL	Carlisle Public Library, Carlisle, IN [*Library symbol*] [*Library of Congress*] (LCLS)
Incalz	Incalzando [*Music*]
InCam	Camden-Jackson Township Public Library, Camden, IN [*Library symbol Library of Congress*] (LCLS)
INCAM	Inducible Cell Adhesion Molecule [*Immunochemistry*]
INCAMS	Individual Cassette Manufacturing System (AAEL)
InCan	Cannelton Public Library, Cannelton, IN [*Library symbol Library of Congress*] (LCLS)
incan	Incandescent (WDMC)
InCanCR	Perry County Recorder's Office, Cannelton, IN [*Library symbol Library of Congress*] (LCLS)
INCAND	Incandescent (MSA)
INCAP	Instituto de Nutricion de Centro America y Panama [*Institute of Nutrition of Central America and Panama*] [*Guatemala, Guatemala*] (EAIO)
InCar	Carmel Public Library, Carmel, IN [*Library symbol Library of Congress*] (LCLS)
INCAR	International Committee Against Racism (EA)
Incarnate Word C	Incarnate Word College (GAGS)
InCarNJ	Carmel News Journal, Carmel, IN [*Library symbol Library of Congress*] (LCLS)
InCarS	Carmel Clay Schools, Carmel IN [*Library symbol*] [*Library of Congress*] (LCLS)
INCAS	Integrated Navigation and Collision Avoidance System (PDAA)
INCAS	International Center for Advanced Studies [*Russia*]
InCayHN	Cayuga Herald News, Cayuga, IN [*Library symbol Library of Congress*] (LCLS)

IncB	Inclusion Body [*Cytology*]
INCB	Indiana Cmnty Bk SB [*NASDAQ symbol*] (TTSB)
INCB	Indiana Community Bank A Savings Bank [*NASDAQ symbol*] (SAG)
INCB	International Narcotics Control Board (DMAA)
INCB	International Nuclear Credit Bank (NRCH)
INCBE	Israel National Committee on the Biosphere and Environment
INCBR	Incubator (MSA)
InCc	Cambridge City Public Library, Cambridge City, IN [*Library symbol Library of Congress*] (LCLS)
INCC	Institut National du Cancer du Canada [*National Cancer Institute of Canada*] (EAIO)
INCC	Interim National Coordinating Committee [*Ghana*] (PPW)
INCC	International Network Controlling Center [*Telecommunications*] (TEL)
INCC	International Newspaper Collector's Club (EA)
INCC	International Nippon Collectors Club (EA)
INCC	Internet Communications [*NASDAQ symbol*] (SAG)
InCcNR	National Road Traveler, Cambridge City, IN [*Library symbol Library of Congress*] (LCLS)
INCD	Incandescent
INCD	Incendiary (AABC)
INCD	Incorporated [*Legal term*] (EY)
INCD	Infantile Nuclear Cerebral Degeneration [*Medicine*] (DMAA)
INCDT	Incident (MSA)
InCe	Centerville and Center Township Library, Centerville, IN [*Library symbol Library of Congress*] (LCLS)
INCE	Institute of Noise Control Engineering (EA)
INCE	Insurance
INCE	International Network for Chemical Education [*Samoa*] (EAIO)
INCEP	Interceptor
INCEPT	Inception (ROG)
INCERFA	Uncertainty Phase Code (Alerting Service) [*Aviation*] (FAAC)
IncFB	Increase Feedback
INCFO	Institute of Newspaper Controllers and Finance Officers [*Later, INFE*] (EA)
INCH	Inchoative (WGA)
INCH	Independent Channel Handler (IAA)
INCH	Integrated Chopper
INCH	Interaction Checklist for Augmentative Communication, Revised Edition [*Test*] (TMMY)
INCH	Interim Charging [*Electric vehicle technology*]
INCH	International Center for High Quality Scrap [*Scrap salvage*]
InCha	Charlestown Township Public Library, Charlestown, IN [*Library symbol Library of Congress*] (LCLS)
InChe	Westchester Public Library, Chesterton, IN [*Library symbol Library of Congress*] (LCLS)
InCheT	Chesterton Tribune, Chesterton, IN [*Library symbol Library of Congress*] (LCLS)
INCHO	Inchoate (ADA)
IN CH Q	Indian Church Quarterly Review [*A publication*] (ROG)
INCID	Incide [*Cut*] [*Pharmacy*]
incid	Incide [*Cut*] [*Latin*] (STED)
INCIDI	Institut International des Civilisations Differentes [*International Institute of Differing Civilizations*]
INCIN	Incinerator (MSA)
InCINC	International Chemometrics Internet Conference
INCINC	International Copyright Information Center (EA)
INCIRS	International Communication Information Retrieval System [*University of Florida*] (PDAA)
INCIS	Incisus [*Being Cut*] [*Pharmacy*] (ROG)
INCJHS	International Network of Children of Jewish Holocaust Survivors (EA)
InCJR	Crawfordsville Journal and Review, Crawfordsville, IN [*Library symbol Library of Congress*] (LCLS)
INCL	Inclination [*Angular distance from equator in degrees*]
INCL	Inclosure (AFM)
INCL	Include [*or Including*] (EY)
Incl	Include (TBD)
incl	Included (REAL)
incl	Including (WDMC)
incl	Inclusive (WDMC)
INCL	Inclusive
INCL	Incoming Line (IAA)
INCL	Inconclusive
INCL	In Control, Inc. [*NASDAQ symbol*] (SAG)
INCL	Infantile Neuronal Ceroid Lipofuscinoses [*Medicine*]
InClcN	Clay City News, Clay City, IN [*Library symbol Library of Congress*] (LCLS)
INCLD	Including [*Freight*]
InCli	Clinton Public Library, Clinton, IN [*Library symbol Library of Congress*] (LCLS)
InCliC	Daily Clintonian, Clinton, IN [*Library symbol Library of Congress*] (LCLS)
INCLN	Inclined (MSA)
INCLN	Inclusion
INCLR	Intercooler
INCLS	Inclosure (MSA)
INCLU	Inclusive (ROG)
INCLUDE	Implementing New Concepts of the Library for Urban Disadvantaged Ethnics [*Cleveland Public Library*] (NITA)
INCLV	Inclusive (FAAC)
InCLW	General Lew Wallace Studio, Crawfordsville, IN [*Library symbol Library of Congress*] (LCLS)
INCM	Income
INCM	Incoming (MSA)
INCMG	Incoming
INCND	Incendiary (MSA)

INCNIA......... Integrated Communications-Navigation-Identification Avionics (MUSM)
INCNR.......... Increment Number (DOMA)
InCo............ Connersville Public Library, Connersville, IN [Library symbol Library of Congress] (LCLS)
INCO .... INCO Ltd. [Formerly, International Nickel Co. of Canada] [Associated Press] (SAG)
INCO .... Installation and Checkout [Military] (CAAL)
INCO .... Instrumentation and Communications Officer [NASA]
INCO .... International Chamber of Commerce (IEEE)
INCO .... International Nickel Co.
InCoa........... Coatesville Public Library, Coatesville, IN [Library symbol Library of Congress] (LCLS)
InCODA......... International Congress of Dealers Associations (EA)
INCODEL...... Interstate Commission on the Delaware River Basin
incog .... Incognito [Unknown] [Latin]
INCOG.......... Indian Nations Council of Governments
INCOH.......... Incoherent (MSA)
IncoHm......... Inco Homes Corp. [Associated Press] (SAG)
InColc.......... Peabody Library, Columbia City, IN [Library symbol Library of Congress] (LCLS)
InColcCR...... Whitley County Recorder's Office, Columbia City, IN [Library symbol Library of Congress] (LCLS)
InColf.......... Colfax Public Library, Colfax, IN [Library symbol] [Library of Congress] (LCLS)
InColo.......... Bartholomew County Library, Columbus, IN [Library symbol Library of Congress] (LCLS)
INCOLR........ Intercooler
INCOLSA...... Indiana Cooperative Library Services Authority [Indianapolis, IN] [Library network]
InColu .... Bartholomew County Library, Columbus, IN [Library symbol Library of Congress] (LCLS)
InColuHi ...... Bartholomew County Historical Society, Columbus, IN [Library symbol Library of Congress] (LCLS)
InColuR........ Columbus Republic, Columbus, IN [Library symbol] [Library of Congress] (LCLS)
INCOM .... Incomplete (AABC)
INCOM .... Indicator Compiler (IAA)
INCOM .... Input Compiler (IAA)
INCOMEX..... International Computer Exhibition
INCOMINDIOS... International Committee for the Indians of the Americas [Kaiseraugst, Switzerland] (EAIO)
Incomnt .... INCOMNET, Inc. [Associated Press] (SAG)
INCOMP........ Incomplete (MSA)
INCOMPAT... Incompatible [Medicine]
INCOMPL..... Incomplete
incompl .... Incomplete (WDMC)
InCon .... Converse Jackson Township Public Library, Converse, IN [Library symbol Library of Congress] (LCLS)
INCON.......... Installation Console (MCD)
INCONCRYO-ISC... International Conference on Cryogenics - International Steering Committee (EAIO)
InCoNE........ Connersville News-Examiner, Connersville, IN [Library symbol Library of Congress] (LCLS)
incont .... Incontinent [Medicine] (DAVI)
InControl...... InControl, Inc. [Associated Press] (SAG)
IncOp2 .... Income Opportunities Fund II, Inc. [Associated Press] (SAG)
IncOp2000 ... Income Opportunities Fund 2000 [Associated Press] (SAG)
IncOpRT....... Income Opportunity Realty Trust [Associated Press] (SAG)
InCor........... Corydon Public Library, Corydon, IN [Library symbol Library of Congress] (LCLS)
INCOR.......... Incorporated [Legal term]
INCOR.......... Incorrect (MSA)
INCOR.......... Intergovernmental Conference on Oceanographic Research (MCD)
InCorCP ...... Harrison County Press, Corydon, IN [Library symbol Library of Congress] (LCLS)
InCorCR ...... Harrison County Recorder's Office, Corydon, IN [Library symbol Library of Congress] (LCLS)
InCorD .... Corydon Democrat, Corydon, IN [Library symbol Library of Congress] (LCLS)
INCORE......... International Programme on Conflict Resolution and Ethnicity
INCORP........ Incorporated [Legal term] (EY)
INCORPN..... Incorporation [Legal term] (ROG)
INCORR........ Incorrect (ADA)
INCOS.......... Integrated Control System [Navy] (NVT)
INCOSAI...... International Congress of Supreme Audit Institutions (PDAA)
INCOSE........ International Council on Systems Engineering (NTPA)
INCOT .... In-Core Test Facility [Nuclear energy] (NRCH)
INCOTEC...... International Committee for Training and Education of Co-Operators (EAIO)
INCOTERM... International Commerce Term [International Chamber of Commerce]
INCOTERMS... International Contracting Terms (AAGC)
InCov .... Covington Public Library, Covington, IN [Library symbol Library of Congress] (LCLS)
InCovFS .... Fountain County Star, Covington, IN [Library symbol Library of Congress] (LCLS)
INCPD ACCT... Incorporated Accountant [British] (ROG)
INCPEN....... Industry Committee for Packaging and the Environment [British] (DI)
INCPT .... Intercept
INCR .... Increase (AFM)
incr .... Increase (WDMC)
inc(r) .... Increase (Relative) (AAMN)
INCR .... Increment (AFM)
INCR .... Interrupt Control Register [Computer science] (MSA)
INCRA.......... International Copper Research Association [Research center British] (IRC)

INCRAPLAN... Integrated Crew and Aircraft Planning (PDAA)
INCRE .... Increment
INCREM .... Incremental
INCREP........ Incident Report [Military] (CINC)
INCRNTN ..... Incarnation
InCrp........... Crown Point Center Public Library, Crown Point, IN [Library symbol Library of Congress] (LCLS)
InCrpCS....... Crown Point Community Schools, Crown Point, IN [Library symbol Library of Congress] (LCLS)
InCrpLS........ Lake County Star, Crown Point, IN [Library symbol Library of Congress] (LCLS)
INCS .... Incomplete Resolution, Scan to Follow [Radiology] (DAVI)
INCS .... Integrated Battlefield Control System (MCD)
INCS .... International Netsuke Collectors Society [Commercial firm] (EA)
INCSEA........ Incident at Sea [Navy] (NVT)
inc sed .... Incertae Sedis [Uncertain Position] [Biology, taxonomy]
INCSR .... International Narcotics Control Strategy Report [Department of State]
Incstar .... Incstar Corp. [Associated Press] (SAG)
INCT .... Incumbent (ROG)
Inc Tax Cas... Reports of Cases Relating to Income Tax [A publication] (DLA)
Inc Tax LJ ... Income Tax Law Journal [India] [A publication] (DLA)
Inc Tax R..... Income Tax Reports [India] [A publication] (DLA)
INCTN .... Incorporation
InCtPd........ Inter-City Products Corp. [Associated Press] (SAG)
INCTRL........ Installation Control [Computer science] (PCM)
InCu .... Culver Public Library, Culver, IN [Library symbol Library of Congress] (LCLS)
INCUMB....... Incumbent
INCUMBCE... Incumbrance (ROG)
INCUMBD.... Incumbered (ROG)
INCUN......... Incunabula (ADA)
INCUR.......... Incurable [Medicine]
INCV .... Inclusive (MSA)
InCW .... Wabash College, Crawfordsville, IN [Library symbol Library of Congress] (LCLS)
INCWF .... Indian National Cement Workers' Federation
INCX .... INFOCURE Corp. [NASDAQ symbol]
INCY .... Incendiary Bomb (DSUE)
INCY .... INCYTE Pharmaceuticals [NASDAQ symbol] (TTSB)
InCyA.......... Cynthiana Argus, Cynthiana, IN [Library symbol Library of Congress] (LCLS)
Incyte........... Incyte Pharmaceuticals, Inc. [Associated Press] (SAG)
Ind .... Adversus Indoctum [of Lucian] [Classical studies] (OCD)
IND .... American Industrial Properties [Formerly, Trammell Crow Real Estate Investment] [NYSE symbol] (SPSG)
IND .... Amer Industrial Prop [NYSE symbol] (TTSB)
IND .... Immigration and Nationality Directorate
IND .... Improvised Nuclear Device
IND .... Indecent [FBI standardized term]
IND .... Independent
ind .... Independent (WDMC)
Ind .... Independents [Pakistan] [Political party]
IND .... Index
ind .... Index (WDMC)
IND .... India [IYRU nationality code] [ANSI three-letter standard code] (CNC)
IND .... Indian (AABC)
IND .... Indiana
IND .... Indianapolis [Indiana] [Airport symbol] (OAG)
Ind .... Indiana Supreme Court Reports [A publication] (DLA)
IND .... Indicate [or Indicator] (KSC)
IND .... Indicative (ROG)
ind .... Indicator (IDOE)
IND .... Indies
IN D............ In Dies [Daily] [Pharmacy]
IND .... Indigo
ind .... Indigo (WDMC)
IND .... Indirect
IND .... Indomethacin [An analgesic]
ind .... Indonesian [MARC language code Library of Congress] (LCCP)
IND .... Indoors (ROG)
IND .... Indorse [Legal term] (AABC)
IND .... Induced Nuclear Disintegration
IND .... Inductance
ind .... Inductance (IDOE)
IND .... Induction (MSA)
ind .... Inductor (IDOE)
Ind .... Indus [Constellation]
IND .... Industrial
ind .... Industrial (WDMC)
Ind .... Industrial (AL)
IND .... Industrial Medicine (DMAA)
IND .... Industry (AL)
IND .... Industry (AFM)
IND .... Industry Division [Census] (OICC)
IND .... In Nomine Dei [In the Name of God] [Latin]
IND .... Intercept Director [Military]
IND .... Inter Mountain Development, Inc. [Vancouver Stock Exchange symbol]
IND .... International Number Dialing [Telecommunications] (TEL)
IND .... Investigational New Device [U.S. Food and Drug Administration]
IND .... Investigational New Drug [Application] [FDA]
IND .... Iona National Airways Ltd. [Republic of Ireland] [ICAO designator] (FAAC)
IND .... University of Notre Dame, Notre Dame, IN [OCLC symbol] (OCLC)

INDA...........	INDA, Association of the Nonwoven Fabrics Industry [*Formerly, International Nonwovens and Disposables Association*]
INDAC.........	Industrial Data Acquisition and Control [*Computer science*] (MHDI)
Ind Acc Com...	Decisions of the Industrial Accident Commission of California [*A publication*] (DLA)
Ind Acts.......	Acts of Indiana [*A publication*] (DLA)
Ind A Dig......	United States Indian Affairs Office, Digest of Decisions [*A publication*] (DLA)
IndAdmin.....	Industrial Administration (DD)
Ind Admin R...	Burns' Indiana Administrative Rules and Regulations [*A publication*] (DLA)
InDaDN........	Dale News, Dale, IN [*Library symbol*] [*Library of Congress*] (LCLS)
Ind Advocate..	Indian Advocate [*A publication*] (DLA)
INDAIR........	Identification of Aircraft
InDair..........	International Dairy Queen, Inc. [*Associated Press*] (SAG)
InDairA........	International Dairy Queen [*Associated Press*] (SAG)
InDairB........	International Dairy Queen [*Associated Press*] (SAG)
InDaN..........	Dale News, Dale, IN [*Library symbol Library of Congress*] (LCLS)
InDan...........	Danville Public Library, Danville, IN [*Library symbol Library of Congress*] (LCLS)
InDanCR	Hendricks County Recorder's Office, Danville, IN [*Library symbol Library of Congress*] (LCLS)
Ind & Intell Prop Aust...	Industrial and Intellectual Property in Australia [*A publication*] (DLA)
InDanN	Central Normal College, Danville, IN [*Library symbol Library of Congress Obsolete*] (LCLS)
InDanR	Danville Republican, Danville, IN [*Library symbol Library of Congress*] (LCLS)
Ind App........	Indiana Court of Appeals Reports [*A publication*] (DLA)
Ind App........	Law Reports, Indian Appeals [*A publication*] (DLA)
Ind App Ct ...	Indiana Appellate Court Reports [*A publication*] (DLA)
Ind App Supp...	Supplemental Indian Appeals, Law Reports [*A publication*] (DLA)
InDar	Darlington Public Library, Darlington, IN [*Library symbol Library of Congress*] (LCLS)
INDASAT......	Indian Scientific Satellite
INDAT	Incoming Data (MCD)
Ind Awards...	Industrial Awards Recommendations [*New Zealand*] [*A publication*] (DLA)
INDB	Independent Bank Corp. [*NASDAQ symbol*] (NQ)
INDB	Independent Bank(MA) [*NASDAQ symbol*] (TTSB)
IndBc	Independence Bancorp, Inc. [*Associated Press*] (SAG)
IndBkMA......	Independent Bank Corp. Massachusetts [*Associated Press*] (SAG)
IndBkMI......	Independent Bank Corp. Michigan [*Associated Press*] (SAG)
IndBnk	Independent Bankshares, Inc. [*Associated Press*] (SAG)
INDC	Indian National Democratic Congress (BARN)
INDC	Indicate (FAAC)
INDC	International Nuclear Data Committee [*of International Atomic Energy Agency*]
Ind Can L P Lit...	Index to Canadian Legal Periodical Literature [*A publication*] (DLA)
Ind Cas........	Indian Cases [*India*] [*A publication*] (DLA)
Ind C Aw......	Industrial Court Awards [*England*] [*A publication*] (DLA)
Ind Chem Eng...	Industrial Engineering Chemical Research (MEC)
Ind Code Ann...	Burns' Indiana Statutes, Annotated Code Edition [*A publication*] (DLA)
Ind Com Law...	Indermaur and Thwaites' Principles of the Common Law [*12th ed.*] [*1914*] [*A publication*] (DLA)
Ind Court Aw...	Industrial Court Awards [*England*] [*A publication*] (DLA)
Ind Ct Awards...	Industrial Court Awards [*England*] [*A publication*] (DLA)
Indctd..........	Inducted [*Army*]
INDCTR........	Indicator
Ind Dec........	Indiana Decisions [*A publication*] (DLA)
Ind Dec........	Indiana Decisions and Law Reporter [*A publication*] (DLA)
Ind Dig	All India Reporter, Indian Digest [*1946-52*] [*A publication*] (DLA)
Ind Div.........	Inderwick's Divorce and Matrimonial Causes Acts [*1862*] [*A publication*] (DLA)
INDE	IndeNet Inc. [*NASDAQ symbol*] (TTSB)
INDE	Independence National Historical Park
INDE	Independent TeleMedia Group [*NASDAQ symbol*] (SAG)
Ind E	Industrial Engineer
INDE	Integrated Nondestructive Evaluation (MCD)
Indebt..........	Indebtedness [*Legal term*] (DLA)
InDec	Decatur Public Library, Decatur, IN [*Library symbol Library of Congress*] (LCLS)
indec	Indeclinable (BJA)
INDEC	Independent Nuclear Disarmament Election Committee [*British*] (DI)
INDEC	Interdepartmental Committee
InDecD.........	Decatur Daily Democrat, Decatur, IN [*Library symbol*] [*Library of Congress*] (LCLS)
INDECL........	Indeclinable [*Grammar*]
INDECS........	Immigration and Nationality Department Electronic Computer System (BARN)
INDECS........	Interactive Design of Control Systems (DI)
INDEF	Indefinite (AABC)
INDEFOPS....	Indefinite Operations (NVT)
InDel...........	Delphi Public Library, Delphi, IN [*Library symbol Library of Congress*] (LCLS)
INDEL	Industry Education Liaison (AIE)
InDelCC	Carroll County Comet, Delphi, IN [*Library symbol Library of Congress*] (LCLS)
InDelCHi	Carroll County Historical Museum, Delphi, IN [*Library symbol Library of Congress*] (LCLS)
InDelCR	Carroll County Recorder's Office, Delphi, IN [*Library symbol Library of Congress*] (LCLS)
INDELISA.....	Indirect Enzyme-Linked Immunosorbent Assay

INDELSEC	Industrial Electronic Security (AABC)
Indem	Indemnity [*Legal term*] (DLA)
INDEMFY	Indemnify [*Legal shorthand*] (LWAP)
INDEMTY	Indemnity [*Legal shorthand*] (LWAP)
INDEMY	Indemnity (ROG)
IndeNet........	IndeNet, Inc. [*Associated Press*] (SAG)
IndEng	Industrial Engineering (DD)
Ind Eng 1922-1931 (NY)...	Industrial Engineering 1922-1931 (New York) [*A publication*]
INDENT........	Indenture (ROG)
Indent.........	Indenture (EBF)
INDEP	Independent (AFM)
IndepBc	Independence Bancorp, Inc. [*Associated Press*] (SAG)
INDEP CONTR...	Independent Contractor (DLA)
IndepHld......	Independence Holding Co. [*Associated Press*] (SAG)
INDEP R	Independent Review [*London*] [*A publication*] (ROG)
INDEPTH......	International Deep Profiling of Tibet and the Himalaya [*Geology*] [*China*]
INDEPTY	Independently (ROG)
INDESYS......	Information Delivery System Inc. [*Information service or system*] (NITA)
INDET	Indeterminate (MSA)
indeterm......	Indeterminative (BJA)
Ind-Eur........	Indo-European
IN-DEV-IL ...	Institute for the Development of Indian Law (EA)
INDEX	Indiana Exchange, Inc.
INDEX	Indian Ocean Experiment
INDEX	Inter-NASA Data Exchange (IEEE)
IndFdg	Industrial Funding Corp. [*Associated Press*] (SAG)
IndFdl	Independence Federal Savings Bank [*Associated Press*] (SAG)
INDGF	Indigo NV [*NASDAQ symbol*] (SAG)
INDH	Independent Insurance Group, Inc. [*NASDAQ symbol*] (NQ)
INDH	Indirect Hire [*Military*]
IndH	Industrial Holdings, Inc. [*Associated Press*] (SAG)
IndHealth.....	Industrial Health (DD)
ind i............	India Ink (VRA)
INDI	Indiana
INDI	Indicate
INDI	Individual Investor Group [*NASDAQ symbol*] (SAG)
Indi	Indus [*Constellation*]
INDI	Irish Nutrition and Dietetics Institute (EAIO)
India AIR Manual...	AIR [*All India Law Reporter*] Manual: Unrepealed Central Acts [*2nd ed.*] [*India*] [*A publication*] (DLA)
India Cen Acts...	Central Acts, India [*A publication*] (DLA)
India Code Civ P...	Code of Civil Procedure [*India*] [*A publication*] (DLA)
India Code Crim P...	Code of Criminal Procedure [*India*] [*A publication*] (DLA)
India Crim LJR...	Criminal Law Journal Reports [*India*] [*A publication*] (DLA)
IndiaFd........	India Fund, Inc. [*Associated Press*] (SAG)
IndiaG.........	India Growth Fund, Inc. [*Associated Press*] (SAG)
India Gen R & O...	General Rules and Orders, India [*A publication*] (DLA)
Indiana........	Indiana Reports [*A publication*] (DLA)
Indian App....	Law Reports, Privy Council, Indian Appeals [*India*] [*A publication*] (DLA)
Indiana Sup Ct Rep...	Indiana Reports [*A publication*] (DLA)
Indian Cas...	Indiana Cases [*A publication*] (DLA)
Indian LJ.....	Indian Law Journal [*A publication*] (DLA)
Indian LR.....	Indian Law Reports [*A publication*] (DLA)
Indian L R Calc...	Indian Law Reports, Calcutta Series [*A publication*] (DLA)
Indian LR Mad...	Indian Law Reports, Madras Series [*A publication*] (DLA)
Indian Rul ...	Indian Rulings [*A publication*] (DLA)
Indian Terr...	Indian Territory Reports [*A publication*] (DLA)
India Pen Code...	Indian Penal Code [*A publication*] (DLA)
India S Ct...	India Supreme Court Reports [*A publication*] (DLA)
India Subs Leg...	Subsidiary Legislation [*India*] [*A publication*] (DLA)
INDIC	Indicate (AABC)
INDIC	Indication Report (MCD)
INDIC	Indicative [*Grammar*]
INDIC	Indicator (WDAA)
IndiCBk.......	Indiana Community Bank a Savings Bank [*Associated Press*] (SAG)
INDICN........	Indication
INDICOM......	Indications Communications (MCD)
indie	Independent [*Filmmaking*] [*Slang*] (WDMC)
Indie	The Independent [*A publication*] (WDAA)
IndiEngy	Indiana Energy, Inc. [*Associated Press*] (SAG)
IndiFdl	Indiana Federal Corp. [*Associated Press*] (SAG)
IndiFedl	Indiana Federal Corp. [*Associated Press*] (SAG)
INDIG	Indigenous (AABC)
INDIGO	Indian Ocean Geochemistry [*France*] [*Marine science*] (OSRA)
INDIGO	Intelligence Division Gaming Operations
IndigoNV......	Indigo NV [*Associated Press*] (SAG)
IndiM.........	Indiana & Michigan Power [*Associated Press*] (SAG)
IND IMP.......	Indiae Imperator [*Emperor of India*] [*Latin*]
Ind Ind LP ...	Index to Indian Legal Periodicals [*A publication*] (DLA)
IndInsr........	Independent Insurance Group, Inc. [*Associated Press*] (SAG)
INDIPEX.......	India International Philatelic Exhibition
INDIR	Indirect Coombs Test [*Hematology*] (DAVI)
INDIRS........	Indiana Information Retrieval System [*Library network*]
INDIS	Industrial Information and Advisory Services [*UNIDO*] (IID)
INDIS	Industrial Information System [*UN Industrial Development Organization*] (NITA)
INDIV	Individual (AFM)
Individul	Individual, Inc. [*Associated Press*] (SAG)
INDIVL	Individual [*Freight*]
Ind J Int'l L...	Indiana Journal of International Law [*A publication*] (DLA)

Ind Jud Pr ...   Indermaur's Practice of the Supreme Court of Judicature [*12th ed.*] [*1919*] [*A publication*] (DLA)

Ind Jur.........   Indian Jurist [*Calcutta or Madras*] [*A publication*] (DLA)

Ind Jur NS...   Indian Jurist, New Series [*A publication*] (DLA)

Ind Jur OS...   Indian Jurist, Old Series [*A publication*] (DLA)

Ind Jur Pr...   Indermaur's Practice of the Supreme Court of Judicature [*12th ed.*] [*1919*] [*A publication*] (DLA)

IND L...........   Independent Liberal (WDAA)

INDL............   Industrial (MSA)

Ind LC Com Law...   Indermaur's Leading Cases in Common Law [*10th ed.*] [*1921*] [*A publication*] (DLA)

Ind LC Eq.....   Indermaur's Leading Cases in Conveyancing and Equity [*A publication*] (DLA)

Ind Led........   Individual Ledger [*Business term*] (MHDW)

Ind LH ....   Indian Law Herald [*A publication*] (DLA)

Ind L Mag...   Indian Law Magazine [*A publication*] (DLA)

Ind LQ ....   Indian Law Quarterly [*A publication*] (DLA)

Ind LQ Rev...   Indian Law Quarterly Review [*A publication*] (DLA)

Ind LR ....   Indiana Law Reporter [*1881*] [*A publication*] (DLA)

Ind LR ....   Indiana Legal Register [*A publication*] (DLA)

Ind LR ....   Indian Law Reports (East) [*A publication*] (DLA)

Ind LR ....   Industrial Law Review [*A publication*] (ILCA)

Ind LR All ...   Indian Law Reports, Allahabad Series [*A publication*] (DLA)

Ind LR Alla...   Indian Law Reports, Allahabad Series [*A publication*] (DLA)

Ind LR And...   Indian Law Reports, Andhra Series [*A publication*] (DLA)

Ind LR Assam...   Indian Law Reports, Assam Series [*A publication*] (DLA)

Ind LR Bomb...   Indian Law Reports, Bombay Series [*A publication*] (DLA)

Ind LR Calc...   Indian Law Reports, Calcutta Series [*A publication*] (DLA)

Ind L Reg ...   Indiana Legal Register [*A publication*] (DLA)

Ind L Rep ...   Indiana Law Reporter [*1881*] [*A publication*] (DLA)

Ind L Rep ....   Indian Law Reporter [*A publication*] (DLA)

Ind LR Hyderabad...   Indian Law Reports, Hyderabad Series [*A publication*] (DLA)

Ind LR Kar...   Indian Law Reports, Karachi Series [*A publication*] (DLA)

Ind LR Ker...   Indian Law Reports, Kerala Series [*A publication*] (DLA)

Ind LR Lah...   Indian Law Reports, Lahore Series [*A publication*] (DLA)

Ind LR Luck...   Indian Law Reports, Lucknow Series [*A publication*] (DLA)

Ind LR Mad...   Indian Law Reports, Madras Series [*A publication*] (DLA)

Ind LR Madhya Bharat...   Indian Law Reports, Madhya Bharat Series [*A publication*] (DLA)

Ind LR Mysore...   Indian Law Reports, Mysore Series [*A publication*] (DLA)

Ind LR Nag...   Indian Law Reports, Nagpur Series [*A publication*] (DLA)

Ind LR Or.....   Indian Law Reports, Orissa Series [*A publication*] (DLA)

Ind LR Pat...   Indian Law Reports, Patna Series [*A publication*] (DLA)

Ind LR Patiala...   Indian Law Reports, Patiala Series [*A publication*] (DLA)

Ind LR Pun...   Indian Law Reports, Punjab Series [*A publication*] (DLA)

Ind LR Rajasthan...   Indian Law Reports, Rajasthan Series [*A publication*] (DLA)

Ind LR Ran...   Indian Law Reports, Rangoon Series [*A publication*] (DLA)

Ind LS........   Indiana Law Student [*A publication*] (DLA)

Ind L Stud ...   Indiana Law Student [*A publication*] (DLA)

Ind LT ....   Indian Law Times [*A publication*] (DLA)

INDM ....   Indemnity [*Legal term*]

Indm...........   Indemnity (EBF)

Ind M ....   Independent Monthly [*A publication*]

INDM ....   Infant of Nondiabetic Mother [*Obstetrics*]

INDMAN.......   Industrial Manager

IND METH...   Independent Methodist (WDAA)

INDMGR ......   Industrial Manager

Ind Mining Stand...   Industrial and Mining Standard [*A publication*]

INDMNTY.....   Indemnity

INDN...........   Indian

INDN...........   Indication (WGA)

INDN...........   Induction

IndNatuz.....   Industrie Natuzzi SA [*Associated Press*] (SAG)

Ind News .....   Industry News [*A publication*]

IndO...........   Indian Ocean

INDO...........   Indomethacin [*An analgesic*]

INDO...........   Indonesia

INDO...........   Intermediate Neglect of Differential Overlap [*Quantum mechanics*]

INDOC........   Indochina [*or Indochinese*] (WDAA)

INDOC........   Indoctrinate (AABC)

INDOC........   Indonesian Documentation and Information Centre [*Leiden, Netherlands*] (EAIO)

INDOC........   Information-Documentation and Communication (PDAA)

INDOCHEM...   Indian Ocean GEOSECS Program (MSC)

INDOCNREGREPCEN...   Indoctrination Naval Regional Reporting Center (DNAB)

INDO-EUR....   Indo-European (ROG)

INDO-GER....   Indo-Germanic [*Language, etc.*] (ROG)

Indo-Germ Forsch...   Indogermanische Forschungen [*A publication*] (OCD)

Indon ....   Indonesia (BARN)

Indones.......   Indonesia Fund [*Associated Press*] (SAG)

INDOR ....   Internuclear Double Resonance

IndoSatel....   Indonesian Satellite Corp. [*Associated Press*] (SAG)

IndoTel ....   Indonesian Telekomunikas [*Associated Press*] (SAG)

Indp ....   Independent (AL)

Ind P...........   Pharmacopoeia of India [*A publication*]

INDPDNC .....   Independence

IND PENS ....   Indian Pension [*Army British*] (ROG)

IND PH ....   Indian Pharmacopoeia (ROG)

INDPNDNT...   Independent

Ind Prog Dev...   Industrial Progress and Development [*A publication*]

Ind Prop .....   Industrial Property [*Legal term*] (DLA)

Ind Prop Q...   Industrial Property Quarterly [*A publication*] (DLA)

INDQ..........   International Dairy Queen, Inc. [*NASDAQ symbol*] (NQ)

INDQA.........   Intl Dairy Queen 'A' [*NASDAQ symbol*] (TTSB)

INDQB.........   Intl Dairy Queen 'B' [*NASDAQ symbol*] (TTSB)

Ind R ....   Indiana Reports [*A publication*] (DLA)

INDR...........   Indicator (IAA)

INDRB.........   Inactive Nondisability Retirement Branch [*BUPERS*]

INDRE.........   Indenture

INDREG.......   Inductance Regulator (IEEE)

Ind Rel J Econ & Soc...   Industrial Relations: Journal of Economy and Society [*A publication*]

Ind Rep.......   Indiana Reports [*A publication*] (DLA)

INDS ....   In-Core Nuclear Detection System [*Nuclear energy*] (IEEE)

INDS ....   Investigational New Drug Submission [*Medicine*] (DB)

Ind SBA ......   Indiana State Bar Association Reports [*A publication*] (DLA)

IndsBc ....   Industrial Bancorp, Inc. [*Associated Press*] (SAG)

INDSCAL.....   Individual Differences Scaling (PDAA)

IndSci ....   Industrial Scientific Corp. [*Associated Press*] (SAG)

INDSL.........   Industrial (WGA)

IndSqS........   Independence Square Income Securities [*Associated Press*] (SAG)

IndSqS.........   Independence Square Income Securities, Inc. [*Associated Press*] (SAG)

Ind St U ......   Indiana State University (GAGS)

Ind Super.....   Wilson's Indiana Superior Court Reports [*A publication*] (DLA)

INDT ....   Indent (MSA)

INDT ....   Induction (DNAB)

INDT ....   Institute for Non-Destructive Testing [*Milwaukee School of Engineering*] (PDAA)

INDT ....   Interceptor Director Technician (SAA)

Ind T Ann St...   Indian Territory Annotated Statutes [*A publication*] (DLA)

IndTc ....   Industrial Technologies, Inc. [*Associated Press*] (SAG)

IndTech.......   Industrial Technologies, Inc. [*Associated Press*] (SAG)

INDTEL ....   Industry and Teacher Education Liaison (AIE)

IND TER ......   Indian Territory

Ind Ter........   Indian Territory Reports [*A publication*] (DLA)

Ind Terr.......   Indian Territory (DLA)

INDTNG.......   Individual Training [*Navy*] (NVT)

INDTR.........   Indicator-Transmitter

IndTrn........   Industrial Training Corp. [*Associated Press*] (SAG)

Indty ....   Indemnity [*Legal term*] (DLA)

Ind U ....   Indiana University (GAGS)

IndUAP ....   Independent United Australia Party [*Political party*]

INDUC........   Induction (AABC)

Ind UCD ......   Indiana Unemployment Compensation Division, Selected Appeal Tribunal Decisions [*A publication*] (DLA)

Ind U Penn...   Indiana University of Pennsylvania (GAGS)

IND U PR....   Indiana University Press (DGA)

Indus ....   Industrialist

INDUS.........   Industry

INDUS.........   Interactive Duct Sizing [*Facet Ltd.*] [*Software package*] (NCC)

Indus & Lab Rel Rev...   Industrial and Labor Relations Review [*A publication*] (AAGC)

Indus Cas R...   Industrial Cases Reports [*Law reports*] [*British*] (DLA)

IndusG........   Indus Group, Inc. (The) [*Associated Press*] (SAG)

IndusHld......   Industrial Holdings, Inc. [*Associated Press*] (SAG)

Indus L Rev...   Industrial Law Review [*A publication*] (DLA)

INDUSMIN...   Industrial Mineral Service [*Midland, ON*]

IndusMt.......   Industir-Matematik International Corp. [*Associated Press*] (SAG)

Indus Rel Guide...   Industrial Relations Guide [*A publication*] (DLA)

INDUSSIM ...   Total Industry Simulation [*Game*]

INDUST........   Industrial [*or Industry*]

Indust........   Industrial (TBD)

INDUST........   Industry

Indust Acc Com...   Decisions of the Industrial Accident Commission of California [*A publication*] (DLA)

Indust Austn & Mining Std...   Industrial Australian and Mining Standard [*A publication*]

Indust Bull...   Industrial Bulletin [*A publication*] (DLA)

Indust C Aw...   Industrial Court Awards [*England*] [*A publication*] (DLA)

Indust Ct Aw...   Industrial Court Awards [*England*] [*A publication*] (DLA)

INDUSTL......   Industrial

Indust Law Rev...   Industrial Law Review [*A publication*] (DLA)

Indust L Rev...   Industrial Law Review [*A publication*] (DLA)

Indust L Soc Bull...   Bulletin. Industrial Law Society [*A publication*] (DLA)

Indust Prop...   Industrial Property [*Legal term*] (DLA)

Indust Prop Q...   Industrial Property Quarterly [*A publication*] (DLA)

Indust Prop'y Yb...   Industrial Property Yearbook [*A publication*] (DLA)

INDUSTR......   Industrial (ROG)

Industr Prop'y Q...   Industrial Property Quarterly [*A publication*] (DLA)

IndUtd.........   Indiana United Bancorp [*Associated Press*] (SAG)

Indv...........   Individual (TBD)

INDV..........   Individual Inc. [*NASDAQ symbol*] (TTSB)

INDV..........   Individually (MSA)

IndvI..........   Individual Investor Group [*Associated Press*] (SAG)

IndvInv........   Individual Investor Group [*Associated Press*] (SAG)

Ind Wills......   Inderwick on Wills [*1866*] [*A publication*] (DLA)

Ind YB Int'l Aff...   Indian Yearbook of International Affairs [*A publication*] (DLA)

INE.............   East Chicago Public Library, East Chicago, IN [*OCLC symbol*] (OCLC)

InE.............   Evansville Public Library and Vanderburgh County Public Library, Evansville, IN [*Library symbol Library of Congress*] (LCLS)

INE.............   Incorrect Negative Expectancy [*Psychometrics*]

ine.............   Indo-European [*MARC language code Library of Congress*] (LCCP)

INE.............   Inertial Navigation Equipment (MCD)

INE.............   Infantile Necrotizing Encephalomyelopathy [*Medicine*] (MAE)

INE.............   Initiatives for Not-for-Profit Entrepreneurship [*Research center*] (RCD)

INE.............   Institution of Nuclear Engineers (PDAA)

INE............... International Kenergy Resource Corp. [*Vancouver Stock Exchange symbol*]

INE............... Missoula, MT [*Location identifier FAA*] (FAAL)

INEA.......... Internationaler Elektronik-Arbeitskreis [*International Electronics Association*]

INEAC .... Institut National pour l'Etude Agronomique du Congo [*National Institute for the Study of Agronomy in the Congo*]

InEaP.......... Earl Park Public Library, Earl Park, IN [*Library symbol Library of Congress*] (LCLS)

InEc .... East Chicago Public Library, East Chicago, IN [*Library symbol Library of Congress*] (LCLS)

INEC........... Institut Europeen d'Ecologie et de Cancerologie [*European Institute of Ecology and Cancer - EIEC*] (EA)

INEC........... Institut Europeen des Industries de la Gomme de Caroube [*European Institute of Carob Gum Industries*] [*EC*] (ECED)

INECA .... Industrial Energy Conservation Abstracts [*UNIDO*] [*United Nations*] (DUND)

InEcIP .... Indiana City Press, Indiana City, IN [*Library symbol Library of Congress*] (LCLS)

InEd .... Edinburg Public Library, Edinburg, IN [*Library symbol*] [*Library of Congress*] (LCLS)

INED .... Inedible

INED .... Inedites [*Unpublished*] [*French*] (ROG)

INED .... Ineditus [*Not Made Known*] [*Latin*]

INED .... Institute for New Enterprise Development (EA)

INED .... International Network for Educational Information (EAIO)

INEEL URC... Idaho National Engineering and Environmental Laboratory University Research Consortium

INEFFCY ...... Inefficiency

INEFFY......... Inefficiency (AABC)

InefMkt........ [*The*] Inefficient-Market Fund [*Associated Press*] (SAG)

INEGI .... Instituto Nacional de Estadistica, Geografia e Informatica [*Main government clearinghouse for statistical information*] [*Mexico*] (CROSS)

INEI............. Insituform East [*NASDAQ symbol*] (TTSB)

INEI............. Insituform East, Inc. [*NASDAQ symbol*] (NQ)

INEI............. International Exhibition of Industrial Electronics (MCD)

INEL............. Idaho National Engineering Laboratory [*Idaho Falls, ID*] [*Department of Energy*]

INEL............. Intelligent Electroncs [*NASDAQ symbol*] (TTSB)

INEL............. Intelligent Electronics, Inc. [*NASDAQ symbol*] (SAG)

InElk .... Elkhart Public Library, Elkhart, IN [*Library symbol Library of Congress*] (LCLS)

InElkB .... Mennonite Biblical Seminary, Elkhart, IN [*Library symbol Library of Congress*] (LCLS)

InElkM .... Miles Laboratories, Inc., Elkhart, IN [*Library symbol Library of Congress*] (LCLS)

InElkT .... Elkhart Truth, Elkhart, IN [*Library symbol Library of Congress*] (LCLS)

InEllJ .... Ellettsville Journal, Ellettsville, IN [*Library symbol Library of Congress*] (LCLS)

INELTEC....... Exhibition of Industrial Electronics, Electrical Engineering, and Technical Installation (TSPED)

InElw .... Elwood Public Library, Elwood, IN [*Library symbol Library of Congress*] (LCLS)

InElwCL .... Elwood Call-Leader, Elwood, IN [*Library symbol Library of Congress*] (LCLS)

InEM .... Mead Johnson Research Center, Evansville, IN [*Library symbol Library of Congress*] (LCLS)

InEng .... Crawford County Public Library, English, IN [*Library symbol Library of Congress*] (LCLS)

InEngD........ Crawford County Democrat, English, IN [*Library symbol Library of Congress*] (LCLS)

InENR .... Northside Reporter, Evansville, IN [*Library symbol Library of Congress*] (LCLS)

InEnt .... Inmark Enterprises, Inc. [*Associated Press*] (SAG)

INEOA .... International Narcotic Enforcement Officers Association (EA)

InEP............. Evansville Press and Courier, Evansville, IN [*Library symbol Library of Congress*] (LCLS)

INEP............. International Nurse Education Program

INep............ Neponset Public Library, Neponset, IL [*Library symbol Library of Congress*] (LCLS)

INepL........... Neponset Public Library, Neponset, IL [*Library symbol*] [*Library of Congress*] (LCLS)

INEPT........... Insensitive Nuclei Enhanced by Polarization Transfer [*Spectroscopy*]

INER .... Inertial (KSC)

INERT .... Index of National Enervation and Related Trends [*Department of Commerce*]

Inertial Gu ... Inertial Guidance [*Aerospace*] (NAKS)

InES............. Indiana State University, Evansville Campus, Evansville, IN [*Library symbol Library of Congress*] (LCLS)

INES............. International Nuclear Event Scale

InESC........... Evansville-Vanderburgh School Corp., Library Services Center, Evansville, IN [*Library symbol Library of Congress*] (LCLS)

INET............. Image Network (DMAA)

INET............. Intelligent Network [*Telecom Canada*] [*Database*]

INET............. Interbank Network for Electronic Transfer

INET............. Intronet, Inc. [*NASDAQ symbol*] (SAG)

InEU .... University of Evansville, Evansville, IN [*Library symbol Library of Congress*] (LCLS)

In Evang Iohan... Tractatus in Evangelium Iohannis [*of Augustine*] [*Classical studies*] (OCD)

INew .... Newman Township Library, Newman, IL [*Library symbol Library of Congress*] (LCLS)

InEW .... Willard Library, Evansville, IN [*Library symbol Library of Congress*] (LCLS)

INEWF .... Indian National Electricity Workers' Federation

INewm .... Newman Township Library, Newman, IL [*Library symbol*] [*Library of Congress*] (LCLS)

INEWS .... Integrated Electronic Warfare System

InEWS.......... West Side Story, Evansville, IN [*Library symbol Library of Congress*] (LCLS)

INewt........... Newton Public Library, Newton, IL [*Library symbol Library of Congress*] (LCLS)

INEX........... Inexperienced (DAVI)

IN EX .... In Extenso [*At Full Length*] [*Latin*] (ROG)

INF.............. Infamous [*FBI standardized term*]

INF.............. Infant

INF.............. Infantile (CPH)

inf.............. Infantile (DMAA)

INF.............. Infantry (AFM)

inf.............. Infected (CPH)

INF.............. Infection [*Medicine*]

INF.............. Inferior

inf.............. Inferior (WDMC)

INF.............. Infield (WGA)

IN F .... In Fine [*Finally*] [*Latin*]

INF.............. Infinite (MSA)

INF.............. Infinite Resources, Inc. [*Vancouver Stock Exchange symbol*]

INF.............. Infinitive

inf.............. Infinitive (WDMC)

INF.............. Infinity

INF.............. Infinity Broadcasting 'A' [*NYSE symbol*] (TTSB)

INFFY........... Infinity Broadcasting Corp. [*NYSE symbol*] (SAG)

INF.............. Infirmary

INF.............. Influence (WDAA)

INF.............. Influenza [*Medicine*]

INF.............. In Folio (DGA)

INF.............. Inform

INF.............. Informaatiopalvelulaitos [*Information Service*] [*Technical Research Center of Finland Espoo*] [*Information service or system*] (IID)

INF.............. Informal

INF.............. Informant (WGA)

INF.............. Information [*Computer science*]

inf.............. Information (WDMC)

Inf.............. Information (AL)

INF.............. Informationszentrum und Bibliotheken [*Information retrieval*]

INF.............. Informed

Inf.............. Infortiatum [*A publication*] (DSA)

INF.............. Infra [*Beneath or Below*] [*Latin*]

INF.............. Infunde [*Pour In*] [*Pharmacy*]

INF.............. Infundibulum of Neurohypophysis [*Pituitary stalk*] [*Medicine*] (DB)

INF.............. Infusion [*Medicine*]

INF.............. Infusum [*Infusion*] [*Pharmacy*] (ROG)

INF.............. Inland Navigation Facility

INF.............. Interceptor Night Fighter (NATG)

INF.............. Interface (KSC)

INF.............. Interference (KSC)

INF.............. Intermediate-Range Nuclear Forces

INF.............. International Naturist Federation [*Antwerp, Belgium*] (EA)

INF.............. International Nuclear Forces (NATG)

INF.............. Iranian National Front (PPW)

INF.............. Irredundant Normal Formula

INF.............. ISDN [*Integrated Services Digital Network*] Numbering Forum (OSI)

INF.............. Parke, Davis & Co. [*Great Britain*] [*Research code symbol*]

infa-- .... Faroe Islands [*MARC geographic area code Library of Congress*] (LCCP)

INFA........... International Federation of Aestheticians [*Brussels, Belgium*] (EAIO)

INFA........... International Nuclear Fuel Authority

INFAC .... Instrumented Factory for Gears [*Illinois Institute of Technology Research Institute*] [*Research center*] (RCD)

INFACON..... International Ferro-Alloys Congress

INFACT .... Infant Formula Action Coalition (EA)

InFai .... Fairmount Public Library, Fairmount, IN [*Library symbol Library of Congress*] (LCLS)

InFaiN.......... Fairmount News, Fairmount, IN [*Library symbol Library of Congress*] (LCLS)

INFANT .... Infants Need to Find Adequate Nourishment Today [*An association*]

INFANT .... Interactive Networks Functioning on Adaptive Neural Topographies [*Robot*]

INFANT .... Iroquois Night Fighter and Night Tracker [*Military*] (MCD)

INFANTS ..... Interested Future Attorneys Negotiating for Tot Safety [*Student legal action organization*]

InFarl .... Farmland Public Library, Farmland, IN [*Library symbol Library of Congress*] (LCLS)

InFb .... Fort Branch Public Library, Fort Branch, IN [*Library symbol Library of Congress*] (LCLS)

INFBAT .... Infantry Battalion [*Army*]

InFbT .... Fort Branch Times, Fort Branch, IN [*Library symbol Library of Congress*] (LCLS)

INF-C .... Influenza-C [*Medicine*]

INFCE.......... Influence (ROG)

INFCE.......... International Nuclear Fuel Cycle Evaluation

INFCO .... Information Committee [*International Organization for Standardization*] (IEEE)

INFCO .... Information Committee of the International Standards Organization (NITA)

INFCY......... Infancy (ROG)

INFD .... Infodata Systems [*NASDAQ symbol*] (TTSB)

INFD .... Infodata Systems, Inc. [*NASDAQ symbol*] (NQ)
INFD .... Informed (ROG)
inf dis .... Infectious Disease (MEDA)
INFE .... Instituto Nacional de Fomento de la Exportacion [*National Institute of Export Development*] [*Spain*] (EY)
INFE .... International Newspaper Financial Executives (EA)
infec dis ...... Infectious Disease [*Medicine*] (CPH)
infect .... Infected (STED)
infect .... Infection [*or Infectious*] (DAVI)
INFEDOP ...... International Federation of Employees in Public Service [*Brussels, Belgium*] (EAIO)
infer .... Inferior (STED)
InFerC .... Sisters of St. Benedict, Convent and Academy of the Immaculate Conception, Ferdinand, IN [*Library symbol*] [*Library of Congress*] (LCLS)
INFEREX ...... Inference Execution Language
InFerN .... Ferdinand News, Ferdinand, IN [*Library symbol Library of Congress*] (LCLS)
Infernce ...... Inference Corp. [*Associated Press*] (SAG)
INF file .... Information File [*Computer science*] (IGQR)
InfFincl .... Infinity Financial Technology, Inc. [*Associated Press*] (SAG)
INFH .... Ischemic Necrosis of Femoral Head [*Orthopedics*] (DAVI)
InfHA .... Influenza Virus Hemagglutinin [*Immunology*]
INFIC .... International Network of Feed Information Centers (EA)
infil .... Infiltrate [*or Infiltrated*] (DAVI)
INFIL/EXFIL .. Infiltration and Exfiltration (DOMA)
INFIN .... Infinitive [*Grammar*]
InfinBr .... Infinity Broadcasting Corp. [*Associated Press*] (SAG)
InfinBrd .... Infinity Broadcasting Corp. [*Associated Press*] (SAG)
INFINET .... International Financial Networks
Infinity .... Infinity, Inc. [*Associated Press*] (SAG)
InFinSv .... Interchange Financial Services Corp. [*Associated Press*] (SAG)
INFINT .... Infinite
INFIRM .... Infirmary
INFIRS .... Invented-File-Search System (DICI)
INFIRS .... Inverted File Information Retrieval System [*UK Chemical Information Service*] (NITA)
INFIS .... Indonesian Aquatic Sciences Fisheries Information System [*Marine science*] (OSRA)
InFl .... Flora-Monroe Public Library, Flora, IN [*Library symbol Library of Congress*] (LCLS)
INFL .... Inflammable
infl .... Inflammation (STED)
INFL .... Inflated (ADA)
infl .... Inflorescence [*Botany*]
INFL .... Influence
infl .... Influence (STED)
infl .... Influx (STED)
INFL .... Influx
In Flacc ...... In Flaccum [*of Philo Judaeus*] [*Classical studies*] (OCD)
INFLAM .... Inflammable
inflam .... Inflammation [*or Inflammatory*] (DAVI)
Inflamm ...... Inflammation (STED)
INFLO .... Integrated Flight Optimization (PDAA)
infl proc ...... Inflammatory Process (STED)
InFlt .... Interactive Flight Technologies, Inc. Cl.A [*Associated Press*] (SAG)
INFM .... Infectious Mononucleosis [*Medicine*] (DAVI)
INFM .... Inform (ROG)
InfMach ...... Infinite Machines Corp. [*Associated Press*] (SAG)
InfMch .... Infinite Machines Corp. [*Associated Press*] (SAG)
InfMgeR ...... Information Management Resources, Inc. [*Associated Press*] (SAG)
InfMgt .... Information Management Technology [*Associated Press*] (SAG)
Inf MI .... Inferior Myocardial Infarction [*Cardiology*]
inf mono ..... Infectious Mononucleosis [*Medicine*] (MAE)
INFMRY ...... Infirmary
INFMTL .... Informational
INFN .... Infinity Financial Technology, Inc. [*NASDAQ symbol*] (SAG)
INFN .... Information (ROG)
InFnDM .... International Finance Corp. [*Associated Press*] (SAG)
InFnDY .... International Finance Corp. [*Associated Press*] (SAG)
INFNET .... Istituto Nazionale Fisica Nucleare Network [*National Institute for Nuclear Physics Network*] [*Italian*] [*Computer science*] (TNIG)
INFNT .... Infant
INFNT .... Iroquois Night Fighter and Night Tracker [*Military*] (DNAB)
InFnYB .... International Finance Corp. [*Associated Press*] (SAG)
InFo .... Benton County Public Library, Fowler, IN [*Library symbol Library of Congress*] (LCLS)
INFO .... Infonautics, Inc. [*NASDAQ symbol*] (SAG)
INFO .... Infonautics Inc.'A' [*NASDAQ symbol*] (TTSB)
info .... Information (DD)
INFO .... Information (AFM)
Info .... Information (TBD)
INFO .... Information Network and File Organization [*Computer science*] (BUR)
INFO .... Information Network for Ontario [*Canada*]
INFO .... Information Network for Operations [*Computer science*]
INFO .... Integrated Fleet Operations
INFO .... Integrated Network Fiber Optics (MCD)
INFO .... International Fortean Organization (EA)
infobit .... Information Bit [*Computer science*] (BARN)
InfoCan .... Information Canada
INFOCEN ...... Information Center (MCD)
INFOCLIMA.. World Climate Data Information Referral Service [*World Meteorological Organization*] [*Information service or system*] (IID)
INFOCOMM... Information and Communications Technology Exposition (ITD)

InFoCR........ Benton County Recorder's Office, Fowler, IN [*Library symbol Library of Congress*] (LCLS)
InFocu .... In Focus System, Inc. [*Associated Press*] (SAG)
InFOCUS ...... Interprofessional Fostering of Opthalmic Care for Underserved Sectors (EA)
Infodat .... Infodata Systems, Inc. [*Associated Press*] (SAG)
INFODATA... Database Information Science and Practice [*Database*]
INFO/DOC ... Information/Documentation [*Information service or system*] (IID)
INFOES .... In-Flight Operational Evaluation of a Space System
INFOEX .... Information Exchange, Inc. [*Telecommunications service*] (TSSD)
INFOHOST ... Database Guide to German Host Operators [*Database*]
INFOHOST ... Information on Hosts (NITA)
InfoIntl........ Information International, Inc. [*Associated Press*] (SAG)
INFOL .... Information Oriented Language [*Information retrieval*]
INFOLAC ..... Information for Latin American Countries Project (NITA)
IN FOL ARG VOLVEND... In Folio Argenti Volvendae [*To Be Silvered*] [*Pharmacy*]
INFOMAG..... Information Magnetics Corp. (EFIS)
INFOMARK... Information Market News [*Database*] [*EC*] (ECED)
INFOMART.. Information Market [*Exhibition and conference centre*] [*Dallas*] (NITA)
Infomed ...... Infomed Holdings, Inc. [*Associated Press*] (SAG)
INFONAC..... Instituto de Fomento Nacional [*Industrial promotion agency*] [*Nicaragua*]
Infonau .... Infonautics, Inc. [*Associated Press*] (SAG)
INFONET...... Information Network [*A federally registered trademark and service mark of Infonet Services Corporation, El Segundo, California*] (TEL)
INFOODS ..... International Network of Food Data Systems [*Massachusets Institute of Technology*] [*Cambridge*] [*Information service or system*] (IID)
INFO PASS... Central Mississippi Library Council [*Library network*]
INFOR......... Information (DSUE)
INFOR......... Information Network and File Organization (MHDB)
INFOR......... Interactive FORTRAN [*Formula Translating System*] [*Computer science*] (IAA)
INFORBW .... Information on Research in Baden-Wurttemberg [*Fachinformationszentrum Karlsruhe GmbH*] [*Germany Information service or system*] (CRD)
INFOREM..... Inventory Forecasting and Replenishment Modules [*IBM Corp.*]
INFOREP..... Information Report (CINC)
INFOREQ..... Information Requested [*or Required*]
InfoRes .... Information Resources, Inc. [*Associated Press*] (SAG)
INFORM....... Information
INFORM....... Information for Optimum Resource Management (MCD)
INFORM....... Information Network for Freight Overhead Billing, Rating, and Message Switching
INFORM....... International Reference Organization in Forensic Medicine and Sciences (EA)
INFORMAC... Immediate Information for Merchant and Customer (PDAA)
INFORMAL... Information for Avionics Laboratory
INFORMALUX... Information Luxembourg (NITA)
INFORMAP... Information Necessary for Optimum Resource Management and Protection (PDAA)
Informed...... Informedics, Inc. [*Associated Press*] (SAG)
INFORMN..... Information
INFORMS..... Information Organization Reporting and Management System (IAA)
INFORMS..... Institute for Operations Research and the Management Sciences (NTPA)
Informx .... Informix Corp. [*Associated Press*] (SAG)
INFOS .... Information Network for Official Statistics [*Department of Statistics*] [*Information service or system*] (IID)
INFOS .... Informationszentrum fuer Schnittwerte [*Cutting Data Information Center*] [*Germany Information service or system*] (IID)
Infosafe ...... Infosafe Systems, Inc. [*Associated Press*] (SAG)
INFOSEC...... Information Security (COE)
INFOSEC...... Information Systems Security (AAGC)
Infoseek...... Infoseek Corp. [*Associated Press*] (SAG)
Infosf .... Infosafe Systems, Inc. [*Associated Press*] (SAG)
Infosfe .... Infosafe Systems, Inc. [*Associated Press*] (SAG)
INFOSOR ..... Information Sources [*Information service or system*] (IID)
Infospecs..... Information Specialists Ltd. [*Information service or system*] (IID)
InfoStor....... Information Storage Devices, Inc. [*Associated Press*] (SAG)
INFOTERM... International Information Centre for Terminology [*UNESCO*] (IID)
INFOTERRA... International Referral System for Sources of Environmental Information [*Formerly, IRS*] [*United Nations Environment Program*] (ASF)
INFOTEX...... Information via Telex [*Telecommunications*] (TEL)
INFP........... Introverted, Intuitive, a Feeler, and Perceiver [*Keirsey Temperament Test Result*] [*Psychology*]
INFR .... Inference Corp. [*NASDAQ symbol*] (SAG)
INFR .... Inference Corp.'A' [*NASDAQ symbol*] (TTSB)
INFR .... Inferior (ROG)
INFRA .... Information Research Analysts [*Database producer*] (IID)
infra........... Infrared (VRA)
INFRA DIG ... Infra Dignitatem [*Undignified*] [*Latin*]
INFRAL .... Information Retrieval Automatic Language [*Computer science*]
INFRAPTUM... Infrascriptum [*Written Below*] [*Latin*] (ROG)
Infrasnc ...... Infrasonics, Inc. [*Associated Press*] (SAG)
InFrem......... Fremont Public Library, Fremont, IN [*Library symbol Library of Congress*] (LCLS)
InFren......... Melton Public Library, French Lick, IN [*Library symbol Library of Congress*] (LCLS)
InFrenSH .... Springs Valley Herald, French Lick, IN [*Library symbol Library of Congress*] (LCLS)
InFrf.......... Frankfort Community Public Library, Frankfort, IL [*Library symbol Library of Congress*] (LCLS)
INF RHEI..... Infusum Rhei [*Infusion of Rhubarb*] [*Pharmacy*] (ROG)

INFRIC .... Infricetur [*Let It Be Rubbed In*] [*Pharmacy*]

InFrl .... Franklin Public Library, Franklin, IN [*Library symbol Library of Congress*] (LCLS)

InFrlC .... Franklin College of Indiana, Franklin, IN [*Library symbol Library of Congress*] (LCLS)

InFrlCR .... Johnson County Recorder's Office, Franklin, IN [*Library symbol Library of Congress*] (LCLS)

InFrlJ .... Franklin Daily Journal, Franklin, IN [*Library symbol Library of Congress*] (LCLS)

InFrlJM .... Johnson County Museum, Franklin, IN [*Library symbol Library of Congress*] (LCLS)

INFRM .... Infirm

INFRMRY ..... Infirmary

INFRN .... Inference (MSA)

INFROSS ...... Information Requirements of the Social Sciences [*British*] (DIT)

INFROSS ...... Investigation into Information Requirements of Social Sciences [*1970s study*] [*British*] (NITA)

InfRsc .... Information Resource Engineering, Inc. [*Associated Press*] (SAG)

InFrv .... Francesville-Salem Township Public Library, Francesville, IN [*Library symbol Library of Congress*] (LCLS)

InFrvT .... Francesville Tribune, Francesville, IN [*Library symbol Library of Congress*] (LCLS)

INFS .... In Focus System, Inc. [*NASDAQ symbol*] (SAG)

INFS .... In Focus Systems [*NASDAQ symbol*] (TTSB)

INFT .... Infant (ROG)

INFT .... Informal Training (NASA)

InFtbh .... United States Army, Post Library, Fort Benjamin Harrison, IN [*Library symbol*] [*Library of Congress*] (LCLS)

InFtbhP .... United States Army, Post Library, Fort Benjamin Harrison, IN [*Library symbol Library of Congress*] (LCLS)

INF Treaty ... Intermediate-Range Nuclear Forces Treaty (MUSM)

InFtv .... Carnegie Public Library District, Fortville, IN [*Library symbol Library of Congress*] (LCLS)

InFtvT .... Fortville Tribune, Fortville, IN [*Library symbol Library of Congress*] (LCLS)

Infty .... Infantry [*British military*] (DMA)

INFU .... Infu-Tech, Inc. [*NASDAQ symbol*] (SAG)

InFu .... Phyllis Meyer Library, Fulton, IN [*Library symbol Library of Congress*] (LCLS)

INFUND .... Infunde [*Pour In*] [*Pharmacy*]

INFUS .... Infusum [*Infusion*] [*Pharmacy*] (ROG)

InfuTech ...... Infu-Tech, Inc. [*Associated Press*] (SAG)

InFw .... Public Library of Fort Wayne and Allen County, Fort Wayne, IN [*Library symbol Library of Congress*] (LCLS)

InFwAHi ...... Allen County-Fort Wayne Historical Society Library, Fort Wayne, IN [*Library symbol Library of Congress*] (LCLS)

InFwB .... Fort Wayne Bible College, Fort Wayne, IN [*Library symbol Library of Congress*] (LCLS)

InFwC .... Concordia Senior College, Fort Wayne, IN [*Library symbol Library of Congress*] (LCLS)

InFwCS .... Fort Wayne Community Schools, Fort Wayne, IN [*Library symbol*] [*Library of Congress*] (LCLS)

InFwCT .... Concordia Theological Seminary, Fort Wayne, IN [*Library symbol Library of Congress*] (LCLS)

InFwGS .... Church of Jesus Christ of Latter-Day Saints, Genealogical Society Library, Fort Wayne Branch, Fort Wayne, IN [*Library symbol Library of Congress*] (LCLS)

InFwI .... Indiana Institute of Technology, Fort Wayne, IN [*Library symbol Library of Congress*] (LCLS)

InFwIP .... Indiana-Purdue University, Fort Wayne, IN [*Library symbol Library of Congress*] (LCLS)

InFwJG .... Fort Wayne Journal-Gazette, Fort Wayne, IN [*Library symbol Library of Congress*] (LCLS)

InFwL .... Lincoln National Life Foundation, Fort Wayne, IN [*Library symbol Library of Congress*] (LCLS)

InFWl-F .... National Life Insurance Co., Lincoln National Life Foundation, Louis A. Warren Lincoln Library and Museum, Fort Wayne, IN [*Library symbol Library of Congress*] (LCLS)

InFwLW ...... Louis A. Warren Lincoln Library and Museum, Fort Wayne, IN [*Library symbol*] [*Library of Congress*] (LCLS)

InFwM .... Magnavox Co., Fort Wayne, IN [*Library symbol Library of Congress*] (LCLS)

InFwSF .... Saint Francis College, Fort Wayne, IN [*Library symbol Library of Congress*] (LCLS)

INFX .... Inspection Fixture

INFY .... Infancy [*Legal shorthand*] (LWAP)

Infy .... Infantry [*British military*] (DMA)

ING .... Ambler, PA [*Location identifier FAA*] (FAAL)

InG .... Gary Public Library, Gary, IN [*Library symbol Library of Congress*] (LCLS)

ING .... Inactive National Guard

ING .... Inertial Navigation and Guidance [*Aerospace*] (AAG)

ING .... Inertial Navigation Gyro

ING .... Ingenieur [*Engineer*] [*French*] (EY)

ing .... Ingenieur (DD)

ING .... Inglis Ltd. [*Toronto Stock Exchange symbol*]

ING .... Ingram Ranch [*California*] [*Seismograph station code, US Geological Survey*] (SEIS)

ING .... Inguinal [*Anatomy*]

ING .... Inside Nazi Germany [*A publication*]

ING .... Integrated News Gathering

ING .... Intense Neutron Generator

ING .... Internationale Nederlanden Groep [*Netherlands*] (ECON)

ING .... International Newspaper Group (EA)

ING .... Isotope Nephrogram (DMAA)

ING .... Lago Argentino [*Argentina*] [*Airport symbol*] (OAG)

INGA .... Indium Gallium Arsenide

INGA .... Inspection Gauge

INGA .... Interactive Graphics Analysis

INGAA .... Interstate Natural Gas Association of America (EA)

INGAALP ..... Indium-Gallium-Aluminum Phosphide [*Light-emitting diode construction*]

InGaAs .... Indium Gallium Arsenide (AAEL)

InGaAs APD ... Indium Gallium Arsenide Avalanche Photodiode

InGaAsP ...... Indium Gallium Arsenide Phosphide (AAEL)

InGaN .... Indium Gallium Nitride (AAEL)

InGar .... Garrett Public Library, Garrett, IN [*Library symbol Library of Congress*] (LCLS)

InGarC .... Garrett Clipper, Garrett, IN [*Library symbol Library of Congress*] (LCLS)

INGAT .... Ingatestone [*Village in England*]

Ing B. .... Ingenium Baccalaureus [*Bachelor of Engineering*]

InGc .... Gas City-Mill Township Public Library, Gas City, IN [*Library symbol Library of Congress*] (LCLS)

Ing Comp .... Ingram's Compensation for Interest in Lands [*2nd ed.*] [*1869*] [*A publication*] (DLA)

Ing D .... Ingenium Doctor [*Doctor of Engineering*]

Ing Dig .... Ingersoll's Digest of the Laws of the United States [*A publication*] (DLA)

InGe .... Geneva Public Library, Geneva, IN [*Library symbol Library of Congress*] (LCLS)

InGeL .... Limberlost State Memorial, Geneva, IN [*Library symbol Library of Congress*] (LCLS)

INGENINST ... Office of the Inspector General Instructions [*Navy*]

INGER .... International Network on Genetic Evaluation in Rice (ECON)

IngerRd .... Ingersoll Rand [*Associated Press*] (SAG)

Ing Hab Corp ... Ingersoll on Habeas Corpus [*A publication*] (DLA)

InGHi .... Gary Historical and Cultural Society, Gary, IN [*Library symbol Library of Congress*] (LCLS)

INGIFPI .... Irish National Group of International Federation of the Phonographic Industry (EAIO)

Ing Insolv .... Ingraham on Insolvency [*Pennsylvania*] [*A publication*] (DLA)

InglMkt .... Ingles Markets, Inc. [*Associated Press*] (SAG)

Ing M .... Ingenium Magister [*Master of Engineering*]

InGo .... Goshen College, Goshen, IN [*Library symbol Library of Congress*] (LCLS)

INGO .... International Non-Governmental Organization

InGoM .... Mennonite Historical Library, Goshen College, Goshen, IN [*Library symbol Library of Congress*] (LCLS)

InGoN .... Goshen News, Goshen, IN [*Library symbol Library of Congress*] (LCLS)

InGoo .... Goodland Public Library (Mitten Memorial Library), Goodland, IN [*Library symbol Library of Congress*] (LCLS)

InGoP .... Goshen Public Library, Goshen, IN [*Library symbol Library of Congress*] (LCLS)

InGP .... Indol Glycerophosphate [*Biochemistry*]

InGPS .... Indoleglycerolphosphate Synthase [*Biochemistry*]

InGPT .... Gary Post-Tribune, Gary, IN [*Library symbol Library of Congress*] (LCLS)

InGr .... Greencastle-Putnam County Library, Greencastle, IN [*Library symbol Library of Congress*] (LCLS)

INGR .... Intergraph Corp. [*NASDAQ symbol*] (NQ)

InGrBG .... Greencastle Banner-Graphic, Greencastle, IN [*Library symbol Library of Congress*] (LCLS)

InGrD .... De Pauw University, Greencastle, IN [*Library symbol Library of Congress*] (LCLS)

INGRD .... Ingredient

InGrD-Ar ..... De Pauw University, Archives, Greencastle, IN [*Library symbol Library of Congress*] (LCLS)

INGRDNT ..... Ingredient

InGreb .... Greensburg Public Library, Greensburg, IN [*Library symbol Library of Congress*] (LCLS)

InGrebCR ..... Decatur County Recorder's Office, Greensburg, IN [*Library symbol Library of Congress*] (LCLS)

InGrebDHi ... Decatur County Historical Society, Greensburg, IN [*Library symbol Library of Congress*] (LCLS)

InGrebHi ..... Decatur County Historical Society, Greensburg, IN [*Library symbol*] [*Library of Congress*] (LCLS)

InGref .... Greenfield Public Library, Greenfield, IN [*Library symbol Library of Congress*] (LCLS)

InGrefL .... Eli Lilly & Co., Library Agricultural Services, Greenfield, IN [*Library symbol Library of Congress*] (LCLS)

InGrefR .... Greenfield Daily Reporter, Greenfield, IN [*Library symbol*] [*Library of Congress*] (LCLS)

INGRES .... Interactive Graphic and Retrieval System

InGretN .... Howard County News, Greentown, IN [*Library symbol Library of Congress*] (LCLS)

InGrew .... Greenwood Public Library, Greenwood, IN [*Library symbol Library of Congress*] (LCLS)

IngrmM .... Ingram Micro, Inc. [*Associated Press*] (SAG)

Ing Roc .... Ingersoll's Edition of Roccus' Maritime Law [*A publication*] (DLA)

InGS .... Gary School System, Gary, IN [*Library symbol Library of Congress*] (LCLS)

INGSOC .... English Socialism [*From George Orwell's novel, "1984"*]

Ing Ves .... Vesey, Junior's, English Chancery Reports, Edited by Ingraham [*A publication*] (ILCA)

INGYO .... International Nongovernmental Youth Organization (PDAA)

INH .... Improved Nike Hercules [*Missile*]

IN/H .... Inches per Hour

INH .... Inhalation

INH .... Inhambane [*Mozambique*] [*Airport symbol*]   (AD)
INH .... Inheritance [*Legal shorthand*]   (LWAP)
INH .... Inhibit   (NASA)
INH .... Isangel [*New Hebrides*] [*Seismograph station code, US Geological Survey*]   (SEIS)
INH .... Isoniazid   (DMAA)
INH .... Isonicotinic Acid Hydrazide [*or Isonicotinylhydrazine*] [*See also INAH, ISONIAZID*] [*Antituberculous agent*]
INHA .... Inhibin Alpha   (DMAA)
INHAB .... Inhabitant
INHABD .... Inhabited   (ROG)
InHag .... Hagerstown Public Library, Hagerstown, IN [*Library symbol Library of Congress*]   (LCLS)
InHagE .... Hagerstown Exponent, Hagerstown, IN [*Library symbol Library of Congress*]   (LCLS)
INHAL .... Inhalatio [*Inhalation*] [*Pharmacy*]
InhalTh .... Inhale Therapeutic Systems [*Associated Press*]   (SAG)
InHam .... Hammond Public Library, Hammond, IN [*Library symbol Library of Congress*]   (LCLS)
InHamP .... Purdue University, Calumet Campus, Hammond, IN [*Library symbol Library of Congress*]   (LCLS)
InHamT .... Hammond Times, Hammond, IN [*Library symbol Library of Congress*]   (LCLS)
InHan .... Hanover College, Hanover, IN [*Library symbol Library of Congress*]   (LCLS)
InHar .... Hartford City Public Library, Hartford City, IN [*Library symbol Library of Congress*]   (LCLS)
InHarBHi ...... Blackford County Historical Society, Hartford City, IN [*Library symbol Library of Congress*]   (LCLS)
InHazN .... White River News, Hazelton, IN [*Library symbol Library of Congress*]   (LCLS)
INHB .... Inhibin Beta   (DMAA)
INHB .... Inhibit   (MSA)
INHBD .... Inhibited
INHCE .... Inheritance [*Legal term*]   (ROG)
InHeb .... Hebron Public Library, Hebron, IN [*Library symbol Library of Congress*]   (LCLS)
InHebPH ...... Porter County Herald, Hebron, IN [*Library symbol Library of Congress*]   (LCLS)
Inher .... Inheritance [*Legal term*]   (DLA)
Inher Est & Gift Tax Rep (CCH)... Inheritance, Estate, and Gift Tax Reports (Commerce Clearing House) [*A publication*]   (DLA)
InHhW .... Workingmen's Institute, New Harmony, IN [*Library symbol Library of Congress*]   (LCLS)
InHi .... Indiana Historical Society, Indianapolis, IN [*Library symbol Library of Congress*]   (LCLS)
INHIB .... Inhibition
INHIGEO ...... International Commission on the History of the Geological Sciences [*ICSU*] [*Paris, France*]   (EAIO)
INHL .... Inhale Therapeutic Sys [*NASDAQ symbol*]   (TTSB)
INHL .... Inhale Therapeutic Systems [*NASDAQ symbol*]   (SAG)
InHld .... Industrial Holdings, Inc. [*Associated Press*]   (SAG)
INHM .... Inco Homes [*NASDAQ symbol*]   (TTSB)
INHM .... Inco Homes Corp. [*NASDAQ symbol*]   (SAG)
INHO .... Independence Hldg [*NASDAQ symbol*]   (TTSB)
INHO .... Independence Holding Co. [*NASDAQ symbol*]   (NQ)
InHobG .... Hobart Gazette, Hobart, IN [*Library symbol*] [*Library of Congress*]   (LCLS)
InHobHi .... Pleak Memorial Library/Hobart Historical Society, Hobart, IN [*Library symbol*] [*Library of Congress*]   (LCLS)
InHoG .... Hobart Gazette, Hobart, IN [*Library symbol Library of Congress*]   (LCLS)
InHoHi .... Pleak Memorial Library/Hobart Historical Society, Hobart, IN [*Library symbol Library of Congress*]   (LCLS)
InHome .... In Home Health, inc. [*Associated Press*]   (SAG)
INHS .... Illinois Natural History Survey [*Illinois Institute of Natural Resources*] [*Research center*]   (RCD)
INHS .... Irish National Hunt Steeplechase   (ROG)
InHu .... Huntington Public Library, Huntington, IN [*Library symbol Library of Congress*]   (LCLS)
InHub .... Huntingburg Public Library, Huntingburg, IN [*Library symbol Library of Congress*]   (LCLS)
InHuCR .... Huntington County Recorder's Office, Huntington, IN [*Library symbol*] [*Library of Congress*]   (LCLS)
InHuH .... Huntington College, Huntington, IN [*Library symbol Library of Congress*]   (LCLS)
InHuHi .... Huntington County Historical Society, Huntington, IN [*Library symbol Library of Congress*]   (LCLS)
InHuHP .... Huntington Herald-Press, Huntington, IN [*Library symbol Library of Congress*]   (LCLS)
INHYX .... IDS High Yield Tax Exempt Cl.A [*Mutual fund ticker symbol*]   (SG)
INI .... Incipient Nonequilibrium Index
InI .... Indianapolis-Marion County Public Library, Indianapolis, IN [*Library symbol Library of Congress*]   (LCLS)
INI .... Industrial Networking, Inc. [*Joint venture of Ungermann-Bass, Inc. and General Electric Corp.*]
INI .... Inner Integument [*Botany*]
INI .... In Nomine Iesu [*In the Name of Jesus*] [*Latin*]
INI .... Instituto Nacional de Industria [*National Institute for Industry*] [*Spain*]
INI .... Interface Noise Inverter
INI .... International Nonviolent Initiatives   (EA)
INI .... Intervideo Network, Inc. [*Beverly Hills, CA*] [*Telecommunications*]   (TSSD)
INI .... Intranuclear Inclusion

InIA .... Indiana Academy of Science, Indianapolis, IN [*Library symbol Library of Congress*]   (LCLS)
InIAL .... American Legion, National Headquarters Library, Indianapolis, IN [*Library symbol Library of Congress*]   (LCLS)
INIAP .... Instituto de Investigacion y Autoformacion Politica [*Guatemala, Guatemala, C.P.*]
InIB .... Butler University, Indianapolis, IN [*Library symbol Library of Congress*]   (LCLS)
INIBAP .... International Network for the Improvement of Banana and Plantain [*Affilia ted with the Consultative Group on International Agricultural Research*] [*France*]
InIBHM .... President Benjamin Harrison Memorial Home, Indianapolis, IN [*Library symbol Library of Congress*]   (LCLS)
InIBHP .... Barnes, Hickam, Pantzer & Boyd, Law Library, Indianapolis, IN [*Library symbol Library of Congress*]   (LCLS)
InIBio .... Bio-Dynamics, Inc., BMC Library, Indianapolis, IN [*Library symbol Library of Congress*]   (LCLS)
InIB-P .... Butler University, College of Pharmacy, Indianapolis, IN [*Library symbol Library of Congress*]   (LCLS)
InIBr .... Everett I. Brown Co., Indianapolis, IN [*Library symbol*] [*Library of Congress*]   (LCLS)
INIC .... Ideal Current Negative Immittance Converter
InIC .... Indianapolis Commercial, Indianapolis, IN [*Library symbol Library of Congress*]   (LCLS)
INIC .... Inverse Negative Impedance Converter   (IAA)
InICC .... Indiana Central University, Indianapolis, IN [*Library symbol Library of Congress*]   (LCLS)
INICE .... Inexpensive In-Circuit Emulator   (NITA)
InICM .... Children's Museum of Indianapolis, Indianapolis, IN [*Library symbol Library of Congress*]   (LCLS)
INICR .... Institute for Childhood Resources   (EA)
InID .... General Motors Corp., Detroit Diesel Allison Division, Plant 8 Library, Indianapolis, IN [*Library symbol Library of Congress*]   (LCLS)
INID .... Institutul National de Informare si Documentare [*National Institute for Information and Documentation*] [*National Council for Science and Technology*] [*Information service or system*]   (IID)
INID/NOD ..... Immediate Network-In Dial/Network-Out Dial   (DNAB)
InIDow .... DOWELANCO, Indianapolis, IN [*Library symbol*] [*Library of Congress*]   (LCLS)
INIDX .... IDS Growth Cl.A [*Mutual fund ticker symbol*]   (SG)
InIFHi .... Franklin Township Historical Society, Indianapolis, IN [*Library symbol Library of Congress*]   (LCLS)
INIG .... International Nutritional Immunology Group   (EA)
InIGS .... Church of Jesus Christ of Latter-Day Saints, Genealogical Society Library, Indianapolis Branch, Indianapolis, IN [*Library symbol Library of Congress*]   (LCLS)
InIH .... Hudson Institute, Indiannapolis, IN [*Library symbol*] [*Library of Congress*]   (LCLS)
InIl .... Indiana Cooperative Library Service Authority (INCOLSA), Indianapolis, IN [*Library symbol Library of Congress*]   (LCLS)
InIIY .... Indiana Youth Institute, Indianapolis, IN [*Library symbol*] [*Library of Congress*]   (LCLS)
InIJ .... Herron School of Art, Indianapolis, IN [*Library symbol Library of Congress*]   (LCLS)
InIL .... Eli Lilly & Co., Scientific Library, Indianapolis, IN [*Library symbol Library of Congress*]   (LCLS)
InILB .... Eli Lilly & Co., Business Library, Indianapolis, IN [*Library symbol Library of Congress*]   (LCLS)
InILL .... Eli Lilly & Co., Law Library, Indianapolis, IN [*Library symbol*] [*Library of Congress*]   (LCLS)
InILS .... Indianapolis Law School, Indianapolis, IN [*Library symbol Library of Congress*]   (LCLS)
InIM .... Marian College, Indianapolis, IN [*Library symbol Library of Congress*]   (LCLS)
InIMa .... Indiana Masonic Library and Museum, Indianapolis, IN [*Library symbol*] [*Library of Congress*]   (LCLS)
InIMu .... Indianapolis Museum of Art, Reference Library, Indianapolis, IN [*Library symbol Library of Congress*]   (LCLS)
ININ .... InStent Inc. [*NASDAQ symbol*]   (TTSB)
IN INIT .... In Initio [*In the Beginning*] [*Latin*]
INIP .... Institute of Non-Numerical Information Processing [*Switzerland*] [*Information service or system*]   (IID)
InIPE .... Indiana University - Purdue University at Indianapolis, School of Physical Education, Indianapolis, IN [*Library symbol Library of Congress*]   (LCLS)
InIR .... James Whitcomb Riley Home, Indianapolis, IN [*Library symbol Library of Congress*]   (LCLS)
InIRCA .... RCA, Selectavision Video Disc Operations Library, Indianapolis, IN [*Library symbol Library of Congress*]   (LCLS)
INIS .... International Nuclear Information System [*International Atomic Energy Agency*]   (IID)
INIS .... Internation Nuclear Information Service [*International Atomic Energy Authority*]   (NITA)
INIS ATOMINDEX... International Nuclear Information System [*International Atomic Energy Agency*] [*Vienna, Austria Bibliographic database*]
InISC .... Indiana Supreme Court Law Library, Indianapolis, IN [*Library symbol*] [*Library of Congress*]   (LCLS)
InISIN .... Sigma Theta Tau International Nursing Library, Indianapolis, IN [*Library symbol*] [*Library of Congress*]   (LCLS)
INIST .... Institute de l'Information Scientifique et Technique [*Institute of Scientific and Technical Information*] [*Information service or system*]   (IID)
INISWF .... Indian National Iron and Steel Workers' Federation
InIT .... Christian Theological Seminary, Indianapolis, IN [*Library symbol Library of Congress*]   (LCLS)

INIT.............	Initial (AFM)
INIT.............	Initialization (KSC)
INIT.............	Initial Training [Aviation] (FAAC)
INIT.............	Initiate (NASA)
INIT.............	Initiation (MSA)
INIT.............	Initio [In the Beginning] [Latin] (ROG)
INIT & REF...	Initiative and Referendum [Legal term] (DLA)
INITCCA	Initial Cash Clothing Allowance [Military] (DNAB)
INITCCCA.....	Initial Civilian Cash Clothing Allowance [Military] (DNAB)
Initio............	Initio, Inc. [Associated Press] (SAG)
INITUNIFALW...	Initial Uniform Allowance [Military]
InIU............	Indiana University - Purdue University at Indianapolis, Downtown Campus, Indianapolis, IN [Library symbol Library of Congress] (LCLS)
InIU-L..........	Indiana University - Purdue University at Indianapolis, School of Law, Indianapolis, IN [Library symbol Library of Congress] (LCLS)
INIVX..........	Van Eck Funds: Intl. Investors [Mutual fund ticker symbol] (SG)
InIWis.........	Wishard Memorial Hospital, Indianapolis, IN [Library symbol Library of Congress] (LCLS)
InIZ............	Indianapolis, Zoological Society, Inc., Indianapolis, IN [Library symbol] [Library of Congress] (LCLS)
INJ..............	Inject
INJ..............	Injectio [An Injection] [Pharmacy]
INJ..............	Injector (KSC)
Inj..............	Injunction [Legal term]
INJ..............	Injure (AABC)
INJ..............	Injury (CPH)
INJ..............	In Nomine Jesu [In the Name of Jesus] [Latin]
INJ..............	Interjet [Greece] [FAA designator] (FAAC)
INJ..............	International North American Resources, Inc. [Vancouver Stock Exchange symbol]
InJ..............	Jasper Public Library, Jasper, IN [Library symbol Library of Congress] (LCLS)
InJa............	Jasonville Public Library, Jasonville, IN [Library symbol] [Library of Congress] (LCLS)
InJaL..........	Jasonville Leader, Jasonville, IN [Library symbol Library of Congress] (LCLS)
InJamP........	Jamestown Press, Jamestown, IN [Library symbol Library of Congress] (LCLS)
INJCT..........	Injunction [Legal term]
INJCTN........	Injection
InJDHi.........	Dubois County Historical Society, Jasper, IN [Library symbol Library of Congress] (LCLS)
InJe............	Jeffersonville Township Public Library, Jeffersonville, IN [Library symbol Library of Congress] (LCLS)
INJECT........	Injection [Medicine]
INJ ENEM	Injiciatur Enema [Let an Enema Be Injected] [Pharmacy]
INJFACS......	Injection Facilities (DNAB)
InJH...........	Jasper Herald, Jasper, IN [Library symbol Library of Congress] (LCLS)
INJ HYP.......	Injectio Hypodermica [Hypodermic Injection] [Pharmacy]
INJIC..........	Injiciatur [Let It Be Given] [Pharmacy] (ROG)
INJICIAT......	Injiciatur [Let It Be Given] [Pharmacy] (ROG)
INJN...........	Injunction [Legal term] (ROG)
InJo...........	Jonesboro Public Library, Jonesboro, IN [Library symbol Library of Congress] (LCLS)
INJON.........	Injunction [Legal term] (ROG)
INK.............	International Coast Minerals Corp. [Vancouver Stock Exchange symbol]
INK.............	Inuvik [Northwest Territories] [Seismograph station code, US Geological Survey] (SEIS)
INK.............	Kentair (International) Ltd. [British ICAO designator] (FAAC)
INK.............	Wink, TX [Location identifier FAA] (FAAL)
INKA	Informationssystem Karlsruhe [Karlsruhe Information System] [Information service or system Germany]
INKA-CONF...	Informationssystem Karlsruhe - Conference [Database]
INKA-CORP...	Informationssystem Karlsruhe - Corporates in Energy [Database] [Defunct]
INKA-DATACOMP...	Informationssystem Karlsruhe - Data Compilations in Energy and Physics [Database]
INKA-MATH...	Informationssystem Karlsruhe - Mathematics [Database]
INKA-MATHDI...	Informationssystem Karlsruhe - Mathematical Education [Database]
INKA-NUCLEAR...	INKA Nuclear Science and Technology [Database] (NITA)
INKA-NUCLEAR PART INIS...	Informationssystem Karlsruhe - Nuclear Database Part: International Nuclear Information System [Database]
INKA-NUCLEAR PART KKK...	Informationssystem Karlsruhe - Nuclear Database Part: Conference Papers: NuclearResearch, Nuclear Technology [Database]
INKA-NUCLEAR PART NSA...	Informationssystem Karlsruhe - Nuclear Database Part: Nuclear Science Abstracts [Database]
INKA-PHYS...	Informationssystem Karlsruhe - Physics [Database]
InKend.........	Kendallville Public Library, Kendallville, IN [Library symbol Library of Congress] (LCLS)
InKendNS	Kendallville News-Sun, Kendallville, IN [Library symbol Library of Congress] (LCLS)
InKent.........	Kentland Public Library, Kentland, IN [Library symbol Library of Congress] (LCLS)
InKentCR	Newton County Recorder's Office, Kentland, IN [Library symbol Library of Congress] (LCLS)
InKentE........	Newton County Enterprise, Kentland, IN [Library symbol Library of Congress] (LCLS)
InKew	Kewanna Public Library, Kewanna, IN [Library symbol Library of Congress] (LCLS)

InKewO........	Kewanna Observer, Kewanna, IN [Library symbol Library of Congress] (LCLS)
InKir...........	Kirklin Public Library, Kirklin, IN [Library symbol Library of Congress] (LCLS)
InKni..........	Knightstown Public Library, Knightstown, IN [Library symbol Library of Congress] (LCLS)
InKniB.........	Knightstown Banner, Knightstown, IN [Library symbol Library of Congress] (LCLS)
InKno..........	Henry F. Schricker Library, Knox, IN [Library symbol Library of Congress] (LCLS)
InKnoCHi	Starke County Historical Museum, Knox, IN [Library symbol Library of Congress] (LCLS)
InKnoCR	Starke County Recorder's Office, Knox, IN [Library symbol Library of Congress] (LCLS)
InKo...........	Kokomo Public Library, Kokomo, IN [Library symbol Library of Congress] (LCLS)
InKoC.........	Cabot Corp., Stellite Division, Kokomo, IN [Library symbol Library of Congress] (LCLS)
InKoT.........	Kokomo Tribune, Kokomo, IN [Library symbol Library of Congress] (LCLS)
InKouT........	Kouts Times, Kouts, IN [Library symbol Library of Congress] (LCLS)
INKT...........	Inktomi [Software provider]
INL.............	Inland Natural Gas Co. Ltd. [Toronto Stock Exchange symbol Vancouver Stock Exchange symbol]
inl.............	Inlay (MAE)
INL.............	Inlet (KSC)
INL.............	Inner Nuclear Layer
INL.............	Internal Noise Level (IEEE)
INL.............	International Falls [Minnesota] [Airport symbol] (OAG)
INL.............	International Falls, MN [Location identifier FAA] (FAAL)
INL.............	Internodal Link (ACRL)
INL.............	Morgan Intertrades Ltd. [Nigeria] [FAA designator] (FAAC)
InL............	tippecanoe County Public Library, Lafayette, IN [Library symbol] [Library of Congress] (LCLS)
InL............	Wells Memorial Library, Lafayette, IN [Library symbol Library of Congress] (LCLS)
INLA...........	International Nuclear Law Association [See also AIDN] [Brussels, Belgium] (EAIO)
INLA...........	Iowa Nursery and Landscape Association (SRA)
INLA...........	Irish National Liberation Army
InLacN........	Lacrosse Regional News, La Crosse, IN [Library symbol Library of Congress] (LCLS)
InLad	Ladoga-Clark Township Public Library, Ladoga, IN [Library symbol Library of Congress] (LCLS)
InLag	LaGrange County Library, LaGrange, IN [Library symbol Library of Congress] (LCLS)
InLagHi.......	LaGrange County Historical Society, LaGrange, IN [Library symbol Library of Congress] (LCLS)
InLagNS.......	LaGrange News and Standard, LaGrange, IN [Library symbol] [Library of Congress] (LCLS)
INLAN	Instant Language [Trademark] [Computer science]
InLap	La Porte Public Library, La Porte, IN [Library symbol Library of Congress] (LCLS)
InLapHA......	LaPorte Herald-Argus, LaPorte, IN [Library symbol Library of Congress] (LCLS)
InLapHi.......	LaPorte County Historical Society, LaPorte, IN [Library symbol Library of Congress] (LCLS)
InLaR.........	Lapel Review, Lapel, IN [Library symbol Library of Congress] (LCLS)
InLasH........	Hygiene Institute, La Salle, IN [Library symbol Library of Congress] (LCLS)
INLAW	Infantry LASER Weapon (MCD)
InLaw..........	Lawrenceburg Public Library, Lawrenceburg, IN [Library symbol Library of Congress] (LCLS)
InLawCR	Dearborn County Recorder's Office, Lawrenceburg, IN [Library symbol Library of Congress] (LCLS)
IN/LB	Inches per Pound
IN-LB	Inch-Pound
In-LB..........	Indiana Legislative Council, State House, Indianapolis, IN [Library symbol Library of Congress] (LCLS)
INLC..........	Initial Launch Capability (IEEE)
InLcLM	Lincoln Boyhood National Memorial, Lincoln City, IN [Library symbol Library of Congress] (LCLS)
INLD	Inland Casino [NASDAQ symbol] (TTSB)
INLD	Inland Casino Corp. [NASDAQ symbol] (SAG)
InldCas	Inland Casino Corp. [Associated Press] (SAG)
InldRs.........	Inland Resources [Associated Press] (SAG)
InldStl.........	Inland Steel Industries, Inc. [Associated Press] (SAG)
INLE..........	Instituto Nacional del Libro Espanol
InLeb	Lebanon Public Library, Lebanon, IN [Library symbol Library of Congress] (LCLS)
InLebCR.......	Boone County Recorder's Office, Lebanon, IN [Library symbol Library of Congress] (LCLS)
InLebR........	Lebanon Reporter, Lebanon, IN [Library symbol Library of Congress] (LCLS)
INLET..........	Inlet [Commonly used] (OPSA)
InLib	Union County Public Library, Liberty, IN [Library symbol Library of Congress] (LCLS)
InLibCN........	College Corner News, Liberty, IN [Library symbol Library of Congress] (LCLS)
InLibH.........	Liberty Herald, Liberty, IN [Library symbol Library of Congress] (LCLS)
INLICA	Indiana Land Improvement Contractors Association (SRA)
InLigAL........	Ligonier Advance-Leader, Ligonier, IN [Library symbol Library of Congress] (LCLS)
IN LIM	In Limine [At the Outset] [Latin]

InLind.......... Linden Public Library, Linden, IN [*Library symbol Library of Congress*] (LCLS)
INLINON ..... Interlineation (ROG)
InLint.......... Linton Public Library, Linton, IN [*Library symbol Library of Congress*] (LCLS)
InLintC....... Linton Daily Citizen, Linton, IN [*Library symbol Library of Congress*] (LCLS)
IN LITT .... In Litteris [*In Correspondence*] [*Latin*]
in litt .... In Litteris [*In Correspondence*] [*Latin*] (EES)
InLJC.......... Lafayette Journal and Courier, Lafayette, IN [*Library symbol Library of Congress*] (LCLS)
INLN .... Inland Resources [*NASDAQ symbol*] (SAG)
INLND.......... Inland
INLO .... In Lieu Of
IN LOC........ In Loco [*In the Place Of*] [*Latin*]
IN LOC CIT... In Loco Citato [*In the Place Mentioned*] [*Latin*] (ROG)
InLog .... Logansport-Cass County Public Library, Logansport, IN [*Library symbol Library of Congress*] (LCLS)
InLogCHi...... Cass County Historical Society Museum Library, Logansport, IN [*Library symbol Library of Congress*] (LCLS)
INLOGOV .... Institute of Local Government [*University of Birmingham*] [*British*] (AIE)
INLOGOV .... Institute of Local Government Studies [*British*]
InLogPT....... Pharos-Tribune, Logansport, IN [*Library symbol Library of Congress*] (LCLS)
InLoo .... Frances L. Folks Memorial Library (Loogootee Public Library), Loogootee, IN [*Library symbol Library of Congress*] (LCLS)
InLooT .... Loogootee Tribune, Loogootee, IN [*Library symbol Library of Congress*] (LCLS)
InLow.......... Lowell Public Library, Lowell, IN [*Library symbol Library of Congress*] (LCLS)
InLowT........ Lowell Tribune, Lowell, IN [*Library symbol Library of Congress*] (LCLS)
INLP............ Integer Non-Linear Programming [*Computer science*] (PDAA)
InLP............ Purdue University, Lafayette, IN [*Library symbol Library of Congress*] (LCLS)
InLP-Ham .... Purdue University, Calumet Campus, Hammond, IN [*Library symbol Library of Congress Obsolete*] (LCLS)
INLQ .... INTERLING Software Corp. [*NASDAQ symbol*] (SAG)
INLQ .... Interlinq Software [*NASDAQ symbol*] (SAG)
INLR .... Item No Longer Required
INLS............ Individualized Learning System (DNAB)
InLS............ Lafayette Schools System, Lafayette, IN [*Library symbol Library of Congress*] (LCLS)
InLSEH........ St. Elizabeth Hospital Medical Center, Bannon Health Science Library, Lafayette, IN [*Library symbol*] [*Library of Congress*] (LCLS)
INLT............ Inlet [*Board on Geographic Names*] (MCD)
InLTHi.......... Tippecanoe County Historical Association, Lafayette, IN [*Library symbol Library of Congress*] (LCLS)
InLv .... Lake Village Library, Lake Village, IN [*Library symbol Library of Congress*] (LCLS)
InLy .... Washington Township Public Library, Lynn, IN [*Library symbol Library of Congress*] (LCLS)
INM............ Imbokodvo National Movement [*Swaziland*] [*Political party*] (PPW)
INM............ Informed Notaries of Maine (SRA)
INM............ Innamincka [*South Australia*] [*Airport symbol*] (AD)
INM............ Inspector of Naval Machinery
INM............ Inspector of Naval Material
INM............ Institute of Naval Medicine [*British*] (DMA)
INM............ Integrated Network Management [*for Companies*]
INM............ Interception Mission [*Air Force*]
INM............ International Narcotics Matters [*Department of State*]
INM............ International Nautical Mile
INM............ International Nuclear Model [*Department of Energy*] (GFGA)
INM............ Istel Network Monitoring System (NITA)
INMA .... International Newspaper Marketing Association (EA)
Inmac .... Inmac Corp. [*Associated Press*] (SAG)
INMAC .... Instant Mini/Micro Computer Accessories and Cables [*Manufacturer/distributor*] [*British*] (NITA)
InMad .... Madison-Jefferson County Public Library, Madison, IN [*Library symbol Library of Congress*] (LCLS)
InMadC....... Madison Daily Courier, Madison, IN [*Library symbol Library of Congress*] (LCLS)
INMAP .... Independent Microelectronics Applications [*British*] (NITA)
InMar.......... Marion Public Library, Marion, IN [*Library symbol Library of Congress*] (LCLS)
InMarC....... Marion College, Marion, IN [*Library symbol Library of Congress*] (LCLS)
InMarCT...... Marion Chronicle Tribune, Marion, IN [*Library symbol Library of Congress*] (LCLS)
InMarGHi..... Grant County Historical Society, Marion, IN [*Library symbol Library of Congress*] (LCLS)
INMARSAT... International Maritime Satellite [*Satellite communications organization*] (NITA)
INMARSAT... International Maritime Satellite Organization
InMart.......... Morgan County Public Library, Martinsville, IN [*Library symbol Library of Congress*] (LCLS)
InMarV........ United States Veterans Administration Hospital, Marion, IN [*Library symbol Library of Congress*] (LCLS)
InMat.......... Matthews Public Library, Matthews, IN [*Library symbol Library of Congress*] (LCLS)
INMC .... Inmac Corp. [*NASDAQ symbol*] (NQ)
INMC .... International Network Management Center [*Telecommunications*] (TEL)

INMD .... IntegraMed America, Inc. [*NASDAQ symbol*] (SAG)
InMe .... Bell Memorial Public Library, Mentone, IN [*Library symbol Library of Congress*] (LCLS)
INMED .... Indians into Medicine (EA)
INMED .... International Medical Services for Health (EA)
InMeIRP...... Richland Press, Mellott, IN [*Library symbol Library of Congress*] (LCLS)
IN MEM .... In Memoriam [*In Memory Of*] [*Latin*] (ROG)
INMEP .... Institute for a New Middle East Policy (EA)
InMerL........ Lake County Public Library, Merrillville, IN [*Library symbol Library of Congress*] (LCLS)
INMETRO .... Instituto Nacional de Metrologia, Normalizacao e Qualidade Industrial [*Government advisory body*] [*Brazil*] (EY)
INMHC .... International Network for Mutual Help Centers (EA)
INMHO........ In My Humble Opinion (BARN)
INMI........... Institute of Microbiology (of the Academy of Sciences, USSR)
InMic .... Michigan City Public Library, Michigan City, IN [*Library symbol Library of Congress*] (LCLS)
InMicLM ...... Old Lighthouse Museum, Michigan City, IN [*Library symbol Library of Congress*] (LCLS)
InMicND ...... Michigan City News-Dispatch, Michigan City, IN [*Library symbol Library of Congress*] (LCLS)
InMid .... Middletown Public Library, Middletown, IN [*Library symbol*] [*Library of Congress*] (LCLS)
InMidb........ Middlebury Public Library, Middlebury, IN [*Library symbol Library of Congress*] (LCLS)
InMidbI........ Middlebury Independent, Middlebury, IN [*Library symbol Library of Congress*] (LCLS)
InMidN........ Middletown News, Middletown, IN [*Library symbol Library of Congress*] (LCLS)
InMil .... Milford Public Library, Milford, IN [*Library symbol Library of Congress*] (LCLS)
InMilMJ........ Milford Mail-Journal, Millford, IN [*Library symbol Library of Congress*] (LCLS)
InMis .... Mishawaka Public Library, Mishawaka, IN [*Library symbol Library of Congress*] (LCLS)
InMisB .... Bethel College, Mishawaka, IN [*Library symbol Library of Congress*] (LCLS)
InMisER ...... Mishawaka Enterprise-Record, Mishawaka, IN [*Library symbol Library of Congress*] (LCLS)
InMit .... Mitchell Community Public Library, Mitchell, IN [*Library symbol Library of Congress*] (LCLS)
InmkEnt ...... Inmark Enterprises, Inc. [*Associated Press*] (SAG)
INMM .... Institute of Nuclear Materials Management (EA)
InMon .... Monon Town and Township Library, Monon, IN [*Library symbol Library of Congress*] (LCLS)
InMonN....... Monon News, Monon, IN [*Library symbol Library of Congress*] (LCLS)
InMont .... Monterrey-Tippecanoe Township Public Library Monterrey, IN [*Library symbol Library of Congress*] (LCLS)
InMoo .... Mooresville Public Library, Mooresville, IN [*Library symbol*] [*Library of Congress*] (LCLS)
InMop .... Montpelier Public Library, Montpelier, IN [*Library symbol Library of Congress*] (LCLS)
InMopH....... Montpelier Herald, Montpelier, IN [*Library symbol Library of Congress*] (LCLS)
InMotc .... Monticello Union Township Public Library, Monticello, IN [*Library symbol Library of Congress*] (LCLS)
InMotz .... Montezuma Public Library, Montezuma, IN [*Library symbol Library of Congress*] (LCLS)
INMR .... Insider Network Market Report [*Information service or system*] (IID)
INMR .... Instrumentarium Corp. [*NASDAQ symbol*] (NQ)
INMRY .... Instrumentarium 'B' ADR [*NASDAQ symbol*] (TTSB)
INMS .... Integrated Network Management System [*Telecommunications*] (ACRL)
INMT .... Intermet Corp. [*NASDAQ symbol*] (NQ)
InMtv .... Alexandrian Free Public Library, Mount Vernon, IN [*Library symbol Library of Congress*] (LCLS)
INMU .... Inertial Navigation Measurement Unit (MCD)
InMu .... Muncie Public Library, Muncie, IN [*Library symbol Library of Congress*] (LCLS)
InMuB .... Ball State University, Muncie, IN [*Library symbol Library of Congress*] (LCLS)
InMuMC....... Minnetrista Cultural Center, Muncie, IN [*Library symbol*] [*Library of Congress*] (LCLS)
InMuP........ Muncie Evening Press, Muncie, IN [*Library symbol Library of Congress*] (LCLS)
InMuSP....... Muncie Morning Star-Evening Press, Muncie, IN [*Library symbol Library of Congress*] (LCLS)
INMUX........ IDS Mutual Cl.A [*Mutual fund ticker symbol*] (SG)
INMWF .... Indian National Mine Workers' Federation
INN .... ImagiNation Network [*Entertainment*]
INN .... Independent Network News [*Television*]
INN .... Inning (WGA)
INN .... Innsbruck [*Austria*] [*Airport symbol*] (OAG)
INN .... Innsbruck [*Austria*] [*Seismograph station code, US Geological Survey Closed*] (SEIS)
INN .... Intermediate Network Node (IAA)
INN .... International Nonproprietary Names [*World Health Organization*]
INN .... Minneapolis, MN [*Location identifier FAA*] (FAAL)
INN .... New Albany-Floyd County Public Library, New Albany, IN [*OCLC symbol*] (OCLC)
INNA .... International Newsreel and News Film Association [*Belgium*] (EAIO)
InNap.......... Nappanee Public Library, Nappanee, IN [*Library symbol Library of Congress*] (LCLS)

InNapAN ...... Nappanee Advance News, Nappanee, IN [*Library symbol Library of Congress*] (LCLS)

InNas .... Brown County Public Library, Nashville, IN [*Library symbol Library of Congress*] (LCLS)

InNasBHi ..... Brown County Historical Society, Nashville, IN [*Library symbol Library of Congress*] (LCLS)

InNasCR ...... Brown County Recorder's Office, Nashville, IN [*Library symbol Library of Congress*] (LCLS)

InNasD .... Brown County Democrat, Nashville, IN [*Library symbol Library of Congress*] (LCLS)

InNcar .... New Carlisle and Olive Township Public Library, New Carlisle, IN [*Library symbol Library of Congress*] (LCLS)

InNcas .... New Castle - Henry County Public Library, New Castle, IN [*Library symbol Library of Congress*] (LCLS)

InNcasCT ..... New Castle Courier Times, New Castle, IN [*Library symbol Library of Congress*] (LCLS)

InNcasHi ...... Henry County Historical Society, Reference Room, New Castle, IN [*Library symbol Library of Congress*] (LCLS)

InNcasNR .... Henry County News-Republican, New Castle, IN [*Library symbol Library of Congress*] (LCLS)

INNCNT .... Innocent

InNd .... University of Notre Dame, Notre Dame, IN [*Library symbol Library of Congress*] (LCLS)

InNd-L .... University of Notre Dame, Law School, Notre Dame, IN [*Library symbol Library of Congress*] (LCLS)

InNd-LS .... University of Notre Dame, Life Sciences Research Library, Notre Dame, IN [*Library symbol Library of Congress*] (LCLS)

InNdS .... Saint Mary's College, Notre Dame, IN [*Library symbol Library of Congress*] (LCLS)

INNDX .... IDS New Dimensions Cl.A [*Mutual fund ticker symbol*] (SG)

InNea .... New Albany-Floyd County Public Library, New Albany, IN [*Library symbol Library of Congress*] (LCLS)

Inn Eas .... Innes on Easements [*8th ed.*] [*1911*] [*A publication*] (DLA)

Inn Ease ..... Innes on Easements [*8th ed.*] [*1911*] [*A publication*] (DLA)

InNeaTL .... New Albany Tribune and Ledger-Tribune, New Albany, IN [*Library symbol Library of Congress*] (LCLS)

InNeb .... Newburgh-Ohio Township Public Library, Newburgh, IN [*Library symbol Library of Congress*] (LCLS)

InNep .... Newport-Vermillion County Library, Newport, IN [*Library symbol Library of Congress*] (LCLS)

Innerdyn ...... Innerdyne, Inc. [*Associated Press*] (SAG)

Inner Gimba... Inner Gimbal [*Aerospace*] (NAKS)

Inner Glide... Inner Glideslope [*Aerospace*] (NAKS)

INNERTAP... Information Network on New and Renewable Energy Resources and Technologies for Asia and the Pacific [*UNESCO*] (DUND)

INNERV .... Innervation [*Medicine*]

Innes .... Innes' Registration of Title [*A publication*] (ILCA)

INNF .... Intermediate Naval Nuclear Forces (DOMA)

InNhvAT .... Allen County Times, New Haven, IN [*Library symbol Library of Congress*] (LCLS)

InNhW .... Workingmen's Institute, New Harmony, IN [*Library symbol*] [*Library of Congress*] (LCLS)

Innisfail Canegr... Innisfail Canegrower [*A publication*]

Innkeepr ...... Innkeepers USA Trust [*Associated Press*] (SAG)

INNKPR .... Innkeeper

INNL .... Improved Nonnuclear LANCE

INNO .... Innocente [*Innocently*] [*Music*] (ROG)

Inno .... Innovations [*Record label*]

INNO .... Innovo Group [*NASDAQ symbol*] (TTSB)

INNO .... Innovo Group, Inc. [*NASDAQ symbol*] (SAG)

InNob .... Noblesville Public Library, Noblesville, IN [*Library symbol Library of Congress*] (LCLS)

InNobL .... Noblesville Daily Ledger, Noblesville, IN [*Library symbol Library of Congress*] (LCLS)

Innodata ...... Innodata Corp. [*Associated Press*] (SAG)

InnoDev .... Innovasive Devices, Inc. [*Associated Press*] (SAG)

InNoj .... North Judson-Wayne Township Public Library, North Judson, IN [*Library symbol Library of Congress*] (LCLS)

InnoM .... Innovative Medical Services [*Associated Press*] (SAG)

InNom .... North Manchester Public Library, North Manchester, IN [*Library symbol*] [*Library of Congress*] (LCLS)

InNoman ...... North Manchester Public Library, North Manchester, IN [*Library symbol Library of Congress*] (LCLS)

InNomanC.... Manchester College, North Manchester, IN [*Library symbol Library of Congress*] (LCLS)

InNomanNJ.. North Manchester News-Journal, North Manchester, IN [*Library symbol Library of Congress*] (LCLS)

InnoMed .... Innovative Medical Services [*Associated Press*] (SAG)

InNomMC ..... Manchester College, North Manchester, IN [*Library symbol*] [*Library of Congress*] (LCLS)

InnoPet .... InnoPet Brands Corp. [*Associated Press*] (SAG)

InnoServe .... InnoServe Technologies, Inc. [*Associated Press*] (SAG)

Innotech ...... Innotech, Inc. [*Associated Press*] (SAG)

Innovex .... Innovex, Inc. [*Associated Press*] (SAG)

InnovirL .... Innovir Laboratories, Inc. [*Associated Press*] (SAG)

InNovJ .... Jennings County Public Library, North Vernon, IN [*Library symbol Library of Congress*] (LCLS)

Innovo .... Innovo Group, Inc. [*Associated Press*] (SAG)

InNovSP ...... North Vernon Sun-Plain Dealer, North Vernon, IN [*Library symbol*] [*Library of Congress*] (LCLS)

InnovT .... Innovative Tech Systems, Inc. [*Associated Press*] (SAG)

InnoVTch ..... Innovative Tech Systems, Inc. [*Associated Press*] (SAG)

Innovus .... Innovus Corp. [*Associated Press*] (SAG)

INNR .... Inner

INNS .... International Neural Network Society (EA)

Inn Sc Leg Ant... Innes' Scotch Legal Antiquities [*A publication*] (DLA)

Innvr .... Innovir Laboratories, Inc. [*Associated Press*] (SAG)

INNVTN .... Innovation

INNVTV .... Innovative

INO .... Inongo [*Zaire*] [*Airport symbol*] (OAG)

Ino .... Inosine [*Also, I*] [*A nucleoside*]

INO .... Inosine (DMAA)

INO .... Inspector of Naval Ordnance [*British*]

INO .... Institute for Naval Oceanography [*Bay St. Louis, MS*] [*Navy*]

INO .... Internuclear Ophthalmoplegia

INO .... Inter-Oceanic Resources Ltd. [*Formerly, Inter-Oceanic Oil & Gas*] [*Vancouver Stock Exchange symbol*]

INO .... Intranuclear Ophthalmolplegia [*Ophthalmology*] (DAVI)

INO .... Irish Nurses Organisation (BI)

INO .... Issue Necessary Orders

INO .... Item Number

INO .... Iterative Natural Orbital [*Atomic physics*]

INO .... Northbrook Public Library, Northbrook, IL [*OCLC symbol*] (OCLC)

INOA .... International Norton Owners' Association (EA)

INOAVNOT... If Not Available Notify This Office at Once

INOC .... Inoculation (AABC)

INOC .... Iraqi National Oil Co. [*Government company*]

INOC .... Isonicotinoyloxycarbonyl [*Medicine*] (DMAA)

InOcC .... Oakland City College, Oakland City, IN [*Library symbol Library of Congress*] (LCLS)

INOD .... Innodata Corp. [*NASDAQ symbol*] (SAG)

InOd .... Odon Winkelpeck Memorial Library, Odon, IN [*Library symbol Library of Congress*] (LCLS)

INODC .... Indian National Oceanographic Data Centre [*Information service or system*] (IID)

INODEP .... Institut Oecumenique pour le Developpement des Peuples [*Ecumenical Institute for the Development of Peoples*] [*Paris, France*] (EAIO)

InOdJ .... Odon Journal, Odon, IN [*Library symbol Library of Congress*] (LCLS)

Inodta .... Innodata Corp. [*Associated Press*] (SAG)

INODW .... Innodata Corp.Wrrt [*NASDAQ symbol*] (TTSB)

INOE .... Internacia Naturista Organizo Esperantista [*International Esperantist Organization of Naturists - IEON*] (EAIO)

IN OEDIB ..... In Oedibus [*In the House Of*] [*Latin*] (ROG)

INOF .... If Not Off (FAAC)

INok .... Nokomis Public Library, Nokomis, IL [*Library symbol Library of Congress*] (LCLS)

INokSD .... Nokomis Community Unit, School District 22, Nokomis, IL [*Library symbol Library of Congress*] (LCLS)

INol .... Northlake Public Library District, Northlake, IL [*Library symbol Library of Congress*] (LCLS)

INOP .... Inoperative

InOr .... Orleans Public Library, Orleans, IN [*Library symbol Library of Congress*] (LCLS)

INORG .... Inorganic

Inorg Chem... Inorganic Chemistry (MEC)

Inorg phos... Inorganic Phosphorus [*Medicine*] (MEDA)

InOrPE .... Orleans Progress-Examiner, Orleans, IN [*Library symbol Library of Congress*] (LCLS)

inor phos ..... Inorganic Phosphorus [*Biochemistry*] (DAVI)

iNOS .... Inducible Nitric Oxide Synthase [*An enzyme*]

INOS .... Isoform of Nitric Oxide Synthase [*An enzyme*]

INOSHAC ..... Indian Ocean and Southern Hemisphere Analysis Center (BARN)

InOsJ .... Osgood Journal, Osgood, IN [*Library symbol Library of Congress*] (LCLS)

InOssJ .... Ossian Journal, Ossian, IN [*Library symbol Library of Congress*] (LCLS)

Inotek .... Inotek Technologies, Inc. [*Associated Press*] (SAG)

INOV .... Association Internationale du Nouvel Objet Visuel [*International Association for New Visual Objects*] [*Paris, France*] (EAIO)

InovGme ...... Innovative Gaming Corp. [*Associated Press*] (SAG)

InOw .... Owensville Public Library, Owensville, IN [*Library symbol Library of Congress*] (LCLS)

InOwSE .... Owensville Star-Echo, Owensville, IN [*Library symbol Library of Congress*] (LCLS)

InOx .... Oxford Public Library, Oxford, IN [*Library symbol Library of Congress*] (LCLS)

InOxG .... Oxford Gazette, Oxford, IN [*Library symbol Library of Congress*] (LCLS)

IN-OZ .... Inch-Ounce

INP .... FA Naval del Peru [*ICAO designator*] (FAAC)

INP .... If Not Possible (FAAC)

INP .... Independent Network Processor [*Computer science*] (CIST)

INP .... Indiana, PA [*Location identifier FAA*] (FAAL)

INP .... Indium Phosphide [*Inorganic chemistry*] (IAA)

InP .... Indium Phosphide (AAEL)

INP .... Inert Nitrogen Protection (IEEE)

INP .... Information-Need-Product [*Sales technique*]

INP .... Initial Program Load [*Computer science*]

INP .... In Pace [*In Peace*] [*Latin*]

INP .... Input (MSA)

INP .... Insulator Nose Projection [*Automotive spark plugs*]

INP .... Integrated Network Processor

INP .... Intelligent Network Processor

INP .... International News Photo

INP .... Internet Nodal Processor [*Computer science*] (ACRL)

INP .... Inter-Net Predicts (MCD)

INPA .... International Newspaper Promotion Association (EA)

InPa .... Paoli Public Library, Paoli, IN [*Library symbol Library of Congress*] (LCLS)

INPADOC ..... INKA Patent Documentation (NITA)
INPADOC ..... International Patent Documentation Center [*Information service or system*] (IID)
InPaN .... Paoli News, Paoli, IN [*Library symbol Library of Congress*] (LCLS)
InPaR........... Paoli Republican, Paoli, IN [*Library symbol Library of Congress*] (LCLS)
INPB .... Irish National Pipe Band
INPBM .... Information Not Provided by Manufacturer
INPC .... Irish National Petroleum Corp.
INPC .... Irish National Productivity Committee (BI)
INPC .... Isopropyl Phenylcarbamate [*Also, IPC, IPPC*] [*Herbicide*]
InPen........... Pendleton and Fall Creek Township Public Library, Pendleton, IN [*Library symbol Library of Congress*] (LCLS)
InPenT......... Pendleton Times, Pendleton, IN [*Library symbol Library of Congress*] (LCLS)
InPer........... Peru and Miami County Public Library, Peru, IN [*Library symbol Library of Congress*] (LCLS)
InPerM......... Miami County Historical Museum, Peru, IN [*Library symbol Library of Congress*] (LCLS)
InPerT.......... Peru Tribune, Peru, IN [*Library symbol Library of Congress*] (LCLS)
InPet........... Barrett Memorial Library, Petersburg, IN [*Library symbol Library of Congress*] (LCLS)
InPetPD .... Petersburg Press-Dispatch, Petersburg, IN [*Library symbol Library of Congress*] (LCLS)
INPEX .... International Postage Stamp Exhibition
INPFC .... International North Pacific Fisheries Commission (EA)
INPFC-US ... International North Pacific Fisheries Commission, United States Section
INPFL........... Independent National Patriotic Front of Liberia [*Political party*] (EY)
IN PH........... Indian Pharmacopoeia [*A publication*] (ROG)
INPH .... Interphase Corp. [*NASDAQ symbol*] (SAG)
INPH .... Interphone
INPH .... Iproniazid Phosphate [*Organic chemistry*]
INPHO......... Information Network for Public Health Officials [*CDC*]
InPHO .... International Photographic Historical Organization (EA)
Inphynet ...... Inphynet Medical Management [*Associated Press*] (SAG)
INPI .... Institut National de la Propriete Industrielle [*National Institute for Industrial Property*] [*France Information service or system*] (IID)
InPi .... Pierceton and Washington Township Library, Pierceton, IN [*Library symbol Library of Congress*] (LCLS)
INPI 1 .... INPI Database 1 [*Database on French patents*] (NITA)
INPI 2 .... INPI Database 2 [*Database on European patents*] (NITA)
InPla........... Plainfield Public Library, Plainfield, IN [*Library symbol Library of Congress*] (LCLS)
InPla-Hi .... Plainfield Public Library, Guilford Township and Hendricks County Historical Collection, Plainfield, IN [*Library symbol Library of Congress*] (LCLS)
InPly .... Plymouth Public Library, Plymouth, IN [*Library symbol Library of Congress*] (LCLS)
InPlyHi........ Marshall County Historical Society Library, Plymouth, IN [*Library symbol Library of Congress*] (LCLS)
INPM .... Integrated Network and Premise Management [*MUX Lab*]
INPO .... Institute for Nonprofit Organizations
INPO .... Institute of Nuclear Power Operations (EA)
INPOLSE...... International Police Services
InPorP .... Portage Press, Portage, IN [*Library symbol Library of Congress*] (LCLS)
InPorS .... Portage Township Schools, Portage, IN [*Library symbol Library of Congress*] (LCLS)
InPosN........ Posey County News, Poseyville, IN [*Library symbol Library of Congress*] (LCLS)
INPOWER .... Independent Power Generation Conference and Exhibition [*British*] (ITD)
IN PR........... In Principio [*In the Beginning*] [*Latin*] (ROG)
INPR .... Inprise Corp. [*NASDAQ symbol*] [*Formerly, Borland International*]
INPR .... In Progress
INPR .... Institute for Natural Products Research [*University of Georgia*] [*Research center*] (RCD)
INPr .... Integon Cp $3.875 Cv Pfd [*NYSE symbol*] (TTSB)
InPr........... Princeton Public Library, Princeton, IN [*Library symbol Library of Congress*] (LCLS)
INPRA......... International Public Relations Association
INPRC......... Item Name Policy Review Committee [*DoD Washington, DC*] (EGAO)
InPrC .... Princeton Daily Clarion, Princeton, IN [*Library symbol Library of Congress*] (LCLS)
INPRIS........ Investment Promotion Information System [*UNIDO*] [*United Nations*] (DUND)
INPRODE ..... Instituto Profesional para el Desarrollo [*Professional Development Institute*] [*Colombia*]
INPRONS...... Information Processing in the Central Nervous System
INPS .... Istituto Nazionale della Previdenza Sociale [*Italy*] (ECON)
IN-PT .... Inpatient [*Medicine*] (DAVI)
INPT........... In Port [*Navy*] (NVT)
INPT........... Input [*Amateur radio shorthand*] (WDAA)
InPtIC......... Jay County Commercial Review, Portland, IN [*Library symbol Library of Congress*] (LCLS)
InPtICR .... Jay County Recorder's Office, Portland, IN [*Library symbol Library of Congress*] (LCLS)
INPUFF........ Gaussian Puff Dispersion Model (COE)
IN PULM...... In Pulmento [*In Gruel*] [*Pharmacy*]
INPUT......... Induced Pulse Transient (PDAA)
INPUT......... International Public Television [*An association*] (NTCM)
InputOut....... Input Output, Inc. [*Associated Press*] (SAG)
INPV .... Intermittent Negative-Pressure Ventilation [*Medicine*]
INQ .... Index of Nutritional Quality

INQ .... Inferior Nasal Quadrant [*Medicine*] (STED)
INQ .... Inquire (ECII)
inq .... Inquiry (WDMC)
INQ .... Inquiry (AFM)
INQ .... Intercontinental Venture [*Vancouver Stock Exchange symbol*]
INQ .... Interior Nasal Quadrant [*Medicine*] (DMAA)
inq .... Query (WDMC)
inq .... Question (WDMC)
INQD .... Inquired (ROG)
INQ PM....... Inquisitio Post-Mortem [*Latin*] (ROG)
IN QRS .... In Quires [*Publishing*] (DGA)
INQSTV ...... Inquisitive
INQT .... Inquest (ROG)
INQUA......... International Union for Quaternary Research [*Research center France*] (IRC)
INQY .... Inquiry (ROG)
INR .... Bureau of Intelligence and Research [*Department of State*]
INR .... Image Navigation and Registration (GAVI)
INR .... Impact Noise Rating [*of insulation*]
INR .... Inertial Reference (MCD)
INR .... Inner (MSA)
INR .... Institute of Natural Resources [*University of Georgia*] [*Research center*] (RCD)
INR .... Institute of Natural Resources [*Montana State University*] [*Research center*] (RCD)
INR .... Institute of Nuclear Research [*Poland*]
INR .... Institut National de Radiodiffusion [*Belgium*]
INR .... Intelligence and Research (DNAB)
INR .... Interaction Resources Ltd. [*Toronto Stock Exchange symbol*]
INR .... Inter Air AB [*Sweden ICAO designator*] (FAAC)
INR .... Interference-to-Noise Ratio
INR .... International Normalized Ratio [*Hematology*]
INR .... Morrisson-Reeves Public Library, Richmond, IN [*OCLC symbol*] (OCLC)
INRA .... Individual Nonrecurrence Action (SAA)
INRA .... Inland Navigational Rules Act of 1980
INRA .... Institut National de la Recherche Agronomique (NITA)
INRA .... International Network for Religion and Animals (EA)
INRAC .... Immigration Nursing Relief Advisory Committee [*Department of Labor*] (EGAO)
INRAD .... Interactive Real-Time Advanced Display
INRC .... Indian Nation Restoration Committee
INRC .... Innovative Naval Reserve Concept (DOMA)
InRCS .... Richmond Community School, Richmond, IN [*Library symbol Library of Congress*] (LCLS)
INRCTN....... Interaction
InRE .... Earlham College, Richmond, IN [*Library symbol Library of Congress*] (LCLS)
IN RE........... In Regard To
IN REF......... In Reference To
INREM .... Internal REM [*Roentgen-Equivalent-Man*] [*Radiation dose*]
InRem.......... Remington Carpenter Township Public Library, Remington, IN [*Library symbol Library of Congress*] (LCLS)
InRen.......... Jasper County Public Library, Rensselaer, IN [*Library symbol Library of Congress*] (LCLS)
InRenS......... Saint Joseph's College, Rensselaer, IN [*Library symbol Library of Congress*] (LCLS)
INREP .... Installation Damage Report [*Air Force*]
INREPL........ Incoming Replacement [*Army*] (AABC)
INREQ......... Information on Request (MCD)
INREQ......... Information Request (COE)
INREQ......... Information Requested
INREQS........ Information Requests [*Army*] (AABC)
INRES .... Independent Reservation System [*Hotels and motels*]
INREX .... Investors Research [*Mutual fund ticker symbol*] (SG)
INRF .... International Nutrition Research Foundation (EA)
INRH .... Institut National de Recherches en Hydrologie [*National Hydrology Research Institute*] [*Canada*]
INRI .... Iesus Nazarenus Rex Iudaeorum [*Jesus of Nazareth, King of the Jews*] [*Latin*]
INRI .... Imperator Napoleon Rex Italiae [*Emperor Napoleon, King of Italy*] [*Latin*]
INRIA........... Institut National de Recherche en Informatique et en Automatique [*National Institute for Research in Informatics and Automation*] [*Research center and database originator*] [*France Information service or system*] (IID)
InRid........... Ridgeville Public Library, Ridgeville, IN [*Library symbol Library of Congress*] (LCLS)
InRis........... Ohio County Public Library, Rising Sun, IN [*Library symbol Library of Congress*] (LCLS)
InRisCN .... Ohio County News, Rising Sun, IN [*Library symbol Library of Congress*] (LCLS)
InRisCR .... Ohio County Recorder's Office, Rising Sun, IN [*Library symbol Library of Congress*] (LCLS)
InRisHi .... Ohio County Historical Society, Rising Sun, IN [*Library symbol Library of Congress*] (LCLS)
InRisR .... Rising Sun Recorder, Rising Sun, IN [*Library symbol Library of Congress*] (LCLS)
InRM........... Morrison-Reeves Public Library, Richmond, IN [*Library symbol Library of Congress*] (LCLS)
InRM........... Wayne Township Library, Richmond, IN [*Library symbol*] [*Library of Congress*] (LCLS)
INRO .... International Natural Rubber Organization [*Kuala Lumpur, Malaysia*] (EAIO)
INRO .... International Naval Research Organization (EA)

InRo............ Roachdale Public Library, Roachdale, IN [*Library symbol Library of Congress*] (LCLS)
InRoa.......... Roanoke Public Library, Roanoke, IN [*Library symbol Library of Congress*] (LCLS)
InRoc........... Fulton County Public Library, Rochester, IN [*Library symbol Library of Congress*] (LCLS)
InRocCR....... Fulton County Recorder's Office, Rochester, IN [*Library symbol Library of Congress*] (LCLS)
InRocFHi..... Fulton County Historical Society, Rochester, IN [*Library symbol Library of Congress*] (LCLS)
InRocS......... Rochester Sentinel, Rochester, IN [*Library symbol Library of Congress*] (LCLS)
InRomS........ Gene Stratton-Porter Memorial, Rome City, IN [*Library symbol Library of Congress*] (LCLS)
InRoyR........ Royal Center Record, Royal Center, IN [*Library symbol Library of Congress*] (LCLS)
InRPI........... Richmond Palladium-Item, Richmond, IN [*Library symbol Library of Congress*] (LCLS)
InRpt........... Rockport-Ohio Township Public Library, Rockport, IN [*Library symbol Library of Congress*] (LCLS)
InRptD......... Rockport Democrat, Rockport, IN [*Library symbol Library of Congress*] (LCLS)
InRptJ......... Rockport Journal, Rockport, IN [*Library symbol Library of Congress*] (LCLS)
INRS............ Institut National de la Recherche Scientifique [*National Institute for Scientific Research*] [*Canada Research center*]
INRS............ Intranet Solutions, Inc. [*NASDAQ symbol*] (SAG)
INRT............ Inertia (KSC)
INRTFLR...... Inert Filler
INRTG.......... Inert Gas
INRTL.......... Inertial (MSA)
INRTLVEL.... Inertial Velocity (MCD)
InRusCR...... Rush County Recorder's Office, Rushville, IN [*Library symbol Library of Congress*] (LCLS)
InRusR......... Rushville Republican, Rushville, IN [*Library symbol Library of Congress*] (LCLS)
InRv............. Rockville Public Library, Rockville, IN [*Library symbol Library of Congress*] (LCLS)
InRvCR........ Parke County Recorder's Office, Rockville, IN [*Library symbol Library of Congress*] (LCLS)
INS............... Idiopathic Nephrotic Syndrome
INS............... Illinois State University, Normal, IL [*Library symbol Library of Congress*] (LCLS)
INS............... Immigration and Naturalization Service [*Department of Justice*]
INS............... Improved Navigational Satellite
INS............... Improved Night Sight
INS............... Inches (EY)
ins................ Inches (ODBW)
IN/S............ Inches per Second
INS............... Independent News Service [*In TV series "The Night Stalker"*]
INS............... Indian Springs, NV [*Location identifier FAA*] (FAAL)
INS............... Indiopahtic Nephrotic Syndrome [*Nephrology*] (DAVI)
INS............... Inelastic Neutron Scattering
INS............... Inertial Navigation Sensor (IAA)
INS............... Inertial Navigation System [*Aviation*]
INS............... Information Network System [*Japan*]
INS............... Information Systems (KSC)
INS............... Initial Navigation System (AABC)
INS............... Inlet Resources Ltd. [*Vancouver Stock Exchange symbol*]
Ins............... Inositol [*Biochemistry*]
INS............... Inrealistic Neutron Scattering [*Physics*]
INS............... Insane (ROG)
INS............... Inscribed
ins............... Inscriber [*MARC relator code*] [*Library of Congress*] (LCCP)
INS............... Inscription (ADA)
INS............... Insect
INS............... Insert (NVT)
ins............... Insertion (STED)
INS............... Insertion Burn [*Orbital Maneuvering Subsystem 1*] [*NASA*] (NASA)
INS............... Insertion Mutation [*Genetics*]
INS............... Insert Shot [*Film production*] (NTCM)
INS............... Inside (MSA)
INS............... In Situ [*In Place*] [*Latin*] (ADA)
Ins............... Insolvency [*Legal term*] (DLA)
INS............... Inspection Division [*Coast Guard*]
INS............... Inspector
INS............... Installation Squadron
ins............... Instant (VRA)
INS............... Institute for Naval Studies
INS............... Institute for Nuclear Study [*Japan*]
INS............... Institute of Neurological Science [*University of Pennsylvania*]
INS............... Institute of Nuclear Studies [*Oak Ridge, TN*]
INS............... Institutional Net Settlements (NUMA)
INS............... Insular
INS............... Insulate
Ins............... Insulin [*Endocrinology*] (DAVI)
INS............... Insulin (STED)
INS............... Insurance (AFM)
Ins............... Insurance (EBF)
ins............... Insurance (ODBW)
ins............... Insurance (WDAA)
INS............... Insure
Ins............... Insured (EBF)
ins............... Insured (STED)
INS............... Integrated Navigation System

INS............... Integrated Network Systems, Inc.
INS............... Integrated Nitrogen System (SSD)
INS............... Intelligent Systems Corp. [*AMEX symbol*] (SPSG)
INS............... Interceptor Simulator (SAA)
INS............... Interchangeable-Substitute Items (AAG)
INS............... Internal Navigation System
INS............... International Navigation System
INS............... International Network for Self-Reliance (EA)
INS............... International Network Service [*Mercury*] [*British*] (TELE)
INS............... International Neuropsychological Society (NTPA)
INS............... International News Service [*Later, UPI*]
INS............... International Numismatic Society (EAIO)
INS............... International Seaway Trading Corp. (MHDW)
I-NS............ Inter-Nation Simulation [*Simulation of international relations*]
INS............... Interstation Noise Suppression
INS............... Intravenous Nurses Society (EA)
INS............... Ion-Neutralization Spectroscopy
INS............... Iron Nickel System
INS............... Iron Soldering
INS............... Isolated Neutron Star [*Astrophysics*]
INS............... Israel Naval Ship (BJA)
INS............... Israel News Service (BJA)
INS............... Northern Illinois Library System, Rockford, IL [*OCLC symbol*] (OCLC)
InS............... South Bend Public Library, South Bend, IN [*Library symbol Library of Congress*] (LCLS)
INSA............ Institut National de Systematique Appliquee [*Canada*]
INSA............ International Naples Sabot Association (EA)
INSA............ International Shipowners' Association [*See also MAS*] [*Gdynia, Poland*] (EAIO)
InSa............ Salem Public Library, Salem, IN [*Library symbol Library of Congress*] (LCLS)
INS AB........ Insulin Antibody [*Endocrinology*] (DAVI)
INS Ab........ Insulin Antibody [*Medicine*] (STED)
INSAB.......... International Numismatic Society Authentication Bureau (EA)
INSAC.......... Interstate Airways Communications (IAA)
InSaCR........ Washington County Recorder's Office, Salem, IN [*Library symbol Library of Congress*] (LCLS)
INSACS........ Interstate Airways Communications Station
INSAG.......... International Nuclear Safety Advisory Group [*United Nations*] (EY)
INSAIR......... Inspector of Naval Aircraft
InSaLD......... Salem Leader/Democrat, Salem, IN [*Library symbol Library of Congress*] (LCLS)
INSAR.......... Instruction Address Register [*Computer science*]
InSAR.......... Interferometric Synthetic Aperture RADAR [*Imaging system*]
INSAT.......... Indian Geostationary Satellite [*Marine science*] (OSRA)
INSAT.......... Indian National Satellite System [*Bangalore, India*] [*Telecommunications*]
INSAT.......... Indian Satellite (USDC)
INSAT.......... India Satellite [*Telecommunications*] (NITA)
INSATRAC... Interception with Satellite Tracking
InsAut......... Insurance Auto Auctions [*Associated Press*] (SAG)
INSAV.......... Interim Shipboard Availability (MCD)
InSaWHi..... Washington County Historical Society, Salem, IN [*Library symbol Library of Congress*] (LCLS)
InSb............ Indium Antimonide (AAEL)
INSB............ Intelligence and Security Board [*Army*] (RDA)
In-SC........... Indiana State Supreme Court, Law Library, Indianapolis, IN [*Library symbol Library of Congress*] (LCLS)
INSC............ Inscribed [*or Inscription*] (MSA)
INSC............ Insulating Concrete [*Technical drawings*]
Ins C........... Insurance Code [*A publication*] (DLA)
INSC............ Internal Shape Components (CINC)
InSc............ Scott County Public Library, Scottsburg, IN [*Library symbol Library of Congress*] (LCLS)
INSCA.......... International Natural Sausage Casing Association (EA)
INSCAIRS.... Instrumentation Calibration Incident Repair Service
INSCE.......... Insurance
in sched...... In Schedula [*On a Herbarium Sheet*] [*Latin*] (EES)
Inschr.......... Inschrift (BJA)
INSCI........... Information Science, Inc. [*Information service or system*] (IID)
Insci............ Insci Corp. [*Associated Press*] (SAG)
INSCO.......... Intercontinental Shipping Corp. (MHDW)
INSCOM...... Intelligence and Security Command [*Army*] (RDA)
INSCOPE..... Information System for Coffee and Other Product Economics [*International Coffee Organization*] (NITA)
Ins Couns J... Insurance Counsel Journal [*A publication*] (DLA)
INSCR.......... Inscription
inscr............ Inscription (VRA)
INSCR.......... Insecure
INSCRPTN... Inscription
INSCRUIT.... Inspector of Navy Recruiting and Naval Officer Procurement
INSD............ Insured
INS Data Base... United States International Air Travel Statistics Data Base [*I. P. Sharp Associates*] [*Canada*] (NITA)
INSDC.......... Indian National Scientific Documentation Centre [*New Delhi*]
INSDEN........ Inspector of Dental Activities
INSDOC........ Indian National Scientific Documentation Centre [*Council of Scientific and Industrial Research*]
Insd Val...... Insured Value [*Business term*] (MHDB)
INSEA.......... International Society for Education through Art [*Corsham, England*]
INSEAD........ Institut Europeen d'Administration des Affaires [*European Business Management Institute*] [*France*] (PDAA)
IN/SEC........ Inches per Second (WDAA)
INSEC.......... Internal Security
INSECTI....... Insecticide(s) [*Freight*]

INSEE.......... Institut National de la Statistique et des Etudes Economiques [*National Institute of Statistics and Economic Research*] [*Paris, France*]

InSelS.......... Sellersburg Star, Sellersburg, IN [*Library symbol Library of Congress*] (LCLS)

INSEM .... Insemination

insem .... Insemination [*Medicine*] (STED)

INSENG........ Inspector of Naval Engineering

INSEP .... Inseparable (MSA)

INSERM....... Institut National de la Sante et de la Recherche Medicale [*National Institute for Health and Medical Research*] [*France Information service or system*] (IID)

Insertion B... Insertion Burn [*Aerospace*] (NAKS)

INSERV....... In Service [*Military*] (CAAL)

INSET.......... In-Service Education and Training [*British*] (DET)

INSET.......... In-service Education for Teachers [*Australia*]

INSET.......... In-Service Training (PDAA)

INSEX .... IDS Selective Cl.A [*Mutual fund ticker symbol*] (SG)

InSey .... Seymour Public Library, Seymour, IN [*Library symbol Library of Congress*] (LCLS)

InSeyT .... Seymour Daily Tribune, Seymour, IN [*Library symbol Library of Congress*] (LCLS)

INSF............ Insulating Fill [*Technical drawings*]

INSGCY....... Insurgency (AABC)

INSGEN....... Inspector General [*Navy*]

INSGENLANTFLT... Inspector General, Atlantic Fleet [*Navy*]

INSGENPAC... Inspector General, Pacific Fleet and Pacific Ocean Areas [*Navy*]

InsgFn......... Insignia Financial Group [*Associated Press*] (SAG)

InSghtH....... InSight Health Services Corp. [*Associated Press*] (SAG)

InsgSol .... Insignia Solutions [*Associated Press*] (SAG)

InsgtEnt ...... Insight Entertainment Corp. [*Associated Press*] (SAG)

INSGY......... Insignia Solutions [*NASDAQ symbol*] (SAG)

INSGY......... Insignia Solutions ADS [*NASDAQ symbol*] (TTSB)

INSH .... Inspection Shell

InShe .... Shelbyville-Shelby County Public Library, Shelbyville, IN [*Library symbol Library of Congress*] (LCLS)

InSheCR ...... Shelby County Recorder's Office, Shelbyville, IN [*Library symbol Library of Congress*] (LCLS)

InSheN........ Shelbyville News, Shelbyville, IN [*Library symbol Library of Congress*] (LCLS)

InSherN ...... Sheridan News, Sheridan, IN [*Library symbol Library of Congress*] (LCLS)

InSho .... Shoals Public Library, Shoals, IN [*Library symbol Library of Congress*] (LCLS)

InShoD........ Martin County Democrat, Shoals, IN [*Library symbol Library of Congress*] (LCLS)

InShoHi....... Martin County Historical Society, Shoals, IN [*Library symbol Library of Congress*] (LCLS)

InShoN........ Shoals News, Shoals, IN [*Library symbol Library of Congress*] (LCLS)

INSHOREPAT... Inshore Patrol

INSHORUNSEAWARGRU... Inshore Undersea Warfare Group [*Navy*]

INSI .... INSCI Corp. [*NASDAQ symbol*] (TTSB)

insid .... Insidious (STED)

Inside Diam... Inside Diameter (NAKS)

Insight .... Insight Enterprises, Inc. [*Associated Press*] (SAG)

INSIGHT....... Interactive System for Investigation by Graphics of Hydrological Trends (PDAA)

Insignia ...... Insignia Systems, Inc. [*Associated Press*] (SAG)

Insilco .... Insilco Corp. [*Associated Press*] (SAG)

INSILCO ...... International Silver Co. [*Acronym now used as firm's name*]

InSIN .... Indianapolis Star and News, Indianapolis, IN [*Library symbol*] [*Library of Congress*] (LCLS)

INSINSTR .... Inspector-Instructor, Naval Reserve

INSIS .... Inter-Institutional Integrated Services Information System

INSITE .... Information on Nuclear Site Data System [*Nuclear Regulatory Commission*] (GFGA)

InsitE .... Insituform East, Inc. [*Associated Press*] (SAG)

INSITE .... Institutional Space Inventory Technique [*Computer science*]

INSITE .... Integrated Sensor Interpretation Techniques

InSiteVis...... InSite Vision, Inc. [*Associated Press*] (SAG)

InsitTc........ Insituform Technology [*Associated Press*] (SAG)

in situ .... In Place (DOG)

INSIU .... Insci Corp. [*NASDAQ symbol*] (SAG)

INSIW .... INSCI Corp.Wrrt [*NASDAQ symbol*] (TTSB)

Ins key........ Insert Key [*Computer science*]

INSL............ Insilco Crop. [*NASDAQ symbol*] (SAG)

INSL .... Insulate

InSL .... South Bend Public Library, South Bend, IN [*Library symbol*] [*Library of Congress*] (LCLS)

INSLAW ...... Institute for Law and Social Research (IID)

Ins Liability Rep... Insurance Liability Reports [*A publication*] (DLA)

Ins LR......... Insurance Law Reporter [*A publication*] (DLA)

Ins L Rep..... Insurance Law Reporter [*A publication*] (DLA)

INSLTD .... Insulated

INSLTN .... Insulation

INSLUG....... Insulating

INSM .... Insituform Mid-America, Inc. [*NASDAQ symbol*] (NQ)

INSMACH..... Inspector of Naval Machinery

INSMARSAT... International Maritime Satellite [*Organization*] (DOMA)

INSMAT ...... Inspector of Naval Material

INSMAT ...... Material Inspection Service [*Navy*] (AAGC)

INSMAT PET... Inspector of Naval Material, Petroleum

INSMATS..... Inspectors of Naval Material (AAGC)

Ins Mon....... Insurance Monitor [*A publication*] (DLA)

InsMuni ...... Insured Municipal Income Fund [*Associated Press*] (SAG)

INSNA......... International Network for Social Network Analysis [*University of Toronto*] [*Toronto, ON*] (EAIO)

INSNAVMAT... Inspector of Navigational Material

InSNHi........ Northern Indiana State Historical Society, South Bend, IN [*Library symbol Library of Congress*] (LCLS)

INSO .... InfoSoft International, Inc. [*NASDAQ symbol*] (SAG)

INSO .... INSO Corp. [*Associated Press*] (SAG)

INSO .... INSO Corp. [*NASDAQ symbol*] (SAG)

INSOL .... Insoluble (MSA)

insol .... Insoluble (STED)

INSOLT .... I've Never Seen One Like That [*Antiques market*]

Insolv......... Insolvency [*Legal term*] (DLA)

INSOLV....... Insolvent [*Legal term*] (ADA)

INSOLVT ..... Insolvent (ROG)

INSORD ...... Inspector of Ordnance

INSORDINC... Inspector of Ordnance in Charge

InSow .... South Whitley Cleveland Township Public Library, South Whitley, IN [*Library symbol Library of Congress*] (LCLS)

InSowTN ..... South Whitley Tribune-News, South Whitley, IN [*Library symbol Library of Congress*] (LCLS)

INSP .... Inspect [*or Inspector*] (AFM)

Insp .... Inspection (STED)

Insp .... Inspector (TBD)

Insp .... Inspiration (STED)

INSP .... Inspiration

INSP .... Internet Name Server Protocol (TNIG)

InSp .... Speedway Public Library, Speedway, IN [*Library symbol Library of Congress*] (LCLS)

INSPAT .... Inshore Patrol

INSPCTN ..... Inspection

INSPCTR ..... Inspector

InSpe .... Spencer Public-Owen County Contractual Library, Spencer, IN [*Library symbol Library of Congress*] (LCLS)

INSPEC .... Information Service: Physics, Electrical and Electronics, and Computers and Con trol [*Information service*] [*British*] (NITA)

INSPEC .... Information Services in Physics, Electronics, and Computers [*Information service or system*]

INSPEC .... Initial Specialty [*Military*] (INF)

INSPEC .... Inspection

INSPEC .... International Information Services for the Physics and Engineering Communities

Inspector Gen Rep... Inspector General Reports (AAGC)

INSPEL .... International Newsletter of Special Libraries [*A publication*]

INSPETRES... Inspector of Petroleum Reserves

InSpeW....... Spencer Evening World, Spencer, IN [*Library symbol Library of Congress*] (LCLS)

INSPEX .... International Measurement and Inspection Technology Exposition

Insp Gen...... Inspector General (WGA)

INSPINSTF... Inspector-Instructor Staff [*Military*] (DNAB)

INSP-INSTR... Inspector-Instruction [*Marine Corps*]

inspir .... Inspiration [*or Inspiratory*] (CPH)

INSPIR........ Inspiretur [*Let It Be Inspired*] [*Pharmacy*]

INSPIRE...... Indiana Spectrum of Information Resources

INSPIRE...... Institute for Public Interest Representation [*Later, CCCIPR*] [*Georgetown University*]

INSP L........ Inspection Laws (DLA)

INSPON....... Inspection (ROG)

INSPR.......... Inspector

INSPR.......... Intelligence Systems Program Review [*Military*] (MCD)

INSP W & M... Inspector of Weights and Measures [*British*] (ROG)

INSR .... Insert (MSA)

INSR .... Insulin Receptor [*Medicine*] (DMAA)

INSRADMAT... Inspector of Radio Material

Ins Rep....... Insurance Reporter [*A publication*] (DLA)

INSRP......... Inter-Agency Network Safety Review Panel [*NASA*] (NASA)

INSRP......... Interagency Nuclear Safety Review Pane (USDC)

INSRP......... Interagency Nuclear Safety Review Panel

InSrvAm...... Industrial Services of America, Inc. [*Associated Press*] (SAG)

INSS .... International Network Services [*NASDAQ symbol*] (SAG)

INSS .... International Neuroblastoma Staging System [*Medicine*] (DMAA)

INSSCC....... Interim National Space Surveillance Control Center

Inst .... Coke's Institutes [*England*] [*A publication*] (DLA)

INST........... Customs and Excise Institutions List [*Database*] (IID)

INST........... In Nomine Sanctae Trinitatis [*In the Name of the Holy Trinity*] [*Latin*]

INST........... Insert Screw Thread

INST........... Installed

INST........... Installment [*Business term*]

Inst .... Installment (EBF)

INST........... Instans [*The Current Month*] [*Latin*]

INST........... Instant

Inst .... Instant [*Of the present month*] [*Business term*] (EBF)

INST........... Instantaneous (MSA)

INST........... Institute [*or Institution*] (AFM)

Inst .... Institutes of England, in Two Parts, or A Commentary upon Littleton by Sir Edward Coke [*A publication*] (DLA)

inst .... Institution (VRA)

Inst .... Institution (AL)

Inst .... Institutional (AL)

Inst .... Institutio Oratoria [*of Quintilian*] [*Classical studies*] (OCD)

INST........... Instruction [*or Instructor*] (AFM)

Inst .... Instructor [*A publication*] (BRI)

INST........... Instrument (AAG)

Inst .... Instrument (EBF)

INST........... Instrumental Delivery [*Obstetrics*] (DAVI)

INST............	International Numbering System for Tides (MSC)
INST............	IPI, Inc. [*NASDAQ symbol*] (SAG)
Inst	Justinian's Institutes [*A publication*] (DLA)
INST............	Revenue Canada - Customs and Excise Institutions List [*Revenue Canada - Customs and Excise*] [*Information service or system*] (CRD)
InST............	South Bend Tribune, South Bend, IN [*Library symbol Library of Congress*] (LCLS)
INSTA	Instruments Authorized (FAAC)
INSTA	Inter-Nordic Standardization
INSTA	Interstate (FAAC)
INSTAAR......	Institute of Arctic and Alpine Research [*University of Colorado*]
INSTAB	Information Service on Toxicity and Biodegradability [*Water Pollution Research Laboratory*] [*British*] (IID)
InstAct	Institute of Actuaries [*British*]
INSTAD	Institute for Training and Development
Inst Ad Legal Stud Ann...	Institute of Advanced Legal Studies. Annals [*A publication*] (DLA)
INSTAL	Installation
Installatio	Installation Notification Certificate (NAKS)
INSTALLN ...	Installation
INSTAR	Inertialess Scanning, Tracking, and Ranging
INSTARS......	Information Storage and Retrieval System [*Computer science*]
in stat pup ...	In Statu Pupillari [*Subject to the Rule of the Institution*] [*Latin*] (BARN)
Inst BE........	Institution of British Engineers
INSTBY	Instability (FAAC)
InstCES	Institution of Civil Engineering Surveyors (DAC)
Inst Cler	Instructor Clericalis (DLA)
Inst Com Com...	Interstate Commerce Commission Reports [*A publication*] (DLA)
INST/COMM...	Instrumentation and Communication (MCD)
INSTCTL......	Instrumentation and Control [*Aerospace*] (IAA)
INSTD	Instead (ROG)
InstD	Institute of Directors [*British*]
InstDokAB....	Institutionendokumentation zur Arbeitsmarkt- und Berufsforschung [*Database*] [*Institut fuer Arbeitsmarkt- und Berufsforschung der Bundesanstalt fuer Arbeit*] [*German*] [*Information service or system*] (CRD)
INSTEAD	Information Service on Technological Alternatives for Development [*ILO*] [*United Nations*] (DUND)
INSTEAD	International Student, Trade, Environment and Development Program (CROSS)
INSTEE........	Institution of Electrical Engineers (IAA)
Insteel	Insteel Industries, Inc. [*Associated Press*] (SAG)
InStent	Instent, Inc. [*Associated Press*] (SAG)
INSTEP	Indian Steel Training and Education Program [*India*]
INSTEP	In-Service Training and Education Panel (AIE)
Inst Epil.......	Epilogue to (a Designated Part or Volume of) Coke's Institutes [*A publication*] (DLA)
InstF...........	Institute of Fuel [*British*]
Inst Fed Tax...	Institute on Federal Taxation (DLA)
INSTFLTNG...	Instrument Flight Training (NVT)
INSTFURASPERS...	Instruction and Further Assignment by Commander, Naval Military Personnel Command (DNAB)
Insti	Institutes of Justinian [*Roman law*] [*A publication*] (DSA)
INSTIA	Instituto Internacional de Andragogia [*International Institute of Andragogy - IIA*] (EAIO)
INSTILL........	Instillandus [*To Be Dropped In*] [*Pharmacy*]
INSTINET	Institutional Networks Corp.
Institutes	Institutes of Justinian [*Roman law*] [*A publication*] (DLA)
Inst Iust	Institutiones Iustiniani [*Classical studies*] (OCD)
InStjN	Saint Joe News, Saint Joe, IN [*Library symbol Library of Congress*] (LCLS)
Inst Jur Angl...	Institutiones Juris Anglicani, by Cowell [*A publication*] (DLA)
INSTL..........	Installation (AFM)
instl	Installation (VRA)
INSTL..........	Installment
Instl	Installment [*Banking*] (TBD)
Inst Lab Rel Bull...	Institute for Labor Relations. Bulletin [*A publication*] (DLA)
INSTL & C/O...	Installation and Checkout (NASA)
Instl LO........	Installment Loan Officer [*Banking*] (TBD)
INSTLLR	Installer
INSTLN........	Installation
INSTLR	Installer
INSTLTN	Installation
INSTM	Instrumentation (MSA)
InStmaS.......	St. Mary-Of-The-Woods College, St. Mary-Of-The-Woods, IN [*Library symbol Library of Congress*] (LCLS)
INSTMC	Institute of Measurement and Control [*British*] (EAIO)
INST ME	Institute of Mechanical Engineers [*British*] (WDAA)
Inst M E.......	Institute of Media Executives [*British*]
InStme	St. Meinrad College and Seminary, St. Meinrad, IN [*Library symbol Library of Congress*] (LCLS)
InstMet	Institute of Metals [*British*]
Inst MM	Institution of Mining and Metallurgy (BARN)
INSTMN	Instrumentation
INSTMNS.....	Instrumentation Squadron [*Military*]
INSTMT........	Instrument (WGA)
INSTN	Institution
INSTN	Instruction [*Computer science*] (TEL)
INSTN	Instrumentation (MUGU)
InSTN	Tri-County News, South Bend, IN [*Library symbol Library of Congress*] (LCLS)
Inst NA	Institution of Naval Architects (BARN)
INSTNL.........	Institutional
INSTNS........	Institutions (ROG)
INSTNS........	Instructions
INSTNT........	Instant
Inst on Plan Zoning & Eminent Domain...	Institute on Planning, Zoning, and Eminent Domain. Proceedings [*Southwestern Legal Foundation*] (DLA)
Inst on Priv Inv & Inv Abroad...	Institute on Private Investments and Investors Abroad. Proceedings [*A publication*] (DLA)
INSTOP........	Instrument or on-Top-of-Clouds Authorized
INST P	Institute of Physics [*British*] (WDAA)
Inst Plan & Zoning...	Institute on Planning, Zoning, and Eminent Domain. Proceedings [*A publication*] (DLA)
Inst Plan Zoning & ED...	Institute on Planning, Zoning, and Eminent Domain. Proceedings [*A publication*] (DLA)
INSTPN........	Instrument Panel
Inst Proem...	Proeme [*Introduction to Coke's Institutes*] [*A publication*] (DLA)
InstPS	Institute of Purchasing and Supply [*British*]
InstPubl	[*The*] Instant Publishers, Inc. [*Associated Press*] (SAG)
INSTR	Instruct [*or Instructor*] (AABC)
INSTR	Instruction
Instr...........	Instruction (AL)
Instr...........	Instructional (AL)
Instr...........	Instructor (AL)
instr...........	Instrument (VRA)
INSTR	Instrument
instr...........	Instrumental [*Grammar*]
INSTR	Instrumentation (NAKS)
INSTRAT	Investment Strategy [*Game*]
INSTRAW.....	International Research and Training Institute for the Advancement of Women [*Dominican Republic*] [*United Nations Research center*] (IRC)
Instr Cler	Instructor Clericalis (DLA)
INSTRCTR.....	Instructor
INSTRD	Instructed (ROG)
INSTRE........	Institute of Radio Engineers [*Later, IEEE*] (IAA)
INSTREF.......	Instrument Reference (IAA)
INSTRL........	Instructional
InstrLab	Instrumentation Laboratory SpA [*Associated Press*] (SAG)
INSTRM	Instrumented
INSTRMNTN...	Instrumentation
INSTRMT	Instrument
INSTRN	Instruction
INSTRNL......	Instructional
Instron	Instron Corp. [*Associated Press*] (SAG)
INSTRONS ...	Instructions (ROG)
INSTRPI........	Instrument Pilot Instructor [*Air Force*]
INSTRPIT	Instructor Pilot [*Air Force*]
INSTRU........	Instrumentation
INSTRUC......	Instruction
InstruCp.......	Instrumentarium Corp. [*Associated Press*] (SAG)
INSTRUCTA...	Intelligent Naval Structures Assistant
INSTRUM......	Instrumentation Subsystem [*NASA*] (NASA)
Instrumenta...	Instrumentation and Communication (NAKS)
Instrumenta...	Instrumentation Group (NAKS)
Inst Sci & Indust Bull...	Australia. Institute of Science and Industry. Bulletin [*A publication*]
Inst Sec Reg...	Institute on Securities Regulation [*A publication*] (DLA)
Inst SMM......	Institute of Sales and Marketing Management [*British*]
INSTSYS.......	Instrumentation System (MCD)
INSTX	IDS Stock Cl.A [*Mutual fund ticker symbol*] (SG)
InSU............	Indiana University at South Bend, South Bend, IN [*Library symbol Library of Congress*] (LCLS)
INSU	Insituform Technology [*NASDAQ symbol*] (SPSG)
INSU	Intensive Neurosurgery Unit (DAVI)
InSu...........	Sullivan County Public Library, Sullivan, IN [*Library symbol Library of Congress*] (LCLS)
INSUA.........	Insituform Technol'A' [*NASDAQ symbol*] (TTSB)
InSuC.........	Sullivan County Public Library, Sullivan, IN [*Library symbol*] [*Library of Congress*] (LCLS)
InSuCR	Sullivan County Recorder's Office, Sullivan, IN [*Library symbol Library of Congress*] (LCLS)
INSUF	Insufficient (AABC)
INSUF	Insufficient Scheduled Time Available [*Aviation*] (FAAC)
INSUFF........	Insufflatio [*An Insufflation*] [*Pharmacy*]
InSuHi	Sullivan County Historical Society, Sullivan, IN [*Library symbol Library of Congress*] (LCLS)
INSUL	Insulated [*or Insulation*]
INSULR	Insulator
INSUPGENCRUIT...	Inspect, Supervise, Generally Superintend Recruitment Methods
Insur..........	Insurance
INSURE........	Industry Network for Social, Urban, and Rural Efforts
Insur L Rep...	Insurance Law Reporter [*A publication*] (DLA)
INSURPAC ...	Independent Insurance Agents of America, Inc. Political Action Committee
INSURR	Insurrection (DLA)
Insur Rec Aust NZ...	Insurance Record of Australia and New Zealand [*A publication*]
INSURV........	Board of Inspection and Survey [*Navy*]
INSURVINST...	Board of Inspection and Survey, Instructions [*Navy*]
InSuT	Sullivan Daily Times, Sullivan, IN [*Library symbol Library of Congress*] (LCLS)
INSUWG	Inshore Undersea Warfare Group [*Navy*]
INSV	InSite Vision [*NASDAQ symbol*] (TTSB)
INSV	InSite Vision, Inc. [*NASDAQ symbol*] (SAG)

InSw .... Swayzee Public Library, Swayzee, IN [*Library symbol Library of Congress*] (LCLS)
InSy .... Syracuse Public Library, Syracuse, IN [*Library symbol Library of Congress*] (LCLS)
INSYD .... Instantaneous Systems Display [*Computer science*] (MHDB)
INT .... Ad Interim Specification [*Navy*]
Int .... De Interpretatione [*of Aristotle*] [*Classical studies*] (OCD)
INT .... Greensboro/High Point/West Salem [*North Carolina*] Reynolds [*Airport symbol*] (OAG)
INT .... Image 'N Transfer [*Developed by 3M Co.*] (WDMC)
INT .... Individual Needs Test (DNAB)
INT .... Induction Neutralizing Transformer [*Computer science*]
INT .... Infrared Nondestructive Testing [*Electrical technique*]
INT .... Initial (IAA)
INT .... Intair, Inc. [*Canada ICAO designator*] (FAAC)
INT .... Intake
INT .... Integer
INT .... Integral (MSA)
INT .... Integrase [*Biochemistry*]
INT .... Integrated (MCD)
INT .... Integrated Test (NASA)
INT .... Integrated Testing (NASA)
INT .... Intelligence
int .... Intelligence (WDAA)
INT .... Intelligence and Law Enforcement Division [*Coast Guard*]
int .... Intense [*Philately*]
INT .... Intensifier [*Linguistics*]
INT .... Intensity
INT .... Intent [*FBI standardized term*]
INT .... Intercept [*or Interceptor*] (CINC)
INT .... Interchange
Int .... Interchange: Papers on Biblical and Current Questions [*A publication*] (APTA)
INT .... Interest [*Finance, Law*] (AFM)
Int .... Interest (EBF)
int .... Interest (WDMC)
INT .... Interface
INT .... Interim (MSA)
INT .... Interior (KSC)
int .... Interior (VRA)
INT .... Interjection
INT .... Interleaved (WGA)
int .... Interlingua [*MARC language code Library of Congress*] (LCCP)
INT .... INTERMARC [*International Machine-Readable Cataloging*] [*French National Library*] [*UTLAS symbol*]
INT .... Intermediate (MCD)
INT .... Intermetco Ltd. [*Toronto Stock Exchange symbol*]
INT .... Intermittent
INT .... Internal (AAG)
Int .... Internal (TBD)
int .... Internal (WDMC)
int .... International (WDMC)
INT .... International (EY)
INT .... Interne [*Medicine British*]
INT .... Interned (AABC)
INT .... Internist [*Medicine*]
INT .... Internship (DAVI)
int .... Internus [*Internal*] [*Latin*]
INT .... Interphone (MDG)
INT .... Interpreter
INT .... Interrogate (MDG)
INT .... Interrogation [*British naval signaling*]
INT .... Interrupt
INT .... Interrupter (MSA)
INT .... Interstate [*Railroad*] (MHDW)
INT .... Interstate Railroad Co. [*AAR code*]
INT .... Interval
int .... Interval (WDMC)
INT .... Interview
int .... Interviewer
Int .... Intestinal (AAMN)
INT .... Intransitive
Int .... Introduction (DLA)
INT .... Introit
int .... Introit (WDAA)
INT .... Iodonitrotetrazolium Violet
INT .... Irrigated, No Tillage [*Agriculture*]
INT .... Isaac Newton Optical Telescope
INT .... North Texas State University, Denton, TX [*OCLC symbol*] (OCLC)
INT .... Winston-Salem [*North Carolina*] [*Airport symbol*] (AD)
INT .... Winston-Salem, NC [*Location identifier FAA*] (FAAL)
INT .... World Fuel Services [*NYSE symbol*] (TTSB)
INT .... World Fuel Services Corp. [*NYSE symbol*] (SAG)
INTA .... Intasys Corp. [*NASDAQ symbol*] (SAG)
INTA .... International Association for the Development and Management of Existing and NewTowns (EAIO)
INTA .... International New Thought Alliance (EA)
INTA .... International Trademark Association (NTPA)
INTA .... Interrupt Acknowledge [*Computer science*]
INTAAS ...... Integrated Aircraft Armament System (MCD)
in-tab .... In-Tabulation [*Broadcasting*] (WDMC)
IntAbs .... International Absorbents [*Associated Press*] (SAG)
INTABS ...... International Terminal Accounting and Banking Service [*Computer science*] (MHDB)
INTAC .... Individual Terrorism Awareness Course (COE)

INTAC .... Intercept Tracking and Control Group
INTACK .... Interrupt-Acknowledge [*Intel Corp.*] (CIST)
IntACom ...... InterAmericas Communications Corp. [*Associated Press*] (SAG)
INTACS .... Integrated Tactical Communications Study [*or System*] [*Army*] (AABC)
INTAG .... Intaglio [*Engraving*] (ROG)
INTAG .... International Advisory Group on Technology Management [*Information broker and consultancy*] (NITA)
INTAGCY ...... Interagency
INTAL .... Instituto para la Integracion de America Latina [*Institute for Latin American Integration*] (EAIO)
INT AL .... Inter Alia [*Among Other Things*] [*Latin*]
IntAlu .... International Aluminum Corp. [*Associated Press*] (SAG)
INTAMEL ...... International Association of Metropolitan City Libraries [*The Hague, Netherlands*] (EA)
INTAMIC ...... International Microcircuit Card Association [*Paris, France*] [*Defunct*] (EAIO)
INTAMP .... Intermediate Amplifier (IAA)
INTAP .... Interoperatbility Technology Association for Information Technology (OSI)
INTAPUC ...... International Association of Public Cleansing [*Later, ISWA*]
INTAR .... International Arts Relations
Int Arb J ..... International Arbitration Journal [*A publication*] (DLA)
INTASAFCON... International Tanker Safety Conference (DS)
INTASAT ...... Instituto Nacional de Tecnica Aeroespacial Satellite [*Spain*]
INTASGRO ... Interallied Tactical Study Group [*NATO*] (NATG)
Intasys .... Intasys Corp. [*Associated Press*] (SAG)
INTAV .... Interim Availability (DNAB)
INTAVA .... International Aviation Association
INTAX .... IDS Tax Exempt Bond Cl.A [*Mutual fund ticker symbol*] (SG)
Int Bar J ..... International Bar Journal [*A publication*] (DLA)
IntBas .... International Basic Resources, Inc. [*Associated Press*] (SAG)
INTBUL .... Intelligence Bulletin (CINC)
Int Bull Indust Prop... International Bulletin of Industrial Property [*A publication*] (DLA)
Int Bus Lawy... International Business Lawyer [*A publication*] (DLA)
IntBusSch .... International Business Schools [*Associated Press*] (SAG)
INTC .... Intel Corp. [*NASDAQ symbol*] (NQ)
INTC .... Intelligence Corps [*Army*]
INTC .... Intercept (GAVI)
INTC .... International Nick Tate Club (EAIO)
InTc .... Tell City-Perry County Public Library, Tell City, IN [*Library symbol Library of Congress*] (LCLS)
IntCabl .... International Cablecasting Technologies, Inc. [*Associated Press*] (SAG)
IntcapIn .... Intercapital Insurance Municipal Bond Fund [*Associated Press*] (SAG)
IntcapIns ...... InterCapital Insured Municipal Securities [*Associated Press*] (SAG)
IntCAQI .... Intercapital California Quality Municipal Security Trust [*Associated Press*] (SAG)
Intcardia ...... Intercardia, Inc. [*Associated Press*] (SAG)
Int Cas .... Rowe's Interesting Cases [*England and Ireland*] [*A publication*] (DLA)
Int Case ...... Rowe's Interesting Cases [*England and Ireland*] [*A publication*] (DLA)
IntCble .... International Cabletel, Inc. [*Associated Press*] (SAG)
INTCHC .... Interchanger (NAKS)
INTCHG .... Interchange (NAKS)
INTCHG .... Interchangeable (MSA)
INTCHGR ...... Interchanger (NASA)
INT CIB .... Inter Cibos [*Between Meals*] [*Pharmacy*]
IntCm .... Interdigital Communications Corp. [*Associated Press*] (SAG)
InTcN .... Tell City News, Tell City, IN [*Library symbol Library of Congress*] (LCLS)
INTCNTL ...... Intercontinental
INTC/O .... Integrated Checkout (NASA)
INTCO .... International Code of Signals
INTCOL .... Intelligence Collection [*Military*] (NVT)
IntColng ...... International Colin Energy [*Associated Press*] (SAG)
Int Com Com... Interstate Commerce Commission. Reports [*A publication*] (DLA)
Int Com Commn... Interstate Commerce Commission [*Independent government agency*] (DLA)
Int Com Rep... Interstate Commerce Commission Reports [*A publication*] (DLA)
INTCON .... Interconnection (MSA)
INTCP .... Intercept (AFM)
IntcpIM .... Intercapital Insured Municipal Income Trust [*Associated Press*] (SAG)
INTCP RNG... Intercept Range
IntCpt .... Intersciences Computer Corp. [*Associated Press*] (SAG)
InTCS .... Commercial Solvents Corp., Terre Haute, IN [*Library symbol Library of Congress Obsolete*] (LCLS)
IntctlBk .... Intercontinental Bank [*Associated Press*] (SAG)
INTCW .... Intel Corp.Wrrt [*NASDAQ symbol*] (TTSB)
INTCYL .... Intercylinder
InTD .... Eugene V. Debs Foundation, Terre Haute, IN [*Library symbol Library of Congress*] (LCLS)
INTD .... Institut National des Techniques de la Documentation [*National Institute for Information Science*] [*France Information service or system*] (IID)
INTD .... InteliData Technologies Corp. [*NASDAQ symbol*] (SAG)
INTD .... Intend (FAAC)
INTDD .... Intended
INTDEPT .... Interdepartmental
INTDISP .... Interdisciplinary
INTE .... Interactive Group [*NASDAQ symbol*] (TTSB)
INTE .... Interactive Group, Inc. [*NASDAQ symbol*] (SAG)
INTE .... Interrupt Enable [*Computer science*]
INTEC .... Interface Technology [*British*] (NITA)

INTEC......... Interference [*Telecommunications*] (MDG)
INTEC......... International Technology Underwriters [*Consortium, Washington*] (NITA)
INTECH .... Instrument Technology-Journal of ISA (ACII)
INTECH .... Integrated Information Technology Conference and Exposition [*National Trade Productions*] (TSPED)
INTECOL ...... International Association for Ecology [*University of Georgia*] [*Athens, GA*] (EAIO)
Integ .... Integ Inc. [*Associated Press*] (SAG)
INTEG .... Integrate [*or Integrating*] (MSA)
INTEG .... Integument [*Dermatology*] (DAVI)
IntegCirc...... Integrated Circuit Systems [*Associated Press*] (SAG)
IntegFn........ Integra Financial Corp. [*Associated Press*] (SAG)
IntegMed ..... IntegraMed America, Inc. [*Associated Press*] (SAG)
Integn .... Integon Corp. [*Associated Press*] (SAG)
Integon .... Integon Corp. [*Associated Press*] (SAG)
INTEGR .... Integrate [*or Integration*] (NASA)
Integral........ Integral Systems, Inc. [*Associated Press*] (SAG)
Integrity ...... Integrity, Inc. [*Associated Press*] (SAG)
IntegSrg....... Integrated Surgical Systems, Inc. [*Associated Press*] (SAG)
IntegTc .... Integrated Technology USA, Inc. [*Associated Press*] (SAG)
Intek........... INTEK Diversified Corp. [*Associated Press*] (SAG)
Intel............ Intel Corp. [*Associated Press*] (SAG)
INTEL......... Intelligence (AABC)
Intelcal .... Intellicall, Inc. [*Associated Press*] (SAG)
INTELCAST... Intelligence Broadcast (DOMA)
INTELCEN .... Intelligence Center
INTELCENPAC... Intelligence Center, Pacific Ocean Areas [*Obsolete*]
Intelcm .... Intelcom Group [*Associated Press*] (SAG)
INTELCOM ... Worldwide Intelligence Communication (MCD)
Intelect .... Intelect Communications Systems Ltd. [*Associated Press*] (SAG)
IntelEl......... Intellignet Electronics, Inc. [*Associated Press*] (SAG)
INTELEVENT... International Televent (EA)
InteliDta ...... InteliData Technologies Corp. [*Associated Press*] (SAG)
INTELL......... Intelligence (ROG)
Intellectual Property L Rev... Intellectual Property Law Review [*A publication*] (DLA)
Intellgrp....... Intelligroup, Inc. [*Associated Press*] (SAG)
Intelli.......... Intelli Corp., Inc. [*Associated Press*] (SAG)
INTELLIVISION... Intelligent Television [*Home video game*] [*Mattel, Inc.*]
INTELNET .... Intelligence Network (DOMA)
INTELO .... Intelligence Officer [*Military*]
INTELPOST... International Electronic Post [*Postal Service*]
INTELPOST... International Telecommunications Post [*Facsimile transmission service*] (NITA)
INTELSA ...... International Telecommunications Satellite Consortium [*Later, International Telecommunications Satellite Organization*] (IAA)
INTELSAT .... International Telecommunications Satellite Consortium (NITA)
Intelsat .... International Telecommunications Satellite Organization [*Washington, D.C.*] (WDMC)
INTELSAT .... International Telecommunications Satellite Organization (EA)
INTELTNG .... Intelligence Training [*Military*] (NVT)
INTEN .... Intensity (MSA)
Int Enc Comp Law... International Encyclopedia of Comparative Law [*A publication*] (DLA)
INTENS .... Intensive
Intensva...... Intensiva Healthcare Corp. [*Associated Press*] (SAG)
INTENT .... Initial Teacher Education and New Technology [*Project*] (AIE)
INTENTN...... Intention (ROG)
INTER .... Interception [*Football*]
INTER .... Interdenominational
Inter............ Interiors, Inc. [*Associated Press*] (SAG)
INTER .... Interleave (DGA)
INTER .... Intermediate (AAG)
inter............ Intermediate (WDMC)
INTER .... Intermittent
INTER .... Internal (KSC)
INTER .... Interphone (MCD)
INTER .... Interrogation (ADA)
INTER .... Interrogative
INTER .... Interrupt
INTER .... Intertype (DGA)
Intera.......... Intera Information Technologies Corp. [*Associated Press*] (SAG)
INTERACT .... Integrated Research Aircraft Control Technology (MCD)
InterAct........ InterAction Media Corp. [*Associated Press*] (SAG)
Interact........ Interactive Group, Inc. [*Associated Press*] (SAG)
InteracT .... Interactive Technologies Corp., Inc. [*Associated Press*] (SAG)
INTERACT .... Interactive Television Network [*Dartmouth-Hitchcock Medical Center*] [*Hanover, NH*] [*Telecommunications*] (TSSD)
INTERACTA... Associazione Italiana della Communicazione Interattiva [*Organization for multimedia professionals*] [*Italy*] (DDC)
INTERALIS ... International Advanced Life Information System (BUR)
INTERALP.... Intercultural Action Learning Program
Inter American U... Inter American University (GAGS)
INTER ARTS... Intermediate of Arts [*British*] (ROG)
INTERASMA... International Association of Asthmology [*Lisbon, Portugal*] (EAIO)
INTERATOM... Internationale Atomreactorbau [*German*]
INTER BA..... Intermediate Bachelor of Arts [*British*] (ROG)
INTERBEV.... International Beverage Industry Exhibition and Congress [*National Soft Drink Association*]
INTERBOR ... Union Internationale des Techniciens Orthopedistes [*International Association of Orthotists and Prosthetists*] (EA)
INTERBRIGHT... International Literary and Information Centre in Science Extension (IID)
INTERCARGO... International Association of Dry Cargo Shipowners (EAIO)

INTERCEDE... International Coalition to End Domestics' Exploitation
Intercel........ Intercel, Inc. [*Associated Press*] (SAG)
INTERCENTRE... International Centre for the Terminology of the Social Sciences [*Grand-Saconnex, Switzerland*] (EA)
Interchange... Interchangeability and Replacement (NAKS)
Interco .... Interco, Inc. [*Formerly, International Shoe Co.*] [*Associated Press*] (SAG)
INTERCO ...... International Code of Signals (PDAA)
INTERCO ...... International Council on Jewish Social and Welfare Services [*Geneva, Switzerland*] (EAIO)
INTERCO ...... International Shoe Co. (EFIS)
INTERCODE... International CODEN Service [*Chemical Abstracts Service*] [*Information service or system*] (IID)
INTERCOL .... Intercolonial (ADA)
INTERCOM.... Intercommunication System
INTERCOM.... Intertribal Christian Communications
Intercommun... Intercommunications (NAKS)
Intercommun... Intercommunication System (NAKS)
INTERCON ... Interconnection (KSC)
INTERCON ... Intercontinental
INTERCON ... Intermediate-Size Cargo Container
INTERCON ... International Convention
INTERCOOP... International Organization for Consumer Co-Operative Distributive Trade (EAIO)
INTERCOSMOS... Council on International Cooperation in the Study and Utilization of Outer Spac e
INTERDACO... Intercontinental Data Control Corp. Ltd. [*Ottawa, ON*] [*Telecommunications*] (TSSD)
INTERDEPT... Interdepartmental (KSC)
INTERDICT... Interference Detection and Interdiction Countermeasures Team [*Electromagnetic compatibility programs*]
InterDig .... Interdigital Communications Corp. [*Associated Press*] (SAG)
INTERDOC ... Integrated Terminology Document Management System (IAA)
INTERDOK .. International Documentation and Information Centre
INTEREG ...... Internationales Institut fuer Nationalitatenrecht und Regionalismus [*International Institute for Ethnic Group Rights and Regionalism*] (EA)
INTEREGEN... Internal Regenerative (KSC)
INTEREST .... Interactive Estimating [*Camic Ltd.*] [*Software package*] (NCC)
INTEREX ...... International Exchangors Association (EA)
Interf.......... Interface Systems, Inc. [*Associated Press*] (SAG)
INTERF .... Interference (IAA)
INTERF .... Interferometer
Interface C... Interface Compatibility Record (NAKS)
Interface C... Interface Control Drawing (NAKS)
Interface C... Interface Control Specification (NAKS)
Interface C... Interface Control Unit (NAKS)
Interface D... Interface Document (NAKS)
Interface F... Interface Functional Analysis (NAKS)
INTERFAIS ... International Food Aid Information System [*World Food Program*] [*United Nations*] (DUND)
Interfc......... Interface Systems, Inc. [*Associated Press*] (SAG)
INTERFER .... Interference
INTERFILM... International Inter-Church Film Center [*Hilversum, Netherlands*] (EAIO)
INTERFOOD... International Exhibition of Foodstuffs, Fast Food, and Traditional and Mass Catering
INTERFRIGO... International Railway-Owned Company for Refrigerated Transport (EAIO)
INTERGALVA... International Galvanizing Conference (MCD)
INTERGOVT... Intergovernmental
INTERGU..... Internationale Gesellschaft fuer Urheberrecht [*International Copyright Society*] (EAIO)
INTERHYBRID... Association Intercontinentale du Mais Hybride
Interim........ Interim Services, Inc. [*Associated Press*] (SAG)
Interior Dec... Decisions of the Department of the Interior [*A publication*] (DLA)
Interiors...... Interiors, Inc. [*Associated Press*] (SAG)
INTERJ......... Interjection
interj........... Interjection (WDMC)
Inter-L .... Interlibrary (AL)
INTERLAINE... Comite des Industries Lainieres de la CEE [*Committee of the Wool Textile Industry in the EEC*] (EAIO)
Interlink...... Interlink Electronics, Inc. [*Associated Press*] (SAG)
Interlinq...... INTERLINQ Software Corp. [*Associated Press*] (SAG)
INTERMAC... International Association of Merger and Acquisition Consultants (EA)
INTERMAG... International Conference on Magnetics (MCD)
INTERMAMA... International Congress for Measurement and Automation (IEEE)
INTERMARC... International Machine Readable Catalogue
INTERMED... Intermediate (ADA)
Intermed...... Intermediate (EBF)
INTERMET ... International Association for Metropolitan Research and Development
Intermex...... International Mexican Bank Ltd. [*British*] (EY)
INTERMILPOL... International Military Police [*NATO*]
INTERMORGEO... International Organization for Marine Geology [*Council for Mutual Economic Assistance*] [*Riga, Union of Soviet Socialist Republics Defunct*] (EAIO)
INTERMSTA... Intermediate Station
INTERMTRA... Intermediate Training [*Naval Air*]
INTERN........ Internal
INTERN........ International
Interna LN ... International Law Notes [*London*] [*A publication*] (DLA)
INTERNAT... International
Internat Bar Assoc... International Bar Association (DLA)
Internat J of Leg Res... International Journal of Legal Research [*A publication*] (DLA)

INTERNATL... International
Internat LN... International Law Notes [*A publication*] (DLA)
Interneur...... Interneuron Pharmaceuticals, Inc. [*Associated Press*] (SAG)
InterNIC....... Internet Network Information Center [*Computer science*]
INTERNL...... Internal
INTER NOCT... Inter Noctem [*During the Night*] [*Pharmacy*]
INTERNST.... Intenist
Internt......... Internet Communications [*Associated Press*] (SAG)
INTEROBS... International Observations (DNAB)
INTEROG...... Interrogate (NASA)
INTEROP...... Interoperability
INTERP....... Interpreter
INTERPET.... International Petroleum Co.
INTERPEX.... International Philatelic Exhibition [*American Stamp Dealers Association*]
INTERPHES... International Pharmaceutical Cosmetics, Toiletry, and Allied Industries Exhibition [*England*]
INTERPHIL... International Standing Conference on Philanthropy [*Yalding, Kent, England*] (EAIO)
INTERPL...... Interplead [*Legal shorthand*] (LWAP)
INTERPLAN... International Group for Studies in National Planning
INTERPLAS... International Plastics and Rubber Exhibition [*British Plastics Federation*] (TSPED)
INTERPOL.... International Criminal Police Organization
Interpol........ International Police Organisation (WDAA)
Interpol........ Interpool, Inc. [*Associated Press*] (SAG)
Interp Op..... Interpretative Opinion [*Legal term*] (DLA)
INTERPR...... Interpreter (WGA)
INTERPRO .. International Probation Organization (EA)
INTERPRON... Photointerpretation Squadron [*Military*]
interr........... Interrogative (BJA)
INTERROG ... Interrogation
INTERROGS... Interrogatories (ROG)
INTERROGY... Interrogatory (ROG)
Inters Com Rep... Interstate Commerce Commission Reports [*A publication*] (DLA)
INTERSEARCH... International Productions and Safety Research [*Auto accident reconstruction*]
INTERSEC.... Intermediate Section
INTERSECT... International Security Technics [*Organization in TV series "The Gemini Man"*]
Interslv........ Intersolv, Inc. [*Associated Press*] (SAG)
INTERSPACE... Interactive System for Pattern Analysis, Classification, and Enhancement (PDAA)
INTERSPUTNIK... International Organization of Space Communications [*Moscow, USSR*] (EAIO)
INTERST...... Interstate [*Legal shorthand*] (LWAP)
Interstate Com R... Interstate Commerce Reports [*A publication*] (DLA)
Interst Com R... Interstate Commerce Commission Reports [*A publication*] (DLA)
INTERSTENO... Federation Internationale de Stenographie et de Dactylographie [*International Federation of Shorthand and Typewriting*] [*Bonn, Federal Republic of Germany*] (EAIO)
INTERSTOL... Inter-City Short Takeoff and Landing [*Aviation*]
INTERTANKO... International Association of Independent Tanker Owners [*Oslo, Norway*] (EAIO)
INTERTEL .... International Intelligence, Inc.
INTERTEL .... International Legion of Intelligence [*Acronym is used as official name of association*] (EA)
INTERTEST... Interactive Test Controller (MHDI)
INTERTEX.... International Textile and Fabrics Trade Fair
INTERV .... Interval
INTERV .... Interview
INTERV .... Interviewer
INTERVISION... International Television (IAA)
INTER/W...... Intersection With (WDAA)
INTERWOOLABS... International Association of Wool and Textile Laboratories (EAIO)
INTESCA...... Internacional de Ingenieria y Estudios Tecnicos SA [*Spain*] (PDAA)
INTEST......... Intestinal
Intevac......... Intevac, Inc. [*Associated Press*] (SAG)
INTEX.......... Integer Extraction (PDAA)
INTEX.......... International Exploration, Inc. (EFIS)
INTEX.......... International Fallout Warning Exercise (NATG)
INTEXT........ International Textbook Co.
INTF........... Interface (NASA)
INTF........... Interface Systems [*NASDAQ symbol*] (TTSB)
INTF........... Interface Systems, Inc. [*NASDAQ symbol*] (NQ)
INTF........... Internal Frosted (IAA)
IntF............. International Finance Corp. [*Associated Press*] (SAG)
IntFam........ International Family Entertainment [*Associated Press*] (SAG)
IntFast........ International Fast Food Corp. [*Associated Press*] (SAG)
INTFC.......... Interface (MSA)
INTFC.......... Interference (FAAC)
INTFER .... Interference (AABC)
Int FHR....... Internatl Fetal Heart Rate [*Medicine*] (MEDA)
IntFib.......... International Fibercom, Inc. [*Associated Press*] (SAG)
IntFibcm...... International Fibercom, Inc. [*Associated Press*] (SAG)
IntFlav .... International Flavors & Fragrances, Inc. [*Associated Press*] (SAG)
INTFR .... Interference (KSC)
Intfrn.......... Interferon Sciences, Inc. [*Associated Press*] (SAG)
INTFU......... Interface Unit [*Computer science*]
intg............ Intaglio (VRA)
INTG .... Integration (NASA)
INTG .... Intergroup Corp. [*NASDAQ symbol*] (TTSB)
INTG .... Interrogate (AABC)
IntGame...... International Game Technology [*Associated Press*] (SAG)

IntgDv........ Integrated Device Technology, Inc. [*Associated Press*] (SAG)
INTGEN...... Interpreter Generator
IntgHS .... Integrated Health Services, Inc. [*Associated Press*] (SAG)
INTGL .... Integral (KSC)
IntgMed...... Integrated Medical Resources, Inc. [*Associated Press*] (SAG)
IntgMic ...... Integrated Micro Products [*Associated Press*] (SAG)
IntgMus ..... Integrity Music, Inc. [*Associated Press*] (SAG)
Intgph......... Intergraph Corp. [*Associated Press*] (SAG)
INTGR .... Integrate (AABC)
IntgrBr .... Integrated Brands [*Associated Press*] (SAG)
INTGRD....... Integrated
Intgrp........ [*The*] Inner Group Corp. [*Associated Press*] (SAG)
INTGRTD..... Integrated
IntgSc .... Integrated Security Systems [*Associated Press*] (SAG)
IntgSec ...... Integrated Security Systems [*Associated Press*] (SAG)
IntgSrg .... Integrated Surgical Systems, Inc. [*Associated Press*] (SAG)
IntgWst ...... Integrated Waste Services, Inc. [*Associated Press*] (SAG)
INTH .... Intrathecal [*Medicine*]
InTho .... Thorntown Public Library, Thorntown, IN [*Library symbol Library of Congress*] (LCLS)
InThr.......... International Thoroughbred Breeders, Inc. [*Associated Press*] (SAG)
InTI .... Indiana State University, Terre Haute, IN [*Library symbol Library of Congress*] (LCLS)
INTI .... Industrial Technologies [*NASDAQ symbol*] (TTSB)
INTI .... Industrial Technologies, Inc. [*NASDAQ symbol*] (SAG)
InTi .... Tipton County Public Library, Tipton, IN [*Library symbol Library of Congress*] (LCLS)
INTIB .... Industrial and Technological Information Bank [*UNIDO*] (IID)
INTIM .... Interrupt and Timing [*Telecommunications*] (TEL)
IntImag....... International Imaging Materials, Inc. [*Associated Press*] (SAG)
InTIMC....... IMC Chemical Group, Inc., Technical Library, Terre Haute, IN [*Library symbol Library of Congress*] (LCLS)
Intime......... Information on Technology in Manufacturing Engineering [*Society of Manufacturing Engineers*] [*Dearborn, MI*]
INTIME....... Interactive Textual Information Management Experiment (PDAA)
Intime......... Intime Systems International, Inc. [*Associated Press*] (SAG)
IntIMT........ Intercapital Insured Municipal Trust [*Associated Press*] (SAG)
Intimte........ Intimate Brands, Inc. [*Associated Press*] (SAG)
IntIns CA..... InterCapital Insured California Municipal Securities [*Associated Press*] (SAG)
INTIP .... Integrated Information Processing
InTip .... Tipton County Public Library, Tipton, IN [*Library symbol*] [*Library of Congress*] (LCLS)
INTIPS .... Integrated Information Processing System [*Air Development Center, Rome, NY*]
INTIW .... Industrial Technol Wrrt'A' [*NASDAQ symbol*] (TTSB)
INTIZ.......... Industrial Technol Wrrt'B' [*NASDAQ symbol*] (TTSB)
Int J Criminol... International Journal of Criminology and Penology [*A publication*] (DLA)
IntJen .... International Jensen, Inc. [*Associated Press*] (SAG)
IntJhn .... Interstate/Johnson Lane, Inc. [*Formerly, Interstate Securities, Inc.*] [*Associated Press*] (SAG)
Int J Pol ..... International Journal of Politics [*A publication*] (DLA)
Int J Quantum Chem... International Journal of Quantum Chemistry (MEC)
Int J Quantum Chem Symp... International Journal of Quantum Chemistry Symposium (MEC)
Int Jurid Assn Bull... International Juridical Association. Bulletin [*A publication*] (DLA)
INTK.......... Inotek Technologies [*NASDAQ symbol*] (TTSB)
INTK.......... Inotek Technologies, Inc. [*NASDAQ symbol*] (SAG)
INTK.......... Intake (MSA)
INTK.......... Intertank (KSC)
INTL........... Internal
INTL........... International (AFM)
intl .... International (VRA)
INTL........... International Movement of Catholic Students [*France*]
INTL........... Inter-Tel Inc. [*NASDAQ symbol*] (TTSB)
IntIAffairs ... International Affairs (DD)
IntIAllSv...... International Alliance Services, Inc. [*Associated Press*] (SAG)
Int'l & Comp L Bull... International and Comparative Law Bulletin [*A publication*] (DLA)
Int'l Arb Awards... Reports of International Arbitral Awards [*A publication*] (DLA)
Int'l Arb J.... International Arbitration Journal [*A publication*] (DLA)
Int'l Assoc L Lib Bull... International Association of Law Libraries. Bulletin [*A publication*] (DLA)
IntIAsst ...... International Assets Holding Corp. [*Associated Press*] (SAG)
IntIAst........ International Assets Holding Corp. [*Associated Press*] (SAG)
Int Law Tr... International Law Tracts [*A publication*] (DLA)
Int'l BA Bull... International Bar Association. Bulletin [*A publication*] (DLA)
Int'l Bar J.... International Bar Journal [*A publication*] (DLA)
Int'l BJ....... International Bar Journal [*A publication*] (DLA)
Int L Bull ... International Law Bulletin [*A publication*] (DLA)
IntIBus........ International Business Schools, Inc. [*Associated Press*] (SAG)
Int'l Bus Lawyer... International Business Lawyer [*London, England*] [*A publication*] (DLA)
Int'l Bus Ser... International Business Series [*A publication*] (DLA)
IntICable...... International Cabletel, Inc. [*Associated Press*] (SAG)
IntICer........ Internacional de Ceramica SA de CV [*Associated Press*] (SAG)
INTL COMB... Internal Combustion [*Freight*]
Int'l Crim Pol Rev... International Criminal Police Review [*A publication*] (DLA)
IntICt......... International Cutlery Ltd. [*Associated Press*] (SAG)
IntICut........ International Cutlery Ltd. [*Associated Press*] (SAG)
Int'l Dig Health Leg... International Digest of Health Legislation [*A publication*] (DLA)
Int Legal Materials... International Legal Materials [*A publication*] (DLA)

IntLeisr........ International Leisure Hosts Ltd. [*Associated Press*] (SAG)
IntlElec........ International Electronics, Inc. [*Associated Press*] (SAG)
Int'l Encycl Comp L... International Encyclopedia of Comparative Law [*A publication*] (DLA)
IntLfe........... Intercontinental Life Corp. [*Associated Press*] (SAG)
Int'l Fin L Rev... International Financial Law Review [*A publication*] (DLA)
IntlgC........... Intelligent Controls, Inc. [*Associated Press*] (SAG)
IntlgSys........ Intelligent Systems Corp. [*Associated Press*] (SAG)
Int Lib.......... Intrationum Liber [*A publication*] (DSA)
INTLINE....... International Online Data Base [*The WEFA Group*] [*Information service or system*]
IntLivC......... Integrated Living Communities, Inc. [*Associated Press*] (SAG)
Int'l J Crim & Pen... International Journal of Criminology and Penology [*A publication*] (DLA)
Int'l J Crimin & Penol... International Journal of Criminology and Penology [*A publication*] (DLA)
Int'l J Legal Res... International Journal of Legal Research [*A publication*] (DLA)
Int'l J Off Ther & Comp Crim... International Journal of Offender Therapy and Comparative Criminology [*A publication*] (DLA)
Int'l Jurid Ass'n Bull... International Juridical Association. Bulletin [*A publication*] (DLA)
INTLK.......... Interlock (MSA)
Int'l Lab Reports... International Labour Reports [*A publication*] (DLA)
Int'l L Ass'n... Reports of the International Law Association [*A publication*] (DLA)
Int'l L Ass'n Bull... Bulletin. International Law Association [*1936-38*] [*A publication*] (DLA)
Int'l Law...... International Law [*A publication*] (DLA)
Intllcll.......... Intellicell Corp. [*Associated Press*] (SAG)
Int'l L Comm'n... International Law Commission [*United Nations*] (DLA)
Int'l L Doc... International Law Documents [*A publication*] (DLA)
Int'l Legal Ed Newsl... International Legal Education Newsletter [*A publication*] (DLA)
INTLLGNC... Intelligence
Int'l LLL....... International Lutheran Laymen's League (EA)
Int'l L Persp... International Law Perspective [*A publication*] (DLA)
Int'l LR....... International Law Reports [*A publication*]
Int'l L Rep... International Law Reports [*A publication*] (DLA)
Int'l L Stud... International Law Studies [*Naval War College*] [*A publication*] (DLA)
Int LN........ International Law Notes [*A publication*] (DLA)
Int L Notes... International Law Notes [*England*] [*A publication*] (DLA)
IntlNtwk....... International Network Services [*Associated Press*] (SAG)
IntlNurs....... International Nursing Services, Inc. [*Associated Press*] (SAG)
INTLOC........ Interdiction of Lines of Communication (PDAA)
IntLotry........ International Lottery, Inc. [*Associated Press*] (SAG)
IntLotTot....... International Lottery & Totalizator Systems [*Associated Press*] (SAG)
IntlPizza........ International Pizza Co. [*Associated Press*] (SAG)
IntlPlatin...... International Platinum Corp. [*Associated Press*] (SAG)
IntlPost........ International Post Ltd. [*Associated Press*] (SAG)
IntlPrec........ International Precious Metals [*Associated Press*] (SAG)
IntlPrecM...... International Precious Metals [*Associated Press*] (SAG)
Int'l Prop Inv J... International Property Investment Journal [*A publication*] (DLA)
IntLR.......... International Law Reports [*A publication*] (DI)
Int'l Rev Ad Sci... International Review of Administrative Sciences [*A publication*] (DLA)
Int'l Rev Crim Policy... International Review of Criminal Policy [*United Nations*] (DLA)
Int'l Soc'y of Barr Q... International Society of Barristers. Quarterly [*A publication*] (DLA)
IntlSpdw....... International Speedway Corp. [*Associated Press*] (SAG)
IntlSpr......... International Sports Wagering, Inc. [*Associated Press*] (SAG)
IntlSrgL........ Intelligent Surgical LASERs, Inc. [*Associated Press*] (SAG)
Int'l Surv LDLL... International Survey of Legal Decisions on Labour Law [*1925-38*] [*A publication*] (DLA)
Int'l Sym Comp L... International Symposium on Comparative Law [*A publication*] (DLA)
Int'l Tax & Bus Law... International Tax and Business Lawyer [*A publication*] (DLA)
IntlTDS........ International Telecommunication Data Systems, Inc. [*Associated Press*] (SAG)
IntlVit........... International Vitamin Corp. [*Associated Press*] (SAG)
INTLVR........ Interleaver (MCD)
Int'l Woman Law... International Woman Lawyer [*A publication*] (DLA)
INTM.......... Interim Services [*NASDAQ symbol*] (TTSB)
INTM........... Intermediate (KSC)
INTMA........ International Mail [*A publication*]
INTMD........ Intermediate (MSA)
INTMED....... Intermediate (AFM)
INTMED....... Internal Medicine (AABC)
IntMedI........ Intelligent Medical Imaging, Inc. [*Associated Press*] (SAG)
IntMet........ International Metals Acquisition Corp. [*Associated Press*] (SAG)
IntmetC........ Intermet Corp. [*Associated Press*] (SAG)
IntMicr........ International Microcomputer Software, Inc. [*Associated Press*] (SAG)
IntMJ.......... International Microfilm Journal of Legal Medicine, New York, NY [*Library symbol Library of Congress*] (LCLS)
IntMP......... International Micro-Print Preservation, Inc., New York, NY [*Library symbol Library of Congress*] (LCLS)
INTMS........ Internal Messenger Service [*Hotels*]
INTMT........ Intermittent (MSA)
IntMult........ International Multifoods Corp. [*Associated Press*] (SAG)
IntMur........ International Murex Technologies [*Associated Press*] (SAG)
INTN.......... InStent, Inc. [*NASDAQ symbol*] (SAG)
INTN.......... Intention
IntNDS........ Interstate National Dealer Services, Inc. [*Associated Press*] (SAG)
IntnetS......... Intranet Solutions, Inc. [*Associated Press*] (SAG)
IntnetSol....... Intranet Solutions, Inc. [*Associated Press*] (SAG)
INTNEW....... International News [*Database*] (IT)

INTN'L......... International
INT NOCT.... Inter Noctem [*During the Night*] [*Pharmacy*]
INTNS........ Intentions (FAAC)
INTNS........ In Transit
INTNTNL...... Intentional
IntNur........ International Nursing Services, Inc. [*Associated Press*] (SAG)
IntNur........ Interntional Nursing Services, Inc. [*Associated Press*] (SAG)
IntNYQ........ Intercapital New York Quality Municipal Security Trust [*Associated Press*] (SAG)
INTO.......... Industrial Training Opportunities Exhibition (ITD)
INTO.......... Inhibited Nitrogen Tetroxide
INTO.......... Initio, Inc. [*NASDAQ symbol*] (SAG)
INTO.......... Intelligence Officer [*Army*]
INTO.......... Intuitive Network Total Office [*Benchmark Associates*] [*Computer science*]
INTO.......... Iran National Tourist Organization
INTO.......... Irish National Teachers' Organisation
int obst........ Intestinal Obstruction [*Medicine*] (MAE)
INTOP........ International Operations Simulation (IEEE)
INTOPS....... Interdiction Operations [*Navy*] (NVT)
INTOR........ International TOKAMAK Reactor [*Thermonuclear-fusion system*]
INTOR........ International Torus Design [*Nuclear energy*] (NUCP)
INTOSAI...... International Organization of Supreme Audit Institutions [*Vienna, Austria*] (EA)
InTour......... International Tourist Entertainment Corp. [*Associated Press*] (SAG)
INTOX........ Intoxication
INTOX L...... Intoxicating Liquor [*Legal term*] (DLA)
Int P.......... International Pharmacopoeia [*A publication*]
INTP.......... Interpoint [*NASDAQ symbol*] (SAG)
INTP.......... Interpoint Corp. [*NASDAQ symbol*] (TTSB)
INTP.......... Interport Trucking [*MTMC*] (TAG)
IntPack....... Integrated Packaging Assembly Corp. [*Associated Press*] (SAG)
IntPap........ International Paper Co. [*Associated Press*] (SAG)
IntpbGp....... [*The*] Interpublic Group of Companies, Inc. [*Associated Press*] (SAG)
INTPH........ Interphone
INTPHIBRFT... Interim Amphibious Refresher Training [*Navy*] (NVT)
Intphse........ Interphase Corp. [*Associated Press*] (SAG)
INTPHTR...... Interphase Transformer [*Electronics*]
INTPLDR...... Interpleader [*Legal*] [*British*] (ROG)
IntPly.......... Intertape Polymer Group [*Associated Press*] (SAG)
INTPN........ Interpretation (AFM)
Intpnt......... Interpoint Corp. [*Associated Press*] (SAG)
INTPO........ Interpole [*Electromagnetics*]
IntPoly........ Intertape Polymer Group [*Associated Press*] (SAG)
Intpore........ Interpore International [*Associated Press*] (SAG)
INTPR......... Interpret (AFM)
Intpr.......... Interpretation: A Journal of Bible and Theology [*A publication*] (BRI)
Int Private Law... Private International Law [*A publication*] (DLA)
IntPtr......... International Petroleum Corp. [*Associated Press*] (SAG)
Int Qk......... Interrupted Quick [*Flashing*] Light [*Navigation signal*]
INTQKFL...... Interrupted Quick Flashing Light [*Navigation signal*]
IntQuest....... IntelliQuest Information Group, Inc. [*Associated Press*] (SAG)
intr........... Intarsia (VRA)
INTR.......... Interior (KSC)
INTR.......... Intermittent (AFM)
INTR.......... Internal (KSC)
INTR.......... Interrupt [*Computer science Telecommunications*]
INTR.......... Interrupt Register [*Computer science*] (CIST)
INTR.......... Interrupt Request [*Computer science*] (CIST)
INTR.......... Interscience Computer [*NASDAQ symbol*] (TTSB)
INTR.......... Intersciences Computer Corp. [*NASDAQ symbol*] (SAG)
INTR.......... Intransitive
INTR.......... Introduction
intr........... Introduction (WDAA)
INTR.......... Intruder
InTR.......... Rose Polytechnic Institute, Terre Haute, IN [*Library symbol Library of Congress*] (LCLS)
INTRA........ International Travel (MCD)
Intra.......... Intramural (DLA)
INTRACONS... In-Transit Control System (PDAA)
IntrAct........ InterAction Media Corp. [*Associated Press*] (SAG)
INTRAFAX.... Facsimile System [*Western Union trade name*]
INTRAFILM... International Travel-Adventure Film Guild [*Defunct*] (EA)
Intra L Rev (St LU)... Intramural Law Review (St. Louis University) [*A publication*] (DLA)
Intramural LJ... Intramural Law Journal [*A publication*] (DLA)
Intramural L Rev... Intramural Law Review [*A publication*] (DLA)
INTRAN....... Infrared Transmitting
INTRAN....... Input Translator [*IBM Corp.*] [*Computer science*]
In trans........ In Transit (EBF)
INTRANS...... Intransitive (ROG)
IN TRANS.... In Transitu [*In Transit*] [*Latin*] (ROG)
INTRANST.... International Transportation Tracking System [*Department of Transportation*]
INTRAST...... Intrastate [*Legal shorthand*] (LWAP)
Intrav.......... Intrav, Inc. [*Associated Press*] (SAG)
INTRC......... Intricate (MSA)
IntrCal........ Intercapital California Insured Municipal Income Trust [*Associated Press*] (SAG)
INTRCHNG... Interchange
IntrCm........ Intermedia Communications of Florida, Inc. [*Associated Press*] (SAG)
Intrcrgo........ Intercargo Corp. [*Associated Press*] (SAG)
INTRCTV..... Interactive
IntRect........ International Rectifier Corp. [*Associated Press*] (SAG)
INTREDIS..... International Tree Disease Register [*US Forest Service*] (NITA)

INTREDIS..... International Tree Disease Register System for Literature Retrieval in Forest Pathology [*National Agricultural Library*]
INTREP........ Intelligence Report (NATG)
INTREPT...... Intelligence Report
INT REV...... Internal Revenue (ROG)
Int Rev Bull... Internal Revenue Bulletin [*A publication*] (DLA)
Int Rev Crim Pol... International Review of Criminal Policy [*United Nations*] (DLA)
INTREX........ Information Transfer Exchange [*Library science*]
INTREX........ Information Transfer Experiment [*Massachusetts Institute of Technology*] (DIT)
INTRF......... Interference [*Telecommunications*] (MSA)
IntrfcIn....... Interface, Inc. [*Associated Press*] (SAG)
IntrFlt.......... Interactive Flight Technologies, Inc. [*Associated Press*] (SAG)
IntrFlt.......... Interactive Flight Technologies, Inc. Cl.A [*Associated Press*] (SAG)
INTRFT........ Interim Refresher Training [*Navy*]
INTRFTH...... Interfaith
INTRG......... Integrate (AFIT)
INTRG......... Interrogate (MSA)
Intrirs......... Interiors, Inc. [*Associated Press*] (SAG)
INTRLCD...... Interlaced
Intrleaf........ Interleaf, Inc. [*Associated Press*] (SAG)
Intrlk.......... Interlink Electronics, Inc. [*Associated Press*] (SAG)
INTRLKD...... Interlocked
Intrlke......... [*The*] Interlake Corp. [*Associated Press*] (SAG)
Intrlne......... Interline Resources Corp. [*Associated Press*] (SAG)
INTRLVR...... Interleaver (NASA)
Intrmagn....... Intermagnetics General Corp. [*Associated Press*] (SAG)
intr-md........ Inter-media (VRA)
INTRMT........ Interment (AABC)
INTRMTRGN... Inter-Mountain Region (FAAC)
Intrn........... Interneuron Pharmaceuticals, Inc. [*Associated Press*] (SAG)
INTRN......... Intravenous [*Medicine*]
Intrnt.......... Intranet, Inc. [*Associated Press*] (SAG)
INTRNTL...... International
Intrnu......... Interneuron Pharmaceuticals, Inc. [*Associated Press*] (SAG)
INTRO......... Introduction (MSA)
intro........... Introduction (WDMC)
intro........... Introductory (WDMC)
INTROD....... Introduction
INTROD....... Introduzione [*Introductory Movement*] [*Music*] (ROG)
INTROPTA..... Introscripta [*Written Within*] [*Latin*] (ROG)
int rot......... Internal Rotation [*Orthopedics*] (DAVI)
INTRP......... Interrupt
INTRPL........ Interpolation (MSA)
INTRPLRY.... Interpupillary
Intrpol......... Interpool, Inc. [*Associated Press*] (SAG)
INTRPT....... Interrupt (MSA)
INTRQ......... Interrupt Request [*Computer science*] (MHDI)
INTRST....... Interest
INTRSTG...... Interstage (KSC)
Intrsy......... Intersystems, Inc. [*Associated Press*] (SAG)
Intrsystm..... Intersystems, Inc. [*Associated Press*] (SAG)
Intrtan......... Intertan, Inc. [*Associated Press*] (SAG)
IntrTel......... Inter-Tel, Inc. [*Associated Press*] (SAG)
INTRW......... Interscience Computer Wrrt [*NASDAQ symbol*] (TTSB)
IntrWBcp...... InterWest Bancorp [*Associated Press*] (SAG)
INTS........... Integrated Systems, Inc. [*NASDAQ symbol*] (SAG)
INTS........... Intense
InTS........... Terre Haute Spectator, Terre Haute, IN [*Library symbol Library of Congress*] (LCLS)
IntscCpt....... Intersciences Computer Corp. [*Associated Press*] (SAG)
INTSCT........ Intersect (MSA)
INTSF......... Intensify
IntShip........ International Shipholding Corp. [*Associated Press*] (SAG)
INTSHP........ Intership
IntSilSy....... Integrated Silicon Systems [*Associated Press*] (SAG)
INTSORMIL... International Sorghum and Millet Research
INTSOY....... International Soybean Program
IntSpclty...... International Specialty Products [*Associated Press*] (SAG)
IntSr.......... Intelligent Surgical Lasers, Inc. [*Associated Press*] (SAG)
INTST......... Intensity
INTST.......... Interest [*Finance, Law*] (ROG)
IntStand...... International Standards Group Ltd. [*Associated Press*] (SAG)
IntstBak...... Interstate Bakeries Corp. [*Formerly, Interstate Brands Corp.*] [*Associated Press*] (SAG)
INTSTDTHD... International Standard Thread (MCD)
INTSTE....... Interstate
INTSTG....... Interstage
IntstGC........ Interstate General Ltd. [*Associated Press*] (SAG)
IntstNDS...... Interstate National Dealer Services, Inc. [*Associated Press*] (SAG)
IntstPw........ Interstate Power Co. [*Associated Press*] (SAG)
INTSTY....... Intestacy [*Legal shorthand*] (LWAP)
INTSUM...... Intelligence Summary
INTSV......... Intensive (WGA)
INTSY......... Intensify (DNAB)
IntSysC........ Integrated Systems Consulting Group, Inc. [*Associated Press*] (SAG)
INTT........... Interest [*Finance, Law*] (ROG)
Int Tax Jour... International Tax Journal [*A publication*] (DLA)
IntTest....... International Testing Services Inc. [*Associated Press*] (SAG)
IntThr......... International Thoroughbred Breeders, Inc. [*Associated Press*] (SAG)
IntThrgh....... International Throughbred Breeders, Inc. [*Associated Press*] (SAG)
IntTourE....... International Tourist Entertainment Corp. [*Associated Press*] (SAG)
Int Trade LJ... International Trade Law Journal [*A publication*] (DLA)
InTTS........... Terre Haute Tribune-Star, Terre Haute, IN [*Library symbol Library of Congress*] (LCLS)

INTU........... Intuit, Inc. [*NASDAQ symbol*] (SAG)
INTUC......... Indian National Trades Union Congress
INTUG......... International Telecommunications Users Group [*Telecommunications Information service or system*] (IID)
Intuit.......... Intuit, Inc. [*Associated Press*] (SAG)
INTURISMO... Instituto Nicaraguense de Turismo (EY)
INTV........... Association of Independent Television Stations (EA)
INTV........... Instrumentation Television (AFM)
INTV........... Interview (CINC)
INTV........... InterVoice [*NASDAQ symbol*] (TTSB)
INTV........... InterVoice, Inc. [*NASDAQ symbol*] (NQ)
InTV........... Vigo County Public Library, Terre Haute, IN [*Library symbol Library of Congress*] (LCLS)
IntVer......... International Verifact, Inc. [*Associated Press*] (SAG)
IntVerif........ International Verifact, Inc. [*Associated Press*] (SAG)
IntvisB........ Intervisual Books, Inc. [*Associated Press*] (SAG)
INTVL......... Interval (MSA)
INTVLM....... Intervalometer [*Military ordnance*]
Intvoice....... InterVoice, Inc. [*Associated Press*] (SAG)
InTVS......... Vigo County School Corp., Instructional Materials Center, Terre Haute, IN [*Library symbol Library of Congress*] (LCLS)
INTVW......... Interview (AFM)
INTWF........ Indian National Textile Workers' Federation
InTWHi........ Wabash Valley Historical Society, Terre Haute, IN [*Library symbol Library of Congress*] (LCLS)
Int Woman L... International Woman Lawyer [*A publication*] (DLA)
INTWORLSA... International Third World Legal Studies Association (EA)
INTXA......... Interiors, Inc. [*NASDAQ symbol*] (SAG)
INTXA......... Interiors Inc.'A' [*NASDAQ symbol*] (TTSB)
INTXL......... Interiors Inc. Wrrt [*NASDAQ symbol*] (TTSB)
INTXP......... Interiors Inc.Cv'A'Pfd [*NASDAQ symbol*] (TTSB)
INTXW......... Interiors Inc. Wrrt'A' [*NASDAQ symbol*] (TTSB)
INTXZ......... Interiors Inc.Wrrt'B' [*NASDAQ symbol*] (TTSB)
INTY........... Intestacy [*Legal*] (ROG)
IntYog......... International Yogurt Co. [*Associated Press*] (SAG)
inu............ Indiana [*MARC country of publication code Library of Congress*] (LCCP)
InU............ Indiana University, Bloomington, IN [*Library symbol Library of Congress*] (LCLS)
INU............ Inertial Navigation Unit
INU............ Integration Unit
INU............ International Nutrition & Genetics Corp. [*Vancouver Stock Exchange symbol*]
INU............ Inuyama [*Japan*] [*Seismograph station code, US Geological Survey*] (SEIS)
INU............ Nauru [*Nauru*] [*Airport symbol*] (OAG)
InU-A......... Indiana University, Anatomy-Physiology Laboratory, Bloomington, IN [*Library symbol Library of Congress*] (LCLS)
InU-AT......... Indiana University, Archive of Traditional Music, Bloomington, IN [*Library symbol*] [*Library of Congress*] (LCLS)
InU-B......... Indiana University, Biology Library, Bloomington, IN [*Library symbol Library of Congress*] (LCLS)
InU-BA....... Indiana University, School of Business Administration, Bloomington, IN [*Library symbol Library of Congress*] (LCLS)
InUc........... Union City Public Library, Union City, IN [*Library symbol Library of Congress*] (LCLS)
INucE......... Institution of Nuclear Engineers [*British*]
InU-D......... Indiana University, School of Dentistry, Indianapolis, IN [*Library symbol Library of Congress*] (LCLS)
InU-Fw........ Indiana University, Fort Wayne Regional Campus, Fort Wayne, IN [*Library symbol Library of Congress*] (LCLS)
InU-I......... Indiana University, Indianapolis Regional Campus, Indianapolis, IN [*Library symbol Library of Congress*] (LCLS)
InU-ISR....... Indiana University, Institute for Sex Research, Bloomington, IN [*Library symbol Library of Congress*] (LCLS)
InU-K......... Indiana University, Kokomo Regional Campus, Kokomo, IN [*Library symbol Library of Congress*] (LCLS)
InU-L......... Indiana University, Law Library, Indianapolis, IN [*Library symbol Library of Congress*] (LCLS)
InU-Li......... Indiana University, Lilly Library, Bloomington, IN [*Library symbol Library of Congress*] (LCLS)
InU-M......... Indiana University, School of Medicine, Indianapolis, IN [*Library symbol Library of Congress*] (LCLS)
INUMRC....... Northwest Indiana Health Science Library Consortium [*Library network*]
InU-Mu....... Indiana University at Bloomington, Music Library, Bloomington, IN [*Library symbol*] [*Library of Congress*] (LCLS)
InU-N......... Indiana University, Northwest Regional Campus, Gary, IN [*Library symbol Library of Congress*] (LCLS)
InU-Nea....... Indiana University Southeast, New Albany, IN [*Library symbol Library of Congress*] (LCLS)
InU-O......... Indiana University, Optometry Library, Bloomington, IN [*Library symbol Library of Congress*] (LCLS)
InUpT.......... Taylor University, Upland, IN [*Library symbol Library of Congress*] (LCLS)
InU-R......... Indiana University at Bloomington, Lilly Rare Books, Bloomington, IN [*Library symbol Library of Congress*] (LCLS)
INUS........... Innovus Corp. [*NASDAQ symbol*] (SAG)
INUS........... Inside the United States
InU-Sb......... Indiana University, South Bend Regional Campus, South Bend, IN [*Library symbol Library of Congress*] (LCLS)
InU-Se......... Indiana University, Southeastern Regional Campus, Jeffersonville, IN [*Library symbol Library of Congress*] (LCLS)
INUW......... Irish National Union of Woodworkers (BI)
INV............. Inductive Null Voltage

INV.............. In-Line Needle Valve
INV.............. Invalid (IAA)
INV.............. Invasion
INV.............. Invective
INV.............. Invenit [*He, or She, Designed It*] [*Latin*]
INV.............. Invent (AABC)
INV.............. Inventory (AFM)
INV.............. Inventory Management (NAKS)
INV.............. Inveralochy [*Australia Seismograph station code, US Geological Survey*] (SEIS)
INV.............. Inverness [*Scotland*] [*Airport symbol*] (OAG)
INV.............. Inverse [*or Invert*]
inv............... Inverse (IDOE)
INV.............. Inversia [*Latvia*] [*ICAO designator*] (FAAC)
inv............... Inversion (DAVI)
INV.............. Inverter (KSC)
INV.............. Investigation
Inv............... Investing (EBF)
Inv............... Investment (EBF)
INV.............. Investment
INV.............. Invitation
INV.............. Invitational Race [*Harness racing*]
INV.............. Invoice [*Billing*] (AFM)
Inv............... Invoice (EBF)
inv............... Invoice [*Billing*] (ODBW)
INV.............. Involuntary
INV.............. Iris Neovascularization [*Opthalmology*]
INVAC.......... Investment Account [*Postal Service*] [*British*]
INVADJ........ Inventory Adjustment (MCD)
INVAL.......... Invalid (IAA)
InVal............ Valparaiso-Porter County Public Library System, Valparaiso, IN [*Library symbol Library of Congress*] (LCLS)
InValCR .... Porter County Recorder's Office, Valparaiso, IN [*Library symbol Library of Congress*] (LCLS)
InValHi .... Historical Society of Porter County, Valparaiso, IN [*Library symbol Library of Congress*] (LCLS)
InValU .... Valparaiso University, Valparaiso, IN [*Library symbol Library of Congress*] (LCLS)
InValVM....... Valparaiso Vidette-Messenger, Valparaiso, IN [*Library symbol Library of Congress*] (LCLS)
INVAR.......... Invariant
InVb .... Van Buren Public Library, Van Buren, IN [*Library symbol Library of Congress*] (LCLS)
InvBank....... Investors Bank Corp. [*Associated Press*] (SAG)
Invcare .... Invacare Corp. [*Associated Press*] (SAG)
INVCE .... Invoice [*Billing*] (ROG)
INVCURR ..... Inverse Current [*Electronics*] (IAA)
INVD .... Invalidate Data [*Cache*] [*Computer instruction*] (PCM)
INV DOC ATTACH... Invoice with Documents Attached [*Billing*] (ROG)
InVe .... Switzerland County Public Library, Vevay, IN [*Library symbol Library of Congress*] (LCLS)
InVeCR .... Switzerland County Recorder's Office, Vevay, IN [*Library symbol Library of Congress*] (LCLS)
INVECS .... Innovative Vehicle Electronic Control System [*Motor vehicles*]
INVECS .... Intelligent and Innovative Vehicle Electronic Control System
INVENT .... Institute for Ventures in New Technology
Inventory C.. Inventory Control Point (NAKS)
inver .... Inversion (DAVI)
InVeRE .... Vevay Reville-Enterprise, Vevay, IN [*Library symbol Library of Congress*] (LCLS)
INVERN........ Inverness [*County in Scotland*]
InVerR .... Versailles Republican, Versailles, IN [*Library symbol Library of Congress*] (LCLS)
InVerRHi...... Ripley County Historical Society, Versailles, IN [*Library symbol Library of Congress*] (LCLS)
INVERT .... Invertebrate (WGA)
INVERTEB .... Invertebrate
Inverter As... Inverter Assembly [*Aerospace*] (NAKS)
INVES .... Investigate [*or Investigation*] (AFM)
Invesco .... Invesco PLC [*Associated Press*] (SAG)
InvescoF...... Invesco Funding [*Associated Press*] (SAG)
InVeSD .... Switzerland Democrat, Vevay, IN [*Library symbol Library of Congress*] (LCLS)
INVEST .... Integrated Vehicle System Technology (MCD)
INVEST .... Investigation
Invest........... Investigation (STED)
INVEST .... Investment
invest........... Investment (DD)
INVESTIG ..... Investigation
Invet .... Inveterate (STED)
INVEX .... International Exhibition of Inventions and Novel Features (TSPED)
InvFnSv....... Investors Financial Services Corp. [*Associated Press*] (SAG)
InvGrMu...... Investment Grade Municipal Income Fund [*Associated Press*] (SAG)
INVI .... Invitro International [*Formerly, Ropak Laboratories*] [*NASDAQ symbol*] (SPSG)
InVi .... Vincennes and Knox County Public Libraries, Vincennes, IN [*Library symbol Library of Congress*] (LCLS)
inv ins .... Inverted Insertion (STED)
InvIns.......... Investors Insurance Group [*Associated Press*] (SAG)
InViSC .... Vincennes Sun Commercial, Vincennes, IN [*Library symbol Library of Congress*] (LCLS)
InVision .... InVision Technologies, Inc. [*Associated Press*] (SAG)
INVIT .... Invitation (KSC)
Invitr............ Invitro International [*Associated Press*] (SAG)

InViU .... Vincennes University, Vincennes, IN [*Library symbol Library of Congress*] (LCLS)
InViU-Hi....... Vincennes University, Byron R. Lewis Historical Collections Library, Vincennes, IN [*Library symbol Library of Congress*] (LCLS)
Invivo.......... Invivo Corp. [*Associated Press*] (SAG)
INVLT.......... Involute
INV MGT...... Inventory Management (MCD)
INVN .... Inventory (MSA)
INVN .... InVision Technologies [*NASDAQ symbol*] (TTSB)
INVN .... InVision Technologies, Inc. [*NASDAQ symbol*] (SAG)
InVnCR .... Jennings County Recorder's Office, Vernon, IN [*Library symbol Library of Congress*] (LCLS)
INVOF .... In the Vicinity Of (FAAC)
INVOG......... Information Officers Working in Voluntary Organisations (AIE)
INVOL .... Involuntary
invol .... Involuntary (STED)
INVOLEX...... Involuntary Extension
INVOLV....... Involve [*Coat*] [*Pharmacy*]
involv.......... Involvement (STED)
INVPX......... IDS Equity Select Cl.A [*Mutual fund ticker symbol*] (SG)
INVR .... Innovir Laboratories [*NASDAQ symbol*] (TTSB)
INVR .... Innovir Laboratories, Inc. [*NASDAQ symbol*] (SAG)
INVREC....... Inventory Record (MCD)
Inv Reg Cas... Notes of Decisions of Appeal Court of Registration at Inverness [*1835-53*] [*Scotland*] [*A publication*] (DLA)
Inv Rhet...... De Inventione Rhetorica [*of Cicero*] [*Classical studies*] (OCD)
INVRN........ Inversion [*NWS*] (FAAC)
INVRW........ Innovir Laboratories Wrrt'A' [*NASDAQ symbol*] (TTSB)
INVRZ......... Innovir Laboratories Wrrt'B' [*NASDAQ symbol*] (TTSB)
INVS .... Inverse (MSA)
INVST .... Invest
INVSTAR...... Investigate and Report (FAAC)
INVSTD .... Invested
INVSTGTN.... Investigation
INVSTGTV.... Investigative
INVSTMNT... Investment
INVSTR .... Investigator
INVT............ Invenit [*He, or She, Designed It*] [*Latin*] (ROG)
INVT............ Inventory (AABC)
INVT............ Invert (MSA)
INVT............ Investext [*Business Research Corp.*]
InvTech....... Investment Technology Group [*Associated Press*] (SAG)
InvTitl .... Investors Title Insurance Co. [*Associated Press*] (SAG)
INVTNL........ Invitational
INVTR .... Inverter
INVTY .... Inventory
INVV .... Inverse Voltage [*Electronics*] (IAA)
INVX .... Innovex, Inc. [*NASDAQ symbol*] (NQ)
INVY .... Inventory (ROG)
INW .... Internet World
INW .... Winslow [*Arizona*] [*Airport symbol*] (OAG)
INW .... Winslow, AZ [*Location identifier FAA*] (FAAL)
InWab......... Wabash Carnegie Public Library, Wabash, IN [*Library symbol Library of Congress*] (LCLS)
InWabHi ...... Wabash County Historical Museum, Wabash, IN [*Library symbol Library of Congress*] (LCLS)
InWabPD .... Wabash Plain Dealer, Wabash, IN [*Library symbol Library of Congress*] (LCLS)
InWak......... Wakarusa Public Library, Wakarusa, IN [*Library symbol Library of Congress*] (LCLS)
InWal.......... Walkerton-Lincoln Township Public Library, Walkerton, IN [*Library symbol Library of Congress*] (LCLS)
InWalIN ...... Walkerton Independent-News, Walkerton, IN [*Library symbol Library of Congress*] (LCLS)
InWan......... Wanatah Public Library, Wanatah, IN [*Library symbol Library of Congress*] (LCLS)
InWars........ Warsaw Public Library, Warsaw, IN [*Library symbol Library of Congress*] (LCLS)
InWarsR ...... Kosciusko County Recorder's Office, Warsaw, IN [*Library symbol Library of Congress*] (LCLS)
InWarsTU.... Warsaw Times-Union, Warsaw, IN [*Library symbol Library of Congress*] (LCLS)
InWas .... Carnegie Public Library, Washington, IN [*Library symbol Library of Congress*] (LCLS)
INWAS .... Inertial Navigation and Weapons Attack System (MCD)
InWasTH...... Washington Times-Herald, Washington, IN [*Library symbol Library of Congress*] (LCLS)
InWat......... Waterloo-Grant Township Public Library, Waterloo, IN [*Library symbol Library of Congress*] (LCLS)
INWATE ...... Integrating Waveguide Technology (PDAA)
INWATS .... Inward Wide Area Telecommunications Service (CIST)
INWATS .... Inward Wide Area Telephone Service [*Bell System*]
InWav......... Waveland Public Library, Waveland, IN [*Library symbol Library of Congress*] (LCLS)
INWD .... Inward (MSA)
InWebaC...... West Baden College, West Baden Springs, IN [*Library symbol Library of Congress*] (LCLS)
InWefG .... GTE North, Inc., Westfield, IN [*Library symbol*] [*Library of Congress*] (LCLS)
InWele......... West Lebanon Pike Township Public Library, West Lebanon, IN [*Library symbol Library of Congress*] (LCLS)
InWevP........ Purdue University, North Central Campus, Westville, IN [*Library symbol Library of Congress*] (LCLS)
INWG.......... International Network Working Group [*International Federation for Information Processing*]

InWh............	Whiting Public Library, Whiting, IN [*Library symbol Library of Congress*] (LCLS)
InWhC..........	Calumet College, Whiting, IN [*Library symbol Library of Congress*] (LCLS)
InWhHi	Whiting-Robertsdale Historical Society, Whiting, IN [*Library symbol Library of Congress*] (LCLS)
InWil............	Williamsport-Washington Township Public Library, Williamsport, IN [*Library symbol Library of Congress*] (LCLS)
InWilCR	Warren County Recorder's Office, Williamsport, IN [*Library symbol Library of Congress*] (LCLS)
InWilR	Williamsport Review-Republican, Williamsport, IN [*Library symbol Library of Congress*] (LCLS)
InWina.........	Pulaski County Public Library, Winamac, IN [*Library symbol Library of Congress*] (LCLS)
InWincCR	Randolph County Recorder's Office, Winchester, IN [*Library symbol Library of Congress*] (LCLS)
InWinFM......	Free Methodist Historical Center, Winona Lake, IN [*Library symbol Library of Congress*] (LCLS)
InWinG	Grace College, Winona Lake, IN [*Library symbol Library of Congress*] (LCLS)
INWL	International Network of Women Liberals (EAIO)
InWo	Worthington Jefferson Township Public Library, Worthington, IN [*Library symbol Library of Congress*] (LCLS)
InWol..........	Wolcott Public Library, Wolcott, IN [*Library symbol Library of Congress*] (LCLS)
InWolE........	New Wolcott Enterprise, Wolcott, IN [*Library symbol Library of Congress*] (LCLS)
InWoT.........	Worthington Times, Worthington, IN [*Library symbol Library of Congress*] (LCLS)
INX..............	Inanwatan [*West Irian, Indonesia*] [*Airport symbol*] (AD)
INX..............	Index Character [*Computer science*]
INX..............	Inexco Oil Co. [*Toronto Stock Exchange symbol*]
INX..............	Ion Exchange (NRCH)
INXLTR........	Input Translator [*IBM Corp.*] [*Computer science*] (MSA)
INY..............	Batesville, AR [*Location identifier FAA*] (FAAL)
INY..............	Ithaca [*New York*] [*Seismograph station code, US Geological Survey*] (SEIS)
INZ..............	In Salah [*Algeria*] [*Airport symbol*] (OAG)
INZ..............	Istituto Nazionale ADS [*NYSE symbol*] (TTSB)
INZ..............	Istituto Nazionale Delle Assicoraziono SPA [*NYSE symbol*] (SAG)
InZSM........	Sullivan Museum, Zionsville, IN [*Library symbol Library of Congress*] (LCLS)
IO................	Air Paris [*ICAO designator*] (AD)
IO................	British Indian Ocean Territory [*ANSI two-letter standard code*] (CNC)
IO................	Image Orthicon
IO................	Immediate Office (COE)
I/O..............	In and Out (STED)
I/O..............	Inboard-Outboard [*Boating*]
IO................	Incisal Opening [*Medicine*] (MAE)
IO................	Incoming Orders
IO................	Indian Ocean
IO................	India Office [*British*]
io................	Indonesia [*pt (Portuguese Timor) used in records cataloged before January 1978*] [*MARC country of publication code Library of Congress*] (LCCP)
IO................	Industrial Operations (MCD)
I/O..............	Industry/Occupation (OICC)
IO................	Infant Orphan [*British*] (ROG)
IO................	Infantry Officer [*British military*] (DMA)
IO................	Inferior Oblique [*Muscle*] [*Anatomy*]
IO................	Inferior Olive [*Neuroanatomy*]
IO................	Information Objectives (COE)
IO................	Information Officer
IO................	Information Operation [*Military*] (RDA)
IO................	Information Overload
IO................	Initial Only (AFM)
IO................	Initial Opening [*Pressure*] [*Measurement*] (DAVI)
IO................	Injector Orifice
IO................	In Order
I/O..............	In-Port Operations [*USCG*] (TAG)
I/O..............	Input/Output [*Computer science*]
IO................	Input/Output Inc. [*NYSE symbol*] (TTSB)
IO................	Inside-Out [*Vesicle*] (DB)
IO................	Inside-Out [*Vesicle*] (STED)
IO................	Inspection Opening (ADA)
IO................	Inspection Order (NATG)
IO................	Inspection Outline
IO................	Institute for Oceanography [*Environmental Science Services Administration*]
I/O..............	Instructor/Operator
I/O..............	Intake and Output (STED)
I/O..............	Intake Opens [*Valve position*]
IO................	Intelligence Office [*or Officer*]
IO................	Intelligence Oversight (DOMA)
IO................	Intensive Observation (STED)
IO................	Intercept Officer
IO................	Interest Only [*Finance*]
IO................	Interest Only Strip [*Mortgage security*]
IO................	Intermediary Organization [*Physiology*]
IO................	Internal Os [*or Orifice*] [*Medicine*] (DAVI)
IO................	International Octal (IAA)
IO................	International Organization
IO................	International Organizations [*A publication*]
IO................	Interpersonal Orientation (BARN)
IO................	Interpreter Officer [*Military British*]

IO................	Interpretive Operation
IO................	Intestinal Obstruction [*Medicine*]
IO................	Intraocular
IO................	Inventory Objective
IO................	Investigating Officer
io................	Iodo [*As substituent on nucleoside*] [*Biochemistry*]
IO................	Ion Engine (AAG)
Io................	Ionium [*Th^{230}, radioactive isotope of thorium*]
IO................	Iowa
IO................	Irish Office
IO................	Iron Overload [*Medicine*]
IO................	Issuing Office
IO................	Iterative Operation
IOA.............	Illinois Optometric Association (SRA)
IOA.............	Imaging Optics Assembly (MCD)
IOA.............	Indiana Optometric Association (SRA)
IOA.............	Indian Ocean Area (MCD)
IOA.............	Indian Ocean Arts Association [*Australia*]
IOA.............	Indian Overseas Airways
IOA.............	Inflammatory Osteoarthritis [*Medicine*]
IOA.............	Initial Outfitting Allowance [*Navy*]
IOA.............	Inner Optic Anlage (STED)
IOA.............	Input-Output Adapter [*Computer science*] (NASA)
IOA.............	Input-Output Address [*Computer science*] (KSC)
IOA.............	Input-Output Analysis [*Economics*]
IOA.............	Input-Output Assembly [*Computer science*] (MCD)
IOA.............	Input/Output or Assembly [*Aerospace*] (NAKS)
IOA.............	Institute of Acoustics [*British*] (DBA)
IoA.............	Institute of Administration [*University of New South Wales*] [*Australia*]
IOA.............	Institute of Outdoor Advertising [*New York, NY*] (EA)
IOA.............	Institute on Aging [*University of Wisconsin - Madison*] [*Research center*] (RCD)
IOA.............	Institute on Aging [*Portland State University*] [*Research center*] (RCD)
IOA.............	Instrumentation Operating Area
IOA.............	Instrument Operating Assembly
IOA.............	Interfaith Office on Accompaniment (EA)
IOA.............	International Office for Audiophonology (EA)
IOA.............	International Olympic Academy
IOA.............	International Omega Association (EA)
IOA.............	International Order of the Armadillo (EA)
IOA.............	International Orthoptic Association [*British*] (EAIO)
IOA.............	International Osteopathic Association (EA)
IOA.............	International Ozone Association (EA)
IOA.............	Interocular Asynchrony [*Ophthalmology*]
IOA.............	Intraoperative Autotransfusion [*Medicine*]
IOA.............	Ioannina [*Greece*] [*Airport symbol*] (OAG)
IOA.............	Iona Industries, Inc. [*Vancouver Stock Exchange symbol*]
IOA.............	Iowa Airways, Inc. [*ICAO designator*] (FAAC)
IOA.............	Irish Orienteering Association (EAIO)
IOa.............	Oak Park Public Library, Oak Park, IL [*Library symbol Library of Congress*] (LCLS)
IOAA	Immediate Office of Assistant Administrator (COE)
IOAA	Independent Offices Appropriation Act of 1952 (COE)
IOAC...........	Infantry Officer Advanced Course [*Army*] (INF)
IOAC/RC......	Infantry Officer Advanced Correspondence Course/Reserve Component (INF)
IOa-D	Oak Park Public Library, Dole Branch, Oak Park, IL [*Library symbol Library of Congress*] (LCLS)
IOaHS	Oak Park-River Forest High School, Oak Park, IL [*Library symbol Library of Congress*] (LCLS)
IOakSD	Oakland Unit School District, Oakland, IL [*Library symbol*] [*Library of Congress*] (LCLS)
IOa-M	Oak Park Public Library, Maze Branch, Oak Park, IL [*Library symbol Library of Congress*] (LCLS)
IOAN...........	Inspect [*and Repair*] Only as Needed [*MTMC*] (TAG)
IOA-PAGB	International Ozone Association-Pan American Group Branch (NTPA)
IOAT...........	International Organization Against Trachoma [*Creteil, France*] (EA)
IOAU...........	Input/Output Access Unit [*Computer science*]
IOAU...........	Input/Output Arithmetic Unit [*Computer science*] (IAA)
IOaWH.........	West Suburban Hospital, Oak Park, IL [*Library symbol Library of Congress*] (LCLS)
IOB.............	Briar Cliff College, Sioux City, IA [*OCLC symbol*] (OCLC)
IOB.............	Industrial Order of Battle (MCD)
IOB.............	Information Officer, Basic [*DoD Information School*] (DNAB)
IOB.............	Input/Output Block [*Computer science*] (CMD)
IOB.............	Input-Output Box [*Computer science*] (MCD)
IOB.............	Input-Output Buffer [*Computer science*]
I/OB............	Input/Output Bus [*Computer science*] (NASA)
IOB.............	Installation Operation Budget (AABC)
IOB.............	Institute of Bankers [*Later, CIB*] [*British*] (EAIO)
IOB.............	Institute of Brewing [*Also, IB*] [*British*]
IOB.............	Institute of Building [*or Builders*] [*British*]
IOB.............	Insurance Ombudsman Bureau (PDAA)
IOB.............	Intelligence Oversight Board [*Federal government*]
IOB.............	Internal Operating Budget
IOB.............	Inter-Organization Board for Information Systems [*United Nations*] (IID)
IOB.............	Inter-Organization Board for Information Systems and Related Activities (NITA)
IOB.............	Iron Ore Beneficiation (COE)
IOBB	Independent Order of B'nai B'rith [*Later, BBI*]
IOBB	International Organization of Biotechnology and Bioengineering [*Guatemala, Guatemala*]

IObC .... Chicago Bridge & Iron Co., Oak Brook, IL [*Library symbol Library of Congress*] (LCLS)
IOBC .... Indian Ocean Biological Center (BARN)
IOBC .... Infantry Officer Basic Course [*Army*]
IOBC .... International Organization for Biological Control of Noxious Animals and Plants [*See also OILB*] [*ICSU Montpellier, France*] [*Research center*] (EAIO)
IOBC-RC ...... Infantry Officer Basic Course-Reserve Component (INF)
IOBFR .... Input/Output Buffer (NITA)
IOBPS .... Input-Output Box and Peripheral Simulator [*Computer science*] (MCD)
IOBS .... Input/Output Buffering System [*Computer science*]
IOBS .... Institute of Bankers in Scotland (DI)
IObSE .... Swift-Eckrich, Research and Development Information Center Library, Oak Brook, IL [*Library symbol*] [*Library of Congress*] (LCLS)
IObT .... Bethany and Northern Baptist Theological Seminaries Library, Oak Brook, IL [*Library symbol Library of Congress*] (LCLS)
IOC .... Clarke College, Dubuque, IA [*OCLC symbol*] (OCLC)
IOC .... Image Orthicon Camera
IOC .... Image Orthicon Control
IOC .... Immediate-or-Cancel Order [*Stock exchange term*]
IOC .... Imperial Owners Club, International (EA)
IOC .... Index of Cooperation
IOC .... Indian Ocean Commission [*Port Louis, Mauritius*] (EAIO)
IOC .... Indirect Operating Costs
ioc .... Indirect Operating Costs (NAKS)
IOC .... Initial Operating Capability
IOC .... Initial Operational Capability [*Military*]
ioc .... Initial Operational Capability (NAKS)
IOC .... Initial Operational Capacity
IOC .... Initial Orbital Configuration (MCD)
IOC .... Initial Order Condition (MCD)
IOC .... Inorganic Chemical [*Environmental science*]
IOC .... In Our Culture
IOC .... In-Out Converter
IOC .... Input Offset Current
IOC .... Input-Output Channel [*Computer science*] (DIT)
IOC .... Input-Output Comparator [*Computer science*]
IOC .... Input/Output Connector (NITA)
I/OC .... Input/Output Console [*Computer science*] (CAAL)
IOC .... Input/Output Control (NITA)
IOC .... Input/Output Controller [*Computer science*]
ioc .... Input-Output Controller (NAKS)
IOC .... Input-Output Converter [*Computer science*]
IOC .... Installation and Operational Checkout
IOC .... Institute of Carpenters [*British*] (DBA)
IOC .... Institute of Chemistry [*British*] (DAS)
IOC .... Institute of Commerce [*British*] (DBA)
IOC .... Institutes for Oceanography [*Marine science*] (MSC)
IOC .... Integrated Optical Circuit [*or Component*]
IOC .... Integrated Optimization Control [*Engineering*]
IOC .... Integrated Optoelectronic Circuit
IOC .... Intelligence Operations Center [*Air Force*] (DOMA)
IOC .... INTELSAT Operations Center
IOC .... Intergovernmental Oceanographic Commission [*See also COI*] [*ICSU Paris, France*] (EAIO)
IOC .... Interim Operational Capability
IOC .... Internationaal Ontmoetings Centrum [*International Network for Self-Reliance - INS*] (EA)
IOC .... International Oceanographic Commission [*NASA*]
IOC .... International Olympic Committee
IOC .... International Ornithological Congress [*New Zealand*]
IOC .... International Ozone Commission [*IAMAP*] (NOAA)
IOC .... Intern on Call (HGAA)
IOC .... Inter-Office Channel [*Telecommunications*] (TSSD)
IOC .... Interoffice Correspondence
IOC .... Interstate Oil Compact
IOC .... Intraoperative Cholangiogram [*Radiology*] (DAVI)
IOC .... Iron Ore Co. of Canada Ltd.
IOC .... ISDN [*Integrated Services Digital Network*] Ordering Code (PCM)
IOC .... Iterative Orbit Calculator
IOC .... Kiowa, CO [*Location identifier FAA*] (FAAL)
IOCA .... Image Object Content Architecture (CDE)
IOCA .... Independent Oil Compounders Association [*Later, ILMA*] (EA)
IOCA .... Intercollegiate Outing Club Association (EA)
IOCARIBE ..... IOC [*Intergovernmental Oceanographic Commission*] Sub-commission for the Caribbean and Adjacent Region [*Marine science*] (OSRA)
IOC/B & CC ... Intergovernmental Oceanographic Commission - Bureau and Consultative Council [*UNESCO*]
IOCC .... Infantry Officer Career Course [*Army*]
IOCC .... Input-Output Control Center [*or Command*] [*Computer science*]
I/OCC .... Input/Output Control Console [*Computer science*] (CAAL)
IOCC .... International Office of Cocoa and Chocolate [*Later, IOCCSC*] (EAIO)
IOCC .... Interstate Oil Compact Commission (EA)
IOCC Bull. .... Interstate Oil Compact Commission. Bulletin [*A publication*] (DLA)
IOCCC .... International Office of Cocoa, Chocolate, and Sugar Confectionary [*Belgium*] (EAIO)
IOCCSC .... International Office of Cocoa, Chocolate, and Sugar Confectionary [*IOCC a nd International Sugar Confectionary Manufacturers Association*] [*Formed by a merger of*] (EAIO)
IOCD .... Initial Operation Capability Date [*Military*] (AABC)
IOCD .... Input Output under Count Control and Disconnect [*Computer science*] (SAA)

IOCD .... International Organization for Chemical Sciences in Development [*Brussels, Belgium*] (EA)
I/OCE .... Input/Output Control Element [*Computer science*] (MCD)
IOC/EC .... Intergovernmental Oceanographic Commission/Executive Council (MSC)
IOCF .... International Oil Compensation Fund
IOC-FDTE ..... Initial Operational Capability - Force Development Testing and Experimentation
IOCG .... Industrial Oil Consumers Group (EA)
IOCG .... Intraoperative Cholecystogram [*Radiology*] (DAVI)
IOCHC .... International Organization for Cooperation in Health Care [*See also MMI*] [*Nijmegen, Netherlands*] (EAIO)
IOCHS .... International Organization for Cultivating Human Spirit [*Later, OISCA*]
IOCI .... Imperial Order of the Crown of India [*British*] (ROG)
IOCI .... Interstate Organized Crime Index [*Computer databank*]
IOCP .... Indian Overseas Communication Project
IOCP .... Input/Output Control Processor [*Computer science*]
IOCP .... Input/Output Control Program [*Computer science*]
IOCP .... Input/Output under Count Control and Proceed [*Computer science*] (IAA)
IOCR .... Input/Output Control Routine [*Computer science*] (IAA)
IOCS .... Input/Output Computer Service (IAA)
IOCS .... Input-Output Control System [*Computer science*]
IOCS .... Instant Ocean Culture System
IOCS .... Interoffice Comment Sheet (NATG)
IOCTL .... Indian Ocean Conventional Target List (MCD)
IOCTR .... Input/Output Controller (NITA)
IOCU .... Input/Output Control Unit [*Computer science*]
iocu .... Input/Output Control Unit (NAKS)
IOCU .... International Organization of Consumers Unions [*The Hague, Netherlands*] (EA)
IOCV .... International Organization of Citrus Virologists (EA)
IOC/VAP .... Intergovernmental Oceanographic Commission/Voluntary Assistance Program (MSC)
IOC-VCP .... Intergovernmental Geographic Commission Voluntary Cooperation Program [*Marine science*] (OSRA)
IOD .... Drake University, Des Moines, IA [*OCLC symbol*] (OCLC)
IOD .... Identified Outward Dialing [*Telecommunications*] (TEL)
IOD .... Immediate Oxygen Demand [*Marine science*] (MSC)
IOD .... Imperial Order of the Dragon (EA)
IOD .... Information on Demand, Inc. [*Information service or system*] (IID)
IOD .... Injured on Duty
IOD .... Input/Output Device [*Telecommunications*] (TEL)
IOD .... Input/Output Dump Program [*Computer science*] (IAA)
IOD .... Institute of Directors [*British*] (DCTA)
IoD .... Institute of Directors [*British*] (ODBW)
IOD .... Institute of Diving (EA)
IOD .... Institute of Outdoor Drama (EA)
IOD .... Integrated Observation Device (MCD)
IOD .... Integrated Optical Density [*Instrumentation*]
IOD .... Interorbital Distance [*Ophthalmology*] (DAVI)
IOD .... Iron Overload Diseases Association (EA)
IOD .... Issue of Data
IODA .... Iron Overload Diseases Association (EA)
IODC .... Input-Output Data Channel [*Computer science*]
IODC .... Input-Output Delay Counter [*Computer science*]
IODD .... Ideal One-Dimensional Device (IAA)
IODD .... Input-Output Data Document [*Computer science*] (MCD)
IODE .... Imperial Order of Daughters of the Empire [*Canada*]
IODE .... International Oceanographic Data and Information Exchange [*Marine science*] (OSRA)
IODE .... International Oceanographic Data Exchange
IODHRI .... International Organization for the Defense of Human Rights in Iraq (EA)
IODM .... Infant of Diabetic Mother [*Neonatology*] (DAVI)
IODMM .... International Office of Documentation on Military Medicine (EA)
IODS .... International Ocean Disposal Symposium (EA)
IODSTR .... Input and Output Driven Selt-Timing Repeater (PDAA)
IOE .... Buena Vista College, Storm Lake, IA [*OCLC symbol*] (OCLC)
IOE .... Industrial and Operations Engineer (PGP)
IOE .... Inlet Over Exhaust [*Automotive engineering*]
IOE .... Input-Output Error Log Table [*Computer science*] (MCD)
IOE .... Institute for the Officialization of Esperanto
IOE .... Institute of Ecology [*Research center*] (RCD)
IOE .... Institute of Offshore Engineering [*Heriot-Watt University*] [*Information service or system*] (IID)
IOE .... Instrumentation Operations Engineer (MCD)
IOE .... Intake Opposite Exhaust (IAA)
IOE .... Intensity of Operational Employment [*Army*] (RDA)
IOE .... International Office of Epizootics
IOE .... International Organization of Employers [*Geneva, Switzerland*]
IOE .... International Organization of Experts (EAIO)
IOEBT .... Irregular Outer Edge [*Army*] (ADDR)
IOEBT .... Intraoperative Electron Beam Therapy [*Medicine*] (DAVI)
IOEH .... Institute of Occupational and Environmental Health [*See also IMTA, IMTE*]
IOEHI .... International Organization for the Education of the Hearing Impaired (EA)
IOEMTFS ...... Independent Order of Engineers and Machinists Trade and Friendly Society [*A union*] [*British*]
IOf .... Acorn Library District, Oak Forest, IL [*Library symbol Library of Congress*] (LCLS)
IOF .... Graceland College, Lamoni, IA [*OCLC symbol*] (OCLC)
IOF .... Income Opportunities Fd 1999 [*NYSE symbol*] (TTSB)
IOF .... Income Opportunities Fund [*NYSE symbol*] (SPSG)

IOF.............. Independent Order of Foresters [*Buffalo, NY*] (EA)
IOF.............. Infrared Optical Film
IOF.............. Initial Operational Flight (MCD)
IOF.............. Input/Output Front End [*Computer science*]
IOF.............. Institute of Fuel [*British*] (BI)
IOF.............. Interactive Operations Facility [*Honeywell, Inc.*]
IOF.............. Internationale Orientierungslauf Foderation [*International Orienteering Federation*] (EA)
IOF.............. International Oceanographic Foundation (EA)
IOF.............. Intraocular Fluid [*Ophthalomology*] (DAVI)
I of A.......... Instructor of Artillery [*British*]
IOfa.............. O'Fallon Public Library, O'Fallon, IL [*Library symbol Library of Congress*] (LCLS)
IOfaCD .... O'Fallon Community Consolidated District 90, O'Fallon, IL [*Library symbol Library of Congress*] (LCLS)
IOfaSD .... O'Fallon Township High School District 203, O'Fallon, IL [*Library symbol Library of Congress*] (LCLS)
IOFB............ Intraocular Foreign Body [*Ophthalmology*]
IOFC............ Income Over Feed Cost [*Livestock*] (OA)
IOFC............ Indian Ocean Fishery Commission [*FAO*] [*Italy United Nations*]
IofE.............. Institute of Electrolysis [*British*] (DBA)
IOfH............ Oak Forest Hospital, Oak Forest, IL [*Library symbol Library of Congress*] (LCLS)
IOFI.............. International Organization of the Flavor Industry [*Geneva, Switzerland*] (EAIO)
I of M.......... Instructor of Musketry [*British*]
I of M.......... Isle of Man [*England*]
IOFOS .... International Organization for Forensic Odonto-Stomatology [*Formerly, International Society of Forensic Odonto-Stomatology*] (EA)
IOFS............ International Organ Festival Society (EA)
IOFSG .... International Orienteering Federation, Scientific Group [*See also IOFWA*] (EAIO)
IOFSI .... Independent Order of the Free Sons of Israel [*Freemasonry*] (ROG)
IOFT............ Institution on Farm Training
I of W.......... Isle of Wight
IOFWA .... Internationale Orientierungslauf Foderation, Wissenschaftliche Arbeitsgruppe [*International Orienteering Federation, Scientific Group - IOFSG*] (EAIO)
IOG .... Grinnell College, Grinnell, IA [*OCLC symbol*] (OCLC)
IOG .... Input-Output Gate [*Computer science*]
IOG .... Institute of Groundsmanship [*British*] (ITD)
IOG .... Intercollegiate Opera Group [*Defunct*] (EA)
IOg.............. Oglesby Public Library, Oglesby, IL [*Library symbol Library of Congress*] (LCLS)
IOGA .... Industry-Organized Government-Approved
IOGAWV...... Independent Oil and Gas Association of West Virginia (SRA)
IOGCC .... Interstate Oil and Gas Compact Commission (NTPA)
IOgd............ Rose Library, Ogden, IL [*Library symbol Library of Congress*] (LCLS)
IOGE .... Integrated Operational Ground Equipment
IOGEN .... Input-Output Generation [*Computer science*]
IOgIV .... Illinois Valley Community College, Oglesby, IL [*Library symbol Library of Congress*] (LCLS)
IOGP .... Independent Oil and Gas Producers (COE)
IOGP .... International Outboard Grand Prix
IOgPS .... Oglesby Public Schools, Oglesby, IL [*Library symbol Library of Congress*] (LCLS)
IOGR............ International Order of the Golden Rule [*Springfield, IL*] (EA)
IOGT............ International Organization of Good Templars [*Oslo, Norway*] (EAIO)
IOH .... Idiopathic Orthostatic Hypotension [*Medicine*]
IOH .... Indication of Hostilities [*Military*]
IOH .... Inside-Out Helmholtz
IOH .... [*The*] Institute of Heraldry [*Military*]
IOH .... Institute of Housing [*British*] (DBA)
IOH .... Inventory on Hand
IOH .... Item [*or Items*] on Hand
IOH .... Luther College, Decorah, IA [*OCLC symbol*] (OCLC)
IOh.............. Ohio Township Library, Ohio, IL [*Library symbol Library of Congress*] (LCLS)
IOHE .... Inter-American Organization for Higher Education [*See also OUI*]
IOHE .... International Organization for Human Ecology (EAIO)
IOHFI .... International Organization for Housing Finance Institutions (EA)
IOHH............ International Order of Hoo-Hoo (EA)
IOHS............ Integrated Operational Hydrological System [*Marine science*] (MSC)
IOI................ Indication of Interest [*Business term*] (MHDW)
IOI................ Interest on Investment (AFIT)
IOI................ Interim Operating Instructions
IOI................ Internal Operating Instruction
IOI................ International Ocean Institute [*Valetta, Malta*] (EAIO)
IOI................ International Ombudsman Institute [*University of Alberta*] [*Edmonton, AB*] [*Research center*] (EAIO)
IOI................ International Orphans, Inc. (EA)
IOI................ International Ozone Institute [*Later, IOA*] (EA)
IOI................ Iori Enterprises, Inc. [*Vancouver Stock Exchange symbol*]
IOI................ Iowa Wesleyan College, Mount Pleasant, IA [*OCLC symbol*] (OCLC)
IOIC............ Integrated Operational Intelligence Center
IOICS............ Integrated Operational Intelligence Center System [*Military*] (DNAB)
IOIH............ Input/Output Interrupt Handler [*Computer science*]
IOIRS .... International Online Information Retrieval Service [*Institute of Scientific and Technical Information of China*] [*Beijing*] [*Information service or system*] (IID)
IOIS .... Integrated Operational Intelligence System (MCD)
IOITBAG ...... International Oil Industry TBA Group (EA)
IOJ.............. Institute of Journalists [*British*]

IOJ.............. International Organization of Journalists [*See also OIJ*] [*Prague, Czechoslovakia*] (EAIO)
IOJ.............. St. Ambrose College, Davenport, IA [*OCLC symbol*] (OCLC)
IOJD............ International Order of Job's Daughters (EA)
IOJD............ International Organization for Justice and Development (EAIO)
IOK.............. Industrial and Occupational Knowledge (AIE)
IOK.............. International Order of Kabbalists (EA)
IOK.............. Iokea [*Papua New Guinea*] [*Airport symbol*] (OAG)
IOK.............. Simpson College, Indianola, IA [*OCLC symbol*] (OCLC)
IOkCD .... West Washington County Community District 10, Okawville, IL [*Library symbol Library of Congress*] (LCLS)
IOKDS........ International Order of the King's Daughters and Sons (EA)
IOL.............. India Office Library and Records [*British*]
IOL.............. Induction of Labor [*Obstetrics*] (DMAA)
IOL.............. Initial Outfitting List [*for advanced naval bases*]
IOL.............. Instantaneous Overload
IOL.............. Intermediate Objective Lens
IOL.............. International Old Lacers (EA)
IOL.............. Intraocular Lens [*Ophthalmology*]
IOL.............. Loras College, Dubuque, IA [*OCLC symbol*] (OCLC)
IOI.............. Oak Lawn Public Library, Oak Lawn, IL [*Library symbol Library of Congress*] (LCLS)
IOLA.......... Input/Output Line Adaptor (NITA)
IOLA.......... Input/Output Link Adapter [*Computer science*]
IOIC .... Christ Hospital, Oak Lawn, IL [*Library symbol Library of Congress*] (LCLS)
IOLC.......... Input/Output Link Control [*Computer science*]
IOLC.......... Input/Output Link Controller (NITA)
IOLC.......... Integrated Optical Logic Circuit
IOL/CR ...... Initial Outfitting List / Complete Repair, Parts, and Tools (SAA)
IOIE .... Evangelical School of Nursing, Oak Lawn, IL [*Library symbol Library of Congress*] (LCLS)
IOLI.......... International Old Lacers, Inc. (EA)
IOLIM.......... International Online Information Meeting
IOLM.......... International Organization for Legal Metrology
IOln.......... Olney Carnegie Public Library, Olney, IL [*Library symbol Library of Congress*] (LCLS)
IOLS.......... Input/Output Label System [*Computer science*] (OA)
IOLS.......... Integrated Online Library Systems
IOLS.......... Iterated Ordinary Least Squares [*Statistics*]
IOLTA.......... Interest on Lawyers' Trust Accounts
IOLV.......... Independent Order Ladies of Vikings (EA)
IOM.......... Index and Options Market (NUMA)
IOM.......... Indian Order of Merit
IOM.......... Inert Operational Missile (NG)
IOM.......... Inferior Orbitomeatal Line [*Brain anatomy*]
IOM.......... Innovator of the Month
IOM.......... Input-Output Module [*Computer science*] (MCD)
I/OM.......... Input-Output Multiplexer [*Computer science*]
IOM.......... Insoluble Organic Material [*or Matter*] [*Analytical chemistry*]
IOM.......... Inspector of Ordnance Machinery [*British military*] (DMA)
IOM.......... Installation, Operation, and Maintenance (COE)
IOM.......... Institute of Materials [*British*] (EAIO)
IOM.......... Institute of Meat [*British*] (DBA)
IoM.......... Institute of Medicine
IOM.......... Institute of Medicine [*National Academy of Sciences*] (EA)
IOM.......... Institute of Metals [*Institution of Metallurgists - IM and Metals Society - MS*] [*Formed by a merger of*]
IOM.......... Institute of Occupational Medicine [*British*] (IRUK)
IOM.......... Institute of Office Management [*British*] (BI)
IOM.......... International Options Market [*Australian Options Market, European Options Exchange in Amsterdam, Montreal Exchange, and Vancouver Stock Exchange*]
IOM.......... International Organization for Migration (EAIO)
IOM.......... International Organization for Mycoplasmology (EA)
IOM.......... Interoffice Memorandum
IOM.......... Island Aviation & Travel Ltd. [*British ICAO designator*] (FAAC)
IOM.......... Isle of Man [*England*] [*Airport symbol*] (OAG)
IOM.......... Morningside College, Sioux City, IA [*OCLC symbol*] (OCLC)
IOMA.......... Idaho Oil Marketers Association (SRA)
IOMA.......... Independent Oil Marketer's Association of New England (SRA)
IOMA.......... International Oxygen Manufacturers Association (EA)
IOMACI ...... Indian Ocean Marine Affairs Cooperation Conference
IOMC.......... International Organization for Medical Cooperation
IOME.......... Irgun Olej Merkas Europa (BJA)
Iomega ...... Iomega Corp. [*Associated Press*] (SAG)
IOMF.......... Inactive-Officer Master File (DNAB)
IOMG.......... Iomega Corp. [*NASDAQ symbol*] (NQ)
I/OMI.......... Integration/Operations and Maintenance Instruction [*NASA*] (NASA)
IOML.......... Infraorbitomeatal Line [*Anatomy*] (DAVI)
IOMMP ...... International Organization of Masters, Mates, and Pilots
IOMO.......... Invitation of Member Only
IOMP .... Input/Output Message Processor [*Computer science*] (IAA)
IOMP .... Input/Output Microprocessor [*Computer science*]
IOMP .... International Organization for Medical Physics (DAVI)
IOMR.......... Isle Of Man Railways [*British*] (ROG)
IOMS.......... Input-Output Management System [*Computer science*] (MHDI)
IOMS.......... Interim Operation Meteorological System
IOMS.......... International Organization for Masoretic Studies
IOMSA.......... International Oil Mill Superintendents Association (NTPA)
IOMSPCo ...... Isle of Man Steam Packet Co. [*British*] (ROG)
IOMT.......... Isomet Corp. [*NASDAQ symbol*] (NQ)
IOMTR .... International Organization for Motor Trades and Repairs [*Rijswljk, Netherlands*] (EAIO)
IOMVM .... International Organization of Motor Vehicle Manufacturers (EAIO)

ION .... Bionaire, Inc. [Toronto Stock Exchange symbol]
ION .... Biotech Electronics Ltd. [Toronto Stock Exchange symbol]
ION .... Coe College, Cedar Rapids, IA [OCLC symbol] (OCLC)
ION .... Impfondo [Congo] [Airport symbol] (OAG)
ION .... Indian Ocean Newsletter [A publication]
ION .... Inferior Olivary Nucleus [Neuroanatomy]
ION .... Institute for Optimum Nutrition [British]
ION .... Institute of Navigation (EA)
ION .... Institute of Neuroscience [University of Oregon] [Research center] (RCD)
ION .... Institute of Neurotoxicology [Yeshiva University] [Research center] (RCD)
ION .... International Organization of Nerds (EA)
ION .... Ione, WA [Location identifier FAA] (FAAL)
ION .... Ionic
ION .... Ionics, Inc. [NYSE symbol] (SPSG)
ION .... Ionosphere and Aural Phenomena Advisory Committee [European Space Research Organization] (IEEE)
ION .... Ischemic Optic Neuropathy [Medicine]
ION .... Isthmo-Optic Nucleus [or Nuclei] [In midbrain of chick]
Iona .... De Iona [Philo] (BJA)
IOna .... Onarga Public Library, Onarga, IL [Library symbol Library of Congress] (LCLS)
IonaApp ...... Iona Appliances, Inc. [Associated Press] (SAG)
Iona C .... Iona College (GAGS)
IONDS .... Initial Operational Nuclear Detection System
IONDS .... Integrated Operational Nuclear Detonation Detection System
IONDT .... Ischemic Optic Neuropathy Decompression Trial
Ionic .... Ionic Fuel Technology, Inc. [Associated Press] (SAG)
IonicFuel ..... Ionic Fuel Technology, Inc. [Associated Press] (SAG)
Ionics .... Ionics, Inc. [Associated Press] (SAG)
IonLaser ...... Ion Laser Technology [Associated Press] (SAG)
IonLsr .... Ion Laser Technology, Inc. [Associated Press] (SAG)
ION-M .... Integrated On-Line Non-Stop Manufacturing [Safe Computing Ltd.] [Software package] (NCC)
IONO .... Ionosphere (MSA)
IONS .... Institute of Noetic Sciences (EA)
IONS .... Institute of Oceanography Nova Scotia [Canada] [Marine science] (OSRA)
IONS .... Intraoperative Neurosonography [Radiology]
IOO .... ICOR Oil & Gas Co. Ltd. [Toronto Stock Exchange symbol]
IOO .... Idaho Operations Office [Energy Research and Development Administration]
IOO .... Input/Output Operation (HGAA)
IOO .... Inspecting Ordnance Officer
IOO .... Northwestern College, Orange City, IA [OCLC symbol] (OCLC)
IOOC .... Integrated Optics and Optical Fiber Communications (MCD)
IOOC .... International Conference on Integrated Optics and Optical Fiber Communication (PDAA)
IOOC .... International Olive Oil Council [See also COI] [Madrid, Spain] (EAIO)
IOOC .... Iranian Oil Operating Companies
IOOF .... Independent Order of Odd Fellows (EA)
IOOL .... International Optometric and Optical League [British] (EAIO)
IOOP .... Input/Output Operation [Computer science]
IOOSF .... Integrated Orbital Operations Simulation Facility
IOOTS .... International Organization of Old Testament Scholars
IOOW .... In Our Own Way (EA)
IOP .... Caliop [France ICAO designator] (FAAC)
IOP .... Central College, Pella, IA [OCLC symbol] (OCLC)
IOP .... Ibero-American Organization of Pilots [See also OIP] [Mexico City, Mexico] (EAIO)
I/OP .... Inboard/Outboard Profile (NASA)
IOP .... Initial Operating Production (MCD)
IOP .... In-Orbit Plane (KSC)
IOP .... Input-Output Package [IBM Corp.] [Computer science]
IOP .... Input-Output Port [Computer science] (MCD)
IOP .... Input-Output Processor [Computer science]
IOP .... Input-Output Pulse [Computer science]
IOP .... Inspection Operation Procedure (MCD)
IOP .... Installation Operating Program (AABC)
IOP .... Institute of Packaging [British] (BI)
IOP .... Institute of Painters in Oil Colours [British]
IOP .... Institute of Petroleum [British] (BI)
IOP .... Institute of Physics [British] (EAIO)
IOP .... Institute of Plumbing (EAIO)
IoP .... Institute of Plumbing (WDAA)
IOP .... Institute of Printing [British]
IOP .... Institute of Pyramidology [Harpenden, Hertfordshire, England] (EA)
IOP .... Integrated Obstacle Plan [Military]
IOP .... Integrated Operation Plan [NASA] (NASA)
IOP .... Integrated Ordnance Package (MCD)
IOP .... Intensive Observation Period [Marine science] (OSRA)
IOP .... Intensive Observing Period (USDC)
IOP .... Interface Operating Procedures (TELE)
IOP .... Interim Operating Procedure (NVT)
IOP .... Internal Operating Procedure
IOP .... International Organization of Palaeobotany [British]
IOP .... International Organization of Psychophysiology [See also IPO] [Montreal, PQ] (EAIO)
IOP .... International Potter Distilling Corp. [Toronto Stock Exchange symbol Vancouver Stock Exchange symbol]
IOP .... Intraocular Pressure [Ophthalmology]
IOP .... Ioma [Papua New Guinea] [Airport symbol] (OAG)
IOP .... Iranian Oil Participants Ltd.

IOp .... Orland Park Public Library, Orland Park, IL [Library symbol Library of Congress] (LCLS)
IOPA .... International Organizations Procurement Act of 1947
IOPAB .... International Organization for Pure and Applied Biophysics
IOPB .... International Organization of Plant Biosystematists [St. Anne De Bellevue, PQ] (EA)
IOPC .... Institute of Paper Conservation (EA)
IOPC .... Interagency Oil Policy Committee
IOPC .... International Oil Pollution Compensation [In association name IOPC Fund] [See also FIPOL]
IOPEC .... International Oil Pollution Exhibition and Conference (PDAA)
IO/PG .... Indian Ocean/Persian Gulf
IOPG .... Input/Output Processor Group (NITA)
IOPI .... International Organization for Plant Information
IOPKG .... Input/Output Package [IBM Corp.] [Computer science]
IOPL .... Instructional Objectives Preference List (AEBS)
IOPL .... Integrated Open Problem List (NASA)
IOPL .... Intermittent Operating Life (IAA)
IOPL .... I/O [Input/Output] Privilege Level [Computer science]
IOPN .... In Operation (IAA)
IOPO .... Interest-Only/Principal-Only [Stock exchange term]
IoPP .... Institute of Packaging Professionals (EA)
IoPP .... Institute of Physics Publishing (TELE)
IOPP .... International Oil Pollution Prevention
IOPS .... Input-Output Programming System [Computer science]
IOQ .... Input-Output Queue [Computer science] (IBMDP)
IOQ .... Installational and Operational Qualifications [Manufacturing]
IOQ .... Institute of Quarrying [British]
IOQ .... Iowa State Historical Society, Iowa City, IA [OCLC symbol] (OCLC)
IOQE .... Input-Output Queue Element [Computer science] (MCD)
IOQE .... Input/Output Queue Element (NAKS)
IOR .... Immediate Operational Requirement (MCD)
IOR .... Independent Order of Rechabites
IOR .... Index of Refraction (MCD)
IOR .... Index of Response [Medicine] (DMAA)
IOR .... Indian Ocean Region [INTELSAT]
IOR .... Indian Other Rank [British military] (DMA)
IOR .... Input-Output Register [SAGE]
IOR .... Institute of Religion (HGEN)
IoR .... Institute of Roofing [British] (DBA)
IOR .... Instituto per le Opere di Religione [Institute for Religious Works] [The Vatican bank]
IOR .... International Offshore Rule [Yachting]
IOR .... International Order of Runeberg (EA)
IOR .... Iowa Resources, Inc. (EFIS)
IOR .... Issue on Request [or Requisition]
IOR .... Marycrest College, Davenport, IA [OCLC symbol] (OCLC)
IORB .... Input/Output Record Block [Computer science]
IORC .... Input-Output Read Control [Computer science] (MHDI)
IORD .... International Organization for Rural Development
IOREG .... Input/Output Register (IAA)
IOREQ .... Input/Output Request [Computer science]
IORL .... Input Output Requirements Language [Teledyne Braun Engineering] (NITA)
IORM .... Improved Order of Red Men
IORS .... Inflatable Occupant Restraint System
IORS .... Input-Output Request Subroutine [Computer science] (MHDI)
IORT .... Input Output of a Record and Transfer [Computer science] (SAA)
IORT .... Input-Output Remote Terminal [Computer science] (MHDI)
IORT .... Intraoperative Radiation Therapy [Medicine]
IORV .... Inadvertently Opened Relief Valve [Environmental science] (COE)
IORV .... Inadvertent Opening of a Safety Relief Valve [Nuclear energy] (NRCH)
IOS .... Davenport Public Library, Davenport, IA [OCLC symbol] (OCLC)
Ios .... De Iosepho [Philo] (BJA)
IOS .... IGOSS [Integrated Global Ocean Station System] Observing System [Marine science] (MSC)
IOS .... Ilheus [Brazil] [Airport symbol] (OAG)
IOS .... Image Optical Scanner
IOS .... Image Orthicon System
IOS .... Independent Order of Svithiod (EA)
IOS .... Indian Ocean Ship
IOS .... Indian Ocean Station (MCD)
IOS .... Input-Output Selector [Computer science] (IEEE)
IOS .... Input-Output Sense [Computer science] (KSC)
IOS .... Input-Output Skip [Computer science]
IOS .... Input/Output Subsystem (NITA)
IOS .... Input-Output Supervision [Computer science] (NASA)
IOS .... Input-Output Switch [Computer science]
IOS .... Input/Output System [General Automation] [Computer science]
IOS .... Inspection Operation Sheet (AAG)
IOS .... Inspection Operation System (AAG)
IOS .... Inspector of Schools [British] (DAS)
IOS .... Institute for Objectivist Studies (EA)
IOS .... Institute of Oceanographic Sciences [British Research center] (IRC)
IOS .... Institute of Ocean Sciences [Canadian Department of Fisheries and Oceans] [Research center] (RCD)
IOS .... Institute of Optimization and Systems Theory [Stockholm]
IOS .... Institute of Statisticians [British] (DBA)
IOS .... Instructor Operation Station [Army] (NASA)
IOS .... Instrumentation Operation Station
IOS .... Instrument Operating System
IOS .... Integrated Observation System (MCD)
IOS .... Integrated Office System [JSB Computer Systems/Olivetti] (NITA)
IOS .... Integrated Operator System [Telecommunications]

IOS............. Intelligence Operations Specialist [*Military*] (MCD)
IOS............. Intelligence Oversight
IOS............. Interactive Operating System [*Computer science*]
IOS............. Interceptor Operator Simulator (IAA)
IOS............. Interim Operational System
IOS............. Internationale Organisation fuer Sukkulentenforschung [*International Organization for Succulent Plant Study - IOS*] (EAIO)
IOS............. International Oculoplastic Society (NTPA)
IOS............. International Officer School [*Military*]
IOS............. International Oleander Society (EA)
IOS............. International Organization for Standardization [*Official initialism is ISO*]
IOS............. International Orthokeratology Society (EA)
IOS............. Internetwork Operating System [*Computer science*] (IGQR)
IOS............. Intraoperative Sonography [*Radiology*] (DAVI)
IOS............. Investors Overseas Services Ltd. [*Firm which sells mutual funds in foreign countries*]
IOS............. Isle Of Skye [*Scotland*]
IOS............. Isles of Scilly Skybus Ltd. [*British ICAO designator*] (FAAC)
IOs............. Oswego Township Library, Oswego, IL [*Library symbol Library of Congress*] (LCLS)
IOSA .... Input/Output Systems Association [*Defunct*] (EA)
IOSA .... Integrated Optical Spectrum Analyzer (CAAL)
IOSA .... International Oil Scouts Association (EA)
IOSA .... Irish Offshore Services Association (EAIO)
IOSC .... Integrated Operations Support Center [*NASA*] (NASA)
iosc............. Integrated Operations Support Center [*NASA*] (NAKS)
IOSCS .... International Organization for Septuagint and Cognate Studies (EA)
IOSD .... Information and Office Systems Division [*Exxon Research and Engineering Co.*] [*Information service or system*] (IID)
IOSD .... Initial Operational Support Date (MCD)
IOSDL .... Institute of Oceanographic Sciences Deacon Laboratory [*Natural Environment Research Council*] [*British*] (IRC)
IOSEWR .... International Organization for the Study of the Endurance of Wire Ropes [*Paris, France*] (EAIO)
IOSGT .... International Organization for the Study of Group Tensions (EA)
IOSH .... Independent Order Sons of Hermann
IOSH .... Institution of Occupational Safety and Health [*British*] (DBA)
IOSHD .... International Organization for the Study of Human Development [*Defunct*] (EA)
IOSI .... International Oculoplastic Society, Inc. (EA)
IOSL .... Independent Order of St. Luke [*Defunct*] (EA)
IOSM .... Independent Order of Sons of Malta
IOSN .... Indian Ocean Standard Net
IOS/OSI .... International Organization for Standardization Open Systems Interconnection Model
IOSOT .... International Organization for the Study of the Old Testament [*British*]
IOSP .... Input/Output under Signal and Proceed [*Computer science*] (IAA)
IOSS .... Indian Ocean Station Support
IOSS .... Input/Output Subsystem [*NCR Corp.*]
IOSS .... Integrated Ocean Surveillance System [*Navy*] (NG)
IOSS .... Integrated Operational Support Study (MCD)
IOSS .... Intelligence Organization Stationing Study [*Army*] (MCD)
IOSS .... Intraoperative Spinal Sonography [*Radiology*]
IOST .... Input/Output under Signal and Transfer [*Computer science*] (IAA)
IOSTA .... Comission Internationale de l'Organisation Scientifique du Travail [*International Committee of Work Study and Labour Management in Agriculture*] (EAIO)
IOSTE........... International Organisation for Science and Technology Education (AIE)
IOSV .... Interorbital Space Vehicle (MCD)
IOT .... British Indian Ocean Territory [*ANSI three-letter standard code*] (CNC)
IOT............... Dordt College, Sioux Center, IA [*OCLC symbol*] (OCLC)
IOT............... Image Output Terminal [*Computer science*] (HGAA)
IOT............... Income Opportunity Realty [*AMEX symbol*] (SPSG)
IOT............... Income Opportunity Rlty [*AMEX symbol*] (TTSB)
IOT............... Individual Operation Test
IOT............... Induction Output Tube
IOT............... Information Origination/Termination Equipment [*Telecommunications*] (OTD)
IOT............... Initial Operational Test [*Army*]
IOT............... Initial Orbit Time [*Aerospace*]
IOT............... Input/Output and Transfer (NITA)
IOT............... Input-Output Termination [*Computer science*]
I/OT............. Input/Output Test [*Computer science*] (NASA)
IOT............... Input-Output Transfer [*Computer science*]
IOT............... Input-Output Trap [*Computer science*] (MHDI)
IOT............... Input/Output Trunk (NITA)
IOT............... Inspection Operation Tag
IOT............... Institute of Operating Theatre Technicians [*British*]
IOT............... International Optical Telecommunications, Inc. [*Information service or system*] (IID)
IOT............... Interocular Transfer [*Ophthalmology*]
IOT............... Interoffice Trunk (IAA)
IOT............... Interorganizational Transfer (AAGC)
IOT............... Intraocular Tension [*Ophthalmology*] (DAVI)
IOT............... Intraocular Transfer [*Ophthalmology*] (DAVI)
IOT............... Ipsilateral Optic Tectum [*Medicine*]
IOT............... Iron Ore Transport [*Steamship*] (MHDW)
IOt............... Reddick's Library, Ottawa, IL [*Library symbol Library of Congress*] (LCLS)
IOTA............ Inbound/Outbound Traffic Analysis [*Military*] (AABC)
IOTA............ Inbound Tourism Organisation of Australia
IOTA............ Information Overload Testing Aid [*or Apparatus*]

IOTA............ Information Overload Testing Apparatus (NITA)
IOTA............ Instant Oxide Thickness Analyzer (IAA)
IOTA............ Institute of Theoretical Astronomy [*University of Cambridge*]
IOTA............ Institute of Transport Administration [*British*] (DCTA)
IOTA............ Integrated On-Line Text Arrangement
IOTA............ Interest on Trust Accounts Program
IOTA............ International Occultation Timing Association (EA)
IOTAE........... Initial Operating Test and Evaluation (IAA)
IOT & E....... Independent Operational Test and Evaluation [*Military*]
IOT & E....... Initial Operating Test and Evaluation (MCD)
IOT & E....... Initial Operational Test and Evaluation [*Army*] (DOMA)
IOtBD .... LaSalle County Board for Developmentally Disabled, Ottawa, IL [*Library symbol Library of Congress*] (LCLS)
IOTC............ Infantry Officers Training Camp
IOTC............ International Originating Toll Center [*Bell System*]
IOtCE .... LaSalle County Cooperative Extension, Ottawa, IL [*Library symbol Library of Congress*] (LCLS)
IOTCG .... International Organization for Technical Cooperation in Geology (EAIO)
IOtCH .... Community Hospital of Ottawa, Ottawa, IL [*Library symbol Library of Congress*] (LCLS)
IOtDSD......... Deer Park Consolidated Community School District 82, Ottawa, IL [*Library symbol Library of Congress*] (LCLS)
IOTE............ Individual Operator Training Equipment (MCD)
IOTE............ Initial Outfitting Technical Evaluation (MCD)
IOTEP........... Initial Operating Test and Evaluation Period [*Navy*]
IOtES .... LaSalle County Educational Service Region, Ottawa, IL [*Library symbol Library of Congress*] (LCLS)
IOtF .... Friendship Facilities, Ottawa, IL [*Library symbol Library of Congress*] (LCLS)
IOTF............ International Obesity Task Force
IOTG .... Input/Output Task Group [*CODASYL*]
IOTG .... Isooctyl Thioglycolate [*Organic chemistry*]
IOtGH .... Ottawa General Hospital, Ottawa, IL [*Library symbol Library of Congress*] (LCLS)
IOtHS .... Ottawa Township High School District 140, Ottawa, IL [*Library symbol Library of Congress*] (LCLS)
IOtM .... Marquette High School, Ottawa, IL [*Library symbol Library of Congress*] (LCLS)
IOTPD .... International Organization for the Transition of Professionals Dancers [*Switzerland*]
IOTR .... Intratrabecular Osteoclastic Tunneling Resorption [*Medicine*]
IOTR .... Item Operation Trouble Report (AAG)
IOtRP .... LaSalle County Regional Planning Commission, Ottawa, IL [*Library symbol Library of Congress*] (LCLS)
IOtRSD......... Rutland Consolidated Community School District 230, Ottawa, IL [*Library symbol Library of Congress*] (LCLS)
IOtS .... Starved Rock Library System, Ottawa, IL [*Library symbol Library of Congress*] (LCLS)
IOTT & E...... Improved Operational Test, Training, and Evaluation [*Military*]
IOTTSG......... International Oil Tanker Terminal Safety Group (PDAA)
IOtWSD......... Wallace Consolidated Community School District 195, Ottawa, IL [*Library symbol Library of Congress*] (LCLS)
IOU .... Immediate Operation Use
IOU .... Input-Output Unit [*Computer chip*]
IOU .... Input-Output Utility [*Computer science*]
IOU .... Intensive Care Observation Unit [*Medicine*] (DMAA)
IOU .... Intensive Therapy Observation Unit (MAE)
IOU .... International Opacity Unit (DB)
IOU .... Investor-Owned Utilities (BARN)
IOU .... I Owe You [*Slang*]
IOU .... Public Library of Des Moines, Des Moines, IA [*OCLC symbol*] (OCLC)
IOUBC .... Institute of Oceanography, University of British Columbia
IOUBC.......... International Office for Universal Bibliographic Control (TELE)
IOV .... Independent Order of Vikings [*Des Plaines, IL*] (EA)
IOV............... Initial Office Visit [*Medicine*] (DAVI)
IOV............... Input Offset Voltage
IOV............... Inside-Out Vesicle [*Biochemistry*]
IOV............... Institute of Virology [*British*] (ARC)
IOV............... University of Dubuque, Dubuque, IA [*OCLC symbol*] (OCLC)
IOVC .... In the Overcast [*Aviation*]
IOVST .... International Organization for Vacuum Science and Technology
IOW .... Inert Ordnance Warehouse
IOW .... In Other Words
IOW .... Input-Output Write [*Computer science*] (MHDI)
IOW .... Iowa City [*Iowa*] [*Airport symbol*] (AD)
IOW .... Iowa City, IA [*Location identifier FAA*] (FAAL)
Iow............... Iowa Reports [*A publication*] (DLA)
IOW .... Isle Of Wight
IOW .... Wartburg College, Waverly, IA [*OCLC symbol*] (OCLC)
IOWA .... Interorganizational Work Authorization (KSC)
IOWA .... Iowa Bancorporation, Inc. [*NASDAQ symbol*] (SAG)
Iowa............. Iowa Supreme Court Reports [*A publication*] (DLA)
Iowa Acts... Acts and Joint Resolutions of the State of Iowa [*A publication*] (DLA)
Iowa Admin Bull... Iowa Administrative Bulletin [*A publication*] (DLA)
Iowa Admin Code... Iowa Administrative Code [*A publication*] (DLA)
Iowa Bar Rev... Iowa Bar Review [*A publication*] (DLA)
IowaBcp....... Iowa Bancorporation, Inc. [*Associated Press*] (SAG)
Iowa B Rev... Iowa Bar Review [*A publication*] (DLA)
Iowa Code... Code of Iowa [*A publication*] (AAGC)
Iowa LB ...... Iowa Law Bulletin [*A publication*] (DLA)
Iowa L Bull... Iowa Law Bulletin [*A publication*] (DLA)
Iowa Legis Serv... Iowa Legislative Service (West) [*A publication*] (DLA)
Iowa RC....... Iowa Railroad Commissioners Reports [*A publication*] (DLA)

Iowa SBA.....	Iowa State Bar Association. Proceedings [*A publication*] (DLA)
Iowa St BAQ...	Iowa State Bar Association. Quarterly [*A publication*] (DLA)
Iowa St U	Iowa State University of Science and Technology (GAGS)
Iowa Univ L Bull...	Iowa University. Law Bulletin [*A publication*] (DLA)
IOWE	International Office for Water Education [*Utah State University*]
IOWE	International Organization of Women Executives [*Defunct*] (EA)
IOWIT	International Organization of Women in Telecommunications [*Defunct*] (TSSD)
IOWMC	International Organization of Wooden Money Collectors (EA)
IOWQ	Input-Output Wait Queue [*Computer science*] (MHDI)
IOWT	International Organization of Women in Telecommunications [*Defunct*] (EA)
IOX..............	Input-Output Executive [*Computer science*] (MHDI)
IOX..............	William Penn College, Oskaloosa, IA [*OCLC symbol*] (OCLC)
IOY..............	Upper Iowa University, Fayette, IA [*OCLC symbol*] (OCLC)
IOZ..............	State Library Commission of Iowa, Des Moines, IA [*OCLC symbol*] (OCLC)
IOZP............	Indian Ocean Zone of Peace
IP...............	Airlines of Tasmania [*ICAO designator*] (AD)
IP...............	Cathode-Ray Tube Indicators [*JETDS nomenclature*] [*Military*] (CET)
I/P..............	Current/Pneumatic [*Nuclear energy*] (NRCH)
I/P..............	Current to Pressure [*Electropneumatic*] (ACII)
IP...............	Empresa AVIAIMPORT [*Cuba ICAO designator*] (ICDA)
IP...............	Ice Plow [*Coast Guard*] (DNAB)
IP...............	Ice Point
IP...............	Icterus Precox [*Medicine*]
IP...............	Identification of Position
IP...............	Identification Peculiarity
IP...............	Identification Point
IP...............	Identified Patient [*Medicine*] (DHP)
IP...............	Identity Preserved [*Wheat*] [*Department of Agriculture*]
IP...............	Igloo Pallet [*Spacelab*] [*NASA*] (NASA)
IP...............	Ignition Point [*Chemistry*] (IAA)
IP...............	Iliopsoas [*Muscle*] [*Anatomy*] (DAVI)
IP...............	Image Previewer (DGA)
IP...............	Image Process
IP...............	Imaginary Part [*of a complex number*] (DEN)
IP...............	Immediate Permanent Incapacitation [*Radiation casualty criterion*] [*Army*]
IP...............	Immune Precipitate [*Immunology*]
IP...............	Immunoperoxidase (Technique) [*Clinical chemistry*]
IP...............	Impact Point (AFM)
IP...............	Impact Predictor [*NASA*]
IP...............	Impact Printer [*Computer science*]
IP...............	Impact Prognosticator [*Aerospace*] (AAG)
IP...............	Impedance Probe
IP...............	Imperial Preference (ADA)
IP...............	Impingement Point
IP...............	Implementation of Plan (NG)
IP...............	Implementation Period
IP...............	Import Penetration
IP...............	Impostor Phenomenon [*Subject of book "If I'm So Successful, Why Do I Feel Like a Fake - The Impostor Phenomenon" by Joan C. Harvey*] [*Psychology*]
IP...............	Improvement Program (AFM)
IP...............	Improvement Purchase (ADA)
iP	Impulse P Wave [*Earthquakes*] [*Exclamation point signifies a very sharp earthquake*]
IP...............	Inca Pacific Resources [*VS, exchange symbol*] (TTSB)
IP...............	Incentive Pay
IP...............	Incisoproximal [*Dentistry*]
IP...............	Incisopulpal [*Dentistry*]
IP...............	Incontinentia Pigmenti (DB)
IP...............	Incubation Period [*Medicine*]
IP...............	Index of Performance
IP...............	Index of Preprogramming [*Computer science*] (PDAA)
IP...............	Indian Pattern [*British military*] (DMA)
IP...............	Indian Preference [*Civil Service*]
IP...............	India Paper
IP...............	Indicator Panel
IP...............	Indirect Proof [*Method in logic*]
IP...............	Indium Phosphide [*Materials science*]
IP...............	Indochina Project [*An association*] (EA)
IP...............	Induced Polarization [*Geophysical prospecting*]
IP...............	Induced Protein [*Biochemistry*] (DAVI)
IP...............	Induction Period [*Medicine*]
IP...............	Industrial Participation [*Civil Defense*]
IP...............	Industrial Planning
IP...............	Industrial Police
IP...............	Industrial Policy
IP...............	Industrial Production
IP...............	Industry Program [*Defense Systems Management College*] (DOMA)
IP...............	Inertial Platform
IP...............	Inertial Processing (MCD)
IP...............	Infection Prevention
IP...............	Information Packets [*or Packages*] (GNE)
IP...............	Information Paper
IP...............	Information Pool (IAA)
IP...............	Information Processing (BUR)
IP...............	Information Provider
IP...............	Information Publication [*HUD*]
IP...............	Information Publications [*Singapore, Hong Kong, Australia*]
IP...............	Information Publishing
IP...............	Infundibular Process [*Medicine*] (DMAA)
IP...............	Infundibulopelvic [*Ligament*] [*Anatomy*] (DAVI)

IP...............	Inhalable Particulates [*Environmental science*] (COE)
IP...............	Inhaled Particles [*or Particulates*] [*Environmental chemistry*]
IP...............	Inhouse Publishing (IAA)
IP...............	Initial Phase [*IEEE*]
IP...............	Initial Point [*Military*]
IP...............	Initial Position
IP...............	Initial Post [*Military*]
IP...............	Initial Pressure [*On lumbar puncture*] [*Neurosurgery*] (DAVI)
IP...............	Initial Production
IP...............	Initial Provisioning (MCD)
IP...............	Inland Postage (IAA)
IP...............	Innings Pitched [*Baseball*]
Ip...............	Innings Played [*Baseball*]
IP...............	Innovative Project
IP...............	Inorganic Phosphorus (OA)
IP...............	Inosine Phosphorylase [*An enzyme*] (MAE)
IP...............	Inpatient [*Medicine*]
IP...............	In-Phase [*Gynecology*]
IP...............	In Place [*Dancing*]
IP...............	In Plaster [*Medicine*] (DAVI)
IP...............	In Process
I/P..............	In Progress (MCD)
I/P..............	Input [*Computer science*]
IP...............	Input Power [*Computer science*]
IP...............	Input Processor [*Computer science*]
IP...............	Insolated Platform
IP...............	Inspection Pit [*Motor garage*] (ROG)
IP...............	Inspection Procedure [*Nuclear energy*] (NRCH)
IP...............	Installation Procedure
IP...............	Installment Paid [*Business term*]
IP...............	Instantaneous Pressure [*Medicine*] (MAE)
IP...............	Institute for Psychohistory (EA)
IP...............	Institute of Petroleum [*British*]
IP...............	Institute of Physics [*British*] (EAIO)
IP...............	Institute of Printing [*British*]
IP...............	Instructional Psychologist (MCD)
IP...............	Instruction Pamphlet
IP...............	Instruction Plate (MSA)
IP...............	Instruction Pointer [*Computer science*]
IP...............	Instruction Processor [*Computer science*]
IP...............	Instruction Pulse (MSA)
IP...............	Instructor-Patient [*Medicine*]
IP...............	Instructor Pilot [*Air Force*] (AFM)
IP...............	Instrumentation Papers [*Air Force*] (MCD)
IP...............	Instrumentation Payload (NASA)
IP...............	Instrumentation PCM [*Power Control Mission*] [*NASA*]
IP...............	Instrumentation Plan (MUGU)
IP...............	Instrumentation Power (MCD)
IP...............	Instrumentation/Pulse Code Modulation Master Unit Data Bus (NAKS)
IP...............	Instrument Panel [*Automotive engineering*]
IP...............	Insulated Platform (MCD)
IP...............	Insurance Patient [*Medicine*]
IP...............	Integrated Processor [*Computer science*]
IP...............	Intellectual Property (MCD)
IP...............	Intelligence Publications (MCD)
IP...............	Intelligent Peripheral [*Computer science*] (ACRL)
IP...............	Interactive Processing (IAA)
IP...............	Intercept Point [*Air Force*]
IP...............	Interchangeable Solid and Screen Panels [*Technical drawings*]
IP...............	Interdigital Pause [*Telecommunications*] (TEL)
IP...............	Interelement Protection (IAA)
IP...............	Interface Processor [*Computer science*]
IP...............	Interface Program [*Computer science*] (IAA)
IP...............	Interference Pattern (CAAL)
IP...............	Intermediate Pallet (NASA)
IP...............	Intermediate Pressure
IP...............	Intermediate Processor (SSD)
IP...............	Internal Phloem [*Botany*]
IP...............	Internal Protocol (SSD)
IP...............	International Paper Co. [*NYSE symbol*] (SPSG)
IP...............	International Pharmacopoeia
IP...............	International Programming (IAA)
IP...............	Internet Protocol [*Computer science*] (PCM)
IP...............	Interphalangeal [*Anatomy*]
IP...............	Interplanetary
IP...............	Interpositive [*Photography*] (WDMC)
IP...............	Interpupillary (DB)
IP...............	Interscience Publishers
IP...............	Intl Paper [*NYSE symbol*] (TTSB)
IP...............	Intraperitoneal [*Medicine*]
IP...............	Invalid Pension
IP...............	Inverse Photoemission [*Spectroscopy*]
IP...............	Ionization Potential
IP...............	Ion-Pair [*Physical chemistry*]
IP...............	Ipatropium [*Pharmacology*]
IP...............	Irate Parent (ADA)
IP...............	Irish Party (ROG)
IP...............	Iron Pipe
I/P..............	Irregular Input Process [*Telecommunications*] (TEL)
IP...............	Isidis Planitia [*A filamentary mark on Mars*]
IP...............	Isoelectric Point [*Also, IEP, PH$_1$, pI*] [*Chemistry*]
IP...............	Isolation Pulse
IP...............	Isoproterenol [*An adrenergic*]
IP...............	Israeli Pound (BJA)
IP...............	Issue Paper

IP .... Issue Price [Business term]
IP .... Issuing Point
IP .... Italian Patent (IAA)
IP .... Item Processing
IP .... Izquierda de los Pueblos [Spain] [Political party] (ECED)
IP .... Office of International Programs [Nuclear energy National Science Foundation] (NRCH)
IP .... Peer of Ireland (ROG)
IP .... Peoria Public Library, Peoria, IL [Library symbol Library of Congress] (LCLS)
IP .... Positive Identification (ECII)
IPA .... Allied Agencies Center, Peoria, IL [Library symbol Library of Congress] (LCLS)
IPA .... Image Power Amplifier (IAA)
IPA .... Image Processing Applications [Computer graphics]
IPA .... Immunoperoxidase Antibody Assay [Clinical chemistry]
IPA .... Imperial Pale Ale
IPA .... Including Particular Average [Insurance]
IPA .... Incontienentia Pigmenti Achromians (STED)
IPA .... Incorporeal Personal Agency [Parapsychology]
IPA .... Independent Physician Association (HCT)
IPA .... Independent-Practice Association [Medical insurance]
IPA .... Independent Product Assurance (SSD)
IPA .... Independent Public Accountant
IPA .... Independent Publishers' Association [Canada]
IPA .... India Pale Ale
IPA .... India Press Agency
IPA .... Indicated Pressure Altitude
IPA .... Individual, Partnership, and Corporation [Deposits] (EBF)
IPA .... Individual Practice Association [Medicine]
IPA .... Indole, Pyruvic Acid (STED)
IPA .... Indolepyruvic Acid [Biochemistry] (DB)
IPA .... Industrial Participation Association [British]
IPA .... Industrial Perforators Association (EA)
IPA .... Industrial Property Administration
IPA .... Industrial Publicity Association (EA)
IPA .... Information for Public Affairs, Inc. [Information service or system] (IID)
IPA .... Information Process Analysis (BUR)
IPA .... Information Processing Architecture (IAA)
IPA .... Information Processing Association [Israel]
IPA .... Information-technology Promotion Agency [Japan] (NITA)
IPA .... In-Principle Agreement
IPA .... Insolvency Practitioners Association [British] (EAIO)
IPA .... Institute for Physics of the Atmosphere
IPA .... Institute for Policy Analysis [University of Toronto] [Canada] (IRC)
IPA .... Institute for Polyacrylate Absorbents (EA)
IPA .... Institute of Practitioners in Advertising
IPA .... Institute of Public Administration (EA)
IPA .... Institute of Public Affairs [Dalhousie University] [Canada Research center]
IPA .... Institutional Patent Agreements [General Services Administration]
IPA .... Instrument Performance Assessment
IPA .... Integrated Peripheral Adapter
IPA .... Integrated Photodetection Assemblies (IEEE)
IPA .... Integrated Plan of Action (MCD)
IPA .... Integrated Printer Adapter
IPA .... Intelligence Production Activity [Military] (MCD)
IPA .... Intelligence Production Agency (COE)
IPA .... Interamerican Press Association
IPA .... Intergovernmental Personnel Act [1970]
IPA .... Intergovernmental Personnel Agreement (COE)
IPA .... Interior Plantscape Association [Later, ALCA/IPD] (EA)
IPA .... Intermediate Power Amplifier [Electronics]
IPA .... International Association for the Child's Right to Play [International PI ayground Association] [Acronym is based on former name,] (EA)
IPA .... International Paddleball Association [Later, AARA] (EA)
IPA .... International Palaeontological Association (EA)
IPA .... International Patent Agreement
IPA .... International Peace Academy (EA)
IPA .... International Peach Academy (BUAC)
IPA .... International Pediatric Association [See also AIP] [Paris, France] (EAIO)
IPA .... International Permafrost Association (BUAC)
IPA .... International Petroleum Annual [Department of Energy] [Database]
IPA .... International Phonetic Alphabet
IPA .... International Phonetic Association [University College] [Leeds, England] (EA)
IPA .... International Photographers Association (BUAC)
IPA .... International Phototherapy Association (EA)
IPA .... International Pietenpol Association (EA)
IPA .... International Pinball Association (EA)
IPA .... International Pipe Association [Later, TPF] (EA)
IPA .... International Platform Association (EA)
IPA .... International Police Academy [Formerly, Inter-American Police Academy]
IPA .... International Police Association [Maidstone, Kent, England] (EAIO)
IPA .... International Polka Association (EA)
IPA .... International Porcelain Artist (EA)
IPA .... International Prepress Association (EA)
IPA .... International Press Association [Defunct] (EA)
IPA .... International Psycho-Analytical Association [British] (EAIO)
IPA .... International Psychogeriatric Association (EA)
IPA .... International Psychohistorical Association (EA)

IPA .... International Publishers Association [See also UIE] [Geneva, Switzerland] (EAIO)
IPA .... International Publishers Audio-Visual Association (BUAC)
IPA .... International Pumpkin Association (EA)
IPA .... Inter-Pacific Resource Corp. [Vancouver Stock Exchange symbol]
IPA .... Interstate Pollution Abatement Notice (COE)
IPA .... Intrapulmonary Artery (STED)
IPA .... Invasive Pulmonary Aspergillosis [Medicine] (DAVI)
IPA .... Investment Partnership Association (EA)
IPA .... Investment Program Association (NTPA)
IPA .... Involvement & Participation Association (BUAC)
IPA .... Ipec Aviation Pty Ltd. [Australia ICAO designator] (FAAC)
IPA .... Ipota [Vanuatu] [Airport symbol] (OAG)
IPA .... Isopentenyladenosine [Biochemistry]
IPA .... Isophthalic Acid [Organic chemistry]
IPA .... Isopropane [Organic chemistry]
IPA .... Isopropyl Alcohol [Organic chemistry]
IPA .... Issue-Position-Argument [Computer science] (BYTE)
IPAA .... Independent Petroleum Association of America (EA)
IPAA .... Industrial Photographers Association of America [Later, Industrial Photographers of New Jersey] (EA)
IPAA .... Instrumental Photon Activation Analysis [National Institute of Standards and Technology]
IPAA .... International Pesticide Applicators Association (EA)
IPAA .... International Prisoners Aid Association (EA)
IPAA .... Inventario del Patrimonio Arquitectonico [Database] [Ministerio de Cultura] [Spanish] [Information service or system] (CRD)
IPAB .... International Program for Antarctic Buoys [Marine science] (OSRA)
IPAC .... Independent Petroleum Association of Canada
IPAC .... Information Processing and Control [Systems Laboratory] [Northwestern University]
IPAC .... Institute of Public Administration of Canada
IPAC .... Integrated Packaging Assembly [NASDAQ symbol] (TTSB)
IPAC .... Integrated Packaging Assembly Corp. [NASDAQ symbol] (SAG)
IPAC .... Intelligence Center, Pacific [Military] (MCD)
IPAC .... Intelligence, Pacific Area Command (MCD)
IPAC .... International Peace Academy Committee (BUAC)
IPACE .... Interprovincial Advisory Council on Energy [Canada]
IPACK .... International Packaging Material Suppliers (DGA)
IPACK .... International Packaging Material Suppliers Association (PDAA)
IPACS .... Integrated Power and Attitude-Control System [NASA]
IPACS .... Interactive Pattern Analysis and Classification System (PDAA)
IPAD .... Incoming Procurement Authorization Document [Air Force] (AFM)
IPAD .... Integrated Program Aircraft Design
IPAD .... Integrated Programs for Aerospace-Vehicle Design
IPAD .... International Plastics Association Directors
IPADAE ...... Integrated Passive Action Detection Acquisition Equipment
IPADD .... Intra-Governmental Professional Advisory Council on Drugs and Devices [Inactive] [FDA] (EGAO)
IP address ... Internet Protocol Address [Computer science] (IGQR)
IPADE .... Instituto Panamericano de Alta Direccion de Empresa [Panamerican Institute for Business Management] [Mexico] (PDAA)
IPADS .... Interactive Processing and Display System (MCD)
IPAE .... (Isopropylamino)ethanol [Organic chemistry]
IPAF .... International Powered Access Federation (EAIO)
IPAFUG ...... International PAF User's Group (EA)
IPAHGEIS .... Inter-Professional Ad Hoc Group for Environmental Information Sharing
IPAI .... International Primary Aluminium Institute [British] (EAIO)
IPAL .... Index to Periodical Articles Related to Law [A publication] (DLA)
IP/AL .... Inland Printer / American Lithographer [A publication] (DGA)
IPAL .... Integrated Program on Arid Lands (BUAC)
IPal .... Palatine Public Library District, Palatine, IL [Library symbol Library of Congress] (LCLS)
Ipalco .... IPALCO Enterprises, Inc. [Associated Press] (SAG)
IPale .... La Motte Township Library, Palestine, IL [Library symbol Library of Congress] (LCLS)
IPalH .... William Rainey Harper College, Palatine, IL [Library symbol Library of Congress] (LCLS)
IPalmSD ...... Northwestern Community Unit, School District 2, Palmyra, IL [Library symbol Library of Congress] (LCLS)
IPALS .... Integrated Pathology Audio-Visual Learning System (PDAA)
IPALSS .... Information Processing Adinstrators of Large School Systems (NTPA)
IPAMS .... Independent Petroleum Association of Mountain States
IPANA .... Indian People's Association in North America (EA)
IP & BE .... Initial Program and Budget Estimate [Army]
IP & C .... Instrumentation Program and Component (KSC)
IP & T .... Intellectual Property and Technology
IPANY .... Individual Psychology Association of New York
IPAO .... Insulin-Induced Peak Acid Output (STED)
IPAP .... Inspiratory Positive Airway Pressure [Medicine] (DMAA)
IPAP .... Interagency Placement Assistance Program [Office of Personnel Management]
IPAP .... Iodophenyl(piperidinoacetyl)piperazine [Biochemistry]
IPAR .... Improved Pulse Acquisition RADAR (AABC)
IPAR .... Innovative Photovoltaics Applications for Residences
IPAR .... Institute of Personality Assessment and Research [University of California] [Research center]
IPAR .... Institute of Policy Analysis and Research [Nairobi, Kenya] [Research center] (ECON)
IPAR .... Intercepted Photosynthetically Active Radiation [Photosynthesis]
IPar .... Paris Carnegie Public Library, Paris, IL [Library symbol Library of Congress] (LCLS)

IPAR .... United States Department of Agriculture, Agricultural Research Service, NorthernResearch Center Library, Peoria, IL [*Library symbol Library of Congress*] (LCLS)
IPARA .... International Publishers Advertising Representatives Association
I-Para .... Primipara [*Obstetrics*] (DAVI)
I-para .... Primipara (STED)
IPARC .... International Pesticide Application Research Centre [*Imperial College at Silwood Park*] [*British*] (CB)
IPARCOM ..... Interim Paris Commission [*British*]
IparF .... Edgar County Film Library, Paris, IL [*Library symbol*] [*Library of Congress*] (LCLS)
IParH .... Paris Community Hospital, Paris, IL [*Library symbol Library of Congress*] (LCLS)
Ipark .... Park Ridge Public Library, Park Ridge, IL [*Library symbol*] [*Library of Congress*] (LCLS)
IParkA .... American Society of Anesthesiologists, Park Ridge, IL [*Library symbol Library of Congress*] (LCLS)
IParkD .... Dames and Moore Chicago Branch Library, Park Ridge, IL [*Library symbol Library of Congress*] (LCLS)
IParkL .... Lutheran General Hospital, Park Ridge, IL [*Library symbol Library of Congress*] (LCLS)
IParP .... Paris Carnegie Public Library, Paris, IL [*Library symbol*] [*Library of Congress*] (LCLS)
IPARS .... International Passenger Airline Reservations System
IParSD .... Paris Union School District, Paris, IL [*Library symbol*] [*Library of Congress*] (LCLS)
IPART .... Institute of Photographic Apparatus Repair Technicians (BUAC)
IPAS .... Independants et Paysans d'Action Sociale [*Independents and Peasants of Social Action*] [*French*] (PPE)
IPAS .... Institute of Psychology, Academia Sinica (BUAC)
IPAS .... Integrated Pneumatic Air System (MCD)
IPAS .... International Projects Assistance Services (BUAC)
IPAS .... Interplatform Alignment System (MCD)
IPASS .... Interactive Policy Analysis Simulation System [*Department of Agriculture*]
IPAST .... IGOSS [*Integrated Global Ocean Services System*] Pilot Project on AlimetricSea-Surface Topography Data [*Marine science*] (OSRA)
IPAT .... Institute for Personality and Ability Testing [*Champaign, IL*]
IPAT .... International Conference on Ion Plating and Allied Techniques (BUAC)
IPAT .... International Porcelain Artist Teachers (BUAC)
IPAT .... International Porcelain Art Teachers [*Later, IPA*] (EA)
IPAT .... Inventario del Patrimonio Historico Artistico Espanol [*Ministerio de Cultura*] [*Spain Information service or system*] (CRD)
IPAT .... Iowa Pressure Articulation Test (DMAA)
IPat .... Patoka Public Library, Patoka, IL [*Library symbol Library of Congress*] (LCLS)
IPATA .... Independent Pet and Animal Transportation Association (EA)
IPAT CPQ ..... Institute for Personality and Ability Testing, Children's Personality Questionnaire [*Psychology*] (AEBS)
IPAT NPFT ... Institute for Personality and Ability Testing, Neurotic Personality Factor Test [*Psychology*] (AEBS)
IPAV .... Institute of Professional Auctioneers and Valuers [*Ireland*] (BUAC)
IPAVS .... International Project of the Association for Voluntary Sterilization
IPax .... Paxton Carnegie Library, Paxton, IL [*Library symbol Library of Congress*] (LCLS)
IPaxH .... Paxton Community Hospital, Paxton, IL [*Library symbol Library of Congress*] (LCLS)
IPB .... Bradley University, Peoria, IL [*Library symbol Library of Congress*] (LCLS)
IPB .... Ice-Penetrating Communications Buoy (DWSG)
IPB .... Illuminated Push Button (NASA)
IPB .... Illustrated Parts Book (IAA)
IPB .... Illustrated Parts Breakdown (AFIT)
IPB .... Inert Processing Building
IPB .... Information Parts Breakdown (MCD)
IPB .... Infrapopliteal Bypass (STED)
IPB .... Injury-Prone Behavior [*Medicine*] (DMAA)
IPB .... Installation Property Book [*Military*] (AABC)
IPB .... Institute of Practitioners in Beauty (BUAC)
IPB .... Institute of Professional Businesswomen (EA)
IPB .... Instruction Prefetch Buffer [*IBM Corp.*] (CIST)
IPB .... Integrated Processor Board
IPB .... Intelligence Preparation of the Battlefield [*Army*] (RDA)
IPB .... Intelligence Preparatory Brief [*Army*] (DOMA)
IPBD .... Intelligence Property Book [*Army*] (ADDR)
IPB .... Intercept Priorities Board [*Armed Forces Security Agency*]
IPB .... Interconnection and Program Bay (IAA)
IPB .... International Pathfinder, Inc. [*Toronto Stock Exchange symbol*]
IPB .... International Peace Bureau [*Geneva, Switzerland*] (EA)
IPB .... Interprocessor Buffer
IPB .... Irish Peat Board (EAIO)
IPB .... Jenner & Block, Chicago, IL [*OCLC symbol*] (OCLC)
IPBA .... India, Pakistan, and Bangladesh Association (PDAA)
IPBA .... Irish Paper Box Association (BI)
IPBC .... India, Pakistan, Bangladesh Conference (DS)
IPBC .... Iodopropynyl Butyl Carbamate [*Wood preservative*]
IPBM .... Integrated Program, Budget, Manpower [*System*] [*Defense Supply Agency*]
IPBM .... Interplanetary Ballistic Missile [*Air Force*]
IPBMM .... International Permanent Bureau of Motor Manufacturers (BARN)
IPBNet .... International Plant Biotech Network (EA)
IPBS .... Israel Plate Block Society (EA)
IPC .... Easter Island [*Chile*] [*Airport symbol*] (OAG)
IPC .... Idaho Potato Commission (EA)

IPC .... Illinois Power Co. [*NYSE symbol*] (SPSG)
IPC .... Illinois Power Financing I [*NYSE symbol*] (SAG)
IPC .... Illustrated Parts Catalog (AAG)
IPC .... Image Processing Center [*Drexel University*] [*Research center*] (RCD)
IPC .... Image Products Co.
IPC .... Imaging Proportional Counter [*Astronomy*]
IPC .... Impact Program Committee (TELE)
IPC .... Impurity Photoconductivity (PDAA)
IPC .... Index of Personality Characteristics [*Test*] [*Brown and Coleman*] (TES)
IPC .... Indicative Planning Council (BUAC)
IPC .... Indirect Photometric Chromatography
IPC .... Indirect Pulp Capping [*Dentistry*]
IPC .... Individual Plan of Care
IPC .... Industrial Personal Computer (NITA)
IPC .... Industrial Planning Committee [*NATO*] (NATG)
IPC .... Industrial Policy Council [*Washington, DC*] (EA)
IPC .... Industrial Pollution Control (EFIS)
IPC .... Industrial Process Control [*by computers*]
IPC .... Industrial Production Corp. [*Sudan*] (BUAC)
IPC .... Industrial Programmable Controller (IAA)
IPC .... Industrial Property Committee [*US Military Government, Germany*]
IPC .... Industrial Publishing Co.
IPC .... Industry Planning Council (EA)
IPC .... Information Processing Center [*of General Motors Corp.*]
IPC .... Information Processing Code (DIT)
IPC .... Information Publishing Corp. [*Telecommunications service*] (TSSD)
IPC .... Initial Planning Conference [*Military*] (INF)
IPC .... Institute for Interconnecting and Packaging Electronic Circuits [*Formerly, Institute of Printed Circuits*] (EA)
IPC .... Institute for Personal Computing (EA)
IPC .... Institute of Paper Chemistry [*Lawrence University*] [*Research center*] (EA)
IPC .... Institute of Paper Conservation [*Formerly, International Institute for Conservation of Historic and Artistic Works Paper Group*] (EA)
IPC .... Institute of Pastoral Care (EA)
IPC .... Institute of Philippine Culture (BUAC)
IPC .... Institute of Printed Circuits (MCD)
IPC .... Institute of Production Control [*British*]
IPC .... Institute of Pure Chiropractic [*British*] (DBA)
IPC .... Institutional Population Component [*National Medical Expenditure Survey*] [*Department of Health and Human Services*] (GFGA)
IPC .... Instrumentation Package Container
IPC .... Instrument Panel Cluster [*Automotive engineering*]
IPC .... Integral Plate Chamber
IPC .... Integrated Peripheral Channel
IPC .... Integrated Peripheral Controller [*Computer chip*]
IPC .... Integrated Pest Control
IPC .... Integrated Pollution Control
IPC .... Integrated Procedures Control
IPC .... Integrated Process Control (IAA)
IPC .... Integrated Programme for Commodities [*UNCTAD*] (EY)
IPC .... Intelligence Priorities Committee [*British World War II*]
IPC .... Intelligent Peripheral Controller [*Computer science*]
IPC .... Inter-African Phytosanitary Commission
IPC .... Intercalated Polymer-Derived Carbon [*Chemistry*]
IPC .... Interconnections Packaging Circuitry (MCD)
IPC .... Intermediate Processing Centers
IPC .... Intermittent Positive Control [*Aviation*]
IPC .... Internal Positive Control [*Genetics*]
IPC .... International Pacific Cypress Minerals Ltd. [*Vancouver Stock Exchange symbol*]
IPC .... International Paralympic Committee (BUAC)
IPC .... International Patent Classification
IPC .... International PBX [*Private Branch Exchange*]/Telecommunicators (EA)
IPC .... International Peace Campaign
IPC .... International Penpal Club (EAIO)
IPC .... International People's College in Denmark (BUAC)
IPC .... International Pepper Community [*Indonesia*] [*Research center*] (IRC)
IPC .... International Petroleum Cartel
IPC .... International Photographic Council (BUAC)
IPC .... International Photosynthesis Committee [*Stockholm, Sweden*] (EAIO)
IPC .... International Planning Corp.
IPC .... International Plasma Corp.
IPC .... International Poliomyelitis Congress
IPC .... International Poplar Commission [*FAO*] [*Rome, Italy*] [*United Nations*] (EA)
IPC .... International Potato Centre [*Peru*] (BUAC)
IPC .... International Press Centre (BUAC)
IPC .... International Prison Commission (BUAC)
IPC .... International Procurement Committee [*ABA*] (AAGC)
IPC .... International Publishing Corp. [*England*]
IPC .... Interpenduncular Cistern [*Medicine*] (DAVI)
IPC .... Interplanetary Communications (AAG)
IPC .... Inter-Process Communication (NITA)
IPC .... Interprocess Controller
IPC .... Inter-Process Coupler (NITA)
IPC .... Interprocessor Channel (IAA)
IPC .... Interprocessor Communication (BUR)
IPC .... Interstate Pollution Control (EFIS)
IPC .... Interstate Processing Center [*Department of Labor*]
IPC .... Investment Promotion Centre [*Tanzania*]
IPC .... Investors Planning Corp.

1588   Acronyms, Initialisms & Abbreviations Dictionary • 27th Edition

IPC .... Ion-Pair Chromatography (STED)
IPC .... Ion-Pair Comonomers [*Organic chemistry*]
IPC .... Iraqi Petroleum Co.
IPC .... Irish Peace Council (EAIO)
IPC .... Irish Presbyterian Church (ROG)
IPC .... Irish Productivity Centre (BUAC)
IPC .... Irish Productivity Council (ACII)
IPC .... Iron Phosphate Coating
IPC .... Islamic Peace Committee (BUAC)
IPC .... Isolation-Physiological Characterization [*Microbiology*]
IPC .... Isopropyl Carbanilate [*Also, INPC, IPPC*] [*Herbicide*]
IPC .... Isopropyl Chlorophenyl [*Medicine*] (MAE)
IPC .... Item Processing Card
IPC .... Purdue University, Calumet Campus, Hammond, IN [*OCLC symbol*] (OCLC)
IPCA .... Independent Parametric Cost Analysis (MCD)
IPCA .... Independent Police Complaints Authority [*British*]
IPCA .... Industrial Pest Control Association [*British*] (BI)
IPCA .... International Petroleum Co-Operative Alliance (BUAC)
IPCA .... International Petroleum Credit Association (NTPA)
IPCA .... International Plate Collectors Association (EA)
IPCA .... International Postcard Collectors Association (EA)
IPC-ASA ...... Intermittent Positive Control - Automatic Seperation [*Aviation*] (PDAA)
IPCC .... Infantry Precommand Course [*Army*] (INF)
IPCC .... Information Processing in Command and Control [*Air Force*]
IPCC .... Institute of Political Campaign Consultants (NTPA)
IPCC .... Intergovernmental Panel on Climate Change [*World Meteorological Organization*]
IPCC .... International Peace Communication and Coordination Centre (BUAC)
IPCC .... International Pin Collectors Club (EA)
IPCC .... Irish Peatland Conservation Council (BUAC)
IPCCB .... Inter-Parliamentary Consultative Council of Benelux (EA)
IPCCC .... International Peace, Communication, and Coordination Center [*The Hague, Netherlands*] (EAIO)
IPCCIOS ...... Indo-Pacific Council of the International Committee of Scientific Management
IPCCS .... Information Processing in Command and Control Systems [*Air Force*]
IPCD .... Infantile Polycistic Disease (DAVI)
IPCDA .... International Penguin Class Dinghy Association (EA)
IPCE .... Independent Parametric Cost Estimate (AABC)
IPCEA .... Insulated Power Cable Engineers Association [*Later, ICEA*] (EA)
IPCF .... Interprocess Communication Facility [*Digital Equipment Corp.*]
IPCF .... Interprogram Communication Facility [*Prime Computer, Inc.*]
IPCG .... International Plate Collectors Guild (EA)
IPCHold ...... IPC Holdings Ltd. [*Associated Press*] (SAG)
IPCI .... IPC Information Systems [*NASDAQ symbol*] (TTSB)
IPCI .... IPC Information Systems, Inc. [*NASDAQ symbol*] (SAG)
IPCI .... Islamic Propagation Centre International (BUAC)
IPC Info ...... IPC Information Systems, Inc. [*Associated Press*] (SAG)
IPCIS .... Integrated Plant Control and Information System [*Nuclear energy*] (NUCP)
IPCL .... Central Illinois Light Co., Resource Center, Peoria, IL [*Library symbol Library of Congress*] (LCLS)
IPCL .... India Petrochemicals Ltd. (BUAC)
IPCL .... Instrumentation Program and Component List (NASA)
IPCL .... International Postal Collectors League [*Commercial firm*] (EA)
IPCO .... Idaho Power Co.
IPCO .... In-Place Cleanable Oilfilter
IPCO .... International Paper Co. (WDMC)
IPCOG .... Informal Policy Committee for Germany
IPCOG .... Interdepartmental Planning Committee on Germany [*US*]
IPCP .... Integrated Printing Collating Processing (DGA)
IPCP .... Interdisciplinary Patient Care Plan (HCT)
IPCPA .... Institute of Private Clinical Psychologists of Australia
IPCPP .... International Physicians Commission for the Protection of Prisoners (EA)
IPCPrA ...... Illinois Pwr 4.08% Pfd [*NYSE symbol*] (TTSB)
IPCPrB ...... Illinois Pwr 4.20% Pfd [*NYSE symbol*] (TTSB)
IPCPrC ...... Illinois Pwr 4.26% Pfd [*NYSE symbol*] (TTSB)
IPCPrD ...... Illinois Pwr 4.42% Pfd [*NYSE symbol*] (TTSB)
IPCPrE ...... Illinois Pwr 4.70% Pfd [*NYSE symbol*] (TTSB)
IPCPrL ...... Illinois Pwr Adj Rt A Pfd [*NYSE symbol*] (TTSB)
IPCPrM ...... Illinois Pwr Cap 9.45%'MIPS' [*NYSE symbol*] (TTSB)
IPCPrT ...... Illinois Pwr Fin I 8%'TOPrS' [*NYSE symbol*] (TTSB)
IPCR .... Institute for Physical and Chemical Research [*Japan*] (BUAC)
IPCR .... Inverse Polymerase Chain Reaction [*Genetics*]
IPCR .... IPC Holdings Ltd. [*NASDAQ symbol*] (SAG)
IPCRA .... Irish Professional Conservators and Restorers Association (BUAC)
IPC Rept ...... International Procurement Committee Report [*ABA*] [*A publication*] (AAGC)
IPCRESS ...... Induction of Psychoneuroses by Conditioned Reflex under Stress [*In book and film "The Ipcress File"*]
IPCRF .... IPC Holdings [*NASDAQ symbol*] (TTSB)
IPCS .... Image Photon Counting System [*Instrumentation*]
IPCS .... Infrapatellar Contracture Syndrome [*Sports medicine*]
IPCS .... Institute of Professional Civil Servants [*British*]
IPCS .... Institution of Professional Civil Servants [*British*] (BI)
IPCS .... Integrated Powertrain Control System [*Automotive engineering*]
IPCS .... Integrated Propulsion Control System [*Air Force*]
IPCS .... Interactive Problem-Control System [*IBM Corp.*]
IPCS .... International Petula Clark Society (EAIO)
IPCS .... International Playing-Card Society (EA)
IPCS .... International Programme on Chemical Safety (EA)
IPCS .... International Program on Chemical Safety (GNE)
IPCS .... Interproject Control Station (IAA)

IPCS .... Intrauterine Progesterone Contraceptive System [*Gynecology*]
IPCT .... Caterpillar Tractor Co., Business Library, Peoria, IL [*Library symbol Library of Congress*] (LCLS)
IPCT-T .... Caterpillar Tractor Co., Technical Information Center, Peoria, IL [*Library symbol Library of Congress*] (LCLS)
IPCV .... Indian Peanut Clump Virus [*Plant pathology*]
IPCWN .... Irish Permaculture Worknet (BUAC)
IPD .... Idiopathic Parkinson's Disease [*Medicine*] (CPH)
IPD .... Illustrated Provisioning Document (MCD)
IPD .... Immediate Pigment Darkening [*Dermatology*]
IPD .... Impact Prediction Data (AFM)
IPD .... Implicit Price Deflator
IPD .... Improved Point Defense
IPD .... Individual Package Delivery [*Shipping*]
IPD .... Individual Protective Device [*Toxicology*]
IPD .... Inflammatory Pelvic Disease [*Medicine*] (MAE)
IPD .... Information Processing Division [*NASA*] (NASA)
IPD .... Initial Performance Data
IPD .... In Praesentia Dominorum [*In the Presence of the Lords of Session*] [*Latin*]
IPD .... Insertion Phase Delay
IPD .... Inspection Planning Document [*Military*] (MCD)
IPD .... Institute for Professional Development (EA)
IPD .... Institute of Personnel Development (WDAA)
IPD .... Institute of Professional Designers
IPD .... Instructional Program Development (NVT)
IPD .... Integrated Pin Diode
IPD .... Integrated Process Demonstration [*Nuclear energy*]
IPD .... Integrated Product Development [*Business term*] (RDA)
IPD .... Intelligence Planning Document [*Military*] (MCD)
IPD .... Intelligent Power Device (CIST)
IPD .... Intelligent Protection Device [*American Solenoid Co.*] [*Somerset, NJ*]
IPD .... Interaural Phase Disparity [*Audiology*]
IPD .... Intermediate Peritoneal Dialysis [*Medicine*] (BARN)
IPD .... Intermittent Peritoneal Dialysis [*Medicine*]
IPD .... International Police Dogs (EA)
IPD .... Inter-Provincial Diversified Holding Ltd. [*Toronto Stock Exchange symbol*]
IPD .... Interpupillary Distance
IPD .... Intra-Penile Device [*Contraceptive*] (DI)
IPD .... Inventory of Psychosocial Development
IPD .... Investment Property Databank [*London, England*]
IPD .... Isophorone Diamine [*Organic chemistry*]
IPD .... Isotope-Powered Device
IPD .... Issue Priority Designator
IPD .... Iterated Prisoner's Dilemma [*Psychology*]
IPDA .... International Periodical Distributors Association (EA)
IPDA .... Intrapulse Demodulation Analysis
IPD/AC .... Institut Panafricain pour le Developpement, Afrique Centrale [*Pan African Institute for Development, Central Africa*] [*Cameroun*] (PDAA)
IPDB .... Intelligence Production Database [*Military*] (MCD)
IPDC .... International Program for the Development of Communications [*UNESCO*]
IPDD .... Initial Project Design Description (NRCH)
IPDF .... Intensity Probability Density Function (PDAA)
IPDH .... In-Service Planned Derated Hours [*Electronics*] (IEEE)
IPDI .... Implicit Price Deflator Index [*Economics*]
IPDI .... Isophorone Diisocyanate [*Organic chemistry*]
IPDL .... Isotopes Process Development Laboratory [*AEC*]
IPDM .... Institute of Physical Distribution Management [*British*]
IPDMS .... Integrated Point Defense Missile System [*Military*] (CAAL)
IPDN .... International Paleoclimatic Data Network
IPDP .... Intervals of Pulsations of Diminishing Period
IPDP .... Isopropylphenyl(diphenyl)phosphate [*Fire-resistant hydraulic fluid*]
IPDR .... Incremental Preliminary Design Review (MCD)
IPDR .... Inter-Plan Data Reporting System [*Health insurance*] (GHCT)
IPDS .... IBM Personal Dication System [*Computer science*]
IPDS .... Imagery Processing and Dissemination System (DOMA)
IPDS .... Improved Point Defense Missile System [*Navy*] (DOMA)
IPDS .... Inland Petroleum Distribution System (COE)
IPDS .... Integrated Product Development System [*FAA*] (TAG)
IPDS .... Integrated Program Development Support System [*Allen Bradley*] (NITA)
IPDS .... Intelligent Printer Data Stream [*IBM Corp.*] (CIST)
IPDS .... Intelligent Printer Data Stream [*Computer science*]
IPDS .... Intelligent Printer Data Systems
IPDSMS .... Improved Point Defense Surface Missile System
IPDT .... Inventory of Piaget's Developmental Tasks (DB)
IPDTAS .... Interim Point Defense Target Acquisition System [*Military*] (IAA)
IPDU .... Instantaneous Panoramic Display Unit
IPE .... Incentive PERT [*Program Evaluation and Review Technique*] Events
IPE .... Incorporated Plant Engineers (BUAC)
IPE .... Individual Plant Examination [*Environmental science*] (COE)
IPE .... Individual Protective Equipment
IPE .... Industrial Plant [*or Production*] Equipment
IPE .... Infectious Porcine Encephalomyelitis [*Medicine*] (DMAA)
IPE .... Information Processing Equipment
IPE .... Initial Portable Equipment
IPE .... Initial Psychiatric Evaluation (DAVI)
IPE .... Inscriptiones Orae Septentrionalis Ponti Euxini [*A publication*] (OCD)
IPE .... Institute for Program Evaluation (AAGC)
IPE .... Institute of Petroleum Engineers (BUAC)
IPE .... Institute of Production Engineers [*British*]
IPE .... Institute of Public Enterprise [*India*] (BUAC)

IPE	Institution of Plant Engineers [*British*]
IPE	Intelligent Peripheral Equipment [*Telecommunications*] (ITD)
IPE	Intelligent Program Editor (PDAA)
IPE	International Partners Facility
IPE	International Petroleum Exchange [*British*]
IPE	International Prism Exploration Ltd. [*Vancouver Stock Exchange symbol*]
IPE	Interpret Parity Error
IPE	Interstitial Pulmonary Emphysema [*Medicine*] (AAMN)
IPE	Inverse Photoelectric Effect
IPE	Isopropyl Ether [*Organic chemistry*]
IPe	Peotone Township Library, Peotone, IL [*Library symbol Library of Congress*] (LCLS)
IPEA	Independent Poster Exchanges of America (EA)
IPEA	Ireland-Poland Economic Association (BUAC)
IPEC	Integrated Process Equipment [*NASDAQ symbol*] (SAG)
IPEC	International Patient Education Council (EAIO)
IPEC	International Pharmaceutical Excipients Council (EA)
IPEC	International Police Exhibition and Conference [*British*] (ITD)
IPEC	International Power and Engineering Consultants
IPECAC	Ipecacuanha [*Pharmacy*] (ROG)
IPECS	Integrated Power and Environmental Control System (MCD)
IPEDS	Integrated Postsecondary Education Data System [*National Center for Education Statistics*] (OICC)
IPEE	Inclination of a Plane to the Plane of the Earth's Equator [*Aerospace*]
IPEE	International Peace, Economy, and Ecology (EA)
IPEE	International Programme on Environmental Education [*UNESCO*] (BUAC)
IPEH	Intravascular Papillary Endothelial Hyperplasia [*Medicine*]
IPek	Pekin Public Library, Pekin, IL [*Library symbol Library of Congress*] (LCLS)
IPekC	Pekin Community High School District No. 30, Pekin, IL [*Library symbol Library of Congress*] (LCLS)
IPekH	Pekin Memorial Hospital, Pekin, IL [*Library symbol Library of Congress*] (LCLS)
IPEL	International Pipeline Engineering Ltd. [*Canada*] (BUAC)
IPEMB	Institute of Physics & Engineering in Medicine & Biology (WDAA)
IPEME	International Program in Environmental Management Education
IPEN	Pan American Institute of Naval Engineering (EAIO)
IPENEB	International PEN [*Poets, Playwrights, Editors, Essayists, Novelists*]-Estonian Center (EAIO)
IPENHKE	International PEN - Hong Kong English (EAIO)
IPENI	International PEN - Ireland (EAIO)
IPENS	International PEN - Scotland (EAIO)
IPENUS	International PEN - United States [*Later, PCUSAW*] (EA)
IPENWIE	International PEN [*Poets, Playwrights, Editors, Essayists, Novelists*]-Writers inExile [*British*] (EAIO)
IPENY	International PEN - Yiddish (EA)
IPEP	Integrated Performance Evaluation Program
IPER	Industrial Production Equipment Reserve (NG)
IPer	Peru Public Library, Peru, IL [*Library symbol Library of Congress*] (LCLS)
IPerIH	Illinois Valley Community Hospital, Peru, IL [*Library symbol Library of Congress*] (LCLS)
i-periton	Intraperitoneal [*Medicine*] (MEDA)
IPERS	Industrial Plant Equipment Reutilization System [*DoD*]
IPerSD	Peru Consolidated Community School District 124, Peru, IL [*Library symbol Library of Congress*] (LCLS)
IPerStB	Saint Bede Academy, Peru, IL [*Library symbol Library of Congress*] (LCLS)
IPES	Inverse Photoemission Spectroscopy
IPE/T	Improved Protective Entrance/Tent [*Army*]
IPET	Independent Professional Electronic Technicians
IPetM	Edgar Lee Masters Memorial Museum, Petersburg, IL [*Library symbol Library of Congress*] (LCLS)
IPEU	International Photo-Engravers Union [*Later, GAIU*] (EA)
IPEX	Instant Purchase Excursion Fares [*Aviation*]
IPEX	International Printing Exhibition
IPEX	Organization for International Professional Exchanges, Inc. (EA)
IPF	Idiopathic Pulmonary Fibrosis [*Medicine*]
IPF	Inches per Foot (IAA)
IPF	Indicative Planning Figure
IPF	Individual Project Fellowships
IPF	Infection Potentiating Factor (AAMN)
IPF	Information Processing Facility (MHDI)
IPF	Initial Production Facilities (AABC)
IPF	Initial Protective Force
IPF	In-Process Factor
IPF	Institute of Public Finance [*British*] (ECON)
IPF	Insulin Promoter Factor [*Biochemistry*]
IPF	Intaken Piled Fathom [*Shipping*] (DS)
IPF	Integrated Processing Facility [*DoD*]
IPF	Intellectual Property Forum [*A publication*]
IPF	Interactive Productivity Facility (HGAA)
IPF	Intermediate Plot File
IPF	International Pain Foundation (EA)
IPF	International Pharmaceutical Federation [*Netherlands*] (EAIO)
IPF	International Pigeon Federation [*See also FCI*] (EAIO)
IPF	International Podrabinek Fund [*Defunct*] (EA)
IPF	International Poetry Forum (EA)
IPF	International Powerlifting Federation [*Hagersten, Sweden*] (EAIO)
IPF	International Prayer Fellowship (EA)
IPF	Interstitial Pulmonary Fibrosis [*Medicine*] (DMAA)
IPF	Iodine Protection Factor [*Nuclear energy*] (GFGA)
IPF	Irish Printing Federation (BI)

IPF	Isotope Production Facility
IPF	IUS Processing Facility [*NASA*] (NASA)
IPf	Park Forest Public Library, Park Forest, IL [*Library symbol Library of Congress*] (LCLS)
IPFA	Information Project for Africa [*Washington, D.C.*] (EA)
IPFA	Institute for Psychiatry and Foreign Affairs [*Defunct*] (EA)
IPFA	Insurance Premium Finance Association (EA)
IPFA	International Physical Fitness Association (EA)
IPFA	International Population and Family Association (EA)
IPFA	Member of the Chartered Institute of Public Finance and Accountancy [*British*]
IPFAA	International Police and Fire Athletic Association [*Defunct*] (EA)
iPFC	Indirect Plaque-Forming Cell [*Immunology*]
IPFC	Indo-Pacific Fisheries Commission [*or Council*] [*FAO ICSU Bangkok, Thailand*] [*United Nations*] (ASF)
IPFC	Indo-Pacific Fishery Commission (EAIO)
IPFD	Incident Power Flux Density (NITA)
IPFD	Intrapartum Fetal Distress [*Obstetrics*] (DAVI)
IPFEO	Institut des Producteurs de Ferro-Alliages d'Europe Occidentale [*Institute of Ferro-Alloy Producers in Western Europe - IFAPWE*] [*Defunct*] (EA)
IPFM	Integral Pulse Frequency Modulation (IEEE)
IPFP	Institut Professionnel de la Fonction Publique du Canada [*Professional Institute of the Public Service of Canada - PIPS*]
IPFP	Iterated Proportional Fitting Procedure [*Statistics*]
IPFR	Institute of Plasma and Fusion Research [*University of California, Los Angeles*] [*Research center*] (RCD)
IPFS	Integrated Polygenerator Fertilizer System
IPFS	International Pen Friend Service (EA)
IPfs	Park Forest South Public Library, Park Forest South, IL [*Library symbol Library of Congress*] (LCLS)
IPFSC	International Pacific Salmon Fisheries Commission [*Marine science*] (OSRA)
IPfsG	Governors State University, Park Forest South, IL [*Library symbol Library of Congress*] (LCLS)
IPfsI	Inolex Pharmaceutical Co., Park Forest South, IL [*Library symbol Library of Congress*] (LCLS)
IPFW	Indiana University - Purdue University at Fort Wayne
IPG	Immediate Participation Guarantee Plan [*Insurance*]
IPG	Immobilized pH Gradients [*Chemistry*]
IPG	Impedance Plethysmography [*Medicine*]
IPG	In-Circuit Program Generator [*Computer science*] (PDAA)
IPG	Independent Publishers Group
IPG	Independent Publishers' Guild [*British*]
IPG	Individually Polymerized Grass [*Organic chemistry*] (DAVI)
IPG	Induction Plasma Gun
IPG	Industrial Painters Group [*British*] (BI)
IPG	Industrial Physics Group [*University of Essex*] [*British*] (IRUK)
IPG	Information Planning Group (SSD)
IPG	Information Policy Group (NITA)
IPG	Information Publishing Group [*The Thomson Corp.*]
IPG	Inositol-Phosphoglycan [*Biochemistry*]
IPG	INPADOC Patent Gazette (NITA)
IPG	Inspiration-Phase Gas (DMAA)
IPG	Institut de Physique du Globe [*France*]
IPG	Institute of Professional Goldsmiths [*British*] (DBA)
IPG	Interactive Presentation Graphics [*IBM Corp.*]
IPG	Internal Problem Generator (IAA)
IPG	International Pagurian Corp. Ltd. [*Toronto Stock Exchange symbol Vancouver Stock Exchange symbol*]
IPG	International Parliamentary Group for Human Rights in the Soviet Union (EA)
IPG	International Payments Group (NATG)
IPG	International Piano Guild (EA)
IPG	International Planning Group [*Belgium, Germany, Netherlands*] (AABC)
IPG	International Portrait Gallery
IPG	International Professional Groomers (NTPA)
IPG	Interproject Group
IPG	[*The*] Interpublic Group of Companies, Inc. [*NYSE symbol*] (SPSG)
IPG	Interpublic Grp Cos. [*NYSE symbol*] (TTSB)
IPG	Isopropylidene Glycerol [*Biochemistry*]
IPG	Isopropylthiogalactoside [*Also, IPTG*] [*Organic chemistry*]
IPG	Isotope Power Generator
IPG	Issue Priority Group [*Army*]
IPG	Phoolbagh [*India*] [*Airport symbol*] (AD)
IPGA	Illinois Propane Gas Association (SRA)
IPGA	Indiana Propane Gas Association (SRA)
IPGA	Island Park Geothermal Area
IPGCU	International Printing and Graphic Communications Union
iPGE	Prostaglandin E, immunoreactive [*Biochemistry*]
IPGEN	Intersection Point Generator (PDAA)
IPGF	Immobilized pH Gradient Isoelectric Focusing [*Analytical biochemistry*]
IPGH	Instituto Panamericano de Geografia e Historia [*Panamerican Institute of Geography and History*] [*Peru*]
IPGI	Institute on Pluralism and Group Identity (EA)
IPGP	Illegal Possession of Government Property
IPGRI	International Plant Genetic Resources Institute [*Italy*]
IPGS	Intercollegiate Program of Graduate Studies
IPGS	Internationale Paracelsus-Gesellschaft zu Salzburg (EAIO)
IPGS	International Percy Grainger Society (EA)
IPH	Idiopathic Portal Hypertension [*Medicine*]
IPH	Idiopathic Pulmonary Hemosiderosis [*Medicine*]
IPH	Impressions per Hour [*Printing*]

iph	Impressions per Hour (WDAA)
IPH	Inches per Hour (TEL)
IPH	Industrial and Pastoral Holdings (ADA)
IPH	Industrial Process Heat
IPH	Inflammatory Papillary Hyperplasia [*Dentistry*]
IPH	Interdisciplinary Programs in Health [*Harvard University*]
IPH	International Association of Paper Historians
IPH	International Pharmadyne Ltd. [*Vancouver Stock Exchange symbol*]
IPH	Interphalangeal [*Anatomy*]
IPH	Intraparenchymal Hemorrhage [*Medicine*]
IPH	Ipoh [*Malaysia*] [*Airport symbol*] (OAG)
IPh	Peoria Heights Public Library, Peoria Heights, IL [*Library symbol Library of Congress*] (LCLS)
IphA	Illinois Pharmacists Association (SRA)
IPHA	Illinois Public Health Association (SRA)
IPHC	International Pacific Halibut Commission (EA)
IPHE	Individual Personal Hygiene Equipment (KSC)
IPHE	Institute of Public Health Engineers [*British*]
IPhe	Palos Heights Public Library, Palos Heights, IL [*Library symbol Library of Congress*] (LCLS)
IP/HHCL	Initial Point/H-Hour Control Line [*Aviation*]
IPhi	Green Hills Public Library District, Palos Hills, IL [*Library symbol Library of Congress*] (LCLS)
IPHi	Peoria Historical Society, Peoria, IL [*Library symbol Library of Congress*] (LCLS)
IPhil	Philo Township Public Library, Philo, IL [*Library symbol Library of Congress*] (LCLS)
IPhiM	Moraine Valley Community College, Palos Hills, IL [*Library symbol Library of Congress*] (LCLS)
IPhiP	Green Hills Public Library District, Palos Hills, IL [*Library symbol*] [*Library of Congress*] (LCLS)
IPHM	Individual Personal Hygiene Module (KSC)
IP-HPLC	Ion-Pair High-Performance Liquid Chromatography [*Medicine*]
IPHR	Inverted Polypoid Hamartoma of the Rectum [*Medicine*] (DMAA)
IPHRD	International Program for Human Resource Development [*Defunct*] (EA)
IPHT	Institute of Physical High Technology [*Germany*]
IPI	Identified Friendly Prior to Interception [*Military*]
IPI	Image Processing Interface [*Computer science*] (PCM)
IPI	Imagined Process Inventory (STED)
IPI	Immigration Patrol Inspector [*Immigration and Naturalization Service*]
IPI	Implicit Price Index (MHDW)
IPI	Improved Processing Inspection [*Food Safety and Inspection Service*] [*Department of Agriculture*]
IPI	Income and Price Index (DICI)
IPI	INCYTE Pharmaceuticals, Inc. [*AMEX symbol*] (SPSG)
IPI	Index of Production Industries [*Department of Employment*] [*British*]
IPI	Individually Planned [*or Prescribed*] Instruction [*Education*]
IPI	Individually Presented Instruction (NITA)
IPI	Industrial Production Index (PDAA)
IPI	Infinite Position Indicator (PDAA)
IPI	Inflation Protected Income (DICI)
IPI	Information Professionals Institute (IID)
IPI	Information Publications International [*Publisher*] [*British*]
IPI	Initial Product Inspection
IPI	Initial Protocol Identifier [*Computer science*] (TNIG)
IPI	In Partibus Infidelium [*In the Countries, Lands, or Regions of Unbelievers*] [*Latin*]
IPI	Institute for Practical Idealism (EA)
IPI	Institute for Public Information
IPI	Institute of Patentees and Inventors [*British*] (ILCA)
IPI	Institute of Physical Medicine and Rehabilitation, Peoria, IL [*Library symbol Library of Congress*] (LCLS)
IPI	Institute of Poultry Industries
IPI	Institute of Professional Investigators (EA)
IPI	Insurance Periodicals Index [*Nils Publishing Co.*] [*Chatsworth, CA*] [*Information service or system*] (IID)
IPI	Integrated Position Indicator
IPI	Intelligence Publications Index [*Published January, 1953, through February, 1968, by the Defense Intelligence Agency*]
IPI	Intelligent Peripheral Interface [*Computer science*]
IPI	Intelligent Printer Interface
IPI	Intense Product Inspection
IPI	Interchemical Printing Inks
IPI	Internal Procedures Instruction
IPI	International Patent Institute [*Later, EPO*]
IPI	International Pesticide Institute
IPI	International Phototherapy Institute [*Defunct*] (EA)
IPI	International Population Institute [*Defunct*] (EA)
IPI	International Potash Institute [*See also IIP*] (EAIO)
IPI	International Press Institute [*Switzerland*] (PDAA)
IPI	International Press Institute [*British*]
IPI	International Press Institute, American Committee (EA)
IPI	International Psychosomatics Institute (EA)
IPI	Interphonemic Interval (STED)
IPI	Interpulse Interval
IPI	Intrapair Interval
IPI	Inventory, Print, and Index [*System*]
IPI	Inwald Personality Inventory [*Test*] (TES)
IPI	Inwald Personality Inventory [*Psychology*] (DHP)
IPI	Iolani Place Irregulars (EA)
IPI	Ipiales [*Colombia*] [*Airport symbol*] (OAG)
IPIA	Immunoperoxidase Infectivity Assay (DB)
IpIA	Independent Primary Inspection Agency [*Department of Housing and Urban Development*] (GFGA)
IPIA	Induced Psycho-Intellectual Activity (PDAA)
IPIACFA	International Private Investment Advisory Council on Foreign Aid [*Agency for International Development*] (EGAO)
IPiaMCD	Macoupin Community Unit, District 9, Piasa, IL [*Library symbol Library of Congress*] (LCLS)
IPiaSD	Southwestern Community Unit, School District 9, Piasa, IL [*Library symbol Library of Congress*] (LCLS)
IPIC	Institute of Personal Image Consultants (EA)
IPIC	Intelligent Power Integrated Circuit [*Electronics*]
IPIC	Interneuron Pharmaceuticals [*NASDAQ symbol*] (TTSB)
IPIC	Interneuron Pharmaceuticals, Inc. [*NASDAQ symbol*] (SAG)
IPICS	Initial Production and Information Control System [*Computer science*] (PDAA)
IPIE	Institute of Profit Improvement Executives [*British*] (DBA)
IPIECA	International Petroleum Industry Environmental Conservation Association [*British*] (EAIO)
IPIF	Institute of Pacific Islands Forestry [*Honolulu, HI*] [*Department of Agriculture*] (GRD)
IPI/IMPC	International Parking Institute (NTPA)
IPI Inc.	IPI, Inc. [*Associated Press*] (SAG)
IPI/MIS	Individually Planned Instruction/Management and Information System
IPI/MIS	International Press Institute/Management and Information System [*Switzerland*]
IPIN	Instituto Panamericano de Ingenieria Naval [*Pan American Institute of Naval Engineering*] (EAIO)
IPIN	Integrated Photogrammetric Instrument Network (PDAA)
IP/IN	Interpositive/Internegative [*Photography*] (WDMC)
IPIP	Implantable Programmable Infusion Pump [*Medicine*]
IPIP	Information Processing Improvement Program
IPip	Piper City Public Library, Piper City, IL [*Library symbol Library of Congress*] (LCLS)
IPIPS	Interactive Planetary Image Processing System
IPipSD	Ford Central Community Unit Shool District, Piper City, IL [*Library symbol*] [*Library of Congress*] (LCLS)
IPIR	Immediate Photograph Intelligence Report [*Military*] (AFM)
IPIR	Initial Photographic Interpretation Report [*Air Force*]
IPIR	Institute for Public Interest Representation [*Later, CCCIPR*] [*Georgetown University*]
IPIR	Integrated Personnel Information Report (AAG)
IPIS	Individually Prescribed Instructional Systems (OICC)
IPIS	Institute for Peace and International Security (EA)
IPIS	Instrument Pilot Instructor School [*Air Force*]
IPIS	International Peace Information Service [*Belgium*]
IPISD	Interservice Procedures for Instructional Systems Development
IPit	Pittsfield Public Library, Pittsfield, IL [*Library symbol Library of Congress*] (LCLS)
IPIV	Illinois Valley Library System, Peoria, IL [*Library symbol Library of Congress*] (LCLS)
IPJ	Institute for Peace and Justice (EA)
IPJ	Intellectual Property Journal [*A publication*]
IPJ	International Pursuit Corp. [*Toronto Stock Exchange symbol*]
IPJ	Interphalangeal Joint [*Anatomy*] (DAVI)
IPJP	Interpost Junction Panel
IPJT	Interplant Job Ticket
IPK	Interactive Press Kit [*Public relations*] (WDMC)
IPK	International Prototype Kilogram
IPK	Interphalangeal Keratosis [*Orthopedics*] (DAVI)
IPK	Intractable Plantar Keratosis [*Orthopedics*] (DAVI)
IPK	Painter Creek, AK [*Location identifier FAA*] (FAAL)
IPK	Peoria Kindergarten Primary Training School, Peoria, IL [*Library symbol Library of Congress*] (LCLS)
IPKC	International Pot and Kettle Clubs (EA)
IPKD	Infantile Polycystic Kidney Disease [*Medicine*] (STED)
IPKF	Indian Peace-Keeping Force [*Army*]
IPKO	International Information on Peace-Keeping Operations
IPL	Air Charter Services (Pty) Ltd. South Africa [*ICAO designator*] (FAAC)
IPL	El Centro/Imperial [*California*] [*Airport symbol*] (OAG)
IPL	Identified Parts List
IPL	Illustrated Parts List (NATG)
IPL	Illustrated Pocket Library [*A publication*]
IPL	Image Processing Laboratory [*University of Houston*] [*Research center*] (RCD)
IPL	Imperial, CA [*Location identifier FAA*] (FAAL)
IPL	Improved Position Locator (PDAA)
IPL	Indentured Parts List
IPL	Independent Publishers League [*Defunct*] (EA)
IPL	Individual Protection Laboratory [*Natick, MA*] [*Army*] (RDA)
IPL	Inferior Parietal Lobule [*Anatomy*]
IPL	Information Processing Language [*Computer science*]
IPL	Initial Program Load [*Computer science*]
IPL	Initial Provisioning List (MCD)
IPL	Inner Plexiform Layer [*Retina*]
IPL	Installation Parts List (AAG)
IPL	Institute of Professional Librarians [*Canada*]
IPL	Instrumentation Program List
IPL	Instrument Panel Lighting (MCD)
IPL	Instrument Pool Laboratory (IAA)
IPL	Integrated Payload [*NASA*]
IPL	Integrated Perceived Level [*Acoustics*]
IPL	Integrated Priority List [*DoD*]
IPL	Interconnected Porosity Level
IPL	Interested Parties List
IPL	Interim Parts List [*Navy*]
IPL	Interim Policy Letter [*Air Force*] (AAGC)

IPL	Internet Public Library [*University of Michigan*] (TELE)
IPL	Interprovincial Pipe Line Ltd. [*Toronto Stock Exchange symbol*]
IPL	Interpupillary Line (STED)
IPL	Interrupt Priority Level
IPL	Intrapleural
IPL	Ion Projection Lithography (AAEL)
IPL	Iota Phi Lambda Sorority (AEBS)
IPL	IPALCO Enterprises [*NYSE symbol*] (TTSB)
IPL	IPALCO Enterprises, Inc. [*NYSE symbol*] (SPSG)
IPL	Purdue University, Lafayette, IN [*OCLC symbol*] (OCLC)
IPLA	Institute of Public Loss Assessors [*British*] (DBA)
IPLA	Instituto Pastoral Latinoamericano
IPLA	Interstate Producers Livestock Association (EA)
IPLAN	Joint IOC/WMO Planning Group for IGOSS [*Marine science*] (MSC)
IPlantE	Institution of Plant Engineers [*British*] (EAIO)
IPLC	International Private Leased Circuits [*British Telecom International*] (NITA)
IPLCA	International Pipe Line Contractors Association [*Later, IPOCA*] (EA)
IPLE	Institution of Public Lighting Engineers [*British*]
IPL En	IPL Energy, Inc. [*Associated Press*] (SAG)
IPLF	Isogrid Payload Fairing (MCD)
IPLGY	Institute for the Protection of Lesbian and Gay Youth (EA)
IPLOCA	International Pipe Line and Offshore Contractors Association [*Belgium*] (EAIO)
IPLS	IPL Systems CI'A' [*NASDAQ symbol*] (TTSB)
IPLS	IPL Systems, Inc. [*NASDAQ symbol*] (NQ)
IPL Sy	IPL Systems, Inc. [*Associated Press*] (SAG)
IPLV	Information Processing Language Five
IPLV	Intermediate Payload Launch Vehicle
IPIx	International Plant Index [*A publication*]
IPM	Illumination per Minute
IPM	Immediate Past Master [*Freemasonry*]
IPM	Imperial Metals Corp. [*Toronto Stock Exchange symbol Vancouver Stock Exchange symbol*]
IPM	Impulses per Minute [*Telecommunications*]
IPM	Inches Penetration per Month (IAA)
IPM	Inches per Minute
ipm	Inches per Minute (IDOE)
IPM	Incidental Phase [*or Pulse*] Modulation
IPM	Incident Power Monitor [*Military*] (CAAL)
IPM	Incremental Phase Modulation (CIST)
IPM	Indomethacin-Treated Platelet Microsomes
IPM	Industrial Preparedness Measures
IPM	Infant Passive Mitt (STED)
IPM	Infusible Platelet Membrane [*Substitute for blood tranfusion*]
IPM	Inhalable Particulate Matter (GNE)
IPM	Inner Peace Movement (EA)
IPM	Input Position Map [*Computer science*] (OA)
IPM	Insect Populations Management Research Unit [*Department of Agriculture*] (GRD)
IPM	Institute of Personnel Management [*British*] (DCTA)
IPM	Institute of Practical Mathematics [*Germany*]
IPM	Institute of Precious Metals [*China*]
IPM	Institute of Printing Management [*British*]
IPM	Instructional Programming Model [*Individually-guided education*] (AEE)
IPM	Integrated Pest Management [*Agronomy*]
IPM	Intelligent Power Management [*Laptop computers*] (BYTE)
IPM	Intelligent Power Module (CIST)
IPM	Intelligent Processing of Materials [*Computer science*]
IPM	Intel Power Monitor (PCM)
IPM	Interaction Place Map (EDAC)
IPM	Interaural Phase Modulation [*Audiology*]
IPM	Interference Prediction Model
IPV	Internal Polarization Modulation (IEEE)
IPM	International Prison Ministry (EA)
IPM	International Prototype Meter
IPM	Internet Protection Module [*Computer science*]
IPM	Interpersonal Mail System [*Computer science*] (TNIG)
IPM	Interpersonal Messaging [*Telecommunications*] (OSI)
IPM	Interpersonal Messaging Service
IPM	Interpersonal Perception Method [*Psychology*]
IPM	Interphotoreceptor Matrix [*Ophthalmology*]
IPM	Interplanetary Medium
IPM	Inter-Processor/Multiplexer (MCD)
IPM	Interruptions per Minute
IPM	Inventory Policy Model (MHDI)
IPM	Isopropyl Myristate [*Pharmacology*]
IPM	Morrison and Mary Wiley Public Library, Elmwood, IL [*OCLC symbol*] (OCLC)
IPM	Peoria Masonic Temple, Peoria, IL [*Library symbol Library of Congress*] (LCLS)
IPMA	In-Plant Management Association (EA)
IPMA	In-Plant Printing Management Association
IPMA	Interlocking Paving Manufacturers Association [*Defunct*] (EA)
IPMA	International Personnel Management Association (EA)
IPMA	International Planned Music Association (EA)
IPMA	International Primary Market Association (EAIO)
IPMA	International Publishing Management Association (NTPA)
IPMANA	Interstate Postgraduate Medical Association of North America (EA)
IPMCF	International Precious Metals [*NASDAQ symbol*] (SAG)
IPMDH	Isopropylmalate Dehydrogenase [*An enzyme*]
IPMH	Methodist Hospital of Central Illinois, Peoria, IL [*Library symbol Library of Congress*] (LCLS)
IPMH-M	Methodist Medical Center of Illinois, Medical Library, Peoria, IL [*Library symbol Library of Congress*] (LCLS)
IPMI	Inferoposterior Myocardial Infarct [*or Infarction*] [*Cardiology*] (DAVI)
IPMI	Intelligent Platform Management Interface [*Computer science*]
IPMI	International Precious Metals Institute (EA)
IPMLF	Intl Precious Metals [*NASDAQ symbol*] (TTSB)
IPMP	IEEE [*Institute of Electrical and Electronics Engineers*] Parts, Materials and Packaging (IAA)
IPMP	Industrial Plant Modernization Program [*Air Force*]
IP/MP	Inphase/Midphase (MHDI)
IPMP	Isopropyl(methoxy)pyrazine [*Organic chemistry*]
IPMPCS	Integrated Pest Management and Program Coordination Staff [*Environmental Protection Agency*] (GFGA)
IPMS	Impact Predictor Monitor Set [*NASA*] (AAG)
IPMS	Infinite Periodic Minimal Surface
IPMS	Institute for Problems of Materials Science [*Ukraine*]
IPMS	Institute of Physical Scientists in Medicine (WDAA)
IPMS	Institution of Professionals, Managers, and Specialists [*British*]
IPMS	Integrated Program Management System [*Navy*]
IPMS	International Plastic Modelers Society (EA)
IPMS	International Polar Motion Service
IPMS	International Primitive Money Society (EA)
IPM/S	Interruptions per Minute/Second (DEN)
IPMS	Investment Performance Monitoring Service [*British*]
IPMS/USA	International Plastic Modelers Society/US Branch (EA)
IPN	Impulse Noise
IPN	Indigenous People's Network (EA)
IPN	Industri Pesawat Terbang Nusantara PT [*Indonesia*] [*ICAO designator*] (FAAC)
IPN	Infantile Periarteritis Nodosa [*Cardiology*] (DAVI)
IPN	Infectious Pancreatic Necrosis [*Medicine*]
IPN	Information Processing Network
IPN	Initial Priority Number [*Computer science*] (OA)
IPN	Initial Processing Number (NITA)
IPN	Inspection Progress Notification
IPN	Instant Private Network
IPN	Instrumentation Plan Number (MUGU)
IPN	Integrated Packet Network [*Hughes Network Systems, Inc.*]
IPN	Intellectual Property Network, Ltd. [*Information service or system*] (IID)
IPN	Interim Progress Note (STED)
IPN	International Platinum Corp. [*Toronto Stock Exchange symbol*]
IPN	International Polio Network (EA)
IPN	International Publishing Newsletter (NITA)
IPN	Intern's Progress Note [*Medical records*] (DAVI)
IPN	Interpeduncular Nucleus [*Cytology*]
IPN	Interpenetrating Polymer Network [*Organic chemistry*]
IPN	Interplanetary Network [*Astronomy*]
IPn	Interstitial Pneumonitis [*Medicine*] (STED)
IPN	Ipatinga [*Brazil*] [*Airport symbol*] (OAG)
IPN	Isophthalonitrile [*Organic chemistry*]
IPN	Purdue University, North Central Campus, Westville, IN [*OCLC symbol*] (OCLC)
IPNA	International Pediatric Nephrology (EA)
IPNA	Isopropylnoradrenaline [*Isoproterenol*] (STED)
IPNC	Independence Plan for Neighborhood Councils (EA)
IPNC	International Council of Plant Nutrition [*Australia*] (EAIO)
IPNFC	International Peter Noone Fan Club (EA)
IPng	Internet Protocol Next Generation (CDE)
IPNJ	Industrial Photographers of New Jersey (EA)
I/PNL	Instrument Panel [*Automotive engineering*]
IPNL	Integrated Perceived Noise Level [*Acoustics*]
IPNS	Intense Pulsed Neutron Source
IPNS	Interpenetrating Networks of Samples [*Statistics*]
IPNS	Isopenicillin N Synthase [*An enzyme*]
IPNV	Infectious Pancreatic Necrosis Virus
IPO	Crown Point Community Schools, Crown Point, IN [*OCLC symbol*] (OCLC)
IPO	Improved Pregnancy Outcome [*Medicine*] (DMAA)
IPO	Indophenol Oxidase [*An enzyme*]
IPO	Information Program Officer [*Foreign service*]
IPO	Initial Planning Option [*Medicine*] (DAVI)
IPO	Initial Public Offering [*Business term*]
IPO	Initial Public Offering [*Stock exchange term*]
IPO	Input, Process, and Output (MHDB)
IPO	Inspection Planning Order
IPO	Installation Planning Order
IPO	Installation Production Order
IPO	Installation Productivity Option [*IBM Corp.*]
IPO	Instantaneous Power Output
IPO	Intellectual Property Owners (EA)
IPO	International Pact Organization
IPO	International Parents' Organization [*Later, PS*] (EA)
IPO	International Payment Order (DCTA)
IPO	International Progress Organization [*Vienna, Austria*] (EAIO)
IPO	Ipora [*Brazil*] [*Airport symbol*] (AD)
IPOC	Iberian Peninsula Operating Committee [*World War II*]
IPOCA	International Pipe Line and Offshore Contractors Association [*Belgium*] (EAIO)
IPOD	International Program of Ocean Drilling [*Formerly, DSDP*] [*National Science Foundation*]
IPO/E	Installation Productivity Option/Extended [*IBM Corp.*]
IPOEE	Institute of Post Office Electrical Engineers [*British*]
IPOFA	Integrated Programmed Operational and Functional Appraisals

IPoH............	Saint James Hospital, Pontiac, IL [*Library symbol Library of Congress*] (LCLS)
IpOHA.........	Isopropyl Oxalyl Hydroxamate [*Organic chemistry*]
IPOL............	Institute of Polarology [*British*]
IPOM	Intelligent Plant Operating Manual [*Combustion Engineering Simcon, Inc.*]
IPOMS	International Polar-Orbiting Meteorological Satellite
IP/OP	Input/Output Interface Element [*Computer science*] (NITA)
IPOP	Installer Point of Purchase
IPOR	International Population Research Center [*University of California*] [*Defunct*]
IPOSA.........	International Photo Optical Show Association [*Defunct*] (EA)
IPOSS.........	Interim Pacific Oceanographic Support System (DNAB)
IPOT............	Inductive Potential Divider [*Electronics*] (ECII)
IPOT............	Inductive Potentiometer (MDG)
IPot.............	Potomac Public Library, Potomac, IL [*Library symbol Library of Congress*] (LCLS)
IPOTMS	Isopropenyloxytrimethylsilane [*Organic chemistry*]
IPP...............	British Institute of Practical Psychology
IPP...............	Imaging Polarimeter [*or Photopolarimetry*] [*NASA*]
IPP...............	Immediate Past President (ADA)
IPP...............	Imminent Peril to the Public (MHDB)
IPP...............	Impact Prediction Point [*NASA*]
IPP...............	Impaired Physician Program (EA)
IPP...............	Implementation Planning Program [*Environmental Protection Agency*] (GFGA)
IPP...............	Import Parity Pricing (ADA)
IPP...............	Inanities per Page [*Facetious criterion for determining insignificance of Supreme Court Justices*] [*Proposed by University of Chicago professor David P. Currie*]
IPP...............	Independent People's Party [*Political party Germany*] (EAIO)
IPP...............	Independent Power Producer
IPP...............	Independent Power Projects (AAGC)
IPP...............	Index of Prices Paid [*Economics*]
IPP...............	Indianapolis Public Schools, Indianapolis, IN [*OCLC symbol*] (OCLC)
IPP...............	Indian Print and Paper [*A publication*] (DGA)
IPP...............	India Paper Proofs
IPP...............	Individual Parameter Perturbation
IPP...............	Individual Program Plan
IPP...............	Industrial Partnering Program [*Department of Energy*]
IPP...............	Industrial Preparedness Planning [*DoD*]
IPP...............	Industrial Preparedness Program [*Environmental science*] (COE)
IPP...............	Inferior Point [*of the*] Pubic [*Bone*] [*Anatomy*] (DAVI)
IPP...............	Inflatable Penile Prosthesis [*Urology*] (DAVI)
IPP...............	Information Privacy Principle
IPP...............	Information Processing Professional
IPP...............	Infrared Pointer Package
IPP...............	Injury Prevention Program
IPP...............	In Propria Persona [*In Person*] [*Latin Legal term*] (DLA)
IPP...............	Input Processor Programs [*Computer science*]
IPP...............	Inspired Partial Pressure [*Physiology*]
IPP...............	Institute of Print Purchasing (DGA)
IPP...............	Integrated Plotting Package (NRCH)
IPP...............	Interface Program Plan (MCD)
IPP...............	Intermedia Priority Pollutant (GNE)
IPP...............	Intermittent Positive Pressure [*Medicine*]
IPP...............	Internal Packet Protocol [*Telecommunications*]
IPP...............	Internationally Protected Person (ADA)
IPP...............	International Partners in Prayer (EA)
IPP...............	International Phototelegraph Position [*Telecommunications*] (TEL)
IPP...............	International Price Program [*Bureau of Labor Statistics*] (GFGA)
IPP...............	International Priority Paid (ADA)
IPP...............	Interprocessor Process [*Telecommunications*] (TEL)
IPP...............	Intrapleural Pressure [*Biology*]
IPP...............	Inverse Polarity Protection
IPP...............	Investment Promotion Program
IPP...............	Ionospheric Propagation Path
IPP...............	Ipplepen [*England*]
IPP...............	Isopentenyl Pyrophosphate [*Organic chemistry*]
IPP...............	Isopropyl Percarbonate [*or Diisopropyl Peroxydicarbonate*] [*Organic chemistry*]
IPP...............	Isotactic Polypropylene [*Organic chemistry*]
IPP...............	Isothermal Pressure Profile
IPP...............	Itek Positive Plate [*Publishing*] (DGA)
IPp...............	Paw Paw Public Library, Paw Paw, IL [*Library symbol Library of Congress*] (LCLS)
IPPA............	Independent Professional Painting Contractors Association of America (NTPA)
IPPA............	Independent Programme Producers' Association [*British*]
IPPA............	Inspection, Palpation, Percussion, Auscultation [*Medicine*]
IPPA............	Instant Potato Products Association [*Defunct*] (EA)
IPPA............	Institute for Public Policy and Administration [*Later, CPPUI*] (EA)
IPPA............	Intensive Pig Producers of Australia
IPPA............	Intercontinental Press Publishing Association [*Defunct*] (EA)
IPPA............	International Paintball Players Association (EA)
IPPA............	International Pectin Producers Association [*Switzerland*] (EAIO)
IPPA............	International Pentecostal Press Association (EA)
IPPA............	International Printing Pressmen and Assistants' Union of North America [*Later, IPGCU*]
IPPA............	International Program for Population Analysis
IPPA............	Isopropylphenyl Acetate [*Organic chemistry*]
IPpa............	Palos Park Public Library, Palos Park, IL [*Library symbol Library of Congress*] (LCLS)
IPPAU	International Printing Pressmen and Assistants' Union of North America [*Later, IPGCU*] (EA)

IPPB............	Incremental Provisioning Parts Breakdown (SAA)
IPPB............	Intermittent Positive Pressure Breathing [*Medicine*]
IPPBA	Intermittent Positive-Pressure Breathing Apparatus [*Medicine*] (MEDA)
IPPB/I	Intermittent Positive Pressure Breathing/Inspiratory
IPPBS	Integrated Personnel Planning and Budgeting System
IPPC...........	Infrastructure Payments and Progress Committee [*NATO*] (NATG)
IPPC...........	Integrated Pollution Prevention and Control [*Environmental science*]
IPPC...........	International Penal and Penitentiary Commission [*Later, IPPF*]
IPPC...........	International Philatelic Press Club (EA)
IPPC...........	International Plant Protection Center [*Oregon State University*] [*Research center*] (RCD)
IPPC...........	Isopropyl N-phenylcarbamate [*Also, INPC, IPC*] [*Herbicide*]
IPPCA.........	Independent Professional Painting Contractors Association of America (EA)
IPPD...........	Integrated Product and Process Development [*Business term*] (RDA)
IPPD...........	Intermittent Positive Pressure Dialysis [*Medicine*] (DB)
IPPD...........	Isopropyl(phenyl)para-phenylene Diamine [*Organic chemistry*]
IPPDSEU	International Plate Printers, Die Stampers, and Engravers' Union of North America (EA)
IPPDT	Integrated Product and Process Development Team [*Military*] (RDA)
IPPF...........	Instruction Preprocessing Function
IPPF...........	International Penal and Penitentiary Foundation [*See also FIPP*] [*Bonn, Federal Republic of Germany*] (EAIO)
IPPF...........	International Planned Parenthood Federation (EA)
IPPF/WHR....	International Planned Parenthood Federation, Western Hemisphere Region (EA)
IPPH	Proctor Community Hospital, Peoria, IL [*Library symbol Library of Congress*] (LCLS)
IPPHA.........	International Peruvian Paso Horse Association (EA)
IPPI............	Instructional Procedures Preference Inventory
IPPI............	International Public Policy Institute
IPPI............	Interruption of Pregnancy for Psychiatric Indication
IPPIA	International Plasma Products Industry Association (NTPA)
IPPIF	IPL Energy [*NASDAQ symbol*] (TTSB)
IPPIF	IPL Energy, Inc. [*NASDAQ symbol*] (SAG)
IPPJ...........	Institute of Plasma Physics, Japan
IPPL...........	Indentured Parts Price List (MCD)
IPPL...........	Industrial Preparedness Planning List
IPPL...........	Integrated Planning Parts List (MCD)
IPPL...........	International Primate Protection League (EA)
IPPM	Integrated Product and Process Management [*Military*]
IPPMA	In-Plant Powder Metallurgy Association (EA)
IPPMA	In-Plant Printing Management Association
IPPMHN	International Post-Partum Mental Health Network (EA)
IPPNO	International Philosophers for the Prevention of Nuclear Omnicide (EA)
IPPNW	International Physicians for the Prevention of Nuclear War (EA)
IPPO	Intermittent Positive Pressure with Oxygen [*Medicine*]
IPPP...........	Industrial Preparedness Production Planning [*DOD*] (AAGC)
IPPP...........	Industrial Property Policy Program [*Insurance*]
IPPP...........	Institute for Philosophy and Public Policy (EA)
IPPP...........	Institute of Private Practicing Psychologists [*Australia*]
IPPR...........	Industrial Production Performance Reporting
IPPR...........	Institute for Public Policy Research [*British*] (ECON)
IPPR...........	Integrated Pancreatic Polypeptide Response [*Medicine*] (DMAA)
IPPR...........	Intermittent Positive Pressure Respiration
IPPS...........	Improved Processing System (MCD)
IPPS...........	Infiniti Personalized Protection System
IPPS...........	Institute of Physics and the Physical Society [*British*] (DI)
IPPS...........	International Philippine Philatelic Society (EAIO)
IPPS...........	International Plant Propagators Society, Eastern Region (EA)
IPpS...........	Paw Paw School System, Paw Paw, IL [*Library symbol Library of Congress*] (LCLS)
IPPSA	Israel-Palestine Philatelic Society of America [*Later, SIP*]
IPPSF	Isolated Perfused Porcine Skip Flap [*Clinical chemistry*]
IPPT...........	Inter-Person Perception Test [*Personality development test*] [*Psychology*]
IPPUAD........	Immediate Postprandial Upper Abdominal Distress
IPPV...........	Intermittent Positive Pressure Ventilation
IPQ.............	International Philosophical Quarterly [*A publication*] (BRI)
IPQ.............	International Praxis Resources [*Vancouver Stock Exchange symbol*]
IPQ.............	Intimacy Potential Quotient
IPQC............	In-Process Quality Control
IPQI.............	Intermediate Personality Questionnaire for Indian Pupils [*Personality development test*] [*Psychology*]
IPR.............	Icar Airlines [*Ukraine*] [*FAA designator*] (FAAC)
IPR.............	Imposter Pass Rate (MHDI)
IPR.............	Inches per Revolution
IPR.............	Independent Professional Review [*Medicaid*] (DHSM)
IPR.............	Index of Prices Received [*Economics*]
IPR.............	Individual Pay Record [*Military*]
IPR.............	Individual Performance Review (WDAA)
IPR.............	Indochina Postwar Reconstruction
IPR.............	Industry Planning Representative [*DoD*]
IPR.............	Inflation Pressure Retention [*Tire technology*]
IPR.............	Informal Progress Report
IPR.............	Initial Pressure Regulator [*Nuclear energy*] (NRCH)
IPR.............	In-Place Repair
IPR.............	In-Process Report
IPR.............	In-Process Review
IPR.............	In-Progress Review (DOMA)
IPR.............	In Pulse to Register [*Telecommunications*] (TEL)
IPR.............	Inspection Planning and Reliability (SAA)

IPR.............. Institute for Policy Research [*University of Wyoming*] [*Research center*] (RCD)
IPR.............. Institute for Policy Research [*University of Cincinnati*] [*Research center*] (RCD)
IPR.............. Institute for Public Research (AAGC)
IPR.............. Institute for Puerto Rican Policy, Inc. [*Research center*] (RCD)
IPR.............. Institute of Pacific Relations
IPR.............. Institute of Peace Research [*La Trobe University*] [*Australia*]
IPR.............. Institute of Population Registration [*British*]
IPR.............. Institute of Psychophysical Research [*British*]
IPR.............. Institute of Public Relations [*British*]
IPR.............. Insulin Production Rate [*Medicine*] (DMAA)
IPR.............. Intellectual Property Rights
IPR.............. Intelligence Production Requests
IPR.............. Intelligence Production Requirement (AFIT)
IPR.............. Interactive Photorealistic Rendering [*Computer-assisted design*]
IPR.............. Inter-City Products [*AMEX symbol*] (TTSB)
IPR.............. Inter-City Products Corp. [*AMEX symbol*] (SPSG)
IPR.............. Interdepartmental Procurement Request
IPR.............. Interdepartmental Purchase Request [*DoD*] (AFIT)
IPR.............. Interim Problem Report (NASA)
IPR.............. Interim Progress Report
IPR.............. Interior Procurement Regulations [*Department of the Interior*]
IPR.............. Internal Progress Report
IPR.............. International Public Relations (ADA)
IPR.............. Interpersonal Process Recall [*Psychology*]
IPR.............. Inward Processing Relief (DCTA)
IPR.............. Ion Production Rate
IPR.............. Irish Publishing Record (TELE)
IPR.............. Isolated Pentagon Rule [*Physical chemistry*]
iPr.............. Isopropyl (DB)
IPR.............. Isoproterenol [*An adrenergic*]
IPRA............ Illinois Park and Recreation Association (SRA)
IPRA............ Imaging Products Remanufacturing Association (NTPA)
IPRA............ Indigenious Peoples Rights Act [*Philippines*]
IPRA............ In-Place Repairable Assembly (MCD)
IPRA............ Institute of Park and Recreation Administration [*British*] (BI)
IPRA............ International Paddle Racket Association [*Later, AARA*]
IPRA............ International Peace Research Association (EA)
IPRA............ International Professional Rodeo Association (EA)
IPRA............ International Public Relations Association [*London, England*] (WDMC)
IPRA............ International Public Relations Association, US Section (EA)
IPRA............ Iowa Park and Recreation Association (SRA)
IPra............. Vernon Area Library District, Prairie View, IL [*Library symbol*] [*Library of Congress*] (LCLS)
IPRB............ Installations Planning and Review Board [*DoD*]
IPRB............ Inter-Allied Postwar Requirements Bureau [*World War II*]
IPRC............ Information Privacy Research Center [*Purdue University*] (PDAA)
IPRE............ Incorporated Practitioners in Radio and Electronics Ltd. [*British*] (BI)
IPRE............ International Professional Association for Environmental Affairs (EA)
IPRI............ International Plant Research Institute (PDAA)
IPri.............. Matson Public Library, Princeton, IL [*Library symbol Library of Congress*] (LCLS)
IPriBSD........ Bureau Township Consolidated School District 250, Princeton, IL [*Library symbol Library of Congress*] (LCLS)
I-PRIDE........ Interracial-Intercultural Pride (EA)
IPriDS.......... Douglas Elementary School, Princeton, IL [*Library symbol Library of Congress*] (LCLS)
IPriHi........... Bureau County Historical Society, Princeton, IL [*Library symbol Library of Congress*] (LCLS)
IPriJS........... Jefferson Elementary School, Princeton, IL [*Library symbol Library of Congress*] (LCLS)
IPriLH.......... Logan Junior High School, Princeton, IL [*Library symbol Library of Congress*] (LCLS)
IPriPH.......... Perry Memorial Hospital, Princeton, IL [*Library symbol Library of Congress*] (LCLS)
IPriv............ Lillie M. Evans Memorial Library, Princeville, IL [*Library symbol Library of Congress*] (LCLS)
IPriWS......... Washington Middle School, Princeton, IL [*Library symbol Library of Congress*] (LCLS)
IPRL............ Interceptor Pilot Research Laboratory (SAA)
IPRL............ Isolated Perfused Rabbit Lung (STED)
IPRL............ Isolated Perfused Rat Liver (DB)
IPRM........... Indium Phosphide Related Materials (AAEL)
I-PRO........... Independent Professional Representatives Organization (EA)
I/Pro............ Interactive Profiles [*Computer science*]
IPRO............ International Pallet Recycling Organization (PDAA)
IPRO............ International Patent Research Office (IAA)
I/PRO........... Internet Profiles Corp.
IProD........... Prospect Heights Public Library District, Prospect Heights, IL [*Library symbol Library of Congress*] (LCLS)
IProdE.......... Institute of Production Engineers [*British*] (DI)
I Prod E....... Institution of Production Engineers [*British*]
IPROP.......... Ionic Propulsion (IAA)
IPRP............ Institute for Puerto Rican Policy (EA)
IP-RPLC....... Ion-Pair-Reversed-Phase Liquid Chromatography
IPRR............ Integrated Personnel Requirement Report (AAG)
IPRS............ Inmate Personal Record System (WDAA)
IPRS............ International Confederation for Plastic and Reconstructive Surgery [*Montreal, PQ*] (EAIO)
IPRSF.......... Interim Protocol for Radon Screening and Followup [*Environmental science*] (COE)
IPRT............ Industrial Platinum Resistance Thermometer (PDAA)
IPRT............ Interpersonal Reaction Test [*Medicine*] (MAE)
IPS.............. Ibero-American Philosophical Society [*Madrid, Spain*] (EAIO)
IPS.............. Idiopathic Pain Syndrome [*Medicine*] (DMAA)
IPS.............. Idiopathic Postprandial Syndrome [*Medicine*] (DMAA)
IPS.............. Ignition Pressure Switch [*Automotive engineering*]
IPS.............. Illinois Psychiatric Society (SRA)
IPS.............. Illustrative Planning Scenario [*DoD*]
IPS.............. Image Processing System (MCD)
IPS.............. Impact Polystyrene (EDCT)
IPS.............. Impact Predictor System [*NASA*]
IPS.............. Imperial Parliament Series [*A publication*]
IPS.............. Improved Plow Steel (PDAA)
IPS.............. Improved Processing System
IPS.............. Impulses per Second [*Telecommunications*] (TEL)
IPS.............. Inches per Second
ips............... Inches per Second (DOM)
IPS.............. Incorporated Phonographic Society [*British*] (BI)
IPS.............. Incremental Purchasing System (SAA)
IPS.............. Index Preparation System [*Foxon-Maddocks Associates*] [*Information service or system*] (IID)
IPS.............. Indian Point Station [*Nuclear energy*] (NRCH)
IPS.............. Indian Police Service [*British*]
IPS.............. Indian Political Service [*British*]
IPS.............. Industrial Planning Specification
IPS.............. Inertial Positioning System (PDAA)
IPS.............. Information Processing System
IPS.............. Infundibular Pulmonic Stenosis [*Medicine*] (DAVI)
IPS.............. Initial Prognostic Score [*Medicine*] (MAE)
IPS.............. Initial Program Specification (SAA)
IPS.............. Inlet Particle Separator (MCD)
IPS.............. Inner Polar Site [*Cytology*]
IPS.............. In-Pavement System
IPS.............. In-Plant Support (MCD)
IPS.............. In Pulse to Sender [*Telecommunications*] (TEL)
IPS.............. Inside Pipe Size (DAC)
IPS.............. Installation Performance Specification [*Computer science*] (IBMDP)
IPS.............. Institute for Palestine Studies (EA)
IPS.............. Institute for Policy Studies (EA)
IPS.............. Institute of Plant Science [*Australia*]
IPS.............. Institute of Polar Studies [*Ohio State University*] [*Later, BPRC*]
IPS.............. Institute of Population Studies (BARN)
IPS.............. Institute of Purchasing and Supply [*British*]
IPS.............. Institutional Payment Summary [*Pell Grant Program*] [*Department of Education*] (GFGA)
IPS.............. Instructions per Second [*Computer science*]
IPS.............. Instrumentation Power Supply
IPS.............. Instrumentation Power System [*or Subsystem*] [*NASA*] (NASA)
IPS.............. Instrument Pointing System (MCD)
IPS.............. Integrated Planning Summary (MCD)
IPS.............. Integrated Power Semiconductors Ltd. [*British*] (NITA)
IPS.............. Integrated Power System
IPS.............. Integrated Procurement System [*Army*]
IPS.............. Integrated Program Study (MCD)
IPS.............. Integrated Program Summary [*Military*] (CAAL)
IPS.............. Integrated Project Support (IAA)
IPS.............. Integrated Propulsion System (MCD)
IPS.............. Intelligent Power Management System [*Laptop computers*] (BYTE)
IPS.............. Intelligent Power Switch [*Electronics*]
IPS.............. Intelligent Printing System [*Dataroyal, Inc.*]
IPS.............. Interactive Pictures Systems [*In IPS Dance, a computer program for choreographers*]
IPS.............. Interceptor Pilot Simulator [*SSTM*]
IPS.............. Interface Problem Sheet (NASA)
IPS.............. Interim Policy Statement (NRCH)
IPS.............. Interim POMSEE [*Performance, Operating, and Maintenance Standards for Electronic Equipment*] Sheet
IPS.............. Interlink Press Service (EA)
IPS.............. Intermittent Photic Stimulation [*Electroencephalography*] (STED)
IPS.............. Intermolecular Pair Potential Surface [*Physical chemistry*]
IPS.............. Intermolecular Potential (Energy) Surface [*Spectroscopy*]
IPS.............. Internal Plate Screen (IAA)
IPS.............. Internal Power Supply [*Computer science*]
IPS.............. International Confederation for Plastic Surgery
IPS.............. Internationale Paracelsus-Gesellschaft zu Salzburg [*International Paracelsus Society*] (EA)
IPS.............. International Palm Society (EA)
IPS.............. International Paracelsus Society [*Salzburg, Austria*] (EA)
IPS.............. International Peat Society [*See also IMTG*] [*Helsinki, Finland*] (EAIO)
IPS.............. International Perimetric Society (EA)
IPS.............. International Phenomenological Society (EA)
IPS.............. International Phycological Society (EA)
IPS.............. International Pipe Standard
IPS.............. International Planetarium Society (EA)
IPS.............. International Plastics Selector, Inc. [*Information service or system*] (IID)
IPS.............. International Polaris Energy Corp. [*Toronto Stock Exchange symbol*]
IPS.............. International Preview Society (EA)
IPS.............. International Primatological Society (EA)
IPS.............. International Processes Simulation [*Game*]
IPS.............. Internet Printing System [*Computer science*]
IPS.............. Interpersonal Perception Scale (STED)
IPS.............. Interplanetary Scintillation
IPS.............. Inter/Press Service - Third World News Agency (EA)
IPS.............. Interpretive Programming System
IPS.............. Interruptions per Second
IPS.............. Intractable Pain Society of Great Britain and Ireland
IPS.............. Intrapartum Stillbirth [*Medicine*] (DMAA)

IPS............. Intraperitoneal Shock [Psychology]
IPS............. Introductory Physical Science [Project] [Education]
IPS............. Inventing and Patenting Sourcebook [A publication]
IPS............. Inventory of Perceptual Skills [Visual and auditory test]
IPS............. Inverse Photoemission Spectroscopy
IPS............. Inverter Power Supply (NASA)
IPS............. Investors Protection Scheme (DCTA)
IPS............. Iodophenylsulfonyl [Pipsyl] (STED)
IPS............. Ionospheric Prediction Service [Telecommunications] (TEL)
IPS............. Ion Plating Supply
IPS............. Iron Pipe Size (WGA)
IPS............. Ischiopubic Synchondrosis (STED)
IPS............. Isopenicillin N-Synthetase (DB)
IP's............ Issue Priority Designators (AFIT)
IPS............. Item Processing System (BUR)
IPS............. Office of Information Programmes and Services [UNESCO] (IID)
IPSA........... Incremental Microwave Power Spectrum Analyzer [Air Force]
IPSA........... Independent Postal System of America [Alternative to US Postal Service]
IPSA........... Industrial Police and Security Association [British] (BI)
IPSA........... Institute for Psychological Study of the Arts [University of Florida] [Research center] (RCD)
IPSA........... International Passenger Ship Association [Merger of Atlantic Passenger St eamship Conference, Trans-Atlantic Passenger Steamship Conference, Caribbean Cruise Association] [Defunct]
IPSA........... International Political Science Association (EA)
IPSA........... International Professional Security Association [Paignton, Devonshire, England] (EAIO)
IPSA........... International Professional Surrogates Association (EA)
IPSAM .... International Presort Airmail [US Postal Service]
IPSANET ...... Sharp [I. P.] Communications Network [I.P. Sharp Associates Ltd.] [Toronto, ON] (TSSD)
IPSAR.......... Integrated Plant Safety Assessment Report [Nuclear energy] (NRCH)
IPSB........... Interprocessor Signal Bus
IPSB........... Intrapartum Stillbirth (STED)
IPSC........... Information Processing Standards for Computers
IPSC........... Information Processing Supplies Council [Defunct] (EA)
IPSC........... Inhibitory Postsynaptic Current [Neurophysiology]
IPSC........... Interagency Primate Steering Committee [National Institutes of Health]
IPSC........... Inventory of Psychic and Somatic Complaints [Medicine] (DB)
IPSC........... Ipsco, Inc. [NASDAQ symbol] (SAG)
IPSCF......... IPSCO Inc. [NASDAQ symbol] (TTSB)
Ipsco.......... Ipsco, Inc. [Associated Press] (SAG)
IPSD........... Interservice Procedures for Systems Development [Military]
IPSE........... Implementing Primary Science Education (AIE)
IPSE........... Integrated Programming Support Environment [BIS Applied Systems] [British]
IPSE........... Integrated Project Support Environment (NITA)
IPSE........... Intelligent Program Support Environment (TELE)
IPSEP......... International Project for Soft Energy Paths [Defunct] (EA)
IPSF........... Immediate Postsurgical Fitting of Prosthesis (STED)
IPSF........... Intermediate Postsurgical Fitting [Medicine]
IPSF........... International Pharmaceutical Students' Federation [Jerusalem, Israel] (EAIO)
IPSFC......... International Pacific Salmon Fisheries Commission [Canada] (EA)
IPSG........... International Programs Steering Group [DoD]
IPSICM....... International PSI Committee of Magicians [See also CIEPP] (EAIO)
IPSID .... Immunoproliferative Small Intestinal Disease (MAE)
IPSJ........... Information Processing Society of Japan (NITA)
IPSL........... Interface Problem Status Log (NASA)
IPSLN .... Indo-Pacific Sea Level Network [Marine science] (OSRA)
IPSM........... Improved Performance Space Motor (MCD)
IPSM........... Institute of Physical Sciences in Medicine [British] (DBA)
IPSN........... Institute for Protection and Nuclear Safety (NUCP)
IPSO........... Initiating Production by Sales Order (PDAA)
IPSO........... Interface Peripheral Standard Olivetti (MCD)
IPSO........... International Programs and Studies Office [Later, DIA] (EA)
IPSOC......... Information Processing Society of Canada
IPSP........... Inhibitory Postsynaptic Potential [Neurophysiology]
IPSP........... Intelligence Priorities for Strategic Planning [Military]
IPSP........... Internet Protocol Security Protocol [Computer science]
IPSR........... Institute of Plant Science Research [Research center British] (IRC)
IPSRA......... International Professional Ski Racers Association (EA)
IPSS........... Information Processing System Simulator [Computer science] (MHDI)
IPSS........... Initial Pre-planned Supply Support (DOMA)
IPSS........... Institute of Planetary and Space Science (MCD)
IPSS........... Interactive Population Statistical System [Computer science]
IPSS........... Intermediate Plutonium Storage System [Nuclear energy] (NUCP)
IPSS........... International Packet Switched Service [Telecommunications system] (NITA)
IPSS........... International Packet Switching Service [British Telecom International, Inc.] [Telecommunications service] (TSSD)
IPSS........... International Packet Switch Stream [Computer science]
IPSS........... International Pilot Study of Schizophrenia [WHO]
I-PSS........... International Prostate Symptoms Score [Medicine] (WDAA)
IPSS........... Interprocessor Signaling System [Telecommunications] (TEL)
IPSSB .... Information Processing Systems Standards Board [Later, Board of Standards Review of ANSI] [American Standards Association]
IPSSG .... International Printers Supply Salesmen's Guild (EA)
IPST........... In-Process Self Test (MCD)
IPST........... Institute for Physical Science and Technology [University of Maryland] [Research center] (RCD)
IPST........... Institute of Paper Science and Technology (NTPA)
IPST........... International Practical Scale of Temperature (PDAA)

IPST........... Israel Program for Scientific Translations [An agency of the Government of Israel]
IPStF........... Saint Francis Hospital, Peoria, IL [Library symbol Library of Congress] (LCLS)
IPSW .... Ipswich [City in England] (ROG)
IPSW .... Ipswich Savings Bank [NASDAQ symbol] (SAG)
IPSW .... Ipswich Svgs Bk Mass [NASDAQ symbol] (TTSB)
IpswchSv ..... Ipswich Savings Bank [Associated Press] (SAG)
IpswichSv .... Ipswich Savings Bank [Associated Press] (SAG)
IPSY .... Interactive Planning System (MHDI)
IPT............. Icelandic Pony Trekkers [Later, IHT] (EA)
IPT............. Ideal Process Time (AAEL)
IPT............. Image Processing Technology [Computer graphics]
IPT............. Immunoprecipitation Technique [Clinical chemistry]
IPT............. Improved Programming Technologies (BUR)
IPT............. Inches per Tooth (IAA)
IPT............. Incremental Proof Testing
IPT............. Indexed, Paged, and Titled (ADA)
IPT............. Individual Perception Threshold (PDAA)
IPT............. Induction Plasma Torch
IPT............. Industrial and Performance Technology [Human performance analysis]
IPT............. Industrial Power Tube
IPT............. Information Presentation Technologies, Inc.
IPT............. Information Processing Technology
IPT............. Infrared Plume Target
IPT............. Initial Production Test [Army] (AABC)
IPT............. In-Plant Test (KSC)
IPT............. In-Plant Training
IPT............. In-Plant Transporter (MCD)
IPT............. In Port [Navy] (NVT)
IPT............. In-Process Testing
IPT............. Installation Preflight Test
IPT............. Institute for Paralegal Training [Later, Philadelphia Institute] [Commercial firm] (EA)
IPT............. Institute of Petroleum Technologists
IPT............. Institute of Property Taxation (EA)
IPT............. Instituto de Promocao Turistica [Portugal] (EY)
IPT............. Integrated Process Team [Business term]
IPT............. Integrated Product Team [Business term] (RDA)
IPT............. Intellectual Property Transfer
IPT............. Intermediate Phase Training (DOMA)
IPT............. Intermittent Pelvic Traction (DAVI)
IPT............. Internal Pipe Thread
IPT............. International Pipe Thread (NASA)
IPT............. International Planning Team [NATO] (NATG)
IPT............. International Production Technology (IAA)
IPT............. Interpersonal Therapy [Mental health treatment technique]
IPT............. Interphase Transformer [Electronics] (IAA)
IPT............. Interplanetary Travel (AAG)
IPT............. Interport Corp. [ICAO designator] (FAAC)
IPT............. Io Plasma Torus [Cosmology]
IPT............. IP Timberlands Cl'A' [NYSE symbol] (TTSB)
IPT............. IP Timberlands Ltd. [NYSE symbol] (SAG)
IPT............. Iron Pipe Thread (MSA)
IPT............. Isopentenyl Transferase [An enzyme]
IPT............. MAP International, Wheaton, IL [OCLC symbol] (OCLC)
IPT............. Williamsport [Pennsylvania] [Airport symbol] (OAG)
IPT 1........... Williamsport, PA [Location identifier FAA] (FAAL)
IPT 1........... Idea Oral Language Proficiency Test (TES)
IPTA........... International Patent and Trademark Association [Later, IIPA] (EA)
IPTA........... International Piano Teachers Association [Defunct]
IPTAR......... Institute for Psychoanalytic Training and Research
IPTC........... International Polar Transportation Conference
IPTC........... International Press Telecommunications Council [See also CIPT] [Telecommunications An association Defunct] (EA)
IPTCS......... Igloo Passive Thermal Control Section [Aerospace] (MCD)
IPTEA......... Internacia Postista kaj Telekomunikista Esperanto-Asocio [International Esperanto Association of Post and Telecommunication Workers] (EAIO)
IPTF........... Indo-Pacific Theosophical Federation (EAIO)
IPTG........... Isopropylthiogalactoside [Also, IPG] [Organic chemistry]
IPTH........... Immunoreactive Parathyroid Hormone [Endocrinology]
IPTIC......... International Pulse Trade and Industry Confederation [FAO]
IP Timb....... IP Timberlands Ltd. [Associated Press] (SAG)
IPTM........... Interval Pulse Time Modulation
IPTN........... Independent Professional Typists Network (EA)
IPTO........... International Pet Trade Organization [Defunct] (EAIO)
IPTP........... In-Plant Test Program (IAA)
IPTPA......... International Professional Tennis Players Association (BARN)
IPTS........... Integrated Powertrain Test System
IPTS........... International Practical Temperature Scale [National Institute of Standards and Technology]
IPTS/PS .... Improved Programmer Test Station / Power Station (SAA)
IPTT........... Internationale du Personnel des Postes, Telegraphes, et Telephones [Postal, Telegraph, and Telephone International - PTTI] [Geneva, Switzerland] (EAIO)
IPTV........... Initial Propulsion Test Vehicle
IPTX........... Intermittent Pelvic Traction [Medicine] (DMAA)
IPU............. Eastern New Mexico University, Portales, NM [OCLC symbol] (OCLC)
IPU............. Immediate Pick-Up (DNAB)
IPU............. Individual Patient Usage
IPU............. Information Processing Utility
IPU............. Initial Production Unit

IPU............	Inpatient Unit [*Medicine*]
IPU............	Input Preparation Unit [*Computer science*] (WDAA)
IPU............	Institute for Public Understanding (EA)
IPU............	Institute of Public Utilities (EA)
IPU............	Instruction Processing Unit (BUR)
IPU............	Integrated Physiological Unit
IPU............	Intelligent Processing Unit [*Canon, Inc.*] [*Computer science*] (PCM)
IPU............	Interface and Priority Unit
IPU............	International Paleontological Union
IPU............	International Peasant Union
IPU............	Inter-Parliamentary Union [*See also UI*] [*Switzerland*]
IPU............	Interphase Unit
IPU............	Interprocessor Unit
IPU............	Irish Postal Union
IPU............	Irish Print Union (DGA)
IPU............	Isotope Power Unit
IPV............	Imperative (WGA)
IPV............	Inaccessible Pore Volume [*Petroleum technology*]
IPV............	Inactivated Polio Vaccine [*Also, Salk vaccine*] (PAZ)
IPV............	Inactivated Poliovirus Vaccine
IPV............	Infectious Pustular Vaginitis [*Medicine*]
IPV............	Infectious Pustular Vulvovaginitis [*Veterinary medicine*]
IPV............	Injectable Polio Vaccine [*Medicine*]
IPV............	Inner Pilot Valve
IPV............	In-Plant Verification (AFIT)
IPV............	Internal Podalic Version [*Obstetrics*]
IPV............	International Prime Tech [*Vancouver Stock Exchange symbol*]
IPV............	Inter-Prison Visit (WDAA)
IPV............	Intrinsic Payload Value
IPV............	Inverse Peak Voltage (CIST)
IPV............	Isopycnic Potential Vorticity [*Oceanography*]
IPV............	Italian Polydor Variable Microgroove [*Record label*]
IPV............	Poliovirus Vaccine Inactivated [*Medicine*] (TAD)
IPVG............	Isopycnic Potential Vorticity Gradient [*Oceanography*]
IPVRA	International Professional Vinyl Repair Association (EA)
IPVS............	International Pig Veterinary Society [*Amer, Spain*] (EAIO)
IPVS............	Ion Pump Vacuum System
IPW............	International Peace Walk [*An association*] (EA)
IPW............	International Powertech Systems, Inc. [*Vancouver Stock Exchange symbol*]
IPW............	Interpole Winding [*Wiring*] (DNAB)
IPW............	Interrogation Prisoner of War
IPW............	Interstate Power [*NYSE symbol*] (TTSB)
IPW............	Interstate Power Co. [*NYSE symbol*] (SPSG)
IPW............	Ipswich [*England*] [*Airport symbol*] (AD)
IPWA............	Invisible Panel Warming Association [*British*] (BI)
IPWF............	International Public Works Federation (EA)
IPWI............	Infrared Proximity Warning Indicator
IPWO............	Interplant Work Order (MCD)
IPWR............	Integrated Pressurized Water Reactor (PDAA)
IPWS............	Iron Plate Workers' Society [*A union*] [*British*]
IPWSOM......	Institute of Practitioners in Work Study, Organisation, and Management (AIE)
IPX............	International Phasor Telecom [*Vancouver Stock Exchange symbol*]
IPX............	Internet Package Exchange [*Computer science*] (DDC)
IPX............	Internetwork Packet Exchange
IPX............	Internetwork Protocol Exchange [*Novell, Inc.*] [*Computer science*] (PCM)
IPX............	Interpool, Inc. [*NYSE symbol*] (SPSG)
IPXI............	Intrinsic Peroxidase Inhibition Solution [*Clinical chemistry*]
IPXPrA........	Interpool Inc. 5.75% Cv Pfd [*NYSE symbol*] (TTSB)
IPX/SPX......	Internet Packet Exchange / Sequenced Packet [*Computer science*] (PCM)
IPY............	Inches per Year
IPY............	International Phoenix Energy [*Vancouver Stock Exchange symbol*]
IPY............	International Polar Year
IPY............	Ion Pair Yield
IPZ............	George A. Zeller Zone Center, Professional Library, Peoria, IL [*Library symbol Library of Congress*] (LCLS)
IPZ............	Insulin Protamine Zinc (DMAA)
IPZ............	Investment Promotion Zone
IPZ............	IPC International Prospector [*Vancouver Stock Exchange symbol*]
IPZ............	World Book - Childcraft International, Inc., Research Library, Chicago, IL [*OCLC symbol*] (OCLC)
IPZP...........	Iranian Peace Zebra Program [*Military*] (MCD)
IQ............	Caribbean Airways [*ICAO designator*] (AD)
IQ............	Ideal Quota [*Vitamin supplement*] [*British*]
IQ............	Idem Quod [*The Same As*] [*Latin*]
IQ............	Ideon Group, Inc. [*NYSE symbol*] (SAG)
IQ............	Indefinite Quantity (AFM)
IQ............	Inflation Quotient
IQ............	Information Quick (PDAA)
I/Q............	In Phase/Quadrature (MCD)
IQ............	Inquix Consulting Ltd. [*Information service or system*] (IID)
IQ............	Installation Qualification (ACII)
IQ............	Institute of Quarrying [*British*]
IQ............	Instrument Quality (IAA)
IQ............	Intelligence Quotient [*Psychological and educational testing*]
IQ............	Intelligent Query
IQ............	Intelligent Quisine [*Campbell Soup Co.*]
IQ............	Internal Quality
IQ............	International Quorum of Film and Video Producers (EA)
IQ............	Interrupted Quick [*Flashing*] Light [*Navigation signal*]
IQ............	Investment Quotient
IQ............	Iowa Quality [*of pigs*]
IQ............	I Quit [*Smoking*]
iq............	Iraq [*MARC country of publication code Library of Congress*] (LCCP)
IQ............	Iraq [*ANSI two-letter standard code*] (CNC)
IQ............	Quincy Free Public Library, Quincy, IL [*Library symbol Library of Congress*] (LCLS)
IQA............	Inertial Quality Attitude
IQA............	Inspection Quality Assurance
IQA............	Institute of Quality Assurance [*British*]
IQA............	International Quality Award [*LIMRA*]
IQA............	Irish Quality Association (ACII)
IqAF............	Iraqi Air Force
IQ & S............	Iron, Quinine, and Strychnine [*Elixir*]
IQB............	Individual Quick Blanching (DICI)
IQC............	Indefinite-Quantity Contract (AAGC)
IQC............	Industrial Quality Control
IQC............	Institutional Quality Control [*Department of Education*] (GFGA)
IQC............	Integrated Quality Control [*Department of Health and Human Services*] (GFGA)
IQC............	InterCapital California Quality Municipal Securities [*NYSE symbol*] (SPSG)
IQC............	InterCapital Cal Qual Muni Sec [*NYSE symbol*] (TTSB)
IQC............	International Quality Centre
IQC............	Quincy College, Quincy, IL [*Library symbol Library of Congress*] (LCLS)
IQCDPS........	Integrated Quality Control Data Processing System [*Department of Health and Human Services*] (GFGA)
IQCODE........	Informant Questionnaire on Cognitive Decline in the Elderly
IQCPP............	Institutional Quality Control Pilot Project [*Department of Education*] (GFGA)
IQE............	Interruption Queue Element [*Computer science*] (MHDI)
IQEC............	International Quantum Electronics Conference (CIST)
IQED	Id Quod Erat Demonstrandum [*That Which Was to Be Proved*] [*Latin*]
IQF............	Individually Quick-Frozen [*Food technology*]
IQF............	Interactive Query Facility [*Computer science*]
IQF............	International Quail Foundation [*Defunct*] (EA)
IQG............	Great River Library System, Quincy, IL [*Library symbol Library of Congress*] (LCLS)
IQHE	Integer Quantum Hall Effect [*Solid state physics*]
IQHE	Integral Quantum Hall Effect [*Solid-state physics*]
IQI............	Image Quality Indicator
IQI............	Industrial Quality, Inc.
IQI............	Instructional Quality Inventory
IQI............	InterCapital Quality Municipal Income [*NYSE symbol*] (SPSG)
IQI............	InterCapital Qual Muni Income [*NYSE symbol*] (TTSB)
IQIQ............	Applied Intelligence Group, Inc. [*NASDAQ symbol*] (SAG)
IQISA	Interest Questionnaire for Indian South Africans [*Vocational guidance test*]
I Qk............	Interrupted Quick [*Flashing*] Light [*Navigation signal*]
I Qk Fl............	Interrupted Quick Flashing Light [*Navigation signal*]
IQL............	Information Query Language (NITA)
IQL............	Interactive Query Language [*Digital Equipment Corp.*] [*Computer science*]
IQL............	Intermediate Query Language [*Computer science*]
IQM............	Input Queue Manager (NITA)
IQM............	InterCapital Quality Municipal Securities [*NYSE symbol*] (SPSG)
IQM............	InterCapital Qual Muni Sec [*NYSE symbol*] (TTSB)
IQM............	Qiemo [*China*] [*Airport symbol*] (OAG)
IQMF............	Image Quality Merit Function [*Color image*]
IQMH............	Input Queue Message Handler [*Computer science*]
IQMInc............	Intercapital Quality Municipal Income Trust [*Associated Press*] (SAG)
IQMInv........	Intercapital Quality Municipal Investment Trust [*Associated Press*] (SAG)
IQMS	Industrial Quality Management Science [*Quality control*]
IQMSec........	InterCapital Quality Municipal Securities [*Associated Press*] (SAG)
IQN............	Inner Quantum Number
IQN............	Intercapital New York Quality Municipal Securities [*NYSE symbol*] (SAG)
IQN............	InterCapital N.Y.Qual Muni Sec [*NYSE symbol*] (TTSB)
IQN............	Qingyang [*China*] [*Airport symbol*] (OAG)
IQO............	Initial Quantity Order (NG)
IQPF............	International Quick Printing Foundation [*Defunct*] (EA)
IQPP............	Interactive Query Pre-Processor (NITA)
IQPS	Institute of Qualified Private Secretaries Ltd. [*British*] (BI)
IQQ............	Caribbean Airways [*Barbados*] [*ICAO designator*] (FAAC)
IQQ............	Iquique [*Chile*] [*Airport symbol*] (OAG)
IQQ............	Iquique [*Chile*] [*Seismograph station code, US Geological Survey*] (SEIS)
IQR............	Interquartile Range
IQRC............	Institut Quebecois de la Recherche sur la Culture [*Database producer*]
IQRP	Interactive Query and Report Processor [*IBM Corp.*] [*Computer science*]
IQS............	Initial Quality Survey
IQS............	Institute of Quantity Surveyors [*Later, RICS*]
IQS............	Interactive Query System [*Computer science*] (IAA)
IQS............	International ™Q∫ Signal
IQSoft............	IQ Software Corp. [*Associated Press*] (SAG)
IQST............	IntelliQuest Information Group, Inc. [*NASDAQ symbol*] (SAG)
IQST............	IntelliQuest Info Group [*NASDAQ symbol*] (TTSB)
IQSU	International Quiet Sun Year [*1964-65*] [*Also, IQSY, IYQS*] (IAA)
IQSW	IQ Software [*NASDAQ symbol*] (TTSB)
IQSW	IQ Software Corp. [*NASDAQ symbol*] (SAG)
IQSY	International Quiet Sun Year [*1964-65*] [*Also, IYQS*]
IQT............	Initial Qualification Training

IQT.............. Intercapital Quality Municipal Investment Trust [*NYSE symbol*] (SPSG)
IQT.............. InterCapital Qual Muni Inv [*NYSE symbol*] (TTSB)
IQT.............. Interquest Resources Corp. [*Toronto Stock Exchange symbol*]
IQT.............. Iquitos [*Peru*] [*Airport symbol*] (OAG)
IQU.............. University of New Mexico, Albuquerque, NM [*OCLC symbol*] (OCLC)
IQUE.......... In-Plant Quality Evaluation Program (AAGC)
IQV.............. Illinois Veterans Home, Quincy, IL [*Library symbol*] [*Library of Congress*] (LCLS)
IQV.............. Pekin Community High School, Pekin, IL [*OCLC symbol*] (OCLC)
IQW............ Individuelle Quantitative Wert [*Mean Total Ridge Count*] [*Anatomy*]
IQW............ John Wood Community College, Quincy, IL [*Library symbol Library of Congress*] (LCLS)
IQW............ Western New Mexico University, Silver City, NM [*OCLC symbol*] (OCLC)
IQX.............. Bradford Public Library, Bradford, IL [*OCLC symbol*] (OCLC)
IQY.............. Internet Query [*Computer science*]
IQY.............. Limestone High School, Bartonville, IL [*OCLC symbol*] (OCLC)
IQZ.............. Farmington East High School, Farmington, IL [*OCLC symbol*] (OCLC)
IR................. Ice on Runway [*NWS*] (FAAC)
IR................. Ice Rinks [*Public-performance tariff class*] [*British*]
IR................. Illumination Rate (CAAL)
IR................. Illuminator RADAR (NATG)
IR................. Illustration Request
IR................. Image Readout [*Computer graphics*]
IR................. Image Rejection
IR................. Imaging RADAR (MCD)
IR................. Imitation Russia [*Bookbinding*] (DGA)
IR................. Immediate Reserve [*Air Force British*]
IR................. Immune Response [*Also, Ir*] [*Genetics*]
IR................. Immunization Rate (AFM)
IR................. Immunoreactive
IR................. Immunoreagent (DB)
IR................. Improved Retrofit (CAAL)
IR................. Impurity Removal Subsystem (MCD)
IR................. Incidence Rate (WDAA)
IR................. Incident Report
IR................. Inclination of the Ascending Return [*Aviation*] (NASA)
IR................. Indent Right [*Typography*] (DGA)
ir................. Indent Right (WDMC)
IR................. Independent Research (NG)
IR................. Index of Response [*Medicine*] (MAE)
IR................. Index Register (WDAA)
IR................. Indiana Railroad System
IR................. Indiana Register [*A publication*] (AAGC)
IR................. Indian Rulings [*A publication*] (DLA)
IR................. India-Rubber (DEN)
IR................. Indicating Recorder [*Electronics*] (ECII)
IR................. Indicator Reading (IAA)
IR................. Indicator Register (IAA)
IR................. Individual Recorder [*Sports*]
IR................. Individual Referral (OICC)
IR................. Industrial Registry [*New South Wales, Australia*]
IR................. Industrial Relations
IR................. Industrial Reports [*Australia A publication*]
I-R............... Industrial Research
IR................. Industry Remarketer (CDE)
IR................. Inferior Rectus [*Muscle*] [*Anatomy*]
IR................. Informal Report
IR................. Information and Technology [*Educational Resources Information Center (ERIC) Clearinghouse*] [*Syracuse University*] (PAZ)
IR................. Information Release (DLA)
IR................. Information Report
IR................. Information Request (AAG)
IR................. Information Requirement [*Military intelligence*] (INF)
IR................. Information Retrieval [*Computer science*]
IR................. Infrared
IR................. Infrared Radiation
IR................. Infrared Radiometer
IR................. Infrared Reconnaissance
IR................. Infrared Reflectance (IAA)
IR................. Infra-Red Spectroscopy (EDCT)
Ir................. Ingenieur [*Engineer*] [*French*]
IR................. Ingersoll-Rand [*NYSE symbol*] (TTSB)
IR................. Ingersoll-Rand Co. [*NYSE symbol*] (SPSG)
IR................. Ingram-Rude Information Researchers [*Information service or system*] (IID)
IR................. Ingreee Router (ACRL)
IR................. Initial Reactive Results
IR................. Initial Release (MCD)
IR................. Initial Reserve
IR................. Initiation Region [*Genetics*]
IR................. Ink Receptivity
IR................. Inland Revenue [*British*]
IR................. Inner Roll Gimbal (NASA)
I/R............... Inquiry/Response [*Automotive engineering Electronics*]
IR................. Inside Radius [*Technical drawings*]
IR................. Inside Right [*Soccer position*]
IR................. Insoluble Residue
IR................. Inspection Record (MCD)
IR................. Inspection Rejection
IR................. Inspection Release
IR................. Inspection [*or Inspector's*] Report
IR................. Inspection Request (IAA)
IR................. Installation Report

IR................. Installation Restoration (MCD)
IR................. Instantaneous Relay
IR................. Instantaneous Release (IAA)
IR................. Instant Release [*Typography*] (DGA)
IR................. Institute of Refrigeration [*British*]
IR................. Instruction Register [*Computer science*]
IR................. Instrumentation Report
IR................. Instrumentation Requirements (MUGU)
I/R............... Instrument Rating [*Aviation*] (AIA)
IR................. Instrument Reading (AFM)
IR................. Instrument Register (IAA)
IR................. Instrument Restricted Controlled Airspace (DA)
IR................. Insulation Resistance
IR................. Intake Restriction [*Automotive engineering*]
IR................. Intelligence Ratio
IR................. Intelligence Report
IR................. Intelligence Request (DOMA)
IR................. Intelligence Requirement [*Military*] (INF)
IR................. Intelligence Review
IR................. Intensive Reading
IR................. Interaction Resistance [*Plant pathology*]
IR................. Interagency Report (PDAA)
IR................. Intergovernmental Relations (OICC)
IR................. Interim Report
IR................. Intermediate Range (MCD)
IR................. Intermediate Register [*Telecommunications*] (OA)
IR................. Intermediate Review (NATG)
IR................. Internal Register (IAA)
IR................. Internal Reliability
IR................. Internal Repeat [*Genetics*]
IR................. Internal Report
IR................. Internal Resistance
IR................. Internal Revenue
IR................. Internal Revenue Decisions [*Department of the Treasury*] [*A publication*] (DLA)
IR................. Internal Review [*Army*] (AABC)
IR................. Internal Rotation [*Myology*]
IR................. Internationale de la Resistance [*Resistance International - RI*] (EAIO)
IR................. International Randonneurs [*An association*] (EA)
IR................. International Rectifier Corp. (EFIS)
IR................. International Registration (BARN)
IR................. International Rendezvous (MCD)
IR................. International Rice (IIA)
IR................. Interpretation Report
IR................. InterRent [*Car rental group*]
IR................. Interrogation Report
IR................. Interrogator-Responder
IR................. Interrupt Register (IAA)
IR................. Interrupt Request [*Computer science*] (MHDB)
IR................. Interval Rate [*Army*] (AABC)
ir................. Intrarectal [*Medicine*] (DB)
ir................. Intrarenal [*Medicine*] (DB)
IR................. Invention Report
IR................. Inversion Recovery [*NMR imaging*]
IR................. Inverted Repeat [*Genetics*]
IR................. Investigation Record
IR................. Investment Recurring (MCD)
IR................. Investor Relations
ir................. Iran [*MARC country of publication code Library of Congress*] (LCCP)
IR................. Iran [*ANSI two-letter standard code*] (CNC)
IR................. Iran Air [*ICAO designator*] (AD)
IR................. Iran Air [*Airline flight code*] (ODBW)
IR................. Iran National Airlines [*ICAO designator*] (AD)
Ir................. Iredell's North Carolina Equity Reports [*A publication*] (DLA)
Ir................. Iredell's North Carolina Law Reports [*A publication*] (DLA)
IR................. Ireland [*IYRU nationality code*] (ROG)
Ir................. Iridium [*Chemical element*]
IR................. Irish
IR................. Irish Law Reports [*A publication*] (DLA)
Ir................. Irnerius [*Flourished, 1113-18*] [*Authority cited in pre-1607 legal work*] (DSA)
ir................. Iron [*CIPW classification*] [*Geology*]
IR................. Irradiance [*Electromagnetism*] (IAA)
IR................. Irrelevancy [*Used in correcting manuscripts, etc.*]
IR................. Isoprene Rubber
IR................. Isotope Ratio (DB)
IR................. Isotope Reactor [*Former USSR*]
IR................. Item Record (AFIT)
I-R............... Ito-Reenstierna [*Reaction*] [*Medicine*]
IR................. Izquierda Republicana [*Republican Left*] [*Spain Political party*] (PPE)
IR................. Rock Island Public Library, Rock Island, IL [*Library symbol Library of Congress*] (LCLS)
IR1.............. Iran Long-Period Array [*Iran*] [*Seismograph station code, US Geological Survey*] (SEIS)
IR2.............. Iran Long-Period Array [*Iran*] [*Seismograph station code, US Geological Survey*] (SEIS)
IR3.............. Iran Long-Period Array [*Iran*] [*Seismograph station code, US Geological Survey*] (SEIS)
IR4.............. Iran Long-Period Array [*Iran*] [*Seismograph station code, US Geological Survey*] (SEIS)
IR5.............. Iran Long-Period Array [*Iran*] [*Seismograph station code, US Geological Survey*] (SEIS)
IR6.............. Iran Long-Period Array [*Iran*] [*Seismograph station code, US Geological Survey*] (SEIS)

IR7 .... Iran Long-Period Array [*Iran*] [*Seismograph station code, US Geological Survey*] (SEIS)

IRA .... Augustana College, Rock Island, IL [*Library symbol Library of Congress*] (LCLS)

IRA .... Ileorectal Anastomosis [*Medicine*]

IRA .... Immunoradioassay (STED)

IRA .... Immunoregulatory alpha-Globulin [*Immunology*]

IRA .... Impact Ratio (AAGC)

IRA .... Inactive Renin Activity [*Medicine*] (DMAA)

IRA .... Independent Regulatory Agency [*US Government*]

IRA .... Indian Registration Act [*British*] (ROG)

IRA .... Indian Reorganization Act (OICC)

IRA .... Indian Rights Association (EA)

IRA .... Individual Retirement Account

IRA .... Individual Retirement Annuity [*Insurance*]

IRA .... Industrial Relations Act [*1971*] [*British*] (DCTA)

IRA .... Information Resource Administration

IRA .... Input Reference Axis (IEEE)

IRA .... Inspector of the Royal Artillery [*British*]

IRA .... Inspector's Report Addendum (AAG)

IRA .... Institute of Registered Architects [*British*]

IRA .... Instruction Register, Address Portion [*Computer science*] (MHDI)

IRA .... Integrated RADOME [*RADAR Dome*] Antenna

IRA .... Intelligence Related Activities [*Military*] (MCD)

IRA .... Intercollegiate Rowing Association (EA)

IRA .... Interim Remedial Action (BCP)

IRA .... Interim Response Actions [*Army*] (DOMA)

IRA .... Internal Release Agent

IRA .... Internal Revenue Act

IRA .... International Racquetball Association [*Later, AARA*] (EA)

IRA .... International Reading Association (EA)

IRA .... International Recreation Association [*Later, WLRA*]

IRA .... International Registration Authority [*Botany*] (PDAA)

IRA .... International Reprographics Association (EA)

IRA .... International Rodeo Association (EA)

IRA .... International Roleo Association [*Later, International Log Rolling Association*] (EA)

IRA .... International Rubber Association [*Kuala Lumpur, Malaysia*] (EAIO)

IRA .... Investment Recovery Association (EA)

IRA .... Investment-Return Assumption [*Finance*] (PDAA)

ira .... Iranian [*MARC language code Library of Congress*] (LCCP)

IRA .... Iranian Airways Co.

IRA .... Iran National Airlines Corp. [*ICAO designator*] (FAAC)

IRA .... Irish Republican Army

IRA .... Ithaca Railroad Association [*Defunct*] (EA)

IRA .... Kira Kira [*Solomon Islands*] [*Airport symbol*] (OAG)

IRA .... Rutland, VT [*Location identifier FAA*] (FAAL)

IRAA .... Independent Refiners Association of America [*Later, AIRA*] (EA)

IRAA & A ..... Increase and Replacement of Armor, Armament, and Ammunition [*Naval budget appropriation title*]

IRAAM .... Improved Remote-Area Armor Mine (MCD)

IRAB .... Index to Reviews of Australian Books [*A publication*]

IRAC .... Indochina Resource Action Center (EA)

IRAC .... Industrial Relations Advisory Council [*Australia*]

IRAC .... Information Resources Administration Councils [*General Services Administration*] [*Washington, DC*] (EGAO)

IRAC .... Infrared Advisory Center

IRAC .... Infrared Array Camera

IRAC .... Institut Royal d'Architecture du Canada [*Royal Architectural Institute of Canada*] (EAIO)

IRAC .... Integrated Random Access Channel (PDAA)

IRAC .... Intelligence Resources Advisory Committee [*To supervise US intelligence budget*]

IRAC .... Interagency Research Animal Committee [*Department of Health and Human Services*] (GFGA)

IRAC .... Interdepartment Radio Advisory Committee [*Department of Commerce*] (EGAO)

IRAC .... Interfraternity Research and Advisory Council [*Defunct*] (EA)

IRAC .... Interim Rapid Action Change (MCD)

IRAC .... Issue, Rule, Application, Conclusions (AAGC)

IRACOR .... Infrared Acquisition RADAR (MSA)

IRACQ .... Infrared Acquisition RADAR

IRACQ .... Instrumentation RADAR and Acquisition

IRACQ .... Instrumented Range Acquisition (KSC)

IRACT .... Incident Response Action Coordination Team [*Nuclear energy*] (NRCH)

IR-ACTH ...... Immunoreactive Adrenocorticotropic Hormone [*Medicine*] (DMAA)

IRAD .... Independent Research and Development

IRAD .... Infrared Ambush Device

IRAD .... Institute for Research on Animal Diseases [*British*]

IRAD .... Institutional Research and Development Office [*Kirksville College of Osteopathic Medicine*] [*Research center*] (RCD)

IRAD .... International Research & Development Corp. (EFIS)

IRADDS .... Infrared Air Defense Detection System

IRADS .... Infrared Acquisition and Designation System (DOMA)

IRA-EEA ...... Ileorectal Anastomosis with End-to-End Anastomosis (STED)

IRAF .... Individual Retirement Account File [*IRS*]

IRAH .... Infrared Active Homing (MCD)

IRAH .... Infrared Alternate Head

IR All .... Indian Rulings, Allahabad Series [*A publication*] (DLA)

IRAM .... Improved Random Access Memory [*Computer science*]

IRAM .... Improved Reliability and Maintainability

IRAM .... Improved Repairables Asset Management (DNAB)

IRAM .... Indexed Random Access Memory (NITA)

IRAM .... Institut de Recherches et d'Applications des Methodes de Developpement [*Institute of Research and Application of Development Methods - IRAM*] (EAIO)

IRAM .... Integrated Random-Access Memory [*Computer science*]

IRAMS .... Infrared Automatic Mass Screening [*Electronics*]

IRAN .... Inspect and Repair as Necessary [*Aviation*]

IRAN .... Iranian [*Language, etc.*] (ROG)

IRanASD ...... Allen Township Consolidated Community School District 65, Ransom, IL [*Library symbol Library of Congress*] (LCLS)

IR & A .... Information Research and Analysis [*Oak Ridge National Laboratory*] [*Oak Ridge, TN*] [*Department of Energy*] (GRD)

IR & AC .... Internal Review and Audit Compliance [*Army*]

IR & D .... Independent Research and Development

IR&D .... Independent Research and Development (AAGC)

IR & D .... Industrial Research and Development

IR & D .... Internal Research and Development [*Army*]

IR & D/B & P... Independent Research and Development/Bid and Proposal

IRANDOC .... Iranian Documentation Centre [*Ministry of Culture and Higher Education*] [*Tehran*]

IRANF .... Immunoreactive Atrial Natriuretic Factor

IRANSAT ...... Iranian Government Communications Satellite [*NASA*] (NASA)

IRant .... Rantoul Public Library, Rantoul, IL [*Library symbol Library of Congress*] (LCLS)

IRAP .... Industrial Research Assistance Program [*Canada*]

IRAP .... Interagency Radiological Assistance Program [*Nuclear Regulatory Commission*] (NRCH)

IRAP .... Interleukin Receptor Antagonist Protein [*Biochemistry*]

IRAR .... Impulse Response Area Ratio

IRAR .... Individual Retirement Account Register [*IRS*]

IRAR .... Infrared Airborne RADAR (PDAA)

IRAR .... Infrared Augmentation Reliability (MCD)

IRAR .... Integrated Random Access Reservation [*Computer science*] (CIST)

IRAR .... Integrator Register Address Register (PDAA)

IRAS .... Information Retrieval Advisory Services Limited [*British*] (NITA)

IRAS .... Infrared Astronomical Satellite [*NASA*] (MCD)

IRAS .... Infrared Attack System

IRAS .... Infrared Automatic System (DNAB)

IRAS .... Infrared Reflection Absorption Spectroscopy [*Also, IRRAS, RAIR, RAIRS, RAIS*]

IRAS .... Institute on Religion in an Age of Science (EA)

IRAS .... Integrated RADOME [*RADAR Dome*] Antenna Structure

IRAS .... Interdiction Reconnaissance Attack System (PDAA)

IRAS .... Internet Routing and Access Service [*Computer science*] (ACRL)

IRASA .... International Radio Air Safety Association

IRASER .... Infrared Amplification by Stimulated Emission of Radiation

IRASER .... Infrared MASER (CET)

IRASI .... Internal Review and System Improvement [*Army*]

IRAT .... Institut de Recherche Appliquee sur le Travail [*Canada*]

IRAT .... Institut de Recherches Agronomiques Tropicales et des Cultures Vivrieres [*Food and agricultural research foundation supported by France and several African states*]

IRATA .... Industrial Rope Access Trade Association [*British*] (DBA)

IRATA .... Irata, Inc. [*NASDAQ symbol*] (SAG)

IRATA .... Irata Inc.'A' [*NASDAQ symbol*] (TTSB)

IRATE .... Inertial Range Atmospheric Turbulence Entrainment (PDAA)

IRATE .... Intelligence Review and Assessment Task Element [*Study of the effectiveness of the air war in Southeast Asia*]

IRATE .... Interactive Retrieval and Text Editor [*Computer science*] (PDAA)

IRATE .... Interim Remote Area Terminal Equipment [*Air Force*]

IRATW .... Irata Inc.Wrrt [*NASDAQ symbol*] (TTSB)

IRAWS .... Infrared Attack Weapon System

IRayL .... Lincolnwood Community Reading Center, Raymond, IL [*Library symbol Library of Congress*] (LCLS)

IRaySD .... Panhandle Community Unit, School District 2, Raymond IL [*Library symbol Library of Congress*] (LCLS)

IRB .... Improved Ribbon-Type Bridge [*Military*] (RDA)

IRB .... Improved Rotor Blade [*Rotorcraft*]

IRB .... Impulse Resistance Bridge

IRB .... Individual Records Brief [*Military*] (AABC)

IRB .... Inducto-Ratio Bridge

IRB .... Industrial Readjustment Branch

IRB .... Industrial Relations Board [*Navy*]

IRB .... Industrial Relations Bulletin [*A publication*] (AAG)

IRB .... Industrial Revenue Bond

IRB .... Infinitely Rigid Beam [*Engineering*] (OA)

IRB .... Inflatable Rescue Boat

IRB .... Informationsverbundzentrum Raum und Bau [*Germany*] (NITA)

IRB .... Informationszentrum Raum und Bau [*Information Center for Regional Planning and Building Construction*] [*Germany Information service or system*] (IID)

IRB .... Infrared Binocular [*Military*] (VNW)

IRB .... Infrared Brazing

IRB .... Inner Radiation Belt

IRB .... Inside Reactor Building (NRCH)

IRB .... Inspection Review Board (KSC)

IRB .... Institutional Review Board

IRB .... Insurance Rating Board [*Later, ISO*]

IRB .... Internal Revenue Bulletin

IRB .... International Resources Bank

IRB .... International Rice Bran Industries Ltd. [*Vancouver Stock Exchange symbol*]

IRB .... International Rugby Board [*Australia*]

IRB .... Interrupt Request Block (CMD)

IRB .... Iranair Tours Co. [*Iran*] [*ICAO designator*] (FAAC)

IRB .... Irish Republican Brotherhood

IRB..............	Iron Rotating Band
IRB..............	Irregular Route Motor Carriers Bureau, Oklahoma City OK [STAC]
IRb..............	Red Bud Public Library, Red Bud, IL [Library symbol Library of Congress] (LCLS)
IRBA	International Rhythm and Blues Association (EA)
IRBAA.........	Institute of Rural Business Administration of Australasia
IRBBB	Incomplete Right Bundle Branch Block [Cardiology]
IRBC	Immature Red Blood Cell (STED)
IRBC	Infected Red Blood Cell (STED)
IRBEL...........	Indexed References to Biomedical Engineering Literature [A publication] (IID)
IRBM	Intermediate-Range Ballistic Missile
IRBO	Infrared Homing Bomb (IEEE)
IR Bom	Indian Rulings, Bombay Series [A publication] (DLA)
IRBP	Interphotoreceptor Retinoid-Binding Protein [Biochemistry]
IRBP	Interstitial Retinol-Binding Protein [Biochemistry]
IRbSCH.......	Saint Clement Hospital, Red Bud, IL [Library symbol Library of Congress] (LCLS)
IRBT...........	Infrared Brightness Temperature
IRBT...........	Intelligent Remote Batch Terminal [Computer science] (IAA)
IRC..............	Circle [Alaska] [Airport symbol] (OAG)
IRC..............	Immediate Reaction Company [Military] (INF)
IRC..............	Incident Response Center [Nuclear Regulatory Commission] (NRCH)
IRC..............	Incrementally Related Carriers [Telecommunications] (OTD)
IRC..............	Independent Record Charts (EA)
IRC..............	Indicating Recording Controller [Electronics] (ECII)
IRC..............	Indications Review Committee [Military] (CINC)
IRC..............	Inductance, Resistance, Capacitance [Electronics] (BARN)
IRC..............	Industrial Relations Center [University of Minnesota] [Research center] (RCD)
IRC..............	Industrial Relations Council for the Plumbing and Pipe Fitting Industry [Chicago, IL] (EA)
IRC..............	Industrial Relations Counselors [New York, NY] (EA)
IRC..............	INEL [Idaho National Engineering Laboratory] Research Center [Idaho Falls, ID] [Department of Energy] (GRD)
IRC..............	Infantry Reserve Corps (WDAA)
IRC..............	Information Recovery Capsule
IRC..............	Information Research Center (DIT)
IRC..............	Information Resource Consultants [Information service or system] (IID)
IRC..............	Information Resources Center [of Mental Health Materials Center]
IRC..............	Information Retrieval Center [BBDO International] [Information service or system] (IID)
IRC..............	Infrared Coagulator [Hematology] (DAVI)
IRC..............	Infrared Countermeasures [Military electronics]
IRC..............	Initiative Resource Center [Defunct] (EA)
IRC..............	Inland Revenue Commissioners [British]
IRC..............	Inspection Record Card [Navy] (NG)
IRC..............	Inspiration Resources (EFIS)
IRC..............	Inspiratory Reserve Capacity [Physiology] (MAE)
IRC..............	Institute for Research in Construction [National Research Council of Canada] [Database producer] (IID)
IRC..............	Institutional Research Council [Defunct] (EA)
IRC..............	Institutional Review Committee [Generic term]
IRC..............	Insurance Research Council (EA)
IRC..............	Integrated Radio Control (NVT)
IRC..............	Integrator Register Counter (PDAA)
IRC..............	Interchange Resource Center (EA)
IRC..............	Interdisciplinary Research Centre [British]
IRC..............	Intergovernmental Refugee Committee [London] [World War II]
IRC..............	Interline Resources Corp. [AMEX symbol] (SAG)
IRC..............	Internal Revenue Code
IRC..............	Internal Revenue Code of 1986 (COE)
IRC..............	International Radiation Commission [of the International Association of Meteorology and Atmospheric Physics] (EAIO)
IRC..............	International Radio Carrier (NTCM)
IRC..............	International Rainwear Council
IRC..............	International Rating Class [Yachting]
IRC..............	International Record Carrier [Telecommunication companies providing international service] (TSSD)
IRC..............	International Red Cross and Red Crescent Movement (EAIO)
IRC..............	International Reference Centre [Community water supply and sanitation] (NITA)
IRC..............	International Relations Committee [American Library Association]
IRC..............	International Relations Committee [Library Association of Australia]
IRC..............	International Reply Coupon
IRC..............	International Rescue Committee (EA)
IRC..............	International Research Council [Later, ICSU]
IRC..............	International Resistance Co. (AAG)
IRC..............	International Resistor Center
IRC..............	International Revenue Code (WDAA)
IRC..............	International Rice Commission [See also CIR] (EAIO)
IRC..............	Internet Relay Chat [Computer science]
IRC..............	Inter-Regional Capital Account [Inter-American Development Bank]
IRC..............	Interservice Recruiting Committee [Military] (DNAB)
IRC..............	Intrinsic Reaction Coordinate [Physical chemistry]
IRC..............	Ionosphere Research Committee (MCD)
IRC..............	Ion Recombination Chamber
IRC..............	Iran Asseman Airline [ICAO designator] (FAAC)
IRC..............	Iraqi Communist Party [Also, ICP] [Political party] (MENA)
IRC..............	IRC International Water and Sanitation Centre [International Reference Ce ntre for Community Water Supply and Sanitation] [Acronym is based on former name,] (EAIO)
IRC..............	Iron Canyon [California] [Seismograph station code, US Geological Survey] (SEIS)

IRC..............	Ironclad
IRC..............	Irregular Route Carrier
IRC..............	Issue Restriction Code (MCD)
IRC..............	Item Responsibility Code
IRCA	[The] Immigration Reform and Control Act [1986] (ECON)
IRCA	Immigration Reform and Control Act of 1986
IRCA	International Radio Club of America (EA)
IRCA	International Ragdoll Cat Association (EA)
IRCA	International Railway Congress Association [Belgium]
IRCA	International Remodeling Contractors Association (EA)
IRCA	Intravascular Red Cell Aggregation [Medicine] (DMAA)
IR Cal	Indian Rulings, Calcutta Series [A publication] (DLA)
IRC & M	Increase and Replacement of Construction and Machinery [Naval budget appropriation title]
IRCAR.........	International Reference Center for Abortion Research (IID)
IRCAS	Information Requirements Control Automated System [Defense Supply Service/Pentagon] (AABC)
IRCAT.........	Infrared Radiometer Clear Air Turbulence [Instrument]
IRCC	Instruction and Research Computer Center [Ohio State University] [Research center] (RCD)
IRCC	International Radio Consultative Committee
IRCC	International Record Collectors' Club [Record label]
IRCC	International Red Cross Committee [World War II]
IRCCCOB.....	Inter Research Council Coordinating Committee on Biotechnology (NITA)
IRCCD.........	Infrared Charge-Coupled Device
IRCCM........	Infrared Counter-Countermeasures [Military electronics]
IRCCOPR	Inter-Research Council Committee on Pollution Research [British]
IRCCS	Intrusion Resistant Communications Cable System (DNAB)
IRCD	Information Retrieval Center on the Disadvantaged [ERIC]
IRCD	International Research Centers Directory [A publication]
IRCDP.........	International Research Career Development Program [Public Health Service]
IRC.EC........	Interline Resources [Exchange symbol] (TTSB)
IRCert	Industrial Relations Certificate (ODBW)
Ir Ch	Irish Chancery Reports [A publication] (DLA)
Ir Ch Rep ...	Irish Chancery Reports [A publication] (DLA)
IRCICA	Research Centre for Islamic History, Art, and Culture [of the Organization of the Islamic Conference] (EAIO)
IRCIHE........	International Referral Center for Information Handling Equipment [Former Yugoslavia] [UNESCO] (IID)
Ir Cir..........	Irish Circuit Reports [1841-43] [A publication] (DLA)
Ir Cir Cas ...	Crawford and Dix's Irish Circuit Court Cases [A publication] (DLA)
Ir Circ Cas ..	Irish Circuit Cases [A publication] (DLA)
Ir Circ Rep..	Irish Circuit Reports [1841-43] [A publication] (DLA)
Ir Cir Rep ...	Reports of Irish Circuit Cases [A publication] (DLA)
IRCL...........	International Research Centre on Lindane [See also CIEL] [Brussels, Belgium] (EAIO)
Ir CL	Irish Common Law Reports [A publication] (DLA)
IRCL...........	Irish Reports, Common Law Series [A publication] (DLA)
IRCM	Infrared Countermeasures [Military electronics] (NVT)
IRCM	Integrated Relay Controller Module [Ford Motor Co.] [Automotive engineering]
IRCM	Intermediate Range Cruise Missile [Military] (CAAL)
IRCN	Interagency Report Control Number
IRCND	International Research Council of Neuromuscular Disorders (EA)
IRCNSW.......	Industrial Relations Commission of New South Wales [Australia]
IRCO	International Rubber Conference Organization (EAIO)
IRCOBI........	International Research Committee on the Biokinetics of Impacts [Later, International Research Council on the Biokinetics of Impacts] (EAIO)
IRCOL	Institute for Information Retrieval and Computational Linguistics [Bar Ilam University] [Israel] (NITA)
Ir Com Law Rep...	Irish Common Law Reports [A publication] (DLA)
Ir Com L Rep...	Irish Common Law Reports [A publication] (DLA)
IR Comrs	Inland Revenue Commissioners [England] (DLA)
IRCOPPS......	Interprofessional Research Commission on Pupil Personnel Services [Defunct]
IRCP	Intermediate Range Construction Program [Military]
IRCPAL........	International Research Council on Pure and Applied Linguistics (EA)
IRCPPFI	Industrial Relations Council for the Plumbing and Pipe Fitting Industry (EA)
IRCPUBS......	Publications of the Institute for Research in Construction [National Research Council of Canada] [Information service or system] (IID)
IRCQ	Industrial Relations Commission of Queensland [Australia]
IRCR	Integrator Register Control Register (PDAA)
IRCS	Inertial Reference and Control System [Aerospace] (AAG)
IRCS	Infrared Communications System
IRCS	Interceptor Reaction Control System
IRCS	Intercomplex Radio Communications System (IAA)
IRCS	Interdisciplinary Research Center on Suicide [Italy] (EAIO)
IRCS	International Radio Call Sign
IRCS	International Research Communications System [Electronic journal publisher] [British]
IRCS	Intersite Radio Communications System (MCD)
IRCS	Italian Red Cross Society
IRCSA	International Reference Collection of Soybean Arthropods [INTSOY]
IRCSI	International Rabbinic Committee for the Safety of Israel (EA)
IRCT...........	International Research on Communist Techniques
IRCV	Industrial Relations Commission of Victoria [Australia]
IRD	Ice-Rafted Debris [Oceanography]
IRD	Immune Renal Disease [Medicine]
IRD	Income in Respect of a Decedent [Banking]
IRD	Information Requirements Description [or Document] (KSC)

IRD	Infrared Detector
IRD	Infrared Display
IRD	Initiating Reference Document (MCD)
IRD	Inland Rail Depot (DCTA)
IRD	Institute on Religion and Democracy (EA)
I/RD	Institutes and Research Divisions [*National Institutes of Health*]
IRD	Integrated Receiver Decoder [*Telecommunications*]
IRD	Interface Requirements Document
IRD	Internal Revenue Department
IRD	International Radiation Detectors [*Marine science*] (OSRA)
IRD	International Research and Development
IRD	International Research & Development Co. Ltd. [*Northern Engineering Industries*] [*British*] (IRUK)
IRD	International Resource Development, Inc. [*Norwalk, CT*] [*Telecommunications Information service or system*] (IID)
IRD	Iron Lady Resources [*Vancouver Stock Exchange symbol*]
IRD	Ishurdi [*Bangladesh*] [*Airport symbol*] (OAG)
IRD	Isotopes and Radiation Division [*American Nuclear Society*]
IRD	Itinerant Recruiting Detail
IRDA	Independent Reinol Distributors Association [*British*] (DBA)
IRDA	Industrial Research & Development Authority (WDAA)
IRDA	Infraed Data Association (PS)
IrDA	Infrared Data Association (PCM)
IRDA	Infrared Detection Array
IRDA	Infrared Developers Association (PCM)
IRDA	Interactive Route Development and Analysis (CAAL)
IRDAC	Industrial Research and Development Advisory Committee [*European Union*]
IRD & S	International Research, Development, and Standardization [*Division*] [*Army*] (RDA)
IRDB	Information Retrieval Databank (IEEE)
IRDC	Improved RADAR Data Correlator (DWSG)
IRDC	Industrial Research and Development Center [*University of Virginia*] (PDAA)
IRDC	Intelligence Research and Development Council (MCD)
IRDC	International Development Research Centre (GNE)
IRDC	International Road Documentation Center
IRDC	International Rubber Development Committee
IRDF	Interactive Report Definition Facility (MCD)
IRDG	Inter-Range Documentation Group [*White Sands Missile Range*]
IRDHS	Imagery Related Data Handling System (MCD)
IRDIA	Industrial Research and Development Investment Assistance [*Department of Industry*] [*Canada*] (PDAA)
IRDL	Information Retrieval and Display Language [*Computer science*] (AABC)
IRDLO	Infantry Research and Development Liaison Office [*Army*] (RDA)
IRDM	Illuminated Runway Distance Marker (PDAA)
IRDM	International Rendezvous and Docking Mission [*Aerospace*]
IRDN	Illinois Resource and Dissemination Network [*Illinois State Board of Education*] [*No longer in operation*] [*Information service or system*] (IID)
IRDN	Important Risk Data Notice [*Insurance*]
IRDO	Infrared Drying Oven
IRDO	Intermediate Retention of Differential Overlap [*Physics*]
IRDOE	Institute for Research and Development in Occupational Education [*City University of New York*] [*Research center*] (RCD)
irdome	Infrared Dome (MED)
IRDP	Icelandic Research Drilling Project
IRDP	Industrial Regional Development Program [*Canada*]
IRDP	Integrated Regional Development Planning (GNE)
IRDS	Idiopathic Respiratory Distress Syndrome [*Pediatrics*]
IRDS	Infant Respiratory Distress Syndrome [*Medicine*]
IRDS	Information Resources Dictionary System (SSD)
IRDS	Infrared Detecting Set [*or System*] (MCD)
IRDS	Integrated Reliability Data System (AAG)
IRDS	International Road Documentation Scheme (NITA)
IRDU	Infrared Detection Unit
IRE	Governor & Co. of the Bank of Ireland [*NYSE symbol*] (SAG)
IRE	IFF Reply Evaluator
IRE	Immediate Ready Element [*Military*] (AABC)
IRE	Infrared Emission
IRE	Institute for Responsive Education (EA)
IRE	Institute of Radio Engineers [*Later, IEEE*]
IRE	Institute of Refractories Engineers [*British*] (DBA)
IRE	Instrument Rating Examiner [*Aviation*] (DA)
IRE	Intelligence Resources [*Program*] [*Department of State*]
IRE	Interferon Regulatory Element [*Biochemistry*]
IRE	Internal Reflection Element [*Spectroscopy*]
IRE	Internal Rotation in Extension [*Orthopedics*] (DAVI)
IRE	International Association of Railway Employees
IRE	International Relations Exercise (DNAB)
IRE	International Research and Evaluation [*Research Center*] [*Also, an information service or system*] (IID)
IRE	International Retail Systems, Inc. [*Toronto Stock Exchange symbol Vancouver Stock Exchange symbol*]
IRE	International Royal Enterprises (EA)
IRE	Investigative Reporters and Editors (EA)
IRE	Ireland
Ire	Ireland (VRA)
IRE	Iron Replacement Element [*Biosynthesis*]
IRE	Iron-Responsive Element [*Genetics*]
i-re--	Reunion [*MARC geographic area code Library of Congress*] (LCCP)
IREB	Intense Relativistic Electron Beams [*Physics*]
IRE-BP	Iron-Responsive Element - Binding Protein

IREC	Increase and Replacement of Emergency Construction [*Ships*] [*Naval budget appropriation title*]
IREC	International Registry of Early Corvettes (EA)
IREC	International Rotary Engine Club [*Later, RX-7 Club of America*] (EA)
IRECA	International Rescue and Emergency Care Association (EA)
Ir Eccl	Irish Ecclesiastical Reports, by Milward [*1819-43*] [*A publication*] (DLA)
IRECUS	Sherbrooke University Institut de Recherche et d'Enseignement pour les Cooperatives [*Canada Research center*] (RCD)
IRED	Infrared-Emitting Diode (IEEE)
IRED	Innovations et Reseaux pour le Developpement [*Development Innovations and Networks*] [*Geneva, Switzerland*] (EAIO)
IRED	International Real Estate Directory [*Real estate computer site*]
Ired	Iredell's North Carolina Equity Reports [*36-43 North Carolina*] [*A publication*] (DLA)
IREDA	International Radio and Electrical Distributors Association (MHDB)
Ired Dig	Iredell's North Carolina Digest [*A publication*] (DLA)
Ired Eq	Iredell's North Carolina Equity Reports [*36-43 North Carolina*] [*A publication*] (DLA)
Ired Eq (NC)	Iredell's North Carolina Equity Reports [*36-43 North Carolina*] [*A publication*] (DLA)
Ired L	Iredell's North Carolina Equity Reports [*36-43 North Carolina*] [*A publication*] (DLA)
Ired L (NC)	Iredell's North Carolina Law Reports [*A publication*] (DLA)
IreDNCA	National College of Art and Design, Dublin, Ireland [*Library symbol*] [*Library of Congress*] (LCLS)
IreDNL	National Library of Ireland, Dublin, Ireland [*Library symbol Library of Congress*] (LCLS)
IreDR	Royal Dublin Society, Ballsbridge, Dublin, Ireland [*Library symbol Library of Congress*] (LCLS)
IreDT	Trinity College, University of Dublin, Dublin, Ireland [*Library symbol Library of Congress*] (LCLS)
IREE	Institut de Recherches et d'Etudes Europeennes [*Institute of European Research and Studies*] (EAIO)
IREF	International Real Estate Federation
IREF	Ischemia Research and Education Foundation
IREFAC	International Real Estate Federation Australian Chapter
IREG	Industriradets Industriregister [*Federation of Danish Industries' Register of Industries*] (EY)
IREG	Information Res Engineering [*NASDAQ symbol*] (TTSB)
IREG	Information Resource Engineering, Inc. [*NASDAQ symbol*] (SAG)
IREH	Institute for Rural Environmental Health [*Colorado State University*] [*Research center*] (RCD)
IREHR	Institute for Research and Education on Human Rights [*Defunct*] (EA)
IREI	International Real Estate Institute (EA)
IRE-ITTD	International Research and Evaluation - Information and Technology Transfer Database [*International Research and Evaluation*] [*Information service or system*] (CRD)
IREM	Incorporation of Readiness into Effectivenss Modeling (MCD)
IREM	Institut de Recherche en Exploration Minerale [*Mineral Exploration Research Institute*] [*Canada Research center*] (RCD)
IREM	Institute of Real Estate Management [*Chicago, IL*] (EA)
IREM	Integrated Regional Environmental Management Project (EA)
IREMAM	Institut de Recherches et d'Etudes sur le Monde Arabe et Musulman [*Institute for Research and Studies on the Arab and Muslim World*] [*France Information service or system*] (IID)
IREM-BASS	Improved Remotely Monitored Battlefield Sensor System
IRENE	Industrial Restructuring and Education Network Europe
IREP	Integrated Reliability Evaluation Program [*Nuclear energy*] (NRCH)
IREP	Interdisciplinary Research Equipment Program
IREP	Interim Reliability Evaluation Program [*Nuclear energy*]
IREP	Internal Representation (MHDB)
IREPS	Integrated Refractive Effects Prediction System [*Military*] (CAAL)
IREQ	Institut de Recherche d'Hydro-Quebec [*Canada*]
IR Eq	Irish Reports, Equity Series [*A publication*] (DLA)
Ir Eq Rep	Irish Equity Reports [*A publication*] (DLA)
IRER	Infrared Extra Rapid (ADA)
IRES	Institute for Resource and Environmental Studies [*Dalhousie University*] [*Canada Research center*] (RCD)
IRES	Internal Ribosomal Entry Site [*Genetics*]
IRES	Internal Ribosome Entry Sequence [*To 21st site sequence*]
IRES	IOC [*Intergovernmental Oceanographic Commission*] Group of Experts on Oceanographic Research as It Relates to IGOSS [*Marine science*] (MSC)
IRET	Institute for Rational-Emotive Therapy (EA)
IRET	Institute for Research on the Economics of Taxation [*Research center*] (RCD)
IRET	Interrupt Return [*PC instruction*] (PCM)
IRETIJ	Institut de Recherches et d'Etudes pour le Traitement de l'Information Juridique [*Institute of Research and Study for the Treatment of Legal Information*] [*University of Montpellier*] [*Information service or system*] (IID)
IRETP	Innovative Rural Education and Training Program
IRETS	Infantry Remote Targeting System [*Army*] (RDA)
IREW	Infrared Electronic Warfare
IREWS	Infrared Early Warning System
IREX	Ideas, Resources, Exchange [*Computer*] [*British*]
IREX	International Research and Exchanges Board (EA)
IRF	Idiopathic Retroperitoneal Fibrosis [*Medicine*] (DMAA)
IRF	Immediate Reaction Force [*Military*] (AABC)
IRF	Impedance-Reduction Factor (IAA)
IRF	Induced Radiation Flux
IRF	Inducing Resistance Factor [*Plant pathology*]
IRF	Inherited Rights Filter [*Computer science*]

IRF............. Input Register Full
IRF............. Instrument Reliability Factor (PDAA)
IRF............. Instrument Response Function
IRF............. Interferon Regulatory Factor [Biochemistry]
IRF............. Intermittent Reinforcement [Psychology]
IRF............. Internal Rotation in Flexion [Orthopedics] (DAVI)
IRF............. International Racquetball Federation (EAIO)
IRF............. International Rectifier Corp. [NYSE symbol] (SPSG)
IRF............. International Reform Federation (EA)
IRF............. International Religious Fellowship (EA)
IRF............. International Research Fellowship Program [Department of Health
      and Human Services] (GFGA)
IRF............. International Road Federation (EA)
IRF............. International Rowing Federation (EA)
IRF............. Interrogation Repetition Frequency [RADAR beacon]
IRF............. Intl Rectifier [NYSE symbol] (TTSB)
IRF............. Intrinsic Rectifying Factor [Biochemistry]
IRF............. Islamic Research Foundation (EA)
IRF............. Island Resources Foundation (EA)
IRF............. Islands Research Foundation [Inactive] (EA)
IRFA.......... Initial Regulatory Flexibility Analysis (AAGC)
IRFA.......... Institut de Recherches sur les Fruits et Agrumes [Institute of
      Research on Fruits and Citrus Fruits] [International Cooperation
      Center of Agricultural Research for Development Database
      producer]
IRFAA .... International Rescue and First Aid Association [Later, IRECA] (EA)
IRFAP .... International Religious Fine Art Program (EA)
IRFB........... International Radio Frequency Board
IRFC........... Intermediate-Range Function Test (IAA)
IR Fed Ct .... Indian Rulings, Federal Court [A publication] (DLA)
IRFF .... International Relief Friendship Foundation (EA)
IRFIS .... Inertial Referenced Flight Inspection System [Aviation] (PDAA)
IRFITS .... Infrared Fault Isolation Test System
IRFL........... Integral Red Fluorescence (DMAA)
IRFM .... Integral Reactor Flow Model [Nuclear energy] (NRCH)
IRFMS .... Interservice Radio Frequency Management School (DOMA)
IRFNA .... Inhibited Red Fuming Nitric Acid [Rocket fuel]
IRFN/UDMH... Inhibited Red Fuming Nitric Acid and Unsymmetrical
      Dimethylhydrazine [Rocket fuel]
IRFO .... International Road Freight Office (WDAA)
IRFP .... International Relations and Foreign Policy [Army British]
IRFPA .... Infrared Focal Plane Array [DoD]
IRFRH......... Institut de Recherche et de Formation aux Relations Humaines
      [Institute for Research and Training in Human Relations]
      [Research center France] (IRC)
IRFT........... Interim Refresher Training [Navy] (NVT)
IRFU .... Irish Rugby Football Union (EAIO)
IRG .... Immunoreactive Gastrin [Medicine] (DMAA)
IRG .... Immunoreactive Glucagon [Immunochemistry]
IRG .... Indian Resources Group (WDAA)
IRG .... Industrial Reprocessing Group (SAA)
IRG .... Inertial Rate Gyro (KSC)
IRG .... Information Resource Group [Information service or system] (IID)
IRG .... Infrared Generator
IRG .... Initial Review Group [National Institutes of Health]
IRG .... Inner Roll Gimbal (MCD)
IRG .... Institut de Reescompte et de Garantie [Development bank]
      [Belgium] (EY)
IRG .... Interagency Regulatory Group
IRG .... Interagency Review Group [Nuclear Regulatory Commission] (NRCH)
IRG .... Interdepartmental Regional Group [Army] (AABC)
IRG .... Interest Rate Guarantee (NUMA)
IRG .... Internationale des Resistants a la Guerre [War Resisters International
      - WRI] [British] (EA)
IRG .... International Register (IAA)
IRG .... International Research Group on Wear of Engineering Materials
      (PDAA)
IRG .... International Research Group on Wood Preservation [Stockholm,
      Sweden] (EAIO)
IRG .... Inter-Record Gap [Computer science Telecommunications] (MCD)
IRG .... Interrelationship Graph (PDAA)
IRG .... Iron Range [Queensland] [Airport symbol] (AD)
IRG .... Lockhart Rivers [Australia Airport symbol] (OAG)
IRG .... Naft Air Lines [Iran] [FAA designator] (FAAC)
IRGA.......... Infrared Gas Analyzer
IRgA.......... International Reprographics Association (EA)
IRGAR......... Infrared Gas Radiation
IRGB.......... Infrared Guided Bomb [DoD]
IRGBA......... International Repro Graphic Blueprint Association [Later, IRA] (EA)
IRGCVD....... International Research Group on Colour Vision Deficiencies [Ghent,
      Belgium] (EAIO)
IRGH.......... Immunoreactive Growth Hormone [Immunology]
IR-GIP......... Immunoreactive Gastric Inhibitory Peptide [Biochemistry]
IRGI........... Immunoreactive Glucagon [Immunochemistry]
IRGL .... Indentation Residual Gauge Level [Automotive engineering]
IRGL .... Infrared Gunfire Locator
IRGMA........ Information Retrieval Group of the Museums Association [British]
      (NITA)
IRGP .... Infrared Guided Projectile (MCD)
IRGPG........ Inter-Range and Global Planning Group [White Sands Missile
      Range] (MUGU)
IRGRD .... International Research Group on Refuse Disposal [Later, ISWA]
IRGT.......... Insulin-Regulatable Glucose Transporter [Biochemistry]
IRH .... Inductive Recording Head
IRH .... Infrared Heater

IRH .... Inspection Requirements Handbook [Navy] (NG)
IRH .... Institute for Reproductive Health (EA)
IRH .... Institute for Research in History
IRH .... Institute for Research in Hypnosis [Later, IRHP] (EA)
IRH .... Institutes of Religion and Health (EA)
IRH .... International Rhodes Resources [Vancouver Stock Exchange symbol]
IRHA .... Injured as Result of Hostile Action [Military] (NVT)
IRHA .... Interchurch Response for the Horn of Africa (EA)
IRHC .... Isolated Rat Hepatocyte Complex
IRHCS .... Immunoradioassayable Human Chorionic Somatomammotropin
      [Medicine] (MAE)
IRHD .... Internationaler Rat der Hauspflegedienste [International Council of
      Home-Help Services]
IRHD .... International Rubber Hardness Degree
IRHF .... Integral Radiative Heat Flux
IRHGH .... Immunoreactive Human Growth Hormone [Immunology] (AAMN)
IRHP .... Institute for Research in Hypnosis and Psychotherapy (EA)
IRHP .... Institute for Responsible Housing Preservation (NTPA)
IRHR .... Institute for Research in Human Relations (MCD)
IRHS .... Intact Reentry Heat Source (OA)
IRHS .... Intraoral Recurrent Herpes Simplex [Medicine]
IRI .... Image Resources, Inc. [Winter Park, FL] [Telecommunications]
      (TSSD)
IRI .... Immunobiology Research Institute [Annandale, NJ]
IRI .... Immunoreactive Insulin
IRI .... Inca Resources, Inc. [Toronto Stock Exchange symbol Vancouver
      Stock Exchange symbol]
IRI .... Industrial Research Institute [Canada Research center] (RCD)
IRI .... Industrial Risk Insurers (EA)
IRI .... Informal Reading Inventory [Education]
IRI .... Information Researchers, Inc. [Information service or system] (IID)
IRI .... Information Resources, Inc. [Information service or system] (IID)
IRI .... Information Retrieval, Inc.
IRI .... Infrared Imagery
IRI .... Infrared Instrumentation
IRI .... Innovative Resources, Inc.
IRI .... Institution of the Rubber Industry [British]
IRI .... Insulin Radioimmunoassay
IRI .... Insulin Resistance Index [Medicine] (DMAA)
IRI .... Integrated Range Instrumentation
IRI .... Interfaculty Reactor Institute [Netherlands]
IRI .... International Industrial Relations Institute
IRI .... International Reference Ionosphere
IRI .... International Relay, Inc. [New York, NY] [Telecommunications]
      (TSSD)
IRI .... International Remote Imaging Systems, Inc. [AMEX symbol] (SPSG)
IRI .... International Republican Institute (ECON)
IRI .... International Robotmotion Intelligence (NITA)
IRI .... International Roughness Index [BTS] [FHWA] (TAG)
IRI .... Intl Remote Imaging [AMEX symbol] (TTSB)
IRI .... Intravehicular Referenced Information [NASA]
IRI .... Inveresk Research International Ltd. [British] (IRUK)
IRI .... Iringa [Tanzania] [Airport symbol] (OAG)
iri .... Irish [MARC language code Library of Congress] (LCCP)
IRI .... Istituto per la Ricostruzione Industriale [Institute for Industrial
      Reconstruction] [Government holding company Italy]
IRIA .... Indirect Radioimmunoassay (DB)
IRIA .... Infrared Information and Analysis Center [University of Michigan]
IRIA .... Institut de Recherche d'Informatique et d'Automatique [French
      Research center]
IRIAC .... Infrared Information and Analysis Center [University of Michigan]
IRIBS .... Inclination Removal Ionospheric Beacon Satellite (PDAA)
IRIC .... Information Resources [NASDAQ symbol] (TTSB)
IRIC .... Information Resources, Inc. [NASDAQ symbol] (NQ)
IRIC .... Infrared Image Converter
IRIC .... Inter-Regional Insurance Conference [Later, ISO]
IRICBM .... Intermediate-Range Interceptor Intercontinental Ballistic Missile
IRICON........ Infrared Vidicon Tube
IRICON........ International Information Service via a Computer-Oriented Network
      (TSSD)
IRICP .... International Research Institute for Climate Prediction [Marine
      science] (OSRA)
IRICU .... Intermountain Respiratory Intensive Care Unit [Medicine] (BABM)
IRicv .... Richview Township Public Library, Richview, IL [Library symbol
      Library of Congress] (LCLS)
IRid........... Elwood Township Carnegie Library, Ridge Farm, IL [Library symbol
      Library of Congress] (LCLS)
IRID .... Iridescent (WGA)
irid............. Irridescent (VRA)
Iridex .... Iridex Corp. [Associated Press] (SAG)
IRidSD .... Ridge Farm Community Unit School District, Ridge Farm, IL [Library
      symbol] [Library of Congress] (LCLS)
IRIE .... Infrared Information Exchange
IR/IED .... Independent Research/Independent Exploratory Development
IRIG .... Inertial Rate Integrating Gyro (NASA)
IRIG .... Inertial Reference Integrating Gyro [NASA] (NASA)
IRIg........... Insulin-Reactive Immunoglobulin [Endocrinology] (DAVI)
IRIG .... Inter-Range Instrumentation Group [White Sands Missile Range]
IRI/G .... Ratio of Immunoreactive Insulin to Serum or Plasma Glucose
      [Medicine] (STED)
IRIG-B......... Inter-Range Instrumentation Group B [NASA] (GFGA)
IRIG-MWG... Inter-Range Instrumentation Group - Meteorological Working Group
      [White Sands Missile Range]
IR/IOD........ Independent Research/Independent Objectives Document [Military]
      (DNAB)

IRIRC	International Refugee Integration Resource Centre [*Later, CDR*] (EAIO)
IRIS	Center for Institutional Reform and the Informal Sector [*University of Maryland*] (ECON)
IRIS	IBM [*International Business Machines Corp.*] Recruitment Information System
IRIS	Imaging of Radicals Interacting with Surfaces [*Electronics*] (AAEL)
IRIS	Incident Resource and Information System [*Police*] [*British*] (NITA)
IRIS	Incorporated Research Institutions for Seismology
IRIS	Increased Readiness Information System
IRIS	Industrial Relations Information Service [*Labour Canada*]
IRIS	Inertial Reactor with Internal Separation [*Coal furnace*] [*Tecogen, Inc.*]
IRIS	Inertia Resonance Induction System [*Automotive engineering*]
IRIS	Information Relayed Instantly from the Source [*Project*]
IRIS	Information Resources Information System [*Library of Congress*]
IRIS	Infrared Image Scanner
IRIS	Infrared Imaging Seeker
IRIS	Infrared Imaging System
IRIS	Infrared Information System [*Sadtler Research Laboratories, Inc.*] [*Philadelphia, PA Database*]
IRIS	Infrared Interferometer Spectrometer
IRIS	Infrared Intruder System
IRIS	Infrared Research Information Symposium (AAG)
IRIS	Instant Response Information System (IEEE)
IRIS	Institute for Regional and International Studies (EA)
IRIS	Institute for Research in Information and Scholarship [*Brown University*] [*Research center*] (RCD)
IRIS	Institute for Research on Interactive Systems [*Research center*] (TSSD)
IRIS	Institute for Robotics and Intelligent Systems [*Research center*] (RCD)
IRIS	Instructional Resources Information System [*Ohio State University*] [*Information service or system*]
IRIS	Instruction and Research Information Systems [*Computer science*]
IRIS	Insurance Regulatory Information System [*National Association of Insurance Commissioners*]
IRIS	Integrated Radio and Intercommunications System [*Canada*]
IRIS	Integrated Reconnaissance Intelligence System (IEEE)
IRIS	Integrated Risk Information System [*Environmental Protection Agency*]
IRIS	Intelligence Report Index Summary
IRIS	Intelligence Reports Information Subsystem [*Computer science*]
IRIS	Intelligent Remote Input Stand [*Computer science*]
IRIS	Interactive Real-Time Information System [*Marine science*] (MSC)
IRIS	Interactive Recorded Information Service [*British Telecommunications*] (TEL)
IRIS	Interleukin Regulation of Immune System [*Medicine*] (DMAA)
IRIS	International Radiation Investigation Satellite [*NASA*]
IRIS	International Radio Interferometric Surveying [*International Association of Geodesy*]
IRIS	International Recruitment Investigation in the Subarctic [*Marine science*] (OSRA)
IRIS	International Recruitment Investigations in the Subarctic (USDC)
IRIS	International Relations Information System [*Forschungsinstitut fuer Internationale Politik und Sicherheit*] [*Germany*] (IID)
IRIS	International Remote Imaging Systems, Inc. [*Associated Press*] (SAG)
IRIS	International Reporting and Information Services [*International Private Intelligence Service*] [*Terminated, 1983*]
IRIS	International Reporting Information Systems
IRIS	International Research Information Service [*American Foundation for the Blind*]
IRIS	International Research on the Interior of the Sun
IRIS	International REST [*Restricted Environmental Stimulation Techniques*] Investigators Society (EA)
IRIS	International Rights Information Service
IRIS	Internet Reach and Involvement Scale [*Advertising value of an Internet site*]
IRIS	Interrogation Requirements Information System [*DoD*] (AFIT)
IRIS	Italian Research Interim Stage (NASA)
IRISH	Infrared Imaging Seeker Head (MCD)
IrishIn	Irish Investment Fund [*Associated Press*] (SAG)
IRIS-M	Infrared Interferometer Spectrometer - Michelson
IRISS	Institute for Research in the Social Sciences [*University of York*] [*British*] (IRC)
IRIV	Immunopotentiating Reconstituted Influenza Virosome [*Immunochemistry*]
IRIV	Immunostimulating Reconstituted Influenza Virosome [*Immunochemistry*]
IRivd	Riverdale Library District, Riverdale, IL [*Library symbol Library of Congress*] (LCLS)
IRivf	River Forest Public Library, River Forest, IL [*Library symbol Library of Congress*] (LCLS)
IRivfR	Rosary College, River Forest, IL [*Library symbol Library of Congress*] (LCLS)
IRivfT	Concordia Teachers College, River Forest, IL [*Library symbol Library of Congress*] (LCLS)
IRivg	River Grove Public Library, River Grove, IL [*Library symbol Library of Congress*] (LCLS)
IRivgT	Triton College, River Grove, IL [*Library symbol Library of Congress*] (LCLS)
IRivs	Riverside Public Library, Riverside, IL [*Library symbol Library of Congress*] (LCLS)
IRIX	IRIDEX Corp. [*NASDAQ symbol*] (TTSB)
IRJ	Infrared Jammer
IRJ	La Rioja [*Argentina*] [*Airport symbol*] (OAG)
IRJE	Infrared Jammer Equipment
IRJE	Interactive Remote Job Entry
IR Jour	Indian Rulings, Journal Section [*A publication*] (DLA)
Ir Jur	Irish Jurist Reports [*1849-66*] [*A publication*] (DLA)
Ir Jur Rep	Irish Jurist Reports [*1849-66*] [*A publication*] (DLA)
IRK	Infrared Kit
IRK	Insulin Receptor Kinase [*An enzyme*]
IRK	Interlake Development [*Vancouver Stock Exchange symbol*]
IRK	Irkutsk [*Former USSR Seismograph station code, US Geological Survey*] (SEIS)
IRK	Kirksville [*Missouri*] [*Airport symbol*] (OAG)
IRK	Kirksville, MO [*Location identifier FAA*] (FAAL)
IRK	Kish Air [*Iran*] [*ICAO designator*] (FAAC)
IRL	Immigration Restriction League
IRL	Indexed Repayment Loan
IRL	Index Retrieval Language [*Computer science*] (PDAA)
IRL	Industrial Reactor Laboratories [*New Jersey*]
IRL	Industrial Research Laboratories [*A publication*]
IRL	Indy Racing League [*Automobile racing*]
IRL	Information Requirements List (KSC)
IRL	Information Research Ltd. [*Information service or system*] (IID)
IRL	Information Retrieval Language [*Computer science*]
IRL	Information Retrieval Ltd. [*Database originator*] [*British Information service or system*]
IRL	Infrared Lamp [*or Light*]
IRL	Infrared Lens
IRL	Initiating Reference Letter (MCD)
IRL	In Real Life [*Computer hacker terminology*]
IRL	Institute for Rational Living [*Absorbed by IRET*]
IRL	Institute of Rural Life at Home and Overseas [*British*] (BI)
IRL	Institute on Religious Life (EA)
IRL	Interactive Reader Language [*Computer science*]
IRL	Interactive Root Locus (PDAA)
IRL	Interface Requirement List (NASA)
IRL	Internationaler Ring fuer Landarbeit [*International Committee of Scientific Management in Agriculture*]
IRL	International Meridian Resources [*Vancouver Stock Exchange symbol*]
IRL	Interrogation and Locating
IRL	Intersection of Range Legs
IRL	Ionosphere Research Laboratory [*Pennsylvania State University*] (PDAA)
IRL	Ireland [*ANSI three-letter standard code*] (CNC)
IRL	Irish Air Corps [*ICAO designator*] (FAAC)
IRL	Irish Investment Fund [*NYSE symbol*] (SAG)
IrL	Irish Law Reports [*A publication*] (DLA)
IRLA	Independent Research Libraries Association (EA)
IRLA	Information Retrieval & Library Automation [*A publication*] (BRI)
IRLA	International Religious Liberty Association (EA)
IRLah	Item Repair Level Analysis [*DoD*]
IR Lah	Indian Rulings, Lahore Series [*A publication*] (DLA)
IrL & Eq	Irish Law and Equity Reports [*1838-50*] [*A publication*] (DLA)
IRLAS	Infrared LASER
Ir Law & Ch	Irish Common Law and Chancery Reports, New Series [*1850-53*] [*A publication*] (DLA)
Ir Law & Eq	Irish Law and Equity Reports [*1838-50*] [*A publication*] (DLA)
Ir Law Rec	Irish Law Recorder [*1827-38*] [*A publication*] (DLA)
Ir Law Rec NS	Irish Law Recorder, New Series [*1833-38*] [*A publication*] (DLA)
Ir Law Rep	Irish Law Reports [*A publication*] (DLA)
Ir Law Rep NS	Irish Common Law Reports, New Series [*A publication*] (DLA)
IRLC	Illinois Regional Library Council [*Library network*]
IRLCO-CSA	International Red Locust Control Organization for Central and Southern Africa (EAIO)
IRLCS	International Red Locust Control Service
IRLD	Institute for Research on Learning Disabilities [*University of Minnesota*] [*Research center*] (RCD)
IRLDA	Independent Retail Lumber Dealers Association
IRLED	Infrared Light Emitting Diode (PDAA)
IRLG	Interagency Regulatory Liaison Group [*Comprising several federal agencies*] [*Terminated, 1981*]
Ir LJ	Irish Law Journal [*1895-1902*] [*A publication*] (DLA)
Ir L NS	Irish Common Law Reports, New Series [*A publication*] (DLA)
IRLR	Industrial Relations Law Reports [*British*] (DCTA)
IRLR	Infrared LASER Ranger (MCD)
Ir LR	Irish Law Reports [*A publication*] (DLA)
Ir L Rec	Irish Law Recorder, First Series [*1827-31*] [*A publication*] (DLA)
Ir L Rec 1st Ser	Law Recorder, First Series [*Ireland*] [*A publication*] (DLA)
Ir L Rec NS	Law Recorder, New Series [*Ireland*] [*A publication*] (DLA)
IRLS	Infrared LASER Spectrometer
IRLS	Infrared Line Scanner (MCD)
IRLS	Interrogation, Recording, and Locating System [*Naval Oceanographic Office*]
IRLSC	Industrial Relations and Labor Studies Center [*University of Maryland*] [*Research center*] (RCD)
Ir LTJ	Irish Law Times Journal [*A publication*] (DLA)
Ir LT Jour	Irish Law Times Journal [*A publication*] (DLA)
Ir LTR	Irish Law Times Reports [*A publication*] (DLA)
Ir LT Rep	Irish Law Times Reports [*A publication*] (DLA)
IRLWR	Institute for Research on Land and Water Resources [*Pennsylvania State University*] (PDAA)
IRM	Illinois Railway Museum (EA)
IRM	Image Rejection Mixer [*Electronics*] (OA)
IRM	Improved Risk Mutuals (EA)

IRM............. Induced Remanent Magnetization
IRM............. Information and Records Management
IRM............. Information Research Management (MCD)
IRM............. Information Resource Management [*Computer science*]
IRM............. Information Resources Management [*Marine science*] (OSRA)
IRM............. Infrared Mapper
IRM............. Infrared Measurement
IRM............. Inherited Releasing Mechanism [*Psychiatry*]
IRM............. Inherited Rights Mask (ACRL)
IRM............. Initial Release Memorandum
IRM............. Innate Release Mechanism [*Endocrinology*]
IRM............. Innate Releasing Mechanism (STED)
IRM............. Inspection Requirements Manual (AAG)
IRM............. Institute for Resource Management (EA)
IRM............. Institute of Rehabilitation Medicine (DAVI)
IRM............. Institute of Religion and Medicine [*British*] (DBA)
IRM............. Institute of Risk Management (EAIO)
IRM............. Integrated Range Missile (MCD)
IRM............. Integrated Range Mission [*Military*]
IRM............. Integrated Review Model
IRM............. Intelligent Remote Multiplexer [*Computer science*] (MHDI)
IRM............. Interactive Request Modification (IAA)
IRM............. Interference Reflection Microscopy
IRM............. Interim Remedial Measure (EPA)
IRM............. Interim Research Memo
IRM............. Intermediate Range Monitor (NRCH)
IRM............. Intermediate Remedial Measures (GNE)
IRM............. Intermediate Restorative Material [*Dentistry*]
IRM............. Internal Revenue (Service) Manual [*A publication*] (AAGC)
IRM............. International Royalon Minerals, Inc. [*Vancouver Stock Exchange symbol*]
IRM............. Iodine Radiation Monitor (IEEE)
IRM............. Ion Rate Monitoring (AAEL)
IRM............. Ion Release Module [*Spacecraft*] [*Germany*]
IRM............. Iron Mountain [*NYSE symbol*]
IRM............. Isothermal Remanent Magnetization
IRMA .... Immunoradiometric Assay [*Immunology*]
IRMA .... Individual Retirement Mortgage Account
IRMA .... Individual Reverse Mortgage Account [*American Homestead, Inc.*]
IRMA .... Information Referral Manual
IRMA .... Information Revision and Manuscript Assembly
IRMA .... Infrared Milk Analyzer (PDAA)
IRMA .... Infrared Miss-Distance Approximator
IRMA .... Interactive Real-Time Music Assembler (PDAA)
IRMA .... International Regional Magazine Association (NTPA)
IRMA .... International Rehabilitation Medicine Association (EA)
IRMA .... International Rock 'n' Roll Music Association (EA)
IRMA .... Intraretinal Microangiopathy [*Ophthalmology*]
IRMA .... Intraretinal Microvascular Abnormality [*Ophthalmology*]
IRMA .... Inverted Roof Membrane Assembly [*Construction*]
IRMAC....... Information Resource Management Association of Canada (EAIO)
IR Mad ...... Indian Rulings, Madras Series [*A publication*] (DLA)
IRMAE .... Ius Romanum Medii Aevi [*Latin*]
IRMC .... Information Resource Management Council [*DoD*]
IRMC .... Information Resources Management College (USGC)
IRMC .... Institute of Risk Management Consultants [*Later, SRMC*] (EA)
IRMC .... Interagency Risk Management Council [*Environmental Protection Agency*] (EPA)
IRME.......... Initiator Resistance Measuring Equipment (NASA)
IRMFSG...... Inter-Range Missile Flight Safety Group [*White Sands Missile Range*]
IRMGSG...... Inter-Range Missile Ground Safety Group [*White Sands Missile Range*] (KSC)
IRMI........... Indirect Reading Measuring Instruments (DICI)
IRMI........... International Risk Management Institute [*Dallas, TX*] (EA)
IR Mim ...... Internal Revenue Service Mimeographed Ruling (AAGC)
IR-MIM ...... Published Internal Revenue Mimeograph [*A publication*] (DLA)
IRMJ.......... Infrared Miniaturized Jammer
IRMM......... Institute for Reference Materials and Measurement [*Belgium*]
IRMMH...... Institute for Research into Mental and Multiple Handicap [*British*]
IRMO .... Information Resources Management Office [*Army Corps of Engineers*]
IRMP .... Industrial Readiness and Mobilization Production Planning [*Military*]
IRMP .... Infrared Measurement Program
IRMP .... Infrared Multiple-Photon [*Physics*]
IRMP .... Intermountain Regional Medical Program (BABM)
IRMP .... Interservice Radiation Measurement Program
IRMP .... Iron-Regulated Membrane Protein [*Biochemistry*]
IRMPC....... Industrial Raw Materials Planning Committee [*NATO*] (NATG)
IRMPD....... Infrared Multiple-Photon Dissociation [*Physics*]
IRMR......... Institute for Research into Mental Retardation
IRMRA....... Infrared Monochromatic Radiation (MSA)
IR/MRBM .... Intermediate-Range/Medium-Range Ballistic Missile (NG)
IRMS .... Information Resource Management Service [*Veterans Administration Medical Center*] [*Information service or system*] (IID)
IRMS .... Information Retrieval and Management System (IAA)
IRMS .... Infrared Mapping System
IRMS .... Integrated Radio Management System (MCD)
IRMS .... International Robert Musil Society [*See also SIRM*] [*Saarbrucken, Federal Republic of Germany*] (EAIO)
IRMS .... Isotope Ratio Mass Spectrometry
IRMT.......... International Register of Manipulative Therapists
IRN .... Illinois Resource Network [*University of Illinois*] [*Urbana*] [*Information service or system*] (IID)
IRN .... Import Release Note (DS)
IRN .... Interface Revision Notice [*NASA*] (KSC)

IRN .... Interim Revision Notice (SAA)
IRN .... Internal Recurrent Neural Network (AAEL)
IRN .... Internal Reference Number
IRN .... Internal Routing Network
IRN .... International Rivers Network (EA)
IRN .... Invoice Register Number [*Business term*] (MCD)
IRN .... Iran [*ANSI three-letter standard code*] (CNC)
IRN .... Iron [*Chemical element*] (DAVI)
IRN .... Iron or Steel [*Freight*]
IRN .... Iron River Resources [*Vancouver Stock Exchange symbol*]
IRN .... [*The*] Ironton Railroad Co. [*Absorbed into Consolidated Rail Corp.*] [*AAR code*]
IRN .... Item Removal Notice [*Nuclear energy*] (NRCH)
IRNA .... Immune Ribonucleic Acid (STED)
IRNA .... Informational Ribonucleic Acid (STED)
iRNA .... Information Ribonucleic Acid [*Biochemistry*] (DB)
IRNA .... Iranian [*or Islamic Republic*] News Agency
I-RNA .... Ribonucleic Acid, Immune [*Biochemistry, genetics*]
IR Nag ...... Indian Rulings, Nagpur Series [*A publication*] (DLA)
IRNDT........ Infrared Nondestructive Testing [*Electrical technique*]
IRNES .... Institut de Recherches et de Normalisation Economiques en Scientifiques [*Canada*]
IRNS .... Inertial Reference Navigational System
IRNU .... Institut de Recherche des Nations Unies pour le Developpement Social [*United Nations Research Institute for Social Development*]
IRNV .... Increase and Replacement of Naval Vessels [*Naval budget appropriation title*]
IRNWRK ...... Ironwork
IRO .... Birao [*Central African Republic*] [*Airport symbol*] (AD)
IRO .... CSA Air, Inc. [*ICAO designator*] (FAAC)
IRO .... Independent Retailer Organisation (EAIO)
IRO .... Industrial Relations Office [*Army*]
IRO .... Inflight Refueling Operator
IRO .... Infrared Oven
IRO .... Inland Revenue Office [*or Officer*] [*British*]
IRO .... Institute of Rent Officers [*British*] (DBA)
IRO .... Interim Range Operations (MUGU)
IRO .... Internal Revenue Office [*or Officer*]
IRO .... International Reception Operators [*Defunct*] (EA)
IRO .... International Refugee Organization [*Later, UNHCR*]
IRO .... International Relations Office [*American Library Association*]
IRO .... International Relief Organization [*Post-World War II*]
IRO .... Inventory Research Office [*Army*]
iro .... Iroquoian [*MARC language code Library of Congress*] (LCCP)
IRo .... Rockford Public Library, Rockford, IL [*Library symbol Library of Congress*] (LCLS)
IROA .... Independent Rabbinate of America
IRoAH .... Auburn High School, Rockford, IL [*Library symbol*] [*Library of Congress*] (LCLS)
IROAN........ Inspect and Repair Only as Necessary [*or Needed*] [*Military*]
IRob .... Robinson Public Library, Robinson, IL [*Library symbol Library of Congress*] (LCLS)
IRoBaE....... Barbour Elementary School, Rockford, IL [*Library symbol*] [*Library of Congress*] (LCLS)
IRobb .... Robbins Public Library District, Robbins, IL [*Library symbol Library of Congress*] (LCLS)
IRoBeE........ Beyer Elementary School, Rockford, IL [*Library symbol*] [*Library of Congress*] (LCLS)
IRoBIE .... Bloom Elementary School, Rockford, IL [*Library symbol*] [*Library of Congress*] (LCLS)
IRoBrE........ Brookview Elementary School, Rockford, IL [*Library symbol*] [*Library of Congress*] (LCLS)
IRobSD....... Robinson Community School District 2, Robinson, IL [*Library symbol Library of Congress*] (LCLS)
IROC .... International Race of Champions [*Auto racing*]
IROC .... International Rose O'Neill Club (EA)
IRoC .... Rockford College, Rockford, IL [*Library symbol Library of Congress*] (LCLS)
IRoCaE....... Carlson Elementary School, Rockford, IL [*Library symbol*] [*Library of Congress*] (LCLS)
IRoChE........ Church Elementary School, Rockford, IL [*Library symbol*] [*Library of Congress*] (LCLS)
IRockt .... Talcott Free Public Library, Rockton, IL [*Library symbol Library of Congress*] (LCLS)
IRocL .... Flagg Township Library, Rochelle, IL [*Library symbol*] [*Library of Congress*] (LCLS)
IRocN.......... Rochelle News, Rochelle, IL [*Library symbol*] [*Library of Congress*] (LCLS)
IRoCoE....... Conklin Elementary School, Rockford, IL [*Library symbol*] [*Library of Congress*] (LCLS)
IROD .... Instantaneous Readout Detector [*Satellite instrument*]
IRoDE .... Dennis Elementary School, Rockford, IL [*Library symbol*] [*Library of Congress*] (LCLS)
IRODP......... International Registry of Organization Development Professionals (EA)
IRODS......... Inertial Rate of Descent Sensor (MCD)
IRoEE......... Ellis Elementary School, Rockford, IL [*Library symbol*] [*Library of Congress*] (LCLS)
IRoEH .... East High School, Rockford, IL [*Library symbol*] [*Library of Congress*] (LCLS)
IRoEM........ Einsehower Middle School, Rockford, IL [*Library symbol*] [*Library of Congress*] (LCLS)
IROF .... Imagery Requirement Objectives File (MCD)

IRoFE.......... Froberg Elementary School, Rockford, IL [*Library symbol*] [*Library of Congress*] (LCLS)

IRO-FIET...... Interamerican Regional Organization of the International Federation of Commercial, Clerical, Professional, and Technical Employees [*Willemstad, Netherlands Antilles*] (EAIO)

IRoFM.......... B. W. Flinn Middle School, Rockford, IL [*Library symbol*] [*Library of Congress*] (LCLS)

IRoFP........... Fairview Preschool, Rockford, IL [*Library symbol*] [*Library of Congress*] (LCLS)

IRoGaE........ Garrison Elementary School, Rockford, IL [*Library symbol*] [*Library of Congress*] (LCLS)

IRoGH.......... Guilford High School, Rockford, IL [*Library symbol*] [*Library of Congress*] (LCLS)

IRoGrE......... Gregory Elementary School, Rockford, IL [*Library symbol*] [*Library of Congress*] (LCLS)

IRoHaE........ Haskell Elementary School, Rockford, IL [*Library symbol*] [*Library of Congress*] (LCLS)

IRoHgE........ Haight Elementary School, Rockford, IL [*Library symbol*] [*Library of Congress*] (LCLS)

IRoHiE......... Hillman Elementary School, Rockford, IL [*Library symbol*] [*Library of Congress*] (LCLS)

IRoHlE......... Hallstrom Elementary School, Rockford, IL [*Library symbol*] [*Library of Congress*] (LCLS)

IRoJaE......... Jackson Elementary School, Rockford, IL [*Library symbol*] [*Library of Congress*] (LCLS)

IRoJH.......... Jefferson High School, Rockford, IL [*Library symbol*] [*Library of Congress*] (LCLS)

IRoJoE......... Johnson Elementary School, Rockford, IL [*Library symbol*] [*Library of Congress*] (LCLS)

IRoKE.......... King Elementary School, Rockford, IL [*Library symbol*] [*Library of Congress*] (LCLS)

IRoKiE......... Kishwaukee Elementary School, Rockford, IL [*Library symbol*] [*Library of Congress*] (LCLS)

IRoKM......... John F. Kennedy Middle School, Rockford, IL [*Library symbol*] [*Library of Congress*] (LCLS)

IROL............ Imagery Requirements Objectives List (MCD)

IRoLE........... Lathrop Elementary School, Rockford, IL [*Library symbol*] [*Library of Congress*] (LCLS)

IRoLM.......... Lincoln Middle School, Rockford, IL [*Library symbol*] [*Library of Congress*] (LCLS)

IRoMcE........ McIntosh Elementary School, Rockford, IL [*Library symbol*] [*Library of Congress*] (LCLS)

IRoMH......... Rockford Memorial Hospital, Rockford, IL [*Library symbol Library of Congress*] (LCLS)

IROMM........ International Register of Microform Masters (TELE)

IRoMuE........ Muhl Center Elementary School, Rockford, IL [*Library symbol*] [*Library of Congress*] (LCLS)

IRON............ Infrared Optical Noise (IAA)

Iron............. Ironical (ROG)

IRoN............ Northern Illinois Library for Mental Health, Rockford, IL [*Library symbol Library of Congress*] (LCLS)

IRoNaE........ Nashold Elementary School, Rockford, IL [*Library symbol*] [*Library of Congress*] (LCLS)

IRoNeE........ Nelson Elementary School, Rockford, IL [*Library symbol*] [*Library of Congress*] (LCLS)

IRoNL.......... Rockford Northern Illinois Library System, Rockford, IL [*Library symbol Library of Congress*] (LCLS)

IRONMAN .... Improving Reliability of New Machines at Night (AAEL)

IRoNmE........ New Milford Elementary School, Rockford, IL [*Library symbol*] [*Library of Congress*] (LCLS)

IronMnt....... Iron Mountain, Inc. [*Associated Press*] (SAG)

IRONS.......... Iron and Total Iron Binding Capacity [*Hematology*] (DAVI)

Irons Pol Law... Irons on Police Law [*A publication*] (DLA)

Irons Pub H... Irons on Public Houses [*A publication*] (DLA)

IRoo............ Roodhouse Public Library, Roodhouse, IL [*Library symbol Library of Congress*] (LCLS)

IROP............ Imagery Requirements Objectives Plan (MCD)

IROP............ Infrared Optical Intelligence (MCD)

IROPG.......... Inter-Range Operations Planning Group [*White Sands Missile Range*]

IRoPpE........ Page Park Center Elementary School, Rockford, IL [*Library symbol*] [*Library of Congress*] (LCLS)

IROQ............ Iroquois Bancorp [*NASDAQ symbol*] (TTSB)

IROQ............ Iroquois Bancorp, Inc. [*NASDAQ symbol*] (SAG)

Iroquoi......... Iroquois Bancorp, Inc. [*Associated Press*] (SAG)

IroquoisB..... Iroquois Bancorp [*Associated Press*] (SAG)

IROR............ Improved Range-Only RADAR (MCD)

IROR............ Inspection, Repair, Overhaul, and Rebuild

IROR............ Interest Rate of Return [*Finance*]

IROR............ Internal Rate of Return [*Telecommunications*] (TEL)

IRoR............ Rockford Newspapers, Inc., Rockford, IL [*Library symbol Library of Congress*] (LCLS)

IRoRC.......... Teacher Resource Center, Rockford, IL [*Library symbol*] [*Library of Congress*] (LCLS)

IRoRgE......... Rolling Green Elementary School, Rockford, IL [*Library symbol*] [*Library of Congress*] (LCLS)

IRoRrE......... Rock River Elementary School, Rockford, IL [*Library symbol*] [*Library of Congress*] (LCLS)

IRoRvE......... Riverdahl Elementary School, Rockford, IL [*Library symbol*] [*Library of Congress*] (LCLS)

IROS............ Improved Reliability Operational System (MCD)

IROS............ Increase Reliability of Operational Systems (AFM)

IROS............ Infrared Operational Satellite (NOAA)

IROS............ Instant Response Ordering System [*Teleordering system*] [*Information service or system*] (IID)

IROS............ Ipsilateral Routing of Signal

IRoSA......... Sundstrand Aviation, Engineering Library, Rockford, IL [*Library symbol Library of Congress*] (LCLS)

IROSB......... Inactive Reserve Officer Status Branch [*BUPERS*]

IRoScE........ Spring Creek Elementary School, Rockford, IL [*Library symbol*] [*Library of Congress*] (LCLS)

IRoSH......... Swedish-American Hospital, Rockford, IL [*Library symbol Library of Congress*] (LCLS)

IRoStA........ Saint Anthony Hospital, Rockford, IL [*Library symbol Library of Congress*] (LCLS)

IRoStE........ Stiles Elementary School, Rockford, Il [*Library symbol*] [*Library of Congress*] (LCLS)

IRoStT........ Saint Thomas High School, Rockford, IL [*Library symbol Library of Congress*] (LCLS)

IRoSuE........ Summerdale Elementary School, Rockford, IL [*Library symbol*] [*Library of Congress*] (LCLS)

IRoSvE........ Sky View Center Elementary School, Rockford, IL [*Library symbol*] [*Library of Congress*] (LCLS)

IROT............ Infrared on Target

IRoTE.......... Thompson Elementary School, Rockford, IL [*Library symbol*] [*Library of Congress*] (LCLS)

IR Oudh...... Indian Rulings, Oudh Series [*A publication*] (DLA)

IRoVC.......... Rockford Area Vocational Center, Rockford, IL [*Library symbol*] [*Library of Congress*] (LCLS)

IRoVE.......... Vandercook Elementary School, Rockford, IL [*Library symbol*] [*Library of Congress*] (LCLS)

IRoWaE....... Walker Elementary School, Rockford, IL [*Library symbol*] [*Library of Congress*] (LCLS)

IRoWC........ Washington Center, Rockford, IL [*Library symbol*] [*Library of Congress*] (LCLS)

IRoWeE....... Welsh Elementary School, Rockford, IL [*Library symbol*] [*Library of Congress*] (LCLS)

IRoWH........ West High School, Rockford, IL [*Library symbol*] [*Library of Congress*] (LCLS)

IRoWhE....... Whitehead Elementary School, Rockford, IL [*Library symbol*] [*Library of Congress*] (LCLS)

IRoWM....... Winnebago County Medical Society, Rockford, IL [*Library symbol Library of Congress*] (LCLS)

IRoWMS..... Wilson Middle School, Rockford, IL [*Library symbol*] [*Library of Congress*] (LCLS)

IRoWsE....... White Swan Elementary School, Rockford, IL [*Library symbol*] [*Library of Congress*] (LCLS)

IRoWvE....... West View Elementary School, Rockford, IL [*Library symbol*] [*Library of Congress*] (LCLS)

IRox........... Roxana Public Library, Roxana, IL [*Library symbol Library of Congress*] (LCLS)

IRoxCU....... Roxana Community Unit 1, Roxana, IL [*Library symbol Library of Congress*] (LCLS)

IRP............. Ice on Runway - Patchy [*Aviation*]

IRP............. Immunoglobulin Reference Preparation [*Clinical chemistry*]

IRP............. Immunoreactive Peptides [*Biochemistry*]

IRP............. Immunoreactive Plasma [*Immunochemistry*] (DMAA)

IRP............. Immunoreactive Proinsulin [*Immunochemistry*]

IRP............. Improved Replenishment-at-Sea Program (MCD)

IRP............. Incus Replacement Prosthesis [*Medicine*] (DMAA)

IRP............. Independent Routing Processor [*Telecommunications*] (ACRL)

IRP............. Indianapolis Raceway Park [*Auto racing venue*]

IRP............. Individualized Reading Program [*Education*]

IRP............. Individual Responsibility Program [*Medicine*] (DHSM)

IRP............. Industrial Readiness Planning [*Military*] (NG)

IRP............. Industry Recognition Program (MCD)

IRP............. Inertial Reference Package (MCD)

IRP............. Information Reporting Program [*IRS*] (EGAO)

IRP............. Information Resources Press [*Washington, DC*]

IRP............. Information Return Program [*IRS*]

IRP............. Information Returns Processing [*Computer science*]

IRP............. Infrared Preamplifier

IRP............. Infrared Projector (MCD)

IRP............. Infrared Radiation Profile

IRP............. Infrared Responsive Phosphor

IRP............. Inhibitor of Radical Processes (STED)

IRP............. Initial Receiving Point

IRP............. Installation Restoration Program [*Army*] (RDA)

IRP............. Institute for Research on Poverty [*University of Wisconsin - Madison*] [*Research center*] (RCD)

IRP............. Institute for Retired Professionals (EA)

IRP............. Institutional Revolutionary Party [*Mexico Political party*]

IRP............. Instructional Resource Package (ACII)

IRP............. Insulin-Releasing Polypeptide [*Medicine*] (DMAA)

IRP............. Intelligence Report Plan (NATG)

IRP............. Interference Reporting Point (NATG)

IRP............. Intermediate Rated Power (MCD)

IRP............. Intermediate Related Power

IRP............. Intermediate Rotating Plug (NRCH)

IRP............. Internal Reflection Plate

IRP............. International Petroleum Corp. [*Vancouver Stock Exchange symbol Toronto Stock Exchange symbol*]

IRP............. International Reference Preparation [*World Health Organization*]

IRP............. International Registered Profile (TELE)

IRP............. International Rostrum of Young Performers [*See also TIJE*] (EAIO)

IRP............. International Routing Plan [*Telecommunications*] (TEL)

IRP............. Interrupt Processor (IAA)

IRP............. Interstitial Radiation Pneumonitis [*Medicine*] (DMAA)

IRP............. Inventory and Requirements Planning (MHDI)

IRP............. Iron Regulatory Protein [*Biochemistry*]

IRP............. Isiro [*Zaire*] [*Airport symbol*] (OAG)

IRP............ Islahat Refah Partisi [*Reformation and Welfare Party*] [*Turkish Cypriot*] (PPE)

IRP............ Islamic Renaissance Party [*Commonwealth of Independent States*] (ECON)

IRP............ Islamic Republican Party [*Iran*] [*Political party*] (PPW)

IRP............ Payam (Air Center Service) [*Iran*] [*FAA designator*] (FAAC)

IRp............ Richton Park Library District, Richton Park, IL [*Library symbol Library of Congress*] (LCLS)

IRPA.......... Institut de Recherche sur le Profil d'Apprentissage [*Canada*]

IRPA.......... International Radiation Protection Association [*Vienna, Austria*] (EAIO)

IR Pat........ Indian Rulings, Patna Series [*A publication*] (DLA)

IRPC.......... Indian Rulings, Privy Council [*1929-47*] [*A publication*] (DLA)

IRPC.......... Indirect Reading Pocket Chamber

IRPC.......... Industrial Relations Policy Committee [*General Council of British Shipping*] (DS)

IRPD.......... Industrial Relations and Personnel Development [*A publication*]

IR-PERS-REC... Industrial Relations Personnel Record [*Military*] (DNAB)

IR Pesh....... Indian Rulings, Peshawar Series [*1933-47*] [*A publication*] (DLA)

IR Peshawar... Indian Rulings, Peshawar Series [*1933-47*] [*A publication*] (DLA)

Ir Pet SJ...... Irish Petty Sessions Journal [*A publication*] (DLA)

IRPF.......... Independent Racing Pigeon Federation [*Australia*]

IRPFC......... International Ray Price Fan Club (EA)

IRPG.......... Iranian Research and Publication Group

IRPI........... Individual Rod Position Indicator [*Nuclear energy*] (NRCH)

IRPIA......... Intelligence Information Report Photo Index [*Military*] (MCD)

IRPL.......... Index to Religious Periodical Literature [*Database*]

IRPL.......... Interim Repair Parts List

IRPL.......... Interservice Radio Propagation Laboratory (MCD)

IRPM.......... Individual Risk Premium Modification [*Insurance*]

IRPM.......... Infrared Physical Measurement

IRPMR........ Information Resources Procurement and Management Review (AAGC)

IRPOD........ Individual Repair Parts Ordering Data [*Program*] [*DoD*]

IRPOS......... Interdisciplinary Research Relevant to Problems of Our Society [*Later, RANN*] [*National Science Foundation*]

IRPP.......... Industrial Readiness Planning Program

IRPP.......... Infrared Pointer Package

IRPP.......... Institute for Research on Public Policy [*Canada*]

IRPP.......... International Petroleum Corp. [*NASDAQ symbol*] (SAG)

IRPPF......... Intl Petroleum [*NASDAQ symbol*] (TTSB)

IR Pr C....... Indian Rulings, Privy Council [*1929-47*] [*A publication*] (DLA)

IRPRI......... International Relations and Peace Research Institute [*Guatemala*] (EAIO)

IRPRL......... Initial Repair Parts Requirements List (MCD)

IRPS.......... Individual Resource Protection Sensor

IRPS.......... Institute for Research in Public Safety [*Indiana University*] [*Research center*] (RCD)

IRPS.......... Institute of Reconstructive Plastic Surgery [*New York University*] [*Research center*] (RCD)

IRPS.......... International Review of Publications in Sociology [*Sociological Abstracts, Inc.*] [*Information service or system*] (CRD)

IRPT.......... Inland Rivers Ports and Terminals (EA)

IRPTC......... International Register of Potentially Toxic Chemicals [*United Nations Environment Program*] [*Geneva, Switzerland*]

IRQ............ Faraz Qeshm Airlines [*Iran*] [*FAA designator*] (FAAC)

IRQ............ Interpersonal Relations Questionnaire [*Personality development test*] [*Psychology*]

IRQ............ Interrupt Request [*Computer science*]

IRQ............ Interrupt Request Line [*Computer science*]

IRQ............ Intimate Relationship Questionnaire

IRQ............ Iraq [*ANSI three-letter standard code*] (CNC)

IRQ............ Rose-Hulman Institute of Technology Library, Terre Haute, IN [*OCLC symbol*] (OCLC)

IRQC.......... Infrared Quantum Counter

IRQR.......... Information Requirement [*Military*]

IRR............ Immediate Ready Reserve [*Army*]

IRR............ Improved Rearming Rates [*Military*] (NG)

IRR............ Incidence Rate Ratio [*Mathematics*]

IRR............ Indian Reservation Roads System [*Bureau of Indian Affairs*]

IRR............ Indian River Resources, Inc. [*Vancouver Stock Exchange symbol*]

IRR............ Individual Ready Reserve [*Army*]

IRR............ Individual Retirement Record [*Air Force*] (AFM)

IRR............ Industrial Retaining Ring Co.

IRR............ Information Reduction Research [*Information service or system*] (IID)

IRR............ Information Resource Repository

IRR............ Infrared Radiometer

IRR............ Infrared Receiver

IRR............ Initial Rate of Return [*Finance*] (MCD)

IRR............ Initial Reliability Review

IRR............ Inspection Rejection Report [*NASA*] (KSC)

IRR............ Installation and Removal Record [*NASA*] (KSC)

IRR............ Institute for Reactor Research [*Switzerland*]

IRR............ Institute for Rehabilitation and Research [*Baylor College of Medicine*] [*Research center*] (RCD)

IRR............ Institute for Risk Research [*University of Waterloo*] [*Canada Research center*] (RCD)

IRR............ Institute of Race Relations [*British*] (EAIO)

IRR............ Institute of Resource Recovery (GNE)

IRR............ Institute of Rubber Research (MCD)

IRR............ Instrumentation Revision Record (IAA)

IRR............ Integral Rocket Ramjet [*Navy*]

IRR............ Integrated Radio Room (MCD)

IRR............ Integrated Readiness Report (COE)

IRR............ Intelligence RADAR Reporting

IRR............ Interface Requirements Review (SSD)

IRR............ Interim Release Request (MCD)

IRR............ Internal Rate of Return [*Finance*]

IRR............ Internal Revenue Looseleaf Regulations System

IRR............ International Rate of Return [*Finance*]

IRR............ International Revenue Record [*New York City*] [*A publication*] (DLA)

IRR............ Interrupt Return Register

IRR............ Intrarenal Reflux [*Medicine*] (AAMN)

Ir R........... Irish Law Reports [*A publication*] (DLA)

IRR............ Irish Royal Rifles [*Military British*] (ROG)

IRR............ Iron Range Research Center, Chisholm, MN [*OCLC symbol*] (OCLC)

irr............. Irradiation

IRR............ Irredeemable [*Banking*]

IRR............ Irregular (WGA)

irr............. Irrigate [*or Irrigated*] (DAVI)

IRR............ Irrigation [*Type of water project*]

IRR............ Irritant

IRR............ Irritation (DAVI)

IRR............ Israeli Research Reactor

IRR............ Tara Air Line [*Iran*] [*FAA designator*] (FAAC)

IRRA.......... Industrial Relations Reform Act [*Australia*]

IRRA.......... Industrial Relations Research Association (EA)

IRRA.......... International Routing and Reporting Activity (DNAB)

IRRAD........ Infrared Range and Detection

IRRADN...... Irradiation

IR Ran........ Indian Rulings, Rangoon Series [*A publication*] (DLA)

IRR & L...... Irish Reports, Registry and Land Cases [*A publication*] (DLA)

IRRAPST..... Individual Ready Reserve - Alternative Preassignment System Test (MCD)

IRRAS......... Infrared Reflection Absorption Spectroscopy [*Also, IRAS, RAIR, RAIRS, RAIS*]

IRRB.......... International Rubber Research Board

IRRC.......... International Relief and Rescue Committee [*Post-World War II*]

IRRC.......... International Rubber Regulation Committee [*World War II*]

IRRC.......... Investor Responsibility Research Center (EA)

Ir R Ch....... Irish Chancery Reports [*A publication*] (DLA)

Ir RCL........ Irish Reports, Common Law Series [*A publication*] (DLA)

IRRCS......... Institute for Regional, Rural, and Community Studies [*Western Illinois University*] [*Research center*] (RCD)

IRRD.......... Institute for Research of Rheumatic Diseases [*Defunct*] (EA)

IRRD.......... International Raod Research Documentation (NITA)

IRRDB......... International Rubber Research and Development Board [*Brickendonbury, Hertford, England*] (EAIO)

IRRED........ Irredeemable (ROG)

Irred.......... Irredeemable (EBF)

IRREG........ Irregular (KSC)

irreg........... Irregular (WDMC)

Irreg.......... Irregular Light [*Navigation signal*]

irreg........... Irregularly (WDMC)

IR Rep........ Reports of Inland Revenue Commissioners [*A publication*] (DLA)

Ir Rep Ch..... Irish Chancery Reports [*A publication*] (DLA)

Ir Rep CL..... Irish Reports, Common Law Series [*A publication*] (DLA)

Ir Rep Eq..... Irish Reports, Equity Series [*A publication*] (DLA)

Ir Rep NS .... Irish Common Law Reports, New Series [*A publication*] (DLA)

Ir Rep VR .... Irish Reports, Verbatim Reprint [*A publication*] (DLA)

Ir R Eq........ Irish Reports, Equity Series [*A publication*] (DLA)

IRREV......... Irrevocable

Irrev.......... Irrevocable (EBF)

IRRF.......... Institut pour la Repression des Ravageurs Forestiers [*Forest Pest Management Institute*] [*Canada*]

IRRG.......... Irrigation

IRRGTN....... Irrigation

IRRI.......... Industrial Relations Research Institute [*University of Wisconsin - Madison*] [*Research center*] (RCD)

IRRI.......... Interagency Rehabilitation Research Information System [*National Institute on Disability and Rehabilitation Research*] [*Washington, DC Information service or system*] (IID)

IRRI.......... International Rice Research Institute [*Philippines*]

IRRICAB...... Current Annotated Bibliography of Irrigation [*Bet Dagan, Israel*] [*A publication*]

IRRIG......... Irrigate

IRRIS......... International Rehabilitation Research Information System [*National Institute of Handicapped Research*] [*Database*]

IRRL.......... Information Retrieval Research Laboratory [*University of Illinois*] [*Urbana*] [*Information service or system*] (IID)

IRRM.......... Information Requested in Above Referenced Message [*Army*] (AABC)

IRRMA........ Institut Romand de Recherche Numerique en Physique des Materiaux

IRRMP........ Infrared RADAR Measurement Program

IRRN.......... Illinois Research and Reference Center Libraries

Irr N.......... Tasmanian Irregular Notes [*A publication*]

IRR Newsl ... Individual Rights and Responsibilities Newsletter [*A publication*] (DLA)

IRRP.......... Icefield Ranges Research Project

IRRP.......... Improved Rearming Rate Program [*Military*] (NVT)

IRRPOS....... Interdisciplinary Research Relevant to Problems of Our Society [*Later, RANN*] [*National Science Foundation*]

IRRR.......... Industrial Relations Review and Report [*A publication*]

IRRR.......... Interest Rate Reduction Refinancing [*Veterans Administration*]

Ir R Reg & L... Irish Reports, Registry and Land Cases [*A publication*] (DLA)

Ir R Reg App... Irish Reports, Registration Appeals [*1868-76*] [*A publication*] (DLA)

IRRS.......... Individual Ready Reserve System [*Military*]

IRRS.......... Infrared Reconnaissance Set

IRRS.......... Infrared Reconnaissance System (MCD)

IRRS	Infrared Reflection Spectroscopy
IRRS	Irish Railway Record Society
IRRSAM	Integral Rocket Ramjet Surface-to-Air Missile (MCD)
IRRSSM	Integral Rocket Ramjet Surface-to-Surface Missile (MCD)
IRRT	International Relations Round Table [American Library Association]
IRRTS	Infrared Resolution Target System (MCD)
IRRTTM	Integral Rocket Ramjet Torpedo Tube Missile (MCD)
IRRV	Institute of Revenues, Rating, and Valuation [British]
IRS	Identification and Reference Sheets (MCD)
IRS	Immunoreactive Secretin [Endocrinology]
IRS	Immunoreactive Somatostatin [Endocrinology]
IRS	Improved RADAR Simulation (DWSG)
IRS	Impurity Removal System
IRS	Inactive Reserve Section [Military]
IRS	Inboard Rotating Shield
IRS	Incident Reporting System [IAEA] (NUCP)
IRS	Incremental Range Summary
IRS	Independent Rear Suspension [Automotive engineering]
IRS	Independent Research Service [Defunct]
IRS	Indian Remote-Sensing Satellite
IRS	Indirect Representative Supplement [British]
IRS	Induction and Recruiting Station [Marine Corps]
IRS	Industrial Relations Section [Princeton University] [Research center] (RCD)
IRS	Industrial Relations Services [Eclipse Group Ltd.] [British] (ECON)
IRS	Ineligible Reserve Section
IRS	Inertial Reference Sensor
IRS	Inertial Reference System [Aviation]
IRS	Inertial Retical System
IRS	Infant Rating Scale [Child development test]
IRS	Infinitely Rigid System [Engineering] (OA)
IRS	Inflatable Restraint System [Automotive engineering]
IRS	Informal Routing Slip
IRS	Information Recovery [or Retrieval] System [or Subsystem]
IRS	Information Research Services [Information service or system] (IID)
IRS	Information Resources Specialists [Information service or system] (IID)
IRS	Information Retrieval Service [Memphis State University Libraries] (OLDSS)
IRS	Information Retrieval Service [European Space Agency] (IID)
IRS	Information Retrieval System (OICC)
IRS	Infrared RADAR Suppressor (MCD)
IRS	Infrared Reconnaissance Set (MCD)
IRS	Infrared Reflective Spectra
IRS	Infrared Soldering
IRS	Infrared Source
IRS	Infrared Spectrometer [or Spectroscopy]
IRS	Infrared Star (BARN)
IRS	Inorganic Resin System [Fire-resistant cement]
IRS	Input Read Submodule
IRS	Inquiry and Reporting System
IRS	Inspection Record Sheet
IRS	Inspector of Radio Services [Military] (IAA)
IRS	Installation Readiness System [Army]
IRS	Institute of Religious Studies [Australia]
IRS	Instructional Review System
IRS	Instrumentation RADAR Set
IRS	Instrument Retrieval System [Containers] [Medicine] (DAVI)
IRS	Insulin Receptor Species [Medicine] (DMAA)
IRS	Insulin Receptor Substrate [Biochemistry]
IRS	Intact Rock Strength [Mining]
IRS	Integrated Rate System
IRS	Integrated Record System (KSC)
IRS	Integrated Review Schedule [Department of Health and Human Services] (GFGA)
IRS	Integration Review Section [Social Security Administration]
IRS	Intelligence Research Specialist [Military] (MCD)
IRS	Interchange Record Separator [Computer science] (BUR)
IRS	Interface Requirements Document [DoD]
IRS	Interface Requirements Specification (MCD)
IRS	Interferon Response Sequence [Genetics]
IRS	Intergroup Rhabdomyosarcoma Study [Oncology]
IRS	Intermedia Ranking Staff (COE)
IRS	Intermediate Reference Structure
IRS	Internal Reflection Spectroscopy
IRS	Internal Revenue Service [Department of the Treasury] [Washington, DC]
IRS	Internal Revenue Service Library, Washington, DC [OCLC symbol] (OCLC)
IRS	International Radio Silence
IRS	International Records Syndicate, Inc.
IRS	International Referral System [United Nations Environment Programme]
IRS	International Repeater Station [Telecommunications] (TEL)
IRS	International Rhinologic Society (EA)
IRS	International Rorschach Society [Strasbourg, France] (EA)
IRS	Internetwork Routing Service [Telecommunications] (OSI)
IRS	Interpersonal Relationship Scale (EDAC)
IRS	Interspersed Repetitive Sequence [Genetics]
IRS	Inverse Raman Scattering [Spectroscopy]
IRS	Iodine Removal System [Nuclear energy] (NRCH)
IRS	Ionospheric Radio Signal
IRS	Irish Standard (IAA)
IRS	IRSA Inversiones y Rep GDS [NYSE symbol] (TTSB)
IRS	IRSA Inversions y Representaciones SA [NYSE symbol] (SAG)
IRS	Isoleucyl-tRNA Synthetase [An enzyme]
IRS	Isotope Radiography System
IRS	Isotope Removal Service (IEEE)
IRS	Item Reduction Studies (MSA)
IRS	Sturgis, MI [Location identifier FAA] (FAAL)
IRS	Transavia Ltd. [Romania] [FAA designator] (FAAC)
IRSA	Idiopathic Refractory Sideroblastic Anemia [Medicine] (MAE)
IRSA	Immigration and Refugee Services of America (EA)
IRSA	Improved Radiator Standards Association (EA)
IRSA	Independent Road Service Association (EA)
IRSA	International Racquet Sports Association [Later, IRSAAQC] (EA)
IRSA	International Rett Syndrome Association (EA)
IRSA	International Rural Sociology Association (EA)
IRSA	Iodinated Rat Serum Albumin (DMAA)
IRSA	Irish Research Scientists Association
IRSA	IRSA Inversiones y Representaciones SA [Associated Press] (SAG)
IRSAAQC	IRSA [International Racquet Sports Association], the Association of Quality Clubs (EA)
IRSAC	Institut pour la Recherche Scientifique en Afrique Centrale [Brussels]
IRSB	Institute for Research in Social Behavior [Research center] (RCD)
IRSC	Institut de Recherches Scientifiques au Congo
IRSC	Internal Revenue Service Centers
IRSC	Inter-Regional Subject Coverage Scheme [Libraries cooperative scheme] [British] (NITA)
IRSCAN	Infrared Scanner
IRSCC	International Relief Service of Caritas Catholica [Belgium] (EAIO)
IRSCL	International Research Society for Children's Literature [Cadaujac, France] (EA)
IRSCOT	Infrared Structural Correlation Tables [A publication]
IRSD	Information and Regulatory Systems Division [Environmental Protection Agency] (GFGA)
IRSE	Infrared Systems Engineering
IRSE	Institution of Railway Signal Engineers [British]
IRSF	Inland Revenue Staff Federation [A union] [British] (DCTA)
IRSF	International Roller Skating Federation (EA)
IRSFC	International Rayon and Synthetic Fibres Committee [See also CIRFS] [Paris, France] (EAIO)
IRSG	Information Retrieval Specialist Group [British Computer Society] (NITA)
IRSG	Internationale Richard Strauss Gesellschaft [An association] (EAIO)
IRSG	International Rubber Study Group [London, England] (EAIO)
IRSG	Internet Research Steering Group [Computer science] (ACRL)
IRSGHL	Infrared Systems and Guidance Heads Laboratory
IRSH	Infrared Spectral Hygrometer (PDAA)
IRSI	Industrial Research and Service Institute
IRSI	International Remote Sensing Institute (MCD)
IR Sind	Indian Rulings, Sind Series [A publication] (DLA)
IRSIO	International Rationalization, Standardization, and Interoperability Office (MCD)
IRSLL	Image Recording System, Low Light
IRSM	Immunoreactive Somatomedin [Endocrinology]
IRSM	Infrared Systems Manufacturing
IRSN	Irvine Sensors [NASDAQ symbol] (TTSB)
IRSN	Irvine Sensors Corp. [NASDAQ symbol] (NQ)
IRSO	Infrared Solder Oven
IRSO	Institute of Road Safety Officers [British]
IRSO	International Rope Skipping Organization
IRSP	Infrared Spectrometer [or Spectroscopy]
IRSP	Irish Republican Socialist Party [Pairti Poblachtach Soisialach na h-Eireann] (PPW)
IRSPECT	Infrared Spectrometer [or Spectroscopy] (MCD)
IRSR	Immediate Replacement Support Requirement (MCD)
IRSS	Inertial Reference Stabilization System
IRSS	Infrared Search Set
IRSS	Infrared Search System [Database] [Environmental Protection Agency Information service or system] (CRD)
IRSS	Infrared Search System [Institut za Nuklearne Nauke Boris Kidric] [Former Yugoslavia] [Information service or system] (CRD)
IRSS	Infrared Sensor System
IRSS	Infrared Smoke Simulator (MCD)
IRSS	Infrared Surveillance Subsystem
IRSS	Institute for Religious and Social Studies (EA)
IRSS	Institute for Research in Social Science [University of North Carolina at Chapel Hill] [Research center] (RCD)
IRSS	Institute for Resource and Security Studies (EA)
IRSS	Instrumentation and Range Safety System [NASA] (KSC)
IRSS	Integrated Range Safety System (IAA)
IRSSO	Infrared Search Set Operator
IRST	Infrared Search and Track
Ir Stat	Irish Statutes [A publication] (DLA)
IRSTDS	Infrared Surveillance and Target Designation System (PDAA)
IRSTS	Infrared Search and Track System
Ir St Tr	Irish State Trials (Ridgeway's) [A publication] (DLA)
IRSU	International Radio Scientific Union (DEN)
IRSU	International Religious Studies Unit [American Topical Association] (EA)
IRSU	ISDN [Integrated Services Digital Network] Remote Subscriber Unit [Telecommunications]
IRT	Icing Research Tunnel [Built at Lewis Research Center in 1944 by the National Advisory Committee for Aeronautics]
IRT	Image Rejection Technology [RADAR detection]
IRT	Immunoreactive Trypsin
IRT	Index Return Character [Computer science]
IRT	Indicating Round Technique [British]
IRT	Individual Reliability Test

IRT	Industrial Reading Test
IRT	Infinite-Resolution Trimmer
IRT	Information Retrieval Technique (AAG)
IRT	Infrared Radiation Thermometer (NOAA)
IRT	Infrared Telescope
IRT	Infrared Temperature
IRT	Infrared Thermography
IRT	Infrared Thermometer
IRT	Infrared Tracker
IRT	Infrared Tube
IRT	Initialize Reset Tape
IRT	Input Revision Typewriter
IRT	In-Reactor Thimble (IEEE)
IRT	In Reference To (NVT)
IRT	In Regard To (MCD)
IRT	In Reply To (NVT)
IRT	In Response To (NVT)
IRT	[*The*] Inscriptions of Roman Tripolitania (BJA)
IRT	Institute for Radiological Technologists
IRT	Institute for Rapid Transit [*Later, APTA*] (EA)
IRT	Institute for Reality Therapy (EA)
IRT	Institute for Research on Teaching [*East Lansing, MI*] [*Department of Education*] (GRD)
IRT	Institute of Reprographic Technology
IRT	Instrument Retrieval Containers [*Medicine*] (DAVI)
IRT	Integrated Readiness Testing
IRT	Intelcom Radiation Technology, Inc.
IRT	Interboro Rapid Transit [*A New York City subway line*]
IRT	Interim Remote Terminals (MCD)
IRT	Intermediate-Range Technology
IRT	Intermediate Rated Thrust [*Military*] (CAAL)
IRT	Internal Reflection Technique
IRT	International Research and Technology, Inc.
IRT	Interot Air Service [*Germany ICAO designator*] (FAAC)
IRT	Interresponse Time [*Psychometrics*]
IRT	Interrogator-Responder-Transducer
IRT	Interrupted Ring Tone [*Telecommunications*] (TEL)
IRT	Interstitial Radiotherapy (DMAA)
IRT	Inverse Reflex Tetrode [*Physics*]
IRT	IRT Properties [*Formerly, Investors Realty Trust*] [*Associated Press*] (SAG)
IRT	IRT Property [*NYSE symbol*] (TTSB)
IRT	IRT Property Co. [*Formerly, Investors Realty Trust*] [*NYSE symbol*] (SPSG)
IRT	Isometric Relaxation Time [*Medicine*] (DAVI)
IRT	Isotope Ratio Tracer (PDAA)
IRT	Isovolumic Relaxation Time [*Cardiology*]
IRT	Item Response Theory (GFGA)
IRT	Richmond Community Schools, Richmond, IN [*OCLC symbol*] (OCLC)
IRTA	Independent Retail Tobacconists Association of America [*Defunct*] (EA)
IRTA	International Reciprocal Trade Association (EA)
IRTA	Intramural Research Training Award [*National Institutes of Health*]
IRTAC	International Round Table for the Advancement of Counseling [*British*]
IRTAFS	International Ready-to-Assemble Furniture Show (ITD)
IRTC	Infantry Replacement Training Center
IRTC-1	Interconnect Reliability Test Chip-1 (AAEL)
IRTCES	International Research and Training Center on Erosion and Sedimentation [*China*] (EAIO)
IRTCG	Installation Restoration Technology Coordinating Group [*Army*] (RDA)
IRTCM	Integrated Real-Time Contamination Monitor [*Module*]
IRTD	Infantry Reinforcement Training Depot [*British military*] (DMA)
IRTD	Infrared Target Detector
IrTD	Iranian Documentation Centre, Tehran, Iran [*Library symbol Library of Congress*] (LCLS)
IRTE	Institut de Radio-Telediffusion pour Enfants [*Children's Broadcast Institute*] [*Canada*]
IRTE	Institute of Road Transport Engineers (EAIO)
Ir Term Rep	Irish Term Reports, by Ridgeway, Lapp, and Schoales [*A publication*] (DLA)
IRTF	Industry Restructuring Task Force
IRTF	Infrared Telescope Facility
IRTF	Intermediate-Range Task Force
IRTF	International Radio and Television Foundation, Inc. [*International Radio and Television Society*] (NTCM)
IRTF	Internet Research Task Force
IRTF	Inter-Religious Task Force on Central America [*Defunct*] (EA)
IRTGSM	Infrared Terminally-Guided Submunition
IRTI	Islamic Research & Training Institute [*Saudi Arabia*]
IRTIS	Inter-Regional Training Information System [*International Labor Organization*] [*United Nations*] (DUND)
IRTM	Infrared Thermal Mapper [*NASA*]
IRTP	Initial Recruiting and Training Plan [*Military*]
IRTP	Integrated Reliability Test Program
Ir TR	Irish Term Reports, by Ridgeway, Lapp, and Schoales [*A publication*] (DLA)
IRTRAN	Infrared Transmitting
IRTRN	Infrared Transmission
IRTS	Infrared Target Seeker (MSA)
IRTS	Infrared Temperature Sounder (PDAA)
IRTS	Interim Recovery Technical Specification (IEEE)
IRTS	International Radio and Television Society (EA)
IRTTD	Infrared Transmission through the Diffusion (PDAA)

IRTU	Integrating Regulatory Transcription Units [*Genetics*]
IRTU	Intelligent Remote Terminal Unit
IRTU	International Railway Temperance Union
IRTV	Information Retrieval Television [*Tele-education project*] (NITA)
IRTWG	Interrange Telemetry Working Group
IRTWS	Infrared Tail Warning Set (MCD)
IRU	Immediate Response Unit [*Police*] [*British*] (DI)
IRU	Indefeasible Right of User [*Telecommunications*] (TEL)
IRU	Industrial Rehabilitation Units [*British*]
IRU	Inertial Reference Unit
IRU	Information Retrieval Unit (NITA)
IRU	Interferon Reference Unit
IRU	Intergenic Repeat Unit [*Genetics*]
IRU	Internationale Raiffeisen-Union [*International Raiffeisen Union*] (EAIO)
IRU	International Radium Unit
IRU	International Raiffeisen Union (EA)
IRU	International Relief Union
IRU	International Road Transport Union [*Geneva, Switzerland*] (EAIO)
IRU	International Romani Union (EA)
IRU	Irvine Research Unit [*University of California, Irvine*]
IRU	IVA [*Intravehicular Activity*] Replacement Unit (SSD)
IRU	New Mexico State University, Las Cruces, NM [*OCLC symbol*] (OCLC)
IRUC	Information and Research Utilization Center in Physical Education and Recreation for the Handicapped [*American Association for Health, Physical Education, and Recreation*]
IRUC	Intermediate Resource Usage Condition (MHDI)
IRUS	Infantry Rifle Unit Study [*Army*]
IRut	Rutland Community Library, Rutland, IL [*Library symbol Library of Congress*] (LCLS)
IR/UV-LS	Infrared/Ultraviolet Line Scanner (PDAA)
IRV	Improved Recovery Vehicle [*Army*] (RDA)
IRV	Inglewood [*Forest*] Rifle Volunteers [*British military*] (DMA)
IRV	Inspiratory Reserve Volume [*Physiology*]
IRV	Internationale Rat fuer Vogelschutz [*International Council for Bird Preservation*]
IRV	International Reference Version (OSI)
IRV	International Rex Ventures, Inc. [*Vancouver Stock Exchange symbol*]
IRV	Inter-Range Vector [*NASA*] (KSC)
IRV	Interrupt Request Vector
IRV	Inversed Ratio of Ventilation
Irv	Irvine's Scotch Justiciary Reports [*1851-68*] [*A publication*] (DLA)
IRV	Isotope Reentry Vehicle [*NASA*] (NASA)
IRV	Item Rating Value (DNAB)
IRVAT	Infrared Video Automatic Tracking (PDAA)
IRVAT	Infrared Video-Auto Tracker (DWSG)
IRVB	India-Rubber Vulcanized, Braided [*Wire insulation*] (IAA)
IRVC	Indian Remount and Veterinary Corps [*British military*] (DMA)
Irv Civ Law	Irving's Civil Law [*A publication*] (DLA)
IRVH	Integrated Reactor Vessel Head [*Nuclear energy*] (NRCH)
Irvine	Irvine Sensors Corp. [*Associated Press*] (SAG)
IrvineApt	Irvine Apartment Communities [*Associated Press*] (SAG)
Irvine Just Cas	Irvine's Justiciary Cases [*England*] [*A publication*] (DLA)
Irving Civ Law	Irving's Civil Law [*A publication*] (DLA)
Irv Just	Irvine's Justiciary Cases [*England*] [*A publication*] (DLA)
IRVR	Instrumented Runway Visual Range [*Aviation*] (DA)
IRVSS	Infrared Vertical Sounding System [*Oceanography*] (MSC)
IRVW	Integrated Research Volkswagen [*Automotive engineering*]
IRW	Index of Relative Worth (MCD)
IRW	Indirect Reference Word (BUR)
IRW	Infrared Window
IRW	Institute for Rural Water (EA)
IRW	International Rehabilitation Week [*Trade show*]
IRW	International Rocket Week
IRW	Inverted Rib Waveguide (NITA)
IRWA	International Right of Way Association (EA)
IRWA	International Rodeo Writers Association [*Later, RMA*] (EA)
IRWC	Institute of Roofing and Waterproofing Consultants International (NTPA)
IRWC	International Registry of World Citizens
Ir WCC	Irish Workmen's Compensation Cases [*A publication*] (DLA)
IRWEP	International Register for the White Eared Pheasant (EAIO)
IRWG	Interface Requirements Working Group (SSD)
IrwinFin	Irwin Financial Corp. [*Associated Press*] (SAG)
Irwin's Code	Clark, Cobb, and Irwin's Code [*Georgia*] [*A publication*] (DLA)
Ir WLR	Irish Weekly Law Reports [*1895-1902*] [*A publication*] (DLA)
IRWN	Irwin Financial Corp. [*NASDAQ symbol*] (SAG)
IrwnFn	Irwin Financial Corp. [*Associated Press*] (SAG)
IRWR	Infrared Warning Receiver [*Aviation*] (MCD)
IRX	Interactive Resource Executive [*NCR Corp.*]
IRY	Iron Bay Trust [*Toronto Stock Exchange symbol*]
IRZ	Inner Radiation Zone
IRZ	International Reference Zero [*Level for pure-tone audiometers*]
IS	Eagle Air [*ICAO designator*] (AD)
IS	Ibbi-Sin
IS	Iceland [*ANSI two-letter standard code*] (CNC)
IS	Ice Screamers (EA)
IS	Ideological Survey [*Psychology*]
IS	IDS Aircraft Ltd. [*British ICAO designator*] (ICDA)
IS	Ignition and Separation (IAA)
IS	Image Stabilization [*Technology from Canon*]
IS	Image Stabilizer [*Canon's technology for binoculars*]
IS	Imaging Spectrometer (SSD)
IS	Immediate Sensitivity [*Medicine*] (DB)

IS...............	Immittance Spectroscopy (EDCT)
IS...............	Immortalist Society (EA)
IS...............	Immune Serum [*Also, ImS*]
IS...............	Immunological Similarity
IS...............	Immunology Status [*Medicine*] (DB)
IS...............	Immunosuppressive [*Immunochemistry*]
IS...............	Impact Switch (SAA)
IS...............	Improved Suspension (MCD)
IS...............	Incentive Spirometer [*or Spirometry*] [*Medicine*] (DMAA)
IS...............	Including Sheeting
IS...............	Incoherent Scatter
IS...............	Income Statement [*Business term*]
IS...............	Incomplete Sequence (MSA)
IS...............	Independent School (BARN)
IS...............	Independent Sector (EA)
IS...............	Independent Shoemen of America [*Defunct*] (EA)
IS...............	Independent Spherical Aluminum Tank [*on a ship*] (DS)
IS...............	Indexed Sequential [*Computer science*]
IS...............	Indexing in Source
IS...............	Indian Standard (IAA)
IS...............	Indicating Switch (NRCH)
IS...............	Induced Sputum [*Otorhinolaryngology*] (DAVI)
IS...............	Induction Soldering
IS...............	Industrial School [*British*] (ROG)
IS...............	Industrial Service [*Equipment specifications*]
IS...............	Industrial Society (AIE)
IS...............	Industrial Source (GNE)
IS...............	Industrial Specialist
IS...............	Industrial Systems (DS)
IS...............	Industry Standard (BCP)
IS...............	Inertial Systems (AFIT)
IS...............	[*The*] Infantry School [*Army*] (MCD)
IS...............	Infant Size (DB)
IS...............	Infection Structure [*Plant pathology*]
IS...............	Information Science (IEEE)
IS...............	Information Seekers
IS...............	Information Separation (NITA)
IS...............	Information Separator [*Control character*] [*Computer science*]
IS...............	Information Service
IS...............	Information Services [*Portion of InterNIC General Atomics Corporation*]
IS...............	Information System
IS...............	Information Systems [*Ori, Inc.*] [*Information service or system*] (IID)
IS...............	Infrared Spectrometer [*or Spectroscopy*] (IAA)
IS...............	Infrasonic
IS...............	Ingglish Speling 3soesiaesh3n [*An organization to reform spelling*] [*See also IS3*] (EA)
IS...............	Initial Shortage (AFM)
IS...............	Initiation Supervisor
IS...............	Inner Sheath [*Botany*]
IS...............	Inorganic Semiconductor [*Materials science*]
IS...............	Input Secondary [*Electronics*]
IS...............	Input Simulator
IS...............	Insect Screen (AAG)
IS...............	Insertion Sequence [*Genetics*]
IS...............	In Service [*Telecommunications*] (TEL)
IS...............	In Shop (MCD)
I/S...............	Inside [*Automotive engineering*]
IS...............	Inside Sentinel [*Freemasonry*]
IS...............	In Situ [*In Place*] [*Latin*]
IS...............	Inspection Services, Inc. (EA)
IS...............	Installation of Systems (IAA)
IS...............	Installation Start [*Telecommunications*] (TEL)
IS2...............	Installation Start [*Telecommunications*] (TEL)
IS...............	Installation Support (KSC)
is...............	Installation Support [*Aerospace*] (NAKS)
IS...............	Institute of Statisticians [*British*]
IS...............	Instruction Section [*Association of College and Research Libraries*] [*American Library Association*]
IS...............	Instruction Sheet
IS...............	Instructions to Ship (AAG)
IS...............	Instructor Squadron
IS...............	Instrument (IAA)
IS...............	Instrumentation Ships Project [*Navy*]
IS...............	Instrumentation Summary (MUGU)
IS...............	Instrumentation System (KSC)
IS...............	Insufficiently Stamped [*Post office*] [*British*] (ROG)
IS...............	Insulating Sleeve
IS...............	Integrally Stiffened
IS...............	Integrated Satellite [*Military spacecraft*]
IS...............	Integrating Support
IS...............	Intelligence in the Sky [*An extraterrestrial intelligence with whom Dr. Andrija Puharich and psychic Uri Geller claim to have communicated*]
IS...............	Intelligence Service (IAA)
IS...............	Intelligence Specialist [*Navy*]
IS...............	Intelligence Support [*Program*] [*Department of State*]
IS...............	Intelligence Systems [*Military*] (MCD)
IS...............	Intercellular Space (DB)
IS...............	Interchangeability and Substitution
IS...............	Interconnecting Station (MCD)
IS...............	Intercostal Space [*Medicine*]
IS...............	Interface Specifications (AAEL)
IS...............	Interference Suppressor (IEEE)
IS...............	Interim Standard (ACRL)
IS...............	Interim Status (GNE)

IS...............	Interior Surface
IS...............	Intermediate School
IS...............	Intermediate Suppression (MCD)
IS...............	Intermediate System [*Computer science*] (TNIG)
IS...............	Internal Security [*Military British*]
IS...............	Internal Shield [*Electronics*]
IS...............	Internal Standard [*Chemistry*]
IS...............	Internal Surface (AAG)
IS...............	Internationaler Suchdienst [*International Tracing Service*] (EAIO)
IS...............	Internationale Schutzenunion [*International Shooting Union*] (EAIO)
IS...............	International Services [*Red Cross*]
IS...............	International Socialists
IS...............	International Society of Sculptors, Painters, and Gravers
IS...............	International Staff (NATG)
IS...............	International Standard
IS...............	International Stock [*Business term*]
IS...............	Intersegmental
IS...............	Interservice
IS...............	Intership [*Freight forwarding company*] [*British*]
IS...............	Interspace
I/S...............	Interstage
IS...............	Interstate
IS...............	Interstate/Johnson Lane [*Formerly, Interstate Securities, Inc.*] [*NYSE symbol*] (SPSG)
IS...............	Interval Signal
IS...............	Intracardial Shunt [*Medicine*] (DB)
IS...............	Intraspinal [*Injection*]
IS...............	Intrasplenic (DB)
IS...............	Intrastriatal (DB)
IS...............	Intraventricular Septum [*Cardiology*] (AAMN)
IS...............	Invalided from Service [*Medicine Navy*]
IS...............	Inventory Schedule
I/S...............	Inventory to Sales Ratio [*Business term*]
IS...............	Investment-Savings [*Economics*]
I-S...............	Investment-Savings Curve [*Economics*]
I-S...............	Ionescu-Shiley [*Artificial cardiac valve*] [*Medicine*] (STED)
IS...............	Ion Source [*Spectroscopy*]
IS...............	Irish Society
IS...............	Irish Standard (IAA)
Is...............	Isaiah [*Old Testament book*]
Is...............	Isidore [*Authority cited in pre-1607 legal work*] (DSA)
Is...............	Islam (BJA)
IS...............	Island (DA)
is...............	Island (STED)
Is...............	Islands [*Maps and charts*]
IS...............	Isle (EY)
I/S...............	Isle Of Skye [*Scotland*] (ROG)
is...............	Islet (STED)
IS...............	Isolated Step
IS...............	Isolation
is...............	Isolation (STED)
IS...............	Isomeric Shift (OA)
IS...............	Isotopic Separation [*Subsystem*] (MCD)
is...............	Israel [*MARC country of publication code Library of Congress*] (LCCP)
Is...............	Israel [*IYRU nationality code*] (BJA)
IS...............	ISSN [*International Standard Serial Number*] [*Online database field identifier*]
IS...............	Issue Code [*Online database field identifier*]
IS...............	Issue Number [*Dialog*] [*Searchable field*] (NITA)
IS1...............	Istituto Superiore di Sanita [*Italy*] [*Research code symbol*]
IS1...............	Intelligence Specialist, First Class [*Navy*] (DNAB)
IS2...............	Intelligence Specialist, Second Class [*Navy*] (DNAB)
IS3...............	Ingglish Speling 3soesiaesh3n [*English Spelling Association*] (EA)
IS3...............	Intelligence Specialist, Third Class [*Navy*] (DNAB)
ISA...............	Ibsen Society of America (EA)
ISA...............	Idle Speed Actuator [*Automotive engineering*]
ISA...............	Ignition and Separation Assembly
ISA...............	Illinois Sheriffs Association (SRA)
ISA...............	Illinois Sign Association (SRA)
ISA...............	Illinois Soybean Association (SRA)
ISA...............	Incest Survivors' Association [*Australia*]
ISA...............	Independent Scholars of Asia (EA)
ISA...............	Independent Schools Association [*British*] (AEBS)
ISA...............	Independent Shoemen of America [*Defunct*]
ISA...............	Independent Signcrafters of America (EA)
ISA...............	Independent Stores Association Ltd. [*British*] (BI)
ISA...............	Index of Spouse Abuse
ISA...............	Indiana Sheriffs' Association (SRA)
ISA...............	Individual Savings Account [*Proposed*]
ISA...............	Inductee Special Assignment
ISA...............	Industrial Security Acquisition (MCD)
ISA...............	Industry Standard Architecture [*Computer hardware*] (PCM)
ISA...............	Inertial Sensor Assembly [*Military*] (CAAL)
ISA...............	Infantry Sailing Association [*British*]
ISA...............	Information Systems Architecture [*AT & T*]
ISA...............	Information Systems Association (EA)
ISA...............	Innkeepers Society of America [*Defunct*] (EA)
ISA...............	Inorganic Sampling and Analysis
ISA...............	Insecta Research [*Vancouver Stock Exchange symbol*]
ISA...............	Installations and Services Agency [*Army Materiel Command*]
ISA...............	Installation Supply Accounting
ISA...............	Installation Supply Activity
ISA...............	Institute for Scientific Analysis (EA)
ISA...............	Institute for Sustainable Agriculture [*Australia*]

ISA .... Institute of Systems Analysis [*Army*]
ISA .... Institut Superieur des Affaires [*Chamber de Commerce et d'Industrie de Paris*] (ECON)
ISA .... Instructional Systems Association (EA)
ISA .... Instruction Set Architecture [*Computer science Army*] (RDA)
ISA .... Instrumentation Society of America (AAEL)
ISA .... Instrument Society of America (EA)
ISA .... Instruments, Systems and Automation (ACII)
ISA .... Instrument Subassembly (IEEE)
ISA .... Insulating Siding Association [*Defunct*] (EA)
ISA .... Insurance Service Associates [*Later, Assurex International*]
ISA .... Integrated Support Area (NVT)
ISA .... Intelligence Support Activity [*Military*]
ISA .... Interactive Services Association (NTPA)
ISA .... Interactive Survey Analysis (IAA)
ISA .... Intercoastal Steamship Freight Association, New York NY [*STAC*]
ISA .... Interconexion Electrica, Sociedad Anonima
ISA .... Interface Switching Assembly
ISA .... Intergalactic SYSOP [*System Operator*] Alliance (EA)
ISA .... Interim Stowage Assembly
ISA .... Intermediate Specific Activity [*Radioisotope*]
ISA .... Intermediate Supply Activity [*Marine Corps*] (DOMA)
ISA .... Internal Storage Area [*Computer science*] (BYTE)
ISA .... International Safety Academy
ISA .... International Schools Association [*Geneva, Switzerland*] (EA)
ISA .... International Seabed Authority
ISA .... International Security Affairs [*DoD*]
ISA .... International Security Agency
ISA .... International Service Agencies
ISA .... International Shakespeare Association (EA)
ISA .... International Shipmasters Association of the Great Lakes (EA)
ISA .... International Shuffleboard Association (EA)
ISA .... International Sign Association [*NESA*] [*Absorbed by*] (EA)
ISA .... International Silk Association - USA (EA)
ISA .... International Silo Association (EA)
ISA .... International Skateboard Association (EA)
ISA .... International Skeeter Association
ISA .... International Society for Measurement and Control (NTPA)
ISA .... International Society of Appraisers [*Hoffman Estates, IL*] (EA)
ISA .... International Society of Arboriculture (EA)
ISA .... International Society of Women Airline Pilots (EA)
ISA .... International Sociological Association [*Research center Spain*] (IRC)
ISA .... International Soling Association [*Bordon, Hampshire, England*] (EAIO)
ISA .... International Songwriters' Association (EAIO)
ISA .... International Standard Atmosphere [*ICAO*] (FAAC)
ISA .... International Standards Association
ISA .... International Stiltwalkers Association (EA)
ISA .... International Strabismological Association (EAIO)
ISA .... International Studies Association (EA)
ISA .... International Sugar Agreement [*1958*]
ISA .... International Surfing Association [*Swansea, England*] (EAIO)
ISA .... International Swift Association (EA)
ISA .... International Symbol of Access [*Department of Transportation*] (EGAO)
ISA .... Interplant Shipping Authority
ISA .... Interrupt Storage Area
ISA .... Intersecting Storage Accelerator [*In name of atomic reactor, Isabelle*]
ISA .... Interservice Agreement [*DoD*]
ISA .... Interservice Support Agreement [*Military*]
ISA .... Intrinsic Stimulating Activity (DB)
ISA .... Intrinsic Sympathomimetic Activity [*Biochemistry*]
ISA .... Investment Savings Account (ADA)
ISA .... Iodinated Serum Albumin [*Medicine*]
ISA .... Ion Scattering Analysis
ISA .... Iowa Soybean Association (SRA)
ISA .... Irregular Serials and Annuals [*A publication*]
ISA .... Irregular Spiking Activity [*Electrophysiology*]
ISA .... Isabella [*California*] [*Seismograph station code, US Geological Survey*] (SEIS)
Isa .... Isaiah [*Old Testament book*]
ISA .... Isaias [*Old Testament book*] [*Douay version*]
ISA .... Island Airlines, Inc. [*ICAO designator*] (FAAC)
ISA .... Israel Space Agency [*Israel*]
ISA .... Mount Isa [*Australia Airport symbol*] (OAG)
ISA .... Santa Isabel ADS [*NYSE symbol*] (TTSB)
ISA .... Santa Isabel SA [*NYSE symbol*] (SAG)
ISA .... UNRWA [*United Nations Relief and Works Agency*] International Staff Association (EAIO)
ISA_5 .... Internal Surface Area of Lung at Volume of 5 Liters [*Medicine*] (MAE)
ISA + 21 .... International Social Affiliation of Women Airline Pilots [*Later, ISWAP*] (EA)
ISAA .... Institute of Shops Acts Administration [*British*] (BI)
ISAA .... Insurance Service Association of America [*Later, Assurex International*] (EA)
ISAA .... Intercollegiate Soccer Association of America (EA)
ISAAA .... International Service for the Acquisition of Agri-Biotech Applications
ISAAC .... Information System for Advanced Academic Computing (IID)
ISAAC .... Integrated System for Automated Acquisition and Control
ISAAC .... International Society for Alternative and Augmentative Communication (EA)
ISAAI .... Illinois Society of Allergy, Asthma, and Immunology (SRA)
IS/A AMPE ... Inter-Service Agency Automated Message Processing Exchange
ISAARE .... Information System for Adaptive, Assistive, and Rehabilitation Equipment [*For the handicapped*]
ISAB .... Institute for the Study of Animal Behavior (BARN)
ISABC .... International Society Against Breast Cancer (EAIO)
ISABEL .... ISO [*International Organization for Standardization*] Status Accumulating Binaries Extraordinary Logic [*Using*]
ISABP .... International South Atlantic Buoy Program [*Marine science*] (OSRA)
ISABPS .... Integrated Submarine Automated Broadcasting Processing System (MCD)
ISABR .... International Society for Animal Blood Group Research [*Australia*] (EAIO)
ISABR .... International Society for Animal Genetics [*Australia*] (EAIO)
ISABS .... Integrated Submarine Automated Broadcast Processing System [*Navy*] (CAAL)
ISAC .... Industrial Safety Advisory Council [*British*]
ISAC .... Industrial Security Association of Canada
ISAC .... Industry Sector Advisory Committee [*Established by Trade Reform Act for industry-to-government advice*]
ISAC .... Industry Sector Advisory Council [*Department of Commerce*] (WPI)
ISAC .... Information Systems Advisory Committee
ISAC .... In Service, Active [*Vessel status*] [*Navy*] (DNAB)
ISAC .... Institute for the Study of American Cultures (EA)
ISAC .... Instrumentation System Assessment Center (MCD)
ISAC .... International Security Affairs Committee
ISAC .... International Society for Analytical Cytology (EAIO)
ISAC .... International Society for Autistic Children [*Defunct*] (EA)
ISAC .... Interuniversity Southeast Asia Committee [*of the Association for Asia*]
ISACA .... Information Systems Audit and Control Association (NTPA)
ISACC .... Initial Satellite Command and Control Center (MCD)
ISACCC .... Initial Satellite Communications Control Center (MCD)
ISACMETU ... International Secretariat of Arts, Communications Media, and Entertainment TradeUnions (EAIO)
ISACS .... Independent Schools Association of the Central States (AEBS)
ISAD .... Information Science and Automation Division [*Later, LITA*] [*American Library Association*]
ISAD .... Integrate Sample and Dump [*Telecommunications*] (IAA)
ISADC .... Interim Standard Airborne Digital Computer (MCD)
ISADH .... Inappropriate Secretion of Antidiuretic Hormone [*Endocrinology*] (MAE)
ISADPM .... International Society for the Abolition of Data Processing Machines (EA)
ISADS .... Innovative Strategic Aircraft Design Studies (IEEE)
ISAE .... Internacia Scienca Asocio Esperantista [*International Association of Esperanto-Speaking Scientists*] [*Oslo, Norway*] (EA)
ISAE .... International Society for AIDS Education (EA)
Isae .... Isaeus [*Fourth century BC*] [*Classical studies*] (OCD)
ISAeM .... International Society for Aerosols in Medicine [*See also IGAeM*] (EAIO)
ISAF .... Intermediate Super-Abrasion Furnace
ISAF .... Isotopic Source Adjustable Fissometer [*Nuclear energy*] (NRCH)
IsAF .... Israeli Air Force
ISAG .... IGOSS [*Integrated Global Ocean Services System*] Scientific Advisory Group [*Marine science*] (OSRA)
ISAG .... International Society for Animal Genetics (HGEN)
ISAG .... Office of the Auditor General, Springfield, IL [*Library symbol Library of Congress*] (LCLS)
ISAGA .... International Simulation and Gaming Association (EA)
ISAGE .... International Symposium on Antarctic Glaciological Exploration
ISAGEX .... International Satellite Geodesy Experiment
ISAGL .... International Shipmasters Association of the Great Lakes
ISAGUG .... International Software AG Users Group (EA)
ISAI .... Independent Schools Association [*British*]
ISAI .... Independent Schools Association Inc. (AIE)
ISAI .... ISA [*Instruments, Systems and Automation*] International (ACII)
ISAKOS .... International Society of Arthroscopy, Knee Surgery and Orthopaedic Sports Medicine (NTPA)
ISal .... Bryan-Bennett Public Library, Salem, IL [*Library symbol Library of Congress*] (LCLS)
ISAL .... Information System Access Lines [*Computer science*]
ISALC .... International Society of Animal License Collectors (EA)
ISalCD .... Selmaville Community Consolidated District 10, Salem, IL [*Library symbol Library of Congress*] (LCLS)
ISALPA .... Incorporated Society of Auctioneers and Landed Property Agents [*British*] (ILCA)
ISAM .... Indexed Sequential Access Method [*Pronounced "i-sam"*] [*Computer science*]
ISAM .... Index Sequential Access Method [*Telecommunications*] (ACRL)
ISAM .... Infant of Substance-Abusing Mother [*Pediatrics*]
ISAM .... Institute for Studies in American Music (EA)
ISAM .... Integrated Switching and Multiplexing [*IBM Corp.*]
ISAM .... International Society for Aerosols in Medicine (EAIO)
ISAM .... Intravenous Streptokinase in Acute Myocardial Infarction [*Cardiology study*]
ISAM .... Israeli Society for the Application of Mathematics (MCD)
ISAMS .... Improved Stratospheric and Mesospheric Sounder (MCD)
ISan .... Sandwich Township Public Library, Sandwich, IL [*Library symbol Library of Congress*] (LCLS)
ISanCH .... Sandwich Community Hospital, Sandwich, IL [*Library symbol Library of Congress*] (LCLS)
IS & CG .... Information Systems and Communications Group (HGAA)
IS&DN .... Illustrated Sporting & Dramatic News [*A publication*] (WDAA)
ISandSD .... Sandoval Community Unit School District 501, Sandoval, IL [*Library symbol Library of Congress*] (LCLS)
IS & T .... Industry, Science, and Technology
IS & T .... Innovative Science and Technology (DOMA)
IS&T .... Society for Imaging Science and Technology (NTPA)

ISanH..........　Lynn G. Haskin School, Sandwich, IL [*Library symbol Library of Congress*] (LCLS)

ISanHS ....　Sandwich Community High School, Sandwich, IL [*Library symbol Library of Congress*] (LCLS)

ISanJS ....　Sandwich Junior High School, Sandwich, IL [*Library symbol Library of Congress*] (LCLS)

ISanP...........　Prairie View School, Sandwich, IL [*Library symbol Library of Congress*] (LCLS)

I-SANTA.......　Industrial Stapling and Nailing Technical Association (EA)

ISANTA ....　International Staple, Nail, and Tool Association (EA)

ISanW..........　W. W. Woodbury School, Sandwich, IL [*Library symbol Library of Congress*] (LCLS)

ISAO ....　International Society for Artificial Organs (EA)

ISAP.............　Individual System Automation Plans [*Military*]

ISAP.............　Information Sort and Predict

ISAP.............　Institute for the Study of Animal Problems [*Defunct*] (EA)

ISAP.............　Instituto Sudamericano del Petroleo [*South American Petroleum Institute*]

ISAP.............　Integrated Safety Assessment Program [*Nuclear energy*] (NRCH)

ISAP.............　Interactive Survey Analysis Package (IAA)

ISAP.............　International School Art Program [*Defunct*]

ISAP.............　International Society for Adolescent Psychiatry (NTPA)

ISAP.............　International Society of Art and Psychopathology [*Paris, France*] (EA)

ISAPA ....　International Screen Advertising Producer's Association [*Defunct*] (EA)

ISAPC ....　Incorporated Society of Authors, Playwrights, and Composers (BARN)

ISAPI ....　Internet Server API [*All-Purpose Interface*] [*Microsoft and Process Software Corp.*] [*Computer science*]

ISAPI ....　Internet Server Application Program Interface [*Computer science*] (IGQR)

ISAPI ....　Internet Services API [*Computer science*]

ISAR ....　Information Storage and Retrieval [*Computer science*] (DIT)

ISAR ....　Institute for Soviet-American Relations (EA)

ISAR ....　International Society for Animal Rights (EA)

ISAR ....　International Society for Astrological Research (EA)

ISAR ....　Inter-Seamount Acoustic Range

ISAR ....　Inverse Synthetic Aperture RADAR [*Navy*] (ANA)

ISARC ....　Installation Shipping and Receiving Capability [*Army*] (AABC)

ISAS ....　Illinois State Academy of Science (PDAA)

ISAS ....　Infrared Small Astronomical Spacecraft

ISAS ....　Institute of Space and Aeronautical Science [*Japan*]

ISAS ....　Integrated Smart Artillery Synthesis (RDA)

ISAS ....　Integrated Spacecraft Avionics System (IAA)

ISAS ....　International Society of African Scientists (EA)

ISAS ....　Isotopic Source Assay System

ISAS ....　Iterative Single Wavelength Anomalous Scattering [*Crystallography*]

ISASC ....　International Society of Antique Scale Collectors (EA)

ISASI ....　International Society of Air Safety Investigators (EA)

ISASNP........　International Symposium on Aerospace Nuclear Propulsion (MCD)

ISAST...........　International Society for the Arts, Sciences, and Technology (EA)

ISAT.............　Initial Surface Absorption Test

ISAT ....　International Society of Analytical Trilogy [*See also SITA*] [*Sao Paulo, Brazil*] (EAIO)

ISAT ....　Interrupt Storage Area Table [*Computer science*] (OA)

ISAT ....　Invite, Show, and Test [*Military*] (SDI)

ISAUS ....　Indonesian Students Association in the United States (EA)

ISAUS ....　Iranian Students Association in the United States

ISAV ....　Institute of Sound and Vibration (MCD)

ISAV............　Instituto de Sistemas Audio-Visuales [*Institute of Audio-Visual Media*] [*Colombia*]

ISAVVT ....　International Symposium on the Aerodynamics and Ventilation of Vehicle Tunnels (PDAA)

ISAW ....　International Society of Aviation Writers

ISAZ.............　Isolation Accommodation Zone [*Geology*]

ISB...........　Illinois Baptist Historical Library, Springfield, IL [*Library symbol Library of Congress*] (LCLS)

ISB.............　Incentive Spirometry Breathing [*Medicine*] (DAVI)

ISB.............　Independent Sideband

ISB.............　Independent Society of Bricklayers [*A union*] [*British*]

ISB.............　Industry Service Bureaus

ISB.............　Information Services Branch [*SHAPE Technical Center*] [*The Hague, Netherlands*]

ISB.............　Information Services Branch [*Chalk River Nuclear Laboratories*] [*Atomic Energy of Canada Ltd.*] [*Information service or system*] (IID)

ISB.............　Information Systems Branch [*National Institutes of Health*] (IID)

ISB.............　Initial Staging Base [*Army*] (DOMA)

ISB.............　Institute of Scientific Business [*British*]

ISB.............　Institute of Small Business [*British*]

ISB.............　Intelligence and Security Board [*Military*] (MCD)

ISB.............　Intelligence Systems Branch [*Military*] (IAA)

ISB.............　Interchangeability Survey Board

ISB.............　Interchange Financial Services Corp. [*Formerly, Interchange State Bank*] [*AMEX symbol*] (SPSG)

ISB.............　Interchange Finl Svcs [*AMEX symbol*] (TTSB)

ISB.............　Intermediate Sideband (NATG)

ISB.............　Intermediate Staging Base

ISB.............　Intermediate Support Base [*Military*] (NVT)

ISB.............　Internationaler Studentenbund [*International Union of Students*]

ISB.............　International Sinabarb [*Vancouver Stock Exchange symbol*]

ISB.............　International Society of Bassists (EA)

ISB.............　International Society of Biometeorology [*See also SIB*] [*Zurich, Switzerland*] (EAIO)

ISB.............　International Society of Biorheology [*Germany*] (EAIO)

ISB.............　International Symposium on Biomembranes

ISB.............　Internet3D Space Builder

ISB.............　Interstate Tariff Bureau, Inc., Lakewood OH [*STAC*]

ISB.............　Investors Service Bureau [*Investment term*]

ISB.............　Islamabad/Rawalpindi [*Pakistan*] [*Airport symbol*] (OAG)

ISB.............　Nisab [*South Arabia*] [*Airport symbol*] (AD)

ISB.............　Southern Methodist University, Bridwell Library, Dallas, TX [*OCLC symbol*] (OCLC)

ISBA.............　Incorporated Society of British Advertisers [*British*]

ISBA.............　Independent Safety Board Act of 1974

ISBA.............　Independent Schools Bursars' Association [*British*]

ISBA.............　International Sea-Bed Authority [*Marine science*] [*United Nations*] (OSRA)

ISBA.............　International Ships-in-Bottles Association (EA)

ISBB.............　International Society of Bioclimatology and Biometeorology (IEEE)

ISBC.............　Infantry Squad Battle Course [*Army*]

ISBC.............　Institute of Certified Business Counselors (EA)

ISBC.............　Interdepartmental Savings Bond Committee [*Military*] (AABC)

ISBC.............　International Society of Bible Collectors (EA)

ISBD.............　International Soap Box Derby, Inc. (EA)

ISBD.............　International Standard Bibliographic Description [*Library of Congress*]

ISBD(A)........　International Standard Bibliographic Description - Antiquarian

ISBD(CM).....　International Standard Bibliographic Description for Cartographic Materials [*Library of Congress*]

ISBD(CP).....　International Standard Bibliographic Description (Component Parts)

ISBD(G).......　International Standard Bibliographic Description - General

ISBD(M).......　International Standard Bibliographic Description for Monographs [*Library of Congress*]

ISBD(NBM)...　International Standard Bibliographic Description for Non-Book Materials

ISBD(PM).....　International Standard Bibliographic Description for Printed Music

ISBD(S)........　International Standard Bibliographic Description for Serials [*Library of Congress*]

ISBE.............　Independent Small Business Employers of America (EA)

ISBE.............　International Society for Boundary Elements (EAIO)

ISBE.............　International Society for Business Education, US Chapter [*Reston, VA*] (EA)

ISBE.............　International Standard Bible Encyclopaedia [*A publication*] (BJA)

ISBEA...........　Independent Small Business Employers of America [*Later, ISBE*] (EA)

ISBF.............　Interactive Search of Bibliographic Files

ISBF.............　ISB Financial [*NASDAQ symbol*] (TTSB)

ISBF.............　ISB Financial Corp. [*NASDAQ symbol*] (SAG)

ISB Fn ....　ISB Financial Corp. [*Associated Press*] (SAG)

ISBGFH.......　International Society for British Genealogy and Family History (EA)

ISBI.............　International Savings Banks Institute [*See also IICE*] [*Geneva, Switzerland*] (EAIO)

ISBI.............　International Society for Burn Injuries (EAIO)

ISBIC............　Interservice Balkan Intelligence Committee [*World War II*]

ISBL.............　Information System Base Language

ISBL.............　Inside Battery Limits [*Chemical engineering*]

ISBM............　Institute for the Study of Business Markets [*Pennsylvania State University*] [*Research center*] (RCD)

ISBM............　International Society of Biophysical Medicine [*British*] (IRUK)

ISbM............　Motorola Communications Sector Library, Schaumburg, IL [*Library symbol*] [*Library of Congress*] (LCLS)

ISBN............　International Standard Book Number [*Library of Congress*]

ISBO............　Islamic States Broadcasting Organization [*Jeddah, Saudi Arabia*] (EAIO)

ISBP.............　International Society for Biochemical Pharmacology

ISBRA..........　International Society Biomedical Research on Alcoholism (EAIO)

ISBS.............　Integrated Small Business Software (NITA)

ISBS.............　International Specialized Books Services [*Book distributor*]

ISBT.............　International Society of Beverage Technologists (NTPA)

ISBT.............　International Society of Blood Transfusion (EA)

ISBX.............　Integrated Services Branch Exchange [*Telecommunications*] (OSI)

ISC..............　Concordia Theological Seminary, Springfield, IL [*Library symbol Library of Congress Obsolete*] (LCLS)

ISC..............　Duneland School Corp., Chesterton, IN [*OCLC symbol*] (OCLC)

ISc..............　Iconic Store, Central [*Psychophysiology*]

ISC..............　Idaho State College [*Later, Idaho State University*] (AEBS)

ISC..............　Idle Speed Control [*Automotive engineering*]

I-SC...........　Illinois Supreme Court, Springfield, IL [*Library symbol Library of Congress*] (LCLS)

ISC..............　Immune Spleen Cell

ISC..............　Immunoglobulin-Secreting Cell [*Medicine*] (DB)

ISC..............　Immunoglobulin-Secreting Cell (STED)

ISC..............　Imperial Service College [*British*]

ISC..............　Improved Submarine Communication (MCD)

ISC..............　Incorporated Staff Sight-Singing College [*London*]

ISC..............　Independent Search Consultants [*An association*] (EA)

ISC..............　Index of Status Characteristics

ISC..............　Indian Staff Corps [*British*] (ROG)

ISC..............　Indirect Strike Control

ISC..............　Individual Soldier's Computer [*Army*] (RDA)

ISC..............　Indoor Sports Club (EA)

ISC..............　Industrial Source Complex [*Environmental science*] (GFGA)

ISC..............　Industrial Support Contractor (KSC)

ISC..............　Industry Steering Council (AAEL)

ISC..............　Inertial Start Command

ISC..............　Infiltration Surveillance Center (CINC)

ISC..............　Information Science Center (MCD)

ISC..............　Information Science Corporation (NITA)

ISC............... Information Services Control Branch [*Control Commission for Germany*] [*World War II*]
ISC............... Information Services of Cranston [*Information service or system*] (IID)
ISC............... Information Society of Canada (MCD)
ISC............... Information Specialties Corp. (IID)
ISC............... Information Systems Command [*DoD*]
ISC............... Information Systems Committee [*Universities Funding Council*] (AIE)
ISC............... Infrared Sightline Control
ISC............... Infrastructure Special Committee [*NATO*] (NATG)
ISC............... Initial Slope Circuit [*Telecommunications*] (OA)
ISC............... Initial Software Configuration Map (MCD)
isc............... Initial Software Configuration Map (NAKS)
ISC............... Initial Student Characteristics
ISC............... In Situ Combustion [*Engineering*]
ISC............... Insoluble Collagen [*Biochemistry*]
ISC............... Inspection and Safety Center [*Military*]
ISC............... Institute for the Study of Conflict [*British*]
ISC............... Instruction Staticizing Control (IEEE)
ISC............... Instrumentation System Corp. (MCD)
ISC............... Instrumentation Systems Center [*University of Wisconsin - Madison*] [*Research center*] (RCD)
ISC............... Insulated Signal Coupler (IAA)
ISC............... Integrated Stage Concept (MCD)
ISC............... Integrated Storage Control
ISC............... Intelligence Subject Code
ISC............... Intelligence Support Center
ISC............... Intelligent Synchronous Controller [*Computer science*] (NITA)
ISC............... Intelligent Systems Corp.
ISC............... Intensive Supportive Care (STED)
ISC............... Interactive Sciences Corp. [*Information service or system*] (IID)
ISC............... Interagency Staff Committee on Public Law 480 [*Department of Agriculture*] (EGAO)
ISC............... Inter-American Society of Cardiology [*Mexico City, Mexico*] (EAIO)
ISC............... Interceptor Subsystem Controller
ISC............... Intercompany Services Coordination [*Telecommunications*] (TEL)
ISC............... Intercomponent Subcontractor (MCD)
ISC............... Interdisciplinary Scientific Commission [*COSPAR*]
ISC............... Interface Signal Chart
ISC............... International Cruiseships [*Vancouver Stock Exchange symbol*]
ISC............... International Salmonella Center
ISC............... International Salon of Cartoons (EA)
ISC............... International Scientific Publications [*Tel Aviv, Israel*]
ISC............... International Security Conference and Exposition (ITD)
ISC............... International Security Council (EA)
ISC............... International Seismological Centre [*ICSU*] [*Newbury, Berkshire, England*] (EAIO)
ISC............... International Serials Catalogue [*A publication*]
ISC............... International Sericultural Commission [*See also CSI*] [*La Mulatiere, France*] (EAIO)
ISC............... International Signal and Control [*Army*]
ISC............... International Society for Chronobiology (EA)
ISC............... International Society of Cardiology [*Later, ISFC*]
ISC............... International Society of Chemotherapy [*Bad Heilbrunn, Federal Republic of Germany*] (EAIO)
ISC............... International Society of Citriculture (EA)
ISC............... International Society of Copoclephologists [*British*] (EAIO)
ISC............... International Society of Cryosurgery [*Turin, Italy*] (EAIO)
ISC............... International Society of Cryptozoology (EA)
ISC............... International Softball Congress (EA)
ISC............... International Space Congress
ISC............... International Space Corp.
ISC............... International Statistical Classification
ISC............... International Student Conference
ISC............... International Sugar Council [*London*] [*Later, ISO*]
ISC............... International Supply Committee [*World War II*]
ISC............... International Supreme Council of World Masons (EA)
ISC............... International Switching Center [*Communications*]
ISC............... International Symposium on Chemiluminescence
ISC............... Inter-Service Communication [*British World War II*]
ISC............... Inter-Service Sports Council [*Military*]
ISC............... Interservice Support Code [*Military*]
ISC............... Inter-Shift Coordination [*Medicine*] (DMAA)
ISC............... Intersociety Committee on Methods for Air Sampling and Analysis
ISC............... Interstage Section Container
ISC............... Interstate Commerce
ISC............... Interstellar Communications (AAG)
ISC............... Interstitial Cells [*Histology*]
ISC............... Inter-System Communication (NITA)
ISC............... Inter-System Crossing [*Chemical Kinetics*]
ISC............... Interval Selection Circuit
ISC............... Interview Schedule for Children
ISC............... Intrasite Cabling (CET)
ISC............... Intrinsic Stimulating Activity (STED)
ISC............... Intuit Services Corp.
ISC............... Invention Submission Corp. [*Information service or system*] (IID)
ISC............... Iowa Safety Council (SRA)
ISC............... Iowa State College of Agriculture and Mechanic Arts [*Later, Iowa State University*] (MCD)
ISC............... Irreversibly Sickled Cell [*Hematology*]
ISC............... Island Air Charters, Inc. [*ICAO designator*] (FAAC)
ISC............... Isles Of Scilly [*England*] [*Airport symbol*] (OAG)
ISC............... Italian Space Commission
ISC............... Item Status Code (NATG)
ISCA............ Idle Speed Control Actuator [*Automotive engineering*]

ISCA............ Independent Safety Consultants Association (DBA)
ISCA............ Industrial Specialty Chemical Association (EA)
ISCA............ Information Systems Consultants Association (NTPA)
ISCA............ Interest Standby Credit Arrangement
ISCA............ Interlake Sailing Class Association (EA)
ISCA............ International Sailing Craft Association [*Exeter, Devonshire, England*] (EAIO)
ISCA............ International Scientific Collectors Association (EA)
ISCA............ International Senior Citizens Association (EA)
ISCA............ International Shooting Coaches Association (EA)
ISCA............ International Show Car Association (EA)
ISCA............ International Society of Copier Artists (EA)
ISCA............ International Speedway Corp. [*NASDAQ symbol*] (SAG)
ISCA............ International Sunfish Class Association (EA)
ISCA............ Ionization Spectroscopy for Chemical Analysis (DB)
ISCA............ Irish Setter Club of America (EA)
ISCAC.......... Interstate Collegiate Athletic Conference (PSS)
IScAF........... United States Air Force, Base Library, Scott AFB, IL [*Library symbol Library of Congress*] (LCLS)
IScAF-A........ United States Air Force, Airlift Operations School, Scott Air Force Base, IL [*Library symbol Library of Congress*] (LCLS)
IScAF-E........ United States Air Force, Environmental Technical Applications Center, Air Weather Service Technical Library, Scott Air Force Base, IL [*Library symbol Library of Congress*] (LCLS)
ISCAMPME...... Iodosuccinyl CAMP Tyrosine Methyl Ester [*Biochemistry*]
ISCAMS ...... Installation Standard Command Automated Data Processing Management System [*Army*]
ISCAN .... Inertialess Steerable Communications Antenna
ISCAN .... International Sanitary Convention for Air Navigation
ISCAS .... Integrated Submarine Communications Antenna System [*Navy*] (CAAL)
ISCAS .... International Symposium on Circuits and Systems [*IEEE*] (MCD)
ISCAY .... International Solidarity Committee with Algerian Youth
ISCB............ Interallied Staff Communications Board [*World War II*]
ISCB............ International Society for Cell Biology [*Later, IFCB*] (ASF)
ISCB............ International Society for Classical Bibliography [*Paris, France*] (EAIO)
ISCB............ International Society for Clinical Biostatistics (EAIO)
ISCBA.......... Insulating Siding Core Board Association [*Defunct*] (EA)
ISCBMC ...... International Single Comb Black Minorca Club (EA)
ISCC............ International Service Coordination Center [*Communications*]
ISCC............ International Somali Cat Club
ISCC............ International Standard Commodity Classification of All Goods and Services
ISCC............ Inter-Society Color Council (EA)
ISCC............ Inter-Society Cytology Council [*Later, American Society of Cytology - ASC*]
ISCC............ Interstate Solar Coordination Council (EA)
ISCC............ Iranian Students Counseling Center (EA)
ISCCED .... Independent Sector Coordinating Committee on Environment and Development (GNE)
ISCCP .... International Satellite Cloud Climatology Project
ISCD .... Interface Specification Control Document (KSC)
ISCD .... International Society for Community Development (EA)
ISCDD .... International Scheme for the Coordination of Dairy Development (EAIO)
ISCDP .... International Standing Committee on Distribution Problems [*International Water Supply Association*]
ISCDS.......... International Stop Continental Drift Society [*Defunct*] (EA)
ISCE .... Institute for the Study of Conscious Evolution [*Defunct*] (EA)
ISCE .... International Society for a Complete Earth
ISCE .... International Society for Clinical Enzymology [*Hanover, Federal Republic of Germany*] (EAIO)
ISCE .... International Society of Chemical Ecology (EA)
ISCE .... International Society of Christian Endeavor (EA)
ISCE .... Interstate Substitute Cost Estimate [*Federal Highway Administration*]
ISCEBS .... International Society of Certified Employee Benefit Specialists [*Brookfield, WI*] (EA)
ISCED .... International Society of Continuing Education in Dentistry [*See also SIECD*] [*Brussels, Belgium*] (EAIO)
ISCED .... International Standard Classification of Education (MCD)
ISCEH .... International Society for Clinical and Experimental Hypnosis [*Charles University*] (EA)
ISCERG .... International Society for Clinical Electroretinography
ISCET .... International Society of Certified Electronics Technicians (EA)
ISCF............ Industrial Sentence Completion Form [*Psychology*]
ISCF............ Inter-School Christian Fellowship [*British*] (BI)
ISCF............ Interstitial Cell Fluid (DMAA)
ISCG .... Institute of School and College Governors [*British*] (EAIO)
ISCG .... Integrated Sys Consulting Gp [*NASDAQ symbol*] (TTSB)
ISCG .... Integrated Systems Consulting Group, Inc. [*NASDAQ symbol*] (SAG)
ISCh............ Incorporated Society of Chiropodists [*British*] (DI)
ISch............ Steger-South Chicago Heights Library District, South Chicago Heights, IL [*Library symbol Library of Congress*] (LCLS)
ISCHDR......... Inter-Society Commission for Heart Disease Resources
ISCHE .... International Standing Conference for the History of Education (AIE)
ISCI............ Information Systems Consultants, Inc. [*Information service or system*] (IID)
ISCII........... International Standard Code for Information Interchange (NATG)
ISCJ............ International Ski Club of Journalists
ISCL............ Interim Status Compliance Letter [*Environmental Protection Agency*] (GFGA)
ISCLC.......... International Symposium on Column Liquid Chromatography [*1986*] [*San Francisco, CA*]
ISCLT.......... Industrial Source Complex Long-Term Model [*Environmental Protection Agency*] (GFGA)

ISCLT........ International Society for Clinical Laboratory Technology (EA)
ISCM........ International Society for Contemporary Music (EA)
ISCM........ International Society of Cybernetic Medicine (EA)
ISCME........ International Society for Computational Methods in Engineering (EAIO)
ISCN........ International System for Human Cytogenetic Nomenclature
ISCO........ Illinois Superconductor [*NASDAQ symbol*] (TTSB)
ISCO........ Illinois Superconductor Corp. [*NASDAQ symbol*] (SAG)
ISCO........ Independent Schools Careers Organisation [*British*]
ISCO........ Indicated Specific Carbon Monoxide
ISCO........ Initial Systems Checkout
ISCO........ Instrumentation Specialties Co.
ISCO........ International Society of Corvette Owners
ISCO........ International Standard Classification of Occupations (WDAA)
Isco........ Isco, Inc. [*Associated Press*] (SAG)
ISCO........ Istituto Nazionale per lo Studio della Congiuntura [*Data Resources, Inc.*] [*Database*]
ISCOM........ Immunostimulatory Complex [*Immunochemistry*]
ISCOM........ Island Commander
ISCOMADEIRA... Island Commander Madeira (AABC)
ISCOMAZORES... Island Commander Azores
ISCOMBERMUDA... Island Commander Bermuda
ISCOMFAROES... Island Commander Faroes
ISCOMGREENLAND... Island Commander Greenland
ISCOMICELAND... Island Commander Iceland
ISCOMS........ Immunity-Stimulating Complexes (DB)
ISCOR........ South African Iron & Steel Corp.
ISCORE........ Intelligence Score (MCD)
ISCOS........ Institute for Security and Cooperation in Outer Space (EA)
ISCOSS........ International Symposium on the Chemistry of the Organic Solid State
ISCP........ India Study Circle for Philately (EA)
ISCP........ Infection Surveillance and Control Program [*Medicine*] (DMAA)
ISCP........ Installation Spill Contingency Plan [*DoD*] (AFIT)
ISCP........ Integrated Subsystem Calibration Plan (SAA)
ISCP........ Intermediate Sodium Characterization Package [*Nuclear energy*] (NRCH)
ISCP........ International Society for Chinese Philosophy (EA)
ISCP........ International Society for Comparative Psychology (EA)
ISCP........ International Society of Clinical Pathology [*Later, WASP*]
ISCP........ International Society of Comparative Pathology (DMAA)
ISCP........ Inventory Stock Cataloging Program
ISCPET........ Illinois Statewide Curriculum Study Center in the Preparation of Secondary School English Teachers
ISCPLN........ International Society of Psychiatric Consultation Liaison Nurses (NTPA)
ISCPP........ International Society of Crime Prevention Practitioners (EAIO)
ISCPVS........ Istituto Sindacale per la Cooperazione con i Paesi in Via di Sviluppo [*Trade Union Institute for Cooperation with Developing Countries*] [*Italy*] (EAIO)
ISC/R........ Individual Soldier's Computer/Radio [*Army*] (INF)
ISCRE........ International Symposium on Chemical Reaction Engineering
ISCRO........ Industrial Security Clearance Review Office [*DoD*]
ISCRP........ International Society of City and Regional Planners [*See also AIU*]
ISCS........ Inferred Self-Concept Scale [*Psychology*] (DHP)
ISCS........ Information Service Computer System (DIT)
ISCS........ Integrated Submarine Communications System (MCD)
ISCS........ Interim Sea Control Ship (MCD)
ISCS........ Intermediate Science Curriculum Study
ISCS........ International Sand Collectors Society (EA)
ISCS........ International Society for Cardiovascular Surgery (DAVI)
ISCS........ International Society of Communications Specialists (EA)
ISCS........ International Stamp Collectors Society (EA)
ISCS........ International Symposium on Cooling Systems (PDAA)
ISCS........ Interservice/Cross Service [*Support*]
ISCSA........ Industrial Sports Clubs Secretaries' Association [*British*] (BI)
ISCSC........ International Society for the Comparative Study of Civilizations (EA)
ISCSH........ Independent Scientific Committee on Smoking and Health [*British*]
ISCST........ Industrial Source Complex Short-Term Model [*Environmental Protection Agency*] (GFGA)
ISCST2........ Industrial Source Complex Short-Term Model Version 2
ISCSTM........ Industrial Source Complex Short-Term Model (COE)
ISCT........ Inner Seal Collar Tool [*Nuclear energy*] (NRCH)
ISCT........ International Society for Cleaning Technicians (NTPA)
ISCT........ Ito System Color Television [*Japan*]
ISCTF........ Interservice Committee on Technical Facilities [*Aerospace*] (AAG)
ISCTP........ International Study Commission for Traffic Police
ISC/USO........ Intercompany Services Coordination/Universal Service Order [*Telecommunications*] (TEL)
ISCV........ Idle Speed Control Valve [*Exhaust emissions*] [*Automotive engineering*]
ISCVS........ International Society for Cardiovascular Surgery (EA)
ISCVS........ International Society of Cardiovascular Surgeons
ISCVS-NA........ International Society for Cardiovascular Surgery - North American Chapter (NTPA)
ISCWFD........ Intergovernmental Steering Committee on World Food Day (EA)
ISCWQT........ International Standing Committee on Water Quality and Treatment [*International Water Supply Association*]
ISCX........ Industrial Scientific [*NASDAQ symbol*] (TTSB)
ISCX........ Industrial Scientific Corp. [*NASDAQ symbol*] (SAG)
ISCYRA........ International Star Class Yacht Racing Association (EA)
ISD........ Cabot Corp., Stellite Division, Kokomo, IN [*OCLC symbol*] (OCLC)
ISD........ IBM [*International Business Machines Corp.*] Standard Data (IAA)
ISD........ Immunosuppressive Drug [*Medicine*] (DMAA)
ISD........ Independent Sealing Distributors (NTPA)
ISD........ Indian Stores Depot [*British military*] (DMA)
ISD........ Induction System Deposit
ISD........ Information Services Department [*Ohio State University Libraries*] [*Columbus*] [*Information service or system*] (IID)
ISD........ Information Services Division [*Scottish Health Service*] [*Research center*]
ISD........ Information Services Division [*Mississippi State Research and Development Center*] [*Information service or system*] (IID)
ISD........ Information Structure Design
ISD........ Information System Development [*Telecommunications*] (TEL)
ISD........ Information Systems Department [*Franklin Research Center, Inc.*] [*Information service or system*] (IID)
ISD........ Information Systems Division [*Ori, Inc.*] [*Bethesda, MD*]
ISD........ Infrared Suppression Device
ISD........ Inhibited Sexual Desire [*Sex therapy*]
ISD........ Initial Search Depth
ISD........ Initial Selection Done
ISD........ Initial Ship Design
ISD........ Innovative Software Design [*South Africa ICAO designator*] (FAAC)
ISD........ Insert Subcaliber Device [*Weaponry*] (INF)
ISD........ Installation Specification Drawing (MCD)
ISD........ Installation Start Date (CET)
ISD........ Installation Supply Division [*Military*] (AABC)
ISD........ Institute for Security Design (EA)
ISD........ Institute of Single Dynamics (EA)
ISD........ Institute of Surplus Dealers (EA)
ISD........ Instructional System Design Model
ISD........ Instructional Systems Design (DOM)
ISD........ Instructional Systems Development (AFM)
ISD........ Integrated Symbolic Debugger [*Computer science*] (IID)
ISD........ Integrated Systems Demonstrator (MCD)
ISD........ Intensity, Severity, and Discharge [*Medicine*] (DHSM)
ISD........ Interactive Screen Definition (IAA)
ISD........ Interface State Density (AAEL)
ISD........ Interim Simulation Display [*FAA*] (TAG)
ISD........ Interim Status Document [*Environmental Protection Agency*] (GFGA)
ISD........ Intermediate School District (AEE)
ISD........ Intermediate Storage Device
ISD........ Internal Security Division [*Abolished 1973; functions transferred to Criminal Division*] [*Department of Justice*]
ISD........ Internal Symbol Dictionary [*Computer science*] (OA)
ISD........ International Society of Dermatology: Tropical, Geographic, and Ecologic (EA)
ISD........ International Society of Differentiation (EA)
ISD........ International Society of Dramatists (EA)
ISD........ International Subscriber Dialing [*Later, IDD*] [*Telecommunications*]
ISD........ Intersystem Designation (CAAL)
ISD........ Invoice Shipping Documentation [*Business term*]
ISD........ Isosorbide Dinitrite [*Coronary vasodilator*]
ISD........ MENU - the International Software Database [*Menu the International Software Database Corp.*] [*Information service or system*] (CRD)
ISD........ Winner, SD [*Location identifier FAA*] (FAAL)
ISDA........ Indian Self-Determination Act [*1975*]
ISDA........ Institute for the Study of Drug Addiction [*Later, ISDM*] (EA)
ISDA........ International Sculpteurs et Designers Associes [*Paris, France*] (EAIO)
ISDA........ International Security and Detective Alliance (EA)
ISDA........ International Swap Dealers' Association
ISDA........ International Swaps and Derivatives Association (ECON)
ISDAIC........ International Staff Disaster Assistance Information Coordinator [*NATO*] (NATG)
ISDB........ Initial Subordinate Dominates Bystander [*Sociology*]
ISDB........ Integrated Satellite Communications Database (COE)
ISDB........ International Society of Development Biologists [*Formerly, IIE*] [*Nogent-Sur-Marne, France*]
ISDC........ Indiana State Data Center [*Indiana State Library*] [*Indianapolis*] [*Information service or system*] (IID)
ISDC........ Intense Sample Data Collection System (MCD)
ISDCC........ Illinois State Data Center Cooperative [*Illinois State Bureau of the Budget*] [*Springfield*] [*Information service or system*] (IID)
ISDCI........ International Society of Developmental and Comparative Immunology (EA)
ISDD........ Information Systems Development Division (SAA)
ISDD........ Institute for the Study of Drug Dependence [*London*]
ISDE........ Integral Square Delay Error (IAA)
ISDE........ International Seismic Data Exchange [*Geology*]
ISDE........ International Six Days Enduro [*Motorcycle racing*]
ISDE........ International Society for Diseases of the Esophagus [*Tokyo, Japan*] (EAIO)
ISDF........ Impact Short Delay Fuze (MCD)
ISDF........ Intermediate Sodium Disposal Facility [*Nuclear energy*] (NRCH)
ISDF........ International Shooter Development Fund [*National Rifle Association*]
ISDG........ Information Science Discussion Group [*British*] (NITA)
ISDI........ Information Storage Devices [*NASDAQ symbol*] (TTSB)
ISDI........ Information Storage Devices, Inc. [*NASDAQ symbol*] (SAG)
ISDI........ Insulated Steel Door Institute (NTPA)
ISDI........ International Social Development Institute
ISDI........ International Society of Dietetic Including All Infant and Young Children Food Industries (EAIO)
ISDI........ International Special Dietary Foods Industries [*France*] (EAIO)
ISDIN........ Isosorbide Dinitrate [*Also, ISDN*] [*Coronary vasodilator*]
ISDM........ Indian Self-Determination Memorandum [*Indian Health Service*] [*Department of Health and Human Services*] (GFGA)
ISDM........ Institute for the Study of Drug Misuse [*Formerly, ISDA*] (EA)
ISDM........ International Society for Disaster Medicine (EA)
ISDN........ Information Service Data Network [*Telecommunications*]
ISDN........ Institute for the Study of Developing Nations (EA)

ISDN	Integrated Services Digital Network [*Telecommunications*]
ISDN	International Society for Developmental Neuroscience (EA)
ISDN	International Standard Data Network (NITA)
ISDN	Isosorbide Dinitrate [*Also, ISDIN*] [*Coronary vasodilator*]
ISDN	It Still Does Nothing [*Facetious translation for ISDN - Integrated Services Digital Network*]
ISDNA	Inverse Standard Deviation of Nucleolar Area [*Oncology*]
ISDO	Institute for Systems Design and Optimization
ISDO	International Staff Duty Officer [*NATO*] (NATG)
ISDOS	Information Systems Design Optimization System
ISDP	Income Survey Development Program [*Department of Health and Human Services*] (GFGA)
ISDP	International Society for Developmental Psychobiology (EA)
ISDPG	Independent Social Democratic Party of Germany [*Political party*] (EAIO)
ISDRA	International Sled Dog Racing Association (EA)
ISDS	Inadvertent Separation and Destruct System [*Aerospace*]
ISDS	Institute for Social Dance Studies [*Defunct*] (EA)
ISDS	Institute for the Study of Defects in Solids [*State University of New York at Albany*] [*Research center*] (RCD)
ISDS	Instructional Systems Development Squadron
ISDS	Instruction Set Design System (PDAA)
ISDS	Integrated Ship Design System (IEEE)
ISDS	Integrated Software Development System
ISDS	Integrated Switched Data Service [*Telecommunications*] (TEL)
ISDS	Intelligence Support Display System [*Military*] (MCD)
ISDS	International Serials Data System [*Database*] (EA)
ISDS	International Sheep Dog Society [*Bedford, England*] (EAIO)
ISDS	International Society of Dermatologic Surgery (EA)
ISDSI	Insulated Steel Door Systems Institute (EA)
ISDS/IC	International Center of the International Serials Data System [*UNESCO*] (PDAA)
ISDT	Instructional Systems Development Team [*Air Force*]
ISDT	International Six Days Trial [*Motorcycling*]
ISDT	International Symposium on Dredging Technology (PDAA)
ISDTS	Iron and Steel Dressers Trade Society [*A union*] [*British*]
ISDU	International Standard Density Unit (DGA)
ISDX	Integrated Services Digital Exchange [*British*]
ISE	Illogical Sequence Error (IAA)
ISE	Independent Scheduled Exercises
ISE	Independent Ship Exercise [*Navy*]
ISE	Indiana State University, Evansville Campus, Evansville, IN [*OCLC symbol*] (OCLC)
ISE	Indian Service of Engineers [*British*]
ISE	Individual Ship Exercises [*Navy*]
ISE	Individual Soldier Energy [*Military*] (RDA)
ISE	Induced Surface Effect
ISE	Influence Strategies Exercise [*Test*] (TMMY)
ISE	Information in Science Extension [*INTERBRIGHT database*] [*Budapest, Hungary*] [*Information service or system*] (IID)
ISE	Information Services to Education [*American Society for Information Science*]
ISE	Inhibited Sexual Excitement [*Medicine*] (DMAA)
ISE	Initial Support Element (MCD)
ISE	In-Service Education (ADA)
ISE	In-Service Engineering [*Navy*]
ISE	Installation Support and Evaluation (AAG)
ISE	Institute for Software Engineering (EA)
ISE	Institute of Sanitary Engineers [*British*] (DAS)
ISE	Institute of Social Ethics (EA)
ISE	Institution of Sales Engineers [*British*] (BI)
ISE	Institution of Structural Engineers [*British*] (EAIO)
ISE	Instrumentation Suitability Evaluation (MCD)
ISE	In System Evaluator [*National Semiconductor Company*] (NITA)
ISE	Integral Squared Error
ISE	Integrated Safeguards Experiment
ISE	Integrated Solid Effect (AAEL)
ISE	Integrated Space Experiment (MCD)
ISE	Integrated Storage Element [*Computer science*]
ISE	Intelligence Support Element [*Military*] (MCD)
ISE	Interactive Software Engineering
ISE	Intercept System Environment [*Army*] (AABC)
ISE	Intermountain Stock Exchange [*Salt Lake City, UT*]
ISE	International Semi-Tech Microelectronics, Inc. [*Toronto Stock Exchange symbol*]
ISE	International Society for Electrostimulation (EA)
ISE	International Society of Electrochemistry [*Graz, Austria*] (EA)
ISE	International Society of Endocrinology (EA)
ISE	International Society of Endoscopy
ISE	International Sports Exchange (EA)
ISE	International Stock Exchange
ISE	International Stock Exchange of the United Kingdom and the Republic of Ireland (DFIT)
ISE	Interpret Sign Error
ISE	Interrupt System Enable
ISE	Inter System Emulator (NITA)
ISE	Ion-Selective Electrode [*Instrumentation*]
ISE	Ion-Sensitive Electrode [*Instrumentation*] (IAA)
ISE	Ion-Specific Electrode (COE)
ISE	Irish School of Ecumenics
ISE	Ise [*Japan*] [*Seismograph station code, US Geological Survey*] (SEIS)
i-se--	Seychelles [*MARC geographic area code Library of Congress*] (LCCP)
ISEA	Industrial Safety Equipment Association [*Arlington, VA*] (EA)
ISEA	Industrial Safety Equipment Association, Inc.
ISEA	Inland Seas Education Association
ISEA	Inservice Engineering Agent [*Military*] (CAAL)
ISEA	Institute for Spiritual and Environmental Awareness (EA)
ISEA	International Stamp Exchange Association
ISEANSW	Institute of Senior Educational Administrators of New South Wales [*Australia*]
ISEAS	Institute of Southeast Asian Studies
ISEB	Independent Schools Education Board [*Later, National Association of IndependentSchools*] (AEBS)
ISEB	Interim Support Equipment Bulletin (MCD)
ISEC	Information System Electronic Command [*Army*]
ISEC	Information Systems Engineering Command (SSD)
ISEC	Institute for Social Economic Change
ISEC	International Solvent Extraction Conference [*Toronto, ON, 1977*] [*Canada*]
ISEC	International Standard Electric Corp. (NATG)
ISEC	International Statistical Education Centre [*India*]
ISECCo	International Space Exploration and Colonization Company [*An association*] (EA)
ISECS	International Society for Eighteenth-Century Studies [*See also SIEDS*] [*Oxford, England*] (EAIO)
ISED	Institute for Social Evaluation and Design
ISEE	Incident-Shock Equilibrium Expansion
ISEE	Initial System Evaluation Experiment [*Photovoltaic energy systems*]
ISEE	International Society for Engineering Education [*Austria*] (EAIO)
ISEE	International Society of Explosives Engineers (NTPA)
ISEE	International Sun-Earth Explorer [*NASA/ESRO satellite*]
ISEE	Sterling Vision [*NASDAQ symbol*] (TTSB)
ISEE	Sterling Vision, Inc. [*NASDAQ symbol*] (SAG)
ISEEM	International Society for Economic Evaluation of Medicines
ISEEP	Infrared Sensitive Element Evaluation Program
ISEERB	Inter-Service Environmental Education Review Board (BCP)
ISEF	International Science and Engineering Fair
ISEG	Independent Safety Engineering Group [*Nuclear energy*] (NRCH)
ISEGR	Institute of Social, Economic, and Governmental Research [*Later, ISER*] [*University of Alaska*]
ISEH	International Society of Experimental Hematology (NTPA)
ISEI	International Standard Engineering, Inc. (NATG)
ISEK	International Society of Electromyographic Kinesiology (EA)
ISEK	International Society of Electrophysiological Kinesiology [*Montreal, PQ*] (EA)
ISEL	Institute of Shipping Economics and Logistics [*See also ISL*] [*Bremen, Federal Republic of Germany*] (EAIO)
IS-ELEMENT	Insertion Sequence Element (DB)
ISELS	Institute of Society, Ethics, and Life Sciences [*Later, HC*] (EA)
ISEM	Immunosorbent Electron Microscopy
ISEM	Improved Standard Electronic Module (MHDB)
ISEM	Inspection/Review Specific Equipment Model (AAEL)
ISEM	Institute for the Study of Earth and Man [*Southern Methodist University*] [*Research center*] (RCD)
ISEM	Integrated Simulation Evaluation Model
ISEM	International Society for Ecological Modelling [*Vaerloese, Denmark*] (EAIO)
ISEMS	International Society of Emergency Medical Services (EA)
ISEN	Interactive Satellite Education Network [*IBM Corp.*] [*New York, NY*] (TSSD)
ISen	Seneca Public Library, Seneca, IL [*Library symbol Library of Congress*] (LCLS)
ISenMS	Miller Township Consolidated Community, School District 210, Seneca, IL [*Library symbol*] [*Library of Congress*] (LCLS)
ISEO	Institute of Shortening and Edible Oils (EA)
ISEP	Instructional Scientific Equipment Program [*National Science Foundation*]
ISEP	International Society for Educational Planning (EA)
ISEP	International Society for Evolutionary Protistology (EA)
ISEP	International Society of Esperantist-Philologists [*See also IUEFI*] (EAIO)
ISEP	International Standard Equipment Practice (MHDB)
ISEP	International Student Exchange Program [*United States Information Agency*]
ISEP	Interservice Experiments Program
ISEPS	International Sun-Earth Physics Satellite
ISEQ	Irish Stock Exchange Equity Index (NUMA)
ISER	InnoServe Technologies, Inc. [*NASDAQ symbol*] (SAG)
ISER	InnoServ Technologies [*NASDAQ symbol*] (TTSB)
ISER	Institute of Sex Education and Research [*British*] (DBA)
ISER	Institute of Social and Economic Research [*Memorial University of Newfoundland*] [*Research center Canada*] (RCD)
ISER	Institute of Social and Economic Research [*Formerly, ISEGR*] [*University of Alaska*]
ISER	Integral Systems Experimental Requirements (NRCH)
ISerSD	Serena Consolidated High School District 390, Serena, IL [*Library symbol Library of Congress*] (LCLS)
ISES	In Silentio et Spe [*In Silence and in Hope*] [*Motto of Bernhard, Prince of Anhalt (1572-96)*] [*Latin*]
ISES	Institute for Socioeconomic Studies (EA)
ISES	International Ship Electric Service Association [*British*] (EAIO)
ISES	International Society of Explosives Specialists (EA)
ISES	International Solar Energy Society [*Australia*] (EAIO)
ISES	International Special Events Society (EA)
ISES	Iron Safe Engineers' Society [*A union*] [*British*]
ISESCO	Islamic Educational, Scientific, and Cultural Organization [*United Nations*]

ISETAP......... Intergovernmental Science, Engineering, and Technology Advisory Panel [*National Science Foundation*]
ISETC.......... International Society for Environmental Toxicology and Cancer (EAIO)
ISETU.......... International Secretariat of Entertainment Trade Unions [*Geneva, Switzerland*]
ISEU............ International Stereotypers and Electrotypers Union [*Later, IPGCU*]
ISEW........... Index of Sustainable Economic Welfare (PS)
ISEW........... Intelligence, Security, and Electronic Warfare [*DoD*]
ISF.............. Alpha Park Public Library District, Pekin, IL [*OCLC symbol*] (OCLC)
ISF.............. Imperial Smelting Furnace [*Zinc and lead*]
ISF.............. Incremental Stretch Forming
ISF.............. Indian States Force [*British military*] (DMA)
ISF.............. Individual Store and Forward
ISF.............. Industrial Space Facility [*Space Industries, Inc.*]
ISF.............. Infant Soy Formula
ISF.............. Information Systems Factory (NITA)
ISF.............. Information Systems Flight [*Military*]
ISF.............. Infrasonic Frequency
ISF.............. Instrument Standards Foundation (ACII)
ISF.............. Insurance, Surety, and Fidelity (MHDB)
ISF.............. Integrated Subject File
ISF.............. Integrated Support Facility (DWSG)
ISF.............. Interdistrict Settlement Fund [*Banking*]
ISF.............. Intermediate Scale Facility [*Department of Energy*]
ISF.............. Internationale Schulsport Foderation [*International School Sport Federation*] (EAIO)
ISF.............. International School Sport Federation (EAIO)
ISF.............. International Science Foundation (EA)
ISF.............. International Scleroderma Federation [*Later, SF*] (EA)
ISF.............. International Shipping Federation [*British*] (EAIO)
ISF.............. International Ski Federation
ISF.............. International Snowshoe Federation (EA)
ISF.............. International Society for Fat Research
ISF.............. International Society of Financiers (EA)
ISF.............. International Softball Federation (EA)
ISF.............. International Spiritualist Federation [*British*]
ISF.............. International Spring Fair [*British*] (ITD)
ISF.............. Intersection of the Shift Fringes (PDAA)
ISF.............. Interstitial Fluid [*Physiology*]
ISF.............. Ionizer, Slab Fabrication
ISF.............. Isfjord [*Norway*] [*Seismograph station code, US Geological Survey Closed*] (SEIS)
ISF.............. Isotope Separation Factor (MCD)
ISFA........... Intercoastal Steamship Freight Association (EA)
ISFA........... International Scientific Film Association
ISFA........... Isaac Garrison Family Association (EA)
ISFAA.......... Intercollegiate Soccer-Football Association of America [*Later, ISAA*] (EA)
ISFAA.......... International Society of Fine Arts Appraisers (EA)
IS-FACT....... Irwin Stone Foundation for Ascorbate Capability and Therapy
ISFAHSIG..... International Society for the Advancement of Humanistic Studies in Gynecology (EA)
ISFC........... Indicated Specific Fuel Consumption
ISFC........... International Short Film Conference (EAIO)
ISFC........... International Society and Federation of Cardiology [*International Cardiol ogy Federation and International Society of Cardiology - ISC*] [*Formed by a merger of*] (EAIO)
ISFC........... International Symposium on Fluorine Chemistry
ISFD........... Integrated Software Functional Design
ISFE........... Incident-Shock Frozen Expansion
ISFE........... Integrated Site Facilities and Equipment (MCD)
ISFE........... International Society of Facilities Executives (NTPA)
ISFE........... International Society of Flying Engineers [*Defunct*] (EA)
ISFEA.......... Infosafe Systems'A' [*NASDAQ symbol*] (TTSB)
ISFEA.......... Infosafe Systems, Inc. [*NASDAQ symbol*] (SAG)
ISFET.......... Ion-Selective Field Effect Transistor
ISFEU.......... Infosafe Sys Units'99 [*NASDAQ symbol*] (TTSB)
ISFEW......... Infosafe Sys Wrrt'A' [*NASDAQ symbol*] (TTSB)
ISFEZ.......... Infosafe Sys Wrrt'B [*NASDAQ symbol*] (TTSB)
ISFFSR .... Institute for the Study of Fatigue Fracture and Structural Reliability [*George Washington University*]
ISFGW .... International Society of Friendship and Good Will (EA)
ISFHC .... International Society of Folk Harpers and Craftsmen (EA)
ISFIS........... Selective Fisheries Information Service (IID)
ISFL............ International Scientific Film Library
ISFL............ International Society of Family Law [*Cambridge, England*] (EAIO)
ISFM........... Indexed Sequential File Manager [*Computer science*]
ISFMP......... Interstate Fisheries Management Program (GNE)
ISFMS.......... Indexed Sequential File Management System [*Computer science*] (BUR)
ISFNR .... International Society for Folk-Narrative Research [*Turku, Finland*] (EA)
ISFR............ International Society for Fluoride Research
ISFSC.......... International Society of Food Service Consultants [*Later, FCSI*] (EA)
ISFSC.......... International Society of Free Space Colonizers [*Superseded by Political Action Caucus*] (EA)
ISFSF.......... Independent Spent Fuel Storage Facility [*Department of Energy*] [*Nuclear energy*]
ISFSI........... Independent Spent Fuel Storage Installation [*Nuclear energy*] (NRCH)
ISFSI........... International Society of Fire Service Instructors (EA)
ISFSM.......... Incompletely-Specified Finite State Machine (MHDB)
ISFV........... Interstitial Fluid Volume [*Medicine*] (DMAA)
ISG.............. Ayer Public Library, Delavan, IL [*OCLC symbol*] (OCLC)

ISG............ Idaho State Grange (SRA)
ISG............ Immune Serum Globulin
ISG............ Imperial Standard Gallon
ISG............ Indiana State Grange (SRA)
ISG............ Inland Shipping Group [*British*]
ISG............ Institute for the Study of Genocide (EA)
ISG............ Insurance Services Group
ISG............ Integrated Survey Grid
ISG............ Interchangeable and Substitute Group [*Military*] (AFIT)
ISG............ Interconnected Systems Group
ISG............ Interfacial Surface Generation [*Instrumentation*]
ISG............ Internal Shutter Grid
ISG............ International SYSOP [*System Operator*] Guild
ISG............ Interservice Group [*Military*]
ISG............ Intersubblock Gap
ISG............ Ishigaki [*Japan*] [*Airport symbol*] (OAG)
ISG............ ISS International Service Systems AS [*NYSE symbol*] (SAG)
ISG............ ISS-Intl Service Sys ADS [*NYSE symbol*] (TTSB)
ISGA .... Idaho Sugarbeet Growers Association (SRA)
ISGA .... Illinois Specialty Growers' Association (SRA)
ISGA .... Indiana Soybean Growers Association (SRA)
ISGA .... International Stained Glass Association (EA)
ISGA .... International Study Group for Aerogrammes
ISGC .... International Society of Guatemala Collectors (EA)
ISGC .... International Steel Guitar Convention (EA)
ISGD .... International Study Group of Diabetes in Children and Adolescents [*Linkoping, Sweden*] (EAIO)
ISGE .... International Society for Geothermal Engineering [*Defunct*] (EA)
ISGE .... International Society of Gastroenterology
ISGF .... Interferon-Stimulated Gene Factor [*Biochemistry*]
ISGI .... International Sheep and Goat Institute [*Utah State University*] [*Research center*] (RCD)
ISGI .... International Standards Group Ltd. [*NASDAQ symbol*] (SAG)
ISGI .... Intl Standards Group Ltd [*NASDAQ symbol*] (TTSB)
ISG Intl .... ISG International Software Group [*Associated Press*] (SAG)
ISGML .... International Study Group for Mathematics Learning [*British*]
ISGN .... Insignia (MSA)
ISGO .... International Society of Geographic Ophthalmology [*Montreal, PQ*] (EAIO)
ISGOTT .... International Safety Guide for Oil Tankers and Terminals (DS)
ISGP .... International Society of General Practice [*Germany*] (PDAA)
ISGP .... International Society of Geographical Pathology [*Australia*] (EY)
ISGRA .... International Study Group on Risk Analysis
ISGS .... Illinois State Geological Survey [*Champaign*] [*Information service or system*] (IID)
ISGS .... International Society for General Semantics (EA)
ISGSH .... International Study Group for Steroid Hormones [*Rome, Italy*] (EAIO)
ISGT .... ISG Technologies, Inc. [*NASDAQ symbol*] (SAG)
ISG Tech..... ISG Technologies, Inc. [*Associated Press*] (SAG)
ISGTF .... I.S.G. Technologies [*NASDAQ symbol*] (TTSB)
ISgW .... Waubonsee Community College, Sugar Grove, IL [*Library symbol Library of Congress*] (LCLS)
ISGWRCA .... International Study Group for Waterworks in the Rhine Catchment Area [*See also IAWR*] (EAIO)
ISH............. Caterpillar Tractor Co., Technical Information Center, Peoria, IL [*OCLC symbol*] (OCLC)
ISH............. Icteric Serum Hepatitis [*Medicine*]
ISH............. Information Superhighway [*Telecommunications*] (PCM)
ISH............. Inner Self-Helper [*Mulitple personality*] [*Psychology*]
ISH............. In Situ Hybridization [*Biology*]
ISH............. Institute for Scientific Humanism [*Later, WISH*]
ISH............. Interim Scout Helicopter (MCD)
ISH............. Intermediate System Hello [*Computer science*] (TNIG)
ISH............. International Shipholding Corp. [*NYSE symbol*] (NQ)
ISH............. International Society of Hematology (DAVI)
ISH............. International Society of Hypertension (EA)
ISH............. International Sterling [*Vancouver Stock Exchange symbol*]
ISH............. Intl Shipholding [*NYSE symbol*] (TTSB)
ISH............. Ishtion [*Former USSR Seismograph station code, US Geological Survey*] (SEIS)
ISH............. Isolated Systolic Hypertension [*Cardiology*] (DAVI)
ISHA........... National Subacute Care Association (NTPA)
ISHAE .... International Society of Hotel Association Executives (EA)
ISHAM .... International Society for Human and Animal Mycology [*London School of Hygiene and Tropical Medicine*] [*British*]
ISHBSS .... International Society for the History of Behavioral and Social Sciences (NTPA)
ISHC .... Indicated Specific Hydrocarbon [*Automotive exhaust emission testing*]
ISHC .... International Siberian Husky Club
ISHC .... International Symposium on Homogeneous Catalysis
IShCoH .... Shelby County Memorial Hospital, Shelbyville, IL [*Library symbol Library of Congress*] (LCLS)
ISHE........... International Safety and Health Exhibition [*British*] (ITD)
ISHE........... International Society for Human Ethology (EA)
ISHE........... International Society of Healthcare Executives (EA)
IShe........... Sheldon Township Public Library, Sheldon, IL [*Library symbol Library of Congress*] (LCLS)
ISherESD .... Sheridan Elementary School District 272, Sheridan, IL [*Library symbol Library of Congress*] (LCLS)
ISHG .... Indian Society of Human Genetics
ISHH .... In Situ Hybridization Histochemistry
ISHI .... Institute for the Study of Human Issues (EA)
ISHI .... International Society for the History of Ideas (EA)
ISHK .... Institute for the Study of Human Knowledge (EA)

ISHL............ International Society for Historical Linguistics (EAIO)
ISHLT.......... International Society for Heart and Lung Transplantation (EAIO)
ISHM .... International Society for Hybrid Microelectronics (EA)
ISho............ South Holland Public Library, South Holland, IL [*Library symbol Library of Congress*] (LCLS)
ISHOF......... International Swimming Hall of Fame (EA)
IShoSHi....... South Suburban Genealogical and Historical Society, South Holland, IL [*Library symbol Library of Congress*] (LCLS)
IShoT.......... Thornton Community College, South Holland, IL [*Library symbol Library of Congress*] (LCLS)
ISHOW......... Information System for Hazardous Organics in Water [*Database*] [*Environmental Protection Agency Information service or system*] (CRD)
(I)SHP......... (Intermediate) Shaft Horsepower
ISHPES .... International Society for the History of Physical Education and Sport [*Belgium*] (EAIO)
ISHR .... Intermediate Scale Homogeneous Reactor
ISHR .... International Society for Heart Research [*Winnipeg, MB*] (EA)
ISHR .... International Society for Human Rights [*See also IGM*] [*Frankfurt, Federal Republic of Germany*] (EAIO)
ISHR .... International Society for the History of Rhetoric (EA)
ISHRA......... Iron and Steel Holdings and Realisation Agency [*British*]
ISHS .... Improved Spartan Homing Sensor [*Missiles*]
ISHS .... International Society for Horticultural Science [*See also SISH*] [*ICSU Wageningen, Netherlands*] (EAIO)
ISHS .... International Society for Humor Studies (EA)
ISHT .... International Society for Heart Transplantation (EA)
ISHTAR .... Inner Shelf Transfer and Recycling [*Marine science*] (OSRA)
ISHTCP .... Inventory of Sources for History of Twentieth Century Physics [*University of California, Berkeley*] [*Information service or system*] (IID)
ISHTE.......... In-Situ Heat Transfer Experiment [*Nuclear energy*] (NUCP)
ISHVBS .... International Society for Hildegard Von Bingen Studies (EA)
ISI................ Chillicothe Township Free Public Library, Chillicothe, IL [*OCLC symbol*] (OCLC)
ISI............... Indian Standards Institution
ISI............... Indian Statistical Institute
ISI............... Induced Spatial Incoherence [*Physics*]
ISI............... Industrial Security International
ISI............... Industrial Static Inverter
ISI............... Industry Standard Item (AAG)
ISI............... Infarct Size Index [*Cardiology*]
ISI............... Infodata Systems, Inc. [*Information service or system*] (IID)
ISI............... Informal Spelling Inventory [*Education*]
ISI............... Information Science, Inc.
ISI............... Information Sciences Institute [*University of Southern California, Marina Del Rey*]
ISI............... Information Service of India
ISI............... Information Services, Inc. [*Information service or system*] (IID)
ISI............... Information Services International [*Information service or system*] (IID)
ISI............... Information Storage, Inc.
ISI............... Information Systems Inventory (AEPA)
ISI............... Inhibited Sporozoite Invasion [*Immunology*]
ISI............... Initial Shipping Instructions (MCD)
ISI............... Initial Slope Index (STED)
ISI............... Initial Support Increments [*Army*] (AABC)
ISI............... Initial Support Item
ISI............... Initial Systems Installation (NASA)
ISI............... Injury Severity Index (MCD)
ISI............... In-Service Inspection (NRCH)
ISI............... In-Service Institute [*National Science Foundation*]
ISI............... Institute for Scientific Information [*Philadelphia, PA*] [*Database producer*]
ISI............... Institute for Social Inquiry [*University of Connecticut*] [*Storrs*] [*Information service or system*] (IID)
ISI............... Instructional Styles Inventory [*Test*] [*Canfield and Canfield*] (TES)
ISI............... Instrumentation Support Instruction (KSC)
isi............... Instrumentation Support Instruction [*NASA*] (NAKS)
ISI............... Insurance Selection Inventory [*Test*] [*London House, Inc.*] (TES)
ISI............... Integra Systems, Inc. [*Toronto Stock Exchange symbol Vancouver Stock Exchange symbol*]
ISI............... Intelligent Serial Interface [*Computer science*]
ISI............... Intercollegiate Studies Institute (EA)
ISI............... Interim Support Item (MCD)
ISI............... Internally Specified Index
ISI............... International Safety Institute [*Defunct*] (EA)
ISI............... International Satellite for Ionospheric Studies [*NASA-Canada*] (NOAA)
ISI............... International Satellite, Inc. [*Telecommunications*]
ISI............... International Sensitivity Index [*Hematology*]
ISI............... International Slope Index (STED)
ISI............... International Statistical Institute [*ICSU*] [*Voorburg, Netherlands*] (EA)
ISI............... International Students, Inc. (EA)
ISI............... Interpersonal Style Inventory [*Personality development test*] [*Psychology*]
ISI............... Inter-Sound Interval (EDAC)
ISI............... Interspike Interval [*Neurophysiology*]
ISI............... Interstimulus Interval
ISI............... Intersymbol Interference
ISI............... Ion Source Injector
ISI............... Iron and Steel Institute (MCD)
ISI............... Ishigakijima [*Ryukyu Islands*] [*Seismograph station code, US Geological Survey*] (SEIS)
ISI............... Isisford [*Australia Airport symbol*] (OAG)

ISI................ Italic Studies Institute (EA)
ISI................ Item Station and Indenture (AAG)
ISIA............. Ice Skating Institute of America (EA)
ISIA............. International Ski Instructors' Association (ECON)
ISIA............. International Snowmobile Industry Association (EA)
ISIA............. Italo Svevo International Association [*Defunct*] (EA)
ISIAL........... Incorporated Society of Irish/American Lawyers (EA)
ISIAME........ International Symposium on the Industrial Applications of the Mossbauer Effect
ISIB............. Institute for the Study of Intellectual Behavior [*University of Colorado*] (PDAA)
ISIB............. Inter-Service Ionosphere Bureau [*Military*]
ISIC............. Immediate Superior in Command [*Military*]
ISIC............. Intelligence Support and Indications Center [*Military*] (MCD)
ISIC............. International Standard Industrial Classification (EY)
ISIC............. International Student Identity Card (BARN)
ISIC............. Intersymbol Interference Corrector
ISICCE........ International Society of India Chemists and Chemical Engineers (EA)
ISICS .... Indian Self-Identified Certified Staff (EDAC)
ISID............. International Society for Infectious Diseases (NTPA)
ISID............. International Society of Interior Designers (EA)
ISid............. Sidell District Library, Sidell, IL [*Library symbol Library of Congress*] (LCLS)
ISIDHI......... International Society on Infectious Diseases and Human Infertility (EA)
ISIdn........... Sidney Community Library, Sidney, IL [*Library symbol Library of Congress*] (LCLS)
ISIDPP........ Initial Shut-In Drill Pipe Pressure
ISIdSD........ Jamaica Community Unit School District, Sidell, IL [*Library symbol*] [*Library of Congress*] (LCLS)
ISIE............. Integral Square Ideal Error (IAA)
ISIFM.......... International Society of Industrial Fabric Manufacturers (EA)
ISIG .... Implementation Special Interest Group [*Association for the Development of Computer-Based Instructional Systems*] (EDAC)
ISIG .... Insignia Sys [*NASDAQ symbol*] (TTSB)
ISIG .... Insignia Systems, Inc. [*NASDAQ symbol*] (SAG)
ISIG .... Irish Special Interest Group of American Mensa (EA)
ISIH .... Interspike Interval Histogram [*Neurophysiology*]
ISII............. International Society for Individualized Instruction (AIE)
ISI/IST .... In-Service Inspections and In-Service Testing
ISI/ISTP & B... ISI/Index to Scientific and Technical Proceedings and Books [*Institute for Scientific Information*] [*Philadelphia, PA Bibliographic database*]
ISIJ .... Iron and Steel Institute of Japan
ISIL .... Interim Support Items List (NASA)
ISIL .... International Society for Individual Liberty (EAIO)
ISILT........... Information Science Index Language Text (NITA)
ISIM............ Inhibit Simultaneity (IAA)
ISIM............ [*The*] International School of Inforamtion Management, Inc. [*Denver, CO*] (ECON)
ISIM............ [*The*] International School of Information Management, Inc. [*Denver, CO*] (ECON)
ISIM............ International Society of Internal Medicine [*Langenthal, Switzerland*] (EA)
ISIM............ Inventory Simulation (IAA)
ISIMC.......... International Study Institution of the Middle Classes [*Brussels, Belgium*] (EAIO)
ISIMEP........ International Symposium on Identification and Measurement of Environmental Pollutants (PDAA)
ISIMM......... International Society for the Interaction of Mechanics and Mathematics (EA)
ISINC .... Immediate Superior in Command [*Military*]
ISIP............. Indexed Security Investment Plan [*Canada*]
ISIP............. Intelligence Support Interface Program
ISIP............. Isis Pharmaceuticals [*NASDAQ symbol*] (SPSG)
ISIPP.......... Information System for Improved Plant Protection [*FAO*] [*United Nations*] (DUND)
ISIR .... Initial Sample Inspection Report
ISIR .... In Service, In Reserve [*Vessel status*] [*Navy*]
ISIR .... Interactive Single Isomorphous Replacement [*Crystallographic procedure*]
ISIR .... International Satellite for Ionospheric Research [*NASA Canada*] (IAA)
ISIR .... International Society for the Immunology of Reproduction (EA)
ISIR .... International Society of Invertebrate Reproduction (EA)
ISIR .... International Symposium on Industrial Robots (PDAA)
ISIR .... Iterative Single Isomorphous Replacement [*Crystallography*]
ISIRC .... International Statistical Institute Research Center [*Research center Netherlands*] (IRC)
ISIRS .... International Sorption Information Retrieval System [*Nuclear Energy Agency*] (EY)
ISIRTA .... I'm Sorry, I'll Read That Again [*BBC radio comedy program*]
ISIS............ Image-Selected in Vivo Spectroscopy
ISIS............ Impact Shock Isolation System [*Tennis-racket technology*] [*Dunlop Slazenger Corp.*]
ISIS............ Independence Square Income Securities [*NASDAQ symbol*] (SAG)
ISIS............ Independence Square Income Securities, Inc. [*NASDAQ symbol*] (NQ)
ISIS............ Independent Schools Information Service [*British*]
ISIS............ Indian School of International Studies [*Delhi*]
ISIS............ Individualized Science Instructional System [*National Science Foundation project*]
ISIS............ Information System Indexing System [*Federal Judicial Center*] [*Database*]
ISIS............ Instant Sales Indicator System (IAA)
ISIS............ Institute for the Study of Inquiring Systems

ISIS............ Institute of Scrap Iron and Steel [*Later, ISRI*] (EA)

ISIS............ Institute of Strategic and International Studies [*Malaysia*] (ECON)

ISIS............ Institutional Sector Investment Services [*Chase Manhattan Securities*] [*British*]

ISIS............ Integral Service Information System (IAA)

ISIS............ Integral Spar Inspection System

ISIS............ Integrated Safeguard Information System (NRCH)

ISIS............ Integrated Scientific Information System

ISIS............ Integrated Set of Information Systems (IAA)

ISIS............ Integrated Ship Instrumentation System (IAA)

ISIS............ Integrated Side-Impact System [*Automotive safety*]

ISIS............ Integrated Software Invocation System [*Computer science*] (MHDI)

ISIS............ Integrated Statistical Information Service (WDAA)

ISIS............ Integrated Strike and Interceptor System

ISIS............ Integrated Surface Irradiance Study [*Marine science*] (OSRA)

ISIS............ Integrated System for Improved Separations [*Membrane filtration*]

ISIS............ Integriertes Statistisches Informationssystem [*Integrated Statistical Information System*] [*Central Statistical Office Vienna, Austria*] [*Information service or system*] (IID)

ISIS............ Interchangeability and Substitutability Item Subgroup (MCD)

ISIS............ Intermarket Surveillance Information System (DFIT)

IS-IS........... Intermediate System-to-Intermediate System [*Telecommunications*]

ISIS............ Internally Switched Interface System [*Tymnet, Inc.*]

ISIS............ Internationale de Services Industriels and Scientifiques

ISIS............ Internationally Syndicated Information Services [*Information service or system Defunct*] (IID)

ISIS............ International Satellite for Ionospheric Studies [*NASA-Canada*]

ISIS............ International Science Information Services [*Earth sciences data center*] [*Dallas, TX*]

ISIS............ International Shipping Information Service (DS)

ISIS............ International Society for Intelligent Systems (NTPA)

ISIS............ International Society of Introduction Services (EA)

ISIS............ International Space Information System [*United Nations*] (DUND)

ISIS............ International Species Information System (IID)

ISIS............ International Species Inventory System [*Data processing for animal mating*] [*Minnesota Zoological Gardens Apple Valley, MN*]

ISIS............ International Student Information Service

ISIS............ International Study of Infarct Survival [*Medicine*]

ISIS............ International Superconductivity Industry Summit [*Conference*]

ISIS............ Interstate Settlement Information System [*AT & T*]

ISIS............ Investigative Support Information System [*Federal Bureau of Investigation*]

Isis............. Isis Pharmaceuticals, Inc. [*Associated Press*] (SAG)

ISIS............ Item Standardization Information System [*DoD*]

ISIS............ Women's International Information and Communication Service [*Italy and Switzerland*]

ISISA .... Individual Scale for Indian South Africans [*Intelligence test*]

ISISC .... Istituto Superiore Internazionale di Scienze Criminali [*Italy*]

ISISSAPORCI... International Section of ISSA [*International Social Security Association*] on the Prevention of Occupational Risks in the Construction Industry [*Boulogne-Billancourt, France*] (EAIO)

ISIS-WICCE... ISIS [*Women's International Information Communication Service*] - Women's International Cross-Cultural Exchange (EAIO)

ISIS-X .... International Satellites for Ionosphere Studies - Experimental [*NASA/Canada*] (SAA)

ISIT............ Intensified Silicon Intensifier Target (MCD)

ISITB.......... Iron and Steel Industry Training Board [*British*] (BI)

ISIUP.......... Islamic Society for International Unity and Peace [*Pakistan*] (EAIO)

ISIYM.......... International Society of Industrial Yarn Manufacturers [*Later, ISIFM*] (EA)

ISJ............. Institute for Social Justice (EA)

ISJ............. Saint Joseph's College, Rensselaer, IN [*OCLC symbol*] (OCLC)

ISJAC.......... Independent Schools Joint Action Committee (AIE)

ISJC........... Independent Schools Joint Council [*British*]

ISJCT.......... International Symposium on Jet Cutting Technology (PDAA)

IsJJNL .... Jewish National and University Library, Hebrew University, Jerusalem, Israel [*Library symbol Library of Congress*] (LCLS)

ISJL........... International Society of Jewish Librarians (EA)

ISJP........... International Society for Japanese Philately (EA)

ISJTA.......... Intensive Student Jet Training Area

ISK............ Galva Township Public Library, Galva, IL [*OCLC symbol*] (OCLC)

ISK............ Insert Storage Key (IEEE)

ISK............ Instruction Space Key

ISK............ Internacia Scienca Kolegio [*International College of Scientists - ICS*] [*Paderborn, Federal Republic of Germany*] (EAIO)

ISK............ Internationale Seidenbau Kommission [*International Sericultural Commission*]

ISK............ International Society of the Knee (EA)

ISK............ Ion Source Kit

ISK............ Iskenderon [*Turkey*] [*Airport symbol*] (AD)

ISK............ Iskut Gold Corp. [*Vancouver Stock Exchange symbol*]

ISK............ Istanbul-Kandilli [*Turkey*] [*Seismograph station code, US Geological Survey*] (SEIS)

ISK............ Nasik [*India*] [*Airport symbol*] (OAG)

ISk............ Skokie Public Library, Skokie, IL [*Library symbol Library of Congress*] (LCLS)

ISKA........... International Saw and Knife Association (EA)

ISKCON........ International Society for Krishna Consciousness (EA)

ISKDC......... International Study of Kidney Disease in Children

ISkH.......... Hebrew Theological College, Skokie, IL [*Library symbol Library of Congress*]

ISKI........... International Secretariat of the Knitting Industries [*Paris, France*] (EAIO)

ISKO .... International Society for Knowledge Organization [*Germany*] (EAIO)

ISKO .... Isco, Inc. [*NASDAQ symbol*] (NQ)

ISkS.......... G. D. Searle & Co., Inc., Skokie, IL [*Library symbol Library of Congress*] (LCLS)

ISkT .... Triodyne, Skokie, IL [*Library symbol Library of Congress*] (LCLS)

ISL............ Eagle Air Ltd. [*Iceland*] [*ICAO designator*] (FAAC)

ISL............ First Israel Fund [*NYSE symbol*] (TTSB)

ISL............ Iceland [*ANSI three-letter standard code*] (CNC)

ISL............ Immunodeficiency-Virus-Suppressing Lymphokine [*Virology*]

ISL............ Inactive Status List (MUGU)

ISL............ Indiana State Library, Indianapolis, IN [*OCLC symbol*] (OCLC)

ISL............ Industrial Security Letter [*DoD*]

ISL............ Inertial Systems Laboratory [*NASA*] (GFGA)

ISL............ Informatics Services [*Oakville, ON*] [*Telecommunications service*] (TSSD)

ISL............ Information Search Language

ISL............ Information Services Ltd. [*Publisher*] [*British*]

ISL............ Information System Language [*Computer science*] (IEEE)

ISL............ Information Systems Laboratories, Inc.

ISL............ Initial Spare Parts List (IAA)

ISL............ Initial Stocks List

ISL............ Initial System Loading

ISL............ Injection Coupled Synchronous Logic (IAA)

ISL............ Inner Scapular Line [*Medicine*] (DMAA)

ISL............ In Situ Leaching (GAAI)

ISL............ Institute of Space Law

ISL............ Institut fuer Seeverkehrwirtschaft und Logistik [*Institute of Shipping Economics and Logistics - ISEL*] [*Bremen, Federal Republic of Germany*] (EAIO)

ISL............ Instructional Systems Language [*Computer science*] (IEEE)

ISL............ Instrument Standards Laboratory [*Space Flight Operations Facility, NASA*]

ISL............ Integrated Schottky Logic (IEEE)

ISL............ Integrated Stock Listing

ISL............ Integrated Synthesis Logic [*Computer science*]

ISL............ Interactive Simulation Language [*Computer science*] (IEEE)

ISL............ Intermountain Swim League (PSS)

ISL............ Internally-Silvered Lamp [*Light bulb*] (DI)

ISL............ Internal Standard Line

ISL............ International Soccer League

ISL............ International Society of Literature [*Ilkley, Yorkshire, England*] (EAIO)

ISL............ International Society of Lymphology (EA)

ISL............ International Subcommittee on Lactobacilli and Closely Related Organisms

ISL............ Intersatellite Link

ISL............ Interscapular Line (STED)

ISL............ Interspinous Ligament [*Medicine*] (DMAA)

ISL............ Intersystem Link

ISL............ Island [*Board on Geographic Names*]

ISL............ Isle

ISL............ Islington (ROG)

ISL............ Isolated Signal Line (IAA)

ISL............ Item Selection List

ISL............ Item Study Listings

ISL............ Item Survey List (DNAB)

ISL............ Lincoln Library, Springfield, IL [*Library symbol Library of Congress*] (LCLS)

ISLA.......... Information Services on Latin America (EA)

ISLA.......... International Survey Libraries Association [*University of Connecticut*] (NITA)

ISLA.......... International Survey Library Association (EA)

ISLADE .... Interactive Structural Layout and Design [*Module*]

ISLAN .... Integrated Services Local Area Network [*Telecommunications*] (ACRL)

ISLAND....... Island [*Commonly used*] (OPSA)

ISLANDS...... Islands [*Commonly used*] (OPSA)

ISLAR........ International Symposium on Laboratory Automation and Robotics

ISLC.......... International Sporting and Leisure Club

ISLC.......... Lincoln Land Community College, Springfield, IL [*Library symbol Library of Congress*] (LCLS)

ISLCBS .... International Seal, Label, and Cigar Band Society (EA)

ISLD.......... Institute for the Study of Learning Difficulties [*Flinders University*] [*Australia*]

ISLD.......... International Special Librarians Day

ISLD.......... Inter-Services Liaison Department [*World War II*]

ISLE.......... Integral Square Linear Error (IAA)

ISLE.......... Integrated Simulation Language Environment [*Computer science*]

ISLE.......... Isle [*Postal Service standard*] (OPSA)

ISLEC......... Institute for the Study of Labor and Economic Crisis (EA)

ISLER......... Islander

ISLES......... Isle [*Commonly used*] (OPSA)

ISLF.......... Improved Saturn Launch Facility

ISLFD........ Incorporated Society of London Fashion Designers

ISLI.......... INTERSOLV [*NASDAQ symbol*] (TTSB)

ISLI.......... Intersolv, Inc. [*NASDAQ symbol*] (SAG)

ISLIC......... Israel Society of Special Libraries and Information Centers

ISLL.......... International Survey of Legal Decisions on Labour Law [*1925-38*] [*A publication*] (DLA)

ISL/LAR ...... Integrated Logistics System and Logistics Assessment Review

ISLLSL........ International Society for Labor Law and Social Legislation [*Later, International Society for Labor Law and Social Security United States National Branch*] (EA)

ISLLSS........ International Society for Labor Law and Social Security [*International Congresses of Labour Law and International Society for Social Law*] [*Formed by a merger of*] (EAIO)

ISLM.......... Integration Shop/Laboratory Manager (MCD)

ISLM.......... Investment-Savings, Liquidity-Money [*Economics*] (ODBW)

ISLMA — Illinois School Library Media Association (SRA)
ISLN — Isolation (MSA)
ISLND — Island [*Commonly used*] (OPSA)
ISLNDS — Islands [*Commonly used*] (OPSA)
ISLP — IGOSS [*Integrated Global Ocean Services System*] Sea Level Project [*Marine science*] (OSRA)
ISLP-Pac — GOSS [*Integrated Global Ocean Station System*] Sea Level Project in the Pacific (USDC)
ISLP-Pac — IGOSS [*Integrated Global Ocean Services System*] Sea Level Project in the Pacific [*Marine science*] (OSRA)
ISLR — Initial Sample Laboratory Report
ISLR — Integrated Side-Lobe Ratio
ISLR — International Symposium on Laboratory Robotics
ISLR — Isolator (MSA)
ISLRS — Inactive Status List Reserve Section
ISLS — Improved Side-Lobe Supression (PDAA)
ISLS — Intelligent Surgical Lasers, Inc. [*NASDAQ symbol*] (SAG)
ISLS — Interrogation Side-Lobe Suppression
ISLS — Islands [*Board on Geographic Names*]
ISLSCP — International Satellite Land Surface Climatology Project [*Federal government*]
ISLT — International Snow Leopard Trust (EA)
ISLTS — Incorporated Society of Licensed Trade Stocktakers [*British*] (DBA)
ISLW — Indian Spring Low Water [*Tides and currents*]
ISLWF — International Shoe and Leather Workers' Federation
ISLWG — Working Group on International Shipping Legislation [*UNCTAD*] (DS)
ISM — Iesus Salvator Mundi [*Jesus, Savior of the World*] [*Latin*]
ISM — Imperial Service Medal [*British*]
ISM — Improved Sensing Munitions (RDA)
ISM — Incorporated Society of Musicians [*British*]
ISM — Independent Subcarrier Method (PDAA)
ISM — Indian Supply Mission [*World War II*]
ISM — Inductor Super Magnetron [*Electronics*] (AAEL)
ISM — Industrial, Scientific and Medical [*Band*] (AAEL)
ISM — Industrial, Scientific, and Medical (IAA)
ISM — Industrial, Scientific and Medical Applications
ISM — Industrial Security Manual (MCD)
ISM — Information System Manager (NATG)
ISM — Information Systems for Management (IEEE)
ISM — Information Systems Marketing, Inc. [*Information service or system*] (IID)
ISM — Infrared Systems Manufacturing
ISM — Initial Segment Membrane
ISM — Inside of Metal
ISM — Institute for the Study of Man (EA)
ISM — Institute of Sanitation Management [*Later, EMA*] (EA)
ISM — Institute of Spiritualist Mediums [*British*] (DBA)
ISM — Institute of Sports Medicine [*British*]
ISM — Institute of Supervisory Management [*British*]
ISM — Instructional Systems in Mathematics Program (EDAC)
ISM — Insulation System Module [*Engineering*] (OA)
ISM — Integrated Sander Machine [*Disk controller*] [*Apple Computer, Inc.*] (BYTE)
ISM — Integrated Skills Method [*Education*]
ISM — Integrated Sustainment Maintenance
ISM — Interactive Siting Method (PDAA)
ISM — Interavia Space Markets [*Interavia Publications*] [*Information service or system*] (CRD)
ISM — Interim Surface Missile (PDAA)
ISM — International Camero Resources [*Vancouver Stock Exchange symbol*]
ISM — International Society for Metaphysics (EA)
ISM — International Society of Microbiologists (DAVI)
ISM — International Software Marketing (HGAA)
ISM — International Soil Museum
ISM — International Standards Method (IAA)
ISM — International Sweets Market [*Trade fair*] [*Cologne, West Germany 1982*]
ISM — International Symposium on Microchemistry
ISM — International Symposium on Microtechniques
ISM — International Systems Meeting [*Computer science*]
ISM — Interpretive Structural Modeling [*A computer-assisted learning process for structuring information*]
ISM — Intersegmental Muscles [*Anatomy*] (DAVI)
ISM — Interstellar Medium [*Planetary science*]
ISM — Ion-Selective Material [*Chemistry*]
ISM — Ion Selective Microelectrodes [*Instrumentation*]
ISM — Irish School of Music (ROG)
ISM — ISDN [*Integrated Services Digital Network*] Subscriber Module [*Telecommunications*]
ISM — Istituto Internazionale Suore di Santa Marcellina [*Also, Instituto Marcelline*] [*Italy*] (EAIO)
ISM — Kissimmee, FL [*Location identifier FAA*] (FAAL)
ISM — Southern Methodist University, Central Library, Dallas, TX [*OCLC symbol*] (OCLC)
ISMA — Indiana State Medical Association (SRA)
ISMA — Industrial Silencer Manufacturers Association (EA)
ISMA — Infantile Spinal Muscular Atrophy [*Medicine*] (DAVI)
ISMA — Institute of Sisters of Mercy of Australia
ISMA — International Securities Market Association (NUMA)
ISMA — International Security Management Association [*Boston, MA*] (EA)
ISMA — International Shipmasters Association (EA)
ISMA — International Snowmobile Manufacturers Association (NTPA)
ISMA — International Stress Management Association (NTPA)
ISMA — International Superphosphate Manufacturers' Association [*Later, IFA*]

Is Mag — Island Magazine [*A publication*]
ISMAP — Indirect Source Model for Air Pollution [*Environmental Protection Agency*] (GFGA)
ISMAR — International Society of Magnetic Resonance
ISMB — Information System Management Board [*NATO*] (NATG)
ISMB — Intelligent Systems for Molecular Biology (HGEN)
ISMB — International Society of Mathematical Biology [*See also SIBM*] [*Antony, France*] (EAIO)
ISMC — Independent Schools Microelectronics Centre [*British*]
ISMC — International Switching Maintenance Center [*Communications*]
ISMD — Indian Subordinate Medical Department [*British military*] (DMA)
ISMDA — Independent Sewing Machine Dealers Association (EA)
ISMDKTS — Iron, Steel, Metal Dressers, and Kindred Trades Society [*A union*] [*British*]
ISME — Institute of Sheet Metal Engineering [*British*]
ISME — International Society for Music Education (EA)
ISME — International Society of Marine Engineers
ISME — International Society of Mechanical Engineers
ISME — International Sysmposium on Marine Engineering (PDAA)
ISMEC — Information Service in Mechanical Engineering [*Cambridge Scientific Abstracts*] [*British Information service or system*] (IID)
ISMED — International Society on Metabolic Eye Disease (EA)
ISMES — Experimental Institute for Models and Structures [*Italy*]
ISMET — Inter-Service Metallurgical Research Council [*British*] (MCD)
ISMF — Inactive Ship Maintenance Facility
ISMF — International Sports Massage Federation (EA)
ISMG — International Scientific Management Group [*GARP*] (NOAA)
ISMGF — International Stoke Mandeville Games Federation [*Aylesbury, Buckinghamshire, England*] (EA)
ISMGR — Island Manager (FAAC)
ISMH — Input Source Message Handler
ISMH — International Society of Medical Hydrology and Climatology
ISMHC — International Society of Medical Hydrology and Climatology (EA)
ISMI — Improved Space Manned Interceptor (IAA)
ISMIS — Improved SAGE [*Semiautomatic Ground Environment*] Manned Intercept System (IAA)
ISMIS — Interservice Depot Maintenance Interrogation Systems
ISMIT — International Society for Mental Imagery Techniques [*France*] (EAIO)
ISmK — Kaskaska Library System, Smithton, IL [*Library symbol Library of Congress*] (LCLS)
ISML — Institute for the Study of Matrimonial Laws (EA)
ISML — Intermediate System Mock-Up Loop (IEEE)
ISMLS — Interim Standard Microwave Landing System [*Aviation*]
ISMM — International Society for Music in Medicine (EAIO)
ISMM — International Society of Mini- and Micro-Computers [*Calgary, AB*] (EAIO)
ISMMRRI — Iowa State Mining and Mineral Resources Research Institute [*Iowa State University*] [*Research center*] (RCD)
ISMMS — Integrated Stores Monitor and Management System [*Later, Armament Control Panel*] (MCD)
ISMN — Isosorbide Mononitrate [*Coronary vasodilator*]
ISMO — Ion-Sieve-Type Manganese Oxide [*Inorganic chemistry*]
ISMO — Isosorbide-5-Mononitrate (DB)
ISMOD — Index Sequential Module (IAA)
ISMPH — International Society for Medical and Psychological Hypnosis (EA)
ISMPMI — International Society for Molecular Plant Microbe Interactions (NTPA)
ISMR — Independent Snowmobile Medical Research [*An association*] (EA)
ISMRC — Inter-Services Metallurgical Research Council [*British*]
ISMRM — International Society for Magnetic Resonance in Medicine (NTPA)
ISMS — Illinois State Medical Society (SRA)
ISMS — Image Store Management System
ISMS — Improved SPRINT [*Solid-Propellant Rocket Intercept*] Missile Subsystem [*Army*]
ISMS — Industrial Standards and Military Specifications [*Information Handling Services*] [*Information service or system*] (CRD)
ISMS — Information Systems and Media Services [*Eastern Illinois University*] [*Information service or system*] (IID)
ISMS — Infrared Spectral Measurement System (MCD)
ISMS — Inherently Safe Mining Systems (PDAA)
ISMS — Integrated Software Maintenance System
ISMS — Interactive Solids Modeling System [*Gould Electronics Ltd. Computer Systems*] [*Software package*] (NCC)
ISMS — International Society for Mushroom Science [*Braunschweig, Federal Republic of Germany*] (EA)
ISMS-D — Improved SPRINT [*Solid-Propellant Rocket Intercept*] Missile Subsystem - Derated [*Army*]
ISMSD — Istituto delle Suore Maestre di Santa Dorotea [*Rome, Italy*] (EAIO)
ISmSD — Smithton Community Consolidated School District 130, Smithton, IL [*Library symbol Library of Congress*] (LCLS)
ISMT — Indoor Simulated Marksmanship Trainer [*Military*]
ISMT — Integrated System Maintenance Trainer (MCD)
ISMUN — International Youth and Student Movement for the United Nations [*Geneva, Switzerland*] (EA)
ISMV — Iris Severe Mosaic Virus
ISMX — Integrated Subrate Data Multiplexer (TEL)
ISN — Information Systems Network [*AT & T*] [*Telecommunications*]
ISN — Initial Sequence Number (IAA)
ISN — Instron Corp. [*AMEX symbol*] (SPSG)
ISN — Internal Statement Number (IAA)
ISN — International Society for Neurochemistry [*Kjeller, Norway*] (EA)
ISN — International Society of Nephrology
ISN — International Suneva Resources [*Vancouver Stock Exchange symbol*]
ISN — Internment Serial Number
ISN — Interplant Shipping Notice

ISN............. Ishinomaki [*Japan*] [*Seismograph station code, US Geological Survey*] (SEIS)
ISN............. Item Sequence Number (MCD)
ISN............. Saint Mary's College, Notre Dame, IN [*OCLC symbol*] (OCLC)
ISN............. Williston [*North Dakota*] [*Airport symbol*] (OAG)
ISN............. Williston, ND [*Location identifier FAA*] (FAAL)
ISNA......... International Society for New Atlantis (EA)
ISNA......... International Space: 1999 Alliance (EA)
ISNA......... International Symposium on Novel Aromatic Compounds
ISNAC........ Inactive Ships Navy Custody (NVT)
ISNAR........ International Service for National Agricultural Research [*The Hague, Netherlands*]
ISNE............ International Scale of Nuclear Events
ISNI............ Idependent Service Network, International (NTPA)
ISNOX........ Indicated Specific Oxides of Nitrogen [*Automotive exhaust emission testing*]
ISNP .... Independent Scholarship National Program [*Defunct*] (EA)
ISNP .... International Society of Naturopathic Physicians
ISNR .... State of Illinois, Institute of Natural Resources, Energy Information Library, Springfield, IL [*Library symbol Library of Congress*] (LCLS)
ISNR-E........ State of Illinois, Institute of Natural Resources, Division of Environmental Management, Chicago, IL [*Library symbol Library of Congress*] (LCLS)
ISNS .... Image Sensing Systems [*NASDAQ symbol*] (TTSB)
ISNS .... Image Sensing Systems, Inc. [*NASDAQ symbol*] (SAG)
ISNS .... Institute for the Study of Natural Systems (EA)
ISNS .... International Society for Neoplatonic Studies (EA)
ISNSE .... International School for Nuclear Science and Engineering
ISNSL .... Incremental Stock Number Sequence List [*Military*] (CAAL)
ISNSPM ...... International Standard Numbering System for Printed Music (TELE)
ISNT .... Informal Single Negotiating Text [*Marine science*] (MSC)
ISNU .... Illinois State Normal University
ISNV .... Institute for the Study of Nonviolence [*Defunct*] (EA)
ISNY .... Insurance Society of New York [*New York, NY*] (EA)
ISO .... Illegal Support Officer [*CIA*] (LAIN)
ISO .... Imaging Spectrometric Observatory (MCD)
ISO .... Imperial Service Order [*British*]
ISO .... I'm So Optimistic [*Dance company*]
ISO .... Incentive Stock Option
ISO .... Independent Sales Organization (HGAA)
ISO .... Individual System Operation
ISO .... Industrial Safety Office
ISO .... Information Services Officer
ISO .... Information Systems Office [*Library of Congress*]
ISO .... Infrared Space Observatory
ISO .... In Search Of [*Classified advertising*]
ISO .... Inside-Out [*Biochemistry*]
ISO .... Installation Supply Officer [*Military*]
ISO .... Insurance Services Office [*An association*] (EA)
IS(O) .... Intelligence Section, Operations [*Control Commission for Germany*] [*World War II*]
ISO .... Intermediate Station Operation (IAA)
ISO .... Internal Standard Organization Code (CMD)
ISO .... Internal System Organization (ECII)
ISO .... International Organization for Standardization [*Geneva, Switzerland*] [*United Nations*]
ISO .... International Science Organization
ISO .... International Self-Service Organization
ISO .... International Shopfitting Organization [*Zurich, Switzerland*] (EAIO)
ISO .... International Sikh Organization (EA)
ISO .... International Socialist Organization (EA)
ISO .... International Society of Organbuilders [*Levallois-Perret, France*] (EAIO)
iso .... International Standardization Organizations (NAKS)
ISO .... International Standards Institute (WPI)
ISO .... International Standards Organization [*Communications*] (PCM)
ISO .... International Sugar Organization [*See also OIA*] [*British*] (EAIO)
ISO .... Interplant Shipping Order
ISO .... Intraseasonal Atmospheric Oscillation (USDC)
ISO .... ISG Technologies, Inc. [*Toronto Stock Exchange symbol*]
ISO .... Isochromatic (ROG)
ISO .... Isoflurane [*An anesthetic*]
ISO .... Isola [*France*] [*Seismograph station code, US Geological Survey*] (SEIS)
iso .... Isolated [*Slang*] (WDMC)
ISO .... Isolated Camera (NTCM)
ISO .... Isolation
ISO .... Isomedix Inc. [*NYSE symbol*] (TTSB)
iso .... Isometric (VRA)
ISO .... Isometric (MSA)
Iso .... Isophase
ISO .... Isoproterenol [*An adrenergic*]
Iso .... Isoproterenol (STED)
ISO .... Isotope
ISO .... Isotropic (KSC)
Iso .... Isotropic (STED)
ISO .... Isotype
ISO .... Israel Students Organization
ISO .... Kinston [*North Carolina*] [*Airport symbol*] (OAG)
ISO .... Kinston, NC [*Location identifier FAA*] (FAAL)
ISO .... South Bend Public Library, South Bend, IN [*OCLC symbol*] (OCLC)
ISO-30 .... Inventory of Suicide Orientation-30 [*Test*] (TMMY)
ISOA .... Improved State-of-the-Art (PDAA)

ISO-ALPHABET... International Standards Organization-Authorized Alphabetic Characters (MCD)
ISOB .... Incorporated Society of Organ Builders [*British*] (BI)
ISOB .... International Society of Barristers (EA)
iso-BTX....... Isobatrachotoxin [*Toxicology*] (LDT)
Isoc........... De Isocrate [*of Dionysius Halicarnassensis*] [*Classical studies*] (OCD)
ISOC .... Individual System/Organization Cost (MHDB)
ISOC .... Instituto de Informacion y Documentacion en Ciencias Sociales y Humanidades [*Institute for Information and Documentation in the Social Sciences and Humanities*] [*Higher Council for Scientific Research*] [*Information service or system*] (IID)
ISOC .... Internal Security Operations Command
ISOC .... Internet Society
Isoc........... Isocrates [*436-338BC*] [*Classical studies*] (OCD)
ISoCaRP ..... International Society of City and Regional Planners [*See also AIU*] [*The Hague, Netherlands*] (EAIO)
ISOCC .... Input System for Operator Connected Calls (PDAA)
ISO-CMOS ... Isolated Fully Recessed Complementary Metal-Oxide Semiconductor (TEL)
ISOD .... International Society for Orbital Disorders (EAIO)
ISOD .... International Sports Organization for the Disabled [*Farstn, Sweden*] (EA)
ISODARCO ... International School of Disarmament and Research on Conflicts
ISODATA..... Iterative Self-Organizing Data Analysis Technique A [*Computer science*]
ISODIS........ International Organization for Standardization Draft International Standard (IAA)
ISODOC....... International Information Centre for Standards in Information and Documentation (ADA)
ISOE .... International Society for Optical Engineering (EA)
IsoENET ...... Isochronous Ethernet [*Computer science*] (CDE)
isoenz........ Isoenzyme (AAMN)
ISOF .... International Society for Ocular Fluorophotometry (EAIO)
IS of LANG... Islets of Langerhans [*Anatomy*]
Is of Lang... Islets of Langerhans (STED)
ISOHP .... International Society for Organ History and Preservation (EA)
ISOL .... IMAGE Software [*NASDAQ symbol*] (TTSB)
ISOL .... Image Software, Inc. [*NASDAQ symbol*] (SAG)
isol .... Isolate [*or Isolated*] (DAVI)
ISOL .... Isolate (NAKS)
isol .... Isolation (STED)
ISOL .... Isolation (KSC)
Isol .... Isolette (STED)
ISOLDE .... Isotopic Low-Weight Device (IAA)
ISOLN .... Isolation
ISOLR .... Isolationer
Isolyser....... Isolyser Co., Inc. [*Associated Press*] (SAG)
ISOM .... International Standard Orthopaedic Measurements [*Medicine*]
ISOM .... Isometric (KSC)
isom .... Isometric (STED)
isom .... Isometrophic (STED)
ISom........... Somonauk Public Library, Somonauk, IL [*Library symbol Library of Congress*] (LCLS)
ISOMATA ..... Idyllwild School of Music and the Arts [*California*]
Isomdx....... Isomedix, Inc. [*Associated Press*] (SAG)
Isomet .... Isomet, Corp. [*Associated Press*] (SAG)
ISOMITE ...... Isotope Miniature Thermionic Electric (IAA)
ISomSD ...... Somonauk Community Unit, School District 432, Somonauk, IL [*Library symbol Library of Congress*] (LCLS)
ISON .... Isolation Network (PDAA)
ISONET .... International Organization for Standardization Information Network [*United Nations*] [*Geneva, Switzerland*] (IID)
ISONG .... International Society of Nurses in Genetics (HGEN)
ISONIAZID ... Isonicotinic Acid Hydrazide [*See also INAH, INH*] [*Antituberculous agent*]
ISOO .... Information Security Oversight Office [*National Archives and Records Service*]
ISO OSI....... International Standards Organisation Open Standards Interconnect [*Computer science*]
ISO/OSI....... International Standards Organization/Open System Interface [*Motorola, Inc.*]
ISOP .... Integrated Spacecraft Operations Plan [*NASA*]
ISOP .... Internal Standard Operating Procedure [*Military*] (MCD)
ISOPAR....... Improved Symbolic Optimizing Assembly Routine
ISOPE .... International Society of Offshore and Polar Engineers
ISOPEDAC.... Integrated System of Pipework Estimating, Detailing, and Control (PDAA)
ISOPEP .... Isometric Piping Efficiency Program
ISOPGU....... International Security Officer's Police and Guard Union (EA)
IsoPPC........ Isopropylphenylcarbamate (DB)
IS(Ops) .... Intelligence Section, Operations [*Joint Intelligence Subcommittee of Chiefs of Staff*] [*World War II*]
Iso-RAS....... Isorenin-Angiotensin System (DB)
ISORID........ International Information System on Research in Documentation [*International Federation for Documentation*] [*UNESCO*] (IID)
ISORT .... Interdisciplinary Student-Originated Research Training [*National Science Foundation*]
ISOS .... International Southern Ocean Study [*National Science Foundation*]
ISOS .... Interplanetare Sonnensonde
ISOS .... Isosceles [*Triangle*]
ISOSC .... International Society for Soilless Culture [*Wageningen, Netherlands*] (EAIO)
ISOSJ........ Institute of Social Order of the Society of Jesus [*Later, JCSS*] (EA)
ISOSS .... Immobile Suspension Feeders on Soft Substrata [*Oceanography*]
ISOT .... International Symposium on Olfaction and Taste

ISOTAP........ Interservice Occupational Task Analysis Program [*Military*] (NVT)
ISOTEC .... Isotope Thermoelectric Converter
ISOTH .... Isothermal (KSC)
ISOU .... International Society for Ophthalmic Ultrasound (EA)
ISOW .... Iceland-Scotland Overflow Water [*Oceanography*]
Isoworg........ International Society for World Government (WDAA)
ISP................. Distance between Iliac Spines [*Anatomy*] (DAVI)
ISP................. Henry Public Library, Henry, IL [*OCLC symbol*] (OCLC)
ISp................. Iconic Store, Peripheral [*Psychophysiology*]
ISP................. Image Stabilization Program [*Photography*]
ISP................. Image Storage Panel [*Computer science*] (PDAA)
ISP................. Image Store Processor [*Computer science*]
ISP................. Image Synthesis Processor [*Computer science*]
ISP................. Immunoreactive Substance P [*Immunology*]
ISP................. Imperial Smelting Process
ISP................. Implementation Support Package [*Army*]
ISp................. Impulse, Specific (KSC)
ISP................. Independent Service Provider [*Telecommunications*]
ISP................. Independent Smallholders' Party [*Hungary Political party*] (EY)
ISP................. Independent Studies Project [*Navy*]
ISP................. Independent Study Program [*IBM Corp.*]
ISP................. Indexed Sequential Processor
ISP................. Index of Social Position [*Advertising*] (DOAD)
ISP................. Individual Seal Packaging [*Food technology*]
ISP................. Individual Service Plan
ISP................. Industrial Security Plan [*Nuclear energy*] (NRCH)
ISP................. Industrial Security Program [*Air Force, Army*]
ISP................. Industry Service Package
ISP................. Information Search and Processing [*Database search service*] (OLDSS)
ISP................. Information System Plan (MCD)
ISP................. Information Systems Plan [*USAID*] (ECON)
ISP................. Information Systems Professional (DD)
ISP................. Information Systems Professional of Canada (ASC)
ISP................. Information Systems Program [*University of Oklahoma*] [*Norman, OK*]
ISP................. Infrared Spectrophotometer
ISP................. Initial Specific Impulse (MCD)
ISP................. Initial Support Package (MCD)
ISP................. Instantaneous Sound Pressure
ISP................. Instant-Set Polymer (PDAA)
ISP................. Institute for Studies in Pragmaticism [*Texas Tech University*] [*Research center*] (RCD)
ISP................. Institute of Sales Promotion [*ICSU*] [*British*]
ISP................. Institute of Store Planners (EA)
ISP................. Instituto de Seguros de Portugal [*Insurance regulatory agency*] [*Portugal*] (EY)
ISP................. Institut pour une Synthese Planetaire [*Institute for Planetary Synthesis - IPS*] [*Geneva, Switzerland*] (EAIO)
ISP................. In-Store Processor [*Computer science*] (CIST)
ISP................. In-Store Promotions [*Marketing events for US goods held by retail establishments in foreign countries*] [*Department of Commerce*]
ISP................. Instructional System Package (MCD)
ISP................. Instruction Set Processor [*1971*] [*Computer science*]
ISP................. Instrumentation Support Plan (MCD)
ISP................. Integrated Scientific Processor [*Sperry*] (NITA)
ISP................. Integrated Shear Plate
ISP................. Integrated Support Plan (MCD)
ISP................. Integrated System Peripheral [*Computer science*]
ISP................. Integrated Systems Planning, Inc. [*Baltimore, MD*] (TSSD)
ISP................. Intensively Supervised Probation [*Legal term*] (BARN)
ISP................. Interamerican Society of Psychology (EA)
ISP................. Interface Strain Parameter (AAEL)
ISP................. Intergovernmental Science Programs
ISP................. Interim Support Period
ISP................. Interim Support Plan (MCD)
ISP................. Internally Stored Program (AAG)
ISP................. Internal Security Plan (CINC)
ISp................. Internationale des Services Publics [*Public Service International - PSI*] [*Ferney Voltaire, France*] (EAIO)
ISP................. International Shadow Project (EA)
ISP................. International Society for Photogrammetry [*Later, ISPRS*]
ISP................. International Society for Plastination (EA)
ISP................. International Society of Postmasters [*Montreal, PQ*] (EAIO)
ISP................. International Solar Polar [*Mission*] [*NASA*]
ISP................. International Specialty Products [*NYSE symbol*] (SPSG)
ISP................. International Streptomyces Project
ISP................. International Stretch Products, Inc. (EFIS)
ISP................. International Student Pugwash [*Formerly, USSPC*] [*Later, Student Pugwash (USA)*] (EA)
ISP................. International Study Program
ISP................. Internet Service Provider
ISP................. Internet Service Providers [*Telecommunications*]
ISP................. Interoperable Systems Project [*Computer science*]
ISP................. Interspace (MAE)
ISP................. Interspinal [*Anatomy*] (DAVI)
ISP................. Intl Specialty Products [*NYSE symbol*] (TTSB)
ISP................. Intraspinal
ISP................. Inverse Sampling Procedure
ISP................. Ipsco, Inc. [*Toronto Stock Exchange symbol*]
ISP................. Islip, NY [*Location identifier FAA*] (FAAL)
ISP................. Isolated Safflower Protein [*Food technology*]
ISP................. Isolated Soy Protein [*Food technology*]
ISP................. Isoproterenol (DMAA)
ISP................. Isotope Separation Power

ISP................. Italian Society of Physics
ISP................. Long Island [*New York*] MacArthur [*Airport symbol*] (OAG)
ISp................. Schiller Park Public Library, Schiller Park, IL [*Library symbol Library of Congress*] (LCLS)
ISP................. Specific Impulse (MCD)
ISPA............. International Screen Publicity Association
ISPA............. International Sleep Products Association (NTPA)
ISPA............. International Society for the Performing Arts (NTPA)
ISPA............. International Society for the Protection of Animals [*Later, WSPA*] [*British*] (EA)
ISPA............. International Society of Parametric Analysts (EA)
I/SPA............ International Spa and Fitness Association
ISPA............. International Sporting Press Association
ISPA............. International Squash Players Association [*Cardiff, Wales*] (EAIO)
ISPA............. Internet Service Provider Association
ISPA............. Inverted Socket Process Architecture [*Computer science*]
ISPAA........... International Society of Performing Arts Administrators (EA)
ISPAA........... International Society of Plastic and Audio-Visual Art
ISPBX........... Integrated Services PBX [*Telecommunications*] (NITA)
ISPC............. International Society for the Philosophy of Chemistry
ISPC............. International Sound Programming Center [*Telecommunications*]
ISPC............. International Spotted Pony Club [*Defunct*] (EA)
ISPC............. International Statistical Programs Center [*Department of Commerce*] (IID)
ISPCA........... Irish Society for the Prevention of Cruelty to Animals (DBA)
ISPCAN........ International Society for Prevention of Child Abuse and Neglect (EA)
ISPCC .... Irish Society for the Prevention of Cruelty to Children (DI)
ISPCON .... Internet Service Provider Convention [*Annual trade show*] (IGQR)
ISPD .... International Society for Peritoneal Dialysis (EA)
ISPE .... Improved SONAR Processing Equipment [*Military*] (CAAL)
ISPE .... Institute and Society of Practictioners in Electrolysis Ltd. [*British*] (BI)
ISPE .... Institute of Swimming Pool Engineers [*British*] (DBA)
ISPE .... International Society for Philosophical Enquiry (EA)
ISPE .... International Society of Pharmaceutical Engineers (EA)
ISPEC.......... Independent Schools Physical Education Conference (AIE)
ISPEC.......... Insulation Specification (MSA)
ISPER .... IPAC [*Intelligence, Pacific Area Command*] Special Report
ISPES........... Inner-Shell Photoelectron Spectroscopy
ISPF.............. Integral Skinned Polyurethane Foam (PDAA)
ISPF.............. Interactive System Productivity Facility [*Computer science*]
ISPF.............. International Save the Pun Foundation (EA)
ISPF.............. International Science Policy Foundation (EAIO)
ISPF/PDF .... Interactive System Productivity Facility/Program Development Facility [*Computer science*]
ISPG .... Institute of Sedimentary and Petroleum Geology [*Geological Survey of Canada*] [*Research center*] (RCD)
ISPG .... Institutional Support Planning Group [*NASA*] (NASA)
ISPH .... International Society for Professional Hypnosis (EA)
ISPH .... International Society for the Protection of Horses (DI)
ISPH .... International Society of Psychology of Handwriting [*Milan, Italy*] (EA)
ISPHS .... International Society for Phenomenology and Human Sciences (EA)
ISPhS .... International Society of Phonetic Sciences (EA)
ISPI.............. Illinois State Psychiatric Institute
ISPI.............. International Society for Prevention of Infertility (EAIO)
ISPICE .... Interactive Simulation Program with Integrated Circuit Emphasis [*Computer science*] (MHDI)
ISPK............. Insulin-Stimulated Protein Kinase [*An enzyme*]
ISPK............. Isolated Spontaneous Psychokinesis [*Parapsychology*]
ISPL.............. Incremental System Programming Language [*Computer science*]
ISPL.............. Initial Spare Parts List (IAA)
ISPL.............. Instruction Set Processor Language [*Computer science*]
ISPL.............. Interim Spare Parts List (AAG)
ISPL.............. International Society for Phenomenology and Literature (EA)
ISPLS........... International Society of Podiatric Laser Surgery (EA)
ISPM............ In Situ Particle Monitor (AAEL)
ISPM............ International Society of Plant Morphologists [*Delhi, India*] (EAIO)
ISPM............ International Solar Polar Mission [*NASA*]
ISPM............ International Staff Planners Message [*NATO*] (NATG)
ISPM............ Interplanetary Shock Propagation Model (USDC)
ISPMB.......... International Society for the Protection of Mustangs and Burros (EA)
ISPMB.......... International Society of Plant Molecular Biology (EA)
ISPMEMO ... International Staff Planners Memo [*NATO*] (NATG)
ISPMM.......... International Symposium on Purine Metabolism in Man
ISPN............. Integrated Surveys Processing Network [*Bureau of the Census*] (GFGA)
ISPN............. International Society for Pediatric Neurosurgery (EA)
ISPN............. International Standard Program Number [*Numbering system for software*]
ISPN............. International Students Peace Network (EA)
ISPO............. Industrial Staffing Plan Occupations (MCD)
ISPO............. Information Society Project Office (DDC)
ISPO............. Instrumentation Ships Project Office [*Navy*]
ISPO............. International Society for Preventive Oncology (EA)
ISPO............. International Society for Prosthetics and Orthotics - US National Member Society (EA)
ISPO............. International Sports Equipment Fair [*Germany*]
ISPO............. International Statistical Programs Office [*Department of Commerce*] (IEEE)
ISPO .... Irradiation Special Purchase Order (SAA)
ISPOG.......... International Society of Psychosomatic Obstetrics and Gynaecology (PDAA)
ISPOUSC...... International Society for Prosthetics and Orthotics - US Committee [*Later, ISPO*] (EA)

ISPP...........	Internationale Studiengemeinschaft fuer Pranatale Psychologie [*International Society for the Study of Prenatal Psychology - ISPP*] (EAIO)
ISPP...........	International Society for Plant Pathology (EAIO)
ISPP...........	International Society for Portuguese Philately (EA)
ISPP...........	International Society for Retirement Planning [*Later, ISRP*] (EA)
ISPP...........	International Society for the Study of Prenatal Psychology (EAIO)
ISPP...........	International Society of Political Psychology (EA)
ISPP...........	International Society of Prenatal and Perinatal Psychology and Medicine (EAIO)
ISPPP.........	International Symposium on HLtd. of Proteins, Peptides, and Polynucleotides
ISPPS........	Item Support Plan Policies Statement (AFIT)
ISPR..........	Infantry Systems Program Review [*Army*] (AABC)
ISPR..........	Information Security Program Regulation (MCD)
ISPR..........	Integrated Support Parts Requirement (KSC)
ISPR..........	International Special Commission on Radio Interference (MCD)
ISPRS........	International Society for Photogrammetry and Remote Sensing [*Royal Institute of Technology*] [*Research center Sweden*] (IRC)
ISprv.........	Spring Valley Public Library, Spring Valley, IL [*Library symbol Library of Congress*] (LCLS)
ISprvHSD.....	Hall Township High School District 502, Spring Valley, IL [*Library symbol Library of Congress*] (LCLS)
ISprvSD.......	Spring Valley Consolidated Community School District 99, Spring Valley, IL [*Library symbol Library of Congress*] (LCLS)
ISPS..........	Instruction Set Processor Specification [*1977*] [*Computer science*] (CSR)
ISPS..........	Integrated Secondary Propulsion System (MCD)
ISPS..........	International Society of Phonetic Sciences (EA)
ISPS..........	International Standard Paper Sizes
ISPT..........	Industry Superannuation Property Trust
ISPT..........	Initial Satisfactory Performance Test (AAG)
ISPT..........	Institute for Studies in Psychological Testing
ISPT..........	Intergovernmental Science and Public Technology [*of ASRA*] [*National Science Foundation*]
ISPT..........	Interspecies Ovum Penetration Test [*Medicine*] (BABM)
ISPW.........	International Society for the Psychology of Writing (EA)
ISPWP.......	International Society for the Prevention of Water Pollution [*Alton, Hampshire, England*] (EAIO)
ISPX..........	Secular Institute of Pius X (EA)
ISQ...........	In Status Quo
ISQ...........	Lillie M. Evans Memorial Library, Princeville, IL [*OCLC symbol*] (OCLC)
ISQ...........	Manistique, MI [*Location identifier FAA*] (FAAL)
ISQD.........	Identification System for Questioned Documents [*Book title*]
ISQL..........	Interactive SQL [*Computer science*]
ISQL..........	Interactive Standard Query Language (HGEN)
ISQOLS.......	International Society for Quality-of-Life Studies (NTPA)
ISR...........	Ice Sounding RADAR
ISR...........	Identification Safety Range [*Military*] (NVT)
ISR...........	Image Storage Retrieval
ISR...........	Impulse Sequencing Relay
ISR...........	Incoherent Scatter RADAR [*Instrumentation*]
ISR...........	Incstar Corp. [*AMEX symbol*] (SPSG)
ISR...........	Indian State Railway (ROG)
ISR...........	Indirect Source Review [*Environmental Protection Agency*] (FFDE)
ISR...........	Individual Soldier Radio [*Military*] (INF)
ISR...........	Individual Soldier's Report
ISR...........	Industrial Security Regulations [*DoD*]
ISR...........	Information Service Representative [*Veterans Administration*]
ISR...........	Information Storage and Retrieval [*Computer science*]
ISR...........	Infrared Scanning Radiometer (KSC)
ISR...........	Initial Sample Report
ISR...........	Initial System Release (MCD)
ISR...........	Innovative Systems Research (NITA)
ISR...........	Input Select and Reset (IAA)
ISR...........	Input Shift Register
ISR...........	In-Service Recruiter [*Army*]
ISR...........	In Situ Rinse (AAEL)
ISR...........	Institute for Sex Research, Inc. [*National Institute of Mental Health*] (IID)
ISR...........	Institute for Social Research [*University of Michigan*] (EA)
ISR...........	Institute for Social Research [*York University*] [*Information service or system*] (IID)
ISR...........	Institute for Storm Research (MCD)
ISR...........	Institute for Study of Regulation [*Defunct*] (EA)
ISR...........	Institute of Seaweed Research [*British*]
ISR...........	Institute of Semiconductor Research [*Former USSR*]
ISR...........	Institute of Social Research [*Indiana University*] [*Information service or system*] (IID)
ISR...........	Institute of Surgical Research [*San Antonio, TX*] [*Army*]
ISR...........	Instructional System Review
ISR...........	Instrumentation Status Report (MUGU)
ISR...........	Insulin Secretion Rate [*Medicine*] (DMAA)
ISR...........	Integral Superheat Reactor
ISR...........	Integrated Secretory Response [*Biochemistry*] (DAVI)
ISR...........	Integrated Support Requirements (AAG)
ISR...........	Interagency Source Register [*Intelligence*] (MCD)
ISR...........	Interim Scientific Report
ISR...........	Interim System Review (SSD)
ISR...........	Intermediate Session Routing (ACRL)
ISR...........	Intermediate Sodium Removal [*Nuclear energy*] (NRCH)
ISR...........	Internal Scientific Report
ISR...........	International Sacred Recordings, Christian Artists' Record Corp. [*Record label*]
ISR...........	International Sanitary Regulations [*World Health Organization*]
ISR...........	International Shasta Resources [*Vancouver Stock Exchange symbol*]
ISR...........	International Society of Radiology [*Berne, Switzerland*] (EA)
ISR...........	International Sourdough Reunion (EA)
ISR...........	International Star Registry
ISR...........	International Student Relief [*Later, WUS*]
ISR...........	International Survey Research [*London consultancy firm*]
ISR...........	International Synthetic Rubber Co. [*United Kingdom*]
ISR...........	Interrupt Service Routine (IEEE)
ISR...........	Interrupt Status Register (IAA)
ISR...........	Intersecting Storage Ring [*High-energy physics*]
ISR...........	Inventory Status Report
ISR...........	Israel [*ANSI three-letter standard code*] (CNC)
Isr............	Israel (VRA)
ISR...........	Istra Air [*Slovakia*] [*ICAO designator*] (FAAC)
ISR...........	Methodist Medical Center of Illinois, Peoria, IL [*OCLC symbol*] (OCLC)
ISRA	Installment Sales Revision Act of 1980
ISRA	Intercollegiate Squash-Racquet Association (PSS)
ISRA	International Seabed Research Authority
ISRA	International Service Robot Association (NTPA)
ISRA	International Ski Racers Association [*Later, WPS-RA*]
ISRA	International Society for Research on Aggression (EA)
ISRA	Irish Squash Rackets Association (EAIO)
ISRAC	ITT [*International Telephone & Telegraph Corp.*] Secure Ranging and Communications System
ISRAD	Institute for Social Research and Development [*University of New Mexico*]
ISRAD	Integrated Software Research and Development Program (MCD)
Israel Ch......	Israel Chemical Ltd. [*Associated Press*] (SAG)
Israel Stud Criminol...	Israel Studies in Criminology [*Jerusalem, Israel*] [*A publication*] (DLA)
Isramc........	Isramco, Inc. [*Associated Press*] (SAG)
ISRB	Inter-Service Research Bureau [*British*]
ISRC	International Service Robot Congress
ISRC	International Society of Radiology Congress
ISRC	International Standard Recording Code (TELE)
ISRC	International Survey Research Corp.
ISRCDVS......	International Society for Research on Civilization Diseases and Vital Substances (PDAA)
ISRD	Information Storage Retrieval and Dissemination (NITA)
ISRD	International Society for Rehabilitation of the Disabled [*Later, RehabilitationInternational*]
ISRDS	Istituto di Studi sulla Ricerca e Documentazione Scientifica [*Institute for Study of Scientific Research and Documentation*] [*National Research Council*] [*Information service or system*] (IID)
ISRE..........	Interferon-Stimulated Response Element [*Medicine*]
ISRF..........	International Squash Rackets Federation [*Cardiff, Wales*] (EAIO)
ISRF..........	International Sugar Research Foundation [*Later, WSRO*] (EA)
ISRG	Independent Space Research Group (EA)
ISRGLU.......	Independent Ship, Riverside, and General Labourers' Union [*British*]
ISRHAI........	International Secretariat for Research on the History of Agricultural Implements [*Lyngby, Denmark*] (EAIO)
ISRI	Institute of Scrap Recycling Industries (NTPA)
ISRIC	International Soil Reference and Information Centre [*Research center Netherlands*] (IRC)
ISRL	Isramco, Inc. [*NASDAQ symbol*] (NQ)
IsrlLd.........	Israel Land & Development Co. [*Associated Press*] (SAG)
ISRLW........	Isramco Inc.Wrrt'A' [*NASDAQ symbol*] (TTSB)
ISRLZ.........	Isramco Inc.Wrrt'B' [*NASDAQ symbol*] (TTSB)
ISRM	Index of Stability of Relative Magnitudes [*Statistics*]
ISRM	Information Systems Resource Manager
ISRM	International Society for Range Management (EA)
ISRM	International Society for Rock Mechanics [*Lisbon, Portugal*] (EA)
ISRM	International Society of Reproductive Medicine (EA)
ISRM	Inter-Service Radio Measurements [*British World War II*]
Isrm..........	Isramco, Inc. [*Associated Press*] (SAG)
ISRN	Incorporated Society of Registered Naturopaths [*British*]
ISRNI	Incest Survivors Resource Network, International (EA)
ISRO	Indian Space Research Organization
ISRO	International Securities Regulatory Organisation [*London, England*] [*Business term*]
ISRO	Isle Royale National Park
ISRP	Indirect Source Review Program (COE)
ISRP	Initial Spares and Repair Parts
ISRP	Internal Surface Reverse Phase [*Chromatography column*]
ISRP	International Society for Respiratory Protection (EA)
ISRP	International Society for Retirement Planning (EA)
ISRR	International Soundex Reunion Registry (EA)
ISRREC........	Institute for Sex Research Library Records [*Database*] [*Kinsey Institute for Research in Sex, Gender, and Reproduction*] [*Information service or system*] (CRD)
ISRRT	International Society of Radiographers and Radiological Technicians [*Don Mills, ON*] (EA)
ISRS	Impulsive Stimulated Raman Scattering [*Physics*]
ISRS	Information Search and Recording System [*of UMREL*]
ISRS	Integrated Status Reporting System (MCD)
ISRS	International Society for Reef Studies
ISRS	International Society of Refractive Surgery (NTPA)
ISRSM	International Symposium on Rocket and Satellite Meteorology
ISRT..........	International Spinal Research Trust [*British*]
ISRT..........	Iowa Silent Reading Tests [*Education*]
ISRT..........	Isotopes and Radiation Technology [*A publication*]
ISRU	Intergovernmental Science and Research Utilization [*National Science Foundation*]

ISRU .... International Scientific Radio Union [*Also, URSI*]
IsRW .... Weizmann Institute of Science, Rehovot, Israel [*Library symbol Library of Congress*] (LCLS)
ISS .... Ideal Solidus Structures (IEEE)
ISS .... Idiopathic Short Stature [*Medicine*] (DMAA)
ISS .... Ignition Shielding System
ISS .... Image Sensor System
ISS .... Image Sharpness Scale [*Photography*] (OA)
ISS .... Imaging Science Subsystem
ISS .... Imperfect Single Stamp [*Philately*]
ISS .... Imperial Service Sappers [*British military*] (DMA)
ISS .... Independent Schools Section [*American Association of School Libraries*] [*American Library Association*]
ISS .... Independent Sweep System
ISS .... Index of Specifications and Standards (MCD)
ISS .... Individual Style Survey [*Test*] (TMMY)
ISS .... Inductive Storage Switch
ISS .... Industrial Security Section [*NATO*] (NATG)
ISS .... Industrial Systems Service (EFIS)
ISS .... Industry Sole Source (AFIT)
ISS .... Industry Standard Specifications (AAG)
ISS .... Inertial Sensor System (KSC)
ISS .... Inertial Subsystem (MCD)
iss .... Inertial Subsystem (NAKS)
ISS .... Information Sharing System (NITA)
ISS .... Information Storage System (IEEE)
ISS .... Information Support System [*Nondestructive Testing Information Analysis Center - NTIAC*] [*Southwest Research Institute*] [*Information service or system*] (CRD)
ISS .... Information Systems Section [*Battelle Memorial Institute*] [*Information service or system*] (IID)
ISS .... Information Systems Security
ISS .... Information Systems Services [*Brigham Young University*] [*Research center*] (RCD)
ISS .... Information Systems Specialists Office [*Library of Congress*] (NITA)
ISS .... Information Systems Subdivision (MCD)
ISS .... Infrared Sensor System
ISS .... Infrared Surveillance Set
iss .... Inhibit/Override Summary Snapshot (NAKS)
ISS .... Inhibit/Override Summary Snapshot Display (NASA)
ISS .... Initial Space Station (KSC)
ISS .... Injury Severity Score [*Auto safety research*]
ISS .... Input Subsystem
ISS .... Inside Skin (MCD)
ISS .... Inside Surface (MCD)
ISS .... Installation Site Survey (MCD)
ISS .... Installation Support School [*Army*]
ISS .... Installation Support Services (NASA)
iss .... Installation Support Services (NAKS)
ISS .... Institute for Socioeconomic Studies (EA)
ISS .... Institute for Southern Studies (EA)
ISS .... Institute for Space Studies [*NASA*]
ISS .... Institute for Strategic Studies [*Later, IISS*] [*Obsolete*]
ISS .... Institute of Salesian Studies
ISS .... Institute of Social Studies [*Netherlands*]
ISS .... Institute of Special Studies [*Army*]
ISS .... Institute of Sports Sponsorship [*British*] (DBA)
ISS .... Institute of Systems Science [*Singapore*] (DDC)
ISS .... Institutional Shareholder Services
ISS .... Instruction Summary Sheet (NASA)
iss .... Instruction Summary Sheet (NAKS)
ISS .... In-Structure Shock [*Army*] (RDA)
ISS .... Instrumentation Support Service
ISS .... Instrument Servo System
ISS .... Integrated Satellite System
ISS .... Integrated Sealift Study [*Army*] (AABC)
ISS .... Integrated Separation Systems [*Electrophoresis*]
ISS .... Integrated Sounding System [*Marine science*] (OSRA)
ISS .... Integrated Start System (AAG)
ISS .... Integrated Storage System (NITA)
ISS .... Integrated Structural Seat [*Automotive engineering*]
ISS .... Integrated Switch Stick (IAA)
ISS .... Integrated System Schematic (NASA)
iss .... Integrated System Schematic (NAKS)
ISS .... Integration Support Service
ISS .... Intelligence Support System
ISS .... Intelligent Support System
ISS .... INTERCO, Inc. [*Formerly, International Shoe Co.*] [*NYSE symbol*] (SPSG)
ISS .... Intercommunication Service System Inc. [*Information service or system*] (IID)
ISS .... Interface Signal Simulator (SAA)
ISS .... Interface Simulation System (CAAL)
ISS .... Interface Supply Support (SAA)
ISS .... Interim Standard Set
ISS .... Interim Status Standards (GNE)
ISS .... Interim Stowage Shelf (KSC)
ISS .... Intermediate Service School [*Military*] (AFM)
ISS .... Internal Switching System
ISS .... Internationale Gesellschaft fuer Stereologie [*International Society for Stereology*] (EAIO)
ISS .... International Savant Society (EA)
ISS .... International School of Sailing
ISS .... International Schools Services (EA)
ISS .... International Scientific Series [*A publication*]

ISS .... International Scotist Society [*See also SIS*] [*Rome, Italy*] (EAIO)
ISS .... International Seaweed Association (EAIO)
ISS .... International Seaweed Symposium [*Trondheim, Norway*] (MSC)
ISS .... International Self-Service Organization [*Cologne, Federal Republic of Germany*] (EAIO)
ISS .... International Sinatra Society (EA)
ISS .... International Skeletal Society (EA)
ISS .... International Social Service [*See also SSI*] [*Geneva, Switzerland*] (EAIO)
ISS .... International Society for Stereology (EA)
ISS .... International Society of Shropshires (EA)
ISS .... International Society of Surgery (DAVI)
ISS .... International Softbill Society (EA)
ISS .... International Space Station
ISS .... International Steamboat Society (EA)
ISS .... International Students Society [*Defunct*] (EA)
ISS .... International Sunshine Society (EA)
ISS .... Interrupt Service Subroutine (CMD)
ISS .... Interservice Supply Support [*Military*] (AABC)
ISS .... Interstage Section Shell
ISS .... Interstellar Scattering [*of radio waves in the galaxy*]
ISS .... Interstellar [*Phase*] Scintillation [*Galactic science*]
ISS .... Intra-List Stimulus Similarity (PDAA)
ISS .... Inventory Service System (AFIT)
ISS .... Involuntary Servitude and Slavery
ISS .... Ionospheric Sounding Satellite [*Japan*]
ISS .... Ion-Scattering Spectrometer [*or Spectrometry*]
ISS .... Ion-Scattering Spectroscopy (EDCT)
ISS .... Ion Silicon System (IAA)
ISS .... Ion Spectroscopy Scattering [*Surface analysis*]
ISS .... Ion Surface Scattering (DB)
ISS .... Iraqi Intelligence Service
ISS .... Iron and Steel Society - of AIME (EA)
ISS .... Islands [*Postal Service standard*] (OPSA)
ISS .... Isotopic Separation Subsystem
ISS .... Issue (AABC)
ISS .... Issy-Les Moulineaux Airport [*France*]
ISS .... Meridiana SpA [*Italy ICAO designator*] (FAAC)
ISS .... Sangamon State University, Springfield, IL [*Library symbol Library of Congress*] (LCLS)
ISS .... St. Meinrad College, St. Meinrad, IN [*OCLC symbol*] (OCLC)
ISS .... Wiscasset, ME [*Location identifier FAA*] (FAAL)
ISS .... YMCA [*Young Men's Christian Association*] International Student Service (EA)
ISSA .... Association Internationale des Ecoles de Voile [*International Sailing Schools Association*] [*France*] (EAIO)
ISSA .... Information Systems Security Association (EA)
ISSA .... Institute for the Study of Sexual Assault [*Defunct*] (EA)
ISSA .... Institute of Social Services Alternatives [*Defunct*] (EA)
ISSA .... Intelligence Specialist, Seaman Apprentice [*Navy*] (DNAB)
ISSA .... International Sailing Schools Association (EA)
ISSA .... International Sanitary Supply Association (EA)
ISSA .... International Ship Suppliers Association [*Wimbledon, England*] (EA)
ISSA .... International Slurry Seal Association (EA)
ISSA .... International Slurry Surfacing Association (EAIO)
ISSA .... International Social Security Association [*Geneva, Switzerland*] (EA)
ISSA .... International Society of Stress Analysts (EA)
ISSA .... International Strategic Studies Association (EA)
ISSA .... Interservice Supply Support Agreements [*Military*]
ISSA .... Inter-Service Support Agreement (COE)
ISSA .... Irish Schools Swimming Association (EAIO)
ISSAA .... Information Systems Selection and Acquisition Agency (AAGC)
ISS/AB .... International Social Service, American Branch (EA)
ISSAB .... International Social Service, Australian Branch [*An association*]
ISSAC .... Integrated Surface Search and Attack Coordinate
ISSAS .... Interactive Structural Sizing and Analysis System [*Computer science*]
ISSB .... Information Systems Standards Board [*American National Standards Institute*] [*Telecommunications*]
ISSB .... Interservice Security Board [*World War II*]
ISSBB .... Inertial Sensor System Breadboard
ISSBD .... International Society for the Study of Behavioural Development [*Nijmegen, Netherlands*] (EAIO)
ISSC .... Information Systems Software Center [*Fort Belvoir, VA*] [*Army*] (RDA)
ISSC .... International Ship Structures Congress (NOAA)
ISSC .... International Smart Shoppers Club (EA)
ISSC .... International Snowshoe Council [*Defunct*] (EA)
ISSC .... International Social Science Council [*See also CISS*] [*Paris, France*] [*Research center*] (EAIO)
ISSC .... Interservice Sports Council [*Later, ISC*]
ISSC .... Interservice Supply Support Committee [*or Coordinator*] [*Military*] (AABC)
ISSC .... Interstate Shellfish Sanitation Conference
ISSCA .... International Swizzle Stick Collectors Association (EA)
ISSCAAP ..... International Standard Statistical Classification of Aquatic Animals and Plants
ISSCB .... International Society for Sandwich Construction and Bonding
ISSCC .... International Solid State Circuits Conference (MCD)
ISSCM .... International Society for the Study of Church Monuments [*Later, CMS*] (EA)
ISSCO .... Integrated Software Systems Corp.
ISSCT .... International Society of Sugar Cane Technologists [*Piracicaoa, Brazil*] (EA)
ISSD .... Information Systems and Services Division [*Department of Commerce*] (IID)

ISSD .... International Society for Social Defence [See also SIDS] [Paris, France] (EAIO)
ISSD .... International Society for the Study of Dissociation (NTPA)
ISSDF .... International Society for the Study of Dendrobatid Frogs (EA)
ISSDN .... Integrated Services Satellite Digital Network (MCD)
ISSE .... In Situ Spectroscopic Ellipsometry (AAEL)
ISSE .... International Sight and Sound Exposition
ISSE .... International Society for the Study of Expressionism [Formerly, ETMS] (EA)
ISSEC .... Internal Spectral Shifter and Energy Converter (MCD)
ISSE-ETMS... International Society for the Study of Expressionism - Ernst Toller Memorial Society (EA)
ISSEL .... University of Illinois Solid State Electronics Laboratory [Research center] (RCD)
ISSEM .... Information System Security Evaluation Method (IAA)
ISSEP .... Integrated System Safety Engineering Plan
ISSEP .... International Soros Science Education Program [Privately-funded program for former Soviet Republics] (EA)
ISSES .... International Stationary Steam Engine Society (EAIO)
ISSET .... International Symposium on Space Electronics (MCD)
ISSF .... Industry Satellite Services Facility (SSD)
ISSG .... Illustrated Shipboard Shopping Guide [Navy]
ISSG .... Information Systems Support Group (AAGC)
ISSGA .... International Society for the Study of Ghosts and Apparitions (EA)
ISSHCAB ...... International Society for the Study of the Human-Companion Animal Bond [Later, IAHAIO] (EA)
ISSI .... Integrated Silicon Solution [NASDAQ symbol] (TTSB)
ISSI .... Integrated Silicon Solution, Inc. [NASDAQ symbol] (SAG)
ISSI .... International Social Science Institute [Later, International Academy at Santa Barbara] (EA)
ISSI .... Interswitching System Interface [Telecommunications] (ACRL)
ISSID .... International Society for the Study of Individual Differences (EAIO)
ISS Int .... ISS International Service Systems AS [Associated Press] (SAG)
ISSIP .... Interswitching System Interface Protocol [Telecommunications] (ACRL)
ISSK .... International Society for the Sociology of Knowledge [St. John's, NF] [Defunct] (EAIO)
ISSL .... Initial Spares Support List (AFM)
ISSLS .... International Symposium on Subscribers' Loops and Services [Telecommunications] (TEL)
ISSM .... Incompletely Specified Sequential Machine (PDAA)
ISSM .... Independent Society of Stick Makers [A union] [British]
ISSM .... Initialized Stochastic Sequential Machine (IAA)
ISSM .... Institute of Sterile Services Management [British] (DBA)
ISSM .... Interim Surface-to-Surface Missile [Military] (CAAL)
ISSM .... Sangamon County Medical Society, Springfield, IL [Library symbol Library of Congress] (LCLS)
ISSM .... Secular Institute of Schoenstatt Sisters of Mary (TOCD)
ISSMB .... Information Systems Standards Management Board
ISSMC .... Interim Surface-to-Surface Missile Capability [Military] (CAAL)
ISSMFE .... International Society for Soil Mechanics and Foundation Engineering [See also SIMSTF] (EA)
ISSMIS .... Integrated Support Services Management Information System (AABC)
ISSMPD .... International Society for the Study of Multiple Personality and Dissociation (EA)
ISSMS .... Interim Surface-to-Surface Missile System [Military] (NVT)
ISSN .... Intelligence Specialist, Seaman [Navy] (DNAB)
ISSN .... International Standard Serial Number [Library of Congress]
ISSO .... Institute of Strategic and Stability Operations [Army]
ISSO .... International Side-Saddle Organization (EA)
ISSO .... International Small Satellite Organization (NTPA)
ISSOL .... International Society for the Study of the Origin of Life (EA)
ISSOP .... Intra-Fleet Supply Support Operations Program [Navy] (DNAB)
ISSOT .... Inactive Ship Supply Overhaul Team
ISSOT .... Intra-Fleet Supply Support Operations Team [Navy] (DNAB)
ISSP .... Individual Service Strategy Portfolio [Test] (TMMY)
ISSP .... Information Sciences and Systems Planning (SAA)
ISSP .... International Society of Sports Psychology (EA)
ISSP .... Interservice Supply Support Program [Military] (AABC)
ISSPA .... International Sport Show Producers Association (EA)
ISSPP .... Integrated System Safety Program Plan [DoD]
ISSR .... Information Storage, Selection, and Retrieval [Computer science]
ISSR .... Information System Service Request (DNAB)
ISSR .... Institute for Social Science Research [Research center] (RCD)
ISSR .... International Society for the Sociology of Religion [Italy] (EAIO)
ISSRO .... Interservice Supply Support Records Office [Military] (AABC)
ISSRT .... Illinois State Society of Radiologic Technologists (SRA)
ISSRU .... Information Science and Scientometrics Research Unit [Hungarian Academy of Sciences Library] [Budapest] [Information service or system] (IID)
ISSS .... IBM Speech Server Series
ISSS .... Inherent Secondary Shutdown System (PDAA)
ISSS .... Installation Service Supply Support
ISSS .... Institute for Space and Security Studies (EA)
ISSS .... Institute for the Study of Sport and Society
ISSS .... Integrated Silicon Systems [NASDAQ symbol] (SAG)
ISSS .... Integrated Support System Sort [Computer science] (MHDB)
ISSS .... International Seebeck Study Society (EA)
ISSS .... International Seminars Support Scheme
ISSS .... International Society for Socialist Studies
ISSS .... International Society for the Study of Symbols
ISSS .... International Society for the Systems Sciences (NTPA)
ISSS .... International Society of Soil Science [See also AISS] [ICSU Wageningen, Netherlands] (EAIO)

ISSS .... International Society of Sport Sponsors (EA)
IS-SS .... International Society of Statistical Science (NTPA)
ISSS .... Schoenstatt Institute of Secular Priests (TOCD)
ISSSA .... International Society for Strategic Studies (Africa) [Formerly, Africa Society forStrategic Studies] (EA)
ISSSC .... Interservice Supply Support Subcommittee [Military] (CINC)
ISSSE .... International Society of Statistical Science in Economics (EA)
ISSSEEM ...... International Society for the Study of Subtle Energies and Energy Medicine (NTPA)
ISSSM .... Imaging Seeker Surface-to-Surface Missile (PDAA)
ISSSP .... International Sacerdotal Society Saint Pius X (EA)
ISSSS .... Integrated SONAR System for Surface Ships (SAA)
ISSST .... Integrated Submarine SONAR System Technician
ISST .... Infrared Surveillance of Surface Targets [Military] (CAAL)
ISST .... Institute for Space Science and Technology, Inc. [Research center] (RCD)
ISST .... International Society for the Study of Time (EA)
ISST .... Involuntary Second SEA [Southeast Asia] Tour [Air Force]
ISSTA .... Israel Student Tourist Association
ISSTDR .... International Society for STD [Sexually Transmitted Diseases] Research (EA)
ISStH .... Saint John's Hospital, Science Library, Springfield, IL [Library symbol] [Library of Congress] (LCLS)
ISSU .... Inter-Services Signals Unit [British military] (DMA)
ISSUE .... Information System Software Update Environment
Issuing Age... Issuing Agency (NAKS)
ISSVD .... International Society for the Study of Vulvar Disease (DAVI)
ISSX .... International Society for the Study of Xenobiotics
IST .... Improved System Technology (NITA)
IST .... Incompatible Simultaneous Transfer (IAA)
IST .... Incredibly Small Transistor (IAA)
IST .... Incremental System Test
IST .... Indexing Slide Table
IST .... Indian Standard Time (IAA)
IST .... Individualized Study by Telecommunications [Alaska] (EDAC)
IST .... Individual Sales Transaction
IST .... Indonesian Speaking Test [Center for Applied Linguistics] (TES)
IST .... Industrielle-Services Techniques Inc. [Industrial Life-Technical Services Inc.] [Information service or system] (IID)
IST .... Information Science and Technology (BUR)
IST .... Information Society Technology (TELE)
IST .... Initial Service Test (AABC)
IST .... Initial Support Team [Military] (AFM)
IST .... Innovative Science and Technology [DoD]
IST .... Input Stack Tape (IAA)
IST .... Inside Trim (DAC)
IST .... In Situ Transcription (DB)
IST .... In Situ Treatment (COE)
IST .... Instantaneous Spatial Transference
IST .... Institute for Simulation and Training [University of Central Florida] [Research center] (RCD)
IST .... Institute of Science and Technology [University of Michigan] [Research center] (RCD)
IST .... Institutional Skill Training (OICC)
IST .... Instruction-Set Translator [IBM Corp.]
IST .... Instrumentation Support Team (KSC)
IST .... Instrumented Sensor Technologies
IST .... Insulin Sensitivity Test
IST .... Insulin Shock Therapy [Psychiatry]
IST .... Integral Simulation Test [Nuclear energy] (NRCH)
IST .... Integrated Switching and Transmission [Telecommunications] (TEL)
IST .... Integrated System (NITA)
IST .... Integrated Systems Technology (IAA)
IST .... Integrated Systems Test [NASA] (KSC)
IST .... Integrated System Trainer (MCD)
IST .... Integrated System Transformer (IEEE)
IST .... Intelligent Sports Technology Ltd.
IST .... International Institute for Safety in Transportation [Later, IIST] (EA)
IST .... International Society on Toxicology (EA)
IST .... International Standard [Vancouver Stock Exchange symbol]
IST .... International Standard Thread (MSA)
IST .... Interstation Transmission (KSC)
IST .... Interstellar Travel (AAG)
IST .... Intraspecific Antigenic Typing (PDAA)
IST .... Iron, Steel and Heavy Transporters Association, Cleveland OH [STAC]
IST .... Isothermal Storage Test [For hazardous chemicals]
IST .... Istanbul [Turkey] [Seismograph station code, US Geological Survey] (SEIS)
IST .... Istanbul [Turkey] [Airport symbol] (OAG)
IST .... Istanbul Airlines [Turkey] [ICAO designator] (FAAC)
ISt .... Morton Public Library, Morton, IL [OCLC symbol] (OCLC)
ISt .... Stickney-Forest View Library District, Stickney, IL [Library symbol Library of Congress] (LCLS)
ISTA .... Illinois School Transportation Association (SRA)
ISTA .... Illinois Seed Trade Association (SRA)
ISTA .... Independent Secretarial Training Association [British]
ISTA .... Indiana State Techers Association (SRA)
ISTA .... Intelligence, Surveillance, and Target Acquisition [Military]
ISTA .... International Safe Transit Association (NTPA)
ISTA .... International Seed Testing Association [Switzerland]
ISTA .... International Sightseeing and Tours Association [Defunct] (EA)
ISTA .... International Society for Technology Assessment (CIST)
ISTA .... International Special Tooling Association [Frankfurt, Federal Republic of Germany] (EA)

ISTA............ Intertank Structural Test Assembly [*NASA*] (NASA)
ISTAC......... International Science and Technology Advisory Committee [*Australia*]
ISTAC......... International Skilled Trades Advisory Committee [*UAW*]
ISTAIA .... Institute for the Study of Traditional American Indian Arts (EA)
ISTAR .... Image Storage Translation and Reproduction
ISTAR .... Information Science Technology Assessment for Research [*Army*]
ISTAT.......... International Society of Transport Aircraft Trading (EA)
I-STAT .... I-STAT Corp. [*Associated Press*] (SAG)
IStau.......... Staunton Public Library, Staunton, IL [*Library symbol Library of Congress*] (LCLS)
IStauMCD .... Macoupin Community District 6, Staunton, IL [*Library symbol Library of Congress*] (LCLS)
ISTB............ Integrated Subsystem Test Bed (NASA)
ISTB............ Interstate Tariff Bureau, Inc.
ISTB............ Introductory Science Text-Books [*A publication*]
ISTC............ Incunable Short Title Catalogue [*British Library*] [*Information service or system*] (IID)
ISTC............ Industry, Science, and Technology Canada [*Government agency*]
ISTC............ Institute of Scientific and Technical Communicators [*British*]
ISTC............ Interdepartmental Screw Thread Committee [*Departments of Commerce and Defense*]
ISTC............ International Science & Technology Center
ISTC............ International Shade Tree Conference [*Later, ISA*] (EA)
ISTC............ International Society for Training and Culture
ISTC............ International Spa and Tub Council [*Defunct*] (EA)
ISTC............ International Stress and Tension Control Association (EA)
ISTC............ International Student Travel Confederation [*Switzerland*] (EAIO)
ISTC............ International Switching and Testing Center [*Communications*]
ISTC............ Iron and Steel Trades Confederation [*British*]
IStc .... Saint Charles Public Library District, Saint Charles, IL [*Library symbol Library of Congress*] (LCLS)
ISTD............ Imperial Society of Teachers of Dancing
ISTD............ Institute for the Study and Treatment of Delinquency [*British*]
ISTD............ International Society of Tropical Dermatology [*Later, International Society of Dermatology: Tropical, Geographic, and Ecologic - ISD*]
ISTD............ Inter-Service Topographical Department [*British*]
ISTDA.......... Institutional and Service Textile Distributors Association (EA)
ISTDF.......... Istec-Industries Technologies [*NASDAQ symbol*] (SAG)
ISTE............ International Society for Technology in Education (EAIO)
ISTE............ International Society for Tropical Ecology (EA)
ISte .... Saint Elmo Public Library, St. Elmo, IL [*Library symbol Library of Congress*] (LCLS)
ISTEA.......... Initial Screening Training Effectiveness Analysis
ISTEA.......... Intermodal Surface Transportation Efficiency Act [*1990*]
ISTEA.......... Iron and Steel Trades Employers' Association [*British*] (BI)
ISTEC.......... International Superconductivity Technology Center [*Japan*]
Istecln .... Istec-Industries Technologies [*Associated Press*] (SAG)
ISter .... Sterling Public Library, Sterling IL [*Library symbol*] [*Library of Congress*] (LCLS)
ISteSD .... Saint Elmo Community Unit, School District 202, Saint Elmo, IL [*Library symbol Library of Congress*] (LCLS)
ISTES TEMP.. Istesso Tempo [*Same Time*] [*Music*] (ROG)
ISTF............ Integrated Servicing and Test Facilities [*Canada*]
ISTF............ Integrated System Test Flow (NASA)
ISTF............ International Social Travel Federation [*See also FITS*] [*Brussels, Belgium*] (EAIO)
ISTF............ International Society of Tropical Foresters [*See also SIIFT*] (EA)
ISTFA.......... International Society for Testing and Failure Analysis (MCD)
ISTFA.......... International Symposium for Testing and Failure Analysis [*Annual electronics symposium*] (NITA)
ISTH............ International Society on Thrombosis and Hemostasis (EA)
ISTH............ Isthmus [*Board on Geographic Names*]
ISTHM......... Isthmian (ROG)
Isthm .... Isthmian Odes [*of Pindar*] [*Classical studies*] (OCD)
ISTI............. International Spa and Tub Institute (EA)
ISTIC.......... Institute of Scientific and Technical Information of China [*INFOTERM*] [*Beijing*]
ISTIG .... Intercooled Steam-Injected Gas Turbine
ISTIM.......... Interchange of Scientific and Technical Information in Machine Language [*Office of Science and Technology*]
ISTIP.......... Information Systems Technical Integration Panel (SSD)
ISTIS.......... International Scientific and Technical Information System (EAIO)
IStjo........... Saint Joseph Township Library (Swearingen Memorial Library), St. Joseph, IL [*Library symbol Library of Congress*] (LCLS)
IStJSD .... Tiraid Community Unit, School District 2, St. Jacob, IL [*Library symbol Library of Congress*] (LCLS)
ISTM........... Institute of Strata Title Management [*Australia*]
ISTM........... International Society for Testing Materials
ISTMC......... Instrumentation Section Test and Monitor Console (SAA)
ISTMH .... Indefinite Substitute Temporary Mail Handler [*US Postal Service employee classification*]
IstMobl .... Istituto Mobiliare Italiano [*Associated Press*] (SAG)
ISTN........... Integrated Switching and Transmission Network [*Telecommunications*] (TEL)
ISTN........... Interstate National Dealer Services, Inc. [*NASDAQ symbol*] (SAG)
ISTN........... Interstate Natl Dealer Svcs [*NASDAQ symbol*] (TTSB)
ISTNW......... Interstate Natl Dealer Wrrt [*NASDAQ symbol*] (TTSB)
ISTO........... Information Science and Technology Office [*Arlington, VA*] [*DoD*] (TSSD)
ISTP........... Index of Scientific and Technical Publications (TELE)
ISTP........... Information System Theory Project (IAA)
ISTP........... Interagency Solar Terrestrial Programme [*European Space Agency*]
ISTP........... International Society of Tropical Pediatrics [*Philippines*] (EAIO)
ISTP........... International Solar Terrestrial Physics [*Proposed NASA mission*]

ISTP........... Isotope
ISTP & B .... Index to Scientific and Technical Proceedings and Books [*Institute for Scientific Information*] [*Database*]
ISTPW .... Impact Signature Training Practice Warhead [*Army*]
ISTR .... Incstar Corp. [*NASDAQ symbol*] (TTSB)
ISTR .... Indexed Sequential Table Retrieval
ISTR .... Institute for Science Training and Research (HGEN)
ISTR .... International Society for Third-Sector Research (NFD)
IStr........... Streator Public Library, Streator, IL [*Library symbol Library of Congress*] (LCLS)
ISTRA .... Interplanetary Space Travel Research Association
ISTRACON ... Interstation Supersonic Track Conferences (MCD)
IStrESD ...... Eagle Elementary Consolidated School District 43, Streator, IL [*Library symbol Library of Congress*] (LCLS)
IStrHSD....... Streator Township High School District 40, Streator, IL [*Library symbol Library of Congress*] (LCLS)
ISTRO .... International Soil Tillage Research Organization [*Netherlands*] (EAIO)
IStrOSD....... Otter Creek Elementary School District 56, Streator, IL [*Library symbol Library of Congress*] (LCLS)
ISTRS .... Index of Submarine Technical Repair Standards [*Military*] (DNAB)
IStrSD .... Streator Elementary School District 45, Streator, IL [*Library symbol Library of Congress*] (LCLS)
IStrSMH ...... Saint Mary's Hospital, Henegen Medical Library, Streator, IL [*Library symbol Library of Congress*] (LCLS)
ISTRUCTE .... Institution of Structural Engineers [*British*]
ISTS .... Institute for Space and Terrestrial Science [*Research center Canada*] (RCD)
ISTS .... International Simultaneous Translation Service
ISTS .... International Society for Twin Studies [*Rome, Italy*] (EA)
ISTS .... International Symposium on Space Technology and Science (MCD)
ISTS .... Intersite Transmission Subsystem [*Ground Communications Facility, NASA*]
ISTS .... Intradermal Skin Test Score [*Immunology*]
ISTSP......... Independent Schools Talent Search Program [*Later, A Better Chance*] (EA)
ISTSR .... International Society for Third-Sector Research (EA)
ISTSS .... International Society for Traumatic Stress Studies (NTPA)
ISTT .... In-Service Training of Teachers [*Scottish National Committee*]
ISTT .... International Society for Trenchless Technology (EAIO)
ISTT .... Intersegmental Travel Time [*Zoology*]
ISTU .... Isometric Strength Testing Unit [*Medicine*] (DMAA)
IsTU .... Tel Aviv University, Tel Aviv, Israel [*Library symbol Library of Congress*] (LCLS)
ISTV .... Insight Entertainment Corp. [*NASDAQ symbol*] (SAG)
ISTVS .... International Society for Terrain-Vehicle Systems (EA)
IStw .... Popular Creek Public Library District, Streamwood, IL [*Library symbol*] [*Library of Congress*] (LCLS)
ISU/CCL ...... In-Arm Suspension Unit [*Tank Technology*]
ISU .... Independent Signal Unit [*Telecommunications*] (TEL)
ISU .... Indiana State University [*Terre Haute*]
ISU .... Indiana State University, Terre Haute, IN [*OCLC symbol*] (OCLC)
ISU .... Inertial Sensing Unit
ISU .... Information Service Unit [*International Potato Center*] [*Information service or system*] (IID)
ISU .... Initial Signal Unit [*Telecommunications*] (TEL)
ISU .... Instruction Storage Unit
ISU .... Instruction Stream Unit (IAA)
ISU .... Integrated Sight Unit [*Weaponry*] (INF)
ISU .... Interface Sharing Unit
ISU .... Interface Surveillance Unit (SAA)
ISU .... Interface Switching Unit (BUR)
ISU .... Interference Suppression Unit (IAA)
ISU .... Internal Airlift/Helicopter Slingable Container Unit [*MTMC*] (TAG)
ISU .... International Salvage Union (PDAA)
ISU .... International Scientific Union
ISU .... International Seaman's Union
ISU .... International Shooting Union
ISU .... International Sigma Security, Inc. [*Vancouver Stock Exchange symbol*]
ISU .... International Skating Union [*See also UIP*] [*Davos-Platz, Switzerland*] (EAIO)
ISU .... International Society of Urology [*See also SIU*] [*Lille, France*] (EAIO)
ISU .... International Space University [*Strasbourg, France*]
ISU .... International Stereoscopic Union (PDAA)
ISU .... International System of Units
ISU .... Iowa Southern Utilities [*Southern Industrial Railroad, Inc.*] [*AAR code*]
ISU .... Iowa State University [*Ames*]
ISU .... Italian Service Unit [*Italian prisoners of war who became volunteers in the Allied war effort*]
ISu .... Summit-Argo Public Library, Summit, IL [*Library symbol Library of Congress*] (LCLS)
I-Sub........... Inhibitor Substance [*Medicine*] (DMAA)
ISU/CCL ...... Iowa State University / Cyclone Computer Laboratory (PDAA)
ISUDO......... International Symposium on Ultrasonic Diagnostics in Ophthalmology [*Later, ISO U*] (EA)
ISUDS .... Iterative Scheme Using a Direct Solution
ISU-ERI ...... Iowa State University - Engineering Research Institute (PDAA)
ISUH .... Institute for the Study of Universal History through Arts and Artifacts [*Defunct*] (EA)
ISUM .... Intelligence Summary
ISUM .... Southern Illinois University, School of Medicine, Springfield, IL [*Library symbol Library of Congress*] (LCLS)
ISumSD .... Red Hill Community Unit, School District 10, Sumner, IL [*Library symbol Library of Congress*] (LCLS)

ISUP	Integrated Services User Part
ISUP	Iowa State University Press (DGA)
ISUP	ISDN [*Integrated Services Digital Network*] User Part [*Telecommunications*]
ISUPTTS	International Sports Union of Post, Telephone, and Telecommunications Service (EA)
ISURSL	Indiana State University Remote Sensing Laboratory [*Research center*] (RCD)
ISUS	International Society for Utilitarian Studies [*British*] (EAIO)
ISUSAIC	Intelligence School, United States Army Intelligence Center
ISUSE	International Secretariat for the University Study of Education
ISV	Independent Software Vendor [*Computer science*]
ISV	Input Signal Voltage
ISV	In Situ Vitrification [*Radioactive waste cleanup*]
ISV	Instantaneous Speed Variation [*Tape recorders*]
ISV	International Scientific Vocabulary
ISV	International Society for Vaccines [*Gaithersburg, MD*]
ISV	International Society of Videographers (EA)
ISV	Interorbital Space Vehicle
ISV	Interval Service Value (BUR)
ISV	Iron-Solution Value (PDAA)
ISV	Irradiated Silicon Vidicon
ISV	Islena de Inversiones SA [*Honduras*] [*ICAO designator*] (FAAC)
ISV	Iso Ventures, Inc. [*Vancouver Stock Exchange symbol*]
ISV	Neponset Public Library, Neponset, IL [*OCLC symbol*] (OCLC)
ISv	Sauk Village Library District, Sauk Village, IL [*Library symbol Library of Congress*] (LCLS)
ISVA	Incorporated Society of Valuers and Auctioneers (EAIO)
ISVA	International Satellite Verification Agency
ISVA	International Society for Vibroacoustics (EAIO)
ISVBM	International Society of Violin and Bow Makers [*Basel, Switzerland*] (EAIO)
ISVCS	Improved Secure Voice Conferencing System [*Military*] (MCD)
ISVD	Information System for Vocational Decisions Program
ISVE	Istituto di Studi per lo Sviluppo Economico [*Institute for the Study of Economic Development*] [*Italy*]
ISVESTA	Individual Survival Vest for Aircrew [*Army*] (RDA)
ISVL	Vachel Lindsay Association, Springfield, IL [*Library symbol Library of Congress*] (LCLS)
ISVP	International Society for Vehicle Preservation (EA)
ISVR	Institute of Sound and Vibration Research [*Southampton University, England*]
ISVR3	Intel Smart Video Recorder III
ISVS	In Situ Vapro Stripping [*Environmental science*]
ISVS	Integrated Secure Voice System
ISVS	International Secretariat for Volunteer Service [*Defunct*]
ISVSK	Internationaler Staendiger Verband fuer Schiffahrt-Kongresse [*Permanent International Association of Navigation Congresses*]
ISW	Ice Shelf Water [*Oceanography*]
ISW	Information Services of Warwick [*Rhode Island*] [*Information retrieval*] (IID)
ISW	Initial Status Word (IAA)
ISW	Institute for Solid Wastes
ISW	Institute of Social Welfare [*British*] (BI)
ISW	Integrated Sachs-Wolfe [*Effect in cosmic microwave background*]
ISW	Integrated Software
ISW	Intermediate Scale Warfare
ISW	Internal Status Word (IAA)
ISW	Interstitial Water [*Physiology*]
ISW	Ion Switch (IAA)
ISW	Serib Wings [*Italy ICAO designator*] (FAAC)
ISW	Toulon Public Library, Toulon, IL [*OCLC symbol*] (OCLC)
ISW	Wisconsin Rapids [*Wisconsin*] [*Airport symbol*] (OAG)
ISW	Wisconsin Rapids, WI [*Location identifier FAA*] (FAAL)
ISWA	Association Internationale pour les Residus Solides et le Nettoiement des Vil les [*International Solid Wastes and Public Cleansing Association*] [*INTAPUC and IRGRD*] [*Formed by a merger of*] [*Denmark*] (EAIO)
ISWA	Insect Screening Weavers Association (EA)
ISWA	International Science Writers Association
ISWA	International Ski Writers Association [*Riehen, Switzerland*] (EA)
ISWAP	International Society of Women Airline Pilots (EA)
ISWBBHA	Iron, Steel, and Wood Barge Builders' and Helpers' Association [*A union*] [*British*]
ISWC	Industrial Social Welfare Center [*Columbia University*] [*Research center*] (RCD)
ISWC	International Society for the Welfare of Cripples [*Later, Rehabilitation International*]
ISWG	Imperial Standard Wire Gauge
ISWG	Independent Schools Working Group (AIE)
ISWG	Integrated Support Working Group (SDI)
ISWG	Item Selection Working Group [*NATO*] (NATG)
ISWI	Incisional Surgical Wound Infection [*Medicine*] (DMAA)
ISWI	International Sports Wagering, Inc. [*NASDAQ symbol*] (SAG)
ISWIM	If You See What I Mean (PDAA)
ISWL	Isolated Single Wheel Load (AIA)
ISWM	Institute of Solid Waste Management [*British*] (DCTA)
ISWM	International Society of Weighing and Measurement (EA)
ISWNE	International Society of Weekly Newspaper Editors (EA)
ISWRRI	Iowa State Water Resources Research Institute [*Iowa State University*] [*Department of the Interior Research center*] (RCD)
ISWS	Illinois State Water Survey [*Illinois Department of Energy and Natural Resources*] [*Research center*] (RCD)
ISWSC	International Society of Worldwide Stamp Collectors [*Formerly, Worldwide Collectors' Club - WCC*]

ISWT	International Society of Wine Tasters [*Defunct*] (EA)
ISWU	International Society of Wang Users (EA)
ISWU	Iron and Steel Workers' Union [*India*]
ISX	Impurity Study Experiment [*Oak Ridge National Laboratory*]
ISX	Information Switching Exchange (IAA)
ISX	Wyoming Public Library, Wyoming, IL [*OCLC symbol*] (OCLC)
ISY	Black Hawk College, East Campus, Gustav E. Lundberg Learning Center, Kewanee, I L [*OCLC symbol*] (OCLC)
ISY	City Air Ltd. [*British ICAO designator*] (FAAC)
ISY	Instrument Systems Corp. [*NYSE symbol*] (SAG)
ISY	International Space Year [*1992*]
ISY	Intrasynovial [*Medicine*]
ISy	Sycamore Public Library, Sycamore, IL [*Library symbol Library of Congress*] (LCLS)
IsYAEC	Israel Atomic Energy Commission, Soreq Nuclear Research Centre, Yavne, Israel [*Library symbol Library of Congress*] (LCLS)
ISYN	Inductosyn
ISYS	Integral Sys MD [*NASDAQ symbol*] (TTSB)
ISYS	Integral Systems, Inc. [*NASDAQ symbol*] (SAG)
ISYSCON	Integrated System Control [*Military*]
ISYVC	International Sivananda Yoga Vedanta Center (EAIO)
ISYVO	International Sivananda Yoga Vedanta Organization [*Val Morin, PQ*] (EAIO)
ISZ	Increment and Skip on Zero [*Computer science*]
ISZ	Interplate Shear Zone [*Geology*]
ISZ	Iskustvennyi Sputnik Zemil [*Former USSR*]
IT	Air Inter [*ICAO designator*] (AD)
It	Air Inter, Societe [*France ICAO designator*] (ICDA)
It	Biblioteca Nazionale Centrale, Rome, Italy [*Library symbol Library of Congress*] (LCLS)
IT	Gartner Group ™A∫ [*NYSE symbol*]
IT	Idaho Territory [*Obsolete*] (ROG)
IT	Identification and Traceability (IAA)
IT	Identification Transponder (MCD)
IT	Iliotibial [*Anatomy*] (DAVI)
IT	Illusion Theater (EA)
IT	Immediate Transient Incapacitation [*Radiation casualty criterion*] [*Army*]
IT	Immediate Transportation
IT	Immunity Test
IT	Immunoreactive Tag [*Clinical chemistry*]
IT	Immunotherapy [*Medicine*]
IT	Immunotoxin
IT	Immunoturbidimetry [*Analytical biochemistry*]
IT	Implantation Test [*Medicine*] (MAE)
IT	Implosive Therapy [*Type of behavior therapy*]
IT	Improved Tartar
IT	Improved Touring [*Class of racing cars*]
IT	Incentive Travel [*Travel industry*]
IT	Inclusive Tour (MCD)
IT	Income Tax
IT	Income Tax Unit Rulings [*US Internal Revenue Service*]
IT	Incomplete Translation [*Telecommunications*] (TEL)
IT	Indent Tab Character [*Computer science*]
IT	Independent Tank (DS)
IT	Index Term [*Computer science*]
IT	Index Translationum [*UNESCO*]
IT	Indian Territory [*in United States*]
IT	Individual Therapy
IT	Individual Training [*Army*]
IT	Individual Transportation [*Urban planning*]
IT	Industrial Technology
IT	Industrial Training
IT	Industrial Tribunal [*British*] (DCTA)
IT	Industry Telephone Maintenance [*FCC*] (IEEE)
IT	Industry Transistor [*Electronics*] (IAA)
IT	Infection Type [*Pathology*]
IT	Inferior Temporal [*Anatomy*]
IT	Inferior Turbinate [*Otorhinolaryngology*] (DAVI)
IT	Information Technology [*Computer science*] (ECON)
IT	Information Theory (MCD)
IT	Information Transform [*Information service or system*] (IID)
IT	Information Type (ACRL)
IT	Inhalation Test [*Clinical medicine*] (MAE)
IT	Inhalation Therapy [*or Therapist*] [*Medicine*]
I/T	Initial Track (MCD)
IT	Initiation Technician (SAA)
IT	Inner Targets (COE)
IT	Inner Temple
IT	Innovative Test
IT	Input Terminal
IT	Input Translator [*IBM Corp.*] [*Computer science*]
IT	Inspection and Test (IAA)
IT	Inspection Tag
IT	Inspiratory Time [*Medicine*] (DAVI)
IT	Installation Test (NASA)
IT	Instant Transaction (IAA)
IT	Institut du Textile [*Textile Institute*] (EAIO)
IT	Institute of Technology [*Air Force*]
IT	Institute of Trichologists (EAIO)
IT	Institutional Training (OICC)
IT	Instructional Technologist (EDAC)
IT	Instructional Technology
IT	Instruction Tag (MSA)
IT	Instructor Trainer [*Red Cross*]

IT	Instrumented Laboratory Training
IT	Instrument Technician
IT	Instrument Test [or Tree] [Nuclear energy] (NRCH)
IT	Instrument Transformer
IT	Insulated Tank Container [Shipping] (DCTA)
IT	Insulating Transformer (KSC)
IT	Intact (DAVI)
IT	Intelligent Terminal [Computer science]
IT	Intelligent Transaction Router [Telecommunications]
IT	Intelligent Transmitter (ACII)
IT	Intensity of Telephone Interference (IAA)
I/T	Intensity/Time [Duration of contractions] [Medicine] (STED)
IT	Intensive Therapy [Medicine] (MAE)
IT	Intention Tremor [Medicine] (DB)
IT	Interactive Television
IT	Interceptor Trap
IT	Interesting Transcript [genetics]
IT	Interfacial Tension [Physical chemistry] (IAA)
IT	Interfering Transmitter (IAA)
IT	Intermediate Technology [An association] (EA)
IT	Intermediate Treatment [Special provision of British law for juvenile offenders]
IT	Internal Thread
IT	Internal Translator [Carnegie Institute] [IBM Corp.]
IT	International Steam Table Calorie (IIA)
IT	International Technology Corp. [Associated Press] (SAG)
IT	International Tolerance
IT	International Traders Association (EA)
IT	International Travellers [YWCA]
IT	Interrogator-Transponder (KSC)
IT	Interstate Theft
I/T	Intertank (NASA)
IT	Intertoll [Trunk] [Telecommunications] (TEL)
IT	Intertuberous [Diameter] [Medicine]
IT	Interval Timer [Computer science]
IT	Interval Training [Physical fitness program]
IT	Intestinal Type [of epithelium]
IT	Intimal Thickening [Medicine] (MEDA)
IT	Intradermal Test [Medicine] (MAE)
IT	In Transitu [In Transit] [Latin]
IT	Intrathecal [Medicine]
IT	Intrathoracic [Medicine]
IT	Intratracheal [Medicine]
IT	Intratracheal Tube [Medicine]
IT	Intratumoral [Medicine] (MAE)
IT	Inventory Transfer
IT	Ion Trap [Instrumentation]
IT	Iphigenia Taurica [of Euripides] [Classical studies] (OCD)
IT	Irrelevant Talk [Slang]
IT	Ischial Tuberosity [Medicine]
IT	Island Telephone Co. Ltd. [Toronto Stock Exchange symbol]
It	Islet [Maps and charts]
IT	Isomeric Transition [Radioactivity]
IT	Isothermal Transformation [Metallurgy]
IT	Isotocin [Endocrinology]
IT	Italian
IT	Italic (IAA)
IT	Italy [ANSI two-letter standard code] (CNC)
it	Italy [MARC country of publication code Library of Congress] (LCCP)
IT	Item (MCD)
IT	Item Transfer
IT	National Organization of Industrial Trade Unions
IT	Tour-Based Fare [Airline fare code]
it	Vetus Itala (BJA)
IT-95	Information Technology 1995 [Marine science] (OSRA)
ITA	Great River Library System, Quincy, IL [OCLC symbol] (OCLC)
ITA	Illinois Motor Truck Operators Association, Chicago IL [STAC]
ITA	Imagining Technologies Association (NTPA)
IT-A	Immunotoxin with A-Chain
ITA	Income Tax Act Regulations [Commerce Clearing House Canadian Ltd.] [Information service or system] (CRD)
ITA	Independent Telecommunications Analysts [Boulder, CO] (TSSD)
ITA	Independent Television Association [British] (DBA)
ITA	Independent Television Authority [Later, IBA] [British]
ITA	Individual Task Authorization
ITA	Individual Treatment Assessment [Medicine] (STED)
ITA	Indoor Tennis Association [Later, NTA] (EA)
ITA	Industrial Technological Associates, Inc. [Information service or system]
ITA	Industrial Telecommunications Association (NTPA)
ITA	Industrial Truck Association [Washington, DC] (EA)
ITA	Industry and Trade Administration [Later, International Trade Administration] [Department of Commerce]
ITA	Inferior Temporal Artery [Medicine] (DMAA)
ITA	Inferior Tympanic Artery [Anatomy]
i/t/a	Initial Teaching Alphabet [A 44-symbol alphabet planned to simplify beginning reading by representing sounds more precisely]
ITA	Inner Transport Area
ITA	Inside Wheel Turning Angle [Automotive engineering]
ITA	Inspection Test Assembly (MCD)
ITA	Institut du Transport Aerien [Institute of Air Transport] [Research center France] (IRC)
ITA	Institute for Telecommunications and Aeronomy [ESSA] (MCD)
ITA	Institute of the Arts [Australian National University]
ITA	Institute of Theoretical Astronomy [Leningrad, USSR]

ITA	Institute of Traffic Administration [British]
ITA	Institute of Transactional Analysis [British] (DBA)
ITA	Institute of Transport Administration [Later, IoTA] (EAIO)
ITA	Institute of Transport Aviation (KSC)
ITA	Institute of Travel Agents [British] (BI)
ITA	Instrumentation Technology Associates, Inc.
ITA	Instrument Time (Actual)
ITA	Integrated Test Area (MCD)
ITA	Integrated Test Article (NAKS)
ITA	Integrated Thruster Assembly (KSC)
ITA	Interactive Television Association
ITA	Inter-Air, Inc. [ICAO designator] (FAAC)
ITA	Intercollegiate Tennis Association (NTPA)
ITA	Interface Test Adapters (MCD)
ITA	Intermediate Teachers Association
ITA	Intermediate Thrust Arc
ITA	Intermediate Training Assessment (DOMA)
ITA	Intermodal Transportation Association (EA)
ITA	International 210 Association (EA)
ITA	International Alphabet
ITA	International Tap Association (EA)
ITA	International Tape Association (NITA)
ITA	International Tape/Disc Association (EA)
ITA	International Taxicab Association (EA)
ITA	International Telegraph Alphabet (NATG)
ITA	International Temperance Association [Later, IHTA] (EA)
ITA	International Texcan Tech [Vancouver Stock Exchange symbol]
ITA	International Thermographers Association (EA)
ITA	International Tin Agreement
ITA	International Tire Association (EA)
ITA	International Titanium Association (NTPA)
ITA	International Tornado Association [Germany] (EAIO)
ITA	International Touring Alliance [Belgium] (EAIO)
ITA	International Track Association [Defunct]
ITA	International Trade Administration [Washington, DC Department of Commerce]
ITA	International Trade Association [BTS] (TAG)
ITA	International Trombone Association (EA)
ITA	International Tube Association [Leamington Spa, Warwickshire, England] (EAIO)
ITA	International Tuberculosis Association (DAVI)
ITA	International Tunnelling Association (EA)
ITA	International Turquoise Association (EA)
ITA	International Twins Association [Defunct] (EA)
ITA	International Typographic Association (MCD)
ITA	Interstate Towing Auxiliary (EA)
ITA	Interstate Truckers Association
ITA	Ionization Test Apparatus
ITA	Itacoatiara [Brazil] [Airport symbol] (AD)
ITA	Itaconic Acid [Organic chemistry]
ita	Italian [MARC language code Library of Congress] (LCCP)
ITA	Italy [ANSI three-letter standard code] (CNC)
ITA	Italy Fund [NYSE symbol] (TTSB)
ITA	Italy Fund, Inc. [NYSE symbol] (SPSG)
ITA	Itapemirim Transportes Aereos SA [Brazil] [ICAO designator] (FAAC)
ITAA	Independent Travel Agencies of America Association (EA)
ITAA	Information Technology Association of America [Arlington, VA] (CDE)
ITAA	International Textile and Apparel Association (NTPA)
ITAA	International Theatrical Agencies Association (EA)
ITAA	International Transactional Analysis Association (EA)
ITAADS	Installation the Army Authorization Document System
ITAADS	Interim Target Acquisition and Designation System
ITAAP	Inspection Test and Analysis Plan (IAA)
ITAB	Information Technology Advisory Board [British]
ITAB	International Transportation Advisory Board [BTS] (TAG)
ITAC	Information Technology Acquisition Center [Navy] (CIST)
ITAC	Information Technology Advisory Committee [Office of Management and Budget] (GFGA)
ITAC	Integrated Tactical Aircraft Control [Air Force] (DOMA)
ITAC	Intelligence and Threat Analysis Center [Air Force] (DOMA)
ITAC	Intelligence Tracking Analysis and Correlation (MCD)
ITAC	Interagency Textile Administrative Committee
ITAC	International Target Audience Code [International Federation of Library Associations]
ITAC	Intestinal Type Adenocarcinoma [Oncology]
ITACC	Incremental Tactical Communications Capability Study [Military] (MCD)
ITACCS	International Trauma Anesthesia and Critical Care Society (EA)
ITACO	Integration Trade and Analysis-Cycle O (SSD)
ITACS	Integrated Tactical Air Control System
ITAC-T	International Telecommunication Advisory Committee-Telecommunications (ACRL)
ITAD	Individual Training Analysis and Design (MCD)
ITAD	Information, Training and Agricultural Development [British consultancy and training service] (ECON)
ITAD	Intelligence Threat Analysis Detachment [Army] (RDA)
ITAE	Integrated Time and Absolute Error
ITAffi2	Internationality Alphabet ffi2 (MCD)
ITAG	Intelligence Threat Analysis Group [Military] (DNAB)
ITAG	Internal Thoracic Artery (STED)
ITAG	Invalid Tricycle Action Group [British] (DI)
ITAK	Illankai Tamil Arasu Kadchi [Federal Party] [Sri Lanka] [Political party] (PPW)
ITAL	Information Technology and Libraries [A publication]

ITAL	Information Technology for Libraries [*Formerly, JOLA*] [*A publication*] (NITA)
ITAL	Initial Task Assignment List
ITAL	Introductory Trials Allowance List [*Military*] (AFIT)
ITAL	Inventory Trial Allowance List
ITAL	Italian
Ital	Italian (ODCC)
ITAL	Italic [*or Italics*]
ital	Italic (WDMC)
ITALD	Improved Tactical Air-Launched Decoy (DWSG)
Ital Dial	Italic Dialects [*A publication*] (OCD)
Italian Yb of Int'l L	Italian Yearbook of International Law [*A publication*] (DLA)
Italy	Italy Fund, Inc. [*Associated Press*] (SAG)
ITALY	I Trust and Love You [*Correspondence*] (DSUE)
ITAM	Immunoreceptor Tyrosine Activation Motif [*Biochemistry*]
ITAM	Immunoreceptor Tyrosine-Based Activation Motif [*Immunology*]
ITAM	Instituto Tecnologico Autonomo de Mexico [*Economic research*] [*Mexico*] (CROSS)
ITAM	Integrated Training Area Management [*Military*] (INF)
ITAM	Interactive Med Tech Ltd [*NASDAQ symbol*] (TTSB)
ITAM	Interdata Telecommunications Access Method [*Computer science*] (MHDB)
ITAMA	Information Technology Acquisition and Marketing Association [*Defunct*] (EA)
ITAM VETS	Italian American War Veterans of the United States [*Defunct*] (EA)
IT & AP	Inspection Test and Analysis Plan (NRCH)
IT & ME	Incentive Travel and Meeting Executives Show [*Trade show*]
IT and T	International Telephone & Telegraph Corp. [*New York, NY*] [*Facetious translation: International Travel and Talk*]
IT & TS	International Turtle and Tortoise Society (EA)
ITAP	Information Technology Advisory Panel [*British*]
ITAP	Integrated Technical Assessment Panel [*NASA*] (NASA)
ITAR	International Trade and Arms Regulations
ITAR	International Traffic in Arms Regulation [*US*]
ITAR	Interstate Transportation in Aid of Racketeering
ITARS	Integrated Terrain Access and Retrieval System [*Hughes Aircraft*] [*Digital mapping project*] (NITA)
ITARS	Integrated Terrain Retrieval System (MCD)
ITAS	Improved Tactical Attack System
ITAS	Improved Target Acquisition System [*Army*]
ITAS	Indicated True Air Speed [*Aviation*] (AFM)
ITAS	Integrated Tactical Attack System (MCD)
ITAS	Integrated Test and Alignment System
ITAS	Inter-American Travel Agents Society (EA)
ITASS	Interim Towed Array Surveillance System [*Military*] (NVT)
ITATLIS	Indian Association of Teachers of Library Science (BUAC)
ITAV	Individual Tactical Air Vehicle
ITAVS	Integrated Testing, Analysis, and Verification System
ITAWDS	Integrated Tactical Amphibious Warfare Data System [*Navy*] (NVT)
ITAX	Intermountain Aviation, Inc. [*Air carrier designation symbol*]
ITAX	Italics
ITB	Abbott Laboratories, North Chicago, IL [*OCLC symbol*] (OCLC)
ITB	Iliotibial Band [*Anatomy*]
ITB	Individual Tour Basing [*Fares*]
ITB	Industrial Test Battery (TES)
ITB	Industrial Training Board [*British*]
ITB	Instantaneous Trip Block [*Computer science*] (IAA)
ITB	Institute of Technology at Bandung [*Indonesia*]
ITB	Institut Technique du Batiment [*Technical Institute for Building*] [*France Information service or system*] (IID)
ITB	Integral Terminal Block
ITB	Integrated Test Block
ITB	Integrated Training Brigade [*Navy*]
ITB	Integrated Tug Barge (DS)
ITB	Interbrasil Star, SA [*Brazil*] [*FAA designator*] (FAAC)
ITB	Intermediate Text Block
ITB	Intermediate Transmission Block [*Computer science*] (BUR)
ITB	Intermountain Tariff Bureau, Inc.
ITB	Internal Transfer Bus
ITB	Internationaler Turnerbund [*International Gymnastic Federation*]
ITB	International Thomson Books
ITB	International Thoroughbred Breeders, Inc. [*AMEX symbol*] (SPSG)
ITB	International Time Bureau
ITB	International Training Branch [*Office of Education*]
ITB	Internet Transaction Broker [*Computer science*]
ITB	In the Business [*Refers to television and film industries*]
ITB	Intl ThoroughBred [*AMEX symbol*] (TTSB)
ITB	Invisible Trade Balance [*Business term*] (MHDW)
ITB	Invitation to Bid
ITB	Ion Thruster Beam
ITB	Irish Tourist Board (EA)
ITB	Island Tug & Barge [*AAR code*]
ItBa	Biblioteca Comunale ™Angelillo∫, Servizio Prestito, Bari, Italy [*Library symbol Library of Congress*] (LCLS)
ITBA	Idaho Thoroughbred Breeders Association (SRA)
ITBA	International Toy Buff's Association (EA)
ITBA	Irish Ten Pin Bowling Association (EAIO)
ItBar	Biblioteca Comunale di Barletta, Barletta, Italy [*Library symbol Library of Congress*] (LCLS)
ItBaU	Universita degli Studi di Bari, Bari, Italy [*Library symbol Library of Congress*] (LCLS)
ITBC	Instructional Television Funding Cooperative (NTCM)
ITBE	Interchannel Time Base Error
ITB-ID	International Thomson Books - International Division
ITBL	Incompressible Turbulent Boundary Layer
ITBOF	Illinois Thoroughbred Breeders and Owners Foundation (SRA)
ITBP	International Thomson Business Press, Inc. [*Publisher*]
ITBPrA	Intl ThoroughBred A Pfd [*AMEX symbol*] (TTSB)
ITBS	Iowa Tests of Basic Skills
ITBTP	Institut Technique du Batiment et des Travaux Publics [*Technical Institute for Building and Public Works*] [*Information service or system*] (IID)
ITC	Concordia Theological Seminary, Fort Wayne, IN [*OCLC symbol*] (OCLC)
ITC	Ideal Toy Corp. (EFIS)
ITC	Igloo Thermal Control [*Aerospace*] (MCD)
ITC	Illinois Terminal Railroad Co. [*AAR code*]
ITC	Imidazolyl-Thioguanine Chemotherapy [*Medicine*] (MAE)
ITC	Immediate Track Control [*Automotive engineering*]
ITC	Imperial Tobacco Co. [*of Great Britain and Ireland*] Ltd.
ITC	Inclusive Tour Charter
ITC	Incontinence Treatment Center [*Medicine*] (STED)
ITC	Independent Tank Center [*of a ship*] (DS)
ITC	Independent Television Commission [*British*] (ECON)
ITC	Industrial Technology Centre [*Manitoba Research Council*] [*Canada Research center*] (RCD)
ITC	Industrial Training Council
ITC	Infantry Training Center [*Army*]
ITC	Information Technology Ltd. [*British*] (NITA)
ITC	Inland Transport Committee [*United Nations*]
ITC	Institute of Tax Consultants (EA)
ITC	Instructional Telecommunications Consortium (EA)
ITC	Instructor Training Course
ITC	Instrumentation Tracking Controller
ITC	Integral Tube Component (IAA)
ITC	Integrated Telemetry Complex
ITC	Integrated Terminal Controller (NITA)
ITC	Integrated Trajectory Computations
ITC	Intelligent Controls, Inc. [*AMEX symbol*] (SAG)
ITC	Intelligent Tape Controller (PDAA)
ITC	Intelligent Telecommunication Controller (IAA)
ITC	Intelligent Transaction Controller (MHDB)
ITC	Intent to Change
ITC	Interagency Testing Committee [*Toxicology*]
ITC	Inter-American Travel Congresses
ITC	Intercept [*Telecommunications*] (TEL)
ITC	Interchurch Transportation Council [*Defunct*] (EA)
ITC	Intercontinental Trailsea Corp.
ITC	Interdata Transaction Controller [*Perkin-Elmer*]
ITC	Intermediate Toll Center [*Telecommunications*] (TEL)
ITC	Internationaal Instituut voor Lucht-en Ruimtekaartering an Aardkunde [*International Institute for Aerospace Survey and Earth Sciences*] [*Netherlands*] (EAIO)
ITC	International Air Carrier Association [*ICAO designator*] (FAAC)
ITC	International Chemalloy Corp. [*Toronto Stock Exchange symbol*]
ITc	International Table Calorie [*Dietetics*] (DAVI)
ITC	International Tar Conference [*See also CIG*] [*Paris, France*] (EAIO)
ITC	International Tea Committee (EAIO)
ITC	International Technology Council [*Defunct*] (EA)
ITC	International Telemetering Conference
ITC	International Telepresence Corp. (ECON)
ITC	International Teletraffic Congress [*Telecommunications*]
ITC	International Television Center [*Communications*]
ITC	International Tin Council [*See also CIE*] [*Defunct*] (EAIO)
ITC	International Toastmistress Clubs (EA)
ITC	International Trade Centre [*Switzerland United Nations*] (MCD)
ITC	International Trade Club of Chicago [*Later, IBCM*] (EA)
ITC	International Trade Commission [*Databank originator*]
ITC	International Trade Council
ITC	International Traders Club (EA)
ITC	International Trading Certificate (DS)
ITC	International Training College [*Salvation Army*]
ITC	International Training in Communication (EA)
ITC	International Trans Asia [*Vancouver Stock Exchange symbol*]
ITC	International Translations Centre [*Formerly, ETC*] (EA)
ITC	International Transport Commission (COE)
ITC	International Trypanotolerance Centre [*Gambia*]
ITC	International Tuberculosis Campaign
ITC	International Typeface Corp.
ITC	Intern Training Center [*DARCOM*]
ITC	Intertropical Convergence [*Trade winds*] [*Meteorology*]
ITC	Interval Time Control [*Computer science*] (OA)
ITC	In-Track Contiguous
ITC	Investment Tax Credit
ITC	Ionic Thermoconductivity [*or Thermocurrent*]
ITC	Isothermal Titration Calorimetry [*Analytical chemistry*]
ITC	Israel Trade Commission
ITC	Italian Tile Center (EA)
ITC	Italian Trade Commission (EA)
ITC	Spinivasan's Reports of Income Tax Cases [*India*] [*A publication*] (DLA)
ITC	Srinivasan's Reports of Income Tax Cases [*India*] [*1886-*] [*A publication*] (ILCA)
ITCA	Independent Television Companies Association [*British*]
ITCA	Indian Transcontinental Airways
ITCA	Inspector of Training Corps and Cadets [*Military British*]
ITCA	Instituto Tecnologico Centroamericano [*El Salvador*]
ITCA	Inter-American Technical Council on Archives (DIT)
ITCA	Intercollegiate Tennis Coaches Association (EA)
ITCA	International Technical Caramel Association (EA)

IT/CA...........	International Tele/Conferencing Association (EA)
ITCA.............	International Thunderbird Class Association (EA)
ITCA.............	International Typographic Composition Association [*Later, TIA*] (EA)
ITCA.............	Invest to Compete Alliance [*Washington, DC*] (EA)
ITCA.............	Irish Terrier Club of America (EA)
ITCABIC	Inter-Territorial Catholic Bishops' Conference (EAIO)
ITCAL...........	International Table Calorie
ITCAN..........	Inspect, Test, and Correct as Necessary (MCD)
ItCaU	Universita di Cagliari, Sardinia, Italy [*Library symbol Library of Congress*] (LCLS)
ITCC.............	Industrial Training [*NASDAQ symbol*] (TTSB)
ITCC.............	Industrial Training Corp. [*NASDAQ symbol*] (NQ)
ITCC.............	International Technical Communications Conference [*Society for Technical Communication*]
ITCC.............	Interstate Truckload Carriers Conference
ITCCU	Information Technology Centre Consultancy Unit [*British*] (AIE)
ITCG.............	Information Technology Co-Ordinating Group [*International Electrotechnical Commission*] [*ISO*] (DS)
ITCH.............	Information Technology for Children in Hospital (WDAA)
ITCI..............	International Tree Crops Institute USA (EA)
ITCIS............	Integrated Telephone Customer Information System [*Telecommunications*] (IAA)
ITCK.............	Issue Time Check [*Aviation*] (FAAC)
ITCM............	Integrated Tactical Countermeasures [*Army*]
ITCOM	Information Technology and Communications Bureau [*United Nations*] (ECON)
IT Corp	International Technology Corp. [*Associated Press*] (SAG)
ITCP.............	Idiopathic Thrombocytopenic Purpura [*Hematology*] (DAVI)
ITCP.............	Integrated Test and Checkout Procedures (MCD)
ItcpSe	Intercapital Income Securities, Inc. [*Associated Press*] (SAG)
ItCr..............	Biblioteca Statale di Cremona, Cremona, Italy [*Library symbol Library of Congress*] (LCLS)
ITCS.............	Installation Training/Coordination Section [*Social Security Administration*]
ITCS.............	Institute for 21st Century Studies [*Defunct*] (EA)
ITCS.............	Integrated Target Central System [*Military*] (CAAL)
ITCS.............	Integrated Target Command [*or Control*] System (IAA)
ITCS.............	Integrated Target Control System (MCD)
ITCSA...........	Institute of Technical Communicators of Southern Africa (EAIO)
ITCTLA.........	ITC [*International Trade Commission*] Trial Lawyers Association (EA)
ITCU............	Information Technology Consultancy Unit (NITA)
ITCU............	Intensive Thoracic Cardiovascular Unit [*Medicine*] (STED)
ITCUA	Information Technologies Credit Union Association (NTPA)
ITCUA	International Telephone Credit Union Association (EA)
ITCZ.............	Intertropical Convergence Zone [*Trade winds*] [*Meteorology*]
ITD..............	Idiopathic Torsion Dystonia [*Medicine*]
ITD..............	Idiopathic Torsion Dytonia [*Medicine*]
ITD..............	Inception-to-Date
ITD..............	Individual'naya Trudovaya Deyatel'nost' [*Individual Labor Activity*] [*Government program designed to foster private enterprise*] [*Russian*]
ITD..............	Industrial Technology Division [*Environmental Protection Agency*] (GFGA)
ITD..............	Information and Technology for the Disabled
ITD..............	Information Technology Development [*Project*] [*DoD*] (RDA)
ITD..............	Information Technology Directorate [*British*]
ITD..............	Information Technology Division [*Naval Research Laboratory*]
ITD..............	Information Trade Directory [*Gale Research Co.*] (NITA)
ITD..............	Infrared Target Detector
ITD..............	Inhalation Toxicology Division [*Environmental Protection Agency*] (GFGA)
ITD..............	Initial Temperature Difference (IAA)
ITD..............	Institute of Training and Development (EAIO)
ITD..............	Integral Trap Door [*Technical drawings*]
ITD..............	Integrated Technology Demonstration
ITD..............	Integrated Test Document (MCD)
ITD..............	Integration Test and Demonstration (SDI)
ITD..............	Intensely Transfused Dialysis [*Medicine*] (DMAA)
ITD..............	Interactive Terminal Display [*Computer science*] (DGA)
ITD..............	Interactive Typographic Display [*Computer science*] (DGA)
ITD..............	Interaural Time Difference [*Andiology*]
ITD..............	Interchannel Time Displacement [*Magnetic recording*]
ITD..............	Intercontinental Data [*Vancouver Stock Exchange symbol*]
ITD..............	Interface Timing Diagram
ITD..............	Interim Technical Directive (MCD)
ITD..............	Internal Test Directive (KSC)
ITD..............	Intertropical Discontinuity [*Meteorology*]
ITD..............	Ion Trap Detector [*Spectroscopy*]
ITD..............	Isothermal Desorption Spectrometry (AAEL)
ITD..............	University of Texas at Dallas, Richardson, TX [*OCLC symbol*] (OCLC)
ITDA............	Independent Truckers and Drivers Association (EA)
ITDA............	Indirect Target Damage Assessment (AAG)
ITDA............	Integrated Tunnel Diode Amplifier
ITDAC	Interagency Trade Data Advisory Committee [*Department of Commerce*] (EGAO)
ITDC............	International Trade Development Center (WPI)
ITDD............	Integrated Tunnel Diode Device (IAA)
ITDE............	Interchannel Time Displacement Error [*Magnetic recording*]
ITDE............	Intertrack Time Displacement Error (IAA)
ITDF............	Interactive Transaction Dump Facility [*Computer science*] (MHDB)
ITDG	Intermediate Technology Development Group [*Rugby, Warwickshire, England*] (EAIO)
ITDG/NA.......	Intermediate Technology Development Group of North America (EA)
ITDM............	Intelligent Time-Division Multiplexer
ITDN	Integrated Tactical-Strategic Data Network (DOMA)
ITDNS.........	Integrated Tour Operating Digital Network Service (MHDI)
ITDP...........	Individual Training and Development Plan (COE)
ITDP...........	Institute for Transportation and Development Policy (EA)
ITDR...........	Institute for Training and Demographic Research (EA)
ITDS...........	Integrated Technical Data System (PDAA)
ITDS...........	International Telecommunication Data Systems, Inc. [*NASDAQ symbol*] (SAG)
ITDT...........	Integrated Technical Documentation and Training
ITDU...........	Infantry Trials and Development Unit [*British military*] (DMA)
ITDU...........	Infrared Tracking Display Unit
ITE.............	Indicated Terminal Efficiency (DNAB)
ITE.............	Indicated Thermal Efficiency [*Automotive engineering*]
ITE.............	Individual Training Evaluation (MCD)
ITE.............	Information Technology in Engineering [*British*]
ITE.............	Input Test Equipment
ITE.............	Institute of Telecommunications Engineers
ITE.............	Institute of Terrestrial Ecology [*Research center British*] (IRC)
ITE.............	Institute of Traffic Engineers (EA)
ITE.............	Institute of Transportation Engineers (EA)
ITE.............	Instrumentation Test Equipment (KSC)
ITE.............	Insufficient Therapeutic Effect [*Medicine*] (DAVI)
ITE.............	Integration Test Equipment (MCD)
ITE.............	Intercity Transportation Efficiency (OA)
ITE.............	Interestatal de Aviacion SA de CV [*Mexico ICAO designator*] (FAAC)
ITE.............	International Telephone Exchange [*Telecommunications*] (TEL)
ITE.............	Intersite Transportation Equipment [*NASA*] (NASA)
ITE.............	Interstrat Resources, Inc. [*Vancouver Stock Exchange symbol*]
ITE.............	In the Ear [*Hearing aid*]
ITE.............	Intrapulmonary Interstitial Emphysema [*Medicine*] (DMAA)
ITE.............	Inverse Time Element (MUGU)
ITEA............	Infraestructura Teatral [*Ministerio de Cultura*] [*Spain Information service or system*] (CRD)
ITEA............	International Technology Education Association (EA)
ITEA............	International Test and Evaluation Association (EA)
ITEA............	International Theatre Equipment Association (NTPA)
ITEC............	Information Technology Centre [*Training centres*] [*British*] (NITA)
ITEC............	Information Technology Electronics and Computers [*A publication*]
ITEC............	Integral Throat/Exit Cone (MCD)
ITEC............	International Thoroughbred Exposition and Conference [*Kentucky Thoroughbred Association, Inc.*] (TSPED)
ITEC............	International Tourist Entertainment Corp. [*NASDAQ symbol*] (SAG)
ITEC............	International Transport Exhibition
ITEC............	International Turbine Engine Corp. (EFIS)
ITECH..........	Joint IOC/WMO Group of Experts on IGOSS Technical Systems Design and Developmentand Service Requirements [*Marine science*] (MSC)
ITED............	Integrated Trajectory Error Display [*Aviation*]
ITED............	Iowa Tests of Educational Development
ITEF............	Integrated Test Equipment Facility (MCD)
I-TEF...........	International Toxicity Equivalency Factor [*Toxicology*]
ITEF............	International Trade Exhibitions in France (EA)
ITEG............	Individual Training Evaluation Group (MCD)
ITEG............	Isotope-Powered Thermoelectric Generator (PDAA)
ITEL............	Joint WMO/IOC Group of Experts on Telecommunications (MSC)
ITEL............	Wavetech Inc. [*NASDAQ symbol*] (TTSB)
ITELIS.........	Irish Times Eurolex Legal Information Service [*Database*] (NITA)
ITEM............	Integrated Test and Maintenance (PDAA)
ITEM............	Integrated Theater Engagement Model
ITEM............	Intelligence Threat Evaluation Model [*Military*] (MCD)
ITEM............	Interference Technology Engineer's Master (IEEE)
ITEME..........	Institution of Technician Engineers in Mechanical Engineering [*British*]
ITeMS..........	Ideas in the Teaching of Mathematics and Science (AIE)
ITEMS.........	INCOTERM [*International Commerce Term*] Transaction Entry Management System
ITEMS.........	In-Service Inspection, Testing, Evaluation, and Monitoring Service
ITEP...........	Individual Training and Evaluation Program [*Army*] (INF)
ITEP...........	Institute of Theoretical and Experimental Physics [*Moscow*]
ITEP...........	Integrated Test/Evaluation Program (AABC)
ITEP...........	Interim Tactical ELINT [*Electronic Intelligence*] Processor
ITEP...........	International Trade Enhancement Program
ITER...........	International Thermonuclear Experimental Reactor
Iterative G ...	Iterative Guidance Mode [*Aerospace*] (NAKS)
ITES...........	Inelastic Tunnelling Electron Spectroscopy
ITESM..........	Instituto Tecnologico de Estudios Superiores de Monterrey [*Research institute onMexico/US relations*] [*Mexico*] (CROSS)
ITEST..........	Institute for Theological Encounter with Science and Technology (EA)
ITeuS	Saint Joseph Seminary, Teutopolis, IL [*Library symbol Library of Congress*] (LCLS)
ITeuSD........	Teutopolis Community Unit, School District 50, Teutopolis, IL [*Library symbol Library of Congress*] (LCLS)
ITEWS..........	Integrated Tactical Electronic Warfare System
ITEX............	Information Technology Exchange Exhibition [*British*] (ITD)
ITEX............	Internal Tide Experiment [*Marine science*] (MSC)
ITEX............	Itex Corp. [*NASDAQ symbol*] (SAG)
ItexCp	Itex Corp. [*Associated Press*] (SAG)
ITF.............	Air Inter, Societe [*France ICAO designator*] (FAAC)
ITF.............	Impulse Transfer Function (KSC)
ITF.............	Indian Territorial Force [*British military*] (DMA)
ITF.............	Industrial and Trade Fairs Ltd. [*Solihull, West Midlands, England*] (TSSD)
ITF.............	Industrial Technology Fund [*British*]
ITF.............	Information Technology Fund (AAGC)

ITF	Instant Transference
ITF	Institute of Tropical Forestry [*Rio Piedras, PR*] [*Department of Agriculture*] [*Research center*]
ITF	Institut Textile de France [*French Textile Institute*] [*Boulogne-Billancourt*] [*Information service or system*] (IID)
ITF	Integrated Test Facility [*Computer science*]
ITF	Integrated Thermal Flux (AAG)
ITF	Intelligence Task Force (DOMA)
ITF	Intelligence Terminal Family [*Military*] (MCD)
ITF	Interactive Terminal Facility
ITF	Interagency Task Force (AAGC)
ITF	Interferon (DMAA)
ITF	Interim [*Contact*] File (MCD)
ITF	Intermediate Test Facility (MCD)
ITF	International Tennis Federation [*Formerly, ILTF*] (EA)
ITF	International Toll Free [*Telecommunications*]
ITF	International Trade Fair [*New Zealand*]
ITF	International Transport Workers' Federation [*London, England*] (EAIO)
ITF	International Tremor Foundation (EA)
ITF	Interstate Transportation of Fireworks
ITF	Interstitial Transfer Facility [*Nuclear energy*] (NRCH)
ITF	Intertropical Front [*Meteorology*] (BARN)
ITF	Intestinal Trefoil Factor [*Biochemistry*]
ITF	In Trust For [*Banking*]
ITF	Inverse Trigonometric Function
ITF	Italfarmaco [*Italy*] [*Research code symbol*]
ITFA	Installation, Testing, and Firing Apparatus [*Military*] (INF)
ItFB	Biblioteca Berenson, Florence, Italy [*Library symbol Library of Congress*] (LCLS)
ItFBM	Biblioteca Marucelliana di Firenze, Servizio Prestito, Florence, Italy [*Library symbol Library of Congress*] (LCLS)
ITFCA	International Track and Field Coaches Association [*Athens, Greece*] (EAIO)
ITFCC	Initial [*or Interim*] Tactical Flag Command Center (MCD)
ITFCS	Institute for Twenty-First Century Studies (EA)
ITFF	Intertrochanteric Femoral Fracture [*Medicine*] (MEDA)
ITFMC	Indian Territorial Force Medical Corps [*British military*] (DMA)
ITFMSG	Interscience Technological Forecasting Methodology Study Group
ITFO	International Trade Fairs Office [*Department of Commerce*]
ITFS	Incomplete Testicular Feminization Syndrome [*Medicine*] (AAMN)
ITFS	Instructional Television Fixed Service [*Educational TV*]
ITFS	International Tropical Fern Society [*Defunct*] (EA)
ITFTRIA	Instrument Tree Flow and Temperature Removal Instrument Assembly [*Nuclear energy*] (NRCH)
ITFW	Industry Training Fund for Women [*Australia*]
ITG	Australian Income Tax Guide [*A publication*]
ITG	Industrial Tachometer Generator
ITG	Industry Technology Group [*Air Force*] (MCD)
ITG	Industry Test Group [*Air Force*]
ITG	Information and Telecommunications Technologies Group [*Electronic Industries Association*] [*Washington, DC*] (TSSD)
ITG	Innovationstechnik GmbH & Co. [*Database producer*] (IID)
ITG	Institute Technical Group
ITG	Integra Financial Corp. [*NYSE symbol*] (SPSG)
ITG	Integrated Terminal Guidance
ITG	Integrin (DMAA)
ITG	Inter-Continental Energy [*Vancouver Stock Exchange symbol*]
ITG	Interdiction Target Graphic (MCD)
ITG	Interlace Airlines Ltd. [*Gambia*] [*FAA designator*] (FAAC)
ITG	International Trumpet Guild (EA)
ITG	Investment Tech Group [*NYSE symbol*]
ITG	Ion Temperature Gradient [*Physics*]
ITGA	Integrin Alpha (DMAA)
ITGA	Isothermogravimetric Analysis
ITGB	Institute of Transport of Great Britain
ITGB	Integrin Beta (DMAA)
ITGBL	International through Government Bill of Lading
ItgCom	Integrated Communications Network, Inc. [*Associated Press*] (SAG)
ITGD	Interstate Transportation of Gambling Devices
ITGI	Investment Tech Group [*NASDAQ symbol*] (TTSB)
ITGI	Investment Technology Group [*NASDAQ symbol*] (SAG)
ItgLfSci	Integra LifeSciences Corp. [*Associated Press*] (SAG)
ITGLWF	International Textile, Garment, and Leather Workers' Federation [*See also FITTHC*] [*Brussels, Belgium*] (EAIO)
ItgPrc	Integrated Process Equipment [*Associated Press*] (SAG)
ITGR	Integrity, Inc. [*NASDAQ symbol*] (SAG)
ITGR	Integrity Music 'A' [*NASDAQ symbol*] (TTSB)
ITGR	Integrity Music, Inc. [*NASDAQ symbol*] (SAG)
ItgSys	Integrated Systems, Inc. [*Associated Press*] (SAG)
ITGWF	International Textile and Garment Workers' Federation [*Later, ITGLWF*]
ITGWU	Irish Transport and General Workers' Union (DCTA)
ITH	Integrated Technology USA, Inc. [*AMEX symbol*] (SAG)
ITH	Interstitial Hyperthermia [*Medicine*] (DMAA)
ITh	Interthecal [*Anesthesiology*]
Ith	Intrathecal [*Medicine*] (CPH)
Ith	Intrathoracic [*Anatomy*]
ITH	Island Technologies Corp. [*Vancouver Stock Exchange symbol*]
ITH	Ithaca [*New York*] [*Airport symbol*] (OAG)
ITH	Ithaca [*New York*] [*Seismograph station code, US Geological Survey Closed*] (SEIS)
ITH	Ithaca, NY [*Location identifier FAA*] (FAAL)
ITh	Thornton Public Library, Thornton, IL [*Library symbol Library of Congress*] (LCLS)
Ithaca C	Ithaca College (GAGS)
ITHE	International Travel Host Exchange
i thec	Intrathecal [*Medicine*] (AAMN)
ITHI	International Thomson Holdings, Inc.
ITHI	International Travelers Health Institute (EA)
ITHL	Internal Triangular Hinge Ligament [*of scallops*]
ITHOF	International Tennis Hall of Fame (EA)
ITHP	Increased Take-Home Pay
ITI	Iceberg Transport International Ltd. [*Saudi Arabia*] (PDAA)
ITI	Immediate Transient Incapacitation [*Radiation casualty criterion*] [*Army*] (AABC)
ITI	Indian Telephone Industries (NITA)
ITI	Industrial Technology Institute [*Research center*] (RCD)
ITI	Infaunal Trophic Index [*Marine pollution*]
ITI	Information Technology Industry Council [*Formerly, Computer and Business Equipment Manufacturers Association*] (IGQR)
ITI	Information Transform, Inc. [*Information service or system*] (IID)
ITI	Initial Task Index (AAG)
ITI	Inspection and Test Instruction (NASA)
ITI	Institute of Translation and Interpreting [*British*] (DBA)
ITI	Instituut TNO voor Toegepaste Informatica [*TNO Institute of Applied Computer Science*] [*Information service or system*] (IID)
ITI	Insurance Testing Institute [*Malvern, PA*] (EA)
ITI	Integrated Task Index (AAG)
ITI	Intelligent Transportation Infrastructure
ITI	Interactive Terminal Interface [*Computer science*] (IEEE)
ITI	Inter-Alpha-Trypsin Inhibitor (DB)
ITI	Interceptor Technology Integration
ITI	Intermittent Trouble Indication [*Telecommunications*] (TEL)
ITI	International Tax Institute (EA)
ITI	International Technical Institute of Flight Engineers
ITI	International Technology Institute (EA)
ITI	International Telesis Industries Corp. [*Vancouver Stock Exchange symbol*]
ITI	International Theatre Institute [*Paris, France*] (EAIO)
ITI	International Thrift Institute
ITI	International Training Institute
ITI	Intertrial Interval [*Psychology*]
ITI	Itapetinga [*Brazil*] [*Airport symbol*] (AD)
ITIA	International Trade and Investment Act [*1984*]
ITIA	International Tungsten Industry Association (EAIO)
ITIAL	Items Troop Installed or Authorized List (MCD)
ITIC	Information Technology Industry Council (AAGC)
ITIC	International Tsunami Information Center (EA)
ITIC	Inter-Tribal Indian Ceremonial Association (EA)
ITIC	Investors Title Co. [*NASDAQ symbol*] (TTSB)
ITIC	Investors Title Insurance Co. [*NASDAQ symbol*] (SAG)
ITIES	Interfaced between Two Immiscible Electrolyte Solutions [*Physical chemistry*]
ITIES	Interservice Technical Information Exchange System [*Military*] (AFIT)
ITIF	Individual Taxpayer Information File [*IRS*]
ITIG	Intelligroup, Inc. [*NASDAQ symbol*] (SAG)
ITII	Internal-to-Internal Interface (MCD)
ITII	International Thomson Information, Inc. [*Later, ITLS*]
ITII	ITI Technologies [*NASDAQ symbol*] (TTSB)
ITII	ITI Technologies, Inc. [*NASDAQ symbol*] (SAG)
ITIM	Immunoreceptor Tyrosine-Based Inhibitory Motif [*Immunology*]
ITIM	Itonut Yisrael Meugedet [*ITIM News Agency of the Associated Israel Press Ltd.*]
I-time	Inspiratory Time (STED)
ITIN	Individual Taxpayer Identification Number
ITIN	Itinerary (AFM)
ITIN	Itinerating (ROG)
IT Info	Income Tax Information Release (DLA)
ITIP	Improved Transtage Injector Program (MCD)
ITIP	International Technical Integration Panel
ITIP	International Thomson Industrial Press
ITIPAT	Institute for the Technology and Industrialization of Tropical Agricultural Products [*Ivory Coast*]
ITIPI	Interim Tactical Information Processing and Interpretation
ITIR	Intermediate Thermal Infrared Radiometer (SSD)
ITIRC	IBM Technical Information Retrieval Center [*International Business Machines Corp.*] [*Armonk, NY*]
ITIS	Industrial Technical Information Service [*Singapore*] (IID)
ITIS	Integrated Tank Insulation System
ITIS	Integrated Technical Information System [*Department of Energy Information service or system*] (IID)
ITIS	Interagency Taxonomy Information System [*A database of all the flora and fauna in North America*] [*Created by the EPA and other agencies*]
IT-IS	Intermediate Technology Industrial Services [*ITDG*] [*British*]
ITIS	Internal Translation Information Subsystem [*Computer science*]
ITIS	International Trade Information Service
ITIS	Italians in Service of the US [*World War II*]
ITis	Tiskilwa Township Library, Tiskilwa, IL [*Library symbol Library of Congress*] (LCLS)
ITISN	Information Technology Information Services Network [*British*] (NITA)
ITisP	Plow Creek Commune Library, Tiskilwa, IL [*Library symbol Library of Congress*] (LCLS)
ITISS	Integrated Tactical Intelligence Support System (MCD)
ITisSD	Tiskilwa Community Unit, School District 300, Tiskilwa, IL [*Library symbol Library of Congress*] (LCLS)
ITI Tech	ITI Technologies, Inc. [*Associated Press*] (SAG)
ITIU	Inventory Temporarily in Use [*Army*] (AABC)
ITI/US	International Theatre Institute of the United States (EA)

ITJ	Indian Tax Journal [*A publication*] (DLA)
ITJ	International Trojan Development Corp. [*Vancouver Stock Exchange symbol*]
ITJ	Itajai [*Brazil*] [*Airport symbol*] (AD)
ITJ	Societa' Italjet [*Italy ICAO designator*] (FAAC)
ITK	Itokama [*Papua New Guinea*] [*Airport symbol*] (OAG)
ITKF	International Traditional Karate Federation (EA)
ITL	Ignition Transmission Line
ITL	Incoming Transaction Listing (AFM)
ITL	Incomplete Task Log (AAG)
ITL	Industrial Test Laboratory [*Philadelphia Navy Yard*] [*Navy*]
ITL	Information Technology Laboratory [*Army Corps of Engineers*]
ITL	Information Technology Ltd. [*British*] (NITA)
ITL	Institute of Tape Learning [*British*] (DBA)
ITL	Instrumented Team Learning (ADA)
ITL	Integrate-Transfer-Launch [*Complex*] [*NASA*]
ITL	Intent to Launch (NG)
ITL	Interactive Technology Laboratory [*New York Institute of Technology*] [*Research center*] (RCD)
ITL	Interceptor/Transporter/Loader
ITL	Intermediate Text Language (NITA)
ITL	Intermediate Transfer Language
ITL	International Theological Library [*A publication*]
ITL	Inverse Taper Lens
ITL	Inverse Time Limit (MSA)
ITL	Isomeric Transition Level [*Radioactivity*]
ITL	Isothermal Luminescence (PDAA)
Itl	Italian (BARN)
ITL	ITL Industries Ltd. [*Toronto Stock Exchange symbol*]
ITL	Mikma Ltd. [*Moldova*] [*FAA designator*] (FAAC)
ITLA	Imperial Thrift & Loan [*NASDAQ symbol*] (TTSB)
ITLA	Imperial Thrift & Loan Association [*NASDAQ symbol*] (SAG)
ITLA	International Taxicab and Livery Association (NTPA)
ITLB	Instruction Translation Lookaside Buffer [*Computer science*] (PCM)
ITLB	International Trade Law Branch [*United Nations*] (DUND)
ITLBV	Individual Tactical Load Bearing Vest [*Army*] (INF)
ITLC	Instant Thin-Layer Chromatography
ITLC	Integrated Transfer Launch Complex (IAA)
ITLGSWF	Interamerican Textile, Leather, Garment, and Shoe Workers Federation (EA)
ITLJ	Income Tax Law Journal [*India*] [*A publication*] (DLA)
ITLMCF	Instrument Technicians Labor-Management Cooperation Fund (EA)
ItlOven	[*The*] Italian Oven, Inc. [*Associated Press*] (SAG)
ITLS	International Thomson Library Services
ITLSA	Integrated Torso Limb Suit Assembly [*NASA*] (KSC)
ITLT	Interstate Transportation of Lottery Tickets
ITM	Improved Thayer-Martin [*Medium*] (DMAA)
ITM	Inch Trim Moment [*Nautical*]
ITM	Index of Technical Manuals [*Military*] (DNAB)
ITM	Indirect Tag Memory
ITM	Induction Tube Modulation
ITM	Infantry Target Mechanism [*Army*]
ITM	Information Transfer Module [*Telecommunications*] (NITA)
ITM	Inspector of Torpedoes and Mines [*Navy*]
ITM	Institute of Thread Machiners [*Defunct*]
ITM	Integral Telemetry
ITM	Intelligent Tutoring Media [*Artificial intelligence*]
ITM	Interceptor Tactical Missile [*Air Force*]
ITM	Intercommunication Teleprocessing Monitor (IAA)
ITM	Interim Technical Memorandum
ITM	Internal Technical Memorandum
ITM	Internal Tympaniform Membrane [*Zoology*]
ITM	International Tourism Management [*Australia*]
ITM	In the Money [*Options*] [*Investment term*] (NUMA)
ITM	Investment Trust Funds under Management
ITM	ISDN [*Integrated Services Digital Network*] Trunk Module [*Telecommunications*]
ITM	Israel Turkey Meningoencephalitis [*Medicine*] (DB)
ITM	ITA [*Itapemirim Transportes Aereos SA*] [*Brazil*] [*ICAO designator*] (FAAC)
ITM	Item [*Online database field identifier*]
ITM	Ithomi [*Greece*] [*Seismograph station code, US Geological Survey*] (SEIS)
ITMA	Institute for Training in Municipal Administration (EA)
ITMA	Institute of Trade Mark Agents [*British*] (DI)
ITMA	International Tanning Manufacturers Association [*Defunct*] (EA)
ITMA	Investigation on Teaching Using Microcomputers as an Aid
ITMA	Irradiation Test Management Activity (NRCH)
ITMA	It's That Man Again [*Long-running English radio comedy, 1939-1949*]
ITMC	International Transmission Maintenance Center [*Communications*]
IT/ME	Incentive Travel and Meeting Executives Show [*Trade show*] (ITD)
ITMF	International Textile Manufacturers Federation [*Zurich, Switzerland*] (EA)
ITMG	Integrated Thermal Micrometeoroid Garment [*Spacesuit*]
ItMGM	Italian MGM [*Record label*]
ITMI	Industrial Technology and Machine Intelligence (NITA)
ITMID	Item Identification File
ITMIS	Integrated Transportation Management Information System [*Army*]
ITMJ	Incoming Trunk Message Junction [*Telecommunications*] (OA)
ITMRA	Information Technology Management Reform Act of 1996 (AAGC)
ITMRC	International Travel Market Research Council
ITMS	In-Core Temperature Monitoring System [*Nuclear energy*] (NRCH)
ITMS	Ingestible Thermal Monitoring System
ITMS	Integrated Training Management System [*DoD*]
ITMS	Interactive Tsunami Modeling System [*Marine science*] (OSRA)
ITMS	International Tax Management System [*Price Waterhouse & Co.*]
ITMS	Ion Trap Mass Spectrometer
ITMT	Intermediate Thermomechanical Treatment (MCD)
ITN	Image Transmission Network [*Computer science*] (CIST)
ITN	Independent Telecommunication Network (ACRL)
ITN	Independent Television News [*British*]
ITN	Industrias Titan SA [*Spain ICAO designator*] (FAAC)
ITN	Institute for TransPacific Networking [*Oakland, CA*] [*Telecommunications service*] (TSSD)
ITN	Integrated Telecommunications Network (CIST)
ITN	Integrated Teleprocessing Network
ITN	Interim Technical Note
ITN	International Television News [*A publication*] (EAAP)
ITN	International Turbine Tech [*Vancouver Stock Exchange symbol*]
ITN	Internegative [*Photography*] (NTCM)
ITN	InterTan, Inc. [*NYSE symbol*] (CTT)
ITN	In Touch Networks (EA)
ITN	Itabuna [*Brazil*] [*Airport symbol*] (OAG)
ITNA	Independent Television News Association [*News service*]
ITNC	In-Track Noncontiguous
ITND	International Trade Names Dictionary [*Later, IBTC*] [*A publication*]
ITNFSA	International Tanker Nominal Freight Scale Association
ITNL	Interactive Tech [*NASDAQ symbol*] (TTSB)
ITNL	Interactive Technologies Corp. [*NASDAQ symbol*] (SAG)
ITNL	Internal (ECII)
ITNOTGAOTU	In the Name of the Great Architect of the Universe [*Freemasonry*] (ROG)
ITNRNT	Itinerant (FAAC)
ITNS	Integrated Tactical Navigation System [*Navy*]
ITNS	International Transplant Nurses Society (EA)
ITNS/D-AHRS	Integrated Tactical Navigation System/Doppler - Altitude Heading Reference System
ItNU	Universita di Napoli, Naples, Italy [*Library symbol Library of Congress*] (LCLS)
ItNU-IC	Universita di Napoli, Istituto Chimico, Naples, Italy [*Library symbol Library of Congress*] (LCLS)
ITO	Hilo [*Hawaii*] [*Airport symbol*] (OAG)
ITO	Hilo, HI [*Location identifier FAA*] (FAAL)
ITO	Impulse Transfer Orbit
ITO	Income Tax Office (DAS)
ITO	Income Tax Order
ITO	Independent Television Organization (NTCM)
ITO	Indian Tribal Organization (GFGA)
ITO	Indium Tin Oxide
ITO	Individual Travel Order [*Military*] (CINC)
ITO	Industrial Therapy Organisation [*British*]
ITO	Inspecting Torpedo Officer [*Navy*]
ITO	Installation Transportation Office [*or Officer*] [*Air Force*] (AFM)
ITO	Institution of Training Officers [*British*]
ITO	Instrument Takeoff
ITO	Integration and Test Order (MCD)
ITO	Interim Technical Order (AFM)
ITO	Intermediate Training Objective [*Army*] (INF)
ITO	International Thomson Organisation [*Later, The Thomson Corp.*]
ITO	International Trade Organization
ITO	International Travel Orders
ITO	Invitational Travel Order [*Army*] (AABC)
ITO	Irish Tourist Office (BI)
ITO	Ito [*Japan*] [*Seismograph station code, US Geological Survey Closed*] (SEIS)
ITOA	Inbound Tourism Organisation of Australia
ITOA	Independent Tanker Owners Association (DS)
ITOA	Independent Terminal Operators Association (EA)
ITODA	Independent Turf and Ornamental Distributors Association (NTPA)
ITOF	Ion Time of Flight
ITOFCN	Interim Technical Order Field Change Notice [*Air Force*] (MCD)
ITOI	International Thomson Organisation, Inc.
ITOL	International Thomson Organisation Ltd. [*Later, TTC*]
ITol	Toluca City Library, Toluca, IL [*Library symbol Library of Congress*] (LCLS)
ITolo	Tolono Township Library, Tolono, IL [*Library symbol Library of Congress*] (LCLS)
ITolSD	Toluca Community Unit, School District 2306, Toluca, IL [*Library symbol Library of Congress*] (LCLS)
ITOM	Interstate Transportation of Obscene Matter
ITONA	Iveco Trucks of North America, Inc.
ITonSD	Tonica Consolidated Community School District 79 and Consolidated High School District 360, Tonica, IL [*Library symbol Library of Congress*] (LCLS)
I-TOO	Independent Truck Owner/Operator Association (EA)
ITOO	Independent Truck Owner-Operators Association
ITOP	Integrated Test Operate Panel
ITOP	International Test Operations Procedure [*DoD*]
ITOPF	International Tanker Owners Pollution Federation
ITOPLC	International Thomson Organisation Public Limited Co.
ITOR	Intercept Target Optical Reader
ITOS	Improved TIROS [*Television Infrared Observation Satellite*] Operational Satellite [*or System*] [*National Oceanic and Atmospheric Administration*]
ITOS	Interactive Terminal Operating System (NITA)
ITOS	Iterative Time Optimal System
ITOSS	Integrated Toolkit for Operating System Security [*Computer security system*]
ITOU	Intensive Therapy Observation Unit [*Medicine*] (DMAA)

ITou	Toulon Public Library, Toulon, IL [*Library symbol Library of Congress*] (LCLS)
ITOW	Improved Tube-Launched, Optically Tracked, Wire-Guided [*Weapon*] (RDA)
ITOY	International Truck of the Year
ItoYokd	Ito-Yokado Co. Ltd. [*Associated Press*] (SAG)
ITP	Idiopathic Thrombocytopenic Purpura [*Medicine*]
ITP	Immune Thrombocytopenic Purpura [*Medicine*]
ITP	Income Tax Professional (ADA)
ITP	Independent Television Publications [*British*] (ECON)
ITP	Index of Technical Publications [*Military*] (DNAB)
ITP	Index to Proceedings [*Information service or system United Nations*] (DUND)
ITP	Individual Training Plan [*Army*]
ITP	Individual Training Program (MCD)
ITP	Individual Treatment Plan [*For the medical care and the education of a handicapped person*]
ITP	Inferior Thalamic Peduncle [*Anatomy*]
ITP	Initial Trial Phase (NG)
ITP	Innovative Training Project
ITP	Inosine Triphosphate [*Biochemistry*]
ITP	Input Translator Program [*Computer science*]
ITP	Inspection Test Procedure
ITP	Installation Test Program
ITP	Instruction to Proceed (NATG)
ITP	Integrated Test Package (CAAL)
ITP	Integrated Test Plan (AAGC)
ITP	Integrated Test Program
ITP	Integrated Transaction Processor (MHDI)
ITP	Intelligence Town Plan
ITP	Intensive Training Program
ITP	Interactive Terminal Protocol [*Computer science*]
ITP	Interceptor Technology Program
ITP	Intercon Petroleum, Inc. [*Vancouver Stock Exchange symbol*]
ITP	Interim Test Procedure (MCD)
ITP	Interim Training Program [*Army*] (INF)
ITP	Intermin Treatment Plan [*Medicine*] (DAVI)
ITP	International Test Pilot School [*British ICAO designator*] (FAAC)
ITP	International Thomson Publishing [*Also, ITPI*]
ITP	Interrupted Task Paradigm [*Psychometrics*]
ITP	Intertape Polymer Group [*AMEX symbol*] (SAG)
ITP	Intrathoracic Pressure [*Medicine*]
ITP	Isotachophoresis [*Analytical biochemistry*]
ITP	Italian Patent (IAA)
It P	Italian Pharmacopoeia [*A publication*]
ITp	Tinley Park Public Library, Tinley Park, IL [*Library symbol Library of Congress*] (LCLS)
ITPA	Illinois Test of Psycholinguistic Abilities
ITPA	Independent Telephone Pioneer Association (EA)
ITPA	International Tea Promotion Association [*Defunct*] (EAIO)
ITPA	International Trotting and Pacing Association (EA)
ITPA	International Truck Parts Association (EA)
ITPA	Irish Trade Protection Association (DBA)
ITPAC	Imported Tobacco Products Advisory Council [*British*] (DBA)
ITPAIS	Image Technology Patent Information System [*Printing technology*] [*Rochester Institute of Technology Rochester, NY*]
ItPavU	Universita degli Studi, Pavia, Italy [*Library symbol Library of Congress*] (LCLS)
ITPB	Integrated Test Program Board
ITPC	International Television Program Center [*Telecommunications*] (TEL)
ITPFF	Interstate Transportation of Prize Fight Films
ITPI	International Thomson Publishing, Inc. [*Also, ITP*]
ITPI	International Transfer Printing Institute (EA)
ITPIAL	Infrared Target Pointer/Illuminator/Aiming Laser [*Military*] (INF)
ITP-ID	International Thomson Publishing - International Division
ITpM	Tinley Park Mental Health Center, Tinley Park, IL [*Library symbol Library of Congress*] (LCLS)
ITPMG	Interstate Transportation of Prison-Made Goods
ITP-NSS	Innovative Training Projects - National Skills Shortage
ITPO	International TOGA [*Tropical Ocean Global Atmosphere*] Project Office [*Geneva, Switzerland*] (EAIO)
ITPP	Individual Training Plan Proposal [*Army*]
ITPP	Institute of Technical Publicity and Publications [*British*] (BI)
ITPP	International Thomson Professional Publishing
ITPR	Infrared Temperature Profile Radiometer
ITPRL	Individual Training and Performance Research Laboratory [*Army*] (RDA)
ITPS	Income Tax Payers' Society [*British*] (BI)
ITPS	Institute for Theological and Philosophical Studies (EA)
ITPS	Integrated Technical Processing System (NITA)
ITPS	Integrated Teleprocessing System (IEEE)
ITPS	Interactive Teleprocessing System (NITA)
ITPS	Interactive Test Preparation System [*Computer science*] (MHDI)
ITPS	Interactive Text Processing System (NITA)
ITPS	Internal Teleprocessing System (CMD)
ITPS	International Thomson Publishing Services
ITQ	Individual Transferable Quota
ITQ	Infant Temperament Questionnaire
ITQ	Inferior Temporal Quadrant [*Medicine*] (DMAA)
ITQ	International Thesaurus of Quotations [*A publication*]
ITQ	Invitation to Quote (MCD)
ITQ	Itaqui [*Brazil*] [*Airport symbol*] (AD)
ITR	Australian Income Tax Reports [*A publication*] (DLA)
ITR	Ignition Test Reactor (MCD)
IT-R	Immunotoxin with Ricin
ITR	Improved Tartar Retrofit [*Missile*] (MCD)
ITR	Income Tax Reports [*India*] [*A publication*] (DLA)
ITR	In-Core Thermionic Reactor [*Nuclear energy*]
ITR	Incremental Tape Recorder
ITR	Indian Tax Reports [*A publication*] (ILCA)
ITR	Individual Training Record [*Military*] (INF)
ITR	Indoor Testing Range [*Golf*] (PS)
ITR	Industrial Target Report [*Later, IDR*] [*British World War II*]
ITR	Industrial Tribunal Reports (DCTA)
ITR	Infantry Training Replacement
ITR	Information Technology Research [*Waltham, MA*] [*Telecommunications*] (TSSD)
ITR	Initial Training Requirement
ITR	Initial Trouble Report (IAA)
ITR	Inlet Temperature Rise
ITR	Inspection Test Report
ITR	Instrumentation Tape Recorder
ITR	Instrumented Test Range [*Fort Huachuca, AZ*] [*United States Army Electronic Proving Ground*] (GRD)
ITR	Instrument Test Rig [*Liquid Metal Engineering Center*] [*Energy Research and Development Administration*] (IEEE)
ITR	Integrated Technology Rotor
ITR	Integrated Telephone Recorder [*Telecommunications*] (TEL)
ITR	Integrated Test Requirements
ITR	Integrated Thyristor Rectifier (IAA)
ITR	Integrated Tourism Resort
ITR	Intelcom Group [*AMEX symbol*] (SPSG)
ITR	Intense Thermal Radiation
ITR	Interim Technical Report
ITR	Interim Test Report
ITR	Internal Technical Report
ITR	Interstate Transport Region
ITR	In-Transit Rendezvous
ITR	Intraocular Tension Recorder
ITR	Intratracheal [*Medicine*]
IT/R	Inventory Transfer Receipt
ITR	Inverse Time Relay (KSC)
ITR	Inverted Terminal Repeat [*Genetics*]
ITR	Invitation to Register (ADA)
ITR	Irish Term Reports, by Ridgeway, Lapp, and Schoales [*A publication*] (DLA)
ITR	Isolation Test Routine (IAA)
ITRA	Integrated Test Requirements Analysis (CAAL)
ITRA	International Tire and Rubber Association (NTPA)
ITRA	International Truck Restorers Association (EA)
i trach	Intratracheal [*Medicine*] (AAMN)
ITRAM	International [*Passenger*] Traffic Management System [*MTMC*] (TAG)
ITRB	Interservice Training Review Board (MCD)
ItRC	Consiglio Nazionale delle Ricerche, Rome, Italy [*Library symbol Library of Congress*] (LCLS)
ITRC	Information Technology Requirements Council (CIST)
ITRC	Intercardia Inc. [*NASDAQ symbol*] (TTSB)
ITRC	International Tin Research Council [*Middlesex, England*] (EAIO)
ITRC	Interstate Transport Region Commission
ITRD	Integrated Test Requirements Documents (MCD)
ITRDB	International Tree-Ring Data Bank [*University of Arizona*] (IID)
ITRDS	Integrated Test Requirements Documents (MCD)
ITRE	Institute for Transportation Research and Education [*University of North Carolina*] [*Research center*] (RCD)
ITre	Trenton Public Library, Trenton, IL [*Library symbol Library of Congress*] (LCLS)
ITreWHS	Weslin Junior-Senior High School, Trenton, IL [*Library symbol Library of Congress*] (LCLS)
ITRI	Industrial Technology Research Institute [*Integrated Circuit Design Centre*] [*Taiwan*] (NITA)
ITRI	Inhalation Toxicology Research Institute [*Albuquerque, NM*] [*Department of Energy*]
ItRI	Institute Centrale Catalogo Unico delle Bibliotheche Italiane e per le Informazioni Bibliografiche, Rome, Italy [*Library symbol*] [*Library of Congress*] (LCLS)
ITRI	Interconnection Technology Research Institute (AAEL)
ITRI	International Tin Research Institute (EAIO)
ITRI	Invitation to Register Interest
ITRI	Itron, Inc. [*NASDAQ symbol*] (SAG)
ITRIA	Instrument Tree Removable Instrument Assembly [*Nuclear energy*] (NRCH)
ITRIS	Integrated Tsunami Research Information System [*Marine science*] (OSRA)
ITRIS	International Trade and Resource Information System [*University of Alaska at Anchorage*] [*Information service or system*] (CRD)
ITRL	Instrument Test Repair Laboratory (AAG)
ITRM	Inverse Thermoremanent Magnetization
ITRO	Installation Test Requirements Outline (MCD)
ITRO	Integrated Test Requirements Outline
ITRO	Interservice Training Review Organization [*Military*] (NVT)
ITro	Tri-Township Library, Troy, IL [*Library symbol Library of Congress*] (LCLS)
ITROD	Incendiary Torch Remote Opening Device (MCD)
ITRON	Industrial TRON (NITA)
Itron	Itron, Inc. [*Associated Press*] (SAG)
ITRP	Institute of Transportation and Regional Planning (EA)
ITRPF	International Tyre, Rubber, and Plastic Federation (EAIO)
ITRU	Industrial Training and Research Unit (ACII)

ItRU .... Universita degli Studi, Biblioteca Alessandrina, Rome, Italy [*Library symbol Library of Congress*] (LCLS)
IT Rulings.... Income Tax Rulings [*A publication*]
ItRUN.......... Centro di Documentazione Umberto Nobile, Museo Storico, Rome, Italy [*Library symbol*] [*Library of Congress*] (LCLS)
ITRY............ Itinerary (FAAC)
ITS.............. Aeronautica Interespacial SA de CV [*Mexico ICAO designator*] (FAAC)
ITS.............. AmericaIntelligent Transportation Society of America [*Formerly, IVHS America*]
ITS.............. Idaho Test Station [*Nuclear energy*] (NRCH)
ITS.............. Idle Tracking Switch [*Automotive engineering*]
ITS.............. IEEE Information Theory Society (EA)
ITS.............. Ignition Test Simulator
ITS.............. Imaginary Transition Structure [*Organic chemistry*]
ITS.............. Import Tabulation System [*United Nations*] (PDAA)
ITS.............. Improved Third Stage [*of Minuteman rocket*]
ITS.............. Incident Tracking System
ITS.............. Inclusive Tour Service (ADA)
ITS.............. Incompatible Time-sharing System (NHD)
ITS.............. Independent Triggering System
ITS.............. Index to Speeches [*Information service or system United Nations*] (DUND)
ITS.............. Industrial Technology Securities [*Investment firm*] [*British*]
ITS.............. Industrial Television Society [*Later, ITVA*] (EA)
ITS.............. Industrial Training Service (AIE)
ITS.............. Industry Training Support
ITS.............. Indus Tsangpo Suture [*Paleogeography*]
ITS.............. Inertial Timing Switch (IAA)
ITS.............. Infective Toxic Shock [*Medicine*] (DMAA)
ITS.............. Infinite Time Span
ITS.............. Information Technology Services [*National Library of Canada*] (TSSD)
ITS.............. Information Technology Services [*California State University, Long Beach*] [*Research center*] (RCD)
ITS.............. Information Technology Services [*Stanford University*] [*Information service or system*] (IID)
ITS.............. Information Technology Systems
ITS.............. Information Transfer Satellite (KSC)
ITS.............. Information Transfer [*or Transmission*] System
ITS.............. Infrared Tracking System
ITS.............. Initial Training School [*British military*] (DMA)
ITS.............. Insertion Test Signal [*Telecommunications*] (TEL)
ITS.............. Institute for Telecommunication Sciences [*Formerly, ITSA*] [*Boulder, CO*] [*Department of Commerce*]
ITS.............. Institute for Transportation Studies [*University of Calgary*] [*Canada Research center*] (RCD)
ITS.............. Institute of Telecommunications Services (MSC)
ITS.............. Institute of Temporary Services [*Later, National Association of Temporary Services*] (EA)
ITS.............. Institute of Theoretical Science [*University of Oregon*] [*Research center*] (RCD)
ITS.............. Institute of Transportation Studies [*University of California*] [*Research center*] (RCD)
ITS.............. Institute of Turkish Studies (EA)
ITS.............. Instrumentation Telemetry Station [*NASA*] (NASA)
ITS.............. Instrumentation Telemetry System [*NASA*] (IAA)
ITS.............. Instrument Time (Simulated)
ITS.............. Insulation Test Specification (MSA)
ITS.............. In-Tank Solidification
ITS.............. Integrated Target System
ITS.............. Integrated Termination System (IAA)
ITS.............. Integrated Test Schedule [*Army*]
ITS.............. Integrated Test Software (CAAL)
ITS.............. Integrated Tracking System [*ARTRAC*] [*Obsolete*] (MCD)
ITS.............. Integrated Trajectory System
ITS.............. Intelligent Terminal System [*IBM Corp.*]
ITS.............. Intelligent Transportation Society [*formerly, IVHS, Intelligent Vehicle-Highway Society*]
ITS.............. Intelligent Transportation System [*FTA*] [*NHTSA*] (TAG)
ITS.............. Intelligent Transport System [*Traffic management*] (ECON)
ITS.............. Intelligent Tutoring System (RDA)
ITS.............. Interactive Terminal Service (NITA)
ITS.............. Interactive Terminal Support [*Computer science*]
ITS.............. Interim Table Simulation (SAA)
ITS.............. Interim Teleprinter System
ITS.............. Intermarket Trading System (IEEE)
ITS.............. Intermediate Tape Store (CET)
ITS.............. Intermediate-Term Standby [*Business term*] (EMRF)
ITS.............. Internal Time Sharing (IAA)
ITS.............. Internal Transcribed Spacer [*Genetics*]
ITS.............. International Technogeographical Society
ITS.............. International Technologies & Systems [*Computer science*]
ITS.............. International Telecommunications Society (EA)
ITS.............. International Telecom Systems, Inc. [*Madison, WI*] [*Telecommunications*] (TSSD)
ITS.............. International Teleproduction Society (EA)
ITS.............. International Television Service [*Turner Teleport, Inc.*] [*Atlanta, GA*] [*Telecommunications service*] (TSSD)
ITS.............. International Temperature Scale (MUGU)
ITS.............. International Tesla Society (EA)
ITS.............. International Thespian Society (EA)
ITS.............. International Time-Sharing Corporation [*Telecommunications*] (NITA)
ITS.............. International Totalizator Systems, Inc. (EFIS)
ITS.............. International Tracing Service [*Arolsen, Germany*] (EAIO)
ITS.............. International Trade Secretariats [*ICFTU*]
ITS.............. International Training School
ITS.............. International Travel Show (ITD)
ITS.............. International Trucking Show (ITD)
ITS.............. International Turfgrass Society (EA)
ITS.............. International Twin Study [*University of Southern California*] [*Research center*] (RCD)
ITS.............. Intersectional Transportation Service
ITS.............. Interstate Energy [*Vancouver Stock Exchange symbol*]
ITS.............. Intertime Switch [*Connection or Call*] [*Telecommunications*] (TEL)
ITS.............. Invitation to Send [*Western Union*] [*Data communications*]
ITS.............. Ion Thrust System
ITS.............. Ion Trap System
ITS.............. Iowa Transfer System
ITS.............. Irish Texts Society (EAIO)
ITS.............. Islamic Texts Society [*British*] (DBA)
ITS.............. Tri-State University, Angola, IN [*OCLC symbol*] (OCLC)
ITSA............ Information Technology Skills Agency (NITA)
ITSA............ Information Technology Strategic Alliances Database (IID)
ITSA............ Insider Trading Sanctions Act of 1984
ITSA............ Installation and Test Support Associate Contractor [*Air Force*]
ITSA............ Institute for Telecommunication Sciences and Aeronomy [*Later, ITS*] [*National Oceanic and Atmospheric Administration*]
ITSA............ Institute of Trading Standards Administration [*British*]
ITSA............ Interstate Transportation of Stolen Aircraft
ITSAADCOTFOIK... International Twelve-Star Admiral and Deputy Custodian of the Fountain of Inexhaustible Knowledge [*Rank in Junior Woodchucks organization mentioned in Donald Duck comic by Carl Barks*]
ITSAC.......... International Thermal Storage Advisory Council (EAIO)
ITSB............ Interstate Transportation of Strikebreakers
ITSC............ International Telecommunications Satellite Consortium [*Superseded by International Telecommunications Satellite Organization*]
ITSC............ International Telephone Services Center [*Telecommunications*] (TEL)
ITSC............ Interstate Transportation of Stolen Cattle
ITSC............ It Scale for Children [*Psychology*]
ITSDC.......... Interagency Toxic Substances Data Committee [*Washington, DC*] [*Environmental Protection Agency*] (EGAO)
ITSE............ Integral of Time Squared Error [*Statistics*] (PDAA)
ITSEC.......... Information Technology Standards Unit [*British*]
ITSH............ Internal Transport, Storage, and Handling
ITSHD.......... Isolated Thyroid Stimulating Hormone Deficiency [*Medicine*] (STED)
ITSI............ International Lottery & Totalizator Systems [*NASDAQ symbol*] (SAG)
ITSI............ International Totalizator Systems, Inc. [*NASDAQ symbol*] (NQ)
ITSI............ Intl Lottery & Totalizator [*NASDAQ symbol*] (TTSB)
ITSL............ Integrated Two-Step Liquefaction [*Chemical engineering*]
ITSL............ International Translator (IAA)
ITSMV.......... Interstate Transportation of Stolen Motor Vehicle
ITSO............ Instrument Technician Service Organization
IT/SP.......... Instrument Tree/Spool Piece [*Nuclear energy*] (NRCH)
ITSP............ Integrated Training System Plan [*Army*]
ITSP............ Interstate Transportation of Stolen Property
ITSS............ Integrated Tactical Surveillance System
ITSS............ Integrated Target Sensor Suite (MCD)
ITSS............ Investment Trust Savings Scheme [*British*]
ITSTC.......... International Telecommunictaions Standards Technical Council (OSI)
ITSU............ Information Technology Standards Unit (NITA)
ITSU............ International Coordination Group for the Tsunami Warning System in the Pacific [*Marine science*] (OSRA)
ITSY............ Innovative Tech Systems, Inc. [*NASDAQ symbol*] (SAG)
ITSYLF.......... Interactive Synthesizer of Letterforms
ITSYW.......... Innovative Tech Sys Wrrt'A' [*NASDAQ symbol*] (TTSB)
ITT.............. Federal Reserve Bank of Chicago Library, Chicago, IL [*OCLC symbol*] (OCLC)
ITT.............. Identical Twins Raised Together (STED)
ITT.............. Iliotibial Tract [*Orthopedics*] (DAVI)
ITT.............. Image Intensification Tube (MCD)
ITT.............. Impact Transition Temperature (MCD)
ITT.............. Incoming Teletype
ITT.............. Incoming Trunk Terminal [*Telecommunications*] (IAA)
ITT.............. Indicator Time Test [*Chemistry*]
ITT.............. Individual Technical Training [*Military*]
ITT.............. Infrared Tympanic Thermometer [*Medicine*]
ITT.............. Initial Teacher Training (AIE)
ITT.............. Inside Trim Template (MSA)
ITT.............. Institute of Textile Technology (EA)
ITT.............. Institute of Travel and Tourism [*British*] (DBA)
ITT.............. Insulin Tolerance Test [*Physiology*]
ITT.............. Internal Tibial Torsion [*Orthopedics*] (DAVI)
ITT.............. International Trade in Textiles [*Textile trade agreement*]
ITT.............. Interpretative Trace and Trap Program (SAA)
ITT.............. Interrogation-Translation Team [*Military*] (CINC)
ITT.............. Inter-Test Time (AAEL)
ITT.............. Inter-Theater Transfer [*Army*] (AABC)
ITT.............. Intertoll Trunk [*Telecommunications*]
ITT.............. Inter-Turbine Temperature (ADA)
ITT.............. Intertype Training [*Navy*] (NVT)
ITT.............. Inventaire des Tablettes de Tello. Mission Francaise en Chaldee [*Paris*] [*A publication*] (BJA)
ITT.............. Invitation to Tender (SSD)
ITT.............. Iron Tolerance Test (STED)
ITT.............. ITT Canada Ltd. [*Toronto Stock Exchange symbol*]
ITT.............. ITT Corp. [*Formerly, International Telephone & Telegraph Corp.*] [*Wall Street slang name: "It Girl," the sobriquet for early movie star Clara Bow*] [*NYSE symbol*] (SPSG)

ITT .... Wittenoom Gorge [*Western Australia*] [*Airport symbol*] (AD)
ITTA............. Independent Taxation with Transferable Allowance [*British*] (DI)
ITTA............. International Tropical Timber Agreement (ECON)
ITTA............. ITT [*Institute of Textile Technology*] Austria (NITA)
ITTAC.......... Information Technology Training Accreditation Council [*British*] (NITA)
ITTAC.......... International Telegraph and Telephonic Advisory Committee (AABC)
ITTAP.......... ITT [*Institute of Textile Technology*] Testability Analysis Program (NITA)
ITTC .... Inter-American Tropical Tuna Commission [*Scripps Institution of Oceanography*]
ITTC .... International Travel and Trailer Club (EA)
ITTC .... International Tropical Timber Council [*Australia*]
ITTCCS........ ITT Corporate Communications Services, Inc.
ITTCOINS ..... ITT [*Institute of Textile Technology*] Communications and Information Services Inc. (NITA)
ITTCOM....... International Telephone & Telegraph World Communications, Inc.
ITT Corp ..... ITT Corp. [*Associated Press*] (SAG)
ITT Cp.......... ITT Corp. [*Formerly, International Telephone & Telegraph Corp.*] [*Wall Street slang name: "It Girl," the sobriquet for early movie star Clara Bow*] [*Associated Press*] (SAG)
ITTCS .... International Telephone and Telegraph Communication System
ITTD .... Information and Technology Transfer Database [*International Research and Evaluation*]
ITTE .... Institute for the Transfer of Technology to Education (EA)
ITTE .... Institute of Transportation and Traffic Engineering [*UCLA*]
ITTE .... Interim Terminal Test Environment [*FAA*]
ITT Ed .... ITT Educational Services, Inc. [*Associated Press*] (SAG)
ITTETS .... ITT Employment & Training Systems, Inc. [*Telecommunications service*] (TSSD)
ITTF .... International Table Tennis Federation [*British*]
ITTF .... International Telephone and Telegraph Federal Laboratories
ITTFA .... Iterative Target Transformation Factor Analysis [*Computer science*]
ITTFL .... International Telephone and Telegraph Federal Laboratories
ITTG .... Interdisciplinary Team Training in Geriatrics [*Veterans Administration*] (GFGA)
ITTGATC ...... ITT [*Institute of Textile Technology*] Gallium Arsenide Technology Center (NITA)
ITT Inds .... ITT Industries, Inc. Indiana [*Associated Press*] (SAG)
ITTL .... International Table Tennis League (EA)
ITTL .... International Telephone and Telegraph Laboratories (SAA)
ITTO .... International Tropical Timber Organization [*Yokohama, Japan*] [*United Nations*]
ITTP .... Instrument Technician Training Program (ACII)
ITT/PMD ...... Interpretative Trace and Trap Program Plus Modifications (SAA)
ITTS .... Instrumentation, Target, and Threat Simulator [*Army*] (RDA)
ITTT .... Individual Tactical Technical Training [*Military*] (MCD)
ITTT .... Institute of Transportation, Travel, and Tourism
ITTTA .... International Technical Tropical Timber Association
ItTU .... Biblioteca Nazional Universitaria di Torino, Servizio Prestito, Turin, Italy [*Library symbol Library of Congress*] (LCLS)
ITT-USTS ..... ITT United States Transmission Systems, Inc. [*Telecommunications service*] (TSSD)
ITU.............. Income Tax Unit
ITU.............. Input Terminal Unit (SSD)
ITU.............. Instructional Technologist Unit
ITU.............. Intensive Therapy Unit [*Medicine*] (MAE)
ITU.............. Interface Transformation Unit (SAA)
ITU.............. International Taurus Resources [*Vancouver Stock Exchange symbol*]
ITU.............. International Telecommunications Union [*An association*] (PCM)
ITU.............. International Telecommunication Union [*Formerly, International Telegraphic Union*] [*A specialized agency of the United Nations*] [*Switzerland Research center*]
ITU.............. International Temperance Union
ITU.............. International Triathlon Union (EAIO)
ITU.............. International Typographical Union (EA)
ITU.............. Inventory Temporarily in Use [*Army*] (AFIT)
ITU.............. Investment Trust Unit [*British*]
ITU.............. Taylor University, Upland, IN [*OCLC symbol*] (OCLC)
ITu.............. Tuscola Public Library, Tuscola, IL [*Library symbol Library of Congress*] (LCLS)
ITUA............ Independent Trade Union Association [*Turkey*]
ITUC............ Irish Trade Union Congress
ITuCoH......... Douglas County Jarman Memorial Hospital, Tuscola, IL [*Library symbol Library of Congress*] (LCLS)
ITUCSTL ...... International Trade Unions Committee of Social Tourism and Leisure [*See also CSITSL*] [*Prague, Czechoslovakia*] (EAIO)
ITU-D .... International Telecommunication Union-Telecommunication Development Sector (ACRL)
ITUG .... Information Technology Users Group [*Exxon Corp.*]
ITUG .... International Tandem Users' Group (EA)
i-Tumor........ Intratumoral (STED)
ITU-R .... International Telecommunication Union-Radio Communication Sector (ACRL)
ITUR .... Interstate Transportation of Unsafe Refrigerators
ITURM .... International Typographical Union Ruling Machine
ITUS............ Institute of Totally Useless Skills [*An association*] (EA)
ITUSA .... Information Technology Users' Standards Association [*British*]
ITUSAF .... Institute of Technology, United States Air Force [*Wright-Patterson Air Force Base, Dayton, OH*] (AAG)
ITUSFP .... Interreligious Taskforce on US Food Policy (EA)
ITU-T .... International Telecommunication Union-Telecommunication Standardization Sector (ACRL)
ITU-TSS .... International Telecommunications Union - Telecommunications Switching System (PCM)

ITV .... Improved TOW [*Tube-Launched, Optically Tracked, Wire-Guided (Weapon)*] Vehicle
ITV .... Independently Targeted Vehicle [*Military*] (DA)
ITV .... Independent Television
ITV .... Industrial Television
ITV .... Inferior Temporal Vein [*Medicine*] (DMAA)
ITV .... Instructional Television
ITV .... Instrumental Test Vehicle
ITV .... Integrated Technology Validation
ITV .... Interactive Television
ITV .... Intermediate Test Vessel (NRCH)
ITV .... Intervuelo SA [*Mexico ICAO designator*] (FAAC)
ITV .... Intranet Visability [*Army*]
ITV .... In-Transit Visibility (COE)
ITV .... Israel Television (BJA)
ItV .... Italian RCA [*Victor*] [*Record label*]
ITVA .... International Industrial Television Association (NTCM)
ITVA .... International Television Association (EA)
ITVAC.......... Industrial Transistor Value Automatic Computer
ITVAD .... Indwelling Transcutaneous Vascular Access Device [*Pharmacology*] (DAVI)
ITVB............ International Television Broadcasting
ITVETS........ Improved TOW [*Tube-Launched, Optically Tracked, Wire-Guided (Weapon)*] Vehicle Evasive Target Simulator [*Military*] (MCD)
ItVox........... Italian Vox [*Record label*]
ITVS............ Ignition Timing Vacuum Switch [*Automotive engineering*]
ITVS............ Independent Television Service
ITVSDA .... Independent Television Service Dealers' Association
ITVTP.......... Internationale Tieraerztliche Vereinigung fuer Tierproduktion [*International Veterinary Association for Animal Production*]
ITW .... Illinois Tool Works [*NYSE symbol*] (TTSB)
ITW .... Illinois Tool Works, Inc. [*NYSE symbol*] (SPSG)
ITW .... Independent Tank Wing [*of a ship*] (DS)
ITW .... Independent True Whig Party [*Liberia*] [*Political party*]
ITW .... Inertia Test Weight [*Exhaust emissions*] [*Automotive engineering*]
ITW .... Initial Training Wing [*British military*] (DMA)
ITW .... Introducing the World [*An association Canada*]
ITWA .... International Tug-of-War Association (EA)
ITW/AA .... Integrated Tactical Warning/Attack Assessment (COE)
ITWC............ Inland Transport War Council [*World War II*]
ITWEA .... International Travel Writers and Editors Association (NTPA)
ITWF .... International Transport Workers' Federation
ITWG .... Interface Technical Working Group
ITWI............ Interstate Transmission of Wagering Information
ITWO .... i2 Technologies [*NASDAQ symbol*] (TTSB)
ITWO .... Inspection Test Work Order (SAA)
ITWP............ Interstate Transportation of Wagering Paraphernalia
ITWS .... Integrated Terminal Weather System [*Marine science*] (OSRA)
ITX .... Iberiotoxin [*Biochemistry*]
ITX .... Imair [*Azerbaijan*] [*FAA designator*] (FAAC)
ITX .... Inclusive Tour Excursion [*Airline fare*]
ITX .... Independent Tank Common [*of a ship*] (DS)
ITX .... Information Transfer Exchange (PDAA)
ITX .... Interactive Transaction
ITX .... International Technology Corp. [*NYSE symbol*] (SPSG)
ITX .... International Tillex Enterprises Ltd. [*Vancouver Stock Exchange symbol*]
ITX .... Intertriginous Xanthoma [*Medicine*] (AAMN)
ITX .... Intl Technology [*NYSE symbol*] (TTSB)
ITY .... Fort Riley, KS [*Location identifier FAA*] (FAAL)
ITY .... Information Technology Year [*1982*]
ITY .... Intensity Resources Ltd. [*Toronto Stock Exchange symbol*]
Ity .... Interchangeability
ITY .... International Tourist Year
ITyr............ Monoiodotryrosine (STED)
ITZ .... Inter-Tropical Convergence Zone
ITZN............ International Trust for Zoological Nomenclature (EES)
IU................ Identification Unit (MSA)
IU................ Immunizing Unit [*Medicine*]
IU................ Impedance Unit (MCD)
IU................ Indianapolis Union [*AAR code*]
IU................ Indiana University
IU................ Industrial User (ERG)
IU................ Infectious Unit
IU................ Information Unit
IU................ Information Unlimited [*Information service or system*] (IID)
IU................ Input Unit
IU-D .... Instant Update [*Professional Farmers of America*] [*Information service or system*] (TSSD)
IU................ Instruction Unit [*Computer science*]
IU................ Instrument Unit [*NASA*]
iu................ Instrument Unit (NAKS)
IU................ Integer Unit [*Computer science*]
IU................ Interface Unit [*Computer science*] (MCD)
iu................ Interface Unit (NAKS)
IU................ Interference Unit [*Military*]
IU................ Interlingue Union
IU................ International Unit
IU................ Internet University [*Computer science*]
IU................ Interval of Uncertainty [*Psychology*]
IU................ Intrauterine [*Medicine*]
IU................ In Utero [*Gynecology*]
iu................ Israel-Syria Demilitarized Zones [*is (Israel) used in records cataloged after January 1978*] [*MARC country of publication code Library of Congress*] (LCCP)

IU................. Izquierda Unida [*United Left*] [*Spain*] [*Political party*] (ECED)
IU................. Izquierda Unida [*United Left*] [*Bolivia*] [*Political party*] (EY)
IU................. Izquierda Unida [*United Left*] [*Peru*] [*Political party*]
IU................. Midstate Airlines [*ICAO designator*] (AD)
IU................. University of Illinois, Urbana, IL [*Library symbol Library of Congress*] (LCLS)
IUA............... Image Understanding Architecture [*Computer science*]
IUA............... Individual Unit Action Model
IUA............... Inertial Unit Assembly
IUA............... Information User Association (NTPA)
IUA............... Inter-American University Association
IUA............... Interface Unit Adapter [*Computer science*] (MCD)
IUA............... Interlibrary Users Association [*University of Maryland*] [*College Park, MD*] [*Library network*]
IUA............... International Union of Academies (EA)
IUA............... International Union of Architects
IUA............... International University of America [*San Francisco, CA*] (ECON)
IUA............... Intrauterine Adhesion [*Medicine*] (DMAA)
IUA............... IOMEC Users Association [*Formerly, DUA*] [*Defunct*] (EA)
IUA............... University of Texas at Arlington, Arlington, TX [*OCLC symbol*] (OCLC)
IUAA .... International Union of Advertisers Associations [*Later, WFA*] (EAIO)
IUAA .... International Union of Alpine Associations
IUAC .... International Union Against Cancer [*An association*] (CDI)
IUACE .... Indian University Association for Continuing Education
IUADM .... International Union of Associations of Doctor-Motorists
IUAES .... International Union of Anthropological and Ethnological Sciences [*See also UISAE*] [*ICSU Gwynedd, Wales*] (EAIO)
IUAI .... International Union of Aviation Insurers [*British*] (EAIO)
IUAJ .... International Union of Agricultural Journalists
IUAM .... Islamic Unity of Afghan Mujahadeen [*Afghanistan*] [*Political party*]
IUANPW .... International Union of Allied Novelty and Production Workers (EA)
IUAO .... Internationalen Union fuer Angewandte Ornithologie [*International Union for Applied Ornithology*] (EAIO)
IUAPPA .... International Union of Air Pollution Prevention Associations [*See also UIAPPA*] [*England*] (EAIO)
IUAR .... Institute for Urban Affairs and Research [*Howard University*] [*Research center*] (RCD)
IU-Ar............ University of Illinois, Archives, Urbana, IL [*Library symbol Library of Congress*] (LCLS)
IUAT............. International Union Against Tuberculosis [*Later, IUATLD*] (EAIO)
IUATLD .... International Union Against Tuberculosis and Lung Disease [*See also UICTMR*] (EAIO)
IUB............... Baltimore, MD [*Location identifier FAA*] (FAAL)
IUB............... Indiana University, School of Law Library, Bloomington, IN [*OCLC symbol*] (OCLC)
IUB............... Instruction Used BIT [*Binary Digit*] [*Computer science*] (MHDI)
IUB............... International Union of Biochemistry (EA)
IUB............... International Universities Bureau
IU-B .... University of Illinois, Biology Library, Urbana, IL [*Library symbol Library of Congress*] (LCLS)
IUBC .... Indiana United Bancorp [*NASDAQ symbol*] (SAG)
IUBCTW .... International Union of Bakery, Confectionery, and Tobacco Workers (BARN)
IUBMB .... International Union of Biochemistry and Molecular Biology (HGEN)
IUBS .... International Union of Biological Sciences [*Paris, France*]
IUBS-CBE..... IUBS Commission on Biological Education (AIE)
IUBSSA........ International Union of Building Societies and Savings Associations [*Later, IOHFI*] [*Chicago, IL*] (EA)
IUC............... Association for Higher Education, Dallas, TX [*OCLC symbol*] (OCLC)
IUC............... Idiopathic Ulcerative Colitis [*Medicine*]
IUC............... Immediate Unit Commander [*Navy*] (NVT)
IUC............... Incurred but Unreported Claims [*Health insurance*] (GHCT)
IUC............... Initial User Capability (SSD)
IUC............... Instructor Utilization Course (MCD)
IUC............... International Underwater Contractors, Inc.
IUC............... International Union of Chemistry (MEC)
IUC............... International Union of Crystallography
IUC............... International University Consortium for Telecommunications in Learning [*Later, IUC*] (EA)
IUC............... International University Contact for Management Education
IUC............... International University of Communication [*Washington, DC*]
IUC............... Inter-University Committee for Debate on Foreign Policy [*Defunct*]
IUC............... Inter-University Council
IUCAA .... Inter-University Center for Astronomy and Astrophysic [*India*]
IUCAB .... International Union of Commercial Agents and Brokers [*EC*] (ECED)
IUCADC........ Inter-Union Commission of Advice to Developing Countries [*of the International Union of Geodesy and Geophysics*] [*Mississauga, ON*] (EAIO)
IUCAF .... Inter-Union Commission on Frequency Allocations for Radio Astronomy and Space Science (EA)
IUCD .... Intrauterine Contraceptive Device [*Medicine*]
IUCED .... Inter-Union Commission of European Dehydrators [*See also CIDE*] [*Paris, France*] (EAIO)
IUCESD .... Inter-American University Council for Economic and Social Development (EA)
IUCF............. Indiana University Cyclotron Facility [*Research center*] (RCD)
IUCFA .... Inter-Union Commission on Frequency Allocations for Radio Astronomy and Space Science (EA)
IUCI .... Inter-University Committee on Israel [*Later, America-Israel Cultural Foundation*] (EA)
IUCME .... International University Contact for Management Education
IUCN .... International Union for Conservation of Nature [*World Conservation Union*] (USDC)

IUCN .... International Union for Conservation of Nature and Natural Resources [*Research Center*] [*ICSU*] [*Switzerland*] (EA)
IUCN .... World Conservation Union
IUCNNR .... International Union for Conservation of Nature and Natural Resources [*ICS U*] [*Research center Switzerland*]
IUCNPSG ..... International Union for the Conservation of Nature's Primate Specialist Group (EA)
IU Cr .... International Union of Crystallography [*See also UIC*] (EA)
IUCRC.......... Industry/University Cooperation Research Center [*National Science Foundation*]
IUCRCB........ Inter-University Committee for Research on Consumer Behavior (EA)
IUCRM .... Inter-Union Commission on Radio Meteorology [*International Council of Scientific Unions*] [*Research center*]
IUCS .... Instruction Update Command System
IUCS .... Instrumentation Unit Update Command System [*NASA*] (NASA)
IUCS .... Inter-Union Commission on Spectroscopy [*International Council of Scientific Unions*]
IUCSTP .... Inter-Union Commission on Solar-Terrestrial Physics (MCD)
IUCTG .... Inter-University Committee on Travel Grants
IUCW .... International Union for Child Welfare [*Geneva, Switzerland*] [*Defunct*]
IUD .... Indiana University, School of Dentistry, Indianapolis, IN [*OCLC symbol*] (OCLC)
IUD .... Industrial Union Department [*of AFL-CIO*] (EA)
IUD .... Institute for Urban Design (EA)
IUD .... Institute for Urban Development
IUD .... Internal Unstable Damper (MCD)
IUD .... Intrauterine Death [*Medicine*]
IUD .... Intrauterine Device [*A contraceptive*] [*Medicine*]
IUDH .... In-Service Unplanned Derated Hours [*Electronics*] (IEEE)
IUdR .... Iodouracildeoxyriboside [*Biochemistry*]
IUDWC......... Irish Union of Distributive Workers and Clerks (BI)
IUDZG .... International Union of Directors of Zoological Gardens [*Canada*] (EAIO)
IUE............... Interface Unit Error Count Table (MCD)
IUE............... International Thunderwood Explorations Ltd. [*Vancouver Stock Exchange symbol Toronto Stock Exchange symbol*]
IUE............... International Ultraviolet Explorer [*NASA*]
IUE............... International Union for Electroheat [*Also, IUE-H*]
IUE............... International Union of Electrical, Radio, and Machine Workers
IUE............... International Union of Electronic [*Electrical, technical, salaried and machine workers*] (NITA)
IUE............... International Union of Electronic, Electrical, Technical, Salaried, Machine, andFurniture Workers (EA)
IUE............... Iron Use Efficiency [*Metabolism*]
IUE............... Niue Island [*Niue*] [*Airport symbol*] (OAG)
IUE............... University of Evansville, Evansville, IN [*OCLC symbol*] (OCLC)
IUEC............ International Union of Elevator Constructors (EA)
IUEF............. Internacia Unuigo de la Esperantistoj-Filologoj [*International Union of Esperantist-Philologists - IUEP*] [*Sofia, Bulgaria*] (EAIO)
IUEFI............ Internacia Unuigo de la Esperantistoj-Filologoj [*International Union of Esperantist-Philologists - IUEP*] [*Sofia, Bulgaria*] (EA)
IUEGS .... International Union of European Guides and Scouts [*See also UIGSE*] [*Chateau Landon, France*] (EAIO)
IUE-H .... International Union for Electroheat [*Also, IUE*]
IUEP............. International Union of Esperantist-Philologists [*Sofia, Bulgaria*] (EAIO)
IUERMW ...... International Union of Electrical, Radio, and Machine Workers (IAA)
IUEW .... International Union of Electrical Workers
IUF............... Interamerican Underwater Festival
IUF............... International Unicycling Federation (EA)
IUF............... International Union of Food and Allied Workers' Associations [*See also IUL*] [*Petit-Lancy, Switzerland*] (EAIO)
IUF............... International University Foundation (EA)
IUF............... Isolated Ultrafiltration [*Organic chemistry*] (DAVI)
IUF............... Southern Methodist University, Law Library, Dallas, TX [*OCLC symbol*] (OCLC)
IUFB............. Intrauterine Foreign Body [*Gynecology*]
IUFD............. Intrauterine Fetal Death [*or Demise*] [*Obstetrics*] (DAVI)
IUFDT .... International Union of Food, Drink, and Tobacco Workers' Associations
IUFGR .... Intrauterine Fetal Growth Retardation [*Obstetrics*] (DAVI)
IUFLJP.......... International Union of French-Language Journalists and Press [*See also UIJPLF*] [*Paris, France*] (EAIO)
IUFO............. International Union of Family Organizations [*Paris, France*]
IUFoST........ International Union of Food Science and Technology [*ICSU*] [*Dublin, Republic of Ireland*] (EAIO)
IUFRO .... International Union of Forestry Research Organizations [*Vienna, Austria*] [*Research center*] (EAIO)
Iug .... Bellum Iugurthinum [*of Sallust*] [*Classical studies*] (OCD)
IUG .... ICES [*Integrated Civil Engineering System*] Users Group [*Defunct*] (EA)
IUG .... Infusion Urogram [*Medicine*] (DMAA)
IUG .... Intelligence Users' Guide (MCD)
IUG .... Intercomm Users' Group (EA)
IUG .... Intrauterine Gestation [*Obstetrics*] (DAVI)
IUGB .... International Union of Game Biologists [*Canada*] (EAIO)
IUGG .... International Union of Geodesy and Geophysics [*Brussels, Belgium*]
IUGGTC........ International Union of Geodesy and Geophysics Tsunami Commission [*Marine science*] (OSRA)
IUGG/TC....... IUGG Tsunami Commission (USDC)
IUGM .... International Union of Gospel Missions (EA)
IUGR .... Intrauterine Growth Rate [*Medicine*] (MAE)
IUGR .... Intrauterine Growth Retardation [*Medicine*]
IUGRI........... International Union of Graphic Reproduction Industries [*Later, IUI*] (EAIO)

IUGS .... International Union of Geological Sciences [*ICSU*] [*Trondheim, Norway*] (EA)
IU-GS .... University of Illinois, Illinois State Geological Survey, Urbana, IL [*Library symbol Library of Congress*] (LCLS)
IUH .... Indiana University, School of Medicine, Health Library Cooperative, Indianapolis, IN [*OCLC symbol*] (OCLC)
IUH .... Instantaneous Unit Hydrograph
IU-H .... University of Illinois, School of Basic Medical Sciences, Library of Public Health Sciences, Urbana, IL [*Library symbol Library of Congress*] (LCLS)
IUHE .... International Union of Health Education [*See also UIES*] [*Paris, France*] (EAIO)
IUHFI .... International Union of Housing Finance Institutions (EAIO)
IUHPS .... International Union of the History and Philosophy of Science [*ICSU*] [*Uppsala, Sweden*] (EAIO)
IUHR .... International Union of Hotel, Restaurant, and Bar Workers
IU-HS .... Illinois Historical Survey, University of Illinois, Urbana, IL [*Library symbol Library of Congress*] (LCLS)
IUI .... Interim Use Item (MCD)
IUI .... Intrauterine Insemination [*Medicine*] (DMAA)
IUI .... Shawnee Library System, Carterville, IL [*OCLC symbol*] (OCLC)
IUIEC .... Inter-University Institute of Engineering Control (PDAA)
IUIN .... International Union for Inland Navigation [*Strasbourg, France*] (EA)
IUIS .... International Union of Immunological Societies (EA)
IUISTHE .... International Union of Industrial Service Transport Health Employees (NTPA)
IUJ .... International University of Japan (ECON)
IUJ .... John Marshall Law School, Chicago, IL [*OCLC symbol*] (OCLC)
IUJCD .... Internationale Union Junger Christlicher Demokraten [*International Union of Young Christian Democrats*]
IUJHUSC ...... International Union of Journeymen Horseshoers of the United States and Canada (EA)
IUKADGE ...... Improved United Kingdom Air Defense Ground Environment
Iul .... Divus Iulius [*of Suetonius*] [*Classical studies*] (OCD)
IUL .... Indiana University, Bloomington, IN [*OCLC symbol*] (OCLC)
IUL .... Indian Unattached List [*British military*] (DMA)
IUL .... Information Utilization Laboratory [*University of Pittsburgh*] (NITA)
IUL .... Institute of Urban Life (EA)
IUL .... Internationale Union der Lebens- und Genussmittelarbeiter-Gewerkschaften [*International Union of Food and Allied Workers Associations - IUF*] [*Petit-Lancy, Switzerland*] (EAIO)
IU/L .... International Units per Liter
IU-L .... University of Illinois, Lincoln Room, Urbana, IL [*Library symbol Library of Congress*] (LCLS)
IULA .... International Union of Local Authorities [*The Hague, Netherlands*] (EA)
IULC .... Committee on Instruction in the Use of Libraries [*Later, CUILL*] (EA)
IULC .... Independent United Labor Congress [*Nigeria*]
IULC-RAILS ... Interuniversity Library Council: Reference and Interlibrary Loan Service [*Library network*]
IULCS .... International Union of Leather Chemists Societies
IULCW .... International Union of Liberal Christian Women
IULD .... International Union of Lorry Drivers [*See also UICR*] [*Munich, Germany*] (EAIO)
IULEC .... Inter-University Labor Education Committee
IULIA .... International Union of Life Insurance Agents [*Milwaukee, WI*] (EA)
IULS .... Indiana Union List of Serials
IU-LS .... University of Illinois, Graduate School of Library Science, Urbana, IL [*Library symbol Library of Congress*] (LCLS)
IULVTFT .... International Union for Land Value Taxation and Free Trade [*British*] (EAIO)
IUM .... Honolulu, HI [*Location identifier FAA*] (FAAL)
IUM .... Indiana University, School of Medicine, Indianapolis, IN [*OCLC symbol*] (OCLC)
IUM .... Interim Use Material (MCD)
IUM .... Intrauterine Fetally Malnourished [*Medicine*] (MAE)
IUM .... Intrauterine Membrane [*Medicine*] (DB)
IU-M .... University of Illinois at the Medical Center, Chicago, IL [*Library symbol Library of Congress*] (LCLS)
IUMA .... Interim Use Material Authorization (MCD)
IUMA .... Internet Underground Music Archive (WDAA)
IU-MG .... University of Illinois, Map and Geography Library, Urbana, IL [*Library symbol*] [*Library of Congress*] (LCLS)
IUMI .... International Union of Marine Insurance [*Basel, Switzerland*]
IUMMSW ...... International Union of Mine, Mill, and Smelter Workers [*Later, USWA*]
IUMP .... International Union of Master Painters [*See also UNIEP*] [*Brussels, Belgium*] (EAIO)
IUMP .... International Union of the Medical Press (DIT)
IUMS .... International Union for Moral and Social Action
IUMS .... International Union of Microbiological Societies [*University of Newcastle*] (EA)
IUMSBD .... International Union of Microbiological Societies Bacteriology Division [*B eckenham, Kent, England*] (EAIO)
IUMSWA ...... Industrial Union of Marine and Shipbuilding Workers of America (EA)
IU-Mu .... University of Illinois, Music Library, Urbana, IL [*Library symbol Library of Congress*] (LCLS)
IUNA .... Irish United Nations Association (EAIO)
IUNDH .... In-Service Unit Derated Hours [*Electronics*] (IEEE)
IU-Ne .... University of Illinois at Urbana-Champaign, University of Illinois Newspaper Library, Urbana-Champaign, IL [*Library symbol Library of Congress*] (LCLS)
IU-NH .... University of Illinois, Illinois Natural History Survey, Urbana, IL [*Library symbol Library of Congress*] (LCLS)
IUNS .... International Union of Nutritional Sciences [*Wageningen, Netherlands*]
IUNT .... Interservice Undergraduate Navigator Training
IUO .... ICG Utilities (Ontario) Ltd. [*Toronto Stock Exchange symbol*]
IUOE .... International Union of Operating Engineers (EA)
IUOMWH ..... Independent United Order of Mechanics - Western Hemisphere (EA)
IUOTO .... International Union of Official Travel Organisations [*Later, WTO*]
IUP .... Indiana University of Pennsylvania
IUP .... Indiana University Press
IUP .... Indiana University - Purdue University at Indianapolis, Indianapolis, IN [*OCLC symbol*] (OCLC)
IUP .... Industrial Union Party (EA)
IUP .... Installed User Program [*Computer science*]
IUP .... International Union of Phlebology [*Paris, France*] (EA)
IUP .... Intrauterine Pregnancy (CPH)
IUP .... Intrauterine Pressure [*Gynecology*]
IUP .... Irish University Press
IUP .... Israel Universities Press
IUPA .... International Union of Police Associations (EA)
IUPA .... International Union of Practitioners in Advertising
IUPAB .... International Union of Pure and Applied Biophysics [*ICSU*] [*Pecs, Hungary*] [*Research center*] (EA)
IUPAC .... International Union of Pure and Applied Chemistry [*Research center British*] (IRC)
IUPAP .... International Union of Pure and Applied Physics [*ICSU*] [*Goteborg, Sweden*] (EA)
IUPD .... Intrauterne Pregnancy, Delivered [*Obstetrics*] (DAVI)
IUPESM .... International Union for Physical and Engineering Sciences in Medicine [*ICSU*] [*Ottawa, ON*] (EAIO)
IUPHAR .... International Union of Pharmacology [*ICSU*] [*Buckingham, England*] (MSC)
IUPIW .... International Union of Petroleum and Industrial Workers (EA)
IUPLAW .... International Union for the Protection of Literary and Artistic Works
IUPM .... International Union for Protecting Public Morality [*Later, International Union for Moral and Social Action*]
IUPN .... International Union for the Protection of Nature [*Later, IUCN*]
IUPOV .... International Union for the Protection of New Varieties of Plants (GNE)
IUPPE .... Independent Union of Plant Protection Employees (EA)
IUPPR .... Institute for Urban and Public Policy Research [*University of Colorado - Denver*] [*Research center*] (RCD)
IUPPS .... International Union of Prehistoric and Protohistoric Sciences [*Ghent, Belgium*] (EAIO)
Iupp Trag ..... Iuppiter Tragoedus [*of Lucian*] [*Classical studies*] (OCD)
IUPS .... International Union of Physiological Sciences [*ICSU*] [*Gif-sur-Yvette, France*] (ASF)
IUPS .... International Union of Psychological Science (EA)
IUPsyS .... International Union of Psychological Science (EA)
IUPT .... International Union of Public Transportation
IUPUI .... Indiana University - Purdue University at Indianapolis
IUPW .... International Union of Petroleum Workers [*Later, IUPIW*] (EA)
IUQ .... Interrupted Ultraquick [*Flashing*] Light [*Navigation signal*]
IUQ .... Quaker Oats Co., Research Library, Barrington, IL [*OCLC symbol*] (OCLC)
IUR .... Insured Unemployment Rate (OICC)
IUR .... International Union of Radioecologists (EA)
IUR .... International Union of Railways [*Paris*]
IUR .... International Union Resources, Inc. [*Vancouver Stock Exchange symbol*]
IUR .... Inter-User Reliability
IUR .... Inventory Update Rule [*Environmental Protection Agency*]
IU-R .... University of Illinois, Rare Book Room, Urbana, IL [*Library symbol Library of Congress*] (LCLS)
IUr .... Urbana Free Library, Urbana, IL [*Library symbol Library of Congress*] (LCLS)
IURAP .... International Users Resource Allocation Panel
IURC .... International Underwater Research Corp.
IURC .... International Union for Research of Communication [*Berne, Switzerland*] (EAIO)
IUrCD .... Clark Dietz Engineers, Urbana, IL [*Library symbol*] [*Library of Congress*] (LCLS)
IUrCH .... Carle Foundation Hospital, Urbana, IL [*Library symbol Library of Congress*] (LCLS)
IURD .... Institute of Urban and Regional Development [*University of California, Berkeley*] [*Research center*] (RCD)
IUrE-E .... Educational Resources Information Center, Elementary and Early Childhood Education (ERIC/ECE), Urbana, IL [*Library symbol Library of Congress*] (LCLS)
IUrE-NC .... Educational Resources Information Center, National Council of Teachers of English, Urbana, IL [*Library symbol Library of Congress*] (LCLS)
IUREP .... International Uranium Resources Evaluation Project
IURES .... International Union of Reticuloendothelial Societies (EA)
IUrG .... Illinois State Geological Survey, Urbana, IL [*Library symbol Library of Congress*] (LCLS)
IURGRQR ..... Item Urgently Required [*Army*] (AFIT)
IUrH .... Mercy Hospital, Urbana, IL [*Library symbol Library of Congress*] (LCLS)
IURMS .... International Union of Railway Medical Services (EA)
IURP .... Integrated Unit Record Processor
IURP .... International Union of Roofing and Plumbing (EAIO)
IURS .... Institute of Urban and Regional Studies [*Washington University*] [*Research center*] (RCD)
IURS .... International Union of Radio Science (MSC)
IUrSD .... Urbana Community Unit School District, Urbana, IL [*Library symbol*] [*Library of Congress*] (LCLS)

IUrW .... Illinois State Water Survey, Urbana, IL [*Library symbol Library of Congress*] (LCLS)

IUS .... Inertial [*formerly, Interim*] Upper Stage [*Air Force*]

ius .... Inertial Upper Stage [*NASA*] (NAKS)

IUS .... Information Unit Separator [*Computer science*]

IUS .... Initial Upper Stage [*NASA*]

IUS .... Initial Upper State (IEEE)

IUS .... Installed User System [*Computer science*] (IAA)

IUS .... Institute of Urban Studies, University of Winnipeg [*UTLAS symbol*]

IUS .... Interchange Unit Selector (NITA)

IUS .... Interchange Unit Separator [*Computer science*] (BUR)

ius .... Interim/Intermediate Upper State [*NASA*] (NAKS)

IUS .... Interim Upper Stage [*Missile*]

IUS .... Interim Use Sheet (NASA)

ius .... Interim Use Sheet (NAKS)

IUS .... Interior Upper Stage (NASA)

IUS .... International Union of Speleology [*See also UIS*] [*Vienna, Austria*] (EAIO)

IUS .... International Union of Students [*See also UIE*] [*Prague, Czechoslovakia*] (EAIO)

IUS .... Inter-University Seminar on Armed Forces and Society (EA)

IUSA .... International Underwater Spearfishing Association (EA)

IUSA .... Interserve/USA [*An association*] (EA)

IUSAMH .... International Union of Societies for the Aid of Mental Health [*Bordeaux, France*] (EAIO)

IUSB .... Indiana University at South Bend

IUSB .... International Universities' Sports Board [*Defunct*] (EA)

IUSC .... Inter-University Software Committee [*Inter-University Committee on Computing*] (AIE)

IUSDT .... International Union of Socialist Democratic Teachers (EAIO)

IUSF .... India-US Foundation (EA)

IUSF .... International Union for Surface Finishing (EAIO)

IUSF .... International Union of Societies of Foresters [*See also UISIF*] [*Ottawa, ON*] (EAIO)

IUSO .... Institute of University Safety Officers [*British*] (DBA)

IUSO .... International Union of Security Officers (EA)

IUSS .... Integrated Undersea-Surveillance System [*Oceanography*] (ECON)

IUSS .... Integrated Underwater Surveillance System [*Navy*] [*Marine science*] (OSRA)

IUSSI .... International Union for the Study of Social Insects [*Utrecht, Netherlands*]

IUSSP .... International Union for the Scientific Study of Population [*Liege, Belgium*]

IUSTFI .... Institute on United States Taxation of Foreign Income [*Later, ITI*] (EA)

IUSTOC .... Independent US Tanker Owners Committee [*Defunct*] (EA)

IUSUHM .... International Union of School and University Health and Medicine [*See also UIHMSU*] [*Brussels, Belgium*] (EAIO)

IUSY .... International Union of Socialist Youth

IUT .... Implementation Under Test [*Telecommunications*] (OSI)

IUT .... Industrial Unit of Tribology [*University of Leeds*] [*An association Research center British*] (EA)

IUT .... Instructor Under Training [*Navy*] (NVT)

IUT .... International Union of Tenants [*Stockholm, Sweden*] (EAIO)

IUT .... Intrauterine Transfusion [*Gynecology*]

IUt .... Utica Public Library, Utica, IL [*Library symbol Library of Congress*] (LCLS)

IUTAM .... International Union of Theoretical and Applied Mechanics [*Germany*]

IUTAO .... International Union of Technical Associations and Organizations [*France*] (EAIO)

IUTCA .... International Union of Technical Cinematograph Associations [*See also UNIATEC*] [*Paris, France*] (EAIO)

IUTDM .... International Union of Tool, Die, and Mold Makers (EA)

IUTDMM .... International Union of Tool, Die, and Mold Makers (EA)

IUTM .... International Union Against Tuberculosis (DAVI)

IUTOX .... International Union for Toxicology

IUTS .... Inter-University Transit System [*Interlibrary loan service*] [*Canada*] (NITA)

IUUCLGW .... International Union, United Cement, Lime and Gypsum Workers (MHDB)

IU-UPGWA ... International Union, United Plant Guard Workers of America (NTPA)

IUUU .... Industrial Unit, University of Ulster [*British*] (IRUK)

IUUW .... International Union, United Welders [*Later, IUOE*]

IUV .... IATA [*International Air Transport Association*] Unit of Value [*International airline currency*]

IU-V .... University of Illinois, Veterinary Medicine Library, Urbana, IL [*Library symbol Library of Congress*] (LCLS)

IUVDT .... International Union Against Venereal Diseases and Treponematoses (EAIO)

IUVSTA .... International Union for Vacuum Science, Technique, and Applications [*See also UISTAV*] (EAIO)

IUW .... Inshore Undersea Warfare [*Navy*]

IUWA .... International Union of Women Architects [*See also UIFA*] [*Paris, France*] (EAIO)

IUWC .... Inshore Undersea Warfare Craft [*Navy*]

IUWCC .... Inshore Undersea Warfare Control Center [*Navy*] (NVT)

IUWDS .... International URSI [*Union Radio Scientifique Internationale*]-gram and World Day Service

IUWG .... Inshore Undersea Warfare Group [*Navy*]

IU-WS .... University of Illinois, Illinois State Water Survey, Champaign, IL [*Library symbol Library of Congress*] (LCLS)

IUWSU .... Inshore Undersea Warfare Surveillance Unit [*Navy*] (DNAB)

IUWWML ..... International Union of Wood, Wire, and Metal Lathers (MHDB)

IUYCD .... International Union of Young Christian Democrats [*Rome, Italy*]

iv .... Air Gambia [*Airline flight code*] (ODBW)

IV .... British Island Airways [*ICAO designator*] (AD)

IV .... Evans Public Library, Vandalia, IL [*Library symbol Library of Congress*] (LCLS)

IV .... Iceland Veterans [*Defunct*] (EA)

IV .... Ichthyosis Vulgaris (STED)

IV .... Improved Value (ADA)

IV .... Increased Value

IV .... Independent Variable (IAA)

IV .... Induct Vent

IV .... Information Victoria [*Australia An association*]

IV .... Initial Value

IV .... Initial Velocity [*Ballistics*]

iv .... Initial Velocity (NAKS)

I/V .... Inlet Valve (MCD)

IV .... Input Voltage

I/V .... Instrument/Visual Controlled Airspace (DA)

IV .... Insurance Value (IAA)

IV .... Integrated Vehicle (MCD)

iv .... Integrated Vehicle [*NASA*] (NAKS)

IV .... Intensifier Vidicon

IV .... Interactive Video (PDAA)

IV .... Interceptor Vehicle

IV .... Interface Volume (MCD)

iv .... Interface Volume (NAKS)

iv .... Interior Upper Stage [*NASA*] (NAKS)

IV .... Intermediate Voltage (MSA)

IV .... Internal Velocity

IV .... Interval (IAA)

IV .... Interventricular [*Medicine*]

IV .... Intervertebral [*or Intravertebral*] [*Medicine*]

IV .... Intravascular [*Medicine*]

IV .... Intravehicular (MCD)

iv .... Intravehicular (NAKS)

IV .... Intravenous [*Medicine*]

IV .... Intraventricular [*Cardiology*]

IV .... Intravertebral [*Anatomy*] (DAVI)

IV .... In Vapour (ROG)

IV .... Invasive (MAE)

IV .... In Verbo [*Under the Word*] [*Latin*]

IV .... Inverted Vertical [*Aircraft engine*]

IV .... Inverter

IV .... Investigation [*Dialog*] [*Searchable field*] [*Information service or system*] (NITA)

IV .... In View

IV .... In Vitro [*Medicine*] (MAE)

IV .... In Vivo [*Medicine*] (MAE)

IV .... Invoice Value [*Business term*]

iv .... Invoice Value (ODBW)

IV .... Iodine Value [*Analytical biochemistry*]

iv .... Iodine Value (STED)

IV .... Irish Viscount (ROG)

IV .... Irish Volunteers [*British military*] (DMA)

iv .... Ivory (VRA)

iv .... Ivory Coast [*MARC country of publication code Library of Congress*] (LCCP)

IV .... Mark IV Industries [*NYSE symbol*] (TTSB)

IV .... Mark IV Industries, Inc. [*NYSE symbol*] (SPSG)

IVA .... Ambanja [*Madagascar*] [*Airport symbol*] (OAG)

IVA .... Evansville-Vanderburgh School Corp., Evansville, IN [*OCLC symbol*] (OCLC)

IVA .... Illinois Vocational Association (SRA)

IVA .... Imposta sul Valore Aggiunto [*Value-Added Tax*] [*Italian*]

IVA .... Independent Voters Association [*Political organization in North Dakota, 1918-1932*]

IVA .... Indiana Veal Association (SRA)

IVA .... Industrial Veterinarians' Association [*Later, AAIV*] (EA)

IVA .... Inlet Vane Actuator

IVA .... Innotech Aviation Ltd. [*Canada ICAO designator*] (FAAC)

IVA .... Inspection Visual Aid (AAG)

IVA .... Integrated Vulnerability Assessment [*Military*]

IVA .... Interactive Video Association (EA)

IVA .... Intermediate Volitility Agents (MCD)

IVA .... Internationaler Verband fuer Arbeiterbildung [*International Federation of Workers' Educational Associations - IFWEA*] (SAG)

IVA .... Internationale Vereinigung der Anschlussgeleise-Benuetzer [*International Association of Users of Private Sidings*]

IVA .... International Volleyball Association [*Defunct*] (EA)

IVA .... International Voyage Alliance (EA)

IVA .... Intraoperative Vascular Angiography [*Cardiology*]

IVA .... Intravehicular Activity

IVA .... Inventory Valuation Adjustment [*Business term*]

IVA .... Isovaleric Acid (DMAA)

IVA .... Ivac [*Intravenous monitor*] [*Medicine*] (DHSM)

IVA .... Ivaco, Inc. [*Toronto Stock Exchange symbol*]

IVAAP .... International Veterinary Association for Animal Production [*See also AIVPA*] [*Brussels, Belgium*] [*Research center*] (EAIO)

IVAC .... International Video and Communications Exhibition [*British*] (ITD)

IVAC .... Intevac, Inc. [*NASDAQ symbol*] (SAG)

IVAC .... Intravenous Accurate Control [*Pharmacology*] (DAVI)

IVACG .... International Vitamin A Consultative Group (EA)

IVAD .... Implantable Vascular Access Device [*Medicine*] (STED)

IVAG .... Institutionenverzeichnis Auslaendischer Gesellschaften [*NOMOS Database*] [*Information service or system*]

IVag .... Intravaginal [*Medicine*] (MAE)

IVAK .... Igloo Vertical Access Kit [*Aerospace*] (NASA)

IVALA........... Integrated Visual Approach and Landing Aid [*System*] [*RADAR*]
IValSD........ Valmeyer Community Unit School District 3, Valmeyer, IL [*Library symbol Library of Congress*] (LCLS)
IVAM........... Interorbital Vehicle Assembly Mode
IVAML.......... Instrumental Variable-Approximate Maximum Likelihood (PDAA)
IV & T.......... Independent Verification and Test
IV & V.......... Independent Validation and Verification (CAAL)
IV-ANES....... Intravenous Anesthetic [*Medicine*]
IVANS......... Insurance Value-Added Network Services [*Insurance Institute for Research*] (TSSD)
IVAP........... In Vivo Adhesive Platelet [*Medicine*] (MAE)
IVAR........... Insertion Velocity Adjust Routine [*NASA*]
IVAR........... Insulin Variable [*Medicine*] (STED)
IVAR........... Internal Variable (NASA)
IVAR........... International Voluntary Action and Voluntary Association Research Organization [*Defunct*] (EA)
IVAS........... International Veterinary Acupuncture Society (EA)
IVAS........... Internet Value-Added Service (PCM)
IvaxCp........ Ivaco Industries [*Associated Press*] (SAG)
IvB.............. Innenstadt von Babylon [*A publication*] (BJA)
IVB.............. Intermediate Vector Boson [*Physics*]
IVB.............. Internationaler Verband fuer Arbeiterbildung [*International Federation of Workers' Educational Associations - IFWEA*] (EAIO)
IVB.............. Intraventricular Block [*Medicine*] (DMAA)
IVB.............. Intravitreal Blood (STED)
IVB.............. Mason Memorial Public Library, Buda, IL [*OCLC symbol*] (OCLC)
IVBA........... International Veteran Boxers Association (EA)
IVBA........... International Volleyball Association [*Defunct*]
IVBAT.......... Intravascular Bronchoalveolar Tumor [*Oncology*]
IVBC........... Integrated Vehicle Baseline Configuration (MCD)
IVBC........... Intravascular Blood Coagulation [*Medicine*] (DMAA)
IVBF........... International Volleyball Federation (EA)
IVBH........... Internationale Vereinigung fuer Brueckenbau und Hochbau [*International Association for Bridge and Structural Engineering*]
IVBK........... Intervisual Books'A' [*NASDAQ symbol*] (TTSB)
IVBK........... Intervisual Books, Inc. [*NASDAQ symbol*] (SAG)
IVC.............. Imperial Valley College [*California*]
IVC.............. Independent Viewing Console
IVC.............. Individual Viable Cells [*Metabolic studies*]
IVC.............. Industrial View Camera
IVC.............. Inferior Vena Cava [*Anatomy*]
IVC.............. Inferior Venacavogram [*Cardiology*] (DAVI)
IVC.............. Inspection Validation Center [*Nuclear energy*] (NUCP)
IVC.............. Inspired Vital Capacity (AAMN)
IVC.............. Installation Volunteer Coordinator
IVC.............. Intake Valve Closing [*Automotive engineering*]
IVC.............. Integrated Vacuum Circuit
IVC.............. Integrated Visual Computing [*Computer science*]
IVC.............. Interactive Videodisc Consortium [*Defunct*] (EA)
IVC.............. Intermediate Velocity Cloud [*Astronomy*] (OA)
IVC.............. Intervehicular Communication (KSC)
ivc............... Intervehicular Communications [*NASA*] (NAKS)
IVC.............. Intravaginal Culture [*Alternative to traditional in-vitro fertilization (IVF)*] (PAZ)
IVC.............. Intravascular Coagulation [*Medicine*] (DB)
IVC.............. Intravenous Cholangiography [*Medicine*]
IVC.............. Intraventricular Cannula [*Medicine*]
IVC.............. Intraventricular Catheter [*Cardiology*] (DAVI)
IVC.............. Invercargill [*New Zealand*] [*Airport symbol*] (OAG)
IVC.............. Invesco PLC [*NYSE symbol*] (SAG)
IVC.............. INVESCO PLC ADS [*NYSE symbol*] (TTSB)
IVC.............. Isovolumic Confraction [*Cardiology*]
IVC.............. Permanent Committee for the International Veterinary Congresses
IVC.............. Vandalia Correctional Center, Vandalia, IL [*Library symbol Library of Congress*] (LCLS)
IVC.............. Vigo County Public Library, Terre Haute, IN [*OCLC symbol*] (OCLC)
IVCAP......... International Video Contest for Amateurs and Professionals [*British*]
IVCC........... Illinois Vocational Curriculum Center (EDAC)
IVCC........... Intravascular Consumption Coagulopathy [*Medicine*]
IVCD........... Indian Veterinary Convalescent Depot [*British military*] (DMA)
IVCD........... Intraventricular Conduction Defect [*Cardiology*]
IVCD........... Intraventricular Conduction Delay [*Cardiology*] (AAMN)
IVCD........... In-Vehicle Communications Device [*Highway safety research*]
IVCE........... International Video and Communications Exhibition (NITA)
IVCF........... Inter-Varsity Christian Fellowship of the United States of America (EA)
IVCh........... Intravenous Cholangiography [*or Cholangiogram*] [*Medicine*] (DAVI)
IVCH........... Intravenous Cholangiography [*Medicine*] (DMAA)
IVCI............ International Venture Capital Institute (EA)
IVCO........... International Vitamin Corp. [*NASDAQ symbol*] (SAG)
IVCO........... IVC Industries [*NASDAQ symbol*] [*Formerly, International Vitamin*] (SG)
Iv Co........... Ivory Coast (VRA)
IVCOW........ I V C Industries Wrrt [*NASDAQ symbol*] (TTSB)
IVCP........... Inferior Vena Cava Pressure [*Medicine*]
IVCR........... Inferior Vena Cava Reconstruction [*Medicine*] (DMAA)
IVCR........... Invacare Corp. [*NASDAQ symbol*] (NQ)
IVCS........... Integrated Vehicular Communication System (MCD)
IVCS........... Integrated [*or Interior*] Voice Communications System (MCD)
Iv Cst.......... Ivory Coast
IVCT........... Inferior Vena Cava Thrombosis [*Medicine*] (DMAA)
IVCT........... Intervalence Charge-Transfer [*Phyical chemistry*]
IVCT........... Isovolumic Contraction Time (DB)
IVCU........... Isotope-Voiding Cystourethrogram [*Urology*] (DAVI)
IVCV........... Inferior Venacavography [*Medicine*]
IVCV........... Ivy Vein Clearing Virus [*Plant pathology*]
IVD............. Image Velocity Detector
IVD............. Indirect Video Display (MCD)
IVD............. Inductive Voltage Divider [*Electromagnetism*] (IAA)
IVD............. Information Viewing Device
IVD............. Intake Valve Detergent [*Automotive fuels*]
IVD............. Interactive Videodisc (INF)
IVD............. Internal Vapor Deposition (ACRL)
IVD............. International Vending Technologies Corp. [*Vancouver Stock Exchange symbol*]
IVD............. Interpolated Voice Data (IAA)
IVD............. Intervertebral Disc [*Medicine*]
IVD............. Intravenous Drip [*Pharmacology*] (DAVI)
IVD............. Invalid Decimal (IAA)
IVD............. In Vitro Diagnostics [*Clinical chemistry*]
IVD............. Ionized Vacuum Deposit (MCD)
IVD............. Ion Vapor Deposition [*Coating technology*]
IVD............. University of Dallas, Irving, TX [*OCLC symbol*] (OCLC)
IVDA........... Intravenous Drug Abuser
IVDA........... Investors Daily [*JA Micropublishing, Inc.*]
IVDBA......... Imperial Valley Dune Buggy Association
iv Dei.......... Institut Voluntas Dei (EA)
IVD-IR/-MR... In-Vitro Dissolution-Immediate Release, or Modified Release [*Drug evalution*]
IVDM........... Integrated Voice Data Multiplexer [*Telecommunications*] (ACRL)
IVDP........... Initial Vector Display Point (IAA)
IVDS........... Independent Variable Depth SONAR
IVDS........... Interactive Video and Data Service
IVDSA......... Intravenous Digital Subtraction Angiography
IVDT........... Integrated [*or Interactive*] Voice Data Terminal [*Telecommunications*]
IVDTS......... Integrated Voice and Data Telecommunications System (AAGC)
IVDU........... Intravenous Drug User
IVE.............. Image of Vocational Education [*ERIC*]
IVE.............. Institute of Vitreous Enamellers [*British*]
IVE.............. Integrated Visualization Environment [*Computer science*] (BTTJ)
IVE.............. Interactive Video Enterprises [*US West, Inc.*] (PCM)
IVE.............. Interface Verification Equipment (NASA)
IVE.............. Internationale Vereinigung der Eisenwaren- und Eisenhaendlerverbaende [*International Federation of Ironmongers and Iron Merchants Association*]
IVE.............. Internationale Vereinigung von Einkaufsverbanden [*International Association of Buying Groups - IABG*] (EAIO)
IVE.............. International Video Entertainment
IVE.............. Investment Equipment (MCD)
IVE.............. Isobutyl Vinyl Ether [*Organic chemistry*]
IVE.............. University of Chicago, Graduate Library School, Chicago, IL [*OCLC symbol*] (OCLC)
IVEC........... In Vitro Expression Cloning [*Analytical biochemistry*]
IVen............ Venice Public Library, Venice, IL [*Library symbol Library of Congress*] (LCLS)
IVenCU....... Venice Community Unit 3, Venice, IL [*Library symbol Library of Congress*] (LCLS)
Iv Ersk........ Ivory. Notes on Erskine's Institutes [*A publication*] (ILCA)
IVES........... Information Vending Encryption System [*An AT&T security system*]
IVES........... Internationaler Verband fuer Erziehung zu Suchtmittelfreiem Leben [*International Association for Education to a Life without Drugs*] (EAIO)
IVES........... International Teachers Temperance Association [*Denmark*] (EAIO)
Ives Mil Law... Ives on Military Law [*A publication*] (DLA)
IVESS......... Interactive Vehicle Scheduling System (MHDI)
IVET........... In Vivo Expression Technology [*Genetics*]
IVETA......... International Vocational Education and Training Association (EA)
IvexPkg....... Ivex Packaging Corp. [*Associated Press*] (SAG)
IVF.............. Idiopathic Ventricular Fibrillation [*Cardiology*]
IVF.............. Internationale Viola Forschunggesellschaft [*International Viola Society*] [*Germany*] (EAIO)
IVF.............. Inter-Varsity Fellowship of Evangelical Unions [*British*] (BI)
IVF.............. Interventricular Foramen [*Medicine*] (DMAA)
IVF.............. Intravascular Fluid [*Medicine*]
IVF.............. Intravenous Fluid [*Pharmacology*] (DAVI)
IVF.............. In Vitro Fertilization [*Gynecology*]
IVF.............. IVF America, Inc. [*Associated Press*] (SAG)
IVF.............. Triodyne, Inc., Information Center, Skokie, IL [*OCLC symbol*] (OCLC)
IVFA........... IVF America [*NASDAQ symbol*] (TTSB)
IVFA........... IVF America, Inc. [*NASDAQ symbol*] (SAG)
IVF Am....... IVF America, Inc. [*Associated Press*] (SAG)
IVFE........... Intravenous Fat Emulsion [*Pharmacology*] (DAVI)
IVFET......... In Vitro Fertilization with Embryo Transfer [*Gynecology*]
IVFGR......... Internationale Vereinigung fuer Gewerblichen Rechtsschultz [*International Association for the Protection of Industrial Property*]
IVFZ........... International Veterinary Federation of Zootechnics [*Later, IVAAP*]
IVg............. Camargo Township Library, Villa Grove, IL [*Library symbol Library of Congress*] (LCLS)
IVG.............. Internationale Vereinigung fuer Germanische Sprach - und Literaturwissenschaft [*International Association of Germanic Studies - IAGS*] [*Tokyo, Japan*] (EAIO)
IVG.............. Interrupt Vector Generator
IVG.............. Isotopic Ventriculogram [*Cardiology*] (DAVI)
IVGG........... Institute of Volcanic Geology and Geochemistry [*Commonwealth of Independent States*]
IVGGD......... Internationale Vereinigung fuer Geschichte und Gegenwart der Druckkunst [*International Association for Past and Present History of the Art of Printing*] (EAIO)
IVGMA........ International Violin and Guitar Makers Association (EA)
IVGT........... Intravenous Glucose Tolerance [*Medicine*] (DB)

IVGTT.......... Intravenous Glucose Tolerance Test [*Clinical medicine*]
IVGWP........ Internationaler Verband der Gastronomie- und Weinbau-Presse [*International Federation of Gastronomical and Vinicultural Press*]
IVH.............. Independent Variable Hull [*Statistics*]
IVH.............. Indian Veterinary Hospital [*British military*] (DMA)
IVH.............. Intravenous Hyperalimentation [*Medicine*]
IVH.............. Intraventricular Hemorrhage [*Cardiology*]
IVH.............. Ivishak, AK [*Location identifier FAA*] (FAAL)
IVHESM ...... International Voluntary Historical Enlightenment Society Memorial (EAIO)
IVHH .... Intravenous Gamma-Globulin [*Medicine*] (DB)
IVHM .... In-Vessel Handling Machine [*Nuclear energy*] (NRCH)
IVHM-EM .... In-Vessel Handling Machine-Engineering Model [*Nuclear energy*] (NRCH)
IVHP .... Intraventricular Hemorrhage Parents (EA)
IVHS .... Intelligent Vehicle Highway System (USGC)
IVHW .... Internationaler Verband fuer Hauswirtschaft [*International Federation for Home Economics*]
IVHX .... In-Vessel Heat Exchanger [*Nuclear energy*] (NRCH)
IVI................. American Conservatory of Music, Chicago, IL [*OCLC symbol*] (OCLC)
IVI................. Ice-Core Volcanic Index
IVI................. Incremental Velocity Indicator [*NASA*]
IVI................. Indeo Video Interactive [*Computer science*]
IVI................. Initial Ventricular Impulse
IVI................. Initial Voluntary Indefinite [*Status*] [*Army*] (INF)
IVI................. Instant Visual Index
IVI................. Internal Vibration Isolator
IVI................. International Vaccine Institute [*Korea*]
IVI................. International Verifact, Inc. [*Toronto Stock Exchange symbol*]
IVI................. Inventory Index (MCD)
IVI................. In Vitro International, Inc. (DB)
IVI................. Ivigtut [*Greenland*] [*Seismograph station code, US Geological Survey Closed*] (SEIS)
IVI................. Tucson, AZ [*Location identifier FAA*] (FAAL)
IVIA............. Interactive Video Industry Association (EA)
IVIA............. International Videotex Industry Association
IVIAF........... International Verifact, Inc. [*NASDAQ symbol*] (SAG)
IVIAF........... Intl Verifact [*NASDAQ symbol*] (TTSB)
IVIAW .... International Verifact Wrrt [*NASDAQ symbol*] (TTSB)
IVIE............. Independent Visually Impaired Enterprisers (EA)
IVIE............. Interactive Video in Education [*National Interactive Video Centre*] (AIE)
IVIG .... Intravenous Immunoglobulin [*Medicine*] (CPH)
IVIM............ Intravoxel Incoherent Motion [*Imaging technique*]
IVING .... Ivinghoe [*England*]
IVINX .... Ivy International Cl.A [*Mutual fund ticker symbol*] (SG)
IVIP............. Internationale Vereinigung fuer Individualpsychologie [*International Association of Individual Psychology*]
IVIP............. IVI Publishing [*NASDAQ symbol*] (TTSB)
IVIP............. IVI Publishing, Inc. [*NASDAQ symbol*] (SAG)
IVIPA .... International Videotex Information Providers' Association [*British Information service or system*] (IID)
IVI Pub ...... IVI Publishing, Inc. [*Associated Press*] (SAG)
IVird........... Virden Public Library, Virden, IL [*Library symbol Library of Congress*] (LCLS)
IVirdMCD..... Macoupin Community District 4, Virden, IL [*Library symbol Library of Congress*] (LCLS)
IVIS............. Integrated Vehicular Information System [*Army*] (RDA)
IVIS............. International Visitors Information Service (EA)
IVIS............. Intervehicular Information System [*Army*] (RDA)
IViS............. Shawnee Correctional Center, Vienna, IL [*Library symbol*] [*Library of Congress*] (LCLS)
IV/IVC .... In-Vitro/In-Vivo Correlation [*Drug evaluation*]
IVIZ............. Institutionenverzeichnis fuer Internationale Zusammenarbeit [*Institutions for International Cooperation*] [*NOMOS Datapool Database*] (IID)
IVJ.............. Oak Lawn Public Library, Oak Lawn, IL [*OCLC symbol*] (OCLC)
IVJC............ Intervertebral Joint Complex [*Medicine*]
IVJH............ Internationale Vereinigung fuer Jugendhilfe [*International Union for Child Welfare*]
IVJS .... International Jewish Vegetarian Society [*Formerly, Jewish Vegetarian Society*] (EA)
IVKMH .... Internationale Vereinigung der Klein- und Mittelbetriebe des Handels [*International Federation of Small and Medium-Sized Commercial Enterprises*]
IVL.............. Internationale Vereinigung der Lehrerverbaende [*International Federation of Teachers' Associations*]
IVL.............. Internationale Vereinigung fuer Theoretische und Angewandte Limnologie [*International Association of Theoretical and Applied Limnology*]
IVL.............. Intervalometer (KSC)
IVL.............. Intravenous Lock (STED)
IVL.............. Invader Resources Ltd. [*Vancouver Stock Exchange symbol*]
IVL.............. Inventory Validation Listing [*Computer science*]
IVL.............. Involucrin (DMAA)
IVL.............. Ivalo [*Finland*] [*Airport symbol*] (OAG)
IVLA............ International Visual Literacy Association (EA)
IVLBW .... Infant of Very Low Birth Weight [*Neonatology*] (DAVI)
IVLD............ Internationale Vereinigung der Organisationen von Lebensmittel-Detail-Listen [*International Federation of Grocers' Associations - IFGA*] (EAIO)
IVLS .... Illinois Valley Library System [*Library network*]
IVM............. Immediate Visual Memory (STED)
IVM............. Improved Visible Marker

IVM............. Initial Virtual Memory
IVM............. Institute of Value Management [*British*]
IVM............. Integrated Vector Management [*Insect control*]
IVM............. Interface Virtual Machine [*Computer science*]
IVM............. Intravascular Mass (MAE)
IVM............. Inventory Verification Manual
IVMA........... Idaho Veterinary Medical Association (SRA)
IVMA........... Indiana Veterinary Medical Association (SRA)
IVMA........... Industrial Vegetation Management Association [*Defunct*] (EA)
IVMA........... Intermountain Veterinary Medical Association (EA)
IVMA........... Iodovinylmethoprenol Analog [*Organic chemistry*]
IVMA........... Iowa Veterinary Medical Association (SRA)
IVMB........... Internationale Vereinigung der Musikbibliotheken, Musikarchive, und Dokumentationszentren [*International Association of Music Libraries, Archives, and Documentation Centers*]
IVMF........... Inter-Varsity Missions Fellowship (EA)
IVMMD .... Interim Vehicle Mounted Mine Detection System [*Military*]
IVMP........... Intravenous Methylprednisolone [*Medicine*]
IVMS........... Instrumented Vibration Measuring System
IVMS........... Integrated Vehicle Management Subsystem (MCD)
IVMS........... Integrated Voice Messaging System [*Commterm, Inc.*] [*Atlanta, GA*] (TSSD)
IVMU .... Inertial Velocity Measurement Unit (IEEE)
IVN............. Intercity Voice Network [*FTS*] (DNAB)
IVN............. Internationale Vereniging voor Neerlandistiek [*International Association of Dutch Studies*] (EAIO)
IVNAA .... In Vivo Neutron Activation Analysis [*Analytical chemistry*]
IVNF............ Intravitreal Neovascular Frond (STED)
IVNTG .... Intravenous Nitroglycerin [*Medication order*] (CPH)
IVO............. Improved Virtual Orbitals [*Atomic physics*]
IVO............. Inova Optics, Inc. [*Vancouver Stock Exchange symbol*]
IVO............. Input Voltage Offset
IVO............. Intake Valve Open [*Automotive engineering*]
IVOX .... Intravascular Oxygenator [*Artificial lung*] [*Medicine*]
IVP............. Imitation Vegetable Parchment [*Paper*] (DGA)
IVP............. Implied Valve Position (ACII)
IVP............. Initial Vapor Pressure
IVP............. Insecticidal Viral Product [*Agricultural chemistry*]
IVP............. Inspected Variety Purity [*Agriculture*]
IVP............. Installation Verification Procedure (MCD)
IVP............. Integrated Vacuum Processing (AAEL)
IVP............. Interactive Voice Response (TELE)
IVP............. Interface Verification Procedure [*NASA*] (IAA)
IVP............. Internationaler Verband der Pektinproduzenten [*International Pectin Producers Association*] [*Switzerland*] (EAIO)
IVP............. Inter-Varsity Press [*British*]
IVP............. Intravenous Pitocin [*Pharmacology*] (DAVI)
IVP............. Intravenous Push [*Medicine*]
IVp............. Intravenous Push [*Dose*] [*Medicine*] (STED)
IVP............. Intravenous Pyelogram [*Radiology*]
IVP............. Intraventricular Pressure [*Cardiology*] (AAMN)
IVP............. Intravesical Pressure (STED)
IVP............. Ion Vacuum Pump
IVPA........... Independent Video Programmers Association [*Defunct*] (EA)
IVPB........... Intravenous Piggyback [*Method of drug administration*] [*Pharmacology*]
IVPC........... Internationaler Verband der Petroleum- und Chemiearbeiter [*International Federation of Petroleum and Chemical Workers*]
IV-PCA .... Intravenous-Patient-Controlled-Analgesia
IVPD........... In Vitro Protein Digestibility [*Nutrition*]
IVPF........... Isovolume Pressure Flow Curve [*Cardiology*] (MAE)
IVPO .... Inside Vapor Phase Oxidation [*Glass technology*]
IVPP........... Institute of Vertebrate Palaeontology and Palaeoanthropology [*China*]
IVPT........... Inter-Vehicle Power Transfer (MCD)
IVQ............. Individual Vessel Quota [*Fisheries management*]
IVQ............. Interrupted Very Quick [*Flashing*] Light [*Navigation signal*]
IVR............. Idioventricular Rhythm [*Cardiology*] (DMAA)
IVR............. Inner Vertical Resonance [*Physics*]
IVR............. Instant Video Receiver [*Electronics*]
IVR............. Instrumented Visual Range (IAA)
IVR............. Instrument Voltage Regulator [*Automotive engineering*]
IVR............. Integrated Voltage Regulator (IEEE)
IVR............. Interactive Voice Response
IVR............. Internal Visual Reference [*Motion sickness*]
IVR............. International Association for the Rhine Vessels Register [*Netherlands*] (EY)
IVR............. Internationale Vereinigung fuer Rechts- und Sozialphilosophie [*International Association for Philosophy of Law and Social Philosophy*] (EAIO)
IVR............. Interventional Radiography [*Medicine*]
IVR............. Intramolecular Vibrational Redistribution [*Chemistry*]
IVR............. Intramolecular Vibrational Relaxation [*Organic chemistry*]
IVR............. Intravaginal Ring [*Medicine*] (DB)
IVR............. Inverell [*Australia Airport symbol*] (OAG)
IVR............. Irvco Resources [*Vancouver Stock Exchange symbol*]
IVR............. Isolated Volume Responders [*Physiology*]
IVR............. Isovolumic Relaxation [*Time*] [*Cardiology*] (DAVI)
IVRD........... In Vitro Rumen Digestibility [*Nutrition*]
IVRET.......... Intramolecular Vibration-Rotation Energy Transfer [*Chemistry*]
IVRG .... International Verticillium Research Group (EAIO)
IVRG .... In-Vehicle Route Guidance System [*FHWA*] (TAG)
IVRS .... Interactive Voice Response System [*Military*] (INF)
IVRT........... Isovolumic Relaxation Time (DMAA)
IVS............. Air Evasion [*France ICAO designator*] (FAAC)

IVS	Idle Validation Switch [*Automotive electronics*]
IVS	Inappropriate Vasopressin Secretion (DB)
IVS	Independent Vertical System
IVS	Infrared Viewing Set
IVS	Input Voltage Supply
IVS	Insect Visual System
IVS	Intact Ventricular System [*Cardiology*]
IVS	Integrated Versaplot Software (PDAA)
IVS	Interactive Video Service (LAIN)
IVS	Interactive Voice System [*Electronics*]
IVS	Interchange Units Separation (ECII)
IVS	International Vestor Resources [*Vancouver Stock Exchange symbol*]
IVS	International Voluntary Services (EA)
IVS	Intervening Sequence [*Genetics*]
IVS	Interventricular Septum [*Cardiology*]
IVS	In-Vessel Storage [*Nuclear energy*] (NRCH)
IVS	Vigo County School Corp., Terre Haute, IN [*OCLC symbol*] (OCLC)
IVSA	International Veterinary Students Association [*Utrecht, Netherlands*] (EAIO)
IVSAWS	In-Vehicle Safety Advisory and Warning System [*FHWA*] (TAG)
IVSD	Interventricular Septal Defect [*Cardiology*]
IVSD	Vandalia Community Unit, School District 203, Vandalia, IL [*Library symbol Library of Congress*] (LCLS)
IVSET	Interactive Videodisc for Special Education Technology (EDAC)
IVSI	Inertial Lead Vertical Speed Indicator (IAA)
IVSI	Instantaneous Vertical Speed Indicator [*NASA*]
ivsi	Instantaneous Vertical Speed Indicator (NAKS)
IVSK	Intravenous Streptokinase [*An enzyme*]
IVSM	In-Vessel Storage Module [*Nuclear energy*] (NRCH)
IVSN	Initial Voice Switched Network [*NATO integrated communications system*] (NATG)
IVSP	In Vitro Synthesized Protein [*Biochemistry*]
IVSS	Internationale Vereinigung fuer Soziale Sicherheit [*International Social Security Association*]
IVSS	Intravenous Solu-Set [*Medicine*] (MEDA)
IVSU	International Veterinary Students Union [*Later, IVSA*]
IVT	Index of Vertical Transmission [*Cultural evolution*]
IVT	Inferential Value Testing (KSC)
IVT	Infinitely Variable Transmission [*Automotive engineering*] (PS)
IVT	Input Value Table [*Computer science*] (ECII)
IVT	Inspection Verification Tag
IVT	Institute for Victims of Trauma (EA)
IVT	Integrated Video Terminal
IVT	Interactive Video Technology [*Database*] [*Heartland Communications*] [*Information service or system*] (CRD)
IVT	Internationale Vereinigung der Textileinkaufsverbande [*International Association of Textile Purchasing Societies*]
IVT	Intervalve Transformer (IAA)
IVT	Intervehicular Transfer (KSC)
IVT	Intravenous Transfusion [*Medicine*]
IVT	Intraventricular [*Cardiology*]
IVT	Isovolumetric Time (DB)
IVT	Iventronics Ltd. [*Toronto Stock Exchange symbol*]
IVTC	International Visitors and Travel Coordinator (COE)
IVTD	Integrated Visual Testing Device
IVTM	In-Vessel Transfer Machine [*Nuclear energy*] (NRCH)
IVTTT	Intravenous Tolbutamide Tolerance Test [*Clinical medicine*] (MAE)
IVU	International Vegetarian Union [*Stockport, Cheshire, England*]
IVU	Intravehicular Umbilical [*NASA*] (KSC)
IVU	Intravenous Urogram [*or Urography*] [*Medicine*]
IVU	In-Vehicle Unit [*Electronic system for charging for road usage*] [*Singapore*] (ECON)
IVU	Valparaiso University, Valparaiso, IN [*OCLC symbol*] (OCLC)
IVUS	Intravascular Ultrasound [*Medicine*]
IVV	Idle Vacuum Valve [*Exhaust emissions*] [*Automotive engineering*]
IVV	Instantaneous Vertical Velocity
IVV	Internationaler Volkssportverband [*International Federation of Popular Sports - IFPS*] (EAIO)
IVV	Internationale Vereinigung fuer Vegetationskunde [*International Association for Vegetation Science - IAVS*] (EAIO)
IVV	Intravenous Vasopressin [*Endocrinology*]
IVV	Lebanon, NH [*Location identifier FAA*] (FAAL)
IVV	Vincennes University, Vincennes, IN [*OCLC symbol*] (OCLC)
IVVI	Instantaneous Vertical Velocity Indicator
IV vol	Intravenous Volume [*Pharmacology*] (DAVI)
IVVS	Instantaneous Vertical Velocity Sensor (NATG)
IVW	International Vintage Wines (EFIS)
IVWO	International Vine and Wine Office
IVWSR	Internationaler Verband fuer Wohnungswesen, Staedtebau und Raumordnung [*International Federation for Housing and Planning*]
IVX	Columbus, OH [*Location identifier FAA*] (FAAL)
IVX	Imperial Valley College, Imperial, CA [*OCLC symbol*] (OCLC)
IVX	IVAX Corp. [*AMEX symbol*] (SAG)
IVY	Ivory Oil & Minerals [*Vancouver Stock Exchange symbol*]
IVYBR	Ivybridge [*England*]
IVYFX	Ivy Growth Cl.A [*Mutual fund ticker symbol*] (SG)
IVYIX	Ivy Growth with Income Cl.A [*Mutual fund ticker symbol*] (SG)
IVZ	Valparaiso University, Law Library, Valparaiso, IN [*OCLC symbol*] (OCLC)
IW	Impulse Weight (IAA)
IW	Index Word [*Online database field identifier*]
IW	Indications and Warning [*Subsystems*] [*Military*] (MCD)
IW	Indirect Waste
IW	Individual Weapon (MCD)

IW	Induction Welding
IW	Inertia Weight [*Exhaust emissions*] [*Automotive engineering*]
IW	Information Warfare
IW	Information World [*A publication*]
IW	Inland Waterways [*Organization that administered British canals during World War II*] [*Facetious translation: "Idle Women," due to high female workforce*]
IW	Inner Wall [*Medicine*] (DMAA)
IW	Inpatient Ward [*Medicine*] (DMAA)
IW	Inside Width
IW	Inside Wire [*Telecommunications*] (TEL)
IW	Inspector of Works
IW	Instruction Word [*Computer science*] (IAA)
I/W	Interchangeable With (AAG)
IW	Interior Width (IAA)
IW	International Air Bahama [*ICAO designator*] (AD)
IW	International Wattier [*Process*] [*A method of making transparencies for rotogravure plates*]
I/W	Interway Corp. (EFIS)
IW	Iron-Wustite [*Geology*]
IW	Isle of Wight
IW	Isotopic Weight
iw	Israel-Jordan Demilitarized Zones [*is (Israel) used in records cataloged after January 1978*] [*MARC country of publication code Library of Congress*] (LCCP)
IW	Wheaton Public Library, Wheaton, IL [*Library symbol Library of Congress*] (LCLS)
IWA	Independent Watchmen's Association (EA)
IWA	Inland Waterways Association [*British*] (DCTA)
IWA	Inland Waterways Authority (WDAA)
IWA	Institute of World Affairs [*Later, UFSI-IWA*] (EA)
IWA	Interdivisional Work Authorization (AAGC)
IWA	International Waterproofing Association [*See also AIE*] [*Brussels, Belgium*] (EAIO)
IWA	International Wheat Agreement [*London*]
IWA	International Women's Auxiliary to the Veterinary Profession
IWA	International Woodworkers of America (EA)
IWA	Iowa State University of Science and Technology, Ames, IA [*OCLC symbol*] (OCLC)
IWA	Iwakuni [*Japan*] [*Airport symbol*] (AD)
IWAAC	Inland Waterways Amenity Advisory Council [*British*] (DCTA)
I/WAC	Interface/Weapon Aiming Computer (MCD)
IWAC	International Women's Anthropology Conference (EA)
IWAHMA	Industrial Warm Air Heater Manufacturers
IWAK	Improved Water Analysis Kit
IWal	Walnut Township Library, Walnut, IL [*Library symbol Library of Congress*] (LCLS)
IWalHSD	Walnut Consolidated High School District 508, Walnut, IL [*Library symbol Library of Congress*] (LCLS)
IWalSD	Walnut Consolidated Community School District 285, Walnut, IL [*Library symbol Library of Congress*] (LCLS)
IWaltSD	Waltonville Community Unit, School District 1, Waltonville, IL [*Library symbol Library of Congress*] (LCLS)
IWARDS	Iowa Water Resources Data System [*Iowa State Geological Survey*] [*Iowa City*] [*Information service or system*] (IID)
IWARS	Installation Worldwide Ammunition Reporting System [*Army*]
IWas	Washington Township Library, Washington, IL [*Library symbol Library of Congress*] (LCLS)
IWas-Su	Washington Township Library, Sunnyland Branch, Sunnyland, IL [*Library symbol Library of Congress*] (LCLS)
IWat	Watseka Public Library, Watseka, IL [*Library symbol Library of Congress*] (LCLS)
IWatF	Iroquois County Film Library, Watseka, IL [*Library symbol*] [*Library of Congress*] (LCLS)
IWatH	Iroquois Memorial Hospital, Watseka, IL [*Library symbol Library of Congress*] (LCLS)
IWatl	Morrison-Talbott Library, Waterloo, IL [*Library symbol Library of Congress*] (LCLS)
IWatlGHS	Gibault High School, Waterloo, IL [*Library symbol Library of Congress*] (LCLS)
IWatlSD	Waterloo Community School District 3, Waterloo, IL [*Library symbol Library of Congress*] (LCLS)
IWau	Waukegan Public Library, Waukegan, IL [*Library symbol Library of Congress*] (LCLS)
i-way	Information Superhighway (CDE)
IWayc	Wayne City Public Library, Wayne City, IL [*Library symbol Library of Congress*] (LCLS)
IWaycCD	Wayne City Community Unit, District 100, Wayne City, IL [*Library symbol Library of Congress*] (LCLS)
IWB	C. Berger & Co., Wheaton, IL [*Library symbol*] [*Library of Congress*] (LCLS)
IWB	Council Bluffs Free Public Library, Council Bluffs, IA [*OCLC symbol*] (OCLC)
IWB	Industry-Wide Bargaining (MHDB)
IWB	Instruction Word Buffer (NITA)
IWB	Intergalactic World Brain [*Underground press service*] (IIA)
IWBC	Interim Wideband Communications (MCD)
IWBK	InterWest Bancorp [*NASDAQ symbol*] (TTSB)
IWBK	InterWest Savings Bank [*NASDAQ symbol*] (SAG)
IWBNI	It Would Be Nice If [*Computer hacker terminology*] (NHD)
IWBP	Integration with Britain Party [*Gibraltar*] (PPE)
IWBS	Congregation of the Incarnate Word and the Blessed Sacrament [*Roman Catholic women's religious order*]
IWBS	Indirect Work Breakdown Structure (NASA)
IWBS	Integral Weight and Balance System [*Aviation*]

IWC	Ice Water Content
IWC	Imperial War Cabinet [*British military*] (DMA)
IWC	Incarnate Word College [*Texas*]
IWC	Individual Weapons Captured
IWC	Inland Waterways Corp. [*Later, Federal Barge Lines, Inc.; liquidated, 1963*]
IWC	Institute for Workers' Control
IWC	In-Stream Waste Concentration [*Environmental science*] (GFGA)
IWC	Interim Wilderness Committee [*Australia*]
IWC	International Whaling Commission [*Cambridge, England*]
IWC	International Wheat Council [*See also CIB*] [*British*] (EAIO)
IWC	International Wildcat Resources [*Vancouver Stock Exchange symbol*]
IWC	International Wildlife Coalition (EA)
IWC	International Willow Collectors [*An association*] (EA)
IWC	Iowa Wesleyan College
IWC	IWC Resources Corp. [*Associated Press*] (SAG)
IWC	Wabash College, Crawfordsville, IN [*OCLC symbol*] (OCLC)
IWCA	Inside Wiring Cable [*Telecommunications*] (TEL)
IWCA	International Window Cleaning Association (NTPA)
IWCA	International Windsurfer Class Association (EA)
IWCA	International World Calendar Association (EA)
IWCA	Irish Wolfhound Club of America (EA)
IWCB	Internal Web Channel Bus (IAA)
IWCC	International Women's Cricket Council [*Australia*] (EAIO)
IWCC	International Wrought Copper Council [*British*] (EAIO)
IWCCA	Inland Waterways Common Carriers Association [*Defunct*] (EA)
IWCHL	Illinois-Wisconsin Collegiate Hockey League (PSS)
IWCI	Industrial Water Conditioning Institute
IWCI	Industrial Wire Cloth Institute [*Later, AWCI*] (EA)
IWCP	Integrated Work Control Program (COE)
IWCR	IWC Resources Corp. [*NASDAQ symbol*] (NQ)
IWCS	Integrated Weapons Control System
IWCS	Integrated Wideband Communications System [*Military*]
IWCS	Interceptor Weapon Control System
IWCS	International Wood Collectors Society (EA)
IWCS/SEA	Integrated Wideband Communications System/Southeast Asia (IEEE)
IWCT	International War Crimes Tribunal
IWCTF	Interdepartmental Workers' Compensation Task Force [*Department of Labor*] [*Terminated, 1976*] (EGAO)
IW/CW	Infectious Waste / Chemotherapeutic Waste
IWD	Drake University, Law Library, Des Moines, IA [*OCLC symbol*] (OCLC)
IWD	Inland Waters Directorate [*Canada*]
IWD	Integrated Weapons Display
IWD	Intermediate Water Depth (MCD)
IWD	International Women's Day
IWD	International Women's Decade
IWD	Iron or Wood [*Freight*]
IWD	Ironwood [*Michigan*] [*Airport symbol*] (OAG)
IWD	Ironwood, MI [*Location identifier FAA*] (FAAL)
IWDA	Independent Wire Drawers Association [*Later, AWPA*]
IWDCC	Inter-Industry Wood Dust Coordinating Committee (WPI)
IWDM	Intermediate Water Depth Mine (MCD)
IWDS	Interactive Wholesale Distribution System (MHDI)
IWDS	International World Day Service
IWE	Camden, AL [*Location identifier FAA*] (FAAL)
IWE	Illustrated World Encyclopedia [*A publication*]
IWE	Instantaneous Word Encoder (IAA)
IWE	Institute for Wholistic Education [*Later, SCIWE*] (EA)
IWE	Institute of Water Engineers [*British*]
IWE	Institution of Water Engineers [*British*] (BI)
IWE	Interpolated Water Elevation (PDAA)
IWe	Westchester Public Library, Westchester, IL [*Library symbol Library of Congress*] (LCLS)
IWE	Winnetka Public Library, Winnetka, IL [*OCLC symbol*] (OCLC)
IWedSD	Wedron Consolidated Community School District 201, Wedron, IL [*Library symbol Library of Congress*] (LCLS)
IWEM	Institution of Water and Environmental Management (EAIO)
IWem	Westmont Public Library, Westmont, IL [*Library symbol Library of Congress*] (LCLS)
IWen	Bond Public Library, Wenona, IL [*Library symbol Library of Congress*] (LCLS)
IWenSD	Wenona Community Unit, School District 1, Wenona, IL [*Library symbol Library of Congress*] (LCLS)
IWERC	Industrial Waste Elimination Research Center [*Illinois Institute of Technology*] [*Research center*] (RCD)
Iwerks	Iwerks Entertainment, Inc. [*Associated Press*] (SAG)
IWERRI	Idaho Water and Energy Resources Research Institute [*University of Idaho*] [*Research center*] (RCD)
IWES	Inhibited White Fuming Nitric Acid (PDAA)
IWES	International Waste Energy Systems (EFIS)
IWes	West Salem Public Library, West Salem, IL [*Library symbol Library of Congress*] (LCLS)
IWesp	Thomas Ford Memorial Library, Western Springs, IL [*Library symbol Library of Congress*] (LCLS)
IWev	Westville Public Library, Westville, IL [*Library symbol Library of Congress*] (LCLS)
IWEWSULOTATDTO	I Wish Everyone Would Stop Using Letters of the Alphabet to Designate Their Organizations [*Originated by Bea von Boeselager in "Line o' Type," Chicago Tribune*]
IWEX	Internal Wave Experiment (NOAA)
IWF	International Weightlifting Federation [*See also FHI*] [*Budapest, Hungary*] (EAIO)
IWF	International Woodworking Machinery and Furniture Supply Fair (ITD)
IWF	Internetworking Function [*Computer science*] (ACRL)
IWFA	Inhibited White Fuming Nitric Acid [*Rocket fuel*] (SAA)
IWFA	Intercollegiate Women's Fencing Association [*Later, NIWFA*]
IWFA	International Wholesale Furniture Association (NTPA)
IWFA	International Window Film Association (EA)
IWFA	International Women's Fishing Association (EA)
IWFAI	International Watch Fob Association, Inc. (EA)
IWFI	Italian Wine and Food Institute (EA)
IWFNA	Inhibited White Fuming Nitric Acid [*Rocket fuel*] (IAA)
IWFP	International Women's Film Project (EA)
IWFS	Industrial Waste Filter System (IEEE)
IWFS	Integrated Waste Fluid System (SSD)
IWFS	International Wine and Food Society [*British*] (EAIO)
IWG	Grand View College, Des Moines, IA [*OCLC symbol*] (OCLC)
IWG	Imperial Wire Gauge (ROG)
IWG	Implementation Work Group [*DoD*]
IWG	Implementation Work Group on Justice Information and Statistics [*See also GMO*] [*Canada*]
IWG	Industry Working Group
IWG	Intelligence Working Group [*Military*] (CINC)
IWG	Interface Working Group [*NASA*] (NASA)
IWG	Intergovernmental Working Group [*United Nations*]
IWG	International Working Group [*NATO*] (NATG)
IWG	International Writers Guild
IWG	Investigator's Working Group [*Spacelab mission*]
IWG	Iron Wire Gauge
IWGA	International Wheat Gluten Association (EA)
IWGA	International World Games Association (EA)
IWGC	Imperial War Graves Commission [*British*]
IWGCS	International Working Group in Clinical Sociology (EAIO)
IWGCSFIPERM	Inter-Service Working Group for Cooperation and Standardization of Foto Interpretation Procedures, Equipment, and Related Matters
IWGDE	Interlaboratory Working Group for Data Exchange [*Computer science*] (MHDI)
IWGFR	International Working Group on Fast Reactors (NRCH)
IWGGDM	International Working Group on Graminaceous Downy Mildews [*Defunct*] (EAIO)
IWGIA	International Work Group for Indigenous Affairs [*Copenhagen, Denmark*] (EAIO)
IWGM	Intergovernmental Working Group on Monitoring or Surveillance [*United Nations*] (ASF)
IWGMP	Intergovernmental Working Group on Marine Pollution [*Inter-Governmental Maritime Consultative Organization*]
IWGMS	Intergovernmental Working Group on Monitoring or Surveillance [*United Nations*] (MSC)
IWH	Wabash, IN [*Location identifier FAA*] (FAAL)
IWHC	International Women's Health Coalition (EA)
IWhh	White Hall Township Library, White Hall, IL [*Library symbol Library of Congress*] (LCLS)
IWhhB	Beecham Laboratories, White Hall, IL [*Library symbol Library of Congress*] (LCLS)
IWhhSD	North Greene Community Unit, School District 3, White Hall, IL [*Library symbol Library of Congress*] (LCLS)
IWhl	Indian Trails Public Library District, Wheeling, IL [*Library symbol Library of Congress*] (LCLS)
IWHM	Institution of Works and Highways Management [*British*] (DBA)
IWHM	Interwest Home Medical [*NASDAQ symbol*] (TTSB)
IWHM	Interwest Home Medical, Inc. [*NASDAQ symbol*] (SAG)
IWhN	North Suburban Library System, Wheeling, IL [*Library symbol Library of Congress*] (LCLS)
IWHS	Institute of Works and Highways Superintendents [*British*]
IWHSD	Irish War Hospital Supply Depot [*British military*] (DMA)
IWI	International Werner Tech [*Vancouver Stock Exchange symbol*]
IWI	Inventors' Workshop International [*Later, IWIEF*] (EA)
IWI	Irreversible Warmup Indicator [*To detect whether frozen foods have risen above an acceptable temperature level*] [*Pronounced "ee-wee"*]
IWI	Wishard Memorial Hospital, Indianapolis, IN [*OCLC symbol*] (OCLC)
IWi	Witt Memorial Library, Witt, IL [*Library symbol Library of Congress*] (LCLS)
IWIEF	Inventors Workshop International Education Foundation (EA)
IWI Hold	IWI Holding Ltd. [*Associated Press*] (SAG)
IWilB	National Baha'i Museum, Wilmette, IL [*Library symbol*] [*Library of Congress*] (LCLS)
IWilGS	Church of Jesus Christ of Latter-Day Saints, Genealogical Society Library, Wilmette Branch, Wilmette, IL [*Library symbol Library of Congress*] (LCLS)
IWin	Winnetka Public Library, Winnetka, IL [*Library symbol Library of Congress*] (LCLS)
IWinfC	Central DuPage Hospital, Medical Library, Winfield, IL [*Library symbol*] [*Library of Congress*] (LCLS)
IWin-N	Winnetka Public Library District, Northfield Branch, Northfield, IL [*Library symbol Library of Congress*] (LCLS)
IWIPC	Interim Wool Industry Policy Council [*Australia*]
IWIS	Interceptor Weapons Instructor School [*Air Force*]
IWiSD	Witt Community Unit, School District 66, Witt, IL [*Library symbol Library of Congress*] (LCLS)
IWISTK	Issue While in Stock
IWIU	Insurance Workers International Union
IWL	Infant Water Loss [*Medicine*] (CPH)
IWL	Insensible Water Loss [*Medicine*]
IWL	Institute Warranty Limits [*Shipping*] (DS)
IWL	International Walther League (EA)
IWL	Italian Welfare League (EA)

IWL............ Willard Library, Evansville, IN [*OCLC symbol*] (OCLC)
IWLA.......... Izaak Walton League of America (EA)
IWLAE........ Izaak Walton League of America Endowment (EA)
IWLE.......... Individual Whole of Life and Endowment [*Insurance*] (ADA)
IWLF.......... International Wilderness Leadership Foundation
IWLS.......... International Water Lily Society (NTPA)
IWLS.......... Iterative Weighted Least Squares [*Statistics*]
IWM........... Bluffton-Wells County Public Library, Bluffton, IN [*OCLC symbol*] (OCLC)
IWM........... Imperial War Museum [*England*]
IWM........... Industrial Waste Management (MCD)
IWM........... Institute of Wastes Management [*British*]
IWM........... Institution of Works Managers [*British*]
IWM........... Integrated Woz Machine [*Apple Computer, Inc.*]
IWM........... Internal Waste Manifest [*Stanford University*]
IWM........... MAP International, Wheaton, IL [*Library symbol Library of Congress*] (LCLS)
IWMA......... Institute of Weights and Measures Administration [*Wales*]
IWMA......... International Wire and Machinery Association [*Leamington Spa, Warwickshire, England*] (EAIO)
IWMA......... International Working Men's Association (WDAA)
IWMI.......... Inferior Wall Myocardial Infarction [*Cardiology*]
IWMP......... International Women's Media Project [*Defunct*] (EA)
IWMS......... Integrated Weed Management System [*Agriculture*]
IWN........... Indigenous Women's Network (EA)
IWN........... North Iowa Area Community College, Mason City, IA [*OCLC symbol*] (OCLC)
IWO .... Institute for World Order (EA)
IWO .... Intelligence Watch Officer [*Military*] (MCD)
IWO .... Interdivisional Work Order (AAGC)
IWo............ Worth Public Library District, Worth, IL [*Library symbol Library of Congress*] (LCLS)
IWOC......... International Wizard of Oz Club (EA)
IWor.......... Wood River Public Library, Wood River, IL [*Library symbol Library of Congress*] (LCLS)
IWordR .... Worden Reading Center, Worden, IL [*Library symbol Library of Congress*] (LCLS)
IWordSD ..... Worden Community Unit, School District 16, Worden, IL [*Library symbol Library of Congress*] (LCLS)
IWorH .... Wood River Township Hospital, Medical Library, Wood River, IL [*Library symbol Library of Congress*] (LCLS)
IWorHS .... East Alton-Wood River Community High School 14, Wood River, IL [*Library symbol Library of Congress*] (LCLS)
IWori .... Woodridge Public Library, Woodridge, IL [*Library symbol Library of Congress*] (LCLS)
IWOSC........ International Working-Group of Soilless Culture
IWP............ Idaho White Pine [*Lumber*]
IWP............ Illawarra Workers Party [*Political party Australia*]
IWP............ Indicative World Plan for Agricultural Development [*United Nations*]
IWP............ Indo-West Pacific [*Biogeographic region*]
IWP............ Internal Working Paper
IWP............ Internationale Weltfriedens Partei [*International World Peace Party*] [*Germany Political party*] (PPW)
IWP............ International Information/Word Processing Association [*Formerly, IWPA*] (EA)
IWP............ International Word Processing Association (NITA)
IWP............ International Working Party
IWP............ Inverse Wulff Plot (PDAA)
IWP............ Irish Workers' Party [*Political party*] (PPW)
IWP............ Sioux City Public Library, Sioux City, IA [*OCLC symbol*] (OCLC)
IWPA .... Independent Wire Producers Association [*Later, AWPA*] (EA)
IWPA .... International Word Processing Association [*Later, IIWPA, IWP*]
IWPA .... Irish Water Polo Association (EAIO)
IWPC .... Institute of Water Pollution Control [*Later, IWEM*] (EAIO)
IWPPA .... Independent Waste Paper Processors Association [*British*] (DBA)
IWQ .... Individual Weapons Qualification [*Military*]
IWR .... Cedar Rapids Public Library, Cedar Rapids, IA [*OCLC symbol*] (OCLC)
IWR .... Connecticut Institute of Water Resources [*Storrs, CT*] [*Department of the Interior*] (GRD)
IWR .... Improved Weather Reconnaissance
IWR .... Information World Review [*A publication Information service or system*] (IID)
IWR .... Infrared Warning Receiver [*Aviation*] (DNAB)
IWR .... Institute for Water Resources [*Fort Belvoir, VA*] [*Army*] (MSC)
IWR .... Institute for Wildlife Research [*Defunct*] (EA)
IWR .... Institute of Water Research [*Michigan State University*]
IWR .... Isle Of Wight Railway [*British*]
IWR .... Isle Of Wight Rifles [*British military*] (DMA)
IWR .... Isolated Word Recognition (MCD)
IWRA .... International Water Resources Association (EA)
IWRA .... International Wild Rice Association (EA)
IWRAW........ International Women's Rights Action Watch (EAIO)
IWRB .... International Waterfowl and Wetlands Research Bureau (EAIO)
IWRC.......... Independent Wire Rope Center [*or Core*]
IWRC.......... International Wildlife Rehabilitation Council (EA)
IWRC.......... Iron Wire Rope Core [*Nuclear energy*] (NRCH)
IWRI........... Informal World Recognition Inventory [*Education*] (EDAC)
IWRK.......... Iwerks Entertainment [*NASDAQ symbol*] (TTSB)
IWRK.......... Iwerks Entertainment, Inc. [*NASDAQ symbol*] (SAG)
IWRM .... Integrated Warfare Requirements Methodology
IWRMA........ Independent Wire Rope Manufacturers Association (EA)
IWRMA........ Irish Wholesale Ryegrass Machiners Association (BI)
IWRO.......... Interdepartmental Work Release Order

IWRP .... Individualized Written Rehabilitation Program [*Department of Education*]
IWRP .... Industrial Waste Reduction Program [*Environmental science*]
IWRRC......... International Wheelchair Road Racers Club (EA)
IWS............. Impact Warning System
IWS............. Industrial Water Society [*British*] (DBA)
IWS............. Industrial Water Supply
IWS............. Industrial Water System (KSC)
IWS............. Industrial Welfare Society [*British*] (ILCA)
IWS............. Information Warfare Squadron [*Air Force*]
IWS............. Inland Waterway Service
IWS............. Institute of Wood Science [*British*] (BI)
IWS............. Instruction Work Stack (MHDB)
IWS............. Integrated Water System (SSD)
IWS............. Integrated Weapon System
IWS............. Integrated Work Statement (MCD)
IWS............. Interactive Work Station (MHDB)
IWS............. International Wildrose Resources, Inc. [*Vancouver Stock Exchange symbol*]
IWS............. International Wine Society (EA)
IWS............. International Wool Secretariat [*British*]
IWS............. Ionizing Wet Scrubber [*Environmental science*] (GFGA)
IWS............. Western Iowa Technical Community College, Sioux City, IA [*OCLC symbol*] (OCLC)
IWSA .... Integrated Waste Services Association (NTPA)
IWSA .... International Water Supply Association [*British*] (EAIO)
IWSA .... International Workers Sport Association
IWSAW .... Institute for Women's Studies in the Arab World [*Beirut, Lebanon*] (EAIO)
IWSB .... Insect Wire Screening Bureau [*Later, Insect Screening Weavers Association*] (EA)
IWSc .... Institute of Wood Science Ltd. [*British*]
IWSC .... Internet & Web Services Corp.
IWSCA .... Irish Water Spaniel Club of America (EA)
IWSF .... Irish Waterski Federation (EAIO)
IWSG .... International Wool Study Group [*British Defunct*] (EAIO)
IWSI .... Integrated Waste Services, Inc. [*NASDAQ symbol*] (SAG)
IWSI .... Integrated Waste Svcs [*NASDAQ symbol*] (TTSB)
IWSI .... Irish Work Study Institute Ltd. (BI)
IWS/IT .... Integrated Work Sequence/Inspection Traveler (NRCH)
IWSM .... Integrated Weapon Support Management (AFM)
IWSO .... Instructor Weapons System Officer [*Military*]
IWSOE .... International Weddell Sea Oceanographic Expedition
IWSP .... Institute of Work Study Practitioners [*British*] (BI)
IWSP .... Integrated Weapon Secret Panel (MCD)
IWSR .... Integrated Weapon System Representative [*or Review*] (MCD)
IWSR .... International Wine and Spirit Record
IWSRA .... Irish Women's Squash Rackets Association (EAIO)
IWSS .... International Weed Science Society (EA)
IWSSA .... Interservice Warehousing Support Services Agreement
IWST .... Integrated Weapon System Training [*Air Force*]
IwstHM .... Interwest Home Medical, Inc. [*Associated Press*] (SAG)
IWT............. Industrial Waste Treatment Management (MCD)
IWT............. Inland Water Transport [*British*]
IWT............. Institute of Women Today (EA)
IWT............. Integrated Waste Water Treatment
IWT............. Internationaal Watertribunaal [*International Water Tribunal*] [*Netherlands*] (EAIO)
IWT............. International Working Team [*NATO*] (NATG)
IWT............. Irwin Toy Ltd. [*Toronto Stock Exchange symbol*]
IWT............. I Was There
IWT............. Schools of Theology in Dubuque, Dubuque, IA [*OCLC symbol*] (OCLC)
IWTC .... International Women's Tribune Centre (EA)
IWTF .... Inland Waterways Trust Fund (COE)
IWTF .... International Water Tribunal Foundation [*Netherlands*] (EAIO)
IWTO .... International Wool Testing Organisation [*Australia*]
IWTO .... International Wool Textile Organization [*See also FLI*] [*Brussels, Belgium*] (EAIO)
IWTP .... Industrial Waste Treatment Plant (BCP)
IWTS.......... Indications and Warning Training System [*Military*] (MCD)
IWTS.......... Individual Weapon Thermal Sight [*Army*] (INF)
IWTS.......... Industrial Waste Treatment System (NRCH)
IWTS.......... Integrated Wire Termination System (IAA)
IWTS.......... Integrated Worldwide Topographic System (PDAA)
IWTT.......... Industrial Wastewater Treatment Plant
IWU............ Illegal Wearing of Uniform
IWU............ Illinois Wesleyan University [*Bloomington*]
IWU............ Interworking Unit [*Computer science*] (TNIG)
IWU............ Isolation Working Unit [*Telecommunications*] (TEL)
IWU............ Texas Woman's University, Denton, TX [*OCLC symbol*] (OCLC)
IWUL.......... Irrigators and Water Users' League [*Australia*]
IWV............. Internationale Warenhaus-Vereinigung [*International Association of Department Stores*]
IWV............. Waterloo Public Library, Waterloo, IA [*OCLC symbol*] (OCLC)
IWVA .... International War Veterans' Alliance (EA)
IWVMTS ...... Interim Water Velocity Meter Test Set
IWW........... Industrial Workers of the World (EA)
IWW........... Inland Waterway (AABC)
IWW........... International Westward Development Corp. [*Vancouver Stock Exchange symbol*]
IWW........... International Who's Who [*A publication*]
IWW........... Intracoastal Waterway
IWW........... Kenai, AK [*Location identifier FAA*] (FAAL)
IWW........... Westmar College, Le Mars, IA [*OCLC symbol*] (OCLC)

IWW............ Wheaton College, Wheaton, IL [*Library symbol Library of Congress*] (LCLS)
IWWA......... International Wild Waterfowl Association (EA)
IWWCS....... International Who's Who in Community Service [*A publication*]
IWWG........ International Women's Writing Guild (EA)
IWW-G........ Wheaton College, Billy Graham Center, Wheaton, IL [*Library symbol*] [*Library of Congress*] (LCLS)
IWWM......... International Who's Who in Music and Musicians Directory [*A publication*]
IWWP......... International Who's Who in Poetry [*A publication*]
IWWRB....... International Waterfowl and Wetlands Research Bureau (EAIO)
IWY............. International Women's Year [*1975*]
IWY............. New York, NY [*Location identifier FAA*] (FAAL)
IWya .... Raymond A. Sapp Memorial Library, Wyanet, IL [*Library symbol Library of Congress*] (LCLS)
IWyaSD....... Wyanet Consolidated High School District 510, Wyanet, IL [*Library symbol Library of Congress*] (LCLS)
IWyo .... Wymoning Public Library, Wymoning, IL [*Library symbol Library of Congress*] (LCLS)
IX................ Flandre Air [*ICAO designator*] (AD)
IX................ Iesus Christus [*Jesus Christ*] [*Latin*]
IX................ In Christo [*In Christ*] [*Latin*]
IX................ Index [*Computer science*] (BUR)
IX................ Industry Manufacturers [*FCC*] (MCD)
IX................ Information Exchange [*Advanced photo system*]
ix................ Interactive Executive (HGAA)
IX................ Inter-Exchange [*Telecommunications*] (NITA)
IX................ Inverted Index (NITA)
IX................ Ion Exchanger (NRCH)
IX................ Unclassified Miscellaneous [*Navy ship symbol*]
IXA............. Agartala [*India*] [*Airport symbol*] (OAG)
i-xa-- .... Christmas Island [*Indian Ocean*] [*MARC geographic area code Library of Congress*] (LCCP)
IXA............. Ion-Excited X-Ray Analysis
IXA............. University of Texas at Austin, Austin, TX [*OCLC symbol*] (OCLC)
IXAE........... International X-Ray Astrophysics Explorer
IXB............. Bagdogra [*India*] [*Airport symbol*] (OAG)
i-xb-- .... Cocos [*Keeling*] Islands [*MARC geographic area code Library of Congress*] (LCCP)
IXC............. Chandigarh [*India*] [*Airport symbol*] (OAG)
IXC............. Interexchange Carrier [*Telecommunications*] (PCM)
IXC............. Interexchange Channel [*Telecommunications*]
IXC............. Interexchange Circuit [*Telecommunications*] (TSSD)
IXC............. Inter-Exchange Control (NITA)
IXC............. Interexchange Mileage (CET)
IXC............. Ixora Communications System [*Vancouver Stock Exchange symbol*]
i-xc-- .... Maldives [*MARC geographic area code Library of Congress*] (LCCP)
IXD............. Allahabad [*India*] [*Airport symbol*] (OAG)
IXD............. Olathe, KS [*Location identifier FAA*] (FAAL)
IXE............. Mangalore [*India*] [*Airport symbol*] (OAG)
IXEE........... International X-Ray and Extreme Ultraviolet Explorer
IXES........... Information Exchange System [*or Subsystem*] [*Military*] (DNAB)
IXF............. Industrial X-Ray Film
IXG............. Belgaum [*India*] [*Airport symbol*] (OAG)
IXH............. Kailashahar [*India*] [*Airport symbol*] (AD)
IXI............. Lilabari [*India*] [*Airport symbol*] (OAG)
IXJ............. Jammu [*India*] [*Airport symbol*] (OAG)
IXK............. Keshod [*India*] [*Airport symbol*] (OAG)
IXL............. Leh [*India*] [*Airport symbol*] (OAG)
IXM............. Index Manager (MHDI)
IXM............. Madurai [*India*] [*Airport symbol*] (OAG)
IXN............. Khowai [*India*] [*Airport symbol*] (AD)
IXO............. Inlet and Outlet
i-xo-- .... Socotra Island [*MARC geographic area code Library of Congress*] (LCCP)
IXOH .... Inlet and Outlet Head
IXP............. Information Exchange Protocol [*Telecommunications*] (NTCM)
IXP............. Ivex Packaging Corp. [*AMEX symbol*] (SAG)
IXP............. Pathankot [*India*] [*Airport symbol*] (AD)
IXQ............. Kamalpur [*India*] [*Airport symbol*] (AD)
IXR............. Integrated X-Ray Reflection
IXR............. Intelligent Transparent Restore [*Computer science*] (CIST)
IXR............. Intersection of Runways [*Aviation*]
IXR............. Ranchi [*India*] [*Airport symbol*] (OAG)
IXRALM....... Imaging Soft X-Ray LASER Microscope
IXS............. Inelastic X-Ray Scattering [*Physics*]
IXS............. Information Exchange System [*or Subsystem*] [*Military*] (CAAL)
IXS............. Silchar [*India*] [*Airport symbol*] (OAG)
IXSD........... International Telex Subscriber Dialling (NITA)
IXSS........... Unclassified Miscellaneous Submarine [*Navy symbol*] (NVT)
IXT............. Christian Theological Seminary, Indianapolis, IN [*OCLC symbol*] (OCLC)
IXT............. Interaction Cross Talk [*Telecommunications*] (TEL)
IXT............. Interexchange Channel [*Computer science*]
IXT............. Ixtapalapa [*Mexico*] [*Seismograph station code, US Geological Survey Closed*] (SEIS)
IXT............. Lineas Aereas de Ixtlan SA de CV [*Mexico ICAO designator*] (FAAC)
IXT............. Pasighat [*India*] [*Airport symbol*] (AD)
IXTR........... Intelligible Crosstalk Ratio
IXU............. Aurangabad [*India*] [*Airport symbol*] (OAG)
IXU............. Index Translation Unit [*Computer science*] (MHDB)
IXV............. Along [*India*] [*Airport symbol*] (AD)
IXW............. Jamshedpur [*India*] [*Airport symbol*] (AD)
IXX............. Dolphin Express Airlines, Inc. [*FAA designator*] (FAAC)
IXY............. Kandla [*India*] [*Airport symbol*] (AD)

IXZ............. Port Blair [*Andaman Islands*] [*Airport symbol*] (OAG)
IY............... Imperial Yeomanry [*British*]
IY............... Ionized Yeast
iy............... Iraq-Saudi Arabia Neutral Zone [*MARC country of publication code Library of Congress*] (LCCP)
IY............... Yemen Airlines [*Airline flight code*] (ODBW)
IY............... Yemen Airways [*ICAO designator*] (AD)
IYA............. Indian Youth of America (EA)
IYA............. Irish Yachting Association (EAIO)
IYB............. Imperial Yeomanry Bearer Corps [*British military*] (DMA)
IYC............. Individual Yield Coverage Program [*Department of Agriculture*]
IYC............. International Year of the Child [*United Nations*] (AEE)
IYC............. International Youth Congress
IYC............. International Youth Council (EA)
IYCM........... International Year of Canadian Music [*1986*]
IYCO........... Ito-Yokado Co. Ltd. [*NASDAQ symbol*] (NQ)
IYCOY......... Ito Yokado Ltd ADR [*NASDAQ symbol*] (NQ)
IYCW .... International Young Christian Workers [*See also JOCI*] (EAIO)
IYDP........... International Year of the Disabled Person [*1981*]
IYDU........... International Young Democratic Union [*Defunct*] (EAIO)
IYE............. Intrest Yield Equivalent (EBF)
IYE............. Yemenia, Yemen Airways [*ICAO designator*] (FAAC)
IYF............. International Year of the Family
IYF............. International Youth Federation for Environmental Studies and Conservation (EAIO)
IYF............. International Youth Foundation (EA)
IYFS........... International Young Fish Survey [*Denmark, Great Britain, Norway, West Germany*] [*1987-88 Oceanography*]
IYFS........... International Young Friends Society [*Pakistan*] (EAIO)
IYH............. Imperial Yeomanry Hospitals [*Military British*] (ROG)
IY'H............ Im Yirtseh Hashem (BJA)
IYHA........... Irish Youth Hostel Association (EAIO)
IYHF........... International Youth Hostel Federation [*See also FAIJ*] [*Welwyn Garden City, Hertfordshire, England*] (EAIO)
IYK............. Inyokern [*California*] [*Airport symbol*] (OAG)
IYK............. Inyokern, CA [*Location identifier FAA*] (FAAL)
IYL............. International Youth Library [*See also IJB*] [*Munich, Federal Republic of Germany*] (EAIO)
IYP............. Instant Yellow Pages [*Information service or system*]
IYPD........... International Year for the Preparation of Disarmament [*Pugwash Conference*]
IYQS........... International Year of the Quiet Sun [*1964-65*] [*Also, IQSY*] (KSC)
IYRA........... Intercollegiate Yacht Racing Association (PSS)
IYRU........... International Yacht Racing Union [*British*]
IYS............. Inverted Y-Suspensor [*Medicine*]
IYSH........... International Year of Shelter for the Homeless [*1987*]
IYTA........... International Yoga Teachers Association (ADA)
IYU............. Baylor University, Waco, TX [*OCLC symbol*] (OCLC)
IYWIP .... International Year of the World's Indigenous People
IYY............. International Youth Year [*1985*] (AIE)
IYYC........... International Youth Year Commission [*Defunct*] (EA)
IZ............... Arkia-Israel Inland Airlines [*ICAO designator*] (AD)
IZ............... Informationszentrum Sozialwissenschaften [*Social Sciences Information Center*] [*Information service or system*] (IID)
IZ............... Inspection Zone
IZ............... Interfacial Zone
IZ............... Intermediate Zone
IZ............... Ischemic (DB)
IZ............... Isolation Zone [*Nuclear energy*] (NRCH)
IZ............... Spofa Ltd. [*Czechoslovakia*] [*Research code symbol*]
IZ............... Zion-Benton Public Library District, Zion, IL [*Library symbol Library of Congress*] (LCLS)
IZA............. International Zen Association [*Formerly, European Zen Association*] (EA)
IZA............. International Zeolite Association
IZAA........... Independent Zinc Alloyers Association (EA)
IZAA........... Isotope-Shift, Zeeman-Effect Atomic Absorption
IZBA........... International Zebu Breeders Association (EA)
IZBB........... Interagency Zero-Based Budgeting [*Federal government*]
IZC............. International Zetcentrum [*International Typesetting Center, The Netherlands*]
IZCA........... International Zuma Class Association (EA)
IZD............. Implanted Zener Diode (MCD)
IZD............. Internationaler Zivildienst [*International Voluntary Service*]
IZE............. Elizabeth City, NC [*Location identifier FAA*] (FAAL)
IZE............. International Association of Zoo Educators (EA)
IZK............. Iizuka [*Japan*] [*Seismograph station code, US Geological Survey Closed*] (SEIS)
IZK............. Wilkes-Barre/Scranton, PA [*Location identifier FAA*] (FAAL)
IZL............. Irgun Zeva'i Le'umi (BJA)
IZM............. Izmir [*Turkey*] [*Airport symbol*] (OAG)
IZM............. Izmir [*Turkey*] [*Seismograph station code, US Geological Survey*] (SEIS)
IZN............. International Trust for Zoological Nomenclature
IZN............. Izone International Ltd. [*Vancouver Stock Exchange symbol*]
IZO............. Izumo [*Japan*] [*Airport symbol*] (OAG)
iZQC........... Intermolecular Zero-Quantum Coherence [*Physics*]
IZR............. San Antonio, TX [*Location identifier FAA*] (FAAL)
IZS............. Insulin Zinc Suspension
IZT............. Ixtepec [*Mexico*] [*Airport symbol*] (AD)
IZTO........... Interzonal Trade Office [*NATO*] (NATG)
IZU............. Izuhara [*Japan*] [*Seismograph station code, US Geological Survey*] (SEIS)
IZY............. Intermediate Zone Yaw
IZY............. International Zoo Yearbook [*A publication*]

IZZI .... Integrated Security Sys [*NASDAQ symbol*] (TTSB)
IZZI .... Integrated Security Systems [*NASDAQ symbol*] (SAG)
IZZIW .... Integrated Sec Sys Wrrt [*NASDAQ symbol*] (TTSB)

J
By Acronym

J .... Action Variable [*Physics*] (BARN)
J .... Air Force Training Category [*Officer training program*]
J .... Angular Momentum [*Physics*] (BARN)
J .... Australian Journalist [*A publication*]
J .... Business Class [*Also, C*] [*Airline fare code*]
J .... Cable Jointing [*Section of the British Royal Navy*]
J .... Chain [*Symbol*] [*A part of the immunoglobulin molecular structure*] (DAVI)
J .... Clubs [*Public-performance tariff class*] [*British*]
j .... Dissenting Opinion Citation in Dissenting Opinion [*Used in Shepard's Citations*] [*Legal term*] (DLA)
J .... Dynamic Movement of Inertia (STED)
J .... Electric Current Density [*Symbol*] [*IUPAC*] (DEN)
J .... Electromechanical [*JETDS nomenclature*]
J .... Flux [*Symbol*] [*IUPAC*]
J .... Institutes of Justinian [*Roman law*] [*A publication*] (DLA)
J .... Irradiation Correction
J .... Jack [*Technical drawings*]
J .... Jack [*In card game*]
J .... Jackpot Enterprises [*NYSE symbol*] (TTSB)
J .... Jackpot Enterprises, Inc. [*NYSE symbol*] (CTT)
J .... Jacobeian Determinant (ROG)
J .... Jacobus de Porta Ravennate [*Deceased, 1178*] [*Authority cited in pre-1607 legal work*] (DSA)
J .... January
J .... Japan [*IYRU nationality code*]
J .... Jargon [*Used in correcting manuscripts, etc.*]
j .... Jaundice [*Medicine*] (DMAA)
J .... Jerusalem Talmud (BJA)
J .... Jesus (ROG)
J .... Jet [*Aircraft*]
J .... Jet Fuel
J .... Jet Route [*Followed by identification*]
J .... Jewels Horology (BARN)
J .... Jewish
J .... Jewish Chaplain [*Territorial Force*] [*Military British*] (ROG)
J .... Jewish School [*British*]
J .... Jig [*Phonetic alphabet*] [*World War II*] (DSUE)
J .... Job (IEEE)
J .... Jobber [*Merchant middleman*]
J .... Johannes Galensis [*Flourished, 13th century*] [*Authority cited in pre-1607 legal work*] (DSA)
J .... Johnnie [*Phonetic alphabet*] [*Royal Navy World War I*] (DSUE)
J .... Johnny [*Phonetic alphabet*] [*Pre-World War II*] (DSUE)
J .... Johnson's New York Reports [*A publication*] (DLA)
J .... Join
J .... Joinable Containers [*Shipping*] (DCTA)
J .... Joiner [*Machinery*]
J .... Joining [*Also, JNG*] [*Genetics*]
J .... Joint
J .... Joint Matriculation Board [*British*]
J .... Joist [*Technical drawings*]
J .... Jonckheere Test [*Fisheries*]
J .... Joshua [*Old Testament book*] [*Freemasonry*]
J .... Joule [*Symbol*] [*SI unit of energy*] (GPO)
j .... Jour [*Day*] [*French*]
J .... Journal
J .... Journalism
J .... Judaeo-Persian
J .... Judean or Yahwistic [*Used in biblical criticism to designate Yahwistic material*]
J .... Judex [*Judge*] [*Latin*]
J .... Judge
J .... Judgment
J .... Juice
J .... Juliett [*Phonetic alphabet*] [*International*] (DSUE)
J .... July
J .... Junction
J .... Junction Devices [*JETDS nomenclature*] [*Military*] (CET)
J .... June
J .... Jungle
J .... Junior
J .... Jupiter
J .... Juris [*Of Law*] [*Latin*] (ADA)
J .... Jus [*Law*] [*Latin*]
J .... Justice [*i.e., a judge; plural is JJ*]

J .... Justiciary Cases [*Scotland*] [*A publication*] (DLA)
J .... Justification (WDMC)
J .... Juta's South African Reports [*A publication*] (DLA)
J .... Jute-Asphalted [*Nonmetallic armor*] (AAG)
J .... Juvenile
J .... Juvenile (Amaurotic Idiocy) [*Medicine*] (DAVI)
J .... Kansas City [*Branch in the Federal Reserve regional banking system*] (BARN)
J .... Lower Canada Jurist, Quebec [*1848-91*] [*A publication*] (DLA)
·J .... Magnetic Poparization [*Physics*] (BARN)
J .... Massieu Function [*Symbol*] [*IUPAC*]
J .... Mechanical Equivalent of Heat [*Symbol*]
J .... Polypeptide Chain in Polymeric Immunoglobulins (STED)
J .... Radiant Intensity [*Symbol*]
J .... Scottish Jurist [*1829-73*] [*A publication*] (DLA)
J .... Sound Intensity (STED)
J .... Special Test, Temporary [*Aircraft classification letter*]
j .... Total Angular Momentum Quantum Number of a Single Particle [*Symbol*] [*Spectroscopy*]
J .... Total Angular Momentum Quantum Number of a System [*Symbol*] [*Spectroscopy*]
J .... VEB Fahlberg-List [*East Germany*] [*Research code symbol*]
J .... Yahwist Source [*Biblical scholarship*]
j .... Yellow [*Symbol*] (DAVI)
J-1 .... Jaeger Test Type One [*Ophthalmology*]
J-1 .... Personnel Section [*of a joint military staff; also, the officer in charge of this section*]
J2 .... Djibouti [*Aircraft nationality and registration mark*] (FAAC)
J-2 .... Intelligence Section [*of a joint military staff; also, the officer in charge of this section*]
J2 .... JTwo Communications [*Associated Press*] (SAG)
J2 Com .... JTwo Communications [*Associated Press*] (SAG)
J3 .... Grenada [*Aircraft nationality and registration mark*] (FAAC)
J-3 .... Operations and Training Section [*of a joint military staff; also, the officer in charge of this section*]
J-4 .... Logistics Section [*of a joint military staff; also, the officer in charge of this section*]
J-5 .... General Administration Section [*of a joint military staff; also the officer in charge of this section*]
J5 .... Guinea-Bissau [*International civil aircraft marking*] (ODBW)
J-6 .... Communications-Electronics Section [*of a joint military staff; also, the officer in charge of this section*]
J6 .... St. Lucia [*Aircraft nationality and registration mark*] (FAAC)
J7 .... Dominica [*Aircraft nationality and registration mark*] (FAAC)
J8 .... St. Vincent and the Grenadines [*Aircraft nationality and registration mark*] (FAAC)
J-14/CA........ Jet 14 Class Association (EA)
J31 .... British Aerospace Jetstream 31 [*Airplane code*]
JA .... Bankair [*ICAO designator*] (AD)
JA .... Jack Adapter
Ja .... Jacobus Balduini [*Deceased, 1235*] [*Authority cited in pre-1607 legal work*] (DSA)
Ja .... Jacobus de Albenga [*Flourished, 13th century*] [*Authority cited in pre-1607 legal work*] (DSA)
Ja .... Jacobus de Ravanis [*Deceased, 1296*] [*Authority cited in pre-1607 legal work*] (DSA)
ja .... Jade (VRA)
JA .... Jama'at Ahmadiyyah [*Ahmadiyya Muslim Association*] (EAIO)
JA .... Jamaica
JA .... January
ja .... Japan [*ry (Ryukyu Islands, Southern) used in records cataloged before January 1978*] [*MARC country of publication code Library of Congress*] (LCCP)
JA .... Jetevator Assembly
JA .... Jewelers of America (EA)
JA .... Jewish Art, An Illustrated History [*A publication*] (BJA)
JA .... Job Aid
JA .... Job Analysis
JA .... Jockey's Association [*Defunct*] (EA)
JA .... John Adams [*US president, 1735-1826*]
JA .... John Alden Financial [*NYSE symbol*] (SPSG)
JA .... Joint Account
JA .... Joint Agent
JA .... Journal Announcement [*Dialog*] [*Searchable field*] [*Information service or system*] (NITA)
JA .... Judge Advocate

JA	Judge of Appeal
JA	Judicature Act (ROG)
JA	Judicial Authority [British]
JA	Jump Address
JA	Jump If Above [Computer science] (PCM)
JA	Junior Achievement [Stamford, CT] (EA)
JA	Junior Ambassadors [Defunct] (EA)
JA	Justice of Appeal [Legal term] (DLA)
JA	Juvenile Atrophy [Medicine] (DAVI)
JA	Juxta-Articular [Orthopedics] (DAVI)
JAA	American Dental Association, Chicago, IL [OCLC symbol] (OCLC)
JAA	Jamiat Adduwal Alarabia [League of Arab States - LAS] (EAIO)
JAA	Japan Asia Airways
JAA	Japan Asia Airways Co. Ltd. [ICAO designator] (FAAC)
JAA	Joint Airworthiness Authority [Aviation]
JAA	Joint Aviation Authorities (BUAC)
JAA	Judge Advocates Association (EA)
JAAA	Jabara Award for Airmanship [Military decoration]
JAAB	Joint Airlift Allocations Board
JAAC	Joint Airlift Allocations Committee
JAAC	Journal of Aesthetics and Art Criticism [A publication] (BRI)
JAACS	John A. Andrew Clinical Society (EA)
JA(ACT)	Jobless Action (Australian Capital Territory) [An association]
JAAF	Japanese Army Air Force
JAAF	Joint Action Armed Forces
JAAF	Joint Army-Air Force
JAAFAR	Joint Army-Air Force Adjustment Regulations
JAAFCTB	Joint Army-Air Force Commercial Traffic Bulletin
JAAFPC	Joint Army-Air Force Procurement Circular
JAAFU	Joint Anglo-American Foul Up [World War II slang] [Bowdlerized version]
JAAL	Jewish Anti-Abortion League (EA)
JAAL	Journal of Adolescent & Adult Literacy [A publication] (BRI)
JAAML	Journal. American Academy of Matrimonial Lawyers [A publication] (DLA)
JAAMRS	Joint Air-to-Air Missile Requirement Study (MCD)
JAAOC	Joint Antiaircraft Operation Center [NATO] (NATG)
JAAP	Joint Airborne Advance Party [Military] (AFM)
JAAP	Joliet Army Ammunition Plant (AABC)
JAAR	Job Area Acceptance Range (AAGC)
JAAR	Journal of the American Academy of Religion [A publication] (BRI)
Ja Are	Jacobus de Arena [Deceased, 1297] [Authority cited in pre-1607 legal work] (DSA)
JAARS	Joint After-Action Reporting System (COE)
JAARS	Jungle Aviation & Radio Service, Inc. [Mission plane service]
JAAS	Jewish Academy of Arts and Sciences (EA)
JAAS	Journal of Analytical Atomic Spectrometry [Formerly, ARAAS] [A publication]
JAAT	Joint Air Attack Team [Military] (INF)
JAATT	Joint Air Attack Team Tactics (MCD)
JA/ATT	Joint Airborne/Air Transportability Training
JAAW	Juvenile Arthritis Awareness Week [Arthritis Foundation]
JAB	American Library Association, Booklist, Chicago, IL [OCLC symbol] (OCLC)
JAB	January Assumption Budget [Budget based on economic forecasts available as of January]
JAB	Jet Business Airlines [Belgium ICAO designator] (FAAC)
JAB	Joint Activity Briefing [Military] (AFM)
JABE	Joint Amphibious Board [Military]
JABES	Just Another Break-Even Situation [Slang]
Jabil	Jabil Circuit, Inc. [Associated Press] (SAG)
JABOWA	Janak-Botkin-Wallis [Data processing program regarding forest growth; named for three men involved in program]
JABPPC	Joint Animal By Products Parliamentary and Advisory Committee [British] (DBA)
JABQC	Job Assembly Breakdown and Quality Control Section [Social Security Administration]
JABRO	James Broadwell [Custom-built racing car]
JABS	Justice, Awareness & Basic Support (WDAA)
JABUP	Joint Air Base Utilization Plan (MCD)
JAC	CEGEP [College d'Enseignement General et Professionnel] John Abbott College Library [UTLAS symbol]
JAC	Jackson [Wyoming] [Airport symbol] (OAG)
JAC	Jacksonville [Florida] [Seismograph station code, US Geological Survey Closed] (SEIS)
JAC	Jackson, WY [Location identifier FAA] (FAAL)
JAC	Jacobean (WDAA)
Jac	Jacob's English Chancery Reports [1821-22] [A publication] (DLA)
Jac	Jacob's Law Dictionary [A publication] (DLA)
Jac	Jacobus [James] [King of England] (DLA)
Jac	Jacobus Balduini [Deceased, 1235] [Authority cited in pre-1607 legal work] (DSA)
JAC	Japan Air Commuter Co. Ltd. [ICAO designator] (FAAC)
JAC	Jet Age Conference
JAC	Jet Aircraft Coating
JAC	Jeunesse Anarchiste Communiste [French student group]
JAC	Jewellery Advisory Centre (BUAC)
JAC	Job Assistance Center (DOMA)
JAC	Johnstown American Co. (MHDW)
JAC	Joint Action Co. [Marine Corps]
JAC	Joint Advisory Committee [Military]
JAC	Joint Aircraft Committee [World War II]
JAC	Joint Apprenticeship Committee
JAC	Joint Arms Control
JAC	Journal of Applied Chemistry [A publication]

JAC	Junior American Citizens [An association] (EA)
JAC	Junior Association of Commerce (BARN)
JACADS	Johnston Atoll Chemical Agents Disposal System
Jac & W	Jacob and Walker's English Chancery Reports [37 English Reprint] (DLA)
Jac & Walk	Jacob and Walker's English Chancery Reports [37 English Reprint] (DLA)
Jac & W (Eng)	Jacob and Walker's English Chancery Reports [37 English Reprint] [A publication] (DLA)
JACARI	Joint Action Committee Against Racial Interference (BUAC)
JACB-E	Joint Acquisition Coordinating Board-Europe (AAGC)
Jacbn	Jacobean (VRA)
Jacbsn	Jacobson Stores, Inc. [Associated Press] (SAG)
JACC	Jayhawk Acceptance [NASDAQ symbol] (TTSB)
JACC	Jayhawk Acceptance Corp. [NASDAQ symbol] (SAG)
JACC	Joint Airborne Communications Center (MCD)
JACC	Joint Air Command Center [Army] (DOMA)
JACC	Joint Alternate Command Center [Military] (CINC)
JACC	Joint Automatic Control Conference [IEEE]
JACC	Journalism Association of Community Colleges (EA)
JACCC	Joint Air Control and Coordination Center [Air Force] (AFM)
JACC/CP	Joint Airborne Communications Center/Command Post (AFM)
JACCI	Joint Allocation Committee Civil Intelligence [of US and Great Britain] [World War II]
J Account	Journal of Accountancy [A publication] (BRI)
JACCP	Joint Airborne Communication and Command Post (IAA)
J Acct	Journal of Accountancy [A publication] (DLA)
Jac Dict	Jacob's Law Dictionary [A publication] (DLA)
JACE	Joint Allied Communications Element (AFM)
JACE	Joint Alternate Command Element
JACE	Just Another Confused Elephant
JACES	Joint Advisory Committee for Engineering Services (BUAC)
Jac Fish Dig	Jacob's American Edition of Fisher's English Digest [A publication] (DLA)
JACFU	Joint American-Chinese Foul Up [World War II slang] [Bowdlerized version]
JACGUAR	Johns and Call Girls United Against Repression (EA)
Jac Int	Jacob's Introduction to the Common, Civil, and Canon Law [A publication] (DLA)
JACK	Golden Bear Golf, Inc. [NASDAQ symbol] (SAG)
JACK	Junior American Coin Klub (EA)
JACK	Junior Assistant Cook [British military] (DMA)
Jack & G Landl & Ten	Jackson and Gross' Treatise on the Law of Landlord and Tenant in Pennsylvania [A publication] (DLA)
Jack & L	Jackson and Lumpkin's Reports [59-64 Georgia] [A publication] (DLA)
Jack Geo Ind	Jackson's Index to the Georgia Reports [A publication] (DLA)
JackHwt	Jackson Hewitt [Associated Press] (SAG)
JACKPHY	Japanese, Arabic, Chinese, Korean, Persian, Hebrew, Yiddish [Nonroman languages] [Library of Congress]
Jack Pl	Jackson on Pleadings [1933] [A publication] (DLA)
Jackpot	Jackpot Enterprises, Inc. [Associated Press] (SAG)
JACKPOT	Joint Airborne Communications Center and Command Post
Jackpt	Jackpot Enterprises [Associated Press] (SAG)
Jackson	Jackson's Reports [1-29 Texas Court of Appeals] [A publication] (DLA)
Jackson	Jackson's Reports [46-58 Georgia] [A publication] (DLA)
Jackson & Lumpkin	Jackson and Lumpkin's Reports [59-64 Georgia] [A publication] (DLA)
Jackson St U	Jackson State University (GAGS)
Jacksonville St U	Jacksonville State University (GAGS)
Jacksonville U	Jacksonville University (GAGS)
Jack Tex App	Jackson's Reports [A publication] (DLA)
JACL	Japanese American Citizens League (EA)
Jac Law Dict	Jacob's Law Dictionary [A publication] (DLA)
Jac LD	Jacob's Law Dictionary [A publication] (DLA)
Jac L Dict	Jacob's Law Dictionary [A publication] (DLA)
Jac Lex Mer	Jacob's Lex Mercatoria [A publication] (DLA)
Jac LG	Jacob's Law Grammar [A publication] (DLA)
Jaclyn	Jaclyn, Inc. [Associated Press] (SAG)
JACNE	Joint Advisory Committee on Nutrition Education [British]
JACO	Jaco Electronics [NASDAQ symbol] (TTSB)
JACO	Jaco Electronics, Inc. [NASDAQ symbol] (NQ)
JACO	Joint Actions Control Office (AABC)
Jacob	Jacob's English Chancery Reports [1821-22] [A publication] (DLA)
Jacob	Jacob's Law Dictionary [A publication] (DLA)
Jacob Ardiz	Jacobus de Ardizone [Flourished, 1213-50] [Authority cited in pre-1607 legal work] (DSA)
Jacobs	Jacobs Engineering Group, Inc. [Associated Press] (SAG)
JacoEl	Jaco Electronics, Inc. [Associated Press] (SAG)
JacoElec	Jaco Electronics, Inc. [Associated Press] (SAG)
JACOPIS	Joint Advisory Committee on Pets in Society [British] (DI)
JacorC	Jacor Communications, Inc. [Associated Press] (SAG)
JacorCm	Jacor Communications, Inc. [Associated Press] (SAG)
JACP	Japanese American Curriculum Project (EA)
JacrCm	Jacor Communications, Inc. [Associated Press] (SAG)
JACRD	Joint Committee for Agricultural Research and Development (BUAC)
JACS	Japan-American Cultural Society (EAIO)
JACS	Jet Attitude Control System (KSC)
JACS	Jewish Alcoholics, Chemically Dependent Persons, and Significant Others
JACS	Joint Action in Community Service (EA)
JACS	JUMPS Army Coding System (MCD)
Jac Sea Laws	Jacobsen's Law of the Sea [A publication] (DLA)
JACSPAC	Joint Air Communications of the Pacific

JACT	[The] Joint Association of Classical Teachers [British]
JACTRU	Joint Air Traffic Control RADAR Unit (IAA)
JACWA	Joint Allied Command Western Approaches [NATO] (LAIN)
JAD	Joint Application Design [Computer science]
JAD	Joint Application Development [Computer science] (CIST)
JAD	Joint Resource Assessment Database
JAD	Wheaton Public Library, Wheaton, IL [OCLC symbol] (OCLC)
JADA	Journal of American Dental Association [A publication] (DHP)
JADB	Joint Air Defense Board
JADC	Joint Administrative Committee [Military]
JADD	Joint Air Defense Division (SAA)
JADE	Japan Area Defense Environment
JADE	Japan Asian Dance Event
JADE	Japanese Air Defense Environment
JADE	Junior Administrator Development Examination (AFM)
JADF	Japan Air Defense Force
JADF	Joint Air Defense Force (AAG)
JADIS	Joint Air Defense Interoperability Study
JADITBHKNYC	Just a Drop in the Basket Helps Keep New York Clean [Antilitter campaign]
JADO	Joint Air Defense Operations [Marine Corps] (DOMA)
JADOC	Joint Air Defense Operation Center
JADOR	Joint Advertising Directors of Recruiting [Navy] (NVT)
JADPU	Joint Automatic Data Processing Unit
JAD/RAD	Joint Application Design/Rapid Application Design [Computer science]
JADREP	Joint Resource Assessment Data Base Report [Military] (AABC)
JADS	Joint Advanced Distributed Simulation [Military]
JADS	Journal Article Delivery Service [Carnegie Mellon University]
jadt	Jadeite (VRA)
J Adv	Judge Advocate [Legal term] (DLA)
J Adv Ed	Journal of Advanced Education [A publication]
J ADV GEN	Judge Advocate General [Military] (WDAA)
JADW	Joint Air Defense Wing (SAA)
JAE	Illinois Agricultural Association & Affiliated Co., Bloomington, IL [OCLC symbol] (OCLC)
JAE	Jacksonville [Illinois] [Airport symbol] (AD)
JAE	Japan Aviation Electronics Industry Ltd.
JAE	Joint Atomic Exercise [NATO] (NATG)
JAE	Journal of Advanced Education [A publication] (ADA)
JAE	Journal of Agricultural Economics [A publication]
JAE	Jump If Above or Equal [Computer science] (PCM)
JAEC	Japan Atomic Energy Commission
JAEC	Joint Atomic Energy Commission
JAEG	Jaegdtiger [Tank-destroyer] [German military - World War II]
Jaeger Labor Law	Jaeger's Cases and Statutes on Labor Law [A publication] (DLA)
JAEH	Journal of Aquatic Ecosystem Health [A publication]
JAEIC	Joint Atomic Energy Intelligence Center [Military]
JAEIC	Joint Atomic Energy Intelligence Committee (KSC)
JAEIP	Japan Atomic Energy Insurance Pool
JAERI	Japan Atomic Energy Research Institute [Tokyo]
JAES	Japan Atomic Energy Society (BUAC)
J Aes Ed	Journal of Aesthetic Education [A publication] (BRI)
JAEW	Japanese Airborne Early Warning
JAF	Corn Belt Library System, Normal, IL [OCLC symbol] (OCLC)
JAF	Jaffna [Ceylon] [Airport symbol] (AD)
JAF	James A. Fitzpatrick [Nuclear power plant] (NRCH)
JAF	Jamestown Area Furniture Haulers Association, Inc., Buffalo NY [STAC]
JAF	Japan-Australia Foundation
JAF	Japan Automobile Federation
JAF	Job Accounting Facility
JAF	John Augustus Foundation (EA)
JAF	Joint Attack Fighter [Air Force] [Navy] [DoD] (DOMA)
JAF	Jordanian Air Force
JAF	Journal of American Folklore [A publication] (BRI)
JAF	Judge Advocate of the Fleet
JAFC	James Allen Fan Club (EA)
JAFC	Jammie Ann Fan Club (EA)
JAFC	Japan Atomic Fuel Corp.
JAFC	John Anderson Fan Club [Defunct] (EA)
JAFC	Junior Acting Field Captain [Military British] (ROG)
JAFE	Joint Advanced Fighter Engine
JAFF	Electronic and Chaff Jamming (IEEE)
JAFHRO	Joint Armed Forces Housing Referral Office (MCD)
JAFNA	Joint Air Force-NASA
JAFNC	Joint Air Force-Navy Committee
JAFO	Junior Acting Field Officer [Military British] (ROG)
JAFP	Jewish Agency for Palestine
JAFPUB	Joint Armed Forces Publication
J African L	Journal of African Law [A publication] (DLA)
JAFS	Japan Asian Association and Asian Friendship Society (BUAC)
JAG	Indian Trails Public Library District, Wheeling, IL [OCLC symbol] (OCLC)
JAG	Jaguar [Automobile]
JAG	James Abram Garfield [US president, 1831-1881]
JAG	Jetag AB [Switzerland ICAO designator] (FAAC)
JAG	Jobs for America's Graduates [An association] (EA)
JAG	Judge Advocate General [Air Force, Army, Navy]
JAGA	Military Affairs Division, Office of Judge Advocate General, United States Army (DLA)
JAGAR	Judge Advocate General's Area Representatives
JAGB	Jockeys' Association [British] (DBA)
JAGB	Jockeys Association of Great Britain (BUAC)
JAG Bull	Judge Advocate General Bulletin [Air Force A publication] (DLA)
JAGC	Judge Advocate General's Corps
JAG CMR (AF)	Judge Advocate General Court-Martial Reports [Air Force A publication] (DLA)
JAG Comp CMO (Navy)	Judge Advocate General Compilation of Court-Martial Orders [Navy A publication] (DLA)
JAGD	Judge Advocate General's Department [Air Force, Army]
JAG Dig Op	Judge Advocate General Digest of Opinions [A publication] (DLA)
JAGDR	Judge Advocate General's Department Reserve
JAGET	Judge Advocates General Network
Jagg Torts	Jaggard on Torts [A publication] (DLA)
JAGINST	Office of the Judge Advocate General Instructions [Navy]
JAGIT	Joint Air-Ground Instruction Team
JAG L Rev	United States. Air Force Judge Advocate General. Law Review [A publication] (DLA)
JAG Man	Judge Advocate General Manual (Navy) [A publication] (DLA)
JAGN	Judge Advocate General of the Navy
JAGO	Judge Advocate General's Office
JAGOS	Joint Air-Ground Operations System [Military]
J Agric W Aust	Journal of Agriculture of Western Australia [A publication]
J Agr Ind SA	Journal of Agricultural Industry, South Australia [A publication]
J Agr Tax'n & L	Journal of Agricultural Taxation and Law [A publication] (DLA)
JAGRY	Jaguar PLC (MHDW)
JAGS	Joint Army-Air Force Air-Ground Study
JAGS	Judge Advocate General's School (DLA)
JAGT	Procurement Division, Judge Advocate General, United States Army (DLA)
Ja Guara	Jacobus Guaraguilia [Authority cited in pre-1607 legal work] (DSA)
JAGUAR-V	Jamming Guarded Radio - VHF [Very High Frequency] (PDAA)
JAH	Glencoe Public Library, Glencoe, IL [OCLC symbol] (OCLC)
JAH	Journal of African History [A publication]
JAH	Journal of American History [A publication] (BRI)
JAHI	Jordan Amer Hldgs [NASDAQ symbol] (TTSB)
JAHI	Jordan American Holdings, Inc. [NASDAQ symbol] (SAG)
JAHIW	Jordan Amer Hldgs Wrrt [NASDAQ symbol] (TTSB)
Jahrb f Cl Phil Suppl	Jahrbucher fuer Classische Philologie. Supplementband [A publication] (OCD)
Jahresb	Jahresberichte ueber die Fortschritte der Altertumswissenschaft [1873-] [A publication] (OCD)
JAHWGS	Joint Ad Hoc Working Group on Shipping [ASEAN]
JAI	JAI Press [Division of Johnson Associates, Inc.]
JAI	Jaipur [India] [Airport symbol] (OAG)
JAI	Jaipur [India] [Geomagnetic observatory code]
JAI	Jami'at Al Islan [Defunct] (EA)
JAI	Japan-America Institute [Defunct] (EA)
JAI	Jewish Agency for Israel [United Israel Appeal] [Absorbed by] (EA)
JAI	Job Accounting Interface
JAI	Johnson Associates Inc. (GAAI)
Jai	Johnson Associates, Incorporated, Greenwich, CT [Library symbol Library of Congress] (LCLS)
JAI	Joint Administrative Instruction
JAI	Joint Staff Administrative Instruction [Military]
JAI	Juvenile Amaurotic Idiocy [Medicine]
JAI	Lake Forest Library, Lake Forest, IL [OCLC symbol] (OCLC)
JAI	M/S Jet Airways Ltd. [India] [FAA designator] (FAAC)
JAIA	Japan Automobile Importers Association
JAIA	Journal. Australian Indonesian Association [A publication]
JAIC	Joint Air Intelligence Center (DOMA)
JAICC	Joint Arab-Irish Chamber of Commerce (BUAC)
JAICI	Japanese Association for International Chemical Information [Tokyo]
JAIEA	Joint Atomic Information Exchange Agency (SAA)
JAIEG	Joint Atomic Information Exchange Group [DoD]
JAIF	Japan Atomic Industrial Forum
JAII	Johnstown America Indus [NASDAQ symbol] (TTSB)
JAII	Johnstown America Industries, Inc. [NASDAQ symbol] (SAG)
JAIM	Job Analysis and Interest Measurement
JAIMS	Japan-American Institute of Management Science
JAIO	Joint Assessment and Initiatives Office [Military]
Jaipur LJ	Jaipur Law Journal [India] [A publication] (DLA)
JAIS	Japan Aircraft Industry Society (BUAC)
JAJ	Waubonsee Community College, Sugar Grove, IL [OCLC symbol] (OCLC)
JAJC	Journalism Association of Junior Colleges [Later, JACC]
JAJO	January, April, July, and October [Denotes quarterly payments of interest or dividends in these months] [Business term]
Jakarta	Jakarta Growth Fund [Associated Press] (SAG)
JAKE	Jakes Pizza International [NASDAQ symbol] (SAG)
JAKE	Jakes Pizza Intl [NASDAQ symbol] (TTSB)
JakePza	Jakes Pizza International [Associated Press] (SAG)
JAKFORCE	Jammu and Kashmir Force [British military] (DMA)
JAKIS	Japanese Keyword Indexing Simulator
JAKK	JAKKS Pacific [NASDAQ symbol] (TTSB)
JAKK	Jakks Pacific, Inc. [NASDAQ symbol] (SAG)
JAL	Japan Air Lines
JAL	Japan Air Lines Ltd. [ICAO designator] (FAAC)
JAL	Jet Approach Landing Charts (FAAC)
JAL	Jewish Apocryphal Literature [A publication] (BJA)
JAL	Journal of Academic Librarianship [A publication] (BRI)
JAL	Judge Advocate Library, Department of the Navy, Alexandria, VA [OCLC symbol] (OCLC)
JALAP	Jalapae [Jalap] [Pharmacology] (ROG)
Jalate	Jalate, Inc. [Associated Press] (SAG)
JALC	Japan American Lumber Conference (BUAC)
JALC	Jet Approach and Landing Chart (AFM)
JAlden	Alden [John] Financial Corp. [Associated Press] (SAG)

JALMA.........	Japan Leprosy Mission for Asia (BUAC)
JALPG.........	Joint Automatic Language Processing Group
JALT	Journal. Association of Law Teachers [*A publication*] (DLA)
JAM	Jail Accounting Microcomputer System
JAM	Jamaica [*ANSI three-letter standard code*] (CNC)
JAM	James [*New Testament Book*] (WDAA)
JaM	J A Micropublishing, Inc., Eastchester, NY [*Library symbol Library of Congress*] (LCLS)
JAM	Jamieson Scotch Dictionary [*A publication*] (ROG)
JAM	Jamming [*Military*] (NVT)
JAM	Jet Age Malfunction (IAA)
JAM	Job Analysis Memorandum
JAM	Job Assignment Memorandum
JAM	Joint Analysed Make-up [*Computer-controlled attachment*] (PDAA)
JAM	JUMPS [*Joint Uniform Military Pay System*] Action Memorandum (NVT)
JAM	Just a Minute [*Computer hacker terminology*] (NHD)
JAM	Moraine Valley Community College, Palos Hills, IL [*OCLC symbol*] (OCLC)
Jama	Jamaica (VRA)
JAMA...........	Japan Automobile Manufacturers Association, Washington Office (EA)
JAMA...........	Journal of the American Medical Association [*A publication*]
JAMA...........	Moslem People's Revolutionary Movement [*Iran*] [*Political party*] (PPW)
JAMAC.........	Job Analysis Memorandum Activity Chart
JAMAC.........	Joint Aeronautical Materials Activity [*Military*] (AABC)
JAMAG.........	Joint American Military Advisory Group
JAMAL.........	Jamaican Movement for the Advancement of Literacy (BUAC)
JAMASS........	Japanese Medical Abstract Scanning System [*International Medical Information Center*] [*Japan*] (NITA)
JAMB	Joint Air Movements Board [*Military*]
J Am Bankers' Assn...	Journal. American Bankers Association [*A publication*] (DLA)
JAMC...........	Japan Aircraft Manufacturing Corp. (BUAC)
J Am Chem Soc...	Journal of American Chemical Society (MEC)
J Am Cult	Journal of American Culture [*A publication*] (BRI)
James..........	James' Reports [*2 Nova Scotia*] [*A publication*] (DLA)
JAMES.........	Java Architecture for Mobile Extended Service [*Computer science*]
James & Mont...	Jameson and Montagu's English Bankruptcy Reports [*Vol. 2 of Glyn and Jameson*] [*1821-28*] [*A publication*] (DLA)
James Bk L...	James' Bankrupt Law PB (DLA)
James Const Con...	Jameson's Constitutional Convention [*A publication*] (DLA)
James Ct Mar...	James on Courts-Martial [*A publication*] (DLA)
James Fr Soc...	James' Guide to Friendly Societies [*A publication*] (DLA)
James JS.....	James' Law of Joint Stock Companies [*A publication*] (DLA)
James Madison U...	James Madison University (GAGS)
JamesnIn.....	Jameson Inns, Inc. [*Associated Press*] (SAG)
James (N Sc)...	James' Reports [*2 Nova Scotia*] [*A publication*] (DLA)
James Op	James' Opinions, Charges, Etc. [*A publication*] (DLA)
James Salv...	James on Salvage [*1867*] [*A publication*] (DLA)
James Sel Cas...	James' Select Cases [*1835-55*] [*Nova Scotia*] [*A publication*] (DLA)
James Sel Cases...	James' Select Cases [*1835-55*] [*Nova Scotia*] [*A publication*] (DLA)
James Sh	James' Merchant Shipping [*1866*] [*A publication*] (DLA)
JAMEX.........	Jamming Exercise [*Military*] (NVT)
JAMG..........	Jamming
JAMG..........	Juvenile Autoimmune Myasthenia Gravis [*Medicine*] (DAVI)
JAMHEP......	Joint Aircraft Hurricane Plan
JAMIA	Journal of the American Medical Informatics Association [*A publication*] (DMAA)
JAMINTEL....	Jamaica International Telecommunications Ltd. [*Kingston*] [*Telecommunications service*]
JamKI-L.......	Institute of Jamaica, National Library of Jamaica, Kingston, Jamaica [*Library symbol*] [*Library of Congress*] (LCLS)
JamKLS.......	Jamaica Library Service, Kingston, Jamaica [*Library symbol Library of Congress*] (LCLS)
JamKU........	University of the West Indies, Mona, Kingston, Jamaica [*Library symbol Library of Congress*] (LCLS)
JAML	Journal of Arts Management, Law & Society [*A publication*] (BRI)
Jam LJ	Jamaica Law Journal [*A publication*] (DLA)
JAMMAT......	Joint American Military Mission for Aid to Turkey (MUGU)
JAMOT........	Julie/Jezebel [*Sonobuoy Systems*] Airborne Maintenance Operator Trainee [*Navy*] (MCD)
JAMP	JINTACCS [*Joint Interoperability of Tactical Command and Control System*] Army Management Plan (MCD)
JAMPAC......	Jamming Package [*Air Force*]
JAMPACK	Jamming Package [*Air Force*] (MCD)
JAMPO........	Joint Allied Military Petroleum Office [*NATO*]
JAMPRESS...	Jamaican Government News Agency (BUAC)
JAMPS........	JINTACCS [*Joint Interoperability of Tactical Command and Control Systems*] Automated Message Preparation System (MCD)
JAMREP......	Jamming Report
JAMS	Jameson Inns [*NASDAQ symbol*] (TTSB)
JAMS	Jameson Inns, Inc. [*NASDAQ symbol*] (SAG)
JAMS	Joint Agency for Municipal Securities Dealers
JAMS	Journal. Academy of Marketing Science [*A publication*]
JAMS	Journal of the American Musicological Society [*A publication*] (WDAA)
JAMSAT.......	Japan Radio Amateur Satellite Corp. (BUAC)
Jam St........	Jamaica Statutes [*A publication*] (DLA)
J Am St	Journal of American Studies [*A publication*] (BRI)
JAMSTEC.....	Japan Marine Science and Technology Center
JAMTO........	Joint Airlines Military Traffic Office
JAMTRAC	Jammers Tracked by Azimuth Crossings [*RADAR*]
JAMTS.........	Japan Association of Motor Trade and Service (BUAC)
JAN.............	Emerald Airways Ltd. [*British*] [*FAA designator*] (FAAC)
JAN.............	Jackson [*Mississippi*] [*Airport symbol*] (OAG)
JAN.............	Jackson, MS [*Location identifier FAA*] (FAAL)
JAN.............	Janes Aviation 748 Ltd. [*British ICAO designator*] (FAAC)
JAN.............	Janina [*Greece*] [*Seismograph station code, US Geological Survey*] (SEIS)
JAN.............	Janitor
JAN.............	Jantar Resources Corp. [*Vancouver Stock Exchange symbol*]
JAN.............	January (EY)
Jan.............	January (ASC)
jan	Janvier [*January*] [*French*] (ASC)
JAN.............	Japanese Accepted Name (DMAA)
JAN.............	Japanese Animation Network (EA)
JAN.............	Jet Aircraft Noise
JAN.............	Job Accommodation Network [*President's Committee on Employment of the Handicapped*] [*Information service or system*] (IID)
JAN.............	Joint Army and Navy
JAN.............	Judgment Analysis [*Psychology*]
JAN.............	Justification for Authority to Negotiate [*Military*]
JAN.............	Lincoln Christian College, Lincoln, IL [*OCLC symbol*] (OCLC)
JANA..........	Jamahiriyah News Agency [*Libya*]
JANAC........	Joint Army-Navy Assessment Committee [*World War II*]
JANAF........	Joint Army-Navy-Air Force
JANAFPAC ...	Joint Army-Navy-Air Force, Pacific General Message [*Serially numbered*] (CINC)
JANAIA	Joint Army-Navy Aircraft Instrument Action (MCD)
JANAIR	Joint Army-Navy Aircraft Instrument Research
JANALP.......	Joint Army-Navy-Air Force Logistics Policy
JANALP.......	Joint Army-Navy-Air Force Logistics Publication
Jan Angl	Jani Anglorum Facies Nova [*1680*] [*A publication*] (DLA)
JANAP........	Joint Army-Navy-Air Force Procedure [*NATO*] (NATG)
JANAP........	Joint Army-Navy-Air Force Publication
JANARS.......	Joint Army-Navy-Air Force Radiotelephone System (IAA)
JANAST.......	Joint Army-Navy-Air Force Sea Transportation Message
JanBell.......	Jan Bell Marketing, Inc. [*Associated Press*] (SAG)
JANBMC......	Joint Army-Navy Ballistic Missile Committee
JANC..........	Junior Army and Navy Club [*British*] (DSUE)
JANCOM	Joint Army-Navy Communications
JANCWR	Joint Army and Navy Committee on Welfare and Recreation
J & A	Justification and Approval [*Army*]
J&A	Justification and Approval (AAGC)
J & B	Justerini and Brooks [*Scotch*]
J & C	Jones and Cary's Irish Exchequer Reports [*1838-39*] [*A publication*] (DLA)
J & D	June and December [*Denotes semiannual payments of interest or dividends in these months*] [*Business term*]
J & E	Jehovistic and Elohistic [*Theology*]
J & F	Job and Function [*Air Force*] (AAG)
J & H	Johnson and Hemming's English Vice-Chancellors' Reports [*A publication*] (DLA)
J & H Hind L...	Johnson and Houghton's Institutes of Hindoo Law [*A publication*] (DLA)
J & J	January and July [*Denotes semiannual payments of interest or dividends in these months*] [*Business term*]
J & J	Johnson and Johnson [*Commercial firm*] (DAVI)
J & J Sn.......	J & J Snack Foods Corp. [*Associated Press*] (SAG)
J & K	All India Reporter, Jammu and Kashmir [*A publication*] (DLA)
J & L	Jones and La Touche's Irish Chancery Reports [*A publication*] (DLA)
J & La T.......	Jones and La Touche's Irish Chancery Reports [*A publication*] (DLA)
J & L SpSt...	J & L Specialty Steel [*Associated Press*] (SAG)
J & P	Joannou & Paraskevaides [*Construction company*] [*British*]
J & P	Joists and Planks [*Technical drawings*]
J & P	Journal and Proceedings [*Australia A publication*]
J & P	Justice and Peace [*An association Scotland*] (EAIO)
J & Proc Aust Chem Inst...	Journal and Proceedings. Australian Chemical Institute. [*A publication*]
J & Proc Roy Soc WA...	Journal and Proceedings. Royal Society of Western Australia [*A publication*]
J & S	Jebb and Symes' Irish Queen's Bench Reports [*A publication*] (DLA)
J & S	Jones and Spencer's Superior Court Reports [*33-61 New York*] [*A publication*] (DLA)
J & S	Judah and Swan's Jamaica Reports [*1839*] [*A publication*] (DLA)
J & S Jam ...	Judah and Swan's Jamaica Reports [*1839*] [*A publication*] (DLA)
J & V	Jones and Varick's Laws of New York [*A publication*] (DLA)
J & W	Jacob and Walker's English Chancery Reports [*A publication*] (DLA)
J & WO........	Jettison and Washing Overboard
JANE..........	Joint Air Force-Navy Experiment (MUGU)
JANE..........	Journalists Against Nuclear Extermination [*British*] (DI)
JANET.........	Joint Academic Network [*Proposed supercomputer network*]
JANET.........	Joint Army-Navy Experimental and Testing Board
JANET.........	Just Another Network [*University of Waterloo*] [*Canada*]
Janex..........	Janex International, Inc. [*Associated Press*] (SAG)
JANFU	Joint Army-Navy Foul Up [*Military slang*] [*Bowdlerized version*]
JANGO	Junior Army-Navy Guild Organization [*Organization of teenage daughters of military officers, who helped out in war work*] [*World War II*]
JANGRID......	Joint Army-Navy Grid System [*NATO*]
JANIC.........	Joint Army-Navy Information Center
JANIS.........	Joint Army-Navy Intelligence Studies
JANMAT.......	Joint Army-Navy Machine Tools Committee (AAG)
JANMAT.......	Joint Army-Navy Material
JANMB........	Joint Army and Navy Munitions Board [*Terminated, 1947*]

JANNAF.......	Joint-Army-Navy-NASA-Air Force Interagency Propulsion Committee (MCD)
JANNF.........	Jannock Ltd. [*NASDAQ symbol*] (SAG)
Jannock........	Jannock Ltd. [*Associated Press*] (SAG)
JANOT........	Joint Army-Navy Ocean Terminal
JANP..........	Joint Army-Navy Procedure
JANP..........	Joint Army-Navy Publication
JANPPA.......	Joint Army-Navy Petroleum Purchase Agency
JANS..........	Jet Aircraft Noise Survey
JANS..........	Joint Army-Navy Specification (IAA)
JANSA.........	Janatorial Supplies Association (BUAC)
JANSPEC.....	Joint Army-Navy Specification
JANSRP.......	Jet Aircraft Noise Survey Research Program
JANSTD.......	Joint Army-Navy Standard [*NATO*] (NATG)
JANSX........	Janus Fund [*Mutual fund ticker symbol*] (SG)
JANTA.........	Journal of the Australian Natural Therapists Association [*A publication*]
JANTAB.......	Joint Army and Navy Technical Aeronautical Board
JANTRL.......	Janitorial
JANTX........	Joint Army-Navy Tested Extra
JANUS........	Joint Analog Numeric Understanding System
JANV..........	Janvier [*January*] [*French*]
JANWSA......	Joint Army-Navy War Shipping Administration
JANX..........	Janex International, Inc. [*NASDAQ symbol*] (SAG)
JANX..........	Janex Intl. [*NASDAQ symbol*] (TTSB)
JANXW	Janex Intl. Wrrt [*NASDAQ symbol*] (TTSB)
JANY..........	January (ROG)
JAO............	Joint Area of Operations (DOMA)
JAO............	Prospect Heights Public Library District, Prospect Heights, IL [*OCLC symbol*] (OCLC)
JAOC..........	Joint Air Operations Center [*Air Force*]
JAp............	Against Apion [*Josephus*] (BJA)
JAP............	G. D. Searle & Co., Inc., Skokie, IL [*OCLC symbol*] (OCLC)
JAP............	Jamaica American Party [*Political party*] (BUAC)
JAP............	Japan (KSC)
Jap............	Japan (VRA)
Jap............	Japanese (ODBW)
JAP............	Japanese (ROG)
jap	Japanned [*Finished with a hard, glossy varnish*] (BARN)
JAP............	Japan Photo [*Norway*] [*FAA designator*] (FAAC)
JAP............	J. A. Prestwick [*British auto and motorcycle engine maker*]
JAP............	Jerusalem Academic Press (BJA)
JAP............	Jewish Agency for Palestine
JAP............	Jewish-American Princess [*Slang*]
JAP............	Joint Acceptance Plan (AAG)
JAP............	Joint Apprenticeship Program [*Department of Labor*]
JAP............	Judicial Appointments Project (EA)
JAP............	Juntas de Accao Patriotica [*Patriotic Action Boards*] [*Portuguese Political party*] (PPE)
JAP............	Jupiter Atmospheric Probe
JAP............	Juventudes de Accion Popular [*Spanish*] (PPE)
JAPA..........	Jane Addams Peace Association (EA)
JAPA..........	Japan Aircraft Pilots Association (BUAC)
JAPA..........	Japan Area
JAPACS.......	Japanese Pacific Climate Study [*Marine science*] (OSRA)
JAPACS.......	Japanese Pacific Ocean Climate Studies (USDC)
Japan Ann L & Pol...	Japan Annual of Law and Politics [*A publication*] (DLA)
JAPANMEC...	Japan International Measuring and Control Industry Show
JapARE.......	Japanese Antarctic Research Expedition [*1956-*]
JAPATIC......	Japan Patient Information Center [*Information service or system*] (IID)
JAPC..........	Joint Air Photo Center [*NATO*] (NATG)
JAPCO........	Jamestown Paint & Varnish Co.
JAPCO........	Japan Atomic Power Co.
JAPCo.........	Japan Atomic Power Company (BUAC)
JAPEX........	Japan Petroleum Exploration Co. (BUAC)
JAPIA.........	Japan Auto Parts Industries Association
JAPIC.........	Japan Pharmaceutical Information Center [*Tokyo*] [*Information service or system*] (IID)
JAPIO.........	Japan Patent Information Organization [*Database producer*]
JAPIT.........	Japanese Association for the Promotion of International Trade (EY)
JAPN..........	Japan Air Lines Co. Ltd. [*NASDAQ symbol*] (NQ)
JapnAr........	Japan Airlines [*Associated Press*] (SAG)
JapnAr........	Japan Airlines Co. Ltd. [*Associated Press*] (SAG)
JapnEq........	[*The*] Japan Equity Fund, Inc. [*Associated Press*] (SAG)
JAPNY	Japan Airlines Co. Ltd ADR [*NASDAQ symbol*] (TTSB)
JAPO..........	Joint Area Petroleum Office
JAPOS........	JAPOS Study Group [*Defunct*] (EA)
JAPOS	Journalists, Authors and Poets on Stamps Study Unit (EA)
JAPP..........	Japanese Patent (IAA)
Jap P..........	[*The*] Pharmacopoeia of Japan [*A publication*]
JAPRRCC.....	Japan Authors' and Publishers' Reprographic Rights Clearance Centre (BUAC)
JAPRW	Japanese Association of Photosynthesis Research Workers (BUAC)
JAPS..........	Japanese American Philatelic Society [*Later, JASP*]
JAPS..........	Joint Administrative Planning Section [*Joint Planning Staff*] [*World War II*]
JAPSS.........	Joint Automated Planning Support System [*of JOPS*] [*Military*]
JAQ............	Jacquinot Bay [*Papua New Guinea*] [*Airport symbol*] (OAG)
JAQ............	Job Activities Questionnaire
JAQ............	Passionist Academic Institute, Chicago, IL [*OCLC symbol*] (OCLC)
JAR............	Airlink Luftverkehrsgesellschaft GmbH [*Austria ICAO designator*] (FAAC)
JAR............	Jamming Avoidance Response
JAR............	Jargon (WDAA)
JAR............	J. Arthur Rank [*Motion picture company in England*]
JAR............	Java Archive [*Computer science*] (IGQR)
JAR............	JavaSoft Java Archive [*Computer science*]
JAr............	Jewish Aramaic (BJA)
JAR............	Jewish Autonomous Region [*Eastern Siberia*]
JAR............	Jews for Animal Rights (EA)
JAR............	Job Appraisal Review (PDAA)
JAR............	Joint Airworthiness Requirements (MCD)
JAR............	Joint Aviation Requirement [*FAA*] (TAG)
JAR............	Journal of Advertising Research [*Advertising Research Foundation*] [*A publication*]
JAR............	Jump Address Register
JAR............	Junior Admitting Resident [*Medicine*] (DAVI)
JAR............	Justice Acquisition Regulation [*A publication*] (AAGC)
JAR............	Zion-Benton Library District, Zion, IL [*OCLC symbol*] (OCLC)
JARA..........	Japan Antibiotics Research Association (BUAC)
Jar & By Conv...	Jarman and Bythewood's Conveyancing [*A publication*] (DLA)
JARB..........	Joint Acquisition Review Board [*Army*]
JARC..........	Jewish Association for Retarded Citizens (EA)
JARC..........	Joint Air Reconnaissance Center [*NATO*] (NATG)
JARCC........	Joint Air Reconnaissance Coordination Center [*Military*] (MCD)
Jar Chy Pr...	Jarman's Chancery Practice [*A publication*] (DLA)
Jar Cr Tr...	Jardine's Criminal Trials [*A publication*] (DLA)
JARD..........	Jardines
JardFICh......	Jardine Fleming China Region [*Associated Press*] (SAG)
Jard Ind......	Jardine's Index to Howell's State Trials [*A publication*] (DLA)
JARE..........	Japanese Antarctic Research Expedition [*1956-*]
JARI..........	Japan Automobile Research Institute
JARI..........	Japan Automotive Research Institute
JARI..........	Japanese Association of Railway Industries (BUAC)
JARI..........	Jute Agricultural Research Institute [*India*] (BUAC)
JARIB.........	Joint Air Reconnaissance Intelligence Board [*Australia*]
JARIC.........	Joint Aerial Reconnaissance Interpretation Center (MCD)
JARIC.........	Joint Air Reconnaissance Intelligence Centre [*British*]
JARL..........	Japan Amateur Radio League (BUAC)
Jar Pow Dev...	Jarman's Edition of Powell on Devises [*A publication*] (DLA)
JARRP.........	Japan Association for Radiation Research on Polymers
JARS..........	Alltrista Corp. [*NASDAQ symbol*] (SAG)
JARS..........	Job Accounting Report System (MHDI)
JARS..........	Journalization and Recovery System (PDAA)
JARTRAN.....	James A. Ryder Transportation [*Acronym is trade name of truck-rental firm*]
JARTS.........	Japan Railway Technical Service (BUAC)
Jar Wills......	Jarman on Wills [*8 eds.*] [*1841-51*] [*A publication*] (DLA)
JAS............	Jamaica Agricultural Society (BUAC)
Jas............	James [*New Testament book*]
JAS............	Jamestown [*California*] [*Seismograph station code, US Geological Survey*] (SEIS)
JAS	Jane Austen Society [*Basingstoke, Hampshire, England*] (EAIO)
JAS	Japan Air System Co. Ltd. [*ICAO designator*] (FAAC)
JAS	Japan Association of Shipbuilders (BUAC)
JAS	Jasper, TX [*Location identifier FAA*] (FAAL)
JAS	Jazz Arts Society
JAS	Jenkins Activity Survey [*Personality development test*] [*Psychology*]
JAS	Jewish Agricultural Society (EA)
JAS	Job Accounting System
JAS	Job Activity Survey
JAS	Job Analysis Schedule [*Department of Labor*]
JAS	Job Analysis System [*Computer program*]
JAS	Job Attitude Scale [*Employment test*]
JAS	Johnny Alfalfa Sprout [*Defunct*] (EA)
JAS	Joint Administration Services
JAS	Joint Airmiss Section [*Aviation*] (DA)
JAS	Joint Association Survey [*American Petroleum Institute, Independent Petroleum Association of America, and Mid-Continent Oil and Gas Association*]
JAS	Journal Access Service [*Center for Research Libraries*]
JAS	Journal of Aerospace Science [*A publication*] (NAKS)
JAS	Journal of Asian Studies [*A publication*] (BRI)
JAS	Journal of Atmospheric Sciences [*A publication*] (SSD)
JAS	Journals Access Service [*Center for Research Libraries*]
J As	Judicial Assessor [*Ghana*] [*A publication*] (DLA)
JAS	Junior Astronomical Society (EAIO)
JAS	Juvenile Ankylosing Spondylitis [*Medicine*] (DMAA)
JAS	Lake Villa District Library, Lake Villa, IL [*OCLC symbol*] (OCLC)
JAS-1.........	Japan Amateur Satellite-1
JASA..........	Jewish Association for Services for the Aged (EA)
JASA..........	Jo-Ann Stores ™A∫ [*Formerly, Fabri-Centers Amer. "B"*] [*NYSE symbol*]
JASA..........	Joint Antisubmarine Action
JASA..........	Junior Assistant Stores Accountant [*British military*] (DMA)
JASAP........	Julie [*Sonobuoy System*] Automatic Search and Attack Plotter [*Navy*] (MCD)
JASAR........	Jittered and Swept Active RADAR
JASASA......	Joint Air-Surface Antisubmarine Action
JASB..........	Jo-Ann Stores ™B∫ [*Formerly, Fabri-Centers Amer. "A"*] [*NYSE symbol*]
JASB..........	Joint Advisory Survey Board [*British*]
JASC..........	Japan-America Student Conference (EA)
JASC..........	Japan Asia Sea Cable
JASC..........	JPL [*Jet Propulsion Laboratory*] Astronautical Star Catalog (KSC)
JASCO........	Joint Assault Signal Co. [*Small unit in Pacific amphibious warfare*] [*World War II*]
JASDA........	Julie [*Sonobuoy System*] Automatic Sonic Data Analyzer [*Navy*]
JASDF........	Japanese Air Self-Defense Force

JASG............	Joint Advanced Study Group
JASGP........	Joint Advanced Study Group
JASIN..........	Joint Air Sea Interaction [*National Science Foundation/United Kingdom*]
JASIN.........	Joint Air-Sea Interaction Program [*Global Atmospheric Research Program*] (USDC)
JASLS........	Japanese American Society for Legal Studies (EA)
JASMMM....	Joint Aviation Supply and Maintenance Material Management (DNAB)
JASMU........	Journal pour l'Avancement des Soins Medicaux d'Urgence [*A publication*]
JASN...........	Jason, Inc. [*NASDAQ symbol*] (NQ)
JASNA	Jane Austen Society of North America (EA)
Jason...........	Jason, Inc. [*Associated Press*] (SAG)
JASORS........	Joint Advanced Special Operations Radio System [*Military*] (RDA)
JASP...........	Japanese American Society for Philately (EA)
JASPA........	Jesuit Association of Student Personnel Administrators (EA)
JASPA.........	Jobs and Skills Programme for Africa (BUAC)
JASPER.......	Joint Academic Services Providers to Education and Research (AIE)
JASPR	Jasper [*Gem*] (ROG)
JASR............	JTPA [*Job Training and Partnership Act*] Annual Status Report (OICC)
JASS...........	Joint Antisatellite Study
JASS...........	Joint Anti-Submarine School [*British military*] (DMA)
JASS...........	JUMPS [*Joint Uniform Military Pay System*] Automated Support System [*or Supplemental*] [*Military*]
JASS-AC	JUMPS [*Joint Uniform Military Pay System*] Automated Supplemental System-Active Component [*Military*]
JASSC..........	Japan-America Society of Southern California
JASSCC.......	Japan Academic Society System for Copyright Clearance (BUAC)
JASSM........	Joint Acoustic Surveillance System Model [*Military*] (CAAL)
J Ass'n L Teachers...	Journal. Association of Law Teachers [*A publication*] (DLA)
J Assoc L Teachers...	Journal. Association of Law Teachers [*A publication*] (DLA)
JASS-RC	JUMPS [*Joint Uniform Military Pay System*] Automated Support System - Reserve Corps
JAST............	Jamaican Association of Sugar Technologists (BUAC)
JAST............	Jazz Action Society of Tasmania
JAST............	Joint Advanced Strike Technology [*Program*] [*Air Force*] [*Navy*] (DOMA)
JAST............	Joint Air Support Tactics [*Military*]
JASTD........	Junior Assistant Steward [*British military*] (DMA)
JASTOP.......	Jet Assist Stop
JASU...........	Jet Aircraft Starting Unit (AFM)
JASW...........	Japan-America Society of Washington (EA)
JAT	Jabat [*Marshall Islands*] [*Airport symbol*] (OAG)
JAT	Jam Angle Tracking
JAT	Job Accounting Table
JAT	Joint Agency Training
JAT	Jugoslovenski Aerotransport [*Yugoslav Air Transport*] [*ICAO designator*]
JAT	Junior Aptitude Tests [*Educational test*]
JAT	Mennonite Hospital, Health Sciences Library, Bloomington, IL [*OCLC symbol*] (OCLC)
JATAN........	Japan Tropical Rainforest Action Network
JATC...........	Japan Association for Tissue Culture (BUAC)
JATC...........	Joint Apprenticeship and Training Committee [*Bureau of Apprenticeship and Training*] [*Department of Labor*]
JATCC.........	Joint Air Traffic Control Center [*Military*]
JATCC.........	Joint Aviation Telecommunications Coordination Committee (BUAC)
JATCCCP......	Joint Advanced Tactical Command, Control, and Communications Program [*Military*]
JATCCCS......	Joint Advanced Tactical Command, Control, and Communications System [*Military*] (MCD)
JATCCS........	Joint Advanced Tactical Command and Control System [*Military*] (SAA)
JATCO..........	Japan Automatic Transmission Co.
JATE	Joint Air Transport Establishment [*Military British*]
JATEC.........	Japan Technical Committee to Aid US Anti-War Deserter (BUAC)
JATES.........	Japan Techno-Economics Society (EA)
JATF	Joint Amphibious Task Force (NVT)
JATLA.........	Journal. American Trial Lawyers Association [*A publication*] (DLA)
JATM...........	Joint Antitactical Missile System (Provisional) [*Army*] (RDA)
JATMA........	Japan Automobile Tire Manufacturers Association
J Atmos Sci...	Journal of Atmospheric Science (MEC)
JATO...........	Jet-Assisted Takeoff
JATP...........	Jazz at the Philharmonic
JATP...........	Joint Air Training Plan
JATP...........	Joint Air Transportation Plan (AABC)
JATS...........	Joint Air Transportation Service
JAU.............	American Hospital Supply Corp., Evanston, IL [*OCLC symbol*] (OCLC)
JAU.............	Jacksboro, TN [*Location identifier FAA*] (FAAL)
JAUN	Jaundice [*Medicine*]
JAUND........	Jaundice [*Medicine*]
J Aust Stud...	Journal of Australian Studies [*A publication*]
J Aus War M...	Journal. Australian War Memorial [*A publication*]
JAUW..........	Japanese Association of Unversity Women (BUAC)
JAV.............	Chicago, IL [*Location identifier FAA*] (FAAL)
JAV.............	Dr. William M. Scholl College of Podiatric Medicine, Chicago, IL [*OCLC symbol*] (OCLC)
JAV.............	Janes Aviation Ltd. [*British ICAO designator*] (FAAC)
JAV.............	Java
jav	Javanese [*MARC language code Library of Congress*] (LCCP)
Jav.............	Javolenus Priscus [*Flourished, 60-120*] [*Authority cited in pre-1607 legal work*] (DSA)
JAV.............	Job Analysis Vocabulary (OICC)
JAVA	Jamaica Association of Villas and Apartments [*Later, JRJ*]
JAVA	Jamming Amplitude Versus Azimuth (NVT)
JAVA	Jandel Video Analysis System
JavaCt	Java Centrale, Inc. [*Associated Press*] (SAG)
JavaCtrl	Java Centrale, Inc. [*Associated Press*] (SAG)
JAVC	Java Centrale [*NASDAQ symbol*] (TTSB)
JAVC	Java Centrale, Inc. [*NASDAQ symbol*] (SAG)
JAVCF	Japan Australia Venture Capital Fund
Javelin........	Javelin Systems, Inc. [*Associated Press*] (SAG)
JAVIC.........	Japan Audio-Visual Information Centre (BUAC)
JAVLX........	Janus Twenty Fund [*Mutual fund ticker symbol*] (SG)
Javole........	Javolenus Priscus [*Flourished, 60-120*] [*Authority cited in pre-1607 legal work*] (DSA)
JAVS	JOVIAL Automated Verification System (MCD)
JAVTX........	Janus Venture Fund [*Mutual fund ticker symbol*] (SG)
JAW	Jamahiriya Airways [*Libya*] [*ICAO designator*] (FAAC)
JAW	Standard Oil Co. (Indiana), Central Research Library, Naperville, IL [*OCLC symbol*] (OCLC)
JAWC	Joint Animal Welfare Council (BUAC)
JAWF	Jet Augmented Wing Flap
JAWF	Joint Agriculture Weather Facility [*Marine science*] (OSRA)
JAWG	Joint Airmiss Working Group (BUAC)
JAWPB........	Joint Atomic Weapons Publications Board (AABC)
JAWPM........	Joint Atomic Weapons Planning Manual (AFM)
JAWPS	Joint Atomic Weapons Publication System
JAWS	Jamming and Warning System (MCD)
JAWS	Japan Animal Welfare Society [*London, England*]
JAWS	Jet Advance Warning System (PDAA)
JAWS	Joint Action for Water Services (BUAC)
JAWS	Joint Airport Weather Studies [*National Center for Atmospheric Research*]
JAWS	Joint Arctic Weather Stations [*Canada-US*]
JAWS	Joint Attack Weapon System [*Military*] (MCD)
JAWS	Josephson AttoWeber Switch [*Data processor circuitry*]
JAWS	Junk Acronyms When Speaking [*Program*]
JAWS	Just Another Work Station [*Jargon*] (NITA)
JAWTR	Junior Assistant Writer [*British military*] (DMA)
JAWYS	Join Airways (FAAC)
JAX	Chicago School of Professional Psychology, Chicago, IL [*OCLC symbol*] (OCLC)
JAX	Jacksonville [*Florida*] [*Airport symbol*] (OAG)
JAX	JanAir, Inc. [*ICAO designator*] (FAAC)
JAX	Mister Jax Fashions, Inc. [*Toronto Stock Exchange symbol*]
JAY	J & J Air Charters Ltd. [*British ICAO designator*] (FAAC)
JAY	Jayapura [*Indonesia*] [*Seismograph station code, US Geological Survey*] (SEIS)
JAY	Travenol Laboratories, Morton Grove, IL [*OCLC symbol*] (OCLC)
JAYA	Jayark Corp. [*NASDAQ symbol*] (NQ)
Jayark........	Jayark Corp. [*Associated Press*] (SAG)
Jayhwk.......	Jayhawk Acceptance Corp. [*Associated Press*] (SAG)
JAYJ	Jay Jacobs [*NASDAQ symbol*] (TTSB)
JAYJ	Jay Jacobs, Inc. [*NASDAQ symbol*] (NQ)
JAYT	Jacobs [*Jay*], Inc. (MHDW)
JAZ	Japan Air Charter Co. Ltd. [*ICAO designator*] (FAAC)
JB	IML Air Services Ltd. [*British ICAO designator*] (ICDA)
Jb	Jaarboek [*Yearbook*] [*Netherlands*] (BJA)
JB	Jahrbuch [*Yearbook*] [*German*]
JB	James Boswell [*Initials used as pseudonym*]
JB	James Buchanan [*US president, 1791-1868*]
JB	Jerusalem Bible
J-B	Jet Barrier
JB	Jet Black [*Derogatory nickname for a black person*]
JB	Jet Bomb
JB	Jiffy Bag
JB	Job (MCD)
Jb	Job [*Old Testament book*]
JB	Job Bank (OICC)
JB	Job Book
JB	Joggle Blocks (MCD)
JB	Johannes Baptista [*John the Baptist*] [*Authority cited in pre-1607 legal work*] (DSA)
JB	John Bull [*The typical Englishman*]
JB	Johore Bahru [*Refers to Europeans named after Malaysian towns*] (DSUE)
JB	Joint Army-Navy Board
JB	Joint Bond
JB	Juggle Box
JB	Jukeboxes [*Public-performance tariff class*] [*British*]
JB	Jump If Below [*Computer science*] (PCM)
JB	Junction Box [*Technical drawings*]
JB	Junior Beadle [*Ancient Order of Foresters*]
JB	Junior Birdman [*Slang*]
JB	Junior Bookshelf [*A publication*] (BRI)
JB	Juris Baccalaureus [*Bachelor of Laws*]
JB	Lakeside Laboratories, Inc. [*Research code symbol*]
JB	Pioneer Airways [*ICAO designator*] (AD)
JB	Stetson Hat [*After John Batterson Stetson, 19th-century American hat manufacturer*] [*Slang*]
JBA.............	Helijet Airways [*Canada ICAO designator*] (FAAC)
JBA.............	Japan Bankers Association (BUAC)
JBA.............	Japanese Bioindustry Association (BUAC)
JBA.............	Jewel Bearing Assembly
JBA.............	John Burroughs Association (EA)
JBA.............	Junction Box Assembly
JBA.............	Junior Bluejackets of America (EA)

JBAA	Journal of the British Archaeological Association [A publication] (WDAA)
JBAFC	Jan Berry and the Alohas Fan Club (EA)
JBAK	Baker [J.], Inc. [NASDAQ symbol] (NQ)
JBAKC	John Brown Anti-Klan Committee (EA)
JBANC	Joint Baltic American National Committee (EA)
J-Bar	Jet Runway Barrier [Aviation] (FAAC)
JBAS	Jussi Bjorling Appreciation Society [British] (DBA)
JBBF	Judo Black Belt Federation [Later, USJE]
JBBFC	James Bond British Fan Club (EAIO)
JBBL	Jamming of Beacons and Blind Landing [Aviation] (IAA)
JBC	Jamaica Broadcasting Corp.
JBC	Japanese Broadcasting Corporation (BUAC)
JBC	[The] Jerome Biblical Commentary [Englewood Cliffs, NJ] [A publication] (BJA)
JBC	Jesness Behavior Checklist [Psychology] (DAVI)
JBC	Jewelers' Book Club (EA)
JBC	Jewish Book Council [of the National Jewish Welfare Board] [Later, JWBJBC] (EA)
JBC	Johnson Bible College [Tennessee]
JBC	Joint Blood Council [Defunct] (EA)
JBC	Joint Budget Committee (OICC)
JBC	Journal. State Bar of California [A publication] (DLA)
JBCPS	Journeyman Bakers' and Confectioners Pension Society [British] (BI)
JBCS	James Branch Cabell Society (EA)
JBCSA	Joint British Committee for Stress Analysis (BUAC)
JBD	Becton, Dickinson & Co., Paramus, NJ [OCLC symbol] (OCLC)
JBD	James Brake [Aviation] (DA)
JBD	Jet Blast Deflector
JBD	Jewish Board of Deputies [Australia]
JBDAAFES	Joint Board of Directors, Army-Air Force Exchange Service (AABC)
JBDFC	James Bond 007 Fan Club [Defunct] (EA)
JBE	Japanese B Encephalitis [Medicine]
JBE	Jump If Below or Equal [Computer science] (PCM)
Jber	Jahresbericht [Journal, Annual Report] [German] (BJA)
JBES	Jodrell Bank Experimental Station [British]
JBF	James Beard Foundation (EA)
JBF	James Buchanan Foundation (EA)
JBF	Japan Booksellers' Federation (BUAC)
JBF	Jeune Ballet de France
JBFC	James Bond 007 Fan Club [British] (EAIO)
JBFC	Jennifer Bassey Fan Club (EA)
JBFC	Jennifer Burnett Fan Club (EA)
JBFC	Johnny Bernard Fan Club (EA)
JBFCI	Jon Beryl Fan Club International (EA)
JBFLP	Journal of Banking and Finance Law and Practice [A publication]
JBFSAW	Joint Board on Future Storage of Atomic Weapons
JBG	Jewish Board of Guardians (EA)
JBHCPIUA	Journeymen Barbers, Hairdressers, Cosmetologists and Proprietors' International Union of America (EA)
JBHT	Hunt(JB)Transport [NASDAQ symbol] (TTSB)
JBHT	Hunt [J. B.] Transport Services, Inc. [NASDAQ symbol] (NQ)
JBI	Jacob Blaustein Institute for the Advancement of Human Rights (EA)
JBI	Jamaica Bauxite Institute (BUAC)
JBI	Jewish Braille Institute of America (EA)
JBIA	Jewish Braille Institute of America (EA)
JBIC	Journal of Biological Inorganic Chemistry [A publication]
JBIL	Jabil Circuit [NASDAQ symbol] (TTSB)
JBIL	Jabil Circuit, Inc. [NASDAQ symbol] (SAG)
Jb Int R	Jahrbuch fuer Internationales und Auslaendisches Oeffentliches Recht [1948-] [A publication German] (ILCA)
JBJ	Bellum Judaicum [Josephus] [Classical studies] (BJA)
JBJ	James Bond Journalism [Term coined by leader Sinnathamby Bajaratman of Singapore and referring to Western journalism]
JBK	Berkeley, CA [Location identifier FAA] (FAAL)
JBL	James B. Lansing Sound, Inc.
JBL	Jonesboro, LA [Location identifier FAA] (FAAL)
JBL	Journal of Biblical Literature [A publication] (BRI)
JBL	Jubilee
JBL	Junior Bird League [British] (BI)
J/BLK	Junction Block [Automotive engineering]
J Bl St	Journal of Black Studies [A publication] (BRI)
JBM	Jan Bell Marketing [AMEX symbol] (TTSB)
JBM	Jan Bell Marketing, Inc. [AMEX symbol] (SPSG)
JBMA	John Burroughs Memorial Association (EA)
JBMI	Journalist Biographies Master Index [A publication]
JBMTO	Joint Bus Military Traffic Office (AABC)
JBNC	Jefferson Bancorp (FL) [NASDAQ symbol] (TTSB)
JBNC	Jefferson Bancorp, Inc. [NASDAQ symbol] (NQ)
JBNK	Jefferson Bankshares, Inc. [NASDAQ symbol] (NQ)
JBOD	Just a Bunch of Disks [Computer science]
JBOH	Oxford [J. B.] Oxford Holdings [NASDAQ symbol] (SAG)
JBOR	Job Bank Operations Review [Employment and Training Administration] [Department of Labor]
JBOS	Job Banks Opening Summary [Department of Labor]
JB Oxfrd	JB Oxford Holdings [Associated Press] (SAG)
JBP	Jettison Booster Package [NASA]
JBP	John B. Pierce Foundation Laboratory [New Haven, CT]
JBP	Joint Blood Program (COE)
JBP	Junior Bowhunter Program (EA)
JBPA	Japan Book Publishers Association (BUAC)
JBPO	Joint Blood Program Office (DOMA)
JBPVE	Joint Board for Pre-Vocational Education (BUAC)
JBR	Job Air Ltd. [Czechoslovakia] [FAA designator] (FAAC)
JBR	Jonesboro [Arkansas] [Airport symbol] (OAG)
JBR	Jonesboro, AR [Location identifier FAA] (FAAL)
J BRANNAM	Just Brand Names [Division of F. W. Woolworth Co.]
J Broadcst	Journal of Broadcasting and Electronic Media [A publication] (BRI)
JBS	Jane Badler Society (EA)
JBS	Japanese Biochemical Society (BUAC)
JBS	Jewish Burial Society [Australia]
JBS	Job Search [Job Training and Partnership Act] (OICC)
JBS	John Birch Society (EA)
JBS	Joly Black Screen
JBS	Josephine Butler Society (EAIO)
JBSS	Sanfilippo [John B.] & Son [NASDAQ symbol] (SPSG)
JBT	Bethel, AK [Location identifier FAA] (FAAL)
JBT	Jewelers Board of Trade (EA)
JBU	John Brown University [Siloam Springs, AR]
JBUSDC	Joint Brazil-United States Defense Commission [Terminated, 1977]
JBUSMC	Joint Brazil-United States Military Commission
JBV	Jolt Beverage Co. Ltd. [Vancouver Stock Exchange symbol]
JC	Community Colleges [Educational Resources Information Center (ERIC) Clearinghouse] [University of California at Los Angeles (UCLA)] (PAZ)
JC	Jack Connection [Electronics] (IAA)
JC	Jack Cover
JC	Jakob-Creutzfeldt [Disease or syndrome] [Neurology] (DAVI)
JC	Janitor Closet (MSA)
JC	Jayhawk Conference (PSS)
JC	J. C. Smith Marketing Corp. [Vancouver Stock Exchange symbol]
JC	Jeanswear Communication (EA)
JC	Jefferson City [Diocesan abbreviation] [Missouri] (TOCD)
JC	Jenny Craig [NYSE symbol] (SPSG)
JC	Jersey Central Railroad
JC	Jesus Christ
JC	Jesus College [Oxford or Cambridge] [England] (DAS)
JC	Jewish Care [British] (EAIO)
JC	[The] Jewish Community: Its History and Structure to the American Revolution [A publication] (BJA)
JC	Jimmy Carter [James Earl Carter, Jr.] [US president, 1924-]
JC	Job Center
JC	Job Club
JC	Job Corps [Department of Labor]
JC	Jockey Club [Later, TJC] (EA)
JC	Johnson's New York Cases [or Reports] [A publication] (DLA)
JC	Joint Compound [Plumbing]
JC	Joule Cycle [Physics]
J/C	Joule per Coulomb [Physics] (DAVI)
JC	Journal Citation (NITA)
JC	Journal Code [Online database field identifier]
JC	Journal Coden [Searchable fields] (NITA)
JC	Journalists' Club [Australia]
JC	Journal of Chromatography [A publication]
JC	Journal of Communication [A publication] (BRI)
JC	JOVIAL Compiler [Computer science]
Jc	Juglans cinerea [Butternut tree]
jc	Juice
JC	Juice
JC	Julius Caesar [Shakespearean work]
JC	Jump on Condition [Computer science] (BUR)
JC	Jump-to-Contact [Physics]
JC	Junction (ADA)
JC	Junction Center [Civil engineering] (IAA)
JC	Junior Chamber of Commerce (WDAA)
JC	Junior Clinicians [Medical students] (DAVI)
JC	Junior College
JC	Jurisconsult
JC	Just Compensation [Business term] (MHDB)
JC	Justice Clerk
JC	Justiciary Cases [Scotland] [A publication] (DLA)
JC	Juvenile Court
JC	Rocky Mountain Airways [ICAO designator] (AD)
JCA	Jamming Control Authority (NATG)
JCA	Japan Container Association (BUAC)
JCA	Javelin Class Association (EA)
JCA	Jetcom SA [Switzerland ICAO designator] (FAAC)
JCA	Jewelry Crafts Association [Later, JMA]
JCA	Jewish Ceremonial Art [A publication] (BJA)
JCA	Jewish Colonization Association [British]
JCA	Johnston(e) Clan in America (EA)
JCA	Joint Church Aid [Biafra relief program in late 1960's] [Defunct]
JCA	Joint Commission on Accreditation of Universities [Military]
JCA	Joint Communication Activity
JCA	Joint Communications Agency [Military]
JCA	Joint Construction Agency
JCA	Joint Cultural Appeal (EA)
JCA	Joint Custody Association (EA)
JCA	Junior Catering Accountant [British military] (DMA)
JCA	Juvenile Chronic Arthritis [Medicine] (DAVI)
JCAAI	Joint Council of Allergy, Asthma, and Immunology (NTPA)
JCAB	Japan Civil Aviation Bureau (MCD)
JCAC	Joint Civil Affairs Committee
JCACC	Joint Combat Airspace Command and Control Course (DOMA)
JCADIS	Joint Continental Aerospace Defense Integration Staff [Military] (AABC)
JCADR	Japan Centre for Area Development (BUAC)
JCAE	Joint Committee on Atomic Energy [of the US Congress] [Terminated]
JCAEC	Joint Congressional Atomic Energy Commission (MUGU)

JCAH............ Joint Commission on Accreditation of Hospitals [Later, JCAHO] (EA)
JCAHCA....... Joint Commission on Accreditation of Health Care Organizations
JCAHO .... Joint Commission on Accreditation of Healthcare Organizations [An association]
JCAHPO .... Joint Commission on Allied Health Personnel in Ophthalmology (EA)
JCAI............. Joint Council of Allergy and Immunology (EA)
JCALM......... Joint Committee on Aboriginal Lands and Mining [Australia]
JCALS.......... Joint Computer-Aided Acquisition and Logistic Support [DoD]
JCALS.......... Joint Computer-Aided Acquisition Logistics System [Army] (RDA)
JCAM........... Joint Commission on Atomic Masses
JCAN........... Jewish Children's Adoption Network (EA)
J Can B........ Juris Canna Baccalaureus [Bachelor of Canon Law]
J Cancer Res Comm... Journal. Cancer Research Committee. University of Sydney [A publication]
J Can D .... Juris Canna Doctor [Doctor of Canon Law]
J Can M...... Juris Canna Magister [Master of Canon Law]
JCAP............ Joint Committee on Aviation Pathology [BUAC]
JCAP............ Joint Conventional Ammunition Program [Army]
JCAP............ Joint Coordinated Ammunition Production (MCD)
JCAP-CG ..... Joint Conventional Ammunition Program Coordinating Group [Army]
JCAR............ Joint Commission on Applied Radioactivity
J card .... Jacket Card [A printed card inside the box holding a cassette tape or compact disc] (WDMC)
JCARD .... Joint Committee on Agricultural Research and Development [Agency for International Development]
JCarlFut....... Jack Carl/312 Futures, Inc. [Associated Press] (SAG)
J Car P & E... Journal of Career Planning and Employment [A publication] (BRI)
JCAT .... Joint Crisis Action Team [Environmental science] (COE)
J Catal......... Journal of Catalysis (MEC)
J-CATCH ..... Joint Countering Attack Helicopter Exercises (RDA)
JCA-USA...... Joint Church Aid - United States of America [See also JCA] [Defunct] (EA)
JCB .... Japan Convention Bureau (EA)
JCB .... J. C. Bamford Excavators [British]
JCB .... Joacaba [Brazil] [Airport symbol] (AD)
JCB .... Job Control Block [Computer science] (BUR)
JCB .... Joint Coal Board (BUAC)
JCB .... Joint Communications Board
JCB .... Joint Computer Bureau [Office of Population Census and Surveys] [British]
JCB .... Joint Consultative Board [NATO] (NATG)
JCB .... Joseph Cyril Bamford (WDAA)
JCB .... Juris Canonici Baccalaureus [Bachelor of Canon Law]
JCB .... Juris Civilis Baccalaureus [Bachelor of Civil Law]
JCBA............ Jewish Conciliation Board of America (EA)
JCBC............ Joint Committee on Building Codes [Later, Model Code Standardization Council] (EA)
JCBC............ Jute Carpet Backing Council (EA)
JCBMI.......... Joint Committee for the British Memorial Industry (DBA)
JCBS............ Jacobson Stores, Inc. [NASDAQ symbol] (NQ)
JCBSF.......... Joint Commission for Black Sea Fisheries
JCBSSA........ Jersey Cattle Breeders Society of South Africa (BUAC)
JCC .... Jamestown Community College [New York]
JCC .... Janney Cylinder Co.
JCC .... Japanese Chamber of Commerce of New York [Later, JCCINY] (EA)
JCC .... Jarvis Christian College [Hawkins, TX]
JCC .... Jarvis Christian College, Hawkins, TX [OCLC symbol] (OCLC)
JCC .... Jesus College, Cambridge [England] (ROG)
JCC .... Jet Circulation Control
JCC .... Jewish Chaplains Council (EA)
JCC .... Jewish Community Center
JCC .... Jharkhand Coordination Committee [Jharkhand Samanvaya Samiti] [India] [Political party]
JCC .... Jilin Chemical Inc ADS [NYSE symbol] (TTSB)
JCC .... Jilin Chemical Industrial Co. Ltd. [NYSE symbol] (SAG)
JCC .... Job Control Card (MCD)
JCC .... Job Corps Camp [Department of Labor]
JCC .... Joint Committee on Contraception (DMAA)
JCC .... Joint Communications Center (MCD)
JCC .... Joint Computer Conference
JCC .... Joint Consultative Committee [of the National Joint Advisory Council] [British World War II]
JCC .... Joint Consultative Council of the Fresh Fruit and Vegetable Industry (BUAC)
JCC .... Joint Control Center (MCD)
JCC .... Joint Coordination Center (NVT)
JCC .... Jowett Car Club (EA)
JCC .... Junior Chamber of Commerce
JCC .... Junior Command Course [British military] (DMA)
JCC .... San Francisco [California] China Bas [Airport symbol] (OAG)
JCCA........... Japanese Canadian Citizens' Association
JCCA........... Japanese Chin Club of America (EA)
JCCA........... Jewish Community Centers Association of North America (NTPA)
JCCA........... Joint CONEX [Container Express] Control Agency
JCCANA ...... Jewish Community Centers Association of North America (EA)
JCCB........... Joint Configuration Control Board [DoD]
JCCBI.......... Joint Committee for the Conservation of British Insects (BUAC)
JCCBI.......... Joint Committee for the Conservation of British Invertebrates (BUAC)
JCCC........... Japanese Canadian Citizens' Council
JCCC........... Joint Committee on Contemporary China (EA)
JCCC........... Joint Communications Control Center (COE)
JCCC........... Joint COMSEC Coordination Center (MCD)
JCCC........... Joint Configuration Control Committee [DoD]
JCCD........... Japanese Canadian Committee for Democracy
JCCDG .... Joint Command and Control Development Group [DoD]

JCCEM .... Joint Committee of Cultural and Education Ministers [Australia]
JCCEP .... Joint Crisis Communications Exercise Program (MCD)
JCCF........... Jamaica Combined Cadet Force (BUAC)
JCCFC .... June Carter Cash Fan Club (EA)
JCCFE .... Joint Coordination Center, Far East [Military] (CINC)
JCCFEP........ Joint Commission on Cooperation in the Field of Environmental Protection [US-USSR] [Marine science] (OSRA)
JCC-FPM...... Joint Coordinating Committee on Fundamental Properties of Matter [US Department of Energy and USSR State Committee on Peaceful Uses of Atomic Energy]
JCCI .... Japan Chamber of Commerce and Industry (BUAC)
JCCIS.......... Japan Chamber of Commerce and Industry, Sydney [Australia]
JCCIUK .... Japanese Chamber of Commerce and Industry in the United Kingdom (DS)
JCCL .... Japanese Canadian Citizens' League
JCCLE .... Joint Committee on Continuing Legal Education [Later, ALI-ABA Committee on Continuing Professional Education] (EA)
JCCMI .... Joint Committee for the Church Music in Ireland (BUAC)
JCCO .... Joint Container Control Office (MCD)
JCCom .... Japan Computers and Communication
JCCOMNET... Joint Coordination Center Communications Network
JCCP .... Joint Casualty Collection Point [Environmental science] (COE)
JCCR .... Joint Command and Control Requirements [Military] (GFGA)
JCCRG .... Joint Command and Control Requirements Group [Joint Chiefs of Staff] [DoD]
JCCS .... Jewish Cultural Clubs and Societies (EA)
JCCSA......... Joint Communications Contingency Station Activity (MCD)
JCCSC......... Joint Command and Control Standards Committee (AFM)
JCCSMAS .... Joint Commission on Competitive Safeguards and the Medical Aspects of Sports [Later, JCSMS] (EA)
JCCSWO ...... Joint Committee on Cooperation in Studies of the World Ocean [US-USSR] [Marine science] (OSRA)
JCCSWO ...... Joint Committee on Cooperation on Studies of the World Ocean [US-USSR] (USDC)
JCCTC .... Joint Customs Consultative Technical Committee [British] (DCTA)
JCD .... John Chard Decoration [British military] (DMA)
JCD .... Journal of Community Development [A publication]
JCD .... Journal of Counseling and Development [A publication] (DHP)
JCD .... Junior College District
JCD .... Juris Canonici Doctor [Doctor of Canon Law] [Latin]
JCD .... Juris Civilis Doctor [Doctor of Civil Law] [Latin]
JCDA .... Junior Catholic Daughters of the Americas [Defunct] (EA)
JCDSG .... Joint Civil Defense Support Group
JCDSIPS ...... Joint Continental Defense Systems Integration Planning Staff [Air Force]
JCDT .... Jamaica Conservation and Development Trust (BUAC)
JCDTA......... Joint Commission on Dance and Theatre Accreditation (EA)
JCE .... Joint Cadet Executive [British military] (DMA)
JCE .... Journal of Chemical Education [A publication] (WDAA)
JCEA .... Jesuit Conference of East Asia (BUAC)
JCEA .... Joint Committee for European Affairs [Defunct] (EA)
JCEADF........ Joint Central Air Defense Force (SAA)
JCEAG .... Joint Civilian Employee Advisory Group [Military] (CINC)
JCEB .... Joint Council on Educational Broadcasting [Later, JCET] (EA)
JCEC .... Joint Chapters - Educational Council
JCEC .... Joint Communications-Electronics Committee [Military]
JCECPAC..... Joint Communications-Electronics Committee, Pacific [Military] (CINC)
JCEE .... Joint Council on Economic Education (EA)
JCEG .... Joint Communications-Electronics Group [Military]
JCEG .... Joint Concepts and Evaluation Group [Military] (CINC)
JCEGP .... Joint Communications-Electronics Group [Military]
JCEM .... Joint Center for Energy Management [Research center] (RCD)
JCEM .... Junior Control Electrical Mechanic [British military] (DMA)
JCENS......... Joint Communications-Electronics Nomenclature System [Military]
JCEOI .... Joint Communications-Electronics Operating Instructions [Military] (CET)
JCEPC......... Joint United States/Canada Civil Emergency Planning Committee
JCET .... Joint Council on Educational Telecommunications [Defunct] (EA)
JCEW .... Joint Communications Electronic Warfare Simulation
JCEWG........ Joint Communications and Electronics Working Group [NATO] (NATG)
JCEWS........ Joint Command, Control, and Electronic Warfare School
J Ceylon Law... Journal of Ceylon Law [A publication] (ILCA)
JCF .... Jamaican Constabulary Force (BUAC)
JCF .... Jaycees Community Foundation [Australia]
JCF .... Jet Center Flight Training SA [Spain ICAO designator] (FAAC)
JCF .... Juvenile Calcaneal Fracture [Medicine] (DMAA)
JCFA .... Japan Chemical Fibres Association (BUAC)
JCFBC......... Joint Committee on Fire Brigade Communications (WDAA)
JCFBO......... Joint Committee on Fire Brigade Operations (WDAA)
JCFBS......... Joint Commission on the Fisheries in the Black Sea (BUAC)
JCFC .... Jesse Couch Fan Club (EA)
JCFC .... John Conlee Fan Club (EA)
JCFC .... Judaica Captioned Film Center (EA)
JCFI .... Job Control File Internal (IAA)
JCFR .... Junior College of Flat River [Missouri]
JCFS .... Job Control File Source (IAA)
JCFSBFC ..... Jerry Campbell and Five Star Band Fan Club (EA)
JCFSO......... Joint Council of Fire Service Organizations [Defunct] (EA)
JCG .... Joint Conservation Group
JCG .... Joint Coordinating Group [Military] (AFIT)
JCGRO........ Joint Central Graves Registration Office [Military] (CINC)
JCGS .... Joint Center for Graduate Study [Research center] (RCD)
J Ch .... Johnson's New York Chancery Reports [A publication] (DLA)

JCHA............ Joint Commission on Hospital Accreditation
J Chem Ed... Journal of Chemical Education [A publication] (BRI)
J Chem Phys... Journal of Physical Chemistry (MEC)
J Chem Soc... Journal of the Chemical Society (MEC)
J Chem Tech and Biotech... Journal of Chemical Technology and Biotechnology (MEC)
JCHMT............ Joint Committee for Higher Medical Training (CMD)
JCHPME....... Joint Committee on the Higher Professional Medical Education [Nigeria] (BUAC)
JCHST.......... Joint Committe on Higher Surgical Training [Royal College of Surgeons] (PDAA)
J Ch St .... Journal of Church and State [A publication] (BRI)
J Church S... Journal of Church and State [A publication] (DLA)
JCI .... Jaycees International (EA)
JCI .... Job Characteristics Inventory
JCI .... Johnson Controls [NYSE symbol] (TTSB)
JCI .... Johnson Controls, Inc. [NYSE symbol] (SPSG)
JCI .... Joint Communications Instruction
JCI .... Junior Chamber International (EAIO)
JCI .... Jute Corp. of India
JCI .... Olathe [Kansas] [Airport symbol] (OAG)
JCIAMR........ Joint Commission on the International Aspects of Mental Retardation (BUAC)
JCIC .... Jewish Community Information Center [Australia]
JCIC .... Joint Committee on Intersociety Coordination [Defunct] (EA)
JCIE/USA ..... Japan Center for International Exchange (EA)
JCIFC .... Johnny Comfort International Fan Club [Defunct] (EA)
JCIHCA .... Joint Council to Improve Health Care of the Aged [Defunct] (EA)
JCII .... Japan Camera and Optical Instruments Inspection and Testing Institute (BUAC)
JCIM .... Joint Council of Immunohistochemical Manufacturers
J Cin BA .... Journal. Cincinnati Bar Association [A publication] (DLA)
JCIPP.......... Jewish Committee for Israeli-Palestinian Peace (EA)
JCIWG .... Joint Cutover Integrated Working Group [Military] (RDA)
JCJ .... Journalist Committee of Japan (BUAC)
JCJC .... Jefferson City Junior College [Discontinued operation, 1958] [Missouri]
JCJC .... Jones County Junior College [Ellisville, MS]
JCJCCIFC..... Johnny Cash and June Carter Cash International Fan Club (EA)
JCJDMU...... Jewel Case & Jewellery Display Makers' Union (WDAA)
JCK .... Jackson Air Services Ltd. [Canada ICAO designator] (FAAC)
JCK .... Joint Commission on Korea
JCK .... Julia Creek [Australia Airport symbol] (OAG)
JCL .... Jackson County Library System, Medford, OR [OCLC symbol] (OCLC)
JCL .... Jet Cargo-Liberia [ICAO designator] (FAAC)
JCL .... Job Command Language (NITA)
JCL .... Job Control Language [High-level programming language] [1979] [Computer science]
JCL .... John Crerar Library [National Translation Center]
JCL .... Johnny Come Lately [Slang]
JCL .... Journal of Contract Law [Australia A publication]
JCL .... Junior Classical League (EA)
JCL .... Juris Canonici Lector [Reader in Canon Law]
JCL .... Juris Canonici Licentiatus [Licentiate in Canon Law]
JCL .... Juris Civilis Licentiatus [Licentiate of Civil Law]
JCLA .... Joint Council of Language Associations [British]
JCLC .... Joint Committee [of Congress] on the Library of Congress
JCLE .... Joint Committee on Library Education
JCLGEN........ Job Control Language Generation [Computer science] (MHDB)
JCLI .... Joint Council for Landscape Industries (BUAC)
JCLIL .... Journal of Comparative Legislation and International Law [A publication]
J ClinPsyc ... Journal of Clinical Psychiatry [A publication] (BRI)
JCLL .... Joint Center for Lessons Learned (DOMA)
JCL-OMATIC... Job Control Language Automatic Generator [Computer science]
JCLOT .... Joint Closed Loop Operations Test (SAA)
JCLPREP...... Job Control Language Preprocessor [Computer science] (MHDB)
JCLS .... Junior College Libraries Section [Association of College and Research Libraries]
JCM .... Jacobina [Brazil] [Airport symbol] (OAG)
JCM .... Jettison Control Module
JCM .... Jeunesse Canada Monde (AC)
JCM .... Jeunesse Chretienne Malgache [Malagasy Christian Youth]
JCM .... Job Cylinder Map [Computer science] (IBMDP)
JCM .... Joint Conflict Model [Military]
JCM .... Joule Ceramic Melter (PDAA)
JCM .... Juris Civilis Magister [Master of Civil Law]
JCMA .... Junior Clergy Missionary Association [British]
JCMBS......... Journeymen Curriers' Mutual Benefit Society [A union] [British]
JCMC .... Joint Conference on Medical Conventions (BUAC)
JCMC .... Joint Crisis Management Capability [DoD]
JCMC .... Junta Civico-Militar Cubana [An association] (EA)
JCMD .... Joint Committee on Mobility for the Disabled [British]
JCMEB .... Joint Civil-Military Engineering Board (COE)
JCMHC .... Joint Commission on Mental Health of Children
JCMIH......... Joint Commission on Mental Illness and Health [Defunct] (EA)
JCML .... Juvenile Chronic Myelogenous [or Myelocytic] Leukemia [Medicine] (DMAA)
JCMPO........ Joint Cruise Missile Program [or Project] Office (MCD)
JCMRFA....... Joseph Cox and Mary Rue Family Association (EA)
JCMST........ Journal of Computers in Math and Science Teaching (NITA)
JCMT.......... James Clerk Maxwell Telescope [Mauna Kea, HI] [Operated by the Royal Observatory in Edinburgh, Scotland]
JCMT.......... Joint Collection Management Tools [Army] (RDA)

JCMWA....... Joint Christian Ministry in West Africa (BUAC)
JCN .... Job Change Notice [Form] (AAG)
JCN .... Job Control Number
JCN .... Joint Communications Network (COE)
JCN .... Joint Control Number
JCN .... Jump on Condition [Computer science]
JCN .... Junction (NITA)
JCNA .... Jaguar Clubs of North America (EA)
JCNFC......... Jimmy C. Newman Fan CLub (EA)
JCNMT........ Joint Committee of Nordic Marine Technology [See also NSTM] (EAIO)
JCNMT........ Joint Committee of Nordic Master Tailors (EA)
JCNNSRC..... Joint Committee of the Nordic Natural Science Research Councils (EA)
JCNSW .... Judicial Commission of New South Wales [Australia]
JCO............. Jesus College, Oxford [England] (ROG)
JCO............. Joint Contracting Offices [Army]
JCO............. Justification for Continued Operation [Nuclear energy] (NRCH)
JCOA.......... Jazz Composers Orchestra Association (EA)
J-COARE ..... Japanese COARE [Coupled Ocean-Atmosphere Response Experiment] (USDC)
JCOARE ...... Japanese Coupled Ocean-Atmosphere Response Experiment [Marine science] (OSRA)
JCOC........... Joint Civilian Orientation Conference [DoD]
JCOC........... Joint Combat Operations Center [Navy] (NVT)
JCOC........... Joint Command Operations Center [NATO] (NATG)
JCOCG .... Joint Cadre Operation Control Group [Military]
J-CODE .... Justification Code (LAIN)
JC of C .... Junior Chamber of Commerce
JCOMCEN ... Joint Communications Center
JCOME........ Jewish Committee on the Middle East (EA)
J Comm Mt Stud... Journal of Common Market Studies [A publication] (DLA)
J Comp Corp L... Journal of Comparative Corporate Law and Securities Regulation [A publication] (ILCA)
J Comp Leg... Journal. Society of Comparative Legislation [A publication] (DLA)
J Con A....... Journal of Consumer Affairs [A publication] (BRI)
J Conat Law... Journal of Conational Law [A publication] (DLA)
J Contemp RDL... Journal of Contemporary Roman-Dutch Law [A publication] (DLA)
J Copr Soc'y.... Journal. Copyright Society of the USA [A publication] (DLA)
J Copyright Ent & Sports L... Journal of Copyright, Entertainment, and Sports Law [A publication] (DLA)
J Copyright Entertainment Sports L... Journal of Copyright, Entertainment, and Sports Law [A publication] (DLA)
JCOR .... Jacor Communications [NASDAQ symbol] (TTSB)
JCOR .... Jacor Communications, Inc. [NASDAQ symbol] (NQ)
J Corp Tax'n... Journal of Corporate Taxation [A publication] (DLA)
JCORW .... Jacor Communications Wrrt [NASDAQ symbol] (TTSB)
JCOS.......... Job Corps Opportunity Specialist [Department of Labor]
JCOS.......... Joint Chiefs of Staff [Military]
JCOT .... Joint Committee on College Teaching
JCP .... Jamaican Communist Party [Political party] (BUAC)
JCP .... Janna Contact Personal [Janna Systems] [Computer interface] (PCM)
JCP .... Japan Communist Party [Nikon Kyosanto] [Political party] (PPW)
JCP .... Jetcopter [Denmark ICAO designator] (FAAC)
JCP .... Jettison Control Panel
JCP .... Jewish Communist Party [Political party] (BJA)
JCP .... Job Content Protection [UAW]
JCP .... Job Control Program (CMD)
JCP .... Job Creation Programme [Manpower Services Commission] (AIE)
JCP .... John Crowe Productions, Inc. [Houston, TX] [Telecommunications] (TSSD)
JCP .... Joint Chiefs of Staff Publications [Military]
JCP .... Joint Committee for Palestine (BUAC)
JCP .... Joint [Congressional] Committee on Printing
JCP .... Joint Contact Point Division [Desert Test Center] [Fort Douglas, UT]
JCP .... Joint Power Conditions [NASA] (LAIN)
JCP .... Jordanian Communist Party [Political party] (PD)
JCP .... JOVIAL [Joule's Own Version of the International Algorithmic Language] Control Program [Computer science]
JCP .... Jungle Canopy Penetration
JCP .... Junior Collegiate Players [Later, Associate Collegiate Players] (EA)
JCP .... Justice of the Common Pleas [Legal term] (DLA)
JCP .... Juvenile Chronic Polyarthritis [Medicine] (DB)
JCP .... Penney [J. C.] Co., Inc. [NYSE symbol] (SPSG)
JCP .... Penney (J.C.) [NYSE symbol] (TTSB)
JCPC .... J. C. Penney Communications, Inc. [J. C. Penney Co., Inc.] [Telecommunications service] (TSSD)
JCPCap........ JCP & L Capital LP [Associated Press] (SAG)
JCPDS .... Joint Committee on Powder Diffraction Standards (MCD)
JCPDS .... Joint Committee on Power Diffraction Standards (BUAC)
JCPES .... Joint Center for Political and Economic Studies (EA)
JCPI .... Japan Cotton Promotion Institute (BUAC)
JCPOA .... Joint Council of Post Office Associations [South Africa]
JCPPRFNA.... Joint Commission on Political Prisoners and Refugees in French North Africa [World War II]
JCPS .... Joint Center for Political Studies [Later, JCPES] (EA)
JCPX .... Joint Command Post Exercise [Military] (AABC)
JCQ .... Jacqueline Gold [Vancouver Stock Exchange symbol]
JCQ .... Jefferson City, MO [Location identifier FAA] (FAAL)
JCQE........... Joint Council on Quantum Electronics (MCD)
JCR............. Jack Criswell Resources [Vancouver Stock Exchange symbol]
JCR............. Jesus Cares Refuge Incorporated [Australia An association]
JCR............. Johnson's New York Chancery Reports [A publication] (DLA)

JCR............. Joint Council for Repatriation (EA)
JCR............. Journal of Court Reporting [A publication]
JCR............. Judicial Council Reports [A publication] (DLA)
JCR............. Junction Current Recovery [in silicon devices]
JCR............. Junior Common Room [in British colleges and public schools]
JCR............. Junta for Revolutionary Coordination [Argentina] [Political party]
                  (BUAC)
JCRA.......... Jewish Committee for Relief Abroad
JCRC........... Jewish Community Relations Council (BARN)
JCRC........... Joint Casualty Resolution Center (MCD)
JCRC........... Joint Concept Review Committee (AAGC)
JCRe........... Judentum im Christlichen Religionsunterricht (BJA)
JC Rettie .... Rettie, Crawford, and Melville's Session Cases, Fourth Series
                  [1873-98] [Scotland] [A publication] (DLA)
JCRFC......... Jeannie C. Riley Fan Club (EA)
J Crim L & Crim... Journal of Criminal Law and Criminology [A publication] (DLA)
J Crim Sci ... Journal of Criminal Science [A publication] (DLA)
JCRPCC .... Joint Council on Research in Pastoral Care and Counseling [Later,
                  COMISS] (EA)
JCRR .... Joint Commission on Rural Reconstruction
JCRS........... Joint Casualty Resolution Center [Established in 1973 to coordinate
                  U.S. military activities regarding American MIA/POWs] (VNW)
JCRWD .... Jersey Committee of Resistance Workers and Deportees (EAIO)
JCS .... Jaicos [Brazil] [Airport symbol] (AD)
JCS .... James Connolly Society (BUAC)
JCS .... Japan Club of Sydney [Australia]
JCS .... Jazz Centre Society [British]
JCS .... Jersey Cattle Society [British] (DBA)
JCS .... Jersey Cattle Society of the United Kingdom (BUAC)
JCS .... Jewish Chautauqua Society (EA)
JCS .... Job Control Statement [Computer science]
JCS .... Job Control System (IAA)
JCS .... Job Cost Sheet (DGA)
JCS .... Job Creation Scheme [Department of Employment] [British]
JCS .... Joint Chiefs of Staff [United States] [Military]
JCS .... Joint Commonwealth Societies (BUAC)
JCS .... Journal of Chromatographic Science [A publication]
JCS .... Justices' Clerks' Society [British] (DBA)
JCSA........... Jewish Communal Service Association of North America (EA)
JCSA........... Joseph Conrad Society of America (EA)
JCS-ACA ..... Joint Chiefs of Staff Automatic Conference Arranger [Military] (CET)
JCSAN .... Joint Chiefs of Staff Alerting Network [Military]
JCSAS......... Joint Chiefs of Staff Alerting System (MCD)
JCSC........... Joint Communications Satellite Center (COE)
JC/SCAMEP... Joint Commonwealth/States Committee on the Adult Migration
                  Education Program [Australia]
JCSCCF....... Joint Commission of the Socialist Countries on Cooperation in the
                  Field of Fisheries (PDAA)
JCSE .... Joint Communications Support Element [DoD]
JCSE .... Joint Communications Systems Elements (MCD)
JCSI........... Joint Combat Systems Integrating
JCSIDBAD.... Joint Chiefs of Staff Identification Badge [Military decoration] (GFGA)
JCSIdentBad.. Joint Chiefs of Staff Identification Badge [Military decoration]
                  (AABC)
JCSIDTN ...... Joint Chiefs of Staff Interim Data Transmission Network [Military]
                  (CET)
JCSIR.......... Journal. Council for Scientific and Industrial Research (Australia)
                  [A publication]
JCSLHG ...... Joint Center for the Study of Law and Human Genetics
JCSM .... Joint Chiefs of Staff Memorandum [Military]
J/CSM .... Junior Company Sergeant-Major [British military] (DMA)
JCSMS........ Joint Commission on Sports Medicine and Science (EA)
JCSNMCC .... Joint Chiefs of Staff National Military Command Center (DNAB)
JCSO .... Joint Chiefs of Staff Organization [Military] (MCD)
JCSOS .... Joint and Combined Staff Officer School
JCSP.......... Joint Chiefs of Staff Plans
JCSP.......... Journal of College Student Personnel [A publication] (DHP)
JCSPUB ...... Joint Chiefs of Staff Publications [Military]
JCSRE .... Joint Chiefs of Staff Representative, Europe [NATO] (NATG)
JCSS........... Jaffee Center for Strategic Studies [Israel] (BUAC)
JCSS........... Jesuit Center for Social Studies [Defunct] (EA)
JCSS........... Jesus Christ Superstar [Rock opera]
JCSS........... Joint Communications Support Squadron
JCSSAB....... Joint Committee of the States to Study Alcoholic Beverage Laws
                  (EA)
JCS(SASM)... Joint Chiefs of Staff (Special Assistant for Strategic Mobility) (DNAB)
JCST .... Joint Combined System Test (KSC)
JCSTC......... Joint Council for Scientific and Technical Communication [British]
JCSTELECON... Joint Chiefs of Staff Teletypwriter Conference Network [Military]
                  (MCD)
JCSTR......... Joint Commission on Solar and Terrestrial Relationships (BUAC)
JCT .... Jacket (ROG)
JCT .... Jewett-Cameron [Vancouver Stock Exchange symbol]
JCT .... Jewish Cemetery Trust [Australia]
JCT .... Job Control Table (CMD)
JCT .... Johnstown/Consolidated Realty Trust (MHDW)
JCT .... Joint Committee on Taxation [US Congress]
JCT .... Joint Contracts Tribunal for the Standard Form of Building Contract
                  (BUAC)
JCT .... Jordan Cosmological Theory
JCT .... Journal Control Table (IAA)
JCT .... Junction (AFM)
JCT .... Junction [Texas] [Seismograph station code, US Geological
                  Survey] (SEIS)
Jct.............. Junction (TBD)

JCT .... Junction, TX [Location identifier FAA] (FAAL)
JCT .... Jurisconsult (ROG)
JCT & M ...... Jordan, Case, Taylor & McGrath [Advertising agency]
JCTC.......... Jewett-Cameron Trading Co. Ltd. [NASDAQ symbol] (SAG)
JCTCF .... Jewett-Cameron Trading [NASDAQ symbol] (TTSB)
JCTG .... Joint Contingency Task Group [Military] (VNW)
JCTI .... James Crowe Traders International [Commercial firm British]
JCTI .... Jurisconsulti [Counselors at Law] [Latin] (ROG)
JCTION .... Junction [Commonly used] (OPSA)
JCTN .... Junction [Commonly used] (OPSA)
JCTNS......... Junctions [Commonly used] (OPSA)
JCTPT .... Junction Point (IAA)
JCTS.......... Junctions [Postal Service standard] (OPSA)
JCTUS......... Jurisconsultus [Counselor at Law] [Latin] (ROG)
JCU........... John Carroll University [University Heights, OH]
JCU........... John Carroll University, Grasselli Library, University Heights, OH
                  [OCLC symbol] (OCLC)
JCUDI .... Japan Computer Usage Development Institute (BUAC)
JCULS......... Joint Committee on the Union List of Serials
JCUNQ .... James Cook University of North Queensland (BUAC)
JCUS......... Joint Center for Urban Studies of MIT [Massachusetts Institute of
                  Technology] and Harvard University [Research center] (RCD)
JCUSD .... Joint Committee on Urban Storm Drainage (BUAC)
JCV........... Jamestown Canyon Virus [Medicine] (DMAA)
JCV........... Jentech Ventures Corp. [Vancouver Stock Exchange symbol]
JCV........... Joule-Clausius Velocity [Physics]
JCVI.......... Joint Committee on Vaccination and Immunisation (BUAC)
JCVS......... JOVIAL Compiler Validation System [Computer science]
JCW.......... Jim Creek [Washington] [Seismograph station code, US Geological
                  Survey] (SEIS)
JCWA......... Japan Clock and Watch Association (BUAC)
JCWG......... Joint Checklist Working Group [Military] (AFIT)
JCWI.......... Joint Council for the Welfare of Immigrants [British] (DI)
JCWP......... Joint Conservation Working Party [Australia Political party]
JCY........... Johnson City, TX [Location identifier FAA] (FAAL)
JD............. Diploma in Journalism (ADA)
JD............. Doctor of Jurisprudence (DD)
JD............. Jack Daniels [A brand name of whiskey]
JD............. J-Band Detector
JD............. Jejunal Diverticulitis [Gastroenterology] (DAVI)
JD............. Jet Driver (KSC)
JD............. Jewish Division [New York Public Library] (BJA)
JD............. Job Description [Department of Labor]
JD............. Job Development (OICC)
JD............. Joggle Die (MCD)
JD............. Joined (AABC)
JD............. Joint Determination (AFM)
JD............. Joint Dictionary [Dictionary of US Military Terms for Joint Usage]
                  [A publication] (AFM)
JD............. Jordanian Dinar [Monetary unit] (BJA)
Jd............. Jude [New Testament book] (BJA)
JD............. Jugulodigastric [Node] [Gastroenterology] (DAVI)
JD............. Julian Date [or Day]
JD............. Junior Deacon [Freemasonry]
JD............. Junior Dean
JD............. Junior Division [British military] (DMA)
JD............. Junta Democratica [Democratic Junta] [Spain Political party] (PPE)
JD............. Jurisdiction [Legal shorthand] (LWAP)
JD............. Juris Doctor [Doctor of Jurisprudence] [Latin]
JD............. Jurum Doctor [Doctor of Laws] [Latin]
JD............. Jury Duty (WGA)
JD............. Justice Department
JD............. Juvenile Delinquency [or Delinquent]
JD............. Juvenile Diabetes [Medicine] (DAVI)
JD............. Toa Domestic Airlines [ICAO designator] (AD)
JDA........... Japan Domestic Airlines (PDAA)
JDA........... Japanese Defense Agency (MCD)
JDA........... Jefferson Davis Association (EA)
JDA........... Jewelery Distributors Association [British] (DBA)
JDA........... Jewellery Distributors Association of the United Kingdom (BUAC)
JDA........... Joint Defense Appeal [Defunct] (EA)
JDA........... Joint Deployment Agency [DoD]
JDA........... Joint Development Agency [DoD]
JDA........... Joint Development Agreement [Business term] (PCM)
JDA........... Joint Duty Assignment (DOMA)
JDA........... Juvenile Delinquency Act
JDAL......... Joint Duty Assignment List (DOMA)
JDAL......... Jurisdictional [Legal shorthand] (LWAP)
JDAM......... Joint Direct Attack Munition (DOMA)
JDAM......... Joint Direct Attack Munitions [DoD]
JDAMIS....... Joint Duty Assignment Management Information System (DOMA)
JDAP......... Joint Direct Attack Program [Air Force] (DOMA)
JDAS......... JDA Software Group [NASDAQ symbol] (TTSB)
JDAS......... JDA Software Group, Inc. [NASDAQ symbol] (SAG)
JDASoft....... JDA Software Group, Inc. [Associated Press] (SAG)
JDB........... Japan Development Bank (PDAA)
JDBC......... Java Database Connect [Computer science]
JDBC......... Java Data Base Connectivity [Computer science] (IGQR)
JDC........... American Jewish Joint Distribution Committee (EA)
JDC........... Deere & Co. [ICAO designator] (FAAC)
JDC........... Japan Airlines Development Co.
JDC........... Japan Documentation Center [Columbia University]
JDC........... Jet Deflection Control (AAG)
JDC........... Jeunesse Democratique Camerounaise [Cameroonian Democratic
                  Youth]

JDC............	Jewish Documentation Centre [*See also BJVN*] (EAIO)
JDC............	Job Description Card
JDC............	Joint Deployment Community [*Military*] (INF)
JDC............	Joint Development Community [*DoD*]
JDC............	Joint Doctrine Center (COE)
JDC............	Joslin Diabetes Center (EA)
JDC............	Junction Diode Circuit
JDC............	Just Discriminable Change (IAA)
JDCA..........	Japan Designer and Craftsman Association (BUAC)
JDCE..........	Jeunes Democrates Chretiens Europeens [*European Young Christian Democrats - EYCD*] (EA)
JDCMC........	Joint Department of Defense Configuration Management Committee (MCD)
JDCS..........	Joint Deputy Chiefs of Staff [*Military*]
JDD............	Joint Doctrine Division (COE)
JDDD..........	Judicial Discipline and Disability Digest [*American Judicature Society*] [*Information service or system*] (CRD)
JDE............	Air Med Jetoperations [*Austria ICAO designator*] (FAAC)
JDEG..........	Joules per Degree [*Physics*] (IAA)
JDENL........	Joined by Enlistment [*Military*]
J Denning LS...	Journal. Denning Law Society [*Tanzania*] [*A publication*] (DLA)
J Denning L Soc'y...	Journal. Denning Law Society [*Tanzania*] [*A publication*] (DLA)
JDEP..........	Juvenile Delinquency Evaluation Project
JDES..........	Joint Density of Electronic State [*Semiconductor technology*] (OA)
JDEWN.......	John Denver Early Warning Network (EA)
JDF............	Jamaican Defense Forces
JDF............	Jamming Direction Finder [*Military*] (CAAL)
JDF............	Juiz De Fora [*Brazil*] [*Airport symbol*] (OAG)
JDF............	Juvenile Diabetes Foundation [*Later, JDFI*] (EA)
JDFC..........	James Darren Fan Club [*Defunct*] (EA)
JDFC..........	Jimmie Dale Fan Club (EA)
JDFC..........	Joanie Dale Fan Club (EA)
JDFC..........	Joint Danube Fishery Commission [*See also ZKRVD*] [*Zilina, Czechoslovakia*] (EAIO)
JDFI..........	Joslin Diabetes Foundation, Inc. [*Later, JDC*] (EA)
JDFI..........	Juvenile Diabetes Foundation International (EA)
JDFR..........	Joined From [*Military*]
JdFR..........	Juan de Fuca Ridge [*Marine science*] (OSRA)
JDFR..........	Juan de Fuca Ridge (USDC)
JDG............	Judge
JDH............	Jodhpur [*India*] [*Airport symbol*] (OAG)
JDHE..........	Joint Directory of Higher Education [*A publication*]
JDHHFC.......	John Denver Heart to Heart Fan Club (EA)
JDHTC	Jaguar-Daimler Heritage Trust Collection
JDI............	JDS Investments Ltd. [*Toronto Stock Exchange symbol*]
JDI............	Job Description Index
JDI............	Joint Declaration of Interest (DS)
JDIND.........	Joined by Induction [*Military*]
JDipMA........	Joint Diploma in Management Accounting Services [*British*]
JDK............	Java Developer's Kit (PCM)
JDK............	Joodsch-Democratische Kiespartij [*Political party*] (BJA)
JDL............	Jewish Defense League (EA)
JDL............	Job Description Language [*Computer science*]
JDL............	Job Description Library
JDL............	Job Descriptor Language (NITA)
JDL............	Job Drawing List (MCD)
JDL............	Joint Directors of Laboratories [*Military*]
JDL............	Juneau, AK [*Location identifier FAA*] (FAAL)
JDL............	Lynn-01, AK [*Location identifier FAA*] (FAAL)
JDM............	Juvenile Diabetes Mellitus [*Medicine*]
JDMA..........	Japan Diet Marketing Association (BUAC)
JDMAG	Joint Depot Maintenance Analysis Group [*Military*]
JDMC..........	James Dean Memory Club (EA)
JDMP..........	Joint Deployment Master Plan [*Military*] (MUSM)
JDMS..........	Juvenile Dermatomyositis [*Medicine*] (DAVI)
JDN............	JDN Realty [*NYSE symbol*] (TTSB)
JDN............	JDN Realty Corp. [*NYSE symbol*] (SAG)
JDN............	Jordan, MT [*Location identifier FAA*] (FAAL)
JDN............	Jordan Petroleum Ltd. [*Toronto Stock Exchange symbol*]
JDN............	Julian Day Number
JDO............	Jewish Defense Organization (EA)
JDO............	Job Delivery Orders (MCD)
JDO............	Junior Duty Officer (MCD)
JDOP	Joint Development Objectives Plan (SAA)
JDOP	Joint Doppler Operational Project [*For tornado warning*] [*Meteorology*]
JDOYM........	Jewish Defense Organization Youth Movement (EA)
JDP............	Covington/Cincinnati, OH [*Location identifier FAA*] (FAAL)
JDP............	Job Development Program
JDP............	Joint Declaration of Principles
JDP............	Joint Development Program
JDP............	Paris-Moulineaux [*France*] [*Airport symbol*] (OAG)
JDPA..........	Japan Directory of Professional Associations [*Japan Publications Guide Service*] [*Information service or system*] (CRD)
JDPA..........	Juvenile Justice Planning Agency (OICC)
JDPC..........	Joint Defense Production Committee [*Later, Joint War Production Committee*] [*World War II*]
JDPC..........	Junior Daughters of Peter Claver (EA)
JDR............	Juta's Daily Reporter, Cape Provincial Division [*South Africa*] [*A publication*] (DLA)
JDR3..........	John D. Rockefeller III [*American philanthropist, 1906-1978*]
JDREENL......	Joined by Reenlistment [*Military*]
JDREMC	Joint Departmental Radio and Electronics Measurements Committee (BUAC)

JDRMA	Japanese Digital Road Mapping Association
JDRP	Joint Dissemination Review Panels
JDS............	Doctor of Juridical Science
JDS............	Jaguar Diagnostic System [*Automotive engineering*]
JDS............	JDS Capital Ltd. [*Toronto Stock Exchange symbol*]
JDS............	Job Data Sheet (IEEE)
JDS............	Job Diagnosis Survey (PDAA)
JDS............	John Dewey Society (EA)
JDS............	Joint Defense Staff [*NATO*] (NATG)
JDS............	Joint Deployment System
JDS............	Joint Disciplinary Scheme [*British*]
JDS............	Jugoslovenska Demokratska Stranka [*Yugoslav Democratic Party*] [*Political party*] (PPE)
JDS............	Julian Day of Spring
JDSCS	Joint Defense Space Communications Station
JDSSC	Joint Data Systems Support Center [*Military*]
JDT............	Joint Design Team [*Military*]
JDT............	Joint Development Team (MCD)
JDT............	Joint Development Testing
Jdt............	Judith [*Old Testament book*] [*Roman Catholic canon*]
JDT............	Judson Dance Theater
JDW............	Jacket Decladding Waste (PDAA)
JDWC	Jazz Dance World Congress
JDY............	Downey, CA [*Location identifier FAA*] (FAAL)
JDYD	Juvenile Delinquency and Youth Development Office [*Federal government*]
JDZ............	Jingdezhen [*China*] [*Airport symbol*] (OAG)
JE..............	Jamin Effect [*Electronics*]
JE..............	Jamming Equipment
JE..............	Japanese Encephalitis [*Medicine*]
Je..............	Jeremiah [*Old Testament book*] (BJA)
JE..............	Jerseyville & Eastern [*AAR code*]
JE..............	Jet Engine
JE..............	Jet Exhaust
JE..............	Jewish Encyclopaedia [*A publication*] (BJA)
JE..............	Job Enlargement (MHDB)
JE..............	Job Enrichment (MHDB)
JE..............	Job Estimate (AAG)
JE..............	Joint Engineers [*Army*] (RDA)
JE..............	Joshi Effect [*Physics*]
JE..............	Joule Effect [*Physics*]
JE..............	Journal of Education [*A publication*] (BRI)
JE..............	Jump If Equal [*Computer science*] (PCM)
JE..............	Junctional Escape [*Cardiology*] (DAVI)
JE..............	Junction Exchange [*Telecommunications*] (OA)
JE..............	June
JE..............	Manx Airlines [*Airline flight code*] (ODBW)
JE..............	Yosemite Airlines [*ICAO designator*] (AD)
JEA............	Jamaica Exporters Association (BUAC)
JEA............	Japan Electric Association (BUAC)
JEA............	Jersey European Airways [*British ICAO designator*] (FAAC)
JEA............	Jesuit Educational Association [*Later split into AJCU and JSEA*] (EA)
JEA............	Jewish Educators Assembly (EA)
JEA............	Joint Endeavor Agreement
JEA............	Joint Engineering Agency
JEA............	Joint Export Agent
JEA............	Joint Export Association [*Department of Commerce*]
JEA............	Journalism Education Association (EA)
JEAC..........	Journal of Electroanalytical Chemistry [*A publication*]
JEADF.........	Joint Eastern Air Defense Force (MUGU)
Jeaf..........	Jeaffreson's Book about Lawyers [*A publication*] (DLA)
JEAH..........	Jewish Endowment for the Arts and Humanities
JEAL..........	Junction Emitting Avalanche Light
JEAN..........	Jean Philippe Fragrances [*NASDAQ symbol*] (TTSB)
JEAN..........	Jean Philippe Fragrances, Inc. [*NASDAQ symbol*] (NQ)
JEAN..........	JOSS-Based Expression Analyser for the Nineteen Hundred (NITA)
JeanPhI.......	Jean Philippe Fragrances, Inc. [*Associated Press*] (SAG)
JEARD	Journal of Eastern African Research and Development [*A publication*]
JEASC	Journal. East African Swahili Committee [*A publication*]
JEAT..........	Joint Emergency Airlift Traffic Management Plan [*DoD*]
JEB	James Ewell Brown Stuart [*American Confederate general known as Jeb Stuart, 1833-1864*]
JEB	Jewish Education Bureau [*British*] (CB)
JEB	Joint Economy Board [*Abolished, 1947*] [*Army-Navy*]
JEB	Joint Electronics Board
JEB	Junctional Epidermolysis Bullosa [*Medicine*]
Jebb..........	Jebb's Irish Crown Cases [*1822-40*] [*A publication*] (DLA)
Jebb & B	Jebb and Bourke's Irish Queen's Bench Reports [*1841-42*] [*A publication*] (DLA)
Jebb & B (Ir)...	Jebb and Bourke's Irish Queen's Bench Reports [*1841-42*] [*A publication*] (DLA)
Jebb & S	Jebb and Symes' Irish Queen's Bench Reports [*A publication*] (DLA)
Jebb & S (Ir)...	Jebb and Symes' Irish Queen's Bench Reports [*A publication*] (DLA)
Jebb & Sym...	Jebb and Symes' Irish Queen's Bench Reports [*A publication*] (DLA)
Jebb CC......	Jebb's Irish Crown Cases [*1822-40*] [*A publication*] (DLA)
Jebb CC (Ir)...	Jebb's Irish Crown Cases [*1822-40*] [*A publication*] (DLA)
Jebb Cr & Pr Cas...	Jebb's Irish Crown and Presentment Cases [*A publication*] (DLA)
JEBC..........	Jefferson Bancorp, Inc. (Los Angeles) [*NASDAQ symbol*] (SAG)
JEBC..........	Jefferson Banc(LA) [*NASDAQ symbol*] (TTSB)
JEBM..........	Jet Engine Base Maintenance
JEBM-RR	Jet Engine Base Maintenance - Return Rate (PDAA)

JEC .... Jacobs Engineering Group, Inc. [*NYSE symbol*] (SPSG)
JEC .... Jacobs Engr Group [*NYSE symbol*] (TTSB)
JEC .... Japanese Electrotechnical Committee
JEC .... Jersey Electric Co. [*British*]
JEC .... Jeunesse Etudiante Catholique Internationale [*International Young Catholic Students*] (EAIO)
JEC .... Joint Economic Committee (COE)
JEC .... Joint Economic Committee of Congress
JEC .... Joint European Committee of Paper Exporters (BUAC)
JEC .... Joint Evaluation Committee [*NSF-UCAR*]
JEC .... Joint Exchanges Committee [*British*] (NUMA)
JEC .... Journal Editorial Committee (ACII)
JECA .... Jewel Cave National Monument
JECB .... Jet Engine Control Bearing
JECC .... Japan Electric Computer Corporation [*Japan*] (NITA)
JECC .... Japanese Electronic Computer Co.
JECC .... Joint Economic Committee of Congress (MCD)
JECC .... Joint Egyptian Cotton Committee (BUAC)
JECC .... Joint Exercise Control Center (MCD)
JECFA .... Joint Expert Committee on Food Additives [*FDA/WHO*]
JECFI .... Joint Expert Committee on Food Irradiation (BUAC)
JECI .... Jeunesse Etudiante Catholique Internationale [*International Young Catholic Students*]
JECL .... Job Entry Control Language
JECMA .... Japan Export Clothing Makers Association (BUAC)
JECMB .... Joint Executive Committee on Medicine and Biology
JECMOS ...... Joint Electronic Countermeasures Operation Section [*NATO*] (NATG)
JECNS .... Joint Electronic Communications Nomenclature System [*Military*] (IAA)
JECS .... Job Entry Central Services (MCD)
JECSS .... Japan and East China Seas Study [*Marine science*] (OSRA)
JED .... Japan Economic Daily [*Database*] [*Kyodo News International, Inc.*] [*Information service or system*] (CRD)
JED .... Jeddah [*Saudi Arabia*] [*Airport symbol*] (OAG)
Jed. .... Jedediah (BJA)
JED .... Jet East, Inc. [*ICAO designator*] (FAAC)
JED .... Jet Engine Duct
JED .... Joint Educational Development (EA)
JED .... Julian Ephemeris Data (MCD)
JEDA .... Joint Environmental Data Analysis Center [*Army*] [*Marine science*] (OSRA)
JEDEC .... Joint Electron Device Engineering Council (EA)
JEDI .... Jobs for Employable Dependent Individuals Program [*Federal government*]
JEDI .... Joint Electronic Data Interchange [*International trade*]
JEDMICS .... Joint Engineering and Data Management Information and Control System [*Military*]
JEDPE .... Joint Emergency Defense Plan Europe [*NATO*] (NATG)
JEDS .... Japanese Expeditions to the Deep Sea
JEDS .... Jedburgh Teams [*Allied intelligence-gathering units in Europe*] [*World War II*]
JEE .... Japanese Equine Encephalitis [*Medicine*]
JEE .... Jet Engine Exhaust
JEEC .... Kenneth E. Johnson Environmental and Energy Center [*University of Alabama in Huntsville*] [*Research center*] (RCD)
JEEP .... General-Purpose Quarter-Ton Military Utility Vehicle
Jeep .... Graduated Payment Mortgage (DFIT)
JEEP .... Joint Effort Evaluation Program [*Military*] (AFM)
JEEP .... Joint Emergency Evacuation Plan [*Military*] (AABC)
JEEP .... Joint Environmental Effects Program [*Military*] (AFM)
JEEP .... Joint Establishment Experimental Pile [*Nuclear reactor*] [*Norway*]
JEEP .... Joint Export Establishment Promotion [*Trade exhibition*] [*Department of Commerce*]
JEEPS .... GNMA Graduated Payment Mortgage Securities (EBF)
JEF .... Jacobi Elliptic Function [*Mathematics*]
JEF .... Jefferies Group [*NYSE symbol*] (TTSB)
JEF .... Jefferson City [*Missouri*] [*Airport symbol*] (OAG)
JEF .... Jefferson City, MO [*Location identifier FAA*] (FAAL)
JEF .... Jefferson Educational Foundation (EA)
JEF .... Jefjen Capital [*Vancouver Stock Exchange symbol*]
JEF .... Jet Engine Fuel
JEF .... Jetflite OY [*Finland ICAO designator*] (FAAC)
JEF .... Jeunesses Europeennes Federalistes
JefBsh .... Jefferson Bankshares, Inc. [*Associated Press*] (SAG)
JEFF .... JeffBanks, Inc. [*NASDAQ symbol*] (SAG)
JEFF .... Jefferson National Expansion Memorial National Historic Site
Jeff .... Jefferson's Virginia General Court Reports [*A publication*] (DLA)
JEFF .... Judiciously Efficient Fixed Frame [*Computer science*] (MCD)
JeffBanks .... JeffBanks, Inc. [*Associated Press*] (SAG)
JeffBcLA .... Jefferson Bancorp, Inc. [*Los Angles*] [*Associated Press*] (SAG)
JeffBcp ...... Jefferson Bancorp, Inc. [*Associated Press*] (SAG)
Jeff Man ...... Jefferson's Manual of Parliamentary Law [*A publication*] (DLA)
JeffPilot ...... Jefferson-Pilot Corp. [*Associated Press*] (SAG)
JeffPlt ...... Jefferson Pilot [*Associated Press*] (SAG)
JeffPOO ...... Jefferson Pilot [*Associated Press*] (SAG)
JeffrGp ...... Jefferies Group, Inc. [*Associated Press*] (SAG)
JeffSvg ...... Jefferson Savings Bancorp [*Associated Press*] (SAG)
Jeff (VA) ...... Jefferson's Virginia General Court Reports [*A publication*] (DLA)
JEFG .... Jefferies Group, Inc. [*NASDAQ symbol*] (NQ)
JEFM .... Jet Engine Field Maintenance
JefSmrf ...... Jefferson Smurfit Corp. [*Associated Press*] (SAG)
JEG .... Joint Exploratory Group [*NATO*] (NATG)
JEGP .... Journal of English and Germanic Philology [*A publication*] (BRI)
JEH .... Journal of Ecclesiastical History [*A publication*] (ODCC)
JEH .... Journal of Economic History [*A publication*] (BRI)

JEHFC .... Jon-Erik Hexum Fan Club (EA)
JEHO .... Jehosaphat [*Biblical*] (ROG)
JEHU .... Joint Experimental Helicopter Unit [*British military*] (DMA)
JEI .... Japan Economic Institute of America (EA)
JEI .... Jones Environmental, Inc. (EFIS)
JEIA .... Japanese Electronic Industries Association
JEIA .... Joint Electronics Information Agency
JEIA .... Joint Export-Import Agency [*Munich*] [*Allied German Occupation Forces*]
JEIDA .... Japanese Electronic Industry Development Association (CDE)
JEIM .... Jet Engine Intermediate Maintenance
JEIPAC ...... JICST [*Japan Information Center of Science and Technology*] Electronic Information Processing Automatic Computer (NITA)
JEIT .... Joint Equipment Identification Team [*Military*] (CINC)
JEJ .... Jejunum [*Medicine*]
JEJ .... Jets Ejecutivos SA [*Mexico ICAO designator*] (FAAC)
JEJUN .... Jejunectomy (ABBR)
JEJUN .... Jejunitis (ABBR)
JEL .... Aerojelk, SA de CV [*Mexico*] [*FAA designator*] (FAAC)
JEL .... Jackson Estuarine Laboratory [*University of New Hampshire*] [*Research center*] (RCD)
JEL .... Jeunesses Europeennes Liberales [*Liberal European Youth*]
JEL .... Joint Electronic Library [*Military*]
JEL .... Journal of Economic Literature [*A publication*] (BRI)
JELC .... Joint Effort Against Lefthanded Complications
J Electrochem Soc... Journal of the Electrochemical Society (MEC)
JELOS .... Jealous (ABBR)
JELOSY ...... Jealousy (ABBR)
JEM .... Japanese Experiment Module
JEM .... Jerusalem and the East Mission
JEM .... Jet Engine Modulation (MCD)
JEM .... Joint Endeavor Manager
JEM .... Joint Exercise Manual (MCD)
JEM .... Journey's End Motel Corp. [*Toronto Stock Exchange symbol*]
JEMA .... Japan Electronic Messaging Association (DDC)
JEM(A) .... Junior Electrical Mechanic (Air) [*British military*] (DMA)
JEM(AW) .... Junior Electrical Mechanic (Air Weapon) [*British military*] (DMA)
JEMC .... Joint Engineering Management Conference
JEMIC .... Japan Electric Meters Inspection Corp. (BUAC)
JEMIMA ...... [*The*] Japan Electrical Measurements Manufacturers' Association (ACII)
JEMP .... Joint Engineers Management Panel [*Army*] (RDA)
JEMRB .... Joint European Medical Research Board (BUAC)
JEN .... Japan Economic Newswire [*Kyodo News International, Inc.*] [*Information service or system*] (CRD)
JEN .... Jena [*German Democratic Republic*] [*Seismograph station code, US Geological Survey Closed*] (SEIS)
JEN .... Jenair Ltd. [*Cyprus*] [*ICAO designator*] (FAAC)
JEN .... Junta de Energia Nuclear [*Spanish nuclear agency*]
JENAKAT .... Jeunesse Nationale Katangaise [*Katangan National Youth*]
Jenck Bills ... Jencken's Bills of Exchange [*1880*] [*A publication*] (DLA)
Jenck Neg S... Jencken's Negotiable Securities [*1880*] [*A publication*] (DLA)
JenCrg ...... Jenny Craig [*Associated Press*] (SAG)
JENDRPC .... Joint Euratom Nuclear Data and Reactor Physics Committee (BUAC)
JENER .... Joint Establishment for Nuclear Energy Research
J Energy & Devel... Journal of Energy and Development [*A publication*] (DLA)
JENEX .... Japanese El Nino Experiment [*Marine science*] (OSRA)
JenfCv ...... Jennifer Convertibles, Inc. [*Associated Press*] (SAG)
Jenk .... Jenkins' Eight Centuries of Reports, English Exchequer [*145 English Reprint*] [*1220-1623*] [*A publication*] (DLA)
Jenk & Formoy... Jenkinson and Formoy's Select Cases in the Exchequer of Pleas [*Selden Society Publication, Vol. 48*] [*A publication*] (DLA)
Jenk Cent .... Jenkins' Eight Centuries of Reports, English Exchequer [*145 English Reprint*] [*1220-1623*] [*A publication*] (DLA)
Jenkins (Eng)... Jenkins' Eight Centuries of Reports, English Exchequer [*145 English Reprint*] [*1220-1623*] [*A publication*] (DLA)
Jenks .... Jenks' Reports [*58 New Hampshire*] [*A publication*] (DLA)
Jenn .... Jennison's Reports [*14-18 Michigan*] [*A publication*] (DLA)
Jenn Sug A... Jennett's Sugden Acts [*A publication*] (DLA)
JENTACN .... Jentaculum [*Breakfast*] [*Pharmacy*]
JEOCN .... Joint European Operations Communications Network
JEOL .... Japan Electron Optics Laboratory Co. (BUAC)
JEOP .... Jeopardy (ABBR)
JEOPZ .... Jeopardize (ABBR)
JEOPZD ...... Jeopardized (ABBR)
JEOPZG ...... Jeopardizing (ABBR)
Jep .... Jeopardy (BARN)
JEP .... Jet Engine Processor
JEP .... Jewish Elite Person
JEP .... Jupiter Entry Probe
JEPA .... Job Evaluation Policy Act of 1970
JEPAP .... Joint Emergency Personnel Augmentation Plan [*Military*] (CINC)
JEPES .... Joint Engineer Planning and Execution System [*Environmental science*] (COE)
JEPG .... Joint Exercise Planning Group [*Military*]
JEPI .... Joint Electronic Payment Intitiative [*Proposed*] [*Computer science*]
JEPI .... Joint Electronic Payments Initiative
JEPI .... Junior Eysenck Personality Inventory [*Psychology*]
JEPIA .... Japan Electronic Parts Industry Association
JEPO .... Joint Engine Project Office (MCD)
JEPP .... Japan English Publications in Print [*Japan Publications Guide Service*] [*Japan Information service or system*] (CRD)
JEPP .... Japanese Earthquake Prediction Plan
JEPS .... Job Effectiveness Prediction System [*Test for insurance company employees*]

JEPS	Job Entry Peripheral Services [*IBM Corp.*] (MCD)
JEPS	Joint Exercise Planning Staff [*NATO*] (NATG)
JEQ	Japan Equity Fund [*NYSE symbol*] (SPSG)
JEQ	Jequie [*Brazil*] [*Airport symbol*] (OAG)
JER	Japan Economic Review [*A publication*] (WDAA)
JER	Japanese Erection Ring [*Medicine*] (BABM)
Jer	Jeremiah [*Old Testament book*]
Jer	Jeremias (BJA)
Jer	Jericho (BJA)
JER	Jersey [*Channel Islands*] [*Airport symbol*] (OAG)
JER	Jerusalem [*Israel*] [*Seismograph station code, US Geological Survey*] (SEIS)
Jer	Jerusalem Talmud (BJA)
Jer	Jerushalmi (BJA)
JER	Junctional Escape Rhythm (STED)
JERA	James E. Rush Associates, Inc. [*Also, an information service or system*] (IID)
JERC	Japan Economic Research Centre (BUAC)
JerC	Jersey Central Power & Light [*Associated Press*] (SAG)
Jerc	Junior Executive Research Consultant [*Fictitious position in Commerce Bank of Beverly Hills created for Jethro Bodine on the television show "The Beverly Hillbillies"*]
Jer Car	Jeremy on Carriers [*A publication*] (DLA)
Jer Dig	Jeremy's Digest [*1817-49*] [*A publication*] (DLA)
Jeremy Eq	Jeremy's Equity Jurisdiction [*A publication*] (DLA)
Jeremy Eq Jur	Jeremy's Equity Jurisdiction [*A publication*] (DLA)
Jer Eq Jur	Jeremy's Equity Jurisdiction [*A publication*] (DLA)
JERI	Japan Economics Research Institute (BUAC)
JerM	Jersey Microfilming, Clifton, NJ [*Library symbol Library of Congress*] (LCLS)
JEROB	Jeroboam (WDAA)
JerPes	Jerusalem Talmud. Pesahim (BJA)
Jerr Copyr	Jerrold on Copyright [*A publication*] (DLA)
JERS	Japan Earth Remote Sensing Satellite
JERS	Japan Ergonomics Research Society (BUAC)
JERS	Joint Emergency Relocation Site
Jersey City St C	Jersey City State College (GAGS)
JERS-I	Japan Earth Resources Satellite [*Marine science*] (OSRA)
JERU	Joint Environmental Research Unit (MCD)
Jerus	Jerusalem (BJA)
Jerv Cor	Jervis. Coroners [*9th ed.*] [*1957*] [*A publication*] (DLA)
Jerv NR	Jervis' New Rules [*A publication*] (DLA)
JerW	Jerusalemer Warte (BJA)
JerYeb	Jerusalem Talmud. Yebamoth (BJA)
Jes	Analysis and Digest of the Decisions of Sir George Jessel, by A. P Peter [*England*] [*A publication*] (DLA)
JES	Japan Electronics Show
JES	Japan Environmental Systems
JES	Japanese Electroplating Society (BUAC)
JES	Japanese Export Standard
JES	Jes Air [*Bulgaria*] [*ICAO designator*] (FAAC)
JES	Jesuit (DSUE)
JES	Jesup, GA [*Location identifier FAA*] (FAAL)
JES	Jesus
JES	Jet Ejector System
JES	Job Entry System [*or Subsystem*] [*IBM Corp.*] [*Computer science*]
JES	John Ericsson Society (EA)
JES	Joint Efficiency Study (AIE)
JESA	Japanese Engineering Standards Association (BUAC)
JESAP	Jet Engine Smoke Abatement Program
JESC	Japanese Engineering Standards Committee (BUAC)
JESC	Joint Electronics Standardisation Committee (BUAC)
JES COLL	Jesus College [*Oxford or Cambridge*] [*England*] (ROG)
JESCOM	Jesuits in Communication in the US (EA)
JESNA	Jewish Education Service of North America (EA)
JESS	Joint Exercise Simulation System [*DoD*]
JESS	Joint Exercise Support System [*Military*]
JESSI	Joint European Semiconductor Silicon Initiative
JESSI	Joint European Submicron Silicon [*Project*]
JESSI	Joint European Submicron Silicon Initiative (BUAC)
JESSI	Junior Engineers' and Scientists' Summer Institute
JEST	Jungle Environmental Survival Training [*Military*]
JET	European Jet Ltd. [*British ICAO designator*] (FAAC)
JET	Frankfort, KY [*Location identifier FAA*] (FAAL)
JET	Jam Exceeds Threshold
JET	Jetronic Industries, Inc. [*AMEX symbol*] (SPSG)
JET	Jetsam (ABBR)
JET	Jettison
JET	Job Element Text (AFM)
JET	Job English Training
JET	Jobs Evaluation and Training
JET	Joint Economic Team
JET	Joint Effort for Talent [*Navy*] (NG)
JET	Joint European TOKAMAK [*Toroidal Kamera Magnetic*] [*or Torus Nuclear reactor*]
JET	Joint European Torus (EDCT)
JET	Jointly Endorsed Training [*Union-management*]
JET	Journal Entries Transfer [*Computer science*] (MHDI)
JET	Judicial Education Teleseminar System [*Defunct*] (TSSD)
JET	Junior Enlisted Travel [*Entitlement*] (MCD)
JETAM	Jet Engine Thrust Augmentation Mix (SAA)
JETAV	Jet Aviation (SAA)
JETD	Jetted (ABBR)
JETD	Joint Electronics Type Designator [*Military*] (AABC)
JETDS	Joint Electronics Type Designation System [*Military*] (AFM)
JETEC	Joint Electron Tube Engineering Council [*Later, JEDEC*] (MCD)
JetForm	Jet Form Corp. [*Associated Press*] (SAG)
JETG	Jetting (ABBR)
J Eth L	Journal of Ethiopian Law [*A publication*] (DLA)
JETLNR	Jetliner (ABBR)
JETN	Jettison
JETP	Jet-Propelled
JETR	Japan Engineering Test Reactor
JETR	Jetevator
JETRO	Japan External Trade Organization [*New York, NY*] (EA)
Jetronic	Jetronic Industries, Inc. [*Associated Press*] (SAG)
JETS	Jet Express Ticketing System
JETS	Job Executive and Transport Satellite [*NCR Corp.*]
JETS	Joint Electronics Type [*Designation*] System [*Military*] (NASA)
JETS	Joint Enroute Terminal System [*Canada*] (MCD)
JETS	Junior Engineering Technical Society
JETSB	Joint European Torus Supervisory Board (BUAC)
JET Scheme	Jobs, Education & Training Scheme [*Australia*] (WDAA)
JETT	Jettison (KSC)
JEV	Japanese Encephalitis Virus [*Medicine*]
JEV	Jesuit European Volunteers [*An association*] (BUAC)
Jev Cr Law	Jevons on Criminal Law [*A publication*] (DLA)
JEW	Jewellery [*British*] (ROG)
JEW	Jewish
JEWC	Joint Electronic Warfare Center (MCD)
JEW COLL LOND	Jewish College, London [*England*] (ROG)
JEWEL	Joint Endeavor for Welfare, Education, and Liberation [*Part of Grenadian political party, the New JEWEL Movement*]
JewettC	Jewett-Cameron Trading Co. Ltd. [*Associated Press*] (SAG)
JEWLF	IWI Holding Ltd. [*NASDAQ symbol*] (SAG)
JEWSOC	Joint Electronic Warfare Staff Officer Course (DOMA)
JEWT	Jungle Exercise without Trees [*British military*] (DMA)
Jew YB Int'l L	Jewish Yearbook of International Law [*A publication*] (DLA)
JEX	Jenks, OK [*Location identifier FAA*] (FAAL)
JEX	Jet Express, Inc. [*ICAO designator*] (FAAC)
JEX	Joint Exercise (NVT)
JEZ	Joint Engagement Zone [*Marine Corps*] (DOMA)
JEZEX	Jezebel [*Sonobuoy*] Exercise [*Navy*] (NVT)
JF	Jack Field
JF	Jackstone Froster Ltd. [*Commercial firm British*]
JF	Jamestown Foundation (EA)
JF	Japan Foundation [*Also, Kokusai Koryu*] (EA)
JF	Jefferson Foundation (EA)
JF	Jet Flap
JF	John Flanagan [*Designer's mark, when appearing on US coins*]
JF	Joint Filler [*Technical drawings*]
JF	Joint Fluid [*Orthopedics*] (DAVI)
JF	Joint Force [*Military*]
JF	Journal Folio (ROG)
JF	Jugular Forainen [*Anatomy*] (DAVI)
JF	Jugular Foramen (STED)
JF	Junctional Fold [*Anatomy*] (DAVI)
JF	Junction Frequency [*Telecommunications*] (TEL)
JF	Junctor Frame [*Telecommunications*] (TEL)
JF	Jundt Growth Fund [*NYSE symbol*] (SPSG)
JF	Junior Fiction [*Library science*] (TELE)
JF	Justice Fellowship (EA)
JF	LAB Flying Service [*ICAO designator*] (AD)
JF	Trehaven Aviation Ltd. [*British ICAO designator*] (ICDA)
JFA	Aviones Ejecutivos, JFA [*Mexico*] [*FAA designator*] (FAAC)
JFA	Jaffa [*Israel*] [*Airport symbol*] (AD)
JFA	Japan Fishery Agency (BUAC)
JFA	Judkins Family Association (EA)
JFAAD	Joint Forward-Area Air Defense (MCD)
JFAADS	Joint Forward-Area Air Defense System
JFAC	Joint Flight Acceptance Composite Test [*Gemini*] [*NASA*] (IAA)
JFACC	Joint Force Air Component Commander (DOMA)
J-FACT	Joint Flight Acceptance Composite Test [*Gemini*] [*NASA*]
JFACTSU	Joint Forward Air Controllers Training and Standards Unit [*British*]
JFAI	Joint Formal Acceptance Inspection [*NATO*] (NATG)
JFAP	Joint Frequency Allocation Panel
JFAST	Joint Flow and Analysis System for Transportation [*Model USA*]
JFAST	Joint Flow and Analysis System Test [*Environmental science*] (COE)
JFB	Jet Flying Belt (PDAA)
JFC	Jardine Fleming China Reg Fd [*NYSE symbol*] (TTSB)
JFC	Jardine Fleming China Regular Fund [*NYSE symbol*] (SPSG)
JFC	Java Foundation Classes [*Sun Microsystems, Inc.*] (IGQR)
JFC	Jewish Folk Center [*Australia*]
JFC	John Forsyth Co., Inc. [*Toronto Stock Exchange symbol*]
JFC	Joint Force Commander [*DoD*]
JFC	Jupiter-family Comets [*Astronomy*]
JFC	LTV Jet Fleet Corp. [*ICAO designator*] (FAAC)
JFCB	Job File Control Block [*Computer science*] (BUR)
JFCC	Japanese Federation of Culture Collections of Microorganisms (BUAC)
JFCL	Jump if Flag Set and Then Clear the Flag [*Computer science*] (NHD)
JFDA	Jewish Funeral Directors of America (EA)
JFDP	Joint Force Development Process [*or Program*] [*Army*]
JFE	Joint Fighter Engine (DWSG)
JFEA	Japan Federation of Employers Association
JFEA	Joint Foreign Exchange Agency [*Berlin*] [*Post-World War II, Germany*]
JFED	Junction Field-Effect Device
JFEO	Japanese Federation of Economic Organizations

J Ferment Technol (1944-1976)... Journal of Fermentation Technology (1944-1976) [*Japan*] [*A publication*]
JFET............ Junction Field-Effect Transistor
JFEW .... Jewish Foundation for Education of Women (EA)
JFF.............. Aguadilla, PR [*Location identifier FAA*] (FAAL)
JFF.............. Jobs for the Future [*An association*]
JFF.............. Junior Fashion Fair International [*British*] (ITD)
JFf.............. Junior Firefighter (WDAA)
JFFC .... Jewish Fighting Force Committee [*British*]
JFFC .... John Fricke Fan Club [*Defunct*] (EA)
JFFC .... Judy Fields Fan Club (EA)
JFG .... Jumbogroup Frequency Generator [*Bell System*]
JFH .... Jam Frequency Hopper
JFHQ.......... Joint Force Headquarters [*Military*]
JFI .... James Franck Institute [*University of Chicago*] [*Research center*] (RCD)
JFI .... Japanese Fermentation Institute
JFI .... Jardine Fleming India Fund [*NYSE symbol*] (SAG)
JFI .... Jet Flight Information (AFM)
JFI .... John La Farge Institute
JFI .... New Orleans, LA [*Location identifier FAA*] (FAAL)
JFIAP .... Joint Foreign Intelligence Assistance Program (AFM)
JFIF .... JPEG [*Joint Photographic Experts Group*] File Interchange Format [*Computer science*] (CDE)
J Film & Vid... Journal of Film & Video [*A publication*] (BRI)
JFIndia .... Jardine Fleming India Fund [*Associated Press*] (SAG)
JFIT .... Joint Framework for Information Technology [*British*]
JFJ .... Jewish Fund for Justice (EA)
JFJ .... Jews for Jesus (EA)
JFK .... John Fitzgerald Kennedy [*US president, 1917-1963*]
JFK .... Kennedy International Airport [*New York*] [*Airport symbol*]
JFKC .... John Fitzgerald Kennedy Center for the Performing Arts
JFKCTRMA... John F. Kennedy Center for Military Assistance (MCD)
JFK FDC SU... John F. Kennedy First Day Cover Study Unit (EA)
JFKL .... John F. Kennedy Library
JFKLF .... John F. Kennedy Library Foundation (EA)
JFKPS .... John F. Kennedy Philatelic Society (EA)
JFKSC.......... John Fitzgerald Kennedy Spaceflight Center [*Also known as KSC*] [*NASA*]
JFL.............. Joint Frequency List
JFL.............. Judy Farquharson Ltd. [*British*]
JFLA .... Jewish Free Loan Association (EA)
JFLC .... Joint Forces Land Component (DOMA)
JFLCC .... Joint Forces Land Component Commander (DOMA)
JFM .... Jet Flap Model
JFM .... Jews for Morality (EA)
JFM .... Job Function Manual (AAG)
JFM .... Joint Force Memorandum [*Military*]
JFM .... Jupiter Flyby Mission [*Aerospace*]
JFMIP .... Joint Financial Management Improvement Program
JFMO .... Joint Frequency Management Office (MCD)
JFMU .... Joint Force Meteorological and Oceanographic Forecast Unit (COE)
JFN .... Jefferson, OH [*Location identifier FAA*] (FAAL)
JFN .... Job File Number
JFNF .... Jewish Family Name File [*Association for the Study of Jewish Languages*] [*Information service or system*] (CRD)
JFNP............ Joseph M. Farley Nuclear Plant (NRCH)
JFNPP.......... James A. FitzPatrick Nuclear Power Plant (NRCH)
JFO............... Just for Openers [*An association*] (EA)
J For Sci Soc... Journal. Forensic Science Society [*A publication*] (DLA)
JFP .... Jewish Family Purity (BJA)
JFP .... Joint Frequency Panel
JFPA .... Jamaica Family Planning Association (BUAC)
JFPC .... Joint Fire Prevention Committee (WDAA)
JFPH............ JUMPS [*Joint Uniform Military Pay System*] Field Procedures Handbook (NVT)
JFPS .... Japan Fire Prevention Society (BUAC)
JFR .... Jamie Frontier Resources, Inc. [*Toronto Stock Exchange symbol*]
JFR .... Jet Flap Rotor
JFR .... Joint Fiction Reserve
JFRC .... James Forrestal Research Center [*Princeton University*] (MCD)
JFRCA.......... Japanese Fisheries Resources Conservation Association (BUAC)
JFRF .... Japan Frame Relay Forum (DDC)
JFRO............ Joint Fisheries Research Organisation [*Malawi, Zambia*] (BUAC)
JFS .... Jamaica Freight and Shipping Co. Ltd. (EY)
JFS .... Jet Fuel Starter
JFS .... Jewish Family Service (EA)
JFS .... Jewish Friends Society (EA)
JFS .... Job Finder System
JFS .... Johnston & Frye [*Vancouver Stock Exchange symbol*]
JFS .... Joint Foundation Support (EA)
JFS .... Juanda Flying School [*Indonesia*] [*ICAO designator*] (FAAC)
JFS .... Jugular Foramen Syndrome [*or Vernet's syndrome*] [*Medicine*] (DAVI)
JFS .... Jumbogroup Frequency Supply [*Bell System*]
JFSEO .... Japan Federation of Smaller Enterprises (BUAC)
JFSG .... Joint Feasibility Study Group [*Air Force*] (MCD)
JFSNY.......... Jewish Folk Schools of New York (EA)
JFSP .... Joint Forecast System Project [*Marine science*] (OSRA)
JFSS .... Joint Force Signals Staff [*Military*]
JFT .... Jet Fret [*France ICAO designator*] (FAAC)
JFT .... Job File Table (PCM)
JFT .... Joint Field Trial (NATG)
JFTC .... Japan Foreign Trade Council (BUAC)
JFTC .... Joint Fur Trade Committee (BUAC)

JFTCG.......... Joint Flight Test Control Group (AAG)
JFTG .... Joint Fuze Task Group [*Army*]
JFTOT .... Jet Fuel Thermal Oxidation Test [*or Tester*] [*Analytical chemistry*] [*Air Force*]
JFTR .... Joint Federal Travel Regulations (DOMA)
JFTS .... Jet Fuel Thermal Stability
JFTU .... Jordan Federation of Trade Unions
JFTX .... Joint Field Training Exercise [*Military*]
JFU .... Jersey Farmers' Union [*British*] (DBA)
JFUB .... Joint Facilities Utilization Board [*Military*]
JFuU .... Fukui University, Fukui-shi, Japan [*Library symbol Library of Congress*] (LCLS)
JFV .... Jobs for Veterans National Committee [*Defunct*] (EA)
JFV .... Jupiter Flyby Vehicle [*Aerospace*]
JFW .... Jamaica Federation of Women (BUAC)
JFW .... Justice for Women (EA)
JFY .... Foster Yeoman Ltd. [*British ICAO designator*] (FAAC)
JFY .... Japanese Fiscal Year (CINC)
JFY .... Jiffy (ABBR)
JG .... Jahrgang [*Year of Publication/Volume*] [*German*]
JG .... Jerusalem und Seine Gelaende [*A publication*] (BJA)
JG .... Jockeys' Guild (EA)
JG .... Joules per Gram [*Physics*] (IAA)
Jg .... Judges [*Old Testament book*] (BJA)
JG .... Judgment [*Legal shorthand*] (LWAP)
JG .... Juedisches Gemeindeblatt fuer die Britische Zone [*A publication*] (BJA)
JG .... Junction Grammar [*Computer science*]
JG .... Junction Grammar [*Machine translation term*] (NITA)
JG .... June Grass [*Test*] [*Medicine*] (DAVI)
JG .... Junior Girls [*School department*] [*British*] (DI)
JG .... Junior Grade
JG .... Juxtaglomerular [*Histology*]
jg .... Juxtaglomerular (STED)
JG .... Swedair [*ICAO designator*] (AD)
JGA .... Jamnagar [*India*] [*Airport symbol*] (OAG)
JGA .... Japan Gas Association (BUAC)
JGA .... Japan Golf Association (BUAC)
JGA .... Jojoba Growers Association (EA)
JGA .... Joseph Guzman & Associates, Inc. [*Palatine, IL*] [*Telecommunications Defunct*] (TSSD)
JGA .... Juxtaglomerular Apparatus [*Histology*]
JGAB .... Joint Government Agencies Board (SSD)
JG & C......... Joint Guidance and Control (KSC)
JG-APP .... Joint Group on Acquisition Pollution Prevention (BCP)
JGB .... Japanese Government Bond (ECON)
JGB .... Jewish Guild for the Blind (EA)
JGC .... Grand Canyon [*Arizona*] [*Airport symbol*] (OAG)
JGC .... Jacob Gold Corp. [*Vancouver Stock Exchange symbol*]
JGC .... JGC Corp. [*Formerly, Japan Gasoline Co. Ltd.*]
JGC .... Juxtaglomerular Cells [*Histology*]
JGCC .... Juxtaglomerular Cell Count [*Endocrinology*]
JGCT........... Juxtaglomerular Cell Tumor [*Histology*] (DAVI)
JG/D............ Judgement for the Defendant [*Legal shorthand*] (LWAP)
JGD .... Junior Grand Deacon [*Freemasonry*]
J/Gdsmn ..... Junior Guardsman [*British military*] (DMA)
JGE .... Jaguar Equity, Inc. [*Vancouver Stock Exchange symbol*]
JGE .... Joint Group of Experts [*Marine science*] (MSC)
JGF .... Jakarta Growth Fund [*NYSE symbol*] (SPSG)
JGF .... Junctor Grouping Frame [*Telecommunications*] (TEL)
JGFC........... Joe Gallison Fan Club (EA)
JGFC........... John Gilbert Fan Club (EA)
JGFC........... John Gill Fan Club (EA)
JGFET .... Junction Gate Field-Effect Transistor [*Electronics*] (IAA)
JGH .... Jig Grinder Head
JGI .... Jejunogastric Intussusception [*Gastroenterology*] (DAVI)
JGI .... Joint Genome Institute (HGEN)
JGI .... Juxtaglomerular Granulation Index [*Endocrinology*]
JGI .... Juxtaglomerular Index [*Endocrinology*]
JGIFC .... John Gary International Fan Club (EA)
JGIN............ JG Industries [*NASDAQ symbol*] (TTSB)
JGIN............ JG Industries, Inc. [*NASDAQ symbol*] (NQ)
JG Ind .... JG Industries, Inc. [*Associated Press*] (SAG)
JGLC .... Joint Government Liaison Committee [*Composed of Association of Brass and Bronze Ingot Manufacturers and Brass and Bronze Ingot Institute*] (EA)
JGM .... Jig Grinding Machine
JGM .... Job Guide Manual (PDAA)
JGMC........... Judy Garland Memorial Club (EA)
JGN .... Junction Gate Number
JGOFS .... Joint Global Ocean Flux Study [*International experiment*]
JGO-US....... Job Guarantee Office of the United States (OICC)
J Gov Info... Journal of Government Information [*A publication*] (BRI)
JGP............. Houston [*Texas*] Greenway [*Airport symbol*] (OAG)
JGP............. Jem Group Products [*Vancouver Stock Exchange symbol*]
JG/P............ Judgement for the Plaintiff [*Legal shorthand*] (LWAP)
JGP............. Juvenile General Paralysis [*Medicine*] (DAVI)
JGP............. Juvenile General Paresis [*Medicine*] (DMAA)
JGPA............ Jobbing Grinders' Provident Association [*A union*] [*British*]
JGQ............. Houston [*Texas*] Guest Quarters [*Airport symbol*] (OAG)
JGR .... Belize Trans Air [*ICAO designator*] (FAAC)
JGR .... Journal of Geophysical Research
JGRIP .... Japanese Government and Public Research in Progress [*International database*]
JGS............. James Griffiths & Sons [*AAR code*]

JGS............. Jewish Genealogical Society (EA)
JGS............. Joint General Staff [Military] (NATG)
Jgs............. Judges [Old Testament book]
JGSDF......... Japanese Ground Self-Defense Forces (AABC)
JGSW.......... Jigsaw (ABBR)
JGT............. Judgment [Legal term] (ROG)
JGT............. Junction Growth Technique
JGTC........... Junior Girls' Training Corps [British World War II]
JGTL........... Job Grading System for Trades and Labor Occupations
JGTOI......... [The] Judge GTO International (EA)
JGW............. Junior Grand Warden [Freemasonry]
JGWTC......... Jungle and Guerrilla Warfare Training Center [Army]
JH.............. Echovirus 28 [Virology] (DAVI)
JH.............. Harland [John H.] Co. [NYSE symbol] (SPSG)
JH.............. Harland (John H.) [NYSE symbol] (TTSB)
JH.............. Jacob's Horse [British military] (DMA)
JH.............. Journal of the House of Representatives [United States]
              [A publication] (DLA)
JH.............. Juvenile Hormone [Entomology]
JH.............. Nordeste-Lineas Aereas Regionais [ICAO designator] (AD)
JHA............. Japan Hour Association [Later, JHB] (EA)
JHA............. Job Hazard Analysis (PDAA)
JHA............. John Howard Association (EA)
JHA............. Juvenile Hormone Analog [Entomology]
JHB............. Japan Hour Broadcasting (EA)
JHB............. Johannesburg [South Africa] (ABBR)
JHB............. Johore Bahru [Malaysia] [Airport symbol] (OAG)
JHBP........... Juvenile Hormone Binding Protein [Entomology]
JHC............. Garden City [New York] [Airport symbol] (OAG)
JHC............. Johnson Canyon [California] [Seismograph station code, US
              Geological Survey] (SEIS)
JHC............. Joint High Command (DNAB)
JHCNHS........ John Henry Cardinal Newman Honorary Society [Defunct] (EA)
JHD............. Jehuda [On Hebrew coins of the fourth century]
JHD............. Joint Hypocenter Determination [Earthquake study]
JHDA .... Junior Hospital Doctors Association [British]
JHe............. Jewish Heritage [A publication] (BJA)
JHE............. Johns Hopkins University, Baltimore, MD [OCLC symbol] (OCLC)
JHE............. Juvenile Hormone Esterase [An enzyme]
JHF............. Jackson, MS [Location identifier FAA] (FAAL)
JHFC........... Jan Howard Friends Club (EA)
JHFC........... Jeff Healey Fan Club (EA)
JHG............. Joule Heat Gradient (IEEE)
JHGA.......... Jewish Historical General Archives [Jerusalem] (BJA)
JHGSOWA.... Joint Household Goods Shipping Office, Washington Area [Military]
              (AABC)
JHHGSO....... Joint Household Goods Shipping Office [Military]
JHI............. Hancock, John, Investors Trust [NYSE symbol] (SAG)
JHI............. Jeffreys Henry International (BUAC)
JHI............. John Hancock Investors Trust [NYSE symbol] (SPSG)
JHI............. John Hancock Inv Tr [NYSE symbol] (TTSB)
JHI............. Journal of the History of Ideas [A publication] (BRI)
J Hi E......... Journal of Higher Education [A publication] (BRI)
J Hist G....... Journal of Historical Geography [A publication] (BRI)
J Hist Soc SA... Journal. Historical Society of South Australia [A publication]
JHjelm......... Hjelms [Jim] Private Collection [Associated Press] (SAG)
JHjelm......... Jim Hjelms Private Collection [Associated Press] (SAG)
JHL............. Jet Heritage Ltd. [British ICAO designator] (FAAC)
JHM............. Juvenile Hormone Mimic [Entomology]
JHMCO .... J. H. Morgan Consultants [Morristown, NJ] [Information service or
              system Telecommunications] (TSSD)
JHMO.......... Junior Hospital Medical Officer
JHN............. John Henry Newman [Initials used as pseudonym]
JHN............. Johnson Air, Inc. [ICAO designator] (FAAC)
JHN............. Johnson, KS [Location identifier FAA] (FAAL)
JHNBX .... Hancock(J) Bond Cl.A [Mutual fund ticker symbol] (SG)
JHO............. Junior House Officer [Military]
J Homosex... Journal of Homosexuality [A publication] (BRI)
JHP............. Jacketed Hollow-Point [Ammunition]
JHP............. Jackson Hole Preserve (EA)
JHP............. Peabody Institute of Johns Hopkins University, Conservatory Library,
              Baltimore, MD [OCLC symbol] (OCLC)
JHPC........... Jim Hielms Private Coll'n [NASDAQ symbol] (TTSB)
JHPC........... Jim Hjelms Private Collection [NASDAQ symbol] (SPSG)
JHPS........... Judaica Historical Philatelic Society (EA)
JHQ............. Joint Headquarters [British military] (DMA)
JHQ............. Shute Harbour [Australia Airport symbol]
JHR............. Jarisch-Herxheimer Reaction [Immunology] (DAVI)
JHR............. Journal Holdings Report (AEPA)
JHRP .... Joint Highway Research Project [Purdue University] [Research
              center] (RCD)
JHS............. Hancock, John, Income Securities Trust [NYSE symbol] (SAG)
JHS............. Jesus Hominum Salvator [Jesus, Savior of Men] (ROG)
JHS............. Job Hunter's Sourcebook [A publication]
JHS............. John Hampden Society (BUAC)
JHS............. John Hancock Income Securities Trust [NYSE symbol] (SPSG)
JHS............. John Hancock Inc. Sec [NYSE symbol] (TTSB)
JHS............. Junior High School
JHS............. School of Advanced International Studies, Johns Hopkins University,
              Washington, DC [OCLC symbol] (OCLC)
JHSE........... Jewish Historical Society of England
JHSF........... Japan Health Sciences Foundation (BUAC)
JHSN........... Journal. Historical Society of Nigeria [A publication]
JHTR........... Japan High Tech Review [Database] [Kyodo News International,
              Inc.] [Information service or system] (CRD)

JHU............ Johns Hopkins University [Maryland]
JHU/APL ..... Johns Hopkins University Applied Physics Laboratory [Laurel, MD]
JHU-CRSC ... Johns Hopkins University - Center for Research in Scientific
              Communication (PDAA)
JHU-DDB .... Johns Hopkins University - Dyslexia and Dysgraphia Batteries
JHVA.......... Jehovah (ROG)
JHVH.......... Jehovah (ABBR)
JHW........... Jamestown [New York] [Airport symbol] (OAG)
JHW........... Jamestown, NY [Location identifier FAA] (FAAL)
JHW........... Johns Hopkins University, Welch Medical Library, Baltimore, MD
              [OCLC symbol] (OCLC)
JHWC......... Joint Hurricane Warning Center (CINC)
JI .... Air Balear [ICAO designator] (ICDA)
JI .... Gull Air [ICAO designator] (AD)
JI .... Jamaat-i-Islami [Pakistan] [Political party] (FEA)
JI .... Japan Institute [Defunct] (EA)
JI .... Jazz Interactions (EA)
JI .... Jazz International
JI .... Jejunal Intestinal [Medicine] (DB)
JI .... Jejunoileitis [Gastroenterology] (DAVI)
JI .... Jejunoileostomy [Gastroenterology] (DAVI)
JI .... Jersey Institute
JI .... Jesness Inventory [Psychology]
JI .... Jet Express [ICAO designator] (AD)
JI .... Jet Interaction (RDA)
JI .... Jigging Information
JI .... Job Instruction
JI .... Job Insurance [Job Service] (OICC)
ji .... Johnston Atoll [MARC country of publication code Library of
              Congress] (LCCP)
JI .... Joint Identification (DNAB)
JI .... Josephson Interferometer [Optics] (IAA)
JI .... Junction Isolation [Electronics]
JI .... Jupiter Inlet [NASA] (KSC)
JIA............. Jetstream International Airlines [ICAO designator] (FAAC)
JIA............. Joint Interest Audiovisual Requirements (MCD)
JIA............. Jordan International Airline
JIA............. Jute Importers' Association [British] (DBA)
JIAA.......... Joint Institute for Aeronautics and Acoustics [Stanford University]
              (PDAA)
JIAD.......... Joint Integrated Avionics Directorate (DOMA)
JIAFS......... Joint Institute for Acoustics and Flight Sciences (MCD)
JIAFS......... Joint Institute for Advancement of Flight Science [Research center]
              (RCD)
JIAWG .... Joint Integrated Avionics Working Group [DoD]
JIB............. Djibouti [Airport symbol] (OAG)
JIB............. Jack-in-the-Box Dummy [CIA]
JIB............. Jejunoileal Bypass [Gastroenterology] (DAVI)
JIB............. Jewish Information Bureau [Defunct] (EA)
JIB............. Job Information Block [Computer science] (BUR)
JIB............. Jobs Impact Bulletin [National Committee for Full Employment]
              [A publication]
JIB............. Joint Information Bureau [Military] (MCD)
JIB............. Joint Intelligence Bureau [British] (MCD)
JIB............. Jordan Information Bureau (EA)
JIB............. Journal of International Business Studies [A publication] (BRI)
JIBA.......... Japanese Institute of Business Administration (BUAC)
JIBECI........ Joint Industry Board for the Electrical Contracting Industry (BUAC)
JIBEI......... Joint Industry Board of the Electrical Industry (EA)
JIBG.......... Jibing (ABBR)
JIBICO .... Japan International Bank and Investment (BUAC)
JIC............. Jet-Induced Circulation [Combustor]
JIC............. Jet Interaction Control (MCD)
JIC............. Jewelry Industry Council (EA)
JIC............. Jewelry Information Center (NTPA)
JIC............. Job Information Centre [Canada]
JIC............. Job Instruction and Communication (PDAA)
JIC............. Joint Ice Center [US Navy] [Marine science] (OSRA)
JIC............. Joint Implementation Committee [Military] (SAA)
JIC............. Joint Industrial Council [Defunct] (EA)
JIC............. Joint Industry Council (EAIO)
JIC............. Joint Insurance Committee [under the Trading with the Enemy Act]
              [World War II]
JIC............. Joint Intelligence Center
JIC............. Joint Intelligence Committee
JIC............. Joint Interrogation Center (MCD)
JIC............. Junior International Club (EA)
JIC............. Just in Case (WDMC)
JIC............. Juventudes Inconformes de Colombia [Political party] (EY)
JIC............. Morgan Stanley Group, Inc. [AMEX symbol] (SAG)
JICA.......... Japan International Cooperation Agency
JICA.......... Jiangsu Provincial Institute of Culture and Art [China] (BUAC)
JICA.......... Joint Intelligence Center, Africa
JICA.......... Joint Intelligence Collecting Agency
JICACBI...... Joint Intelligence Collecting Agency, China, Burma, India [World War
              II]
JICAME...... Joint Intelligence Collecting Agency, Middle East [World War II]
JICANA...... Joint Intelligence Collecting Agency, North Africa [World War II]
JICARC ...... Joint Intelligence Collecting Agency, Reception Committee [Navy]
JICC.......... Japan Information and Cultural Centre (BUAC)
JICC.......... Job Item Cost Code (MCD)
JICCAR ...... Joint Industry Committee for Cable Audience Research [Television]
              [British]
JICG.......... Joint International Coordination Group (MSC)
JICHS......... Joint Industrial Conference on Hydraulic Standards

JICI	Jeunesse Independante Chretienne Internationale [*International Independant Christian Youth - IICY*] (EA)
JICJ	Journal. International Commission of Jurists [*A publication*] (DLA)
Jick Est	Jickling. Legal and Equitable Estates [*1829*] [*A publication*] (DLA)
JICMARS	Joint Industry Committee of Medical Advertisers for Readership Surveys (BUAC)
JICNARS	Joint Industry Committee for National Readership Surveys [*British*]
JICOA	Japan Information and Communication Association [*Information service or system*] (IID)
JICPAC	Joint Intelligence Center Pacific (DOMA)
JICPAR	Joint Industry Committee for Postal Audience Research (BUAC)
JICPAS	Joint Industry Committee for Poster Audience Surveys [*British*]
JICPOA	Joint Intelligence Center, Pacific Ocean Areas
JICRAR	Joint Industry Committee for Radio Audience Resarch (BUAC)
JICRAR	Joint Industry Committee for Radio Audience Research [*British*]
JICS	Joint Intelligence Coordination Staff [*Central Intelligence Agency*] (AABC)
JICS	Joint Interpreting and Conference Service (BUAC)
JICST	Japan Information Center for Science and Technology
JICST	Japan Information Center of Science and Technology [*Tokyo*] (IID)
JICST	Japan International Center of Science and Technology (USGC)
JICTAR	Joint Industry Committee for Television Advertising Research [*Database producer*]
JICUF	Japan International Christian University Foundation (EA)
JID	Air Condal SA [*Spain ICAO designator*] (FAAC)
JIDA	Japan Industrial Designers Association (BUAC)
JIDA	Jewelry Industry Distributors Association (EA)
JIDC	Jamaica Industrial Development Corp. (BUAC)
JIDS	Job Information Delivery System [*US Employment Service*] [*Department of Labor*]
JIE	Japan Information Exchange [*Comtex Scientific Corp.*] [*Information service or system Defunct*] (CRD)
JIE	Jobs in Energy (EA)
JIE	Junior Institute of Engineers
JIEA	Japan Industrial Explosives Association (BUAC)
JIEE	Japanese Institute of Electrical Engineers
JIEO	Joint Interoperability and Engineering Organization [*DoD*]
JIEP	Joint Intelligence Estimate for Planning (AFM)
JIF	French Lick, IN [*Location identifier FAA*] (FAAL)
JIF	Janus Information Facility [*Later, J2CP Information Services*] (EA)
JIF	Jet Interaction Fuel
JIF	Joint Integrated Firepower [*Task force*] (MCD)
JIF	Joint Interrogation Facility (DOMA)
JIFA	Japanese Institute for Foreign Affairs (BUAC)
JIFC	Janis Ian Fan Club (EA)
JIFC	Julio Iglesias Fan Club [*Defunct*] (EA)
JIFDATS	Joint In-Flight Data Transmission System [*Army*] (MCD)
JIFE	Junta Internacional de Fiscalizacion de Estupefacientes [*International Narcotics Control Board*]
JIFS	Jerusalem Institute for Federal Studies (BUAC)
JIFSAN	Joint Institute of Food Safety and Applied Nutrition
JIFTS	Joint In-Flight Transmission System [*Army*] (IEEE)
JIG	Jinotega [*Nicaragua*] [*Seismograph station code, US Geological Survey*] (SEIS)
JIG	Joint Industry Group [*An association*] (EA)
JIG	Joint Intelligence Group [*Military*]
JIG	Joule Impulse Generator [*Physics*]
JIGFET	Junction and Insulated Gate Field Effect Transistor (MCD)
JIGG	Jet Interaction Gas Generator
JIGL	Jiggle (ABBR)
JIGLD	Jiggled (ABBR)
JIGLG	Jiggling (ABBR)
JIGLY	Jiggly (ABBR)
JIGR	Jigger (ABBR)
JIGS	Joule Impulse Generator System [*Physics*]
JIGTSC	Joint Industry-Government Tall Structures Committee
JIH	Joint Interval Histogram [*Histology*] (DAVI)
JIH	Journal of Interdisciplinary History [*A publication*] (BRI)
JII	John Innes Institute [*British*] (ARC)
JII	Johnston Industries [*NYSE symbol*] (TTSB)
JII	Johnston Industries, Inc. [*NYSE symbol*] (SPSG)
JIIA	Japan Institute of International Affairs (BUAC)
JIIB	Jewish Immigrants Information Bureau (BJA)
JIIG-CAL	Job Ideas and Information Generator - Computer Assisted Learning (AIE)
JIII	Japan Institute of Invention and Innovation (BUAC)
JIIKS	Joint Imagery Interpretation Key Structure (MCD)
JIIP	Joint Interface Implementation Program [*Army*] (MCD)
JIIST	Japan Institute for International Studies and Training
JIL	Jet-Induced Lift
JIL	Joy Industries Ltd. [*Vancouver Stock Exchange symbol*]
JILA	Japanese Institute of Landscape Architects (BUAC)
JILA	Joint Institute for Laboratory Astrophysics [*University of Colorado, National Bureau of Standards*] (EA)
JILA-IC	Joint Institute for Laboratory Astrophysics-Information Center [*University of Colorado*] (PDAA)
JILE	Joint Intelligence Liaison Element (MCD)
JilinCh	Jilin Chemical Industrial Co. Ltd. [*Associated Press*] (SAG)
JILL	Jobs Illustrated [*CD-ROM*]
JillEnt	Jillians Entertainment Corp. [*Associated Press*] (SAG)
JILO	Joint Information Liaison Office [*Military*]
JILTA	Journal. Indian Law Teachers Association [*A publication*] (DLA)
JIM	Jevreiski Istoriski Muzej (BJA)
JIM	Jimma [*Ethiopia*] [*Airport symbol*] (OAG)
JIM	Job Instruction Manual
JIM	Memphis, TN [*Location identifier FAA*] (FAAL)
JIM	Sark International Airways Ltd. [*British ICAO designator*] (FAAC)
JIMA	Japan Industrial Management Association (BUAC)
JIMA	John Innes Manufacturers Association (DBA)
JIMAR	Joint Institute for Marine and Atmospheric Research [*Honolulu, HI*] [*National Oceanic and Atmospheric Administration*] (GRD)
JIMC	Japan Immuno-Monitoring Centre (BUAC)
JIMI	Jimi Hendrix Information Management Institute (EA)
JIMPP	Joint Industrial Mobilization Planning Process [*Environmental science*] (COE)
JIMS	Joint Industrial Measurement Programme (ACII)
JIN	Japanese Institution of Navigation (BUAC)
JIN	Jindabyne [*Australia Seismograph station code, US Geological Survey Closed*] (SEIS)
JIN	Jinja [*Uganda*] [*Airport symbol*] (AD)
JIN	Jump Indirectly [*Computer science*]
JIN	Justice Institute of British Columbia, Instructional Service [*UTLAS symbol*]
J Ind L Inst	Journal. Indian Law Institute [*A publication*] (DLA)
J Ind R	Journal of Industrial Relations [*A publication*]
J Indust Rel	Journal of Industrial Relations [*A publication*]
JINGLD	Jingled (ABBR)
JINGLG	Jingling (ABBR)
J INOR NUCL CHEM	Journal of Inorganic and Nuclear Chemistry [*A publication*] (WDAA)
JINR	Joint Institute of Nuclear Research [*Dubna, USSR*]
JINS	Juveniles in Need of Supervision [*Classification for delinquent children*]
JINSA	Jewish Institute for National Security Affairs (EA)
JINSTE	Junior Institution of Engineers [*British*]
J Inst Electr Eng (1949-63)	Journal. Institution of Electrical Engineers (1949-63) [*A publication*]
J Inst Electr Eng (1889-1940)	Journal. Institution of Electrical Engineers (1889-1940) [*A publication*]
J Instn Eng Aust	Journal. Institution of Engineers of Australia. [*A publication*]
JINTACCS	Joint Interoperability of Tactical Command and Control Systems (MCD)
JINTCCS	Joint Interoperability of Tactical Command and Control Systems (DOMA)
J Int'l & Comp L	Journal of International and Comparative Law [*A publication*] (DLA)
J Int'l Comm Jur	Journal. International Commission of Jurists [*A publication*] (DLA)
J Int'l L & Dipl	Journal of International Law and Diplomacy [*A publication*] (DLA)
J Int'l L & Pol	Journal of International Law and Politics [*A publication*] (DLA)
JIO	Joint Information Office [*Military*]
JIO	Joint Integration Office [*Department of Energy*] [*Albuquerque, NM*] (GAAI)
JIO	Joint Intelligence Organization (BUAC)
JIO	Ontario, CA [*Location identifier FAA*] (FAAL)
JIOA	Joint Intelligence Objectives Agency (MCD)
JIOC	Jensen Interceptor Owners Club (EA)
JIOP	Joint Interface Operational Procedures (COE)
JIP	Jipijapa [*Ecuador*] [*Airport symbol*] (AD)
JIP	Job Improvement Plan
JIP	Job the Impatient (BJA)
JIP	Join in Progress [*Broadcasting*] (WDMC)
JIP	Joint Implementation Plan [*Military*]
JIP	Joint Input
JIP	Joint Input Processing (IEEE)
JIP	Joint Installation Plan (AAG)
JIP/AMD	JIP/Areal Marketing Database [*Toyo Keizai Shinposha Co. Ltd.*] [*Japan Information service or system*] (CRD)
JIPC	Joint Imagery Production Complex (DOMA)
JIPC	Jordan Is Palestine Committee (EA)
JIPDEC	Japan Information Processing Development Center (NITA)
JIPID	Japanese International Protein Information Database
JIPMER	Jawahrlal Institute of Postgraduate Medical Education and Research [*India*]
JIR	Jewish Institute of Religion
JIR	Jiri [*Nepal*] [*Airport symbol*] (OAG)
JIR	Job Improvement Request
JIRA	Japanese Industrial Robot Association (CIST)
JIRA	Japan Industrial Robot Association (BUAC)
JIRC	Journal of Information Research Communications [*British*] (NITA)
JIRCSM	Joint Industry Research Committee for Standardization of Miniature Precision Coaxial Connectors
JIRI	Johnson Informal Reading Inventory (EDAC)
JIRP	Juneau Icefield Research Project [*University of Idaho*] [*Research center*]
JIRS	Jewish Information and Referral Service Directory [*A publication*] (EAAP)
JIRS	Joint Information and Retrieval System [*DoD*] (MCD)
JIS	Jamaica Information Service (BUAC)
JIS	Japanese Industrial Standards
JIS	Japan Investment Service [*Reuters Holdings Ltd.*] [*British Information service or system*] (CRD)
JIS	Jet Inlet System
JIS	Jet Interaction Steering
JIS	Jewish Information Society of America (EA)
JIS	Job Information Service [*Department of Labor*]
JIS	Job Information Station [*Department of Labor*] (IAA)
JIS	Job Information System (NITA)
JIS	Job Input System (NITA)
JIS	Joint Integrated Simulation (NASA)

JIS .... Joint Intelligence Staff
JIS .... Joint Operations Interim Software (MCD)
JIS .... Journal of Information Science [*A publication*] (NITA)
JIS .... Juvenile Idiopathic Scoliosis [*Medicine*] (DMAA)
JISAO .... Joint Institute for Study of the Atmosphere and Ocean [*Seattle, WA*] [*University of Washington, NOAA*] (GRD)
JISC .... Japanese Industrial Standards Committee [*Agency of Industrial Science and Technology, Ministry of International Trade and Industry*]
JISC .... Joint Information Services Committee (BUAC)
JISC .... Joint Information Systems Committee [*British*] (TELE)
JISEA .... Japan Iron and Steel Exporters Association (BUAC)
JISETA .... Joint Investigation of the Southeastern Tropical Atlantic [*Angola, US*] (MSC)
JISF .... Japan Iron and Steel Federation (BUAC)
JISHA .... Japan Industrial Safety and Health Association (BUAC)
JI/SI .... Jet Interaction / Secondary Injection
J Islam & Comp L... Journal of Islamic and Comparative Law [*Nigeria*] [*A publication*] (DLA)
JISO .... Japanese International Satellite Organization [*Cable-television system*]
JISPB .... Joint Intelligence Studies Publishing Board
JISR .... Joint Information Search Unit Retrieval System (MCD)
JISS .... Jet Impurity Survey Spectrometer [*Nuclear energy*] (NUCP)
JISTEC .... Japan International Science and Technology Exchange Center
JIT .... Jamiat-i-Talaba [*Pakistan*] [*Political party*] (PD)
JIT .... Job Information Test [*Military*] (AFM)
JIT .... Job Instruction Training
JIT .... Joint Interest Test [*Navy*] (NG)
JIT .... Just in Time
jit .... Just-In-Time [*Industry*] (ODBW)
JIT .... Just-in-Time Inventory (TDOB)
JITA .... Japanese Industrial Technology Association
JITA .... Jet Interaction Test Apparatus (MCD)
JITC .... Jewelry Industry Tax Committee [*Defunct*] (EA)
JIT compiler... Just-in-Time Compiler [*Computer science*] (IGQR)
JITF .... Joint Interface Test Facility [*Army*] (RDA)
JITF .... Joint Interface Test Force [*Military*] (RDA)
JITF .... Joint Interservice Task Force (MCD)
JITPA .... Japanese International Trade Promotion Association (BUAC)
JITR .... Jitter (ABBR)
JITRBG .... Jitterbug (ABBR)
JITRY .... Jittery (ABBR)
JIU .... Joint Inspection Unit [*United Nations*]
JIW .... J. Inglis Wright [*Advertising agency*] [*New Zealand*]
JIW .... Jiwani [*Pakistan*] [*Airport symbol*] (OAG)
JIWP .... Joint Interim Working Party
JJ .... Coddair Air East [*ICAO designator*] (AD)
JJ .... Jaw Jerk [*Medicine*]
JJ .... Jeep Junior [*Automobile model designation*]
JJ .... Jejunojejunostomy [*Gastroenterology*] (DAVI)
JJ .... Jennifer Jo [*In TV series "The Governor and JJ"*]
JJ .... Jews for Jews [*Defunct*] (EA)
JJ .... Josephson Junction [*Cryogenics*] (IAA)
JJ .... Judges [*Old Testament book*]
JJ .... Junior Judge [*Legal term*] (DLA)
JJ .... Justices
JJA .... Jack and Jill of America (EA)
JJA .... Judges of Appeal [*Legal term*]
JJA .... June-July-August [*Marine science*] (OSRA)
JJA .... Justices of Appeal [*Legal term*] (DLA)
JJAF .... Jack and Jill of America Foundation (EA)
JJAMD .... Jaw Joints and Allied Musculo-Skeletal Disorders Foundation (EA)
JJC .... Jackson Junior College [*Florida; Michigan*]
JJC .... Jiffy Junction Connector
JJC .... Joliet Junior College [*Illinois*]
JJDP .... Juvenile Justice and Delinquency Prevention
JJDPA .... Juvenile Justice and Delinquency Prevention Act
JJ FAD .... Just Jammin' Fresh and Def [*Rap recording group*]
JJFC .... Jana Jae Fan Club (EA)
JJFC .... Jim and Jesse Fan Club (EA)
JJFC .... Joan Jett Fan Club (EA)
JJFC .... Johnny and Jack Fan Club (EA)
JJI .... Juanjui [*Peru*] [*Airport symbol*] (OAG)
JJITC .... Jayco Jafari International Travel Club (EA)
JJM .... John Judkyn Memorial
JJ Marsh (KY)... Marshall's Reports [*Kentucky*] [*A publication*] (DLA)
JJMAS .... Jack Jones Music Appreciation Society [*Defunct*] (EAIO)
JJN .... Jinjiang [*China*] [*Airport symbol*] (OAG)
JJO .... Mountain City, TN [*Location identifier FAA*] (FAAL)
JJP .... Jatiya Janata Party [*National People's Party*] [*Bangladesh*] [*Political party*] (PPW)
JJS .... James Joyce Society (EA)
JJSC .... Jefferson Smurfit [*NASDAQ symbol*] (TTSB)
JJSC .... Jefferson Smurfit Corp. [*NASDAQ symbol*] (SAG)
JJSC .... Justices of the Supreme Court [*Legal term*] (DLA)
JJSF .... J&J Snack Foods [*NASDAQ symbol*] (TTSB)
JJSF .... J & J Snack Foods Corp. [*NASDAQ symbol*] (NQ)
J-J S-S ...... Jean-Jacques Servan-Schreiber [*French publisher*]
JJSSPA .... Jewish Social Service Professionals Association (NTPA)
JJSWC .... Jiffy Junction Single Wire Connector
JJT .... Josephson Junction Transistor [*Electronics*] (AAEL)
JJT .... Jumbo Jet Transport
JJU .... Julienhaab [*Greenland*] [*Airport symbol*] (AD)
J Jur .... Journal of Jurisprudence [*A publication*] (DLA)

J Jur Papyrol... Journal of Juristic Papyrology [*A publication*] (DLA)
JJW .... Sternair, Inc. [*FAA designator*] (FAAC)
JJWC .... Jiffy Junction Wire Connector
JJWFC .... Jerry Jeff Walker Fan Club (EA)
JK .... Flip-Flop Circuit [*Computer science*]
JK .... Jack (MSA)
JK .... Jishu Kanri [*Voluntary Management*] [*Japanese method for increasing productivity of industrial workers by involving them in planning*]
J/K .... Joule per Kelvin [*Physics*]
JK .... Junk [*Ship's rigging*] (ROG)
JK .... Sun World [*ICAO designator*] (AD)
JK .... Trabajos Aereos y Enlaces SA [*Spain ICAO designator*] (ICDA)
JKA .... Jakarta [*Indonesia*] (ABBR)
Jkᵃ .... Kidd A [*Blood group*] (DAVI)
JKAA .... Japan Karate Association of Australia
J Kan B Ass'n... Journal. Kansas Bar Association [*A publication*] (DLA)
JK & A .... John Krucek & Associates [*Telecommunications service*] (TSSD)
JKAS .... Jackass (ABBR)
JKAS .... Jack Knight Airmail Society (EA)
JKB .... Justice of the King's Bench (ROG)
Jkᵇ .... Kidd B [*Blood group*] (DAVI)
JKBIR .... Justice of the King's Bench, Ireland (ROG)
JKBT .... Jackboot (ABBR)
JKBX .... Jukebox (ABBR)
JKC .... Jidosha Kiki Co. Ltd.
JKC .... Shreveport, LA [*Location identifier FAA*] (FAAL)
JKCL .... Jockey Club, Inc. [*NASDAQ symbol*] (SAG)
JKD .... Jacked (ABBR)
JKET .... Jacket (ABBR)
JKETD .... Jacketted (ABBR)
JKFC .... Japan-Republic of Korea Joint Fisheries Commission [*Marine science*] (OSRA)
JKFCFC .... Jimmy Kish ™The Flying Cowboy∫ Fan Club (EA)
JKG .... Jacking (ABBR)
JKG .... Jonkoping [*Sweden*] [*Airport symbol*] (OAG)
J/kg .... Joule per Kilogram [*Physics*]
J/(KG K)...... Joules per Kilogram Kelvin
JKH .... Chios [*Greece*] [*Airport symbol*] (OAG)
JKHY .... Henry (Jack) & Assoc [*NASDAQ symbol*] (TTSB)
JKHY .... Henry, Jack Associates [*NASDAQ symbol*] (SAG)
JKKB .... Jeunesse du Kwilu-Kwango-Bateke [*Kwilu-Kwango-Bateke Youth*]
JkksPac ...... Jakks Pacific, Inc. [*Associated Press*] (SAG)
JKL .... Jackal (ABBR)
JKL .... Jackson, KY [*Location identifier FAA*] (FAAL)
JKLF .... Jammu and Kashmir Liberation Front [*India*] [*Political party*] (ECON)
JKMR .... Jackhammer (ABBR)
JKMS .... Jack Knight Air Mail Society (EA)
JKNC .... Jammu and Kashmir National Conference [*India*] [*Political party*] (PPW)
JKNC .... Jammu and Kashmir National Congress (BUAC)
JKNIF .... Jackknife (ABBR)
JKP .... James Knox Polk [*US president, 1795-1849*]
JKPC .... Junior Knights of Peter Claver (EA)
JKPMA .... James K. Polk Memorial Association (EA)
JKPT .... Jackpot (ABBR)
JKPT .... Jackpot Enterprises [*NASDAQ symbol*] (SAG)
JKPTW .... Jackpot Enterprises Wrrt [*NASDAQ symbol*] (TTSB)
JKR .... Janakpur [*Nepal*] [*Airport symbol*] (OAG)
JKS .... Jacks (ABBR)
JKS .... Jacks Creek, TN [*Location identifier FAA*] (FAAL)
JKS .... Jackson [*Diocesan abbreviation*] [*Mississippi*] (TOCD)
JKSCR .... Jackscrew [*Mechanical engineering*]
JksnvII .... Jacksonville Bancorp, Inc. [*Associated Press*] (SAG)
JksnvlSL ..... Jacksonville Savings & Loan Association [*Texas*] [*Associated Press*] (SAG)
JksnvSB ...... Jacksonville Savings Bank (Illinois) [*Associated Press*] (SAG)
JKST .... Johnson-Kenney Screening Test [*Psychology*] (DAVI)
JKT .... Djakarta [*Java, Indonesia*] [*Airport symbol*] (AD)
JKT .... Jacket (KSC)
JKT .... Jakarta [*Indonesia*] [*Airport symbol*] (OAG)
JKT .... Job Knowledge Test [*Military*] (AFM)
JKTD .... Jacketed (ABBR)
JKTG .... Jacketing (ABBR)
JKU .... Kyoto University, Kyoto, Japan [*Library symbol Library of Congress*] (LCLS)
JKW .... Juvonen, K. W., Winnipeg, Manitoba CDA [*STAC*]
JL .... Jadassohn-Lewandowsky [*Syndrome*] [*Thickening of the nails*] [*Medicine*] (DAVI)
JL .... Jaffe-Lichtenstein [*Syndrome*] [*or Fibrous dysplasia Orthopedics*] (DAVI)
JL .... JAG Listing [*Military*]
JL .... Jaksch-Luzet [*Disease*] [*Medicine*] (DB)
JL .... J & L Specialty Steel [*NYSE symbol*] (SPSG)
JL .... Japan Air Lines [*ICAO designator*] (OAG)
JL .... Javan LASER
JL .... Jazz-Lift [*Provides jazz records to persons in Iron Curtain countries*] [*Defunct*] (EA)
JL .... Jefferson Lyons [*Commercial firm British*]
Jl .... Jejunoileal [*Medicine*] (MEDA)
Jl .... Joel [*Old Testament book*]
Jl .... Joliotium [*Chemistry*] (MEC)
JL .... Joule's Law [*Physics*]
JL .... Journal [*Online database field identifier*]
JL .... July

JL	Junior Leaders Regiment [*British military*] (DMA)
JL	Jurin Law [*Electronics*]
JL	JustLife [*Defunct*] (EA)
JL	Just Looking [*A browser*] [*Retail slang*]
JL	Lab. Jacques Logeais [*France*] [*Research code symbol*]
JLA	Cooper Landing, AK [*Location identifier FAA*] (FAAL)
JLA	Jack L. Ahr [*Designer's mark on US bicentennial quarter*]
JLA	Jalna Resources [*Vancouver Stock Exchange symbol*]
JLA	Japanese Library Association (BUAC)
JLA	Jet Lift Aircraft
JLA	Jewish Law Association (BUAC)
JLA	Jewish Librarians Association [*Later, AJL*] (EA)
JLA	Jordan Library Association (BUAC)
JLAF	Joint Lithuanian-American Fund (BUAC)
JL & Com Soc	Journal. Law and Commerce Society [*Hong Kong*] [*A publication*] (DLA)
JL & Information Science	Journal of Law and Information Science [*A publication*]
JL & Pol	Journal of Law and Politics [*A publication*] (DLA)
JL & Religion	Journal of Law and Religion [*A publication*] (DLA)
J Laryng Otol	Journal of Laryngology and Otology (MEC)
JLAS	JUMPS [*Joint Uniform Military Pay System*] Leave Accounting System (DNAB)
J Law & Ed	Journal of Law and Education [*A publication*] (DLA)
J Law Reform	Journal of Law Reform [*A publication*] (DLA)
J Law Soc'y Scotland	Law Society of Scotland. Journal [*A publication*] (DLA)
JLB	Jewish Labor Bund (EA)
JLB	Jewish Lads' Brigade [*British*] (DI)
JLBD	Jailbird (ABBR)
JLBRK	Jailbreak (ABBR)
JLBTS	Japanese Land-Based Test Site (MCD)
JLC	Houston [*Texas*] Allen Center [*Airport symbol*] (OAG)
JLC	Japanese Linear Collider [*High energy physics*]
JLC	Jewish Labor Committee (EA)
JLC	Joint Logistics Commanders [*Military*]
JLC	Joint Logistics Committee [*Military*]
JLC	Junction Latching Circulator
JLC	Justification for Limited Competition (COE)
JLC & E	Jonesboro, Lake City & Eastern Railroad
JLCAT	Joint Logistics Commanders' Action Team [*Military*]
JLCD	Joint Liaison Committee on Documents [*Used in the international carriage of goods*] (BUAC)
J/L/Cpl	Junior Lance-Corporal [*British military*] (DMA)
J/Ldr	Junior Leader [*British military*] (DMA)
JLE	Jet Lift Engine
JLEM	Jerusalem (ABBR)
JLEN	Julienne (ABBR)
JLEP	Julep (ABBR)
JLF	Joint Landing Force
JLFB	Joint Landing Force Board
JLFC	Joan Lunden Fan Club [*Defunct*] (EA)
JLFC	Johnny Len Fan Club (EA)
JLG	Jewish Lawyers Guild (EA)
JLG	JLG Industries, Inc. [*Associated Press*] (SAG)
JLG	Joint Liaison Group (ECON)
JLGA	James L. Grant and Associates (EFIS)
JLGI	JLG Indus [*NASDAQ symbol*] (TTSB)
JLH	Arlington Heights, IL [*Location identifier FAA*] (FAAL)
JLHC	Just Like Home [*NASDAQ symbol*] (TTSB)
JLHC	Just Like Home, Inc. [*NASDAQ symbol*] (SAG)
JLI	Jiffy Lube International, Inc. (EFIS)
JLI	Julian, CA [*Location identifier FAA*] (FAAL)
JLIA	Japan Lumber Importers Association (BUAC)
JLIOOF	Junior Lodge, Independent Order of Odd Fellows (EA)
JLIRI	Jinan Light Industry Research Institute (EA)
JLM	Junior Legacy Melbourne [*Australia An association*]
JLMC	Joint Labor Management Committee of the Retail Food Industry (EA)
JLMIC	Japan Light Machinery Information Center (EA)
JLMSA	Jewish Liturgical Music Society of America (EA)
JLN	Jaclyn, Inc. [*AMEX symbol*] (SPSG)
JLN	Joplin [*Missouri*] [*Airport symbol*] (OAG)
JLN	Joplin, MO [*Location identifier FAA*] (FAAL)
JLO	Jesolo [*Italy*] [*Airport symbol*] (AD)
JLO	Junction Light Output
JLOIC	Joint Logistics, Operations, Intelligence Center [*NATO*] (NATG)
JLOTS	Joint Logistics Over-the-Shore [*Military*] (RDA)
JLP	Jamaica Labour Party [*Political party*] (PPW)
JLP	Jazz for Life Project [*Defunct*] (EA)
JLP	John Lewis Partnership [*British*] (ECON)
JLP	Juan-les-Pins [*France*] [*Airport symbol*] (AD)
JLP	Juvenile Laryngeal Papilloma [*Medicine*] (DAVI)
JLPB	Joint Logistics Planning Board
JLPC	Joint Logistics Plans Committee [*Military*]
JLPG	Joint Logistics Plans Group [*Military*]
JLPPG	Joint Logistics and Personnel Policy Guidance [*Military*] (AFM)
JLR	Jabalpur [*India*] [*Airport symbol*] (OAG)
JLR	Jailer (ABBR)
JLR	Jamaica Law Reports [*1953-55*] [*A publication*] (DLA)
JLR	Jeweler (ABBR)
JLR	Johore Law Reports [*India*] [*A publication*] (DLA)
JLR	Junior Leaders Regiment [*British military*] (DMA)
JLRB	Joint Labor Relations Board
JLRB	Joint Logistics Review Board [*Military*]
JLRC	Jack London Research Center (EA)
JLREID	Joint Long-Range Estimative Intelligence Document [*Military*]
JLRPG	Joint Long-Range Proving Ground (KSC)
JLRRT	Jordan Left-Right Reversal Test [*Educational test*]
JLRSA	Joint Long-Range Strategic Appraisal [*Military*]
JLRSE	Joint Long-Range Strategic Estimates [*Military*]
JLRSS	Joint Long-Range Strategic Study [*Military*] (AFM)
jlry	Jewelry (VRA)
JLS	Jet Alsace [*France ICAO designator*] (FAAC)
JLS	Jet Lift System
JLS	Jewels (ADA)
JLS	Joint Least Squares [*Statistics*]
JLSC	Joint Logistics System Command (DOMA)
J/L/Sgt	Junior Lance-Sergeant [*British military*] (DMA)
JL Soc	Journal. Law Society of Scotland [*A publication*] (DLA)
JLSP	Joint Logistics Support Plan
JLT	Jalate, Inc. [*AMEX symbol*] (SAG)
JLT	Jalate Ltd [*AMEX symbol*] (TTSB)
JLT	Junior Lord of the Treasury
JLTF	Jewish Librarians Task Force (EA)
JLTPB	Joint Logistics Techniques and Procedures Board [*Military*]
JLTR	Jilter (ABBR)
JLU	Jilin University (BUAC)
JLUAC	Joint Land Use Advisory Committee
JLUS	Jealous (ABBR)
JLUSLY	Jealously (ABBR)
JLUSNS	Jealousness (ABBR)
JLUSY	Jealousy (ABBR)
JLW	Jahrbuch fuer Liturgiewissenschaft [*A publication*] (ODCC)
JLW-155	Joint Lightweight 155mm Howitzer (RDA)
JLY	Jelly (ABBR)
JLY	Jena, LA [*Location identifier FAA*] (FAAL)
JLYBN	Jellybean (ABBR)
JLYD	Jellied (ABBR)
JLYFSH	Jellyfish (ABBR)
JLYLK	Jellylike (ABBR)
JM	Air Jamaica Ltd. [*ICAO designator*] (OAG)
JM	Jactitation of Marriage [*Legal*] [*British*] (ROG)
JM	Jamaica [*ANSI two-letter standard code*] (CNC)
jm	Jamaica [*MARC country of publication code Library of Congress*] (LCCP)
Jm	James [*New Testament book*] (BJA)
JM	James Madison [*US president, 1751-1836*]
JM	James Monroe [*US president, 1758-1831*]
JM	Jesuit Missions (EA)
J/M	Jettison Motor (KSC)
JM	Jewish Male [*Classified advertising*]
JM	Jiyu-Minshuto [*Liberal-Democratic Party*] [*Japan Political party*]
JM	John Mercanti [*Designer's mark, when appearing on US coins*]
JM	Johns Manville Corp. (MCD)
JM	Journal of Marketing [*A publication*] (BRI)
JM	Journal of Micrographics (NITA)
JM	Jugomaxillary [*Dentistry*] (DAVI)
JM	Julia MacRae [*Publisher*] [*British*]
JM	Julian Messner [*Publisher's imprint*]
JM	Junction Module [*Deep Space Instrumentation Facility, NASA*]
JM	Juris Magister [*Master of Laws*]
JM	Justizminister [*Minister of Justice*] [*German*] (ILCA)
JM	Justizministerium [*Ministry of Justice*] [*German*] (ILCA)
JM	Juxtamembrane Domain
jM	Mass Transfer Factor [*Physics*] (DAVI)
J/M²	Joules per Square Meter
J/M³	Joules per Cubic Meter [*Physics*]
JMA	Houston [*Texas*] Astrodome [*Airport symbol*] (OAG)
JMA	Jamaica Manufacturers Association (BUAC)
JMA	Jamara Memorial Association (BUAC)
JMA	James Martin Associates [*Database consulting group*] [*British*]
JMA	Jamming Modulation Analysis
JMA	Japanese Military Administration
JMA	Japan Management Association (BUAC)
JMA	Japan Meteorological Agency
JMA	Japan Microphotography Association
JMA	Jewelry Manufacturers Association (EA)
JMA	Jewish Music Alliance (EA)
JMA	John More Association (EA)
JMA	Joinery Managers' Association [*British*] (BI)
JMA	Joint Mission Analysis
JMA	Julia Morgan Association [*Defunct*] (EA)
JMA	Junior Management Assistant
JMA	Junior Medical Assistant [*British military*] (DMA)
JMA	Junior Military Aviator
JMAAD	Juvenile Missionary Association [*British*] (BI)
JMAAD	Joint Military Assistance Affairs Division (CINC)
JMAC	Joint Munitions Allocation Committee
JMAHEP	Joint Military Aircraft Hurricane Evacuation Plan (AFM)
J MAN GS	Journal of the Manchester Geographical Society [*A publication*] (ROG)
JMAPI	Java Management Application Program Interface [*Computer science*] (IGQR)
JMAR	JMAR Industries [*NASDAQ symbol*] (SPSG)
JMAR	JMAR Technologies [*NASDAQ symbol*] [*Formerly, JMAR Industries*]
JMARW	JMAR Inds Wrrt [*NASDAQ symbol*] (TTSB)
JMAS	Joint Manpower Automation System (COE)
J-Mass	Joint-Modeling and Simulation System
J Math Physics	Journal of Mathematical Physics (MEC)
JMB	Jamb (ABBR)
JMB	Jewelers Memorandum Bureau (EA)
JMB	Johnson Matthey Bankers [*Commercial firm British*]

JMB	Joint Matriculation Board [*British*] (DCTA)
JMB	Joint Meteorological Board (AAG)
JMB	Joint Movements Branch [*NATO*] (NATG)
JMBL	Jumble (ABBR)
JMBLD	Jumbled (ABBR)
JMBLG	Jumbling (ABBR)
JMBRE	Jamboree (ABBR)
JMC	James Mitchell & Co. (EFIS)
JMC	Japan Monopoly Corp. (BUAC)
JMC	Jewish Marriage Council (BUAC)
JMC	Jiangxi Medical College [*China*] (BUAC)
JMC	Joint Maritime Commission
JMC	Joint Maritime Congress [*Washington, DC*] (EA)
JMC	Joint Mathematical Council of the United Kingdom (BUAC)
JMC	Joint Message Center
JMC	Joint Meteorological Committee
JMC	Joint Military Commission [*US, North Vietnam, South Vietnam, Viet Cong*]
JMC	Joint Movement Center (COE)
JMC	Justice Mining Corp. [*Vancouver Stock Exchange symbol*]
JMC	Sausalito, CA [*Location identifier FAA*] (FAAL)
JMCA	Jewish Ministers Cantors Association of America and Canada (EA)
JMCA	Joint Movement Coordination Agency
JMCA	Judges, Marshals, and Constables Association
JMCAA	Jewish Minister and Cantors Association of America [*Later, JMCA*] (EA)
JMCAAC	Jewish Ministers Cantors Association of America and Canada (EA)
JMCC	Joint Mobile Communications Center [*NATO*] (NATG)
JMCC	Joint Movements Coordinating Committee [*British*]
JMCG	JMC Group [*NASDAQ symbol*] (TTSB)
JMCG	JMC Group, Inc. [*NASDAQ symbol*] (SAG)
JMC Gp	JMC Group, Inc. [*Associated Press*] (SAG)
JMCOL	JUMPS [*Joint Uniform Military Payment System*] Monthly Compute Output Listing [*Military*] (AABC)
JMCP	Jefferson Medical College of Philadelphia
JMCQ	Journalism & Mass Communication Quarterly [*A publication*] (BRI)
JMCY	Joseph Malins Crusade of Youth [*British*] (BI)
JMD	Joint Managing Director (DCTA)
JMD	Joint Monitor Display
JMD	Justice Management Division [*U.S. Department of Justice*] (BARN)
JMD	Juvenile Macular Degeneration [*Medicine*] (MEDA)
JMDC	Joint Manual Direction Center [*Air Force*]
JME	James Industries [*Vancouver Stock Exchange symbol*]
JME	Joint Maximum Effort
JME	Juvenile Myoclonic Epilepsy [*Medicine*]
JMEA	Japan Machinery Exporters Association (BUAC)
JMEA	Jewish Music Educators Association [*Defunct*] (EA)
JMED	Jones Medical Indus [*NASDAQ symbol*] (TTSB)
JMED	Jones Medical Industries, Inc. [*NASDAQ symbol*] (NQ)
JMED	Jones Pharma [*NASDAQ symbol*] [*Formerly, Jones Medical Indus.*]
JMED	Jungle Message Encoder-Decoder (MCD)
J Medicinal Chem...	Journal of Medicinal Chemistry (MEC)
JMEM	Job Memory [*Computer science*] (MHDB)
JMEM	Joint Munitions Effectiveness Manual [*Military*] (AFM)
JMEM	Junior Marine Engineering Mechanic [*British military*] (DMA)
J Membrane Sci...	Journal of Membrane Science (MEC)
JMEMS	Joint Munition Effectiveness Manual [*Navy*] (DOMA)
JMEMT	John Morgan Evans of Merthyr Tydil [*An association*] (EA)
JMEMTF	Joint Munitions Effectiveness Manual Task Force (MCD)
JMENS	Joint Mission Element Need Statement (MCD)
JMETL	Joint Mission Essential Task List (DOMA)
JMF	James Madison Foundation (EA)
JMF	Java Media Framework [*Computer science*]
JMF	Jet Mixing Flow
JMF	Jewish Music Forum
JMF	John Marshall Foundation (EA)
JMF	Journal of Marriage and the Family [*A publication*] (BRI)
JMFC	Jared Martin Fan Club [*Defunct*] (EA)
JMFC	Jayne Mansfield Fan Club (EA)
JMFC	Jimmy Murphy Fan Club (EA)
JMG	Jewelry Manufacturers Guild (EA)
JMG	Joint Meteorological Group [*DoD*]
JMH	John Milton Hagen [*Antibody*] [*Immunology*] (DAVI)
JMH	Journal of Modern History [*A publication*] (BRI)
JMI	Jackson & Moreland, Inc. (MCD)
JMI	Jan Mayen Island [*Seismograph station code, US Geological Survey*] (SEIS)
JMI	Japan Management Institute (BUAC)
JMI	John Muir Institute for Environmental Studies [*Defunct*] (EA)
JMI	Jones Medical Industries, Inc. (EFIS)
JMI	Jorm Microlab, Inc., Cedar Rapids, IA [*Library symbol*] [*Library of Congress*] (LCLS)
JMI	Justice Management Institute
JMIA	Japan Mining Industry Association (BUAC)
JMIE	Joint Maritime Information Element [*Coast Guard*]
JMIE	Joint Maritime Information Exchange
JMIF	Japan Motor Industrial Federation (BUAC)
JMIFC	Jeanette MacDonald International Fan Club (EA)
JMIFC	Johnny Mathis International Fan Club (EA)
J Mil H	Journal of Military History [*A publication*] (BRI)
JMJ	James J. Johnston [*FAA designator*] (FAAC)
JMJ	Jesus, Mary, and Joseph
JMK	Mikonos [*Greece*] [*Airport symbol*] (OAG)
JML	James Madison Ltd. (EFIS)
JML	Job Method Learning (PDAA)
JML	Taxi Aereo de Jimulco SA de CV [*Mexico ICAO designator*] (FAAC)
JMLS	John Marshall Law School [*Chicago, IL*] (DLA)
JMLS	John Menzies Library Services [*Information service or system*] (IID)
JMM	Jacobi Matrix Method [*Mathematics*]
JMM	Jamaica Merchant Marine (EY)
JMM	Joint Man Machine (IAA)
JMM	Journal of Molecular Medicine [*A publication*]
JMMA	Japan Materials Management Association (BUAC)
JMMA	Japan Microscope Manufacturers Association (BUAC)
JMMF	James Monroe Memorial Foundation (EA)
JMMII	Japan Machinery and Metals Inspection Institute (BUAC)
JMN	Jeweled-Orifice Misting Nozzle
JMN	Johan Mangku Negara [*Malaysian Honour*]
JMNA	Joint Military Net Assessment [*A publication*] (RDA)
JMNCL	Jeunesse du Mouvement National Congolaise - Lumumba [*Youth of the Lumumba Wing of the Congolese National Movement*]
J/Mne	Junior Marine [*British military*] (DMA)
JMO	Jesuit Mission Office [*Australia*]
JMO	Joint Force Meteorological and Oceanographic Officer (COE)
JMO	Joint Maritime Operations (COE)
JMO	Jomsom [*Nepal*] [*Airport symbol*] (OAG)
JMO	Jugoslovenska Muslimanska Organizacija [*Yugoslav Moslem Organization*] [*Political party*] (PPE)
J/MOL	Joules per Mole [*Physics*]
J Molec Struct...	Journal of Molecular Structure (MEC)
J/(MOL K)	Joules per Mole Kelvin [*Physics*]
J Mol Med...	Journal of Molecular Medicine (MEC)
JMOS	Job Management Operations System (PDAA)
JMP	Jack Morton Productions, Inc. [*New York, NY*] [*Telecommunications*] (TSSD)
JMP	Jen Min Piao [*or Yuan*] [*Peoples money of China*] (BARN)
JMP	John M. Poindexter [*National Security Advisor during the Reagan Administration*]
JMP	Johnson Matthey Public Ltd. Co. [*Toronto Stock Exchange symbol*]
JMP	Joint Manpower Program [*Military*] (CINC)
JMP	Jump [*Computer science*]
JMPAB	Joint Materiel Priorities and Allocation Board [*Military*] (AABC)
JMPC	Joint Military Procurements Control [*World War II*]
JMPD	Jumped (ABBR)
JMPG	Jumping (ABBR)
JMPI	Jumpmaster Personnel Inspection [*Army*] (ADDR)
JMPNS	Jumpiness (ABBR)
JMPOF	Jumpoff (ABBR)
JMPP	Joint Munitions Production Panel (MCD)
JMPR	Jumper (MSA)
JMPT	Joint Military Potential Test (MCD)
JMPTC	Joint Military Packaging Training Center
JMR	Alexandair, Inc. [*Canada ICAO designator*] (FAAC)
JMR	Johannesburg Mounted Rifles [*British military*] (DMA)
JMRC	Joint Mobile Relay Center
JMRO	Joint Medical Regulating Office (AABC)
JMRO	Joint Military Regulating Office
JMRP	Joint Meteorological Radio Propagation Committee [*British*] (MCD)
JMRP	Joint Meteorological Radio Propagation Sub-Committee (BUAC)
JMRT	Junior Members Round Table [*American Library Association*]
JMS	Jacob More Society (EA)
JMS	Jamestown [*North Dakota*] [*Airport symbol*] (OAG)
JMS	Jamestown, ND [*Location identifier FAA*] (FAAL)
JMS	Jewish Media Service [*Defunct*] (EA)
JMS	John Milton Society for the Blind [*Later, JMSB*] (EA)
JMS	Joint Movements Staff [*British*]
JMS	Jump to Subroutine Instruction [*Computer science*]
JMS	Junior Medical Student (DAVI)
JMS	Morgan Stanley Group, Inc. [*AMEX symbol*] (SAG)
JMSA	Japan Marine Safety Agency [*Marine science*] (OSRA)
JMSAC	Joint Meteorological Satellite Advisory Committee
JMSB	John Milton Society for the Blind
JmSC	Japan Microfilm Service Center Co. Ltd., Tokyo, Japan [*Library symbol Library of Congress*] (LCLS)
JMSDC	Joint Merchant Shipping Defence Committee [*General Council of British Shipping*] (DS)
JMSDF	Japanese Maritime Self-Defense Force
JMSEP	Joint Modeling and Simulation Executive Panel [*DoD*]
JMSLS	Joliet Three-Minute Speech and Language Screen [*Test*]
JMSNS	Justification of Major System New Start [*Military*]
JMSPO	Joint Meteorological Satellite Program Office
JMSW	Journal of Multicultural Social Work [*A publication*] (BRI)
JMSX	Job Memory Switch Matrix
JMT	Job Methods Training
JMT	Joint Management Team (MCD)
JMT	Judgment (DCTA)
JMTB	Joint Military Transportation Board
JMTBA	Japan Machine Tool-Builders Association (BUAC)
JMTC	Joint Military Transportation Committee
JMTG	Joint Military Task Group (MUGU)
JMTG	Joint Military Terminology Group (AFM)
JMTSS	Joint Multichannel Trunking and Switching System (MCD)
JMU	James Madison University [*Virginia*]
JMU	Jamshedpur Mazdoor Union [*India*]
JMU	John Moores University [*British*]
JMUA	Joint Meritorious Unit Award [*Military decoration*] (GFGA)
JMUSDC	Joint Mexican-United States Defense Commission
J/Musn	Junior Musician [*British military*] (DMA)
JMV	Justice for Murder Victims [*An association*]
JMVB	Joint Merchant Vessels Board [*World War II*]

JMW .... James McNeill Whistler [*Nineteenth-century American painter and etcher*]
JMX .... Jumbogroup Multiplex [*Bell System*]
JMY .... Jimmy (ABBR)
JMYG .... Jimmying (ABBR)
jn .... Jan Mayen [*MARC country of publication code Library of Congress*] (LCCP)
JN .... Jannock Ltd. [*Toronto Stock Exchange symbol*]
J-N .... Jet Navigation (AAG)
JN .... Jet Navigation Chart
JN .... Jim's Neighbors (EA)
JN .... Job Number
Jn .... John [*New Testament book*]
JN .... Johnson Noise [*Thermal noise, that made by a resistor at a temperature above absolute zero*]
JN .... Join (MSA)
JN .... Journal Name [*Online database field identifier*]
Jn .... Juglans nigra [*Eastern black walnut*]
JN .... Junction
JN .... June (ROG)
JN .... Junior (ROG)
JN .... Justice Now [*An association*]
Jn .... King John [*Shakespearean work*]
JNA .... Januaria [*Brazil*] [*Airport symbol*] (AD)
JNA .... Jena Nomina Anatomica [*Also, INA*] [*Anatomy*]
JNA .... Jewish News Agency (BJA)
JNA .... John Nurminen, OY [*Finland*] [*FAA designator*] (FAAC)
JNA .... Joint Navy (IAA)
JNA .... Jordanian News Agency
JNA .... Jump If Not Above [*Computer science*] (PCM)
JNA .... Junior Naval Airman [*British military*] (DMA)
JNA .... Northern Illinois University, De Kalb, IL [*OCLC symbol*] (OCLC)
JNA .... Yugoslav People's Army
JNAC .... Japan-North American Commission on Cooperative Mission (EA)
JNACC .... Joint Nuclear Accident Coordinating Center
JNADPI .... Japan National Assembly of Disabled Peoples' International (EAIO)
JNAE .... Jump If Not Above or Equal [*Computer science*] (PCM)
JNAF .... Japanese Navy Air Force
JNAF .... Joint Navy-Air Force
JNAM .... Junior Naval Air Mechanic [*British military*] (DMA)
JNA Referees Bank... Journal. National Association of Referees in Bankruptcy [*A publication*] (DLA)
JNAU .... Jawaharlal Nehru Agricultural University [*India*] (BUAC)
JNB .... Johannesburg [*South Africa*] [*Airport symbol*] (OAG)
JNB .... Joinable (ABBR)
JNB .... Jump If Not Below [*Computer science*] (PCM)
JNBE .... Jump If Not Below or Equal [*Computer science*] (PCM)
JNC .... Jet Navigation Chart
JNC .... John Nuveen 'A' [*NYSE symbol*] (TTSB)
JNC .... Joint National Council (AIE)
JNC .... Joint Negotiating Council [*British*] (DCTA)
JNC .... Jump If No Carry [*Computer science*] (PCM)
JNC .... Junction (ADA)
JNC .... Nuveen [*John*] & Co. [*NYSE symbol*] (SPSG)
JNCC .... Joint Nature Conservation Committee (BUAC)
JNCC .... Junior Naval Command Course
JNCG .... Japan Nuclear Codes Group
JNCIMC .... Japanese National Committee of the International Music Council (EAIO)
JNCL .... Joint National Committee for Languages (EA)
JNCN .... Junction (ABBR)
JNCO .... Junior Non-Commissioned Officer [*British military*] (DMA)
JNCP .... Justification for Non-Competitive Procurement (GFGA)
JNC Referees Bank... Journal. National Conference of Referees in Bankruptcy [*A publication*] (DLA)
JNCUR .... Juncture (ABBR)
JND .... Air East Africa Ltd. [*Kenya*] [*FAA designator*] (FAAC)
JND .... Joined (ABBR)
JND .... Just Noticeable Difference [*Psychology*]
JNDR .... Joinder (ABBR)
JNE .... Ja Niin Edespain [*And So On*] [*Finnish*]
JNE .... Journal of Negro Education [*A publication*] (BRI)
JNE .... Jump Not Equal [*Computer science*] (OA)
JNE .... June (ABBR)
JNEC .... Jamaica National Export Corp. (BUAC)
JNF .... Japan Nuclear Fuel Co. (BUAC)
JNF .... Jewish National Fund (EA)
JNF .... Junior Non-Fiction [*Library science*] (TELE)
JNFA .... Jewish National Fund of Australia
JNFC .... Juice Newton Fan Club (EA)
JNFI .... Japan's Nuclear Fuel Industries (BUAC)
JNG .... [*The*] Jews in NAZI Germany; A Handbook of Facts Regarding Their Present Situation [*A publication*] (BJA)
JNG .... Joining [*Also, J*]
JNGL .... Jonquil (ABBR)
JNGL .... Jungle (ABBR)
JNHAC .... Jewish National Home for Asthmatic Children
JNI .... Java Native Interface [*Computer science*] (IGQR)
JNIB .... Jamaica National Investment Bank (BUAC)
JNIP .... Jamaica National Investment Promotions (BUAC)
JNJ .... Johnson & Johnson [*NYSE symbol*] (SPSG)
JNKD .... Junked (ABBR)
JNKG .... Junking (ABBR)
JNKI .... Junkie (ABBR)
JNKMA........ Junkman (ABBR)

JNKT .... Junket (ABBR)
JNKTD .... Junketed (ABBR)
JNKTG .... Junketing (ABBR)
JNKTR .... Junketer (ABBR)
JNL .... Atchison, KS [*Location identifier FAA*] (FAAL)
JNL .... Japanese National Laboratory
JNL .... Jefferson National Life Insurance Co. (EFIS)
JNL .... Jenolan [*Australia Seismograph station code, US Geological Survey*] (SEIS)
JNL .... Journal
JNLS .... Journals (ADA)
JNLST .... Journalist
JNMR .... Joint National Media Research [*Database producer*]
JNND .... Just Not Noticeable Difference (MSA)
JNNS .... Japanese Neural Network Society (BUAC)
JNOC .... Japan National Oil Corp. (BUAC)
JNOV .... Judgment Not Withstanding Verdict (HGAA)
JNP .... Jasper National Park [*Alberta*] [*Airport symbol*] (AD)
JNP .... Joint Nuclear Plot (CINC)
JNP .... Newport Beach, CA [*Location identifier FAA*] (FAAL)
JNPE .... Joint Nuclear Planning Element (MCD)
JNPI .... Jetevator Null Position Indicator
JNPR .... Juniper (ABBR)
JNR .... Japanese National Railways (BARN)
JNR .... Joiner (ABBR)
JNR .... June Resources, Inc. [*Vancouver Stock Exchange symbol*]
JNR .... Junior (EY)
JNR .... Unalakleet, AK [*Location identifier FAA*] (FAAL)
JNRC .... Joint Nuclear Research Center [*EURATOM*]
JNRI .... Joint Nuclear Research Institute [*Former USSR*]
JNROTC ...... Junior Naval Reserve Officer Training Corps
JNS .... Chic by HIS, Inc. [*NYSE symbol*] (SPSG)
JNS .... International Graduate School, St. Louis, MO [*OCLC symbol*] (OCLC)
JNS .... Jet Noise Survey
JNS .... Jugoslovenska Nacionalna Stranka [*Yugoslav National Party*] [*Political party*] (PPE)
JNS .... Just Noticeable Shift (PDAA)
JNS .... Minneapolis, MN [*Location identifier FAA*] (FAAL)
JNSC .... Japan Nuclear Safety Commission (BUAC)
JNSC .... Joint Navigation Satellite Committee
JNSRDA....... Japan Nuclear Ship Research and Development Agency (BUAC)
JNT .... Jaunt (ABBR)
JNT .... Joint
JNT .... Joint Network Scheme [*British*]
JNT .... Joint Network Team [*British*] (NITA)
JNT .... Jonathan [*Italy*] [*FAA designator*] (FAAC)
JNT .... Junction (ABBR)
JNT .... Juncture (ABBR)
JNT .... New York, NY [*Location identifier FAA*] (FAAL)
JNTA .... Japan National Tourist Association (BUAC)
JNTD .... Jointed (ABBR)
JNTINS .... Jauntiness (ABBR)
JNTIR........... Jauntier (ABBR)
JNTLY.......... Jauntily (ABBR)
JNTLY.......... Jointly (ABBR)
JNTO .... Japan National Tourist Organization (EA)
JNTR .... Janitor (ABBR)
JNTR .... Jointer (ABBR)
JNTST .... Jauntiest (ABBR)
JNT STK CO... Joint Stock Co. (DLA)
JNTUR .... Jointure (ABBR)
JNTURD....... Jointured (ABBR)
JNTURG....... Jointuring (ABBR)
JNT VEN ...... Joint Venture [*Legal term*] (DLA)
JNTY .... Jaunty (ABBR)
JNTY .... Jointly (ABBR)
JNU .... Jiangnan University [*China*] (BUAC)
JNU .... Jiangxi Normal University [*China*] (BUAC)
JNU .... Juneau [*Alaska*] [*Airport symbol*] (OAG)
JNU .... Juneau, AK [*Location identifier FAA*] (FAAL)
JNU .... Universal Jet Navigation Charts [*Air Force*]
JNUL .... Jewish National and University Library
JNuveen ...... Nuveen [*John*] Co. [*Associated Press*] (SAG)
JNVOA .... Jewish Nazi Victims Organization of America (EA)
JNW .... Joint Committee on New Weapons and Equipment
JNW .... Newport, OR [*Location identifier FAA*] (FAAL)
JNWOC .... Joint Warfare Operations Center
JNWP .... Joint Numerical Weather Prediction Unit (IAA)
JNWPS .... Joint Nuclear Weapons Publication Systems (MCD)
JNWPU .... Joint Numerical Weather Prediction Unit
JNX .... Jackson [*Michigan*] [*Airport symbol*] (AD)
JNY .... January (ABBR)
JNY .... Jenney Beechcraft, Inc. [*ICAO designator*] (FAAC)
JNY .... Jones Apparel Group [*NYSE symbol*] (SPSG)
JNZ .... Jennings, LA [*Location identifier FAA*] (FAAL)
JNZ .... Jump on Not Zero [*Computer science*] (PCM)
JO .... Holiday Airlines [*ICAO designator*] (AD)
JO .... Job Order
Jo .... Joel [*Old Testament book*] (BJA)
Jo .... Johannes Faventinus [*Deceased circa 1187*] [*Authority cited in pre-1607 legal work*] (DSA)
JO .... Joint Organization
JO .... Joint Ownership [*Business term*]
Jo .... Jones' Irish Exchequer Reports [*A publication*] (DLA)
JO .... Jordan [*ANSI two-letter standard code*] (CNC)

jo .... Jordan [*MARC country of publication code Library of Congress*] (LCCP)

Jo .... Joseph (BJA)

JO .... Journalist [*Navy rating*]

JO .... Journal Officiel des Communautes Europeennes [*Official Journal of the European Communities*] [*A publication*] (ILCA)

JO .... Judicial Officer [*Department of Agriculture*] (GFGA)

JO .... Junction Office [*Telecommunications*] (OA)

JO .... Junior Officer

JO .... Jupiter Orbiter [*NASA*]

JO .... Juvenile Offenders

JO1 .... Journalist, First Class [*Navy rating*]

JO2 .... Journalist, Second Class [*Navy rating*]

JO3 .... Journalist, Third Class [*Navy rating*]

JOA .... Joint Objective Area (NVT)

JOA .... Joint Oceanographic Assembly [*Marine science*] (MSC)

JOA .... Joint Operating Agreement

JOA .... Joint Operations Area (COE)

Joa Bologne... Johannes Bolognetus [*Deceased, 1575*] [*Authority cited in pre-1607 legal work*] (DSA)

JOAC .... Joachim Bancorp [*NASDAQ symbol*] (TTSB)

JOAC .... Joachim Bancorp, Inc. [*NASDAQ symbol*] (SAG)

Joachim ...... Joachim Bancorp, Inc. [*Associated Press*] (SAG)

JOAD .... Junior Olympic Archery Development

JOAG .... Juvenile Open Angle Glaucoma [*Ophthalmology*]

JO AI .... Jahreshefte des Oesterreichischen Archaeologischen Instituts in Wien [*A publication*] (OCD)

Joa Imo ...... Johannes de Imola [*Deceased, 1436*] [*Authority cited in pre-1607 legal work*] (DSA)

Joan Andr .... Johannes Andreae [*Deceased, 1348*] [*Authority cited in pre-1607 legal work*] (DSA)

Joan Bapt Villalob... Johannes Baptista Villalobos [*Authority cited in pre-1607 legal work*] (DSA)

Joan Bologne... Johannes Bolognetus [*Deceased, 1575*] [*Authority cited in pre-1607 legal work*] (DSA)

Joan Borcholt... Johannes Borcholten [*Deceased, 1593*] [*Authority cited in pre-1607 legal work*] (DSA)

Jo & Car .... Jones and Cary's Irish Exchequer Reports [*1838-39*] [*A publication*] (DLA)

Joan de Ces... Johannes de Cesena [*Flourished, 13th century*] [*Authority cited in pre-1607 legal work*] (DSA)

Joan de Lign... Johannes de Lignano [*Deceased, 1383*] [*Authority cited in pre-1607 legal work*] (DSA)

Jo & La T .... Jones and La Touche's Irish Chancery Reports [*A publication*] (DLA)

Joan Fan ..... Johannes Faventinus [*Deceased circa 1187*] [*Authority cited in pre-1607 legal work*] (DSA)

Joan Mon .... Johannes Monachus [*Deceased, 1313*] [*Authority cited in pre-1607 legal work*] (DSA)

Joann .... Johannes Teutonicus [*Deceased circa 1246*] [*Authority cited in pre-1607 legal work*] (DSA)

Joannes .... Johannes Franciscus Pavinus [*Flourished, 1448-82*] [*Authority cited in pre-1607 legal work*] (DSA)

Joann Teut... Johannes Teutonicus [*Deceased, 1246*] [*Authority cited in pre-1607 legal work*] (DSA)

Joan Vaud ... Johannes Vaudus [*Flourished, 16th century*] [*Authority cited in pre-1607 legal work*] (DSA)

JOAP .... Joint Oil Analysis Program [*Military*] (NVT)

JOAP-CG .... Joint Oil Analysis Program Coordinating Group (MCD)

JOAP-TSC .... Joint Oil Analysis Program Technical Support Center (MCD)

JOB .... Aerojobeni SA de CV [*Mexico ICAO designator*] (FAAC)

JOB .... General Employment Enterprises, Inc. [*AMEX symbol*] (SPSG)

JOB .... Genl Employ Enterpr [*AMEX symbol*] (TTSB)

JOB .... Jobber

Jo B .... Johannes Bassianus [*Flourished, 12th century*] [*Authority cited in pre-1607 legal work*] (DSA)

JOB .... Judicial Officers Bulletin [*A publication*]

JOB .... Just One Break (EA)

JOBAPT....... John the Baptist

JOBCAT....... Job Catalog (HGAA)

JOBD .... Jobbed (ABBR)

JOBG .... Jobbing (ABBR)

JOBHLDR.... Jobholder (ABBR)

JOBLIB........ Job Library [*Computer science*]

JOBR .... Jobber (ABBR)

JOBS .... Job Opportunities in the Business Sector (WDAA)

JOBS .... Job Oriented Basic Skills [*Program*] [*Military*]

JOBTAP....... Job Training Assessment Program [*Vocational guidance test*]

JOC .... Cambria County Library System, Johnstown, PA [*OCLC symbol*] (OCLC)

JOC .... Chief Journalist [*Navy rating*]

JOC .... Jewett Owners Club (EA)

JOC .... Jewish Occupational Council [*Later, NAJVS*] (EA)

JOC .... Job Order Contracting

JOC .... Job Order Costing (MHDI)

JOC .... Jocose [*or Jocular*]

JOC .... Jocular (ABBR)

JOC .... John Coutts Library Services [*ACCORD*] [*UTLAS symbol*]

JOC .... Joint Operations Center

JOC .... Joint Organizing Committee [*Global Atmospheric Research Program*]

JOC .... Journal of Organic Chemistry [*A publication*]

JOC .... Junior Officer Council [*Army*]

JOC .... Junior Optimist Clubs (EA)

JOC .... New York, NY [*Location identifier FAA*] (FAAL)

JOCARG .... Joint Wideband Circuit Allocation and Requirement Group, Thailand [*Military*] (CINC)

JOCAS .... Job Order Cost Accounting System (MCD)

JOCC........... Jeunesse Ouvriere Catholique Canadienne [*Young Canadian Catholic Workers*] [*Established 1930*]

JOCC........... Joint Operations Control Center

J Occ Health Safety Aust... Journal of Occupational Health and Safety in Australia [*A publication*]

J Occup Health Safety... Journal of Occupational Health and Safety - Australia and New Zealand [*A publication*]

JOCG .... Joint Ordnance Commanders Group

Jo Ch .... Johnson's New York Chancery Reports [*A publication*] (DLA)

JOCI............ Jeunesse Ouvriere Chretienne Internationale [*International Young Christian Workers - IYCW*] (EAIO)

JOCIT.......... JOVIAL Compiler Implementation Tool [*Computer science*] (MCD)

JOCK.......... Jockey (ABBR)

JOCK.......... Jockstrap (ABBR)

JockeyC ...... Jockey Club, Inc. [*Associated Press*] (SAG)

JOCM.......... Master Chief Journalist [*Navy rating*]

JOCO.......... Jointly-Owned Contractor-Operated Facility (MCD)

Jo Comm Eur... Journal Officiel des Communautes Europeennes [*Official Journal of the European Communities*] [*A publication*] (ILCA)

JOCOTAS..... Joint Committee on Tactical Shelters (MCD)

JOCR........... Joint Observation for Cometary Research (MCD)

Jo Cre .... Johannes Bassianus de Cremona [*Flourished, 12th century*] [*Authority cited in pre-1607 legal work*] (DSA)

JOCS .... Senior Chief Journalist [*Navy rating*]

JOCSG .... Joint Ordnance Commanders Supply Group [*DoD*]

J-OCT.......... Joint Operational Compatibility Tests

JOCT........... Junior Officers Common Training

JOD............ Joint Occupancy Data (NAKS)

JOD............ Joint Occupancy Date (MCD)

JOD............ Juvenile Onset Diabetes [*Medicine*]

JODC .... Japan Oceanographic Data Center [*Information service or system*] (IID)

JODC .... Juvenile Osteochondrititis Dissecans [*Medicine*]

JODCO .... Japan Oil Development Co. (BUAC)

Jo de Ana .... Johannes de Anania [*Deceased, 1457*] [*Authority cited in pre-1607 legal work*] (DSA)

Jo de Anna... Johannes de Anania [*Deceased, 1457*] [*Authority cited in pre-1607 legal work*] (DSA)

Jo de Bor.... Johannes de Borbonio [*Flourished, 1317-30*] [*Authority cited in pre-1607 legal work*] (DSA)

Jo de Cre.... Johannes Bassianus de Cremona [*Flourished, 12th century*] [*Authority cited in pre-1607 legal work*] (DSA)

Jo de F .... Johannes de Fintona [*Flourished, 13th century*] [*Authority cited in pre-1607 legal work*] (DSA)

Jo de Fi....... Johannes de Fintona [*Flourished, 13th century*] [*Authority cited in pre-1607 legal work*] (DSA)

Jo de Imol .... Johannes de Imola [*Deceased, 1436*] [*Authority cited in pre-1607 legal work*] (DSA)

Jo de Mo .... Johannes de Monciaco [*Flourished, 1263-66*] [*Authority cited in pre-1607 legal work*] (DSA)

JODIN .... Iodinium [*Iodine*] [*Symbol is I*] [*Chemical element Pharmacy*] (ROG)

JODIV .... John the Divine

JODM........... Juvenile Onset Diabetes Mellitus [*Medicine*]

joe .... Java Objects Everywhere [*Computer science*] (IGQR)

Joe .... Java Objects Everywhere [*Computer science*]

JOE .... Joensuu [*Finland*] [*Airport symbol*] (OAG)

JOE .... Joensuu [*Finland*] [*Seismograph station code, US Geological Survey Closed*] (SEIS)

JOE .... Juvenile Opportunities Endeavor

JOEG .... Joint Operations Evaluation Group (AABC)

JOEG-V .... Joint Operations Evaluation Group, Vietnam [*Air Force*] (MCD)

JOEM .... Junior Ordnance Electrical Mechanic [*British military*] (DMA)

JOERA .... Japan Optical Engineering Research Association (BUAC)

JOERS .... Joint Opto-Electronics Research Scheme [*British*]

JOEVANG.... John the Evangelist

Jo Ex Ir....... Jones' Irish Exchequer Reports [*A publication*] (DLA)

Jo Ex Pro W... Jones' Exchequer Proceedings Concerning Wales [*1939*] [*A publication*] (DLA)

JOF .... Japan OTC Equity Fund [*NYSE symbol*] (TTSB)

JOF .... Japan OTC Equity Fund, Inc. [*NYSE symbol*] (SPSG)

Jo F .... Johannes de Fintona [*Flourished, 13th century*] [*Authority cited in pre-1607 legal work*] (DSA)

Jo Fa .... Johannes Faventinus [*Deceased circa 1187*] [*Authority cited in pre-1607 legal work*] (DSA)

Jo Fav .... Johannes Faventinus [*Deceased circa 1187*] [*Authority cited in pre-1607 legal work*] (DSA)

J of Ceylon L... Journal of Ceylon Law [*Colombo, Ceylon*] [*A publication*] (DLA)

J of E .... Journal of Education [*A publication*] (ROG)

J of EL .... Journal of Electric Lighting [*A publication*] (ROG)

J of Ethiop L... Journal of Ethiopian Law [*Addis Ababa, Ethiopia*] [*A publication*] (DLA)

J of Ins of Arbitrators... Journal. Institute of Arbitrators [*A publication*] (DLA)

JOFL............ Johnstown Flood National Memorial

JOFOC .... Justification for Other than Full and Open Competition (SSD)

JOG............. Joggle [*Engineering*]

JOG............. Jogyakarta [*Indonesia*] [*Airport symbol*] (OAG)

JOG............. Joint Operating Group [*SLA/ASIS*]

JOG............. Joint Operations Graphics [*Military*]

JOG............. Joint Operations Group [*DoD*]

JOG............. Junior Offshore Group [*Racing*] [*British*]

JOG-A .... Joint Operations Graphics - Air [*Military*] (PDAA)

JOGD .... Jogged (ABBR)

JOGG .... Jogging (ABBR)

JOG-G .... Joint Operations Graphics - Ground (PDAA)

JOGL............ Joggle (ABBR)
JOGLD .... Joggled (ABBR)
JOGLG .... Joggling (ABBR)
JOGR .... Jogger (ABBR)
JOGS .... Joint Operation Graphics System (COE)
JOH............. Johannesburg [South Africa] [Seismograph station code, US Geological Survey Closed] (SEIS)
Joh............... Johannine (BJA)
Joh............... John [New Testament book] (BJA)
JOH.............. Johnstone Point, AK [Location identifier FAA] (FAAL)
JOH.............. St. John's College [Cambridge, England] (DAS)
Joh Ch Rep... Johnson's New York Chancery Reports [A publication] (DLA)
John............. Chase's United States Circuit Court Decisions, Edited by Johnson [A publication] (DLA)
John............. Johnson's English Vice-Chancellors' Reports [A publication] (DLA)
John............. Johnson's Maryland Chancery Reports [A publication] (DLA)
John............. Johnson's New York Reports [A publication] (DLA)
John............. Johnson's New York Supreme Court Reports [A publication] (DLA)
John Am Not... John's American Notaries [A publication] (DLA)
John & H ..... Johnson and Hemming's English Chancery Reports [70 English Reprint] [A publication] (DLA)
John Carroll U... John Carroll University (GAGS)
John Cas .... Johnson's New York Cases [A publication] (DLA)
John Chan ... Johnson's New York Chancery Reports [A publication] (DLA)
John Ch Rep... Johnson's New York Chancery Reports [A publication] (DLA)
JohnCn .... Johnson Controls, Inc. [Associated Press] (SAG)
John Dict..... Johnson's English Dictionary [A publication] (DLA)
John Eng Ch... Johnson's English Vice-Chancellors' Reports [A publication] (DLA)
John Jay C (CUNY)... John Jay College of Criminal Justice of The City University of New York (GAGS)
JohnJn.......... Johnson & Johnson [Associated Press] (SAG)
John Marshall Law Sch... John Marshall Law School (GAGS)
John Marshall LQ... John Marshall Law Quarterly [A publication] (DLA)
John Marsh LJ... John Marshall Law Journal [A publication] (DLA)
John Marsh LQ... John Marshall Law Quarterly [A publication] (DLA)
JOHNNIAC ... John's [Von Neumann] Integrator and Automatic Computer [An early computer]
John Oxley J... John Oxley Journal [A publication]
Johns............ Chase's United States Circuit Court Decisions, Edited by Johnson [A publication] (DLA)
Johns............ Johnson's English Vice-Chancellors' Reports [A publication] (DLA)
Johns............ Johnson's Maryland Chancery Reports [A publication] (DLA)
Johns............ Johnson's New York Supreme Court Reports [A publication] (DLA)
Johns & H ... Johnson and Hemming's English Chancery Reports [70 English Reprint] [A publication] (DLA)
Johns & Hem... Johnson and Hemming's English Chancery Reports [70 English Reprint] [A publication] (DLA)
Johns & H (Eng)... Johnson and Hemming's English Chancery Reports [70 English Reprint] [A publication] (DLA)
Johns Bills... Johnson's Bills of Exchange [2nd ed.] [1839] [A publication] (DLA)
Johns C .... Johnson's New York Cases [A publication] (DLA)
Johns Cas ... Johnson's New York Cases [A publication] (DLA)
Johns Cases... Johnson's New York Cases [A publication] (DLA)
Johns Cas (NY)... Johnson's New York Cases [A publication] (DLA)
Johns Ch ..... Johnson's English Vice-Chancellors' Reports [A publication] (DLA)
Johns Ch ..... Johnson's Maryland Chancery Decisions [A publication] (DLA)
Johns Ch ..... Johnson's New York Chancery Reports [A publication] (DLA)
Johns Ch Cas... Johnson's New York Chancery Reports [A publication] (DLA)
Johns Ch (NY)... Johnson's New York Chancery Reports [A publication] (DLA)
Johns Civ L Sp... Johnson's Civil Law of Spain [A publication] (DLA)
Johns Ct Err... Johnson's New York Court of Errors Reports [A publication] (DLA)
Johns Dec ... Johnson's Maryland Chancery Decisions [A publication] (DLA)
Johns Eccl L... Johnson's Ecclesiastical Law [A publication] (DLA)
Johns Eng Ch... Johnson's English Chancery Reports [A publication] (DLA)
Johns Hopkins U... [The] Johns Hopkins University (GAGS)
Johns HRV... Johnson's English Chancery Reports [A publication] (DLA)
Johns Mar R... Johnson on Maritime Rights [A publication] (DLA)
Johns (NY)... Johnson's New York Reports [A publication] (DLA)
Johns NZ... Johnson's New Zealand Reports [A publication] (DLA)
Johnson...... Johnson's English Vice-Chancellors' Reports [A publication] (DLA)
Johnson...... Johnson's Maryland Chancery Decisions [A publication] (DLA)
Johnson...... Johnson's New York Reports [A publication] (DLA)
Johnson NYR... Johnson's New York Reports [A publication] (DLA)
Johnson R... Johnson's New York Reports [A publication] (DLA)
Johnson's Quarto Dict... Johnson's Quarto Dictionary [A publication] (DLA)
Johnson's Rep... Johnson's New York Reports [A publication] (DLA)
Johns Pat Man... Johnson's Patent Manual [A publication] (DLA)
Johns R....... Johnson's New York Reports [A publication] (DLA)
Johns Rep ... Johnson's New York Supreme Court Reports [A publication] (DLA)
Johnst Inst... Johnston's Institutes of the Laws of Spain [A publication] (DLA)
JohnstnA....... Johnstown America Industries, Inc. [Associated Press] (SAG)
Johnst (NZ).... Johnston's New Zealand Reports [A publication] (DLA)
Johnston...... Johnston Industries, Inc. [Associated Press] (SAG)
Johns Tr ...... Johnson's Impeachment Trial [A publication] (DLA)
Johns US..... Johnson's Reports of Chase's United States Circuit Court Decisions [A publication] (DLA)
Johns VC ..... Johnson's English Vice-Chancellors' Reports [A publication] (DLA)
Johns VC (Eng)... Johnson's English Vice-Chancellors' Reports [A publication] (DLA)
Johs............. Johannes Galensis [Flourished, 13th century] [Authority cited in pre-1607 legal work] (DSA)
Joh Teut ...... Johannes Teutonicus [Deceased circa 1246] [Authority cited in pre-1607 legal work] (DSA)
JOHX .... Johnson Flying Service [Air carrier designation symbol]
JOI............... Joint Oceanographic Institution (USDC)

JOI............... Joint Oceanographic Institutions, Inc. [Research center] (RCD)
JOI............... Joinville [Brazil] [Airport symbol] (OAG)
JOIA............. Japan Ocean Industries Association (BUAC)
JOICFP........ Japanese Organisation for International Cooperation in Family Planning (BUAC)
JOIDES .... JODC [Japan Oceanographic Data Center] On-Line Information and Data Exchange Service [Marine science] (OSRA)
JOIDES .... Joint Oceanographic Institutions for Deep Earth Sampling
JOIN............ Job Orientation in Neighborhoods (AEBS)
JOIN............ Jobs or Income Now [Students for a Democratic Society] [Defunct]
JOIN............ Joinery (ADA)
JOIN............ Joint Optical Information Network [Army]
JOIN............ Jones Intercable [NASDAQ symbol] (TTSB)
JOIN............ Jones Intercable, Inc. [NASDAQ symbol] (NQ)
JOINA.......... Jones Intercable CI'A' [NASDAQ symbol] (TTSB)
JOINREP ...... Joining Report (MCD)
JOIP............. Joint Operations Interface Procedure (NASA)
JOIS............. Japan Online Information System [Database]
JOJA............ July, October, January, and April [Denotes quarterly payments of interest or dividends in these months] [Business term]
Jo Jur .... Journal of Jurisprudence [A publication] (DLA)
JOK.............. Airtaxi Bedarfsluftverkehrsges GmbH [Austria ICAO designator] (FAAC)
JOKG .... Joking (ABBR)
JOKGLY ...... Jokingly (ABBR)
JOKGY .... Jokingly (ABBR)
JOKI............. John Fitzgerald Kennedy National Historical Site
JOKING .... Joint Kinematics and Geometry (PDAA)
JOKP............ Junior Order, Knights of Pythias (EA)
JOKSTR ...... Jokester (ABBR)
JOL.............. Job Organization Language [1979] [Computer science] (CSR)
JOL.............. Joliet in Illinois [Diocesan abbreviation] [Illinois] (TOCD)
JOL.............. Jolo [Philippines] [Airport symbol] (OAG)
JOL.............. Jolon [California] [Seismograph station code, US Geological Survey] (SEIS)
JOL.............. Joule, Inc. [AMEX symbol] (SPSG)
JOLD............ Jollied (ABBR)
Jo Le .... Johannis Lectura [A publication] (DSA)
JOLT............ Juvenile Offenders Learn the Truth [Program]
JOLTGLY...... Joltingly (ABBR)
JOM............. Jeunesse Ouvriere Marocaine [Moroccan Working Youth]
JOM............. Job Operation Manual (AAG)
JOM............. Job-Oriented Manual (AAG)
JOM............. Johnson-O'Malley Act [1934]
JOM............. Njombe [Tanzania] [Airport symbol] (AD)
JOMA........... Japan Oriental Music Association (BUAC)
JOMAC......... Judgement, Orientation, Memory, Abstraction, and Calculation [Medicine] (DAVI)
JOMACI........ Judgment, Orientation, Memory, Abstraction, and Calculation Intact [Medicine] (DAVI)
JOMAR .... John and Margaret Seidel [Children of US importer after whom British sports car was named]
JOMN........... Jeweled-Orifice Misting Nozzle
JOMO........... Job Mix Optimization [Computer science] (MHDB)
Jo Mon .... Johannes Monachus [Deceased, 1313] [Authority cited in pre-1607 legal work] (DSA)
JOMU........... John Muir National Historic Site
JON............. Jeweled-Orifice Nozzle
JON............. Job Order Number (MCD)
JON............. Johnston Island [Airport symbol] (OAG)
Jon.............. Jonah [Old Testament book]
JON.............. Jonas [Old Testament book] [Douay version]
Jon.............. Jones' Irish Exchequer Reports [A publication] (DLA)
JON.............. Jonpol Explorations Ltd. [Toronto Stock Exchange symbol]
JONAH.......... Jews Organised for a Nuclear Arms Halt [An association] (BUAC)
Jon & Car.... Jones and Cary's Irish Exchequer Reports [1838-39] [A publication] (DLA)
Jon & L .... Jones and La Touche's Irish Chancery Reports [A publication] (DLA)
Jon & La T... Jones and La Touche's Irish Chancery Reports [A publication] (DLA)
Jonel .... Jones Intercable, Inc. [Associated Press] (SAG)
JoneInt .... Jones Intercable Investors Ltd. [Associated Press] (SAG)
Jones.......... Jones' Irish Exchequer Reports [A publication] (DLA)
Jones.......... Jones' North Carolina Equity Reports [54-59] [1853-63] [A publication] (DLA)
Jones.......... Jones' North Carolina Law Reports [A publication] (DLA)
Jones.......... Jones' Reports [22-30 Missouri] [A publication] (DLA)
Jones.......... Jones' Reports [11, 12 Pennsylvania] [A publication] (DLA)
Jones.......... Jones' Reports [43-48, 52-57, 61, 62 Alabama] [A publication] (DLA)
Jones.......... Jones' Upper Canada Common Pleas Reports [A publication] (DLA)
Jones & C ... Jones and Cary's Irish Exchequer Reports [1838-39] [A publication] (DLA)
Jones & H Hind Law... Jones and Haughton's Hindoo Law [A publication] (DLA)
Jones & L.... Jones and La Touche's Irish Chancery Reports [A publication] (DLA)
Jones & La T... Jones and La Touche's Irish Chancery Reports [A publication] (DLA)
Jones & L (Ir)... Jones and La Touche's Irish Chancery Reports [A publication] (DLA)
Jones & McM... Jones and McMurtrie's Pennsylvania Supreme Court Reports [A publication] (DLA)
Jones & McM (PA)... Jones and McMurtrie's Pennsylvania Supreme Court Reports [A publication] (DLA)
Jones & S ... Jones and Spencer's Superior Court Reports [33-61 New York] [A publication] (DLA)
Jones & Sp... Jones and Spencer's Superior Court Reports [33-61 New York] [A publication] (DLA)

Jones & Spen... Jones and Spencer's Superior Court Reports [*33-61 New York*] [*A publication*] (DLA)
Jones & V Laws... Jones and Varick's Laws of New York [*A publication*] (DLA)
JonesAp....... Jones Apparel Group, Inc. [*Associated Press*] (SAG)
Jones B ...... Jones' Law of Bailments [*A publication*] (DLA)
Jones Bailm... Jones' Law of Bailments [*A publication*] (DLA)
Jones B & W (MO)... Jones, Barclay, and Whittelsey's Reports [*31 Missouri*] [*A publication*] (DLA)
Jones Barclay & Whittelsey... Jones, Barclay, and Whittelsey's Reports [*31 Missouri*] [*A publication*] (DLA)
Jones Ch Mort... Jones on Chattel Mortgages [*A publication*] (DLA)
Jones Easem... Jones' Treatise on Easements [*A publication*] (DLA)
Jones Eq...... Jones' North Carolina Equity Reports [*54-59*] [*1853-63*] [*A publication*] (DLA)
Jones Eq (NC)... Jones' North Carolina Equity Reports [*54-59*] [*1853-63*] [*A publication*] (DLA)
Jones Exch.. Jones' Irish Exchequer Reports [*A publication*] (DLA)
Jones Fr Bar... Jones' History of the French Bar [*A publication*] (DLA)
Jones French Bar... Jones' History of the French Bar [*A publication*] (DLA)
Jones Inst.... Jones' Institutes of Hindoo Law [*A publication*] (DLA)
Jones Intr... Jones' Introduction to Legal Science [*A publication*] (DLA)
Jones Ir ... Jones' Irish Exchequer Reports [*A publication*] (DLA)
Jones L....... Jones' Law Reports [*A publication*] (DLA)
Jones Law... Jones' North Carolina Law Reports [*A publication*] (DLA)
Jones Lib... Jones on Libel [*1812*] [*A publication*] (DLA)
Jones L Of T... Jones on Land and Office Titles [*A publication*] (DLA)
JonesM....... Jones Medical Industries, Inc. [*Associated Press*] (SAG)
Jones Mort... Jones on Mortgages [*A publication*] (DLA)
Jones NC... Jones' North Carolina Law Reports [*A publication*] (DLA)
Jones PA..... Jones' Reports [*11, 12 Pennsylvania*] [*A publication*] (DLA)
JonesPl....... Jones Plumbing Systems, Inc. [*Associated Press*] (SAG)
Jones Pledges... Jones on Pledges and Collateral Securities [*A publication*] (DLA)
Jones Ry Sec... Jones on Railway Securities [*A publication*] (DLA)
Jones Salv... Jones' Law of Salvage [*A publication*] (DLA)
Jones Securities... Jones on Railroad Securities [*A publication*] (DLA)
JonesSp....... Jones Spacelink Ltd. [*Associated Press*] (SAG)
Jones UC.... Jones' Upper Canada Common Pleas Reports [*A publication*] (DLA)
Jones Uses... Jones' Law of Uses [*A publication*] (DLA)
Jon Ex ...... Jones' Irish Exchequer Reports [*A publication*] (DLA)
Jon Exch...... Jones' Irish Exchequer Reports [*A publication*] (DLA)
JonIcbl....... Jones Intercable, Inc. [*Associated Press*] (SAG)
Jon Ir Exch.. Jones' Irish Exchequer Reports [*A publication*] (DLA)
JONR .... Joiner (ABBR)
JONS .... Juntas de Ofensiva Nacional Sindicalista [*Syndicalist Juntas of the National Offensive*] [*Spain Political party*] (PPE)
JONSDAP..... Joint North Sea Data Acquisition Project [*An informal group of Belgian, German, British, Dutch, and Swedish scientific institutes*] (PDAA)
JONSIS .... Joint North Sea Information Systems (PDAA)
JONSWAP... Joint North Sea Wave Atmosphere Program [*Global Atmospheric Research Program*] (USDC)
JONSWAP... Joint North Sea Wave Project [*An informal group of Belgian, German, British, Dutch, and Swedish scientific institutes*] (PDAA)
JOO .... Jonesboro, GA [*Location identifier FAA*] (FAAL)
JOOD .... Junior Officer of the Day [*or Deck*] [*Navy*]
JOOI........... Junior Optimist Octagon International [*An association*] (EA)
JOOMS .... Junior Observers of Meteorology [*Trainees for government service to replace Weather Bureau men who had gone to war*] [*World War II*]
JOOS .... Job-Oriented Organizational Structure (AAG)
JOOW .... Junior Officer of the Watch [*Navy*]
JOP .... Job Opportunity Program (OICC)
JOP .... Jobs Optional Program [*Combination job opportunities in the business sector and on the job training*] (OICC)
JOP .... Joint Observing Program [*NASA*]
JOP .... Joint Operating Plan
JOP .... Joint Operation Procedure (AAG)
JOP .... Joint Optoelectronics Project [*Japan*] [*Agreement for conducting cooperative global research*]
JOp .... Jupiter Orbiter Probe [*Later, Project Galileo*] [*NASA*]
JOPA .... Junior Officers and Professional Association
JOPA .... Juventud Organizada del Pueblo en Armas [*Armed People's Organized Youth*] [*Guatemala*] (PD)
JOPC .... Junior Olympic Pistol Championship [*National Rifle Association*]
JO/PCN ...... Job Order/Program Control Number [*Army*]
JOPD .... Junior Officer Professional Development Program [*Army*] (RDA)
JOPES .... Joint Operation Planning and Execution System [*DoD*]
JOPES .... Joint Operations Planning and Execution System [*Military*]
JOPM .... Joint Occupancy Plan Memorandum (AAG)
JOPM .... Joint Operation Procedure Memorandum (AAG)
JOPP .... Joint Operational Policies and Procedures (MCD)
JOPR .... Joint Operation Procedure Report (AAG)
JOPREP ...... Joint Operational Report [*Military*] (AFM)
JOPS .... Joint Operational Planning System [*Military*]
JOQ .... Job Order Quantity [*Military*] (AFIT)
JOR........... Jet Operations Requirements
JOR........... Job Operations Report
JOR........... Job Order Request (AAG)
JOR........... Joint Operations Requirements [*Military*] (AFM)
JOR........... Jordan [*ANSI three-letter standard code*] (CNC)
Jor .... Jordan (VRA)
JOR........... Yorkshire European Airways Ltd. [*British ICAO designator*] (FAAC)
Jo Radio Law... Journal of Radio Law [*A publication*] (DLA)
JORC .... Jeddah Oil Refinery Co. [*Saudi Arabia*] (BUAC)
JORC .... Junior Olympic Rifle Championship [*National Rifle Association*]

JORD .... Jordan (ABBR)
Jordan .... Jordan American Holdings, Inc. [*Associated Press*] (SAG)
Jord Jt St Comp... Jordan on Joint Stock Companies [*A publication*] (DLA)
Jord PJ ...... Jordan's Parliamentary Journal [*A publication*] (DLA)
JORG .... Joint Oceanographic Research Group
J Org Chem... Journal of Organic Chemistry (MEC)
JORITDS...... Joint Optical Range Instrumentation Type Designation System
JOS........... Jeunesse Ouvriere du Senegal [*Senegalese Working Youth*]
JOS........... Job Order Supplement (MCD)
JOS........... Joint Operations Staff [*Military*]
JOS........... Jos [*Nigeria*] [*Airport symbol*] (OAG)
Jos........... Joseph (BJA)
Jos........... Joseph's Reports [*21 Nevada*] [*A publication*] (DLA)
Jos........... Josephus (BJA)
Jos........... Joshua [*Old Testament book*]
Jos........... Josiah (BJA)
JOS........... Joss Energy Ltd. [*Toronto Stock Exchange symbol*]
JOS........... Jostens, Inc. [*NYSE symbol*] (SPSG)
JOS........... Josvafo [*Hungary*] [*Seismograph station code, US Geological Survey*] (SEIS)
JOSA .... Seaman Apprentice, Journalist, Striker [*Navy rating*]
JOSAF .... Joint Operations Support Activity Frankfurt [*National Security Agency*]
Jos & Bev.... Joseph and Beven's Digest of Decisions [*Ceylon*] [*A publication*] (DLA)
JosAnt .... Jewish Antiquities [*Josephus*] (BJA)
JosApion...... Against Apion [*Josephus*] (BJA)
JOSB .... Bank [*Joseph A.*] Clothiers, Inc. [*NASDAQ symbol*] (SAG)
JOSB .... Jos.A. Bank Clothiers [*NASDAQ symbol*] (TTSB)
JOSB .... Joseph A Bank Clothiers [*NASDAQ symbol*] (SAG)
JosBank...... Bank [*Joseph A.*] Clothiers, Inc. [*Associated Press*] (SAG)
JosBank...... Joseph A. Bank Clothers [*Associated Press*] (SAG)
JOSCO .... Joint Overseas Shipping Control Office
Joseph........ Josephus [*First century AD*] [*Classical studies*] (OCD)
JOSH .... Job Safety and Health [*Bureau of National Affairs*] [*Information service or system*] (CRD)
Josh .... Joshua [*Old Testament book*]
JOSHUA ...... Joint Sticking Hemoglobin Universal Assay [*Sickle cell anemia test*]
JO/SL .... Jupiter Orbiter Satellite Lander [*NASA*]
JosLife........ Life of Josephus (BJA)
JOSM .... Jesuit Office of Social Ministry [*Later, NOJSM*] (EA)
JOSN .... Seaman, Journalist, Striker [*Navy rating*]
JOSO .... Joint Organization for Solar Observations
JOSP .... Junior Olympic Shooting Program [*National Rifle Association*]
JOSPRO ...... Joint Ocean [*or Overseas*] Shipping Procedure
JOSS .... JOHNNIAC [*John's Integrator and Automatic Computer*] Open Shop System [*Time-sharing language*] [*Rand Corp. 1962*] [*Computer science*]
JOSS .... Joint Ocean Surface Study
JOSS .... Joint Overseas Switching System [*Military*] (AABC)
Jostens....... Jostens, Inc. [*Associated Press*] (SAG)
JosWars ...... Wars [*Josephus*] (BJA)
JOT .... Jam on Target
Jo T .... John of Tynemouth [*Deceased, 1221*] [*Authority cited in pre-1607 legal work*] (DSA)
JOT .... Joint Operational Test
JOT .... Joliet, IL [*Location identifier FAA*] (FAAL)
JOTA .... Jamboree on the Air [*Boy Scouts of America*]
JOT & E...... Joint Operational Test and Evaluation (MCD)
JOTB .... Jungle Operations Training Battalion [*Military*]
JOTC .... Joint Oil Targets Committee [*World War II*]
JOTC .... Jungle Operations Training Center [*Army*] (INF)
JOTD .... Jotted (ABBR)
Jo Te .... Johannes Teutonicus [*Deceased circa 1246*] [*Authority cited in pre-1607 legal work*] (DSA)
JOTFOC....... Justification for Other than Full and Open Competition (AAGC)
JOTG .... Jotting (ABBR)
JOTR .... Joint Operational and Technical Reviews [*Military*] (AFIT)
JOTR .... Joshua Tree National Monument
JOTS .... Job-Oriented Training Standards (AFM)
JOTS .... Joint Operational Tactical System [*Navy*] (DOMA)
JOU........... Osaka University, Kita-ku, Osaka, Japan [*Library symbol Library of Congress*] (LCLS)
JOU........... Sioux Falls, SD [*Location identifier FAA*] (FAAL)
JOUAM .... Junior Order United American Mechanics
Joule .... Joules, Inc. [*Associated Press*] (SAG)
JOU-N .... Osaka University, Nakanishima Library, Osaka, Japan [*Library symbol Library of Congress*] (LCLS)
JOUR .... Journal (ABBR)
Jour .... Journal (EBF)
JOUR .... Journey (WGA)
JOUR .... Journeyman
Jour Comp Leg... Journal. Society of Comparative Legislation [*A publication*] (DLA)
Jour Conat Law... Journal of Conational Law [*A publication*] (DLA)
Jour Jur ...... Journal of Jurisprudence [*A publication*] (DLA)
Jour Juris .... Hall's Journal of Jurisprudence [*A publication*] (DLA)
Jour Jur Sc.. Journal of Jurisprudence and Scottish Law Magazine [*A publication*] (DLA)
Jour Law .... Journal of Law [*A publication*] (DLA)
JOURN........ Journal
Journ .... Journalism (DD)
JOURN........ Journey (ABBR)
Journ Bib Lit... Journal of Biblical Literature [*A publication*] (OCD)
Journ Jur ..... Journal of Jurisprudence [*A publication*] (DLA)
Journ Phil .... Journal of Philology [*A publication*] (OCD)
Journ Sav .... Journal des Savants [*A publication*] (OCD)

Jour Ps Med...	Journal of Psychological Medicine and Medical Jurisprudence [*A publication*] (DLA)
Jour Soc Civ...	Journal des Societes Civiles et Commerciales [*A publication*] (DLA)
Jour Trib Com...	Journal des Tribunaux de Commerce [*A publication*] (DLA)
Jov.	Hymnus in Jovem [*of Callimachus*] [*Classical studies*] (OCD)
JOVE	Jupiter Orbiting Vehicle for Exploration (MCD)
JOVIAL	Joule's Own Version of the International Algebraic [*or Algorithmic*] Language [*1958*] [*Computer science*]
Jow Dict	Jowitt's Dictionary of English Law [*2nd ed.*] [*1977*] [*A publication*] (DLA)
JOWIP	Joint Ocean Wave Investigation Project [*US and Canadian venture*]
JOWOG	Joint Working Group
JOY	Job Opportunity for Youth [*NASA employment program*]
JOY	Joy [*Poland ICAO designator*] (FAAC)
Joy Acc	Joy's Evidence of Accomplices [*1836*] [*A publication*] (DLA)
Joyce Ins	Joyce on Insurance [*A publication*] (DLA)
Joyce Lim	Joyce on Limitations [*A publication*] (DLA)
Joyce Prac Inj...	Joyce's Law and Practice of Injunctions [*1872*] [*A publication*] (DLA)
Joyce Prin Inj...	Joyce's Doctrines and Principles of Injunctions [*1877*] [*A publication*] (DLA)
Joy Chal	Joy's Peremptory Challenge of Jurors [*1844*] [*A publication*] (DLA)
Joy Conf	Joy. Admissibility of Confessions [*1842*] [*A publication*] (DLA)
Joy Ev	Joy's Evidence of Accomplices [*1836*] [*A publication*] (DLA)
Joy Leg Ed	Joy on Legal Education [*A publication*] (DLA)
Joyn Lim	Joynes on Limitations [*A publication*] (DLA)
JOYS	Journal of Youth Services in Libraries [*American Library Association*]
JOZ	Jozini [*South Africa*] [*Seismograph station code, US Geological Survey*] (SEIS)
JP	Adria Airways [*Airline flight code*] (ODBW)
JP	Die Juedische Presse [*The Jewish Press*] [*German*] (BJA)
JP	Fighter [*Russian aircraft symbol*]
JP	Indo-Pacific International [*ICAO designator*] (AD)
JP	Jack Panel
JP	Jackson-Pratt [*Drain*] [*Surgery*] (DAVI)
JP	Jacobi Polynomial [*Mathematics*]
JP	James M. Peed [*Designer's mark when appearing on US coins*]
JP	Janata Party [*India*] [*Political party*] (PPW)
JP	Japan [*ANSI two-letter standard code*] (CNC)
JP	Japan Paper
JP	Jarrow Press, Inc.
JP	Jatiya Party [*Bangladesh*] [*Political party*]
JP	Jean Pierre Cosmetiques, Inc. [*Vancouver Stock Exchange symbol*]
JP	Jefferson Pilot [*NYSE symbol*] (SAG)
JP	Jefferson-Pilot Corp. [*NYSE symbol*] (SPSG)
JP	Jet Penetration
JP	Jet Petroleum (AFM)
JP	Jet Pilot
JP	Jet Pipe
JP	Jet Power
JP	Jet Propellant [*or Propulsion*]
jp	Jet Propellant (NAKS)
jp	Jet Propulsion (NAKS)
JP	Jet Propulsion Fuel
JP	Jet Publications [*DoD*]
JP	Jet Pump [*Bioinstrumentation*]
JP	Jewish Press [*Brooklyn, NY*] [*A publication*] (BJA)
JP	Jobbing Printer [*A publication*] (DGA)
JP	Job Placement [*Job Service*] (OICC)
JP	Job Processor
JP	Jobst Pump [*Medicine*]
JP	Job the Patient (BJA)
JP	Joining Peptide [*Medicine*] (DMAA)
JP	Joint Pacific [*Military*] (CINC)
JP	Joint Protection (STED)
JP	Joint Publication [*Military*]
JP	Jones Party [*Malta*] [*Political party*] (PPE)
JP	Jones Plug [*Electricity*] (IAA)
JP	Joseph Pennell [*Specification-made paper*]
JP	Journal of Parapsychology [*A publication*] (BRI)
JP	Judge of Probate [*British*] (ROG)
JP	Jumper (IAA)
JP	Junction Panel [*or Point*] [*Electronics*]
JP	Junge Pioniero
JP	Jungle Penetrator [*A helicopter rescue device*] [*Military*] (VNW)
JP	Junior Partner [*i.e., a husband*] [*Slang*]
JP	Junior Principal [*Freemasonry*] (ROG)
JP	Junior Probationer [*British*] (ROG)
JP	Justice of the Peace
JP	Justice of the Peace and Local Government Review [*A publication*] (DLA)
JP	Justice of the Peace. Weekly Notes of Cases [*England*] [*A publication*] (DLA)
JP	Justice Party [*Turkey*] [*Political party*]
JP	Jute Protection [*Telecommunications*] (TEL)
JP	Juvenile Periodontist [*Dentistry*] (DAVI)
JP	Juventud Peronista [*Peronist Youth*] [*Argentina*]
JP	Kim Jong Pil [*South Korean politician*]
JPA	Jack Panel Assembly
JPA	Jamaica Press Association (BUAC)
JPA	Japan Petroleum Association (BUAC)
JPA	Japan Procurement Agency
JPA	Jesuit Philosophical Association of the United States and Canada (EA)
JPA	Jet Pioneers Association of the United States of America (EA)

JPA	Jewish Palestinian Aramaic (BJA)
JPA	Joao Pessoa [*Brazil*] [*Airport symbol*] (OAG)
JPA	Job Pack Area [*Computer science*] (IBMDP)
JPA	Job Performance Aid
JPA	Joint Passover Association of the City of New York (EA)
JPA	Joint Permitting Agreement (COE)
JPA	Joint Planning Activity [*DoD*]
JPA	Junior Philatelists of America (EA)
JPA	Justices of the Peace Association [*Australia*]
JPA	Juvenile Pilocytic Astrocytoma [*Medicine*] (DMAA)
JPA	La Porte, TX [*Location identifier FAA*] (FAAL)
J-PAAS	Jubilation - Paul Anka Admiration Society [*Defunct*] (EA)
J Pac H	Journal of Pacific History [*A publication*]
JPAM	Joint Program Assessment Memorandum (MCD)
JPAO	Joint Public Affairs Office (DOMA)
JPAP	Jet Penetration Approach
JPAT	Joint Process Action Team
JPATS	Joint Primary Aircraft Training System [*Air Force*] [*Navy*] (DOMA)
JPB	Joint Planning Board
JPB	Joint Procurement Board [*Military*] (AABC)
JPB	Joint Production Board [*US and Great Britain*]
JPB	Joint Purchasing Board
JPB	Junctional Premature Beat [*Cardiology*]
JPBS	Jettison Pushbutton Switch
JPC	Jack Patch Cord
JpC	Japanese Columbia [*Record label*]
JPC	Japan Productivity Centre (BUAC)
JPC	Jeunesse pour Christ [*Youth for Christ International - YFCI*] (EA)
JPC	Jeunesse Progressiste Casamancaise [*Casamance Progressive Youth*] [*Senegal*]
JPC	Johnson Products (EFIS)
JPC	Joint Pensions Committee (WDAA)
JPC	Joint Planning Center
JPC	Joint Planning Committee
JPC	Joint Power Condition [*Aerospace*] (NAKS)
JPC	Joint Power Conditioner
JPC	Joint Production Committee [*British*] (DCTA)
JPC	Journal of Popular Culture [*A publication*] (BRI)
JPC	Judgement Purchase Corp.
JPC	Judge of the Prize Court (DLA)
JPC	Judicial Planning Council (OICC)
JPC	Junctional Premature Contraction [*Cardiology*]
JPC	Justice of the Peace Clerk [*British*] (ROG)
JPC	Just Prior Condition [*Computer science*]
JPC	Polar Air Co. [*Russian Federation*] [*ICAO designator*] (FAAC)
JPCA	Japan Petrochemical Industry Association (BUAC)
JPCA	Jewish Penicillin Connoisseurs Association (EA)
JPCC	Joint Pacific Command Control Network (MCD)
JPCC	Joint Petroleum Coordination Center/Committee [*NATO*] (NATG)
JPCD	Just Perceptible Color Difference [*Telecommunications*] (TEL)
JPCG-CRM...	Joint Policy Coordinating Group on Computer Resources Management (MCD)
JPCG/DIMM...	Joint Policy Coordinating Group on Defense Integrated Materiel Management (AFIT)
JPCG-DMI...	Joint Policy Coordinating Group on Depot Maintenance Interservicing
JP Ct	Justice of the Peace's Court [*Legal term*] (DLA)
JPD	Japan Publishers Directory [*Japan Publications Guide Service*] [*Japan Information service or system*] (CRD)
JPD	Joint Planning Document (COE)
JPD	Joint Potential Designator [*DoD*]
JPDC	Juvenile Plantar Dermatosis [*Medicine*] (DAVI)
JPDC	Japan Petroleum Development Co.
JPDR	Japan Power Demonstration Reactor
JPE	Job Performance Evaluation (PDAA)
JPE	Journal of Political Economy [*A publication*] (BRI)
JPE	JPE, Inc. [*Associated Press*] (SAG)
JPEC	Joint Planning and Execution Community (DOMA)
JP ECON	Journal of Political Economy [*A publication*] (ROG)
J PED	Journal of Pedagogy [*New York*] [*A publication*] (ROG)
JPEG	Joint Photographic Experts Group [*International video standard*] (PCM)
JPEG	Joint Photographic Experts Group [*Antineoplastic drug*]
jpeg	Joint Photographic Experts Group [*Computer science*]
JPEI	JPE, Inc. [*NASDAQ symbol*] (SAG)
JPERSTAT	Joint Personnel Status and Casualty Report (COE)
JPESJ	Jewish Palestine Exploration Society. Journal [*A publication*] (BJA)
JPET	Job Placement and Employment Training
JPF	Jewish Peace Fellowship (EA)
JPF	Jewish Philanthropic Fund of 1933 (EA)
JPF	Job Planning Form
JPF	Justice of the Peace Fiscal [*British*] (ROG)
JPFC	Jane Powell Fan Club (EA)
JPFC	Jeanne Pruett Fan Club (EA)
JPFC	Judas Priest Fan Club (EA)
JPFFI	Jiangsu Provincial Freshwater Fisheries Institute [*China*] (BUAC)
JPFO	Jews for the Preservation of Firearms Ownership (EA)
JP Food	JP Foodservice, Inc. [*Associated Press*] (SAG)
JPFS	JP Foodservice [*NASDAQ symbol*] (TTSB)
JPFS	JP Foodservice, Inc. [*NASDAQ symbol*] (SAG)
JPFT	Joiner Pilaster Fumetight [*Technical drawings*]
JPG	Jefferson Proving Ground [*Madison, IN*] [*Army*] (AABC)
JPG	Job Performance [*or Proficiency*] Guide (AFM)
JPG	Joint Planning Group [*NATO*] (NATG)
JPGC	Joint Power Generation Conference

JPGS............ Japan Publications Guide Service [Information service or system] (IID)
JPH............. Jones, Paul H., Romulus MI [STAC]
JPHA............ John Pelham Historical Association (EA)
J Pharm Sci... Journal of Pharmaceutical Science (MEC)
J Phil........... Journal of Philosophy [A publication] (BRI)
J Phys Chem... Journal of Physical Chemistry (MEC)
JPI .... Jackson Personality Inventory [Personality development test] [Psychology]
JPI .... Japan Packaging Institute (BUAC)
JPI .... Jianghan Petroleum Institute [China] (BUAC)
JPI .... Job Performance Illustrations (MCD)
JPI .... Joint Packaging Instruction
JPI .... Joint Precision Interdiction [NATO] (DOMA)
JPI .... Jupiter National, Inc. (SPSG)
JPI .... Sitka, AK [Location identifier FAA] (FAAL)
JPIA .... Japan Plastics Industry Association (BUAC)
JPIC............. Joint Program Integration Committee [NASA] (NASA)
JPIC............. Joint Public Information Center (COE)
JPIM .... Journal of Product Innovation Management [Product Development and Management Association] [A publication]
JPJ............... Justice of the Peace and Local Government Review [A publication] (DLA)
JPJ............... Justice of the Peace Journal [A publication]
JPJ............... Justice of the Peace. Weekly Notes of Cases [England] [A publication] (DLA)
JPJ............... Paterson, NJ [Location identifier FAA] (FAAL)
JPJo............. Justice of the Peace. Weekly Notes of Cases [England] [A publication] (DLA)
JPL .... Jacksonville Public Library System, Jacksonville, FL [OCLC symbol] (OCLC)
JPL .... Jet Propulsion Laboratory [Renamed H. Allen Smith Jet Propulsion Laboratory, 1973, after a retiring congressman. However, JPL is used officially] [California Institute of Technology Pasadena, CA] [NASA] [Research center]
JPL .... Jewish Peace Lobby (EA)
JPL .... Job Parts List (AAG)
JPLE .... Journal of Professional Legal Education [Australia A publication]
JPL/ETR........ Jet Propulsion Laboratory Field Station, Air Force Eastern Test Range
JPL/PODS ..... Jet Propulsion Laboratory/Pilot Ocean Data System (MCD)
JPL-STAR .... Jet Propulsion Laboratory Self Testing and Repairing Computer [California Institute of Technology] (PDAA)
JPM .... Jet-Piercing Machine
JPM .... Job Performance Manual (MCD)
JPM .... Job Performance Measure
JPM .... Joint Project Manager
JPM .... Morgan [J. P.] & Co., Inc. [NYSE symbol] (SPSG)
JPM .... Morgan (J.P.) [NYSE symbol] (TTSB)
JPMA........... Japan Plywood Manufactures Association (BUAC)
JPMA........... Juvenile Products Manufacturers Association (EA)
JPMC............ JPM Co. [NASDAQ symbol] (TTSB)
JPMCo .... JPM Co. (The) [Associated Press] (SAG)
JPMO............ Jersey Potato Marketing Organisation (BUAC)
JPMO............ Joint Program Management Office (MCD)
JPMPrA......... Morgan(JP) Adj Rt A Pfd [NYSE symbol] (TTSB)
JPMPrH......... Morgan(JP)6.625% Dep'H'Pfd [NYSE symbol] (TTSB)
JPMR .... Joint Projected Manpower Requirements [Military] (AABC)
JPMS .... J. P. Morgan Securities
JPMX .... JPM Co. (The) [NASDAQ symbol] (SAG)
JPN .... Japan [ANSI three-letter standard code] (CNC)
jpn .... Japanese [MARC language code Library of Congress] (LCCP)
JPN............. Memrykord Ltd. [British ICAO designator] (FAAC)
JPN............. Washington, DC [Location identifier FAA] (FAAL)
JPNL............ Judged Perceived Noise Level (OA)
JPNT............ Joiner Pilaster Nontight [Technical drawings]
JPO .... Japanese Patent Office (TELE)
JPO .... Joint Petroleum Office
JPO .... Joint Program Office [Military] (SDI)
JPO .... Joint Project Office [or Officer]
JPO .... Junior Professional Officer [United Nations]
JPO .... Juvenile Probation Officer (OICC)
JPO .... Pomona [California] [Airport symbol] (AD)
JPOAA .... Junior Panel Outdoor Advertising Association [Later, ESOAA]
JPO-BD........ Joint Program Office for Biological Defense [Army] (RDA)
JPOC............ JSC [Johnson Space Center] Payload Operations Center (MCD)
J Pol........... Journal of Politics [A publication] (BRI)
J Pol Sci & Admin... Journal of Police Science and Administration [A publication] (DLA)
J Pop F&TV... Journal of Popular Film and Television [A publication] (BRI)
JpOTC.......... Japan OTC Equity Fund, Inc. [Associated Press] (SAG)
JPOTS.......... Joint Panel on Oceanographic Tables and Standards [Marine science] [United Nations] (OSRA)
JPO-TT......... Joint Program Offrice-Transition Team [DoD]
JPP .... Jalkeen Puolenpaiuan [Afternoon] [Finland]
JPP .... Japan Paper Proofs
JPP .... Joint Planning Process [Military] (NVT)
JPP .... Joint Program Plan (NASA)
jpp .... Joint Program Plan (NAKS)
JPPL............ Joint Personnel Priority List
JpPol........... Japanese Polydor-Deutsche Grammophon [Record label]
JPPP .... Jewish People, Past and Present [Jewish Encyclopedic Handbooks] [A publication] (BJA)
JPPRI........... Jewish Planning Policy and Research Institute (BUAC)

JPPRI........... Jewish Policy Planning and Research Institute [Synagogue Council of America]
JPPS .... Jack Point Preservation Society (EA)
JPPSO .... Joint Personal Property Shipping Office [Military] (DNAB)
JPPSOWA .... Joint Personal Property Shipping Office, Washington, DC [Military] (AABC)
JPPSST........ Joseph Preschool and Primary Self-Concept Screening Test [Child development test] [Psychology]
JpPV .... Japanese Polydor Variable Microgroove [Record label]
JPQ .... Jung Personality Questionnaire [Personality development test] [Psychology]
JPR............. Air International (Holdings) PLC [British ICAO designator] (FAAC)
JPR............. Inversiones Ayacucho, SA, ™Jet Privado∫[Peru] [FAA designator] (FAAC)
JPR............. Joint Procurement Regulations [of Army and Air Force]
JPR............. Journal of Peace Research [A publication] (BRI)
JPR............. Journal of Purchasing and Materials Management [A publication] (AAGC)
JPR............. JP Realty [NYSE symbol] (SPSG)
jpr.............. Judaeo-Persian [MARC language code Library of Congress] (LCCP)
JPR............. Justice of the Peace and Local Government Review Reports [A publication] (DLA)
JPR............. Justice Procurement Regulation [A publication] (AAGC)
JPRA............ Japanese Phonograph Record Association [An association] (NITA)
JPRC............ Joint Personnel Recovery Center [Military]
J PR CT .... Judge Prerogative Court, Canterbury [British] (ROG)
JPRDY .... Jeopardy (ABBR)
JPRDZ .... Jeopardize (ABBR)
JPRDZG .... Jeopardizing (ABBR)
JP Rlty........ JP Realty [Associated Press] (SAG)
JPRO .... Joint Photographic Reconnaissance Organization [World War II]
JPROB .... Judge of Probate [British] (ROG)
J Prod L ...... Journal of Products Law (DLA)
JPRS .... Joint Publications Research Service [Department of Commerce]
JPRS-GUO ... Joint Publications Research Service Translations - Government Use Only [Department of Commerce]
JPS .... Japan Press Service
JPS .... Jean Piaget Society [Later, JPSSSKD] (EA)
JPS .... Jet Plume Simulation
JPS .... Jeunesse Populaire Senegalaise [Senegalese People's Youth]
JPS .... Jewish Publication Society (EA)
JPS .... John Player Special [Sponsor of British Lotus Formula I racing car]
JPS .... Joint Planning Staff [US and Great Britain] [World War II]
JPS .... Joint Position Sense [Medicine]
JPS .... Jones Plumbing Systems, Inc. [AMEX symbol] (SPSG)
JPS .... Junior Philatelic Society [British] (BI)
JPS .... Juvenile Polyposis Syndrome [Medicine]
JPSA............ Jacob's Prevocational Skills Assessment
JPSA............ Japanese Plating Supplier's Association [Environmetal science]
JPSA............ Jewish Pharmaceutical Society of America (EA)
JPSA............ Jewish Publication Society of America (DGA)
JPSA............ Joint Program for the Study of Abortion
JPSA............ Junior Philatelic Society of America [Later, JPA] (EA)
JPSC............ Joint Production Survey Committee
JPSG............ Joint Planning and Scheduling Group
JPSP............ Journal of Personality and Social Psychology [A publication] (DHP)
JPSS............ Just, Participatory, and Sustainable Society [World Council of Churches]
JPSSSKD...... Jean Piaget Society: Society for the Study of Knowledge and Development (EA)
JPST .... Journal of Parenteral Science and Technology [A publication] (EAAP)
JPSTH.......... Joint Peristimulus Time Histograms [For study of physiology]
J Psycho Drugs... Journal of Psychoactive Drugs (MEC)
J Psychological Medicine... Journal of Psychological Medicine and Medical Jurisprudence [A publication] (DLA)
JPT .... Houston [Texas] Park-Ten [Airport symbol] (OAG)
JPT .... Japanese Proficiency Test [Educational test]
JPT .... Jet Pipe Temperature
JPT .... Job Progress Ticket
JPT .... Joint Planning Team (COE)
JPT .... Jupitor Resources Ltd. [Vancouver Stock Exchange symbol]
JPTDS.......... Joint Photographic Type Designation System [Military]
JPTDS.......... Junior Participating Tactical Data System [Also known as "Jeep"] (MCD)
JPTF .... Joint Parachute Test Facility [DoD]
JPTL............ Jet Pipe Temperature Limiter (MCD)
JPTO............ Jet-Propelled Takeoff
JPTS............ Jet Petroleum, Thermally Stable (DOMA)
JPU .... Job Processing Unit
JPU .... Just Publishable Unit
JpV .... Japanese Victor [Record label]
JPV .... Joint Pacific Voice [Military] (CINC)
JPW .... Job Processing Word
JPWC............ Joint Postwar Committee
JPWC............ Joint Psychological Warfare Committee (LAIN)
JQ .... Job Questionnaire
JQ .... Journalism Quarterly [A publication] (BRI)
JQ .... J-Q Resources, Inc. [Toronto Stock Exchange symbol]
JQ .... Trans-Jamaican Airlines [ICAO designator] (AD)
JQA .... John Quincy Adams [US president, 1767-1848]
JQA .... Trans Jamaican Airlines Ltd. [ICAO designator] (FAAC)
JQB .... Justice of the Queen's Bench [Legal term] (DLA)
JQC .... Dayton, OH [Location identifier FAA] (FAAL)
JQE .... Jaque [Panama] [Airport symbol] (OAG)
JQH .... Hammons [John Q.] Hotels, Inc. [NYSE symbol] (SAG)

JQHamm......	Hammons [*John Q.*] Hotel, Inc. [*Associated Press*] (SAG)
JQP..............	Josephson Quasi Particle (AAEL)
JQR..............	Hammons(John Q)Hotels'A' [*NYSE symbol*] (TTSB)
JQR..............	Jewish Quarterly Review [*A publication*] (ODCC)
JR...............	Jacobus Rex [*King James*]
JR...............	James River Corp. [*NYSE symbol*] (TTSB)
JR...............	James River Corp. of Virginia [*NYSE symbol*] (SPSG)
JR...............	Jam Resistant
JR...............	Jar (MCD)
Jr...............	Jeremiah [*Old Testament book*] (BJA)
JR...............	[*The*] Jewish Right (EA)
JR...............	Jigger [*Ship's rigging*] (ROG)
JR...............	Job Rotation [*Computer science*] (MHDB)
JR...............	Job Routed [*Military*] (AFIT)
JR...............	John Ross Ewing, Jr. [*Character in TV series "Dallas"*]
JR...............	Johnson's New York Reports [*A publication*] (DLA)
JR...............	Joint Resolution [*Usually, of the US Senate and House of Representatives*]
JR...............	Joint Return (MHDB)
JR...............	Joint Review
JR...............	Jolly Reaction (STED)
JR...............	Jolly's Reaction [*Neurology*] (DAVI)
JR...............	Jordan Register (EA)
JR...............	Jour [*Day*] [*French*]
JR...............	Journal (ADA)
JR...............	Journal of Religion [*A publication*] (BRI)
JR...............	Judge's Remand (WDAA)
JR...............	Judges' Rules [*A publication*] (DLA)
Jr...............	Juglans regia [*Persian walnut*]
JR...............	Junctional Rhythm [*Cardiology*]
JR...............	Junction Rack (KSC)
JR...............	Junior
Jr...............	Junior (ASC)
JR...............	Jurist Reports [*1873-78*] [*New Zealand*] [*A publication*] (DLA)
JR...............	Juror
JR...............	Juvenile Rheumatoid Arthritis [*Also, JRA*] [*Medicine*] (DAVI)
JRA.............	Jam-Resistant Antenna
JRA.............	Japanese Racing Association
JRA.............	Japan Racing Association (ECON)
JRA.............	Jewish Royalty Association (EA)
JRA.............	Job Release Analysis
JRA.............	Juvenile Rheumatoid Arthritis [*Medicine*]
JRA.............	New York, NY [*Location identifier FAA*] (FAAL)
JRAD	Joint Resource Assessment Data
JRAD	Judicial Recommendation against Deportation
J Radio L....	Journal of Radio Law [*A publication*] (DLA)
JRAN	Junior Resident Admission Note (STED)
JRAS...........	Journal of the Royal Agricultural Society [*A publication*] (ROG)
JRATA.........	Joint Research and Test Activity (MCD)
JRATA.........	Joint Research and Test Agency [*Terminated, 1966*] [*Military*]
JRB.............	Joint Radio Board
JRB.............	Joint Reconnaissance Board [*Military*] (AABC)
JRB.............	Joint Review Board (MCD)
jrb.............	Judaeo-Arabic [*MARC language code Library of Congress*] (LCCP)
JRB.............	New York, NY [*Location identifier FAA*] (FAAL)
Jr BF	Junior Baby Food (STED)
JRBK...........	James River Bankshares [*NASDAQ symbol*] (TTSB)
JRBK...........	James River Bankshares, Inc. [*NASDAQ symbol*] (SAG)
JRC.............	Jet Reaction Control
JrC.............	Jewish Refugees Committee (EAIO)
JrC.............	Johnson Reprint Corporation, New York, NY [*Library symbol Library of Congress*] (LCLS)
JRC.............	Joint Railroad Conference
JRC.............	Joint Reconnaissance Center [*Military*] (AFM)
JRC.............	Joint Recovery Center (MCD)
JRC.............	Joint Replacement Center [*Medicine*] (STED)
JRC.............	Joint Representation Committee [*British*] (DCTA)
JRC.............	Joint Research Center [*Commission of the European Communities*]
JRC.............	Junior Red Cross
JRCAT.........	Joint Research Center for Atom Technology [*Japan*]
JRCC...........	Joint Reconnaissance Control Center (MCD)
JRCC...........	Joint Regional Continuing Committee [*Later, RCEAC*] [*Civil Defense*]
JRCC...........	Joint Rescue Coordination Center [*Military*] (AFM)
JRC-CVT	Joint Review Committee on Education in Cardiovascular Technology (DAVI)
JRCDMS	Joint Review Committee on Education in Diagnostic Medical Sonography (EA)
JRC-EEG	Joint Review Committee on Education in Electroencephalographic [*Technology*] (DAVI)
JRCEMT-P ...	Joint Review Committee on Educational Programs for the EMT [*Emergency MedicalTechnician*]-Paramedic (EA)
JRCEPEP.....	Joint Review Committee on Educational Programs for the EMT [*Emergency MedicalTechnician*]-Paramedic (EA)
JRCEPPA	Joint Review Committee on Educational Programs for Physician Assistants (EA)
JRCERT.......	Joint Review Committee on Education in Radiologic Technology (EA)
JRCEST.......	Joint Review Committee on Education for the Surgical Technologist (EA)
JRCI............	Jamming RADAR Coverage Indicator (MSA)
JRCI............	Journal of the Royal Colonial Institute (ROG)
JRC-NMT	Joint Review Committee on Educational Programs in Nuclear Medicine Technology (DAVI)
JRCOMA	Joint Review Committee for the Ophthalmic Medical Assistant (EA)
JRCOMP	Joint Review Committee for Ophthalmic Medical Personnel (EA)
JRCP...........	Joint Reinforced Concrete Pavement
JRC-PA	Joint Review Committee on Educational Programs for Physician Assistants (EA)
JRCPE.........	Joint Review Committee for Perfusion Education (DAVI)
JRCRTE.......	Joint Review Committee for Respiratory Therapy Education (EA)
JRCS...........	Jet Reaction Control System
JRCS...........	John Reich Collectors Society (EA)
JRC-ST	Joint Review Committee on Education for the Surgical Technologist (DAVI)
JRD............	Jarred (ABBR)
JRD............	Justification Review Document (AAGC)
JRD............	Riverside, CA [*Location identifier FAA*] (FAAL)
JRDA...........	Jeunesse du Rassemblement Democratique Africain [*Youth of the African Democratic Rally*]
JRDACI	Jeunesse du Rassemblement Democratique Africain de Cote d'Ivoire [*Youth of the African Democratic Rally of the Ivory Coast*]
JRDB...........	Joint Research and Development Board [*1946-1947*]
JRDF...........	Joint Rapid Development Force [*Military*] (WDAA)
JRDOD.........	Joint Research and Development Objectives Document [*Military*] (AABC)
JRE.............	JR Energy Ltd. [*Vancouver Stock Exchange symbol*]
JRE.............	New York [*New York*] E. 60th Street [*Airport symbol*] (OAG)
JREA...........	James Robison Evangelistic Association (EA)
J receptor...	Juxtapulmonary-Capillary Receptor [*Medicine*] (STED)
J Rehab RD...	Journal of Rehabilitation Research and Development [*A publication*] (BRI)
JREM..........	Junior Radio Electrical Mechanic [*British military*] (DMA)
J Rep..........	Johnson's Maryland Chancery Reports [*A publication*] (DLA)
J Rep..........	Johnson's New York Reports [*A publication*] (DLA)
J Rep..........	Johnson's Reports of Chase's United States Circuit Court Decisions [*A publication*] (DLA)
J Reprints Antitrust L & Econ...	Journal of Reprints for Antitrust Law and Economics [*A publication*] (DLA)
JRF.............	Jackie Robinson Foundation (EA)
JRF.............	Jewish Reconstructionist Foundation (EA)
JRF.............	John-Roger Foundation (EA)
JRF.............	Judicial Research Foundation [*Defunct*]
JRFC...........	Jerry Reed Fan Club [*Defunct*] (EA)
JRFC...........	Johnny Rodriguez Fan Club (EA)
JRFL...........	Jarful (ABBR)
JRFTNG	Jet Refresher Training [*Navy*] (NVT)
JRG............	Jarring (ABBR)
JRG............	Junction Register (IAA)
JRGN..........	Jargon (ABBR)
JRH............	Jorhat [*India*] [*Airport symbol*] (OAG)
JR HS	Junior High School (WDAA)
JRHSQ........	Journal. Royal Historical Society of Queensland [*A publication*]
JRI.............	Jail Release Information
JRI.............	Jewel Resources [*Vancouver Stock Exchange symbol*]
JRISDON......	Jurisdiction (ROG)
JRivBsh.......	James River Bankshares, Inc. [*Associated Press*] (SAG)
JRiver.........	James River Corp. of Virginia [*Associated Press*] (SAG)
JRJ	JAVA [*Jamaica Association of Villas and Apartments*] Reservations Jamaica (EA)
JRKD	Jerked (ABBR)
JRKG	Jerking (ABBR)
JRKIR	Jerkier (ABBR)
JRKLY.........	Jerkily (ABBR)
JRKN	Jerkin (ABBR)
JRKNS	Jerkiness (ABBR)
JRKR	Jerker (ABBR)
JRKST.........	Jerkiest (ABBR)
JRL.............	Cincinnati G&E8.28%JrSubDebs [*NYSE symbol*] (TTSB)
JRL.............	Cincinnati Gas & Electric [*NYSE symbol*] (SAG)
JRL.............	Jarvis Resources [*Vancouver Stock Exchange symbol*]
JRL.............	Jet Research Laboratory (MCD)
jrl.............	Journal (DAVI)
JRLI............	Life Outreach International (EA)
Jr LS	Junior Life Saving [*Red Cross*]
JRM............	Jettison Release Mechanism
JRM............	Joule-Rowland Method [*Physics*]
JRM............	McDermott [*J. Ray*] SA [*NYSE symbol*] (SAG)
JRMB..........	Joint Requirements and Management Board [*Later, JROC*] [*Military*]
JRMB..........	Joint Resources Management Board [*Military*]
JRMF..........	Joseph R. McCarthy Foundation (EA)
JRMTO........	Joint Rail Military Traffic Office (AABC)
JRN............	Jet Rent SA [*Mexico ICAO designator*] (FAAC)
JRN............	Junior Resident Note [*Medical records*] (DAVI)
JrNAD	Junior National Association for the Deaf [*Defunct*] (EA)
JRNDEX	Journal Index
JRNIST	Journalist
JRNL	Journal
JRNLM........	Journalism (ABBR)
JRNLSM	Journalism (ABBR)
JRNLST	Journalist (ABBR)
JRNLSTC	Journalistic (ABBR)
JRNLT.........	Journalist (ABBR)
JRNLTC.......	Journalistic (ABBR)
JRNLTCY	Journalistically (ABBR)
JRNLZ.........	Journalize (ABBR)
JRNLZD........	Journalized (ABBR)
JRNLZG	Journalizing (ABBR)
JRNLZR	Journalizer (ABBR)
JRNSCA.......	Jurist Reports, New Series, Court of Appeal [*New Zealand*] [*A publication*] (DLA)

JRNSML	Jurist Reports, New Series, Cases in Mining Law [*New Zealand*] [*A publication*] (DLA)
JRNSSC	Jurist Reports, New Series, Supreme Court [*New Zealand*] [*A publication*] (DLA)
JRNY	Journey (ABBR)
JRNYD	Journeyed (ABBR)
JRNYG	Journeying (ABBR)
JRNYMAN ...	Journeyman (ABBR)
JRO	Jicamarca Radar Observatory [*Peru*]
JRO	Junior Radio Operator [*British military*] (DMA)
JRO	Kilimanjaro [*Tanzania*] [*Airport symbol*]
JROC	Joint Requirements Oversight Council [*Military*]
JROFC	James ™Rebel∫O'Leary Fan Club (EA)
JROJATCC....	James ™Rebel∫O'Leary and Jammie Ann Tape Club [*Defunct*] (EA)
JROTC	Junior Reserve Officers' Training Corps (AABC)
JRP	Job Readiness Posture (OICC)
JRP	Joint Requirements Planning (CDE)
JRPG	Joint RADAR Planning Group [*Military*] (CET)
JRPM	Joint Registered Publications Memorandum
JRPO	Joint Research Projects Office [*Army and NASA joint operation*] (RDA)
JRPrK	James River$3.375Cv Ex K Pfd [*NYSE symbol*] (TTSB)
JRPrL..........	James River Dep Cv Ex Pfd [*NYSE symbol*] (TTSB)
JRPrO	James River 8.25% Dep Pfd [*NYSE symbol*] (TTSB)
JRPrP	James River 9% 'DECS' [*NYSE symbol*] (TTSB)
JRR	Japanese Research Reactor
JRR	Juror (ABBR)
JRRC	Joint Regional Reconnaissance Center [*NATO*] (NATG)
JRRT	John Ronald Renel Tolkien [*British author, 1892-1973*]
JRS	Japanese Rocket Society
JRS	Jersey [*Channel Islands*] [*Seismograph station code, US Geological Survey Closed*] (SEIS)
JRS..............	Jerusalem [*Israel*] [*Airport symbol*] (OAG)
JRS	Jet Repair Service
JRS	Job Rehearsal Scheme (AIE)
JRS	Job Release Scheme (PDAA)
JRS	John R. Sinnock [*Designer's mark, when appearing on US coins*]
JRS	Joint Reporting Structure [*Military*] (AFM)
JRS	Journal. Roentgen Society [*A publication*] (ROG)
JRS	Junction Relay Set (IAA)
JRSA..........	Justice Research and Statistics Association (NTPA)
JRSC..........	Jam-Resistant Secure Communications
JRSC..........	Joint Rescue Sub-Center (COE)
JRSC..........	Joint Resistant Secure Communications [*DoD*]
JRSDCNL....	Jurisdictional (ABBR)
J/RSM..........	Junior Regimental Sergeant-Major [*British military*] (DMA)
JRSO	Jewish Restitution Successor Organization (EA)
J R Soc Med...	Journal of the Royal Society of Medicine (MEC)
JRSPDN.......	Jurisprudent (ABBR)
JRSPDNC.....	Jurisprudence (ABBR)
JRSPDTL	Jurisprudential (ABBR)
JRST	Jurist (ABBR)
JRS/USA	Jesuit Refugee Service/USA (EA)
JRSVC	Jam-Resistant Secure Voice Communications (MCD)
JRSWG	Joint Reentry System Working Group
JRSY	Jersey (ABBR)
JRT	Jaguar-Rover-Triumph
JRT	Job Relations Training
JRT	Jugoslovenska Radiotelevizija [*Association of Yugoslav Radio and Television Organizations*] (EY)
JRT	Junctional Recovery Time [*Medicine*] (DMAA)
JRT	Tampa, FL [*Location identifier FAA*] (FAAL)
JRTC..........	Joint Readiness Training Center [*Fort Chaffee, AR*] (INF)
JRTCA........	Jack Russell Terrier Club of America (EA)
JRTC-IS	Joint Readiness Training Center Instrumentation System [*DoD*]
JRUSI	Journal of the Royal United Service Institution [*A publication*] (ROG)
JRV	Javelin Rocket Vehicle
JRvr	James River Corp. of Virginia [*Associated Press*] (SAG)
JRWG	Job Redesign Working Group
JRX	Joint Readiness Exercise (MCD)
JRY	Jury (ABBR)
JRYBLD	Jerrybuild (ABBR)
JRYBLDG.....	Jerrybuilding (ABBR)
JRYBLDR.....	Jerrybuilder (ABBR)
JRYBLT.......	Jerrybuilt (ABBR)
JryDeli........	Jerrys Famous Deli, Inc. [*Associated Press*] (SAG)
JRYMA........	Juryman (ABBR)
JRZ	Jugoslovenska Radikalna Zajednica [*Yugoslav Radical Union*] [*Political party*] (PPE)
JS	Jack Screw
JS	Jamestowne Society (EA)
J/S	Jamming to Signal
JS	Jam Strobe (IEEE)
J/S	Jam to Signal Ratio
JS	Japan Society (EA)
JS	Jargon Society (EA)
JS	JCS [*Joint Chiefs of Staff*] Support (MCD)
JS	Jefferson Smurfit Group PLC [*NYSE symbol*] (SAG)
JS	Jefferson Smurfit Grp ADS [*NYSE symbol*] (TTSB)
JS	Jejunal Segment [*Gastroenterology*] (DAVI)
JS	Jetevator Sensor
JS	Jet Stabilization
JS	Jet Stream
JS	Jet Study (AAG)
JS	Jettison Signal
JS	Job Search [*Job Training and Partnership Act*] (OICC)
JS	Job Service (OICC)
JS	Job Specification [*Department of Labor*]
JS	Job Stream [*Computer science*]
JS	John R. Sinnock [*Designer's mark, when appearing on US coins*]
JS	Johnson Society (EA)
JS	Joint Services [*British military*] (DMA)
JS	Joint Spacing [*Mining technology*]
JS	Joint Staff [*Military*] (CINC)
JS	Joint Support [*Military*] (AFM)
JS	Jones and Spencer's Superior Court Reports [*33-61 New York*] [*A publication*] (DLA)
JS	Joshua [*Old Testament book*]
J/s	Joules per Second (IDOE)
JS	Jourdain Society [*British*]
JS	Judaisme Sepharadi (BJA)
JS	Judean Society (EA)
JS	Judgment Summons [*British*] (ROG)
JS	Judicial Separation [*British*] (ROG)
JS	Junctional Slowing [*Cardiology*] (DAVI)
JS	Junior Seaman [*British military*] (DMA)
JS	Junkman-Shoeller Unit (MAE)
JS	Jury Sittings (Faculty Cases) [*Scotland*] [*A publication*] (DLA)
J/S	Justified
JS	Justifying Space [*Typography*] (DGA)
JS	Just Scale
JS	Korean Airways [*ICAO designator*] (AD)
JS	Sea of Japan
JSA	Jammer System Analysis
JSA	Japanese Standards Association (NTCM)
JSA	Japan Silk Association (EA)
JSA	Jesuit Seismological Association (EA)
JSA	Jet Show Assembly
JSA	Jewelers Security Alliance of the US (EA)
JSA	Jewelers Shipping Association (EA)
JSA	Jewish Society of America
JSA	Job Safety Analysis
JSA	Job Search Allowance
JSA	Job Seekers' Allowance (WDAA)
JSA	Joint Security Area (MCD)
JSA	Joint Supportability Assessment [*Army*]
JSA	Journeymen Stone Cutters Association of North America [*Defunct*]
JSA	Junior Statesmen of America (EA)
Jsᵃ	Sutter Antigen [*Of Kell system blood group*] [*Hematology*] (DAVI)
JSAAE	Japanese Society for Alternatives to Animal Experiments
JSAC	Jet Strategic Airlift Capability [*of Military Air Command*] (AAG)
JSAC	Joint Strategy and Action Committee [*Defunct*] (EA)
JSAG	Joint Service Advisory Group
JSAIS	Junior South African Individual Scales [*Intelligence test*]
J-SAK	Joint Attack of the Second Echelon (MCD)
JSAL	Journal of South African Law [*A publication*] (ILCA)
JSAM	Joint Security Assistance Memorandum [*Military*]
JSAM	Joint Service Achievement Medal [*Military decoration*]
JSAMSA......	Joint Security Assistance Memorandum Supporting Analysis (MCD)
JSAP	Joint Statement of Agreed Principles [*US-USSR*]
JSAR	Joint Search and Rescue [*Military*] (DNAB)
JSAR	Joint Service Agreement Report [*Defense Supply Agency*]
JSARC	Joint Search and Rescue Center [*Military*] (AABC)
JSAS	Jammer System Analysis Simulator
JSAS	Journal Supplement Abstract Service [*American Psychological Association*]
JSAT	Japan Satellite Systems [*Commercial firm*]
JSAT	Joint System Acceptance Test (MCD)
JSAT	Junior Scholastic Aptitude Test [*Education*] (AEBS)
JSATG	Joint Services Actions Task Group (MCD)
JSATP	Joint Services Automatic Testing Panel (AAGC)
JSA-US	Jewelers' Security Alliance of the United States (NTPA)
JSB	Bachelor of Judicial Science
JSB	Japanese Society in Brisbane [*Australia*]
JSB	Jaswant Singh and Bhattacharji [*Staining method for blood cells, named for its discoverers*] [*Medicine*]
JSB	Jewish Society for the Blind (EA)
JSB	Jewish Statistical Bureau (EA)
JSB	Joint-Stock Bank [*Banking*]
JSBA..........	Jefferson Savings Bancorp [*NASDAQ symbol*] (SAG)
JSBF..........	JSB Financial [*NASDAQ symbol*] (TTSB)
JSBF..........	JSB Financial, Inc. [*NASDAQ symbol*] (SPSG)
JSB Fn........	JSB Financial, Inc. [*Associated Press*] (SAG)
JSBS	Joint Strategic Bomber Study
JSC	Jackson State College [*Later, Jackson State University*] [*Mississippi*]
JSC	Japanese Studies Center [*Monash University*] [*Australia*]
JSC	Jascan Resources, Inc. [*Toronto Stock Exchange symbol*]
JSC	Jenkinsville [*South Carolina*] [*Seismograph station code, US Geological Survey*] (SEIS)
JSC	Job-Site Component
JSC	Johnson Space Center (USDC)
JSC	Johnstown & Stony Creek Rail Road Co. [*AAR code*]
JSC	Joint Scientific Committee [*WMO/ICSU*]
JSC	Joint Security Control
JSC	Joint Selection Committee
JSC	Joint Service Committee [*Military*]
JSC	Joint Setup Cost
JSC	Joint Staff Council [*Japanese*] [*Military*] (CINC)
JSC	Joint Standing Committee (ADA)

JSC .... Joint Steering Committee for Revision of Anglo-American Cataloging Rules (AL)
JSC .... Joint-Stock Company
JSC .... Joint Strategic Capabilities [Military]
JSC .... Joint Strategic Committee [Military]
JSC .... Joint Support Command [Navy]
JSC .... Joly Steam Calorimeter
JSC .... Judgments of the Supreme Court of Cyprus [A publication] (ILCA)
JSC .... Junior Staff Course [British]
JSC .... Justice of the Supreme Court
JSCA .... Japanese Spaniel Club of America [Later, JCCA] (EA)
JSCA .... Journeymen Stone Cutters Association of North America [Defunct] (EA)
JSCAACR ..... Joint Steering Committee for Revision of AACR [Anglo-American Cataloging Rules]
JSCAEN .... Joint Schools Committee for Academic Excellence Now (EA)
JSCAMPS .... Joint Service Common Airframe Multiple Purpose System [Military] (MCD)
JSCAT .... Joint Staff Crisis Action Team [Environmental science] (COE)
JSCB .... Job Step Control Block [Computer science] (BUR)
JSCC .... Joint Service Coordination Committee [Military] (DOMA)
JSCC .... Joint Staff Consultative Committee [British] (DI)
JSCCB .... Joint Services Configuration Control Board [Military] (AFIT)
J Sc D .... Doctor of Juridical Science
JScE .... Eimac [Division of Varian Associates] Technical Library, San Carlos, CA [Library symbol Library of Congress] (LCLS)
JSCERDCG... Joint Service Civil Engineering Research and Development Coordination Group [Military] (RDA)
J school .... Journalism School (WDMC)
J School Libr Ass Qd... Journal. School Library Association of Queensland [A publication]
JSCIC .... Joint Space Command Intelligence Center [Air Force]
JSCLC .... Joint Standing Committee on Library Cooperation [British] (NITA)
JSCM .... Joint Service Commendation Medal [Military decoration] (AFM)
JSCM .... JSC [Johnson Space Center] Manual [NASA] (NASA)
JSCMPO ...... Joint Service Cruise Missile Program Office (MCD)
JSCO .... Joint Staff Communications Office [Military] (AABC)
JSCO .... Journal Status Central Operations Table (SAA)
JSCOM .... Joint Services Commendation Medal (RDA)
JS Com Ind L... Journal. Society of Commercial and Industrial Law [A publication] (ILCA)
J Scott .... Reporter, English Common Bench Reports [A publication] (DLA)
JSCP .... Joint Strategic Capabilities Plan [Military]
JSCR .... Job Schedule Change Request
Jscript .... Java Script [Microsoft Corp.]
JSCS .... Job Shop Control System (MHDI)
JSCS .... Joint Strategic Connectivity Committee [Joint Chiefs of Staff]
JSCS .... Joint Strategic Connectivity Staff
JSCS .... Junior Slovak Catholic Sokol (EA)
JSCU .... Joint Supply Council for Union of South Africa [World War II]
JSD .... Doctor of Judicial [or Juridical] Science [or Doctor of the Science of Law]
JSD .... Jackson Structured Design (COE)
JSD .... Jackson System Development [Systems development methodology] (NITA)
JSD .... Jatiya Samajtantrik Dal [National Socialist Party] [Bangladesh] [Political party] (PPW)
JSD .... Jeunesse Social Democrate [Social Democratic Youth] [Malagasy]
JSD .... Jewish Society for the Deaf [Later, New York Society for the Deaf] (EA)
JSD .... JiJi Securities Data Service [JiJi Press Ltd.] [Japan Information service or system] (CRD)
JSD .... Justification Service Digit [Telecommunications] (TEL)
JSD .... Stratford, CT [Location identifier FAA] (FAAL)
JSDA .... Japanese Securities Dealers Association (ECON)
JSDA .... Japanese Self-Defense Agency
JSDF .... Japan Self-Defense Force (CINC)
JSDF .... Jin Shin Do Foundation for Bodymind Acupressure (EA)
JSDM .... June, September, December, and March [Denotes quarterly payments of interest or dividends in these months] [Business term]
JSDP .... Jewish Social Democratic Party [Political party] (BJA)
JSE .... Jam Strobe Extractor
JSEA .... Jesuit Secondary Education Association (EA)
JSEAC .... Joint Societies Employment Advisory Committee
J-SEAD .... Joint Suppression of Enemy Air Defenses [Military] (INF)
JSEI .... Joint Second Echelon Interdiction
JSEP .... Job Skills Education Program [Military]
JSEP .... Joint Services Electronics Program [Military]
JSESPO........ Joint [Maritime Administration - Navy] Surface-Effects Ship Program Office
JSeTU .... Tohoku University, Sendai, Japan [Library symbol] [Library of Congress] (LCLS)
JSEXP .... Joint Services Explosives Program (MCD)
JSEY .... Jersey [One of the Channel Islands] (ROG)
JSF .... Japan Scholarship Foundation (EA)
JSF .... Jesse Stuart Foundation (EA)
JSF .... Job Services File
JSF .... Joint Security Force [Army] (INF)
JSF .... Joint Stipulated Facts and Figures (AAGC)
JSF .... Joint Strike Fighter
JSF .... Junctor Switch Frame [Telecommunications] (TEL)
JSF .... Junior Statesmen Foundation (EA)
JSFC .... Jack Scalia Fan Club (EA)
JSFC .... Japanese-Soviet Fisheries Commission for the Northwest Pacific

JSFC .... Joe Stampley Fan Club [Defunct] (EA)
JSFP .... Joint Service Fuze Plan [Army]
JSG .... Jamaica (BWI) Study Group [Defunct] (EA)
JSG .... Job Seekers Guide to Private and Public Companies [A publication]
JSG .... Jugoslavia Study Group (EA)
JSGCC .... Joint Service Guidance and Control Committee
JSGOMRAM... Joint Study Group on Military Resources Allocation Methodology (MCD)
JSGRP .... Jewish Symbols in the Greco-Roman Period [A publication] (BJA)
JSH .... Jetstream Ltd. [Hungary ICAO designator] (FAAC)
JSH .... Journal of Southern History [A publication] (BRI)
JSHA .... Johannes Schwalm Historical Association (EA)
J Shaw .... John Shaw's Justiciary Reports [1848-52] [Scotland] [A publication] (DLA)
J Shaw Just... John Shaw's Justiciary Reports [1848-52] [Scotland] [A publication] (DLA)
JSHDFC ...... Jean S. Harris Defense Fund Committee (EA)
JSHG .... Hokkai Gakuen University, Sapporo, Japan [Library symbol Library of Congress] (LCLS)
JSHS .... Jewish Society for Human Service [British]
JSHS .... Junior Science and Humanities Symposia [Terminated, 1977]
JSI .... Jansky Screening Index [Psychology] (DAVI)
JSI .... Job Satisfaction Inventory [Guidance]
JSI .... Job Schedule Items (MCD)
JSI .... Job Search Information
JSI .... Job Search Inventory [Test] (TMMY)
JSI .... Job Sensitivity Inventory [Interpersonal skills and attitudes test]
JSI .... Job Step Index [Computer science] (IAA)
JSI .... Job Style Indicator [Test] (TMMY)
JSI .... Joint Support Item (DNAB)
JSI .... Skiathos [Greece] [Airport symbol] (OAG)
JSIA .... Japan Software Industry Association (CIST)
JSIA .... Joint Service Induction Area
JSIA .... Justice System Improvement Act [1979]
JSIC .... Joint Space Intelligence Center
J-SIDS .... Joint Service Intrusion Detection System [Military] (INF)
JSIID .... Joint Service Interior Intrusion Detection Devices [Military] (MCD)
JSIIDS .... Joint Service Interior Intrusion Detection System [Military]
JSIM .... Joint Service Intelligence Manual
JSIMS .... Joint Simulation System [DoD]
JSIP .... Job Service Improvement Program [Department of Labor]
JSIPS .... Joint Services Imagery Processing System [Military]
JSIPS .... Joint Systems Integration Planning Staff [Air Force]
JSK .... St. Cloud, MN [Location identifier FAA] (FAAL)
JSL .... Jet Select Logic (MCD)
JSL .... Job Specification Language
JSL .... Johnson Society of London (EA)
JSL .... Joint Stock List [Military] (AFIT)
JSL .... Joint Support List [Military]
JSLB .... Joint Stock Land Banks [New Deal]
JSLGWCM .... Joint Services LASER-Guided Weapons Countermeasures (MCD)
JSLI .... Johnson-Sea-Link I [A submersible for deep sea studies]
JSLPC .... Joint Service Local Planning Committee
JSLRMDO ..... Joint Service Large Rocket Motor Disposal Office [Army]
JSLS .... Japan Society of Library Science (NITA)
JSLS .... Joint Services Liaison Staff [British]
JSLWG .... Joint Spacelab Working Group [NASA] (NASA)
JSM .... Jesus Salvator Mundi [Jesus the Savior of the World] [Latin] (ROG)
JSM .... Job Stream Manager [Computer science] (IAA)
JSM .... Joint Staff Memorandum (MCD)
JSM .... Joint Staff Mission [British World War II]
JSM .... Jose de San Martin [Argentina] [Airport symbol] (OAG)
JSM .... Master of Judicial Science
JSMA .... Joint Sealer Manufacturers Association
JSMB .... Joint Sealift Movements Board [Military] (AFM)
JSME .... Japan Society of Mechanical Engineers
JSME .... Joint Soil Moisture Experiment
JSMIN .... Jasmine (ABBR)
JSMP .... JSIMS [Joint Simulation (System)] Master Plan [DoD]
JSmrfG .... Jefferson Smurfit Group PLC [Associated Press] (SAG)
JSMS .... Job Service Matching Systems [US Employment Service] [Department of Labor]
JSMSM .... Joint Service Meritorious Service Medal [Military decoration]
JSN .... Job Sequence Number
JSN .... Joint Space Narrowing [Medicine]
JSNA .... Jaspers Society of North America (EA)
JSNM .... Japan Society of New Metals (AAEL)
JSNOOFC ..... Judson Scott Is Number 1 Official Fan Club (EA)
JSNPE .... Joint Staff Nuclear Planning Element (MCD)
JSO .... Jacksonville, TX [Location identifier FAA] (FAAL)
JSO .... Joint Service Office
JSO .... Joint Specialty Officer (DOMA)
JSOA .... Joint Special Operations Area [Military] (INF)
JSOC .... Joint Ship Operations Center
JSOC .... Joint Ship Operations Committee
JSOC .... Joint Special Operations Center (MCD)
JSOC .... Joint Special Operations Command [Military]
JSOC .... Joint Strategic Operations Command (MCD)
J Soc H .... Journal of Social History [A publication] (BRI)
J Soc'y Comp Leg... Journal. Society of Comparative Legislation [A publication] (DLA)
JSOFI.......... Joint Special Operations Force Institute [DoD]
JSON .... Joint Services Operational Notice
JSONOM ...... Joint Specialty Officer Nominee (DOMA)
JSOP........... Dominican Oblates of Jesus (Spain) (TOCD)

JSOP	Joint Strategic Objectives Plan [*Military*]
JSOR	Joint Services Operational Requirement [*Military*]
JSOR	Joint Statements of Requirements (DOMA)
JSORD	Joint System Operational Requirements [*Document*] (DOMA)
JSORS	Joint Service Operational Requirement Statement (MCD)
JSOSE	Joint Special Operations Support Element [*DoD*]
JSOTF	Joint Special Operations Task Force [*DoD*]
JSOW	Joint Standoff Weapons Program
JSP	Jacketed Soft-Point [*Ammunition*]
JSP	Jackson Structured Programming [*Program design tool*] (NITA)
JSP	Japan Socialist Party [*Nikon Shakaito*] [*Political party*] (PPW)
jsp	Jasper (VRA)
JSP	Job Support Program
JSP	Joint Services Development Program
JSP	Joint Services Publication
JSP	Joint Staff Planners [*Joint Chiefs of Staff*]
JSP	Judicial Selection Project (EA)
JSP	Jupiter, Saturn, and Pluto Mission (MCD)
JSP	Jurisdictional Separation Process
J Space L	Journal of Space Law (AAGC)
JSPB	Joint Staff Pension Board [*United Nations*]
JSPC	Japan Sports Prototype Championship [*Auto racing*]
JSPC	Joint Sobe Processing Center [*Okinawa*] [*Military*]
JSPC	Joint Strategic Plans Committee [*Military*]
JSPD	Joint Strategic Planning Document (MCD)
JSPD	Joint Subsidiary Plans Division [*Military*] (MUGU)
JSPDSA	Joint Strategic Planning Document Supporting Analysis [*Military*] (AABC)
JSPF	Joint Staff Pension Fund [*United Nations*]
JSPFL	Jointly Sponsored Program for Foreign Libraries [*Defunct*]
JSPG	Joint Strategic Plans Group [*Military*]
JSPMRC	Joint Service Program Management Review Committee [*Military*]
JSPOG	Joint Strategic Plans and Operations Group
JSPP	Joint Service Program Plan [*Military*] (RDA)
JSPS	Japan Society for the Promotion of Science
JSPS	Jewish Student Press Service (EA)
JSPS	Joint Strategic Planning System [*Military*]
JSR	Jackson Resources Ltd. [*Vancouver Stock Exchange symbol*]
JSR	Jam to Signal Ratio (MCD)
JSR	Japan Science Review [*A publication*]
JSR	Japan Synthetic Rubber Co. Ltd.
JSR	Jessore [*Bangladesh*] [*Airport symbol*] (OAG)
JSR	Joint Staffing Review
JSR	Joint Strategic Review (DOMA)
JSR	Journal of Ship Research [*A publication*] (DNAB)
JSR	Journal of Spacecraft and Rockets [*A publication*] (AAGC)
JSR	Jump to Subroutine [*Computer science*] (BUR)
JSRA	Job Search and Relocation Assistance Projects (OICC)
JSRA	Joint Sponsored Research Agreement (GAVI)
JSRC	Joint Services Review Committee
JSRC	Joint Ship Repair Committee
JSRCC	Joint Search and Rescue Coordination Center (MCD)
JSRK	Jeunesse Socialiste Royale Khmere [*Royal Cambodian Socialist Youth*] [*Political party*]
JSRP	Joint Services Reading Panel [*Military British*]
JSRS	Jury System Reform Society [*British*]
JSRT	Joint Short-Range Technology (MCD)
JSRU	Joint Speech Research Unit [*British*] (NITA)
JSRWG	JSIMS [*Joint Simulation (System)*] Requirements Working Group [*Military*]
JSS	Jacob Sheep Society [*British*] (DBA)
JSS	Japanese Society of Sydney [*Australia*]
JSS	Jet Steering System
JSS	Jet Strip System (PDAA)
JSS	Jewish Social Studies [*A publication*] (BRI)
JSS	Jim Smith Society (EA)
JSS	Job Schedule Status (SAA)
JSS	Job Shop Simulator
JSS	Joint Surveillance System [*FAA Air Force*]
JSS	Junior Secondary School
JSSA	John Steinbeck Society of America (EA)
JSSA	Joint Stealth Strike Aircraft [*DoD*] (DOMA)
JSSAM	Joint Service Small Arms Management Committee (MCD)
JSSAP	Joint Service Small Arms Panel (MCD)
JSSAP	Joint Service Small Arms Program (RDA)
JSSAP	Joint Service Small Arms Program Office [*Dover, NJ*] [*Military*]
JSSC	Joint Services Staff College [*or Course*] [*Obsolete British*]
JSSC	Joint Shop Stewards Committee [*British*]
JSSC	Joint Strategic Survey Committee [*or Council*] [*DoD*]
JSSE	Japanese Software Support Environment
JSSIS	Joint Staff Support Information System [*Military*] (GFGA)
JSSM	Joint Services Staff Manual [*Military British*]
JSSPA	Jewish Social Services Professional Association (EA)
JSSPG	Job Shop Simulation Program Generator (KSC)
JSSS	Job Seeking Skills Survey [*Test*] [*Donald S. Tackley*] (TES)
JSST	Job Seeking Skills Training (OICC)
JSSUP	Japanese Space Shuttle Utilization Program (MCD)
JSS/US	Japanese Sword Society of the United States (EA)
JST	Jamming Station (IAA)
JST	Japanese Standard Time
JST	Japan Universal System Transport Co. Ltd. [*ICAO designator*] (FAAC)
JST	Jet STOL [*Short Takeoff and Landing*] Transport [*Aircraft*]
JST	Job Skills Training
JST	Johnstown [*Pennsylvania*] [*Airport symbol*] (OAG)

JST	Johnstown, PA [*Location identifier FAA*] (FAAL)
JST	Joint Systems Test (KSC)
JSTA	Justice System Training Association [*Defunct*] (EA)
JSTARS	Joint Surveillance and Target Attack RADAR System
JSTARS	Joint Surveillance Target Attack Radar System
JSTARS-GSM	Joint Surveillance/Target Attack RADAR System Ground Station Module (RDA)
J St Bar Calif	Journal. State Bar of California [*A publication*] (DLA)
JSTC	Job Skills Training Course
JSTC	Justice
JSTE	Joint System Training Exercise [*Military*]
JstFeet	Just For Feet, Inc. [*Associated Press*] (SAG)
JSTN	Justin Indus [*NASDAQ symbol*] (TTSB)
JSTN	Justin Industries, Inc. [*NASDAQ symbol*] (NQ)
JSTOR	Journal Storage Project
JSTP	Job Search Training Program
JSTP	Joint System Test Plan [*Initial Defense Communications Satellite Program*] (DNAB)
JSTPA	Joint Strategic Target Planning Agency (NATG)
JSTPPC	Joint Services Technical Publication Policy Committee [*Ministry of Defence*] (PDAA)
JSTPS	Joint Strategic Target Planning Staff [*DoD*]
JSTR	Joint Systematic Troop Review [*Military*]
J Struct Chem	Journal of Structural Chemistry (MEC)
J St Tax'n	Journal of State Taxation [*A publication*] (DLA)
JSTU	Tohoku University, Sendai, Japan [*Library symbol Library of Congress*] (LCLS)
JSTX	Joro Spider Toxin [*Biochemistry*]
JSU	Hokkaido University, Sapporo, Japan [*Library symbol Library of Congress*] (LCLS)
JSU	Jacksonville State University [*Jacksonville, AL*]
JSU	Junta Socialista Unida [*United Socialist Party*] [*Spain*]
JSU	Sukkertoppen [*Greenland*] [*Airport symbol*] (AD)
JSUN	Jupiter, Saturn, Uranus, and Neptune (PDAA)
JSV	Jerry-Slough Virus [*Medicine*] (DMAA)
JSVA	Jewish Socialist Verband of America [*Defunct*] (EA)
JSWAP	Job Swapping Memory [*Computer science*] (MHDB)
JSWDL	Joint Services Weapon Data Link (MCD)
JSWPB	Joint Special Weapons Publications Board
JSYB	Jewish Socialist Youth Bund [*Later, MJSG*] (EA)
J Syd Univ Eng Soc	Journal. Sydney University Engineering Society. [*A publication*]
JT	Iowa Airways [*ICAO designator*] (AD)
JT	Jahn-Teller (AAEL)
JT	James Taylor [*Singer*]
JT	Japan Times [*A publication*] (BARN)
JT	Jejunostomy Tube [*Medicine*] (DMAA)
JT	Jerusalem Talmud (BJA)
JT	Jig Template (MSA)
JT	Job Table [*Computer science*] (IAA)
JT	John Tyler [*US president, 1790-1862*]
Jt	Joint (EBF)
JT	Joint Tenancy (MHDW)
J-T	Joule-Thomson [*Physics*]
JT	Junction Transistor [*Electronics*] (IAA)
JT	Juridisk Tidsskrift [*A publication*] (ILCA)
JT	Juvenile Templar [*Freemasonry*]
JTA	Azia Keizai Kenkyujo [*Institute for Developing Economies*], Tokyo, Japan [*Library symbol Library of Congress*] (LCLS)
JTA	Japanese Technical Abstracts [*A publication*]
JTA	Japan Transocean Air Co. Ltd. [*ICAO designator*] (FAAC)
JTA	Jewish Telegraphic Agency (EA)
JTA	Job Task Analysis
JTA	Joint Table of Allowance
JTA	Joint Technical Architecture [*Office of the Secretary of Defense*]
JTA	Joint Tenancy Agreement [*Military*]
JTA-Army	Joint Technical Architecture-Army
JTAC	Joint Technical Advisory Committee [*Electronics*]
JTACC	Joint Tactical Air Control Center
JTACMIS-A	Joint Tactical Missile System - Army
JTACMS	Joint Tactical Missile System
JTACMS-A	Joint Tactical Missile System - Army
JTACS	Joint Tactical Area Communications System [*Army*] (RDA)
JTAD	Joint Tactical Aids Detachment [*Military*]
JTAG	Japan Trade Advisory Group [*British Overseas Trade Board*] (DS)
JTAG	Joint Test Action Group [*European automotive industry*]
JTAGG	Joint Turbine Advanced Gas Generator [*DoD*]
JTAGS	Joint Tactical Ground Station [*Army*] (RDA)
JTAGS	Joint Target Acquisition Ground Station [*Military*]
JT AGT	Joint Agent (WDAA)
JTA-M	Jewish Teachers Association - Morim (EA)
JT & E	Joint Test and Evaluation [*DoD*]
JT & SEV	Joint and Several [*Legal shorthand*] (LWAP)
JTARS	Joint Tactical Aerial Reconnaissance/Surveillance [*Military*] (DNAB)
JTARS MISREP	Joint Tactical Aerial Reconnaissance/Surveillance Mission Report [*Military*] (DNAB)
JTASB	Joint Tactical Air Support Board
jt asp	Joint Aspiration [*Orthopedics*] (DAVI)
jt auth	Joint Author
JTAWG	Joint Targeting and Weapon Guidance (MCD)
JTAX	Jackson Hewitt [*NASDAQ symbol*] (SAG)
JTB	Japanese Tourist Board
JTB	Joint Bar
JTB	Joint Transportation Board [*Military*]

JTBSMHS	Jacques Timothe Boucher Sieur de Montbrun Heritage Society (EA)
JTC	Houston [*Texas*] Town/Country [*Airport symbol*] (OAG)
JTC	Jets Corporativos SA de CV [*Mexico ICAO designator*] (FAAC)
JTC	Jewish Thought and Civilization (BJA)
JTC	Joint Technical Committee (CDE)
JTC	Joint Telecommunications Committee [*Military*] (AFM)
JTC	Joint Training Committee (WDAA)
JTC	Joint Transform Correlator [*Instrumentation*]
JTC	Joke to Come (WDMC)
JTC	Joule-Thomson Coefficient [*Physics*]
JTC	Junior Training Corps [*British*]
JTC	Jurong Town Corp. [*Singapore*]
JTC3A	Joint Tactical Command, Control, and Communications Agency (USGC)
JTC³A	Joint Tactical Command, Control, and Communications Agency [*Military*]
JTC³S	Joint Tactical Command and Control and Communications System [*Military*] (RDA)
JTCC	Joint Test Coordinating Committee (MCD)
JTCCCS	Joint Tactical Command, Control, and Communications System [*Military*] (MCD)
JTCCG	Joint Technical Configuration Control Group [*Military*] (AABC)
JTCG	Joint Technical Coordinating Group [*Military*] (MCD)
JTCG/ALNNO...	Joint Technical Coordinating Group for Air Launched Non-Nuclear Ordnance [*Military*] (AFM)
JTCG/AS	Joint Technical Coordinating Group for Aircraft Survivability [*Military*]
JTCG-DLA	Joint Technical Coordinating Group for Data Link Acquisitions (MCD)
JTCG-DMI	Joint Technical Coordinating Group for Depot Maintenance Interservicing [*Military*] (AFIT)
JTCG-EER	Joint Technical Coordinating Group for Electronic Equipment Reliability (MCD)
JTCG-ESR	Joint Technical Coordinating Group for Electronics Systems Reliability (MCD)
JTCG/MD	Joint Technical Coordinating Group for Munitions Development [*Military*]
JTCG/ME......	Joint Technical Coordinating Group for Munitions Effectiveness [*Military*] (AFM)
JTCG/MS......	Joint Technical Coordinating Group on Munitions Survivability [*Military*] (RDA)
JTCGP.........	Joint Technical Coordinating Group [*Military*]
JTCGP/ME....	Joint Technical Coordinating Group for Munitions Effectiveness [*Military*]
JTCGP-TACS...	Joint Technical Coordinating Group for Tactical Air Control System [*Military*]
JTCG-STD	Joint Technical Coordinating Group on Simulators and Training Devices (MCD)
JTCO	Jacksonville Terminal Co. [*AAR code*]
JTCP	JOVIAL [*Joule's Own Version of the International Algorithmic Language*] Test Control Program [*Computer science*] (SAA)
JTCTS	Joint Tactical Combat Training System [*Military*]
JTCY-P........	Jig Transit Central Y-Plane
JTD	Joint Table of Distribution [*Military*] (AFM)
JTD	Joint Test Directorate [*Military*] (CAAL)
JTDA	Joint Track Data Storage
JTDARMVAL...	Joint Test Directorate Advanced Antiarmor Vehicle Evaluation [*Military*] (DNAB)
JTDE	Joint Technology Demonstrator Engine [*Air Force*] (MCD)
JTDP	Joint Technical Development Plan
JTDS..........	Joint Track Data Storage
JTE	Jamming Tactics Evaluation
JTE	Joint Technical Evaluation (MCD)
JTE	Joint Test Element
JTE	Joule-Thomson Effect [*Physics*]
JTE	Junction Tandem Exchange [*Electronics*] (IAA)
JTE	Junction Termination Extension (PDAA)
J Teach Ed...	Journal of Teacher Education [*A publication*] (BRI)
JTEC	Japan Telecommunications Engineering and Consultancy
JTEC	Jeep-Truck Engine Controller
JTEC	Joint Training Enhancement Committee [*Military*]
JT ED..........	Joint Editor
J-TENS.......	Joint Tactical Exploitation of National Systems [*Army*] (ADDR)
J Tert Ed Admin...	Journal of Tertiary Educational Administration [*A publication*]
JTETF..........	Joint Test and Evaluation Task Force [*Air Force*]
JTEV	Joint Tactical Electric Vehicle [*Military*]
JTF.............	Japan Textile Federation
JTF.............	Jet Tear-Down Facility (MCD)
JTF.............	Joint Tactical Fusion [*Army*] (RDA)
JTF.............	Joint Task Force [*Military*]
JTF.............	Joint Test Force [*Military*]
JTF2..........	Joule-Thomson Flow [*Physics*]
JTF2..........	Joint Task Force Two [*Sandia Base, NM*]
JTFAK	Joint Task Force Alaska [*Military*]
JTF/ASAS.....	Joint Tactical Fusion/All Source Analysis System (AAGC)
JTF-FA........	Joint Task Force-Full Accounting [*DoD*]
JTFHQ........	Joint Task Force Headquarters [*Military*] (MCD)
JTFME........	Joint Task Force Middle East (DOMA)
JTFOA........	Joint Task Force Operating Area [*Military*] (NVT)
JTFP..........	Joint Tactical Fusion Program [*Military*] (RDA)
JTFPMO.......	Joint Tactical Fusion Program Management Office [*Army*] (RDA)
JTFREP........	Joint Task Force Report [*Military*]
JTFS	Joint Tactical Fusion System [*Military*] (LAIN)
JTFS	JTF [*Joint Task Force*] Simulation [*Model*] [*DoD*]
JTG	Joint Task Group [*Military*]
JTG	Joint Test Group [*Nuclear energy*] (NRCH)
JTG	Joint Training Group [*NASA*] (NASA)
Jth	Judith [*Old Testament book*] [*Roman Catholic canon*] (BJA)
JTHP	Joule-Thomson High Pressure [*Physics*]
JTI	Jatai [*Brazil*] [*Airport symbol*] (AD)
JTI	Jydsk Teknologisk Institut [*Technological Institute of Jutland*] [*Denmark*]
JTIC	Joint Transportation Intelligence Center (COE)
JTIDS.........	Joint Tactical Information Distribution System [*DoD*]
J-TIES.........	Japan Technology Information and Evaluation Service (IID)
JTIG	Joint Target Intelligence Group [*Military*] (CINC)
JTIS	Japanese Technical Information Service [*University Microfilms International*] [*Information service or system*] (IID)
JTJ	Japan Information Center of Science and Technology, Tokyo, Japan [*Library symbol Library of Congress*] (LCLS)
JTKU	Keio University, Tokyo, Japan [*Library symbol Library of Congress*] (LCLS)
JTL.............	Jetall Holdings, Corp. [*Canada ICAO designator*] (FAAC)
JTL.............	Josephson Transmission Line [*Physics*]
JTL.............	Joutel Resources Ltd. [*Toronto Stock Exchange symbol*]
JTLAS.........	Jet Transport Landing Approach Simulator
JTLS	Joint Theater Level Simulation [*Model*] [*DoD*]
JTLY	Jointly
JTM	Job Transfer and Management (ACRL)
JTM	Job Transfer and Manipulation [*Telecommunications*] (OSI)
JTMA	Joint Traffic Management Agency (MCD)
JTM & H......	Journal of Tropical Medicine and Hygiene [*A publication*] (WDAA)
JTMB	Joint Transportation Movements Board [*Military*] (CINC)
JTMD	Joint Table of Mobilization Distribution (COE)
JTMD	Joint Theater Missile Defense [*DoD*]
JTML	Junior Town Meeting League (EA)
JTMLS	Joint Tactical Microwave Landing System (MCD)
JTMP	Job Transfer and Manipulation Protocol (NITA)
JTMSS	Joint Tactical Multichannel Switch System (MCD)
JTN	Jewish Television Network
JTNDL	Kokuritsu Kokkai Toshokan [*National Diet Library*], Tokyo, Japan [*Library symbol Library of Congress*] (LCLS)
JTNS	Nihon Shinbun Kyokai [*Japanese Newspaper Association*], Tokyo, Japan [*Library symbol Library of Congress*] (LCLS)
JTO	Jeunesse Travailleuse Oubanguienne [*Ubangi Working Youth*]
JTO	Joint Technical Operations (AAG)
JTO	Joint Test Organization [*Joint Tactical Communications Office*] [*Fort Huachuca, AZ*]
JTO	JOPES [*Joint Operations, Planning, and Execution System*] Training Organization (DOMA)
JTO	Jump Takeoff (WDAA)
JTO	Junction Temperature, Operating
JTOC	Joint Tactical Operations Center
JTOR	Joint Terms of Reference (MCD)
JTP	Job Training Package
JTP	Job Training Program (OICC)
JTP	Joint Technical Panel [*Aerospace*]
JTP	Joint Training Package
JTP	Journeyman Training Program
JTP	Juventud Trabajadora Peronista [*Working Peronist Youth*] [*Argentina*]
JTPA	Job Training Partnership Act [*Formerly, CETA*] [*1982*]
JTPA	Job Training Partnership Administration
JTPS	Job and Tape Planning System
JTPS	Juvenile Tropical Pancreatitis Syndrome [*Medicine*] (DMAA)
JTPT	Job Task Performance Test
JTQ	Wrightstown, NJ [*Location identifier FAA*] (FAAL)
JTR	Jet-Air Bedarfsflugunternehmen [*Austria ICAO designator*] (FAAC)
JTR	Joint Tactical Radio [*Army*]
JTR	Joint Termination Regulation
JTR	Joint Travel Regulations
JTR	Santorini [*Thira Islands*] [*Airport symbol*] (OAG)
JTR	Thira [*Greece*] [*Airport symbol*] (AD)
JTRA	Job Task Requirements Analysis (PDAA)
JTRAC.........	JPL [*Jet Propulsion Laboratory*] Transient Radiation Analysis by Computer Program [*NASA*]
JTRB	Joint Telecommunications Resource Board [*Office of Science and Technology Policy*] [*Washington, DC*] (EGAO)
JTRC	Joint Theatre Reconnaissance Committee [*NATO*] (NATG)
JTRCP.........	Joint Travel Regulations, Department of Defense Civilian Personnel
JTRE	JIMAP [*Joint Institute for Marine and Atmospheric Research*] Tsunami Research Effort [*Marine science*] (OSRA)
JTRE	JIMAR [*Joint Institute for Marine and Atmospheric Research*] Tsunami Research Effort (USDC)
JTRE	Joint Tsunami Research Effort
JTRL	Janitorial (ABBR)
JTRS	Joint Tenant with Right of Survivorship [*Legal term*] (DLA)
JTRU	Joint Tropical Research Unit [*Australia*]
JTRUS	Joint Travel Regulations
JTS	Arrendamiento de Aviones Jets, SA [*Mexico*] [*FAA designator*] (FAAC)
JTS	Jahn-Teller Stripes [*Solid state physics*]
JTS	Japan Troposcatter Systems
JTS	Job Training Scheme [*Government initiative*] [*British*]
JTS	Job Training Standard
JTS	Joint Training Scheme (AIE)
JTS	Joint Training Standards [*Military*] (KSC)
JTS	Journal of Theological Studies [*A publication*] (ODCC)
JTS	JTS Corp. [*AMEX symbol*] [*Formerly, Atari Corp.*] (SG)
JTS	Justice Telecommunications Service [*Department of Justice*] (TSSD)
JTSA	Jewish Theological Seminary of America
JTSA	Joint Tactical Support Activity
JTSA	Joint Technical Support Activity

JTSCC......... Joint Telecommunications Standards Coordinating Committee [*American National Standards Institute*] [*Telecommunications*]
JTS Corp...... JTS Corp. [*Associated Press*] (SAG)
JTSG.......... Joint Trials Subgroup [*NATO*] (NATG)
JTSN.......... Jettison (MSA)
JTST.......... Jet Stream
JTSTR......... Jet Stream
JTT/CIBSM... Joint Tactical Terminal/Common Integrated Broadcast System Module [*Military*] (RDA)
JTTCW........ Jesus to the Communist World [*Later, CMCW*] (EA)
JTTP.......... Joint Tactics, Techniques, and Procedures (DOMA)
JTTPRG....... Joint Tactics, Techniques, and Procedures Review Group
JTTU.......... Jet Transitional Training Unit [*Navy*]
JTU........... Jackson Turbidity Unit [*Water pollution*]
JTU........... Jet Training Unit
JTUAC........ Joint Trade Union Advisory Committee
JT-UAV....... Joint Tactical Unmanned Aerial Vehicle [*DoD*]
JTV........... Jet Test Vehicle
JTV........... Jones Intercable Inv CI'A' [*AMEX symbol*] (TTSB)
JTV........... Jones Intercable Investors Ltd. [*AMEX symbol*] (SPSG)
J-T-W......... Journey to Work [*FHWA*] (TAG)
JTWC......... Joint Typhoon Warning Center
JTWO......... J2 Communications [*NASDAQ symbol*] (TTSB)
JTWO......... JTwo Communications [*NASDAQ symbol*] (SAG)
JTWOW....... J2 Communications Wrrt'A' [*NASDAQ symbol*] (TTSB)
JTWROS...... Joint Tenants with Right of Survivorship [*Legal term*]
JTWS......... Journal of Third World Studies [*A publication*]
JTX........... Jet Aspen Air Lines, Inc. [*FAA designator*] (FAAC)
JTX........... Joint Test Exercises
JTX........... Joint Training Exercise [*Military*]
JTZ........... Oklahoma City, OK [*Location identifier FAA*] (FAAL)
JU............ Jeunesse Universelle
JU............ Joint Use [*Military*] (AFIT)
JU............ Joint User [*Telecommunications*] (TEL)
JU............ Joygerms Unlimited (EA)
Ju............ Judges [*Old Testament book*] (BJA)
JU............ Julep (ROG)
JU............ Jump Unit
JU............ June
JU............ Junker [*German aircraft type*] [*World War II*]
JU............ Jure Uxoris [*In Right of His Wife*] [*Latin*] (ROG)
JU............ Yugoslav Airlines [*ICAO designator*] (AD)
JUA........... Joint Underwriting Association [*Generic term*] (DHSM)
JUA........... Joint Underwriting Authority [*Insurance*]
JUB........... Job Unit Block [*Computer science*] (IAA)
JUB........... Juba [*Sudan*] [*Airport symbol*] (OAG)
JUB........... Jubilate
Jub........... Jubilees [*Pseudepigrapha*] (BJA)
JUB........... Justice of the Upper Bench [*Legal term*] (DLA)
JUBU......... Journalistutbildningsutredningen [*Sweden*]
JUCG......... Joint Utilization Coordination Group [*DoD*]
JUCO......... Junior College (OICC)
JUCUND...... Jucunde [*Pleasantly*] [*Latin*]
JUD.......... Duluth, MN [*Location identifier FAA*] (FAAL)
JUD.......... Jeunesse d'Union Dahomeene [*Dahomean Youth Union*]
JUD.......... Judah (WDAA)
Jud.......... Judaic (BJA)
JUD.......... Judea (WDAA)
Jud.......... Judean (BJA)
JUD.......... Judge (WDAA)
JUD.......... Judges [*Old Testament book*] (ROG)
JUD.......... Judgment
JUD.......... Judicial
Jud.......... Judith [*Old Testament book*] [*Roman Catholic canon*]
JUD.......... Juris Utriusque Doctor (DD)
JUD.......... Juris Utriusque Doctor [*Doctor of Both Laws; i.e., Canon and Civil Law*]
JUD.......... US Department of Justice [*ICAO designator*] (FAAC)
Jud & Sw..... Judah and Swan's Jamaica Reports [*1839*] [*A publication*] (DLA)
Jud Chr...... Judicial Chronicle [*A publication*] (DLA)
Jud Com PC... Judicial Committee of the Privy Council [*A publication*] (DLA)
Jud Conduct Rep... Judicial Conduct Reporter [*A publication*] (DLA)
Jud Coun (NY)... Judicial Council (New York). Annual Reports [*A publication*] (DLA)
Judd.......... Judd's Reports [*4 Hawaii*] [*A publication*] (DLA)
JUDE......... Judicature (ROG)
JUDG........ Judge
Judg......... Judges [*Old Testament book*]
JUDG........ Judicate, Inc. [*NASDAQ symbol*] (NQ)
Jud GCC..... Judgments, Gold Coast Colony [*A publication*] (DLA)
JUDGE....... Judged Utility Decision Generator
JUDGT....... Judgment
Judg UB..... Judgments of Upper Bench [*England*] [*A publication*] (DLA)
JUDIC....... Judicial
Judicate..... Judicate, Inc. [*Associated Press*] (SAG)
JUDL........ Judicial (ROG)
Jud Pan Mult Lit... Rulings of the Judicial Panel on Multidistrict Litigation [*A publication*] (DLA)
Jud QR...... Judicature Quarterly Review [*1896*] [*A publication*] (DLA)
JUDr........ Juris Utriusque Doctor [*Doctor of Both Laws; i.e., Canon and Civil Law*]
JUDRE...... Judicature
Jud Rep..... New York Judicial Repository [*A publication*] (DLA)
Jud Repos... Judicial Repository [*New York*] [*A publication*] (DLA)
JUDY........ Just a Useful Device for You (PDAA)

JUE.......... Julich [*Federal Republic of Germany*] [*Seismograph station code, US Geological Survey*] (SEIS)
JUG.......... Joint Users Group [*Computer science*]
JUG.......... Jugenheim [*Federal Republic of Germany*] [*Seismograph station code, US Geological Survey Closed*] (SEIS)
JUG.......... Jugoslav (DSUE)
Jug.......... Jugoton [*Former Yugoslavia*] [*Record label*]
jug.......... Jugular [*Anatomy*] (DAVI)
JUG.......... Jugulo [*To the Throat*] [*Pharmacy*]
JUG.......... Junction Gate (IAA)
jug comp..... Jugular Compression [*Test*] [*Neurology*] (DAVI)
JUGFET..... Junction Gate Field-Effect Transistor (TEL)
Jughead...... Jonzy's Universal Gopher Hierachy Excavation and Display [*Internet*]
JUI.......... Jamiatul Ulama-i-Islam [*Pakistan*] [*Political party*] (FEA)
JUI.......... Juist [*Germany Airport symbol Obsolete*] (OAG)
Juilliard...... [*The*] Juilliard School (GAGS)
JUJ.......... Jujuy [*Argentina*] [*Airport symbol*] (OAG)
JUJ.......... Jujuy [*Argentina*] [*Seismograph station code, US Geological Survey*] (SEIS)
JUJAMCYN... Jujamcyn Theaters [*Established by William McKnight, and named for his three grandchildren, Judy, James, and Cynthia*]
JUKE........ Video Jukebox Network [*NASDAQ symbol*] (SAG)
JUKE........ Video Jukebox Ntwk [*NASDAQ symbol*] (TTSB)
JUL.......... Joint University Libraries
JUL.......... Julepus [*Julep*] [*Pharmacy*] (ROG)
JUL.......... Juliaca [*Peru*] [*Airport symbol*] (OAG)
JUL.......... Julian [*Calendar*]
JUL.......... Julianehab [*Denmark*] [*Later, NAQ*] [*Geomagnetic observatory code*]
JUL.......... July (AFM)
Jul.......... July (ODBW)
JUL.......... Juris Utriusque Licentiatus [*Licentiate in Both Laws; i.e., Canon and Civil Law*]
Jul Caes..... Julius Caesar [*Shakespearean work*] (BARN)
Jul Frontin... Julius Frontinus [*Roman soldier and author, 40-103*] (DLA)
Julian........ Julianus Imperator [*332-363AD*] [*Classical studies*] (OCD)
JULIE........ Joint Utility Locating Information for Excavators [*Telecommunications*] (TEL)
JULIEX...... Julie [*Sonobuoy System*] Exercise [*Navy*] (NVT)
JULLS....... Joint Universal Lessons Learned System (DOMA)
JUM......... Jumla [*Nepal*] [*Airport symbol*] (OAG)
JUMO....... Junkers-Motor [*Junkers aircraft engine*] [*German military - World War II*]
JUMP....... Joint UHF Modernization Project (MCD)
JUMPER..... Joint Unit for Minorities Policy & Research (WDAA)
JUMPS...... Joint Uniform Military Pay Service [*or System*]
JUMPS/MMS... Joint Uniform Military Pay System/Manpower Management System (DNAB)
JUMPS-RC... Joint Uniform Military Pay System - Reserve Components (MCD)
JUN......... Jump Unconditionally [*Computer science*]
JUN......... Jundah [*Queensland*] [*Airport symbol*] (AD)
Jun......... June (ODBW)
JUN......... June (AFM)
JUN......... Juneau [*Diocesan abbreviation*] [*Alaska*] (TOCD)
JUN......... Junior
Jun......... Junior (EBF)
JUN......... Junius (ROG)
JUNAC...... Grupo Andino - Junta del Acuerdo de Cartagena [*Andean Group - Cartagena Agreement Board - ANCOM*] (EAIO)
JUNC....... Jeunesse d'Union Nationale Congolaise [*Congolese National Youth Union*]
JUNC....... Junction
JUNCT...... Junction
JUNCTION... Junction [*Commonly used*] (OPSA)
JUNCTIONS... Junctions [*Commonly used*] (OPSA)
JUNCTN..... Junction [*Commonly used*] (OPSA)
JUNCTON.... Junction [*Commonly used*] (OPSA)
Jundt....... Jundt Growth Fund [*Associated Press*] (SAG)
JUNE....... Joint Utility Notification for Excavators (IEEE)
JUNET..... Japanese University Network (ACRL)
JUNET..... Japan UNIX Network [*Japan*] [*Computer science*] (TNIG)
JunF....... Juniper Features Ltd. [*Associated Press*] (SAG)
JUNI....... Juniper Features Ltd. [*NASDAQ symbol*] (SAG)
JUNIP...... Juniperus [*Juniper*] [*Pharmacy*] (ROG)
JuniprF..... Juniper Features Ltd. [*Associated Press*] (SAG)
JUNIW..... Juniper Features Wrr'A' [*NASDAQ symbol*] (TTSB)
JUNIZ..... Juniper Features Wrrt'B' [*NASDAQ symbol*] (TTSB)
JUNO....... Juno Lighting [*NASDAQ symbol*] (TTSB)
JUNO....... Juno Lighting, Inc. [*NASDAQ symbol*] (NQ)
JunoLt...... Juno Lighting, Inc. [*Associated Press*] (SAG)
JUNR....... Junior
JUNT....... Juntae (ROG)
Junta del Acuer... Grupo Andino - Junta del Acuerdo de Cartagena [*Andean Group - Cartagena Agreement Board - ANCOM*] (EA)
JUO........ Junior Under-Officer [*British military*] (DMA)
JUP........ Jamiatul Ulama-i-Pakistan [*Political party*] (FEA)
JUP........ Jupiter (KSC)
JUP........ Juventud Universitaria Peronista [*University Peronist Youth*] [*Argentina*]
JUP........ Juventud Uruguaya de Pie [*Upstanding Uruguayan Youth*] (PD)
JUP........ Upland, CA [*Location identifier FAA*] (FAAL)
JUPITER..... Judicial Precedent Information Trace by Electronic Retrieval [*Database*] [*Toyo Information Systems Co.*] [*Information service or system*] (CRD)
JupNatl...... Jupiter National, Inc. [*Associated Press*] (SAG)
JUPPIE...... Japanese Urban Professional [*Lifestyle classification*]

JUR.............	Julia Resources [*Vancouver Stock Exchange symbol*]
JUR.............	Jurassic [*Period, era, or system*] [*Geology*]
JUR.............	Juridical (ROG)
JUR.............	Jurisprudence (ROG)
Jur	[*The*] Jurist [*Washington, DC*] [*A publication*] (DLA)
Jur	Jurist Reports [*18 vols.*] [*England*] [*A publication*] (DLA)
Jur	London Jurist [*1854*] [*A publication*] (DLA)
J Urban H ...	Journal of Urban History [*A publication*] (BRI)
JUR D	Juris Doctor [*Doctor of Law*] [*Latin*] (ADA)
JUR DIG	Jure Dignitatis [*By Right of Rank*] [*Latin*] (ROG)
JURE............	Junta Revolucionaria Cubana [*Exile action group*]
Jur Ex	Hargrave's Francis-Jurisconsult Exercitations [*A publication*] (DLA)
JURG	Joint Users Requirements Group (NASA)
Jurid Soc'y Pap...	Juridical Society Papers [*England*] [*A publication*] (DLA)
JURIS	Jurisdiction (AABC)
JURIS	Jurisprudence (ADA)
JURIS	Juristisches Informationssystem [*Judicial Information System*] [*Federal Ministry of Justice Legal database*] [*Germany*] (IID)
JURIS	Justice Retrieval and Inquiry System [*Department of Justice*] [*Legal databank*] [*Information service or system*] (IID)
JURISD.......	Jurisdiction
JURISDN.....	Jurisdiction (ROG)
JURISDON	Jurisdiction (ROG)
JURISP	Jurisprudence
Jurispr	Jurisprudence (DLA)
Jur M	Master of Jurisprudence
Jur Mar.......	Molloy's De Jure Maritimo [*A publication*] (DLA)
Jur NY	Jurist, or Law and Equity Reporter [*New York*] [*A publication*] (DLA)
Jur Ros	Roscoe's Jurist [*London*] [*A publication*] (DLA)
Jur (Sc)	[*The*] Scottish Jurist [*Edinburgh*] [*A publication*] (DLA)
Jur Sc D	Doctor of Judicial Science [*or Doctor of the Science of Jurisprudence*]
Jur Soc P....	Juridical Society Papers [*1858-74*] [*Scotland*] [*A publication*] (DLA)
Jur St...........	Juridical Styles [*Scotland*] [*A publication*] (DLA)
JURUE.........	Joint Unit for Research on the Urban Environment [*British*]
Jur Utr Dr	Juris Utriusque Doctor [*Doctor of Both Laws; i.e., Canon and Civil Law*]
JUS.............	Active Aero Charter [*FAA designator*] (FAAC)
JUS.............	Department of Justice Library [*UTLAS symbol*]
Jus..............	Jacobus de Porta Ravennate [*Deceased, 1178*] [*Authority cited in pre-1607 legal work*] (DSA)
JUS.............	Justice
JUS.............	Nenana, AK [*Location identifier FAA*] (FAAL)
JUS AVEN ...	Jusculum Avenaceum [*Gruel*] [*Pharmacy*] (ROG)
JUSC..........	Jusculum [*Broth*] [*Pharmacy*] (ROG)
JUSCIMPC ..	Joint United States/Canada Industrial Mobilization Planning Committee [*NATO*] (NATG)
JUS/CIV	Department of Justice, Civil Division
Jus Code	Code of Justinian [*A publication*] (DLA)
Jus Code	Justices' Code [*Oregon*] [*A publication*] (DLA)
Juscul........	Jusculum [*Broth*] [*Pharmacy*]
JUSE...........	Japanese Union of Scientists and Engineers [*Databank originator*] (NITA)
JUSE...........	Japan Union of Scientists and Engineers (BARN)
JUSE-AESOPP...	JUSE [*Japanese Union of Scientists and Engineers*] an Estimator of Phy sical Properties (NITA)
Jus Inst.......	Institutes of Justinian [*Roman law*] [*A publication*] (DLA)
JUSMAAG	Joint United States Military Assistance Advisory Group
JUSMAG	Joint United States Military Advisory Group
JUSMAG	Joint U.S. Military Assistance Group
JUSMAGG	Joint United States Military Aid Group, Greece
JUSMAG-K...	Joint United States Military Advisor Group-Korea (DOMA)
JUSMAGPHIL...	Joint United States Military Advisory Group to the Republic of the Philippines [*World War II*]
JUSMAGTHAI...	Joint United States Military Assistance Group, Thailand
JUSMAP	Joint United States Military Advisory and Planning Group
JUSMG	Joint United States Military Group
JUSMGP	Joint United States Military Group
JUSMMAT....	Joint United States Military Mission for Aid to Turkey
Jus Nav Rhod...	Jus Navale Rhodiorum [*A publication*] (DLA)
JUSO...........	Jungsozialist [*Young Socialist*] [*Germany*]
JUSPAO	Joint United States Public Affairs Office [*Vietnam*]
JUSS...........	Jussien (ROG)
JUSS...........	Jussive
JUSSC	Joint United States Strategic Committee
JUSSIM.......	Justice System Interactive Model (PDAA)
JUST..........	Justice (ROG)
Just.............	Justices' Law Reporter [*Pennsylvania*] [*A publication*] (DLA)
Just.............	Justiciary [*Legal term*] (DLA)
JUST..........	Justification (AABC)
Just.............	Justin (BJA)
JUST..........	Justinian (ROG)
JUST..........	Just Toys [*NASDAQ symbol*] (TTSB)
JUST..........	Just Toys, Inc. [*NASDAQ symbol*] (SAG)
JUST ANGL...	Justiciarius Anglie [*Chief Justiciary of England*] [*Latin*] (ROG)
JUST CP	Justice of the Common Pleas (ROG)
Just Dig.......	Digest of Justinian [*A publication*] (DLA)
JUSTICE......	Journeymen Under Specific Training in Construction Employment (PDAA)
Justices' LR (PA)...	Justices' Law Reporter [*Pennsylvania*] [*A publication*] (DLA)
JUSTIFON......	Justification (ROG)
Justin..........	Justinian [*483-565, Byzantine emperor*] [*Authority cited in pre-1607 legal work*] (DSA)
Justin..........	Justin Industries, Inc. [*Associated Press*] (SAG)
Just Inst	Justinian's Institutes (DLA)

JUSTIS........	Judicial State Information System (OICC)
JUST ITIN	Justice Itinerant [*Legal term*] (DLA)
JUST KB	Justice of the King's Bench [*British*] (ROG)
JustLHo.......	Just Like Home, Inc. [*Associated Press*] (SAG)
Just LR........	Justices' Law Reporter [*Pennsylvania*] [*A publication*] (DLA)
Justn..........	Justinian [*Australia A publication*]
Just P	Justice of the Peace and Local Government Review [*A publication*] (DLA)
Just Peace...	Justice of the Peace and Local Government Review [*A publication*] (DLA)
Just SL	Justice's Sea Law [*A publication*] (DLA)
JustToys	Just Toys, Inc. [*Associated Press*] (SAG)
JUT.............	Jet Utility Transport
JUT.............	Jeunesse de l'Unite Togolaise [*Togolese Unity Youth*]
Juta	Juta's Daily Reporter [*South Africa*] [*A publication*] (DLA)
Juta	Juta's Prize Cases [*South Africa*] [*A publication*] (DLA)
Juta	Juta's Supreme Court Reports [*1880-1910*] [*Cape Of Good Hope, South Africa*] [*A publication*] (DLA)
JUTCPS........	Joint Uniform Telephone Communications Precedence System (DNAB)
JUV.............	Juvenal [*Roman poet, 60-140AD*] [*Classical studies*] (ROG)
JUV.............	Juvenile
Juv.............	Juvenile (AL)
JUV.............	Juvenis [*Young*] [*Latin*]
Juv & Dom Rel Ct...	Juvenile and Domestic Relations Court [*Legal term*] (DLA)
Juv Ct J	Juvenile Court Journal [*A publication*] (DLA)
JUVE...........	Juvenile
juvenile SMA...	Spinal Muscular Atrophy [*Kugelberg-Welander disease*] (PAZ)
JUV JUST	Juvenile Justice [*Legal term*] (DLA)
JUVOS........	Joint Unemployment, Vacancy, and Operating Statistics [*Department of Employment*] [*British*]
JUWAT........	Joint Unconventional Warfare Assessment Team [*Military*]
JUWC.........	Joint Unconventional Warfare Command (MCD)
JUWTF........	Joint Unconventional Warfare Task Force
JUWTFA.......	Joint Unconventional Warfare Task Force, Atlantic
JUX............	Juxtaposition (WDAA)
JUXT..........	Juxta [*Near*] [*Pharmacy*]
JUY............	Andalusia, AL [*Location identifier FAA*] (FAAL)
JV	Air Charters [*Senegal*] [*ICAO designator*] (ICDA)
JV	Bearskin Lake [*ICAO designator*] (AD)
JV	Jagdverband [*German aircraft fighter unit*] [*World War II*]
JV	Janesbury Valve [*Aerospace*] (KSC)
JV	Japanese Vellum
JV	Jersey European Airways [*ICAO designator*] (AD)
JV	Jet Ventilation [*Medicine*]
JV	Jewish Vegetarians of North America (EA)
JV	Joint Venture [*Legal term Business term*]
JV	Journal Voucher [*Accounting*]
JV	Jugular Vein [*Anatomy*]
JV	Jugular Venous [*Pressure and pulse*] [*Cardiology*] (DAVI)
JV	Junin Virus [*Medicine*] (DMAA)
JV	Junior Varsity
JVA	Ankavandra [*Madagascar*] [*Airport symbol*] (OAG)
JVA	Genavia SRL [*Italy ICAO designator*] (FAAC)
JVA	Jet Vane Actuators
JVA	Jewish Vacation Association [*Superseded by Association of Jewish Sponsored Camps*] (EA)
JVA	Junior Victory Army [*World War II*]
JVAA	Jewish Visual Artists Association [*Defunct*] (EA)
JVAS	Jandel Video Analysis System
JVB	James V. Brown Library of Williamsport and Lycoming County, Williamsport, PA [*OCLC symbol*] (OCLC)
JVB	Joint Vulnerability Board
JVC	Japan Victor Co.
JVC	Jesuit Volunteer Corps: Northwest (EA)
JVC	Jet Vane Control (MCD)
JVC	Jewelers Vigilance Committee (EA)
JVC	Jewelry Valuers' Council [*Australia*]
JVC	Jugular Venous Catheter [*Medicine*] (DMAA)
JVC	Jules Verne Circle (EA)
JVC	Junior Vice Commander
JVD	Jet Vapor Deposition [*Coating technology*]
JVD	Jugular Venous Distention [*Medicine*]
JVD	Juris Utriusque Doctor [*Doctor of Both Laws; i.e., Canon and Civil Law*]
JVDHS	Jahresverzeichnis der Deutschen Hochschulschriften [*A bibliographic publication*] [*Germany*]
JVE	Jeans Viscosity Equation [*Physics*]
JVER	Journal of Vocational Education Research [*A publication*] (EAAP)
JVH	Bangor, ME [*Location identifier FAA*] (FAAL)
JVIDS	Joint Visually Integrated Display System (DOMA)
JVIS	Jackson Vocational Interest Survey [*Vocational guidance test*]
JVIS	Joint Visual Information Services [*DoD*] (DOMA)
JVita	Life of Josephus (BJA)
JVL	Beloit/Janesville [*Wisconsin*] [*Airport symbol*] (OAG)
JVL	Janesville, WI [*Location identifier FAA*] (FAAL)
JVLN	Javelin Systems, Inc. [*NASDAQ symbol*] (SAG)
JVM	Java Virtual Machine [*Computer science*]
JVNC	John Von Neumann National Supercomputer Center [*Princeton, NJ*] (GRD)
JvNCnet.......	John Von Neumann Computer Center Network (ACRL)
JVNL	Juvenile
J Voet Com ad Pand...	Jan Voet's Commentarius ad Pandectas [*A publication*] (DLA)

JVP .... Janatha Vimukhti Peramuna [*People's Liberation Front*] [*Sri Lanka*] [*Political party*] (PPW)
JVP .... Japanese Vellum Proofs
JVP .... Joint Venture Partners
JVP .... Juedische Volkspartei (BJA)
JVP .... Jugular Vein Pressure (WDAA)
JVP .... Jugular Vein [*or Venous*] Pulse [*Medicine*]
JVP .... Jugular Venous Pressure [*Cardiology*] (DAVI)
JVP .... Junior Vice-President [*Freemasonry*] (ROG)
JVPT .... Jugular Venous Pulse Tracing [*Medicine*]
JVR .... Jury Verdict Research, Inc. [*Information service or system*] (IID)
JVS .... Jewish Vegetarian Society - America [*Later, JVSNA*] (EA)
JVS .... Jewish Vocational Services
JVS .... Joint Venture Scheme
JVS .... Joint Vocational School
JVSNA .... Jewish Vegetarian Society-North America (EA)
JVSPLNMQNSC... Je Vous Salue par les Noms Maconniques que Nous Seul Connoissons [*I Salute You by the Masonic Names, Which We Only Know*] [*Freemasonry*] [*French*]
JVVVA.......... Justice for Veteran Victims of the Veterans Administration (EA)
JVX .... Joint Service Vertical-Lift Aircraft, Experimental [*Military*] (RDA)
JVY .... Jeffersonville, IN [*Location identifier FAA*] (FAAL)
JW .... Jacket Water
JW .... Jehovah's Witnesses (ADA)
JW .... [*The*] Jewish War [*A publication*] (BJA)
JW .... John Wiley [*& Sons*] [*Publisher*]
JW .... Joint Warfare
JW .... Jordan Watch [*Database*] [*Jordan & Sons Ltd.*] [*Information service or system*] (CRD)
JW .... Jump Walker [*Rehabilitation*] (DAVI)
JW .... Junction Wide [*Telecommunications*] (OA)
JW .... Junior Warden [*Freemasonry*]
JW .... Junior Wolf [*A young philanderer*] [*Slang*]
JW .... Junior Woodward [*Ancient Order of Foresters*]
JW .... Polar Avia [*ICAO designator*] (AD)
JW .... Royal American [*ICAO designator*] (AD)
JW .... Wiley [*John*] & Sons [*NYSE symbol*] (SAG)
JWA .... Jetworld Airways Ltd. [*Antigua and Barbuda*] [*ICAO designator*] (FAAC)
JWA .... Johnson Worldwide Associates, Inc. [*Associated Press*] (SAG)
JWA .... Jwalamukhi [*India*] [*Seismograph station code, US Geological Survey Closed*] (SEIS)
JWADF........ Joint Western Air Defense Force (MUGU)
JWAI............ Johnson Worldwide Associates, Inc. [*NASDAQ symbol*] (NQ)
JWAIA......... Johnson Worldwide'A' [*NASDAQ symbol*] (TTSB)
JW & NW .... Jamestown, Westfield & Northwestern Railroad (IIA)
JWAR.......... Jehovah's Witnesses for Animal Rights [*An association*] (EA)
JWB .... Joint Wages Board (DAS)
JWB .... National Jewish Welfare Board [*Later, JCCANA*] (EA)
JWBC .... Joint Whole Blood Center [*Military*]
JWBCA........ Joint Whole Blood Control Agency (MCD)
JWBJBC...... JWB [*Jewish Welfare Board*] Jewish Book Council (EA)
JWBJCC....... JWB Jewish Chaplains Council (NTPA)
JWC .... Jayhawk Western Conference (PSS)
JWC .... Joint Warfare Center [*DoD*]
JWC .... Junction Wire Connector
JWC .... Jungle Warfare Course [*Military*] (MCD)
JWD .... Journal of Workforce Diversity [*A publication*]
JWE .... Joint Warfare Establishment [*British*]
JWEF .... Joinery and Woodwork Employers' Federation [*British*] (BI)
JWF .... Job Work Folder (AABC)
JWFC .... Jacky Ward Fan Club [*Defunct*] (EA)
JWFC .... Jimmy Wakely Fan Club [*Defunct*] (EA)
JWFC .... Joe Waters Fan Club (EA)
JWFC .... Joint Warfighting Center [*DoD*]
JWG .... Joint Working Group [*Military*]
JWG .... Jugendwohlfahrtsgesetz [*Youth Welfare Law*] [*German*] (ILCA)
JWG .... JWGenesis Financial [*AMEX symbol*] [*Formerly, Charles Financial Services*]
JWGA.......... Joint War Games Agency [*JCS*] [*DoD*]
JWGCG .... Joint War Games Control Group [*Military*] (CINC)
JWGM......... Joint Working Group Meeting [*NASA*] (KSC)
JWI .... Jewish Women International (EA)
JWICS......... Joint Worldwide Intelligence Communications System (COE)
JWKB.......... Jordan-Wentzel-Kramers-Brillouin [*Physics*]
JWLR.......... Jeweler
JWLR.......... Jeweller [*British*] (ADA)
JWLRY........ Jewelry (WDAA)

JWNS.......... Jewish News Service (BJA)
jwo............. Jettisoning and Washing Overboard [*Inventor*] (ODBW)
JWO............ Job Work Order
JWOD .... Javits-Wagner-O'Day Act
JWP............ Jamaican Workers' Party [*Political party*] (PPW)
JWP............ Jamaica Water Properties (EFIS)
JWP............ Joint Working Paper
JWP............ Joint Working Party (ADA)
JWPC.......... Joint War Plans Committee
JWPC.......... Joint War Production Committee
JWPNN........ Jobs with Peace National Network [*Later, NJWPC*] (EA)
JWPS .... Joint War Production Staff
JWPT .... Jersey Wildlife Preservation Trust (EAIO)
JWR............ Joint War Room [*Military*]
JWRA .... Joint War Room Annex [*Military*] (CINC)
JWRC.......... Jewish Women's Resource Center (EA)
JWRC.......... Joint Warfighter Range Complex [*Army*]
JWS .... Japanese Weekend School
JWS .... Jazz World Society (EA)
JWS .... Jewish Welfare Society [*Australia*]
JwS .... John Wiley & Sons, New York, NY [*Library symbol Library of Congress*] (LCLS)
JWS .... Joint Warfare Staff [*British*]
JWS .... Judson Welliver Society (EA)
JWSOL........ Joint Warfare Simulation Object Library [*DoD*]
JWSS.......... James Willard Schultz Society (EA)
JWS/TD ...... Jungle Warfare School Trial and Development Wing [*Johore Bahru, Malaysia*]
JWSTP........ Joint Warfighting Science and Technology Plan [*Defense Technical Information Center*]
JWT .... J. Walter Thompson (WDAA)
JWTC.......... Jungle Warfare Training Center [*Army*]
JWU............ International Jewelry Workers Union [*Later, Service Employees International Union*]
JWU............ Sumter, SC [*Location identifier FAA*] (FAAL)
JWV............ Jewish War Veterans (WDAA)
JWV............ Jewish War Veterans of the USA (EA)
JWVA.......... Jewish War Veterans of the USA - National Ladies Auxiliary (EA)
JWV-NMI .... National Museum of American Jewish Military History (EA)
JWVUSANM... Jewish War Veterans USA National Memorial (EA)
JWY .... Jet Way, Inc. [*ICAO designator*] (FAAC)
JWYCC........ Jamestown-Williamsburg-Yorktown Celebration Committee
JX .... Bougair [*ICAO designator*] (AD)
JX .... Jesus Christus [*Jesus Christ*] [*Latin*] (ROG)
JX .... Jorex Ltd. [*Toronto Stock Exchange symbol*]
JXCG .... Joint Exercise Control Group [*Military*] (AABC)
JXG .... Juvenile Xanthogranuloma [*Ophthalmology*]
JXN .... Jackson [*Michigan*] [*Airport symbol*] (OAG)
JXSB .... Jacksonville Savings Bank (Illinois) [*NASDAQ symbol*] (SAG)
JXT .... Morristown, TN [*Location identifier FAA*] (FAAL)
JXVL .... Jacksonville Bancorp, Inc. [*NASDAQ symbol*] (SAG)
JXVL .... Jacksonville Savings & Loan Association [*Texas*] [*NASDAQ symbol*] (SAG)
J XXII.......... Extravagantes Johannes XXII [*A publication*] (DSA)
Jy .... Jansky [*A unit of electromagnetic flux density*]
JY .... Japanese Yen [*Monetary unit*]
JY .... Jersey European [*ICAO designator*] (AD)
JY .... July
JY .... Jury [*Ship's rigging*] (ROG)
JYA .... Junior Year Abroad [*Collegiate term*]
JYC .... Jacques-Yves Cousteau [*French marine explorer*] [*Initialism pronounced "Jheek" when used as nickname*]
JYP .... JCP & L Capital LP [*NYSE symbol*] (SAG)
JYP .... Jersey Central Power & Light Co. [*NYSE symbol*] (SAG)
JYPPr.......... Jersey Cent P&L 4%cmPfd [*NYSE symbol*] (TTSB)
JYPPrE........ Jersey Cent P&L7.88% Pfd [*NYSE symbol*] (TTSB)
JYPPrZ........ JCP&L Cap L.P.8.56%'MIPS' [*NYSE symbol*] (TTSB)
JYV .... Houston, TX [*Location identifier FAA*] (FAAL)
JYV .... Jyvaskyla [*Finland*] [*Airport symbol*] (OAG)
JZ .... Alamo Commuter Airlines [*ICAO designator*] (AD)
JZ .... Jazz [*A radio station format*] (WDMC)
JZ .... Juedische Zeremonialkunst [*A publication*] (BJA)
JZ .... Jump on Zero [*Computer science*] (PCM)
JZF .... Jannasch-Zafirion-Farrington [*Marine sediment trap*]
JZG .... Juedische Zeitschrift fuer Wissenschaft und Leben (A. Geiger) [*A publication*] (BJA)
JZI .... Charleston, SC [*Location identifier FAA*] (FAAL)
JZM .... Jazzman Resources, Inc. [*Vancouver Stock Exchange symbol*]
JZQ .... Norfolk, VA [*Location identifier FAA*] (FAAL)

K
By Acronym

K	Absolute Zero [Temperature] (MAE)
K	Amphibious [JETDS]
K	Black (WDMC)
k	Boltzmann Constant [Symbol] [IUPAC]
k	Bulk Modulus of Elasticity [Symbol] (DEN)
K	Calcium in the Solar Spectrum [Astronomy] (BARN)
K	Calix [Anatomy] (MAE)
K	Capacity (AAG)
K	Capital [Factor of production]
K	Capsular Antigen [Immunology] (MAE)
K	Cara [Dear One] [Latin]
K	Carat [Unit of measure for precious stones or gold]
K	Care
K	Carissimus [Dearest] [Latin]
K	Carlo Erba [Italy] [Research code symbol]
K	Carrying Capacity [Genetics] (DAVI)
K	Carus
K	Cathode [Electron device] (MSA)
K	Cellophane (AAG)
K	Certified Kosher [Food labeling]
K	Chritiania Bank og Kreditkasse [Bank] [Norway]
K	Circuses [Public-performance tariff class] [British]
k	Coefficient of Alienation [Psychology]
K	Coefficient of Scleral Rigidity [Ophthalmology] (DAVI)
k	Cold Air Mass [Meteorology] (BARN)
K	Computer [JETDS nomenclature]
K	Consonantal [Linguistics]
K	Constant
K	Contract [Legal shorthand] (LWAP)
K	Cretaceous [Period, era, or system] [Geology]
K	Cumulus [Cloud] [Meteorology]
K	Dallas [Branch in the Federal Reserve regional banking system] (BARN)
K	Declared or Paid This Year on a Cumulative Issue with Dividends in Arrears [Investment term] (DFIT)
K	Degrees Kelvin
K	Dielectric Constant
K	Electrostatic Capacity [Symbol] (AAMN)
K	Equilibrium Constant [Symbol] [Chemistry]
K	Ionization Constant [Symbol] [Chemistry]
K	Kadenz [Cadence] [Music]
K	Kaempferol [Biochemistry]
K	Kainic Acid [Biochemistry]
K	Kaiser [In radio call signs west of the Mississippi River] (ROG)
K	Kaken Chemical Co. [Japan] [Research code symbol]
K	Kalendas [Calends]
K	Kalium [Potassium] [Chemical element]
K	Kallikrein [or Kininogenin] Inhibiting Unit [Hematology]
K	Kanamycin [Antibacterial compound]
K	Kanone [Gun] [German military - World War II]
K	Kansas State Library, Topeka, KS [Library symbol Library of Congress] (LCLS)
K	Kappa [Tenth letter of the Greek alaphabet] (DAVI)
K	Karat [A twenty-fourth part; unit of value for gold]
K	Karolus de Tocco [Flourished, 13th century] [Authority cited in pre-1607 legal work] (DSA)
K	Karyotype [Clinical chemistry]
K	Kathode [Cathode]
K	Kayak
K	Kayser
K	K Capture [A type of radioactive decay]
K	Keel
K	Keg
K	Kell [Blood group]
K	Kell Factor (DMAA)
K	Kellogg Co. [NYSE symbol] (SPSG)
K	Kelp [Quality of the Bottom] [Nautical charts]
K	Kelvin [Symbol] [SI unit of thermodynamic temperature]
K	Kennedy Space Center [NASA]
K	Kensal Press [Publisher] [British]
K	Kentish
K	Kenyon's English King's Bench Reports [A publication] (DLA)
K	Kerma (DMAA)
K	Kern Wave [Earthquakes]
K	Kerosene (AAG)
K	Kerr Constant [Optics]
K	Ketamine [An anesthetic]
K	Ketch (ROG)
k	Ketib (BJA)
K	Ketotifen [Pharmacology]
K	Key
K	Keyes' New York Court of Appeals Reports [A publication] (DLA)
K	KGB [Komitet Gossudarstvennoi Bezopasnosti] Agent
K	Kicker [Football]
K	Kidney [Anatomy] (MAE)
K	Killed
K	Killer [Cells] [Cytology] (DAVI)
k	Kilo [A prefix meaning multiplied by 10^3] [SI symbol]
K	Kilo [Phonetic alphabet] [International] (DSUE)
k	Kilo (WDMC)
K	Kilobyte [10^3 bytes] [Computer science]
K	Kilocycle
k	Kilogram [Also, kg] [Symbol SI unit for mass]
k	Kilohm
K	Kilometer (WDAA)
K	Kilowatt (WDMC)
K	Kindergarten
K	Kinesthetic (AAG)
K	Kinetic Energy [Symbol] [IUPAC]
K	King [Phonetic alphabet] [Royal Navy] (DSUE)
K	King [Chess, card games]
K	King [Monetary unit] [Papua, New Guinea] (BARN)
K	Kingdom (ROG)
K	Kings [Old Testament book] (BJA)
K	Kip [Monetary unit] [Laos]
K	Kip [1000 lbs.]
K	Kirk (ROG)
K	Kirschner [Wire] [Orthopedics] (DAVI)
K	Kitchen
K	Klebsiella [Genus of microorganisms] (DAVI)
K	Klinge [Germany] [Research code symbol]
K	Klystron
K	Knee [Anatomy] (DAVI)
K	Knight [Chess, card games]
K	Knighthood
K	Knit
K	Knock [Cardiology]
K	Knots [Also, KT] [Nautical speed unit]
K	Knudsen Number
K	Koechel [Catalogue of Mozart's works] (ODBW)
K	Koechel Numeration [Of Mozart's Works] [Music] (WA)
K	Kollaborateur [Nickname given Alain Robbe-Grillet] [World War II]
K	Kontra [Contra] [Music]
K	Kopeck [Monetary unit] [Former USSR]
k	K-Orbital (MEC)
K	Koruna [Monetary unit] [Former Czechoslovakia]
K	Kosher
K	Kosmos [Publisher] [Holland]
K	Kotze's Transvaal High Court Reports [South Africa] [A publication] (DLA)
K	Kouyunjik [or Kuyounjik] [Collection of cuneiform tablets from Kuyounjik in the British Museum, London] (BJA)
K	Kraft [Paper] (DGA)
K	Kraftfahrwesen [Motor transport] [German military - World War II]
K	Kraftrad [Motorcycle] [German military - World War II]
K	Krazy Kat [Cartoon character by George Herriman]
K	Krona [Monetary unit] [Iceland, Sweden]
K	Krone [Crown] [Monetary unit Denmark, Norway]
K	Kroon [Monetary unit] [Estonia]
K	Krupp Gun
K	Kurus [Monetary unit] [Turkey]
K	Kwacha [Monetary unit] [Malawi, Zambia]
K	Kyat [Monetary unit] [Myanmar]
K	Luminous Efficiency [Physics] (BARN)
K	Lysine [One-letter symbol; see Lys]
k	Magnetic Susceptibility (STED)
k	Mass Transfer Coefficient [Symbol] [IUPAC]
K	Motor Coordination [Neurology and orthopedics] (DAVI)
K	Multiplication Factor [or Constant]
K	NCO Logistics Program [Army skill qualification identifier] (INF)
K	One Thousand (NASA)
K	Phylloquinone [Vitamin K] [Also, PMQ] [Biochemistry]

K .... Potassium [*Chemical element*]
K .... Promotional Fare [*Also, L, Q, V*] [*Airline fare code*]
K .... Radius of Curvature of Flattest Meridian of Apical Cornea [*Ophthalmology*] (DAVI)
k .... Rate (DAVI)
k .... Rate Constant [*Symbol*] [*Chemistry*]
k .... Reaction Rate Constant [*Chemistry*] (DAVI)
K .... Red Star of Maximum Intensity of Metal [*Astronomy*] (BARN)
K .... Relay (CET)
K .... Required Rate of Return [*Finance*]
K .... Smoke [*Weather charts*]
K .... Solar Absorption Index (CET)
K .... Strikeout [*Baseball symbol*]
K .... Tanker [*Designation for all US military aircraft*]
K .... Telemetering [*JETDS*]
k .... Thermal Conductivity [*Symbol*] [*IUPAC*]
K .... Thousand (ADA)
k .... Torsion Constant [*Physics*] (BARN)
K .... United Kingdom [*IYRU nationality code*] (IYR)
K .... Velocity [*Physics*] (DAVI)
K .... Wetboek van Koophandel [*Commercial Code*] [*Dutch*] (ILCA)
K1 .... Kayak, Single Person (ADA)
K2 .... Kayak, Two Person (ADA)
K2 .... Mount Godwin-Austen [*Initialism denotes that mountain is second highest (to Everest) in the Karakoram range in the Himalayas*] [*Initialism also used as brand name of skiing equipment*]
K2Desgn ...... K2 Design, Inc. [*Associated Press*] (SAG)
K2Dsgn .... K2 Design, Inc. [*Associated Press*] (SAG)
K-3 .... Krasnogorsk-3 [*A 16mm film camera*] (WDMC)
K-3 .... Kummer, Kneser, and Kodaira [*Surfaces*] [*Mathematics*]
K$_3$ .... Menadione [*Vitamin K$_3$*] (DAVI)
K4 .... Kayak, Four Person (ADA)
K$_4$ .... Menadiol Sodium Diphosphate [*Vitamin K$_4$*] (DAVI)
K9 .... Canine [*K9 Corps - Army Dogs*] [*World War II*]
K-10 .... Gastric Tube [*Medicine*] (STED)
K-12 .... Kindergarten through 12th Grade (WDAA)
K24H .... Potassium, Urine 24 Hour [*Biochemistry*] (DAVI)
K-25 .... Oak Ridge K-25 Site [*Department of Energy*] [*Oak Ridge, TN*] (GAAI)
K25 .... Oak Ridge Uranium Separation Plant [*Code designation*] (DEN)
K$_a$ .... Acid Ionization Constant [*Physics*] (DAVI)
KA .... Alkair [*Denmark ICAO designator*] (ICDA)
KA .... Alkaline Phosphatase [*An enzyme*] (DAVI)
KA .... Auroral Absorption Index (CET)
KA .... Australia [*IYRU nationality code*] (IYR)
Ka .... Cathode [*Electron device*] (AAMN)
KA .... Coastal Plains Commuter [*ICAO designator*] (AD)
KA .... Concrete Arch [*Bridges*]
KA .... Eha-Kibbuts ha-Artsi (BJA)
KA .... HMS King Alfred [*British military*] (DMA)
KA .... Kainic Acid [*Biochemistry*]
Ka .... Kallikrein (MEDA)
KA .... Kamov [*Former USSR ICAO aircraft manufacturer identifier*] (ICAO)
Ka .... Kaolinite [*A mineral*]
Ka .... Karolus de Tocco [*Flourished, 13th century*] [*Authority cited in pre-1607 legal work*] (DSA)
KA .... Kathode [*Cathode*] (AAG)
KA .... Keratoacanthoma [*Dermatology*] (DAVI)
KA .... Keren Ami (BJA)
KA .... Keto Acid (DMAA)
KA .... Ketoacidosis [*Medicine*]
K/A .... Ketogenic to Anti-Ketogenic [*Ratio*] [*In diets*]
KA .... Keyed Address (IAA)
KA .... Keyed Alike [*Locks*] (ADA)
ka .... Killed in Action
KA .... Kilmarnock [*Postcode*] (ODBW)
kA .... Kiloampere
KA .... King-Armstrong Unit [*Clinical chemistry*]
KA .... King of Arms
KA .... King Pin Angle [*Automotive engineering*]
KA .... Knight of St. Andrew [*Russia*] [*Obsolete*]
KA .... Knight of the Order of Australia (WDAA)
K/A .... Knights of the Altar (EA)
K-A .... Kuhlmann-Anderson Intelligence Tests [*Education*]
KA .... Kuwait Airways Corp.
KA .... Kynurenic Acid [*Biochemistry*] (OA)
KA .... Kypriakes Aerogrammes [*Cyprus Airlines*]
KA .... Thousands of Amperes
KAA .... Asia Aero Survey & Consulting Engineers, Inc. [*Korea*] [*ICAO designator*] (FAAC)
Ka A .... Kansas Appeals Reports [*A publication*] (DLA)
kaa .... Karakalpak [*MARC language code Library of Congress*] (LCCP)
KAA .... Karratha [*Australia Seismograph station code, US Geological Survey Closed*] (SEIS)
KAA .... Kasama [*Zambia*] [*Airport symbol*] (OAG)
KAA .... Keep-Alive Anode
KAAA .... Kingman, AZ [*AM radio station call letters*]
KAAB .... Batesville, AR [*AM radio station call letters*]
KAAD .... Kerosene, Alcohol, Acetic Acid, and Dioxane (DMAA)
KAAH .... Honolulu, HI [*Television station call letters*] (BROA)
KAAK .... Great Falls, MT [*FM radio station call letters*]
KAAL .... Austin, MN [*Television station call letters*]
KAAM .... Huntsville, MO [*FM radio station call letters*]
KAAM .... Plano, TX [*AM radio station call letters*] (RBYB)
KAAN .... Bethany, MO [*AM radio station call letters*]
KAAN-FM ..... Bethany, MO [*FM radio station call letters*]

KAAO .... Kabul [*Afghanistan*] [*Seismograph station code, US Geological Survey*] (SEIS)
KAAP .... Kansas Army Ammunition Plant (AABC)
KAAQ .... Alliance, NE [*FM radio station call letters*]
KAAR .... Butte, MT [*FM radio station call letters*]
KAAS .... Keele Assessment of Auditory Style (DMAA)
KAAS .... Salina, KS [*Television station call letters*]
KAAT .... Oakhurst, CA [*FM radio station call letters*]
KAAX .... Avenal, CA [*FM radio station call letters*]
KAAY .... Little Rock, AR [*AM radio station call letters*]
KAb .... Abilene Free Public Library, Abilene, KS [*Library symbol Library of Congress*] (LCLS)
KAB .... Kabansk [*Former USSR Seismograph station code, US Geological Survey*] (SEIS)
KAB .... Kaneb Services [*NYSE symbol*] (TTSB)
KAB .... Kaneb Services, Inc. [*NYSE symbol*] (SPSG)
KAB .... Kariba Dam [*Zimbabwe*] [*Airport symbol*] (OAG)
KAB .... Katholieke Arbeidersbeweging [*Netherlands*]
KAB .... Keep America Beautiful (EA)
KAB .... Knowledge, Attitudes, and Behavior Survey [*Department of Health and Human Services*] (GFGA)
KABB .... San Antonio, TX [*Television station call letters*]
K-ABC .... Kaufman Assessment Battery for Children [*Diagnostic assessment test*] (PAZ)
KABC .... Los Angeles, CA [*AM radio station call letters*]
KABCC .... Korea Australia Business Cooperation Council
KABC-TV ...... Los Angeles, CA [*Television station call letters*]
KAbE .... Dwight D. Eisenhower Library, Abilene, KS [*Library symbol Library of Congress*] (LCLS)
KABF .... Little Rock, AR [*FM radio station call letters*]
KABG-FM ...... Los Alamos, NM [*FM radio station call letters*] (BROA)
KABH .... Shawnee, OK [*FM radio station call letters*]
KABI .... Abilene, KS [*AM radio station call letters*]
KABI .... Abilene/Municipal [*Texas*] [*ICAO location identifier*] (ICLI)
KABINS .... Knowledge, Attitude, Behavior, and Improvement in Nutritional Status (STED)
KABIR .... Kapitalist Birokrat [*Capitalist Bureaucrat*] [*Term for foreigner Indonesia*]
KABK .... Augusta, AR [*FM radio station call letters*]
KABL .... Oakland, CA [*AM radio station call letters*]
KABN .... Long Island, AK [*AM radio station call letters*]
KABPrA .... Kaneb Svc Adj Rt A Pfd [*NYSE symbol*] (TTSB)
KABQ .... Albuquerque/International [*New Mexico*] [*ICAO location identifier*] (ICLI)
KABQ .... Albuquerque, NM [*AM radio station call letters*]
KABR .... Alamo Community, NM [*AM radio station call letters*]
KABS .... Great Falls, MT [*FM radio station call letters*]
KABU-FM ...... Fort Totten, ND [*FM radio station call letters*] (RBYB)
KABX .... Merced, CA [*FM radio station call letters*]
KABY .... Aberdeen, SD [*Television station call letters*]
kac .... Kachin [*MARC language code Library of Congress*] (LCCP)
KAC .... Kaman Aircraft Corp. (MCD)
KAC .... Kameshli [*Syria*] [*Airport symbol*] (OAG)
KAC .... Kamishli [*Syria*] [*Airport symbol*] (AD)
KAC .... Kinetics and Catalysis
KAC .... Komatsu America Corp.
KAC .... Korean American Coalition (EA)
KAC .... Kuwait Airways Corp. [*ICAO designator*] (FAAC)
KACB .... San Angelo, TX [*Television station call letters*]
KACC .... Alvin, TX [*FM radio station call letters*]
KACC .... Kaiser Aluminum & Chemical Corp. (MCD)
KACC .... Korean-American Chamber of Commerce [*Later, AAACC*]
KACD .... Kansas Association of Soil Conservation Districts (SRA)
KACD .... Santa Monica, CA [*FM radio station call letters*]
KACE .... Inglewood, CA [*FM radio station call letters*]
KACEE .... Kansas Advisory Council on Environmental Education (EDAC)
KACF .... Korean-American Cultural Foundation (EA)
KACH .... Preston, ID [*AM radio station call letters*]
KACHA .... Kentuckiana Automated Clearing House (TBD)
KACHAPAG... Karlsruhe Charged Particle Group (NITA)
KACI .... The Dalles, OR [*AM radio station call letters*]
KACIA .... Korea-American Commerce and Industry Association [*Later, KS*]
KACI-FM ...... The Dalles, OR [*FM radio station call letters*]
KACK .... Nantucket [*Massachusetts*] [*ICAO location identifier*] (ICLI)
KACL-FM ...... Bismarck, ND [*FM radio station call letters*] (RBYB)
KACO-FM ...... Ardmore, OK [*FM radio station call letters*] (RBYB)
KACP .... Custer, SD [*FM radio station call letters*]
KACP .... Kansas Association of Chiefs of Police (SRA)
KACQ .... Lometa, TX [*FM radio station call letters*] (RBYB)
KACS .... Chehalis, WA [*FM radio station call letters*]
KACT .... Andrews, TX [*AM radio station call letters*]
KACT .... Waco/Waco Municipal [*Texas*] [*ICAO location identifier*] (ICLI)
KACT-FM ...... Andrews, TX [*FM radio station call letters*]
KACU .... Abilene, TX [*FM radio station call letters*]
KACV .... Amarillo, TX [*FM radio station call letters*]
KACV-TV ...... Amarillo, TX [*Television station call letters*]
KACW .... North Bend, OR [*FM radio station call letters*]
KACY .... Atlantic City/Atlantic City [*New Jersey*] [*ICAO location identifier*] (ICLI)
KACY .... Lafayette, LA [*AM radio station call letters*]
KAD .... Kadena Air Base, Ryuku Islands (NASA)
KAD .... Kadrey Energy [*Vancouver Stock Exchange symbol*]
KAD .... Kaduna [*Nigeria*] [*Airport symbol*] (OAG)
KAD .... Karad [*India*] [*Seismograph station code, US Geological Survey*] (SEIS)

KAD	Keyboard and Display [*Computer science*]
KADA	Ada, OK [*AM radio station call letters*]
KADA-FM	Ada, OK [*FM radio station call letters*]
KADD	Laughlin, NV [*FM radio station call letters*]
KADE	San Luis Obispo, CA [*Television station call letters*]
KaDeWe	Kaufhaus des Westens [*Department Store of the West*] [*Germany*]
KADF	Kuwait Air Defense Force (MCD)
KADI	Republic, MO [*FM radio station call letters*]
KADM	Ardmore [*Oklahoma*] [*ICAO location identifier*] (ICLI)
KADM	Odessa, TX [*FM radio station call letters*]
KADN	Lafayette, LA [*Television station call letters*]
KADOS	Knowledge-Based Automated Design of Silencers [*Automotive engineering*]
KADP	Kaduna State Agricultural Development Project [*Nigeria*] (ECON)
KADQ	Rexburg, ID [*FM radio station call letters*]
KADR	Elkader, IA [*AM radio station call letters*]
KADS	Elk City, OK [*AM radio station call letters*]
KADS	Korea Air Defense System (CINC)
KADU	Hibbing, MN [*FM radio station call letters*]
KADU	Kenya African Democratic Union [*Political party*] (PPW)
KADV	Modesto, CA [*FM radio station call letters*]
KADW	Camp Springs/Andrews Air Force Base [*Maryland*] [*ICAO location identifier*] (ICLI)
KADX	Houston, AK [*FM radio station call letters*]
KADY	Oxnard, CA [*Television station call letters*]
KAE	Kaena [*Hawaii*] [*Seismograph station code, US Geological Survey*] (SEIS)
KAE	Kake [*Alaska*] [*Airport symbol*] (OAG)
KAE	Knitting Arts Expo (TSPED)
KAEC	Kentucky Association of Electric Cooperatives (SRA)
KAEDS	Keystone Association for Educational Data Systems (HGAA)
KAEF	Arcata, CA [*Television station call letters*]
KAEH	Beaumont, CA [*FM radio station call letters*]
KAEP	Spokane, WA [*FM radio station call letters*] (RBYB)
KAET	Phoenix, AZ [*Television station call letters*]
KAEX	Alexandria/England Air Force Base [*Louisiana*] [*ICAO location identifier*] (ICLI)
KAEZ	Amarillo, TX [*FM radio station call letters*]
KAF	Conglutinogen-Activating Factor (STED)
KAF	Kafue International Air Services Ltd. [*Zambia*] [*FAA designator*] (FAAC)
KAF	Karato [*Papua New Guinea*] [*Airport symbol*] (OAG)
KAF	Kenya Air Force
KAF	Khmer [*Cambodia*] Air Force (VNW)
KAF	Killer-Assistng Factor (DAVI)
KAF	Kinase-Activating Factor [*Organic chemistry*] (DAVI)
KAF	Kuwaiti Air Force (DOMA)
KAFB	Keesler Air Force Base [*Mississippi*]
KAFB	Kirtland Air Force Base [*New Mexico*]
KAFC	Kenny Antcliff Fan Club (EA)
KAFE	Bellingham, WA [*FM radio station call letters*]
KAFF	Flagstaff, AZ [*AM radio station call letters*]
KAFF-FM	Flagstaff, AZ [*FM radio station call letters*]
KAFFR	Kaffaria [*South Africa*] (ROG)
KAFH	Ku-Band Antenna Feed Horn
KAFN-FM	Gould, AR [*FM radio station call letters*] (BROA)
KAFO	Knee-Ankle-Foot Orthosis [*Medicine*]
KAFP	Kansas Academy of Family Physicians (SRA)
KAFP	Kentucky Academy of Family Physicians (SRA)
KAFR	Angel Fire, NM [*FM radio station call letters*]
KAFT	Fayetteville, AR [*Television station call letters*]
KAFU	Enid, OK [*Television station call letters*]
KAFW	Wilson, AR [*FM radio station call letters*] (RBYB)
KAFX-FM	Diboll, TX [*FM radio station call letters*]
KAFY	Bakersfield, CA [*AM radio station call letters*]
KAG	Cryptographic Aid, General Publication (CET)
KAG	Kagoshima [*Japan*] [*Seismograph station code, US Geological Survey*] (SEIS)
KAG	Kagoshima Space Center [*Japan*]
KAG	Kelvin Astatic Galvanometer [*Electronics*]
KAGA	Santa Ynez, CA [*FM radio station call letters*]
KAGC	Bryan, TX [*AM radio station call letters*]
KAGE	Winona, MN [*AM radio station call letters*]
KAGE-FM	Winona, MN [*FM radio station call letters*]
KAGG	Madisonville, TX [*FM radio station call letters*]
KAGH	Crossett, AR [*AM radio station call letters*]
KAGH-FM	Crossett, AR [*FM radio station call letters*]
KAGI	Grants Pass, OR [*AM radio station call letters*]
KAGI	Kesatuan Aksi Guru Indonesia [*Action Front of Indonesian Teachers*]
KAGJ	Ephraim, UT [*FM radio station call letters*]
KAGL	El Dorado, AR [*FM radio station call letters*] (RBYB)
KAGM	Strasburg, CO [*FM radio station call letters*]
KAGO	Klamath Falls, OR [*AM radio station call letters*]
KAGO-FM	Klamath Falls, OR [*FM radio station call letters*]
KAGP	Grants, NM [*FM radio station call letters*]
KAGR	Bemidji, MN [*Television station call letters*] (BROA)
KAGR	Morro Bay, CA [*FM radio station call letters*] (RBYB)
KAGU	Spokane, WA [*FM radio station call letters*]
KAGY	Port Sulphur, LA [*AM radio station call letters*]
KAH	Keilschrifttexte aus Assur Historischen Inhalts [*A publication*] (BJA)
KAH	Kent Aviation Ltd. [*Canada ICAO designator*] (FAAC)
KAH	Kiloampere Hour (IAA)
KAHF-FM	Ortonville, MN [*FM radio station call letters*] (RBYB)
KAHI	Auburn, CA [*AM radio station call letters*]
KAHI	Keilschrifttexte aus Assur Historischen Inhalts [*A publication*] (BJA)

KAHK-FM	Georgetown, TX [*FM radio station call letters*] (BROA)
Kahler	Kahler Corp. [*Associated Press*] (SAG)
KAHM	Prescott, AZ [*FM radio station call letters*]
KAHO	Junction, TX [*FM radio station call letters*]
KAHP	Kentucky Allied Health Project (EDAC)
KAHR	Poplar Bluff, MO [*FM radio station call letters*]
KAHRP	Knob-Associated Histidine-Rich Protein [*Cytology*]
KAHS	Thousand Oaks, CA [*AM radio station call letters*] (RBYB)
KAHSLC	Knoxville Area Health Science Consortium [*Library network*]
KAHU	Hilo, HI [*AM radio station call letters*]
KAHX-FM	Ingleside, TX [*FM radio station call letters*] (RBYB)
KAHY	Myrtle Point, OR [*FM radio station call letters*]
KAHZ	Fort Worth, TX [*AM radio station call letters*]
KAI	Kaieteur [*Guyana*] [*Airport symbol*] (OAG)
KAI	Kaimata [*New Zealand*] [*Seismograph station code, US Geological Survey*] (SEIS)
KAI	Kanaanaeische und Aramaeische Inschriften [*A publication*] (BJA)
KAI	Kazan Aviation Institute
KAI	Keep America Independent [*Defunct*] (EA)
KAI	Korean Affairs Institute (EA)
KAI	Kurzweil Applied Intelligence [*Computer science*]
KAIC	Komatsu America Industries Corp.
KAID	Boise, ID [*Television station call letters*]
KAIE	Honolulu, HI [*Television station call letters*] (BROA)
KAIG	Kearfott Acceleration Integrating Gyroscope
KAIH	Jacksboro, TX [*FM radio station call letters*] (RBYB)
KAII	Kiddie Academy International, Inc. [*NASDAQ symbol*] (SAG)
KAII	Kiddie Academy Intl [*NASDAQ symbol*] (TTSB)
KAII	Wailuku, HI [*Television station call letters*]
KAIIW	Kiddie Academy Intl Wrrt [*NASDAQ symbol*] (TTSB)
KAIL	Fresno, CA [*Television station call letters*]
KAIM	Honolulu, HI [*AM radio station call letters*]
KAIM-FM	Honolulu, HI [*FM radio station call letters*]
KAIN	Vidalia, LA [*FM radio station call letters*]
KAIO	Rio Grande City, TX [*Television station call letters*] (BROA)
KAIR-AM	Atchison, KS [*AM radio station call letters*] (RBYB)
KAIR-FM	Horton, KS [*FM radio station call letters*] (RBYB)
KAIS	Korean Air Intelligence System (MCD)
KaisA	Kaiser Aluminum & Chemical Corp. [*Associated Press*] (SAG)
KaisAl	Kaiser Aluminum & Chemical Corp. [*Associated Press*] (SAG)
KAIST	Korea Advanced Institute of Science and Technology [*Seoul*] [*Information service or system*] (IID)
KaisVent	Kaiser Ventures, Inc. [*Associated Press*] (SAG)
KAIT	Jonesboro, AR [*Television station call letters*]
KAIT	Katzman Automatic Imaging Telescope [*University of California*]
KAIU-FM	Grants, NM [*FM radio station call letters*] (BROA)
KAJ	Kajaani [*Finland*] [*Airport symbol*] (OAG)
KAJ	Kashiwara [*Japan*] [*Seismograph station code, US Geological Survey*] (SEIS)
KAJ	Keilschrifttexte aus Assur Juridischen Inhalts [*A publication*] (BJA)
KAJA	San Antonio, TX [*FM radio station call letters*]
KAJB	Calipatria, CA [*Television station call letters*] (BROA)
KAJF	Kids Against Junk Food [*An association*] (EA)
KAJI	Keilschrifttexte aus Assur Juridischen Inhalts [*A publication*] (BJA)
KAJI	Point Comfort, TX [*FM radio station call letters*] (RBYB)
KAJK	Fortuna, CA [*AM radio station call letters*]
KAJK-FM	Ferndale, CA [*FM radio station call letters*] (RBYB)
KAJL	Winters, TX [*FM radio station call letters*] (RBYB)
KAJN	Crowley, LA [*FM radio station call letters*]
KAJO	Grants Pass, OR [*AM radio station call letters*]
KAJP	Firebaugh, CA [*FM radio station call letters*] (RBYB)
KAJQ	Sibley, IA [*FM radio station call letters*] (RBYB)
KAJW	Tolleson, AZ [*Television station call letters*] (RBYB)
KAJX	Aspen, CO [*FM radio station call letters*]
KAJZ-FM	Killeen, TX [*FM radio station call letters*] (RBYB)
KAK	Kakioka [*Japan*] [*Seismograph station code, US Geological Survey*] (SEIS)
KAK	Key-Auto-Key [*Computer science*]
KAK	Kungliga Automobil Klubben
KAKA-FM	Salina, KS [*FM radio station call letters*] (BROA)
KAKC	Tulsa, OK [*AM radio station call letters*]
KAKD	Eureka, CA [*FM radio station call letters*] (RBYB)
KAKE	Wichita, KS [*Television station call letters*]
KAKJ	Marianna, AR [*FM radio station call letters*]
KAKM	Anchorage, AK [*Television station call letters*]
kakm	Kakemono (VRA)
KAKN	Naknek, AK [*FM radio station call letters*]
KAKO	Gooding, ID [*FM radio station call letters*] (RBYB)
KAKP	Bagdad, AZ [*FM radio station call letters*] (RBYB)
KAKP-FM	Chino Valley, AZ [*FM radio station call letters*] (BROA)
KAKQ	Fairbanks, AK [*FM radio station call letters*]
KAKQ-FM	Fairbanks, AK [*FM radio station call letters*]
KAKR	Akron [*Ohio*] [*ICAO location identifier*] (ICLI)
KAKR-FM	Sterling City, TX [*FM radio station call letters*] (RBYB)
KAKT-FM	Phoenix, OR [*FM radio station call letters*] (RBYB)
KAKU-FM	Springfield, MO [*FM radio station call letters*] (RBYB)
KAKV-FM	Lompoc, CA [*FM radio station call letters*] (RBYB)
KAKW	Kileen, TX [*TV station call letters*] (RBYB)
KAKX	Mendocino, CA [*FM radio station call letters*] (RBYB)
KAKZ	Juneau, AK [*FM radio station call letters*] (RBYB)
KAL	Caltech Data Ltd. [*Vancouver Stock Exchange symbol*]
KAL	Kalamazoo [*Diocesan abbreviation*] [*Michigan*] (TOCD)
KAL	Kalamein [*Trademark*]
KAL	Kalendae [*The Kalends*] [*First day of the ancient Roman month*]
KAL	Kalium [*Potassium*] [*Pharmacy*]

Kal	Kalium [*Potassium*] (STED)
Kal	Kallah (BJA)
KAL	Kallmann [*Syndrome*] [*Medicine*] (DMAA)
KAL	Kalocsa [*Hungary*] [*Seismograph station code, US Geological Survey Closed*] (SEIS)
KAL	Kaltag [*Alaska*] [*Airport symbol*] (OAG)
KAL	Kappa Application Language [*Artificial intelligence system*] [*IntelliCorp*] (PCM)
KAL	Key Assets List (COE)
KAL	Keywords and Learning (AIE)
KAL	Korean Air Lines Co. Ltd. [*ICAO designator*] (FAAC)
KAL	Korean Air Lines, Inc.
KALA	Davenport, IA [*FM radio station call letters*]
KALB	Albany/Albany [*New York*] [*ICAO location identifier*] (ICLI)
KALB-TV	Alexandria, LA [*Television station call letters*]
KALC	Denver, CO [*FM radio station call letters*]
KALC	Krypton Absorption in Liquid Carbon Dioxide [*Nuclear energy*] (NRCH)
KALD	Kalamein [*Trademark*] Door
KALDAS	Kidsgrove ALGOL [*Algorithmic Language*] Digital Analogue Simulation [*Computer science British*]
KALE	Richland, WA [*AM radio station call letters*]
KALF	Red Bluff, CA [*FM radio station call letters*]
KALG	Chadron, NE [*FM radio station call letters*] (RBYB)
KALI	Alice/International [*Texas*] [*ICAO location identifier*] (ICLI)
KALI	San Gabriel, CA [*AM radio station call letters*]
KALI-FM	Santa Ana, CA [*FM radio station call letters*] (RBYB)
KALK	Winfield, TX [*FM radio station call letters*]
KALL	Salt Lake City, UT [*AM radio station call letters*]
KALM	Thayer, MO [*AM radio station call letters*]
KALN	Iola, KS [*AM radio station call letters*]
KALO	Port Arthur, TX [*AM radio station call letters*]
KALP	Alpine, TX [*FM radio station call letters*]
KAL PPT	Kali Praeparatum [*Prepared Kali*] [*Carbonate of potash*] [*Pharmacy*] (ROG)
KALQ	Alamosa, CO [*FM radio station call letters*]
KALR	Hot Springs, AR [*FM radio station call letters*]
KalR	Kallah Rabbati (BJA)
KALS	Kalispell, MT [*FM radio station call letters*]
KALT	Atlanta, TX [*AM radio station call letters*]
KALT-FM	Alturas, CA [*FM radio station call letters*] (BROA)
KALU	Langston, OK [*FM radio station call letters*]
KALV	Alva, OK [*AM radio station call letters*]
KALW	San Francisco, CA [*FM radio station call letters*]
KALX	Berkeley, CA [*FM radio station call letters*]
KALY	Los Ranchos de Albuquerque, NM [*AM radio station call letters*]
KAM	Benedictine College, South Campus, Atchison, KS [*Library symbol Library of Congress*] (LCLS)
KAM	Kamaran Island [*South Arabia (Yemen)*] [*Airport symbol*] (AD)
kam	Kamba [*MARC language code Library of Congress*] (LCCP)
Kam	Kames' Dictionary of Decisions, Scotch Court of Session [*A publication*]
Kam	Kames' Remarkable Decisions, Scotch Court of Session [*2 vols.*] [*1716-52*] [*A publication*] (DLA)
KAM	Kameyama [*Japan*] [*Seismograph station code, US Geological Survey*] (SEIS)
KAM	Keep-Alive Memory [*Computer science*]
KAM	Kehillath Anshe Mayriv (BJA)
KAM	Kenya African Movement
KAM	Kinematic Analysis Method
KAM	Knudsen Absolute Manometer [*Physics*]
KAM	Kolmogorov-Arnold-Moser [*Statistical mechanics*]
KAMA	Amarillo/Amarillo Air Terminal [*Texas*] [*ICAO location identifier*] (ICLI)
KAMA	El Paso, TX [*AM radio station call letters*]
KAMA	Korean-American Medical Association (EA)
Kaman	Kaman Corp. [*Associated Press*] (SAG)
KAMB	Merced, CA [*FM radio station call letters*]
KAMC	Komatsu America Manufacturing Corp. [*Chattanooga, TN*]
KAMC	Lubbock, TX [*Television station call letters*]
KAMD	Camden, AR [*AM radio station call letters*]
KAMD-FM	Camden, AR [*FM radio station call letters*] (RBYB)
KAME	Reno, NV [*Television station call letters*]
Kam Eluc	Kames' Elucidation of the Laws of Scotland [*A publication*] (DLA)
Kam Eq	Kames' Principles of Equity [*A publication*] (DLA)
Kames	Kames' Dictionary of Decisions, Scotch Court of Session [*A publication*] (DLA)
Kames	Kames' Remarkable Decisions, Scotch Court of Session [*2 vols.*] [*1716-52*] [*A publication*] (DLA)
Kames Dec	Kames' Dictionary of Decisions, Scotch Court of Session [*A publication*] (DLA)
Kames Dict Dec	Kames' Dictionary of Decisions, Scotch Court of Session [*A publication*] (DLA)
Kames Elucid	Kames' Elucidation of the Laws of Scotland [*A publication*] (DLA)
Kames Eq	Kames' Principles of Equity [*A publication*] (DLA)
Kames Rem	Kames' Remarkable Decisions, Scotch Court of Session [*2 vols.*] [*1716-52*] [*A publication*] (DLA)
Kames Rem Dec	Kames' Remarkable Decisions [*Scotland*] [*A publication*] (DLA)
Kames Sel Dec	Kames' Select Decisions [*Scotland*] [*A publication*] (DLA)
KAMFES	Kentucky Association of Milk, Food, and Environmental Sanitarians (SRA)
KAMFR	Kinesthetic Application of Mechanical Force Reflection
KAMFT	Kansas Association of Marriage and Family Therapy (SRA)
KAMFT	Kentucky Association for Marriage and Family Therapy (SRA)
KAMG	Victoria, TX [*AM radio station call letters*]
KAMI	Cozad, NE [*AM radio station call letters*]
KAMI	Kasatuan Aksi Mahasiswa Indonesia [*Political party*] (BARN)
KAMI-FM	Cozad, NE [*FM radio station call letters*]
KAMJ	Gosnell, AR [*FM radio station call letters*] (RBYB)
KAMK-FM	Forest City, IA [*FM radio station call letters*] (RBYB)
KAML	Gillette, WY [*FM radio station call letters*]
KAML	Kenedy-Karnes City, TX [*AM radio station call letters*]
Kam L Tr	Kames' Historical Law Tracts [*Scotland*] [*A publication*] (DLA)
KAMM	Madison, SD [*FM radio station call letters*] (RBYB)
KAMN	Kaman Corp. [*NASDAQ symbol*] (NQ)
KAMNA	Kaman Corp. Cl'A' [*NASDAQ symbol*] (TTSB)
KAMNZ	Kaman Cp $3.25 Ser 2 Cv Dep Pfd [*NASDAQ symbol*] (TTSB)
KAMO	Rogers, AR [*AM radio station call letters*]
KAMO-FM	Rogers, AR [*FM radio station call letters*]
KAMP	El Centro, CA [*AM radio station call letters*]
KAMQ	Carlsbad, NM [*AM radio station call letters*]
KAMR	Amarillo, TX [*Television station call letters*]
Kam Rem	Kames' Remarkable Decisions, Scotch Court of Session [*2 vols.*] [*1716-52*] [*A publication*] (DLA)
KAMS	Korea Ammunition Management System (MCD)
KAMS	Mammoth Spring, AR [*FM radio station call letters*]
Kam Sel	Kames' Select Decisions [*Scotland*] [*A publication*] (DLA)
Kam Sel Dec	Kames' Select Decisions [*Scotland*] [*A publication*] (DLA)
KAMT	Juneau, AK [*FM radio station call letters*] (RBYB)
KAMU	College Station, TX [*FM radio station call letters*]
KAMU-TV	College Station, TX [*Television station call letters*]
KAMX	Luling, TX [*FM radio station call letters*] (RBYB)
KAMY	Lubbock, TX [*FM radio station call letters*]
KAN	Kanazawa [*Japan*] [*Seismograph station code, US Geological Survey*] (SEIS)
kan	Kannada [*MARC language code Library of Congress*] (LCCP)
KAN	Kano [*Nigeria*] [*Airport symbol*] (OAG)
KAN	Kansas
Kan	Kansas (ODBW)
Kan	Kansas Supreme Court Reports [*A publication*] (DLA)
Kan	Kantorei [*Record label*] [*Germany*]
KAN	Kriegsausruestungsnachweisung [*Table of Basic Allowances*] [*German military - World War II*]
KANA	Kamut Association of North America (NTPA)
Kan Admin Regs	Kansas Administration Regulations [*A publication*] (DLA)
Kan Ann	Vernon's Kansas Statutes, Annotated [*A publication*] (DLA)
Kan App	Kansas Appeals Reports [*A publication*] (DLA)
Kanb	Kaneb Services, Inc. [*Associated Press*] (SAG)
Kan City L Rep	Kansas City Law Reporter [*A publication*] (DLA)
Kan City L Rev	Kansas City Law Review [*A publication*] (DLA)
Kan Civ Pro Stat Ann	Vernon's Kansas Statutes, Annotated, Code of Civil Procedure [*A publication*] (DLA)
Kan Civ Pro Stat Ann (Vernon)	Vernon's Kansas Statutes, Annotated, Code of Civil Procedure [*A publication*] (DLA)
Kan CL & IWC	Kansas Commission of Labor and Industry Workmen's Compensation Department Reports [*A publication*] (DLA)
Kan CL Rep	Kansas City Law Reporter [*A publication*] (DLA)
Kan Crim Code & Code of Crim Proc	Criminal Code and Code of Criminal Procedure [*Kansas*] [*A publication*] (DLA)
Kan Crim Code & Code of Crim Proc (Vernon)	Vernon's Kansas Statutes, Annotated, Criminal Code and Code of Criminal Procedure [*A publication*] (DLA)
Kan Ct App	Kansas Appellate Reports [*A publication*] (DLA)
KAND	Corsicana, TX [*AM radio station call letters*]
K & B	Kotze and Barber's Transvaal (High Court) Reports [*1885-88*] [*A publication*] (DLA)
K & B Dig	Kerford and Box's Victorian Digest [*A publication*] (DLA)
K & CL	Kensington and Chelsea Law Group [*British*]
K & D	Kitchen and Dining Room [*Real estate terminology*]
K & E Conv	Key and Elphinstone's Conveyancing [*15th ed.*] [*1953-54*] [*A publication*] (DLA)
K & F NSW	Knox and Fitzhardinge's New South Wales Reports [*A publication*] (DLA)
K & G	Keane and Grant's English Registration Appeal Cases [*1854-62*] [*A publication*] (DLA)
K & G	Kerbing and Guttering [*British*] (ADA)
K & Gr	Keane and Grant's English Registration Appeal Cases [*1854-62*] [*A publication*] (DLA)
K & GRC	Keane and Grant's English Registration Appeal Cases [*1854-62*] [*A publication*] (DLA)
KANDIDATS	Kansas Digital Data System
Kan Dig	Hatcher's Kansas Digest [*A publication*] (DLA)
K & J	Kay and Johnson's English Vice-Chancellors' Reports [*69, 70 English Reprint*] [*A publication*] (DLA)
K & J	Kenrick & Jefferson (DGA)
K & O	Knapp and Ombler's English Election Cases [*A publication*] (DLA)
K & R	Kent and Radcliff's Law of New York, Revision of 1801 [*A publication*] (DLA)
K and R	Kidnaping and Ransom [*Insurance policy*]
K & W	Kames and Woodhouselee's Folio Dictionary, Scotch Court of Session [*A publication*] (DLA)
K & W Dic	Kames and Woodhouselee's Folio Dictionary, Scotch Court of Session [*A publication*] (DLA)
K & Z	Kipp and Zonen Recorders
KANE	New Iberia, LA [*AM radio station call letters*]
Kaneb	Kaneb Services, Inc. [*Associated Press*] (SAG)
Kanex	Kansai Agricultural Commodities Exchange (NUMA)
KANGA	Kangaroo (DSUE)
KANG-FM	Carrington, ND [*FM radio station call letters*] (RBYB)
KANI	Wharton, TX [*AM radio station call letters*]
KANJ-FM	Giddings, TX [*FM radio station call letters*] (RBYB)

KankakB ...... Kankakkee Bancorp, Inc. [*Associated Press*] (SAG)
KANL .... Elko, NV [*Television station call letters*] (RBYB)
Kan Law ...... Kansas Lawyer [*A publication*] (DLA)
Kan LJ .... Kansas Law Journal [*A publication*] (DLA)
KANM .... Winnemucca, NV [*Television station call letters*] (RBYB)
KANN .... Roy, UT [*AM radio station call letters*]
KANO-FM ..... Hilo, HI [*FM radio station call letters*] (BROA)
KANP .... St. Charles, MN [*FM radio station call letters*] (RBYB)
KanPip .... Kaneb Pipe Line Partners Ltd. [*Associated Press*] (SAG)
KanPipSn ...... Kaneb Pipe Line Partners LP [*Associated Press*] (SAG)
KANQ .... Grand Marais, MN [*FM radio station call letters*] (RBYB)
KANR .... Belle Plaine, KS [*FM radio station call letters*]
KANr .... Kanamycin Resistant [*Genetics*]
KANS .... Kansas (AFM)
Kans .... Kansas (ODBW)
Kans .... Kansas Reports [*A publication*] (DLA)
KANS .... Larned, KS [*AM radio station call letters*]
KANS .... Osage City, KS [*FM radio station call letters*] (RBYB)
Kans App ..... Kansas Appeals Reports [*A publication*] (DLA)
Kansas LJ .... Kansas Law Journal [*A publication*] (DLA)
Kansas R ..... Kansas Reports [*A publication*] (DLA)
Kans BA .... Kansas City Bar Journal [*A publication*] (DLA)
Kan SCC ...... Kansas State Corporation Commission Reports [*A publication*] (DLA)
Kan Sess Laws ... Session Laws of Kansas [*A publication*] (DLA)
Kans R .... Kansas Reports [*A publication*] (DLA)
Kans St U .... Kansas State University of Agriculture and Applied Science (GAGS)
Kan Stat ...... Kansas Statutes [*A publication*] (DLA)
Kan Stat Ann ... Kansas Statutes Annotated [*A publication*] (AAGC)
Kan St LJ ..... Kansas State Law Journal [*A publication*] (DLA)
Kan Subject Ann Vernon's ... Vernon's Kansas Statutes, Annotated [*A publication*] (DLA)
KANT .... Roseau, MN [*FM radio station call letters*] (RBYB)
KANU .... Kenya African National Union [*Political party*] (PPW)
KANU .... Lawrence, KS [*FM radio station call letters*]
Kan UCC Ann (Vernon) ... Vernon's Kansas Statutes, Annotated, Uniform Commercial Code [*A publication*] (DLA)
Kan U Lawy ... Kansas University Lawyer [*A publication*] (DLA)
Kan Univ Lawy ... Kansas University Lawyer [*A publication*] (DLA)
KANW .... Albuquerque, NM [*FM radio station call letters*]
KANX-FM ..... Pine Bluff, AR [*FM radio station call letters*] (RBYB)
KANZ .... Garden City, KS [*FM radio station call letters*]
KANZUS .... Korea, Australia, New Zealand, and the United States
kao .... Kaolin (BARN)
KAO .... Kappa Alpha Order
KAO .... Kinesthetic Anharmonic Oscillator [*Facetious term for a swing*]
KAO .... Kirtland Area Office [*Department of Energy*]
KAO .... Knee-Ankle Orthosis [*Medicine*] (DAVI)
KAO .... Knights of Aquarius Order (EAIO)
KAO .... Kuiper Airborne Observatory [*NASA*]
KAO .... Kuusamo [*Finland*] [*Airport symbol*] (OAG)
KAOA EXP STN ... New Orleans, LA [*Radio expansion station*] (RBYB)
KAOB .... Devils Lake, ND [*FM radio station call letters*] (RBYB)
KAOC .... Cavalier, ND [*FM radio station call letters*] (RBYB)
KAOD .... Babbitt, MN [*FM radio station call letters*] (RBYB)
KAOE .... Hilo, HI [*FM radio station call letters*]
KAOG .... Jonesboro, AR [*FM radio station call letters*] (RBYB)
KAOH-FM ..... Lompoc, CA [*FM radio station call letters*] (RBYB)
KAOI .... Kihei, HI [*AM radio station call letters*]
KAOI-FM ...... Wailuku, HI [*FM radio station call letters*]
KAOK .... Lake Charles, LA [*AM radio station call letters*]
KAOL .... Carrollton, MO [*AM radio station call letters*]
KAOM .... Kansas Association of Osteopathic Medicine (SRA)
KAOR .... Vermillion, SD [*FM radio station call letters*]
KAOS .... Killer as an Organized Sport [*Campus game*]
KAOS .... Olympia, WA [*FM radio station call letters*]
KAOW-FM .... Fort Smith, AR [*FM radio station call letters*] (RBYB)
KAOX-FM ..... Kemmerer, WY [*FM radio station call letters*] (RBYB)
KAOY .... Kealakekua, HI [*FM radio station call letters*]
KAP .... CapMAC Holdings [*NYSE symbol*] (SAG)
KAP .... Hyannis Air Service, Inc. [*ICAO designator*] (FAAC)
KAP .... Kaphearst Resources [*Vancouver Stock Exchange symbol*]
KAP .... Kids Against Pollution
KAP .... Kinematical Analysis Program
KAP .... Knowledge, Aptitudes, and Practices [*Fertility*] (STED)
KAP .... Knowledge, Attitudes, and Practice [*Sociology*]
KAP .... Kuwait Action Plan [*Advisory Committee on Pollution of the Sea*]
KAPA .... Kaneohe, HI [*TV station call letters*] (RBYB)
KAPA .... Potassium Aminopropylamide [*Organic chemistry*]
KAPB .... Marksville, LA [*AM radio station call letters*]
KAPB-FM ..... Marksville, LA [*FM radio station call letters*]
KAPC-FM ..... Butte, MT [*FM radio station call letters*] (RBYB)
KAPCS .... Kansas Association of Private Career Schools (SRA)
KAPE .... Cape Girardeau, MO [*AM radio station call letters*]
KAPE .... Kansas Association of Public Employees (SRA)
KAPE .... Keeping the Army in the Public Eye [*British military*] (DMA)
KAPF-FM ..... Taos, NM [*FM radio station call letters*] (RBYB)
KAPI .... Kasatuan Aksi Peladjar Indonesia [*Political party*] (BARN)
KAPI-FM ...... Ruston, LA [*FM radio station call letters*] (RBYB)
KAPK-FM ..... Grants Pass, OR [*FM radio station call letters*] (RBYB)
KAPL .... Kennedy Approved Parts List [*NASA*] (KSC)
KAPL .... Knolls Atomic Power Laboratory [*Schenectady, NY*] [*Department of Energy*]
KAPL .... Phoenix, OR [*AM radio station call letters*] (RBYB)
K-APM .... Kennedy Space Center Automated Payloads Plan/Requirement (NAKS)
KAPM-FM .... Alexandria, LA [*FM radio station call letters*] (RBYB)
K-APN .... KSC [*Kennedy Space Center*] Automated Payloads Notice [*NASA*] (NASA)
KAPN .... Salt Lake City, UT [*AM radio station call letters*]
KAPO .... Kameradschaftpolizei (BJA)
KAPP .... Key Asset Protection Plan [*National Guard*] (INF)
KAPP .... Knolls Atomic Power Plant
KAPP .... Yakima, WA [*Television station call letters*]
K-APPS .... KSC [*Kennedy Space Center*] Automated Payloads Project Specification [*NASA*] (NASA)
KAPR .... Douglas, AZ [*AM radio station call letters*]
KAPS .... Kawasaki Automatic Power-Drive System [*Kawasaki Motors Corp.*]
KAPS .... Kuopio Atherosclerosis Prevention Study
KAPS .... Mount Vernon, WA [*AM radio station call letters*]
KAPSE .... Kernel APSE [*ADA Program Support Environment*] [*Computer science*]
KapsnSn ...... Kapson Senior Quarters Corp. [*Associated Press*] (SAG)
KAPU-FM ..... Amarillo, TX [*FM radio station call letters*] (RBYB)
KAPV-FM ..... Elma, WA [*FM radio station call letters*] (RBYB)
KAPY .... Port Angeles, WA [*AM radio station call letters*]
KAPZ .... Bald Knob, AR [*AM radio station call letters*]
KAQA-FM ..... Kilauea, HI [*FM radio station call letters*] (RBYB)
KAQD-FM ..... Abilene, TX [*FM radio station call letters*] (RBYB)
KAQE-FM ..... St. Martinville, LA [*FM radio station call letters*] (RBYB)
KAQF-FM ..... Clovis, NM [*FM radio station call letters*] (RBYB)
KAQQ .... Spokane, WA [*AM radio station call letters*]
KAQR-FM ..... Helena, MT [*FM radio station call letters*] (RBYB)
KAQS .... Shawnee, OK [*TV station call letters*] (RBYB)
KAQU .... Huntington, TX [*FM radio station call letters*]
KAQX-FM ..... Bonanza, OR [*FM radio station call letters*] (RBYB)
KAQY .... Columbia, LA [*Television station call letters*] (BROA)
Kar .... Indian Law Reports, Karachi Series [*A publication*] (DLA)
KAR .... Kamarang [*Guyana*] [*Airport symbol*] (OAG)
KAR .... Kansas Administrative Regulations [*A publication*]
KAR .... Kap Resources [*Vancouver Stock Exchange symbol*]
KAR .... Karabiner [*Carbine*] [*German military - World War II*]
KAR .... Karachi [*Pakistan*] [*Seismograph station code, US Geological Survey*] (SEIS)
KAR .... Kar-Air OY [*Finland ICAO designator*] (FAAC)
kar .... Karen [*MARC language code Library of Congress*] (LCCP)
Kar .... Karolus de Tocco [*Flourished, 13th century*] [*Authority cited in pre-1607 legal work*] (DSA)
KAR .... Kars [*Turkey*] [*Airport symbol*] (AD)
KAR .... Keilschrifttexte aus Assur Religioesen Inhalts [*A publication*] (BJA)
KAR .... Kentucky Administrative Regulations [*A publication*] (AAGC)
KAR .... King's African Rifles [*Military unit*] [*British*]
KAR .... Knot Area Ratio (PDAA)
KAR .... Kodak Automated Registration [*Eastman Kodak Co.*] (CIST)
KAR .... Kodak Automated Retrieval [*Kodak*] [*Microfilm office information system*] (NITA)
Kar .... Pakistan Law Reports, Karachi Series [*A publication*] (DLA)
KARA .... Santa Clara, CA [*FM radio station call letters*]
KARAC .... Kustoms and Rodders Association of Canada
KARB .... Price, UT [*FM radio station call letters*]
KARD .... West Monroe, LA [*Television station call letters*]
KARE .... Koala Corp. [*NASDAQ symbol*] (SAG)
KARE .... Minneapolis, MN [*Television station call letters*]
KARF .... Washington [*District of Columbia*] [*ICAO location identifier*] (ICLI)
KARF-FM ..... Independence, KS [*Television station call letters*] (BROA)
KARG-FM ..... Poteau, OK [*Television station call letters*] (BROA)
KARH-FM ..... Forrest City, AR [*FM radio station call letters*] (BROA)
KARI .... Blaine, WA [*AM radio station call letters*]
KARI .... Keilschrifttexte aus Assur Religioesen Inhalts [*A publication*] (BJA)
KARI .... Ketol-Acid Reductoisomerase [*An enzyme*]
KARK .... Little Rock, AR [*Television station call letters*]
KARL .... Karlsruhe Architectural Language [*Computer science*] (CSR)
KARL .... Tracy, MN [*FM radio station call letters*]
KARM .... Visalia, CA [*FM radio station call letters*]
KARN .... Humnoke, AR [*FM radio station call letters*] (RBYB)
KARN .... Little Rock, AR [*AM radio station call letters*]
KARO .... Caldwell, ID [*FM radio station call letters*] (RBYB)
KARP .... Glencoe, MN [*FM radio station call letters*]
KARPEN .... Karyawan Pegawai Negeri [*Indonesia*]
KARQ .... Ashdown, AR [*FM radio station call letters*]
KARR .... Karrington Health, Inc. [*NASDAQ symbol*] (SAG)
KARR .... Kirkland, WA [*AM radio station call letters*]
KarrHlth .... Karrington Health, Inc. [*Associated Press*] (SAG)
KARS .... Belen, NM [*AM radio station call letters*]
KARS .... Kansas Applied Remote Sensing Program [*University of Kansas*] [*Research center*] (RCD)
KARS .... Kennedy Athletic Recreation and Social [*NASA*] (KSC)
KART .... Jerome, ID [*AM radio station call letters*]
KART .... Watertown/International [*New York*] [*ICAO location identifier*] (ICLI)
KARV .... Russellville, AR [*AM radio station call letters*]
KARV-FM ..... Ola, AR [*FM radio station call letters*] (BROA)
KARW .... Longview, TX [*AM radio station call letters*]
KARX .... Claude, TX [*FM radio station call letters*]
KARY .... Grandview, WA [*FM radio station call letters*]
KARY .... Prosser, WA [*AM radio station call letters*]
KARZ .... Burney, CA [*FM radio station call letters*]
KARZ-FM ..... Marshall, MN [*FM radio station call letters*] (BROA)
KAS .... Benedictine College, North Campus, Atchison, KS [*Library symbol Library of Congress*] (LCLS)
KAS .... Kansas [*Obsolete*] (ROG)
Kas .... Kansas Reports [*A publication*] (DLA)

kas..............	Kashmiri [*MARC language code Library of Congress*] (LCCP)
KAS..............	Kaskada Resources Ltd. [*Vancouver Stock Exchange symbol*]
KAS..............	Kasler Holdings [*NYSE symbol*] (SPSG)
KAS..............	Kastamonu [*Turkey*] [*Seismograph station code, US Geological Survey*] (SEIS)
KAS..............	Katz Adjustment Scales [*Psychology*]
KAS..............	Kenya-Australia Society
KAS..............	Ketoacyl-ACP Synthase [*An enzyme*]
KAS..............	Kingston Air Services [*Canada ICAO designator*] (FAAC)
KAS..............	Kiva Administrative Server [*Computer science*]
KAS..............	Knowledge Access System [*Interface*]
KAS..............	Knowledge Acquisition System
KAS..............	Konrad Adenauer Stiftung [*Germany Political party*]
KAS..............	Kroeber Anthropological Society (EA)
KAS..............	Kulanka Afka Somalyed
KASA	Kentucky Association of School Administrators (SRA)
KASA	Phoenix, AZ [*AM radio station call letters*]
KASA	Santa Fe, NM [*Television station call letters*]
KASB	Bellevue, WA [*FM radio station call letters*]
KASB	Kansas Association of School Boards (SRA)
KASC	Knowledge Availability Systems Center [*University of Pittsburgh*]
KASE	Austin, TX [*FM radio station call letters*]
KASF	Alamosa, CO [*FM radio station call letters*]
KASH	Anchorage, AK [*FM radio station call letters*]
Kash	Kashmir (VRA)
KASH	Kash n'Karry Food Stores [*NASDAQ symbol*] (TTSB)
KASH	Kash n Karry Food Stores, Inc. [*NASDAQ symbol*] (SAG)
KASH	Knowledge, Abilities, Skills, and Habits (STED)
KASH	Knowledge, Attitude, Skills, Habits [*Formula*] [*LIMRA*]
Kashmir LJ...	Kashmir Law Journal [*India*] [*A publication*] (DLA)
KashrK........	Kash n Karry Food Stores, Inc. [*Associated Press*] (SAG)
KASI...........	Ames, IA [*AM radio station call letters*]
KASI...........	Kesatuan Aksi Sardjana Indonesia [*Action Front of Indonesian Scholars*]
KASK-FM	Fairfield, CA [*FM radio station call letters*] (BROA)
KASL	Kansas Association of School Librarians (SRA)
KASL	Newcastle, WY [*AM radio station call letters*]
Kasler Holding Co....	Kasler Corp. [*Associated Press*] (SAG)
KASM........	Albany, MN [*AM radio station call letters*]
KASM-FM ...	Albany, MN [*FM radio station call letters*]
KASN	Pine Bluff, AR [*Television station call letters*]
KASO	Minden, LA [*AM radio station call letters*]
KASO-FM ...	Minden, LA [*FM radio station call letters*]
KASP	Kehr-Activated Sludge Process (PDAA)
Kas R	Kansas Reports [*A publication*] (DLA)
KASR	Perry, OK [*AM radio station call letters*]
KASR-FM	Conway, AR [*FM radio station call letters*] (BROA)
KASR-FM	Perry, OK [*FM radio station call letters*]
KASS	Casper, WY [*FM radio station call letters*] (RBYB)
KASS	Kagan Affective Sensitivity Scales [*Psychology*] (DHP)
Kass...........	Kassinin [*Biochemistry*]
KASS	Kent Automated Serials System [*Kent State University*] [*Automated library system*] (NITA)
KASSP	Kentucky Association of Secondary School Principals (SRA)
KAST..........	Astoria, OR [*AM radio station call letters*]
KAST..........	Kalman Automatic Sequential TMA [*Military*] (CAAL)
KAST..........	Kindergarten Auditory Screening Test [*Otorhinolaryngology*] (DAVI)
KAST-FM	Astoria, OR [*FM radio station call letters*]
KASU	Jonesboro, AR [*FM radio station call letters*]
KASV-FM	Borger, TX [*FM radio station call letters*] (BROA)
KASW	Phoenix, AZ [*Television station call letters*]
KASX-FM	Pine Bluffs, WY [*FM radio station call letters*] (BROA)
KASY	Albuquerque, NM [*FM radio station call letters*]
KASY-TV	Albuquerque, NM [*Television station call letters*]
KAT.............	Asbury Theological Seminary, Wilmore, KY [*OCLC symbol*] (OCLC)
KAT.............	Die Keilinschriften und das Alte Testament [*A publication*] (BJA)
KAT.............	Kaitaia [*New Zealand*] [*Airport symbol*] (OAG)
KAT.............	Kanamycin Acetyltransferase [*An enzyme*]
KAT.............	Kappa Alpha Theta [*Sorority*]
kat	Katal [*Unit of enzyme activity*]
KAT.............	Kattegat Air, AS [*Denmark ICAO designator*] (FAAC)
KAT.............	Key-to-Address Transformation [*Computer science*] (PDAA)
KAT.............	Kizyl-Arvat [*Former USSR Seismograph station code, US Geological Survey*] (SEIS)
KAT.............	Kommentar zum Alten Testament [*A publication*] (BJA)
KATA	Arcata, CA [*AM radio station call letters*]
KATB	Anchorage, AK [*FM radio station call letters*]
KATC	Katz Digital Technologies [*NASDAQ symbol*] (TTSB)
KATC	Katz Digital Technologies, Inc. [*NASDAQ symbol*] (SAG)
KATC	Korean Army Training Center
KATC	Lafayette, LA [*Television station call letters*]
KATCA	Korean-American Technical Cooperation Association
Katch Pr Law...	Katchenovsky's Prize Law [*2nd ed.*] [*1867*] [*A publication*] (DLA)
KATD	Pittsburg, CA [*AM radio station call letters*]
KATE	Albert Lea, MN [*AM radio station call letters*]
KatechBR....	Katechetische Blaetter [*Berlin-Grunewald*] [*A publication*] (BJA)
KATF	Dubuque, IA [*FM radio station call letters*]
KATH	Bozeman, MT [*FM radio station call letters*]
KathM	Die Katholischen Missionen (BJA)
KATI	California, MO [*FM radio station call letters*] (RBYB)
KATJ	George, CA [*FM radio station call letters*]
KATK	Carlsbad, NM [*AM radio station call letters*]
KATK-FM	Carlsbad, NM [*FM radio station call letters*]
KATL..........	Atlanta/The William B. Hartsfield Atlanta International [*Georgia*] [*ICAO location identifier*] (ICLI)
KATL..........	Miles City, MT [*AM radio station call letters*]
KATM	Katmai National Monument
KATM	Modesto, CA [*FM radio station call letters*]
KATN	Fairbanks, AK [*Television station call letters*]
KATO	Safford, AZ [*AM radio station call letters*]
KATP	Amarillo, TX [*FM radio station call letters*]
KATQ	Plentywood, MT [*AM radio station call letters*]
KATQ-FM	Plentywood, MT [*FM radio station call letters*]
KATR	Wray, CO [*FM radio station call letters*]
KATS	Kennedy Space Center Avionics Test Set [*NASA*] (NASA)
KATS	Yakima, WA [*FM radio station call letters*]
KatShing	Katorikku Shingaku [*Catholic Theology*] [*Tokyo*] [*A publication*] (BJA)
KATSI	Kommentar zum Alten Testament [*E. Sellin*] [*A publication*] (BJA)
KATT	Oklahoma City, OK [*FM radio station call letters*]
KATU	Portland, OR [*Television station call letters*]
KATUSA	Korean Augmentation to the United States Army
KATV..........	Little Rock, AR [*Television station call letters*]
KATW..........	Lewiston, ID [*FM radio station call letters*]
KATY..........	Idyllwild, CA [*FM radio station call letters*]
KatyInd	Katy Industries, Inc. [*Formerly, Missour-Kansas-Texas R.R. Co., with Wall Street slang name of "Kathy"*] [*Associated Press*] (SAG)
KATYP	Kallitype (VRA)
KATZ	St. Louis, MO [*AM radio station call letters*]
KatzDig	Katz Digital Technologies, Inc. [*Associated Press*] (SAG)
KatzM	Katz Media Group, Inc. [*Associated Press*] (SAG)
kau.............	Kanuri [*MARC language code Library of Congress*] (LCCP)
KAU	Kaohsiung [*Takao*] [*Republic of China*] [*Seismograph station code, US Geological Survey*] (SEIS)
KAU	Kauhava [*Finland*] [*Airport symbol*] (AD)
KAU	Kenya African Union [*1944*] [*Political party*] (PPW)
KAU	Keystation Adapter Unit [*Computer science*]
KAU	Kilo Accounting Units (NASA)
KAU	King-Armstrong Unit [*Clinical chemistry*]
KAUB-FM	Reedsport, OR [*FM radio station call letters*] (BROA)
KaufBH	Kaufman & Broad Home Corp. [*Associated Press*] (SAG)
KAUF-FM	Kennett, MO [*FM radio station call letters*] (BROA)
KaufHW	Kaufman [*H. W.*] Financial Group [*Associated Press*] (SAG)
Kauf Mack ..	Kaufmann's Edition of Mackeldey's Civil Law [*A publication*] (DLA)
Kaufm Mackeld Civ Law...	Kaufmann's Edition of Mackeldey's Civil Law [*A publication*] (DLA)
KAUFX	Kaufmann Fund [*Mutual fund ticker symbol*] (SG)
KAUG	Augusta [*Maine*] [*ICAO location identifier*] (ICLI)
KAUG-FM	El Dorado, AR [*FM radio station call letters*] (BROA)
KAUI	Kekaha, HI [*FM radio station call letters*]
KAUL-FM	Ellington, MO [*FM radio station call letters*] (BROA)
KAUM	Colorado City, TX [*FM radio station call letters*]
KAUN	Sioux Falls, SD [*Television station call letters*] (BROA)
KAUO	Santa Fe, NM [*Television station call letters*] (BROA)
KAUP	Pendleton, OR [*Television station call letters*] (BROA)
KAUQ-FM	Omak, WA [*FM radio station call letters*] (BROA)
KAUR	Sioux Falls, SD [*FM radio station call letters*]
KAUS	Austin, MN [*AM radio station call letters*]
KAUS	Austin/Robert Mueller Municipal [*Texas*] [*ICAO location identifier*] (ICLI)
KAUS-FM	Austin, MN [*FM radio station call letters*]
KAUV-FM	Viola, AR [*FM radio station call letters*] (BROA)
KAUY-FM	LaJunta, CO [*FM radio station call letters*] (BROA)
KAUZ	Wichita Falls, TX [*Television station call letters*]
KAV.............	Cambourne Resources [*Vancouver Stock Exchange symbol*]
KAV.............	Kavieng [*New Ireland*] [*Seismograph station code, US Geological Survey Closed*] (SEIS)
KAV.............	Keilschrifttexte aus Assur Verschiedenen Inhalts [*A publication*] (BJA)
KAVA	Burney, CA [*AM radio station call letters*]
KAVC	Rosamond, CA [*FM radio station call letters*]
KAVD-FM	Limon, CO [*FM radio station call letters*] (BROA)
KAVE.........	Oakridge, OR [*FM radio station call letters*]
KAVG-FM	Beulah, ND [*FM radio station call letters*] (BROA)
KAVH-FM	Eudora, AR [*FM radio station call letters*] (BROA)
KAVI	Keilschrifttexte aus Assur Verschiedenen Inhalts [*A publication*] (BJA)
KAVJ-FM	Sutherlin, OR [*FM radio station call letters*] (BROA)
KAVK-FM	Many, LA [*FM radio station call letters*] (BROA)
KAVL.........	Lancaster, CA [*AM radio station call letters*]
KAVO-FM	Borger, TX [*FM radio station call letters*] (BROA)
KAVP-AM	Colona, CO [*AM radio station call letters*] (BROA)
KAVS	Mojave, CA [*FM radio station call letters*]
KAVT-AM	Fresno, CA [*AM radio station call letters*] (BROA)
KAVU	Victoria, TX [*Television station call letters*]
KAVV	Benson, AZ [*FM radio station call letters*]
KAW	Kawthaung [*Myanmar*] [*Airport symbol*] (OAG)
KAWA	Floydada, TX [*AM radio station call letters*]
KAWAD	Karnataka Watersheds Development
KAWB	Brainerd, MN [*Television station call letters*]
KAWC	Yuma, AZ [*AM radio station call letters*]
KAWC-FM	Yuma, AZ [*FM radio station call letters*]
KAWD-FM	Tahoka, TX [*FM radio station call letters*] (BROA)
KAWE	Bemidji, MN [*Television station call letters*]
KAWF-FM	Los Molinos, CA [*FM radio station call letters*] (BROA)
KAWJ	Hutchinson, KS [*Television station call letters*] (BROA)
KAWJ	Korrespondenzblatt des Vereins zur Gruendung und Erhaltung der Akademie fuer dieWissenschaft des Judentums [*A publication*] (BJA)
KAWK-FM	Custer, SD [*FM radio station call letters*] (RBYB)
KAWL	York, NE [*AM radio station call letters*]
KAWN	Carswell [*Texas*] [*ICAO location identifier*] (ICLI)
KAWOL	Knowledge, Absent Without Leave [*Army*] (ADDR)

KAWQ-FM — Bridgeport, NE [*FM radio station call letters*] (BROA)
KAWS — Hemphill, TX [*AM radio station call letters*]
KAWT-FM — Princeville, HI [*FM radio station call letters*] (BROA)
KAWU-FM — Newberry Springs, CA [*FM radio station call letters*] (BROA)
KAWW — Heber Springs, AR [*AM radio station call letters*]
KAWW-FM — Heber Springs, AR [*FM radio station call letters*]
KAWX-FM — Weaverville, CA [*FM radio station call letters*] (BROA)
KAWY-FM — Denver City, TX [*FM radio station call letters*] (BROA)
KAWZ — Twin Falls, ID [*FM radio station call letters*]
KAX — Kalbarri [*Australia Airport symbol*] (OAG)
KAXA-FM — Pioche, NV [*FM radio station call letters*] (BROA)
KAXB-FM — Tuba City, AZ [*FM radio station call letters*] (BROA)
KAXE — Grand Rapids, MN [*FM radio station call letters*]
KAXF-FM — Huntsville, TX [*FM radio station call letters*] (BROA)
KAXG-FM — Gillette, WY [*FM radio station call letters*] (BROA)
KAXH-FM — Pampa, TX [*FM radio station call letters*] (BROA)
KAXI-FM — Willcox, AZ [*FM radio station call letters*] (BROA)
KAXJ-FM — Sunrise Beach, MO [*FM radio station call letters*] (BROA)
KAXL — Green Acres, CA [*FM radio station call letters*]
KAXM — Agana, Guam [*Television station call letters*] (BROA)
KAXR-FM — Arkansas City, KS [*FM radio station call letters*] (BROA)
KAXT — Hollister, CA [*FM radio station call letters*] (RBYB)
KAXW-AM — Merced, CA [*AM radio station call letters*] (BROA)
KAXX — Ventura, CA [*FM radio station call letters*]
KAXX-AM — Eagle River, AK [*AM radio station call letters*] (BROA)
KAXY-AM — Waco, TX [*AM radio station call letters*] (BROA)
KAY — Katlanovo [*Yugoslavia*] [*Seismograph station code, US Geological Survey*] (SEIS)
Kay — Kay's English Vice-Chancellors' Reports [*69 English Reprint*] [*A publication*] (DLA)
KAY — Wakaya [*Fiji*] [*Airport symbol Obsolete*] (OAG)
KAYA-FM — Hubbard, NE [*FM radio station call letters*] (BROA)
Kay & J — Kay and Johnson's English Vice-Chancellors' Reports [*69, 70 English Reprint*] [*A publication*] (DLA)
Kay & J (Eng) — Kay and Johnson's English Vice-Chancellors' Reports [*69, 70 English Reprint*] [*A publication*] (DLA)
Kay & John — Kay and Johnson's English Vice-Chancellors' Reports [*69, 70 English Reprint*] [*A publication*] (DLA)
Kay & Johns — Kay and Johnson's English Vice-Chancellors' Reports [*69, 70 English Reprint*] [*A publication*] (DLA)
KAYB-FM — Sunnyside, WA [*FM radio station call letters*] (BROA)
KAYC-FM — Durant, OK [*FM radio station call letters*] (BROA)
KAYD — Beaumont, TX [*AM radio station call letters*] (RBYB)
KAYD-FM — Beaumont, TX [*FM radio station call letters*]
Kaydon — Kaydon Corp. [*Associated Press*] (SAG)
KAYE — Kaye Group [*NASDAQ symbol*] (TTSB)
KAYE — Kaye Group, Inc. [*NASDAQ symbol*] (SAG)
KAYE — Tonkawa, OK [*FM radio station call letters*]
KayeGrp — Kaye Group, Inc. [*Associated Press*] (SAG)
KayeK — Kaye Kotts Associates, Inc. [*Associated Press*] (SAG)
Kay (Eng) — Kay's English Vice-Chancellors' Reports [*69 English Reprint*] [*A publication*] (DLA)
KAYF-FM — Starbuck, MN [*FM radio station call letters*] (BROA)
KAYG-FM — Camp Wood, TX [*FM radio station call letters*] (BROA)
KAYH-FM — Fayetteville, AR [*FM radio station call letters*] (BROA)
KAYI-FM — Princeville, HI [*FM radio station call letters*] (BROA)
KAYK-AM — Arvada, CO [*AM radio station call letters*] (BROA)
KAYL — Storm Lake, IA [*AM radio station call letters*]
KAYL-FM — Storm Lake, IA [*FM radio station call letters*]
KAYO-FM — Aberdeen, WA [*FM radio station call letters*]
KAYP-FM — Mount Pleasant, IA [*FM radio station call letters*] (BROA)
KAYQ — Warsaw, MO [*FM radio station call letters*]
KAYR — Van Buren, AR [*AM radio station call letters*]
KAYS — Hays, KS [*AM radio station call letters*]
KAYSEE — Kansas City [*Missouri*] [*Slang*]
Kay Ship — Kay. Shipmasters, and Seamen [*2nd ed.*] [*1894*] [*A publication*] (DLA)
KAYU — Spokane, WA [*Television station call letters*]
KAYW-FM — Meeker, CO [*FM radio station call letters*] (BROA)
KAYX — Richmond, MO [*FM radio station call letters*]
KAYY-FM — Clearwater, KS [*FM radio station call letters*] (BROA)
KAZ — Karuizawa [*Also, KRZ*] [*Japan*] [*Seismograph station code, US Geological Survey*] (SEIS)
kaz — Kazakh [*MARC language code Library of Congress*] (LCCP)
KAZA — Gilroy, CA [*AM radio station call letters*]
KAZAIR — Kazakhstan Airlines [*ICAO designator*] (FAAC)
KAZB-FM — Coalinga, CA [*FM radio station call letters*] (BROA)
KAZC-FM — Tishomingo, OK [*FM radio station call letters*] (BROA)
KAZD-FM — Montrose, CO [*FM radio station call letters*] (BROA)
KAZE-FM — Coalgate, OK [*FM radio station call letters*] (BROA)
KAZF-FM — Hebronville, TX [*FM radio station call letters*] (BROA)
KAZG — Ogden, UT [*Television station call letters*] (BROA)
KAZI — Austin, TX [*FM radio station call letters*]
KAZL — Castle Rock, WA [*FM radio station call letters*]
KAZM — Sedona, AZ [*AM radio station call letters*]
KAZN — Pasadena, CA [*AM radio station call letters*]
KAZP-AM — Bellevue, NE [*AM radio station call letters*] (BROA)
KAZQ — Albuquerque, NM [*Television station call letters*]
KAZR-FM — Pella, IA [*FM radio station call letters*] (RBYB)
KazSSR — Kazakh Soviet Socialist Republic
KAZT-AM — Redding, CA [*AM radio station call letters*] (BROA)
KAZU — Pacific Grove, CA [*FM radio station call letters*]
KAZW-AM — College Station, TX [*AM radio station call letters*] (BROA)
KAZY-FM — Winfield, KS [*FM radio station call letters*] (BROA)
KAZZ — Deer Park, WA [*FM radio station call letters*]
KB — Bermuda [*IYRU nationality code*] (IYR)
KB — Burnthills [*ICAO designator*] (AD)
KB — English Law Reports, King's Bench Division [*1901-52*] [*A publication*] (DLA)
KB — Kashin-Bek Disease [*Medicine*] (DMAA)
KB — Kaufman & Broad, Inc. (MHDW)
KB — Kauri-Butanol Value [*Measure of relative solvent power*]
KB — Keel Bending (SSD)
KB — Keilinschriftliche Bibliothek [*Berlin*] [*A publication*] (BJA)
KB — Kelly Bushing [*Drilling*] (DICI)
KB — Ketone Bodies [*Clinical chemistry*]
KB — Keyboard [*Computer science*]
KB — Kickback (MHDB)
kb — Kilobar
kb — Kilobase
KB — Kilobaud (IAA)
kb — KiloBIT [*Binary Digit*] [*Computer science*]
KB — Kilobit (NAKS)
KB — Kilo BTU [*British Thermal Unit*]
KB — Kilobyte [*10^3 bytes*] [*Computer science*]
Kb — Kilobyte (NFD)
KB — Kincheng Banking Corp. [*Hong Kong*]
KB — King's Bench [*of law courts*] [*British*]
KB — King's Bishop [*Chess*]
KB — Kitchen and Bathroom
KB — Kitchen Biddy [*Female kitchen worker*] [*Restaurant slang*]
KB — Kite Balloon [*Air Force*]
K-B — Kleihauer-Betke [*Stain*] [*Medicine*] (MEDA)
KB — Knee Bearing [*Prosthesis*]
KB — Knee Brace [*Technical drawings*]
KB — Knight Bachelor [*or Knight Companion*] of the Order of the Bath [*British*]
Kb — Knit into Back [*of Stitch*] [*Knitting*] (BARN)
Kb — Knit into Back of Stitch [*Knitting*] (BARN)
KB — Knockback (WDAA)
KB — Knowledgeability Brief (MCD)
KB — Knowledge Base [*Computer science*] (IAA)
KB — Knuckle-Bender Splint [*Orthopedics*] (DAVI)
KB — Komercni Bank [*Czech Republic Bank*]
KB — Komercni Banka AS [*Czech Republic*] [*Banking*]
KB — Kommanditbolaget [*Limited Partnership*] [*German*] (ILCA)
KB — Koninklijk Besluit [*Royal Decree*] [*Dutch*] (ILCA)
KB — Kontrabass [*Double Bass*] [*Music*]
Kb — Kontrabass [*Double Bass*] [*German*] [*Music*] (WDAA)
KB — Korpus Bezpieczenstwa (BJA)
KB — Korrespondenz-Blatt des Verbandes der Deutschen Juden [*A publication*] (BJA)
KB — Kuiper Belt [*Planetary science*]
KB — Kulturbund
KB — Kunstgeschichte in Bildern [*A publication*] (OCD)
KBA — Barbados [*IYRU nationality code*] (IYR)
KBA — Beni Abbes [*Algeria*] [*Airport symbol*] (AD)
KBA — Kabala [*Sierra Leone*] [*Airport symbol*] (OAG)
KBA — Kansas Bankers Association (SRA)
KBA — Kansas Bar Association (SRA)
KBA — Kenn Borek Air Ltd. [*Canada ICAO designator*] (FAAC)
KBA — Kentucky Bar Association (SRA)
KBA — Kentucky Broadcasters Association (SRA)
KBA — Ketobutyraldehyde Dimethyl Acetal [*Biochemistry*]
KBA — Keyboard Assembly (DWSG)
KBA — Killed by Action [*In reference to the enemy*] [*Vietnam*] (VNW)
KBA — Killed by Air [*Military*]
KBA — Killed by Artillery [*In reference to the enemy*] [*Vietnam*] (VNW)
KBA — Kleinwort Benson Aus [*NYSE symbol*] (TTSB)
KBA — Kleinwort Benson Australian Income Fund, Inc. [*NYSE symbol*] (SPSG)
KBA — Knight of St. Benedict of Avis
KBAB — Marysville/Beale Air Force Base [*California*] [*ICAO location identifier*] (ICLI)
KBAB-FM — Kerrville, TX [*FM radio station call letters*] (BROA)
KBAC — Kennedy Booster Assembly Contractor (MCD)
KBAC — Las Vegas, NM [*FM radio station call letters*]
KBAD — Shreveport/Barksdale Air Force Base [*Louisiana*] [*ICAO location identifier*] (ICLI)
KBAD-AM — Las Vegas, NV [*AM radio station call letters*] (BROA)
KBAE — Llano, TX [*FM radio station call letters*] (RBYB)
KBAH-FM — Plainview, TX [*FM radio station call letters*] (BROA)
KBAI — Morro Bay, CA [*AM radio station call letters*]
KBAK — Bakersfield, CA [*Television station call letters*]
KBAL — Kimball International, Inc. [*NASDAQ symbol*] (NQ)
KBAL — Kleine Beitraege zum Assyrischen Lexikon [*A publication*]
KBAL — San Saba, TX [*AM radio station call letters*]
KBALB — Kimball Intl Cl'B' [*NASDAQ symbol*] (TTSB)
KBAL-FM — San Saba, TX [*FM radio station call letters*] (RBYB)
K-BALL — Cannibalize (MCD)
KBAM — Longview, WA [*AM radio station call letters*]
KBAQ — Phoenix, AZ [*FM radio station call letters*]
KBAR — Burley, ID [*AM radio station call letters*]
KBAR — Kilobar
KBART — Kings Bay Army Terminal
KBAS — Bullhead City, AZ [*AM radio station call letters*]
KBAT — Midland, TX [*FM radio station call letters*]
KBAU — Big Sandy, TX [*FM radio station call letters*] (RBYB)
KBAust — Kleinwort Benson Australian Income Fund, Inc. [*Associated Press*] (SAG)

KBAW-FM .... Zapata, TX [*FM radio station call letters*] (BROA)
KBAX .... Fallbrook, CA [*FM radio station call letters*]
KBAY .... San Jose, CA [*FM radio station call letters*]
KBB .... Baker University, Baldwin City, KS [*Library symbol Library of Congress*] (LCLS)
KBB .... Bear Stearns Companies, Inc. [*AMEX symbol*] (SAG)
KBB .... Bear Stearns Cos.'CUBS"98 [*AMEX symbol*] (TTSB)
KBB .... King's Bad Bargain [*Undesirable serviceman*] [*Slang British*] (DSUE)
KBB .... Kitchens, Bedrooms, and Bathrooms Equipment Exhibition [*British*] (ITD)
KBBA .... Abilene, TX [*AM radio station call letters*]
KBBB-FM .... Billings, MT [*FM radio station call letters*] (RBYB)
KBBC .... Lake Havasu City, AZ [*FM radio station call letters*]
KBBE .... McPherson, KS [*FM radio station call letters*]
KBBF .... Santa Rosa, CA [*FM radio station call letters*]
KBBG .... Waterloo, IA [*FM radio station call letters*]
KBBI .... Homer, AK [*AM radio station call letters*]
KBBJ .... Havre, MT [*Television station call letters*] (BROA)
KBBK .... Rupert, ID [*AM radio station call letters*]
KBBL .... Cabot, AR [*AM radio station call letters*]
KBBL-FM .... Cabot, AR [*FM radio station call letters*]
KBBN .... Broken Bow, NE [*FM radio station call letters*]
KBBO .... Yakima, WA [*AM radio station call letters*]
KBBQ .... Fort Smith, AR [*FM radio station call letters*]
KBBR .... North Bend, OR [*AM radio station call letters*]
KBBS .... Buffalo, WY [*AM radio station call letters*]
KBBT .... Portland, OR [*AM radio station call letters*]
KBBT-FM .... Banks, OR [*FM radio station call letters*] (BROA)
KBBV .... Big Bear Lake, CA [*AM radio station call letters*]
KBBW .... Waco, TX [*AM radio station call letters*]
KBBX .... Omaha, NE [*AM radio station call letters*]
KBBY-FM .... Ventura, CA [*FM radio station call letters*]
KBBZ .... Kalispell, MT [*FM radio station call letters*]
KBC .... Bellarmine College, Louisville, KY [*OCLC symbol*] (OCLC)
KBC .... Birch Creek [*Alaska*] [*Airport symbol*] (OAG)
KBC .... K-Band Circulator
KBC .... King's Bench Court [*British*]
KBC .... Kiowa Business Committee [*An association*]
KBCA .... Elk City, OK [*Television station call letters*] (BROA)
KBCA .... Keystone Bituminous Coal Association
KBCB .... Bellingham, WA [*Television station call letters*]
KBCC .... Helena, MT [*Television station call letters*] (BROA)
KBCD .... Newport Beach, CA [*FM radio station call letters*]
KBCE .... Boyce, LA [*FM radio station call letters*]
KBCH .... Kings Beach, CA [*FM radio station call letters*] (RBYB)
KBCH .... Lincoln City, OR [*AM radio station call letters*]
KBCI .... Boise, ID [*Television station call letters*]
KBCJ .... Vemal, UT [*Television station call letters*] (BROA)
KBCK .... Diamondville, WY [*FM radio station call letters*]
KBCL .... Shreveport, LA [*AM radio station call letters*]
KBCN .... Marshall, AR [*FM radio station call letters*]
KBCO .... Boulder, CO [*AM radio station call letters*]
KBCO-FM .... Boulder, CO [*FM radio station call letters*]
KBCQ .... Roswell, NM [*FM radio station call letters*]
KBCR .... Steamboat Springs, CO [*AM radio station call letters*]
KBCR-FM .... Steamboat Springs, CO [*FM radio station call letters*] (RBYB)
KBCS .... Bellevue, WA [*FM radio station call letters*]
KBCT .... Boca Raton [*Florida*] [*ICAO location identifier*] (ICLI)
KBCT-FM .... Waco, TX [*FM radio station call letters*] (RBYB)
KBCU .... North Newton, KS [*FM radio station call letters*]
KBCY .... Tye, TX [*FM radio station call letters*]
KBD .... Kaschin-Beck Disease [*Medicine*]
KBD .... Keyboard
kbd .... Keyboard (WDAA)
KBD .... King's Bench Division [*of law courts*] [*British*] (ROG)
KBD .... Thousand Barrels per Day [*Also, TBD*]
KBDC .... King's Bench Divisional Court [*British*]
KBDE .... Baudette [*Minnesota*] [*ICAO location identifier*] (ICLI)
KBDG .... Turlock, CA [*FM radio station call letters*]
KBDI .... Broomfield, CO [*Television station call letters*]
KB Div'l Ct .... King's Bench Divisional Court [*England*] (DLA)
KBDL .... Windsor Locks/Bradley International [*Connecticut*] [*ICAO location identifier*] (ICLI)
KBDN .... Bandon, OR [*FM radio station call letters*] (RBYB)
KBDR .... Mirando City, TX [*FM radio station call letters*]
KBDZ .... Perryville, MO [*FM radio station call letters*]
KBE .... Bell Island, AK [*Location identifier FAA*] (FAAL)
KBE .... Berea College, Berea, KY [*OCLC symbol*] (OCLC)
KBE .... Keyboard Encoder [*Computer science*]
KBE .... Keyboard Entry [*Computer science*]
KBE .... Key British Enterprises [*Dun & Bradstreet Ltd.*] [*Information service or system*] (IID)
KBE .... Knight Commander of the [*Order of the*] British Empire
KBE .... Knight of the Black Eagle [*Russia*] [*Obsolete*]
KBE .... Knowledge-Based Engineering [*Expert systems*] [*Computer-aided design*]
KBEC .... Waxahachie, TX [*AM radio station call letters*]
KBED .... Bedford/Laurence G. Hanscom Field [*Massachusetts*] [*ICAO location identifier*] (ICLI)
KBEE .... Modesto, CA [*AM radio station call letters*]
KBEE .... Salt Lake City, UT [*FM radio station call letters*] (RBYB)
KBEH .... Bellevue, WA [*Television station call letters*]
KBEK .... Mora, MN [*FM radio station call letters*]
KBEL .... Idabel, OK [*AM radio station call letters*]
KBEL-FM .... Idabel, OK [*FM radio station call letters*]
KBEM .... Minneapolis, MN [*FM radio station call letters*]
KBEN .... Carrizo Springs, TX [*AM radio station call letters*]
KBENC .... Keyboard Encoder (NITA)
KB (Eng) .... English Law Reports, King's Bench Division [*1901-52*] [*A publication*] (DLA)
KBEQ .... Blue Springs, MO [*AM radio station call letters*]
KBEQ .... Kansas City, MO [*FM radio station call letters*]
KBER .... Ogden, UT [*FM radio station call letters*]
KBES .... Ceres, CA [*FM radio station call letters*]
KBES .... Knowledge-Based Expert System
KBET .... Canyon Country, CA [*AM radio station call letters*]
KBEW .... Blue Earth, MN [*AM radio station call letters*]
KBEW-FM .... Blue Earth, MN [*FM radio station call letters*]
KBEZ .... Tulsa, OK [*FM radio station call letters*]
KBF .... K-Band Feed
KBF .... Kyburz Flat [*California*] [*Seismograph station code, US Geological Survey*] (SEIS)
KBFB-FM .... Dallas, TX [*FM radio station call letters*] (BROA)
KBFC .... Forrest City, AR [*FM radio station call letters*]
KBFC .... Karen Brooks Fan Club (EA)
KBFC .... Kippe Brannon Fan Club [*Defunct*] (EA)
KBFD .... Honolulu, HI [*Television station call letters*]
KBFG-FM .... Santa Fe, NM [*FM radio station call letters*] (BROA)
KBFI .... Bonners Ferry, ID [*AM radio station call letters*]
KBFI .... Seattle Boeing Field/King Country International [*Washington*] [*ICAO location identifier*] (ICLI)
KBFL .... Bakersfield/Meadows Field [*California*] [*ICAO location identifier*] (ICLI)
KBFL .... Buffalo, MO [*FM radio station call letters*]
KBFM .... Edinburg, TX [*FM radio station call letters*]
KBFM .... Mobile/Aerospace [*Alabama*] [*ICAO location identifier*] (ICLI)
KBFN-FM .... Big Sky, MT [*FM radio station call letters*] (BROA)
KBFS .... Belle Fourche, SD [*AM radio station call letters*]
KBFW .... Bellingham-Ferndale, WA [*AM radio station call letters*]
KBFX .... Anchorage, AK [*FM radio station call letters*]
KBGA-FM .... Missoula, MT [*FM radio station call letters*] (RBYB)
KBGE .... Bellevue, WA [*Television station call letters*] (RBYB)
KBGG .... San Francisco, CA [*FM radio station call letters*] (RBYB)
KBGH .... Filer, ID [*Television station call letters*]
KBGN .... Caldwell, ID [*AM radio station call letters*]
KBGO-FM .... Las Vegas, TX [*FM radio station call letters*] (RBYB)
KBGR .... Bangor/International [*Maine*] [*ICAO location identifier*] (ICLI)
KBGS .... Big Spring/Webb Air Force Base [*Texas*] [*ICAO location identifier*] (ICLI)
KBH .... Kaufman & Broad Home [*NYSE symbol*] (TTSB)
KBH .... Kaufman & Broad Home Corp. [*NYSE symbol*] (SPSG)
KBH .... Killed by Helicopter [*In reference to the enemy*] [*Vietnam*]
KBHB .... Sturgis, SD [*AM radio station call letters*]
KBHC .... Nashville, AR [*AM radio station call letters*]
KBHE .... Rapid City, SD [*FM radio station call letters*]
KBHE-TV .... Rapid City, SD [*Television station call letters*]
KBHK .... San Francisco, CA [*Television station call letters*]
KBHL .... Osakis, MN [*FM radio station call letters*]
KBHM .... Birmingham [*Alabama*] [*ICAO location identifier*] (ICLI)
KBHP .... Bemidji, MN [*FM radio station call letters*]
KBHR .... Big Bear City, CA [*FM radio station call letters*]
KBHS .... Hot Springs, AR [*AM radio station call letters*]
KBHT .... Crockett, TX [*FM radio station call letters*]
KBHU .... Spearfish, SD [*FM radio station call letters*]
KBHW .... International Falls, MN [*FM radio station call letters*]
KBHZ-FM .... Willmar, MN [*FM radio station call letters*] (RBYB)
KBI .... Keyboard Immortals [*Recording label*]
KBI .... Key Buying Influence (WDMC)
KBI .... Kribi [*Cameroon*] [*Airport symbol*] (OAG)
KBIA .... Columbia, MO [*FM radio station call letters*]
KBIA .... Kent Barlow Information Associates [*British*] (NITA)
KBIB .... Marion, TX [*AM radio station call letters*]
KBIC .... Raymondville, TX [*FM radio station call letters*] (RBYB)
KBID .... Bakersfield, CA [*AM radio station call letters*]
KBIF .... El Paso/Biggs Air Force Base [*Texas*] [*ICAO location identifier*] (ICLI)
KBIF .... Fresno, CA [*AM radio station call letters*]
KBIG .... Los Angeles, CA [*FM radio station call letters*]
KBIL .... Breckenridge, TX [*AM radio station call letters*]
KBIM .... Keyboard Interface Module (MCD)
KBIM .... Roswell, NM [*AM radio station call letters*]
KBIM-FM .... Roswell, NM [*FM radio station call letters*]
KBIM-TV .... Roswell, NM [*Television station call letters*]
KBIN .... Council Bluffs, IA [*Television station call letters*]
KBIQ .... Fountain, CO [*FM radio station call letters*]
KBIQ-FM .... Manitou Springs, CO [*FM radio station call letters*] (RBYB)
KBIS .... Kitchen and Bath Industry Show West (ITD)
KBISKK .... Kodak Business Information Services K.K. (EFIS)
Kbit .... Kilobit
KBIT/S .... KiloBITS [*Binary Digits*] per Second [*Transmission rate*] [*Computer science*] (TEL)
KBIU .... Lake Charles, LA [*FM radio station call letters*]
KBIX .... Biloxi/Keesler Air Force Base [*Mississippi*] [*ICAO location identifier*] (ICLI)
KBIX .... Muskogee, OK [*AM radio station call letters*]
KBIZ .... Ottumwa, IA [*AM radio station call letters*]
KBJ .... Kentucky State Bar Journal [*A publication*] (DLA)
KBJJ .... Marshall, MN [*FM radio station call letters*]
KBJM .... Lemmon, SD [*AM radio station call letters*]
KBJR .... Superior, WI [*Television station call letters*]
KBJS .... Jacksonville, TX [*FM radio station call letters*]

KBJT .... Fordyce, AR [*AM radio station call letters*]
KBK .... KBK Capital [*AMEX symbol*] (TTSB)
KBK .... KBK Capital Corp. [*AMEX symbol*] (SAG)
KBK .... Kirkjubaejar [*Iceland*] [*Airport symbol*] (AD)
KBKB .... Fort Madison, IA [*AM radio station call letters*]
KBKB-FM ..... Fort Madison, IA [*FM radio station call letters*]
KBKC .... KBK Capital Corp. [*NASDAQ symbol*] (SAG)
KBK Cap ..... KBK Capital Corp. [*Associated Press*] (SAG)
KBKG .... Corning, AR [*FM radio station call letters*]
KBKK .... Spanish Fork, UT [*FM radio station call letters*] (RBYB)
KBKL .... Grand Junction, CO [*FM radio station call letters*]
KBKO .... Billings, MT [*FM radio station call letters*] (RBYB)
KBKO-AM .... Santa Barbara, CA [*AM radio station call letters*] (BROA)
KBKR .... Baker City, OR [*AM radio station call letters*]
KBKS-FM ..... Tacoma, WA [*FM radio station call letters*] (RBYB)
KBKW .... Aberdeen, WA [*AM radio station call letters*] (RBYB)
KBL .... Hebraeisches und Aramaeisches Lexikon zum Alten Testament [*L. Koehler and W. Baumgarther*] [*A publication*] (BJA)
KBL .... Kabul [*Afghanistan*] [*Airport symbol*] (OAG)
KBL .... Kabul [*Afghanistan*] [*Seismograph station code, US Geological Survey*] (SEIS)
KBL .... Keyboard Listener [*Computer science*] (MHDI)
KBL .... Kilusan ng Bangong Lipunan [*New Society Movement*] [*Philippines*] (PD)
KBL .... Kraft Black Liquor [*Pulping technology*]
KBL .... Kredietbank Luxembourgeoise [*Luxembourg*]
KBL .... Lexicon in Veteris Testamenti Libros. Supplementum [*L. Koehler and W. Baumgartner*] [*A publication*] (BJA)
KBLA .... Santa Monica, CA [*AM radio station call letters*]
KBLE .... Seattle, WA [*AM radio station call letters*]
KBLF .... Red Bluff, CA [*AM radio station call letters*]
KBLG .... Billings, MT [*AM radio station call letters*]
KBLH .... Keel Blade Height [*Botany*]
KBLI .... Bellingham/International [*Washington*] [*ICAO location identifier*] (ICLI)
KBLJ .... La Junta, CO [*FM radio station call letters*]
KBLK .... Burnet, TX [*FM radio station call letters*]
KBLL .... Helena, MT [*AM radio station call letters*]
KBLL .... Keel Blade Length [*Botany*]
KBLL-FM ..... Helena, MT [*FM radio station call letters*]
KBLP .... Lindsay, OK [*FM radio station call letters*]
KBLPS .... Knowledge-Based Logistics Planning Shell
KBLQ .... Logan, UT [*FM radio station call letters*]
KBLR .... Paradise, NV [*Television station call letters*]
KBLS .... North Fort Riley, KS [*FM radio station call letters*]
KBLU .... Yuma, AZ [*AM radio station call letters*]
KBLV .... Bellerville/Scott Air Force Base [*Illinois*] [*ICAO location identifier*] (ICLI)
KBLV .... Bellevue, WA [*AM radio station call letters*]
KBLX .... Berkeley, CA [*FM radio station call letters*] (RBYB)
KBLZ .... Kaneohe, HI [*FM radio station call letters*]
KBM .... Kabwum [*Papua New Guinea*] [*Airport symbol*] (OAG)
KBM .... Karissimo Bene Merenti [*To the Most Dear and Well-Deserving*] [*Correspondence*]
KBM .... Keyboard Monitor [*Computer science*]
KBM .... Knowledge Base Machine [*Computer science*]
KBMA .... Bryan, TX [*FM radio station call letters*]
KBMB-FM .... Sacramento, CA [*FM radio station call letters*] (BROA)
KBMC .... Bozeman, MT [*FM radio station call letters*]
KBME .... Bismarck, ND [*Television station call letters*]
KBMG .... Hamilton, MT [*FM radio station call letters*]
KBMI .... Roma, TX [*FM radio station call letters*]
KBMJ .... Hardin, MT [*FM radio station call letters*]
KBMR .... Bismarck, ND [*AM radio station call letters*]
KBMS .... Knowledge Based Management System
KBMS .... Knowledge Base Management System [*Computer science*]
KBMS .... Vancouver, WA [*AM radio station call letters*]
KBMT .... Beaumont, TX [*Television station call letters*]
KBMT .... Knowledge-Based Machine Translation [*Computer science*]
KBMV .... Birch Tree, MO [*AM radio station call letters*]
KBMV-FM .... Birch Tree, MO [*FM radio station call letters*]
KBMW .... Breckenridge, MN [*AM radio station call letters*]
KBMX .... Eldon, MO [*FM radio station call letters*]
KBMY .... Bismarck, ND [*Television station call letters*]
KBN .... Kill Bad Name [*Marketing*] (WDMC)
KBNA .... El Paso, TX [*AM radio station call letters*]
KBNA .... Nashville/Metropolitan [*Tennessee*] [*ICAO location identifier*] (ICLI)
KBNA-FM ..... El Paso, TX [*FM radio station call letters*]
KBNB-AM .... Gilmer, TX [*AM radio station call letters*] (RBYB)
KBND .... Bend, OR [*AM radio station call letters*]
KBNJ .... Corpus Christi, TX [*FM radio station call letters*]
KBNL .... Laredo, TX [*FM radio station call letters*]
KBNN-AM .... Lebanon, MO [*AM radio station call letters*] (BROA)
KBNO .... Denver, CO [*AM radio station call letters*]
KBNP .... Portland, OR [*AM radio station call letters*]
KBNR .... Brownsville, TX [*FM radio station call letters*]
KBNU-FM .... Uvalde, TX [*FM radio station call letters*] (RBYB)
KBO .... Kabalo [*Zaire*] [*Airport symbol*] (AD)
KBO .... Keep Buggering On [*Perseverance*] [*Slang British*] (DSUE)
KBo .... Keilschrifttexte aus Boghazkoi [*A publication*] (BJA)
KBO .... Kite and Balloon Officer [*Navy*]
KBO .... Kommunistischer Bund Oesterreichs [*Communist League of Austria*] [*Political party*] (PPW)
KBO .... Kuiper Belt Objects [*Planetary science*]
KBO .... Organization for the Management and Development of the Kagera River Basin (EA)

KBOA .... Kennett, MO [*AM radio station call letters*]
KBOA .... Piggott, AR [*FM radio station call letters*] (RBYB)
KBOB .... Muscatine, IA [*FM radio station call letters*]
KBOC .... Bridgeport, TX [*FM radio station call letters*]
KBOE .... Oskaloosa, IA [*AM radio station call letters*]
KBOE-FM .... Oskaloosa, IA [*FM radio station call letters*]
KBOF .... Washington/Bolling Air Force Base [*District of Columbia*] [*ICAO location identifier*] (ICLI)
KBOI .... Boise/Boise Air Terminal [*Idaho*] [*ICAO location identifier*] (ICLI)
KBOI .... Boise, ID [*AM radio station call letters*]
KBOK .... Malvern, AR [*AM radio station call letters*]
KBOK-FM .... Malvern, AR [*FM radio station call letters*]
KBOM .... Los Alamos, NM [*FM radio station call letters*]
KBON-FM .... Mamou, LA [*FM radio station call letters*] (BROA)
KBOO .... Portland, OR [*FM radio station call letters*]
KBOP .... Pleasanton, TX [*AM radio station call letters*]
KBOQ .... Carmel, CA [*FM radio station call letters*] (RBYB)
KBOR .... Brownsville, TX [*AM radio station call letters*]
KBOS .... Boston/Logan International [*Massachusetts*] [*ICAO location identifier*] (ICLI)
KBOS .... Tulare, CA [*FM radio station call letters*]
KBOT .... Kansas City Board of Trade
KBOT .... Pelican Rapids, MN [*FM radio station call letters*]
KBOV .... Bishop, CA [*AM radio station call letters*]
KBOW .... Butte, MT [*AM radio station call letters*]
KBOX .... Lompoc, CA [*FM radio station call letters*]
KBOY .... Medford, OR [*FM radio station call letters*]
KBOZ .... Bozeman, MT [*AM radio station call letters*]
KBP .... Kainate-Binding Protein [*Biochemistry*]
KBP .... Kappa Beta Pi [*Society*]
KBP .... Kent-Barlow Publications Ltd. [*Information service or system*] (IID)
KBP .... Keyboard Process [*Computer science*]
KBP .... Kiev Borispol Airport [*Former USSR Airport symbol*] (OAG)
kbp .... Kilobase Pairs [*Genetics*]
KBP .... King's Bishop's Pawn [*Chess*] (IIA)
KBP .... Kite Balloon Pilot
KBP .... Koala Bear Park [*Adelaide*] [*Airport symbol*] (AD)
KBPA .... Knowledge-Based Programming Assistant (PDAA)
KBPA-AM .... Palo Alto, CA [*AM radio station call letters*] (BROA)
KBPAP .... Kidney Bean Purple Acid Phosphatase [*An enzyme*]
KBPI .... Denver, CO [*FM radio station call letters*]
KBPK .... Buena Park, CA [*FM radio station call letters*]
KBPL .... Communist League Proletarian Left [*Netherlands Political party*] (PPW)
KBPR .... Brainerd, MN [*FM radio station call letters*]
KBPRC .... Keyboard and Printer Controller [*Computer science*] (NITA)
Kbps .... Kilobits per Second [*Computer science*]
kbps .... KiloBITS [*Binary Digits*] per Second [*Transmission rate*] [*Computer science*]
KBPS .... Kilobits per Second (NAKS)
KBps .... Kilobytes per Second [*Computer science*] (DOM)
KBPS .... Kilobytes Per Second (NITA)
KBPS .... Portland, OR [*AM radio station call letters*]
KBPS-FM .... Portland, OR [*FM radio station call letters*]
KBPT .... Beaumont Port-Arthur/Jefferson County [*Texas*] [*ICAO location identifier*] (ICLI)
KBPX .... Flagstaff, AZ [*Television station call letters*] (BROA)
KBQQ .... Minot, ND [*FM radio station call letters*]
KBR .... Kaaba Resources [*Vancouver Stock Exchange symbol*]
KBR .... Kota Bharu [*Malaysia*] [*Airport symbol*] (OAG)
KBr .... Potassium Bromide [*An anticonvulsant and sedative*] (DAVI)
KBRA-FM .... Freer, TX [*FM radio station call letters*] (BROA)
KBRB .... Ainsworth, NE [*AM radio station call letters*]
KBRB-FM .... Ainsworth, NE [*FM radio station call letters*]
KBRC .... Mount Vernon, WA [*AM radio station call letters*]
KBRD .... Lacey, WA [*AM radio station call letters*] (RBYB)
KBRE .... Cedar City, UT [*AM radio station call letters*]
KBRE-FM .... Cedar City, UT [*FM radio station call letters*]
KBRF .... Fergus Falls, MN [*AM radio station call letters*]
KBRG .... Fremont, CA [*FM radio station call letters*]
KBRH .... Baton Rouge, LA [*AM radio station call letters*]
KBRI .... Brinkley, AR [*AM radio station call letters*]
KBRJ .... Anchorage, AK [*FM radio station call letters*]
KBRK .... Brookings, SD [*AM radio station call letters*]
KBRK-FM .... Brookings, SD [*FM radio station call letters*]
KBRL .... McCook, NE [*AM radio station call letters*]
KBRN .... Boerne, TX [*AM radio station call letters*]
KBRO .... Bremerton, WA [*AM radio station call letters*]
KBRO .... Brownsville/International [*Texas*] [*ICAO location identifier*] (ICLI)
KBRQ .... Hillsboro, TX [*FM radio station call letters*]
KBRR .... Thief River Falls, MN [*Television station call letters*]
KBRS .... Springdale, AR [*FM radio station call letters*]
KBRT .... Avalon, CA [*AM radio station call letters*]
KBRU .... Fort Morgan, CO [*FM radio station call letters*]
KBRV .... Soda Springs, ID [*AM radio station call letters*]
KBRW .... Barrow, AK [*AM radio station call letters*]
KBRW-FM .... Barrow, AK [*FM radio station call letters*] (RBYB)
KBRX .... O'Neill, NE [*AM radio station call letters*]
KBRX-FM .... O'Neill, NE [*FM radio station call letters*]
KBRZ .... Freeport, TX [*FM radio station call letters*]
KBS .... Bo [*Sierra Leone*] [*Airport symbol Obsolete*] (OAG)
KBS .... Gamair Ltd. [*Gambia*] [*ICAO designator*] (FAAC)
KBS .... Kellogg Biological Station [*Michigan State University*]
kbs .... KiloBITS [*Binary Digits*] per Second [*Transmission rate*] [*Computer science*]

KBS............ Kilobytes per Second [*Computer science*]
KBS............ Kinematic Bombing System
KBS............ Kingsbay [*Spitsbergen*] [*Seismograph station code, US Geological Survey*]   (SEIS)
KBS............ Kluver-Bucy Syndrome [*Psychiatry*]   (DAVI)
KBS............ Knight of the Blessed Sacrament
KBS............ Knowledge-Based System [*Computer model*] [*Computer science*]
KBS............ Korean Broadcasting System [*South Korea*]   (FEA)
KBS............ Stites, McElwain & Fowler, Bellarmine College Library, Louisville, KY [*OCLC symbol*]   (OCLC)
KBSA .... El Dorado, AR [*FM radio station call letters*]
KBSA .... Kassian Benevolent Society in America   (EA)
KBSA .... Knowledge-Based Software Assistant [*Computer science*]
KBSB .... Bemidji, MN [*FM radio station call letters*]
KBSC .... Knowledge-Based Systems Centre [*Polytechnic of the South Bank*] [*British*]   (CB)
KBSD .... Ensign, KS [*Television station call letters*]
KBSF .... Springhill, LA [*AM radio station call letters*]
KBSG .... Auburn, WA [*AM radio station call letters*]
KBSG .... Tacoma, WA [*FM radio station call letters*]
KBSH .... Hays, KS [*Television station call letters*]
KBSI .... Cape Girardeau, MO [*Television station call letters*]
KBSL .... Goodland, KS [*Television station call letters*]
KBSM .... Austin/Bergstrom Air Force Base [*Texas*] [*ICAO location identifier*]   (ICLI)
KBSM .... McCall, ID [*FM radio station call letters*]
KBSN .... Moses Lake, WA [*AM radio station call letters*]
KBSO .... Corpus Christi, TX [*FM radio station call letters*]
KBSP .... Salem, OR [*Television station call letters*]
KBSR .... Kankakee, Beaverville & Southern Railroad Co. [*AAR code*]
KBSR .... Laurel, MT [*AM radio station call letters*]
KBST .... Big Spring, TX [*AM radio station call letters*]
KBST-FM .... Big Spring, TX [*FM radio station call letters*]
KBSU .... Boise, ID [*AM radio station call letters*]
KBSU-FM .... Boise, ID [*FM radio station call letters*]
KBSV-TV ..... Ceres, CA [*TV station call letters*]   (RBYB)
KBSW .... Twin Falls, ID [*FM radio station call letters*]
KBSY-FM .... Burley, ID [*FM radio station call letters*]   (BROA)
KBSZ .... Wickenburg, AZ [*FM radio station call letters*]   (RBYB)
KBTA .... Batesville, AR [*AM radio station call letters*]
KBTC .... Houston, MO [*AM radio station call letters*]
KBTC .... Tacoma, WA [*FM radio station call letters*]
KBTC-TV ..... Tacoma, WA [*Television station call letters*]
KBTD .... Knee Board Training Device [*Military*]   (MCD)
KBTG .... Keep Britain Tidy Group   (DCTA)
KBTM .... Jonesboro, AR [*AM radio station call letters*]
KBTN .... Neosho, MO [*AM radio station call letters*]
KBTN-FM .... Neosho, MO [*FM radio station call letters*]   (RBYB)
KBTO .... Bottineau, ND [*FM radio station call letters*]
KBTR .... Baton Rouge/Ryan Field [*Louisiana*] [*ICAO location identifier*]   (ICLI)
KBTS .... Big Spring, TX [*FM radio station call letters*]
KBTT .... Bridgeport, TX [*FM radio station call letters*]
KBTU .... Kilo British Thermal Unit   (WDAA)
KBTV .... Burlington/International [*Vermont*] [*ICAO location identifier*]   (ICLI)
KBTX .... Bryan, TX [*Television station call letters*]
KBU .... Keyboard Unit [*Computer science*]   (NASA)
KBU .... Knuckle Buster University [*Facetious term*]
KBU .... Kotabaru [*West Irian, Indonesia*] [*Airport symbol*]   (AD)
KBUA-FM .... San Fernando, CA [*FM radio station call letters*]   (BROA)
KBUB-FM .... Brownwood, TX [*FM radio station call letters*]   (BROA)
KBUC .... Pleasonton, TX [*FM radio station call letters*]
KBUC .... Upper Canada King's Bench Reports [*A publication*]   (DLA)
KBUE .... Long Beach, CA [*FM radio station call letters*]   (RBYB)
KBUF .... Buffalo/Greater Buffalo International [*New York*] [*ICAO location identifier*]   (ICLI)
KBUF .... Holcomb, KS [*AM radio station call letters*]
KBUG .... Osceola, MO [*FM radio station call letters*]
KBUK .... La Grange, TX [*FM radio station call letters*]
KBUL .... Carson City, NV [*FM radio station call letters*]
KBUL-AM .... Modesto, CA [*AM radio station call letters*]   (BROA)
KBUN .... Bemidji, MN [*AM radio station call letters*]
KBUQ-FM .... Paradise Valley, AZ [*FM radio station call letters*]   (RBYB)
KBUR .... Burbank/Hollywood-Burbank [*California*] [*ICAO location identifier*]   (ICLI)
KBUR .... Burlington, IA [*AM radio station call letters*]
KBUS .... Paris, TX [*FM radio station call letters*]
KBUT .... Crested Butte, CO [*FM radio station call letters*]
KBUX .... Quartzsite, AZ [*FM radio station call letters*]
KBUY .... Ruidoso, NM [*AM radio station call letters*]
KBUY-FM .... Amarillo, TX [*FM radio station call letters*]
KBUZ .... Topeka, KS [*FM radio station call letters*]
KBV .... Kobold Resources Ltd. [*Vancouver Stock Exchange symbol*]
KBV .... Kustbevakningen [*Sweden ICAO designator*]   (FAAC)
KBVA .... Bella Vista, AR [*AM radio station call letters*]
KBVC-FM .... Buena Vista, CO [*FM radio station call letters*]   (BROA)
KBVI .... Boulder, CO [*AM radio station call letters*]   (RBYB)
KBVM .... Portland, OR [*FM radio station call letters*]
KBVR .... Corvallis, OR [*FM radio station call letters*]
KBVU .... Eureka, CA [*Television station call letters*]
KBVU-FM .... Alta, IA [*FM radio station call letters*]   (BROA)
KBVV .... Enid, OK [*FM radio station call letters*]
KBW .... Kommunistischer Bund Westdeutschland [*Communist League of West Germany*] [*Political party*]   (PPW)
KBWC .... Marshall, TX [*FM radio station call letters*]
KBWD .... Brownwood, TX [*AM radio station call letters*]

KBWI .... Baltimore/Baltimore-Washington International [*Maryland*] [*ICAO location identifier*]   (ICLI)
KBWS .... Sisseton, SD [*FM radio station call letters*]
KBXB-FM ..... Sikeston, MO [*FM radio station call letters*]   (RBYB)
KBXL .... Caldwell, ID [*FM radio station call letters*]
KBXR .... Ashland, MO [*FM radio station call letters*]
KBXX .... Houston, TX [*FM radio station call letters*]
KBXY .... Baker, CA [*FM radio station call letters*]
KBY .... Streaky Bay [*Australia Airport symbol*]   (OAG)
KBYB .... El Dorado, AR [*FM radio station call letters*]
KBYE .... Oklahoma City, OK [*AM radio station call letters*]
KBYG .... Big Spring, TX [*AM radio station call letters*]
KBYG .... Coahoma, TX [*FM radio station call letters*]
KBYH .... Blytheville Air Force Base [*Arkansas*] [*ICAO location identifier*]   (ICLI)
KBYN .... Arnold, CA [*AM radio station call letters*]
KBYO .... Tallulah, LA [*AM radio station call letters*]
KBYO-FM .... Tallulah, LA [*FM radio station call letters*]
KBYR .... Anchorage, AK [*AM radio station call letters*]
Kbytes/sec .. Kilobytes per Second [*Computer science*]   (IGQR)
KBYU .... Provo, UT [*AM radio station call letters*]
KBYU-TV .... Provo, UT [*Television station call letters*]
KBYZ .... Bismarck, ND [*FM radio station call letters*]
KBZE .... Berwick, LA [*FM radio station call letters*]
KBZK-FM .... Morro Bay, CA [*FM radio station call letters*]   (BROA)
KBZN .... Ogden, UT [*FM radio station call letters*]
KBZO .... Lubbock, TX [*AM radio station call letters*]   (RBYB)
KBZQ .... Lawton, OK [*FM radio station call letters*]
KBZR .... Coolidge, AZ [*FM radio station call letters*]   (RBYB)
KBZS-AM .... Grand Junction, CO [*AM radio station call letters*]   (RBYB)
KBZT .... San Diego, CA [*AM radio station call letters*]
KBZX-FM .... Paso Robles, CA [*FM radio station call letters*]   (BROA)
KBZY .... Salem, OR [*AM radio station call letters*]
KBZZ .... La Junta, CO [*AM radio station call letters*]
KC .... Canada [*IYRU nationality code*]   (IYR)
KC .... Cook Islands International [*ICAO designator*]   (AD)
KC .... [*The*] Kanawha Central Railway Co. [*AAR code*]
KC .... Kansas City [*Missouri*] [*Slang*]
KC .... Kansas City-St. Joseph [*Diocesan abbreviation*] [*Missouri*]   (TOCD)
KC .... Karman Constant [*Physics*]
KC .... Kartell Convent Deutscher Studenten Juedischen Glaubens   (BJA)
KC .... Kathodal Closing [*Medicine*]
KC .... Kennel Club
KC .... Keratoconjunctivitis [*Ophthalmology*]
KC .... Keratoconus [*Ophthalmology*]   (DAVI)
KC .... Keratoma Climacterium [*Dermatology*]   (DAVI)
KC .... Kerr Cell [*Optics*]
KC .... Ketocyclazocine [*Biochemistry*]
KC .... Keystone Center [*An association*]   (EA)
kc .... Kilocalorie
KC .... Kilocharacter   (BUR)
KC .... Kilocurie   (IAA)
kc .... Kilocurie   (IDOE)
kc .... Kilocycle [*Radio*]
KC .... Kilograms per Square Centimeter   (DS)
KC .... King's Colonials [*British military*]   (DMA)
KC .... King's Counsel [*British*]
KC .... Kings County [*Sussex, New Brunswick*]   (DAS)
KC .... King's Cross [*British*]   (ADA)
KC .... Kiting Check [*Investment*]   (MHDB)
KC .... Knees to Chest [*Position*] [*Medicine*]   (DAVI)
KC .... Knickerbocker Conference   (PSS)
KC .... Knight Club   (EA)
KC .... Knight Commander
KC .... Knight of the Crescent [*Turkey*]
KC .... Knights of Columbus
KC .... Knuckle Cracking [*Orthopedics*]   (DAVI)
Kc .... Koruna [*Czech Coin*]   (BARN)
Kc .... Kupffer Cell [*Histology*]
KC .... Kyle Classification [*Library science*]
KCA .... Kansas Chiropractic Association   (SRA)
KCA .... Kansas Contractors Association   (SRA)
KCA .... Keeshond Club of America   (EA)
KCA .... Keesings Contemporary Archives [*A publication Also, an information service or system*]
KCA .... Kentucky Callers Association   (EA)
KCA .... Kentucky Cattlemen's Association   (SRA)
KCA .... Kentucky Coal Association   (SRA)
KCA .... Kiowa-Comanche-Apache
KCA .... Komondor Club of America   (EA)
KCA .... Kuvasz Club of America   (EA)
KCAB .... Dardanelle, AR [*AM radio station call letters*]
KCAC .... Camden, AR [*FM radio station call letters*]
KCAC .... Kansas Collegiate Athletic Conference   (PSS)
KCAD-FM .... Dickinson, ND [*FM radio station call letters*]   (RBYB)
KCAH .... Watsonville, CA [*Television station call letters*]
KCAILUC ..... Kiowa-Commanche-Apache Intertribal Land Use Committee
KCAJ-FM .... Roseau, MN [*FM radio station call letters*]   (BROA)
kcal .... Kilocalorie
KCAL .... Redlands, CA [*AM radio station call letters*]   (RBYB)
KCAL-FM .... Redlands, CA [*FM radio station call letters*]
KCAL-TV .... Los Angeles, CA [*Television station call letters*]
KCAM .... Glennallen, AK [*AM radio station call letters*]
KCAN .... Albion, NE [*Television station call letters*]
KCAO .... Kansas City Area Office [*Energy Research and Development Administration*]

KCAP .... Helena, MT [*AM radio station call letters*]
KCAQ .... Oxnard, CA [*FM radio station call letters*]
KCAR .... Caribou [*Maine*] [*ICAO location identifier*] (ICLI)
KCAR .... Clarksville, TX [*AM radio station call letters*]
KCAS .... Knots Calibrated Airspeed (MCD)
KCAT .... Kemptville College of Agricultural Technology [*Canada*] (ARC)
KCAT .... Pine Bluff, AR [*AM radio station call letters*]
KCAU .... Sioux City, IA [*Television station call letters*]
KCAW .... Sitka, AK [*FM radio station call letters*]
KCAY .... Russell, KS [*FM radio station call letters*]
KCAZ .... Mission, KS [*AM radio station call letters*] (RBYB)
KCB .... Kansas City Ballet
KCB .... Kartell Convent Blaetter (BJA)
KCB .... Keyboard Change Button [*Computer science*]
KCB .... Knight Commander of the [*Order of the*] Bath [*British*] (GPO)
KCBA .... Salinas, CA [*Television station call letters*]
KCBC .... Riverbank, CA [*AM radio station call letters*]
KCBD .... Lubbock, TX [*Television station call letters*]
KCBF .... Fairbanks, AK [*AM radio station call letters*]
KCBI .... Dallas, TX [*FM radio station call letters*]
KCBL-AM .... Fresno, CA [*AM radio station call letters*] (BROA)
KCBM .... Colombus Air Force Base [*Mississippi*] [*ICAO location identifier*] (ICLI)
KCBN .... Reno, NV [*AM radio station call letters*]
KCBQ .... San Diego, CA [*AM radio station call letters*]
KCBQ-FM .... San Diego, CA [*FM radio station call letters*]
KCBR .... Monument, CO [*AM radio station call letters*]
KCBS .... Los Angeles, CA [*FM radio station call letters*]
KCBS .... San Francisco, CA [*AM radio station call letters*]
KCBS-TV .... Los Angeles, CA [*Television station call letters*]
KCBT .... Board of Trade of Kansas City, MO (EA)
KCBX .... San Luis Obispo, CA [*FM radio station call letters*]
KCBY .... Coos Bay, OR [*Television station call letters*]
KCBZ .... Cannon Beach, OR [*FM radio station call letters*] (RBYB)
KCC .... Centre College of Kentucky, Danville, KY [*OCLC symbol*] (OCLC)
KCC .... Coffman Cove, AK [*Location identifier FAA*] (FAAL)
KCC .... Kansas City Connecting Railroad Co. [*AAR code*]
KCC .... Kansas Co-Operative Council (SRA)
KCC .... Kathodal Closure Contraction [*Medicine*]
KCC .... Kentucky Chamber of Commerce (SRA)
KCC .... Keokuk Community College [*Iowa*]
KCC .... Keyboard Common Contact [*Computer science*]
KCC .... Key Control Characteristic
KCC .... K-III Communications [*NYSE symbol*] (TTSB)
KCC .... K-III Communications Corp. [*NYSE symbol*] (SPSG)
KCC .... Knapp Communications Corp.
KCC .... Knife Collectors Club (EA)
KCC .... Knight Commander of the [*Order of the*] Crown [*Belgium*]
KCC .... Kona Coffee Council [*Defunct*] (EA)
KCC .... Koplar Communications Center [*St. Louis, MO*] [*Telecommunications*] (TSSD)
KCC .... Korea Church Coalition for Peace, Justice and Reunification (EA)
KCCA .... Colorado City, AZ [*FM radio station call letters*]
KCCB .... Corning, AR [*AM radio station call letters*]
KCCC .... Carlsbad, NM [*AM radio station call letters*]
KCCC .... Key Chain Collectors Club (EA)
KCCD .... Moorhead, MN [*FM radio station call letters*]
KCCF .... Cave Creek, AZ [*AM radio station call letters*]
KCCG-FM .... Ingleside, TX [*FM radio station call letters*] (BROA)
KCCH .... Knight Commander of Court of Honor [*British*]
KCCI .... Des Moines, IA [*Television station call letters*]
KCCI .... Kansas Chamber of Commerce and Industry (SRA)
KCCK .... Cedar Rapids, IA [*FM radio station call letters*]
KCCM .... Kupffer Cell Conditioned Medium
KCCM .... Moorhead, MN [*FM radio station call letters*]
KCCN .... Honolulu, HI [*AM radio station call letters*]
KCCN .... Monterey, CA [*Television station call letters*]
KCCN-FM .... Honolulu, HI [*FM radio station call letters*]
KCCO .... Alexandria, MN [*Television station call letters*]
KCCPr .... K-III Commun$2.875SrExPfd [*NYSE symbol*] (TTSB)
KCCQ .... Ames, IA [*FM radio station call letters*]
KCCR .... Pierre, SD [*AM radio station call letters*]
KCCS .... Salem, OR [*AM radio station call letters*]
KCCT .... Corpus Christi, TX [*AM radio station call letters*]
KCCT .... Kaolin Cephalin Clotting Time (PDAA)
KCCU .... Lawton, OK [*FM radio station call letters*]
KCCV .... Overland Park, KS [*AM radio station call letters*]
KCCV-FM .... Olathe, KS [*FM radio station call letters*]
KCCW .... Walker, MN [*Television station call letters*]
KCCX-FM .... Lexington, MO [*FM radio station call letters*] (BROA)
KCCY .... Pueblo, CO [*FM radio station call letters*]
KCDA .... Coeur D'Alene, ID [*FM radio station call letters*]
KCDC .... Longmont, CO [*FM radio station call letters*]
KCDD .... Hamlin, TX [*FM radio station call letters*]
KCDI .... Oro Valley, AZ [*FM radio station call letters*]
KCDL .... Cordell, OK [*FM radio station call letters*]
KCDQ .... Monahans, TX [*FM radio station call letters*]
KCDR .... Turlock, CA [*AM radio station call letters*] (RBYB)
KCDS .... Angwin, CA [*FM radio station call letters*]
KCDS .... Childress [*Texas*] [*ICAO location identifier*] (ICLI)
KCDT .... Coeur D'Alene, ID [*Television station call letters*]
KCDU-FM .... Hollister, CA [*FM radio station call letters*] (RBYB)
KCDV-FM .... Cordova, KS [*FM radio station call letters*] (RBYB)
KCDX .... San Carlos, AZ [*FM radio station call letters*]
KCDY .... Carlsbad, NM [*FM radio station call letters*]
KCDZ .... Twentynine Palms, CA [*FM radio station call letters*]
KCE .... Collinsville [*Australia Airport symbol*] (OAG)
KCE .... Key Configuration Element (DNAB)
KCEA .... Atherton, CA [*FM radio station call letters*]
KCEC .... Denver, CO [*Television station call letters*]
KCED .... Centralia, WA [*FM radio station call letters*]
KCEE .... Tucson, AZ [*AM radio station call letters*]
KCEF .... Chicopee Falls/Westover Air Force Base [*Massachusetts*] [*ICAO location identifier*] (ICLI)
KCEL-FM .... California City, CA [*FM radio station call letters*] (BROA)
KCEN .... Temple, TX [*Television station call letters*]
KCEO .... Vista, CA [*AM radio station call letters*]
KCEP .... Las Vegas, NV [*FM radio station call letters*]
KCER .... Kananaskis Centre for Environmental Research [*University of Calgary*] [*Research center*] (RCD)
KCES .... Eufaula, OK [*FM radio station call letters*]
KCET .... Los Angeles, CA [*Television station call letters*]
KCEW .... Crestview/Bob Sikes [*Florida*] [*ICAO location identifier*] (ICLI)
KCEY .... Huntsville, TX [*FM radio station call letters*]
KCEZ .... Corning, CA [*FM radio station call letters*]
KCF .... Key-Click Filter
KCF .... Key Clinical Finding [*Medicine*] (HCT)
KCF .... Thousand Cubic Feet
KCFA .... Amold, CA [*FM radio station call letters*]
KCFB .... St. Cloud, MN [*FM radio station call letters*]
KCFC .... Karen Carpenter Fan Club [*Defunct*] (EA)
KCFD .... Bryan/Coulter Field [*Texas*] [*ICAO location identifier*] (ICLI)
KCFE .... Eden Prairie, MN [*FM radio station call letters*]
KCFF .... Korean Cultural and Freedom Foundation (EA)
KCFG .... Flagstaff, AZ [*Television station call letters*] (BROA)
KCFMC .... Kevin Collins Foundation for Missing Children (EA)
KCFM-FM .... Okmulgee, OK [*FM radio station call letters*] (BROA)
KCFN .... Wichita, KS [*FM radio station call letters*]
KCFO .... Tulsa, OK [*AM radio station call letters*]
KCFP-FM .... Pueblo, CO [*FM radio station call letters*] (RBYB)
KCFR .... Denver, CO [*FM radio station call letters*]
KCFS .... Sioux Falls, SD [*FM radio station call letters*]
KCFV .... Ferguson, MO [*FM radio station call letters*]
KCFW .... Kalispell, MT [*Television station call letters*]
KCFX .... Harrisonville, MO [*FM radio station call letters*]
KCFY .... Yuma, AZ [*FM radio station call letters*]
KCG .... Chignik, AK [*Location identifier FAA*] (FAAL)
KCG .... Key Calling [*Telecommunications*] (IAA)
KCG .... Kinetocardiogram [*Cardiology*]
KCGB .... Hood River, OR [*FM radio station call letters*]
KCGM .... Scobey, MT [*FM radio station call letters*]
KCGN .... Sioux Falls, SD [*AM radio station call letters*]
KCGN-FM .... Ortonville, MN [*FM radio station call letters*]
KCGQ .... Cape Girardeau, MO [*AM radio station call letters*]
KCGQ-FM .... Gordonville, MO [*FM radio station call letters*]
KCGR .... Cottage Grove, OR [*FM radio station call letters*]
KCGS .... Marshall, AR [*AM radio station call letters*]
KCGX .... Broken Bow, OK [*FM radio station call letters*] (RBYB)
KCGY .... Laramie, WY [*FM radio station call letters*]
KCH .... Ketch
kch .... Kilocharacter (MHDB)
KCH .... King's College Hospital
KCH .... Knight Commander of the Guelphic Order of Hanover [*British*]
KCH .... Kuching [*Malaysia*] [*Airport symbol*] (OAG)
KCHA .... Charles City, IA [*AM radio station call letters*]
KCHA .... Chattanooga/Lovell [*Tennessee*] [*ICAO location identifier*] (ICLI)
KCHA-FM .... Charles City, IA [*FM radio station call letters*]
KCHC-FM .... Conroe, TX [*FM radio station call letters*] (RBYB)
KCHD .... Chandler/Williams Air Force Base [*Arizona*] [*ICAO location identifier*] (ICLI)
KCHE .... Cherokee, IA [*AM radio station call letters*]
KCHE-FM .... Cherokee, IA [*FM radio station call letters*]
KCHF .... Santa Fe, NM [*Television station call letters*]
KCHG .... Somerset, TX [*AM radio station call letters*]
KCHI .... Chicago/Metropolitan Area [*Illinois*] [*ICAO location identifier*] (ICLI)
KCHI .... Chillicothe, MO [*AM radio station call letters*]
KCHI-FM .... Chillicothe, MO [*FM radio station call letters*]
KCHJ .... Delano, CA [*AM radio station call letters*]
KCHK .... New Prague, MN [*AM radio station call letters*]
KCHK-FM .... New Prague, MN [*FM radio station call letters*]
KCHL .... San Antonio, TX [*AM radio station call letters*]
KCHN-AM .... Liberty, TX [*AM radio station call letters*] (BROA)
KCHO .... Chico, CA [*FM radio station call letters*]
KCHQ .... Altamont, OR [*FM radio station call letters*]
KCHR .... Charleston, MO [*AM radio station call letters*]
kchr .... Kilocharacter (MHDB)
KCHS .... Charleston/Municipal and Air Force Base [*South Carolina*] [*ICAO location identifier*] (ICLI)
KCHS .... Kilo Characters per Second (IAA)
KCHS .... Knight Commander of the Holy Sepulchre
KCHS .... Truth or Consequences, NM [*AM radio station call letters*]
KCHT .... Kechabta [*Tunisia*] [*Seismograph station code, US Geological Survey*] (SEIS)
KCHT-AM .... Selah, WA [*AM radio station call letters*] (RBYB)
KCHU .... Valdez, AK [*AM radio station call letters*]
KCHX .... Midland, TX [*FM radio station call letters*]
KCHZ-FM .... Ottawa, KS [*FM radio station call letters*] (RBYB)
KCI .... Key Club International (EA)
KCI .... Key Collectors International (EA)
kCi .... Kilocurie (DEN)

KCI	Kit Collectors International (EA)
KCIA	Medford, OR [*FM radio station call letters*]
KCIA	South Korean Central Intelligence Agency [*Later, Agency for National Security Planning*] (PD)
KCIB	Milan, NM [*AM radio station call letters*] (RBYB)
KCIC	Grand Junction, CO [*FM radio station call letters*]
KCID	Caldwell, ID [*AM radio station call letters*]
KCID-FM	Caldwell, ID [*FM radio station call letters*]
KCIE	Dulce, NM [*FM radio station call letters*]
KCIE	Knight Commander of the [*Order of the*] Indian Empire [*British*]
KCIF-FM	Hilo, HI [*FM radio station call letters*] (BROA)
KCII	Washington, IA [*AM radio station call letters*]
KCII-FM	Washington, IA [*FM radio station call letters*]
KCIJ	North Fort Polk, LA [*FM radio station call letters*]
KCIL	Houma, LA [*FM radio station call letters*]
KCIM	Carroll, IA [*AM radio station call letters*]
KCIN	Tacoma, WA [*AM radio station call letters*] (RBYB)
KCIO	King's Commissioned Indian Officer [*British military*] (DMA)
KCIR	Twin Falls, ID [*FM radio station call letters*]
KCIS	Edmonds, WA [*AM radio station call letters*]
KCIT	Amarillo, TX [*Television station call letters*]
K-CITEM	Kennedy Space Center Cite Plan/Requirement (NAKS)
KCIV	Mount Bullion, CA [*FM radio station call letters*]
KCIX	Garden City, ID [*FM radio station call letters*]
KCIY	Liberty, MO [*FM radio station call letters*] (RBYB)
KCJ	Kolel Chibas Jerusalem [*An association*] (EA)
KCJB	Minot, ND [*AM radio station call letters*]
KCJC	Dardanelle, AR [*FM radio station call letters*] (RBYB)
KCJH	Stockton, CA [*FM radio station call letters*]
KCJJ	Iowa City, IA [*AM radio station call letters*]
KCJZ	Terrell Hills, TX [*FM radio station call letters*] (RBYB)
KCK	Kansas City, KS [*Location identifier FAA*] (FAAL)
KCKA	Centralia, WA [*Television station call letters*]
KCKC	San Bernardino, CA [*AM radio station call letters*]
KCKI	Henryetta, OK [*FM radio station call letters*]
KCKL	Malakoff, TX [*FM radio station call letters*]
KCKN	Roswell, NM [*AM radio station call letters*]
KCKR	Waco, TX [*FM radio station call letters*]
KCKS	Concordia, KS [*FM radio station call letters*]
KCKX	Stayton, OR [*AM radio station call letters*]
KCKY	Coolidge, AZ [*AM radio station call letters*]
KCL	Chignik, AK [*Location identifier FAA*] (FAAL)
KCL	Keystation Control Language [*Computer science*] (MHDI)
KCL	King's College, London
KCL	Kirchhoff's Current Law [*Electronics*] (IAA)
KCL	Kitchen, Company Level
KCL	Klamath County Library, Klamath Falls, OR [*OCLC symbol*] (OCLC)
KCL	Knitting Cylinder Lubrication (PDAA)
KCL	Knudsen Cosine Law [*Physics*]
KCLA	Pine Bluff, AR [*FM radio station call letters*]
KCLB	Coachella, CA [*AM radio station call letters*]
KCLB-FM	Coachella, CA [*FM radio station call letters*]
KCLC	Kinder-Care Learning Centers, Inc. [*NASDAQ symbol*] (SAG)
KCLC	Kinder-Care Learning Ctrs [*NASDAQ symbol*] (TTSB)
KCLC	St. Charles, MO [*FM radio station call letters*]
KCLCW	Kinder-Care Lrng Ctr Wrrt [*NASDAQ symbol*] (TTSB)
KCLD	St. Cloud, MN [*FM radio station call letters*]
KCLE	Cleburne, TX [*AM radio station call letters*]
KCLE	Cleveland/Cleveland-Hopkins International [*Ohio*] [*ICAO location identifier*] (ICLI)
KCLE	Continuing Legal Education, University of Kentucky College of Law (DLA)
KCLE	Glen Rose, TX [*FM radio station call letters*] (RBYB)
KCLI	Clinton, OK [*FM radio station call letters*]
KCLI	Kansas City Life Ins [*NASDAQ symbol*] (TTSB)
KCLI	Kansas City Life Insurance Co. [*NASDAQ symbol*] (NQ)
KCLI-AM	Clinton, OK [*AM radio station call letters*] (RBYB)
KCLJ	Knight Commander of the Order of St. Lazarus of Jerusalem (DD)
KCLJ	Knight Commander, Order of St. Lazarus of Jerusalem [*British*] (WA)
KCLK	Asotin, WA [*AM radio station call letters*]
KCLK	Clarkston, WA [*FM radio station call letters*]
KCLL	College Station/Easterwood Field [*Texas*] [*ICAO location identifier*] (ICLI)
KCLL	Lompoc, CA [*AM radio station call letters*]
KCLM	Newport, OR [*FM radio station call letters*]
KCLN	Clinton, IA [*FM radio station call letters*]
KCLO	Rapid City, SD [*Television station call letters*]
KCLQ	Lebanon, MO [*FM radio station call letters*]
KCLR	Boonville, MO [*FM radio station call letters*]
KCLR	Ralls, TX [*AM radio station call letters*]
KCLS	Flagstaff, AZ [*AM radio station call letters*]
KCLS	Kern County Library System [*Library network*]
KCLS	Knight Commander of the Lion and the Sun
KCLT	West Helena, AR [*FM radio station call letters*]
KCLU	Korean Council of Organization [*South Korea*]
KCLU	Thousand Oaks, CA [*FM radio station call letters*]
KCLV	Clovis, NM [*AM radio station call letters*]
KCLV-FM	Clovis, NM [*FM radio station call letters*]
KCLW	Hamilton, TX [*AM radio station call letters*]
KCLX	Colfax, WA [*AM radio station call letters*]
KCLY	Clay Center, KS [*FM radio station call letters*]
KCLY	Kent and County of London Yeomanry [*Military unit*] [*British*]
KCM	Kam Creed Mines Ltd. [*Vancouver Stock Exchange symbol Toronto Stock Exchange symbol*]
KCM	Keratinocyte-Conditioned Medium [*Biochemistry*]
KCM	Key Center for Mines [*University of Wollongong*] [*Australia*]
KCM	Kilenge Mission [*New Britain*] [*Seismograph station code, US Geological Survey*] (SEIS)
KCM	Kirchhoff Coda Migration [*For seismic wave imaging*]
KCM	Kupffer Cell Medium
KCMA	Holdenville, OK [*FM radio station call letters*] (RBYB)
KCMA	Kitchen Cabinet Manufacturers Association (EA)
KCM & B	Kansas City, Memphis & Birmingham Railroad
KCMB	Baker City, OR [*FM radio station call letters*]
KCMC	Texarkana, TX [*AM radio station call letters*]
KCME	Kuznetsk Commodity and Raw Materials Exchange [*Russian Federation*] (EY)
KCME	Manitou Springs, CO [*FM radio station call letters*]
KCMG	Knight Commander of St. Michael and St. George [*Facetiously translated, "Kindly Call Me God"*] [*British*]
KCMG	Mountain Grove, MO [*AM radio station call letters*]
KCMG-FM	Mountain Grove, MO [*FM radio station call letters*]
KCMH	Columbus/Port Columbus International [*Ohio*] [*ICAO location identifier*] (ICLI)
KCMH	Mountain Home, AR [*FM radio station call letters*]
KCMI	Terrytown, NE [*FM radio station call letters*]
KCMJ	Indio, CA [*FM radio station call letters*]
KCMJ	Palm Springs, CA [*AM radio station call letters*]
KCMLN	Kansas City Metropolitan Library Network Council [*Library network*]
KCMN	Colorado Springs, CO [*AM radio station call letters*]
KCMO	Kansas City, Mexico & Orient [*AAR code*]
KCMO	Kansas City, MO [*AM radio station call letters*]
KCMO-FM	Kansas City, MO [*FM radio station call letters*]
KCMQ	Columbia, MO [*FM radio station call letters*]
KCMR	Mason City, IA [*FM radio station call letters*]
KCMS	Edmonds, WA [*FM radio station call letters*]
KCMS	Kodak Color Management System [*Eastman Kodak Co.*] (PCM)
KCMT	Chester, CA [*FM radio station call letters*]
KCMU	Seattle, WA [*FM radio station call letters*]
KCMW	Warrensburg, MO [*FM radio station call letters*]
KCMX	Ashland, OR [*AM radio station call letters*]
KCMX	Keyset Central Multiplexer
KCMX-FM	Ashland, OR [*FM radio station call letters*]
KCMY	Sacramento, CA [*Television station call letters*]
KCN	Chernofski Harbor, AK [*Location identifier FAA*] (FAAL)
KCN	Intetnational Colin Energy [*NYSE symbol*] (SAG)
KCN	Intl Colin Energy [*NYSE symbol*] (TTSB)
KCN	Kids' Clubs Network (AIE)
KCN	Kit Configuration Notice (MCD)
KCN	Kit Control Number [*Navy*] (NG)
KCNA	Cave Junction, OR [*FM radio station call letters*]
KCNA	Korean Central News Agency [*North Korea*]
KCNC	Denver, CO [*Television station call letters*]
KCND	Bismarck, ND [*FM radio station call letters*]
KCNE	Chadron, NE [*FM radio station call letters*]
KCNF	Fort Worth [*Texas*] [*ICAO location identifier*] (ICLI)
KCNI	Broken Bow, NE [*AM radio station call letters*]
KCNM	Carlsbad/Cavern City Air Terminal [*New Mexico*] [*ICAO location identifier*] (ICLI)
KCNM	San Jose, Philippines [*AM radio station call letters*]
KCNN	East Grand Forks, MN [*AM radio station call letters*]
KCNO	Alturas, CA [*AM radio station call letters*]
KCNO-FM	Alturas, CA [*FM radio station call letters*] (RBYB)
KCNQ	Kernville, CA [*FM radio station call letters*]
KCNR	Salt Lake City, UT [*AM radio station call letters*]
KCNS	San Francisco, CA [*Television station call letters*]
KCNT	Hastings, NE [*FM radio station call letters*]
KCNW	Fairway, KS [*AM radio station call letters*]
KCNW	Kelly's Creek & Northwestern Railroad Co. [*AAR code*]
KCNW	Waco/James Connally [*Texas*] [*ICAO location identifier*] (ICLI)
KCNZ	Cedar Falls, IA [*AM radio station call letters*] (RBYB)
KCO	Keep Cost Order [*Telecommunications*] (TEL)
KCOB	Newton, IA [*AM radio station call letters*]
KCOB-FM	Newton, IA [*FM radio station call letters*]
KCOF	Cocoa/Patrick Air Force Base [*Florida*] [*ICAO location identifier*] (ICLI)
KCOG	Centerville, IA [*AM radio station call letters*]
KCOH	Houston, TX [*AM radio station call letters*]
KCOL	Fort Collins, CO [*AM radio station call letters*]
KColC	Colby Community College, Colby, KS [*Library symbol Library of Congress*] (LCLS)
KCole	Kenneth Cole Productions, Inc. [*Associated Press*] (SAG)
KColePd	Kenneth Cole Productions, Inc. [*Associated Press*] (SAG)
KCOM	Comanche, TX [*AM radio station call letters*]
KCOMZ	Korean Communications Zone [*Military*]
KCON	Conway, AR [*AM radio station call letters*]
KCOO-FM	Shafter, CA [*FM radio station call letters*] (BROA)
KCOP	Los Angeles, CA [*Television station call letters*]
KCOR	San Antonio, TX [*AM radio station call letters*]
KCOS	Colorado Springs/Peterson Field [*Colorado*] [*ICAO location identifier*] (ICLI)
KCOS	El Paso, TX [*Television station call letters*]
KCOT	Cotulla/Municipal [*Texas*] [*ICAO location identifier*] (ICLI)
KCOT	San Augustine, TX [*FM radio station call letters*]
KCOU	Columbia, MO [*FM radio station call letters*]
KCOW	Alliance, NE [*AM radio station call letters*]
KCOY	Santa Maria, CA [*Television station call letters*]
KCOZ	Point Lookout, MO [*FM radio station call letters*] (RBYB)
KCP	Kansas City Plant [*Department of Energy*] [*Kansas City, MO*] (GAAI)
KCP	Kansas City Public Library, Kansas City, MO [*OCLC symbol*] (OCLC)

KCP	Keene's Cement Plaster [Technical drawings]
KCP	Kenneth Cole Productions'A' [NYSE symbol] (TTSB)
KCP	Kenneth Cole Productions, Inc. [NYSE symbol] (SAG)
KCP	Keyboard-Controlled Phototypesetter
KCP	Key Crude Prices [Database] [Petroleum Intelligence Weekly] [Information service or system] (CRD)
KCP	Kirghiz Communist Party [Political party]
KCP	Knight Commander of [the Order of] Pius IX
KCPA	Korean Communist Party [Political party North Korea] (FEA)
KCPA	Kaolin Clay Producers Association (DGA)
KCP & G	Kansas City, Pittsburgh & Gulf Railroad
KCPB	Thousand Oaks, CA [FM radio station call letters]
KCPC	Keene's Cement Plaster Ceiling [Technical drawings]
KCPCA	Kansas Committee for Prevention of Child Abuse (EDAC)
KCPI	Albert Lea, MN [FM radio station call letters]
KCPL	Kansas City Power & Light Co. [Associated Press] (SAG)
KCPL	Olympia, WA [AM radio station call letters]
KCPM	Chico, CA [Television station call letters]
KCPQ	Tacoma, WA [Television station call letters]
KCPR	San Luis Obispo, CA [FM radio station call letters]
KCPS	Burlington, IA [AM radio station call letters]
KCPS	Kansas City Public Service R. R. [AAR code]
kcps	Kilocycles per Second
KCPT	Kansas City, MO [Television station call letters]
KCPW	Salt Lake City, UT [FM radio station call letters]
KCPX	Centerville, UT [FM radio station call letters]
KCPX-AM	Centerville, UT [FM radio station call letters] (RBYB)
KCQL	Aztec, NM [AM radio station call letters]
KCQQ	Davenport, IA [FM radio station call letters] (RBYB)
KCQV	Arthur, ND [FM radio station call letters]
KCR	Colorado Creek, AK [Location identifier FAA] (FAAL)
KCR	Kansas City Law Review [A publication] (DLA)
KCR	Key Call Receiver [Telecommunications] (TEL)
KCR	[The] Kowloon Canton Railway [Hong Kong] (DCTA)
KCR	Reports Tempore Chancellor King [A publication] (DLA)
KCRA	Sacramento, CA [Television station call letters]
KCRB	Bemidji, MN [FM radio station call letters]
KCRC	Enid, OK [AM radio station call letters]
KCRC	Kansas City Records Center [Military]
KCRC	Kowloon-Canton Railway Corp. [Commercial firm] [Hong Kong]
KCRCHE	Kansas City Regional Council for Higher Education [Library network]
KCRE	Crescent City, CA [FM radio station call letters]
KCRF	Korean Conflict Research Foundation [Defunct]
KCRF	Newport, OR [FM radio station call letters] (RBYB)
KCRG	Cedar Rapids, IA [AM radio station call letters]
KCRG-TV	Cedar Rapids, IA [Television station call letters]
KCRH	Hayward, CA [FM radio station call letters]
KCRI-FM	Mojave, CA [FM radio station call letters] (BROA)
KCRK	Colville, WA [FM radio station call letters]
KCRL	Rayne, LA [FM radio station call letters]
KCRM-FM	Lubbock, TX [FM radio station call letters] (BROA)
KCRN	San Angelo, TX [AM radio station call letters]
KCRN-FM	San Angelo, TX [FM radio station call letters]
KCRO	Omaha, NE [AM radio station call letters]
KCRP	Corpus Christi/International [Texas] [ICAO location identifier] (ICLI)
KCRR	Grundy Center, IA [FM radio station call letters] (RBYB)
KCRS	Midland, TX [AM radio station call letters]
KCRS-FM	Midland, TX [FM radio station call letters]
KCRT	Keyboard Cathode Ray Tube (MCD)
KCRT	Trinidad, CO [AM radio station call letters]
KCRT-FM	Trinidad, CO [FM radio station call letters]
KCRU	Oxnard, CA [FM radio station call letters]
KCRV	Caruthersville, MO [AM radio station call letters]
KCRW	Santa Monica, CA [FM radio station call letters]
KCRX	Roswell, NM [AM radio station call letters]
KCRY	Indio, CA [FM radio station call letters]
KCRZ	Tucson, AZ [FM radio station call letters]
KCS	[The] Kansas City Southern Railway Co. [AAR code]
KCS	Kansas City Standard [Audio tape technology] (EECA)
KCS	KCS Energy, Inc. [Formerly, KCS Group, Inc.] [NYSE symbol] (SPSG)
KCS	Keratoconjunctivitis Sicca [Ophthalmology]
KCS	Keyboard Configuration Studies (NASA)
KCS	Keyboard Controlled Sequencer [Computer science]
KCS	Keyboards, Computers, and Software [A publication]
KCS	Key Configuration Studies (NASA)
KCS	Kilocharacters per Second (IAA)
kcs	Kilocycles per Second
KCS	King's College School [British]
KCS	Knight of [the Order of] Charles III of Spain
KCS	Knight of the Order of Charles XIII of Sweden [Freemasonry]
KCS	Korean Chemical Society
KCS	Thousand Characters per Second
KCSA	Kerr Center for Sustainable Agriculture [Research center] (RCD)
KCSB	Santa Barbara, CA [FM radio station call letters]
KCSC	Edmond, OK [FM radio station call letters]
KCSC	Kansas City Service Center [IRS]
KCSC	Kansas Cosmosphere and Space Center [Hutchinson, KS]
KCSD	Sioux Falls, SD [FM radio station call letters]
KCSD-TV	Sioux Falls, SD [FM radio station call letters] (RBYB)
KCSE-FM	Ballinger, TX [FM radio station call letters] (RBYB)
KCSF	Stanton Foundation (EA)
KCSG	Knight Commander of the [Order of] St. Gregory [British]
KCSI	Knight Commander of the [Order of the] Star of India [British]
KCSI	Red Oak, IA [FM radio station call letters]
KCSJ	Pueblo, CO [AM radio station call letters]
KCSM	San Mateo, CA [FM radio station call letters]
KCSM-TV	San Mateo, CA [Television station call letters]
KCSN	Northridge, CA [FM radio station call letters]
KCSo	Kansas City Southern Industries, Inc. [Associated Press] (SAG)
KCSO	Modesto, CA [Television station call letters]
KCSou	Kansas City Southern Industries, Inc. [Associated Press] (SAG)
KCSP	Casper, WY [FM radio station call letters]
KCSR	Chadron, NE [AM radio station call letters]
KCSS	Key Center for Statistical Services [Deakin University] [Australia]
KCSS	Knight Commander of [the Order of] St. Sylvester
KCSS	Turlock, CA [FM radio station call letters]
KCS/SO	Keyboard Class Select / Statistics Output [Computer science] (MHDI)
KCST	Florence, OR [AM radio station call letters]
KCST-FM	Florence, OR [FM radio station call letters]
KCStJ & CB	Kansas City, St. Joseph & Council Bluffs Railroad
KCSU	Fort Collins, CO [FM radio station call letters]
KCT	Kansas City Terminal Railway Co. [AAR code]
KCT	Kaolin Cephalin Time [Clinical chemistry]
KCT	Kaolin Clotting Time [Clinical chemistry]
KCT	Kathodal Closing Tetanus [Medicine]
KCT	Kelvin Circulation Theorem [Physics]
KCT	Knight Commander of the Temple [Freemasonry] (ROG)
KCT	Knox's Cube Test [Short-term memory and attention span test]
KCTA	Corpus Christi, TX [AM radio station call letters]
KCTAX	Kemper State TF Inc. Ser: Cal. Cl.A [Mutual fund ticker symbol] (SG)
KCTB	Cut Bank [Montana] [ICAO location identifier] (ICLI)
KCTC	Sacramento, CA [AM radio station call letters]
KCTD-AM	Los Angeles, CA [AM radio station call letters] (BROA)
KCTE	Independence, MO [AM radio station call letters]
KCTE	Kathodal Closure Tetanus [Medicine]
KCTF	Waco, TX [Television station call letters]
KCTG	Ozark, MO [FM radio station call letters] (RBYB)
KCTI	Gonzales, TX [AM radio station call letters]
KCTI-FM	Gonzales, TX [FM radio station call letters] (RBYB)
KCTM	Rio Grande City, TX [FM radio station call letters]
KCTMLPCC	Key Chain Tag and Mini License Plate Collectors Club [Later, LPKCMLPCC] (EA)
KCTN	Garnavillo, IA [FM radio station call letters]
KCTO	Columbia, LA [AM radio station call letters]
KCTO-FM	Columbia, LA [FM radio station call letters]
KCTR-FM	Billings, MT [FM radio station call letters]
KCTS	Knight Commander of the Tower and Sword [Portugal] (ROG)
KCTS	Seattle, WA [Television station call letters]
KCTT	Yellville, AR [FM radio station call letters]
KCTV	Kansas City, MO [Television station call letters]
KCTX	Childress, TX [AM radio station call letters]
KCTY	Salinas, CA [AM radio station call letters]
KCtyPL	Kansas City Power & Light Co. [Associated Press] (SAG)
KCTZ	Bozeman, MT [Television station call letters]
KCU	Keyboard Control Unit
KCU	Kilocurie (IAA)
KCUA	Coalville, UT [FM radio station call letters]
KCUB	Stephenville, TX [FM radio station call letters]
KCUB	Tucson, AZ [AM radio station call letters]
KCUE	Red Wing, MN [AM radio station call letters]
KCUI	Pella, IA [FM radio station call letters]
KCUK	Chevak, AK [FM radio station call letters]
KCUL-AM	Marshall, TX [AM radio station call letters] (BROA)
KCUL-FM	Marshall, TX [FM radio station call letters] (BROA)
KCUR	Kansas City, MO [FM radio station call letters]
KCUS	Columbus/Municipal [New Mexico] [ICAO location identifier] (ICLI)
KCUV	Englewood, CO
KCUZ	Clifton, AZ [AM radio station call letters]
KCV	Kancana Ventures Ltd. [Vancouver Stock Exchange symbol]
KCVG	Cincinnati/Greater Cincinnati [Ohio] [ICAO location identifier] (ICLI)
KCVI	Blackfoot, ID [FM radio station call letters]
KCVL	Colville, WA [AM radio station call letters]
KCVM-FM	Hudson, IA [FM radio station call letters] (BROA)
KCVO	Camdenton, MO [FM radio station call letters]
KCVO	Knight Commander of the Royal Victorian Order [British]
KCVP	Konservativ-Christlichsoziale Volkspartei [Conservative Christian-Social Party] [Switzerland Political party] (PPE)
KCVQ-FM	Knob Noster, MO [FM radio station call letters] (BROA)
KCVR	Lodi, CA [AM radio station call letters]
KCVS	Clovis/Cannon Air Force Base [New Mexico] [ICAO location identifier] (ICLI)
KCVS	Salina, KS [FM radio station call letters]
KCVT-FM	Silver Lake, KS [FM radio station call letters] (RBYB)
KCVU	Paradise, CA [Television station call letters]
KCVW-FM	Kingman, KS [FM radio station call letters] (RBYB)
KCWA	Arnold, MO [FM radio station call letters]
KCWB	Kansas City Westport Belt [AAR code]
KCWB-TV	Kansas City, MO [TV station call letters] (RBYB)
KCWC	Lander, WY [Television station call letters]
KCWC	Riverton, WY [FM radio station call letters]
KCWD	Harrison, AR [FM radio station call letters]
KCWD	Kaleidoscope: Current World Data [ABC-CLIO] [Information service or system] (IID)
KCWM	Hondo, TX [AM radio station call letters] (RBYB)
KCWM-FM	Hondo, TX [FM radio station call letters] (RBYB)
KCWN	New Sharon, IA [FM radio station call letters]
KCWR	Bakersfield, CA [AM radio station call letters]
KCWS	Merkel, TX [FM radio station call letters]
KCWT	Wenatchee, WA [Television station call letters]

KCWW	Tempe, AZ [AM radio station call letters]
KCWX	Columbia Falls, MT [FM radio station call letters]
KCXL	Calexico/International [California] [ICAO location identifier] (ICLI)
KCXL	Liberty, MO [AM radio station call letters] (RBYB)
KCXX	Lake Arrowhead, CA [FM radio station call letters] (RBYB)
KCXY	Camden, AR [FM radio station call letters]
KCYC	King's Cheshire Yeomanry Cavalry [British military] (DMA)
KCYL	Lampasas, TX [AM radio station call letters]
KCYN-FM	Moab, UT [FM radio station call letters] (RBYB)
KCYQ-FM	Richfield, UT [FM radio station call letters] (BROA)
KCYS	Cheyenne [Wyoming] [ICAO location identifier] (ICLI)
KCYS-FM	Seaside, OR [FM radio station call letters] (BROA)
KCYT-FM	Houston, AK [FM radio station call letters] (RBYB)
KCYY	San Antonio, TX [FM radio station call letters]
KCZ	Kochi [Japan] [Airport symbol] (OAG)
KCZE	New Hampton, IA [FM radio station call letters]
KCZO	Carrizo Springs, TX [FM radio station call letters]
KCZQ	Cresco, IA [FM radio station call letters]
KCZY	Osage, IA [FM radio station call letters]
KD	Cathodal Duration [Medicine] (DMAA)
Kd	Coefficient of Soil-Water Absorption (GNE)
K_d	Dissociation Constant [Physics] (DAVI)
K_d	Distribution Coefficient [Partition coefficient] [Physics] (DAVI)
KD	Kallidin [Biochemistry]
KD	Kathodal Duration [Medicine]
KD	Kawasaki Disease [Also, KS, MLNS] [Medicine]
KD	Keep It Dark [Say nothing about it] [Slang]
KD	Kendell Airlines [ICAO designator] (AD)
KD	Kennnedy Disease [Medicine] (DMAA)
KD	Kentucky Dam [TVA]
KD	Keto-Diastix [Miles Inc.] [Pharmacology] (DAVI)
KD	Kettledrum
KD	Keyboard and Display [Computer science] (MHDB)
K/D	Keyboard/Display (ACRL)
KD	Key Definition (MHDB)
KD	Keyed to Differ [Locks] (ADA)
KD	Khaki Drill [British military] (DMA)
KD	Kidney Donor (STED)
KD	Killed (AABC)
KD	Kiln-Dried [Lumber]
KD	Kilodalton [Molecular mass measure]
kd	Kilodalton (STED)
KD	Kilter Diagram
KD	Klinge [Germany] [Research code symbol]
KD	Knee Disarticulation [Medicine]
KD	Knitted Dacron (MEDA)
KD	Knocked Down [i.e., disassembled]
kd	Knocked Down (EBF)
KD	Known-Distance [Range] [Weaponry] (INF)
KD	Komitet Domowy. Warsaw Ghetto (BJA)
KD	Korsakoff's Disease [Medicine]
KD	Kriegs Dekoration [War Decoration] [German]
KD	Kuwaiti Dinar [Monetary unit] (BJA)
KD	Pilotless Aerial Target [Navy]
KDA	Kendall Airlines [Australia ICAO designator] (FAAC)
kDa	Kilodalton [Physics] [Chemistry] (DOG)
KDA	Kit Design Approach
KDA	Known Drug Allergies [Medicine] (DMAA)
KDA	Kolda [Senegal] [Airport symbol] (AD)
KDA	Kuranda [Australia Seismograph station code, US Geological Survey Closed] (SEIS)
KDAA	Rolla, MO [FM radio station call letters] (RBYB)
KDAB	Prairie Grove, AR [FM radio station call letters]
KDAC	Fort Bragg, CA [AM radio station call letters]
KDAE	Sinton, TX [AM radio station call letters]
KDAF	Dallas, TX [Television station call letters]
KDAG	Farmington, NM [FM radio station call letters]
KDAK	Carrington, ND [AM radio station call letters]
KDAL	Dallas/Dallas-Love Field [Texas] [ICAO location identifier] (ICLI)
KDAL	Duluth, MN [AM radio station call letters]
kdal	Kilodalton (STED)
KDAL-FM	Duluth, MN [FM radio station call letters]
KDAM	Monroe City, MO [FM radio station call letters]
KDAO	Marshalltown, IA [AM radio station call letters]
KDAO-FM	Eldora, IA [FM radio station call letters]
KDAP	Douglas, AZ [AM radio station call letters]
KDAP-FM	Douglas, AZ [FM radio station call letters]
KDAQ	Shreveport, LA [FM radio station call letters]
KDAR	Oxnard, CA [FM radio station call letters]
KDAT	Cedar Rapids, IA [FM radio station call letters] (RBYB)
KDAT	Kiln-Dried After Treatment [Lumber]
KDAY	Dayton/James M. Coxdayton Municipal [Ohio] [ICAO location identifier] (ICLI)
KDAY	Independence, CA [FM radio station call letters]
KDAZ	Albuquerque, NM [AM radio station call letters]
KDB	Kambalda [Australia Airport symbol] (OAG)
KDB	Keller-Dorian, Berthon [Method] [Photography]
KDB	Kelvin Double Bridge [Physics]
KDB	Konedobu [Papua New Guinea] [Seismograph station code, US Geological Survey] (SEIS)
KDB	Korea Development Bank
KDB	Santa Barbara, CA [FM radio station call letters]
KDBB	Bonne Terre, MO [FM radio station call letters]
KDBC	El Paso, TX [Television station call letters]
KDBH	Natchitoches, LA [FM radio station call letters]

KDBM	Dillon, MT [AM radio station call letters]
KDBM-FM	Dillon, MT [FM radio station call letters]
KDBR	Kalispell, MT [FM radio station call letters]
KDBS-AM	Alexandria, LA [AM radio station call letters] (RBYB)
KDBX	Banks, OR [FM radio station call letters]
KDc	Dodge City Public Library, Dodge City, KS [Library symbol Library of Congress] (LCLS)
KDC	Kathodal Duration Contraction [Medicine]
KDC	KD Air Corp. [ICAO designator] (FAAC)
KDC	Keil and Delitzsch Commentaries [A publication] (BJA)
KDC	Key Distribution Center (MCD)
KDC	Keyed Display Console
KDC	Kidney Disease Treatment Center (DMAA)
KDC	Kodak Digital Camera [Image format] (AAEL)
KDC	Kodiak [Alaska] [Seismograph station code, US Geological Survey] (SEIS)
KDC	Kosher Dining Club (BJA)
KDCA	Washington/National [District of Columbia] [ICAO location identifier] (ICLI)
KDCC	Dodge City, KS [AM radio station call letters]
KDCC	Washington [District of Columbia] [ICAO location identifier] (ICLI)
KDCD	San Angelo, TX [FM radio station call letters]
KDCE	Espanola, NM [AM radio station call letters]
KDCG	San Diego Coast Guard Air Base [California] [ICAO location identifier] (ICLI)
KDCK	Dodge City, KS [Television station call letters] (BROA)
KDCL	Knocked Down, in Carloads
KDCP	Kidney Disease Control Program [Public Health Service]
KDCQ	Coos Bay, OR [FM radio station call letters] (RBYB)
KDCR	Sioux Center, IA [FM radio station call letters]
KDCV	Blair, NE [FM radio station call letters]
KDD	Kokusai Denshin Denwa Co. Ltd. [Telegraph & Telephone Corp.] [Tokyo, Japan] [Telecommunications]
KDDA	Dumas, AR [AM radio station call letters]
KDDB	Paso Robles, CA [FM radio station call letters]
KDDD	Dumas, TX [AM radio station call letters]
KDDG-FM	Albany, MN [FM radio station call letters] (BROA)
KDDK	Jacksonville, AR [FM radio station call letters]
KDDQ	Comanche, OK [FM radio station call letters]
KDDR	Oakes, ND [AM radio station call letters]
KDDS-AM	Duluth, MN [AM radio station call letters] (BROA)
KDDX	Spearfish, SD [FM radio station call letters] (RBYB)
KDDZ-AM	San Diego, CA [AM radio station call letters] (RBYB)
KDe	Derby Public Library, Derby, KS [Library symbol Library of Congress] (LCLS)
KDE	Kappa Delta Epsilon [An association] (NTPA)
KDE	Keyboard Data Entry
KDE	Kinetic Depth Effect [Cognitive science]
KDE	Koroba [Papua New Guinea] [Airport symbol Obsolete] (OAG)
KDEA	New Iberia, LA [FM radio station call letters]
KDEB	Springfield, MO [Television station call letters]
KDEC	Decorah, IA [AM radio station call letters]
KDEC-FM	Decorah, IA [FM radio station call letters]
KDEF	Albuquerque, NM [AM radio station call letters]
KDEL	Arkadelphia, AR [FM radio station call letters]
KDEM	Deming, NM [FM radio station call letters]
KDEM	Kurzweil Data Entry Machine [for optical character recognition]
KDEN	Denver/Stapleton International [Colorado] [ICAO location identifier] (ICLI)
KDEN-TV	Longmont, CO [TV station call letters] (RBYB)
KDEO-FM	Waipahu, HI [FM radio station call letters]
KDEP	Kentucky Department of Environmental Protection
KDEP	Smoke Layer Estimated (Feet) Deep [Meteorology] (FAAC)
KDEP-FM	Depoe Bay, OR [FM radio station call letters] (RBYB)
KDES	Palm Springs, CA [AM radio station call letters] (RBYB)
KDES-FM	Palm Springs, CA [FM radio station call letters]
KDET	Center, TX [AM radio station call letters]
KDET	Detroit/Detroit City [Michigan] [ICAO location identifier] (ICLI)
KDET-FM	Center, TX [FM radio station call letters]
KDEW	De Witt, AR [AM radio station call letters] (RBYB)
KDEW-FM	De Witt, AR [FM radio station call letters] (RBYB)
KDEX	Dexter, MO [AM radio station call letters]
KDEX-FM	Dexter, MO [FM radio station call letters]
KDEZ	Jonesboro, AR [FM radio station call letters]
KDF	Kalamein [Trademark] Door and Frame
KDF	Knob Door Fastener
KDF	Knocked Down Flat
KDF	Kraft durch Freude [Strength through Joy Movement] [Pre-World War II] [German]
KDFC	Kenny Dale Fan Club (EA)
KDFC	Korea Development Finance Corp.
KDFC	Palo Alto, CA [AM radio station call letters]
KDFC	San Francisco, CA [FM radio station call letters]
KDFI	Dallas, TX [Television station call letters]
KDFN	Doniphan, MO [AM radio station call letters]
KDFR	Des Moines, IA [FM radio station call letters]
KDFT	Ferris, TX [AM radio station call letters]
KDFW	Dallas-Fort Worth/Regional Airport [Texas] [ICAO location identifier] (ICLI)
KDFW	Dallas, TX [Television station call letters]
KDFX	Dallas, TX [AM radio station call letters] (RBYB)
KDG	Kedougou [Senegal] [Seismograph station code, US Geological Survey Closed] (SEIS)
KDG	King's Dragoon Guards [Later, QDG] [Military unit] [British]
KDGB	Dodge City, KS [FM radio station call letters]

KDGE .... Gainesville, TX [*FM radio station call letters*]
KDGO .... Durango, CO [*AM radio station call letters*]
KDGS .... Andover, KS [*FM radio station call letters*] (RBYB)
KDH .... Kandahar [*Afghanistan*] [*Airport symbol*] (OAG)
KDH .... Key Depression per Hour [*Computer science*] (IAA)
KDH .... Korean Direct Hire
KDH .... Kosher Dining Hall (BJA)
KDHI .... Twentynine Palms, CA [*FM radio station call letters*]
KDHL .... Faribault, MN [*AM radio station call letters*]
KDHN........... Dimmitt, TX [*AM radio station call letters*]
KDHN........... Dothan [*Alabama*] [*ICAO location identifier*] (ICLI)
KDHT........... Dalhart [*Texas*] [*ICAO location identifier*] (ICLI)
KDHX........... St. Louis, MO [*FM radio station call letters*]
KDI .... Kendari [*Indonesia*] [*Airport symbol*] (OAG)
KDI .... Knowledge and Distributed Intelligence
KDI .... Korea Development Institute (ECON)
KDI .... Kuwaiti Dinar [*Monetary unit*] (DS)
KDIA .... Oakland, CA [*AM radio station call letters*]
KDIC .... Grinnell, IA [*FM radio station call letters*]
KDIF............ Riverside, CA [*AM radio station call letters*]
KDIG .... Orland, CA [*FM radio station call letters*]
KDII .... Key Defense Intelligence Issue (MCD)
KDIN .... Des Moines, IA [*Television station call letters*]
KDIO .... Ortonville, MN [*AM radio station call letters*]
KDIS-AM...... Los Angeles, CA [*AM radio station call letters*] (BROA)
KDIU .... Dimmitt, TX [*FM radio station call letters*]
KDIX .... Dickinson, ND [*AM radio station call letters*]
KDIZ-AM...... Golden Valley, MN [*AM radio station call letters*] (RBYB)
KDJ .... Njdole [*Gabon*] [*Airport symbol*] (AD)
KDJI .... Holbrook, AZ [*AM radio station call letters*]
KDJK .... Oakdale, CA [*FM radio station call letters*]
KDJR .... De Soto, MO [*FM radio station call letters*]
KDJS .... Willmar, MN [*AM radio station call letters*]
KDJS-FM...... Willmar, MN [*FM radio station call letters*]
KDJW........... Amarillo, TX [*AM radio station call letters*]
KDK .... Khodzhikent [*Former USSR Seismograph station code, US Geological Survey Closed*] (SEIS)
KDK .... Knit de Knit Texturing (IAA)
KDK .... Kodiak [*Alaska*] Municipal Airport [*Airport symbol Obsolete*] (OAG)
KDKA .... Pittsburgh, PA [*First station to broadcast a baseball game, August 5, 192 1*] [*AM radio station call letters*]
KDKA-TV..... Pittsburgh, PA [*Television station call letters*]
KDKB-FM..... Mesa, AZ [*FM radio station call letters*] (RBYB)
KDKD .... Clinton, MO [*AM radio station call letters*]
KDKD-FM..... Clinton, MO [*FM radio station call letters*]
KDKF........... Klamath Falls, OR [*Television station call letters*]
KDKK .... Park Rapids, MN [*FM radio station call letters*]
KDKO .... Littleton, CO [*AM radio station call letters*]
KDKR-FM..... Decatur, TX [*FM radio station call letters*] (RBYB)
KDKS-FM..... Haughton, LA [*FM radio station call letters*]
KDL............. Kerrisdale Resources Ltd. [*Vancouver Stock Exchange symbol*]
KDL............. Koronadal [*Mindanao, Philippines*] [*Airport symbol*] (AD)
KDL............. Kreisinger Development Laboratory (KSC)
KDLA .... De Ridder, LA [*AM radio station call letters*]
KDLB .... Henryetta, OK [*AM radio station call letters*]
KD lcl .... Knocked Down in Less Than Carload Lots (EBF)
KDLCL .... Knocked Down, in Less than Carloads
KDLF........... Del Rio/Laughlin Air Force Base [*Texas*] [*ICAO location identifier*] (ICLI)
KDLG .... Dillingham, AK [*AM radio station call letters*]
KDLH .... Duluth/International [*Minnesota*] [*ICAO location identifier*] (ICLI)
KDLH .... Duluth, MN [*Television station call letters*]
KDLK .... Del Rio, TX [*AM radio station call letters*] (RBYB)
KDLK-FM..... Del Rio, TX [*FM radio station call letters*]
KDLL .... Kenai, AK [*FM radio station call letters*] (RBYB)
KDLM........... Detroit Lakes, MN [*AM radio station call letters*]
KDLO .... Watertown, SD [*FM radio station call letters*]
KDLO-TV...... Florence, SD [*Television station call letters*]
KDLP .... Bayou Vista, LA [*AM radio station call letters*]
KDLR .... Devils Lake, ND [*AM radio station call letters*]
KDLS .... Perry, IA [*AM radio station call letters*]
KDLS-FM..... Perry, IA [*FM radio station call letters*]
KDLT........... Mitchell, SD [*Television station call letters*]
kdlth .... Kodalith (VRA)
KDLV........... Sioux Falls, SD [*Television station call letters*] (BROA)
KDLX........... Makawao, HI [*FM radio station call letters*]
KDLY........... Lander, WY [*FM radio station call letters*]
KDM............. Kingdom (WGA)
KDM............. Kyrgyzstan Democratic Movement [*Political party*]
KDMA .... Montevideo, MN [*AM radio station call letters*]
KDMA .... Tucson/Davis Monthan Air Force Base [*Arizona*] [*ICAO location identifier*] (ICLI)
KDMD .... Anchorage, AK [*Television station call letters*]
KDMG .... Burlington, IA [*AM radio station call letters*]
KDMI .... Des Moines, IA [*FM radio station call letters*]
KDMI .... Thousands of Delivered Machine Instructions [*Computer science*]
KDMI-AM..... Des Moines, IA [*AM radio station call letters*] (RBYB)
KDMM .... Herington, KS [*FM radio station call letters*]
KDMM .... Highland Park, TX [*AM radio station call letters*]
KDMN .... Buena Vista, CO [*AM radio station call letters*]
KDMO .... Carthage, MO [*AM radio station call letters*]
KDMS .... El Dorado, AR [*AM radio station call letters*]
KDMS .... Kennedy Space Center Data Management System [*NASA*] (NASA)
KDMX .... Dallas, TX [*FM radio station call letters*]
KDN .... Kaydon Corp. [*NYSE symbol*] (SAG)

K/DN .... Kickdown [*Automotive engineering*]
KDN .... Kinetically Designed Nozzle (NASA)
KdN.............. Koninkrijk der Nederlanden [*Kingdom of the Netherlands*] [*Dutch*] (BARN)
KDN .... N'Dende [*Gabon*] [*Airport symbol*] (OAG)
K-DNA......... Deoxyribonucleic Acid - Kinetoplast [*Biochemistry, genetics*]
kDNA .... Kinetoplast DNA[*Deoxyribonucleic Acid*] [*Genetics*] (DOG)
KDNA .... Yakima, WA [*FM radio station call letters*]
KDNE .... Crete, NE [*FM radio station call letters*]
KDNI .... Duluth, MN [*FM radio station call letters*]
KDNK .... Carbondale, CO [*FM radio station call letters*]
KDNL .... St. Louis, MO [*Television station call letters*]
KDNO........... Delano, CA [*FM radio station call letters*]
KDNP........... Keresztenydemokrata Neppart [*Christian Democratic People's Party*] [*Hungary Political party*] (EY)
KDNR........... Los Lunas, NM [*FM radio station call letters*] (RBYB)
KDNS .... Downs, KS [*AM radio station call letters*]
KDNW.......... Duluth, MN [*FM radio station call letters*]
KDO .... Ketodeoxyoctonate [*Biochemistry*]
KDO .... Ketodeoxyoctonic Acid (STED)
KDO .... Key District Office [*IRS*]
KDOC .... Anaheim, CA [*Television station call letters*]
K-DODM ...... Kennedy Space Center Department of Defense Plan/Requirement (NAKS)
KDOG........... North Mankato, MN [*FM radio station call letters*]
KDOK........... Tyler, TX [*FM radio station call letters*]
KDOL .... Henderson, NV [*AM radio station call letters*]
KDOM .... Windom, MN [*AM radio station call letters*]
KDOM-FM..... Windom, MN [*FM radio station call letters*]
KDON........... Salinas, CA [*FM radio station call letters*]
KDOR........... Bartlesville, OK [*Television station call letters*]
KDOS .... Key Display Operating System
KDOS .... Key to Disk Operating System
KDOS .... Laredo, TX [*AM radio station call letters*]
KDOT-FM..... Reno, NV [*FM radio station call letters*] (RBYB)
KDOV........... Dover Air Force Base [*Delaware*] [*ICAO location identifier*] (ICLI)
KDOV........... Medford, OR [*FM radio station call letters*] (RBYB)
KDP .... Kandep [*Papua New Guinea*] [*Airport symbol Obsolete*] (OAG)
KDP .... Kappa Delta Pi [*Honor society*] (AEE)
KDP .... Keyboard, Display, and Printer [*Computer science*]
KDP .... Key Data Points (MCD)
KDP .... Key Decision Point [*USCG*] (TAG)
KDP .... Key Development Plan [*Telecommunications*] (TEL)
KDP .... Known Datum Point
KDP .... Korean Democratic Party [*North Korea Political party*] (FEA)
KDP .... Kurdish Democratic Party [*Iran*] [*Political party*]
KDP .... Potassium Dideuterium Phosphate
KDP .... Potassium [*Kalium*] Dihydrogen Phosphate [*Inorganic chemistry*]
KDPA .... Knitgoods Dyers and Processors Association
KDPA .... West Chicago/Du Page County [*Illinois*] [*ICAO location identifier*] (ICLI)
KDPI .... Kurdish Democratic Party of Iran [*Political party*] (PPW)
K-DPM .... Kennedy Space Center Department of Defense Payloads Plan/Requirement (NAKS)
K-DPN .... Kennedy Space Center Department of Defense Payloads Notice (NAKS)
K-DPN .... KSC [*Kennedy Space Center*] DOD Payloads Notice [*Department of Defense*] [*NASA*] (NASA)
K-DPPS........ Kennedy Space Center Department of Defense Payloads Project Specification (NAKS)
K-DPPS........ KSC [*Kennedy Space Center*] DOD Payloads Projects Specification [*Department of Defense*] [*NASA*] (NASA)
KDPR........... Dickinson, ND [*FM radio station call letters*]
KDPS .... Des Moines, IA [*FM radio station call letters*]
KDPS .... Kurdish Democratic Party of Syria [*Political party*]
KDQN........... De Queen, AR [*AM radio station call letters*]
KDQN-FM..... De Queen, AR [*FM radio station call letters*]
KDR .... Kandrian [*Papua New Guinea*] [*Airport symbol*] (OAG)
KDR .... Kangeld Resources Ltd. [*Vancouver Stock Exchange symbol*]
KDR .... Kappa Delta Rho [*Fraternity*]
KDR .... Keyboard Data Recorder [*Computer science*]
KDR .... Kidderminster [*British depot code*]
K/DR .... Kitchen/Dining Room [*Classified advertising*] (ADA)
KDR .... Knockdown Resistance [*Pesticide technology*]
KDRE .... North Little Rock, AR [*FM radio station call letters*]
KDRG........... Deer Lodge, MT [*AM radio station call letters*]
KDRH........... Glenwood Springs, CO [*FM radio station call letters*]
KDRK........... Spokane, WA [*FM radio station call letters*]
KDRM........... Moses Lake, WA [*FM radio station call letters*]
KDRO........... Sedalia, MO [*AM radio station call letters*]
KDRQ........... Wishek, ND [*AM radio station call letters*]
KDRS .... Paragould, AR [*AM radio station call letters*]
KDRT........... Del Rio/International [*Texas*] [*ICAO location identifier*] (ICLI)
KDRV........... Medford, OR [*Television station call letters*]
KDRY........... Alamo Heights, TX [*AM radio station call letters*]
KDS .... K2 Del Aire SA de CV [*Mexico ICAO designator*] (FAAC)
KDS .... Kamad Silver Co. Ltd. [*Vancouver Stock Exchange symbol*]
KDS .... Kathode Dark Space
KDS .... Kaufman Developmental Scale [*Child development test*]
KDS .... Kedougou [*Senegal*] [*Seismograph station code, US Geological Survey*] (SEIS)
KDS .... Keel Depth Simulator
KDS .... Keyboard Display Station [*Computer science*] (DA)
KDS .... Key Data Station (NITA)
KDS .... Key Display System [*Computer science*] (MDG)

KDS .... Key to Disc System
KDS .... Kiting Detection System (HGAA)
KDS .... Knowledge Directory Server
KDS .... Komma Dimokratikou Sosialismou [*Party for Democratic Socialism*] [*Greek Political party*] (PPE)
KDS .... Kristen Demokratisk Samling [*Christian Democratic Union*] [*Sweden Political party*] (PPE)
KDSD .... Aberdeen, SD [*Television station call letters*]
KDSD .... Pierpont, SD [*FM radio station call letters*]
KDSE .... Dickinson, ND [*Television station call letters*]
kd/sec .... Kilocycles per Second [*Measurement*] (DAVI)
KDSI .... Alice, TX [*AM radio station call letters*]
KDSI .... Thousands of Delivered Source Instructions [*Computer science*]
KDSJ .... Deadwood, SD [*AM radio station call letters*]
KDSL .... Thousands of Delivered Source Lines of Code [*Computer science*]
KDSM .... Des Moines [*Iowa*] [*ICAO location identifier*] (ICLI)
KDSM .... Des Moines, IA [*Television station call letters*]
KDSM .... Keratinizing Desquamative Squamous Metaplasia [*Medicine*]
KDSN .... Denison, IA [*AM radio station call letters*]
KDSN-FM..... Denison, IA [*FM radio station call letters*]
KDSR .... Williston, ND [*AM radio station call letters*]
KDSS .... Ely, NV [*FM radio station call letters*]
KDSS .... Key-to-Disk Subsystem [*Computer science*] (MHDB)
KDST .... Dyersville, IA [*FM radio station call letters*]
KDSU .... Fargo, ND [*FM radio station call letters*]
KDSX .... Denison-Sherman, TX [*AM radio station call letters*]
KDT............. Kammer der Technik
KDT............. Kathodal Duration Tetanus [*Medicine*]
KDT............. Keyboard and Display Test (MCD)
KDT............. Keyboard Display Terminal (MCD)
KDT............. Key Data Terminal
KDT............. Key Definition Table [*Computer science*] (PCM)
KDT............. Key-to-Disk-to-Tape (MCD)
KDTA .... Delta, CO [*AM radio station call letters*]
KDTE .... Kathodal Duration Tetanus [*Medicine*] (ROG)
KDTH .... Dubuque, IA [*AM radio station call letters*]
KDTK .... Prescott Valley, AZ [*FM radio station call letters*]
KDTL-FM ..... Lake Village, AR [*FM radio station call letters*] (RBYB)
KDTN .... Denton, TX [*Television station call letters*]
KDTV .... San Francisco, CA [*Television station call letters*]
KDTW .... Detroit/Metropolitan Wayne County [*Michigan*] [*ICAO location identifier*] (ICLI)
KDTX .... Dallas, TX [*Television station call letters*]
KDU .... Christian Democratic Union [*Czechoslavakia*] [*Political party*] (ECON)
KDU .... Keyboard Display Unit (MCD)
KDU .... Skardu [*Pakistan*] [*Airport symbol*] (AD)
KDUC .... Barstow, CA [*FM radio station call letters*]
KDUG .... Douglas/Bisbee International [*Arizona*] [*ICAO location identifier*] (ICLI)
KDUH .... Scottsbluff, NE [*Television station call letters*]
KDUK .... Eugene, OR [*AM radio station call letters*]
KDUK .... Florence, OR [*FM radio station call letters*]
KDUN .... Reedsport, OR [*AM radio station call letters*]
KDUQ .... Ludlow, CA [*FM radio station call letters*]
KDUR .... Durango, CO [*FM radio station call letters*]
KDUS .... Cadus Pharmaceutical Corp. [*NASDAQ symbol*] (SAG)
KDUS-AM .... Tempe, AZ [*AM radio station call letters*] (BROA)
KDUV .... Visalia, CA [*FM radio station call letters*]
KDUX .... Aberdeen, WA [*FM radio station call letters*]
KDUZ .... Hutchinson, MN [*AM radio station call letters*]
KDV .... Kandavu [*Fiji*] [*Airport symbol*] (OAG)
KdV............. Korteweg-deVries [*Equation*] [*Mathematics*]
kDVC.......... Kilovolts, Direct Current (KSC)
KDVE-FM ..... Denison-Sherman, TX [*FM radio station call letters*] (RBYB)
KDVL .... Devils Lake, ND [*FM radio station call letters*]
KDVR .... Denver, CO [*Television station call letters*]
KDVS .... Davis, CA [*FM radio station call letters*]
KDVV .... Topeka, KS [*FM radio station call letters*]
KDWA .... Hastings, MN [*AM radio station call letters*]
KDWB .... Richfield, MN [*FM radio station call letters*]
KDWG .... Billings, MT [*AM radio station call letters*] (RBYB)
KDWN .... Las Vegas, NV [*AM radio station call letters*]
KDX .... Klondike Mines [*Vancouver Stock Exchange symbol*]
KDX .... Klondex Mines Ltd [*VS, exchange symbol*] (TTSB)
KDX .... Knock Down Export [*Automotive engineering*]
KDXE .... Sulphur Springs, TX [*FM radio station call letters*]
KDXL .... St. Louis Park, MN [*FM radio station call letters*]
KDXU .... St. George, UT [*AM radio station call letters*]
KDXY-FM..... Lake City, AR [*FM radio station call letters*] (RBYB)
KDY .... Kennedy Resources [*Vancouver Stock Exchange symbol*]
KDYL .... Salt Lake City, UT [*AM radio station call letters*]
KDYN .... Ozark, AR [*AM radio station call letters*]
KDYN-FM..... Ozark, AR [*FM radio station call letters*]
KDYS .... Abilene/Dyess Air Force Base [*Texas*] [*ICAO location identifier*] (ICLI)
KDyS-AM.... Lafayette, LA [*AM radio station call letters*] (RBYB)
KdyWils ..... Kennedy Wilson, Inc. [*Associated Press*] (SAG)
KDZ .... Kurdzhali [*Bulgaria*] [*Seismograph station code, US Geological Survey*] (SEIS)
KDZA .... Pueblo, CO [*AM radio station call letters*]
KDZA-FM..... Pueblo, CO [*FM radio station call letters*] (RBYB)
KDZN .... Glendive, MT [*FM radio station call letters*]
KDZZ .... Albuquerque, NM [*AM radio station call letters*]
K$_e$............ Exchangeable Body Potassium [*Biochemistry*] (DAVI)
KE............... Kaiser Engineers (NRCH)

Ke............... Keen's English Rolls Court Reports [*48 English Reprint*] [*A publication*] (DLA)
KE............... Kendall's Compound E [*Cortisone*]
ke............... Kenya [*MARC country of publication code Library of Congress*] (LCCP)
KE............... Kenya [*ANSI two-letter standard code*] (CNC)
KE............... Kerr Effect [*Optics*]
KE............... Key Equipment [*Telecommunications*] (TEL)
KE............... Kinetic Energy
KE............... King Edward (ROG)
KE............... Kitchen Exhaust (OA)
KE............... Knight of the Eagle
KE............... Knight of the Elephant [*Denmark*]
KE............... Knights of Equity (EA)
KE............... Knowledge Engineer [*Computer science*]
KE............... Koger Equity [*AMEX symbol*] (TTSB)
KE............... Koger Equity, Inc. [*AMEX symbol*] (CTT)
KE............... Korea Fund [*NYSE symbol*] (TTSB)
KE............... Korean Air [*Airline flight code*] (ODBW)
KE............... Korean Air Lines [*ICAO designator*] (AD)
KEA............ Kanada Esperanto-Asocio [*Canadian Esperanto Association*]
KEA............ Kealakomo [*Hawaii*] [*Seismograph station code, US Geological Survey Closed*] (SEIS)
KEA............ Keane, Inc. [*AMEX symbol*] (SPSG)
KEA............ Kent Executive Aviation Ltd. [*British ICAO designator*] (FAAC)
KEA............ Knitwear Employers Association (EA)
KEAG .... Anchorage, AK [*FM radio station call letters*]
KEAL-FM..... Douglas, AZ [*FM radio station call letters*] (RBYB)
KEAN .... Abilene, TX [*AM radio station call letters*]
Kean C NJ ... Kean College of New Jersey (GAGS)
Keane .... Keane, Inc. [*Associated Press*] (SAG)
Keane & Gr... Keane and Grant's English Registration Appeal Cases [*1854-62*] [*A publication*] (DLA)
Keane & GRC... Keane and Grant's English Registration Appeal Cases [*1854-62*] [*A publication*] (DLA)
KEAN-FM .... Abilene, TX [*FM radio station call letters*]
KEAR .... San Francisco, CA [*FM radio station call letters*]
KEAS.......... Eastland, TX [*AM radio station call letters*]
KEAS.......... Knots Equivalent Airspeed (MCD)
KEASAT...... Kinetic Energy Anti-Satellite
KEAS-FM..... Eastland, TX [*FM radio station call letters*]
Keat Fam Sett... Keatinge's Family Settlements [*1810*] [*A publication*] (DLA)
KEAZ.......... De Ridder, LA [*FM radio station call letters*]
KEB............ English Bay, AK [*Location identifier FAA*] (FAAL)
KEB............ Keban [*Turkey*] [*Seismograph station code, US Geological Survey*] (SEIS)
Keb............ Keble's English King's Bench Reports [*83, 84 English Reprint*] [*A publication*] (DLA)
KEB............ Korea Exchange Bank (IMH)
KEBC.......... Oklahoma City, OK [*FM radio station call letters*]
KEB COLL .... Keble College [*Oxford University*] (ROG)
KEBE.......... Jacksonville, TX [*AM radio station call letters*]
KEBI........... Kentucky Enterprise Bancorp [*NASDAQ symbol*] (SAG)
Keb J.......... Keble's Justice of the Peace [*A publication*] (DLA)
Kebl........... Keble's English King's Bench Reports [*83, 84 English Reprint*] [*A publication*] (DLA)
Keble .... Keble's English King's Bench Reports [*83, 84 English Reprint*] [*A publication*] (DLA)
Keble (Eng)... Keble's English King's Bench Reports [*83, 84 English Reprint*] [*A publication*] (DLA)
KEBN .... Salem, OR [*Television station call letters*]
KEBR .... North Highlands, CA [*FM radio station call letters*]
KEBR .... Rocklin, CA [*AM radio station call letters*]
Keb Stat ..... Keble's Statutes [*A publication*] (DLA)
KEC............ KDD Engineering and Consulting Inc. (NITA)
KEC............ Kecskemet [*Hungary*] [*Seismograph station code, US Geological Survey*] (SEIS)
KEC............ Klebsiella, Enterobacter, Citrobacter [*Bacteriae*] [*Microbiology*] (DAVI)
KECC.......... Keystone Empire Collegiate Conference (PSS)
KECC.......... Miles City, MT [*FM radio station call letters*]
KECG.......... El Cerrito, CA [*FM radio station call letters*]
KECG.......... Elizabeth City Coast Guard Air Base/Municipal [*North Carolina*] [*ICAO location identifier*] (ICLI)
KECH .... Sun Valley, ID [*FM radio station call letters*]
KECI.......... Missoula, MT [*Television station call letters*]
KECME........ Kuzbass Commodity and Raw Materials Exchange [*Russian Federation*] (EY)
KECN-AM..... Blackfoot, ID [*AM radio station call letters*] (RBYB)
KECO.......... Elk City, OK [*FM radio station call letters*]
KECO.......... Korea Electric Co. (BUAC)
KECP.......... Kit Engineering Change Proposal (KSC)
KECR.......... El Cajon, CA [*AM radio station call letters*]
KECS.......... Gainesville, TX [*FM radio station call letters*] (RBYB)
KECY.......... El Centro, CA [*Television station call letters*] (RBYB)
KED............ Kaedi [*Mauritania*] [*Airport symbol*] (OAG)
KED............ Kedougou [*Senegal*] [*Seismograph station code, US Geological Survey Closed*] (SEIS)
KED............ Known Enemy Dead [*Military*]
KEDA .... San Antonio, TX [*AM radio station call letters*]
KEDDS .... Kansas Education Dissemination/Diffusion System (EDAC)
KEDG .... Las Vegas, NV [*FM radio station call letters*]
KEDI........... Korean Education Development Institute (BUAC)
KEDJ........... Sun City, AZ [*FM radio station call letters*]
KEDM.......... Monroe, LA [*FM radio station call letters*]

KEDO	Korea Energy Development Organisation [*A consortium formed by the US, North Korea, and South Korea to finance and build reactors*] (ECON)
KEDO	Longview, WA [*AM radio station call letters*]
KEDP	Las Vegas, NM [*FM radio station call letters*]
KEDR	Sacramento, CA [*FM radio station call letters*]
KEDS	Knowledge Express Data Systems
KEDT	Corpus Christi, TX [*FM radio station call letters*]
KEDT-TV	Corpus Christi, TX [*Television station call letters*]
KEDW	Edwards Air Force Base [*California*] [*ICAO location identifier*] (ICLI)
KEE	Emporia State University, School of Library Science, Emporia, KS [*OCLC symbol*] (OCLC)
KEE	Kelle [*Congo*] [*Airport symbol*] (OAG)
KEE	Kerr Electro-Optical Effect [*Optics*]
KEE	Keychart Educational Equipment [*for use with an electronic typewriter*]
KEE	Keystone Air Services Ltd. [*Canada ICAO designator*] (FAAC)
KEE	Knowledge Engineering Environment [*An artificial intelligence system*]
KEED	Eugene, OR [*AM radio station call letters*] (RBYB)
KEEE	Nacogdoches, TX [*AM radio station call letters*]
KEEF	Los Angeles, CA [*Television station call letters*]
KEEH	Spokane, WA [*FM radio station call letters*]
KEEL	Kent European Enterprises Ltd. [*British*]
KEEL	Shreveport, LA [*AM radio station call letters*]
Keen	Keen's English Rolls Court Reports [*48 English Reprint*] [*A publication*] (DLA)
KEEN	Palmer, AK [*FM radio station call letters*] (RBYB)
Keen Ch	Keen's English Rolls Court Reports [*48 English Reprint*] [*A publication*] (DLA)
Keen (Eng)	Keen's English Rolls Court Reports [*48 English Reprint*] [*A publication*] (DLA)
Keener Quasi Contr	Keener's Cases on Quasi Contracts [*A publication*] (DLA)
Keene St C	Keene State College (GAGS)
KEEP	Bandera, TX [*FM radio station call letters*]
KEEP	Kamehameha Early Education Program [*Hawaii*] (EDAC)
KEEP	Kentucky Environmental Education Program (EDAC)
KEEP	Kyosato Education Experiment Project [*Self-help program for Japanese farmers established by Americans in 1948*]
KEEPS	Kodak Ektaprint Electronic Publishing System [*Hardware and software components*] [*Eastman Kodak Co.*]
KEES	Gladewater, TX [*AM radio station call letters*]
KEET	Eureka, CA [*Television station call letters*]
KEEY	St. Paul, MN [*FM radio station call letters*]
KEEZ	Mankato, MN [*FM radio station call letters*]
KEF	Keflavik [*Iceland*] [*Airport symbol*] (AD)
KEF	Korea Equity Fund [*NYSE symbol*] (SPSG)
KEF	Reykjavik [*Iceland*] Keflavik Airport [*Airport symbol*] (OAG)
KEFD	Houston/Ellington Air Force Base [*Texas*] [*ICAO location identifier*] (ICLI)
KEFE	Los Alamos, NM [*FM radio station call letters*]
KEFH-FM	Clarendon, TX [*FM radio station call letters*] (BROA)
KEFM	Omaha, NE [*FM radio station call letters*]
KEFR	Le Grand, CA [*FM radio station call letters*]
KEFX-FM	Twin Falls, ID [*FM radio station call letters*] (BROA)
KEG	Keg Restaurants Ltd. [*Toronto Stock Exchange symbol Vancouver Stock Exchange symbol*]
KEG	Key Energy Group [*AMEX symbol*] (SPSG)
KEG	Key Gap [*Computer science*] (MHDI)
KEGE	Richfield, MN [*AM radio station call letters*]
KEGE-FM	Minneapolis, MN [*FM radio station call letters*]
KEGG	Daingerfield, TX [*AM radio station call letters*]
KEGG	Kyoto Encyclopedia of Genes and Genomes [*Computer network*]
KEGL	Fort Worth, TX [*FM radio station call letters*]
KEGP	Eagle Pass/Municipal [*Texas*] [*ICAO location identifier*] (ICLI)
KEGR	Red Bluff, CA [*FM radio station call letters*] (RBYB)
KEGS	Kenworth Engine Governing System [*Automotive engineering*]
KEGT	Lake Village, AR [*AM radio station call letters*]
KEGX	Richland, WA [*FM radio station call letters*]
KEH	King Edward's Horse Regiment [*Military unit*] [*British*]
KEH	Kurzgefasstes Exegetisches Handbuch zum Alten Testament [*Leipzig*] [*A publication*] (BJA)
KEHK-FM	Brownsville, OR [*FM radio station call letters*] (RBYB)
KEI	Keithley Instruments [*NYSE symbol*] (TTSB)
KEI	Keithley Instruments, Inc. [*AMEX symbol*] (SPSG)
KEI	Kepi [*Indonesia*] [*Airport symbol*] (OAG)
KEI	Kresge Eye Institute
KEIA	Korea Economic Institute of America (EA)
Keil	Keilway's English King's Bench Reports [*72 English Reprint*] [*A publication*] (DLA)
KEIL	Key Essential Item List [*Defense Supply Agency*]
Keilw	Keilway's English King's Bench Reports [*72 English Reprint*] [*A publication*] (DLA)
Keilway	Keilway's English King's Bench Reports [*72 English Reprint*] [*A publication*] (DLA)
Keilw (Eng)	Keilway's English King's Bench Reports [*72 English Reprint*] [*A publication*] (DLA)
KEIN	Great Falls, MT [*AM radio station call letters*]
KEIN-FM	Conrad, MT [*FM radio station call letters*] (BROA)
KEIS	Kentucky Economic Information System [*University of Kentucky*] [*Lexington Database producer*] [*Information service or system*]
Keith Ch PA	Registrar's Book, Keith's Court of Chancery [*Pennsylvania*] [*A publication*] (DLA)
Keithly	Keithley Instruments, Inc. [*Associated Press*] (SAG)
KEJC	Modesto, CA [*FM radio station call letters*] (RBYB)

KEJJ-FM	Gunnison, CO [*FM radio station call letters*] (BROA)
KEJO	Corvallis, OR [*FM radio station call letters*]
KEJS	Lubbock, TX [*FM radio station call letters*]
KEK	Ekwok [*Alaska*] [*Airport symbol*] (OAG)
KEK	Kappa Eta Kappa [*Fraternity*]
KEK	Konferenz Europaeischer Kirchen [*Conference of European Churches - CEC*] (EA)
KEK	Kypriakon Ethnikon Komma [*Cypriot National Party (1944-1960)*] [*Greek Cypriot*] [*Political party*] (PPE)
KEKA	Eureka, CA [*FM radio station call letters*]
KEKB	Fruita, CO [*FM radio station call letters*]
Ke/Kg	Exchangeable Potassium per Kilogram of Body Weight [*Biochemistry*] (DAVI)
KEL	Karntner Einheitsliste [*Carinthian Unity List*] [*Austria Political party*] (PPE)
KEL	Keles [*Later, TKT*] [*Former USSR Geomagnetic observatory code*]
Kel	Kelim (BJA)
KEL	Kelsey-Hayes Canada Ltd. [*Toronto Stock Exchange symbol*]
KEL	Kelud [*Java*] [*Seismograph station code, US Geological Survey Closed*] (SEIS)
KEL	Known Enemy Location [*Military*]
KEL	Koroska Enotna Lista [*Carinthian Unity List*] [*Austria Political party*] (PPE)
KELA	Centralia-Chehalis, WA [*AM radio station call letters*]
Kel An	Kelly's Life Annuities [*1835*] [*A publication*] (DLA)
Kel Cont	Kelly on Contracts of Married Women [*A publication*] (DLA)
KELD	El Dorado, AR [*AM radio station call letters*]
KELD	El Dorado/Goodwin Field [*Arkansas*] [*ICAO location identifier*] (ICLI)
Kel Draft	Kelly's Draftsman [*14th ed.*] [*1978*] [*A publication*] (DLA)
KELE-AM	Mountain Grove, MO [*AM radio station call letters*] (RBYB)
KELE-FM	Mountain Grove, MO [*FM radio station call letters*] (BROA)
Kel-f	Polymonochlorotrifluoroethylene (IDOE)
KELG	Elgin, TX [*AM radio station call letters*]
Kel GA	Kelly's Reports [*1-3 Georgia*] [*A publication*] (DLA)
Kelh	Kelham's Norman French Law Dictionary [*A publication*] (DLA)
Kelham	Kelham's Norman French Law Dictionary [*A publication*] (DLA)
Kelh Dict	Kelham's Norman French Law Dictionary [*A publication*] (DLA)
KELI	Kristana Esperantista Ligo Internacia [*International Christian Esperanto Association*] (EAIO)
KELI	San Angelo, TX [*FM radio station call letters*]
K-ELISA	Kinetic Measurement of Enzyme-Linked Immunosorbant Assay
KELK	Elko, NV [*AM radio station call letters*]
Kelk Jud Acts	Kelke's Judicature Acts [*A publication*] (DLA)
KELL	Kellstrom Industries [*NASDAQ symbol*] (TTSB)
KELL	Kellstrom Industries, Inc. [*NASDAQ symbol*] (SAG)
Kellen	Kellen's Reports [*146-55 Massachusetts*] [*A publication*] (DLA)
Kel Life Ann	Kelly on Life Annuities [*A publication*] (DLA)
KellOG	Kelley Oil and Gas Corp. [*Associated Press*] (SAG)
Kellogg	Kellogg Co. [*Associated Press*] (SAG)
KELLW	Kellstrom Inds Wrrt [*NASDAQ symbol*] (TTSB)
Kellwood	Kellwood Co. [*Associated Press*] (SAG)
Kelly	Kelly's Reports [*1-3 Georgia*] [*A publication*] (DLA)
Kelly & C	Kelly and Cobb's Reports [*4, 5 Georgia*] [*A publication*] (DLA)
Kelly & Cobb	Kelly and Cobb's Reports [*4, 5 Georgia*] [*A publication*] (DLA)
KellyRus	Kelly Russell Studios, Inc. [*Associated Press*] (SAG)
KellyS	Kelly Services, Inc. [*Associated Press*] (SAG)
KELN	Kell Negative [*Hematology*] (DAVI)
KELN	North Platte, NE [*FM radio station call letters*]
KELO	Sioux Falls, SD [*AM radio station call letters*]
KELO-FM	Sioux Falls, SD [*FM radio station call letters*]
KELO-TV	Sioux Falls, SD [*Television station call letters*]
KELP	El Paso/International [*Texas*] [*ICAO location identifier*] (ICLI)
KELP	El Paso, TX [*AM radio station call letters*]
KELP	Kindergarten Evaluation for Learning Potential [*McGraw Hill*]
KELR	Chariton, IA [*FM radio station call letters*]
KELS	Kohlman Evaluation of Living Skills [*Occupational therapy*]
Kel Sc Fac	Kelly's Scire Facias [*2nd ed.*] [*1849*] [*A publication*] (DLA)
Kelstr	Kellstrom Industries, Inc. [*Associated Press*] (SAG)
Kelstrm	Kellstrom Industries, Inc. [*Associated Press*] (SAG)
KELT-FM	Riverside, CA [*FM radio station call letters*] (BROA)
KELU	Kuching Employees and Labourers' Union [*Sarawak*]
Kel Us	Kelly on Usury [*1835*] [*A publication*] (DLA)
KELY	Ely, NV [*AM radio station call letters*]
KELY	Kelly Services, Inc. [*NASDAQ symbol*] (NQ)
KELYA	Kelly Services'A' [*NASDAQ symbol*] (TTSB)
KELYB	Kelly Services'B' [*NASDAQ symbol*] (TTSB)
KELY-FM	Ely, NV [*FM radio station call letters*]
KEm	Emporia Public Library, Emporia, KS [*Library symbol Library of Congress*] (LCLS)
KEM	Kemi [*Finland*] [*Airport symbol*] (OAG)
KEM	Kemper Corp. [*NYSE symbol*] (SPSG)
KEM	Kinetic Energy Missile (INF)
KEMAR	Knowles Electronics Manikin for Acoustic Research
KEMB	Emmetsburg, IA [*FM radio station call letters*]
Kemble Sax	Kemble's The Saxons in England [*A publication*] (DLA)
KEMC	Billings, MT [*FM radio station call letters*]
KEmC	College of Emporia, Emporia, KS [*Library symbol Library of Congress*] (LCLS)
KEMC	Kemper Corp. (MHDW)
Kemet	Kemet Corp. [*Associated Press*] (SAG)
KEMM	Commerce, TX [*FM radio station call letters*]
KEMO	Kennesaw Mountain National Battlefield Park
Kemo Tx	Chemical Therapy [*or Chemotherapy*] [*Pharmacology*] (DAVI)
Kemper	Kemper Corp. [*Associated Press*] (SAG)
KEMRI	Kenya Medical Research Institute (BUAC)

KEmT............ Kansas State Teachers College, Emporia, KS [*Library symbol Library of Congress Obsolete*] (LCLS)

KEmU........... Emporia State University, Emporia, KS [*Library symbol Library of Congress*] (LCLS)

KEM-V........... Kinetic Energy Missile Vehicle [*Army*]

KEMV.......... Mountain View, AR [*Television station call letters*]

KEMX.......... Locust Grove, OK [*FM radio station call letters*]

Ken................ Kendall [*Record label*]

KEN............... Kenema [*Sierra Leone*] [*Airport symbol*] (OAG)

KEN............... Kenridge Mineral [*Vancouver Stock Exchange symbol*]

KEN............... Kentucky

Ken................ Kentucky (ODBW)

Ken................ Kenya (VRA)

KEN............... Kenya [*ANSI three-letter standard code*] (CNC)

KEN............... Kenyon College, Gambier, OH [*OCLC symbol*] (OCLC)

Ken................ Kenyon's English King's Bench Reports [*A publication*] (DLA)

KENA............ Mena, AR [*AM radio station call letters*]

KENA-FM...... Mena, AR [*FM radio station call letters*]

Kenan.......... Kenan's Reports [*76-91 North Carolina*] [*A publication*] (DLA)

Kenan.......... Kenan Transportation Co. [*Associated Press*] (SAG)

KENATCO...... Kenya National Transport Co. (BUAC)

KENCLIP...... Kentucky Cooperative Library and Information Project [*Library network*]

KENCO.......... Kendrick & Co. [*Telecommunications service*] (TSSD)

KEND............ Enid/Vance Air Force Base [*Oklahoma*] [*ICAO location identifier*] (ICLI)

KEND............ Roswell, NM [*FM radio station call letters*]

Ken Dec....... Kentucky Decisions (Sneed) [*2 Kentucky*] [*A publication*] (DLA)

KENE............ Toppenish, WA [*AM radio station call letters*]

Kenetech...... Kenetech Corp. [*Associated Press*] (SAG)

KENGO.......... Kenya Energy and Environment Organisations (BUAC)

KENI............. Anchorage, AK [*AM radio station call letters*]

Ken LR.......... Kentucky Law Reporter [*A publication*] (DLA)

Ken L Re....... Kentucky Law Reporter [*A publication*] (DLA)

KENN............ Farmington, NM [*AM radio station call letters*]

KENN............ Kennecott Co. Railroad [*AAR code*]

Kenn Ch........ Kennedy's Chancery Practice [*2nd ed.*] [*1852-53*] [*A publication*] (DLA)

Kenn C Mar... Kennedy on Courts-Martial [*A publication*] (DLA)

Kennett......... Kennett's Glossary [*A publication*] (DLA)

Kennett......... Kennett upon Impropriations [*A publication*] (DLA)

Kennett Gloss... Kennett's Glossary [*A publication*] (DLA)

Kennett Par Ant... Kennett's Parochial Antiquities [*A publication*] (DLA)

Kenn Gloss... Kennett's Glossary [*A publication*] (DLA)

Kenn Imp....... Kennett upon Impropriations [*A publication*] (DLA)

Kenn Jur....... Kennedy on Juries [*A publication*] (DLA)

Kennmtl........ Kennametal, Inc. [*Associated Press*] (SAG)

Kenn Par Antiq... Kennett's Parochial Antiquities [*A publication*] (DLA)

Kenn Pr........ Kennedy's Chancery Practice [*2nd ed.*] [*1852-53*] [*A publication*] (DLA)

KENO............ Las Vegas, NV [*AM radio station call letters*]

Ken Opin...... Kentucky Opinions [*A publication*] (DLA)

Kenora.......... Keewatin, Norman, and Rat Portage [*Communities that merged to form town in Ontario, Canada*]

KENPRO........ Kenyan Committee on Trade Procedures (BUAC)

KENR............ Hudson, TX [*AM radio station call letters*]

Ken R............ Kenyon Review [*A publication*] (BRI)

KENS............ Kensington [*West London*] (ROG)

KENS............ San Antonio, TX [*AM radio station call letters*]

KenseyN....... Kensey Nash Corp. [*Associated Press*] (SAG)

KENS-TV........ San Antonio, TX [*Television station call letters*]

KENT............ Kent Financial Services [*NASDAQ symbol*] (SPSG)

KENT............ Kent Financial Svcs [*NASDAQ symbol*] (TTSB)

Kent.............. Kent's Commentaries on American Law [*A publication*] (DLA)

KENT............ Odessa, TX [*AM radio station call letters*]

Kent & R St... Kent and Radcliff's Law of New York, Revision of 1801 [*A publication*] (DLA)

Kentch.......... Kenetech Corp. [*Associated Press*] (SAG)

Kent Com...... Kent's Commentaries on American Law [*A publication*] (DLA)

Kent Comm.... Kent's Commentaries on American Law [*A publication*] (DLA)

Kentekl......... Kentek Information Systems, Inc. [*Associated Press*] (SAG)

KentEl.......... Kent Electronics [*Associated Press*] (SAG)

KentEnt......... Kentucky Enterprise Bancorp [*Associated Press*] (SAG)

KENT-FM....... Odessa, TX [*FM radio station call letters*]

KentFn.......... Kent Financial Services, Inc. [*Associated Press*] (SAG)

Kent's Commen... Kent's Commentaries on American Law [*A publication*] (DLA)

Kent St U....... Kent State University (GAGS)

KENU............ Enumclaw, WA [*AM radio station call letters*]

KENV............ Wendover/Wendover Auxiliary Air Base [*Utah*] [*ICAO location identifier*] (ICLI)

KENV-TV........ Elko, NV [*TV station call letters*] (RBYB)

KENW............ Portales, NM [*FM radio station call letters*]

KENW-TV....... Portales, NM [*Television station call letters*]

Ke:nx........... Connects [*Macintosh*] [*Computer science*]

Keny............. Kenyon's English King's Bench Reports [*A publication*] (DLA)

Kenya LR....... Kenya Law Reports [*A publication*] (DLA)

Keny Ch........ Chancery Cases [*2 Notes of King's Bench Cases*] [*England*] [*A publication*] (DLA)

KENZ-FM....... Orem, UT [*FM radio station call letters*] (RBYB)

KEO.............. Keld'Or Resources, Inc. [*Vancouver Stock Exchange symbol*]

KEO.............. King Edward's Own [*British military*] (DMA)

KEO.............. Odienne [*Ivory Coast*] [*Airport symbol*] (OAG)

KEOC............ King Edward's Own Cavalry [*British military*] (DMA)

KEOJ............ Caney, KS [*FM radio station call letters*]

KEOK............ Tahlequah, OK [*FM radio station call letters*]

KEOL............ King Edward's Own Lancers [*British military*] (DMA)

KEOL............ La Grande, OR [*FM radio station call letters*]

KEOM............ Mesquite, TX [*FM radio station call letters*]

KEOR............ Atoka, OK [*AM radio station call letters*]

KEOS............ College Station, TX [*FM radio station call letters*] (RBYB)

KEP............... Kaneb Energy Partners Ltd. (MHDW)

KEP............... Kellner Eye Piece

KEP............... Key Entry Processing

KEP............... King Edward Point [*South Georgia Island*] [*Seismograph station code, US Geological Survey*] (SEIS)

KEP............... Knight of the Eagle and Pelican [*Freemasonry*]

KEP............... Korea Electric Power ADS [*NYSE symbol*] (TTSB)

KEP............... Korea Electric Power Corp. [*NYSE symbol*] (SAG)

KEP............... Nepalganj [*Nepal*] [*Airport symbol*] (OAG)

KEPB............ Eugene, OR [*Television station call letters*]

KEPC............ Colorado Springs, CO [*FM radio station call letters*]

KEPE............ Kentron Programmatismou kai Oikonomikon Ereunon [*Centre of Planning and Economic Research*] [*Greece*]

KEPG............ Victoria, TX [*FM radio station call letters*]

KEPI............. Eagle Pass, TX [*FM radio station call letters*] (RBYB)

KEPOA.......... Keep This Office Advised

KEPR............ Pasco, WA [*Television station call letters*]

KEPROM........ Keyed-Access, Erasable, Programmable Read-Only Memory [*Computer science*]

KEPS............ Eagle Pass, TX [*AM radio station call letters*]

KEPX............ Eagle Pass, TX [*FM radio station call letters*]

KEPZ............ Kaohsiung Export Processing Zone [*Reexport manufacturing complex*] [*Taiwan*]

KEQ............... Kebar [*Indonesia*] [*Airport symbol*] (OAG)

KEQU............ Kewaunee Scientific [*NASDAQ symbol*] (TTSB)

KEQU............ Kewaunee Scientific Corp. [*Formerly, Kewaunee Science Equipment*] [*NASDAQ symbol*] (NQ)

Ker............... Indian Law Reports, Kerala Series [*A publication*] (DLA)

Ker............... Kerithoth (BJA)

KER............... Kerman [*Iran*] [*Airport symbol*] (OAG)

KER............... Kermanshah [*Iran*] [*Seismograph station code, US Geological Survey*] (SEIS)

KER............... Kerr-Addison Mines [*TS, exchange symbol*] (TTSB)

KER............... Kerr Addison Mines Ltd. [*Toronto Stock Exchange symbol*]

KER............... Kerry [*County in Ireland*] (ROG)

KER............... Kinetic Energy Release

KERA............ Dallas, TX [*FM radio station call letters*]

KERA............ Kentucky Education Reform Act

Kera............. Keratitis [*Ophthalmology*] (DAVI)

KERA............ KeraVision, Inc. [*NASDAQ symbol*] (SAG)

Kerala.......... All Indian Law Reports, Kerala Series [*A publication*] (DLA)

Kerala LJ....... Kerala Law Journal [*A publication*] (DLA)

KERA-TV........ Dallas, TX [*Television station call letters*]

KeraVis......... KeraVision, Inc. [*Associated Press*] (SAG)

KeraVs.......... KeraVision, Inc. [*Associated Press*] (SAG)

KERB............ Kermit, TX [*AM radio station call letters*]

KERB-FM....... Kermit, TX [*FM radio station call letters*]

KERC............ Marked Tree, AR [*FM radio station call letters*]

KERD............ Kinetic Energy Release Distribution [*Of ions for spectral studies*]

KERE............ Atchison, KS [*AM radio station call letters*]

KERE-FM....... Horton, KS [*FM radio station call letters*]

KEREN-OR... Jerusalem Institutions for the Blind (EA)

KERI............. Wasco, CA [*AM radio station call letters*]

KERM............ Torrington, WY [*FM radio station call letters*]

KERMA.......... Kinetic Energy Released per Unit Mass (DEN)

KERN............ Bakersfield, CA [*AM radio station call letters*]

Kern............. Kernan's Reports [*11-14 New York*] [*A publication*] (DLA)

Kern............. Kern's Reports [*100-116 Indiana*] [*A publication*] (DLA)

KERN-FM....... Bakersfield, CA [*FM radio station call letters*]

KERO............ Bakersfield, CA [*Television station call letters*]

KERO............ Kerosine [*British*]

KERP............ Pueblo, CO [*FM radio station call letters*]

Kerr............. Kerr Group [*Associated Press*] (SAG)

KERR............ Kerrier [*England*]

Kerr............. Kerr's New Brunswick Reports [*A publication*] (DLA)

Kerr............. Kerr's Reports [*27-29 New York Civil Procedure*] [*A publication*] (DLA)

Kerr............. Kerr's Reports [*18-22 Indiana*] [*A publication*] (DLA)

KERR............ Polson, MT [*AM radio station call letters*]

Kerr Act........ Kerr's Actions at Law [*3rd ed.*] [*1861*] [*A publication*] (DLA)

Kerr Anc L.... Kerr on Ancient Lights [*A publication*] (DLA)

Kerr Black.... Kerr's Blackstone [*12th ed.*] [*1895*] [*A publication*] (DLA)

Kerr Disc...... Kerr's Discovery [*1870*] [*A publication*] (DLA)

Kerr Ext........ Kerr on Inter-State Extradition [*A publication*] (DLA)

Kerr F & M.... Kerr's Fraud and Mistake [*7th ed.*] [*1952*] [*A publication*] (DLA)

Kerr Fr.......... Kerr's Fraud and Mistake [*7th ed.*] [*1952*] [*A publication*] (DLA)

KerrGp.......... Kerr Group [*Associated Press*] (SAG)

Kerr Inj......... Kerr on Injunctions [*A publication*] (DLA)

KerrMc.......... Kerr McGee Corp. [*Associated Press*] (SAG)

Kerr (NB)....... Kerr's New Brunswick Reports [*A publication*] (DLA)

Kerr Rec....... Kerr on Receivers [*A publication*] (DLA)

Kerr Stu Black... Kerr's Student's Blackstone [*A publication*] (DLA)

Kerr W & M Cas... Kerr's Water and Mineral Cases [*A publication*] (DLA)

Kerse........... Kerse's Manuscript Decisions, Scotch Court of Session [*A publication*] (DLA)

KERUK-NASI... Kerukunan Nasional [*Campaign for National Harmony*] [*Indonesia*]

KERV............ Kentucky Equine Respiratory Virus [*Veterinary science*] (DMAA)

KERV............ Kerrville, TX [*AM radio station call letters*]

Kerwin.......... Kerwin Shops, Inc. [*Associated Press*] (SAG)

KERX............ Paris, AR [*FM radio station call letters*]

KES	Karg-Elert Society (BUAC)
KES	Key Element Search (MCD)
KES	Keystone Consolidated Industries, Inc. [*NYSE symbol*] (SPSG)
KES	Keystone Consol Ind [*NYSE symbol*] (TTSB)
KES	Knigovedenie: Entsiklopedicheskil Slovar [*A publication*]
KES	Knowledge Engineering System [*Software Architecture and Engineering Inc.*] (NITA)
KES	Ksar Es Souk [*Seismograph station code, US Geological Survey Closed*] (SEIS)
KES	Kvakera Esperantista Societo [*Quaker Esperanto Society - QES*] (EAIO)
KESC	Karachi Electric Supply Corp. (BUAC)
KESD	Brookings, SD [*FM radio station call letters*]
KESD-TV	Brookings, SD [*Television station call letters*]
KESE	Bentonville-Bella Vista, AR [*AM radio station call letters*] (RBYB)
KESF	Alexandria/Esler Field [*Louisiana*] [*ICAO location identifier*] (ICLI)
KESH	State Electricity Cooperative of Albania (BUAC)
KESI	Kentucky Electric Steel [*NASDAQ symbol*] (TTSB)
KESI	Kentucky Electric Steel Co. [*NASDAQ symbol*] (SAG)
KESI	Kurzweil Educational Systems, Inc.
KESM	El Dorado Springs, MO [*AM radio station call letters*]
KESM-FM	El Dorado Springs, MO [*FM radio station call letters*]
KESP-FM	Payson, AZ [*FM radio station call letters*] (BROA)
KESQ	Palm Springs, CA [*Television station call letters*]
KESS	Fort Worth, TX [*AM radio station call letters*]
KESS	Kesselring Site [*Knolls Atomic Power Laboratory*] (GAAI)
KESS	Kinetic Energy Storage System
KEST	Kestrel Energy [*NASDAQ symbol*] (TTSB)
KEST	Kestrel Energy, Inc. [*NASDAQ symbol*] (SAG)
KEST	San Francisco, CA [*AM radio station call letters*]
Kestrel	Kestrel Energy, Inc. [*Associated Press*] (SAG)
KESY	Omaha, NE [*FM radio station call letters*]
KESZ	Phoenix, AZ [*FM radio station call letters*]
KET	Cat Kargo Hava Tasima, AS [*Turkey*] [*FAA designator*] (FAAC)
KET	Kengtung [*Myanmar*] [*Airport symbol*] (OAG)
KET	Keravat [*New Britain*] [*Seismograph station code, US Geological Survey Closed*] (SEIS)
KET	Ketamine [*An anesthetic*]
Ket	Kethuboth (BJA)
KET	Kiel Electron Telescope
KET	Krypton Exposure Technique (MCD)
KETA	Kenya External Trade Authority (BUAC)
KETA	Oklahoma City, OK [*Television station call letters*]
KETAL	Kalamazoo Area Library Consortium [*Library network*]
KET BD	Ketone Bodies [*Endocrinology*] (DAVI)
KETC	St. Louis, MO [*Television station call letters*]
KETG	Arkadelphia, AR [*Television station call letters*]
KETH	Houston, TX [*Television station call letters*]
Keth	Kethuboth (BJA)
KETK	Jacksonville, TX [*Television station call letters*]
keto	Ketosteroid [*Endocrinology*]
KETO-AM	Rupert, ID [*AM radio station call letters*] (BROA)
KE-TP	Kinetic Energy-Training Projectile (MCD)
KETR	Commerce, TX [*FM radio station call letters*]
KETRI	Kenya Trypanosomiasis Research Institute
KETS	Little Rock, AR [*Television station call letters*]
K'ETTE	Kitchenette [*Classified advertising*] (ADA)
KETV	Omaha, NE [*Television station call letters*]
KETX	Livingston, TX [*AM radio station call letters*]
KETX-FM	Livingston, TX [*FM radio station call letters*]
KEU	Eastern Kentucky University, Richmond, KY [*OCLC symbol*] (OCLC)
KEUN	Eunice, LA [*AM radio station call letters*]
KEV	Kevo [*Finland*] [*Seismograph station code, US Geological Survey*] (SEIS)
keV	Kiloelectron Volt
KEV	Kilo Electron Volt (AAEL)
KEV	King's Empire Veterans [*British military*] (DMA)
KEV	Komisarstvo za Evreiskiie Vuprosi [*Bulgaria*] (BJA)
KEVA	Evanston, WY [*AM radio station call letters*]
KEVAS	Key Educational Vocational Assessment System (TES)
KEVII	King Edward VII [*British*]
KEVIII	King Edward VIII [*British*]
Kevlin	Kevlin Corp. [*Associated Press*] (SAG)
KEVN	Rapid City, SD [*Television station call letters*]
KEVT	Cortaro, AZ [*AM radio station call letters*]
KEVU	Eugene, OR [*Television station call letters*]
KEW	Kew [*England*] [*Seismograph station code, US Geological Survey Closed*] (SEIS)
KEW	Kewatin
keW	Kiloelectron Watt
KEW	Kinetic Energy Weapons [*Military*] (RDA)
KEWB	Anderson, CA [*FM radio station call letters*]
KEWB	Kinetic Experiment on Water Boiler [*Nuclear reactor*]
KEWE	Oroville, CA [*FM radio station call letters*]
KEWI	Benton, AR [*AM radio station call letters*]
KEWL	New Boston, TX [*FM radio station call letters*] (RBYB)
KEWN	New Bern/Simmons-Nott [*North Carolina*] [*ICAO location identifier*] (ICLI)
KewnSc	Kewaunee Scientific Corp. [*Associated Press*] (SAG)
KEWR	Newark/International [*New Jersey*] [*ICAO location identifier*] (ICLI)
KEWS	Koger Equity Wrrt [*AMEX symbol*] (TTSB)
KEWS-AM	Portland, OR [*AM radio station call letters*] (BROA)
KEWS-FM	Arlington, WA [*FM radio station call letters*] (RBYB)
KEWU	Cheney, WA [*FM radio station call letters*]
KEX	Kanabea [*Papua New Guinea*] [*Airport symbol*] (OAG)
KEX	Kirby Corp. [*AMEX symbol*] (SPSG)
KEX	Portland, OR [*AM radio station call letters*]
KEXL	Norfolk, NE [*FM radio station call letters*]
KEXO	Grand Junction, CO [*AM radio station call letters*]
KEXS	Excelsior Springs, MO [*AM radio station call letters*]
KEXT	Bosque Farms, NM [*FM radio station call letters*] (RBYB)
KEY	Key [*Commonly used*] (OPSA)
KEY	Key Anacon Mines Ltd. [*Toronto Stock Exchange symbol*]
KEY	KeyCorp [*NYSE symbol*] (SPSG)
Key	Keyes' New York Court of Appeals Reports [*A publication*] (DLA)
KEYA	Belcourt, ND [*AM radio station call letters*]
Key & Elph Conv	Key and Elphinstone's Conveyancing [*15th ed.*] [*1953-54*] [*A publication*] (DLA)
KEYB	Altus, OK [*FM radio station call letters*]
KEYBD	Keyboard [*Computer science*]
KEYC	Key Centurion Bancshares (EFIS)
KEYC	Mankato, MN [*Television station call letters*]
Key Ch	Keyes on Future Interest in Chattels [*A publication*] (DLA)
KeyCon	Keystone Consolidated Industries [*Associated Press*] (SAG)
Keycorp	Keycorp [*Associated Press*] (SAG)
Keycp	Keycorp [*Associated Press*] (SAG)
KEYE	Perryton, TX [*AM radio station call letters*]
KEYE-FM	Perryton, TX [*FM radio station call letters*]
KeyEng	Key Energy Group [*Associated Press*] (SAG)
Keyes	Keyes' New York Court of Appeals Reports [*A publication*] (DLA)
KEYE-TV	Austin, TX [*Television station call letters*] (RBYB)
KEYF	Cheney, WA [*FM radio station call letters*]
KEYF	Dishman, WA [*AM radio station call letters*]
KeyFn	Keyston Financial, Inc. [*Associated Press*] (SAG)
KEYG	Grand Coulee, WA [*AM radio station call letters*]
KEYG-FM	Grand Coulee, WA [*FM radio station call letters*]
KEYH	Houston, TX [*AM radio station call letters*]
KEYI	San Marcos, TX [*FM radio station call letters*]
KeyInt	Keystone International [*Associated Press*] (SAG)
KEYJ	Abilene, TX [*FM radio station call letters*]
Keyl	Keylway's [*or Keilway's*] English King's Bench Reports [*A publication*] (DLA)
KEYL	Long Prairie, MN [*AM radio station call letters*]
Key Lands	Keyes on Future Interest in Lands [*A publication*] (DLA)
Keylway	Keylway's [*or Keilway's*] English King's Bench Reports [*A publication*] (DLA)
KEYMAT	Keying Material [*Computer science*] (NVT)
KEYN	Wichita, KS [*FM radio station call letters*]
KEYPER	Keywords Permuted (DIT)
KEYPrA	KeyCorp 10% cm Dep Pfd [*NYSE symbol*] (TTSB)
KeyPrd	Key Production Co., Inc. [*Associated Press*] (SAG)
KEYQ	Fresno, CA [*AM radio station call letters*]
KEYR	Marlin, TX [*FM radio station call letters*]
Key Rem	Keyes on Remainders [*A publication*] (DLA)
KEYS	Corpus Christi, TX [*AM radio station call letters*]
KEYS	Keys [*Commonly used*] (OPSA)
KEYS	Keystone Automotive Industries, Inc. [*NASDAQ symbol*] (SAG)
KeysAut	Keystone Automotive Industries, Inc. [*Associated Press*] (SAG)
KeysHer	Keystone Heritage Group, Inc. [*Associated Press*] (SAG)
Keys St Ex	Keyser's Stock Exchange [*1850*] [*A publication*] (DLA)
KeystFn	Keystone Financial [*Associated Press*] (SAG)
KEYSTN	Keystone
KEYT	Santa Barbara, CA [*Television station call letters*]
KeyTech	Key Technology, Inc. [*Associated Press*] (SAG)
KEYTECT	Keyword Detection (NITA)
Key Trn	Key Tronics Corp. [*Associated Press*] (SAG)
KEYV	Las Vegas, NV [*FM radio station call letters*]
KEYW	Key West/Key West International [*Florida*] [*ICAO location identifier*] (ICLI)
KEYW	Pasco, WA [*FM radio station call letters*]
KEYY	Provo, UT [*AM radio station call letters*]
KEYZ	Williston, ND [*AM radio station call letters*]
KEZA	Fayetteville, AR [*FM radio station call letters*]
KEZB	Hempstead, TX [*FM radio station call letters*]
KEZC	Yuma, AZ [*AM radio station call letters*]
KEZD	Windsor, CA [*AM radio station call letters*]
KEZE-FM	Spokane, WA [*FM radio station call letters*] (RBYB)
KEZF	Tigard, OR [*AM radio station call letters*]
KEZF-FM	Albuquerque, NM [*FM radio station call letters*] (BROA)
KEZG	Lincoln, NE [*FM radio station call letters*]
KEZH	Hastings, NE [*FM radio station call letters*]
KEZI	Eugene, OR [*Television station call letters*]
KEZJ	Twin Falls, ID [*AM radio station call letters*]
KEZJ-FM	Twin Falls, ID [*FM radio station call letters*]
KEZK	St. Louis, MO [*FM radio station call letters*]
KEZL	Fowler, CA [*FM radio station call letters*]
KEZM	Sulphur, LA [*AM radio station call letters*]
KEZN	Palm Desert, CA [*FM radio station call letters*]
KEZO	Omaha, NE [*AM radio station call letters*]
KEZO-FM	Omaha, NE [*FM radio station call letters*]
KEZP	Bunkie, LA [*FM radio station call letters*]
KEZQ	Little Rock, AR [*AM radio station call letters*] (RBYB)
KEZQ	Sheridan, AR [*FM radio station call letters*]
KEZR	San Jose, CA [*FM radio station call letters*]
KEZS	Cape Girardeau, MO [*FM radio station call letters*]
KEZT	Ames, IA [*FM radio station call letters*]
KEZU	Booneville, AR [*FM radio station call letters*]
KEZW	Aurora, CO [*AM radio station call letters*]
KEZX	Seattle, WA [*AM radio station call letters*]
KEZY	Anaheim, CA [*FM radio station call letters*]

KEZZ .... Aitkin, MN [*FM radio station call letters*]
KF .... Catskill Airways [*ICAO designator*] (AD)
KF .... Fiji [*IYRU nationality code*] (IYR)
kf .... Flocculation Speed in Antigen-Antibody Reactions [*Immunology*] (DAVI)
KF .... Gold Coast Judgments and the Masai Cases, by King-Farlow [*1915-17*] [*Ghana*] [*A publication*] (DLA)
KF .... Karl Fischer [*Reagent*] [*Analytical chemistry*]
KF .... Kenner-Fecal Medium [*Organic chemistry*] (DAVI)
KF .... Keramos Fraternity [*An association*] (NTPA)
KF .... Kerr-Fourier [*Imaging*]
KF .... Key Field
KF .... Kidney Function [*Nephrology*] (DAVI)
KF .... KIDS Fund (EA)
KF .... Kleine Flote [*Piccolo*] [*German*]
KF .... Klenow Fragment [*Genetics*]
KF .... Klippel-Feil [*Syndrome*] [*Neurology*] (DAVI)
KF .... Knight of Ferdinand [*Spain*]
KF .... Knudsen Flow [*Physics*]
KF .... Koff [*Type of ship*] (DS)
KF .... Koinonia Foundation (EA)
KF .... Konservative Folkeparti [*Conservative People's Party (Commonly called the Conservative Party)*] [*Denmark Political party*] (PPE)
KF .... Kontrafagott [*Double Bassoon*] [*Organ stop Music*]
KF .... Korea Fund, Inc. [*NYSE symbol*] (SPSG)
KF .... Kosciuszko Foundation (EA)
KF .... Kossuth Foundation (EA)
KF .... Rhine Air AG [*Sweden ICAO designator*] (ICDA)
KFA .... Keep Fit Association [*British*]
KFA .... Kelowna Flightcraft Air Charter Ltd. [*Canada ICAO designator*] (FAAC)
KFA .... Kenya Farmers Association (BUAC)
KFA .... Kernforschungsanlage [*Julich, Germany*]
KFA .... Kiffa [*Mauritania*] [*Airport symbol*] (OAG)
KFA .... Kinesthetic Figural Aftereffects [*Also, KFAE*] [*Psychometrics*]
KFA .... Krishnamurti Foundation of America (EA)
KFAA .... Rogers, AR [*Television station call letters*]
KFAB .... Kidney-Fixing Antibody [*Immunology*]
KFAB .... Omaha, NE [*AM radio station call letters*]
KFAC .... Santa Barbara, CA [*AM radio station call letters*]
KFAD .... Alexandria, LA [*FM radio station call letters*]
KFAE .... Kinesthetic Figural Aftereffects [*Also, KFA*] [*Psychometrics*]
KFAE .... Richland, WA [*FM radio station call letters*]
KFAED .... Kuwait Fund for Arab Economic Development
KFAI .... Minneapolis, MN [*FM radio station call letters*]
KFAL .... Fulton, MO [*AM radio station call letters*]
KFAM .... Keyed File Access Method [*Computer science*] (PDAA)
KFAM .... North Salt Lake City, UT [*AM radio station call letters*]
KFAN .... Johnson City, TX [*FM radio station call letters*]
KFAN .... Minneapolis, MN [*AM radio station call letters*]
KF&R .... Knight, Frank & Rutley (WDAA)
KFAO .... Knee-Foot-Ankel Orthosis [*Orthopedics*] (DAVI)
KFAR .... Fairbanks, AK [*AM radio station call letters*]
KFAS .... Casa Grande, AZ [*AM radio station call letters*]
KFAS .... Keyed File Access System
KFAS .... Kuwait Foundation for the Advancement of Science (BUAC)
K-FAST .... Kaufman Functional Academic Skills Test (TMMY)
KFAT .... Corvallis, OR [*FM radio station call letters*]
KFAT .... Fresno/Fresno Air Terminal [*California*] [*ICAO location identifier*] (ICLI)
KFAV .... Warrenton, MO [*FM radio station call letters*]
KFAX .... San Francisco, CA [*AM radio station call letters*]
KFAY .... Bentonville, AR [*FM radio station call letters*] (RBYB)
KFAY .... Farmington, AR [*AM radio station call letters*]
KFB .... Air Botnia OY, AB, Finland [*FAA designator*] (FAAC)
KFB .... Bethany College, Lindsborg, KS [*OCLC symbol*] (OCLC)
KFB .... Kuwait French Bank
KFBB .... Great Falls, MT [*Television station call letters*]
KFBC .... Cheyenne, WY [*AM radio station call letters*]
KFBD .... Waynesville, MO [*AM radio station call letters*]
KFBG .... Fort Bragg/Simons Auxiliary Air Base [*North Carolina*] [*ICAO location identifier*] (ICLI)
KfBH .... Kaufman & Broad Home Corp. [*Associated Press*] (SAG)
KfBI .... Klamath First Bancorp [*NASDAQ symbol*] (TTSB)
KfBI .... Klamath First Bancorp, Inc. [*NASDAQ symbol*] (SAG)
KFBI .... Pahrump, NV [*FM radio station call letters*]
KFBK .... Sacramento, CA [*AM radio station call letters*]
KFBN .... Lincoln, NE [*FM radio station call letters*]
KFBQ .... Cheyenne, WY [*FM radio station call letters*]
KFBT .... Las Vegas, NV [*Television station call letters*]
KFC .... Kajagoogoo Fan Club [*Defunct*] (EA)
KFC .... Katholieke Film-Centrale [*Netherlands*]
KFC .... Kentfield [*California*] [*Seismograph station code, US Geological Survey*] (SEIS)
KFC .... Kentucky Fried Chicken Corp. [*Later, KFC Corp.*] (ADA)
KFC .... Korea Friendship Committee [*British*] (EAIO)
KFCA .... Conway, AR [*AM radio station call letters*]
KFCB .... Concord, CA [*Television station call letters*]
KFCC .... Bay City, TX [*AM radio station call letters*] (RBYB)
KFCF .... Fresno, CA [*FM radio station call letters*]
KFCI .... Knife and Fork Club International (EA)
KFCM .... Cherokee Village, AR [*FM radio station call letters*]
KFCR .... Custer, SD [*AM radio station call letters*]
KFCT .... Fort Collins, CO [*FM radio station call letters*]
KFD .... Key Financial Data (ADA)

KFD .... Kinetic Family Drawing [*Psychology*]
KFD .... Kyasanur Forest Disease
KFDA .... Amarillo, TX [*Television station call letters*]
KFDC .... Washington/National Flight Data Center [*District of Columbia*] [*ICAO location identifier*] (ICLI)
KFDF .... Van Buren, AR [*AM radio station call letters*]
KFDI .... Wichita, KS [*AM radio station call letters*]
KFDI-FM ..... Wichita, KS [*FM radio station call letters*]
KFDM .... Beaumont, TX [*Television station call letters*]
KfdO .... Komitee fuer den Osten (BJA)
KFDT .... Kinetic Family Drawing Test [*Psychology*] (DAVI)
KFDX .... Wichita Falls, TX [*Television station call letters*]
KFE .... Kathode Flicker Effect
KFEA .... Korean Federation of Education Associations
KFEL .... Pueblo, CO [*AM radio station call letters*]
KFEQ .... St. Joseph, MO [*AM radio station call letters*]
KFER .... Santa Cruz, CA [*FM radio station call letters*]
KFEZ .... Kansas City, MO [*AM radio station call letters*]
KFF .... Kvinnenes Frie Folkevalgte [*Women's Freely Elected Representatives*] [*Norway Political party*] (PPE)
KFFA .... Helena, AR [*AM radio station call letters*]
KFFA-FM ..... Helena, AR [*FM radio station call letters*] (RBYB)
KFFB .... Fairfield Bay, AR [*FM radio station call letters*]
KFFG .... Los Altos, CA [*FM radio station call letters*] (RBYB)
KFFLBA .... Konglomerati Florida Foundation for Literature and the Book Arts (EA)
KFFM .... Yakima, WA [*FM radio station call letters*]
KFFN-AM ..... Tucson, AZ [*AM radio station call letters*] (RBYB)
KFFO .... Dayton/Wright-Patterson Air Force Base [*Ohio*] [*ICAO location identifier*] (ICLI)
KFFR .... Eagle River, AK [*AM radio station call letters*]
KFFX .... Emporia, KS [*FM radio station call letters*]
KFGA-FM ..... Clayton, LA [*FM radio station call letters*] (BROA)
KFGE .... Lincoln, NE [*FM radio station call letters*]
KFGG .... Corpus Christi, TX [*FM radio station call letters*]
KFGI-FM ...... Brainerd, MN [*FM radio station call letters*] (RBYB)
KFGO .... Fargo, ND [*AM radio station call letters*]
KFGO-FM ..... Fargo, ND [*FM radio station call letters*]
KFGQ .... Boone, IA [*AM radio station call letters*]
KFGQ-FM ..... Boone, IA [*FM radio station call letters*]
KFGX-FM ..... Detroit Lakes, MN [*FM radio station call letters*] (RBYB)
KFGY-FM ..... Healdsburg, CA [*FM radio station call letters*] (RBYB)
KFH .... Fort Hays State University, Hays, KS [*OCLC symbol*] (OCLC)
KFH .... Ku-Band Feed Horn
KFH .... Kuwait Finance House (BUAC)
KFH .... Wichita, KS [*AM radio station call letters*]
KFI .... Kinetic Fluid Induction
KFI .... Los Angeles, CA [*AM radio station call letters*]
KFIA .... Carmichael, CA [*AM radio station call letters*]
KFIA .... King Fahd International Airport [*Saudi Arabia*]
KFIE .... Merced, CA [*FM radio station call letters*]
KFIG .... Fresno, CA [*AM radio station call letters*]
KFIL .... Preston, MN [*AM radio station call letters*]
KFIL-FM ...... Preston, MN [*FM radio station call letters*]
KFIN .... Jonesboro, AR [*FM radio station call letters*]
KFIR .... Sweet Home, OR [*AM radio station call letters*]
KFIS .... Soda Springs, ID [*FM radio station call letters*]
KFIT .... Lockhart, TX [*AM radio station call letters*]
KFIT EXP STN... San Antonio, TX [*Radio expansion station*]
KFIV .... Modesto, CA [*AM radio station call letters*]
KFIX-FM ...... Plainville, KS [*FM radio station call letters*] (RBYB)
KFIZ .... Fond Du Lac, WI [*AM radio station call letters*]
KFIZ-FM ...... Fond du Lac, WI [*FM radio station call letters*] (RBYB)
KFJB .... Marshalltown, IA [*AM radio station call letters*]
KFJC .... Los Altos, CA [*FM radio station call letters*]
KFJM .... Grand Forks, ND [*AM radio station call letters*]
KFJM-FM ..... Grand Forks, ND [*FM radio station call letters*]
KFJY .... Grand Forks, ND [*FM radio station call letters*] (RBYB)
KFJZ .... Fort Worth, TX [*AM radio station call letters*]
KFKA .... Greeley, CO [*AM radio station call letters*]
KFKF .... Kansas City, KS [*FM radio station call letters*]
KFKQ .... New Holstein, WI [*FM radio station call letters*]
KFKX-FM ..... Hastings, NE [*FM radio station call letters*] (RBYB)
KFL .... Kenya Federation of Labour
KFL .... Kenya Flamingo Airways Ltd. [*ICAO designator*] (FAAC)
KFL .... Key Facilities List [*AEC*]
KFL .... University of Kansas, Law Library, Lawrence, KS [*OCLC symbol*] (OCLC)
KFLA .... Scott City, KS [*AM radio station call letters*]
KFIAH .... United States Army Hospital, Fort Leavenworth, KS [*Library symbol Library of Congress*] (LCLS)
KFLD .... Pasco, WA [*AM radio station call letters*] (RBYB)
KFLG .... Bullhead City, AZ [*AM radio station call letters*]
KFLG-FM ..... Bullhead City, AZ [*FM radio station call letters*]
KFIGS .... United States Army, Command and General Staff College Library, Fort Leavenworth,KS [*Library symbol Library of Congress*] (LCLS)
KFLL .... Floydada, TX [*FM radio station call letters*]
KFLL .... Fort Lauderdale/Fort Lauderdale-Hollywood International [*Florida*] [*ICAO location identifier*] (ICLI)
KFLN .... Baker, MT [*AM radio station call letters*]
KFLO .... Florence/Municipal [*South Carolina*] [*ICAO location identifier*] (ICLI)
KFLO .... Shreveport, LA [*AM radio station call letters*]
KFLOPS .... Kilo Floating Point Operations per Second [*Computer science*] (CiST)
KFLP-AM ..... Floydada, TX [*AM radio station call letters*] (RBYB)

KFLQ............ Albuquerque, NM [*FM radio station call letters*]
KFLR............ Phoenix, AZ [*FM radio station call letters*]
KFLS............ Klamath Falls, OR [*AM radio station call letters*]
KFLS............ Tulelake, CA [*FM radio station call letters*]
KFLT............ Tucson, AZ [*AM radio station call letters*]
KFLW............ St. Robert, MO [*FM radio station call letters*] (RBYB)
KFLX............ Kachina Village, AZ [*FM radio station call letters*]
KFLY............ Corvallis, OR [*FM radio station call letters*]
KFLZ............ Bishop, TX [*FM radio station call letters*]
KFM............. Klystron Frequency Multiplier
KFM............. Knight of St. Ferdinand and Merit [*Italy*]
KFMA-FM .... Green Valley, AZ [*FM radio station call letters*] (RBYB)
KFMB............ San Diego, CA [*AM radio station call letters*]
KFMB-FM .... San Diego, CA [*FM radio station call letters*]
KFMB-TV .... San Diego, CA [*Television station call letters*]
KFMC............ Fairmont, MN [*FM radio station call letters*]
KFMD............ Delta, UT [*FM radio station call letters*]
KFME............ Fargo, ND [*Television station call letters*]
KFMF............ Chico, CA [*FM radio station call letters*]
KFMG............ Pella, IA [*FM radio station call letters*]
KFMH............ Falmouth/Otis Air Force Base [*Massachusetts*] [*ICAO location identifier*] (ICLI)
KFMI............ Eureka, CA [*FM radio station call letters*]
KFMJ-FM .... Ketchikan, AK [*FM radio station call letters*] (RBYB)
KFMK............ Winton, CA [*FM radio station call letters*]
KFML............ Kommunistiska Foerbundet Marxist-Leninisterna [*Communist League of Marxist-Leninists*] [*Sweden Political party*] (PPE)
KFML............ Little Falls, MN [*FM radio station call letters*]
KFMM............ Thatcher, AZ [*FM radio station call letters*]
KFMN............ Farmington [*New Mexico*] [*ICAO location identifier*] (ICLI)
KFMN............ Lihue, HI [*FM radio station call letters*]
KFMO............ Park Hills, MO [*AM radio station call letters*]
KFMQ-FM .... Gallup, NM [*FM radio station call letters*] (RBYB)
KFMR-FM .... Winslow, AZ [*FM radio station call letters*] (RBYB)
KFMS-FM .... Las Vegas, NV [*FM radio station call letters*]
KFMT............ Fremont, NE [*FM radio station call letters*]
KFMU............ Oak Creek, CO [*FM radio station call letters*]
KFMV............ Franklin, LA [*FM radio station call letters*]
KFMW............ Waterloo, IA [*FM radio station call letters*]
KFMX............ Lubbock, TX [*FM radio station call letters*]
KFMY............ Fort Myers/Page Field [*Florida*] [*ICAO location identifier*] (ICLI)
KFMY-FM .... South Bend, WA [*FM radio station call letters*] (RBYB)
KFMZ............ Columbia, MO [*FM radio station call letters*]
KFNA............ El Paso, TX [*AM radio station call letters*]
KFNB............ Casper, WY [*Television station call letters*]
KFNE............ Riverton, WY [*Television station call letters*]
KFNF............ Oberlin, KS [*FM radio station call letters*]
KFNN............ Mesa, AZ [*AM radio station call letters*]
KFNO............ Fresno, CA [*FM radio station call letters*]
KFNR............ Rawlins, WY [*Television station call letters*]
KFNS............ Wood River, IL [*AM radio station call letters*]
KFNV............ Ferriday, LA [*AM radio station call letters*]
KFNV-FM .... Ferriday, LA [*FM radio station call letters*]
KFNW............ West Fargo, ND [*AM radio station call letters*]
KFNW-FM .... Fargo, ND [*FM radio station call letters*]
KFNZ-AM .... Salt Lake, UT [*AM radio station call letters*] (RBYB)
KFO............. Killing Federal Officer
KFO............. King Solomon Resources [*Vancouver Stock Exchange symbol*]
KFO............. Klamath Falls [*Oregon*] [*Seismograph station code, US Geological Survey*] (SEIS)
KFOC........... Kaiser-Frazer Owners Clubs of America [*Later, KFOCI*] (EA)
KFOCI.......... Kaiser-Frazer Owners Club International (EA)
KFOE............ Topeka/Forbes Air Force Base [*Kansas*] [*ICAO location identifier*] (ICLI)
KFOG........... San Francisco, CA [*FM radio station call letters*]
KFOK........... West Hampton Beach/Suffolk County [*New York*] [*ICAO location identifier*] (ICLI)
KFON........... Austin, TX [*AM radio station call letters*]
KFOR........... Lincoln, NE [*AM radio station call letters*]
KFOR-TV...... Oklahoma City, OK [*Television station call letters*]
KFOX........... Redondo Beach, CA [*FM radio station call letters*]
KFOX-TV...... El Paso, TX [*Television station call letters*]
KFP............. False Pass [*Alaska*] [*Airport symbol*] (OAG)
KFP............. Konstitutionella Folkpartiet [*Constitutional People's Party*] [*Finland Political party*] (PPE)
KFP............. Korean Fighter Program
KFP............. Pittsburg State University, Pittsburg, KS [*OCLC symbol*] (OCLC)
KFPR........... Redding, CA [*FM radio station call letters*]
KFPW........... Fort Smith, AR [*AM radio station call letters*]
KFQC........... Davenport, IA [*AM radio station call letters*]
KFQD........... Anchorage, AK [*AM radio station call letters*]
KFQX-FM..... Merkel, TX [*FM radio station call letters'*] (BROA)
KFQX-TV...... Grand Junction, CO [*TV station call letters*] (RBYB)
KFR............. Kayser-Fleischer Ring [*Medicine*] (DMAA)
KFR............. Keefer Resources, Inc. [*Vancouver Stock Exchange symbol*]
KFRA........... Franklin, LA [*AM radio station call letters*]
KFRB-FM ..... Bakersfield, CA [*FM radio station call letters*] (RBYB)
KFRC........... San Francisco, CA [*AM radio station call letters*]
KFRC-FM ..... San Francisco, CA [*FM radio station call letters*]
KFRD........... Bellville, TX [*AM radio station call letters*]
KFRE........... Fresno, CA [*AM radio station call letters*]
KFRG........... San Bernardino, CA [*FM radio station call letters*]
KFRL........... Kansas Flight Research Laboratory
KFRM........... Salina, KS [*AM radio station call letters*]
KFRN........... Long Beach, CA [*AM radio station call letters*]

KFRO .... Gilmer, TX [*FM radio station call letters*]
KFRO .... Longview, TX [*AM radio station call letters*]
KFRQ .... Harlingen, TX [*FM radio station call letters*]
KFRQ-FM..... Harlingen, TX [*FM radio station call letters*]
KFRR .... Woodlake, CA [*FM radio station call letters*]
KFRST .... Killing Frost [*NWS*] (FAAC)
KFRU .... Columbia, MO [*AM radio station call letters*]
KFRX .... Lincoln, NE [*FM radio station call letters*]
KFRY-FM ..... Manteca, CA [*FM radio station call letters*] (BROA)
KFS............. Kalitta Flying Service, Inc. [*FAA designator*] (FAAC)
KFS............. Kalman Filtering System
KFS............. Keyed File System [*Computer science*]
KFS............. Klippel-Feil Syndrome [*Medicine*]
KFS............. Kohles, F. S., Montebello CA [*STAC*]
KFS............. University of Kansas, Spencer Library, Lawrence, KS [*OCLC symbol*] (OCLC)
KFSA........... Fort Smith, AR [*AM radio station call letters*]
KFSA........... Keep Fit South Australia
KFSB........... Joplin, MO [*AM radio station call letters*]
KFSB........... Korean Federation of Small Businesses (BUAC)
KFSD........... Keratosis Follicularis Spinulosa Decalvans [*Medicine*] (DMAA)
KFSD........... San Diego, CA [*FM radio station call letters*]
KFSG........... Los Angeles, CA [*FM radio station call letters*]
KFSH-AM..... Seward, AK [*AM radio station call letters*] (BROA)
KFSH & RC... King Faisal Specialist Hospital and Research Center [*Saudi Arabia*]
KFSI........... Rochester, MN [*FM radio station call letters*]
KFSK........... Petersburg, AK [*FM radio station call letters*]
KFSM........... Fort Smith, AR [*Television station call letters*]
KFSM........... Fort Smith/Municipal [*Arkansas*] [*ICAO location identifier*] (ICLI)
KFSN........... Fresno, CA [*Television station call letters*]
KFSO........... Visalia, CA [*FM radio station call letters*]
KFSR........... Fresno, CA [*FM radio station call letters*]
KFSR........... Karakul Fur Sheep Registry [*Later, AKFSR*] (EA)
KFST........... Fort Stockton, TX [*AM radio station call letters*]
KFST-FM...... Fort Stockton, TX [*FM radio station call letters*]
KFT............. Kalman Filter Theory
KFTCIC........ Kuwait Foreign Trading, Contracting & Investment Co.
KFTE........... Breaux Bridge, LA [*FM radio station call letters*]
KFTG........... Pasadena, TX [*FM radio station call letters*] (RBYB)
KFTH........... Marion, AR [*FM radio station call letters*]
KFTL........... Stockton, CA [*Television station call letters*]
KFTM........... Fort Morgan, CO [*AM radio station call letters*]
KFTS........... Klamath Falls, OR [*Television station call letters*]
KFTU........... Korean Federation of Trade Unions [*North Korea*]
KFTV........... Hanford, CA [*Television station call letters*]
KFTW........... Fort Worth/Meacham [*Texas*] [*ICAO location identifier*] (ICLI)
KFTW........... Fredericktown, MO [*AM radio station call letters*]
KFTX........... Kingsville, TX [*FM radio station call letters*] (RBYB)
KFTY........... Santa Rosa, CA [*Television station call letters*]
KFTZ........... Idaho Falls, ID [*FM radio station call letters*]
KFU............. Friends University, Wichita, KS [*OCLC symbol*] (OCLC)
KFU............. King Faisal University [*Saudi Arabia*] (BUAC)
KFUK........... Kristelig Forening for Unge Kvinder [*Young Women's Christian Associations - YWCA*] [*Denmark*]
KFUM........... Kristelig Forening for Unge Maend [*Young Men's Christian Associations - YMCA*] [*Denmark*]
KFUN........... Las Vegas, NM [*AM radio station call letters*]
KFUO........... Clayton, MO [*AM radio station call letters*]
KFUO-FM..... Clayton, MO [*FM radio station call letters*]
KFV............. Quest for Value Dual Fd [*NYSE symbol*] (TTSB)
KFV............. Quest for Value Fund [*NYSE symbol*] (SAG)
KFVE........... Honolulu, HI [*Television station call letters*]
KFVPr......... Quest For Value Income Shrs [*NYSE symbol*] (TTSB)
KFVR........... Crescent City, CA [*AM radio station call letters*]
KFVS........... Cape Girardeau, MO [*Television station call letters*]
KfW............. Kreditanstalt fur Wiederaufbau [*Finance*] [*Germany*]
KFW............. Wichita Public Library, Wichita, KS [*OCLC symbol*] (OCLC)
KFWB........... Los Angeles, CA [*AM radio station call letters*]
KFWD......... Fort Worth, TX [*Television station call letters*]
KFWH........... Fort Worth/Carswell Air Force Base [*Texas*] [*ICAO location identifier*] (ICLI)
KFWJ........... Lake Havasu City, AZ [*AM radio station call letters*]
KFWU........... Fort Bragg, CA [*Television station call letters*]
KFX............. KFX Inc. [*AMEX symbol*] (TTSB)
KFX............. Korean Foreign Exchange (IMH)
KFXA........... Cedar Rapids, IA [*Television station call letters*] (RBYB)
KFXB........... Dubuque, IA [*Television station call letters*] (RBYB)
KFXD........... Nampa, ID [*AM radio station call letters*]
KFXD-FM..... Nampa, ID [*Television station call letters*]
KFXE........... Cuba, MO [*AM radio station call letters*]
KFXE........... Fort Lauderdale/Executive [*Florida*] [*ICAO location identifier*] (ICLI)
KFXF........... Fairbanks, AK [*Television station call letters*] (RBYB)
KFXI........... KFx, Inc. [*NASDAQ symbol*] (SAG)
KFXI........... Marlow, OK [*FM radio station call letters*]
KFX Inc....... KFx, Inc. [*Associated Press*] (SAG)
KFXJ........... Abilene, TX [*FM radio station call letters*]
KFXK........... Longview, TX [*Television station call letters*]
KFXR........... Chinle, AZ [*FM radio station call letters*] (RBYB)
KFXS........... Rapid City, SD [*FM radio station call letters*] (RBYB)
KFXT........... Sulphur, OK [*FM radio station call letters*]
KFXX........... Hugoton, KS [*FM radio station call letters*]
KFXX........... Oregon City, OR [*AM radio station call letters*]
KFXY........... Morgan City, LA [*FM radio station call letters*]
KFXZ........... Maurice, LA [*FM radio station call letters*]

KFY.............. KISS [*Knights in the Service of Satan*] - Flaming Youth [*Defunct*] (EA)

KFYI............. Phoenix, AZ [*AM radio station call letters*]

KFYN........... Bonham, TX [*AM radio station call letters*]

KFYO........... Lubbock, TX [*AM radio station call letters*]

KFYR........... Bismarck, ND [*AM radio station call letters*]

KFYR-TV...... Bismarck, ND [*Television station call letters*]

KFYV........... Fayetteville/Drake Field [*Arkansas*] [*ICAO location identifier*] (ICLI)

KFYZ........... Bonham, TX [*FM radio station call letters*]

KG............... Catalina Airlines [*ICAO designator*] (AD)

KG............... Center of Gravity above Keel (MCD)

KG............... Kammergericht [*District Court, Berlin*] [*German*] (DLA)

KG............... Kampfgeschwader [*Bombardment wing*] [*German military - World War II*]

KG............... Karmann-Ghia [*Volkswagen model designation*]

KG............... Keg

KG............... Ketoglutarate (DMAA)

KG............... Ketoglutaric [*Biochemistry*]

KG............... Key Generator (MCD)

kG............... Kilogauss

kg .... Kilogram [*Also, k*] [*Symbol SI unit for mass*]

Kg............... Kilogram (EBF)

KG............... Kilogram (GAVI)

KG............... Kindergarten

KG............... Kinder, Gentler [*America*] [*In a George Bush speech during the 1989 Republican Convention*]

KG............... King

KG............... Kininogen [*Biochemistry*]

KG............... Knifemakers Guild (EA)

KG............... Knight of [*the Order of*] the Garter [*British*]

KG............... Known Gambler [*Police slang*]

KG............... Kommanditgesellschaft [*Limited Partnership*] [*German*]

KG............... Kultusgemeinde (BJA)

KG............... Kumagai Gumi Co. (EFIS)

KG............... Kyrgyzstan [*Internet country code*]

KG-1 .... Koeffler Golde-1 [*Cell line*] [*Cytology*] (DAVI)

KG5............. HMS King George V [*British military*] (DMA)

KGA .... Kananga [*Zaire*] [*Airport symbol*] (OAG)

KGA .... King's German Artillery [*British military*] (DMA)

KGA .... Kitchen Guild of America

KGA .... Kyrghyzstan Airlines [*ICAO designator*] (FAAC)

KGA .... Spokane, WA [*AM radio station call letters*]

KGAB-AM..... Orchard Valley, WY [*AM radio station call letters*] (BROA)

KGAC .... Kentucky Guild of Artists and Craftsmen (SRA)

KGAC .... St. Peter, MN [*FM radio station call letters*]

KGAF .... Gainesville, TX [*AM radio station call letters*]

KGAG .... Gage [*Oklahoma*] [*ICAO location identifier*] (ICLI)

KgAG .... Kurzgefasste Assyrische Grammatik [*A publication*] (BJA)

KGAK .... Gallup, NM [*AM radio station call letters*]

KGAL .... Lebanon, OR [*AM radio station call letters*] (RBYB)

KGAL/MIN .... Kilogallons per Minute (MCD)

kgal/min ...... Kilogallons per Minute (NAKS)

KGAM-AM.... Palm Springs, CA [*AM radio station call letters*] (BROA)

KGAN .... Cedar Rapids, IA [*Television station call letters*]

KGAP .... Clarksville, TX [*FM radio station call letters*]

KGAS .... Carthage, TX [*AM radio station call letters*]

KGAS-FM..... Carthage, TX [*FM radio station call letters*]

KGB .... Kewaunee, Green Bay & Western R. R. [*AAR code*]

KGB .... Kindly Gunn Bunch [*Refers to the Metropolitan Transit Authority of New York City; Gunn is the MTA chairman*]

KGB .... Known Good Board (AAEL)

KGB .... Komitet Gosudarstvennoi Bezopasnosti [*Committee of State Security*] [*Russian Secret Police Also satirically interpreted as Kontora Grubykh Banditov, or "Office of Crude Bandits"*]

KGB .... Konge [*Papua New Guinea*] [*Airport symbol*] (OAG)

KGB .... San Diego, CA [*FM radio station call letters*]

KGBA .... Holtville, CA [*FM radio station call letters*]

KGbB .... Barton County Community College, Great Bend, KS [*Library symbol Library of Congress*] (LCLS)

KGBC .... Galveston, TX [*AM radio station call letters*]

KGBI .... Omaha, NE [*FM radio station call letters*]

KGbLS .... Central Kansas Library System, Great Bend, KS [*Library symbol Library of Congress*] (LCLS)

KGbMC .... Central Kansas Medical Center, Great Bend, KS [*Library symbol Library of Congress*] (LCLS)

KGBR .... Gold Beach, OR [*FM radio station call letters*]

KGBS .... Krypton Gas Bottling Station [*Nuclear energy*] (NRCH)

KGBT .... Harlingen, TX [*AM radio station call letters*]

KGBT-TV...... Harlingen, TX [*Television station call letters*]

KGBX .... Nixa, MO [*FM radio station call letters*]

KGBY .... Sacramento, CA [*FM radio station call letters*]

KGC .... Keflin, Gentamicin, and Carbenicellin [*Antibiotics*] (DAVI)

kgc............. Kilogram-Calorie (IDOE)

KGC .... Kingscote [*Australia Airport symbol*] (OAG)

KGC .... Kinross Gold [*NYSE symbol*] (TTSB)

KGC .... Kinross Gold Corp. [*NYSE symbol*] (SAG)

KGC .... Kiwi Growers of California (EA)

KGC .... Knight Grand Commander

KGC .... Knight of the Golden Circle

KGC .... Knight of the Grand Cross

KGC .... W. M. Krogman Center for Research in Child Growth and Development [*University of Pennsylvania*] [*Research center*] (RCD)

kgcal........... Kilogram-Calorie

KGCB .... Knight Grand Cross of the [*Order of the*] Bath [*British*]

KGCB .... Prescott, AZ [*FM radio station call letters*]

KGCF .... Kahlil Gibran Centennial Foundation (EA)

KGCK .... Garden City [*Kansas*] [*ICAO location identifier*] (ICLI)

KGCR .... Goodland, KS [*FM radio station call letters*]

KGCSG .... Knight Grand Cross of the Order of St. Gregory the Great [*British*] (ADA)

kg/cum .... Kilograms per Cubic Meter

KGD .... Karaganda [*Former USSR Geomagnetic observatory code*]

KGD .... Known Good Die (AAEL)

KGDC .... Walla Walla, WA [*AM radio station call letters*] (RBYB)

KGDD .... Paris, TX [*AM radio station call letters*]

KGDE .... Lincoln, NE [*FM radio station call letters*] (RBYB)

KGDN .... Pasco, WA [*FM radio station call letters*]

KGDP .... Orcutt, CA [*AM radio station call letters*]

KGE .... King-Errington Resources Ltd. [*Vancouver Stock Exchange symbol*]

KGE .... Klein-Gordon Equation [*Physics*]

KGE .... Knights of the Golden Eagle (EA)

KGEE .... Monahans, TX [*FM radio station call letters*]

KGEG .... Spokane/International [*Washington*] [*ICAO location identifier*] (ICLI)

KGEM .... Boise, ID [*AM radio station call letters*]

KGEN .... Hanford, CA [*FM radio station call letters*] (RBYB)

KGEN .... Tulare, CA [*AM radio station call letters*]

KGEO .... Bakersfield, CA [*AM radio station call letters*]

KGER .... Long Beach, CA [*AM radio station call letters*]

KGER-AM.... Yakima, WA [*AM radio station call letters*] (BROA)

KGET .... Bakersfield, CA [*Television station call letters*]

KGEZ .... Kalispell, MT [*AM radio station call letters*]

KGF .... Keilinschriften und Geschichtsforschung [*A publication*] (BJA)

KGF.f .... Keratinocyte Growth Factor [*Biochemistry*]

kg-f .... Kilogram-Foot

kgf .... Kilogram-Force [*Unit of force*]

KGF .... Knight of the Golden Fleece [*Spain and Austria*]

KGF .... Kriegsgefangener [*Prisoner of War*] [*German*]

KGFA .... Great Falls/Malmstrom Air Force Base [*Montana*] [*ICAO location identifier*] (ICLI)

KGFC-FM ..... Great Falls, MT [*FM radio station call letters*] (RBYB)

KGF/CM² .... Kilogram Force per Square Centimeter

KGFE .... Grand Forks, ND [*Television station call letters*]

KGFF .... Shawnee, OK [*AM radio station call letters*]

KGFJ .... Los Angeles, CA [*AM radio station call letters*]

KGFJ-FM..... Markham, TX [*FM radio station call letters*] (BROA)

KGFK .... Grand Forks/International [*North Dakota*] [*ICAO location identifier*] (ICLI)

KGFL .... Clinton, AR [*AM radio station call letters*]

KGFM .... Bakersfield, CA [*FM radio station call letters*]

KGF/M .... Kilogram Force per Meter

KGF/M² ...... Kilogram Force per Square Meter

KGFR .... Keratinocyte Growth Factor Receptor [*Biochemistry*]

KGFS .... King George's Fund for Sailors [*British*]

KGFT .... Pueblo, CO [*FM radio station call letters*]

KGFW .... Kearney, NE [*AM radio station call letters*]

KGFX .... Pierre, SD [*AM radio station call letters*]

KGFX-FM..... Pierre, SD [*FM radio station call letters*]

KGFY .... Stillwater, OK [*FM radio station call letters*]

KGG .... Consolidated Goldwest [*Vancouver Stock Exchange symbol*]

KGG .... Kedougou [*Senegal*] [*Airport symbol*] (OAG)

KgGBAS ...... Kurzgefasste Grammatik der Biblisch Aramaeischen Sprache [*A publication*] (BJA)

KGGF .... Coffeyville, KS [*AM radio station call letters*]

KGGG .... Longview/Gregg County [*Texas*] [*ICAO location identifier*] (ICLI)

KGGG .... Sterling, KS [*AM radio station call letters*] (RBYB)

KGGI .... Riverside, CA [*FM radio station call letters*]

KGGK-FM .... Winner, SD [*FM radio station call letters*] (RBYB)

KGGL .... Missoula, MT [*FM radio station call letters*] (RBYB)

KGGM .... Delhi, LA [*FM radio station call letters*] (RBYB)

KGGN .... Gladstone, MO [*AM radio station call letters*]

KGGO .... Des Moines, IA [*FM radio station call letters*]

KGGR .... Dallas, TX [*AM radio station call letters*]

KGGY .... Dubuque, IA [*FM radio station call letters*]

KGH .... Kidney Goldblatt Hypertension Scale

KGH .... Knight of the Guelphic Order of Hanover [*British*]

KGHF .... Pueblo, CO [*AM radio station call letters*]

KGHL .... Billings, MT [*AM radio station call letters*]

KGHO-AM ... Olympia, WA [*AM radio station call letters*] (RBYB)

KGHO-FM ... Hoquiam, WA [*FM radio station call letters*]

KGHP .... Gig Harbor, WA [*FM radio station call letters*]

KG/HR......... Kilograms per Hour (WDAA)

KGHR .... Tuba City, AZ [*FM radio station call letters*]

KGHS .... International Falls, MN [*AM radio station call letters*]

KGHT .... Kidney Goldblatt Hypertension [*Medicine*] (DAVI)

KGHT .... Sheridan, AR [*AM radio station call letters*]

KGI .... Cryderman Gold, Inc. [*Vancouver Stock Exchange symbol*]

KGI .... Kalgoorlie [*Australia Airport symbol*] (OAG)

KGI............. Kellogg [*Idaho*] [*Seismograph station code, US Geological Survey*] (SEIS)

KGII .... King George II [*British*]

KGIL-AM...... Beverly Hills, CA [*AM radio station call letters*] (BROA)

KGIM .... Aberdeen, SD [*AM radio station call letters*]

KGIN .... Grand Island, NE [*Television station call letters*]

KGIR-AM..... Cape Giradeau, MO [*AM radio station call letters*] (RBYB)

KGIW .... Alamosa, CO [*AM radio station call letters*]

KGJ .... Karonga [*Malawi*] [*Airport symbol*] (OAG)

KG/J........... Kilograms per Joule

KGJ .... King Jack Resources [*Vancouver Stock Exchange symbol*]

KGK .... Kabushiki Goshi Kaisha [*Partnership*] [*Japan*]

KGK	Koliganek [Alaska] [Airport symbol] (OAG)
KGKL	San Angelo, TX [AM radio station call letters]
KGKL-FM	San Angelo, TX [FM radio station call letters]
KGL	Kaufel Group Ltd. [Toronto Stock Exchange symbol]
KGL	Kigali [Rwanda] [Airport symbol] (OAG)
kg/L	Kilogram Per Liter (STED)
KGL	King's German Legion [British military] (DMA)
KGL	Koeniglich [Royal] [German]
KGL	Port-Aux-Francais [Formerly, Kerguelen] [France] [Geomagnetic observatory code]
KGLA	Gretna, LA [AM radio station call letters]
KGLB	Okmulgee, OK [Television station call letters]
KGLC	Miami, OK [FM radio station call letters]
KGLD	Tyler, TX [AM radio station call letters]
KGLE	Glendive, MT [AM radio station call letters]
KGLE	South Lake Tahoe, CA [FM radio station call letters]
KGLF	Robstown, TX [AM radio station call letters]
KGLI	Sioux City, IA [FM radio station call letters]
KGLL	Greeley, CO [FM radio station call letters]
KGLM	Anaconda, MT [FM radio station call letters]
KGLN	Glenwood Springs, CO [AM radio station call letters]
KGLO	Mason City, IA [AM radio station call letters]
KGLP	Gallup, NM [FM radio station call letters]
KGLQ-FM	Phoenix, AZ [FM radio station call letters] (BROA)
KGLS	Galveston/Scholes Field [Texas] [ICAO location identifier] (ICLI)
KGLS	Pratt, KS [FM radio station call letters]
KGLT	Bozeman, MT [FM radio station call letters]
KGLW	San Luis Obispo, CA [AM radio station call letters]
KGLX	Gallup, NM [FM radio station call letters]
KGLY	Tyler, TX [FM radio station call letters]
KGM	Keratinocyte Growth Medium [Cell culture]
KGM	Kerr Glass Mfg. (EFIS)
KGM	Kerr Group [NYSE symbol] (SPSG)
KGM	Key Generator Module
KGM	Kiena Gold Mines Ltd. [Toronto Stock Exchange symbol]
kgm	Kilogram [Also, k, kg] [SI unit for mass] (DAVI)
kgm	Kilogram-Meter (IDOE)
KGM	Kluang [Malaysia] [Seismograph station code, US Geological Survey] (SEIS)
KG/M²	Kilograms per Square Meter
KG/M³	Kilograms per Cubic Meter
kg/m³	Kilograms per Cubic Meter (IDOE)
KGMB	Honolulu, HI [Television station call letters]
KGMC	Clovis, CA [Television station call letters]
KGMD	Hilo, HI [Television station call letters]
KGME	Glendale, AZ [AM radio station call letters]
KGMens	K & G Mens Center, Inc. [Associated Press] (SAG)
KGMI	Bellingham, WA [AM radio station call letters]
KGMN	Kingman, AZ [FM radio station call letters]
KGMO	Cape Girardeau, MO [FM radio station call letters]
KGMS	Green Valley, AZ [FM radio station call letters]
KGMT	Fairbury, NE [AM radio station call letters]
KGMV	Wailuku, HI [Television station call letters]
KGMX	Lancaster, CA [FM radio station call letters]
KGMY	Aurora, MO [FM radio station call letters]
KGMY	Springfield, MO [AM radio station call letters]
KGMZ	Aiea, HI [FM radio station call letters]
KGNB	New Braunfels, TX [AM radio station call letters]
KGNC	Amarillo, TX [AM radio station call letters]
KGNC-FM	Amarillo, TX [FM radio station call letters]
KGND	Ketchum, OK [FM radio station call letters]
KGNM	St. Joseph, MO [AM radio station call letters]
KGNN	Cuba, MO [AM radio station call letters]
KGNN-FM	Cuba, MO [FM radio station call letters] (RBYB)
KGNO	Dodge City, KS [AM radio station call letters]
KGNS	Laredo, TX [Television station call letters]
KGNT	Grants/Grants-Milan [New Mexico] [ICAO location identifier] (ICLI)
KGNU	Boulder, CO [FM radio station call letters]
KGNV	Gainesville [Florida] [ICAO location identifier] (ICLI)
KGNV	Washington, MO [FM radio station call letters]
KGNW	Burien-Seattle, WA [AM radio station call letters]
KGNZ	Abilene, TX [FM radio station call letters]
KGO	Kasongo [Zaire] [Airport symbol] (AD)
KGO	King's Gurkha Officer [British military] (DMA)
KGO	San Francisco, CA [AM radio station call letters]
KGOE	Eureka, CA [FM radio station call letters]
KGOK	Pauls Valley, OK [FM radio station call letters]
KGOL	Humble, TX [AM radio station call letters]
KGON	Portland, OR [FM radio station call letters]
KGOR	Omaha, NE [FM radio station call letters]
KGOS	Torrington, WY [AM radio station call letters]
KGOT	Anchorage, AK [FM radio station call letters]
KGO-TV	San Francisco, CA [Television station call letters]
KGOU	Norman, OK [FM radio station call letters]
KGOZ	Gallatin, MO [FM radio station call letters]
KGP	Komma Georgiou Papandreou [Party of George Papandreou] [Greek Political party] (PPE)
KG/(PA S M²)	Kilograms per Pascal Second Square Meter
KGPL	Dermott, AR [AM radio station call letters]
KGPQ-FM	Monticello, AR [FM radio station call letters] (RBYB)
KGPR	Great Falls, MT [FM radio station call letters]
kgps	Kilograms per Second
KGPZ	Coleraine, MN [FM radio station call letters]
KGR	Kanonengranate [Shell for a gun] [German military - World War II]
KGR	Kengate Resources [Vancouver Stock Exchange symbol]
KGR	Key Generator Receiver (MCD)
kgr	Kilograin (BARN)
kgr	Kirghiz Soviet Socialist Republic [MARC country of publication code Library of Congress] (LCCP)
KGR	Klydonograph Type Gradient Recorder (IAA)
KGRA	Jefferson, IA [FM radio station call letters]
KGRA	Known Geothermal Resource Area [Department of the Interior]
KGRAX	Kemper Growth Cl.A [Mutual fund ticker symbol] (SG)
KGRB	Greenbay/Austin Straubel [Wisconsin] [ICAO location identifier] (ICLI)
KGRB	West Covina, CA [AM radio station call letters]
KGRBX	Kemper Growth Cl.B [Mutual fund ticker symbol] (SG)
KGRC	Hannibal, MO [FM radio station call letters]
KGRD	Orchard, NE [AM radio station call letters]
KGRE	Greeley, CO [AM radio station call letters]
KGRG	Auburn, WA [FM radio station call letters]
KGRI	Henderson, TX [FM radio station call letters]
KGRK	Killeen/Robert Gray Army Air Field [Texas] [ICAO location identifier] (ICLI)
KGRM	Grambling, LA [FM radio station call letters]
KGRN	Grinnell, IA [AM radio station call letters]
KGRO	Pampa, TX [AM radio station call letters]
KGRP-FM	Calistoga, CA [FM radio station call letters] (BROA)
KGRR	Epworth, IA [FM radio station call letters]
KGRR	Grand Rapids/Kent County Cascade [Michigan] [ICAO location identifier] (ICLI)
KGRS	Burlington, IA [FM radio station call letters]
KGRT	Las Cruces, NM [AM radio station call letters]
KGRT-FM	Las Cruces, NM [FM radio station call letters]
KGRV	Winston, OR [AM radio station call letters]
KGRW	Friona, TX [FM radio station call letters]
KGRZ	Missoula, MT [AM radio station call letters]
KGS	Kate Greenaway Society (EA)
KGS	Ketogenic Steroid [Endocrinology]
kg/s	Kilograms per Second
Kgs	Kings [Old Testament book]
KGS	Kos [Greece] [Airport symbol] (OAG)
KGSB	Goldsboro/Seymour-Johnson Air Force Base [North Carolina] [ICAO location identifier] (ICLI)
KGSG-FM	Pasco, WA [FM radio station call letters] (BROA)
KGSP	Parkville, MO [FM radio station call letters]
KGSR	Bastrop, TX [FM radio station call letters]
KGST	Fresno, CA [AM radio station call letters]
kgst	Kilograms Static Thrust (DOMA)
KGStJ	Knight of Grace, Order of St. John of Jerusalem
KGT	Kemper Intermediate Government Trust [NYSE symbol] (SPSG)
KGT	Kemper Interm Gvt Tr [NYSE symbol] (TTSB)
KGTF	Agana, GU [Television station call letters]
KGTF	Great Falls/International [Montana] [ICAO location identifier] (ICLI)
KGTL	Homer, AK [AM radio station call letters]
KGTM	Rexburg, ID [FM radio station call letters]
KGTO	Tulsa, OK [AM radio station call letters]
KGTR	Larned, KS [FM radio station call letters] (RBYB)
KGTS	College Place, WA [FM radio station call letters]
KGTV	San Diego, CA [Television station call letters]
KGTW	Ketchikan, AK [FM radio station call letters]
KGU	Honolulu, HI [AM radio station call letters]
KGU	Keningau [Malaysia] [Airport symbol] (OAG)
KGU	Kobe Gakuin University [UTLAS symbol]
KGUL	Port Lavaca, TX [AM radio station call letters]
KGUM	Agana, GU [AM radio station call letters]
KGUN	Tucson, AZ [Television station call letters]
KGUS	Peru/Grisson Air Force Base [Indiana] [ICAO location identifier] (ICLI)
KGV	King George V [British]
KGV	Knight of Gustavus Vasa [Sweden]
KGVA	Fort Belknap Agency, MT [FM radio station call letters] (RBYB)
KGVE	Grove, OK [FM radio station call letters]
KGVL	Greenville, TX [AM radio station call letters]
KGVM	Gardnerville-Minden, NV [FM radio station call letters]
KGVO	King George the Fifth's Own [British military] (DMA)
KGVO	Missoula, MT [AM radio station call letters]
KGVT	Greenville/Majors Field [Texas] [ICAO location identifier] (ICLI)
KGVW	Belgrade, MT [AM radio station call letters]
KGVW	Grandview/Richards-Gebaur Air Force Base [Missouri] [ICAO location identifier] (ICLI)
KGVY	Green Valley, AZ [AM radio station call letters]
KGW	Kagi [Papua New Guinea] [Airport symbol] (OAG)
KGW	Kreeger, George W., Atlanta GA [STAC]
KGW	Portland, OR [Television station call letters]
KGWA	Enid, OK [AM radio station call letters]
KGWB	Wahpeton, ND [FM radio station call letters]
KGWC	Casper, WY [Television station call letters]
KGWC	Offutt Air Force Base, Omaha [Nebraska] [ICAO location identifier] (ICLI)
KGWL	Lander, WY [Television station call letters]
KGWN	Cheyenne, WY [Television station call letters]
KGWO	Greenwood-Leflore [Mississippi] [ICAO location identifier] (ICLI)
KGWR	Rock Springs, WY [Television station call letters]
KGWT	Kilogram Weight (IAA)
KGWY	Gillette, WY [FM radio station call letters]
KGX	Grayling [Alaska] [Airport symbol] (OAG)
KGXL-AM	Costa Mesa, CA [AM radio station call letters] (BROA)
KGXY	Lenwood, CA [FM radio station call letters]
kGy	Kilo Gray [Absorbed dose] [Radiology]
KGY	Kingaroy [Australia Airport symbol] (OAG)

KGY .... Olympia, WA [*AM radio station call letters*]
KGY-FM .... McCleary, WA [*FM radio station call letters*]
KGYN .... Guymon, OK [*AM radio station call letters*]
kg/yr .... Kilograms per Year (COE)
KGZ .... Glacier Creek, AK [*Location identifier FAA*] (FAAL)
KGZC .... Folsom, LA [*FM radio station call letters*]
KGZF .... Emporia, KS [*FM radio station call letters*]
KGZH .... Nyssa, OR [*FM radio station call letters*]
KGZO-FM .... Shafter, CA [*FM radio station call letters*] (RBYB)
KH .... Cambodia [*ANSI two-letter standard code*] (CNC)
KH .... Cook Islandair [*ICAO designator*] (AD)
KH .... Hong Kong [*IYRU nationality code*] (IYR)
KH .... Hungary [*License plate code assigned to foreign diplomats in the US*]
KH .... Kadosh [*Freemasonry*] (ROG)
KH .... Kawasaki Heavy Industries Ltd. [*Japan ICAO aircraft manufacturer identifier*] (ICAO)
KH .... Kelvin-Helmholtz [*Waves*] [*Meteorology*]
KH .... Keren Hayesod (BJA)
KH .... Kersten Hurik Group [*Commercial firm British*]
KH .... Key Hole [*Reconnaissance satellite series*] (DOMA)
KH .... Keyhole Series [*Optical reconnaissance satellites*]
Kh .... Khirbet (BJA)
KH .... Kilohenry
kH .... Kilohertz
KH .... King's Hussars [*Military unit*] [*British*]
KH .... Kneller Hall [*British military*] (DMA)
KH .... Knight of Honor
KH .... Knight of the Guelphic Order of Hanover [*British*]
KH .... Kramers-Henneberger [*Coordinate frame for electron movement*] [*Physics*]
KH .... Krebs-Henseleit [*Cycle*] [*or Ornithine cycle Analytical biochemistry*] (DAVI)
KH .... Krebs-Henseleit Buffer [*Analytical biochemistry*] (DMAA)
KH .... Kupat Holim (BJA)
KHA .... Kansas Hospital Association (SRA)
KHA .... Khancoban [*Australia Seismograph station code, US Geological Survey*] (SEIS)
kha .... Khasi [*MARC language code Library of Congress*] (LCCP)
KHA .... Killed by Hostile Action [*Military*]
KHA .... Kitty Hawk Airways, Inc. [*ICAO designator*] (FAAC)
KHAC .... Tse Bonito, NM [*AM radio station call letters*]
KHAD .... De Soto, MO [*AM radio station call letters*]
KHAK-FM .... Cedar Rapids, IA [*FM radio station call letters*]
KHalH .... Hertzler Research Foundation, Halstead, KS [*Library symbol Library of Congress*] (LCLS)
KHAM-FM .... Saint Ansgar, IA [*FM radio station call letters*] (BROA)
KHAP .... Chico, CA [*FM radio station call letters*]
KHAR .... Anchorage, AK [*AM radio station call letters*]
KHAR .... Harrisburg/Capital City [*Pennsylvania*] [*ICAO location identifier*] (ICLI)
KHAS .... Hastings, NE [*AM radio station call letters*]
KHAS-TV .... Hastings, NE [*Television station call letters*]
KHAT .... Kurzer Handkommentar zum Alten Testament [*Tuebingen*] [*A publication*] (BJA)
KHAT .... Lincoln, NE [*AM radio station call letters*]
KHAW .... Hilo, HI [*Television station call letters*]
KHAY .... Ventura, CA [*FM radio station call letters*]
KHayF .... Fort Hays State University, Hays, KS [*Library symbol Library of Congress*] (LCLS)
KHayv .... Haysville Community Library, Haysville, KS [*Library symbol Library of Congress*] (LCLS)
KHAZ .... Hays, KS [*FM radio station call letters*]
KHB .... Khabarovsk [*Former USSR Geomagnetic observatory code*]
KHB .... King's Hard Bargain [*British military slang for undesirable sailor or soldier*]
KHB .... Korea Housing Bank (IMH)
KHB .... Krebs-Henseleit Bicarbonate [*A buffer*] [*Analytical biochemistry*]
KHB .... KSC [*Kennedy Space Center*] Handbook [*NASA*] (KSC)
KHB .... Kurzgefasstes Exegetisches Handbuch zum Alten Testament [*Leipzig*] [*A publication*] (BJA)
KHb .... Potassium Hemoglobinate (AAMN)
KHBC .... Hilo, HI [*Television station call letters*]
KHBG .... Healdsburg, CA [*FM radio station call letters*] (RBYB)
KHBM .... Monticello, AR [*AM radio station call letters*]
KHBM-FM .... Monticello, AR [*FM radio station call letters*]
KHBR .... Hillsboro, TX [*AM radio station call letters*]
KHBR .... Hobart [*Oklahoma*] [*ICAO location identifier*] (ICLI)
KHBS .... Fort Smith, AR [*Television station call letters*]
KHBT .... Humboldt, IA [*FM radio station call letters*]
KHC .... 135 Airways [*FAA designator*] (FAAC)
KHC .... Karen Horney Clinic (EA)
KHC .... Kasperske Hory [*Czechoslovakia*] [*Seismograph station code, US Geological Survey*] (SEIS)
KHC .... Kinesin Heavy Chain [*Physiology*]
KHC .... Kinesin Heavy Chain [*Cytology*]
KHC .... Kinetic Hemolysis Curve [*Biochemistry*] (DAVI)
KHC .... King's Honorary Chaplain [*British*]
KHCA .... Wamego, KS [*FM radio station call letters*]
KHCB .... Galveston, TX [*AM radio station call letters*]
KHCB .... Houston, TX [*FM radio station call letters*]
KHCC .... Hutchinson, KS [*FM radio station call letters*]
KHCD .... Kenya High Court Digest [*A publication*] (DLA)
KHCD .... Salina, KS [*FM radio station call letters*]
KHCE .... Khabarovsk Commodity Exchange [*Russian Federation*] (EY)
KHCE .... San Antonio, TX [*Television station call letters*]
KHCK .... Denton, TX [*FM radio station call letters*] (RBYB)
KHCME .... Kharkov Commodity and Raw Materials Exchange [*Ukraine*] (EY)
KHCR .... Potosi, MO [*FM radio station call letters*]
KHCS .... Palm Desert, CA [*FM radio station call letters*]
KHCT .... Great Bend, KS [*FM radio station call letters*]
KHCV .... Seattle, WA [*Television station call letters*]
KHD .... Kinky Hair Disease [*Medicine*] (DMAA)
KHDC .... Chualar, CA [*FM radio station call letters*]
KHDN .... Hardin, MT [*AM radio station call letters*] (RBYB)
KHDR-FM .... Victorville, CA [*FM radio station call letters'*] (BROA)
KHDS .... King's Honorary Dental Surgeon [*British*]
KHDT .... Caldwell, ID [*Television station call letters*]
KHDX .... Conway, AR [*FM radio station call letters*]
KHDY-FM .... Plainview, TX [*FM radio station call letters*] (RBYB)
KHE .... Kanfey-Ha'Emek Aviation [*Israel*] [*FAA designator*] (FAAC)
KHE .... Kheis [*Former USSR Seismograph station code, US Geological Survey*] (SEIS)
KHE .... Kherson [*USSR*] [*Airport symbol*] (AD)
KHEP .... Phoenix, AZ [*AM radio station call letters*]
KHER .... Crystal City, TX [*FM radio station call letters*]
KHET .... Honolulu, HI [*Television station call letters*]
KHEY .... El Paso, TX [*AM radio station call letters*]
KHEY-FM .... El Paso, TX [*FM radio station call letters*]
KHF .... Know How Fund [*European economic development fund*]
KHF .... Korean Hemorrhagic Fever [*Medicine*]
KHFD .... Hartford/Brainard Field [*Connecticut*] [*ICAO location identifier*] (ICLI)
KHFD-FM .... Hereford, TX [*FM radio station call letters*] (BROA)
KHFI .... Georgetown, TX [*FM radio station call letters*]
KHFM .... Albuquerque, NM [*FM radio station call letters*]
KHFN .... Los Ranchos de Albuquerque, NM [*AM radio station call letters*] (RBYB)
KHFS-AM .... Fort Smith, AR [*AM radio station call letters*] (BROA)
KHFT .... Hobbs, NM [*Television station call letters*]
KHG .... Kashi [*China*] [*Airport symbol*] (OAG)
KHG .... Keystone Heritage Group [*AMEX symbol*] (TTSB)
KHG .... Keystone Heritage Group, Inc. [*AMEX symbol*] (SAG)
K hgb .... Potassium Hemoglobinate [*Organic chemistry*] (DAVI)
KHGI .... Kearney, NE [*Television station call letters*]
KHGN-FM .... Kirksville, MO [*FM radio station call letters*] (BROA)
KHH .... Kaohsiung [*Taiwan*] [*Airport symbol*] (OAG)
KHH .... Kirchoff, H. H., St. Paul MN [*STAC*]
KHHK-FM .... Naches, WA [*FM radio station call letters*] (RBYB)
KHHO-AM .... Tacoma, WA [*AM radio station call letters*] (RBYB)
KHHT .... Killeen, TX [*FM radio station call letters*]
KHI .... Kakhk [*Iran*] [*Seismograph station code, US Geological Survey*] (SEIS)
KHi .... Kansas State Historical Society, Topeka, KS [*Library symbol Library of Congress*] (LCLS)
KHI .... Karachi [*Pakistan*] [*Airport symbol*] (OAG)
KHI .... Kelvin-Helmholtz Instability (PDAA)
KHI .... Kemper High Income [*NYSE symbol*] (SPSG)
KHIB .... Durant, OK [*FM radio station call letters*]
KHIB .... Hibbing/Chisholm-Hibbing [*Minnesota*] [*ICAO location identifier*] (ICLI)
KHID .... McAllen, TX [*FM radio station call letters*]
KHIF .... Keeping House of Ill Fame
KHIF .... Ogden/Hill Air Force Base [*Utah*] [*ICAO location identifier*] (ICLI)
KHIH-FM .... Denver, CO [*FM radio station call letters*] (RBYB)
KHII .... Security, CO [*FM radio station call letters*]
KHIL .... Willcox, AZ [*AM radio station call letters*]
KHilT .... Tabor College, Hillsboro, KS [*Library symbol Library of Congress*] (LCLS)
KHIM-TV .... Conroe, TX [*TV station call letters*] (RBYB)
KHIN .... Red Oak, IA [*Television station call letters*]
KHIP .... Felton, CA [*FM radio station call letters*]
KHIS .... Bakersfield, CA [*AM radio station call letters*]
KHIS-FM .... Bakersfield, CA [*FM radio station call letters*]
KHIT .... Reno, NV [*FM radio station call letters*]
KHIT-AM .... Reno, NV [*AM radio station call letters*] (RBYB)
KHIZ .... Barstow, CA [*Television station call letters*]
KHJJ .... Lancaster, CA [*AM radio station call letters*]
KHJM .... Taft, OK [*FM radio station call letters*]
KHK .... Khark [*Iran*] [*Airport symbol Obsolete*] (OAG)
KHK .... Kurzer Handkommentar zum Alten Testament [*A publication*] (BJA)
KHKC .... Atoka, OK [*FM radio station call letters*]
KHKE .... Cedar Falls, IA [*FM radio station call letters*]
KHKI .... Des Moines, IA [*FM radio station call letters*]
KHKK-FM .... Modesto, CA [*FM radio station call letters*] (RBYB)
KHKR .... East Helena, MT [*AM radio station call letters*]
KHKR-FM .... East Helena, MT [*FM radio station call letters*]
KHKS .... Denton, TX [*FM radio station call letters*]
KHKY .... Hickory/Municipal [*North Carolina*] [*ICAO location identifier*] (ICLI)
KHL .... Kennedy-Heaviside Layer [*Electronics*]
KHL .... Keren Hajesod Ljisroel (BJA)
KHL .... Khulna [*Bangladesh*] [*Airport symbol*] (AD)
KHL .... Kupat Holim Le-'Ovdim Le'umiyim [*A publication*] (BJA)
KHLA .... Lake Charles, LA [*FM radio station call letters*]
KHLB .... Burnet, TX [*AM radio station call letters*]
KHLB-FM .... Burnet, TX [*FM radio station call letters*]
KHLL .... Richwood, LA [*FM radio station call letters*]
KHLO .... Hilo, HI [*AM radio station call letters*]
KHLR .... Cameron, TX [*FM radio station call letters*]
KHLR .... Kahler Corp. [*NASDAQ symbol*] (NQ)
KHLR .... KahlerRealty [*NASDAQ symbol*] (TTSB)
KHLS .... Blytheville, AR [*FM radio station call letters*]

KHLT.......... Hallettsville, TX [*AM radio station call letters*] (RBYB)
KHM.......... Cambodia [*ANSI three-letter standard code*] (CNC)
KHM.......... Khamtis [*Myanmar*] [*Airport symbol*] (OAG)
KHM.......... King's Harbour Master [*Obsolete British*]
KH-M.......... Yad V'Kidush Hashem, House of Martyrs (EA)
KHMA.......... Kentucky Hotel and Motel Association (SRA)
KHMB.......... Hamburg, AR [*FM radio station call letters*]
KHMC.......... Goliad, TX [*FM radio station call letters*]
KHME.......... Winona, MN [*FM radio station call letters*]
KHMG.......... Barrigada, GU [*FM radio station call letters*] (RBYB)
KHMN.......... Alamogordo/Holloman Air Force Base [*New Mexico*] [*ICAO location identifier*] (ICLI)
KHMO.......... Hannibal, MO [*AM radio station call letters*]
KHMS.......... Victorville, CA [*FM radio station call letters*]
KHMT.......... Hardin, MT [*Television station call letters*] (RBYB)
KHMX.......... Houston, TX [*FM radio station call letters*]
KHN.......... Knoop Hardness Number
KHN.......... Nanchang [*China*] [*Airport symbol*] (OAG)
KHN.......... Northern Kentucky University, Highland Heights, KY [*OCLC symbol*] (OCLC)
KHNC.......... Johnstown, CO [*AM radio station call letters*]
KHND.......... Harvey, ND [*AM radio station call letters*]
KHNE.......... Hastings, NE [*FM radio station call letters*]
KHNE-TV.......... Hastings, NE [*Television station call letters*]
KHNL.......... Honolulu, HI [*Television station call letters*]
KHNR.......... Honolulu, HI [*AM radio station call letters*]
KHNS.......... Haines, AK [*FM radio station call letters*]
KHNS.......... King's Honorary Nursing Sister [*British*]
KHO.......... Khorog [*Former USSR Seismograph station code, US Geological Survey*] (SEIS)
KHO.......... Khors Aircompany [*Ukraine*] [*FAA designator*] (FAAC)
kho.......... Khotanese [*MARC language code Library of Congress*] (LCCP)
KHOB.......... Hobbs/Les County [*New Mexico*] [*ICAO location identifier*] (ICLI)
KHOB.......... Hobbs, NM [*AM radio station call letters*]
KHOE.......... Fairfield, IA [*FM radio station call letters*]
KHOG.......... Fayetteville, AR [*Television station call letters*]
KHOK.......... Hoisington, KS [*FM radio station call letters*]
KHOL.......... Beulah, ND [*AM radio station call letters*]
KHOM.......... Houma, LA [*FM radio station call letters*]
KHON.......... Honolulu, HI [*Television station call letters*]
KHOP.......... Hopkinsville/Campbell Army Air Field [*Kentucky*] [*ICAO location identifier*] (ICLI)
KHOP.......... Modesto, CA [*FM radio station call letters*]
KHOS.......... Sonora, TX [*AM radio station call letters*]
KHOS-FM.......... Sonora, TX [*FM radio station call letters*]
KHOT.......... Globe, AZ [*FM radio station call letters*] (RBYB)
KHOT.......... Madera, CA [*AM radio station call letters*]
KHOU.......... Houston, TX [*Television station call letters*]
KHOU.......... Houston/William P. Hobby [*Texas*] [*ICAO location identifier*] (ICLI)
KHOW.......... Denver, CO [*AM radio station call letters*]
KHOX.......... Hoxie, AR [*FM radio station call letters*]
KHOY.......... Laredo, TX [*FM radio station call letters*]
KHOZ.......... Harrison, AR [*AM radio station call letters*]
KHOZ-FM.......... Harrison, AR [*FM radio station call letters*]
KHP.......... Honorary Physician to the King [*British*]
KHP.......... Koppers Hydrate Process
KHPA.......... Hope, AR [*FM radio station call letters*]
KHPE.......... Albany, OR [*FM radio station call letters*]
KHPN.......... White Plains/Westchester [*New York*] [*ICAO location identifier*] (ICLI)
KHPQ.......... Clinton, AR [*FM radio station call letters*]
KHPR.......... Honolulu, HI [*FM radio station call letters*]
KHPU-FM.......... Brownwood, TX [*FM radio station call letters*] (BROA)
KHPY.......... Moreno Valley, CA [*AM radio station call letters*]
KHQ.......... Spokane, WA [*Television station call letters*]
KHQA.......... Hannibal, MO [*Television station call letters*]
KHQN.......... Spanish Fork, UT [*AM radio station call letters*]
KHR.......... Khazar [*Turkmenistan*] [*ICAO designator*] (FAAC)
KHR.......... Khorongon [*Former USSR Seismograph station code, US Geological Survey Closed*] (SEIS)
KHRI.......... Kresge Hearing Research Institute [*University of Michigan*] [*Research center*]
KHRL.......... Harlingen/Industrial Airpack [*Texas*] [*ICAO location identifier*] (ICLI)
KHRN.......... Hearne, TX [*FM radio station call letters*] (RBYB)
KHRO.......... Harrison/Boone County [*Arkansas*] [*ICAO location identifier*] (ICLI)
KHRP.......... Kurdish Human Rights Project (BUAC)
KHRR.......... Tucson, AZ [*Television station call letters*]
KHRT.......... Mary Esther/Eglin Air Field Auxiliary [*Florida*] [*ICAO location identifier*] (ICLI)
KHRT.......... Minot, ND [*AM radio station call letters*]
KHS.......... Honorary Surgeon to the King [*British*]
KHS.......... Kinky Hair Syndrome [*Medicine*] (DMAA)
KHS.......... Knight of the Holy Sepulchre
KHS.......... Knight of the Holy Sepulchre of Jerusalem (DD)
KHS.......... Krebs-Henseleit Solution (DB)
KHS.......... Kushtia [*Bangladesh*] [*Airport symbol*] (AD)
KHSA.......... Kentucky Human Services Association (SRA)
KHSC.......... Ontario, CA [*Television station call letters*]
KHSD.......... Lead, SD [*Television station call letters*]
KHSH.......... Alvin, TX [*Television station call letters*]
KHSL.......... Paradise, CA [*FM radio station call letters*]
KHSL-TV.......... Chico, CA [*Television station call letters*]
KHSN.......... Coos Bay, OR [*AM radio station call letters*]
KHSP.......... Ashdown, AR [*FM radio station call letters*]
KHSP.......... Texarkana, TX [*AM radio station call letters*]
KHSR-FM.......... Crescent City, CA [*FM radio station call letters*] (BROA)
KHSS.......... Walla Walla, WA [*FM radio station call letters*]
KHST.......... Homestead/Homestead Air Force Base [*Florida*] [*ICAO location identifier*] (ICLI)
KHST.......... Lamar, MO [*FM radio station call letters*]
KHSU.......... Arcata, CA [*FM radio station call letters*]
KHSX.......... Irving, TX [*Television station call letters*]
KHT.......... Kathode Heating Time
KHT.......... Khost [*Afghanistan*] [*Airport symbol Obsolete*] (OAG)
KHTC.......... Phoenix, AZ [*FM radio station call letters*] (RBYB)
KHTH.......... Dillon, CO [*AM radio station call letters*]
KHTK.......... Sacramento, CA [*AM radio station call letters*]
KHTL.......... Albuquerque, NM [*AM radio station call letters*] (RBYB)
KHTL.......... Houghton Lake/Roscommon [*Michigan*] [*ICAO location identifier*] (ICLI)
KHTN.......... Los Banos, CA [*FM radio station call letters*]
KHTO.......... Mount Vernon, MO [*FM radio station call letters*]
KHTQ.......... Hayden, ID [*FM radio station call letters*] (RBYB)
KHTR.......... Pullman, WA [*FM radio station call letters*]
KHTS.......... El Cajon, CA [*FM radio station call letters*] (RBYB)
KHTT.......... Muskogee, OK [*FM radio station call letters*]
KHTTA.......... Kanata High Technology Training Association [*Canada*] (EDAC)
KHTV.......... Houston, TX [*Television station call letters*]
KHTW-FM.......... Caledonia, MN [*FM radio station call letters*] (BROA)
KHTX.......... Salinas, CA [*AM radio station call letters*] (RBYB)
KHTY.......... Santa Barbara, CA [*FM radio station call letters*]
KHTZ.......... Albuquerque, NM [*FM radio station call letters*] (RBYB)
KHu.......... Hutchinson Public Library, Hutchinson, KS [*Library symbol Library of Congress*] (LCLS)
KHU.......... Kahuku [*Hawaii*] [*Seismograph station code, US Geological Survey*] (SEIS)
KHUB.......... Fremont, NE [*AM radio station call letters*]
KHuC.......... Hutchinson Community Junior College, Hutchinson, KS [*Library symbol Library of Congress*] (LCLS)
KHUG.......... Rocky Ford, CO [*FM radio station call letters*]
KHUG-FM.......... England, AR [*FM radio station call letters*] (BROA)
KHUL.......... Houlton/International [*Maine*] [*ICAO location identifier*] (ICLI)
KHUL-FM.......... Waipahu, HI [*FM radio station call letters*] (BROA)
KHUM.......... Garberville, CA [*FM radio station call letters*] (RBYB)
KHUT.......... Hutchinson, KS [*FM radio station call letters*]
KHV.......... Khabarovsk [*Former USSR Airport symbol*] (OAG)
KhV.......... Khranit' Vechno [*To be Kept in Perpetuity*] [*KGB file status*]
KhV.......... Khristianski Vostok (BJA)
KHVH.......... Honolulu, HI [*AM radio station call letters*]
KHVN.......... Fort Worth, TX [*AM radio station call letters*]
KHVO.......... Hilo, HI [*Television station call letters*]
KHVR.......... Havre [*Montana*] [*ICAO location identifier*] (ICLI)
KHWG-FM.......... Kings Beach, CA [*FM radio station call letters*] (RBYB)
KHWI.......... Hilo, HI [*FM radio station call letters*]
KHWK.......... Tonopah, NV [*FM radio station call letters*]
KHWO.......... Hollywood/North Perry [*Florida*] [*ICAO location identifier*] (ICLI)
KHWS-FM.......... North Pole, AK [*FM radio station call letters*] (BROA)
KHWY.......... Essex, CA [*FM radio station call letters*]
KHWZ-FM.......... Ludlow, CA [*FM radio station call letters*] (RBYB)
KHX.......... Hugo Rizzuto [*ICAO designator*] (FAAC)
KHXS.......... Abilene, TX [*FM radio station call letters*]
KHYAX.......... Kemper High Yield Cl.A [*Mutual fund ticker symbol*] (SG)
KHYB.......... Kupat Holim Year Book [*A publication*] (BJA)
KHYBX.......... Kemper High Yield Cl.B [*Mutual fund ticker symbol*] (SG)
KHYF-FM.......... Taos, NM [*FM radio station call letters*] (BROA)
KHYI.......... Howe, TX [*FM radio station call letters*]
KHYL.......... Auburn, CA [*FM radio station call letters*]
KHYM.......... Gilmer, TX [*AM radio station call letters*]
KHYM-FM.......... Copeland, KS [*FM radio station call letters*] (BROA)
KHYS.......... Port Arthur, TX [*FM radio station call letters*]
KHYT-FM.......... Tucson, AZ [*FM radio station call letters*] (RBYB)
KHYZ.......... Mountain Pass, CA [*FM radio station call letters*]
kHz.......... Kilohertz [*Electronics*]
KHZ.......... Kilohertz [*FAA*] (TAG)
KHZL.......... Shingletown, CA [*FM radio station call letters*] (RBYB)
KI.......... Kach International (EA)
KI.......... Kanaanaeische Inschriften [*A publication*] (BJA)
KI.......... Karyopyknotic Index [*Cytology*] (MAE)
KI.......... Karyotype Instability [*Genetics*]
KI.......... Kennarasamband Islands [*Iceland*] (BUAC)
KI.......... Keyette International (EA)
KI.......... Key Industry [*Business term*]
KI.......... Khmer Insurgents [*Cambodian rebel force*]
KI.......... Kilo (WDAA)
KI.......... Kinase Insert
Ki.......... Kings [*Old Testament book*]
KI.......... Kiribati [*Internet country code*]
KI.......... Kitchen (AABC)
KI.......... Kiwanis International (EA)
KI.......... Knesset Israel (BJA)
KI.......... Know, Inc. (EA)
KI.......... Knowledge Integrity [*Electronic information*] (IT)
KI.......... Kovats [*Retention*] Index
KI.......... Kroenig's Isthmus [*Of resonance*] [*Medicine*]
KI.......... Potassium Iodide (AAMN)
KiA.......... Die Keilinschriften der Achaemeniden [*A publication*] (BJA)
KIA.......... Kachin Independence Army [*Myanmar*] [*Political party*] (EY)
KIA.......... Kaiapit [*New Guinea*] [*Airport symbol*] (AD)
KIA.......... Kansai International Airport [*Japan*]
KIA.......... Kent International Airport [*British*]
KIA.......... Kenya Institute of Administration (BUAC)

KIA............	Kibbutz Industries Association [*Israel*] (BUAC)
KIA............	Killed in Action [*Military*]
KIA............	KIWI International Air Lines, Inc. [*ICAO designator*] (FAAC)
KIA............	Kligler Iron Agar [*Medium*]
KIA............	Kotoka International Airport [*Ghana*]
KIAA..........	Kangaroo Industries Association of Australia
KIAB..........	Wichita/McConnell Air Force Base [*Kansas*] [*ICAO location identifier*] (ICLI)
KIA - BNR....	Killed in Action - Body Not Recovered (MCD)
KIAC..........	Kansai International Airport Co. [*Japan*]
KIAC..........	Kerr Industrial Applications Center [*Southeastern Oklahoma State University*] [*Durant*] [*Information service or system*] (IID)
KIAD..........	Washington/Dulles International [*District of Columbia*] [*ICAO location identifier*] (ICLI)
KIAG..........	Niagara Falls/International [*New York*] [*ICAO location identifier*] (ICLI)
KIAH..........	Houston/Intercontinental [*Texas*] [*ICAO location identifier*] (ICLI)
KIAI...........	Mason City, IA [*FM radio station call letters*]
KIAK..........	Fairbanks, AK [*AM radio station call letters*]
KIAK-FM......	Fairbanks, AK [*FM radio station call letters*]
KIAL..........	Unalaska, AK [*AM radio station call letters*]
KIAM..........	Nenana, AK [*AM radio station call letters*]
KIAQ..........	Clarion, IA [*FM radio station call letters*]
KIAR..........	Kiwanis International Accredited Representative
KIAR..........	Kuzell Institute for Arthritis Research [*Medical Research Institute at Pacific Medical Center*] [*Research center*] (RCD)
KIAS..........	Knots Indicated Airspeed (MCD)
KIAS..........	Korea Advanced Institute of Science
KIB............	Ivanof Bay, AK [*Location identifier FAA*] (FAAL)
KiB............	Keilinschriftliche Bibliothek [*A publication*] (BJA)
kib............	Kilopounds (NAKS)
KIBB-FM......	Los Angeles, CA [*FM radio station call letters*] (RBYB)
KIBC..........	Burney, CA [*FM radio station call letters*]
KIBG-FM......	Merced, CA [*FM radio station call letters*] (RBYB)
KIBIC.........	Karolinska Institutets Bibliotek och Informationscentral [*Karolinska Institute Library and Information Center*] [*Sweden Information service or system*] (IID)
KIBL..........	Beeville, TX [*AM radio station call letters*]
KIBN..........	Wichita, KS [*FM radio station call letters*]
KIBS..........	Bishop, CA [*FM radio station call letters*]
KIBZ..........	Lincoln, NE [*FM radio station call letters*]
KIC............	Kansas Information Circuit [*Library network*]
KIC............	Karlsruhe Isochronous Cyclotron
KIC............	Kart Industry Council
KIC............	Kernal Input Controller [*Computer science*] (CIST)
KIC............	Ketoisocaproate [*Biochemistry*]
KIC............	Keto Isocaproic Acid (DMAA)
KIC............	King City, CA [*Location identifier FAA*] (FAAL)
KIC............	Knight of the Iron Crown [*British*] (ROG)
KIC............	Kosan Boka [*Ivory Coast*] [*Seismograph station code, US Geological Survey*] (SEIS)
KIC............	Kurdistan Information Centre (BUAC)
KIC............	Kuwait Insurance Co. (BUAC)
KICA..........	Clovis, NM [*AM radio station call letters*]
KICA..........	Farwell, TX [*FM radio station call letters*]
KICAX........	Kemper Inc. Cap. Pres. Cl.A [*Mutual fund ticker symbol*] (SG)
KICB..........	Fort Dodge, IA [*FM radio station call letters*]
KICB..........	Killed Intracellular Bacteria [*Microbiology*] (DAVI)
KICD..........	Spencer, IA [*AM radio station call letters*]
KICD-FM......	Spencer, IA [*FM radio station call letters*]
KICE..........	Bend, OR [*FM radio station call letters*]
KICI..........	Corsicana, TX [*FM radio station call letters*] (RBYB)
KICI..........	Denton, TX [*AM radio station call letters*] (RBYB)
KICK.........	Master Glaziers Karate Intl. [*NASDAQ symbol*] (SAG)
KICK.........	Palmyra, MO [*FM radio station call letters*]
KICKW........	Master Glaziers Karate Wrrt'A' [*NASDAQ symbol*] (TTSB)
KICKZ.........	Master Glaziers Karate Wrrt'B' [*NASDAQ symbol*] (TTSB)
KICM..........	Healdton, OK [*FM radio station call letters*]
KICN..........	Idaho Falls, ID [*AM radio station call letters*]
KICO..........	Calexico, CA [*AM radio station call letters*]
KICR..........	Oakdale, LA [*AM radio station call letters*]
KICR-FM......	Oakdale, LA [*FM radio station call letters*]
KICS..........	Hastings, NE [*AM radio station call letters*]
KICS..........	Kansas Individualized Curriculum Sequencing (EDAC)
KICT..........	Wichita, KS [*FM radio station call letters*]
KICT..........	Wichita/Mid-Continent [*Kansas*] [*ICAO location identifier*] (ICLI)
KICU..........	Keyboard Interface Control Unit [*Computer science*]
KICU..........	San Jose, CA [*Television station call letters*]
KICX..........	McCook, NE [*FM radio station call letters*]
KICY..........	Nome, AK [*AM radio station call letters*]
KICY-FM......	Nome, AK [*FM radio station call letters*]
KID............	Idaho Falls, ID [*AM radio station call letters*]
KID............	Kent Infant Development Scale (EDAC)
KID............	Keratitis, Ichthyosis, and Deafness Syndrome [*Medicine*] (DMAA)
KID............	Keyboard Input Device (MCD)
KID............	Key Industry [*Business term*] (DS)
KID............	Khmer Institute of Democracy [*Phnom Penh, Cambodia*]
KID............	Kiddie
KID............	Kidd Resources Ltd. [*Vancouver Stock Exchange symbol*]
Kid............	Kiddushin (BJA)
KID............	Kidnaping [*FBI standardized term*]
KID............	Kidney [*Anatomy*] (DAVI)
KID............	Kildare [*County in Ireland*] (ROG)
KID............	Kinase-Inducible Domain [*Biochemistry*]
KID............	Kristianstad [*Sweden*] [*Airport symbol*] (OAG)
KIDA.........	Ida Grove, IA [*FM radio station call letters*]
KIDA.........	Korean International Development Agency (BUAC)
KidAInt......	Kiddie Academy International, Inc. [*Associated Press*] (SAG)
KIDC.........	Kentucky Industrial Development Council (SRA)
KIDC.........	Kiowa Industrial Development Commission
KIDD.........	First Yars Inc. (The) [*NASDAQ symbol*] (SAG)
KIDD.........	First Years [*NASDAQ symbol*] (TTSB)
KIDD.........	Kiddie Products, Inc. [*NASDAQ symbol*] (NQ)
KIDD.........	Monterey, CA [*AM radio station call letters*]
KiddAcInt....	Kiddie Academy International, Inc. [*Associated Press*] (SAG)
KIDDCOS.....	Kitchens Design Drawing and Costing [*Kitchens International DMS Electronics Ltd.*] [*Software package*] (NCC)
KIDE.........	4 Kids Entertainment [*NASDAQ symbol*] (TTSB)
KIDE.........	For Kids Entertainment, Inc. [*NASDAQ symbol*] (SAG)
KIDE.........	Hoopa, CA [*FM radio station call letters*]
Kideo........	Kideo Productions [*Associated Press*] (SAG)
KID-FM.......	Idaho Falls, ID [*FM radio station call letters*]
KIDH.........	Eagle, ID [*AM radio station call letters*]
KIDI..........	Guadalupe, CA [*FM radio station call letters*]
KIDK.........	Idaho Falls, ID [*Television station call letters*]
KIDN.........	Hayden, CO [*FM radio station call letters*]
KIDO.........	Boise, ID [*AM radio station call letters*]
KIDO.........	Kideo Productions [*NASDAQ symbol*] (SAG)
KIDQ.........	New Horizon Kids Quest [*NASDAQ symbol*] (TTSB)
KIDQ.........	New Horizon Kids Quest, Inc. [*NASDAQ symbol*] (SAG)
KIDR.........	Phoenix, AZ [*AM radio station call letters*]
KIDS.........	Children's Comprehensive Services [*NASDAQ symbol*] (SAG)
KIDS.........	Children's Comp Svcs [*NASDAQ symbol*] (TTSB)
KIDS.........	Kent Infant Development Scale [*Neonatology*] (DAVI)
KIDS.........	Kestrel Interactive Development System [*Computer science*]
KIDS.........	Kindergarten Inventory of Developmental Skills [*Child development test*]
KIDS.........	Knowledge-Based Integrated Design System (DOMA)
KIDS.........	Springfield, MO [*AM radio station call letters*]
Kidult.......	Kid-Adult [*Television viewer aged 12-34*]
KIDWE.......	Direct Connect Intl Wrrt [*NASDAQ symbol*] (TTSB)
KIDX.........	Billings, MT [*FM radio station call letters*]
KIDY.........	San Angelo, TX [*Television station call letters*]
KIE...........	Kennedy Institute of Ethics, Washington, DC [*OCLC symbol*] (OCLC)
KIE...........	Kieta [*Papua New Guinea*] [*Airport symbol*] (OAG)
KIE...........	Kinetic Isotope Effect [*Physical chemistry*]
KIE...........	Kirklees Information Exchange [*Formerly, Huddersfield and District Information*] (NITA)
KIE...........	Kodak Image Enhancement
KIEE.........	Knoxville International Energy Exposition [*1982*]
KIEE.........	Korean Institute of Electrical Engineers
KI-EF........	Kiwanis International - European Federation [*An association*]
KIEI.........	Kundu Introversion-Extraversion Inventory [*Personality development test*] [*Psychology*]
KIEM.........	Eureka, CA [*Television station call letters*]
KIEMP.......	Kenya Industrial Energy Management Program (BUAC)
KIER.........	Korea Institute of Energy and Resources (BUAC)
KIET.........	Korea Institute for Economics and Technology (BUAC)
KIET.........	Korea Institute for Industrial Economics and Trade (ECON)
KIEV.........	Glendale, CA [*AM radio station call letters*]
KIEZ.........	Carmel Valley, CA [*AM radio station call letters*]
KIF...........	Kiwanis International Foundation [*An association*]
KIF...........	Knitting Industries Federation (BUAC)
KIF...........	Knitting Industries Foundation [*British*] (DBA)
KIF...........	Knowledge Interchange Format [*Computer science*]
KIF...........	Kodak Industrial Film
KIF...........	Korean Investment Fund [*NYSE symbol*] (SAG)
KIF...........	Name and Address Key Index File [*IRS*]
Kif Aus......	Kiffa Australis [*Constellation*] (WDAA)
Kif Bor......	Kiffa Borealis [*Constellation*] (WDAA)
KIFG.........	Iowa Falls, IA [*AM radio station call letters*]
KIFG-FM.....	Iowa Falls, IA [*FM radio station call letters*]
KIFI.........	Idaho Falls, ID [*Television station call letters*]
KIFIS........	Kollsman Integrated Flight Instrumentation System [*Aviation*]
KIFM.........	San Diego, CA [*FM radio station call letters*]
KIFO.........	Pearl City, HI [*AM radio station call letters*]
KIFP.........	Korean Institute for Family Planning (BUAC)
KIFTSG......	Kiftsgate [*England*]
KIFW.........	Sitka, AK [*AM radio station call letters*]
KIFX.........	Roosevelt, UT [*FM radio station call letters*]
KIG...........	Koingnaas [*South Africa*] [*Airport symbol*] (OAG)
KIGC.........	Oskaloosa, IA [*FM radio station call letters*]
KIGL.........	Spencer, IA [*FM radio station call letters*]
KIGN-FM.....	Cheyenne, WY [*FM radio station call letters*] (RBYB)
KIGO.........	St. Anthony, ID [*AM radio station call letters*]
KIGS.........	Hanford, CA [*AM radio station call letters*]
KIH...........	Coast Independent Hi-Tech [*Vancouver Stock Exchange symbol*]
KIH...........	Kaisar-I-Hind [*Indian medal*]
KIH...........	Kilometres in the Hour [*Rate of march*] [*Military British*]
KIH...........	Kish Island [*Iran*] [*Airport symbol*] (OAG)
KIHASA......	Korea Institute for Health and Social Affairs (BUAC)
KIHK-FM.....	Rock Valley, IA [*FM radio station call letters*] (BROA)
KIHM-AM.....	Sun Valley, NV [*AM radio station call letters*] (BROA)
KIHN.........	Hugo, OK [*AM radio station call letters*]
KIHR.........	Hood River, OR [*AM radio station call letters*]
KIHR.........	Korean Institute for Human Rights (EA)
KIHT.........	St. Louis, MO [*FM radio station call letters*]
K-II..........	Karyovirus-II (ECON)
KII...........	Keystone International, Inc. [*NYSE symbol*] (SPSG)
KII...........	Kuder Interest Inventory [*Occupational information*] (OICC)

KIIC............ Kuwait International Investment Co.
KIIC-FM .... Lamoni, IA [FM radio station call letters] (BROA)
KIII............. Corpus Christi, TX [Television station call letters]
K-III .... K-III Communications Corp. [Associated Press] (SAG)
KIIK............ Fairfield, IA [FM radio station call letters]
KIIM............ Tucson, AZ [FM radio station call letters]
KIIN .... Iowa City, IA [Television station call letters]
KIIS............ Korean Institute of International Studies
KIIS............ Los Angeles, CA [AM radio station call letters]
KIIS-FM .... Los Angeles, CA [FM radio station call letters]
KIIX............ Wellington, CO [AM radio station call letters]
KIIZ............ Killeen, TX [FM radio station call letters]
KIJ .... Independence Community Junior College, Independence, KS [Library
                symbol Library of Congress] (LCLS)
KIJ .... Kawah Idjen [Java] [Seismograph station code, US Geological
                Survey Closed] (SEIS)
KIJ .... Niigata [Japan] [Airport symbol] (OAG)
KIJK............ Prineville, OR [FM radio station call letters]
KIJN............ Farwell, TX [AM radio station call letters]
KIJN-FM .... Farwell, TX [FM radio station call letters]
KIJV............ Huron, SD [AM radio station call letters]
KIK .... Kentucky's Individualized Kindergartens (EDAC)
kik.............. Kikuyu [MARC language code Library of Congress] (LCCP)
KIK .... Kirkuk [Iraq] [Airport symbol] (AD)
KIK .... Kozawa, Iwatsuru, and Kawaguchi [Factor involving injection of
                cancerous gastric juices into rabbits, named for its discoverers]
                [Medicine]
KIKC............ Forsyth, MT [AM radio station call letters]
KIKC-FM ...... Forsyth, MT [FM radio station call letters]
KIKD-FM ...... Lake City, IA [FM radio station call letters] (BROA)
KIKF............ Garden Grove, CA [FM radio station call letters]
KIKI............ Honolulu, HI [AM radio station call letters]
KIKI-FM .... Honolulu, HI [FM radio station call letters]
KIKK............ Pasadena, TX [AM radio station call letters]
KIKK-FM ...... Houston, TX [FM radio station call letters]
KIKM............ Sherman, TX [FM radio station call letters]
KIKN............ Salem, SD [FM radio station call letters]
KIKO............ Claypool, AZ [FM radio station call letters]
KIKO............ Miami, AZ [AM radio station call letters]
KIKR............ Asbury, IA [FM radio station call letters]
KIKS............ Iola, KS [FM radio station call letters]
KIKT............ Greenville, TX [FM radio station call letters]
KIKU............ Honolulu, HI [Television station call letters]
KIKV............ Alexandria, MN [FM radio station call letters]
KIKX............ Manitou Springs, CO [FM radio station call letters]
KIKX-FM ...... Ketchum, ID [FM radio station call letters] (BROA)
KIKY............ Hutto, TX [FM radio station call letters] (RBYB)
KIKY-FM ...... Hutto, TX [FM radio station call letters] (RBYB)
KIKZ............ Seminole, TX [AM radio station call letters]
KIL .... Keyed Input Language
KIL .... Keystone Intl [NYSE symbol] (TTSB)
Kil.............. Kil'aim (BJA)
KIL .... Kilderkin [Unit of measurement] [British] (ROG)
KIL .... Kilembe Resources Ltd. [Vancouver Stock Exchange symbol]
KIL .... Kilogram
KIL .... Kilometer
KIL .... Krypton Ion LASER
KILA............ Las Vegas, NV [FM radio station call letters]
Kilamco ...... Kilwa Ammonia Co. [Tanzania] (BUAC)
Kilb............. Kilburn's English Magistrates' Cases [A publication] (DLA)
KILD............ Kildare [County in Ireland] (ROG)
KILD............ Kilderkin [Unit of measurement] [British]
KILE-AM ...... Port Lavaca, TX [AM radio station call letters] (RBYB)
Kilern.......... Killearn Properties, Inc. [Associated Press] (SAG)
KILG............ Wilmington/Greater Wilmington [Delaware] [ICAO location identifier]
                (ICLI)
KILJ............ Mount Pleasant, IA [AM radio station call letters]
KILJ-FM .... Mount Pleasant, IA [FM radio station call letters]
KILK............ Kilkenny [County in Ireland]
Kilk............. Kilkerran's Scotch Court of Session Decisions [A publication] (DLA)
Kilkerran...... Kilkerran's Scotch Court of Session Decisions [A publication] (DLA)
kill .... Kilowatt (NAKS)
KILLS.......... Ka-Inertial Launch and Leave System
KILM............ Wilmington/New Hannover County [North Carolina] [ICAO location
                identifier] (ICLI)
KILN............ Kirlin Holding [NASDAQ symbol] (TTSB)
KILN............ Kirlin Holding Corp. [NASDAQ symbol] (SAG)
KILO............ Colorado Springs, CO [FM radio station call letters]
KILO............ Kilogram
KILO............ Kilometer
KILOL.......... Kiloliter
KILOM .... Kilometer
kilovar .... Kilovolt-Ampere Reactive Hour (BARN)
KILR............ Estherville, IA [AM radio station call letters]
KILR-FM ...... Estherville, IA [FM radio station call letters]
KILS............ Minneapolis, KS [FM radio station call letters]
KILT............ Houston, TX [AM radio station call letters]
KILT-FM....... Houston, TX [FM radio station call letters]
KILU............ Paauilo, HI [FM radio station call letters] (RBYB)
KIM .... Kenya Institute of Management (BUAC)
KIM .... Keyboard Input Matrix [Computer science]
KIM .... Kimberley [South Africa] [Airport symbol] (OAG)
KIM .... Kimberley [South Africa] [Seismograph station code, US Geological
                Survey] (SEIS)
KIM .... Kimco Realty [NYSE symbol] (SPSG)

KIM .... Knowledge-Based Integrated Machine [Computer science]
KIMA........... Yakima, WA [Television station call letters]
KIMB........... Kimball, NE [AM radio station call letters]
Kimbal......... Kimball International, Inc. [Associated Press] (SAG)
KimbClk....... Kimberly Clark [Associated Press] (SAG)
Kimc........... Kimco Realty Corp. [Associated Press] (SAG)
Kimco.......... Kimco Realty Corp. [Associated Press] (SAG)
KIMCODE...... Kimble Method for Controlled Devacuation
KimEnv .... Kimmins Environmental Services [Associated Press] (SAG)
KIML........... Gillette, WY [AM radio station call letters]
KIMM.......... Rapid City, SD [AM radio station call letters]
KIMMA........ Kongres Indian Muslim Malaysia [Malaysia Indian Moslem Congress]
                [Political party] (PPW)
KIMN .... Fort Collins, CO [FM radio station call letters]
KIMO .... Anchorage, AK [Television station call letters]
KIMO .... Kings Mountain National Military Park
KIMP.......... Mount Pleasant, TX [AM radio station call letters]
KIMPrA .... Kimco Rlty 7.75% Sr'A'Dep Pfd [NYSE symbol] (TTSB)
KIMPrB .... Kimco Rlty 8.50% Sr'B'Dep Pfd [NYSE symbol] (TTSB)
KIMPrC .... Kimco Rlty 8.375% Sr'C'Dep [NYSE symbol] (TTSB)
KIMS........... Kennedy Inventory Management System [NASA] (SSD)
KIMS........... Kodak Image Management System (HGAA)
KIMSA .... Kirsten Murine Sarcoma [Virus] [Oncology] (DAVI)
KiMSV .... Kirsten Murine Sarcoma Virus
KIMT .... Mason City, IA [Television station call letters]
KI MUSV...... Kirsten Murine Sarcoma Virus
KIMX........... Laramie, WY [FM radio station call letters]
KIMY........... Watonga, OK [FM radio station call letters]
KIN .... Association of Kinsmen Clubs (EA)
KIN .... Kinark Corp. [AMEX symbol] (SPSG)
KIN .... Kinescope
kin .... Kinetic (VRA)
KIN .... Kingston [Jamaica] [Airport symbol] (OAG)
KIN .... Kingston [Jamaica] [Seismograph station code, US Geological
                Survey] (SEIS)
Kin .... Kinnim (BJA)
KIN .... Kinross-Shire [Former county in Scotland] (WGA)
kin .... Kinyarwanda [MARC language code Library of Congress] (LCCP)
KIN .... K Mart Information Network (EFIS)
KINA .... Salina, KS [AM radio station call letters]
Kinark......... Kinark Corp. [Associated Press] (SAG)
KINC .... Las Vegas, NV [Television station call letters] (RBYB)
KIND.......... Independence, KS [AM radio station call letters]
KIND.......... Indianapolis/International [Indiana] [ICAO location identifier] (ICLI)
KIND.......... Kindergarten (WDAA)
KIND.......... Kindness in Nature's Defense [Elementary school course]
KINDERGTN... Kindergarten
KIND-FM...... Independence, KS [FM radio station call letters]
KINE........... Honolulu, HI [FM radio station call letters]
KINE........... Kinescope
KINE........... Kingsville, TX [AM radio station call letters] (RBYB)
Kinetic........ Kinetic Concepts, Inc. [Associated Press] (SAG)
KINF-AM ...... Denton, TX [AM radio station call letters] (RBYB)
KING .... Kinetic Intense Neutron Generator
King .... King's Reports [5, 6 Louisiana] [A publication] (DLA)
King .... Select Cases in Chancery Tempore King, Edited by Macnaghten
                [1724-33] [England] [A publication] (DLA)
King Cas...... Cases in King's Colorado Civil Practice [A publication] (DLA)
King Cas Temp... Select Cases in Chancery Tempore King [1724-33] [England]
                [A publication] (DLA)
KINGD......... Kingdom
King Dig ...... King's Tennessee Digest [A publication] (DLA)
King-Farlow... Gold Coast Judgments and the Masai Cases, by King-Farlow
                [1915-17] [Ghana] [A publication] (DLA)
KING-FM...... Seattle, WA [FM radio station call letters]
KINGMAP..... King's Music Analysis Package [King's College] [University of
                London] [British] (NITA)
Kings .... Kingsway [Record label]
KINGSBR ..... Kingsbridge [England]
King's Con Cs... King's Conflicting Cases [Texas] [A publication] (DLA)
King's Conf Ca... King's Conflicting Cases [Texas] [A publication] (DLA)
KING-TV...... Seattle, WA [Television station call letters]
KingWd....... King World Productions [Associated Press] (SAG)
KINI .... Crookston, NE [FM radio station call letters]
KINIT .... Korea Institute of Industry & Technology Information [South Korea]
                (DDC)
KINK .... Portland, OR [FM radio station call letters]
KINK .... Wink/Winkler County [Texas] [ICAO location identifier] (ICLI)
KINL .... Eagle Pass, TX [FM radio station call letters]
KINL .... International Falls [Minnesota] [ICAO location identifier] (ICLI)
KINN .... Alamogordo, NM [AM radio station call letters]
KINN .... Kinnard Investments [NASDAQ symbol] (TTSB)
KINN .... Kinnard Investments, Inc. [NASDAQ symbol] (NQ)
Kinnard....... Kinnard Investments, Inc. [Associated Press] (SAG)
Kinney Law Dict & Glos... Kinney's Law Dictionary and Glossary [A publication]
                (DLA)
KINO .... Winslow, AZ [AM radio station call letters]
Kinross........ Kinross Gold Corp. [Associated Press] (SAG)
KINS .... Eureka, CA [AM radio station call letters]
KINS .... Indian Springs/Indian Springs Army Air Field [Nevada] [ICAO location
                identifier] (ICLI)
KINSA .... Kodak International Newspaper Snapshot Awards
KINSYM....... Kinematic Synthesis (PDAA)
KINT........... El Paso, TX [Television station call letters]

KINT............ Winston Salem/Smith-Reynolds [*North Carolina*] [*ICAO location identifier*] (ICLI)
KINTB.......... Kintbury [*England*]
KINT-FM ...... El Paso, TX [*FM radio station call letters*]
KINY .... Juneau, AK [*AM radio station call letters*]
KINZ-TV ...... Arlington, TX [*TV station call letters*] (RBYB)
KIo............. Iola Free Public Library, Iola, KS [*Library symbol Library of Congress*] (LCLS)
KIO............. Kachin Independence Organization [*Myanmar*] [*Political party*] (EY)
KIO............. Kenya Information Office (BUAC)
KIO............. Kick It Off [*Slang*] (DOMA)
KIO............. Kili [*Marshall Islands*] [*Airport symbol*] (OAG)
KIO............. Kraiaero [*Russian Federation*] [*ICAO designator*] (FAAC)
KIO............. Kuwait Investment Office (BUAC)
KIOA .... Des Moines, IA [*AM radio station call letters*]
KIOA-FM ..... Des Moines, IA [*FM radio station call letters*]
KIOC .... Orange, TX [*FM radio station call letters*]
KIOI........... San Francisco, CA [*FM radio station call letters*]
KIOK .... Richland, WA [*FM radio station call letters*]
KIOL .... Lamesa, TX [*FM radio station call letters*]
KION .... Monterey, CA [*Television station call letters*] (BROA)
KIOO .... Porterville, CA [*FM radio station call letters*]
KIOPI .... Kienzle Input/Output Peripheral Interface
KIOPI .... Kienzle Input/Output Processor Interface (NITA)
KIOQ .... Folsom, CA [*AM radio station call letters*]
KIOS .... Omaha, NE [*FM radio station call letters*]
KIoS .... Southeast Kansas Library System, Iola, KS [*Library symbol Library of Congress*] (LCLS)
KIOT........... Los Lunas [*FM radio station call letters*]
KIOU .... Shreveport, LA [*AM radio station call letters*]
KIOV .... Payette, ID [*AM radio station call letters*]
KIOW .... Forest City, IA [*FM radio station call letters*]
KIOX .... El Campo, TX [*FM radio station call letters*]
KIOZ .... Oceanside, CA [*FM radio station call letters*]
KIP............. Keyboard Input Processor [*Computer science*] (NASA)
KIP............. Key Indigenous Personnel (MCD)
KIP............. Key Intelligence Position (AFM)
KIP............. Key Intermediary Proteins (DAVI)
KIP............. Kilopound (IAA)
KIP............. Kipapa [*Hawaii*] [*Seismograph station code, US Geological Survey*] (SEIS)
KIP............. Kit, Individual Protection [*British army*] (INF)
KIP............. Knowledge Industry Publications, Inc. [*Telecommunications*]
KIP............. Knowledge Information Processing [*Computer science*]
KIP............. Thousand Pounds
KIPA........... Hilo, HI [*AM radio station call letters*]
KIP-FT .... Thousand Foot-Pounds
KIPI .... Knowledge Industry Publications, Inc. [*White Plains, NY*] [*Telecommunications Information service or system*]
KIPIC .... Kuwait International Petroleum Investment Co. (BUAC)
KIPL .... Imperial/Imperial County [*California*] [*ICAO location identifier*] (ICLI)
Kiplinger...... Kiplinger's Personal Finance Magazine [*A publication*] (BRI)
KIPO .... Honolulu, HI [*FM radio station call letters*]
KIPO .... Keyboard Input Printout [*Computer science*] (IEEE)
KIPR .... Pine Bluff, AR [*FM radio station call letters*]
KIPS........... 10³ (K) of Instructions Per Second [*Unit of computer processing speed*] (NITA)
KIPS........... Kaufman Infant and Preschool Scale [*Child development test*] [*Psychology*]
KIPS........... Key Indicators, Probes, and a Scoring Method [*Health care*] (HCT)
KIPS........... Kilo-Instructions per Second
KIPS........... Kilowatt Isotope Power System (IEEE)
KIPS........... Knowledge Information Processing Systems [*Computer science*]
KIPT.......... Twin Falls, ID [*Television station call letters*]
KIQ........... Key Intelligence Question [*CIA*]
KIQ........... Key Intelligence Requirement [*Military*] (MUSM)
KIQ........... Kira [*Papua New Guinea*] [*Airport symbol*] (OAG)
KIQI .... San Francisco, CA [*AM radio station call letters*]
KIQK .... Rapid City, SD [*FM radio station call letters*]
KIQO .... Atascadero, CA [*FM radio station call letters*]
KIQQ .... Barstow, CA [*AM radio station call letters*]
KIQS .... Willows, CA [*AM radio station call letters*]
KIQX .... Durango, CO [*FM radio station call letters*]
KIQZ.......... Rawlins, WY [*FM radio station call letters*]
KIR........... Key Intelligence Requirement (MCD)
KIR........... Killer-Cell Inhibitory Receptor [*Immunology*]
Kir............. Kirby's Connecticut Reports and Supplement [*1785-89*] [*A publication*] (DLA)
kir .... Kirghiz [*MARC language code Library of Congress*] (LCCP)
KIR........... Kiruna [*Sweden*] [*Seismograph station code, US Geological Survey*] (SEIS)
KIR........... Knight's Industrial Reports [*A publication*] (DLA)
Kirb........... Kirby's Connecticut Reports and Supplement [*1785-89*] [*A publication*] (DLA)
KIRBS .... Korean Institute for Research in the Behavioral Sciences
Kirby.......... Kirby Exploration Co., Inc. [*Associated Press*] (SAG)
Kirby.......... Kirby's Connecticut Reports and Supplement [*1785-89*] [*A publication*] (DLA)
Kirby's Conn R... Kirby's Connecticut Reports [*A publication*] (DLA)
Kirby's R ..... Kirby's Connecticut Reports [*A publication*] (DLA)
Kirby's Rep... Kirby's Connecticut Reports [*A publication*] (DLA)
KIRC .... Seminole, OK [*FM radio station call letters*]
KIRDI .... Kenya Industrial Research and Development Institute (BUAC)
KirinBr........ Kirin Brewery Co. Ltd. [*Associated Press*] (SAG)
KIRK .... Kirkcaldy [*Seaport in Scotland*]

KIRK .... Lebanon, MO [*FM radio station call letters*]
KIRK-AM..... Bethany, MO [*AM radio station call letters*] (BROA)
KIRKCUDB... Kirkcudbrightshire [*County in Scotland*]
KIRL........... St. Charles, MO [*AM radio station call letters*]
Kirlin .... Kirlin Holding Corp. [*Associated Press*] (SAG)
KIRO .... Seattle, WA [*AM radio station call letters*]
KIRO-FM..... Seattle, WA [*FM radio station call letters*]
KIRO-TV ..... Seattle, WA [*Television station call letters*]
KIRP .... Kodak Infrared Phosphor
KIRQ .... Lawton, OK [*FM radio station call letters*] (RBYB)
KIRS .... Kodak Infrared Scope
KIRS .... Sun Valley, NV [*AM radio station call letters*] (RBYB)
KirSeph....... Kirjath Sepher [*Jerusalem*] (BJA)
KirSSR........ Kirghiz Soviet Socialist Republic
KIRT........... Mission, TX [*AM radio station call letters*]
KIRTAK .... Kirghiz Telegraph Agency, Frunze (BUAC)
Kirt Sur Pr... Kirtland on Practice in Surrogates' Courts [*A publication*] (DLA)
KIRV .... Fresno, CA [*AM radio station call letters*]
KIRX .... Kirksville, MO [*AM radio station call letters*]
KIS .... Contactair Flugdienst & Co. [*Germany ICAO designator*] (FAAC)
KIS .... Keep It Simple (ADA)
KIS .... Kenny Information Systems [*Database producer*] (IID)
KIS .... Kenya Independent Squadron [*British military*] (DMA)
KIS .... Kenya Inspection Service (BUAC)
KIS .... Keyboard Input Simulation [*Computer science*]
KIS .... Kishinev [*Former USSR Seismograph station code, US Geological Survey*] (SEIS)
KIS .... Kisumu [*Kenya*] [*Airport symbol*] (OAG)
KIS .... Kitting Instruction Sheet [*NASA*] (NASA)
KIS .... Kodak Infrared Scope
KIS .... Krankenhaus Information System (DAVI)
KISA .... Honolulu, HI [*AM radio station call letters*]
KISA .... Karaoke International Sing-Along Association (EA)
KISA .... Korean International Steel Associates (BUAC)
KISA .... Voluntary International Service Assignments [*of the Society of Friends*]
Kisb Ir Land L... Kisbey on the Irish Land Law [*A publication*] (DLA)
KISC........... Knowledge Industry Systems Concept [*Publishing and education*] [*Pronounced "kiss"*]
KISC........... Knowledge Information Skills and Curriculum [*Project*] (AIE)
KISC........... Spokane, WA [*FM radio station call letters*]
KISD .... Pipestone, MN [*FM radio station call letters*]
KISE-FM ...... Seaside, CA [*FM radio station call letters*] (RBYB)
KISF .... Lexington, MO [*FM radio station call letters*]
KISI........... Malvern, AR [*FM radio station call letters*]
KISL .... Avalon, CA [*FM radio station call letters*]
KISM-FM ..... Bellingham, WA [*FM radio station call letters*] (RBYB)
KISMIF....... Keep It Simple, Make It Fun
KISN .... Salt Lake City, UT [*AM radio station call letters*]
KISN .... Williston/International [*North Dakota*] [*ICAO location identifier*] (ICLI)
KISN-FM ..... Salt Lake City, UT [*FM radio station call letters*]
KISNOPI ...... Keyboard Input Stimulation Noise Problem Input (IAA)
KISO .... Phoenix, AZ [*AM radio station call letters*]
KISP .... Blair, NE [*FM radio station call letters*]
KISP .... Islip/MacArthur Field [*New York*] [*ICAO location identifier*] (ICLI)
KISQ-FM ..... San Francisco, CA [*FM radio station call letters*] (BROA)
KISR .... Fort Smith, AR [*FM radio station call letters*]
KISR .... Kuwait Institute for Scientific Research (BUAC)
KISS .... Keep It Short and Simple (MCD)
KISS .... Keep It Short and Sweet [*Radio messages*]
KISS .... Keep It Simple, Sir (SAA)
KISS .... Keep It Simple, Stupid [*Bridge bidding term*]
KISS .... Keep It Straight and Simple [*Computer science*]
KISS .... Keyed Indexed Sequential Search
KISS .... Key Integrative Social Systems
KISS .... Knights in the Service of Satan [*Rock music group*]
KISS .... Knowledge Integrating Simulation System
KISS .... Korean Intelligence Support System (DOMA)
KISS .... San Antonio, TX [*FM radio station call letters*]
KISS .... Saturated Solution of Potassium Iodide [*Pharmacology*] (DAVI)
KIST .... Keyword Index to Serial Titles [*A publication*]
KIST .... Korean Institute for Science and Technology
KIST .... Santa Barbara, CA [*AM radio station call letters*]
KISU .... Pocatello, ID [*Television station call letters*]
KiSV........... Kirsten Sarcoma Virus
KISV-FM ..... Bakersfield, CA [*FM radio station call letters*] (BROA)
KISW .... Seattle, WA [*FM radio station call letters*]
KISX .... Whitehouse, TX [*FM radio station call letters*]
KISZ .... Cortez, CO [*FM radio station call letters*]
KISZ .... Kommunista Ifjusagi Szovetseg [*Communista Youth Organization*] [*Hungary*]
KIT.............. Kahn Intelligence Test (DMAA)
KIT.............. Kaufman Ion Thrustor
KIT.............. Keep in Touch [*Slang*] (DNAB)
KIT.............. Kent Information Technology Conference (NITA)
KIT.............. Kentucky & Indiana Terminal Railroad Co. [*AAR code*]
KIT.............. Kermit [*Texas*] [*Seismograph station code, US Geological Survey*] (SEIS)
KIT.............. Key Intelligence Topic (AAEL)
KIT.............. Key Issue Tracking [*Database*]
KIT.............. Kitchen (ADA)
KIT.............. Kitchen [*Classified advertising*]
Kit.............. Kitchin's Retourna Brevium [*4 eds.*] [*1581-92*] [*A publication*] (DLA)
KIT.............. Kithira [*Greece*] [*Airport symbol*] (OAG)
KIT.............. Kit Manufacturing Co. [*AMEX symbol*] (SPSG)

KIT	Kit Mfg [*AMEX symbol*] (TTSB)
KIT	Kittrell Junior College, Kittrell, NC [*Inactive*] [*OCLC symbol*] (OCLC)
KIT	KWIC Interactive Tagger [*University of Minnesota*] [*Text editing system*] (NITA)
KIT	Yakima, WA [*AM radio station call letters*]
KITA	Kesatuan Insaf Tanah Air [*National Consciousness Party*] [*Malaysia*] [*Political party*] (PPW)
KITA	Kick in the Afterdeck [*Bowdlerized version*]
KITA	Little Rock, AR [*AM radio station call letters*]
KITC	Kentucky-Indiana-Tennessee Conference (PSS)
kitch	Kitchen (BARN)
Kitch	Kitchin on Jurisdictions of Courts-Leet, Courts-Baron, Etc. [*A publication*] (DLA)
Kitch Courts	Kitchin on Jurisdictions of Courts-Leet, Courts-Baron, Etc. [*A publication*] (DLA)
Kitch Cts	Kitchin on Courts [*A publication*] (DLA)
Kitchen	Griqualand West Reports [*Cape Colony, South Africa*] [*A publication*] (DLA)
KITCO	Kenala Industry and Technical Consultancy Organisation [*India*] (BUAC)
Kit Ct	Kitchin on Jurisdictions of Courts-Leet, Courts-Baron, Etc. [*A publication*] (DLA)
KITE	Kerrville, TX [*FM radio station call letters*]
KITE	Kinetic Energy Weapon Integrated Test Experiment (MCD)
KITES	Kinescope Image Test and Evaluation System (MCD)
KITG	Kiting (ABBR)
KITI	Centralia-Chehalis, WA [*AM radio station call letters*]
KITI	Winlock, WA [*FM radio station call letters*] (RBYB)
Kit Jur	Kitchin on Jurisdictions of Courts-Leet, Courts-Baron, Etc. [*A publication*] (DLA)
Kit Mfg	Kit Manufacturing Co. [*Associated Press*] (SAG)
KITN	Kitten (ABBR)
KITN	Worthington, MN [*FM radio station call letters*] (RBYB)
KITO	Vinita, OK [*AM radio station call letters*]
KITO-FM	Vinita, OK [*FM radio station call letters*]
KITR	Creston, IA [*FM radio station call letters*]
Kit Rd Trans	Kitchin's Road Transport Law [*19th ed.*] [*1978*] [*A publication*] (DLA)
KITS	Meridian Diagnostics [*NASDAQ symbol*] (TTSB)
KITS	San Francisco, CA [*FM radio station call letters*]
KITT	Kinetic Tree Theory (PDAA)
KITT	Knight Industries Two Thousand [*Acronym is name of computerized car in TV series "Knight Rider"*]
KITT	Korean International Telephone & Telegraph
KITT	Shreveport, LA [*FM radio station call letters*]
KITTY	Kentucky-Illinois-Tennessee League [*Old baseball league*]
KittyHk	Kitty Hawk, Inc. [*Associated Press*] (SAG)
KITU	Beaumont, TX [*Television station call letters*]
KITV	Honolulu, HI [*Television station call letters*]
KITX	Hugo, OK [*FM radio station call letters*]
KITZ	Silverdale, WA [*AM radio station call letters*]
KIU	Kainantu [*New Guinea*] [*Airport symbol*] (AD)
KIU	Kallikrein Inactivator Unit [*Analytical biochemistry*]
KIU	Kallikrein-Inhibiting Unit [*Analytical biochemistry*] (DAVI)
KIU	Krein Inactivator Unit (DB)
KIUL	Garden City, KS [*AM radio station call letters*]
KIUN	Pecos, TX [*AM radio station call letters*]
KIUP	Durango, CO [*AM radio station call letters*]
KIV	Air Kiev [*Ukraine*] [*FAA designator*] (FAAC)
KIV	Kali Venture Corp. [*Vancouver Stock Exchange symbol*]
KIV	Keep in View
KIV	Ketoisovalerate [*Biochemistry*]
KIV	Kiev [*Former USSR Geomagnetic observatory code*]
KIV	Kishinev [*Former USSR Airport symbol*] (OAG)
KIVA	Corrales, NM [*AM radio station call letters*]
KIVA	Workgroup for Indians of North America [*Acronym is based on foreign phrase Netherlands*]
KIVI	Koninklijk Instituut van Inginieurs [*Netherlands*] (ACII)
KIVI	Nampa, ID [*Television station call letters*]
KIVV	Lead, SD [*Television station call letters*]
KIVY	Crockett, TX [*AM radio station call letters*]
KIVY-FM	Crockett, TX [*FM radio station call letters*]
KIW	Kitwe [*Zambia*] [*Airport symbol*] (OAG)
KIW	Royal New Zealand Air Force [*FAA designator*] (FAAC)
KIWA	Keuringsinstituut voor Waterleidingartikelen
KIWA	Sheldon, IA [*AM radio station call letters*]
KIWA-FM	Sheldon, IA [*FM radio station call letters*]
KIWI	Bakersfield, CA [*FM radio station call letters*]
KIWR	Council Bluffs, IA [*FM radio station call letters*]
KIWW	Harlingen, TX [*FM radio station call letters*]
KIXA	Lucerne Valley, CA [*FM radio station call letters*]
KIXB	El Dorado, AR [*FM radio station call letters*]
KIXC	Quanah, TX [*FM radio station call letters*]
KIXE	Redding, CA [*Television station call letters*]
KIXF	Baker, CA [*FM radio station call letters*]
KIXF	Kodak Industrial X-Ray Film
KIXI	Mercer Island-Seattle, WA [*AM radio station call letters*]
KIXK	Canton, SD [*FM radio station call letters*] (RBYB)
KIXL	Del Valle, TX [*AM radio station call letters*]
KIXN	Hobbs, NM [*FM radio station call letters*] (RBYB)
KIXQ	Webb City, MO [*FM radio station call letters*]
KIXR	Ponca City, OK [*FM radio station call letters*]
KIXS	Victoria, TX [*FM radio station call letters*]
KIXT-FM	Grover City, CA [*FM radio station call letters*]
KIXV	Brady, TX [*FM radio station call letters*]
KIXW	Apple Valley, CA [*AM radio station call letters*] (RBYB)
KIXW	Lenwood, CA [*FM radio station call letters*]
KIXX	Watertown, SD [*FM radio station call letters*]
KIXY	San Angelo, TX [*FM radio station call letters*]
KIXZ	Amarillo, TX [*AM radio station call letters*]
KIY	Kilwa [*Tanzania*] [*Airport symbol*] (OAG)
KIY	Kiyosumi [*Japan*] [*Seismograph station code, US Geological Survey Closed*] (SEIS)
KIYS	Jonesboro, AR [*FM radio station call letters*]
KIYU	Galena, AK [*AM radio station call letters*]
KIYX-FM	Sageville, IA [*FM radio station call letters*] (RBYB)
KIZ	Kanaf-Arkia Airlines Ltd. [*Israel*] [*ICAO designator*] (FAAC)
KIZ	Kunming Institute of Zoology (BUAC)
KIZN	Boise, ID [*FM radio station call letters*]
KIZZ	Minot, ND [*FM radio station call letters*]
KJ	Air Guyane [*ICAO designator*] (AD)
KJ	Jamaica [*IYRU nationality code*] (IYR)
kJ	Kilojoule
KJ	King James [*Version of the Bible*] (WDAA)
KJ	Kirchenmusikalisches Jahrbuch [*A publication*]
KJ	Knee Jerk [*Medicine*]
KJ	Knight of St. Joachim
KJ	Knights of Jurisprudence
KJA	Avistar (Cyprus) Ltd. [*ICAO designator*] (FAAC)
KJAA	Globe, AZ [*AM radio station call letters*]
KJAB	Mexico, MO [*FM radio station call letters*]
KJAC	Port Arthur, TX [*Television station call letters*]
KJAE	Leesville, LA [*FM radio station call letters*]
KJAK	Slaton, TX [*FM radio station call letters*]
KJAM	Madison, SD [*AM radio station call letters*]
KJAM-FM	Madison, SD [*FM radio station call letters*]
KJAN	Atlantic, IA [*AM radio station call letters*]
KJAN	Jackson/Allen C. Thompson Field [*Mississippi*] [*ICAO location identifier*] (ICLI)
KJAS-FM	Jasper, TX [*FM radio station call letters*] (RBYB)
KJAV	Alamo, TX [*FM radio station call letters*]
KJAX	Jacksonville/International [*Florida*] [*ICAO location identifier*] (ICLI)
KJAX	Stockton, CA [*AM radio station call letters*]
KJAY	Sacramento, CA [*AM radio station call letters*]
KJAZ	McFarland, CA [*AM radio station call letters*]
KJBC	Midland, TX [*AM radio station call letters*]
KJBN	Little Rock, AR [*AM radio station call letters*]
KJBR-FM	Marked Tree, AR [*FM radio station call letters*] (RBYB)
KJBX-FM	Trumann, AR [*FM radio station call letters*] (BROA)
KJBZ	Laredo, TX [*FM radio station call letters*]
KJC	Jefferson Community College, Louisville, KY [*OCLC symbol*] (OCLC)
KJC	Keystone Junior College [*Pennsylvania*]
KJCB	Lafayette, LA [*AM radio station call letters*]
KJCC	Lake Havasu City, AZ [*FM radio station call letters*]
KJCCC	Kansas Jayhawk Community College Conference (PSS)
KJCE	Rollingwood, TX [*AM radio station call letters*]
KJCF	Festus, MO [*AM radio station call letters*]
KJCK	Junction City, KS [*AM radio station call letters*]
KJCK-FM	Junction City, KS [*FM radio station call letters*]
KJCPL	Koninklijke Java-China-Paketvaart Lijnen
KJCR	Keene, TX [*FM radio station call letters*]
KJCS	Nacogdoches, TX [*FM radio station call letters*]
KJCT	Grand Junction, CO [*Television station call letters*]
KJDJ	San Luis Obispo, CA [*AM radio station call letters*]
KJDX	Susanville, CA [*FM radio station call letters*]
KJDY	John Day, OR [*AM radio station call letters*]
KJDY-FM	Canyon City, OR [*FM radio station call letters*] (RBYB)
KJEE	Montecito, CA [*FM radio station call letters*]
KJEF	Jennings, LA [*AM radio station call letters*]
KJEF-FM	Jennings, LA [*FM radio station call letters*]
KJEL	Lebanon, MO [*AM radio station call letters*]
KJEM	Seligman, MO [*FM radio station call letters*] (RBYB)
KJEO	Fresno, CA [*Television station call letters*]
KJET	Hoquiam, WA [*AM radio station call letters*] (RBYB)
KJEZ	Poplar Bluff, MO [*FM radio station call letters*]
KJF	Kajaani [*Finland*] [*Seismograph station code, US Geological Survey*] (SEIS)
KJF	Karl-Jaspers Foundation (EA)
KJF	Kutta-Joukowski Force
KJFA	Grass Valley, CA [*FM radio station call letters*]
KJFF-AM	Festus, MO [*AM radio station call letters*] (RBYB)
KJFK	New York/John F. Kennedy International [*New York*] [*ICAO location identifier*] (ICLI)
KJFM	Louisiana, MO [*FM radio station call letters*]
KJFX	Fresno, CA [*FM radio station call letters*]
KJGM	Fredonia, KS [*FM radio station call letters*] (RBYB)
KJHK	Lawrence, KS [*FM radio station call letters*]
KJHY	Emmett, ID [*FM radio station call letters*]
KJIB	South Padre Island, TX [*FM radio station call letters*]
KJIL	Copeland, KS [*FM radio station call letters*]
KJIM	Sherman, TX [*AM radio station call letters*]
KJIN	Houma, LA [*AM radio station call letters*]
KJIW	West Helena, AR [*AM radio station call letters*]
KJIW-FM	West Helena, AR [*FM radio station call letters*]
KJJ	Kuhner, J. J., Cleveland OH [*STAC*]
KJJB	Eunice, LA [*FM radio station call letters*]
KJJD	Osceola, IA [*FM radio station call letters*]
KJJJ-FM	Seligman, AZ [*FM radio station call letters*] (RBYB)
KJJK	Fergus Falls, MN [*AM radio station call letters*]
KJJK-FM	Fergus Falls, MN [*FM radio station call letters*]

KJJL-AM ...... Cheyenne, WY [*AM radio station call letters*]   (RBYB)
KJJO .... St. Louis Park, MN [*AM radio station call letters*]
KJJQ .... Volga, SD [*AM radio station call letters*]
KJJR .... Whitefish, MT [*AM radio station call letters*]
KJJY .... Ankeny, IA [*FM radio station call letters*]
KJJZ .... Kodiak, AK [*FM radio station call letters*]
KJKB-FM ..... Jacksboro, TX [*FM radio station call letters*]   (RBYB)
KJKJ .... Grand Forks, ND [*FM radio station call letters*]
KJKS .... Cameron, TX [*FM radio station call letters*]
KJKT .... Joplin, MO [*FM radio station call letters*]
KJL .... Kenneth J. Lane [*Jewelry designer*]
KJLF .... El Paso, TX [*Television station call letters*]
KJLH .... Compton, CA [*FM radio station call letters*]
KJLO .... Monroe, LA [*FM radio station call letters*]
KJLS .... Hays, KS [*FM radio station call letters*]
KJLT .... North Platte, NE [*AM radio station call letters*]
KJLT-FM ..... North Platte, NE [*FM radio station call letters*]
KJLU .... Jefferson City, MO [*FM radio station call letters*]
KJLY .... Blue Earth, MN [*FM radio station call letters*]
KJMB .... Blythe, CA [*FM radio station call letters*]
KJME .... Denver, CO [*AM radio station call letters*]
KJMH .... Burlington, IA [*Television station call letters*]
KJMK-FM ..... Webb City, MO [*FM radio station call letters*]   (BROA)
KJML-FM ..... Columbus, KS [*FM radio station call letters*]   (BROA)
KJMM .... Bixby, OK [*FM radio station call letters*]
KJMN-FM ..... Castle Rock, CO [*FM radio station call letters*]   (RBYB)
KJMO .... Jefferson City, MO [*FM radio station call letters*]
kJ mol .... Kilojoule Mole [*Chemistry*]   (MEC)
KJMS .... Memphis, TN [*FM radio station call letters*]
KJMX .... Tulia, TX [*FM radio station call letters*]
KJMY .... Seaside, CA [*FM radio station call letters*]   (RBYB)
KJMZ .... Henderson, NV [*FM radio station call letters*]   (RBYB)
KJMZ-FM ..... Lawton, OK [*FM radio station call letters*]   (RBYB)
KJN .... Kajaani [*Finland*] [*Seismograph station code, US Geological Survey Closed*]   (SEIS)
KJNA .... Jena, LA [*AM radio station call letters*]
KJNA-FM ..... Jena, LA [*FM radio station call letters*]
KJNO .... Juneau, AK [*AM radio station call letters*]
KJNP .... North Pole, AK [*AM radio station call letters*]
KJNP-FM ..... North Pole, AK [*FM radio station call letters*]
KJNP-TV ...... North Pole, AK [*Television station call letters*]
KJNT .... Hempsted [*New York*] [*ICAO location identifier*]   (ICLI)
KJO .... Kommunistische Jugend Oesterreich [*Communist Youth of Austria*]
KJOC .... Davenport, IA [*AM radio station call letters*]
KJOE .... Slayton, MN [*FM radio station call letters*]   (RBYB)
KJOI .... Dinuba, CA [*FM radio station call letters*]
KJOJ .... Conroe, TX [*AM radio station call letters*]
KJOJ-FM ..... Freeport, TX [*FM radio station call letters*]
KJOK .... Yuma, AZ [*FM radio station call letters*]
KJOL .... Grand Junction, CO [*FM radio station call letters*]
KJON-AM ..... Anadarko, OK [*AM radio station call letters*]   (BROA)
KJOP .... Lemoore, CA [*AM radio station call letters*]
KJOT .... Boise, ID [*FM radio station call letters*]
KJOV-FM ..... Woodward, OK [*FM radio station call letters*]   (RBYB)
KJOX-AM ..... Yakima, WA [*AM radio station call letters*]   (RBYB)
KJOY .... Stockton, CA [*FM radio station call letters*]
KJPN .... Waipahu, HI [*AM radio station call letters*]
KJPW .... Waynesville, MO [*AM radio station call letters*]
KJPW-FM ..... Waynesville, MO [*FM radio station call letters*]
KJQN-FM ..... Stockton, CA [*FM radio station call letters*]   (BROA)
KJQY .... San Diego, CA [*FM radio station call letters*]
KJR .... Seattle, WA [*AM radio station call letters*]
KJRB .... Spokane, WA [*AM radio station call letters*]
KJRE .... Ellendale, ND [*Television station call letters*]
KJR-FM ...... Seattle, WA [*FM radio station call letters*]
KJRG .... Newton, KS [*AM radio station call letters*]
KJRH .... Tulsa, OK [*Television station call letters*]
KJRR .... Jamestown, ND [*Television station call letters*]
KJRT .... Amarillo, TX [*FM radio station call letters*]
KJS .... Kansas Journal of Sociology
KJS .... Karl-Jaspers Stiftung [*Karl-Jaspers Foundation - KJF*]   (EA)
KJS .... Kiva Java Server [*Computer science*]
KJS .... Kodak Job Sheet
KJS .... V-Groove on One Side [*Lumber*]
KJSA .... Mineral Wells, TX [*AM radio station call letters*]
KJSK .... Columbus, NE [*AM radio station call letters*]
KJSL .... St. Louis, MO [*AM radio station call letters*]
KJSN .... Modesto, CA [*FM radio station call letters*]
KJSR .... Tulsa, OK [*FM radio station call letters*]   (RBYB)
KJStJ .... Knight of Justice, Order of St. John of Jerusalem
KJTA .... Flagstaff, AZ [*FM radio station call letters*]
KJTL .... Wichita Falls, TX [*Television station call letters*]
KJTT .... Oak Harbor, WA [*FM radio station call letters*]
KJTV .... Lubbock, TX [*Television station call letters*]
KJTX .... Jefferson, TX [*FM radio station call letters*]
KJTY .... Topeka, KS [*FM radio station call letters*]
KJU .... Kamiraba [*Papua New Guinea*] [*Airport symbol Obsolete*]   (OAG)
KJUD .... Juneau, AK [*Television station call letters*]
KJUG .... Tulare, CA [*AM radio station call letters*]
KJUG-FM ..... Tulare, CA [*FM radio station call letters*]
KJUL .... North Las Vegas, NV [*FM radio station call letters*]
KJUN .... Eatonville, WA [*FM radio station call letters*]
KJUN .... Puyallup, WA [*AM radio station call letters*]
KJUS .... Beaumont, TX [*AM radio station call letters*]   (RBYB)
KJV .... King James Version [*or Authorized Version of the Bible, 1611*]

KJVC .... Mansfield, LA [*FM radio station call letters*]
KJVD .... Kommunistischer Jugendverband Deutschlands [*Communist Youth Club of Germany*]
KJVH .... Longview, WA [*FM radio station call letters*]
KJVI .... Jackson, WY [*Television station call letters*]
KJWA .... Grand Junction, CO [*Television station call letters*]
KJWL .... Fresno, CA [*FM radio station call letters*]
KJWY-TV ..... Jackson, WY [*TV station call letters*]   (RBYB)
KJYE .... Grand Junction, CO [*FM radio station call letters*]
KJYL .... Eagle Grove, IA [*FM radio station call letters*]
KJYO .... Oklahoma City, OK [*FM radio station call letters*]
KJZY .... Sebastopol, CA [*FM radio station call letters*]   (RBYB)
KJZZ .... Phoenix, AZ [*FM radio station call letters*]
KJZZ-TV ...... Salt Lake City, UT [*Television station call letters*]
KK .... Die Welt der Bibel. Kleinkommentare zur Heiligen Schrift [*Duesseldorf*] [*A publication*]   (BJA)
KK .... Kabushiki Kaishi [*Joint stock company*] [*Japan*]
KK .... Kahal Kadosh. Holy Congregation   (BJA)
KK .... Kallikrein   (DB)
KK .... Kaluza-Klein [*Theories*] [*Physics*]
KK .... Kar-Kraft [*Automotive industry supplier*]
KK .... Kenya [*IYRU nationality code*]   (IYR)
KK .... Keren Kayemeth   (BJA)
kK .... Kilokayser
KK .... Kilokelvin
KK .... Kings
KK .... Kingston Korner   (EA)
KK .... Kirov-Kiev [*Former USSR*]
K-K .... Kleinkaliber [*Small Caliber*] [*German military*]
KK .... Knee Kick [*Neurology*]
KK .... Kokusai Koryu [*Japan Foundation*]   (EAIO)
KK .... Komisja Koordynacyjna. Zydowskie Instytucje Opiekuncze   (BJA)
KK .... Kosher Kitchen   (BJA)
KK .... Kremlin Kommandant
KK .... Kulutusosuuskuntien Keskusliitto [*Co-Operative Union*] [*Finland*]   (EY)
KK .... Kurtis-Kraft [*US racecar maker*]
KK .... Kurzgefasster Kommentar zu den Heiligen Schriften Alten und Neuen Testaments [*Munich*] [*A publication*]   (BJA)
KKA .... Benedictine College, Atchison, KS [*OCLC symbol*]   (OCLC)
KKA .... Kelsey Kindred of America   (EA)
KKA .... Kitchen Klutzs of America [*Inactive*]   (EA)
KKA .... Knights of King Arthur   (EA)
KKA .... Koyukuk [*Alaska*] [*Airport symbol*]   (OAG)
KKAA .... Aberdeen, SD [*AM radio station call letters*]
KKAG .... Porterville, CA [*Television station call letters*]
KKAJ-FM ..... Ardmore, OK [*FM radio station call letters*]
KKAL .... Arroyo Grande, CA [*AM radio station call letters*]
KKAM .... Lubbock, TX [*AM radio station call letters*]
KKAN .... Phillipsburg, KS [*AM radio station call letters*]
KKAQ .... Thief River Falls, MN [*AM radio station call letters*]
KKAR .... Omaha, NE [*AM radio station call letters*]
KKAS .... Silsbee, TX [*AM radio station call letters*]
KKAT .... Ogden, UT [*FM radio station call letters*]
KKAY .... Donaldsonville, LA [*FM radio station call letters*]
KKAY .... White Castle, LA [*AM radio station call letters*]
KKAZ .... Cheyenne, WY [*FM radio station call letters*]
KKB .... Baker University, Baldwin City, KS [*OCLC symbol*]   (OCLC)
KKB .... Kitoi [*Alaska*] [*Airport symbol*]   (OAG)
KKBA .... Kingsville, TX [*FM radio station call letters*]   (RBYB)
KKBB .... Bakersfield, CA [*FM radio station call letters*]
KKBC .... Baker City, OR [*FM radio station call letters*]
KKBC .... Korea Kuwait Banking Corp.
KKBE-FM ..... Ojai, CA [*FM radio station call letters*]   (BROA)
KKBG .... Hilo, HI [*FM radio station call letters*]
KKBH .... San Diego, CA [*FM radio station call letters*]   (RBYB)
KKBI .... Broken Bow, OK [*FM radio station call letters*]
KKBJ .... Bemidji, MN [*AM radio station call letters*]
KKBJ-FM ..... Bemidji, MN [*FM radio station call letters*]
KKBL .... Monett, MO [*FM radio station call letters*]
KKBN .... Twain Harte, CA [*FM radio station call letters*]
KKBQ .... Houston, TX [*AM radio station call letters*]
KKBQ .... Pasadena, TX [*FM radio station call letters*]
KKBR .... Billings, MT [*FM radio station call letters*]
KKBS .... Guymon, OK [*FM radio station call letters*]
KKBT .... Los Angeles, CA [*FM radio station call letters*]
KKBY-AM ..... Puyallup, WA [*AM radio station call letters*]   (RBYB)
KKBY-FM ..... Eatonville, WA [*FM radio station call letters*]   (RBYB)
KKBZ .... Clarinda, IA [*FM radio station call letters*]
KKc .... Kansas City Public Library, Kansas City, KS [*Library symbol Library of Congress*]   (LCLS)
KKC .... Kansas City Public Library, Kansas City, KS [*OCLC symbol*]   (OCLC)
KKC .... Khon Kaen [*Thailand*] [*Airport symbol*]   (OAG)
KKC .... Knox College Library, University of Toronto [*UTLAS symbol*]
KKCA .... Fulton, MO [*FM radio station call letters*]
KKcB .... Central Baptist Theological Seminary, Kansas City, KS [*Library symbol Library of Congress*]   (LCLS)
KKCB-FM ..... Duluth, MN [*FM radio station call letters*]   (RBYB)
KKcBM .... Bethany Medical Center, Kansas City, KS [*Library symbol Library of Congress*]   (LCLS)
KKcD .... Donnelly College, Kansas City, KS [*Library symbol*] [*Library of Congress*]   (LCLS)
KKCD .... Omaha, NE [*FM radio station call letters*]
KKCH-FM ..... Glenwood Springs, CO [*FM radio station call letters*]   (BROA)
KKCI .... Goodland, KS [*FM radio station call letters*]

KKcJS .... Jensen-Salsbery Laboratories, Kansas City, KS [*Library symbol Library of Congress*] (LCLS)
KKCK .... Marshall, MN [*FM radio station call letters*]
KKCL .... Lorenzo, TX [*FM radio station call letters*]
KKCM .... Shakopee, MN [*AM radio station call letters*]
KKCN .... Trumann, AR [*FM radio station call letters*] (RBYB)
KKCO-TV ...... Grand Junction, CO [*TV station call letters*] (RBYB)
KKcP .... Providence - Saint Margaret Health Center, Kansas City, KS [*Library symbol Library of Congress*] (LCLS)
KKcPS .... Kansas City Kansas Public Schools, Kansas City, KS [*Library symbol*] [*Library of Congress*] (LCLS)
KKCQ .... Fosston, MN [*AM radio station call letters*]
KKCQ-FM ...... Fosston, MN [*FM radio station call letters*]
KKCR-FM ...... Hanalei, HI [*FM radio station call letters*] (RBYB)
KKCS .... Colorado Springs, CO [*AM radio station call letters*]
KKCS-FM ...... Colorado Springs, CO [*FM radio station call letters*]
KKCT .... Bismarck, ND [*FM radio station call letters*]
KKCV .... Cedar Falls, IA [*FM radio station call letters*]
KKCW .... Beaverton, OR [*FM radio station call letters*]
KKCY .... Colusa, CA [*FM radio station call letters*]
KKD .... Kokoda [*Papua New Guinea*] [*Airport symbol*] (OAG)
KKD .... Korintji-Kaba-Dempo [*Sumatra*] [*Seismograph station code, US Geological Survey Closed*] (SEIS)
KKDA .... Dallas, TX [*FM radio station call letters*]
KKDA .... Grand Prairie, TX [*AM radio station call letters*]
KKDD .... Katalog Kandidatskikh i Doktorskikh Dissertatsii [*A bibliographic publication*]
KKDD .... North Las Vegas, NV [*AM radio station call letters*] (RBYB)
K K-D-H ...... Knight Kadosch [*Freemasonry*]
KKDJ .... Fresno, CA [*FM radio station call letters*]
KKDL .... Detroit Lakes, MN [*FM radio station call letters*]
KKDM .... Des Moines, IA [*FM radio station call letters*]
KKDQ .... Thief River Falls, MN [*FM radio station call letters*]
KKDS .... South Salt Lake, UT [*AM radio station call letters*]
KKDY .... West Plains, MO [*FM radio station call letters*]
KKDZ .... Seattle, WA [*AM radio station call letters*]
KKE .... Kerikeri [*New Zealand*] [*Airport symbol*] (OAG)
KKE .... Kleena Kleene Gold Mines [*Vancouver Stock Exchange symbol*]
KKE .... Kommunistiko Komma Ellados [*Communist Party of Greece*] [*Political party*] (PPW)
KKEE .... Long Beach, WA [*FM radio station call letters*]
KKEes .... Kommunistiko Komma Ellados - Esoterikou [*Communist Party of Greece - Interior*] [*Political party*] (PPE)
KKEex .... Kommunistiko Komma Ellados - Exoterikou [*Communist Party of Greece - Exterior*] [*Political party*] (PPE)
KKEG .... Fayetteville, AR [*FM radio station call letters*]
KKEL .... Hobbs, NM [*AM radio station call letters*]
KKEQ-FM ...... Fosston, MN [*FM radio station call letters*] (RBYB)
KKES .... Kommunistiko Komma Ellados - Esoterikou [*Communist Party of Greece - Interior*] [*Political party*] (PPW)
KKEX .... Preston, ID [*FM radio station call letters*]
KKEY .... Portland, OR [*AM radio station call letters*]
KKEZ .... Fort Dodge, IA [*FM radio station call letters*]
KKFC .... KISS [*Knights in the Service of Satan*] Konnection Fan Club (EA)
KKFG .... Bloomfield, NM [*FM radio station call letters*]
KKFI .... Kansas City, MO [*FM radio station call letters*]
KKFJ-AM ...... Alturas, CA [*AM radio station call letters*] (RBYB)
KKFM .... Colorado Springs, CO [*FM radio station call letters*]
KKFN .... Denver, CO [*AM radio station call letters*]
KKFO .... Coalinga, CA [*AM radio station call letters*]
KKFR .... Glendale, AZ [*FM radio station call letters*]
KKG .... Kappa Kappa Gamma [*Sorority*]
KKG .... Konawaruk [*Guyana*] [*Airport symbol Obsolete*] (OAG)
KKG .... Kootenay King Resources [*Vancouver Stock Exchange symbol*]
KKG .... Thousand Kilograms (EG)
KKGB .... Sulphur, LA [*FM radio station call letters*]
KKGL-FM ...... Nampa, ID [*FM radio station call letters*] (BROA)
KKGM .... Grand Junction, CO [*AM radio station call letters*] (RBYB)
KKGO .... Frazier Park, CA [*AM radio station call letters*]
KKGO-FM ...... Los Angeles, CA [*FM radio station call letters*]
KKGR-AM ...... East Helena, MT [*AM radio station call letters*] (BROA)
KKH .... Kailua-Kona [*Hawaii*] [*Seismograph station code, US Geological Survey*] (SEIS)
KKH .... Karakoram Highway [*Asia*]
KKH .... Kongiganak [*Alaska*] [*Airport symbol*] (OAG)
KKHB-FM ...... Eureka, CA [*FM radio station call letters*] (RBYB)
KKHG .... Tucson, AZ [*FM radio station call letters*]
KKHI .... San Rafael, CA [*AM radio station call letters*]
KKHI-FM ...... San Rafael, CA [*FM radio station call letters*]
KKHJ .... Los Angeles, CA [*AM radio station call letters*]
KKHK-FM ...... Denver, CO [*FM radio station call letters*] (RBYB)
KKHL .... Klung Kidney-Heart-Lung [*Machine*]
KKHQ .... Odem, TX [*FM radio station call letters*]
KKHR .... Anson, TX [*FM radio station call letters*]
KKHT .... Conroe, TX [*FM radio station call letters*] (RBYB)
KKI .... Akiachak [*Alaska*] [*Airport symbol*] (OAG)
KKI .... Karkar Island [*Papua New Guinea*] [*Seismograph station code, US Geological Survey*] (SEIS)
KKIC .... Boise, ID [*AM radio station call letters*]
KKID .... Sallisaw, OK [*AM radio station call letters*]
KKIFC .... Kris Kristofferson International Fan Club (EA)
KKIH .... King Khalid International Hospital [*Saudi Arabia*] (WDAA)
KKIK .... Temple, TX [*FM radio station call letters*] (RBYB)
KKIM .... Albuquerque, NM [*AM radio station call letters*]
KKIN .... Aitkin, MN [*AM radio station call letters*]
KKIN-FM ...... Aitkin, MN [*FM radio station call letters*] (RBYB)
KKIQ .... Livermore, CA [*FM radio station call letters*]
KKIS .... Concord, CA [*AM radio station call letters*]
KKIS .... Soldotna, AK [*FM radio station call letters*]
KKIT .... Taos, NM [*AM radio station call letters*]
KKIX .... Fayetteville, AR [*FM radio station call letters*]
KKJ .... Kita Kyushu [*Japan*] [*Airport symbol Obsolete*] (OAG)
KKJG .... San Luis Obispo, CA [*FM radio station call letters*]
KKJI .... Gallup, NM [*FM radio station call letters*]
KKJJ-FM ...... Ashland, OR [*FM radio station call letters*] (RBYB)
KKJL .... San Luis Obispo, CA [*AM radio station call letters*] (RBYB)
KKJM .... St Joseph, MN [*FM radio station call letters*]
KKJO .... St. Joseph, MO [*FM radio station call letters*]
KKJQ .... Garden City, KS [*FM radio station call letters*]
KKJR .... Hutchison, MN [*FM radio station call letters*]
KKJT .... Joshua Tree, CA [*FM radio station call letters*]
KKJW-FM ...... Stanton, TX [*FM radio station call letters*] (BROA)
KKJY-AM ...... Lake Oswego, OR [*AM radio station call letters*] (BROA)
KKJZ .... Lake Oswego, OR [*FM radio station call letters*]
KKK .... Invisible Empire Knights of the Ku Klux Klan (EA)
KKK .... Kissel Kar Klub (EA)
KKK .... Knight of the Ku Klux Klan (EA)
KKK .... Kolmer, Kline, Kahn [*Test for syphilis*] [*Medicine*] (DAVI)
KKK .... Kuehnle, Kopp, & Kausch [*Auto industry supplier*]
KKKIS .... K.K. Kodak Information Systems (EFIS)
KKKK .... Knights of the Ku Klux Klan (BUAC)
KKKK .... Odessa, TX [*FM radio station call letters*]
KKL .... Kam-Kotia Mines Ltd. [*Toronto Stock Exchange symbol*]
KKL .... Karluk Lake, AK [*Location identifier FAA*] (FAAL)
KKL .... Keren Kayemeth Leisrael (BJA)
KKL .... Kol-Kol Airlines Ltd. [*Nigeria*] [*FAA designator*] (FAAC)
KKLA .... Los Angeles, CA [*FM radio station call letters*]
KKLA .... San Bernardino, CA [*AM radio station call letters*] (RBYB)
KKLB .... Elgin, TX [*FM radio station call letters*]
KKLD-FM ...... Prescott Valley, az [*FM radio station call letters*] (RBYB)
KKLE .... Winfield, KS [*AM radio station call letters*]
KKLH-FM ...... Marshfield, MO [*FM radio station call letters*] (RBYB)
KKLI .... Widefield, CO [*FM radio station call letters*]
KKLK-FM ...... Daingerfield, TX [*FM radio station call letters*] (BROA)
KKLL .... Webb City, MO [*AM radio station call letters*]
KKLL-FM ...... Webb City, MO [*FM radio station call letters*]
KKLO .... Leavenworth, KS [*AM radio station call letters*]
KKLQ .... Oceanside, CA [*AM radio station call letters*] (RBYB)
KKLQ-FM ...... San Diego, CA [*FM radio station call letters*]
KKLR .... Poplar Bluff, MO [*FM radio station call letters*]
KKLS .... Rapid City, SD [*AM radio station call letters*]
KKLS-FM ...... Sioux Falls, SD [*FM radio station call letters*]
KKLT .... Phoenix, AZ [*FM radio station call letters*]
KKLV .... Honolulu, HI [*FM radio station call letters*]
KKLX .... Worland, WY [*FM radio station call letters*]
KKLY-FM ...... Pecos, TX [*FM radio station call letters*] (RBYB)
KKLZ .... Las Vegas, NV [*FM radio station call letters*]
KKM .... Kota Kinabalu [*Malaysia*] [*Seismograph station code, US Geological Survey*] (SEIS)
KKM .... North Central Kansas Library, Manhattan, KS [*OCLC symbol*] (OCLC)
KKMA .... Le Mars, IA [*FM radio station call letters*]
KKMC .... Gonzales, CA [*AM radio station call letters*]
KKMC .... King Khalid Military City [*Saudi Arabia*] (DOMA)
KKMG .... Pueblo, CO [*FM radio station call letters*]
KKMI .... Burlington, IA [*FM radio station call letters*]
KKMJ .... Austin, TX [*FM radio station call letters*]
KKMK .... Rapid City, SD [*FM radio station call letters*]
KKMO .... Tacoma, WA [*AM radio station call letters*]
KKMS-AM ...... Richfield, MN [*AM radio station call letters*] (BROA)
KKMT-FM ...... Columbia Falls, MT [*FM radio station call letters*] (BROA)
KKMV .... Rupert, ID [*FM radio station call letters*]
KKMX .... Tri City, OR [*FM radio station call letters*]
KKMY .... Orange, TX [*FM radio station call letters*]
KKN .... Kansas Newman College, Wichita, KS [*OCLC symbol*] (OCLC)
KKN .... Kirkenes [*Norway*] [*Airport symbol*] (OAG)
KKNB .... Crete, NE [*FM radio station call letters*]
KKND .... Tucson, AZ [*AM radio station call letters*] (RBYB)
KKND-FM ...... Port Sulphur, LA [*FM radio station call letters*] (RBYB)
KKNG .... Laramie, WY [*FM radio station call letters*]
KKNN .... Delta, CO [*FM radio station call letters*] (RBYB)
KKNO .... Gretna, LA [*AM radio station call letters*]
KKNU .... Springfield-Eugene, OR [*FM radio station call letters*]
KKNW-AM ...... Port Angeles, WA [*AM radio station call letters*] (BROA)
KKNX-AM ...... Eugene, OR [*AM radio station call letters*] (RBYB)
KKO .... Kaikohe [*New Zealand*] [*Airport symbol Obsolete*] (OAG)
KKO .... National Citizens' Committee [*Poland*] [*Political party*]
KKO .... Ottawa University, Ottawa, KS [*OCLC symbol*] (OCLC)
KKOA .... Kustom Kemps of America (EA)
KKOA .... Volcano, HI [*FM radio station call letters*]
KKOB .... Albuquerque, NM [*AM radio station call letters*]
KKOB Exp Stn ... Santa Fe, NM [*Radio expansion station*] (RBYB)
KKOB-FM ...... Albuquerque, NM [*FM radio station call letters*]
KKOH .... Reno, NV [*AM radio station call letters*] (RBYB)
KKOJ .... Jackson, MN [*AM radio station call letters*]
KKOK .... Morris, MN [*FM radio station call letters*]
KKOL .... Hampton, AR [*FM radio station call letters*]
KKOL-AM ...... Seattle, WA [*AM radio station call letters*] (BROA)
KKON .... Kealakekua, HI [*AM radio station call letters*]
KKOR .... Gallup, NM [*FM radio station call letters*]

KKOS-FM..... Palacios, TX [*FM radio station call letters*] (RBYB)
KKOT.......... Columbus, NE [*FM radio station call letters*]
KKOW......... Pittsburg, KS [*AM radio station call letters*]
KKOW-FM..... Pittsburg, KS [*FM radio station call letters*]
KKOY.......... Chanute, KS [*AM radio station call letters*]
KKOY-FM..... Chanute, KS [*FM radio station call letters*]
KKOZ.......... Ava, MO [*AM radio station call letters*]
KKOZ-FM..... Ava, MO [*FM radio station call letters*]
KKP............. Canadian Communist Party [*Political party*]
KKP............. Chinese Communist Party [*Political party*]
KKP............. Cuban Communist Party [*Political party*]
KKP............. Cypriot Communist Party [*Political party*]
KKP............. Kappa Kappa Psi [*Society*]
KKP............. Kina Kommunista Partja [*Communist Party of China*] [*Political party*]
KKP............. King's Knight's Pawn [*Chess*] (IIA)
KKP............. University of Kansas, Medical Library, Kansas City, KS [*OCLC symbol*] (OCLC)
KKPC.......... Pueblo, CO [*FM radio station call letters*]
KKPC-AM..... Pueblo, CO [*AM radio station call letters*] (RBYB)
KKPL.......... Opportunity, WA [*AM radio station call letters*]
KKPN-FM..... Houston, TX [*FM radio station call letters*] (BROA)
KKPR.......... Kearney, NE [*AM radio station call letters*]
KKPR-FM..... Kearney, NE [*FM radio station call letters*]
KKPS.......... Brownsville, TX [*FM radio station call letters*]
KKPT.......... Little Rock, AR [*FM radio station call letters*]
KKPX.......... San Jose, CA [*Television station call letters*] (BROA)
KKPZ.......... Portland, OR [*AM radio station call letters*] (RBYB)
KKQ............ Sterling College, Sterling, KS [*OCLC symbol*] (OCLC)
KKQQ.......... Volga, SD [*FM radio station call letters*]
KKQY-FM..... HillCity, KS [*FM radio station call letters*] (RBYB)
KKR............ Emporia State University, Emporia, KS [*OCLC symbol*] (OCLC)
KKR............ Kaukura [*French Polynesia*] [*Airport symbol*] (OAG)
KKR............ Kohlberg Kravis Roberts (BUAC)
KKR............ Kohlberg Kravis Roberts & Co.
KKR............ Kokanee Resources Ltd. [*Vancouver Stock Exchange symbol*]
KKR............ Kurtis-Kraft Register [*Defunct*] (EA)
KKR............ Kurukshetra [*India*] [*Seismograph station code, US Geological Survey*] (SEIS)
KKRB.......... Klamath Falls, OR [*FM radio station call letters*]
KKRC.......... Granite Falls, MN [*FM radio station call letters*]
KKRD.......... Wichita, KS [*FM radio station call letters*]
KKRF.......... Stuart, IA [*FM radio station call letters*]
KKRH.......... Salem, OR [*FM radio station call letters*] (RBYB)
KKRK.......... Douglas, AZ [*FM radio station call letters*]
KKRL.......... Carroll, IA [*FM radio station call letters*]
KKRN-FM..... Cabot, AR [*FM radio station call letters*] (RBYB)
KKRO.......... Anchorage, AK [*FM radio station call letters*]
KKRO.......... Koo Koo Roo [*NASDAQ symbol*] (TTSB)
KKRO.......... Koo Koo Roo, Inc. [*NASDAQ symbol*] (SAG)
KKRQ.......... Iowa City, IA [*FM radio station call letters*]
KKRR-FM..... Casper, WY [*FM radio station call letters*] (BROA)
KKRT.......... Wenatchee, WA [*AM radio station call letters*]
KKRV-FM..... Wenatchee, WA [*FM radio station call letters*]
KKRW.......... Houston, TX [*FM radio station call letters*]
KKRX.......... Lawton, OK [*AM radio station call letters*]
KKRX-FM..... Lawton, OK [*FM radio station call letters*]
KKRY-FM..... Miles City, MT [*FM radio station call letters*] (BROA)
KKRZ.......... Portland, OR [*FM radio station call letters*]
KKS............ Kansas State University, Farrell Library, Manhattan, KS [*OCLC symbol*] (OCLC)
KKSA.......... Keith Keating Society for the Arts [*Defunct*] (EA)
KKSA.......... San Angelo, TX [*AM radio station call letters*] (RBYB)
KKSF.......... San Francisco, CA [*FM radio station call letters*]
KKSI........... Eddyville, IA [*FM radio station call letters*]
KKSJ........... San Jose, CA [*AM radio station call letters*]
KKSL.......... Lake Oswego, OR [*AM radio station call letters*] (RBYB)
KKSM-AM..... Oceanside, CA [*AM radio station call letters*] (RBYB)
KKSN.......... Portland, OR [*FM radio station call letters*]
KKSN.......... Vancouver, WA [*AM radio station call letters*]
KKSO.......... Des Moines, IA [*AM radio station call letters*]
KKSR.......... Sartell, MN [*FM radio station call letters*]
KKSS.......... Santa Fe, NM [*FM radio station call letters*]
KKST-FM..... Oakdale, LA [*FM radio station call letters*] (BROA)
KKSU.......... Manhattan, KS [*AM radio station call letters*]
KKSY.......... Bald Knob, AR [*FM radio station call letters*]
KKT............ King's Knight [*Chess*]
KKTK-AM..... Waco, TX [*AM radio station call letters*] (RBYB)
KKTO-FM..... Tahoe City, CA [*FM radio station call letters*] (RBYB)
KKTP.......... King's Knight's Pawn [*Chess*] (IIA)
KKTR.......... Fresno, CA [*FM radio station call letters*]
KKTU.......... Cheyenne, WY [*Television station call letters*]
KKTV.......... Colorado Springs, CO [*Television station call letters*]
KKTX.......... Kilgore, TX [*AM radio station call letters*]
KKTX-FM..... Kilgore, TX [*FM radio station call letters*]
KKTY.......... Douglas, WY [*AM radio station call letters*]
KKTY-FM..... Douglas, WY [*FM radio station call letters*]
KKTZ.......... Mountain Home, AR [*FM radio station call letters*]
KKU............ Ekuk [*Alaska*] [*Airport symbol*] (OAG)
KKU............ Keanakolu [*Hawaii*] [*Seismograph station code, US Geological Survey*] (SEIS)
KKU............ University of Kansas, Lawrence, KS [*OCLC symbol*] (OCLC)
KKUA.......... Wailuku, HI [*AM radio station call letters*]
KKUB.......... Brownfield, TX [*AM radio station call letters*]
KKUH.......... King Khalid University Hospital [*Saudi Arabia*]
KKUL-FM..... Lincoln, NE [*FM radio station call letters*] (RBYB)

KKUP.......... Cupertino, CA [*FM radio station call letters*]
KKUS.......... Tyler, TX [*FM radio station call letters*]
KKUZ.......... Sallisaw, OK [*FM radio station call letters*]
KKUZ-AM..... Sallisaw, OK [*AM radio station call letters*] (RBYB)
KKV............ Central Kansas Library System, Book Processing Center, Great Bend, KS [*OCLC symbol*] (OCLC)
KKV............ Kinetic-Kill Vehicle [*Military*] (SDI)
KKVI.......... Twin Falls, ID [*Television station call letters*]
KKVO.......... Altus, OK [*FM radio station call letters*]
KKVV.......... Las Vegas, NV [*AM radio station call letters*]
KKW............ Kainokawa [*Japan*] [*Seismograph station code, US Geological Survey*] (SEIS)
KKW............ Kikwit [*Zaire*] [*Airport symbol*] (OAG)
KKW............ Washburn University of Topeka, Topeka, KS [*OCLC symbol*] (OCLC)
KKWM......... Winfield, KS [*FM radio station call letters*]
KKWQ.......... Warroad, MN [*FM radio station call letters*]
KKWS.......... Wadena, MN [*FM radio station call letters*]
KKWZ.......... Richfield, UT [*FM radio station call letters*]
KKX............ Kikaiga Shima [*Japan*] [*Airport symbol*] (OAG)
KKX............ Southwestern College, Winfield, KS [*OCLC symbol*] (OCLC)
KKXK.......... Montrose, CO [*FM radio station call letters*]
KKXL.......... Grand Forks, ND [*AM radio station call letters*]
KKXL-FM..... Grand Forks, ND [*FM radio station call letters*]
KKXO.......... Eugene, OR [*AM radio station call letters*]
KKXX.......... Delano, CA [*FM radio station call letters*]
KKXX.......... Paradise, CA [*AM radio station call letters*]
KKYA.......... Yankton, SD [*FM radio station call letters*]
KKYC.......... Muleshoe, TX [*FM radio station call letters*]
KKYD.......... Denver, CO [*AM radio station call letters*]
KKYN.......... Plainview, TX [*AM radio station call letters*]
KKYN-FM..... Plainview, TX [*FM radio station call letters*]
KKYR.......... Texarkana, AR [*AM radio station call letters*]
KKYR-FM..... Texarkana, TX [*FM radio station call letters*]
KKYS.......... Bryan, TX [*FM radio station call letters*]
KKYT.......... McCook, NE [*FM radio station call letters*]
KKYX.......... San Antonio, TX [*AM radio station call letters*]
KKYY.......... Gunnison, CO [*FM radio station call letters*]
KKYZ.......... Sierra Vista, AZ [*FM radio station call letters*]
KKZIS......... Komisja Koordynacyjna Zydowskich Instytucji Spolecznych (BJA)
KKZN-FM..... Haltom City, TX [*FM radio station call letters*] (BROA)
KKZQ.......... Lowell, AR [*FM radio station call letters*]
KKZX.......... Spokane, WA [*FM radio station call letters*]
KKZZ.......... Santa Paula, CA [*AM radio station call letters*]
KL............. Air Atlantique [*ICAO designator*] (AD)
KL............. Kaliszer Leben (BJA)
KL............. Kansalaisvallen Liitto [*League of Civil Power*] [*Finland Political party*] (PPW)
K-L............ Kansas State Library, Law Department, Topeka, KS [*Library symbol Library of Congress*] (LCLS)
KL............. Karl Lagerfeld [*Fashion designer*]
K-L............ Karl-Lorimar Home Video, Inc.
KL............. Keel (ROG)
KL............. Keller's Language [*1977*] [*Computer science*] (CSR)
KL............. Kelvin Law [*Physics*]
KL............. Kerley Lines [*Radiology*]
KL............. Key Length [*Computer science*] (BUR)
KL............. Key Lever (IAA)
KL............. Key Locker
KL............. Kidney Lobe
kL............. Kilolambert
kL............. Kiloliter
KL............. Klaeger [*Plaintiff*] [*German*] (ILCA)
kl............. Klang [*Musical Overtone*] [*German*]
KI............. Klarinette [*Clarinet*] [*German*] [*Music*] (WDAA)
KL............. Klebs-Loeffler [*Bacteriology*]
KL............. Kleine-Levin [*Syndrome*] [*Medicine*] (DAVI)
KL............. Kleinmann-Low [*Astronomy*]
KL............. Klemm Flugzeugbau GmbH & Apparatebau Nabern [*Germany ICAO aircraft manufacturer identifier*] (ICAO)
KL............. KLM [*Koninklijke Luchtvaart Maatschappij*] Royal Dutch Airlines [*ICAO designator*] (OAG)
KL............. Knight of Leopold [*Austria, Belgium*] (ROG)
KL............. Knight of [*the Order of*] Leopold of Austria
KL............. Knights of Lithuania
KL............. Konzentrationslager [*Concentration Camp*] [*German*] (BJA)
KL............. Kuala Lumpur [*Malaysia*]
KL............. Kullback-Leibler [*Mathematics*]
KLA........... Air Lietuva [*Lithuania*] [*ICAO designator*] (FAAC)
KLA........... Ka-Ahari Resources [*Vancouver Stock Exchange symbol*]
KLA........... Kampala [*Uganda*] [*Airport symbol*] (AD)
KLA........... Karachi Library Association [*Pakistan*] (BUAC)
KLA........... Kenya Library Association (BUAC)
KLA........... Key Learning Area [*Education*]
KLA........... KLA Instruments Corp. [*Associated Press*] (SAG)
KLA........... Klystron Amplifier
KLA........... Knight of [*the Order of*] Leopold of Austria
KLA........... Korean Library Association (BUAC)
KLA........... Kosovo Liberation Army [*Yugoslavia*]
KLAA.......... Tioga, LA [*FM radio station call letters*]
KLAC.......... KLA Instruments [*NASDAQ symbol*] (TTSB)
KLAC.......... KLA Instruments Corp. [*NASDAQ symbol*] (NQ)
KLAC.......... Los Angeles, CA [*AM radio station call letters*]
KLAD.......... Klamath Falls, OR [*AM radio station call letters*]
KLAD-FM..... Klamath Falls, OR [*FM radio station call letters*]
KLAK.......... Durant, OK [*FM radio station call letters*]

KLAL-FM...... Wrightsville, AR [*FM radio station call letters*] (BROA)
KLAM........... Cordova, AK [*AM radio station call letters*]
Klamath....... Klamath First Bancorp, Inc. [*Associated Press*] (SAG)
KLAN........... Glasgow, MT [*FM radio station call letters*]
KLAN .... Lansing/Capital Region [*Michigan*] [*ICAO location identifier*] (ICLI)
KLANSS ...... Keep That Local Area Network Simple, Stupid [*Telecommunications*]
KLAQ .... El Paso, TX [*FM radio station call letters*]
KLAR .... Laredo, TX [*AM radio station call letters*]
KLAS........... Las Vegas/McCarran International [*Nevada*] [*ICAO location identifier*] (ICLI)
KLAS........... Las Vegas, NV [*Television station call letters*]
KLaSH .... Larned State Hospital, Larned, KS [*Library symbol Library of Congress*] (LCLS)
Klass Phil Stud... Klassische Philologische Studien [*A publication*] (OCD)
KLAT........... Houston, TX [*AM radio station call letters*]
KLAV.......... Las Vegas, NV [*AM radio station call letters*]
KLaw .... Lawrence Free Public Library, Lawrence, KS [*Library symbol Library of Congress*] (LCLS)
KLAW......... Lawton, OK [*FM radio station call letters*]
K Law Rep... Kentucky Law Reporter [*A publication*] (DLA)
KLAX.......... Long Beach, CA [*FM radio station call letters*]
KLAX.......... Los Angeles/International [*California*] [*ICAO location identifier*] (ICLI)
KLAX-TV ..... Alexandria, LA [*Television station call letters*]
KLAY .... Lakewood, WA [*AM radio station call letters*]
KLAZ.......... Hot Springs, AR [*FM radio station call letters*]
KLB .... Kalabo [*Zambia*] [*Airport symbol*] (OAG)
KLB .... Kilopound (MCD)
KLB .... Knight of [*the Order of*] Leopold [*Belgium*]
KLB .... Korea Longterm Credit Bank (BUAC)
KLBA.......... Albia, IA [*AM radio station call letters*]
KL Bac .... Klebs-Loeffler Bacillus (AAMN)
KLBA-FM .... Albia, IA [*FM radio station call letters*]
KLBB.......... Lubbock/Regional [*Texas*] [*ICAO location identifier*] (ICLI)
KLBB.......... St. Paul, MN [*AM radio station call letters*]
KLBC.......... Durant, OK [*FM radio station call letters*]
KLBF.......... Kilopound-Force (WDAA)
KLBG.......... Alexandria, LA [*AM radio station call letters*] (RBYB)
KLBJ .... Austin, TX [*AM radio station call letters*]
KLBJ-FM ..... Austin, TX [*FM radio station call letters*]
KLBK.......... Lubbock, TX [*Television station call letters*]
KLBM.......... La Grande, OR [*AM radio station call letters*]
KLBN .... Auberry, CA [*FM radio station call letters*] (RBYB)
KLBO.......... Monahans, TX [*AM radio station call letters*]
KLBQ.......... El Dorado, AR [*FM radio station call letters*]
KLBS.......... Los Banos, CA [*AM radio station call letters*]
KLBY.......... Colby, KS [*Television station call letters*]
KLC .... Kaolack [*Senegal*] [*Airport symbol*] (AD)
KLC .... Kern County Library System, Bakersfield, CA [*OCLC symbol*] (OCLC)
KLC .... Kinesin Light Chain [*Cytology*]
KLC .... Kirkland Lake [*Ontario*] [*Seismograph station code, US Geological Survey Closed*] (SEIS)
KLC .... KLM Cityhopper BV [*Netherlands ICAO designator*] (FAAC)
KLCB.......... Libby, MT [*AM radio station call letters*]
KLCC.......... Eugene, OR [*FM radio station call letters*]
KLCC.......... Kuala Lumpur City Center [*Malaysia*] (ECON)
KLCCL......... Kilocycle (ABBR)
KLCD .... Decorah, IA [*FM radio station call letters*]
KLCE .... Blackfoot, ID [*FM radio station call letters*]
KLCE .... Kuala Lumpur Commodity Exchange [*Malaia*] (NUMA)
KLCH .... Lake Charles/Lake Charles [*Louisiana*] [*ICAO location identifier*] (ICLI)
KLCI............ Nampa, ID [*FM radio station call letters*]
KLCK.......... Goldendale, WA [*AM radio station call letters*]
KLCK.......... Rickenbacker Air Force Base [*Ohio*] [*ICAO location identifier*] (ICLI)
KLCL.......... Lake Charles, LA [*AM radio station call letters*]
KLCM.......... Lewistown, MT [*FM radio station call letters*]
KLCN.......... Blytheville, AR [*AM radio station call letters*]
KLCO .... Newport, OR [*FM radio station call letters*]
KLCQ.......... Healdsburg, CA [*FM radio station call letters*]
KLCR-FM ..... Lakeview, OR [*FM radio station call letters*] (BROA)
KLCS.......... Los Angeles, CA [*Television station call letters*]
KLCU-FM .... Ardmore, OK [*FM radio station call letters*] (BROA)
KLCV-FM .... Lincoln, NE [*FM radio station call letters*] (RBYB)
KLCX.......... Indio, CA [*FM radio station call letters*] (RBYB)
KLCY.......... East Missoula, MT [*AM radio station call letters*]
KLCY-FM .... Vernal, UT [*FM radio station call letters*]
KLCZ.......... Corcoran, CA [*FM radio station call letters*]
KLD........... Kelly, Douglas & Co. Ltd. [*Toronto Stock Exchange symbol*]
KLD........... King's Light Dragoons [*British military*] (DMA)
KLD........... Kongres Liberalno-Demokratyczny [*Liberal Democratic Congress*] [*Poland Political party*] (EY)
KLDC .... Commerce City, CO [*AM radio station call letters*] (RBYB)
KLDC-AM .... Brighton, CO [*AM radio station call letters*] (RBYB)
KLDE.......... Houston, TX [*FM radio station call letters*]
KLDG .... Liberal, KS [*FM radio station call letters*]
KLDI........... Laramie, WY [*AM radio station call letters*]
KLDJ-FM..... Duluth, MN [*FM radio station call letters*] (RBYB)
KLDN.......... Lufkin, TX [*FM radio station call letters*]
KLDO.......... Laredo, TX [*Television station call letters*]
KLDR .... Harbeck-Fruitdale, OR [*FM radio station call letters*]
KLDR .... Killdeer (ABBR)
KLDS-AM .... Falfurrias, TX [*AM radio station call letters*] (BROA)
KLDSOP...... Kaleidoscope (ABBR)
KLDSOPC.... Kaleidoscopic (ABBR)
KLDT.......... Lake Dallas, TX [*Television station call letters*]

KLDY-AM .... Lacey, WA [*AM radio station call letters*] (BROA)
KLDZ.......... Lincoln, NE [*FM radio station call letters*]
KLE .... Kaele [*Cameroon*] [*Airport symbol*] (AD)
KLE .... Kala Explorations [*Vancouver Stock Exchange symbol*]
KLe .... Leavenworth Public Library, Leavenworth, KS [*Library symbol Library of Congress*] (LCLS)
KLEA.......... Lovington, NM [*AM radio station call letters*]
KLEA-FM ..... Lovington, NM [*FM radio station call letters*]
KLEB.......... Golden Meadow, LA [*AM radio station call letters*]
Kleb........... Klebsiella [*Genus of microorganisms*] (MAH)
KleBl.......... Klerusblatt [*Munich*] [*A publication*] (BJA)
Klebs......... Klebsiella [*A genus of bacteria*]
KLEE.......... Ottumwa, IA [*AM radio station call letters*]
KleerVu....... Kleer-Vu Industries, Inc. [*Associated Press*] (SAG)
KLEF.......... Anchorage, AK [*FM radio station call letters*]
KLEH.......... Anamosa, IA [*AM radio station call letters*]
KLEI........... Kailua-Kona, HI [*AM radio station call letters*]
Kleinrt........ Kleinert's, Inc. [*Associated Press*] (SAG)
KLEL.......... San Jose, CA [*FM radio station call letters*]
KLEM.......... Le Mars, IA [*AM radio station call letters*]
KLEN.......... Cheyenne, WY [*FM radio station call letters*]
KLEO.......... Kahaluu, HI [*FM radio station call letters*]
KLEP.......... Newark, AR [*Television station call letters*]
KLEPTO...... Kleptomania (ABBR)
KLER.......... Orofino, ID [*AM radio station call letters*]
KLER-FM ..... Orofino, ID [*FM radio station call letters*]
KLeS.......... Saint Mary College, Leavenworth, KS [*Library symbol Library of Congress*] (LCLS)
KLES-FM ..... Mabton, WA [*FM radio station call letters*] (BROA)
KLeVA........ United States Veterans Administration Center, Leavenworth, KS [*Library symbol Library of Congress*] (LCLS)
KLEW.......... Lewiston, ID [*Television station call letters*]
KLEX.......... Lexington, MO [*AM radio station call letters*]
KLEY.......... Wellington, KS [*AM radio station call letters*]
KLFA.......... King City, CA [*FM radio station call letters*]
KLFB.......... Lubbock, TX [*AM radio station call letters*]
KLFC.......... Branson, MO [*FM radio station call letters*]
KLFD.......... Litchfield, MN [*AM radio station call letters*]
KLFE.......... Seattle, WA [*AM radio station call letters*] (RBYB)
KLFF.......... San Luis Obispo, CA [*FM radio station call letters*] (RBYB)
KLFI............ Hampton/Langley Air Force Base [*Virginia*] [*ICAO location identifier*] (ICLI)
KLFJ.......... Springfield, MO [*AM radio station call letters*]
KLFK.......... Lufkin/Angelina County [*Texas*] [*ICAO location identifier*] (ICLI)
KLFM.......... Great Falls, MT [*FM radio station call letters*]
KLFT.......... Lafayette/Regional [*Louisiana*] [*ICAO location identifier*] (ICLI)
KLFX.......... Nolanville, TX [*FM radio station call letters*] (RBYB)
KLFY.......... Lafayette, LA [*Television station call letters*]
KLG........... Kalgoorlie [*Australia Seismograph station code, US Geological Survey*] (SEIS)
KLG........... Kalskag [*Alaska*] [*Airport symbol*] (OAG)
KLG........... Keto-Laevo-Gulonic Acid [*Organic chemistry*]
KLG........... Keto-L-glutonic (Acid) [*Biochemistry*]
KLG........... Killing (ABBR)
KLG........... Knudsen Leaf Gauge [*Physics*]
KLG........... University of Louisville, Louisville, KY [*OCLC symbol*] (OCLC)
KLGA.......... Algona, IA [*AM radio station call letters*]
KLGA.......... New York/La Guardia [*New York*] [*ICAO location identifier*] (ICLI)
KLGA-FM .... Algona, IA [*FM radio station call letters*]
KLGB.......... Long Beach [*California*] [*ICAO location identifier*] (ICLI)
KLGM.......... Kilogram (ABBR)
KLGN.......... Logan, UT [*AM radio station call letters*]
KLGR.......... Knight's Local Government Reports [*A publication*] (DLA)
KLGR.......... Redwood Falls, MN [*AM radio station call letters*]
KLGR-FM ..... Redwood Falls, MN [*FM radio station call letters*]
KLGT.......... Buffalo, WY [*FM radio station call letters*]
KLGT-TV ..... Minneapolis, MN [*Television station call letters*]
KLH........... Kapapala Ranch [*Hawaii*] [*Seismograph station code, US Geological Survey*] (SEIS)
KLH........... Keyhole Limpet Hemocyanin [*Immunology*]
KLH........... Kingdom of Lesotho Handicrafts (BUAC)
KLH........... KLM Helicopters NV [*Netherlands ICAO designator*] (FAAC)
KLH........... Kloss, Low, and Hofmann [*Initialism is name of electronics company and brand name of its products*]
KLH........... Knight of the Legion of Honor [*France*]
KLH........... Knight of the Legion of Honour (DD)
KLH........... Long Akha [*Malaysia*] [*Airport symbol*] (AD)
KLHB-FM ..... Odem, TX [*FM radio station call letters*] (RBYB)
KLHI........... Lahaina, HI [*FM radio station call letters*]
KLHS.......... Lewiston, ID [*FM radio station call letters*]
KLHT.......... Honolulu, HI [*AM radio station call letters*]
KLI........... Kaliber Resources Ltd. [*Vancouver Stock Exchange symbol*]
KLI........... King's Light Infantry [*Military unit*] [*British*]
KLI........... Klingon Language Institute
KLI........... Kolyma-Avia [*Former USSR*] [*FAA designator*] (FAAC)
Kliatt......... Kliatt Young Adult Paperback Book Guide [*A publication*] (BRI)
KLIAU .... Korea Land Improvement Association Union (BUAC)
KLIC.......... Keyletter-in-Context [*Computer science*]
KLIC.......... Kulicke & Soffa Ind [*NASDAQ symbol*] (TTSB)
KLIC.......... Kulicke & Soffa Industries, Inc. [*NASDAQ symbol*] (NQ)
KLIC.......... Monroe, LA [*AM radio station call letters*]
KLID.......... Poplar Bluff, MO [*AM radio station call letters*]
KLIF.......... Dallas, TX [*AM radio station call letters*]
KLIH-AM ..... Little Rock, AR [*AM radio station call letters*] (BROA)
KLIK.......... Jefferson City, MO [*AM radio station call letters*]

KLIL............ Moreauville, LA [*FM radio station call letters*]
KLIM............ Limon, CO [*AM radio station call letters*] (RBYB)
KLIN............ Lincoln, NE [*AM radio station call letters*]
KLINA.......... K, Li, and Na [*For the chemical elements potassium, lithium, and sodium*] [*Beckman flame system Trademark*]
KLindB........ Bethany College, Lindsborg, KS [*Library symbol Library of Congress*] (LCLS)
KLIP............ Monroe, LA [*FM radio station call letters*]
KLIR............ Columbus, NE [*FM radio station call letters*]
KLIS............ Palestine, TX [*FM radio station call letters*]
KLIT............ Little Rock/Adams Field [*Arkansas*] [*ICAO location identifier*] (ICLI)
KLIT-FM...... Avalon, CA [*FM radio station call letters*] (BROA)
KLIV............ San Jose, CA [*AM radio station call letters*]
KLIX............ Twin Falls, ID [*AM radio station call letters*]
KLIX-FM ...... Twin Falls, ID [*FM radio station call letters*]
KLIZ............ Brainerd, MN [*AM radio station call letters*]
KLIZ............ Korea Limited Identification Zone
KLIZ............ Limestone/Loring Air Force Base [*Maine*] [*ICAO location identifier*] (ICLI)
KLIZ-FM...... Brainerd, MN [*FM radio station call letters*]
KLJ .... Jewish Hospital, Louisville, KY [*OCLC symbol*] (OCLC)
KLJ .... Knight of [*the Order of*] St. Lazarus of Jerusalem [*British*]
KLJ .... Knight of the Military and Hospitalier Order of St. Lazarus (DD)
KLJB............ Davenport, IA [*Television station call letters*]
KLJC............ Kansas City, MO [*FM radio station call letters*]
KLJY .... Killjoy (ABBR)
KLJZ .... Port Sulphur, LA [*FM radio station call letters*] (RBYB)
KLK .... Kealakekua [*Hawaii*] [*Seismograph station code, US Geological Survey Closed*] (SEIS)
KLK .... Killick Gold Co. [*Vancouver Stock Exchange symbol*]
KLKC........... Parsons, KS [*AM radio station call letters*]
KLKC-FM ..... Parsons, KS [*FM radio station call letters*]
KLKE........... Albion, NE [*Television station call letters*] (RBYB)
KLKI............ Anacortes, WA [*AM radio station call letters*]
KLKK........... Clear Lake, IA [*FM radio station call letters*]
KLKL........... Benton, LA [*FM radio station call letters*]
KLKN-TV...... Lincoln, NE [*TV station call letters*] (RBYB)
KLKO .... Elko, NV [*AM radio station call letters*]
KLKS........... Breezy Point, MN [*FM radio station call letters*]
KLKX........... Rosamond, CA [*FM radio station call letters*]
KLKY .... Milton-Freewater, OR [*AM radio station call letters*]
KLKY-FM ..... Milton-Freewater, OR [*FM radio station call letters*] (RBYB)
KLL .... Kalltalsperre [*Federal Republic of Germany*] [*Seismograph station code, US Geological Survey*] (SEIS)
KLL .... Levelock [*Alaska*] [*Airport symbol*] (OAG)
KLLA........... Leesville, LA [*AM radio station call letters*]
KLLB........... West Jordan, UT [*AM radio station call letters*]
KLLC-FM..... San Francisco, CA [*FM radio station call letters*] (RBYB)
KLLF........... Wichita Falls, TX [*AM radio station call letters*]
KLLI............ Hooks, TX [*FM radio station call letters*]
KLLK........... Fort Bragg, CA [*FM radio station call letters*]
KLLK........... Willits, CA [*AM radio station call letters*]
KLLL............ Lubbock, TX [*AM radio station call letters*]
KLLL-FM...... Lubbock, TX [*FM radio station call letters*]
KLLM........... Forks, WA [*FM radio station call letters*]
KLLM........... KLLM Transport Services, Inc. [*NASDAQ symbol*] (NQ)
KLLM........... KLLM Transport Sv [*NASDAQ symbol*] (TTSB)
KLLN........... Newark, AR [*AM radio station call letters*]
KLLR........... Amarillo, TX [*FM radio station call letters*] (RBYB)
KLLS........... Augusta, KS [*AM radio station call letters*]
KLLT........... Vinton, IA [*FM radio station call letters*]
KLLU-AM..... Reedsport, OR [*AM radio station call letters*] (BROA)
KLLV........... Breen, CO [*AM radio station call letters*]
KLLY........... Oildale, CA [*FM radio station call letters*]
KLLZ........... Walker, MN [*AM radio station call letters*]
KLLZ-FM...... Walker, MN [*FM radio station call letters*]
KL/M........... Kiloliters per Minute
KLM............ Kilometer
KLM............ KLM Royal Dutch Air [*NYSE symbol*] (TTSB)
KLM............ KLM Royal Dutch Airlines [*Netherlands ICAO designator*] (FAAC)
KLM............ KLM [*Koninklijke Luchtvaart Maatschappij*] Royal Dutch Airlines [*NYSE symbol*] (SPSG)
KLM............ Koninklijke Luchtvaart Maatschappij [*Royal Dutch Airlines*]
KLM............ Kuala Lumpur [*Malaysia*] [*Seismograph station code, US Geological Survey*] (SEIS)
KLM............ University of Louisville, School of Music Library, Louisville, KY [*OCLC symbol*] (OCLC)
KLMA.......... Hobbs, NM [*FM radio station call letters*]
KLMB-FM..... Bastrop, LA [*FM radio station call letters*] (RBYB)
KLMC.......... Knights of Life Motorcycle Club (EA)
KLME.......... Kuala Lumpur Metal Exchange (BUAC)
KLMJ........... Hampton, IA [*FM radio station call letters*]
KLMN........... Amarillo, TX [*FM radio station call letters*]
KLMO........... Longmont, CO [*AM radio station call letters*]
KLMP........... Rapid City, SD [*FM radio station call letters*]
KLMR........... Lamar, CO [*AM radio station call letters*]
KLMS-AM..... Lincoln, NE [*AM radio station call letters*] (BROA)
KLMTR......... Kilometer (ABBR)
KLMX-AM..... Clayton, NM [*AM radio station call letters*] (RBYB)
KLMY........... Seaside, CA [*FM radio station call letters*]
KLN .... Kelan Resources [*Vancouver Stock Exchange symbol*]
KLN .... Larsen Bay [*Alaska*] [*Airport symbol*] (OAG)
KLN .... Norton-Children's Hospital Medical Library, Louisville, KY [*OCLC symbol*] (OCLC)

KLNA .... West Palm Beach/Palm Beach County Park [*Florida*] [*ICAO location identifier*] (ICLI)
KLNA-FM .... Dunnigan, CA [*FM radio station call letters*] (RBYB)
KLND .... Little Eagle, SD [*FM radio station call letters*] (RBYB)
KLNE .... Lexington, NE [*FM radio station call letters*]
KLNE-TV ..... Lexington, NE [*Television station call letters*]
KLNG .... Council Bluffs, IA [*AM radio station call letters*]
KLNI .... Decorah, IA [*FM radio station call letters*]
KLNITE........ Knitting, Lace, and Net Industry Training Board (BUAC)
KLNK .... Lincoln/Municipal [*Nebraska*] [*ICAO location identifier*] (ICLI)
KLNR .... Panaca, NV [*FM radio station call letters*]
KLNT .... Clinton, IA [*AM radio station call letters*]
KLO .... Kalibo [*Philippines*] [*Airport symbol*] (OAG)
KLO .... Klystron Oscillator
KLO .... Ogden, UT [*AM radio station call letters*]
KLOA .... Ridgecrest, CA [*AM radio station call letters*]
KLOA-FM ..... Ridgecrest, CA [*FM radio station call letters*]
KLOB .... Thousand Palms, CA [*FM radio station call letters*]
KLOC .... Ceres, CA [*AM radio station call letters*]
KLOC .... Kilo Lines of Code [*Computer science*] (IGQR)
KLOC .... Kush Locke [*NASDAQ symbol*] (SAG)
KLOC .... Kushner-Locke [*NASDAQ symbol*] (TTSB)
KLOC .... [*The*] Kushner-Locke Co. [*NASDAQ symbol*] (NQ)
KLOCW........ Kushner-Locke Wrrt [*NASDAQ symbol*] (TTSB)
KLOD .... Shafter, CA [*FM radio station call letters*]
KLOE .... Goodland, KS [*AM radio station call letters*]
KLOF .... Kloof Gold Mining Co. Ltd. [*NASDAQ symbol*] (NQ)
KLOFFE........ Kuala Lumpur Options and Financial Futures Exchange [*Maylaysia*] (NUMA)
KLOFY .... Kloof Gold Mining ADR [*NASDAQ symbol*] (TTSB)
KLOG .... Kelso, WA [*AM radio station call letters*]
KLOH .... Pipestone, MN [*AM radio station call letters*]
KLOK .... San Jose, CA [*AM radio station call letters*]
KLOK-FM ..... Greenfield, CA [*FM radio station call letters*] (RBYB)
KLOL .... Houston, TX [*FM radio station call letters*]
KLOM .... Lompoc, CA [*AM radio station call letters*]
KLON .... Long Beach, CA [*FM radio station call letters*]
KLOO .... Corvallis, OR [*AM radio station call letters*]
KLoofG .... Kloof Gold Mining Co. Ltd. [*Associated Press*] (SAG)
KLOO-FM ..... Corvallis, OR [*FM radio station call letters*] (BROA)
KLOQ .... Merced, CA [*AM radio station call letters*]
KLOQ-FM ..... Winton, CA [*FM radio station call letters*] (RBYB)
KLOR .... Ponca City, OK [*FM radio station call letters*]
KLOS .... Los Angeles, CA [*FM radio station call letters*]
KLOU .... Louisville/Bowman [*Kentucky*] [*ICAO location identifier*] (ICLI)
KLOU .... St. Louis, MO [*FM radio station call letters*]
KLOV .... Loveland, CO [*AM radio station call letters*]
KLOW .... Caruthersville, MO [*FM radio station call letters*]
KLOZ .... Eldon, MO [*FM radio station call letters*]
KLP .... Korean Labor Party [*Political party*]
KLP .... Louisville Free Public Library, Louisville, KY [*OCLC symbol*] (OCLC)
KLP .... Redding Aero Enterprises, Inc. [*FAA designator*] (FAAC)
KLPA .... Alexandria, LA [*Television station call letters*]
KLPA .... Khan-Lewis Phonological Analysis [*Speech evaluation test*]
KI Pauly...... Der Kleine Pauly [*A publication*] (OCD)
KLPB .... Lafayette, LA [*Television station call letters*]
KLPI .... Ruston, LA [*FM radio station call letters*]
KLPL .... Lake Providence, LA [*AM radio station call letters*]
KLPL-FM...... Lake Providence, LA [*FM radio station call letters*]
KLPQ .... Sherweood, AR [*FM radio station call letters*]
KLPR-FM ..... Keamey, NE [*FM radio station call letters*] . (RBYB)
KLPTMN ...... Kleptomania (ABBR)
KLPTMNC ... Kleptomaniac (ABBR)
KLPW .... Union, MO [*AM radio station call letters*]
KLPW-FM ..... Union, MO [*FM radio station call letters*]
KLPX .... Tucson, AZ [*FM radio station call letters*]
KLPZ .... Parker, AZ [*AM radio station call letters*]
KLQB .... Oracle, AZ [*FM radio station call letters*]
KLQL .... Luverne, MN [*FM radio station call letters*]
KLQP .... Madison, MN [*FM radio station call letters*]
KLQZ .... Paragould, AR [*FM radio station call letters*]
KLR .... Columbus Air Transport, Inc. [*ICAO designator*] (FAAC)
KLR .... Kalmar [*Sweden*] [*Airport symbol*] (OAG)
KLR .... Kathiawar Law Reports [*India*] [*A publication*] (DLA)
KLR .... Kentucky Law Reporter [*A publication*] (DLA)
KLRA .... England, AR [*AM radio station call letters*]
KLRA-FM ..... England, AR [*FM radio station call letters*]
KLRB .... Aurora, NE [*FM radio station call letters*]
KLRC .... Siloam Springs, AR [*FM radio station call letters*]
KLRD .... Laredo/International [*Texas*] [*ICAO location identifier*] (ICLI)
KLRD .... Yucaipa, CA [*FM radio station call letters*]
KLRE .... Little Rock, AR [*FM radio station call letters*]
KLRF .... Brownsville, OR [*FM radio station call letters*]
KLRF .... Jacksonville/Little Rock Air Force Base [*Arkansas*] [*ICAO location identifier*] (ICLI)
KLRG .... North Little Rock, AR [*AM radio station call letters*]
KLRK .... Vandalia, MO [*FM radio station call letters*]
KLRN .... San Antonio, TX [*Television station call letters*]
KLRO-FM ..... Nile, WA [*FM radio station call letters*] (BROA)
KLRQ .... Clinton, MO [*FM radio station call letters*]
KLRR .... Redmond, OR [*FM radio station call letters*]
KLRS .... Chico, CA [*FM radio station call letters*]
KLRT .... Kleinert's, Inc. [*NASDAQ symbol*] (NQ)
KLRU .... Little Rock, AR [*FM radio station call letters*]
KLRU .... Austin, TX [*Television station call letters*]

KLRX-FM	Madrid, IA [*FM radio station call letters*] (BROA)
KLRZ	Larose, LA [*FM radio station call letters*]
KLS	Faculty of Library and Information Science, University of Toronto [*UTLAS symbol*]
KLS	Karlskrona [*Sweden*] [*Seismograph station code, US Geological Survey Closed*] (SEIS)
KLS	Kaskaskia Library System [*Library network*]
KLS	Kelso Resources [*Vancouver Stock Exchange symbol*]
KLS	Kelso, WA [*Location identifier FAA*] (FAAL)
KLS	Key Lock Switch
KLS	Kidney, Liver, Spleen [*Medicine*]
KLS	Knight of the Lion and Sun [*Persia*] (ROG)
KLS	Knotted List Structure (BUR)
KLS	Kreuzbein Lipomatous Syndrome [*Medicine*] (DMAA)
KLS	Kreuzbein's Lipomatous Syndrome [*Medicine*] (DB)
KLS	Krypton LASER System
KLSA	Alexandria, LA [*FM radio station call letters*]
KLSB	Nacogdoches, TX [*Television station call letters*]
KLSC	Korean Logistic Service Corps (CINC)
KLSC-FM	Fayette, MO [*FM radio station call letters*] (RBYB)
Kl Schr	Kleine Schriften [*of various authors*] [*Classical studies*] (OCD)
KLSE	Kuala Lumpur Stock Exchange
KLSE	Rochester, MN [*FM radio station call letters*]
KLSIFC	Kathy Lynn Sacra International Fan Club (EA)
KLSK	Santa Fe, NM [*FM radio station call letters*]
KLSN	New London, MO [*FM radio station call letters*] (RBYB)
KLSP	Angola, LA [*FM radio station call letters*]
KLSQ	Laughlin, NV [*AM radio station call letters*] (RBYB)
KLSQ EXP STN	East Las Vegas, NV [*Radio expansion station*] (RBYB)
KLSR	Memphis, TX [*AM radio station call letters*]
KLSR-FM	Memphis, TX [*FM radio station call letters*]
KLSR-TV	Eugene, OR [*Television station call letters*] (BROA)
KLSS	Korean Library Science Society (BUAC)
KLSS-FM	Mason City, IA [*FM radio station call letters*]
KLST	Kindergarten Language Screening Test
KLST	San Angelo, TX [*Television station call letters*]
KLSU	Baton Rouge, LA [*FM radio station call letters*]
KLSV	Las Vegas/Nellis Air Force Base [*Nevada*] [*ICAO location identifier*] (ICLI)
KLSX	Los Angeles, CA [*FM radio station call letters*]
KLSY	Bellevue, WA [*FM radio station call letters*]
KLSZ	Van Buren, AR [*FM radio station call letters*]
KLT	Kansas City Power & Light Co. [*NYSE symbol*] (SPSG)
KLT	Kansas City Pwr & Lt [*NYSE symbol*] (TTSB)
KLT	Karhunen-Loeve Transform [*Mathematics*]
KLT	Kiloton [*Nuclear equivalent of 1000 tons of high explosives*] (AAG)
KlT	Kleine Texte fuer Theologische und Philosophische Vorlesungen [*A publication*] (BJA)
KLT	Klystron Life Test
KLTA	Breckenridge, MN [*FM radio station call letters*]
KLTB	Boise, ID [*FM radio station call letters*]
KLTC	Dickinson, ND [*AM radio station call letters*]
KLTCB	Korean Long Term Credit Bank
KLTD	Temple, TX [*FM radio station call letters*]
KLTE	Kirksville, MO [*FM radio station call letters*]
KLTF	Little Falls, MN [*AM radio station call letters*]
KLTG	Corpus Christi, TX [*FM radio station call letters*]
KLTH	Kansas City, MO [*FM radio station call letters*]
KLTI	Macon, MO [*AM radio station call letters*]
KLTJ	Galveston, TX [*Television station call letters*]
KLTK	South West City, MO [*AM radio station call letters*]
KLTL	Lake Charles, LA [*Television station call letters*]
KLTM	Monroe, LA [*Television station call letters*]
KLTN	Kiloton (ABBR)
KLTN	Port Arthur, TX [*FM radio station call letters*]
KLTO	Knurling Tool
KLTO	Rosenberg, TX [*FM radio station call letters*] (RBYB)
KLTP-FM	Galveston, TX [*FM radio station call letters*] (RBYB)
KLTPrA	Kansas City P&L 3.80% Pfd [*NYSE symbol*] (TTSB)
KLTPrD	Kansas City P&L 4.35% Pfd [*NYSE symbol*] (TTSB)
KLTPrE	Kansas City P&L 4.50% Pfd [*NYSE symbol*] (TTSB)
KLTQ	Sparta, MO [*FM radio station call letters*]
KLTR	Franklin, TX [*FM radio station call letters*] (RBYB)
KLTR	Kilter (ABBR)
KLTS	Altus Air Force Base [*Oklahoma*] [*ICAO location identifier*] (ICLI)
KLTS	Shreveport, LA [*Television station call letters*]
KLTT	Brighton, CO [*AM radio station call letters*]
KLTV	Tyler, TX [*Television station call letters*]
KLTW-AM	Sierra Vista, AZ [*AM radio station call letters*] (RBYB)
KLTX	Harker Heights, TX [*FM radio station call letters*]
KLTY	Fort Worth, TX [*FM radio station call letters*]
KLTZ	Glasgow, MT [*AM radio station call letters*]
KLU	Kaiser Aluminum [*NYSE symbol*] (TTSB)
KLU	Kaiser Aluminum & Chemical Corp. [*NYSE symbol*] (SPSG)
KLU	Key and Lamp Units [*Telecommunications*]
KLU	Klagenfurt [*Austria*] [*Airport symbol*] (OAG)
KLU	Klutina [*Alaska*] [*Seismograph station code, US Geological Survey*] (SEIS)
KLUA	Kailua-Kona, HI [*FM radio station call letters*]
KLUB	Bloomington, IN [*FM radio station call letters*]
KLUC-FM	Las Vegas, NV [*FM radio station call letters*]
KLUE	Knowledge Legacy of the Unavailable Expert [*Computer science*] (BTTJ)
KLUE	Soledad, CA [*FM radio station call letters*]
KLUF	Phoenix/Luke Air Force Base [*Arizona*] [*ICAO location identifier*] (ICLI)
KLUH	Poplar Bluff, MO [*FM radio station call letters*]
KLUJ	Harlingen, TX [*Television station call letters*]
KLUK	Cincinnati/Municipal-Lunken Field [*Ohio*] [*ICAO location identifier*] (ICLI)
KLUK	Laughlin, NV [*FM radio station call letters*] (RBYB)
KLUP	Terrell Hills, TX [*AM radio station call letters*]
KLUPrD	Kaiser Alum 8.255% 'PRIDES' [*NYSE symbol*] (TTSB)
KLUR	Wichita Falls, TX [*FM radio station call letters*]
KLUV	Dallas, TX [*FM radio station call letters*]
KLUX	Robstown, TX [*FM radio station call letters*]
KLUZ	Albuquerque, NM [*Television station call letters*]
KLV	Karlovy Vary [*Former Czechoslovakia*] [*Airport symbol*] (OAG)
KLVA	Casa Grande, AZ [*FM radio station call letters*] (RBYB)
KLVB-AM	Medford, OR [*AM radio station call letters*] (BROA)
KLVC	Magalia, CA [*FM radio station call letters*]
KLVE	Los Angeles, CA [*FM radio station call letters*]
KLVF	Las Vegas, NM [*FM radio station call letters*]
KLVG	Garberville, CA [*FM radio station call letters*] (RBYB)
KLVH-FM	Leavenworth, WA [*FM radio station call letters*] (BROA)
KLVI	Beaumont, TX [*AM radio station call letters*]
KLVJ	Mountain Home, ID [*AM radio station call letters*]
KLVJ-FM	Mountain Home, ID [*FM radio station call letters*]
KLVK	Dimmitt, TX [*FM radio station call letters*] (RBYB)
KLVL	Pasadena, TX [*AM radio station call letters*]
KLVM	Prunedale, CA [*FM radio station call letters*]
KLVN	Chowchilla, CA [*FM radio station call letters*] (RBYB)
KLVO	Belen, NM [*FM radio station call letters*] (RBYB)
KLVQ	Athens, TX [*AM radio station call letters*]
KLVR	Santa Rosa, CA [*FM radio station call letters*]
KLVS	Las Vegas [*New Mexico*] [*ICAO location identifier*] (ICLI)
KLVS-FM	Kingsburg, CA [*FM radio station call letters*] (RBYB)
KLVT	Levelland, TX [*AM radio station call letters*]
KLVT-FM	Levelland, TX [*FM radio station call letters*]
KLVU	Haynesville, LA [*AM radio station call letters*]
KLVV	Ponca City, OK [*FM radio station call letters*]
KLVW	Julian, CA [*FM radio station call letters*] (RBYB)
KLVX	Las Vegas, NV [*Television station call letters*]
KLVY-FM	Fairmead, CA [*FM radio station call letters*] (BROA)
KLW	Claw Resources Ltd. [*Vancouver Stock Exchange symbol*]
KLW	Faculty of Law Library, University of Toronto [*UTLAS symbol*]
KLW	Klawock [*Alaska*] [*Airport symbol*] (OAG)
KLWD-FM	Gillette, WY [*FM radio station call letters*] (BROA)
KLWJ	Umatilla, OR [*AM radio station call letters*]
KLWN	Lawrence, KS [*AM radio station call letters*]
KLWS-FM	Moses Lake, WA [*FM radio station call letters*] (BROA)
KLWT	Kilowatt (ABBR)
KLWT	Lebanon, MO [*AM radio station call letters*]
KLWY	Cheyenne, WY [*Television station call letters*]
KLX	Kalamata [*Greece*] [*Airport symbol*] (OAG)
KLX	Kalix Air [*Nigeria*] [*FAA designator*] (FAAC)
KLX	Kidney and Lung Extract
KLXK	Duluth, MN [*FM radio station call letters*]
KLXM-FM	Salinas, CA [*FM radio station call letters*] (BROA)
KLXO	El Centro, CA [*Television station call letters*]
KLXQ	Hot Springs, AR [*FM radio station call letters*]
KLXR	Redding, CA [*AM radio station call letters*]
KLXS	Pierre, SD [*FM radio station call letters*]
KLXV	San Jose, CA [*Television station call letters*]
KLXX	Bismarck-Mandan, ND [*AM radio station call letters*]
KLY	Kalima [*Zaire*] [*Airport symbol*] (AD)
KLY	Klyuchi [*Former USSR Seismograph station code, US Geological Survey*] (SEIS)
KLYC	McMinnville, OR [*AM radio station call letters*]
KLYD	Shafter, CA [*FM radio station call letters*] (RBYB)
KLYF	Des Moines, IA [*FM radio station call letters*]
KLYK	Longview, WA [*FM radio station call letters*]
KLYN	Lynden, WA [*FM radio station call letters*]
KLYQ	Hamilton, MT [*AM radio station call letters*]
KLYR	Clarksville, AR [*AM radio station call letters*]
KLYR	Smoke Layer Aloft [*Meteorology*] (FAAC)
KLYR-FM	Clarksville, AR [*FM radio station call letters*]
KLYT	Albuquerque, NM [*FM radio station call letters*]
KLYV	Dubuque, IA [*FM radio station call letters*]
KLYY-FM	Arcadia, CA [*FM radio station call letters*] (RBYB)
KLZ	Denver, CO [*AM radio station call letters*]
KLZ	Kleinzee [*South Africa*] [*Airport symbol*] (OAG)
KLZA-FM	Falls City, NE [*FM radio station call letters*] (BROA)
KLZE	Owensville, MO [*FM radio station call letters*]
KLZK	Brownfield, TX [*FM radio station call letters*]
KLZR	Lawrence, KS [*FM radio station call letters*]
KLZX-FM	Brigham City, UT [*FM radio station call letters*] (RBYB)
KLZY	Powell, WY [*FM radio station call letters*]
KLZZ	Waite Park, MN [*FM radio station call letters*]
KM	Air Malta [*ICAO designator*] (AD)
KM	Comoros [*ANSI two-letter standard code*] (CNC)
KM	Draepelin-Morel [*Disease*] [*Psychiatry*] (DAVI)
KM	Ha-Kibbuts ha-Me'uhad (BJA)
KM	Kabataang Makabayan [*Nationalist Youth*] [*Philippines*]
KM	Kanamycin [*Antibacterial compound*]
KM	[*The*] Kansas & Missouri Railway & Terminal Co. [*Formerly, KMRT*] [*AAR code*]
kM	Kilomega
km	Kilometer

Km	Kilometer (TBD)
KM	Kilometer [BTS] (TAG)
KM	K-Immunoglobulin Light Chains [Immunology] (DAVI)
KM	Kinetic Momentum
KM	King and Martyr [Church calendars]
KM	Kingdom
KM	King's Medal [or Medallist] [British]
KM	King's Messenger [British] (ROG)
KM	Kirchoff Method [Telecommunications] (OA)
KM	Kitchen Mechanic [Restaurant slang]
KM	Klystron Mount
KM	Kmart [NYSE symbol] (TTSB)
KM	K Mart Corp. [NYSE symbol] (SPSG)
KM	K mart Financing Trust I [NYSE symbol] (SAG)
KM	Knight of Malta
KM	Knight of the Sovereign and Military Order of Malta (DD)
KM	Knowledge Manager
KM	Kraepelin-Morel [Disease] [Psychiatry] (DAVI)
KM	Kubelka-Munk [Optics]
KM	Kurram Militia [British military] (DMA)
KM	Manhattan Public Library, Manhattan, KS [Library symbol Library of Congress] (LCLS)
Km	Michaelis Constant [In enzyme assays] (STED)
Km	Michaelis-Menten Dissociation Constnat (DAVI)
KM2	Kermit [Texas] [Seismograph station code, US Geological Survey] (SEIS)
km²	Square Kilometer (CDAI)
km2	Square Kilometer
K M²/W	Kelvin Square Meters per Watt
KM³	Cubic Kilometer
KM5	Kermit [Texas] [Seismograph station code, US Geological Survey] (SEIS)
KM6	Kermit [Texas] [Seismograph station code, US Geological Survey] (SEIS)
KM9	Kermit [Texas] [Seismograph station code, US Geological Survey] (SEIS)
KMA	Kerema [Papua New Guinea] [Airport symbol] (OAG)
KMA	Korea Military Academy
KMA	Ku-Band Multiple Access (MCD)
KMA	Shenandoah, IA [AM radio station call letters]
KMAA	Kart Marketing Association of America (EA)
KMAC	Gainesville, MO [FM radio station call letters]
KMAC	Kushi Macrobiotic Corp. [NASDAQ symbol] (SAG)
KMAC	Kushi Macrobiotics [NASDAQ symbol] (TTSB)
KMACW	Kushi Macrobiotics Wrrt [NASDAQ symbol] (TTSB)
KMAD	Madill, OK [AM radio station call letters]
KMAD-FM	Madill, OK [FM radio station call letters]
KMAF	Midland/Regional Air Terminal [Texas] [ICAO location identifier] (ICLI)
KMAG	Fort Smith, AR [FM radio station call letters]
KMAG	Komag, Inc. [NASDAQ symbol] (NQ)
KMAG	Korea Military Advisory Group [United States]
KMAGV	Korean Military Assistance Group, Vietnam (VNW)
KMAJ	Topeka, KS [AM radio station call letters]
KMAJ-FM	Topeka, KS [FM radio station call letters]
KMAK	Orange Cove, CA [FM radio station call letters]
KMAL	Malden, MO [FM radio station call letters]
KMAM	Butler, MO [AM radio station call letters]
KMAN	Manhattan, KS [AM radio station call letters]
KMAQ	Marquoketa, IA [AM radio station call letters]
KMAQ-FM	Maquoketa, IA [FM radio station call letters]
KMAR	Winnsboro, LA [AM radio station call letters]
KMAR-FM	Winnsboro, LA [FM radio station call letters]
K mart	K Mart Corp. [Associated Press] (SAG)
KmartF	K mart Financing Trust I [Associated Press] (SAG)
KMAS	Korean Medical Association of America (EA)
KMAS	Shelton, WA [AM radio station call letters]
KMAT-FM	Seadrift, TX [FM radio station call letters] (BROA)
KMAV	Mayville, ND [AM radio station call letters]
KMAV-FM	Mayville, ND [FM radio station call letters]
KMAX	Arcadia, CA [FM radio station call letters]
KMAX-AM	Opportunity, WA [AM radio station call letters] (RBYB)
KMAY	Billings, MT [AM radio station call letters]
KMAZ	Las Cruces, NM [Television station call letters] (BROA)
KMB	Kimbe [New Britain] [Seismograph station code, US Geological Survey Closed] (SEIS)
KMB	Kimberly-Clark [NYSE symbol] (TTSB)
KMB	Kimberly-Clark Corp. [NYSE symbol] (SPSG)
KMB	Koinambe [Papua New Guinea] [Airport symbol] (OAG)
KMBAX	Kemper Municipal Bond CI.A [Mutual fund ticker symbol] (SG)
KMBC	Kansas City, MO [Television station call letters]
KMBD	Tillamook, OR [AM radio station call letters]
KMBH	Harlingen, TX [Television station call letters]
KMBH-FM	Harlingen, TX [FM radio station call letters]
KMBI	Spokane, WA [AM radio station call letters]
KMBI-FM	Spokane, WA [FM radio station call letters]
KMBL	Junction, TX [AM radio station call letters]
KMBO	Keith Martin Ballet Oregon
KMBQ	Wasilla, AK [FM radio station call letters]
KMBR-FM	Butte, MT [FM radio station call letters] (BROA)
KMBS	West Monroe, LA [AM radio station call letters]
KMBV	Navasota, TX [FM radio station call letters]
KMBY	Capitola, CA [FM radio station call letters] (RBYB)
KMBY-FM	Gonzales, CA [FM radio station call letters] (RBYB)
KMBZ	Kansas City, MO [AM radio station call letters]
KMC	Kamloops CableNet [Vancouver Stock Exchange symbol]
KMC	Kane-Miller Corp. (EFIS)
KMC	Kenya Meat Commission (BUAC)
KMC	Kernel Migration Coefficient (PDAA)
kMc	Kilomegacycle
KMC	Kinetic Monte Carlo [Simulation]
KMC	Korean Marine Corps [North Korea]
KMC	Manhattan Christian College, Manhattan, KS [Library symbol] [Library of Congress] (LCLS)
KMCA-AM	Burney, CA [AM radio station call letters] (BROA)
KMCC	Lake Havasu City, AZ [Television station call letters] (BROA)
KMCC	Sacramento/McClellan Air Force Base [California] [ICAO location identifier] (ICLI)
KMCD	Fairfield, IA [AM radio station call letters]
KMCF	Tampa/MacDill Air Force Base [Florida] [ICAO location identifier] (ICLI)
KMCG-FM	Carlsbad, CA [FM radio station call letters] (BROA)
KMCH	Manchester, IA [FM radio station call letters]
KMCI	Kansas City/International [Missouri] [ICAO location identifier] (ICLI)
KMCI	Lawrence, KS [Television station call letters]
KMCK	Siloam Springs, AR [FM radio station call letters]
KMCL	McCall, ID [AM radio station call letters]
KMCL-FM	McCall, ID [FM radio station call letters]
KMCM	Miles City, MT [FM radio station call letters]
K-MCM	Potassium-Containing Minimal Capacitation Medium [Medicine] (BABM)
KMCO	McAlester, OK [FM radio station call letters]
KMCO	Orlando/McCoy Air Force Base [Florida] [ICAO location identifier] (ICLI)
KMCP	Kodak Metal Clad Plate (IAA)
KMcpC	McPherson College, McPherson, KS [Library symbol Library of Congress] (LCLS)
kMcps	Kilomegacycle per Second (STED)
kMcps	Kilomegacycles per Sound [Measurement] (DAVI)
KMCQ	The Dalles, OR [FM radio station call letters]
KMCR	Montgomery City, MO [FM radio station call letters]
kMcs	Kilomegacycles per Second (AABC)
KMCT	West Monroe, LA [Television station call letters]
KMCX	Ogallala, NE [FM radio station call letters]
KMCY	Minot, ND [Television station call letters]
KMD	Kamlode Resources, Inc. [Vancouver Stock Exchange symbol]
KMDAT	KeyMath Diagnostic Arithmetic Test
KMDC	Kirschner Medical Corp. (EFIS)
KMDL	Kaplan, LA [FM radio station call letters]
KMDO	Fort Scott, KS [AM radio station call letters]
KMDT	Middletown/Harrisburg International-Olmsted Field [Pennsylvania] [ICAO location identifier] (ICLI)
KMDW	Chicago/Chicago Midway [Illinois] [ICAO location identifier] (ICLI)
KME	Kappa Mu Epsilon [Society]
KME	Kermit [Texas] [Seismograph station code, US Geological Survey Closed] (SEIS)
KME	Kerr Magneto-Optical Effect [Optics]
KME	Kraft Mill Effluent [Pulp and paper processing]
KME	Media Center, Audio Visual Library, University of Toronto [UTLAS symbol]
KMEB	Wailuku, HI [Television station call letters]
KMED	Medford, OR [AM radio station call letters]
KMEF	Keratin, Myosin, Epidermin, Fibrin [Biochemistry]
KMEG	Sioux City, IA [Television station call letters]
KMEIA	Kodaly Music Education Institute of Australia
KMEL	San Francisco, CA [FM radio station call letters]
KMEM	Lincoln, NE [AM radio station call letters]
KMEM	Memphis/International [Tennessee] [ICAO location identifier] (ICLI)
KMEM	Memphis, MO [FM radio station call letters]
KMEN	San Bernardino, CA [AM radio station call letters]
KMER	Kemmerer, WY [AM radio station call letters]
KMER	Kodak Metal Etch Resist
KMER	Merced/Castle Air Force Base [California] [ICAO location identifier] (ICLI)
KMET	Banning, CA [AM radio station call letters]
KMET	Kemet Corp. [NASDAQ symbol] (SAG)
KMEX	Los Angeles, CA [Television station call letters]
KMEZ	Belle Chasse, LA [FM radio station call letters]
KMF	Kamina [Papua New Guinea] [Airport symbol] (OAG)
KMF	Koussevitzky Music Foundation (EA)
KMFA	Austin, TX [FM radio station call letters]
KMFB	Mendocino, CA [FM radio station call letters]
KMFC	Centralia, MO [FM radio station call letters]
KMFC	Kimberly McCullough Fan Club (EA)
KMFE	McAllen/Miller International [Texas] [ICAO location identifier] (ICLI)
KMFG-FM	Nashwauk, MN [FM radio station call letters] (BROA)
KMFM	Premont, TX [FM radio station call letters]
KMFX	Lake City, MN [FM radio station call letters]
KMFX	Wabasha, MN [AM radio station call letters]
KMFY	Grand Rapids, MN [FM radio station call letters]
KMG	Kerr-McGee [NYSE symbol] (TTSB)
KMG	Kerr-McGee Corp. [NYSE symbol Toronto Stock Exchange symbol] (SPSG)
KMG	Kumagaya [Japan] [Seismograph station code, US Geological Survey] (SEIS)
KMG	Kunming [China] [Airport symbol] (OAG)
KMGA	Albuquerque, NM [FM radio station call letters]
KMGC	Camden, AR [FM radio station call letters] (RBYB)
KMGE	Eugene, OR [FM radio station call letters]

KMGE........... Marietta/Dobbins Air Force Base [*Georgia*] [*ICAO location identifier*] (ICLI)
KMGG......... Monte Rio, CA [*FM radio station call letters*]
KMGH......... Denver, CO [*Television station call letters*]
KMGI........... Pocatello, ID [*FM radio station call letters*]
KMGK......... Glenwood, MN [*FM radio station call letters*]
KMGL......... Oklahoma City, OK [*FM radio station call letters*]
KMGM......... Montevideo, MN [*FM radio station call letters*]
KMGN......... Flagstaff, AZ [*FM radio station call letters*]
KMGO......... Centerville, IA [*FM radio station call letters*]
KMGPrD...... Kerr Group $1.70 Cv Pfd [*NYSE symbol*] (TTSB)
KMGQ......... Goleta, CA [*FM radio station call letters*]
KMGR......... Murray, UT [*AM radio station call letters*]
KMGW......... Casper, WY [*FM radio station call letters*]
KMGX......... Rio Dell, CA [*FM radio station call letters*] (RBYB)
KMGZ......... Lawton, OK [*FM radio station call letters*] (RBYB)
kmh............ Kilometers per Hour
KMH........... Knight of Merit of Holstein
KMHA......... Four Bears, ND [*FM radio station call letters*]
KMHD......... Gresham, OR [*FM radio station call letters*]
KMHI-AM..... Mountain Home, ID [*AM radio station call letters*] (BROA)
KMHK-FM.... Hardin, MT [*FM radio station call letters*] (RBYB)
KMHL......... Marshall, MN [*AM radio station call letters*]
KMHM-FM.... Lutesville, MO [*FM radio station call letters*] (RBYB)
KM/HR........ Kilometers per Hour
KMHR......... Sacramento/Mather Air Force Base [*California*] [*ICAO location identifier*] (ICLI)
KMHS-AM..... Coos Bay, OR [*AM radio station call letters*] (BROA)
KMHT......... Marshall, TX [*AM radio station call letters*]
KMHX-FM.... Windsor, CA [*FM radio station call letters*] (BROA)
kMHZ.......... Kilomega Hertz (MCD)
KMI........... Keilschrifttexte Medizinischen Inhalts [*A publication*] (BJA)
KMI........... Kessler Marketing Intelligence [*Information service or system*] (IID)
KMI........... KSC [*Kennedy Space Center*] Management Instruction [*NASA*] (KSC)
KMI........... Miyazaki [*Japan*] [*Airport symbol*] (OAG)
KMIA......... Jasper, TX [*FM radio station call letters*]
KMIA......... Miami/International [*Florida*] [*ICAO location identifier*] (ICLI)
KMIB.......... Minot/Minot Air Force Base [*North Dakota*] [*ICAO location identifier*] (ICLI)
KMID......... Midland, TX [*Television station call letters*]
KMIH......... Mercer Island, WA [*FM radio station call letters*]
KMIJ......... Johnson County Mental Health Center, Mission, KS [*Library symbol Library of Congress*] (LCLS)
KMIL......... Cameron, TX [*AM radio station call letters*]
KMIN......... Grants, NM [*AM radio station call letters*]
KMIQ......... Robstown, TX [*FM radio station call letters*]
KMIR......... Palm Springs, CA [*Television station call letters*]
KMIS......... New Madrid, MO [*FM radio station call letters*]
KMIS......... Portageville, MO [*AM radio station call letters*]
KMIT......... Mitchell, SD [*FM radio station call letters*]
KMIV......... Millville/Millville [*New Jersey*] [*ICAO location identifier*] (ICLI)
KMIX......... Tracy, CA [*FM radio station call letters*] (RBYB)
KMIZ......... Columbia, MO [*Television station call letters*]
KMJ........... Fresno, CA [*AM radio station call letters*]
KMJ........... Knight of Maximilian Joseph [*Bavaria*]
KMJ........... Kumamoto [*Japan*] [*Airport symbol*] (OAG)
KMJ........... Kume Jima [*Ryukyu Islands*] [*Seismograph station code, US Geological Survey*] (SEIS)
KMJC......... Mount Shasta, CA [*AM radio station call letters*] (RBYB)
KMJC-FM.... Mount Shasta, CA [*FM radio station call letters*] (RBYB)
KMJE-FM..... Gridley, CA [*FM radio station call letters*] (RBYB)
KMJI......... Sacramento, CA [*FM radio station call letters*] (RBYB)
KMJJ......... Shreveport, LA [*FM radio station call letters*]
KMJK......... Buckeye, AZ [*FM radio station call letters*]
KMJM......... St. Louis, MO [*FM radio station call letters*]
KMJQ......... Houston, TX [*FM radio station call letters*]
KMJX......... Conway, AR [*FM radio station call letters*]
KMJY......... Newport, WA [*AM radio station call letters*]
KMJY-FM..... Newport, WA [*FM radio station call letters*]
KMJZ-FM..... St. Louis Park, MN [*FM radio station call letters*] (RBYB)
KMK.......... Kamakura [*Japan*] [*Seismograph station code, US Geological Survey Closed*] (SEIS)
KMK.......... Kansas State University, Manhattan, KS [*Library symbol Library of Congress*] (LCLS)
KMK.......... Keren Mif'alim Konstruktiviyim [*Constructive Enterprises Fund*] (BJA)
KMK.......... Konyvtartudomanyi es Modszertani Kozpont [*Center for Library Science and Methodology*] [*Hungary*] [*Information service or system*] (IID)
KMK.......... Makabana [*Congo*] [*Airport symbol*] (AD)
KMK.......... Perhaps...Kids Meeting Kids Can Make A Difference [*An association*] (EA)
KMKC......... Kansas City/Kansas City [*Missouri*] [*ICAO location identifier*] (ICLI)
KMKE......... Grand Junction, CO [*FM radio station call letters*]
KMKE......... Milwaukee/General Mitchell Field [*Wisconsin*] [*ICAO location identifier*] (ICLI)
KMKF......... Manhattan, KS [*FM radio station call letters*]
KMKM......... Kansas City [*Missouri*] [*ICAO location identifier*] (ICLI)
KMKO......... Muskogee/Davis [*Oklahoma*] [*ICAO location identifier*] (ICLI)
KMKRY........ Kvutzat Mesahake Kadur Regel Yehudit (BJA)
KMKS......... Bay City, TX [*FM radio station call letters*]
KMKT-FM .... Bells, TX [*FM radio station call letters*] (BROA)
KMK-V .... Kansas State University, Veterinary Medicine Library, Manhattan, KS [*Library symbol Library of Congress*] (LCLS)
KMKX......... San Diego, CA [*FM radio station call letters*] (RBYB)

KMKZ......... Lahoma, OK [*FM radio station call letters*]
KML.......... Carmel Container Sys [*AMEX symbol*] (TTSB)
KML.......... Carmel Container Systems Ltd. [*AMEX symbol*] (SPSG)
KML.......... Kamileroi [*Australia Airport symbol*] (OAG)
KML.......... Kamuela [*Hawaii*] [*Seismograph station code, US Geological Survey Closed*] (SEIS)
KMLA-FM .... El Rio, CA [*FM radio station call letters*] (RBYB)
KMLB......... Melbourne/Cape Kennedy Regional [*Florida*] [*ICAO location identifier*] (ICLI)
KMLB......... Monroe, LA [*FM radio station call letters*]
KMLC......... McAlester/Municipal [*Oklahoma*] [*ICAO location identifier*] (ICLI)
KMLD-FM .... Casper, WY [*FM radio station call letters*] (BROA)
KMLE......... Chandler, AZ [*FM radio station call letters*]
KMLM......... Odessa, TX [*Television station call letters*]
KMLO-FM .... Lowry, SD [*FM radio station call letters*] (RBYB)
KMLT......... Millinocket/Millinocke [*Maine*] [*ICAO location identifier*] (ICLI)
KMLU......... Monroe/Monroe Municipal [*Louisiana*] [*ICAO location identifier*] (ICLI)
KMLW........ Moses Lake, WA [*FM radio station call letters*] (RBYB)
KMM......... Kamigamo [*Japan*] [*Seismograph station code, US Geological Survey Closed*] (SEIS)
KMM......... Kemper Multi-Market Income [*NYSE symbol*] (SPSG)
KMM......... Kimam [*Indonesia*] [*Airport symbol*] (OAG)
KMM......... Knight of the Order of Military Merit [*Prussia*] (ROG)
KMM......... Morehead State University, Morehead, KY [*OCLC symbol*] (OCLC)
KMMA......... Knitting Machine Manufacturers Association [*Defunct*] (EA)
KMMC......... Kangaroo Marketing and Management Committee [*Australia*]
KMMC......... Kerala Minerals and Metals Corp. [*India*] (BUAC)
KMMC......... Salem, MO [*FM radio station call letters*]
KMMJ......... Grand Island, NE [*AM radio station call letters*]
KMML......... Amarillo, TX [*FM radio station call letters*]
KMMM......... Madera, CA [*FM radio station call letters*]
KMMO......... Marshall, MO [*AM radio station call letters*]
KMMO-FM .... Marshall, MO [*FM radio station call letters*]
KMMPI........ Khatena-Morse Multitalent Perception Inventory [*Test*] (TMMY)
KMMR......... Malta, MT [*FM radio station call letters*]
KMMS......... Bozeman, MT [*AM radio station call letters*]
K-MMSEN.... KSC [*Kennedy Space Center*] MMSE Notice [*Multiuse Mission Support Equipment*] [*NASA*] (NASA)
K-MMSEPS... KSC [*Kennedy Space Center*] MMSE Project Specification [*Multiuse Mission Support Equipment*] [*NASA*] (NASA)
KMMS-FM ... Bozeman, MT [*FM radio station call letters*]
KMMT......... Mammoth Lakes, CA [*FM radio station call letters*]
KMMX......... Lamesa, TX [*FM radio station call letters*]
KMMY......... Muskogee, OK [*FM radio station call letters*]
KMN.......... Kamina [*Zaire*] [*Airport symbol*] (OAG)
KMN.......... Kumano [*Japan*] [*Seismograph station code, US Geological Survey*] (SEIS)
KMNC......... North Central Kansas Libraries, Manhattan, KS [*Library symbol Library of Congress*] (LCLS)
KMND......... Midland, TX [*AM radio station call letters*]
KMNE......... Bassett, NE [*FM radio station call letters*]
KMNE-TV .... Bassett, NE [*Television station call letters*]
KMNO......... Kimono (ABBR)
KMnO........ Potassium Permanganate [*Pharmacology*] (DAVI)
KMNR......... Rolla, MO [*FM radio station call letters*]
KMNS......... Sioux City, IA [*AM radio station call letters*]
KMNT......... Centralia, WA [*FM radio station call letters*]
KMNY......... Pomona, CA [*AM radio station call letters*]
KMNZ......... Oklahoma City, OK [*Television station call letters*]
KMO.......... Kobe Marine Observatory (BARN)
KMO.......... Manokotak [*Alaska*] [*Airport symbol*] (OAG)
KMOB......... Mobile/Bates Field [*Alabama*] [*ICAO location identifier*] (ICLI)
KMOC......... Wichita Falls, TX [*FM radio station call letters*]
KMOD......... Tulsa, OK [*FM radio station call letters*]
KMOE......... Butler, MO [*FM radio station call letters*]
KMOG......... Payson, AZ [*AM radio station call letters*]
KMOH......... Kingman, AZ [*Television station call letters*]
KMOJ......... Minneapolis, MN [*FM radio station call letters*]
KMOK......... Lewiston, ID [*FM radio station call letters*]
KMOL......... San Antonio, TX [*Television station call letters*]
KMOM......... Monticello, MN [*AM radio station call letters*]
KMON......... Great Falls, MT [*AM radio station call letters*]
KMON......... Keyboard Monitor [*Digital Equipment Corp.*]
KMON-FM.... Great Falls, MT [*FM radio station call letters*]
KMOO-FM.... Mineola, TX [*FM radio station call letters*]
KMOQ......... Baxter Springs, KS [*FM radio station call letters*]
KMOR......... Scottsbluff, NE [*FM radio station call letters*]
KMOS......... Sedalia, MO [*Television station call letters*]
KMOT......... Minot/International [*North Dakota*] [*ICAO location identifier*] (ICLI)
KMOT......... Minot, ND [*Television station call letters*]
KMOU......... Roswell, NM [*FM radio station call letters*]
KMOV......... St. Louis, MO [*Television station call letters*]
KMOX......... St. Louis, MO [*AM radio station call letters*]
KMOZ......... Rolla, MO [*AM radio station call letters*]
KMP.......... Kangaroo Management Program [*Australia*]
KMP.......... Keetmanshoop [*South-West Africa*] [*Airport symbol*] (OAG)
KMP.......... Kent Mathematics Project [*British*] (AIE)
KMP.......... Kilusang Mabubukid ng Pilipinas [*Philippine Peasant Federation*] [*Political party*]
KMP.......... Kommunistak Magyarorszagi Partja [*Communist Party of Hungary*] [*Political party*] (PPE)
KMP.......... Policy and Regulations Division, Information Resources Management Service (AAGC)
KMPC......... Los Angeles, CA [*AM radio station call letters*]
KMPD......... Kingston Military Products Division (SAA)

KMPG	Hollister, CA [*AM radio station call letters*]
KMPH	Hanford, CA [*FM radio station call letters*]
kmph	Kilometers per Hour (AABC)
KMPH	Visalia, CA [*Television station call letters*]
KmpHi	Kemper High Income Trust [*Associated Press*] (SAG)
KmpIGv	Kemper Intermediate Government Trust [*Associated Press*] (SAG)
KMPL	Sikeston, MO [*AM radio station call letters*]
KmpMl	Kemper Multi-Market Income Trust [*Associated Press*] (SAG)
KmpMu	Kemper Municipal Income Fund [*Associated Press*] (SAG)
KMPO	Modesto, CA [*FM radio station call letters*]
KMPP	Kisan Mazdoor Praja Party [*India*] [*Political party*]
KMPQ	Rosenberg-Richmond, TX [*AM radio station call letters*]
KMPQ-FM	Woodward, OK [*FM radio station call letters*] (BROA)
KMPR	Minot, ND [*FM radio station call letters*]
KMPS	Kernel Multiple Processing System [*Computer science*]
kmps	Kilometers per Second
KMPS	Seattle, WA [*AM radio station call letters*]
KMPS-FM	Seattle, WA [*FM radio station call letters*]
KmpSInc	Kemper Strategic Income Fund [*Associated Press*] (SAG)
KmpStr	Kemper Strategic Municipal Income Trust [*Associated Press*] (SAG)
KMP-TUCP	Katipunang Manggagawang Pilipino [*Trade Union Congress of the Philippines*] (EY)
KMPV	Montpelier/Edward F. Knapp [*Vermont*] [*ICAO location identifier*] (ICLI)
KMPX	Decatur, TX [*Television station call letters*]
KMQ	Komatsu [*Japan*] [*Airport symbol*] (OAG)
KMQA	West Covina, CA [*FM radio station call letters*]
KMQT	Marquette/Marquette County [*Michigan*] [*ICAO location identifier*] (ICLI)
KMQUT	Kumquat (ABBR)
KMQX	Springtown, TX [*FM radio station call letters*] (RBYB)
KMR	Cambria Resources Ltd. [*Vancouver Stock Exchange symbol*]
KMR	Kafrarian Mounted Rifles [*British military*] (DMA)
KMR	Karimui [*Papua New Guinea*] [*Airport symbol*] (OAG)
KMR	Kremsmuenster [*Austria*] [*Seismograph station code, US Geological Survey*] (SEIS)
KMR	Kwajalein Missile Range (AABC)
KMR	Western Pacific Airlines, Inc. [*FAA designator*] (FAAC)
KMRA	Knitwear Mill Representatives Association [*Defunct*] (EA)
KMRC	Morgan City, LA [*AM radio station call letters*]
KMRE	Dumas, TX [*FM radio station call letters*]
KMRF	Keyswitch Magic Relay Finder (IAA)
KMRF	Marshfield, MO [*AM radio station call letters*]
KMRI-AM	West Valley City, UT [*AM radio station call letters*] (BROA)
KMrJ	Johnson County Library, Merriam, KS [*Library symbol Library of Congress*] (LCLS)
KMRJ-FM	Rancho Mirage, CA [*FM radio station call letters*] (RBYB)
KMRK	Odessa, TX [*FM radio station call letters*]
KMRL	Buras, LA [*FM radio station call letters*] (RBYB)
KMRN	Cameron, MO [*AM radio station call letters*]
KMRO	Camarillo, CA [*FM radio station call letters*]
KMRR	South Tucson, AZ [*AM radio station call letters*]
KMRS	Morris, MN [*AM radio station call letters*]
KMrS	Shawnee Mission Medical Center, Merriam, KS [*Library symbol Library of Congress*] (LCLS)
KMRT	Dallas, TX [*AM radio station call letters*]
KMRT	[*The*] Kansas & Missouri Railway & Terminal Co. [*Later, KM*] [*AAR code*]
KMRT-FM	Granbury, TX [*FM radio station call letters*] (RBYB)
KMRV-FM	Blair, NE [*FM radio station call letters*] (RBYB)
KMRX-FM	Collinsville, OK [*FM radio station call letters*] (BROA)
KMRY	Cedar Rapids, IA [*AM radio station call letters*]
KMRZ-AM	San Bernadino, CA [*AM radio station call letters*] (BROA)
KMS	Camas Resources Ltd. [*Vancouver Stock Exchange symbol*]
KMS	Kabuki Make-Up Syndrome [*Medicine*] (DMAA)
KMS	Karitane Mothercraft Society [*Australia*]
KMS	Keysort Multiple Selector
km/s	Kilometers per Second
KMS	King's Magnetic Ore Separator (ROG)
KMS	Knowledge Management System [*Computer science*]
KMS	Komatsu Mining Systems [*Japan*]
KMS	Kumasi [*Ghana*] [*Airport symbol*] (OAG)
KMS	Kwashiorkormarasmus Syndrome [*Medicine*] (DMAA)
KMS	K-Words Times Millions of Seconds [*Unit of measure*] (GFGA)
KMS	Murray State University, Murray, KY [*OCLC symbol*] (OCLC)
KMSA	Grand Junction, CO [*FM radio station call letters*]
KMSB	Tucson, AZ [*Television station call letters*]
KMSC	Sioux City, IA [*FM radio station call letters*]
KMSD	Milbank, SD [*AM radio station call letters*]
KMSG	Sanger, CA [*Television station call letters*]
KMSI	Moore, OK [*FM radio station call letters*]
KMSK	Austin, MN [*FM radio station call letters*]
KMSL	Great Falls, MT [*AM radio station call letters*]
KMSM	Butte, MT [*FM radio station call letters*]
KMSN	Madison/Truax Field [*Wisconsin*] [*ICAO location identifier*] (ICLI)
KMSO	Missoula, MT [*FM radio station call letters*]
KMSP	Minneapolis/Minneapolis-St. Paul International [*Minnesota*] [*ICAO location identifier*] (ICLI)
KMSP	Minneapolis, MN [*Television station call letters*]
KMSR	Sauk Centre, MN [*FM radio station call letters*]
KMSS	Massena/Richards Field [*New York*] [*ICAO location identifier*] (ICLI)
KMSS	Shreveport, LA [*Television station call letters*]
KMSU	Mankato, MN [*FM radio station call letters*]
KMSV	Kirsten Murine Sarcoma Virus [*Medicine*] (DB)
KMSY	New Orleans/International [*Louisiana*] [*ICAO location identifier*] (ICLI)

KMT	Kennametal, Inc. [*NYSE symbol*] (SPSG)
KMT	Kinomoto [*Japan*] [*Seismograph station code, US Geological Survey Closed*] (SEIS)
KMT	Knight of St. Maria Theresa [*Austria*] (ROG)
KMT	Kuomintang [*Nationalist Party of Taiwan*] [*Political party*] (PD)
KMTA	Miles City, MT [*AM radio station call letters*]
KMTB	Kibris Milli Turk Birligi [*Cypriot National Turkish Union*] (PPE)
KMTB	Murfreesboro, AR [*FM radio station call letters*]
KMTC	Mount Clemens/Selfridge Air Force Base [*Michigan*] [*ICAO location identifier*] (ICLI)
KMTC	Russellville, AR [*FM radio station call letters*]
KMTH	Maljamar, NM [*FM radio station call letters*]
KMTI	Manti, UT [*AM radio station call letters*]
KMTL	Sherwood, AR [*AM radio station call letters*]
KMTN	Jackson, WY [*FM radio station call letters*]
KMTNC	King Mahendra Trust for Nature Conservation [*Nepal*] (BUAC)
KMTP	San Francisco, CA [*Television station call letters*]
KMTPS	Key Makers' Trade Protection Society [*A union*] [*British*]
KMTR	Eugene, OR [*Television station call letters*]
KMTS	Glenwood Springs, CO [*FM radio station call letters*]
KMTT	Tacoma, WA [*AM radio station call letters*]
KMTT-FM	Tacoma, WA [*FM radio station call letters*]
KMTV	Omaha, NE [*Television station call letters*]
KMTX	Helena, MT [*AM radio station call letters*]
KMTX-FM	Helena, MT [*FM radio station call letters*]
KMTX-TV	Roseburg, OR [*Television station call letters*]
KMTY-FM	Holdrege, NE [*FM radio station call letters*] (RBYB)
KMTZ	Coos Bay, OR [*Television station call letters*]
KMU	Kamikineusu Station [*Japan*] [*Seismograph station code, US Geological Survey*] (SEIS)
KMU	Kilusang Mayo Uno [*May First Movement*] [*Philippines*] [*Political party*]
KMU	Kismayu [*Somalia*] [*Airport symbol*] (OAG)
KMU	Kit Munition Unit [*Air Force*] (MCD)
KMUD	Garberville, CA [*FM radio station call letters*]
KMUE-FM	Eureka, CA [*FM radio station call letters*] (RBYB)
KMUL	Muleshoe, TX [*AM radio station call letters*]
KMUN	Astoria, OR [*FM radio station call letters*]
KMUO	Mountain Home/Mountain Home Air Force Base [*Idaho*] [*ICAO location identifier*] (ICLI)
KMUS	Burns, WY [*FM radio station call letters*]
KMUS-AM	Muskogee, OK [*AM radio station call letters*] (RBYB)
KMUW	Wichita, KS [*FM radio station call letters*]
KMUZ	Gresham, OR [*AM radio station call letters*] (RBYB)
KMV	Kalemyo [*Myanmar*] [*Airport symbol*] (OAG)
KMV	Keen Mountain [*Virginia*] [*Seismograph station code, US Geological Survey Closed*] (SEIS)
KMV	Killed Measles-Virus Vaccine
KMVC	Marshall, MO [*FM radio station call letters*]
KMVI	Wailuku, HI [*AM radio station call letters*]
KMVI-FM	Pukalani, HI [*FM radio station call letters*]
KMVK	Benton, AR [*FM radio station call letters*]
KMVL	Madisonville, TX [*AM radio station call letters*]
KMVL-FM	Madisonville, TX [*FM radio station call letters*] (RBYB)
KMVP-AM	Phoenix, AZ [*AM radio station call letters*] (BROA)
KMVR	Mesilla Park, NM [*FM radio station call letters*]
KMVT	Twin Falls, ID [*Television station call letters*]
KMVU	Medford, OR [*Television station call letters*]
KMVX	Jerome, ID [*FM radio station call letters*]
kmw	Kilomegawatt (WGA)
kmwh	Kilomegawatt-Hour (WGA)
KMWL	Mineral Wells [*Texas*] [*ICAO location identifier*] (ICLI)
KMWX	Yakima, WA [*AM radio station call letters*]
KMXA-AM	Aurora, CO [*AM radio station call letters*] (RBYB)
KMXA-FM	Minot, ND [*FM radio station call letters*] (RBYB)
KMXB	Orem, UT [*FM radio station call letters*]
KMXC	Sioux Falls, SD [*FM radio station call letters*]
KMXD	Ankeny, IA [*FM radio station call letters*]
KMXE	Red Lodge, MT [*FM radio station call letters*]
KMXF	Montgomery/Maxwell Air Force Base [*Alabama*] [*ICAO location identifier*] (ICLI)
KMXG	Clinton, IA [*FM radio station call letters*]
KMXI	Chico, CA [*FM radio station call letters*] (RBYB)
KMXJ-FM	Sallisaw, OK [*FM radio station call letters*] (RBYB)
KMXK	Cold Spring, MN [*FM radio station call letters*]
KMXL	Carthage, MO [*FM radio station call letters*]
KMXM-FM	Gooding, ID [*FM radio station call letters*] (RBYB)
KMXN	Santa Rosa, CA [*AM radio station call letters*]
KMXO	Merkel, TX [*AM radio station call letters*]
KMXQ	Socorro, NM [*FM radio station call letters*]
KMXR	Corpus Christi, TX [*FM radio station call letters*]
KMXS	Anchorage, AK [*FM radio station call letters*] (RBYB)
KMXT	Kodiak, AK [*FM radio station call letters*]
KMXU	Manti, UT [*FM radio station call letters*]
KMXV	Kansas City, MO [*FM radio station call letters*]
KMXX	Imperial, CA [*FM radio station call letters*]
KMXY-FM	Grand Junction, CO [*FM radio station call letters*] (RBYB)
KMXZ-FM	Tucson, AZ [*FM radio station call letters*] (RBYB)
KMY	Moser Bay [*Alaska*] [*Airport symbol*] (OAG)
KMYC	Marysville, CA [*AM radio station call letters*]
KMYI	Kirtland, NM [*FM radio station call letters*]
KMYL-AM	Tolleson, AZ [*AM radio station call letters*] (BROA)
KMYL-FM	Wickenburg, AZ [*FM radio station call letters*] (BROA)
KMYR	Myrtle Beach/Myrtle Beach Air Force Base [*South Carolina*] [*ICAO location identifier*] (ICLI)

KMYX............ Taft, CA [*AM radio station call letters*]
KMYX-FM .... Taft, CA [*FM radio station call letters*]
KMYY.......... Monroe, LA [*FM radio station call letters*]
KMYZ.......... Pryor, OK [*AM radio station call letters*]
KMYZ-FM .... Pryor, OK [*FM radio station call letters*]
KMZ............ Kangaroo Management Zone
KMZA.......... Seneca, KS [*FM radio station call letters*]
KMZE.......... Woodward, OK [*FM radio station call letters*]
KMZK-AM .... Billings, MT [*AM radio station call letters*] (BROA)
KMZN.......... Farwell, TX [*Television station call letters*]
KMZQ.......... Henderson, NV [*FM radio station call letters*]
KMZU.......... Carrollton, MO [*FM radio station call letters*]
KMZX.......... Lonoke, AR [*FM radio station call letters*]
KN.............. Air Kentucky [*ICAO designator*]
KN.............. GKN Group Services Ltd. [*British ICAO designator*] (ICDA)
KN.............. Kenya Navy
KN.............. Khan (ABBR)
kN.............. Kilonewton
KN.............. Kinetics of Neutralization [*Chemistry*]
KN.............. Kings Norton Mint [*British*]
KN.............. Kitting Notice [*NASA*] (NASA)
KN.............. Klamath Northern Railway Co. [*Later, KNOR*] [*AAR code*]
Kn.............. Knapp's Privy Council Appeal Cases [*1829-36*] [*England*]
               [*A publication*] (DLA)
kn.............. Knee
KN.............. Knight (ABBR)
KN.............. Knot
KN.............. Known
kn.............. Known (VRA)
KN.............. Know-Nothing [*American political party, 1855-60*]
Kn.............. Knudsen Number [*IUPAC*]
KN.............. Kol Nidre (BJA)
kn.............. Korea, North [*MARC country of publication code Library of
               Congress*] (LCCP)
KN.............. Krone (ABBR)
KN.............. Kronen (ABBR)
KN.............. KSC [*Kennedy Space Center*] Notice [*NASA*] (NASA)
KN.............. St. Christopher-Nevis [*ANSI two-letter standard code*] (CNC)
KN.............. Temsco Airlines [*ICAO designator*] (AD)
KNA............ Katholische Nachrichten-Agentur [*Catholic Press Agency*] [*Germany*]
KNA............ Kenar Resources [*Vancouver Stock Exchange symbol*]
KNA............ Kenya News Agency
KNA............ Kex National Association (EA)
KNA............ Killed; Not Enemy Action [*Military*]
KNA............ Knight Air Ltd. [*Canada ICAO designator*] (FAAC)
KNA............ Knogo North America [*AMEX symbol*] (TTSB)
KNA............ Knogo North America, Inc. [*AMEX symbol*] (SAG)
KNA............ Korean National Airlines
KNA............ Korean National Association (EA)
KNA............ Kuki National Assembly [*India*] [*Political party*] (PPW)
KNA............ Kununurra [*Australia Seismograph station code, US Geological
               Survey*] (SEIS)
KNA............ St. Christopher-Nevis [*ANSI three-letter standard code*] (CNC)
KNAA-FM .... Show Low, AZ [*FM radio station call letters*] (BROA)
KNAB.......... Albany/Albany Naval Air Station [*Georgia*] [*ICAO location identifier*]
               (ICLI)
KNAB.......... Burlington, CO [*AM radio station call letters*]
KNAB-FM .... Burlington, CO [*FM radio station call letters*]
KNAC.......... Earlimart, CA [*FM radio station call letters*] (RBYB)
Kn AC .... Knapp's Privy Council Appeal Cases [*1829-36*] [*England*]
               [*A publication*] (DLA)
KNAD-FM .... Page, AZ [*FM radio station call letters*] (BROA)
KNAF.......... Fredricksburg, TX [*AM radio station call letters*]
KNAI.......... Phoenix, AZ [*FM radio station call letters*]
KNAIR........ Kuehne & Nagel Air Cargo Ltd. [*British*]
KNAK.......... Delta, UT [*AM radio station call letters*]
KNAL.......... Victoria, TX [*AM radio station call letters*]
Kn & O ...... Knapp and Ombler's English Election Cases [*A publication*] (DLA)
Kn & Omb ... Knapp and Ombler's English Election Cases [*A publication*] (DLA)
KNAP.......... Knape & Vogt Manufacturing Co. [*NASDAQ symbol*] (NQ)
KNAP.......... Knape & Vogt Mfg [*NASDAQ symbol*] (TTSB)
KNAP.......... Knapwell [*England*]
KnapeV........ Knape & Vogt Manufacturing Co. [*Associated Press*] (SAG)
Knapp........ Knapp's Privy Council Reports [*England*] [*A publication*] (DLA)
Knapp & O... Knapp and Ombler's English Election Cases [*A publication*] (DLA)
KNAQ.......... Flagstaff, AZ [*FM radio station call letters*] (RBYB)
KNAS.......... Kenya National Academy of Arts and Sciences (BUAC)
KNAS.......... Nashville, AR [*FM radio station call letters*]
KNAT.......... Albuquerque, NM [*Television station call letters*]
KNAU.......... Flagstaff, AZ [*FM radio station call letters*]
KNAX.......... Fresno, CA [*FM radio station call letters*]
KNAZ.......... Flagstaff, AZ [*Television station call letters*]
KNB............ Kanab [*Utah*] [*Seismograph station code, US Geological Survey*]
               (SEIS)
KNB............ Kanab [*Utah*] [*Airport symbol*] (OAG)
KNB............ Kanab, UT [*Location identifier FAA*] (FAAL)
KNBA-FM .... Anchorage, AK [*FM radio station call letters*] (RBYB)
KNBC.......... Beaufort/Beaufort Marine Corps Air Station [*South Carolina*] [*ICAO
               location identifier*] (ICLI)
KNBC.......... Los Angeles, CA [*Television station call letters*]
KNBE.......... Dallas/Hensley Field Naval Air Station [*Texas*] [*ICAO location
               identifier*] (ICLI)
KNBG.......... New Orleans/Alvin Callender Naval Air Station [*Louisiana*] [*ICAO
               location identifier*] (ICLI)
KNBJ........... Bemidji, MN [*FM radio station call letters*]

KNBL .... Knife Blade
KNBO .... New Boston, TX [*AM radio station call letters*]
KNBR .... Knobbier (ABBR)
KNBR .... San Francisco, CA [*AM radio station call letters*]
KNBR-FM .... Haltom City, TX [*FM radio station call letters*] (RBYB)
KNBST .... Knobbiest (ABBR)
KNBT .... New Braunfels, TX [*FM radio station call letters*]
KNBU .... Baldwin City, KS [*FM radio station call letters*]
KNBW .... Kirin Brewery Co. Ltd. [*NASDAQ symbol*] (NQ)
KNBWY ...... Kirin Brewery ADS [*NASDAQ symbol*] (TTSB)
KNBY .... Knobby (ABBR)
KNBY .... Newport, AR [*AM radio station call letters*]
KNBZ-FM .... Redfield, SD [*FM radio station call letters*] (BROA)
KNC .... Canadian Crew Energy [*Vancouver Stock Exchange symbol*]
KNC .... Kamerun National Congress
KNC .... Kansas Newman College [*Formerly, Sacred Heart College*] [*Wichita*]
KNC .... Karenni National Council [*Burma*] (BUAC)
KNC .... Kingcome Navigation [*AAR code*]
KNCA .... Burney, CA [*FM radio station call letters*]
KNCA .... Jacksonville/New River Marine Corps Air Station [*North Carolina*]
               [*ICAO location identifier*] (ICLI)
KNCB .... Vivian, LA [*AM radio station call letters*]
KNCB-FM .... Vivian, LA [*FM radio station call letters*]
KNCC .... Elko, NV [*FM radio station call letters*]
KNCCI .... Kenya National Chamber of Commerce and Industry (BUAC)
KNCI .... Kinetic Concepts [*NASDAQ symbol*] (TTSB)
KNCI .... Kinetic Concepts, Inc. [*NASDAQ symbol*] (NQ)
KNCI .... Sacramento, CA [*FM radio station call letters*]
KNCIAWPRC... Korean National Committee of the International Association on
               Water Pollution Research and Control (EAIO)
KNCIAWPRC... Kuwaiti National Committee of the International Association on
               Water Pollution Research and Control (EAIO)
Kn Civ Proc... Knox on Civil Procedure in India [*A publication*] (DLA)
KNCK .... Concordia, KS [*AM radio station call letters*]
KNCK-AM .... Concordia, KS [*AM radio station call letters*] (BROA)
KNCKBT .... Knockabout (ABBR)
KNCKDN ...... Knockdown (ABBR)
KNCKKN .... Knock-knee (ABBR)
KNCKOT .... Knockout (ABBR)
KNCKR .... Knocker (ABBR)
KNCM-FM .... Appleton, MN [*FM radio station call letters*] (RBYB)
KNCN .... Sinton, TX [*FM radio station call letters*]
KNCO .... Grass Valley, CA [*AM radio station call letters*]
KNCO .... Quonset Point/Quonset Point Naval Air Station [*Rhode Island*] [*ICAO
               location identifier*] (ICLI)
KNCO-FM .... Grass Valley, CA [*FM radio station call letters*]
KNCQ .... Redding, CA [*FM radio station call letters*]
KNCR .... Paso Robles, CA [*FM radio station call letters*] (RBYB)
Kn Cr Law ... Knox on Bengal Criminal Law [*A publication*] (DLA)
KNCT .... Belton, TX [*Television station call letters*]
KNCT .... Killeen, TX [*FM radio station call letters*]
KnCtyL........ Kansas City Life Insurance [*Associated Press*] (SAG)
KNCY .... Nebraska City, NE [*AM radio station call letters*]
KNCY-FM .... Auburn, NE [*FM radio station call letters*] (RBYB)
KND .... Kindu [*Zaire*] [*Airport symbol*] (OAG)
KNDA .... Alice, TX [*FM radio station call letters*] (RBYB)
KNDC .... Hettinger, ND [*AM radio station call letters*]
KNDD .... Seattle, WA [*FM radio station call letters*]
KNDGTN ...... Kindergarten (ABBR)
KNDHTD ...... Kindhearted (ABBR)
KNDHTDNS... Kindheartedness (ABBR)
KNDI .... Honolulu, HI [*AM radio station call letters*]
KNDK .... Langdon, ND [*AM radio station call letters*]
KNDK-FM .... Langdon, ND [*FM radio station call letters*]
KNDL .... Kindle (ABBR)
KNDLD .... Kindled (ABBR)
KNDLES .... Kindless (ABBR)
KNDLG .... Kindling (ABBR)
KNDLIR........ Kindlier (ABBR)
KNDLNS....... Kindliness (ABBR)
KNDLST .... Kindliest (ABBR)
KNDLY........ Kindly (ABBR)
KNDN .... Farmington, NM [*AM radio station call letters*]
KNDNS........ Kindness (ABBR)
KNDO .... Karen National Defense Organization [*Burma*]
KNDO .... Yakima, WA [*Television station call letters*]
KNDP .... Kamerun National Democratic Party [*Later, UNC*]
KNDR .... Kinder (ABBR)
KNDR .... Mandan, ND [*FM radio station call letters*]
KNDRD .... Kindred (ABBR)
KNDRG .... Kindergarten (ABBR)
KNDRGR ...... Kindergartener (ABBR)
KndrCr........ Kinder-Care Learning Centers, Inc. [*Associated Press*] (SAG)
KndrLr........ Kinder-Care Learning Centers, Inc. [*Associated Press*] (SAG)
KNDST........ Kindest (ABBR)
KNDU .... Richland, WA [*Television station call letters*]
KNDY .... Kindly (ABBR)
KNDY .... Marysville, KS [*AM radio station call letters*]
KNDY-FM.... Marysville, KS [*FM radio station call letters*]
KNE .... KN Energy [*NYSE symbol*] (TTSB)
KNE .... KN Energy, Inc. [*NYSE symbol*] (SPSG)
KNE............ Knie Resources, Inc. [*Vancouver Stock Exchange symbol*]
KNEA .... Brunswick/Glynco Naval Air Station [*Georgia*] [*ICAO location
               identifier*] (ICLI)
KNEA .... Jonesboro, AR [*AM radio station call letters*]

KNEB .... Scottsbluff, NE [*AM radio station call letters*]
KNEB-FM .... Scottsbluff, NE [*FM radio station call letters*]
KNEB-TV ..... Ketchikan, AK [*Television station call letters*] (RBYB)
KNECP .... Kneecap (ABBR)
KNED .... Knife Edge
KNED .... McAlester, OK [*AM radio station call letters*]
KNEDP .... Kneedeep (ABBR)
KNEI .... Waukon, IA [*AM radio station call letters*]
KNEI-FM ..... Waukon, IA [*FM radio station call letters*]
KNEK .... Washington, LA [*AM radio station call letters*]
KNEK-FM .... Washington, LA [*FM radio station call letters*]
KNEL........... Brady, TX [*AM radio station call letters*]
KNEL........... Lakehurst/Lakehurst Naval Air Station [*New Jersey*] [*ICAO location identifier*] (ICLI)
KNEL-FM .... Brady, TX [*FM radio station call letters*] (RBYB)
KNELG .... Kneeling (ABBR)
KNELR .... Kneller (ABBR)
KNEM.......... Nevada, MO [*AM radio station call letters*]
KNEN .... Norfolk, NE [*FM radio station call letters*]
KN Engy...... KN Energy, Inc. [*Associated Press*] (SAG)
KNEO .... Neosho, MO [*FM radio station call letters*]
KNeo........... W. A. Rankin Memorial Library, Neodesha, KS [*Library symbol Library of Congress*] (LCLS)
KNES .... Fairfield, TX [*FM radio station call letters*]
KNET .... Palestine, TX [*AM radio station call letters*]
KNET-FM .... Lincoln, NE [*FM radio station call letters*] (RBYB)
KNEU .... Roosevelt, UT [*AM radio station call letters*]
KNEV .... Reno, NV [*FM radio station call letters*]
KNEW .... New Orleans [*Louisiana*] [*ICAO location identifier*] (ICLI)
KNEW .... Oakland, CA [*AM radio station call letters*]
KNEX-FM .... Laredo, TX [*FM radio station call letters*] (BROA)
KNEZ-AM .... Creedmoor, TX [*AM radio station call letters*] (BROA)
KNF............. Klein-Nishina Formula [*Physics*]
KNF............. Knife (ABBR)
KNFC .... Kenya National Federation of Cooperatives (BUAC)
KNFD .... Knifed (ABBR)
KNFG .... Knifing (ABBR)
KNFL........... Tremonton, UT [*AM radio station call letters*]
KNFL-FM ..... Tremonton, UT [*FM radio station call letters*]
KNFLK .... Kinfolk (ABBR)
KNFLK .... Knifelike (ABBR)
KNFM.......... Midland, TX [*FM radio station call letters*]
KNFO .... Basalt, CO [*FM radio station call letters*] (RBYB)
KNFP .... Kellogg National Fellowship Program
KNFR .... Opportunity, WA [*FM radio station call letters*]
KNFT........... Bayard, NM [*AM radio station call letters*]
KNFT-FM ..... Bayard, NM [*FM radio station call letters*]
KNFX........... Austin, MN [*AM radio station call letters*]
KNFX-FM .... Spring Valley, MN [*FM radio station call letters*]
KNG .... Kaimana [*Indonesia*] [*Airport symbol*] (OAG)
KNG .... Kaliningrad [*Former USSR Geomagnetic observatory code*]
KNG .... King Aviation [*British ICAO designator*] (FAAC)
KNG .... Kininogen (DMAA)
KNG .... Konigsberg [*Kaliningrad*] [*Former USSR Seismograph station code, US Geological Survey Closed*] (SEIS)
KNGA.......... St. Peter, MN [*FM radio station call letters*]
KNGDM........ Kingdom (ABBR)
KNGDM........ Kinhdom
KNGFSH....... Kingfish (ABBR)
KNGFSHR...... Kingfisher (ABBR)
KNGHT......... Knight
KnghtR........ Knight Ridder, Inc. [*Associated Press*] (SAG)
KNGL .... McPherson, KS [*AM radio station call letters*]
KNGLNS....... Kingliness (ABBR)
KNGLR .... Kinglier (ABBR)
KNGLST....... Kingliest (ABBR)
KNGLY .... Kingly (ABBR)
KNGM.......... Emporia, KS [*FM radio station call letters*]
KNGN.......... McCook, NE [*AM radio station call letters*]
KNGP.......... Corpus Christi/Corpus Christi Naval Air Station [*Texas*] [*ICAO location identifier*] (ICLI)
KNGPN......... Kingpin (ABBR)
KNGR.......... Kangaroo (ABBR)
KNGS .... Coalinga, CA [*FM radio station call letters*]
KngsRd........ Kings Road Entertainment, Inc. [*Associated Press*] (SAG)
KNGSZ .... Kingsize (ABBR)
KNGT .... Jackson, CA [*FM radio station call letters*]
KNGT .... Knight (ABBR)
KNGT .... Knight Transportation [*NASDAQ symbol*] (SAG)
KNGTHD....... Knighthood (ABBR)
KNGTLY .... Knightly (ABBR)
KNGT-RNT ... Knight-Errant (ABBR)
KNGU.......... Norfolk/Norfolk Naval Air Station [*Virginia*] [*ICAO location identifier*] (ICLI)
KNGY .... Kingly (ABBR)
KNGZ .... Alameda/Alameda Naval Air Station [*California*] [*ICAO location identifier*] (ICLI)
KNH .... Kipuka Nene [*Hawaii*] [*Seismograph station code, US Geological Survey*] (SEIS)
KNHC .... Seattle, WA [*FM radio station call letters*]
KNHD-AM .... Camden, AR [*AM radio station call letters*] (BROA)
KNHK .... Patuxent River/Patuxent River Naval Air Station [*Maryland*] [*ICAO location identifier*] (ICLI)
KNHN .... Kansas City, KS [*AM radio station call letters*]
KNHT .... Knight (ABBR)

KNHZ .... Brunswick/Brunswick Naval Air Station [*Maryland*] [*ICAO location identifier*] (ICLI)
KNI.............. Kalallit Niuerfiat [*Greenland Trade*] (EY)
KNI.............. Kantorberita Nasional Indonesia [*News service*] [*Indonesia*] (EY)
KNI.............. Katmai New Instructions [*Computer science*]
KNI.............. Koyna Nagar [*India*] [*Seismograph station code, US Geological Survey Closed*] (SEIS)
KNI.............. Kyodo News International, Inc. [*Information service or system*] (IID)
KNIA .... Knoxville, IA [*AM radio station call letters*]
KNIC .... [*The*] Knickerbocker [*L.L.*] Company, Inc. [*NASDAQ symbol*] (SAG)
Knick .... [*The*] Knickerbocker [*L.L.*] Co., Inc. [*Associated Press*] (SAG)
KnickL .... [*The*] Knickerbocker [*L. L.*] Company, Inc. [*Associated Press*] (SAG)
KNID .... Enid, OK [*FM radio station call letters*]
Knight Mech Dict... Knight's American Mechanical Dictionary [*A publication*] (DLA)
Knight's Ind... Knight's Industrial Reports [*A publication*] (DLA)
KnightTr..... Knight Transportation [*Associated Press*] (SAG)
KNIK .... Anchorage, AK [*FM radio station call letters*]
KNIL........... Koninklijk Nederlandsch-Indisch Leger [*Royal Dutch Indies Army*]
KNIM .... Maryville, MO [*AM radio station call letters*]
KNIM-FM ..... Maryville, MO [*FM radio station call letters*]
KNIN-FM ..... Wichita Falls, TX [*FM radio station call letters*]
KNIN-TV...... Caldwell, ID [*TV station call letters*] (RBYB)
KNIP .... Jacksonville/Jacksonville Naval Air Station [*Florida*] [*ICAO location identifier*] (ICLI)
KNIR .... Beeville/Chase Field Naval Air Station [*Texas*] [*ICAO location identifier*] (ICLI)
KNIR .... New Iberia, LA [*AM radio station call letters*]
KNIS .... Carson City, NV [*FM radio station call letters*]
KNIT........... Techknits, Inc. [*NASDAQ symbol*] (SAG)
KNITG .... Knitting (ABBR)
KNITR .... Knitter (ABBR)
KNIX .... Phoenix, AZ [*FM radio station call letters*]
KNJ .... Kindamba [*Congo*] [*Airport symbol*] (OAG)
KNJK .... El Centro Naval Air Station [*California*] [*ICAO location identifier*] (ICLI)
KNJO .... Thousand Oaks, CA [*FM radio station call letters*]
KNJP........... Sargent, NE [*FM radio station call letters*]
KNJU .... Raton, NM [*FM radio station call letters*]
KNJY .... Spokane, WA [*FM radio station call letters*]
KNJZ .... Alton, IL [*FM radio station call letters*]
KNK .... Kakhonak [*Alaska*] [*Airport symbol*] (OAG)
KNK .... Kankakee Bancorp [*AMEX symbol*] (TTSB)
KNK .... Kankakee Bancorp, Inc. [*AMEX symbol*] (SAG)
KNK .... Knik Glacier [*Alaska*] [*Seismograph station code, US Geological Survey*] (SEIS)
KNKA .... Kansas City [*Missouri*] [*ICAO location identifier*] (ICLI)
KNKE .... Jasper, TX [*FM radio station call letters*]
KNKI-FM ..... Sherman, TX [*FM radio station call letters*] (BROA)
KNKK-FM .... Needles, CA [*FM radio station call letters*] (BROA)
KNKL .... Knuckle (ABBR)
KNKLD .... Knuckled (ABBR)
KNKLG .... Knuckling (ABBR)
KNKN .... Pueblo, CO [*FM radio station call letters*]
KNKR .... Kinkier (ABBR)
KNKRS......... Knickers (ABBR)
KNKST .... Kinkiest (ABBR)
KNKT .... Armijo, NM [*FM radio station call letters*] (RBYB)
KNKT .... Cherry Point Marine Corps Air Station [*North Carolina*] [*ICAO location identifier*] (ICLI)
KNKX .... Miramar Naval Air Station [*California*] [*ICAO location identifier*] (ICLI)
KNL .... Centaur Resources Ltd. [*Vancouver Stock Exchange symbol*]
KNL .... Darrow's Solution [*For antidiarrhea potassium therapy*] (DAVI)
KNL .... Keller, N. L., Washington DC [*STAC*]
KNL .... Kennel (ABBR)
KNL .... Knight of the Netherlands Lion
KNL .... Knoll (ABBR)
KNLA .... Karen National Liberation Army [*Myanmar*] [*Political party*]
KNLA .... White Rock, NM [*FM radio station call letters*]
KNLB .... Lake Havasu City, AZ [*FM radio station call letters*]
KNLC .... Hanford/Lemoore Naval Air Station [*California*] [*ICAO location identifier*] (ICLI)
KNLC .... St. Louis, MO [*Television station call letters*]
KNLD .... Duluth, MN [*Television station call letters*]
KNLD .... Kenneled (ABBR)
KNLE .... Round Rock, TX [*FM radio station call letters*]
KNLF .... Karen National Liberation Front [*Myanmar*] [*Political party*] (PD)
KNLF .... Quincy, CA [*FM radio station call letters*]
KNLG .... Kenneling (ABBR)
Kn LGR........ Knight's Local Government Reports [*A publication*] (DLA)
KNLH-FM ..... Cedar Hill, MO [*FM radio station call letters*] (BROA)
KNLJ .... Jefferson City, MO [*Television station call letters*]
KNLM-FM ..... Marshfield, MO [*FM radio station call letters*] (BROA)
KNLP-FM ..... Potosi, MO [*FM radio station call letters*] (BROA)
KNLR .... Bend, OR [*FM radio station call letters*]
KNLS .... Kenya National Library Service (BUAC)
KNLS .... Knolls (MCD)
KNLT .... Walla Walla, WA [*FM radio station call letters*]
KNLU .... Monroe, LA [*FM radio station call letters*]
KNLV .... Ord, NE [*AM radio station call letters*]
KNLV-FM ..... Ord, NE [*FM radio station call letters*]
KNM........... Keene State College, Keene, NH [*OCLC symbol*] (OCLC)
KNM........... Kenya National Museum
KNM........... Mennonite Historical Society, Newton, KS [*Library symbol Library of Congress*] (LCLS)
KNMA-FM .... Reserve, NM [*FM radio station call letters*] (BROA)

KNMC .... Havre, MT [*FM radio station call letters*]

KNME.......... Albuquerque, NM [*Television station call letters*]

KNMH .... Coast Guard Station, Washington [*District of Columbia*] [*ICAO location identifier*] (ICLI)

KNMI .... Farmington, NM [*FM radio station call letters*]

KNML-AM .... Los Ranchos de Albuquerque, NM [*AM radio station call letters*] (RBYB)

KNMO .... Nevada, MO [*FM radio station call letters*]

KNMT.......... Portland, OR [*Television station call letters*]

KNMTCS ...... Kinematics

KNMX .... Las Vegas, NM [*AM radio station call letters*]

KNMZ-FM .... Alamogordo, NM [*FM radio station call letters*] (RBYB)

KNN .... Kankan [*Guinea*] [*Airport symbol*] (AD)

KNN .... Kenton Natural Resources Corp. [*Vancouver Stock Exchange symbol*]

KNN .... K-Nearest-Neighbor [*Algorithm*]

KNnB .... Bethel College, North Newton, KS [*Library symbol Library of Congress*] (LCLS)

KNNB .... Whiteriver, AZ [*FM radio station call letters*]

KNNC .... Georgetown, TX [*FM radio station call letters*]

KNND .... Cottage Grove, OR [*AM radio station call letters*]

KNNG .... Sterling, CO [*FM radio station call letters*]

KNNK-FM .... Dimmitt, TX [*FM radio station call letters*] (RBYB)

KNNN .... Central Valley, CA [*FM radio station call letters*]

KNNS .... Beverly Hills, CA [*AM radio station call letters*] (RBYB)

Kn NSW ...... Knox's New South Wales Reports [*A publication*] (DLA)

KNNZ .... Costa Mesa, CA [*AM radio station call letters*] (RBYB)

KNO .... Kano, Nigeria [*Remote site*] [*NASA*] (NASA)

KNO .... Keep Needle Open [*Reference to intravenous fluid lines*] (DAVI)

KNO .... Kennedy Space Center Notice (NAKS)

KNO .... Knox Ranch [*California*] [*Seismograph station code, US Geological Survey Closed*] (SEIS)

KNO .... Koch, Neff, Oetlinger [*Germany*] (NITA)

KNO .... Korrespondenzblatt der Nachrichtenstelle fuer den Orient [*A publication*] (BJA)

KNOB .... San Rafael, CA [*AM radio station call letters*] (RBYB)

KNOBS .... Knowledge-Based System

KNOC .... Natchitoches, LA [*AM radio station call letters*]

KNOD .... Harlan, IA [*FM radio station call letters*]

KNOE .... Monroe, LA [*AM radio station call letters*]

KNOE-FM .... Monroe, LA [*FM radio station call letters*]

KNOE-TV .... Monroe, LA [*Television station call letters*]

KNOF .... St. Paul, MN [*FM radio station call letters*]

KNOG-FM .... Nogales, AZ [*FM radio station call letters*] (RBYB)

KnogNA........ Knogo North America, Inc. [*Associated Press*] (SAG)

KNOL .... Knoll [*Commonly used*] (OPSA)

KNOLL .... Knoll [*Commonly used*] (OPSA)

KNOLLS .... Knolls [*Commonly used*] (OPSA)

KNOM .... Nome, AK [*AM radio station call letters*]

KNOM-FM .... Nome, AK [*FM radio station call letters*]

KNON .... Dallas, TX [*FM radio station call letters*]

KNOP .... North Platte, NE [*Television station call letters*]

KNOR .... Klamath Northern Railway Co. [*AAR code*]

KNOR .... Norman, OK [*AM radio station call letters*]

knork .... Knife and Fork [*Pharmacology*] (DAVI)

KNOS .... Albuquerque, NM [*AM radio station call letters*] (RBYB)

KNOS-FM .... Omaha, NE [*AM radio station call letters*] (RBYB)

KNoSH .... Norton State Hospital, Norton, KS [*Library symbol Library of Congress*] (LCLS)

KNOT .... Prescott, AZ [*AM radio station call letters*]

KNOT-FM .... Prescott, AZ [*FM radio station call letters*]

Know .... Knowledge [*Record label*]

KNOW .... Port Angeles Coast Guard Air Station [*Washington*] [*ICAO location identifier*] (ICLI)

KNOW-FM .... Minneapolis-St. Paul, MN [*FM radio station call letters*]

Knowles........ Knowles' Reports [*3 Rhode Island*] [*A publication*] (DLA)

KNOWLT ...... Knowlton [*England*]

KNOW-NET... Knowledege Network of Washington (EDAC)

KNOX .... Grand Forks, ND [*AM radio station call letters*]

Knox .... Knox's New South Wales Reports [*A publication*] (DLA)

Knox & F ...... Knox and Fitzhardinge's New South Wales Reports [*A publication*] (DLA)

KNOX-FM .... Grand Forks, ND [*FM radio station call letters*]

KNOZ .... Cameron, MO [*FM radio station call letters*]

KNP .... Katholieke Nationale Partij [*Catholic National Party*] [*Netherlands Political party*] (PPE)

KNP .... Katholisch Nederlands Persbureau [*Catholic Netherlands Press Agency*] [*Netherlands*]

KNP .... Kinetics of Nonhomogeneous Processes

KNP .... King's Knight's Pawn [*Chess*] (BARN)

KNP .... Korea National Party [*South Korea Political party*] (PPW)

KNP .... Koshkonong Nuclear Plant (NRCH)

KNPA .... Pensacola/Pensacola Naval Air Station [*Florida*] [*ICAO location identifier*] (ICLI)

KNPB .... Reno, NV [*Television station call letters*]

Kn PC .... Knapp's Privy Council Appeal Cases [*1829-36*] [*England*] [*A publication*] (DLA)

KNPC .... Korea National Party [*Political party*] (BUAC)

KNPC .... Kuwait National Petroleum Co.

KNPI .... Kundu's Neurotic Personality Inventory [*Psychology*]

KNPP .... Karenni National Progressive Party [*Myanmar*] [*Political party*] (EY)

KNPP .... Kewaunee Nuclear Power Plant (NRCH)

KNPR .... Las Vegas, NV [*FM radio station call letters*]

KNPSK .... Knapsack (ABBR)

KNPT .... Newport, OR [*AM radio station call letters*]

KNQ .... Kone [*New Caledonia*] [*Airport symbol Obsolete*] (OAG)

KNQI .... Kingsville Naval Air Station [*Texas*] [*ICAO location identifier*] (ICLI)

KNQX .... Key West/Key West Naval Air Station [*Florida*] [*ICAO location identifier*] (ICLI)

KNR .... Kalaallit Nunaata Radioa [*Greenland*] (EY)

KNR .... Kidnap and Ransom [*Insurance terminology*]

KNR .... King's National Roll

KNR .... Klamath Northern Railway (MHDW)

KNR .... Korean National Railroad (DCTA)

KNRB .... Mayport/Mayport Naval Station [*Florida*] [*ICAO location identifier*] (ICLI)

KNRC .... Reno, NV [*AM radio station call letters*] (RBYB)

KNRK .... Camas, WA [*FM radio station call letters*] (RBYB)

KNRK .... Kirsten Sarcoma Virus in Normal Rat Kidney [*Medicine*] (DMAA)

KNRL .... Kernel (ABBR)

KNRL .... Knurl [*Engineering*]

KNRO .... Redding, CA [*AM radio station call letters*]

KNRQ .... Springfield, OR [*AM radio station call letters*] (RBYB)

KNRQ-FM .... Creswell, OR [*FM radio station call letters*] (RBYB)

KNRR .... Pembina, ND [*Television station call letters*]

KNRV-FM .... Harker Heights, TX [*FM radio station call letters*] (RBYB)

KNRX .... Castle Rock, CO [*FM radio station call letters*] (RBYB)

KNRX-FM .... Oklahoma City, OK [*FM radio station call letters*] (RBYB)

KNRY .... Monterey, CA [*AM radio station call letters*]

KNS .... Kazan [*Formerly, Kazanskaya*] [*Former USSR Geomagnetic observatory code*]

KNS .... Kenuz Airlines Ltd. [*Nigeria*] [*ICAO designator*] (FAAC)

KNS .... King Island [*Tasmania*] [*Airport symbol*] (OAG)

KNS .... Knight of [*the Order of*] the Royal Northern Star [*Sweden*]

KNSA .... Unalakleet, AK [*AM radio station call letters*]

KNSCP .... Kinescope (ABBR)

KNSD .... San Diego, CA [*Television station call letters*]

KNSE .... Ontario, CA [*AM radio station call letters*]

KNSF .... Washington Naval Air Facility [*District of Columbia*] [*ICAO location identifier*] (ICLI)

KNSG .... Springfield, MN [*FM radio station call letters*] (RBYB)

KNSHP .... Kinship (ABBR)

KNSI .... San Nicolas Island/San Nicolas Auxiliary Air Base [*California*] [*ICAO location identifier*] (ICLI)

KNSI .... St. Cloud, MN [*AM radio station call letters*]

KNSMN .... Kinsman (ABBR)

KNSN .... Chico, CA [*AM radio station call letters*] (RBYB)

KNSO .... Merced, CA [*Television station call letters*]

KNSP .... Staples, MN [*AM radio station call letters*]

KNSP-FM .... Staples, MN [*FM radio station call letters*]

KNSQ .... Mount Shasta, CA [*FM radio station call letters*]

KNSR .... Collegeville, MN [*FM radio station call letters*]

KNSS .... Wichita, KS [*AM radio station call letters*]

KNST .... Tucson, AZ [*AM radio station call letters*]

KNSU .... Thibodaux, LA [*FM radio station call letters*]

KNSW .... Knife Switch

KNSWMN ...... Kinswoman (ABBR)

KNSX-FM .... Steelville, MO [*FM radio station call letters*] (BROA)

KNSY .... Kensey Nash [*NASDAQ symbol*] (TTSB)

KNSY .... Kensey Nash Corp. [*NASDAQ symbol*] (SAG)

KNT .... Kent Electronics [*NYSE symbol*] (TTSB)

KNT .... Kent Electronics Corp. [*NYSE symbol*] (SPSG)

KNT .... Knight [*British title*]

KNT .... Knightway Air Charter Ltd. [*British ICAO designator*] (FAAC)

KNT .... Knitting

KNT .... Sanandaj [*Iran*] [*Airport symbol*] (AD)

KNTA .... Santa Clara, CA [*AM radio station call letters*]

KNTB .... Los Alamitos/Los Alamitos Naval Air Station [*California*] [*ICAO location identifier*] (ICLI)

KNTB-FM .... Lakewood, WA [*FM radio station call letters*] (RBYB)

KNTC .... Kenya National Trading Corp. (BUAC)

KNTC .... Kinetic (ABBR)

KNTC .... Korea National Tourism Corp. (BUAC)

KntckyEl...... Kentucky Electric Steel Co. [*Associated Press*] (SAG)

KNTD .... Knotted (ABBR)

KNTD .... Point Mugu Naval Air Station [*California*] [*ICAO location identifier*] (ICLI)

KNTE .... Lakewood, WA [*AM radio station call letters*]

KNTG .... Knotting (ABBR)

KNTHL .... Knothole (ABBR)

KNTI .... Lakeport, CA [*FM radio station call letters*]

KNTK .... Kentek Information Sys [*NASDAQ symbol*] (TTSB)

KNTK .... Kentek Information Systems, Inc. [*NASDAQ symbol*] (SAG)

KNTL .... Bethany, OK [*FM radio station call letters*]

KNTLK .... Knotlike (ABBR)

KNTLS .... Knotless (ABBR)

KNTN .... Thief River Falls, MN [*FM radio station call letters*]

KNTO .... Livingston, CA [*FM radio station call letters*]

KNTR .... Ferndale, WA [*AM radio station call letters*]

KNTS .... Abilene, TX [*AM radio station call letters*]

KNTTD .... Knitted

KNTU .... Denton, TX [*FM radio station call letters*]

KNTU .... Virginia Beach/Oceana Naval Air Station [*Virginia*] [*ICAO location identifier*] (ICLI)

KNTV .... San Jose, CA [*Television station call letters*]

KNTWR .... Knitwear

KNTY .... Knotty (ABBR)

KNU .... Kanpur [*India*] [*Airport symbol*] (OAG)

KNU .... Karen National Union [*Myanmar*] (PD)

KNU .... Knuckle [*Automotive engineering*]

KNUC.......... Smithfield, UT [*FM radio station call letters*]
KNUE .... Tyler, TX [*FM radio station call letters*]
KNUFNS...... Kampuchean National United Front for National Salvation (PD)
KNUI .... Kahului, HI [*AM radio station call letters*]
KNUI-FM...... Kahului, HI [*FM radio station call letters*]
KNUJ .... New Ulm, MN [*AM radio station call letters*]
KNUJ .... Sleepy Eye, MN [*FM radio station call letters*]
KNUP .... Karen National Unity Party [*Burma*]
KNUQ .... Mountain View/Moffett Naval Air Station [*California*] [*ICAO location identifier*] (ICLI)
KNUQ-FM .... Paauilo, HI [*FM radio station call letters*] (RBYB)
KNUS .... Denver, CO [*AM radio station call letters*]
KNUU .... Paradise, NV [*AM radio station call letters*]
KNUW .... Whidbey Island/Whidbey Island Naval Air Station [*Washington*] [*ICAO location identifier*] (ICLI)
KNUW-FM.... Central, NM [*FM radio station call letters*] (RBYB)
KNUZ .... Houston, TX [*AM radio station call letters*]
KNUZ Exp Stn... Houston, TX [*Radio expansion station*]
KNV .... Knave (ABBR)
KNVA .... Austin, TX [*Television station call letters*]
KNVC .... Consolidated Nevada Goldfields Corp. [*NASDAQ symbol*] (SAG)
KNVCF .... Consolidated Nev Goldfields [*NASDAQ symbol*] (TTSB)
KNVH .... Knavish (ABBR)
KNVHLY ...... Knavishly (ABBR)
KNVO .... McAllen, TX [*Television station call letters*]
KNVRY .... Knavery (ABBR)
KNW .... Konawaena [*Hawaii*] [*Seismograph station code, US Geological Survey Closed*] (SEIS)
KNW .... New Stuyahok [*Alaska*] [*Airport symbol*] (OAG)
KNWA .... Bellefonte, AR [*AM radio station call letters*]
KNWB .... Hilo, HI [*FM radio station call letters*] (RBYB)
KNWB .... Knowable (ABBR)
KNWC .... Sioux Falls, SD [*AM radio station call letters*]
KNWC-FM..... Sioux Falls, SD [*FM radio station call letters*]
KNWD .... Natchitoches, LA [*FM radio station call letters*]
KNWDV........ Knickerbocker L L Wrrt [*NASDAQ symbol*] (TTSB)
KNWG .... Knowing (ABBR)
KNWGNS ..... Knowingness (ABBR)
KNWGY .... Knowingly (ABBR)
KNWHW ...... Know-How (ABBR)
KNWL .... Knowledge (ABBR)
KNWLB .... Knowledgeable (ABBR)
KNWLDG...... Knowledge (ABBR)
KNWLDGB .. Knowledgeable (ABBR)
KNWNTHG ... Know-Nothing (ABBR)
KNWO .... Cottonwood, ID [*FM radio station call letters*]
KNWR .... Ellensburg, WA [*FM radio station call letters*] (RBYB)
KNWR .... Knower (ABBR)
KNWS .... Waterloo, IA [*AM radio station call letters*]
KNWS-FM.... Waterloo, IA [*FM radio station call letters*]
KNWS-TV...... Katy, TX [*Television station call letters*]
KNWV-FM.... Clarkston, WA [*FM radio station call letters*] (RBYB)
KNWX .... Seattle, WA [*AM radio station call letters*] (RBYB)
KNWY .... Yakima, WA [*FM radio station call letters*]
KNWZ .... Thousand Palms, CA [*AM radio station call letters*]
KNWZ-FM.... Yucca Valley, CA [*FM radio station call letters*]
KNX .... Knighthawk Air Express Ltd. [*Canada ICAO designator*] (FAAC)
KNX .... Knoxville [*Diocesan abbreviation*] [*Tennessee*] (TOCD)
KNX .... Kununurra [*Australia Airport symbol*] (OAG)
KNX .... Los Angeles, CA [*AM radio station call letters*]
KNXN .... Sierra Vista, AZ [*AM radio station call letters*]
KNXR .... Rochester, MN [*FM radio station call letters*]
KNXT .... Visalia, CA [*Television station call letters*]
KNXV .... Knoxville [*Tennessee*] (ABBR)
KNXV .... Phoenix, AZ [*Television station call letters*]
KNXX .... Willow Grove/Willow Grove Naval Air Station [*Pennsylvania*] [*ICAO location identifier*] (ICLI)
KNY .... Kanoya [*Japan*] [*Geomagnetic observatory code*]
KNY .... Kenergy Resource Corp. [*Vancouver Stock Exchange symbol*]
KNYC .... New York (City) [*New York*] [*ICAO location identifier*] (ICLI)
KNYD .... Broken Arrow, OK [*FM radio station call letters*]
KNYL .... Yuma/Vincent Marine Corps Air Station [*Arizona*] [*ICAO location identifier*] (ICLI)
KNYN .... Santa Fe, NM [*FM radio station call letters*]
KNYZ .... Kanozan [*Japan*] [*Geomagnetic observatory code*]
KNZ .... Kenieba [*Mali*] [*Airport symbol*] (OAG)
KNZA .... Hiawatha, KS [*FM radio station call letters*]
KNZJ .... El Toro Marine Corps Air Station [*California*] [*ICAO location identifier*] (ICLI)
KNZR .... Bakersfield, CA [*AM radio station call letters*]
KNZS .... Montecito, CA [*AM radio station call letters*]
KNZW .... South Weymouth/South Weymouth Naval Air Station [*Massachusetts*] [*ICAO location identifier*] (ICLI)
KNZY .... San Diego/North Island Naval Air Station [*California*] [*ICAO location identifier*] (ICLI)
KNZZ .... Grand Junction, CO [*AM radio station call letters*]
Ko .... C. H. Boehringer Sohn, Ingelheim [*Germany*] [*Research code symbol*]
KO............ [*The*] Coca-Cola Co. [*NYSE symbol*] (SPSG)
KO............ Commanding Officer [*Military slang*]
KO............ Contracting Officer [*Also, CO, CONTRO*]
KO............ Kashrut Observance (BJA)
KO............ Kattoo [*Ship's rigging*] (ROG)
KO............ Keep Off [*i.e., avoid assuming the risk on an application, pending further investigation*] [*Insurance*]

KO............ Keep On [*Continue*] [*Medicine*] (DAVI)
K/O............ Keep Open [*Medicine*]
KO............ Kickoff (MSA)
KO............ Killarney Oscillation [*Climatology*]
KO............ Killed Organism [*Medicine*] (DMAA)
KO............ Kilogram (ROG)
KO............ Kilohm (ABBR)
KO............ King's Own [*Military unit*] [*British*]
KO............ Klystron Oscillator
KO............ Knee Orthosis [*Medicine*]
K/O............ Knocked Out [*To write or produce something quickly*] [*Also called knock off*] (WDMC)
KO............ Knockout [*Boxing*]
KO............ Knockout [*Partly cut out or loosened area which can be easily removed, as in a junction box*] [*Technical drawings*]
ko............ Knock Out [*Boxing*] (WA)
KO............ Kodiak-Western Alaska Airlines, Inc. [*CAB official abbreviation*]
ko............ Korea, South [*MARC country of publication code Library of Congress*] (LCCP)
KO............ Kraus-Thomson Organization [*Publisher*]
KOA............ Communications on Alternatives in Education [*Defunct*] (EA)
KOA............ Denver, CO [*AM radio station call letters*]
KOA............ Kailua-Kona, HI [*Location identifier FAA*] (FAAL)
KOA............ Kampground Owners Association [*Phoenix, AZ*] (EA)
KOA............ Kampgrounds of America
KOA............ Kentucky Optometric Association (SRA)
KOA............ Knocked-on-Atom
KOA............ Kobuan [*Solomon Islands*] [*Seismograph station code, US Geological Survey Closed*] (SEIS)
KOA............ Kona [*Hawaii*] [*Airport symbol*] (OAG)
KOA............ Kone Air Ltd. [*Finland ICAO designator*] (FAAC)
KOAA.......... Pueblo, CO [*Television station call letters*]
KOAB.......... Bend, OR [*FM radio station call letters*]
KOAB-TV..... Bend, OR [*Television station call letters*]
KOAC.......... Corvallis, OR [*AM radio station call letters*]
KOAC-TV...... Corvallis, OR [*Television station call letters*]
KOAI.......... Fort Worth, TX [*FM radio station call letters*]
KOAK.......... Oakland/Metropolitan Oakland International [*California*] [*ICAO location identifier*] (ICLI)
KOAK.......... Red Oak, IA [*AM radio station call letters*]
KOAL.......... Price, UT [*AM radio station call letters*]
KOALA.......... Keyfile Open Access Layer [*Workflow automation software*] (PCM)
Koala.......... Koala Corp. [*Associated Press*] (SAG)
KOAM.......... Korean-American Oil Co.
KOAM.......... Pittsburg, KS [*Television station call letters*]
KO & G.......... Kansas, Oklahoma & Gulf Railway Co.
KOAQ.......... Terrytown, NE [*AM radio station call letters*]
KOAS.......... Broken Arrow, OK [*FM radio station call letters*] (RBYB)
KOAT .... Albuquerque, NM [*Television station call letters*]
KOAZ-FM...... Glendale, AZ [*FM radio station call letters*] (RBYB)
KOB............ Albuquerque, NM [*Television station call letters*]
KOB............ King's Own Borderers [*British military*] (DMA)
KOB............ Kob Air Ltd. [*Uganda*] [*ICAO designator*] (FAAC)
KOB............ Kobe [*Japan*] [*Seismograph station code, US Geological Survey*] (SEIS)
KoB............ Koehler and Baumgartner Lexikon in Veteris Testamenti Libros [*Leiden*] [*A publication*] (BJA)
KOB............ Koutaba [*Cameroon*] [*Airport symbol*] (OAG)
KOB............ Kriegsoffizier-Bewerber [*Applicant for Wartime Commission*] [*German military - World War II*]
KOBB.......... Bozeman, MT [*AM radio station call letters*]
KOBC.......... Joplin, MO [*FM radio station call letters*]
KOBE.......... Las Cruces, NM [*AM radio station call letters*]
Kobe UL Rev... Kobe University. Law Review [*A publication*] (DLA)
KOBF.......... Farmington, NM [*Television station call letters*]
KOBI.......... Medford, OR [*Television station call letters*]
KOBN.......... Honolulu, HI [*Television station call letters*]
KOBO.......... Yuba City, CA [*AM radio station call letters*]
KOBOL.......... Keystation On-Line Business-Oriented Language [*Computer science*]
KOBR.......... Roswell, NM [*Television station call letters*]
Koc............ Coefficient of Organic Carbon Partition (GNE)
KOC............ Kathodal Opening Contraction [*Medicine*]
KOC............ Key Operational Capability [*Military*] (RDA)
KOC............ Knight of the [*Order of the*] Oak Crown
KOC............ Kochi [*Japan*] [*Seismograph station code, US Geological Survey*] (SEIS)
KOC............ Koumac [*New Caledonia*] [*Airport symbol*] (OAG)
KOC............ Kuwait Oil Co.
Koc .... Measure of Soil Absorption (GNE)
KOC............ Occupational and Environmental Health Unit, University of Toronto [*UTLAS symbol*]
KOC............ TCC Beverages Ltd. [*Toronto Stock Exchange symbol*]
KOCB.......... Oklahoma City, OK [*Television station call letters*]
KOCC.......... Oklahoma City, OK [*FM radio station call letters*]
KOCCCG...... Kunia Operations Control Center Coordination Group (CINC)
KOCD.......... Columbus, KS [*FM radio station call letters*]
KOCE.......... Huntington Beach, CA [*Television station call letters*]
KOCE.......... Komi Commodity Exchange [*Russian Federation*] (EY)
Koch............ Koch's Supreme Court Decisions [*Ceylon*] [*A publication*] (DLA)
KOCN.......... Pacific Grove, CA [*FM radio station call letters*]
KOCO.......... Korea Oil Corp.
KOCO.......... Oklahoma City, OK [*Television station call letters*]
KOCP.......... Camarillo, CA [*FM radio station call letters*] (RBYB)
KOCR-AM...... Joplin, MO [*AM radio station call letters*] (BROA)
KOCT.......... Carlsbad, NM [*Television station call letters*]

KOCV	Odessa, TX [*FM radio station call letters*]
KOCV-TV	Odessa, TX [*Television station call letters*]
KOCY-FM	Hoxie, AR [*FM radio station call letters*] (RBYB)
KO'd	Knocked Out [*Boxing*] (DAVI)
KOD	Kodaikanal [*India*] [*Geomagnetic observatory code*]
KOD	Kodaikanal [*India*] [*Seismograph station code, US Geological Survey*] (SEIS)
KODA	Houston, TX [*FM radio station call letters*]
KODC	Korea Oceanographic Data Center [*Marine science*] (OSRA)
KODCH	Kodachrome (VRA)
KODCO	Korean Overseas Development Co. [*Korean government agency*]
KODE	Joplin, MO [*Television station call letters*]
KODI	Cody, WY [*AM radio station call letters*]
KODJ	Salt Lake City, UT [*FM radio station call letters*]
KODL	The Dalles, OR [*AM radio station call letters*]
KODM	Odessa, TX [*FM radio station call letters*]
KODR	King's Overseas Dominions Regiment [*British military*] (DMA)
KODS	Carnelian Bay, CA [*FM radio station call letters*]
KODY	North Platte, NE [*AM radio station call letters*]
KODZ	Eugene, OR [*FM radio station call letters*]
KOE	Kilograms Oil Equivalent [*Petroleum industry*]
kOe	Kilooersted
KOE	Koppel [*Federal Republic of Germany*] [*Seismograph station code, US Geological Survey*] (SEIS)
KOE	Kupang [*Indonesia*] [*Airport symbol*] (OAG)
KOE	MER Leasing [*FAA designator*] (FAAC)
KOE	Northland Aviation, Inc. [*ICAO designator*] (FAAC)
KOEA	Doniphan, MO [*FM radio station call letters*]
KOEBES	Koelner Bibliothekserschliessungssystem [*Automated library system*] (NITA)
KOED	Tulsa, OK [*Television station call letters*]
KOEL	Oelwein, IA [*AM radio station call letters*]
KOEL-FM	Oelwein, IA [*FM radio station call letters*]
KOEO	Key-On Engine-Off [*Automotive engineering*]
KOER	Key-On Engine-Running [*Automotive engineering*]
KOET	Eufaula, OK [*Television station call letters*]
KOEX	Oklahoma City [*Oklahoma*] [*ICAO location identifier*] (ICLI)
KOEZ	Newton, KS [*FM radio station call letters*]
KOF	Coca-Cola FEMSA [*NYSE symbol*] (SPSG)
KOF	Coca-Cola FEMSA ADS [*NYSE symbol*] (TTSB)
KOF	Knitted Outerwear Foundation (EA)
KOF	Kofu [*Japan*] [*Seismograph station code, US Geological Survey*] (SEIS)
KOFC	Fayetteville, AR [*AM radio station call letters*]
K of C	Knights of Columbus (EA)
KofC	Knights of Columbus (WDAA)
KOFE	St. Maries, ID [*AM radio station call letters*]
KOFF	Offutt Air Force Base, Omaha [*Nebraska*] [*ICAO location identifier*] (ICLI)
K of H	Knight of Hanover
KOFH-FM	Nogales, AZ [*FM radio station call letters*] (BROA)
KOFI	Kalispell, MT [*AM radio station call letters*]
KOFI-FM	Kalispell, MT [*FM radio station call letters*]
K of L	Knights of Labor
K of L	Knights of Lithuania (EA)
KOFM	Enid, OK [*FM radio station call letters*]
KOFO	Ottawa, KS [*AM radio station call letters*]
K of P	Knights of Pythias
KOFS	Key Officers of Foreign Service Posts [*A publication*]
KOFST	Korean Federation of Science and Technology
KOFT	Gallup, NM [*Television station call letters*]
KOFX	El Paso, TX [*FM radio station call letters*]
KOFY	San Francisco, CA [*Television station call letters*]
KOFY	San Mateo, CA [*AM radio station call letters*]
KOG	Kansas, Oklahoma & Gulf Railway Co. [*AAR code*]
KOG	Kindly Old Gentleman [*Slang*]
KOGA	Ogallala, NE [*AM radio station call letters*]
KOGA-FM	Ogallala, NE [*FM radio station call letters*]
KOGC	Kelley Oil and Gas Corp. [*NASDAQ symbol*] (SAG)
KogEq	Koger Equity, Inc. [*Associated Press*] (SAG)
KOGG	Wailuku, HI [*Television station call letters*]
KOGM	Opelousas, LA [*FM radio station call letters*]
KOGO	San Diego, CA [*AM radio station call letters*]
KogrEq	Koger Equity, Inc. [*Associated Press*] (SAG)
KOGS	Ogdensburg [*New York*] [*ICAO location identifier*] (ICLI)
KOGT	Orange, TX [*AM radio station call letters*]
KOH	King's Own Hussars [*British military*] (DMA)
KOH	Kohala [*Hawaii*] [*Seismograph station code, US Geological Survey*] (SEIS)
Koh	Kohelet (BJA)
KOH	Koolatah [*Australia Airport symbol Obsolete*] (OAG)
KOH	Potassium Hydroxide [*Organic chemistry*]
KOHEPFC	King of Our Hearts Elvis Presley Fan Club (EA)
KOHI	St. Helens, OR [*AM radio station call letters*]
KOHL	Fremont, CA [*FM radio station call letters*]
Kohls	Kohls Corp. [*Associated Press*] (SAG)
KOHM	Kilohm (MCD)
KOHM	Lubbock, TX [*FM radio station call letters*]
KOHO	Honolulu, HI [*AM radio station call letters*]
KohR	Kohelet Rabbah (BJA)
KOHS	Orem, UT [*FM radio station call letters*]
KOHT	Marana, AZ [*FM radio station call letters*]
KOHU	Hermiston, OR [*AM radio station call letters*]
KOI	Kennedy Operating Instructions [*NASA*] (KSC)
K-OI	Keren-OR, Inc. [*An association*] (EA)
KOI	Kirkwall [*Orkney Islands*] [*Airport symbol*] (OAG)
KOI	KSC [*Kennedy Space Center*] Operation Instruction [*NASA*] (NASA)
KOI	Ontario Institute for Studies in Education Library [*UTLAS symbol*]
KOICA	Korea International Cooperation Agency (BUAC)
KOIL	Bellevue, NE [*AM radio station call letters*]
KOIN	Portland, OR [*Television station call letters*]
KOIR	Edinburg, TX [*FM radio station call letters*]
KOIS	Kuder Occupational Interest Survey [*Aptitude and skills test*]
KOIT	San Francisco, CA [*AM radio station call letters*]
KOIT-FM	San Francisco, CA [*FM radio station call letters*]
KOJ	Kagoshima [*Japan*] [*Airport symbol*] (OAG)
KOJ	Keen on the Job (ADA)
KOJJ	East Porterville, CA [*FM radio station call letters*]
KOJM	Havre, MT [*AM radio station call letters*]
KOJO	Lake Charles, LA [*FM radio station call letters*]
KOK	Horizon Cargo Transport, Inc. [*ICAO designator*] (FAAC)
KOK	Kansallinen Kokoomus [*National Coalition Party*] [*Finland*] [*Political party*] (EAIO)
KOK	Kokkola [*Finland*] [*Airport symbol*] (OAG)
kok	Konkani [*MARC language code Library of Congress*] (LCCP)
KOKA	Shreveport, LA [*AM radio station call letters*]
KOKB	Blackwell, OK [*AM radio station call letters*]
KOKC	Guthrie, OK [*AM radio station call letters*]
KOKC	Oklahoma City/Will Rogers World [*Oklahoma*] [*ICAO location identifier*] (ICLI)
KOKE	Giddings, TX [*FM radio station call letters*]
KOKF	Edmond, OK [*FM radio station call letters*]
KOKH	Oklahoma City, OK [*Television station call letters*]
KOKI	Tulsa, OK [*Television station call letters*]
KOKK	Huron, SD [*AM radio station call letters*]
KOKL	Okmulgee, OK [*AM radio station call letters*]
KO-KO	Kommerzielle Koordination [*Former East German political party*]
KOKO	Warrensburg, MO [*AM radio station call letters*]
KOKR	Newport, AR [*FM radio station call letters*]
KOKS	Poplar Bluff, MO [*FM radio station call letters*]
KOKU	Agana, GU [*FM radio station call letters*]
KOKX	Keokuk, IA [*AM radio station call letters*]
KOKX-FM	Keokuk, IA [*FM radio station call letters*]
KOKY-FM	Sherwood, AR [*FM radio station call letters*] (BROA)
KOKZ	Waterloo, IA [*FM radio station call letters*]
KOL	King's College, Wilkes-Barre, PA [*OCLC symbol*] (OCLC)
KOL	Knights of Lithuania (EA)
KOL	Kollmorgen Corp. [*NYSE symbol*] (SPSG)
KOl	Olathe Public Library, Olathe, KS [*Library symbol Library of Congress*] (LCLS)
KOLA	San Bernardino, CA [*FM radio station call letters*]
KOLD	Tucson, AZ [*Television station call letters*]
KOLE	Port Arthur, TX [*AM radio station call letters*]
KOlH	Olathe Community Hospital, Olathe, KS [*Library symbol Library of Congress*] (LCLS)
KOLI	King's Own Light Infantry [*Military unit*] [*British*]
KOlJL	Johnson County Law Library, Olathe, KS [*Library symbol Library of Congress*] (LCLS)
KOLK-FM	Onawa, IA [*FM radio station call letters*] (RBYB)
KOLL	Maumelle, AR [*FM radio station call letters*]
KollRE	Koll Real Estate Group [*Associated Press*] (SAG)
KollRI	Koll Real Estate Group [*Associated Press*] (SAG)
KOLM	Rochester, MN [*AM radio station call letters*]
KOlMN	Mid-America Nazarene College, Olathe, KS [*Library symbol Library of Congress*] (LCLS)
Kolmor	Kollmorgen Corp. [*Associated Press*] (SAG)
KOLN	Lincoln, NE [*Television station call letters*]
KOLO	Reno, NV [*Television station call letters*]
KOLR	Springfield, MO [*Television station call letters*]
KOLS	Dodge City, KS [*FM radio station call letters*]
KOLS	Nogales/International [*Arizona*] [*ICAO location identifier*] (ICLI)
KOLT	Scottsbluff, NE [*AM radio station call letters*]
KOLT-FM	Santa Fe, NM [*FM radio station call letters*]
KOLU	Pasco, WA [*FM radio station call letters*]
KOLV	Olivia, MN [*FM radio station call letters*]
KOLX	Barling, AR [*FM radio station call letters*]
KOLY	Mobridge, SD [*AM radio station call letters*]
KOLY-FM	Mobridge, SD [*FM radio station call letters*]
Kolze	Transvaal Reports, by Kolze [*A publication*] (DLA)
KOLZ-FM	Cheyenne, WY [*FM radio station call letters*] (BROA)
KOM	Kansas-Oklahoma-Missouri League [*Old baseball league*]
KOM	Kentucky, Ohio, Michigan [*Medical library network*]
KOM	Kilometric Wavelength [*Radio astronomy*]
KOM	Knight of the Order of Malta (WDAA)
KOM	Komaba [*Japan*] [*Seismograph station code, US Geological Survey Closed*] (SEIS)
KOM	Komitet Opiekunczy Miejski (BJA)
KOM	Komo-Manda [*Papua New Guinea*] [*Airport symbol Obsolete*] (OAG)
KoM	Korea Microforms, Seoul, Korea [*Library symbol Library of Congress*] (LCLS)
KOM	KSC [*Kennedy Space Center*] Organizational Manual [*NASA*] (NASA)
KOMA	Oklahoma City, OK [*AM radio station call letters*]
KOMA	Omaha/Eppley Air Field [*Nebraska*] [*ICAO location identifier*] (ICLI)
KOMA-FM	Oklahoma City, OK [*FM radio station call letters*]
Komag	Komag, Inc. [*Associated Press*] (SAG)
KOMB	Fort Scott, KS [*FM radio station call letters*]
KomBeiANT	Kommentare und Beitraege zum Alten und Neuen Testament [*Duesseldorf*] [*A publication*] (BJA)
KOMC	Branson, MO [*AM radio station call letters*]
KOME	San Jose, CA [*FM radio station call letters*]

KOMH-AM.... Pawhuska, OK [AM radio station call letters] (RBYB)
KOMO........ Seattle, WA [AM radio station call letters]
KOMO-TV.... Seattle, WA [Television station call letters]
KOMP........ Las Vegas, NV [FM radio station call letters]
KOMRMLN... Kentucky-Ohio-Michigan Regional Medical Library [Library network]
KOMS........ Poteau, OK [FM radio station call letters]
KOMSOMOL... Communist Youth League [From the Russian]
KOMU........ Columbia, MO [Television station call letters]
KOMW........ Omak, WA [AM radio station call letters]
KOMW-FM... Omak, WA [FM radio station call letters]
KOMX........ Pampa, TX [FM radio station call letters]
KOMY-AM.... Watsonville, CA [AM radio station call letters] (BROA)
kon............. Kongo [MARC language code Library of Congress] (LCCP)
KON........... Kongsberg [Norway] [Seismograph station code, US Geological Survey] (SEIS)
KON........... Kontum [South Vietnam] [Airport symbol] (AD)
KONA......... Kennewick, WA [AM radio station call letters]
KONA-FM.... Kennewick, WA [FM radio station call letters]
KOND-FM.... Cleveland, TX [FM radio station call letters] (RBYB)
KONE......... Lubbock, TX [FM radio station call letters]
KONG......... Everett, WA [Television station call letters]
KONI.......... Lanai City, HI [FM radio station call letters]
KONO......... San Antonio, TX [AM radio station call letters]
KONO-FM.... Fredericksburg, TX [FM radio station call letters]
KONP......... Port Angeles, WA [AM radio station call letters]
KONQ......... Dodge City, KS [FM radio station call letters]
Konst & W Rat App... Konstam and Ward's Rating Appeals [1909-12] [A publication] (DLA)
Konst Rat App... Konstam's Rating Appeals [1904-08] [A publication] (DLA)
KONT.......... Ontario/International [California] [ICAO location identifier] (ICLI)
KONY......... Washington, UT [AM radio station call letters]
KONY-FM.... Kanab, UT [FM radio station call letters]
KONZ.......... Arizona City, AZ [FM radio station call letters]
KOO........... Kongolo [Zaire] [Airport symbol] (OAG)
KOOC......... Belton, TX [FM radio station call letters]
KOOD......... Hays, KS [Television station call letters]
KOOG......... Ogden, UT [Television station call letters]
KOOI.......... Jacksonville, TX [FM radio station call letters]
KOOJ.......... Riverside, CA [FM radio station call letters]
KOOKR........ Kookier (ABBR)
KooKR......... Koo Koo Roo, Inc. [Associated Press] (SAG)
KOOKST....... Kookiest (ABBR)
KOOL......... Phoenix, AZ [AM radio station call letters]
KOOL......... Thermagenesis Corp. [NASDAQ symbol] (SAG)
KOOL......... Thermogenesis Corp. [NASDAQ symbol] (SAG)
KOOL-FM..... Phoenix, AZ [FM radio station call letters]
KOOO-AM.... Dallas, TX [AM radio station call letters] (BROA)
KOOP......... Hornsby, TX [FM radio station call letters]
KOOQ......... North Platte, NE [AM radio station call letters]
Koor........... Koor Industries Ltd. [Associated Press] (SAG)
KOOS.......... North Bend, OR [FM radio station call letters]
KOOU......... Hardy, AR [FM radio station call letters]
KOOV.......... Copperas Cove, TX [FM radio station call letters]
KOOZ.......... Great Falls, MT [FM radio station call letters]
KOP........... Kansallis-Osake-Pankki [National Capital Stock Bank] [Finland]
KOP........... Kickoff Point [Diamond drilling]
KOP........... Kopeck [Monetary unit in Russia]
KOP........... Nakhon Phanom [Thailand] [Airport symbol Obsolete] (OAG)
KOPA......... Scottsdale, AZ [AM radio station call letters]
KOPB......... Portland, OR [FM radio station call letters]
KOPB-TV..... Portland, OR [Television station call letters]
KOPCC........ Kunzang Odsal Palyul Changchub Choling [An association] (EA)
KOPE......... Medford, OR [FM radio station call letters]
KOPF......... Miami/Opa Locka [Florida] [ICAO location identifier] (ICLI)
Kopin......... Kopin Corp. [Associated Press] (SAG)
KOPN......... Columbia, MO [FM radio station call letters]
KOPN......... Kopin Corp. [NASDAQ symbol] (SAG)
KOPR......... Butte, MT [FM radio station call letters]
KOPS......... K (10³) Operations Per Second (NITA)
KOPS......... Keep Off Pounds Sensibly [Club]
KOPS......... Thousands of Operations per Second (NASA)
KOPX......... Oklahoma City, OK [Television station call letters] (BROA)
KOPY-AM.... Alice, TX [AM radio station call letters] (RBYB)
KOPY-FM.... Alice, TX [FM radio station call letters] (RBYB)
KOQI.......... Soquel, CA [AM radio station call letters]
KOQL.......... Columbia, MO [FM radio station call letters]
KOQO......... Clovis, CA [AM radio station call letters]
KOQO......... Fresno, CA [FM radio station call letters]
KOR........... Air Koryo [North Korea] [ICAO designator] (FAAC)
KOR........... Contracting Officer
KOR........... King's Own Royal [Military unit] [British]
KOR........... Klein Offset Rotation [Typography] (DGA)
KOR........... Knowledge of Results [Visual monitoring]
KOR........... Koala Resources Ltd. [Vancouver Stock Exchange symbol]
KOR........... Kodak Ortho Resist
KOR........... Kokoro [Papua New Guinea] [Airport symbol] (OAG)
KOR........... Koor Indus Ltd ADS [NYSE symbol] (TTSB)
KOR........... Koor Industries Ltd. [NYSE symbol] (SAG)
KOR........... Koran (ROG)
Kor........... Korea (VRA)
kor........... Korean [MARC language code Library of Congress] (LCCP)
KOR........... Koror [Palau Islands] [Seismograph station code, US Geological Survey Closed] (SEIS)
KOR........... Republic of Korea [ANSI three-letter standard code] (CNC)
KOR........... Seaplane [Russian symbol]

KOR........... Social Self-Defense Committee [Also, SSDC] [Poland] (PD)
KORA......... Bryan, TX [FM radio station call letters]
KORB......... Bettendorf, IA [FM radio station call letters] (RBYB)
KORC......... Waldport, OR [FM radio station call letters]
KORD......... Chicago/O'Hare [Illinois] [ICAO location identifier] (ICLI)
KORD-FM.... Richland, WA [FM radio station call letters]
KORDI........ Korea Ocean Research and Development Institute (USDC)
KORE......... Kinetic Analysis Using Over-Relaxation [FORTRAN computer program] [Physical chemistry]
KORE......... Springfield-Eugene, OR [AM radio station call letters]
Korea........ Korea Fund, Inc. [Associated Press]
KoreaElc..... Korea Electric Power Corp. [Associated Press] (SAG)
KoreaEqt..... Korea Equity Fund [Associated Press] (SAG)
KoreaInv..... Korean Investment Fund [Associated Press] (SAG)
Korea LR..... Korea Law Review [A publication] (DLA)
KoreaM...... Korea Mobile Telecommunications [Associated Press] (SAG)
Korean J Comp L... Korean Journal of Comparative Law [A publication] (DLA)
Korean J Int'l L... Korean Journal of International Law [A publication] (DLA)
Korean J of Internat L... Korean Journal of International Law [A publication] (DLA)
Korean L..... Korean Law [A publication] (DLA)
KorEIN....... Korea Electric Power Corp. [Associated Press] (SAG)
KORF......... Norfolk/Norfolk Regional Airport [Virginia] [ICAO location identifier] (ICLI)
KORG......... Anaheim, CA [AM radio station call letters]
KORI......... Mansfield, LA [FM radio station call letters]
KORK......... Las Vegas, NV [AM radio station call letters]
KORL......... Honolulu, HI [AM radio station call letters]
KORL......... Orlando [Florida] [ICAO location identifier] (ICLI)
KORL-FM.... Honolulu, HI [FM radio station call letters] (RBYB)
KORN......... Mitchell, SD [AM radio station call letters]
KORO......... Corpus Christi, TX [Television station call letters]
KOROC........ Keep Out of Reach of Children (DI)
KORP......... Charles, [J. W.] Financial Services [NASDAQ symbol] (SAG)
KORP......... Charles (JW) Finl Svcs [NASDAQ symbol] (TTSB)
KORQ-FM.... Abilene, TX [FM radio station call letters]
KORR......... American Falls, ID [FM radio station call letters] (RBYB)
KORR......... King's Own Royal Regiment [Military unit] [British]
KORSTIC...... Korea Scientific and Technical Information Centre (NITA)
KORSTIC...... Korea Scientific and Technological Information Center [INSPEC operator]
KORT......... Grangeville, ID [AM radio station call letters]
KORT-FM.... Grangeville, ID [FM radio station call letters]
KORV......... Oroville, CA [AM radio station call letters]
KOS........... Kent University On-Line System [Computer science] (PDAA)
KO's.......... Knockout Drops [A drug producing unconsciousness] [Slang]
KOS........... Kosmodemyansk [Former USSR Seismograph station code, US Geological Survey Closed] (SEIS)
KOS........... Kosovaair [Yugoslavia] [ICAO designator] (FAAC)
KOSA......... Odessa, TX [Television station call letters]
KOSB......... King's Own Scottish Borderers [Military unit] [British]
KOSC......... Oscoda/Wurtsmith Air Force Base [Michigan] [ICAO location identifier] (ICLI)
KOSCO....... Korea Oil Storage Co. (CINC)
KOSCOT...... Cosmetics for the Community of Tomorrow [Acronym used as brand name]
KOSE......... Osceola, AR [AM radio station call letters]
KOSE-FM.... Osceola, AR [FM radio station call letters]
KOSG......... Camden, AR [AM radio station call letters]
KOSH......... Osawatomie State Hospital, Osawatomie, KS [Library symbol Library of Congress] (LCLS)
KOSI......... Denver, CO [FM radio station call letters]
KOSJ......... Nebraska City, NE [FM radio station call letters] (RBYB)
KoSNU....... Seoul National University, Seoul, Korea [Library symbol Library of Congress] (LCLS)
KOSO......... Patterson, CA [FM radio station call letters]
KOSP......... Willard, MO [FM radio station call letters]
KOSR-AM.... Omaha, NE [AM radio station call letters] (RBYB)
KOSS......... Koss Corp. [NASDAQ symbol] (SAG)
KOST......... Los Angeles, CA [FM radio station call letters]
KOSU......... Stillwater, OK [FM radio station call letters]
KOSY-FM.... Spanish Fork, UT [FM radio station call letters] (BROA)
KoSYU....... Yonsei University, Seoul, Korea [Library symbol Library of Congress] (LCLS)
KOSZ......... Vermillion, SD [AM radio station call letters]
KOSZ-FM.... Idaho Falls, ID [FM radio station call letters]
KOT........... Knowledge of Occupations Test [Psychology] (DAVI)
KOT........... Kotlik [Alaska] [Airport symbol] (OAG)
KOTA......... Rapid City, SD [AM radio station call letters]
KOTA-TV..... Rapid City, SD [Television station call letters]
KOTB......... Evanston, WY [FM radio station call letters]
KOTC......... Kennett, MO [AM radio station call letters] (RBYB)
KOTC......... Kuwait Oil Tanker Co. (BUAC)
KOTD......... Plattsmouth, NE [AM radio station call letters]
KOTD-FM.... Plattsmouth, NE [FM radio station call letters]
KOTE......... Eureka, KS [FM radio station call letters]
KOTI......... Klamath Falls, OR [Television station call letters]
KOTK......... Portland, OR [AM radio station call letters] (RBYB)
KOTM......... Ottumwa, IA [FM radio station call letters]
KOTN......... Keep on Truckin' News [A publication] (EAAP)
KOTN......... Pine Bluff, AR [AM radio station call letters]
KOTO......... Telluride, CO [FM radio station call letters]
KOTR......... Cambria, CA [FM radio station call letters]
KOTRA........ Korea Trade Promotion Center (EA)
KOTRA........ Korea Trade Promotion Co. (BUAC)
KOTS......... Deming, NM [AM radio station call letters]

KOTT...........	Otterville, MO [*FM radio station call letters*]
KOtU	Ottawa University, Ottawa, KS [*Library symbol Library of Congress*] (LCLS)
KOTV	Tulsa, OK [*Television station call letters*]
KOTZ...........	Kotzebue, AK [*AM radio station call letters*]
Kotze	Kotze's Transvaal High Court Reports [*South Africa*] [*A publication*] (DLA)
Kotze & B	Supreme Court Reports, Transvaal [*1885-88*] [*South Africa*] [*A publication*] (DLA)
Kotze & Barb...	Supreme Court Reports, Transvaal [*1885-88*] [*South Africa*] [*A publication*] (DLA)
Kotze & Barber...	Transvaal Court Reports [*A publication*] (DLA)
KOU	Koula Moutou [*Gabon*] [*Airport symbol*] (OAG)
KOU	Koumac [*New Caledonia*] [*Seismograph station code, US Geological Survey*] (SEIS)
KOUL	Sinton, TX [*FM radio station call letters*]
KOUT	Rapid City, SD [*FM radio station call letters*]
KOUU	American Falls, ID [*FM radio station call letters*]
KOUZ	Alexandria, LA [*FM radio station call letters*] (RBYB)
KOV	Key Operated Valve
Kov	N. A. Kovach, Los Angeles, CA [*Library symbol Library of Congress*] (LCLS)
KOVC	Valley City, ND [*AM radio station call letters*]
KOVC-FM	Valley City, ND [*FM radio station call letters*]
KOVE	Lander, WY [*AM radio station call letters*]
KOVO	Provo, UT [*AM radio station call letters*]
KOvpJ	Johnson County Community College, Overland Park, KS [*Library symbol Library of Congress*] (LCLS)
KovpST	St. Thomas High School, Overland Park, KS [*Library symbol*] [*Library of Congress*] (LCLS)
KOVR	Stockton, CA [*Television station call letters*]
KOVT	Silver City, NM [*Television station call letters*]
Kow	Coefficient of Octanolwater Partition (GNE)
KOW	Ghanzhou [*China*] [*Airport symbol*] (OAG)
KOW	Keen on Waller [*A coterie of women admirers of British stage actor, Lewis Waller (1860-1915)*] (ROG)
KOW	Knock-Off Wheels [*Automotive accessory*]
KOW	Kowkash Gold [*Vancouver Stock Exchange symbol*]
KOWB	Laramie, WY [*AM radio station call letters*]
KOWF	Escondido, CA [*FM radio station call letters*]
KOWL	South Lake Tahoe, CA [*AM radio station call letters*]
KOWO	Waseca, MN [*AM radio station call letters*]
KOWS-FM	Ashdown, AR [*FM radio station call letters*] (BROA)
KOWW-AM	Blue Springs, MO [*AM radio station call letters*] (RBYB)
KOWZ-FM	Blooming Prairie, MN [*FM radio station call letters*] (RBYB)
KOX	Kokonao [*West Irian, Indonesia*] [*Airport symbol*] (AD)
KOXE	Brownwood, TX [*FM radio station call letters*]
KOXR	Oxnard, CA [*AM radio station call letters*]
KOY	Koyama [*Japan*] [*Seismograph station code, US Geological Survey Closed*] (SEIS)
KOY	Olga Bay [*Alaska*] [*Airport symbol*] (OAG)
KOY	Phoenix, AZ [*AM radio station call letters*]
KOYE	Laredo, TX [*FM radio station call letters*]
KOYLI	King's Own Yorkshire Light Infantry [*Military unit*] [*British*]
KOYN	Paris, TX [*FM radio station call letters*]
KOZ...........	Kozyrevsk [*Former USSR Seismograph station code, US Geological Survey*] (SEIS)
KOZ...........	Ouzinkie, AK [*Location identifier FAA*] (FAAL)
KOZA	Odessa, TX [*AM radio station call letters*]
KOZE	Lewiston, ID [*AM radio station call letters*]
KOZE-FM	Lewiston, ID [*FM radio station call letters*]
KOZI	Chelan, WA [*AM radio station call letters*]
KOZI-FM	Chelan, WA [*FM radio station call letters*]
KOZJ	Joplin, MO [*Television station call letters*]
KOZK	Springfield, MO [*Television station call letters*]
KOZN-FM	Kansas City, MO [*FM radio station call letters*] (BROA)
KOZO-FM	Branson, MO [*FM radio station call letters*] (RBYB)
KOZQ	Waynesville, MO [*AM radio station call letters*]
KOZT	Fort Bragg, CA [*FM radio station call letters*]
KOZX	Cabool, MO [*FM radio station call letters*]
KOZY	Grand Rapids, MN [*AM radio station call letters*]
KOZZ...........	Reno, NV [*AM radio station call letters*]
KOZZ-FM	Reno, NV [*FM radio station call letters*]
KP	Democratic People's Republic of Korea [*ANSI two-letter standard code*] (CNC)
K-P	Kaiser-Permanente [*Diet*]
kp	Kaliophilite [*CIPW classification*] [*Geology*]
KP	Kaufmann-Peterson Base [*Medicine*] (DMAA)
KP	Kensington Palace [*British*]
KP	Keogh Plan [*Business term*]
KP	Keratitic Precipitate [*Ophthalmology*]
KP	Keratitis Punctata [*Ophthalmology*]
KP	Keskustapuolue [*Center Party of Finland*] [*Political party*] (PPW)
KP	Keyboard Perforator
KP	Key Personnel
KP	Key Production Co. [*NYSE symbol*] (SAG)
KP	Key Pulsing
KP	Keypunch [*Computer science*]
KP	Kickpipe [*Building construction*]
KP	Kick Plate
KP	Kidder, Peabody & Co. (EFIS)
KP	Kidney Pore
KP	Kidney Protein [*Nephrology*] (DAVI)
KP	Kidney Punch [*Medicine*] (DAVI)
KP	Kids of Preachers

KP	Killed Parenteral [*Vaccine*] [*Immunology*] (DAVI)
KP	Kill Probability (MCD)
KP	Kilometer Post
KP	Kilopond
kp	Kilopulse
KP	Kinetic Percolation
KP	Kinetic Potential
KP	King Post
KP	King's Parade [*British*] (DSUE)
KP	King's Pawn [*Chess*] (ADA)
KP	King's Pleasure [*British*]
KP	King's Proctor [*British*]
KP	Kitchen Police [*Kitchen helpers*] [*Military*]
KP	Klebsiella Pneumonia [*Genus of microorganism*] (DAVI)
KP	Klein Paradox [*Physics*]
KP	Knight of Pius IX
KP	Knight of St. Patrick [*British*]
KP	Knights of Pythias (EA)
KP	Knotty Pine
KP	Kodak Process Resist [*Photography*] (DICI)
KP	Komma Proodeftikon [*Progressive Party*] [*Greek Political party*] (PPE)
KP	Kommunistesch Partei [*Communist Party*] [*Luxembourg*] [*Political party*] (PPE)
KP	Kommunistische Partei [*Communist Party*] [*German Political party*]
KP	Kurdish Heritage Foundation of America
KP	Kurdish Program (EA)
KP	Kurie Plot [*Physics*]
KP	North Korea [*Internet country code*]
KP	Papua New Guinea [*IYRU nationality code*] (IYR)
KP	Safair [*ICAO designator*] (AD)
KPA	Innkeepers USA Trust [*NYSE symbol*] (SAG)
KPA	Key-Process Area (AAEL)
KPA	Key Pulse Adapter [*Telecommunications*] (TEL)
KPA	Kidney Plasminogen Activator [*Anticlotting agent*]
kPa	Kilopascal
KPA	Klystron Power Amplifier
KPA	Kopiago [*Papua New Guinea*] [*Airport symbol*] (OAG)
KPA	Korean People's Army [*Democratic People's Republic of Korea*] (BUAC)
KPA	Korea Procurement Agency
KPA	Kraft Paper Association [*Later, API*] (EA)
KPAC-FM	San Antonio, TX [*FM radio station call letters*]
KPAE	Erwinville, LA [*FM radio station call letters*]
KPAE	Everett/Snohomish County-Paine Field [*Washington*] [*ICAO location identifier*] (ICLI)
KPAG	Pagosa Springs, CO [*AM radio station call letters*]
KPAL-AM	North Little Rock, AR [*AM radio station call letters*] (RBYB)
KPAM	Panama City/Tyndall Air Force Base [*Florida*] [*ICAO location identifier*] (ICLI)
KPAN	Hereford, TX [*AM radio station call letters*]
KP & D	Kick Plate and Drip (AAG)
KPAN-FM	Hereford, TX [*FM radio station call letters*]
KPAR	Granbury, TX [*AM radio station call letters*]
KParSH	Parsons State Hospital, Parsons, KS [*Library symbol Library of Congress*] (LCLS)
KPAS	Fabens, TX [*FM radio station call letters*]
KPAT-FM	San Luis Obispo, CA [*FM radio station call letters*] (BROA)
KPAW	Fort Collins, CO [*FM radio station call letters*] (RBYB)
KPAWU	Kenya Plantation and Agricultural Workers Union (BUAC)
KPAX	Missoula, MT [*Television station call letters*]
KPAY	Chico, CA [*AM radio station call letters*]
KPAZ	Phoenix, AZ [*Television station call letters*]
KPB	Kalium [*Potassium*] Phosphate Buffer [*Biochemistry*] (DAVI)
KPB	Kenai Peninsula Borough [*Alaska*]
KPB	Kenya Pyrethrum Board (BUAC)
KPB	Ketophenylbutazone [*or Kebuzone*] [*An antirheumatic*] (DAVI)
KPB	Kommunistische Partij van Belgie [*Communist Party of Belgium*] [*See also PCB*] [*Political party*] (PPE)
KPB	Point Baker, AK [*Location identifier FAA*] (FAAL)
KPBA	Pine Bluff, AR [*AM radio station call letters*]
KPBC	Garland, TX [*AM radio station call letters*]
KPBF	Pine Bluff/Grider Field [*Arkansas*] [*ICAO location identifier*] (ICLI)
KPBG	Plattsburg/Plattsburg Air Force Base [*New York*] [*ICAO location identifier*] (ICLI)
KPBI...........	Greenwood, AR [*AM radio station call letters*]
KPBI...........	West Palm Beach/Palm Beach International [*Florida*] [*ICAO location identifier*] (ICLI)
KPBL-AM	Hemphill, TX [*AM radio station call letters*] (BROA)
KPBQ	Pine Bluff, AR [*FM radio station call letters*]
KPBRS	Korean Peace Bioreserves System
KPBS	San Diego, CA [*Television station call letters*]
KPBS-FM	San Diego, CA [*FM radio station call letters*]
KPBX	Spokane, WA [*FM radio station call letters*]
KPC	Kappa Resources [*Vancouver Stock Exchange symbol*]
KPC	Kembata People's Congress [*Ethiopia*]
KPC	Kentucky Power Co. [*NYSE symbol*] (SAG)
KPC	Kentucky Pwr 8.72% Sr'A'Debs [*NYSE symbol*] (TTSB)
KPC	Keratinocyte Precursor Cell
KPC	Keratoconus Posticus Circumscriptus [*Medicine*] (DMAA)
KPC	Keyboard/Printer Control [*Computer science*]
KPC	Keyboard Priority Controller [*Computer science*] (HGAA)
KPC	Key Personnel Course (MCD)
KPC	Key Product Characteristic
KPC	Keypunch Cabinet [*Computer science*]

KPC .... Khapcheranga [*Former USSR Seismograph station code, US Geological Survey*] (SEIS)
kpc .... Kiloparsec [*Astronomy*]
KPC .... Kinetic Process Control
KPC .... Klystron Phase Control
KPC .... Knights of Peter Claver (EA)
KPC .... Koblenz Procurement Center [*Federal Republic of Germany*] [*Military*] (NATG)
KPC .... Kodak Photofabrication Center
KPC .... Kohn Problem Checklist (TES)
KPC .... Korea Productivity Centre (BUAC)
KPC .... Kuwait Petroleum Corp. (BUAC)
KPC .... Paducah Junior College, Paducah, KY [*OCLC symbol*] (OCLC)
KPC .... Port Clarence [*Alaska*] [*Airport symbol*] (OAG)
KPC .... Port Clarence, AK [*Location identifier FAA*] (FAAL)
KPCB-TV ..... Snyder, TX [*TV station call letters*] (RBYB)
KPCC .... Pasadena, CA [*FM radio station call letters*]
KPCH .... Dubach, LA [*FM radio station call letters*]
KPCI .... Key Production [*NASDAQ symbol*] (TTSB)
KPCI .... Key Production Co., Inc. [*NASDAQ symbol*] (NQ)
KPCK .... Kopeck (ABBR)
KPC/KSC ..... Kohn Problem Checklist/Kohn Social Competence Scale [*Test*] (TMMY)
KPCL .... Farmington, NM [*FM radio station call letters*]
KPCO .... Quincy, CA [*AM radio station call letters*]
KPCR .... Bowling Green, MO [*AM radio station call letters*]
KPCR-FM .... Bowling Green, MO [*FM radio station call letters*]
KPCU .... Kenyan Planters Co-Operative Union (BUAC)
KPCW .... Park City, UT [*FM radio station call letters*]
KPD .... Kennedy Program Directive [*NASA*] (NASA)
KPD .... Knowledge-Based Producibility Decision-Maker [*Productivity technology*] (RDA)
KPD .... Kommunistische Partei Deutschlands [*Communist Party of Germany*] [*Political party*] (PPW)
KPD-ML .... Kommunistische Partei Deutschlands/Marxisten-Leninisten [*Communist Party of Germany/Marxists-Leninists*] [*Political party*] (PPW)
KPDQ .... Portland, OR [*AM radio station call letters*]
KPDQ-FM .... Portland, OR [*FM radio station call letters*]
KPDR .... Korean People's Democratic Republic (BUAC)
KPDR .... Wheeler, TX [*FM radio station call letters*]
KPDU .... Kaffa People's Democratic Union [*Ethiopia*] [*Political party*] (EY)
KPDX .... Portland/International [*Oregon*] [*ICAO location identifier*] (ICLI)
KPDX .... Vancouver, WA [*Television station call letters*]
KPE .... Kelman Phakoemulsification [*Ophthalmology*] (DAVI)
KPE .... Key Point Error [*Computer science*] (IAA)
KPE .... Kilman Phacoemulsification [*Medicine*] (MEDA)
kpe .... Kpelle [*MARC language code Library of Congress*] (LCCP)
KPEJ .... Odessa, TX [*Television station call letters*]
KPEK-FM .... Albuquerque, NM [*FM radio station call letters*] (RBYB)
KPEL .... Lafayette, LA [*AM radio station call letters*]
KPEL-FM .... Erath, LA [*FM radio station call letters*]
KPENC .... Korean Centre of International PEN (EAIO)
KPEN-FM .... Soldotna, AK [*FM radio station call letters*]
KPER .... Hobbs, NM [*FM radio station call letters*]
KPET .... Lamesa, TX [*AM radio station call letters*]
KPEZ .... Austin, TX [*FM radio station call letters*]
KPF .... Kangaroo Protection Foundation (EA)
KPF .... Katadyn Pocket Filter
KPF .... Kenya Patriotic Front [*Political party*] (BUAC)
KPF .... Key Pulse on Front Cord [*Telecommunications*] (TEL)
KPFA .... Berkeley, CA [*FM radio station call letters*]
KPFA .... Knackery and Pet Food Association [*Australia*]
KPFB .... Berkeley, CA [*FM radio station call letters*]
KPFK .... Los Angeles, CA [*FM radio station call letters*]
KPFM .... Mountain Home, AR [*FM radio station call letters*]
KPFSM .... King's Police & Fire Services Medal for Gallantry [*British*] (WDAA)
KPFT .... Houston, TX [*FM radio station call letters*]
KPFX .... Fargo, ND [*FM radio station call letters*]
KPG .... Keeping
KPG .... Kurupung [*Guyana*] [*Airport symbol*] (OAG)
KPGE .... Page, AZ [*AM radio station call letters*]
KPGR .... Pleasant Grove, UT [*FM radio station call letters*]
KPH .... Kaena Point [*Hawaii*] [*Seismograph station code, US Geological Survey Closed*] (SEIS)
KPH .... Keystrokes Per Hour (NITA)
kph .... Kilometers per Hour
KPH .... Know Problems of Hydrocephalus (EA)
KPH .... Komunisticka Partija Hrvatske [*Communist Party of Croatia*] [*Political party*]
KPH .... Ktav Publishing House, Inc. [*New York*] (BJA)
KPH .... Pauloff Harbor/Sanak Island, AK [*Location identifier FAA*] (FAAL)
KPhA .... Kansas Pharmacists Association (SRA)
KPhA .... Kentucky Pharmacists Association (SRA)
KPHF .... Newport News/Patrick Henry [*Virginia*] [*ICAO location identifier*] (ICLI)
KPHF .... Phoenix, AZ [*FM radio station call letters*]
KPHL .... Philadelphia/International [*Pennsylvania*] [*ICAO location identifier*] (ICLI)
KPHN .... Pittsburg, KS [*AM radio station call letters*]
KPHN .... Port Huron [*Michigan*] [*ICAO location identifier*] (ICLI)
KPHO .... Phoenix, AZ [*Television station call letters*]
KPHR .... Milbank, SD [*FM radio station call letters*]
KPHS-FM .... Plains, TX [*FM radio station call letters*] (RBYB)
KPHT .... Kindred, ND [*FM radio station call letters*]

KPHX .... Phoenix, AZ [*AM radio station call letters*]
KPHX .... Phoenix/Sky Harbor International [*Arizona*] [*ICAO location identifier*] (ICLI)
KPI .... Kapit [*Malaysia*] [*Airport symbol*] (OAG)
KPI .... Karyopyknotic Index [*Cytology*]
KPI .... Kernel Programming Interface [*Computer science*]
KPI .... Key Performance Indicator (EBF)
KPI .... Killearn Properties, Inc. [*AMEX symbol*] (SPSG)
KPI .... King Pin Inclination [*Automotive engineering*]
kpi .... Kips [*Thousands of Pounds*] per Square Inch
KPI .... Kontron Personal Instrumentation [*Kontron Electronics*] (NITA)
KPI .... Kunitz Protease Inhibitor [*Medicine*]
KPI .... Kuwait Petroleum International (BUAC)
KPI .... KWIK Products International Corp. [*Vancouver Stock Exchange symbol*]
KPIC .... Key Phrase in Context
KPIC .... Roseburg, OR [*Television station call letters*]
KPICO .... Kuwait Pharmaceutical Industries Co. (BUAC)
KPIE .... St. Petersburg/Clearwater International [*Florida*] [*ICAO location identifier*] (ICLI)
KPIG .... Freedom, CA [*FM radio station call letters*]
KPIK .... Beebe, AR [*FM radio station call letters*]
KPIN-FM ..... Pinedale, WY [*FM radio station call letters*] (RBYB)
KPIT .... Pittsburgh/Greater Pittsburgh [*Pennsylvania*] [*ICAO location identifier*] (ICLI)
KPIX .... San Francisco, CA [*AM radio station call letters*] (RBYB)
KPIX-FM ..... San Francisco, CA [*AM radio station call letters*] (RBYB)
KPIX-TV ...... San Francisco, CA [*Television station call letters*]
KPJ .... Komunisticka Partija Jugoslavije [*Communist Party of Yugoslavia*] [*Political party*] (PPE)
KPK .... Communist Party of Kazakhstan [*Political party*] (BUAC)
KPK .... Kanaka Peak [*California*] [*Seismograph station code, US Geological Survey*] (SEIS)
KPK .... Kapok (ABBR)
KPK .... Kappa Phi Kappa [*Fraternity*]
KPK .... Parks [*Alaska*] [*Airport symbol*] (OAG)
KPK .... Parks, AK [*Location identifier FAA*] (FAAL)
KPKE-AM ..... Gunnison, CO [*AM radio station call letters*] (RBYB)
KPKX .... Livingston, MT [*FM radio station call letters*] (RBYB)
KPKY .... Pocatello, ID [*FM radio station call letters*]
KPL .... Copeland Resources [*Vancouver Stock Exchange symbol*]
KPL .... Khao San Pathet Lao [*News agency*] [*Laos*] (FEA)
KPL .... Kick Plate [*Building construction*]
KPL .... Killearn Properties [*AMEX symbol*] (TTSB)
KPL .... Kommunistisch Partei vu Leetzebuerg [*Communist Party of Luxembourg*] [*Political party*] (PPW)
K-PL .... Potassium-Plasma [*Biochemistry*] (DAVI)
KPLA .... Columbia, MO [*FM radio station call letters*] (RBYB)
KPLC .... Lake Charles, LA [*Television station call letters*]
KPLG-FM .... Plains, MT [*FM radio station call letters*] (BROA)
KPLM .... Palm Springs, CA [*FM radio station call letters*]
KPLN-FM ..... Plains, TX [*FM radio station call letters*]
KPLO .... Reliance, SD [*FM radio station call letters*]
KPLO-TV ..... Reliance, SD [*Television station call letters*]
KPLR .... St. Louis, MO [*Television station call letters*]
KPLS .... Key Pulsing (MSA)
KPLS .... Orange, CA [*AM radio station call letters*]
KPLT .... Paris, TX [*AM radio station call letters*]
KPLT-FM ..... Paris, TX [*FM radio station call letters*]
KPLU .... Tacoma, WA [*FM radio station call letters*]
KPLV .... Port Lavaca, TX [*FM radio station call letters*]
KPLW-FM .... Wenatchee, WA [*FM radio station call letters*] (RBYB)
KPLX .... Fort Worth, TX [*FM radio station call letters*]
KPLY .... Sparks, NV [*AM radio station call letters*]
KPLZ .... Seattle, WA [*FM radio station call letters*]
KPM .... Kahler Process Model [*Computer science*]
KPM .... Kathode Pulse Modulation
KPM .... Kensington Palace Gardens [*British interrogation center*]
Kpm .... Kilopondmeter
KPM .... Kilo/Pound/Meters (STED)
KPM .... King's Police Medal
KPM .... Kronig-Penny Model
KPMB .... Pembina [*North Dakota*] [*ICAO location identifier*] (ICLI)
KPMD .... Palmdale/Air Force Plant No. 42 [*California*] [*ICAO location identifier*] (ICLI)
KPMG .... Klynveld Peat Marwick Goerdeler [*Commercial firm British*]
KPMI .... Kraner Preschool Math Inventory [*Educational test*]
KPMO .... Mendocino, CA [*AM radio station call letters*]
KPMW .... Hallimaile, HI [*FM radio station call letters*]
KPMX .... Sterling, CO [*FM radio station call letters*]
KPN .... Confederation for an Independent Poland (PD)
KPN .... Kipnuk [*Alaska*] [*Airport symbol*] (OAG)
KPN .... Kipnuk, AK [*Location identifier FAA*] (FAAL)
KPN .... Koninklijke PTT Nederland [*Post and telecommunications company*] (ECON)
KPN .... KPN [*NYSE symbol*] (SAG)
KPN .... Kupiano [*Papua New Guinea*] [*Seismograph station code, US Geological Survey*] (SEIS)
KPN .... Royal PTT Nederland ADS [*NYSE symbol*] (TTSB)
KPNC .... Ponca City [*Oklahoma*] [*ICAO location identifier*] (ICLI)
KPNC .... Ponca City, OK [*FM radio station call letters*]
KPND .... Sandpoint, ID [*FM radio station call letters*]
KPNE .... North Platte, NE [*Television station call letters*]
KPNE .... Philadelphia/North Philadelphia [*Pennsylvania*] [*ICAO location identifier*] (ICLI)

KPNE-FM ..... North Platte, NE [*FM radio station call letters*]

KPNLF .... Khmer People's National Liberation Front [*Cambodia*] [*Political party*] (PD)

KPNO .... Kitt Peak National Observatory [*Tucson, AZ*] [*National Science Foundation*]

KPNO .... Norfolk, NE [*FM radio station call letters*]

KPNOB .... Kitt Peak National Observatory [*Tucson, AZ*]

KPNS .... Pensacola/Regional [*Florida*] [*ICAO location identifier*] (ICLI)

KPNT-FM ...... Ste. Genevieve, MO [*FM radio station call letters*] (RBYB)

KPNW .... Eugene, OR [*AM radio station call letters*]

KPNX-TV ...... Mesa, AZ [*Television station call letters*]

KPNY .... Alliance, NE [*FM radio station call letters*]

KPO .... Keypunch Operator [*Computer science*]

KPO .... King Pin Offset [*Automotive engineering*]

KPO .... Kitt Peak National Observatory, Tucson, AZ [*OCLC symbol*] (OCLC)

KPO .... Kommunistische Partei Oesterreichs [*Communist Party of Austria*] [*Political party*] (PPW)

KPOA .... Lahaina, HI [*FM radio station call letters*]

KPOB .... Fayetteville/Pope Air Force Base [*North Carolina*] [*ICAO location identifier*] (ICLI)

KPOB .... Poplar Bluff, MO [*Television station call letters*]

KPOC .... Key Prep on Campus [*Slang*]

KPOC .... Pocahontas, AR [*AM radio station call letters*]

KPOC-FM ..... Pocahontas, AR [*FM radio station call letters*]

KPOD .... Crescent City, CA [*AM radio station call letters*]

KPOD-FM ..... Crescent North, CA [*FM radio station call letters*]

KPOF .... Denver, CO [*AM radio station call letters*]

KPOI .... Honolulu, HI [*FM radio station call letters*]

KPOK .... Bowman, ND [*AM radio station call letters*]

KPOM .... Fort Smith, AR [*Television station call letters*]

KPOO .... San Francisco, CA [*FM radio station call letters*]

KPOP .... San Diego, CA [*AM radio station call letters*]

KPOS .... Post, TX [*AM radio station call letters*]

KPOS-FM ..... Post, TX [*FM radio station call letters*]

KPOW .... Powell, WY [*AM radio station call letters*]

KPOWU .... Kenya Petroleum and Oil Workers' Union

KPOZ-AM ..... San Antonio, TX [*AM radio station call letters*] (BROA)

KPP .... Kaneb Pipeline Partnership LP [*NYSE symbol*] (SPSG)

KPP .... Kaneb Pipe Line PtnrsL.P. [*NYSE symbol*] (TTSB)

KPP .... Keeper of the Privy Purse [*British*]

KPP .... Komunistyczna Partia Polski [*Communist Party of Poland (1925-1938)*] [*Political party*] (PPE)

KPPA .... Kosovo Patriotic and Political Association (BUAC)

KPPC .... Pasadena, CA [*AM radio station call letters*]

KPPL .... Colusa, CA [*FM radio station call letters*]

KPPR .... Williston, ND [*FM radio station call letters*]

KPPS .... Kilopackets per Second [*Telecommunications*]

kpps .... Kilopulses per Second

KPPS .... Kilopulses per Second (NAKS)

KPPT-AM ..... Toledo, OR [*AM radio station call letters*] (BROA)

KPPT-FM ..... Toledo, OR [*FM radio station call letters*] (BROA)

KPPV .... Prescott Valley, AZ [*FM radio station call letters*]

KPQ .... Wenatchee, WA [*AM radio station call letters*]

KPQ-FM .... Wenatchee, WA [*FM radio station call letters*]

KPQI .... Presque Isle/Presque Isle [*Maine*] [*ICAO location identifier*] (ICLI)

KPQX .... Havre, MT [*FM radio station call letters*]

KPR .... Keeper (ABBR)

KPR .... Kenya Police Reserve

KPR .... Key Pulse Rate [*Cardiology*] (DAVI)

KPR .... Keypunch Replacement [*Computer science*] (MHDI)

KPR .... Knight of Polonia Restituta [*British*]

KPR .... Knots per Revolution

KPR .... Kodak Photo Resist

KPR .... Krasnaya Polyana [*Former USSR Seismograph station code, US Geological Survey Closed*] (SEIS)

KPR .... Kuder Preference Record [*Psychology*] (DAVI)

KPR .... Port Williams [*Alaska*] [*Airport symbol*] (OAG)

KPR .... Port Williams, AK [*Location identifier FAA*] (FAAL)

KPRA .... Ukiah, CA [*FM radio station call letters*]

KPRC .... Houston, TX [*AM radio station call letters*]

KPRC-TV ...... Houston, TX [*Television station call letters*]

KPRD .... Hays, KS [*FM radio station call letters*] (RBYB)

KPRD .... KSC [*Kennedy Space Center*] Program Requirements Document [*NASA*] (NASA)

KPRE .... Vail, CO [*FM radio station call letters*] (RBYB)

KPRG .... Agana, GU [*FM radio station call letters*] (RBYB)

KPRI .... Fagaitua, AS [*FM radio station call letters*] (RBYB)

KPRJ .... Jamestown, ND [*FM radio station call letters*]

KPRK .... Livingston, MT [*AM radio station call letters*]

KPRL .... Paso Robles, CA [*AM radio station call letters*]

KPRM .... Park Rapids, MN [*AM radio station call letters*]

KPRN .... Grand Junction, CO [*FM radio station call letters*]

KPRO .... Riverside, CA [*AM radio station call letters*]

KPRP .... Kampuchean [*or Khmer*] People's Revolutionary Party [*Political party*] (PD)

KPR-P .... Kuder Preference Record - Personal [*Psychology*]

KPRQ .... Price, UT [*FM radio station call letters*]

KPRR .... El Paso, TX [*FM radio station call letters*]

KPRS .... Kansas City, MO [*FM radio station call letters*]

KPRT .... Kansas City, MO [*AM radio station call letters*]

KPRV .... Heavener, OK [*FM radio station call letters*]

KPR-V .... Kuder Preference Record - Vocational [*Psychology*] (DAVI)

KPRV .... Poteau, OK [*AM radio station call letters*]

KPRW-FM ..... Perham, MN [*FM radio station call letters*] (RBYB)

KPRX .... Bakersfield, CA [*FM radio station call letters*]

KPRY .... Pierre, SD [*Television station call letters*]

KPRZ .... San Marcos, CA [*AM radio station call letters*]

KPRZ-FM ..... Fountain, CO [*FM radio station call letters*] (RBYB)

KPS .... Kempsey [*Australia Airport symbol*] (OAG)

KPS .... Keypunch Performance System [*Computer science*] (PDAA)

KPS .... Kilometers per Second (NASA)

KPS .... Kirbati Philatelic Society (EA)

KPS .... Klystron Power Supply

KPS .... Knight of the (Order of the) Polar Star [*Sweden*] (ROG)

KPS .... Knowledge Processing System [*Expert system shell*] (NITA)

KPS .... Kommunistische Partei der Schweiz [*Communist Party of Switzerland*] [*Political party*] (PPE)

KPS .... Kommunistische Partij Suriname [*Communist Party of Surinam*] [*Political party*] (PPW)

KPS .... One Thousand Pulses per Second (KSC)

KPSA .... Alamogordo, NM [*AM radio station call letters*]

KPSA .... La Luz, NM [*FM radio station call letters*]

KPSC .... Palm Springs, CA [*FM radio station call letters*]

KPSD .... Faith, SD [*FM radio station call letters*]

KPSD-TV ...... Eagle Butte, SD [*Television station call letters*]

KPSI .... Kip [*Thousands of Pounds*] per Square Inch

KPSI .... Palm Springs, CA [*AM radio station call letters*]

KPSI-FM ...... Palm Springs, CA [*FM radio station call letters*]

KPSK .... Keepsake (ABBR)

KPSL .... Thousand Palms, CA [*AM radio station call letters*]

KPSM .... Brownwood, TX [*FM radio station call letters*]

KPSM .... Klystron Power Supply Modulator

KPSM .... Portsmouth/Pease Air Force Base [*New Hampshire*] [*ICAO location identifier*] (ICLI)

KPSNSW ...... Koala Preservation Society of New South Wales [*Australia*]

KPSO .... Falfurrias, TX [*AM radio station call letters*]

KPSO-FM ..... Falfurrias, TX [*FM radio station call letters*]

KPSQ .... Kapson Senior Quarters Corp. [*NASDAQ symbol*] (SAG)

KPSS .... Kommunisticheskaya Partiya Sovietskogo Soyuza [*Communist Party of the Soviet Union*] [*Political party*]

KPST .... Vallejo, CA [*Television station call letters*]

KPSU .... Goodwell, OK [*FM radio station call letters*]

KPSX .... Palacios [*Texas*] [*ICAO location identifier*] (ICLI)

KPT .... Kaena Point Station [*Hawaii*] [*Military*]

KPT .... Kai's Power Tools for Windows [*HSC Software*] (PCM)

KPT .... Karpatair [*Hungary ICAO designator*] (FAAC)

KPT .... Keeprite, Inc. [*Toronto Stock Exchange symbol*]

KPT .... Kidney Punch Test [*or Murphy's test*] (DAVI)

KPT .... Kidney Punch Test [*Physical exam*] (STED)

KPT .... Konover Property [*Formerly, FAC Realty Trust*] [*NYSE symbol*]

KPT .... Kuder Performance Test [*Psychology*] (DAVI)

KPT .... Pittsburg State University, Pittsburg, KS [*Library symbol Library of Congress*] (LCLS)

KPT3 .... Kai's Power Tools [*Computer science*]

KPTB .... Lubbock, TX [*Television station call letters*] (RBYB)

KPTC .... Kuwait Public Transport Co. (BUAC)

KPTH .... Sioux City, IA [*Television station call letters*] (BROA)

KPTI .... Kunitz Pancreatic Trypsin Inhibitor [*Medicine*] (MAE)

KPTL .... Carson City, NV [*AM radio station call letters*]

KPTM .... Omaha, NE [*Television station call letters*]

KPTS .... Hutchinson, KS [*Television station call letters*]

KPTT .... Kaolin Partial Thromboplastin Time [*Clinical chemistry*] (MAE)

KPTV .... Portland, OR [*Television station call letters*]

KPTX .... Pecos, TX [*FM radio station call letters*]

KPTY-FM ..... Gilbert, AZ [*FM radio station call letters*] (BROA)

KPU .... Kaneb Pipe Line Partners LP [*NYSE symbol*] (SAG)

KPU .... Kaneb Pipe Ln Ptnrs LP Pref Ut [*NYSE symbol*] (TTSB)

KPU .... Kaszubian Pomeranian Union [*Poland*] [*Political party*] (BUAC)

KPU .... Khapalu [*Pakistan*] [*Airport symbol*] (AD)

KPU .... Kommunisticheskaia Partiia Ukrainy [*Communist Party of the Ukraine*] [*Political party*]

KPUA .... Hilo, HI [*AM radio station call letters*]

KPUB .... Pueblo Memorial [*Colorado*] [*ICAO location identifier*] (ICLI)

KPUC .... Korean Presidential Unit Citation [*Military award*]

KPUG .... Bellingham, WA [*AM radio station call letters*]

KPUP .... Key Personnel Upgrade Program [*National Guard*]

KPUR .... Amarillo, TX [*AM radio station call letters*]

KPUR-FM ..... Canyon, TX [*FM radio station call letters*]

KPUZ .... Kommunisticheskaia Partiia Uzbekistana [*Communist Party of Uzbekistan*] [*Political party*]

KPV .... Kid-Powered Vehicle

KPV .... Killed Parenteral Vaccine [*Immunology*] (DAVI)

KPV .... Killed Polio Vaccine [*Medicine*] (STED)

KPVD .... Providence/Theodore Francis Greene State [*Rhode Island*] [*ICAO location identifier*] (ICLI)

KPV HMG .... Krupnokalibernyi Pulemyoy Vladimirova Heavy Machine Gun [*Soviet-made weaponry used extensively by the People's Army of North Vietnam*] (VNW)

KPVI .... Pocatello, ID [*Television station call letters*]

KPVS .... Hilo, HI [*FM radio station call letters*]

KPVU .... Prairie View, TX [*FM radio station call letters*]

KPVY .... Amarillo, TX [*FM radio station call letters*]

KPWA .... Korean Patriotic Women's Association in America [*Defunct*] (EA)

KPWB .... Piedmont, MO [*AM radio station call letters*]

KPWB-FM ..... Piedmont, MO [*FM radio station call letters*]

KPWB-TV ..... Sacramento, CA [*Television station call letters*] (RBYB)

KPWM .... Portland/International Jetport [*Maine*] [*ICAO location identifier*] (ICLI)

KPWR .... Los Angeles, CA [*FM radio station call letters*]

KPWS .... Crowley, LA [*AM radio station call letters*]

KPWU .... Korean Port Worker's Union (BUAC)

KPXA .... Sisters, OR [*FM radio station call letters*]
KPXB .... Conroe, TX [*Television station call letters*] (BROA)
KPXC .... Indian Springs, NV [*FM radio station call letters*]
KPXE .... Liberty, TX [*AM radio station call letters*]
KPXF .... Lacombe, LA [*FM radio station call letters*]
KPXH .... Garapan-Saipan, MP [*FM radio station call letters*]
KPXI .... Mount Pleasant, TX [*FM radio station call letters*]
KPXM .... St. Cloud, MN [*Television station call letters*] (BROA)
KPXN .... San Bernardino, CA [*Television station call letters*] (BROA)
KPXP .... Garapan-Saipan, MP [*FM radio station call letters*]
KPXQ-AM .... Phoenix, AZ [*AM radio station call letters*] (RBYB)
KPY .... Port Bailey [*Alaska*] [*Airport symbol*] (OAG)
KPY .... Port Bailey, AK [*Location identifier FAA*] (FAAL)
KPYK .... Terrell, TX [*AM radio station call letters*]
KPYN .... Atlanta, TX [*FM radio station call letters*]
KPZA .... Espanola, NM [*FM radio station call letters*] (RBYB)
KQ .... Air South, Inc. [*Airline code*]
KQ .... Kenya Airways [*ICAO designator*] (AD)
KQ .... Kenya Airways [*Airline flight code*] (ODBW)
KQ .... Line Squall [*Meteorology*] (WDAA)
KQA .... Akutan [*Alaska*] [*Airport symbol*] (OAG)
KQA .... Akutan, AK [*Location identifier FAA*] (FAAL)
KQA .... Kenya Airways Ltd. [*ICAO designator*] (FAAC)
KQAA .... Aberdeen, SD [*FM radio station call letters*]
KQAB-AM .... Lake Isabella, CA [*AM radio station call letters*] (BROA)
KQAC .... Amarillo, TX [*FM radio station call letters*]
KQAD .... Luverne, MN [*AM radio station call letters*]
KQAK .... Bend, OR [*FM radio station call letters*]
KQAL .... Winona, MN [*FM radio station call letters*]
KQAM .... Wichita, KS [*AM radio station call letters*]
KQAR-FM .... Jacksonville, AR [*FM radio station call letters*] (BROA)
KQAY .... Tucumcari, NM [*FM radio station call letters*]
KQAZ .... Springerville-Eager, AZ [*FM radio station call letters*]
KQBE .... Ellensburg, WA [*FM radio station call letters*]
KQBR .... Davis, CA [*FM radio station call letters*]
KQC .... King's College London [*British*] (IRUK)
KQCA .... Stockton, CA [*Television station call letters*] (RBYB)
KQCD .... Dickinson, ND [*Television station call letters*]
KQCL .... Faribault, MN [*FM radio station call letters*]
KQCP .... King's and Queen's College of Physicians [*Ireland*]
KQCT .... Davenport, IA [*Television station call letters*]
KQCV .... Oklahoma City, OK [*AM radio station call letters*]
KQDI-FM ..... Great Falls, MT [*FM radio station call letters*]
KQDJ .... Jamestown, ND [*AM radio station call letters*]
KQDJ-FM ..... Valley City, ND [*FM radio station call letters*] (RBYB)
KQDS .... Duluth, MN [*AM radio station call letters*]
KQDS-FM .... Duluth, MN [*FM radio station call letters*]
KQDY .... Bismarck, ND [*FM radio station call letters*]
KQED .... San Francisco, CA [*FM radio station call letters*]
KQED-TV .... San Francisco, CA [*Television station call letters*]
KQEG .... La Crescent, MN [*FM radio station call letters*]
KQEN .... Roseburg, OR [*AM radio station call letters*]
KQEO-FM .... Grants, NM [*FM radio station call letters*] (BROA)
KQEP .... Rock Valley, IA [*FM radio station call letters*]
KQEQ .... Fowler, CA [*AM radio station call letters*] (RBYB)
KQEW .... Fordyce, AR [*FM radio station call letters*]
KQEX .... Fortuna, CA [*FM radio station call letters*]
KQEZ-FM .... Houston, AK [*FM radio station call letters*] (BROA)
KQF .... Krupp Quick-Firing Gun
KQFC .... Boise, ID [*FM radio station call letters*]
KQFE .... Springfield, OR [*FM radio station call letters*]
KQFM .... Hermiston, OR [*FM radio station call letters*]
KQFN .... Fargo, ND [*AM radio station call letters*] (RBYB)
KQFX .... Borger, TX [*FM radio station call letters*]
KQHC-FM .... Burns, OR [*FM radio station call letters*] (RBYB)
KQHN .... Nederland, TX [*AM radio station call letters*]
KQHT .... Crookston, MN [*FM radio station call letters*]
KQIC .... Willmar, MN [*FM radio station call letters*]
KQID .... Alexandria, LA [*FM radio station call letters*]
KQIK .... Lakeview, OR [*AM radio station call letters*]
KQIK-FM ..... Lakeview, OR [*FM radio station call letters*]
KQIL .... Grand Junction, CO [*AM radio station call letters*]
KQIP .... Odessa, TX [*FM radio station call letters*]
KQIX .... Grand Junction, CO [*FM radio station call letters*]
KQIZ .... Amarillo, TX [*FM radio station call letters*]
KQJM .... King, Queen, Jack Meld [*Canasta*]
KQKD .... Redfield, SD [*AM radio station call letters*]
KQKD-FM .... Redfield, SD [*FM radio station call letters*]
KQKI .... Bayou Vista, LA [*FM radio station call letters*]
KQKQ .... Council Bluffs, IA [*FM radio station call letters*]
KQKS .... Longmont, CO [*FM radio station call letters*]
KQKY .... Kearney, NE [*FM radio station call letters*]
KQL .... Kol [*Papua New Guinea*] [*Airport symbol*] (OAG)
KQLA .... Ogden, KS [*FM radio station call letters*]
KQLB .... Los Banos, CA [*FM radio station call letters*]
KQLL .... Owasso, OK [*FM radio station call letters*]
KQLL .... Tulsa, OK [*AM radio station call letters*]
KQLM-FM .... Odessa, TX [*FM radio station call letters*] (RBYB)
KQLO .... Reno, NV [*AM radio station call letters*]
KQLS .... Colby, KS [*FM radio station call letters*]
KQLT .... Casper, WY [*FM radio station call letters*]
KQLX .... Lisbon, ND [*AM radio station call letters*]
KQLX-FM .... Lisbon, ND [*FM radio station call letters*]
KQM .... Kolson Quick Modality Test [*Education*]
KQMA .... Phillipsburg, KS [*FM radio station call letters*]

KQMB-FM .... Midvale, UT [*FM radio station call letters*] (RBYB)
KQMC .... Brinkley, AR [*FM radio station call letters*]
KQMG .... Independence, IA [*AM radio station call letters*]
KQMG-FM .... Independence, IA [*FM radio station call letters*]
KQML .... Knowledge Query and Manipulation Language [*Computer science*]
KQMN .... Thief River Falls, MN [*FM radio station call letters*]
KQMO-FM .... Ash Grove, MO [*FM radio station call letters*] (RBYB)
KQMQ .... Honolulu, HI [*AM radio station call letters*]
KQMQ-FM .... Honolulu, HI [*FM radio station call letters*]
KQMS .... Redding, CA [*AM radio station call letters*]
KQMX-FM .... Clinton, OK [*FM radio station call letters*] (RBYB)
KQNA .... Prescott Valley, AZ [*AM radio station call letters*]
KQNC .... Quincy, CA [*FM radio station call letters*]
KQNG .... Lihue, HI [*AM radio station call letters*]
KQNG-FM .... Lihue, HI [*FM radio station call letters*]
KQNK .... Norton, KS [*AM radio station call letters*]
KQNK-FM .... Norton, KS [*FM radio station call letters*]
KQNN .... Alice, TX [*FM radio station call letters*]
KQNS .... Lindsborg, KS [*FM radio station call letters*]
KQNV .... Sparks, NV [*FM radio station call letters*] (RBYB)
KQOD .... Stockton, CA [*FM radio station call letters*]
KQOL .... Boulder City, NV [*FM radio station call letters*] (RBYB)
KQPM .... Ukiah, CA [*FM radio station call letters*]
KQPR .... Albert Lea, MN [*FM radio station call letters*]
KQPT .... Sacramento, CA [*FM radio station call letters*]
KQQK .... Galveston, TX [*FM radio station call letters*]
KQQL .... Anoka, MN [*FM radio station call letters*]
KQQQ .... Pullman, WA [*AM radio station call letters*]
KQR .... Cobequid Resources Ltd. [*Vancouver Stock Exchange symbol*]
KQR .... Kit Quotation Request (MCD)
KQRC-FM .... Leavenworth, KS [*FM radio station call letters*]
KQRK .... Ronan, MT [*FM radio station call letters*]
KQRN .... Mitchell, SD [*FM radio station call letters*]
KQRS .... Golden Valley, MN [*AM radio station call letters*]
KQRS-FM .... Golden Valley, MN [*FM radio station call letters*]
KQRX .... Midland, TX [*FM radio station call letters*]
KQSB .... Santa Barbara, CA [*AM radio station call letters*]
KQSC .... Willows, CA [*FM radio station call letters*]
KQSD .... Lowry, SD [*Television station call letters*]
KQSK .... Chadron, NE [*FM radio station call letters*]
KQSN-FM .... Toppenish, WA [*FM radio station call letters*] (BROA)
KQSR-FM .... Oklahoma City, OK [*FM radio station call letters*] (BROA)
KQSS .... Miami, AZ [*FM radio station call letters*]
KQST .... Sedona, AZ [*FM radio station call letters*]
KQSW .... Rock Springs, WY [*FM radio station call letters*]
KQSY .... Nowata, OK [*FM radio station call letters*] (RBYB)
KQT .... Konkordanz zu den Qumrantexten [*A publication*] (BJA)
KQTL .... Sahuarita, AZ [*FM radio station call letters*]
KQTN-FM .... Lordsburg, NM [*FM radio station call letters*] (BROA)
KQTP .... St. Marys, KS [*FM radio station call letters*]
KQTV .... St. Joseph, MO [*Television station call letters*]
KQTY .... Borger, TX [*AM radio station call letters*]
KQTZ .... Hobart, OK [*FM radio station call letters*]
KQUA .... Lutesville, MO [*FM radio station call letters*]
KQUE .... Houston, TX [*FM radio station call letters*]
KQUL .... Lake Ozark, MO [*FM radio station call letters*]
KQUS .... Hot Springs, AR [*FM radio station call letters*]
KQUY .... Butte, MT [*FM radio station call letters*]
KQV .... Pittsburgh, PA [*AM radio station call letters*]
KQVO .... Calexico, CA [*FM radio station call letters*]
KQWB .... Moorhead, MN [*FM radio station call letters*]
KQWC .... Webster City, IA [*AM radio station call letters*]
KQWC-FM .... Webster City, IA [*FM radio station call letters*]
KQWK-FM .... Wallace, ID [*FM radio station call letters*] (BROA)
KQWS-FM .... Omak, WA [*FM radio station call letters*] (BROA)
KQXC .... Wichita Falls, TX [*FM radio station call letters*]
KQXI .... Aruada, CO [*AM radio station call letters*]
KQXL .... New Roads, LA [*FM radio station call letters*]
KQXR .... Payette, ID [*FM radio station call letters*] (RBYB)
KQXT .... San Antonio, TX [*FM radio station call letters*]
KQXX .... McAllen, TX [*FM radio station call letters*]
KQXY .... Beaumont, TX [*FM radio station call letters*]
KQYB .... Spring Grove, MN [*FM radio station call letters*]
KQYN .... Twentynine Palms, CA [*FM radio station call letters*]
KQYX .... Joplin, MO [*AM radio station call letters*]
KQZE .... St. Johns, AZ [*FM radio station call letters*]
KQZZ-FM .... Devils Lake, ND [*FM radio station call letters*] (RBYB)
KR .... Contractor [*Navy*]
KR .... Kallah Rabbati (BJA)
KR .... Kar-Air [*ICAO designator*] (AD)
KR .... Karat (ABBR)
KR .... Keesom Relationship
K-R .... Kent-Rosanoff Free Association Test [*Psychology*]
KR .... Kenya Railways
KR .... Ketoaldonate Reductase [*An enzyme*]
KR .... Ketoreductase [*An enzyme*]
KR .... Keying Relay
KR .... Key Records [*Record label*]
KR .... Key Register
KR .... Khmer Rouge (BARN)
kR .... Kilorayleigh
kR .... Kiloroentgen
KR .... Kinetic Reaction
KR .... King's Regiment [*Military unit*] [*British*]
KR .... King's Regulations for the Army and the Army Reserves [*British*]

KR	King's Remembrancer [*British*]
KR	King's Rook [*Chess*]
KR	Kipp Relay
KR	Kirkus Review [*A publication*] (BRI)
KR	Knight of the [*Order of the*] Redeemer [*Greece*]
KR	Knight-Ridder
KR	Knowledge of Results
KR	Knowledge Representation [*Computer science*]
KR	Koloniale Rundschau (BJA)
KR	Kopper Reppart [*Medium*] [*Biochemistry*] (DAVI)
KR	Kreuzer [*Monetary unit*] [*German*]
KR	Kroger Co. [*NYSE symbol*] (TTSB)
KR	Krona [*Crown*] [*Monetary unit Iceland, Sweden*] (EY)
KR	Krone [*Crown*] [*Monetary unit Denmark, Norway*] (EY)
K-R	Krueger-Ringier [*Book manufacturer*]
Kr	Krypton [*Chemical element*]
K-R	Kuder-Richardson Formula [*Education*] (AEE)
KR	Republic of Korea [*ANSI two-letter standard code*] (CNC)
KR20	Kuder-Richardson Formula 20
KR21	Kuder-Richardson Formula 21
KRA	Contractor Responsible Action (MCD)
KRA	Karenni Revolutionary Army [*Myanmar*] [*Political party*] (EY)
KRA	Kerang [*Victoria, Australia*] [*Airport symbol*] (AD)
KRA	Key Result Area
KRA	Kickback Racket Act
KRA	Klinefelter-Reifenstein-Albright [*Syndrome*] [*Medicine*] (DAVI)
KRA	Krakow [*Poland*] [*Seismograph station code, US Geological Survey*] (SEIS)
KRAB	Greenacres, CA [*FM radio station call letters*]
KRAD	Kilorad (WDAA)
KRAD	Portland, TX [*FM radio station call letters*]
KRAE	Cheyenne, WY [*AM radio station call letters*]
KRAF	Holdenville, OK [*AM radio station call letters*]
KRAG-JORG...	Krag-Jorgensen Rifle
KRAI	Craig, CO [*AM radio station call letters*]
KRAI-FM	Craig, CO [*FM radio station call letters*]
KR Air	King's Regulations and Orders for the Royal Canadian Air Force
KRAJ	Johannesburg, CA [*FM radio station call letters*]
KRAK-FM	Sacramento, CA [*FM radio station call letters*]
KRAL	Rawlins, WY [*AM radio station call letters*]
KRAM	St. Louis, MO [*AM radio station call letters*] (RBYB)
KRAN	Krantor Corp. [*NASDAQ symbol*] (SAG)
KR & ACI	King's Regulations and Air Council Instructions [*British military*] (DMA)
KR & AI	King's Regulations and Admiralty Instructions [*Navy British*]
KR & O (Can)...	King's Regulations and Orders for the Royal Canadian Army
Krantor	Krantor Corp. [*Associated Press*] (SAG)
Krantr	Krantor Corp. [*Associated Press*] (SAG)
KRANW	Krantor Corp.Wrrt'A' [*NASDAQ symbol*] (TTSB)
Kranzc	Kranzco Realty Trust [*Associated Press*] (SAG)
KRAO	Colfax, WA [*FM radio station call letters*]
KRAQ	Jackson, MN [*FM radio station call letters*]
KRAS	Keyworded References to Archaeological Science [*Department of Archaeology*] [*University of Leicester British*] [*Database*] (NITA)
KRAT-FM	Altamont, OR [*FM radio station call letters*] (BROA)
Krause	Krauses Furniture, Inc. [*Associated Press*] (SAG)
KrauseF	Krauses Furniture, Inc. [*Associated Press*] (SAG)
KRAV	Tulsa, OK [*FM radio station call letters*]
KRAW-FM	Lake Arthur, LA [*FM radio station call letters*] (BROA)
KRAY	Salinas, CA [*FM radio station call letters*]
KRAZ	Sutter Creek, CA [*FM radio station call letters*]
KRB	Kansas River Basin
KRB	Kariba [*Zimbabwe*] [*Seismograph station code, US Geological Survey Closed*] (SEIS)
KRB	Karumba [*Australia Airport symbol*] (OAG)
KRB	Krebs-Ringer-Bicarbonate [*Buffer solution*]
KRB	Krebs-Ringer Bicarbonate Buffer [*Biochemistry*] (DAVI)
KRB	MBNA Corp. [*NYSE symbol*] (SPSG)
KRBA	Lufkin, TX [*AM radio station call letters*]
KRBB	Krebs-Ringer Bicarbonate Buffer [*Biochemistry*] (DAVI)
KRBB	Wichita, KS [*FM radio station call letters*]
KRBC	Abilene, TX [*Television station call letters*]
KRBD	Ketchikan, AK [*FM radio station call letters*]
KRBE	Houston, TX [*FM radio station call letters*]
KRBF	Bonners Ferry, ID [*FM radio station call letters*]
KRBFC	Kenny Roberts and Bettyanne Fan Club [*Defunct*] (EA)
KRBG	Canadian, TX [*AM radio station call letters*]
KRBG	Krebs-Ringer Bicarbonate Buffer [*Containing*] Glucose (DAVI)
KRBG-GA	Krebs-Ringer Bicarbonate Buffer with Glucose [*Medicine*] (DMAA)
KRB-GA	Krebs-Ringer-Bicarbonate Glucose-Albumin [*Buffer solution*]
KRBH-FM	Hondo, TX [*FM radio station call letters*] (RBYB)
KRBI	St. Peter, MN [*AM radio station call letters*]
KRBI-FM	St. Peter, MN [*FM radio station call letters*]
KRBL	Idalou, TX [*FM radio station call letters*] (RBYB)
KRBM	Pendleton, OR [*FM radio station call letters*]
KRBN	Boston [*Massachusetts*] [*ICAO location identifier*] (ICLI)
KRBO	Las Vegas, NV [*FM radio station call letters*]
KRBPrA	MBNA Corp.7.50% Sr'A'Pfd [*NYSE symbol*] (TTSB)
KRBR-FM	Superior, WI [*FM radio station call letters*] (RBYB)
KRBS	Krebs-Ringer Bicarbonate Solution
KRBSG	Krebs-Ringer Bicarbonate Solution with Glucose
KRBT	Fresno, CA [*FM radio station call letters*]
KRBV	Dallas, TX [*FM radio station call letters*] (RBYB)
KRBW-FM	Ottawa, KS [*FM radio station call letters*] (BROA)
KRBZ	Reedsport, OR [*FM radio station call letters*]

KRC	Keweenaw Research Center [*Houghton, MI*] [*Army Research center*] (GRD)
KRC	King Ranch [*California*] [*Seismograph station code, US Geological Survey Closed*] (SEIS)
KRC	Knight of the Red Cross [*Freemasonry*]
KRC	Knowledge Resource Center [*Computer-based information delivery system in libraries*] [*Generic term*]
KRC	Kodak Reflex Camera
KRC	Regis College Library, University of Toronto [*UTLAS symbol*]
KRCA	Rapid City/Ellsworth Air Force Base [*South Dakota*] [*ICAO location identifier*] (ICLI)
KRCA	Riverside, CA [*Television station call letters*]
KRCB	Santa Rosa, CA [*FM radio station call letters*]
KRCB-TV	Cotati, CA [*Television station call letters*]
KRCC	Colorado Springs, CO [*FM radio station call letters*]
KRCC	Kingston Regional Cancer Center [*Canada*] (PDAA)
KRCD	Chubbuck, ID [*AM radio station call letters*]
KRCG	Jefferson City, MO [*Television station call letters*]
KRCH	Rochester, MN [*FM radio station call letters*]
KRCHF	Kerchief (ABBR)
KRCI	Avalon, CA [*FM radio station call letters*]
KRCK	Burbank, CA [*AM radio station call letters*]
KRCL	Salt Lake City, UT [*FM radio station call letters*]
KRCN	King's Regulations and Orders for the Royal Canadian Navy
KRCO	Prineville, OR [*AM radio station call letters*]
KRCQ	Detroit Lakes, MN [*FM radio station call letters*] (RBYB)
KRCR	Redding, CA [*Television station call letters*]
KRCRA	Known Recoverable Coal Resource Area (PDAA)
KRCS	Sturgis, SD [*FM radio station call letters*]
KRCU	Cape Girardeau, MO [*FM radio station call letters*]
KRCW	Royal City, WA [*FM radio station call letters*]
KRCX	Roseville, CA [*AM radio station call letters*]
KRCY	Kingman, AZ [*FM radio station call letters*]
KRD	Kourday [*Former USSR Seismograph station code, US Geological Survey Closed*] (SEIS)
KRD	Krieger Data International Corp. [*Vancouver Stock Exchange symbol*]
KRDC	St. George, UT [*FM radio station call letters*]
KRDD	Roswell, NM [*AM radio station call letters*]
KRDE	Denver [*Colorado*] [*ICAO location identifier*] (ICLI)
KRDF	Spearman, TX [*FM radio station call letters*]
KRDG	Redding, CA [*AM radio station call letters*]
KRDO	Colorado Springs, CO [*AM radio station call letters*]
KRDO-FM	Colorado Springs, CO [*FM radio station call letters*]
KRDO-TV	Colorado Springs, CO [*Television station call letters*]
KRDR	Red River/Grand Forks Air Force Base [*North Dakota*] [*ICAO location identifier*] (ICLI)
KRDS	Tolleson, AZ [*AM radio station call letters*]
KRDS	Wickenburg, AZ [*FM radio station call letters*]
KRDU	Dinuba, CA [*AM radio station call letters*]
KRDU	Raleigh/Raleigh-Durham [*North Carolina*] [*ICAO location identifier*] (ICLI)
KRDZ	Wray, CO [*AM radio station call letters*]
KRE	Aerosucre, SA [*Colombia*] [*FAA designator*] (FAAC)
KRE	Capital Re [*NYSE symbol*] (TTSB)
KRE	Capital Real Estate [*NYSE symbol*] (SPSG)
KRE	Capital Re Corporation1 [*NYSE symbol*] (SAG)
KRE	Consolidated Regal Resources Ltd. [*Vancouver Stock Exchange symbol*]
KRE	Knight of the Red Eagle [*Prussia*]
KRE	Kobe Rubber Exchange (NUMA)
KRE	Kure [*Japan*] [*Seismograph station code, US Geological Survey Closed*] (SEIS)
KREA	Ontario, CA [*FM radio station call letters*]
KREB	Huntsville, AR [*FM radio station call letters*]
KREC	Brian Head, UT [*FM radio station call letters*]
KRED-FM	Eureka, CA [*FM radio station call letters*]
KREE	Lubbock/Reese Air Force Base [*Texas*] [*ICAO location identifier*] (ICLI)
KREEP	Potassium [*Chemical symbol: K*], Rare-Earth Elements, and Phosphorus [*Acronym used to describe crust material brought from the moon by astronauts*]
KREG	Glenwood Springs, CO [*Television station call letters*]
KREG	Koll Real Estate Group [*NASDAQ symbol*] (SAG)
KREG	Koll Real Estate Grp [*NASDAQ symbol*] (TTSB)
KREGP	Koll Real Estate Cv'A'Pfd [*NASDAQ symbol*] (TTSB)
KREH	Oakdale, LA [*FM radio station call letters*]
KREI	Farmington, MO [*AM radio station call letters*]
KREIC	Kuwait Real Estate Investment Consortium (BUAC)
Kreislr	Kreisler Manufacturing Co. [*Associated Press*] (SAG)
KREJ	Medicine Lodge, KS [*FM radio station call letters*]
KREK	Bristow, OK [*FM radio station call letters*]
KREL	California, MO [*AM radio station call letters*] (RBYB)
KREM	Spokane, WA [*Television station call letters*]
KREMS	Kiernan Reentry Measurement Site
KREMU	Kenya Department of Resources Surveys and Remote Sensing (BUAC)
KREMU	Kenya Rangeland Ecological Monitoring Unit
KREN	Kings Road Entertainment, Inc. [*NASDAQ symbol*] (NQ)
KREN	Kings Road Entmt [*NASDAQ symbol*] (TTSB)
KREN	Reno, NV [*Television station call letters*]
KREP	Belleville, KS [*FM radio station call letters*]
KREPrL	Capital Re LLC'MIPS' [*NYSE symbol*] (TTSB)
KRES	Moberly, MO [*FM radio station call letters*]
KRESS	Kinetic Ring Energy Storage System

Kress	Kress' Reports [2-12 Pennsylvania Superior Court] [166-194 Pennsylvania] [A publication] (DLA)
KREU-FM	Roland, OK [FM radio station call letters] (RBYB)
KREUZ	Kreuzer [Monetary unit] [German] (ROG)
KREV	Lakeville, MN [FM radio station call letters]
KREW	Sunnyside, WA [AM radio station call letters]
KREW-FM	Sunnyside, WA [FM radio station call letters]
KREX	Grand Junction, CO [Television station call letters]
KREX	Keel Blade Tip Reflex [Botany]
KREY	Montrose, CO [Television station call letters]
KREZ	Durango, CO [Television station call letters]
KRF	Kathode Ray Furnace
KRF	Kerf Petroleums [Vancouver Stock Exchange symbol]
KRF	Knowledge of Results Feedback
KRF	Kramfors [Sweden] [Airport symbol] (OAG)
KrF	Kristelig Folkpartiet [Christian People's Party] [Norway Political party] (PPE)
KrF	Kristeligt Folkeparti [Christian People's Party] [Denmark Political party] (PPE)
KRF	No. 32 (The Royal) Squadron [British] [FAA designator] (FAAC)
KRFA	Moscow, ID [FM radio station call letters]
KRFC	KISS [Knights in the Service of Satan] Rocks Fan Club (EA)
KRFE	Lubbock, TX [AM radio station call letters] (RBYB)
KRFM	Show Low, AZ [FM radio station call letters]
KRFN	Knight-Ridder Financial News [Database] (IT)
KRFO	Owatonna, MN [AM radio station call letters]
KRFO-FM	Owatonna, MN [FM radio station call letters]
KRFS	Superior, NE [AM radio station call letters]
KRFS-FM	Superior, NE [FM radio station call letters]
KRFT	Knowledge of Results Feedback Task (SAA)
KRFW	Fort Worth [Texas] [ICAO location identifier] (ICLI)
KRFX	Denver, CO [FM radio station call letters]
KRG	Karasabai [Guyana] [Airport symbol] (OAG)
KRG	Kerema [Papua New Guinea] [Seismograph station code, US Geological Survey Closed] (SEIS)
KRG	Knight of the Redeemer of Greece (ROG)
KRG	Krebs-Ringer-Glucose [Buffer solution and growth medium]
KRG	KRG Management, Inc. [Toronto Stock Exchange symbol]
KrG	Kriegsgericht [War Tribunal] [German]
KRG	Krug International Corp. [AMEX symbol] (SAG)
KRG	Quantum Restaurant Group, Inc. [NYSE symbol] (SPSG)
KRGC	Chicago [Illinois] [ICAO location identifier] (ICLI)
KRGD-FM	Burlington, CO [FM radio station call letters] (BROA)
KRGE	Weslaco, TX [AM radio station call letters]
KRGI	Grand Island, NE [AM radio station call letters]
KRGI-FM	Grand Island, NE [FM radio station call letters]
KRGN	Amarillo, TX [FM radio station call letters]
KRGO	Fowler, CA [AM radio station call letters]
KRGQ	West Valley City, UT [AM radio station call letters]
KRGQ-FM	Roy, UT [FM radio station call letters]
KRGS	Rifle, CO [AM radio station call letters]
KRGV	Weslaco, TX [Television station call letters]
KRH	Redhill [England] [Airport symbol]
KRHCF	Rich Coast Res Ltd [NASDAQ symbol] (TTSB)
KRHCF	Rich Coast Resouces [NASDAQ symbol] (SAG)
KRHD	Duncan, OK [AM radio station call letters]
KRHD-FM	Duncan, OK [FM radio station call letters]
KRHS	Overland, MO [FM radio station call letters]
KRHT-AM	Concord, CA [AM radio station call letters] (RBYB)
KRHV	Big Pine, CA [FM radio station call letters] (RBYB)
KRHW-AM	Sikeston, MO [AM radio station call letters] (BROA)
KRI	Karin Lake Explorations [Vancouver Stock Exchange symbol]
KRI	Kikori [Papua New Guinea] [Airport symbol] (OAG)
KRI	King Research, Inc. [Computer consultant] [Information service or system] (IID)
KRI	King's Royal Irish [Military unit] [British]
KRI	Knight-Ridder, Inc. [NYSE symbol] (SPSG)
KRI	Krilo [Former USSR] [FAA designator] (FAAC)
KRIB	Mason City, IA [AM radio station call letters]
KRIC	Rexburg, ID [FM radio station call letters]
KRIC	Richmond/Richard Evelyn Byrd International [Virginia] [ICAO location identifier] (ICLI)
KRIG	Nowata, OK [FM radio station call letters]
KRIG	Pawhuska, OK [AM radio station call letters] (RBYB)
KRIH	King's Royal Irish Hussars [British military] (DMA)
KRII	Knight-Ridder Information Inc.
KRIL	Odessa, TX [AM radio station call letters]
KRIM	Payson, AZ [FM radio station call letters]
KRIN	Waterloo, IA [Television station call letters]
KRIO	Floresville, TX [FM radio station call letters]
KRIO	McAllen, TX [AM radio station call letters]
KRIPA	Korean Research Institute of Public Administration (BUAC)
KRIPES	K-Resolved Inverse Photoelectron Spectroscopy
KRIPO	Kriminalpolizei [Ordinary Criminal Police] [German]
KRIS	Corpus Christi, TX [Television station call letters]
KRISO	Korea Research Institute of Ship and Ocean (BUAC)
KRISP	Kenya Rift International Seismic Project
KRIV	Houston, TX [Television station call letters]
KRIV	Riverside/March Air Force Base [California] [ICAO location identifier] (ICLI)
KRIZ	Renton, WA [AM radio station call letters]
KRJ	Kamimuroga [Japan] [Seismograph station code, US Geological Survey] (SEIS)
KRJB	Ada, MN [FM radio station call letters]
KRJC	Elko, NV [FM radio station call letters]

KRJT	Bowie, TX [AM radio station call letters]
KRJT-FM	Bowie, TX [FM radio station call letters]
KRK	Kirkenes [Norway] [Seismograph station code, US Geological Survey Closed] (SEIS)
KRK	Krakow [Poland] [Airport symbol] (OAG)
KRKC	Kansas City [Missouri] [ICAO location identifier] (ICLI)
KRKC	King City, CA [AM radio station call letters]
KRKC-FM	King City, CA [FM radio station call letters]
KRKE	Aspen, CO [AM radio station call letters]
KRKI	Estes Park, CO [AM radio station call letters]
KRKK	Rock Springs, WY [AM radio station call letters]
KRKL	Yountville, CA [AM radio station call letters]
KRKM	Kremmling, CO [FM radio station call letters]
KRKN	Eldon, IA (RBYB)
KRKN	Kraken (ABBR)
KRKO	Everett, WA [AM radio station call letters]
KRKQ-FM	Boone, IA [FM radio station call letters] (RBYB)
KRKR-FM	Roy, UT [FM radio station call letters] (RBYB)
KRKS	Boulder, CO [FM radio station call letters]
KRKS	Denver, CO [AM radio station call letters]
KRKT	Albany, OR [AM radio station call letters]
KRKT-FM	Albany, OR [FM radio station call letters]
KRKX	Billings, MT [FM radio station call letters]
KRKY	Granby, CO [AM radio station call letters]
KRKZ	Altus, OK [FM radio station call letters]
KRL	Karlsruhe [Federal Republic of Germany] [Seismograph station code, US Geological Survey] (SEIS)
KRL	Kathode Ray Lamp
KRL	Kingdom Resources Ltd. [Vancouver Stock Exchange symbol]
KRL	Kirchhoff Radiation Law [Physics]
KRL	Knowledge Representation Language
KRL	Korla [China] [Airport symbol] (OAG)
KRL	Kryla [Ukraine] [FAA designator] (FAAC)
KRLA	Los Angeles [California] [ICAO location identifier] (ICLI)
KRLA	Pasadena, CA [AM radio station call letters]
KRLB	Lubbock, TX [FM radio station call letters]
KRLC	Lewiston, ID [AM radio station call letters]
KRLD	Dallas, TX [AM radio station call letters]
KRLF	Pullman, WA [FM radio station call letters]
KRLI	Malta Bend, MO [FM radio station call letters]
KRLK	Cassville, MO [FM radio station call letters]
KRLN	Canon City, CO [AM radio station call letters]
KRLN-FM	Canon City, CO [FM radio station call letters]
KRLR	Las Vegas, NV [Television station call letters]
KRLS	Keweenaw Rocket Launch Site [University of Michigan]
KRLS	Knoxville, IA [FM radio station call letters]
KRLT	South Lake Tahoe, CA [FM radio station call letters]
KRLV	Las Vegas, NV [AM radio station call letters] (RBYB)
KRLW	Walnut Ridge, AR [AM radio station call letters]
KRLW-FM	Walnut Ridge, AR [FM radio station call letters]
KRLX	Northfield, MN [FM radio station call letters]
KRM	Karma (ABBR)
KRM	Klein-Rydberg Method [Physics]
KRM	Kurmenty [Former USSR Seismograph station code, US Geological Survey] (SEIS)
KRM	Kurzweil Reading Machine
KRM	Royal Ontario Museum Library [UTLAS symbol]
KRMA	Denver, CO [Television station call letters]
KRMB-FM	Bisbee, AZ [FM radio station call letters] (RBYB)
KRMC	Douglas, AZ [FM radio station call letters] (RBYB)
KRMC	Karmic (ABBR)
KRMD	Shreveport, LA [AM radio station call letters]
KRMD-FM	Shreveport, LA [FM radio station call letters]
KRME	Rome/Griffiss Air Force Base [New York] [ICAO location identifier] (ICLI)
KRME-FM	Shafter, CA [FM radio station call letters] (RBYB)
KRMG	Tulsa, OK [AM radio station call letters]
KRMH-FM	Red Mesa, AZ [FM radio station call letters] (BROA)
KRMJ-FM	Grand Junction, CO [FM radio station call letters] (RBYB)
KRML	Carmel, CA [AM radio station call letters]
KRMN-FM	Shamrock, TX [FM radio station call letters] (BROA)
KRMO	Monett, MO [AM radio station call letters]
KRMS	Osage Beach, MO [AM radio station call letters]
KRMS-FM	Osage Beach, MO [FM radio station call letters] (BROA)
KRMT	Denver, CO [Television station call letters] (RBYB)
KRMX	Pueblo, CO [AM radio station call letters]
KRMY	Kileen, TX [AM radio station call letters]
KRN	Kiruna [Sweden] [Airport symbol] (OAG)
KRN	Knight Ridder Newspapers [Viewdata Corp.] [Videotex producer] (NITA)
KRNA	Iowa City, IA [FM radio station call letters]
KRNB	Decatur, TX [FM radio station call letters] (RBYB)
KRNC-FM	Fresno, CA [FM radio station call letters] (BROA)
KRND	San Antonio/Randolf Air Force Base [Texas] [ICAO location identifier] (ICLI)
KRNE	Merriman, NE [FM radio station call letters]
KRNE-TV	Merriman, NE [Television station call letters]
KRNG	Fallon, NV [FM radio station call letters] (RBYB)
KRNH	Comfort, TX [FM radio station call letters]
KRNI	Mason City, IA [AM radio station call letters]
KRNL	Kernel (ABBR)
KRNL	Mount Vernon, IA [FM radio station call letters]
KRNN-AM	North Little Rock, AR [AM radio station call letters] (RBYB)
KRNO	Reno/International [Nevada] [ICAO location identifier] (ICLI)
KRNO	Reno, NV [FM radio station call letters]

KRNQ-FM .... Keokuk, IA [*FM radio station call letters*] (RBYB)
KRNR.......... Roseburg, OR [*AM radio station call letters*]
KRNT .... Des Moines, IA [*AM radio station call letters*]
KRNU .... Lincoln, NE [*FM radio station call letters*]
KRNV .... Reno, NV [*Television station call letters*]
KRNV-FM..... Reno, NV [*FM radio station call letters*] (RBYB)
KRNW .... Chillicothe, MO [*FM radio station call letters*]
KRNY .... Kearney, NE [*FM radio station call letters*]
KRNY .... New York [*New York*] [*ICAO location identifier*] (ICLI)
KRO .... Aliblu Airways SpA [*Italy ICAO designator*] (FAAC)
KRO .... Kathode Ray Oscilloscope
KRO .... Katholieke Radio Omroep [*Catholic Broadcasting Association*]
                  [*Netherlands*]
kro .... Kru [*MARC language code Library of Congress*] (LCCP)
KROA .... Grand Island, NE [*FM radio station call letters*]
KROAG........ Committee for the Revolution in Oman and the Arabian Gulf
                  [*Denmark*]
KROC .... Rochester, MN [*AM radio station call letters*]
KROC .... Rochester/Rochester-Monroe County [*New York*] [*ICAO location
                  identifier*] (ICLI)
KROC-FM.... Rochester, MN [*FM radio station call letters*]
KROD.......... El Paso, TX [*AM radio station call letters*]
KROE .... Sheridan, WY [*AM radio station call letters*]
KROE-FM..... Sheridan, WY [*FM radio station call letters*]
KROF .... Abbeville, LA [*AM radio station call letters*]
KROF-FM..... Abbeville, LA [*FM radio station call letters*]
KROG.......... Kroll-O'Gara [*Stock market symbol*]
KROG.......... Phoenix, OR [*FM radio station call letters*]
Kroger .... [*The*] Kroger Co. [*Associated Press*] (SAG)
KROK.......... De Ridder, LA [*FM radio station call letters*]
KROL .... Las Cruces, NM [*FM radio station call letters*]
KROM .... San Antonio, TX [*FM radio station call letters*]
KRON .... Kronos, Inc. [*NASDAQ symbol*] (SAG)
KRON .... San Francisco, CA [*Television station call letters*]
Kronos .... Kronos, Inc. [*Associated Press*] (SAG)
KROO.......... Breckenridge, TX [*FM radio station call letters*]
KROP.......... Brawley, CA [*AM radio station call letters*]
KROQ.......... Pasadena, CA [*FM radio station call letters*]
KROS .... Clinton, IA [*AM radio station call letters*]
KROU.......... Spencer, OK [*FM radio station call letters*]
KROW.......... Mariposa, CA [*FM radio station call letters*]
KROW.......... Roswell/Industrial Air Center [*New Mexico*] [*ICAO location
                  identifier*] (ICLI)
KROX .... Crookston, MN [*AM radio station call letters*]
KROX-FM..... Giddings, TX [*FM radio station call letters*] (RBYB)
KROY .... Victorville, CA [*AM radio station call letters*] (RBYB)
KROZ .... Roseburg, OR [*Television station call letters*]
KRP .... Karapiro [*New Zealand*] [*Seismograph station code, US Geological
                  Survey*] (SEIS)
KRP .... Karup [*Denmark*] [*Airport symbol*] (OAG)
KRP .... Key Resource People [*US Chamber of Commerce*]
KRP .... Kinesin-Related Polypeptide [*Biochemistry*]
KRP .... King's Rook's Pawn [*Chess*]
KRP .... Known Reference Point
KRP .... Kodak Relief Plate
KRP .... Kolmer [*Test with*] Reiter Protein [*Serology*]
KRP .... Krebs-Ringer-Phosphate [*Buffer solution*]
KRP .... Kurdistan Revolutionary Party [*Iraq*] [*Political party*] (PPW)
KRPA .... Rancho Palos Verdes, CA [*Television station call letters*]
KRPB .... Krebs-Ringer-Phosphate Buffer [*Solution*]
KRPH-FM..... Dodge City, KS [*FM radio station call letters*] (BROA)
KRPL .... Moscow, ID [*AM radio station call letters*]
KRPM .... Tacoma, WA [*FM radio station call letters*]
KRPM-AM.... Seattle, WA [*FM radio station call letters*] (RBYB)
KRPQ .... Rohnert Park, CA [*FM radio station call letters*]
KRPR .... Rochester, MN [*FM radio station call letters*]
KRPS .... Krebs-Ringer-Phosphate Buffer Solution (MAE)
KRPS .... Pittsburg, KS [*FM radio station call letters*]
KRPT .... Anadarko, OK [*AM radio station call letters*]
KRPT-FM..... Anadarko, OK [*FM radio station call letters*]
KRPV .... Roswell, NM [*Television station call letters*]
KRPX .... Price, UT [*AM radio station call letters*]
KRQ .... Crimsonstar Resources [*Vancouver Stock Exchange symbol*]
KRQC.......... Marina, CA [*FM radio station call letters*]
KRQE .... Albuquerque, NM [*Television station call letters*]
KRQK.......... Lompoc, CA [*FM radio station call letters*]
KRQQ.......... Tucson, AZ [*FM radio station call letters*]
KRQR.......... San Francisco, CA [*FM radio station call letters*]
KRQS .... Pagosa Springs, CO [*FM radio station call letters*]
KRQT-FM..... Castle Rock, WA [*FM radio station call letters*] (RBYB)
KRQU.......... Laramie, WY [*FM radio station call letters*]
KRQX .... Mexia, TX [*AM radio station call letters*]
KRQZ-FM..... Wagoner, OK [*FM radio station call letters*] (RBYB)
KRR .... Kansai Research Reactor [*Japan*]
KRR .... Karoi [*Zimbabwe*] [*Seismograph station code, US Geological
                  Survey*] (SEIS)
KRR .... Kettle River Resources Ltd. [*Vancouver Stock Exchange symbol*]
KRR .... King's Royal Rifles [*Military unit*] [*British*]
KRR .... Krasnodar [*Former USSR Airport symbol*] (OAG)
KRRA-AM..... West Covina, CA [*AM radio station call letters*] (BROA)
KRRB .... Dickinson, ND [*FM radio station call letters*]
KRRC .... King's Royal Rifle Corps [*Military unit*] [*British*]
KRRC .... Portland, OR [*FM radio station call letters*]
KRRD .... Dickinson, ND [*FM radio station call letters*]
KRRF-AM..... Denver, CO [*AM radio station call letters*] (RBYB)

KRRG.......... Laredo, TX [*FM radio station call letters*]
KRRK .... Bennington, NE [*FM radio station call letters*]
KRRM .... Rogue River, OR [*FM radio station call letters*]
KRRO.......... Sioux Falls, SD [*FM radio station call letters*]
KRRP.......... Coushatta, LA [*AM radio station call letters*]
KRRQ.......... Lafayette, LA [*FM radio station call letters*]
KRRR-FM..... Cheyenne, WY [*FM radio station call letters*] (RBYB)
KRRS .... Kinetic Resonance Raman Spectroscopy (DAVI)
KRRS .... Santa Rosa, CA [*AM radio station call letters*]
KRRT .... Kerrville, TX [*Television station call letters*]
KRRU.......... Pueblo, CO [*AM radio station call letters*]
KRRV .... Alexandria, LA [*AM radio station call letters*]
KRRV-FM..... Alexandria, LA [*FM radio station call letters*]
KRRW .... Dallas, TX [*FM radio station call letters*]
KRRY .... Canton, MO [*FM radio station call letters*] (RBYB)
KRRZ .... Minot, ND [*AM radio station call letters*]
KRS .... Kearney State College, Kearney, NE [*OCLC symbol*] (OCLC)
KRS .... Kentucky Revised Statutes [*A publication*]
KRS .... Kerato-Refractive Society (EA)
KRS .... Kinematograph Renter's Society
KRS .... Knowledge Retrieval System [*KnowledgeSet Corp.*]
KRS .... Korsar [*Russian Federation*] [*ICAO designator*] (FAAC)
KRS .... Krasnogorka [*Former USSR Seismograph station code, US
                  Geological Survey Closed*] (SEIS)
KRS .... Kristiansand [*Norway*] [*Airport symbol*] (OAG)
KRSA .... Petersburg, AK [*AM radio station call letters*]
KRSB .... Roseburg, OR [*FM radio station call letters*]
KRSC .... Claremore, OK [*Television station call letters*]
KRSC .... Kaiser Resources, Inc. [*NASDAQ symbol*] (SAG)
KRSC .... Kaiser Ventures [*NASDAQ symbol*] (TTSB)
KRSC .... Kaiser Ventures, Inc. [*NASDAQ symbol*] (SAG)
KRSC .... Othello, WA [*AM radio station call letters*]
KRSC-FM..... Claremore, OK [*FM radio station call letters*] (RBYB)
KRSD .... Sioux Falls, SD [*FM radio station call letters*]
KRSE .... Seattle [*Washington*] [*ICAO location identifier*] (ICLI)
KRSE .... Yakima, WA [*FM radio station call letters*]
KRSEN .... Kerosene (ABBR)
KRSH .... Middletown, CA [*FM radio station call letters*]
KRSI .... Garapan-Saipan, MP [*FM radio station call letters*]
KRSI .... Kelly Russell Studios, Inc. [*NASDAQ symbol*] (SAG)
KRSI .... Kreisler Mfg [*NASDAQ symbol*] (TTSB)
KRSJ .... Durango, CO [*FM radio station call letters*]
KRSL .... Kreisler Manufacturing Co. [*NASDAQ symbol*] (NQ)
KRSL .... Russell, KS [*AM radio station call letters*]
KRSM .... Dallas, TX [*FM radio station call letters*]
KRSN .... Kerosene (MSA)
KRSN .... Los Alamos, NM [*AM radio station call letters*]
KRS-ONE ..... Knowledge Reigns Supreme Over Nearly Everyone [*Rap recording
                  artist*]
KRSP .... Salt Lake City, UT [*FM radio station call letters*]
KRSQ .... Laurel, MT [*FM radio station call letters*]
KRSR .... Coos Bay, OR [*AM radio station call letters*]
KRSS .... Chubbuck, ID [*FM radio station call letters*]
KRST .... Albuquerque, NM [*FM radio station call letters*]
KRSTL .... Knowledge Representation Systems Trials Laboratory [*Pronounced
                  "crystal"*] [*Artificial intelligence*]
KRSU.......... Appleton, MN [*FM radio station call letters*]
KRSV .... Afton, WY [*AM radio station call letters*]
KRSV-FM..... Afton, WY [*FM radio station call letters*]
KRSW .... Worthington-Marshall, MN [*FM radio station call letters*]
KRSY .... Roswell, NM [*AM radio station call letters*]
KRT............. Cretan Airlines SA [*Greece*] [*ICAO designator*] (FAAC)
KRT............. Karate
KRT............. Kathode Ray Tube (AAG)
KRT............. Keratin (DMAA)
KRT............. Keravat [*New Britain*] [*Seismograph station code, US Geological
                  Survey Closed*] (SEIS)
KRT............. Khartoum [*Sudan*] [*Airport symbol*] (OAG)
KRT............. Kranzco Realty Trust [*NYSE symbol*] (SPSG)
KRTA .... Medford, OR [*AM radio station call letters*] (RBYB)
KRTE .... Karate (ABBR)
KRTH .... Los Angeles, CA [*FM radio station call letters*]
KRTI .... Grinnell, IA [*FM radio station call letters*]
KRTL .... Atlanta [*Georgia*] [*ICAO location identifier*] (ICLI)
KRTM .... Temecula, CA [*FM radio station call letters*]
KRTN .... Karatin (ABBR)
KRTN .... Raton, NM [*AM radio station call letters*]
KRTN-FM..... Raton, NM [*FM radio station call letters*]
KRTO .... Kathode Ray Tube Oscillograph
KRTO-FM..... West Covina, CA [*FM radio station call letters*] (RBYB)
KRTR .... Kailua, HI [*FM radio station call letters*]
KRTS .... Kathode Ray Tube Shield
KRTS .... Seabrook, TX [*FM radio station call letters*]
KRTT .... Kathode Ray Tube Tester
KRTU .... San Antonio, TX [*FM radio station call letters*]
KRTV .... Great Falls, MT [*Television station call letters*]
KRTX .... Galveston, TX [*FM radio station call letters*]
KRTY .... Los Gatos, CA [*FM radio station call letters*]
KRTZ .... Cortez, CO [*FM radio station call letters*]
KRU .... Karasu [*Former USSR Seismograph station code, US Geological
                  Survey*] (SEIS)
kru .... Kurukh [*MARC language code Library of Congress*] (LCCP)
KRUA .... Anchorage, AK [*FM radio station call letters*]
KRUC-FM..... Las Cruces, NM [*FM radio station call letters*] (BROA)
KRUE .... Waseca, MN [*FM radio station call letters*]

KRUF-FM..... Shreveport, LA [*FM radio station call letters*] (RBYB)
KRUG.......... KRUG International [*NASDAQ symbol*] (TTSB)
KRUG.......... KRUG International Corp. [*NASDAQ symbol*] (NQ)
KRUGW....... KRUG Intl Wrrt [*NASDAQ symbol*] (TTSB)
KRUI........... Iowa City, IA [*FM radio station call letters*]
KRUI........... Ruidoso Downs, NM [*AM radio station call letters*]
Krummeck ... Decisions of the Water Courts [*1913-36*] [*South Africa*]
              [*A publication*] (DLA)
KRUN.......... Ballinger, TX [*AM radio station call letters*]
KRUN-FM .... Ballinger, TX [*FM radio station call letters*]
KRUP.......... Dillingham, AK [*FM radio station call letters*] (RBYB)
KRUS.......... Ruston, LA [*AM radio station call letters*]
KRUU.......... Boone, IA [*FM radio station call letters*]
KRUX.......... Las Cruces, NM [*FM radio station call letters*]
KRUZ .... Europa Cruises [*NASDAQ symbol*] (TTSB)
KRUZ .... Europa Cruises Corp. [*NASDAQ symbol*] (SAG)
KRUZ .... Santa Barbara, CA [*FM radio station call letters*]
KRV .... Kilham Rat Virus [*Medicine*]
KRV .... Kirovabad [*Former USSR Seismograph station code, US Geological*
              Survey] (SEIS)
KRVA .... Cockrell Hill, TX [*AM radio station call letters*]
KRVA .... McKinney, TX [*FM radio station call letters*]
KRVC .... Medford, OR [*AM radio station call letters*]
KRVE .... Brusly, LA [*FM radio station call letters*]
KRVH .... Rio Vista, CA [*FM radio station call letters*]
KRVL .... Kerrville, TX [*FM radio station call letters*]
KRVM .... Eugene, OR [*FM radio station call letters*]
KRVN .... Lexington, NE [*AM radio station call letters*]
KRVN-FM .... Lexington, NE [*FM radio station call letters*]
KRVR .... Copperopolis, CA [*FM radio station call letters*] (RBYB)
KRVS .... Lafayette, LA [*FM radio station call letters*]
KRVV .... Bastrop, LA [*FM radio station call letters*]
KRVZ .... Springerville-Eager, AZ [*AM radio station call letters*]
KRW .... Karlsruhe - West [*Federal Republic of Germany*] [*Seismograph*
              station code, US Geological Survey] (SEIS)
KRWA .... Waldron, AR [*FM radio station call letters*]
KRWA .... Washington [*District of Columbia*] [*ICAO location identifier*] (ICLI)
KRWB .... Roseau, MN [*AM radio station call letters*]
KRWB-FM .... Roseau, MN [*FM radio station call letters*] (RBYB)
KRWC .... Buffalo, MN [*AM radio station call letters*]
KRWF .... Redwood Falls, MN [*Television station call letters*]
KRWG .... Las Cruces, NM [*FM radio station call letters*]
KRWG-TV .... Las Cruces, NM [*Television station call letters*]
KRWM .... Bremerton, WA [*FM radio station call letters*]
KRWN .... Farmington, NM [*FM radio station call letters*]
KRWQ .... Gold Hill, OR [*FM radio station call letters*]
KRWV-FM .... Emporia, KS [*FM radio station call letters*] (BROA)
KRX .... Christina Exploration [*Vancouver Stock Exchange symbol*]
KRX .... Kar Kar [*Papua New Guinea*] [*Airport symbol*] (OAG)
KRXI .... Reno, NV [*Television station call letters*]
KRXK .... Rexburg, ID [*AM radio station call letters*]
KRXL .... Kirksville, MO [*FM radio station call letters*]
KRXO .... Oklahoma City, OK [*FM radio station call letters*]
KRXQ .... Roseville, CA [*FM radio station call letters*]
KRXR .... Gooding, ID [*AM radio station call letters*]
KRXS .... Globe, AZ [*FM radio station call letters*]
KRXT .... Rockdale, TX [*FM radio station call letters*]
KRXV .... Yermo, CA [*FM radio station call letters*]
KRXX-FM.... Kodiak, AK [*FM radio station call letters*] (RBYB)
KRXZ .... Ardmore, OK [*AM radio station call letters*] (RBYB)
KRY .... Karamay [*China*] [*Airport symbol*] (OAG)
KRYD .... Telluride, CO [*FM radio station call letters*]
KRYK .... Chinook, MT [*FM radio station call letters*]
KRYL .... Gatesville, TX [*FM radio station call letters*]
KRYPN .... Krypton (ABBR)
KRYS .... Corpus Christi, TX [*AM radio station call letters*]
KRYS .... Krystal Co. [*NASDAQ symbol*] (SAG)
KRYS-FM .... Corpus Christi, TX [*FM radio station call letters*]
KRYSQ .... Krystal Company [*NASDAQ symbol*] (TTSB)
Krystal .... Krystal Co. [*Associated Press*] (SAG)
KRZ............ Karuizawa [*Japan*] [*Also, KAZ*] [*Seismograph station code, US*
              Geological Survey] (SEIS)
KRZ............ Kiri [*Zaire*] [*Airport symbol*] (OAG)
KRZA.......... Alamosa, CO [*FM radio station call letters*]
KRZB-FM..... Olney, TX [*FM radio station call letters*] (BROA)
KRZE.......... Farmington, NM [*AM radio station call letters*]
KRZI........... Waco, TX [*AM radio station call letters*]
KRZK.......... Branson, MO [*FM radio station call letters*]
KRZN.......... Albuquerque, NM [*FM radio station call letters*]
KRZQ.......... Tahoe City, CA [*FM radio station call letters*]
KRZR.......... Hanford, CA [*FM radio station call letters*]
KRZY .... Albuquerque, NM [*AM radio station call letters*]
KRZY-FM .... Santa Fe, NM [*FM radio station call letters*] (RBYB)
KRZZ........... Derby, KS [*FM radio station call letters*]
KS.............. Kafus Environmental Industries [*AMEX symbol*] [*Formerly, Kafus*
              Capital] (SG)
KS.............. Kansas [*Postal code*]
KS.............. Kansas Reports [*A publication*] (DLA)
KS.............. Kaposi's Sarcoma [*Medicine*]
KS.............. Kartagener's Syndrome [*Medicine*] (DAVI)
KS.............. Katoptric System [*Optics*]
KS.............. Kawasaki Syndrome [*Also, KD, MLNS*]
KS.............. Keep Type Standing [*Printing*]
KS.............. Kelly-Springfield Tire Co.
KS.............. Keltic Society and the College of Druidism (EA)

KS.............. Ketosteroid [*Endocrinology*]
KS.............. Key Seated [*Freight*]
KS.............. Keyset [*Navy*] (NVT)
KS.............. Key Stage [*Of National Curriculum*] [*British*] (AIE)
KS.............. Keystone (IAA)
K/S............. Kick Stage [*NASA*] (NASA)
KS.............. Kidney Sac
KS.............. Kilostere
KS.............. King Solomon [*Freemasonry*] (ROG)
KS.............. King's Scholar [*British*]
KS.............. King's Serjeant [*British*] (ROG)
KS.............. King's Speech [*British*]
KS.............. Kipling Society of North America - USA and Canada (EA)
KS.............. Kirjath Sepher [*Jerusalem*] (BJA)
KS.............. Kiting Stock [*Investment term*]
KS.............. Klinefelter's Syndrome [*Medicine*]
KS.............. Knife Switch
KS.............. Knight of the Sword [*of Sweden*]
KS.............. Knock Sensor [*Automotive engineering*]
KS.............. Knowledge Source (IAA)
KS.............. Kodak Standard [*Photography*]
KS.............. Kokoxili Suture [*Paleogeography*]
KS.............. Kolmogorov - Smirnov Test [*Statistics*]
KS.............. Konungariket Sverige [*Kingdom of Sweden*] (BARN)
KS.............. Korea Society (EA)
KS.............. Korsakoff Syndrome [*Medicine Medicine*] (DMAA)
KS.............. Kraemer System
KS.............. Kugel-Stoloff [*Syndrome*] [*Medicine*] (DAVI)
KS.............. Kurze Sicht [*Short Sight*] [*German*]
Ks.............. Kush (BJA)
KS.............. Kveim-Seltzback (Test) [*Medicine*]
KS.............. Peninsula Airways [*ICAO designator*] (AD)
ks.............. Potassium Metasilicate [*CIPW classification*] [*Geology*]
KS.............. Singapore [*IYRU nationality code*] (IYR)
KS.............. Storm of Drifting Snow [*Meteorology*] (WDAA)
KSA........... Kafka Society of America (EA)
KSA........... Kansas Motor Carriers Association, Topeka KS [*STAC*]
KSA........... Kansas Statutes, Annotated [*A publication*]
KSA........... Kindle, Stone & Associates, Inc. (EFIS)
KSA........... Kitchen Specialists Association [*British*] (DBA)
KSA........... Kite-Supported Antenna
KSA........... Klinefelter's Syndrome Association (BUAC)
KSA........... Klinefelter Syndrome and Associates (EA)
KSA........... Knight of St. Anne [*Russia*] [*Obsolete*]
KSA........... Knowledge, Skills, and Abilities [*Psychology*] (DAVI)
KSA........... Ksara [*Lebanon*] [*Seismograph station code, US Geological*
              Survey] (SEIS)
KSA........... Ku-Band Single Access (MCD)
KSA........... Kwajalein Standard Atmosphere
KSA........... St. Augustine's Seminary Library, University of Toronto [*UTLAS*
              symbol]
KSAA .... Keats-Shelley Association of America (EA)
KSAB .... Robstown, TX [*FM radio station call letters*]
KSAC .... Kingston and Saint Andrew Corp. [*Jamaica*] (BUAC)
KSAC .... Sacramento/Executive [*California*] [*ICAO location identifier*] (ICLI)
KSAC .... Sutter Creek, CA [*FM radio station call letters*] (RBYB)
KSAE .... Kansas Society of Association Executives (SRA)
KSAE .... Kentucky Society of Association Executives (SRA)
KSAF .... K-Band, Single Access Forward (SSD)
KSAF .... Santa Fe [*New Mexico*] [*ICAO location identifier*] (ICLI)
KSAH .... Universal City, TX [*AM radio station call letters*]
KSAI .... Saipan, MP [*AM radio station call letters*]
KSAJ .... Abilene, KS [*FM radio station call letters*]
KSAK .... Walnut, CA [*FM radio station call letters*]
KSAL .... Salina, KS [*AM radio station call letters*]
KSal .... Salina Public Library, Salina, KS [*Library symbol Library of*
              Congress] (LCLS)
KSalM .... Marymount College, Salina, KS [*Library symbol Library of*
              Congress] (LCLS)
KSalW .... Kansas Wesleyan University, Salina, KS [*Library symbol Library of*
              Congress] (LCLS)
KSAM .... Huntsville, TX [*AM radio station call letters*]
KSAM .... Keyed Sequential Access Method [*Computer science*] (CMD)
KSAM .... Key Field Sequential Access Method (NITA)
KSAM-FM .... Huntsville, TX [*FM radio station call letters*]
KSAN .... San Diego/International-Lindbergh Field [*California*] [*ICAO location*
              identifier] (ICLI)
KSAN .... San Francisco, CA [*FM radio station call letters*]
KSANG........ Kansas Air National Guard (MUSM)
KSAR .... K-Band, Single Access Return (SSD)
KSAR .... Salem, AR [*FM radio station call letters*]
KSAS .... Wichita, KS [*Television station call letters*]
KSAT .... San Antonio/International [*Texas*] [*ICAO location identifier*] (ICLI)
KSAT .... San Antonio, TX [*Television station call letters*]
KSAU .... Nacogdoches, TX [*FM radio station call letters*]
KSAV .... KS Bancorp [*NASDAQ symbol*] (TTSB)
KSAV .... KS Bancorp, Inc. [*NASDAQ symbol*] (SAG)
KSAV .... Savannah/Municipal [*Georgia*] [*ICAO location identifier*] (ICLI)
KSAW .... Gwinn/K. I. Sawyer Air Force Base [*Michigan*] [*ICAO location*
              identifier] (ICLI)
KSAX .... Alexandria, MN [*Television station call letters*]
KSAY .... Fort Bragg, CA [*FM radio station call letters*]
KSAZ .... Tucson, AZ [*AM radio station call letters*]
KSAZ-TV ...... Phoenix, AZ [*Television station call letters*]

KSB.............. Kradschuetzen-Bataillon [*Motorcycle Battalion*] [*German military - World War II*]
KSBA .... Coos Bay, OR [*FM radio station call letters*]
KSB Bc .... KSB Bancorp [*Associated Press*] (SAG)
KSBC .... Hot Springs, AR [*FM radio station call letters*]
KS Bcp .... KS Bancorp, Inc. [*Associated Press*] (SAG)
KSBD .... San Bernardino/Norton Air Force Base [*California*] [*ICAO location identifier*] (ICLI)
KSBH .... Coushatta, LA [*FM radio station call letters*]
KSBI .... Oklahoma City, OK [*Television station call letters*]
KSBJ .... Humble, TX [*FM radio station call letters*]
KSBK .... KSB Bancorp [*NASDAQ symbol*] (SAG)
KSBL .... Carpinteria, CA [*FM radio station call letters*]
KSBN .... Spokane, WA [*AM radio station call letters*]
KSBN .... Springdale, AR [*Television station call letters*]
KSBQ .... Santa Maria, CA [*AM radio station call letters*]
KSBR .... Mission Viejo, CA [*FM radio station call letters*]
KSBS .... Pago Pago, AS [*AM radio station call letters*]
KSBS .... Steamboat Springs, CO [*Television station call letters*]
KSBT .... Steamboat Springs, CO [*FM radio station call letters*]
KSBW .... Salinas, CA [*Television station call letters*]
KSBY .... Salisbury/Wicomico County [*Maryland*] [*ICAO location identifier*] (ICLI)
KSBY .... San Luis Obispo, CA [*Television station call letters*]
KSBZ .... Sitka, AK [*FM radio station call letters*]
KSC.............. Council of State Governments, Lexington, KY [*OCLC symbol*] (OCLC)
KSC.............. Kagoshima Space Center [*Japan*]
KSC.............. Kathodal Closing Contraction [*Medicine*] (DAVI)
KSC.............. Kennedy Space Center [*NASA*]
KSC.............. King's School, Canterbury (ROG)
KSC.............. Knight of St. Columba
KSC.............. Knights of St Columbanus (BUAC)
KSC.............. Kohn Social Competence Scale [*Psychology*] (DHP)
KSC.............. Komunisticka Strana Ceskoslovenska [*Communist Party of Czechoslovakia*] [*Political party*] (PPW)
KSC.............. Korean Service Corps
KSC.............. Kosice [*Former Czechoslovakia*] [*Airport symbol*] (OAG)
KSCA .... Glendale, CA [*FM radio station call letters*]
KSCAP .... Kennedy Space Center Area Permit [*NASA*] (MCD)
KSCAX .... Kemper Small Cap. Equity Cl.A [*Mutual fund ticker symbol*] (SG)
KSCB .... Khe Sanh Combat Base [*Vietnam*] [*Marine Corps*] (VNW)
KSCB .... Liberal, KS [*AM radio station call letters*]
KSCB-FM .... Liberal, KS [*FM radio station call letters*]
KSCE .... El Paso, TX [*Television station call letters*]
KSCF .... Thousand Standard Cubic Feet
KSch (Alt).... Kleine Schriften zur Geschichte de Volkes Israel [*A. Alt*] [*A publication*] (BJA)
KSCI .... San Bernardino, CA [*Television station call letters*]
KSCI .... San Clemente Naval Auxiliary Air Base [*California*] [*ICAO location identifier*] (ICLI)
KSCJ .... Sioux City, IA [*AM radio station call letters*]
KSCK .... Stockton/Stockton Metropolitan [*California*] [*ICAO location identifier*] (ICLI)
KSCL .... Shreveport, LA [*FM radio station call letters*]
KSCN .... Potassium Thiocyanate [*Broth*] [*A reagent*] [*Pharmacology*] (DAVI)
KSCO .... Santa Cruz, CA [*AM radio station call letters*]
KSCQ .... Silver City, NM [*FM radio station call letters*]
KSCR .... Benson, MN [*AM radio station call letters*]
KSCR-FM .... Benson, MN [*FM radio station call letters*]
KSCS .... Fort Worth, TX [*FM radio station call letters*]
KSCU .... Santa Clara, CA [*FM radio station call letters*]
KSC/ULO ..... Kennedy Space Center/Unmanned Launch Operations [*NASA*]
KSCV .... Kearney, NE [*FM radio station call letters*]
KSC-WTROD... Kennedy Space Center - Western Test Range Operations Division [*NASA*]
KSCY .... Belgrade, MT [*FM radio station call letters*]
KSD .... C. H. Boehringer Sohn, Ingelheim [*Germany*] [*Research code symbol*]
KSD .... Karlstad [*Sweden*] [*Airport symbol*] (OAG)
KSD .... St Louis, MO [*AM radio station call letters*]
KSDA .... Agat, GU [*FM radio station call letters*]
KSDA .... Korean Securities Dealers' Association (ECON)
KSDB .... Kommunal Statistisk DataBank [*Danmarks Statistik*] [*Denmark Information service or system*] (CRD)
KSDB .... Manhattan, KS [*FM radio station call letters*]
KSD-FM .... St. Louis, MO [*FM radio station call letters*]
KSDIC .... Kerala State Industrial Development Corp. [*India*] (BUAC)
KSDJ .... Brookings, SD [*FM radio station call letters*]
KSDK .... St. Louis, MO [*Television station call letters*]
KSDL .... Sedalia, MO [*FM radio station call letters*]
KSDM .... International Falls, MN [*FM radio station call letters*]
KSDN .... Aberdeen, SD [*AM radio station call letters*]
KSDN-FM .... Aberdeen, SD [*FM radio station call letters*]
KSDO .... San Diego, CA [*AM radio station call letters*]
KSDP .... Sand Point, AK [*AM radio station call letters*]
KSDR .... Watertown, SD [*AM radio station call letters*]
KSDR-FM .... Watertown, SD [*FM radio station call letters*]
KSDS .... Key Sequenced Data Set (CMD)
KSDS .... San Diego, CA [*FM radio station call letters*]
KSDT .... Hemet, CA [*AM radio station call letters*] (RBYB)
KSDZ .... Gordon, NE [*FM radio station call letters*]
KSE.............. Karachi Stock Exchange [*Pakistan*]
KSE.............. Kasese [*Uganda*] [*Airport symbol*] (OAG)

KSE.............. Keyspan Energy [*NYSE symbol*] [*Formerly, Brooklyn Union Gas*] (SG)
KSE.............. Kids for Saving Earth [*An association*] (EA)
KSE.............. Kisbee Air Ltd. [*New Zealand*] [*ICAO designator*] (FAAC)
KSE.............. Knight of Saint-Esprit [*France*]
KSE.............. Knight of the Star of the East (ROG)
KSE.............. Korea Stock Exchange (ECON)
KSEA .... Greenfield, CA [*FM radio station call letters*]
KSEA .... Korean Scientists and Engineers Association in America (EA)
KSEA .... Seattle/Seattle-Tacoma International [*Washington*] [*ICAO location identifier*] (ICLI)
KSEC .... Lamar, CO [*FM radio station call letters*]
KSED .... Sedona, AZ [*FM radio station call letters*]
KSEE .... Fresno, CA [*Television station call letters*]
KSEG .... Sacramento, CA [*FM radio station call letters*]
KSEI .... Pocatello, ID [*AM radio station call letters*]
KSEK .... Girard, KS [*FM radio station call letters*]
KSEL .... Portales, NM [*AM radio station call letters*]
KSEL-FM..... Portales, NM [*FM radio station call letters*]
KSEM .... Selma/Craig Air Force Base [*Alabama*] [*ICAO location identifier*] (ICLI)
KSEM .... Seminole, TX [*FM radio station call letters*]
KSEN .... Shelby, MT [*AM radio station call letters*]
KSEO .... Durant, OK [*AM radio station call letters*]
KSEQ .... Visalia, CA [*FM radio station call letters*]
KSER .... Everett, WA [*FM radio station call letters*]
KSES .... Selma/Selfield [*Alabama*] [*ICAO location identifier*] (ICLI)
KSES-FM ..... Yucca Valley, CA [*FM radio station call letters*] (RBYB)
KSET .... El Paso, TX [*FM radio station call letters*]
KSEV .... Tomball, TX [*AM radio station call letters*]
KSEY .... Seymour, TX [*AM radio station call letters*]
KSEY-FM ..... Seymour, TX [*FM radio station call letters*]
KSEZ .... Sioux City, IA [*FM radio station call letters*]
KSF .... Karen Silkwood Fund (EA)
KSF .... Kashmiri Students Federation (BUAC)
KSF .... Kassel [*Germany Airport symbol*] (OAG)
KSF .... K-Band Shuttle Forward (SSD)
KSF .... Keel Shock Factor (NATG)
ksf .... Kips [*Thousands of Pounds*] per Square Foot
KSF .... Knight of San Fernando [*Spain*]
KSF .... Knight of St. Ferdinand [*Sicily*] (ROG)
KSF .... Quaker State Corp. [*NYSE symbol*] (SPSG)
KSFA .... Nacogdoches, TX [*AM radio station call letters*]
KSFC .... Karnataka State Financial Corp. [*India*] (BUAC)
KSFC .... Keith Sewell Fan Club (EA)
KSFC .... Spokane, WA [*FM radio station call letters*]
KSFF .... Spokane/Felts [*Washington*] [*ICAO location identifier*] (ICLI)
KSFH .... Mountain View, CA [*FM radio station call letters*]
KSFI .... Salt Lake City, UT [*FM radio station call letters*]
KSFM .... Knight of St. Ferdinand and Merit [*Italy*]
KSFM .... Woodland, CA [*FM radio station call letters*]
KSFN-AM .... North Las Vegas, NV [*AM radio station call letters*] (BROA)
KSFO .... San Francisco, CA [*AM radio station call letters*]
KSFO .... San Francisco/International [*California*] [*ICAO location identifier*] (ICLI)
KSFQ-FM .... White Rock, NM [*FM radio station call letters*] (BROA)
KSFR .... Santa Fe, NM [*FM radio station call letters*]
KSFS .... San Francisco Coast Guard Air Station [*California*] [*ICAO location identifier*] (ICLI)
KSFT .... St. Joseph, MO [*AM radio station call letters*]
KSFT-FM..... South Sioux City, NE [*FM radio station call letters*] (RBYB)
KSFUS .... Korean Student Federation of the United States (EA)
KSFX .... Roswell, NM [*FM radio station call letters*]
KSFY .... Sioux Falls, SD [*Television station call letters*]
KSG .... Harvard University, Kennedy School for Government, Cambridge, MA [*OCLC symbol*] (OCLC)
KSG .... Knight of St. George [*Russia*] [*Obsolete*]
KSG .... Knight of St. Gregory
KSGB .... Kite Society of Great Britain (BUAC)
KSGC .... Tusayan, AZ [*FM radio station call letters*]
KSGI .... Cedar City, UT [*Television station call letters*]
KSGI .... St. George, UT [*AM radio station call letters*]
KSGI-FM ..... St George, UT [*FM radio station call letters*]
KSGL .... Wichita, KS [*AM radio station call letters*]
KSGM .... Chester, IL [*AM radio station call letters*]
KSGN .... Riverside, CA [*FM radio station call letters*]
KSGS-AM .... St. Louis Park, MN [*AM radio station call letters*] (RBYB)
KSGT .... Jackson, WY [*AM radio station call letters*]
KSGW .... Sheridan, WY [*Television station call letters*]
KSH .... K-Band Shuttle (SSD)
KSH .... Kenya Shilling [*Monetary unit*] (IMH)
KSh .... Kenya Shilling [*Monetary unit*] (ODBW)
KSH .... Kermanshah [*Iran*] [*Airport symbol*] (AD)
KSH .... Key Strokes per Hour
KSH .... Knight of St. Hubert [*Bavaria*]
KSH .... Kolel Shomre Hachomos [*An association*] (EA)
KSH .... Kuh Shi [*Republic of China*] [*Seismograph station code, US Geological Survey*] (SEIS)
KSHA .... Redding, CA [*FM radio station call letters*]
KSHB .... Kansas City, MO [*Television station call letters*]
KSHE .... Crestwood, MO [*FM radio station call letters*]
KSHI .... Zuni, NM [*FM radio station call letters*]
KSHL .... Gleneden Beach, OR [*FM radio station call letters*]
KshLc.......... Kush Locke [*Associated Press*] (SAG)

KShm............ Johnson County Public Library, Shawnee Mission, KS [*Library symbol Library of Congress*] (LCLS)
KSHN............ Liberty, TX [*FM radio station call letters*]
KSHO............ Lebanon, OR [*AM radio station call letters*]
KSHP-AM.... North Las Vegas, Nv [*AM radio station call letters*] (RBYB)
KSHR............ Coquille, OR [*FM radio station call letters*]
KSHR............ Kosher (ABBR)
KSH/RMBH.... Kolel Shomre Hachomos/Reb Meir Baal Haness (EA)
KSHS............ Kansas State Historical Society (BUAC)
KSHU............ Huntsville, TX [*FM radio station call letters*]
KSHV............ Kaposi's Sarcoma Associated Herpesvirus [*Medicine*]
KSHV............ Shreveport, LA [*Television station call letters*] (RBYB)
KSHV............ Shreveport/Regional Airport [*Louisiana*] [*ICAO location identifier*] (ICLI)
KSHY............ Cheyenne, WY [*AM radio station call letters*]
KSI............... Karsanskaya [*Later, TFS*] [*Former USSR Geomagnetic observatory code*]
KSI............... Kemgas Sydney, Inc. [*Vancouver Stock Exchange symbol*]
KSI............... Kilopounds per Square Inch (SAA)
KSI............... Kips [*Thousands of Pounds*] per Square Inch (MCD)
KSI............... Kissidougou [*Guinea*] [*Airport symbol*] (AD)
KSI............... Kleine Schriften zur Geschichte des Volkes Israel [*A. Alt*] [*A publication*] (BJA)
KSI............... Knight of [*the Order of*] the Star of India [*British*]
KSIB............. Creston, IA [*AM radio station call letters*]
KSID............. Sidney, NE [*AM radio station call letters*]
KSID-FM...... Sidney, NE [*FM radio station call letters*]
KSIG............. Basile, LA [*FM radio station call letters*]
KSIG............. Crowley, LA [*AM radio station call letters*]
KSII.............. El Paso, TX [*FM radio station call letters*] (RBYB)
KSIIMK......... Kratkie Soobshcheniia o Dokladakh i Polevykh Issledovaniiakh Instituta Istorii Materialnoi Kulturi [*A publication*] (BJA)
K-SIM.......... K-Band Simulation (SSD)
KSIM............ Sikeston, MO [*AM radio station call letters*]
KSIN............. Sioux City, IA [*Television station call letters*]
KSIP............. Kent Scientific & Industrial Projects Ltd. [*University of Kent*] [*Research center British*] (IRUK)
KSIQ............. Brawley, CA [*FM radio station call letters*]
KSIR............. Brush, CO [*AM radio station call letters*]
KSIR-FM...... Brush, CO [*FM radio station call letters*]
KSIS............. Sedalia, MO [*AM radio station call letters*]
KSIT............. Rock Springs, WY [*FM radio station call letters*]
KSIV............. Clayton, MO [*AM radio station call letters*]
KSIV-FM...... St. Louis, MO [*FM radio station call letters*] (RBYB)
KSIW............ Woodward, OK [*AM radio station call letters*]
KSIX............. Corpus Christi, TX [*AM radio station call letters*]
KSIZ............. Jacksonville, TX [*FM radio station call letters*]
KSJ.............. Kashima [*Japan*] [*Seismograph station code, US Geological Survey*] (SEIS)
KSJ.............. Kasos Island [*Greece*] [*Airport symbol*] (OAG)
KSJ.............. Knight of St. Januarius [*Naples*]
KSJ.............. Knights of St. John (EA)
KSJB............ Jamestown, ND [*AM radio station call letters*]
KSJC............ Stockton, CA [*FM radio station call letters*]
KSJD............ Cortez, CO [*FM radio station call letters*]
KSJE............ Farmington, NM [*FM radio station call letters*]
KSJJ............ Redmond, OR [*FM radio station call letters*]
KSJK............ Talent, OR [*AM radio station call letters*]
KSJL............ San Antonio, TX [*FM radio station call letters*]
KSJM-FM...... Oro Valley, AZ [*FM radio station call letters*] (RBYB)
KSJN............ Minneapolis, MN [*FM radio station call letters*]
KSJO............ San Jose, CA [*FM radio station call letters*]
KSJQ............ Savannah, MO [*FM radio station call letters*]
KSJR............ Collegeville, MN [*FM radio station call letters*]
KSJS............ San Jose, CA [*FM radio station call letters*]
KSJSC.......... Knights of St. John Supreme Commandery (EA)
KSJT............ San Angelo/Mathis Field [*Texas*] [*ICAO location identifier*] (ICLI)
KSJT............ San Angelo, TX [*FM radio station call letters*]
KSJV............ Fresno, CA [*FM radio station call letters*]
KSJX............ San Jose, CA [*AM radio station call letters*]
KSJY............ Lafayette, LA [*FM radio station call letters*]
KSJZ............ Jamestown, ND [*FM radio station call letters*]
KSK.............. Kappa Sigma Kappa [*Later, Theta Xi*] [*Fraternity*]
KSK.............. Karlskoga [*Sweden*] [*Airport symbol*] (OAG)
KSK.............. Kathodenschliessungs-Kontaktion [*or kathodal closing contraction*] [*Medicine*] (DAVI)
KSK.............. Kiosk (ABBR)
KSKA............ Anchorage, AK [*FM radio station call letters*]
KSKA............ Spokane/Fairchild Air Force Base [*Washington*] [*ICAO location identifier*] (ICLI)
KSKB............ Brooklyn, IA [*FM radio station call letters*]
KSKD............ Sweet Home, OR [*FM radio station call letters*]
KSKE............ Vail, CO [*AM radio station call letters*]
KSKE-FM...... Vail, CO [*FM radio station call letters*]
KSKF............ Klamath Falls, OR [*FM radio station call letters*]
KSKF............ San Antonio/Kelly Air Force Base [*Texas*] [*ICAO location identifier*] (ICLI)
KSKG............ Salina, KS [*FM radio station call letters*]
KSKI............. Sun Valley, ID [*FM radio station call letters*]
KSKJ............ American Slovenian Catholic Union of the USA (EA)
KSKK............ Staples, MN [*FM radio station call letters*]
KSKL............ Scott City, KS [*FM radio station call letters*]
KSKN............ Spokane, WA [*Television station call letters*]
KSKO............ McGrath, AK [*AM radio station call letters*]
KSKS............ Fresno, CA [*FM radio station call letters*]

KSKU............ Lyons, KS [*FM radio station call letters*]
KSKX-FM...... Security, CO [*FM radio station call letters*] (RBYB)
KSKY........... Balch Springs, TX [*AM radio station call letters*]
KSKY........... Sandusky/Griffing [*Ohio*] [*ICAO location identifier*] (ICLI)
KSKZ............ Leoti, KS [*FM radio station call letters*] (RBYB)
KSL.............. Kanadska Slovenska Liga [*Canadian Slovak League - CSL*]
KSL.............. Kassala [*Sudan*] [*Airport symbol*] (OAG)
KSL.............. Keio University [*EDUCATSS*] [*UTLAS symbol*]
KSL.............. Kentucky Department of Libraries, Library Extension Division, Frankfort, KY [*OCLC symbol*] (OCLC)
KSL.............. Keyboard Simulated Lateral Telling [*Computer science*]
KSL.............. Knight of the Sun and Lion [*Persia*]
KSL.............. Salt Lake City, UT [*AM radio station call letters*]
KSLA............ Shreveport, LA [*Television station call letters*]
KSLC............ McMinnville, OR [*FM radio station call letters*]
KSLC............ Salt Lake City/International [*Utah*] [*ICAO location identifier*] (ICLI)
KSLD............ Soldotna, AK [*AM radio station call letters*]
KSLI............. King's Shropshire Light Infantry [*Military unit*] [*British*]
KSLJ............ Knight of [*the Order of*] St. Lazarus of Jerusalem [*British*]
KSLK............ Visalia, CA [*FM radio station call letters*]
K-SLM......... Kennedy Space Center Spacelab Plan/Requirement (NAKS)
KSLM........... Salem, OR [*AM radio station call letters*]
K-SLN.......... KSC [*Kennedy Space Center*] Spacelab Notice [*NASA*] (NASA)
KSLO........... Opelousas, LA [*AM radio station call letters*]
K-SLPS........ KSC [*Kennedy Space Center*] Spacelab Project Specification [*NASA*] (NASA)
KSLQ........... Washington, MO [*AM radio station call letters*]
KSLQ-FM...... Washington, MO [*FM radio station call letters*]
KSLR............ San Antonio, TX [*AM radio station call letters*]
KSLS............ Liberal, KS [*FM radio station call letters*]
KSLT............ Spearfish, SD [*FM radio station call letters*]
KSL-TV........ Salt Lake City, UT [*Television station call letters*]
KSLU............ Hammond, LA [*FM radio station call letters*]
KSLV............ Monte Vista, CO [*AM radio station call letters*]
KSLV-FM...... Monte Vista, CO [*FM radio station call letters*]
KSLX............ Scottsdale, AZ [*FM radio station call letters*]
KSLY............ San Luis Obispo, CA [*FM radio station call letters*]
KSLZ-FM...... St. Louis, MO [*FM radio station call letters*] (BROA)
KSM............. Kane Security Monitor [*Computer security device*]
KSM............. Katubsanan sa Mamumio [*Philippine United Labor Congress*]
KSM............. Kemper Strategic Municipal Trust [*NYSE symbol*] (SPSG)
KSM............. Kemper Strategic Muni Tr [*NYSE symbol*] (TTSB)
KSM............. Kooperative Serbaguna Malaysia [*Bank*]
KSM............. Korean Service Medal [*Military decoration*]
K-SM........... KSC [*Kennedy Space Center*] Shuttle Management [*Document*] [*NASA*] (NASA)
KSM............. Saint Mary's [*Alaska*] [*Airport symbol*] (OAG)
KSM............. Saint Mary's, AK [*Location identifier FAA*] (FAAL)
KSM............. Shawnee Medical Center Medical Library, Shawnee Mission, KS [*OCLC symbol*] (OCLC)
KSM............. St. Michael's College Library, University of Toronto [*UTLAS symbol*]
KSMA........... Keats-Shelley Memorial Association (BUAC)
K-SMA......... Keats-Shelley Memorial Association [*British*] (DBA)
KSMA........... Santa Maria, CA [*AM radio station call letters*]
KSM & SG... Knight of Saint Michael and Saint George [*Ionian Islands*]
KSMB........... Lafayette, LA [*FM radio station call letters*]
KSMC........... Moraga, CA [*FM radio station call letters*]
KSMF........... Ashland, OR [*FM radio station call letters*]
KSMF........... Sacramento/Sacramento Metropolitan [*California*] [*ICAO location identifier*] (ICLI)
KSMG........... Seguin, TX [*FM radio station call letters*]
KSMJ-FM...... Bakersfield, CA [*FM radio station call letters*] (BROA)
KSML........... Diboll, TX [*AM radio station call letters*] (RBYB)
KSML........... Kosher Meal [*Airline notation*]
KSMMP........ Kin Seeking Missing Military Personnel [*Organization of parents with sons missing in action with purpose of supplementing US government search for missing personnel*] [*Post-World War II*]
KSMN........... Worthington, MN [*Television station call letters*] (RBYB)
KSMO........... Kansas City, MO [*Television station call letters*]
KSMO........... Salem, MO [*AM radio station call letters*]
KSMQ........... Austin, MN [*Television station call letters*]
KSMR........... Winona, MN [*FM radio station call letters*]
KSMS........... Point Lookout, MO [*FM radio station call letters*]
KSMS-TV...... Monterey, CA [*Television station call letters*]
KSMT........... Breckenridge, CO [*FM radio station call letters*]
KSMT........... Kismet (ABBR)
KSMU........... Komunistycha Spilka Molodi Ukrainy
KSMU........... Springfield, MO [*FM radio station call letters*]
KSMX........... Clovis, NM [*FM radio station call letters*] (RBYB)
KSN............. Kassan Resources [*Vancouver Stock Exchange symbol*]
KSN............. Kit Shortage Notice
KSN............. Sam Neua [*Laos*] [*Airport symbol*] (AD)
KSNA-FM...... Laramie, WY [*FM radio station call letters*] (BROA)
K-SNAP....... Kaufman Short Neuropsychological Assessment Procedure [*Test*] (TMMY)
KSNB........... Superior, NE [*Television station call letters*]
KSNC........... Great Bend, KS [*Television station call letters*]
KSND........... Lincoln City, OR [*Television station call letters*]
KSNE-FM...... Las Vegas, NV [*FM radio station call letters*] (RBYB)
KSNF............ Joplin, MO [*Television station call letters*]
KSNG........... Garden City, KS [*Television station call letters*]
KSNI............ Santa Maria, CA [*FM radio station call letters*]
KSNK........... McCook, NE [*Television Edition*]
KSNN........... Truth or Consequences, NM [*FM radio station call letters*]
KSNN........... Arlington, TX [*FM radio station call letters*]

KSNO .... Snowmass Village, CO [*FM radio station call letters*]
KSNOPI .... Keyboard Input Simulation-Noise-Problem Input [*Computer science*] (SAA)
KSNP .... Burlington, KS [*FM radio station call letters*]
KSNR .... Thief River Falls, MN [*FM radio station call letters*]
KSNS-FM ..... Medicine Lodge, KS [*FM radio station call letters*] (BROA)
KSNT .... Topeka, KS [*Television station call letters*]
KSNU-FM ..... Roy, UT [*FM radio station call letters*] (BROA)
KSNW .... Wichita, KS [*Television station call letters*]
KSNY .... Snyder, TX [*AM radio station call letters*]
KSNY-FM ..... Snyder, TX [*FM radio station call letters*]
KSO .... Kastoria [*Greece*] [*Airport symbol*] (OAG)
KSOC .... Key Symbol Out of Context [*Computer science*] (DIT)
KSOF .... Caledonia, MN [*FM radio station call letters*]
KSOH .... Wapato, WA [*FM radio station call letters*]
KS/OI .... Kaposi's Sarcoma and Opportunistic Infection [*Infectious disease*] (DAVI)
KSOK .... Arkansas City, KS [*AM radio station call letters*]
KSOK-FM ..... Winfield, KS [*FM radio station call letters*] (RBYB)
KSOL .... San Francisco, CA [*FM radio station call letters*]
KSOM .... Audubon, IA [*FM radio station call letters*] (RBYB)
KSON .... San Diego, CA [*AM radio station call letters*]
KSON-FM ..... San Diego, CA [*FM radio station call letters*]
KSOO .... Sioux Falls, SD [*AM radio station call letters*]
KSOP .... Salt Lake City, UT [*FM radio station call letters*]
KSOP .... South Salt Lake, UT [*AM radio station call letters*]
KSOR .... Ashland, OR [*FM radio station call letters*]
KSOS .... Brigham City, UT [*AM radio station call letters*]
KSOS-FM ..... Brigham City, UT [*FM radio station call letters*]
KSOU-AM ... Sioux Center, IA [*AM radio station call letters*] (RBYB)
KSOU-FM ... Sioux Center, IA [*FM radio station call letters*] (RBYB)
KSOX .... Raymondville, TX [*AM radio station call letters*]
KSOX-FM ..... Raymondville, TX [*FM radio station call letters*]
KSP .... Karolinska Scales of Personality [*Medicine*] (DMAA)
KSP .... Kentucky Department of Libraries, Processing Center, Frankfort, KY [*OCLC symbol*] (OCLC)
KSP .... Keyset Panel
KSP .... Kidney-Specific Protein [*Medicine*] (DAVI)
KSP .... Knight of St. Stanislaus of Poland
KSP .... Kodak Special Plate
KSP .... Ksiaz [*Poland*] [*Seismograph station code, US Geological Survey*] (SEIS)
Ksp .... Potassium Solubility Product [*Biochemistry*] (DAVI)
KSP .... Servicios Aereos Especializados en Transportes Petroleros [*Colombia*] [*ICAO designator*] (FAAC)
KSPA .... Escondido, CA [*AM radio station call letters*]
KSPB .... Pebble Beach, CA [*FM radio station call letters*]
KSPC .... Claremont, CA [*FM radio station call letters*]
KSPC .... Kuwait Spanish Petroleum Co. (BUAC)
KSPD .... Boise, ID [*AM radio station call letters*]
KSPE .... Santa Barbara, CA [*AM radio station call letters*]
KSPE-FM ..... Ellwood, CA [*FM radio station call letters*] (RBYB)
KSPG .... Clearwater, KS [*FM radio station call letters*]
KSPG .... St. Petersburg/Albert Whitted [*Florida*] [*ICAO location identifier*] (ICLI)
KSPI .... Stillwater, OK [*AM radio station call letters*]
KSPI-FM ...... Stillwater, OK [*FM radio station call letters*]
KSPK .... Walsenburg, CO [*FM radio station call letters*]
KSPL-FM ..... Kalispell, MT [*FM radio station call letters*] (RBYB)
KSPN .... Aspen, CO [*FM radio station call letters*]
K-SPN .... KSC [*Kennedy Space Center*] Shuttle Project Notice [*NASA*] (NASA)
KSPO .... Spokane, WA [*FM radio station call letters*]
KSPQ .... West Plains, MO [*FM radio station call letters*]
KSPR .... Springfield, MO [*Television station call letters*]
KSPS .... Kilo Symbols per Second (MCD)
K-SPS .... KSC [*Kennedy Space Center*] Shuttle Project Specification [*NASA*] (NASA)
KSPS .... Spokane, WA [*Television station call letters*]
KSPS .... Wichita Falls/Sheppard Air Force Base and Municipal [*Texas*] [*ICAO location identifier*] (ICLI)
K-SPT .... Potassium-Urine [*Spot*] [*Biochemistry*] (DAVI)
KSPT .... Sandpoint, ID [*AM radio station call letters*]
KSPT-FM ..... Sandpoint, ID [*FM radio station call letters*] (RBYB)
KSPX .... Sacramento, CA [*Television station call letters*] (BROA)
KSPY .... Quincy, CA [*FM radio station call letters*]
KSPZ .... Colorado Springs, CO [*FM radio station call letters*]
KSQA .... Wallace, ID [*AM radio station call letters*]
KSQD .... Lowry, SD [*FM radio station call letters*]
KSQQ .... Morgan Hill, CA [*FM radio station call letters*]
KSQR .... Sacramento, CA [*AM radio station call letters*] (RBYB)
KSQY .... Deadwood, SD [*FM radio station call letters*]
KSR .... Kaiser (ABBR)
KSR .... K-Band Shuttle Return (SSD)
KSR .... Keyboard Send and Receive [*Computer science*]
KSR .... Koster [*South Africa*] [*Seismograph station code, US Geological Survey*] (SEIS)
KSR .... Sandy River, AK [*Location identifier FAA*] (FAAL)
KSRA .... Salmon, ID [*AM radio station call letters*]
KSRA-FM ..... Salmon, ID [*FM radio station call letters*]
KSRC .... Kuwait Shipbuilding and Repairyard Co. (BUAC)
KSRE .... Minot, ND [*Television station call letters*]
KSRF .... Poipu, HI [*FM radio station call letters*]
KSRG .... Ashland, OR [*FM radio station call letters*] (RBYB)
KSRH .... San Rafael, CA [*FM radio station call letters*]
KSRM .... Soldotna, AK [*AM radio station call letters*]

KSRN .... Sparks, NV [*FM radio station call letters*]
KSRO .... Santa Rosa, CA [*AM radio station call letters*]
KSRQ .... Thief River Falls, MN [*FM radio station call letters*]
KSRR .... Provo, UT [*AM radio station call letters*]
KSRS .... Roseburg, OR [*FM radio station call letters*]
KSR/T .... Keyboard Send/Receive Terminal [*Computer science*] (MHDI)
KSRTC .... Karnataka State Road Transport Corp. [*India*] (BUAC)
KSR terminal... Keyboard Send Receive Terminal [*Computer science*]
KSRV .... Ontario, OR [*AM radio station call letters*]
KSRV-FM .... Ontario, OR [*FM radio station call letters*]
KSRW .... Childress, TX [*FM radio station call letters*]
KSRX .... El Dorado, KS [*AM radio station call letters*]
KSS .... Kearns-Sayre Syndrome [*Ophthalmology*]
KSS .... Keep Sunday Special [*Campaign*] (BUAC)
KSS .... Kellogg Switchboard and Supply
KSS .... Kent State University, School of Library Science, Kent, OH [*OCLC symbol*] (OCLC)
KSS .... Keying Switching Station
KSS .... Knee Signature System [*Orthopedics*]
KSS .... Knight of St. Sylvester
KSS .... Knight of the Southern Star [*Brazil*]
KSS .... Knight of the Sword of Sweden
KSS .... Kohl's Corp. [*NYSE symbol*] (SPSG)
KSS .... Komunisticka Strane Slovenska [*Communist Party of Slovakia*] [*Former Czechoslovakia*] [*Political party*] (PPW)
KSS .... Korea Stamp Society (EA)
KSSB .... Calipatria, CA [*FM radio station call letters*]
KSSB .... Kissable (ABBR)
KSSC .... KSC [*Kennedy Space Center*] Security Steering Committee [*NASA*] (SSD)
KSSC .... Sumter/Shaw Air Force Base [*South Carolina*] [*ICAO location identifier*] (ICLI)
KSSD .... Cedar City, UT [*FM radio station call letters*]
KSSE .... Kurdish Students' Society in Europe (BUAC)
KSSI .... China Lake, CA [*FM radio station call letters*]
KSSJ .... Shingle Springs, CA [*FM radio station call letters*]
KSSK .... Honolulu, HI [*AM radio station call letters*]
KSSK .... Waipahu, HI [*FM radio station call letters*]
KSSM .... Sault Ste. Marie/Sault Ste. Marie Municipal [*Michigan*] [*ICAO location identifier*] (ICLI)
KSSN .... Little Rock, AR [*FM radio station call letters*]
KSSQ .... Conroe, TX [*AM radio station call letters*]
KSSR .... Kisser (ABBR)
KSSR .... Santa Rosa, NM [*AM radio station call letters*]
KSSS .... Bismarck, ND [*FM radio station call letters*]
K-SSS .... KSC [*Kennedy Space Center*] Shuttle Project Station Set Specification [*NASA*] (NASA)
KSST .... Sulphur Springs, TX [*AM radio station call letters*]
KSSU-FM ..... Durant, OK [*FM radio station call letters*] (RBYB)
KST .... Kallistatin (DMAA)
KST .... Kathodenschilessungs-Tetanus [*or Kathodal closing tetanus*] [*Medicine*] (DAVI)
KST .... Keilinschriftliche Studien [*A publication*] (BJA)
KST .... Kemper Strategic Income [*AMEX symbol*] (TTSB)
KST .... Kemper Strategic Income Fund [*NYSE symbol*] (SAG)
KST .... Keyboard Skills Test (TES)
KST .... Keyseat (KSC)
KST .... Key Station Terminal [*Computer science*]
KST .... King Solomon's Temple [*Freemasonry*]
KST .... Known Segment Table [*Computer science*] (IAA)
KST .... Kolcsonos Segito Takarekpenztarak [*Mutual Savings Banks*] [*Hungarian*]
KST .... Kosti [*Sudan*] [*Airport symbol*] (AD)
KSTA .... Coleman, TX [*AM radio station call letters*]
KSTA-FM ..... Coleman, TX [*FM radio station call letters*]
KSTB-FM .... Crystal Beach, TX [*FM radio station call letters*] (RBYB)
KSTC .... Kansas State Teachers College
KSTC .... Sterling, CO [*AM radio station call letters*]
KSTE .... Rancho Cordova, CA [*AM radio station call letters*]
KSteC .... Sterling College, Sterling, KS [*Library symbol Library of Congress*] (LCLS)
KSTF .... Scottsbluff, NE [*Television station call letters*]
KSTG .... Sikeston, MO [*FM radio station call letters*]
KStJ .... Knight Commander [*of the Order of*] St. John of Jerusalem [*British*]
KStJ .... Knight of the Order of St. John of Jerusalem (DD)
KStJ .... Knight Venerable, Order of St. John of Jerusalem [*Decoration*] (CMD)
K ST J of J... Knight of St. John of Jerusalem [*Freemasonry*] (ROG)
KSTK .... Wrangell, AK [*FM radio station call letters*]
KSTL .... St. Louis/Lambert-St. Louis International [*Missouri*] [*ICAO location identifier*] (ICLI)
KSTL .... St. Louis, MO [*AM radio station call letters*]
KSTM .... Indianola, IA [*FM radio station call letters*]
KSTN .... Keystone Financial [*NASDAQ symbol*] (TTSB)
KSTN .... Keystone Financial, Inc. [*NASDAQ symbol*] (NQ)
KSTN .... Kriegsstaerke-Nachweisung [*Table of Organization*] [*German military - World War II*]
KSTN .... Stockton, CA [*AM radio station call letters*]
KSTN-FM ..... Stockton, CA [*FM radio station call letters*]
KSTO .... Agana, GU [*FM radio station call letters*]
K stoff .... Chloromethyl Chloroformate [*Organic chemistry*] (DAVI)
KSTP .... St. Paul, MN [*AM radio station call letters*]
KSTP-FM ..... St. Paul, MN [*FM radio station call letters*]
KSTP-TV ..... St. Paul, MN [*Television station call letters*]
KSTQ .... Alexandria, MN [*FM radio station call letters*]

KSTR .... Montrose, CO [*FM radio station call letters*]
KSTRL .... Kestrel (ABBR)
KSTS........... San Jose, CA [*Television station call letters*]
K-STSM .... KSC [*Kennedy Space Center*] Space Transportation System Management [*Document*] [*NASA*] (NASA)
K-STSN .... KSC [*Kennedy Space Center*] Shuttle Test Station Notice [*NASA*] (GFGA)
K-STSPS ...... KSC [*Kennedy Space Center*] Shuttle Test Station Project Specification [*NASA*] (GFGA)
KSTT........... Los Osos-Baywood Park, CA [*FM radio station call letters*]
KSTU .... Salt Lake City, UT [*Television station call letters*]
KSTV .... Stephenville, TX [*AM radio station call letters*]
KSTV .... Ventura, CA [*Television station call letters*]
KSTW .... Tacoma, WA [*Television station call letters*]
KSTX .... San Antonio, TX [*FM radio station call letters*]
KSTY .... Canon City, CO [*FM radio station call letters*]
KSTZ........... Des Moines, IA [*FM radio station call letters*]
ksu .... Kansas [*MARC country of publication code Library of Congress*] (LCCP)
KSU .... Kansas City So. Ind. [*NYSE symbol*] (TTSB)
KSU .... Kansas City Southern Industries, Inc. [*NYSE symbol*] (SPSG)
KSU .... Kansas State University
KSU .... Kent State University [*Ohio*]
KSU .... Kent State University, Kent, OH [*OCLC symbol*] (OCLC)
KSU .... Key Service Unit (IEEE)
KSU .... Key System Control Unit [*Telecommunications*]
KSU .... Kousour [*Djibouti*] [*Seismograph station code, US Geological Survey*] (SEIS)
KSU .... Kristiansund [*Norway*] [*Airport symbol*] (OAG)
KSUA .... Kyoto Sangyo University [*UTLAS symbol*]
KSUA .... College, AK [*FM radio station call letters*]
KSUB .... Cedar City, UT [*AM radio station call letters*]
KSUD .... West Memphis, AR [*AM radio station call letters*]
KSUE .... Susanville, CA [*AM radio station call letters*]
KSUI .... Iowa City, IA [*FM radio station call letters*]
KSUM .... Fairmont, MN [*AM radio station call letters*]
KSUN .... Phoenix, AZ [*AM radio station call letters*]
KSUP .... Juneau, AK [*FM radio station call letters*]
KSUPr......... Kansas City So. Ind 4% Pfd [*NYSE symbol*] (TTSB)
KSUT .... Ignacio, CO [*FM radio station call letters*]
KSUU .... Cedar City, UT [*FM radio station call letters*]
KSUU .... Fairfield/Travis Air Force Base [*California*] [*ICAO location identifier*] (ICLI)
KSUV-FM..... McFarland, CA [*FM radio station call letters*]
KSUW-FM.... Sheridan, WY [*FM radio station call letters*] (BROA)
KSUX .... Sioux City [*Iowa*] [*ICAO location identifier*] (ICLI)
KSUX .... Winnebago, NE [*FM radio station call letters*]
KSVA .... Corrales, NM [*FM radio station call letters*]
KSVC .... Richfield, UT [*AM radio station call letters*]
KSVE........... El Paso, TX [*AM radio station call letters*]
KSVI........... Billings, MT [*Television station call letters*]
KSVN .... Ogden, UT [*AM radio station call letters*]
KSVP .... Artesia, NM [*AM radio station call letters*]
KSVR........... Mount Vernon, WA [*FM radio station call letters*]
KSVY .... Opportunity, WA [*AM radio station call letters*]
KSW............ C. H. Boehringer Sohn, Ingelheim [*Germany*] [*Research code symbol*]
KSW............ Wichita State University, Wichita, KS [*OCLC symbol*] (OCLC)
KSWA .... Graham, TX [*AM radio station call letters*]
KSWA .... Swan Islands [*ICAO location identifier*] (ICLI)
KSWB .... Seaside, OR [*AM radio station call letters*] (RBYB)
KSWB-TV..... San Diego, CA [*TV station call letters*] (RBYB)
KSWC .... Winfield, KS [*FM radio station call letters*]
KSWD .... Seward, AK [*AM radio station call letters*]
KSWF .... Newburgh/Stewart [*New York*] [*ICAO location identifier*] (ICLI)
KSWG-FM.... Wickenburg, AZ [*FM radio station call letters*] (RBYB)
KSWH .... Arkadelphia, AR [*FM radio station call letters*]
K Swiss ...... K Swiss, Inc. [*Associated Press*] (SAG)
KSWK .... Lakin, KS [*Television station call letters*]
KSWM .... Aurora, MO [*AM radio station call letters*]
KSWO .... Lawton, OK [*AM radio station call letters*]
KSWO-TV..... Lawton, OK [*Television station call letters*]
KSWP .... Lufkin, TX [*FM radio station call letters*]
KSWR........... Clinton, OK [*FM radio station call letters*]
KSWS .... K Swiss, Inc. [*NASDAQ symbol*] (SAG)
KSWS .... K Swiss Inc. 'A' [*NASDAQ symbol*] (TTSB)
KSWS .... Sisseton, SD [*AM radio station call letters*]
KSWT .... Yuma, AZ [*Television station call letters*]
KSWV .... Santa Fe, NM [*AM radio station call letters*]
KSWW .... Raymond, WA [*FM radio station call letters*]
KSXX .... Marysville, CA [*FM radio station call letters*]
KSYC .... Yreka, CA [*AM radio station call letters*]
KSYC-FM ..... Yreka, CA [*FM radio station call letters*] (RBYB)
KSYD........... Reedsport, OR [*AM radio station call letters*]
KSYE........... Frederick, OK [*FM radio station call letters*]
KSYG .... Little Rock, AR [*AM radio station call letters*] (RBYB)
KSYG-FM..... Little Rock, AR [*FM radio station call letters*] (RBYB)
KSYL........... Alexandria, LA [*AM radio station call letters*]
KSYM........... San Antonio, TX [*FM radio station call letters*]
KSYM........... Smyrna/Sewart Air Force Base [*Tennessee*] [*ICAO location identifier*] (ICLI)
KSYN .... Joplin, MO [*FM radio station call letters*]
KSYR .... Syracuse/Hancock International [*New York*] [*ICAO location identifier*] (ICLI)
KSYS .... Medford, OR [*Television station call letters*]

KSYV .... Solvang, CA [*FM radio station call letters*]
KSYY-FM .... Fallbrook, CA [*FM radio station call letters*] (RBYB)
KSYZ.......... Grand Island, NE [*FM radio station call letters*]
KSZL.......... Barstow, CA [*AM radio station call letters*]
KSZL.......... Knobnoster/Whiteman Air Force Base [*Missouri*] [*ICAO location identifier*] (ICLI)
KSZZ.......... San Bernardino, CA [*AM radio station call letters*] (RBYB)
KT .... British Airtours Ltd. [*British ICAO designator*] (ICDA)
KT .... Canadian-Tech Industries, Inc. [*Vancouver Stock Exchange symbol*]
KT .... Contract [*Navy*]
KT .... Cretaceous-Tertiary [*Geology*]
KT .... Kangmar Thrust [*Geophysics*]
KT .... Karat [*Also, CT*]
KT .... Karuna Trust [*Multinational association based in England*] (EAIO)
KT .... Katy Indus [*NYSE symbol*] (TTSB)
KT .... Katy Industries, Inc. [*Formerly, Missouri-Kansas-Texas R. R. Co., with Wall Street slang name of "Kathy"*] [*NYSE symbol*] (SPSG)
KT .... Keel Torsion (SSD)
KT .... Kentucky & Tennessee Railway [*AAR code*]
KT .... Kenya Times [*A publication*]
KT .... Kermit [*Texas*] [*Seismograph station code, US Geological Survey*] (SEIS)
KT .... Ketamine [*An anesthetic*]
KT .... Keying Time [*Computer order entry*]
KT .... Khaksar Tehrik [*Pakistan*] [*Political party*] (FEA)
KT .... Khotanese Texts (BJA)
KT .... Kidney Transplant [*Medicine*] (DMAA)
kt .... Kiloton [*Nuclear equivalent of 1000 tons of high explosives*]
KT .... Kinetic Theory
KT .... Kinetin [*Plant growth regulator*]
KT .... Kingston-upon-Thames [*Postcode*] (ODBW)
KT .... Kit
KT .... Klippel-Trenaunay [*Syndrome*] [*Medicine*] (DAVI)
KT .... Knight [*British title*]
KT .... Knight [*Chess*]
Kt. .... Knight [*British title*] (WA)
KT .... Knighted
KT .... Knight of Tabor [*Freemasonry*] (ROG)
KT .... Knight of the Thistle [*British*]
KT .... Knights Templar
kt .... Knot (COE)
KT .... Knots [*Also, K*] [*Nautical speed unit*]
K-T .... Kosterlitz-Thouless Theory [*Physics*]
KT .... Kuder Test [*Psychology*] (DAVI)
KT .... Kungtang [*Labor party*] [*Taiwan*] [*Political party*] (EY)
KT .... Topeka Public Library, Topeka, KS [*Library symbol Library of Congress*] (LCLS)
KT .... Trinidad and Tobago [*IYRU nationality code*] (IYR)
KT .... Turtle Airways [*ICAO designator*] (AD)
KTA .... Kansas Telecommunications Association (SRA)
KTA .... Karratha [*Australia Airport symbol*] (OAG)
KTA .... Kentucky Telephone Association (SRA)
KTA .... Kentucky Thoroughbred Association (SRA)
KTA .... Keyboard Teachers Association (EA)
KTA .... Key Telephone Adapter [*Telecommunications*] (TEL)
KTA .... Kindergarten Teachers Association (BARN)
KTA .... Kite Trade Association International (EA)
KTA .... Knitted Textile Association (EA)
KTA .... Knots True Airspeed
KTA .... Korea Tourist Association (EAIO)
KTA .... Kotzebue [*Alaska*] [*Seismograph station code, US Geological Survey*] (SEIS)
KTA .... Potassium Turbo-Alternator
KTAA .... Kerman, CA [*FM radio station call letters*]
KTAB .... Abilene, TX [*Television station call letters*]
KTAC .... Ephrata, WA [*FM radio station call letters*] (RBYB)
KTAE .... Taylor, TX [*AM radio station call letters*]
KTAG .... Cody, WY [*FM radio station call letters*]
KTAG .... Korea Trade Advisory Group [*British Overseas Trade Board*] (DS)
KTAI .... Keyboard Teachers Association International (NTPA)
KTAI .... Kingsville, TX [*FM radio station call letters*]
KTAI .... Kite Trade Association International [*Later, KTA*] (EA)
KTAJ .... St. Joseph, MO [*Television station call letters*]
KTAK .... Riverton, WY [*FM radio station call letters*]
KTAL .... Texarkana, TX [*FM radio station call letters*]
KTAL-TV ..... Texarkana, TX [*Television station call letters*]
KTAM .... Bryan, TX [*AM radio station call letters*]
KTAN .... Sierra Vista, AZ [*AM radio station call letters*]
KTAO .... Taos, NM [*FM radio station call letters*]
KTAP .... Santa Maria, CA [*AM radio station call letters*]
KTAQ .... Greeneville, TX [*Television station call letters*]
KTAR .... Phoenix, AZ [*AM radio station call letters*]
KTAS .... Knots True Airspeed [*Navy*] (NVT)
KTAT .... Frederick, OK [*AM radio station call letters*]
KTAX .... Kaye Kotts Associates, Inc. [*NASDAQ symbol*] (SAG)
KTAX .... Kay Kotts Assoc [*NASDAQ symbol*] (TTSB)
KTAXW .... Kaye Kotts Assoc Wrrt [*NASDAQ symbol*] (TTSB)
KTB .... Kosterlitz-Thouless-Berezinskii Layers [*Physics*]
KTB .... Kriegstagebuch [*War Diary*] [*German military - World War II*]
KTB .... Thorne River, AK [*Location identifier FAA*] (FAAL)
KTBA .... Ketothiomethylbutyric Acid [*Organic chemistry*]
KTBA .... Tuba City, AZ [*AM radio station call letters*]
Kt Bach....... Knight Bachelor
KTBB........... Tyler, TX [*AM radio station call letters*]
KTBC .... Austin, TX [*Television station call letters*]

KTBI............ Ephrata, WA [*AM radio station call letters*]
KTBJ-FM...... Festus, MO [*FM radio station call letters*] (RBYB)
KTBL-FM...... Albuquerque, NM [*FM radio station call letters*] (RBYB)
KTBN............ Santa Ana, CA [*Television station call letters*]
KTBO............ Oklahoma City, OK [*Television station call letters*]
KTBQ............ Nacogdoches, TX [*FM radio station call letters*]
KTBR............ Roseburg, OR [*AM radio station call letters*]
KTBS............ Shreveport, LA [*Television station call letters*]
KTBT-FM...... New Iberia, LA [*FM radio station call letters*] (BROA)
KTBW............ Tacoma, WA [*Television station call letters*]
KTBY............ Anchorage, AK [*Television station call letters*]
KTBZ............ Lake Jackson, TX [*FM radio station call letters*] (RBYB)
KTC............ Kellogg Telecommunications Corp. [*Littleton, CO*] [*Telecommunications*] (TSSD)
KTC............ Kentucky Tourism Council (SRA)
KTC............ Kutchino [*Later, MOS*] [*Former USSR Geomagnetic observatory code*]
KTC............ Somerset Community College, Somerset, KY [*OCLC symbol*] (OCLC)
KTC............ Trinity College Library, University of Toronto [*UTLAS symbol*]
KTCA............ St. Paul, MN [*Television station call letters*]
KTCAX.......... Kemper Technology Cl.A [*Mutual fund ticker symbol*] (SG)
KTCB............ Malden, MO [*AM radio station call letters*]
KTCC............ Colby, KS [*FM radio station call letters*]
KTCC............ Key Tronic Corp. [*NASDAQ symbol*] (TTSB)
KTCC............ Key Tronics Corp. [*NASDAQ symbol*] (NQ)
KTCC............ Tucumcari [*New Mexico*] [*ICAO location identifier*] (ICLI)
KTCCA.......... Kotwali Thana Central Cooperative Association [*Bangladesh*] (BUAC)
KTCE............ Payson, UT [*FM radio station call letters*]
KTCF............ Crosby, MN [*FM radio station call letters*]
KTCH............ Wayne, NE [*AM radio station call letters*]
KTCH-FM...... Wayne, NE [*FM radio station call letters*]
KTCHN.......... Kitchen
KTCHP.......... Ketchup (ABBR)
KTCI............ St. Paul, MN [*Television station call letters*]
KTCJ............ Minneapolis, MN [*AM radio station call letters*]
KTCK............ Dallas, TX [*AM radio station call letters*]
KTCL............ Fort Collins, CO [*FM radio station call letters*]
KTCM............ Kingman, KS [*FM radio station call letters*]
KTCM............ Tacoma/McChord Air Force Base [*Washington*] [*ICAO location identifier*] (ICLI)
KTCN............ Eureka Springs, AR [*FM radio station call letters*]
KTCN............ Kitchen (ABBR)
KTCNET........ Kitchenette (ABBR)
KTCNWR........ Kitchenware (ABBR)
KTCO............ Duluth, MN [*FM radio station call letters*]
KTCO............ Kenan Transport [*NASDAQ symbol*] (TTSB)
KTCO............ Kenan Transportation Co. [*NASDAQ symbol*] (NQ)
KTCR............ Kennewick, WA [*AM radio station call letters*]
KTCS............ Fort Smith, AR [*AM radio station call letters*]
KTCS............ Truth Or Consequences/Municipal [*New Mexico*] [*ICAO location identifier*] (ICLI)
KTCS-FM...... Fort Smith, AR [*FM radio station call letters*]
KTCT-AM...... San Mateo, CA [*AM radio station call letters*] (BROA)
KTCU............ Fort Worth, TX [*FM radio station call letters*]
KTCV............ Kennewick, WA [*FM radio station call letters*]
KTCWAO........ Kenya Thirsty Child and Women Aid Organisation (BUAC)
KTCX-FM...... Beaumont, TX [*FM radio station call letters*] (RBYB)
KTCY............ Denison, TX [*FM radio station call letters*]
KTCZ............ Minneapolis, MN [*FM radio station call letters*]
KTD............ Killed Target Detector [*Military*] (PDAA)
KTD............ Kita-Daito [*Japan*] [*Airport symbol*] (OAG)
KTDA............ Kenya Tea Development Authority (BUAC)
KTDB............ Ramah, NM [*FM radio station call letters*]
KTDC............ Kenya Tourist Development Corp. (BUAC)
KTDO............ Columbia, CA [*FM radio station call letters*] (RBYB)
KTDR............ Del Rio, TX [*FM radio station call letters*]
KTDS............ Key to Disk Software
KTDX............ Mountain Pine, AR [*FM radio station call letters*] (RBYB)
KTDY............ Lafayette, LA [*FM radio station call letters*]
KTE............ Kennedy-Thorndike Experiment
KTE............ Kermit [*Texas*] [*Seismograph station code, US Geological Survey*] (SEIS)
K-TEA......... Kaufman Test of Educational Achievement
KTEB............ Teterboro [*New Jersey*] [*ICAO location identifier*] (ICLI)
KTEC............ Key Technologies, Inc. [*NASDAQ symbol*] (SAG)
KTEC............ Key Technology [*NASDAQ symbol*] (TTSB)
KTEC............ Klamath Falls, OR [*FM radio station call letters*]
KTEG............ Albuquerque, NM [*FM radio station call letters*] (RBYB)
KTEH............ San Jose, CA [*Television station call letters*]
KTEJ............ Jonesboro, AR [*Television station call letters*]
KTEK............ Alvin, TX [*AM radio station call letters*]
K-TEL......... Kives-Television [*In company name K-Tel International. Derived from name of company president and fact that it markets its products on television*]
KTEL............ K-Tel International [*NASDAQ symbol*] (TTSB)
KTEL............ K-tel International, Inc. [*NASDAQ symbol*] (SAG)
K-Tel......... K-tel International, Inc. [*Associated Press*] (SAG)
KTEL............ Walla Walla, WA [*AM radio station call letters*]
KTEL-FM...... Walla Walla, WA [*FM radio station call letters*]
KTEM............ Temple, TX [*AM radio station call letters*]
KTEN............ Ada, OK [*Television station call letters*]
KTEO............ Wichita Falls, TX [*FM radio station call letters*]
KTEP............ El Paso, TX [*FM radio station call letters*]
KTEQ............ Rapid City, SD [*FM radio station call letters*]
KTEX............ Brownsville, TX [*FM radio station call letters*]

KTF............ Kansas Turfgrass Foundation (EA)
KTF............ Kauai Test Facility [*AEC*]
KTF............ Kemper Municipal Income Fund [*NYSE symbol*] (CTT)
KTF............ Kemper Muni Income [*NYSE symbol*] (TTSB)
KTF............ Kuwaiti [*Civil Affairs*] Task Force (DOMA)
KTFA............ Groves, TX [*FM radio station call letters*]
KTFC............ Sioux City, IA [*FM radio station call letters*]
KTFG............ Sioux Rapids, IA [*FM radio station call letters*]
KTFH............ Conroe, TX [*Television station call letters*]
KTFI............ Twin Falls, ID [*AM radio station call letters*]
KTFJ............ Dakota City, NE [*AM radio station call letters*]
KTFL............ Flagstaff, AZ [*Television station call letters*] (BROA)
KTFM............ San Antonio, TX [*FM radio station call letters*]
KTFN-AM...... Merced, CA [*AM radio station call letters*] (BROA)
KTFO............ Tulsa, OK [*Television station call letters*]
KTFR............ Claremore, OK [*FM radio station call letters*]
KTFR............ Kodak Thin-Film Resist [*Cathode coating*]
KTFS-AM...... Texarkana, TX [*AM radio station call letters*] (RBYB)
KTFW-FM...... Stamford, TX [*FM radio station call letters*] (BROA)
KTFX............ Sand Springs, OK [*FM radio station call letters*] (RBYB)
KTG............ Kap Tobin [*Greenland*] [*Seismograph station code, US Geological Survey*] (SEIS)
KTG............ Ketapang [*Indonesia*] [*Airport symbol*] (OAG)
KTGA............ Kenya Tea Growers Association (BUAC)
KTGE............ Salinas, CA [*AM radio station call letters*]
KTGF............ Great Falls, MT [*Television station call letters*]
KTGF............ Keratinocyte T-Cell Growth Factor [*Immunology*]
KTGG............ Spring Arbor, MI [*AM radio station call letters*]
KTGIFC........ Karen Taylor-Good International Fan Club [*Defunct*] (EA)
KTGL............ Beatrice, NE [*FM radio station call letters*]
KTGM............ Tamuning, GU [*Television station call letters*]
KTGO............ Tioga, ND [*AM radio station call letters*]
KTGP-FM...... Pawhuska, OK [*FM radio station call letters*] (RBYB)
KTGR............ Columbia, MO [*AM radio station call letters*]
KTH............ Kungliga Tekniska Hoegskolan [*Royal Institute of Technology*] [*Stockholm, Sweden*] (ARC)
KTHB............ Kungliga Tekniska Hogskolans Bibliotek [*Royal Institute of Technology Library*] [*Information service or system*] (IID)
KTHC............ Sidney, MT [*FM radio station call letters*] (RBYB)
KTHE............ Thermopolis, WY [*AM radio station call letters*]
KTHK............ Okmulgee, OK [*AM radio station call letters*]
KTHN-FM...... Hooks, TX [*FM radio station call letters*] (BROA)
KTHO............ South Lake Tahoe, CA [*AM radio station call letters*]
KTHQ-FM...... Eagar, AZ [*FM radio station call letters*] (RBYB)
KTHR-FM...... Grants, NM [*FM radio station call letters*] (RBYB)
KTHS............ Berryville, AR [*AM radio station call letters*]
KTHS-FM...... Berryville, AR [*FM radio station call letters*]
KTHT............ Fresno, CA [*FM radio station call letters*]
KTHV............ Little Rock, AR [*Television station call letters*]
KTHX............ Visalia, CA [*AM radio station call letters*]
KTHX-FM...... Carson City, NV [*FM radio station call letters*]
KTI............ Kallikrein-Trypsin Inhibitor (DB)
KTI............ Kano Transport International Ltd. KATI Air [*Nigeria*] [*ICAO designator*] (FAAC)
KTI............ Kinai Technologies, Inc. [*Formerly, Kinai Resources Corp.*] [*Vancouver Stock Exchange symbol*]
KTI............ Kirsch Technologies, Inc. [*Software manufacturer*] [*St. Clair, MI*]
KTI............ Kitchen Table International [*David D. Busch's vaporware software company*]
KTI............ Kratie [*Cambodia*] [*Airport symbol*] (AD)
KTI............ KTI, Inc. [*Associated Press*] (SAG)
KTI............ Kunitz Trypsin Inhibitor (DB)
KTIB............ Thibodaux, LA [*AM radio station call letters*]
KTIC............ West Point, NE [*AM radio station call letters*] (RBYB)
KTIE............ Bakersfield, CA [*FM radio station call letters*]
KTIE............ KTI, Inc. [*NASDAQ symbol*] (SAG)
KTIG............ Pequot Lakes, MN [*FM radio station call letters*]
KTII............ K-Tron International, Inc. [*NASDAQ symbol*] (NQ)
KTII............ K-Tron Intl [*NASDAQ symbol*] (TTSB)
KTIJ............ Elk City, OK [*FM radio station call letters*]
KTIK............ Nampa, ID [*AM radio station call letters*]
KTIK............ Oklahoma City/Tinker Air Force Base [*Oklahoma*] [*ICAO location identifier*] (ICLI)
KTIL-FM...... Tillamook, OR [*FM radio station call letters*]
KTIM............ Wickenburg, AZ [*AM radio station call letters*]
KTIN............ Fort Dodge, IA [*Television station call letters*]
KTIP............ Porterville, CA [*AM radio station call letters*]
KTIS............ Minneapolis, MN [*AM radio station call letters*]
KTIS-FM...... Minneapolis, MN [*FM radio station call letters*]
KTIV............ Sioux City, IA [*Television station call letters*]
KTIX............ Pendleton, OR [*AM radio station call letters*]
KTJC............ Rayville, LA [*FM radio station call letters*]
KTJJ............ Farmington, MO [*FM radio station call letters*]
KTJN............ Mercedes, TX [*FM radio station call letters*]
KTJO............ Ottawa, KS [*FM radio station call letters*]
KTJS............ Hobart, OK [*AM radio station call letters*]
KTJX............ Mission, TX [*FM radio station call letters*]
KTKA............ Topeka, KS [*Television station call letters*]
KTKC............ Springhill, LA [*FM radio station call letters*]
KTKK............ Sandy, UT [*AM radio station call letters*]
KTKN............ Ketchikan, AK [*AM radio station call letters*]
KTKO............ Beeville, TX [*FM radio station call letters*]
KTKR............ San Antonio, TX [*AM radio station call letters*]
KTKS............ Versailles, MO [*FM radio station call letters*]
KTKT............ Tucson, AZ [*AM radio station call letters*]

KTKU	Juneau, AK [*FM radio station call letters*]
KTKX	Crystal Beach, TX [*FM radio station call letters*]
ktl	Kai ta Loipa [*And the Rest, And So Forth*]
KTL	Kettle (ABBR)
KTL	Key-Edit Terminal Language [*Computer science*] (MHDI)
KTL	Kitale [*Kenya*] [*Airport symbol*] (AD)
KTL	K-Tel International, Inc. [*Toronto Stock Exchange symbol*] (SPSG)
KTL	Kuratorium fuer Technik in der Landwirtschaft
KTLA	Los Angeles, CA [*Television station call letters*]
KTLB	Twin Lakes, IA [*FM radio station call letters*]
KTLC	Oklahoma City, OK [*Television station call letters*]
KTLD	Pineville, LA [*AM radio station call letters*]
KTLDR	Kettledrum (ABBR)
KTLE	Tooele, UT [*FM radio station call letters*]
KTLF	Colorado Springs, CO [*FM radio station call letters*]
KTLH	Tallahassee/Dale Mabry Field [*Florida*] [*ICAO location identifier*] (ICLI)
KTLI	El Dorado, KS [*FM radio station call letters*]
KTLK	Thornton, CO [*AM radio station call letters*]
KTLN	Thibodaux, LA [*FM radio station call letters*] (RBYB)
KTLO	Mountain Home, AR [*AM radio station call letters*]
KTLO-FM	Mountain Home, AR [*FM radio station call letters*]
KTLQ	Tahlequah, OK [*AM radio station call letters*]
KTLR	Terrell, TX [*FM radio station call letters*]
KTLS	Ada, OK [*FM radio station call letters*]
KTLT	Wichita Falls, TX [*FM radio station call letters*]
KTLU	Rusk, TX [*AM radio station call letters*]
KTLV	Midwest City, OK [*AM radio station call letters*]
KTLW	Lancaster, CA [*FM radio station call letters*] (RBYB)
KTLX	Columbus, NE [*FM radio station call letters*]
KTM	Katmai [*Alaska*] [*Seismograph station code, US Geological Survey*] (SEIS)
KTM	Katmandu [*Nepal*] [*Airport symbol*] (OAG)
KTM	Key Transport Module
KTM	Menninger Clinic Library, Topeka, KS [*Library symbol Library of Congress*] (LCLS)
KTM	Thomas More College, Fort Mitchell, KY [*OCLC symbol*] (OCLC)
KT MAR SC	Knight Mareschal of Scotland (ROG)
KTMB	Miami/New Tamiami [*Florida*] [*ICAO location identifier*] (ICLI)
KTMC	McAlester, OK [*AM radio station call letters*]
KTMC-FM	McAlester, OK [*FM radio station call letters*]
KTMD	Galveston, TX [*Television station call letters*]
KTME	Lompoc, CA [*AM radio station call letters*]
KTMF	Missoula, MT [*Television station call letters*]
KTMG	Deer Trail, CO [*AM radio station call letters*]
KTMN	Los Alamos, NM [*FM radio station call letters*]
KTMO	Kennett, MO [*AM radio station call letters*]
KTMP	Heber City, UT [*AM radio station call letters*]
KTMR	Edna, TX [*AM radio station call letters*]
KTMS	Knapp Time Metaphor Scale
KTMS	Santa Barbara, CA [*AM radio station call letters*]
KTMT	Medford, OR [*FM radio station call letters*]
KTMT	Phoenix, OR [*AM radio station call letters*]
KTMX	York, NE [*FM radio station call letters*]
KTN	Keltic, Inc. [*Toronto Stock Exchange symbol*]
KTN	Ketchikan [*Alaska*] [*Airport symbol*] (OAG)
KTN	Ketchikan, AK [*Location identifier FAA*] (FAAL)
KTN	Kitten (ABBR)
KTN	Kuratorium fuer die Tagungen der Nobelpreistrager [*Standing Committee for Nobel Prize Winners' Congresses - SCNPWC*] [*Germany*] (EA)
KTN	Potassium Tantalate Niobate (MCD)
KTNA	Talkeetna, AK [*FM radio station call letters*]
KTNC	Falls City, NE [*AM radio station call letters*]
KTNC-TV	Concord, CA [*TV station call letters*] (RBYB)
KTND	Ojai, CA [*FM radio station call letters*] (RBYB)
KTNE	Alliance, NE [*FM radio station call letters*]
KTNE-TV	Alliance, NE [*Television station call letters*]
KTNF	Kodak Timing Negative Film
KTNH	Kittenish (ABBR)
KTNI	Kansas Neurological Institute, Topeka, KS [*Library symbol Library of Congress*] (LCLS)
KTNL	Sitka, AK [*Television station call letters*]
KTNM	Tucumcari, NM [*AM radio station call letters*]
KTNN	Window Rock, AZ [*AM radio station call letters*]
KTNO	Fort Worth, TX [*AM radio station call letters*]
KTNP-FM	Bennington, NE [*FM radio station call letters*] (RBYB)
KTNQ	Los Angeles, CA [*AM radio station call letters*]
KTNR	Kenedy, TX [*FM radio station call letters*]
KTNS	Oakhurst, CA [*AM radio station call letters*]
KTNT	Edmund, OK [*FM radio station call letters*]
KTNT	Miami/Dade-Collier Training and Transition Airport [*Florida*] [*ICAO location identifier*] (ICLI)
KTNV	Las Vegas, NV [*Television station call letters*]
KTNW	Richland, WA [*Television station call letters*]
KTNY	Libby, MT [*FM radio station call letters*]
KTNZ	Amarillo, TX [*AM radio station call letters*] (RBYB)
KTO	K2, Inc. [*NYSE symbol*] [*Formerly, Anthony Industries*] (SG)
KTO	Kato [*Guyana*] [*Airport symbol*] (OAG)
KTO	Kraus-Thomson Organization [*Publishing*]
KtO	KTO Microform, Millwood, NY [*Library symbol Library of Congress*] (LCLS)
KTO	Kuwaiti Theatre of Operation [*Operation Desert Storm*]
KTOB	Petaluma, CA [*AM radio station call letters*]
KTOC	Jonesboro, LA [*AM radio station call letters*]
KTOC-FM	Jonesboro, LA [*FM radio station call letters*]
KTOD	Conway, AR [*FM radio station call letters*]
KTOE	Mankato, MN [*AM radio station call letters*]
KTOF	Cedar Rapids, IA [*FM radio station call letters*]
KTOK	Oklahoma City, OK [*AM radio station call letters*]
KTOL	Lacey, WA [*AM radio station call letters*]
KTOM	Salinas, CA [*AM radio station call letters*]
KTOM-FM	Salinas, CA [*FM radio station call letters*]
KTON	Belton, TX [*AM radio station call letters*]
KTON	Ketone [*Organic chemistry*] (ABBR)
KTOO	Juneau, AK [*FM radio station call letters*]
KTOO-TV	Juneau, AK [*Television station call letters*]
KTOP	Topeka, KS [*AM radio station call letters*]
KTOQ	Rapid City, SD [*AM radio station call letters*]
KTOW	Sand Springs, OK [*AM radio station call letters*]
KTOW-FM	Sand Springs, OK [*FM radio station call letters*]
KTOX	Needles, CA [*AM radio station call letters*]
KTOZ	Marshfield, MO [*FM radio station call letters*]
KTOZ	Springfield, MO [*AM radio station call letters*]
KTP	Kentucky Truck Plant [*Ford Motor Co.*]
KTP	Keyboard Typing Perforator (NITA)
KTP	Kingston-Tinson [*Jamaica*] [*Airport symbol*] (OAG)
KT P	Knight's Pawn [*Chess*] (ROG)
KTP	Kommunistinen Tyovaenpuolue [*Communist Workers' Party*] [*Finland*] [*Political party*] (EY)
KTPA	Prescott, AR [*AM radio station call letters*]
KTPA	Tampa/International [*Florida*] [*ICAO location identifier*] (ICLI)
KTPB	Kilgore, TX [*FM radio station call letters*]
KTPH	Tonopah, NV [*FM radio station call letters*]
KTPI	Kaum-Tani Persatuan Indonesia [*Indonesian Farmers' Party*] [*Surinam*] [*Political party*] (PPW)
KTPI	Tehachapi, CA [*FM radio station call letters*]
KTPK	Topeka, KS [*FM radio station call letters*]
KTPR	Fort Dodge, IA [*FM radio station call letters*]
KTPX	Okmulgee, OK [*Television station call letters*] (BROA)
KTPZ-FM	Mountain Home, ID [*FM radio station call letters*] (BROA)
KTQM	Clovis, NM [*AM radio station call letters*]
KTQX	Bakersfield, CA [*FM radio station call letters*]
KTR	Contractor
KTR	Helikoptertransport AB [*Sweden ICAO designator*] (FAAC)
KTR	K-2 Resources, Inc. [*Vancouver Stock Exchange symbol*]
KTR	Katherine [*Northern Territory, Australia*] [*Airport symbol*] (AD)
KTR	Katuura [*Japan*] [*Later, HTY*] [*Geomagnetic observatory code*]
KTR	Keyboard Typing Reperforator [*Computer science*]
KTRA	Farmington, NM [*FM radio station call letters*]
KTRAX	Kemper Total Return Cl.A [*Mutual fund ticker symbol*] (SG)
KTRB	Modesto, CA [*AM radio station call letters*]
KTRBX	Kemper Total Return Cl.B [*Mutual fund ticker symbol*] (SG)
KTRC	Santa Fe, NM [*AM radio station call letters*]
KTRE-TV	Lufkin, TX [*Television station call letters*]
KTRF	Thief River Falls, MN [*AM radio station call letters*]
KTRG	Del Rio, TX [*Television station call letters*]
KTRH	Houston, TX [*AM radio station call letters*]
KTRI	Mansfield, MO [*FM radio station call letters*]
KTRJ-AM	Frazier Park, CA [*AM radio station call letters*] (RBYB)
KTRK	Houston, TX [*Television station call letters*]
KTRM-FM	Kirksville, MO [*FM radio station call letters*] (BROA)
KTRN	Silverton, CO [*FM radio station call letters*]
KTRO	Port Hueneme, CA [*AM radio station call letters*]
KTron	K-Tron International, Inc. [*Associated Press*] (SAG)
KTRQ-FM	Quincy, WA [*FM radio station call letters*] (RBYB)
KTRR	Loveland, CO [*FM radio station call letters*]
KTRS	Casper, WY [*FM radio station call letters*]
KTRT	Claremore, OK [*AM radio station call letters*]
KTRU	Houston, TX [*FM radio station call letters*]
KTRV	Nampa, ID [*Television station call letters*]
KTRW	Spokane, WA [*AM radio station call letters*]
KTRX	Tarkio, MO [*FM radio station call letters*]
KTRY	Bastrop, LA [*AM radio station call letters*]
KTRY-FM	Bastrop, LA [*FM radio station call letters*]
KTRZ	Riverton, WY [*FM radio station call letters*]
KTS	Brevig Mission [*Alaska*] [*Airport symbol*] (OAG)
KTS	Kelvin Temperature Scale
KTS	Kethoxal Thiosemicarbazone [*An antiviral*] [*Pharmacology*] (DAVI)
KTS	Key Telephone System [*Telecommunications*] (AAG)
KTS	Kiersley Temperament Sorter [*Psychiatry*] (DAVI)
KTS	Klippel-Trenaunay Syndrome [*Medicine*] (DMAA)
KTS	Knight of the Tower and Sword [*Portugal*]
KTS	Knots (ADA)
KTS	Kodiak Tracking Station [*NASA*] (MCD)
KTS	Kotas Joint Civil Aviation Enterprise [*Former USSR*] [*FAA designator*] (FAAC)
KTS	Kwajalein Test Site (MCD)
KTS	Southern Baptist Theological Seminary, Louisville, KY [*OCLC symbol*] (OCLC)
KTS	Teller Mission, AK [*Location identifier FAA*] (FAAL)
KTSA	Kahn Test of Symbol Arrangement [*Psychology*]
KTSA	San Antonio, TX [*AM radio station call letters*]
KTSB	Sioux Center, IA [*FM radio station call letters*]
KTSC	Kitsch (ABBR)
KTSC	Pueblo, CO [*FM radio station call letters*]
KTSC-TV	Pueblo, CO [*Television station call letters*]
KTSD	Reliance, SD [*FM radio station call letters*]
KTSD-TV	Pierre, SD [*Television station call letters*]
KTSF	San Francisco, CA [*Television station call letters*]

KTSG	Klippel-Trenaunay Support Group (EA)
KTSH	Tishomingo, OK [*FM radio station call letters*]
KTSH	Topeka State Hospital, Topeka, KS [*Library symbol Library of Congress*] (LCLS)
KTSJ	Pomona, CA [*AM radio station call letters*]
KTSL	Medical Lake, WA [*FM radio station call letters*]
KTSM	El Paso, TX [*AM radio station call letters*]
KTSM-FM	El Paso, TX [*FM radio station call letters*]
KTSM-TV	El Paso, TX [*Television station call letters*]
KTSN-AM	Elko, NV [*AM radio station call letters*] (RBYB)
KTSR	College Station, TX [*FM radio station call letters*]
KTST	Oklahoma City, OK [*FM radio station call letters*] (RBYB)
KTSU	Houston, TX [*FM radio station call letters*]
KTSV	Stormont-Vail Hospital, Topeka, KS [*Library symbol Library of Congress*] (LCLS)
KTSW	San Marcos, TX [*FM radio station call letters*]
KTSY	Caldwell, ID [*FM radio station call letters*]
KTT	Kermit [*Texas*] [*Seismograph station code, US Geological Survey Closed*] (SEIS)
KTT	Kittila [*Finland*] [*Airport symbol*] (OAG)
KTTC	Keesler Technical Training Center
KTTC	Rochester, MN [*Television station call letters*]
KTTG	Mena, AR [*FM radio station call letters*] (RBYB)
KTTI	Yuma, AZ [*FM radio station call letters*]
KTTL	Alva, OK [*FM radio station call letters*]
KTTL	Korea Tactical Target List (MCD)
KTTM	Huron, SD [*Television station call letters*]
KTTN	Trenton/Mercer County [*New Jersey*] [*ICAO location identifier*] (ICLI)
KTTN	Trenton, MO [*AM radio station call letters*]
KTTN-FM	Trenton, MO [*FM radio station call letters*]
KTTR	Rolla, MO [*AM radio station call letters*]
KTTR	St. James, MO [*FM radio station call letters*]
KTTS	Springfield, MO [*AM radio station call letters*]
KTTS-FM	Springfield, MO [*FM radio station call letters*]
KTTT	Columbus, NE [*AM radio station call letters*]
KTTU	Tucson, AZ [*Television station call letters*]
KTTV	Los Angeles, CA [*Television station call letters*]
KTTW	Sioux Falls, SD [*Television station call letters*]
KTTX	Brenham, TX [*FM radio station call letters*]
KTTY	Kitty Hawk, Inc. [*NASDAQ symbol*] (SAG)
KTTY	San Diego, CA [*Television station call letters*]
KTTZ	Ajo, AZ [*FM radio station call letters*]
KTU	Key Telephone Unit
KTU	Kidney Transplant Unit [*National Health Service*] [*British*] (DI)
KTU	Kota [*India*] [*Airport symbol*] (OAG)
KTU	Kutaisi [*USSR*] [*Airport symbol*] (AD)
KTU	Transylvania University, Lexington, KY [*OCLC symbol*] (OCLC)
KTUC	Kiribati Trades Union Congress (BUAC)
KTUC	Tucson, AZ [*AM radio station call letters*]
KTUE	Tulia, TX [*AM radio station call letters*]
KTUF	Kirksville, MO [*FM radio station call letters*]
KTUH	Honolulu, HI [*FM radio station call letters*]
KTUI	Sullivan, MO [*AM radio station call letters*]
KTUI-FM	Sullivan, MO [*FM radio station call letters*]
KTUL	Tulsa/International [*Oklahoma*] [*ICAO location identifier*] (ICLI)
KTUL	Tulsa, OK [*Television station call letters*]
KTUN-FM	Eagle, CO [*FM radio station call letters*] (RBYB)
KTUO	Sonora, CA [*FM radio station call letters*]
KTUR	Tooele, UT [*AM radio station call letters*]
KTUS	Tucson/International [*Arizona*] [*ICAO location identifier*] (ICLI)
KTUU-TV	Anchorage, AK [*Television station call letters*]
KTUX	Carthage, TX [*FM radio station call letters*]
KTV	Kamarata [*Venezuela*] [*Airport symbol*] (OAG)
KTV	Kuwait Television
KTVA	Anchorage, AK [*Television station call letters*]
KTVA	United States Veterans Administration Hospital, Topeka, KS [*Library symbol Library of Congress*] (LCLS)
KTVB	Boise, ID [*Television station call letters*]
KTVC	Cedar Rapids, IA [*Television station call letters*]
KTVD	Denver, CO [*Television station call letters*]
KTVE	El Dorado, AR [*Television station call letters*]
KTVF	Fairbanks, AK [*Television station call letters*]
KTVG	Grand Island, NE [*Television station call letters*]
KTVH	Helena, MT [*Television station call letters*]
KTVI	St. Louis, MO [*Television station call letters*]
KTVJ	Boulder, CO [*Television station call letters*]
KTVK	Phoenix, AZ [*Television station call letters*]
KTVL	Medford, OR [*Television station call letters*]
KTVM	Butte, MT [*Television station call letters*]
KTVN	Reno, NV [*Television station call letters*]
KTVO	Kirksville, MO [*Television station call letters*]
KTVQ	Billings, MT [*Television station call letters*]
KTVR	La Grande, OR [*Television station call letters*]
KTVS	Keystone Telebinocular Visual Survey (STED)
KTVS	Sterling, CO [*Television station call letters*]
KTVT	Fort Worth, TX [*Television station call letters*]
KTVU	Oakland, CA [*Television station call letters*]
KTVW	Phoenix, AZ [*Television station call letters*]
KTVX	Salt Lake City, UT [*Television station call letters*]
KTVZ	Bend, OR [*Television station call letters*]
KTW	Katowice [*Poland*] [*Airport symbol*] (OAG)
KTW	Klippel-Trenaunay-Weber Syndrome [*Medicine*] (DMAA)
KTW	Washburn University of Topeka, Topeka, KS [*Library symbol Library of Congress*] (LCLS)
KTWA	Ottumwa, IA [*FM radio station call letters*]
KTWB	Sioux Falls, SD [*FM radio station call letters*]
KTWC	Glendale, AZ [*FM radio station call letters*]
KTWG	Agana, GU [*AM radio station call letters*]
KTWI	Warm Springs, OR [*FM radio station call letters*]
KTWK	Colorado Springs, CO [*AM radio station call letters*]
KTW-L	Washburn University of Topeka, School of Law, Topeka, KS [*Library symbol Library of Congress*] (LCLS)
KTWN	Texarkana, TX [*AM radio station call letters*]
KTWN-FM	Texarkana, AR [*FM radio station call letters*]
KTWO	Casper, WY [*AM radio station call letters*]
KTWO	K2 Design, Inc. [*NASDAQ symbol*] (SAG)
KTWO-TV	Casper, WY [*Television station call letters*]
KTWS	Bend, OR [*FM radio station call letters*]
KTWS	Klippel-Trenaunay-Weber Syndrome [*Medicine*] (DMAA)
KTWU	Topeka, KS [*Television station call letters*]
KTWV	Los Angeles, CA [*FM radio station call letters*]
KTWY-FM	Walla Walla, WA [*FM radio station call letters*] (RBYB)
KTX	Keith Railway Equipment Co. [*AAR code*]
KTX	Kermit [*Texas*] [*Seismograph station code, US Geological Survey*] (SEIS)
KTXA	Arlington, TX [*Television station call letters*]
KTXB	Beaumont, TX [*FM radio station call letters*]
KTXC	Cuero, TX [*AM radio station call letters*] (RBYB)
KTXH	Houston, TX [*Television station call letters*]
KTXJ	Jasper, TX [*AM radio station call letters*]
KTXK	Texarkana/Municipal-Webb Field [*Arkansas*] [*ICAO location identifier*] (ICLI)
KTXK	Texarkana, TX [*FM radio station call letters*]
KTXL	Sacramento, CA [*Television station call letters*]
KTXN	Victoria, TX [*FM radio station call letters*]
KTXQ	Fort Worth, TX [*FM radio station call letters*]
KTXR	Springfield, MO [*FM radio station call letters*]
KTXS	Sweetwater, TX [*Television station call letters*]
KTXT	Lubbock, TX [*FM radio station call letters*]
KTXT-TV	Lubbock, TX [*Television station call letters*]
KTXX	Devine, TX [*FM radio station call letters*]
KTXY	Jefferson City, MO [*FM radio station call letters*]
KTXZ	West Lake Hills, TX [*AM radio station call letters*]
KTY	Kitty (ABBR)
KTY	Terror Bay [*Alaska*] [*Airport symbol*] (OAG)
KTY	Terror Bay, AK [*Location identifier FAA*] (FAAL)
KTYCR	Kitty-Corner (ABBR)
KTYD	Katydid (ABBR)
KTYD	Santa Barbara, CA [*FM radio station call letters*]
KTYL	Tyler, TX [*FM radio station call letters*]
KTYM	Inglewood, CA [*AM radio station call letters*]
KTYN	Minot, ND [*FM radio station call letters*]
KTYR	Tyler/Pounds Field [*Texas*] [*ICAO location identifier*] (ICLI)
KTYS	Knoxville/McGee Tyson [*Tennessee*] [*ICAO location identifier*] (ICLI)
KTYX-FM	Jonesville, LA [*FM radio station call letters*] (BROA)
KTZ	Katz Media [*AMEX symbol*] (TTSB)
KTZ	Katz Media Group, Inc. [*AMEX symbol*] (SAG)
KTZ	Kutztown [*Pennsylvania*] [*Seismograph station code, US Geological Survey*] (SEIS)
KTZA	Artesia, NM [*FM radio station call letters*]
KTZR	Tucson, AZ [*AM radio station call letters*]
KTZZ	Seattle, WA [*Television station call letters*]
KU	Kallikrein Unit (DMAA)
KU	Kapuskasing Uplift [*Geology*] [*Canada*]
KU	Karmen Unit [*Medicine*] (MAE)
KU	Keep Up [*Typography*] (DGA)
KU	Kentucky University (PDAA)
KU	Kentucky Utilities Co. (EFIS)
KU	Keyboard Unit [*Computer science*] (NASA)
KU	Kilourane (ABBR)
KU	Kimbel Unit (AAMN)
KU	Kimbrel Unit (STED)
KU	Kitvei Ugarit (BJA)
KU	Knightsbridge University [*Denmark*] (ECON)
KU	Knowledge Universe
K-U	Kremers-Urban Co. (DAVI)
KU	KU Energy [*NYSE symbol*] (TTSB)
KU	KU Energy Co. [*NYSE symbol*] (SPSG)
Ku	Kurchatovium [*See also Rf*] [*Proposed name for chemical element 104*]
Ku	Kurtosis [*The relative degree of flatness in the region about the mode of a frequency curve*]
ku	Kuwait [*MARC country of publication code Library of Congress*] (LCCP)
KU	Kuwait Airways [*ICAO designator*] (AD)
KU	University of Kansas, Lawrence, KS [*Library symbol Library of Congress*] (LCLS)
KUA	Kit Upkeep Allowance [*British*]
KUA	Kuantan [*Malaysia*] [*Airport symbol*] (OAG)
KUAB-FM	Fairbanks, AK [*FM radio station call letters*] (BROA)
KUAC	Fairbanks, AK [*FM radio station call letters*]
KUAC-TV	Fairbanks, AK [*Television station call letters*]
KUAD	Windsor, CO [*FM radio station call letters*]
KUAF	Fayetteville, AR [*FM radio station call letters*]
KUAI	Eleele, HI [*AM radio station call letters*]
KUAM	Agana, GU [*AM radio station call letters*]
KUAM-FM	Agana, GU [*FM radio station call letters*]
KUAM-TV	Agana, GU [*Television station call letters*]
KUAP	Pine Bluff, AR [*FM radio station call letters*]
KUAR	Little Rock, AR [*FM radio station call letters*]

KUAS .... Tucson, AZ [Television station call letters]
KUAT .... Tucson, AZ [AM radio station call letters]
KUAT-FM .... Tucson, AZ [FM radio station call letters]
KUAT-TV .... Tucson, AZ [Television station call letters]
KUAU .... Haiku, HI [AM radio station call letters]
KUAZ .... Tucson, AZ [FM radio station call letters]
KUB .... Keilschrifturkunden aus Boghazkoi [A publication] (BJA)
KUB .... Kidney and Upper Bladder
KUB .... Kidney and Urinary Bladder (STED)
KUB .... Kidney, Ureter, Bladder [X-ray]
KUB .... Kubota Corp. ADR [NYSE symbol] (SPSG)
KUBA .... Yuba City, CA [AM radio station call letters]
KUBB .... Mariposa, CA [FM radio station call letters]
KUBC .... Montrose, CO [AM radio station call letters]
KUBD .... Denver, CO [Television station call letters]
KUBE .... Seattle, WA [FM radio station call letters]
KUBL .... Salt Lake City, UT [FM radio station call letters] (RBYB)
KUBO .... Calexico, CA [FM radio station call letters]
Kubota .... Kubota Corp. [Associated Press] (SAG)
KUBQ .... La Grande, OR [FM radio station call letters]
KUBR .... San Juan, TX [AM radio station call letters]
KUBS .... Newport, WA [FM radio station call letters]
KUC .... Kucino [Former USSR Seismograph station code, US Geological
              Survey Closed] (SEIS)
KUC .... Kuria [Kiribati] [Airport symbol] (OAG)
KUCA .... Conway, AR [FM radio station call letters]
KUCB .... Des Moines, IA [FM radio station call letters]
KUCD .... Pearl City, HI [FM radio station call letters]
KUCE .... Kiev Universal Commodity Exchange [Ukraine] (EY)
KUCI .... Irvine, CA [FM radio station call letters]
KUCOG .... Kunia Coordinating Group (SAA)
KUCR .... Riverside, CA [FM radio station call letters]
KUCU-AM .... Hobbs, NM [AM radio station call letters] (RBYB)
KUCV .... Lincoln, NE [FM radio station call letters]
KUD .... Kudat [Malaysia] [Airport symbol] (OAG)
KUDL .... Kansas City, KS [FM radio station call letters]
KUDU-FM .... Tok, AK [FM radio station call letters] (RBYB)
KUDY .... Spokane, WA [AM radio station call letters]
KUED .... Kodak Unitized Engineering Data
KUED .... Salt Lake City, UT [Television station call letters]
KUEL .... Fort Dodge, IA [AM radio station call letters]
KU Engy ...... KU Energy Corp. [Associated Press] (SAG)
KUER .... Salt Lake City, UT [FM radio station call letters]
KUES .... Richfield, UT [Television station call letters] (BROA)
KUET .... Black Canyon, AZ [AM radio station call letters] (RBYB)
KUEZ .... Lufkin, TX [FM radio station call letters]
KUF .... Kabul Union of Furriers [Afghanistan] (BUAC)
KUF .... Kidney Ultrafiltration Rate [Nephrology] (DAVI)
KUFM .... Missoula, MT [FM radio station call letters]
KUFM-TV .... Missoula, MT [Television station call letters]
KUFNCD ...... Kampuchean United Front for National Construction and Defence
              [Political party] (PPW)
KUFN-FM .... Hamilton, MT [FM radio station call letters] (RBYB)
KUFNS .... Kampuchean National United Front for National Salvation
KUFO .... Portland, OR [FM radio station call letters]
KUFPEC ...... Kuwait Foreign Petroleum Exploration Co. (BUAC)
KUFR .... Salt Lake City, UT [FM radio station call letters]
KUFX .... Gilroy, CA [FM radio station call letters]
KUG .... Kupang [Timor] [Seismograph station code, US Geological Survey]
              (SEIS)
KUGB .... Karate Union of Great Britain
KUGBNC ...... Karate Union of Great Britain National Championship
KUGN .... Eugene, OR [AM radio station call letters]
KUGN-FM .... Eugene, OR [FM radio station call letters]
KUGR .... Green River, WY [AM radio station call letters]
KUGS .... Bellingham, WA [FM radio station call letters]
KUGT .... Jackson, MO [AM radio station call letters]
KUH .... Kaapuna [Hawaii] [Seismograph station code, US Geological
              Survey] (SEIS)
KUH .... Kuhlman Corp. [NYSE symbol] (SPSG)
KUH .... Kushiro [Japan] [Airport symbol] (OAG)
KUHB .... St. Paul Island, AK [FM radio station call letters]
KUHD .... Port Neches, TX [AM radio station call letters]
KUHF .... Houston, TX [FM radio station call letters]
KUHG .... Milford, NE [FM radio station call letters]
KUHL .... Santa Maria, CA [AM radio station call letters]
Kuhlm .... Kuhlman Corp. [Associated Press] (SAG)
KUHM-FM .... Helena, MT [FM radio station call letters] (RBYB)
KUHT .... Houston, TX [Television station call letters]
KUIC .... Vacaville, CA [FM radio station call letters]
KUID .... Moscow, ID [Television station call letters]
KUIK .... Hillsboro, OR [AM radio station call letters]
KUJ .... Walla Walla, WA [AM radio station call letters]
KUK .... Kasigluk [Alaska] [Airport symbol] (OAG)
KUK .... University of Kentucky, Lexington, KY [OCLC symbol] (OCLC)
KUKA .... San Diego, TX [FM radio station call letters]
KUKI .... Ukiah, CA [AM radio station call letters]
KUKI-FM ...... Ukiah, CA [FM radio station call letters]
KUKL .... Kalispell, MT [FM radio station call letters] (RBYB)
KUKN .... Kelso, WA [FM radio station call letters]
KUKQ .... Tempe, AZ [AM radio station call letters]
KUKU .... Willow Springs, MO [AM radio station call letters]
KUKU-FM .... Willow Springs, MO [FM radio station call letters]
KUL .... Kinjo Gakuin University Library [UTLAS symbol]
KUL .... Kuala Lumpur [Malaysia] [Airport symbol] (OAG)

KUL .... Kulyab [Former USSR Seismograph station code, US Geological
              Survey] (SEIS)
KUL .... Sterling Central Union List of Serials, Sterling, KS [OCLC symbol]
              (OCLC)
KU-L .... University of Kansas, School of Law, Lawrence, KS [Library symbol
              Library of Congress] (LCLS)
KULA .... Maunawili, HI [AM radio station call letters]
KULC .... Ogden, UT [Television station call letters]
Kulcke .... Kulicke & Soffa Industries, Inc. [Associated Press] (SAG)
KULE .... Ephrata, WA [AM radio station call letters]
KULE-FM .... Ephrata, WA [FM radio station call letters]
KULF .... Brenham, TX [FM radio station call letters]
KULM .... Columbus, TX [FM radio station call letters]
KULP .... El Campo, TX [AM radio station call letters]
Kulp .... Kulp's Luzerne Legal Register Reports [Pennsylvania]
              [A publication] (DLA)
KULR .... Billings, MT [Television station call letters]
KULS .... Kentucky Union List of Serials [Library network]
KULY .... Ulysses, KS [AM radio station call letters]
KUM .... Kumamoto [Japan] [Seismograph station code, US Geological
              Survey] (SEIS)
KU-M .... University of Kansas, School of Medicine, Kansas City, KS [Library
              symbol Library of Congress] (LCLS)
KUM .... University of Kentucky, Medical Center, Lexington, KY [OCLC
              symbol] (OCLC)
KUM .... Yaku Shima [Japan] [Airport symbol] (OAG)
KUMA .... Pendleton, OR [AM radio station call letters]
KUMA-FM .... Pendleton, OR [FM radio station call letters]
KUMBX .... Kemper U.S. Mtge Cl.B [Mutual fund ticker symbol] (SG)
KUMD .... Duluth, MN [FM radio station call letters]
KUMM .... Morris, MN [FM radio station call letters]
KUMMI .... Kobe University Medical Mission to Indonesia
KUMR .... Rolla, MO [FM radio station call letters]
KUMT .... Centerville, UT [FM radio station call letters]
KUMU .... Honolulu, HI [AM radio station call letters]
KUMU-FM .... Honolulu, HI [FM radio station call letters]
KUMV .... Williston, ND [Television station call letters]
KU-MW .... University of Kansas, School of Medicine-Witchita, Witchita, KS
              [Library symbol] [Library of Congress] (LCLS)
KUN .... Kunia, Oahu, HI [Location identifier FAA] (FAAL)
KUN .... Kunming [Republic of China] [Seismograph station code, US
              Geological Survey] (SEIS)
KUNA .... Indio, CA [AM radio station call letters]
KUNA .... Kuwait News Agency (BUAC)
KUNA-FM .... La Quinta, CA [FM radio station call letters]
KUNC .... Greeley, CO [FM radio station call letters]
KUND-AM .... Grand Forks, ND [AM radio station call letters] (BROA)
KUND-FM .... Grand Forks, ND [FM radio station call letters] (BROA)
KUNI .... Cedar Falls, IA [FM radio station call letters]
KUNM .... Albuquerque, NM [FM radio station call letters]
KUNO .... Corpus Christi, TX [AM radio station call letters]
KUNQ .... Houston, MO [FM radio station call letters]
KUNR .... Reno, NV [FM radio station call letters]
KUNV .... Las Vegas, NV [FM radio station call letters]
KUNY .... Mason City, IA [FM radio station call letters]
KUO .... Kuopio [Finland] [Airport symbol] (OAG)
KUOA .... Siloam Springs, AR [AM radio station call letters]
KUOI .... Moscow, ID [FM radio station call letters]
KUOL .... San Marcos, TX [AM radio station call letters]
KUOM .... Minneapolis, MN [AM radio station call letters]
KUON .... Lincoln, NE [Television station call letters]
KUOO .... Spirit Lake, IA [FM radio station call letters]
KUOP .... Stockton, CA [FM radio station call letters]
KUOR .... Redlands, CA [FM radio station call letters]
KUOW .... Seattle, WA [FM radio station call letters]
KUP .... Kupang [Timor] [Seismograph station code, US Geological Survey
              Closed] (SEIS)
KUP .... Kupiano [Papua New Guinea] [Airport symbol] (OAG)
KUP .... Kwacha United Press [Angola] (BUAC)
KUP .... University of Kentucky, Prestonburg Community College,
              Prestonburg, KY [OCLC symbol] (OCLC)
KUPC .... Carlsbad, NM [Television station call letters] (BROA)
KUPD .... Tempe, AZ [FM radio station call letters]
KUPH-FM .... Mountain View, MO [FM radio station call letters] (BROA)
KUPI .... Idaho Falls, ID [AM radio station call letters]
KUPI-FM ...... Idaho Falls, ID [FM radio station call letters]
KUPK-TV .... Garden City, KS [Television station call letters]
KUPL-FM .... Portland, OR [FM radio station call letters]
KUPN .... Las Vegas, NV [Television station call letters] (RBYB)
KUPR .... Carlsbad, CA [FM radio station call letters] (RBYB)
KUPS .... Tacoma, WA [FM radio station call letters]
KUQQ-FM .... Milford, IA [FM radio station call letters] (RBYB)
KUR .... Kit Use Ratio [Statistics]
kur .... Kurdish [MARC language code Library of Congress] (LCCP)
KUR .... Kurilsk [Former USSR Seismograph station code, US Geological
              Survey] (SEIS)
KUR .... Kyoto University Reactor
KURA .... Ouray, CO [FM radio station call letters]
KURB .... Little Rock, AR [AM radio station call letters]
KURB-FM .... Little Rock, AR [FM radio station call letters]
KURE .... KURE Foundation
KURE-FM .... Ames, IA [FM radio station call letters] (RBYB)
KURL .... Billings, MT [AM radio edition call letters]
KURM .... Rogers, AR [AM radio station call letters]
KURR-FM .... Bountiful, UT [FM radio station call letters] (RBYB)

KURRI............ Kyoto University Research Reactor Institute [*Japan*] (BUAC)
KURS........... San Diego, CA [*AM radio station call letters*]
KURV........... Edinburg, TX [*AM radio station call letters*]
KURY........... Brookings, OR [*AM radio station call letters*]
KURY-FM....... Brookings, OR [*FM radio station call letters*]
KURZ........... Kurzweil Applied Intelligence, Inc. [*NASDAQ symbol*] (SAG)
Kurzweil....... Kurzweil Applied Intelligence, Inc. [*Associated Press*] (SAG)
KUS .... Kidney, Ureter, and Spleen [*Anatomy*] (MAH)
KUS .... Kulusuk Island [*Greenland*] [*Airport symbol*] (AD)
KUS .... Kursk State Air Enterprise [*Former USSR*] [*FAA designator*] (FAAC)
KUS .... Kushiro [*Japan*] [*Seismograph station code, US Geological Survey*] (SEIS)
KU-S .... University of Kansas, Kenneth Spencer Research Library, Lawrence, KS [*Library symbol Library of Congress*] (LCLS)
KUS .... University of Kentucky, Southeast Center, Cumberland, KY [*OCLC symbol*] (OCLC)
KUSA........... Denver, CO [*Television station call letters*]
KUSAX......... Kemper U.S. Govt. Secs. Cl.A [*Mutual fund ticker symbol*] (SG)
KUSC .... Los Angeles, CA [*FM radio station call letters*]
KUSD .... Vermillion, SD [*AM radio station call letters*]
KUSD-FM....... Vermillion, SD [*FM radio station call letters*]
KUSD-TV..... Vermillion, SD [*Television station call letters*]
KUSF .... San Francisco, CA [*FM radio station call letters*]
KUSG .... St. George, UT [*Television station call letters*]
KUSH .... Cushing, OK [*AM radio station call letters*]
Kush .... Kushan (VRA)
Kushi .... Kushi Macrobiotic Corp. [*Associated Press*] (SAG)
KushLc......... Kush Locke [*Associated Press*] (SAG)
KushLc......... [*The*] Kushner-Locke Co. [*Associated Press*] (SAG)
KushLk......... Kush Locke [*Associated Press*] (SAG)
KushLk......... [*The*] Kushner-Locke Co. [*Associated Press*] (SAG)
KUSI .... San Diego, CA [*Television station call letters*]
KUSK .... Prescott, AZ [*Television station call letters*]
KUSM .... Bozeman, MT [*Television station call letters*]
KUSN .... Coffeyville, KS [*FM radio station call letters*]
KUSP .... Ku-Band Signal Processor (MCD)
KUSP .... Ku-Band Single Processor (MCD)
KUSP .... Santa Cruz, CA [*FM radio station call letters*]
KUSR .... Ames, IA [*FM radio station call letters*]
KUSU .... Logan, UT [*FM radio station call letters*]
KUSZ .... Proctor, MN [*FM radio station call letters*] (RBYB)
KUT............. Austin, TX [*FM radio station call letters*]
KUT............. Kutahya [*Turkey*] [*Airport symbol*] (AD)
kut.............. Kutenai [*MARC language code Library of Congress*] (LCCP)
KUT............. Kutsu-Ga-Hara [*Japan*] [*Seismograph station code, US Geological Survey*] (SEIS)
Kut.............. Kuttim (BJA)
KUT............. Lexington Technical Institute, Lexington, KY [*OCLC symbol*] (OCLC)
KUT............. University of Toronto Union Catalogue Section [*UTLAS symbol*]
KUTA .... Blanding, UT [*AM radio station call letters*]
Kutch .... All India Reporter, Kutch [*1949-56*] [*A publication*] (DLA)
KUTD .... Keep Up to Date (KSC)
KUTE-FM....... Ignacio, CO [*FM radio station call letters*] (BROA)
KUTGW........ Keep Up the Good Work
KUTI .... Selah, WA [*AM radio station call letters*]
KUTP .... Phoenix, AZ [*Television station call letters*]
KUTQ .... Bountiful, UT [*FM radio station call letters*]
KUTT........... Fairbury, NE [*FM radio station call letters*]
KUTV .... Salt Lake City, UT [*Television station call letters*]
KUTX .... San Angelo, TX [*FM radio station call letters*] (RBYB)
KUTY .... Palmdale, CA [*AM radio station call letters*]
KUTZ........... Lampasas, TX [*FM radio station call letters*]
Kutztown U.... Kutztown University of Pennsylvania (GAGS)
KUU .... Kulu [*India*] [*Airport symbol*] (AD)
KUUL .... Davenport, IA [*FM radio station call letters*]
KUUY .... Orchard Valley, WY [*AM radio station call letters*]
KUUZ .... Lake Village, AR [*FM radio station call letters*]
KUVA .... Uvalde, TX [*FM radio station call letters*]
KUVI .... Bakersfield, CA [*Television station call letters*] (BROA)
KUVN .... Garland, TX [*Television station call letters*]
KUVO .... Denver, CO [*FM radio station call letters*]
KUVR .... Holdrege, NE [*AM radio station call letters*]
KUVR-FM....... Holdrege, NE [*FM radio station call letters*]
KUVS .... Modesto, CA [*Television station call letters*] (BROA)
KUW .... Kuwait (ABBR)
Kuw .... Kuwait (VRA)
KUWA-FM....... Afton, WY [*FM radio station call letters*] (BROA)
KUWC-FM....... Casper, WY [*FM radio station call letters*] (BROA)
KUWG-FM....... Gillette, WY [*FM radio station call letters*] (BROA)
KUWJ........... Jackson, WY [*FM radio station call letters*]
KUWL .... Fairbanks, AK [*FM radio station call letters*]
KUWN-FM....... Newcastle, WY [*FM radio station call letters*] (BROA)
KUWR .... Laramie, WY [*FM radio station call letters*]
KUWS .... Superior, WI [*FM radio station call letters*]
KUWZ .... Rock Springs, WY [*FM radio station call letters*]
KUX .... Kumix Resources Corp. [*Vancouver Stock Exchange symbol*]
KUY .... Kuyper [*Indonesia*] [*Later, TNG*] [*Geomagnetic observatory code*]
KUY .... Uyak [*Alaska*] [*Airport symbol*] (OAG)
KUY .... Uyak, AK [*Location identifier FAA*] (FAAL)
KUYO .... Evansville, WY [*AM radio station call letters*]
KUZZ .... Bakersfield, CA [*FM radio station call letters*]
KUZZ-TV..... Bakersfield, CA [*Television station call letters*]
KV .... British Virgin Island [*IYRU nationality code*] (IYR)
KV .... Kanamycin-Vancomycin [*An antibiotic*] (DAVI)
KV .... Kerr Vector [*Optics*]

KV............... Key Verifier [*Computer science*]
KV............... Kidney Valve
KV............... Killed Vaccine [*Immunology*] (MAE)
KV............... Killed Virus [*Pharmacology*] (DAVI)
KV............... Kill Vehicle
kV............... Kilovolt
KV............... Kilovolt (AAEL)
KV............... Kinematic Viscosity
KV............... Knights of Vartan (EA)
KV............... Kochel-Verzeichnis [*List of Mozart's works*] (IIA)
KV............... Kriegsverwendungsfaehig [*Fit for Active Service*] [*German military - World War II*]
KV............... K-V Pharmaceutical Co. [*AMEX symbol*] (SPSG)
KV............... Transkei Airways [*ICAO designator*] (AD)
KV1............. Kalanchoe Virus 1 [*Plant pathology*]
KVA............ Karavia [*Zaire*] [*Geomagnetic observatory code*]
KVA............ Kavala [*Greece*] [*Airport symbol*] (OAG)
kVA............ Kilovolt Ampere
KVAB-FM....... Clarkston, WA [*FM radio station call letters*] (RBYB)
KVAC.......... Forks, WA [*AM radio station call letters*]
KVAC.......... Kilovolt Alternating Current (IAA)
KVAD.......... Valdosta/Moody Air Force Base [*Georgia*] [*ICAO location identifier*] (ICLI)
KVAG-FM....... Rugby, ND [*FM radio station call letters*] (RBYB)
kVAH.......... Kilovolt-Ampere Hour
kVAhm......... Kilovolt-Ampere Hour Meter (MSA)
KVAK.......... Valdez, AK [*AM radio station call letters*]
KVAL.......... Eugene, OR [*Television station call letters*]
kVAM.......... Kilovolt-Ampere Meter
KVAN.......... Vancouver, WA [*AM radio station call letters*]
kvar........... Kilovar
kVAr.......... Kilovolt-Ampere Reactive
KVAR.......... Riverside, CA [*FM radio station call letters*]
kvarh.......... Kilovar-Hour
kVARh......... [*Reactive*] Kilovolt-Ampere-Hour (IDOE)
KVAS.......... Astoria, OR [*AM radio station call letters*]
KVAW.......... Eagle Pass, TX [*Television station call letters*]
KVAY.......... Lamar, CO [*FM radio station call letters*]
KVAZ.......... Henryetta, OK [*FM radio station call letters*]
KVBA.......... Kanamycin-Vancomycin Blood Agar [*Microbiology*]
KVBC.......... Las Vegas, NV [*Television station call letters*]
KVBC-FM....... Las Vegas, NV [*FM radio station call letters*] (RBYB)
KVBG.......... Lompoc/Vandenberg Air Force Base [*California*] [*ICAO location identifier*] (ICLI)
KVBM.......... Minneapolis, MN [*Television station call letters*]
KVBR.......... Brainerd, MN [*AM radio station call letters*]
KVBR-FM....... Brainerd, MN [*FM radio station call letters*]
KVC............ King Cove [*Alaska*] [*Airport symbol*] (OAG)
KVC............ King Cove, AK [*Location identifier FAA*] (FAAL)
KVCA-AM....... Simi Valley, CA [*AM radio station call letters*] (BROA)
KVCE.......... Fallon, NV [*FM radio station call letters*]
KVCI.......... Mineola, TX [*AM radio station call letters*]
KVCK.......... Wolf Point, MT [*AM radio station call letters*]
KVCK-FM....... Wolf Point, MT [*FM radio station call letters*]
KVCL.......... Winnfield, LA [*AM radio station call letters*]
KVCL-FM....... Winnfield, LA [*FM radio station call letters*]
KVCM.......... Helena, MT [*FM radio station call letters*]
KVCO.......... Concordia, KS [*FM radio station call letters*]
kVCP.......... Kilovolt Constant Potential
kVcp.......... Kilovolt Constant Potential (STED)
KVCQ.......... Cuero, TX [*FM radio station call letters*] (RBYB)
KVCR.......... San Bernardino, CA [*FM radio station call letters*]
KVCR-TV..... San Bernardino, CA [*Television station call letters*]
KVCS.......... KXE6S Verein Chess Society (EA)
KVCS-AM....... Perry, OK [*AM radio station call letters*] (RBYB)
KVCS-FM....... Perry, OK [*FM radio station call letters*] (RBYB)
KVCT.......... Victoria, TX [*Television station call letters*]
KVCV.......... Victorville/George Air Force Base [*California*] [*ICAO location identifier*] (ICLI)
KVCX.......... Gregory, SD [*FM radio station call letters*]
KVCY.......... Fort Scott, KS [*FM radio station call letters*]
KVDA.......... San Antonio, TX [*Television station call letters*]
KVDB.......... Sioux Center, IA [*AM radio station call letters*]
kVdc.......... Kilovolt Direct Current (IEEE)
KVDL.......... Quanah, TX [*AM radio station call letters*]
KVDP.......... Dry Prong, LA [*FM radio station call letters*]
KVDT.......... Keyboard Visual Display Terminal (MCD)
KVE............ Kaposi's Varicelliform Eruption [*Medicine Medicine*] (DMAA)
KVEA.......... Corona, CA [*Television station call letters*]
KVEC.......... San Luis Obispo, CA [*AM radio station call letters*]
KVEG.......... North Las Vegas, NV [*AM radio station call letters*]
KVEL.......... Vernal, UT [*AM radio station call letters*]
KVEN.......... Ventura, CA [*AM radio station call letters*]
KVEO.......... Brownsville, TX [*Television station call letters*]
KVER.......... El Paso, TX [*FM radio station call letters*]
KVET.......... Austin, TX [*AM radio station call letters*]
KVET-FM....... Austin, TX [*FM radio station call letters*]
KVEW.......... Kennewick, WA [*Television station call letters*]
KVEZ-FM....... Parker, AZ [*FM radio station call letters*] (RBYB)
KVF............ Kent Volunteer Fencibles [*British military*] (DMA)
KVFC.......... Cortez, CO [*AM radio station call letters*]
KVFD.......... Fort Dodge, IA [*AM radio station call letters*]
KVFM.......... Logan, UT [*FM radio station call letters*]
K-V Funds.... Knutson-Vandenberg Funds (WPI)
KVFX........... Manteca, CA [*FM radio station call letters*]

KVG	Kavieng [*Papua New Guinea*] [*Seismograph station code, US Geological Survey*] (SEIS)
KVG	Kavieng [*Papua New Guinea*] [*Airport symbol*] (OAG)
KVG	Kavieng [*New Ireland*] [*Airport symbol*] (AD)
KVG	Keyed Video Generator
KVG	Key Variable Generator (COE)
KVGB	Great Bend, KS [*AM radio station call letters*]
KVGB-FM	Great Bend, KS [*FM radio station call letters*]
KVGO-FM	Spring Valley, MN [*FM radio station call letters*] (RBYB)
KVHI	KVH Industries [*NASDAQ symbol*] (TTSB)
KVHI	KVH Industries, Inc. [*NASDAQ symbol*] (SAG)
KVHInd	KVH Industries, Inc. [*Associated Press*] (SAG)
KVHP	Lake Charles, LA [*Television station call letters*]
KVHS	Concord, CA [*FM radio station call letters*]
KVHT	Vermillion, SD [*FM radio station call letters*]
KVI	Carlsbad Ventures [*Vancouver Stock Exchange symbol*]
KVI	Korean Veterans International (EA)
KVI	Seattle, WA [*AM radio station call letters*]
KVIA	El Paso, TX [*Television station call letters*]
KVIC	Victoria, TX [*FM radio station call letters*]
KVIE	Sacramento, CA [*Television station call letters*]
KVIH	Clovis, NM [*Television station call letters*]
KVII	Amarillo, TX [*Television station call letters*]
KVIK	Decorah, IA [*FM radio station call letters*] (RBYB)
KVIL-FM	Highland Park, TX [*FM radio station call letters*]
KVIN-AM	Turlock, CA [*AM radio station call letters*] (BROA)
KVIP	Redding, CA [*AM radio station call letters*]
KVIP-FM	Redding, CA [*FM radio station call letters*]
KVIQ	Eureka, CA [*Television station call letters*]
KVIS	Miami, OK [*AM radio station call letters*]
KVIV	El Paso, TX [*AM radio station call letters*]
KVJY	Pharr, TX [*AM radio station call letters*]
KVK	Kriegsverdienstkreuz [*War Service Cross*] [*German military decoration - World War II*]
KVKI	Shreveport, LA [*FM radio station call letters*]
KVL	Kingsvale Resources [*Vancouver Stock Exchange symbol*]
KVL	Kirchhoff's Voltage Law (PDAA)
KVL	Kivalina [*Alaska*] [*Airport symbol*] (OAG)
KVL	Kivalina, AK [*Location identifier FAA*] (FAAL)
KVLA	Vidalia, LA [*AM radio station call letters*]
KVLBA	Kanamycin-Vancomycin Labeled Blood Agar [*Microbiology*]
KVLC	Hatch, NM [*FM radio station call letters*] (RBYB)
KVLD	Valdez, AK [*AM radio station call letters*]
KVLE	Gunnison, CO [*FM radio station call letters*]
KVLF	Alpine, TX [*AM radio station call letters*]
KVLG	La Grange, TX [*AM radio station call letters*]
KVLH	Pauls Valley, OK [*AM radio station call letters*]
KVLI	Lake Isabella, CA [*AM radio station call letters*]
KVLI-FM	Lake Isabella, CA [*FM radio station call letters*]
KVLL	Woodville, TX [*AM radio station call letters*]
KVLL-FM	Woodville, TX [*FM radio station call letters*]
KVLM	Kevlin Corp. [*NASDAQ symbol*] (NQ)
KVLO-FM	Sheridan, AR [*FM radio station call letters*] (RBYB)
KVLR	Twisp, WA [*FM radio station call letters*]
KVLT	Victoria, TX [*FM radio station call letters*]
KVLU	Beaumont, TX [*FM radio station call letters*]
KVLV	Fallon, NV [*AM radio station call letters*]
KVLV-FM	Fallon, NV [*FM radio station call letters*]
KVLY	Edinburg, TX [*FM radio station call letters*]
KVLY-TV	Fargo, ND [*Television station call letters*] (RBYB)
KVM	Keyboard-Video-Mouse [*Computer science*]
kVM	Kilovolt Meter
KVM	Rusaerolizing Airling [*Former USSR*] [*FAA designator*] (FAAC)
KVMA	Magnolia, AR [*AM radio station call letters*]
KVMA-FM	Magnolia, AR [*FM radio station call letters*]
KVMC	Colorado City, TX [*AM radio station call letters*]
KVMD-TV	Twentynine Palms, CA [*TV station call letters*] (RBYB)
KVML	Sonora, CA [*AM radio station call letters*]
KVMR	Nevada City, CA [*FM radio station call letters*]
KVMV	McAllen, TX [*FM radio station call letters*]
KVMX	Eastland, TX [*FM radio station call letters*]
KVN	Kaiserville [*Nevada*] [*Seismograph station code, US Geological Survey*] (SEIS)
KVN	Kimmins Corp. [*NYSE symbol*] (TTSB)
KVN	Kimmins Environmental Services [*NYSE symbol*] (SPSG)
KVNA	Flagstaff, AZ [*AM radio station call letters*]
KVNA-FM	Flagstaff, AZ [*FM radio station call letters*]
KVNE	Tyler, TX [*FM radio station call letters*]
KVNF	Paonia, CO [*FM radio station call letters*]
KVNI	Coeur D'Alene, ID [*AM radio station call letters*]
KVNO	Omaha, NE [*FM radio station call letters*]
KVNU	Logan, UT [*AM radio station call letters*]
KVO	Keep Vein Open [*Medicine*]
KVO	Kraftverkehrsordnung fuer den Gueterfernverkehr mit Kraftfahrzeugen [*Regulation for the Carriage of Goods by Motor Vehicles*] [*German Business term*] (ILCA)
KVOA	Tucson, AZ [*Television station call letters*]
KVOC	Casper, WY [*AM radio station call letters*]
KVO C D5W	Keep Vein Open Cum [*with*] Dextrose 5% in Water [*Pharmacology*] (DAVI)
KVOD	Denver, CO [*AM radio station call letters*]
KVOE	Emporia, KS [*AM radio station call letters*]
KVOE-FM	Emporia, KS [*FM radio station call letters*]
KVOI	Oro Valley, AZ [*AM radio station call letters*]
KVOK	Kodiak, AK [*AM radio station call letters*]
KVOL	Lafayette, LA [*AM radio station call letters*]
KVOL	Opelousas, LA [*FM radio station call letters*]
KVOM	Morrilton, AR [*AM radio station call letters*]
KVOM-FM	Morrilton, AR [*FM radio station call letters*]
KVON	Napa, CA [*AM radio station call letters*]
KVOO	Tulsa, OK [*AM radio station call letters*]
KVOO-FM	Tulsa, OK [*FM radio station call letters*]
KVOP	Plainview, TX [*AM radio station call letters*]
KVOR	Colorado Springs, CO [*AM radio station call letters*]
KVOS-TV	Bellingham, WA [*Television station call letters*]
KVOU	Uvalde, TX [*AM radio station call letters*]
KVOW	Riverton, WY [*AM radio station call letters*]
KVOX	Moorhead, MN [*AM radio station call letters*]
KVOX-FM	Moorhead, MN [*FM radio station call letters*]
KVOY	Mojave, CA [*AM radio station call letters*]
KVOZ	Laredo, TX [*AM radio station call letters*]
KVP	Katholieke Volkspartij [*Catholic People's Party*] [*Netherlands Political party*] (PPE)
kVP	Kilovolt Peak
KVP	Kodak Vacuum Probe
KVP	Kodak Versamat Processor
KVPA	Port Isabel, TX [*FM radio station call letters*]
KVPC	San Joaquin, CA (RBYB)
KV Ph	K-V Pharmaceutical Co. [*Associated Press*] (SAG)
KVPI	Ville Platte, LA [*AM radio station call letters*]
KVPI-FM	Ville Platte, LA [*FM radio station call letters*]
KVPR	Fresno, CA [*FM radio station call letters*]
KVPS	Valparaiso/Eglin Air Force Base [*Florida*] [*ICAO location identifier*] (ICLI)
KVPT	Fresno, CA [*Television station call letters*]
KVRB	Vero Beach/Vero Beach [*Florida*] [*ICAO location identifier*] (ICLI)
KVRC	Arkadelphia, AR [*AM radio station call letters*]
KVRD	Cottonwood, AZ [*AM radio station call letters*]
KVRD-FM	Cottonwood, AZ [*FM radio station call letters*]
KVRE	Hot Springs Village, AR [*FM radio station call letters*]
KVRG	Seaside, CA [*FM radio station call letters*]
KVRG	Soledad, CA [*FM radio station call letters*] (RBYB)
KVRH	Salida, CO [*AM radio station call letters*]
KVRH-FM	Salida, CO [*FM radio station call letters*]
KVRP	Haskell, TX [*FM radio station call letters*]
KVRP	Stamford, TX [*AM radio station call letters*]
KVRQ	Atwater, CA [*FM radio station call letters*]
KVRR	Fargo, ND [*Television station call letters*]
KVRS	Lawton, OK [*AM radio station call letters*]
KVRT	Victoria, TX [*FM radio station call letters*] (RBYB)
KVRW	Lawton, OK [*FM radio station call letters*]
KVRX	Austin, TX [*FM radio station call letters*]
KVRY	Mesa, AZ [*FM radio station call letters*]
KVS	Kansanvalistusseura [*Society for Culture and Education*] [*Finland*] (EAIO)
KVS	Kelvin-Varley Slide [*Electronics*]
KVS	Keyboard/Video Switch [*Computer science*]
KVS	Kurzweil VoiceSystem [*Voice-recognition computer device*]
KVSA	McGehee, AR [*AM radio station call letters*]
KVSC	St. Cloud, MN [*FM radio station call letters*]
KVSF	Santa Fe, NM [*AM radio station call letters*]
KVSH	Valentine, NE [*AM radio station call letters*]
KVSI	Montpelier, ID [*AM radio station call letters*]
KVSL	Show Low, AZ [*AM radio station call letters*]
KVSN	Tumwater, WA [*AM radio station call letters*]
KVSO	Ardmore, OK [*AM radio station call letters*] (RBYB)
KVSP	Oklahoma City, OK [*AM radio station call letters*]
KVSR-FM	Fresno, CA [*FM radio station call letters*] (BROA)
KVST	Huntsville, TX [*FM radio station call letters*]
KVST	Keystone Visual Survey Test [*Ophthalmology*]
KVSV	Beloit, KS [*AM radio station call letters*]
KVSV-FM	Beloit, KS [*FM radio station call letters*]
KVT	Kavak [*Turkey*] [*Seismograph station code, US Geological Survey*] (SEIS)
KVTF	Williams, AZ [*FM radio station call letters*]
KVTH	Hot Springs, AR [*Television station call letters*] (RBYB)
KVTI	Tacoma, WA [*FM radio station call letters*]
KVTJ-TV	Jonesboro, AR [*TV station call letters*] (RBYB)
KVTN	Pine Bluff, AR [*Television station call letters*]
KVTO	Berkeley, CA [*AM radio station call letters*]
KVTT	Dallas, TX [*FM radio station call letters*]
KVTV	Laredo, TX [*Television station call letters*]
KVU	Kleer-Vu Industries [*AMEX symbol*] (TTSB)
KVU	Kleer-Vu Industries, Inc. [*AMEX symbol*] (SPSG)
KVU	Victoria University Library, University of Toronto [*UTLAS symbol*]
KVUE	Austin, TX [*Television station call letters*]
KVUT	Little Rock, AR [*Television station call letters*]
KVUU	Pueblo, CO [*FM radio station call letters*]
KVVA	Phoenix, AZ [*AM radio station call letters*]
KVVA-FM	Apache Junction, AZ [*FM radio station call letters*]
KVVP	Leesville, LA [*FM radio station call letters*]
KVVQ	Hesperia, CA [*AM radio station call letters*]
KVVQ	Victorville, CA [*FM radio station call letters*]
KVVS	Windsor, CO [*AM radio station call letters*]
KVVU	Henderson, NV [*Television station call letters*]
KVVV	Baytoun, TX [*Television station call letters*]
KVW	Kansas City, Kaw Valley R. R., Inc. [*AAR code*]
KVW	Kurzweil Voice Writer
KVWC	Vernon, TX [*AM radio station call letters*]
KVWC-FM	Vernon, TX [*FM radio station call letters*]

KVWG .... Pearsall, TX [*AM radio station call letters*]
KVWG-FM .... Pearsall, TX [*FM radio station call letters*]
KVWM .... Show Low, AZ [*AM radio station call letters*]
KVWM-FM ... Show Low, AZ [*FM radio station call letters*]
KVY .... CAI [*Compagnia Aeronautica Italiana SpA*] [*Italy ICAO designator*] (FAAC)
KVYE-TV ...... El Centro, CA [*TV station call letters*] (RBYB)
KVYF .... Wilson Creek, WA [*AM radio station call letters*]
KVYN .... St. Helena, CA [*FM radio station call letters*]
KVYS .... St. George, UT [*FM radio station call letters*]
KVYY-FM ..... Ventura, CA [*FM radio station call letters*] (RBYB)
KVZK-2 .... Pago Pago, AS [*Television station call letters*]
KVZK-4 .... Pago Pago, AS [*Television station call letters*]
KVZK-5 .... Pago Pago, AS [*Television station call letters*]
K_w .... Dissociation Constant of Water [*Physics*] (DAVI)
KW .... Dorado Wings [*Airline code*]
KW .... Kaiser Wilhelm [*King William*] [*Name of two Prussian kings and emperor of Germany*] (ROG)
KW .... Kaliszer Woch (BJA)
KW .... Kampfwagen [*Tank*] [*German military - World War II*]
KW .... Katabatic Wind
KW .... Keith-Wagener [*Ophthalmology*]
KW .... Kenworth Truck Co.
KW .... Key West [*Florida*]
KW .... Key Word [*Online database field identifier*]
KW .... Killer Weed [*Slang for phencyclidine; also called PCP and Sernyl*] (DAVI)
kW .... Kilohm [*Formerly, K*] [*Unit of electrical resistance*] (DAVI)
kW .... Kilowatt
Kw .... Kilowatt (EBF)
KW .... Kilowatt [*DOE*] (TAG)
KW .... Kiloword (BUR)
KW .... Kimmelstiel-Wilson [*Medicine*]
KW .... Kirkwall, Orkney [*Postcode*] (ODBW)
KW .... Knight of William [*Netherlands*]
KW .... Knight of Windsor (ROG)
KW .... Knitwise [*Knitting*]
KW .... Korean War
KW .... Kraftwagen [*Motor Vehicle*] [*German*]
KW .... Kruskal-Wallis Test [*Fisheries*]
KW .... Kugelberg-Welander Disease (DAVI)
KW .... Kuwait [*ANSI two-letter standard code*] (CNC)
KWA .... Keyword Adapted [*Computer science*]
KWA .... Kwajalein [*Marshall Islands*] [*Airport symbol*] (OAG)
KWA .... Kwantlen College Library [*UTLAS symbol*]
KWA .... Kweiyang [*Republic of China*] [*Seismograph station code, US Geological Survey*] (SEIS)
KWAB .... Big Spring, TX [*Television station call letters*]
KWAC .... Bakersfield, CA [*AM radio station call letters*]
KWAC .... Keyword and Context [*Indexing*] (DIT)
KWAD .... Wadena, MN [*AM radio station call letters*]
KWADE .... Key Word as a Dictionary Entry [*IBM*] [*Indexing system*] (NITA)
KWAI .... Honolulu, HI [*AM radio station call letters*]
KWAJ .... Kwajalein Atoll (AABC)
KWAK .... Stuttgart, AR [*AM radio station call letters*]
KWAK-FM .... Stuttgart, AR [*FM radio station call letters*]
KWAL .... Wallace, ID [*AM radio station call letters*]
KWAL .... Wallops Island/Wallops Station [*Virginia*] [*ICAO location identifier*] (ICLI)
KWAM .... Memphis, TN [*AM radio station call letters*]
KWAN .... Gualala, CA [*FM radio station call letters*]
Kwansei Gak L Rev... Kwansei Gakuin University. Law Review [*A publication*] (DLA)
KWAR .... Waverly, IA [*FM radio station call letters*]
KWAS .... Joplin, MO [*AM radio station call letters*]
KWAT .... Watertown, SD [*AM radio station call letters*]
KWAU .... Korea Women's Associations United (BUAC)
KWAV .... Monterey, CA [*FM radio station call letters*]
KWAX .... Eugene, OR [*FM radio station call letters*]
KWAY .... Waverly, IA [*AM radio station call letters*]
KWAY-FM .... Waverly, IA [*FM radio station call letters*]
KWAZ .... Needles, CA [*FM radio station call letters*]
KWB .... Keith, Wagener, Barker [*Ophthalmology*]
KWBA .... Sierra Vista, AZ [*Television station call letters*] (BROA)
KWBC .... Navasota, TX [*AM radio station call letters*]
KWBC .... Washington [*District of Columbia*] [*ICAO location identifier*] (ICLI)
KWBE .... Beatrice, NE [*AM radio station call letters*]
KWBF .... Flagstaff, AZ [*Television station call letters*] (RBYB)
KWBF .... Katholische Welt-Bibelfoderation [*World Catholic Federation for the Biblical Apostolate - WCFBA*] (EAIO)
KWBG .... Boone, IA [*AM radio station call letters*]
KWBH .... Rexburg, ID [*FM radio station call letters*]
KWBI .... Morrison, CO [*FM radio station call letters*]
KWBK-AM ... Beaumont, TX [*AM radio station call letters*] (BROA)
KWBN .... Honolulu, HI [*Television station call letters*] (BROA)
KWBP .... Salem, OR [*Television station call letters*] (RBYB)
KWBR .... Pismo Beach, CA [*FM radio station call letters*]
KWBU .... Waco, TX [*FM radio station call letters*]
KWBW .... Hutchinson, KS [*AM radio station call letters*]
KWBY .... Woodburn, OR [*AM radio station call letters*]
KWC .... K-Band Waveguide Circulator
KWC .... Kentucky Wesleyan College [*Owensboro*]
KWC .... Kierownictwo Walki Cywilnej (BJA)
KWC .... Wycliffe College Library, University of Toronto [*UTLAS symbol*]
KWCB .... Floresville, TX [*FM radio station call letters*]

KWCC-FM .... Muscatine, IA [*FM radio station call letters*] (RBYB)
KWCD .... Bisbee, AZ [*FM radio station call letters*]
KWCH .... Hutchinson, KS [*Television station call letters*]
KWCK .... Searcy, AR [*AM radio station call letters*]
KWCK-FM .... Searcy, AR [*FM radio station call letters*]
KWCL .... Oak Grove, LA [*FM radio station call letters*]
KWCM .... Appleton, MN [*Television station call letters*]
KWCO .... Chickasha, OK [*AM radio station call letters*]
KWCR .... Ogden, UT [*FM radio station call letters*]
KWCV .... Wichita, KS [*Television station call letters*]
KWCW .... Walla Walla, WA [*FM radio station call letters*]
KWCX .... Wilcox, AZ [*FM radio station call letters*]
KWD .... Consolidated Westrex Development [*Vancouver Stock Exchange symbol*]
KWD .... Draco [*Sweden*] [*Research code symbol*]
KWD .... Kellwood Co. [*NYSE symbol*] (SPSG)
KWDA .... White Hall, AR [*FM radio station call letters*]
KWDF .... Ball, LA [*AM radio station call letters*]
KWDK .... Tacoma, WA [*Television station call letters*]
KWDM .... West Des Moines, IA [*FM radio station call letters*]
KWDQ .... Woodward, OK [*FM radio station call letters*]
KWDX .... Silsbee, TX [*FM radio station call letters*]
KWE .... Guiyang [*China*] [*Airport symbol*] (OAG)
KWE .... Keith-Welti-Ernst [*Method*] [*Radiology*] (DAVI)
KWE .... Kilowatt Electric [*DOE*]
kWe .... Kilowatts of Electric Energy
KWE .... Knight of the White Eagle [*Poland*]
KWE .... Kweiyang [*China*] [*Airport symbol*] (AD)
KWEB .... Rochester, MN [*AM radio station call letters*]
KWED .... Seguin, TX [*AM radio station call letters*]
KWEI .... Weiser, ID [*AM radio station call letters*]
KWEI-FM ..... Fruitland, ID [*FM radio station call letters*] (RBYB)
KWEL .... Midland, TX [*AM radio station call letters*]
KWEN .... Tulsa, OK [*FM radio station call letters*]
KWEO .... Garberville, CA [*FM radio station call letters*]
KWES .... Ruidoso, NM [*FM radio station call letters*]
KWES-TV ..... Odessa, TX [*Television station call letters*]
KWET .... Cheyenne, OK [*Television station call letters*]
KWEX .... San Antonio, TX [*Television station call letters*]
KWEY .... Weatherford, OK [*AM radio station call letters*]
KWEY-FM .... Weatherford, OK [*FM radio station call letters*]
KWEZ-FM .... Santa Margarita, CA [*FM radio station call letters*] (BROA)
KWF .... Waterfall, AK [*Location identifier FAA*] (FAAL)
KWFC .... Kelli Warren Fan Club [*Defunct*] (EA)
KWFC .... Springfield, MO [*FM radio station call letters*]
KWFH .... Parker, AZ [*FM radio station call letters*]
KWFJ .... Roy, WA [*FM radio station call letters*]
KWFL .... Roswell, NM [*FM radio station call letters*]
KWFM .... Kurt Weill Foundation for Music (EA)
KWFM-FM .... Tucson, AZ [*FM radio station call letters*]
KWFR .... San Angelo, TX [*FM radio station call letters*] (RBYB)
KWFS .... Wichita Falls, TX [*FM radio station call letters*]
KWFS-FM .... Wichita Falls, TX [*FM radio station call letters*] (RBYB)
KWFT .... Kilowatt Foot (IAA)
KWFT .... Wichita Falls, TX [*AM radio station call letters*]
KWFX .... Woodward, OK [*FM radio station call letters*]
KWG .... Stockton, CA [*AM radio station call letters*]
KWGDF .... KWG Resources, Inc. [*NASDAQ symbol*] (SAG)
KWGN .... Denver, CO [*Television station call letters*]
KWG Rs ...... KWG Resources, Inc. [*Associated Press*] (SAG)
KWGS .... Tulsa, OK [*FM radio station call letters*]
kWh .... Kilowatt-Hour
Kwh .... Kilowatt Hour (EBF)
KWH .... Kilowatt Hour [*DOE*] (TAG)
KWHB .... Tulsa, OK [*Television station call letters*]
KWHD .... Castle Rock, CO [*Television station call letters*]
KWHE .... Honolulu, HI [*Television station call letters*]
kWhe .... Kilowatt-Hour Electric
KWHH .... Hilo, HI [*Television station call letters*]
KWHI .... Brenham, TX [*AM radio station call letters*]
KWHL .... Anchorage, AK [*FM radio station call letters*]
KWHM .... Kilowatt-Hour Meter
KWHM .... Wailuku, HI [*Television station call letters*]
KWHN .... Fort Smith, AR [*AM radio station call letters*]
KWHN .... Haynesville, LA [*FM radio station call letters*]
KWHO .... Weed, CA [*FM radio station call letters*]
KWHQ .... Kenai, AK [*FM radio station call letters*]
KWHR .... Kilowatthour (ABBR)
kWhr .... Kilowatt-Hour
KWHT .... Pendleton, OR [*FM radio station call letters*]
KWHW .... Altus, OK [*AM radio station call letters*]
KWHY .... Los Angeles, CA [*Television station call letters*]
KWI .... Kosher Wine Institute (EA)
KWI .... Kuwait [*Airport symbol*] (OAG)
KWi .... Wichita Public Library, Wichita, KS [*Library symbol Library of Congress*] (LCLS)
KWiB .... [*The*] Boeing Co., Wichita Division Library, Wichita, KS [*Library symbol Library of Congress*] (LCLS)
KWIC .... Kennedy Wilson, Inc. [*NASDAQ symbol*] (SAG)
KWIC .... Kentucky Women's Intercollegiate Conference (PSS)
KWIC .... Keyword in Context [*Indexing*]
KWIC .... Topeka, KS [*FM radio station call letters*]
KWiF .... Friends University, Wichita, KS [*Library symbol Library of Congress*] (LCLS)

KWiGS .... Church of Jesus Christ of Latter-Day Saints, Genealogical Society Library, Wichita Branch, Wichita, KS [*Library symbol Library of Congress*] (LCLS)
KWiIL .... Institute of Logopedics, Wichita, KS [*Library symbol Library of Congress*] (LCLS)
KWiK .... Kansas Newman College, Wichita, KS [*Library symbol Library of Congress*] (LCLS)
KWIK .... Pocatello, ID [*AM radio station call letters*]
KWIL .... Albany, OR [*AM radio station call letters*]
KWIM .... Window Rock, AZ [*FM radio station call letters*]
KWIN .... Lodi, CA [*FM radio station call letters*]
KWIP .... Dallas, OR [*AM radio station call letters*]
KWIP .... Keyword Word in Permutation [*Indexing*] (PDAA)
KWIQ .... Moses Lake, WA [*AM radio station call letters*]
KWIQ-FM ..... Moses Lake, WA [*FM radio station call letters*]
KWiSF .... Saint Francis Hospital, Wichita, KS [*Library symbol Library of Congress*] (LCLS)
KWiSJ .... Saint Joseph Hospital, Wichita, KS [*Library symbol Library of Congress*] (LCLS)
KWIT .... Keyword in Title [*Indexing*]
KWIT .... Sioux City, IA [*FM radio station call letters*]
KWiU .... Wichita State University, Wichita, KS [*Library symbol Library of Congress*] (LCLS)
KWiVA .... United States Veterans Administration Hospital, Wichita, KS [*Library symbol Library of Congress*] (LCLS)
KWiWC .... Wichita Clinic, Wichita, KS [*Library symbol Library of Congress*] (LCLS)
KWiWM .... Wesley Medical Center, Wichita, KS [*Library symbol Library of Congress*] (LCLS)
KWIX .... Moberly, MO [*AM radio station call letters*]
KWIZ .... Santa Ana, CA [*AM radio station call letters*]
KWIZ-FM ..... Santa Ana, CA [*FM radio station call letters*]
KWJC .... Liberty, MO [*FM radio station call letters*]
KWJJ .... Portland, OR [*AM radio station call letters*]
KWJJ-FM ..... Portland, OR [*FM radio station call letters*]
KWJM .... Farmerville, LA [*FM radio station call letters*]
KWJZ .... Seattle, WA [*FM radio station call letters*] (RBYB)
KWK .... Kampfwagenkanone [*Tank Gun*] [*German military - World War II*]
KWK .... Kwigillingok [*Alaska*] [*Airport symbol*] (OAG)
KWK .... Kwigillingok, AK [*Location identifier FAA*] (FAAL)
KWKA .... Clovis, NM [*AM radio station call letters*]
KWKB-TV ..... Iowa City, IA [*TV station call letters*] (RBYB)
KWKH .... Shreveport, LA [*AM radio station call letters*]
KWKH-FM .... Shreveport, LA [*FM radio station call letters*]
KWKK .... Dardanelle, AR [*FM radio station call letters*]
KWKM-FM .... St. Johns, AZ [*FM radio station call letters*] (BROA)
KWKQ .... Graham, TX [*FM radio station call letters*]
KWKT .... Waco, TX [*Television station call letters*]
KWKW .... Los Angeles, CA [*AM radio station call letters*]
KWKY .... Des Moines, IA [*AM radio station call letters*]
KWKZ .... Charleston, MO [*FM radio station call letters*]
KWL .... Guilin [*China*] [*Airport symbol*] (OAG)
KWLA .... Many, LA [*AM radio station call letters*]
KWLC .... Decorah, IA [*AM radio station call letters*]
KWLD .... Plainview, TX [*FM radio station call letters*]
KWLF .... Fairbanks, AK [*FM radio station call letters*]
KWLF .... Kodak Wratten Light Filter
KWLL .... Casa Grande, AZ [*AM radio station call letters*]
KWLM .... Willmar, MN [*AM radio station call letters*]
KWLO .... Waterloo, IA [*AM radio station call letters*]
KWLS .... Pratt, KS [*AM radio station call letters*]
KWLT .... North Crossett, AR [*FM radio station call letters*]
KWLV .... Many, LA [*FM radio station call letters*]
kWm .... Kilowatt Meter
KWM .... Korean War Memorial (EA)
KWM .... Kowanyama [*Australia Airport symbol*] (OAG)
KW/M² .... Kilowatts per Square Meter
KWMC .... Del Rio, TX [*AM radio station call letters*]
KWME .... Wellington, KS [*FM radio station call letters*]
KWMJ .... Tulsa, OK [*Television station call letters*]
KWMQ .... Southwest City, MO [*FM radio station call letters*]
KWMT .... Fort Dodge, IA [*AM radio station call letters*]
KWMU .... St. Louis, MO [*FM radio station call letters*]
KWMW .... Maljamar, NM [*FM radio station call letters*]
KWMX .... Lakewood, CO [*FM radio station call letters*]
KWN .... Kenwin Shops [*AMEX symbol*] (TTSB)
KWN .... Kenwin Shops, Inc. [*AMEX symbol*] (SPSG)
KWN .... Korean Wideband Network [*Communications*] [*Military*] (MCD)
KWN .... Quinhagak [*Alaska*] [*Airport symbol*] (OAG)
KWN .... Quinhagak, AK [*Location identifier FAA*] (FAAL)
KWNA .... Winnemucca, NV [*AM radio station call letters*]
KWNA-FM .... Winnemucca, NV [*FM radio station call letters*]
KWNB .... Hayes Center, NE [*Television station call letters*]
KWNC .... Quincy, WA [*AM radio station call letters*]
KWND .... Kenetech Corp. [*NASDAQ symbol*] (SAG)
KWND .... Springfield, MO [*FM radio station call letters*]
KWNDZ .... KENETECH Cp 8.25% Cv Dep Pfd [*NASDAQ symbol*] (TTSB)
KWNE .... Ukiah, CA [*FM radio station call letters*]
KWNG .... Red Wing, MN [*FM radio station call letters*]
KWNK .... Simi Valley, CA [*AM radio station call letters*]
KWNN .... Turlock, CA [*FM radio station call letters*] (RBYB)
KWNO .... Rushford, MN [*FM radio station call letters*]
KWNO .... Winona, MN [*AM radio station call letters*]
KWNR .... Henderson, NV [*FM radio station call letters*]
KWNS .... Winnsboro, TX [*FM radio station call letters*]
KWNV-TV ..... Winnemucca, NV [*TV station call letters*] (RBYB)
KWNZ .... Carson City, NV [*FM radio station call letters*]
KWOA .... Worthington, MN [*AM radio station call letters*]
KWOA-FM .... Worthington, MN [*FM radio station call letters*]
KWOC .... Keyword out of Context [*Indexing*]
KWOC .... Poplar Bluff, MO [*AM radio station call letters*]
KWOCA .... Key Word Online Catalogue Access
KWOD .... Sacramento, CA [*FM radio station call letters*]
KWOF .... Waterloo, IA [*AM radio station call letters*] (RBYB)
KWOK .... Novato, CA [*Television station call letters*] (BROA)
KWOM .... Watertown, MN [*AM radio station call letters*] (RBYB)
KWON .... Bartlesville, OK [*AM radio station call letters*]
KWOR .... Worland, WY [*AM radio station call letters*]
KWOS .... Jefferson City, MO [*AM radio station call letters*]
KWOT .... Keyword out of Title [*Indexing*]
KWOT .... Kilometer-Wave Orbiting Telescope [*NASA*]
KWOW .... Clifton, TX [*FM radio station call letters*]
KWOX .... Woodward, OK [*FM radio station call letters*]
KWOZ .... Mountain View, AR [*FM radio station call letters*]
KWP .... Kierowinctwo Walki Podziemnej (BJA)
KWP .... King World Prod'ns [*NYSE symbol*] (TTSB)
KWP .... King World Productions, Inc. [*NYSE symbol*] (SPSG)
KWP .... Korean Workers' Party [*North Korea Political party*] (PD)
KWP .... West Point [*Alaska*] [*Airport symbol*] (OAG)
KWP .... West Point, AK [*Location identifier FAA*] (FAAL)
KWPA-AM .... Pomona, CA [*AM radio station call letters*] (RBYB)
KWPC .... Muscatine, IA [*AM radio station call letters*]
KWPM .... West Plains, MO [*AM radio station call letters*]
KWPN-FM .... West Point, NE [*FM radio station call letters*]
KWPZ-FM .... Lynden, WA [*FM radio station call letters*] (RBYB)
KWQC .... Davenport, IA [*Television station call letters*]
KWQH-FM .... San Luis Obispo, CA [*FM radio station call letters*] (RBYB)
KWQJ-FM .... Anchorage, AK [*FM radio station call letters*] (RBYB)
KWQL .... Dishman, WA [*FM radio station call letters*]
kWr .... Kilowatts Reactive
KWR .... KW Resources Ltd. [*Vancouver Stock Exchange symbol*]
KWRB .... Bisbee, AZ [*FM radio station call letters*] (RBYB)
KWRB .... Macon/Robins Air Force Base [*Georgia*] [*ICAO location identifier*] (ICLI)
KWRD .... Henderson, TX [*AM radio station call letters*]
KWRE .... Warrenton, MO [*AM radio station call letters*]
KWRF .... Warren, AR [*AM radio station call letters*]
KWRF-FM .... Warren, AR [*FM radio station call letters*]
KWRI .... Wrightstown/McGuire Air Force Base [*New Jersey*] [*ICAO location identifier*] (ICLI)
KWRK .... Window Rock, AZ [*FM radio station call letters*]
KWRL .... La Grande, OR [*FM radio station call letters*]
KWRM .... Corona, CA [*AM radio station call letters*]
KWRN .... Apple Valley, CA [*AM radio station call letters*] (RBYB)
KWRO .... Coquille, OR [*AM radio station call letters*]
KWRP .... San Jacinto, CA [*FM radio station call letters*]
KWRQ .... Clifton, AZ [*FM radio station call letters*] (RBYB)
KWRR-FM .... Ethete, WY [*FM radio station call letters*] (RBYB)
KWRRI .... Kansas Water Resources Research Institute [*Kansas State University*] [*Department of the Interior Research center*] (RCD)
KWRRI .... Kentucky Water Resources Research Institute [*University of Kentucky*] [*Lexington, KY*] [*Department of the Interior*] [*Research center*] (RCD)
KWRS .... Spokane, WA [*FM radio station call letters*]
KWRT .... Boonville, MO [*AM radio station call letters*]
KWRV .... Sun Valley, ID [*FM radio station call letters*]
KWRW .... Rusk, TX [*FM radio station call letters*]
KWS .... Kenya Wildlife Service
KWS .... Kenya Wildlife Service
KWS .... Korean Welfare Society [*Australia*]
KWS .... Southwestern College, Winfield, KS [*Library symbol Library of Congress*] (LCLS)
KWSA .... West Klamath, OR [*AM radio station call letters*]
KWSB .... Gunnison, CO [*FM radio station call letters*]
KWSC .... Wayne, NE [*FM radio station call letters*]
KWSD .... White Sands/Condron Army Air Field [*New Mexico*] [*ICAO location identifier*] (ICLI)
KWSE .... Williston, ND [*Television station call letters*]
KWSH .... Wewoka, OK [*AM radio station call letters*]
KWSJ .... Saint John's College, Winfield, KS [*Library symbol Library of Congress*] (LCLS)
KWSJ-FM .... Haysville, KS [*FM radio station call letters*] (RBYB)
KWSK-FM .... Daingerfield, TX [*FM radio station call letters*] (RBYB)
KWSL .... Sioux City, IA [*AM radio station call letters*] (RBYB)
KWSM .... Sherman, TX [*FM radio station call letters*]
KWSN .... Sioux Falls, SD [*AM radio station call letters*]
KWSO .... Warm Springs, OR [*FM radio station call letters*]
KWSP .... Santa Margarita, CA [*FM radio station call letters*]
KWST .... Brawley, CA [*FM radio station call letters*]
KWSU .... Pullman, WA [*AM radio station call letters*]
KWSU-TV ..... Pullman, WA [*Television station call letters*]
KWSW .... Eureka, CA [*AM radio station call letters*]
KWSWA .... Kansas Wine and Spirits Wholesalers Association (SRA)
kWt .... Kilowatt, Thermal
KWT .... Kuwait [*ANSI three-letter standard code*] (CNC)
KWT .... Kwethluk [*Alaska*] [*Airport symbol*] (OAG)
KWT .... Kwethluk, AK [*Location identifier FAA*] (FAAL)
kW(th) .... Kilowatt, Thermal
KWTO .... Springfield, MO [*AM radio station call letters*]
KWTO-FM .... Springfield, MO [*FM radio station call letters*]

KWTR .... Georgetown, TX [*AM radio station call letters*]
KWTS .... Canyon, TX [*FM radio station call letters*]
KWTV .... Oklahoma City, OK [*Television station call letters*]
KWTX .... Waco, TX [*AM radio station call letters*]
KWTX-FM .... Waco, TX [*FM radio station call letters*]
KWTX-TV .... Waco, TX [*Television station call letters*]
KWTY .... Cartago, CA [*FM radio station call letters*]
KWU .... Kansas Wesleyan University [*Salina*]
KWU .... Kawau Island [*New Zealand*] [*Airport symbol*] (AD)
KWU .... Kraftwerksunion [*Germany*]
KWUA .... Clovis, NM [*FM radio station call letters*]
KWUC .... Keyword and Universal Decimal Classification (PDAA)
KWUF-AM .... Pagosa Springs, CO [*AM radio station call letters*] (BROA)
KWUF-FM .... Pagosa Springs, CO [*FM radio station call letters*] (BROA)
KWUN-AM .... Murray, UT [*AM radio station call letters*] (BROA)
KWUR .... Clayton, MO [*FM radio station call letters*]
KWVA .... Eugene, OR [*FM radio station call letters*]
KWVA .... Korean War Veterans Association (EA)
KWVE .... San Clemente, CA [*FM radio station call letters*]
KWVM .... Korean War Veterans Memorial [*Defunct*] (EA)
KWVR .... Enterprise, OR [*AM radio station call letters*]
KWVR-FM .... Enterprise, OR [*FM radio station call letters*]
KWVV .... Homer, AK [*FM radio station call letters*]
KWW .... Asbury College, Wilmore, KY [*OCLC symbol*] (OCLC)
KWWC .... Columbia, MO [*FM radio station call letters*]
KWWD .... Wildwood/Cape May County [*New Jersey*] [*ICAO location identifier*] (ICLI)
KWWF-FM ... West Yellowstone, MT [*FM radio station call letters*] (RBYB)
KWWJ .... Baytown, TX [*AM radio station call letters*]
KWWK .... Rochester, MN [*FM radio station call letters*]
KWWL .... Waterloo, IA [*Television station call letters*]
KWWR .... Mexico, MO [*FM radio station call letters*]
KWWS-FM .... Walla Walla, WA [*FM radio station call letters*] (RBYB)
KWwUT .... United Telecommunications/U.S. Sprint, Westwood, KS [*Library symbol*] [*Library of Congress*] (LCLS)
KWWV .... Morro Bay, CA [*FM radio station call letters*]
KWWW .... Quincy, WA [*FM radio station call letters*]
KWWX .... Wenatchee, WA [*AM radio station call letters*]
KWX .... Kiwai Island [*Papua New Guinea*] [*Airport symbol*] (OAG)
KWXA .... Durango, CO [*FM radio station call letters*]
KWXD .... Asbury, MO [*FM radio station call letters*]
KWXE .... Glenwood, AR [*FM radio station call letters*]
KWXH .... Sun City, CA [*FM radio station call letters*]
KWXI .... Glenwood, AR [*AM radio station call letters*]
KWXI-AM .... Glenwood, AR [*AM radio station call letters*] (RBYB)
KWXT .... Dardanelle, AR [*AM radio station call letters*]
KWXX .... Hilo, HI [*FM radio station call letters*]
KWXY .... Cathedral City, CA [*AM radio station call letters*]
KWXY-FM .... Cathedral City, CA [*FM radio station call letters*]
KWY .... Key Way
KWYB .... Butte, MT [*Television station call letters*]
KWYD .... Colorado Springs, CO [*AM radio station call letters*]
KWYI .... Kawaihae, HI [*FM radio station call letters*]
KWYK .... Aztec, NM [*FM radio station call letters*]
KWYN .... Wynne, AR [*AM radio station call letters*]
KWYN-FM .... Wynne, AR [*FM radio station call letters*]
KWYO .... Sheridan, WY [*AM radio station call letters*]
KWYO-FM .... Sheridan, WY [*FM radio station call letters*]
KWYR .... Winner, SD [*AM radio station call letters*]
KWYR-FM .... Winner, SD [*FM radio station call letters*]
KWYS .... West Yellowstone, MT [*AM radio station call letters*]
KWYX .... Jasper, TX [*FM radio station call letters*]
KWYZ .... Everett, WA [*AM radio station call letters*]
KWZ .... Kolwezi [*Zaire*] [*Airport symbol*] (AD)
KX .... Cayman Airways [*ICAO designator*] (AD)
KX .... Cayman Airways [*Airline flight code*] (ODBW)
KX .... [*The*] Holy Bible (1955) [*R.A. Knox*] [*A publication*] (BJA)
KXA .... Kasaan, AK [*Location identifier FAA*] (FAAL)
KXAA .... Rock Island, WA [*FM radio station call letters*]
KXAC .... St. James, MN [*FM radio station call letters*]
KXAL .... Pittsburg, TX [*FM radio station call letters*]
KXAM .... Mesa, AZ [*AM radio station call letters*]
KXAM-TV .... Llano, TX [*Television station call letters*]
KXAN .... Austin, TX [*Television station call letters*]
KXAR .... Hope, AR [*AM radio station call letters*]
KXAR-FM .... Hope, AR [*FM radio station call letters*]
KXAS .... Fort Worth, TX [*Television station call letters*]
KXAX .... St. James, MN [*FM radio station call letters*]
KXAZ .... Page, AZ [*FM radio station call letters*]
KXBJ .... Victoria, TX [*FM radio station call letters*]
KXBR-AM .... Minneapolis, MN [*AM radio station call letters*] (BROA)
KXBS .... Santa Paula, CA [*FM radio station call letters*]
KXBT .... Vallejo, CA [*AM radio station call letters*]
KXBX .... Lakeport, CA [*AM radio station call letters*]
KXBX-FM .... Lakeport, CA [*FM radio station call letters*]
KXBZ-FM .... Manhattan, KS [*FM radio station call letters*] (RBYB)
KXC .... Keleket X-Ray Corp.
KXCC .... Rockport, TX [*FM radio station call letters*]
KXCI .... Tucson, AZ [*FM radio station call letters*]
KXCL .... Yuba City, CA [*FM radio station call letters*]
KXCR .... El Paso, TX [*FM radio station call letters*]
KXCV .... Maryville, MO [*FM radio station call letters*]
KXDA .... Las Cruces, NM [*FM radio station call letters*] (RBYB)
KXDC .... Carmel, CA [*FM radio station call letters*] (RBYB)
KXDD .... Yakima, WA [*FM radio station call letters*]

KXDG .... Webb City, MO [*FM radio station call letters*] (RBYB)
KXDL .... Browerville, MN [*FM radio station call letters*]
KXEB .... Sherman, TX [*FM radio station call letters*]
KXED .... Los Angeles, CA [*AM radio station call letters*]
KXEG .... Tolleson, AZ [*AM radio station call letters*]
KXEI .... Havre, MT [*FM radio station call letters*]
KXEL .... Waterloo, IA [*AM radio station call letters*]
KXEM .... Bakersfield, CA [*AM radio station call letters*] (RBYB)
KXEN .... Festus-St. Louis, MO [*AM radio station call letters*]
KXEO .... Mexico, MO [*AM radio station call letters*]
KXEQ .... Reno, NV [*AM radio station call letters*]
KXEW .... South Tucson, AZ [*AM radio station call letters*]
KXEX .... Fresno, CA [*AM radio station call letters*]
KXEZ .... Los Angeles, CA [*FM radio station call letters*]
KXF .... Kodak X-Ray Film
KXF .... Koro [*Fiji*] [*Airport symbol*] (OAG)
KXFE .... Dumas, AR [*FM radio station call letters*]
KXFG-FM ..... Sun City, CA [*FM radio station call letters*] (RBYB)
KXFM .... Santa Maria, CA [*FM radio station call letters*]
KXFX .... Santa Rosa, CA [*FM radio station call letters*]
KXGA .... Glennallen, AK [*FM radio station call letters*] (RBYB)
KXGE-FM ..... Dubuque, IA [*FM radio station call letters*] (BROA)
KXGF .... Great Falls, MT [*AM radio station call letters*]
KXGJ .... Bay City, TX [*FM radio station call letters*]
KXGL-FM ..... San Diego, CA [*FM radio station call letters*] (BROA)
KXGM .... Muenster, TX [*FM radio station call letters*]
KXGN .... Glendive, MT [*AM radio station call letters*]
KXGN-TV ..... Glendive, MT [*Television station call letters*]
KXGO .... Arcata, CA [*FM radio station call letters*]
KXGR .... Green Valley, AZ [*Television station call letters*]
KXGT-FM ..... Jamestown, ND [*FM radio station call letters*] (RBYB)
KXHA .... Shafter, CA [*FM radio station call letters*]
KXHT-FM ..... Marion, AR [*FM radio station call letters*] (BROA)
KXHV .... Sacramento, CA [*FM radio station call letters*]
KXIA .... Marshalltown, IA [*FM radio station call letters*]
KXIC .... Iowa City, IA [*AM radio station call letters*]
KXII .... Sherman, TX [*Television station call letters*]
KXIL-FM ..... Sanger, TX [*FM radio station call letters*] (BROA)
KXIO .... Clarksville, AR [*FM radio station call letters*]
KXIT .... Dalhart, TX [*AM radio station call letters*]
KXIT-FM ..... Dalhart, TX [*FM radio station call letters*]
KXIX .... Bend, OR [*FM radio station call letters*]
KXJB .... Valley City, ND [*Television station call letters*]
KXJK .... Forrest City, AR [*AM radio station call letters*]
KXJZ .... Sacramento, CA [*FM radio station call letters*]
KXKB .... Tahoe City, CA [*FM radio station call letters*]
KXKC .... New Iberia, LA [*FM radio station call letters*]
KXKK .... Lordsburg, NM [*FM radio station call letters*]
KXKL .... Denver, CO [*AM radio station call letters*]
KXKL-FM ..... Denver, CO [*FM radio station call letters*]
KXKM .... McCarthy, AK [*FM radio station call letters*] (RBYB)
KXKQ .... Safford, AZ [*FM radio station call letters*]
KXKS .... Albuquerque, NM [*AM radio station call letters*]
KXKT .... Atlantic, IA [*FM radio station call letters*]
KXKX .... Knob Noster, MO [*FM radio station call letters*]
KXKZ .... Ruston, LA [*FM radio station call letters*]
KXL .... Portland, OR [*AM radio station call letters*]
KXLA .... Rayville, LA [*AM radio station call letters*]
KXLC .... La Crescent, MN [*FM radio station call letters*]
KXLE .... Ellensburg, WA [*AM radio station call letters*]
KXLE-FM ..... Ellensburg, WA [*FM radio station call letters*]
KXLF .... Butte, MT [*Television station call letters*]
KXLI .... St. Cloud, MN [*Television station call letters*]
KXLK .... Haysville, KS [*FM radio station call letters*]
KXLM .... Oxnard, CA [*FM radio station call letters*]
KXLN .... Rosenburg, TX [*Television station call letters*]
KXLO .... Lewistown, MT [*AM radio station call letters*]
KXLP .... New Ulm, MN [*FM radio station call letters*]
KXLQ .... Indianola, IA [*AM radio station call letters*] (RBYB)
KXLR .... Fairbanks, AK [*FM radio station call letters*]
KXLS .... Alva, OK [*AM radio station call letters*]
KXLT .... Eagle, ID [*FM radio station call letters*]
KXLT-TV ..... Rochester, MN [*Television station call letters*]
KXLU .... Los Angeles, CA [*FM radio station call letters*]
KXLY .... Spokane, WA [*AM radio station call letters*]
KXLY-FM ..... Spokane, WA [*FM radio station call letters*]
KXLY-TV ..... Spokane, WA [*Television station call letters*]
KXMA .... Dickinson, ND [*Television station call letters*]
KXMB .... Bismarck, ND [*Television station call letters*]
KXMC .... Minot, ND [*Television station call letters*]
KXMD .... Williston, ND [*Television station call letters*]
KXMG-AM ..... Los Angeles, CA [*AM radio station call letters*] (RBYB)
KXMR .... Bismarck, ND [*AM radio station call letters*] (RBYB)
KXMS .... Joplin, MO [*FM radio station call letters*]
KXMX .... Cedar Rapids, IA [*FM radio station call letters*] (RBYB)
KXNE .... Norfolk, NE [*FM radio station call letters*]
KXNE-TV ..... Norfolk, NE [*Television station call letters*]
KXNO .... North Las Vegas, NV [*AM radio station call letters*]
KXNP .... North Platte, NE [*FM radio station call letters*]
KXO .... El Centro, CA [*AM radio station call letters*]
KXOA .... Sacramento, CA [*AM radio station call letters*]
KXOA-FM ..... Sacramento, CA [*FM radio station call letters*]
KXOF .... Bloomfield, CO [*FM radio station call letters*]
KXO-FM ...... El Centro, CA [*FM radio station call letters*]
KXOI .... Crane, TX [*AM radio station call letters*]

KXOJ............ Sapulpa, OK [*AM radio station call letters*]
KXOJ-FM .... Sapulpa, OK [*FM radio station call letters*]
KXOK .... Florissant, MO [*FM radio station call letters*]
KXOL .... Clinton, OK [*AM radio station call letters*]
KXOO .... Elk City, OK [*FM radio station call letters*] (RBYB)
KXOQ .... Kennett, MO [*FM radio station call letters*] (RBYB)
KXOR .... Thibodaux, LA [*FM radio station call letters*]
KXOW .... Hot Springs, AR [*AM radio station call letters*]
KXOX .... Sweetwater, TX [*AM radio station call letters*]
KXOX-FM .... Sweetwater, TX [*FM radio station call letters*]
KXOZ .... Mountain View, MO [*FM radio station call letters*]
KXPA-AM .... Pasadena, CA [*AM radio station call letters*] (RBYB)
KXPC .... Lebanon, OR [*FM radio station call letters*]
KXPK .... Evergreen, CO [*FM radio station call letters*]
KXPO .... Grafton, ND [*AM radio station call letters*]
KXPO-FM .... Grafton, ND [*FM radio station call letters*]
KXPR .... Sacramento, CA [*FM radio station call letters*]
KXPT .... Las Vegas, NV [*FM radio station call letters*]
KXPW .... Belle Plaine, IA [*FM radio station call letters*]
KXPX .... Stillwater, OK [*FM radio station call letters*] (RBYB)
KXPZ .... Lytle, TX [*FM radio station call letters*]
KXRA .... Alexandria, MN [*AM radio station call letters*]
KXRA-FM .... Alexandria, MN [*FM radio station call letters*]
KXRB .... Sioux Falls, SD [*AM radio station call letters*]
KXRD .... Victorville, CA [*FM radio station call letters*]
KXRE .... Manitou Springs, CO [*AM radio station call letters*]
KXRJ .... Russellville, AR [*FM radio station call letters*]
KXRK .... Provo, UT [*FM radio station call letters*]
KXRM .... Colorado Springs, CO [*Television station call letters*]
KXRO .... Aberdeen, WA [*AM radio station call letters*]
KXRQ-FM .... Roosevelt, UT [*FM radio station call letters*] (BROA)
KXRS .... Hemet, CA [*FM radio station call letters*]
KXRX .... Walla Walla, WA [*FM radio station call letters*]
KXS .... Kiva Executive Server [*Computer science*]
KXSA-FM .... Dermott, AR [*FM radio station call letters*]
KXSB .... Big Bear Lake, CA [*FM radio station call letters*] (RBYB)
KXSM .... Saint Mary College, Xavier, KS [*Library symbol Library of Congress*] (LCLS)
KXSP .... Ventura, CA [*AM radio station call letters*] (RBYB)
KXSR .... Groveland, CA [*FM radio station call letters*]
KXSS .... Waite Park, MN [*AM radio station call letters*]
KXST-FM .... Oceanside, CA [*FM radio station call letters*] (RBYB)
KXTC .... Thoreau, NM [*FM radio station call letters*]
KXTD .... Wagoner, OK [*FM radio station call letters*]
KXTE-FM .... Rahrump, NV [*FM radio station call letters*] (RBYB)
KXTF .... Twin Falls, ID [*Television station call letters*] (BROA)
KXTJ .... Beaumont, TX [*FM radio station call letters*]
KXTK-AM .... Des Moines, IA [*AM radio station call letters*] (RBYB)
KXTL .... Butte, MT [*AM radio station call letters*]
KXTN .... San Antonio, TX [*AM radio station call letters*]
KXTN-FM .... San Antonio, TX [*FM radio station call letters*]
KXTO .... Reno, NV [*AM radio station call letters*]
KXTP .... Superior, WI [*AM radio station call letters*]
KXTQ .... Lubbock, TX [*AM radio station call letters*]
KXTQ-FM .... Lubbock, TX [*FM radio station call letters*]
KXTR .... Kansas City, MO [*FM radio station call letters*]
KXTV .... Sacramento, CA [*Television station call letters*]
KXTX .... Dallas, TX [*Television station call letters*]
KXU .... Kastamonu [*Turkey*] [*Airport symbol*] (AD)
KXU .... Keyword Transformation Unit [*Computer science*] (MHDI)
KXUS .... Springfield, MO [*FM radio station call letters*]
KXUX .... Bend, OR [*AM radio station call letters*]
KXVO .... Omaha, NE [*Television station call letters*] (RBYB)
KXXI .... Gallup, NM [*FM radio station call letters*]
KXXK .... Chickasha, OK [*FM radio station call letters*]
KXXL .... Crane, TX [*FM radio station call letters*]
KXXO .... Olympia, WA [*FM radio station call letters*]
KXXR-FM .... Minneapolis, MN [*FM radio station call letters*] (BROA)
KXXS .... Toppenish, WA [*FM radio station call letters*]
KXXV .... Waco, TX [*Television station call letters*]
KXXX .... Colby, KS [*AM radio station call letters*]
KXXY .... Oklahoma City, OK [*AM radio station call letters*]
KXXY-FM .... Oklahoma City, OK [*FM radio station call letters*]
KXXZ .... Barstow, CA [*FM radio station call letters*]
KXYL .... Brownwood, TX [*AM radio station call letters*]
KXYL-FM .... Brownwood, TX [*FM radio station call letters*]
KXYQ .... Milwaukie, OR [*FM radio station call letters*]
KXYZ .... Houston, TX [*AM radio station call letters*]
KXZZ .... Lake Charles, LA [*AM radio station call letters*]
KY .... Cayman Islands [*ANSI two-letter standard code*] (CNC)
KY .... Kabaka Yekka [*The King Alone*] [*Uganda Suspended*] [*Political party*]
KY .... Kapustin Yar [*Test Facility*] [*US prefix for Soviet-Russian developmental missiles*] (DOMA)
Ky .... Kentucky (ODBW)
KY .... Kentucky [*Postal code*] (AFM)
Ky .... Kentucky Department of Libraries, Frankfort, KY [*Library symbol Library of Congress*] (LCLS)
Ky .... Kentucky Reports [*A publication*] (AAGC)
KY .... Kentucky Supreme Court Reports [*1879-1951*] [*A publication*] (DLA)
KY .... Kent Yeomanry [*Military unit*] [*British*]
KY .... Key
KY .... Keyhole [*United States reconnaissance satellite*] (DOMA)
KY .... Keying Devices [*JETDS nomenclature*] [*Military*] (CET)
KY .... Kol Yisroel [*Israeli Broadcasting Service*]

KY .... Kyrie [*Liturgical*]
KY .... Sun West [*ICAO designator*] (AD)
KyA .... Ashland Public Library, Ashland, KY [*Library symbol Library of Congress*] (LCLS)
KYA .... Konya [*Turkey*] [*Airport symbol*] (AD)
KYA .... Kyakhta [*Former USSR Seismograph station code, US Geological Survey Closed*] (SEIS)
KYA .... Yana Air Cargo (Kenya) Ltd. [*ICAO designator*] (FAAC)
KY Admin Reg... Kentucky Administrative Register [*A publication*] (DLA)
KY Admin Regs... Kentucky Administration Regulations Service [*A publication*] (DLA)
Ky Admin Regs... Kentucky Administrative Regulations [*A publication*] (AAGC)
KYAJ .... Merced, CA [*FM radio station call letters*]
KYAK .... Anchorage, AK [*AM radio station call letters*]
Ky-Ar .... Kentucky Department of Libraries and Archives, Kentucky State Archives, Frankfort, KY [*Library symbol*] [*Library of Congress*] (LCLS)
KYAT .... Keokuk, IA [*FM radio station call letters*]
KYAX .... Alturas, CA [*FM radio station call letters*]
KYB .... Kayaba Industry Co. [*Auto industry supplier*]
KYB .... Know Your Body (DAVI)
KYBA .... Stewartville, MN [*FM radio station call letters*]
KyBB .... Berea College, Berea, KY [*Library symbol Library of Congress*] (LCLS)
KYBC-AM .... Cottonwood, AZ [*AM radio station call letters*] (RBYB)
KYBD .... Copeland, KS [*FM radio station call letters*]
KYBD .... Keyboard (MSA)
KYBE .... Frederick, OK [*FM radio station call letters*]
KYBG .... Aurora, CO [*AM radio station call letters*]
KyBgW .... Western Kentucky University, Bowling Green, KY [*Library symbol Library of Congress*] (LCLS)
KyBgW-K .... Western Kentucky University, Kentucky Library, Bowling Green, KY [*Library symbol Library of Congress*] (LCLS)
KYBI-FM ..... Huntington, TX [*FM radio station call letters*] (RBYB)
KYBJ .... Lake Jackson, TX [*AM radio station call letters*] (RBYB)
Ky-BPH .... Kentucky Library for the Blind and Physically Handicapped, Frankfort, KY [*Library symbol Library of Congress*] (LCLS)
KYBRD .... Keyboard
KYBR-FM ..... Espanola, NM [*FM radio station call letters*] (RBYB)
KyBvU .... Union College, Barbourville, KY [*Library symbol Library of Congress*] (LCLS)
KYC .... HCL Aviation, Inc. [*ICAO designator*] (FAAC)
KYC .... Know Your Customer [*Investment term*] (DFIT)
KYCA .... Prescott, AZ [*AM radio station call letters*]
KyCambC ..... Campbellsville College, Campbellsville, KY [*Library symbol Library of Congress*] (LCLS)
KyCarD .... Dow Corning Corp., TIS Library, Carrollton, KY [*Library symbol Library of Congress*] (LCLS)
KYCC-FM ..... Livingston, CA [*FM radio station call letters*] (BROA)
KYCH .... Convent General of the Knights York Cross of Honour (EA)
KYCK .... Crookston, MN [*FM radio station call letters*]
KYCN .... Wheatland, WY [*AM radio station call letters*]
KYCN-FM ..... Wheatland, WY [*FM radio station call letters*]
KyColW .... Lindsey Wilson College, Columbia, KY [*Library symbol Library of Congress*] (LCLS)
KY Comment'r... Kentucky Commentator [*A publication*] (DLA)
KyCov .... Kenton County Public Library, Covington, KY [*Library symbol Library of Congress*] (LCLS)
KyCovStE .... Saint Elizabeth Medical Center, Covington, KY [*Library symbol Library of Congress*] (LCLS)
KYCR .... Golden Valley, MN [*AM radio station call letters*]
KYCS .... Rock Springs, WY [*FM radio station call letters*]
KYCW .... Seattle, WA [*FM radio station call letters*]
KYCX .... Mexia, TX [*FM radio station call letters*]
KYCY .... San Francisco, CA [*FM radio station call letters*]
KYD .... Kilo Yard
Kyd .... Kyd on Bills of Exchange [*A publication*] (DLA)
Kyd Aw .... Kyd on Awards [*A publication*] (DLA)
Kyd Bills..... Kyd on Bills of Exchange [*A publication*] (DLA)
KyDC .... Centre College of Kentucky, Danville, KY [*Library symbol Library of Congress*] (LCLS)
Kyd Corp..... Kyd on Corporations [*A publication*] (DLA)
KYDE .... Pine Bluff, AR [*AM radio station call letters*]
KY Dec .... Sneed's Kentucky Decisions [*2 Kentucky*] [*A publication*] (DLA)
KYDS .... Kiloyards (MCD)
KYDS .... Sacramento, CA [*FM radio station call letters*]
KYDT-FM ..... Sundance, WY [*FM radio station call letters*] (RBYB)
KYDZ .... Cody, WY [*FM radio station call letters*]
KYEA .... West Monroe, LA [*FM radio station call letters*]
KYEE .... Alamogordo, NM [*FM radio station call letters*]
KYEG-FM ..... Canadian, TX [*FM radio station call letters*] (RBYB)
KyeKtts ...... Kaye Kotts Associates, Inc. [*Associated Press*] (SAG)
KYERI .... Know Your Endorsers - Require Identification [*Advice to businessmen and others who cash checks for the public*]
KyErP .... Seminary of Saint Pius X, Erlanger, KY [*Library symbol Library of Congress*] (LCLS)
KYES .... Anchorage, AK [*Television station call letters*]
KYET .... Williams, AZ [*AM radio station call letters*]
KYEZ .... Salina, KS [*FM radio station call letters*]
KYF .... Kentucky First Bancorp [*AMEX symbol*] (TTSB)
KYF .... Kentucky First Bancorp, Inc. [*AMEX symbol*] (SAG)
KYF .... Yeelirie [*Australia Airport symbol*] (OAG)
KYFA .... Amarillo, TX [*FM radio station call letters*]
KYFC .... Kansas City, MO [*Television station call letters*]

KyFc............. United States Army, Fort Campbell Post Library (R. F. Sink Memorial Library), Fort Campbell, KY [*Library symbol Library of Congress*] (LCLS)

KyFCE......... Kentucky Council on Higher Education, Frankfort, KY [*Library symbol*] [*Library of Congress*] (LCLS)

KyFkAS....... United States Army Armor School, Fort Knox, KY [*Library symbol Library of Congress*] (LCLS)

KYFL........... Monroe, LA [*FM radio station call letters*]

KyFLR......... Legislative Research Commission, Library, Frankfort, KY [*Library symbol*] [*Library of Congress*] (LCLS)

KYFM.......... Bartlesville, OK [*FM radio station call letters*]

KyFmTM...... Thomas More College, Fort Mitchell, KY [*Library symbol Library of Congress*] (LCLS)

KYFO .... Ogden, UT [*AM radio station call letters*]

KYFO-FM..... Ogden, UT [*FM radio station call letters*]

KYFP-FM..... Palestine, TX [*FM radio station call letters*] (BROA)

KYFR.......... Shenandoah, IA [*AM radio station call letters*]

KYFS........... San Antonio, TX [*FM radio station call letters*]

KyFSC......... Kentucky State University, Frankfort, KY [*Library symbol Library of Congress*] (LCLS)

KY Fst........ Kentucky First Bancorp, Inc. [*Associated Press*] (SAG)

KY FstB....... Kentucky First Bancorp, Inc. [*Associated Press*] (SAG)

KYFT........... Lubbock, TX [*FM radio station call letters*]

KYFW.......... Wichita, KS [*FM radio station call letters*]

KYFX........... Little Rock, AR [*FM radio station call letters*]

Ky-G........... Kentucky Department of Libraries and Archives, Kentucky Guide Project, Frankfort, KY [*Library symbol*] [*Library of Congress*] (LCLS)

KyGeC........ Georgetown College, Georgetown, KY [*Library symbol Library of Congress*] (LCLS)

KYGL .... Texarkana, AR [*FM radio station call letters*] (RBYB)

KYGO .... Lakewood, CO [*AM radio station call letters*]

KYGO-FM.... Denver, CO [*FM radio station call letters*]

KyHaHi....... Harrodsburg Historical Society, Harrodsburg, KY [*Library symbol Library of Congress*] (LCLS)

KyHhN .... Northern Kentucky University, Highland Heights, KY [*Library symbol Library of Congress*] (LCLS)

KyHhN-L..... Northern Kentucky University, B. P. Chase College of Law, Covington, KY [*Library symbol Library of Congress*] (LCLS)

KyHi........... Kentucky Historical Society, Frankfort, KY [*Library symbol Library of Congress*] (LCLS)

KYHL .... Keyhole (ABBR)

KyHopC....... Hopkinsville Community College, Hopkinsville, KY [*Library symbol*] [*Library of Congress*] (LCLS)

KYHT.......... Yermo, CA [*FM radio station call letters*]

KyHzC........ Hazard Community College, Hazard, KY [*Library symbol Library of Congress*] (LCLS)

KYIN .... Mason City, IA [*Television station call letters*]

KYIP........... Detroit/Willow Run [*Michigan*] [*ICAO location identifier*] (ICLI)

KYIS........... Oklahoma City, OK [*FM radio station call letters*]

KYIX........... South Oroville, CA [*FM radio station call letters*] (RBYB)

KYJC-FM...... Grants Pass, OR [*FM radio station call letters*]

KYJT .... Yuma, AZ [*FM radio station call letters*] (RBYB)

KYK .... Karluk [*Alaska*] [*Airport symbol*] (OAG)

KYK .... Karluk, AK [*Location identifier FAA*] (FAAL)

KYK .... Kayak (ABBR)

KYK .... Kayak Island [*Alaska*] [*Seismograph station code, US Geological Survey*] (SEIS)

KYK .... Kelley-Kerr Energy [*Vancouver Stock Exchange symbol*]

KYKA .... Naches, WA [*FM radio station call letters*]

KYKC .... Byng, OK [*FM radio station call letters*]

KYKD .... Bethel, AK [*FM radio station call letters*]

KYKF .... San Fernando, CA [*FM radio station call letters*]

KYKK .... Hobbs, NM [*AM radio station call letters*]

KYKM........... Yoakum, TX [*FM radio station call letters*] (RBYB)

KYKN .... Keizer, OR [*AM radio station call letters*]

KYKN .... Nephi, UT [*FM radio station call letters*]

KYKN .... Pknocytes [*Hematology*] (DAVI)

KYKR .... Beaumont, TX [*FM radio station call letters*]

KYKS .... Lufkin, TX [*FM radio station call letters*]

KYKX .... Longview, TX [*FM radio station call letters*]

KYKY .... St. Louis, MO [*FM radio station call letters*]

KYKZ.......... Lake Charles, LA [*FM radio station call letters*]

KY L .... Kentucky Law Reporter [*A publication*] (DLA)

KYL........... Kyle Resources, Inc. [*Vancouver Stock Exchange symbol*]

KY Law Rep... Kentucky Law Reporter [*A publication*] (DLA)

KYLC........... Osage Beach, MO [*FM radio station call letters*]

KYLD........... San Mateo, CA [*FM radio station call letters*]

KYLE........... Bryan, TX [*Television station call letters*]

KyLo........... Louisville Free Public Library, Louisville, KY [*Library symbol Library of Congress*] (LCLS)

KyLoB......... Bellarmine College, Louisville, KY [*Library symbol Library of Congress*] (LCLS)

KyLoB-M..... Bellarmine College, Thomas Merton Studies Center, Louisville, KY [*Library symbol Library of Congress*] (LCLS)

KyLoBW...... Brown & Williamson Tobacco Corp., Research Department Library, Louisville, KY [*Library symbol Library of Congress*] (LCLS)

KyLoC......... Courier-Journal & Louisville Times Co., Inc., Louisville, KY [*Library symbol Library of Congress*] (LCLS)

KyLoF......... Filson Club, Louisville, KY [*Library symbol Library of Congress*] (LCLS)

KyLoJ.......... Jefferson Community College, Louisville, KY [*Library symbol Library of Congress*] (LCLS)

KyLoL .... Louisville Presbyterian Seminary, Louisville, KY [*Library symbol Library of Congress*] (LCLS)

KyLoM........ Louisville Medical Library, Louisville, KY [*Library symbol Library of Congress*] (LCLS)

KyLoN......... Spalding College, Louisville, KY [*Library symbol Library of Congress*] (LCLS)

KyLoS .... Southern Baptist Theological Seminary, Louisville, KY [*Library symbol Library of Congress*] (LCLS)

KyLoU .... University of Louisville, Louisville, KY [*Library symbol Library of Congress*] (LCLS)

KyLoU-Ar .... University of Louisville, University Archives and Records Center, Louisville, KY [*Library symbol Library of Congress*] (LCLS)

KyLoU-HS ... University of Louisville, Health Sciences Library, Louisville, KY [*Library symbol Library of Congress*] (LCLS)

KyLoU-L ..... University of Louisville, Law Library, Louisville, KY [*Library symbol*] [*Library of Congress*] (LCLS)

KyLoU-Mu.... University of Louisville, Dwight Anderson Music Library, Louisville, KY [*Library symbol*] [*Library of Congress*] (LCLS)

KyLoV .... United States Veterans Administration Hospital, Louisville, KY [*Library symbol Library of Congress*] (LCLS)

KYLR .... Huntsville, TX [*AM radio station call letters*]

KY LR .... Kentucky Law Reporter [*A publication*] (DLA)

KY L Rep..... Kentucky Law Reporter [*A publication*] (DLA)

KY L Rev .... Kentucky Law Review [*A publication*] (DLA)

KY L Rptr.... Kentucky Law Reporter [*A publication*] (DLA)

KYLS-AM ..... Fredericktown, MO [*AM radio station call letters*] (BROA)

KYLS-FM ..... Ironton, MO [*FM radio station call letters*] (BROA)

KYLT .... Missoula, MT [*AM radio station call letters*]

KyLx .... Lexington Public Library, Lexington, KY [*Library symbol Library of Congress*] (LCLS)

KyLxCB ...... Lexington Theological Seminary, Lexington, KY [*Library symbol Library of Congress*] (LCLS)

KyLxCS ...... Council of State Governments, State Information Center, Lexington, KY [*Library symbol Library of Congress*] (LCLS)

KyLxI .... IBM Corp., Office Products Division, Lexington, KY [*Library symbol Library of Congress*] (LCLS)

KyLxIMM..... Institute for Mining and Minerals Research, Lexington, KY [*Library symbol Library of Congress*] (LCLS)

KyLxK .... Keeneland Association, Inc., Lexington, KY [*Library symbol Library of Congress*] (LCLS)

KyLxT.......... Transylvania University, Lexington, KY [*Library symbol Library of Congress*] (LCLS)

KyLxTI .... Lexington Technical Institute, Lexington, KY [*Library symbol Library of Congress*] (LCLS)

KyLxV .... United States Veterans Administration Hospital, Lexington, KY [*Library symbol Library of Congress*] (LCLS)

KYLZ .... Santa Cruz, CA [*FM radio station call letters*]

KYMA.......... Yuma, AZ [*Television station call letters*]

KyMadC ..... Madisonville Community College, Media Center, Madisonville, KY [*Library symbol Library of Congress*] (LCLS)

KyMan .... Clay County Public Library, Manchester, KY [*Library symbol Library of Congress*] (LCLS)

KYMC.......... Ballwin, MO [*FM radio station call letters*]

KYMD .... Kentucky Medical Insurance Co. [*NASDAQ symbol*] (NQ)

KyMdC........ Midway Junior College and Pinkerton High School, Midway, KY [*Library symbol Library of Congress*] (LCLS)

KyMed .... Kentucky Medical Insurance Co. [*Associated Press*] (SAG)

KYMG .... Anchorage, AK [*FM radio station call letters*]

KYMI .... Los Ybanez, TX [*FM radio station call letters*]

KYMN .... Northfield, MN [*AM radio station call letters*]

KYMO .... East Prairie, MO [*AM radio station call letters*]

KYMO .... Kymograph (ABBR)

KYMO-FM..... East Prairie, MO [*FM radio station call letters*]

KyMoreU..... Morehead State University, Morehead, KY [*Library symbol Library of Congress*] (LCLS)

KYMS .... Keep Your Mouth Shut

KYMS.......... Santa Ana, CA [*FM radio station call letters*]

KyMurT....... Murray State University, Murray, KY [*Library symbol Library of Congress*] (LCLS)

KYMV .... Kennedya Yellow Mosaic Virus [*Plant pathology*]

KYMX .... Sacramento, CA [*FM radio station call letters*]

KyMyC .... Maysville Community College, Maysville, KY [*Library symbol*] [*Library of Congress*] (LCLS)

KYN .... Kynurenic Acid (DMAA)

KYN .... Kynurenine [*Biochemistry*]

KYN .... Kyrnair [*France ICAO designator*] (FAAC)

KyNaM........ Nazareth Mother House Archives, Nazareth, KY [*Library symbol Library of Congress*] (LCLS)

KYND .... Cypress, TX [*AM radio station call letters*]

KYNE .... Omaha, NE [*Television station call letters*]

KYNG .... Dallas, TX [*FM radio station call letters*]

KYNG .... Youngstown [*Ohio*] [*ICAO location identifier*] (ICLI)

KYNO .... Fresno, CA [*AM radio station call letters*]

KYNT .... Keynote (ABBR)

KYNT .... Yankton, SD [*AM radio station call letters*]

KYNTG .... Keynoting (ABBR)

KYNU .... Jamestown, ND [*FM radio station call letters*]

KYNZ .... Lone Grove, OK [*FM radio station call letters*]

KYO .... Kyocera Corp. [*NYSE symbol*] (SPSG)

KYO .... Kyocera Corp.ADR [*NYSE symbol*] (TTSB)

KYO .... Kyoto [*Japan*] [*Seismograph station code, US Geological Survey*] (SEIS)

Kyocer .... Kyocera Corp. [*Associated Press*] (SAG)

KYOD-FM..... Casper, WY [*FM radio station call letters*] (BROA)

KYOK .... Houston, TX [*FM radio station call letters*]

KYOO .... Bolivar, MO [*AM radio station call letters*]

KYOO-FM..... Halfway, MO [*FM radio station call letters*]

KY Op .... Kentucky Court of Appeals Opinions [*A publication*] (DLA)
KY Opin .... Kentucky Opinions [*A publication*] (DLA)
KYOS .... Merced, CA [*AM radio station call letters*]
KYOT-FM ..... Phoenix, AZ [*FM radio station call letters*]
Kyoto L Rev... Kyoto Law Review [*A publication*] (DLA)
KYOU .... Wendover, NV [*FM radio station call letters*]
KYOU-TV..... Ottumwa, IA [*Television station call letters*]
KyOw .... Owensboro-Daviess County Public Library, Owensboro, KY [*Library symbol Library of Congress*] (LCLS)
KyOwB .... Brescia College, Owensboro, KY [*Library symbol Library of Congress*] (LCLS)
KyOwC .... Owensboro Community College, Owensboro, KY [*Library symbol*] [*Library of Congress*] (LCLS)
KyOwK .... Kentucky Wesleyan College, Owensboro, KY [*Library symbol Library of Congress*] (LCLS)
KYP .... Kyaukpyu [*Myanmar*] [*Airport symbol*] (OAG)
KYPA-AM ..... Los Angeles, CA [*AM radio station call letters*] (RBYB)
KyPad .... Paducah Public Library, Paducah, KY [*Library symbol Library of Congress*] (LCLS)
KyPadC .... Paducah Community College, Paducah, KY [*Library symbol Library of Congress*] (LCLS)
KyParF .... John Fox, Jr. Memorial Library, Paris, KY [*Library symbol Library of Congress*] (LCLS)
kyph............ Kyphosis [*Orthopedics*] (DAVI)
KyPikC .... Pikeville College, Pikeville, KY [*Library symbol Library of Congress*] (LCLS)
KYPL-FM ..... Yakima, WA [*FM radio station call letters*] (RBYB)
KyPpA.......... Alice Lloyd College, Pippa Passes, KY [*Library symbol*] [*Library of Congress*] (LCLS)
KyPrbC........ Prestonburg Community College, Prestonsburg, KY [*Library symbol*] [*Library of Congress*] (LCLS)
KyPw25 .... Kentucky Power Co. [*Associated Press*] (SAG)
KYQQ .... Arkansas City, KS [*FM radio station call letters*]
KYQX .... Weatherford, TX [*FM radio station call letters*] (RBYB)
KY R .... Kentucky Reports [*A publication*] (DLA)
KYR .... Kyber Resources [*Vancouver Stock Exchange symbol*]
KyRE............ Eastern Kentucky University, Richmond, KY [*Library symbol Library of Congress*] (LCLS)
KY Rev Stat... Kentucky Revised Statutes [*A publication*] (DLA)
KY Rev Stat & Rules Serv... Kentucky Revised Statutes and Rules Service (Baldwin) [*A publication*] (DLA)
KY Rev Stat Ann... Baldwin's Kentucky Revised Statutes, Annotated [*A publication*] (DLA)
KYRK-FM ..... Eunice, NM [*FM radio station call letters*] (RBYB)
KYRM-FM ..... Yuma, AZ [*FM radio station call letters*] (BROA)
KYRO .... Potosi, MO [*AM radio station call letters*]
KYRS .... Atwater, NM [*FM radio station call letters*]
KYRV-FM ..... Concordia, MO [*FM radio station call letters*] (BROA)
KYRX .... Chaffee, MO [*FM radio station call letters*]
KYS .... Kayes [*Mali*] [*Airport symbol*] (OAG)
KYS .... Kentucky State University, Frankfort, KY [*OCLC symbol*] (OCLC)
KYS .... Keycorp Industries [*Vancouver Stock Exchange symbol*]
KYS .... Keys
KYS .... Kiyosumi - Telemeter [*Japan*] [*Seismograph station code, US Geological Survey*] (SEIS)
KY SBJ .... Kentucky State Bar Journal [*A publication*] (DLA)
KYSC .... Yakima, WA [*FM radio station call letters*]
KYSG .... Coos Bay, OR [*FM radio station call letters*] (RBYB)
Kyshe.......... Kyshe's Reports [*1808-90*] [*A publication*] (DLA)
KYSL........... Frisco, CO [*FM radio station call letters*]
KYSM .... Mankato, MN [*AM radio station call letters*]
KYSM-FM ..... Mankato, MN [*FM radio station call letters*]
KYSN .... East Wenatchee, WA [*FM radio station call letters*]
KySoC .... Somerset Community College, Somerset, KY [*Library symbol Library of Congress*] (LCLS)
Kysor .... Kysor Industrial Corp. [*Associated Press*] (SAG)
KYSR .... Los Angeles, CA [*FM radio station call letters*]
KYSS-FM ..... Missoula, MT [*FM radio station call letters*]
kyst............. Keystone (VRA)
KYST........... Texas City, TX [*AM radio station call letters*]
KY St BJ ...... Kentucky State Bar Journal [*A publication*] (DLA)
KY St Law ... Morehead and Brown. Digest of Kentucky Statute Laws [*A publication*] (DLA)
KYSTN .... Keystone (ABBR)
KYT............. Corporate High Yield Fd II [*NYSE symbol*] (TTSB)
KYT............. Corporate High Yield II [*NYSE symbol*] (SAG)
KYT............. Keystone Explorations [*Vancouver Stock Exchange symbol*]
KYT............. Kyauktaw [*Myanmar*] [*Airport symbol*] (OAG)
KYTC........... Northwood, IA [*FM radio station call letters*]
KYTE........... Newport, OR [*FM radio station call letters*]
KYTI-FM ...... Sheridan, WY [*FM radio station call letters*] (BROA)
KYTN .... Wrightsville, AR [*FM radio station call letters*]
KYTOON....... Kite Balloon [*Air Force*]
KyTrA.......... Abbey of Gethsemani, Trappist, KY [*Library symbol Library of Congress*] (LCLS)
KYTT........... Coos Bay, OR [*FM radio station call letters*]
KYTV .... Springfield, MO [*Television station call letters*]
KYTX........... Beeville, TX [*FM radio station call letters*]
kyu .... Kentucky [*MARC country of publication code Library of Congress*] (LCCP)
KYU .... Koyukuk [*Alaska*] [*Airport symbol*] (OAG)
KYU .... Koyukuk, AK [*Location identifier FAA*] (FAAL)
KyU .... University of Kentucky, Lexington, KY [*Library symbol Library of Congress*] (LCLS)

KyU-A .... University of Kentucky, Ashland Community College, Ashland, KY [*Library symbol Library of Congress*] (LCLS)
KyU-ASC ..... University of Kentucky, Agricultural Science Center, Lexington, KY [*Library symbol Library of Congress*] (LCLS)
KYUC .... Roland, OK [*FM radio station call letters*]
KyU-C .... University of Kentucky, Southeast Center, Cumberland, KY [*Library symbol Library of Congress*] (LCLS)
KyU-E .... University of Kentucky, Elizabethtown Community College, Elizabethtown, KY [*Library symbol Library of Congress*] (LCLS)
KyU-F .... University of Kentucky, Fort Knox Center, Fort Knox, KY [*Library symbol Library of Congress*] (LCLS)
KYUF .... Uvalde, TX [*FM radio station call letters*]
KyU-H .... University of Kentucky, Northwest Center, Henderson, KY [*Library symbol Library of Congress*] (LCLS)
KYUK .... Bethel, AK [*AM radio station call letters*]
KYUK-TV ..... Bethel, AK [*Television station call letters*]
KyU-L .... University of Kentucky, Law Library, Lexington, KY [*Library symbol Library of Congress*] (LCLS)
KyU-M .... University of Kentucky, Medical Center, Lexington, KY [*Library symbol Library of Congress*] (LCLS)
KYUM .... Yuma/Yuma Marine Corps Air Station, Yuma International [*Arizona*] [*ICAO location identifier*] (ICLI)
KyU-N .... University of Kentucky, Northern Center, Covington, KY [*Library symbol Library of Congress*] (LCLS)
KyU-P .... University of Kentucky, Prestonburg Community College, Prestonburg, KY [*Library symbol Library of Congress*] (LCLS)
KYUS .... Miles City, MT [*Television station call letters*]
KYUU .... Liberal, KS [*AM radio station call letters*]
KYV .... Kibris Turk Hava Yollari Ltd. [*Turkey*] [*FAA designator*] (FAAC)
KYVA .... Gallup, NM [*AM radio station call letters*]
KYVE........... Yakima, WA [*Television station call letters*]
KYW .... Philadelphia, PA [*AM radio station call letters*]
KyWA.......... Asbury College, Wilmore, KY [*Library symbol Library of Congress*] (LCLS)
KyWAT........ Asbury Theological Seminary, Wilmore, KY [*Library symbol Library of Congress*] (LCLS)
KyWavH....... Waverly Hills Tuberculosis Sanatorium, Waverly Hills, KY [*Library symbol Library of Congress*] (LCLS)
KY WC Dec... Kentucky Workmen's Compensation Board Decisions [*A publication*] (DLA)
KyWilC......... Cumberland College, Williamsburg, KY [*Library symbol Library of Congress*] (LCLS)
KyWn .... Clark County Public Library, Winchester, KY [*Library symbol Library of Congress*] (LCLS)
KyWnS......... Southeastern Christian College, Winchester, KY [*Library symbol Library of Congress*] (LCLS)
KYW-TV .... Philadelphia, PA [*Television station call letters*]
KYX .... Yalumet [*Papua New Guinea*] [*Airport symbol*] (OAG)
KYXE........... Selah, WA [*AM radio station call letters*]
KYXK .... Gurdon, AR [*FM radio station call letters*]
KYXS .... Mineral Wells, TX [*FM radio station call letters*]
KYXX .... Ozona, TX [*FM radio station call letters*]
KYXY .... San Diego, CA [*FM radio station call letters*]
KYYA .... Billings, MT [*FM radio station call letters*]
KYYD .... Abilene, TX [*AM radio station call letters*]
KYYI........... Burkburnett, TX [*FM radio station call letters*]
KYYK .... Palestine, TX [*FM radio station call letters*]
KYYS .... Kansas City, MO [*FM radio station call letters*]
KYYT .... Goldendale, WA [*FM radio station call letters*]
KYYX .... Minot, ND [*FM radio station call letters*]
KYYY .... Bismarck, ND [*FM radio station call letters*]
KYYZ .... Williston, ND [*FM radio station call letters*]
KYZ .... Kayseri [*Turkey*] [*Airport symbol*] (AD)
Kyzen.......... Kyzen Corp. [*Associated Press*] (SAG)
KYZN .... Kyzen Corp. [*NASDAQ symbol*] (SAG)
KYZN .... Kyzen Corp.'A' [*NASDAQ symbol*] (TTSB)
KYZNW........ Kyzen Corp.Wrrt'A' [*NASDAQ symbol*] (TTSB)
KYZS .... Tyler, TX [*AM radio station call letters*]
KYZX........... Pueblo, CO [*FM radio station call letters*]
KYZZ .... San Angelo, TX [*FM radio station call letters*]
KZ .... Dust/Sand Storm [*Meteorology*] (WDAA)
KZ .... Kaplan-Zuelzer [*Syndrome*] (DAVI)
KZ .... Kazakhstan [*Internet country code*]
KZ .... Ketoconazole (DMAA)
KZ .... Killing Zone [*Military British*]
KZ .... Kilohertz [*Preferred form is kHz*] [*Electronics*] (MCD)
KZ .... Konzentrationslager [*Concentration Camp*] [*Initials also used in medicine to indicate a psychiatric syndrome found in surviving victims of the World War II camps*] [*German*]
KZ .... Kuhns Zeitschrift fuer Vergleichende Sprachforschung [*A publication*] (BJA)
Kz .... Kwanza [*Monetary Unit*] [*Angola*] (BARN)
KZ .... Kysor Indl [*NYSE symbol*] (TTSB)
KZ .... Kysor Industrial Corp. [*NYSE symbol*] (SPSG)
KZ .... New Zealand [*IYRU nationality code*] (IYR)
KZ .... Oriens & King [*ICAO designator*] (AD)
KZA .... Kazakhstan Airlines [*ICAO designator*] (FAAC)
KZAB .... Albuquerque [*New Mexico*] [*ICAO location identifier*] (ICLI)
KZAC........... Esparto, CA [*FM radio station call letters*] (RBYB)
KZAK .... Incline Village, NV [*FM radio station call letters*]
KZAL .... Desert Center, CA [*FM radio station call letters*]
KZAM-FM .... Ganado, TX [*FM radio station call letters*] (RBYB)
KZAP .... Paradise, CA [*FM radio edition call letters*] (RBYB)
KZAR-TV ...... Provo, UT [*Television station call letters*] (RBYB)
KZAT........... Kommentar zum Alten Testament [*A publication*] (BJA)

KZAU .... Chicago, Aurora [*Illinois*] [*ICAO location identifier*] (ICLI)
KZAZ .... Bellingham, WA [*FM radio station call letters*]
KZB .... Zachar Bay [*Alaska*] [*Airport symbol*] (OAG)
KZB .... Zachar Bay, AK [*Location identifier FAA*] (FAAL)
KZBA .... Shafter, CA [*FM radio station call letters*]
KZBB .... Poteau, OK [*FM radio station call letters*]
KZBE .... Pleasant Hope, MO [*FM radio station call letters*] (RBYB)
KZBK .... Brookfield, MO [*AM radio station call letters*]
KZBK-FM .... Brookfield, MO [*FM radio station call letters*]
KZBL .... Natchitoches, LA [*FM radio station call letters*]
KZBN .... Santa Barbara, CA [*FM radio station call letters*] (RBYB)
KZBQ-FM .... Pocatello, ID [*FM radio station call letters*]
KZBR-FM .... Mountain Pine, AR [*FM radio station call letters*] (RBYB)
KZBW .... Boston, Nashua [*New Hampshire*] [*ICAO location identifier*] (ICLI)
KZBZ .... Salina, KS [*FM radio station call letters*]
KZCD .... Lawton, OK [*FM radio station call letters*]
KZCO-FM .... Oroville, CA [*FM radio station call letters*] (RBYB)
KZCR .... Fergus Falls, MN [*FM radio station call letters*]
KZDC .... San Antonio, TX [*AM radio station call letters*] (RBYB)
KZDC .... Washington, Leesburg [*Virginia*] [*ICAO location identifier*] (ICLI)
KZDG .... Greeley, CO [*FM radio station call letters*]
KZDV .... Denver, Longmont [*Colorado*] [*ICAO location identifier*] (ICLI)
KZDX .... Burley, ID [*FM radio station call letters*]
KZEE .... Weatherford, TX [*AM radio station call letters*]
KZEL .... Eugene, OR [*FM radio station call letters*]
KZEN .... Central City, NE [*FM radio station call letters*]
KZEP-FM .... San Antonio, TX [*FM radio station call letters*]
KZEY .... Tyler, TX [*AM radio station call letters*]
KZEY-FM .... Marshall, TX [*FM radio station call letters*]
KZEZ .... St. George, UT [*FM radio station call letters*]
KZF .... Kaintiba [*Papua New Guinea*] [*Airport symbol*] (OAG)
KZFM .... Corpus Christi, TX [*FM radio station call letters*]
KZFN .... Moscow, ID [*FM radio station call letters*]
KZFO .... Madera, CA [*FM radio station call letters*]
KZFR .... Chico, CA [*FM radio station call letters*]
KZFT .... Merced, CA [*FM radio station call letters*] (RBYB)
KZFW .... Fort Worth, Euless [*Texas*] [*ICAO location identifier*] (ICLI)
KZGL .... Cottonwood, AZ [*FM radio station call letters*]
KZGO .... Glenwood Springs, CO [*FM radio station call letters*] (RBYB)
KZGT .... Great Falls [*Montana*] [*ICAO location identifier*] (ICLI)
KZGZ .... Agana, GU [*FM radio station call letters*]
KZHE .... Stamps, AR [*FM radio station call letters*]
KZHK-FM .... St. George, UT [*FM radio station call letters*] (BROA)
KZHR .... Dayton, WA [*FM radio station call letters*]
KZHT .... Provo, UT [*FM radio station call letters*]
KZHU .... Houston, Humble [*Texas*] [*ICAO location identifier*] (ICLI)
KZI .... Kozani [*Greece*] [*Airport symbol*] (OAG)
KZIA .... Las Cruces, NM [*Television station call letters*]
KZID .... Indianapolis [*Indiana*] [*ICAO location identifier*] (ICLI)
KZIG .... Cave City, AR [*FM radio station call letters*]
KZII .... Lubbock, TX [*FM radio station call letters*]
KZIM .... Cape Girardeau, MO [*AM radio station call letters*]
KZIN .... Shelby, MT [*FM radio station call letters*]
KZIO .... Superior, WI [*FM radio station call letters*]
KZIP .... Amarillo, TX [*AM radio station call letters*]
KZIQ .... Ridgecrest, CA [*AM radio station call letters*]
KZIQ-FM .... Ridgecrest, CA [*FM radio station call letters*]
KZIZ .... Sumner, WA [*AM radio station call letters*]
KZJC .... Flagstaff, AZ [*Television station call letters*]
KZJG .... Longmont, CO [*Television station call letters*]
KZJH .... Jackson, WY [*FM radio station call letters*]
KZJL .... Houston, TX [*Television station call letters*]
KZJM-FM .... Rockport, TX [*FM radio station call letters*] (BROA)
KZJX .... Jacksonville Hillard [*Florida*] [*ICAO location identifier*] (ICLI)
KZKC .... Kansas City Olathe [*Kansas*] [*ICAO location identifier*] (ICLI)
KZKE .... Seligman, AZ [*FM radio station call letters*] (RBYB)
KZKI .... San Bernardino, CA [*Television station call letters*]
KZKK .... Huron, SD [*FM radio station call letters*]
KZKL .... Rio Rancho, NM [*FM radio station call letters*]
KZKS .... Rifle, CO [*FM radio station call letters*]
KZKX .... Seward, NE [*FM radio station call letters*]
KZKZ .... Greenwood, AR [*FM radio station call letters*]
KZLA .... Los Angeles, CA [*FM radio station call letters*]
KZLA .... Los Angeles Palmdale [*California*] [*ICAO location identifier*] (ICLI)
KZLC .... Salt Lake City [*Utah*] [*ICAO location identifier*] (ICLI)
KZLE .... Batesville, AR [*FM radio station call letters*]
KZLN .... Othello, WA [*FM radio station call letters*]
KZLO .... Bozeman, MT [*AM radio station call letters*]
KZLS .... Great Bend, KS [*FM radio station call letters*]
KZLT .... East Grand Forks, MN [*FM radio station call letters*]
KZLZ .... Keamy, AZ [*FM radio station call letters*]
KZMA .... Miami [*Florida*] [*ICAO location identifier*] (ICLI)
KZMA .... Poplar Bluff, MO [*FM radio station call letters*]
KZME .... Hudson, IA [*FM radio station call letters*]
KZME .... Memphis [*Tennessee*] [*ICAO location identifier*] (ICLI)
KZMG .... New Plymouth, ID [*FM radio station call letters*]
KZMI .... San Jose, MP [*FM radio station call letters*]
KZMK .... Sierra Vista, AZ [*FM radio station call letters*]
KZMM .... Troy, MO [*FM radio station call letters*]
KZMP .... Minneapolis, Farmington [*Minnesota*] [*ICAO location identifier*] (ICLI)
KZMQ .... Greybull, WY [*AM radio station call letters*]
KZMQ-FM .... Greybull, WY [*FM radio station call letters*]
KZMS .... Patterson, CA [*FM radio station call letters*]
KZMT .... Helena, MT [*FM radio station call letters*]
KZMU .... Moab, UT [*FM radio station call letters*]
KZMX .... Hot Springs, SD [*AM radio station call letters*]
KZMX-FM .... Hot Springs, SD [*FM radio station call letters*]
KZMZ .... Alexandria, LA [*FM radio station call letters*]
KZN .... Kazan [*Former USSR Airport symbol*] (OAG)
KZN .... Kozani [*Greece*] [*Seismograph station code, US Geological Survey*] (SEIS)
KZN .... KwaZulu Natal [*South Africa*]
KZN .... Zaimische [*Later, KNS*] [*Former USSR Geomagnetic observatory code*]
KZNA .... Hill City, KS [*FM radio station call letters*]
KZNC .... Huron, SD [*FM radio station call letters*]
KZNG .... Hot Springs, AR [*AM radio station call letters*]
KZNM .... Grants, NM [*FM radio station call letters*]
KZNN .... Rolla, MO [*FM radio station call letters*]
KZNO .... Nogales, AZ [*FM radio station call letters*] (RBYB)
KZNT-FM .... Cambridge, MN [*FM radio station call letters*] (BROA)
KZNX-FM .... Astoria, OR [*FM radio station call letters*] (BROA)
KZNY .... New York, Ronkonkoma [*New York*] [*ICAO location identifier*] (ICLI)
KZOA .... KZ Owners' Association [*Defunct*] (EA)
KZOA .... Oakland, Freemont [*California*] [*ICAO location identifier*] (ICLI)
KZOB .... Cleveland, Oberlin [*Ohio*] [*ICAO location identifier*] (ICLI)
KZOE .... Longview, WA [*FM radio station call letters*]
KZOK .... Seattle, WA [*FM radio station call letters*]
KZOL-FM .... Santa Cruz, CA [*FM radio station call letters*] (RBYB)
KZON .... Phoenix, AZ [*FM radio station call letters*]
KZOO .... Honolulu, HI [*AM radio station call letters*]
KZOQ .... Missoula, MT [*FM radio station call letters*]
KZOR .... Hobbs, NM [*FM radio station call letters*]
KZOT .... Marianna, AR [*AM radio station call letters*]
KZOZ .... San Luis Obispo, CA [*FM radio station call letters*]
KZP .... Kwartalnik dla Historji Zydow w Polsce [*A publication*] (BJA)
KZPA .... Fort Yukon, AK [*AM radio station call letters*]
KZPD .... Ash Grove, MO [*FM radio station call letters*]
KZPE .... Ford City, CA [*FM radio station call letters*]
KZPH .... Cashmere, WA [*FM radio station call letters*]
KZPI-FM .... Deming, NM [*FM radio station call letters*] (RBYB)
KZPK .... Paynesville, MN [*FM radio station call letters*]
KZPM .... Bakersfield, CA [*AM radio station call letters*]
KZPN .... Bayside, CA [*FM radio station call letters*]
KZPO .... Lindsay, CA [*FM radio station call letters*]
KZPR .... Minot, ND [*FM radio station call letters*]
KZPS .... Dallas, TX [*FM radio station call letters*]
KZPT-FM .... Tucson, AZ [*FM radio station call letters*] (BROA)
KZQD .... Liberal, KS [*FM radio station call letters*]
KZQZ-FM .... San Francisco, CA [*FM radio station call letters*] (BROA)
kzr .... Kazakh Soviet Socialist Republic [*MARC country of publication code Library of Congress*] (LCCP)
KZR .... Khuzdar [*Pakistan*] [*Airport symbol*] (AD)
KZRA .... Springdale, AR [*AM radio station call letters*]
KZRB .... New Boston, TX [*FM radio station call letters*]
KZRK .... Canyon, TX [*AM radio station call letters*] (RBYB)
KZRK-FM .... Canyon, TX [*FM radio station call letters*] (RBYB)
KZRO .... Dunsmuir, CA [*FM radio station call letters*]
KZRQ .... Santa Fe, NM [*FM radio station call letters*]
KZRR .... Albuquerque, NM [*FM radio station call letters*]
KZS .... Kutztown State College, Kutztown, PA [*OCLC symbol*] (OCLC)
KZSA .... Placerville, CA [*FM radio station call letters*]
KZSC .... Santa Cruz, CA [*FM radio station call letters*]
KZSD .... Martin, SD [*FM radio station call letters*]
KZSD-TV .... Martin, SD [*Television station call letters*]
KZSE .... Rochester, MN [*FM radio station call letters*]
KZSE .... Seattle, Auburn [*Washington*] [*ICAO location identifier*] (ICLI)
KZSF .... Alameda, CA [*FM radio station call letters*] (RBYB)
KZSJ .... San Martin, CA [*AM radio station call letters*] (RBYB)
KZSN .... Hutchinson, KS [*FM radio station call letters*]
KZSN .... Wichita, KS [*AM radio station call letters*]
KZSP .... South Padre Island, TX [*FM radio station call letters*]
KZSQ .... Sonora, CA [*FM radio station call letters*]
KZSR .... Reno, NV [*FM radio station call letters*]
KZSS .... Albuquerque, NM [*AM radio station call letters*]
KZST .... Santa Rosa, CA [*FM radio station call letters*]
KZSU .... Stanford, CA [*FM radio station call letters*]
KZTA .... Yakima, WA [*AM radio station call letters*]
KZTA-FM .... Yakima, WA [*FM radio station call letters*]
KZTB-FM .... Sunnyside, WA [*FM radio station call letters*] (RBYB)
KZTL .... Atlanta, Hampton [*Georgia*] [*ICAO location identifier*] (ICLI)
KZTO .... Ottawa, KS [*FM radio station call letters*]
KZTQ .... Laredo, TX [*FM radio station call letters*]
KZTS-AM .... Tacoma, WA [*AM radio station call letters*] (BROA)
KZTU .... Eugene, OR [*AM radio station call letters*] (RBYB)
KZTU-AM .... Eugene, OR [*AM radio station call letters*] (RBYB)
KZTV .... Corpus Christi, TX [*Television station call letters*]
KZTW .... Fairview, OR [*AM radio station call letters*] (RBYB)
KZTX .... Refugio, TX [*FM radio station call letters*]
KZTY .... Winchester, NV [*AM radio station call letters*]
KZUA .... Holbrook, AZ [*FM radio station call letters*]
KZUB .... Tahoka, TX [*FM radio station call letters*]
KZUE .... El Reno, OK [*FM radio station call letters*]
KZUL .... Lake Havasu City, AZ [*FM radio station call letters*]
KZUM .... Lincoln, NE [*FM radio station call letters*]
KZUN .... Zuni Pueblo/Blackrock [*New Mexico*] [*ICAO location identifier*] (ICLI)
KZUS .... Toledo, OR [*AM radio station call letters*]
KZUS-FM .... Toledo, OR [*FM radio station call letters*]
KZUU .... Pullman, WA [*FM radio station call letters*]
KZV .... Kartell Zionistischer Verbindungen (BJA)

KZWA........... Lake Charles, LA [*FM radio station call letters*]
KZWC.......... Walnut Creek, CA [*FM radio station call letters*]
KZWY-FM .... Sheridan, WY [*FM radio station call letters*] (BROA)
KZXA........... Santa Fe, NM [*FM radio station call letters*]
KZXB........... Homer, LA [*FM radio station call letters*]
KZXC........... Anchorage, AK [*Television station call letters*]
KZXR .... Prosser, WA [*FM radio station call letters*]
KZXX........... Kenai, AK [*AM radio station call letters*]
KZXY-FM ..... Apple Valley, CA [*FM radio station call letters*]
KZYP........... Pine Bluff, AR [*FM radio station call letters*]
KZYR .... Avon, CO [*FM radio station call letters*]
KZYX........... Philo, CA [*FM radio station call letters*]
KZYZ........... Willits, CA [*FM radio station call letters*] (RBYB)
KZZB........... Beaumont, TX [*AM radio station call letters*]
KZZC-FM...... Tipton, CA [*FM radio station call letters*] (RBYB)

KZZE........... Eagle Point, OR [*FM radio station call letters*] (RBYB)
KZZF-FM...... South Lake Tahoe, CA [*FM radio station call letters*] (RBYB)
KZZI .... Belle Fourche, SD [*FM radio station call letters*] (RBYB)
KZZJ .... Rugby, ND [*AM radio station call letters*] (RBYB)
KZZK-FM...... New London, MO [*FM radio station call letters*] (RBYB)
KZZL .... Pullman, WA [*FM radio station call letters*]
KZZN........... Littlefield, TX [*AM radio station call letters*]
KZZO-FM ..... Sacramento, CA [*FM radio station call letters*] (BROA)
KZZP........... Winner, SD [*FM radio station call letters*] (RBYB)
KZZQ........... Winterset, IA [*FM radio station call letters*] (RBYB)
KZZR........... Burns, OR [*AM radio station call letters*]
KZZT........... Moberly, MO [*FM radio station call letters*]
KZZU........... Spokane, WA [*FM radio station call letters*]
KZZX........... Alamogordo, NM [*FM radio station call letters*]
KZZY........... Devils Lake, ND [*FM radio station call letters*]
KZZZ........... Kingman, AZ [*FM radio station call letters*]

L
By Acronym

L .... Angle
L .... Angular Momentum [*Symbol*] [*IUPAC*]
I----- .... Atlantic Ocean [*MARC geographic area code Library of Congress*] (LCCP)
L .... Avogadro Constant [*Symbol*] [*IUPAC*]
I .... Azimuthal Quantum Number [*or Orbital Angular Momentum Quantum Number*] [*Symbol*]
L .... Azimuthal Quantum Number [*or Orbital Angular Momentum Quantum Number*] - Total [*Symbol*]
L .... Coefficient of Physics [*Physics*]   (DAVI)
L .... Concerts and Recitals of Serious Music (Permits) [*Public-performance tariff class*] [*British*]
L .... Countermeasures [*JETDS nomenclature*]
L .... Days before Launch [*Usually followed by a number*] [*NASA*]   (KSC)
L .... Difference of Latitude [*Navigation*]
L .... Drizzle [*Meteorology*]
L .... Electrical [*in British naval officers' ranks*]
L .... Electromagnet Radiance [*Astronomy*]   (BARN)
L .... Element
L .... Elevated [*Railway*] [*Also, EL*]
L .... Equipped with Search Light [*Suffix to plane designation*] [*Navy*]
L .... Fifty [*Roman numeral*]
L .... Finland [*IYRU nationality code*]   (IYR)
L .... Glider Aircraft [*When first letter in Navy aircraft designation*]
L .... Inductance [*Symbol*]   (AAG)
L .... Kinetic Potential [*Symbol*]
L .... Labaz [*Belgium, France*] [*Research code symbol*]
L .... Label   (MDG)
L .... Labetalol [*Pharmacology*]
L .... Labor
L .... Laboratory
L .... Laboratory Attendant [*Ranking title*] [*British Royal Navy*]
L .... Lactobacillus
L .... Ladestreifen [*Ammunition Clip*] [*German military - World War II*]
L .... Ladinian [*Geology*]
L .... Lady [*or Ladyship*]
L .... Lagrangian Function
L .... Lake [*Maps and charts*]
L .... Lambda   (WDAA)
L .... Lambert [*Unit of luminance*] [*Preferred unit is lx, Lux*]
L .... Lameness [*Used by immigration officials*] [*Obsolete*]
L .... Laminated
L .... Lamp
L .... Lancashire Flats [*British*]   (DCTA)
L .... Lancers
L .... Land
L .... Landing
L .... Landplane
L .... Land Transportation [*FCC*]   (NTCM)
L .... Landulfus Acconzaioco [*Flourished, 13th century*] [*Authority cited in pre-1607 legal work*]   (DSA)
L .... Lane
L .... Langmuir [*Unit of measure*]
L .... Language
L .... Lansing's New York Supreme Court Reports [*A publication*]   (DLA)
L .... Lansing's Select Cases in Chancery [*1824, 1826*] [*New York*] [*A publication*]   (DLA)
L .... Lanthanum [*Chemical element; symbol is La*]
L .... Larceny [*FBI standardized term*]
L .... Large [*Size designation for clothing, etc.*]
I .... Large   (WDMC)
L .... Larva [*Biology*]
L .... Laser
L .... L-Asparaginase [*Also, A, L-ase, L-asnase, L-Asp*] [*An enzyme, an antineoplastic*]
L .... Lat [*Monetary unit*] [*Latvia*]
L .... Latching [*Electronics*]
L .... Late
L .... Late   (WDMC)
L .... Latent Heat
L .... Lateral   (IAA)
L .... Latex   (DMAA)
L .... Latin
L .... Latitude
L .... Laudatur [*Latin*]
L .... Launch [*or Launcher*]

L .... Laurentius Hispanus [*Deceased, 1248*] [*Authority cited in pre-1607 legal work*]   (DSA)
L .... Lavender [*Botany*]
L .... Law
L .... Lawson's Notes of Decisions, Registration [*A publication*]   (DLA)
L .... Layer [*Officer's rating*] [*British Royal Navy*]
L .... ™Lay∫ Source   (BJA)
L .... Leader   (ADA)
L .... Leader Sequence   (DMAA)
L .... Lead Sheath   (AAG)
L .... Leaf [*Bibliography*] [*Botany*]
L .... Leaflet
L .... League
L .... Learner
L .... Learning [*Denotes learning drivers before they receive their automobile driving licenses*] [*British*]
L .... Leasehold   (ROG)
L .... Leather
L .... Leave
L .... Lederle Laboratories [*Research code symbol*]
L .... Leeward
L .... Left [*Direction*]
L .... Left [*Politics*]
I .... Left   (WDMC)
L .... Left Eye [*Opthalmology*]   (DAVI)
L .... Left Hand [*Music*]   (ROG)
L .... Legal Division [*Coast Guard*]
L .... Leges [*Laws*] [*Latin*]   (ROG)
L .... Legge [*Law, Act, Statute*] [*Italian*]   (ILCA)
L .... Legionella [*A bacteria*]   (DAVI)
L .... Legitimate
L .... Leishmania [*Microbiology*]   (MAE)
L .... Lek [*Monetary unit*] [*Albania*]   (BARN)
L .... Lempira [*Monetary unit*] [*Honduras*]
L .... Lenad Subgroup [*Leucite, nephelite, halite, thenardite*] [*CIPW classification Geology*]
L .... Length [*or Lengthwise*]
I .... Length [*Symbol*] [*IUPAC*]
L .... Lens
L .... Lente Insulin [*Pharmacology*]   (DAVI)
L .... Leo   (WDAA)
L .... Lepetit [*Italy*] [*Research code symbol*]
L .... Lepidocrocite [*A mineral*]
L .... Leptospira [*A bacteria*]   (DAVI)
L .... Leptotrichia [*A bacteria*]   (DAVI)
L .... Lesser   (DAVI)
L .... Lethal
L .... Letter
L .... Leu [*Monetary unit*] [*Romania*]
L .... Leucine [*One-letter symbol; see Leu*] [*An amino acid*]
L .... Leuconostoc [*An algae*] [*Biochemistry*]   (DAVI)
L .... Lev [*Monetary unit*] [*Bulgaria*]
L .... Level   (KSC)
L .... Lever
L .... Levo [*or Laevo*] [*Configuration in chemical structure*]
I .... Levorotary [*or Levorotatory*] [*Chemistry*]
L .... Levorotatory [*Optics*] [*Chemistry*]   (DOG)
L .... Lewisite [*War gas*] [*Army symbol*]
L .... Lexical Rule [*Linguistics*]
L .... Liaison [*Airplane designation*]
L .... Liber [*Book*] [*Latin*]
L .... Liberal [*Politics*]
L .... Liberty Financial Companies, Inc. [*NYSE symbol*]   (SAG)
L .... Liberty Financial Cos. [*NYSE symbol*]   (TTSB)
L .... Libra [*Pound*]
L .... Library
L .... Libration [*Space exploration*]
L .... Licenciatus [*Academic Qualification*] [*Latin*]
L .... License
L .... Licensed to Practice [*Medicine*]
L .... Licentiate
L .... Lidocaine [*Topical anesthetic*]
L .... Lidoflazine [*A vasodilator*]
L .... Lies [*Read*] [*German*]
L .... Lieutenant [*Navy British*]
L .... Life [*Insurance*]

L .... Lifestyle [*Wire service code*] (NTCM)
L .... Lift
L .... Ligament [*or Ligamentum*]
L .... Ligand [*Chemistry*]
L .... Light [*Chain*] [*Biochemistry, immunochemistry*]
L .... Lighting [*As part of a code*]
L .... Lightning [*Meteorology*]
L .... Light Sense
L .... Lignite (WDAA)
L .... Lilac
L .... Lilangeni [*Monetary unit*] [*Swaziland*] (BARN)
L .... Lima [*Phonetic alphabet*] [*International*] (DSUE)
L .... Lime
L .... Limen or Threshold [*Psychology*]
L .... Limes [*Boundary*] [*Pharmacology*] (DAVI)
L .... Limestone [*Petrology*]
L .... Limit
L .... Limited (DLA)
L .... Lincomycin (STED)
L .... Line
l .... Line (WDMC)
L .... Line Assembly (AAG)
L .... Linen [*Deltiology*]
L .... Line (of Print) [*Publishing*] (NTCM)
L .... Liner [*Nautical*]
L .... Lines Dose [*Medicine*]
L .... Lingual [*Dentistry*]
L .... Link
L .... Linnaean
L .... Lip
L .... Lipoid [*Biochemistry*]
(l) .... Liquid [*Chemistry*]
L .... Liquidity [*Business term*]
L .... Liquor (STED)
L .... Liquor (DAVI)
L .... Lira [*Monetary unit*] [*Italy*]
L .... List (MSA)
L .... Listed [*Stock exchange term*]
L .... Listening Post [*In symbol only*]
L .... Listeria [*A bacteria*] (DAVI)
L .... Lit
L .... Litas [*Monetary unit*] [*Lithuania*]
L .... Liter [*Also, l*] [*Metric measure of volume*]
l .... Liter
L .... Literate
L .... Lithium [*Chemical element*] (ROG)
L .... Little
L .... Live [*Wiring code*] [*British*]
L .... Liver (MAE)
L .... Liverpool [*Postcode*] (ODBW)
L .... Living (DAVI)
L .... Living Room (ROG)
L .... Livre [*Monetary unit*] [*Obsolete French*]
L .... Load (MDG)
L .... Loam [*Agronomy*]
L .... Lobe [*Of a leaf*] [*Botany*]
L .... Loblaw Companies Ltd. [*Toronto Stock Exchange symbol Vancouver Stock Exchange symbol*]
L .... Loblaw Cos. [*TS, exchange symbol*] (TTSB)
l .... Local (WDMC)
l .... Local [*Broadcasting program*] (NTCM)
l .... Locative (Case) [*Linguistics*]
L .... Locator [*Compass*]
L .... Locator Beacon
L .... Loch
L .... Lockheed Aircraft Corp. [*ICAO aircraft manufacturer identifier*] (ICAO)
L .... Locking [*Lamp base type*] (NTCM)
L .... Locus [*Place*] [*Latin*]
L .... Lodge
L .... Logarithm [*Mathematics*]
L .... London [*England*]
L .... London [*Phonetic alphabet*] [*Royal Navy World War I Pre-World War II*] (DSUE)
L .... Long
L .... Longacre [*James B.*] [*Designer's mark, when appearing on US coins*]
L .... Longitude
L .... Long, Rolling Sea [*Meteorology*]
L .... Loop [*Fingerprint description*]
L .... Looper [*Computer science*] (MDG)
L .... LORAN [*Long-Range Navigation*] (IAA)
L .... Lorazepam [*A tranquilizer*]
L .... Lord [*or Lordship*]
L .... Lorentz Unit [*Electronics*]
L .... loss (WDAA)
L .... Lost [*RADAR*]
L .... Lost [*Sports statistics*]
L .... Loti [*Monetary unit*] [*Lesotho*] (BARN)
L .... Lough [*Maps and charts*]
L .... Louisiana Reports [*A publication*] (DLA)
L .... Louisiana State Library, Baton Rouge, LA [*Library symbol Library of Congress*] (LCLS)
L .... Louisville [*Diocesan abbreviation*] [*Kentucky*] (TOCD)
L .... Love [*Phonetic alphabet*] [*World War II*] (DSUE)
L .... Low [*or Lower*]

L .... Low (IDOE)
L .... Lower Bow [*Music*] (ROG)
l .... Lower Limit of a Class Interval [*Psychology*]
L .... Low Season [*Airline fare code*]
L .... Loyalty
L .... Lues [*or Syphilis*] [*Medicine*] (DAVI)
L .... Luitingh [*Holland*]
L .... Lumbar [*Medicine*]
L .... Lumen [*Unit of luminous flux*]
L .... Lumen [*Anatomy*] (DAVI)
L .... Lumen (IDOE)
L .... Luminance (DMAA)
L .... Lunch (CDAI)
L .... Lung [*Anatomy*] (DAVI)
L .... Luteolin [*Botany*]
L .... Luxembourg
L .... Luxury [*In automobile model name "Cordia L"*]
L .... Lymph (STED)
L .... Lymph [*A fluid*] [*Biochemistry*] (DAVI)
L .... Lymphocyte [*Biochemistry*] (DAVI)
L .... Lymphocyte (STED)
L .... Lymphogranuloma [*Pathology*] (DAVI)
L .... Lysosome [*Biochemistry*] (DAVI)
l .... Lyxose [*As substituent on nucleoside*] [*Biochemistry*]
l .... Mean Free Path [*Symbol*] [*IUPAC*]
L .... Merck & Co., Inc. [*Research code symbol*]
L .... Promotional Fare [*Also, K, Q, V*] [*Airline fare code*]
L .... Quinquaginta [*Fifty*] [*Latin*]
L .... Radiance [*Symbol*] [*IUPAC*]
L .... Requires Fuel and Oil [*Search and rescue symbol that can be stamped in sand or snow*]
L .... Sandoz Pharmaceuticals [*Research code symbol*]
L .... San Francisco [*Branch in the Federal Reserve regional banking system*] (BARN)
L .... Searchlight Control [*JETDS nomenclature*]
L .... Self-Inductance [*Symbol*] [*IUPAC*]
L .... Shape Descriptor [*Dining el, for example. The shape resembles the letter for which it is named*]
L .... Silo Launched [*Missile launch environment symbol*]
L .... Single Acetate (AAG)
L .... Timber [*Lumber*] [*Vessel load line mark*]
L .... Time of Launch [*NASA*]
L1 .... First Language (ADA)
L₁ .... First Lumbar Nerve [*Second lumbar nerve is L₂, etc., through L₅*] [*Medicine*] (DAVI)
L₁ .... First Lumbar Vertebra [*Second lumbar vertebra is L₂, etc., through L5*] [*Medicine*]
L1TC .... Level 1 Trauma Center [*Medicine*] (DMAA)
LO2 .... Liquid Oxygen (NAKS)
L/3 .... Lower Third [*Referring to long bones*] [*Orthopedics*] (DAVI)
L3S .... LNG [*Liquefied Natural Gas*] Seabed Supported System
L4 .... Automatic Lockup Four Speed [*DOE*] (TAG)
L5 .... Long Quinto [*Pt. 10 of Year Books*] [*A publication*] (DSA)
L-5HTP .... L-5-Hydroxytryptophan [*Pharmacology*] (DAVI)
L6 .... Laboratories Low-Level Linked List Language [*Bell Systems*] (DIT)
L-10-W .... Levulose (10 Percent) in Water
L123UA .... Lotus 1-2-3 Users' Association
LA .... Concerts and Recitals of Serious Music (Annual Licence) [*Public-performance tariff class*] [*British*]
LA .... Fighter [*Russian aircraft symbol*]
LA .... Hoffmann-La Roche, Inc. [*Research code symbol*]
La .... [*The*] Holy Bible from Ancient Eastern Manuscripts [*G. M. Lamsa*] [*A publication*] (BJA)
LA .... Lab. Aron [*France*] [*Research code symbol*]
La .... Labial [*Dentistry*]
LA .... Labor Arbitration Reports [*A publication*] (DLA)
LA .... Labor Area
La .... Laches [*of Plato*] [*Classical studies*] (OCD)
La .... Lactalbumin [*Biochemistry*]
LA .... Lactic Acid [*Biochemistry*]
LA .... Lag Amplifier
LA .... Lag Angle (IAA)
LA .... LA Gear, Inc. [*NYSE symbol*] (CTT)
La .... Lagulanda (BJA)
LA .... Laira [*Plymouth*] [*British depot code*]
La .... Lake Aircraft [*ICAO aircraft manufacturer identifier*] (ICAO)
LA .... Lama Foundation (EA)
LA .... Lambda Alpha
La .... Lambert [*Unit of luminance*] [*Preferred unit is lx, Lux*] (ADA)
La .... Lamellar Phase [*Physical chemistry*]
LA .... Lamentations [*Old Testament book*] (BJA)
LA .... Lancaster [*Postcode*] (ODBW)
LA .... Lancastrian [*Of the royal house of Lancaster*] [*British*] (ROG)
LA .... Lan Chile [*Airline flight code*] (ODBW)
LA .... Land Agent [*Ministry of Agriculture, Fisheries, and Food*] [*British*]
L/A .... Landing Account [*Shipping*]
La .... Landulfus Acconzaioco [*Flourished, 13th century*] [*Authority cited in pre-1607 legal work*] (DSA)
LA .... Lane
La .... Lane's English Exchequer Reports [*1605-12*] [*A publication*] (DLA)
La .... Lanfrancus [*Deceased, 1089*] [*Authority cited in pre-1607 legal work*] (DSA)
La .... Lanfrancus Cremensis [*Deceased, 1229*] [*Authority cited in pre-1607 legal work*] (DSA)
LA .... Language [*Online database field identifier*]

LA	Language Age [Score]
LA	Language Arts [A publication] (BRI)
La	Lanthanum [Chemical element]
LA	Lanthanum (NAKS)
LA	Laos [or Lao People's Democratic Republic] [ANSI two-letter standard code] (CNC)
La	Lapus de Castiglionchio [Flourished, 1353-81] [Authority cited in pre-1607 legal work] (DSA)
La	Lapus Tatti [Flourished, 14th century] [Authority cited in pre-1607 legal work] (DSA)
LA	Lard Association (BUAC)
LA	Large Amount [Medicine]
LA	Large Aperture [Photography] (ROG)
LA	LASER Altimeter [NASA]
LA	LASER Angioplasty [Cardiology] (DMAA)
LA	LASER [Gyro] Axis (IEEE)
LA	Last [Wool weight]
la	Late (VRA)
LA	Late Abortion [Medicine] (DMAA)
LA	Late Antigen [Biochemistry] (DAVI)
LA	Latex Agglutination [Test] [Clinical chemistry]
LA	Lathe [Division in the county of Kent] [British]
LA	Latin America
LA	Launch Abort [NASA] (KSC)
LA	Launch Aft
LA	Launch Analyst [Aerospace] (AAG)
LA	Launch Area [NASA] (KSC)
LA	Launch Azimuth [NASA] (KSC)
LA	Laureate in Arts
La	Laurentius Hispanus [Deceased, 1248] [Authority cited in pre-1607 legal work] (DSA)
LA	Lava [Maps and charts]
LA	Lavatory (DSUE)
LA	Lavochkin [USSR aircraft type] [World War II]
LA	Law Agent
LA	Lawyers' Reports, Annotated [A publication] (DLA)
LA	Lead Adapter [Electric equipment]
LA	Lead Agent (COE)
LA	Lead Amplifier
LA	Lead Angle (MSA)
LA	Leading Aircraftsman [RAF] [British]
LA	Leading Article (ROG)
LA	Leaf Abscission [Botany]
LA	Learning Activity (ADA)
LA	Leasehold Area (ADA)
L/A	Leave Address (DNAB)
L/A	Leave Advance [Military]
LA	Lebanese Army (BUAC)
LA	Lebensalter [Chronological Age] [Psychology]
LA	Ledger Account (ROG)
LA	Ledger Asset
LA	Left Angle
LA	Left Angulation [Orthopedics] (DAVI)
LA	Left Arm [Medicine]
LA	Left Ascension
LA	Left Atrial [or Avricular] Appendage [Cardiology] (DAVI)
LA	Left Atrium [Anatomy]
LA	Left Auricle [Anatomy]
LA	Left Axilla (KSC)
LA	Legal Adviser
LA	Legal Asset [Business term]
LA	Lege Artis [According to the Art] [Pharmacy]
LA	Legislative Affairs
LA	Legislative Assembly
LA	Legislative Assistant [US Congress]
LA	Legitimate Access [British police term]
LA	Legum Allegoriae [Philo] (BJA)
LA	LeMans America (EA)
LA	Lemko Association [Poland] (BUAC)
LA	Lemko Association of US and Canada (EA)
LA	Lesbian Activities (WDAA)
LA	Leschetizky Association (EA)
LA	Lethal Area [Of indirect-fire weapon systems] [Military]
LA	Letter of Activation [Military]
L/A	Letter of Authority (EBF)
LA	Letters Abroad (EA)
L/A	Lettre d'Avis [Letter of Advice] [French]
LA	Leucine Aminopeptidase [Also, LP, LPAP] [An enzyme]
LA	Leukemia Antigen [Immunochemistry] (DAVI)
LA	Leukoagglutinating [Immunochemistry]
LA	Leukogglutination (DMAA)
LA	Leuprolide Acetate (DMAA)
LA	Levator Ani [Anatomy]
LA	Level Absolute (SSD)
LA	Level Alarm [Engineering]
LA	Level Amplifier (IAA)
LA	Levulinic Acid [Organic chemistry]
LA	Liberal Arts
LA	Liberator Atlanta [An association] (EA)
LA	Libertarian Alliance [British] (EAIO)
LA	Library Association [British] (NITA)
LA	Library Automation
LA	Library of Art [A publication]
LA	Licensing Act (DLA)
LA	Licensing Assistant (NRCH)
LA	Licensing Authority (DCTA)
LA	Licentiate in Arts
LA	Lichen Amyloidosis [Dermatology] (DAVI)
LA	Lieutenant-at-Arms [British]
LA	Light Ale (ADA)
LA	Light Alloy
LA	Light Armor [Telecommunications] (TEL)
LA	Light Artillery
LA	Lighter Association (EA)
LA	Lighter-than-Air [Aircraft]
LA	Lightning Arrester
LA	Lightwood-Albright [Syndrome] (STED)
LA	Lightwood-Albright [Syndrome] [Nephrology] (DAVI)
LA	Limited Area
LA	Linea Aerea Nacional de Chile [Chilean airline] [ICAO designator] (OAG)
LA	Line Adapter [Computer science] (CMD)
LA	Line Adaptor (NITA)
LA	Linear Arithmetic [Computer science]
LA	Linear Assembly
LA	Linguoaxial [Dentistry]
LA	Link Address (IAA)
LA	Link Allotter
LA	Link Analysis
LA	Linnaean Society
LA	Linoleic Acid (AAMN)
LA	Liquid Asset [Business term]
LA	Listed Address [Telecommunications] (TEL)
LA	Listing Agent [Classified advertising] (ADA)
la	Listing Agent [Real estate] (REAL)
LA	Literate in Arts
LA	Live Action (NTCM)
LA	Liverpool Academy [British]
LA	Living Allowance
L/A	Lloyd's Agent
LA	Load Address (IAA)
LA	Load Adjuster (CET)
LA	Load Allocation [Environmental science] (FFDE)
LA	Loan Amount [Dialog] [Searchable field] [Information service or system] (NITA)
LA	Lobuloalveolar [Medicine] (DAVI)
LA	Local Address
LA	Local Agent
LA	Local Alarm (NRCH)
LA	Local Anesthetic [Medicine]
LA	Local Authority
LA	Lock Actuator (MCD)
LA	Locus Allowed (ROG)
LA	Lodging Allowance [British military] (DMA)
LA	Log Analyzer Processor [Computer science]
LA	Logarithmic Amplifier
LA	Logical Address
LA	Loners of America [An association] (EA)
LA	Long-Acting [Pharmacy]
LA	Long-Arm [Cast] [Orthopedics] (DAVI)
LA	Longitudinal Acoustic [Spectroscopy]
LA	Look Ahead (IAA)
LA	Loop Antenna (DEN)
LA	Lord Advocate of Scotland (DLA)
LA	Los Alamos Scientific Laboratory [USAEC] (MCD)
LA	Los Angeles [California] [Slang]
LA	Louisiana [Postal code] (AFM)
LA	Louisiana & Arkansas Railway Co. [AAR code]
LA	Louisiana Reports [A publication] (DLA)
LA	Louisiana Supreme Court Reports [A publication] (DLA)
LA	Low Alcohol [Trademark of Anheuser-Busch, Inc.]
LA	Low Altitude
LA	Low Angle [RADAR] (DEN)
LA	Low Anxiety (MAE)
LA	Lower Arm
LA	Ludwig's Angina [Medicine] (DAVI)
LA	Luscombe Association (EA)
LA	Lymphadenopathy [Medicine]
La	Old Latin Version (BJA)
LAA	Amphibious Assault Ship [Military]
LAA	Jamahiriya Libyan Arab Airlines [ICAO designator] (FAAC)
LAA	Lamar [Colorado] [Airport symbol] (OAG)
LAA	Lamar, CO [Location identifier FAA] (FAAL)
LAA	Laser Association of America [Later, LEMA] (EA)
LAA	LASER Attenuator Assembly
LAA	Lateral Accelerometer Assembly (MCD)
LAA	Latex Advisors Association (NTPA)
LAA	Latin American Association (BUAC)
LAA	Launch Area Antenna (MCD)
LAA	Laundrette Association of Australia
LAA	League of Advertising Agencies [New York, NY] (EA)
LAA	Leather Apparel Association (EA)
LAA	Left Atrial Abnormality [Medicine] (STED)
LAA	Left Atrial Appendage [Medicine] (STED)
LAA	Left Auricular Appendage [Medicine] (STED)
LAA	Leukemia-Associated Antigen [Medicine] (STED)
LAA	Leukemia-Associated Antigen [Immunochemistry] (DAVI)
LAA	Leukocyte Ascorbic Acid [Clinical chemistry] (AAMN)
LAA	Library Association of Alberta [Canada] (BUAC)
LAA	Library Association of Australia (BUAC)

LAA............. Libyan Arab Airlines (BUAC)
LAA............. Lieutenant-at-Arms [*British*] (DMA)
LAA............. Life Insurance Advertisers Association [*Later, LCA*] (EA)
LAA............. Light Antiaircraft [*Guns*]
LAA............. Light Army Aircraft
LAA............. Lighterage Assembly Area
LAA............. Limited Access Authorization [*Military*] (GFGA)
LAA............. Lipizzan Association of America (EA)
LAA............. Lithuanian Agriculture Academy (BUAC)
LAA............. Lithuanian Alliance of America (EA)
LAA............. Little America [*Antarctica*] [*Seismograph station code, US Geological Survey Closed*] (SEIS)
LAA............. Little Athletics Association [*Australia*]
LAA............. Live Assembly Area (MCD)
LAA............. Liverpool Academy of Arts [*England*]
LAA............. Local Airport Advisory [*Aviation*] (FAAC)
LAA............. Locally Administered Address [*Computer science*] (CIST)
LAA............. Los Angeles Airways, Inc.
LA A............. Louisiana Annual Reports [*A publication*] (DLA)
LA A............. Louisiana Courts of Appeal Reports [*A publication*] (DLA)
LAA............. Low-Altitude Attack
LAAA............ Latin American Association of Archives [*See also ALA*] (EAIO)
LAAAAS...... Latin American Association for Afro-Asian Studies [*Mexico*] (EAIO)
LAAAS .... Low-Altitude Airfield Attack System (MCD)
LAAB........... Landscape Architectural Accreditation Board (GAGS)
LAAB........... Light Armored Assault Battalion [*Marine Corps*]
LAABAM ..... Latin American Association of Behavior Analysis and Modification [*Uruguay*] (EAIO)
LAABF......... Ladies' Auxiliary of the American Beekeeping Federation (EA)
LAAC........... Library Association's Annual Conference [*British*]
LAAC........... Lord Chancellor's Legal Aid Advisory Committee [*British*] (DLA)
LAACC........ Light Antiaircraft Control Center (NATG)
LAACT......... Legislative Assembly of the Australian Capital Territory
LA Acts....... State of Louisiana: Acts of the Legislature [*A publication*] (DLA)
LAAD .... Latin American Agribusiness Development Corp.
LAAD .... Los Angeles Aircraft Division [*Rockwell International*]
LAADBN...... Low Altitude Air Defense Battalion [*Navy*] (ANA)
LAADIW ..... Latin American Association for the Development and Integration of Women [*See also ALADIM*] [*Chile*] (EAIO)
LA Admin Code... Louisiana Administrative Code [*A publication*] (DLA)
LA Admin Reg... Louisiana Administrative Register [*A publication*] (DLA)
LAADS .... Los Angeles Air Defense Sector [*ADC*]
LAADS .... Low-Altitude Air Defense [*or Delivery*] System
LAADS .... Low-Altitude Air Dropped Stores (MCD)
LAAEMCTS... Latin American Association of Environmental Mutagens, Carcinogens, and Teratogens Societies [*Mexico*] (EAIO)
LAAF........... Lawson Army Airfield [*Fort Benning, GA*] (MCD)
LAAF........... Libby Army Airfield
LAAF........... Libyan Arab Air Force (BUAC)
LAAFS......... Los Angeles Air Force Station
LAAG .... Latin American Anthropology Group (EA)
LAAGOWRNAFE... Local Authority Associations Group of Work Related Non-Advanced Further Education (AIE)
LAAI........... Licentiate of the Institute of Administrative Accountants [*British*] (DBQ)
LAAIB......... Latin American Air Intelligence Brief (MCD)
LAAM.......... Large-Animal Anesthesia Machine [*Instrumentation*]
LAAM.......... Levo-alpha-Acetylmethadol [*Drug alternative to methadone*]
LAAM.......... Light Antiaircraft Missile
LAAMBN...... Light Antiaircraft Missile Battalion (MUGU)
LAAMSF...... Latin American Association of Medical Schools and Faculties [*See also ALAFEM*] [*Ecuador*] (EAIO)
La An.......... Lawyers' Reports, Annotated [*A publication*] (DLA)
LA & LR ...... Livonia Avon & Lakeville Railroad (MHDB)
LA & M....... Library Administration and Management
LAANG........ Louisiana Air National Guard (MUSM)
LA Ann........ Louisiana Annual Reports [*A publication*] (DLA)
LA Ann Reps... Louisiana Annual Reports [*A publication*] (DLA)
LA An R..... Louisiana Annual Reports [*A publication*] (DLA)
LA An Rep .. Louisiana Annual Reports [*A publication*] (DLA)
L A Ant .... Latin America Antiquity [*A publication*]
LA Ant .... Latin American Antiquity [*A publication*] (BRI)
LAAO.......... L-Amino Acid Oxidase [*An enzyme*]
LAAO .... Los Alamos Area Office [*Energy Research and Development Administration*]
LA A (Orleans)... Louisiana Court of Appeals (Parish of Orleans) (DLA)
LAAP........... Language Arts Assessment Portfolio [*Test*] (TMMY)
LAAP........... Law Association for Asia and the Pacific [*Australia*]
LAAP........... Longhorn Army Ammunition Plant (MCD)
LAAP........... Louisiana Army Ammunition Plant (AABC)
LAAPD........ Los Angeles Air Procurement District
LAAPI......... Latin American Association of Pharmaceutical Industries [*See also ALIFAR*] (EAIO)
LA App........ Louisiana Courts of Appeal Reports [*A publication*] (DLA)
LA App (Orleans)... Louisiana Court of Appeals (Parish of Orleans) (DLA)
LAAPS .... Laptop Automated Aid Positioning System [*Coast Guard*] [*Computer science*] (DOMA)
LAAR .... Liquid Air Accumulator Rocket
LAARD......... Long-Acting Antirheumatic Drug [*Medicine*] (STED)
LAARS .... LASER-Augmented Air-Rescue System (PDAA)
LAAS........... Light Armor Antitank System (MCD)
LAAS........... Los Angeles Air Service, Inc.
LAAS........... Low-Altitude Alerting System
LAASCA ...... Long-Range Antisubmarine Capability Aircraft
LAASL......... Latin American Association for the Study of the Liver [*Mexico*] (EAIO)

LAASP .... Latin American Association for Social Psychology [*Formerly, Latin American Social Psychology Committee*] (EA)
LAAT........... LASER-Augmented Airborne TOW Sight [*Army*] (MCD)
LAAT........... LASER-Augmented Airborne Track
LAAT........... Logistics Assessment and Assistance Team (MCD)
LAATC......... Latin American Association of Trading Companies [*Brazil*] (BUAC)
LAAV........... Light Airborne ASW [*Antisubmarine Warfare*] Vehicle
LAAW.......... Legal Automated Army-Wide
LAAW.......... Light Assault Antitank Weapon
LAAW.......... Local Antiair Warfare (NVT)
LAAWC .... Local Antiair Warfare Commander (NVT)
LAAWS .... Legal Automation Army-Wide Systems
Lab .... Labatt's California District Court Reports [*1857-58*] [*A publication*] (DLA)
LAB .... Label [*or Labelling*] (IAA)
LAB .... Lablab [*Papua New Guinea*] [*Airport symbol*] (OAG)
LAB .... Labmin Resources Ltd. [*Toronto Stock Exchange symbol*]
LAB .... Labor
LAB .... Labor Advisory Board [*New Deal*]
LAB .... Laboratories for Applied Biology Ltd. (WDAA)
Lab .... Laboratory (AL)
LAB .... Laboratory
lab .... Laboratory (WDMC)
LAB .... Laboratory Animals Bureau (BUAC)
LAB .... Laboratory for Applied Biophysics [*MIT*] (MCD)
LAB .... Labor Officer [*Foreign service*]
LAB .... Labour Party [*British Political party*]
LAB .... Labrador [*Canada*]
LAB .... Labrador Retriever [*Dog breed*]
LAB .... Labuan [*Island in Malaysia*] (ROG)
LAB .... Lactic Acid Bacteria [*Food microbiology*]
Lab .... Lambertus de Ramponibus [*Deceased, 1304*] [*Authority cited in pre-1607 legal work*] (DSA)
LAB .... Latin America Bureau [*British*] (EAIO)
LAB .... Lead Acid Battery
LAB .... Leave Authorization Balance [*Air Force*] (AFM)
LAB .... Legal Advisory Board (TELE)
LAB .... Legal Aid Board (BUAC)
LAB .... Leisure Activities Blank [*Vocational guidance test*]
LAB .... Level of Aspiration Board [*Psychology*]
LAB .... Liber Antiquitatum Biblicarum. Pseudo-Philo (BJA)
LAB .... Library Association of Barbados (BUAC)
LAB .... Licentiate of the Associated Board of Royal Schools of Music [*British*]
LAB .... Light Assault Bridge [*Military program*] (INF)
LAB .... Light Attack Battalion (INF)
LAB .... Linear Alkylbenzene [*Organic chemistry*]
LAB .... Lithosphere-Asthenosphere Boundary [*Geology*]
LAB .... Live Animals Board [*IATA*] (DS)
LAB .... Lloyd Aereo Boliviano SA [*Lloyd Bolivian Air Line*]
LAB .... Local Area Broadcast (NVT)
LAB .... Los Angeles Branch [*AEC*]
LAB .... Low-Altitude Bombing [*Military*]
LABA .... Laboratory Animal Breeders Association (EA)
Lab AC........ Labour Appeal Cases [*India*] [*A publication*] (DLA)
LABAC......... Licentiate Member of the Association of Business and Administrative Computing [*British*] (DBQ)
LABAN......... Lakas ng Bayan [*Peoples' Power Movement - Fight*] [*Philippines*] [*Political party*] (PPW)
Lab & Auto Bull... Labor and Automation Bulletin [*A publication*] (DLA)
LA Bar .... Louisiana Bar. Official Publication of the Louisiana State Bar Association [*A publication*] (DLA)
Lab Arb........ Labor Arbitration Reports [*Bureau of National Affairs*] [*A publication*] (DLA)
Lab Arb & Disp Settl... Labor Arbitration and Dispute Settlements [*A publication*] (DLA)
Lab Arb Awards... Labor Arbitration Awards [*Commerce Clearing House*] [*A publication*] (DLA)
LaBarg......... La Barge, Inc. [*Associated Press*] (SAG)
LABB........... Legal Abbreviations [*Database*]
LABBS.......... Ladies Association of British Barbershop Singers (BUAC)
LabChile....... Laboratorio Chile SA [*Associated Press*] (SAG)
LABCOM ...... Laboratory Command [*Adelphi, MD*] [*Army*] (RDA)
LAB-CO-OP... Labour and Co-Operative Party [*British*]
LabCp.......... Laboratory Corp. of America Holdings [*Associated Press*] (SAG)
LABE........... Lava Beds National Monument
LABE........... Louisiana Association of Business Educators (EDAC)
LABECO....... Laboratory Equipment Corp. [*Auto industry supplier*]
LABEL......... Law Students Association for Buyers' Education in Labeling [*Student legal action organization*]
LABEX......... Laboratory Equipment Exhibition (TSPED)
LABF.......... Latin American Banking Federation [*Bogota, Colombia*] (EA)
Lab His........ Labour History [*A publication*]
LABIB......... LASER Bibliography (MCD)
LABIL......... Light Aircraft Binary Information Link
LABIM........ Licentiate, American Board of International Medicine (CMD)
Lab Ind........ Labour and Industry [*A publication*]
LABIS......... Laboratory Information Systems (DNAB)
Lab J Aust... Laboratory Journal of Australasia [*A publication*]
LABK.......... Lafayette American Bank & Trust [*NASDAQ symbol*] (SAG)
LABK.......... Lafayette American Bk & Tr [*NASDAQ symbol*] (TTSB)
LABL.......... Australian Co. Secretary's Business Law Manual [*A publication*]
LABL.......... Multi-Color Corp. [*NASDAQ symbol*] (NQ)
Lab L Rep ... Labor Law Reporter [*Commerce Clearing House*] [*A publication*] (DLA)
LABMIS........ Laboratories Management Information System

LABN	Lake Ariel Bancorp [*NASDAQ symbol*] (SAG)
LABO	Licentiate, American Board of Ophthalmology (CMD)
LabOne	LabOne, Inc. [*Associated Press*] (SAG)
Labor C	Labor Code [*A publication*] (DLA)
LABORDOC	International Labour Documentation [*International Labour Office*] [*Geneva, Switzerland Bibliographic database*]
LABORINFO	Labour Information Database [*International Labour Office*] [*Information service or system*] (IID)
LABORSTAT	International Labor Organization, Bureau of Statistics Database (GFGA)
LABP	Latin American Book Programs [*Defunct*]
LABP	Lethal Aid for Bomber Penetration (MCD)
LABP	Licentiate, American Board of Pediatrics (CMD)
LABPIE	Low-Altitude Bombing Position Indicator Equipment [*Military*]
LABPR	Local Advisory Board Procedural Regulation (Office of Rent Stabilization) [*Economic Stabilization Agency*] [*A publication*] (DLA)
LAB PROC	Laboratory Procedure [*Medicine*] (BABM)
LabPU	Labour Party of Ukraine [*Political party*] (BUAC)
LABR	Laborer
LABR	Licentiate, American Board of Radiology (CMD)
L Abr	Lilly's Abridgment [*England*] [*A publication*] (DLA)
LABRAPS	Laboratoire de Recherche en Administration et Politique Scolaires [*Canada*]
Lab Rel Guide (P-H)	Labor Relations Guide (Prentice-Hall, Inc.) [*A publication*] (DLA)
LABREV	Laboratoire de Recherche sur l'Emploi, la Repartition, et la Securite du Revenu [*University of Quebec at Montreal*] [*Research center*] (RCD)
LABROC	Laboratory Rocket
LABS	LabOne, Inc. [*NASDAQ symbol*] (SAG)
LABS	Laboratory Admission Baseline Studies
LABS	LASER Active Boresight System (PDAA)
LABS	Learning about Basic Science [*Education program*]
LABS	Linear Alkylbenzene Sulfonate (EDCT)
LABS	Low-Altitude Bombing System [*Air Force*]
LABSAP	Laboratoire des Sciences de l'Activite Physique [*Laval University*] [*Canada Research center*] (RCD)
LabSpc	Laboratory Specialists of America, Inc. [*Associated Press*] (SAG)
LabSpec	Laboratory Specialists of America, Inc. [*Associated Press*] (SAG)
LABSTAT	Labor Statistics [*Database*] [*Department of Labor*]
LAB TECH	Laboratory Technologies Corp. (PCM)
LABU	Latin American Blind Union [*See also ULAC*] [*Uruguay*] (EAIO)
LABUT	Labor Utilization (MCD)
LAbV	Vermilion Parish Library, Abbeville, LA [*Library symbol Library of Congress*] (LCLS)
LabVIEW	Laboratory Virtual Instrument Engineering Workbench
LABVT	Left Atrial Ball-Valve Thrombus [*Medicine*] (STED)
LABVT	Left Atrial Ball-Valve Thrombus [*Cardiology*] (DAVI)
LABZ	Laboratory Specialists Amer [*NASDAQ symbol*] (TTSB)
LABZ	Laboratory Specialists of America, Inc. [*NASDAQ symbol*] (SAG)
LABZW	Laboratory Specialists Wrrt [*NASDAQ symbol*] (TTSB)
LAC	AB Bofors [*Sweden*] [*Research code symbol*]
LAC	Fort Lewis, WA [*Location identifier FAA*] (FAAL)
LaC	Labiocervical [*Dentistry*]
LAC	Laboratory Animals Centre (BUAC)
LAC	Labour Appeal Cases [*India*] [*A publication*] (ILCA)
LAC	Labour Arbitration Cases [*Canada Law Book, Inc.*] [*Information service or system A publication A publication*] (CRD)
LAC	Laceration [*Medicine*]
Lac	Lacerta [*Constellation*]
LAC	Lacquer (WDAA)
lac	Lacquer (VRA)
LAC	La Crosse [*A bunyavirus*]
LAC	Lactation (WDAA)
LAC	Lactose [*Cardiology*] (DAVI)
LAC	Lae-City [*Papua New Guinea*] [*Airport symbol*] (OAG)
LAC	Landers [*California*] [*Seismograph station code, US Geological Survey*] (SEIS)
LAC	Landscape Advisory Committee (BUAC)
LAC	Large Acrocentric Chromosome [*Medicine*]
LAC	Large-Area-Counter [*Astronomy*] [*Instrumentation*]
LAC	Large Area Coverage [*Marine science*] (OSRA)
LAC	LASER Amplifier Chain
LAC	Latin American Center (BUAC)
LAC	Latvian Academy of Culture (BUAC)
LAC	Launch Analyst's Console [*Aerospace*] (AAG)
LAC	Launcher Assignment Console
LAC	Law-abiding Citizen (BARN)
LAC	Leading Aircraftsman [*RAF*] [*British*]
LAC	Learning Assistance Center [*Stanford University*]
LAC	Left Atrial Contraction [*Cardiology*] (DAVI)
LAC	Legal Advisory Committee [*of NYSE*]
LAC	Lemon Administrative Committee (EA)
LAC	Liberal Academic Complex
LAC	Liberated Areas Committee [*World War II*]
LAC	Liberty Amendment Committee of the USA (EA)
LAC	Library Advisory Council [*Department of Education and Science*] [*British*] (NITA)
LAC	Library Assistants Certificate [*City and Guilds Institute*] [*British*] (NITA)
LAC	Library Association of China (BUAC)
LAc	Licensed Acupuncturist [*Medicine*]
LAC	Licentiate of the Apothecaries' Company [*British*]
LAC	Lights Advisory Committee [*General Council of British Shipping*] (DS)
LAC	Limited Area Coverage [*Data*]
LAC	Limiting Admissible Concentration
LAC	Limits to Acceptable Change [*Park tourism management*]
LAC	Lindamood Auditory Conceptualization Test [*Psychology*] (DAVI)
LAC	Linear Absorption Coefficient
LAC	Linear Aeronautical Chart (BARN)
LAC	Linear Amplitude-Continuous (PDAA)
LAC	Linguoaxiocervical [*Dentistry*]
LAC	Liposome-Antibody-Complement [*Immunochemistry*]
LAC	Liquid Affinity Chromatography
LAC	List of Assessed Contractors [*Military*] (RDA)
LAC	Lithuanian American Community (EA)
LAC	Lithuanian American Council
LAC	Live Action Camera (WDMC)
LAC	Load Accumulator
LAC	Local Advisory Council [*British labor*]
LAC	Local Agency Check (AFM)
LAC	Local Area Coverage [*Meteorology*]
LAC	Local Arrangements Committee [*National Court Reporters Association*]
LAC	Lockheed Aircraft Corp. [*ICAO designator*] (FAAC)
LAC	Logistics Area Coordinator (MCD)
LAC	Long Arm Cast [*Medicine*] (MEDA)
LAC	Longitudinal Aerodynamic Characteristics
LAC	Long-Run Average Cost Curve [*Economics*]
LAC	Low-Altitude Cruise (MCD)
LAC	Low Amplitude Contraction [*Neurology*] (DAVI)
LAC	Lunar Aeronautical Chart [*Air Force*]
LAC	Lunar Atlas Chart [*Aerospace*] (SAA)
LAC	Lung Adenocarcinoma Cell [*Medicine*] (STED)
LAC	Lupus Anticoagulant [*Immunochemistry*]
LACA	Ladies Apparel Contractors Association (EA)
LACA	Latin America Coffee Agreement (BUAC)
LACA	Life Agency Cashiers Association of the United States and Canada (EA)
LACA	Local Authority Caterers Association (BUAC)
LACA	Low-Altitude Control Area
LACAC	Latin American Civil Aviation Commission [*See also CLAC*] (EAIO)
lac & cont	Lacerations and Contusions [*Medicine*] (STED)
lac & cont	Lacerations and Contusions [*Medicine*] (DAVI)
LACAP	Latin American Cooperative Acquisitions Program [*or Project*]
LACAS	LASER Applications in Close Air Support [*Air Force*]
LACas	Latin American Casinos, Inc. [*Associated Press*] (SAG)
LACAS	Lineas Aereas Costarricenses SA [*Costa Rica*] [*ICAO designator*] (FAAC)
LACAS	Local Authority Catering Advisory Service (AIE)
LACAS	Low-Altitude Close Air Support [*Military*]
LACASA	Latin American and Caribbean Solidarity Association (EA)
LACAT	Legislative Alliance of Creative Arts Therapies [*Defunct*] (EA)
LACATA	Laundry and Cleaners Allied Trades Association [*Later, TCATA*] (EA)
LACATE	Lower Atmosphere Composition and Temperature Experiment [*National Science Foundation*]
LACB	Landing Aids Control Building [*NASA*] (NASA)
LACB	Look Angles of Celestial Bodies (KSC)
LACBWR	LaCrosse Boiling Water Reactor [*Also, LCBWR*]
LACC	Latin American and Caribbean Center [*Florida International University*] [*Research center*] (RCD)
LACC	Latin-American Council of Churches (BUAC)
LACC	Lloyd's Aviation Claims Centre (AIA)
LACC	Los Angeles City College [*California*]
l'ACCAB	L'Association Canadienne des Centres d'Action Benevole (AC)
LACCB	Latin American Confederation of Clinical Biochemistry [*Colombia*] (EAIO)
LACCSM	Latin American and Caribbean Council for Self-Management (EAIO)
LACD	Limited-Amplitude, Controlled-Decay (PDAA)
LACDL	Louisiana Association of Criminal Defense Lawyers (SRA)
LACE	Alpine Lace Brands [*NASDAQ symbol*] (SPSG)
LACE	Language for ALGOL [*Algorithmic Language*] Compiler Extension [*Computer science*] (CSR)
LACE	LASER Aerospace Communications Experiment
LACE	Launch Angle Condition Evaluator
LACE	Launch Automatic Checkout Equipment
LACE	Library Advisory Council for England (NITA)
LACE	[*The*] Lingerie and Corsetry Exhibition [*British*] (ITD)
LACE	Linkage Assistance and Cooperation for the European Border Regions (BUAC)
LACE	Liquid Air Collection Engine
LACE	Liquid Air Cycle Engine [*Aerospace plane engine concept*]
LACE	Local Automatic Circuit Exchange [*Telecommunications*]
LACE	Low-Power Atmospheric Compensation Experiment [*Strategic Defense Initiative*]
LACE	Lunar Atmospheric Composition Experiment [*Apollo*] [*NASA*]
LACE	Luton Analogue Computing Engine [*British*] (DEN)
LACE	Lysergic Acid Cryptoethelane (IIA)
LACES	London Airport Cargo Electronic-Data-Processing Scheme
Lacey Dig	Lacey's Digest of Railroad Decisions [*A publication*] (DLA)
LACFFP	Latin-American Commission on Forestry and Forestry Products (BUAC)
Lach	Laches [*of Plato*] [*Classical studies*] (OCD)
LACH	Lightweight Amphibious Container Handler (MCD)
LACI	Latin Amer Casinos [*NASDAQ symbol*] (TTSB)
LACI	Latin American Casinos, Inc. [*NASDAQ symbol*] (SAG)
LACI	Lipoprotein-Associated Coagulation Inhibitor [*Hematology*]
LACIE	Large Area Crop Inventory Experiment [*NASA*]
LACIM	Latin American and Caribbean International Moving [*Panama*] (EAIO)

LACIP............ Large Area Crop Inventory Program [*NASA*] (NASA)
LA Civ Code Ann (West)... West's Louisiana Code of Civil Procedure, Annotated [*A publication*] (DLA)
LACIW .... Latin Amer Casinos Wrrt [*NASDAQ symbol*] (TTSB)
L'ACJE .... L'Association Canadienne pour les Jeunes Enfants (AC)
Lacka Leg News... Lackawanna Legal News [*Pennsylvania*] [*A publication*] (DLA)
Lackawanna B... Lackawanna Bar Reporter [*Pennsylvania*] [*A publication*] (DLA)
Lack Bar R... Lackawanna Bar Reporter [*Pennsylvania*] [*A publication*] (DLA)
Lack Co (PA)... Lackawanna County Reports [*Pennsylvania*] [*A publication*] (DLA)
Lack Leg N... Lackawanna Legal News [*Pennsylvania*] [*A publication*] (DLA)
Lack Leg News (PA)... Lackawanna Legal News [*Pennsylvania*] [*A publication*] (DLA)
Lack Leg R... Lackawanna Legal Record [*Pennsylvania*] [*A publication*] (DLA)
Lack Leg Rec... Lackawanna Legal Record [*Pennsylvania*] [*A publication*] (DLA)
Lack LN ...... Lackawanna Legal News [*Pennsylvania*] [*A publication*] (DLA)
Lack LR .... Lackawanna Legal Record [*Pennsylvania*] [*A publication*] (DLA)
LACLA .... Latin American Constitutional Law Association [*Argentina*] (EAIO)
LacledeSt ... Laclede Steel Co. [*Associated Press*] (SAG)
LaclGas ..... Laclede Gas Co. [*Associated Press*] (SAG)
LACM .... Latin America Common Market [*Proposed*]
LACM .... Load Accumulator with Magnitude (HGAA)
LACMA .... Latin American and Caribbean Movers Association (EAIO)
LACMA .... Los Angeles County Museum of Art
LACMN .... Leading Aircrewman [*British military*] (DMA)
lac-mRNA .... Ribonucleic Acid, Messenger - lac operon [*Biochemistry, genetics*]
LACN .... Local Area Communications Network (DMAA)
LACNSW ...... Legal Aid Commission of New South Wales [*Australia*]
LACNT .... Legal Aid Commission of the Northern Territory [*Australia*]
LACO .... LASER Communication (SSD)
LACO .... Los Angeles College of Optometry [*California*]
LA Code Civ Pro Ann... West's Louisiana Code of Civil Procedure, Annotated [*A publication*] (DLA)
LA Code Crim Pro Ann... West's Louisiana Code of Criminal Procedure, Annotated [*A publication*] (DLA)
LAC of AMFC... Library Affairs Committee of the Associated Mid-Florida Colleges [*Library network*]
LACOM .... Low-Altitude Contour Matching (MCD)
LACONIQ ...... Laboratory Computer Online Inquiry
LA Const Art... Louisiana Constitution [*A publication*] (DLA)
LACOTS .... Local Authorities' Coordinating Body on Training Standards [*British*]
LACP .... Lignes Aeriennes Canadiennes Pacifiques
LACQ .... Lacquer
LACQLD .... Legal Aid Commission of Queensland [*Australia*]
Lacr .... Lacerta [*Constellation*]
lacr .... Lacrimal [*Ophthalmology*] (DAVI)
LACR .... Low-Altitude Coverage RADAR
LACRC .... Locally Assigned Convoy Route Carrier Code
LAC REC ..... Lactis Recentis [*New Milk*] [*Pharmacy*] (ROG)
LaCrose ...... LaCrosse Footwear, Inc. [*Associated Press*] (SAG)
Lac RR Dig... Lacey's Digest of Railroad Decisions [*A publication*] (DLA)
LACS............ Laboratory Automated Calibration System (MCD)
LACS............ League Against Cruel Sports (EA)
LACS............ Listener Active State (IAA)
LACS............ Lithuanian-American Catholic Services [*Defunct*] (EA)
LACS............ Los Angeles Catalyst Study [*Environmental Protection Agency*]
LACS............ Los Angeles Copyright Society (EA)
LACSA .... Lineas Aereas Costarricenses Sociedad Anonima [*Airline*] [*Costa Rica*]
LACSAB .... Local Authorities' Conditions of Service Advisory Board [*British*] (DCTA)
L'ACSQ .... Association Canadienne des Cinq Quilles [*Formerly, Canadian Bowling Congress*] (AC)
lact .... Lactate [*or Lactating*] (AAMN)
lact .... Lactating [*Medicine*] (MAE)
LACT............ Lactic Acid [*Biochemistry*] (DAVI)
LAC T.......... Lactose Tolerance [*Gastroenterology*] (DAVI)
LAC T.......... Lactose Tolerance [*Medicine*] (STED)
LACT............ Lease Automatic Custody Transfer
LACT............ Legal Aid Commission of Tasmania [*Australia*]
LACT............ Library of Anglo-Catholic Theology [*A publication*] (ODCC)
LACT............ Lindamood Auditory Conceptualization Test [*Psychology*] (STED)
LACT-ART .... Low-Affinity Choline Transport
Lactate Arterial (STED)
lact hyd ...... Lactalbumin Hydrolysate (STED)
LACUS .... Linguistic Association of Canada and the United States (EA)
LACUSA....... Liberty Amendment Committee of the USA (EA)
LACUSA....... Lithuanian-American Community of the USA [*Later, LAC*] (EA)
LAC/USC ...... Los Angeles County/University of Southern California Medical Center (DAVI)
LACV............ Light Amphibious Cargo Vehicle (MCD)
LACV............ Light Armored Combat Vehicle
LACV............ Lighter, Air-Cushion Vehicle [*Usually used in combination with numerals*] [*Military*] (RDA)
LACV-30 .... Lighter, Air Cushion Vehicle, 30 Tons [*Military*] (MCD)
LACW........... Leading Aircraft Woman [*RAF*] [*British*]
LACWA .... Legal Aid Commission of Western Australia
LACYMCA .... Latin American Confederation of YMCAs [*See also CLACJ*] (EAIO)
LAD............. Lactate Dehydrogenase [*Also, LD, LDH*] [*An enzyme*]
LAD............. Lactic Acid Dehydrogenase [*See also LDH*] [*An enzyme*]
LAD............. Ladder (MSA)
lad .... Ladino [*MARC language code Library of Congress*] (LCCP)
LAD............. Ladron Mountain [*New Mexico*] [*Seismograph station code, US Geological Survey*] (SEIS)
LAD............. Landing Assist Device [*Aviation*] (NG)
LAD............. Language Acquisition Device

LAD............. Large Area Detector [*Instrumentation*]
LAD............. Large Area Display
LAD............. LASER Acoustic Delay
LAD............. LASER Acquisition and Direction
LAD............. LASER Acquisition Device (MCD)
LAD............. LASER Air Defense
LAD............. Last Appearance Datum [*Geology*]
LAD............. Lateral Awareness and Directionality Test [*Sensorimotor skills test*]
LAD............. Latest Arrival Date (AABC)
LAD............. Leaf Area Duration [*Botany*]
LAD............. Lebanon Airport Development Corp. [*ICAO designator*] (FAAC)
LAD............. Left Anterior Descending [*Artery*]
LAD............. Left Anterior Digestive [*Gland*]
LAD............. Left Axis Deviation [*Medicine*]
LAD............. Leukocyte Adhesion Deficiency [*Medicine*]
LAD............. Library Administration Division [*American Library Association*] [*Later, LAMA*] (EA)
LAD............. Ligament Augmentation Device [*Sports medicine*]
LAD............. Light Aid Detachment [*Military British*]
LAD............. Light Area Defense (MCD)
LAD............. Linoleic Acid Depression [*Clinical chemistry*] (AAMN)
LAD............. Lipoamide Dehydrogenase [*An enzyme*]
LAD............. Liquid Agent Detector (AABC)
LAD............. Lithium Aluminum Deuteride [*Inorganic chemistry*]
LAD............. Lloyd's Aviation Department (AIA)
LAD............. Load Address (IAA)
LAD............. Location Aid Device (MCD)
LAD............. Logical Analysis Device
LAD............. Logical Aptitude Device (BUR)
LAD............. Logic and Adder (IAA)
LAD............. Logistic Approval Data
LAD............. Logistics Anchor Desk [*Military*]
LAD............. Lookout Assist Device [*Navigation*] (OA)
LAD............. Low-Accuracy Data/Designation [*System*] (MUGU)
LAD............. Low Alcohol Drinking [*Rat strain*]
LAD............. Low-Altitude Dispenser
LAD............. Low-Angle Dolly
LAD............. Luanda [*Angola*] [*Airport symbol*] (OAG)
LAD............. Lunar Atmosphere Detector [*Aerospace*]
LAD............. Lymphocyte-Activating Determinant (DAVI)
LAD............. Lymphocyte-Activating Determinate (STED)
LAD............. Our Lady of Angels College, Aston, PA [*OCLC symbol*] (OCLC)
LADA........... Laboratory Animal Dander Allergy (DAVI)
LADA........... Left Acromio-Dorso-Anterior [*A fetal position*] [*Obstetrics*]
LADA........... Left Anterior Descending Artery [*Anatomy*] (DAVI)
LADA........... Lesson Analysis Design Approach
LADA........... Light Air Defense Artillery [*Army*]
LADA........... London Air Defence Area [*British military*] (DMA)
LADAPT .... Lookup Dictionary Adaptor Program (IEEE)
LADAR .... LASER Detection and Ranging
LADAR .... LASER Doppler RADAR (MCD)
LADB .... Laboratory Animal Data Bank [*Battelle Memorial Institute*] [*Columbus, OH No longer available online*] [*Information service or system*] (IID)
LADB .... Latin American Data Bank [*University of Florida*] (IID)
LADB .... Latin American Data Base [*An association*] (EA)
LADB .... Lesotho Agricultural Development Bank (BUAC)
LADC .... LASER Advanced Development Center (IAA)
L'ADC .... L'Association Dentaire Canadienne (AC)
LADC .... Left Anterior Descending Coronary Artery [*Anatomy*]
LADCA .... Left Anterior Descending Coronary Artery [*Medicine*] (STED)
Ladd .... Ladd's Reports [*59-64 New Hampshire*] [*A publication*] (DLA)
LADD .... Left Anterior Descending Diagonal [*Branch of coronary artery*] [*Anatomy*] (DAVI)
LADD .... Low-Altitude Drogue Delivery (AFM)
LADDER...... Language Access to Distributed Data with Error Recovery
LaddFr....... Ladd Furniture, Inc. [*Associated Press*] (SAG)
LADDR........ Layered Device Driver Architecture [*Microsoft Corp.*] [*Computer science*] (PCM)
LADDS .... Laundry and Decontamination Drycleaning System [*Military*] (DWSG)
LADE .... Lineas Aereas del Estada [*Argentine Air Force airline*]
La de Castigl... Lapus de Castiglionchio [*Flourished, 1353-81*] [*Authority cited in pre-1607 legal work*] (DSA)
LADECO ...... Linea Aerea del Cobre SA [*Chile*] (EY)
La de Rampo... Lambertus de Ramponibus [*Deceased, 1304*] [*Authority cited in pre-1607 legal work*] (DSA)
LADF........... Ladd Furniture [*NASDAQ symbol*] (SAG)
LADH .... Lactic Acid Dehydrogenase [*An enzyme*] (DAVI)
LADH .... Liver Alcohol Dehydrogenase [*An enzyme*]
LADIES .... Life after Divorce Is Eventually Sane (EA)
LADIES .... Los Alamos Digital Image Enhancement Software (PDAA)
LADIES .... Low-Altitude Air Defense Identification and Engagement Study
LADIR .... Low-Cost Arrays for Detection of Infrared (PDAA)
LADIZ .... Leaving Air Defense Identification Zone
LADLE......... Librarians Antidefamation League
LAD-LOMS... Library Administration Division, Library Organization and Management Section [*American Library Association*] (AEBS)
LADM .... Laboratory Automated Data Management
LADME........ Liberation, Absorption, Distribution, Metabolism, and Excretion [*Medicine*] (STED)
LADME........ Liberation, Absorption, Distribution, Metabolism, Excretion [*Medicine*] (DAVI)
LAD-MIN..... Left Axis Deviation Minimal [*Cardiology*] (DAVI)
LADOG........ Low-Altitude Drive on Ground (IAA)
Ladp .... Ladyship (BARN)

LADP	Leadership Assessment and Development Program [*Army*] (INF)
LADP	Left Acromio-Dorso-Posterior [*A fetal position*] [*Obstetrics*]
LADP	Locally-Acting Drug Product [*Drug evalution*]
LADPOP	Lethal Agent Disposal Process Optimization Program (MCD)
LADR	Linear Accelerator-Driven Reactor (BARN)
LADRAP	Lethal Area Data Reduction and Plotting (SAA)
LADS	LASER Actuator Director System [*DoD*]
LADS	LASER Airborne Depth Sounder
LADS	LASER Air Defense System
LADS	Light Area Defense System (MCD)
LADS	Lightweight Air Defense System (MCD)
LADS	Limited Attack Defense System
LADS	Linear Analysis and Design of Structure (IAA)
LADS	Listener Addressed State (IAA)
LADS	Local Area Data Service [*Telecommunications*] (ACRL)
LADS	Local Area Data Set
LADS	Low-Altitude Defense System (MCD)
LADS	Low-Altitude Detection System [*Air Force*]
LADS	Low-Altitude Dispensing System [*Missiles*]
LADSIRLAC	Liverpool and District Scientific Industrial and Research Library Advisory Council [*Library cooperative scheme*] [*British*] (NITA)
LADT	Local Area Data Transport [*AT & T*]
LADT	Local Area Digital Transmission (WGA)
LADT	Low-Altitude Drop Test [*NASA*]
LADu	Lobuloalveolar-Ductal (STED)
LADu	Lobuloalveolar-Ductal [*Medicine*] (DAVI)
L Adv	Lord Advocate [*British*] (DAS)
L Advertiser	Law Advertiser [*1823-31*] [*A publication*] (DLA)
LadyLuck	Lady Luck Gaming Corp. [*Associated Press*] (SAG)
LAE	Lae [*Papua New Guinea*] [*Seismograph station code, US Geological Survey Closed*] (SEIS)
LAE	Lae [*Papua New Guinea*] [*Airport symbol*] (OAG)
LAE	Launcher Adapter Electronics (MCD)
LAE	Lead Angle Error
LAE	Leadership Ability Evaluation [*Psychology*]
LAE	Left Arithmetic Element
LAE	Left Atrial Enlargement [*Cardiology*]
LAE	Lethal Area Estimate
LAE	Linear Alcohol Ethoxylate [*Surfactant*]
LAE	Lineas Aereas Colombianas Ltd. [*Colombia*] [*ICAO designator*] (FAAC)
LAE	London Association of Engineers [*England*] (BUAC)
LAE	Long Above-Elbow [*Cast*] (STED)
LAE	™Love Is All ∫ for Enge (EA)
LAECC	Groupe International Laicat et Communaute Chretienne [*International Laity and Christian Community Group - ILCCG*] [*Defunct*] (EA)
LAECG	Local Aboriginal Education Consultative Group [*Australia*]
LAED	Large Area Electronic Display
LAED	Low Angle Electron Diffraction (PDAA)
LAEDP	Large Area Electronic Display Panel
LAEDV	Left Atrial End-Diastolic Volume [*Medicine*] (STED)
LAEDV	Left Atrial Volume in End Diastole [*Medicine*] (DMAA)
LAEE	Lithuanian Association for Energy Economics (BUAC)
LAEF	Luso-American Education Foundation (EA)
LAEI	Left Atrial Emptying Index [*Medicine*] (STED)
LAEI	Left Atrial Emptying Index [*Medicine*] (DMAA)
LAE NOTE	Licensed Aircraft Engineers' Notice (DNAB)
LAEP	Large Area Electronic Panel
LAEPC	Local Aboriginal Employment Promotion Committee [*Australia*]
LAER	Lowest Achievable Emission Rate [*Environmental Protection Agency*]
LAERF	Lewisville Aquatic Ecosystem Research Facility [*Texas*]
LAES	Latin American Economic System
LAESV	Left Atrial End-Systolic Volume [*Medicine*] (STED)
LAET	Limiting Actual Exposure Time (KSC)
LAETRILE	Laevo-Mandelonitrile-beta-glucuronic Acid [*Possible anticancer compound*]
LAEV	Laevus [*Left*] [*Pharmacy*]
LAF	Lafarge Corp. [*NYSE symbol*] (SPSG)
LAF	Lafayette [*Rhode Island*] [*Seismograph station code, US Geological Survey Closed*] (SEIS)
LAF	Lafayette [*Indiana*] [*Airport symbol*] (OAG)
LAF	Lafayette [*Diocesan abbreviation*] [*Louisiana*] (TOCD)
LAF	Lafayette College, Easton, PA [*OCLC symbol*] (OCLC)
LAF	Lafayette, IN [*Location identifier FAA*] (FAAL)
LAF	Laminar Airflow (KSC)
LAF	Landscape Architecture Foundation (EA)
Laf	Lanfrancus [*Deceased, 1089*] [*Authority cited in pre-1607 legal work*] (DSA)
Laf	Lanfrancus Cremensis [*Deceased, 1229*] [*Authority cited in pre-1607 legal work*] (DSA)
LAF	Latin American Female [*Classified advertising*] (DMAA)
LAF	Left Anterior Fascicle [*Anatomy*]
LAF	Leukocyte-Activating Factor [*Immunochemistry*]
LAF	Limited Amplifier Filter
LAF	Limits and Fits [*System*] [*Precision of tolerance*] [*Automotive engineering*]
LAF	Live Aid Foundation (EA)
LAF	Living Arts Foundation (EA)
LAF	Logistic Availability Factor (CAAL)
LAF	Long Address Form (NITA)
LAF	Low Animal Fat (STED)
LAF	Luteal Angiogenic Factor [*Biochemistry*]
LAF	Lymphocyte Activating Factor [*Immunology*]
LAF	Lyophilized Allantoic Fluid [*Endocrinology*]
Lafarge	Lafarge Corp. [*Associated Press*] (SAG)

Lafay	Lafayette Industries, Inc. [*Associated Press*] (SAG)
LafayABk	Lafayette American Bank & Trust [*Associated Press*] (SAG)
Lafaye	Lafayette Industries, Inc. [*Associated Press*] (SAG)
LAFB	Langley Air Force Base (MCD)
LAFB	Left Anterior Fascicular Block [*Cardiology*]
LAFB	Libyan Arab Foreign Bank
LAFB	Light Assault Floating Bridge [*British military*] (DMA)
LAFB	Lincoln Air Force Base (AAG)
LAFB	Local Authority Fire Brigade [*British*]
LAFB	Lowry Air Force Base (SAA)
LAFC	Latin-American Forestry Commission
LAFC	Lynn Anderson Fan Club (EA)
LAFF	Launcher Air Filtration Facility
LAFF	Luso-American Fraternal Federation (EA)
LAFFX	Lord Abbett: Affiliated Cl.A [*Mutual fund ticker symbol*] (SG)
LAFI	Lafayette Industries, Inc. [*NASDAQ symbol*] (SAG)
Lafico	Libyan Arab Foreign Investment (BUAC)
LAFIE	Lafayette Industries [*NASDAQ symbol*] (TTSB)
LAFIS	Local Authority Financial Information System (PDAA)
LAFIS	Local Authority Financial Institution System (AIE)
LAFL	Latin American Football League [*British*]
LAFM	Los Alamos Fuel Model [*Department of Energy*] (GFGA)
LA FONT	La Fontaine [*French author, 1621-1695*] (ROG)
LAFR	Laminar Air Flow Room (STED)
LAFR	Laminar Air Flow Room (DMAA)
LaFr	Laminar Airflow Room [*Medicine*] (DAVI)
LAFTA	Latin American Association of Freight and Transport Agents [*Paraguay*] (EAIO)
LAFTA	Latin-American Free Trade Association [*Later, LAIA*]
LAFTC	Latin American Federation of Thermalism and Climatism [*See also FLT*] [*Argentina*] (EAIO)
LAFTO	Latin American Confederation of Tourist Organizations [*Argentina*] (EAIO)
LAFTS	LASER and FLIR [*Forward-Looking Infrared*] Test Set [*Air Force*]
LAFTS	Los Alamos Fourier Transform Spectrometer [*Department of Energy*] (GRD)
LAFU	Ladies Amateur Fencing Union [*British*] (DBA)
LAFU	Laminar Airflow Unit [*Medicine*] (DAVI)
LAFUS	Latvian Association of Foresters in the United States [*Defunct*] (EA)
LAFV	Light Armoured Fighting Vehicle [*British military*] (DMA)
LAFWE	Lafayette Industries Wrrt [*NASDAQ symbol*] (TTSB)
LAG	Aerovias de Lagos SA de CV [*Mexico ICAO designator*] (FAAC)
LaG	Labiogingival [*Dentistry*]
Lag	Lagena [*Flask*] [*Latin*]
LAG	Lagging [*Engineering*]
LAG	Lagoon [*Maps and charts*]
LAG	La Guaira [*Venezuela*] [*Airport symbol*] (AD)
LAG	LaGuardia Community College Library [*UTLAS symbol*]
LAG	Langila [*Cape Gloucester*] [*New Britain*] [*Seismograph station code, US Geological Survey*] (SEIS)
LAG	LASER Absolute Gravimeter
LAG	Lastenausgleichsgesetz (BJA)
LAG	Legal Action Group [*British*] (DBA)
LAG	Librarians Automation Group [*Australia*] (NITA)
LAG	Liga Armada Gallega [*Armed Galician League*] [*Spain*] (PD)
LAG	Line of Arrested Growth [*Biology*]
LAG	Linguoaxiogingival [*Dentistry*]
LAG	[*A*] Literary Atlas and Gazetteer of the British Isles [*A publication*]
LAG	Livermore Action Group [*Defunct*] (EA)
LAG	Load and Go (NITA)
LAG	Load and Go Assembler (BUR)
LAG	Logical Applications Group [*Social Security Administration*]
LAG	London Amusement Guide
LAG	Lympangiosium [*Medicine*]
LAG	Lymphangiogram [*or Lymphangiography*]
LAGB	Linguistics Association of Great Britain
LAGB	Linhas Aereas da Guine-Bissau [*Airline*] [*Guinea-Bissau*]
LAGE	Los Angeles Grain Exchange (EA)
LA Gear	LA Gear, Inc. [*Associated Press*] (SAG)
LAGEO	LASER Geodynamic Satellite [*NASA*] (PDAA)
LAGEOS	LASER Geodynamic Satellite [*NASA*]
LAGER	Lesbian and Gay Employment Rights (BUAC)
LAGER	Liberal Action Group for Electoral Reform [*British*] (DI)
LAGEX	Lord Abbett: Global Equity Cl.A [*Mutual fund ticker symbol*] (SG)
LAGG	Fighter [*Russian aircraft symbol*]
LaGIN	Louisiana Government Information Network [*Louisiana State Library*] [*Baton Rouge*] [*Information service or system*] (IID)
LAGIX	Lord Abbett: Global Income Cl.A [*Mutual fund ticker symbol*] (SG)
LAGLG	Library Association Government Libraries Group (PDAA)
LAGMA	Lawn and Garden Manufacturers Association [*Defunct*] (EA)
LAGN	Lagoon [*Board on Geographic Names*]
LAGO	Light Atomic Gas Oil [*Petroleum product*]
Lagos HCR	Lagos High Court Reports [*A publication*] (DLA)
Lagos R	Judgments in the Supreme Court, Lagos [*1884-92*] [*Nigeria*] [*A publication*] (DLA)
LaGrange C	LaGrange College (GAGS)
LAGS	LASER-Activated Geodetic Satellite [*AFCRL*]
LAGS	Launch Abort Guide Simulation [*NASA*] (NASA)
LAGUMS	LASER-Guided Missile System (MCD)
LAGVX	Lord Abbett: U.S. Govt. Secs. Cl.A [*Mutual fund ticker symbol*] (SG)
LAGWX	Lord Abbett: Developing Growth Cl.A [*Mutual fund ticker symbol*] (SG)
Lah	Indian Law Reports, Lahore Series [*A publication*] (DLA)
Lah	Indian Rulings, Lahore Series [*A publication*] (DLA)
LAH	Labuha [*Indonesia*] [*Airport symbol*] (OAG)

LAH	Lactalbumin Hydrolysate [*Biochemistry*] (MAE)
LAH	LA Helicopter, Inc. [*ICAO designator*] (FAAC)
lah	Lahnda [*MARC language code Library of Congress*] (LCCP)
LAH	Lahore [*Pakistan*] [*Seismograph station code, US Geological Survey Closed*] (SEIS)
LAH	Latex Agglutination-Inhibition (DB)
LAH	Launch Axis, Horizontal (MCD)
LAH	Lebanon, NH [*Location identifier FAA*] (FAAL)
LAH	Left Anterior Hemiblock [*Cardiology*]
LAH	Left Atrial Hypertrophy [*Cardiology*]
LAH	Licentiate of the Apothecaries' Hall [*Dublin*]
LAH	Light-Armed Helicopter [*Military*] (PDAA)
LAH	Lithium Aluminum Hydride [*Inorganic chemistry*]
LAH	Logical Analyzer of Hypothesis [IEEE]
LAH	Low-Altitude Hold [*Military*] (CAAL)
Lah	Pakistan Law Reports, Lahore Series [*A publication*] (DLA)
LAHA	Linear Array Hybrid Assembly (PDAA)
LAHAWS	LASER Homing and Warning System [*Military*] (PDAA)
LAHB	Left Anterior Hemiblock [*Medicine*] (STED)
LAHB	Local Authorities Historic Buildings Act [*Town planning*] [*British*]
LAHC	Low Affinity-High Capacity [*Medicine*] (DMAA)
Lah Cas	Lahore Cases [*India*] [*A publication*] (DLA)
LAHCG	Look Ahead Carry Generator [*Computer science*] (NITA)
LAHF	Latin American Hospital Federation [*Mexico*] (EAIO)
Lahhs	Large Hydrofoil Hybrid Ship
LAHIVE	Low-Altitude/High-Velocity Experiment
Lah LJ	Lahore Law Journal [*India*] [*A publication*] (DLA)
Lah LT	Lahore Law Times [*India*] [*A publication*] (DLA)
LAHM	Limited Area HIBU [*Hydrological Institute and Belgrade University*] (USDC)
Lahore	All India Reporter, Lahore Series [*A publication*] (ILCA)
Lahore L Times	Lahore Law Times [*India*] [*A publication*] (DLA)
LAHPERD	Louisiana Association for Health, Physical Education, Recreation, and Dance (SRA)
LAHRC	Libyan Arab Human Rights Committee (BUAC)
LAHS	Local Authority Health Services [*British*]
LAHS	Low-Altitude, High-Speed
LAHV	Leukocyte-Associated Herpesvirus [*Medicine*] (STED)
LAHV	Leukocyte-Associates Herpes Virus [*Medicine*] (DAVI)
LAI	LaBat-Anderson, Inc. (EFIS)
LAI	Labioincisal [*Dentistry*]
LAI	Lact-Aid International [*Commercial firm*] (EA)
LAI	LAN [*Linked Access Network*] Automatic Inventory [*Brightwork Development, Inc.*] [*Computer science*] (PCM)
LAI	Lannion [*France*] [*Airport symbol*] (OAG)
LAI	Lasir Gold, Inc. [*Vancouver Stock Exchange symbol*]
LAI	Latex Agglutination-Inhibition (PDAA)
LAI	Latin American Institute [*University of New Mexico*] [*Research center*] (RCD)
LAI	Leaf Area Index [*Forestry*]
LAI	Left Artrial Involvement [*Medicine*] (MEDA)
LAI	Left Atrial Involvement [*Medicine*] (STED)
LAI	Lesotho Airways Corp. [*ICAO designator*] (FAAC)
LAI	Lesson Administrative Instructions [*Military*]
LAI	Leukocyte Adherence Inhibition [*Immunochemistry*]
LAI	Library Association of Ireland (EAIO)
LAI	Life Adjustment Inventory [*Psychology*]
LAI	Light Armored Infantry [*Marine Corps*] (DOMA)
L-A-I	Linkage, Ability, Interest [*Fundraising term*] (NFD)
LAI	Load Address Immediate (BUR)
LAI	Loaded Applicator Impedance
LAI	Location-Activity Inventory (DB)
LAI	Love Attitudes Inventory [*Premarital relations test*] [*Psychology*]
LAI	Low-Altitude Indicator
LAIA	Latin American Industrialists Association [*Uruguay*] (EAIO)
LAIA	Latin American Integration Association [*Formerly, LAFTA*] [*See also ALADI Uruguay*] (EAIO)
LAIC	Latin America Information Centre (BUAC)
LAIC	Lesbian Archive and Information Centre (BUAC)
LAIC	Lithuanian-American Information Center [*Defunct*]
LA-ICP-MS	LASER Ablation-Inductively Coupled Plasma-Mass Spectrometry [*Analytical chemistry*]
LaidlwA	Laidlaw, Inc. [*Associated Press*] (SAG)
LaidlwB	Laidlaw, Inc. [*Associated Press*] (SAG)
LAIEC	Latin American Institute of Educational Communication [*Mexico*] (EAIO)
LAIF	Leukocyte Adherence Inhibition Factor (DAVI)
LAIFS	Los Angeles International Fern Society (EA)
LAIG	LA Industrial Group (NITA)
LAIG	Library Association Industrial Group (BUAC)
LAIICS	Latin American Institute for Information and Computer Sciences [*Chile*] (PDAA)
LAILA	Latin American Indian Literatures Association (EA)
LAIMP	Lunar-Anchored Interplanetary Monitoring Platform [*Aerospace*] (MCD)
LAINS	Low-Altitude Inertial Navigation System [*Air Force*]
LAIR	Letterman Army Institute of Research [*San Francisco, CA*]
LAIR	Liquid Air (NASA)
LAIRS	Labor Agreement Information Retrieval System [*Office of Management and Budget*]
LAIRS	Land-Air Integrated Reduction System (MUGU)
LAIRS	Lightweight Advanced Inertial Reference Sphere
LAIRTS	Large Aperture Infrared Telescope System
LAIS	Labor Arbitration Information System [*LRP Publications*] [*Information service or system*] (CRD)
LAIS	Labyrinth Air Induction Silencer [*Automotive engineering*]
LAIS	Labyrinth Air Induction System [*Automotive engineering*]
LAIS	Leiter Adult Intelligence Scale [*Intelligence test*] [*Psychology*]
LAIS	Library Acquisitions Information System
LAIS	Loan Accounting Information System [*Agency for International Development*]
LAISDSS	Latin American Institute of Social Doctrine and Social Studies [*Chile*] (EAIO)
LAIT	Langdon Adult Intelligence Test (TES)
LAIT	Latex Agglutination Inhibition Test [*for pregnancy*] [*Medicine*]
LAIT	Library Association Information Technology Group [*British*] (NITA)
LAIT	Logistics Assistance and Instruction Team [*Military*] (AABC)
LAITG	Library Association Information Technology Group (AIE)
LAITS	Latin American Institute for Transnational Studies (EA)
LAIU	Launch Abort Interface Unit [*NASA*] (MCD)
LAIWS	Land-Air White Sands (MUGU)
LAJ	British Mediterranean Airways Ltd. [*FAA designator*] (FAAC)
LAJ	Lajes [*Brazil*] [*Airport symbol*] (OAG)
LAJ	London Airtours Ltd. [*British ICAO designator*] (FAAC)
LAJ	Los Angeles Junction Railway Co. [*AAR code*]
LAJC	Latin American Jewish Congress (BUAC)
LaJollPh	La Jolla Pharmaceutical [*Associated Press*] (SAG)
LaJolP	La Jolla Pharmaceutical [*Associated Press*] (SAG)
LAJPEL	Latin American Journal of Politics, Economics, and Law [*A publication*] (DLA)
LAK	Aklavik [*Canada*] [*Airport symbol*] (OAG)
LAK	Laker Resources [*Vancouver Stock Exchange symbol*]
LAK	Lennox Airways [*Kenya*] [*ICAO designator*] (FAAC)
LAK	Leukocyte-Activated Killer [*Cells*] [*Oncology*] (DAVI)
LAK	Lightweight Antenna Kit
LAK	Lymphokine-Activated Killer [*Cells*] [*Immunotherapy*]
LAKE	Lake [*Commonly used*] (OPSA)
LAKE	Lakeland Indus [*NASDAQ symbol*] (TTSB)
LAKE	Lakeland Industries, Inc. [*NASDAQ symbol*] (SAG)
LakeAriel	Lake Ariel Bancorp [*Associated Press*] (SAG)
LakehdP	Lakehead Pipe Line Partners Ltd. [*Associated Press*] (SAG)
LakeInd	Lakeland Industries, Inc. [*Associated Press*] (SAG)
LAKES	Lakes [*Commonly used*] (OPSA)
LakevwF	Lakeview Financial Corp. [*Associated Press*] (SAG)
LAKFC	Los Angeles Kings Fan Club (EA)
LakldFt	Lakeland First Fianancial Group, Inc. [*Associated Press*] (SAG)
LaL	Labiolingual [*Dentistry*]
LAL	Labrador Airways Ltd. [*Canada ICAO designator*] (FAAC)
LAL	Lakeland [*Florida*] [*Airport symbol*] (AD)
LAL	Lakeland, FL [*Location identifier FAA*] (FAAL)
LAL	Lana Gold Corp. [*Vancouver Stock Exchange symbol*]
LAL	Langley Aeronautical Laboratory [*NASA*]
LAL	Launch and Leave [*Military*] (MUSM)
LAL	Left Axillary Line [*Medicine*] (DMAA)
LAL	Limulus Amebocyte Lysate
LAL	Livonia, Avon & Lakeville Railroad Corp. [*AAR code*]
LAL	Local Adjunct Language (PDAA)
LAL	Loudspeaker Acoustical Labyrinth
LAL	Low Air Loss
LAL	Lower Acceptance Level
LAL	Lysinoalanine [*An amino acid*]
L-Ala	L-Alanine [*Biochemistry*] (DAVI)
LALA	Large Amplitude Late Arrival [*Seismology*]
LALA	Linoletic Acid-Like Activity (PDAA)
LA(L)A	Local Authorities (Land) Act [*Town planning*] [*British*]
LALA	Low-Altitude Alert [*Air traffic control*]
LaLand	Louisiana Land & Exploration Co. [*Associated Press*] (SAG)
LALD	Low-Angle Low-Drag
L Alem	Law of the Alemanni [*A publication*] (DLA)
LALI	Labiolingual [*Dentistry*]
LALI	Latin American-Caribbean Labor Institute (EA)
LALI	Lymphocyte Antibody-Lymphocytolytic Interaction [*Medicine*] (DMAA)
LALIS	Luso-American Life Insurance Society
LA LJ	Louisiana Law Journal [*New Orleans*] [*A publication*] (DLA)
LALLL	Low-Altitude Low-Light Level
LALLS	Low-Angle LASER Light Scattering
LALM	Limulus Amebocyte Lysate Method
LALO	Low-Altitude Observation
Lalor	Lalor's Supplement to Hill and Denio's New York Reports [*A publication*] (DLA)
Lalor Pol Econ	Lalor's Cyclopaedia of Political Science, Political Economy, Etc. [*A publication*] (DLA)
Lalor's Supp	Lalor's Supplement to Hill and Denio's New York Reports [*A publication*] (DLA)
Lalor's Supp (Hill and Denio)	Lalor's Supplement to Hill and Denio's New York Reports [*A publication*] (DLA)
Lalor Supp	Lalor's Supplement to Hill and Denio's New York Reports [*A publication*] (DLA)
LALP	Longest Activity from Longest Project
LALR	Lookahead Left to Right [*Computer science*]
LAIR	Rapides Parish Library, Alexandria, LA [*Library symbol Library of Congress*] (LCLS)
Lal RP	Lalor's Law of Real Property [*A publication*] (DLA)
LALS	LaGuardia Automated Library System [*LaGuardia Community College*] [*Information service or system*] (IID)
LALS	LASER Alarm Locator System
LALS	Linkless Ammunition Loading System (MCD)
LALSD	Language for Automated Logic and System Design [*Computer science*] (CSR)
LALUC	Local Authority Land Use Classification (PDAA)

LALV............ Lucerne Australian Latent Virus [Plant pathology]
L'AM............ L'Alliance Monarchiste (EA)
Lam............. Lamarck [Biology] (BARN)
lam.............. Lamba [MARC language code Library of Congress] (LCCP)
Lam.............. Lambert [Unit of luminance] [Preferred unit is lx, Lux]
Lam.............. Lambertus de Ramponibus [Deceased, 1304] [Authority cited in pre-1607 legal work] (DSA)
Lam.............. Lamentations [Old Testament book]
Lam.............. Lamina (STED)
LAM............. Lamina [Medicine] (DAVI)
LAM............. Laminate (MSA)
lam.............. Laminated (WDMC)
LAM............. Laminectomy [Medicine]
lam.............. Laminogram (MAE)
LAM............. Land Attack Mode [Navy] (CAAL)
LAM............. Laramide Resources Ltd. [Vancouver Stock Exchange symbol]
LAM............. LASER [Light Amplification by Stimulated Emission of Radiation] Aiming Module
LAM............. L-Asparaginase and Methotrexate [Antineoplastic drug regimen] (DAVI)
LAM............. Late Ambulatory Monitoring [Medicine]
LAM............. Latin America Inv Fd [NYSE symbol] (TTSB)
LAM............. Latin America Mission (EA)
LAM............. Latin American Investment Fund [NYSE symbol] (SPSG)
LAM............. Latin American Male (DAVI)
LAM............. Latin American Mission [Air Force]
LAM............. Leading Air Mechanic [British military] (DMA)
LAM............. Learner-Approved Motorcycle
LAM............. Left Anterior Measurement [Medicine] (STED)
LAM............. Left Atrial Myxoma [Cardiology] (DAVI)
LAM............. Left Atrial Myxoma [Medicine] (STED)
LAM............. Liberal Alliance of Montenegro (BUAC)
LAM............. Liberalium Artium Magister [Master of the Liberal Arts]
LAM............. Library Association of Malaysia (BUAC)
LAM............. Life Action Ministries (EA)
LAM............. Light-Absorbing Molecules
LAM............. Lightweight Analog Motor (MCD)
LAM............. Limited Area Model [Marine science] (OSRA)
LAM............. Limpet Assembly Modular [Navy] (CAAL)
LAM............. Linhas Aereas de Mocambique [Mozambique] [ICAO designator] (FAAC)
LAM............. Lipoarabinomannan [Biochemistry]
LAM............. Lithuanian Academy of Music (BUAC)
LAM............. Load Acceptance Module
LAM............. Load Accumulator with Magnitude
LAM............. Lobe Attachment Module [Computer science]
LAM............. Lobe Attachment Unit [Computer science] (ACRL)
LAM............. Logical Acknowledgement Message [Aviation] (DA)
LAM............. London Academy of Music
LAM............. Long Aerial Mine [Military]
LAM............. Longitudinal Acoustic [or Acoustical] Mode [Spectroscopy]
LAM............. Look at Me (IAA)
LAM............. Loop Adder and Multiplier (NITA)
LAM............. Loop Addition and Modification [Computer science]
LAM............. Los Alamos [New Mexico] [Airport symbol] (OAG)
LAM............. Los Alamos, NM [Location identifier FAA] (FAAL)
LAM............. Louisiana Motor Freight Bureau [STAC]
LAM............. Lousiana Maneuvers [Military]
LAM............. Low-Altitude Missile (MCD)
LAM............. Low-Attack Mode (MCD)
LAM............. Lymphangioleiomyomatosis [Medicine]
LAM............. Master of Liberal Arts
LAMA........... Laboratory Animal Management Association (EA)
LAMA........... Laminin A (DMAA)
LAMA........... Latin American Manufacturers Association [Washington, DC] (EA)
LAMA........... Lead Air Materiel Area [Air Force]
LAMA........... Legal Assistant Management Association (EA)
LAMA........... Library Administration and Management Association (EA)
LAMA........... Light Aircraft Manufacturers' Association (EA)
LAMA........... Livestock Auction Markets Association (EA)
LAMA........... Local Authority Members Association [Ireland] (BUAC)
LAMA........... Local Automatic Message Accounting [Telecommunications] (TEL)
LAMA........... Locomotive and Allied Manufacturers' Association [British] (BI)
LAMA BES ... LAMA [Library Administration and Management Association] Buildings and Equipment Section
LAMACHA.... Louisiana-Alabama-Mississippi Automated Clearing House Association
LAMA FRFDS... LAMA [Library Administration and Management Association] Fund Raising and Financial Development Section
LAMA LOMS... LAMA [Library Administration and Management Association] Library Organization and Management Section
LaMan......... LaMan Corp. [Associated Press] (SAG)
lam & fus... Laminectomy and Fusion [Medicine] (DAVI)
LAMA PAS ... LAMA [Library Administration and Management Association] Personnel Administration Section
LAMA PRS ... LAMA [Library Administration and Management Association] Public Relations Section
Lamar......... Lamar's Reports [25-40 Florida] [A publication] (DLA)
LAMAR .... Large Area Modular Array of Reflectors [Astronomy]
LAMAR .... Linear-Elastic Matrix Analysis Routine
LAMARS....... Large Amplitude Multimode Aerospace Research Simulator
Lamar U ..... Lamar University (GAGS)
LAMAS........ Location and Movement Analysis System (MCD)
LAMAS........ London and Middlesex Archaeological Society [England] (BUAC)

LAMA SASS... LAMA [Library Administration and Management Association] Systems and Services Section
LAMA SS ..... LAMA [Library Administration and Management Association] Statistics Section
LAMA SSS ... LAMA [Library Administration and Management Association] Systems and Services Section
LA-MAX ...... Maximal Left Atrial [Dimension] [Medicine] (STED)
LA-MAX ...... Maximal left Atrial [Dimension] [Cardiology] (DAVI)
Lamb .... Lambard's Archaionomia [A publication] (DLA)
Lamb .... Lambard's Archeion [1635] [A publication] (DLA)
Lamb .... Lambard's Eirenarcha [A publication] (DLA)
Lamb .... Lambard's Explication [A publication] (DLA)
LAMB.......... Lambeth [Degrees granted by Archbishop of Canterbury] [British] (ROG)
LAMB.......... Lambourne [England]
Lamb .... Lamb's Reports [103-105 Wisconsin] [A publication] (DLA)
LAMB.......... Light Armoured Motor Brigade [British military] (DMA)
LAMB.......... Local Area Multiuser Board [American Micronics] [Computer science]
LAMB.......... Los Alamos Water Boiler (NRCH)
LAMB.......... Low-Altitude Multiburst Code (MCD)
Lamb Arch... Lambard's Archaionomia [A publication] (DLA)
Lamb Arch... Lambard's Archeion [1635] [A publication] (ILCA)
Lamb Archaion... Lambard's Archaionomia [A publication] (DLA)
Lamb Const... Lambard's Duties of Constables, Etc. [A publication] (DLA)
LAMBDA...... Language for Manufacturing Business and Distribution Activity (IAA)
Lamb de Ramp... Lambertus de Ramponibus [Deceased, 1304] [Authority cited in pre-1607 legal work] (DSA)
Lamb Dow ... Lambert's Law of Dower [A publication] (DLA)
Lamb Eir...... Lambard's Eirenarcha [A publication] (DLA)
Lamb Eiren... Lambard's Eirenarcha [A publication] (DLA)
Lamber de Sal... Lambertus de Salinis [Flourished, 14th century] [Authority cited in pre-1607 legal work] (DSA)
Lamb Explic... Lambard's Explication [A publication] (DLA)
Lam Bk Rpt... Lambda Book Report [A publication] (BRI)
LAMBR......... Laminin B Receptor (DMAA)
LAMBS......... Laboratory Animal Management and Business Systems [Computer science]
LAMC.......... Laminin C (DMAA)
LAMC.......... Language and Mode Converter [Computer science] (TEL)
LAMC.......... Last Maneuver Calculation [Orbit identification]
LAMC.......... Letterman Army Medical Center (AABC)
LAMC.......... Lima Army Modification Center (RDA)
LAMC.......... Livestock Auctioneers' Market Committee [British] (DBA)
LAMC.......... Livestock Auctioneers Market Committee for England and Wales (BUAC)
LAMCIS....... Los Angeles Multiple Corridor Identification System (SAA)
LAMCO....... Liberian American-Swedish Minerals Co.
LAMCS........ Latin American-American Communications Systems (PDAA)
LAMCS........ Latin American Military Communications System
LAMDA....... [The] London Academy of Music and Dramatic Art
LAME .... Lake Mead National Recreation Area
LAME .... Licensed Aircraft Maintenance Engineer (ADA)
LAMEF........ Los Alamos Medium Energy Facility
LAMG......... Laban Art of Movement Guild [Later, LG] (EA)
lami............ Laminotomy [Medicine] (STED)
lami............ Laminotomy [Medicine] (DAVI)
Lamin........ Laminating Technologies, Inc. [Associated Press] (SAG)
Laminat...... Laminating Technologies, Inc. [Associated Press] (SAG)
LAMIS........ Local Authority Managaement Information System (PDAA)
LAMIT........ Local Authorities' Mutual Investment Trust [British]
LAMMA....... LASER Microprobe Mass Analyzer [Spectrometry]
LAMMP....... Lower Acceptable Mean Maximum Pressure (SAA)
LAMMR....... Large Antenna Multifrequency Microwave Radiometer (MCD)
LAMMS....... LASER Microprobe Mass Spectrometry [or Spectroscopy]
LAMN......... La Man Corp. [NASDAQ symbol] (TTSB)
LAMOPH...... Ladies Auxiliary, Military Order of the Purple Heart, United States of America (EA)
LAMOST ...... Large Area Multi Object Fiber Spectroscopic Telescope [Proposed, China]
LAMOST ...... Large Sky Area Multi-Objects Fiber Spectoscopic Telescope [China]
LAMP.......... Center for the Study of Legal Authority and Mental Patient Status (EA)
LAMP.......... Lake Acidification Mitigation Project [Environmental Protection Agency] (GFGA)
LAMP.......... Lakewide Management Plan [Great Lakes] [Environmental Protection Agency]
LAMP.......... Lanier Academic Motivational Program [Military]
LAMP.......... Laos Ammunition Procedures (CINC)
LAMP.......... Large Advanced Mirror Program [Military] (SDI)
LAMP.......... LASER and MASER Patents
LAMP.......... LASER and Mixing Program
LAMP.......... Laser Microbeam Program [Research center] (RCD)
LAMP.......... Latin America Mass Media Project (BUAC)
LAMP.......... Latin American Market Planning Centre (BUAC)
LAMP.......... Leap and Stamp [Dance terminology]
LAMP.......... Library Addition and Maintenance Program
LAMP.......... Life Agency Management Program [GAMC]
LAMP.......... Light Airborne Multipurpose System [Navy] (MCD)
LAMP.......... Lighthouse Automation and Modernization Project [US Coast Guard] (PDAA)
LAMP.......... Logic Analysis for Maintenance Planning (MHDB)
LAMP.......... Logistics Automation Master PLan [Military]
LAMP.......... Louis Armstrong Memorial Project
LAMP.......... Low-Altitude Manned Penetrator
LAMP.......... Lunar Analysis and Mapping Program [NASA] (IAA)

LAMP......... Lysosome-Associated Membrane Protein [Biochemistry]
LAMPF...... Los Alamos Meson Physics Facility [Later, Clinton P. Anderson Meson Physics Facility at Los Alamos] [Department of Energy]
LAMP-H...... Lighter, Amphibian Heavy Lift
LAMPP...... Los Alamos Molten Plutonium Program
LAMPRE...... Los Alamos Molten Plutonium Reactor Experiment
LAMPS........ Large Amplitude SLOSH [Sea, Lake, Overland Surge from Hurricanes] [NASA]
LAMPS........ Light Airborne Multiple Package System
LAMPS........ Light Airborne Multipurpose System [Navy]
LAMPS........ Limited Area Mesoscale Prediction System (MCD)
LAMPSOP.... Light Airborne Multipurpose System Standard Operating Procedures Manual [Navy] (DNAB)
LA/MPSS ..... Large Area/Mobile Projected Smoke System [Military] (RDA)
LamR........... Lamentations Rabbah (BJA)
LAMR.......... Large Aperture Microwave Radiometer (SSD)
LAMRL........ Logistic Area Material Readiness List [Military] (AFIT)
LamRsch ..... Lam Research Corp. [Associated Press] (SAG)
LAMRTPI ..... Legal Associate Member of the Royal Town Planning Institute [British] (DBQ)
LAMS........... Land Acoustical Monitoring System [NASA]
LAMS........... Land Acquisition and Management Schemes [British]
LAMS........... Large Atypical Mole Syndrome [Medicine]
LAMS........... Load Alleviation and Mode Stabilization
LAMS........... London Aero Motor Services
LAMS........... Los Alamos Scientific Laboratory [USAEC] (MCD)
LAMSA........ Lineas Aereas Mexicana, Sociedad Anonima
LAMSAC ...... Local Authorities' Management Services and Computer Committee [British]
LAMSAC ...... Local Authorities Management Services and Computer Committee (BUAC)
LAMSAS....... Linguistic Atlas of the Middle and South Atlantic States
LamSes .... [The] Lamson & Sessions Co. [Associated Press] (SAG)
LAMSIM....... Launcher and Missile Simulator
L Am Soc.... Law in American Society [A publication] (DLA)
L Am Soc'y.. Law in American Society [A publication] (DLA)
LAMT .... Laminating Technologies, Inc. [NASDAQ symbol] (SAG)
LAmT .... Tangipahoa Parish Library, Amite, LA [Library symbol Library of Congress] (LCLS)
LAMTD........ Laminated
LAMTS........ Launcher Adapter Missile Test Set
LAN.............. Inland [Aviation code]
LAN.............. Lanarkshire [County in Scotland]
LAN.............. Lancer Corp. [AMEX symbol] (SPSG)
LAN.............. Lanchow [Republic of China] [Seismograph station code, US Geological Survey Closed] (SEIS)
LAN.............. Landing Aid [Navigation] (IAA)
Lan .... Landulfus Acconzaioco [Flourished, 13th century] [Authority cited in pre-1607 legal work] (DSA)
Lan .... Lanfrancus [Deceased, 1089] [Authority cited in pre-1607 legal work] (DSA)
Lan .... Lanfrancus Cremensis [Deceased, 1229] [Authority cited in pre-1607 legal work] (DSA)
LAN.............. Langley [Unit of sun's heat] (IAA)
lan .... Langue d'Oc [MARC language code Library of Congress] (LCCP)
LAN.............. Lansing [Michigan] [Airport symbol] (OAG)
LAN.............. Lansing, MI [Location identifier FAA] (FAAL)
Lan .... Lanthionine (DB)
LAN.............. Lateral Access Network (NITA)
LAN.............. Latin American Newsletters [British Information service or system] (IID)
LAN.............. Library Advocacy Now [American Library Association]
LAN.............. Library Automation and Networks
LAN.............. Lime-Ammonium-Nitrate [Fertilizer]
LAN.............. Linea Aerea Nacional [National Airline] [Chile]
LAN.............. Linea Aerea Nacional de Chile [ICAO designator] (FAAC)
LAN.............. Linked Access Network
LAN.............. Local Apparent Noon [Navigation]
LAN.............. Local Area Network [Telecommunications]
LAN.............. Local Area Networks [Information Gatekeepers, Inc.] [No longer available online] [Information service or system] (CRD)
LAN.............. Long-Acting Neuroleptic [Pharmacology] (DAVI)
LAN.............. Longitude of the Ascending Node
LAN.............. Lymphadenopathy (STED)
LAN.............. Mesa Public Library, Los Alamos, NM [OCLC symbol] (OCLC)
LANA .... Language Analog [Project]
LANA .... Lipizzan Association of North America (NTPA)
LANA .... Lithuanian American National Alliance (EA)
LANA .... Llama Association of North America (EA)
LANA .... Local Area Network Accelerator [Computer science] (CIST)
LANA .... Low-Altitude Night Attack (DOMA)
LANABS ...... Light Attack Navigation and Bombing System (MCD)
LANAC........ Laminar Air Navigation and Anticollision [Air Force]
LANAC........ Lawyers Alliance for Nuclear Arms Control [Later, LAWS] (EA)
Lan Acon .... Landulfus Acconzaioco [Flourished, 13th century] [Authority cited in pre-1607 legal work] (DSA)
LANAP........ Latin American Natural Areas Program (BUAC)
LANBY........ Large Automatic Navigational Buoy [Shipping] (DS)
LANC .... Lancaster [England] (ROG)
LANC .... Lancaster Colony [NASDAQ symbol] (SAG)
Lanc............ Lancellottus [Authority cited in pre-1607 legal work] (DSA)
LANC .... Lancer [Military British] (ROG)
LANC .... Liga Apararii Nationale Crestine [League of National Christian Defense] [Romania] [Political party] (PPE)
LANC .... Local Application Numerical Control [Sony Corp.] (DOM)

LANC .... Long-Arm Navicular Cast [Orthopedics] (DAVI)
Lancastr ...... Lancaster Colony [Associated Press] (SAG)
Lance.......... Lance, Inc. [Associated Press] (SAG)
LANCE .... Local Area Network Controller for Ethernet [Mostek] (NITA)
Lancell Giaiaul... Lancellottus Galiaula [Flourished, 16th century] [Authority cited in pre-1607 legal work] (DSA)
Lancer .... Lancer Corp. [Associated Press] (SAG)
LANCET........ Library Association National Council for Educational Technology (NITA)
Lancit .... Lancit Media Productions Ltd. [Associated Press] (SAG)
Lanc Law Rev... Lancaster Law Review [A publication] (DLA)
Lanc L Rev... Lancaster Law Review [A publication] (DLA)
LANCO .... Landscape Nursery Council (EA)
LANCRA....... Landing Craft
LANCRAB..... Landing Craft and Bases [Military]
LANCRABEU... Landing Craft and Bases, Europe [Navy]
LANCRABNAW... Landing Craft and Bases, Northwest African Waters [World War II Navy]
Lan Cre........ Lanfrancus Cremensis [Deceased, 1229] [Authority cited in pre-1607 legal work] (DSA)
Lanc Rev ..... Lancaster Review [Pennsylvania] [A publication] (DLA)
LANCS .... Lancashire [County in England]
LAND .... Land [Postal Service standard] (OPSA)
LAND .... Landair Services [NASDAQ symbol] (SAG)
LAND .... League Against Nuclear Dangers [Defunct] (EA)
LAND .... Local Access Network Directory [Frye Computer Systems] [Telecommunications] (PCM)
LANDA .... Ladies Auxiliary to the National Dental Association [Later, ANDA] (EA)
LANDA .... LAN [Local Area Network] Dealers Association (CDE)
L & A.......... Landing and Ascent [NASA]
L & A.......... Leembruggen and Asirvatham's Appeal Court Reports [Ceylon] [A publication] (DLA)
L & A.......... Light and Accommodation [Ophthalmology] (DAVI)
L & A.......... Living and Active (DAVI)
L & A.......... Louisiana & Arkansas Railway Co.
LANDAC....... Land Development Accounting System (MHDB)
Landair........ Landair Services [Associated Press] (SAG)
LANDATA..... Land Division Data Base [Australia] (BUAC)
Landaur....... Landauer, Inc. [Associated Press] (SAG)
L & B.......... Leadam and Baldwin's Select Cases before the King's Council [England] [A publication] (DLA)
L & B.......... Left and Below [Medicine]
L & B.......... Lothians and Border Horse [British military] (DMA)
L & Bank ..... Lawyer and Banker [A publication] (DLA)
L & B Bull.... Daily Law and Bank Bulletin [Ohio] [A publication] (DLA)
L & B Fin..... L & B Financial, Inc. [Associated Press] (SAG)
L & B Ins Dig... Littleton and Blatchley's Insurance Digest [A publication] (DLA)
LandBnc....... Landmark Bancshares [Associated Press] (SAG)
L & B Prec.... Leake and Bullen's Precedents of Pleading [A publication] (DLA)
L & BR........ London & Blackwall Railway [British] (ROG)
L & C.......... Laboratory and Checkout (NASA)
L&C............. Laboratory and Checkout (NAKS)
L & C.......... Lefroy and Cassel's Practice Cases [1881-83] [Ontario] [A publication] (ILCA)
L & C.......... Leigh and Cave's English Crown Cases Reserved [1861-65] [A publication] (DLA)
L & CCC...... Leigh and Cave's English Crown Cases Reserved [1861-65] [A publication] (DLA)
LANDCENT... Allied Land Forces Central Europe [NATO]
L & CM....... Lime and Cement Mortar (DAC)
L & Comm.... Law and Communication [A publication] (DLA)
Land Comp Rep... Land Reports, by Roche, Dillon, and Kehoe [1881-82] [Ireland] [A publication] (DLA)
L & Computer Tech... Law and Computer Technology [A publication] (DLA)
Land Com Rep... Land Reports, by Roche, Dillon, and Kehoe [1881-82] [Ireland] [A publication] (DLA)
L & CONTEM PROB... Law and Contemporary Problems [A publication] (LWAP)
LANDCRA..... Landing Craft and Bases [Military] (AFIT)
LANDCRAB... Landing Craft and Bases [Military] (AABC)
L & D.......... Labor and Delivery [Area of a hospital]
L & D.......... Landing and Deceleration [NASA] (NASA)
L & D.......... Loans and Discounts [Banking]
l&d............... Loans and Discounts (EBF)
l&d............... Loss and Damage (EBF)
L & D.......... Loss and Damage
L & D Conv... Leigh and Dalzell. Conversion of Property [1825] [A publication] (DLA)
Land Dec..... Land Decisions, United States [A publication] (DLA)
L & E.......... English Law and Equity Reports [American Reprint] [A publication] (DLA)
LANDENMARK... Allied Land Forces Denmark [NATO]
L & Eq Rep... Law and Equity Reporter [United States] [A publication] (DLA)
L & E Rep ... English Law and Equity Reports [American Reprint] [A publication] (DLA)
Land Est C... Landed Estates Court [England] (DLA)
LANDEX....... Landing Exercise [Navy] (CAAL)
LANDFAE..... Large Area Nozzle Delivery of Fuel Air Explosive (RDA)
LANDFOR..... Landing Force [Military]
LANDFORASCU... Landing Force Air Support Control Unit [Navy]
L & G Temp Plunk... Lloyd and Good's Irish Chancery Reports Tempore Plunkett [A publication] (DLA)
L & G Temp Sugd... Lloyd and Good's Irish Chancery Reports Tempore Sugden [1835] [A publication] (DLA)

L & GTP ...... Lloyd and Goold's Irish Chancery Reports Tempore Plunkett [*A publication*] (DLA)
L & GT Plunk... Lloyd and Goold's Irish Chancery Reports Tempore Plunkett [*A publication*] (DLA)
L & GTS ...... Lloyd and Goold's Irish Chancery Reports Tempore Sugden [*1835*] [*A publication*] (DLA)
L & GT Sug... Lloyd and Goold's Irish Chancery Reports Tempore Sugden [*1835*] [*A publication*] (DLA)
L & H........... Lamport & Holt Line [*Steamship*] (MHDB)
L & H........... Laurel and Hardy [*The film comedy team of Stan Laurel and Oliver Hardy*]
L&H .... Lernout & Hauspie [*A speech products manufacturer*] (PCM)
L & HR .... [*The*] Lehigh & Hudson River Railway Co. [*Absorbed into Consolidated Rail Corp.*]
L & HTC ...... Line and Halftone Combined [*Illustration*] (DGA)
L & I........... Launch and Impact (AFM)
L&I............. Liver and Iron (DMAA)
L & ID......... London and India Docks [*Shipping*] [*British*] (ROG)
LANDING ..... Landing [*Commonly used*] (OPSA)
LANDIS........ Low-Approach Navigation Director System [*Aircraft landing aid*] [*Air Force*]
L & J Tr Mar... Ludlow and Jenkyns on the Law of Trade-Marks [*A publication*] (DLA)
LANDJUT ..... Allied Land Forces Schleswig-Holstein and Jutland [*NATO*] (NATG)
L & K........... Love and Kisses [*Correspondence*]
L & L........... Latch and Lock (DAC)
L&L............. Launch and Landing [*Aerospace*] (NAKS)
L & L........... Leave and Liberty (WDAA)
L & L........... Legislative and Liaison [*Military*]
L&L............. Lerner and Loewe [*Composers*]
L & L........... Lewd and Lascivious
L & L........... Love and Liquor (IIA)
L&L............. Lyrics and Lyricists [*Long running New York show*]
L & LC .... Leeds and Liverpool Canal [*Shipping*] [*British*] (ROG)
L & LC......... Lift and Lift Cruise (MCD)
LANDLD....... Landlord (ROG)
L & Leg GDR... Law and Legislation in the German Democratic Republic [*A publication*] (DLA)
L & Legis in GDR... Law and Legislation in the German Democratic Republic [*A publication*] (DLA)
L & LeM ...... Leigh and Le Marchant. Elections [*4th ed.*] [*1885*] [*A publication*] (DLA)
L & Lib........ Law and Liberty [*A publication*] (DLA)
L & M........... Labor and Material Bond
L & M........... Layout and Manuscript [*Advertising*] (WDMC)
L&M........... Layout and Manuscript [*Publishing*] (WDMC)
L & M........... Legal and Magnanimous Side [*Sarcastic reference to the government of Vietnam and its allies*] (VNW)
L & M........... [*The*] Librarian and the Machine [*A publication*]
L & M........... Lowndes and Maxwell's English Practice Cases [*1852-54*] [*A publication*] (DLA)
L&N............. Lomas & Nettleton Financial Corp. (EFIS)
L & N........... Louisville & Nashville Railroad Co.
L & NE......... Lehigh & New England Railway Co. [*Absorbed into Consolidated Rail Corp.*]
LANDNON .... Allied Land Forces North Norway [*NATO*] (NATG)
LANDNORTH... Allied Land Forces Northern Europe [*NATO*] (NATG)
LANDNORWAY... Allied Land Forces Norway [*NATO*]
L & NRR....... Louisville & Nashville Railroad Co.
L & OD .... Lester & Orpen Dennys [*Canadian publisher*]
L & Order..... Law and Order [*A publication*] (DLA)
L & P........... Latch and Plaster (DAC)
L & P........... Lighting and Power
L & PA......... Lodging and Pay Allowance [*British military*] (DMA)
L & PP........ Lunar and Planetary Program
L & Psychology Rev... Law and Psychology Review [*A publication*] (DLA)
L & Psych Rev... Law and Psychology Review [*A publication*] (DLA)
L & R........... Lake and Rail
L & R........... Landing and Recovery (KSC)
L & R........... Larceny and Receiving
L & R........... Left and Right
L & R........... Loring and Russell's Election Cases in Massachusetts [*A publication*] (DLA)
L & R Election Cases... Loring and Russell's Election Cases in Massachusetts [*A publication*] (DLA)
Landrys........ Landrys Seafood Restaurants, Inc. [*Associated Press*] (SAG)
L & S........... Launch and Servicing (AAG)
L & S........... Laurinburg & Southern Railroad Co. (IIA)
L & S........... Laverne and Shirley [*Television program*]
L & S........... Logistics and Support (NASA)
LANDSAT...... Land Remote Sensing Satellite System (GFGA)
LANDSAT...... Land Satellite [*Marine science*] (OSRA)
LANDSC....... Landscape
LANDSCPG.... Landscaping
LandsE........ Land's End, Inc. [*Associated Press*] (SAG)
LANDSONOR... Allied Land Forces South Norway [*NATO*] (NATG)
LANDSOUTH... Allied Land Forces Southern Europe [*NATO*]
LANDSOUTHEAST... Allied Land Forces Southeastern Europe [*NATO*]
Landstr .... Landstar Systems, Inc. [*Associated Press*] (SAG)
L & SWR ...... London & South-Western Railway (ROG)
L & T........... Laboratories and Test (NASA)
L & T........... Landlord and Tenant [*A publication*] (DLA)
L & T........... Line and Terminal [*Telecommunications*] (TEL)
L & T........... Longfield and Townsend's Irish Exchequer Reports [*1841-42*] [*A publication*] (DLA)

L & TH........... Lethality and Target Hardening [*Military*] (SDI)
L & U........... Loading and Unloading
L & U........... Lower and Upper [*Anatomy*]
LANDUP....... Alberta Land Use Planning Data Bank [*Alberta Municipal Affairs*] [*Information service or system Defunct*] (IID)
Land U Pl Rep... Land Use Planning Reports [*A publication*] (DLA)
Land Use & Env't L Rev... Land Use and Environment Law Review [*A publication*] (DLA)
L & W........... Living and Well
L & W........... Lloyd and Welsby's English Commercial and Mercantile Cases [*1829-30*] [*A publication*] (DLA)
L & Welsb..... Lloyd and Welsby's English Commercial and Mercantile Cases [*1829-30*] [*A publication*] (DLA)
LANDZEALAND... Allied Land Forces Zealand [*NATO*] (NATG)
LANE........... Lane [*Commonly used*] (OPSA)
Lane .... Lane's English Exchequer Reports [*1605-12*] [*A publication*] (DLA)
LANE........... Local Area Network Emulation [*Telecommunications*] (ACRL)
LANES .... Lane [*Commonly used*] (OPSA)
LANFORTRACOMLANT... Landing Force Training Command, Atlantic [*Navy*]
LANFORTRAU... Landing Force Training Unit [*Marine Corps*] (DNAB)
LANG .... Langley [*England*]
LANG .... Language (AFM)
lang .... Language (WDAA)
Lang .... Language (AL)
Lang Ca Cont... Langdell's Cases on Contracts [*A publication*] (DLA)
Lang Ca Sales... Langdell's Cases on the Law of Sales [*A publication*] (DLA)
Lang Cont..... Langdell's Cases on Contracts [*A publication*] (DLA)
Lang Cont..... Langdell's Summary of the Law of Contracts [*A publication*] (DLA)
Langd Cont... Langdell's Cases on Contracts [*A publication*] (DLA)
Langd Cont... Langdell's Summary of the Law of Contracts [*A publication*] (DLA)
Lang Eq Pl... Langdell's Cases in Equity Pleading [*A publication*] (DLA)
Lang Eq Pl... Langdell's Summary of Equity Pleading [*A publication*] (DLA)
Langer......... [*The*] Langer Biomechanics Group, Inc. [*Associated Press*] (SAG)
Lang Sales.... Langdell's Cases on the Law of Sales [*A publication*] (DLA)
Lang Soc ..... Language in Society [*A publication*] (BRI)
Lang Sum Cont... Langdell's Summary of the Law of Contracts [*A publication*] (DLA)
Lang Tr........ Langley's Trustees' Act [*A publication*] (DLA)
LANH .... Launch (MSA)
LANIC .... LAN [*Local Area Network*] Interface Card (PCM)
LANICA .... Lineas Aereas de Nicaragua, SA [*Nicaraguan airline*]
LANL .... Los Alamos National Laboratory [*Los Alamos, NM*] [*Department of Energy*]
L Ann .... Louisiana Annual Reports [*A publication*] (DLA)
Lannet .... Lannet Data Communictions Ltd. [*Associated Press*] (SAG)
LANNET .... Large Artificial Nerve [*or Neuron*] Network
Lanoptic ...... Lanoptics Ltd. [*Associated Press*] (SAG)
LANP .... Leucine-Rich Acidic Nuclear Protein [*Biochemistry*]
LAnP .... Louisiana State Penitentiary, Angola, LA [*Library symbol Library of Congress*] (LCLS)
LANP .... Plaintree Systems Inc. [*NASDAQ symbol*] (SAG)
LAN/PDL ...... Local Area Network / Program Design Language (LAIN)
LANPF .... Plaintree Systems [*NASDAQ symbol*] (TTSB)
LANRES .... Linked Access Network Resource Extension and Service
LANRES .... Local Network Resource Extension [*Computer science*] (CIST)
LAN/RM ...... Local Area Network Reference Model
Lans............ Lansing's New York Supreme Court Reports [*A publication*] (DLA)
LANS .... Large Atypical Nevus Syndrome [*Medicine*]
LANS .... Latin America News Service (BUAC)
LANS .... Lightweight Airborne Navigation System (MCD)
LANS .... Local Area Network System [*Telecommunications*]
LANS .... LORAN Airborne Navigation System (IEEE)
LANSA .... Lineas Aereas Nacionales Consolidadas Sociedad Anonima
LANSCE .... Los Alamos Neutron Scattering Center
Lans Ch .... Lansing's Select Cases in Chancery [*1824, 1826*] [*New York*] [*A publication*] (DLA)
Lansg.......... New York Supreme Court Reports (Lansing) [*A publication*] (DLA)
LANSHIPRON... Landing Ship Squadron (CINC)
Lansing....... New York Supreme Court Reports (Lansing) [*A publication*] (DLA)
LANSL .... Los Alamos National Scientific Laboratories [*New Mexico*]
Lans Sel Cas... Lansing's Select Cases in Chancery [*1824, 1826*] [*New York*] [*A publication*] (DLA)
LANSW .... Laryngectomee Association of New South Wales [*Australia*]
LANSW .... Legislative Assembly of New South Wales [*Australia*]
LANSW .... Lupus Association of New South Wales [*Australia*]
LANSX .... Lord Abbett: Tax Free Inc.: National Cl.A [*Mutual fund ticker symbol*] (SG)
LANT........... Atlantic
LANT........... Lannet Data Communications Ltd. [*NASDAQ symbol*] (SAG)
L ANT .... Left Anterior (STED)
LANT........... Legislative Assembly of the Northern Territory [*Australia*]
LANTCOM..... Atlantic Command [*Navy*]
LANTCOMINSGEN... Atlantic Command Inspector General (DNAB)
LANTCOMMBPO... Atlantic Command Military Blood Program Office (DNAB)
LANTCOMOPCONCEN... Atlantic [*Fleet*] Commander Operational Control Center [*Navy*]
LANTCOMOPSUPPFAC... Atlantic Command Operations Support Facility (DNAB)
LANTFAP ...... Allied Command Atlantic Frequency Allocation Panel [*Obsolete NATO*] (NATG)
LANTFAST..... Atlantic Forward Area Support Team [*Military*] (DNAB)
LANTFLEASWTACSCOL... Atlantic Fleet Antisubmarine Warfare Tactical School [*Navy*]
LANTFLT....... Atlantic Fleet
LANTFLTHEDSUPPACT... Atlantic Fleet Headquarters Support Activity [*Navy*] (DNAB)

LANTFLTMATCONOFF... Atlantic Fleet Material Control Office [*Navy*] (DNAB)
LANTFLTPEB... Atlantic Fleet Propulsion Examining Board [*Navy*] (DNAB)
LANTFLTRANSUPPFAC... Atlantic Fleet Training Support Facilities
LANTFLTWPNRAN... Atlantic Fleet Weapons Range [*Later, AFRSF*] [*Navy*]
LANTFLTWPNTRAFAC... Atlantic Fleet Weapons Training Facility [*Navy*] (DNAB)
L Anti Antilles (VRA)
L Anti Lesser Antilles (VRA)
LANTICOMIS... LANTCOM Integrated Command and Control Management Information System (MCD)
LANTINTCEN... Atlantic Intelligence Center [*Navy*]
LANTIRN... Low-Altitude Navigation and Targeting Infrared [*System*] for Night [*Aviation*]
LANTMS Linked Access Network Transport Management System [*Telecommunications*]
LANTNAVFACENGCOM... Atlantic Division Naval Facilities Engineering Command
LANTOPS... Atlantic Operations Supply Facilities (MCD)
LANTOPSSUPFAC... Atlantic Operations Supply Facilities
LANTREADEX... Atlantic Readiness Exercise (MCD)
LANTREPCNAVRES... Atlantic Fleet Chief of Naval Reserve Representative (DNAB)
LANTREPCOMNAVSURFRES... Atlantic Representative for Commander Naval Surface Reserve Force (DNAB)
LANTRESFLT... Atlantic Reserve Fleet
LANTSAR... Atlantic International Air and Surface Search and Rescue Seminar (PDAA)
LANTSOC... Atlantic Fleet Signals Security Operations Center [*Navy*] (DNAB)
LANTWWMCCS... Atlantic Fleet Worldwide Military Command Control System [*Navy*] (DNAB)
LANV LanVision Systems [*NASDAQ symbol*] (TTSB)
LANV Left Atrial Neovascularization [*Cardiology*] (DAVI)
LANV Left Atrial Neovascularization [*Medicine*] (STED)
LANX Local Area Network Exchange
LANYX Lord Abbett: Tax Free Inc.: N.Y. Cl.A [*Mutual fund ticker symbol*] (SG)
LANZ Lancer Orthodontics [*NASDAQ symbol*] (TTSB)
LANZ Lancer Orthodontics, Inc. [*NASDAQ symbol*] (SAG)
lao Lao [*MARC language code Library of Congress*] (LCCP)
LAO Laoag [*Philippines*] [*Airport symbol*] (OAG)
LAO Lao Aviaton [*Laos*] [*ICAO designator*] (FAAC)
LAO Laos [*or Lao People's Democratic Republic*] [*ANSI three-letter standard code*] (CNC)
LAO Large Assembly Order (MCD)
LAO Lasa Array [*Montana*] [*Seismograph station code, US Geological Survey*] (SEIS)
LAO La Teko Resources Ltd. [*Vancouver Stock Exchange symbol*]
LAO Lateral Anterior Oblique (DB)
LAO Lead Agency Official (MHDB)
LAO Left Anterior Oblique [*Cardiology*]
LAO Left Anterior Occipital [*Medicine*] (STED)
LAO Left Anterior Occipital [*Position*] [*Obstetrics*] (DAVI)
LAO Left Atrial Overloading [*Cardiology*] (DAVI)
LAO Left Atrial Overloading [*Medicine*] (STED)
LAO Legal Aid Office
LAO Legal Assistance Officer
LAO Licensing Authorities Office
LAO Licentiate in Obstectric Science (DAVI)
LAO Licentiate of the Art of Obstetrics [*British*]
LAO Limited Attack Option (COE)
LAO Logistics Area Officer (MCD)
LAO Logistics Assistance Office [*or Officer*] [*Army Materiel Command*]
LAOAR Latin American Office of Aerospace Research [*Air Force*]
LAOCIF Logistic Assistance Office Command Interest Flasher [*Military*] (AABC)
LAOCP Limited Amateur Operator's Certificate of Proficiency [*Radio*]
LAOD Los Angeles Ordnance District [*Military*] (AAG)
LAOOC Los Angeles Olympic Organizing Committee (EA)
LAOR La Teko Resources Ltd. [*NASDAQ symbol*] (SAG)
LAORF La Teko Resources Ltd [*NASDAQ symbol*] (TTSB)
LAOS Laymen's Overseas Service [*Acronym is now used as official name of the organization*]
LAOSA Librarianship and Archives Old Students' Association (DGA)
LAOSC Local Authorities Ordnance Survey Committee [*British*]
LAP Laboratory Accreditation Program [*Department of Commerce*]
LAP Laboratory of Advertising Performance [*McGraw-Hill*]
LAP Laboratory of Architecture and Planning [*Massachusetts Institute of Technology*] [*Research center*] (RCD)
LAP Labour Action for Peace [*Political party*] (BUAC)
LAP Lakewood Public Library, Lakewood, OH [*OCLC symbol*] (OCLC)
lap Laparoscopy [*Medicine*]
LAP Laparotomy [*Sponges*] (DAVI)
LAP La Paz [*Mexico*] [*Seismograph station code, US Geological Survey*] (SEIS)
LAP La Paz [*Mexico*] [*Airport symbol*] (OAG)
LAP Lapland
lap Lapp [*MARC language code Library of Congress*] (LCCP)
Lap Lapus de Castiglionchio [*Flourished, 1353-81*] [*Authority cited in pre-1607 legal work*] (DSA)
LAP Large Area Panel
LAP Large-Area Processing [*For fabricating multichip modules*]
LAP Latin American Parliament [*See also PLA*] [*Colombia*] (EAIO)
LAP Lattice Assessment Program [*Civil Defense*]
LAP Launch Analyst Panel [*Aerospace*] (AAG)
LAP Learning Ability Profile [*Margarita Henning*] (TES)
LAP Learning Accomplishment Profile [*Psychology*]
LAP Learning Activity Package (EDAC)
LAP Learning Activity Packet (AEE)

LAP Leased Attached Pallet (SSD)
LAP Left Arterial Pressure [*Cardiology*] (DAVI)
LAP Left Atrial Pressure [*Cardiology*]
LAP Lesson Assembly Program (IEEE)
LAP Lethality Assessment Program
LAP Leucine Aminopeptidase [*Also, LA, LP*] [*An enzyme*]
LAP Leukocyte Alkaline Phosphatase [*An enzyme*]
LAP Liberation Action Party [*Trinidad and Tobago*] [*Political party*] (PPW)
LAP Liberian Action Party [*Political party*] (BUAC)
LAP Library Access Program
LAP Library Awareness Program [*FBI*]
LAP Line Access Point [*Telecommunications*] (TEL)
LAP Linear Arithmetic Processor (IAA)
LAP Lineas Aereas Paraguayas [*Paraguay*] [*ICAO designator*] (FAAC)
LAP Lingual Antimicrobial Peptide [*Biochemistry*]
LAP Link Access Procedure [*Telecommunications*] (TEL)
LAP Link Access Protocol [*Telecommunications*]
LAP Link Asynchronous Protocol [*Telecommunications*]
LAP List Assembly Programming [*Computer science*]
LAP Load, Assemble, Pack [*Army*] (AABC)
LAP Loading Assembling and Packing
LAP Local Access Port [*Telecommunications*] (ACRL)
LAP Local Analysis and Prediction [*Marine science*] (OSRA)
LAP Local Analysis and Prediction [*Branch*] (USDC)
LAP Local Area Power [*Computer science*] (CIST)
LAP Location Audit Program [*Navy*] (NG)
LAP Logistics Assistance Program
LAP Loide Aereo Nacional, SA [*Brazilian airline*]
LAP London Airport
LAP Lord's Acre Plan (EA)
LAP Loudspeaker Acoustical Phase-Inverter
L Ap Louisiana Courts of Appeal Reports [*A publication*] (DLA)
LAP Low Achievers Project [*Education*] (AIE)
LAP Low-Altitude Penetration
LAP Low-Altitude Performance
LAP Low Atmospheric Pressure (DAVI)
LAP Lyophilized Anterior Pituitary [*Endocrinology*]
LAPA Latin America Parents Association (EA)
LAPA Leukocyte Alkaline Phosphatase Activity [*Biochemistry*]
LAPA Lightweight Aggregate Producers Association (EA)
LAPA Los Angeles Procurement Agency [*Army*]
LAPAC Life Amendment Political Action Committee [*Defunct*] (EA)
LaPac Louisiana-Pacific Corp. [*Associated Press*] (SAG)
LAPADA London and Provincial Antique Dealers Association [*England*] (BUAC)
LAPADS Lightweight Acoustic Processing and Display System [*British military*] (DMA)
LAPAM Low-Altitude Penetrating Attack Missile [*Proposed*]
LAPAR Large Phased-Array RADAR
LAPB Laboratories' Applied Physiology Branch [*Army*]
LAPB Link Access Procedure [*or Protocol*] Balanced [*Telecommunications*]
LAPB Link Access Protocol, B Channel [*Telecommunications*]
LAPC Land and Agriculture Policy Centre [*South Africa*]
LAPC Landmarks of American Popular Culture [*A publication*]
LAPC Los Angeles Pacific College [*California*]
LAPCO Lavan Petroleum Co. [*Iran*] (BUAC)
LAPD Limited Axial Power Distribution (IEEE)
LAPD Link Access Procedure-D [*Telecommunications*] (DOM)
LAPD Link Access Protocol, D Channel [*Telecommunications*]
LAPD Los Angeles Air Procurement District
LAPD Los Angeles Police Department (WDAA)
Lap Dec Laperriere's Speaker's Decisions [*Canada*] [*A publication*] (DLA)
LAPDOG Low-Altitude Pursuit Dive on Ground (MCD)
LAPDRY Lapidary
LAPE Lineas Aereas Postales Espanoles [*Airline*] [*Spain*]
LAPERS Labor and Production Effectiveness Reporting System [*DoD*]
LAPES Low-Altitude Parachute Extraction System [*Military*]
LAPF Link Access Procedure to Frame Mode Bearer Services [*Telecommunications*] (ACRL)
LAPF Low-Affinity Platelet Factor (STED)
LAPFO Los Angeles Procurement Field Office
LAPH Lithium Aluminum Pentahydride (MCD)
lapid Lapideum [*Stony*] [*Latin*] (MAE)
LAPIS LASER Photoionization Spectroscopy
LAPIS Legislative Authorization Program Information System [*General Accounting Office*] [*Defunct*] (IID)
LAPIS Local Automated Personnel Information System (DNAB)
LAPL Lead Allowance Parts List
LAPL Library Association Publishing Ltd. [*British*]
LAPL Los Angeles Public Library
LaPL Louisiana Power & Light Co. [*Associated Press*] (SAG)
LAPLS Lead Allowance Parts List System (DNAB)
LAPM Last Premidcourse Orbit
LAPM Link Access Procedure for MODEMs [*Communications protocol*] [*Computer science*] (PCM)
LAPMS Latin American Paper Money Society (EA)
LAPMS Long Arm Posterior Molded Splint [*Medicine*] (MEDA)
LAPMS Long-Arm Posterior-Molded Splint (STED)
LAPOCA L-Asparaginase, Prednisone, Oncovin [*Vincristine*], Cytarabine, Adriamycin [*Antineoplastic drug regimen*]
LAPP Lappish [*Language, etc.*] (ROG)
LAPP Lower Achieving Pupils Project [*British*]
LAPPES Large Power Plant Effluent Study (NRCH)
Lappie Live-Alone Person [*Lifestyle classification*]
LAPR Life Assurance Premium Relief [*Business term*]

LAPR	Los Alamos Power Reactor
LAPRE	Los Alamos Power Reactor Experiment
LAPS	LASER Profile System
LAPS	Latin American Philatelic Society (EA)
LAPS	Latin American, Portuguese, and Spanish [*Division*] [*Library of Congress*]
LAPS	Launcher Avionics Packages (MCD)
LAPS	Left Aft Propulsion System [*or Subsystem*] (NASA)
LAPS	Light-Addressable Potentiometric Sensor [*Semiconductor*]
LAPS	Literary, Artistic, Political, or Scientific [*Value*] [*In obscenity law, a criterion established by the 1973 case of Miller Versus California*]
LAPS	Loan Application Processing System
LAPS	Local Analysis and Prediction System [*Marine science*] (OSRA)
LAPS	Louis-Allen Power Supply
LAPS	Lovelace Aerosol Particle Separator [*Lovelace Foundation for Medical Education and Research*] (PDAA)
LAPS	Low-Altitude Proximity Sensor (MCD)
LAPS	Low Attaining Pupils in Secondary Schools (AIE)
LAPSA	Lineas Aereas Paraguayas Sociedad Anonima [*Airline*] [*Paraguay*]
LAPSE	Longterm Ambulatory Physiological Surveillance Equipment (PDAA)
LAPSS	LASER Airborne Photographic Scanning System [*Navy*]
LAPSS	Low-Angle Polycrystalline Silicon Sheet [*Photovoltaic energy systems*]
LAPT	Library Acquisitions: Practice and Theory [*A publication*]
LAPT	Local Apparent Time (MSA)
LAPT	Los Angeles Union Passenger Terminal [*AAR code*]
LAPUT	Light-Activated Programmable Unijunction Transistor
LAPW	Left Atrial Posterior Wall [*Medicine*] (STED)
LAPW	Left Atrial Posterior Wall [*Cardiology*] (DAVI)
LAPW	Linear Augmented Plane-Wave [*Physics*]
LAPW	Linearized Augmented Plane Wave [*Physical chemistry*]
LAPX	Link Access Procedure Half-Duplex [*Telecommunications*] (ACRL)
LAQ	Al Bayda [*Libya*] [*Airport symbol*] (AD)
LAQ	Beida [*Libya*] [*Airport symbol*] (OAG)
LAQ	Lacquer (KSC)
LAQ	Latin America Equity Fd [*NYSE symbol*] (TTSB)
LAQ	Latin America Equity Fund [*NYSE symbol*] (SPSG)
LAQ	Leathercrafters' Association of Queensland [*Australia*]
LAQ	Lebanese Air Transport [*ICAO designator*] (FAAC)
LAQ	Legislative Assembly of Queensland [*Australia*]
L'AQORCD	L'Association Quebecoise des Organismes Regionaux de Concertation et de Developpement (AC)
LAQT	Low-Altitude Qualification Test [*Balloon*]
LaQuinta	La Quinta Motor Inns Ltd. [*Associated Press*] (SAG)
LAR	Labor Arbitration Reports [*Bureau of National Affairs*] [*A publication*] (DLA)
LAR	Land Registry [*British*]
LAR	Laramie [*Wyoming*] [*Seismograph station code, US Geological Survey*] (SEIS)
LAR	Laramie [*Wyoming*] [*Airport symbol*] (OAG)
LAR	Laramie, WY [*Location identifier FAA*] (FAAL)
LAR	Larceny [*Legal shorthand*] (LWAP)
LAR	Lariat Oil & Gas Ltd. [*Toronto Stock Exchange symbol*]
LAR	Laryngology
lar	Larynx [*Anatomy*] (DAVI)
LAR	LASER-Aided Rocket (MCD)
LAR	Late Asthmatic Response [*Medicine*] (DAVI)
LAR	Late Reaction [*Medicine*] (DMAA)
LAR	Launch Acceptability Region (MCD)
LAR	Launch Alert Receiver (DNAB)
LAR	Launcher Adapter Rail (MCD)
LAR	Lawrence Aviation, Inc. [*ICAO designator*] (FAAC)
LAR	Leaf Area Ratio [*Botany*]
LAR	Leaflet Artillery Round [*PSYOP*] (RDA)
LAR	Left Arm Reclining [*or Recumbent*] [*Medicine*]
LAR	Leukocyte Adhesion Receptor [*Immunology*]
LAR	Leukocyte Antigen-Related [*Medicine*] (DMAA)
LAR	Library Association Record [*A publication*] (BRI)
LAR	Libyan Arab Republic (BUAC)
LAR	Life Assurance Relief [*British*]
LAR	Light Artillery Rocket (MCD)
LAR	Light Attendant Station [*Coast Guard*]
LAR	Limit Address Register [*Computer science*]
LAR	Linhas Aereas Regionais SA [*Portugal ICAO designator*] (FAAC)
LAR	Liquid Air Rocket
LAR	Local Acquisition RADAR (CET)
LAR	Locus Activation Region [*Genetics*]
LAR	Logistics Assistance Representative [*Army*] (DOMA)
LAR	Loita Armada Revolucionaria [*Armed Revolutionary Struggle*] [*Spain*] (PD)
LAR	Long-Range Aircraft Rocket (NG)
LAR	Long-Range Assessments and Research [*Program*] [*Department of State*] [*Washington, DC*]
LAR	Lot Age Report (AAEL)
L-Ar	Louisiana Department of State, State Archives and Records, Baton Rouge, LA [*Library symbol Library of Congress*] (LCLS)
LA R	Louisiana Reports [*A publication*] (DLA)
LAR	Low-Altitude Release
LAR	Low-Angle Reentry [*Aerospace*] (MCD)
LAR	Low-Aspect Ratio
LARA	Land Access Rights Association (BUAC)
LARA	Latin American Railways Association (EA)
LARA	Light Armed Reconnaissance Aircraft [*Air Force*]
LARA	Low-Altitude RADAR Altimeter [*Air Force*]
LARAC	Local Authority Recycling Advisory Council (BUAC)
LARAM	Line Addressable Random Access Memory [*Computer science*] (MDG)
LArB	Bienville Parish Library, Arcadia, LA [*Library symbol Library of Congress*] (LCLS)
LArbG	Landesarbeitsgericht [*Provincial Labor Court of Appeal*] [*German*] (ILCA)
LARC	Association for Library Automation Research Communications (EA)
LARC	Lambda Amateur Radio Club (EA)
LARC	Langley Research Center [*NASA*]
LaRC	Langley Research Center [*Hampton, VA*] (NAKS)
LARC	Larceny [*FBI standardized term*]
LARC	Large Automatic Research Computer [*or Calculator*]
LARC	LASER-Activated Recession Compensator (MCD)
LARC	LASER Applications Research Center (RCD)
LARC	Legal Aid Review Committee
LARC	Leukocyte Automatic Recognition Computer [*Blood counting*]
LARC	Library Automation Research and Consulting Association (NITA)
LARC	Library Automation Research and Consulting Services (IAA)
LARC	Libyan-American Reconstruction Commission
LARC	Light Amphibious Resupply Craft
LARC	Lighter, Amphibious, Resupply, Cargo [*Vessel*]
LARC	Lindheimer Astronomical Research Center [*Northwestern University*]
LARC	Livermore Atomic Research Computer
LARC	Local Alcoholism Reception Center
LARC	Locally Assigned Reporting Code [*Munitions reports*] (AFM)
LARC	Loose Actors Revolving Company [*for producing plays; members include actors George C. Scott and Rod Steiger*]
LARC	Low-Altitude Ride Control [*Shock-absorbing system*] [*Aviation*] (MCD)
LARC	Regional Conference for Latin America [*UN Food and Agriculture Organization*]
LARCCH	Latin America Resource Center and Clearinghouse [*Defunct*] (EA)
LARCF	Lithuanian American Roman Catholic Federation (EA)
LARCT	Last Radio Contact [*Aviation*]
LARC-V	Lighter, Amphibious, Resupply, Cargo-Five Ton [*Vessel*] (DNAB)
LARD	Load Adjuster Reference Datum (IAA)
LarDav	Larson-Davis [*Associated Press*] (SAG)
LARDS	Low-Accuracy RADAR Data Transmission System
LARE	Local Asymptotic Relative Efficiency [*Statistics*]
LAREHS	Laboratory of Research in Human and Social Ecology [*University of Quebec at Montreal*] [*Canada Research center*] (RCD)
LA Rep	Louisiana Reports [*A publication*] (DLA)
LA Rev Stat Ann (West)	West's Louisiana Revised Statutes, Annotated [*A publication*] (DLA)
LARF	Latin American Reserve Fund (BUAC)
LARF	Lebanese Armed Revolutionary Faction
LARF	Low-Altitude RADAR Fuzing (CET)
LARG	Largamente [*Easily*] [*Music*]
LARG	Largo [*Very Slow*] [*Music*] (ROG)
LARG	Library-Anthropology Resource Group
LARGO	Larghetto [*Slow*] [*Music*] (ROG)
LARGOS	LASER-Activated Reflecting Geodetic Optical Satellite
LARIA	Local Authorities Research and Intelligence Association [*British*]
LARIAT	LASER RADAR Intelligence Acquisition Technology
LARIAT	Long-Range Area RADAR for Intrusion Detection and Tracking
LARIS	Low-Altitude RADAR Interface System (MCD)
Larizz	Larizza Industries, Inc. [*Associated Press*] (SAG)
LARK	Landmark Bancshares [*NASDAQ symbol*] (TTSB)
LARL	Laurel Cap Group [*NASDAQ symbol*] (TTSB)
LARL	Laurel Capital Group [*NASDAQ symbol*] (SAG)
LARM	Logistics Assets Requirements Model (PDAA)
LARM	Low-Angle Re-Entry Maneuvering Re-Entry Vehicle (PDAA)
LARMC	Landstuhl Army Regional Medical Center [*Germany*]
LARO	Latin American Regional Office [*United Nations Food and Agricultural Organization*] (BARN)
LAROO	Lackland Aircraft Reactors Operations Office (SAA)
LARP	Launch and Recovery Platform (DNAB)
LARP	Line Automatic Reperforator (CET)
LARP	Local and Remote Printing [*Computer science*]
LARP	Local Approvals Review Program
LARPS	Local and Remote Printing Station [*Computer science*]
LARR	Large Area Record Reader (IAA)
LARR	Linear Accelerator Regenerator Reactor (BARN)
LARRIE	Local Authorities Race Relations Information Exchange (BUAC)
LARRL	Fort Keogh Livestock and Range Research Laboratory [*Miles City, MT*] [*Department of Agriculture*] (GRD)
LARRS	Livestock and Range Research Station [*Department of Agriculture*] (GRD)
LARRS	Low-Altitude Retro Rocket System (DWSG)
LARS	Laboratory for Agricultural Remote Sensing
LARS	Laboratory for Applications of Remote Sensing [*Purdue University*] [*Research center*] (RCD)
LARS	Laminar Angular Rate Sensor [*Navy*]
LARS	Language-Structured Auditory Retention Span Test
LARS	Larscom Inc. [*NASDAQ symbol*] (SAG)
LARS	LASER-Aided Rocket System [*Military*] (CAAL)
LARS	LASER Angular Rate Sensor [*or Scanner*]
LARS	LASER-Articulated Robotic System
LARS	Launch and Recovery System [*NASA*]
LARS	Learning and Recognition System [*GTE*]
LARS	Left Add, Right Subtract [*Army field artillery technique*] (INF)
LARS	Leucyl-Transfer Ribonucleic Acid [*Biochemistry*] (DAVI)
LARS	Light Artillery Rocket System (NATG)
LARS	Living Aquatic Resources Sector [*Aquaculture*]
LARS	Low-Altitude RADAR System (NATG)
LARS	Lower Airspace RADAR Advisory Service [*British*] (DA)

LARS	Lower Atmosphere Research Satellite (SSD)
LARSA	Latin American Rural Sociological Association (EAIO)
Larscom	Larscom Inc. [*Associated Press*] (SAG)
LARSI	Laboratoire de Recherche en Sciences Immobilieres [*University of Quebec at Montreal*] [*Research center*] (RCD)
LA RSIS	LA Reference, Special and Information Section [*British*] (NITA)
LARSIS	Library Association Reference and Special Information Section (PDAA)
LARSP	Language Assessment Remediation and Screening Procedure [*for the language impaired*]
LARSSYAA	Laboratory for Applications of Remote Sensing System for Aircraft Analysis [*NASA*] (GFGA)
LART	Lateral Acceleration Response Time
LARV	Low-Altitude Research Vehicle (IAA)
LARVA	Low-Altitude Research Vehicular Advancements
laryn	Laryngeal [*Medicine*] (STED)
laryn	Laryngeal [*Otorhinolaryngology*] (DAVI)
laryn	Laryngitis [*Otorhinolaryngology*] (DAVI)
laryn	Laryngoscopy [*Otorhinolaryngology*] (DAVI)
Laryng	Laryngology
LARYNGLGST	Laryngologist
LARYNGLGY	Laryngology
Laryngol	Laryngologist (DAVI)
LARYNGOL	Laryngology
LAS	Almirall [*Spain*] [*Research code symbol*]
LAS	Label as Such [*Pharmacology*] (CDAI)
las	Label as Such [*Medicine*] (WDAA)
LAS	Labor Area Summary [*Employment and Training Administration*] [*Department of Labor*]
LAS	Laboratories of Applied Sciences [*University of Chicago*] (MCD)
LAS	Laboratory Automation System
LAS	Laboratory of Atmospheric Sciences [*National Science Foundation*]
LAS	Land Agents' Society [*British*] (DI)
LAS	Landing Approach Simulator
LAS	LANDSAT [*Land Remote Sensing Satellite System*] Sensor [*NASA*] (SSD)
LAS	Language Assessment Scales [*Test*]
LAS	Lapidus Airfloat System (DAVI)
LAS	Large Amplitude Simulator
LAS	Large Astronomical Satellite [*ESRO*]
LAS	Large-Probe Atmospheric Structure [*NASA*]
LAS	La Salle College, Philadelphia, PA [*OCLC symbol*] (OCLC)
LAS	LASER Absorption Spectrometer
LAS	LASER Antiflash System
LAS	LASER Attack System
LAS	Laser Indus Ltd, Ord [*AMEX symbol*] (TTSB)
LAS	Laser Industries Ltd. [*AMEX symbol*] (SPSG)
LAS	Las Vegas [*Nevada*] [*Airport symbol*] (OAG)
LAS	Las Vegas, NV [*Location identifier FAA*] (FAAL)
LAS	Lateral Amyotrophic Sclerosis [*Medicine*] (STED)
LAS	Launch Area Supervisor (AFM)
LAS	Launch Auxiliary System
las	Laxative [*Medicine*] (DAVI)
LAS	Laxative Abuse Syndrome [*Medicine*] (DAVI)
LAS	Leader Authenticity Scale [*Psychology*] (EDAC)
LAS	Leadership Appraisal Survey [*Interpersonal skills and attitudes test*]
LAS	League of Arab States [*Tunis, Tunisia*]
LAS	Lebanese-American Society of Greater New York [*Defunct*] (EA)
LAS	Left Anterior-Superior [*Anatomy*] (DAVI)
LAS	Left Arm Sitting [*Blood pressure and pulse measurement*] [*Cardiology*] (DAVI)
LAS	Legal Aid Society (WDAA)
LAS	Leipziger Aegyptologische Studien [*A publication*] (BJA)
LAS	Leucine Acetylsalicylate [*Biochemistry*] (DAVI)
LAS	Library Association of Singapore (BUAC)
LAS	Library Automation Services [*Oxford University*]
LAS	Life Assurance of Scotland [*Commercial firm*]
LAS	Light-Activated Switch
LAS	Lignes Aerienne Seychelles [*ICAO designator*] (FAAC)
LAS	Limited Assignment Status [*Military*]
LAS	Limited Assortment Store (WDMC)
LAS	Line Apparatus Shop [*Telecommunications*] (OA)
LAS	Linear Alkylbenzene Sulfonate [*Surfactant*]
LAS	Linear Alkyl Sulfonate (EDCT)
LAS	Linear Alkyl Sulfonate (STED)
LAS	Link Active Scheduler (ACII)
LAS	Litha-Alumina-Silicate [*Inorganic chemistry*]
LAS	Lithuanian Academy of Sciences (BUAC)
LAS	Liturgical Arts Society (EA)
LAS	Local Adaptation Syndrome [*Medicine*]
LAS	Local Address Space
LAS	Local Alignment System [*Optics*]
LAS	Local Area Screening
LAS	Logical Address Strobe
LAS	Logical Compare Accumulator with Storage (SAA)
LAS	Logic Analysis System [*Rohde and Schwartz*] [*Germany*] (NITA)
LAS	London Appreciation Society
LAS	Long-Arm Splint [*Orthopedics*] (DAVI)
LAS	Longitudinal Air Spring
LAS	Long-Range Assistance Strategy (CINC)
LAS	Look-Out Aiming Sight [*Military*] (PDAA)
LAS	Loop Actuating Signal (SAA)
LAS	Lord Advocate of Scotland
LAS	Low Air Speed (MCD)
LAS	Low-Alloy Steel

LAS	Low-Altitude Satellite
LAS	Lower Abdominal Surgery (DAVI)
LAS	Lower Airspace (WDAA)
LAS	Lunar Attitude System [*Aerospace*]
LAS	Lutheran Academy for Scholarship [*Defunct*] (EA)
LAS	Lymphadenopathy Syndrome [*Medicine*]
LAS	Lymphangioscintigraphy (STED)
LAS	Lysine Acetylsalicylate [*Biochemistry*]
LAS	McCarran International Airport [*FAA*] (TAG)
LAS	Saskatchewan Libraries Retrospective Conversion [*UTLAS symbol*]
LASA	Laboratory Animal Science Association [*British*]
LASA	Large Aperture Seismic Array [*Nuclear detection device*]
LASA	Large Area Solar Array
LASA	LASER Anti-Satellite Weapon (LAIN)
LASA	Latin American Shipowners Association (BUAC)
LASA	Latin American Studies Association (EA)
LA(SA)	Latvian Association of South Australia
LASA	LIDAR [*Light Detection and Ranging*] Atmospheric Sounder and Altimeter
LASA	Linear-Analogue Self Assessment (DMAA)
LASA	London Advice Services Alliance [*England*] (BUAC)
LaSalle	La Salle Re Holdings Ltd. [*Associated Press*] (SAG)
LASAM	LASER Semiactive Missile
LASA-P	Linear-Analogue Self-Assessment-Pristman (DMAA)
LASAR	Logic Automated Stimulus and Response (MCD)
LASARS	Low Probability of Intercept Antijam Secure Airborne Radio System (MCD)
LASAS	Latin American Secretariat for Academic Services [*Defunct*]
LASA-S	Linear-Analogue Self-Assessment-Selby (DMAA)
LASB	Lackawaxen & Stourbridge Railroad Corp. [*AAR code*]
LASC	Light Armored Squad Carrier
LASCA	Large Area Solar Cell Array
LASCAR	Language for Simulation of Computer Architecture (CSR)
Lasc H War	Lascelles' Horse Warranty [*2nd ed.*] [*1880*] [*A publication*] (DLA)
Lasc Juv Off	Lascelles on Juvenile Offenders [*A publication*] (DLA)
LASCO	Large Angle and Spectrometric Coronagraph Experiment [*For observation of the sun*]
LASCO	Large-Angle Spectrometric Coronagraph [*Marine science*] (OSRA)
LASCO	Large-Angle Spectroscopic Coronagraph [*Instrumentation*]
LASCO	Latin America Science Cooperation Office (MSC)
LASCODOCS	Linguistic Analysis of Spanish Colonial Documents
LASCOT	Large Screen Color Television System (NASA)
LASCR	Light-Activated Silicon-Controlled Rectifier
LASCS	Light-Activated Silicon-Controlled Switch (MCD)
LASD	Labor Agreement Settlement Data [*Cast Metals Association*] [*A publication*]
LASD	Latin American Serial Documents
LASE	LAMPS Shipboard Element (MCD)
LASE	Large Aperture Seismic Experiment [*Geophysical survey*]
LASE	Laser Sight, Inc. [*NASDAQ symbol*] (SAG)
L-Ase	L-Asparaginase [*Also, A, L, L-Asp, L-asnase*] [*An enzyme, an antineoplastic*]
LASE	LIDAR [*Light Detection and Ranging*] Atmosphere Sensing Experiment
LASE	Logistics Asset Support Estimate
LASEDECO	Land Settlement and Development Corp. [*Philippines*] (BUAC)
Laser	Laser Industries Ltd. [*Associated Press*] (SAG)
LASER	League for the Advancement of States' Equal Rights (EA)
LASER	Learning Achievement through Saturated Educational Resources
LASER	Light Amplification by Stimulated Emission of Radiation [*Acronym was coined in 1957 by scientist Gordon Gould*]
laser	Light Amplification by Stimulated Emission of Radiation (WDMC)
LASER	London and South East Advisory Council [*England*] (BUAC)
LASER	London and South Eastern Library Region [*Information service or system*] (IID)
LASERCOM	LASER Communications (MCD)
LASERCOM	Light Amplification by Stimulated Emission of Radiation Computer Output Microfilm (EECA)
Lasergte	Lasergate Systems, Inc. [*Associated Press*] (SAG)
LaserSt	Laser Storm, Inc. [*Associated Press*] (SAG)
Lasertech	Laser Technics [*Associated Press*] (SAG)
LA Sess Law Serv	Louisiana Session Law Service [*A publication*] (DLA)
LASFB	Left Anterior-Superior Fascicular Block [*Medicine*] (STED)
LASFB	Left Anterior-Superior Fascicular Block [*Cardiology*] (DAVI)
LASH	LASER Antitank Semiactive Homing
LASH	Latin American Society of Hepatology [*See also SLH*] (EAIO)
LASH	Left Anterior-Superior Hemiblock [*Medicine*] (STED)
LASH	Left Anterosuperior Hemiblock [*Cardiology*] (DAVI)
LASH	Legislative Action on Smoking and Health (EA)
LASH	Lighter Aboard Ship [*Barge-carrying ship*]
LASHST	Latin American Society for the History of Sciences and Technology (BUAC)
LASHUP	Land-Air Synergic Homogeneous Ultra-Processor (SAA)
LASI	Landing-Site Indicator [*Aviation*]
LASI	Library of Ancient Semitic Inscriptions (BJA)
LASI	Licentiate of the Ambulance Service Institute [*British*] (DBQ)
LASIE	Library Automated Systems Information Exchange [*Australia*] (NITA)
LASIK	Laser Assisted In-Situ Keratomileusis [*Ophthalmology*]
LASIL	Land and Sea Interaction Laboratory [*Environmental Science Services Administration*]
LASIM	LASER Aiming Simulation (PDAA)
LASIM	Los Angeles Society of Internal Medicine (BUAC)
LASINT	LASER Intelligence (MCD)
LASL	Los Alamos Scientific Laboratory [*USAEC*]

LASLA.......... Laboratoire d'Analyse Statistique des Langues Anciennes [*Laboratory for the Statistical Analysis of Ancient Languages*] [*University of Liege, Belgium*]
LASM.......... Land-Attack Standard Missile
LASM.......... LASER Semiactive Missile (DNAB)
LASMEC.......... Local Authorities School Meals Equipment Consortium
Lasmo.......... Lasmo Ltd. [*Associated Press*] (SAG)
LASMO........ London & Scottish Marine Oil [*British*]
L-Asnase..... L-Asparaginase [*Also, A, L, L-ase, L-Asp*] [*An enzyme, an antineoplastic*]
LASO.......... Latin American Solidarity Organization (BUAC)
LASO.......... Low-Altitude Search Option [*Search mode of the BOMARC guidance system*]
LASOR......... LASER Spillover and Reflectivity (MCD)
LASP.......... Laboratory for Atmospheric and Space Physics [*University of Colorado*] [*Research center*]
L-Asp.......... L-Asparaginase [*Also, A, L, L-ase, L-asnase*] [*An enzyme, an antineoplastic*]
LASP.......... Local Attached Support Processor
LASP.......... Low-Altitude Space Platform (MCD)
LASP.......... Low-Altitude Surveillance Platform (MCD)
LASPAC....... Landing Gear, Avionics Systems Package (MCD)
LASPAU....... Latin American Scholarship Program of American Universities (EA)
LasPMd....... Laser Pacific Media Corp. [*Associated Press*] (SAG)
LASR.......... Laboratories for Astrophysics and Space Research [*University of Chicago*] [*Research center*]
LASR.......... Letter Writing with Automatic Send-Receive (IAA)
LASR.......... Low-Altitude Surveillance RADAR
LASR-2........ Litton Airborne Search RADAR Mark Two [*Canada*] (PDAA)
LASRA......... Leather and Shoe Research Association [*New Zealand*] (BUAC)
LASRAM....... Low-Altitude Short-Range Missile
LasrCp......... Laser Corp. [*Associated Press*] (SAG)
LASRE......... Lightweight Advanced Super-Responsive Engine [*Automotive engineering*]
Lasrgt.......... Lasergate Systems, Inc. [*Associated Press*] (SAG)
LASRM........ Low-Altitude Short-Range Missile
LASRM........ Low-Altitude Supersonic Research Missile
LasrmTc....... LaserMaster Technologies, Inc. [*Associated Press*] (SAG)
Lasrscp........ Laserscope, Inc. [*Associated Press*] (SAG)
Lasrtch........ Laser Technics, Inc. [*Associated Press*] (SAG)
LASS.......... Labile Aggregation-Stimulating Substance [*Hematology*]
LASS.......... Language and Assembly Language [*Computer science*] (DNAB)
LASS.......... Large Aircraft Start System (DWSG)
LASS.......... Large Aperture Solenoid Spectrometer [*Stanford Linear Accelerator Center*]
LASS.......... Large Area Screening Systems (MCD)
LASS.......... Large Area Sky Survey
LASS.......... LASER-Activated Semiconductor Switch (IAA)
LASS.......... LASER-Activated Silicon Switch (MCD)
LASS.......... LASER Applications System Study [*Military*]
LASS.......... Lateral Acceleration Sensing System (PDAA)
LASS.......... Launch Area Support Ship
LASS.......... Liaoning Academy of Social Sciences (BUAC)
LASS.......... Library Access and Sixth-Form Studies [*British*] (AIE)
LASS.......... Library Automated Service System (IAA)
LASS.......... Light-Activated Silicon Switch
LASS.......... Lighter-than-Air Submarine Simulator
LASS.......... Line Amplifier and Super Sync Mixer
LASS.......... Linguistic Analysis of Speech Samples (DAVI)
LASS.......... Linked Administrative Statistical Sample [*Social Security Administration*] (GFGA)
LASS.......... Local Area Sensor System [*Military*] (LAIN)
LASS.......... Local Area Signaling Service [*Bell Laboratories*]
LASS.......... Local Area Signaling Services [*Telecommunications*] (ACRL)
LASS.......... Local Authority Social Services [*British*]
LASS.......... Lockheed Airline System Simulation (PDAA)
LASS.......... Logistic-Automated Support System (SSD)
LASS.......... Logistics Analysis Simulation System
LASS.......... Logistics Automated Supply System
LASS.......... Low-Altitude Space Surveillance System [*Military*] (MUSM)
LASS.......... Low-Angle Silicon Sheet [*Photovoltaic energy systems*]
LASS.......... Lunar Applications of a Spent Stage [*Aerospace*] (MCD)
LASSA......... Licensed Animal Slaughterers and Salvage Association [*British*] (BI)
LASSC......... Latin American Social Sciences Council [*Argentina Database producer*] (EA)
LASSI.......... Latin American Secretariat of the Socialist International (BUAC)
LASSI-HS..... Learning and Study Strategies Inventory-High School Version [*Test*] (TMMY)
LASSII........ Low-Altitude Satellite Studies of Ionospheric Irregularities
LASSM........ Line Amplifier and Super Sync Mixer (MSA)
LASSO......... Landing and Approach System, Spiral-Oriented
LASSO......... LASER Search and Secure Observer (CET)
LASSO......... LASER Synchronization from Stationary Orbit (IEEE)
LASSO......... Library Acquisition Services System Online [*Suggested name for the Library of Cogress computer system*]
LASSO......... Light Air-to-Surface Semiautomatic Optical [*French missile*]
LASSO......... Light Aviation Special Support Operations
LASSO......... Lunar Applications of a Spent Stage in Orbit [*Aerospace*] (MCD)
LASSOS....... Library Automation Systems and Services Options Study [*Advisory committee*] (NITA)
LASSP......... Laboratory for Atomic and Solid State Physics [*Cornell University*] [*Research center*] (RCD)
LASST......... Laboratory for Surface Science and Technology [*University of Maine at Orono*] [*Research center*] (RCD)
LASSV........ Land and Approach System for Space Vehicles [*NASA*] (KSC)

LAST.......... Language and Systems Together [*Programming language*] [*Baytec Bay City, MI*]
LAST.......... Large Aperture Scanning Telescope (TEL)
LAST.......... Last Satellite Position [*Navy Navigation Satellite System*] (DNAB)
LAST.......... Left Anterior Small Thoracotomy [*Medicine*] (DMAA)
LAST.......... Leukocyte-Antigen Sensitivity Testing [*Medicine*] (MEDA)
LAST.......... Local Area System Transport [*Computer science*] (CIST)
LAST.......... Low-Altitude Supersonic Target (RDA)
LASTE......... Low-Altitude Safety and Targeting Equipment (DWSG)
LASU.......... Local Air Supply Unit [*British military*] (DMA)
LA SUQ....... Louisiana State University. Quarterly [*A publication*] (DLA)
LASV.......... Low-Altitude Supersonic Vehicle [*Formerly, SLAM*] [*Air Force*]
LASV.......... Low-Altitude Surface Vehicle (WDAA)
LasVDsc...... Las Vegas Discount Golf & Tennis, Inc. [*Associated Press*] (SAG)
LasVE......... Las Vegas Entertainment Network [*Associated Press*] (SAG)
LasVEE....... Las Vegas Entertainment Network [*Associated Press*] (SAG)
LASVEM...... Lightly Armored Structure Vulnerability Estimation Methodology (MCD)
LasVEnt...... Las Vegas Entertainment Network [*Associated Press*] (SAG)
LasVMaj..... Las Vegas Major League Sports [*Associated Press*] (SAG)
LASWMMR... London Association of Scale and Weighing Machine Manufacturers and Repairers [*England*] (BUAC)
LASX.......... Laser Technics [*NASDAQ symbol*] (SAG)
LASX.......... Lasertechnics Inc. [*NASDAQ symbol*] (TTSB)
LAT.......... Aviation Legere de l'Armee de Terre [*France ICAO designator*] (FAAC)
LaT.......... Lactate Threshold [*Biochemistry*]
LAT.......... Lae [*Papua New Guinea*] [*Seismograph station code, US Geological Survey*] (SEIS)
LAT.......... Language Aptitude Test [*Military*] (AFM)
LAT.......... Large Angle Tagger (MCD)
LAT.......... Large Angle Torque (MCD)
LAT.......... LASER Acquisition and Tracking (OA)
LAT.......... Latch (NASA)
Lat.......... Latch's English King's Bench Reports [*1625-28*] [*A publication*] (DLA)
LAT.......... Latent
LAT.......... Lateral (KSC)
lat.......... Lateral (VRA)
LAT.......... Latex Agglutination Test [*Clinical chemistry*]
LAT.......... Lathwell Resources Ltd. [*Vancouver Stock Exchange symbol*]
LAT.......... Latin
lat.......... Latin [*MARC language code Library of Congress*] (LCCP)
lat.......... Latissimus [*Dorsi*] (STED)
LAT.......... Latitude
Lat.......... Latitude (WA)
LAT.......... Latitude of Target
LAT.......... Latrine (DSUE)
LAT.......... Latus [*Wide*] [*Pharmacy*]
lat.......... Latus [*Broad*] [*Latin*] (EES)
LAT.......... Latvia
LAT.......... Learning Ability Test [*Military*] (AFM)
LAT.......... Left Anterior Thigh [*Medicine*]
LAT.......... Less Active Tetragonal (PDAA)
LAT.......... Level above Threshold
LAT.......... Licensing Appeals Tribunal [*Australia*]
LAT.......... Light Artillery Tractor [*British military*] (DMA)
LAT.......... Linear Accelerator Tube
LAT.......... Linseed Association Terms [*Shipping*]
LAT.......... Local Apparent Time
LAT.......... Local Area Transport [*Telecommunications*]
LAT.......... Lockheed Air Terminal, Inc. [*Subsidiary of Lockheed Aircraft Corp.*]
LAT.......... Logistics Assistance Team (MCD)
LAT.......... Long-Acting Theophylline [*Pharmacology*]
LAT.......... Los Angeles Times [*A publication*]
LAT.......... Lot Acceptance Test (NASA)
LAT.......... Low-Altitude Tactics (DOMA)
LAT.......... Low-Angle Track (CAAL)
LAT.......... Lowest Astronomical Tide (PDAA)
LAT.......... Lumbermen's Association of Texas (SRA)
Lat.......... Valsts Biblioteka [*State Library of Latvia*], Riga, Latvia [*Library symbol Library of Congress*] (LCLS)
LAT-A........ Latrunculin-A [*A toxin*]
LATA......... Local Access and Transport Area
LATA......... Local Access Transport Area [*Telecommunications*]
LATA......... Local-Area Telephone Authority [*Telecommunications*]
LATA......... London Amenity and Transport Association
LatACas...... Latin American Casinos, Inc. [*Associated Press*] (SAG)
LatADis...... Latin American Discovery Fund [*Associated Press*] (SAG)
LatADlr....... Latin America Dollar Income Fund [*Associated Press*] (SAG)
LAT ADMOV.. Lateri Admoveatum [*Let It Be Applied to the Side*] [*Pharmacy*]
LatAEqt...... Latin America Equity Fund [*Associated Press*] (SAG)
LATAF........ Logistics Activation Task Force [*Air Force*] (MCD)
LATAG........ LASER Air-to-Air Gunnery Simulator [*Military*] (CAAL)
LATAG........ Latin American Trade Advisory Group [*British Overseas Trade Board*] (DS)
LatAInv...... Latin American Investment Fund [*Associated Press*] (SAG)
lat & loc...... Lateralizing and Localizing [*Medicine*] (STED)
LATAR........ LASER-Augmented Target Acquisition and Recognition System (MCD)
LATAS........ LASER-Augmented Target Acquisition System
LAT-B........ Latrunculin-B [*A toxin*]
LATB.......... Lithium Aluminum Tri-tert-Butoxyhydride [*Organic chemistry*]
LATBR........ Los Angeles Times Book Review [*A publication*] (BRI)
LATC.......... Los Angeles Theater Center [*California*]
LATCC........ London Air-Traffic Control Center

Latch	Latch's English King's Bench Reports [1625-28] [A publication] (DLA)
LATCH	Literature Attached to Charts [Nursing program]
LATD	Large Area Transmission Density (MCD)
LATD	Latitude (ADA)
LATDISP	Lateral Dispersion (MCD)
LAT DOL	Lateri Dolente [To the Painful Side] [Pharmacy]
LATE	Late Assessment of Thrombolytic Efficacy [Cardiology study]
LATE	Legal Assistance for the Elderly
LATE	London Association for the Teaching of English [British] (AIE)
La Tech U	Louisiana Tech University (GAGS)
LaTeko	La Teko Resources Ltd. [Associated Press] (SAG)
LATER	Ladies' After Thoughts on Equal Rights [Acronym is used as name of association] [Defunct] (EA)
LATER	[The] Life and Times of Eddie Roberts [TV program]
Later Rom Emp...	[The] Later Roman Empire [A publication] (OCD)
Latex	Latex Resources [Associated Press] (SAG)
LATEX	Louisiana-Texas Experiment [Gulf Marine Minerals Management] [Marine science] (OSRA)
LatexRs	Latex Resources [Associated Press] (SAG)
LATF	Legal Aid Task Force
LATF	Lloyd's American Trust Fund (AIA)
LATH	Laos and Thailand Military Assistance
La Th	La Themis [A publication] (DLA)
Lath	Lathrop's Reports [115-145 Massachusetts] [A publication] (DLA)
LATH	Libraries of Affiliated Teaching Hospitals - School of Medicine [Library network]
La Them LC...	La Themis (Lower Canada) [A publication] (DLA)
LATHES	LASER Terminal Homing Engagement Simulator (PDAA)
Lathrop	Lathrop's Reports [115-145 Massachusetts] [A publication] (DLA)
Lath Wind L..	Latham on the Law of Window Lights [A publication] (DLA)
LATI	Linee Aeree Transcontinentali Italiane
LatinAGr	Latin America Growth Fund, Inc. [Associated Press] (SAG)
LATINAH	Latin America Human Settlements Information Network (BUAC)
LATIS	Lightweight Airborne Thermal Imaging System (MCD)
LATIS	Loop Activity Tracking Information System [Telecommunications] (TEL)
LATIX	Lord Abbett: Tax Free Inc: Texas Cl.A [Mutual fund ticker symbol] (SG)
Lat Jus	Latrobe's Justice [A publication] (DLA)
LATK	Local Administrative Tool Kit [AT & T] [Software development and integration tools] (NITA)
LATKWEPSCOLPAC...	Light Attack Weapons School, Pacific (DNAB)
LATL	Lateral (MSA)
LATLI	Latin American Tax Law Institute [Uruguay] (EAIO)
lat men	Lateral Meniscectomy [Medicine] (STED)
lat men	Lateral Meniscectomy [Orthopedics] (DAVI)
LATN	Low-Altitude Tactical Navigation
LATNET	Latvian Academic Network (TELE)
LATNS	Los Angeles Times News Service
LATO	List of Applicable Technical Orders [Military] (AFIT)
LATOFF	Lowest Astronomical Tide of the Foreseeable Future (PDAA)
LATOM	Lowest Astronomical Tide of the Month (PDAA)
LATOY	Lowest Astronomical Tide of the Year (PDAA)
LATP	League of American Theatres and Producers (EA)
LATP	Left Atrial Transmural Pressure [Medicine] (DMAA)
LATP	Lima Army Tank Plant [Ohio]
LATPT	Left Atrial Transesophageal Pacing Test [Medicine] (DMAA)
LATR	Lateral (DNAB)
Latr	Locator [Compass] (DA)
LA TR	Louisiana Term Reports (Martin) [A publication] (DLA)
LATREC	LASER-Acoustic Time Reversal Expansion and Compression (MCD)
lat Rin	Lactated Ringer [Solution] (STED)
LATRL	Lateral
LA TR (NS)...	Louisiana Term Reports, New Series (Martin) [1823-30] [A publication] (DLA)
LATS	Latin-America Thyroid Society (BUAC)
LATS	L.A. T Sportswear [NASDAQ symbol] (TTSB)
LATS	LA T Sportswear, Inc. [NASDAQ symbol] (SAG)
LATS	LDEF [Long-Duration Exposure Facility] Assembly and Transportation System [NASA] (NASA)
LATS	Leather and Associated Trades Show [British] (ITD)
LATS	Light Armored Turret System (MCD)
LATS	Light Attack Turbofan Single Aircraft [Aviation]
LATS	Lightweight Antenna Terminal Seeker
LATS	Long-Acting Thyroid Stimulator [Endocrinology]
LATS	Long-Acting Transmural Stimulator [Medicine] (STED)
LATS-P	Long Acting Thyroid Stimulator-Protector [Endocrinology]
LA T Spt	LA T Sportswear, Inc. [Associated Press] (SAG)
LatSSR	Latvian Soviet Socialist Republic
LATT	LASER Atmospheric Transmission Test
LATT	Library Association of Trinidad and Tobago (BUAC)
Lattice	Lattice Semiconductor Corp. [Associated Press] (SAG)
Latt Pr C Pr...	Lattey's Privy Council Practice [1869] [A publication] (DLA)
LATTU	Latin American Table Tennis Union (BUAC)
LATu	Lobuloalveolar Tumor [Medicine] (DB)
LATUF	Latin America Trade Union Federation (NATG)
Latv	Latvia (VRA)
Latv	Latvian
LATWING	Light Attack Wing [Navy] (NVT)
LATX	Latex Res Inc. [NASDAQ symbol] (TTSB)
LATX	Latex Resources, Inc. [NASDAQ symbol] (SAG)
LAU	Lamu [Kenya] [Airport symbol] (OAG)
LAU	Lauder [New Zealand] [Geomagnetic observatory code]
LAU	Laumontite [A zeolite]
LAU	Launcher Aircraft Unit
LAU	Launcher Armament Unit [Navy] (DOMA)
LAU	Laundry (MSA)
LAU	Laurentian University Library [UTLAS symbol]
Lau	Laurentius Hispanus [Deceased, 1248] [Authority cited in pre-1607 legal work] (DSA)
LAU	Line Access Unit (NITA)
LAU	Line Adapter Unit [Computer science]
LAU	Linear Accelerometer Unit (PDAA)
LAU	Lineas Aereas Suramericanas Ltd. [Colombia] [ICAO designator] (FAAC)
LAU	Lithuanian Artists' Union (BUAC)
lau	Louisiana [MARC country of publication code Library of Congress] (LCCP)
LAU	Lower Arithmetic Unit (IAA)
LAUA	Lloyd's Aviation Underwriters Association [British] (DBA)
LAUD	League of Americans of Ukrainian Descent (EA)
Lau de Pin...	Laurentius de Pinu [Deceased, 1397] [Authority cited in pre-1607 legal work] (DSA)
Lauder	Fountainhall's Session Cases [1678-1712] [Scotland] [A publication] (DLA)
LAUK	Library Association of the United Kingdom
LAUM	Linguistic Atlas of the Upper Midwest
LAUNC	Launceston [Municipal borough in England]
LAUND	Laundry [Classified advertising]
LAUP	LASER-Assisted Uvulopalatoplasty [Medicine] (DMAA)
LAUR	Laurel Bancorp, Inc. [NASDAQ symbol] (SAG)
Laur	Laurentian Library [Classical studies] (OCD)
Laur	Laurentius Hispanus [Deceased, 1248] [Authority cited in pre-1607 legal work] (DSA)
Laur	Reports of the High Court of Griqualand [1882-1910] [South Africa] [A publication] (DLA)
LAURA	Low-Altitude Unmanned Reconnaissance Aircraft (DOMA)
Laur de Palat...	Laurentius de Pallatis [Flourished, 16th century] [Authority cited in pre-1607 legal work] (DSA)
LaurelBc	Laurel Bancorp, Inc. [Associated Press] (SAG)
Lauren	Laurentius Hispanus [Deceased, 1248] [Authority cited in pre-1607 legal work] (DSA)
Laurence	Laurence's Reports of the High Court of Griqualand [1882-1910] [South Africa] [A publication] (DLA)
Lauren de Rodul...	Laurentius de Rodulphis [Flourished, 15th century] [Authority cited in pre-1607 legal work] (DSA)
Laur HC Ca...	Lauren's High Court Cases [South Africa] [A publication] (DLA)
LaurlCa	Laurel Capital Group [Associated Press] (SAG)
Laur Prim	Laurence's Primogeniture [1878] [A publication] (DLA)
LAUS	Local Area Unemployment Statistics (OICC)
LAUSC	Linguistic Atlas of the United States and Canada [1930]
Lauss Eq......	Laussat's Equity Practice in Pennsylvania [A publication] (DLA)
LAUTRO	Life Assurance and Unit Trust Regulatory Organisation [British]
LAV	Las Vegas [Diocesan abbreviation] [Nevada] (TOCD)
lav	Latvian [MARC language code Library of Congress] (LCCP)
LAV	Launch Axis, Vertical (MCD)
LAV	Lavaliere [Lapel microphone] (NTCM)
LAV	Lavatory (KSC)
lav	Lavender [Philately]
LAV	Law Association of Victoria [Australia]
LAV	Leafhopper A Virus [Medicine] (DMAA)
LAV	Legislative Assembly of Victoria [Australia]
LAV	Lifting Ascent Vehicle
LAV	Light Armored Vehicle [Army] (RDA)
LAV	Linea Aeropostal Venezolana [Venezuela] [ICAO designator] (FAAC)
LAV	Lymphadenopathy-Associated Virus
LAV	Lymphocyte-Associated Virus
LAV	Varah [L. A.] Ltd. [Toronto Stock Exchange symbol]
LAVA	Linear Acoustic Vernier Analyzer (CAAL)
LAVA	Linear Amplifier for Various Applications (IEEE)
LAVA	Local Authorities Videotex Association (BUAC)
LAVA	Local Authority Valuers Association [British] (DBA)
LAVA	Look Ahead Variable Acceleration [Computer science] (MHDB)
LAVAC	Low-Frequency Acoustic Vernier Analyzer (NVT)
LAVAC	LASER Atmospheric Visibility and Contamination (PDAA)
LAV/AD	Light Armored Vehicle / Air Defense [Army] (DWSG)
LAV/ADS	Light Armored Vehicle/Air Defense System [Army]
LAV-AF	Light Armored Vehicle, Air Force (LAIN)
LAV-AG	Light Armored Vehicle-Assault Gun [Marine Corps] (DOMA)
LavalTPh	Laval Theologique et Philosophique [Quebec] [A publication] (BJA)
LAV-AT	Light Armored Vehicle - Antitank [Canada]
LAVB	Light Armored Vehicle Battalion [Marine Corps] (DOMA)
LAVc	Local Area Vaxcluster (USDC)
LAVE	Association Vocanologique Europeenne [European Volcanological Association] [Paris, France] (EAIO)
LAVEND	Lavendula [Lavender] [Pharmacology] (ROG)
LAVEPA	Local Administration of Vocational Education and Practical Arts (OICC)
LAVERS	Lake Vessel Reporting System
LAVFWUS	Ladies Auxiliary to the Veterans of Foreign Wars of the United States (EA)
LAVH	Laparoscopically-Assisted Vaginal Hysterectomy [Medicine]
LAVH	Leparoscopically Assisted Vaginal Hysterectomy [Medicine]
LAVI	Lymphadenopathy-Associated Virus (PDAA)
LAVLX	Lord Abbett Mid-Cap Value Cl.A [Mutual fund ticker symbol] (SG)
LAVM	LORAN [Long-Range Navigation] Automatic Vehicle Monitoring (PDAA)
LAVM	Low-Altitude Vulnerability Model [Aerospace] (MCD)
LAVO	Lassen Volcanic National Park
LAVO	Lavatory [Slang] (DSUE)

Lav Pall......	Lavacrum Palladis [of Callimachus] [Classical studies] (OCD)
LAW.............	Ladies Against Women (EA)
LAW.............	Land Authority for Wales
LAW.............	LASER Absorption Wave (PDAA)
LAW.............	Lawrence [Kansas] [Seismograph station code, US Geological Survey] (SEIS)
LAW.............	Lawter International, Inc. [NYSE symbol] (SPSG)
LAW.............	Lawter Intl [NYSE symbol] (TTSB)
LAW.............	Lawton [Oklahoma] [Airport symbol] (OAG)
LAW.............	Lawton, OK [Location identifier FAA] (FAAL)
LAW.............	Lawyer (ADA)
LAW.............	Leading Aircraft Woman [RAF] [British]
LAW.............	League of American Wheelmen
LAW.............	Left Atrial Wall [Medicine] (STED)
LAW.............	Left Attack Wing [Women's lacrosse position]
LAW.............	Left-Handers Against the World [Defunct] (EA)
LAW.............	Legal Action for Women [An association] (BUAC)
LAW.............	Legal Advocates for Women (EA)
LAW.............	Legal Aid Warranty [Fund providing legal services in case of arrest]
LAW.............	Library, Amphibious Warfare (DNAB)
LAW.............	Light Antiarmor Weapon [Military] (RDA)
LAW.............	Light Antitank Weapon
LAW.............	Light Area Weapon
LAW.............	Light Assault Weapon
LAW.............	Light Attack Weapon
LAW.............	Link Airways of Australia [Australia ICAO designator] (FAAC)
LAW.............	Local Air Warning
LAW.............	Local Air Wing (DNAB)
LAW.............	Logistics Action Worksheet
LAW.............	Low-Acid Waste [Nuclear energy] (NRCH)
LAW.............	Low Active Waste [Nuclear energy]
LAW.............	Low-Altitude Warning (MCD)
LAW.............	Loyalist Association of Workers [Trade union] [Northern Ireland]
LAW.............	Lubricant, Arctic, Weapon [Military] (INF)
LAW.............	Quaere Legal Resources Ltd. [UTLAS symbol]
LAW.............	United States Supreme Court Library, Washington, DC [OCLC symbol] (OCLC)
LAWA...........	Legislative Assembly of Western Australia
Law Advert...	Law Advertiser [1823-31] [A publication] (DLA)
Law Alm	Law Almanac [New York] [A publication] (DLA)
Law Amdt J...	Law Amendment Journal [1855-58] [A publication] (DLA)
Law Am Jour...	Law Amendment Journal [1855-58] [A publication] (DLA)
Law & Bank...	Lawyer and Banker [New Orleans] [A publication] (DLA)
Law & Bank...	Lawyers' and Bankers' Quarterly [A publication] (DLA)
Law & Banker...	Lawyer and Banker and Central Law Journal [A publication] (DLA)
Law & Bk Bull...	Weekly Law and Bank Bulletin [Ohio] [A publication] (DLA)
Law & Eq Rep...	Law and Equity Reporter [New York] [A publication] (DLA)
Law & Hist Rev...	Law and History Review [A publication] (DLA)
Law & Legisl in the German Dem Rep...	Law and Legislation in the German Democratic Republic [A publication] (DLA)
Law & Lib ...	Law and Liberty [A publication] (DLA)
Law & Mag...	Lawyer and Magistrate Magazine [1898-99] [Dublin] [A publication] (DLA)
Law & Magis Mag...	Lawyer's and Magistrate's Magazine [A publication] (DLA)
Law & Mag Mag...	Lawyer and Magistrate Magazine [1898-99] [Dublin] [A publication] (DLA)
Law & Psychology Rev...	Law and Psychology Review [A publication] (DLA)
Law & Soc...	Law and Social Change [A publication] (DLA)
LAWASIA.....	LAWASIA. Journal of the Law Association for Asia and the Western Pacific [A publication] (DLA)
LAWASIA.....	Law Association for Asia and the Western Pacific (BUAC)
LAWASIA HRB...	LAWASIA [Law Association for Asia and the Pacific] Human Rights Bulletin [A publication]
LAWASIA LJ...	LAWASIA [Law Association for Asia and the Pacific] Law Journal [A publication] (DLA)
LAWB...........	Los Alamos Water Boiler [Nuclear reactor] (NRCH)
Law Bk Rev Dig...	Law Book Review Digest and Current Legal Bibliography [A publication] (DLA)
Law Bul & Br...	Law Bulletin and Brief [A publication] (DLA)
Law Bull IA...	Law Bulletin. State University of Iowa [A publication] (DLA)
Law Bull......	Law Bulletin [Zambia] [A publication] (DLA)
Law Bull......	Weekly Law Bulletin [Ohio] [A publication] (DLA)
LAW/BUSA...	League of American Wheelman/Bicycle USA (EA)
LAWC...........	Land Air Warfare Committee [Military]
Law Cas Wm I...	Law Cases, William I to Richard I [England] [A publication] (DLA)
Law Ch Bdg Soc...	Law on Church Building Societies [A publication] (DLA)
Law Ch P......	Lawes on Charterparties [1813] [A publication] (DLA)
Law Chr.......	Law Chronicle [England] [A publication] (DLA)
Law Chr.......	Law Chronicle [South Africa] [A publication] (ILCA)
Law Chr & Auct Rec...	Law Chronicle and Auction Record [A publication] (DLA)
Law Chr & Jour Jur...	Law Chronicle and Journal of Jurisprudence [A publication] (DLA)
Law Ch Ward...	Law on Church Wardens [A publication] (DLA)
Law Cl.........	Law Clerk (DLA)
Law Cl Rec...	Law Clerk Record [1910-11] [A publication] (DLA)
Law Com	Law Commission (DLA)
Law Com	Law Commission Report [A publication] (DLA)
Law Committee News...	Lawyers' Committee News [A publication] (DLA)
Law Con	Lawson on Contracts [A publication] (DLA)
Law Dept Bull...	Law Department Bulletin, Union Pacific Railroad Co. [A publication] (DLA)
LAWDS........	LORAN-Aided Weapons Delivery System
LAWEB.........	Lake Warning [or Weather] Bulletin [National Weather Service] [A publication]
Law Ecc Law...	Law's Ecclesiastical Law [2nd ed.] [1844] [A publication] (DLA)
Law Ed........	Lawyer's Edition, United States Supreme Court Reports [A publication] (DLA)
Law Ed 2d ...	United States Supreme Court Reports, Lawyers' Edition, Second Series [A publication] (DLA)
Law Ed Adv Op...	United States Supreme Court Reports, Lawyers' Edition, Advance Opinions [A publication] (DLA)
Lawes Ch.....	Lawes on Charterparties [1813] [A publication] (DLA)
Lawes Pl.....	Lawes on Pleading [A publication] (DLA)
Law Ex J.....	Law Examination Journal [A publication] (DLA)
Law Ex Rep...	Law Examination Reporter [A publication] (DLA)
Law Fr Dict...	Law French Dictionary [A publication] (DLA)
LAWG.........	Latin American Working Group [Canada] (CROSS)
Law Gaz	Law Gazette [A publication] (DLA)
Law Guild M...	Lawyers Guild Monthly [A publication] (DLA)
Law in Cont...	Law in Context [A publication]
Law Int........	Law Intelligencer [United States] [A publication] (DLA)
Law J...........	Law Journal Reports [A publication] (DLA)
Law J Ch	Law Journal, New Series, Chancery [A publication] (DLA)
Law J Exch...	Law Journal, New Series, Exchequer [A publication] (DLA)
Law Jour	Law Journal Reports [A publication] (DLA)
Law Jour (M & W)...	Morgan and Williams' Law Journal [London] [A publication] (DLA)
Law JPD	Law Journal, Probate Division [A publication] (DLA)
Law JPD & A...	Law Journal Reports, New Series, Probate, Divorce, and Admiralty [1875-1946] [A publication] (DLA)
Law JQB	Law Journal, New Series, English Queen's Bench [A publication] (DLA)
Law Jr QB ...	Law Journal, New Series, English Queen's Bench [A publication] (DLA)
Law Jur	Law's Jurisdiction of the Federal Courts [A publication] (DLA)
Law Lat Dic...	Law Latin Dictionary [A publication] (DLA)
Law Lib N...	Law Library News [A publication] (DLA)
Law Lib NS...	Law Library, New Series [Philadelphia, PA] [A publication] (DLA)
Law LJ........	Lawrence Law Journal [A publication] (DLA)
LAW M	Law Magazine and Review [A publication] (ROG)
LawM...........	Lawrence Microfilming Service, Fuquay-Varina, NC [Library symbol Library of Congress] (LCLS)
LAWM...........	Light All-Weather Missile (MCD)
Law Mag	Law Magazine [A publication] (DLA)
Law Mag & Law Rev...	Law Magazine and Law Review [A publication] (DLA)
Law Mag & R...	Law Magazine and Review [A publication] (DLA)
Law Mag & Rev...	Law Magazine and Review [A publication] (DLA)
Law Mo	Western Law Monthly (Reprint) [Ohio] [A publication] (DLA)
Law N	Law News [A publication] (DLA)
LAWN	Local Area Wireless Network [O'Neill Communications, Inc.] [Computer science] (PCM)
Law of Trusts Tiff & Bul...	Tiffany and Bullard on Trusts and Trustees [A publication] (DLA)
Law Pat......	Law's United States Patent Cases [A publication] (DLA)
Law Pat Dig...	Law's Digest of United States Patent Cases [A publication] (DLA)
Law Pl........	Lawes' Pleading in Assumpsit [1810] [A publication] (DLA)
Law Pl........	Lawes' Pleading in Civil Actions [1806] [A publication] (DLA)
Law Pr........	Law's Practice in United States Courts [A publication] (DLA)
Law Q Rev...	Law Quarterly Review [A publication] (BRI)
Lawr..........	Lawrence High Court Reports [Griqualand] [A publication] (DLA)
LAWRC	Limited Air Weather Reporting Certificate (IAA)
Law Rec	Ceylon Law Recorder [A publication] (DLA)
Law Rec	Irish Law Recorder [1827-38] [A publication] (ILCA)
Law Rec	Law Recorder [1827-31] [Ireland] [A publication] (DLA)
Law Rec (NS)...	Law Recorder, New Series [Ireland] [A publication] (DLA)
Law Rec (OS)...	Law Recorder, First Series [Ireland] [A publication] (DLA)
Law Ref Com...	Law Reform Committee (DLA)
Law Ref Cttee...	Law Reform Committee (DLA)
Law Reg......	American Law Register [Philadelphia] [A publication] (DLA)
Law Reg......	Law Register, Chicago [A publication] (DLA)
Law Reg Cas...	Lawson's Registration Cases [England] [A publication] (DLA)
Lawrence.....	Lawrence's Reports [20 Ohio] [A publication] (DLA)
Lawrence Comp Dec...	Lawrence's First Comptroller's Decisions [United States] [A publication] (DLA)
Lawrence Compt Dec...	Lawrence's First Comptroller's Decisions [United States] [A publication] (DLA)
Law Rep......	Law Reporter [England] [A publication] (DLA)
Law Rep......	Law Reporter (Ramsey and Morin) [Canada] [A publication] (DLA)
Law Rep......	Law Reports [England] [A publication] (DLA)
Law Rep......	Louisiana Reports [A publication] (DLA)
Law Rep......	New Zealand Law Reports [A publication] (DLA)
Law Rep......	Ohio Law Reporter [A publication] (DLA)
Law Rep A & E...	Law Reports, Admiralty and Ecclesiastical Cases [1865-75] [A publication] (DLA)
Law Rep App Cas...	Law Reports, Appeal Cases [England] [A publication] (DLA)
Law Rep CC...	Law Reports, Crown Cases [A publication] (DLA)
Law Rep Ch...	Law Reports, Chancery Appeal Cases [England] [A publication] (DLA)
Law Rep Ch App...	Law Reports, Chancery Appeal Cases [England] [A publication] (DLA)
Law Rep Ch D...	Law Reports, Chancery Division [A publication] (DLA)
Law Rep CP...	Law Reports, Common Pleas [England] [A publication] (DLA)
Law Rep CPD...	Law Reports, Common Pleas Division [England] [A publication] (DLA)
Law Rep Dig...	Law Reports Digest [A publication] (DLA)
Law Rep Eq...	Law Reports, Equity Cases [A publication] (DLA)
Law Rep Ex...	Law Reports, Exchequer [A publication] (DLA)
Law Rep Ex D...	Law Reports, Exchequer Division [England] [A publication] (DLA)
Law Rep HL...	Law Reports, House of Lords, English and Irish Appeal Cases [A publication] (DLA)

Law Rep HL Sc... Law Reports, Scotch and Divorce Appeal Cases, House of Lords [*A publication*] (DLA)
Law Rep Ind App... Law Reports, Indian Appeals [*A publication*] (DLA)
Law Rep Ir... Law Reports, Irish [*A publication*] (DLA)
Law Rep Misc D... Law Reports, Miscellaneous Division [*A publication*] (DLA)
Law Rep NS... Law Reports, New Series [*New York*] [*A publication*] (DLA)
Law Repos... Carolina Law Repository [*North Carolina*] [*A publication*] (DLA)
Law Rep P... Law Reports, Probate [*A publication*] (DLA)
Law Rep P & D... Law Reports, Probate and Divorce Cases [*A publication*] (DLA)
Law Rep PC... Law Reports, Privy Council, Appeal Cases [*England*] [*A publication*] (DLA)
Law Rep QB... Law Reports, Queen's Bench [*A publication*] (DLA)
Law Rep QBD... Law Reports, Queen's Bench Division [*A publication*] (DLA)
Law Repr... Law Reporter (Ramsey and Morin) [*Canada*] [*A publication*] (DLA)
Law Rep (Tor)... Law Reporter (Toronto) [*A publication*] (DLA)
Law Rev & Qu J... Law Review and Quarterly Journal [*London*] [*A publication*] (DLA)
Law Rev J... Law Review Journal [*A publication*] (DLA)
Law Rev Qu... Law Review Quarterly [*Albany, NY*] [*A publication*] (DLA)
Law Rev U Det... Law Review. University of Detroit [*A publication*] (DLA)
LawrG... Lawrence Insurance Group, Inc. [*Associated Press*] (SAG)
LAWRS... Limited Aviation Weather Reporting Station [*FAA*] (TAG)
LawrSB... Lawrence Savings Bank [*Associated Press*] (SAG)
Lawr Wh... Lawrence's Edition of Wheaton on International Law [*A publication*] (DLA)
LAWS... Land and Water Systems [*Michigan*]
LAWS... LASER Atmospheric Wind Sounder [*NASA*]
LAWS... Lawson Products [*NASDAQ symbol*] (SAG)
LAWS... Lawyers Alliance for World Security (EA)
LAWS... Leadership and World Society [*Defunct*]
LAWS... Light Antitank Weapon System (LAIN)
LAWS... Low-Altitude Warning System (NVT)
Law School Rec... Law School Record [*Chicago*] [*A publication*] (DLA)
Law School Rev... Law School Review. Toronto University [*A publication*] (DLA)
Laws Cont... Lawson on Contracts [*A publication*] (DLA)
Law Ser MO Bull... University of Missouri. Bulletin. Law Series [*A publication*] (DLA)
Lawsn... Lawson Products, Inc. [*Associated Press*] (SAG)
LAWSO... Lockheed Antisubmarine Warfare Systems Organization
Law Soc ACT NL... Law Society of the Australian Capital Territory. Newsletter [*A publication*]
Law Soc G... Law Society. Gazette [*A publication*]
Law Soc Jo... Law Society of Massachusetts. Journal [*A publication*] (DLA)
Law Soc Tas NL... Law Society of Tasmania. Newsletter [*A publication*]
Law Soc'y Scotl... Law Society of Scotland. Journal [*A publication*] (DLA)
Lawson Exp Ev... Lawson on Expert and Opinion Evidence [*A publication*] (DLA)
Lawson Pres Ev... Lawson on Presumptive Evidence [*A publication*] (DLA)
Lawson Rights Rem & Pr... Lawson on Rights, Remedies, and Practice [*A publication*] (DLA)
Lawson Usages & Cust... Lawson on the Law of Usages and Customs [*A publication*] (DLA)
Laws Reg Cas... Lawson's Registration Cases, Irish [*1885-1914*] [*A publication*] (DLA)
Law Stud... Law Student [*A publication*] (ILCA)
Law Stud Mag... Law Students' Magazine [*A publication*] (DLA)
Law Stud Mag NS... Law Students' Magazine. New Series [*A publication*] (DLA)
Law Stu H... Law Students' Helper [*A publication*] (ILCA)
Law Stu Mag... Law Students' Magazine [*A publication*] (DLA)
Laws Wom... Laws of Women [*A publication*] (DLA)
Law T... Law Times Reports [*A publication*] (DLA)
Law Tchr... Law Teacher [*A publication*] (DLA)
Law Tenn Rep... Tennessee Reports [*A publication*] (DLA)
Lawter... Lawter International, Inc. [*Associated Press*] (SAG)
Law Times (NS)... Law Times. New Series [*Pennsylvania*] [*A publication*] (DLA)
Law Times (OS)... Law Times, Old Series [*Luzerne, PA*] [*A publication*] (DLA)
Law T NS... Law Times. New Series [*Pennsylvania*] [*A publication*] (DLA)
Law T NS... Law Times Reports, New Series [*England*] [*A publication*] (DLA)
Law Tr... Law Tracts [*A publication*] (DLA)
Law T Rep NS... Law Times Reports, New Series [*England*] [*A publication*] (DLA)
Law T Rep OS... Law Times Reports, Old Series [*England*] [*A publication*] (DLA)
Law US Cts... Law's Practice in United States Courts [*A publication*] (DLA)
LAWV... [*The*] Lorain & West Virginia Railway Co. [*AAR code*]
Law V & S... Lawrence's Visitation and Search [*A publication*] (DLA)
Law W... Law Weekly [*A publication*]
Law Wheat... Lawrence's Edition of Wheaton on International Law [*A publication*] (DLA)
Lawy... Lawyer (DLA)
Lawyer & Banker... Lawyer and Banker and Central Law Journal [*A publication*] (DLA)
Lawyers Co-Op... Lawyers Co-Operative Publishing Co. (DLA)
Lawyers' Rep Ann... Lawyers' Reports, Annotated [*A publication*] (DLA)
Lawyers' Rep Annotated... Lawyers' Reports, Annotated [*A publication*] (DLA)
Lawyers' Rev... Lawyers' Review [*A publication*] (DLA)
Lawy Mag... Lawyers' Magazine [*A publication*]
Lawy Rep Ann... Lawyers' Reports, Annotated [*A publication*] (DLA)
Lawy Rev... Lawyers' Review [*A publication*] (DLA)
LAX... Bahia De Los Angeles [*Mexico*] [*Seismograph station code, US Geological Survey*] (SEIS)
LAX... Lacrosse [*British*] (ROG)
LAX... Laurel Explorations Ltd. [*Vancouver Stock Exchange symbol*]
lax... Laxative [*Pharmacy*]
lax... Laxity (STED)
LAX... Los Angeles [*California*] [*Airport symbol*] (OAG)
LAXRAY... Large X-Ray Survey Experiment (PDAA)
LAXS... Large-Angle X-Ray Scattering

LAXS... Low-Angle X-Ray Scattering (MCD)
LAY... Ladysmith [*South Africa*] [*Airport symbol*] (OAG)
LAY... Lanyu [*Republic of China*] [*Seismograph station code, US Geological Survey*] (SEIS)
Lay... Lay's English Chancery Reports [*A publication*] (DLA)
LAY... Look After Yourself Project Centre (BUAC)
LAYB... Library Association Year Book [*A publication*] (DGA)
LAYDET... Layer Detection (SAA)
LAYGEN... Layout Generator [*Ergonomics*]
LAYN... Layne Christensen Co. [*NASDAQ symbol*] (SAG)
LAYN... Layne, Inc. [*NASDAQ symbol*] (SAG)
Layne... Layne Christensen Co. [*Associated Press*] (SAG)
Layne... Layne, Inc. [*Associated Press*] (SAG)
Layos... Layos, Hollywood [*Record label*]
LAZ... Balkan-Bulgarian Airlines [*ICAO designator*] (FAAC)
LAZ... Bom Jesus Da Lapa [*Brazil*] [*Airport symbol*] (OAG)
LAZ... La Luz Mines Ltd. [*Toronto Stock Exchange symbol*]
LaZ Boy... La-Z Boy Chair Co. [*Associated Press*] (SAG)
LazKap... Lazare Kaplan International, Inc. [*Associated Press*] (SAG)
LAZR... Laser Storm [*NASDAQ symbol*] (TTSB)
LAZR... Laser Storm, Inc. [*NASDAQ symbol*] (SAG)
LAZRU... Laser Storm Unit [*NASDAQ symbol*] (TTSB)
LAZRW... Laser Storm Wrrt [*NASDAQ symbol*] (TTSB)
LB... Baccalaureus Literarum [*Bachelor of Literature*] [*Latin*]
LB... Farbwerke Hoechst AG [*Germany*] [*Research code symbol*]
LB... Graduate in Letters
LB... LaBarge, Inc. [*AMEX symbol*] (SPSG)
LB... Laboratory (MAE)
LB... Laboratory Bulletin
LB... Labrador [*Postal code*] [*Canada*]
LB... Lactose Broth [*Microbiology*]
LB... Ladies of Bethany (TOCD)
LB... Lady Boss
LB... Lag Bolt [*Technical drawings*]
LB... Lamellar Body [*Physiology*]
LB... Land Based
LB... Landing Barge
LB... Landing Beach [*Navy*]
L/B... Landing Book [*Tea trade*] (ROG)
LB... Lane Bryant, Inc.
LB... Langmuir-Blodgitt Technique [*Optics*] (EECA)
LB... Large Bowel [*Anatomy*]
LB... Lasa B Ring [*Montana*] [*Seismograph station code, US Geological Survey*] (SEIS)
LB... Last Brochure
LB... Late Babylonian (BJA)
LB... Late Bronze [*Age*] (BJA)
LB... Lateral Bending (STED)
LB... Launch Boost (MCD)
LB... Launch Bunker (MUGU)
LB... Launch Bus (NASA)
LB... Laurentian Bank of Canada [*Toronto Stock Exchange symbol*]
LB... Lavatory Basin
LB... Lebanon [*ANSI two-letter standard code*] (CNC)
LB... Lectori Benevolo [*To the Kind (or Gentle) Reader*] [*Latin*]
LB... Lecture Bottle [*Shipment of gas products*] [*Union Carbide Corp.*]
LB... Lederer-Brill [*Syndrome*] [*Medicine*] (DB)
LB... Left Back [*Football*] (WDAA)
LB... Left Base [*Aviation*] (FAAC)
LB... Left Border [*Genetics*]
LB... Left Breast [*Medicine*] (DMAA)
LB... Left Bundle [*Cardiology*] (DMAA)
LB... Left Buttock [*Medicine*]
LB... Left Fullback [*Soccer*]
LB... Left on Base [*Baseball*]
LB... Legal Bond [*Investment term*]
LB... Leg Bye [*Cricket*]
LB... Legum Baccalaureus [*Bachelor of Laws*]
LB... Leiomyoblastoma [*Medicine*]
L/B... Length/Beam Ratio (DNAB)
Lb... Leptosphaerulinia briosiana [*A fungus*]
LB... Letter Box
LB... Levobunolol [*Also, LBUN*] [*Biochemistry*]
LB... Liaison Branch [*BUPERS*]
lb... Liberia [*MARC country of publication code Library of Congress*] (LCCP)
lb... Libra [*Pound*] [*Latin*] (AAG)
LB... Library Bookseller (NITA)
LB... Library Bulletin
L-B... Liebermann-Burchard [*Reaction*] [*Medicine*] (MEDA)
L-B... Liebermann-Burchard [*Test for cholesterol*] (STED)
LB... Lifeboat (AAG)
LB... Lifeboat Station [*Coast Guard*]
LB... Ligand Binding Domain [*Genetics*]
LB... Light Battalion [*British military*] (DMA)
LB... Light Bombardment [*Air Force*]
LB... Light Bomber [*Air Force*]
LB... Light Bracket (AAG)
LB... Lighted Buoy [*USCG*] (TAG)
LB... Limited Base [*Air Force*] (AFM)
LB... Limited Benefits [*Unemployment insurance*] (OICC)
LB... Limited Partner in Brokers Firm [*London Stock Exchange*]
LB... Linebacker [*Football*]
LB... Line Buffer [*Computer science*]
LB... Line Busy

LB	Link Babler [Telecommunications] (ECII)
LB	Linoleum Base [Technical drawings]
LB	Lipid Body [Biochemistry] (MAE)
LB	Lithium Bromide (DNAB)
LB	Litterarum Baccalaureus [Bachelor of Letters or Literature] [Latin]
LB	Litter Bearer (AABC)
LB	Live Birth
LB	Liver Biopsy [Medicine] (STED)
LB	Living Bank (EA)
LB	Lloyd Aereo Boliviano [ICAO designator] (AD)
LB	Load Bank [Computer science] (KSC)
LB	Local Batch (IAA)
LB	Local Battery [Radio]
LB	Local Board
LB	Logan Brothers Book Co.
LB	Log Book
LB	Logical Block
LB	London Borough [England]
LB	London Bridge
LB	Long Bill [Business term]
Lb	Long Bill (EBF)
LB	Long Binh [Vietnam]
LB	Loose Body [Medicine]
LB	Low Back [Disorder] [Medicine]
LB	Low Band (AAG)
LB	Low Battery [Modem status information light] [Computer science] (IGQR)
LB	Low Bay (KSC)
LB	Low Breakage (STED)
LB	Lower Bearing
LB	Lower Bound [Computer science]
LB	Lower Brace (MCD)
LB	Lunch Break
LB	Lung Biopsy [Medicine] (STED)
LB	Luria Broth [For cultivation of cells]
LB	Photographic Laboratory Specialist [Navy]
lb	Pound [Libra] [Unit of weight]
LBA	Lahr/Bader Area [Germany]
LBA	LASER Beam Analyzer (IAA)
LBA	Latin Business Association (NTPA)
LBA	Leeds/Bradford [England] [Airport symbol] (OAG)
LBA	Left Basal Artery [Medicine] (DMAA)
LBA	Lifting-Body Airship (PDAA)
LBA	Ligand-Binding Assay [Analytical biochemistry]
LBA	Lima Bean Agar [Microbiology]
LBA	Limas Bulgarian Airlines [ICAO designator] (FAAC)
LBA	Limit of Basic Aircraft (MCD)
LBA	Linear-Bounded Automaton
LBA	Little Books on Art [A publication]
LBA	Load-Bearing Axis
LBA	Local Battery Apparatus
LBA	Local Bus Adapter [Computer science]
LBA	Local Bus Adaptor (NITA)
LBA	Logical Block Address [Computer science]
LBA	London Boroughs Association [British] (DCTA)
LBA	Longbow Apache [Helicoptor] [Army] (RDA)
LBA	Louisiana Bankers Association (SRA)
LBA	Lutheran Benevolent Association (EA)
LBA	Luxembourg Brotherhood of America (EA)
LBAB	Lima Bean Advisory Board [Superseded by California Dry Bean Advisory Board] (EA)
LBAD	Lexington-Blue Grass Army Depot [Kentucky] (AABC)
LBAF	Line Width, Black-to-White-Ratio, Area, Fixation Point
LBAK	Lightweight Broadband Antenna Kit
lb ap	Apothecaries' Pound (BARN)
LBAT	Late Babylonian Astronomical and Related Texts (BJA)
LBA-TESS	Longbow Apache-Tactical Engagement Simulation System
lb av	Pound Avoirdupois (BARN)
LBB	Lancaster Bible College, Lancaster, PA [OCLC symbol] (OCLC)
LBB	Left Breast Biopsy [Medicine] (STED)
LBB	Left Bundle-Branch [Cardiology] (DAVI)
Lbb	Leishmania braziliensis braziliensis [Microbiology]
LBB	Life Blower Bearing
LBB	Linear Ball Bushing
LBB	[The] Little Black Book [Cygnet Technologies, Inc.] [Database software]
LBB	Low Back Bend (STED)
LBB	Low Back Bending (DMAA)
LBB	Lubbock [Texas] [Airport symbol] (OAG)
LBB	Lubbock, TX [Location identifier FAA] (FAAL)
LBBA	London Bacon Buyers' Association Ltd. [British]
LBBB	Left Bundle Branch Block [Cardiology]
LBBG	Burgas [Bulgaria] [ICAO location identifier] (ICLI)
LBBM	Ludlow Bone Bed Member [England] [Geology]
LBBP	Laboratory of Blood and Blood Products [Public Health Service]
LBBSB	Left Bundle Branch System Block [Cardiology]
LBB/W	Locks, Bolts & Bars/Windows (WDAA)
LBBX	Left Breast Biopsy Examination [Medicine] (AAMN)
LBBY	Lobby
LBC	Albanian Airline Co. [ICAO designator] (FAAC)
LBC	Laboratoires Bruneau & Cie [France] [Research code symbol]
LBC	Laboratorio Chile ADS [NYSE symbol] (TTSB)
LBC	Laboratorio Chile SA [NYSE symbol] (SAG)
LBC	Land Bank Commission
LBC	Large Bore Cannon (MCD)

LBC	LASER Beam Cutting [Welding]
LBC	Layman's Bible Commentary [London] [A publication] (BJA)
LBC	Left Book Club [Founded in the 1930's by publisher Victor Gollancz] [Defunct British]
LBC	Left Bounded Context [Computer science] (MHDB)
LBC	Levesque, Beaubien & Co. [Toronto Stock Exchange symbol]
LBC	Liberty Baptist College [Virginia]
LBC	Liberty Bell Communications, Inc. [Detroit, MI] [Telecommunications] (TSSD)
LBC	Lidocaine Blood Concentration [Medicine] (STED)
LBC	Lilliputian Bottle Club (EA)
LBC	Line Balance Converter
LBC	Load Bus Contactor [Aviation]
LBC	Local Baggage Committee [IATA] (DS)
LBC	Local Bus Controller
LBC	Logistical Base Command [Korea]
LBC	London Ballet Circle
LBC	London Bankruptcy Court
LBC	London Brick Co. (WDAA)
LBC	London Broadcasting Co.
LBC	Loose Bladder Construction [Ball] (DICI)
LBC	Lothian and Berwick Cavalry [British military] (DMA)
LBC	Lowband Color [Broadcasting] (NTCM)
LBC	Lubudi [Zaire] [Seismograph station code, US Geological Survey] (SEIS)
LBC	Lummer-Brodhun Cube [Physics]
LBC	Lymphadenosis Benigna Cutis [Medicine] (DMAA)
LBC-A	LASER Beam Cutting - Air
LB CAL	Pound Calorie (WDAA)
LBCC	Long Beach City College [California]
LBC/CML	Lymphoid Blast Crisis of Chronic Myeloid Leukemia [Oncology]
LBCD	Left Border Cardiac Dullness [Cardiology]
LBC-EV	LASER Beam Cutting - Evaporative
LBCF	Laboratory Branch Complement Fixation [Clinical chemistry]
LBCI	Liberty Bancorp, Inc. [NASDAQ symbol] (SAG)
LBC-IG	LASER Beam Cutting - Inert Gas
LBCL	Louisville Behavior Check List [Psychology]
LBCL	Lymphoblastoid B-Cell Line [Genetics]
LBCM	Licentiate of the Bandsmen's College of Music (WDAA)
LBCM	Locator at Back Course Marker (PDAA)
LBCO	Lanthanum-Barium-Copper-Oxide [Inorganic chemistry]
LBC-O	LASER Beam Cutting - Oxygen
LBcS	Belle Chasse State School, Belle Chasse, LA [Library symbol Library of Congress] (LCLS)
LBCS	Land-Based Classification Standard (PA)
LBD	Large Bile Duct [Medicine] (DMAA)
LBD	Left Border of Dullness [Cardiology]
LBD	Licensed Beverage Distributors (SRA)
LBD	Lifting Body Development
LBD	Ligand-Binding Domain [Biology]
LBD	Ligand-Binding Domain [Biochemistry]
LBD	Light Beam Deflection
LBD	Little Black Devils [Nickname given to the 90th Battalion of the Winnipeg Rifles during the Northwest Rebellion in 1885]
LBD	Little Black Dress [Women's fashions]
LBD	Logic Block Diagram (IAA)
LBD	Lower Back Disability [Medicine]
LBDA	Lexington Bluegrass Depot Activity [Kentucky] [Army]
LBDI	Liberian Bank for Development and Investment (BUAC)
LBDQ	Leader Behavior Description Questionnaire [Psychology]
L/Bdr	Lance-Bombardier [British military] (DMA)
LBDS	Leiden-Berkeley Deep Survey [Astronomy]
LBDT	Low Bay Dolly Tug (NASA)
LBE	Lakewood Board of Education, Lakewood, OH [Inactive] [OCLC symbol] (OCLC)
LBE	Lance-Bubbling-Equilibrium [Steelmaking]
LBE	Land-Bearing Equipment [Military] (INF)
LBE	Landing Barge, Emergency Repair
LBE	Latrobe [Pennsylvania] [Airport symbol] (OAG)
LBE	Latrobe, PA [Location identifier FAA] (FAAL)
LBE	Libra Energy, Inc. [Vancouver Stock Exchange symbol]
LBE	Load-Bearing Equipment (INF)
LBE	Location-based Entertainment
LBE	Long Below-Elbow [Cast] (STED)
LBE	Long Bill of Exchange [Business term] (MHDW)
LBEA	Lutheran Braille Evangelism Association (EA)
LBeB	Bossier Parish Library, Benton, LA [Library symbol Library of Congress] (LCLS)
LBEB	Laboratory of Brain Evolution and Behavior [National Institute of Mental Health]
LBEF	Land-Based Evaluation Facility [Military] (CAAL)
LBEFM	Low Background Epifluorescence Microscopy
LBEI	Licentiate of the Institution of Body Engineers [British] (DBQ)
LBEN	Low-Byte Enable
Lber	Literaturbericht (BJA)
LBES	Laboratory of Biomedical and Environmental Sciences [Research center] (RCD)
LBES	Lifeboat Enthusiasts Society (BUAC)
LBETV	Les Brown's Encyclopedia of Television [A publication]
LB Eur	Lehman Brothers, Inc. [Associated Press] (SAG)
LBF	Lactobacillus bulgaricus Factor [Biochemistry]
LBF	Landing Barge Flak [British military] (DMA)
LBF	Latin America Dollar Inc.Fd [NYSE symbol] (TTSB)
LBF	Latin America Dollar, Inc. Fund [NYSE symbol] (SPSG)

LBF	Les Buteaux [*France*] [*Seismograph station code, US Geological Survey*] (SEIS)
LBF	Limb Blood Flow (AAMN)
LBF	Lithuanian Basketball Federation (BUAC)
LBF	Liver Blood Flow [*Physiology*]
LBF	Load Bit Field [*Computer science*] (IAA)
LBF	London Book Fair [*England*]
LBF	Louis Braille Foundation for Blind Musicians [*Defunct*] (EA)
LBF	Lyme Borreliosis Foundation (EA)
LBF	North Platte [*Nebraska*] [*Airport symbol*] (OAG)
LBF	North Platte, NE [*Location identifier FAA*] (FAAL)
lbf	Pound-Force (WPI)
LBF	Pounds, Force (MCD)
LBFA	Official Martin Landau-Barbara Bain Fan Association (EA)
LBFC	Lane Brody Fan Club (EA)
LBFC	Laura Branigan Fan Club (EA)
LBFC	Lauralee Bell Fan Club (EA)
LBFCR	Longbow Fire Control RADAR (DWSG)
lbf-ft	Pound Force Foot (STED)
LBFI	L & B Financial, Inc. [*NASDAQ symbol*] (SAG)
LBF/IN^2	Pound-Force per Square Inch (WDAA)
LBFL	L&B Financial [*NASDAQ symbol*] (TTSB)
LBF-S	Pound-Force per Second
LBF S/FT^2	Pound-Force Seconds per Square Foot
lb-ft	Pound-Feet (STED)
LB/FT	Pounds per Foot
LB/FT^2	Pounds per Square Foot
LB/FT^3	Pounds per Cubic Foot
LB/(FT H)	Pounds per Foot-Hour
LB/(FT S)	Pounds per Foot-Second
LBG	Le Bourget Airport [*France*]
LBG	Left Buccal Ganglion [*Medicine*]
LBG	Locust Bean Gum (OA)
LBG	Low BTU Gas (MCD)
LBG	Lucky Break Gold [*Vancouver Stock Exchange symbol*]
LB/GAL	Pounds per Gallon
LBGC	Columbia Lesbian, Bisexual and Gay Coalition (EA)
LBGO	Gorna Orechovitsa [*Bulgaria*] [*ICAO location identifier*] (ICLI)
LBH	Laker Airways (Bahamas) Ltd. [*ICAO designator*] (FAAC)
LBH	LB Ltd. [*FAA designator*] (FAAC)
LBH	Leased Bachelor Housing [*Military*] (DNAB)
LBH	Length, Breadth, Height
LBH	Local Board of Health [*British*]
LBH	Lyman-Birge-Hopfield [*System*] [*Physics*] (MUGU)
LB/H	Pounds per Hour
LBH	Sydney [*Australia Airport symbol*] (OAG)
LBHA	Little Big Horn Associates (EA)
LBHB	Low-Barrier Hydrogen Bond [*Enzymology*]
LB/(HP H)	Pounds per Horsepower-Hour
LBHS	Longbow Hellfire Seeker (DWSG)
LBI	Albi [*France*] [*Airport symbol*] (OAG)
LBI	Last Byte In (ECII)
LBI	Leo Baeck Institute (EA)
LBI	Liberte Investors [*Formerly, Lomas & Nettleton Mortgage Investors*] [*NYSE symbol*] (SPSG)
LBI	Libra Industries, Inc. [*Vancouver Stock Exchange symbol*]
LBI	Library Bibliographies and Indexes [*A publication*]
LBI	Library Binding Institute (EA)
LBI	Licensed Beverage Industries [*Later, DISCUS*] (EA)
LBI	Lima Bean (trypsin) Inhibitor [*Biochemistry*]
LBI	Lloyds & BOLSA [*Bank of London & South America*] International Bank Ltd. [*British*]
LBI	Lloyds Bank International (ADA)
LBI	Long-Baseline Interferometer [*or Interferometry*] (PDAA)
LBI	Lost by Inventory (DNAB)
LBI	Low Back Injury [*Medicine*] (DMAA)
LBI	Low Serum-Bound Iron (MAE)
LBibel	Im Lande der Bibel [*Berlin-Dahlem*] [*A publication*] (BJA)
LBIC	Licensed Beverage Information Council (EA)
LBIMS	Laban/Bartenieff Institute of Movement Studies (EA)
LBIN	Pound-Force per Inch (MSA)
LB/IN^2	Pounds per Square Inch
LB/IN^3	Pounds per Cubic Inch
LBIPP	Licentiate of the British Institute of Professional Photography (DBQ)
LBIR	LASER Beam Image Reproducer
LBIST	Licentiate of the British Institute of Surgical Technologists (DBQ)
LBJ	Lady Bird Johnson [*Mrs. Lyndon Baines Johnson*]
LBJ	Little Brown Job [*Unidentified bird, to a bird watcher*]
LBJ	Load Bank and Jump [*Computer science*]
LBJ	Long Binh Jail [*Vietnam*]
LBJ	Lower Ball Joint [*Automotive engineering*]
LBJ	Lyndon Baines Johnson [*US president, 1908-1973*]
LBJL	Lyndon B. Johnson Library
LBJSC	Lyndon B. Johnson Space Center (MSC)
LBK	Landing Barge, Kitchen
LBK	Left Bank
LBL	Label (MSA)
LBL	Labeled Lymphoblast [*Oncology*] (DMAA)
LBL	Laminar Boundary Layer
LBL	Lawrence Berkeley Laboratory [*Berkeley, CA*] [*Department of Energy*] (GRD)
LBL	Left Buttock Line (MCD)
LBL	Liberal [*Kansas*] [*Airport symbol*] (OAG)
LBL	Liberal, KS [*Location identifier FAA*] (FAAL)
LBL	Limited Broadcasting License [*Australia*]
LBL	Lymphoblastic Lymphoma [*Oncology*]
LBLG	Large Blast Load Generator (PDAA)
LBLS	Laminar Boundary-Layer Separation
LBLTY	Liability
LBM	LASER Beam Machine (IAA)
LBM	Lean Body Mass [*Exercise*]
LBM	Left Buffer Memory (GFGA)
LBM	Liberty-Bell Mines, Inc. [*Vancouver Stock Exchange symbol*]
LBM	Liquid Boost Module (MCD)
LBM	Little Brown Mushroom (LDT)
LBM	Little Butte [*Montana*] [*Seismograph station code, US Geological Survey Closed*] (SEIS)
LBM	Load Buffer Memory [*Computer science*]
LBM	Local Board Memoranda
LBM	Locator Back Marker [*Aviation*] (DA)
LBM	Logic Bus Monitor [*Computer science*] (CET)
LBM	Loose Bowel Movement [*Medicine*] (CPH)
LBM	Lowband Monochrome [*Broadcasting*] (NTCM)
LBM	Lunar Breaking Module [*NASA*] (IAA)
LBM	Lung Basement Membrane [*Medicine*] (DMAA)
LBM	Morehouse Parish Library, Bastrop, LA [*Library symbol Library of Congress*] (LCLS)
LBM	Pounds, Mass (MCD)
LB/M	Pounds per Minute (AAG)
LBMA	London Bullion Market Association
LBMC	Liberty Bell Matchcover Club (EA)
LBMCTX	Local Battery Magneto Call Telephone Exchange (IAA)
LBMI	Lease Base Machine Inventory (MHDB)
LB/MIN	Pounds per Minute
LBMM	Lifetime Book of Money Management [*A publication*]
LBMP	Land-Based Marine Pollution
LBMS	Learmonth & Burchett Management Systems [*British*] (NITA)
LBM/S-IN2	Pounds of Mass per Second per Square Inch
LBMSY	Learmouth & Burchett Management Systems, Inc. [*NASDAQ symbol*] (SAG)
LBMSY	Learmouth & Burchett Mgt ADS [*NASDAQ symbol*] (TTSB)
LbN	Labial Nerve [*Anatomy*]
LBN	Lebanon [*ANSI three-letter standard code*] (CNC)
LBN	Letter Box Number [*Viet Cong equivalent to the US APO*]
LBN	Lewis x Brown Norway [*Rat strain*]
LBN	Liberty Broadcasting Network [*Cable-television system*]
LBN	Line Balancing Network [*Telecommunications*] (TEL)
LBN	Logical Bibliographic Network [*Library science*] (TELE)
LBN	Logical Block Numer [*Computer science*] (CIST)
LBN	Logic Bucket Number (NITA)
LBNA	Liberty Bancorp, Inc., Oklahoma [*NASDAQ symbol*] (SAG)
LBNA	Liberty Bancorp(OK) [*NASDAQ symbol*] (TTSB)
LBNDX	Lord Abbett: Bond Debenture Cl.A [*Mutual fund ticker symbol*] (SG)
LBNL	Lawrence Berkeley National Laboratory (HGEN)
LBNP	Lower Body Negative Pressure [*Boots*] [*Space flight equipment*] [*NASA*]
LBNPD	Lower Body Negative Pressure Device [*Space flight equipment*] [*NASA*]
LBNS	Long Beach Naval Shipyard (DNAB)
LBNSY	Long Beach Naval Shipyard (MUGU)
LBO	Landing Barge Oiler [*British military*] (DMA)
LBO	Lanthanum Boron Oxide [*Inorganic chemistry*]
LBO	Large Bowel Obstruction [*Medicine*]
LBO	Lebanon, MO [*Location identifier FAA*] (FAAL)
LBO	Leveraged Buy-Out
LBO	Liberal Bosnian Organization (BUAC)
LBO	Light Beam Oscillograph
LBO	Line Building Out
LBO	Lithium Boron Oxide [*Inorganic chemistry*]
LBocNS	Northwest State School, Bossier City, LA [*Library symbol Library of Congress*] (LCLS)
L Book Adviser	Law Book Adviser [*A publication*] (DLA)
LBP	Land-Based Plant (NRCH)
LBP	Laser Beam Printer (NITA)
LBP	Length Between Perpendiculars [*Technical drawings*]
LBP	Leucine-Binding Protein [*Biochemistry*]
LBP	Light Beam Pickup
LBP	Line Binder Post (IAA)
LBP	Lipopolysaccharide-Binding Protein [*Biochemistry*]
LBP	Low-Back Pain [*Medicine*]
LBP	Low Blood Pressure [*Medicine*]
LBP	Lumbar Back Pain [*Medicine*] (DMAA)
LBP	Personnel Landing Boat [*Navy symbol Obsolete*]
LBPA	Lysobisphosphatidic Acid [*Biochemistry*]
LBPD	Plovdiv [*Bulgaria*] [*ICAO location identifier*] (ICLI)
LBPF	Long Bone or Pelvic Fracture [*Medicine*] (DMAA)
LBPH	Libraries for the Blind and Physically Handicapped [*Automated system*]
L-BPH	Louisiana State Library, Department for the Blind and Physically Handicapped, Baton Rouge, LA [*Library symbol Library of Congress*] (LCLS)
LBPI	LASER Beam Position Indicator
LBPIS	LASER Beam Position Indicator System
LBPO	Lifting Body Program Office [*NASA*]
LBPQ	Low Back Pain Questionnaire [*Medicine*] (DMAA)
LBPR	Lumped Burnable Poison Rod [*Assembly*] [*Nuclear energy*] (NRCH)
LBPS	Lead-Based Paint Survey [*Environmental science*] (COE)
LBQ	Lambarene [*Gabon*] [*Airport symbol*] (OAG)
LBQS	Large Bright Quasar Survey [*Astronomy*]

LBr	East Baton Rouge Parish Public Library, Baton Rouge, LA [*Library symbol Library of Congress*] (LCLS)
Lbr	Labor
LBR	Laborer
LBR	Labrea [*Brazil*] [*Airport symbol*] (AD)
LBR	Large Business Remote [*Computer science*] (CIST)
LBR	LASER Beam Recorder [*or Recording*]
LBR	LASER Beam Rider (RDA)
LBR	L-Band Radiometer (MCD)
LBR	Liberia [*ANSI three-letter standard code*] (CNC)
LBR	Librarian (WDAA)
LBR	Line of Bomb Release (NATG)
LBR	Little Bear Resources [*Vancouver Stock Exchange symbol*]
LBR	Little Books on Religion [*A publication*]
LBR	Living Benefits Rider [*Insurance*] (WYGK)
LBR	Local Base Rescue [*Air Force*] (AFM)
LBR	Low Birth Rate
LBR	Low BIT [*Binary Digit*] Rate [*Computer science*] (MCD)
LBR	Lower Burma Rulings [*India*] [*A publication*] (DLA)
LBR	Low Rurning Rate (KSC)
LBR	[*The*] Lowville & Beaver River Railroad Co. [*AAR code*]
LBR	Lumber (KSC)
LBRA	Laboratory of Biochemical Risk Analysis (GNE)
LBrAg	Louisiana State Department of Agriculture, Research Library, Baton Rouge, LA [*Library symbol Library of Congress*] (LCLS)
LBRC	Loft Bomb Release Computer (MCD)
LBrC	Louisiana Commerce Department, Research Library, Baton Rouge, LA [*Library symbol Library of Congress*] (LCLS)
LBrCJIS	Commission on Law Enforcement and Criminal Justice, Criminal Justice InformationSystem, Baton Rouge, LA [*Library symbol Library of Congress*] (LCLS)
LBrcTI	Louisiana Training Institute, Bridge City Library, Bridge City, LA [*Library symbol Library of Congress*] (LCLS)
LBrE	Ethyl Corp., Chemical Development Library, Baton Rouge, LA [*Library symbol Library of Congress*] (LCLS)
LBrEd	Louisiana Education Department, Baton Rouge, LA [*Library symbol Library of Congress*] (LCLS)
LBRF	Louse-Borne Relapsing Fever [*Medicine*] (AAMN)
LBRF	Lower Branchial Filament
LBrG	Gulf South Research Institute, Baton Rouge, LA [*Library symbol Library of Congress*] (LCLS)
LBRG	LASER Beam Rider Guidance (MCD)
LBrGS	Church of Jesus Christ of Latter-Day Saints, Genealogical Society Library, BatonRouge Branch, Baton Rouge, LA [*Library symbol Library of Congress*] (LCLS)
LBrHR	Louisiana Department of Health and Human Resources, Policy Planning and Evaluation Office, Baton Rouge, LA [*Library symbol Library of Congress*] (LCLS)
LBrHR-Y	Louisiana Department of Health and Human Resources, Office of Youth Services, Baton Rouge, LA [*Library symbol Library of Congress*] (LCLS)
LBRI	Lake Biwa Research Institute (BUAC)
LBrIPA	Louisiana Information Processing Authority, Baton Rouge, LA [*Library symbol Library of Congress*] (LCLS)
LBrJ	Louisiana Justice Department, Huey P. Long Library, Baton Rouge, LA [*Library symbol Library of Congress*] (LCLS)
LBrJS	Jimmy Swaggart Bible College Library, Baton Rouge, LA [*Library symbol*] [*Library of Congress*] (LCLS)
LBrL	Labor Department, Research Library, Baton Rouge, LA [*Library symbol Library of Congress*] (LCLS)
LBrLAS	Louisiana Arts and Science Center, Baton Rouge, LA [*Library symbol*] [*Library of Congress*] (LCLS)
LBrLC	Louisiana Legislative Council, Reference Division, Baton Rouge, LA [*Library symbol Library of Congress*] (LCLS)
LBrLH	Earl K. Long Hospital, Medical Library, Baton Rouge, LA [*Library symbol Library of Congress*] (LCLS)
LBRM	Large Basin Runoff Model [*Marine science*] (OSRA)
LBrNR	Natural Resources Department, Research and Development Library, Baton Rouge, LA [*Library symbol Library of Congress*] (LCLS)
LBrNR-F	Natural Resources Department, Office of Forestry, Baton Rouge, LA [*Library symbol Library of Congress*] (LCLS)
LBrPS	Public Service Commission, Baton Rouge, LA [*Library symbol Library of Congress*] (LCLS)
LBrR	Louisiana Revenue Department, Research Department, Baton Rouge, LA [*Library symbol Library of Congress*] (LCLS)
LBRS	Rousse [*Bulgaria*] [*ICAO location identifier*] (ICLI)
LBrSP	State Planning Office, Library, Baton Rouge, LA [*Library symbol Library of Congress*] (LCLS)
LBRT	Liberty
LBrTD-Av	Department of Transportation and Development, Aviation Office, Baton Rouge, LA [*Library symbol Library of Congress*] (LCLS)
LBrTD-H	Department of Transportation and Development, Office of Highways, Research and Development Library, Baton Rouge, LA [*Library symbol Library of Congress*] (LCLS)
LBrTD-Pw	Department of Transportation and Development, Office of Public Works, Baton Rouge, LA [*Library symbol Library of Congress*] (LCLS)
LBRTY	Liberty
LBrUC	Department of Urban and Community Affairs, Office of Planning and Technical Assistance, Baton Rouge, LA [*Library symbol Library of Congress*] (LCLS)
LBRV	Lifting Body Research Vehicle
LBRV	Low BIT [*Binary Digit*] Rate Voice [*Telecommunications*]
LBrWF-S	Department of Wildlife and Fisheries, Louisiana Stream Control Commission, BatonRouge, LA [*Library symbol Library of Congress*] (LCLS)
LBRY	Library (MSA)
LBS	Labasa [*Fiji*] [*Airport symbol*] (OAG)
LBS	Lactobacillus Selector [*Microbiology*] (DAVI)
LBS	Laminar Boundary-Layer Separation
LBS	Land-Based Sources [*of Marine Pollution*] [*Marine science*] (OSRA)
LBS	Land-Based Sources of Marine Pollution (USDC)
LBS	Landing Boat, Support [*Navy symbol*]
LBS	Large Blast Simulator
LBS	Large Bulb Ship
LBS	LASER Beam Surgery
LBS	LASER Bombing System
LBS	Launch Base Support [*Air Force*]
LBS	Launch Blast Simulator (MUGU)
LBS	Lead Belly Society (EA)
LBS	Lecithin Bile State [*Medicine*]
LBS	Lectori Benevolo Salutem [*To the Kind (or Gentle) Reader, Greeting*] [*Latin*]
LBS	Liberation Broadcasting Station (CINC)
LBS	Light Bomber Strike [*Air Force*] (NATG)
LBS	Line Buffer System [*Computer science*]
LBS	Lithuanian Boy Scouts (EA)
LBS	Load Balance System [*Telecommunications*] (TEL)
LBS	Load-Bearing Surface (MCD)
LBS	Load Bearing System
LBS	Local Battery Signaling [*Telecommunications*] (IAA)
LBS	Local Battery Supply [*Telecommunications*] (IAA)
LBS	Local Battery Switchboard [*Telecommunications*] (IAA)
LBS	Local Battery System [*Telecommunications*] (IAA)
LBS	Loire Base Section [*World War II*]
LBS	London Business Aviation [*British ICAO designator*] (FAAC)
LBS	London Business School [*England*]
LBS	Low Back Strain (DAVI)
LBS	Low Back Syndrome [*Medicine*] (DMAA)
LBS	Lumbar Back Strain [*Medicine*] (DMAA)
LBS	Lysine-Binding Site [*Hematology*]
LB/S	Pounds per Second
LBSA	Libraries Board of South Australia
LBSA	Lipid-Bound Sialic Acid [*Analytical biochemistry*]
LBSA	Long Binh Subarea [*Vietnam*]
LBSC	Licentiate of the British Society of Commerce (DBQ)
LBSCR	London, Brighton & South Coast Railway [*British*]
LBSD	Lightweight Battlefield Surveillance Device
LBSF	Lions Blind Sports Foundation (EA)
LBSF	Little Brothers of Saint Francis (TOCD)
LBSF	Sofia [*Bulgaria*] [*ICAO location identifier*] (ICLI)
LBSG	Letter Box Study Group [*British*] (DBA)
LBSS	Local Boards of the Selective Service System
lbst	Pounds [*Libra in Latin*] Static Thrust (DOMA)
LBSTR	Lobster
LBSZ	Stara Zagora [*Bulgaria*] [*ICAO location identifier*] (ICLI)
LBT	Air Liberte Tunisie [*Tunisia*] [*ICAO designator*] (FAAC)
LBT	Chemical Laboratory Technician [*or Technology*] [*Navy*]
LBT	Labatt [*John*] Ltd. [*Toronto Stock Exchange symbol Vancouver Stock Exchange symbol*]
LBT	Labete [*Solomon Islands*] [*Seismograph station code, US Geological Survey*] (SEIS)
LBT	Land-Based Tanker [*Aircraft*] (DOMA)
LBT	Large Binocular Telescope
LBT	L-Band Tetrode
LBT	L-Band Transmitter
LBT	Lean Best Torque [*Automotive engineering*]
lbt	Librettist [*MARC relator code*] [*Library of Congress*] (LCCP)
LBT	Light-Beam Transmissometer (PDAA)
LBT	Linear Beam Tube
LBT	Listen before Talk (IAA)
LBT	Local Battery Telephone [*Telecommunications*] (IAA)
LBT	Long-Baseline Tiltmeter [*For earthquake study*]
LBT	Low Back Tenderness [*Medicine*] (DMAA)
LBT	Low Bandpass Transformer
LBT	Low BIT [*Binary Digit*] Test [*Computer science*] (IEEE)
LBT	Lumberton, NC [*Location identifier FAA*] (FAAL)
LBT	Lutheran Bible Translators (EA)
LBT	Pounds Thrust [*NASA*] (KSC)
LBT	Pound Troy
LBT CBS	Local-Battery Talking, Common-Battery Signaling [*Telecommunications*] (TEL)
LBTF	Land-Based Test Facility (DNAB)
LBTF	Long Beach Test Facility [*Missiles*]
LBTI	Lima Bean Trypsin Inhibitor (DB)
LBTI	Long-Burning Target Indicator [*British military*] (DMA)
LBTMA	Listen Before Transmission Multiple Access (PDAA)
LBTS	Land-Based Test Site
LBTS	Local Battery Telephone Set [*Telecommunications*] (IAA)
LBTS	Local Battery Telephone Switchboard [*Telecommunications*] (IAA)
LbtTrm	Liberty Term Trust [*Associated Press*] (SAG)
LBTX	Local Battery Telephone Exchange [*Telecommunications*] (IAA)
LBTY	Tele-Communications Class A [*NASDAQ symbol*] (SAG)
LBTYA	Tele-Comm Inc. 'A' Liberty Media [*NASDAQ symbol*] (TTSB)
LbtyASE	Liberty All-Star Equity [*Associated Press*] (SAG)
LbtyASG	Liberty All Star Growth [*Associated Press*] (SAG)
LBTYB	Tele-Comm'B'Liberty Media [*NASDAQ symbol*] (TTSB)
LbtyBc	Liberty Bancorp, Inc. [*Associated Press*] (SAG)

LbtyH	Liberty Homes, Inc. [Associated Press] (SAG)
LBU	Labuan [Malaysia] [Airport symbol] (OAG)
LBU	Large Base Unit [Telecommunications]
LBU	Launcher Booster Unit
LBUN	Levobunolol [Also, LB] [Biochemistry]
LBuP	Plaquemines Parish Library, Buras, LA [Library symbol Library of Congress] (LCLS)
LBUTX	Federated Utility Cl.A [Mutual fund ticker symbol] (SG)
LBV	La Belle, FL [Location identifier FAA] (FAAL)
LBV	Landing Boat, Vehicle [Navy symbol Obsolete]
LBV	Left Brachial Vein [Cardiology] (DAVI)
LBV	Libreville [Gabon] [Airport symbol] (OAG)
LBV	Load-Bearing Vest [Military] (INF)
LBV	Local Bus Video
LBV	Luminous Blue Variables [Astronomy]
LBW	Landing Barge Water [British military] (DMA)
LBW	LASER Beam Welding
LBW	Lean Body Weight [Medicine] (DMAA)
LBW	Leg before Wicket [Cricket]
lbw	Leg before Wicket [Cricket] (WA)
LBW	Long Bawan [Indonesia] [Airport symbol] (OAG)
LBW	Low Birth Weight [Obstetrics]
LBW	Low Body Weight
LBW	Low-Speed Black and White [Photography]
LBW	Lutheran Braille Workers (EA)
LBWBUZCALTX	Local Battery with Buzzer Calling Telephone Exchange [Telecommunications] (IAA)
LBWI	Low-Birth-Weight Infant [Obstetrics] (MAE)
LBWMABCTX	Local Battery with Magneto and Buzzer Calling Telephone Exchange [Telecommunications] (IAA)
LBWN	Varna [Bulgaria] [ICAO location identifier] (ICLI)
LBWOC	Level Bombing Wind Offset Computer [Military] (IAA)
LBWR	Lung-Body Weight Ratio [Medicine] (MAE)
LBX	Lake Jackson, TX [Location identifier FAA] (FAAL)
LBY	Hattiesburg, MS [Location identifier FAA] (FAAL)
LBY	La Baule [France] [Airport symbol] (AD)
LBY	Libbey, Inc. [NYSE symbol] (SPSG)
LBY	Libya [ANSI three-letter standard code] (CNC)
LB/YD^2	Pounds per Square Yard
LB/YD^3	Pounds per Cubic Yard
LBYR	Labyrinth [Engineering]
LBYRPK	Labyrinth Pack [Engineering]
LC	Deferred Cable (EBF)
LC	Ewell's Leading Cases on Infancy, Etc. [A publication] (DLA)
L/C	Inductance/Capacitance (AAG)
LC	Label Clause
LC	Laboratory Craftsman (ADA)
LC	Labor Cases [A publication] (DLA)
LC	Labor Code (DNAB)
LC	Labour Canada [See also TRAVC]
LC	Labour Corps [British military] (DMA)
LC	La Crosse [Diocesan abbreviation] [Wisconsin] (TOCD)
LC	Lactation Consultant [Medicine] (MEDA)
LC	Laennec's Cirrhosis [Medicine] (MAE)
LC	Lagonda Club, US Section (EA)
LC	Lake Central Airlines
LC	Lake Current (COE)
LC	Lakey Clinic Medical Center [Burlington, MA]
LC	Lamb Committee (EA)
LC	Lancaster & Chester Railway Co. [AAR code]
LC	Lance Corporal
LC	Land Commission [British]
LC	Land Court [Legal] [British]
LC	Landing Craft
LC	Langerhans' Cells [Medicine]
LC	Langmuir Circulation [Geophysics]
LC	Language Code [Online database field identifier]
LC	Lannois-Cleret [Syndrome] [Medicine] (DB)
LC	Large Case [Indicator] [IRS]
LC	Large Cell [Lymphoma classification]
LC	Large Cleaved Cell (DB)
LC	Larval Chamber [Botany]
LC	Lasa C Ring [Montana] [Seismograph station code, US Geological Survey] (SEIS)
LC	Last Card
LC	Late Clamped [Umbilical cord]
LC	Late Commitment [Reason for missed interception] [Military]
LC	Lateral Component
LC	Launch Center
LC	Launch Complex
LC	Launch Conference [Aerospace] (AAG)
L/C	Launch Control [Aerospace] (AAG)
LC	Launch Coordinator [NASA]
LC	Launch Corridor [Aerospace] (AAG)
LC	Launch Cost [Aerospace]
LC	Launch Count [NASA] (KSC)
LC	Launch Countdown [NASA] (NASA)
LC	Launch Critical (MCD)
LC	Launching Control [Military]
LC	Laundry Chute (MSA)
LC	Laureate of Arts
LC	Laureate of Letters
LC	Law Commission (DLA)
LC	Law Courts
LC	Lead Covered [or Coated]

LC	Leading Cases (DLA)
LC	League of Communists [Former Yugoslavia]
LC	League of Composers (EA)
LC	League of the Cross [Roman Catholic religious order] (ROG)
LC	Learning Curve (MSA)
LC	Least Count
LC	Lecithin Cholesterol Acyltransferase (DB)
LC	Leesona Corp. (KSC)
LC	Left Center [A stage direction]
lc	Left Center (WDAA)
LC	Left Chest [Medicine] (KSC)
LC	Left Circumflex (Artery) [Anatomy]
LC	Left Ear, Cold Stimulus [Medicine] (MEDA)
LC	Legal Committee (MCD)
LC	Legal Currency (ADA)
LC	Legionaries of Christ [Roman Catholic men's religious order]
lc	Legionaries of Christ (TOCD)
LC	Legislative Council [British]
LC	Legitimate Child
LC	Leisure Counseling [Medicine] (MEDA)
LC	Length of Chord (MSA)
LC	Lethal Concentration
L/C	Lettera di Credito [Letter of Credit] [Italian Business term]
LC	Letter Contract
LC	Letter of Credit
l/c	Letter of Credit (EBF)
LC	Letters and Cards [US Postal Service]
LC	Lettre de Credit [Letter of Credit] [Business term] [French]
lc	Leucite [CIPW classification] [Geology]
LC	Level Control
LC	Level Crossing
LC	Leverage Contract [Business term]
LC	Leydig's Cells [Endocrinology]
LC	Leyland Cars [Leyland Daf Ltd.]
LC	Liaison-Cargo [Air Force]
LC	Liaison Committee of Rector's Conferences of Member States of the European Communities (BUAC)
LC	Liaison/Communicator (COE)
LC	Liberal Conservative
LC	Liberalt Centrum [Liberal Center] [Denmark Political party] (PPE)
LC	Liberty Corp. [NYSE symbol] (SPSG)
LC	Library of Congress
LC	Library of Congress Card Number (NITA)
LC	Library of Congress Classification
LC	Licensing Country [Dialog] [Searchable field] [Information service or system] (NITA)
LC	Lieutenant Commander
LC	Life Care [Medicine] (BABM)
LC	Light Car [British]
LC	Light Case [Military] (NATG)
LC	Light Chain [Immunoglobulin]
LC	Light Company [British military] (DMA)
LC	Light Control [Technical drawings]
LC	Light Current (IAA)
LC	Lightly Canceled
LC	Limited Coordinating (NG)
LC	Limp Cloth [Bookbinding] (DGA)
LC	Linear Combination
LC	Line-Carrying
LC	Line Circuit [Telecommunications]
LC	Line Collector
LC	Line Concentrator
LC	Line Connection
LC	Line Connector (NITA)
LC	Line Construction Tools [JETDS nomenclature] [Military] (CET)
LC	Line Contractor (MCD)
LC	Line Control
LC	Line Crosser [Deserter] [Military]
LC	Line Length Ciceros [Typography] (DGA)
LC	Line of Communication [Military]
LC	Line of Contact [Military]
L/C	Line of Credit [Business term]
LC	Linguocervical [Dentistry]
LC	Link Circuit
LC	Link Control [Telecommunications] (OSI)
LC	Links and Chargers (NATG)
LC	Lipid Cytosome [Biochemistry] (MAE)
LC	Liquid Capacity
LC	Liquid Chromatography
LC	Liquid Crystal
LC	Literature Criticism from 1400 to 1800 [A publication]
LC	Lithocholate [Biochemistry]
LC	Lithocolic Acid [Biochemistry] (DB)
LC	Liturgical Conference (EA)
LC	Liver Cirrhosis [Medicine]
LC	Living Children
LC	Load Carrier
LC	Load Cell
LC	Load Center (MSA)
LC	Load-Compensating (MSA)
LC	Load Computer [or Controller] (MCD)
LC	Load Contactor
LC	Loading Coil [Telecommunications] (TEL)
LC	Loan Capital [Business term]
LC	Loan Crowd [Investment term]

LC	Local Call [*Followed by telephone number*]
LC	Local Channel (CET)
LC	Localization Code (IAA)
LC	Localized Corrosion (PDAA)
LC	Location Counter [*Computer science*]
LC	Locked Closed
LC	Loco Citato [*In the Place Cited*] [*Latin*]
lc	Loco Citato [*At the Place Cited*] [*Latin*] (EES)
LC	Locomotive and Carriage Institute (BUAC)
LC	Locus Ceruleus [*Brain anatomy*]
LC	Locus of Control [*Psychology*]
LC	Loganair [*ICAO designator*] (AD)
LC	Logical Channel (PDAA)
LC	Logic Cell (IAA)
LC	Logic Corp.
LC	Logistics Command (IAA)
LC	London Clause [*Business term*]
LC	London Club (EA)
LC	Long-Chain [*Triglyceride*] [*Biochemistry*] (MAE)
L/C	Loop Check (MUGU)
LC	Loose Coupler
LC	Lord Chamberlain [*British*]
LC	Lord Chancellor [*British*]
LC	Los Californianos (EA)
LC	Loss of Contact (IAA)
LC	Lotta Continua [*Continuous Struggle*] [*Italy Political party*] (PPE)
LC	Loud and Clear
LC	[*A*] Lover's Complaint [*Shakespearean work*]
LC	Low Calorie (AAMN)
LC	Low Carbon [*Content, as low-carbon steel*]
L/C	Low Compression [*Automotive engineering*]
LC	Low Conditioners [*Psychology*]
LC	Low Cost Color [*Computer science*] (CDE)
LC	Lower California
LC	Lower Canada
LC	Lowercase [*i.e., small letters*] [*Typography*]
lc	Lowercase (WDMC)
LC	Lower Character (IAA)
LC	Lower Control (IAA)
LC	Lower Cylinder
LC	LOX [*Liquid Oxygen*] Clean
LC	Lubrication Chart
LC	Luminosity Class [*Astronomy*] (IAA)
LC	Lutheran Council [*British*] (DBA)
LC	Lutheran Council of Great Britain (BUAC)
LC	Lyman Continuum [*Spectroscopy*] (OA)
LC	Lymphocyte-Mediated Cytotoxicity [*Also, LMC*] [*Immunology*]
LC	Lytic Capacity [*Clinical chemistry*]
LC	Scottish Land Court Reports [*A publication*] (DLA)
L/C	Single Acetate Single Cotton [*Wire insulation*] (AAG)
LC	St. Lucia [*ANSI two-letter standard code*] (CNC)
LC₅₀	Lethal Concentration, Median [*Lethal for 50% of test group*]
LCA	Lacana Mining Corp. [*Toronto Stock Exchange symbol*]
LCA	Lake Carriers' Association (EA)
LCA	Lake Central Airlines
LCA	Lamborghini Club America (EA)
LCA	Laminate Council of America [*Defunct*] (EA)
LCA	Land Compensation Act [*Town planning*] [*British*]
LCA	Landing Craft, Armored [*Used in Vietnam by the French to transport their engineer units*] (VNW)
LCA	Landing Craft, Assault [*Navy ship symbol*]
LCA	Larnaca [*Cyprus*] [*Airport symbol*] (OAG)
LCA	Last Common Ancestor [*Evolution*]
LCA	Latent Class Analysis
LCA	Launch Control Amplifier [*NASA*] (NASA)
LCA	Launch Control Analyst [*NASA*] (AAG)
LCA	Launch [*or Launcher*] Control Area [*Missiles*]
LCA	Lead Contractors Association [*British*] (EAIO)
LCA	Leadership Councils of America (EA)
LCA	Leading Cases, Annotated [*A publication*] (DLA)
LCA	Leading Catering Accountant [*British military*] (DMA)
LCA	Leber's Congenital Amaurosis [*Medicine*] (DAVI)
LCA	LeConte Airlines [*ICAO designator*] (FAAC)
LCA	Left Carotid Artery [*Cardiology*] (DAVI)
LCA	Left Circumflex Artery [*Medicine*] (DB)
LCA	Left Coronary Artery [*Cardiology*]
LCA	Lesson Content Analysis
LCA	Leukocyte Common Antigen [*Immunochemistry*]
LCA	Leveling Control Amplifier
LCA	Library Club of America [*Defunct*] (EA)
LCA	Library-College Associates [*Defunct*] (EA)
LCA	Library of Congress Authority File [*Source file*] [*UTLAS symbol*]
LCA	Licensed Company Auditor [*British*]
LCA	Life Communicators Association [*Des Moines, IA*] (EA)
LCA	Life Cycle Analysis [*or Assessment*] [*Environmental science*]
LCA	Light Combat Aircraft [*Military*]
LCA	Light Contact Assist (STED)
LCA	Lighting Control Assembly [*NASA*] (KSC)
LCA	Line Clearance Airdrome [*Air Force*]
LCA	Line Control Adapter
LCA	Liquid Crystal Analog
LCA	Lithocholic Acid [*Biochemistry*]
LCA	Lithuanian Catholic Alliance (EA)
LCA	Liverpool Cotton Association (BUAC)
LCA	Living Centers of America [*NYSE symbol*] (SAG)

LCA	Load-Carrying Ability (IAA)
LCA	Load Controller Assembly (NASA)
LCA	Local Communications Adapter [*IBM Corp.*]
LCA	Local Communications Area (KSC)
LCA	Local Cooperation Agreement [*Army Corps of Engineers*]
LCA	Local Core Alignment [*Telecommunications*] (NITA)
LCA	Log Cabin [*Alabama*] [*Seismograph station code, US Geological Survey*] (SEIS)
LCA	Logic Cell Array (IAA)
LCA	Logistic Control Activity (AABC)
LCA	Logistics Control Area (IAA)
LCA	London City Airport [*British*]
LCA	Longitudinal Chromatic Aberration
LCA	Louisiana Cattlemen's Association (SRA)
LCA	Louisiana Chemical Association (SRA)
LCA	Low-Cost Automation (WDAA)
LCA	Lowercase Alphabet
lca	Lowercase-Alphabet Length [*Typesetting*] (WDMC)
LCA	Lussazione Congenita dell'Anca [*Congenital Hip Dislocation*] [*Italian Medicine*]
LCA	Lutheran Church in America [*Later, ELCA*]
LCA	Lutheran Collegiate Association [*Defunct*] (EA)
LCA	Lymphocytotoxic Antibody [*Medicine*] (STED)
LCA	St. Lucia [*ANSI three-letter standard code*] (CNC)
LCAA	Licensed Clubs Association of Australia
LCAACT	Licensed Clubs Association of the Australian Capital Territory
LCAAJ	Language and Culture Atlas of Ashkenazic Jewry [*A publication*] (BJA)
LCAAP	Lake City Army Ammunition Plant (AABC)
LCABLS Bull	Law Council of Australia. Business Law Section. Bulletin [*A publication*]
LCaC	Cameron Parish Library, Cameron, LA [*Library symbol Library of Congress*] (LCLS)
LCAC	Landing Craft, Air Cushion [*Navy symbol*]
LCAC	Library of Congress Classification - Additions and Changes [*A publication*]
LCAC	Listed Company Advisory Committee [*of NYSE*]
LCAC	Low-Cost Automation Centre [*British*]
LCACCC	Laymen's Commission of the American Council of Christian Churches (EA)
LCACT	Law Council of the Australian Capital Territory
LCAD	Logistics Cost Analysis Data (MCD)
LC-ADD	Library of Congress - American Doctoral Dissertations [*A bibliographic publication*]
LCAF	Lutheran Church in America Foundation
LCA(FT)	Landing Craft, Assault (Flamethrower) [*British military*] (DMA)
LCA-GB	Lightweight Cycle Association of Great Britain (BUAC)
LCA(H)	Landing Craft, Assault (Hedgerow)
LCAH	London and Continental Advertising Holdings [*British*]
LCAL	Lower Conformance Altitude (SAA)
LCAM	Liver Cell Adhesion Molecule [*Cytology*]
LC & M Gaz	Lower Courts and Municipal Gazette [*Canada*] [*A publication*] (DLA)
LC&TPA	Lighting Column and Transmission Pole Association (BUAC)
LCANSW	Landscape Contractors' Association of New South Wales [*Australia*]
LCANSW	Licensed Clubs Association of New South Wales [*Australia*]
LCAO	Leadership Council of Aging Organizations (EA)
LCAO	Limited Configuration Atomic Orbital (MCD)
LCAO	Linear Combination of Atomic Orbitals [*Physical chemistry*]
LCA(OC)	Landing Craft, Assault (Obstacle Clearance) [*British military*] (DMA)
LCAofGB	Lightweight Cycle Association of Great Britian (DBA)
LCAO-MO	Linear Combination of Atomic Orbital-Molecular Orbital (DB)
LCAO-MO-SCF	Linear Combination of Atomic Orbitals to Form Molecular Orbitals by a Self-Consistent Field [*Quantum mechanics*]
LCAP	Local Combat Air Patrol
LCAP	Loop Carrier Analysis Program [*Bell System*]
LCAR	Late Cutaneous Anaphylactic Reaction [*Immunology*]
LCAR	Launch Complex Assessment Report [*NASA*] (KSC)
LCAR	Lotus Cortina of America Register [*Defunct*] (EA)
LCAR	Low-Cost Attack RADAR
LCAR	Low-Coverage Acquisiton RADAR (PDAA)
LCar	United States Public Health Service Hospital, Carville, LA [*Library symbol Library of Congress*] (LCLS)
LCAS	Lithuanian Catholic Academy of Sciences (EA)
LCASA	Licensed Clubs Association of South Australia
LCAT	Lecithin-Cholesterol Acyltransferase [*An enzyme*]
LCAT	Licensed Clubs Association of Tasmania [*Australia*]
LCAT	Lifts and Cranes Appeals Tribunal [*Australia*]
LCATA	Laundry and Cleaners Allied Trades Association [*Later, TCATA*]
LCAUE	Liaison Committee of the Architects of United Europe [*EC*] (ECED)
LCAUS	Latvian Choir Association of the US (EA)
LCAV	Landscape Contractors Association of Victoria [*Australia*]
LCAV	LCA-Vision [*NASDAQ symbol*] (TTSB)
LCAVAT	Landing Craft and Amphibious Vehicle Assignment Table
LCAX	Landing Craft, Assault, Experimental [*Navy ship symbol*]
LCB	Landing Craft, Vehicle [*Navy symbol*]
LCB	Launch Control Building [*NASA*]
LCB	Least-Common Bigram [*Computer science*] (BYTE)
LCB	Least Common BIT [*Binary Digit*] (MCD)
LCB	Left Cornerback [*Football*]
LCB	Liefdezusters van de H. Carolus Borromeus [*Sisters of Charity of St. Charles Borromeo - SCSCB*] (EAIO)
LCB	Limited Capability Buoy
LCB	Line Control Block [*Computer science*]
LCB	Liquor Control Board [*Canada*]
LCB	Living Country Blues [*A publication*]

LCB	Logic Control Block
LCB	London Centre for Biotechnology [British] (IRUK)
LCB	Long-Chain Branching [Organic chemistry]
LCB	Longitudinal Position of Center of Buoyancy
LCB	Lord Chief Baron [British]
LCBA	Loyal Christian Benefit Association [Erie, PA] (EA)
LCBB	™Life Can Be Beautiful∫ [Old radio program; nicknamed "Elsie Beebee"]
LCBC	Lake Chad Basin Commission [Chad] (BUAC)
LCBF	Local Cerebral Blood Flow [Medicine]
LCBM	Lifecore Biomedical [NASDAQ symbol] (TTSB)
LCBM	LifeCore Biomedical, Inc. [NASDAQ symbol] (SAG)
LCBO	Linear Combination of [Semi-localized] Band Orbitals [Atomic physics]
LCBS	London Classification of Business Studies [Library classification scheme] [British] (NITA)
LCBWR	LaCrosse Boiling Water Reactor [Also, LACBWR]
LCBX	Large Computerized [Private] Branch Exchange (MHDI)
LCC	Amphibious Command Ship [Formerly, AGC] [Navy symbol]
LCC	Charles A. Lindbergh Collectors Club (EA)
LCC	Labor Case Comments [Cast Metals Association] [A publication]
LCC	Labor Class Code (DNAB)
LCC	Labour Coordinating Committee [British]
LCC	Lactose Coliform Count [Medicine] (BABM)
LCC	Land Capability Classes [Agriculture]
LCC	Land Component Commander (MCD)
LCC	Land Court Cases [New South Wales] [A publication] (DLA)
LCC	Landing Control Center
LCC	Landing Craft, Control
LCC	Langley Complex Coordination [Device] [NASA]
LCC	Language for Conversational Computing (MDG)
LCC	Large Capacity Cassette [Electronic printing] (DGA)
LCC	Large Cavitation Channel [Pressurized water tunnel to test submarines and ship models] [Navy]
LCC	Large Compressor Colorimeter (MCD)
LCC	Last Clear Chance [Legal shorthand] (LWAP)
LCC	Late Choice Call (NITA)
LCC	Launch Command and Control
LCC	Launch Commit Criteria (MCD)
LCC	Launch Control Center [NASA]
LCC	Launch Control Console
LCC	Laurie Cox Conference (PSS)
LCC	Leach's English Crown Cases [1730-1815] [A publication] (DLA)
LCC	Lead-Coated Copper (OA)
LCC	Lead Covered Cable [Telecommunications] (TEL)
LCC	Leaded Chip Carrier [Electronics] (AAEL)
LCC	Leadless Chip Carrier [Motorola, Inc.]
LCC	Le Cercle Concours d'Elegance (EA)
LCC	Ledger Card Computer (MHDB)
LCC	Left Circumflex Coronary Artery [Medicine] (DMAA)
LCC	Left Coronary Cusp [Medicine] (STED)
LCC	Legacy Coordinating Council [Australia]
LCC	Legalise Cannabis Campaign [British] (DBA)
LCC	Lesser of Costs or Charges [Medicine] (GFGA)
LCC	Levo-Carnitine Chloride [Biochemistry]
LCC	Liang-Chow [Republic of China] [Seismograph station code, US Geological Survey Closed] (SEIS)
LCC	Libertarian Council of Churches [Defunct] (EA)
LCC	Libraries Consultative Committee [Australia]
LCC	Libraries Copyright Committee [Australia]
LCC	Library of Congress Classification
LCC	Life-Cycle Costing [or Costs] [DoD]
LCC	Lignin-Carbohydrate Complex [Organic chemistry]
LCC	Ligue Canadienne des Composeurs [Canadian League of Composers - CLC]
LCC	Limited Capability Configuration [Army] (DOMA)
LCC	Lincoln Capital Corp. [Toronto Stock Exchange symbol]
LCC	Linear Cutting Cord [Aircraft escape technology] (PDAA)
LCC	Linecaster Control (DGA)
LCC	Link Control Standard Controller [Telecommunications] (ECII)
LCC	Liquid Column Chromatography (EDCT)
LCC	Liquid Crystal Cell (IEEE)
LCC	Liquid-Cushion Electroplating Cell [Steel production]
LCC	Liquor Control Commission
LCC	Lithophane Collectors Club (EA)
LCC	Little Carter Cay [NASA] (KSC)
LCC	Liver Cell Carcinoma [Medicine] (DB)
LCC	Load Controlling Crewman [Helicopter] [Navy]
LCC	Loading Coil Case [Telecommunications] (TEL)
LCC	Local Communications Complex
LCC	Local Communications Console
LCC	Local Control Console (CAAL)
LCC	Local Coordinating Committee
LCC	Lockheed-California Co. [Division of Lockheed Aircraft Corp.]
LCC	Logistic Control Code [Military] (AABC)
LCC	Logistics Control Center [Military] (INF)
LCC	Logistics Coordination Center [NATO]
LCC	London Chamber of Commerce [British] (DAS)
LCC	London Communications Committee [World War II]
LCC	London County Council [or Councillor] [Later, GLC]
LCC	London Cycling Campaign [England] (BUAC)
LCC	Lost Calls Cleared [Telecommunications] (NITA)
LCC	Lost Chord Clubs (EA)
LCC	Low-Cement Castable [Ceramics]
LCC	Low-Cost Classifier (MCD)

LCC	Lundy Collectors Club (EA)
LCCA	Late Cortical Cerebellar Atrophy [Neurology]
LCCA	Lawyers Committee on Central America [Defunct] (EA)
LCCA	Lead Contamination Control Act of 1988 (COE)
LCCA	Left Circumflex Coronary Artery [Anatomy]
LCCA	Left Common Carotid Artery [Cardiology] (DAVI)
LCCA	Leukocytoelastic Angitis [Cardiology] (DAVI)
LCCA	Life Cycle Cost Analysis (MCD)
LCCA	Lionel Collectors Club of America (EA)
LCCA	Lithuanian Chamber of Commerce of America (EA)
LCCA	Load Current Contacting Aiding
LCCA	London Church Choir Association
LCCA	Low-Cost Computer Attachment (IAA)
LCCB	Local Change Control Board (MCD)
LCCB	Local Configuration Control Board (AABC)
LCCB	Low-Cost Controllable Booster (MCD)
LCCC	Leadless Ceramic Chip Carrier [Electronics]
LCCC	Library of Congress Catalogue Card (WDAA)
LCCC	Library of Congress Computer Catalog (NITA)
LCCC	Lower Canada Civil Code [A publication] (DLA)
LCCC	Luzerne County Community College [Nanticoke, PA] (TSSD)
LCCC	Nicosia [Cyprus] [ICAO location identifier] (ICLI)
LCCCN	Library of Congress Catalog Card Number (NITA)
LCCD	Launch Commit Criteria Document [NASA] (NASA)
LCCD	Low Complexity Color Display [Video technology] (EECA)
LCC/DTC	Life Cycle Cost / Design to Cost
LCCE	Lee County Central Electric [AAR code]
LCCE	Life-Cycle Cost Estimate (AABC)
LCCEB	London Chamber of Commerce Examinations Board [British] (AIE)
LCCEP	Logistics Civilian Career Enhancement Program [Military]
LCCFC	Launch Control Complex Facility Console [NASA] (IAA)
LCCI	London Chamber of Commerce and Industry [British] (DCTA)
LCCID	Life Cycle Cost in Design [Computer program released by US Army Construction Engineering Research Laboratory] (RDA)
LCCM	LanClient Control Manager [Computer science]
LCCM	Late Choice Call Meter [Telecommunications] (NITA)
LCCMARC	Library of Congress Current MARC [Machine-Readable Catalog] File (NITA)
LCCMS	Launch Control Center Measuring Station [NASA] (KSC)
LCCN	Library of Congress Catalog-Card Number
LCCO	Landing Craft Control Officer [Military]
LCCO	Leadership Career Counseling Officer (DNAB)
LCCO	Life Cycle Cost of Ownership (MCD)
LCCOGA	Liaison Committee of Cooperating Oil and Gas Associations (EA)
LC Cont	Langdell's Cases on Contracts [A publication] (DLA)
LCCP	Landing Craft Control Primary [Military]
LCCP	LASER Code Control Panel (MCD)
LCCP	Launch Captain's Control Panel [Navy] (CAAL)
LCCP	Lower Canada Civil Procedure [A publication] (DLA)
LCC-PDR	League of Communists of Croatia - Party of Democratic Reform [Political party]
LCCPT	Low-Cost Cockpit Procedures Trainer (MCD)
LCCR	Laboratory for Computer and Communications Research [Simon Fraser University] [Canada Research center] (RCD)
LCCR	Leadership Conference on Civil Rights (EA)
LCCRUL	Lawyers' Committee for Civil Rights under Law (EA)
LCCS	Land Capability Classification System (COE)
LCCS	Large Capacity Core Storage [Computer science] (MDG)
LCCS	Launch Checkout and Countdown System [Aerospace] (IAA)
LCCS	Launch Control and Checkout System [Aerospace] (IAA)
LCCS	Launcher Captain Control System [Military] (NVT)
LCCS	Library of Congress Classification Schedules [A publication]
LCCS	Life Cycle Contractor Support
LCCS	Logistics Control Center System
LCCS	Low Cervical Caesarean Section
LCCTS	Life Cycle Cost Tracking System [Social Security Administration]
LCCU	Lightweight Crewman Communication Umbilical (MCD)
LCCV	Large-Component Cleaning Vessel [Nuclear energy] (NRCH)
LCCW	Low-Cost Composite Weapon (MCD)
LCD	Language for Computer Design (CSR)
LCD	Launch Control Design [NASA] (AAG)
LCD	Launch Countdown [NASA] (NASA)
LCD	Least [or Lowest] Common Denominator [or Divisor] [Mathematics]
LCD	Letter Carrier Depot (DD)
LCD	Lightweight Ceramic Dome
LCD	Line Current Disconnect (HGAA)
LCD	Liquid Crystal Digital [Battery-powered wristwatch]
LCD	Liquid Crystal Diode
LCD	Liquid Crystal Display
LCD	Liquor Carbonis Detergens [Coal tar solution] [Medicine]
LCD	List of Chosen Descriptors (PDAA)
LCD	Liver Cell Dysplasia [Medicine]
LCD	LM [Lunar Module] Change Directive [NASA] (KSC)
LCD	Local Climatological Data [A publication]
LCD	Localized Collagen Dystrophy [Medicine] (DAVI)
LCD	Logistics Communications Division [Military]
LCD	London College of Divinity
LCD	Lord Chancellor's Department [British]
LCD	Loss of Clock Detector
LCD	Louis Trichardt [South Africa] [Airport symbol] (OAG)
LCD	Low Cost Drifter [Marine science] (OSRA)
lcd	Lowest Common Denominator
LCD	Lumped Constant Dispersion
LCD	Ohio Lower Court Decisions [A publication] (DLA)
LCDC	Laboratory Centre for Disease Control [Canada]

LCDD	Light Chain Deposition Disease [*Medicine*] (DMAA)
LCDDS	Leased Circuit Digital Data Service [*British Telecom*] (EECA)
LCDHWIU	Laundry, Cleaning, and Dye House Workers' International Union [*Later, Textile Processors, Service Trades, Health Care, Professional, and Technical Employees International Union*] (EA)
LCDLVC	Library of Congress Digital Library Visiotrs' Center (WDAA)
LCDOSEM	Local Civil Defense Operating Systems Evaluation Model (PDAA)
LCDR	Lieutenant Commander (AAG)
LCDR	London, Chatham & Dover Railway [*British*]
LCDS	Lefschetz Center for Dynamical Systems [*Brown University*] [*Research center*] (RCD)
LCDS	Liquid-Crystal Displays [*Computer science*]
LCDS	Low-Cost Development System [*National Semiconductor Corp.*]
LCDT	London Contemporary Dance Theatre [*Defunct*]
LCDTL	Load-Compensated Diode Transistor Logic [*Computer science*]
LCDTL	Low Current Diode Transistor Logic [*Electronics*] (IAA)
LCE	La Ceiba [*Honduras*] [*Airport symbol*] (OAG)
LCE	Lance (WGA)
LCE	Land-Covered Earth (OA)
LCE	Landing Craft, Emergency Repair
LCE	Latest Cost Estimate (NATG)
LCE	Launch Complex Engineer [*NASA*] (KSC)
LCE	Launch Complex Equipment
LCE	Launch Control Equipment (AAG)
LCE	Launch Countdown Exercise [*NASA*] (AFM)
LCE	Left Center Entrance [*Theater*] (WDMC)
LCE	Legal Counsel for the Elderly (EA)
LCE	Licentiate in Civil Engineering (WDAA)
LCE	Load-Carrying Equipment (MCD)
LCE	Load Circuit Efficiency
LCE	Logistic Capability Estimate (MCD)
LCE	Logistics Capability Estimator (COE)
LCE	London Commodity Exchange (NUMA)
LCE	Lone Star Indus [*NYSE symbol*] (TTSB)
LCE	Lone Star Industries, Inc. [*Formerly, Lone Star Cement Corp.*] [*NYSE symbol*] (SPSG)
LCE	Low-Cost Expendable [*Refers to payload type*] [*NASA*]
LCE	Lyapunov Characteristic Exponent [*Mathematics*]
LCEA	Licentiate of the Association of Cost and Executive Accountants [*British*] (DBQ)
LCEAPL	Lawyers Committee for the Enforcement of Animal Protection Law (EA)
LCEB	Launch Control Equipment Building (AFM)
LCEBM	Liaison Committee of European Bicycle Manufacturers [*Belgium*] (EAIO)
LCEC	Liquid Chromatographs with Electrochemical Detection
LCED	Low-Cost Encryption Device [*Military*] (GFGA)
LCEE	Louisiana Council on Economic Education (EDAC)
LCEECSTI	Liaison Committee of the European Economic Community Steel Tube Industry [*Defunct*] (EAIO)
LCEHV	Low-Cost Expendable Harassment Vehicle [*Air Force*] (MCD)
LCEM	Leading Control Electrical Mechanic [*British military*] (DMA)
LCEMM	Liaison Committee of European Motorcycle Manufacturers [*Belgium*] (EAIO)
LCEOP	Landing Craft, Engine Overhaul Parties
LCEP	Lower Critical End Points [*Supercritical extraction*]
LCEPS	Labor Cooperative Educational and Publishing Society [*Defunct*] (EA)
LC Eq	White and Tudor's Leading Cases in Equity [*A publication*] (DLA)
LCER	Labour Campaign Electoral Reform [*British*] [*An association*] (DBA)
LCES	Least Cost Estimating and Scheduling (IAA)
LCE.WS	Lone Star Indus Wrrt [*NYSE symbol*] (TTSB)
LCEWS	Low-Cost Electronic Warfare Suite (NVT)
LCF	Landing Craft, Flak
LCF	Language Central Facility [*Computer science*] (IEEE)
LCF	Last Chance Filter (MCD)
LCF	Last Chance Forever (EA)
LCF	Latent Cancer Fatalities (PDAA)
LCF	Launch Control Facility
LCF	Law Centres Federation [*British*] (DBA)
LCF	Lawyers Christian Fellowship (EA)
LCF	Learning Curve Factor
LCF	Least [*or Lowest*] Common Factor [*Mathematics*]
LCF	Least Cost Feed Formulation System (ADA)
LCF	Lederberg-Coxeter-Frucht [*Notation*] [*Graph theory, mathematics*]
LCF	Left Circumflex Artery [*Anatomy*]
LCF	Left Common Femoral [*Artery*] [*Anatomy*] (DAVI)
LCF	Leonard Cheshire Foundation (WDAA)
LCF	Level Control Function [*Computer science*]
LCF	Librarians' Christian Fellowship [*British*] (DBA)
LCF	Library of Congress Films [*Source file*] [*UTLAS symbol*]
LCF	Lime, Cement, and Flyash (PDAA)
LCF	Lincomycin Cosynthetic Factor [*Biochemistry*]
LCF	Liquid, Complex Fertilizer (PDAA)
LCF	Little City Foundation (EA)
LCF	Living Church Foundation (EA)
LCF	Local Control Facility [*FAA*] (TAG)
LCF	Local Cycle Fatigue (IEEE)
LCF	Log Cabin Federation (EA)
LCF	Logical Channel Fill
LCF	London College of Fashion [*England*] (WDAA)
LCF	Longitudinal Position of Center of Flotation
LCF	Low Cab Forward [*Truck configuration*]
LCF	Low-Carbon Ferrochrome [*Metallurgy*]
LCF	Low Coefficient of Friction [*Aerodynamics*]
LCF	Low-Cycle Fatigue [*Rocket engine*]
LCF	Lymphocyte Chemoattractant Factor [*Biochemistry*]
LCFA	Lithuanian Catholic Federation Ateitis (EA)
LCFA	Long-Chain Fatty Acids [*Organic chemistry*]
LCFC	Launch Complex Facility Console [*NASA*] (IAA)
LCFC	Leslie Charleson Fan Club (EA)
LCFC	Linear Combination of Fragment Configuration (DB)
LCFC	Living Colour Fan Club (EA)
LCFC	Low-Cycle Fatigue Counter (PDAA)
LC(FF)	Landing Craft, Infantry (Flotilla Flagship) [*Navy symbol*]
LCFIX	Lord Abbett: Cal. Tax-Free Inc. Cl.A [*Mutual fund ticker symbol*] (SG)
LCFLOLS	Laterally Compounded Fresnel Lens Optical Landing System
LCFLOTSPAC	Landing Craft, Flotilla, Pacific Fleet
LCFNM	Lawyers' Campaign to Free Nelson Mandela [*Defunct*] (EA)
LCFS	Last-Come, First-Served
LCFS	Launch Control Facility Simulator [*NASA*] (IAA)
LCFSPR	Last Come, First Served Preemptive Resume (PDAA)
LCFU	Laboratory Configured Fire Units (MCD)
LCG	La Coruna [*Spain*] [*Airport symbol*] (OAG)
LCG	Landing Craft Gun (MCD)
LCG	Landing Craft, Gunboat
LCG	Langerhans' Cell Granule [*Anatomy*]
LCG	Langerhans' Cell Granulomatosis [*Oncology*]
LCG	Lead Computing Gyro (MCD)
LCG	Left Cerebral Ganglion [*Medicine*]
LCG	Leon Cerro Gordo [*Mexico*] [*Seismograph station code, US Geological Survey*] (SEIS)
LCG	Liquid-Cooled Garment [*Spacesuit*]
LCG	Load Classification Group (DA)
LCG	Loads Control Group [*Prepares supplies to be airlifted*] [*Military*]
LCG	Logistics Control Group [*Air Materiel Command*] (AAG)
LCG	Longitudinal Position of Center of Gravity
LCG	Lookahead Carry Generator [*Computer science*] (IAA)
LCG	Low Center of Gravity [*Tractor engineering*]
LCG	Low-Cost Generator
LCG	Lower Courts Gazette [*Ontario*] [*A publication*] (DLA)
LCG	Wayne, NE [*Location identifier FAA*] (FAAL)
LCGB	Letzeburger Chreschtliche Gewerkschaftsbond [*Confederation of Christian Trade Unions of Luxembourg*]
LCGB	Locomotive Club of Great Britain (BI)
LCGF	Longitudinal Ciliated Groove of Filament
LCGIL	Libera Confederazione Generale Italiana dei Lavoratori [*Free Italian General Confederation of Workers*]
LCG(L)	Landing Craft, Gun (Large)
LCG(M)	Landing Craft, Gun (Medium)
LCGME	Liaison Committee on Graduate Medical Education
LCGN	Logical Channel Group Number [*Telecommunications*] (OSI)
LCGO	Linear Combination of Gaussian Orbitals [*Atomic physics*]
LCGP	Landing Craft, Group
LCG(S)	Landing Craft, Gun (Small) [*British military*] (DMA)
LCGS	Lead Computing Gun Sight
LCGT	Listening Comprehension Group Test
LCGT/IGS	Low-Cost Graphics Terminal/Interactive Graphics System (PDAA)
LCGU	Lead Computing Gyroscope Unit (MCD)
LCGU	Local Cerebral Glucose Utilization [*Biochemistry*]
LCGU	Local Rates of Glucose Utilization (DB)
LCH	Lake Charles [*Louisiana*] [*Airport symbol*] (OAG)
LCH	Lake Charles, LA [*Location identifier FAA*] (FAAL)
LCH	Landing Craft Headquarters [*British military*] (DMA)
LCH	Landing Craft (Heavy) (ADA)
LCH	Landing Craft Hospital [*British military*] (DMA)
LCH	Larch Resources Ltd. [*Vancouver Stock Exchange symbol*]
LCH	Latch (MSA)
LCH	Launch
LCH	Launching Charging Header
LCh	Licentiate of the Institute of Chiropodists [*British*]
L Ch	Licentiatus Chirurgiae [*Licentiate in Surgery*]
LCH	Life Cycle Hypothesis [*Economics*]
LCH	Load Channel (IAA)
LCH	Local City Hospital (DAVI)
LCH	Logical Channel Queue [*Computer science*]
L CH	Lord Chancellor [*British*] (ROG)
LCH	Lost Calls Held [*Telecommunications*] (NITA)
Lch	Lunch
LCH	Lynch Flying Service, Inc. [*ICAO designator*] (FAAC)
LCHA	Love Canal Homeowners Association (EA)
LChaMC	Louisiana Universities Marine Consortium, Chauvin, LA [*Library symbol*] [*Library of Congress*] (LCLS)
LCHE	Luton College of Higher Education (AIE)
LCHP	Local Control Hydraulic Panel
LCHQ	Local Command Headquarters [*NATO*] (NATG)
LCHR	Launcher (AAG)
L Chr	Law Chronicle [*England*] [*A publication*] (DLA)
LCHR	Lawyers Committee for Human Rights (EA)
LChr	Liberte Chretienne [*A publication*] (BJA)
L Chron	Law Chronicle [*England*] [*A publication*] (DLA)
L Chron & L Stud Mag	Law Chronicle and Law Students' Magazine [*A publication*] (DLA)
L Chron & L Stud Mag (NS)	Law Chronicle and Law Students' Magazine (New Series) [*A publication*] (DLA)
LCHS	Large Component Handling System [*Nuclear energy*] (NRCH)
LChSt	Saint Bernard Parish Library, Chalmette, LA [*Library symbol Library of Congress*] (LCLS)
LCHTF	Low-Cycle High-Temperature Fatigue [*Rocket engine*]

LCI .... Laboratory of Cellular Immunology [*University of Arizona*] [*Research center*] (RCD)
LCI .... Labor Cost Index
LCI .... Laconia [*New Hampshire*] [*Airport symbol*] (OAG)
LCI .... Laconia, NH [*Location identifier FAA*] (FAAL)
LCI .... Lafarge Canada, Inc. [*Toronto Stock Exchange symbol*]
LCI .... Landing Craft, Infantry [*Obsolete*]
LCI .... Launch Complex Instrumentation (IAA)
LCI .... Launcher Control Indicator [*Missiles*] (AABC)
LCI .... LCI International [*NYSE symbol*] (SAG)
LCI .... Leadership Competency Inventory [*Test*] (TMMY)
LCI .... Learner-Centered Instruction (PDAA)
LCI .... Legally Correct Interpretation [*of the ABM treaty*]
LCI .... Life Cycle Inventory [*Environmental engineering*]
LCI .... Liga Comunista Internacionalista [*International Communist League*] [*Portugal Political party*] (PPE)
LCI .... Lions Clubs International (EA)
LCI .... Liquid Crystal Institute [*Kent State University*] (PDAA)
LCI .... Literary Criticism Index [*A publication*]
LCI .... Livestock Conservation Institute (EA)
LCI .... Locus of Control Interview [*Psychology*]
LCI .... Low-Cost Inertial
LCI .... Lummus Crest, Inc. [*Telecommunications service*] (TSSD)
LCI .... United States Central Intelligence Agency, McLean, VA [*OCLC symbol*] (OCLC)
LCI(A) .... Landing Craft, Infantry (Ammunition)
LCIA .... London Court of International Arbitration
LCIB .... Library of Congress. Information Bulletin [*A publication*]
LCIC .... Leisure Concepts [*NASDAQ symbol*] (SAG)
LCICD .... Liquid Crystal Induced Circular Dichroism [*Spectroscopy*]
LCI(D) .... Landing Craft, Infantry (Demolition) [*British military*] (DMA)
LCIDIV .... Landing Craft, Infantry, Division
LCIFC .... Lou Christie International Fan Club (EA)
LCIFLOT ...... Landing Craft, Infantry, Flotilla [*Obsolete*]
LCI(G) .... Landing Craft, Infantry, Gunboat [*Obsolete*]
LCIGB .... Locomotive and Carriage Institution of Great Britain and Eire (BI)
LCIGRP .... Landing Craft, Infantry, Group
LCIGS .... Low-Cost Inertial Guidance Subsystem (MCD)
LCIHR .... Lawyers Committee for International Human Rights (EA)
LCI Int .... LCI International [*Associated Press*] (SAG)
LCIL .... Landing Craft, Infantry, Large [*Obsolete*]
LCILFLOT .... Landing Craft, Infantry, Large, Flotilla [*Obsolete*]
LCI(M) .... Landing Craft, Infantry (Medium) [*British military*] (DMA)
LCI(M) .... Landing Craft, Infantry (Mortar Ship) [*Obsolete*]
LC Intl .... LCI International [*Associated Press*] (SAG)
LCIOB .... Licentiate of the Chartered Institute of Building [*British*] (DI)
LCIPr .... LCI Intl 5% Cv Exch Pfd [*NYSE symbol*] (TTSB)
LCI(R) .... Landing Craft, Infantry (Rocket Ship) [*Obsolete*]
LC/IR .... Liquid Chromatography/Infrared
LCIR .... London Centre of International Relations [*University of Kent at Canterbury*] [*British*]
LCI(S) .... Landing Craft, Infantry (Small) [*British military*] (DMA)
LCIS .... Lighter Collectors' International Society [*Defunct*] (EA)
LCIS .... Lobular Carcinoma in Situ [*Medicine*] (AAMN)
LCJ .... Lawyers for Civil Justice (EA)
LCJ .... Lord Chief Justice [*British*]
LCJ .... Low Cost Junction [*Optical fibre equipment*] (NITA)
LCJ .... Lower Canada Jurist, Montreal [*1848-91*] [*A publication*] (DLA)
LC Jur .... Lower Canada Jurist [*A publication*] (DLA)
LCK .... Columbus, OH [*Location identifier FAA*] (FAAL)
LCK .... Landing Craft, Kitchen
L Ck .... Leading Cook [*British military*] (DMA)
LCK .... Legion of Christ the King [*Defunct*] (EA)
LCK .... Library Construction Kit [*Microsoft Corp.*] [*Computer science*] (PCM)
LCK .... Lock [*Postal Service standard*] (OPSA)
LCKR .... Locker
LCKS .... Locks
LCKY .... Lucky
LCL .... Labor Congress of Liberia
LCL .... Lambert Cosine Law [*Physics*]
LCL .... Landing Craft, Logistic [*British military*] (DMA)
LCL .... Lateral Collateral Ligament [*Anatomy*]
LCL .... Leading Catholic Layman
LCL .... Lens Culinaris Lectin
LCL .... Less-than-Carload [*Under 60,000 pounds*]
Lcl .... Less than Carload (EBF)
LCL .... Less-than-Carload Lot (DFIT)
lcl .... Less than Carload Lots (WPI)
LCL .... Less-than-Container Load [*Shipping*]
LCL .... Levinthal-Coles-Lillie Bodies [*Microbiology*]
LCL .... Liberal Country League [*Australia*] (BARN)
LCL .... Library Control Language (OA)
LCL .... Library of Congress, Interlibrary Loan Department [*UTLAS symbol*]
LCL .... Licentiate of Canon Law [*British*]
LCL .... Licentiate of Civil Law
LCL .... Lifting Condensation Level [*Meteorology*]
LCL .... Light Center Length
LCL .... Limited Channel Logout
LCL .... Linkage Control Language [*Computer science*] (BUR)
LCL .... Local (AFM)
LCL .... Localizer (CET)
LCL .... Loeb Classical Library. Harvard University Press [*A publication*] (BJA)
LCL .... Logical Comparative LOFAR
LCL .... Loose Container Load [*Shipping*] (IMH)

LCL .... Lot-Car Load
LCL .... Low-Capacity Link [*Telecommunications*] (OA)
LCL .... Lower Confidence Limit [*Statistics*]
LCL .... Lower Control Limit [*QCR*]
LCL .... Lower of Cost or Market (TDOB)
LCL .... Lymphoblastoid Cell Line
LCL .... Lymphocytic Leukemia (MAE)
LCL .... Lymphocytic Lymphosarcoma [*Oncology*]
LCL .... Lymphoma Cell Line [*Oncology*]
LCL .... Mala Services Ltd. [*British*] [*FAA designator*] (FAAC)
LCLA .... Lutheran Church Library Association (EA)
LCLAA .... Labor Council for Latin American Advancement (EA)
LCLC .... Large Cell Lung Carcinoma [*Oncology*] (DAVI)
LCL/CI .... Limited Calendar Life, Controlled Item
LCLD .... Laclede Steel [*NASDAQ symbol*] (TTSB)
LCLD .... Laclede Steel Co. [*NASDAQ symbol*] (SAG)
LCLi .... Audubon Regional Library, Clinton, LA [*Library symbol Library of Congress*] (LCLS)
LCLJ .... Lower Canada Law Journal [*A publication*] (DLA)
LCL Jo .... Lower Canada Law Journal [*A publication*] (DLA)
LCLK .... Larnaca [*Cyprus*] [*ICAO location identifier*] (ICLI)
LCLM .... Low-Cost Lightweight Missile (MCD)
LC^{Lo} .... Lethal Concentration Low (ERG)
LCLO .... Lethal Concentration Low [*Environmental science*] (COE)
LCLS .... Lewis and Clark Library System [*Library network*]
LCLSC .... Life-Cycle Logistic Support Cost (PDAA)
LCLU .... Landing Control Logic Unit [*Aviation*] (OA)
LCLV .... Liberace Club of Las Vegas (EA)
LCLV .... Lilac Chlorotic Leafspot Virus [*Plant pathology*]
LCLV .... Liquid-Crystal Light Valve (IEEE)
LCLV .... Low-Cost Launch Vehicle [*NASA*] (KSC)
LCLZR .... Localizer (IAA)
LCM .... Laboratory Contract Manager (MCD)
LCM .... La Cumbre [*Argentina*] [*Airport symbol*] (AD)
LCM .... Lake Champlain & Moriah Rail Road Co. [*AAR code*]
LCM .... Land Combat Missile
LCM .... Landing Craft, Mechanized [*Navy symbol*]
LCM .... Landing Craft, Medium [*Navy*]
LCM .... Large-Core Memory [*Computer science*]
LCM .... Laser Capture Microdissection [*Biochemistry*]
LCM .... LASER Cloud Mapper
LCM .... LASER Countermeasure
LCM .... Last Calls Meter [*Telecommunications*] (NITA)
LCM .... Late Change Message [*Aviation*] (DA)
LCM .... Latent Cardiomyopathy [*Medicine*] (STED)
LCM .... Launch Control Monitor (MCD)
LCM .... Launch Crew Member (AAG)
LCM .... Lead-Coated Metal [*Technical drawings*]
LCM .... Least Common Multiple [*Mathematics*]
LCM .... Least Concave Majorant [*Statistics*]
LCM .... Left Costal Margin [*Medicine*]
LCM .... Legis Comparativae Magister [*Master of Comparative Law*] [*Latin*] (WGA)
LCM .... Leukocyte-Conditioned Medium [*Microbiology*]
LCM .... Library of Congress Maps [*Source file*] [*UTLAS symbol*]
LCM .... Life Cycle Manager (MCD)
LCM .... Lightning Creek Mines Ltd. [*Vancouver Stock Exchange symbol*]
LCM .... Line Concentrator Module
LCM .... Line Control Module [*Telecommunications*] (TEL)
LCM .... Liquid Composite Molding [*Materials science*]
LCM .... Liquid Curing Medium
LCM .... Little Company of Mary, Nursing Sisters [*Roman Catholic religious order*]
LCM .... LOCA [*Loss-of-Coolant Accident*] Core Melt [*Nuclear energy*] (NRCH)
LCM .... Loer, C. M., Reno NV [*STAC*]
LCM .... London City Mission
LCM .... London College of Music (ROG)
LCM .... Longhaul Customer Modem [*Telecommunications*] (NITA)
LCM .... Loose Cubic Meter (DAC)
LCM .... Lost Circulation Material [*Oil well drilling*]
LCM .... Low Cost Module (IAA)
LCM .... Lower Costal Margin (STED)
LCM .... Lower of Cost or Market
LCM .... Lowest Common Multiple [*Mathematics*]
LCM .... Lymphocyte Conditioned Medium [*Hematology*]
LCM .... Lymphocytic Choriomeningitis [*Medicine*]
LCM(2) .... Landing Craft, Mechanized, MKII [*Navy symbol*]
LCM(3) .... Landing Craft, Mechanized, MKIII [*Navy symbol*]
LCM6 .... Landing Craft, Mechanized, MKVI [*Navy symbol*]
LCM8 .... Landing Craft, Mechanized, MKVIII [*Navy symbol*]
LCMA .... Lightweight Cycle Manufacturers Association [*British*] (DBA)
LCMA .... Longhaul Customer Modem Adapter [*Telecommunications*] (NITA)
LCMA .... Lutheran Campus Ministry Association [*Defunct*] (EA)
LCMA .... Lutheran Church Men of America
LC MARC .... Library of Congress Machine Readable Catalog [*Washington, DC*] [*Bibliographic database*] [*Library of Congress*]
LCMARC ...... Library of Congress MARC [*Machine-Readable Catalog*] Files (NITA)
LCMCFC ...... Liaison Committee for Mediterranean Citrus Fruit Culture [*See also CLAM*] [*Madrid, Spain*] (EAIO)
LCMCS .... Liquid Conditioned Microclimate System [*Army*] (RDA)
LCMD .... Low-Cost Motor Demonstration (MCD)
LCME .... Large Climate-Moderating Envelope [*Energy-conserving form of architecture*]
LCME .... Liaison Committee on Medical Education (EA)

LCM(G)...... Landing Craft, Mechanised (Gun) [*British military*] (DMA)
LCMG.......... Long-Chain Monoglyceride [*Biochemistry*] (MAE)
LCMH.......... Lake Charles Memorial Hospital [*Lake Charles, LA*]
LCMI .... Licentiate of Cost and Management Institute [*British*]
LCML.......... Library of Congress Minimal Level Cataloguing [*Source file*] [*UTLAS symbol*]
LCML.......... Low-Capacity Microwave Link
LC(ML)C ..... Ligue Communiste (Marxiste-Leniniste) du Canada [*Canadian Communist League (Marxist-Leninist)*]
LCMM......... Life-Cycle Management Model (AABC)
LCMM......... Life Cycle Material Manager (MCD)
LCMO.......... Lanthanum/Calcium/Manganese/Oxygen [*Inorganic chemistry*]
LCMP........... Launcher Control and Monitoring Panel
LCMP .... Life Cycle Management Planning [*Army*]
LCMP .... Local Commandant, Military Police [*British military*] (DMA)
LCM-PDR.... League of Communists of Macedonia - Party for Democratic Reform [*Political party*]
LCM(R)......... Landing Craft, Mechanised (Rocket) [*British military*] (DMA)
LCMR......... Local Cerebral Metabolic Rate (DB)
LCMRGlc..... Local Cerebral Metabolic Rate for Glucose [*Brain research*]
LCMS........... LASER Countermeasure System [*Military*] (INF)
LCMS........... Launch Control and Monitoring System [*NASA*] (AAG)
LCMS........... Library Collection Management System (NITA)
LCMS........... Life-Cycle Management System
LC/MS.......... Liquid Chromatography/Mass Spectrometry
LCMS........... Logistics Command Management System
LCMS........... Longshore Case Management System [*Department of Labor*] (GFGA)
LCMS........... Low-Cost Modular Spacecraft [*NASA*]
LCMS........... Lutheran Church - Missouri Synod
LCMSO .... Landing Craft, Material Supply Officer
LCMT.......... London Centre for Marine Technology [*British*] (IRUK)
LCMV.......... Lymphocytic Choriomeningitis Virus
LC-MY .... League of Communists - Movement for Yugoslavia [*Political party*]
LCN............. La Cosa Nostra [*Our Thing*]
LCN............. Landing Craft, Navigation [*Obsolete*]
LCN............. Large Co-Ops Network [*British*]
LCN............. Lateral Cervical Nucleus (STED)
LCN............. Left Caudate Nucleus [*Medicine*] (DMAA)
LCN............. Liaison Change Notice
LCN............. Library of Congress Number (MCD)
LCN............. Lineas Aereas Canarias SA [*Spain ICAO designator*] (FAAC)
LCN............. Linked Cluster Network [*Chemistry*]
LCN............. Load Classification Number (AFM)
LCN............. Local Civil Noon (ADA)
LCN............. Local Communication Network (ACRL)
LCN............. Local Communications Network (GAVI)
LCN............. Local Computer Network
LCN............. Local Control Number (MCD)
LCN............. Logical Channel Number [*Computer science*] (TNIG)
LCN............. Logistics Control Number (MCD)
LCN............. Loosely Coupled Network [*Telecommunications*] (OSI)
LCNA .... Lewis Carroll Society of North America (EA)
LC/NA .... Lutherans Concerned/North America (EA)
LCNADE....... Liquid-Cooled Naturally Aspirated Diesel Engine
LCNC........... Local Cartage National Conference [*Later, LSHCNC*]
LCNC........... Nicosia [*Cyprus*] [*ICAO location identifier*] (ICLI)
LC NGO-EC... Liaison Committee of Development Non-Governmental Organizations to the European Communities [*Belgium*] (EAIO)
LCNI............ Landmark Communications, Inc. (EFIS)
LCNN .... Land Commander, North Norway [*NATO*] (NATG)
LCNP .... Lawyers' Committee on Nuclear Policy (EA)
LCNP .... Licentiate of the National Council of Psychotherapists [*British*]
LCNR .... Liquid Core Nuclear Rocket
LCNSD .... Licensed
LCNSW .... Labor Council of New South Wales [*Australia*]
LCNSW .... Legislative Council of New South Wales [*Australia*]
LCNT .... Link Celestial Navigation Trainer
LCNTR .... Location Counter [*Computer science*]
LC/NUC........ Library of Congress and National Union Catalog Author Lists, 1942-1962 [*A publication*]
LCNVA........ Low-Cost Night Vision Aid (MCD)
LCNVG .... Low-Cost Night Vision Goggles (MCD)
LCO............. Landing Craft Officer [*British*] (ADA)
LCO............. Launch Control Operation (MCD)
LCO............. Launching Control Office [*or Officer*] [*Military*]
LCO............. Light Cycle Oil [*Petrochemical technology*]
LCO............. Limiting Conditions for Operation [*Nuclear energy*] (NRCH)
LCO............. Linea Aerea del Cobre Ltda. [*Chile*] [*ICAO designator*] (FAAC)
LCO............. Lipo-Chitooligosaccharide [*Botany*]
LCO............. Logistics Control Office [*Military*] (AABC)
LCO............. Lord Chancellor's Office [*British*] (DLA)
LCO............. Low Cardiac Output [*Cardiology*]
LCO............. Lowest Cost of Ownership
LCOA .... Logistics Control Office, Atlantic [*Military*]
LCOC........... Launch Control Officer's Console (AAG)
LCOC........... Lincoln Continental Owners Club (EA)
LCOCC........ Atlantic [*Fleet*] Commander Operational Control Center [*Navy*]
LCOCU........ Landing Craft, Obstruction Clearance Unit
LC OFC .... Linear Crystal Oxygen Free Copper [*Cable component*] (NITA)
L/COH......... Lance-Corporal of Horse [*British military*] (DMA)
LCOL........... Lieutenant Colonel
LColC.......... Caldwell Parish Library, Columbia, LA [*Library symbol Library of Congress*] (LCLS)
LColfG......... Grant Parish Library, Colfax, LA [*Library symbol Library of Congress*] (LCLS)

LCOLNT....... Low Coolant
LCOM......... Local Committee Operations Manual [*A publication*] (EAAP)
LCOM......... Logic Control Output Module (MCD)
LCOM......... Logistics Composite Model
LCOMM....... Library Council of Metropolitan Milwaukee [*Wisconsin*] [*Library network*]
L Comment... Law Commentary [*A publication*] (DLA)
L Comment'y... Law Commentary [*A publication*] (DLA)
L COMP RAM... Licentiate in Composition, Royal Academy of Music [*British*] (ROG)
L/COMPT ..... Luggage Compartment [*Automotive engineering*]
LCOP.......... Launch Control Officer's Panel (AAG)
LCOP .... Logistics Control Office, Pacific [*Military*] (AABC)
LCOR .... Lincoln Cosmopolitan Owners Registry [*Defunct*] (EA)
L-CORP........ Lance-Corporal [*Military British*] (ROG)
LCOS .... Lead Computing Optical Sight
LCOS .... Low Cardiac Output Syndrome [*Medicine*] (DMAA)
LCOS .... Lycos Inc. [*NASDAQ symbol*] (TTSB)
LCOSE .... Launch Complex Operational Support Equipment
LCOSS .... Lead Computing Optical Sighting System (MCD)
LCOT.......... Lower Critical Ordering Transition [*Polymer physics*]
LCouRR .... Red River Parish Library, Coushatta, LA [*Library symbol Library of Congress*] (LCLS)
LCovD......... Delta Regional Primate Research Center, Science Information Service, Covington, LA [*Library symbol Library of Congress*] (LCLS)
LCovSt........ Saint Tammany Parish Library, Covington, LA [*Library symbol Library of Congress*] (LCLS)
LCP............ Galbraith Lake Camp, AK [*Location identifier FAA*] (FAAL)
LCP .... Landing Craft, Personnel
LCP .... Language Conversion Program [*Computer science*] (BUR)
LCP .... Large Coil Program [*Physics*]
LCP .... Large Computer Project (IAA)
LCP .... Last Card Program Start (IAA)
LCP .... Last Complete Program (WDAA)
LCP .... Lateral Choroid Plexus (PDAA)
LCP .... Launch Control Panel
LCP .... Launch Control Post (MCD)
LCP .... Laws for Construction of Programs (MHDB)
LCP .... Lawyers Co-Operative Publishing Co. [*Rochester, NY*]
LCP .... Leader, Company Procurement [*Military*] (AFIT)
LCP .... League of Canadian Poets [*Canada*] (EAIO)
LCP .... Left Circular Polarization
L-C-P .... Leg-Calve-Perthes Disease [*Medicine*]
LCP .... Legg-Calve-Perthes [*Disease*] [*Medicine*] (DB)
LCP .... Legislative Council for Photogrammetry [*Later, MAPPS*] (EA)
LCP .... Lehndorff Canadian Prop. [*Limited Partnership Units*] [*Toronto Stock Exchange symbol*]
LCP .... Letter Carrier Presort [*Canadian postal term*] (NFD)
LCP .... Liberal Country Party [*Australia*] (BARN)
LCP .... Licensed Clinical Psychologist
LCP .... Licentiate of the College of Preceptors [*British*]
LCP .... Light Compact Performance [*Filtration systems*] [*Automotive engineering*]
LCP .... Link Control Procedure [*Telecommunications*]
LCP .... Link Control Protocol [*Telecommunications*] (ACRL)
LCP .... Liquid-Crystal Polymer [*Organic chemistry*]
LCP .... Liquid Cyclone Process [*for making high-protein edible cottonseed flour*]
LCP .... Little Computer Person [*Activision computer game*]
LCP .... Load Cell Platform
LCP .... Loading Control Program (IAA)
LCP .... Local Calibration Procedure
LCP .... Local Collaborative Projects [*Between business and education*] [*British*]
LCP .... Local Control Panel (CAAL)
LCP .... Local Control Point [*Telecommunications*] (TEL)
LCP .... Logistic Capability Plan [*Navy*]
LCP .... London College of Printing
LCP .... Long-Chain Polysaturated Fatty Acid [*Biochemistry*] (MAE)
LCP............ Lost Cause Press, Louisville, KY [*Library symbol Library of Congress*] (LCLS)
LCP .... Low-Calcium Pyroxene [*Mineralogy*]
LCP .... Low-Cost Production (WDAA)
LCP .... Lower Cost Processor (MCD)
LCP............. Lymphocyte Cytosol Polypeptide [*Medicine*] (DMAA)
LCPA........... Lincoln Center for the Performing Arts (EA)
LC-PAD........ Liquid Chromatography plus Pulsed Amperometric Detection [*Analytical chemistry*]
LCP & SA .... Licentiate of Physicians and Surgeons of America
LCPC........... Liquid Cyclone Processed Cottonseed Flour
LCPC........... Low-Cost-to-Produce Classifier (MCD)
LCP-FY........ Logistic Capability Plan - Fiscal Year [*Navy*] (NG)
LCPG .... Logic Clock Pulse Generator [*Computer science*]
LCPH .... Paphos [*Cyprus*] [*ICAO location identifier*] (ICLI)
LCPIS.......... Low-Cost Propulsion Integration Study (MCD)
LCPL........... Lance Corporal
L/Cpl........... Lance-Corporal (WDAA)
LCPL............ Landing Craft, Personnel, Large [*Navy symbol*]
LCPL........... Left Circularly Polarized Light
LCPL........... Leon-Jefferson Library System [*Library network*]
LCPLR .... Landing Craft, Personnel Leader
LCP(M)........ Landing Craft, Personnel (Medium)
LCP(N)........ Landing Craft, Personnel (Nested) [*Obsolete*]
LCPO .... Leading Chief Petty Officer (DNAB)

LCP(P)	Landing Craft, Personnel (Plastic)
LCPR	Landing Craft, Personnel, Ramped [*Navy symbol*]
LCPRC	Liquid Crystalline Polymer Research Center [*University of Connecticut*] [*Research center*] (RCD)
LCP(S)	Landing Craft, Personnel (Small) [*British military*] (DMA)
LCPS	Large Cloud Particle-Size Spectrometer
LCPS	Licentiate of the College of Physicians and Surgeons [*British*]
LCPS	Lithuanian Catholic Press Society (EA)
LCP(SY)	Landing Craft, Personnel (Survey)
LCPT	Lightweight Collapsible Pillolo Tank
LCPTT	Low-Cost Part Task Trainer (MCD)
LCP(U)	Landing Craft, Personnel (Utility) [*British military*] (DMA)
LCQ	Launch Crew Quarters (AFM)
LCQ	Learning Climate Questionnaire [*Medicine*] (DMAA)
LCQ	Liquid Crystal Quartz (WGA)
LCQ	Logical Channel Queue [*Computer science*] (BUR)
LCR	Inductance-Capacitance-Resistance (CET)
LCR	La Lucha [*Costa Rica*] [*Seismograph station code, US Geological Survey*] (SEIS)
LCR	Land Compensation Reports [*A publication*] (ILCA)
LCR	Landing Craft, Raiding [*British*]
LCR	Landing Craft, Rocket [*British military*] (DMA)
LCR	Landing Craft, Rubber
LCR	Las Cruces, NM [*Location identifier FAA*] (FAAL)
LCR	Late Cutaneous Reaction [*Immunology*]
LCR	Launch Control Room (MCD)
LCR	Least-Cost Routing [*Telecommunications*]
LCr	Letter of Credit
L/CR	Lettre de Credit [*Letter of Credit*] [*French*]
LCR	Leurocristine [*Oncovin, Vincristine*] [*Also, O, V, VC, VCR*] [*Antineoplastic drug*]
LCR	Level Crossing Rate (IAA)
LCR	Level Crossing Resonance [*Physical chemistry*]
LCR	Libyan Arab Company for Air Cargo [*ICAO designator*] (FAAC)
LCr	Lieutenant Commander [*Navy British*]
LCR	Ligase Chain Reaction [*Genetics*]
LCR	Light Chopping Reticle
LCR	Ligue Communiste Revolutionnaire [*Revolutionary Communist League*] [*France Political party*] (PPW)
LCR	Limit Control Register [*Navy Navigation Satellite System*] (DNAB)
LCR	Liquid Chromatographic Reactor
LCR	Liquide Cephalo-Rachidien [*Cerebrospinal Fluid*] [*French*]
LCR	Liquido Cefaloraquideo [*Cerebrospinal Fluid*] [*Spanish*]
LCR	Load Complement Register (IAA)
LCR	Locus Control Region [*Genetics*]
LCR	Logarithmic Correlators Ratiometer (PDAA)
LCR	Log Cabin Republicans (EA)
LCR	Log Count Rate [*Nuclear energy*] (NRCH)
LCR	Logistic Change Report [*Military*] (AFM)
LCR	London & Continental Railways Ltd.
LCR	Low Compression Ratio [*Automotive engineering*] (IAA)
LCR	Low Cost Range
LCR	Low-Cost Reusable [*Refers to payload type*] [*NASA*]
LCR	Low Count Range [*Nuclear energy*] (NUCP)
LCR	Low Cross Range
LCR	Lower Canada Reports [*A publication*] (DLA)
LCR	Lower Circulating Reflux [*Chemical engineering*]
LCR	Lucero Resources Corp. [*Vancouver Stock Exchange symbol*]
LCR	Lung Configuration Recorder
LCR	Lutheran Churches of the Reformation
LCrA	Acadia Parish Library, Crowley, LA [*Library symbol Library of Congress*] (LCLS)
LCRA	Akrotiri [*Cyprus*] [*ICAO location identifier*] (ICLI)
LCRA	Labour Cost Research Associates Ltd. [*British*] (ECON)
LCRA	Lithuanian Catholic Religious Aid (EA)
LCRA	Lower Colorado River Authority
LCRC	Lake Champlain Research Consortium [*Marine science*] (OSRA)
LCRC	Laotian Cultural and Research Center (EA)
LCRC	Lenawee County Railroad Co., Inc. [*AAR code*]
LCRE	Lithium Cooled Reactor Experiment
LC Rep S Qu...	Lower Canada Seignorial Questions Reports [*A publication*] (DLA)
LCRES	Letter Carrier Route Evaluation System [*Postal Service*]
LCRF	L'Association Canadienne des Ludotheques et des Centres de Ressources pour la Famille [*Canadian Association of Toy Libraries and Parent Resource Centers*] [*See also TLRC*] (EAIO)
LCRIS	Loop Cable Record Inventory System (MCD)
LCR(L)	Landing Craft, Rubber (Large) [*Obsolete*]
LCRL	Lewis and Clark Regional Library [*Library network*]
LCRM	Launch Control Room (AAG)
LCRM	Linear Count Rate Meter (NRCH)
LCRO	Episkopi [*Cyprus*] [*ICAO location identifier*] (ICLI)
LCRO	Linear Combination of Rydberg Orbitals [*Atomic physics*]
LCRO	Low Cross-Range Orbiter (KSC)
LCR(R)	Landing Craft, Rubber (Rocket)
LCRR	Low-Cost Risk Reduction (PDAA)
LCRR	Nicosia [*Cyprus*] [*ICAO location identifier*] (ICLI)
LCR(S)	Landing Craft, Rubber (Small) [*Obsolete*]
LCRS	Leachate Control and Removal System [*Environmental science*] (COE)
LCRS	Low-Cost Readout Station [*NASA*]
LCRSMEEC	Liaison Committee of the Rice Starch Manufacturers of the EEC [*Belgium*] (EAIO)
LCRT	Low-Contrast Resolution Test [*Optics*]
LCRU	Landing Craft, Recovery Unit
LCRU	Lunar Communications Relay Unit [*Apollo*] [*NASA*]
LCRV	Length of Curve (MSA)
LCRY	LeCroy Corp. [*NASDAQ symbol*] (SAG)
LCS	Laboratory-Certifying Scientist [*Analytical chemistry*]
LCS	Laboratory for Computational Statistics [*Stanford University*] (PDAA)
LCS	Laboratory for Computer Science [*Massachusetts Institute of Technology*] [*Research center*] (RCD)
LCS	Lancaster Resources [*Vancouver Stock Exchange symbol*]
LCS	Land Combat System
LCS	Landing Craft, Support
LCS	Lane Control Signal
LCS	Large Capacity [*or Core*] Storage [*Computer science*]
LCS	Large Core Storage [*Computer science*] (OA)
LCS	LASER Communications System
LCS	LASER Crosswind System (RDA)
LCS	Last Cast Syndrome [*Fictitious fishing malady*]
LCS	Lateral Channel Stop (IAA)
LCS	Lateral Control System (MUGU)
LCS	Lathe Control System
LCS	Launch Complex Set
LCS	Launch Control Sequence (AAG)
LCS	Launch Control Simulator
LCS	Launch Control Station
LCS	Launch Control System [*or Subsystem*]
LCS	Law of Corresponding States [*Physics*]
LCS	LCS Industries, Inc. [*Associated Press*] (SAG)
LCS	League Championship Series [*Baseball*]
LCS	Leakage Collection System [*Nuclear energy*] (NRCH)
LCS	Leak Control System [*Nuclear energy*] (NRCH)
LCS	Learning Classifier System [*Computer science*]
LCS	Leveling Control System
LCS	Liaison Call Sheet
LCS	Library Cat Society (EA)
LCS	Library Computer System [*University of Illinois*] [*Library network*]
LCS	Library Control System [*Ohio State Library*] [*Columbus*] [*Information service or system*] (IID)
LCS	Lichen Chronicus Simplex [*Dermatology*] (DAVI)
LCS	Life Care Services
LCS	Life-Cycle Survivability (MSA)
LCS	Light Cruiser Squadron [*British military*] (DMA)
LCS	Lincoln Calibration Sphere
LCS	Linear Collision Sequence (MCD)
LCS	Line Coding Storage
LCS	Link Control Station [*Telecommunications*] (ECII)
LCS	Linked Cross Sectional (PDAA)
LCS	Liquid Controlled Solid (KSC)
LCS	Liquid Cooling System
LCS	Liquid Crystal Shutter [*Epson*] [*Printer technology*]
LCS	List of Command Signals (MCD)
LCS	Lithuanian Cultural Society [*Defunct*] (EA)
LCS	Litton Computer Services [*Information service or system*] (IID)
LCS	Lladro Collectors Society (EA)
LCS	Loadable Control Storage [*Computer science*] (NITA)
LCS	Local Communications Services [*British*]
LCS	London Controlling Section [*British military*] (DMA)
LCS	Loop Control System [*Nuclear energy*] (NRCH)
LCS	LOPO [*Local Post*] Collectors Society (EA)
LCS	Lottery Collectors Society (EA)
LCS	Loudness Contour Selector
LCS	Low Constant [*or Continuous*] Suction [*Surgical procedure*] (DAVI)
LCS	Low-Cost LASER Seeker (MCD)
LCS	Low-Cost Sonobuoy
LCS	Statewide Library Computer System [*University of Illinois*] [*Information service or system*] (IID)
LCSA	Legislative Council of South Australia
LCSA	Lewis and Clark Society of America (EA)
LCSA	Lotteries Commission of South Australia
LC Sales	Langdell's Cases on the Law of Sales [*A publication*] (DLA)
LCSB	Launch Control Support Building [*Missiles*]
LCSCU	Launch Coolant System Control Unit (AAG)
LC-SDP	League of Communists-Social Democratic Party [*Bosnia-Hercegovina*] [*Political party*] (BUAC)
LCSE	LASER Communication Satellite Experiment [*NASA*]
LCSE	Life-Cycle Software Engineering [*Army*] (RDA)
LCSEC	Life-Cycle Software Engineering Center [*Army*]
LCSEFE	Labor Committee for Safe Energy and Full Employment [*Defunct*] (EA)
LCSH	Library of Congress National Union Catalogue Subject Headings (TELE)
LCSH	Library of Congress Subject Headings [*Formerly, SHDC*] [*A publication*]
LCSI	Launch Critical Support Items [*NASA*] (KSC)
LCSI	LCS Industries [*NASDAQ symbol*] (SAG)
LCSI	Licentiate of the Construction Surveyors' Institute [*British*] (DBQ)
LCSI	Logistic Control Shipping Instruction (AAG)
LCSIE	Liquid-Cooled Spark Ignition Engine
LCS/IS	Local Communications Services/Information Services (NITA)
LCS(L)	Landing Craft, Support (Large) [*Obsolete*]
LCSLT	Low-Cost Solid Logic Technology (IAA)
LCS(M)	Landing Craft, Support (Medium)
LCSM	Launch Control and Status Monitor
LCSMM	Life-Cycle Systems Management Model
LCSN	Local Circuit Switched Network
LCSO	Launch Complex Safety Officer (IAA)
LCSO	Launch Control Safety Officer (MCD)
LCSO	Local Communications Service Order

LCSO .... Low-Cost Systems Office [*NASA*] (PDAA)
LCSP .... Logical Channels Switching Program (MHDB)
LCS-PDR ...... League of Communists of Slovenia - Party of Democratic Reform [*Political party*]
LCSPL .... Launch Critical Spare Parts List [*NASA*] (KSC)
LCSR .... Laboratory for Computer Science Research [*Rutgers University*] [*Research center*] (RCD)
LCS(R) .... Landing Craft, Support (Rocket)
LCSR .... Landing Craft, Swimmer Reconnaissance [*Navy symbol*]
LCSR .... Large Caliber Soft Recoil [*Weaponry*] (MCD)
LCSR(L) .... Landing Craft, Swimmer Recovery (Light) [*Navy symbol*] (NVT)
LCSRM .... Loop Current Step Response Method (IEEE)
LCSS .... Land Combat Support Set (NATG)
LCSS .... Land Combat Support System (DWSG)
LCSS .... Land Combat Support Systems
LCSS .... Land Combat System Study (AFIT)
LCS(S) .... Landing Craft, Support (Small), MKI [*Navy symbol Obsolete*]
LCSS .... Launch Control and Sequencer System
LCSS .... Launch Control System Simulator [*NASA*] (IAA)
LCSS .... Life Cycle Software Support
LCSS .... Lightweight Camouflage Screen System (MCD)
LCSS .... London Council of Social Service
LCSSAP .... Low-Cost Silicon Solar Array Project
LCSSC .... Life-Cycle Software Support Center [*Army*]
LCSSE .... Life-Cycle Software Support Environment [*Army*]
LCSSP .... Laboratory of Chemical and Solid-State Physics [*MIT*] (MCD)
LCST .... Licentiate of the College of Speech Therapists [*British*]
LCST .... Lower Critical-Solution-Temperature
LCSU .... Lao Civil Servants' Union
LCSU .... Local Concentrator Switching Unit [*Telecommunications*] (TEL)
LCSVF .... Logistics Combat Support Vehicle Family (MCD)
LCSW .... Latch Checking Switch (MSA)
LCSW .... Licensed Clinical Social Worker [*Medicine*]
LCT .... Landing Craft, Tank [*Navy symbol*]
LCT .... Laplace-Carson Transform [*Mathematics*]
LCT .... Last Card Total (IAA)
LCT .... Latest Closing Time
LCT .... Launch Control Trailer
LCt .... Launch Countdown [*NASA*] (NASA)
L Ct .... Law Court (DLA)
LCT .... Legislative Council of Tasmania [*Australia*]
LCT .... Lencourt Ltd. [*Toronto Stock Exchange symbol*]
LCT .... Less than Truckload Lot [*Under 24,000 pounds*] (MHDW)
LCT .... Licensing Commission of Tasmania [*Australia*]
LCT .... Life Component Tester
LCT .... Light Capital Technology (PDAA)
LCT .... Ligue Communiste des Travailleurs [*Communist Workers' League*] [*Senegal*] [*Political party*] (PPW)
LCT .... Linear Combination Technique [*Nuclear science*] (OA)
LCT .... Linkage Control Table [*Telecommunications*] (IAA)
LCT .... Liquid Crystal Thermography
LCT .... Listening Comprehension Test (TES)
LCT .... Liver Cell Tumor [*Medicine*] (DMAA)
LCT .... Local Civil Time
LCT .... Local Correlation-Tracking [*Instrumental technique*]
LCT .... Locate (MSA)
LCT .... Location, Command, and Telemetry (IAA)
LCT .... Locust (MSA)
LCT .... Logical Channel Termination
LCT .... Long Calcined Ton [*Bauxite, etc.*]
LCT .... Long-Chain Triglyceride [*Biochemistry*]
LCT .... Louis Comfort Tiffany [*Signature on the art glass designed by Tiffany*]
LCT .... Low Cervical Transverse [*Position*] [*Obstetrics*] (DAVI)
LCT .... Low-Cost Technology (PDAA)
LCT .... Low Cost Terminal [*Telecommunications*] (LAIN)
LCT .... Luscher Color Test [*Psychology*] (DAVI)
LCT .... Lymphocytotoxicity [*Medicine*] (DMAA)
LCT-1 .... Lymphocytotoxicity Test [*Hematology*]
LCT-1 .... Lunar Cycle Test One [*Aerospace*]
LCTA .... Land Condition-Trend Analysis [*Army*] (RDA)
LCT(A) .... Landing Craft, Tank (Armored)
LCTA .... London Corn Trade Association
LCTA .... Lymphocytotoxic Antibodies [*Immunochemistry*]
LCTB .... Launch Control Training Building [*NASA*] (IAA)
LC/TC .... Livonia Career/Technical Center
LCTCDE .... Liquid-Cooled Turbocharged Diesel Engine
LCTD .... Located (AFM)
LCTF .... Large Coil Test Facility (MCD)
LCTF .... Lloyd's Canadian Trust Fund (AIA)
LCTGM .... Library of Congress Thesaurus for Graphic Materials (TELE)
LCT(H) .... Landing Craft, Tank (Hospital) [*British military*] (DMA)
LCTHF .... Lewis and Clark Trail Heritage Foundation (EA)
LCTI .... Large Components Test Installation [*Nuclear energy*] (NRCH)
LCTL .... Large Component Test Loop [*Nuclear energy*]
LCTMP .... Little Change in Temperature [*NWS*] (FAAC)
LCTN .... Location
LCTP .... Launcher Control Test Panel
LCT(R) .... Landing Craft, Tank (Rocket)
LCTR .... Locator
LCT(S) .... Landing Craft, Tank (Slow)
LCTS .... LASER Coherence Techniques Section
LCTSU .... Launch Control Transfer Switching Unit [*Aerospace*] (AAG)
LCTT .... Launch Complex Telemetry Trailer
LCTV .... Liquid Crystal Television (CIST)

LCU .... Lac-Coated Urea Fertilizer
LCU .... Landing Craft, Utility [*Navy symbol*]
LCU .... Large Close-Up (ADA)
LCU .... LASER Cooling Unit (MCD)
LCU .... Launch Control Unit (MCD)
LCU .... Level Converter Unit [*Computer science*] (CIST)
LCU .... Library of Congress Music [*Source file*] [*UTLAS symbol*]
LCU .... Life Change Unit [*Psychometrics*]
LCU .... Lightweight Computer Unit [*Computer science*] (CIST)
LCU .... Line Control Unit [*Data communications*]
LCU .... Line Coupling Unit (NASA)
LCU .... Link Control Unit [*Telecommunications*] (TEL)
LCU .... Local Control Unit (IAA)
LCU .... Lower Control Unit (WDAA)
LCU .... Lucin, UT [*Location identifier FAA*] (FAAL)
LCUC .... Letter Carriers' Union of Canada
LCuC .... Liver Copper Concentration [*Physiology*]
LCUG .... Liquid-Cooled Undergarment (MCD)
LCUSA .... Ladies of Charity of the United States of America [*An association*] (EA)
LC/USA .... Lutheran Council in the USA [*Defunct*] (EA)
LCUT .... Lifetime Hoan [*NASDAQ symbol*] (TTSB)
LCUT .... Lifetime Hoan Corp. [*NASDAQ symbol*] (SAG)
LCV .... La Cueva [*New Mexico*] [*Seismograph station code, US Geological Survey*] (SEIS)
LCV .... Landing Craft, Vehicle [*Navy symbol*]
LCV .... Large Compound Vesicle [*Biochemistry*]
LCV .... LASER Compatible Vidicon
LCV .... League of Conservation Voters (EA)
LCV .... Legislative Council of Victoria [*Australia*]
LCV .... Level Control Valve (MCD)
LCV .... Light Commercial Vehicle
LCV .... Llymphocryptovirus
LCV .... Load Control Valve [*Engineering*]
LCV .... Local Control Valve [*Nuclear energy*] (NRCH)
LCV .... Longer Combination Vehicle [*Trucks hauling multiple trailers*]
LCV .... Lorry Command Vehicle [*British military*] (DMA)
LCV .... Low Calorific Value [*of a fuel*]
LCV .... Low Cervical Vertical [*Incision*] [*Obstetrics*] (DAVI)
LCV .... Lymphocytic Choriomeningitis Virus [*Medicine*] (DB)
LCVA .... Light Commercial Vehicle Association (EA)
LCVAO .... Linear Combination of Virtual Atomic Orbitals [*Physical chemistry*]
LCVASI .... Low-Cost Visual-Approach Slope Indicator (DNAB)
LCVD .... Laser-Assisted Chemical Vapor Deposition [*Coating technology*]
LCVD .... LASER Chemical Vapor Deposition [*Coating technology*]
LCVD .... Least Coincidence Voltage Detection (MDG)
LCVG .... Liquid Cooling and Ventilation Garment [*NASA*] (NASA)
LCVIP .... Licensee Contractor Vendor Inspection Report Program [*Nuclear energy*] (NRCH)
LCVM .... Log Conversion Voltmeter
LCVP .... Landing Craft, Vehicle, Personnel [*Navy symbol NATO*]
LCW .... Limited Conventional War [*Description of Vietnam War*] [*DoD*] (VNW)
LCW .... Line Control Word
LCW .... Lithuanian American Roman Catholic Women's Alliance
LCW .... Lithuanian Catholic Women (EA)
LCW .... Lutheran Church Women [*Defunct*] (EA)
LCWA .... Legislative Council of Western Australia
LCWA .... Lotteries Commission of Western Australia
LCWDS .... Low-Cost Weapon Delivery System (MCD)
LCWF .... Launch Complex Work Flow (IAA)
LCWHN .... Latin American and Caribbean Women's Health Network (EAIO)
LCWI .... Left Ventricular Cardiac Work Index [*Physiology*]
LCWIO .... Liaison Committee of Women's International Organisations [*British*] (DI)
LCWP .... Law Commission Working Paper [*A publication*] (DLA)
LCWR .... Leadership Conference of Women Religious of the USA (EA)
LCWSL .... Large Caliber Weapon Systems Laboratory [*ARRADCOM*] (RDA)
LCX .... Higginsville, MO [*Location identifier FAA*] (FAAL)
LCX .... Launch Complex
LCx .... Left Circumflex [*Artery*] [*Medicine*] (DB)
LCX .... Left Circumflex Coronary Artery [*Cardiology*] (DAVI)
LCXT .... Large Cosmic X-Ray Telescope (PDAA)
LCY .... Guthrie, OK [*Location identifier FAA*] (FAAL)
LCY .... League of Communists of Yugoslavia [*Savez Komunista Jugoslavije*] [*Political party*] (PPW)
LCY .... Loose Cubic Yard (DAC)
LCZ .... Laws of the Canal Zone [*A publication*] (DLA)
LCZR .... Localizer
LD .... Decisions Lost [*Boxing*]
LD .... Doctor of Letters
LD .... Lab. Dausse [*France*] [*Research code symbol*]
LD .... Label Definition (IAA)
LD .... Labor and Delivery [*Obstetrics*] (DAVI)
LD .... Laboratory Data (MAE)
LD .... Labor Daily [*A publication*]
LD .... Labor Department
LD .... Labor Dispute (DLA)
LD .... Labyrinthine Defect [*Physiology*] (MAE)
LD .... Lactate Dehydrogenase [*Also, LAD, LDH*] [*An enzyme*]
LD .... Lady Day [*March 25, the Feast of the Annunciation*] [*British*]
LD .... Lamina Densa [*Dermatology*]
LD .... Lamp Driver
LD .... Land
LD .... Landing Distance [*Aviation*] (IAA)
LD .... Land Office Decisions, United States [*A publication*] (DLA)

LD	Large Dollar [Indicator] [IRS]
LD	Lasa D Ring [Montana] [Seismograph station code, US Geological Survey] (SEIS)
LD	LASER Desorption [of ions for analysis]
LD	LASER Diode
LD	LASER Discectomy [Spinal surgery]
LD	Lateral Direction (MCD)
LD	Lateral Dorsal [Anatomy]
LD	Lateral Drift
LD	Lateralis Dorsalis [Neuroanatomy]
LD	Launch Director [NASA] (KSC)
LD	Launching Division [Missiles] (MUGU)
LD	Laus Deo [Praise to God] [Latin]
LD	Law Dictionary [A publication] (DLA)
LD	Layer Depth
LD	Lead [or Leads] [Publishing]
ld	Lead (WDMC)
ld	Leading (WDMC)
ld	Leading (MSA)
LD	Leading Edge Delay [Aviation] (IAA)
LD	Leak Detection [Nuclear energy] (IAA)
LD	Learning Disabilities/Differences
LD	Learning Disability [or Learning-Disabled]
LD	Learning Disorder (DB)
LD	Least Depth [Nautical charts]
LD	Lectio Divina [Paris] [A publication] (BJA)
LD	Left Defense
LD	Left Deltoid [Medicine]
LD	Left Door [Theater]
LD	Legal Deposit (ADA)
LD	Legal Discriminator (MCD)
LD	Legionnaire's Disease
LD	Legislative Department [Generic term] (ROG)
L-D	Leishman-Donovan (Bodies) [Microbiology]
LD	Length-Diameter Ratio
LD	Lepide Dictum [Wittily Said] [Latin] (ADA)
LD	Letdown [Nuclear energy] (NRCH)
LD	Lethal Dose
LD	Let's Discuss
LD	Letter Description (PDAA)
L/D	Letter of Deposit [Banking]
LD	Level Detector
LD	Level Discriminator
LD	Levodopa [Obstetrics] (DAVI)
LD	Liberal Democrat (WA)
LD	Library of Devotion [A publication]
LD	Libyan Dinar [Monetary unit] (BJA)
LD	Licentiate in Dentistry [British] (ROG)
LD	Licentiate in Divinity (DAS)
LD	Lifeboat Deck
L:D	Lift-Drag [Ratio]
LD	Light-Dark [Cycles]
L/D	Light-Dark [Ratio] [Ophthalmology] (DAVI)
LD	Light Difference [Difference between amounts of light perceptible to the two eyes] [Ophthalmology]
LD	Light Dragoons [Military unit] [British]
LD	Light Driver (IAA)
L/D	Light Duty [Automotive engineering]
LD	Lighting Designer (NTCM)
LD	Lighting Director (NTCM)
LD	Light on Dark
LD	Limited
LD	Limited Disease [Medicine]
LD	Limited Partner in Dual Capacity Firm [London Stock Exchange]
LD	Linear Decision
LD	Linear Dichroism [Spectra]
LD	Line Dolly (MCD)
LD	Line Drawing (MSA)
LD	Line Driver
LD	Line of Departure [Military]
LD	Line of Duty [Military]
LD	Linguodistal [Dentistry]
LD	Linkage Disequilibrium [Genetics]
LD	Linker Directive [Telecommunications] (TEL)
LD	Linz and Donawetz [Furnace] [Metallurgy Named after two plant sites in Austria]
LD	Liquid Drop
LD	List Down
LD	List of Drawings [USN] (MCD)
LD	Litera Dominicalis [Sunday Letter]
LD	Litterarum Doctor [Doctor of Letters or Literature] [Latin] (ROG)
lD	Liver Disease [Gastroenterology] (DAVI)
LD	Living Donor [Medicine]
LD	Load [or Loader] (AAG)
ld	Load (WDAA)
LD	Load Draught (IAA)
LD	Loaded Deployability [Posture] [Military] (DOMA)
LD	Loading Dock (MCD)
LD	Loading Dose
LD	Local Delivery
LD	Local Director (DCTA)
LD	Local Directory (ACRL)
LD	Loft Dried Paper (DGA)
LD	Logical Design
LD	Logic Driver [Computer science]
LD	Logistics Demonstration (MCD)
LD	Logistics Document (MCD)
LD	Lombard-Dowell [Broth medium] [Microbiology]
LD	London Docks
LD	Long Day [Botany]
LD	Long Delay
LD	Long Distance
LD	Long Duration
LD	Longitudinal Diameter
LD	Longitudinal Division [Cytology]
LD	Loop Diagram
LD	Loop-Disconnect [Telecommunications] (TEL)
LD	Lord
LD	Loss and Damage (IAA)
LD	Louis Dreyfus Natural Gas [NYSE symbol] (TTSB)
LD	Louis Dreyfus Natural Gas Holdings Corp. [NYSE symbol] (SPSG)
LD	Low Density
LD	Low Dispersion [Optics]
LD	Low Door (WDAA)
LD	Low Dose [Medicine]
LD	Low Drag
LD	Low Dust
LD	Low Dutch [Language, etc.]
LD	Low Dynamic
LD	Lower Deck
LD	Luminescence Detector (SSD)
LD	Luminescence Diode (IAA)
LD	Lunar Day (KSC)
LD	Lunar Docking [NASA] (IAA)
LD	Lunar Drill [NASA] (KSC)
LD	Lyme Disease [Medicine]
LD	Lymphocyte Defined [Immunology]
LD	Lymphocyte Depletion [Hematology]
LD	Lymphocytical Determined [Hematology] (DAVI)
LD	Vietnam [License plate code assigned to foreign diplomats in the US]
LD$_{50}$	Lethal Dose, Median [Also, MLD] [Lethal for 50% of test group]
LD 50	Low Dose, Fifty Percent Fatality [Environmental science] (COE)
LDA	Ascension Parish Library, Donaldsonville, LA [Library symbol Library of Congress] (LCLS)
LDA	Laboratory Designated Area (AFIT)
LDA	Labor Developments Abroad [A publication]
LDA	Land Development Aircraft (PDAA)
LDA	Landing Directional Aid [FAA] (TAG)
LDA	Landing Distance Available [ICAO] (FAAC)
LDA	Laser Disc Association (NTPA)
LDA	LASER Doppler Anemometry
LDA	Last Day of Attendance
LDA	Late-Differentiation Antigen [Immunology]
LDA	Lauda Air [Austria ICAO designator] (FAAC)
LDA	Lauryl Diethanolamide [Also, LDE] [Organic chemistry]
LDA	Lead Development Association [British] (EAIO)
LDA	Learning Disabilities Association of America (EA)
LDA	Left Dorso-Anterior [A fetal position] [Obstetrics]
LDA	Legitimacy Declaration Act [British] (ROG)
LDA	Lesson Design Approach (MCD)
LDA	Limited Depository Account
LDA	Limiting Dilution Analyses [Analytical biochemistry]
LDA	Linear Discriminant Analysis
LDA	Linear Displacement Analysis (DAVI)
LDA	Linear Dynamic Analyzer (IAA)
LDA	Line Driving Amplifier
LDA	Lithium Diisopropylamide [Organic chemistry]
LDA	Local Data Administrator
LDA	Local-Density (Functional) Approximation [Physical chemistry]
LDA	Local Design Agency (MCD)
LDA	Local Display Adapter (MHDB)
LDA	Localizer Directional Aid [Aviation]
LDA	Locate Drum Address (CET)
LDA	Logical Device Address [Computer science] (IBMDP)
LDA	Logic Design Automation (AAEL)
LDA	Lord's Day Alliance of the United States (EA)
LDA	Low-Density Amorph [Materials science]
LDA	Lower-Deck Attitude [British military] (DMA)
LDA	Lowest Designated Assembly
LDA	Lutheran Deaconess Association (EA)
LDA	Lymphocyte-Dependent Antibody [Immunology]
LDAC	Learning Disabilities Association of Canada (EAIO)
LDAC	Lunar Surface Data Acquisition Camera [Aerospace]
LDAI	Low-Dose Oral Alpha Interferon [Medicine] (TAD)
LDAK	Lidak Pharmaceuticals [NASDAQ symbol] (SAG)
LDAKA	LIDAK Pharmaceuticals'A' [NASDAQ symbol] (TTSB)
LDAM	Local Damage Assessment Model (PDAA)
LDAO	Lauryldimethylamine Oxide [Detergent]
LDAP	Lightweight Directory Access Protocol [Computer utility tool] (PCM)
LDAPS	Long-Duration Auxiliary Power System (NG)
LDAQ	Association Quebecoise pour les Troubles d'Apprentissage (AC)
LDAQ	Learning Disabilities Association of Quebec (AC)
LDAR	Latex Direct Agglutination Reaction [Medicine] (DMAA)
LDAR	Leak Detection and Repair [Chemical engineering]
LDAR	Lightning Detection and Ranging System [Meteorology]
LDAS	LASER Detection and Analysis System (MCD)
LDASE	Large Deployable Antenna Shuttle Experiment [NASA] (PDAA)
LdB	Das Land der Bibel (BJA)
LDB	Lamb Dysentery Bacillus [Medicine] (DMAA)
LDB	Launch Data Bus [Computer science] (MCD)

LDB.............	Leader Dogs for the Blind (EA)
LDB.............	Legionnaires Disease Bacillus [*Medicine*] (DMAA)
LDB.............	Legionnaire's Disease Bacterium
LDB.............	Legislative Data Base [*Department of Energy*] [*Information service or system*] (IID)
LDB.............	Leisure Diagnostic Battery [*Psychology*] (EDAC)
LDB.............	Lexington Development Branch (SAA)
LDB.............	Light Distribution Box (AAG)
LDB.............	Limited Data Block (KSC)
LDB.............	Liquidity Data Bank (NUMA)
LDB.............	Load Determining Bolt
LDB.............	Local Data Buffer (IAA)
LDB.............	Logical Database
LDB.............	Logistics Data Bank (NASA)
LDB.............	Londrina [*Brazil*] [*Airport symbol*] (OAG)
LDB.............	Low-Drag Bomb
LDBE............	London Diocesan Board of Education
Ld Birk........	Lord Birkenhead's Judgments, House of Lords [*England*] [*A publication*] (DLA)
LDBLC........	Low-Drag Boundary Layer Control [*Military*]
LDBOS........	LASER Designation Battlefield Obscuration Simulator (RDA)
Ld Br Sp.....	Lord Brougham's Speeches [*A publication*] (DLA)
LDBS..........	Local Data Base System (MHDI)
LDC...........	Laboratory Data Control [*Commercial firm*]
LDC...........	Labor Data Collection (MCD)
LDC...........	Labor Day Committee [*Australia*]
LDC...........	Ladeco Cargo, SA [*Chile*] [*FAA designator*] (FAAC)
LDC...........	Large Diameter Core (SAA)
LDC...........	LASER Discharge Capacitor (IAA)
LDC...........	Latitude Data Computer
LDC...........	Laundry and Dry Cleaning International Union
LDC...........	Learning Disability Center
LDC...........	Learning Disordered Children
LDC...........	Less Developed Country
LDC...........	Leukocyte Differential Count [*Medicine*] (MEDA)
LDC...........	Level Decision Circuit
LDC...........	Libertarian Defense Caucus [*Defunct*] (EA)
LDC...........	Library Development Center [*Columbia University*]
LDC...........	Library Development Consultants, Inc. [*Information service or system*] (IID)
LDC...........	Light Direction Center [*Military*]
LDC...........	Lightweight Deployable Communications System [*Army*]
LDC...........	Limiting Dilution Cloning [*Biochemistry*]
LDC...........	Lindeman Island [*Australia Airport symbol*]
LDC...........	Linear Detonating Cord (MSA)
LDC...........	Line Directional Coupler
LDC...........	Line-Drop Compensator (MSA)
LDC...........	Linguistic Data Consortium [*Defense Advanced Research Projects Agency*]
LDC...........	Linguistics Documentation Center [*University of Ottawa*] [*Database*] [*Canada*] (NITA)
LDC...........	Load Drawer Computer (MCD)
LDC...........	Local Damping Control [*Automotive engineering*]
LDC...........	Local Data Concentrator [*Telecommunications*]
LDC...........	Local Defense Center
LDC...........	Local Departmental Committee [*British labor*]
LDC...........	Local Development Company
LDC...........	Local Display Controller
LDC...........	Local Distribution Company
LDC...........	Logistics Data Center [*Army*] (AABC)
LDC...........	London Diagnostic Centre [*England*] (WDAA)
LDC...........	London Dumping Convention [*Sets standards for disposal of wastes in oceans*]
LDC...........	Long Day Care
LDC...........	Long-Distance Call
LDC...........	Long-Distance Communications
LDC...........	Lower Dead Center
LDC...........	Low-Speed Data Channel
LDC...........	Lutheran Deaconess Conference (EA)
LDCA..........	Land Development Contractors' Association [*Australia*]
LDCC..........	Large Diameter Component Cask [*Nuclear energy*] (NRCH)
LDCC..........	Lectin-Dependent Cell-Mediated Cytotoxicity [*Biochemistry*]
LDCF..........	Lymphocyte Derived Chemotactic Factor [*Biochemistry*]
LDCIU........	Laundry and Dry Cleaning International Union (NTPA)
LDCM..........	LANDesk Client Manager Technology [*Intel*] [*Computer science*]
LDCO..........	Laundry and Dry Cleaning Operations [*Military*]
LDCP..........	Landing Dynamics Computer Program [*NASA*]
L(D)CRS......	Leachate (Detection) Collection and Removal System (GNE)
LDCS..........	Long-Distance Control System (IEEE)
LDCT..........	Late Distal Cortical Tubule [*Medicine*] (DMAA)
LDCT..........	Linear Discriminant Classification Tree [*Mathematics*]
LDCV..........	Large Dense-Core Vesicle [*Neurobiology*]
LDD............	LASER Detector Diode
LDD............	LASER Diode Driver
LDD............	Late Dedifferentiation (DB)
LDD............	Letter of Determination of Dependency
LDD............	Light-Dark Discrimination [*Ophthalmology*]
LDD............	Light-Dependent Diode [*Instrumentation*]
LDD............	Light Duty Diesel (COE)
LDD............	Lightly Doped Drain (MCD)
LDD............	Little Diomede Island, AK [*Location identifier FAA*] (FAAL)
LDD............	Loaded
LDD............	Local Data Distribution
LDD............	Local Development District
LDD............	Logical Database Designer [*Computer science*]
LDD............	Logic Design Data [*Telecommunications*] (TEL)
LDD............	Long-Distance Dispersal [*Botany*]
LDD............	Low-Density Data (KSC)
LDD............	Luminaire Dirt Depreciation [*Floodlighting*]
LDD............	Lunar Dust Detector [*NASA*]
LDDC..........	Least-Developed Developing Country [*Trade status*]
LDDC..........	London Docklands Development Corp. [*British*] (ECON)
LDDC..........	Long-Distance Dialing Center (IAA)
LDDC..........	Long Distance Direct Current [*Telecommunications*] (CIST)
LDDCS........	Laundry and Decontamination Drycleaning System [*Military*] (DWSG)
LDDI...........	Local Distributed Data Interface [*Telecommunications*]
LDDL..........	Logical Data Definition Language (IAA)
LDDM..........	LASER Doppler Displacement Meter (AAEL)
LDDO..........	Long-Distance Diesel Oil (PDAA)
LDDS..........	Light Division Direct Support [*Artillery system*] (MCD)
LDDS..........	Limited Distance Data Service [*Telecommunications*]
LDDS..........	Limited Distance Data Set [*Modem*] (NITA)
LDDS..........	Local Dentist (DAVI)
LDDS..........	Local Digital Distribution Subsystem
LDDS..........	Local Doctor of Dental Surgery (MAE)
LDDS..........	Long-Distance Discount Service [*Telecommunications*]
LDDS..........	Low-Density Data System
LDDT..........	Light-Duty Diesel Truck [*Automotive emissions*]
LDDV..........	Light Duty Diesel Vehicle [*VDOT*] (TAG)
LDDVX........	Lindner Dividend [*Mutual fund ticker symbol*] (SG)
LDE............	Lagrange Differential Equation
LDE............	Laminar Defect Examination (IEEE)
LDE............	Lauryl Diethanolamide [*Also, LDA*] [*Organic chemistry*]
LDE............	Les Dames d'Escoffier (EA)
LDE............	Lighting Director Engineer (NTCM)
LDE............	Linear Differential Equation
LDE............	Lineas Aereas del Estado [*Argentina ICAO designator*] (FAAC)
LDE............	Local Dynamics Experiment [*Marine science*] (MSC)
LDE............	Long-Delayed Echo
LDE............	Long-Duration Exposure
LDE............	Lourdes/Tarbes [*France*] [*Airport symbol*] (OAG)
LDeB..........	Beauregard Parish Library, DeRidder, LA [*Library symbol Library of Congress*] (LCLS)
L Dec.........	Land Office Decisions, United States [*A publication*] (DLA)
LDEC..........	Lunar Docking Events Controller [*NASA*] (MCD)
LDEF......,.....	Long-Duration Exposure Facility [*NASA*]
LDEG..........	Laus Deo et Gloria [*Praise and Glory Be to God*] [*Latin*]
LDERRY......	Londonderry [*County in Ireland*] (ROG)
LDET..........	Level Detector (MSA)
LDEX..........	Landing Exercise [*Navy*] (NVT)
LD-EYA.......	Lombard-Dowell Egg Yolk Agar [*Microbiology*]
LDF............	Land Disposal Facility
LDF............	Landed Duty Free
LDF............	Latin American Discovery Fd [*NYSE symbol*] (TTSB)
LDF............	Latin American Discovery Fund [*NYSE symbol*] (SPSG)
LDF............	Light Digital FACSIMILE [*Machine*]
LDF............	Light Distillate Feedstock (PDAA)
LDF............	Linear Discriminant Function [*Mathematics*]
LDF............	Linear Driving Force
LDF............	Load Division Fault
LDF............	Load Factor (IAA)
LDF............	Local Defense Forces
LDF............	Local-Density Functional Equation (MCD)
LDF............	Local Density Functional Theory [*Chemistry*]
LDF............	London Diocesan Fund
LDF............	Lyme Disease Foundation
LDF............	NAACP [*National Association for the Advancement of Colored People*] Legal Defense and Educational Fund (EA)
LDFC..........	Lew DeWitt Fan Club [*Defunct*] (EA)
LDFSTN......	Landing Direction Finding Station [*Aviation*] (IAA)
LDG............	Lactic Dehydrogenase (DMAA)
LDG............	Lading (WDAA)
LDG............	Landing [*Maps and charts*] (AFM)
LDG............	Leading
LDG............	Left Digestive Gland
LDG............	Lexington Design Group (SAA)
LDG............	Libyan Desert Glass [*Archeology*]
LDG............	Linear Displacement Gauge
LDG............	Lingual Developmental Groove (DMAA)
LDG............	Loading
LDG............	Lodge [*or Lodging*] (MCD)
LDG............	Longs Drug Stores [*NYSE symbol*] (TTSB)
LDG............	Longs Drug Stores Corp. [*NYSE symbol*] (SPSG)
LDG............	Low-Density Gas
Ldg & Dly...	Landing and Delivery [*Shipping*] (DS)
LDGE..........	LEM [*Lunar Excursion Module*] Dummy Guidance Equipment [*NASA*] (KSC)
LDGE..........	Lodge [*Commonly used*] (OPSA)
LDGLT........	Leading Light [*Navigation signal*]
L-DGO........	Lamont-Doherty Geological Observatory [*Formerly, LGO*] [*Columbia University*]
LDGO..........	Lamont Doherty Geological Observatory [*Marine science*] (OSRA)
LDGP..........	Low-Drag General Purpose (MCD)
LDGPS........	Local DGPS [*Differential*] [*Global Positioning System*] (GAVI)
LDGSPTBN..	Landing Support Battalion (DNAB)
Ld Gt.........	Land Grant (MHDB)
Ldg Tel.......	Leading Telegraphist
LDGV..........	Light-Duty Gasoline Vehicle
LDH............	Lactate Dehydrogenase [*Also, LAD, LD*] [*An enzyme*]
L d'H..........	Legion d'Honneur [*French decoration*]

LDH	Ligue des Droits de l'Homme [*France*]
LDH	Limiting Dome Height [*Automotive metal stamping*]
LDH	Lord Howe Island [*Australia Airport symbol*] (OAG)
LDHA	Lactic Dehydrogenase A (DB)
LDHB	Lactic Dehydrogenase B (DB)
LDHC	Lactic Dehydrogenase-C (DMAA)
LDHC	Locker Door Hydraulic Cylinder
LDHD	Lymphocyte-Depletion Hodgkin's Disease [*Medicine*]
LDHI	Lactic Dehydrogenase Isoenzymes (DAVI)
LDHK	Lactic Dehydrogenase-K (DMAA)
LDHM	London Diocesan Home Mission [*or Missionary*]
LDHRR	League for the Defense of Human Rights in Romania [*Paris, France*] (EAIO)
LDI	Landing Direction Indicator [*ICAO*] (FAAC)
LDI	LASER Desorption Ionization [*Spectroscopy*]
LDI	Lauda Air [*Italy ICAO designator*] (FAAC)
LDI	Life Detection Instrument
LDI	Lindi [*Tanzania*] [*Airport symbol*] (OAG)
LDI	Linear Displacement Indicator
LDI	Load Indicator
LDI	Lockheed DataPlan, Inc. [*Information service or system*] (IID)
LDI	Loredi Resources Ltd. [*Vancouver Stock Exchange symbol*]
LDI	Lossless Digital Integrator (IAA)
LDIC	Low-Density Indication (MCD)
LDIC	LDI Corp. [*NASDAQ symbol*] (SAG)
LDI Cp	LDI Corp. [*Associated Press*] (SAG)
L Dict	Law Dictionary [*A publication*] (DLA)
LDIH	Left Direct Inguinal Hernia [*Medicine*] (DMAA)
LDII	Larson Davis [*NASDAQ symbol*] (TTSB)
LDIM	Luminescence Digital Imaging Microscopy
LDIN	Lead-In Lighting [*or Lights*] [*Aviation*]
LDIN	Lead-in-Light System [*FAA*] (TAG)
L-Dink	Lower Class - Double [*or Dual*] Income, No Kids [*Lifestyle classification*]
LDIP	Laboratory Data Integrity Program [*Environmental Protection Agency*] (GFGA)
L-DISC	Late Direct Injection Stratified Charge
LDISCR	Level Discriminator (MSA)
LD Is FFD	Line of Departure Is Friendly Forward Disposition [*Army*] (AABC)
LDISO	Lactic Dehydrogenase Isoenzymes (DAVI)
LD Is PPOS	Line of Departure Is Present Positions [*Military*] (AABC)
LDIU	Launch Data Interface Unit (MCD)
L Div	Law Division (DLA)
L Div	Licentiate in Divinity
LDJ	Linden, NJ [*Location identifier FAA*] (FAAL)
LDJ	Load D-Bank and Jump [*Computer science*]
LDJU	Luvers of David Jones United (EA)
LDK	Lower Deck
Ld Ken	Lord Kenyon's English King's Bench Reports [*1753-59*] [*A publication*] (DLA)
Ld Kenyon	Lord Kenyon's English King's Bench Reports [*1753-59*] [*A publication*] (DLA)
Ld Kenyon (Eng)	Lord Kenyon's English King's Bench Reports [*1753-59*] [*A publication*] (DLA)
LDL	Landing Direction Light [*Aviation*] (IAA)
LDL	Language Description Language [*Computer science*]
LDL	Learned Doctor of Laws
LDL	Lighting Design Lumen (PDAA)
LDL	Liquid Delay Line
LDL	Logical Data Language [*Computer science*] (IAA)
LDL	Logical Display List (MCD)
LDL	Long Distance Love [*An association*] (EA)
LDL	Loudness Discomfort Level (MAE)
LDL	Low-Density Lipoprotein [*Biochemistry*]
LDL	Lower Detectable Limit [*Chemical analysis*]
LDL	Lower Detection Limit (AAEL)
LDL	Lower Deviation Level (AABC)
LDL	Lydall, Inc. [*NYSE symbol*] (SPSG)
LDL	University of Nebraska, Lincoln, Lincoln, NE [*OCLC symbol*] (OCLC)
LDLA	Limited Distance Line Adapter
LDLA	Low-Density Lipoprotein Apheresis [*Medicine*] (DMAA)
LD/LC	Line of Departure/Line of Contact [*Army*] (ADDR)
LDL-C	Low-Density Lipoprotein-Cholesterol [*Biochemistry*]
LDLE	Light-Duty Lathe Engine
LdLew	Lewisville Public Library, Lewisville, ID [*Library symbol*] [*Library of Congress*] (LCLS)
LD-LISC	Ligand-Driven Light-Induced Spin Changes [*Physics*]
LD LMT	Load Limit (WDAA)
LD^{Lo}	Lethal Dose Low (ERG)
LDLO	Lethal Dose Low [*Environmental science*] (COE)
LDLP	Low Density Lipoprotein [*Biochemistry*]
LDLR	Land Development Law Reporter [*A publication*] (DLA)
LDLR	Low-Density Lipoprotein Receptor [*Biochemistry*]
Ldlw COO	Laidlaw One, Inc. [*Associated Press*] (SAG)
Ldlw000	Laidlaw One, Inc. [*Associated Press*] (SAG)
LDM	Laidlaw Transportation Ltd. [*Toronto Stock Exchange symbol*]
LDM	LASER Drilling Machine
LDM	Last Day of the Month (AFM)
LDM	Lee, David M., Los Angeles CA [*STAC*]
LDM	Libby Dam [*Montana*] [*Seismograph station code, US Geological Survey*] (SEIS)
LDM	Licentiate of Dental Medicine
LDM	Limited-Distance MODEM [*Computer science*]
LDM	Linear Delta Modulation
LDM	Load Distribution Matrix (IAA)

LDM	Local Data Manager
LDM	Long-Delay Monostable [*Circuitry*]
LDM	Lord Mayor
LDM	Low-Density Microsome [*Cytology*]
LDM	Ludington, MI [*Location identifier FAA*] (FAAL)
LDm	Median Lethal Time (EES)
LDMA	London Discount Market Association [*British*] (MHDW)
LDME	LASER Distance Measuring Equipment (DNAB)
LDMI	LASER Distance Measuring Instrument
LDMK	Landmark (KSC)
LdmkBc	Landmark Bancorp [*Associated Press*] (SAG)
LdmkGph	Landmark Graphics Corp. [*Associated Press*] (SAG)
LDMOS	Lateral Double-Diffused Metal-Oxide Semiconductor (MCD)
LDMOS	Laterally Diffused Metal-Oxide Semiconductor (AAEL)
LD-MPT	Ligue Democratique - Mouvement pour le Parti des Travailleurs [*Democratic League - Movement for the Workers' Party*] [*Senegal*] [*Political party*] (PPW)
LDMS	Laboratory Data Management System [*IBM Corp.*]
LDMS	LASER Desorption Mass Spectrometry
LDMS	LASER Distance Measuring System
LDMS	Lunar Distance Measuring System [*Aerospace*]
LDMWR	Limited Depot Maintenance Work Requirements
LDMX	Local Digital Message Exchange (AABC)
LDN	Lamidanda [*Nepal*] [*Airport symbol*] (OAG)
LDN	Lightning Detection Network [*Electric Power Research Institute*]
LDN	Linden, VA [*Location identifier FAA*] (FAAL)
LDN	Listed Directory Number [*Bell System*]
LDN	Locally Defined Neighborhood
LDN	London [*England*]
LDN	London [*Ontario*] [*Seismograph station code, US Geological Survey*] (SEIS)
LDN	London Silver Corp. [*Vancouver Stock Exchange symbol*]
LDNA	Long-Distance Navigation Aid
LD-NEYA	Lombard-Dowell Neomycin Egg Yolk Agar [*Microbiology*]
LDNG	Loading
LDNRX	Lindner Growth Fund [*Mutual fund ticker symbol*] (SG)
LDNS	Lightweight Doppler Navigation System (MCD)
LDO	Ladouanie [*Suriname*] [*Airport symbol*] (OAG)
LDO	Laminated Diatom Ooze [*Oceanography*]
LDO	Launch Division Officer [*Missiles*] (MUGU)
LDO	Light Diesel Oil (IAA)
LDO	Limited Duty Officer [*Navy*]
LDO	Linear Diophantine Object
LDO	Local Dental Officer
LDO	Logical Device Order [*Computer science*] (IBMDP)
LDO	Long-Distance Oil [*Service mark*] [*Amoco Oil Co.*]
LDO	Low-Density Oil [*Petroleum industry*]
LDO	Low-Density Overlay [*Plywood*]
LDO	Low Drop Out
LDO	St. Mary's Dominican College, New Orleans, LA [*OCLC symbol*] (OCLC)
LDOCE	Longman's Dictionary of Contemporary English [*A publication*]
LDOM	Lorenz Domination [*Statistics*]
L-DOPA	Levo-Dihydroxyphenylalanine [*Pharmacology*]
L-dopa	Levodopa (WDAA)
LDOS	Leather Dressers' Old Society [*A union*] [*British*]
LDOS	Local Density of Electron States [*Physical chemistry*]
LDOS	Local Density of States [*Solid state physics*]
LDOS	Lord's Day Observance Society [*British*]
LDP	Laban ng Demokratikong Pilipino [*Democratic Filipino's Struggle*] [*Political party*]
LDP	Laboratory Data Processor (IAA)
LDP	Laboratory Distribution Panel
LDP	Ladyship [*or Lordship*]
LDP	Landed Duty Paid [*Military*]
LDP	Langmuir Diffusion Pump [*Engineering*]
LDP	Language Data Processing (MSA)
LDP	Large Developmental Plant [*Project*] [*Department of Energy*]
LDP	Leadership Development Projects [*National Science Foundation*]
LDP	Leaflet Dispensing Pod
LDP	League for Democracy and Peace [*Myanmar*] [*Political party*] (EY)
LDP	Left Dorso-Posterior [*A fetal position*] [*Obstetrics*]
LDP	Liberal Democratic Party [*Slovenia*] [*Political party*] (EY)
LDP	Liberal-Democratic Party of Japan [*Jiyu-Minshuto*] [*Political party*] (PPW)
LDP	Liberal Demokratische Partei [*Liberal Democratic Party*] [*Germany Political party*] (PPE)
LDP	Lietuviy Demokraty Partija [*Lithuanian Democratic Party*] [*Political party*] (PPE)
L/DP	Living/Dying Project (EA)
LDP	Local Data Package (KSC)
LDP	Local Data Processor (AABC)
LDP	Logistics Data Package
LDP	Logistics Development Program (DOMA)
LDP	Lomas Data Products [*Marlboro, MA*] [*Computer manufacturer*]
LDP	London Daily Price [*British*]
LDP	Long-Day Plant [*Botany*]
LDP	Lordship [*British*]
LDP	Lorentz Doppler Profile [*Physics*]
LDP	Low Density Plasma (AAEL)
LDP	Lung Damaging Particle
LDPD	Liberal-Demokratische Partei Deutschlands [*Liberal Democratic Party of Germany*] [*Political party*] (PPW)
LDPE	Low-Density Polyethylene [*Polymer*]
LDPN	Low-Density Phenolic Nylon [*Polymer*]

LDPS	L-Band Digital Phase Shifter
LDQ	Leaders Equity Corp. [Vancouver Stock Exchange symbol]
LDQ	Lobe-Dominated Quasar [Astronomy]
LDR	Aero Lider SA de CV [Mexico ICAO designator] (FAAC)
LDR	Labor, Delivery, Recovery Room [Medicine]
LDR	Landauer, Inc. [AMEX symbol] (SPSG)
LDR	Land Disposal Restriction (COE)
LDR	Land Disposal Restrictions [Environmental Protection Agency]
LDR	Landmark Resources Ltd. [Vancouver Stock Exchange symbol]
LDR	Large Deployable Reflector [Astronomy]
LDR	LASER Designator Range (MCD)
LDR	Latest Date of Release (WDAA)
LDR	Leader
LDR	Leading Deep Recess [Rotary automotive engine]
LDR	Ledger (ADA)
LDR	Length-Diameter Ratio
LDR	Level Distribution Recorder
LDR	Liberal, Democratic, and Reformist Group [European political movement] (ECON)
LDR	Light Dependent Resistor
LDR	Light-to-Dark Ratio
LDR	Limiting Drawing Ratio (MCD)
LDR	Linear Decision Rule
LDR	Linear Dynamic Range
LDR	Line Driver-Receiver [Computer communication] (TEL)
LDR	Liquid Droplet Radiator (MCD)
LDR	Llandore [Welsh depot code]
LDR	Loader (MSA)
LDR	Lodar [South Arabia] [Airport symbol] (AD)
LDR	Log Dose Response [Biochemical analysis]
LDR	Lorentz Double Refraction [Physics]
L/DR	Lounge/Dining Room [Classified advertising] (ADA)
LDR	Low Data Rate [RADAR]
LDR	Low Data Register [Computer science]
LDR	Low-Density, Recorder
LDR	Low Dose Rate [Medicine]
LDRA	Low Data Rate Auxiliary [RADAR]
Ld Ray	Lord Raymond's King's Bench and Common Pleas Reports [1694-1732] [A publication] (DLA)
Ld Raym	Lord Raymond's King's Bench and Common Pleas Reports [1694-1732] [A publication] (DLA)
LDRC	Libel Defense Resource Center (EA)
LDRC	Lumber Dealers Research Council [Defunct] (EA)
LDRDA	Long Distance Running Directors Association (EA)
LDRER	Launderer
LDRF	Long-Distance Range Finder (SSD)
LDRG	Liberal, Democratic and Reformist Group [See also GLDR] (EAIO)
LDRI	Learning Disabilities Research Institute [University of Virginia] (EDAC)
LDRI	Low Data Rate Input [RADAR]
LDRIACS	Low Data Rate Integrated Acoustic Communications System [Military] (CAAL)
LDRM	LASER Designator Rangefinding Module (RDA)
LDRP	Labor, Delivery, Recovery, Post-Partum [Medicine] (MEDA)
LDRP	Learning Disability Rating Procedure [Educational test]
LDRPS	Labor-Delivery-Recovery-Postpartum Suite (HCT)
LDRRIM	Low-Density Reinforced Reaction Injection Molding [Plastics]
LDRS	Labor-Delivery-Recovery Suite (HCT)
LDRS	LASER Discrimination RADAR System
L/DRS	Level and Density Recorder Switch [Nuclear energy] (NRCH)
LDRSHP	Leadership
LDRSP	Leadership (AFM)
LDRT	[The] Lake Front Dock & Railroad Terminal Co. [Formerly, LDT] [AAR code]
LDRT	Low Data Rate [RADAR] (IAA)
LDRTF	Land Disposal Restrictions Task Force [Environmental Protection Agency] (GFGA)
LDRY	Landry's Seafood Restaurants [NASDAQ symbol] (TTSB)
LDRY	Landrys Seafood Restaurants, Inc. [NASDAQ symbol] (SAG)
LDRY	Laundry (AFM)
LDryNG	Louis Dreyfus Natural Gas [Associated Press] (SAG)
LDS	Havre, MT [Location identifier FAA] (FAAL)
LDS	Landing/Deceleration Subsystem [NASA] (NASA)
LDS	Landing, Deservicing, and Safing [NASA] (KSC)
LDS	Langmuir Dark Space [Electronics]
LDS	Large Disk Storage [Computer science] (IEEE)
LDS	LASER Deep Space
LDS	LASER Designator System [Rangefinder] (MCD)
LDS	Laser Detection System
LDS	LASER Drilling System
LDS	Last Data Sample (IAA)
LDS	Latter-Day Saints [Mormons]
LDS	Launch Data System [NASA] (KSC)
LDS	Launch Detection Satellite [Former USSR]
LDS	Laus Deo Semper [Praise to God Always] [Latin]
LDS	Layered Defense System (MCD)
LDS	Lead Design Supervisor [Engineering]
LDS	Leader Development Study [Army]
LDS	Leak Detection System [Nuclear energy] (NRCH)
LDS	Lethal Defense System (MCD)
LDS	Lexington Developmental Scales [Child development test]
LDS	Licentiate in Dental Surgery
LDS	Lietuviu Darbininku Susivienijimas [Association of Lithuanian Workers] (EA)
LDS	Ligating and Dividing Stapler [Used surgical procedures] (DAVI)
LDS	Light Distillate Spirit (PDAA)
LDS	Lightweight Decontamination System (INF)
LDS	Linear Dynamic System
LDS	Liquid, Diesel-Cycle, Supercharged
LDS	Loads [Military]
LDS	Local Digital Switch [Telecommunications] (TEL)
LDS	Local Distribution Service [Cable TV network] (NITA)
LDS	Local Distribution System [or Service] [Cable television] (MDG)
LDS	Locked Door Seclusion [Medicine] (DMAA)
LDS	Logistics Data Sheet
LDS	Long Distance Savers
LDS	Long Distance Swimmer
LDS	Longitudinal Direct Substitution Imputation Procedure [Bureau of the Census] (GFGA)
LDS	Lunar Drill System [NASA]
LDSA	Logistics Doctrine and Systems Agency [Army] (MCD)
LDSc	Licentiate in Dental Science [British]
ldscp	Landscape (VRA)
LDSD	Lookdown/Shootdown (MCD)
LDSD	Low Dimensional Structures and Devices [British]
LDSI	Licentiate in Dental Surgery (Ireland)
LDSJ	Little Daughters of St. Joseph [Roman Catholic religious order]
LDSO	Logistics Doctrine and Systems Office [Army]
LDSP	Lietuvos Socialdemokratu Partija [Social Democratic Party of Lithuania] [Political party] (EAIO)
LDSR	League of Distilled Spirits Rectifiers [Defunct]
LDSRA	Logistics Doctrine Systems and Readiness Agency [Army] (AABC)
LDSRCPS Glas	Licentiate in Dental Surgery of the Royal College of Physicians and Surgeons of Glasgow [British]
LDSRCS	Licentiate in Dental Surgery of the Royal College of Surgeons [British]
LDSRCSEd	Licentiate in Dental Surgery of the Royal College of Surgeons of Edinburgh (DI)
LDSRCS Edin	Licentiate in Dental Surgery of the Royal College of Surgeons of Edinburgh [British]
LDSRCS Eng	Licentiate in Dental Surgery of the Royal College of Surgeons of England
LDSRCS Irel	Licentiate in Dental Surgery of the Royal College of Surgeons in Ireland
LD-SRIM	Low-Density Structural Reaction Injection Molding [Plastics]
LDSS	LASER Designator Search System
LDSS	Lunar Deep Seismic Sounding [Aerospace] (MCD)
LDSSIG	Learning Disabled Student SIG [Special Interest Group] (EA)
LDST	Letdown Storage Tank [Nuclear energy] (NRCH)
LDSU	Local Distribution Service Unit (IAA)
LDT	[The] Lake Front Dock & Railroad Terminal Co. [Later, LDRT] [AAR code]
LDT	Language Dependent Translator
LDT	LASER Discharge Tube
LDT	Lateral Dorsal Tract [Neuroanatomy]
LDT	L-DOPA Test [Endocrinology]
LDT	Left Dorsotransverse [Medicine] (DMAA)
LDT	Level Delay Time
LDT	Level Detector (KSC)
LDT	Library Development Team
LDT	Licensed Deposit-Taking Institution [British]
LDT	Light Displacement Ton [MARAD] (TAG)
LDT	Light-Duty Truck
LDT	Linear Differential Transformer
LDT	Linear Displacement Transduced (MCD)
LDT	Local Daylight Saving Time
LDT	Local Descriptor Table [Computer science]
LDT	Logical Design Translator (NITA)
LDT	Logical Device Table (IAA)
LDT	Logic Design Translator [Computer science]
LDT	Logistic Delay Time (CAAL)
LDT	London Dipole Theory
LDT	Long Distance Transmission (BUR)
LDT	Long Dry Ton
LDT	Lubbock, TX [Location identifier FAA] (FAAL)
LDTA	Leak Detection Technology Association (EA)
LDTC	Lawndale Transportation Co. [AAR code]
LDTC	Learning Disabilities Teacher Consultant
LD/TE	Line Driver/Terminal Equipment (MCD)
LDTEL	Long Distance Telephone [Telecommunications] (IAA)
LDTF	Light of Divine Truth Foundation (EA)
LDTM	Lander Dynamic Test Model [NASA]
LDTOF	LASER Desorption Time-of-Flight [Spectrometry]
LDTR	Long Dwell Time RADAR (NATG)
LDTTY	Landing Line Teletype
LDU	Lahad Datu [Malaysia] [Airport symbol] (OAG)
LDU	Lamp Dimmer Unit (MCD)
LdU	Landesring der Unabhaengigen [Independent Party] [Switzerland Political party] (PPE)
LDU	Leather Dressers' Union [British]
LDU	Line Driver Unit [Computer communication] (MCD)
LDUB	Long Double Upright Brace [Medicine]
LDUH	Low-Dose Unfractionated Heparin [Medicine] (DMAA)
LD/USA	Long Distance/USA, Inc. [Honolulu, HI] [Telecommunications] (TSSD)
LDV	Lactic Dehydrogenase Virus
LDV	Large Dense-Cored Vesicle [Medicine] (DMAA)
LDV	LASER Doppler Velocimeter
LDV	Leadville [Nevada] [Seismograph station code, US Geological Survey Closed] (SEIS)

LDV............ League of Disabled Voters (EA)
LDV............ Lectus Developments Ltd. [*Vancouver Stock Exchange symbol*]
LDV............ Light-Duty Vehicle
LDV............ Linear Differential Vector
LDV............ Local Defence Volunteers [*Later called Home Guards*] [*British World War II*]
LDV............ Low-Dollar Value
LDVA.......... Lodi District Vintners Association (EA)
LDVE.......... Linear Differential Vector Equation
LDW.......... Laidlaw Inc. [*NYSE symbol*] (SAG)
LDW.......... Left Defense Wing [*Women's lacrosse position*]
LDW.......... Liability Damage Waiver [*Insurance*]
LDW.......... Licensed Driver's Waiver (BARN)
LDWA........ Long Distance Walkers Association [*British*] (DBA)
LDWSS....... LASER Designator Weapon System Simulation (RDA)
LDX........... Long-Distance Xerography [*Xerox Corp.*] [*Communications facsimile system*]
LDY........... Laundry
LDY........... Leicestershire and Derbyshire Yeomanry [*Military unit*] [*British*]
LDY........... Londonderry [*Northern Ireland*] [*Airport symbol*] (OAG)
LDZ........... Lodz [*Poland*] [*Airport symbol*] (AD)
LDZ........... St. Louis, MO [*Location identifier FAA*] (FAAL)
LE .... Antenna Effective Length for Electric-Field Antennas (IEEE)
LE .... Eunice Public Library, Eunice, LA [*Library symbol Library of Congress*] (LCLS)
LE .... Laboratory Evaluation (MUGU)
LE .... Laboratory of Electronics [*Rockefeller University*] [*Research center*] (RCD)
LE .... Labor Exchange
LE .... Lactate Extraction [*Medicine*] (DMAA)
LE .... Lands' End [*NYSE symbol*] (SPSG)
LE .... LAN [*Local Area Network*] Emulation [*Computer science*]
LE .... Large End (OA)
LE .... LASER Electronics (MCD)
LE .... Lateral Element
LE .... Lateral Epicondyle [*Anatomy*]
LE .... Latest Estimate [*Business term*]
LE .... Launch Eject
LE .... Launch Electronics
L/E .... Launch Encounter [*NASA*] (KSC)
LE .... Launch Escape [*NASA*] (KSC)
LE .... Launching Equipment
LE .... Law Enforcement
LE .... Laws of Eshnunna (BJA)
LE .... Lawyers' Edition, United States Supreme Court Reports [*A publication*] (DLA)
LE .... Lead Engineer (AAG)
LE .... Leading Edge [*Aerospace*]
LE .... Lease
LE .... Leave Edge (DGA)
le .... Lebanon [*MARC country of publication code Library of Congress*] (LCCP)
LE .... Lector
Le .... Ledge
LE .... Lee-Enfield [*British military*] (DMA)
LE .... Left Ear (DMAA)
LE .... Left End
LE .... Left Extremity
LE .... Left Eye
LE .... Leg Exercise [*Sports medicine*]
LE .... Length (IAA)
Le .... Leonard [*Unit for cathode rays*]
LE .... Leone [*Monetary unit*] [*Sierra Leone*]
LE .... Less than or Equal
LE .... Leucine Enkephalin [*Biochemistry*]
LE .... Leucocyte Elastase [*An enzyme*]
LE .... Leukemia [*Oncology*]
LE .... Leukoerythrogenetic (MAE)
LE .... Levy Industries Ltd. [*Toronto Stock Exchange symbol*]
Le .... Lewis [*Blood group*]
Le .... Lewis Number [*IUPAC*]
LE .... Library Edition (ADA)
LE .... Lifting Eye
LE .... Light Equipment
LE .... Limited Edition (ADA)
LE .... Limits of Error
LE .... Linear Expansion [*Physics*]
LE .... Line Equipment [*Telecommunications*] (TEL)
LE .... Linkage Editor (IAA)
LE .... Linkage Equilibrium [*Genetics*]
LE .... Local Area Network Emulation [*Computer science*] (DDC)
LE .... Local Exchange [*Telecommunications*] (TEL)
LE .... Locally Engaged
LE .... Locally Excited [*Physical chemistry*]
LE .... Logic Element
LE .... Logistic Effectiveness (CAAL)
LE .... Logistic Evaluation
LE .... Long-Evans Rat
LE .... Loop Extender [*Telecommunications*] (TEL)
LE .... Louisiana Eastern Railroad [*AAR code*]
LE .... Low Efficiency
LE .... Low Energy (CAAL)
LE .... Low Entry [*Truck cab*]
LE .... Lower Epidermis [*Botany*]
LE .... Lower Extremity [*Medicine*]

LE .... Low Explosive [*Military*]
LE .... Lugalbanda and Enmerkar (BJA)
LE .... Lugalbanda Epos (BJA)
LE .... Lunar Ephemeris
LE .... Lupus Erythematosus [*Hematology*]
LE .... Magnum Airlines [*ICAO designator*] (AD)
Le .... [*The*] Twenty-Four Books of the Holy Scriptures (1853) [*I. Leeser*] (BJA)
LE 2d .... Lawyer's Edition, United States Supreme Court Reports, Second Series [*A publication*] (DLA)
LEA .... Landes-Entschaedigungsamt (BJA)
LEA .... Language Experience Approach [*Education*]
LEA .... Latest Epicardial Activation [*Cardiology*]
LEA .... Launch Enable Alarm (MCD)
LEA .... Launch Escape Assembly [*NASA*] (KSC)
LEA .... Law Enforcement Agencies (DOMA)
LEA .... Law Enforcement Assistance Program (EA)
LEA .... Lead [*South Dakota*] [*Seismograph station code, US Geological Survey Closed*] (SEIS)
LEA .... Lead Air Jet Service [*France ICAO designator*] (FAAC)
LEA .... Leader Resources, Inc. [*Vancouver Stock Exchange symbol*]
LEA .... League [*Unit of measurement*]
lea .... League (WDAA)
LEA .... Lear Corp. [*NYSE symbol*] [*Formerly, Lear Seating*] (SG)
LEA .... Learmonth [*Australia Airport symbol*] (OAG)
LEA .... Learning Experience Approach [*Education*] (EDAC)
LEA .... Lear Seating Co. [*NYSE symbol*] (SAG)
Lea .... Lea's Tennessee Reports [*A publication*] (DLA)
LEA .... Leather
lea .... Leather (VRA)
LEA .... Leave
LEA .... Letter Enjoyers Association (EA)
LEA .... Light-Emitting Array
LEA .... Linear Embedding Algorithm (PDAA)
LEA .... Line Equalizing Amplifier (AFM)
LEA .... Load Effective Address [*Computer science*]
LEA .... Local Education Agency [*School district*] [*HEW*] (OICC)
LEA .... Local Education Authority [*British*] (WDAA)
LEA .... Local Employment Act [*Town planning*] [*British*]
LEA .... Logistic Evaluation Agency [*Army*]
LEA .... Logistics Engineering Analysis (NASA)
LEA .... Logistics Evaluation Activity [*Army*]
LEA .... Long-Endurance Aircraft
LEA .... Longitudinally Excited Atmosphere [*LASER technology*] (EECA)
LEA .... Loop Extension Amplifier
LEA .... Loss Executives Association [*Parsippany, NJ*] (EA)
LEA .... Lower Excess Air [*Combustion technology*]
LEA .... Lower Extremity Amputation [*Medicine*] (DMAA)
LEA .... Low-Excess-Air [*Combustion technology*]
LEA .... Lutheran Education Association (EA)
LEAA .... Lace and Embroidery Association of America [*Later, Lace Importers Association*] (EA)
LEAA .... Law Enforcement Assistance Act
LEAA .... Law Enforcement Assistance Administration [*Closed, functions transferred to Office of Justice Assistance, Research, and Statistics*] [*Department of Justice*]
LEAA Legal Op... Law Enforcement Assistance Administration. Legal Opinions [*A publication*] (DLA)
LEAB .... Albacete [*Spain ICAO location identifier*] (ICLI)
LEA/BZ .... Vessel Leased to Brazil [*Navy*]
LEAC .... Levelized Energy Adjustment Clause (NRCH)
LEAC .... Madrid [*Spain ICAO location identifier*] (ICLI)
LEA/CH .... Vessel Leased to China [*Navy*]
Leach CC .... Leach's Crown Cases, King's Bench [*England*] [*A publication*] (DLA)
Leach CL .... Leach's Cases in Crown Law [*A publication*] (DLA)
Leach Cl Cas... Leach's Club Cases [*London*] [*A publication*] (DLA)
Leach Cr Cas... Leach's English Crown Cases [*1730-1815*] [*A publication*] (DLA)
LEAD .... Law Enforcement Activities Division [*National Rifle Association*]
LEAD .... Law Students Exposing Advertising Deceptions [*Student legal action organization*]
LEAD .... Leader Effectiveness and Adaptability Description [*Test*]
Lead .... Leader Law Reports [*Ceylon*] [*A publication*] (DLA)
LEAD .... Leadership and Excellence in Alzheimer's Disease Award Program [*Department of Health and Human Services*] (GFGA)
LEAD .... Leadership, Education, and Development [*US Army Corps of Engineers*]
LEAD .... Leadership for Environment and Development Institute [*Non-profit organization*] (ECON)
LEAD .... Leadership in Educational Administration Development
LEAD .... Leadville Corp. [*NASDAQ symbol*] (SAG)
LEAD .... Learn, Execute, and Diagnose
LEAD .... Lens Electronic Automatic Design (IAA)
LEAD .... Letterkenny Army Depot [*Pennsylvania*] (AABC)
Leadam ...... Leadam's Select Cases before King's Council in the Star Chamber [*Selden Society Publications, Vols. 16, 25*] [*A publication*] (DLA)
Leadam Req... Select Cases in the Court of Requests, Edited by I. S. Leadam [*Selden Society Publications, Vol. 12*] [*A publication*] (DLA)
Lead Cas Am... American Leading Cases, Edited by Hare and Wallace [*A publication*] (DLA)
Lead Cas Eq... Leading Cases in Equity, by White and Tudor [*A publication*] (DLA)
Lead Cas in Eq... Leading Cases in Equity, by White and Tudor [*A publication*] (DLA)
Lead Cas in Eq (Eng)... Leading Cases in Equity, by White and Tudor [*England*] [*A publication*] (DLA)

LEADER .... Lehigh Automatic Device for Efficient Retrieval [*Center for Information Sciences, Lehigh University*] [*Bethlehem, PA*] [*Computer science*]
LEADER .... Logistics Echelons above Division in Europe (MCD)
LEADERMART... LEADER Mechanical Analysis and Retrieval of Text (NITA)
LEADEX....... Lead Experiment [*Marine science*] (OSRA)
Lead LR...... Leader Law Reports [*South Africa*] [*A publication*] (DLA)
LEADR .... Lawyers Engaged in Alternative Dispute Resolution [*Australia An association*]
LeadrFn ...... Leader Financial Corp. [*Associated Press*] (SAG)
LEADS .... Law Enforcement Automated Data System (IEEE)
LEADS .... Library Experimental Automated Demonstration System [*Computer science*]
LEADS .... Line Equipment Assignment and Display System [*GTE Corp.*]
LEAD USA.... Leadership Education and Development USA (EA)
Leadvle....... Leadville Corp. [*Associated Press*] (SAG)
LEA/EC....... Vessel Leased to Ecuador [*Navy*]
LEAF........... Interleaf, Inc. [*Cambridge, MA*] [*NASDAQ symbol*] (NQ)
LEAF........... Land Educational Associates Foundation [*Defunct*] (EA)
LEAF........... Law Enforcement Access Field [*Telecommunications*]
LEAF........... Legal Environmental Assistance Foundation (EA)
LEAF........... Liberal Education for Adoptive Families (EA)
LEAF........... LISP Extended Algebraic Facility
LEAF........... Lotus Extended Applications Facility
LEAF........... Women's Legal Education and Action Fund [*Canada*]
LEA/FR........ Vessel Leased to France [*Navy*]
LEAFS .... LASER-Excited Atomic Fluorescent Spectrometry
LEAG........... Legislative Extended Assistance Group [*University of Iowa*] [*Research center*] (RCD)
LEA/GR .... Vessel Leased to Greece [*Navy*]
LEAGUE ...... Lesbian, Bisexual, and Gay United Employees at AT & T
League of Nations Off J... League of Nations. Official Journal [*A publication*] (DLA)
League of Nations OJ... League of Nations. Official Journal [*A publication*] (DLA)
League of Nations OJ Spec Supp... League of Nations. Official Journal. Special Supplement [*A publication*] (DLA)
LEAH........... Lulov, Esrog, Arrovos, Hadassim (BJA)
LEAHS .... Lifetime Evaluation and Analysis of Heterogeneous System (PDAA)
LEAK........... Leak-X Environmental [*NASDAQ symbol*] (TTSB)
LEAK........... Leak-X Environmental Corp. [*NASDAQ symbol*] (SAG)
LEAK........... Liposome-Encapsulated Amikacin [*Bactericide*]
Leake.......... Leake on Contracts [*1861-1931*] [*A publication*] (DLA)
Leake.......... Leake's Digest of the Law of Property in Land [*A publication*] (DLA)
Leake Cont... Leake on Contracts [*1861-1931*] [*A publication*] (DLA)
Leake Land... Leake's Digest of the Law of Property in Land [*A publication*] (DLA)
LEAKM........ Leak-X Environmental Wrrt [*NASDAQ symbol*] (TTSB)
LeakX .... Leak-X Environmental Corp. [*Associated Press*] (SAG)
LEAL .... Alicante [*Spain ICAO location identifier*] (ICLI)
LEAM .... Almeria [*Spain ICAO location identifier*] (ICLI)
LEAM .... Lunar Ejecta and Meteorites [*Experiment*] [*NASA*]
Leam & Spic... Leaming and Spicer's Laws, Grants, Concessions, and Original Constitutions [*New Jersey*] [*A publication*] (DLA)
LEA/MX........ Vessel Leased to Mexico [*Navy*]
LEAN........... Low-Fat Eating for America Now
Le & Ca...... Leigh and Cave's English Crown Cases Reserved [*1861-65*] [*A publication*] (DLA)
LEA/NE........ Vessel Leased to Netherlands [*Navy*]
LEA/NO........ Vessel Leased to Norway [*Navy*]
LEANON....... Lupus Erythematosus Anonymous (EA)
LEANS .... Lehigh Analog Simulator (IAA)
LEAO........... Almagro [*Spain ICAO location identifier*] (ICLI)
LEAP........... Laboratory Education Advancement Program [*Department of Labor*]
LEAP........... Laboratory Evaluation and Accreditation Program
LEAP........... Laboratory Evening Academic Program (SAA)
LEAP........... Labor Education Advancement Program
LEAP........... Language for Expressing Associative Procedures [*Computer science*]
LEAP........... Large Einsteinium Activation Program
LEAP........... Large Experimental Aquifer Program [*Oregon Graduate Institute of Science and Technology*] [*Research center*] (RCD)
LEAP........... Leadership and Education for Advancement of Phoenix [*Arizona*]
LEAP........... Leading Edge Airborne PANAR
LEAP........... Leap Group, Inc. (The) [*NASDAQ symbol*] (SAG)
LEAP........... Legal and Educational Aid to the Poor [*Center*]
LEAP........... Lewis Expandable Adjustable Prosthesis [*Orthopedics*]
LEAP........... Lifetime Element Advancing Program
LEAP........... Lift-Off Elevation and Azimuth Programmer
LEAP........... Light Exo-Atmospheric Projectile [*Formerly, Lightweight*] (DOMA)
LEAP........... Lightweight Exoatmospheric Advanced Projectile [*Military*] (SDI)
LEAP........... Linear-Elastic Analysis Program [*SIA Computer Services*] [*Software package*] (NCC)
LEAP........... Liquid Engine Air-Augmented Package (MCD)
LEAP........... Loaned Executives Assignment Program [*American Association of Advertising Agencies lobbying group*]
LEAP........... Local Education Authorities Project for School Management Training (AIE)
LEAP........... Lockheed Electronics Assembly Program
LEAP........... Logistic Element Action Proposal (MCD)
LEAP........... Logistic Element Alternatives Process (MCD)
LEAP........... Logistic Event and Assessment Program
LEAP........... Logistics Efficiencies to Increase Army Power (MCD)
LEAP........... Long-Term Equity Anticipations [*Business term*]
LEAP........... Low-Energy All-Purpose (Collimator) [*Radiology*]
LEAP........... Lower Eastside Action Project [*New York City*]
LEAP........... Lower-Extremity Amputation Protocol [*Orthopedics*]
LEAP........... Lunar Escape Ambulance Pack [*Aerospace*]
LEA/PA........ Vessel Leased to Panama [*Navy*]

LEA/PE........ Vessel Leased to Peru [*Navy*]
LEA/PG .... Vessel Leased to Paraguay [*Navy*]
LeapGrp....... Leap Group, Inc. (The) [*Associated Press*] (SAG)
Leap Rom Civ L... Leapingwell on the Roman Civil Law [*A publication*] (DLA)
LEAPS........ LASER Electro-Optical Alignment Pole for Surveying [*NASA*]
LEAPS........ LASER Engineering and Application of Prototype System (MCD)
LEAPS........ Local Exchange Area Planning Simulation [*Bell Laboratories*]
LEAPS........ Long-Term Equity Anticipation Securities [*Investment term*] (DFIT)
LEAR.......... Learn [*Database*]
LEAR.......... Logistics Evaluation and Review
LEAR.......... Low-Energy Antiproton Ring [*Particle physics*]
LEAR.......... Low Erucic Acid Rapeseed [*Plant variety*]
LearBur........ Learmouth & Burchett Management Systems, Inc. [*Associated Press*] (SAG)
LEARN .... Learnng
LEARN .... Los Angeles Educational Alliance for Restructuring Now [*Education-reform project*] (ECON)
Learn & L.... Learning and the Law [*A publication*] (DLA)
Learn & Law... Learning and the Law [*A publication*] (DLA)
LearnI.......... LeaRonal, Inc. [*Associated Press*] (SAG)
LEARS .... Long [*Term*] Equity Anticipation Securities [*Finance*]
LearSeat...... Lear Seating Co. [*Associated Press*] (SAG)
LEARSYN.... Logistics Evaluation and Review Synchronization (IAA)
LEA/RU........ Vessel Leased to Russia [*Navy*]
LEAS.......... Aviles/Asturias [*Spain ICAO location identifier*] (ICLI)
LEAS.......... Lease Electronic Accounting System (IEEE)
LEAs.......... Local Education Agencies (PAZ)
LEAS.......... Local Education Authorities (ECON)
LEAS.......... Lower Echelon Automatic Switchboard
LEAS.......... Pride Automotive Gp [*NASDAQ symbol*] (TTSB)
LEAS.......... Pride Automotive Group, Inc. [*NASDAQ symbol*] (SAG)
LEASAT........ Leased Satellite (NITA)
LEASAT........ Leased Satellite Communications (NVT)
LEASE......... Leasing
LeasEd........ Leasing Edge Corp. [*Associated Press*] (SAG)
LEAS-FACS... Lease-Financial Accounting Control System (MHDB)
LEASIB........ Local Education Authorities and Schools Item Banking [*Project*] (AIE)
L East Eur.... Law in Eastern Europe [*A publication*] (DLA)
LEASW........ Pride Automotive Gp Wrrt [*NASDAQ symbol*] (TTSB)
LEATGS....... Local Education Authority Training Grants Scheme (AIE)
LEATH........ Leather (ROG)
LEATH........ Leatherhead [*City in England*]
LeathFac...... Leather Factory, Inc. [*Associated Press*] (SAG)
LEA/UK........ Vessel Leased to United Kingdom [*Navy*]
LEA/UR........ Vessel Leased to Uruguay [*Navy*]
LEAVERATS... Leave Rations [*Military*]
LEB .... East Baton Rouge Parish Public Library, Baton Rouge, LA [*OCLC symbol*] (OCLC)
LEB .... Lateral Efferent Bundle [*Neuroanatomy*]
LEB .... Lebanon [*New Hampshire*] [*Airport symbol*] (OAG)
Leb .... Lebanon (VRA)
LEB .... Lebanon, NH [*Location identifier FAA*] (FAAL)
LEB .... Lebap [*Turkmenistan*] [*ICAO designator*] (FAAC)
LEB .... Local Ethernet Bridge [*RAD Network Devices, Inc.*]
LEB .... London Electricity Board
LEB .... Low-Emissions Bus
LEB .... Lower Equipment Bay [*Apollo*] [*NASA*]
LEBA .... Cordoba [*Spain ICAO location identifier*] (ICLI)
LEBA .... Long Endurance Breathing Apparatus (PDAA)
Lebanon ...... Lebanon County Legal Journal [*Pennsylvania*] [*A publication*] (DLA)
Lebanon Co LJ (PA)... Lebanon County Legal Journal [*Pennsylvania*] [*A publication*] (DLA)
LeBAU .... American University of Beirut, Beirut, Lebanon [*Library symbol Library of Congress*] (LCLS)
LEBB .... Bilbao [*Spain ICAO location identifier*] (ICLI)
LEBC.......... Letchworth Indep Bancshares [*NASDAQ symbol*] (TTSB)
LEBC.......... Letchworth Independent Bancshares Corp. [*NASDAQ symbol*] (SAG)
LEBCW........ Letchworth Indep Bcshrs Wrrt [*NASDAQ symbol*] (TTSB)
LEBG.......... Burgos [*Spain ICAO location identifier*] (ICLI)
LEBL .... Barcelona [*Spain ICAO location identifier*] (ICLI)
LEBNAP....... Lebanese Kidnap [*Victims*] [*American hostages held in Beirut*]
LEBR.......... Bardenas Reales [*Spain ICAO location identifier*] (ICLI)
LebSeels ..... Lebendige Seelsorge (BJA)
LEBT .... Betera [*Spain ICAO location identifier*] (ICLI)
LEBU .... Large Eddy Breakup Device [*Aerodynamics*]
LEBZ .... Badajoz/Talavera La Real [*Spain ICAO location identifier*] (ICLI)
LEC .... Lake Erie College [*Painesville, OH*]
LEC .... Lake Erie College, Painesville, OH [*OCLC symbol*] (OCLC)
LEC .... LAMPS [*Light Airborne Multipurpose System*] Element Coordinator [*Navy*] (CAAL)
LEC .... Landed Estates Courts Commission [*England*] (DLA)
LEC .... LAN [*Local Area Network*] Emulation Client [*Telecommunications*] (ACRL)
LEC .... LANTCOM ELINT Center (MCD)
LEC .... LASER Electronic Computer
LEC .... Launch Escape Control [*NASA*] (KSC)
LEC .... Lec Refrigeration Ltd. [*British ICAO designator*] (FAAC)
LEC .... Lecture
LEC .... Leukoencephalitis [*Medicine*] (DB)
LEC .... Levelized Energy Cost
LEC .... Library of English Classics [*A publication*]
LEC .... Ligand Exchange Chromatography (DB)
LEC .... Light-Emitting Chemical Compound [*Marking agent for equipment used in night operations*] [*Military*] (VNW)
LEC .... Light-Emitting Electrochemical Cell [*Chemistry*]

LEC .... Light Energy Converter [*Telecommunications*] (TEL)
LEC .... Limited Editions Club
LEC .... Liquid Encapsulated Czochralski [*Crystal growing technique*] (IEEE)
LEC .... List Execution Condition (IAA)
LEC .... Little East Conference (PSS)
LEC .... Livestock Equipment Council [*Defunct*] (EA)
LEC .... Local Employment Committee [*Department of Employment*] [*British*]
LEC .... Local Engineering Change [*DoD*]
LEC .... Local Exchange Carrier [*Telecommunications*] (PCM)
LEC .... Local Export Control [*British*] (DS)
LEC .... Lockheed Electronics Corp. [*Subsidiary of Lockheed Aircraft Corp.*]
LEC .... London Education Classification [*Library classification system*] (NITA)
LEC .... Low-Echo-Centroid [*Geology*]
LEC .... Low Emitter Concentration (PDAA)
LEC .... Lower Epidermal Cell [*Botany*]
LEC .... Lumped Element Circulator
LEC .... Lunar Equipment Conveyor [*Aerospace*]
LECA .... Landed Estate Companies Association [*British*] (BI)
LECA .... Launch Escape Control Area [*NASA*] (KSC)
LECA .... Lehman Caves National Monument
LECA .... Light European Combat Aircraft (PDAA)
LECA .... Light-Expanded Clay Aggregate (DAC)
LECA .... Madrid [*Spain ICAO location identifier*] (ICLI)
LECAM .... Lectin Adhesion Molecule [*Biochemistry*]
LECAM .... Lectin-Cellular Adhesion Molecule [*Biochemistry*]
LECAPSR ..... Llano Estacado Center for Advanced Professional Studies and Research [*Eastern New Mexico University*] [*Research center*] (RCD)
LECB .... Barcelona [*Spain ICAO location identifier*] (ICLI)
LECC .... Lake Erie Cleanup Committee [*Defunct*] (EA)
LECC .... Linear Error Correcting Code (IAA)
LECCAM ...... Leukocyte Endothelial Cell-Cell Adhesion Molecule [*Cytology*]
LECE .... Leasing Edge [*NASDAQ symbol*] (TTSB)
LECE .... Leasing Edge Corp. [*NASDAQ symbol*] (SAG)
LECEL .... Leasing Edge Wrrt'B' [*NASDAQ symbol*] (TTSB)
LECEP .... Leasing Edge cm Cv'A'Pfd [*NASDAQ symbol*] (TTSB)
LECEZ .... Leasing Edge Wrrt'A' [*NASDAQ symbol*] (TTSB)
LECH .... Calamocha [*Spain ICAO location identifier*] (ICLI)
LECH .... Lechters, Inc. [*NASDAQ symbol*] (SAG)
Lechters ...... Lechters, Inc. [*Associated Press*] (SAG)
LECL .... Valencia [*Spain ICAO location identifier*] (ICLI)
LECM .... Madrid [*Spain ICAO location identifier*] (ICLI)
LECNA .... Lutheran Educational Conference of North America (EA)
LECO .... La Coruna [*Spain ICAO location identifier*] (ICLI)
LECO .... Lincoln Electric [*NASDAQ symbol*] (TTSB)
LECO .... [*The*] Lincoln Electric Co. [*NASDAQ symbol*] (SAG)
LECO .... Lincoln Electric Holdings [*NASDAQ symbol*] [*Formerly, Lincoln Electric*]
LECO .... Local Engineering Control Office [*Telecommunications*] (TEL)
LECOA .... Lincoln Electric `A' [*NASDAQ symbol*] (TTSB)
LEconSc ...... License Economic Sciences [*Canada*] (DD)
LECOS .... Lunar-Environment Construction and Operations Simulator [*NASA*] (IAA)
LECP .... Low-Energy Charged Particle [*Atomic physics*]
LECP .... Palma [*Spain ICAO location identifier*] (ICLI)
LECR .... Law Enforcement Candidate Record [*Test*] (TMMY)
LeCroy .... LeCroy Corp. [*Associated Press*] (SAG)
LECS .... LAN [*Local Area Network*] Emulation Configuration Server [*Telecommunications*] (ACRL)
LECS .... Launching Equipment Checkout Set
LECS .... Local Economic Consequences Study [*Military*]
LECS .... Local Enterprise Companies [*Scotland*] (ECON)
LECS .... Sevilla [*Spain ICAO location identifier*] (ICLI)
LECT .... League for the Exchange of Commonwealth Teachers (EA)
LECT .... LecTec Corp. [*NASDAQ symbol*] (SAG)
LECT .... Lectern (ROG)
LECT .... Lecture [*or Lecturer*]
Lect .... Lecturer (AL)
Lectec .... LecTec Corp. [*Associated Press*] (SAG)
Lect LSUC ... Special Lectures. Law Society of Upper Canada [*A publication*] (DLA)
lectn .... Lectionary (VRA)
LECTO .... Lectotype
LECTR .... Lecturer
Lect y V ...... Lectura y Vida [*A publication*]
LECV .... Colmenar Viejo [*Spain ICAO location identifier*] (ICLI)
LED .... Large Electronic Display
LED .... Law Enforcement Division [*National Park Service*]
L Ed .... Lawyers' Edition, United States Supreme Court Reports [*A publication*] (DLA)
LED .... Leaded
LED .... League for Ecological Democracy (EA)
LED .... Ledger
Led .... Ledger (EBF)
led .... Ledger (WDAA)
LED .... Leningrad [*Former USSR Airport symbol*] (OAG)
LED .... Library Education Division [*American Library Association*] [*Defunct*]
LED .... License Expiry Date (WDAA)
LED .... Light-Emitting Diode [*Display component*]
LED .... Light-Emitting diode (NAKS)
LED .... Line Embossing Device [*Computer science*]
LED .... Liquid Element Display
LED .... Logical Error Detection
LED .... Logistics Engineering Directorate [*ARRCOM*] (RDA)
LED .... Longitudinal Establishment Data [*Bureau of the Census*] (GFGA)

LED .... Low-Energy Detector
LED .... Low-Energy Diffraction
LED .... Lower Emissions Dispatch [*Environmental Protection Agency*]
LED .... Lowest Effective Dose [*Medicine*] (DB)
LED .... Lowest Emitting Dose [*Medicine*] (DMAA)
LED .... Lupus Erythematosus Disseminatus [*Medicine*]
LED .... North Platte, NE [*Location identifier FAA*] (FAAL)
L Ed 2d .... Lawyers' Edition, United States Supreme Court Reports, Second Series [*A publication*] (DLA)
LEDA .... LANDSAT Earthnet Data Availability [*ESA-Earthnet Programme Office*] [*Database*]
LEDA .... Low-Energy Deasphalting [*Petroleum refining*]
L Ed (Adv Ops)... United States Supreme Court Reports, Lawyers' Edition, Advance Opinions [*A publication*] (DLA)
LEDC .... League for Emotionally Disturbed Children
LEDC .... Local Economic Development Corp.
LEDC .... Logistics Executive Development Course [*Army*]
LEDC .... Low-Energy Detonating Cord (SAA)
LEDD .... Light-Emitting Diode Display
LEDET .... Law Enforcement Detachment [*Coast Guard*]
LED FO .... Ledger Folio (ROG)
LEDI .... Local Employment Development Initiative [*Australia*]
LEDM .... Valladolid [*Spain ICAO location identifier*] (ICLI)
LEDO .... Long-Term Effects of Dredging Operations [*Coastal Engineering Research Center*]
LEDP .... Large Electronic Display Panel
LEDR .... Laboratory for Environmental Data Research [*National Oceanic and Atmospheric Administration*]
LEDR .... Light-Emitting Diode Recorder (MCD)
LEDS .... Law Enforcement Data System
LEDS .... Liquid Effluents Data System [*Environmental Protection Agency*] (GFGA)
LEDSHP ...... Leadership
LEDT .... Limited Entry Decision Table
L Ed (US) .... Lawyers' Edition, United States Supreme Court Reports [*A publication*] (DLA)
L Ed US ...... Supreme Court Reports, Lawyer's Edition [*A publication*] (NTCM)
LEE .... [*The*] Lake Erie & Eastern Railroad Co. [*AAR code*]
LEE .... LASER Energy Evaluator (PDAA)
LEE .... Launch Electronics Equipment
LEE .... Leading Edge Environment
LEE .... Leeds [*Utah*] [*Seismograph station code, US Geological Survey*] (SEIS)
LEE .... Lee Enterprises [*NYSE symbol*] (TTSB)
LEE .... Lee Enterprises, Inc. [*NYSE symbol*] (SPSG)
LEE .... Leesburg, FL [*Location identifier FAA*] (FAAL)
Lee .... Lee's English Ecclesiastical Reports [*A publication*] (DLA)
Lee .... Lee's Reports [*9-12 California*] [*A publication*] (DLA)
LEE .... Logistics Evaluation Exercise
LEEA .... Lifting Equipment Engineers Association [*British*] (EAIO)
Lee Abs ...... Lee's Abstracts of Title [*1843*] [*A publication*] (DLA)
Lee & H ...... Lee's English King's Bench Reports Tempore Hardwicke [*1733-38*] [*A publication*] (DLA)
Lee Bank .... Lee's Law and Practice of Bankruptcy [*3rd ed.*] [*1887*] [*A publication*] (DLA)
LEEBI .... Low-Energy Electron Beam Irradiation [*Physics*]
LEEC .... LASER-to-Electric Energy Conversion (SSD)
LEEC .... Sevilla-El Copero Base [*Spain ICAO location identifier*] (ICLI)
Lee Cap ...... Lee on Captures [*A publication*] (DLA)
LEED .... LASER-Energized Explosive Device
LEED .... Longitudinal Employer-Employee Data File [*Social Security Administration*]
LEED .... Low-Energy Electron Diffraction [*Spectroscopy*]
Lee Dict ...... Lee's Dictionary of Practice [*A publication*] (DLA)
LEEDS .... Low-Energy Electron Diffraction Spectroscopy (DB)
LeedsFdl ..... Leeds FSB [*Associated Press*] (SAG)
LEEE .... Madrid [*Spain ICAO location identifier*] (ICLI)
Lee Eccl ...... Lee's English Ecclesiastical Reports [*A publication*] (DLA)
LeeEnt .... Lee Enterprises, Inc. [*Associated Press*] (SAG)
LE-EIA .... Leukocyte Esterase Enzyme Immunoassay
LEEIXS .... Low-Energy-Electron-Induced X-Ray Spectrometry
LEEM .... Low-Energy Electron Microscopy
LEEP .... Law Enforcement Education Program [*Department of Justice*]
LEEP .... Law Enforcement Explorer Post [*Boy Scouts*]
LEEP .... Library Education Experimental Project [*Syracuse University*]
LEEP .... Loop Electrosurgical Excision Procedure [*Medicine*]
LeePhr .... Lee Pharmaceuticals [*Associated Press*] (SAG)
LEER .... Low-Energy Electron Reflection (IEEE)
LEERS .... Long-Endurance Experimental Research Submarine (SAA)
LEES .... Laboratory for Electromagnetic and Electronic Systems [*Massachusetts Institute of Technology*] [*Research center*] (RCD)
LEES .... Lake Erie Environmental Studies
LEES .... Launch Equipment Evaluation Set (MCD)
Leese .... Leese's Reports [*26 Nebraska*] [*A publication*] (DLA)
Lee Ship ..... Lee's Laws of Shipping [*A publication*] (DLA)
LEET .... Limiting Equivalent Exposure Time (MUGU)
Lee T Hard... Lee's English King's Bench Cases Tempore Hardwicke [*1733-38*] [*England*] [*A publication*] (DLA)
Lee T Hardw... Lee's English King's Bench Cases Tempore Hardwicke [*1733-38*] [*England*] [*A publication*] (DLA)
LEE W .... Lee White Tritium [*Clotting Time*] [*Hematology*] (DAVI)
LEF .... Lake Erie, Franklin & Clarion Railroad Co. [*AAR code*]
LEF .... Landpower Education Fund
LEF .... LASER Excited Fluorescence
LEF .... Leading Edge Flap [*Aviation*]

LEF .... Left-In Telephone [*Telecommunications*] (TEL)
LEF .... Leukokinesis-Enhancing Factor [*Medicine*] (DMAA)
LEF .... Licentiate in Economics and Finance
LEF .... Life Extension Foundation (EA)
LEF .... Light-Emitting Film (IEEE)
LEF .... Lincoln Educational Foundation [*Defunct*] (EA)
LEF .... Linear-Energy Spectrophotofluorometry
LEF .... Line Expansion Function
LEF .... Liquid Expanded Film
LEF .... Lobby Europeen des Femmes [*European Women's Lobby*] [*Belgium*] (EAIO)
LEF .... Local Education Fund
LEF .... Loss Entry Form [*Insurance*]
LEF .... Lupus Erythematosus Factor [*Medicine*] (DMAA)
LEF .... Lymphoid-Enhanced Binding Factor [*Medicine*] (DMAA)
LEF .... Lymphoid Enhancer Factor [*Biochemistry*]
Lef & Cas .... Lefroy and Cassel's Practice Cases [*1881-83*] [*Ontario*] [*A publication*] (DLA)
LEFC .... L-Band Electronic Frequency Converter
Lef Cr L ...... Lefroy's Irish Criminal Law [*A publication*] (DLA)
LEFCS .... Leading Edge Flap Control System [*Aviation*]
Lef Dec .... Lefevre's Parliamentary Decisions, by Bourke [*England*] [*A publication*] (DLA)
LEFE .... Linear Electric Field Effect (PDAA)
LEFM .... Linear-Elastic Fracture Mechanics
LEFO .... Land's End for Order [*Shipping*]
Lefroy .... Lefroy's Railroad and Canal Cases [*England*] [*A publication*] (DLA)
LEFU .... Light Ends Fractionating Unit [*Petroleum technology*]
LEFW .... Lake Erie & Fort Wayne Railroad Co. [*AAR code*]
LEG .... Aleg [*Mauritania*] [*Airport symbol*] (AD)
Leg .... De Legibus [*of Cicero*] [*Classical studies*] (OCD)
LEG .... Language of Functions and Graphs (AIE)
LEG .... Law Enforcement Group (WDAA)
LEG .... Legal (AFM)
LEG .... Legate
leg .... Legate (WDAA)
Leg .... Legatio ad Gaium [*of Philo Judaeus*] [*Classical studies*] (OCD)
LEG .... Legato [*Smoothly and Connectedly*] [*Music*]
LEG .... Legend [*Numismatics*]
Leg .... Leges [*Laws*] [*Latin*] (ILCA)
LEG .... Leggett & Platt [*NYSE symbol*] (TTSB)
LEG .... Leggett & Platt, Inc. [*NYSE symbol*] (SPSG)
LEG .... Legislation [*or Legislature*]
Leg .... Legislative (PHSD)
LEG .... Legislative Library of British Columbia [*UTLAS symbol*]
Leg .... Legislature (WDAA)
LEG .... Legit [*He, or She, Reads*] [*Latin*]
LEG .... Legunt [*They Read*] [*Latin*] (ADA)
LEG .... Library Education Group of the Library Association (NITA)
LEG .... Liquefied Energy Gas
LEG .... Logistical Expediting Group
LEG .... Logistic Evaluation Group
LEGA........... Granada/Armilla [*Spain ICAO location identifier*] (ICLI)
Legacy......... Legacy: A Journal of American Women Writers [*A publication*] (BRI)
Leg Adv ...... Legal Adviser [*Chicago*] [*A publication*] (DLA)
Leg Agr....... De Lege Agraria [*of Cicero*] [*Classical studies*] (OCD)
LEGAL......... League for Equitable General Aviation Legislation (EA)
Legal Adv ... Legal Advertiser [*Chicago*] [*A publication*] (DLA)
Legal Adv .... Legal Adviser [*Denver*] [*A publication*] (DLA)
Legal Asp Med Prac... Legal Aspects of Medical Practice [*A publication*] (DLA)
Leg Alfred ... Leges Alfredi [*Laws of King Alfred*] [*Latin A publication*] (DLA)
Legal Gaz (PA)... Legal Gazette (Pennsylvania) [*A publication*] (DLA)
Legal Int...... Legal Intelligencer [*A publication*] (DLA)
Legal Intel.... Legal Intelligencer [*A publication*] (DLA)
Legal Intell... Legal Intelligencer [*A publication*] (DLA)
Legal Obser... Legal Observer [*London*] [*A publication*] (DLA)
Legal Observer... New York Legal Observer [*A publication*] (DLA)
LegalR......... Legal Research Center, Inc. [*Associated Press*] (SAG)
Legal Rep.... Legal Reporter [*Australia A publication*]
Legal Rep.... Legal Reporter, New Series [*Tennessee*] [*A publication*] (DLA)
Legal Resp Child Adv Protection... Legal Response; Child Advocacy and Protection [*A publication*] (DLA)
Leg & Ins R... Legal and Insurance Reporter [*Pennsylvania*] [*A publication*] (DLA)
Leg & Ins Rep... Legal and Insurance Reporter [*Philadelphia, PA*] [*A publication*] (DLA)
Leg & Ins Rept... Legal and Insurance Reporter [*Philadelphia, PA*] [*A publication*] (DLA)
Legat .... De Lagatione ad Caium [*Philo*] (BJA)
LEGAT......... Legal Attache [*FBI agent posted at an American embassy*]
Legato .... Legato Systems, Inc. [*Associated Press*] (SAG)
LEGATT....... Legal Attache [*Foreign service*]
Leg Bibl....... Legal Bibliography [*A publication*] (DLA)
Leg Canut.... Leges Canuti [*Laws of King Canute or Knut*].[*Latin A publication*] (DLA)
Leg Ch Forms... Leggo's Chancery Forms [*Ontario*] [*A publication*] (DLA)
Leg Ch Pr.... Leggo's Chancery Practice [*Ontario*] [*A publication*] (DLA)
Leg Chron.... Legal Chronicle Reports, Edited by Foster [*Pennsylvania*] [*A publication*] (DLA)
Leg Chron Rep... Legal Chronicle Reports [*Pottsville, PA*] [*A publication*] (DLA)
Legco.......... Legislative Council [*Hong Kong*] (ECON)
LEG COM .... Legally Committed (BABM)
legd .... Legend
LEGE .... Gerona/Costa Brava [*Spain ICAO location identifier*] (ICLI)
Leg Edm ..... Leges Edmundi [*Laws of King Edmund*] [*Latin A publication*] (DLA)
LEGEN .... Liposome-Encapsulated Gentamicin [*Bactericide*]

LEGEND ...... Legal Electronic Network and Database (IID)
Legend .... Legend Properties, Inc. [*Associated Press*] (SAG)
Leg Ethel .... Leges Ethelredi [*Laws of King Ethelred*] [*Latin A publication*] (DLA)
Leg Exam .... Legal Examiner [*London or New York*] [*1831-35; 1862-68; 1869-72*] [*A publication*] (DLA)
Leg Exam & LC... Legal Examiner and Law Chronicle [*London*] [*A publication*] (DLA)
Leg Exam & Med J... Legal Examiner and Medical Jurist [*London*] [*A publication*] (DLA)
Leg Exam NS... Legal Examiner, New Series [*England*] [*A publication*] (DLA)
Leg Exam WR... Legal Examiner Weekly Reporter [*A publication*] (DLA)
Leg Exch...... Legal Exchange [*Des Moines, IA*] [*A publication*] (DLA)
LEGG .... Launch Eject Gas Generator
Leg G.......... Legal Guide [*A publication*] (DLA)
Legg .... Leggett's Reports [*India*] [*A publication*] (DLA)
LEGG .... Leggiero [*Light and Rapid*] [*Music*]
Leg Gaz...... Legal Gazette [*A publication*] (DLA)
Leg Gaz R ... Campbell's Legal Gazette Reports [*Pennsylvania*] [*A publication*] (DLA)
Leg Gaz Re... Campbell's Legal Gazette Reports [*Pennsylvania*] [*A publication*] (ILCA)
Leg Gaz Rep... Campbell's Legal Gazette Reports [*Pennsylvania*] [*A publication*] (DLA)
Legg Bills L... Leggett on Bills of Lading [*A publication*] (DLA)
LeggMas...... Legg Mason, Inc. [*Associated Press*] (SAG)
Leggo .... Leggiero [*Light and Rapid*] [*Music*]
Legg Out..... Legge on Outlawry [*A publication*] (DLA)
LEGGS .... Loyal Escorts of the Green Garters (EA)
Leg HI .... Laws of King Henry the First [*A publication*] (DLA)
Leg Inf Bul... Legal Information Bulletin [*A publication*] (DLA)
Leg Inq....... Legal Inquirer [*London*] [*A publication*] (DLA)
Leg Int........ Legal Intelligencer [*A publication*] (DLA)
Leg Intel...... Legal Intelligencer [*A publication*] (DLA)
Leg Intell..... Legal Intelligencer [*A publication*] (DLA)
Leg Intl........ Legal Intelligencer [*A publication*] (DLA)
LEGIS.......... Legislative [*or Legislature*]
Legis .... Legislative (AL)
LEGIS.......... Legislative Information and Status System [*for House of Representatives*]
LEGISL........ Legislative (ADA)
LEGISLN ...... Legislation
LEGISN .... Legislation [*Legal shorthand*] (LWAP)
LEGISNET ... National Legislative Network [*National Conference of State Legislatures*] [*Information service or system*] (IID)
LEGISOR...... Legislator [*Legal shorthand*] (LWAP)
Legis Stud Q... Legislative Studies Quarterly [*A publication*] (DLA)
Leg Issues... Legal Issues of European Integration [*A publication*] (ILCA)
LEGISURE.... Legislature [*Legal shorthand*] (LWAP)
LEGISV .... Legislative [*Legal shorthand*] (LWAP)
LEGIT.......... Legitimate (DSUE)
LEGIW .... Co. Counsel Inc. Wrrt [*NASDAQ symbol*] (TTSB)
Leg J .... Pittsburgh Legal Journal [*Pennsylvania*] [*A publication*] (DLA)
Leg Jour ..... Pittsburgh Legal Journal [*Pennsylvania*] [*A publication*] (DLA)
LEGL........... Co-Counsel, Inc. [*NASDAQ symbol*] (SAG)
LEGM.......... Low-Energy Gamma Monitor
Leg Misc ..... Legal Miscellany [*Ceylon*] [*A publication*] (DLA)
Leg Misc & Rev... Legal Miscellany and Review [*India*] [*A publication*] (DLA)
Leg News .... Legal News [*Canada*] [*A publication*] (DLA)
Leg Notes ... Legal Notes on Local Government [*New York*] [*A publication*] (DLA)
LEGO .... Leg Godt [*Play Well*] [*Acronym is brand of child's building toy*] [*Denmark*]
Leg Obs....... Legal Observer [*London*] [*A publication*] (DLA)
Leg Obs....... Legal Observer and Solicitor's Journal [*London*] [*A publication*] (DLA)
LEGOL .... Legally Oriented Language [*Programming language project*] [*British*] (NITA)
Leg Oler ..... Laws of Oleron [*Maritime law*] [*A publication*] (DLA)
Leg Op........ Legal Opinion [*Pennsylvania*] [*A publication*] (DLA)
Leg Ops (PA)... Legal Opinion [*Pennsylvania*] [*A publication*] (DLA)
Leg Out....... Legge on Outlawry [*A publication*] (DLA)
LegPlat....... Leggett & Platt, Inc. [*Associated Press*] (SAG)
Leg Port...... Leges Portuum [*A publication*] (DLA)
Leg Pract & Sol J... Legal Practitioner and Solicitor's Journal [*1846-47, 1849-51*] [*A publication*] (DLA)
LEGR .... Granada [*Spain ICAO location identifier*] (ICLI)
Leg R.......... Legal Record Reports [*Pennsylvania*] [*A publication*] (DLA)
Leg Rec....... Legal Record [*Detroit, MI*] [*A publication*] (DLA)
Leg Rec Rep... Legal Record Reports [*Pennsylvania*] [*A publication*] (DLA)
Leg Ref ...... Legal Reformer [*1819-20*] [*A publication*] (DLA)
Leg Rem...... Legal Remembrancer [*Calcutta*] [*A publication*] (DLA)
Leg Rep....... Legal Reporter [*1840-43*] [*Ireland*] [*A publication*] (DLA)
Leg Rep (Ir)... Legal Reporter, Irish Courts [*A publication*] (DLA)
Leg Rep SL... Legal Reporter Special Leave Supplement [*A publication*]
Leg Rev....... Legal Review [*1812-13*] [*London*] [*A publication*] (DLA)
Leg R (Tenn)... Legal Reporter Parallel to Shannon Cases [*Tennessee*] [*A publication*] (DLA)
LEGS........... Lateral Electronic Guidance System [*Automotive engineering*]
LEGS........... Learning Experience Guides for Nursing Students [*Series of films, games, slides, etc.*]
LEGS........... Legacies (ROG)
LEGS........... Lethality End Game Simulation (MCD)
LEGS........... Lighter Electronics Guidance System (MCD)
LEGS........... Logistic Engine Generator Set (DWSG)
LEGT........... Lycee d'Enseignement General et Technologique [*High School for General and Technical Studies*] [*French*] (BARN)
LEGT........... Madrid/Getafe [*Spain ICAO location identifier*] (ICLI)

Leg T Cas....   Legal Tender Cases [*A publication*]   (DLA)
Legul ....   Leguleian [*1850-65*] [*A publication*]   (DLA)
LEG (UN) .....   Department of Legal Affairs of the United Nations
Legve ....   Legislative
Leg W ....   Legal World [*India*] [*A publication*]   (DLA)
Leg Wisb ....   Laws of Wisby [*Maritime law*] [*A publication*]   (DLA)
LEG WT ....   Legal Weight   (WDAA)
LEGY ....   Legacy   (ROG)
Leg YB ....   Legal Year Book [*London*] [*A publication*]   (DLA)
LEH ....   Launch/Entry Helmet   (MCD)
LEH ....   Leeds Central Helicopters [*British*] [*FAA designator*]   (FAAC)
LEH ....   Le Havre [*France*] [*Airport symbol*]   (OAG)
Leh ....   Lehigh County Law Journal [*Pennsylvania*] [*A publication*]   (DLA)
LEH ....   Lehman Br Holdngs [*NYSE symbol*]   (TTSB)
LEH ....   Lehman Brothers [*NYSE symbol*]   (SAG)
LEH ....   Liposome Encapsulated Hemoglobin [*Biochemistry*]
LehAMGN ...   Lehman Brothers Holdings, Inc. [*Associated Press*]   (SAG)
LehBr35 ....   Lehman Brothers [*Associated Press*]   (SAG)
LEHC ....   Huesca [*Spain ICAO location identifier*]   (ICLI)
Leh Co LJ (PA)...   Lehigh County Law Journal [*Pennsylvania*] [*A publication*]   (DLA)
LehGTel ....   Lehman Brothers, Inc. [*Associated Press*]   (SAG)
LEHI ....   Hinojosa Del Duque [*Spain ICAO location identifier*]   (ICLI)
LEHI ....   Lehame Herut Israel [*Fighters of the Freedom of Israel*]
Lehigh ....   Lehigh Valley Law Reporter [*Pennsylvania*] [*A publication*]   (DLA)
Lehigh Co LJ ..   Lehigh County Law Journal [*Pennsylvania*] [*A publication*]   (DLA)
LehighGp ......   Lehigh Group, Inc. [*Formerly, LUI Group*] [*Associated Press*]   (SAG)
Lehigh LJ ....   Lehigh County Law Journal [*Pennsylvania*] [*A publication*]   (DLA)
Lehigh U .....   Lehigh University   (GAGS)
Lehigh Val Law Rep...   Lehigh Valley Law Reporter [*Pennsylvania*] [*A publication*]   (DLA)
Lehigh Val LR...   Lehigh Valley Law Reporter [*Pennsylvania*] [*A publication*]   (DLA)
Lehigh Val L Rep...   Lehigh Valley Law Reporter [*Pennsylvania*] [*A publication*]   (DLA)
LeHK ....   Lehman Brothers, Inc. [*Associated Press*]   (SAG)
Leh LJ ....   Lehigh County Law Journal [*A publication*]   (DLA)
Lehman C (CUNY)...   Herbert H. Lehman College of The City University of New York   (GAGS)
LehmBr ....   Lehman Brothers [*Associated Press*]   (SAG)
LEHMIC ....   Lumped Element Hybrid Microwave Integrated Circuit [*Electronics*]   (LAIN)
LehMU ....   Lehman Brothers, Inc. [*Associated Press*]   (SAG)
LehORCL ......   Lehman Brothers Holdings, Inc. [*Associated Press*]   (SAG)
LEHPZ ....   Lower Esophageal High Pressure Zone [*Gastroenterology*]   (DAVI)
LEHR ....   Laboratory for Energy-Related Health Research [*University of California-Davis*] [*Department of Energy*]   (GRD)
LehRgBk .....   Lehman Brothers, Inc. [*Associated Press*]   (SAG)
LehSTc ....   Lehman Brothers [*Associated Press*]   (SAG)
Leh VLR (PA)...   Lehigh Valley Law Reporter [*Pennsylvania*] [*A publication*]   (DLA)
LEI ....   Air UK (Leisure) Ltd. [*British ICAO designator*]   (FAAC)
LEI ....   Almeria [*Spain*] [*Airport symbol*]   (OAG)
LEI ....   LASER-Enhanced Ionization [*Spectrometry*]
LEI ....   Leading Economic Indicator
LEI ....   Lehigh Group [*NYSE symbol*]   (TTSB)
Lei ....   Leijona [*Record label*] [*Finland*]
LEI ....   Leipzig [*German Democratic Republic*] [*Seismograph station code, US Geological Survey Closed*]   (SEIS)
LEI ....   Libertarian Education Institute   (EA)
LEI ....   Library Equipment Institute [*American Library Association*]
LEI ....   Life Events [*or Expectancy*] Inventory
LEI ....   Literacy and Evangelism International   (EA)
LEI ....   Lloyd's Electronics, Inc.   (EFIS)
LEI ....   Local Engineering Instruction   (DNAB)
LEI ....   Locher Evers International Ltd.
LEI ....   Raleigh, NC [*Location identifier FAA*]   (FAAL)
LEIA ....   Luminescence Enzyme Immunoassay [*Clinical chemistry*]
LEIB ....   Ibiza [*Spain ICAO location identifier*]   (ICLI)
LEIC ....   Leicestershire [*County in England*]   (ROG)
LEICS ....   Leicestershire [*County in England*]
LEICSC ....   Legal Education Institute, United States Civil Service Commission   (DLA)
LEID ....   Limit of Error on Inventory Difference
LEID ....   Low-Energy Ion Detector
LEIDS ....   Logistics Electronic Information Delivery System
LeIF ....   Leukocyte Interferon [*Genetics*]
LEIFS ....   Lake Erie Information Forecasting System [*Marine science*]   (OSRA)
LEIFX ....   Federated Equity Income Cl.A [*Mutual fund ticker symbol*]   (SG)
Leigh ....   Leigh's Virginia Supreme Court Reports [*1829-42*] [*A publication*]   (DLA)
Leigh ....   Ley's English King's Bench Reports [*1608-29*] [*A publication*]   (DLA)
Leigh Abr .....   Leigh's Abridgment of the Law of Nisi Prius [*1838*] [*A publication*]   (DLA)
Leigh & C ....   Leigh and Cave's English Crown Cases Reserved [*1861-65*] [*A publication*]   (DLA)
Leigh & CCC...   Leigh and Cave's English Crown Cases Reserved [*1861-65*] [*A publication*]   (DLA)
Leigh & D Conv...   Leigh and Dalzell. Conversion of Property [*1825*] [*A publication*]   (DLA)
Leigh & LM Elec...   Leigh and Le Marchant. Elections [*4th ed.*] [*1885*] [*A publication*]   (DLA)
Leigh GA .....   Leigh's Game Act [*A publication*]   (DLA)
Leigh NP .....   Leigh's Abridgment of the Law of Nisi Prius [*1838*] [*A publication*]   (DLA)
Leigh (VA) ...   Leigh's Virginia Supreme Court Reports [*1829-42*] [*A publication*]   (DLA)

LEIM ....   Law Enforcement Information Management Section [*An association*]   (EA)
LEIN ....   Law Enforcement Information Network
LEINS R ....   Leinster Regiment [*Military unit*] [*British*]   (ROG)
leio ....   Leiomyoma [*Gynecology*]   (DAVI)
LEIP ....   Leipzig [*City in East Germany*]   (ROG)
LEIP ....   Link Eleven Improvement Program   (DOMA)
Leipz Stud ...   Leipziger Studien zur Klassischen Philosophie [*A publication*]   (OCD)
LEIS ....   Lander Electrical Interface Simulator [*NASA*]
LEIS ....   LASER-Enhanced Ionization Spectroscopy   (MEC)
Le Is ....   Leeward Islands   (BARN)
LEIS ....   LeisureLine [*Footscray Institute of Technology Library*] [*Database*] [*Information service or system*]   (IID)
LEIS ....   Low-Energy Ion Scattering [*For study of surfaces*]
LeisMkt ....   Leisureways Marketing [*Associated Press*]   (SAG)
LEISS ....   Low-Energy Ion Scattering Spectroscopy
LEIT ....   Leitrim [*County in Ireland*]   (ROG)
LEIT ....   Light Emission via Inelastic Tunnelling   (IAA)
Leith Black ...   Leith. Blackstone on Real Property [*2nd ed.*] [*1880*] [*A publication*]   (DLA)
Leith R Pr ...   Leith's Real Property Statutes [*Ontario*] [*A publication*]   (DLA)
LEITR ....   Leitrim [*County in Ireland*]   (ROG)
LEIU ....   Law Enforcement Intelligence Units [*An association*]   (EA)
LEIX ....   Lowrance Electronics [*NASDAQ symbol*]   (SAG)
LEJ ....   Leipzig [*Germany Airport symbol*]   (OAG)
LEJ ....   Longitudinal Expansion Joint [*Technical drawings*]
LEJR ....   Jerez [*Spain ICAO location identifier*]   (ICLI)
LeJY ....   Lehman Brothers, Inc. [*Associated Press*]   (SAG)
LEK ....   Labe [*Guinea*] [*Airport symbol*]   (AD)
LEK ....   Laiko Enotiko Komma [*Populist Union Party*] [*Greece*] [*Political party*]   (PPE)
LEK ....   LASER Experimental Package
LEK ....   Lexington [*Kentucky*] [*Seismograph station code, US Geological Survey*]   (SEIS)
LEK ....   Liquid Encapsulated Kyropoulos [*Crystal growing technique*]
LEKOTEK ......   Leksaker, Bibliotek [*Program providing meaningful toys for mentally disturbed children; operates on the same principle as a lending library.*] [*Name formed from Swedish words for "playthings" and "library"*]
lekyt ....   Lekythos   (VRA)
LEL ....   Lake Evella [*Australia Airport symbol*]   (OAG)
LEL ....   Lancashire Enterprise Ltd. [*British*]   (ECON)
LEL ....   Large Engineering Loop [*NASA*]   (NRCH)
LEL ....   Laureate in English Literature
LEL ....   League of Empire Loyalists [*British*]
LEL ....   Learning Expectancy Level [*Education*]
LEL ....   Lens-End-Lamp
LEL ....   Letitia Elizabeth Landon [*English poet and novelist, 1802-1839*]
LEL ....   Link-Edit Language [*Computer science*]
LEL ....   Low Energy LASER [*Light Amplification by Stimulated Emission of Radiation*] [*Military*]
LEL ....   Lower Earnings Limit   (MHDB)
LEL ....   Lower Electrical Limit   (NRCH)
LEL ....   Lower Explosive Limit [*of fuel vapor*]
LEL ....   Lowest Effect Level [*Toxicology*]
LELC ....   Murcia/San Javier [*Spain ICAO location identifier*]   (ICLI)
LELL ....   Sabadell [*Spain ICAO location identifier*]   (ICLI)
LELN ....   Leon [*Spain ICAO location identifier*]   (ICLI)
LELO ....   Logrono [*Spain ICAO location identifier*]   (ICLI)
LELS ....   Low-Energy LASER System
LELTS ....   Lightweight Electronic Locating and Tracking System
LELU ....   Launch Enable Logic Unit
LELU ....   Lugo [*Spain ICAO location identifier*]   (ICLI)
Lely & F Elec...   Lely and Foulkes' Elections [*3rd ed.*] [*1887*] [*A publication*]   (DLA)
Lely & F Jud Acts...   Lely and Foulkes' Judicature Acts [*4th ed.*] [*1883*] [*A publication*]   (DLA)
Lely & F Lic Acts...   Lely and Foulkes' Licensing Acts [*3rd ed.*] [*1887*] [*A publication*]   (DLA)
Lely Railw ...   Lely's Regulation of Railway Acts [*1873*] [*A publication*]   (DLA)
LEM ....   Antenna Effective Length for Magnetic-Field Antennas   (IEEE)
LEM ....   Laboratory Environment Model   (MCD)
LEM ....   Laboratory of Electro-Modeling [*Former USSR*]
LEM ....   Lake Exploration Module [*University of Wisconsin*]
LEM ....   LASER Energy Monitor
LEM ....   LASER Exhaust Measurement
LEM ....   Lateral Eye Movement
LEM ....   Launch Enclosure Maintenance [*Aerospace*]   (IAA)
LEM ....   Launcher Electronic Module [*Military*]   (RDA)
LEM ....   Launch Escape Monitor   (MCD)
LEM ....   Launch Escape Motor [*NASA*]
LEM ....   Law Enforcement Manual [*IRS*]
LEM ....   Leading Electrical Mechanician
LEM ....   Legacy Encapsulation Methodology
LEM ....   Leibovitz-Emory Medium [*Microbiology*]
LEM ....   Lembang [*Java*] [*Seismograph station code, US Geological Survey*]   (SEIS)
LEM ....   Lemmon, SD [*Location identifier FAA*]   (FAAL)
lem ....   Lemon [*Philately*]
LEM ....   Length of Effectiveness for Magnetic-Field Antennae
LEM ....   Leukocytic Endogenous Mediator [*Immunochemistry*]
LEM ....   Leukoencephalomalacia [*Veterinary medicine*]
LEM ....   Light Effector Mediator System [*Plant physiology*]
LEM ....   Light Equipment Maintenance   (MCD)
LEM ....   Linear Electric Motor [*Magnetic rapid-transit car*]   (PS)
LEM ....   Liquid Emulsion Membrane [*Separation technology*]

LEM .... Logical End of Media
LEM .... Logic Enhanced Memory
LEM .... Logistic Element Manager
LEM .... Luminescences Emission Monitor
LEM .... Lunar Excursion Module [*Later, LM*] [*NASA*]
LEM .... Lunar Exploration Module [*NASA*] (IAA)
LEMA .... Laser and Electro-Optics Manufacturers' Association (EA)
LEM(A) ...... Leading Electrical Mechanic (Air) [*British military*] (DMA)
LEMA .... Lifting Equipment Manufacturers Association [*British*] (BI)
LEMA .... Lighting Equipment Manufacturers' Association (DAC)
LEMAC .... Leading Edge Mean Aerodynamic Chord
LEMAR .... Legalize Marijuana [*Acronym is used for name of an organization*]
Le Mar. .... Le Marchant's Gardner Peerage Case [*A publication*] (DLA)
LEM(AW) ..... Leading Electrical Mechanic (Air Weapon) [*British military*] (DMA)
LEMCO .... Light Equipment Maintenance Co. (MCD)
LEMD .... Madrid/Barajas [*Spain ICAO location identifier*] (ICLI)
LEMDA .... Lighting-Electrical Materials Distributors Association (EA)
LEMDE .... Lunar Excursion Module Descent Engine [*NASA*] (MCD)
LEMES .... Low-Energy Magnetic Electron Spectrum (IAA)
LEMF .... Labour Exchange Managers' Federation [*A union*] [*British*]
LEMF .... Law Enforcement Memorial Foundation (EA)
LEMF .... Local Effective Mole Fraction [*Chemistry*]
LEMG .... Malaga [*Spain ICAO location identifier*] (ICLI)
LEMH .... Mahon/Menorca [*Spain ICAO location identifier*] (ICLI)
LEML & AIA... Locomotive Engineers Mutual Life and Accident Insurance Association (EA)
LEMM .... Madrid [*Spain ICAO location identifier*] (ICLI)
LEMO .... Local Emergency Management Officer
LEMO .... Lowest Empty Molecular Orbital [*Medicine*] (DMAA)
LEMO .... Sevilla/Moron [*Spain ICAO location identifier*] (ICLI)
LEMPA .... Low-Energy Magnetospheric Particle Analyzer [*Atomic physics*]
LEMRAS ...... Law Enforcement Manpower Resources Allocation [*IBM program product*]
LEMRP .... Law Enforcement Memorial Research Project (EA)
LEMS .... Lambert-Eaton Myasthenic Syndrome [*Medicine*] (DB)
LEMS .... Linear Econometric Modeling System (BUR)
LEMS .... Low-Energy Molecular Scattering (MCD)
LEMSIP ...... Laboratory for Experimental Medicine and Surgery in Primates [*New York University*] [*Research center*]
LEMT .... Lunar Excursion Module Track [*NASA*] (IAA)
LEMUF .... Limits of Error on Material Unaccounted For
LEN .... [*The*] Lake Erie & Northern Railway Co. [*AAR code*]
LEN .... Large Extension Node [*Telecommunications*] (LAIN)
LEN .... Length
LEN .... Leninakan [*Former USSR Seismograph station code, US Geological Survey*] (SEIS)
LEN .... Lennar Corp. [*NYSE symbol*] (SPSG)
LEN .... Lenora Explorations Ltd. [*Toronto Stock Exchange symbol*]
LEN .... Lentini Aviation, Inc. [*ICAO designator*] (FAAC)
LEN .... Leon [*Mexico*] [*Airport symbol*] (OAG)
LEN .... Library of Early Novelists [*A publication*]
LEN .... Light-Emitting Numerics
LEN .... Ligue Europeenne de Natation [*European Swimming Federation*] [*Sweden*] (EAIO)
LEN .... Linear Electrical Network
LEN .... Load Equalization Net [*Aircraft arresting barrier*] [*Trademark*]
LEN .... Local Employment Network (AIE)
LEN .... Local Entry Network (NITA)
LEN .... Low Entry Networking (MCD)
LEND .... Credit Depot [*NASDAQ symbol*] (TTSB)
LEND .... Credit Depot Corp. [*NASDAQ symbol*] (SAG)
L en D .... Licencie en Droit [*Licentiate in Law*] [*French*]
LEND .... Lockheed Engineers for National Deployment (SAA)
LENGTH .... Length
LENGTHD ..... Lengthened (ROG)
LENIT .... Leniter [*Gently*] [*Pharmacy*]
Lennar .... Lennar Corp. [*Associated Press*] (SAG)
LENS .... Concord Camera [*NASDAQ symbol*] (TTSB)
LENS .... Concord Camera Corp. [*NASDAQ symbol*] (NQ)
LENS .... LASER-Engineered Net Shaping
LENS .... LASER Enhanced NMR [*Nuclear Magnetic Resonance*] Spectroscopy
LEntA .... London Enterprise Agency
LENTO .... Lentando [*With Increasing Slowness*] [*Music*] (ROG)
LENWID ...... Length to Width Ratio [*Of a leaf*] [*Botany*]
LEO .... Dreyfus Strategic Municipals [*NYSE symbol*] (SPSG)
LEO .... Law Enforcement Officer (MCD)
LEO .... Lear Oil & Gas Corp. [*Vancouver Stock Exchange symbol*]
Leo .... Leonard's King's Bench Reports [*1540-1615*] [*England*] [*A publication*] (DLA)
Leo .... Leonardus [*Authority cited in pre-1607 legal work*] (DSA)
LEO .... Leoncito [*Argentina*] [*Seismograph station code, US Geological Survey*] (SEIS)
LEO .... Leopair SA [*Switzerland ICAO designator*] (FAAC)
LEO .... Liaison Engineering Order
LEO .... Library Entrance Online
LEO .... Librating Equidistant Observer
LEO .... Littoral Environment Observation [*Program*] [*Oceanography*]
LEO .... Local Elected Official (OICC)
LEO .... Low Earth Orbit
LEO .... Lunar Exploration Office [*NASA*]
LEO .... Lyons Electronic Office [*J. Lyons & Co*] [*British*] (NITA)
Leoc .... Against Leocrates [*of Lycurgus*] [*Classical studies*] (OCD)
LEOC .... Local Emergency Operations Controller
LEOC .... Ocana [*Spain ICAO location identifier*] (ICLI)

LEOCOMM ... Low Earth Orbit Mobile Data Communications
LEOD .... Lens Extraction, Oculus Dexter [*Right eye*] [*Ophthalmology*] (DAVI)
LEOMA .... LASER and Electro-Optics Manufacturers' Association
LEOMA .... LASER/Electro/Optic Measurement Alignment System
Leon .... Leonard's King's Bench, Common Pleas, and Exchequer Reports [*England*] [*A publication*] (DLA)
Leon LA Dig... Leonard's Louisiana Digest of United States Cases [*A publication*] (DLA)
Leon Prec .... Leonard's Precedents in County Courts [*1869*] [*A publication*] (DLA)
LEOPARD ..... Lentigines, EKG Abnormalities, Ocular Hypertelorism, Pulmonary Stenosis, Abnormalities of Genitalia, Retardation of Growth, and Deafness Syndrome [*Medicine*] (DMAA)
LEOPCID ...... Local Elected Officials Project of the Center for Innovative Diplomacy [*Defunct*] (EA)
LEOS .... IEEE [*Institute of Electrical and Electronics Engineers*] LASERS and Electro-Optics Society (EA)
LEOS .... Loral Electro-Optical Systems Corp.
LEOS .... Low Earth Orbit Satellite (MCD)
LEOS .... Low Earth Orbit Satellites (ACRL)
LEOT .... Left-End-of-Tape
LEOV .... Oviedo [*Spain ICAO location identifier*] (ICLI)
LEP .... Air West Airlines, Inc. [*ICAO designator*] (FAAC)
LEP .... Laboratory Evaluation Program [*Environmental Protection Agency*] (GFGA)
LEP .... Large Electronic Panel
LEP .... Large Electron-Positron [*Accelerator*] [*in Europe*]
LEP .... Least Energy Principle
Lep .... Lepidoptera [*Entomology*]
Lep .... Lepus [*Constellation*]
LEP .... Lethal Effective Phase [*Medicine*] (DB)
LEP .... Library of Exact Philosophy
LEP .... Light-Emitting Polymer
LEP .... Light Evaluation Plan (MCD)
LEP .... Lightning-Induced Electron Precipitation [*Atmospheric physics*]
LEP .... Limited English Proficiency
LEP .... Lipoprotein Electrophoresis [*Biochemistry*]
LEP .... List of Effective Pages (NVT)
LEP .... Local Enterprise Program
LEP .... Local Field Potential [*Neurobiology*]
LEP .... Locally Enlisted Personnel [*British military*] (DMA)
LEP .... Low Egg Passage [*Rabies vaccine*]
LEP .... Low Emissions Partnership
LEP .... Lower End Plug (IEEE)
LEP .... Lower Esophageal [*Medicine*] (DB)
LEP .... Lowest Effective Power
LEP .... Low-Frequency Prediction [*Marine science*] (OSRA)
LEP .... Lupus Erythematosus Preparation [*Hematology*] (DAVI)
LEP .... Lycee d'Enseignement Professionel [*Professional Secondary School for AdvancedStudies*] [*French*] (BARN)
LEPA .... Laboratoire d'Etudes Politiques et Administratives [*Universite Laval, Quebec*] [*Canada*]
LEPA .... Palma De Mallorca [*Spain ICAO location identifier*] (ICLI)
LEPC .... Law Enforcement Planning Commission
LEPC .... Local Emergency Planning Committee [*Hazardous waste*]
LEPC .... Low Emissions Paint Consortium
LEPD .... Legal Enforcement Policy Division [*Environmental Protection Agency*] (GFGA)
LEPD .... Low-Energy Photon Detector [*Environmental Protection Agency*]
LEPEDEA ..... Low-Energy Proton-Electron Differential Energy Analyzer [*NASA*]
LEPG .... Lep Group Ltd. [*NASDAQ symbol*] (SAG)
LE/PH .... Local Exchange/Packet Handler (ACRL)
LEPI .... Litton Educational Publishing, Inc.
LEPMA .... Lithographic Engravers and Plate Makers Association (EA)
LEPO .... Low Exercise Price Options (NUMA)
LEPO .... Pollensa [*Spain ICAO location identifier*] (ICLI)
LEPOR .... Long-Term and Expanded Program of Oceanic Exploration and Research
LEPORE .... Long-Term and Expanded Program of Oceanic Research and Exploration (BARN)
LEPP .... Pamplona/Noain-Pamplona [*Spain ICAO location identifier*] (ICLI)
LEPR .... LASER Electron Paramagnetic Resonance
LEPRA .... British Leprosy Relief Association (IRUK)
LEPRA .... Leprosy Relief Association [*British*] (DI)
LE Prep .... Lupus Erythematosus Preparation [*Hematology*] (CPH)
LEPS .... Launch Escape Propulsion System [*NASA*]
Leps .... Lepus [*Constellation*]
LEPS .... London-Eyring-Polanyi-Sato Method [*Reaction dynamics*]
LEPSOC ...... Lepidopterists' Society (EA)
Lept .... Against Leptines [*of Demosthenes*] [*Classical studies*] (OCD)
LEPT .... Leptocytes [*Biochemistry*] (DAVI)
Lept .... Leptospira [*Genus of bacteria*]
LEPT .... Long-Endurance Patrolling Torpedo
LEPT .... Low-Energy Particle Telescope
LEPTOS .... Leptospirosis Agglutinins [*Biochemistry*] (DAVI)
LEPW .... Longitudinal Electric Pressure Wave
LEQ .... Lehman Br Hldg 8.30%'QUICS' [*NYSE symbol*] (TTSB)
LEQ .... Lehman Brothers [*NYSE symbol*] (SAG)
LEQ .... Level Equivalent (SSD)
LEQ .... Life Events Questionnaire [*Psychology*] (EDAC)
LEQ .... Line Equipped [*Telecommunications*] (TEL)
LEQ .... Line of Equipment [*Telecommunications*] (TEL)
Leq .... Loudness Equivalent [*Medicine*] (DMAA)
LER .... Land Equivalent Ratio [*Agriculture*]
LER .... Launcher Equipment Room [*Missiles*]
LER .... Leading Edge Radius (MSA)

LER	Lease Expenditure Request (MCD)
LER	Leinster [*Australia Airport symbol*] (OAG)
LER	Lerwick [*United Kingdom*] [*Geomagnetic observatory code*]
LER	Licensee Event Report [*Nuclear energy*] (NRCH)
LER	Life Elongation Ratio (DB)
LER	Light Efficiency Radiator [*General Motors Corp.*] [*Automotive engineering*]
LER	Light-Emitting Resistor [*Computer hacker terminology*] (NHD)
LER	Lissajous Electron Plasma (AAEL)
LER	London Electric Railway
LER	Long Eye Relief (MCD)
LER	Loss Exchange Ratio (MCD)
LER	Lysozomal Enzyme Release (DB)
LERA	Limited Employee Retirement Account (IEEE)
LERAM	Littoral Ecosystem Risk Assessment Model for Prediction of Risk of Chemical Stressors Entering the Aquatic Environment [*Environmental Protection Agency*] (AEPA)
LERB	Line Error Recording Block (MCD)
LERC	Language for Export Research Center [*University of Western Sydney*] [*Australia*]
LERC	Laramie Energy Research Center [*Department of Energy*]
LERC	Lewis Research Center [*NASA*] (KSC)
LeRC	Lewis Research Center [*Cleveland, OH*] (NAKS)
LERF	Laboratory Experimental Research Facility [*Army*] (RDA)
LERG	Local Electroretingogram (DB)
LERI	Murcia/Alcantarilla [*Spain ICAO location identifier*] (ICLI)
LERIS	Low-Energy Recoil Ion Spectroscopy
LERK	LASER Experimental Research Kit
LERMISTOR	Learning Materials Information Store (PDAA)
LERN	Learning Resources Network (EA)
LERP	Labor Education and Research Project (EA)
LERP	Linear Interpolation [*Computer science*] (NHD)
LERS	Reus [*Spain ICAO location identifier*] (ICLI)
LERSC	Location Evaluation Recognition and Statistical Comparison (PDAA)
LERSO	Low Erucic Acid Rapeseed Oil (PDAA)
LERT	Lockheed Emergency Reset Timer (IAA)
LERT	Rota [*Spain ICAO location identifier*] (ICLI)
LERTCON	Alert Condition [*Military*] (AABC)
LERX	Leading Edge Root Extension [*Aviation*]
L-ERX	Leukoerythroblastic Reaction [*Biochemistry*] (DAVI)
LES	Automotors Salta SACYF [*Argentina ICAO designator*] (FAAC)
LES	Laboratory for Environmental Studies [*Ohio State University*] [*Research center*] (RCD)
LES	Lambert-Eaton Myasthenic Syndrome [*Medicine*]
LES	LAN [*Local Area Network*] Emulation Server [*Telecommunications*] (ACRL)
LES	Large Eddy Simulation [*For modelling fluid flow*]
LES	LASER Excitation Spectroscopy
LES	Lateral Epithelial Space [*Anatomy*] (DAVI)
LES	Launch Effects Simulator
LES	Launch Enabling System
LES	Launch/Entry Suit [*NASA*]
LES	Launch Environmental Simulator (MCD)
LES	Launch Equipment Shop (MCD)
LES	Launch Escape System [*or Subsystem*] [*NASA*]
LES	Law Enforcement Squadron
LES	Lawrence Experiment Station [*Agar*] [*Medicine*] (BABM)
LES	Leading Edge Slats (MCD)
LES	Leave and Earnings Statement [*Military*] (AABC)
LES	Lesbian (DSUE)
LES	Lesobeng [*Lesotho*] [*Airport symbol*] (OAG)
LES	Lesozavodsk [*Former USSR Seismograph station code, US Geological Survey Closed*] (SEIS)
LES	Licensing Executives Society (EA)
LES	Life Experiences Survey [*Psychology*]
LES	Light-Emitting Switch [*Electronics*] (OA)
LES	Light Experimental Supercruiser (MCD)
LES	Light Exposure Speed [*Photography*] (OA)
LES	Lilliput Edison Screw
LES	Limited Early Site [*Nuclear energy*] (NRCH)
LES	Limited English Speaking (OICC)
LES	Lincoln Experimental Satellite [*Lincoln Laboratory, MIT*]
LES	Loaded Equipment Section
LES	Local Engineering Specifications [*DoD*]
LES	Local Engineering Standard (IAA)
LES	Local Excitatory State
LES	Locally Engaged Staff
LES	Locke Egg Serum [*Medicine*] (MAE)
LES	Loop Error Signal
LES	Low-Energy Sputter
LES	Lower Esophageal Sphincter [*Medicine*]
LES	Lunar Escape System [*NASA*]
LES	Lupus Erythematosus, Systemic [*Medicine*] (MAE)
LES	Support Landing Boat [*Navy symbol Obsolete*]
LESA	Lake Erie Steam Association [*Defunct*]
LESA	Land Evaluation and Site Assessment System [*Department of Agriculture*]
LESA	Lunar Exploration System for Apollo [*NASA*]
LESA	Salamanca [*Spain ICAO location identifier*] (ICLI)
LESAP	Law Enforcement Security Access Position
LESAT	Leased Satellite [*Military*] (CAAL)
LESC	Launch Escape System Control [*NASA*] (KSC)
LESC	LE [*Lupus Erythematosus*] Support Club (EA)
LESC	Light-Emitting Switch Control [*Electronics*] (OA)
LESC	Lunar-Environment Sample Container [*Apollo*] [*NASA*]

Lesco	Lesco, Inc. [*Associated Press*] (SAG)
LESCS	Launch Escape Stabilization and Control System [*NASA*] (IAA)
LESD	Letterer-Siwe Disease [*Medicine*] (DMAA)
LESG	Late Effects Study Group [*for Hodgkins disease*]
Lesh	Leshonenu [*Jerusalem*] (BJA)
LESI	Leif Ericson Society International (EA)
LESJ	Son San Juan Air Force Base [*Spain ICAO location identifier*] (ICLI)
LESL	Law Enforcement Standards Laboratory [*National Institute of Standards and Technology*]
LESL	Leslie's Poolmart [*NASDAQ symbol*] (TTSB)
L es L	Licencie es Lettres [*Licentiate in Letters*] [*French*] (EY)
Lesli	List of Eligible Surplus Line Insurers
LESM	Longman's Elementary Science Manuals [*A publication*]
LESM	Murcia [*Spain ICAO location identifier*] (ICLI)
Les Miz	Les Miserables [*Musical based on Victor Hugo's novel*]
LESNW	Lesnwith [*England*]
LESO	San Sebastian [*Spain ICAO location identifier*] (ICLI)
LESOC	Lincoln Experimental Satellite Operations Center (MCD)
LESOP	Leveraged Employee Stock Ownership Plan [*Procter & Gamble Co.*]
LESP	Law Enforcement Standards Program [*National Institute of Law Enforcement and Criminal Justice*]
LESP	Lower Esophageal Sphincter Pressure [*Medicine*]
LESP	Madrid [*Spain ICAO location identifier*] (ICLI)
LesPol	Leslie's Poolmart, Inc. [*Associated Press*] (SAG)
L'Esprit	L'Esprit Createur [*A publication*] (BRI)
LESR	Limited Early Site Review [*Nuclear energy*] (NRCH)
LESS	LASER-Excited Shpol'skii Spectrometry
LESS	Lateral Electrical Spine Stimulation [*Orthopedics*] (DAVI)
LESS	Launch Escape System Simulator [*NASA*] (IAA)
LESS	Law Encounter Severity Scale [*Personality development test*] [*Psychology*]
LESS	Leading Edge Structure Subsystem [*Aviation*] (NASA)
LESS	Leading Edge Structure Subsystem (NAKS)
LESS	Leading Edge Subsystem (NAKS)
LESS	Least-Cost Estimating and Scheduling System
LesS	Licencie es Sciences [*Licentiate in Science*] [*French*] (BARN)
L/ESS	Loads/Environmental Spectra Survey (MCD)
LESS	Lunar Escape System Simulator [*NASA*]
L es SC	Licencie es Sciences [*Licentiate of Sciences*] [*French*]
LesSc	Licencie es Sciences [*Licentiate of Sciences*] [*French*] (ASC)
lessy	lesbian [*Psychology*]
LEST	Large Earth-Based [*formerly, European*] Solar Telescope
LEST	Large Earth Survey Telescope
LEST	Launch Electronics System Test
LEST	Launch Enable System Turret (IAA)
Lest	Licencie es Lettres [*Licentiate in Letters*] [*French*] (BARN)
LEST	Low-Energy Speech Transmission
LEST	Santiago [*Spain ICAO location identifier*] (ICLI)
Lest & But	Lester and Butler's Supplement to Lester's Georgia Reports [*A publication*] (DLA)
Lester	Lester's Reports [*31-33 Georgia*] [*A publication*] (DLA)
Lester & B	Lester and Butler's Supplement to Lester's Georgia Reports [*A publication*] (DLA)
Lester Supp	Lester and Butler's Supplement to Lester's Georgia Reports [*A publication*] (DLA)
Lest PL	Lester's Decisions in Public Land Cases [*A publication*] (DLA)
LESTR	Leukocyte-Expressed Seven-Transmembrane-Domain Receptor [*Biochemistry*]
LESU	Law Enforcement Study Unit [*of the American Topical Association*] (EA)
LESU	Seo De Urgel [*Spain ICAO location identifier*] (ICLI)
LET	Aerolineas Ejecutivas SA [*Mexico ICAO designator*] (FAAC)
LET	Laboratory Electronics Technician (IAA)
LET	Launch Effects Trainer [*Weaponry*] (MCD)
LET	Launch Eject Test
LET	Launch Equipment Test
LET	Launch Escape Tower [*NASA*] (MCD)
LET	Leader Effectiveness Training [*A course of study*]
LET	Leading Edge Tracker
LET	Learning Efficiency Test [*Educational test*]
LET	Legacy Encapsulation Technology
LET	Leticia [*Colombia*] [*Airport symbol*] (OAG)
LET	Letter
LET	Lettish [*Latvian*] (ROG)
LET	Lidocaine, Epinephrine, and Tetracaine Solution [*Medicine*] (DMAA)
LET	Life Environmental Testing (IAA)
LET	Light Equipment Transporter (MCD)
LET	Limited Environmental Test (MCD)
LET	Lincoln Experimental Terminal [*NASA*]
LET	Linear Energy Transfer [*Radiology*]
LET	Lithium Excretion Test [*Clinical chemistry*]
LET	Live Environment Testing
LET	Live Environment Training [*Military*] (ADDR)
LET	Local Enterprise Trust [*British*]
LET	Logical Equipment Table
LET	Logistic Escape Trunk (CAAL)
LET	London and Edinburgh Trust [*British*]
LET	Low-Emissions Truck
LET	Low-End Torque [*Automotive engineering*]
LET	Low-Energy Telescope [*Geophysics*]
LET	Lux e Tenebris [*Light Out of Darkness*] [*Freemasonry*] [*Latin*]
LETA	Latvian Telegraph Agency (EY)
LETA	Sevilla/Tablada [*Spain ICAO location identifier*] (ICLI)
LETATA	Light Edge Tool and Allied Trades Association [*British*] (BI)
LETB	Local Exchange Test Bed [*Telecommunications*] (TEL)

LETC	Laramie Energy Technology Center [*Department of Energy*] (GRD)
Letch	Letchworth Independent Bancshares Corp. [*Associated Press*] (SAG)
LetchInd	Letchworth Independent Bancshares Corp. [*Associated Press*] (SAG)
LETCO..........	Law Engineering Testing Co. (EFIS)
LETCS	Launch Escape Tower Canard System [*NASA*] (IAA)
Let D	Doctor of Letters
LETD	Lowest Effective Toxic Dose [*Medicine*] (DMAA)
LE-TE	Leading Edge - Trailing Edge [*Aerodynamics*]
LETEC	London East Training and Enterprise Council [*British*] (AIE)
LETF	Launch Equipment Test Facility [*NASA*] (NASA)
LETFO..........	Letter Follows (NOAA)
leth	Lethal [*Pharmacology*] (DAVI)
LETHR	Leather
LETIS	Leicestershire Technical Information Service [*British*] (NITA)
LETM	Lake Evaporation and Thermodynamics Model [*Marine science*] (OSRA)
LETN	Law Enforcement Television Network
LETO	Madrid/Torrejon [*Spain ICAO location identifier*] (ICLI)
LETS	Large, External Transformation Sensitive [*Glycoprotein*] [*Also known as CSP Cytochemistry*]
LETS	Launch Equipment Test Set (MCD)
LETS	Law Enforcement Teletype [*or Teletypewriter*] Service [*Phoenix, AZ*]
LETS	Leading Edge Tracker System
LETS	Learning Experience for Technical Students [*NASA*]
LETS	Linear-Energy Transfer Spectrometer [*Radiology*] (KSC)
LETS	Linear-Energy Transfer System [*Radiology*]
LETS	Live Environment Testing with SAGE (MCD)
LETS	Local Exchange Trading Scheme (WDAA)
LETS	Low-Energy Telescope System [*Geophysics*]
LETS	Lunar Experiment Telemetry System [*Aerospace*]
LETT	Letters
LETT	Lettish [*Latvian*] (ROG)
LEU	Emory University, Division of Librarianship, Atlanta, GA [*OCLC symbol*] (OCLC)
LEU	Launch Enable Unit
LEU	Launcher Electronic Unit (MCD)
Leu	Leucine [*Also, L*] [*An amino acid*]
leu	Leucine [*An amino acid*] (DOG)
LEU	Leucovorin (DMAA)
LEU	Leukocyte Equivalent Unit (DMAA)
LEU	Lewis, IN [*Location identifier FAA*] (FAAL)
LEU	License to Export Uranium (NRCH)
LEU	Lions-Air, AG [*Switzerland*] [*FAA designator*] (FAAC)
LEU	Low-Enriched Uranium [*Nuclear energy*]
LEU	Seo De Urgel [*Spain*] [*Airport symbol*] (OAG)
LEUC	Leucotomy [*European term for lobotomy*] (DSUE)
LeucNtl	Leucadia National Corp. [*Associated Press*] (SAG)
Leuk	Leukemia [*Medicine*]
LEUK..........	Leukocyte [*Biochemistry*] (DAVI)
LEUKAP........	Leukocyte Alkaline Phosphatase [*Biochemistry*] (DAVI)
leuko	Leukocyte [*Hematology*]
LEUP	Leuprlide [*Antineoplastic drug*] (CDI)
LEV	Bureta [*Fiji*] [*Airport symbol*] (OAG)
LEV	Grand Isle, LA [*Location identifier FAA*] (FAAL)
LEV	Launch Escape Vehicle [*NASA*]
LEV	Leibovitz-Emory Medium for Viral Cultures [*Microbiology*]
LEV	Leichtverwundet; Leichtverwundeter [*Slightly wounded; minor casualty*] [*German military - World War II*]
LEV	Levamisole [*Antineoplastic drug*] (CDI)
LEV	Levant
lev	Levator [*Muscle*] [*Medicine*] (MEDA)
LEV	Level
LEV	Lever
LEV	Leviathan Gas PL Partners Ltd. [*NYSE symbol*] (SPSG)
LEV	Leviathan Gas PLPtnrs LP [*NYSE symbol*] (TTSB)
Lev............	Levinz's King's Bench and Common Pleas Reports [*1660-97*] [*England*] [*A publication*] (DLA)
LEV	Levis [*Light*] [*Pharmacy*]
Lev............	Leviticus [*Old Testament book*]
lev	Levorotatory [*Optics*] [*Chemistry*] (DOG)
LEV	Lev Scientific Industries Ltd. [*Vancouver Stock Exchange symbol*]
LEV	Levyne [*A zeolite*]
LEV	Lifting Entry Vehicle
LEV	Loader/Editor/Verifier [*Telecommunications*] (TEL)
LEV	Local Exhaust Ventilation [*Hazardous material control*]
LEV	Logistics Entry Vehicle
LEV	Lolium Enation Virus [*Plant pathology*]
LEV	Low-Emissions Vehicle
LEV	Loyal Edinburgh Volunteers [*British military*] (DMA)
LEV	Lunar Escape Vehicle (IAA)
LEV	Lunar Excursion Vehicle [*Aerospace*]
LEVC..........	Valencia [*Spain ICAO location identifier*] (ICLI)
LEVCB..........	Low-Emission Vehicle Certification Board [*Terminated, 1980*] [*Environmental Protection Agency*]
LEVD..........	Valladolid [*Spain ICAO location identifier*] (ICLI)
LevelOne	Level One Communications, Inc. [*Associated Press*] (SAG)
Lev Ent	Levinz's Entries [*England*] [*A publication*] (DLA)
LevGas	Leviathan Gas Pipeline [*Associated Press*] (SAG)
LE-VGF	Liquid Encapsulation-Vertical Gradient Freeze (PDAA)
Levi Com L..	Levi's International Commercial Law [*2nd ed.*] [*1863*] [*A publication*] (DLA)
Levi Merc L..	Levi's Mercantile Law [*1854*] [*A publication*] (DLA)
LEVIT	Leviter [*Lightly*] [*Pharmacy*]
LEVIT	Leviticus [*Old Testament book*] (ROG)
Levitz..........	Levitz Furniture, Inc. [*Associated Press*] (SAG)

Lev JP	Levinge's Irish Justice of the Peace [*A publication*] (DLA)
LEVL	Level One Communications [*NASDAQ symbol*] (TTSB)
LEVL	Level One Communications, Inc. [*NASDAQ symbol*] (SAG)
LEVM	Valencia [*Spain ICAO location identifier*] (ICLI)
LEVMETR.....	Levelometer
LevR	Leviticus Rabbah (BJA)
LEVS	Leaves
LEVS	Madrid/Cuatro Vientos [*Spain ICAO location identifier*] (ICLI)
LEVT	Left Extremity Venous Tracing [*Cardiology*] (DAVI)
LEVT	Lower Extremity Venous Tracing [*Cardiology*] (DAVI)
LEVT	Vitoria [*Spain ICAO location identifier*] (ICLI)
LEVTAB..........	Level Table (MHDB)
LEVVA..........	Lunar Extravehicular Visor Assembly [*NASA*] (KSC)
LEVX..........	Vigo [*Spain ICAO location identifier*] (ICLI)
Levy WTM ...	Woerterbuch ueber die Talmudim und Midraschim [*J. Levy*] [*A publication*] (BJA)
LEW	Auburn-Lewiston [*Maine*] [*Airport symbol*] (AD)
LEW	Auburn/Lewiston, ME [*Location identifier FAA*] (FAAL)
Lew............	Lewin's English Crown Cases Reserved [*1822-38*] [*A publication*] (DLA)
LEW	Lewis [*Rat strain*]
Lew............	Lewis' Reports [*Missouri*] [*A publication*] (DLA)
Lew............	Lewis' Reports [*Nevada*] [*A publication*] (DLA)
LEW	Lewiston [*Maine*] [*Airport symbol*] (OAG)
Lew App	Lewin's Appportionment [*1869*] [*A publication*] (DLA)
Lew B & S..	Lewis on Bonds and Securities [*A publication*] (DLA)
Lew CC	Lewin's English Crown Cases [*A publication*] (DLA)
Lew CL	Lewis' Criminal Law [*A publication*] (DLA)
Lew Conv ...	Lewis' Principles of Conveyancing [*A publication*] (DLA)
Lew Dig Cr L.	Lewis' Digest of United States Criminal Law [*A publication*] (DLA)
Lew Elec	Lewis' Election Manual [*A publication*] (DLA)
Lew Eq Dr ..	Lewis on Equity Drafting [*A publication*] (DLA)
Lewin..........	Lewin on Trusts [*A publication*] (DLA)
Lewin CC	Lewin's English Crown Cases Reserved [*1822-38*] [*A publication*] (DLA)
Lewin CC (Eng)...	Lewin's English Crown Cases [*A publication*] (DLA)
Lewin Cr Cas...	Lewin's English Crown Cases Reserved [*A publication*] (DLA)
Lew Ind Pen...	Lewis' East India Penal Code [*A publication*] (DLA)
Lewis..........	Lewis' Appeals Reports [*29-35 Missouri*] [*A publication*] (DLA)
Lewis..........	Lewis' Kentucky Law Reporter [*A publication*] (DLA)
Lewis..........	Lewis' Reports [*Nevada*] [*A publication*] (DLA)
Lewis & Clark C..	Lewis and Clark College (GAGS)
Lewis Em Dom...	Lewis on Eminent Domain [*A publication*] (DLA)
Lewis Perp ...	Lewis' Law of Perpetuities [*A publication*] (DLA)
Lew L Cas ..	Lewis' Leading Cases on Public Land Law [*A publication*] (DLA)
Lew LT	Lewis on Land Titles in Philadelphia [*A publication*] (DLA)
LEWP..........	Line Echo Wave Pattern
Lew Perp....	Lewis' Law of Perpetuities [*A publication*] (DLA)
Lew St........	Lewis on Stocks, Bonds, Etc. [*A publication*] (DLA)
Lew Tr	Lewin on Trusts [*A publication*] (DLA)
LEWU..........	Lanka Estate Workers' Union [*Ceylon*]
Lew US Cr L..	Lewis' Digest of United States Criminal Law [*A publication*] (DLA)
LEX	Cary Memorial Library, Lexington, MA [*OCLC symbol*] (OCLC)
LEX	Land Exercise [*Marine Corps*]
LEX	Leading Edge Extension [*Aviation*]
LEX	Letter Exchange (EA)
Lex............	Lexical (BJA)
LEX	Lexicographer (ABBR)
LEX	Lexicon
lex	Lexicon (WDAA)
LEX	Lexington [*Virginia*] [*Seismograph station code, US Geological Survey Closed*] (SEIS)
LEX	Lexington [*Diocesan abbreviation*] [*Kentucky*] (TOCD)
LEX	Lexington/Frankfort [*Kentucky*] [*Airport symbol*] (OAG)
LEX	L'Express, Inc. [*ICAO designator*] (FAAC)
LEX	Line Exchange [*Telecommunications*]
LEX	Listing Exchange
LEx............	Liver Extract [*Protein/lipid substance*] [*Immunology*]
LexBLF	Lexington B & L Financial Corp. [*Associated Press*] (SAG)
LexCrpP........	Lexington Corporate Properties [*Associated Press*] (SAG)
Lex Cust	Lex Custumaria [*Latin A publication*] (DLA)
LEXD..........	Lexden [*England*]
LexGlbl........	Lexington Global Asset Managers, Inc. [*Associated Press*] (SAG)
LEXI	Lexical (ABBR)
LEXICO	Lexicographer (ABBR)
LEXICOG......	Lexicography
lexicog........	Lexicography (WDAA)
LEXIS	Legal Research Service [*Registered service mark*] (IID)
LEXIS	Lexicography Information Service [*Germany Computer science*]
LEXJ	Santander [*Spain ICAO location identifier*] (ICLI)
Lex Man	Lex Maneriorum [*Latin A publication*] (DLA)
Lex Mer Am...	Lex Mercatoria Americana [*Latin A publication*] (DLA)
Lex Mess.....	Lexicon Messanense [*Classical studies*] (OCD)
Lexmrk........	Lexmark International Group [*Associated Press*] (SAG)
LEXN..........	Lexicon (ABBR)
LEXOG........	Lexicology (ABBR)
LEXOGL........	Lexicological (ABBR)
LEXOGT........	Lexicologist (ABBR)
LEXP..........	Language Experience
Lex Parl	Lex Parliamentaria [*Latin A publication*] (DLA)
LEXPHR	Lexicographer (ABBR)
LEXPHY	Lexicography (ABBR)
LEXSWG	Lunar Exploration Science Working Group [*NASA*]
LexSyr........	Lexicon Syriacum [*A publication*] (BJA)
L/EXT..........	Lower Extremity [*Medicine*]

Ley	Ley's English Court of Wards Reports [*A publication*] (DLA)
Ley	Ley's English King's Bench Reports [*1608-29*] [*A publication*] (DLA)
LEY	Liberal European Youth
LEYD	Leyden [*Netherlands*] (ROG)
Ley Wards	Ley's English Court of Wards Reports [*A publication*] (DLA)
LEZ	Lunar Equatorial Zone [*Army Map Service*]
LEZA	Zaragoza [*Spain ICAO location identifier*] (ICLI)
LEZG	Zaragoza [*Spain ICAO location identifier*] (ICLI)
LEZL	Sevilla [*Spain ICAO location identifier*] (ICLI)
LEZOR	Liquid Encapsulation Zone-Refining (PDAA)
LF	Labile Factor (DB)
LF	Lacrimatory Factor [*Food technology*]
LF	Lacrosse Foundation (EA)
LF	Lactoferrin [*Biochemistry*]
LF	La Fosse Platinum Group, Inc. [*Toronto Stock Exchange symbol*]
LF	Lama Foundation (EA)
LF	Laminar Flow (AAEL)
LF	[*The*] Lancashire Fusiliers [*Military unit*] [*British*]
LF	Land Forces [*Military British*]
LF	Landing Force [*Navy*] (NVT)
LF	Largest Frame (ACRL)
LF	Laryngofissure (MAE)
LF	Latex Fixation [*Test*] [*Medicine*]
LF	Lathe Fixture (MCD)
LF	Laucks Foundation (EA)
LF	Launch Facility
LF	Launch Forward
LF	Law French (DLA)
LF	Lawn Faucet (MSA)
LF	Lead-Free
lf	Leaf (VRA)
LF	Leaf [*Bibliography*] (ROG)
LF	Leaflet (WGA)
LF	League of Friendship [*Defunct*] (EA)
LF	Leapfrog Configuration [*Circuit theory*] (IEEE)
LF	Least Frequent (AEBS)
LF	Lebanese Forces
LF	Lederer Foundation (EA)
LF	Ledger Folio
LF	Left (ECII)
LF	Left Field [*or Fielder*] [*Baseball*]
LF	Left Foot
LF	Left Forward [*Football*]
LF	Left Front
LF	Left Fullback [*Soccer*]
LF	Legion of Frontiersmen [*British military*] (DMA)
LF	Lettering Faded
LF	Liberty Federation (EA)
LF	Library of Fathers [*A publication*] (ODCC)
LF	Liederkranz Foundation (EA)
LF	Life (ABBR)
LF	Life Float
LF	Lifeline Foundation (EA)
LF	Lifting Fan [*Hovercraft*]
LF	Lightface [*Type*]
lf	Lightface Type (WDMC)
LF	Light Fastness Ink (DGA)
LF	Ligue de Foyer [*Salvation Army Home League - SAHL*] (EAIO)
LF	Limiting Fragmentation [*Physics*] (OA)
LF	Limit of Flocculation
LF	Lineal Feet
LF	Linear File [*Computer file*] (NITA)
LF	Linear Filter
LF	Linear Foot
LF	Line Feed [*Control character*] [*Computer science*]
LF	Line Finder [*Teletype*]
L/F	Linen-Faced Paper (DGA)
LF	Linjeflyg [*ICAO designator*] (AD)
LF	Linoleum Floor [*Technical drawings*]
LF	Lisle Fellowship (EA)
LF	Listener Function (IAA)
LF	Lituanus Foundation (EA)
LF	Live Fire
LF	Live Flying (NATG)
LF	Load Factor
LF	Loaf
LF	Loan Forgiveness (DICI)
LF	Local Film
LF	Local Force [*Viet Cong combat force*]
LF	Locally Funded (AFM)
LF	Lock Forward
LF	Logical File [*Computer science*] (BUR)
LF	Logic Function
LF	Lost on Foul [*Boxing*]
LF	Lovelace Foundation for Medical Education and Research [*Reorganized to form Lovelace Medical Foundation and Lovelace Biomedical and Environmental Research Institute*]
LF	Low Fat [*Diet*]
LF	Low Flange (DICI)
LF	Low-Fluence [*Physics*]
LF	Low Foliage Forager [*Ecology*]
LF	Low Food Density [*Ecology*]
LF	Low Force
LF	Low Forceps [*Delivery*] [*Obstetrics*]
LF	Low Frequency

lf	Low Frequency (WDMC)
lf	Low Rate Forward [*Ecology*]
LF	Siebelwerke ATG GmbH [*Germany ICAO aircraft manufacturer identifier*] (ICAO)
LFA	Air Alfa Hava Yollari Ve Tec, AS [*Turkey*] [*FAA designator*] (FAAC)
LFA	Klamath Falls, OR [*Location identifier FAA*] (FAAL)
LFA	Land Force Adriatic [*British Royal Marines*] [*World War II*]
LFA	Land Force, Airmobility [*NATO*] (NATG)
LFA	Landing Force Aviation
LFA	Language Foundation of Australia
LFA	Large Families of America [*Defunct*] (EA)
LFA	Last Field Address (IAA)
LFA	Lead Federal Agency (COE)
LFA	Leading Field Activity (MCD)
LFA	Left Femoral Artery [*Anatomy*]
LFA	Left Frontal Craniotomy [*Medicine*] (DMAA)
LFA	Left Frontoanterior [*A fetal position*] [*Obstetrics*]
LFA	Less Favored Areas (WDAA)
LFA	Leukocyte Function-Associated Antigen [*Immunology*]
LFA	Leukotactic Factor Activity [*Medicine*] (DMAA)
LFA	Light Freight Agent (ADA)
LFA	Lime Fly Ash [*Aggregate*] (DICI)
LFA	Littlefield, Adams [*AMEX symbol*] (TTSB)
LFA	Littlefield, Adams & Co. [*AMEX symbol*] (SPSG)
LFA	Local Flying Area [*Aviation*] (DA)
LFA	Local Freight Agent
LFA	Louisiana Forestry Association (WPI)
LFA	Low Flow Alarm (IEEE)
LFA	Low Frequency Active (DOMA)
LFA	Low Friction Arthroplasty [*Orthopedics*] (DAVI)
LFA	Low Functioning Autism
LFA	Lupus Foundation of America (EA)
LFA	Lutheran Fraternities of America (EA)
LFA	Luther Family Association
LFA	Lymphocyte Function-Associated Antigen [*Immunochemistry*]
LFAA	Ambleteuse [*France ICAO location identifier*] (ICLI)
LFAAV	Landing Force Assault Amphibious Vehicle (MCD)
LFAB	Dieppe/Saint-Aubin [*France ICAO location identifier*] (ICLI)
LFAC	Calais/Dunkerque [*France ICAO location identifier*] (ICLI)
LFACS	Light Future Armored Combat System [*Tank*]
LFAD	Compiegne/Margny [*France ICAO location identifier*] (ICLI)
LFAE	Eu-Mers/Le Treport [*France ICAO location identifier*] (ICLI)
LFAF	Laon/Chambry [*France ICAO location identifier*] (ICLI)
LFAF	Low-Frequency Accelerometer Flutter (MCD)
LFAG	Leafage (ABBR)
LFAG	Peronne/Saint-Quentin [*France ICAO location identifier*] (ICLI)
LFAH	Soissons/Cuffies [*France ICAO location identifier*] (ICLI)
LFAI	Lifting Fair Air Intake [*Hovercraft*]
LFAI	Nangis/Les Loges [*France ICAO location identifier*] (ICLI)
LFAJ	Argentan [*France ICAO location identifier*] (ICLI)
LFAK	Dunkerque-Ghyvelde [*France ICAO location identifier*] (ICLI)
LFAL	La Fleche/Thoree-Les-Pins [*France ICAO location identifier*] (ICLI)
LFAL	Lutheran Fraternities of America Life
LFAM	Berck-Sur-Mer [*France ICAO location identifier*] (ICLI)
LFAM	Low-Frequency Accelerometer Modes (MCD)
LFAN	Conde-Sur-Noireau [*France ICAO location identifier*] (ICLI)
LFAO	Bagnole-De-L'Orne [*France ICAO location identifier*] (ICLI)
LFAP	Low-Frequency Accelerometer POGO [*Polar Orbiting Geophysical Observatory*] [*NASA*] (NASA)
LFAP	Rethel-Perthes [*France ICAO location identifier*] (ICLI)
LFAQ	Albert/Bray [*France ICAO location identifier*] (ICLI)
LFAR	Last Frame Address Register
LFAR	Libertarians for Animal Rights (EA)
LFAR	Montdidier [*France ICAO location identifier*] (ICLI)
LFAS	Falaise-Monts-D'Eraines [*France ICAO location identifier*] (ICLI)
LFAS	League of Finnish-American Societies (EAIO)
LFAS	Low-Frequency Active Sonar (DOMA)
LFASV	Landing Force Amphibious Support Vehicle (SAA)
LFAT	Le Touquet/Paris-Plage [*France ICAO location identifier*] (ICLI)
LFATDS	Light Field Artillery Tactical Data System (GFGA)
LFaU	Union Parish Library, Farmerville, LA [*Library symbol Library of Congress*] (LCLS)
LFAU	Vauville [*France ICAO location identifier*] (ICLI)
LFAV	Valenciennes/Denain [*France ICAO location identifier*] (ICLI)
LFAW	Villerupt [*France ICAO location identifier*] (ICLI)
LFAX	Mortagne-Au-Perche [*France ICAO location identifier*] (ICLI)
LFAY	Amiens/Glisy [*France ICAO location identifier*] (ICLI)
LFB	Lafayette, TN [*Location identifier FAA*] (FAAL)
LFB	Landing Force Bulletin [*Marine Corps*]
LFB	Lateral Forebrain Bundle
LFB	Left Fullback [*Soccer*]
LFB	Licensed Fishing Boat
LFB	Light Field Battery [*British military*] (DMA)
LFB	Limited Frequency Band
LFB	London Festival Ballet
LFB	London Fire Brigade
LFB	Longview Fibre [*NYSE symbol*] (TTSB)
LFB	Longview Fibre Co. [*NYSE symbol*] (CTT)
LFB	Loop Fluidized Bed [*Chemical engineering*]
LFB	Low-Frequency Beacon
LFB	Luxol Fast Blue [*Biological stain*]
LFB2	London Festival Ballet's Ensemble Group
LFBA	Agen/La Garenne [*France ICAO location identifier*] (ICLI)
LFBA	Licentiate of the Corporation of Executives and Administrators [*British*] (DBQ)

LFBB .... Bordeaux [*France ICAO location identifier*] (ICLI)
LFBC .... Cazaux [*France ICAO location identifier*] (ICLI)
LFBD .... Bordeaux/Merignac [*France ICAO location identifier*] (ICLI)
LFBD .... Letters of the First Babylonian Dynasty [*A publication*] (BJA)
LFBD .... Lifeblood (ABBR)
LFBE .... Bergerac/Roumaniere [*France ICAO location identifier*] (ICLI)
LFBF .... Louisiana Farm Bureau Federation (SRA)
LFBF .... Toulouse/Francazal [*France ICAO location identifier*] (ICLI)
LFBG .... Cognac/Chateau Bernard [*France ICAO location identifier*] (ICLI)
LFBH .... La Rochelle/Laleu [*France ICAO location identifier*] (ICLI)
LFBI .... Little Falls Bancorp [*NASDAQ symbol*] (TTSB)
LFBI .... Poitiers/Biard [*France ICAO location identifier*] (ICLI)
LFBJ .... Saint-Junien [*France ICAO location identifier*] (ICLI)
LFBK .... Montlucon-Gueret [*France ICAO location identifier*] (ICLI)
LFBL .... Limoges/Bellegarde [*France ICAO location identifier*] (ICLI)
LFBM .... Mont-De-Marsan [*France ICAO location identifier*] (ICLI)
LFBN .... Niort/Souche [*France ICAO location identifier*] (ICLI)
LFBO .... Toulouse/Blagnac [*France ICAO location identifier*] (ICLI)
LFBP .... Pau/Pont-Long-Uzein [*France ICAO location identifier*] (ICLI)
LFBQ .... Toulouse [*France ICAO location identifier*] (ICLI)
LFBR .... LASER Fusion Breeder Reactor
LFBR .... Liquid Fluidized Bed Reactor
LFBR .... Muret/Lherm [*France ICAO location identifier*] (ICLI)
LFBR-CX .... Liquid Fluidized Bed Reactor Critical Experiment
LFBS .... Biscarosse/Parentis [*France ICAO location identifier*] (ICLI)
LFBT .... Lifeboat (ABBR)
LFBT .... Tarbes/Ossun-Lourdes [*France ICAO location identifier*] (ICLI)
LFBU .... Angouleme/Brie-Champniers [*France ICAO location identifier*] (ICLI)
LFBV .... Brive/La Roche [*France ICAO location identifier*] (ICLI)
LFBW .... Mont-De-Marsan [*France ICAO location identifier*] (ICLI)
LFBX .... Perigeux/Bassillac [*France ICAO location identifier*] (ICLI)
LFBY .... Dax/Seyresse [*France ICAO location identifier*] (ICLI)
LFBZ .... Biarritz-Bayonne/Anglet [*France ICAO location identifier*] (ICLI)
LFC .... Aero Control Air Ltd. [*Canada ICAO designator*] (FAAC)
LFC .... Concordia Parish Library, Ferriday, LA [*Library symbol Library of Congress*] (LCLS)
LFC .... Lafayette Flying Corps [*World War I*]
LFC .... Lake Forest College [*Illinois*]
LFC .... Lake Fork Canyon [*New Mexico*] [*Seismograph station code, US Geological Survey*] (SEIS)
LFC .... Laminar Flow Control [*Aerodynamics*]
LFC .... Lands and Forests Commission [*Australia*]
LFC .... Large Format Camera [*Space exploration*]
LFC .... Lateral Femoral Condyle [*Anatomy*]
LFC .... L-Band Frequency Converter
LFC .... Level of Free Convection [*Meteorology*]
LFC .... Liberty Financial Corp. (EFIS)
LFC .... Liberty Football Conference (PSS)
LFC .... Light Fighter Course [*Army*]
LFC .... Liquids from Coal
LFC .... Live Fire Component (MCD)
LFC .... Living Female Child [*Medicine*] (DMAA)
LFC .... Load Frequency Control (IEEE)
LFC .... Local Files Check
LFC .... Local Forms Control [*Computer science*] (CMD)
LFC .... Logic Flow Chart [*Computer science*]
LFC .... Logo Forum on Compuserve [*Defunct*] (EA)
LFC .... Lomas Financial Corp. [*NYSE symbol*] (SPSG)
LFC .... Loverboy Fan Club (EA)
LFC .... Low Fat and Cholesterol Diet (DMAA)
LFC .... Low-Frequency Choke (DEN)
LFC .... Low-Frequency Correction (CET)
LFC .... Low-Frequency Current
LFC .... Lunar Facsimile Capsule [*NASA*] (KSC)
LFC .... Lunar Farside Chart [*Air Force*]
LFC .... Lutheran Free Church (WDAA)
LFCA .... Chatellerault/Targe [*France ICAO location identifier*] (ICLI)
LFCB .... Bagneres De Luchon [*France ICAO location identifier*] (ICLI)
LFCB .... Legal Fees and Costs Board [*Australia*]
LFCC .... Cahors/Lalbenque [*France ICAO location identifier*] (ICLI)
LFCD .... Andernos-Les-Bains [*France ICAO location identifier*] (ICLI)
LFCE .... Gueret/Saint-Laurent [*France ICAO location identifier*] (ICLI)
LFCF .... Figeac/Livernon [*France ICAO location identifier*] (ICLI)
LFCG .... Saint-Girons/Antichan [*France ICAO location identifier*] (ICLI)
LFCH .... Arcachon/La Teste De Buch [*France ICAO location identifier*] (ICLI)
LFCI .... Albi/Le Sequestre [*France ICAO location identifier*] (ICLI)
LFCI .... Licentiate of the Faculty of Commerce and Industry [*British*] (DBQ)
LFCJ .... Jonzac/Neulles [*France ICAO location identifier*] (ICLI)
LFCK .... Castres/Mazamet [*France ICAO location identifier*] (ICLI)
LFCL .... Less Than Full Container Load
LFCL .... Toulouse/Lasbordes [*France ICAO location identifier*] (ICLI)
LFCM .... Low-Frequency Cross-Modulation [*Electronics*] (OA)
LFCM .... Millau/Larzac [*France ICAO location identifier*] (ICLI)
LFCN .... Nogaro [*France ICAO location identifier*] (ICLI)
LFCO .... Oloron/Herrere [*France ICAO location identifier*] (ICLI)
LFCOp .... Leading Fire Control Operator (WDAA)
LFCP .... Pons/Avy [*France ICAO location identifier*] (ICLI)
LFCQ .... Graulhet/Mondragon [*France ICAO location identifier*] (ICLI)
LFCR .... Rodez/Marcillac [*France ICAO location identifier*] (ICLI)
LFCS .... Bordeaux/Saucats [*France ICAO location identifier*] (ICLI)
LFCS .... Land Forces Classification System (AABC)
LFCS .... LASER Fire Control System
LFCS .... Licentiate of the Faculty of Secretaries [*British*] (DBQ)
LFCT .... Leader Financial [*NASDAQ symbol*] (TTSB)
LFCT .... Leader Financial Corp. [*NASDAQ symbol*] (SAG)
LFCT .... Thouars [*France ICAO location identifier*] (ICLI)
LFCU .... Ussel/Thalamy [*France ICAO location identifier*] (ICLI)
LFCV .... Villefranche-De-Rouergue [*France ICAO location identifier*] (ICLI)
LFCW .... Villeneuve-Sur-Lot [*France ICAO location identifier*] (ICLI)
LFCX .... Castelsarrasin/Moissac [*France ICAO location identifier*] (ICLI)
LFCY .... Royan/Medis [*France ICAO location identifier*] (ICLI)
LFCZ .... Mimizan [*France ICAO location identifier*] (ICLI)
LFD .... Lactose-Free Diet
LFD .... Latest Finish Date
LFD .... Launch and Flight Division [*Ballistic Research Laboratory*] (RDA)
LFD .... Least Fatal Dose
LFD .... Line Fault Detector [*Telecommunications*] (TEL)
LFD .... Litchfield, MI [*Location identifier FAA*] (FAAL)
LFD .... Local Frequency Distribution
LFD .... Longford [*County in Ireland*] (ROG)
LFD .... Low-Fat Diet
LFD .... Low-Forceps Delivery [*Obstetrics*]
LFD .... Low-Frequency Decoy
LFD .... Low-Frequency Disturbance
LFD .... Lutheran Foundation for Religious Drama (EA)
LFDA .... Aire-Sur-L'Addour [*France ICAO location identifier*] (ICLI)
LFDA .... Land and Facilities Development Administration [*HUD*]
LFDB .... Montauban [*France ICAO location identifier*] (ICLI)
LFDC .... Montendre/Marcillac [*France ICAO location identifier*] (ICLI)
LFDE .... Egletons [*France ICAO location identifier*] (ICLI)
LFDF .... Low-Frequency Direction Finder (MCD)
LFDF .... Sainte-Foy-La-Grande [*France ICAO location identifier*] (ICLI)
LFDG .... Gaillac/Lisle Sur Tarn [*France ICAO location identifier*] (ICLI)
LFDH .... Auch/Lamothe [*France ICAO location identifier*] (ICLI)
LFDI .... Libourne/Artiques De Lussac [*France ICAO location identifier*] (ICLI)
LFDJ .... Pamiers/Les Pujols [*France ICAO location identifier*] (ICLI)
LFDK .... Soulac-Sur-Mer [*France ICAO location identifier*] (ICLI)
LFDL .... Loudun [*France ICAO location identifier*] (ICLI)
LFDM .... Low Flyer, Defense Mode
LFDM .... Marmande/Virazeil [*France ICAO location identifier*] (ICLI)
LFDN .... Rochefort/Saint-Agnant [*France ICAO location identifier*] (ICLI)
LFDO .... Bordeaux/Souge [*France ICAO location identifier*] (ICLI)
LFDP .... Saint-Pierre D'Oleron [*France ICAO location identifier*] (ICLI)
LFDQ .... Castelnau-Magnoac [*France ICAO location identifier*] (ICLI)
LFDR .... La Reole/Floudes [*France ICAO location identifier*] (ICLI)
LFDS .... Sarlat/Domme [*France ICAO location identifier*] (ICLI)
LFDT .... Tarbes/Laloubere [*France ICAO location identifier*] (ICLI)
LFDU .... Lesparre/St. Laurent Du Medoc [*France ICAO location identifier*] (ICLI)
LFDV .... Couhe/Verac [*France ICAO location identifier*] (ICLI)
LFDW .... Chauvigny [*France ICAO location identifier*] (ICLI)
LFDX .... Fumel/Montayral [*France ICAO location identifier*] (ICLI)
LFDY .... Bordeaux-Yvrac [*France ICAO location identifier*] (ICLI)
LFDZ .... Condat-Sur-Vezere [*France ICAO location identifier*] (ICLI)
LFE .... Brotherhood of Locomotive Firemen and Enginemen [*Later, United Transportation Union*] [*AFL-CIO*]
LFE .... Laboratory for Electronics (DNAB)
LFE .... Laminar Flow Element [*Engineering*]
LFE .... Large Flight Envelope (MCD)
LFE .... Logarithmic Feedback Element [*Computer science*]
LFEA .... Delle-Ile [*France ICAO location identifier*] (ICLI)
LFEB .... Dinan/Trelivan [*France ICAO location identifier*] (ICLI)
LFEB .... Launch Facility Equipment Building [*Missiles*]
LFEC .... Ouessant [*France ICAO location identifier*] (ICLI)
Lfecore .... LifeCore Biomedical, Inc. [*Associated Press*] (SAG)
LFED .... Leeds Federal Svgs Bk [*NASDAQ symbol*] (TTSB)
LFED .... Leeds FSB [*NASDAQ symbol*] (SAG)
LFED .... Pontivy [*France ICAO location identifier*] (ICLI)
LFEE .... Reims [*France ICAO location identifier*] (ICLI)
LFEF .... Amboise/Dierre [*France ICAO location identifier*] (ICLI)
LFEG .... Argenton-Sur-Creuse [*France ICAO location identifier*] (ICLI)
LFEH .... Aubigny-Sur-Nere [*France ICAO location identifier*] (ICLI)
LFEI .... Briare/Chatillon [*France ICAO location identifier*] (ICLI)
LFEJ .... Chateauroux/Villers [*France ICAO location identifier*] (ICLI)
LFEK .... Issoudun/Le Fay [*France ICAO location identifier*] (ICLI)
LFEL .... Le Blanc [*France ICAO location identifier*] (ICLI)
LfelneS .... Lifeline Systems, Inc. [*Associated Press*] (SAG)
LFEM .... Montargis/Vimory [*France ICAO location identifier*] (ICLI)
LfeMd .... Life Medical Sciences [*Associated Press*] (SAG)
LfeMed .... Life Medical Sciences [*Associated Press*] (SAG)
LFEN .... Laboratorio de Fisica e Engenharia Nucleores [*Portugal*]
LFEN .... Tours/Sorigny [*France ICAO location identifier*] (ICLI)
LFEO .... Saint-Malo/Saint-Servan [*France ICAO location identifier*] (ICLI)
LFEP .... Pouilly-Maconge [*France ICAO location identifier*] (ICLI)
LFEQ .... Quiberon [*France ICAO location identifier*] (ICLI)
LfeQst .... LifeQuest Medical, Inc. [*Associated Press*] (SAG)
LFER .... Linear Free Energy Relationship
LFER .... Redon/Bains-Sur-Oust [*France ICAO location identifier*] (ICLI)
LFES .... Guiscriff-Scaer [*France ICAO location identifier*] (ICLI)
LFET .... Til-Chatel [*France ICAO location identifier*] (ICLI)
LfeTch .... Life Technologies, Inc. [*Associated Press*] (SAG)
LFETS .... Live Fire Evasive Target System [*Army*] (INF)
LFEU .... Bar-Le-Duc [*France ICAO location identifier*] (ICLI)
LfeUSA .... Life USA Holding, Inc. [*Associated Press*] (SAG)
LFEV .... Gray-Saint-Adrien [*France ICAO location identifier*] (ICLI)
LFEW .... Saulieu-Liernais [*France ICAO location identifier*] (ICLI)
LF-EX .... Life Expectancy [*Military*]
LFEX .... Nancy-Azelot [*France ICAO location identifier*] (ICLI)
LFEY .... Ile-D'Yeu/Le Grand Phare [*France ICAO location identifier*] (ICLI)
LFEZ .... Nancy-Malzeville [*France ICAO location identifier*] (ICLI)

LFF La Frestal [*France*] [*Seismograph station code, US Geological Survey*] (SEIS)
LFF Large Formation Flyer (SSD)
LFf Leading Firefighter (WDAA)
LFF Light Filter Factor
LFF Limited Fanout-Free (MHDB)
LFF Logistic Factors File (DOMA)
LFF London Film Festival
LFF Low-Frequency Filter (IAA)
LFFA CORTA (Orly Ouest) [*France ICAO location identifier*] (ICLI)
LFFB Buno-Bonnevaux [*France ICAO location identifier*] (ICLI)
LFFC Mantes-Cherence [*France ICAO location identifier*] (ICLI)
LFFD Saint-Andre-De L'Eure [*France ICAO location identifier*] (ICLI)
LFFE Enghien-Moisselles [*France ICAO location identifier*] (ICLI)
LFFET Low-Frequency Field-Effect Transistor [*Electronics*] (OA)
LFFF Paris [*France ICAO location identifier*] (ICLI)
LFFG La Ferte-Gaucher [*France ICAO location identifier*] (ICLI)
LFFH Chateau-Thierry-Belleau [*France ICAO location identifier*] (ICLI)
LFFI Ancenis [*France ICAO location identifier*] (ICLI)
LFFJ Joinville-Mussey [*France ICAO location identifier*] (ICLI)
LFFK Fontenay-Le-Conte [*France ICAO location identifier*] (ICLI)
LFFL Bailleau-Armenonville [*France ICAO location identifier*] (ICLI)
LFFM La Motte-Beuvron [*France ICAO location identifier*] (ICLI)
LFFN Brienne-Le-Chateau [*France ICAO location identifier*] (ICLI)
LFFO Tonnerre-Moulins [*France ICAO location identifier*] (ICLI)
LFFP LASER Fusion Feasibility Project [*Nuclear fusion*]
LFFP Pithiviers [*France ICAO location identifier*] (ICLI)
LFFQ La Ferte-Alais [*France ICAO location identifier*] (ICLI)
LFFR Bar-Sur-Seine [*France ICAO location identifier*] (ICLI)
LFFS Suippes [*France ICAO location identifier*] (ICLI)
LFFT Left Front Fluid Temperature [*Brake system*] [*Automotive engineering*]
LFFT Neufchateau-Roucaux [*France ICAO location identifier*] (ICLI)
LFFU Chateauneuf-Sur-Cher [*France ICAO location identifier*] (ICLI)
LFFV Vierzon-Mereau [*France ICAO location identifier*] (ICLI)
LFFW Montaigu-Saint-Georges [*France ICAO location identifier*] (ICLI)
LFFX Tournus-Cuisery [*France ICAO location identifier*] (ICLI)
LFFY Etrepagny [*France ICAO location identifier*] (ICLI)
LFFZ Sezanne-Saint-Remy [*France ICAO location identifier*] (ICLI)
LFG Landfill Gas
LFG Lead-Free Glass
LFG Lexical Functional Grammar [*Artificial intelligence*]
LFG Low-Frequency Generator
LFGA Colmar/Houssen [*France ICAO location identifier*] (ICLI)
LFGB Mulhouse/Habsheim [*France ICAO location identifier*] (ICLI)
LFGC Strasbourg/Neuhof [*France ICAO location identifier*] (ICLI)
LFGD Arbois [*France ICAO location identifier*] (ICLI)
LFGE Avallon [*France ICAO location identifier*] (ICLI)
LFGF Beaune/Challanges [*France ICAO location identifier*] (ICLI)
LFGG Belfort/Chaux [*France ICAO location identifier*] (ICLI)
LFGG Low-Frequency Gravity Gradiometer
LFGH Cosne-Sur-Loire [*France ICAO location identifier*] (ICLI)
LFGI Dijon/Val Suzon [*France ICAO location identifier*] (ICLI)
LFGJ Dole/Tavaux [*France ICAO location identifier*] (ICLI)
LFGK Joigny [*France ICAO location identifier*] (ICLI)
LFGL Lons Le Saunier/Courlaoux [*France ICAO location identifier*] (ICLI)
LFGM Montceau Les Mines/Pouilloux [*France ICAO location identifier*] (ICLI)
LFGN Paray Le Monial [*France ICAO location identifier*] (ICLI)
LFGO Pont-Sur-Yonne [*France ICAO location identifier*] (ICLI)
LFGP Saint-Florentin/Cheu [*France ICAO location identifier*] (ICLI)
LFGQ Semur-En-Auxois [*France ICAO location identifier*] (ICLI)
LFGR Doncourt-Les-Conflans [*France ICAO location identifier*] (ICLI)
LFGRD Lifeguard (ABBR)
LFGS Longuyon/Villette [*France ICAO location identifier*] (ICLI)
LFGT Sarrebourg/Buhl [*France ICAO location identifier*] (ICLI)
LFGU Sarreguemines/Neunkirch [*France ICAO location identifier*] (ICLI)
LFGV Thionville/Yutz [*France ICAO location identifier*] (ICLI)
LFGW Verdun/Rozelier [*France ICAO location identifier*] (ICLI)
LFGX Champagnole/Crotenay [*France ICAO location identifier*] (ICLI)
LFGY Saint-Die/Remoneix [*France ICAO location identifier*] (ICLI)
LFGZ Nuits-Saint-Georges [*France ICAO location identifier*] (ICLI)
LFH Left Femoral Hernia [*Medicine*]
LFH Lower Fascial Height [*Medicine*]
LFH Lunar Far Horizon (KSC)
LFHA Issoire/Le Broc [*France ICAO location identifier*] (ICLI)
LFHB Moulins/Avermes [*France ICAO location identifier*] (ICLI)
LFHC Perouges/Meximieux [*France ICAO location identifier*] (ICLI)
LFHD Pierrelatte [*France ICAO location identifier*] (ICLI)
LFHE Romans/Saint-Paul [*France ICAO location identifier*] (ICLI)
LFHF Ruoms [*France ICAO location identifier*] (ICLI)
LFHG Saint-Chamond/L'Horme [*France ICAO location identifier*] (ICLI)
LFHH Vienne/Reventin [*France ICAO location identifier*] (ICLI)
LFHI Morestel [*France ICAO location identifier*] (ICLI)
LFHJ Lyon/Corbas [*France ICAO location identifier*] (ICLI)
LFHK Camp De Canjuers [*France ICAO location identifier*] (ICLI)
LFHL Langogne/L'Esperon [*France ICAO location identifier*] (ICLI)
LFHL Low-Frequency Hearing Loss (DMAA)
LFHM Megeve [*France ICAO location identifier*] (ICLI)
LFHN Bellegarde/Vouvray [*France ICAO location identifier*] (ICLI)
LFHO Aubenas-Vals-Lanas [*France ICAO location identifier*] (ICLI)
LFHP Le Puy/Loudes [*France ICAO location identifier*] (ICLI)
LFHQ Saint-Flour/Coltines [*France ICAO location identifier*] (ICLI)
LFHR Brioude-Beaumont [*France ICAO location identifier*] (ICLI)
LFHS Bourg/Ceyreziat [*France ICAO location identifier*] (ICLI)
LFHT Ambert-Le-Poyet [*France ICAO location identifier*] (ICLI)
LFHU L'Alpe D'Huez [*France ICAO location identifier*] (ICLI)
LFHV Villefrance/Tarare [*France ICAO location identifier*] (ICLI)
LFHW Belleville-Villie-Morgon [*France ICAO location identifier*] (ICLI)
LFHX Lapalisse-Perigny [*France ICAO location identifier*] (ICLI)
LFHY Moulins/Montbeugny [*France ICAO location identifier*] (ICLI)
LFHZ Sallanches-Mont-Blanc [*France ICAO location identifier*] (ICLI)
LFI Hampton, VA [*Location identifier FAA*] (FAAL)
LFI Last Frame Indicator
LFI Let's Face It [*Later, AFLFI*] [*An association*] (EA)
LFI Levitz Furniture [*NYSE symbol*] (TTSB)
LFI Levitz Furniture, Inc. [*NYSE symbol*] (SPSG)
LFI Licensed Financial Institution
LFI Lifting Fan Intake [*Hovercraft*]
LFI Linear Function Interpolator
L-FI Live-Free, Inc. [*An association*] (EA)
LFI Long Fiber Injection
LFI Low-Frequency Inductor
LFIA Luminescence and Fluorescence Immunoassay [*Clinical chemistry*]
LFIB Belves-Saint-Pardoux [*France ICAO location identifier*] (ICLI)
LFIC Cross Corsen [*France ICAO location identifier*] (ICLI)
LFIC Landing Force Intelligence Center [*Navy*] (DNAB)
LFICS Landing Force Integrated Communications System [*Marine Corps*]
LFID Condom-Valence-Sur-Baise [*France ICAO location identifier*] (ICLI)
LFIE Cross Etel [*France ICAO location identifier*] (ICLI)
LFIF Saint-Afrique-Belmont [*France ICAO location identifier*] (ICLI)
LFIG Cassagnes-Begonhes [*France ICAO location identifier*] (ICLI)
LFIH Chalais [*France ICAO location identifier*] (ICLI)
LFIINST Life Fellow Imperial Institute [*British*] (ROG)
LFIJ Cross Jobourg [*France ICAO location identifier*] (ICLI)
LFIK Riberac-Saint-Aulaye [*France ICAO location identifier*] (ICLI)
LFIL Rion-Des-Landes [*France ICAO location identifier*] (ICLI)
LFILIE Libera Federazione Italiana Lavoratori Industrie Estrattive [*Free Italian Federation of Workers in Mining Industries*]
LFIM Low-Frequency Instruments and Measurement (MCD)
LFIM Saint Gaudens Montrejeau [*France ICAO location identifier*] (ICLI)
LFIN Cross Gris-Nez [*France ICAO location identifier*] (ICLI)
LFINT Low-Frequency Intersection
LFIP Peyresourde-Balestas [*France ICAO location identifier*] (ICLI)
LFIPA Laminated Fiberglass Insulation Producers Association [*Defunct*] (EA)
LFIR Revel-Montgey [*France ICAO location identifier*] (ICLI)
LFIRSS Louis Finkelstein Institute for Religious and Social Studies (EA)
LFISWB Loyal, Free, Industrious Society of Wheelwrights and Blacksmiths [*A union*] [*British*]
LFIT Toulouse-Bourg-Saint-Bernard [*France ICAO location identifier*] (ICLI)
LFIV Vendays-Montalivet [*France ICAO location identifier*] (ICLI)
LFIX Itxassou [*France ICAO location identifier*] (ICLI)
LFIY Saint-Jean-D'Angely [*France ICAO location identifier*] (ICLI)
LFJ Local Feed Junctor [*Telecommunications*] (NITA)
LFJ Low-Frequency Jammer
LFJG Cross La Garde [*France ICAO location identifier*] (ICLI)
LFJV Low Frequency Jet Ventilation [*Medicine*]
LFK Lufkin/Nacogdoches [*Texas*] [*Airport symbol*] (OAG)
LFK Lufkin, TX [*Location identifier FAA*] (FAAL)
LFKA Albertville [*France ICAO location identifier*] (ICLI)
LFKB Bastia/Poretta, Corse [*France ICAO location identifier*] (ICLI)
LFKC Calvi/Sainte-Catherine, Corse [*France ICAO location identifier*] (ICLI)
LFKD Sollieres-Sardieres [*France ICAO location identifier*] (ICLI)
LFKE Saint-Jean-En-Royans [*France ICAO location identifier*] (ICLI)
LFKF Figari, Sud-Corse [*France ICAO location identifier*] (ICLI)
LFKG Ghisonaccia-Alzitone [*France ICAO location identifier*] (ICLI)
LFKH Saint-Jean-D'Avelanne [*France ICAO location identifier*] (ICLI)
LFKJ Ajaccio/Campo Dell'Oro, Corse [*France ICAO location identifier*] (ICLI)
LFKL Lyon-Brindas [*France ICAO location identifier*] (ICLI)
LFKM Saint-Galmier [*France ICAO location identifier*] (ICLI)
LFKO Propriano [*France ICAO location identifier*] (ICLI)
LFKP La Tour-Du-Pin-Cessieu [*France ICAO location identifier*] (ICLI)
LFKS Solenzara, Corse [*France ICAO location identifier*] (ICLI)
LFKT Corte [*France ICAO location identifier*] (ICLI)
LFKY Belley-Peyrieu [*France ICAO location identifier*] (ICLI)
LFKZ Saint-Claude-Pratz [*France ICAO location identifier*] (ICLI)
LFL Lan Chile ADS [*NYSE symbol*] [*Formerly, Linea Aerea Nac'l. Chile ADS*]
LFL LASER Flash Lamp
LFL League for Liberty (EA)
LFL Left Frontolateral [*Medicine*] (DMAA)
LFL Length of Flowering Period [*Botany*]
LFL Lesbian Feminist Liberation (EA)
LFL Leukocyte Feeder Layer [*Medicine*] (DMAA)
LFL Libertarians for Life (EA)
LFL Linear Field Line
LFl Long Flashing Light [*Navigation signal*]
LFL Lower Flammable Limit
LFL Lower Flexibility Limit [*Environmental science*] (COE)
LFL Lutherans for Life (EA)
LFLA Auxerre/Moneteau [*France ICAO location identifier*] (ICLI)
LFLA Landing Force Logistics Afloat (MCD)
LFIAA Laut-und Formenlehre des Aegyptisch-Aramaeisch [*A publication*] (BJA)
LFLB Chambery/Aix-Les-Bains [*France ICAO location identifier*] (ICLI)
LFLC Clermont-Ferrand/Aulnat [*France ICAO location identifier*] (ICLI)
LFLD Bourges [*France ICAO location identifier*] (ICLI)
LFLE Chambery/Challes-Les-Eaux [*France ICAO location identifier*] (ICLI)

LFLEN	Leaf Length [*Botany*]
LFLF	Orleans [*France ICAO location identifier*] (ICLI)
LFLG	Grenoble/Le Versoud [*France ICAO location identifier*] (ICLI)
LFLGTH	Leaf Length [*Botany*]
LFLH	Chalon/Champforgeuil [*France ICAO location identifier*] (ICLI)
LFLI	Annemasse [*France ICAO location identifier*] (ICLI)
LFLJ	Courchevel [*France ICAO location identifier*] (ICLI)
LFLK	Lifelike (ABBR)
LFLK	Oyonnax/Arbent [*France ICAO location identifier*] (ICLI)
LFLL	Lyon/Satolas [*France ICAO location identifier*] (ICLI)
LFLM	Macon/Charnay [*France ICAO location identifier*] (ICLI)
LFLN	Lifeline (ABBR)
LFLN	Saint-Yan [*France ICAO location identifier*] (ICLI)
LFLO	Roanne/Renaison [*France ICAO location identifier*] (ICLI)
LFLOW	Linearized High-Resolution Wind-Field Flow [*Model*] [*Marine science*] (OSRA)
LFLP	Annecy/Meythet [*France ICAO location identifier*] (ICLI)
LFLPU	Libyan Federation of Labor and Professional Unions
LFLQ	Montelimar/Ancone [*France ICAO location identifier*] (ICLI)
LFLR	Saint-Rambert-D'Albon [*France ICAO location identifier*] (ICLI)
LFLS	Grenoble/Saint-Geoirs [*France ICAO location identifier*] (ICLI)
LFLS	Leafless (ABBR)
LFLSY	Lifelessly (ABBR)
LFLT	Left Front Lining Temperature [*Brake system*] [*Automotive engineering*]
LFLT	Montlucon/Domerat [*France ICAO location identifier*] (ICLI)
LFLU	Valence/Chabeuil [*France ICAO location identifier*] (ICLI)
LFLV	Vichy/Charmeil [*France ICAO location identifier*] (ICLI)
LFLW	Aurillac [*France ICAO location identifier*] (ICLI)
LFLWP	Land Forces Logistics Working Party (MCD)
LFLX	Chateauroux/Deols [*France ICAO location identifier*] (ICLI)
LFLY	Lyon/Bron [*France ICAO location identifier*] (ICLI)
LFLZ	Feurs/Chambeon [*France ICAO location identifier*] (ICLI)
LFM	Franklin and Marshall College, Lancaster, PA [*OCLC symbol*] (OCLC)
LFM	Landing Force Manual [*Marine Corps, Navy*]
LFM	LASER Feedback Microscope
LFM	LASER Force Microscope
LFM	Lateral Force Microscopy [*Morphology*]
LFM	Launch First Motion
LFM	Lieutenant Field Marshal
LFM	Limited-Area Fine-Mesh Model [*Marine science*] (OSRA)
LFM	Limited Fine Mesh
LFM	Linear Feet per Minute
LFM	Linear Frequency Modulation (CAAL)
LFM	Local File Manager
LFM	Longitudinal Field Modulator
LFM	Loss Frequency Method [*Insurance*]
LFM	Lower Figure of Merit
LFM	Low-Field Magnetometer [*Instrumentation*]
LFM	Low-Frequency Magnetic [*Field*]
LFM	Low-Frequency Modulation
LFM	Low-Powered Fan Marker (MUGU)
LFM	Lubrecht Forest [*Montana*] [*Seismograph station code, US Geological Survey Closed*] (SEIS)
LFMA	Aix-Les-Milles [*France ICAO location identifier*] (ICLI)
LFMA	Laminated Foil Manufacturers' Association [*Defunct*]
LFMB	Aix-En-Provence [*France ICAO location identifier*] (ICLI)
LFMC	Le Luc/Le Cannet [*France ICAO location identifier*] (ICLI)
LFMD	Cannes/Mandelieu [*France ICAO location identifier*] (ICLI)
LfMd	Life Medical Sciences [*Associated Press*] (SAG)
LFME	Nimes/Courbessac [*France ICAO location identifier*] (ICLI)
LFMER	Lovelace Foundation for Medical Education and Research [*Reorganized to form Lovelace Medical Foundation and Lovelace Biomedical and Environmental Research Institute*] (MCD)
LFMF	Fayence [*France ICAO location identifier*] (ICLI)
LF/MF	Low Frequency, Medium Frequency
LFMG	La Montagne Noire [*France ICAO location identifier*] (ICLI)
LFMH	Saint-Etienne/Boutheon [*France ICAO location identifier*] (ICLI)
LFMI	Istres/Le Tube [*France ICAO location identifier*] (ICLI)
LFMJ	Nice/Mont Agel [*France ICAO location identifier*] (ICLI)
LFMK	Carcassonne/Salvaza [*France ICAO location identifier*] (ICLI)
LFML	Little Flower Mission League (EA)
LFML	Marseille/Marignane [*France ICAO location identifier*] (ICLI)
LFMM	Aix-En-Provence [*France ICAO location identifier*] (ICLI)
LFMN	Nice/Cote D'Azur [*France ICAO location identifier*] (ICLI)
LFMO	Orange/Caritat [*France ICAO location identifier*] (ICLI)
LFMOP	Linear Frequency Modulation on Pulse (MCD)
LFMP	Perpignan/Rivesaltes [*France ICAO location identifier*] (ICLI)
LFM/PD	Local Flow Management/Profile Descent
LFMQ	Le Castellet [*France ICAO location identifier*] (ICLI)
LFMR	Barcelonnette/Saint-Pons [*France ICAO location identifier*] (ICLI)
LFMR	Low-Frequency Microwave Radiometer
LFMS	Ales/Deaux [*France ICAO location identifier*] (ICLI)
LFMS	Laminated Ferrite Memory System (MCD)
LFMT	Montpellier/Frejorgues [*France ICAO location identifier*] (ICLI)
LFMU	Beziers/Vias [*France ICAO location identifier*] (ICLI)
LFMV	Avignon/Caumont [*France ICAO location identifier*] (ICLI)
LFMW	Castelnaudary/Villeneuve [*France ICAO location identifier*] (ICLI)
LFMX	Chateau-Arnoux/Saint-Auban [*France ICAO location identifier*] (ICLI)
LFMY	Salon [*France ICAO location identifier*] (ICLI)
LFMZ	Lezignan-Corbieres [*France ICAO location identifier*] (ICLI)
LFN	Lactoferrin [*Biochemistry*] (MAE)
LFN	Logical File Name
LFN	Logical File Number [*Computer science*] (MCD)

LFN	Long Filename (PCM)
LFN	Louisburg, NC [*Location identifier FAA*] (FAAL)
LFNA	Gap/Tallard [*France ICAO location identifier*] (ICLI)
LFNB	Mende/Brenoux [*France ICAO location identifier*] (ICLI)
LFNC	Mont-Dauphin/Saint-Crepin [*France ICAO location identifier*] (ICLI)
LFND	Pont-Saint-Esprit [*France ICAO location identifier*] (ICLI)
LFNE	Salon/Eyguieres [*France ICAO location identifier*] (ICLI)
LFNF	Vinon [*France ICAO location identifier*] (ICLI)
LFNG	Montpellier/L'Or [*France ICAO location identifier*] (ICLI)
LFNGFT	Landing Force Naval Gunfire Team
LFNH	Carpentras [*France ICAO location identifier*] (ICLI)
LFNI	Conqueyrac [*France ICAO location identifier*] (ICLI)
LFNJ	Aspres-Sur-Buech [*France ICAO location identifier*] (ICLI)
LFNK	Vars-Les-Crosses-Et-Les-Tronches [*France ICAO location identifier*] (ICLI)
LFNL	Saint-Martin-De-Londres [*France ICAO location identifier*] (ICLI)
LFNM	La Mole [*France ICAO location identifier*] (ICLI)
LFNO	Florac-Sainte-Enimie [*France ICAO location identifier*] (ICLI)
LFNP	Pezenas-Nizas [*France ICAO location identifier*] (ICLI)
LFNQ	Mont-Louis-La-Quillane [*France ICAO location identifier*] (ICLI)
LFNR	Berre-La-Fare [*France ICAO location identifier*] (ICLI)
LFNS	Leafiness (ABBR)
LFNS	Low-Frequency Navigation System (NG)
LFNS	Sisteron-Theze [*France ICAO location identifier*] (ICLI)
LFNT	Avignon-Pujaut [*France ICAO location identifier*] (ICLI)
LFNT	Low Frequency Intersection (FAAC)
LFNU	Uzes [*France ICAO location identifier*] (ICLI)
LFNV	Valreas-Visan [*France ICAO location identifier*] (ICLI)
LFNW	Puivert [*France ICAO location identifier*] (ICLI)
LFNX	Bedarieux-La-Tour-Sur-Orb [*France ICAO location identifier*] (ICLI)
LFNY	Saint-Etienne-En-Devoluy [*France ICAO location identifier*] (ICLI)
LFNZ	Le Mazet-De-Romanin [*France ICAO location identifier*] (ICLI)
LFO	Large Follow-On
LFO	LASER/Fiber-Optic (MCD)
LFO	Light Fuel Oil (BARN)
LFO	Low-Frequency Oscillator
LFOA	Avord [*France ICAO location identifier*] (ICLI)
LFOA	Last Frame of Action [*Cinematography*] (WDMC)
LFOB	Beauvais/Tille [*France ICAO location identifier*] (ICLI)
LFOC	Crateaudun [*France ICAO location identifier*] (ICLI)
LFOC	Landing Force Operation Center [*Navy*] (CAAL)
LFOC	Lea-Francis Owners Club [*British*] (EAIO)
LFOD	Saumur/Saint-Florent [*France ICAO location identifier*] (ICLI)
LFOE	Evreux/Fauville [*France ICAO location identifier*] (ICLI)
LFOF	Alencon/Valframbert [*France ICAO location identifier*] (ICLI)
LFOG	Flers/Saint-Paul [*France ICAO location identifier*] (ICLI)
LFOH	Le Havre/Octeville [*France ICAO location identifier*] (ICLI)
LFOI	Abbeville [*France ICAO location identifier*] (ICLI)
LFOJ	Orleans/Bricy [*France ICAO location identifier*] (ICLI)
LFOK	Chalons/Vatry [*France ICAO location identifier*] (ICLI)
LFOL	L'Aigle/Saint-Michel [*France ICAO location identifier*] (ICLI)
LFOM	Lessay [*France ICAO location identifier*] (ICLI)
LFOM	Low-Frequency Outer Marker (MSA)
LFON	Dreux/Vernouillet [*France ICAO location identifier*] (ICLI)
LFOO	Les Sables D'Olonne/Talmont [*France ICAO location identifier*] (ICLI)
LFOP	Landing and Ferry Operations Panel [*NASA*] (NASA)
LFOP	Rouen/Boos [*France ICAO location identifier*] (ICLI)
LFOQ	Blois/Le Breuil [*France ICAO location identifier*] (ICLI)
LFOR	Chartres/Champhol [*France ICAO location identifier*] (ICLI)
LFORM	Landing Force Operational Reserve Material [*Navy*] (NVT)
LFOS	Launch and Flight Operations System
LFOS	Saint-Valery/Vittefleur [*France ICAO location identifier*] (ICLI)
LFOT	Tours/Saint-Symphorien [*France ICAO location identifier*] (ICLI)
LFOU	Cholet/Le Pontreau [*France ICAO location identifier*] (ICLI)
LFOV	Large Field of View [*Radiology*] (DAVI)
LFOV	Laval/Entrammes [*France ICAO location identifier*] (ICLI)
LFOW	Saint-Quentin/Roupy [*France ICAO location identifier*] (ICLI)
LFOX	Etampes/Mondesir [*France ICAO location identifier*] (ICLI)
LFOY	Le Havre/Saint-Romain [*France ICAO location identifier*] (ICLI)
LFOZ	Orleans/Saint-Denis-De-L'Hotel [*France ICAO location identifier*] (ICLI)
LFP	Labor-Force Participation
LFP	Large Flat Plate
LFP	LASER Flash Photolysis (MEC)
LFP	Late Flight Plan
LFP	Left Frontoposterior [*A fetal position*] [*Obstetrics*]
LFP	LFP Holdings, Inc. [*Toronto Stock Exchange symbol*]
LFP	Liberala Folkpartiet [*Liberal People's Party*] [*Finland Political party*] (PPE)
LFP	Libraries for Prisons [*An association*] (EA)
LFP	Listen for Pleasure [*Audio books*]
LFP	Livestock Feed Program
LFP	Local Field Potential [*Electrophysiology*]
LFP	Low-Frequency Prediction (USDC)
LFPA	Persan-Beaumont [*France ICAO location identifier*] (ICLI)
LFPAG	Live Firing Program Analysis Group [*Military*] (CAAL)
LFPB	Paris/Le Bourget [*France ICAO location identifier*] (ICLI)
LFPC	Creil [*France ICAO location identifier*] (ICLI)
LFPD	Bernay/Saint-Martin [*France ICAO location identifier*] (ICLI)
LFPE	Meaux/Esbly [*France ICAO location identifier*] (ICLI)
LFPEF	Low-Frequency Pulsed Electromagnetic Field
LFPER	Leaf Persistence [*Botany*]
LFPF	Beynes/Thiverval [*France ICAO location identifier*] (ICLI)
LFPG	Paris/Charles-De-Gaulle [*France ICAO location identifier*] (ICLI)
LFPH	Chelles/Le Pin [*France ICAO location identifier*] (ICLI)

LFPI .... Paris/Issy-Les-Moulineaux [*France ICAO location identifier*] (ICLI)
LFPJ .... Taverny [*France ICAO location identifier*] (ICLI)
LFPK .... Coulommiers/Voisins [*France ICAO location identifier*] (ICLI)
LFPL .... Lewis Flight Propulsion Laboratory [*NASA*]
LFPL .... Lognes/Emerainville [*France ICAO location identifier*] (ICLI)
LFPM .... Melun/Villaroche [*France ICAO location identifier*] (ICLI)
LFPN .... Toussus-Le-Noble [*France ICAO location identifier*] (ICLI)
LFPO .... Paris/Orly [*France ICAO location identifier*] (ICLI)
LFPP .... Le Plessis-Belleville [*France ICAO location identifier*] (ICLI)
LFPPV .... Low-Frequency Positive Pressure Ventilation [*Medicine*] (DMAA)
LFPQ .... Fontenay-Tresigny [*France ICAO location identifier*] (ICLI)
LFPR .... Guayancourt [*France ICAO location identifier*] (ICLI)
LFPRL .... Lewis Flight Propulsion Research Laboratory [*NASA*] (MUGU)
LFPS .... Licentiate of the Faculty of Physicians and Surgeons [*British*]
LFPS .... Low-Frequency Phase Shifter [*Telecommunications*]
LFPS .... Paris [*France ICAO location identifier*] (ICLI)
LFPSG .... Licentiate of the Faculty of Physicians and Surgeons, Glasgow (ROG)
LFPT .... Pontoise/Cormeilles-En-Vexin [*France ICAO location identifier*] (ICLI)
LFPU .... Moret/Episy [*France ICAO location identifier*] (ICLI)
LFPUB .... Leaf Pubescence [*Botany*]
LFPV .... Villacoublay/Velizy [*France ICAO location identifier*] (ICLI)
LFPW .... Low-Frequency Plasma Wave
LFPW .... Paris, Centre Meteorologique [*France ICAO location identifier*] (ICLI)
LFPX .... Chavenay/Villepreux [*France ICAO location identifier*] (ICLI)
LFPY .... Bretigny-Sur-Orge [*France ICAO location identifier*] (ICLI)
LFPZ .... Saint-Cyre-L'Ecole [*France ICAO location identifier*] (ICLI)
LFQ .... Light Foot Quantizer
LFQ .... Limited Flying Quality
LFQA .... Reims/Prunay [*France ICAO location identifier*] (ICLI)
LFQB .... Troyes/Barberey [*France ICAO location identifier*] (ICLI)
LFQC .... Luneville/Croismare [*France ICAO location identifier*] (ICLI)
LFQD .... Arras/Roclincourt [*France ICAO location identifier*] (ICLI)
LFQE .... Etain/Rouvres [*France ICAO location identifier*] (ICLI)
LFQF .... Autun/Bellevue [*France ICAO location identifier*] (ICLI)
LFQG .... Nevers/Fourchambault [*France ICAO location identifier*] (ICLI)
LFQH .... Chatillon-Sur-Seine [*France ICAO location identifier*] (ICLI)
LFQI .... Cambrai/Epinoy [*France ICAO location identifier*] (ICLI)
LFQJ .... Maubeuge/Elesmes [*France ICAO location identifier*] (ICLI)
LFQK .... Chalons/Ecury-Sur-Coole [*France ICAO location identifier*] (ICLI)
LFQL .... Lens/Benifontaine [*France ICAO location identifier*] (ICLI)
LFQM .... Besancon-La-Veze [*France ICAO location identifier*] (ICLI)
LFQN .... Saint-Omer/Wizernes [*France ICAO location identifier*] (ICLI)
LFQO .... Lille/Marcq-En-Baroeul [*France ICAO location identifier*] (ICLI)
LFQP .... Phalsbourg/Bourscheid [*France ICAO location identifier*] (ICLI)
LFQQ .... Lille/Lesquin [*France ICAO location identifier*] (ICLI)
LFQR .... Romilly-Sur-Seine [*France ICAO location identifier*] (ICLI)
LFQS .... Vitry-En-Artois [*France ICAO location identifier*] (ICLI)
LFQT .... Merville/Calonne [*France ICAO location identifier*] (ICLI)
LFQU .... Sarre-Union [*France ICAO location identifier*] (ICLI)
LFQV .... Charleville/Mezieres [*France ICAO location identifier*] (ICLI)
LFQW .... Vesoul-Frotey [*France ICAO location identifier*] (ICLI)
LFQY .... Saverne-Steinbourg [*France ICAO location identifier*] (ICLI)
LFQZ .... Dieuze-Gueblange [*France ICAO location identifier*] (ICLI)
L FR .... Franc [*Monetary unit*] [*Luxembourg*]
LFR .... Inshore Fire Support Ship [*Navy symbol*]
LFR .... Laboratory Facilities Request (MCD)
LFR .... La Fria [*Venezuela*] [*Airport symbol*] (OAG)
LFR .... Laminar-Flow Reactor [*Engineering*]
LFR .... LASERgraphics Film Recorder (PCM)
L Fr .... Law French (DLA)
LFR .... Leafier (ABBR)
LFR .... Lifer (ABBR)
LFR .... Linear Flow Reactor [*Chemical engineering*]
LFR .... Line Frequency Rejection (IAA)
LFR .... Logical Forms Recognition [*Computer science*]
LFR .... Lowest Fare Routing [*Travel industry*]
LFR .... Low-Flux Reactor
LFR .... Low Frequency Radio Range (TAG)
LFR .... Low-Frequency Range (MCD)
LFR .... Lymphoid Follicular Reticulosis [*Medicine*] (DB)
LFr .... Saint Mary Parish Library, Franklin, LA [*Library symbol Library of Congress*] (LCLS)
LFRA .... Angers/Avrille [*France ICAO location identifier*] (ICLI)
LFRA .... League of Federal Recreation Associations (EA)
LFRA .... Leatherhead Food Research Association [*British*] (ARC)
LFRAP .... Long Feeder Route Analysis Program [*Bell System*]
LFRB .... Brest/Guipavas [*France ICAO location identifier*] (ICLI)
LFRC .... Cherbourg/Maupertus [*France ICAO location identifier*] (ICLI)
LFRC .... Latex Foam Rubber Council [*Defunct*] (EA)
LFRC .... Laurentian Forest Research Center [*Canadian Forestry Service*] [*Research center*] (RCD)
LFRC .... Library Fundraising Resource Center [*American Library Association*]
LFRD .... Dinard/Pleurtuit-Saint-Malo [*France ICAO location identifier*] (ICLI)
LFRD .... Lot Fraction Reliability Deviation [*Quality control*]
LFRE .... La Baule/Escoublac [*France ICAO location identifier*] (ICLI)
LFRED .... Liquid-Fueled Ramjet Engine Demonstration [*Navy*] (MCD)
LFRF .... Granville [*France ICAO location identifier*] (ICLI)
LFRG .... Deauville/Saint-Gatien [*France ICAO location identifier*] (ICLI)
LFRH .... Lorient/Lann-Bihoue [*France ICAO location identifier*] (ICLI)
LFRI .... La Roche-Sur-Yon/Les Ajoncs [*France ICAO location identifier*] (ICLI)
LFRJ .... Landivisiau [*France ICAO location identifier*] (ICLI)
LFRJ .... Liquid-Fueled Ramjet [*Navy*] (MCD)
LFRK .... Caen/Carpiquet [*France ICAO location identifier*] (ICLI)
LFRL .... Lanveoc/Poulmic [*France ICAO location identifier*] (ICLI)
LFRM .... Le Mans/Arnage [*France ICAO location identifier*] (ICLI)
LFRN .... Lavender Families Resource Network [*An association*] (EA)
LFRN .... Rennes/Saint-Jacques [*France ICAO location identifier*] (ICLI)
LFRO .... Lannion/Servel [*France ICAO location identifier*] (ICLI)
LFRP .... Ploermel-Loyat [*France ICAO location identifier*] (ICLI)
LFRQ .... Quimper/Pluguffan [*France ICAO location identifier*] (ICLI)
LFRR .... Brest [*France ICAO location identifier*] (ICLI)
LFRR .... Low-Frequency Radio Range (MCD)
LFRS .... Nantes/Chateau Bougon [*France ICAO location identifier*] (ICLI)
LFRSB .... Loose Fuel-Rod Shipping Basket (GAAI)
LFRT .... Saint-Brieuc Armor [*France ICAO location identifier*] (ICLI)
LFrtW .... Washington Parish Library, Franklinton, LA [*Library symbol Library of Congress*] (LCLS)
LFRU .... Morlaix/Ploujean [*France ICAO location identifier*] (ICLI)
LFRV .... Vannes/Meucon [*France ICAO location identifier*] (ICLI)
LFRW .... Avranches/Le Val Saint-Pere [*France ICAO location identifier*] (ICLI)
LFRX .... Brest [*France ICAO location identifier*] (ICLI)
LFRY .... Cherbourg [*France ICAO location identifier*] (ICLI)
LFRZ .... Saint-Nazaire/Montoir [*France ICAO location identifier*] (ICLI)
LFS .... Amphibious Fire Support Ship [*Navy symbol*]
LFS .... Labour Force Survey [*Canada*]
LFS .... Lancaster Finishing School [*British military*] (DMA)
LFS .... LASER Fluorescence Spectroscopy
LFS .... Launch Facility Simulator
LFS .... League of Filipino Students
LFS .... Leather Finishers' Society [*A union*] [*British*]
LFS .... Libertarian Futurist Society (EA)
LFS .... Licentiate of the Faculty of Architects and Surveyors [*British*] (DBQ)
LFS .... Li-Fraumeni Syndrome [*Oncology*]
LFS .... Liquid Filtration System
LFS .... Liquid Flow System
LFS .... Liver Function Series [*Clinical chemistry*]
LFS .... Local Format Storage
LFS .... Logical File Structure [*Computer science*] (OA)
LFS .... Logical File System (IAA)
LFS .... Logic Fault Simulator [*Computer science*]
LFS .... Logistics Feasibility System
LFS .... Logistics/Ferry Station
LFS .... Loop Feedback Signal
LFS .... Low-Frequency Stimulation [*Neurophysiology*]
LFS .... Luftfahrzeug Service - Aircraft Service [*Austria ICAO designator*] (FAAC)
LFSA .... Besancon/Thise [*France ICAO location identifier*] (ICLI)
LFSA .... Logistical Force Structure Assessment (MCD)
LFSB .... Bale/Mulhouse [*France/Switzerland*] [*ICAO location identifier*] (ICLI)
LFSB .... LFS Bancorp [*NASDAQ symbol*] (SAG)
LFS Bcp .... LFS Bancorp [*Associated Press*] (SAG)
LFSC .... Colmar/Meyenheim [*France ICAO location identifier*] (ICLI)
LFSC .... Limited First-Strike Capability
LFSC .... Louisville Fear Survey for Children [*Psychology*]
LFSCWW .... Live Food Singles Club - World Wide [*Defunct*] (EA)
LFSD .... Dijon/Longvic [*France ICAO location identifier*] (ICLI)
LFSE .... Epinal/Dogneville [*France ICAO location identifier*] (ICLI)
LFSF .... Metz/Frescaty [*France ICAO location identifier*] (ICLI)
LFSG .... Epinal/Mirecourt [*France ICAO location identifier*] (ICLI)
LFSH .... Haguenau [*France ICAO location identifier*] (ICLI)
LFSI .... Saint-Dizier/Robinson [*France ICAO location identifier*] (ICLI)
LFSID .... Local Form Session Identifier (ACRL)
LFSJ .... Sedan/Douzy [*France ICAO location identifier*] (ICLI)
LFSK .... Vitry-Le-Francois/Vauclerc [*France ICAO location identifier*] (ICLI)
LFSL .... Toul/Rosieres [*France ICAO location identifier*] (ICLI)
LFSM .... Montbeliard/Courcelles [*France ICAO location identifier*] (ICLI)
LFSMT/S .... Liquid Fuel Systems Maintenance Technician/Specialist [*Aerospace*] (AAG)
LFSN .... Nancy/Essey [*France ICAO location identifier*] (ICLI)
LFSO .... Nancy/Ochey [*France ICAO location identifier*] (ICLI)
LFSP .... Landing Force Support Party [*Navy*] (ANA)
LFSP .... Pontarlier [*France ICAO location identifier*] (ICLI)
LFSQ .... Belfort/Fontaine [*France ICAO location identifier*] (ICLI)
LFSR .... Linear Feedback Shift Register [*Computer science*] (CIST)
LFSR .... Reims/Champagne [*France ICAO location identifier*] (ICLI)
LFSS .... Landing Force Support Ship [*Navy*]
LFSS .... Launch Facility Security System [*NASA*] (KSC)
LFST .... Largest Feasible Steerable Telescope
LFST .... Lifestyle (ABBR)
LFST .... Strasbourg/Entzheim [*France ICAO location identifier*] (ICLI)
LFSTK .... Leafstalk (ABBR)
LFSU .... Rolampont [*France ICAO location identifier*] (ICLI)
LFSV .... Landing Force Support Vehicle (MCD)
LFSV .... Lifesaver (ABBR)
LFSV .... Pont-Saint-Vincent [*France ICAO location identifier*] (ICLI)
LFSW .... Epernay/Plivot [*France ICAO location identifier*] (ICLI)
LFSW .... Landing Force Support Weapon
LFSX .... Luxeuil/Saint-Sauveur [*France ICAO location identifier*] (ICLI)
LFSY .... Chaumont-La Vendue [*France ICAO location identifier*] (ICLI)
LFSZ .... Lifesize (ABBR)
lf sz .... Life Size (VRA)
LFSZ .... Vittel/Champ De Courses [*France ICAO location identifier*] (ICLI)
LFT .... Aerolift Philippines Corp. [*ICAO designator*] (FAAC)
LFT .... Ladd-Franklin Theory [*Color vision*]
LFT .... Lafayette [*Louisiana*] [*Airport symbol*] (OAG)
LFT .... Lafayette [*Diocesan abbreviation*] [*Indiana*] (TOCD)
LFT .... Lafayette, LA [*Location identifier FAA*] (FAAL)
LFT .... Laminar Flow Torch [*For plasma generation*]
LFT .... LASER Flash Tube

LFT	Late Finish Time
LFT	Latest Finish Time
LFT	Latex Fixation Test [*Medicine*]
LFT	Latex Flocculation Test [*Clinical chemistry*]
LFT	Launch Facility Trainer
LFT	Law Foundation of Tasmania [*Australia*]
LFT	Leafiest (ABBR)
LFT	Leaflet (ADA)
LFT	Leap-Frog Test
LFT	Left (ABBR)
lft	Left (VRA)
LFT	Left Frontotransverse [*A fetal position*] [*Obstetrics*]
LFT	Left Half Indicators, Off Test (SAA)
LFT	Lifting (MSA)
LFT	Ligand-Field Theory [*Physical chemistry*]
LFT	Light Fire Team [*Military*] (CINC)
LFT	Linear Flash Tube
LFT	Linear Foot (ADA)
LFT	Live Fire Test
LFT	Liver Function Test [*Medicine*]
LFT	Long-Fiber Thermoplastic
LFT	Low-Frequency Tetanus [*Medicine*] (DMAA)
LFT	Low-Frequency Transduction
LFT	Low-Frequency Transfer [*Sex factor*] (DB)
L/FT^2	Lumens per Square Foot (WDAA)
LFTA	Low-Frequency Timing Assembly (IAA)
LFT & E	Live Fire Test and Evaluation [*Required testing for major weapon system and munition programs*] [*Military*] (RDA)
LFTC	Landing Force Training Command [*Navy*] (NVT)
LFTC	Toulon [*France ICAO location identifier*] (ICLI)
LFTCPAC	Landing Force Training Command, Pacific [*Navy*] (DNAB)
LFTDWP	Land Force Tactical Doctrine Working Party [*NASA*] (MCD)
LFTEG	Liquid-Fuelled Thermo-Electric Generator (PDAA)
LFTF	Cuers/Pierrefeu [*France ICAO location identifier*] (ICLI)
LFTF	Liftoff (ABBR)
LFTH	Hyeres/Le Palyvestre [*France ICAO location identifier*] (ICLI)
LFTHDD	Lefthanded (ABBR)
LFTHDY	Lefthandedly (ABBR)
LFTINS	Loftiness (ABBR)
LFTIR	Loftier (ABBR)
LFTIT	Loftiest (ABBR)
LFTM	Lifetime (ABBR)
LFTN	La Grand'Combe [*France ICAO location identifier*] (ICLI)
LFTOV	Leftover (ABBR)
LFtp	Library Program, Cataloging Department, Recreation Service, Fort Polk, LA [*Library symbol Library of Congress*] (LCLS)
LFTPR	Long Fiber Thermoplastic Resin
LFTR	Toulon/Saint-Mandrier [*France ICAO location identifier*] (ICLI)
LFTS	Toulon [*France ICAO location identifier*] (ICLI)
LFTT	Leftist (ABBR)
LFTU	Frejus/Saint-Raphael [*France ICAO location identifier*] (ICLI)
LFTU	Landing Force Training Unit [*Marine Corps*]
LFTW	Nimes/Garons [*France ICAO location identifier*] (ICLI)
LFTWF	Luftwaffe (ABBR)
LFTWG	Leftwing (ABBR)
LFTWR	Leftwinger (ABBR)
LFTY	Lofty (ABBR)
LFU	Least Frequency Unit (NITA)
LFU	Least Frequently Used [*Computer science*]
LFU	Leonhartsberger Flugunternchmen GmbH [*Austria ICAO designator*] (FAAC)
LFU	LFU Leonhartsberger Flugunternehmen Gesellschaft MbH [*Austria*] [*FAA designator*] (FAAC)
LFU	Lipid Fluidity Unit (DB)
LFU	Lunar Flying Unit [*NASA*]
LFUS	Littelfuse, Inc. [*NASDAQ symbol*] (SAG)
LFUSS	Landing Force Organizational Systems Study
LFUSW	Littelfuse Inc. Wrrt'A' [*NASDAQ symbol*] (TTSB)
LFV	Large Field of View [*Radiology*] (DAVI)
LFV	Lassa-Fever Virus
LFV	Low-Frequency Vibration
LFV	Lunar Flying Vehicle [*NASA*]
LFV	Northhampton, MA [*Location identifier FAA*] (FAAL)
LFVLF	Low Frequency, Very Low Frequency (IAA)
LFVM	Miquelon [*France ICAO location identifier*] (ICLI)
LFVO	Library Foundation for Voluntary Organizations [*Defunct*] (EA)
LFVP	Saint-Pierre, Saint-Pierre-Et Miquelon [*France ICAO location identifier*] (ICLI)
LFW	Linear Friction Welding [*Environmental science*]
LFW	Lome [*Togo*] [*Airport symbol*] (OAG)
LFW	Looking for Work
LFWB	Sccom Sud-Ouest [*France ICAO location identifier*] (ICLI)
LFWID	Length of Leaf at Widest Portion [*Botany*]
LFWK	Lifework (ABBR)
LFX	Live Fire Exercise [*Army*] (INF)
LFX	Live-Fire Exercises [*Army*] (INF)
LFXA	Amberieu [*France ICAO location identifier*] (ICLI)
LFXB	Saintes/Thenac [*France ICAO location identifier*] (ICLI)
LFXC	Contrexeville [*France ICAO location identifier*] (ICLI)
LFXD	Doullens/Lucheux [*France ICAO location identifier*] (ICLI)
LFXE	Camp De Mourmelon [*France ICAO location identifier*] (ICLI)
LFXF	Limoges/Romanet [*France ICAO location identifier*] (ICLI)
LFXG	Camp De Bitche [*France ICAO location identifier*] (ICLI)
LFXH	Camp Du Valdahon [*France ICAO location identifier*] (ICLI)
LFXI	Apt/Saint-Christol [*France ICAO location identifier*] (ICLI)
LFXJ	Bordeaux [*France ICAO location identifier*] (ICLI)
LFXK	Camp De Suippes [*France ICAO location identifier*] (ICLI)
LFXL	Mailly-Le-Camp [*France ICAO location identifier*] (ICLI)
LFXM	Mourmelon [*France ICAO location identifier*] (ICLI)
LFXN	Narbonne [*France ICAO location identifier*] (ICLI)
LFXO	Tours/Cinq-Mars La Pile [*France ICAO location identifier*] (ICLI)
LFXP	Camp De Sissonne [*France ICAO location identifier*] (ICLI)
LFXQ	Camp De Coetquidan [*France ICAO location identifier*] (ICLI)
LFXR	Rochefort/Soubise [*France ICAO location identifier*] (ICLI)
LFXS	Camp De La Courtine [*France ICAO location identifier*] (ICLI)
LFXT	Camp De Caylus [*France ICAO location identifier*] (ICLI)
LFXU	Les Mureaux [*France ICAO location identifier*] (ICLI)
LFXV	Lyon/Mont-Verdun [*France ICAO location identifier*] (ICLI)
LFXW	Camp Du Larzac [*France ICAO location identifier*] (ICLI)
LFY	Leafy (ABBR)
LFYA	Drachenbronn [*France ICAO location identifier*] (ICLI)
LFYD	Damblain [*France ICAO location identifier*] (ICLI)
LFYF	Centre Meteorologique de Concentration et de Diffusion, French Air Force [*France ICAO location identifier*] (ICLI)
LFYG	Cambrai/Niergnies [*France ICAO location identifier*] (ICLI)
LFYH	Broye-Les-Pesmes [*France ICAO location identifier*] (ICLI)
LFYL	Lure/Malbouhans [*France ICAO location identifier*] (ICLI)
LFYM	Marigny-Le-Grand [*France ICAO location identifier*] (ICLI)
LFYO	Villacoublay [*France ICAO location identifier*] (ICLI)
LFYR	Romorantin/Pruniers [*France ICAO location identifier*] (ICLI)
LFYS	Sainte-Leocadie [*France ICAO location identifier*] (ICLI)
LFYT	Saint-Simon/Clastres [*France ICAO location identifier*] (ICLI)
LFYX	Paris [*France ICAO location identifier*] (ICLI)
LFZ	Laminar Flow Zone
LG	Guidotti & C. [*Italy*] [*Research code symbol*]
LG	Laban Guild [*Formerly, LAMG*] (EA)
LG	Laboratory of Genetics (GNE)
LG	Laclede Gas [*NYSE symbol*] (TTSB)
LG	Laclede Gas Co. [*NYSE symbol*] (SPSG)
LG	Lady [*of the Order of the*] Garter (BARN)
LG	Lagoon [*Maps and charts*] (ROG)
LG	Landed Gentry
LG	Landgericht [*Regional Court*] [*German*] (ILCA)
L/G	Land Grant (DLA)
LG	Landing Gear [*Aircraft*]
LG	Landing Ground [*Navy*]
LG	Landing Group [*Navy*] (NVT)
LG	Lane Grader [*Slang for an army instructor*] (VNW)
LG	Language [*Online database field identifier*]
LG	Large
LG	Large Grain
LG	Laryngectomy [*Medicine*] (MAE)
LG	LASER Gyro (MCD)
LG	Lateral Gastrocnemius
LG	Launcher Group [*Army*]
LG	Law Glossary (DLA)
LG	Leathercraft Guild (EA)
LG	Left Gluteus [*Medicine*]
LG	Left Guard [*Football*]
LG	Leg (IAA)
LG	Leichtgeschuetz [*Light gun for airborne operations*] [*German military - World War II*]
LG	Length (MSA)
LG	Leucylglycine (DB)
LG	Level Gauge
LG	Lewis Gun
LG	Lieutenant General [*British*] (ROG)
LG	Life Guards [*Military unit*] [*British*]
LG	Light Green
LG	Light Gun
LG	Linear Gate
LG	Line Generator [*Computer science*]
LG	Line Graph (OA)
LG	Line-to-Ground (IAA)
LG	Linguogingival [*Dentistry*]
LG	Lining
LG	Linkage Group [*Genetics*] (OA)
LG	Lipoglycopeptide (DB)
LG	Liquid Gas
LG	Liquid Gold (WDAA)
LG	[*The*] Literary Guild
LG	Little Guides [*A publication*]
LG	Local Government (ADA)
LG	Loganiar Ltd. [*British*]
LG	Logistics Group [*Military*]
LG	Long (KSC)
LG	Longold Resources, Inc. [*Vancouver Stock Exchange symbol*]
LG	Longwood Gardens [*Kennett Square, PA*]
LG	Loop Gain
LG	Low German [*Language, etc.*]
LG	Low Glucose [*Medicine*]
LG	Lumen Gentium [*Dogmatic Constitution on the Church*] [*Vatican II document*]
LG	Lymph Glands [*Medicine*]
LGA	Elgaz [*Poland ICAO designator*] (FAAC)
LGA	LaGuardia Airport [*New York*] (CDAI)
LGA	Large for Gestational Age [*Pediatrics*]
LGA	LGA: Local Government Administration [*A publication*]
LGA	Light-Gun Amplifier
LGA	Local Government Administration

LGA	Local Government Area (ADA)
LGA	Local Government Audit [British]
LgA	Lodging Allowance [British military] (DMA)
LGA	Low-Gain Antenna
LGA	New York [New York] La Guardia [Airport symbol] (OAG)
LGAANSW	Local Government Auditors' Association of New South Wales [Australia]
LGAB	Local Government Advisory Board [Tasmania, Australia]
LGAB	Local Government Auditors' Board [Queensland, Australia]
LGAC	Athinai [Greece] [ICAO location identifier] (ICLI)
LgacySft	Legacy Software, Inc. [Associated Press] (SAG)
LGAD	Andravida [Greece] [ICAO location identifier] (ICLI)
LGAES	Lesbian and Gay Associated Engineers and Scientists [Later, NOGLSTP] (EA)
LGAF	Light Ground-Attack Fighter
LGAG	Agrinion [Greece] [ICAO location identifier] (ICLI)
LGAG	Luggage (ABBR)
LGAL	Alexandroupolis [Greece] [ICAO location identifier] (ICLI)
LGAM	Amphiali [Greece] [ICAO location identifier] (ICLI)
LGAM	Lexington Global Asset Managers, Inc. [NASDAQ symbol] (SAG)
LGAM	Lexington Global Assets Mgrs [NASDAQ symbol] (TTSB)
LG&E	Louisville Gas and Electric Co. (EFIS)
LGANSW	Local Government Association of New South Wales [Australia]
LGANT	Local Government Association of the Northern Territory [Australia]
LGAR	Ladies of the Grand Army of the Republic (EA)
LGAS	Louisville Gas & Electric Co. [NASDAQ symbol] (SAG)
LGAS	Low-G Accelerometer System [NASA]
LGASA	Local Government Association of South Australia
LGASP	Louiseville G&E 5% Pfd [NASDAQ symbol] (TTSB)
LGAT	Athinai [Greece] [ICAO location identifier] (ICLI)
LGAX	Alexandria [Greece] [ICAO location identifier] (ICLI)
L Gaz	Law Gazette [A publication] (DLA)
LGB	Landry-Guillain-Barre (Syndrome) [Medicine]
LGB	LASER-Guided Bomb
LGB	Lateral Geniculate Body
LGB	Legible (ABBR)
LGB	Local Government Board
LGB	Long Beach [California] [Airport symbol] (OAG)
LGB	Long Beach, CA [Location identifier FAA] (FAAL)
LGBA	Lesbian and Gay Bands of America (EA)
LGBC	Local Government Boundaries Commission [New South Wales, Australia]
LGBCE	Local Government Boundary Commission for England
LGBL	Nea Anghialos [Greece] [ICAO location identifier] (ICLI)
LGBO	Local Government Board Office [British]
LGBPM	Lesbian, Gay, and Bisexual People in Medicine (EA)
LGBR	Loganberry (ABBR)
LGBRPCV	Lesbian, Gay, and Bisexual Returned Peace Corps Volunteers (EA)
LGBRU	Lugubrious (ABBR)
LGBRUY	Lugubriously (ABBR)
LGBS	Landry-Guillain-Barre Syndrome [Medicine] (DMAA)
LGBT	Legibility (ABBR)
LGBT	Lesbian, Gay, Bisexual, and Transgendered [Lifestyle classifications]
LGBY	Legibly (ABBR)
LGC	Laboratory of the Government Chemist [Research center British] (IRC)
LGC	La Grange, GA [Location identifier FAA] (FAAL)
LGC	Lakewood Golf Course [California] [Seismograph station code, US Geological Survey] (SEIS)
LGC	Large Diameter Gravity Corer [Nuclear energy] (NUCP)
LGC	Large-Probe Gas Chromatograph [NASA]
LGC	Launch Guidance Computer
LGC	Laurentian Group Corp. [Toronto Stock Exchange symbol]
LGC	Leafy Greens Council (EA)
LGC	Left Giant Cell [Medicine] (STED)
LGC	Line Group Controller (ACRL)
LGC	LM [Lunar Module] Guidance Computer [NASA]
LGC	Local Government Center [Database producer] (EA)
LGC	Local Government Chronicle [1855] [A publication] (DLA)
LGC	Local Government Commission [Victoria, Australia]
LGC	Local Government Council
LGC	Logic (MSA)
LGC	Lord Great Chamberlain [British A publication] (DLA)
LGC	Lorry with Gas Containers [British]
LGC	Lunar Gas Chromatograph
LGC	Lunar Geological Camera [NASA] (KSC)
LGCA	Land-Grant College of Agriculture
LGCA	Late Great Chevrolet Association (EA)
LGCA	Local Government Clerks' Association [Australia]
LGCA	London Gregorian Choral Association
LGCANSW	Local Government Clerks' Association of New South Wales [Australia]
LGCB	Local Government Clerks' Board [Queensland, Australia]
LGCC	Local Government Clerks' Certificate
LGCL	Licentiate of the Guild of Cleaners and Launderers [British] (DBQ)
LGCL	Logical (ABBR)
LGCLT	Logicality (ABBR)
LGCLY	Logically (ABBR)
LGCM	Lesbian & Gay Christian Movement (WDAA)
LGCN	Logician (ABBR)
LGCOMB	Large Combatant (DNAB)
LGCP	Lexical-Graphical Composer Printer [Photocomposition]
LGCPHW	Lesbian and Gay Caucus of Public Health Workers (EA)
LGCY	Legacy (ABBR)
LGCY	Legacy Software [NASDAQ symbol] (TTSB)
LGCY	Legacy Software, Inc. [NASDAQ symbol] (SAG)
LGD	Compagnie Aerienne du Languedoc [France ICAO designator] (FAAC)
LGd	Dorsal Lateral Geniculate Nucleus [Also, dLGN] [Anatomy]
LGD	La Grande, OR [Location identifier FAA] (FAAL)
LGD	Lambda Gamma Delta [Society]
LGD	Large Group Display (MCD)
LGD	Leaderless Group Discussion
lgd	Legend (VRA)
LGD	Low-Grade Dysplasia [Medicine]
LGDA	National Lawn and Garden Distributors Association (EA)
LGDHC	Ligue Guineenne des Droits de l'Homme [Guinea] [Political party] (EY)
LGDM	LASER-Guided Dispenser Munition (PDAA)
LGDMN	Legerdemain (ABBR)
LGDR	Labor of Genetic Disease Research [National Institutes of Health]
LGE	Landing Ground, Emergency [British military] (DMA)
LGE	Large (MSA)
lge	Large (REAL)
LGE	League (WDAA)
LGE	LEM [Lunar Excursion Module] Guidance Equipment [NASA] (KSC)
LGE	LG & E Energy [NYSE symbol] (SPSG)
LGE	Light Generation Efficiency (AAEL)
LGE	Local Government Engineer
LGE	Logic Gate Expander [Computer science]
LGE	Lunar Geological Equipment [NASA]
LGEANSW	Local Government Electricity Association of New South Wales [Australia]
LGEANSW	Local Government Engineers' Association of New South Wales [Australia]
LGEC	Lunar Geological Exploration Camera (PDAA)
LGEEQC	Local Government Electrical Engineering Qualifications Committee [Australia]
LGEL	Elefsis [Greece] [ICAO location identifier] (ICLI)
LGEME	Legion of Greeks from Egypt and the Middle East [Australia An association]
LGEMP	Local Government Energy Management Program
LGen	Lieutenant General [Navy British]
LGEQC	Local Government Engineering Qualifications Committee [Australia]
LGER	Low German [Language, etc.] (ROG)
LGF	Lateral Giant Fiber (DB)
LGF	Yuma/Yuma Proving Ground, AZ [Location identifier FAA] (FAAL)
LGFA	Lattice Girder Floor Association [British] (DBA)
LGFC	Lesley Gore Fan Club (EA)
LGFS	Local Government Financial System (MHDB)
LGFSTF	Liquified Gaseous Fuels Spill Test Facility [Department of Energy]
LGFSTP	Liquefied Gaseous Fuels Spill Test Facility (USDC)
LGG	Legging (ABBR)
LGG	Liege [Belgium] [Airport symbol] (OAG)
LGG	Light Gas Gun
LGG	Light-Gun Pulse Generator
LGGBFC	Larry Gatlin and the Gatlin Brothers Fan Club (EA)
LGGBIFC	Larry Gatlin and the Gatlin Brothers International Fan Club (EA)
LGGC	Local Government Grants Commission
LGGE	Laboratory of Glaciology and Geophysics of the Environment [France]
LGGG	Athinai [Greece] [ICAO location identifier] (ICLI)
LGGR	Logger (ABBR)
LGGRHD	Loggerhead (ABBR)
LGH	Lactogenic Hormone [Also, LTH, PR, PRL] [Endocrinology]
LGH	Lansing General Hospital [Michigan]
LGH	Laugh (ABBR)
LGH	Leigh Creek [Australia Airport symbol] (OAG)
LGH	Length
LGH	Liberty Godparent Home [An association] (EA)
LGH	Little Growth Hormone [Medicine] (STED)
LGH	Little Growth Hormone (DB)
LGH	Logarithmic Histogram Scanning [Mass spectrometry]
LGHB	Laughable (ABBR)
LGHBY	Laughably (ABBR)
LGHCS	Lutheran General Health Care System (EA)
LGHD	Laughed (ABBR)
LGHET	Larghetto (ABBR)
LGHG	Laughing (ABBR)
LGHGY	Laughingly (ABBR)
LGHI	Khios [Greece] [ICAO location identifier] (ICLI)
LGHL	Porto Heli [Greece] [ICAO location identifier] (ICLI)
LGHN	Leghorn (ABBR)
LGHP	Large Group Health Plan [Department of Health and Human Services] (GFGA)
LGHR	Laugher (ABBR)
LGHTR	Laughter (ABBR)
LGHTR	Lighter
LGI	Deadman's Cay [Bahamas] [Airport symbol] (OAG)
LGI	Large Glucagon Immunoreactivity [Immunochemistry]
LGI	Lateral Giant Interneuron [Neurobiology]
LGI	Linear Gate and Integrator (MHDB)
LGI	Locally Generated Income (MCD)
LGI	Lower Gastrointestinal [Medicine] (STED)
LGI	Lunar Geology Investigation [NASA]
LGIEE	Liaison Group for International Educational Exchange (EA)
LGIO	Ioannina [Greece] [ICAO location identifier] (ICLI)
LGIR	Iraklion [Greece] [ICAO location identifier] (ICLI)
LGITIT	Legitimist (ABBR)
LGITIZ	Legitimize (ABBR)

LGITIZD	Legitimized (ABBR)
LGITIZG	Legitimizing (ABBR)
LGITMA	Legitimate (ABBR)
LGITMAD	Legitimated (ABBR)
LGITMAG	Legitimating (ABBR)
LGITMC	Legitmacy (ABBR)
LGITMY	Legitimately (ABBR)
LGIU	LASER Gyro Interface Unit (NASA)
LGIU	Local Government Information Unit [British]
LGJ	Local Government Journal [A publication] (ROG)
LGK	Langkawi [Malaysia] [Airport symbol] (OAG)
LGk	Late Greek [or Low Greek] [Language] (BARN)
LGKA	Kastoria [Greece] [ICAO location identifier] (ICLI)
LGKC	Kithira [Greece] [ICAO location identifier] (ICLI)
LGKF	Kefallinia [Greece] [ICAO location identifier] (ICLI)
LGKJ	Kastelorizo [Greece] [ICAO location identifier] (ICLI)
LGKL	Kalamata [Greece] [ICAO location identifier] (ICLI)
LGKM	Kavala/Amigdhaleon [Greece] [ICAO location identifier] (ICLI)
LGKO	Kos [Greece] [ICAO location identifier] (ICLI)
LGKP	Karpathos [Greece] [ICAO location identifier] (ICLI)
LGKR	Kerkira [Greece] [ICAO location identifier] (ICLI)
LGKS	Kasos [Greece] [ICAO location identifier] (ICLI)
LGKV	Kavala/Khrisoupolis [Greece] [ICAO location identifier] (ICLI)
LGKZ	Kozani [Greece] [ICAO location identifier] (ICLI)
LGL	Labioglossolaryngeal [Dentistry] (DAVI)
LGL	La Gloria [Colombia] [Airport symbol] (AD)
LGL	Large Granular Leukocyte [Hematology]
LGL	Large Granular Lymphocyte [Hematology]
LGL	Large Granular Lymphocyte [Medicine] (TAD)
Lgl	Legal (TBD)
LGL	Legal (ABBR)
LGL	Lobular Glomerulonephritis [Medicine] (STED)
LGL	Local Government Library [A publication]
LGL	Local Graphics Library [Cambridge Computer Graphics Ltd.] [Software package] (NCC)
LGL	Long Lellang [Malaysia] [Airport symbol] (OAG)
LGL	Lown-Ganong-Levine [Syndrome] [Medicine]
LGL	Luxair-Societe Luxembourgeoise de Navigation Aerienne SA [Germany ICAO designator] (FAAC)
LGL	Lynch Corp. [AMEX symbol] (SPSG)
LGLA	Legislate (ABBR)
LGLAD	Legislated (ABBR)
LGLAG	Legislating (ABBR)
LGLAN	Legislation (ABBR)
LGLAR	Legislator (ABBR)
LGLAR	Legislature (ABBR)
LGLAY	Legislative (ABBR)
LGLC	Libertarians for Gay and Lesbian Concerns (EA)
LGLE	Leros [Greece] [ICAO location identifier] (ICLI)
LGLM	Legalism (ABBR)
LGLR	Larissa [Greece] [ICAO location identifier] (ICLI)
LGLST	Legalist (ABBR)
LGLSTC	Legalistic (ABBR)
LGLSTCY	Legalistically (ABBR)
LGLT	Legality (ABBR)
LGLTC	Legalistic (ABBR)
LGLY	Legally (ABBR)
LGLZ	Legalize (ABBR)
LGLZD	Legalized (ABBR)
LGLZG	Legalizing (ABBR)
LGLZN	Legalization (ABBR)
LGM	LASER Ground Mapper
LGM	LASER-Guided Munition
LGM	Last Glacial Maximum [Climatology]
LGM	Liberty Godparent Ministry (EA)
LGM	Little Green Men [British term for space signals]
LGM	Little Green Mountain [Idaho] [Seismograph station code, US Geological Survey Closed] (SEIS)
LGM	Local Government Management [A publication]
LGM	Logistic Guidance Memorandum
LGM	Logistics Module [Simulation games] [Army] (SSD)
LGM	Loop Ground Multiplexer (MCD)
LGMA	Lesbian and Gay Medical Association [Defunct] (EAIO)
LGMB	Local Government Management Board (AIE)
LGMD	Limb Girdle Muscular Dystrophy [Medicine]
LGMD	Lobular Giant Movement Detector (PDAA)
LGMG	Lipid and Glycopeptide Modified Derivative (DB)
LGMG	Megara [Greece] [ICAO location identifier] (ICLI)
LGMK	Mikonos [Greece] [ICAO location identifier] (ICLI)
LGML	Milos [Greece] [ICAO location identifier] (ICLI)
LGMN	Ligament (ABBR)
LGMR	Marathon [Greece] [ICAO location identifier] (ICLI)
LGMS	LASER Ground Mapping System
LGMT	Mitilini [Greece] [ICAO location identifier] (ICLI)
LGN	Lagoon (ADA)
LGN	Lagunillas [Venezuela] [Seismograph station code, US Geological Survey] (SEIS)
LGN	Lateral Geniculate Nucleus
LGN	Left Green Network [An association] (EA)
LGN	Legion (ABBR)
LGN	Legion Resources Ltd. [Vancouver Stock Exchange symbol]
LGN	Line Gate Number [Computer science]
LGN	Lobular Glomerulonephritis [Medicine] (MAE)
LGN	Logical Group Number [Computer science] (IBMDP)
LGN	Logicon, Inc. [NYSE symbol] (SPSG)
LGNAP	Lagniappe (ABBR)
LGNAR	Legionaire (ABBR)
LGNBRY	Loganberry (ABBR)
LGND	Lateral Geniculate Nucleus Dorsal [Neuroanatomy]
LGND	Legend (ABBR)
LGND	Ligand Pharmaceuticals `B' [NASDAQ symbol] (TTSB)
LGND	Ligand Pharmaceuticals, Inc. [NASDAQ symbol] (SAG)
LGNDY	Legendary (ABBR)
LGNMVTE	Lignum Vitae [Botany]
LGNS	Largeness (ABBR)
LGNS	Leggoons Inc. [NASDAQ symbol] (TTSB)
LGNY	Legionary (ABBR)
LGO	Lamont Geological Observatory [Later, L-DGO] [Columbia University]
LGO	Largo (ABBR)
LGO	Light Gas Oil [Fuel technology]
LGO	Local Government Office
LGO	Logo Resources Ltd. [Vancouver Stock Exchange symbol]
LGO	Low Gravity Orbit
LGO	Lunar Geoscience Observer (MCD)
LGOC	London General Omnibus Co. [British] (DCTA)
LGOFC	Linda Gray's Official Fan Club (EA)
LGON	Lagoon (ABBR)
LGOR	Langor (ABBR)
LGORU	Langorous (ABBR)
LGORU	Local Government Operational Research Unit [British] (DI)
LGORUY	Langorously (ABBR)
LGP	Labioglossopharyngeal [Dentistry] (DAVI)
LGP	Laboratory Graduate Participation [Oak Ridge National Laboratory]
LGP	LASER-Guided Projectile (MCD)
LGP	Legaspi [Philippines] [Airport symbol] (OAG)
LGP	Legaspi [Philippines] [Seismograph station code, US Geological Survey] (SEIS)
LGP	Low Ground Pressure
LGP	Lummer-Gehreke Plate [Physics]
LGPA	Paros [Greece] [ICAO location identifier] (ICLI)
LGPANSW	Livestock and Grain Producers' Association of New South Wales [Australia]
LGPIM	Lesbian and Gay People in Medicine [Later, LGBPM] (EA)
LGPN	International Leather Goods, Plastic, and Novelty Workers' Union (EA)
LGPZ	Preveza [Greece] [ICAO location identifier] (ICLI)
LGQ	Lago Agrio [Ecuador] [Airport symbol] (OAG)
LGQ	Linear Gaussian Quadratic (AAEL)
LGQB	Local Government Qualifications Board [Victoria, Australia]
LGR	Knight's Local Government Reports [A publication] (DLA)
LGR	Lager (ABBR)
LGR	Laird Group, Inc. [Toronto Stock Exchange symbol]
LGR	Larger (WGA)
LGR	Leasehold Ground Rent (ROG)
LGR	Lethal Ground Range (MCD)
LGR	Letter of General Representation (PDAA)
LGR	Light-Water-Cooled, Graphite-Moderated Reactor (NRCH)
LGR	Local Government Reorganization [British]
LGR	Local Government Reports [England] [A publication] (DLA)
LGR	Localized Gain Region (PDAA)
LGR	Logrono [Spain] [Seismograph station code, US Geological Survey] (SEIS)
LGR	London Grand Rank [Freemasonry]
LGR	Longer (WGA)
LGR	Loop Gap Resonator [Spectrometry]
LGR	Low Greek [Language, etc.]
LGR	Low Group Receiving Unit
LGra	Grambling State University, Grambling, LA [Library symbol Library of Congress] (LCLS)
LGRD	Laggard (ABBR)
LGRD	Rodos/Maritsa [Greece] [ICAO location identifier] (ICLI)
LGR (Eng)	Local Government Reports [England] [A publication] (DLA)
LGRF	Loan Guaranty Revolving Fund
LGrJ	Jefferson Parish Public Library, Gretna, LA [Library symbol Library of Congress] (LCLS)
LGRMG	Lesbian/Gay Rights Monitoring Group (EA)
LGRP	Rodos/Paradisi [Greece] [ICAO location identifier] (ICLI)
LGRX	Araxos [Greece] [ICAO location identifier] (ICLI)
LGS	Grambling State University, Grambling, LA [OCLC symbol] (OCLC)
LGS	Lagoons [Maps and charts] (ROG)
LGS	Landing Guidance System [Aerospace]
LGS	Large Gray Ship [Slang Navy]
LGS	Large Green Soft [Stool] [Gastroenterology] (DAVI)
LGS	LASER Guidance System (MCD)
LGS	Late Glacial Stage [Paleontology]
LGS	Lega dei Giovani Somali [Somali Youth League]
LGS	Limerick Generation Station [Nuclear energy] (NRCH)
LGS	Liquid Asset and Government Securities (ADA)
LGS	Lithogenic Grain Size [An indicator of wind intensity]
LGS	Litton Graphics Standard (MCD)
LGS	Lower Group Stop (NRCH)
LGS	Lunar Geophysical Surface
LGS	Lunar Gravity Simulator [Aerospace]
LGSA	Khania/Souda [Greece] [ICAO location identifier] (ICLI)
LGSB	Local Government Services Bureau [South Australia]
LGSB	Local Government Superannuation Board [Queensland, Australia]
LGSC	Large Scale (ABBR)
LGSD	Sedes [Greece] [ICAO location identifier] (ICLI)
L/GSE	Launch and Ground Support Equipment
LGSIL	Low Grade Squamous Intraepithelial Lesions [Medicine] (WDAA)

LGSK	Skiathos [*Greece*] [*ICAO location identifier*] (ICLI)
LGSL	Lugsail (ABBR)
LGSM	Licentiate of Guildhall School of Music [*British*]
LGSM	Light Ground Station Module
LGSM	Samos [*Greece*] [*ICAO location identifier*] (ICLI)
LGSP	Sparti [*Greece*] [*ICAO location identifier*] (ICLI)
LGSR	Santorini [*Greece*] [*ICAO location identifier*] (ICLI)
LGsSH	Greenwell Springs State Hospital, Greenwell Springs, LA [*Library symbol Library of Congress*] (LCLS)
LGST	Sitia [*Greece*] [*ICAO location identifier*] (ICLI)
LGSTC	Logistic (ABBR)
LGSTCL	Logistical (ABBR)
LGSTCN	Logistician (ABBR)
LGSV	Stefanovikion [*Greece*] [*ICAO location identifier*] (ICLI)
LGSY	Skyros [*Greece*] [*ICAO location identifier*] (ICLI)
LGT	Langat Encephalitis [*Medicine*]
LGT	Largest (ABBR)
LGT	Late Generalized Tuberculosis [*Medicine*]
LGT	Legate (ABBR)
LGT	Liechtenstein Global Trust
LGT	Light
LGT	Liquid Gas Tank
LGT	Local Geomagnetic Time
LGT	Logistec Corp. [*Toronto Stock Exchange symbol*]
LGT	Low Gelling Temperature [*Analytical biochemistry*]
LGT	Low Group Transmitting Unit
LGTA	Ligue Generale des Travailleurs Angolais [*General League of Angolan Workers in Exile*]
LGTB	Local Government Training Board [*British*]
LGTD	Lighted
LGTE	Legatee (ABBR)
LGTFGR	Lightfingered (ABBR)
LGTFTD	Lightfooted (ABBR)
LGTFTY	Lightfootedly (ABBR)
LGTG	Lighting (ABBR)
LGTG	Tanagra [*Greece*] [*ICAO location identifier*] (ICLI)
LGTH	Length (AFM)
lgth	Length (VRA)
LGTH	Lexington Group in Transportation History (EA)
LGTH	Lightning Hole [*Electronics*]
LGTHCOLM...	Length of Column [*Military*] (GFGA)
LGTHD	Lightheaded (ABBR)
LGTHDY	Lightheadedly (ABBR)
LGTHIY	Lengthily (ABBR)
LGTHN	Lengthen (ABBR)
LGTHND	Lengthened (ABBR)
LGTHNG	Lengthening (ABBR)
LGTHNS	Lengthiness (ABBR)
LGTHR	Lengthier (ABBR)
LGTHRTD	Lighthearted (ABBR)
LGTHRTNS...	Lightheartedness (ABBR)
LGTHRTY	Lightheartedly (ABBR)
LGTHS	Lighthouse (ABBR)
LGTHT	Lengthiest (ABBR)
LGTHWS	Lengthwise (ABBR)
LGTHY	Lengthy (ABBR)
LGTI	Lower Genital Tract Infection [*Medicine*] (DMAA)
LGTIC	Logistic (ABBR)
LGTICL	Logistical (ABBR)
LGTL	Kasteli [*Greece*] [*ICAO location identifier*] (ICLI)
LGTMDD	Lightminded (ABBR)
LGTMDY	Lightmindedly (ABBR)
LGTN	Legation (ABBR)
LGTN	Lighten (ABBR)
LG TN	Long Ton [*2240 pounds*] (WDAA)
LGTNG	Lightning (ABBR)
LGTO	Legato (ABBR)
LGTO	Legato Systems [*NASDAQ symbol*] (TTSB)
LGTO	Legato Systems, Inc. [*NASDAQ symbol*] (SAG)
LGTP	Tripolis [*Greece*] [*ICAO location identifier*] (ICLI)
LGTPB	Local Government Town Planners' Board [*Queensland, Australia*]
LG TPR	Long Taper (WDAA)
LGTR	Ligature (ABBR)
LGTR	Lightener (ABBR)
LGTRD	Ligatured (ABBR)
LGTRG	Ligaturing (ABBR)
LGTS	Lights [*Postal Service standard*] (OPSA)
LGTS	Thessaloniki [*Greece*] [*ICAO location identifier*] (ICLI)
LGTT	Dekeleia/Tatoi [*Greece*] [*ICAO location identifier*] (ICLI)
LGTUD	Longitude (ABBR)
LGTUDL	Longitudinal (ABBR)
LGTUDY	Longitudinally (ABBR)
LGTWT	Lightweight (ABBR)
LGTY	Lightly (ABBR)
LGTYR	Lightyear (ABBR)
LGU	Ladies Golf Union
LGU	Land-Grant University
LGU	League (ABBR)
LGU	Legume (ABBR)
LGU	Local Glucose Utilization [*Physiology*]
LGU	Logan [*Utah*] [*Airport symbol*] (OAG)
LGU	Logan, UT [*Location identifier FAA*] (FAAL)
L Guard	Law Guardian [*A publication*] (DLA)
LGUD	Leagued (ABBR)
LGUG	Leaguing (ABBR)

LGUNU	Leguminous (ABBR)
LGV	Large Granular Vesicle (OA)
LGV	Lymphogranuloma Venereum [*Medicine*]
LGVC	Local Government Valuers' Committee [*New South Wales, Australia*]
LGVD	Large Group View Display (MCD)
LGVHD	Lethal Graft-Versus-Host Disease [*Medicine*] (DMAA)
LGVO	Volos [*Greece*] [*ICAO location identifier*] (ICLI)
LGW	Landing Gear Warning
LGW	Laser-Guided Weapon (DOMA)
LGW	London-Gatwick [*England*] [*Airport symbol*] (OAG)
LGW	Love Games Won [*Tennis*]
LGW	Lufttarhtgesellschaft Walter GmbH [*Germany ICAO designator*] (FAAC)
LGWCM	LASER-Guided Weapons Counter-Measure (PDAA)
LGWF	Libyan General Workers' Federation
LGWS	LASER-Guided Weapons Systems (IEEE)
LGWV	Long Wave (FAAC)
LGWX	Logic Works [*NASDAQ symbol*] (TTSB)
LGWX	Logic Works, Inc. [*NASDAQ symbol*] (SAG)
LGX	Lovington, NM [*Location identifier FAA*] (FAAL)
LGY	Lagunillas [*Venezuela*] [*Airport symbol*] (AD)
LGY	Largely (ABBR)
LGY	Leggy (ABBR)
LGZA	Zakinthos [*Greece*] [*ICAO location identifier*] (ICLI)
LH	Deutsche Lufthansa AG [*Germany*] [*ICAO designator*] (OAG)
LH	Laboratory Corp. Amer Hldgs Wrrt [*NYSE symbol*] (TTSB)
LH	Laboratory Corp. of America Holdings [*NYSE symbol*] (SAG)
LH	Labor Historians [*Defunct*] (EA)
LH	Labor Hour [*In contract work*]
LH	Laetolil Hominid
LH	Lamphole (ABBR)
LH	Langmuir-Hinshelwood Mechanism [*Chemistry*]
LH	Large Heavy Seeds [*Botany*]
LH	Larval Heart
LH	Las Hermanas [*Later, LH-USA*] (EA)
LH	Last Half [*of month*] [*Business term*] (DS)
LH	Last Harvest [*An association*] (EA)
LH	Last Hope [*Facetious name for Chrysler's 1993 sedans*]
LH	Late Helladic (BJA)
LH	Latent Heat (IAA)
LH	Lateral Hypothalamic [*or Hypothalamus*]
LH	Learning Handicapped
LH	Learning How [*An association*] (EA)
L/H	Leasehold [*Legal term*] (DLA)
LH	Left Half (WDAA)
LH	Left Halfback [*Soccer*]
LH	Left Hand
LH	Left Hemisphere (DB)
LH	Left Hyperphoria [*Ophthalmology*]
LH	Legal Holiday (MHDW)
LH	Legion d'Honneur [*French decoration*]
LHS	Lewisite-Mustard Gas Mix [*for land mines*] [*Army symbol*]
LHS	L. Hungerford [*Record label*] [*Great Britain*]
lh	Liechtenstein [*MARC country of publication code Library of Congress*] (LCCP)
LH	Light-Harvesting (MEC)
LH	Lighthawk [*An association*] (EA)
LH	Light Helicopter [*Military*] (RDA)
LH	Light Horse [*Cavalry*]
LH	Lighthouse [*Maps and charts*]
LH	Lightly Hinged [*Philately*]
LH	Limited Hold
LH	Linear Hybrid
LH	Link Header (ACRL)
LH	Link House Books [*Publisher*] [*British*]
LH	Lipid Hydrocarbon [*Biochemistry*]
LH	Liquid Helium (IAA)
LH	Liquid Hydrogen
LH	Litter Hook
LH	Little House (WDAA)
LH	Load-High [*Computer science*] (PCM)
LH	Local Horizontal
LH	Locating Head [*Engineering*] (OA)
LH	Loch's Horse [*British military*] (DMA)
LH	Loop of Henle (MEC)
LH	Lower Half
LH	Lower Hemispherical (MCD)
LH	Lower Hold [*Shipping*]
LH	Low Head [*Nuclear energy*] (NRCH)
L/H	Low-to-High (MDG)
LH	Lues Hereditaria [*Medicine*]
LH	Lufthansa (ABBR)
LH	Lufthansa German Airlines [*ICAO designator*] (AD)
LH	Luteinizing-Hormone [*Also, ICSH, LSH*] [*Endocrinology*]
LH$_2$	Liquid Hydrogen [*NASA*]
LH2	Liquid Hydrogen (NAKS)
LHA	Amphibious Assault Carrier [*or Ship*] (Landing Helicopter Assault Ship) [*Navy symbol*]
LHA	Ladies' Hermitage Association (EA)
LHA	Landing Helicopter Assault
LHA	Lanham Housing Act (DLA)
LHA	Lateral Hypothalamic Area
LHA	Lay Helpers' Association [*British*]
LHA	Left Heart Assistance [*Cardiology*]
LHA	Left Hepatic Artery [*Medicine*] (DMAA)

LHA............ Leisure & Hotel Appointments [*Recruitment for the hotel, leisure, and travel industries*] [*British*]

LHA............ Lhasa [*Tibet*] [*Seismograph station code, US Geological Survey Closed*] (SEIS)

LHA............ Libertarian Humanist Association (EA)

LHA............ Licentiate of the Institute of Health Service Administrators [*British*] (DBQ)

LHA............ Light Helicopter, Attack [*Computer test vehicle*]

LHA............ Lincoln Highway Association [*Motoring history organization*]

LHA............ Livestock Husbandry Adviser [*Ministry of Agriculture, Fisheries, and Food*] [*British*]

LHA............ Local Health Authority [*British*]

LHA............ Local Hour Angle [*Navigation*]

LHA............ Local Housing Authority

LHA............ Lord High Admiral [*British*]

LHA............ Lower-Half Assembly

LHA............ Lower Hour Angle [*Navigation*]

LHA............ Lutheran Hospital Association of America (EA)

LHA............ McNeese State University, Lake Charles, LA [*OCLC symbol*] (OCLC)

LHAA.......... Budapest [*Hungary*] [*ICAO location identifier*] (ICLI)

LHAAP........ Longhorn Army Ammunition Plant (AABC)

L/Hadr........ Lance Havidar [*Military British*]

LHAL.......... Lethal (ABBR)

LHAMS........ Local Hour Angle of Mean Sun

LHAR.......... London, Havre, Antwerp, Rouen [*Shipping route*] (ROG)

LHAR.......... London, Hull, Antwerp, or Rotterdam [*Shipping route*]

LHAR.......... Lothario (ABBR)

LHarC......... Catahoula Parish Library, Harrisonburg, LA [*Library symbol Library of Congress*] (LCLS)

LHAS.......... Luteinizing Hormone Antiserum [*Endocrinology*]

LHaSC........ Saint Charles Parish Library, Hahnville, LA [*Library symbol Library of Congress*] (LCLS)

LHAT.......... League of Historic American Theatres (EA)

LHATS........ Local Hour Angle of True Sun

LHAW......... Liquid High Activity Waste [*Nuclear energy*] (NUCP)

LHB............ Bachelor of Humane Letters [*or Bachelor of Literature or Bachelor of the More Humane Letters*]

LHB............ Laboratory Hazards Bulletin [*Royal Society of Chemistry*] [*Information service or system*] (IID)

LHB............ Late Heavy Bombardment [*Planetary history*]

LHb............ Lateral Habenular (Nucleus) [*Neuroanatomy*]

LHB............ Left Halfback [*Soccer*]

LHB............ Lost Heartbeat [*An attractive girl*] [*Slang*]

LHBANA...... Log House Builder's Association of North America (EA)

LHBMA....... Let's Have Better Mottoes Association [*A mythical association*] (EA)

LHBP.......... Budapest/Ferihegy [*Hungary*] [*ICAO location identifier*] (ICLI)

LHBV.......... Left Heart Blood Volume [*Medicine*] (DB)

LHC............ Arlington, TN [*Location identifier FAA*] (FAAL)

LHC............ Heavy Salvage Ship [*Navy symbol*] (VNW)

LHC............ Lakehead University [*Thunder Bay*] [*Ontario*] [*Seismograph station code, US Geological Survey*] (SEIS)

LHC............ Large Hadron Collider [*Nuclear physics*] (ECON)

LHC............ Left-Hand Chain (MHDI)

LHC............ Left-Hand Circular [*Polarization*] (IEEE)

LHC............ Left Hypochondrium [*Medicine*]

LHC............ Light Harvesting Complex

LHC............ Light Hydrocarbon [*Organic chemistry*]

LHC............ Lignin-Hemicellulose-Cellulose [*A complex found in plants*]

LHC............ Lined Hollow Charge

LHC............ Liquid Hydrogen Container

LHC............ LNH Real Estate Investment Trust (SPSG)

LHC............ LNH REIT, Inc. [*NYSE symbol*] (SAG)

LHC............ Local Health Councils [*Scotland*] (DAVI)

LHC............ Log Homes Council (EA)

LHC............ Lord High Chancellor [*British*]

LHC............ Loretto Heights College [*Denver, CO*]

LHC............ Louis, Holland, Callaway [*Advertising agency*]

LHC............ Lovers of the Holy Cross Sisters (TOCD)

LHC............ Lutheran Historical Conference (EA)

LHCA.......... Longshoremen's and Harbor Workers' Compensation Act (DLA)

LHCC.......... Budapest [*Hungary*] [*ICAO location identifier*] (ICLI)

LHCIMA...... Licentiate of the Hotel, Catering, and Institutional Management Association [*British*] (DBQ)

LHCP.......... Left-Hand Circularly Polarized [*LASER waves*]

LHCP.......... Left Hand Circularly Polarized (NAKS)

LHCP.......... Light-Harvesting Chlorophyll A/B-Binding Protein (DB)

LHCTL........ Left-Hand Control (IAA)

LHD............ Anchorage, AK [*Location identifier FAA*] (FAAL)

LHD............ Doctor of Humane Letters (DD)

LHD............ Doctor of Literature (DD)

LHD............ Doctor of the Humanities (DD)

LHD............ Lakehead University Library [*UTLAS symbol*]

LHD............ Large Helical Device [*Plasma physics*]

LHD............ Lateral Head Displacement [*Sperm*] [*Medicine*] (DMAA)

LHD............ Left-Hand Drive [*AEC*]

LHD............ Licentiate in Health, Dublin (ROG)

LHD............ Litterarum Humaniorum Doctor [*Doctor of Humane Letters*] [*Latin*]

LHD............ Load, Haul, Dump [*Mining*]

LHD............ Multipurpose Amphibious Assault Ship

LHDA.......... Lesotho Highlands Development Authority (ECON)

LHDC.......... Debrecen [*Hungary ICAO location identifier*] (ICLI)

LHDC.......... Lateral Homing Depth Charge

LHDDE........ Light Heavy-Duty Diesel Engine [*Motor vehicle specifications*]

LHDPE........ Linear High-Density Polyethylene (EDCT)

LHDR.......... Left-Hand Drive [*AEC*]

LHDS.......... LASER Hole Drilling System

LHE............ Lagrange-Helmholtz Equation

LHE............ Lahore [*Pakistan*] [*Airport symbol*] (OAG)

LHE............ Liquid Helium

LHe............ Liquid Helium (NAKS)

LHEA.......... Laboratory for High Energy Astrophysics [*Greenbelt, MD*] [*NASA*] (GRD)

LHEAA........ Low-Income Home Energy Assistance Act of 1981 (COE)

L HEB......... Late Hebrew (WDAA)

LHEB.......... Left-Hand Equipment Bay [*NASA*] (KSC)

LHEF.......... Lesbian Herstory Educational Foundation (EA)

LHEG.......... Local Healthcare Executive Group (HCT)

LHeT.......... Liquid Helium Temperature (PDAA)

LHF............ Labor Heritage Foundation (EA)

LHF............ Lamp Heat Flux

LHF............ Left Heart Failure [*Medicine*]

LHF............ Lighthouse, Fixed [*Maps and charts*] (ROG)

LHF............ List Handling Facility

LHFA.......... Lung Hageman Factor Activator [*Medicine*] (DMAA)

LHFC.......... Laura Hendler Fan Club (EA)

LHFCS........ Long Haul Fuel Conservation System

LHFEB........ Left-Hand Forward Equipment Bay [*NASA*] (KSC)

LHFI........... Lighthouse, Floating [*Maps and charts*] (ROG)

LHFS.......... Ligand Hyperfine Structure

LHFT.......... Light Helicopter Fireteam [*Navy*] (NVT)

LHG............ Left Hand Grip (DMAA)

LHG............ Licentiate of the Institute of Heraldic and Genealogical Studies [*British*] (DBQ)

LHG............ Local Hemolysis in Gel (PDAA)

LHGR.......... Linear Heat Generation Rate [*Nuclear energy*] (NRCH)

LHH............ League of Home Help [*Australia An association*]

LHH............ Left-Hand Head

LHH............ Lower Hybrid Resonance Heating (MCD)

LHHS.......... Lutheran Hospitals and Homes Society of America (EA)

LHHW......... Langmuir-Hinshelwood-Hougen-Watson Rate Equation [*Chemical kinetics*]

LHI............ Fort Lauderdale, FL [*Location identifier FAA*] (FAAL)

LHI............ Lefthanders International (EA)

LHI............ Leigh Instruments Ltd. [*Toronto Stock Exchange symbol*]

LHI............ Lighthouse, Intermittent [*Maps and charts*] (ROG)

LHI............ Lipid Hydrocarbon Inclusions [*Biochemistry*] (DAVI)

LHi............ Louisiana Historical Society, New Orleans, LA [*Library symbol Library of Congress*] (LCLS)

LHID.......... Logical Hardware Interface Description [*Computer science*]

LHL............ Left Hemisphere Lesion [*Neurology*] (DAVI)

LHL............ Left Hepatic Lobe [*Anatomy*]

LHL............ Line and Half Line [*Illustration*] (DGA)

LHLW......... Liquid High Level Waste [*Nuclear energy*] (NUCP)

LHM............ Lake Helena [*Montana*] [*Seismograph station code, US Geological Survey Closed*] (SEIS)

LHM............ Left-Hand Circularly Polarized Mode (IAA)

LHM............ Licensed Hotel Motel

LHM............ Lisuride Hydrogen Maleate [*Pharmacology*]

LHM............ Loop Handling Machine [*Nuclear energy*] (NRCH)

LHM............ Master of Humane Letters [*or Master of the More Humane Letters*]

LHMC.......... London Hospital Medical College [*British*] (DI)

LHME.......... LASER HELLFIRE Missile Evaluation (MCD)

LHMEL........ LASER-Hardened Materials Evaluation Laboratory

LHMM......... Laymen's Home Missionary Movement (EA)

LHMP.......... Life Health Monitoring Program (BABM)

LHMU......... Ladies' Home Mission Union [*British*] (BI)

LHN............ Express One International, Inc. [*ICAO designator*] (FAAC)

LHN............ Lateral Hypothalamic Nucleus (STED)

LHN............ Lillehammer [*Norway*] [*Seismograph station code, US Geological Survey*] (SEIS)

LHN............ Localized Hypertrophic Neuropathy [*Medicine*]

LHN............ Long-Haul Network (RDA)

LHNCBC...... Lister Hill National Center for Biomedical Communications [*National Library of Medicine*] [*Information service or system*] (IID)

LHO............ Local Head Office [*British*] (DCTA)

LHOB.......... Longworth House Office Building

LHoC.......... Clairborne Parish Library, Homer, LA [*Library symbol Library of Congress*] (LCLS)

LHOLD........ Leasehold (ROG)

LHON.......... Leber's Hereditary Optic Neuropathy [*Ophthalmology*]

LHO ratio.... Library Holdings Ratio per Inhabitant

LHOTS........ Long-Haul Optical Transmission Set [*Telecommunications*] (EECA)

LHouT......... Terrebonne Parish Library, Houma, LA [*Library symbol Library of Congress*] (LCLS)

LHOX.......... Low- and High-Pressure Oxygen

LHP............ Lakehead Pipe Line Partners Ltd. [*NYSE symbol*] (SPSG)

LHP............ Lakehead Pipe Line Ptrs L.P. [*NYSE symbol*] (TTSB)

LHP............ Lamp of Hope Project [*An association*] (EA)

LHP............ Larval Hemolymph Protein [*Entomology*]

LHP............ Late Hyperpolarizing Potential [*Neurophysiology*]

LHP............ Launcher Handling Procedure

LHP............ Left Half Plane (IAA)

LHP............ Left-Handed Pitcher [*Baseball*]

LHP............ Left-Hand Page (DGA)

lhp............ Left-Hand Page (WDMC)

LHP............ Left-Hand Panel

LHP............ Left Hemiparesis [*Medicine*] (MEDA)

LHP............ Left Hemiplegia (STED)

LHP............ Lehu [*Papua New Guinea*] [*Airport symbol*] (OAG)

LHPC.......... Light-Harvesting Chlorophyll Protein Complex [*Botany*]

LHPG	LASER-Heated Pedestal Growth [*Crystal growing technology*]
LHPS	Lead Hydrogen Purge System [*Nuclear energy*] (IEEE)
LHPZ	Lower Esophageal High-Pressure Zone [*Medicine*] (STED)
LHQ	Allied Land Headquarters [*World War II*]
LHQ	Lancaster, OH [*Location identifier FAA*] (FAAL)
LHQ	Life History Questionnaire [*Psychology*] (DAVI)
LHR	Left-Hand Rule
LHR	[*The*] Lehigh & Hudson River Railway Co. [*Absorbed into Consolidated Rail Corp.*] [*AAR code*]
LHR	Leukocyte Histamine Release [*Test*]
LHR	Lighthouse, Revolving [*Maps and charts*] (ROG)
LHR	Liquid-Holding Recovery [*of bacterial cells*]
LHR	London-Heathrow [*England*] [*Airport symbol*] (OAG)
LHR	Long-Term Heart Rate (PDAA)
LHR	Lower Hybrid Resonance
LHR	Low-Heat-Rejection Engine [*Mechanical engineering*] (RDA)
LHR	Low heat Release [*Adiabatic engines*] [*Automotive engineering*]
LHR	Lumen Hour (ADA)
l-hr	Lumen-Hour [*Unit quantity of light*] (STED)
LHRAA	Lutheran Human Relations Association of America (EA)
LHRBI	Luteinizing Hormone Receptor Binding Inhibitor [*Endocrinology*]
LHRE	Low Heat Rejection Engine [*Mechanical engineering*]
LH-RF	Luteinizing-Hormone Releasing Factor [*Also, GnRF, GnRH, LH-RH, LH-RH/FSH-RH, LRF, LRH*] [*Endocrinology*]
LHRF	Luteinizing Hormone-Releasing Factor [*Medicine*] (STED)
LHRF	Luteotropin Hormone-Releasing Factor [*Medicine*] (STED)
LHRH	Left Hand, Right Hand (IAA)
LH-RH	Luteinizing-Hormone Releasing Hormone [*Also, GnRF, GnRH, LH-RF, LH-RH/FSH-RH, LRF, LRH*] [*Endocrinology*]
LHRH	Luteinizing Hormone Releasing Hormone [*Medicine*] (STED)
LH-RH/FSH-RH	Luteinizing-Hormone Releasing Hormone/Follicle-Stimulating Hormone Releasing Hormone [*Also, GnRF, GnRH, LH-RF, LH-RH, LRF, LRH*] [*Endocrinology*]
LHRS	Life History Recorder Set [*or System*] (MCD)
LHRT	Library History Round Table [*American Library Association*]
LHS	Lake Hughes, CA [*Location identifier FAA*] (FAAL)
LHS	Layered Half Space
LHS	Left-Hand Side
LHS	Left Heart Strain [*Medicine*]
LHS	Left Heel Strike
LHS	Liberty Hill [*South Carolina*] [*Seismograph station code, US Geological Survey*] (SEIS)
LHS	Library History Seminar
LHS	Lightweight Hydraulic System [*Navy aviation*]
LHS	Loop Handling System [*Nuclear energy*] (NRCH)
LHS	Lunar Horizon Sensor [*Aerospace*]
LHS	Lymphatic and Hematopoietic System (STED)
LHS	Southeastern Louisiana University, Hammond, LA [*Library symbol Library of Congress*] (LCLS)
LHSC	Left-Hand Side Console [*NASA*] (KSC)
LHSC	Liquid Hydrogen System Complex [*NASA*] (KSC)
LHSC	Luther Hospital Sentence Completions [*Nursing school test*]
LHSI	Low-Head Safety Injection [*Nuclear energy*] (NRCH)
LHSLG	Lincoln Health Sciences Library Group [*Library network*]
LHSP	Lernout & Hauspie Speech Products [*NASDAQ symbol*] (SAG)
LHSPF	Lernout & Hauspie Speech Pds [*NASDAQ symbol*] (TTSB)
LHSSC	Left-Hand Side Storage Container [*NASA*] (KSC)
LHSV	Liquid Hourly Space Velocity [*Fluid dynamics*]
LHT	Left Hypertropia [*Ophthalmology*]
LHT	Library Hi Tech [*Pierian Press, Inc.*] [*Information service or system A publication*] (IID)
LHT	Light (ABBR)
LHT	Lighthouse Tender
LHT	Line and Halftone [*Illustration*] (DGA)
LHT	Line-Haul Tractor (DOMA)
LHT	Lord High Treasurer [*British*]
LHT	Lunar Hand Tool [*NASA*]
LHTD	Lighted (ABBR)
LHTEC	Light Helicopter Turbine Engine Co. [*US Army contractor*]
LHTEN	Lighten (ABBR)
LHTEND	Lightened (ABBR)
LHTENG	Lightening (ABBR)
LHTF	Lincoln Heritage Trail Foundation (EA)
LHTG	Lighting (ABBR)
LHTH	Left-Hand Thread
L-HTL	L-Histidinol [*Biochemistry*]
LHTN	Library Hi Tech News [*A publication*]
LHTNG	Lightning (ABBR)
LHTR	Lighter (ABBR)
LHTR	Lighthouse Transmitter Receiver (IAA)
LHTST	Lightest (ABBR)
LHTY	Lightly (ABBR)
LHU	Lake Havasu City [*Arizona*] [*Airport symbol*] (OAG)
LH-USA	Las Hermanas-United States of America (EA)
LHUSA	Likud-Herut USA (EA)
LHV	Light Horse Volunteers [*British military*] (DMA)
LHV	Liquid Hydrogen Vessel
LHV	Lock Haven [*Pennsylvania*] [*Airport symbol*] (AD)
LHV	Lock Haven, PA [*Location identifier FAA*] (FAAL)
LHV	Low Heat [*or Heating*] Value (MCD)
LHV	Luchtvaart Historische Vereniging [*Society of Aeronautical Historians*] [*Netherlands Defunct*] (EAIO)
LHW	Hinesville, GA [*Location identifier FAA*] (FAAL)
LHW	Lanzhou [*China*] [*Airport symbol*] (OAG)
LHW	Lees-Hromas-Webb [*Theory*]
LHW	Left Half Word
LHW	Left Hand World [*British*] [*An association*] (DBA)
LHW	Lehman Brothers, Inc. [*AMEX symbol*] (SAG)
LHW	Lower High-Water [*Tides and currents*]
LHWCA	Longshore and Harbor Workers' Compensation Act (AAGC)
LHWI	Lower High-Water Interval [*Tides and currents*]
LHWP	Lesotho Highlands Water Project (ECON)
LH.WS	Laboratoy Corp. Amer Hldgs Wrrt [*NYSE symbol*] (TTSB)
LHX	La Junta [*Colorado*] [*Airport symbol*] (AD)
LHX	La Junta, CO [*Location identifier FAA*] (FAAL)
LHX	Light Helicopter, Experimental [*Army*] (RDA)
LHX	Light Helicopters [*Army*] (RDA)
LHX	Lochiel Exploration Ltd. [*Toronto Stock Exchange symbol*]
LHY	Lancashire Hussars Yeomanry [*British military*] (DMA)
LHY	Lohame Herut Yisrael (BJA)
L Hy	Registered Hypnotist
LHY	Wilkes-Barre, PA [*Location identifier FAA*] (FAAL)
LI	Labeling Index [*Measurement of cell labeling*]
L/I	Labindustries [*Commercial firm*]
LI	Labor Intensive (MHDW)
LI	Land Institute [*An association*] (EA)
LI	Landscape Institute [*British*]
LI	Large Intestine [*Medicine*] (DB)
LI	LASER Interferometry (AAEL)
LI	Late Iron [*Age*] (BJA)
LI	Launch Instructions (SAA)
LI	Lawn Institute (EA)
LI	(Laws of) Lipit-Ishtar (BJA)
LI	Leadership Institute (EA)
LI	Leakage of Information [*British World War II*]
LI	Learned Information [*Database originator and marketer*] (NITA)
LI	Leeward Islands (BARN)
LI	Left in Place [*Telecommunications*] (TEL)
LI	Legal Intelligencer [*A publication*] (DLA)
LI	Legislative Instrument [*Ghana*] [*1960-*] [*A publication*] (ILCA)
LI	Leitender Ingenieur [*Chief Engineer*] [*German military - World War II*]
LI	Length Indicator [*Computer science*] (TNIG)
LI	Leptospirosis Icterohemorrhagica [*Medicine*] (DB)
L/I	Letter of Indemnity (DS)
LI	Letter of Intent
LI	Letter of Introduction (ADA)
LI	Level Indicator
LI	Liability [*Insurance*]
LI	Liberal International [*World Liberal Union*] [*British*] (EAIO)
LI	Liberia (ABBR)
LI	Libertarian International (EA)
LI	License Inquiry [*Police*]
LI	Licentiate of Instruction [*or Licentiate Instructor*]
LI	Liechtenstein [*ANSI two-letter standard code*] (CNC)
LI	Lifegain Institute (EA)
LI	Lifting Index [*Ergonometrics*]
LI	Liga International (EA)
LI	Light Infantry
LI	Lightly Included [*Colored gemstone grade*]
LI	Lignin Institute (NTPA)
LI	Ligue Internationale de la Representation Commerciale [*International League of Commercial Travelers and Agents - ILCTA*] (EAIO)
LI	Lilac (ROG)
LI	Lilly Industries`A' [*NYSE symbol*] (TTSB)
LI	Lilly Industries, Inc. [*NYSE symbol*] (SAG)
LI	Lincoln's Inn [*London*] [*One of the Inns of Court*]
LI	Linear Interpolator (IAA)
LI	Line Item (AABC)
li	Lines per Vertical Inch (WDMC)
LI	Linguoincisal [*Dentistry*]
LI	Link
LI	Lions International [*Later, LCI*] (EA)
LI	Liquid Ionization [*Spectrometric instrumentation*]
LI	Litchfield Institute (EA)
Li	Liter [*Metric measure of volume*] (MCD)
Li	Lithium [*Chemical element*]
LI	Lithograph [*or Lithography*] (WDAA)
LI	Lithographer [*Navy rating*]
LI	Load Index [*Tires*] [*Automotive engineering*]
LI	Local Interneuron [*Neuroanatomy*]
LI	Location Identifier (IAA)
LI	Logistic Index (CAAL)
LI	Logistics Instructions [*Military*]
LI	Loglan Institute (EA)
LI	Loitering with Intent [*British*] (DSUE)
LI	London International [*Record label*] [*Great Britain, USA, etc.*]
LI	Long Island
LI	[*The*] Long Island Rail Road Co. [*AAR code*]
LI	Longitudinal Interval (ADA)
LI	Loop of Intestine
LI	Lot Indices
LI	Low Impulsiveness (MAE)
LI	Low Intensity
LI	Lubrication Instructions [*Marine Corps*]
LI	Lubricity Index (IAA)
LI	Lues I [*Primary syphilis*] [*Infectious diseases*] (DAVI)
LI	Lukens, Inc. (EFIS)
LI	Luteinization Inhibitor [*Endocrinology*]
LI	Lymphoid Cellular Infiltration [*Oncology*]
LI1	Lithographer, First Class [*Navy rating*]

LI2	Lithographer, Second Class [*Navy rating*]
LI3	Lithographer, Third Class [*Navy rating*]
LIA	International Union of Life Insurance Agents
LIA	Label Information Area (CMD)
LIA2	Land Information and Analysis [*Program*] [*Department of the Interior*]
LIA	Laser Institute of America (EA)
LIA	Lead Industries Association [*New York, NY*] (EA)
LIA	Leather Industries of America (EA)
LIA	Lebanese International Airways
LIA	Leeward Islands Air Transport (1974) Ltd. [*Antigua and Barbuda*] [*ICAO designator*] (FAAC)
LIA	Leukemia-Associated Inhibiting Activity [*Medicine*]
LIA	Leukemia Cell-Derived Inhibitory Activity [*Hematology*] (DAVI)
LIA2	Level Indicating Alarm [*Engineering*]
LIA	Liaison
LIA	Licensing Industry Association [*Later, ILMA*] (EA)
LIA	Licentiate in Accountancy (DD)
LIA	Life Insurance Act [*Australia*]
LIA	Life Insurance Association [*British*] (DBA)
LIA	Lima [*Ohio*] [*Airport symbol*] (OAG)
LIA	Limited Intelligent Agent [*Virtual reality technology*] (PS)
LIA	Limiting Interval Availability
LIA	Linear Induction Accelerator (MCD)
LIA	Liposome Immunoassay [*Clinical chemistry*]
LIA	Lithographic Institute of Australia
LIA	Little Ice Age [*Geoscience*]
LIA	Liver Infusion Agar [*Germination medium*]
LIA	Localized Induction Approximation [*Mathematics*]
LIA	Lock-In Amplifier (MAE)
LIA	Loop Interface Address
LIA	Low-Impact Aerobics
LIA	Luminescence Immunoassay [*Clinical chemistry*]
LIA	Lymphocyte-Induced Angiogenesis [*Immunology*]
LIA	Lysine Iron Agar [*Microbiology*]
LIAA	Life Insurance Association of America [*Later, ACLI*] (EA)
LIAA	Louisiana Independent Administrators Association (SRA)
LIAB	Liability
Liab	Liability (TBD)
LIAB	Life Insurance Adjustment Bureau [*Defunct*] (EA)
LIABT	Liability (ABBR)
LIAC	Legal Industry Advisory Council (EA)
LIAC	Liberian International American Corporation [*New York*]
LIAC	Light-Induced Absorbance Change
LIAC	Local Industry Advisory Committee [*Civil defense*]
LIADA	Liga Ibero-Americana de Astronomia [*Ibero-American Astronomy League*] (EAIO)
LIADA	Louisiana Independent Automobile Dealers Association (SRA)
LIAFI	Late Infantile Amaurotic Familial Idiocy [*Medicine*] (MAE)
LIAI	Love in Action International (EA)
LIAMA	Life Insurance Agency Management Association [*Later, LIMRA*]
LIAR	Lexicon of Inconspicuously Ambiguous Recommendations [*Term coined by Robert J. Thornton of Lehigh University*]
LIAS	Library Information Access System [*Pennsylvania State University Libraries*] [*University Park*] [*Information service or system*] (IID)
LIASAR	LASER Inertial Aided Synthetic Aperture RADAR (MCD)
LIASE	Linking Industry and School Education (AIE)
LIAT	Leeward Islands Air Transport Services Ltd. [*Humorous interpretation: Luggage in Another Town*] [*Airline*]
LIB	Air Liberte [*France ICAO designator*] (FAAC)
LIB	Federal Liberal Agency of Canada Library [*UTLAS symbol*]
LIB	Laboratory Information Bulletin (GNE)
LIB	Left Inboard (MCD)
LIB	Left in Bottle (MAE)
LIB	Liber [*Book*] [*Latin*]
LIB	Liberal
Lib	Liberal (WDAA)
LIB	Liberation
LIB	Liberator Bomber Aircraft [*British*] (DSUE)
Lib	Liberia
LIB	Liberty [*Geographical division*] [*British*]
lib	Liberty (WDAA)
LIB	Liberty, NC [*Location identifier FAA*] (FAAL)
LIB	Libra [*Pound*]
Lib	Libra [*Constellation*]
Lib	Librarian (DLA)
LIB	Library (AFM)
Lib	Library [*A publication*] (BRI)
Lib	Libretto [*Music*]
lib	Libretto (WDAA)
LIB	Light Ion Beam (PDAA)
LIB	Line Interface Base [*Telecommunications*]
LIBA	Amendola [*Italy ICAO location identifier*] (ICLI)
LIBA	Licentiate of the Institute of Business Administration
LIBA	Long Island Biological Association
LIBACC	Library Acquisition Program [*Computer program*]
Lib & Cult	Libraries & Culture [*A publication*] (BRI)
LIB & SL	Libel and Slander [*Legal term*] (DLA)
Lib Ass	Liber Assisarum [*Book of Assizes, or pleas of the crown*] [*Pt. 5 of Year Books*] [*A publication*] (DLA)
LIBB	Brindisi [*Italy ICAO location identifier*] (ICLI)
Libbey	Libbey, Inc. [*Associated Press*] (SAG)
LIBC	Crotone [*Italy ICAO location identifier*] (ICLI)
LIBC	Latent Iron-Binding Capacity [*Clinical chemistry*]
LIBC	Liberty National Bank [*NASDAQ symbol*] (SAG)
LIBC	Lloyd's Insurance Brokers Committee (AIA)

LIB CAT	Library Catalogue (WDAA)
LIBCEPT	LIBRIS Intercept [*Sweden*] (NITA)
Lib Colon	Libri Coloniarum [*Classical studies*] (OCD)
LIBCON	Libertarian Conservative
LIBCON	Library of Congress
LIBCON/E	Library of Congress/English [*Database on English language monographs*] (NITA)
LIB CONG	Library of Congress (WDAA)
Lib Cong Q	Library of Congress. Quarterly Journal [*A publication*] (DLA)
LI Bcp	Long Island Bancorp, Inc. [*Associated Press*] (SAG)
LIBD	Bari/Palese Macchie [*Italy ICAO location identifier*] (ICLI)
Lib-Dem	Liberal Democrat (WDAA)
LIBE	Library Editor (MHDI)
LIBE	Ligo Internacia de Blindaj Esperantistoj [*International League of Blind Esperantists - ILBE*] (EAIO)
LIBE	Monte S. Angelo [*Italy ICAO location identifier*] (ICLI)
LIBEC	Light Behind Camera [*Photographic technique*]
LIBEDIT	Library Editor (MHDI)
Lib Ent	Old Books of Entries [*A publication*] (DLA)
Liber	Liberia (VRA)
LIBER	Ligue des Bibliotheques Europeennes de Recherche [*League of European Research Libraries*] (EAIO)
LIBERD	Liberated (ABBR)
LIBERG	Liberating (ABBR)
LIBERN	Liberation (ABBR)
LIBERR	Liberator (ABBR)
Liberte	Liberte Investors, Inc. [*Associated Press*] (SAG)
LIBF	Foggia [*Italy ICAO location identifier*] (ICLI)
Lib Feud	Liber Feudorum [*Book of Feuds*] [*At the end of the Corpus Juris Civilis*] [*A publication*] (DLA)
LibFin	Liberty Financial Companies, Inc. [*Associated Press*] (SAG)
LIBG	Grottaglie [*Italy ICAO location identifier*] (ICLI)
LIBGIS	Library General Information Survey [*of the National Center for Educational Statistics*]
LIBH	Liberty Homes, Inc. [*NASDAQ symbol*] (SAG)
LIBH	Marina Di Ginosa [*Italy ICAO location identifier*] (ICLI)
LIBHA	Liberty Homes CI'A' [*NASDAQ symbol*] (TTSB)
LIBHB	Liberty Homes CI'B' [*NASDAQ symbol*] (TTSB)
LIBI	Vieste [*Italy ICAO location identifier*] (ICLI)
LIBID	London Interbank Bid Rate [*Finance British*]
LibInt(BG)	Liberal International (British Group) [*World Liberal Union*] (EAIO)
LIBISAC	Livres Bibliotheque Saclay Database [*Commissariat a l'Energie Atomique*] [*France Information service or system*] (CRD)
LIBJ	Vibo Valentia [*Italy ICAO location identifier*] (ICLI)
LIBK	Caraffa Di Catanzaro [*Italy ICAO location identifier*] (ICLI)
LIBL	Liable (ABBR)
LIBL	Liberal
LIBL	Palascia [*Italy ICAO location identifier*] (ICLI)
LIB LAB	Liberal-Labour Alliance [*British*] (DSUE)
Lib L & Eq	Library of Law and Equity [*A publication*] (DLA)
LIBLZG	Liberalizing (ABBR)
LIBM	Grottammare [*Italy ICAO location identifier*] (ICLI)
LIBMAN	Library Management (MHDB)
LIBMAS	Library Master File [*FORTRAN program*]
LIBMISH	Liberia Military Mission [*US*]
LIBMRG	Library Merge Program [*Computer program*]
LIBN	Lecce [*Italy ICAO location identifier*] (ICLI)
LIBN	Librarian (WGA)
LIBNAT	Library Network Analysis Theory
LibNBk	Liberty National Bank [*Huntington Beach, CA*] [*Associated Press*] (SAG)
LIBO	Lincoln Boyhood National Memorial
LIBO	London Interbank Offered [*Rate*] [*Reference point for syndicated bank loans*]
LIBO	Ortanova [*Italy ICAO location identifier*] (ICLI)
LIB/OL	Librarian/Online [*Database*] (MHDI)
LIBOL	Litton Business-Oriented Language (IAA)
LIBOR	London Interbank Offered Rate [*Reference point for syndicated bank loans*]
LIBORS	LASER Ionization Based on Resonant Saturation [*Physics*]
LIBP	Pescara [*Italy ICAO location identifier*] (ICLI)
Lib Plac	Lilly's Assize Reports [*1688-93*] [*A publication*] (DLA)
LIBQ	Monte Scuro [*Italy ICAO location identifier*] (ICLI)
LIBR	Brindise/Casale [*Italy ICAO location identifier*] (ICLI)
Libr	Libra [*Constellation*]
LIBR	Librarian (EY)
LIBR	Library
libr	Library (VRA)
LIBR	Librium [*Pharmacology*] (DAVI)
Lib Reg	Register Book [*A publication*] (DLA)
LIBRI	Literary Information Bases for Research and Instruction [*American Philological Association*] [*An association*] (NITA)
LIBRIME	Library and Information Management in Europe (TELE)
LIBRIS	Library Information Service [*or System*] [*The Royal Library Database*] [*Information service or system*] (IID)
LIBRLZ	Liberalize (ABBR)
LIBRN	Librarian
LibrtyTc	Liberty Technologies, Inc. [*Associated Press*] (SAG)
LIBRY	Library (ABBR)
LIBS	Campobasso [*Italy ICAO location identifier*] (ICLI)
LIBS	LASER-Induced Breakdown Spectroscopy
LIBS	Library Internet Browsing Software
LIBSET	Library Set [*Computer program*]
LibSIG	Libertarian SIG [*Special Interest Group*] (EA)
LIBSOFT	Library Software Archives [*Computer science*] (TNIG)

LIBSTAD	Working Party on Library and Book Trade Relations [*British*]
LIBSYS	Library System [*Computer program*]
LIBT	Liability (ABBR)
LIBT	Liberty (ABBR)
LIBT	Liberty Technologies [*NASDAQ symbol*] (TTSB)
LIBT	Liberty Technologies, Inc. [*NASDAQ symbol*] (SAG)
LIBT	Termoli [*Italy ICAO location identifier*] (ICLI)
LibtProp	Liberty Property Trust [*Associated Press*] (SAG)
LibtyCp	Liberty Corp. [*Associated Press*] (SAG)
LIBU	Latronico [*Italy ICAO location identifier*] (ICLI)
LIB (UN)	Headquarters Library of the United Nations
LIBV	Gioia Del Colle [*Italy ICAO location identifier*] (ICLI)
LibVT	Libri Veteris Testamenti (BJA)
LIBW	Bonifati [*Italy ICAO location identifier*] (ICLI)
LIBX	Martina Franca [*Italy ICAO location identifier*] (ICLI)
LIBY	Santa Maria Di Leuca [*Italy ICAO location identifier*] (ICLI)
LIBZ	Potenza [*Italy ICAO location identifier*] (ICLI)
LIC	Chief Lithographer [*Navy rating*]
LIC	Lacquer Insulating Compound
LIC	Lamto [*Ivory Coast*] [*Seismograph station code, US Geological Survey*] (SEIS)
LIC	Language Identity Code [*Army*] (INF)
LIC	Large Integrated Circuit [*Electronics*]
LIC	LASER Image Converter
LIC	LASER-Induced Chemistry (RDA)
LIC	LASER Intercept Capability [*Military*] (CAAL)
LIC	Last Instruction Cycle (IAA)
LIC	Launcher Interchange Circuit (IAA)
LIC	Law in Context [*Australia A publication*]
LIC	Lawson, I. C., St. Paul MN [*STAC*]
LIC	League International for Creditors (DCTA)
LIC	Least Incompatible [*Laboratory science*] (DAVI)
LIC	Lecturer in Charge (ADA)
LIC	Left Iliac Crest [*Anatomy*] (DAVI)
LIC	Left Internal Carotid [*Artery*] [*Anatomy*] (DAVI)
LIC	Leisure-Interest Class (MEDA)
LIC	Less Industrialized Country (MHDW)
LIC	Level Indicator Controller (NRCH)
LIC	Library and Information Commission [*British*] (TELE)
LIC	Library Information Center [*Lunar and Planetary Institute*] [*Information service or system*] (IID)
Lic	Licenciado [*Lawyer*] [*Spanish*] (WA)
LIC	License (KSC)
LIC	Licentiate
LIC	Life Insurers Conference [*Richmond, VA*] (EA)
LIC	Limiting Isorrheic Concentration [*Medicine*]
LIC	Limon, CO [*Location identifier FAA*] (FAAL)
LIC	Linear Integrated Circuit
LIC	Lineas Aereas del Caribe [*Colombia*] [*ICAO designator*] (FAAC)
LIC	List of Instruments and Controls (DNAB)
LIC	Lithuanian Information Center [*Defunct*] (EA)
LIC	Load Interface Circuit (MCD)
LIC	Local Import Control [*British*] (DS)
LIC	Local Indigenous Civilian [*Military*]
LIC	Local Interstellar Cloud [*Astronomy*]
LIC	Logistics Indoctrination Course [*Military*] (DNAB)
LIC	London International College [*British*]
LIC	Loop Insertion Cell [*Nuclear energy*] (NRCH)
LIC	Louisiana Insurers' Conference (SRA)
LIC	Low Income Country
LIC	Low Inertia Clutch
LIC	Low-Intensity Conflict [*Military*]
LIC	Lunar Instrument Carrier [*NASA*] (KSC)
LICA	Lamezia/Terme [*Italy ICAO location identifier*] (ICLI)
LICA	Land Improvement Contractors of America (EA)
LICA	Left Internal Carotid Artery [*Anatomy*] (DAVI)
LICA	Licentiate, International College of Anesthetists (CMD)
LICA	Ligue Internationale Contre le Racisme et l'Antisemitisme [*International League Against Racism and Antisemitism*]
LICA	Lithium Isopropylcyclohexylamide [*Organic chemistry*]
LicAc	Licentiate in Acupuncture [*British*]
Lic Agro	Licentiate in Agronomy [*British*]
LICALM	LORAN Inertial Command Air-Launched Missile
LICAP	LASER-Induced Cut and Patch
LICB	Comiso [*Italy ICAO location identifier*] (ICLI)
LICB	Licensable (ABBR)
LICC	Catania/Fontanarossa [*Italy ICAO location identifier*] (ICLI)
LICC	League for Innovation in the Community College (EA)
LICC	Litton Industries, Inc. (EFIS)
LICC	Local Interagency Coordinating Council
LICCD	Ligue Internationale Contre la Concurrence Deloyale [*International League Against Unfair Competition*] (EAIO)
LICD	Lampedusa [*Italy ICAO location identifier*] (ICLI)
LICD	Licensed (ROG)
LICE	Enna [*Italy ICAO location identifier*] (ICLI)
LICE	LASER Interface Control Electronics (MCD)
LICE	License (ROG)
LIC ECON	Licentiate in Economic Sciences (WDAA)
Lic en Der	Licenciado en Derecho [*Licentiate in Law*] [*Spanish*]
Lic en Fil	Licenciado en Filosofia [*Licentiate in Philosophy*] [*Spanish*]
LICET	Library of Industrial and Commercial Education and Training
LICF	Laser-Induced Chlorophyll Fluorescence [*Analytical biochemistry*]
LICF	Messina [*Italy ICAO location identifier*] (ICLI)
LICG	Licensing (ABBR)
LICG	Pantelleria [*Italy ICAO location identifier*] (ICLI)
LICGS	Lightweight Intermediate Caliber Gun System (MCD)
LICH	Capo Spartivento [*Italy ICAO location identifier*] (ICLI)
LICH	Lichfield [*City in England*] (ROG)
LICI	Finale [*Italy ICAO location identifier*] (ICLI)
LICIT	Labor-Industry Coalition for International Trade [*Washington, DC*] (EA)
LICITA	Life Insurance Co. Income Tax Act of 1959
LICJ	Palermo/Punta Raisi [*Italy ICAO location identifier*] (ICLI)
LICK	Lightweight Communication Kit (MCD)
LICL	Gela [*Italy ICAO location identifier*] (ICLI)
LICM	Calopezzati [*Italy ICAO location identifier*] (ICLI)
LICM	Left Intercostal Margin [*Anatomy*]
LICM	Master Chief Lithographer [*Navy rating*]
Lic Med	Licentiate in Medicine
LICND	Life Insurance Committee for a Nuclear Disarmament (EA)
LICNWF	Life Insurance Committee for a Nuclear Weapons Freeze [*Later, LICND*] (EA)
LICO	Cozzo Spadaro [*Italy ICAO location identifier*] (ICLI)
LICO	Low Income Cut-Off [*Canada*]
LiCO₃	Lithium Carbonate [*Pharmacology*] (DAVI)
LICOF	Land Lines Communications Facilities (FAAC)
LICOR	Lightning Correlation
LICP	Lead Inventory Control Point (NG)
LICP	Palermo/Boccadifalco [*Italy ICAO location identifier*] (ICLI)
Lic Phil	Licentiate in Philosophy [*British*]
LICR	Lloyd's Information Casualty Report [*A publication*]
LICR	Reggio Calabria [*Italy ICAO location identifier*] (ICLI)
LICRA	Ligue Internationale Contre le Racisme et l'Antisemitisme [*France*]
LICROSS	League of International Red Cross Societies
LiCrOx	Lithium/Chromium-Oxide [*Type of battery*]
LICS	Left Intercostal Space [*Cardiology*] (MAE)
Lic S	Licentiate in Surgery [*Academic degree*] (WDAA)
LICS	Lotus International Character Set [*Printer technology*] (PCM)
LICS	Sciacca [*Italy ICAO location identifier*] (ICLI)
LICS	Senior Chief Lithographer [*Navy rating*]
LICSR	Life Insurance Committee for Social Responsibility (EA)
LICT	Trapani/Birgi [*Italy ICAO location identifier*] (ICLI)
LICTA	Life Insurance Co. Tax Act of 1955
Lic Tech	Licentiate in Technology [*British*]
Lic Theol	Licentiate in Theology [*British*]
LICU	League of IBM [*International Business Machines Corp.*] Employee Credit Unions (EA)
LICU	Ustica [*Italy ICAO location identifier*] (ICLI)
LICVD	LASER-Induced Chemical Vapor Deposition [*Photovoltaic energy systems*]
LICW	Licentiate of the Institute of Clerks of Works of Great Britain, Inc. (DBQ)
LICX	Prizzi [*Italy ICAO location identifier*] (ICLI)
LICZ	Sigonella [*Italy ICAO location identifier*] (ICLI)
LID	Alidaunia SRL [*Italy ICAO designator*] (FAAC)
LID	Laboratory of Infectious Diseases [*Later, Laboratory of Viral Diseases*] [*NIAID*]
LID	Labor Information Database [*International Labor Office*] [*Information service or system*] (IID)
LID	LASER Image Display (MCD)
LID	LASER Injection Diode
LID	LASER Intrusion Detector
LID	LASER Intrusion Device (MCD)
LID	LASER Isotope Dating
LID	Late Immunoglobulin Deficiency [*Medicine*] (DB)
LID	Leadless Inverted Device
LID	League for Industrial Democracy (EA)
LID	Letters in Digit Strings [*Psychology*]
LID	Library Issue Document (NVT)
LID	Lidco Industries, Inc. [*Toronto Stock Exchange symbol*]
LID	Lift Improvement Device (MCD)
LID	Light Infantry Division [*Army*] (INF)
LID	Limited Instrument Departure (MCD)
LID	Linear Imaging Device (MCD)
LID	Line Isolation Device [*Telecommunications*] (NITA)
LID	Line Item Description (MCD)
LID	Liquid Immersion Development [*Reprography*]
LID	Liquid Interface Diffusion
LID	Literaturdienst Medizin und Umwelt [*Literature Service in Medicine and Environment*] [*Austrian National Institute for Public Health*] [*Information service or system*] (IID)
LID	Local Issue Data [*Telecommunications*] (TEL)
LID	Locked-In Device (MSA)
LID	Logical Identification (MCD)
LID	Logistics Identification Document (NASA)
LID	Low-Iodine Diet [*Medicine*]
LID	Lunar Ionosphere Detector (PDAA)
LIDA	Ligue Internationale des Droits de l'Animal [*International League for Animal Rights*] (EAIO)
LIDA	Lodzer Idishe Dramatishe Aktyorn (BJA)
Lidak	Lidak Pharmaceuticals [*Associated Press*] (SAG)
LIDAR	Atmospheric Light Detection and Ranging Facility [*Los Alamos, NM*] [*Los Alamos National Laboratory*] [*Department of Energy*] (GRD)
LIDAR	LASER Infrared RADAR (IEEE)
LIDAR	LASER Intensity Direction and Ranging (IEEE)
LIDAR	Light Detection and Ranging
LIDAS	Laboratory Instrument Data Acquisition
LIDB	Line Information Database [*Telecommunications*] (ACRL)
LIDB	Logistics Intelligence Data Base (AABC)
LIDC	Lead Industries Development Council [*British*] (DAS)

LIDC............	Ligue Internationale du Droit de la Concurrence [*International League for Competition Law*] [*Paris, France*] (EA)
LIDC............	Low Intensity - Direct Current
LIDE............	LED Light-Emittng Diode Indirect Exposure [*Canon*]
LIDF............	Line Intermediate Distributing Frame
LIDIA	Learning in Dialog (PDAA)
LIDIA	Liaison Internationale des Industries de l'Alimentation [*International Liaison for the Food Industries*]
LIDO	Logic In, Documents Out (PDAA)
LIDO	Logistics Inventory Disposition Order (AAG)
LIDOC	Lidocaine [*Topical anesthetic*] (WDAA)
LIDS............	Laboratory for Information and Decision Systems [*Massachusetts Institute of Technology*] [*Research center*] (RCD)
LIDS............	LASER Illumination Detection System
LIDS............	LASER Infrared Countermeasures Demonstration System [*Air Force*]
LIDS............	Listener Idle State (IAA)
LIDS............	Lithium Ion Drift Semiconductor
LIDS............	Local Inmate Database System (WDAA)
LIDS............	Logistics Item Data Systems [*DoD*]
LIDT............	LASER-Induced Damage Testing
LIDUS..........	Liberal-Demokratische Union der Schweiz [*Liberal Democratic Union of Switzerland*] [*Political party*] (PPE)
LIE..............	Left Inboard Elevon [*Aviation*] (MCD)
LIE..............	Lessio Intellectuale Europeo [*Research Institute*] [*Consiglio Nationale delle Richerche*] [*Italy*] (NITA)
LIE..............	Libenge [*Zaire*] [*Airport symbol Obsolete*] (OAG)
LIE..............	Liechtenstein [*ANSI three-letter standard code*] (CNC)
LIE..............	Limited Information Estimation
LIE..............	Line Islands Experiment [*National Science Foundation*]
LIE..............	Long Island Expressway (BARN)
LIEA............	Alghero [*Italy ICAO location identifier*] (ICLI)
LIEA............	Low Income Energy Assistance [*Later, LIHEAP*] [*Block grant*]
LIEB............	Capo Bellavista [*Italy ICAO location identifier*] (ICLI)
Lieber Civ Lib...	Lieber on Civil Liberty and Self Government [*A publication*] (DLA)
Lieb Herm ...	Lieber's Hermeneutics [*A publication*] (DLA)
Liebigs Ann Chem...	Liebigs Annalen der Chemie (MEC)
LIEC............	Capo Carbonara [*Italy ICAO location identifier*] (ICLI)
LIECH..........	Liechtenstein (ABBR)
Liecht	Liechtenstein
LIECU..........	League of IBM [*International Business Machines Corp.*] Employee Credit Unions [*Later, LICU*] (EA)
LIED............	Decimomannu [*Italy ICAO location identifier*] (ICLI)
LIED............	LASER Initiating Explosive Device
LIED............	Linkage Editor [*Computer science*]
LIEE............	Cagliari/Elmas [*Italy ICAO location identifier*] (ICLI)
LIEE............	Law in Eastern Europe [*A publication*] (DLA)
LIEF............	Capo Frasca [*Italy ICAO location identifier*] (ICLI)
LIEF............	Launch Information Exchange Facility [*NASA*]
LIEFC..........	Long Island Early Fliers Club (EA)
LIEG............	Guardiavecchia [*Italy ICAO location identifier*] (ICLI)
LIEH............	Capo Caccia [*Italy ICAO location identifier*] (ICLI)
LIEL............	Capo S. Lorenzo [*Italy ICAO location identifier*] (ICLI)
LIEM............	Macomer [*Italy ICAO location identifier*] (ICLI)
LIEN............	Fonni [*Italy ICAO location identifier*] (ICLI)
LIENS..........	Ligue Europeenne pour une Nouvelle Societe [*European League for a New Society - ELNS*] [*Paris, France*] (EAIO)
LIEO............	Olbia/Costa Smeralda [*Italy ICAO location identifier*] (ICLI)
LIEP............	LORAN Integrated Engineering Program
LIEP............	Perdasdefogu [*Italy ICAO location identifier*] (ICLI)
LIEPS..........	LORAN Integrated Engineering Program, Shed Light
LIES............	LASER-Induced Emission Spectroscopy (MEC)
LIES............	Library Information and Enquiry System
LIESST.........	Light-Induced Excited Spin State Trapping [*Physics*]
LIETS..........	Land Integrated Equipment for Tactical Systems (MCD)
LIEUT..........	Lieutenant (EY)
Lieut...........	Lieutenant (WDAA)
LIEUTC.........	Lieutenancy (ABBR)
Lieut-Col......	Lieutenant-Colonel [*British military*] (DMA)
LIEUTE.........	Lieutenancy (ABBR)
Lieut-Gen	Lieutenant-General [*British military*] (DMA)
Lieut Jg......	Lieutenant Junior Grade [*Navy*]
LIF..............	LASER-Induced Fluorescence [*Physical chemistry*]
LIF..............	LASER Interference Filter
LIF..............	Layaway of Industrial Facilities (AABC)
LIF..............	Left Iliac Fossa [*Medicine*]
LIF..............	Leukemia Inhibitory Factor [*Oncology*]
LIF..............	Leukocyte Inhibition Factor [*Hematology*]
LIF..............	Leukocytosi-Inducing Factor [*Hematology*] (DAVI)
LIF..............	Lief (ABBR)
LIF..............	Lifu [*Loyalty Islands*] [*Airport symbol*] (OAG)
LIF..............	Lighting Industry Federation [*British*] (DBA)
LIF..............	Logistics Intelligence File (AABC)
LIF..............	Lone Indian Fellowship [*Later, Lone Indian Fellowship and Lone Scout Alumni*] (EA)
LIF..............	Low Insertion Force (AAEL)
LIF..............	Low-Ionization Filament Component [*Galactic science*]
LIFA............	Licentiate of the International Faculty of Arts [*British*]
LIFB............	Life Bancorp [*NASDAQ symbol*] (TTSB)
LIFB............	Life Bancorp, Inc. [*NASDAQ symbol*] (SAG)
LIFC............	Lifecell Corp. [*NASDAQ symbol*] (SAG)
LIFE............	Laboratory for International Fuzzy Engineering Research [*Japan*]
LIFE............	Language Improvement to Facilitate Education of Hearing-Impaired Children [*A project of NEA*]
LIFE............	LASER-Induced Fluorescence Emission
LIFE............	League for International Food Education [*Defunct*] (EA)
LIFE............	Lear Integrated Flight Equipment (MCD)
LIFE............	Learning in a Free Environment [*Education program*]
LIFE............	Less Infant Fatality Everywhere [*In association name, Project LIFE*]
LIFE............	Let's Improve Future Environment
LIFE............	Liberia International Foundation for Elevation
LIFE............	Life Issues in Formal Education (EA)
LIFE............	Lifeline Systems [*NASDAQ symbol*] (TTSB)
LIFE............	Lifetime [*Cable television channel*]
LIFE............	Living in Family Environments
LIFE............	Logistics Evaluation and Review Integrated Flight Equipment [*Aviation*] (IAA)
LIFE............	Logistics Intelligence File Europe
LIFE............	Long Instruction Format Engine [*Computer science*] (CIST)
LIFE............	Longitudinal Interval Follow-Up Evaluation (MEDA)
LIFE............	Love Is Feeding Everyone (EA)
LIFE............	Low Income Family Emancipation Society
LIFE............	Low Income Family Emergency Center
LIFE............	Lung-Imaging Fluorescent Endoscope [*Medicine*] (ECON)
Life and Acc Ins R...	Bigelow's Life and Accident Insurance Reports [*A publication*] (DLA)
Life Bcp.......	Life Bancorp, Inc. [*Associated Press*] (SAG)
Life C..........	Life (Health and Accident) Cases [*Commerce Clearing House*] [*A publication*] (DLA)
Life Cas.......	Life (Health and Accident) Cases [*Commerce Clearing House*] [*A publication*] (DLA)
Life Cas 2d...	Life (Health and Accident) Cases, Second Series [*Commerce Clearing House*] [*A publication*] (DLA)
Lifecell	Lifecell Corp. [*Associated Press*] (SAG)
LifeHoan.....	Lifetime Hoan Corp. [*Associated Press*] (SAG)
LIFEL	Limited Functional English Literacy
LIFEMAN......	Live Fire Evaluation Manikin [*Perceptronics, Inc.*] [*Military*]
LifePart.......	Life Partners [*Associated Press*] (SAG)
LIFER..........	Language Interface Facility with Ellipsis and Recursion [*Computer science*] (MHDI)
LifeRe.........	Life Re Corp. [*Associated Press*] (SAG)
LifeRte........	LifeRate Systems, Inc. [*Associated Press*] (SAG)
LIFES..........	LASER-Induced Fluorescence and Environmental Sensing [*NASA*]
LifeSpir.......	[*The*] Life of the Spirit [*London*] [*A publication*] (BJA)
LIFESTA.......	Lifeboat Station [*Coast Guard*]
Lifeway........	Lifeway Foods, Inc. [*Associated Press*] (SAG)
LIFF	Lifschultz Inds [*NASDAQ symbol*] (TTSB)
LIFF	Lifschultz Industries, Inc. [*NASDAQ symbol*] (SAG)
LIFFE..........	London International Financial Futures and Options Exchange (NUMA)
LIFFE..........	London International Financial Futures Exchange (EBF)
LIFFE..........	London International Financial Futures Exchange Ltd. [*London, England*]
LIFFOE........	London International Financial Futures and Options Exchange (EBF)
LIFHAS........	Libertarian Foundation for Human Assistance (EAIO)
LIFLSA........	Lone Indian Fellowship and Lone Scout Alumni (EA)
LIFMOP.......	Linearly Frequency-Modulated Pulse
LIFO...........	Last In, First Out [*Queuing technique*] [*Accounting*]
LIFO...........	Life Orientation (Survey)
LIFPL.........	Ligue Internationale de Femmes pour la Paix et la Liberte [*Women's International League for Peace and Freedom - WILPF*] (EAIO)
LIFPL/SF.....	Ligue Internationale de Femmes pour la Paix et la Liberte, Section Francaise (EAIO)
LIFR...........	Leukemia Inhibitory Factor Receptor [*Biochemistry*]
LIFRAM.......	Liquid-Fueled Ramjet [*Navy*] (MCD)
LIFS...........	LASER-Induced Fluorescence Spectroscopy
LIFS...........	London International Furniture Show [*British*] (ITD)
Lifschlt	Lifschultz Industries, Inc. [*Associated Press*] (SAG)
LIFSUM........	Airlift Summary Report [*Air Force*]
LIFT...........	Bereavement Services & Community Education (AC)
LIFT...........	Labor Investing for Tomorrow [*Department of Labor*]
LIFT...........	Lead-In Flight Training [*Air Force*] (DOMA)
LIFT...........	Link Intellectual Functions Tester
LIFT...........	Literacy Involves Families Together [*Arizona*]
LIFT...........	Logically Integrated FORTRAN Translator [*UNIVAC*]
LIFT...........	London International Festival of Theatre [*British*]
LIFT...........	London International Freight Terminal (DS)
LIFT...........	Lower Inventory for Tomorrow [*A program of the Canadian government to bring heavy stocks of wheat into line with demand by paying farmers not to produce*]
LIFT	Low Interfacial Tension [*Physical chemistry*]
LIFT...........	Lymphocyte Immunofluorescence Test (STED)
LIFTG.........	Lifting (ABBR)
LIFU..........	Liquid Fuel
LIG............	LASER Image Generator (MCD)
LIG............	LASERS in Graphics (DGA)
LIG............	Last Interglacial Period [*Climatology*]
LIG............	Leichte Infanteriegeschuetz [*Light Infantry Howitzer*] [*German military - World War II*]
LIG............	Liege (ABBR)
LIG............	Ligament [*Anatomy*] (DAVI)
lig.............	Ligamentum (STED)
LIG............	Ligated [*or Ligation*] [*Medicine*]
lig.............	Ligation (STED)
LIG............	Ligature (DGA)
LIG............	Limoges [*France*] [*Airport symbol*] (OAG)
LIG............	London Industrial Group [*British*]
Lig............	Pro Ligario [*of Cicero*] [*Classical studies*] (OCD)
LIGA..........	Liquid Granule Applicator [*Device used to disperse pesticides*]
LIGA..........	Lithographic Galvanoforming Abformung [*Materials science*]
Ligand	Ligand Pharmaceuticals, Inc. [*Associated Press*] (SAG)

LIGCM .... Licentiate of the Incorporated Guild of Church Musicians [*British*] (ROG)
Lig Dig .... Ligon's Digest [*Alabama*] [*A publication*] (DLA)
LIGG .... Ligaments [*or Ligamenti*]
ligg .... Ligaments (STED)
ligg .... Ligature [*Surgery*] (DAVI)
LIGHT .... Light [*Commonly used*] (OPSA)
LIGHT .... Light Industrial Gas Heat Transfer
LIGHT .... Lighting (ABBR)
LIGHT .... Lightning (ABBR)
LIGHTEX ..... Searchlight Illumination Exercise [*Also, LITEX*] [*Military*] (NVT)
LightP .... LightPath Technologies, Inc. [*Associated Press*] (SAG)
LIGHTPHOTORON... Light Photographic Squadron
LIGHTS .... Lights [*Commonly used*] (OPSA)
LightSav ...... Light Savers USA, Inc. [*Associated Press*] (SAG)
Lign .... Lignum [*Wood*] [*Latin*]
LIGO .... LASER Interferometry Gravitational Wave Observatory [*Proposed*]
LIH .... LASER Interferometric Holography
LIH .... Left Inguinal Hernia [*Medicine*]
LIH .... Letters and Inscriptions of Hammurabi [*A publication*] (BJA)
LIH .... Light Intensity High
LIH .... Lihue [*Hawaii*] [*Airport symbol*] (OAG)
LIH .... Line Interface Handler
LIH .... Lithium Hydride
LIHA .... Low Impulsiveness, High Anxiety (MAE)
LIHDC .... Low Income Housing Development Corp. [*North Carolina*] (EA)
LIHE .... Lutheran Institute of Human Ecology (EA)
LIHEAP .... Low Income Home Energy Assistance Program [*Formerly, LIEA*] [*Block grant*]
LIHG .... Ligue Internationale de Hockey sur Glace [*International Ice Hockey Federation*]
LihirGld .... Lihir Gold Ltd. [*Associated Press*] (SAG)
LIHIS .... Low Income Housing Information Service (EA)
LIHM .... Licentiate of the Institute of Housing Managers [*British*] (DI)
LIHN .... Hieronymi Liber Interpretationis Hebraicorum Nominum (BJA)
LIHPRHA ..... Low Income Housing Preservation and Resident Homeownership Act of 1990
LIHRY .... Lihir Gold ADS [*NASDAQ symbol*] (TTSB)
LIHRY .... Lihir Gold Ltd. [*NASDAQ symbol*] (SAG)
LII .... Flight Research Institute, M. Gromov [*Former USSR*] [*FAA designator*] (FAAC)
LII .... Larizza Industries, Inc. [*AMEX symbol*] (SPSG)
LII .... Leisure Interest Inventory (STED)
LII .... Life Insurance Index [*A publication*]
LII .... Livestock Industry Institute (EA)
LII .... Lues II [*or Secondary syphilis*] [*Infectious diseases*] (DAVI)
LII .... Mulia [*Indonesia*] [*Airport symbol*] (OAG)
LIIA .... Italy International NOTAM Office [*Italy ICAO location identifier*] (ICLI)
LIIB .... Roma [*Italy ICAO location identifier*] (ICLI)
LIIC .... Italy Military International NOTAM Office [*Italy ICAO location identifier*] (ICLI)
LIIG .... Logistics Item Identification Guide [*Military*] (AFM)
LIII .... Lues III [*Teritiary syphilis*] [*Infectious diseases*] (DAVI)
LIII .... Roma [*Italy ICAO location identifier*] (ICLI)
li-ion .... Lithium Ion
LIIP .... LASER-Induced Infrared Photochemistry
LIIR .... Italian Agency for Air Navigation Services [*Italy ICAO location identifier*] (ICLI)
LIJ .... Lawyers for an Independent Judiciary [*Defunct*] (EA)
LIJ .... Left Internal Jugular Vein [*Medicine*] (DMAA)
LIJJ .... Roma [*Italy ICAO location identifier*] (ICLI)
LIK .... Leichte Infanteriekolonne [*Light Infantry Supply Column*] [*German military - World War II*]
LIK .... Likiep [*Marshall Islands*] [*Airport symbol*] (OAG)
LIKE .... Learning Inventory of Kindergarten Experience [*Owigns, Mills, and O'Dell*] (TES)
LIL .... Laboratory Interface Language [*Programming language*]
LIL .... Large Immersion Lens
LIL .... Large-Ion Lithophile
LIL .... Law of the Iterated Logarithm (PDAA)
LIL .... Lead-In Light-System [*Aviation*]
LIL .... Light Intensity Low
LIL .... Lilac (ROG)
LIL .... Lille [*France*] [*Seismograph station code, US Geological Survey Closed*] (SEIS)
LIL .... Lille [*France*] [*Airport symbol*] (OAG)
LIL .... Lilliputian (ABBR)
Lil .... Lilly's English Assize Reports [*1688-93*] [*A publication*] (DLA)
LIL .... Lincoln's Inn Library [*A publication*] (DLA)
LIL .... Lithuanian Airlines [*ICAO designator*] (FAAC)
LIL .... Little (ABBR)
LIL .... Live-In Lover [*Slang*] (DSUE)
LIL .... Log-Inject-Log [*Petroleum technology*]
LIL .... Long Island Light'g [*NYSE symbol*] (TTSB)
LIL .... Long Island Lighting Co. [*Formerly, LLT*] [*NYSE symbol*] (SPSG)
LIL .... Low-Input Landscaping
LIL .... Lunar International Laboratory
LILA .... Ligue Internationale de la Librairie Ancienne [*International League of Antiquarian Booksellers - ILAB*] (EAIO)
LILA .... Low Impulsiveness, Low Anxiety (MAE)
Lil Abr .... Lilly's Abridgment [*England*] [*A publication*] (DLA)
LILAC .... Low-Intensity Large Area [*Headlight*]
LILACS .... Latin American and Caribbean Health Sciences Literature (IID)
LILAM .... Licentiate of the Institute of Leisure and Amenity Management [*British*] (DBQ)

LILCo .... Long Island Lighting Co. [*Associated Press*] (SAG)
Lil Conv ...... Lilly's Conveyancer [*A publication*] (DLA)
LILE .... Large Ion Lithophile Element [*Geochemistry*]
Lill Ent .... Lilly's Entries [*England*] [*A publication*] (DLA)
Lilly .... Lilly [*Eli*] and Co. [*Associated Press*] (SAG)
Lilly .... Lilly's Reports and Pleadings of Cases in Assize [*170 English Reprint*] [*1688-93*] [*A publication*] (DLA)
Lilly Abr ...... Lilly's Abridgment [*England*] [*A publication*] (DLA)
Lilly Assize... Lilly's Reports and Pleadings of Cases in Assize [*170 English Reprint*] [*1688-93*] [*A publication*] (DLA)
Lilly Assize (Eng)... Lilly's Reports and Pleadings of Cases in Assize [*170 English Reprint*] [*1688-93*] [*A publication*] (DLA)
LillyE .... Lilly [*Eli*] & Co. [*Associated Press*] (SAG)
LillyEli .... Lilly [*Eli*] [*Associated Press*] (SAG)
LillyInd .... Lilly Industries, Inc. [*Associated Press*] (SAG)
LILO .... Last-In, Last-Out [*Accounting*]
LILO .... Link Loader (IAA)
LILOC .... Light Lyne Optical Correlation (MCD)
LILPrA .... Long Island Ltg 7.95% Pfd [*NYSE symbol*] (TTSB)
LILPrB .... Long Island Ltg 5% B Pfd [*NYSE symbol*] (TTSB)
LILPrC .... Long Island Ltg 7.66% Pfd [*NYSE symbol*] (TTSB)
LILPrE .... Long Island Ltg 4.35% Cv E Pfd [*NYSE symbol*] (TTSB)
LILPrI .... Long Island Ltg, 5.75% Cv I Pfd [*NYSE symbol*] (TTSB)
LILPrQ .... Long Island Ltg 7.05% Pfd [*NYSE symbol*] (TTSB)
LILRC .... Long Island Library Resources Council [*Bellport, NY*] [*Library network*]
Lil Reg .... Lilly's Practical Register [*A publication*] (ILCA)
LilVern .... Lillian Vernon Corp. [*Associated Press*] (SAG)
LIM .... BVBA Lucorp [*Belgium*] [*FAA designator*] (FAAC)
LIM .... Compass Locator of Inner Marker Site
LIM .... Laboratory Institute of Merchandising [*New York, NY*]
LIM .... Language Interface Module (NITA)
LIM .... Language Interpretation Module
LIM .... Latent Image Memory
LIM .... Leg-Inducing Membrane [*Entomology*]
LIM .... Leningrad Institute of Metals [*Former USSR*] (MCD)
LIM .... Light Intensity Medium
LIM .... Lima [*Peru*] [*Seismograph station code, US Geological Survey*] (SEIS)
LIM .... Lima [*Peru*] [*Airport symbol*] (OAG)
LIM .... Lima Public Library, Lima, OH [*OCLC symbol*] (OCLC)
LIM .... Limber (MSA)
LIM .... Limerick [*County in Ireland*] (ROG)
lim .... Limes [*Limit*] [*Latin*]
LIM .... Limit
lim .... Limitation (STED)
lim .... Limiter [*Electronics*] (ECII)
LIM .... Limonene [*Organic chemistry*]
LIM .... Linear Induction Motor [*Magnetic rapid-transit car*]
LIM .... Line Insulation Monitor (PDAA)
LIM .... Line Interface Module
LIM .... Liquid Injection Molding
LIM .... Locator Inner Marker [*Aviation*] (DA)
LIM .... Losing Inventory Manager [*Army*] (AABC)
LIM .... Lotus/Intel/Microsoft [*Computer science*]
LIM .... Lower Inlet Module [*Nuclear energy*] (NRCH)
LIMA .... LASER-Induced Ion-Mass Analyzer [*Instrumentation*]
LIMA .... LASER-Induced Mass Analysis (AAEL)
LIMA .... Left Internal Mammary Artery [*Anatomy*] (AAMN)
LIMA .... Licentiate of the Institute of Mathematics and Its Applications [*British*] (DBQ)
LIMA .... Logic-in-Memory Array
LIMA .... Torino [*Italy ICAO location identifier*] (ICLI)
LIMAC .... Large Integrated Monolithic Array Computer (MCD)
LIM ACT ...... Limitation of Action [*Legal term*] (DLA)
LIMAS .... Lightweight Marking System [*British Army*]
LIMB .... Library Instruction Materials Bank [*Loughborough University of Technology*] [*Information service or system*] (IID)
LIMB .... Limestone Injection/Multistage Burner
LIMB .... Liquid Metal Breeder [*Reactor*]
LIMBE .... Milano/Bresso [*Italy ICAO location identifier*] (ICLI)
LIMC .... Milano/Malpensa [*Italy ICAO location identifier*] (ICLI)
LIMD .... Grigna Settentrionale [*Italy ICAO location identifier*] (ICLI)
LIMD .... Limited (ROG)
LIMDAT .... Limiting Date
LIMDIS .... Limited Distribution [*Military*] (AFIT)
LIMDOW ...... Light Intensity Modulation Direct OverWrite [*Computer science*]
LIMDU .... Limited Duty (MCD)
LIME .... Bergamo/Orio Al Serio [*Italy ICAO location identifier*] (ICLI)
LIME .... Low-Iron, Manganese-Enriched [*Meteorite*]
LIMEA .... Low-Iron-Content Monoethanolamine
LIMEAN .... London Interbank Median Average Rate
LIM-EMS ...... Lotus-Intel-Microsoft Expanded Memory Specification [*Computer science*] (BTTJ)
LIMESCO ..... Line Memory Scan Converter
limest .... Limestone [*Petrology*]
LIMF .... Licentiate of the Institute of Metal Finishing [*British*] (DBQ)
LIMF .... Torino/Caselle [*Italy ICAO location identifier*] (ICLI)
LIMFAC .... Limiting Factor (MCD)
LIMG .... Albenga [*Italy ICAO location identifier*] (ICLI)
LIMH .... Pian Rosa [*Italy ICAO location identifier*] (ICLI)
LIMI .... Colle Del Gigante [*Italy ICAO location identifier*] (ICLI)
LIMI .... Leningrad International Management Institute [*Joint Venture between Bocconi University, Italy and Leningrad University*] (ECON)
LIMIRIS .... LASER-Induced Modulation of Infrared in Silicon

LIMIT .... Leicester Intravenous Magnesium Intervention Trial [*Cardiology study*]
LIMIT .... Lot-Size Inventory Management Interpolation Technique (BUR)
Limitd .... [*The*] Limited, Inc. [*Associated Press*] (SAG)
LIMJ .... Genova/Sestri [*Italy ICAO location identifier*] (ICLI)
LIMK .... Torino/Bric Della Croce [*Italy ICAO location identifier*] (ICLI)
LIML .... Limited Information Maximum Likelihood [*Econometrics*]
LIML .... Milano/Linate [*Italy ICAO location identifier*] (ICLI)
LIMM .... Milano [*Italy ICAO location identifier*] (ICLI)
LIMN .... Cameri [*Italy ICAO location identifier*] (ICLI)
LIMNOL ...... Limnology
LIMO .... Least Input for the Most Output [*Business term*]
LIMO .... Limousine (DSUE)
LIMO .... Limousine Industry Manufacturers Organization (EA)
LIMO .... Monte Bisbino [*Italy ICAO location identifier*] (ICLI)
LIMON .... Limonis [*Of Lemon*] [*Pharmacy*] (ROG)
LIMOS .... Laser Intensity Modulation System [*Computer science*]
LIMOSO ...... Limitation of Supplies Order [*World War II*]
LIMP .... Language-Independent Macro Processor (PDAA)
LIMP .... Louis XIV, James II, Mary, Prince of Wales [*Jacobite toast*]
LIMP .... Lunar-Anchored Interplanetary Monitoring Platform [*Aerospace*]
LIMP .... Lunar Interplanetary Monitoring Probe (IAA)
LIMP .... Parma [*Italy ICAO location identifier*] (ICLI)
LIMPS .... Linear Induction Motor Propulsion System
LIMQ .... Govone [*Italy ICAO location identifier*] (ICLI)
LIMR .... Limiter
LIMR .... Novi Ligure [*Italy ICAO location identifier*] (ICLI)
LIMRA .... Life Insurance Marketing and Research Association [*Hartford, CT*] (EA)
LIMRC .... LRU [*Line Replaceable Unit*] Identification and Maintenance Requirements Catalog (NASA)
LIMRF .... Life Insurance Medical Research Fund [*Defunct*]
LIMRV .... Linear Induction Motor Research Vehicle [*Magnetic rapid-transit car*]
LIMS .... Laban Institute of Movement Studies [*Later, LBIMS*] (EA)
LIMS .... Laboratory Information Management System
LIMS .... LASER-Induced Mass Spectrometry (AAEL)
LIMS .... LASERInduced Microgrough Structures [*Surface Technology*]
LIMS .... Library Information Management System [*University of Maryland*]
LIMS .... Limb Infrared Monitor of the Stratosphere
LIMS .... Limb-Motion Sensor [*System*]
LIMS .... Limb Sounder (SSD)
LiMS .... Lithium Metal Sulfide
LIMS .... Logistic Inventory Management System [*North American Rockwell*]
LIMS .... Piacenza/San Damiano [*Italy ICAO location identifier*] (ICLI)
LIMSS .... Logistics Information Management Support System [*Military*]
LIMSW .... Limit Switch (NRCH)
LIMT .... Passo Della Cisa [*Italy ICAO location identifier*] (ICLI)
LIMTV .... Linear Induction Motor Test Vehicle [*Magnetic rapid-transit car*]
LIMU .... Capo Mele [*Italy ICAO location identifier*] (ICLI)
LIMU .... LASER Inertial Measurement Unit (MCD)
LIMV .... Lilac Mottle Virus [*Plant pathology*]
LIMV .... Passo Dei Giovi [*Italy ICAO location identifier*] (ICLI)
LIMW .... Aosta [*Italy ICAO location identifier*] (ICLI)
LIMY .... Monte Malanotte [*Italy ICAO location identifier*] (ICLI)
LIMZ .... Levaldigi [*Italy ICAO location identifier*] (ICLI)
LIN .... Law Institute News [*Australia A publication*]
LIN .... Linair-Hungarian Regional Airlines [*FAA designator*] (FAAC)
LIN .... Lincoln [*Diocesan abbreviation*] [*Nebraska*] (TOCD)
LIN .... Lincoln [*Nebraska*] [*Seismograph station code, US Geological Survey Closed*] (SEIS)
Lin .... Linden [*Record label*]
LIN .... Linden, CA [*Location identifier FAA*] (FAAL)
LIN .... Line (WDAA)
LIN .... Lineal (MSA)
LIN .... Linear (KSC)
lin .... Linear (STED)
LIN .... Line Item Number (AABC)
LIN .... Linen (ADA)
lin .... Linen (VRA)
LIN .... Liniment
lin .... Liniment (STED)
LIN .... Liquid Nitrogen (AFM)
LIN .... Massachusetts Institute of Technology, Lincoln Laboratory, Lexington, MA [*OCLC symbol*] (OCLC)
LIN .... Milan [*Italy*] Forlanini-Linate [*Airport symbol*] (OAG)
LINA .... Liberian News Agency (EY)
LINA .... Literaturnachweise [*Literature Compilations Database*] [*Fraunhofer Society*] (IID)
LINABOL ..... Lineas Navieras Bolivianas [*Shipping line*] [*Bolivia*] (EY)
LINAC .... Linear [*Electron*] Accelerator
LINAS .... LASER Inertial Navigation Attack System (IAA)
LINAS .... LASER-Integrated Navigation/Attack System (MCD)
LINC .... Laboratory Instrument Computer [*Medical analyzer*]
LINC .... Language Information Network Coordination [*Education*] (AIE)
LINC .... Language in the National Curriculum [*Project*] (WDAA)
LINC .... Learning Institute of North Carolina
LINC .... Legislative Information Network Corp. [*Information service or system*] (IID)
LINC .... Library & Information Consultants Ltd. [*Information service or system*] (IID)
LINC .... Lincolnshire [*County in England*]
LINC .... Lindas Diversified Holdings [*NASDAQ symbol*] (SAG)
LINC .... Lucas Industries Noise Centre [*Research center British*] (IRUK)
LINCA .... Linda's Flame Roasted Chicken [*NASDAQ symbol*] (TTSB)
L'INCA .... L'Institut National Canadien pour les Aveugles (AC)

Lincare .... Lincare Holdings, Inc. [*Associated Press*] (SAG)
LINCE .... LASER-Improved Naval Combat Equipment (PDAA)
LincEl .... [*The*] Lincoln Electric Co. [*Associated Press*] (SAG)
LincElA .... Lincoln Electric Co. (The) [*Associated Press*] (SAG)
LINCLOE ..... Lightweight Individual Combat Clothing and Equipment (AABC)
LinCMOS ..... Linear CMOS [*Complementary Metal Oxide Semiconductor*] [*Texas Instruments*] (NITA)
LINCMOS ..... Linear Complementary Metal-Oxide Semiconductor [*Electronics*] (EECA)
LincN .... Lincoln National Corp. [*Associated Press*] (SAG)
LincN .... Lincoln National Corp. Capital I [*Associated Press*] (SAG)
LincN .... Lincoln National Corp. Capital II [*Associated Press*] (SAG)
LincNatl ...... Lincoln National Corp. [*Associated Press*] (SAG)
LincNIF .... Lincoln National Income Fund, Inc. [*Associated Press*] (SAG)
LINCO .... Linear Composition (PDAA)
LINCO .... Linearly Organized Chemical Code for Use in Computer Systems (DIT)
Lincoln U .... Lincoln University (GAGS)
LINCOMPEX... Linked Compressor and Expander (NATG)
LINCOS .... Lingua Cosmica [*Artificial language consisting of radio signals of varying lengths and frequencies*]
LINCOTT ..... Liaison, Interface, Coupling, Technology Transfer
LINCS .... Language Information Network and Clearinghouse System [*Center for Applied Linguistics*] [*Washington, DC*]
LINCS .... Leased Interfacility Nas Communications System [*FAA*] (TAG)
LINCS .... Lincolnshire [*County in England*]
LINCS .... Literacy Information and Communication System
LincSB .... Lincoln Savings Bank [*Associated Press*] (SAG)
LincSnk ...... Lincoln Snacks Co. [*Associated Press*] (SAG)
LINCT .... Linctus [*Tincture*] [*Pharmacy*] (ROG)
LincTel .... Lincoln Telecommunications Co. [*Associated Press*] (SAG)
LINCW .... Linda's Flame Rstd Ckn Wrrt'A' [*NASDAQ symbol*] (TTSB)
LINCZ .... Linda's Flame Rstd Ckn Wrrt'B' [*NASDAQ symbol*] (TTSB)
LIND .... Lindberg Corp. [*NASDAQ symbol*] (SAG)
Linda .... Lindas Flame Roasted Chicken, Inc. [*Associated Press*] (SAG)
Linda .... Lindasw Diversified Holdings [*Associated Press*] (SAG)
LINDA .... Line Drawing Analyzer [*Cybernetics*]
LindasCh ..... Lindas Flame Roasted Chicken, Inc. [*Associated Press*] (SAG)
LindasDiv .... Lindas Diversified Holdings [*Associated Press*] (SAG)
Lindbrg ...... Lindberg Corp. [*Associated Press*] (SAG)
LINDI .... Line-to-Disk [*Computer science*] (MHDI)
Lind Jur ...... Lindley's Study of Jurisprudence [*A publication*] (DLA)
Lindl Copartn... Lindley on Partnership [*A publication*] (DLA)
Lindley .... Lindley's Law of Companies [*A publication*] (DLA)
Lindley Comp ... Lindley's Law of Companies [*A publication*] (DLA)
Lindley P ..... Lindley on Partnership [*A publication*] (DLA)
Lindley Part... Lindley on Partnership [*A publication*] (DLA)
LindlH .... Lindal Cedar Homes, Inc. [*Associated Press*] (SAG)
Lindl Partn... Lindley on Partnership [*A publication*] (DLA)
Lind Part .... Lindley on Partnership [*A publication*] (DLA)
Lind Pr ...... Lindewoode's Provinciales [*A publication*] (DLA)
Lind Prob.... Lindsay on Probates [*A publication*] (DLA)
Lindsy .... Lindsay Manufacturing Co. [*Associated Press*] (SAG)
lindwd .... Lindenwood (VRA)
LINE .... Lightweight Inertial Northseeking Equipmet (SAA)
LINE .... Long Interspersed Element Sequence [*Genetics*]
LINE .... Long Interspersed Nuclear Element [*Genetics*]
LinearT .... Linear Technology Corp. [*Associated Press*] (SAG)
L in Eastern Eur... Law in Eastern Europe [*A publication*] (DLA)
LINED .... Line Editor [*Computer science*] (MHDI)
LINEII .... Logic and Information Network Compiler II [*Computer science*] (HGAA)
LINER .... Low-Ionization Nuclear Emission-Line Region [*Spectroscopy*]
LINES .... Library Information Network Exchange Services [*Australia A publication*]
LINEs .... Long Inerspered Nuclcotide Elements [*Genetics*]
LINES .... Long-Interspersed Repeated Segments [*of DNA*] [*Genetics*] (DAVI)
Linfield C .... Linfield College (GAGS)
LINFT .... Linear Foot
linft .... Linear Foot (WPI)
Ling .... De Lingua Latina [*of Varro*] [*Classical studies*] (OCD)
LING .... Learning Independence Through Computers, Inc.
LING .... Linguistics
LINGUA .... Linguistic Analysis System (ECII)
LINIM .... Liniment
Lin Ins .... De Lineis Insecabilibus [*of Aristotle*] [*Classical studies*] (OCD)
Linium .... Linium Technology Corp. [*Associated Press*] (SAG)
LINJET .... Liquid Injection Electric Thruster [*NASA*] (NASA)
LINK .... Interlink Electronics [*NASDAQ symbol*] (TTSB)
LINK .... Interlink Electronics, Inc. [*NASDAQ symbol*] (SAG)
LINK .... Lambeth Information Network [*Information service or system*] [*British*] (NITA)
LINK .... Library and Information Network [*Planned Parenthood Federation of America, Inc.*] [*Information service or system*] (IID)
LINK .... Literature in Nursing Kardex
LINKW .... Interlink Electrs Wrrt [*NASDAQ symbol*] (TTSB)
LINLOG .... Linear-Logarithmic (IEEE)
LINMH .... Linear Meters per Hour (IAA)
LINN .... Linnaeus
Linn Ind ...... Linn's Index of Pennsylvania Reports [*A publication*] (DLA)
Linn Laws Prov PA... Linn on the Laws of the Province of Pennsylvania [*A publication*] (DLA)
LINO .... Liaison Officer [*Military*]
lino .... Linocut (VRA)
LINO .... Linoleum

Lino .... Linotronic [*Computer science*]
LINO .... Linotype
LINOL .... Linoleum (MSA)
LINOSCO ...... Libraries in North Staffordshire and South Cheshire in Cooperation [*British*] (NITA)
LINQ .... Literature in North Queensland [*A publication*]
LINS .... Labrador Institute of Northern Studies [*Memorial University of Newfoundland*] [*Canada Research center*] (RCD)
LINS .... LASER Inertial Navigation System (MCD)
LINS .... Lightweight Inertial Navigation System [*Air Force*]
LINS .... LORAN Inertial System
L in Soc'y .... Law in Society [*A publication*] (DLA)
LInstBB .... Licentiate of the Institute of British Bakers (DBQ)
LInstBCA ..... Licentiate of the Institute of Burial and Cremation Administration [*British*] (DBQ)
L Inst P .... Licentiate of the Institute of Physics [*British*]
LInstPRA ..... Licentiate of the Institute of Park and Recreation Administration [*British*] (DI)
LINTEL .... Lincoln Telecommunications Co. (EFIS)
LinTelev ..... Lin Television Corp. [*Associated Press*] (SAG)
L Intell .... Law Intelligencer [*United States*] [*A publication*] (DLA)
L in Trans J ... Law in Transition Journal [*A publication*] (DLA)
L in Trans Q ... Law in Transition Quarterly [*A publication*] (DLA)
LINUS .... Local Information Network for Universal Service [*Telecommunications service*] (TSSD)
LINUS .... Logical Inquiry and Update System
LINX .... Logistics Information Exchange [*Computer science*] (CIST)
LINZ .... Lindsay Manufacturing [*NASDAQ symbol*] (SAG)
LINZ .... Lindsay Mfg [*NASDAQ symbol*] (TTSB)
LIO .... Air Charter Ltd. (Leiguflug Isleifs Ottesen) [*Iceland*] [*FAA designator*] (FAAC)
LIO .... Left Inferior Oblique [*Anatomy*] (DAVI)
LIO .... Lesser Included Offense
LIO .... Liberian Iron Ore Ltd. [*Toronto Stock Exchange symbol*]
LIO .... Limon [*Costa Rica*] [*Airport symbol*] (OAG)
LIO .... Liottite [*A zeolite*]
LIO .... Lithium Organic Battery
LIO .... Local Interconnect Option [*Wang Laboratories, Inc.*] (BYTE)
LIO .... National Restaurant Association Large Independent Operators [*Defunct*] (EA)
LIOAS .... LASER-Induced Optoacoustic Spectroscopy
LIOC .... Lighted Independent of Computer
LIOCS .... Logical Input/Output Control System [*Computer science*]
LIOD .... Lightweight Optronic Director (MCD)
LIODD .... LASER In-Flight Obstacle Detection Device
LiOH .... Lithium Hydroxide (NASA)
LIOL .... Legal Information On-Line [*Ministry of Labour*] [*Hamilton, ON*] [*Information service or system*] (IID)
LION .... Fidelity National [*NASDAQ symbol*] (TTSB)
LION .... Fidelity National Corp. [*NASDAQ symbol*] (SAG)
LION .... Lehman Investment Opportunity Note
LION .... Library Information OnLine [*International Atomic Energy Agency*] [*United Nations*] (DUND)
LION .... Local Input/Output Nozzle [*Computer science*]
LI/ON .... Logicon Input/Output Network
LION .... Lunar International Observer Network [*NASA*]
LionBrw ...... Lion Brewery, Inc. (The) [*Associated Press*] (SAG)
LIONS .... Library Information and On-Line Network Service [*New York Public Library*] [*Information service or system*] (IID)
LIOP .... Life in One Position [*Telecommunications*] (TEL)
LIOP .... Limited Initial Operating Production (MCD)
LIP .... Boston, MA [*Location identifier FAA*] (FAAL)
LIP .... Large Internet Packet [*Computer science*] (PCM)
LIP .... LASER-Induced Plasma [*Spectroscopy*]
LIP .... Latent Information Parameter
LIP .... Lateral Intraparietal Area [*Anatomy*]
LIP .... Launch in Process [*NASA*] (IAA)
LIP .... Legal Inverse Path [*Physics*]
LIP .... Letter Input Procesing [*Printing*] (DGA)
LIP .... Library Information Plan (AIE)
LIP .... Life Insurance Policy
LIP .... Limited Implementation Program [*FAA*] (TAG)
lip .... Lipemic [*Cardiology*] (DAVI)
LIP .... Lipkovo [*Yugoslavia*] [*Seismograph station code, US Geological Survey*] (SEIS)
Lip .... Lipoate [*Also called Lipoic acid*] [*Biochemistry*] (DAVI)
LIP .... Lithium-Induced Polydipsia (DB)
LIP .... Local Initiatives Program [*Canada*]
LIP .... Low Internal Phase [*Emulsion chemistry*]
LIP .... Lunar Impact Probe [*Aerospace*]
LIP .... Lymphoid Interstitial Pneumonitis [*Medicine*]
LIPA .... Aviano [*Italy ICAO location identifier*] (ICLI)
LIPA .... Labor Institute of Public Affairs (EA)
LIPA .... Lauric [*or Lauroyl or Lauryl*] Isopropanolamide [*Also, LPA*] [*Organic chemistry*]
LIPA .... List of Interchangeable Parts and Assemblies
LIPA .... Liverpool Institute of Performing Arts [*England*] (WDAA)
LIPA .... Louisiana Independent Physicians Association, Inc.
LIPAD .... Ligue Patriotique pour le Developpement [*Burkina Faso*] [*Political party*] (EY)
LIPAS .... LASER-Induced Photoacoustic Spectroscopy
LIPB .... Bolzano [*Italy ICAO location identifier*] (ICLI)
LIPB .... Lipase B (DMAA)
LIPB .... Lloyd's International Private Banking [*Finance*]
Lip Bib Jur ... Lipenius' Bibliotheca Juridica [*A publication*] (DLA)

LIPC .... Cervia [*Italy ICAO location identifier*] (ICLI)
LIPC .... Levenson's Internal, Powerful Others, and Chance Scales (EDAC)
LIPC .... Livestock Industry Promotion Council [*Australia*]
LIPD .... Lipase D (DMAA)
LIPD .... Udine/Campoformido [*Italy ICAO location identifier*] (ICLI)
LIPE .... Bologna/Borgo Panigale [*Italy ICAO location identifier*] (ICLI)
LIPES .... LASER-Induced Plasma Emission Spectroscopy (MEC)
LIPF .... Ferrara [*Italy ICAO location identifier*] (ICLI)
LIPF .... LASER-Induced Photodissociation and Fluorescence [*Coal technology*]
LIPFS .... Laser-Induced Plasma Fluorescence Spectroscopy (MEC)
LIPG .... Gorizia [*Italy ICAO location identifier*] (ICLI)
LIPH .... Treviso/San Angelo [*Italy ICAO location identifier*] (ICLI)
LIPHE .... Life Interpersonal History Enquiry [*Test*] [*Psychology*]
LIPI .... Indonesian Institute of Sciences [*Marine science*] (OSRA)
LIPI .... Rivolto [*Italy ICAO location identifier*] (ICLI)
LIPID .... Logical Page Identifier
LIPJ .... Bassano Del Grappa [*Italy ICAO location identifier*] (ICLI)
LIPK .... Forli [*Italy ICAO location identifier*] (ICLI)
LIPL .... Ghedi [*Italy ICAO location identifier*] (ICLI)
LIPL .... Linear Information Processing Language [*High-order programming language*] [*Computer science*] (IEEE)
LIPN .... Verona/Boscomantico [*Italy ICAO location identifier*] (ICLI)
LIPO .... Liposome Co. [*NASDAQ symbol*] (SAG)
LIPO .... Montichiari [*Italy ICAO location identifier*] (ICLI)
Liposm .... [*The*] Liposome Co., Inc. [*Associated Press*] (SAG)
LIPOZ .... Liposome $1.9375 Cv Dep'A'Pfd [*NASDAQ symbol*] (TTSB)
LIPP .... LASER-Induced Pressure Pulse [*Medicine*] (DMAA)
LIP P .... Lipid Profile [*Cardiology*] (DAVI)
LIPP .... Padova [*Italy ICAO location identifier*] (ICLI)
Lipp Cr L .... Lippitt's Massachusetts Criminal Law [*A publication*] (DLA)
LIPQ .... Ronchi De'Legionari [*Italy ICAO location identifier*] (ICLI)
LIPR .... Rimini [*Italy ICAO location identifier*] (ICLI)
LIPS .... Laboratory Interface Peripheral Subsystem [*Computer science*]
LIPS .... Lanthanide Ion Probe Spectroscopy
LIPS .... Leiter International Performance Scale [*Psychology*]
LIPS .... Library and Information Plans [*British*]
LIPS .... Litton Industries Privacy System
LIPS .... Logical Inferences per Second [*Processing power units*] [*Computer science*]
LIPS .... Logic Inference per Second (IAA)
Lips .... Low Income, Parents Supporting [*Lifestyle classification*]
LIPS .... Treviso/Istrana [*Italy ICAO location identifier*] (ICLI)
Lipsm .... [*The*] Liposome Co., Inc. [*Associated Press*] (SAG)
LIPT .... Leiter International Performance Test [*Psychology*] (DAVI)
LIPT .... Vicenza [*Italy ICAO location identifier*] (ICLI)
LIPU .... Padova [*Italy ICAO location identifier*] (ICLI)
LIPV .... Venezia/San Nicolo [*Italy ICAO location identifier*] (ICLI)
LIPX .... Villafranca [*Italy ICAO location identifier*] (ICLI)
LIPY .... Ancona/Falconara [*Italy ICAO location identifier*] (ICLI)
LIPZ .... Venezia/Tessera [*Italy ICAO location identifier*] (ICLI)
LIQ .... Athens, TX [*Location identifier FAA*] (FAAL)
LIQ .... Liquest International Marketing [*Vancouver Stock Exchange symbol*]
liq .... Liqueur [*Solution*] [*Pharmacy*]
LIQ .... Liquid (AAG)
LIQ .... Liquidation (MCD)
LIQ .... Liquor
LIQ .... Lisala [*Zaire*] [*Airport symbol*] (OAG)
LIQ .... Lower Inner Quadrant [*Anatomy*]
LIQB .... Arezzo [*Italy ICAO location identifier*] (ICLI)
LIQB .... Liqui-Box Corp. [*NASDAQ symbol*] (SAG)
LIQC .... Capri [*Italy ICAO location identifier*] (ICLI)
LIQD .... Liquid (ECII)
LIQD .... Passo Della Porretta [*Italy ICAO location identifier*] (ICLI)
LIQDTE .... Liquidate (ROG)
LIQFRKT ...... Liquid Fuel Rocket (IAA)
LIQI .... Gran Sasso [*Italy ICAO location identifier*] (ICLI)
LIQJ .... Civitavecchia [*Italy ICAO location identifier*] (ICLI)
LIQK .... Capo Palinuro [*Italy ICAO location identifier*] (ICLI)
LIQM .... Rifredo Mugello [*Italy ICAO location identifier*] (ICLI)
LIQN .... Rieti [*Italy ICAO location identifier*] (ICLI)
LIQO .... Monte Argentario [*Italy ICAO location identifier*] (ICLI)
LIQOR .... Liquidator (ROG)
LIQP .... Palmaria [*Italy ICAO location identifier*] (ICLI)
LIQQ .... Monte Cavo [*Italy ICAO location identifier*] (ICLI)
LIQR .... Radicofani [*Italy ICAO location identifier*] (ICLI)
LIQS .... Siena [*Italy ICAO location identifier*] (ICLI)
LIQSS .... Liquid Steady State (PDAA)
LIQT .... Circeo [*Italy ICAO location identifier*] (ICLI)
LIQT .... Liquid Transient (PDAA)
LiquiBox ...... Liqui-Box Corp. [*Associated Press*] (SAG)
LIQUID .... Liquidus [*Liquid*] [*Pharmacy*] (ROG)
LIQUON .... Liquidation
Liquor Cont L Serv (CCH) ... Liquor Control Law Service (Commerce Clearing House) [*A publication*] (DLA)
LIQV .... Volterra [*Italy ICAO location identifier*] (ICLI)
LIQW .... Sarzana/Luni [*Italy ICAO location identifier*] (ICLI)
LIQZ .... Ponza [*Italy ICAO location identifier*] (ICLI)
LIR .... Dover, DE [*Location identifier FAA*] (FAAL)
LIR .... Laboratory for Insulation Research [*MIT*] (MCD)
LIR .... Leader Internode Ratio [*Botany*]
LIR .... Left Iliac Region [*Medicine*] (MAE)
LIR .... Left Inferior Rectus [*Muscle*] [*Ophthalmology and surgery*] (DAVI)
LIR .... Level Indicator Recorder [*Electronics*] (ECII)
LIR .... Liberia [*Costa Rica*] [*Airport symbol*] (OAG)

LIR..............	Library and Information Resources (NITA)
LIR..............	Licentiate of the Institute of Population Registration [*British*] (DBQ)
LIR..............	Limiting Interval Reliability
LIR..............	Line Integral Refractometer
LIR..............	Lionair SA [*Luxembourg*] [*ICAO designator*] (FAAC)
lir..............	Lira [*Monetary unit*] [*Italy*]
lir..............	Lithuanian Soviet Socialist Republic [*MARC country of publication code Library of Congress*] (LCCP)
LIR..............	Load-Indicating Relay (IAA)
LIR..............	Load-Indicating Resistor (IAA)
LIR..............	Location Inventory Report (AAEL)
LIR..............	Longitude Independent Reset
LIR..............	Lost Item Replacement (MCD)
LIRA..............	Lambeg Industrial Research Association [*British*] (IRUK)
LIRA..............	Liberal Industrial Relations Association [*British*]
LIRA..............	Linen Industry Research Association [*British*] (BI)
LIRA..............	Little Italy Restoration Association
LIRA..............	Roma/Ciampino [*Italy ICAO location identifier*] (ICLI)
LIRB..............	Liability Insurance Research Bureau (NTPA)
LIRB..............	Vigna Di Valle [*Italy ICAO location identifier*] (ICLI)
LIRBM..............	Liver, Iron, Red Bone Marrow
LIRC..............	Centocelle [*Italy ICAO location identifier*] (ICLI)
LIRC..............	Lebanese Information and Research Center (EA)
LIRC..............	Level Indicator Recorder Controller [*Electronics*] (ECII)
LIRC..............	Ligue Internationale de la Representation Commerciale [*International League of Commercial Travelers and Agents - ILCTA*] (EAIO)
LIRC..............	Low Interest Rate Currency (MHDW)
LIRDP..............	Luangwa Integrated Resource Development Project [*China*] (BUAC)
LIRE..............	Lincoln Institute for Research and Education (EA)
LIRE..............	Pratica Di Mare [*Italy ICAO location identifier*] (ICLI)
LIRES..............	Literature Retrieval System [*Computer science*]
LIRES-MC	Literature Retrieval System - Multiple Searching, Complete Text [*Computer science*]
LIRF..............	Low-Intensity Reciprocity Failure [*Of photographic emulsions*]
LIRF..............	Roma/Fiumicino [*Italy ICAO location identifier*] (ICLI)
LIRG..............	Guidonia [*Italy ICAO location identifier*] (ICLI)
LIRG..............	Landesverband der Israelitischen Religionsgemeinde (BJA)
LIRG..............	Library and Information Research Group [*Bristol Polytechnic Library*] [*British Information service or system*] (IID)
LIRH..............	Frosinone [*Italy ICAO location identifier*] (ICLI)
LIRI..............	Leather Industries Research Institute [*South Africa*] (BUAC)
LIRI..............	Salerno/Pontecagnano [*Italy ICAO location identifier*] (ICLI)
LIRIC..............	Language Instruction for Recent Immigrants through Computer Technology (EDAC)
LIRJ..............	Marina Di Campo [*Italy ICAO location identifier*] (ICLI)
LIRK..............	Monte Terminillo [*Italy ICAO location identifier*] (ICLI)
LIRL..............	Latina [*Italy ICAO location identifier*] (ICLI)
LIRL..............	Low Intensity Runway Edge Lights [*FAA*] (TAG)
LIRL..............	Low-Intensity Runway Lighting
LIRLY..............	Load-Indicating Relay (MSA)
LIRM..............	Grazzanise [*Italy ICAO location identifier*] (ICLI)
LIRMA..............	London Insurance and Reinsurance Market Association (ECON)
LIRN..............	Library and Information for the Northwest [*Program of the Fred Meyer Charitable Trust*]
LIRN..............	Library and Information Research News [*A publication*] (NITA)
LIRN..............	Library Information Enquiry and Referral Network (TELE)
LIRN..............	Napoli/Capodichino [*Italy ICAO location identifier*] (ICLI)
LIROC..............	Last Instruction Readout Cycle (IAA)
LIRP..............	Pisa [*Italy ICAO location identifier*] (ICLI)
LIRQ..............	Firenze [*Italy ICAO location identifier*] (ICLI)
LIRR	[*The*] Long Island Rail Road Co.
LIRR..............	Luoyang Institute of Refractories Research [*China*] (BUAC)
LIRR..............	Roma [*Italy ICAO location identifier*] (ICLI)
LIRS..............	Grosseto [*Italy ICAO location identifier*] (ICLI)
LIRS..............	Lance Information Retrieval System
LIRS..............	Legal Information and Reference Services [*General Accounting Office*] (IID)
LIRS..............	Level Indicator Recording Switch (NRCH)
LIRS..............	Library Information Retrieval Service [*Oregon State University*] [*Information service or system*]
LIRS..............	Library Information Retrieval System [*California Institute of Technology*] [*Pasadena, CA*]
LIRS..............	Low Impact Resistant Supports [*FAA*] (TAG)
LIRS..............	Lutheran Immigration and Refugee Service (EA)
LIRSH..............	List of Items Requiring Special Handling
LIRT..............	Library Instruction Round Table [*American Library Association*]
LIRT..............	Low Input Reduced Tillage [*Cropping systems*] (GNE)
LIRT..............	Trevico [*Italy ICAO location identifier*] (ICLI)
LIRTS..............	Large Infrared Telescope
LIRU..............	Roma/Urbe [*Italy ICAO location identifier*] (ICLI)
LIRV..............	Viterbo [*Italy ICAO location identifier*] (ICLI)
LIRZ..............	Perugia [*Italy ICAO location identifier*] (ICLI)
LIS..............	Airlis SA [*Spain ICAO designator*] (FAAC)
LIS..............	Laboratory Information Systems
LIS..............	Language Implementation System (IAA)
LIS..............	Lanthanide-Induced Shift [*Spectroscopy*]
LIS..............	Lanthanide-Ion Induced Chemical Shift [*Spectroscopy*]
LIS..............	LARC Instruction Simulator
LIS..............	Large Interactive Surface [*Automated drafting table that serves as a computer input and output device*]
LIS..............	Laser Ignition System [*Military*]
LIS..............	LASER Illuminator System
LIS..............	LASER-Induced Separation (MCD)
LIS..............	LASER Interferometer System
LIS..............	LASER Isotope Separation
LIS..............	Lateral Intercellular Space (PDAA)
LIS..............	Launch Instant Selector
LIS..............	Laurentide Ice Sheet [*Climatology*]
LIS..............	Left Intercostal Space [*Cardiology*]
LIS..............	Legislative Information Service [*New Jersey State Legislature*] [*Trenton*] [*Information service or system*] (IID)
LIS..............	Legislative Information System [*National Conference of State Legislatures*] [*Information service or system*] (IID)
LIS..............	Lesbian Information Service (BUAC)
LIS..............	Libertarian Information Service [*An association*] (EA)
LIS..............	Library and Information Science
LIS..............	Library and Information Service
LIS..............	Library and Information Services [*Institution of Mining and Metallurgy*] [*British Information service or system*] (IID)
LIS..............	Library Information System [*Georgetown University*] [*Information service or system*]
LIS..............	Licensing Information Service (IID)
LIS..............	Licensure Information System [*Public Health Service*] [*Georgetown University Medical Center*] (IID)
LIS..............	Light Industries Services [*Singapore*] (BUAC)
LIS..............	Line Information Store [*Telecommunications*] (TEL)
LIS..............	Line Isolation Switch [*Reactor level switch*] (IEEE)
LIS..............	Link Information Sciences (BUR)
LIS..............	Liposome Immunosensor [*Electrochemistry*]
LIS..............	Lisbon [*Portugal*] [*Airport symbol*] (OAG)
LIS..............	Lisbon [*Portugal*] [*Seismograph station code, US Geological Survey*] (SEIS)
LIS..............	List and Index Society [*British*] (NITA)
LIS..............	Lithium Diodosalicylate [*Organic chemistry*]
LIS..............	LM [*Lunar Module*] Interface Control Specification [*NASA*] (KSC)
LIS..............	Load I-Bank and Jump [*Computer science*]
LIS..............	Lobular in Situ [*Medicine*]
LIS..............	Locate in Scotland [*Investment group*] (ECON)
LIS..............	Lockheed Information Systems (NITA)
LIS..............	Loop Input Signal
LIS..............	Loss Information Service [*Insurance*]
LIS..............	Low-Impact Switch (MCD)
LIS..............	Low Inductance Stripline (IAA)
LIS..............	Low-Intensity Sonication [*Chemistry*]
LIS..............	Low Intermittent Suction [*Medicine*] (MEDA)
LIS..............	Low Ionic Strength (DB)
LIS..............	Lutheran Immigration Service [*Later, LIRS*] (EA)
LIS..............	Luxembourg Income Study [*Economics*]
LISA..............	Laboratory for Information Science in Agriculture [*Research center Defunct*] (RCD)
LISA..............	Laboratory for Information Science in Agriculture [*Colorado*] (BUAC)
LISA..............	LARC Instruction Assembly
LISA..............	LASER Indirect Fire Semiactive
LISA..............	Lead-in-Steel Analyser (PDAA)
LISA..............	Leather Industry Suppliers Associates [*British*] (DBA)
LISA..............	Leather Industry Suppliers Association (BUAC)
LISA..............	Library and Information Science Abstracts (TELE)
LISA..............	Library Systems Analysis
LISA..............	Licht Sammler [*Light Collector*] [*Fluorescent plastic used in commercial displays*] [*German*]
LISA..............	Life Insurance Society of America (EA)
LISA..............	Linear Systems Analysis
LISA..............	Line Impedance Stabilization Network
LISA..............	Linked Indexed Sequential Access
LISA..............	Locally Integrated Software Architecture [*Apple microcomputer*] [*Computer science*]
LISA..............	London and International School of Acting [*British*]
LISA..............	Low-Input Sustainable Agriculture
LISA..............	Seaman Apprentice, Lithographer, Striker [*Navy rating*]
LISAN..............	Librarians on the Information Superhighway Advocacy Network (AL)
LISAN..............	Libraries on the Information Superhighway Advocacy Network (TELE)
LISARD..............	Latest Information Selected and Abstracted for Researchers and Decision-Makers [*Database*]
LISARD..............	Library and Information Service Automated Retrieval of Data (NITA)
LISARD..............	Library Information Search and Retrieval Data System [*US Navy*] (NITA)
LISB..............	Lithium Ion Storage Battery (PCM)
LISB..............	Long Island Bancorp [*NASDAQ symbol*] (TTSB)
LISB..............	Long Island Bancorp, Inc. [*NASDAQ symbol*] (SAG)
LISC..............	Library and Information Services Council [*British*]
LISC..............	Lions International Stamp Club (EA)
LISC..............	Local Initiatives Support Corp. (EA)
LISCO..............	Liberian Iron and Steel Corp. (BUAC)
LISD..............	Latest Information Selected and Abstracted for Researchers and Decision-Makers [*Database*]
LISD..............	Library and Information Services Division [*National Oceanic and Atmospheric Administration*] (NITA)
LISDOK..............	Literaturinformationssystem [*Literature Information System*] [*North Rhine-Westphalia Institute for Air Pollution Control*] [*Information service or system*] (IID)
LISDP..............	LOAD [*Low-Altitude Defense*] Interceptor Subsystem Development Plan
LISE..............	Librarians of Institutes and Schools of Education [*British*] (DBA)
LISFA..............	Lost in Space Fannish Alliance (EA)
LISH..............	Last In, Still Here [*Accounting*] (ADA)
LISI..............	Library Interface Systems, Inc. [*Information service or system*] (IID)
LISIC..............	Library and Information Service to Industry and Commerce (NITA)
LISK..............	Liskeard [*Municipal borough in England*]
LISM..............	Licentiate, Institute of Sales and Marketing Executives (ADA)
LISM..............	Licentiate of the Incorporated Society of Musicians (ROG)

LISN.............	Library Services Network [Library network]
LISN.............	Line Impedance Stabilization Network
LISN.............	Load Impedance Stabilization Network [Electrical engineering]
LISN.............	Long Island Sports Network [Cable-television system]
LISN.............	Seaman, Lithographer, Striker [Navy rating]
LISNY	Life Insurance Society of New York (SRA)
LISP.............	LASER Isotope Separation Program
LISP.............	Library and Information Software Package (PDAA)
LISP.............	Lightweight Individual Special Purpose [Weaponry]
LISP.............	Liquid Injector Spray Pattern (MCD)
LISP.............	List Processing [Programming language] [Facetious translation: "Lots of Insane, Stupid Parentheses"] [Computer science]
LISP.............	List Processor [Standard programming language] [1958] [Computer science]
LISPB.........	Lithospheric Seismic Profile in Britain (PDAA)
LISPER	Limited Speech Recognition (PDAA)
LISR...........	Line Information Storage and Retrieval [Information service or system] (NITA)
LISRB	Life Insurance Sales Research Bureau [Later, LIMRA]
LISREL........	Linear Structural Relationships (NITA)
LISRES-A.....	Life Stressors and Social Resources Inventory-Adult Form [Test] (TMMY)
LISRES-Y	Life Stressors and Social Resources Inventory Youth-Form [Test] (TMMY)
LISS.............	Lightweight Integrated Shelter System (DWSG)
LISS.............	Linear/Imaging Self-Scanner Sensor (MCD)
LISS.............	Los-Ionic-Strength Saline Solution [Medicine] (MEDA)
LISS.............	Low-Ionic-Strength Saline [Medicine] (DMAA)
LISSADA......	Library and Information Science Students Attitudes, Demographics, and Aspirations Survey [American Libraries Association]
LISST...........	Library and Information Scholarship Today [A publication]
LIST.............	Last In, Still There [Accounting]
LIST.............	Library and Information Science Trends
LIST.............	Library & Information Selective Targeting (WDAA)
LIST.............	Library and Information Services, Tees-Side (IEEE)
LIST.............	Library and Information Services Today [A publication]
LIST.............	Library Index Search and Transcribe
LIST.............	Low Isotonic Strength Titrator
LISTAR	Lincoln Information Storage and Associative Retrieval System [Lincoln Laboratory] [Massachusetts Institute of Technology] (NITA)
LISTAR	Lincoln Information Storage and Retrieval [MIT]
LISTD..........	Licentiate of the Imperial Society of Teachers of Dancing [British]
LISTED........	Library Integrated Systems for Telematics-Based Education (TELE)
LISTS...........	Library Information System Time-Sharing
LISU.............	Library and Information Statistics Unit (AIE)
LISV.............	Loyal Independent Sheffield Volunteers [British military] (DMA)
LISWG	Land Interface Sub-Working Group [NATO] (NATG)
LIT	Adams Field [FAA] (TAG)
LIT	Air Littoral [France ICAO designator] (FAAC)
LIT	Language Imitation Test
LIT	Language Inventory for Teachers [Child development test]
LIT	Lawrence Institute of Technology [Later, Lawrence Technological University]
LIT	Lead-In Training [Air Force] (DOMA)
LIT	Librarians Inquiry Terminal (IT)
Lit	Lietuvos TSR Valstybine Respublikine Biblioteka [National Library of Lithuania], Vilnius, Lithuania [Library symbol Library of Congress] (LCLS)
LIT	Life Insurance Trust (DLA)
LIT	Light Interface Technology [Signal transmission]
LIT	Light Intratheater Transport [Air Force]
LIT	Light Ion Trough
LIT	Line Insulation Test [Telecommunications]
LIT	Liquid Injection Technique (IEEE)
Lit	Lire Italiane [Italian Lire] [Monetary unit]
LIT	Litany (ROG)
LIT	Liter [Metric measure of volume]
LIT	Literacy
LIT	Literal
LIT	Literary
Lit	Literary (WA)
LIT	Literature
lit	Literature (WDMC)
Lit	Literature (AL)
lit	Lithuanian [MARC language code Library of Congress] (LCCP)
LIT	Lithuanian Apostolate for Lithuanian Catholics [Diocesan abbreviation] (TOCD)
Lit	Littell's Kentucky Reports [A publication] (DLA)
LIT	Litter (WDAA)
Lit	Litterae [Letters] [Latin] (ADA)
Lit	Little
LIT	Little Rock [Arkansas] [Airport symbol] (OAG)
Lit	Littleton's English Common Pleas Reports [A publication] (DLA)
Lit	Littleton's Tenures [A publication] (DLA)
LIT	Litton Indus [NYSE symbol] (TTSB)
LIT	Litton Industries, Inc. [NYSE symbol] (SPSG)
LIT	Liturgy
LIT	Local Inclusive Tour (DCTA)
LIT	Local Income Tax
LIT	Location/Identification Transmitter [NASA]
LIT	London Investment Trust [British]
LIT	Low-Impedance Transmission
LITA.............	Library and Information Technology Association (EA)
LITA.............	LIbrary and Information Technology Associaton of the ALA (NITA)

Lit & Bl Dig...	Littleton and Blatchley's Insurance Digest [A publication] (DLA)
LITAS..........	Low Intensity Two-Color Approach Slope Indicator [Aviation] (DA)
LITASTOR....	Light Tapping Storage (IAA)
Lit B	Litterarum Baccalaureus [Bachelor of Letters or Literature] [Latin]
Lit Brooke....	Brooke's New Cases, English King's Bench [1515-58] [A publication] (DLA)
LITC............	Library Information Technology Centre [British] (TELE)
LITCA..........	Licensing Innovation Technology Consultants Association (BUAC)
LitchFin	Litchfield Financial Corp. [Associated Press] (SAG)
Lit Crit	Literary Criticism (WGA)
LITD............	Laser-Induced Thermal Desorption
Lit D	Litterarum Doctor [Doctor of Letters or Literature] [Latin]
LitDokAB......	Literaturdokumentation zur Arbeitsmarkt- und Berufsforschung [Deutsche Bundesanstalt fuer Arbeit] [Germany Information service or system] (CRD)
LITE	LASER Illuminator Targeting Equipment
LITE	LASER In-Space Technology Experiment
LITE	Legal Information Through Electronics [Air Force]
LITE	Let's Improve Today's Education [Newsletter]
Litelfuse......	Littelfuse, Inc. [Associated Press] (SAG)
LITES	LASER Initiated Transfer Energy Subsystem [Detonator, developed by US Navy]
LITES	LASER Intercept and Technical Exploitation System (MCD)
LITEX	Searchlight Illumination Exercise [Also, LIGHTEX] [Military] (NVT)
LitfldAd.......	Littlefield, [Adams] & Co. [Associated Press] (SAG)
Litfse..........	Littelfuse, Inc. [Associated Press] (SAG)
LITFUND......	Fund for the Relief of Russian Writers and Scientists in Exile (EA)
litg.............	Liturgy (VRA)
LITH	Lithium [Pharmacy] (DAVI)
lith	Lithograph (WDMC)
LITH	Lithograph [or Lithography] (ROG)
lith	Lithographic (WDMC)
lith	Lithography (WDMC)
Lith	Lithuania (VRA)
LITH	Lithuania (ROG)
LITH	Lithuanian [Language, etc.]
LITH BRO....	Lithium Bromide (DNAB)
LITHD	Lithographed (ROG)
LITHO	Lithograph (AABC)
litho	Lithograph (VRA)
litho	Lithographic (WDMC)
litho	Lithography (WDMC)
litho	Lithotripsy [Medicine] (DAVI)
LITHOC	Lithographic
lithog	Lithograph (WDMC)
lithog	Lithographic (WDMC)
LITHOG	Lithographing
lithog	Lithography (WDMC)
LITHOG	Lithography
lithol...........	Lithology (BARN)
LITHOR	Lithographer
LITHOT	Lithotomy [Medicine]
LITHOY	Lithography
LithSSR	Lithuanian Soviet Socialist Republic
LITHUAN......	Lithuanian
Lit Hum	Literae Humaniores [Faculty of Classics and Philosophy, Oxford] [British] (WA)
LIT HUM	Litterae Humaniores [Classic literature] [Latin] (ROG)
Litig	Litigation [A publication] (DLA)
LITIGON.......	Litigation (ROG)
LITINT.........	Literacy International
LITINT.........	Literature Intelligence (MCD)
LITIR...........	Literary Information and Retrieval [Computer science]
LITIR...........	Literature Information and Retrieval [Database on Victorian studies literature] [University of Alberta] [Canada] (NITA)
LIT-LIT........	Committee on World Literacy and Christian Literature [Later, Intermedia] (EA)
Lit M...........	Master of Literature
LitMo..........	Liturgie und Moenchtum [A publication] (BJA)
LITPrB	Litton Indus,$2 B Pfd [NYSE symbol] (TTSB)
LITR...........	Low-Cost Indirect-Fire Training Round [Army] (INF)
LITR...........	Low-Intensity Test Reactor [ORNL]
Lit Sel Ca ...	Littell's Select Kentucky Cases [A publication] (DLA)
Litt.............	Littell's Kentucky Supreme Court Reports [1822-24] [A publication] (DLA)
LITT	Litterateur [French] (ROG)
Litt.............	Littleton's English Common Pleas Reports [A publication] (DLA)
Litt & S St Law...	Littell and Swigert's Digest of Statute Law [Kentucky] [A publication] (DLA)
Litt B	Litterarum Baccalaureus [Bachelor of Letters or Literature] [Latin]
Litt Comp Laws...	Littell's Statute Law [Kentucky] [A publication] (DLA)
Litt D	Litterarum Doctor [Doctor of Letters or Literature] [Latin]
LittD(Econ)...	Doctor of Letters in Economic Studies (ADA)
Littell	Littell's Kentucky Reports [A publication] (DLA)
LittHD ;.......	Doctor of Hebrew Letters (BJA)
Litt (KY)......	Littell [Kentucky] [A publication] (DLA)
Litt L	Licentiate in Letters
Little Brooke...	Brooke's New Cases, English King's Bench [1515-58] [A publication] (DLA)
Littleton.......	Littleton's English Common Pleas and Exchequer Reports [A publication] (DLA)
Litt M..........	Master of Letters
Litton..........	Litton Industries, Inc. [Associated Press] (SAG)
Litt Rep	Littleton's English Common Pleas and Exchequer Reports [A publication] (DLA)

LITTS........... Large Inventory Top-Tier Site [Industrial hazard designation] [British]
Litt Sel Cas... Littell's Select Kentucky Cases [A publication] (DLA)
LITTT........... Luoyang Institute of Tracking and Telecommunication Technology [China] (BUAC)
Litt Ten....... Littleton's Tenures [A publication] (DLA)
LITTY.......... Libraries of Idaho Teletype Network - Academics [Library network]
LITURG........ Liturgies (ROG)
LITVC.......... Liquid Injection Thrust Vector Control
LITW........... Longitudinally in Homogeneous Traveling Waves (MCD)
LITZ........... Litzendraht [Wire] [German]
LIU............. Library and Information Unit
LIU............. Line Interface Unit [Data communications]
LIU............. Line Isolation Unit [Electronics]
LIU............. Link Interface Unit [Telecommunications] (ECII)
LIU............. Littlefield, TX [Location identifier FAA] (FAAL)
LIU............. Long Island University [Brooklyn, NY]
LIU............. Long Island University [Brooklyn Campus] (GAGS)
LIU............. Wood, Wire, and Metal Lathers' International Union [Later, UBC]
LIUNA......... Laborers' International Union of North America (EA)
LIUP........... Long Island University Press (DGA)
Liuski.......... Liuski International, Inc. [Associated Press] (SAG)
LIV............. Law of Initial Value [Joseph Wilder]
LIV............. Left Innominate Vein [Medicine] (MAE)
LIV............. Legislative Indexing Vocabulary
LIV............. Light Infantry Volunteers [Military unit] [British]
LIV............. Linear, Invariant (PDAA)
LIV............. Line Item Value
LIV............. Lived [or Living]
LIV............. Livengood, AK [Location identifier FAA] (FAAL)
LIV............. Liver Battery Test [Gastroenterology] (DAVI)
LIV............. Liverpool (ROG)
LIV............. Living (DAVI)
LIV............. Livingstone Energy [Vancouver Stock Exchange symbol]
Liv .... Livingston's Mayor's Court Reports [New York] [A publication] (DLA)
LIV............. Livorno [Italy] [Seismograph station code, US Geological Survey Closed] (SEIS)
LIV............. Livraison [Delivery] [French]
LIV............. Livre [Book or Pound] [French]
LIV............. Livy [Roman historian, c. 10BC] (ROG)
LIV............. Low-Input Voltage (KSC)
LIV............. Low Investment Vehicle
LIV............. Lunar and Interplanetary Vehicle [Aerospace] (AFM)
Liv Ag......... Livermore on Principal and Agent [A publication] (DLA)
LIVB........... Passo Del Brennero [Italy ICAO location identifier] (ICLI)
LIV-BP .... Leucine, Isoleucine, and Valine Binding Protein [Biochemistry] (DMAA)
LIVC........... Low-Input Voltage Converter
LIVC........... Monte Cimone [Italy ICAO location identifier] (ICLI)
Liv Cas .... Livingston's Cases in Error [New York] [A publication] (DLA)
LIVCR......... Low-Input Voltage Conversion and Regulation
LIVD.......... Dobbiaco [Italy ICAO location identifier] (ICLI)
Liv Dis........ Livermore's Dissertation on the Contrariety of Laws [A publication] (DLA)
LIVE........... Learning through Industry and Voluntary Educators [Community education program]
LIVE........... Live Entertainment [NASDAQ symbol] (TTSB)
LIVE........... Lunar Impact Vehicle [NASA] (KSC)
LIVE........... Passo Resia [Italy ICAO location identifier] (ICLI)
LiveEn .... LIVE Entertainment, Inc. [Associated Press] (SAG)
LiveEnt .... LIVE Entertainment, Inc. [Associated Press] (SAG)
Livent .... Livent, Inc. [Associated Press] (SAG)
LIVEP.......... Live Entmt cm Cv'B' Pfd [NASDAQ symbol] (TTSB)
Liverm Ag.... Livermore on Principal and Agent [A publication] (DLA)
Livermore Ag... Livermore on Principal and Agent [A publication] (DLA)
LIVEX......... Live Exercise [Military exercise in which live forces participate] (NATG)
LIVF........... Frontone [Italy ICAO location identifier] (ICLI)
LIVG.......... Monte Grappa [Italy ICAO location identifier] (ICLI)
Livingston U... Livingston University (GAGS)
Liv Jud Cas... Livingston's Judicial Opinions [New York] [A publication] (DLA)
Liv Judic Op... Livingston's Judicial Opinions [New York] [A publication] (DLA)
Liv Jud Op... Livingston's Judicial Opinions [New York] [A publication] (DLA)
Liv La Cr Code... Livingston's Louisiana Criminal Code [A publication] (DLA)
Liv Law Mag... Livingston's Law Magazine [New York] [A publication] (DLA)
Liv L Mag.... Livingston's Law Magazine [New York] [A publication] (DLA)
Liv L Reg.... Livingston's Law Register [New York] [A publication] (DLA)
LIVM.......... Marino Di Ravenna [Italy ICAO location identifier] (ICLI)
LivngCtr....... Living Centers of America, Inc. [Associated Press] (SAG)
LIVO.......... Tarvisio [Italy ICAO location identifier] (ICLI)
LIVP........... Paganella [Italy ICAO location identifier] (ICLI)
LIVR.......... Low-Input Voltage Regulation
LIVR.......... Passo Rolle [Italy ICAO location identifier] (ICLI)
livrm........... Living Room (REAL)
liv rm........... Living Room (BARN)
LIVT........... Trieste [Italy ICAO location identifier] (ICLI)
Liv US Pen Co... Livingston's System of United States Penal Codes [A publication] (DLA)
LIVV........... Monte Venda [Italy ICAO location identifier] (ICLI)
LIW............. Letters in Words [Psychology]
LIW............. Lightweight Individual Weapon (PDAA)
LIW............. Loikaw [Myanmar] [Airport symbol] (OAG)
LIW............. Long Instruction Word [Teraplex] [Computer science]
LIW............. Loss in Weight
LIWB.......... Livermore Water Boiler [Nuclear reactor] [Dismantled]
LIWMS......... Laura Ingalls Wilder Memorial Society (EA)

LIX............. Liquid Crystal (IDOE)
LIXISCOPE... Low-Intensity X-Ray Imaging Scope
LIY............. Leicestershire Imperial Yeomanry [British military] (DMA)
LIY............. Limay [Nicaragua] [Seismograph station code, US Geological Survey] (SEIS)
LIYP........... Legacy International Youth Program [Later, LIYTP] (EA)
LIYTP......... Legacy International Youth Training Program (EA)
LIYV........... Lettuce Infectious Yellows Virus
LIYW.......... Aviano [Italy ICAO location identifier] (ICLI)
LIZ............. Limestone, ME [Location identifier FAA] (FAAL)
LIZ............. Lizard (MSA)
LIZ............. Liz Claiborne [NYSE symbol] (TTSB)
LIZ............. Liz Claiborne, Inc. [NYSE symbol] (SAG)
LIZARDS..... Library Information Search and Retrieval Data System (IEEE)
Lizars......... Lizar's Scotch Exchequer Cases [A publication] (DLA)
LizClab .... Claiborne [Liz], Inc. [Associated Press] (SAG)
Liz Sc Exch... Lizar's Scotch Exchequer Cases [A publication] (DLA)
LJ............. British Guiana Limited Jurisdiction (Official Gazette) [1899-1955] [A publication] (DLA)
LJ............. Hall's American Law Journal [A publication] (DLA)
LJ............. House of Lords Journals [England] [A publication] (DLA)
LJ............. Jennings Public Library, Jennings, LA [Library symbol Library of Congress] (LCLS)
LJ............. Joullie [France] [Research code symbol]
LJ............. Larsen-Johansson [Disease] [Medicine] (DB)
LJ............. Law Journal Newspaper [1866-1965] [A publication]
LJ............. Law Judge (DLA)
LJ............. Lawson & Jones Ltd. [Toronto Stock Exchange symbol]
LJ............. Lennard-Jones [Physical chemistry]
LJ............. Library Journal [A publication] (BRI)
LJ............. Life Jacket
LJ............. Limited Partner in Jobbers Firm [London Stock Exchange]
LJ............. Line Judge [Football]
LJ............. Little Joe [Early developmental spacecraft] [NASA]
LJ............. Little John [Rocket] [Military] (AABC)
LJ............. Long Jump
LJ............. Lord Justice
L-J............. Lowenstein-Jensen [Growth medium]
LJ............. Lower Canada Law Journal [A publication] (DLA)
LJ............. Sierra Leone Airways [ICAO designator] (AD)
LJA............ Lady Jockeys Association [British] (DBA)
LJA............ Lodja [Zaire] [Airport symbol] (OAG)
LJA............ London Jute Association [England] (BUAC)
LJA............ Lord Justice of Appeal
LJaD........... Dixon Correctional Institute, Jackson, LA [Library symbol Library of Congress] (LCLS)
LJ Adm .... Law Journal, New Series, Admiralty [A publication] (DLA)
LJ Adm NS... Law Journal Reports, Admiralty, New Series [1865-75] [A publication] (DLA)
LJ Adm NS (Eng)... Law Journal Reports, New Series, Admiralty [England] [A publication] (DLA)
LJ App .... Law Journal Reports, New Series, Appeals [A publication] (DLA)
LJ Bank ...... Law Journal Reports, Bankruptcy [A publication] (DLA)
LJ Bank NS... Law Journal Reports, New Series, Bankruptcy [A publication] (DLA)
LJ Bankr...... Law Journal Reports, Bankruptcy [A publication] (DLA)
LJ Bankr NS (Eng)... Law Journal Reports, New Series, Bankruptcy [England] [A publication] (DLA)
LJ Bcy .... Law Journal Reports, New Series, Bankruptcy [A publication] (DLA)
LJ Bk .... Law Journal Reports, Bankruptcy [A publication] (DLA)
LJC............. La Jolla [California] [Seismograph station code, US Geological Survey Closed] (SEIS)
LJC............. Laredo Junior College [Texas]
LJC............. Lasell Junior College [Newton, MA]
LJC............. Law Journal Reports, New Series, Common Pleas [England] [A publication] (DLA)
LJC............. Lees Junior College [Jackson, KY]
LJC............. London Juvenile Court (DAS)
LJC............. Lord Jesus Christ (ROG)
LJC............. Loretto Junior College [Kentucky]
LJC............. Louisville, KY [Location identifier FAA] (FAAL)
LJCC.......... Law Journal, County Courts Reporter [A publication] (DLA)
LJCC.......... Local Joint Consultative Committee [British] (DCTA)
LJCCA......... Law Journal Newspaper, County Court Appeals [England] [A publication] (DLA)
LJCCR........ Law Journal Reports, New Series, Crown Cases Reserved [England] [A publication] (DLA)
LJCCR (NS)... Law Journal Reports, New Series, Crown Cases Reserved [England] [A publication] (DLA)
LJ Ch .... Law Journal Reports, New Series, Chancery [A publication] (DLA)
LJ Ch (Eng)... Law Journal Reports, New Series, Chancery [England] (DLA)
LJ Ch NS (Eng)... Law Journal Reports, New Series, Chancery [England] [A publication] (DLA)
LJ Ch (OS)... Law Journal Reports, Chancery, Old Series [1822-31] [England] [A publication] (DLA)
LJCP.......... Law Journal Reports, Common Pleas Decisions [England] [A publication] (DLA)
LJCPD......... Law Journal Reports, Common Pleas Decisions [England] [A publication] (DLA)
LJCP (Eng)... Law Journal Reports, Common Pleas Decisions [England] [A publication] (DLA)
LJCP NS ...... Law Journal Reports, Common Pleas Decisions, New Series [1831-75] [A publication] (DLA)
LJCP NS (Eng)... Law Journal Reports, Common Pleas, New Series [England] [A publication] (DLA)

LJCP (OS).... Law Journal Reports, Common Pleas, Old Series [*England*]
[*A publication*] (DLA)
LJCRF.......... La Jolla Cancer Research Foundation [*Research center*] (RCD)
LJCS........... Lord Justice Clerk of Scotland (DAS)
LJD........... Doctor of Letters of Journalism
LJD & M..... Law Journal Reports, New Series, Divorce and Matrimonial [*England*]
[*A publication*] (DLA)
LJDFC......... Lacy J. Dalton Fan Club (EA)
LJE........... Local Job Entry
LJ Ecc........ Law Journal Reports, New Series, Ecclesiastical Cases
[*A publication*] (DLA)
LJ Eccl....... Law Journal Reports, New Series, Ecclesiastical Cases
[*A publication*] (DLA)
LJED.......... Large Jet Engine Department [*NASA*] (KSC)
LJeL.......... LaSalle Parish Library, Jena, LA [*Library symbol Library of
Congress*] (LCLS)
LJ Eq .... Law Journal Reports, Chancery, New Series [*1831-1946*]
[*A publication*] (DLA)
LJEWU........ Lanka Jatika Estate Workers' Union [*Ceylon National Estate Workers'
Union*]
LJ Ex .... Law Journal Reports, New Series, Exchequer Division [*England*]
[*A publication*] (DLA)
LJ Exch....... Law Journal Reports, New Series, Exchequer Division [*England*]
[*A publication*] (DLA)
LJ Exch (Eng)... Law Journal Reports, New Series, Exchequer Division [*England*]
[*A publication*] (DLA)
LJ Exch in Eq (Eng)... English Law Journal. Exchequer in Equity [*A publication*]
(DLA)
LJ Exch NS... Law Journal Reports, New Series, Exchequer [*1831-75*]
[*A publication*] (DLA)
LJ Exch NS (Eng)... Law Journal Reports, New Series, Exchequer Division
[*England*] [*A publication*] (DLA)
LJ Exch (OS)... Law Journal Reports, Exchequer, Old Series [*A publication*] (DLA)
LJ Ex D....... Law Journal Reports, New Series, Exchequer Division [*England*]
[*A publication*] (DLA)
LJ Ex Eq ...... Law Journal, Exchequer in Equity [*England*] [*A publication*] (DLA)
LJFC .... Leon Jordan Fan Club (EA)
LJG .... Leading Jewelers Guild (NTPA)
LJG .... Levend Joods Geloof (Liberaal Joodse Gemeente) (BJA)
LJG .... Lord Justice General [*British*]
LJHL........... Law Journal Reports, New Series, House of Lords [*England*]
[*A publication*] (DLA)
LJI .... Legal Journals Index [*Information service or system*] (IID)
LJI .... Library of Jewish Information (BJA)
LJI .... List of Journals Indexed (DMAA)
LJIFS .... Law Journal, Irish Free State [*1931-32*] [*A publication*] (DLA)
LJ Ir .... Law Journal, Irish [*1933-34*] [*A publication*] (DLA)
LJJ.............. Jefferson Davis Parish Library, Jennings, LA [*Library symbol Library
of Congress*] (LCLS)
LJJ.............. Lords Justices
LJK .... Ashland, VA [*Location identifier FAA*] (FAAL)
LJKB .... Law Journal Reports, King's Bench [*A publication*] (DLA)
LJKB (Eng)... Law Journal Reports, King's Bench [*England*] [*A publication*] (DLA)
LJKB NS ...... Law Journal Reports, King's Bench, New Series [*A publication*]
(DLA)
LJKB NS (Eng)... Law Journal Reports, King's Bench, New Series [*England*]
[*A publication*] (DLA)
LJKB OS ...... Law Journal, King's Bench, Old Series [*England*] [*A publication*]
(DLA)
LJL............. Lateral Joint Line [*Orthopedics*] (DAVI)
LJL............. Little John Launcher [*Military*]
LJLC .... Law Journal (Lower Canada) [*A publication*] (DLA)
LJLT .... Law Journal (Law Tracts) [*England*] [*A publication*] (DLA)
LJLV .... Little Joe Launch Vehicle [*NASA*]
LJM .... Limited Joint Mobility [*Medicine*] (DMAA)
LJM .... Lowenstein-Jensen Growth Medium (MAE)
LJ Mag .... Law Journal, New Series, Common Law, Magistrates Cases
(Discontinued) [*A publication*] (DLA)
LJ Mag Cas... Law Journal Reports, Magistrates' Cases [*1822-31*] [*A publication*]
(DLA)
LJ Mag Cas (Eng)... Law Journal Reports, Magistrates' Cases [*England*]
[*A publication*] (DLA)
LJ Mag Cas NS... Law Journal Reports, Magistrates' Cases, New Series [*1831-96*]
[*A publication*] (DLA)
LJ Mag Cas NS (Eng)... Law Journal Reports, Magistrates' Cases, New Series
[*England*] [*A publication*] (DLA)
LJM & W..... Morgan and Williams' Law Journal [*London*] [*A publication*] (DLA)
LJ Mat .... Law Journal, Matrimonial [*England*] [*A publication*] (DLA)
LJ Mat Cas... Law Journal, New Series, Divorce and Matrimonial [*England*]
[*A publication*] (DLA)
LJ Mat (Eng)... Law Journal, Matrimonial [*England*] [*A publication*] (DLA)
LJMC .... Law Journal Reports, New Series, Magistrates' Cases [*England*]
[*A publication*] (DLA)
LJM Cas ..... Law Journal Reports, New Series, Magistrates' Cases [*England*]
[*A publication*] (DLA)
LJMCOS....... Law Journal Reports, Old Series, Magistrates' Cases [*England*]
[*A publication*] (DLA)
LJMPA .... Law Journal Reports, Matrimonial, Probate, and Admiralty [*England*]
[*A publication*] (DLA)
LJN .... Lake Jackson [*Texas*] [*Airport symbol*] (OAG)
LJNC .... Law Journal, Notes of Cases [*A publication*] (DLA)
LJNCCA....... Law Journal Newspaper, County Court Appeals [*England*]
[*A publication*] (DLA)
LJNCCR .... Law Journal Newspaper, County Court Reports [*England*]
[*A publication*] (DLA)

LJNC (Eng)... Law Journal, Notes of Cases [*England*] [*A publication*] (DLA)
LJ News ...... Law Journal Newspaper [*1866-1965*] [*A publication*] (DLA)
LJ News (Eng).. Law Journal Newspaper [*England*] [*A publication*] (DLA)
LJ Newsp..... Law Journal Newspaper [*1866-1965*] [*A publication*] (DLA)
LJ NS .... Law Journal, New Series [*England*] [*A publication*] (DLA)
LJo............. Jackson Parish Library, Jonesboro, LA [*Library symbol Library of
Congress*] (LCLS)
L Jo .... Law Journal Newspaper [*England*] [*A publication*] (DLA)
LJ of the Marut Bunnag Internat L Off... Law Journal. Marut Bunnag International
Law Office [*A publication*] (DLA)
L Jo NC .... Law Journal, Notes of Cases [*England*] [*A publication*] (DLA)
LJ OS.......... Law Journal, Old Series [*1822-31*] [*London*] [*A publication*] (DLA)
LJ OS Ch ..... Law Journal, Old Series, Chancery [*1822-23*] [*A publication*] (DLA)
LJ OS CP..... Law Journal, Old Series, Common Pleas [*1822-31*] [*A publication*]
(DLA)
LJ OS Ex...... Law Journal, Old Series, Exchequer [*1830-31*] [*A publication*] (DLA)
LJ OS KB ..... Law Journal, Old Series, King's Bench [*1822-31*] [*A publication*]
(DLA)
LJOSMC....... Law Journal, Old Series, Magistrates' Cases [*1826-31*]
[*A publication*] (ILCA)
LJP .... Law Journal Reports, New Series, Privy Council [*England*]
[*A publication*] (DLA)
LJP .... Law Journal Reports, Probate, Divorce, and Admiralty [*England*]
[*A publication*] (DLA)
LJP .... Liquid Junction Potential
LJP .... Localized Juvenile Periodontitis [*Dentistry*]
LJP .... Local Job Processing (IAA)
LJP & M...... Law Journal, Probate and Matrimonial [*England*] [*A publication*]
(DLA)
LJPC .... La Jolla Pharmaceutical [*NASDAQ symbol*] (SAG)
LJPC .... Law Journal Reports, Privy Council [*England*] [*A publication*] (DLA)
LJ PC (Eng)... Law Journal Reports, Privy Council [*England*] [*A publication*] (DLA)
LJ PC NS ..... Law Journal Reports, New Series, Privy Council [*England*]
[*A publication*] (DLA)
LJPCW .... La Jolla Pharmaceutical Wrrt [*NASDAQ symbol*] (TTSB)
LJPD & A..... Law Journal Reports, New Series, Probate, Divorce, and Admiralty
[*1875-1946*] [*A publication*] (DLA)
LJPD & Adm... Law Journal Reports, New Series, Probate, Divorce, and Admiralty
[*England*] [*A publication*] (DLA)
LJPM & A..... Law Journal Reports, New Series, Probate, Matrimonial, and
Admiralty [*England*] [*A publication*] (DLA)
LJ Prob........ Law Journal Reports, New Series, Probate and Matrimonial [*1858-59,
1866-75*] [*A publication*] (DLA)
LJ Prob & Mat... Law Journal, Probate and Matrimonial [*England*] [*A publication*]
(DLA)
LJ Prob (Eng)... Law Journal, Probate and Matrimonial [*England*] [*A publication*]
(DLA)
LJ Prob NS... Law Journal Reports, New Series, Probate and Matrimonial
[*1858-59, 1866-75*] [*A publication*] (DLA)
LJ Prob NS (Eng)... Law Journal, Probate and Matrimonial, New Series [*England*]
[*A publication*] (DLA)
LJQB .... Law Journal Reports, New Series, Queen's Bench [*England*].
[*A publication*] (DLA)
LJQBD .... Law Journal Reports, New Series, Queen's Bench Division [*England*]
[*A publication*] (DLA)
LJQBD NS.... Law Journal Reports, New Series, Queen's Bench Division [*England*]
[*A publication*] (DLA)
LJQB (Eng)... Law Journal Reports, New Series, Queen's Bench [*England*]
[*A publication*] (DLA)
LJQB NS ...... Law Journal Reports, New Series, Queen's Bench [*1831-1946*]
[*A publication*] (DLA)
LJQB NS (Eng)... Law Journal Reports, Queen's Bench, New Series [*England*]
[*A publication*] (DLA)
LJR .... Law Journal Reports [*A publication*]
LJR .... Lead Joint Runner
LJR .... Little John Rocket [*Military*]
LJR .... Lone Jack Resources Ltd. [*Vancouver Stock Exchange symbol*]
LJR .... Low Jet Route (ADA)
LJR (Eng) .... Law Journal Reports [*England*] [*A publication*] (DLA)
LJ Rep .... Law Journal Reports [*A publication*] (DLA)
LJ Rep NS ... Law Journal Reports, New Series [*A publication*] (DLA)
LJS .... Lap Joint Strength
LJS .... Lithuanian Journalists' Society (BUAC)
LJ Sm .... Smith's Law Journal [*London*] [*A publication*] (DLA)
LJST .... Library of Japanese Science and Technology [*England*] (BUAC)
LJSU .... Local Junction Switching Unit [*Telecommunications*] (TEL)
LJU .... Lithuanian Journalists' Union (BUAC)
LJU .... Ljubljana [*Slovenia*] [*Seismograph station code, US Geological
Survey*] (SEIS)
LJU .... Ljubljana [*Slovenia*] [*Airport symbol*] (OAG)
LJU .... Oscoda, MI [*Location identifier FAA*] (FAAL)
LJUC........... Law Journal of Upper Canada [*A publication*] (DLA)
LJWG .... Logistic Joint Work Group [*DoD*]
LJZ............ Lajes [*Brazil*] [*Airport symbol*] (AD)
LK............. Arawak Airlines (OAG)
LK............. Laiko Komma [*Populist Party*] [*Greece*] [*Political party*] (PPE)
LK............. Lake
LK............. Lamellar Keratoplasty (STED)
LK............. Landry-Kussmaul [*Syndrome*] [*Medicine*] (DB)
LK............. Leak (KSC)
LK............. Left Kidney [*Medicine*]
LK............. Lek [*Monetary unit*] [*Albania*]
Lk............. Leptosphaeria korrea [*A fungus*]
LK............. Letaba Airways [*ICAO designator*] (AD)
LK............. Lichenoid Keratosis [*Medicine*] (DMAA)

LK............	Liederkranz [*Type of cheese*] (BJA)
L-K............	Linguistic-Kinesic [*Psychiatry*]
LK............	Link (KSC)
LK............	Lock [*Automotive engineering*]
LK............	Loehr-Kindberg [*Syndrome*] [*Medicine*] (DB)
LK............	Looking for Party [*Telecommunications*] (TEL)
LK............	Lord Keeper [*of the Great Seal*] [*British*] (ROG)
LK............	Lowenfeld Kaleidoblocs [*Psychological testing*]
LK............	Low-Priority Key [*Computer science*]
Lk............	Luke [*New Testament book*]
LK............	Lymphokine [*Immunochemistry*]
LK............	Sri Lanka [*ANSI two-letter standard code*] (CNC)
LK1............	Ladies' Kayak, Single Person (ADA)
LK2............	Ladies' Kayak, Two Person (ADA)
LK4............	Ladies' Kayak, Four Person (ADA)
LKA............	Alkair Flight Operations APS [*Denmark ICAO designator*] (FAAC)
LKA............	Amphibious Cargo Ship [*Navy symbol*]
LKA............	Attack Cargo Ship [*Navy symbol*]
LKA............	Ladies Kennel Association [*British*] (BI)
LKA............	Larantuka [*Indonesia*] [*Airport symbol*] (OAG)
LKA............	Last Known Address (LAIN)
LKA............	Lazare-Klerman-Armour [*Personality inventory*] (STED)
LKA............	Lighthouse Keepers Association (EA)
LKA............	Literarische Keilschrifttexte aus Assur [*A publication*] (BJA)
LKA............	Miraloma, CA [*Location identifier FAA*] (FAAL)
LKA............	Sri Lanka [*ANSI three-letter standard code*] (CNC)
LKAA............	Ladies Kennel Association of America (EA)
LKAA............	Praha [*Former Czechoslovakia*] [*ICAO location identifier*] (ICLI)
LK & PRR...	Lahaina-Kaanapali & Pacific Railroad [*Hawaii*]
LKA of A...	Ladies Kennel Association of America (EA)
LKartB........	Landeskartellbehoerde [*Provincial Cartel Authority*] [*German*] (DLA)
LKB............	Lakeba [*Fiji*] [*Airport symbol*] (OAG)
LKBB............	Bratislava [*Former Czechoslovakia*] [*ICAO location identifier*] (ICLI)
LKC............	Lake Chabot [*California*] [*Seismograph station code, US Geological Survey*] (SEIS)
LKC............	Lake Charles [*Diocesan abbreviation*] [*Louisiana*] (TOCD)
LKC............	Lancaster County Library, Lancaster, PA [*OCLC symbol*] (OCLC)
LKC............	Lekana [*Congo*] [*Airport symbol*] (OAG)
LKCL............	LASER Kit Combination Lock
LKD............	Locked (KSC)
LKDM............	Low K Dielectric Material (AAEL)
LKDP	Lietuviu Krikscioniu Demokratu Partija [*Lithuanian Christian Democratic Party*] [*Political party*] (PPE)
LKED............	Linkage Editor [*Computer science*] (CIST)
LKESTR........	Leukocyte Esterase (STED)
LKF............	Linear Kalman Filter
LKG............	League of the Kingdom of God [*Church of England*]
LKG............	Leakage (MSA)
LKG............	Linking (IAA)
LKG............	Locking (KSC)
LKG............	Looking (MSA)
LKG............	Loop Key Generator (MCD)
LKGABKG.....	Leakage and Breakage (IAA)
LKG & BKG...	Leakage and Breakage (WDAA)
LKGE............	Linkage (MSA)
LKHO	Holesov [*Former Czechoslovakia*] [*ICAO location identifier*] (ICLI)
LKI............	Duluth, MN [*Location identifier FAA*] (FAAL)
LKI............	Lazare Kaplan International, Inc. [*AMEX symbol*] (SPSG)
LKI............	Lazare Kaplan Intl [*AMEX symbol*] (TTSB)
LKI............	Loki Gold Corp. [*Vancouver Stock Exchange symbol*]
LKIB............	Bratislava/Ivanka [*Former Czechoslovakia*] [*ICAO location identifier*] (ICLI)
LKID............	Left Kidney [*Anatomy*] (DAVI)
LKJ............	Linton Kwesi Johnson [*British musician*]
LKK............	Kulik Lake, AK [*Location identifier FAA*] (FAAL)
LKK............	Lake Shore Mines Ltd. [*Toronto Stock Exchange symbol*]
LKKS............	Liver, Kidneys, and Spleen (STED)
LKKV............	Karlovy Vary [*Former Czechoslovakia*] [*ICAO location identifier*] (ICLI)
LKKZ............	Kosice [*Former Czechoslovakia*] [*ICAO location identifier*] (ICLI)
LKL............	Lakeland Aviation [*ICAO designator*] (FAAC)
LKL............	Lakselv [*Norway*] [*Airport symbol*] (OAG)
LKLF............	Lung Kruppel-Like Factor [*Immunology*]
LKLY............	Likely (FAAC)
LKM............	Lafayette, LA [*Location identifier FAA*] (FAAL)
LKM............	Liver-Kidney Microsomal [*Antibody*] [*Medicine*] (DMAA)
LKM............	Locke Rich Minerals [*Vancouver Stock Exchange symbol*]
LKM............	Low-Key Maintenance
LKM............	Nekempt [*Ethiopia*] [*Airport symbol*] (AD)
LKMT............	Ostrava [*Former Czechoslovakia*] [*ICAO location identifier*] (ICLI)
LKN............	Leknes [*Norway*] [*Airport symbol*] (OAG)
LKN............	Lock-In
LK-NDV........	Newcastle Disease Virus, L-Kansas Strain
LKNPOS........	Last Known Position (MCD)
LKNPT............	Last Known Port (MCD)
LKNT............	Locknut (MSA)
LKO............	Billings, MT [*Location identifier FAA*] (FAAL)
LKO............	Lucknow [*India*] [*Airport symbol*] (OAG)
LKP............	Lake Placid, NY [*Location identifier FAA*] (FAAL)
LKP............	Lamellar Keratoplasty [*Ophthalmology*]
LKP............	Landelijke Knokplogen [*Netherlands Regional Action Groups*] [*World War II*]
LKP............	Last Known Position [*Aviation*] (NVT)
LKP............	Liberaalinen Kansanpuolue [*Liberal People's Party*] [*Finland Political party*] (PPE)

LKP............	Lietuvos Komunisty Partija [*Communist Party of Lithuania*] [*Political party*] (PPE)
LKPP............	Piestany [*Former Czechoslovakia*] [*ICAO location identifier*] (ICLI)
LKPR............	Praha/Ruzyne [*Former Czechoslovakia*] [*ICAO location identifier*] (ICLI)
LKQ............	Like Kind and Quality (Metal) [*Auto repair*]
LKQCPI............	Licentiate of the King's and Queen's College of Physicians of Ireland
LKR............	Lake Air Helicopters Ltd. [*British ICAO designator*] (FAAC)
LKR............	Lancaster, SC [*Location identifier FAA*] (FAAL)
LKR............	Left Knee Right [*Guitar playing*]
LKR............	LK Resources Ltd. [*Toronto Stock Exchange symbol*]
LKR............	Locker (KSC)
LKROT	Locked Rotor
LKRT............	Loyal Knights of the Round Table (EA)
LKS............	Lakes
LKS............	Lakeside Aviation Ltd. [*British ICAO designator*] (FAAC)
LKS............	Lambda Kappa Sigma (EA)
LKS............	Liberation Kanake Socialiste [*Socialist Kanak Liberation*] [*New Caledonia*] (PD)
LKS............	Liver, Kidneys, and Spleen (DAVI)
LKS............	Liver, Kidney, Spleen [*Medicine*]
LKS............	Logan-Keck-Stickney [*Method*]
LKS............	Louisville, KY [*Location identifier FAA*] (FAAL)
LKS............	Lucky 7 Exploration [*Vancouver Stock Exchange symbol*]
LKSB............	Liver, Kidney, Spleen, Bladder [*Medicine*] (DMAA)
LKSCR	Lockscrew
LKSL............	Sliac [*Former Czechoslovakia*] [*ICAO location identifier*] (ICLI)
LKS NP........	Liver, Kidneys, and Spleen Not Palpable [*On physical examination*] (DAVI)
LKT............	Locket (ROG)
LKT............	Lookout (MSA)
LKT............	Salmon, ID [*Location identifier FAA*] (FAAL)
LKTT............	Poprad/Tatry [*Former Czechoslovakia*] [*ICAO location identifier*] (ICLI)
LKTYP	Like Type (FAAC)
LKU............	Literarische Keilschrifttexte aus Uruk [*A publication*] (BJA)
LKUP	Lockup
LKV............	Laked Kanamycin-Vancomycin [*Agar*] [*Microbiology*]
LKV............	Lake Ventures Ltd. [*Vancouver Stock Exchange symbol*]
LKV............	Lakeview, OR [*Location identifier FAA*] (FAAL)
LKV............	Left Knee Vertical [*Guitar playing*]
LKV............	Lengyel-Kerman-Vargar [*Rating*] [*Psychology*] (DAVI)
LKVY............	Lykens Valley Railroad Co. [*AAR code*]
LKW............	Lake Wisdom [*Papua New Guinea*] [*Seismograph station code, US Geological Survey*] (SEIS)
LKW............	Lakewood Mining [*Vancouver Stock Exchange symbol*]
LKW............	Larkana [*Pakistan*] [*Airport symbol*] (AD)
LK/WA............	Lock Washer [*Automotive engineering*]
LKWASH............	Lock Washer [*Automotive engineering*]
LKX............	La Pryor, TX [*Location identifier FAA*] (FAAL)
LKY............	Lucky Strike Resources [*Vancouver Stock Exchange symbol*]
LKZ............	Letaba Airways [*South Africa ICAO designator*] (FAAC)
LL............	All Is Well [*Search and rescue symbol that can be stamped in sand or snow*]
LL............	Bell-Air [*ICAO designator*] (AD)
LL............	Double-Loop Magnetic Mine Sweep [*Navy British*]
LL............	Lab. Lafon [*France*] [*Research code symbol*]
LL............	Labor Letter [*Cast Metals Association*] [*A publication*]
LL............	Lamina Lucida [*Dermatology*]
LL............	Landline [*Aviation*]
LL............	Land-Line [*Telecommunications*] (TEL)
LL............	Land Locomotion Division [*Army Tank-Automotive Command*] [*Warren, MI*]
LL............	Land Locomotion Laboratory [*Army*]
LL............	Landlord [*Legal shorthand*] (LWAP)
ll............	Lapis Lazuli (VRA)
LL............	Large Letter
LL............	Large Light Seeds [*Botany*]
LL............	Large Lymphocyte [*Medicine*]
LL............	Last (ROG)
LL............	Late Latin [*Language, etc.*]
Ll..............	Latent Lethality [*Radiation casualty criterion*] [*Army*]
LL............	Lateral Lemniscus [*Neuroanatomy*]
LL............	Lateral Line [*Invertebrate zoology*]
LL............	Lateral Lip
L/L............	Latitude/Longitude (IEEE)
LL............	Laugh Lovers (EA)
LL............	Launch and Landing [*NASA*] (NASA)
LL............	Launch Left (MCD)
LL............	Laurentian Life Insurance Co., Inc. [*Toronto Stock Exchange symbol*]
LL............	Law Latin
L-L............	Law Library of Louisiana, New Orleans, LA [*Library symbol Library of Congress*] (LCLS)
LL............	Law List (ILCA)
LL............	Laws (ROG)
LL............	Laymen's League (EA)
LL............	League (ROG)
LL............	Lean Line (EA)
LL............	Leased Line [*Private telephone or Teletype line*] [*Telecommunications*]
LL............	Lease or Loan
LL............	Leaves [*Bibliography*]
LL............	Lederle Laboratories [*Research code symbol*]
LL............	Left Lateral [*Anatomy*] (DAVI)
LL............	Left Leg (MAE)

LL	Left Lower [*Medicine*]
LL	Left Lung [*Medicine*]
LL	Legal Letter (WDAA)
LL	Lega Lombarda [*Italy*] [*Political party*] (ECED)
LL	Leges [*Laws*] [*Latin*]
LL	Legislative Liaison
LL	Legum [*Of Laws*] [*Latin*] (ADA)
L/L	Leigh Light [*British military*] (DMA)
L/L	Lending Library
LL	Lend-Lease [*Bill*] [*World War II*]
LL	Lepromatous-Type Leprosy [*Animal pathology*]
LL	Lessons Learned
LL	Lever Lock (MCD)
LL	Lewandowsky-Lutz [*Syndrome*] [*Medicine*] (DB)
LL	Liberty Lobby (EA)
L/L	Library Labels [*Antiquarian book trade*]
LL	License in Civil Law
LL	Lighterage Limits
LL	Light Line [*Military*]
LL	Light Load (AAG)
LL	Light Lock
LL	Light Lorry [*British*]
LL	Limited Liability [*Finance*]
LL	Limiting Level
LL	Lincoln Laboratory [*MIT*] (MCD)
LL	Lincoln Library of Essential Information
L/L	Line for Line [*Typesetting*] (WDMC)
LL	Line Leg [*Telegraph*] [*Telecommunications*] (TEL)
LL	Line Link (IAA)
LL	Lines
ll	Lines (WDMC)
LL	Lines Layout (MCD)
L-L	Line-to-Line (MCD)
LL	Linking Loader (IAA)
LL	Link Level [*Telecommunications*]
LL	Lipoprotein Lipase (DB)
LL	Liquid Level (ECII)
LL	Liquid Limit (IEEE)
L/L	Liquid/Liquid Extraction [*Laboratory procedure*]
LL	Liquor Law
LL	Literary Lives [*A publication*]
LL	Litre (ROG)
LL	Little League [*Baseball*]
LL	Live Load
LL	Load Line [*Shipping*] (DS)
LL	Load List (MSA)
LL	Local Lesion [*Pathology*]
LL	Local Line [*Telecommunications*]
LL	Local Linearization
LL	Local Loopback (MHDB)
LL	Locator Lists [*Army*]
LL	Loco Laudato [*In the Place Quoted*] [*Latin*]
LL	Lodges [*Freemasonry*] (ROG)
LL	Loft Line (MSA)
LL	Long Lead (NASA)
LL	Long Line [*Telecommunications*] (MCD)
LL	Loose Leaf
LL	Lord Lieutenant
LL	Lords
LL	Loudness Level
LL	Lower Laterals [*Botany*]
LL	Lower Left
LL	Lower Leg
LL	Lower Lid [*Ophthalmology*]
LL	Lower Limb [*Lower edge of sun, moon, etc.*] [*Navigation*]
LL	Lower Limen [*Psychology*]
LL	Lower Limit
LL	Lower Lip [*Anatomy*] (DAVI)
LL	Lower Lobe [*Medicine*]
LL	Low Latin [*Language, etc.*]
LL	Low Level
LL	Low Load [*Finance*]
LL	Lumbar Length [*Anatomy*] (DAVI)
LL	Lunar Landing [*NASA*] (KSC)
LL	Luther League [*Defunct*] (EA)
LL	Lutlag [*Limited Company*] [*Norwegian*]
LL	Lymphoblastic Lymphoma [*Oncology*] (DAVI)
LL	Lymphoid Leukemia [*Medicine*] (DB)
L/L	Lymphoma/Leukemia [*Oncology*]
LL	Lysolecithin [*Biochemistry*]
LLA	Lady Licentiate of Arts [*Scotland*]
LLA	Lady Literate in Arts [*British*]
LLA	Latin Liturgy Association (EA)
LLA	Laubach Literacy Action (EA)
LLA	Leased Line Adapter [*Telecommunications*]
LLA	Leased Line Adaptor (NITA)
LLA	Lebanese Library Association (BUAC)
LLA	Lend-Lease Administration [*Defunct*]
LLA	Lesotho Liberation Army (PD)
LLA	Limited Locus Allowed [*Legal*] (ROG)
LLA	Limiting Lines of Approach [*Navy*] (NVT)
LLA	Limulus Lysate Assay (DMAA)
LLA	Literary Landmarks Association (EA)
LLA	Little Library [*A publication*]

LLA	Llanada [*California*] [*Seismograph station code, US Geological Survey*] (SEIS)
LLA	Louisiana Library Association (BUAC)
LLA	Lower Left Abdomen [*Injection Site*]
LLA	Low-Level Analog (MCD)
LLA	Low Low Alarm (ECII)
LLA	Lulea [*Sweden*] [*Airport symbol*] (OAG)
LLA	Luther League of America [*Later, LL*]
LLA	Servicio Leo Lopez SA de CV [*Mexico ICAO designator*] (FAAC)
LLA	White Lake, LA [*Location identifier FAA*] (FAAL)
LLAA	Israel Airports Authority Headquarters [*Israel*] [*ICAO location identifier*] (ICLI)
LLAAII	Leurs Altesses Imperiales [*Their Imperial Highnesses*] [*French*]
LLAARR	Leurs Altesses Royales [*Their Royal Highnesses*] [*French*]
LLAD	Ben Gurion [*Israel*] [*ICAO location identifier*] (ICLI)
LLAD	Low-Level Air Defence [*Navy British*]
LLafL	Lafayette Public Library, Lafayette, LA [*Library symbol Library of Congress*] (LCLS)
LLafS	University of Southwestern Louisiana, Lafayette, LA [*Library symbol Library of Congress*] (LCLS)
LL Alfredi	Leges Alfredi [*Laws of King Alfred*] [*Latin A publication*] (DLA)
Llam	Lumbar Laminectomy [*Medicine*] (DAVI)
LLAMA	Low-Level Acceleration Measurement Apparatus
LLAN	Llandaff (ROG)
LL & B	Latch, Lock, and Bolt (DAC)
LI & GTP	Lloyd and Goold's Irish Chancery Reports Tempore Plunkett [*A publication*] (DLA)
LI & GT PI	Lloyd and Goold's Irish Chancery Reports Tempore Plunkett [*A publication*] (DLA)
LI & GTS	Lloyd and Goold's Irish Chancery Reports Tempore Sugden [*1835*] [*A publication*] (DLA)
LL & N	Language, Literacy and Numeracy Skills Taskforce [*Australia*]
LI & W	Lloyd and Welsby's English Mercantile Cases [*A publication*] (DLA)
LI & Wels	Lloyd and Welsby's English Commercial Cases [*A publication*] (DLA)
LLAP	LocalTalk Link Access Protocol [*Computer science*] (ACRL)
LLap	Saint John Parish Library, La Place, LA [*Library symbol Library of Congress*] (LCLS)
LLAR	Local Loop Access Ring [*Telecommunications*] (ACRL)
LLAT	Law Latin
LLAT	Lawrence Lowery Apperception Test
LLAT	Left Lateral [*Radiology*] (DAVI)
LL Athelst	Laws of Athelstan [*A publication*] (DLA)
LLATIS	Low Light and Thermal Imaging System (PDAA)
LLAW	Liquid Low Activity Waste [*Nuclear energy*] (NUCP)
LLB	Bachelor of Laws (DD)
LLB	Computrac, Inc. [*AMEX symbol*] (SPSG)
LLB	Lawyers' Law Books [*1977*] [*A publication*] (ILCA)
LLB	Left Lateral Border [*Medicine*] (DMAA)
LLB	Left Linebacker (WGA)
LLB	Legum Baccalaureus [*Bachelor of Laws*] [*Latin*]
LLB	Line Loop Back [*Telecommunications*] (ITD)
LLB	Liquor Licensing Board [*Australian Capital Territory*]
LLB	Little League Baseball (EA)
LLB	Lloyd Aereo Boliviano SA [*Bolivia*] [*ICAO designator*] (FAAC)
LLB	Long Leg Brace [*Orthopedics*]
LLB	Lower Leg Brace [*Medicine*]
LLB	Luluabourg [*Zaire*] [*Airport symbol*] (AD)
LLBA	Language and Language Behavior Abstracts [*Sociological Abstracts*] [*Database*] (NITA)
LLBAM	Lincoln Laboratory Boolean Algebra Minimizer (IAA)
LLBBMA	Loose Leaf and Blank Book Manufacturers Association [*Later, ABPM*] (EA)
LLBC	Liquid Large-Bore Cannon (MCD)
LLBCD	Left Lower Border of Cardiac Dullness [*Cardiology*]
LLBD	Meteorological Service [*Israel*] [*ICAO location identifier*] (ICLI)
LLBG	Tel Aviv/D. Ben Gurion [*Israel*] [*ICAO location identifier*] (ICLI)
LLBS	Beersheba/Teyman [*Israel*] [*ICAO location identifier*] (ICLI)
LLBS	Low-Level Bombsight (NATG)
LL Burgund	Laws of Burgundians [*A publication*] (DLA)
LLc	Lake Charles Public Library, Lake Charles, LA [*Library symbol Library of Congress*] (LCLS)
LLC	Lakeland Library Cooperative [*Library network*]
LLC	La Lucha Farm [*Costa Rica*] [*Seismograph station code, US Geological Survey*] (SEIS)
LLC	Lankalink Aircargo (Pvp) Ltd. [*Sri Lanka*] [*FAA designator*] (FAAC)
LLC	Law Certificate
LLC	Left Line Contactor (MCD)
LLC	Lewis Lung Carcinoma [*Medicine*] (DB)
LLC	Library Learning Center (AL)
LLC	Light Salvage Ship [*Navy symbol*] (VNW)
LLC	Lightweight Leader Computer [*Army*] (INF)
LLC	Limited Liability Company
LLC	Limited Life Component (MCD)
LLC	Liquid Level Control
LLC	Liquid Level Controller (ECII)
LLC	Liquid-Liquid Chromatography
LLC	Local Level Control [*Electronics*]
LLC	Logical Link Control [*Telecommunications*]
LLC	Logic Link Control [*Network interfacing*] (NITA)
LLC	Long Leg Cast [*Orthopedics*]
LLC	Long Lines Coordination (NATG)
LLC	Long-Linking Carbon
LLC	Low Liquid Cutoff
LLC	Loyola University, Career Information Center, New Orleans, LA [*OCLC symbol*] (OCLC)

LLC .... Luneberg Lens Commutator [Physics]
LLC .... Lymphocytic Leukemia, Chronic (MAE)
LLC .... Lyotropic Liquid Crystals [Physical chemistry]
LL Canuti R... Laws of King Canute [or Knut] [A publication] (DLA)
LLcC .... Calcasieu Parish Public Library, Lake Charles, LA [Library symbol Library of Congress] (LCLS)
LLCC .... Leadless Chip Carrier (AAEL)
LI CC Pr ...... Lloyd's County Courts Practice [A publication] (DLA)
LLCF .... Launch and Landing Computational Facilities [NASA] (NASA)
LLCFR .... Lobbyists and Lawyers for Campaign Finance Reform (EA)
LLCM .... Licentiate of the London College of Music [British] (DBQ)
LLCM .... Master of Comparative Law (DLA)
LLcM .... McNeese State University, Lake Charles, LA [Library symbol Library of Congress] (LCLS)
LLCM(TD) .... Licentiate of the London College of Music (Teacher's Diploma) [British]
LLCO .... Licentiate of the London College of Osteopathy
LI Comp ...... Lloyd's Compensation for Lands, Etc. [6th ed.] [1895] [A publication] (DLA)
LL COOL J ... Ladies Love Cool James [Rap recording artist, James Todd Smith]
LLCS .... Link Level Communications Subsystem [NCR Corp.]
LLCS .... Liquid Level Control Switch
LLCS .... Low-Level Compaction Station [Nuclear energy] (NRCH)
LLCSC .... Lower Level Computer Software Component
LLCUNAE ..... Law Library of Congress United Association of Employees
LLD .... Doctor of Laws (CMD)
LLD .... Lactobacillus Lactis Dorner Factor [Vitamin B_{12}] [Also, APA, APAF, EF]
LLD .... Lamp Lumen Depreciation
LLD .... LASER Light Detector
LLD .... Launcher Load Dolly
LLD .... Law and Legal Information Directory [A publication]
LLD .... Left Lateral Decubitus [Medicine] (AAMN)
LLD .... Leg Length Discrepancy [Orthopedics] (DAVI)
LLD .... Legum Doctor [Doctor of Laws] [Latin]
LLD .... Live Letter-Drop [Espionage]
LLD .... Logic Level Driver [Computer science] (MCD)
LLD .... Long-Lasting Depolarization [Neurophysiology]
LLD .... Lower Limit of Detection [Spectrometry]
LLD .... Lowest Lethal Dose [Medicine] (LDT)
LLD .... Low-Level Detector (IEEE)
LLD .... Low-Level Dose [Nuclear energy] (NRCH)
LLDB .... Luc Luong Dac Biet [South Vietnam]
LLDEF .... Lambda Legal Defense and Education Fund (EA)
LLDF .... Lactobacillus Lactis Dormer Factor [Vitamin B12] (STED)
LLDH .... Liver Lactate Dehydrogenase [An enzyme] (DAVI)
LLDL .... Low-Level Differential Logic (IAA)
LLDPE .... Linear Low-Density Polyethylene [Plastics technology]
LLDR .... Lightweight LASER [Light Amplification by Stimulated Emission of Radiation] Designator Range Finder [DoD]
LLDS .... Low-Level Weapons Delivery System (MCD)
LLDV .... Luc-Luong Dac-Viet [Vietnamese special forces]
LLE .... Laboratory for LASER Energetics [University of Rochester] [Research center]
LLE .... Large Local Exchange [Telecommunications] (TEL)
LLE .... Left Lower Extremity [Medicine]
LLE .... Lightning Loss Exclusion [Insurance]
LLE .... Liquid-Liquid Equilibria [Physical chemistry]
LLE .... Liquid-Liquid Extraction
LLE .... Long Line Effect
LLE .... Long Line Equipment [Telecommunications] (TEL)
LLE .... West Bend, WI [Location identifier FAA] (FAAL)
LLEA .... Local Law Enforcement Agency
LL Edw Conf... Laws of Edward the Confessor [A publication] (DLA)
LLEE .... Leurs Eminences [Their Eminences] [French]
LLEE .... Leurs Excellences [Their Excellencies] [French]
LLEIS .... Lower Level End Item Subdivision [Army] (AABC)
LLE Ry .... LL & E Royalty Trust [Associated Press] (SAG)
LLES .... Eyn-Shemer [Israel] [ICAO location identifier] (ICLI)
LLeS .... Leesville State School, Leesville, LA [Library symbol Library of Congress] (LCLS)
LLET .... Elat/J. Hozman [Israel] [ICAO location identifier] (ICLI)
L LETT .... Licentiate of Letters (WDAA)
LLETZ .... Large Loop Excision of the Transformation Zone [Medicine]
LLeV .... Vernon Parish Library, Leesville, LA [Library symbol Library of Congress] (LCLS)
LLF .... Fibrin-Stabilizing Factor [Hematology] (DAVI)
LLF .... Lag Line Filter
LLF .... Laki-Lorand Factor [Factor XIII] [Also, FSF Hematology]
LLF .... Land Level Facility [Navy]
LLF .... Latin American Growth Fd [NYSE symbol] (TTSB)
LLF .... Laubach Literacy Fund [Later, LLI] (EA)
LLF .... Left Lateral Femoral [Site of injection] [Medicine]
LLF .... Left Lateral Flexion [Medicine] (DMAA)
LLF .... Lehman Brothers Latin American Growth Fund [NYSE symbol] (SAG)
LLF .... Light Loss Factor [Floodlighting]
LLF .... Line Link Frame [Telecommunications] (TEL)
LLF .... Little League Foundation (EA)
LLF .... Load List File (AFIT)
LLFA .... Low-Low Frequency Acoustics (DOMA)
LLFC .... Laryssa Lauret Fan Club (EA)
LLFC .... Loretta Lynn Fan Club (EA)
LLFET .... Linear-Load Field Effect Transistor [Electronics] (PDAA)
LLFM .... Land Line Frequency Modulation (AAG)

LLFM .... Low-Level Flux Monitor [Nuclear energy] (NRCH)
LLFPB .... Linear, Lumped, Finite, Passive, Bilateral
LLG .... Chillagoe [Australia Airport symbol Obsolete] (OAG)
LLG .... Labour Life Group (BUAC)
LLG .... Landcare Liaison Group (BUAC)
LLG .... Line-to-Line to Ground (IAA)
LLG .... Logical Language Group [An association] (EA)
LLG .... Logical Line Group [Computer science] (IBMDP)
LLG .... Luggage and Leather Goods Salesmen's Association of America (EA)
LLGA .... Leadless Land Grid Array [Electronics] (EECA)
LLGAF .... Leslie-Lohman Gay Art Foundation (EA)
LLGDS .... Landlocked and Geographically Disadvantaged States [Developing countries]
LLGF .... Leather, Leather Goods, Fur [Department of Employment] [British]
LLGL .... Low-Level Graphical Language (PDAA)
LLGMA .... Luggage and Leather Goods Manufacturers of America (EA)
LLGSA .... Luggage and Leather Goods Salesmen's Association of America (NTPA)
LL-GXT .... Low-Level Graded Exercise Test [Cardiology] (DAVI)
LLH .... Ladies Left Handed
LLH .... Lahore Light Horse [British military] (DMA)
LLH .... Library of Literary History [A publication]
LLH .... Low-Level Heating [Nuclear energy] (OA)
LLHA .... Haifa/U. Michaeli [Israel] [ICAO location identifier] (ICLI)
LL Hen I ...... Laws of Henry I [A publication] (DLA)
LLHZ .... Herzlia [Israel] [ICAO location identifier] (ICLI)
LLI .... Lalibella [Ethiopia] [Airport symbol] (OAG)
LLI .... Language-Based Learning Impairment [Neurology]
LLI .... Late Latent Infection [Medicine]
LLI .... Latitude and Longitude Indicator
LLI .... Laubach Literacy International (EA)
LLI .... Life Line International (EA)
LLI .... Ligula Length Index
LLI .... Limited Life Item (MCD)
LLI .... Link Layer Interface [Computer science] (PCM)
LLI .... Lipari [Lipari Islands] [Seismograph station code, US Geological Survey] (SEIS)
LLI .... Liquid Level Indicator
LLI .... Logical Link Identifier (ACRL)
LLI .... Longitude and Latitude Indicator
LLI .... Long Lead Item (MUGU)
LLI .... Lord Lieutenant of Ireland
LLI .... Low-Level Interface
LLIB .... Load Module Librarian (MHDB)
LLIB .... Rosh Pina/Mahanaim-I. Ben-Yaakov [Israel] [ICAO location identifier] (ICLI)
LLIBC .... Lotus Lantern International Buddhist Center [South Korea] (EAIO)
LLIL .... Long Lead Item List
LLIL .... Long Lead Time Items List (NASA)
LLiLi .... Livingston Parish Library, Livingston, LA [Library symbol Library of Congress] (LCLS)
LL Inse .... Laws of Ina [A publication] (DLA)
LLIT .... Liquid-Like Intermediate Transistory
LLIU .... Launch and Landing Interface Unit (MCD)
LLIV .... Low-Level Input Voltage
LLJ .... Challis, ID [Location identifier FAA] (FAAL)
LLJ .... Lahore Law Journal [India] [A publication] (DLA)
LLJ .... Lalmonirhat [Bangladesh] [Airport symbol] (AD)
LLJ .... LaTrobe Library Journal [A publication]
LLJ .... Low-Level Jet [Marine science] (OSRA)
LLJJ .... Lords Justices
LLJM .... Ministry of Transport [Israel] [ICAO location identifier] (ICLI)
LI Jud Act.... Lloyd's Supreme Court of Judicature Acts [1875] [A publication] (DLA)
LLK .... Liberator Lake, AK [Location identifier FAA] (FAAL)
LLK .... Little Lake Resources Ltd. [Vancouver Stock Exchange symbol]
LLK .... Louis Leakey - Korongo [Anthropological skull]
LLL .... Labour Left Liaison [An association] (BUAC)
LLL .... La Leche League [Local affiliates of LLLI] (EA)
LLL .... Land Locomotion Laboratory [Army]
LLL .... Lawrence Livermore Laboratory [Also, LLNL] [University of California]
LLL .... Lawyers, Layers, and Limos [Television broadcasting industry]
LLL .... Left Liver Lobe (STED)
LLL .... Left Lower Eyelid [Medicine]
LLL .... Left Lower Leg (STED)
LLL .... Left Lower Limb [Anatomy] (DAVI)
LLL .... Left Lower Lobe [of lung] [Medicine]
LLL .... Left Lower Lung (STED)
LLL .... Liberte, Liberation, et Liberation Nationale [French resistance movement] [World War II]
LLL .... Licence en Droit [Licentiate in Law] [French] (ASC)
LLL .... Licentiate in Laws
LLL .... Light Living Library (EA)
LLL .... Lillooet [British Columbia] [Seismograph station code, US Geological Survey Closed] (SEIS)
LLL .... Long Lead List (MCD)
LL/L .... Long Leadtime/Items List
LLL .... Long Line Loiter [Aircraft]
LLL .... Loose Leaf Ledger
LLL .... Love's Labour's Lost [Shakespearean work]
LLL .... Lower Lip Length [Medicine]
LLL .... Low Level Language [Computer programming] (NTCM)
LLL .... Low-Level Logic

LLL	Low Light Level
LLL	Low Liquid Level [Engineering]
LLL	Loyal Lusitanian League [British military] (DMA)
LLL	Lutheran Laymen's League [Later, ILLL] (EA)
LLL	University of Nebraska, Lincoln College of Law, Lincoln, NE [OCLC symbol] (OCLC)
LLLB	Left Long Leg Brace [Medicine]
L LL brace...	Left Long-Leg Brace (STED)
LLLGB	Low-Level-LASER Guided Bomb
LLLI	La Leche League International (EA)
Ll List LR	Lloyd's List Law Reports [England] [A publication] (DLA)
LLLLL	Laboratories Low Level Linked List (NITA)
LLLLLL	Laboratories Low-Level Linked List Language [Bell Systems] (MCD)
Ll LLR	Lloyd's List Law Reports [England] [A publication] (DLA)
LLLM	Low Liquid Level Monitor (STED)
LLLNR	Left Lower Lobe, No Rales [Medicine] (STED)
LLLO	Lend-Lease Liaison Office [World War II]
LL Longobard...	Laws of the Lombards [A publication] (DLA)
Ll L Pr Cas...	Lloyd's List Prize Cases Reports [England] [A publication] (DLA)
Ll LR	Lloyd's List Law Reports [England] [A publication] (DLA)
Ll L Rep	Lloyd's List Law Reports [England] [A publication] (DLA)
LLLT	Low-Light-Level Television [Night vision device] [Military] (RDA)
LLLTV	Low-Level LASER Television
LLLTV	Low-Light-Level Television [Night vision device] [Military]
LLLW	Liquid Low Level Waste [Nuclear energy] (NUCP)
LLLW	Low Level Liquid Waste [Nuclear energy] (NUCP)
LLLWT	Low-Level Liquid Waste Tank [Nuclear energy] (NRCH)
LLM	Launcher Loader Module
LLM	Lawyers Linked by MODEM [Computer bulletin board system] [FIDO]
LLM	Legum Magister [Master of Laws] [Latin]
LLM	Limb Load Monitor
LLM	Linear Learning Machine [Data analysis]
LLM	Load Line Method
LLM	Localized Leukocyte Mobilization
LLM	Local Linear Model (AAEL)
LLM	Long Lama [Malaysia] [Airport symbol] (AD)
LLM	Low-Level Multiplexer
LLM	Loyola University, New Orleans, LA [OCLC symbol] (OCLC)
LLM	Lunar Landing Mission [NASA]
LLM	Lunar Landing Module [NASA] (MCD)
LLM	Master of Law (GAGS)
LLM	Master of Laws
LLMA	Leavers Lace Manufacturers of America [Defunct] (EA)
LL Malcom R Scott...	Laws of Malcolm, King of Scotland [A publication] (DLA)
Ll Mar LN....	Lloyd's Maritime Law Newsletter [A publication] (DLA)
LLM (CL)	Master of Laws in Comparative Law
LLM Com	Master of Commercial Law
LLME	Leuo Leucine Methylester [Biochemistry]
LLMFC	Laura Lee McBride Fan Club (EA)
LLMH	Loyal Legion of the Medal of Honor (EA)
LLMI	Local Labour Market Information/Intelligence [British] (AIE)
LLM (Int L)...	Master of Laws in International Law
LLMM	Leurs Majestes [Their Majesties] [French]
LLMPP	Liquid Level Monitor Port Plug [Nuclear energy] (NRCH)
LLMR	Mitzpe-Ramon [Israel] [ICAO location identifier] (ICLI)
LLMW	Low Level Mixed Waste [Environmental science] (COE)
LLMZ	Metzada/I. Bar Yehuda [Israel] [ICAO location identifier] (ICLI)
LLN	Language, Literacy and Numeracy
LLN	League for Less Noise
LLN	Levelland, TX [Location identifier FAA] (FAAL)
LLN	Line Link Network [Bell System]
LLN	Local Line Network [Telecommunications] (NITA)
LLNE	Law Librarians of New England (BUAC)
LLNL	Lawrence Livermore National Laboratory [Also, LLL] [Livermore, CA] [Department of Energy] (GRD)
LLNO	Low-Level Night Operations [Aviation]
LLNQ	Least Lots Next Queue (AAEL)
LL NS	Law Library, New Series [Philadelphia Reprint of English Treatises] [A publication] (DLA)
LLO	Eliadamello SPA [Italy ICAO designator] (FAAC)
LLO	Legionella-Like Organisms [Medicine]
LLO	Legislative Liaison Office (AAGC)
LLO	Lifer Liaison Officer (WDAA)
LLO	Llano, TX [Location identifier FAA] (FAAL)
LLO	Local Lockout (IAA)
LLO	Low Lunar Orbit
LLOC	Land Line of Communications [Military]
LLOD	Lowe Limit of Detection [Also, LLD] [Analytical chemistry]
LLOS	Landmark Line of Sight (KSC)
LLOV	Low-Level Output Voltage
LLOV	Ovda [Israel] [ICAO location identifier] (ICLI)
Lloyd & Goold (T Plunkett) (Ir)...	Lloyd and Goold's Irish Chancery Reports Tempore Plunkett [A publication] (DLA)
Lloyd & Goold (T Sugden) (Ir)...	Lloyd and Goold's Irish Chancery Reports Tempore Sugden [A publication] (DLA)
Lloyd & W ...	Lloyd and Welsby's English Mercantile Cases [A publication] (DLA)
Lloyd LR	Lloyd's List Law Reports [England] [A publication] (DLA)
Lloyd Pr Cas...	Lloyd's List Prize Cases Reports [England] [A publication] (DLA)
Lloyd Pr Cas NS...	Lloyd's List Prize Cases Reports, Second Series [1939-53] [A publication] (DLA)
Lloyd's List LR...	Lloyd's List Law Reports [England] [A publication] (DLA)
Lloyd's Mar LN...	Lloyd's Maritime Law Newsletter [A publication] (DLA)
Lloyd's Pr Cas...	Lloyd's List Prize Cases Reports [England] [A publication] (DLA)
Lloyd's Prize Cas...	Lloyd's List Prize Cases Reports [London] [A publication] (DLA)

Lloyd's Rep...	Lloyd's List Law Reports [England] [A publication] (DLA)
LLP	Lambda Limiting Process
LLP	LASER Light Pump
LLP	Late Luteal Phase (DB)
LLP	Launch and Landing Project [NASA] (NASA)
LLP	Law and Liberty Project [Defunct] (EA)
LLP	Leased Long Lines Program (NATG)
LLP	Liberian Liberal Party [Political party] (EY)
LLGB	Linear Log Potentiometer
LLP	Line Link Pulsing [Telecommunications]
LLP	Literacy and Learning Program
LLP	Live Load Punch
LLP	Lloyd's of London Press [British]
LLP	Local Language Program
LLP	Lollipop Daycare [Vancouver Stock Exchange symbol]
LLP	London Labour Party [British Political party]
LLP	Long-Lasting Potentiation (DB)
LLP	Long Lead Part
LLP	Lowest Level Processor [Computer science] (CIST)
LLP	Lunar Landing Program [NASA]
LLP	Lyman Laboratory of Physics [Harvard] (MCD)
LLPA	Low Level Waste Policy Act [1980] (NUCP)
LLPDD	Late Luteal Phase Dysphoric Disorder [Gynecology]
LLPE	Labor's League for Political Education [AFL] [Later merged into Committee on Political Education of AFL-CIO]
LLpEC	East Carroll Parish Library, Lake Providence, LA [Library symbol Library of Congress] (LCLS)
LLPI	Linen and Lace Paper Institute [Later, SSI] (EA)
LLPL	Low Low Pond Level (IEEE)
LLPMS.........	Long Leg Posterior Molded Splint [Medicine] (MEDA)
LLPN	Lumped, Linear, Parametric Network
LLPO	Launch and Landing Project Office [NASA] (NASA)
LLPO	Launch and Landing Project Office [Aerospace] (NAKS)
Ll Pr	Lloyd on Prohibition [1849] [A publication] (DLA)
Ll Pr Cas	Lloyd's List Prize Cases Reports [England] [A publication] (DLA)
Ll Pr Cas NS...	Lloyd's List Prize Cases Reports, New Series [1939-53] [A publication] (DLA)
LLPS	Low-Level Pumping Station (ADA)
LL-PTC.........	Liquid Liquid Phase Transfer Catalysis [Physical chemistry]
LLQ	Left Lower Quadrant [of abdomen] [Medicine]
LLQA	Limiting Lines of Quiet Approach [Navy] (NVT)
LLR	High Court of Lagos Law Reports [Nigeria] [A publication] (ILCA)
LLR	Lancaster Law Review [A publication] (DLA)
LLR	Large Lattice Relaxation (AAEL)
LLR	Large Local Reaction [Medicine] (DMAA)
LLR	Leader Law Reports [South Africa] [A publication] (DLA)
LLR	Left Lateral Rectus [Eye muscle] (BABM)
LLR	Left Lateral Rotation [Medicine]
LLR	Left Lumbar Region [Medicine] (MAE)
LLR	Lender of Last Resort
LLR	Leukemia-Like Reaction [Hematology]
LLR	Liberian Law Reports [A publication] (ILCA)
LLR	Line Length Remainder [Graphic arts] (DGA)
LLR	Line of Least Resistance
LLR	Load-Limiting Resistor
LLR	LOFT [Loss-of-Fluid Test] Lead Rod (GAAI)
LLR	Log-Likelihood Ratio (PDAA)
LLR	Long Latency Response [Neurology]
LLR	Long Length Record (IAA)
LLR	Low-Level Radiation
LLR	Low-Level Resistance [to disease]
LLR	Lunar LASER Ranging [Aerospace]
LLRA	LapLink Remote Access [Traveling Software, Inc.] [Computer science] (PCM)
LLRC...........	Luneberg Lens Rapid Commutator [Physics]
LLRDS	Long Life Recording and Data Storage (MCD)
Ll Rep	Lloyd's List Law Reports [England] [A publication] (DLA)
LLRES..........	Load-Limiting Resistor (MSA)
LLRF	Low-Level Radio Frequency
LLRF	Lunar Landing Research Facility [Aerospace]
LLRF	Lunar LASER Range-Finder [Aerospace]
LLRI	Low-Level-Run-In (MCD)
LLRM...........	Low-Level Radio Modulator
LLRP...........	Long Lead Repair Part
Ll R Pr Cas...	Lloyd's List Prize Cases Reports, Second Series [1939-53] [A publication] (DLA)
LLRR	Log-Likelihood Ratio Representation (MHDB)
LLRR	Lowest Level Remove-Replace (SAA)
LLRS	LASER Lightning Rod System (PDAA)
LLRT	Local Leak Rate Test [Nuclear energy] (NRCH)
LLRT	Low-Level Reactor Test (IEEE)
LLRV	Lunar Landing Research Vehicle [Aerospace]
LLRW...........	Low-Level Radiological Waste [U.S. Army Corps of Engineers]
LLRWPA	Low-Level Radioactive Waste Policy Act of 1980 (GAAI)
LLRWPAA.....	Low-Level Radioactive Waste Policy Amendments Act of 1985 (GAAI)
LLS	Land Laws Service [Australia A publication]
LLS	LASER Light Scattering [Physical chemistry]
LLS	LASER Light Source
LLS	LASER Line Scanner
LLS	Launch and Landing Site (MCD)
LLS	Lazy Leukocyte Syndrome [Medicine]
LLS	Linear Least Squares [Mathematics]
LLS	Liquid Level Sensor
LLS	Liquid Level Switch (IAA)

LLS............	Localized Light Scatterer (AAEL)
LLS............	Local Library System [OCLC]
LLS............	Long Left Shift (SAA)
LLS............	Long Leg Splint [Orthopedics] (DAVI)
LLS............	Louisiana State University, Graduate School of Library Science, Baton Rouge, LA [OCLC symbol] (OCLC)
LLS............	Low-Level Sensor (KSC)
LLS............	Low-Level Service [Computer science]
LLS............	Low-Level Solid [Nuclear energy] (NRCH)
LLS............	Lunar Landing Simulator [Aerospace] (AAG)
LLS............	Lunar Logistics System [NASA]
LLS............	Lyman Limit System [Spectroscopy]
LLSA........	Land Lines Assembly [Ground Communications Facility, NASA]
LLSA........	Latin Languages Speaking Allergists [See also GAILL] (EAIO)
LLSA........	Limiting Lines of Surfaced Approach [Navy] (NVT)
LLSAC......	LASER Line Scanner Aerial Camera
LLSAGW...	Low-Level Surface-to-Air Guided Weapon (IAA)
LLSB........	Left Lower Scapular Border [Medicine] (DMAA)
LLSB........	Left Lower Sternal Border [Anatomy] (DAVI)
LLSBA......	Leicester Longwool Sheep Breeders Association [England] (BUAC)
LLSC........	Israel South Control Area Control Center Unit [Israel] [ICAO location identifier] (ICLI)
LLSD........	Tel Aviv/Sde Dov [Israel] [ICAO location identifier] (ICLI)
LLSIL.......	Lower Living Standard Income Level [CETA] [Department of Labor]
LLSNA......	Limiting Lines of Snorkel Approach [Navy] (NVT)
LLSP........	Law Library Service to Prisoners [Minnesota State Law Library]
LLSPT......	Licentiateship of the London School of Polymer Technology [British] (DBQ)
LLSS.........	LASER Light Scattering Spectroscopy
LLSS.........	LASER Light Source Station
LLSS.........	Long Life Space System (IAA)
LLSS.........	Low-Level Sounding System [for measuring weather conditions]
LI St..........	Lloyd's Statutes of Practical Utility [A publication] (DLA)
LLSU........	Low-Level Signaling Unit [Telecommunications] (TEL)
LLSUA......	Limiting Lines of Submerged Approach [Navy] (NVT)
LI Suc.......	Lloyd on Succession Laws [1877] [A publication] (DLA)
LLSV.........	Low-Level Storage Vault [Nuclear energy] (NRCH)
LLSV.........	Lunar Logistics Supply Vehicle [NASA] (IAA)
LLSV.........	Lunar Logistics System Vehicle [NASA]
LLSWV......	Low-Level Solid Waste Storage Vault [Nuclear energy] (NRCH)
LLT...........	Lahore Law Times [India] [A publication] (DLA)
LLT...........	Lander Local Time [NASA]
LLT...........	Land-Line Teletypewriter [Military] (IAA)
LLT...........	Left Lateral [Anatomy] (DAVI)
LLT...........	Left Lateral Thigh [Medicine]
LLT...........	Library of Living Thought [A publication]
LLT...........	London Landed Terms [Shipping]
LLT...........	Long Lead Time
LLT...........	Low-Level Terminal
LLT...........	Low-Level Turbulence
LLT...........	Low-Light Television
LLT...........	Loyola University, Law Library, New Orleans, LA [OCLC symbol] (OCLC)
LLT...........	Lysolecithin (DMAA)
LLTA.........	Tel Aviv [Israel] [ICAO location identifier] (ICLI)
LLTC.........	Linear Technology Corp. [NASDAQ symbol] (TTSB)
LLTCS.......	Low-Limit Temperature Control Systems
LLTD........	Lightweight LASER Target Designator
LLTDS.......	Launch Landing Test Data System (MCD)
LLTI..........	Long Lead Time Items (AAG)
LLTIL........	Long Lead Time Items List [Military] (CAAL)
LLTM........	Long Lead Time Material (DNAB)
LLTR.........	Large Leak Test Rig [Nuclear energy] (NRCH)
LLTR.........	Low-Level Transit Time
LI Tr M.....	Lloyd on Trade-Marks [A publication] (DLA)
LLTT.........	Landline Teletypewriter [Military]
LLTTY.......	Landline Teletypewriter [Military]
LLTV.........	Low-Light-Level Television [Night vision device] [Military]
LLTV.........	Lunar Landing Training Vehicle [Aerospace]
LLTWP......	Low-Level Tritiated Water Processing Subsystem (MCD)
LLU..........	Lamar, MO [Location identifier FAA] (FAAL)
LLU..........	Lending Library Unit
LLU..........	Lithuanian Liberal Union (BUAC)
LLU..........	Loma Linda University, Loma Linda, CA [OCLC symbol] (OCLC)
LLu..........	Saint James Parish Library, Lutcher, LA [Library symbol Library of Congress] (LCLS)
LLV..........	Long Life Valve
LLV..........	Long Life Vehicle [Automotive engineering]
LLV..........	Lonicera Latent Virus [Plant pathology]
LLV..........	Loyal London Volunteers [British military] (DMA)
LLV..........	Lunar Landing Vehicle [NASA]
LLV..........	Lunar Logistics Vehicle [NASA]
LLV..........	Lymphocytic Leukemia Virus
LLVIR.......	Long Line Voice Interface Rack (SSD)
LLVP........	Left Lateral Ventricular Preexcitation [Medicine] (DMAA)
LLVPG......	Large Launch Vehicle Planning Group [NASA]
LLW..........	Lilongwe [Malawi] [Airport symbol] (OAG)
LLW..........	Lower Low Water [Tides and currents]
LLW..........	Low-Level Radioactive Waste
LLW..........	Low-Level Waste [Nuclear energy] (NRCH)
LLWAS......	Low-Level Windshear Alert System (USDC)
LLWC........	Long-Leg Walking Cast [Orthopedics] (DAVI)
LLWDDD...	Low-Level Waste Disposal Development and Demonstration
LLWI.........	Lower Low-Water Interval [Tides and currents]
LL Wisegotho...	Laws of the Visigoths [A publication] (DLA)
LL Wm Conq...	Laws of William the Conqueror [A publication] (DLA)
LL Wm Noth...	Laws of William the Bastard [A publication] (DLA)
LLWMP.......	Low-Level Waste Management Program (GAAI)
LLWS.........	Low Level Wind Shear [Aviation] (FAAC)
LLWSV......	Low-Level Waste Storage Vault [Nuclear energy] (NRCH)
LLX...........	Louisiana Land & Exploration Co. [NYSE symbol Toronto Stock Exchange symbol]
LLX...........	Louisiana Land/Exp [NYSE symbol] (TTSB)
LLX...........	Lyndonville, VT [Location identifier FAA] (FAAL)
LLY...........	Lilly [Eli] & Co. [NYSE symbol] (SPSG)
LLY...........	Lilly (Eli) [NYSE symbol] (TTSB)
LLY...........	Llanelly [Welsh depot code]
LLYP.........	Long Leaf Yellow Pine [Lumber]
LLZ...........	Left Lower Zone [Medicine] (DMAA)
LLZ...........	Localizer [ICAO designator] (CET)
LM............	Labiomental [Lip and chin] [Dentistry] (DAVI)
LM............	Laboratory Manager
LM............	Laboratory Microscope
LM............	Laboratory Module (MCD)
LM............	Labour Mobility [British]
LM............	Lactic Acid Mineral (DMAA)
LM............	Lactose Malabsorption [Gastroenterology]
LM............	Lacus Mortis [Lunar area]
LM............	Lamentations [Old Testament book]
LM............	Landmark (KSC)
LM............	Land Mine [Military]
LM............	Land Mobile
LM............	Large Memory [Computer science]
LM............	Large Mouth Bass [Pisciculture]
LM............	Laryngeal Mask [Medicine] (DMAA)
LM............	Laryngeal Muscle (BABM)
LM............	LASER Machine (IAA)
LM............	Late Model [Class of racing cars]
LM............	Lateral Malleolus [Anatomy]
LM............	Lateral Meniscus [Anatomy]
LM............	Laufenden Monats [Of the Current Month] [German]
LM............	Launch Module
LM............	Launch Mount (AFM)
LM............	Leading Mechanician
LM............	Leave Message [Word processing]
LM............	Lee-Metford [British military] (DMA)
LM............	Left Male (MSA)
LM............	Left Mid (NASA)
LM............	Legal Medicine
LM............	Legg Mason, Inc. [NYSE symbol] (SPSG)
LM............	Legion of Merit [Military decoration]
LM............	Leg Multiple [Telegraph] [Telecommunications] (TEL)
LM............	Lemniscus Medialis (DB)
LM............	Lentigo Maligna [Oncology]
LM............	Leprosy Mission [Australia An association]
LM............	Leptomeningeal Metastasis
LM............	Lethal Material
LM............	Level Meter
LM............	Liability Management (EBF)
LM............	Licentiate in Medicine
LM............	Licentiate in Midwifery
LM............	Licentiate in Music (WDAA)
LM............	Light Machine Gun
LM............	Light Maintenance
LM............	Light Metal
LM............	Light Microscope
LM............	Light Microscopy (AAEL)
LM............	Light Minimum [Medicine]
LM............	Light Music [Canadian Broadcasting Corp. record series prefix]
LM............	Lime Mortar (DAC)
LM............	Limit (IAA)
LM............	Limitation [Dialog] [Searchable field] [Information service or system] (NITA)
LM............	Lincoln Mercury [Division of Ford Motor Co.]
LM............	Linear Meter
LM............	Linear Modulation
LM............	Line Mark (IAA)
L/M...........	Lines per Minute [Computer science]
l/m...........	Lines per Minute (IDOE)
LM............	Linguomesial [Dentistry]
LM............	Link Manager
LM............	Lipid Mobilizing Hormone [Endocrinology]
LM............	Liquidity-Money Supply [Economics]
LM............	Liquid Membrane
LM............	Liquid Metal
Lm............	[Maltese] Lira [Monetary Unit] [Malta] (BARN)
LM............	Listeria Monocytogenes [Microorganism]
LM............	List of Material [DoD]
L/M...........	List of Materials (AAG)
L/M...........	Liters per Minute
LM............	Liturgie und Moenchtum [A publication] (BJA)
LM............	Load Module (MCD)
LM............	Load Multiple [Computer command] (PCM)
LM............	Local Manufacture (AAG)
LM............	Local Memory
LM............	Local Militia [British military] (DMA)
LM............	Locus Monumenti [Place of the Monument] [Latin]
LM............	Logical Module (NITA)
LM............	Logic Module [Computer science] (MCD)

LM	Logistics Manager (MCD)
LM	Logistics Module [*Simulation games*] [*Army*] (SSD)
LM	Longitudinal Muscle [*Anatomy*]
LM	Long Measure (ROG)
LM	Long Meter [*Music*]
LM	Long Module (MCD)
LM	Loop Multiplexer
LM	Looser-Milkman [*Syndrome*] [*Medicine*] (DB)
LM	Lord Mayor
LM	Loss Margin (IAA)
LM	Louisiana Midland Railway Co. (IIA)
L-M	Louisiana State Museum, New Orleans, LA [*Library symbol Library of Congress*] (LCLS)
LM	Lower Magazine [*Typography*]
LM	Lower Motor [*Neurology*]
LM	Low Meaningfulness [*Psychology*]
L/M	Low/Medium (MCD)
LM	Low-Melting (OA)
LM	Low Molecular [*Chemistry*]
LM	Luftmine [*Aerial mine*] [*German military - World War II*]
LM	Lumen [*Symbol*] [*SI unit of luminous flux*]
lm	Lumen (IDOE)
L/M	Luminosity to Mass [*Ratio*] [*Astronomy*]
LM	Lunar Mission
LM	Lunar Module [*Formerly, LEM*] [*NASA*]
LM	Maestretti [*Italy*] [*Research code symbol*]
LM	Middle Latitude [*Navigation*]
LM1A	Late Minoan 1A [*Archaeology*]
LM1B	Late Minoan 1B [*Archaeology*]
LM2	Lima [*Magdalena*] [*Peru*] [*Seismograph station code, US Geological Survey*] (SEIS)
LM2	Liver Microsomal Band 2
L/(M² D)	Liters per Square Meter Day
LMA	Labor Market Area
LMA	Lake Minchumina [*Alaska*] [*Airport symbol*] (OAG)
LMA	Laminating Materials Association [*Oradell, NJ*] (EA)
LMA	Land Mammal Ages [*Paleontology*]
LMA	Large Model Access (MCD)
LMA	LASER Microspectral Analysis
LMA	Last Manufacturers Association [*Defunct*] (EA)
LMA	Latvian Maritime Academy (BUAC)
LMA	Leading Medical Assistant [*British military*] (DMA)
LMA	League for Mutual Aid [*Defunct*] (EA)
LMA	Leased Management Agreement [*Radio*] [*Television*] (WDMC)
LMA	Lebanese Management Association (BUAC)
LMA	Lebanese Moslem Association [*Australia*]
LMA	Left Mentoanterior [*A fetal position*] [*Obstetrics*]
LMA	Licensed Merchandisers' Association [*Later, ILMA*] (EA)
LMA	Limbic Midbrain Area (STED)
LMA	Lingerie Manufacturers Association [*Later, IAMA*] (EA)
LMA	Linoleum Manufacturers Association (BUAC)
LMA	Liquor Merchants' Association [*Australia*]
LMA	Liver Membrane Antibody [*Medicine*] (STED)
LMA	Liver Membrane Autoantibody [*Immunochemistry*]
LMA	Livestock and Meat Authority [*Queensland, Australia*]
LMA	Livestock Marketing Association (EA)
LMA	Local Marshalling Areas (MCD)
LMA	Lock Museum of America (EA)
LMA	Logsplitter Manufacturers Association [*Defunct*] (EA)
LMA	London Mayors Association [*England*] (BUAC)
LMA	Low Moisture Activity [*Brake system*] [*Automotive engineering*]
LMA	Lunar Meteoroid Analyzer [*NASA*]
LMA	Lunar Module Adapter [*NASA*] (MCD)
LMAA	Liquor Merchants' Association of Australia
LMAA	Logistics Management Association of Australia
LMAB	London Munitions Assignments Board [*World War II*]
LMAC	Labor-Management Advisory Committee [*Terminated, 1974*] [*Cost of Living Council*] (EGAO)
LMAC	Labor Market Advisory Councils [*Department of Labor and Department of Health, Education, and Welfare*] [*Terminated, 1982*] (EGAO)
LMaD	DeSoto Parish Library, Mansfield, LA [*Library symbol Library of Congress*] (LCLS)
LMAD	Let's Make a Deal [*TV program*]
LMAE	Lunar Module Ascent Engine [*NASA*]
LMAF	Live Missile Assembly Facility
LMAFS	Lookout Mountain Air Force Station
LM-Ag	Liver Membrane Antigen [*Immunochemistry*]
L Mag & LR	Law Magazine and Law Review [*A publication*] (DLA)
L Mag & Rev	Law Magazine and Review [*A publication*] (DLA)
LMAGB	Locomotive Manufacturers Association of Great Britain (BUAC)
LMAL	Langley Memorial Aeronautical Laboratory [*NASA*] (AAG)
LMAMA	Louisa May Alcott Memorial Association (EA)
LmAN	Limited Area Networks (NITA)
LM & LR	Law Magazine and Law Review [*A publication*] (DLA)
LM & P	Lowndes, Maxwell, and Pollock's English Bail Court Practice Reports [*1850-51*] [*A publication*] (DLA)
LM & Sc R	London, Midland & Scottish Railway [*British*] (DCTA)
LManyS	Sabine Parish Library, Many, LA [*Library symbol Library of Congress*] (LCLS)
LMAQ	Liquor Merchants Association of Queensland [*Australia*]
LMAQ	Livestock and Meat Authority of Queensland [*Australia*]
LMarA	Avoyelles Parish Library, Marksville, LA [*Library symbol Library of Congress*] (LCLS)
LMARS	Library Management and Retrieval System [*Navy Information service or system*] (IID)
LM/ATM	Lunar Module Apollo Telescope Mount [*NASA*] (MCD)
LMAV	LASER Maverick (MCD)
LMAV	Lumber Manufacturers Association of Virginia (WPI)
LMAW	Liquid Medium Active Waste (NUCP)
LMB	Laboratory of Molecular Biophysics (GNE)
LMB	Labor Market Bulletin (OICC)
LMB	Laurence-Moon-Biedl [*Medicine*]
LMB	Left Main-Stem Bronchus [*Medicine*] (MEDA)
LMB	Left Most BIT [*Binary Digit*] [*Computer science*] (MHDB)
LMB	Leiomyblastoma [*Pathology*] (DAVI)
LMB	Leptomycin B [*A cytotoxin*]
LMB	Linear Motion Bearing
LMB	Local Message Box (NATG)
LMB	Low-Maintenance Battery (MCD)
LMBB	Laurence-Moon-Bardet-Biedl Syndrome [*Medicine*] (DMAA)
LMBBS	Laurence-Moon-Bardet-Biedl Syndrome [*Medicine*]
LMBBSN	Laurence-Moon-Bardet-Biedl Syndrome Network [*An association*] (EA)
LMBC	Lady Margaret Boat Club [*of St. John's College, Cambridge*] [*British*]
LMBC	Landmark Bancorp [*NASDAQ symbol*] (SAG)
LMBC	Liverpool Marine Biological Committee [*British*] (BARN)
LMBF	Low and Medium Bleeding Frequency [*Medicine*]
LMBI	Local Memory Bus Interface [*Computer science*]
LMBO	Leveraged Management Buy-Out
LMBR	Lumber
LMBS	Laurence-Moon-Biedl Syndrome [*Medicine*]
LMC	Cleveland-Marshall College of Law, Cleveland, OH [*OCLC symbol*] (OCLC)
LMC	Laboratory of Molecular Carcinogensis (GNE)
LMC	Labor Market Characteristics (OICC)
LMC	Lake Michigan Conference (PSS)
LMC	Lamacarena [*Colombia*] [*Airport symbol Obsolete*] (OAG)
LMC	Lamina Monopolar Cell [*Cytology*]
LMC	Lamocks [*Republic of China*] [*Seismograph station code, US Geological Survey*] (SEIS)
LMC	Lancia Motor Club [*Ledbury, Herefordshire, England*] (EAIO)
LMC	Land Management Code (PA)
LMC	Lanzhou Medical College [*China*] (BUAC)
LMC	Large Magellanic Cloud [*Astronomy*]
LMC	Large Monopolar Cell [*Anatomy*]
LMC	large Motile Cell [*Medicine*] (STED)
LMC	LASER Mirror Coating
LMC	Lateral Motor Column [*of the spinal cord*] [*Neurobiology*]
LMC	Latex-Modified Concrete (PDAA)
LMC	Launch Monitor Console [*or Control*] [*NASA*] (IAA)
LMC	Least Material Condition (MSA)
LMC	Left Main Coronary [*Artery*] [*Medicine*] (STED)
LMC	Left Middle Cerebral [*Artery*] [*Medicine*] (STED)
LMC	Library Media Center
LMC	Ligue Monarchiste du Canada [*Monarchist League of Canada*] (EAIO)
LMC	Lime-Magnesium Carbonate
LMC	Liquid Media Concentrate [*Cell culture*]
LMC	Liquid Metal Cycle
LMC	Living Male Child [*Medicine*] (DMAA)
LMC	Lloyd's Machinery Certificate [*Shipping*]
LMC	Local Management Committee
LMC	Local Mate Competition [*Entomology*]
LMC	Local Medical Committee [*British*]
LMC	Logistic Movement Center [*Military*] (CAAL)
LMC	Logistics Management Center [*Army*] (MCD)
LMC	London Montessori Centre [*British*] (AIE)
LMC	Long-Run Marginal Cost Curve [*Economics*]
LMC	Lon Morris College [*Texas*]
LMC	Loss of Mesodermal Competence [*Developmental biology*]
LMC	Louisville Municipal College [*Kentucky*]
LMC	Low Middling Clause [*Business term*]
LMC	Low-Pressure Molding Compound (MCD)
LMC	Lymphocyte-Mediated Cytolysis [*Medicine*] (STED)
LMC	Lymphocyte-Mediated Cytotoxicity [*Also, LC*] [*Immunology*]
LMC	Lymphocyte Microcytotoxicity [*Medicine*] (STED)
LMC	Lymphomyeloid Complex [*Medicine*]
LMc	Morgan City Public Library, Morgan City, LA [*Library symbol Library of Congress*] (LCLS)
LMCA	Laboratory Materiel Control Activity (AFIT)
LMCA	Left Main Coronary Artery [*Anatomy*]
LMCA	Left Middle Cerebral Artery [*Medicine*] (MAE)
LMCA	Logistics Management Course for Auditors [*Army*]
LMCA	Logistics Material Control Activity [*Military*]
LMCA	Long-Term Medical Conditions Alliance (BUAC)
LMCA	Lorry-Mounted Crane Association [*British*] (BI)
LMCAD	Left Main Coronary Artery Disease
LMCC	Land Mobile Communications Council (EA)
LMCC	Licentiate of Medical Council of Canada
LMCC	Licentiate of the Medical College of Canada (DD)
LMCC	Logistic Movement Coordination Center [*Navy*] (ANA)
LMCC	Low-Mintage Coin Club (EA)
LMCD	Liquid Metal Cooled Demonstration (IAA)
LMCFP	Life Member, College of Family Physicians (CMD)
LMCLQ	Lloyds Maritime and Commercial Law Quarterly [*A publication*] (DLA)
LM/CM²	Lumens per Square Centimeter
LMCMS	Licentiate Ministers and Certified Mediums Society (EA)
LMCN	Launch Maintenance Conference Network [*Aerospace*] (AAG)

LMCN........... Launch Missile Control Network (IAA)
LMCNI .... Livestock Marketing Commission for Northern Ireland (BUAC)
LMCP........... Laboratory Module Computer Program
LMCPA......... London Motor Cab Proprietors Association [England] (BUAC)
LMCR........... Liquid Metal Cooled Reactor
LMCSS......... Letter Mail Code Sort System [Postal Service]
LMCT........... Ligand-to-Metal Charge Transfer [Physical chemistry]
LMD............ Laboratory Management Division
LMD............ Labor Mobility Demonstration
LMD............ Lamda Airlines [Greece] [ICAO designator] (FAAC)
LMD............ LASER Microwave Division [Army]
LMD............ Leaf-Mold (ROG)
LMD............ Left Main Disease [Cardiology] (DB)
LMD............ Left Medial Deltoid [Injection Site]
LMD............ Licensed Motor Dealer
LMD............ Lipid-Moiety Modified Derivative (DB)
LMD............ Liquid Metal Detector
L/(M D)....... Liter per Meter Day
LMD............ Local Medical Doctor
LMD............ Logistics Management Data [Military] (MCD)
LMD............ Long Meter Double [Music]
LMD............ Louisiana Midland Railway Co. [Later, LMT] [AAR code]
LMD............ Low Modulus Direction [Mechanical testing]
LMD............ Low-Molecular-Weight Dextran [Medicine]
LMD............ Lunar Meteoroid Detector [NASA]
LMDA........... Lee's Multidifferential Agar [Brewery bacteria culture medium]
LMDA........... Literary Managers and Dramaturgs of the Americas (NTPA)
LMDA........... Lunar Meteoroid Detector-Analyzer [NASA]
LMDC........... Leadership and Management Development Center [Maxwell Air Force Base, AL]
LMDE........... Lunar Module Descent Engine [NASA]
LMDH.......... Mauritanian Human Rights League (BUAC)
LMDM.......... Little Mission for the Deaf-Mute [See also PMS] [Rome, Italy] (EAIO)
LMDS........... Local Multipoint Distribution Service [Telecommunications]
LMDS........... Local Multipoint Distribution System [Telecommunications] (ACRL)
LMDS........... Local Multipoint Distribution Systems [Broadcasting term]
LM/DUP....... Launch Module / Defense Unit Platform
LMDX.......... Low-Molecular-Weight Dextran (MAE)
LME .... Labor Market Exposure [Work Incentive Program]
LME .... Lambda Mercantile Corp. [Toronto Stock Exchange symbol]
LME .... Large Marine Ecosystem
LME .... Launch Monitor Equipment [NASA] (KSC)
LME .... Layer Management Entity [Telecommunications]
LME .... Left Mediolateral Episiotomy [Obstetrics] (MAE)
LME .... Light Mitochondrial Extract (OA)
LME .... Link Monitor Equipment (MCD)
LME .... Liquid Membrane Extraction [Separation science and technology]
LME .... Liquid Mercury Engine
LME .... Liquid Metal Embrittlement (MCD)
LME .... Locally Manufactured Equipment
LME .... Logistics Management Engineering, Inc. [Annapolis, MD] [Telecommunications] (TSSD)
LME .... London Metal Exchange
LME .... Lunar Module Engine [NASA]
LME .... Lysine Methyl Ester [Biochemistry]
LMEC........... Labour Middle East Council (BUAC)
LMEC........... Line Map Editing Console
LMEC........... Liquid Metal Engineering Center [Energy Research and Development Administration]
LMed & Ch... Licentiate in Medicine and Surgery (DAVI)
LMEE.......... Left Middle Ear Exploration [Otorhinolaryngology] (DAVI)
LMEE.......... Light Military Electronics Equipment
LMEIC......... Life Member of Engineering Institute of Canada
LMER.......... Land Margin Ecosystem Research [Marine science] (OSRA)
LMES.......... Laboratory for Meteorology and Earth Sciences [NASA]
LMES.......... Lockheed Martin Energy Systems, Inc. (GAAI)
LMET.......... Leadership and Management Education and Training [Navy]
LMetJ .... Jefferson Parish Library, Metairie, LA [Library symbol Library of Congress] (LCLS)
LMetR......... Jefferson Parish Recreation Department, Metairie, LA [Library symbol Library of Congress] (LCLS)
LMF .... Lack of Moral Fibre [British military] (DMA)
LMF .... Lake Michigan Federation (EA)
LMF .... Language Media Format (CET)
LMF .... Large Myelinated Fiber [Neuroanatomy]
LMF .... Large-Scale Melt Facility [Nuclear reactor test unit]
LMF .... Last Meal Furnished
LMF .... Last Month's Forecast (MCD)
LMF .... Left Middle Finger (DMAA)
LMF .... Le Mans [France] [Seismograph station code, US Geological Survey Closed] (SEIS)
LMF .... Leukeran [Chlorambucil], Methotrexate, Fluorouracil [Antineoplastic drug regimen]
LMF .... Leukocyte Mitogenic Factor [Medicine]
LMF .... Linear Matched Filter (IEEE)
LMF .... Linear Multistep Formula (PDAA)
LMF .... Liquid Metal Fuel
LMF .... Logical Mainframe (COE)
LMF .... Low and Medium Frequency
LMF .... Lower Mid Fuselage
LMF .... Lymphocyte Mitogenic Factor [Endocrinology, hematology]
LMFA.......... Light Metal Founders Association [British] (DBA)
LMFA.......... Lucky Mee Family Association (EA)
LMFB.......... Liquid-Metal Fast Breeder (MEC)
LMFBR........ Liquid Metal Fast Breeder Reactor

LMFC........... Leigh McCloskey Fan Club (EA)
LMFC........... Liza Minnelli Fan Club (EA)
LMFC........... Louise Mandrell Fan Club (EA)
LMFE........... London Meat Futures Exchange [British]
LMFR.......... Liquid Metal Fueled Reactor
LMFRE........ Liquid Metal Fueled Reactor Experiment
LM/FT²........ Lumen per Square Foot (WDAA)
lm/ft²......... Lumens per Square Foot (IDOE)
LMG........... Laboratory of Molecular Genetics (GNE)
LMG........... Lactic Esters of Mono/Diglycerides
LMG........... Lamington [Papua New Guinea] [Seismograph station code, US Geological Survey] (SEIS)
LMG........... LASER Milling Gauge
LMG........... Laurer Markin Gibbs, Inc. [Maumee, OH] [Telecommunications] (TSSD)
LMG........... Lawson Mardon Group (EFIS)
LMG........... Left Main Gear (MCD)
LMG........... Light Machine Gun
LMG........... Liquid Methane Gas
LMG........... Louisiana Mining Corp. [Vancouver Stock Exchange symbol]
LMGC......... Lunar Module Guidance Computer [NASA] (KSC)
LMGEN....... Load Module Generator (IAA)
LMGR .... Liberation Movement of the German Reich [An association] (EAIO)
LMGSM....... Latin and Mediterranean Group for Sport Medicine (EA)
LMH........... Lady Margaret Hall [Oxford University]
LMH........... Lewis, M. H., Winchester VA [STAC]
LMH........... Light Metal Hydride
LMH........... Light Military Hovercraft (PDAA)
LMH........... Lipid Mobilizing Hormone [Endocrinology]
LMH........... Lumen Hour (IAA)
LMHA......... Lay Mission-Helpers Association (EA)
LMHF......... Lauritz Melchior Heldentenor Foundation (EA)
LMHI......... Liga Medicorum Homoeopathica Internationalis [International Homoeopathic Medical League] (EA)
LMHR......... Lumen Hour (IAA)
lm-hr .... Lumen-Hour (IDOE)
LMHS......... Lancaster Mennonite Historical Society (EA)
LMHX......... Liquid Metal Heat Exchanger (NRCH)
LMI .... Labor Market Information [Department of Labor]
LMI .... Lawn Mower Institute [Later, OPEI]
LMi .... Leo Minor [Constellation]
LMI .... Leukocyte Migration Inhibition [Hematology]
LMI .... Life Management Institute [Life Office Management Association]
LMI .... Link Management Interface [Computer science]
LMI .... Liquid Mercury Isolator
LMI .... Liquid Metal Ionization [Spectrometry]
LMI .... Livestock Merchandising Institute [Later, LII] (EA)
LMI .... Loaded Motional Impedance
LMI .... Local Management Interface [Telecommunications] (ACRL)
LMI .... Local Memory Image
LMI .... Logistics Management Institute [Bethesda, MD] [Research center] (AFM)
LMI .... Low-Molecular-Weight Inhibitor [of protease activity]
LMI .... Lumi [Papua New Guinea] [Airport symbol] (OAG)
LMI .... Luthiers Mercantile International [Healdsburg, CA] [Commercial firm]
LMI .... Lymphocyte Migration Index
LMIA.......... Louisiana Meat Industry Association (SRA)
LMIAA........ Licentiate Architect Member of the Incorporated Association of Architects and Surveyors [British] (DAS)
LMIAS........ Licentiate Surveyor Member of the Incorporated Association of Architects and Surveyors [British] (DAS)
LMI-ATS ..... Labor Market Information - Analytical Table Series [Department of Labor - Employment and Training Administration] (OICC)
LMIB.......... Light Motorized Infantry Battalion (INF)
LMIC.......... Liberty Mutual Insurance Co.
LMIC.......... Liquid Metals Information Center [AEC]
LMIC.......... Lower Middle Income Country
LMIF.......... Leukocyte Migration Inhibition Factor [Hematology] (DMAA)
LMIG.......... Liquid Metal Ion Gun [Surface analysis]
LMIN.......... Laboratory of Molecular and Integrative Neuroscience (GNE)
LMin........... Leo Minor [Constellation]
L/MIN......... Liters per Minute
LMIS.......... Labor Market Information System [Department of Labor]
LMIS.......... Liquid Metal Ion Source
LMIS.......... Lloyd's Maritime Information Services Ltd. [Information service or system] (IID)
LMIS.......... Logistics Management Information System [Marine Corps] (GFGA)
LMIT.......... Lockheed Martin Idaho Technologies (GAAI)
LMiW......... Webster Parish Library, Minden, LA [Library symbol Library of Congress] (LCLS)
LMJ .... Greer, SC [Location identifier FAA] (FAAL)
LMK........... Landmark (NASA)
LMK........... Landmark Corp. [Toronto Stock Exchange symbol]
LML........... Lae [Marshall Islands] [Airport symbol] (OAG)
LML........... Large and Medium Lymphocytes [Medicine]
LML........... Lean Misfire Limb (PDAA)
LML........... Lean Misfire Limit [Automotive engine testing]
LML........... Leesona Moos Laboratory
LML........... Left Mediolateral [Episiotomy] [Obstetrics]
LML........... Left Mentolateral [Episiotomy] [Obstetrics]
LML........... Left Middle Lobe [of lung] (DAVI)
LML........... Logical Memory Level
LML........... Lookout Mountain Laboratories [California] (SAA)
LML........... Lowest Maintenance Level (MCD)
LMLA.......... Leisureways Marketing [NASDAQ symbol] (SAG)

LMLAF......... Leisureways Marketing Ltd [*NASDAQ symbol*] (TTSB)
LMLE.......... Left Mediolateral Episiotomy [*Medicine*] (STED)
LMLE.......... Local Maximum Likelihood Estimates [*Statistics*]
LMLE.......... Long Magazine Lee-Enfield [*British military*] (DMA)
LMLR.......... Load Memory Lockout Register
LM/LRV....... Lunar Module/Lunar Roving Vehicle [*NASA*]
LML scar w/h... Lower Midline Scar with Hernia [*Medicine*] (STED)
LMLV.......... Lockheed Martin Launch Vehicle
LMLW.......... Liquid Medium Level Waste [*Nuclear energy*] (NUCP)
LMM........... Lactobacillus Maintenance Medium [*Microbiology*]
LMM........... Lemming Resources, Inc. [*Vancouver Stock Exchange symbol*]
LMM........... Lentigo Maligna Melanoma [*Oncology*]
LMM........... Library Microfilm & Materials Co.
LMM........... Light Meromyosin [*Biochemistry*]
LMM........... Lights Monitor Module [*Automotive engineering*]
LMM........... Linear Multi-Step Method (PDAA)
LMM........... Lines per Millimeter (AAG)
LMM........... Liquid Money Market [*Banking*]
LMM........... Living Masters of Music [*A publication*]
LMM........... Llanelly & Mynydd Mawr Railway [*Wales*]
LMM........... Locator at Middle Marker [*Aviation*]
LMM........... Los Mochis [*Mexico*] [*Airport symbol*] (OAG)
LMM........... Lourenco Marques [*Mozambique*] [*Seismograph station code, US Geological Survey*] (SEIS)
LMM........... Lumbar Motion Monitor [*Ergonometrics*]
LMM........... Lutheran Men in Mission [*An association*] (EA)
LM/M²........ Lumen per Square Meter (WDAA)
lm/m²......... Lumens per Square Meter (IDOE)
LMMA........ LASER Microprobe Mass Analysis (AAEL)
LMMA........ Lutheran Medical Mission Association [*Defunct*] (EA)
LMMCI........ Labor Management Maritime Committee, Inc. (EA)
LMMF......... Lederer Messianic Ministries (EA)
LMMF......... Lisa Madonia Memorial Fund [*An association*] (EA)
LMMF......... Local Maintenance and Management of Facilities [*Military*] (AABC)
LMMFHR .... Letelier-Moffitt Memorial Fund for Human Rights [*Later, LMMFHR/IPS*] (EA)
LMMFHR/IPS... Letelier-Moffitt Memorial Fund for Human Rights/Institute for Policy Studies (EA)
LMMHD ...... Liquid Metal Magnetohydrodynamics
LMML........ Malta/Luqa [*Malta*] [*ICAO location identifier*] (ICLI)
LMMM....... Malta [*Malta*] [*ICAO location identifier*] (ICLI)
LMMS........ LASER Microprobe Mass Spectrometry [*or Spectroscopy*]
LMMS........ Library Materials Management System
LMMS........ Lightweight Multipurpose Missile System (MCD)
LMMS........ Local Message Metering Service [*Telecommunications*] (TEL)
LMMU........ Latin Mediterranean Medical Union [*See also UMML*] [*Mantua, Italy*] (EAIO)
LMMV......... Lamium Mild Mosaic Virus [*Plant pathology*]
LMN........... Lamoni, IA [*Location identifier FAA*] (FAAL)
LMN........... Lanthanum Magnesium Double Nitrate
LMN........... Lateral Mesencephalic Nucleus [*Brain anatomy*]
LMN........... Lateral Motoneuron [*Neurobiology*]
LMN........... Library Management Network, Inc. [*Information service or system*] (IID)
LMN........... Library Micromation News (NITA)
LMN........... Limbang [*Malaysia*] [*Airport symbol*] (OAG)
LMN........... Lineman (AABC)
LMN........... Load Matching Network
LMN........... Locomotor Neuron [*Neurology*]
LMN........... Lornex Mining Corp. [*Vancouver Stock Exchange symbol*]
LMN........... Lost Music Network [*Defunct*] (EA)
LMN........... Lower Motor Neuron [*Anatomy*]
LMN........... Northeast Louisiana University, Monroe, LA [*Library symbol Library of Congress*] (LCLS)
LMNA......... Label Manufacturers National Association [*Defunct*]
LMNA......... Land-Based Multimission Naval Aircraft (MCD)
LMNA......... Long-Range Multipurpose Naval Aircraft (HGAA)
LMNDF .... Lesbian Mothers National Defense Fund (EA)
LMNED .... Laboratories for Molecular Neuroendocrinology and Diabetes [*Tulane University*] [*Research center*] (RCD)
LMNL......... Lower Motor Neuron Lesion [*Medicine*]
LMNT......... Laminate
LMNTNG ...... Laminating
LMO........... LASER Master Oscillator
LMO........... Lasmo Canada, Inc. [*Toronto Stock Exchange symbol*]
LMO........... Lens-Modulated Oscillator
LMO........... Linear Master Oscillator
LMO........... Living Modified Organism
LMO........... Localized Molecular Orbital (DB)
LMO........... Logistics Management Office [*Army*]
LMO........... Lookout Mountain Observatory [*California*] [*Seismograph station code, US Geological Survey Closed*] (SEIS)
LMO........... Ouachita Parish Public Library, Monroe, LA [*Library symbol Library of Congress*] (LCLS)
LMOA......... Locomotive Maintenance Officers' Association (EA)
LMOI......... Labor Market and Occupational Information (OICC)
L/mole......... Liters per Mole [*Chemistry*] (MEC)
LMOS......... Line-Maintenance Operating System [*Telecommunications*] (ITD)
LMOS......... Loop Maintenance Operations System [*Formerly, MLR*] [*Bell System*]
LMP........... Labor Mobility Project [*Department of Labor*]
LMP........... Lamap [*New Hebrides*] [*Seismograph station code, US Geological Survey*] (SEIS)
LMP........... Laminated Metal Part
LMP........... Lampedusa [*Italy*] [*Airport symbol*] (OAG)
LMP........... Large Multifunctional Protease [*Medicine*] (DMAA)

LMP............. Last Menstrual Period [*Medicine*]
LMP............. Latent Membrane Potential [*Medicine*] (DMAA)
LMP............. Latent Membrane Protein [*Genetics*]
LMP............. Lawson Mardon Group Ltd. [*Toronto Stock Exchange symbol*]
LMP............. Layered Metal Phosphates [*Physical chemistry*]
LMP............. Left Mentoposterior [*A fetal position*] [*Obstetrics*]
LMP............. Library Material Processed
LMP............. Light Marching Pack [*Military*]
LMP............. Light Metal Products
LMP............. Linguistic Minorities Project [*Education*] (AIE)
LMP............. Liquid Metal Plasma Valve (IAA)
LMP............. Liquid Monopropellant
LMP............. Liquid Oxygen Maintenance Panel (AAG)
LMP............. List of Measurement Points (NASA)
LMP............. Literary Market Place [*A publication*]
LMP............. LM [*Lunar Module*] Mission Programmer [*NASA*] (KSC)
LMP............. Longitudinal Muscles of Pinnule
LMP............. Low Melting Point
LMP............. Low-Molecular-Weight Polypeptide [*Biochemistry*]
LMP............. Lumbar Puncture [*Medicine*]
LMP............. Lunar Module Pilot [*Apollo*] [*NASA*]
LMPA......... Methodist Local Preachers Mutual Aid Association (BUAC)
LMPA......... Qualified Member of the Master Photographers Association [*British*] (DBQ)
LMPBLK...... Lampblack
LMPCR....... Ligation-Mediated Polymerase Chain Reaction [*Genetics*]
LMPG........ Light Mobile Protected Gun (INF)
LMPM........ Library Material Preservation Manual
LMPRT....... Locally Most Powerful Rank Test [*Statistics*]
LMPS......... Lift Manufacturers Product Section - Material Handling Institute (NTPA)
LMPS......... Lunar Module Procedures Simulator [*NASA*]
LMPT......... Logistics and Material Planning Team (NATG)
LMQ.......... La Malbaie [*Quebec*] [*Seismograph station code, US Geological Survey*] (SEIS)
LMQ.......... Marsa Brega [*Libya*] [*Airport symbol*] (AD)
LMR.......... Labor-Management Relations
LMR.......... La Mourre [*France*] [*Seismograph station code, US Geological Survey*] (SEIS)
LMR.......... Land Mobile Radio (NITA)
LMR.......... LASER Magnetic Resonance (MCD)
LMR.......... Launch Mission Rules [*NASA*] (KSC)
LMR.......... Launch Monitor Room [*NASA*] (MCD)
LMR.......... Left Medial Rectus [*Eye muscle*] (BABM)
LMR.......... Library Maintenance Routine (IAA)
LMR.......... Licensed Motor Repairer
LMR.......... Light Modulation Recording
LMR.......... Ligue Marxiste Revolutionnaire [*Revolutionary Marxist League*] [*Switzerland Political party*] (PPW)
LMR.......... Linear Multiple Regression (IAA)
LMR.......... Line Monitor/Recorder (MCD)
LMR.......... Linguomandibular Reflex (STED)
LMR.......... Lipman Management Resources Ltd. (NITA)
LMR.......... Liquid Metal Reactor
LMR.......... Liquid Molding Resin [*Organic chemistry*]
LMR.......... Literary Magazine Review [*A publication*] (BRI)
LMR.......... Living Marine Resource [*Marine science*] (OSRA)
LMR.......... Localized Magnetic Resonance (DAVI)
LMR.......... Log Magnitude Ratio (STED)
LMR.......... Longmoor Military Railway [*British military*] (DMA)
LMR.......... Lowest Maximum Range
LMR.......... Lymphocytic Meningpolyradiculitis [*Medicine*] (DMAA)
LMR.......... St. Louis, MO [*Location identifier FAA*] (FAAL)
LMRA......... Labor-Management Relations Act [*1947*]
LMRCP .... Licenciate in Midwifery of the Royal College of Physicians [*British*]
LMRD........ Launch Mission Rules Document [*NASA*] (KSC)
LMRDA....... Labor-Management Reporting and Disclosure Act [*1959*]
LMRDA-IM... Labor-Management Reporting and Disclosure Act - Investigative Matter [*FBI standardized term*]
LMRDFS ...... Lightweight Man-Transportable Radio Direction-Finding System [*Army*]
LMRK........ Landmark Graphics [*NASDAQ symbol*] (SAG)
LMRP........ Lunar Module Replaceable Package [*NASA*] (KSC)
LMRPC....... Linear-Motor Resonant-Piston Compressor [*Navy*]
LMRR........ Lunar Module Rendezvous RADAR [*NASA*]
LMRS........ Labor-Management Relations Service of the US Conference of Mayors (EA)
LMRS........ Labor-Management Relations Staff [*Department of Agriculture*] (GFGA)
LMRS......... Land Mobile Radio Service [*Telecommunications*] (CIST)
LMRS......... Lockheed Maintenance Recording System
LMRS......... Lunar Module Rendezvous Simulator [*NASA*] (IAA)
LMRSH....... Licentiate Member of the Royal Society of Health [*British*]
LMRTPI...... Legal Member of the Royal Town Planning Institute [*British*] (DBQ)
LMRU........ Library Management Research Unit (NITA)
LMS.......... Laboratory for Mathematics and Statistics [*University of California at San Diego*] [*Research center*] (RCD)
LMS.......... Laboratory of Molecular Structure [*Massachusetts Institute of Technology*]
LMS.......... Lamsn & Sessions [*NYSE symbol*] (TTSB)
LMS.......... [*The*] Lamson & Sessions Co. [*NYSE symbol*] (SPSG)
LMS.......... Land Mass Simulator
LMS.......... Land Mobile Service (DA)
LMS.......... LASER Bank Management System [*Computer science*]
LMS.......... LASER Magnetic Stage

LMS............	LASER Magnetic Storage International
LMS............	LASER Mapping System
LMS............	LASER Mass Spectrometer
LMS............	LASER Mass Spectroscopy (EDCT)
LMS............	Lateral Medullary Syndrome [STED]
LMS............	Latin Mass Society (EAIO)
LMS............	Laurence-Moon Syndrome [Medicine]
LMS............	Least Mean Square (IEEE)
LMS............	Leiomyosarcoma [Oncology]
LMS............	LEM [Lunar Excursion Module] Mission Simulator [NASA]
LMS............	Level Measuring Set [for test signals] [Telecommunications] (TEL)
LMS............	Library Maintenance System (PDAA)
LMS............	Library Management System
LMS............	Licentiate in Medicine and Surgery [British]
LMS............	Lightning Mapper Sensor [NASA]
LMS............	Limestone [Technical drawings]
LMS............	Limited Mass Search [Chromatography]
LMS............	Linear Measuring System
LMS............	Liquid Measuring System
LMS............	Liquid Metal System
LMS............	List Management System
LMS............	Literature Management System
LMS............	Loadmaster Systems, Inc. [Vancouver Stock Exchange symbol]
LMS............	Load Matching Switch
LMS............	Load Measurement System (NASA)
LMS............	Local Management of Schools [British]
LMS............	Local Measured Service [Telecommunications] (TEL)
LMS............	Local Missile Selector (IAA)
LMS............	Location and Monitoring Service [Telecommunications] (OTD)
LMS............	Lockheed Missile System (MCD)
LMS............	Logistics Management Specialist (MCD)
LMS............	Logistics Master Schedules (MCD)
LMS............	Logistics Master Schedules (NAKS)
LMS............	Lomas Helicopters Ltd. [British ICAO designator] (FAAC)
LMS............	London Mathematical Society [England] (BUAC)
LMS............	London Medieval Society [England] (BUAC)
LmS............	London Microfilming Services Ltd., London, ON, Canada [Library symbol Library of Congress] (LCLS)
LMS............	London, Midland & Scottish Railway [British]
LMS............	London Missionary Society
LMS............	Lookout Mountain Observatory [California] [Seismograph station code, US Geological Survey] (SEIS)
LMS/...........	Louisville, MS [Location identifier FAA] (FAAL)
LM/S...........	Lumens per Second (MCD)
LMS............	Lunar Mass Spectrometer [NASA]
LMS............	Lunar Measuring System [Aerospace]
LMS............	Lunar Module Simulator [NASA] (SSD)
LMS............	Lutheran Mission Societies (EA)
LMSA...........	Labor-Management Services Administration [Department of Labor]
LMSA...........	Large Metoscale Area (PDAA)
LMSC...........	Let Me See Correspondence [Business term]
LMSC...........	Liquid Metals Safety Committee [AEC] (MCD)
LMSC...........	Little Missionary Sisters of Charity (TOCD)
LMSC...........	Lockheed Missiles & Space Corp. [Subsidiary of Lockheed Aircraft Corp.]
LMSC...........	Logistics Management Systems Center [Military]
LMSD...........	Lockheed Missile and Space Division (IAA)
LMSE...........	Laboratory Module Simulation Equipment
LMSE...........	Liquid Metal Slip Ring
LMSEC.........	Lumen Second (IAA)
LMSFX.........	Federated Municipal Securities Cl.A [Mutual fund ticker symbol] (SG)
LMSG...........	Low Magnetic Saturation Garnet
LMSI...........	Association of Lithuanian Foresters in Exile [Defunct] (EA)
LMSN...........	Local Message Switched Network
LMSQFT.......	Lumen per Square Foot (IAA)
LMSR...........	Large, Medium Speed RO/RO [Roll On/Roll Off] [Navy]
LMSR...........	London, Midland & Scottish Railway [British]
LMSS...........	Land Mobile Satellite Service [Rockwell International Corp.]
LMSS...........	Lunar Mapping and Survey System [NASA] (MCD)
LMSSA.........	Licentiate in Medicine and Surgery of the Society of Apothecaries [British]
LMST...........	Learning of Middle Size Task [Psychology]
lmst............	Limestone (VRA)
LMSWA.......	Land Management Society of Western Australia
LMT............	Air Limousin TA [France ICAO designator] (FAAC)
LMT............	Klamath Falls [Oregon] [Airport symbol] (OAG)
LMT............	Large Millimeter Telescope [US-Mexico project] [Proposed, 1994]
LMT............	LASER Marksmanship Trainer (MCD)
LMT............	Launch Motor Test
LMT............	Leadership and Management Training [Navy] (NVT)
LMT............	Learning Methods Test [Mills] [Education]
LMT............	Left Mentotransverse [A fetal position] [Obstetrics]
LMT............	Lemonthyme [Tasmania] [Seismograph station code, US Geological Survey Closed] (SEIS)
LMT............	Length, Mass, Time [Physics]
LMT............	Length of Mean Turn
LMT............	Levtech Medical Technologies Ltd. [Vancouver Stock Exchange symbol]
LMT............	Licensed Massage Therapist [Medicine]
LMT............	Lifetime Medical Television
LMT............	Limit (AFM)
LMT............	Local Mean Time (AFM)
LMT............	Lockheed Martin [NYSE symbol] (TTSB)
LMT............	Lockheed Martin Corp. [NYSE symbol] (SAG)
LMT............	Logical Mapping Table

LMT............	Logic Master Tape (IAA)
LMT............	Logistic Management of the Turnaround (MCD)
LMT............	Logistics Management Team [Navy]
LMT............	Log Mean Temperature
LMT............	Louisiana Midland Transport [AAR code]
LMT............	Lowenfeld Mosaic Test [Psychology]
LMTA...........	Language Modalities Test for Aphasia [Psychology]
LMTA...........	Library/Media Technical Assistant
LMTA...........	Light Microscopy Trace Analysis
LMTA...........	Louisiana Motor Transport Association (SRA)
LMTAS........	Lockheed Martin Tactical Aircraft Systems
LMTBR........	Liquid Metal Thorium Breeder Reactor
LMTBS........	Lightweight Multifunction Tactical Beacon System (MCD)
LMTC...........	Launcher Maintenance Trainer Course
lmtd...........	Limited (AAMN)
LMTD...........	Logarithmic Mean Temperature Difference
LMTDNS......	Launch Environment, Mission, Type, Design Number, and Series [Missiles] (AFM)
LMTG...........	Limiting (MSA)
LMTI...........	Louisiana Training Institute, Monroe, LA [Library symbol Library of Congress] (LCLS)
LMTLSS.......	Limitless
LMTN...........	Labor Market Training Needs
LMTN...........	Leamington [British depot code]
LMTO...........	Linear Combination of Muffin Tin Orbitals [Atomic physics]
LMTPI.........	Legal Member of the Town Planning Institute [British] (DLA)
LMTR...........	Limiter [Electronics]
LMTS...........	LaserMaster Technologies [NASDAQ symbol] (TTSB)
LMTS...........	LaserMaster Technologies, Inc. [NASDAQ symbol] (SAG)
LMTV...........	Light Medium Tactical Vehicle [Army] (RDA)
LMU............	Lake Mountain [Utah] [Seismograph station code, US Geological Survey] (SEIS)
LMU............	Latin Monetary Union [Established in 1865]
LMU............	Lifer Management Unit (WDAA)
LMU............	Lincoln Memorial University [Tennessee]
LMU............	Line Monitor Unit
LMU............	Loyola Marymount University [Los Angeles, CA]
LMU............	University of Missouri, Law School, Columbia, MO [OCLC symbol] (OCLC)
LMUA...........	Lloyd's Motor Underwriters Association [British] (DBA)
LMus...........	Licentiate of Music
LMusLCM....	Licentiate in Music of the London College of Music [British] (DBQ)
LMusTCL.....	Licentiate in Music, Trinity College of Music, London [British] (DBQ)
LMV............	Lettuce Mosaic Virus
LMV............	Long Market Value [Investment term]
LMV............	Low Mass Vehicle
LMVD..........	Lower Mississippi Valley Division [Army Engineers]
LMVE..........	Linear, Minimum Variance Estimation (PDAA)
LMW............	Ladd Mountain [Washington] [Seismograph station code, US Geological Survey] (SEIS)
LMW............	LASER Microwelder
LMW............	Lower Midwest
LM/W..........	Low-Molecular Weight [Chemistry]
lm/W..........	Lumens per Watt
lmwd..........	Limewood (VRA)
LMWD.........	Low-Molecular-Weight Dextran [Medicine] (AAMN)
LMWH.........	Low-Molecular-Weight Heparin [Biochemistry]
LMWHC.......	Low-Molecular-Weight Hydrocarbon (MCD)
LMWK.........	Low Molecular-Weight Kininogen [Biochemistry]
LMWP.........	Labor-Management Welfare-Pension [Reports] [Department of Labor]
LMWP.........	Low-Molecular-Weight Proteinuria [Medicine]
LMX............	Aerolineas Mexicanas JS SA de CV [Mexico ICAO designator] (FAAC)
LMX............	LMX Resources Ltd. [Vancouver Stock Exchange symbol]
LMX............	London Market Excess of Loss [British] (BUAC)
LMX............	L-Type Multiplex [Telecommunications] (TEL)
LMXB...........	Low-Mass X-Ray Binary [Star system]
LMY............	Lake Murray [Papua New Guinea] [Airport symbol] (OAG)
LN...............	Background Noise Level (CAAL)
In................	Central and Southern Line Islands [gb (Gilbert Islands) used in records cataloged after October 1978] [MARC country of publication code Library of Congress] (LCCP)
LN...............	Labionasal [lip and nose] [Otorhinolaryngology] (DAVI)
LN...............	Lane (MCD)
Ln...............	Lanthanide [Chemical element] (WGA)
LN...............	Large-Probe Nephelometer [NASA]
LN...............	LASER Nephelometry [Analytical biochemistry]
LN...............	Lateen [Ship's rigging] (ROG)
LN...............	Lateral Neuropil [Neurology]
LN...............	Law Notes, American Bar Association Section of General Practice [A publication] (DLA)
LN...............	Law Notes, London [A publication] (DLA)
LN...............	Leading Note [Music] (ROG)
LN...............	League of Nations [1919-1946]
LN...............	Legal News [Canada] [A publication] (DLA)
LN...............	Legal Notice (OICC)
LN...............	Legal Notification [Ghana] [A publication] (DLA)
LN...............	Lepista Nuda [A fungus]
L-N............	Lesch-Nyhan [Medicine]
LN...............	Lesion Number [Pathology]
L/N............	Letter-Numerical [system] (DAVI)
LN...............	Liaison (AFM)
LN...............	Liber Niger [Black Book] [A publication] (DLA)
Ln...............	Librarian (AL)
LN...............	Libyan Arab Airlines [ICAO designator] (AD)

LN	Licensed Nurse
LN	Lien
Ln	Lien (EBF)
LN	Line (AAG)
In	Line (VRA)
LN	Link Number (MHDB)
LN	Lip Nerve
LN	Lipoid Nephrosis (DB)
LN	Liquid Nitrogen
LN	Lira Nuova [Monetary unit] [Italy] (ROG)
LN	Lithuanian Navigation (BUAC)
LN	Load Number
LN	Loan
Ln	Loan (TBD)
LN	Local National
In	Logarithm (Natural) [Mathematics]
LN	Lot Number
LN	Love Notes [An association] (EA)
LN	Low Foliage Nester [Ecology]
LN	Low Noise (IAA)
LN	Luminometer Number [Hydrocarbon fuel rating]
LN	Lupus Network (EA)
LN	Lymph Node [Medicine]
LN	Natural
LN	New Orleans Public Library, New Orleans, LA [Library symbol Library of Congress] (LCLS)
In----	North Atlantic Ocean [MARC geographic area code Library of Congress] (LCCP)
LN₂	Liquid Nitrogen [NASA] (NASA)
LNA	Airlen [Russian Federation] [ICAO designator] (FAAC)
LNA	Lahu National Army [Myanmar] [Political party] (EY)
LNA	Launch Numerical Aperture [Telecommunications] (TEL)
LNA	Leading National Advertiser
LNA	League for National Advancement [Papua New Guinea] [Political party] (EY)
LNA	League of the Norden Associations (EA)
LNA	Leucine Nitroanilide [Biochemistry]
LNA	Liberation News Agency [Vietnam]
LNA	Libyan National Alliance (BUAC)
LNA	Lithium Nitrate Ammoniate [Inorganic chemistry]
LNA	Lithographers National Association
LNA	Lithuanian Numismatic Association (EA)
LNA	Local Navy Authority
LNA	Local Numbering Area [Telecommunications] (TEL)
LnA	London Allowance [British military] (DMA)
LNA	Love-N-Addiction [An association] (EA)
LNA	Low-Noise Amplifier [Satellite communications]
LNA	Low-Noise Antenna
LNA	Lunar Resources Ltd. [Vancouver Stock Exchange symbol]
LNA	New Orleans City Archives, New Orleans, LA [Library symbol Library of Congress] (LCLS)
LNA	West Palm Beach, FL [Location identifier FAA] (FAAL)
LNAA	Large Neutral Amino Acid [Biochemistry] (DB)
LNAC	Amistad Research Center Library, New Orleans, LA [Library symbol] [Library of Congress] (LCLS)
LNAC	Librarians for Nuclear Arms Control [Defunct] (EA)
LNAC	Limited National Agency Check (AFM)
LNAC	Louisville, New Albany & Corydon Railroad Co. [AAR code]
LNADW	Lower North Atlantic Deep Water [Oceanography]
LNAH	League of Night Adoration in the Home [Later, NAH] (EA)
LNaN	Northwestern State University of Louisiana, Natchitoches, LA [Library symbol Library of Congress] (LCLS)
LNaNa	Natchitoches Parish Library, Natchitoches, LA [Library symbol Library of Congress] (LCLS)
LNAP	Low Nonessential Air Pressure (IEEE)
LNapA	Assumption Parish Library, Napoleonville, LA [Library symbol Library of Congress] (LCLS)
LNAPL	Light Non-Aqueous Phase Liquids
LNAV	Lateral Navigation [Provides computer description of aircraft's planned lateral flight path] (GAVI)
Inaz--	Azores Islands [MARC geographic area code Library of Congress] (LCCP)
LNB	Lamen Bay [Vanuata] [Airport symbol] (OAG)
LNB	Large Navigation Buoy [Marine science] (MSC)
LNB	Liberty National Bancorp, Inc. (EFIS)
LNB	Lithium Niobate (PDAA)
LNB	Local Name Base [Computer science]
LNB	Louisiana National Bank [Baton Rouge] (TSSD)
LNB	Low Nitrogen Oxide Burner [Combustion technology]
LNB	Low-Noise Block [Satellite communications]
LNB	Lymph Node Biopsy [Surgical procedure] (DAVI)
LNB	New Orleans Baptist Theological Seminary, New Orleans, LA [Library symbol Library of Congress] (LCLS)
LNBA	Bell Aerospace Co., New Orleans, LA [Library symbol Library of Congress] (LCLS)
LNBA	Laymen's National Bible Association (EA)
LNBC	Laymen's National Bible Committee [Formerly, LNC] [Later, LNBA] (EA)
LNBD	Lens Board [Mechanical engineering]
LNBF	Low-Noise Block Feed [Satellite communications]
Inbm--	Bermuda [MARC geographic area code Library of Congress] (LCCP)
LNBS	Lesotho National Broadcasting Service [South Africa]
LNC	Lancaster, TX [Location identifier FAA] (FAAL)
LNC	Lance
LNC	Lancer Resources [Vancouver Stock Exchange symbol]

LNC	Landscape Nursery Council (EA)
LNC	Laymen's National Committee [Later, LNBC] (EA)
LNC	Lincoln National Corp. [NYSE symbol] (SPSG)
LNC	Lincoln National Corp. Capital I [NYSE symbol] (SAG)
LNC	Lincoln National Corp. Capital II [NYSE symbol] (SAG)
LNC	Lincoln Natl Corp. [NYSE symbol] (TTSB)
LNC	Local Naval Commander
LNC	LORAN Navigation Chart [Air Force]
LNC	Low-Noise Cable
LNC	Low-Noise Converter [Satellite communications]
LNC	Lunacharskoye [Former USSR Seismograph station code, US Geological Survey Closed] (SEIS)
LNC	Lymph Node Cell [Medicine]
LNC	New Orleans Public Library, New Orleans, LA [OCLC symbol] (OCLC)
Inca--	Canary Islands [MARC geographic area code Library of Congress] (LCCP)
LNCE	Lance, Inc. [NASDAQ symbol] (SAG)
LNCFS	Low Nitric Oxide [Combustion technology]
LNCH	Launch (AAG)
LNCHR	Launcher
LncNtC	Lincoln National Convertible Securities Fund, Inc. [Associated Press] (SAG)
L-NCP	Liberal-National Country Party [Australia Political party] (PPW)
LNCPr	Lincln Natl $3.00 Cv Pfd [NYSE symbol] (TTSB)
LNCR	Lincare Holdings [NASDAQ symbol] (TTSB)
LNCR	Lincare Holdings, Inc. [NASDAQ symbol] (SAG)
LncrOrt	Lancer Orthodontics, Inc. [Associated Press] (SAG)
LNCRT	Licentiate of the National College of Rubber Technology [British] (DI)
LNCT	Lancit Media Productions [NASDAQ symbol] (TTSB)
LNCT	Lancit Media Productions Ltd. [NASDAQ symbol] (SAG)
Incv--	Cape Verde [Islands] [MARC geographic area code Library of Congress] (LCCP)
LNCY	Lunacy [FBI standardized term]
LND	Dillard University, New Orleans, LA [Library symbol Library of Congress] (LCLS)
LND	Lander, WY [Location identifier FAA] (FAAL)
LND	Lawyers for Nuclear Disarmament [Defunct] (EAIO)
LND	Limiting Nose Dive [Aerospace]
LND	Lincoln National Income Fund, Inc. [Formerly, Lincoln National Direct Placement Fund, Inc.] [NYSE symbol] (SPSG)
LND	Lincoln Natl Income Fd [NYSE symbol] (TTSB)
LND	Lined
LND	Local Number Dialed [Telecommunications] (TEL)
LND	Local Number Dialling [Telecommunications] (NITA)
LND	London [Ontario] [Seismograph station code, US Geological Survey] (SEIS)
LND	Lymph Node Dissection [Medicine]
LND	Skargardsflyg, AB, Finland [FAA designator] (FAAC)
LNDB	Lesotho National Development Bank (BUAC)
LNDC	Delgado Community College, New Orleans, LA [Library symbol Library of Congress] (LCLS)
LNDC	Landec Corp. [NASDAQ symbol] (TTSB)
LNDC	Lesotho National Development Corp.
LNDCF	Locally-Normalized Discrete Correlation Function [Mathematics]
LNDF	Linear Natural Density Filter (AAEL)
LNDFLL	Landfill
LNDG	Landing [Maps and charts] (KSC)
Lndg	Lending (TBD)
LNDH	Local Nationals, Direct Hire [Military] (AABC)
LNDL	Least Negative Down Level (IAA)
LNDL	Lindal Cedar Homes [NASDAQ symbol] (SAG)
LNDMRK	Landmark
LNDNG	Landing [Commonly used] (OPSA)
LNDO	Local Neglect of Differential Overlap [Physical chemistry]
Lndr	Lender (TBD)
LNDRMT	Laundromat
LNDRY	Laundry
LNDSCP	Landscape
LndsPc	Landsing Pacific Fund [Associated Press] (SAG)
LNDSPTPLT	Landing Support Platoon [Navy] (DNAB)
LNE	Lehigh & New England Railway Co. [Absorbed into Consolidated Rail Corp.] [AAR code]
LNE	Liquid Nitrogen Evaporator
LNE	Local Network Emulator
LNE	Lonorore [Vanuata] [Airport symbol] (OAG)
LNE	Lymph Node Enlargement [Medicine] (DMAA)
LNE	Northeast Louisiana University, Monroe, LA [OCLC symbol] (OCLC)
LNEP	Low-Noise Emission Product (GFGA)
LNER	London & North Eastern Railway [British]
LNERG	London & North Eastern Railway Group [British]
LNESC	LULAC [League of United Latin American Citizens] National Educational Service Centers (EA)
LneSStk	Lone Star Steakhouse & Saloon, Inc. [Associated Press] (SAG)
LNET	LodgeNet Entertainment [NASDAQ symbol] (TTSB)
LNET	Lodgenet Entertainment Corp. [NASDAQ symbol] (SAG)
LNewr	Pointe Coupee Parish Library, New Roads, LA [Library symbol Library of Congress] (LCLS)
LNF	Latvian National Foundation [Stockholm, Sweden] (EAIO)
LNF	Leon's Furniture Ltd. [Toronto Stock Exchange symbol]
LNF	Linfen [Republic of China] [Seismograph station code, US Geological Survey] (SEIS)
LNF	Liposoluble Neutral Fraction (OA)
LNF	Lithuanian National Foundation (EA)

LNF............. Little-Known Fan [of science fiction or fantastic literature] [See also BNF]
LNF............. Local National Forces [SEATO] (CINC)
LNF............. London Flights (Biggin Hill) Ltd. [British ICAO designator] (FAAC)
LNF............. Low-Noise Feed [Satellite communications]
LNFC........... Leonard Nimoy Fan Club (EA)
LNFCS......... Leonard Nimoy Fan Club, Spotlight (EAIO)
LNFM.......... Louisiana Masonic Grand Lodge, New Orleans, LA [Library symbol Library of Congress] (LCLS)
LNG .... Lateral Nasal Gland [Anatomy]
LNG .... Length (IAA)
LNG .... Lese [Papua New Guinea] [Airport symbol] (OAG)
LNG .... Lining (MSA)
LNG .... Liquefied Natural Gas
LNG .... Liquid Natural Gas [BTS] [DOE] (TAG)
LNG .... Liste de Noms Geographiques [A publication] (BJA)
LNG .... Long
LNG .... Lounge
LNG .... Luning [Nevada] [Seismograph station code, US Geological Survey Closed] (SEIS)
Lnge .... Lounge [Classified advertising] (ADA)
LNGR .... Lingerie
LngStk .... Longhorn Steaks, Inc. [Associated Press] (SAG)
LNH .... Large Number Hypothesis [Medicine] (DMAA)
LNH .... Lengeh [Iran] [Airport symbol] (AD)
LNH .... LNH REIT [Real Estate Investment Trust], Inc. [Associated Press] (SAG)
LNH .... Lunar Near Horizon [NASA] (KSC)
LNHA .... Louisiana Historical Association, Memorial Hall, New Orleans, LA [Library symbol Library of Congress] (LCLS)
LNHiC .... [The] Historic New Orleans Collection, New Orleans, LA [Library symbol Library of Congress] (LCLS)
LNI............. Inland Library System, Redlands, CA [OCLC symbol] (OCLC)
LNI............. Log Neutralization Index [Microbiology]
LNI............. Lonely, AK [Location identifier FAA] (FAAL)
LNIAC .... Los Ninos International Adoption Center (EA)
LNIB.......... Loch Ness Investigation Bureau [Inactive] (EA)
LNiI........... Iberia Parish Library, New Iberia, LA [Library symbol Library of Congress] (LCLS)
LNIS........... Atlantic Naval Intelligence Summary (MCD)
LNIT .... Local Nasal Immunotherapy
lnjn-- .... Jan Mayen [MARC geographic area code Library of Congress] (LCCP)
LNK........... Airlink Airlines (Pty) Ltd. [South Africa ICAO designator] (FAAC)
L/Nk .... Lance-Naik [British military] (DMA)
LNK........... Lenkoran [Former USSR Seismograph station code, US Geological Survey] (SEIS)
LNK........... Lincoln [Nebraska] [Airport symbol] (OAG)
LNK........... Link
LNKEDT ...... Linkage Editor [Computer science] (IAA)
LNL............. Land O'Lakes [Wisconsin] [Airport symbol] (AD)
LNL............. Land O' Lakes, WI [Location identifier FAA] (FAAL)
LNL............. Law Library of Louisiana, New Orleans, LA [OCLC symbol] (OCLC)
LNL............. Let Nicaragua Live [An association Defunct] (EA)
LNL............. Loyola University, New Orleans, LA [Library symbol Library of Congress] (LCLS)
LNL............. Lymph Node Lymphocyte [Medicine] (DMAA)
LNLA .... Lithuanian National League of America (EA)
LNLC.......... Ladies' Naval Luncheon Club (WDAA)
LNLI.......... League for National Labor in Israel (EA)
LNL-L .... Loyola University, Law Library, New Orleans, LA [Library symbol Library of Congress] (LCLS)
LNLM.......... Linoleum
LNLM.......... Low-Noise Level Margin
LNLM.......... United States Bureau of Land Management, New Orleans Outer Continental Shelf Office, New Orleans, LA [Library symbol Library of Congress] (LCLS)
LNL-Phar ..... Loyola University, Pharmacy Library, New Orleans, LA [Library symbol Library of Congress] (LCLS)
LNM........... Langimar [Papua New Guinea] [Airport symbol] (OAG)
LNM........... LAN [Linked Access Network] Network Manager
LNM........... Lansdowne Minerals [Vancouver Stock Exchange symbol]
LNM........... Lebanese National Movement [Political party] (PPW)
LNM........... Leon [Mexico] [Seismograph station code, US Geological Survey] (SEIS)
LNM........... Level of No Motion [Oceanography]
LNM........... Library Cooperative of Macomb [Library network]
LNM........... Lithium Nuclear Microprobe
LNM........... Local Notice to Mariners
LNM........... Logical Network Machine (MHDB)
LNM........... Lumen Technologies [NYSE symbol] [Formerly, BEC Group]
LNM........... Lymph Node Metastases [Oncology]
LNM........... Margaret C. Hanson Normal School, New Orleans, LA [Library symbol Library of Congress Obsolete] (LCLS)
lnma-- .... Madeira Islands [MARC geographic area code Library of Congress] (LCCP)
LNMA.......... New Orleans Museum of Art, New Orleans, LA [Library symbol Library of Congress] (LCLS)
LNMC.......... Monaco [Monaco] [ICAO location identifier] (ICLI)
LNME.......... Mobil Exploration and Producing U.S., Inc., New Orleans, LA [Library symbol Library of Congress] (LCLS)
LNMMS....... McMain Magnet Secondary School, New Orleans, LA [Library symbol] [Library of Congress] (LCLS)
LNMP .... Last Normal Menstrual Period [Medicine]
LNMRB .... Laboratory of Nuclear Medicine and Radiation Biology

LNMS........... Large-Probe Neutral Mass Spectrometer [NASA]
LNN .... Leningrad [Former USSR Geomagnetic observatory code]
LNN .... Leningrad [Former USSR Seismograph station code, US Geological Survey Closed] (SEIS)
LNN .... Lincoln Resources, Inc. [Vancouver Stock Exchange symbol]
LNN .... Linear Nearest Neighbor (MHDB)
LNN .... Willoughby, OH [Location identifier FAA] (FAAL)
LNNB .... Luria-Nebraska Neuropsychological Battery
LNND .... Notre Dame Seminary, New Orleans, LA [Library symbol Library of Congress] (LCLS)
LNO .... Laona & Northern Railway Co. [AAR code]
LNO .... Leonora [Australia Airport symbol] (OAG)
LNO .... Liaison Officer [Military]
LNO .... Limited Nuclear Option [Military] (MCD)
LNOC .... Libya National Oil Co.
LNOP .... Lanoptics Ltd. [NASDAQ symbol] (SAG)
LNOP .... Orleans Parish Medical Society, New Orleans, LA [Library symbol Library of Congress] (LCLS)
LNOPF .... LanOptics Ltd [NASDAQ symbol] (TTSB)
L Notes........ Law Notes, England [A publication] (DLA)
L Notes Gen Pract... Law Notes for the General Practitioner [A publication] (DLA)
LNP............. Bibliotheca Parsoniana, New Orleans, LA [Library symbol Library of Congress Obsolete] (LCLS)
LNP............. Chieftain Aviation PC [South Africa ICAO designator] (FAAC)
LNP............. Large Neuronal Polypeptide [Medicine] (DMAA)
LNP............. Least Newtonian Path (IAA)
LNP............. Leg Negative Pressure (PDAA)
LNP............. Liberal/National Party [Political party Australia]
LNP............. Libertarian Party [Australia Political party]
LNP............. Liquefied Natural Petroleum
LNP............. Liquid Nitrogen Processing
LNP............. Loss of Normal Power (IEEE)
LNP............. Low Needle Position [on dial]
LNP............. Lunar Neutron Probe [NASA] (KSC)
LNP............. Lunping [Taiwan] [Geomagnetic observatory code]
LNP............. Wise, VA [Location identifier FAA] (FAAL)
LNP & W ...... Laramie, North Park & Western Railroad (IIA)
LNPF.......... Lebanese National Patriotic Forces [Political party]
LNPF.......... Lymph Node Permeability Factor [Immunology]
LNPIB .... Loch Ness Phenomena Investigation Bureau [Later, LNIB]
LNPo .... Polyanthos, New Orleans, LA [Library symbol Library of Congress] (LCLS)
LNQ .... Longest Queue
LNR .... Lagos Notes and Records [A publication]
LNR .... Linamar Machine Ltd. [Toronto Stock Exchange symbol]
LNR .... Liner
LNR .... Liquid Natural Rubber
LNR .... Liquid Nitrogen Refrigeration
LNR .... Local Nature Reserve (PDAA)
LNR .... Lone Rock, WI [Location identifier FAA] (FAAL)
LNR .... Lonorore [New Hebrides] [Seismograph station code, US Geological Survey] (SEIS)
LNR .... Louisiana Numerical Register [Louisiana State Library] [Baton Rouge, LA] [Library network]
LNR .... Low-Noise Receiver
LNR .... Luftnachrichten-Regiment [Air forces signal regiment] [German military - World War II]
LNR .... Lymph Node Region [Medicine] (DAVI)
LNR .... Sky Liners Air Services Ltd. [Suriname] [ICAO designator] (FAAC)
LNRA.......... Linear Nested Region Analysis (PDAA)
LNRC.......... Little Nash Rambler Club (EA)
LNRS.......... Limited Night Recovery System (PDAA)
LNS............. Laboratory for Nuclear Science [MIT] (MCD)
LNS............. Lancaster [Pennsylvania] [Airport symbol] (OAG)
LNS............. Land Navigation System
LNS............. Lansco Resources [Vancouver Stock Exchange symbol]
LNS............. Lanslevillard [France] [Seismograph station code, US Geological Survey] (SEIS)
LNS............. LASER Night Sensor
LNS............. Lateral Nuclear Stratum [Medicine] (DMAA)
LNS............. Lesch-Nyhan Syndrome [Medicine]
LNS............. Liberation News Service (EA)
LNS............. London Normal School
LNS............. Long Normal Superchron [Geology]
LNS............. Lutheran News Service [Lutheran Church in America] [Information service or system] (IID)
LNS............. Lymph Node Seeking [Medicine] (DB)
LNS............. Lymph Node Seeking [Equivalent] (STED)
LNS............. Nicholls State University, Ellender Memorial Library, Thibodaux, LA [OCLC symbol] (OCLC)
LNSA .... Local Navy Supervising Activity
lnsb-- .... Svalbard and Jan Mayen [MARC geographic area code Library of Congress] (LCCP)
lnscp.......... Landscaped (REAL)
lnsd .... Linseed Oil (VRA)
LNSF....:..... Light Night Striking Force [British military] (DMA)
Lnship .... Librarianship (AL)
LNSL.......... Liberia National Shipping Line (EY)
LNSL.......... Southeast Louisiana Library Network Cooperative (SEALLING), New Orleans, LA [Library symbol Library of Congress] (LCLS)
LNSM.......... Saint Mary's Dominican College, New Orleans, LA [Library symbol Library of Congress] (LCLS)
LNSN .... Local Non-Switched Network
LNSO .... Shell Oil Co., New Orleans, LA [Library symbol Library of Congress] (LCLS)

LNSP .... Lens Speed [*Mechanical engineering*]
LnStr.......... Lone Star Industries [*Associated Press*] (SAG)
LnStrInd...... Lone Star Industries [*Associated Press*] (SAG)
LNSU .... Library Network of SIBIL Users (EAIO)
LNSU .... United States Department of Agriculture, Southern Utilization and Development Division, Agricultural Research Service, New Orleans, LA [*Library symbol Library of Congress*] (LCLS)
LNT.............. Aerolineas Internacionales, SA de CV [*Mexico*] [*FAA designator*] (FAAC)
LNT.............. Launch Network Test
LNT.............. Linear No-Threshold [*Risk model*]
LNT.............. Liquid Nitrogen Temperature (IAA)
LNT.............. Millinocket, ME [*Location identifier FAA*] (FAAL)
LNT.............. Tulane University, New Orleans, LA [*Library symbol Library of Congress*] (LCLS)
LNT-BA .... Tulane University, Graduate School of Business Administration, New Orleans, LA [*Library symbol Library of Congress*] (LCLS)
LNTC.......... International House, Cunningham Library, New Orleans, LA [*Library symbol Library of Congress*] (LCLS)
LNTC.......... Lymph Node T Cells [*Immunology*]
LNTex .... Texas, Inc., New Orleans, LA [*Library symbol*] [*Library of Congress*] (LCLS)
LNTF.......... Lipid Nurse Task Force (NTPA)
LNTL.......... Lintel
LNT-L......... Tulane University, Law Library, New Orleans, LA [*Library symbol Library of Congress*] (LCLS)
LNT-M .... Tulane University, Medical Library, New Orleans, LA [*Library symbol Library of Congress*] (LCLS)
LNT-MC ...... Greater New Orleans Microform Cooperative, Tulane University, New Orleans, LA [*Library symbol Library of Congress*] (LCLS)
LNTO .... Lento [*Very Slow*] [*Music*] (ROG)
LNTP.......... New Orleans Times-Picayune, New Orleans, LA [*Library symbol Library of Congress*] (LCLS)
LNTS.......... League of Nations Treaty Series [*A publication*] (DLA)
LNTS.......... Liquid Nitrogen Transfer System
LNTV.......... Lin Television Corp. [*NASDAQ symbol*] (SAG)
LNTWA ...... Low-Noise Traveling Wave Amplifier
LNTWTA ...... Low-Noise Traveling Wave Tube Amplifier (IAA)
LNU .... Last Name Unknown
LNU .... League of Nations Union
LNU .... University of New Orleans, New Orleans, LA [*Library symbol Library of Congress OCLC symbol*] (LCLS)
LNUCA........ United States Circuit Court of Appeals, Fifth Circuit Law Library, New Orleans, LA [*Library symbol Library of Congress*] (LCLS)
LNUrs .... Ursuline Academy, New Orleans, LA [*Library symbol Library of Congress*] (LCLS)
LNV.......... Lincln Natl Cv Sec [*NYSE symbol*] (TTSB)
LNV.......... Lincoln National Convertible Securities Fund, Inc. [*NYSE symbol*] (SPSG)
LNV.......... Londolovit [*Papua New Guinea*] [*Airport symbol Obsolete*] (OAG)
LNV.......... Longovilo [*Chile*] [*Seismograph station code, US Geological Survey*] (SEIS)
LNV.......... Lonvest Corp. [*Toronto Stock Exchange symbol Vancouver Stock Exchange symbol*]
LNVA .... United States Veterans Administration Hospital, New Orleans, LA [*Library symbol Library of Congress*] (LCLS)
LNVT.......... Launch Network Verification Test (IAA)
LNW.......... [*The*] Louisiana & North West Railroad Co. [*AAR code*]
LNWR .... London & North Western Railway [*British*]
LNX.......... Lenex [*Poland ICAO designator*] (FAAC)
LNX.......... London Executive Aviation Ltd. [*British*] [*FAA designator*] (FAAC)
LNX.......... Xavier University, New Orleans, LA [*Library symbol Library of Congress OCLC symbol*] (LCLS)
LNY.......... Lanai City [*Hawaii*] [*Airport symbol*] (OAG)
LNY.......... Laws of New York [*A publication*] (DLA)
LNYD.......... Lanyard
LNYL.......... Leksikon fun der Nayer Yidisher Literatur [*New York*] [*A publication*] (BJA)
LNYT.......... League of New York Theatres [*Later, LNYTP*] (EA)
LNYTP .... League of New York Theatres and Producers (EA)
LNYV.......... Lettuce Necrotic Yellows Virus
LNZ.......... Linz [*Austria*] [*Airport symbol*] (OAG)
LNZ.......... Litag K.G. [*Austria*] [*FAA designator*] (FAAC)
LO.......... Laboratory Outfitting (SSD)
LO.......... Lamp Oil
LO.......... Landelijke Organistatie [*Netherlands underground organization*] [*World War II*]
LO.......... Landsorganisasjonen i Norge [*Norwegian Federation of Trade Unions*]
LO.......... Landsorganisationen i Sverige [*Swedish Federation of Trade Unions*]
LO.......... Larval Operculum
LO.......... Lateral Oblique [*X-ray view*] (DAVI)
LO.......... Launch Operations [*or Operator*] [*NASA*]
LO.......... Law Observer [*1872*] [*India*] [*A publication*] (DLA)
LO.......... Law Officer
LO.......... Law Opinions [*A publication*] (DLA)
LO.......... Lay Observer (ILCA)
LO.......... Layout [*Graphic arts*]
LO.......... Learning Objective
LO.......... Left Outboard (MCD)
LO.......... Legal Observer [*British*]
LO.......... Legal Officer
LO.......... Legal Opinion [*1870-73*] [*A publication*] (DLA)
LO.......... Lenticular Opacity [*Ophthalmology*] (DAVI)

Lo.............. Lesotho [*MARC country of publication code Library of Congress*] (LCCP)
L/O.......... Letter of Offer
LO.......... Letter Orders
LO.......... Leucine Oxidation (STED)
LO.......... Level Off
LO.......... Liaison Office [*or Officer*]
LO.......... Licensed Officer [*US Merchant Marine*]
LO.......... [*The*] Lifestyles Organization (EA)
LO.......... Lift-Off (AAG)
LO.......... Limerent Object [*One who is the object of obsessional romantic love*]
LO.......... Limited Order [*Business term*]
LO.......... Line Occupancy
LO.......... Line Office (USDC)
LO.......... Linguooclusal [*Dentistry*]
LO.......... Liquid Oxygen
LO.......... Listing Office [*Real estate*] (REAL)
LO.......... Loam [*Type of soil*] (ROG)
LO.......... Loan Officer [*Banking*] (TBD)
Lo.......... Local [*Navy*]
LO.......... Local Office
LO.......... Local Order
LO.......... Local Origination [*Television programming*]
LO.......... Local Oscillator [*Electronics*]
LO.......... Locator File [*Information retrieval*]
LO.......... Locked Open [*Technical drawings*]
LO.......... Locked Oscillator
LO.......... Lock-On
LO.......... Lock-Out
LO.......... Loco [*Place*] [*Latin*]
LO.......... Loco [*As Written*] [*Music*]
LO.......... Logical Operation (AAG)
LO.......... Logistics Offensive
LO.......... London Office
Lo.......... London Stock Exchange [*England*]
LO.......... Longitude
LO.......... Longitudinal Optic
LO.......... Look-Out [*Navy British*]
Lo.......... Lord (WGA)
Lo.............. Lotarius [*Flourished, 1191-1212*] [*Authority cited in pre-1607 legal work*] (DSA)
LO.......... Louisville Orchestra [*Record label*]
LO.......... Louth [*County in Ireland*] (ROG)
LO.......... Love Object
LO.......... Low (KSC)
Io.......... Low (IDOE)
LO.......... Lowest Offer [*Business term*]
LO.......... Low Loaders (DCTA)
LO.......... Low Oblique [*Aerospace*]
LO.......... Low Observable (DOMA)
LO.......... Low Order [*Computer science*] (OA)
LO.......... Low Ordinary (IAA)
LO.......... Lubricating Oil
LO.......... Lubrication Order
LO.......... Lumber Orthosis (STED)
LO.......... Lunar Orbiter [*Aerospace*] (MCD)
LO.......... Lutte Ouvriere [*Workers' Struggle*] [*France Political party*] (PPW)
LO.......... Lysyl Oxidase [*An enzyme*]
LO.......... Opelousas-Eunice Public Library, Opelousas, LA [*Library symbol Library of Congress*] (LCLS)
LO.......... Solicitor's Law Opinion, United States Internal Revenue Bureau [*A publication*] (DLA)
LO$_2$.......... Liquid Oxygen [*Also, LOX*] [*NASA*] (KSC)
LO2.......... Pahute Mesa [*Nevada*] [*Seismograph station code, US Geological Survey Closed*] (SEIS)
LOA.......... Landing Operations Area [*NASA*] (NASA)
LOA.......... LASER Opto-Acoustic
LOA.......... Launch on Assessment [*Military*]
LOA.......... Launch on Attack [*Military*]
LOA.......... Launch Operations Agency [*NASA*] (KSC)
LOA.......... Launch Operations Area (MCD)
LOA.......... Lead Operational Authority (COE)
LOA.......... Leave of Absence
LOA.......... Leber Optic Atrophy (STED)
LOA.......... Left Occipitoanterior [*A fetal position*] [*Obstetrics*]
LOA.......... Length Over-All [*Technical drawings*]
LOA.......... Leona, TX [*Location identifier FAA*] (FAAL)
LOA.......... Letter of Acceptance
LOA.......... Letter of Agreement
LOA.......... Letter of Authorization
LOA.......... Letter of Offer and Acceptance (MCD)
LOA.......... Level of Authority [*Military*] (AFIT)
LOA.......... Life Offices' Association [*British*] (DCTA)
LOA.......... Light Observation Aircraft
LOA.......... Limit of Advance [*Army*] (DOMA)
LOA.......... Line of Assurance
LOA.......... Local Overseas Allowance [*British military*] (DMA)
LOA.......... Log-Out Analysis (NITA)
LOA.......... London Orphan Asylum (ROG)
LOA.......... Looseness of Associations (STED)
LOA.......... Lorcan Resources Ltd. [*Vancouver Stock Exchange symbol*]
LOA.......... Lorraine [*Australia Airport symbol Obsolete*] (OAG)
LOA.......... Los Alamos [*New Mexico*] [*Seismograph station code, US Geological Survey*] (SEIS)
LOA.......... Low Oil Agglomeration [*Coal processing*]

LOA	Low-Speed Output Adapter (MHDB)
LOAA	Letter of Agreement and Acceptance
LOAC	Low Accuracy
LOAD	LASER Optoacoustic Detection
LOAD	Low-Altitude Defense (MCD)
LOADEX	Loading Exercise [Military] (NVT)
LOADS	Lifting of Aerodynamic Decelerators (PDAA)
LOADS	Low-Altitude Defense System
LOAEL	Lowest Observed Adverse Effect Level (EG)
LOAF	Large Open-Area Floor
LOAF	Loaf [Commonly used] (OPSA)
LOAL	Lock-On after Launch [Weaponry] (CAAL)
LOAL	Lock-One After Launch [Military] (MUSM)
LOAM	List of Applicable Material (MCD)
LOAMP	Logarithmic Amplifier (IEEE)
LOAN	Horizon Bancorp, Inc. (TX) [NASDAQ symbol] (SAG)
LOAN	Horizon Bancorp(TX) [NASDAQ symbol] (TTSB)
LOAN	Local Officials' Administration Network [An association]
LOAN/A	Vessels Loaned to Army [Navy]
LOAN/C	Vessels Loaned to Coast Guard [Navy]
LO & DS	London Operatic and Dramatic Society (ROG)
LOAN/M	Vessels Loaned to Miscellaneous Activities [US Maritime Academy, etc.] [Navy]
LOAN/S	Vessels Loaned to States [Navy]
LOAN/W	Vessels Loaned to War Shipping Administration [Terminated, 1946] [Navy]
LOAP	Length of Adjacency Process (MHDB)
LOAP	List of Applicable Publications [Air Force]
LOAPS	Large Order Assembly Planning System (MCD)
LOAS	Lift-Off Acquisition System
LOAS	List of Assessed Spares (MCD)
LOAS	Loyal Order of Ancient Shepherds [British] (BI)
LOAT	Trausdorf [Austria ICAO location identifier] (ICLI)
LOAV	Lift Owners' Association of Victoria [Australia]
LOAV	Voslau [Austria ICAO location identifier] (ICLI)
LOB	Laboratory Office Building
LOB	[The] Land of the Bible: A Historical Geography [A publication] (BJA)
LOB	Launch Operations Branch [NASA]
LOB	Launch Operations Building [NASA]
LOB	Left of Baseline
LOB	Left on Base [Baseball]
LOB	Left Outboard (MCD)
LOB	Left Out of Battle [British]
LOB	Limited Operating Base (AFM)
LOB	Line of Balance
LOB	Line of Bearing [Navy] (NVT)
LOB	Line of Business [Used in corporate reports to Federal Trade Commission]
LOB	Lobito [Angola] [Airport symbol] (AD)
LOB	Location of Offices Bureau [British]
LOB	Logistics Operating Base
LOB	Logistics-over-the-Beach Base [Military] (VNW)
LOB	Loyal Order of the Boar (EA)
LObA	Allen Parish Library, Oberlin, LA [Library symbol Library of Congress] (LCLS)
LOBA	Last Offer Binding Arbitration [Labor negotiations]
LOBAR	Long Baseline RADAR
LOBI	Library Orientation/Bibliographic Instruction [Florida Library Association caucus]
Lobin	Lobingier's Extra-Territorial Cases [United States Court for China] [A publication] (DLA)
LOBL	Lock-On Before Launch [Missile] (DOMA)
LOBSTER	Long-Term Ocean Bottom Settlement Test for Engineering Research [Navy project]
LOBTP	League of Off-Broadway Theatres and Producers [Later, OBL] (EA)
LOC	Landing Operations Center (MCD)
LOC	Large Optical Cavity [LASER design]
LOC	Launch Operations Center [NASA]
LOC	Launch Operations Complex
LOC	Launch Operations Control
LOC	Launch Operator's Console [Aerospace] (AAG)
LOC	Laverda Owner's Club (EA)
LOC	Laxative of Choice [Medicine]
LOC	Le Groupe Opus Communications, Inc. [Vancouver Stock Exchange symbol]
LOC	LeMoyne-Owen College, Memphis, TN [OCLC symbol] (OCLC)
LOC	Letter of Comment
LOC	Letter of Compliance [Program] [Coast Guard]
LOC	Letter of Consent
LOC	Letterpress to Offset Conversion (DGA)
LOC	Letters of Credit
LOC	Level of Care [Medicine] (GFGA)
LOC	Level of Concern [Environmental Protection Agency] (ERG)
LOC	Level of Consciousness [Medicine]
LOC	Liaison Officer Coordinator [Air Force] (AFM)
LOC	Libraries and Our Civilizations [A publication]
LOC	Library of Congress
LoC	Library of Congress Classification (TELE)
LOC	Light-Off Catalyst [Exhaust emissions] [Automotive engineering]
LOC	Limitation of Cost (AAGC)
LOC	Limited Operational Capability (CET)
LOC	Limiting Oxygen Concentration [For ignition]
LOC	Lincoln Owners Club (EA)
LOC	Lincoln School [California] [Seismograph station code, US Geological Survey] (SEIS)

LOC	Line of Code
LOC	Line of Communication [Military]
LOC	Line of Contact (MCD)
LOC	Line of Correction
LOC	Linked Object Code (TEL)
LOC	Linked Operational Capability (DOMA)
LOC	Liquid Organic Compound
LOC	Load Overcurrent
LOC	Local
loc	Localized (STED)
LOC	Localizer (MSA)
LOC	Localizer Line of Sight
LOC	Local Original Channel [Cable television broadcasting]
LOC	Locate (MSA)
loc	Located (REAL)
LOC	Location (AFM)
loc	Location (VRA)
LOC	Location Counter [Computer science]
LOC	Locative (Case) [Linguistics]
LOC	Locavia 49 [France ICAO designator] (FAAC)
LOC	Lock-On Completed (MCD)
LOC	Loco [Place] [Latin] (WGA)
LOC	Loctite Corp. [NYSE symbol] (SPSG)
LOC	Locus of Control (STED)
LOC	Logistic Operation Center [Military]
LOC	Lord of Creation
LOC	Loss of Consciousness [Medicine]
LOC	Loss of Coolant (GAAI)
LOCA	Late Onset Cerebellar Ataxia [Medicine]
LOCA	Loss-of-Coolant Accident [Nuclear energy]
LoCa	Low Calcium (STED)
LOCA	Low-Cost Computer Attachment (IAA)
LOCA	Low Osmolar Contrast Agent [Medicine]
LOCAAS	Low-Cost Anti-Armor Submunitions [Military]
LOC ACC	Location Accuracy [Environmental science] (COE)
LOCAL	Laboratory Program for Computer-Assisted Learning (IAA)
LOCAL	Load On-Call [Computer science]
lo cal	Low Calorie (MAE)
lo cal	Low-Calorie (STED)
lo calc	Low Calcium [Diet] (DAVI)
Local Ct & Mun Gaz	Local Courts and Municipal Gazette [Toronto, ON] [A publication] (DLA)
Local Gov	Local Government and Magisterial Reports [England] [A publication] (DLA)
Local Gov R Aust	Local Government Reports of Australia [A publication] (DLA)
Local Gov't	Local Government and Magisterial Reports [England] [A publication] (DLA)
Local Govt Jl WA	Local Government Journal of Western Australia [A publication]
LOCALS	Low-Cost Alternate LASER Seeker (MCD)
LOCAM	Logistics Cost Analysis Model (MCD)
LOCAP	Low Capacitance [Cable] [Bell System]
LOCAP	Low [Altitude] Combat Air Patrol (NVT)
LOCAS	Local Cataloguing Service (NITA)
LOCAT	Location (DAVI)
LOCAT	Low-Altitude Clear-Air Turbulence (MCD)
LOCAT	Low-Cost Air Target (MCD)
LOCATE	Library of Congress Automation Techniques Exchange
LOCATE	List of Common Abbreviations in Training and Education (AIE)
LOCATE	Local Area Telecommunications, Inc. [Digital microwave carrier] [New York, NY] (TSSD)
LOCATE	LORAN/OMEGA Course and Tracking Equipment (MCD)
LOCATS	Lockheed Optical Communications and Tracking System
LOCC	Launcher Order and Capture Computer (MCD)
LOCC	Launch Operations Control Center
LOCC	Limitation of Cost Clause (AAGC)
Locc	Loccenius. De Jure Maritimo [A publication] (DLA)
LOCC	Logistical Operations Control Center [Army]
loc cit	In the Place Cited [Loco citato] [Latin] (WDMC)
LOC CIT	Loco Citato [In the Place Cited] [Latin]
LOCCOZO	Line of Communication Combat Zone [Military]
LOCCS	Letter of Credit Control System [Department of Housing and Urban Development] (GFGA)
Loc Ct Gaz	Local Courts and Municipal Gazette [Toronto, ON] [A publication] (DLA)
LOCD	Lines of Communication Designators (MCD)
LOCD	Local Disease
LOC DOL	Loco Dolenti [To the Painful Spot] [Pharmacy]
LOCE	Limited Operational Capability for Europe [DoD]
LOCE	Loss-of-Coolant Experiment [Nuclear energy]
LOCF	Location File (MCD)
LOCF	Loss-of-Coolant Flow [Nuclear energy] (NRCH)
Loc Gov Chron	Local Government Chronicle [London, England] [A publication] (DLA)
Loc Govt Chr & Mag Rep	Local Government Chronicle and Magisterial Reporter [London] [A publication] (DLA)
LOCH	London Options Clearing House (NUMA)
LOCI	Ligue des Originaires de Cote d'Ivoire [League of Ivory Coast Natives]
LOCI	List of Cancelled Items
LOCI	Local Course Improvement [National Science Foundation] (EDAC)
LOCI	Logarithmic Computing Instrument
LOCI	Low-Cost Interceptor (MCD)
LOCID	Location Identifier [FAA] (TAG)
LOCIG	Limited-Overs Cricket Information Group [British] (DBA)

LOCIS .... Library of Congress Information System [*Library of Congress Information service or system*] (IID)
LO CIT .... Loco Citato [*In the Place Cited*] [*Latin*]
LOCK .... Lock [*Commonly used*] (OPSA)
LOCK .... Logistical Operational Control Key [*Army*] (AABC)
Lock GL .... Locke's Game Laws [*5th ed.*] [*1866*] [*A publication*] (DLA)
LockhM .... Lockheed Martin Corp. [*Associated Press*] (SAG)
Lock Rev Ca... Lockwood's Reversed Cases [*New York*] [*A publication*] (DLA)
Lock Rev Cas... Lockwood's Reversed Cases [*New York*] [*A publication*] (DLA)
LOCKS .... Locks [*Commonly used*] (OPSA)
LOCL .... Loyal Order of Catfish Lovers (EA)
LOC LAUD ... Loco Laudato [*In the Place Quoted*] [*Latin*]
LOCLED .... Low-Operating Current Light-Emitting Diode
LOC LF .... Local Line Feed [*Telecommunications*] (DNAB)
LOCM .... Low Osmolar Contrast Medium (DB)
LOCMOS ..... Locally-Oxidized Complementary Metal-Oxide Semiconductor (PDAA)
LOCN .... Location
LOCO .... Locomotion (WDAA)
LOCO .... Locomotive (AABC)
LOCO .... Long Core [*Drilling program*]
Loco .... On the Spot (EBF)
LOCOM .... Local Community (ADA)
LOCOM .... Locomotive
LOCOR .... Local Coordinator (FAAC)
LOCOS .... Local Oxidation of Silicon [*Transistor technology*]
LOCOSS ...... Logic of Computers Operating System (MCD)
LOCO TAC.... Low-Cost Tactical RADAR (DNAB)
LOCP .... Launcher Operation Control Panel
LOCP .... Loss-of-Coolant Protection [*Nuclear energy*] (NRCH)
LOCPOD...... Low-Cost Powered Dispenser
LOCPORT..... Lines of Communications Ports (AABC)
Loc Primo Cit... Loco Primo Citato [*In the Place First Cited*] [*Latin*] (ILCA)
LOC PRIUS CIT... Loco Prius Citato [*In the Place First Cited*] [*Latin*] (ADA)
LOCPURO .... Local Purchase Order
LOCS .... Land-Ocean-Climate Satellite [*Marine science*] (OSRA)
LOCS .... Librascope Operations Control System
LOCS .... Logic and Control Simulation (NITA)
LOCS .... Logic and Control Simulator [*Computer science*] (BUR)
LOCT .... Lockheed Command and Tracking (IAA)
Loctite .... Loctite Corp. [*Associated Press*] (SAG)
LOCTRACS... Lockheed Tracking and Control System
LOCUSP....... Low Cost Uncooled Sensor Prototype [*Army*]
Locus Standi... Locus Standi Reports [*England*] [*A publication*] (DLA)
LOCV .... Loss of Condenser Vacuum [*Environmental science*] (COE)
LOD .... Large Organic Debris [*Pisciculture*]
LOD .... Launch Operations Directive [*or Director*] [*NASA*]
LOD .... Launch Operations Division [*NASA*] (KSC)
LOD .... Law Officers' Department [*British*]
LOD .... Leading Ones Detector [*Computer science*]
LOD .... Length of Day
LOD .... Level of Detail (MCD)
LOD .... Light-Off Detector [*Military*] (CAAL)
LOD .... Limit of Detection
LOD .... Limits of Disturbance (PA)
LOD .... Line of Dance
LOD .... Line of Departure [*Military*] (AFM)
LOD .... Line of Direction
LOD .... Line of Duty [*Military*]
LOD .... List of Drawings
LOD .... Little Oxford Dictionary [*A publication*]
LOD .... Locally One-Dimensional [*Engineering*] (OA)
LOD .... Location Dependent
LOD .... Lodi Metals, Inc. [*Vancouver Stock Exchange symbol*]
LOD .... Logarithm of the Odds
lod .... Logarithm of the Odds [*Favoring linkage*] [*Genetics*] (DOG)
LOD .... Longana [*Vanuatu*] [*Airport symbol*] (OAG)
LOD .... Low Density (IAA)
LODACS....... Longitudinal Fame Developing and Conducting System (PDAA)
LODACS....... Low-Dispersion Automatic Cannon System
LODC .... Local Defense District Craft
LODCS......... Lunar Orbiter Data Conversion System [*Aerospace*]
LODE .... Comstock Bank [*NASDAQ symbol*] (SAG)
LODE .... Cornstock Bk Carson City Nev [*NASDAQ symbol*] (TTSB)
LODE .... Large Optics Demonstration Experiment [*DoD*]
LODEM .... Loading Dock Equipment Manufacturers Association (EA)
LODESMP.... Logistics Data Element Standardization and Management Process (IEEE)
LODESTAR... Logically Organized Data Entry, Storage, and Recording
LODG .... Lodge [*Commonly used*] (OPSA)
LODG .... Sholodge, Inc. [*NASDAQ symbol*] (SAG)
LODGE .... Lodge [*Commonly used*] (OPSA)
LodgEnt .... Lodgenet Entertainment Corp. [*Associated Press*] (SAG)
LODI .... List of Deleted Items (NG)
LODIF .... Long Distance Infrared Flash Camera (PDAA)
LODISNAV ... Long Distance Navigation (FAAC)
LODOR .... Loaded, Waiting Orders or Assignment [*Navy*]
LODP .... Lunar Orbiter Data Printer [*Aerospace*]
LODR .... Loader
LODTM .... Large Optics Diamond Turning Machine (SDI)
LODUS......... Low Data Rate UHF [*Ultra-High Frequency*] Satellite [*RADAR*] (MCD)
LODYC......... Laboratoire d'Oceanographie Dynamique et de Climatologie [*France*] [*Marine science*] (OSRA)
LOE............. Left Outboard Elevon [*Aviation*] (MCD)
LOE............. Letter of Evaluation

LOE .... Letter of Execution (MCD)
LOE............. Level of Effort (KSC)
LOE............. Light-Off Examination [*Navy*] (NVT)
LOE............. Line of Effort (MCD)
LOE............. Line Oriented Evaluation (GAVI)
LOE............. Loei [*Thailand*] [*Airport symbol Obsolete*] (OAG)
LOE............. Loeser, Luftfahrtgesellschaft GmbH [*Germany ICAO designator*] (FAAC)
LOEAT.......... Lowest Temperature Equaled for All Time [*NWS*] (FAAC)
LOEC........... List of Effective Cards (NVT)
LOEC........... Lowest Observed Effect Concentration [*Environmental Technology*]
LOEFM......... Lowest Temperature Equaled for the Month [*NWS*] (FAAC)
LOEH .... Loehmann's Inc. [*NASDAQ symbol*] (TTSB)
LOEL........... Lowest-Observed-Effect Level [*Environmental science*] (FFDE)
LOEM(A)...... Leading Ordnance Electrical Mechanic (Air) [*British military*] (DMA)
LOEP........... List of Effective Pages (NVT)
LOEP........... Loss of Electric Power
LOERO .... Large Orbiting Earth Resources Observatory (IEEE)
LOESE......... Lowest Temperature Equaled So Early [*NWS*] (FAAC)
LOESL......... Lowest Temperature Equaled So Late [*NWS*] (FAAC)
Loewen........ Loewen Group, Inc. [*Associated Press*] (SAG)
LoewenG...... Loewen Group Capital LP [*Associated Press*] (SAG)
Loews.......... Loew's Corp. [*Formerly, Loew's Theatres, Inc.*] [*Associated Press*] (SAG)
LOEX........... Library Orientation/Instruction Exchange [*Library network*]
LOF............. Lack of Fusion
LOF............. Lecherous Old Fool [*Slang*]
LOF............. Letter of Finding (GFGA)
LOF............. Libbey-Owens-Ford Glass Co. [*Auto industry supplier*]
LOF............. Limitation of Funds (AAGC)
LOF............. Line of Fire
LOF............. Line-of-Flight (MCD)
LOF............. Line of Force
LOF............. Local Oscillator Filter [*Electronics*]
LOF............. Local Oscillator Frequency [*Electronics*]
LOF............. Lofexidine (DMAA)
LOF............. London and Overseas Freighter
LOF............. Longest Operation First
LOF............. Look Ahead on Fault [*Computer science*] (MHDB)
LOF............. Loss of Feedwater [*Nuclear energy*] (NRCH)
LOF............. Loss of Flow [*Nuclear energy*] (NRCH)
LOF............. Loss of Fluid (BARN)
LOF............. Lowest Operating Frequency (IEEE)
LOF............. Low Outlet Forceps [*Delivery*] [*Obstetrics*] (DAVI)
LOF............. Lube and Oil Filter
LOF............. Lube, Oil, and Filter [*Automobile servicing*]
LOF............. Trans States Airlines, Inc. [*ICAO designator*] (FAAC)
LOFA........... Leisure and Outdoor Furniture Association [*British*] (DBA)
LOFA........... Loss of Flow Accident [*Nuclear energy*] (NRCH)
LOFAAD ...... Low-Altitude Forward Area Air Defense (AABC)
LOFAADS.... Low-Altitude Forward Area Anti-Aircraft Defense System [*Army*]
LOFADS ...... Low-Altitude Forward Air Defense System (PDAA)
LOFAR .... Low-Frequency Acquisition and Ranging
LOFAR .... Low-Frequency Analysis and Recording [*Sonobuoys*] [*Navy*]
LOFAT......... Low-Flying Aerial Target [*Military*] (CAAL)
L of C .... Library of Congress
LOFC........... Loss of Forced Circulation [*Nuclear energy*] (NRCH)
LOFES......... Load Factor Error Sensor (MCD)
LOFEZ.......... Low Fighter Engagement Zone (PDAA)
LOFF........... Leakoff [*Mechanical engineering*]
L Off Econ & Mgt... Law Office Economics and Management [*A publication*] (DLA)
Lofft .... Lofft's English King's Bench Reports [*1772-74*] [*A publication*] (DLA)
Lofft Append... Lofft's Maxims, Appended to Lofft's Reports [*A publication*] (DLA)
Lofft Lib...... Lofft on the Law of Libels [*A publication*] (DLA)
Lofft Max..... Maxims Appended to Lofft's Reports [*A publication*] (DLA)
Lofft's Rep... Lofft's English King's Bench Reports [*1772-74*] [*A publication*] (DLA)
Lofft Un L... Lofft's Elements of Universal Law [*A publication*] (DLA)
L of N .... League of Nations [*1919-1946*]
LOFO........... Low-Frequency Oscillation (MCD)
L of P .... Lodge of Perfection [*Freemasonry*] (DAS)
LOFRECO..... Low Front End Cost [*Engineering*]
LOFS .... London & Overseas Freightliners [*NASDAQ symbol*] (SAG)
LOFSY .... London & Overseas Freight ADS [*NASDAQ symbol*] (TTSB)
LOFT........... Line Oriented Flight Training (MCD)
Loft .... Lofft's English King's Bench Reports [*1772-74*] [*A publication*] (DLA)
LOFT........... Loss of Flow [*or Fluid*] Test Facility [*Nuclear energy*]
LOFT........... Loss-of-Fluid Test (GAAI)
LOFT........... Low-Frequency Telescope [*NASA*]
LOFTI.......... Low-Frequency Transionospheric Satellite
LOFTPS........ Lube Oil Fill, Transfer, and Purification System (DNAB)
LOFW.......... Loss of Feedwater [*Nuclear energy*] (NRCH)
LOG............. Labor Old Guard [*Australia An association*]
LOG .... Lambda Omicron Gamma Medical Society (NTPA)
LOG .... Lawn-O-Gram [*A publication*] (EAAP)
LOG .... Legion of Guardsmen (EA)
LOG .... Logan [*Utah*] [*Seismograph station code, US Geological Survey Closed*] (SEIS)
LOG .... Loganair Ltd. [*British ICAO designator*] (FAAC)
LOG .... Logan Mines Ltd. [*Vancouver Stock Exchange symbol*]
LOG .... Logarithm [*Mathematics*]
log .... Logarithm (IDOE)
LOG .... Loggia (VRA)
LOG .... Logging
LOG .... Logic
LOG .... Logistician

LOG	Logistics (KSC)
log	Logogram (BJA)
log	Logographic (BJA)
LOG	Pago Pago, AQ [Location identifier FAA] (FAAL)
LOG	Rayonier Timberlands CI'A' [NYSE symbol] (TTSB)
LOG	Rayonier Timberlands LP [NYSE symbol] (SPSG)
LOGACS	Low-G Accelerometer Calibration System [NASA]
LOGAIR	Logistics Airlift [Military]
LOGAIRNET	Logistics Air Network [Air Force]
LOGAIS	Logistics Automated Information System [Marine Corps] (DOMA)
LOGAL	Logical Algorithmic Language [Computer science] (CSR)
LogalEd	Logal Educational Software & Systems Ltd. [Associated Press] (SAG)
LOGALGOL	Logical Algorithmic Language [Computer science]
LOGAM	Logistics Analysis Model [Army] (RDA)
LOGAMP	Logarithmic Amplifier (IAA)
LOGAMP	Logistics and Acquisition Management Program [Army] (RDA)
LOGANDS	Logical Commands
Logans	Logan's Roadhouse, Inc. [Associated Press] (SAG)
LOGATAK	Logistics Attack Model [BDM Corp.] (MCD)
LOGBALNET	Logistics Ballistic Missile Network [Air Force]
LOGC	Logic Devices [NASDAQ symbol] (TTSB)
LOGC	Logic Devices, Inc. [NASDAQ symbol] (SAG)
LOGC	Logistics Center [Army]
LOGCAB	Logistics Center Advisory Board (MCD)
LOGC-AMIP	Logistics Center Involvement in Army Model Improvement Program
LOGCAP	Logistic and Command Assessment of Projects [Army]
LOGCAP	Logistics Capability
LOGCAP	Logistics Civil Augmentation Program [Army]
LOGCCIS	Logistics Command Central Information System [British]
LOGCEN	Logistics Center (MCD)
LOGCMD	Logistical Command
LOGCOM	Logistic Communications (CET)
LOGCOM	Logistics Command (MCD)
LOGCOMD	Logistical Command
Log Comp	Logan's Compendium of Ancient Law [A publication] (DLA)
LOGCON	Logistics Readiness Condition System [DARCOM] (MCD)
LOGCOR	Logistics Coordination (NVT)
LOGCOST	Logistics Cost Model (PDAA)
LOG CTR	Logistic Center [Army]
LOGDB	Logistics Database
LOGDEC	Logarithmic Decrement (IAA)
LOGDESMAP	Logistics Data Element Standardization and Management Program [DoD] (AABC)
LOGDESMO	Logistics Data Element Standardization and Management Office [DoD] (AABC)
LOGDIV	Logistics Division [Supreme Headquarters, Allied Powers Europe] (NATG)
log$_e$	Logarithm to the Base e [Mathematics] (DAVI)
LOGEL	Logic Generating Language [Computer science]
LOGEST	Annual Logistic Estimate (NATG)
LOGEX	Logistical Exercise [Army] (AABC)
LOGFED	Log File Editor (NITA)
LOGFED	Log File Editor Processor [Computer science]
LOGFOR	Logistics Force [Military]
LOGFTC	Logarithmic Fast Time Constant
LOGHELO	Logistics Helicopter (NVT)
LOGI	Logarithmic Computing Instrument (HGAA)
LOGIC	LASER Optical Guidance Integration Concept [Missile guidance]
LOGIC	Level of Greatest Item Control [DoD]
LOGIC	Local Government Information Center
Logic	Logic Works, Inc. [Associated Press] (SAG)
LogicD	Logic Devices, Inc. [Associated Press] (SAG)
LOGICOM	Logical Communications, Inc. [East Norwalk, CT] [Telecommunications] (TSSD)
Logicon	Logicon Corp. [Associated Press] (SAG)
LOGIFAMP	Logarithmic Intermediate Frequency Amplifier (IAA)
LOGIK	Logical Organizing and Gathering of Information Knowledge (MHDI)
LOGIMP	Logistic Improvement Program [Military]
LOGIN	Local Government Information Network [Information service or system]
LOGIPAC	Logical Processor and Computer
LOGISTC	Logistic
LOGIT	Logical Inference Tester [NASA]
LOGK	Kapfenberg [Austria ICAO location identifier] (ICLI)
LOGL	Logal Educational Software & Systems Ltd. [NASDAQ symbol] (SAG)
LOGLAN	Logical Language
LOGLAND	Logistics Transport by Land [Military]
LOGLF	Logal Educational Softwr&Sys [NASDAQ symbol] (TTSB)
LOGLISP	Prolog and List Processing
LOGMAP	Logistics System Master Plan [Army]
LOGMAPS	Logistics Master Planning System
LOGMARS	Logistic Applications of Automated Marking and Reading Symbols [DoD]
LOGMET	Logistics Management Engineering Team [Military]
LOGMIS	Logistics Management Information System [USACC]
LOGMOD	Logic Model [Fault isolation device] [Army] (MCD)
LOGMOD	Logistics Module [Simulation games] [Army] (INF)
LOGMTD	Logarithmic Mean Temperature Difference (IAA)
LOGN	Logansort Financial [NASDAQ symbol] (TTSB)
LOGN	Logansport Financial Corp. [NASDAQ symbol] (SAG)
LOGNET	Logistics Network (MCD)
Lognspt	Logansport Financial Corp. [Associated Press] (SAG)
LOGO	Limitation of Government Obligation (MCD)
LOGO	Limit of Government Obligation (NAKS)
LOGO	Logotype [Advertising] (DSUE)
LOGOIS	Logistics Operating Information System (AABC)
LOGP	Logistics Plans
LOGPAC	Logistics Package [Army] (INF)
LOGPARS	Logistics Planning and Requirements Simplification System [Army] (RDA)
LOG PLAN	Logistics System Plan [Navy DoD]
LOGR	Logistical Ratio [Army]
LOGRAM	Logical Program
LOGREC	Log Recording [Computer science]
LOGREP	Logistics Replenishment (NVT)
LOGREP	Logistics Representative [Navy] (NVT)
LOGREQ	Logistics Requirements (NVT)
LOGS	Labor's Old Guard Socialists [Australia An association]
LOGS	Logistics Supportability (AABC)
LOGSACS	Logistics Structure and Composition System (AABC)
LOGSAFE	Logistics Sustainability Analysis Feasibility Estimator (DOMA)
LOGSAM	Logistics Support Alternative [or Analysis] Model (MCD)
LOGSAR	Logistics Storage and Retrieval System (MCD)
LOGSAT	Logistics Special Assistance Team (MCD)
LOGSEA	Logistics Transport by Sea [Military]
LOGSS	Logistics Support Squadron [Military]
LOGSTAT	Logistical Status Report [Military] (INF)
LOGSTCN	Logistician
LOGSUM	Logistics Summary (NVT)
LOGSUP	Logistics Support
LOGSVC	Logistics Service [Military] (NVT)
LOGTAB	Logic Tables (IEEE)
LOGTANBG	Logarithm Tangent Bearing (IAA)
LOgWC	West Carroll Parish Library, Oak Grove, LA [Library symbol Library of Congress] (LCLS)
LOH	™Lady of the House∫ [Advertising] (DOAD)
loh	Lady of the House [Telephone marketing] (WDMC)
LOH	League of Housewives [Also known as HOW]
LOH	Length of Hospitalization
LOH	Light Observation Helicopter
LOH	Line Overhead (ACRL)
LOH	Local Osteolytic Hypercalcemia [Endocrinology]
LOH	Loja [Ecuador] [Airport symbol] (OAG)
LOH	Loop of Henle [Medicine] (DMAA)
LOH	Loss of Heterozygosity [Genetics]
LOHAC	Loading and Handling Corrective Action Program
LOHAP	Light Observation Helicopter Avionics Package (MCD)
LOHET	Linear Output Hall Effect Transducer
LOHO	Longhorn Steaks [NASDAQ symbol] (TTSB)
LOHO	Longhorn Steaks, Inc. [NASDAQ symbol] (SAG)
LOHS	Loss of Heat Sink [Nuclear energy] (NRCH)
LOHTADS	Light Observation Helicopter Target Acquisition Designation System (MCD)
LOI	Laboratory Operating Instructions (MCD)
LOI	Laredo [Texas] [Airport symbol] (AD)
LOI	Laredo, TX [Location identifier FAA] (FAAL)
LOI	Launch-on-Impact [Military] (MUSM)
LOI	Letter of Instruction
LOI	Letter of Intent (MCD)
LOI	Letter of Interest (NG)
LOI	Letter of Introduction
LOI	Level of Incompetence (DMAA)
LOI	Level of Injury [Neurology] (DAVI)
LOI	Limiting Oxygen Index
LOI	Limit of Impurities
LOI	Line of Induction
LOI	List of Items (AABC)
LOI	Lock-On Initiated (MCD)
LOI	Lodge of Instruction [Freemasonry]
LOI	Loss of Imprinting [Genetics]
LOI	Loss-of-Input (COE)
LOI	Loss on Ignition [Analytical chemistry]
LOI	Lunar Orbit Insertion [NASA]
LOICZ	Land-Ocean Interaction in the Costal Zone [International Geosphere Biosphere Programme]
LOID	Location Identifiers [A publication FAA]
LOIH	Hohenems-Dornbirn [Austria ICAO location identifier] (ICLI)
LOIH	Left Oblique Inguinal Hernia [Medicine] (DMAA)
LOIJ	St. Johann, Tirol [Austria ICAO location identifier] (ICLI)
LOIS	Langsam Library Online Information Services [University of Cincinnati] (OLDSS)
LOIS	Legal Office Information System
LOIS	Library Online Information Services [Morehead State University] (OLDSS)
LOIS	Library Order Information System [Computer system] [Library of Congress Obsolete]
LOIS	Loss of Interim Status [Environmental Protection Agency]
Lois Batim	Lois des Batiments [A publication] (DLA)
Lois Rec	Lois Recentes du Canada [A publication] (DLA)
LOIT	Loitering [FBI standardized term]
LOIUSA	Loyal Orange Institution of United States of America (EA)
LOIV	Loyal Orange Institution of Victoria [Australia]
LoJack	Lo-Jack Corp. [Associated Press] (SAG)
LOJN	LoJack Corp. [NASDAQ symbol] (SAG)
LOK	Lockwood Petroleum, Inc. [Vancouver Stock Exchange symbol]
LOKSMTH	Locksmith
LOKTAL	Locked Octal (IAA)
LOL	Laughing Out Loud

LOL..............	Laugh Out Loud [*Internet language*] [*Computer science*]
LOL..............	League of Lefthanders [*Defunct*] (EA)
LOL..............	Left Occipitolateral [*A fetal position*] [*Obstetrics*]
LOL..............	Length of Lead [*Actual*] [*Technical drawings*]
LOL..............	Limited Operating Life
LOL..............	Limit of Liability (MCD)
LOL..............	Line of Launch [*Navy*] (CAAL)
LOL..............	Little Old Lady [*Slang*]
lol..............	Lolo (Bantu) [*MARC language code Library of Congress*] (LCCP)
LOL..............	London-Oiseau-Lyre [*Record label*] [*Great Britain, USA, etc.*]
LOL..............	Longitude of Launch
LOL..............	Lovelock [*Nevada*] [*Airport symbol Obsolete*] (OAG)
LOL..............	Loyal Orange Lodge
LOLA..........	Layman-Oriented Language (IAA)
LOLA..........	Library On-Line Acquisitions [*Washington State University*] [*Data processing system*]
LOLA..........	Light Observation Light-Armored Aircraft·
LOLA..........	London Online Local Authorities (NITA)
LOLA..........	Long Line Azimuth [*Survey*]
LOLA..........	Lower Leg Artery [*Anatomy*]
LOLA..........	Low-Level Oil Alarm (IAA)
LOLA..........	Lunar Orbit and Landing Approach [*Simulator*] [*NASA*]
LOLAD........	Low-Altitude LASER Air Defense System
LOLAS........	Location of Launching Site [*Army*]
LOLEX........	Low-Level Extraction [*Military aviation*]
LOLI..........	Limited Operational-Life Items [*NASA*] (NASA)
LOLI..........	Loyal Orange Ladies Institution (EA)
LOLITA........	Language for the On-Line Investigation and Transformation of Abstractions [*Computer science*]
LOLITA........	Library On-Line Information and Text Access [*Oregon State University*] [*Corvallis, OR Data processing system*]
LOLITS........	Little Old Ladies in Tennis Shoes [*Facetious reference to minor league baseball*]
LO/LO........	Lift-On/Lift-Off
LOLP..........	Loss of Load Probability [*Nuclear energy*] (IEEE)
LOLV..........	Lower Leg Vein [*Anatomy*]
LOLVE........	Lower Leg Venule [*Anatomy*]
LOLW..........	Laid Off, Lack of Work [*Unemployment insurance and the Bureau of Labor Statistics*] (OICC)
LOLW..........	Wels [*Austria ICAO location identifier*] (ICLI)
LOM..........	Laminated Object Manufacturing [*Desktop manufacturing*]
LOM..........	LASER Optical Modulator
LOM..........	Launch Operations Manager [*NASA*]
LOM..........	League of Mercy [*Salvation Army*]
LOM..........	Left Otitis Media [*Medicine*] (CPH)
LOM..........	Legion of Merit [*Military award*]
LOM..........	Level of Maintenance (MCD)
LOM..........	Light-Optic Microscope (MSA)
LOM..........	Limitation of Motion [*Neurology*] (DAVI)
LOM..........	Limitation of Movement
LOM..........	List of Materials (CET)
LOM..........	List of Modifications (AFM)
LOM..........	Little Old Man [*Slang*] (DAVI)
LOM..........	Locator at Outer Marker [*Aviation*]
LOM..........	Loewen, Ondaatje, McCutcheon, Inc. [*Toronto Stock Exchange symbol Vancouver Stock Exchange symbol*]
LOM..........	Lome [*Togo*] [*Seismograph station code, US Geological Survey*] (SEIS)
LOM..........	Loss of Motion [*Medicine*]
LOM..........	Low-Frequency Outer Marker
LOM..........	Low-Order Memory (CET)
LOM..........	Loyal Order of Moose (EA)
LOM..........	Lunar Orbital Map [*Air Force*]
LOM..........	Lunar Orbital Mission [*NASA*] (KSC)
LOM..........	SERTEL [*Servicios Telereservacios SA de CV*] [*ICAO designator*] (FAAC)
LOMA..........	Life Office Management Association [*Atlanta, GA*] (EA)
LOMA..........	Literature on Modern Art
LOMA..........	Lutheran Outdoors Ministry Association [*Later, NLOMA*] (EA)
LOMAC........	Logistic Management Advisory Committee
LOMAD........	Low-to-Medium-Altitude Air Defense (AABC)
LOMAH........	Location of Miss and Hit [*Marksmanship training*] [*Army*] (INF)
Lomak........	Lomak Petroleum, Inc. [*Associated Press*] (SAG)
Loma Linda U...	Loma Linda University (GAGS)
LOMAR........	Local Manual Attempt Recording (TEL)
LOMAR........	Logistics, Maintenance, and Repair (IAA)
LOMAS........	Law Office Managemnt and Accounting System (HGAA)
Lomax Ex'rs...	Lomax on Executors [*A publication*] (DLA)
LOMB..........	Lockheed Missile Beacon (IAA)
LOMC..........	Logistics Management Committee (AAGC)
Lom CH Rep...	Lomas's City Hall Reporter [*New York*] [*A publication*] (DLA)
Lom Dig......	Lomax's Digest of Real Property [*A publication*] (DLA)
Lom Ex........	Lomax on Executors [*A publication*] (DLA)
LOMF..........	Loss of Main Feedwater [*Nuclear energy*] (NRCH)
LOMI..........	Letter of Moral Intent [*Business term*]
LOMI..........	Low Oxidation State Metallic Ion [*Nuclear energy*] (NUCP)
LOMIS........	Locator Map in Source (IAA)
LOMK..........	Lomak Petroleum [*NASDAQ symbol*] (TTSB)
LOMK..........	Lomak Petroleum, Inc. [*NASDAQ symbol*] (SAG)
LOMMIS......	Land Ordnance Maintenance Management Information System (PDAA)
LOMO..........	London Overseas Mail Office
LOMOR........	Long-Distance Medium Frequency Omni Range (IAA)
LOMP..........	Local Office Microcomputer Project (NITA)

LOMS..........	Library Organization and Management Section [*Library Administration Division of ALA*]
LOMSA........	Left Otitis Media Suppurative Acute [*Medicine*]
LOMSACh...	Left Otitis Media Suppurative, Chronic [*Medicine*] (MEDA)
LOMSCH......	Left Otitis Media Suppurative Chronic [*Medicine*]
LOMUSS......	Lockheed Multiprocessor Simulation System (IEEE)
LOMV..........	Lolium Mottle Virus [*Plant pathology*]
LON..........	Avilond, TAC [*Ukraine*] [*FAA designator*] (FAAC)
LON..........	Letter of Notification
LON..........	Line of Nodes
LON..........	London [*England*] [*Airport symbol*] (OAG)
Lon..........	London [*Record label*] [*Export issues of English Decca - mainly USA, Canada, etc.*]
LON..........	London European Airways PLC [*British ICAO designator*] (FAAC)
LON..........	Longitude (KSC)
LON..........	Longmire [*Washington*] [*Seismograph station code, US Geological Survey*] (SEIS)
LON..........	Tupelo, MS [*Location identifier FAA*] (FAAL)
LON..........	University College, London, England [*OCLC symbol*] (OCLC)
LoNa..........	Low Sodium [*Dietetics*] (DAVI)
LONAL.......	Local Off-Net Access Line [*Telecommunications*] (TEL)
LOND..........	London
Lond........	London Encyclopedia [*A publication*] (DLA)
LOND..........	London International Group Ltd. [*NASDAQ symbol*] (SAG)
LondInt......	London International Group PLC [*Associated Press*] (SAG)
Lond Jur......	London Jurist Reports [*England*] [*A publication*] (DLA)
Lond Jur NS...	London Jurist, New Series [*A publication*] (DLA)
Lond LM......	London Law Magazine [*A publication*] (DLA)
LondonP......	London Pacific Group Ltd. [*Associated Press*] (SAG)
LondOvr......	London & Overseas Freightliners [*Associated Press*] (SAG)
LONDY........	London Intl Group plc ADS [*NASDAQ symbol*] (TTSB)
LONESHS.....	Limited- or Non-English Speaking Handicapped Student
LoneStar.....	Lone Star Technologies [*Associated Press*] (SAG)
LoneStr......	Lone Star Technologies, Inc. [*Associated Press*] (SAG)
LONEX........	Laboratory Office Network Experiment [*DoD*]
LONF..........	London Financial [*NASDAQ symbol*] (TTSB)
Long..........	Longford [*County in Ireland*] (WGA)
LONG..........	Longitude (AFM)
Long..........	Longtitude (WA)
LONG..........	Longus [*Long*] [*Pharmacy*]
Long & R....	Long and Russell's Election Cases [*Massachusetts*] [*A publication*] (DLA)
Long & T....	Longfield and Townsend's Irish Exchequer Reports [*1841-42*] [*A publication*] (DLA)
Long Beach B Bull...	Long Beach Bar Bulletin [*A publication*] (DLA)
LongDr......	Longs Drug Stores Corp. [*Associated Press*] (SAG)
LongDrg......	Longs Drug Stores [*Associated Press*] (SAG)
LONGF........	Longford [*County in Ireland*] (ROG)
Longf & T....	Longfield and Townsend's Irish Exchequer Reports [*1841-42*] [*A publication*] (DLA)
LONGFD......	Longford [*County in Ireland*]
Longf Dist...	Longfield on Distress and Replevin [*A publication*] (DLA)
LONGFOG	Long-Range, Fiber-Optic Guided [*Missiles*]
Long Irr......	Long on Irrigation [*A publication*] (DLA)
longit........	Longitudinal (VRA)
LONGN........	Longeron [*Aerospace engineering*]
Long Q........	Long Quinto [*Pt. 10 of Year Books*] [*A publication*] (DLA)
Long Quinto...	Year Books, Part X [*5 Edw. 4, 1465*] [*A publication*] (DLA)
Long S........	Long on Sales of Personal Property [*A publication*] (DLA)
LONGT........	Longtree [*England*]
LONGV........	Longevity (AFM)
LongvF........	Longview Fibre Co. [*Associated Press*] (SAG)
Longwood C...	Longwood College (GAGS)
LONO..........	Letter of No Objection [*FDA*]
LONO..........	Low Noise
Lon R Bks...	London Review of Books [*A publication*] (BRI)
LONS..........	Laboratory Office Network System [*DoD*]
LONS..........	Light of the Night Sky [*Galaxy*]
LONS..........	Local Online Network System
Lons Cr L.....	Lonsdale's Statute Criminal Law [*A publication*] (DLA)
LOO..........	Laghouat [*Algeria*] [*Airport symbol*] (AD)
LOO..........	Leave One Out at a Time [*Data analysis*]
LOO..........	Loumic Resources Ltd. [*Vancouver Stock Exchange symbol*]
LOOM........	Light Opera of Manhattan
LOOM........	Loyal Order of Moose (EA)
LOOP..........	Long-Range Open Ocean Patrol [*Navy*] (NVT)
LOOP..........	Loop [*Postal Service standard*] (OPSA)
LOOP..........	Loss of Offsite Power [*Nuclear energy*] (NRCH)
LOOP..........	Louisiana Offshore Oil Port [*Group of major oil companies*]
LOOPS........	Local Office Online Payment System [*Unemployment insurance*]
LOOPS........	Loop [*Commonly used*] (OPSA)
LOOW........	Lake Ontario Ordnance Works
LOP..........	Lake Ontario Cement Ltd. [*Toronto Stock Exchange symbol*]
LOP..........	Last Operation Completed [*Computer science*]
LOP..........	Launch Operations [*or Operator's*] Panel [*NASA*]
LOP..........	Learning Opportunity [*Education*]
LOP..........	Least Objectionable Program [*Television*]
LOP..........	Leave on Pass
LOP..........	Left Occipitoposterior [*A fetal position*] [*Obstetrics*]
LOP..........	Left Outside Position [*Dancing*]
LOP..........	Letter of Promulgation [*Navy*] (NVT)
LOP..........	Letter of Proposal [*Military*] (AFM)
LOP..........	Levels-of-Processing [*Psychology*]
LOp..........	Lex Operator Gene
LOP..........	Life of Program

LOP	Line of Position [*Electronics*]
LOP	Line of Power (WDAA)
LOP	Line-Oriented Protocol
LOP	Linton-on-Ouse FTU [*British ICAO designator*] (FAAC)
LOP	Loanda [*Brazil*] [*Airport symbol*] (AD)
LOP	Locally-Originated Program [*Broadcasting*] (NTCM)
LOP	Local Office Project [*Department of Health and Social Security*] [*British*]
LOP	Local Operating Procedures (AFM)
LOP	Local Operational Plot
LOP	Logic Processor (IAA)
LOP	Logistics Officer Program [*Army*]
LOP	Lookout Post (IAA)
LOP	Loss of Offsite Power [*Nuclear energy*] (NRCH)
LOP	Loss of Privileges (WDAA)
LOP	Low-Order Position [*Military*] (AFIT)
LOP	Lubricating Oil Pump (MSA)
LOP	Lunar Orbit Plane [*NASA*] (IAA)
LOPA	Layout of Passenger Accommodation (MCD)
LOPA	Local Payment of Airline (MCD)
LOPAC	Load Optimization and Passenger Acceptance Control [*Airport computer*]
LOPAD	Logarithmic Outline [*or Online*] Processing System for Analog Data (IEEE)
LOPAIR	Long Path Infrared
LOP & G	Live Oak, Perry & Gulf Railroad (IIA)
LOPAR	Long Baseline Position and Rates [*Guidance and tracking system*] [*Air Force*]
LOPAR	Low-Power Acquisition RADAR
LOPC	Lunar Orbital Photocraft [*NASA*] (IAA)
LOPC	Lunar Orbit Plane Change [*NASA*]
LOPE	Live on Planet Earth (WDAA)
LOPG	Launch Operations Planning Group
LOP-GAP	Liquid Oxygen Petrol, Guided Aircraft Projectile
LOPI	Loss of Pipe Integrity [*Nuclear energy*] (NRCH)
LOPKGS	Loose or in Packages [*Freight*]
LOPO	Local Post (EA)
LOPO	Low-Power Boiler [*US reactor*]
LOPOS	Local Oxidation of Polysilicon over Silicon [*Transistor technology*]
LOPP	Lunar Orbiter Photographic Project [*Aerospace*]
LOPPLAR	LASER Doppler RADAR (IAA)
LOPRA	Low-Power Reactor Assembly [*University of Illinois*] (NRCH)
LO-PRO	Low-Profile
LOPRPr	Santander Overseas Bk'A' Pfd [*NYSE symbol*] (TTSB)
LOPS	Length of Patient Stay [*Medicine*] (AABC)
LOPS	Lunar Orbiting Photographic System [*Aerospace*]
LOPT	Line Output Transformer (IAA)
LOPU	Logistics Organization Planning Unit
LOQ	Leadership Opinion Questionnaire [*Test*]
LOQ	Limit of Quantitation [*Analytical chemistry*]
LOQ	Lobatsi [*Botswana*] [*Airport symbol*] (AD)
LOQ	Loquitur [*He, or She, Speaks*] [*Latin*]
LOQ	Lower Outer Quadrant [*Anatomy*]
LO-QG	Locked Oscillator-Quadrature Grid [*Computer science*]
LOR	Ladies of Retreads (EA)
LOR	Large Optical Reflector
LOR	Lender's Offered Rate [*Banking*]
LOR	Letter of Request (AFIT)
LOR	Level of Repair
LOR	Licence of Right (DB)
LOR	Light Output Ratio (WDAA)
LOR	Likely Operational Range [*Navy*] (ANA)
LOR	Lockout Relay (MCD)
LOR	Long Open Reading [*Frame*] [*Genetics*]
LOR	Loral Corp. [*NYSE symbol*] (SPSG)
LOR	Loral Space Communications [*NYS*] (TTSB)
LOR	Lorazepam [*A tranquilizer*]
LOR	Lorcainide (STED)
LOR	Lorcha [*Ship's rigging*] (ROG)
LOR	Loricrin (DMAA)
LOR	Lormes [*Somee*] [*France*] [*Seismograph station code, US Geological Survey*] (SEIS)
LOR	Loss of Righting Reflex [*Medicine*] (DMAA)
LOR	Lower Operator Rate [*Telecommunications British*]
LOR	Low-Frequency Omnidirectional Radio Range
LOR	Lunar Orbit [*or Orbital*] Rendezvous [*NASA*]
LOR	Ozark, Fort Rucker, AL [*Location identifier FAA*] (FAAL)
LOR-1	Level of Rehabilitation Scale 1 (STED)
LORA	Lecturer-Oriented Response Analysis (PDAA)
LOR/A	Letter of Repair/Analysis (AAGC)
LORA	Level of Repair Analysis (MCD)
LORA	Long-Range Adaption (MCD)
LORA	Long-Range Addition (NVT)
LORA	Low Out of Range Alarm (ECII)
LORAAS	Long-Range Airborne ASW [*Antisubmarine Warfare*] System (MCD)
LORAC	Long-Range Accuracy [*RADAR*]
LORAD	Long-Range Active Detection
LORAD	Long-Range Air Defense (AABC)
LORADAC	Long-Range Active Detection and Communications System
LORADS	LASER Optical Ranging and Designation System
LORAE	Long-Range Attitude and Event [*Instrumentation system*]
LORAH	Long-Range Area Homing
LORA-HOJ	Long-Range - Home on Jam
Loral	Loral Corp. [*Associated Press*] (SAG)
LORAM	Level of Repair for Aeronautical Material (PDAA)
LORAMS	Long-Range Automatic Measuring Station [*Meteorology*]
LORAN	Long-Range Aid to Navigation [*Military*] (DOMA)
loran	Long-Range Navigation (IDOE)
LORAN	Long-Range Navigation
LORAN	Long-Range Radio Navigation (ACRL)
LORAN D	Long-Range Navigation Doppler Inertial (DNAB)
LORAN DM	Long-Range Navigation Double Master
Lor & Russ	Loring and Russell's Election Cases in Massachusetts [*A publication*] (DLA)
LORAN DS	Long-Range Navigation Double Slave
LORAN M	Long-Range Navigation Master
LORAN S	Long-Range Navigation Slave
LORAP	Level of Repair Analysis Program
LORAPH	Long-Range Passive Homing System
LORAPL	Long-Range Planning Task Group [*Oversaw military strategy in Vietnam*] (VNW)
LORAS	Linear Omnidirectional Airspeed System (PDAA)
LORAS	Low-Range Airspeed System (MCD)
Loras C	Loras College (GAGS)
LORBAS	Large Off-Line Retrieval Text Base Access System
LORBI	Locked-On RADAR Bearing Indicator
LORC	Lockheed Radio Command (MUGU)
LORCS	League of Red Cross and Red Crescent Societies
LORCS	League of Red Cross Societies
LORD	Licensing Online Retrieval Data (NRCH)
LORD	List of Required Documents (NVT)
LORD	Long-Range and Detection RADAR (NATG)
LORD	Lordosis [*Medicine*]
lord	Lordosis (STED)
LORDS	Licensing On-Line Retrieval Data System (NRCH)
Lords Jour	Journals of the House of Lords [*England*] [*A publication*] (DLA)
LORE	Land Ordnance Engineering Branch [*Canada Military*] (PDAA)
LOREC	Long-Range Earth Current Communications
LORELCO	Lower Elevated Serum Cholesterol [*Acronym is trade name of Dow Chemical*]
LORELEI	Long-Range Echo Level Indicator
LORENDAS	Long-Range Energy Development and Supply (PDAA)
Lorenz	Lorenz's Ceylon Reports [*A publication*]
Lorenz App R	Lorenz's Appeal Reports [*Ceylon*] [*A publication*] (DLA)
Lorenz Rep	Lorenz's Ceylon Reports [*A publication*] (ILCA)
LOREORS	Long-Range, Electro-Optical Reconnaissance System
LORES	Long-Route Engineering Study [*Bell System*]
LO-RES	Low Resolution [*Computer science*]
LORI	Limited Operational Readiness Inspection (MCD)
LoriCp	Lori Corp. [*Associated Press*] (SAG)
Loring & Russel El Cases	Loring and Russell's Election Cases in Massachusetts [*A publication*] (DLA)
Loring & Russell	Loring and Russell's Election Cases in Massachusetts [*A publication*] (DLA)
Lor Inst	Lorimer. Institutes of Law [*A publication*] (ILCA)
LORL	Large Orbital Research Laboratory [*NASA*]
LORMODS	Long-Range Metal Object Detection System (MCD)
LORMONSTA	LORAN Monitor Station
LORO	Lobe-On Receive Only [*Electronic counter-countermeasures*]
Loronix	Loronix Information Systems, Inc. [*Associated Press*] (SAG)
LOROP	Long-Range Oblique Photography
LORPGAC	Long-Range Proving Ground Automatic Computer (IEEE)
L or RC	Leather or Rubber Covered [*Freight*]
LORRE	Laboratory of Renewable Resources Engineering [*Purdue University*]
LORS	Labor Organization Reporting System [*Department of Labor*] (GFGA)
LORS	LM [*Lunar Module*] Optical Rendezvous System [*NASA*]
LORS	Long-Range SONAR
LORS	Lunar Orbiting Reconnaissance System [*Aerospace*]
LORSA	Long-Range Steerable Antenna (MCD)
LORSAC	Long-Range Submarine Communications (AAG)
Lor Sc L	Lorimer's Handbook of Scotch Law [*A publication*] (DLA)
LORS-I	Level of Rehabilitation Scale-I [*Medicine*] (DAVI)
LORSTA	LORAN Transmitting Station
LORSU	Long-Range Special Unit [*Military*]
LORT	League of Resident Theaters (EA)
LORTAN	Long-Range and Tactical Navigation System
LORTRAP	Long-Range Training and Rotation Plan
LORV	Low-Observability Reentry Vehicle
LORW	Light Output Ratio Working (PDAA)
LORX	Loronix Information Systems, Inc. [*NASDAQ symbol*] (SAG)
LORX	Loronix Info Systems [*NASDAQ symbol*] (TTSB)
LOS	Laboratory Operating System [*NASA*]
LOS	Lagos [*Nigeria*] [*Airport symbol*] (OAG)
LOS	Land Observation Satellite (PDAA)
LOS	Land Ownership Survey
LOS	Latin Old Style (ADA)
LOS	Launcher Operation Station (MCD)
LOS	Launch on Search [*Navy*] (CAAL)
LOS	Launch Operations System [*NASA*] (KSC)
LOS	Launch Optional Selector (IAA)
LOS	Law of the Sea [*United Nations*] (ASF)
LOS	Length of Service
LOS	Length of Stay
LOS	Level of Service [*BTS*] (TAG)
LOS	Liaison Office Support
LOS	Licentiate in Obstetrical Science
LOS	Lift-Off Simulator [*NASA*] (NASA)
LOS	Limited Operational Strategy
LOS	Limit Order Switching (PDAA)
LOS	Line of Scrimmage [*Football*]

LOS.............	Line of Sight
LOS.............	Line of Supply
LOS.............	Line-Oriented Simulation (GAVI)
LOS.............	Line Out of Service [*Telecommunications*] (TEL)
LOS.............	Live Oak Society (EA)
LOS.............	Local Operating Station (DNAB)
LOS.............	Local Operating System (IAA)
LOS.............	Logistic Operation - Streamline [*Military*] (AABC)
LOS.............	Logistic Oriented Schools [*Army*]
LOS.............	Loop Output Signal (CET)
LOS.............	Lossiemouth FTU [*British ICAO designator*] (FAAC)
LOS.............	Loss of Selectivity (AAEL)
LOS.............	Loss of Sight
LOS.............	Loss of Signal
LOS.............	Loss of Site (STED)
LOS.............	Loss of Sync [*Aerospace*] (NAKS)
LOS.............	Loss of Synchronization
LOS.............	Lower (O)Esophageal Sphincter (STED)
LOS.............	Low Output Syndrome (MAE)
LOS.............	Lunar Orbiting Satellite [*or Spacecraft*] [*Aerospace*] (MCD)
LOS.............	Midwestern Baptist Theological Seminary, Kansas City, MO [*OCLC symbol*] (OCLC)
LOS-AD......	Line-of-Sight - Air Defense [*DoD*]
LOSAM........	Low-Altitude Surface-to-Air Missiles (NATG)
Los Angeles BAB...	Los Angeles Bar Association. Bulletin [*A publication*] (DLA)
Los Angeles L Rev...	Los Angeles Law Review [*A publication*] (DLA)
LOSARP.......	Line-of-Sight - Repeater Placement Program (IAA)
LOSAT........	Language-Oriented System Analysis Table (IAA)
LOS-AT.......	Line-of-Sight - Antitank [*DoD*]
LOSC	Laboratory Operations Support Center [*NASA*] (SSD)
LOSC	Law of the Sea Conference [*United Nations*] (MSC)
LOSC	Law of the Sea Convention [*Australia*]
LOSC	Local On-Scene Commander [*Military*] (DNAB)
LOSD	League of St. Dymphna (EA)
LOSE...........	Let Others Share Equally [*Slogan opposing President Gerald R. Ford's anti-inflation WIN campaign*]
LOSE...........	Let's Omit Superfluous Expenses [*Slogan opposing President Gerald R. Ford's anti-inflation WIN campaign*]
LOSE...........	Line-of-Sight Expendables (DNAB)
LOS-F	Line-of-Sight - Forward [*DoD*]
LOS-FH	Line-of-Sight - Forward Heavy [*DoD*]
LOS-FL	Line of Sight-Forward Light [*DoD*]
LOSIS	Law of the Sea Information System (GNE)
LOSL...........	Saint Landry Parish Library, Opelousas, LA [*Library symbol Library of Congress*] (LCLS)
LOSM..........	Launch Operations Simulation Model
LOS of NA ...	Ladies Oriental Shrine of North America (EA)
LOSOS	Local Oxidation of Silicon on Sapphire [*Transistor technology*] (IAA)
LOSP	Loss of Offsite Power [*Nuclear energy*] (NRCH)
LOSP	Loss of System Pressure [*Nuclear energy*] (NRCH)
LOS(P).......	Lower O-Esophageal Sphincter Pressure [*Medicine*] (DMAA)
LOSP	Lower (O)Esophageal Sphincter Pressure (STED)
LOSR	Limit of Stack Register
LOSR	Line-of-Sight Rate (MCD)
LOS-R	Line-of-Sight - Rear [*DoD*]
LOSREP	Loss Report [*Aircrew/aircraft*]
LOSS	Landing Observer Signal System (MSA)
LOSS	LAPS Observing System Simulation (USDC)
LOSS	LAPS [*Local Analysis and Prediction System*] Observing System Stimulation [*Marine science*] (OSRA)
LOSS	Large Object Salvage System [*Navy*]
LOSS	Lunar Orbital Survey System [*NASA*] (KSC)
LOSS	Lunar Orbit Space Station [*NASA*]
Loss & Dam Rev...	Loss and Damage Review [*A publication*] (DLA)
Loss Sec Reg...	Loss' Security Regulations [*A publication*] (DLA)
LOSSYS	Landing Observer Signal System
LOST...........	Law of the Sea Treaty (MCD)
LOST...........	Linear One-Step Transition [*Mathematical model for social grouping*]
LOST...........	Lommel and Steinkopf [*German name for mustard gas, taken from two of the chemists who helped develop it as a chemical warfare agent*]
LOST...........	Lube Oil Storage Tank (NRCH)
LOST/A	Vessels Lost by Accident, Collision, or Similar Methods [*Navy*]
LOST/E........	Vessels Lost through Enemy Action [*Navy*]
LOSTF.........	Line-of-Sight Test Fixture
LOSTFC.......	Line-of-Sight Task Force Communications [*Military*] (CAAL)
LOSTFCS	Line-of-Sight Task Force Communications System [*Military*]
LOST/P	Vessels Lost Due to Weather, Perils of the Sea, or Similar Reasons [*Navy*]
LOSTW	Lostwithiel [*Municipal borough in England*]
LOT.............	Laminated Overlay Transistor [*Electronics*] (IAA)
LOT.............	Lapped Orthogonal Transform [*Telecommunications*]
LOT.............	Large Orbiting Telescope (MCD)
LOT.............	Lateral Olfactory Tract
LOT.............	Leak-Off Test
LOT.............	Left Occipitotransverse [*A fetal position*] [*Obstetrics*]
LOT.............	Left Outer Thigh [*Injection site*]
LOT.............	Lengthened Off Time (STED)
LOT.............	Letter of Transmittal (MCD)
LOT.............	Life of Type (AFIT)
LOT.............	Lift-Off Time [*Aerospace*] (MCD)
LOT.............	Light-Off Temperature [*For steady-state combustion*]
LOT.............	Light-Off Time [*Exhaust emissions*] [*Automotive engineering*]
LOT.............	Light Operated Typewriter
LOT.............	Limited Operational Test
LOT.............	Linear Optical Trajectory [*Vision*]
LOT.............	List on Tape (IAA)
LOT.............	Load on Top [*Oil tankers*]
LOT.............	Lock on Track
LOT.............	Lodestar Energy, Inc. [*Vancouver Stock Exchange symbol*]
Lot.............	Lotarius Rosario de Cremona [*Deceased, 1227*] [*Authority cited in pre-1607 legal work*] (DSA)
LOT.............	Lotio [*Lotion*] [*Pharmacy*]
lot.............	Lotion (STED)
LOT.............	Lotru [*Romania*] [*Seismograph station code, US Geological Survey*] (SEIS)
LOT.............	Lower Outer Tube
LOT.............	Low-Observable Technology (MCD)
LOT.............	Polskie Linie Lotnicze [*Poland*] [*ICAO designator*] (FAAC)
LOT.............	Romeoville, IL [*Location identifier FAA*] (FAAL)
LOTA..........	Loss of Target Accident [*Environmental science*] (COE)
LOTADS	Long-Term Worldwide Air Defense Study [*Army*] (AABC)
LOTAS........	Large Optical Tracker - Aerospace
LOTAWS	LASER Obstacle Terrain Avoidance Warning System
LOTC..........	London Over-the-Counter Market [*Information service or system*] (IID)
LOTCA	Loewenstein Occupational Therapy Cognitive Assessment [*Test*] (TMMY)
LOTCIP	Long-Term Communications Improvement Plan (NATG)
LOTE..........	Languages Other than English
LOTE..........	Lesser of Two Evils [*Politics*]
LOTH R.......	Lotharian Regiment [*Military British*] (ROG)
LOTIS.........	Logical Structure: The Timing and the Sequencing of Synchronous/Asynchronous Machines [*Computer science*] (CSR)
LOTIS.........	Logical Timing Sequencing (NITA)
LOTMP........	Lowest Temperature [*NWS*] (FAAC)
LO-TO........	Longitudinal-Optic-Transverse-Optic [*Spectral characteristic*]
LOTO	Lottery Enterprises [*NASDAQ symbol*] (TTSB)
LOTON	Long Tons Discharged or Loaded
LOTOS	Language of Temporal Ordering of Specifications [*Computer science*]
LOTR	[*The*] Lord of the Rings [*A trilogy*]
LOTS	Large Overland Transporter System (MCD)
LOTS	Launch Operations Television System
LOTS	Launch Optical Trajectory System [*NASA*] (IAA)
LOTS	LEM [*Lunar Excursion Module*] Optical Tracking System [*NASA*] (KSC)
LOTS	Lighter, Over-the-Shore [*Missions*] [*For air-cushion vehicles*] (RDA)
LOTS	Load over the Side
LOTS	Logistics over the Shore [*Military*]
LOTS	LORAN Operational Training School
LOTSS	Low Overhead Time-Sharing System (CIST)
LOTSS	Libraries of the Social Sciences [*Australia An association*]
LotteryE......	Lottery Enterprises, Inc. [*Associated Press*] (SAG)
LottoW........	Lotto World, Inc. [*Associated Press*] (SAG)
LOTUS........	Long-Term Upper Ocean Study
LOTV..........	Launch Operations and Test Vehicle [*NASA*] (KSC)
LOTW.........	Loaded on Trailers or Wagons [*Freight*]
LOU............	Letter of Understanding [*Nuclear energy*] (NRCH)
LOU............	Letters of Undertaking [*RSPA*] (TAG)
LOU............	Line Output Unit [*Printing*] (DGA)
LOU............	Linomatic Operating Unit [*Printing*] (DGA)
LOU............	Louisiana
LOU............	Louisville, KY [*Location identifier FAA*] (FAAL)
Lou............	Louth [*County in Ireland*] (WGA)
LouG	Louisville Gas & Electric Co. [*Associated Press*] (SAG)
LouG 5.......	Louisville Gas & Electric Co. [*Associated Press*] (SAG)
LOUH.........	Light Observation Utility Helicopter (NATG)
LOUISA.......	Lunar Optical-UVIR [*Ultraviolet Infrared*] Synthesis Array [*NASA*]
Louisiana Ann...	Louisiana Annual Reports [*A publication*] (DLA)
Louisiana Ann Rep...	Louisiana Annual Reports [*A publication*] (DLA)
Louisiana Rep...	Louisiana Reports [*A publication*] (DLA)
Louis Rep...	Louisiana Reports [*A publication*] (DLA)
Lou Leg N ...	Louisiana Legal News [*A publication*] (DLA)
Lou LJ ...	Louisiana Law Journal [*New Orleans*] [*A publication*] (DLA)
Lou L Jour...	Louisiana Law Journal [*A publication*] (DLA)
LOUO.........	Limited Official Use Only [*Military*]
Lou R.........	Louisiana Reports [*A publication*] (DLA)
Lou Rep NS...	Martin's Louisiana Reports, New Series [*A publication*] (DLA)
Lou Reps...	Louisiana Reports [*A publication*] (DLA)
LOV............	Large Opaque Vesicle [*Medicine*] (DMAA)
LOV............	Limit of Visibility
LOV............	London Flight Centre (Stansted) Ltd. [*British ICAO designator*] (FAAC)
LOV............	Loss of Vehicle (KSC)
LOV............	Loss of Visibility (NASA)
LOV............	Loss of Vision (DAVI)
LOV............	Lovo [*Sweden*] [*Geomagnetic observatory code*]
LOV............	Low-Observable Vehicle [*Military*] (MUSM)
LOV............	Monclova [*Mexico*] [*Airport symbol*] (AD)
LOV............	Societe Miniere Louvem, Inc. [*Toronto Stock Exchange symbol*]
LOVA	Low Vulnerability Ammunition [*Military*] (RDA)
Lov Arb	Lovesy on Arbitration [*1867*] [*A publication*] (DLA)
LOVE..........	Language Organization Voicing Esperanto
LOVE..........	Linguistics of Visual English [*Sign language system for the hearing impaired*]
Love Bank ...	Lovesy's Bankruptcy Act [*1869, 1870*] [*A publication*] (DLA)
LOVER........	Lunar Orbiting Vehicle for Emergency Rescue (PDAA)
LOVISIM	Low-Visibility Landing Simulation [*Program*] [*Air Force*]
LOVL..........	Laugh Out Very Loud [*Internet language*] [*Computer science*]
LOVV	Wien [*Austria ICAO location identifier*] (ICLI)

LOW............	Launch on Warning [*Missiles*]
LOW............	Laws of War (MCD)
LOW............	Link Orderwire Project
LOW............	Loners on Wheels (EA)
LOW............	Low Core Threshold (NITA)
Low............	Lowell's District Court Reports [*United States, Massachusetts District*] [*A publication*] (DLA)
low............	Lower (VRA)
LOW............	Lowe's Companies, Inc. [*NYSE symbol*] (SPSG)
LOW............	Lowe's Cos. [*NYSE symbol*] (TTSB)
LOW............	West Yellowstone, MT [*Location identifier FAA*] (FAAL)
LOWBI........	Low-Birth-Weight Infant [*Obstetrics*]
Low Can......	Lower Canada Reports [*A publication*] (DLA)
Low Can Jur...	Lower Canada Jurist [*A publication*] (DLA)
Low Can Jurist...	Lower Canada Jurist [*A publication*] (DLA)
Low Can LJ...	Lower Canada Law Journal [*A publication*] (DLA)
Low Can R...	Lower Canada Reports [*A publication*] (DLA)
Low Can Rep...	Lower Canada Reports [*A publication*] (DLA)
Low Can Rep SQ...	Lower Canada Seignorial Questions Reports [*A publication*] (DLA)
Low C Seign...	Lower Canada Seignorial Questions Reports [*A publication*] (DLA)
Low Dec (F).	Lowell's Decisions [*A publication*] (DLA)
Low Dis.......	Lowell's District Court Reports [*United States, Massachusetts District*] [*A publication*] (DLA)
Low-E.........	Low-Elevation (CAAL)
LOW-E........	Low-Emissivity [*Glass*]
Lowell.........	Lowell's District Court Reports [*United States, Massachusetts District*] [*A publication*] (DLA)
Lower Can Jur...	Lower Canada Jurist [*A publication*] (DLA)
Lower Can SQ...	Lower Canada Seignorial Questions Reports [*A publication*] (DLA)
Lower Ct Dec...	Ohio Lower Court Decisions [*A publication*] (DLA)
Lowes.........	Lowe's Companies, Inc. [*Associated Press*] (SAG)
LOWESS......	Locally-Weighted Scatterplot Smoother [*Medicine*]
LOWFAR......	Low-Frequency Analysis and Recording (MCD)
LOWG.........	Graz [*Austria ICAO location identifier*] (ICLI)
LOWG.........	Landing Operations Working Group [*NASA*] (NASA)
LOWI.........	Innsbruck [*Austria ICAO location identifier*] (ICLI)
LOWK.........	Klagenfurt [*Austria ICAO location identifier*] (ICLI)
LOWL.........	Linz [*Austria ICAO location identifier*] (ICLI)
LOWL.........	Low-Level Language [*Computer programming*]
LOWM.........	Wien [*Austria ICAO location identifier*] (ICLI)
Lown & M...	Lowndes and Maxwell's English Bail Court Reports [*1852-54*] [*A publication*] (DLA)
Lownd & M...	Lowndes and Maxwell's English Bail Court Reports [*1852-54*] [*A publication*] (DLA)
Lownd Av.....	Lowndes' General Average [*10th ed.*] [*1975*] [*A publication*] (DLA)
Lownd Col ...	Lowndes on Collisions at Sea [*A publication*] (DLA)
Lownd Cop...	Lowndes on Copyright [*A publication*] (DLA)
Lowndes & M...	Lowndes and Maxwell's English Bail Court Reports [*1852-54*] [*A publication*] (DLA)
Lowndes & M (Eng)...	Lowndes and Maxwell's English Bail Court Reports [*1852-54*] [*A publication*] (DLA)
Lowndes M & P...	Lowndes, Maxwell, and Pollock's English Bail Court Reports [*1850-51*] [*A publication*] (DLA)
Lownd Ins....	Lowndes on Insurance [*A publication*] (DLA)
Lownd Leg...	Lowndes on Legacies [*A publication*] (DLA)
Lownd M & P...	Lowndes, Maxwell, and Pollock's English Bail Court Reports [*1850-51*] [*A publication*] (DLA)
LownInST	P. W. Lown Institute. Brandeis University. Studies and Texts (BJA)
Lown Leg......	Lowndes on Legacies [*A publication*] (DLA)
Lown M & P...	Lowndes, Maxwell, and Pollock's English Bail Court Reports [*1850-51*] [*A publication*] (DLA)
Low Pr Code...	Lower Provinces Code [*India*] [*A publication*] (DLA)
LOWR.........	Lower
Lowranc......	Lowrance Electronics, Inc. [*Associated Press*] (SAG)
LOWS.........	Salzburg [*Austria ICAO location identifier*] (ICLI)
LOWW........	Wien/Schwechat [*Austria ICAO location identifier*] (ICLI)
LOWZ.........	Zell Am See [*Austria ICAO location identifier*] (ICLI)
LOX...........	Lipoxygenase [*An enzyme*]
LOX...........	Liquid Oxygen [*Also, LO_2*]
lox	Liquid Oxygen (STED)
LOX...........	Liquid Oxygen Expert System (NITA)
LO-X	Low Thermal Expansion [*Synthetic ceramic*]
LOXA	Aigen/Ennstal [*Austria ICAO location identifier*] (ICLI)
LOXAT	Lowest Temperature Exceeded for All Time [*NWS*] (FAAC)
LOXFM.......	Lowest Temperature Exceeded for the Month [*NWS*] (FAAC)
LOXG	Graz [*Austria ICAO location identifier*] (ICLI)
LOXK.........	Klagenfurt [*Austria ICAO location identifier*] (ICLI)
LOXL.........	Horsching [*Austria ICAO location identifier*] (ICLI)
LOX/LH	Liquid Oxygen and Liquid Hydrogen
LOXN.........	Wiener Neustadt [*Austria ICAO location identifier*] (ICLI)
Lox-PLD.....	Loxoseles reclusus - Phospholipase D [*An enzyme*]
LOXS.........	Schwaz, Tirol [*Austria ICAO location identifier*] (ICLI)
LOXSE.......	Lowest Temperature Exceeded So Early [*NWS*] (FAAC)
LOXSL.......	lowest Temperature Exceeded So Late [*NWS*] (FAAC)
LOXT.........	Langenlebarn [*Austria ICAO location identifier*] (ICLI)
LOXT.........	Large Orbital X-Ray Telescope [*NASA*]
LOXZ.........	Zeltweg [*Austria ICAO location identifier*] (ICLI)
LOY...........	Loyalty (AABC)
LOY...........	Loyola - Notre Dame Library, Inc., Baltimore, MD [*OCLC symbol*] (OCLC)
LOYC	Loyola Capital [*NASDAQ symbol*] (SAG)
Loy Con Prot J...	Loyola Consumer Protection Journal [*Los Angeles*] [*A publication*] (DLA)
Loy Dig........	Loyola Digest [*A publication*] (DLA)
Loy Law......	Loyola Lawyer [*A publication*] (DLA)
Loy LJ	Loyola Law Journal [*New Orleans*] [*1920-32*] [*A publication*] (DLA)
Loyola	Loyola Capital Corp. [*Associated Press*] (SAG)
Loyola C (Md)...	Loyola College (Maryland) (GAGS)
Loyola Dig...	Loyola Digest [*A publication*] (DLA)
Loyola LJ....	Loyola Law Journal [*A publication*] (DLA)
Loyola Marymount U...	Loyola Marymount University (Los Angeles) (GAGS)
Loyola U Chicago...	Loyola University of Chicago (GAGS)
Loyola U (La)...	Loyola University (Louisiana) (GAGS)
Loyola ULJ (Chicago)...	Loyola University. Law Review (Chicago) [*A publication*] (DLA)
Loyola Univ L Rev...	Loyola University. Law Review [*Chicago*] [*A publication*] (DLA)
LOZ...........	Liquid Ozone
LOZ...........	London [*Kentucky*] [*Airport symbol*] (OAG)
LOZ...........	Lovozero [*Former USSR Geomagnetic observatory code*]
LOZ...........	Lozenge [*Pharmacy*] (DAVI)
LP	Air Alpes [*ICAO designator*] (AD)
LP	Labile Peptide (DB)
LP	Labile Protein (DB)
LP	Laboratory Procedure
LP	Labour Party of South Africa [*Political party*] (PPW)
L/P	Lactate/Pyruvate [*Ratio*]
LP	Lactoperoxidase (DB)
LP	Ladyship [*or Lordship*]
LP	Laminated Polyethylene Film
LP	Lamp [*Automotive engineering*]
LP	Landing Point [*British military*] (DMA)
LP	Land Plane
LP	Large-Paper Edition [*of a book*]
LP	Large Particle
LP	Large Post
LP	Laryngeal Pharyngeal [*Medicine*]
LP	Last Paid [*Military*]
LP	Last Performance
LP	Last Post (WDAA)
LP	Latent Period [*Physiology*]
LP	Lateral Pyloric [*Neuron*]
LP	Launching Platoon [*Army*]
LP	Launch Pad (KSC)
LP	Launch Panel
LP	Launch Platform
LP	Laureate of Philosophy
LP	Law Pamphlet (ROG)
LP	Lay Preacher
LP	Leadership Project [*Defunct*] (EA)
LP	Leaf Protein [*Food industry*]
LP	Leathery Pocket [*of pineapple*]
LP	Lecturer Practitioner (WDAA)
LP	Left Pectoral Fin [*Fish anatomy*]
LP	Left Traffic Pattern [*Aviation*] (FAAC)
LP	Legal Process [*British*]
LP	Legal Procurator (WDAA)
LP	Legislative Proposal (GFGA)
LP	Lempira [*Monetary unit*] [*Honduras*]
LP	Lesson Plan
LP	Lettering Piece (ROG)
L/P	Letterpress (ADA)
LP	Letters Patent (ROG)
LP	Leucine Aminopeptidase [*Also, LA, LAP*] [*An enzyme*]
LP	Leucocyte Pyrogen [*Immunology*]
LP	Leukocyte-Poor [*Hematology*]
LP	Liability Policy [*Information service or system*] (DOAD)
LP	Liberal Party [*Canada*] (PPW)
LP	Liberator Party [*Guyana*] [*Political party*] (PPW)
LP	Libertarian Party (EA)
LP	Library of Parliament [*Canada*]
LP	Library of Philosophy [*A publication*]
L/P	Life Policy [*Insurance*]
LP	Lighting Panel (IAA)
LP	Light Pen
LP	Light Perception [*Ophthalmology*]
LP	Lightproof [*Technical drawings*]
LP	Light Pulse [*Embryology*]
LP	Limited Partnership
LP	Limited Planning (MCD)
LP	Limited Procurement
LP	Limited Production (AABC)
LP	Limited Proprietorship [*Business term*]
LP	Limit of Proportionality [*Mechanics*] (IAA)
LP	Limp [*Binding*] [*Publishing*]
LP	Linear Phase
LP	Linear Polarization
LP	Linear Prediction [*Computer science*]
LP	Linear Programming [*Computer science*]
LP	Linear Programming Language (NITA)
LP	Linen Press (ADA)
lp	Line Pair [*Philately*]
LP	Line Pressure
LP	Line Printer [*Computer science*]
LP	Linguistic Problems
LP	Linguopulpal [*Dentistry*]
LP	Linker Polypeptide [*Biochemistry*]
LP	Linkport [*Electronics*] (ECII)
LP	Link Printer (ACRL)

Lp	Lipoprotein [*Biochemistry*]
LP	Liquefied Petroleum [*Gas*]
LP	Liquidity Preference [*Economics*]
LP	Liquid Phase [*Chemistry*]
LP	Liquid Propellant
LP	Listening Post
LP	List of Publications [*National Institute of Standards and Technology*]
LP	List Price (BARN)
LP	List Processor [*Standard programming language*] [*1958*] [*Computer science*] (BUR)
LP	Lists of Parts (NATG)
LP	Litter Patient
LP	Livens Projector [*Military*]
LP	Liver Protein [*Medicine*]
LP	Liver to Plasma Concentration Ratio (MAE)
LP	Load Point (BUR)
LP	Local-Pair [*Superconductivity*]
LP	Local Pastors [*British*]
LP	Local Primary (OTD)
LP	Local Procurement [*Military*]
LP	Local Purchase (AFM)
LP	Locating Point [*Optical tooling*]
LP	Lodge-Pole Pine [*Utility pole*] [*Telecommunications*] (TEL)
LP	Loewenthal Papers [*Shanghai/Washington, DC*] [*A publication*] (BJA)
LP	Logic Probe
LP	Log Periodic [*Antenna*] (NATG)
LP	Lollipop Power [*An association*] (EA)
LP	London Particular [*Marsala*]
LP	Longest Path
LP	Longest Perpendicular [*IOR*] [*Yacht racing*]
LP	Longitudinal Parity [*Telecommunications*] (TEL)
LP	Long-Pass [*Absorption cell*]
LP	Long Period
LP	Long Persistence
LP	Long Picot
LP	Long Play [*VHS recorder mode*] (NTCM)
LP	Long Playing [*Phonograph record*]
LP	Long Position [*Investment term*]
LP	Long Primer
LP	Long Provost
LP	Loop [*Knitting*]
LP	Lord President of the Court of Session, Scotland (DLA)
LP	Lord Provost [*British*]
LP	Lorentz-Polarization [*Optics*]
LP	Losing Pitcher [*Baseball*]
LP	Loss of Pay [*Court-martial sentence*] [*Marine Corps*]
LP	Lost Planes [*An association*] (EA)
LP	Love Project (EA)
LP	Lower Panel (IAA)
LP	Lower Peninsula [*Michigan*]
LP	Low Pass [*Electronics*]
LP	Low Performance
LP	Low Point
LP	Low Potency (DB)
LP	Low Power [*Microscopy*]
LP	Low Pressure
LP	Low-Pressure Cylinder [*Especially, a locomotive cylinder*]
LP	Low Primary (IAA)
LP	Low Protein [*Nutrition*]
LP	Lumbar-Peritoneal [*Shunt*] (DAVI)
LP	Lumbar Puncture [*Medicine*]
LP	Lumboperitoneal (DB)
LP	Lunar and Planetary [*Aerospace*] (IAA)
LP	Lunar Prospector [*NASA*]
LP	Luster Paper [*Photography*] (DGA)
L/P	Lymphocyte to Polymorph Ratio [*Hematology*]
LP	Lymphoid Plasma [*Hematology*] (MAE)
LP	Lymphoid Predominance [*Medicine*] (AAMN)
L/P	Lymph-Plasma [*Ratio*] [*Laboratory science*] (DAVI)
LP	Lymph-Plasma Ratio [*Hematology*] (MAE)
LP	Lythway Press [*British*]
LP	Popular Concerts [*Public-performance tariff class*] [*British*]
LP-28	Ligas Populares de 28 de Febrero [*February 28 Popular Leagues*] [*El Salvador*] (PD)
LPA	Amphibious Transport [*Navy ship symbol*]
LPA	Laboratory Products Association (NTPA)
LPA	Labor Policy Association (EA)
LPA	La Plata [*Argentina*] [*Seismograph station code, US Geological Survey*] (SEIS)
LPA	LASER Printer Adapter
LPA	Las Palmas [*Canary Islands*] [*Airport symbol*] (OAG)
LPA	Latex Particle Agglutination [*Immunochemistry*] (DAVI)
LPA	Latvian Privatization Agency
LPA	Launcher Plant Assembly (IAA)
LPA	Launch Phase Analyst
LPA	Lauric [*or Lauroyl or Lauryl*] Isopropanolamide [*Also, LIPA*] [*Organic chemistry*]
LPA	Leaky Pipe Antenna
LPA	Leather Producers' Association for England, Scotland, and Wales (BI)
LPA	Left Pulmonary Artery [*Anatomy*]
LPA	Light Pulser Array
LPA	Limited Period Appointment [*Short-term employment*] [*British*]
LPA	Limited Purpose Agency (OICC)
LPA	Linear Power Amplifier

LPA	Link Pack Area [*Computer science*] (MCD)
LpA	Lipoprotein A [*Biochemistry*]
LPA	Liquid Propellant Analysis
LPA	Literature Primers [*A publication*]
LPA	Lithium Perchlorate Ammoniate [*Inorganic chemistry*]
LPA	Little People of America (EA)
LPA	Loan Production Office (EBF)
LPA	Local Pay Authority (AIE)
LPA	Local Planning Assistance (OICC)
LPA	Local Planning Authority [*British*] (DCTA)
LPA	Local Processing Agency [*Department of Housing and Urban Development*] (GFGA)
LPA	Local Public Agency
LPA	Logarithmic Periodic Antenna (MCD)
LPA	Logistics Pipeline Analysis [*Military*] (MCD)
LPA	Log Periodic Antenna
LPA	London Academy of Performing Arts [*England*] (WDAA)
LPA	Louisiana Pharmacists Association (SRA)
LPA	Louisiana Press Association (SRA)
LPA	Louisiana Psychological Association (SRA)
LPA	Low-Power Amplifier (CET)
LPA	Low-Pressure Alarm (IEEE)
LPA	Lysophosphatidic Acid [*Biochemistry*]
LPA	PAL Aerolineas SA de CV [*Mexico ICAO designator*] (FAAC)
LPAA	League of Pace Amendment Advocates (EA)
LPAAT	Log Periodic Array Antenna
LPAAT	Lysophosphatidic Acid Acyltransferase [*An enzyme*]
LPAB	Legal Practitioners' Admission Board [*Australia*]
LPAC	Labor Policy Advisory Committee for Multilateral Trade Negotiations [*Terminated, 1980*] (EGAO)
LPAC	Laser Pacific Media Corp. [*NASDAQ symbol*] (SAG)
LPAC	Laser-pac Media [*NASDAQ symbol*] (TTSB)
LPAC	Libertarian Party Abolitionist Caucus (EA)
LPAI	Ligue Populaire Africaine pour l'Independance [*African People's League for Independence*] [*Djibouti*]
LPAM	Lisboa [*Portugal ICAO location identifier*] (ICLI)
L-PAM	L-Phenylalanine Mustard [*Melphalan*] [*Also, A, M, MPH, MPL*] [*Antineoplastic drug*]
L-PAM	L-Phenylalanin, Procarbazine, Adriamycin, Methotrexate [*Antineoplastic drug regimen*]
LP & KTF	London Printing and Kindred Trades Federation (DGA)
LP & M	Liverpool Post and Mercury [*A publication*] (ROG)
LP & P	Logistics Policy and Procedures for Contingency Operations [*DARCOM*] (CINC)
LPAR	Alverca [*Portugal ICAO location identifier*] (ICLI)
LPAR	Large Phased-Array RADAR
LPAR	Logical Partition [*Computer science*] (CIST)
LPARM	Liquid Propellant Applied Research Motor
LPAS	Luciano Pavarotti Appreciation Society [*British*] (DBA)
LPASA	Linear Pulse-Height Analyzer Spectrum Analysis (PDAA)
L/PAT	Legislative/Political Action Team
L/PAT	Letters Patent (ROG)
LPATS	Lightning Position and Tracing System (MCD)
LPAV	Aveiro [*Portugal ICAO location identifier*] (ICLI)
LPAZ	Santa Maria, Santa Maria Island [*Portugal ICAO location identifier*] (ICLI)
LPB	La Paz [*Bolivia*] [*Airport symbol*] (OAG)
LPB	La Paz [*Bolivia*] [*Seismograph station code, US Geological Survey*] (SEIS)
LPB	Lighted Pushbutton (ECII)
LpB	Lipoprotein B [*Biochemistry*]
LPB	Lithium Polymer Battery
LPB	Loan Policy Board [*of SBA*] [*Abolished, 1965*]
LPB	Lollipop Power Books (EA)
LPB	[*The*] Louisiana & Pine Bluff Railway Co. [*AAR code*]
LPB	Low-Level Penetration Bomb
LPB	Low-Probability Behavior
LPB	Lunar and Planetary Bibliography [*Lunar and Planetary Institute*] [*Information service or system*] (IID)
LPB	Paper Book of Laurence, J., in Lincoln's Inn Library [*A publication*] (DLA)
LPBA	Lawyer-Pilots Bar Association (EA)
LPBBA	Log Periodic Broadband Antenna
LPBE	Beja [*Portugal ICAO location identifier*] (ICLI)
LPBE	Linear Poisson-Boltzmann Equation [*Physical chemistry*]
LPBG	Braganca [*Portugal ICAO location identifier*] (ICLI)
LPBJ	Beja [*Portugal ICAO location identifier*] (ICLI)
LPBP	Low-Profile Bioprosthesis [*Medicine*] (DMAA)
LPBR	Braga [*Portugal ICAO location identifier*] (ICLI)
LPBT	Ladies Professional Bowlers Tour (EA)
LPC	Laboratory Precision Connector (IAA)
LPC	Laboratory Pulse Compression
LPC	La Cumbre Peak [*California*] [*Seismograph station code, US Geological Survey*] (SEIS)
LPC	Lamina Precursor Cell [*Neurology*]
LPC	Landmarks Preservation Commission [*New York City*]
LPC	Land Protection Council [*Victoria, Australia*]
LPC	LASER Particle Counter (AAEL)
LPC	Laser Photocoagulation [*Ophthalmology*] (DAVI)
LPC	Late Positive Component (MAE)
LPC	Launch Pod Container [*General Support Rocket System*] (MCD)
LPC	Laurylpyridinium Chloride [*Also, DPC*] [*Organic chemistry*]
LPC	Leader Preparation Course
LPC	Leaf Protein Concentrate [*Food industry*]
LPC	League of Professional Craftsmen [*British*] (DBA)

LPC	Least-Preferred Co-Worker [*Management term*]
LPC	Leather Personnel Carriers [*i.e., boots*] [*Slang Army*]
LPC	Less Prosperous Country
LPC	Leukocyte Particle Counter [*Instrumentation*]
LPC	Licensed Professional Counselor
LPC	Lieberman Plasma Cell (DB)
LPC	Light Patrol Car [*British*]
LPC	Linear Power Controller
LPC	Linear Prediction Code
LPC	Linear Predictive Coding [*Digital coding technique*] [*Telecommunications*]
LPC	Linkport Controller [*Electronics*] (ECII)
LPC	Link Priority Change [*NASA*] (KSC)
LPC	Lipocortin (DMAA)
LpC	Lipoprotein C [*Biochemistry*]
LPC	Livestock Publications Council (EA)
LPC	Lockheed Propulsion Co. [*Division of Lockheed Aircraft Corp.*] (KSC)
LPC	Lompoc, CA [*Location identifier FAA*] (FAAL)
LPC	Longitudinal Parity Check [*Telecommunications*] (IAA)
LPC	Longitudinal Primary Care [*Medicine*] (DMAA)
LPC	Loop-Control [*Relay*] (IEEE)
LPC	Loop Preparation Cask [*Nuclear energy*] (NRCH)
LPC	Lord President's Committee [*British*]
LPC	Lords of the Privy Council Lower Provinces Code [*India*] [*A publication*] (DLA)
LPC	Lottery Promotion Co. [*British*] (ECON)
LPC	Lower Pump Cubicle (IEEE)
LPC	Low-Power Channel (IAA)
LPC	Low-Power Counter
LPC	Low-Pressure Chamber Technician [*Navy*]
LPC	Low-Pressure Composite
LPC	Low-Pressure Compressor
LPC	Lumped-Parameter Calorimeter [*Heat measure*]
LPC	Lysophosphatidylcholine [*Also, Lyso-PC*] [*Biochemistry*]
LPCA	Louisiana Pest Control Association (SRA)
LPCA	Louisiana Primary Care Association (SRA)
LPCA	Lunar Pyrotechnic Control Assembly [*Aerospace*]
LPCAT	Laboratory for Pest Control Application Technology [*Ohio State University*] [*Research center*] (RCD)
LPCC	Legal Practitioners Complaints Committee [*South Australia*]
LPCC	Low-Pressure Combustion Chamber
LPCG	LASER Planning and Coordination Group [*Energy Research and Development Administration*]
LPCH	Chaves [*Portugal ICAO location identifier*] (ICLI)
LPCH	Local Process Control Host (IAA)
LPCI	Low-Pressure Coolant Injection [*Nuclear energy*] (NRCH)
LPCIS	Low-Pressure Coolant Injection System [*Nuclear energy*] (NRCH)
LPCL	Laboratory Pulse Compression Loop
LPCM	Linear Phase Code Modulation
LPCM	Linear Pulse-Code Modulation [*Computer science*]
LPCM	Low Placed Conus Medullaris [*Medicine*] (DMAA)
LPCO	Coimbra [*Portugal ICAO location identifier*] (ICLI)
LPCO	Low-Pressure Cut-Off [*Air conditioning system*] [*Automotive engineering*]
LPCP	Launcher Preparation Control Panel
LPCR	Low-Pressure Cooling Recirculation Phase [*Environmental science*] (COE)
LPCRS	Low-Pressure Coolant Recirculation System [*Nuclear energy*] (IEEE)
LPCS	Cascais [*Portugal ICAO location identifier*] (ICLI)
LPCS	Laterally to the Pedunculus Cerebellaris Superior [*Medicine*]
LPCS	Local Post Collectors Society (EA)
LPCS	Low-Pressure Core Spray [*Environmental science*] (COE)
LPCS	Low-Pressure Core Spray System [*Nuclear energy*] (NRCH)
LPCT	Late Proximal Cortical Tubule (DB)
LPCV	Covilha [*Portugal ICAO location identifier*] (ICLI)
LPCVD	Liquid Phase Chemical Vapor Deposition [*Photovoltaic energy systems*]
LPCVD	Liquid Phase Chemical Vapour Deposition (AAEL)
LPCVD	Low-Pressure Chemical Vapor Deposition [*Semiconductor technology*]
LP-CW	Long Pulse - Continuous Wave (NG)
LPD	Amphibious Transport Dock [*Landing Platform, Dock*] [*Navy ship symbol*]
LPD	Labelled Plan Display (PDAA)
LPD	Labour Party of Dominica [*Political party*] (EY)
LPD	Landing Platform, Dock
LPD	Landing Point Designator [*Apollo*] [*NASA*]
LPD	Language Processing and Debugging [*Computer science*] (BUR)
LPD	La Pedrera [*Colombia*] [*Airport symbol*] (OAG)
LPD	Laredo Petroleums [*Vancouver Stock Exchange symbol*]
LPD	LASER Polarization Detector
LPD	LASER Projection Display (AAEL)
LPD	Lateral Photoelectric Detector (PDAA)
LPD	Launch Platform Detected [*Navy*] (CAAL)
LPD	Launch Point Determination
LPD	Launch Procedure Document [*NASA*] (KSC)
LPD	Least Perceptible Difference [*Psychology*]
LPD	Lighting-Power Density
LPD	Light Point Defect (AAEL)
LPD	Linear Phasing Device [*Telecommunications*] (OA)
LPD	Line Printer Daemon (PCM)
LpD	Lipoprotein D [*Biochemistry*]
LPD	Liquid-Protein Diet
LPD	Liters per Day (KSC)
LPD	Local Power Density (NRCH)

LPD	Local Procurement Direct [*Military*]
LPD	Log Periodic Dipole
LPD	Low-Performance Drone
LPD	Low Period Dipole
LPD	Low-Power Difference (IEEE)
LPD	Low-Pressure Difference (IEEE)
LPD	Low Protein Diet
LPD	Luteal Phase Defect [*Gynecology*] (DAVI)
LPD	Lymphoproliferative Disease [*Oncology*]
LPDA	Linear Photodiode Array [*Instrumentation*]
LPDA	Log Periodic Dipole Antenna [*Military*] (CAAL)
LPDA	Log Periodic Dipole Array
LPDC	LASER Plasmadynamic Converter
LPDC	Leonard Peltier Defense Committee (EA)
LPDC	London Parcels Delivery Co.
LPDF	Lipoprotein-Deficient Fraction [*Medicine*] (DMAA)
LpDH	Lysopine Dehydrogenase [*An enzyme*]
LPDM	List of Physical Dimensions (NASA)
LPDR	Lao People's Democratic Republic
LPDR	Local Public Document Room (GFGA)
LPDS	Lipoprotein Deficient Human Serum
LPDT	Legal Practitioners Disciplinary Tribunal [*South Australia*]
LPDT	Low Power Distress Transmitter [*Aviation*] (DA)
LPDTL	Low-Power Diode Transistor Logic [*Electronics*] (IAA)
LPDU	Link Layer Protocol Data Unit [*Telecommunications*] (OSI)
LPE	Launch Preparation Equipment (AABC)
LPE	Layer Primitive Equation (MHDI)
LPE	Lead Piping Engineer
LPE	Limited Paperback Editions
LPE	Linear Parameter Estimation [*Physical chemistry*]
LPE	Linear Polyethylene [*Organic chemistry*]
LPE	Linkport Extension [*Electronics*] (ECII)
LpE	Lipoprotein E [*Biochemistry*]
LPE	Lipoprotein Electrophoresis [*Biochemistry*]
LPE	Liquid Phase Epitaxy [*Magnetic film*]
LPE	London Press Exchange
LPE	Loop Preparation Equipment [*Nuclear energy*] (NRCH)
LPE	Low Probability of Exploitation (PDAA)
LPE	Lunar and Planetary Ephemerides Assembly [*Space Flight Operations Facility, NASA*]
LPE	Lysophosphatidylethanolamine [*Biochemistry*]
LPEA	Luis Palau Evangelistic Association (EA)
LPEC	Launch Preparation Equipment Compartment (AABC)
LPEM	Launch Preparation Equipment Monitor (MCD)
LPEO	Local Public Employment Office
LPerc	Light Perception [*Ophthalmology*]
LPERE	Linear Phase with Equal Ripple Error (IAA)
LPES	Launch Preparation Equipment Set (AABC)
LPEV	Evora [*Portugal ICAO location identifier*] (ICLI)
LPEV	Launch Preparation Equipment Vault (MCD)
LPF	Landsing Pacific Fund [*AMEX symbol*] (CTT)
LPF	Latvian Popular Front [*Political party Defunct*] (EAIO)
LPF	Leach-Precipitate Float (BARN)
LPF	League for Programming Freedom (EA)
LPF	Left Posterior Fascicle [*Anatomy*]
LPF	Le Pertre [*France*] [*Seismograph station code, US Geological Survey*] (SEIS)
LPF	Leukocytosis-Promoting Factor [*Hematology*]
LPF	Leukopenia Factor (STED)
LPF	Life Probability Function
LPF	Light Patrol Frigate (ADA)
LPF	Lipopolysaccharide Factor (STED)
LPF	Liquid Pressure Filter
LPF	Liver Plasma Flow [*Medicine*] (STED)
LPF	Localized Plaque Formation [*Dentistry*] (MAE)
LPF	Logically Passive Function
LPF	Lowest Possible Airfare
LPF	Low-Pass Filter [*Electronics*]
LPF	Low-Power Field [*Microscopy*]
lpf	Low-Power Field (STED)
LPF	Low-Profile Flange
LPF	Lutheran Peace Fellowship (EA)
LPF	Lymphocytosis-Promoting Factor [*Hematology*] (DAVI)
LPF	Pop Festivals [*Public-performance tariff class*] [*British*]
LPFA	Laminated Plastics Fabricators Association [*British*] (BI)
LPFA	London Potato Futures Association [*London Stock Exchange*]
LPFB	Left Posterior Fascicular Block [*Cardiology*]
LPFGEN	Linear Programming File Generator [*Computer science*] (IAA)
LPFL	Flores, Flores Island [*Portugal ICAO location identifier*] (ICLI)
LPFL	Lowpass Filter (MSA)
LPFM	Low-Powered Fan Marker (MSA)
LPFN	Low-Pass-Filtered Noise (STED)
LPFO	London Procurement Field Office
LPFP	Low-Pressure Fuel Pump (KSC)
LPFR	Faro [*Portugal ICAO location identifier*] (ICLI)
LPFR	Liquid Phase Flow Reactor (KSC)
LPFRT	Limited Preliminary Flight Rating Test
LPFS	Low-Pass-Filtered Signal (STED)
LPFSSB	Lone Parents' Family Support Service - Birthright [*Australia*]
LPFT	Low-Pressure Fuel Turbopump
LPFTP	Low-Pressure Fuel Turbopump (NASA)
LPFU	Funchal, Madeira Island [*Portugal ICAO location identifier*] (ICLI)
LPG	Lake Ponask Gold Corp. [*Toronto Stock Exchange symbol*]
LPG	Langage de Programmation et de Gestion [*French computer language*]

LPG............ La Plata [*Argentina*] [*Airport symbol*] (OAG)
LPG............ Lapping [*Electricity*]
LPG............ Last Page Generator (NASA)
LPG............ Launch Preparations Group [*NASA*]
LPG............ Le Parti de la Guadeloupe [*Political party*] (EY)
LPG............ Licentiate of the Physicians Guild [*British*]
LPG............ Life Partners Group [*NYSE symbol*] (TTSB)
LPG............ Life Partners Group, Inc. [*NYSE symbol*] (SPSG)
LPG............ Lipophosphoglycan [*Biochemistry*]
LPG............ Liquefied Petroleum Gas
LPG............ Liquid Propane Gas
LPG............ Liquid Propane-Gas Shutoff [*NFPA pre-fire planning symbol*] (NFPA)
LPG............ Liquid Propellant Gun (NASA)
LPG............ List Program Generator (IAA)
LPG............ Long Path Gas [*Spectroscopy*]
LPG............ Lousy Paying Guest [*Hotel slang*]
LPG............ Low-Pressure Gas (NRCH)
LPGA .... Ladies Professional Golf Association (EA)
LPGA .... Living Plant Growers Association (EA)
LPGA .... Louisiana Pecan Growers' Association (EA)
LPGE.......... LEM [*Lunar Excursion Module*] Partial Guidance Equipment [*NASA*] (KSC)
LPGG .... Liquid Propellant Gas Generator
LPGITA ...... Liquefied Petroleum Gas Industry Technical Association [*British*]
LPGITC .... Liquified Petroleum Gas Industry Technical Committee
LPGL.......... London Pacific Group Ltd. [*NASDAQ symbol*] (SAG)
LPGLY .... London Pacific Grp ADS [*NASDAQ symbol*] (TTSB)
LPGM......... Last Pinedale Glacial Maximum [*Climatology*]
LPGR .... Graciosa, Graciosa Island [*Portugal ICAO location identifier*] (ICLI)
LPGS .... Liquid Pathway Generic Study [*Nuclear energy*] (NRCH)
LPGS .... Liquified Petroleum Gas Report [*American Petroleum Institute*] [*Database*]
LPGTC .... Liquified Petroleum Gas Industry Technical Committee (MCD)
LPH............ Amphibious Assault Ship (Landing Platform, Helicopter) [*Navy symbol*]
LPH............ Assault Hospital Ship [*Navy symbol*] (VNW)
LPH............ Laboratory of Physiological Hygiene [*University of Minnesota*] [*Research center*] (RCD)
LPH............ Landing Personnel Helicopter [*British*] (NATG)
LPh............ Late Phoenician (BJA)
LPH............ Lee Pharmaceuticals [*AMEX symbol*] (SPSG)
LPH............ Left Posterior Hemiblock [*Cardiology*]
LPH............ Legrest Pin Handle
LPh............ Licentiate of Philosophy
LPH............ Lines per Hour [*Printing*]
LPH............ Lipotropic Pituitary Hormone [*Lipotropin*] [*Medicine*] (STED)
LPH............ Lipotropin Hormone [*Endocrinology*]
LPH............ Liters per Hour (KSC)
LPH............ Lochgilphead [*Scotland*] [*Airport symbol*] (OAG)
LPHB .... Left Posterior Hemiblock [*Medicine*] (STED)
LPHB .... Low-Pressure Heating Boiler
LPHLDR ...... Lampholder
LPHR .... Horta, Faial Island [*Portugal ICAO location identifier*] (ICLI)
LPHS .... Lunar and Planetary Horizon Scanner [*Aerospace*]
LPHSW .... Last Pass Heat Sink Welding [*Nuclear energy*] (NUCP)
LPI............ Colorado Springs, CO [*Location identifier FAA*] (FAAL)
LPI............ LASER Peripheral Irridectomy (STED)
LPI............ Latent Photographic Image
LPI............ Launching Position Indicator
LPI............ Leadership Practices Inventory [*Test*] (TMMY)
LPI............ Leaf Plastochron Index [*Botany*]
LPI............ Learning Preference Inventory
LPI............ Left Posterior-Inferior [*Medicine*] (DMAA)
LPI............ Lightning Protection Institute (EA)
LPI............ Linear Partial Information (PDAA)
LPI............ Lines per Inch [*Printing*]
LPI............ Linkoeping [*Sweden*] [*Airport symbol*] (OAG)
LPI............ Linus Pauling Institute of Science and Medicine [*Research center*] (RCD)
LPI............ List per Inch (IAA)
LPI............ Logistics Performance Indicator (PDAA)
LPI............ Lomond Publications, Inc. [*Telecommunications service*] (TSSD)
LPI............ Longitudinally Applied Paper Insulation [*Telecommunications*] (TEL)
LPI............ Long Process of Incus (STED)
LPI............ Louisiana Polytechnic Institute
LPI............ Low-Power Illuminator (NATG)
LPI............ Low-Power Injection [*Nuclear energy*] (NRCH)
LPI............ Low-Power Interrupt (MCD)
LPI............ Low-Pressure Index
LPI............ Low-Pressure Injection [*Nuclear energy*] (NRCH)
LPI............ Low-Pressure Isolation (AAEL)
LPI............ Low Probability of Intercept (NVT)
LPI............ Low Probability of Interest
LPI............ Lunar and Planetary Institute [*University Space Research Association*] [*Research center*] (RCD)
LPI............ Lysinuric Protein Intolerance [*Medicine*] (DMAA)
LPIA.......... Label Printing Industries of America (EA)
LPIA.......... Launch Pad Interface Assembly
LPIA.......... Liquid Propellant Information Agency [*Johns Hopkins Univeristy*]
LPIB.......... Law and Policy in International Business [*ABA*] [*A publication*] (AAGC)
LPIBSS .... Lunar and Planetary Institute Bibliographic Search Service [*University Space Research Association*] [*Information service or system*] (IID)

LPiC............ Central Louisiana State Hospital, Medical Library, Pineville, LA [*Library symbol Library of Congress*] (LCLS)
LPICBM....... Liquid Propellant Intercontinental Ballistic Missile [*Military*] (IAA)
LPID........... Logical Page Identifier (BUR)
LPI/D .... Low Probability of Intercept/Detection [*Environmental science*] (COE)
LPiL........... Louisiana College, Pineville, LA [*Library symbol Library of Congress*] (LCLS)
LPIN.......... Espinho [*Portugal ICAO location identifier*] (ICLI)
LPIR.......... Limited Partnership Investment Review [*Information service or system*] (IID)
LPIR.......... Low-Probability Intercept RADAR
LPIS........... Low-Pressure Injection System [*Nuclear energy*] (NRCH)
LPISM......... Liquid Photo-Imageable Solder Mask [*Electronics*] (AAEL)
LPISS .... Low-Power Illuminator Signal Source (MCD)
LPIU.......... Lithographers and Photoengravers International Union [*Later, Graphic Arts International Union*]
LPIW.......... Lumber, Production, and Industrial Workers (WPI)
LPJF .... Leiria [*Portugal ICAO location identifier*] (ICLI)
LPJO.......... Alijo [*Portugal ICAO location identifier*] (ICLI)
LPK........... Lao Pen Kang [*Laotian Neutralist Party*] (CINC)
LPK........... Liver Pyruvate Kinase [*Medicine*] (DMAA)
LPKCMLPCC... License Plate, Key Chain, and Mini License Plate Collectors Club (EA)
LPL........... Entergy Louisiana, Inc. [*NYSE symbol*] (SAG)
LPL........... Entergy Louisiana, Inc. Capital I [*NYSE symbol*] (SAG)
LPL........... Laborers Political League (EA)
LPL........... Labour Protection League [*A union*] [*British*]
LPL........... Lamina Propria Lymphocyte [*Hematology*]
LPL........... Lamp-Pumped LASER (MCD)
LPL........... LASER-Pumped-LASER
LPL........... Lawton Public Library, Lawton, OK [*OCLC symbol*] (OCLC)
LPL........... Lawyers Professional Liability [*Insurance*]
LPL........... Lease-A-Plane International [*ICAO designator*] (FAAC)
LPL........... Lethbridge Public Library [*UTLAS symbol*]
LPL........... Lichen Planus-Like Lesion [*Medicine*] (DMAA)
LPL........... Lightproof Louver [*Technical drawings*]
LPL........... Linear Programming Language [*Intertechnique*] [*French Computer science*]
LPL........... Lipoprotein Lipase [*An enzyme*]
LPL........... List Processing Language [*Computer science*] (IEEE)
LPL........... Liverpool [*England*] [*Airport symbol*] (OAG)
LPL........... LM [*Lunar Module*] Plan [*NASA*] (KSC)
LPL........... Local Processor Link
LPL........... Long Pulse LASER
LPL........... Louisiana Power & Light Co. [*NYSE symbol*] (SPSG)
LPL........... Low Polar Latitude [*Geophysics*]
LPL........... Low-Power Logic
LPL........... Lunar and Planetary Laboratory [*University of Arizona*] [*Research center*] (MCD)
LPL........... Lunar Projects Laboratory
LPL........... Lysophospholipase [*An enzyme*]
LPLA.......... Lajes, Terceira Island [*Portugal ICAO location identifier*] (ICLI)
LPLA.......... Lao Peoples Liberation Army (CINC)
LPLA.......... Lipoprotein Lipase Activity [*Medicine*] (DMAA)
LPLA.......... Log-Periodic Loop Antenna (PDAA)
LPlaI.......... Iberville Parish Library, Plaquemine, LA [*Library symbol Library of Congress*] (LCLS)
LPLE.......... Leukocyte Pepsin-Like Enzyme (DB)
LPLG.......... Lagos [*Portugal ICAO location identifier*] (ICLI)
LPLG.......... Left Pleural Ganglion [*Medicine*]
LPLIS.......... Lipoprotein Lipase Inactivation System [*Biochemistry*] (DAVI)
LPLM.......... Lowest Planned Level of Maintenance (SAA)
LPLNG .... Low-Pressure Liquefied Natural Gases (NRCH)
LPLPr.......... Entergy Louisiana 12.64% cmPfd [*NYSE symbol*] (TTSB)
LPLPrA........ Entergy Louisiana 9.68% cm Pfd [*NYSE symbol*] (TTSB)
LPLR.......... Lock Pillar (AAG)
LPL?TMC.... Low-Pressure Low-Temperature Molding Compound
LPLWS .... Launch Pad Lightning Warning System [*NASA*] (KSC)
LPM........... Lamap [*Vanuatu*] [*Airport symbol*] (OAG)
LPM........... Lane Photograph Method
LPM........... LASER Particle Monitor (PDAA)
LPM........... LASER Phase Macroscope
LPM........... LASER Precision Microfabrication (IAA)
LPM........... Lateral Pterygoid Muscle (DMAA)
LPM........... Leading Patrolman [*Navy British*] (DI)
lpm........... Letters Per Minute (WDMC)
LPM........... Licensing Project Manager [*Nuclear energy*] (NRCH)
LPM........... Light Pulser Matrix
LPM........... Linearly Polarized Mode [*Telecommunications*] (TEL)
LPM........... Linear Power Module [*Computer science*] (CIST)
LPM........... Lines per Millimeter (WDAA)
LPM........... Lines per Minute [*Computer science*]
lpm........... Lines per Minute (IDOE)
LPM........... Liquid Phase Methanation [*Fuel chemistry*]
lpm........... Liter per Minute (COE)
LPM........... Liters per Minute (MCD)
LPM........... Liver Plasma Membrane
LPM........... Local Processor Memory (IAA)
LPM........... Long Particular [*or Peculiar*] Metre [*Music*]
LPM........... Los Pinos Mountain [*New Mexico*] [*Seismograph station code, US Geological Survey*] (SEIS)
LPM........... Lunar Payload Module [*Aerospace*] (MCD)
LPM........... Lunar Portable Magnetometer [*Apollo*] [*NASA*]
LPMA.......... Lead Pencil Manufacturers Association [*Later, Pencil Makers Association*] (EA)

LPMA............	Loose-Parts-Monitor Assembly [*Nuclear energy*] (NRCH)
LPMAD	Living Personnel Management Authorization Document [*DoD*]
LPMATGEN...	Linear Programming Matrix Generation (IAA)
LPMC............	Low-Pressure Molding Compound
LPMES..........	Logistics Performance Measurement and Evaluation System (AABC)
LPMF.............	Monfortinho [*Portugal ICAO location identifier*] (ICLI)
LPMG............	Lisboa [*Portugal ICAO location identifier*] (ICLI)
LPMI.............	Mirandela [*Portugal ICAO location identifier*] (ICLI)
LPMOSS	Linear Programming Mathematical Optimization Subroutine System (IAA)
LPMR............	Monte Real [*Portugal ICAO location identifier*] (ICLI)
LPM/S...........	Liquid Phase Methanation/Shift Reaction [*Fuel chemistry*]
LPMS............	Lock Performance Monitoring System [*DOD*] [*COE*] (TAG)
LPMS............	Logistics Program Management System [*Air Force*] (AFIT)
LPMS............	Loose-Parts Monitoring System [*Nuclear energy*] (NRCH)
LPMT............	Montijo [*Portugal ICAO location identifier*] (ICLI)
LPN...............	Alpenair GmbH & Co. KG [*Austria ICAO designator*] (FAAC)
LPN...............	Licensed Practical Nurse
LPN...............	Logical Page Number (BUR)
LPN...............	Long Part Number
LPN...............	Longview, Portland & Northern Railway Co. [*AAR code*]
LPN...............	Low-Pass Network [*Electronics*]
LPN...............	National Federation of Licensed Practical Nurses
LPNA............	Lithographers and Printers National Association [*Later, PIA*] (EA)
LPNAF..........	Licensed Practical Nurses Association of Florida (SRA)
LPNGP..........	Low-Pressure Noble Gas Processing (NRCH)
LPO..............	La Porte [*Indiana*] [*Airport symbol*] (OAG)
LPO..............	Laramie Project Office [*Laramie, WY*] [*Department of Energy*] (GRD)
LPO..............	Late Pleistocene Origins [*Ecology*]
LPO..............	Lateral Preoptic [*Brain anatomy*]
LPO..............	Lattice-Preferred Orientation [*Geophysics*]
LPO..............	Lauroyl Peroxide [*Organic chemistry*]
LPO..............	Left Posterio Occipital [*A fetal position*] (DAVI)
LPO..............	Left Posterior Oblique [*Cardiology*] (MAE)
LPO..............	Le Pouchou [*France*] [*Seismograph station code, US Geological Survey*] (SEIS)
LPO..............	Liberale Partei Oesterreichs [*Liberal Party of Austria*] [*Political party*] (PPE)
LPO..............	Liberal Party Organization [*British*]
LPO..............	Light Perception Only [*Ophthalmology*]
LPO..............	Limited Production Option [*Automotive engineering*]
LPO..............	Liquid Phase Oxidation [*Chemical processing*]
LPO..............	Loan Production Office [*Banking*]
LPO..............	Lobus Parolfactorius (PDAA)
LPO..............	Local Purchase Order
LPO..............	London Philharmonic Orchestra
LPO..............	Low Power Output (MSA)
LPO..............	Low-Pressure Oxygen
LPO..............	Lunar Parking Orbit [*Apollo*] [*NASA*]
LPO..............	Lunar Polar Orbiter [*NASA*]
LPO..............	Lunar Program Office [*NASA*] (IAA)
LPOC	Labile Particulate Organic Carbon [*Environmental science*]
LPOF............	Low-Pressure Oil-Filled [*Cable*] (DICI)
LpOH............	Lysopine Dehydrogenase (BABM)
L/POL...........	Life Policy [*Insurance*] (DCTA)
L'POOL.........	Liverpool (ROG)
LPOP............	Low-Pressure Oxidizer Turbopump (NASA)
L POST	Left Posterior [*Medicine*] (MEDA)
LPOT............	Low-Pressure Oxidizer Turbopump (MCD)
LPOT............	Ota [*Portugal ICAO location identifier*] (ICLI)
LPOTP..........	Low-Pressure Oxidizer Turbopump (NASA)
LPOX	Low-Pressure Oxygen (AFM)
LPP..............	Laboratory of Pulmonary Pathobiology (GNE)
LPP..............	Labor Protection Plan
LPP..............	Labour Progressive Party [*Canadian communist party*]
LPP..............	Lanka Prajatantrawadi Party [*Ceylon*]
LPP..............	Lappeenranta [*Finland*] [*Airport symbol*] (OAG)
LPP..............	Large Paper Proofs
LPP..............	LASER-Produced Plasma
LPP..............	Lateral Pterygoid Plate [*Medicine*] (DMAA)
LPP..............	Launcher Preparation Control Panel
LPP..............	Leader Preparation Program
LPP..............	Lebowa People's Party [*South Africa*] [*Political party*] (PPW)
LPP..............	Length of Perpendiculars
LPP..............	Liberian People's Party [*Political party*] (EY)
LPP..............	Lightweight Presentation Protocol [*Telecommunications*] (ACRL)
LPP..............	Linear Photopolymerization [*Organic chemistry*]
LPP..............	Lines per Page
LPP..............	Link Peripheral Processor (ACRL)
LPP..............	Lipoprotein Lipase [*An enzyme*] (DAVI)
LPP..............	Liquid Phase Processing [*Chemistry*]
LPP..............	Local Patching Panel
LPP..............	Long Periodic Perturbation
LPP..............	Long-Period Pulses [*Volcanology*]
LPP..............	Long Plenum Plugs (COE)
LPP..............	Low-Power Physics (IEEE)
LPP..............	Low-Pressure-Pipe System [*Waste water treatment*]
LPP..............	Lunar Precepts Positioner [*Aerospace*]
LPPA............	Licensed Pearl Producers' Association [*Australia*]
LPPC............	Lisboa [*Portugal ICAO location identifier*] (ICLI)
LPPC............	Load Point Photocell
LPPD	Ponta Delgada, Sao Miguel Island [*Portugal ICAO location identifier*] (ICLI)
LPPH	Late Postpartum Hemorrhage [*Medicine*] (DMAA)
LPPH	Leningrad Prison Psychiatric Hospital [*Later, LSPH*]
LPPI.............	Pico, Pico Island [*Portugal ICAO location identifier*] (ICLI)
LPPM...........	Low Pressure Permanent Mould (PDAA)
LPPM...........	Portimao [*Portugal ICAO location identifier*] (ICLI)
LPPMUL	Lawyers Protecting People from Malicious and Unjustified Lawsuits (EA)
LPPO	Santa Maria [*Portugal ICAO location identifier*] (ICLI)
LPPP............	Low-Pressure Pump Pad (COE)
LPPR............	Porto [*Portugal ICAO location identifier*] (ICLI)
LPPS............	Low-Pressure Plasma Sprayed [*Thermal barrier coating*]
LPPS............	Porto Santo, Porto Santo Island [*Portugal ICAO location identifier*] (ICLI)
LPPT............	Lisboa [*Portugal ICAO location identifier*] (ICLI)
LPPT............	Low Pressurization Pressure Test Transmitter (IEEE)
LPPTS..........	[*The*] Library of the Palestine Pilgrims' Text Society (BJA)
LPPV............	Praia Verde [*Portugal ICAO location identifier*] (ICLI)
LPQ..............	Learning Process Questionnaire [*J. Biggs*] (TES)
LPQ..............	Luang Prabang [*Laos*] [*Airport symbol*] (AD)
LPR..............	Amphibious Transport (Small) [*Navy ship symbol*]
LPR..............	Lactate-Pyruvate Ratio (MAE)
LPR..............	Lanpar Technologies, Inc. [*Toronto Stock Exchange symbol*]
LPR..............	La Peregrina [*Puerto Rico*] [*Seismograph station code, US Geological Survey*] (SEIS)
LPR..............	Late Phase Reaction [*or Response*] [*Medicine*]
LPR..............	Late Position Report [*Report of a flight which is off flight plan*]
LPR..............	Late Procurement Request [*Air Force*] (AFM)
LPR..............	Lawful Permanent Resident [*Department of Justice*]
LPR..............	Leadership Potential Rating [*Army*] (AABC)
LPR..............	Licensed Preacher
LPR..............	License Plate Reader
LPR..............	Lilly's Practical Register [*A publication*] (DLA)
LPR..............	Linea Aerea Privadas Argentina [*ICAO designator*] (FAAC)
LPR..............	Linear Polarization Resistance (MCD)
LPR..............	Line Printer [*Computer science*] (NASA)
LPR..............	Line Printer Remote (PCM)
LPR..............	Liquid Propellant Rocket [*Air Force*]
LPR..............	Local Payment Receipt (AABC)
LPR..............	London Property Register [*London Research Centre*] [*British Information service or system*] (IID)
LPR..............	Long-Playing Record (IAA)
LPR..............	Long-Playing Rocket [*Aerospace*]
LPR..............	Looper Position Regulator
LPR..............	Lymphocyte Proliferative Response [*Immunology*]
LPR..............	Lynchburg Pool Reactor
LPR-5	Lease Production Revenue System - 5 File [*Petroleum Information Corp.*] [*Information service or system*] (CRD)
LPR-10	Lease Production Revenue System - 10 File [*Petroleum Information Corp.*] [*Information service or system*] (CRD)
LPRA	Laws of Puerto Rico Annotated [*A publication*]
LPRA	Lost Parts Replacement Authorization (MCD)
LPRB	Loaded Program Request Block [*Computer science*] (BUR)
LPRC	Launch Pitch Rate Control
LPRC	Library Public Relations Council (EA)
LPRCO	Logistics Planning and Reporting Code [*Military*]
LPRD	Launch Program Requirement Document [*NASA*] (IAA)
LPRE	Liquid Propellant Rocket Engine [*Air Force*]
LPRF............	Low-Power Radio Frequency (MCD)
LPRF............	Low Pulse Recurrence Frequency (MCD)
LPRI.............	Licentiate of the Plastics and Rubber Institute [*British*] (DBQ)
LPRINT	Lookup Dictionary Print Program (IEEE)
LPRL	Lentz Peace Research Laboratory (EA)
LPRM...........	Local Power Range Monitor (NRCH)
LPRM...........	Low-Power Range Monitor [*Nuclear energy*] (NRCH)
LPRO...........	Legend Properties, Inc. [*NASDAQ symbol*] (SAG)
LProj............	Light Projection [*Ophthalmology*]
LPRP............	Lao People's Revolutionary Party [*Phak Pasason Pativat Lao*] [*Political party*] (PPW)
LPRPrB........	Santander Overseas Bk `B'Pfd [*NYSE symbol*] (TTSB)
LPRR............	Low-Power Research Reactor
LPRS............	Local Primary Reference Source
LPRS............	Low-Pressure Recirculation System (NRCH)
LPRSVR........	Life Preserver
LPRSX	Low-Pressure Recirculation System Heat Exchanger [*Environmental science*] (COE)
LPRT............	Low Power Relay Transmitter
LPS..............	Laboratory Peripheral System
LPS..............	Laboratory Program Summary (MCD)
LPS..............	Landing Performance Score (MCD)
LPS..............	Language for Programming-in-the-Small [*Computer science*] (MHDI)
LPS..............	Lanterman-Petris-Short Act [*Psychology*] (DAVI)
LPS..............	La Palma [*El Salvador*] [*Seismograph station code, US Geological Survey*] (SEIS)
LPS..............	Large Pointing System (MCD)
LPS..............	LASER Particulate Spectrometer [*NASA*]
LPS..............	LASER Power Supply
LPS..............	Laser Printing System (NITA)
LPS..............	Last Papanicolaou Smear [*Gynecology*] (DAVI)
LPS..............	Last Period Satisfied [*IRS*]
LPS..............	Laterality Preference Schedule [*Psychology*]
LPS..............	Lateral Premotor System (DMAA)
LPS..............	Launch Phase Simulator [*NASA*]
LPS..............	Launch Processing System [*NASA*] (KSC)
LPS..............	L-Band Phase Shifter
LPS..............	Learning Preference Scales [*Test*] (TMMY)
LPS..............	Levator Palpebrae Superioris [*Muscle*] [*Anatomy*] (AAMN)

LPS............. Liberale Partei der Schweiz [*Liberal Party of Switzerland*] [*Political party*] (PPE)
LPS............. Liberian Philatelic Society [*Defunct*] (EA)
LPS............. Library Processes System [*Educomp*] [*Information service or system*] (IID)
LPs............. Licentiate in Psychiatry (CMD)
LPS............. Life-Cycle Productivity System
LPS............. Lightning Protection System [*Boating*]
LPS............. Lightproof Shade [*Technical drawings*]
LPS............. Linear Profile Scan [*Medicine*] (DMAA)
LPS............. Linear Programming System [*Computer science*]
LPS............. Linear Pulse Sector (OA)
LPS............. Line Procedure Specifications (CMD)
LPS............. Line Program Selector (IAA)
LPS............. Lines per Second [*Computer science*]
LPS............. Lipase (MAE)
LPS............. Lipopolysaccharide [*Biochemistry*]
LPS............. Liquid-Phase Sintering (MCD)
LPS............. Liters per Second (KSC)
LPS............. Loan Production System [*Department of Veterans Affairs*]
LPS............. Local Process Specification (NG)
LPS............. Logicon Products [*Vancouver Stock Exchange symbol*]
LPS............. Logistic Policy Statement [*Navy*]
LPS............. Logistics Planning Study (MCD)
LPS............. London & Port Stanley Railway Co. [*AAR code*]
LPS............. London Press Service
LPS............. Longfellow Poetry Society (EA)
Lps............. Loops [*Military decoration*] (AABC)
LPS............. Lopez Island [*Washington*] [*Airport symbol*] (OAG)
LPS............. Lord Privy Seal [*British*]
LPS............. Low-Power Schottky [*Electronics*]
LPS............. Low-Pressure Sand [*Casting*] [*Automotive engineering*]
LPS............. Low-Pressure Scram [*Nuclear energy*] (IEEE)
LPS............. Low-Pressure Separator [*Chemical engineering*]
LPS............. Low-Pressure Sodium
LPS............. Lunar Penetrometer System [*Aerospace*]
LPS............. Lunar Pilotage System [*Aerospace*]
LPS............. Lypopolysaccharide [*Medicine*] (TAD)
LPSA............ Licensed Program Support Agreement [*Computer science*] (CIST)
LPSA............ Lithographic Preparatory Services Association [*Later, GPA*] (EA)
LPSA............ Log Periodic Scattering Array
LPSC............ Lunar and Planetary Science Conference
LPSC............ Luxembourg Philatelic Study Club [*Defunct*] (EA)
LPSC............ Santa Cruz [*Portugal ICAO location identifier*] (ICLI)
LPS/CDS...... Launch Processing System / Central Data Subsystem [*Military*]
LPSCU......... Ladies Pennsylvania Slovak Catholic Union (EA)
LPSD........... Logically Passive Self-Dual
LPSF........... Lens-Pinhole Spatial Filter (PDAA)
LPSG .... Live Oak, Perry & South Georgia Railway Co. [*AAR code*]
LPSI............ Low-Pressure Safety Injection [*Nuclear energy*] (NRCH)
LPSI............ Sines [*Portugal ICAO location identifier*] (ICLI)
LPSIP.......... Low-Pressure Safety Injection Pump [*Nuclear energy*] (NRCH)
LPSJ............ Sao Jorge, Sao Jorge Island [*Portugal ICAO location identifier*] (ICLI)
LPSM........... Levenson Phase Shift Mask (AAEL)
LPSN .... Local Packet Switched Network
LPSNY......... Lithuanian Philatelic Society of New York (EA)
LPSO .... Laboratory Procurement Supply Office
LPSO .... Lloyd's Policy Signing Office [*Lloyd's of London*]
LPSOL......... Linear Programming Solution (IAA)
LPSR........... Lipopolysaccharide Receptor (DB)
LPSS........... Amphibious Transport Submarine [*Landing Platform, Submarine*] [*Navy ship symbol*]
LPSS........... Law and Political Science Section [*Association of College and Research Libraries*]
LPSS........... Line Protection Switching System [*Bell System*]
LPSS........... Local Population Studies Society [*British*]
LPSSNJ........ Low-Power Self-Screening Noise Jammer [*Military*] (CAAL)
LPSSR......... Low-Power Spread Spectrum RADAR (PDAA)
LPST........... Sintra [*Portugal ICAO location identifier*] (ICLI)
LPSTTL........ Low-Power Schottky Transistor-Transistor Logic [*Electronics*] (IAA)
LPSV........... Low-Pressure Solenoid Valve
LPSVD........ Linear Prediction with Singular Value Decomposition [*Computer science*]
LPSW.......... Load Program Status Word (IAA)
LPSW.......... Low-Pressure Service Water [*Nuclear energy*] (NRCH)
LPT............. Lampang [*Thailand*] [*Airport symbol*] (OAG)
LPT............. Lampang [*Thailand*] [*Seismograph station code, US Geological Survey*] (SEIS)
LPT............. Language Proficiency Test [*Military*] (AFM)
LPT............. Largest Processing Time First [*Computer science*] (MHDB)
LPT............. LASER Propulsion Test (SSD)
LPT............. LASER Pyrolysis Technique [*Inorganic synthesis*]
LPT............. Latest Recommended Posting Times [*Business term*] (DCTA)
LPT............. Leading Physical Trainer [*British military*] (DMA)
LPT............. Licensed Physical Therapist
LPT............. Light Pen Tracking (MCD)
LPT............. Limited Procurement Test
LP-T........... Limited Production - Test (AABC)
LPT............. Line Printer [*Computer science*]
LPT............. Lipotropin (DMAA)
LPT............. Liquid Penetrant Testing [*or Examination*] [*Nuclear energy*] (NRCH)
LPT............. Listed Property Trust
LPT............. Local Public Transportation
LPT............. Lock Pointer Table
LPT............. Long-Period Tremor [*Volcanology*]

LPT............. Low Point [*Technical drawings*]
LPT............. Low-Power Test
LPT............. Low-Pressure Test
LPT............. Low-Pressure Transducer
LPT............. Low-Pressure Turbine [*Nuclear energy*] (NRCH)
LPT............. Low Pressure Turbocharger
LPT............. Luminescent Pigment Tattooing
LPT............. Lymphocyte Transfer (DB)
LPtaW........ West Baton Rouge Parish Library, Port Allen, LA [*Library symbol Library of Congress*] (LCLS)
LPTB........... London Passenger Transport Board
LPTB........... Low-Pressure Turbine [*on a ship*] (DS)
LPTD........... Linear Programmed Thermal Degradation [*Instrumentation*]
LPTD........... Long Play Talkdown
LPTD-MS .... Linear Programmed Thermal Degradation - Mass Spectroscopy [*Instrumentation*]
LPTF........... Low-Power Test Facility [*Nuclear energy*]
LPTH........... LightPath Technologies, Inc. [*NASDAQ symbol*] (SAG)
LPTHA .... LightPath Technologes`A' [*NASDAQ symbol*] (TTSB)
LPTHU........ LightPath Technologies Unit [*NASDAQ symbol*] (TTSB)
LPTHW........ LightPath Technol Wrrt `A' [*NASDAQ symbol*] (TTSB)
LPTHZ........ LightPath Technol Wrrt `B' [*NASDAQ symbol*] (TTSB)
LPTIS.......... Laguna Peak Tracking and Injection Station
LPTN........... Tancos [*Portugal ICAO location identifier*] (ICLI)
LPTR........... Line Printer [*Computer science*] (MSA)
LPTR........... Livermore Pool Type Reactor
LPTS........... Louisiana Presbyterian Theological Seminary
LPTTL......... Low-Power Transistor-Transistor Logic
LPTTP......... League of Professional Theatre Training Programs [*Defunct*] (EA)
LPTV........... Large Payload Test Vehicle [*Air Force*]
LPTV........... Low-Power Television
LPTW.......... Lake Providence, Texarkana & Western R. R. [*AAR code*]
LPU............. Language Processor Unit
LPu............. Late Punic (BJA)
LPU............. League of Prayer for Unity [*Defunct*] (EA)
LPU............. Least Publishable Unit [*of research data*]
LPU............. Legal Practices Update [*A publication*]
LPU............. Life Preserver Unit
LP-U........... Limited Procurement, Urgent (MCD)
LP-U........... Limited Production - Urgent (AABC)
LP-U........... Line Printer Unit (COE)
LPU............. Line Processing Unit
LPU............. Lions Philatelic Unit (EA)
LPU............. Liquid Processing Unit
LPU............. Low Pay Unit [*British*]
LPU............. Low-Power Unit (CAAL)
LPUG........... Lasers in Publishing Users Group (EA)
LPUL........... Least Positive Uplevel (IAA)
LPUU.......... Linear Programming under Uncertainty [*Computer science*]
LPV............. Houston, TX [*Location identifier FAA*] (FAAL)
LPV............. Landing Platform Vehicle [*Navy British*]
LPV............. Landing Pontoon Vehicle [*Military*]
LPV............. Laser-Protective Visor (DOMA)
LPV............. Launching Point Vertical (NATG)
LPV............. Left Pulmonary Vein [*Anatomy*]
LPV............. Light Pen Value (IAA)
LPV............. Lightproof Vent [*Technical drawings*]
LPV............. Limiting Pressure Velocity (PDAA)
LPV............. Log Periodic V [*Antenna*]
LPV............. Low-Pressure Vent (AAEL)
LPV............. Lymphopathia Venereum (MAE)
LPV............. Lymphotropic Papovavirus [*Medicine*] (DB)
LPVP........... Left Posterior Ventricular Preexcitation [*Medicine*] (DMAA)
LPVR........... Vila Real [*Portugal ICAO location identifier*] (ICLI)
LPVS........... Link Packetized Voice Subsystem [*Telecommunications*] (ACRL)
LPVT........... Large Print Video Terminal
LPVZ........... Viseu [*Portugal ICAO location identifier*] (ICLI)
LPW............. Lateral Pharyngeal Wall [*Medicine*] (DMAA)
LPW............. Liberal Party of Wales [*Political party*]
LPW............. Linear Polarized Wave
LPW............. Local Point Warning [*Military*]
LPW............. Longitudinal Pressure Wave
lp/W.......... Lumens per Watt (CET)
LPW............. Lumens per Watt (NAKS)
LPWA......... Local Public Works Act (OICC)
LPWG .... Lunar and Planetary Working Group [*Aerospace*] (IAA)
Lp-X........... Lipoprotein-X [*Biochemistry*] (MAE)
LPX............. Louisiana Pacific [*NYSE symbol*] (TTSB)
LPX............. Louisiana-Pacific Corp. [*NYSE symbol*] (SPSG)
LPYS........... Labour Party Young Socialists [*British Political party*]
LPZ............. La Paz [*San Calixto*] [*Bolivia*] [*Seismograph station code, US Geological Survey*] (SEIS)
LPZ............. Leipzig [*City and district in East Germany*] (ROG)
LPZ............. Low Population Zone (NRCH)
LPZ............. Ruston, LA [*Location identifier FAA*] (FAAL)
LQ............... Inland Empire Airlines [*ICAO designator*] (AD)
LQ............... Last Quarter [*Moon phase*]
LQ............... Laterality Quotient [*Neuropsychology*]
LQ............... Learning Quotient
LQ............... Lege Quaeso [*Please Read*] [*Latin*]
LQ............... Lens Quality [*Optics*]
LQ............... Letter Quality (PCM)
LQ............... Library Quarterly [*A publication*] (BRI)
LQ............... Limiting Quality (IAA)
LQ............... Linear Quadratic [*Mathematics*]

lq	Liquid
LQ	Longevity Quotient [Demography]
LQ	Lordosis Quotients [Medicine]
Lq	Love Wave [Earthquakes]
LQ	Lowest Quadrant
LQ	Lowest Quadrille
LQA	La Quiaca [Argentina] [Geomagnetic observatory code]
LQA	La Quiaca [Argentina] [Seismograph station code, US Geological Survey Closed] (SEIS)
LQA	Link Quality Analysis (PDAA)
LQA	Living Quarters Allowance [Air Force] (AFM)
LQD	Liquid
LQD	Lowest Quantity Determinable [Analytical chemistry]
LQDR	Liquidator
LQFD	Liquefied
LQG	Large Quantity Generator (COE)
LQG	Linear Quadratic Gaussian (MCD)
LQG	Lorain, OH [Location identifier FAA] (FAAL)
LQGLS	Liquid in Glass
LQI	La Quinta Inns [NYSE symbol] (SAG)
LQIV	Linear, Quasi Invariant (PDAA)
LQK	Pickens, SC [Location identifier FAA] (FAAL)
LQL	Willoughby, OH [Location identifier FAA] (FAAL)
LQM	La Quinta Motor Inns (EFIS)
LQM	Puerto Leguizamo [Colombia] [Airport symbol] (OAG)
LQMD	LifeQuest Medical [NASDAQ symbol] (TTSB)
LQMD	LifeQuest Medical, Inc. [NASDAQ symbol] (SAG)
LQMETR	Liquidometer
LQN	Boston, MA [Location identifier FAA] (FAAL)
LQN	Qala-Nau [Afghanistan] [Airport symbol Obsolete] (OAG)
LQP	Fort Collins, CO [Location identifier FAA] (FAAL)
LQP	Letter Quality Printer [Computer science]
LQP	Linear Quadratic Problem [Mathematics]
LQQ	Chicago, IL [Location identifier FAA] (FAAL)
LQQ	Larned, KS [Location identifier FAA] (FAAL)
LQR	Liquor
LQR	Local Qualitative Radio [Ratings] (NTCM)
LQRR	Low-Quality Recruiting Report (DNAB)
LQS	Les Quatre Saisons [Record label] [France]
LQS	Lock Haven State College, Lock Haven, PA [OCLC symbol] (OCLC)
LQST	Leadership Q-Sort Test [Psychology]
LQT	Linear Quantizer (IAA)
LQT	Liverpool Quay Terms (DS)
LQT	Los Queltehues [Chile] [Seismograph station code, US Geological Survey] (SEIS)
lqtx	Liquitex (VRA)
LQU	Quilmes Ind(Quinsa)ADS [NYSE symbol] (TTSB)
LQUT	Queensland Unit and Group Titles Law and Practice [Australia A publication]
LQV	Leiurus Quinquestriatus Venom (DB)
LQV	Pennington Gap, VA [Location identifier FAA] (FAAL)
LQX	Lehighton, PA [Location identifier FAA] (FAAL)
LQY	Springfield, IL [Location identifier FAA] (FAAL)
LR	Dealer
Lr	King Lear [Shakespearean work]
LR	Labeled Release [Mars life detection experiment]
LR	Laboratory Reactor
LR	Laboratory Reagent
LR	Laboratory Reference (MAE)
LR	Laboratory Report
LR	Labor Reports (OICC)
LR	Labor Review [A publication]
LR	Labor Room [Obstetrics]
LR	Lactated Ringer [Medicine]
LR	Ladder Rung (AAG)
LR	Lady's Realm [A publication] (ROG)
Lr	Lancer [Military British] (DMA)
LR	Landing RADAR
LR	Landing Report (WDAA)
LR	Land Registry (DLA)
LR	Lapse Ratio [Insurance]
LR	Large Ring
LR	LASER-RADAR (MCD)
LR	Last Record (IAA)
LR	Last Renewal
LR	Latency Reaction [Medicine] (DB)
LR	Latency Relaxation
LR	Lateral Rectus [Muscle] [Anatomy]
LR	Lateral Reversal [Typography] (DGA)
LR	Lateral Root [Botany]
lR	Laufend Rechnung [Current Account] [German Business term]
L/R	Launch/Reentry (MCD)
LR	Launch Reliability (MCD)
LR	Launch Right (MCD)
LR	Lawesson Reagent [Organic chemistry]
LR	Law Record [1911-12] [India] [A publication] (DLA)
LR	Law Recorder [1827-38] [Ireland] [A publication] (DLA)
LR	Law Register [1880-1909] [A publication] (DLA)
Lr	Lawrencium [Original symbol, Lw, changed in 1963] [Chemical element]
LR	Law Reporter [1821-22] [A publication] (DLA)
LR	Layer Rating [British military] (DMA)
LR	Lay Reader (ROG)
LR	Leaching Rate [Nuclear energy] (NUCP)
LR	Leaders of Religion [A publication]
LR	Leaf Rust [Plant Pathology]
LR	Lear [ICAO aircraft manufacturer identifier] (ICAO)
LR	Leave Rations [Military]
LR	Leave to Appeal Refused [Legal term] (ADA)
LR	Ledger (ROG)
L - R	Left minus Right [Stereo signals] (NTCM)
L + R	Left plus Right [Stereo signals] (NTCM)
LR	Left Rear
LR	Left Rudder (MCD)
LR	Left to Right (MAE)
L/R	Left to Right [Ratio] (DAVI)
LR	Legal Reserve (MHDW)
LR	Leicestershire Regiment [Military unit] [British]
LR	Lending Rate [Banking] (MHDW)
LR	Lent Reading (ROG)
LR	Lesion Expansion Rate [Pathology]
LR	Letter [Online database field identifier]
LR	Letter Report
LR	Letter Requirement
LR	Level Recorder
LR	Level Regulator (NRCH)
LR	Leviticus Rabbah (BJA)
LR	Liaison Report (AAG)
LR	Liaison Request (AAG)
LR	Liberia [ANSI two-letter standard code] (CNC)
LR	Library Review [A publication] (BRI)
LR	Licensing Registration [British]
L/R	Life/Revisit [NASA] (KSC)
LR	Lifespan Resources [An association] (EA)
LR	Light Reaction (MAE)
LR	Light Reflex [Medicine] (AAMN)
LR	Likelihood Ratio [Statistics]
Lr	Limes Reacting Dose of Diphtheria Toxin [Medicine] (DMAA)
LR	Limited Recoverable (IEEE)
LR	Limit Register
LR	Lincoln Red [Livestock terminology]
LR	Lindblad Resonance [Planetary science]
LR	Linear Regression [Mathematics]
LR	Lineas Aereas Costarricenses, Sociedad Anonima (LACSA) [Costa Rica] [ICAO designator] (ICDA)
LR	Line Receiver
LR	Line Relay
LR	Link Resources, Inc. [Vancouver Stock Exchange symbol]
LR	Liquid Rocket
LR	Listing Representative (REAL)
lr	Listing Representative [Real estate] (REAL)
LR	Listing Representative [Investment term]
LR	Little Rock [Diocesan abbreviation] [Arkansas] (TOCD)
LR	Living Room
LR	Lloyd's Register of Shipping
LR	Loading Ramp
LR	Load Ratio
LR	Load Rejection (NRCH)
LR	Load-Resistor Relay (MSA)
LR	Loan Rate [Banking]
L/R	Local/Remote [Telecommunications] (TEL)
LR	Lock Rail
LR	Lock Range (IAA)
L/R	Locus of Radius
LR	Logical Record
LR	Logistical Reassignment [Military] (AFIT)
LR	Logistical Requirement
LR	Logistic Regression [Medicine]
LR	Log Run [Lumber]
LR	London Rank [Freemasonry]
LR	Long Range
LR	Long Rifle
LR	Long Run [Economics]
LR	Louisiana Register [A publication] (AAGC)
LR	Louisiana Reports [A publication] (DLA)
LR	Lower (ADA)
LR	Lower Rail [Typography]
LR	Lower Right
LR	Lower Rule
lr	Low Rate Reverse [Ecology]
LR	Low Reduction (NITA)
LR	Low Register (IAA)
LR	Low Resistance (IAA)
LR	Low Risk
LR	Loyal Regiment [Military British]
LR	Lugger [Ship's rigging] (ROG)
LR	New Zealand Law Reports [A publication] (DLA)
LR	Ohio Law Reporter [A publication] (DLA)
LR	Radiolocation Land Station [ITU designation]
Lr	Rayleigh Wave [Earthquakes]
LR3	LASER Ranging Retroreflection [Also, LRRR] [Initialism pronounced "LR-cubed" Apollo 11 experiment] [NASA]
LR³	Logistics Readiness Rating Report [DoD]
LRA	Labor Research Association (EA)
LRA	Lace Research Association [British]
LRA	Lagged Reserve Accounting [Banking]
LRA	Landing Rights Airport [US Customs]
LRA	Larissa [Greece] [Airport symbol] (OAG)
LRA	LASER [Gyro] Reference Axis (IEEE)
LRA	Last Return Amount [IRS]

LRA............. Launcher Relay Assembly [Navy] (CAAL)
LRA............. Lawyers' Reports, Annotated [A publication] (DLA)
LRA............. Lease Rental Agreement (MHDB)
LRA............. Least Restrictive Alternative [For the education of the handicapped]
LRA............. left Renal Artery [Anatomy] (DAVI)
LRA............. Libertarian Republican Alliance (EA)
LRA............. Library of Romance [A publication]
LRA............. Light Replaceable Assemblies
LRA............. Line Receiving Amplifier (MSA)
LRA............. Lithuanian Regeneration Association (EA)
LRA............. Little Red Air Service [Canada ICAO designator] (FAAC)
LRA............. Little Rock [Arkansas] [Seismograph station code, US Geological Survey Closed] (SEIS)
LRA............. Load Real Address (HGAA)
LRA............. Load Reference Axis
LRA............. Local Redevelopment Authority (BCP)
LRA............. Locked-Rotor Amperes (MSA)
LRA............. Logical Record Access [Computer science] (MHDB)
LRA............. Logical Record Address (NITA)
LRA............. Long-Range Aviation [Army] (AABC)
LRA............. Lord Ruthven Assembly [An association] (EA)
LRA............. Lord's Resistance Army [Kampala]
LRA............. Lord's Resistance Army [Uganda] [Political party]
LRA............. Louisiana Realtors Association (SRA)
LRA............. Louisiana Restaurant Association (SRA)
LRA............. Louisiana Retailers Association (SRA)
LRA............. Lower Right Abdomen [Injection site]
LRA............. Low Right Atrium [Anatomy]
LRA............. North Carolina Union List of Serials for Community Colleges [Library network]
LRAA .... Long-Range Air Army [Former USSR] (MCD)
LRAACA...... Long-Range Air Antisubmarine Warfare Capable Aircraft (MCD)
LRAAM .... Long Range Air-to-Air Missile [Air Force]
LRA & E ..... English Law Reports, Admiralty and Ecclesiastical [A publication] (DLA)
LRAAS .... Long-Range Airborne ASW [Antisubmarine Warfare] System (MCD)
LRAC .... English Law Reports, Appeal Cases [A publication] (DLA)
LRAC .... Long-Run Average Costs [Marketing]
LRAD .... Licentiate of the Royal Academy of Dancing [British]
LRADM .... Long-Range Air Defense Missile (MCD)
LR Adm & Ecc... Law Reports, Admiralty and Ecclesiastical Cases [1865-75] [A publication] (DLA)
LR Adm & Eccl.. Law Reports, Admiralty and Ecclesiastical Cases [1865-75] [A publication] (DLA)
LR Adm & Eccl (Eng)... Law Reports, Admiralty and Ecclesiastical Cases [England] [A publication] (DLA)
LRADP .... Long-Range Active Duty Program [Army]
LRAF........... Long-Range Air Force
LRALS .... Long-Range Approach and Landing System (PDAA)
LRAM .... Licentiate of the Royal Academy of Music [British] (EY)
LRAN .... Local Regional Access Node (MCD)
LR Ann .... Lawyers' Reports, Annotated [A publication] (DLA)
LRA NS....... Lawyers' Reports, Annotated, New Series [A publication] (DLA)
LRAO .... Logistics Review and Analysis Office [US Army Defense Ammunition Center and School]
LRAOP .... Long-Range Aerospace Observation Platform
LRAP .... Leucine-Rich Amelogenin Polypeptide [Biochemistry of dental enamel]
LRAP .... Long-Range Acoustic Propagation
LR App .... English Law Reports, Appeal Cases, House of Lords [A publication] (DLA)
LRAPP .... Long-Range Acoustic Propagation Project
LR App Cas... English Law Reports, Appeal Cases, House of Lords [A publication] (DLA)
LR App Cas (Eng)... English Law Reports, Appeal Cases, House of Lords [A publication] (DLA)
LRAR .... Arad [Romania] [ICAO location identifier] (ICLI)
LRaR .... Richland Parish Library, Rayville, LA [Library symbol Library of Congress] (LCLS)
LRAS .... Logistics Requirements Allocation Sheet (SSD)
LRAS .... Long-Range Autonomous Submersible
LRAS .... Lunar Module Replaceable Assembly [NASA] (IAA)
LRASM .... Long-Range Air-to-Surface Missile (MCD)
LRASV .... Long-Range Air-to-Surface Vessel (IAA)
LRAT........... Lecithin-Retinol Acyltransferase [An enzyme]
LRAT........... Long-Range Antitank [Army] (INF)
LRATC .... Long-Run Average Total Costs [Economics]
LRATGW ...... Long-Range Antitank Guided Weapon [British military] (DMA)
LRB............. Labour Relations Board [Canada]
LRB............. Level Reference Base
LRB............. Lissamine Rhodamine B [Fluorescent dye]
LRB............. Load Request Block (IAA)
LRB............. Local Reference Beam [Holography]
LRB............. London Rifle Brigade [Military unit] [British]
LRB............. Loyalty Review Board [Abolished, 1953] [Civil Service Commission]
LRBB .... Bucuresti [Romania] [ICAO location identifier] (ICLI)
LRBC .... Bacau [Romania] [ICAO location identifier] (ICLI)
LRBC .... Lift-Right Bounded-Context [Computer science] (MHDI)
LRBC .... Lloyd's Registry Building Certificate
LRBF .... Longitudinal Ridge of Basal Fold
LRBFM .... National Labor Relations Board Field Manual
LRBG .... Law Reports, British Guiana [1890-1955] [A publication] (DLA)
LRBM........... Baia Mare/Tauti Magherusi [Romania] [ICAO location identifier] (ICLI)
LRBM........... Long-Range Ballistic Missile

LRBR .... Long-Range Ballistic Rocket
LRBR .... Long-Range Bombardment Round
LRBS .... Bucuresti/Baneasa [Romania] [ICAO location identifier] (ICLI)
LRBS .... LASER Ranging Bombing System
LR Burm .... Law Reports, British Burma [A publication] (DLA)
LR Burma .... Law Reports, British Burma [A publication] (DLA)
LRC............ Labour Representation Committee [Northern Ireland] (PPW)
LRC............ Labrador Retriever Club (EA)
LRC............ Langley Research Center [NASA]
LRC............ Launch/Recovery Visual Landing Aid Change (MCD)
LRC............ Law Reform Commission [Canada]
LRC............ Law Reform Committee (DLA)
LRC............ Leaders Reaction Course [Military training] (INF)
LRC............ Lead Resistance Compensator
LRC............ Learning Resource Center
LRC............ Learning Resources Center
LRC............ Lenoir Rhyne College [Hickory, NC]
LRC............ Lesbian Resource Center (EA)
LRC............ Level Recording Controller
LRC............ Lewis Research Center [NASA]
LRC............ Liberia Refining Co.
LRC............ Library Research Center [University of Illinois] (IID)
LRC............ Light Rapid Comfortable [Train system]
LRC............ Light Reflective Capacitor [Electronics] (DA)
LRC............ Light Repair Car [British]
LRC............ Limnological Research Center [University of Minnesota] [Research center] (RCD)
LRC............ Linear Responsibility Charting (PDAA)
LRC............ Lineas Aereas Costarricenses SA [Costa Rica] [ICAO designator] (FAAC)
LRC............ Line Rectifier Circuit
LRC............ Linguistics Research Center [University of Texas at Austin] [Research center] (RCD)
LRC............ Lionel Railroader Club (EA)
LRC............ Lipid Research Center [Washington University] [Research center] (RCD)
LRC............ Lipid Research Clinics
LRC............ Load Ratio Control (MSA)
LRC............ Local Review Committee (WDAA)
LRC............ Locomotor Respiratory Coupling [Physiology]
LRC............ Lode Resources Corp. [Vancouver Stock Exchange symbol]
LRC............ Logistics Readiness Center [Air Force]
LRC............ Logistics to Relay Converter (MCD)
LRC............ London Rowing Club
LRC............ Lone Oak Road [California] [Seismograph station code, US Geological Survey] (SEIS)
LRC............ Longitudinal Redundancy Check [Computer science]
LRC............ Long-Range Climb (MCD)
LRC............ Long Range Communications (NTCM)
LRC............ Long-Range Cruise [Aircraft speed]
LRC............ Lori Corp. [AMEX symbol] (SPSG)
LRC............ Lower Rib Cage [Anatomy]
LRC............ Luneberg Rapid Commutator [Physics]
LRC............ Lung Rate Counter
LRC............ Lutheran Resources Commission (EA)
LRCA .... Law Reports, Court of Appeals of New Zealand [A publication] (DLA)
LRCA .... Lithuanian Roman Catholic Alliance of America [Later, LCA] (EA)
LRCA .... Long-Range Combat Aircraft
LRCA .... Lop Rabbit Club of America (EA)
LRCC .... English Law Reports, Crown Cases Reserved [2 vols.] [1865-75] [A publication] (DLA)
LRCC .... Library Resources Coordinating Committee of the University of London (NITA)
LRCC .... Longitudinal Redundancy Check Character [Telecommunications] (TEL)
LRCC (Eng)... English Law Reports, Crown Cases Reserved [2 vols.] [1865-75] [A publication] (DLA)
LRCCM .... Long-Range Conventional Cruise Missile (MCD)
LRCCPPT ..... Lipid Research Clinics Coronary Primary Prevention Trial [Cardiology]
LRCCR .... Law Reports, Crown Cases Reserved [England] [A publication] (DLA)
LRCD .... Linear Rule of Cumulative Damage (PDAA)
LRCE........... LASER Relay Communication Equipment
LRCE........... Little Rock Cotton Exchange [Defunct]
LRCFA .... Lithuanian Roman Catholic Federation of America (EA)
LR Ch .... Law Reports, Chancery Appeal Cases [England] [A publication] (DLA)
LR Ch App... Chancery Appeal Cases [1865-75] [A publication] (DLA)
LR Ch D ...... English Law Reports, Chancery Division [A publication] (DLA)
LR Ch D (Eng)... Law Reports, Chancery Division, English Supreme Court of Judicature [A publication] (DLA)
LR Ch Div (Eng)... Law Reports, Chancery Division, English Supreme Court of Judicature [A publication] (DLA)
LR Ch (Eng)... Law Reports, Chancery Appeal Cases [England] [A publication] (DLA)
LRCI........... Legal Research Center [NASDAQ symbol] (TTSB)
LRCI........... Legal Research Center, Inc. [NASDAQ symbol] (SAG)
LRCK .... Constanta/M. Kogalniceau [Romania] [ICAO location identifier] (ICLI)
LRCL........... Cluj-Napoca/Someseni [Romania] [ICAO location identifier] (ICLI)
LRCL........... Long-Range Chemical LASER (MCD)
LRCM........... Licentiate of the Royal College of Music [British]
LRCM........... Long-Range Cruise Missile [Navy]
LRCNSW...... Law Reform Commission of New South Wales [Australia]
LRCO........... Limited Remote [or Radio] Communication Outlet

LRCO	Long-Range Capability Objective [Air Force]
LRCP	Laboratory Research Cooperative Program [Scientific Services Program] [Army] (RDA)
LRCP	Law Reports, Common Pleas [1865-75] [England] [A publication] (DLA)
LRCP	Licentiate of the Royal College of Physicians [British]
LRCP	Licentiate, Royal College of Physicians [British] (CMD)
LRCP	Long-Range Construction Program [Military]
LRCP & S	Licentiate of the Royal College of Physicians and the College of Surgeons of Edinburgh, and of the Faculty of Physicians and Surgeons of Glasgow (ROG)
LRCP & SI	Licentiate of the Royal College of Physicians and Surgeons of Ireland (AAMN)
LRCPD	English Law Reports, Common Pleas Division [A publication] (DLA)
LRCP Div	Law Reports, Common Pleas Division [England] [A publication] (DLA)
LRCP Div (Eng)	English Law Reports, Common Pleas Division [A publication] (DLA)
LRCPE	Licentiate of the Royal College of Physicians (Edinburgh)
LRCP (Eng)	Law Reports, Common Pleas [England] [A publication] (DLA)
LRCPI	Licentiate of the Royal College of Physicians of Ireland
LRCP Irel	Licentiate of the Royal College of Physicians of Ireland
LRCPLA	Lithuanian Roman Catholic Priests' League of America (EA)
LRCPSGlasg	Licentiate of the Royal College of Physicians and Surgeons of Glasgow (DI)
LRCR	Longitudinal Redundancy Check Register [Telecommunications] (IAA)
LR Cr Cas Res	Law Reports, Crown Cases Reserved [England] [A publication] (DLA)
LRCS	Caransebes/Caransebes [Romania] [ICAO location identifier] (ICLI)
LRCS	LASER RADAR Cross Section
LRCS	League of Red Cross and Red Crescent Societies [Switzerland] (EA)
LRCS	League of Red Cross Societies
LRCS	Licentiate of the Royal College of Surgeons [British]
LRCS	Lincoln Red Cattle Society [British] (DBA)
LRCSA	Load Relief Control System
LRCSA	Lincoln Red Cattle Society of Australia
LRCSE	Licentiate of the Royal College of Surgeons (Edinburgh)
LRCS (Edin)	Licentiate of the Royal College of Surgeons (Edinburgh) (DI)
LRCSI	Licentiate of the Royal College of Surgeons in Ireland
LRCS Irel	Licentiate of the Royal College of Surgeons in Ireland
LRCSOW	Long-Range Conventional Standoff Weapon [Military]
LRCSW	Long-Range Conventional Standoff Weapon (MCD)
LRCT	Licentiate of the Royal Conservatory of Toronto [Canada]
L/RCU	Local/Remote Control Unit
LRCU	Logic Refresh Control Unit
LRCV	Craiova [Romania] [ICAO location identifier] (ICLI)
LRCVS	Licentiate of the Royal College of Veterinary Surgeons [British]
LRC-W	Lutheran Resources Commission - Washington [Later, LRC] (EA)
LRCX	Lam Research [NASDAQ symbol] (TTSB)
LRCX	Lam Research Corp. [NASDAQ symbol] (SAG)
LRD	Labelled RADAR Display (PDAA)
LRD	Labour Research Department [Trade union] [British]
LRD	Landing and Recovery Division [NASA]
LRD	Laredo [Texas] [Airport symbol] (OAG)
LRD	Laredo Air, Inc. [ICAO designator] (FAAC)
LRD	LASER Ranger and Designator (MCD)
LRD	Launch Readiness Demonstration [NASA] (KSC)
LRD	Lightning and Radio-Emission Detector [Instrumentation]
LRD	Living Related Donor [Medicine]
LRD	Living Renal Donor [Nephrology] (DAVI)
LRD	Logistics Requirements Determination (MCD)
LRD	Long-Range Data [RADAR]
LRD	Long-Reach Detonator [Explosive]
LRD	Lord River Gold [Vancouver Stock Exchange symbol]
LRD	Lysinated Rhodamine Dextran [Cytology]
LRDC	Land Resources Development Centre [British] (ARC)
LRDC	Learning Research and Development Center [University of Pittsburgh] [Research center]
LRDCT	Linear Rotary Differential Capacitance Transducer [Instrumentation]
LRDD	Limited Rights to Delivered Data
LRDE	Long-Run Deal Effect [Marketing]
LRDG	Learning Resources Development Group [British] (DBA)
LRDG	Long Range Desert Group [British Army] [World War II]
LR Dig	Law Reports Digest [A publication] (DLA)
LRDL	Longitudinal Ridge of Dorsal Lip
LRDMM	Long-Range Dual-Mission Missile (MCD)
LRDP	Long-Range Development Program (IAA)
LRDR	Last Revision Date Routine
LRDS	LASER Ranging and Designation System [Military] (CAAL)
LRDSB	Left Minus Right Double Sideband (IAA)
LRDT	Laboratory of Reproductive and Developmental Toxicology (GNE)
LRDT	Living Related Donor Transplant [Medicine] (DMAA)
LRDU	Long-Range Development Unit
LRE	Lafayette Radio Electronics Corp.
LRE	Latest Revised Estimate (MCD)
LRE	Law-Related Education (AEE)
LRE	Least Restrictive Environment [For the education of the handicapped]
LRE	Leukemic Reticuloendotheliosis [Medicine] (AAMN)
LRE	Library Resources Exhibition [British]
LRE	Licentiate in Religious Education
LRE	Life Re [NYSE symbol] (TTSB)
LRE	Life Real Estate [NYSE symbol] (SPSG)
LRE	Light Responsive Element [Chemistry]
LRE	Liquid Rocket Engine

LRE	Local Resource Enhancement [Biology]
LRE	Logistics Readiness Elements (MCD)
LRE	Longreach [Australia Airport symbol] (OAG)
LRE	Lossless Reciprocal Embedding (IAA)
LRE	Low Rate Encoding [Telecommunications] (LAIN)
LRE	Lunar Retrograde Engine [NASA] (KSC)
LRE	Lymphoreticuloendothelial (DB)
LREA	Law Reports, East Africa [A publication] (DLA)
LRE & I App	Law Reports, House of Lords, English and Irish Appeals [1866-75] [A publication] (DLA)
LREB	London Regional Examining Board [British] (AIE)
L Rec	Law Recorder [Dublin, Ireland] [A publication] (DLA)
LREC	Liaison Residency Endorsement Committee [RRCEM] [Superseded by] (EA)
LRECL	Logical Records of Fixed Length (MCD)
L Rec NS	Law Recorder, New Series [Ireland] [A publication] (DLA)
L Record	Law Recorder [Dublin, Ireland] [A publication] (DLA)
L Rec OS	Law Recorder, First Series [Ireland] [A publication] (DLA)
LREDA	Liberal Religious Educators Association (EA)
LREE	Light Rare Earth Elements [Chemistry]
LREG	Leading Regulator [British]
LREH	Low-Renin Essential Hypertension [Medicine]
LREI	Life Role Expectations Inventory (EDAC)
LREM(A)	Leading Radio Electrical Mechanic (Air) [British military] (DMA)
LR Eng & Ir App	Law Reports, English and Irish Appeals [1866-75] [A publication] (DLA)
L Rep	Carolina Law Repository (Reprint) [North Carolina] [A publication] (DLA)
L Rep Mont	Law Reporter, Montreal [A publication] (DLA)
L Repos	Law Repository [A publication] (DLA)
LR Eq	English Law Reports, Equity [1866-75] [A publication] (DLA)
LR Eq (Eng)	English Law Reports, Equity [1866-75] [A publication] (DLA)
L-RERP	Long-Range Effects Research Program (USDC)
LRES	Letters
LRES	Linear Rocket Engine System (PDAA)
LRES	Long-Range Earth Sensor
LRES	Low Rigid Frame (PDAA)
L Rev & Quart J	Law Review and Quarterly Journal [London] [A publication] (DLA)
L Rev Dig	Law Review Digest [A publication] (DLA)
L Rev U Detroit	Law Review. University of Detroit [A publication] (DLA)
LREW	Long-Range Early Warning (NATG)
LREWP	Long-Range Electronic Warfare Plan [Military] (CAAL)
LREWS	Long-Range Early Warning System (NATG)
LR Ex	English Law Reports, Exchequer [1866-75] [A publication] (DLA)
LR Ex Cas	English Law Reports, Exchequer [1866-75] [A publication] (DLA)
LR Exch	English Law Reports, Exchequer [1866-75] [A publication] (DLA)
LR Exch D	English Law Reports, Exchequer Division [A publication] (DLA)
LR Exch Div	Law Reports, Exchequer Division [England] [A publication] (DLA)
LR Exch Div (Eng)	English Law Reports, Exchequer Division [A publication] (DLA)
LR Exch (Eng)	English Law Reports, Exchequer [1866-75] [A publication] (DLA)
LR Ex D	Law Reports, Exchequer Division [England] [A publication] (DLA)
LR Ex Div	English Law Reports, Exchequer Division [A publication] (DLA)
LRF	Jacksonville, AR [Location identifier FAA] (FAAL)
LRF	Ladle Refining Furnace [Nuclear energy] (NUCP)
LRF	LASER RADAR Fuze
LRF	LASER Range-Finder
LRF	Last Return Filed [IRS]
LRF	Late Renal Failure [Medicine]
LRF	Latex and Resorcinol Formaldehyde
LRF	Launch Rate Factor
LRF	Lepidoptera Research Foundation (EA)
LRF	Lincoln Resign Formulation
LRF	Liquid Rocket Fuel (MCD)
LRF	Liver Residue Factor [Molybdenum] [Medicine]
LRF	London Regional Federation [League of Nations Union]
LRF	Long-Range Facility [Telecommunications] (TEL)
LRF	Long-Range Flight
LRF	Low Refraction Layer
LRF	Lumber Recovery Factor
LRF	Luteinizing-Hormone Releasing Factor [Also, GnRF, GnRH, LH-RF, LH-RH, LH-RH/FSH-RH, LRH] [Endocrinology]
LRFA	Lymphoma Research Foundation of America (EA)
LRFAX	Low-Resolution Facsimile [Telecommunications] (TEL)
LRFC	LASER Range-Finder Controller (MCD)
LRF/D	LASER Range-Finder/Designator (MCD)
LRFD	Load and Resistance Factor Design (WPI)
LRFG	Low-Range Force Gauge
LRFI	League for Religious Freedom in Israel [Later, American Friends of Religious Freedom in Israel] (EA)
LRF/MTR	LASER Range-Finder and Marked Target Receiver (MCD)
LRFPS	Licentiate of the Royal Faculty of Physicians and Surgeons [British]
LRFPS(G)	Licentiate of the Royal Faculty of Physicians and Surgeons, Glasgow
LRFS	Long-Range Forecasting System (TEL)
LRF/SSC	LASER Ranger Finder/Solid State Computer (MCD)
LRFT	Left Rear Fluid Temperature [Brake system] [Automotive engineering]
LRG	Land Resources Group
LRG	Landscape Research Group [Lutterworth, Leicestershire, England] (EAIO)
LRG	Large [Classified advertising]
LRG	Leucine-Rich Glycoprotein
LRG	License Review Group [Nuclear energy] (NRCH)
LRG	Lincoln, ME [Location identifier FAA] (FAAL)

LRG .... Liquefied Refinery Gas
LRG .... Logistic Review Group [*Military*] (CAAL)
LRG .... Long Range
LRG .... Long-Range Guidance (MCD)
LRG .... Lorgues [*France*] [*Seismograph station code, US Geological Survey*] (SEIS)
LRGB .... Long-Range Guided Bomb (MCD)
LRGPP .... Long-Range Generation Planning Problem [*Energy*]
LRH .... La Rochelle [*France*] [*Airport symbol*] (OAG)
LRh .... Liquid Rheostat
LRH .... Luteinizing-Hormone Releasing Hormone [*Also, GnRF, GnRH, LH-RF, LH-RH, LH-RH/FSH-RH, LRF*] [*Endocrinology*]
LRHL .... Law Reports, English and Irish Appeals and Peerage Claims, House of Lords [*England*] [*A publication*] (DLA)
LRHL (Eng)... Law Reports, English and Irish Appeals and Peerage Claims, House of Lords [*England*] [*A publication*] (DLA)
LRHL Sc ...... English Law Reports, House of Lords, Scotch and Divorce Appeal Cases [*1866-75*] [*A publication*] (DLA)
LRHL Sc App Cas... Law Reports, House of Lords, Scotch and Divorce Appeal Cases [*1866-75*] [*A publication*] (DLA)
LRHL Sc App Cas (Eng)... English Law Reports, House of Lords, Scotch and Divorce Appeal Cases [*1866-75*] [*A publication*] (DLA)
LRHS .... Large Radioisotope Heat Source [*NASA*] (IAA)
LRHS .... Longitudinal Retirement History Survey [*Social Security Administration*] (GFGA)
LRHSC .... Large Radioisotope Heat Source Capsule [*NASA*] (KSC)
LRI .... Big Lost River [*Idaho*] [*Seismograph station code, US Geological Survey Closed*] (SEIS)
LRI .... Lawndale Railway & Industrial Co. [*Terminated AAR code*]
LRI .... Learning Resources Institute (EA)
LRI .... LeaRonal, Inc. [*NYSE symbol*] (SPSG)
LRI .... Left-Right Indicator
LRI .... Legal Resource Index [*Information Access Corp.*] [*Bibliographic database*] [*Information service or system*] (IID)
LRI .... Library Resources, Inc. [*Subsidiary of Encyclopaedia Britannica*]
Lrl .... Library Resources, Incorporated, Chicago, IL [*Library symbol Library of Congress*] (LCLS)
LRI .... Life Roles Inventory [*Test*] (TMMY)
LRI .... Lighting Research Institute (EA)
LRI .... Limited Range Intercept [*Telecommunications Navy*] (ANA)
LRI .... Literature and Religion of Israel [*A publication*]
LRI .... Longboat Resources, Inc. [*Vancouver Stock Exchange symbol*]
LRI .... Long-Range Indicator
LRI .... Long-Range Input (CET)
LRI .... Long-Range Inspector
LRI .... Long-Range Interceptor
LRI .... Long-Range International (DOMA)
LRI .... Long-Range RADAR Input
LRI .... Lorica [*Colombia*] [*Airport symbol*] (AD)
LRI .... Lower Respiratory Infection [*Medicine*]
LRI .... Lymphocyte Reactivity Index (DB)
LRIA .... English Law Reports, Indian Appeals [*A publication*] (DLA)
LRIA .... Iasi [*Romania*] [*ICAO location identifier*] (ICLI)
LRIA .... Level Removable Instrument Assembly [*Nuclear energy*] (IEEE)
LRIBA .... Licentiate of the Royal Institute of British Architects
LRIC .... Licentiate of the Royal Institute of Chemistry [*British*]
LRIC .... Long-Run Incremental Cost [*Business term*] (ADA)
LRIM .... Liquid Reaction Injection Molding (EDCT)
LRIM .... Long-Range Input Monitor [*RADAR*]
LR Ind App... English Law Reports, Indian Appeals [*A publication*] (DLA)
LR Ind App Supp... English Law Reports, Indian Appeals, Supplement [*A publication*] (DLA)
LR Indian App... English Law Reports, Indian Appeals [*A publication*] (DLA)
LR Indian App (Eng)... English Law Reports, Indian Appeals [*A publication*] (DLA)
LRINF .... Longer-Range Intermediate-Range Nuclear Forces
LRIP .... Language Research in Progress (DIT)
LRIP .... Liberia Research and Information Project (EA)
LRIP .... Long-Range Impact Point (MUGU)
LRIP .... Low-Rate Initial Production (RDA)
L Ripuar ...... Law of the Ripuarians [*A publication*] (DLA)
LRIr .... Law Reports, Ireland [*1878-1893*] [*A publication*]
LR Ir .... Law Reports, Irish [*A publication*] (DLA)
LRIR .... Limb Radiance Inversion Radiometer
LRIR .... Low-Resolution Infrared Radiometer
LRIRR .... Low-Resolution Infrared Radiometer (MSA)
LRIS .... Low Resolution Imaging Spectrograph [*Instrumentation*]
LRJ .... Lemars, IA [*Location identifier FAA*] (FAAL)
LRK .... Kenya Law Reports [*A publication*]
LRK .... LASER Research Kit
LRKB .... English Law Reports, King's Bench Division [*1901-52*] [*A publication*] (DLA)
LRKB .... Quebec Official Reports, King's Bench [*A publication*] (ILCA)
LRL .... Lawrence Radiation Laboratory [*Livermore*] [*Later, Lawrence Livermore Laboratory University of California*]
LRL .... Leakage Resistance Limit
LRL .... Light Railway Loads [*British*]
LRL .... Limited Raman LASER
LRL .... Lincoln Research Laboratory
LRL .... Linguistics Research Laboratory [*Gallaudet College*] [*Research center*] (RCD)
LRL .... Linking Relocating Loader
LRL .... Livermore Research Laboratory [*University of California*] (KSC)
LRL .... Logical Record Length
LRL .... Logical Record Location
LRL .... Lunar Receiving Laboratory [*NASA*]

LRL .... Lunar Research Laboratory [*NASA*] (DAVI)
LRL .... Tulane University, Law Library, New Orleans, LA [*OCLC symbol*] (OCLC)
LRLCX .... Lord Abbett Research: Large Cap [*Mutual fund ticker symbol*] (SG)
LR/LD .... Line Receiver/Line Driver (MCD)
LRLEI .... League for Religious Labor in Eretz Israel (EA)
LRLF .... Local Radio Luminosity Function [*Cosmology*]
LRLG .... Long-Range Logistics Guidance [*Air Force*]
LRL-L .... Lawrence Radiation Laboratory, Livermore [*Later, Lawrence Livermore Laboratory*] [*University of California*]
LRLL .... Longitudinal Ridge of Lateral Lip
LRLM .... Lower Reject Limit Median (SAA)
LRLT .... Left Rear Lining Temperature [*Brake system*] [*Automotive engineering*]
LRLTRAN ..... Lawrence Radiation Laboratory FORTRAN [*Programming language*] [*1961*] (CSR)
LRLTRAN ..... Lawrence Radiation Laboratory Translator (IEEE)
LRM .... Labor Relations Reference Manual [*A publication*] (DLA)
LRM .... Land Resources Management (MCD)
LRM .... La Rassegna Musicale [*A publication*]
LRM .... La Romana [*Dominican Republic*] [*Airport symbol*] (OAG)
LRM .... Latching Relay Matrix
LRM .... Lead Reactor Manufacturer (NRCH)
LRM .... Leaflet Rolling Machine [*PSYOP*] (RDA)
LRM .... Least Recently Used Master [*Computer science*]
LRM .... Left Radical Mastectomy [*Medicine*] (MAE)
LRM .... Lightweight Ramjet Missile (MCD)
LRM .... Limited Register Machine
LRM .... Line Replacement Module
LRM .... Liquid Reaction Molding
LRM .... Liquid Rocket Motor (KSC)
LRM .... Logarithmic Radiation Monitor (NRCH)
LRM .... Logarithmic Ratio Module
LRM .... Long-Range Missile Launcher
LRM .... Lower Reject Limit Median
LRM .... Lunar Reconnaissance [*or Rendezvous*] Mission [*Aerospace*]
LRM .... Lunar Reconnaissance Module [*Aerospace*]
LR Mad .... Indian Law Reports, Madras Series [*A publication*] (DLA)
LRMC .... Lloyd's Refrigerating Machinery Certificate
LRMC .... Long-Run Marginal Costs
LRMCO .... Long Run, Mill Cuts Out [*Forest industry*] (WPI)
LRMG .... Hughes Lockless Rifle/Machine Gun (MCD)
LR Misc D ... Law Reports, Miscellaneous Division [*A publication*] (DLA)
LRML .... Long-Range Missile Launcher [*Military*] (IAA)
LRMP .... Last Regular Menstrual Period [*Gynecology*] (DMAA)
LRMP .... Legacy Resource Management Program (DOMA)
LRMP .... Long-Range Maritime Patrol [*Aircraft*] (NATG)
LRMS .... Library Routine Management System
LRMS .... Low Resolution Mass Spectroscopy (COE)
LRMTS .... LASER Range-Finder and Marked Target Seeker (MCD)
LRMV .... Lilac Ring Mottle Virus [*Plant pathology*]
LRN .... Long-Range Navigation
LRN .... Long Reference Number
LRN .... LORAN [*Long-Range Aid to Navigation*]
LRNA .... Laws Relating to the Navy Annotated [*Military law*]
LRNAV .... Long Range Navigation [*FAA*] (TAG)
LRNBA .... La Raza National Bar Association (EA)
LRNC .... Long Reference Number Code
LRND .... Left Radical Neck Dissection [*Surgical procedure*] (DAVI)
LRNF .... Longer-Range Nuclear Forces (WDAA)
LRNG .... Learning
LRNG .... Learning Co. [*NASDAQ symbol*] (SAG)
LrngCo .... Learning Co. [*Associated Press*] (SAG)
LrnHaus ...... Lernout & Hauspie Speech Products [*Associated Press*] (SAG)
LRNOD .... Long-Range Night Observation Device [*Army*] (AABC)
LRNR .... Low-Resolution Non-Scanning Radiometer (MCD)
LRNRM .... Landowners for Responsible Natural Resource Management [*An association*] (WPI)
LRNS .... Long-Range Navigation System [*Aviation*]
LRNS .... Nova Scotia Law Reports [*A publication*] (DLA)
LRNSW .... Law Reports, New South Wales Supreme Court [*A publication*] (DLA)
LrnTree .... Learning Tree International, Inc. [*Associated Press*] (SAG)
LRNZ .... Law Reports, New Zealand [*A publication*] (DLA)
LRO .... Laboratory Review Office [*Army*] (RDA)
LRO .... Labor Relations Officer (COE)
LRO .... Large Radio Observatory (KSC)
LRO .... Lathrop, CA [*Location identifier FAA*] (FAAL)
LRO .... Leading Radio Operator [*British military*] (DMA)
LRO .... Loan Review Officer [*Banking*] (TBD)
LRO .... Logistics Readiness Officer [*Military*] (AABC)
LRO .... Long-Range Objectives [*Navy*]
LRO .... Long-Range Order
LRO .... Low-Resistance Ohmmeter
LROA .... Land Rover Owners Association (EA)
LROA USA ... Land Rover Owners Association, USA (EA)
LROC .... Libertarian Republican Organizing Committee [*Defunct*] (EA)
LROD .... Long-Range Overwater Diffusion [*Experiment*] [*Marine science*] (OSRA)
LROD .... Oradea [*Romania*] [*ICAO location identifier*] (ICLI)
LRO(G) .... Leading Radio Operator (General) [*British military*] (DMA)
LROG .... Long-Range Objectives Group [*Navy*] (MCD)
LROI .... Legal Rate of Interest [*Business term*] (MHDB)
LROL .... Laboratoire de Recherches en Optique et Laser [*Laval University*] [*Canada Research center*] (RCD)
LROP .... Bucuresti/Otopeni [*Romania*] [*ICAO location identifier*] (ICLI)

LROP .... Lower Radicular Obstetrical Paralysis [*Medicine*] (DMAA)
LROR .... Low-Resolution Omnidirectional Radiometer (MCD)
LRO(W) .... Leading Radio Operator (Warfare) [*British military*] (DMA)
LRP .... English Law Reports, Probate Division [*A publication*] (DLA)
LRP .... Lancaster, PA [*Location identifier FAA*] (FAAL)
LRP .... Large Repairs to Hull
LRP .... Large Rotating Plug [*Nuclear energy*] (NRCH)
LRP .... LASER Retinal Photocoagulator
LRP .... Lateralized Readiness Potential [*Neurophysiology*]
LRP .... Lateralized Readiness Potential [*Psychophysiology*]
LRP .... Late Receptor Potential [*Photoreceptor*] [*Physiology*]
LRP .... Latest Reporting Period [*Business term*]
LRP .... Launching Reference Point
LRP .... LDI [*Low Density Lipoprotein*] Receptor-Related Protein
         [*Biochemistry*]
LRP .... League for the Revolutionary Party (EA)
LRP .... Lebanese Revolutionary Party [*Political party*] (PD)
LRP .... Lesbian Rights Project [*Later, NCLR*] (EA)
LRP .... Lichen Ruber Planus (DMAA)
LRP .... Limited Rate Production
LRP .... Limited Reaction Processing [*Semiconductor technology*]
LRP .... Liporotein Receptor-Related Protein [*Biochemistry*]
LRP .... LM [*Lunar Module*] Replaceable Package [*NASA*]
LRP .... Loan Repayment Program [*Department of Health and Human
         Services*] (GFGA)
LRP .... Logical Record Processor (IAA)
LRP .... Logical Request Package [*Computer science*] (CIST)
LRP .... Logistics Release Point [*Army*] (INF)
LRP .... Long-Range Path (IEEE)
LRP .... Long-Range Patrol [*Pronounced "lurp"*] [*Formerly, LRRP*] [*Army*]
         (AABC)
LRP .... Long-Range Penetration
LRP .... Long-Range Plans (NVT)
LRP .... Low Rate Production (RDA)
LRP .... Low Rigging Penalty [*IOR*] [*Yacht racing*]
LRPA .... Little Rock Port Railroad [*AAR code*]
LRPA .... Long-Range Patrol Aircraft (MCD)
LRP & D ...... Probate and Divorce Cases [*1865-75*] [*England*] [*A publication*]
         (DLA)
LRP & M ..... Law Reports, Probate and Matrimonial [*1866-75*] [*A publication*]
         (DLA)
LRPC .... English Law Reports, Privy Council, Appeal Cases [*1866-75*]
         [*A publication*] (DLA)
LRPC .... Lightweight Remote Procedure Call [*Computer science*]
LRPC .... London Regional Passengers Committee [*British*] (ECON)
LRPC (Eng) ... English Law Reports, Privy Council, Appeal Cases [*1866-75*]
         [*A publication*] (DLA)
LRPD .... Law Reports, Probate Division [*A publication*] (DLA)
LRP Div .... English Law Reports, Probate, Divorce, and Admiralty Division
         [*A publication*] (DLA)
LRPDS .... Long-Range Position-Determining System [*Army*] (RDA)
LRPE .... Long-Range Procurement Estimate (PDAA)
LRPE .... Long-Run Price Effect [*Marketing*]
LRPF .... Liberal Religious Peace Fellowship (EA)
LRPG .... Long-Range Penetration Group [*Military World War II*]
LRPG .... Long-Range Proving Ground [*Air Force*]
LRPGD .... Long-Range Proving Ground Division [*Air Force*]
LRPGR .... Long-Range Planning Ground Rules (AAG)
LRP/GWU .... Logistics Research Project, George Washington University
LRPL .... Liquid Rocket Propulsion Laboratory [*Army*] (IEEE)
LRPLS .... Long-Range Passive Location System (PDAA)
LRPP .... Long-Range Propulsion Plan (MCD)
LRPPD .... Long-Range Planning Purpose Document
LR Prob & M (Eng) ... English Law Reports, Probate, Divorce, and Admiralty
         Division [*A publication*] (DLA)
LR Prob Div ... English Law Reports, Probate, Divorce, and Admiralty Division
         [*A publication*] (DLA)
LR Prob Div (Eng) ... English Law Reports, Probate, Divorce, and Admiralty Division
         [*A publication*] (DLA)
LRPS .... Licentiate of the Royal Photographic Society [*British*] (DBQ)
LRPS .... Long-Range Planning Service [*Stanford Research Institute*] [*Assists
         businesses in investment activities*] (IID)
LRPS .... Long-Range Positioning System
LRPSI .... Long-Range Planning for School Improvement [*Pennsylvania*]
         (EDAC)
LRPT .... Large Repair Parts Transporter (MCD)
LRPT .... Longest Remaining Processing Time (PDAA)
LRQ .... Lower Right Quadrant (MAE)
LRQB .... English Law Reports, Queen's Bench Division [*1865-75*]
         [*A publication*] (DLA)
LRQB .... Quebec Queen's Bench Reports [*Canada*] [*A publication*] (DLA)
LRQBD .... English Law Reports, Queen's Bench Division [*1865-75*]
         [*A publication*] (DLA)
LRQB Div ..... English Law Reports, Queen's Bench Division [*1865-75*]
         [*A publication*] (DLA)
LRQB Div (Eng) ... English Law Reports, Queen's Bench Division [*1865-75*]
         [*A publication*] (DLA)
LRQB (Eng) ... English Law Reports, Queen's Bench Division [*1865-75*]
         [*A publication*] (DLA)
LR-QR .... Letter Requirement - Quick Reaction [*Army*]
LRR .... Labyrinthine Righting Reflex [*Physiology*]
LRR .... Lagged Reserve Requirement [*Finance*]
LRR .... Land-Rover Register 1947-1951 [*Petersfield, Hampshire, England*]
         (EAIO)
LRR .... LASER Radiation Receiver

LRR .... Launch Readiness Report [*or Review*] [*NASA*] (KSC)
LRR .... Launch Readiness Review [*Aerospace*] (NAKS)
LRR .... Leucine-Rich Repeat [*Biochemistry*]
LRR .... Leucine-Rich Repeats [*Genetics*]
LRR .... Logistic Readiness Review [*Navy*]
LRR .... Long-Range RADAR
LRR .... Long-Range Reconnaissance (MCD)
LRR .... Long-Range Requirements [*Navy*]
LRR .... Long-Range Rocket (MUGU)
LRR .... Longreach Resources Ltd. [*Vancouver Stock Exchange symbol*]
LRR .... Long Reduced Rate [*Taxation*] (WDAA)
LRR .... Long Regulatory Region [*Genetics*]
LRR .... Loop Regenerative Repeater
LRR .... Loss of Righting Reflex [*Medicine*]
LRR .... Lot Rejection Report
LRR & MF ... Long-Range Resource and Management Forecast
LRRC .... Labor Relations and Research Center [*University of Massachusetts*]
LRRC .... Land Resource Research Centre [*Canada*] (IRC)
LRRD .... Long-Range Reconnaissance Detachment
LRRDAP ...... Long-Range Research, Development, and Acquisition Plan (RDA)
LRRI .... Land Resources Research Institute [*Agriculture Canada*] [*Formerly,
         Soil Research Institute*] [*Research center*] (RCD)
LRRI .... Long-Range Reference Retroreflectance Instrument [*Bicycle test*]
         [*National Institute of Standards and Technology*]
LRRM .... Labor Relations Reference Manual [*Bureau of National Affairs*]
         [*A publication*] (DLA)
LRRM .... Loss Ratio Reserve Method [*Insurance*]
lrRNA .... Ribonucleic Acid, Light Ribosomal [*Biochemistry, genetics*]
LRRO .... Land Revenue Records and Enrollments Office [*British*]
LRRP .... Law Reports, Restrictive Practices Cases [*1958-72*] [*A publication*]
         (DLA)
LRRP .... Long-Range Reconnaissance Patrol [*Pronounced "lurp"*] [*Later, LRP*]
         [*Army*] (AABC)
LRRP .... Lowest Required Radiated Power
LRRPC .... Restrictive Practices Cases [*1958-72*] [*England*] [*A publication*]
         (DLA)
LRRR .... LASER Ranging Retroreflection [*Also, LR3*] [*Pronounced "LR-cubed"*
         Apollo 11 experiment*] [*NASA*]
LRRS .... Library Reports & Research Service, Inc. [*Information service or
         system*] (IID)
LRRS .... Limited Remaining Radiation Service [*Unit*] [*Military*]
LRRS .... Long-Range RADAR Site (OA)
LRRSA .... Light Railway Research Society of Australia
LRRT .... Library Research Round Table [*American Library Association*]
LRRT .... Light Rail Rapid Transit [*TRB*] (TAG)
LR/RT .... Long-Range Radiotelephone (DNAB)
LRS .... Laboratory Recoil Simulator (MCD)
LRS .... Laboratory Release System (MCD)
LRS .... Labor Relations Specialist (AAGC)
LRS .... Lactated Ringer's Solution [*Intravenous solution*]
LRS .... Lake Reporting Service
LRS .... Lamb-Retherford Shift [*Physics*]
LRS .... Lander Radio Subsystem [*NASA*]
LRS .... Lanyard Release Switch
LRS .... Larder Resources, Inc. [*Toronto Stock Exchange symbol*]
LRS .... Lares [*Puerto Rico*] [*Seismograph station code, US Geological
         Survey*] (SEIS)
LRS .... Large Ring Sparger [*Engineering*]
LRS .... LASER Raman Scattering
LRS .... LASER Raman Spectroscopy
LRS .... LASER Ranging System
LRS .... LASER Raster Scanner
LRS .... LASER Reflectance Spectrometer (SSD)
LRS .... Launch and Recovery Site (COE)
LRS .... Launch Recoil Simulator
LRS .... Laurinburg & Southern Railroad Co. [*AAR code*]
LRS .... Lawyer Referral Service
LRS .... League of Religious Settlements (EA)
LRS .... Legislative Reference Service [*Later, Congressional Research
         Service*] [*Library of Congress*]
LRS .... Level Recording Switch (NRCH)
LRS .... Library Reproduction Service, Microfilm Co. of California, Los
         Angeles, CA [*Library symbol Library of Congress*] (LCLS)
L/R/S .... Library Rubber Stamps [*Antiquarian book trade*]
LRS .... Lifetime Reproductive Success [*Demographics*]
LRS .... Light Radiation Sensor
LRS .... Light Repair Section [*British military*] (DMA)
LRS .... Light's Retention Scale [*Test*]
LRS .... Lightweight RADAR Set
LRS .... Limited Resources Specialty (AFM)
LRS .... Linear Referencing System [*FHWA*] (TAG)
LRS .... Linguistics Research System
LRS .... Liquid RADWASTE System (NRCH)
LRS .... Lloyd's Register of Shipping
LRS .... Logistics Requirements System [*Navy*]
LRS .... London Record Society [*British*] (ILCA)
LRS .... London Research Station [*British Gas*] (WDAA)
LRS .... Long-Range Schedule (SAA)
LRS .... Long-Range Search
LRS .... Long-Range Study
LRS .... Long-Range Surveillance [*Military*] (INF)
LRS .... Long Reversed Superchron [*Geology*]
LRS .... Long Right Shift
LRS .... Low-Rate Station

LRSA .... Laboratoire de Recherche en Sciences de l'Administration [*Laval University*] [*Canada Research center*] (RCD)
LRSA .... Lamprey River Study Act of 1991 (COE)
LRSAGW ...... Long-Range Surface-to-Air Guided Weapon (IAA)
LRSAM .... Long-Range Surface-to-Air Missile (NATG)
LRS & D App... Law Reports, Scotch and Divorce Appeals [*1866-75*] [*A publication*] (DLA)
LRS & TP ... Long-Range Science and Technology Plan [*Army*]
LRSB .... Sibiu/Turnisor [*Romania*] [*ICAO location identifier*] (ICLI)
LRSC .... Law Reports, New Zealand Supreme Court [*A publication*] (DLA)
LRSC .... Licentiate of the Royal Society of Chemistry [*British*] (DBQ)
LRSC .... Long-Range Surveillance Co. [*Military*] (INF)
LRSCA .... Land Remote Sensing Commercialization Act [*1984*]
LRSCA .... Large Retractable Solar Cell Array
LR Sc & D ... English Law Reports, House of Lords, Scotch and Divorce Appeal Cases [*1866-75*] [*A publication*] (DLA)
LR Sc & D App... Scottish and Divorce Appeals [*1866-75*] [*A publication*] (DLA)
LR Sc & D App... Scottish and Divorce Cases before the House of Lords [*A publication*] (DLA)
LR Sc & Div... Scotch and Divorce Appeals [*1866-75*] [*A publication*] (DLA)
LR Sc App ... Law Reports, Scotch Appeals [*A publication*] (DLA)
LR Sc Div App... Law Reports, Scotch Appeals [*A publication*] (DLA)
LRSCX .... Lord Abbett Research: Small Cap [*Mutual fund ticker symbol*] (SG)
LRSD .... Long-Range Surveillance Detachment [*Military*] (INF)
LRSDC .... Lakes Region Sled Dog Club (EA)
LR Sess Cas... English Law Reports, Sessions Cases [*A publication*] (DLA)
LRSF........... Lactating Rat Serum Factor [*Immunology*]
LRSF........... Liver Regenerating Serum Factor [*Medicine*] (DMAA)
LRSF........... Long-Range Systems Forecast
LRSI........... LifeRate Systems [*NQS*] (TTSB)
LRSI........... LifeRate Systems, Inc. [*NASDAQ symbol*] (SAG)
LRSI........... Long-Range SOF [*Special Operation Force*] Insertion (DOMA)
LRSI........... Low-Temperature Reusable Surface Insulation (NASA)
LRSIFC .... Lori Robin Smith International Fan Club (EA)
LRSK .... Long-Range Station Keeping (NG)
LRSL .... Law Reports, Sierra Leone Series [*A publication*] (DLA)
LRSL .... Long-Range Surveillance Leader [*Military*] (INF)
LRSLA .... Long-Range Service Life Analysis (MCD)
LRSLC .... Long Range Surveillance Leaders Course [*Army*]
LRSLP .... Lietuvos Revoliuciniu Socialistu Liaudininkai Partija [*Revolutionary Socialist Populists Party of Lithuania*] [*Political party*] (PPE)
LRSM.......... Laboratory for Research on the Structure of Matter [*University of Pennsylvania*]
LRSM.......... Licentiate of the Royal School of Music, London [*British*]
LRSM.......... Long-Range Seismograph Measurements (MCD)
LRSM.......... Long-Range Standoff Missile [*Military*] (MUSM)
LRSM.......... Satu Mare [*Romania*] [*ICAO location identifier*] (ICLI)
LRSO .... Long-Range Surveillance Outpost (MCD)
LRSOM .... Long-Range Stand-Off Missile
LRSOW .... Long-Range Conventional Standoff Weapon
LRSP .... Long-Range Strategic Planning (PDAA)
LRSR .... Liquid Redox Sulfur Recovery [*Processes for removing hydrogen sulfide from gases*]
LRSR .... Long-Range Sniper Rifle (PDAA)
LRSS .... Long-Range Strategic Studies [*Military*] (AFIT)
LRSS .... Long-Range Survey System [*Military*]
LR Stat .... English Law Reports, Statutes [*A publication*] (DLA)
LRSTPP ...... Long-Range Scientific Technical Planning Program (NG)
LRSU .... Long-Range Surveillance Unit [*Military*] (INF)
LRSUBRS .... Long-Range Surveillance Unit Base Radio Station [*Military*] (INF)
LRSV .... Lychnis Ringspot Virus [*Plant pathology*]
LRSV .... Suceava/Salcea [*Romania*] [*ICAO location identifier*] (ICLI)
LRT............. LASER Range-Finder Theodolite
LRT............. Last Resort Target [*Military*]
LRT............. Launch, Recovery, and Transport [*Vehicle*]
LRT............. Lawrenceburg, TN [*Location identifier FAA*] (FAAL)
LRT............. Light Rail Transit
LRT............. Light Repair Truck [*British*]
LRT............. Likelihood Ratio Test [*Statistics*]
LRT............. Linear Response Theory [*Physics*]
LRT............. LL&E Royalty Tr UBI [*NYSE symbol*] (TTSB)
LRT............. LL & E Royalty Trust UBI [*NYSE symbol*] (SPSG)
LRT............. Load Ratio Transformer (IAA)
LRT............. Local Leak Rate Test [*Nuclear energy*] (IEEE)
LRT............. Local Radiotherapy
LRT............. Loki Ranging Transponder
LRT............. London Reading Test [*Educational test*]
LRT............. London Regional Transport
LRT............. Long-Range Radiotelephone
LRT............. Long-Range Transport [*Navy British*]
LRT............. Long-Range Typhon [*Navy*] (NG)
LRT............. Long Ring Timer
LRT............. Lorentz Reciprocal Theorem
LRT............. Lorient [*France*] [*Airport symbol*] (OAG)
LRT............. Lower Respiratory Tract [*Medicine*]
LRTA........... Lath Renders' Trade Association [*A union*] [*British*]
LRTA........... Leisure, Recreation, and Tourism Abstracts [*Database*] [*Commonwealth Agricultural Bureaux International*] [*Information service or system*] (CRD)
LRTA........... Light Rail Transit Association [*Milton, Keynes, England*] (EAIO)
LRTAP .... Long-Range Transport of Atmospheric Pollutants
LRTC .... Law Reform Commission of Tasmania [*Australia*]
LRTC .... Tulcea/Cataloi [*Romania*] [*ICAO location identifier*] (ICLI)
LRTF .... Linear Radial Transmission Filter [*Photography*]
LRTF .... Long-Range Technical Forecast (IEEE)

LRTG .... Logistics Reassignment Task Group [*DoD*] (MCD)
LRTGT .... Last Resort Target [*Military*]
LRThD .... Lateral Reach-Through Device (PDAA)
LRTI .... Lower Respiratory Tract Illness (DAVI)
LRTI .... Lower Respiratory Tract Infection [*Medicine*] (ADA)
LRTL .... Light Railway Transport League [*British*] (DCTA)
LRTM .... Long-Range Training Mission [*Military*]
LRTM .... Tirgu Mures/Vidrasau [*Romania*] [*ICAO location identifier*] (ICLI)
LRTNF .... Long-Range Theater Nuclear Force [*Military*]
LRTNW .... Long-Range Theater Nuclear Weapons [*Military*]
LRTP .... Long-Range Technical Plan (PDAA)
LRTP .... Long-Running Thermal Precipitation (DICI)
LRTR .... Timisoara/Giarmata [*Romania*] [*ICAO location identifier*] (ICLI)
LRTRO .... Loaded Radial Tire Run-Out [*Automotive engineering*]
LRTS .... LASER Ranging and Tracking System (RDA)
LRTS .... Library Resources & Technical Services [*Association for Library Collections and Technical Services*] [*American Library Association*]
LRTx .... Living Related Renal Transplantation [*Medicine*]
LRU .... Las Cruces [*New Mexico*] [*Airport symbol*] (OAG)
LRU .... Las Cruces, NM [*Location identifier FAA*] (FAAL)
LRU .... Least Recently Used [*Replacement algorithm*] [*Computer science*]
LRU .... Least Repairable Unit
LRU .... Least Replaceable Unit (IAA)
LRU .... Less than Release Unit [*Army*] (AABC)
LRU .... Line Removable Unit
LRU .... Line Replaceable Unit (AFM)
LRU .... Link Retraction Unit (KSC)
LRU .... Little Rock University [*Merged with University of Arkansas*]
LRU .... Lone Replaceable Unit (MCD)
LRU .... Lowest Repairable Unit (MCD)
LRU .... Lowest Replacement Unit (MCD)
LRU .... Tulane University, New Orleans, LA [*OCLC symbol*] (OCLC)
LRuL .... Louisiana Technical University, Ruston, LA [*Library symbol Library of Congress*] (LCLS)
LRuLP .... Lincoln Parish Library, Ruston, LA [*Library symbol Library of Congress*] (LCLS)
LRUP .... La Raza Unida Party (EA)
LRUPS .... Line Replaceable Unit Power Supply (MCD)
LRV........... Lanarkshire Rifle Volunteers [*British military*] (DMA)
LRV........... Lancashire Rifle Volunteers [*British military*] (DMA)
LRV........... Launch Readiness Verification [*NASA*] (NASA)
LRV........... Left Renal Vein [*Anatomy*] (DAVI)
LRV........... Leirvogur [*Iceland*] [*Geomagnetic observatory code*]
LRV........... Lifting Reentry Vehicle (MCD)
LRV........... Light Rail Vehicle
LRV........... Light Reconnaissance Vehicle [*Military*]
LRV........... Light Recreational Vehicle [*Mitsubishi minivan*]
LRV........... Little Rabbit Valley [*California*] [*Seismograph station code, US Geological Survey*] (SEIS)
LRV........... Long-Range Video (MCD)
LRV........... Lunar Rover [*or Roving*] Vehicle [*NASA*]
LRVEP .... League of Rural Voters Education Project (EA)
LRW........... Labor Relations Week [*Bureau of National Affairs*] [*Information service or system*] (CRD)
LRW........... London Radio Workshop [*Independent Local Radio*] [*British*]
LRWRO........ Loaded Radial Wheel Run-Out [*Automotive engineering*]
LRY........... Lady Robyn Resources, Inc. [*Vancouver Stock Exchange symbol*]
LRY........... Latching Relay (IAA)
LRY........... Liberal Religious Youth
LRY........... Liberty Property Trust [*NYSE symbol*] (SAG)
LS .... Labologists Society [*Farnborough, Hampshire, England*] (EAIO)
LS .... Laboratory System
LS .... Labor Service [*Military*]
L/S .... Lactose/Sucrose [*Ratio*]
LS .... Lacus Somniorum [*Lunar area*]
LS .... Lamellar Strip [*Botany*]
LS .... Landesschuetzeneinheit [*Regional defense force*] [*German military - World War II*]
LS .... Landing Ship
LS .... Landing Side [*Air Force*]
LS .... Landing Site (KSC)
LS .... Land Service
LS .... Land Surveying Program [*Association of Independent Colleges and Schools specialization code*]
LS .... Land Surveyor
LS .... Lange Sicht [*Long Sight*] [*German*]
LS .... Language Specification (IEEE)
LS .... Lantern Slide [*Photography*]
ls .... Laos [*MARC country of publication code Library of Congress*] (LCCP)
LS .... Lapped Seam (DNAB)
LS .... Lasallian Sisters (Vietnam) (TOCD)
LS .... LASER System
LS .... Lastensegler; Lastensegelflugzeug [*Cargo transport glider*] [*German military - World War II*]
LS .... Latch Side
LS .... Lateral Septum
LS .... Lateral Subsylvian Cortex [*Neuroanatomy*]
LS .... Lateral Suspensor [*Ligament*] [*Anatomy*] (DAVI)
LS .... Late Scramble [*Reason for missed interception*] [*Military*]
LS .... Late Shock [*Medicine*]
LS .... Launching System
LS .... Launch Sequence (MCD)
LS .... Launch Service
LS .... Launch Set

LS	Launch Simulator	(MUGU)
LS	Launch Site [*NASA*]	(MCD)
LS	Launch Station	(MCD)
LS	Law Society	(WDAA)
LS	Law Student	(DLA)
LS	Leaders of Science [*A publication*]	
LS	Leading Seaman [*Navy British*]	
LS	Leading Stoker	
LS	Lead Sheet [*Military*]	
LS	Lead Survey [*Environmental science*]	(COE)
LS	Leaf Spring [*Automotive engineering*]	
L-S	Leap-Second	
LS	Learning Step	
LS	Lease	
LS	Least Significant	(IEEE)
LS	Least Squares [*Mathematical statistics*]	
L/S	Lecithin/Sphingomyelin [*Ratio*] [*Clinical chemistry*]	
LS	Lectori Salutem [*Latin*]	
LS	Left Sacrum [*Medicine*]	(KSC)
LS	Left Safety [*Football*]	(DICI)
LS	Left Shift	
LS	Left Side	
LS	Left Sign	(IAA)
LS	Legally Separated	(MAE)
LS	Legal Scroll	
LS	Le Gros Scouts [*British military*]	(DMA)
LS	Leiomyosarcoma [*Medicine*]	
LS	Length of Stroke	
LS	Lepidopterists' Society	
LS	Lesotho [*ANSI two-letter standard code*]	(CNC)
LS	Less	
LS	Lessing Society	(EA)
LS	Letterer-Siwe [*Disease*] [*Medicine*]	(DB)
LS	Letter Service	
LS	Letter Signed [*Manuscript descriptions*]	
ls	Letter Signed [*Handwritten signature*]	(WDMC)
LS	Letter Stock	
LS	Leukemia Society of America	
LS	Level Setter	
LS	Level Switch	
LS	Libman-Sacks [*Disease*] [*Medicine*]	(DB)
LS	Library Science	
LS	Library Search	
LS	Library Services	
LS	Licensed Surveyor [*British*]	(ADA)
LS	Licentiate in Science	
LS	Licentiate in Surgery	
L-S	Lifesaving Service [*Coast Guard*]	
LS	Life Science	(NASA)
LS	Life Support	(AAG)
LS	Life System	(MCD)
LS	Lighthouse Service [*Coast Guard*]	
LS	Lighting Supervisor [*Television*]	
LS	Lighting System	
LS	Lightning Sensor [*Aviation*]	
LS	Light Ship	
LS	Light Source	
LS	Light Sussex [*Poultry*]	
LS	Light Switch	
LS	Lignosulfonate [*Pulp and paper processing*]	
LS	Like-Sexed	
LS	Limbic System [*Brain anatomy*]	
LS	Limestone [*Petrology*]	(AAG)
LS	Liminal [*or Least*] Sensation [*Psychology*]	
LS	Limit Switch [*Electronics*]	
LS	Line Scan	(DEN)
LS	Line-Sequential	(IAA)
LS	Line Speed	
L/S	Lines per Second	(WDAA)
LS	Line Stretcher	
LS	Line Switch [*Telecommunications*]	(TEL)
LS	Linker Scanning [*Mutants*] [*Genetics*]	
LS	Linksozialisten [*Left Socialists*] [*Austria Political party*]	(PPE)
LS	Link State	(ACRL)
LS	Linnean Society [*Australia*]	
LS	Liquid Scintillation [*Chemical analysis*]	
LS	Liquid Sensor	(AAG)
LS	Listed Securities	
LS	Listing Salesperson [*Real estate*]	(REAL)
ls	Listing Salesperson [*Real estate*]	(REAL)
LS	List of Specifications	(NATG)
LS	List Total [*Banking*]	
LS	Literature Search	
l/s	Liters per Second [*SI symbol*]	
LS	Little Stock	(MHDW)
LS	Liver and Spleen [*Medicine*]	
LS	Livestock	(DCTA)
LS	Loading Splice [*Telecommunications*]	(TEL)
L/S	Load System	(MCD)
LS	Lobe Switching	(IAA)
LS	Local Store	
LS	Local Sunset	
LS	Local Sunset Time	(WDMC)
LS	Loca Sancta [*A publication*]	(BJA)
LS	Locked Shut	(NRCH)
LS	Lockheed Standards	
LS	Locus Sepulchri [*Place of the Sepulchre*] [*Latin*]	
LS	Locus Sigilli [*Place of the Seal*] [*Legal term Latin*]	
LS	Logical Sum [*Computer science*]	
LS	Logistical Support [*Army*]	
LS	Logistics Squadron [*Military*]	
LS	Log-Skidder [*Tires*]	(DICI)
LS	London Scottish [*Army regiment*]	
LS	[*The*] London Sinfonietta	
Ls	Longear Sunfish [*Ichthyology*]	
LS	Longitudinal Section	
LS	Longitudinal Staggering	(IAA)
LS	Long Service	(ADA)
LS	Long Shot [*A photograph or motion picture sequence taken from a distance*]	
LS	Long Sight	(WDAA)
LS	Long Sleeves [*Dressmaking*]	
LS	Loose Shot	
LS	Lost Seska [*Defunct*]	(EA)
LS	Loudspeaker	
LS	Lovat Scouts [*British military*]	(DMA)
LS	Lower Sprocket	(ECII)
LS	Lower Structure	
LS	Low-Power Schottky [*Electronics*]	
LS	Low Salt [*Dietetics*]	
LS	Low Secondary	(IAA)
LS	Low Similarity [*Psychology*]	
LS	Low-Sodium Diet	(DMAA)
LS	Low-Speed	
LS	Low Spin	(EDCT)
LS	Lumbar Spine [*Medicine*]	(DMAA)
LS	Lumbosacral [*Medicine*]	
LS	Lump Sum	
LS	Lunar Surface	(KSC)
LS	Lung Sounds [*Medicine*]	
LS	Luteinization Stimulator [*Endocrinology*]	
LS	Lute Society [*Harrow, England*]	(EAIO)
LS	Luxury Sport [*In automobile model name "Cordia LS"*]	
LS	Lymphosarcoma [*Medicine*]	
LS	Marco Island Airways [*ICAO designator*]	(AD)
ls----	South Atlantic Ocean [*MARC geographic area code Library of Congress*]	(LCCP)
LS	Sudanese Pound	(IMH)
LS	Summer [*Vessel load line mark*]	
LS3	London Specialist Software Systems	(NITA)
LSA	Labor Services Agency	(AABC)
LSA	Labor Surplus Area	
LSA	Labour Staff Association [*National Coal Board*] [*British*]	
LSA	Lamesa, TX [*Location identifier FAA*]	(FAAL)
LSA	Landing Ship, Assault [*Navy British*]	
LSA	Landing Supply Activity	
LSA	Landmark Savings Association	(EFIS)
LSA	Land Service Assistant [*Ministry of Agriculture, Fisheries, and Food*] [*British*]	
LSA	Land Settlement Association [*British*]	
LSA	Language Sampling and Analysis [*Educational test*]	
LSA	Large Science Aperture [*Spectrometer*]	
LSA	Large Space Antenna	(SSD)
LSA	Large Spherical Array	
LSA	LASER-Supported Absorption	(PDAA)
LSA	Lateral Spherical Aberration	
LSA	Late Stone Age	
LSA	Launch Services Agreement	(MCD)
LSA	Law and Society Association	(EA)
LSA	Law Services Association [*British*]	(DBA)
LSA	Layton School of Art [*Wisconsin*]	
LSA	Leading Stores Accountant [*British military*]	(DMA)
LSA	Leading Supply Assistant	(WDAA)
LSA	Lead Spring Assembly	
LSA	League for Socialist Action [*Canada*]	
LSA	Leaving Scene of an Accident [*Traffic offense charge*]	
LSA	Left Sacroanterior [*A fetal position, the breech position*] [*Obstetrics*]	
LSA	Left Subclavian Artery [*Anatomy*]	(AAMN)
LSA	Leisure Studies Association [*British*]	
LSA	Leukemia Society of America	(EA)
LSA	Leukocyte Specific Activity	(DB)
LSA	Level Shift Amplifier	
LSA	Lhasa [*Tibet*] [*Seismograph station code, US Geological Survey*]	(SEIS)
LSA	Library Science Abstracts [*A publication*]	
LSA	Library Services Act [*1956*]	
LSA	Licentiate in Agricultural Science	
LSA	Licentiate of the Society of Apothecaries [*British*]	
LSA	Lichen Sclerosis et Atrophicus [*Dermatology*]	
LSA	Life Saving Appliance [*or Apparatus*]	(DS)
LSA	Life Style Analysis [*Psychology*]	
LSA	Light Strike Aircraft [*Military*]	(PDAA)
LSA	Limited Space-Charge Accumulation [*Electronics*]	
LSA	Linea Aerea Nacional (Lansa) [*Dominican Republic*] [*ICAO designator*]	(FAAC)
LSA	Linear Servo Actuator	
LSA	Line Sensing Amplifier	(IAA)
LSA	Line-Sharing Adapter	
LSA	Line Sharing Adaptor	(NITA)
LSA	Linguistic Society of America	(EA)

1840 Acronyms, Initialisms & Abbreviations Dictionary • 27th Edition

LSA	Lipid-Bound Sialic Acid [Biochemistry] (DAVI)
LSA	Liquid Scintillation Analyzer [Chemistry]
LSA	List of Sections Affected (AAGC)
LSA	Lithuanian Scouts Association (EA)
LSA	Lithuanian Students Association (EA)
LSA	Little Sisters of the Assumption [See also PSA] [France] (EAIO)
LSA	Livestock Agent
LSA	Local Supervising Authority
LSA	Locksmith Security Association (EA)
LSA	Logic State Analyzer (IAA)
LSA	Logistics Supply Area
LSA	Logistics Support Analysis
LSA	Logistic Support Agreement [Military] (CAAL)
LSA	Logistic Support Aircraft (MCD)
LSA	Logistic Support Analysis
LSA	Logistic Support Area (NVT)
LSA	Logistic Sustainability Analysis [Environmental science] (COE)
LSA	Logistic System Analysis [Navy]
LSA	Longitudinal Spherical Aberration
LSA	Losuia [Papua New Guinea] [Airport symbol] (OAG)
LSA	Loudspeaker Amplifier (DWSG)
LSA	Louisiana Statutes, Annotated [A publication] (DLA)
LSA	Low-Cost Solar Array (IEEE)
LSA	Lowe's Syndrome Association (EA)
LSA	Low Specific Activity [Radioisotope]
LSA	Low-Speed Adapter (IAA)
LSA	Lubricant, Small Arms [Weaponry] [Military] (VNW)
LSA	Lute Society of America (EA)
LSa	Lymphosarcoma [Medicine]
LSA	University of Arizona, Graduate Library School, Tucson, AZ [OCLC symbol] (OCLC)
LSAA	Library Services Authority Act (NITA)
LSAA	Linen Supply Association of America [Later, TRSA] (EA)
LSAAP	Lone Star Army Ammunition Plant (AABC)
LSAB	Learning Systems and Access Branch [Education] (AIE)
LSAC	Labor Sector Advisory Committee [Terminated, 1980] (EGAO)
LSAC	Law School Admission Council (EDAC)
LSAC	London Small Arms Co. [Military]
LSAC	Low-Pressure Suction Air Conveyor (PDAA)
LSAC	Low-Speed Access to a Computer (PDAA)
LSAC/LSAS	Law School Admission Council/Law School Admission Services (EA)
LSACN	Logistic Support Analysis Control Number (MCD)
LSAD	Launch Safe-and-Arm Device
LSAG	Geneve [Switzerland ICAO location identifier] (ICLI)
LSAH	Launch Site Accommodations Handbook [NASA] (NASA)
lsai--	Ascension Island [MARC geographic area code Library of Congress] (LCCP)
LSAL	Left Salivary [Gland]
L Salic	Salic Law [A publication] (DLA)
LSA/LSAR	Logistic Support Analysis/Logistic Support Analysis Record [Army] (RDA)
LSALT	Lowest Safe Altitude [Aviation] (DA)
LSAM	Launcher System Angles Matched [Navy] (CAAL)
LSAM	Logistics Support Alternative [or Analysis] Model (MCD)
LSAM	Lumped Shell Analysis Method
LSA mode	Limited Space Charge Accumulation Mode [Telecommunications] (NITA)
LSANA	Leukocyte-Specific Antinuclear Antibody [Hematology] (DMAA)
LS & GCM	Long Service and Good Conduct Medal [Military decoration British]
LS & MS	Lake Shore & Michigan Southern Railway
LS and MS	Less Sleep and More Speed [Hobo slang]
LSANSW	Limbless Soldiers' Association of New South Wales [Australia]
LSANSW	Liquor Stores Association of New South Wales [Australia]
LSAO	Line Station Assembly Order (MCD)
LSAP	Laboratory Space Allocation Plan (MCD)
LSAP	Launch Sequence Applications Program (MCD)
LSAP	Letzeburger Sozialistesch Arbechter Partei [Socialist Workers' Party of Luxembourg] [Political party] (PPE)
LSAP	Life Space Analysis Profile [Test] (TMMY)
LSAP	Linear Systems Analysis Program [Statistics]
LSAP	Link Layer Service Access Point
LSAP	Local Service Access Point [Telecommunications] (OSI)
LSAP	Logistic Support Analysis Plan [or Program] [Army]
LSAP	Logistic Support Analysis Process [Navy]
LSAPT	Lunar Sample Analysis Planning Team [NASA]
LSAQ	Limbless Soldiers' Association of Queensland [Australia]
LSAR	Local Storage Address Register (IAA)
LSAR	Logistic Support Analysis Record (RDA)
LSAR	Lymphosarcoma Cell [Oncology] (DAVI)
LSA/RCS	Lymphosarcoma - Reticulum Cell Sarcoma [Oncology] (MAE)
LSARS	West's Louisiana Revised Statutes [A publication] (DLA)
LSAS	Law School Admission Services (EDAC)
LSAS	Longitudinal Stability Augmentation System [Aviation] (DA)
LSASA	Limbless Soldiers' Association of South Australia
LSAT	Law School Admission Test
LSAT	Law School Aptitude Test (GAGS)
LSAT	Legal Scholastic Aptitude Test (HGAA)
LSAT	Leveling/Sharpening Aggressions Test [Psychology] (EDAC)
LSAT	Logistic Shelter Air Transportable
LSAV	Limbless Soldiers' Association of Victoria [Australia]
LSAV	Liquor Stores' Association of Victoria [Aerospace]
LSAW	LASER-Supported Absorption-Wave (PDAA)
LSAWA	Liquor Stores' Association of Western Australia
LSAY	Longitudinal Study of American Youth [Northern Illinois University] [Education]

LSAZ	Zurich [Switzerland ICAO location identifier] (ICLI)
LSB	Bachelor of Life Science
LSB	Labour Supply Board [British]
LSB	Landing Ship, Bombardment
LSB	Large-Scale Bypass [Telecommunications] (CIST)
LSB	La Sacra Bibbia (BJA)
LSB	Launcher Support Building
LSB	Launch Service Building
LSB	Learned Society Board (ACII)
LSB	Leased Spacecraft Bus (SSD)
LSB	Least Significant BIT [or Byte] [Data compaction]
LSB	Left Sternal Border
LSB	Lensibavia [Former USSR] [FAA designator] (FAAC)
LSB	Library of Standard Biographies [A publication]
LSB	Life Safety Box
LSB	Lifestyle Beverage Corp. [Vancouver Stock Exchange symbol]
LSB	Line Segment Block [Computer science]
LSB	List of Successful Bidders [DoD]
LSB	Lithuanian Boy Scouts [An association] (EA)
LSB	Logistics Sustaining Base [Military] (RDA)
LSB	Logistic Support Base (NVT)
LSB	London School Board
LSB	Longitudinal Studies Branch [Department of Education] (GFGA)
LSB	Lordsburg, NM [Location identifier FAA] (FAAL)
LSB	Lower Sideband [Data transmission]
LSB	Low Silhouette Blade [Aircraft]
LSB	Low-Speed Breaker Relay (IEEE)
LSB	Low-Speed Buffer (CET)
LSB	Low-Surface-Brightness [Galaxies - astronomy]
LSB	LSB Industries [NYSE symbol] (TTSB)
LSB	LSB Industries, Inc. [NYSE symbol] (SAG)
LSB	Lucas-Sumitomo Brakes [Auto industry supplier]
LSB	Lunar Surface Base [NASA] (KSC)
LSB	Southern University, Library, Baton Rouge, LA [OCLC symbol] (OCLC)
LSBA	Leading Sick Bay Attendant [Navy British]
LSBC	[The] La Salle & Bureau County Railroad Co. [AAR code]
LSB Fn	LSB Financial Corp. [Associated Press] (SAG)
LSB Fncl	LSB Financial Corp. [Associated Press] (SAG)
LSBI	LSB Financial [NASDAQ symbol] (TTSB)
LSBI	LSB Financial Corp. [NASDAQ symbol] (SAG)
LSB Ind	LSB Industries, Inc. [Associated Press] (SAG)
LSB NC	LSB Bancshares, Inc. of North Carolina [Associated Press] (SAG)
LSBPHF	Library Service to the Blind and Physically Handicapped Forum [Association of Specialized and Cooperative Library Agencies]
LSBPrC	LSB Ind $3.25 Cv Exch Pfd [NYSE symbol] (TTSB)
LS BPS	Laparoscopic Bilateral Partial Salpingectomies [Gynecology] (DAVI)
LSBR	Large Seed-Blanket Reactor
LSBR	Liquid Strand Burning Rate (MCD)
LSBRT	Library Service to the Blind Round Table
lsbv--	Bouvet Island [MARC geographic area code Library of Congress] (LCCP)
LSBX	Lawrence Savings Bank [NASDAQ symbol] (SAG)
LSBY	Least Significant Byte [Data compaction] [Computer science]
LSC	Labor Socialist Committee [Australia]
LSC	Labor Studies Center [AFL-CIO]
LSC	Lake Survey Center [National Oceanic and Atmospheric Administration]
LSC	Landing Ship Carrier [British military] (DMA)
LSC	Language and Society Centre [Monash University] [Australia]
LSC	Languages Services Centre [South Australia]
LSC	Large-Scale Computer
LSC	Large Single Copy Region [Of a chromosome] [Genetics]
LSC	Large Solar Concentrator (SSD)
LSC	Large Submetacentric Chromosome [Medicine]
LSC	Las Cruces [Diocesan abbreviation] [New Mexico] (TOCD)
LSC	La Serena [Chile] [Airport symbol] (AD)
LSC	LASER Spectral Control
LSC	LASER-Supported Combustion (MCD)
LSC	Last Significant Character (ECII)
LSC	Late Systolic Click [Cardiology] (DAVI)
LSC	Launch Sequence Control
L/SC	Launch/Storage Container
L Sc	Laureate of Science
LSC	Law of the Sea Conference [United Nations]
LSC	Learning Skills Center Reading and Study Skills Program [Cornell University] [Research center] (RCD)
LSC	Least Significant Character (IEEE)
LSC	Least Square Center (IAA)
LSC	Least Squares Circle [Manufacturing term]
LSC	Least-Squares Collocation [Mathematics]
LSC	Left-Sided Colon Cancer [Oncology]
LSC	Left Stage Center [A stage direction]
LSC	Legal Services Corp. [Government agency]
LSC	Legal Services for Children (EA)
LSC	Legislative Service Center [Washington State Legislature] [Information service or system] (IID)
LSC	Lens Sign Convention
LSC	Liberian Shipowners Council (EA)
LSC	Library Services Center, Midwestern Regional Library System [UTLAS symbol]
LSC	Library Services Center of Missouri [Library network]
LSc	Licentiate in Science (DD)
LSC	Lichen Simplex Chronicus (DB)
LSC	Lid, Sclera, and Conjunctiva [Opthalmology] (DAVI)

LSC	Life Safety Code	LSD	Large Screen Display
LSC	Limit Signaling Comparator	LSD	Large Shallow-Draught [Bulk carrier] (PDAA)
LSC	Lincoln Sesquicentennial Committee [Terminated, 1960] [Government agency]	LSD	Large Steel Desk [Position given to ex-astronauts]
LSC	Linear Sequential Circuit	LSD	Laryngeal Sound Discrimination [Medicine] (DMAA)
LSC	Linear-Shaped Charge	LSD	LASER-Selective Demagnetization [Analytical technique]
LSC	Linear Slope Controlled (PDAA)	LSD	LASER Signal Device
LSC	Liquid Scintillation Cocktail [Analytical chemistry]	LSD	LASER-Supported Detonation Waves (MCD)
LSC	Liquid Scintillation Counter [or Counting]	LSD	Last Safe Date [Marine insurance] (DS)
LSC	Liquid Smoke Condensate	LSD	Latching Semiconductor Diode
LSC	Liquid Solid Chromatography	LSD	Latest Start Date
LSC	Liquids Solids Contact	LSD	Launch Support Division [NASA] (KSC)
LSC	Little Sisters of Carmel	LSD	Launch Systems Data
LSC	LOAD [Low Altitude Defense] Simulation Center	LSD	Law Student Division [American Bar Association] (BARN)
LSC	Load Standardization Crew (MCD)	LSD	Leadless Sealed Device (PDAA)
LSC	Lobbyist Systems Corp. [Information service or system] (IID)	LSD	Lead Sulfide Detection
LSC	Local Supercluster [Cosmology]	LSD	League for Spiritual Discovery (WDAA)
LSC	Local Switching Centre [Telecommunications] (NITA)	LSD	League of Safe Drivers [British] (BI)
LSC	Loco Sub Citato [In the Place Cited Below] [Latin] (ROG)	LSD	Leased (WGA)
LSC	Loco Supra Citato [In the Place Cited Above] [Latin]	LSD	Least Separation Distance (MUSM)
LSC	Logistical Support Center [Army]	LSD	Least Significant Decade (IAA)
LSC	Logistic Support Cadre (MCD)	LSD	Least Significant Difference [Statistics]
LSC	London Salvage Corps	LSD	Least Significant Digit [Data compaction] (MUGU)
LSC	Lone Star Conference (PSS)	LSD	Lesson Specification Document (MCD)
LSC	Loop Station Connector (MHDB)	LSD	Level Sensor Demonstration
LSC	Low-Speed Concentrator	LSD	Lexington, KY [Location identifier FAA] (FAAL)
LSC	LSI Logic Corp. of Canada, Inc. [Toronto Stock Exchange symbol]	Lsd	Librae, Solidi, Denarii [Shillings and Pence] [British] (WA)
LSC	Luminescent Solar Concentrator	LSD	Library Service to the Disadvantaged Committee
LSC	Luminescent Stamp Club [Defunct] (EA)	LSD	Life, Sport, and Drama [A publication British]
LSC	Lump-Sum Contract	LSD	Lightermen, Stevedores, and Dockers
LSC	Luxury Sport Coupe	LSD	Light-Sensing Device (IAA)
LSC	Shopco Laurel Centre L.P. [AMEX symbol] (TTSB)	LSD	Lime Juice, Scotch, Drambuie [A cocktail] (IIA)
LSC	Shopco Laurel Centre Ltd. [AMEX symbol] (SPSG)	LSD	Limited Saturation Device (PDAA)
LSC	Southern University, Law Library, Baton Rouge, LA [OCLC symbol] (OCLC)	LSD	Limited-Slip Differential [Automotive engineering]
		LSD	Limited Space-Charge Drift [Electronics] (IAA)
LScA	Left Scapuloanterior [A fetal position] [Obstetrics]	LSD	Limitswitch Down [Electronics] (IAA)
LSCA	Left Subclavian Artery [Anatomy] (DAVI)	LSD	Line-Sharing Device
LSCA	Library Services and Construction Act [1963]	LSD	Line Signal Detector
LSCA	Logistics Support Cost Analysis (NASA)	LSD	Linkage System Diagnostic (IAA)
LScAdmin	Licence in Administration [Canada] (DD)	LSD	Local Spin Density [Physics]
LSCC	Lattice Semiconductor [NASDAQ symbol] (TTSB)	LSD	Logarithmic Series Distribution [Statistics]
LSCC	Lattice Semiconductor Corp. [NASDAQ symbol] (SAG)	LSD	Logistics Systems Division [Air Force]
LSCC	Liberty Seated Collectors Club (EA)	LSD	Log-Slope Difference [Statistics]
LScC	Licentiate in Commercial Science (DD)	LSD	Lomir Shoyn Davenen (BJA)
LSCC	Line-Sequential Color Composite (IEEE)	LSD	Long Side
LSCC	Local Servicing Control Center [Telecommunications] (TEL)	LSD	Long, Slow Distance [Training method for runners]
LSCC	London Scottish Cadet Corps [British military] (DMA)	LSD	Lowest Significant Dose [Toxicology]
LScCom	Licentiate in Commercial Science	LSD	Low-Salt Diet (STED)
LScComm	Licentiate in Commercial Science (DD)	LSD	Low-Sodium Diet (DMAA)
LScCompt	Licencie en Sciences Comptables [Licentiate of Accounting] (DD)	LSD	Low-Speed Data
L Sc D	Doctor of the Science of Law	LSD	Low-Sulfur Diesel Fuel [Petroleum marketing]
LSCD	Leading Seaman Clearance Diver	LSD	Lump-Sum Distribution [Banking]
LSCE	Launch Sequence and Control Equipment	LSD	Lunar Surface Drill [Aerospace]
LSCE	Least Square Complex Exponential [Mathematics]	LSD	Lysergic Acid Diethylamide [or Lysergsaeure Diethylamid] [Hallucinogenic drug]
LScEco	Licence in Economics [Canada] (DD)	LSD	Lysergide (LDT)
LSc(Econ)	Licence in Science (Economics) [British] (DI)	LSD-25	Lysergic Acid Diethylamide (STED)
LSCG	Law School Computer Group [Defunct] (EA)	LSDA	Licentiate of the Speech and Drama Association (ADA)
LSCI	Large-Scale Compound Integration	LSDA	Louisiana Soft Drink Association (SRA)
LSCI	Lymphosarcoma Cell Leukemia [Medicine] (DMAA)	LSDAS	Law School Data Assembly Service (GAGS)
LSCL	Limit Switch Closed [Electronics] (IAA)	LSDDP	Library Service to Developmentally Disabled Persons [ASCLA] (AL)
LSCL	Lower Surface Center Line	LSDF	Large Sodium Disposal Facility [Nuclear energy] (NRCH)
LSCM	LASER-Scan Confocal Microscope	LSDF	Library Service to the Deaf Forum [Association of Specialized and Cooperative Library Agencies]
LSCM	LASER Scanning Confocal Microscopy		
LSCM	Logistic Support Coordination Meeting [Military] (MCD)	LSDG	Latitudinal Species-Diversity Gradient [Biodiversity]
LSCO	Lanthanum Strontium Copper Oxide [Inorganic chemistry]	LSDH	Ligue Suisse des Droits de l'Homme [Switzerland]
LSCO	Lesco, Inc. [NASDAQ symbol] (SAG)	LSDM	Lagrangian Stochastic Dispersion Model [Marine science] (OSRA)
LScO	Licence in the Science of Optometry [Canada] (DD)	LSDM	Logical Systems Design Methodology (NITA)
LSCP	Laserscope [NASDAQ symbol] (SAG)	LSDP	Lietuvos Socialdemokratu Partija [Lithuanian Social Democratic Party] [Political party] (PPE)
LScP	Left Scapuloposterior [A fetal position] [Obstetrics]		
LSCP	Logistic Support Control Point [Military] (AFM)	LSDP	Lump-Sum Death Payment
LSCP	Low-Speed Card Punch [Computer science] (AABC)	LSDR	Local Store Data Register
LSCP(Assoc)	Associate of the London and Counties Society of Physiologists [British] (DBQ)	LSDRM	Logistic Support Data Responsibility Matrix (MCD)
		LSDS	Large-Scale Dynamical System (PDAA)
LSCRA	Lower Saint Croix River Act of 1972 (COE)	LSDS	Large Screen Display System
LScRel	Licentiate in Religion (DD)	LSDS	Low-Speed Data Service [RCA Global Communications, Inc.] [Piscataway, NJ] [Telecommunications] (TSSD)
LSCRRC	Law Students Civil Rights Research Council (EA)		
LSCS	Lower Segment Caesarean Section [Medicine]	LSDS	Low-Speed Digital System
LScS	Southern University, Scotlandville, Baton Rouge, LA [Library symbol Library of Congress] (LCLS)	LSDSP	Latvijas Socialdemokratiska Stradnieku Partija [Latvian Social Democratic Workers' Party] [Political party] (EAIO)
LScS-N	Southern University at New Orleans, New Orleans, LA [Library symbol Library of Congress] (LCLS)	LSDT	Local Sidereal Time (MSA)
		LSDU	Link Layer Service Data Unit
LScSoc	Licence in Social Science [British]	LS/DW	Life Safety/Disaster Warning [Environmental science] (COE)
LSCT	LASER Spectral Control Technique	LSE	Laboratory Support Equipment (SSD)
LSCT	Loevinger Sentence Completion Test (EDAC)	LSE	La Crosse [Wisconsin]/Winona [Minnesota] [Airport symbol] (OAG)
LSCT	Low-Speed Compound Terminal (CET)	LSE	Landing Ship, Emergency Repair
LSCU	Local Servicing Control Unit [Telecommunications] (TEL)	LSE	Landing Signal Enlisted [Military]
LSCV	Left Subclavian Vein [Anatomy] (DAVI)	LSE	Language-Sensitive Editor [Computer science] (CIST)
LSD	Amphibious Ship, Dock	LSE	Large-Scale Equipment (MCD)
LSD	Doctor of Library Science	LSE	Latex Sphere Equivalent (AAEL)
LSD	Doctor of Life Science	LSE	Lattice Screen Editor [Program editor]
LSD	Landing Ship Deck	LSE	Launch Sequencer Equipment [NASA]
LSD	Landing Ship, Dock [Navy symbol]	LSE	Launch Station Equipment
LSD	Landing-Site Determination [NASA] (KSC)	LSE	Launch Support Equipment [NASA] (AAG)
LSD	Landing, Storage, Delivery [Business term]	LSE	Lease (ROG)
LSD	Language for Systems Development	Lse	Lease (TBD)

LSE	Least Squares Estimator [*Statistics*]
LSE	Left Second Entrance [*Theater*]
LSE	Left Sternal Edge [*Cardiology*]
LSE	Legal Services for the Elderly (EA)
lse	Licensee [*MARC relator code*] [*Library of Congress*] (LCCP)
LSE	Life Science Experiment (MUGU)
LSE	Life Support Equipment (KSC)
LSE	Life Support Evaluator (SAA)
LSE	Limited Signed Edition (ADA)
LSE	Linkage Stack Entry [*Computer science*] (CIST)
LSE	Liquid-Solid Extraction [*Chemistry*]
LSE	Living Skin Equivalent [*Synthetic organ*]
LSE	Local Side Effects [*Pharmacology*] (DAVI)
LSE	Logistics Support Element
LSE	Logistics Support Equipment [*Military*] (MCD)
LSE	London School of Economics
LSE	London Stock Exchange
LSE	Longitudinal-Section Electric (IEEE)
LSE	Loose
LSE	Louisiana Sugar Exchange (EA)
LSE	Lower Sternal Edge [*Cardiology*]
LSE	Low-Speed Encoder (IAA)
LSE	Low-Styrene Emission
LSE	Lunar Support Equipment [*Aerospace*] (IAA)
LSE	Lunar Surface Experiment [*NASA*]
LSE	Luxembourg Stock Exchange
LSE	Luxury Sport Euro [*Automobile model designation*] [*General Motors Corp. - Cadillac*]
LSE	Queen's Bench Library [*Alberta*] [*UTLAS symbol*]
LSEC	Australian Company Secretary's Practice Manual [*A publication*]
LSEC	Life-Cycle Software Engineering Center [*Army*]
l/sec	Liters per Second [*Respiration*] [*Medicine*] (DAVI)
LSECS	Life Support and Environmental Control System (IEEE)
LsEd	Leasing Edge Corp. [*Associated Press*] (SAG)
LSEED	Launch Support Equipment - Engineering Division [*NASA*] (KSC)
LSEG	Low Styrene Emission Gelcoat
LSELR	Low-Styrene-Emission Laminating Resin
LSEP	Left Somatosensory Evoked Potential (STED)
LSEP	Legal Services for the Elderly Poor [*Later, LSE*] (EA)
LSEP	Lifetime Sports Education Project [*of Lifetime Sports Foundation*]
LSEP	Lunar Surface Experiment Package [*NASA*]
LSEQ	Launch Sequencer [*Navy*] (CAAL)
LSER	Laser Corp. [*NASDAQ symbol*] (SAG)
LSER	Linear Solvation Energy Relationship [*Physical chemistry*]
LSER	Raron [*Switzerland ICAO location identifier*] (ICLI)
LSES	Large Surface Effect Ship (PDAA)
LSES	Life Support and Environmental System (IAA)
LSE SKDS	Loose or on Skids [*Freight*]
LSET	Logistics Supportability Evaluation Team [*Military*] (AFIT)
LSEV	Lunar Surface Exploration Vehicle [*Aerospace*]
LSEZ	Zermatt [*Switzerland ICAO location identifier*] (ICLI)
LSF	Fort Benning (Columbus), GA [*Location identifier FAA*] (FAAL)
LSF	Laboratory Simulation Facility (MCD)
LSF	Lande Splitting Factor
LSF	Landing Ship, Fighter Direction [*British military*] (DMA)
LSF	Language System FORTRAN [*Computer science*]
LSF	La Souterraine [*France*] [*Seismograph station code, US Geological Survey*] (SEIS)
LSF	Launch Support Facility [*NASA*] (KSC)
LSF	Least Square Fit
LSF	Lightship Screen File [*Computer science*]
LSF	Lightweight Strike Fighter [*NATO Air Forces*]
LSF	Limit Switch Forward (IAA)
LSF	Line Spread Function (MCD)
LSF	Line Switch Frame [*Telecommunications*] (TEL)
LSF	Liquid-State Submerged Fermentation [*Biochemistry*]
LSF	Literary Society Foundation (EA)
LSF	Lloyd Shaw Foundation (EA)
LSF	Load Sheet Fuel [*Aviation*] (DA)
LSF	Logistic Support Force [*Military*]
LSF	Loss Factor [*Electronics*] (IAA)
LSF	Lower Side Frequency [*Electronics*] (ECII)
LSF	Low Saturated Fat [*Diet*] (DAVI)
LSF	Lumped Selection Filter [*Telecommunications*] (OA)
LSF	Lunar Scientific Facility [*NASA*] (KSC)
LSF	Lymphocyte-Stimulating Factor [*Biochemistry*]
LSFA	Logistic System Feasibility Analysis (AABC)
LSFAE	Low-Speed Fuel Air Explosive
LSFC	Lennon Sisters Fan Club (EA)
LSFE	Life Sciences Flight Experiment [*NASA*] (NASA)
LSFF	Landing Ship, Flotilla Flagship [*Navy symbol Obsolete*]
LSFFAR	Low-Spin Folding Fin Aircraft Rocket (IEEE)
lsfk--	Falkland Islands [*MARC geographic area code Library of Congress*] (LCCP)
LSFN	List of Selected File Numbers (AABC)
LSFO	Logistics Support Field Office [*Federal disaster planning*]
LSFO	Low-Sulfur Fuel Oil
LSFR	Large-Probe Solar Net Flux Radiometer [*NASA*]
LSFR	Local Storage Function Register
LSFS	Lateral Separation Focus Sensor (PDAA)
LSFS	Light Sequence Flasher System (DWSG)
LSFT	Low Steamline Flow Test (IEEE)
LSG	labial Salivary Gland [*Medicine*] (STED)
LSG	Laminated Safety Glass [*Automotive engineering*]
LSG	Landing Ship, Gantry
LSG	Landing Ship, Gun [*British military*] (DMA)
LSG	Language Structure Group [*CODASYL*]
LSG	Large-Scale Geostrophic [*Marine science*] (OSRA)
LSG	Lateral Superior Geniculate Artery [*Anatomy*]
LSG	Legal Services Group
LSG	Legislative Strategy Group [*Reagan administration*]
LSG	Level Sensor Gradiometer
LSG	Ligo Samseksamaj Geesperantistoj [*Richmond, Surrey, England*] (EAIO)
LSG	Limited Subgroup (NATG)
LSG	Little Sisters of the Gospel (France) (TOCD)
LSG	Logistics Support Group (AAG)
LSG	Loh's Sinfully Good Ice Cream & Cookies, Inc. [*Vancouver Stock Exchange symbol*]
LSG	Low-Stress Grinding (DICI)
LSG	Lunar Surface Gravimeter [*Apollo*] [*NASA*]
LSGA	Laminators Safety Glass Association (EA)
LSGC	Les Eplatures [*Switzerland ICAO location identifier*] (ICLI)
LSGC	Long Service and Good Conduct (ADA)
LSGD	Lymphocyte Specific Gravity Distribution [*Medicine*]
LSGE	Ecuvillens [*Switzerland ICAO location identifier*] (ICLI)
LSGG	Geneve/Cointrin [*Switzerland ICAO location identifier*] (ICLI)
LSGK	Saanen [*Switzerland ICAO location identifier*] (ICLI)
LSGL	Lausanne/Blecherette [*Switzerland ICAO location identifier*] (ICLI)
LSG/LSU	Landing Support Group/Logistics Support Unit (DNAB)
LSGN	Neuchatel [*Switzerland ICAO location identifier*] (ICLI)
LSGP	La Cote [*Switzerland ICAO location identifier*] (ICLI)
LSGP	Large-Scale General Purpose
LSGP	Lateral Simulated Ground Plane [*Aerodynamics*]
LSGR	Loose Granular Snow [*Skiing condition*]
LSGS	Left Stellate Ganglion Stimulation [*Physiology*]
LSGS	Sion [*Switzerland ICAO location identifier*] (ICLI)
LsgSolu	Leasing Solutions, Inc. [*Associated Press*] (SAG)
LSGT	Gruyeres [*Switzerland ICAO location identifier*] (ICLI)
L/Sgt	Lance Sergeant [*British military*] (DMA)
LSGT	Lasergate Systems [*NASDAQ symbol*] (TTSB)
LSGT	Lasergate Systems, Inc. [*NASDAQ symbol*] (SAG)
LSGTW	Lasergate Sys Wrrt [*NASDAQ symbol*] (TTSB)
LSGU	Local Spinal Glucose Utilization [*Medicine*]
LSH	Landing Ship, Headquarters
LSH	Landing Ship, Heavy
LSH	Lashio [*Myanmar*] [*Airport symbol*] (OAG)
LSH	Library Services to the Handicapped, Alberta Culture [*UTLAS symbol*]
LSH	Light Ship (IAA)
LSH	London School of Hygiene
LSH	Lowland-Southern Hybrid [*Hemoglobin phenotype of Rana pipiens*]
LSH	Low Section Height [*Automotive engineering*]
LSH	Loyal Suffolk Hussars [*British military*] (DMA)
LSH	Lutein-Stimulating Hormone [*Also, ICSH, LH*] [*Endocrinology*]
LSH	Lymphocytosis-Stimulating Hormone [*Endocrinology*]
LSh	Shreve Memorial and Caddo Parish Extension Library, Shreveport, LA [*Library symbol Library of Congress*] (LCLS)
LSH	Southeastern Louisiana University, Hammond, LA [*OCLC symbol*] (OCLC)
LSHA	Gstaad-Inn Grund [*Switzerland ICAO location identifier*] (ICLI)
LShC	Centenary College of Louisiana, Shreveport, LA [*Library symbol Library of Congress*] (LCLS)
LSHC	Light-Saturated Hydrocarbon [*Organic chemistry*]
LShCa	Caddo Parish Library, Shreveport, LA [*Library symbol Library of Congress*] (LCLS)
LSHCNC	Local and Short Haul Carriers National Conference (EA)
LSHG	Gampel [*Switzerland ICAO location identifier*] (ICLI)
LSHG	Lashing [*Engineering*]
LSHI	Large-Scale Hybrid Integration
LSHIP	Leadership
LSH(L)	Landing Ship, Headquarters (Large)
LSHLD	Leasehold
Lshld	Leasehold (EBF)
LSH/LSF	Landing Ship, Helicopter/Landing Ship, Fighter Direction (DNAB)
LShN	R. W. Norton Art Foundation, Shreveport, LA [*Library symbol Library of Congress*] (LCLS)
LSHQ	Landing Ship, Headquarters [*British military*] (DMA)
LSH(S)	Landing Ship, Headquarters (Small)
LSHS	Low Sulphur Heavy Stock (PDAA)
LSHS	Sezegnin [*Switzerland ICAO location identifier*] (ICLI)
LShTE	Texas Eastern Transmission Corp., Shreveport, LA [*Library symbol Library of Congress*] (LCLS)
LSHTM	London School of Hygiene and Tropical Medicine (DAVI)
LShUG	United Gas Corp., Shreveport, LA [*Library symbol Library of Congress*] (LCLS)
LsHUP	Pennzoil United, Inc., Shreveport, LA [*Library symbol Library of Congress*] (LCLS)
LSHV	Laminated Synthetic High Voltage
LSI	Alis [*Former USSR*] [*FAA designator*] (FAAC)
LSI	Labour Supply Inspector [*British*]
LSI	Lake Superior & Ishpeming Railroad Co. [*AAR code*]
LSI	Landing Ship, Infantry [*Navy symbol*]
LSI	Large-Scale Integration [*of circuits*] [*Electronics*]
LSI	Largest Single Item (AFM)
LSI	LASER Surface Interaction
LSI	Lateral Shear Interferometer (PDAA)
LSI	Launch Success Indicator
LSI	Law of the Sea Institute (EA)
LSI	Laws of the State of Israel (BJA)

LSI	Leadership Skills Inventory [Test] (TMMY)
LSI	Lead Systems Integration
LSI	Learning Style Inventory [Occupational therapy]
LSI	Learning Systems Institute [Florida State University] [Research center] (RCD)
LSI	Lear Siegler Inc. (NITA)
LSI	Legal Support Inspection [Clean Water Act] [Environmental Protection Agency] (EPA)
LSI	Leisure Search Inventory [Test] (TMMY)
LSI	Lerwick [Scotland] [Airport symbol] (OAG)
LSI	Life Satisfaction Index [Medicine] (DMAA)
LSI	Life Space Interviewing [Teaching technique]
LSI	Light Scatter Index
LSI	Light Scattering Index (STED)
LSI	Listing Site Inspection [Environmental science] (FFDE)
LSI	Little Sitkin Island [Alaska] [Seismograph station code, US Geological Survey Closed] (SEIS)
LSI	Logistic Supportability Index
LSI	Logistic Support Impact
LSI	LSI Logic [NYSE symbol] (TTSB)
LSI	LSI Logic Corp. [NYSE symbol] (SPSG)
LSI	Lumbar Spine Index [Medicine] (DMAA)
LSI	Lunar Science Institute [Houston]
LSI	Lunar Surface Instrument [Aerospace]
LSIA	Lamp and Shade Institute of America [Defunct] (EA)
LSIA	Licentiate of the Society of Industrial Artists [British]
LSIB	London Stage Information Bank [Lawrence University] [Information service or system] (IID)
LSIC	Large-Scale Integrated Circuit [Electronics] (KSC)
LSIC	Large-Scale Integration Computer
LSIC	Little Servant Sisters of the Immaculate Conception (TOCD)
LSICA	Liquid and Solid Industrial Control Association (EA)
LSID	Large Scale Integration Development
LSID	Launch Sequence and Interlock Document [NASA] (NASA)
LSID	Local Session Identification [Computer science] (IBMDP)
LSidFW	United States Fish and Wildlife Service, Sidell, LA [Library symbol Library of Congress] (LCLS)
LSIEF	Library Service to the Impaired Elderly Forum [Association of Specialized and Cooperative Library Agencies]
LSI(G)	Landing Craft, Infantry (Gunboat) [Navy symbol Obsolete]
LSIG	Least Significant (IAA)
LSIG	Line Scan Image Generator (OA)
LSI(H)	Landing Ship, Infantry (Hand-Hoisted Boats) [British]
LSI Ind	LSI Industries, Inc. [Associated Press] (SAG)
LSI Inds	LSI Industries, Inc. [Associated Press] (SAG)
LSIL	Land and Sea Interaction Laboratory [Environmental Science Services Administration] (NOAA)
LSI(L)	Landing Ship, Infantry (Large) [Obsolete]
LSIL	Low-Grade Squamous Intraepithelial Lesion [Medicine]
LSI Log	LSI Logic Corp. [Associated Press] (SAG)
LSI(M)	Landing Craft, Infantry (Mortar) [Navy symbol Obsolete]
LSI(M)	Landing Ship, Infantry (Medium) [British]
LSIMS	Liquid Secondary Ion Mass Spectrometry
LSIO	Lumbosacroiliac Orthosis [Medicine]
LSI-P	Learning Styles Inventory-Primary Version [Occupational therapy] (EDAC)
LSI(R)	Landing Craft, Infantry (Rocket) [Navy symbol Obsolete]
LSIR	Limb-Scanning Infrared Radiometer
LSIR	Low-Ship Impact Ranging [Navy] (CAAL)
LSI(S)	Landing Ship, Infantry (Small)
LSIS	LASER Scan Inspection System (PDAA)
LSIS	LASER Shutterable Image Sensor
LSIS	League of Shut-In Sodalists (EA)
LSIS	Learning Style Identification Scale [Educational test]
LSIT	Large-Scale Integration Technology (IAA)
LSIT	Linear Strip Ion Thruster
LSITT	Let's Stick It to Them [Acronym used as book title]
LSITV	Liquid Secondary Injection Thrust Vector Control (PDAA)
LSJ	La Societe Jersiaise (EAIO)
LSJ	Liddell and Scott [Greek-English Lexicon, 9th ed., revised by H. Stuart Jones] [A publication] (OCD)
LSJ	Little Sisters of Jesus [See also PSJ] [Italy] (EAIO)
LSJM	Laus Sit Jesu et Mariae [Praise Be to Jesus and Mary] [Latin]
LSJM	Little Sisters of Jesus and Mary (TOCD)
LSK	Leucosulfakinin [Biochemistry]
LSK	Liquid Sample Kit
LSK	Liuski International [NASDAQ symbol] (TTSB)
LSK	Liver, Spleen, Kidney [Medicine]
LSK	Lusk, WY [Location identifier FAA] (FAAL)
LSKI	Liuski International, Inc. [NASDAQ symbol] (SAG)
LSKM	Liver-Spleen-Kidney Megaly [Medicine]
LSL	Ladder Static Logic
LSL	Landing Ship, Logistic [British]
LSL	Lateral Superlattice [Physics]
LSL	Left Sacrolateral [A fetal position] [Obstetrics]
LSL	Life Sciences Laboratory (AAG)
LSL	Link and Selector Language
LSL	Link Support Layer
LSL	Linnaean Society of London
LSL	Litton Systems Ltd. (MCD)
LSL	Logical Shift Left [Computer science]
LSL	Logistics Spares List (KSC)
LSL	Logistics Systems Laboratory
LSL	Long Service Leave (ADA)
LSL	Los Chiles [Costa Rica] [Airport symbol] (OAG)

LSL	Louisiana State Library, Baton Rouge, LA [OCLC symbol] (OCLC)
LSL	Lower Specified Limit
LSL	Low Sight Lobe
LSL	Low-Speed Logic (IAA)
LSL	Lump Sum Leave (COE)
LSL	Lump-Sum Leave Payment [Military] (DNAB)
LSLA	Low Speed Line Adaptor (NITA)
LSLB	Land Surveyors' Licensing Board [Western Australia]
LSLB	Left Short Leg Brace [Medicine]
LSLBP	Lump-Sum Leave Payment, Basic Pay [Military] (DNAB)
LSLDP	Lietuvos Socialistu Liaudininkai Demokratu Partija [Socialist Populists Democratic Party of Lithuania] [Political party] (PPE)
LSLI	Large-Scale Linear Integration (IAA)
LSLP	Lietuvos Socialistu Liaudininkai Partija [Socialist Populists Party of Lithuania] [Political party] (PPE)
LSLP	Lump-Sum Leave Payment [Air Force] (AFM)
LSL PMA	Lump-Sum Leave Payment, Personal Money Allowance [Military] (DNAB)
LSL QTRS	Lump-Sum Leave Payment, Quarters [Military] (DNAB)
LSL SUBS	Lump-Sum Leave Payment, Subsistence [Military] (DNAB)
LSLT	League to Save Lake Tahoe (EA)
LSM	Laboratory for the Structure of Matter [Navy] (PDAA)
LSM	Lakeside & Marblehead R. R. [AAR code]
LSM	Landing Ship, Medium [Navy symbol]
LSM	Large Solid Motor [Aerospace]
LSM	LASER Scanning Microscope
LSM	LASER Slicing Machine
LSM	Late Systolic Murmur (MAE)
LSM	Launcher Status Multiplexer (MSA)
LSM	Launching System Module
LSM	Launch Site Maintenance [NASA] (IAA)
LSM	Layered Synthetic Microstructure [For optical instruments]
LSM	Learning Systems Model (EDAC)
LSM	Least Square Mean [Mathematical statistics]
LSM	Letter Sorting Machine [US Postal Service]
LSM	Liberation Support Movement Information Center (EA)
LSM	Life Science Module [NASA] (NASA)
LSM	Linear Select Memory
LSM	Linear Sequential Machine
LSM	Linear Synchronous Motor (IAA)
LSM	Line-Scanning Mode [Microscopy]
LSM	Line Selection Module [Telecommunications] (TEL)
LSM	Line Select Module (NITA)
LSM	Line Switch Module [Computer science] (CIST)
LSM	Litera Scripta Manet [The Written Word Remains] [Latin] (ADA)
LSM	Little Skull Mountain [Nevada] [Seismograph station code, US Geological Survey] (SEIS)
LSM	Local Service for Mobiles [Computer science]
LSM	Logistic Support Manager
LSM	Longitudinal Section Magnetic [Electronics] (OA)
LSM	Long Semado [Malaysia] [Airport symbol] (OAG)
LSM	Loop Sampling Module
LSM	Louisiana State Library, Processing Center, Baton Rouge, LA [OCLC symbol] (OCLC)
LSM	Low-Speed MODEM (IAA)
LSM	Low-Sulfate Medium [Microbiology]
LSM	Lunar Surface Magnetometer [NASA]
LSM	Lymphocyte Separation Medium [Medicine]
LSM	Lysergic Acid Morpholide
LSM	Master of Life Science
LSMA	Low-Speed Multiplexer Arrangement
LSMC	Launching System Module Console [Navy] (CAAL)
LSMD	Dubendorf [Switzerland ICAO location identifier] (ICLI)
LSME	Emmen [Switzerland ICAO location identifier] (ICLI)
LSME	Logistic Support Maintenance Equipment (MCD)
LSME	London Society of Music Engravers [British] (DGA)
LS/MFT	Lucky Strike Means Fine Tobacco [Advertising slogan]
LSMHT	List of Standard/Modified Hand Tools (MCD)
LSMI	Logistics Support Management Information [NASA] (NASA)
LSMITH	Locksmith
LSMLC	Low-Speed Multiline Controller (MHDB)
L/Smn	Leading Seaman [Navy British] (DMA)
LSMP	Logistic Support and Mobilization Plan [Military] (NVT)
LSMP	Payerne [Switzerland ICAO location identifier] (ICLI)
LSM(R)	Landing Ship, Medium (Rocket) [Later, LFR] [Navy symbol]
LSMR	Rocket Ship [Navy symbol]
LSMS	Living Standards Management Study [International Monetary Fund]
LSMS	Louisiana State Medical Society (SRA)
LSMSO	Landing Ship, Material Supply Officer
LSMT	Land Site Marshalling Team [Military]
LSMTP	ListServ Simple Mail Transport Protocol [L-Soft International, Inc.] [Computer science]
LSMU	LASERcom Space Measurement Unit (IEEE)
LSM-USA	Lutheran Student Movement - USA (EA)
LSMV	Lettuce Speckles Mottle Virus [Plant pathology]
LSMW	London School of Medicine for Women (ROG)
LSN	Left Substantia Nigra (DB)
LSN	Life Services Network of Illinois (SRA)
LSN	Linear Sequential Network (MUGU)
LSN	Line Stabilization Network
LSN	Listen [Amateur radio shorthand] (WDAA)
LSN	Load Sharing Network
LSN	Local Stock Number
LSN	Los Banos, CA [Location identifier FAA] (FAAL)
LSNB	Lake Shore Bancorp (EFIS)

LSND	Liquid Scintillator Neutrino Detector [*Physics*]
LSNLIS	Lunar Science Natural Language Information System (PDAA)
LSNSR	Line of Bearing Sensor
LSNSW	Law Society of New South Wales [*Australia*]
LSNT	Law Society of the Northern Territory [*Australia*]
LSNY	Linnaean Society of New York (EA)
LSO	Aerolineas del Sol, SA de CV [*Mexico*] [*FAA designator*] (FAAC)
LSO	Kelso, WA [*Location identifier FAA*] (FAAL)
LSO	Landing Safety Officer (MCD)
LSO	Landing Signal Officer
LSO	Landing Support Officer [*Navy*]
LSO	Large Solar Observatory [*NASA*]
LSO	LASER Safety Officer (COE)
LSO	LASMO pic ADS [*NYSE symbol*] (TTSB)
LSO	Lasmo PLC [*NYSE symbol*] (SAG)
LSO	Last Standing Order
LSO	Lateral Superior Olive [*Brain anatomy*]
LSO	Launch/Safety Officer [*NASA*]
LSO	Law Schools On-Line (AAGC)
LSO	Left Salpingo-Oophorectomy [*Gynecology*] (CPH)
LSO	Lesotho [*ANSI three-letter standard code*] (CNC)
lso	Licensor [*MARC relator code*] [*Library of Congress*] (LCCP)
LSO	Life Systems Officer [*NASA*] (KSC)
LSO	Line Stabilized Oscillator
LSO	Linseed Oil (PDAA)
LSO	Local Central Office [*Telecommunications*] (ITD)
LSO	Logistics Studies Office [*Army*] (RDA)
LSO	London Symphony Orchestra
LSO	Lost Lake Resources Ltd. [*Vancouver Stock Exchange symbol*]
LSO	Louisiana Southern Railway Co. [*AAR code*]
LSO	Lumbosacral Orthosis [*Medicine*]
LSOA	Lutetium, Silicon, and Oxygen [*Inorganic chemistry*]
LSOA	Longitudinal Study of the Aging [*Department of Health and Human Services*] (GFGA)
LSOAD	Life Sciences Organizations and Agencies Directory [*A publication*]
LSOC	Launch Support Operations Contractor (SSD)
LSOC	Lockheed Space Operations Co.
LSOC	Logistical Support Operations Center [*Army*]
LSOCE	Linear Stochastic Optimal Control and Estimation [*Computer program*]
LSOMT	Large-Scale Operations Management Test (RDA)
LSOP	Limit Switch Open [*Electronics*] (IAA)
LSOP	L-Serine-O-Phosphate [*Biochemistry*]
LSOP	Lunar Surface Operations Planning [*NASA*] (KSC)
LSOPrA	LASMO plc Sr'A'Pref ADS [*NYSE symbol*] (TTSB)
LSOT	Landing Signal Officer Trainer [*Navy*]
LSOV	Linguistic Survey of the Ottawa Valley [*Carleton University*] [*Canada Research center*] (RCD)
LSP	Landing Ship Personnel [*British military*] (DMA)
LSP	Land Surface Parmeterization [*Environmental science*]
LSP	Las Mesas [*Puerto Rico*] [*Seismograph station code, US Geological Survey*] (SEIS)
LSP	Las Piedras [*Venezuela*] [*Airport symbol*] (OAG)
LSP	Launcher Status Panel (MCD)
LSP	Launch Sequence Plan [*NASA*] (IAA)
LSP	Learning Skills Profile [*Test*] (TMMY)
LSP	Least Significant Portion (MCD)
LSP	Least Significant Position (CMD)
LSP	Left Sacroposterior [*Medicine*] (DB)
LSp	Left Span (MAE)
LSP	Level Set Point (NRCH)
LSP	Levitated Spherator (PDAA)
LSP	Liberale Staatspartij [*Liberal State Party*] [*Netherlands Political party*] (PPE)
LSP	Liberal Socialist Party [*Egypt*] [*Political party*] (PPW)
LSP	Library Software Package (ADA)
LSp	Life Span
LSP	Life Support Package [*Diving apparatus*]
LSP	Light Scattering Photometer
LSP	Lincoln Society of Philately [*Defunct*] (EA)
LSP	Linear Selenium Photocell
LSP	Line Spectrum Pair (IAA)
LSP	Line Synchronizing Pulse
LSP	Linked Systems Project [*of the Library of Congress*]
LSP	Linked Systems Protocol [*Computer science*] (TNIG)
LSP	Link State Packet [*Telecommunications*]
lsp	Liters per Second per Person (ECON)
LSP	Little Sisters of the Poor [*Roman Catholic religious order*]
LSP	Liver-Specific [*Membrane*] Lipoprotein (DAVI)
LSP	Liver-Specific Protein
LSP	LM [*Lunar Module*] Specification [*NASA*] (KSC)
LSP	Local Store Pointer
LSP	Logical Signal Processor (IAA)
LSP	Logistics Support Plan
LSP	Lot Sensitive Plan (PDAA)
LSP	Lower Sequential Permissive (NRCH)
LSP	Lower Solution Point
LSP	Low-Salinity Plume [*Oceanography*]
LSP	Low-Speed Printer
LSP	Low Support Program (OICC)
LSP	Lucas-Sargent Proposition [*Economics*]
LSP	Lumbar Spine [*Medicine*] (DHSM)
LSP	Lunar Spectral Photometrics [*Aerospace*]
LSP	Lunar Surface Probe [*Aerospace*]
LSP	Lunar Survey Probe [*NASA*] (IAA)

LSPA	Amlikon [*Switzerland ICAO location identifier*] (ICLI)
LSPA	Lithuanian State Privatisation Agency
LSPAFRO	Lump-Sum Payment to Air Force Reserve Officers
LSPBP	Large-Solid Propellant Booster Program [*Aerospace*] (IAA)
LSPBV	Load-Sensing Proportioning and Bypass Valve
LSPC	Legal Services for Prisoners with Children (EA)
LSPC	Lewis Space Flight Center (MCD)
LSPC	Linear Selenium Photocell
LSPC	Living Stream Prayer Circle (EA)
LSPC	Logistics Systems Policy Committee [*Navy*]
LSPC	Louisiana Sweet Potato Commission
LSPD	Dittingen [*Switzerland ICAO location identifier*] (ICLI)
LSPDF	Life Science Payloads Development Facility (MCD)
LSPDS	Lunar Survey Probe Delivery System [*NASA*] (SAA)
LSPE	Lunar Seismic Profiling Experiment [*NASA*]
LSPET	Lunar Sample Preliminary Examination Team [*NASA*]
LSPF	Least Square Polynomial Fit (IAA)
LSPF	Library Service to Prisoners Forum [*Association of Specialized and Cooperative Library Agencies*]
LSPF	Schaffhausen [*Switzerland ICAO location identifier*] (ICLI)
LSPH	Leningrad Special Psychiatric Hospital [*Formerly, LPPH*]
LSPH	Winterthur [*Switzerland ICAO location identifier*] (ICLI)
LSPK	Hasenstrick [*Switzerland ICAO location identifier*] (ICLI)
LSPK	Loudspeaker (TEL)
LSPL	Langenthal [*Switzerland ICAO location identifier*] (ICLI)
LSPN	Triengen [*Switzerland ICAO location identifier*] (ICLI)
LSPO	Lunar Surface Project Office [*NASA*] (KSC)
LSPP	Step-by-Step Precedents and Procedures. Companies, Trusts, Superannuation Funds [*Australia A publication*]
LSPPO	Lead Screw Position Pick-Off
LSPPS	Logistic Support Plan for Preoperational Support (MCD)
LSPR	Low-Speed Pulse Restorer (MCD)
LSPS	Limited Serial Project Slip
LSPS	Local Service Planning System [*Telecommunications*] (TEL)
LSPS	Logistic Support Plan Summary
LSPSD	Low-Speed Packet Switched Data [*Computer science*] (ACRL)
LSPT	Limited Scope Performance Test [*Environmental science*] (COE)
LSPT	London School of Polymer Technology [*British*] (AIE)
LSPTP	Low-Speed Paper Tape Punch [*Telecommunications*] (AABC)
LSPTR	Low-Speed Paper Tape Reader [*Telecommunications*] (TEL)
LSPUD	Lietuvos Socialdemokratu Partijos Uzsienio Delegatura [*Lithuanian Social Democratic Party*] (EAIO)
LSPV	Wangen-Lachen [*Switzerland ICAO location identifier*] (ICLI)
LSPVPD	Library Service to People with Visual or Physical Disabilities Forum [*Association of Specialized and Cooperative Library Agencies*] [*American Library Association*]
LSPVPDF	Library Service to People with Visual or Physical Disabilities Forum [*ASCLA*] (AL)
LSPZ	Luzern-Beromunster [*Switzerland ICAO location identifier*] (ICLI)
LSQ	Line Squall [*ICAO*] (FAAC)
LSQ	L'Octogone, Bibliotheque Municipale de LaSalle, Quebec [*UTLAS symbol*]
LSQ	Newark, NJ [*Location identifier FAA*] (FAAL)
LSQA	Local System Queue Area [*Computer science*] (BUR)
LSQCP	Logistic System Quality Control Program [*Military*] (AFIT)
LSR	Alsair Societe [*France ICAO designator*] (FAAC)
LSR	Laboratory for Space Research [*Netherlands*]
LSR	Landing Ship, Rocket (NATG)
LSR	Land Sea Rescue (NASA)
LSR	Land Speed Record [*Auto racing*]
LSR	Lanthanide Shift Reagent [*Spectroscopy*]
LSR	Large Ship Reactor
lsr	Laser (VRA)
LSR	Laser
LSR	Laser Technology [*AMEX symbol*] (TTSB)
LSR	Laser Technology, Inc. [*AMEX symbol*] (SPSG)
LSR	Last Speed Rating [*of a horse*]
LSR	Launch Signal Responder (AAG)
LSR	Launch Site Recovery [*NASA*] (KSC)
LSR	Launch Support Requirement [*NASA*] (KSC)
LSR	League for Socialist Reconstruction [*Later, IUP*] (EA)
LSR	Lecithin/Sphingomyelin Ratio [*Medicine*] (DMAA)
LSR	Left Superior Rectus [*Muscle*] [*Medicine*] (DMAA)
LSR	Life Science Research Ltd. [*British*] (IRUK)
LSR	Lighthouse Resources, Inc. [*Vancouver Stock Exchange symbol*]
LSR	Light-Scattering Response [*Biology*]
LSR	Light-Sensitive Relay
LSR	Light-Sensitive Resistor
LSR	Light Stopping Reticle
LSR	Light, Straight Run [*Petroleum technology*]
LSR	Limited Style Run
LSR	Limited to Searches (MCD)
LSR	Limit Switch Reverse [*Electronics*] (IAA)
LSR	LINAC Stretcher Ring [*Design for an electron accelerator*]
LSR	Linear Seal Ring
LSR	Linear Sedimentation Rate [*Geology*]
LSR	Line Source Range (IAA)
LSR	Lingual Skills Required [*Civil service*]
LSR	Liquid Slip Ring
LSR	Liver/Spleen Ratio [*Medicine*] (DMAA)
LSR	Load Shifting Resistor (MSA)
LSR	Load Storage Register
LSR	Local Shared Resources [*Computer science*] (IBMDP)
LSR	Local Standard of Rest [*Galactic science*]
LSR	Local Storage Register (NITA)

LSR..............	Local Sunrise
LSR..............	Location Stack Register
LSR..............	Locus Standi Reports [*A publication*] (DLA)
LSR..............	Logical Shift Right [*Computer science*]
LSR..............	Logistics Support Requirements (NG)
LSR..............	Logistic Status Review
LSR..............	Loop Shorting Relay (MCD)
LSR..............	Loose Snow on Runway [*NWS*] (FAAC)
LSR..............	Lost River, AK [*Location identifier FAA*] (FAAL)
LSR..............	Lovers of the Stinking Rose (EA)
LSR..............	Low-Speed Reader
LSR..............	Low Stocking Rate [*Agriculture*] (OA)
LSR..............	Luftschutzraum [*Air-Raid Shelter*] [*German military - World War II*]
LSR..............	Lunar Surface Rendezvous [*NASA*] (KSC)
LSR..............	Lynchburg Source Reactor
LSRA	Logistic Support Requirement Analysis (MCD)
LSRB	Linear Sound Ranging Base (PDAA)
LSRC	Launch Site Recovery Commander [*NASA*] (KSC)
LSRC	Logistics Systems Review Committee [*DARCOM*] (MCD)
LSRC	Lunar Surface Return Container [*NASA*] (KSC)
LSRD	Logistic Support Readiness Date
LSRE............	Leisure
LSREF.........	LaSalle Re Holdings Ltd. [*NASDAQ symbol*] (SAG)
LSREF.........	LaSall Re Holdings [*NASDAQ symbol*] (TTSB)
LSRF	LASER Submarine Range-Finder
LSRF	Logistic Support Resource Funds [*Army*]
LSRI	Large Screen RADAR Indicator
LSRM...........	Life Science Research Module (MCD)
LSRO	Life Sciences Research Office [*NASA*] (KSC)
LSRP	Local Switching Replacement Planning [*Telecommunications*] (TEL)
LSR-P	Loose Snow on Runway-Patchy [*Aviation*] (DNAB)
LSRS	LOAD [*Low Altitude Defense*] System Requirements Simulation
LsrSght.......	Laser Sight, Inc. [*Associated Press*] (SAG)
LsrTc..........	Laser Technology, Inc. [*Associated Press*] (SAG)
LsrTech.......	Laser Technology, Inc. [*Associated Press*] (SAG)
LsrV	Laser Video Network, Inc. [*Associated Press*] (SAG)
LSRV	London and Scottish Rifle Volunteers [*Military British*] (ROG)
LSRV	Lunar Surface Roving Vehicle [*Aerospace*]
LsrVd	Laser Video Network, Inc. [*Associated Press*] (SAG)
LsrVide........	Laser Video Network, Inc. [*Associated Press*] (SAG)
LsrVis.........	Laser Vision Centers, Inc. [*Associated Press*] (SAG)
LsrVs	Laser Vision Centers, Inc. [*Associated Press*] (SAG)
LSR.WS........	Laser Technology Wrrt [*AMEX symbol*] (TTSB)
LSS..............	Exec Express II, Inc. [*ICAO designator*] (FAAC)
LSS..............	Laboratory for Surface Studies [*University of Wisconsin, Milwaukee*] [*Research center*] (RCD)
LSS..............	Laboratory Support Service
LSS..............	Ladies Shoemakers' Society [*A union*] [*British*]
LSS..............	Landing, Separation Simulator (MCD)
LSS..............	Landing Ship Sternchute [*British military*] (DMA)
LSS..............	Landing Ship, Support (NATG)
LSS..............	Landing-Site Supervisor
LSS..............	Lane Sensing System [*Automotive engineering*]
LSS..............	Language for Symbolic Simulation
LSS..............	Language Support System (IAA)
LSS..............	Large-Scale Standard (IAA)
LSS..............	Large-Scale Structure [*Cosmology*]
LSS..............	Large Space Structure (IEEE)
LSS..............	Large Space System (IEEE)
LSS..............	Lateral Series Servo (MCD)
LSS..............	Launcher Support Structure [*Navy*] (CAAL)
LSS..............	Launch Sequence Simulator
LSS..............	Launch Signature Simulator (MCD)
LSS..............	Launch Status Summarizer
LSS..............	Launch Support Section [*NASA*]
LSS..............	Launch Support System [*NASA*] (KSC)
LSS..............	Law Society of Scotland
LSS..............	Leipziger Semitische Studien [*A publication*] (BJA)
LSS..............	Leopold Stokowski Society (EA)
LSS..............	Les Saintes [*Guadeloupe*] [*Airport symbol*] (OAG)
LSS..............	Licensing Support System [*Department of Energy*] (EGAO)
LSS..............	Life Saving Service (WDAA)
LSS..............	Lifesaving Station [*Nautical charts*]
LSS..............	Life Services System [*For the disabled*]
LSS..............	Life-Span Study [*Environmental science*] (FFDE)
LSS..............	Life Support System [*or Subsystem*]
LSS..............	Light Spot Scanner
LSS..............	Limited Storage Site (AABC)
LSS..............	Line Scanner System
LSS..............	Linking Segment Subprogram
LSS..............	Liquid Scintillation Spectrometer
LSS..............	Liver-Spleen Scan [*Medicine*] (MEDA)
LSS..............	Local Synchronization Subsystem [*Telecommunications*] (TEL)
LSS..............	Logistic Support Squadron (AAG)
LSS..............	Logistic Support System (AABC)
LSS..............	Longitudinal Static Stability
LSS..............	Loop Switching System [*Telecommunications*]
LSS..............	LOT [*Limited Operational Test*] Support Services [*Military*] (DWSG)
LSS-P..........	Lumbosacral Spine [*Medicine*] (MEDA)
LSS..............	Lunar Soil Stimulant [*NASA*]
LSS..............	Lunar Surveying System [*Aerospace*]
LSS..............	Lunar Survey Sensor [*NASA*] (KSC)
LSS..............	Lung Serum Simulant (PDAA)
LSS..............	Lutheran Social Service System [*An association*]
LSSA............	Law Society of South Australia
LSSA............	Leopold Stokowski Society of America (EA)
LSSA............	Lipid Soluble Secondary Antioxidants [*Biochemistry*]
LSSA............	Lithuanian Student Scout Association [*Later, Lithuanian Scouts Association College Division*] (EA)
LSSA............	Logistic System Support Activity [*Army*]
LSSA............	Logistic System Support Agency
LSSAS	Longitudinal Static Stability Augmentation System (MCD)
LSSB............	Bern Radio [*Switzerland ICAO location identifier*] (ICLI)
LSSB............	Legal Support Services Branch [*General Accounting Office*] [*Information service or system*] (IID)
LSSB............	Light SEAL [*Sea, Air, and Land*] Support Boat [*Navy*] (DNAB)
LSSC............	Lake Superior State College [*Sault Ste. Marie, MI*]
LSSc............	Licentiate in Sacred Scriptures
LSSC............	Licentiate in Sanitary Science [*British*] (ROG)
LSSC............	Light SEAL [*Sea, Air, and Land*] Support Craft [*Navy symbol*]
LSSC............	Logistic Support System Characteristics (AAG)
LSSC............	Logistic System Support Center [*Army*]
LSSC............	Lower-Sideband Suppressed Carrier (IDOE)
LSSD............	Level Sensitive Scan Design (MCD)
LSSD............	Level-Sensitive Scan Detector (CIST)
LSSD............	Lower-Speed Service-Deriving [*Telecommunications*] (TSSD)
LSSD............	Lunar Surface Sampling Device [*Aerospace*]
LSSDDPMAG...	Library Service to Developmentally Disabled Persons Membership Activity Group [*Association of Specialized and Cooperative Library Agencies*] [*American Library Association*]
LSSDPF	Library Service to the Developmentally Disabled Persons Forum [*Association of Specialized and Cooperative Library Agencies*] [*American Library Association*]
LSSE............	Licentiate in Social, Economic, & Political Sciences (DD)
LSSF............	Land Special Security Force [*Army*] (AABC)
LSSF............	Life Sciences Support Facility [*NASA*] (NASA)
LSSF............	Limited Service Storage Facility
LSSG............	Logistics Studies Steering Group (AABC)
LSSGR..........	Local Switching System General Requirement [*Telecommunications*]
LSSI............	Leasing Solutions [*NASDAQ symbol*] (TTSB)
LSSI............	Leasing Solutions, Inc. [*NASDAQ symbol*] (SAG)
LSSI............	Library Systems and Services, Inc. [*Information service or system*] (IID)
LSSL............	Landing Ship Support, Large [*Military*] (VNW)
LSSL............	Life Sciences Space Laboratory [*NASA*] (NASA)
LSSL............	Support Landing Ship (Large) MK III
LSSM............	Launch Site Support Manager [*NASA*] (NASA)
LSSM............	Local Scientific Survey Module [*NASA*]
LSSM............	Lunar Surface Scientific Module [*NASA*]
LSSO............	Bern Office Federal de l'Air [*Switzerland ICAO location identifier*] (ICLI)
LSSO............	Library Science Student Organization
LSSP............	Lanka Sama Samaja Party [*Sri Lanka Equal Society Party*] [*Political party*] (PPW)
LSSP............	Latest Scram Set Point (NRCH)
LSSP............	Launch Site Support Plan (MCD)
LSSP............	Lunar Surveying System Program [*Aerospace*]
LSSPO	Life Support Systems Project Office [*NASA*] (MCD)
LSSPS	Libraries Serving Special Populations Section [*Association of Specialized and Cooperative Library Agencies*]
LSSPSC	Life Sciences Strategic Planning Study Committee [*NASA*]
LSSR............	Amphibious Coastal Reconnaissance Ship [*Navy symbol*]
LSSR............	Berne/Radio Suisse SA [*Switzerland ICAO location identifier*] (ICLI)
LSSR	Lessor
LSSRC..........	Life Sciences Shuttle Research Centrifuge [*NASA*] (NASA)
LSSS............	Geneve [*Switzerland ICAO location identifier*] (ICLI)
LSSS............	LASER Source Signature Simulator
LSSS............	Lightweight Ship SATCOM Set [*Navy*] (CAAL)
LSSS............	Lime-Sulphur-Synthetic-Solution [*Hydrometallurgy*]
LSSS............	Limiting Safety System Setting [*Nuclear energy*] (NRCH)
LSSt............	Launch Site Support Team (MCD)
lsst............	Lead-Sheathed Steel-Taped
LS/ST..........	Light Shield/Star Tracker (NASA)
LSST...........	List of Specifications and Standards (MSA)
LSST...........	Lone Star Technologies [*NASDAQ symbol*] (SAG)
LSSTA..........	Low Supersonic Transport (PDAA)
LSSTA..........	Lunar Space Tug (PDAA)
LSSU...........	Lake Superior State University [*Michigan*]
LSSW...........	Zurich [*Switzerland ICAO location identifier*] (ICLI)
LST.............	Amphibious Ship, Tank
LST.............	Lakewood Forest Products Ltd. [*Vancouver Stock Exchange symbol*]
LST.............	Laminated SONAR Transistor
LST.............	Landing Ship, Tank [*Navy symbol*]
LST.............	Landing Ship Transport (MCD)
LST.............	Laplace-Stieltjes Transform
LST.............	Large Simple Trial [*Medicine*] (TAD)
LST.............	Large Space Telescope [*Later, Space Telescope*] [*NASA*]
LST.............	Large Stellar Telescope (KSC)
LST.............	Large Subsonic Tunnel [*NASA*]
LST.............	LASER Spot Tracker (MCD)
LST.............	Last (BUR)
LST.............	Lateral Sinus Thrombophlebitis [*Medicine*] (MEDA)
LST.............	Lateral Spinothalamic Tract [*Neurology*] (DAVI)
LST.............	Late Start Time
LST.............	Launceston [*Tasmania*] [*Airport symbol*] (OAG)
LST.............	Launch Support Team [*NASA*] (KSC)
LST.............	Lauryl Sulfate Tryptose [*Growth medium*]
LST.............	Law Society of Tasmania [*Australia*]
LST.............	Left Sacrotransverse [*A fetal position*] [*Obstetrics*]
LST.............	Left Store (SAA)

LST .... Licentiate in Sacred Theology [*British*]
LST .... Life-Sustaining Treatment [*Medicine*] (DMAA)
LST .... Light-Sensitive Tube
LST .... Line Scan Tube
LST .... Liquid Oxygen Start Tank (AAG)
LST .... Liquid Storage Tank (AAG)
LST .... Listing of a Program in a File [*Computer science*]
LST .... Living Structures Tank (WDAA)
LST .... Local Sidereal Time
LST .... Local Solar Time
LST .... Local Standard Time
LST .... Local Summer Time [*Astronomy*] (IAA)
LST .... Lone Star [*Missouri*] [*Seismograph station code, US Geological Survey*] (SEIS)
LST .... Lone Star, TX [*Location identifier FAA*] (FAAL)
LST .... Long-Term Stability Test [*Chemistry*]
LST .... Loud Speaking Telephone (NITA)
LST .... Low-Solvent Technology (GNE)
LST .... Lunar Surface Telescope [*NASA*]
LST .... Lunar Surface Transponder [*Aerospace*]
LSTAR .... Limited Scientific and Technical Aerospace Reports [*NASA*] (MCD)
LSTAT .... Life Support for Trauma And Transport [*Northrop Grumman*] (PS)
LSTB .... Bellechasse [*Switzerland ICAO location identifier*] (ICLI)
LSTB .... Long Shoot Terminal Bud [*Botany*]
LStBA .... Saint Joseph's Abbey, St. Benedict, LA [*Library symbol Library of Congress*] (LCLS)
LST/CAM ...... LASER Spot Tracker/Strike Camera (MCD)
LSTD .... Leading Steward [*British military*] (DMA)
LSTD .... Lunar Satellite Tracking Data [*NASA*] (KSC)
lstd-- .... Tristan da Cunha Island [*MARC geographic area code Library of Congress*] (LCCP)
LSTE .... Large Structure Technology Experiment (SSD)
LSTE .... Launch Site Transportation Equipment [*NASA*] (NASA)
LSTF .... Lead Sulfide Thin Film
LST-G .... Large Steam Turbine-Generator
LStgH .... Hunt Correctional Center (Louisiana Correctional Institute for Women), St. Gabriel, LA [*Library symbol Library of Congress*] (LCLS)
LST(H) .... Landing Ship, Tank (Casualty Evacuation) [*Navy symbol Obsolete*]
LST(H) .... Landing Ship, Tank (Hospital) [*British military*] (DMA)
LStjT .... Tensas Parish Library, St. Joseph, LA [*Library symbol Library of Congress*] (LCLS)
LSTL .... Laparoscopic Tubal Ligation [*Gynecology*] (DAVI)
LSTM .... Lander Static Test Model [*NASA*]
LSTM .... Large-Sample Scanning Tunneling Mode [*Microscopy*]
LSTM .... Low Steam
LStmSM .... St. Martin Parish Library, St. Martinville, LA [*Library symbol Library of Congress*] (LCLS)
LSTN .... Light Station [*Coast Guard*] (IAA)
LSTNG .... Lasting
LSTO .... Motiers [*Switzerland ICAO location identifier*] (ICLI)
LSTR .... Landstar System [*NASDAQ symbol*] (TTSB)
LSTR .... Landstar System, Inc. [*NASDAQ symbol*] (SAG)
LSTR .... Montricher [*Switzerland ICAO location identifier*] (ICLI)
LSTS .... Landing Ship (Utility) [*Navy symbol*]
LSTS .... Launch Station Test Set (MCD)
LSTS .... Low-Pressure Side Temperature Sensor [*Air conditioning system*] [*Automotive engineering*]
LSTS .... Lunar Surface Thermal Simulator [*NASA*] (KSC)
LST/SCAM ... LASER Spot Tracker / Strike Camera
LSTSRFA ...... Launch Station Test Set Radio Frequency Adapter (MCD)
LSTT .... Lake Superior Terminal & Transfer Railway Co. [*AAR code*]
LSTTL .... Low-Power Schottky Transistor-Transistor Logic [*Electronics*]
L Stud H ...... Law Students' Helper [*A publication*] (DLA)
L Stud Helper... Law Students' Helper [*A publication*] (DLA)
L Stud J .... Law Students' Journal [*A publication*] (DLA)
L Stu Mag ..... Law Students' Magazine [*A publication*] (DLA)
L Stu Mag NS... Law Students' Magazine. New Series [*A publication*] (ILCA)
L Stu Mag OS... Law Students' Magazine. Old Series [*A publication*] (ILCA)
lstwx .... Lost Wax (VRA)
LSTX .... Bex [*Switzerland ICAO location identifier*] (ICLI)
LSTY .... Yverdon [*Switzerland ICAO location identifier*] (ICLI)
LSU .... Institute of Continuing Legal Education, Louisiana State University Law Center (DLA)
LSU .... Labor Service Unit [*Military*]
LSU .... Lactose Saccharose Urea [*Cell growth medium*]
LSU .... Lamentation over the Destruction of Sumer and Ur (BJA)
LSU .... Landing Ship, Utility [*Navy symbol Obsolete*]
LSU .... LASER Scanning Unit [*Computer science*] (CIST)
LSU .... Launcher Selector Unit
LSU .... Launcher Switching Unit [*Navy*] (CAAL)
LSU .... Law Society of Upper Canada [*UTLAS symbol*]
LSU .... Leading Signal Unit [*Telecommunications*] (TEL)
LSU .... Liberalsoziale Union [*Liberal Social Union*] [*Germany Political party*] (PPW)
LSU .... Library Storage Unit
LSU .... Life Support Umbilical [*NASA*]
LSU .... Life Support Unit [*NASA*] (KSC)
LSU .... Lighthouse Study Unit (EA)
LSU .... Limit Switch Up [*Electronics*] (IAA)
LSU .... Line Selection Unit [*Telecommunications*] (IAA)
LSU .... Line-Sharing Unit
LSU .... Livestock Unit
LSU .... Load Storage Unit [*Computer science*]
LSU .... Local Storage Unit [*Computer science*]
LSU .... Local Switching Unit [*Telecommunications*] (TEL)
LSU .... Local Synchronization Utility [*Telecommunications*] (TEL)
LSU .... Logistics Support Unit [*Military*] (NVT)
LSU .... Lone Signalling Unit (NITA)
LSU .... Lone Signal Unit [*Telecommunications*] (TEL)
LSU .... Long Sukang [*Malaysia*] [*Airport symbol*] (OAG)
LSU .... Louisiana State University
LSU .... Louisiana State University and Agricultural and Mechanical College (GAGS)
LSU .... Southern University at New Orleans, New Orleans, LA [*OCLC symbol*] (OCLC)
LSU Med Cent... Louisiana State University Medicine Center (GAGS)
LSUNO .... Louisiana State University in New Orleans [*Later, University of New Orleans*]
L Sup .... Lake Superior (BARN)
LSUP .... Loader Storage Unit Support Program [*Computer science*] (MHDI)
L Sup H & D... Lalor's Supplement to Hill and Denio's New York Reports [*A publication*] (DLA)
LSUR .... Leisure
LSU Shreveport... Louisiana State University Shreveport (GAGS)
LSUV .... Lunar Surface Ultraviolet [*Camera*] [*NASA*]
LSUV .... Luxury Sport Utility Vehicle
LSV .... Alak [*Former USSR ICAO designator*] (FAAC)
LSV .... Landing Ship, Vehicle [*Navy symbol*]
LSV .... Las Vegas, NV [*Location identifier FAA*] (FAAL)
LSV .... Left Subclavian Vein [*Anatomy*]
LSV .... Lily Symptomless Virus [*Plant pathology*]
LSV .... Linear Shift-Varying (PDAA)
LSV .... Linear Sweep Voltammograms [*Electrochemistry*]
LSV .... Line Status Verifier [*Telecommunications*] (TEL)
LSV .... Logistics Support Vessel [*Military*]
LSV .... Low-Signature Vehicle [*Hazardous materials control*]
LSV .... Lunar Shuttle Vehicle [*Aerospace*] (AAG)
LSV .... Lunar Surface Vehicle [*Aerospace*]
LSV .... Lunar Survey Viewfinder [*Aerospace*]
LSVC .... Left Superior Vena Cava [*Medicine*] (STED)
LSVC .... Lunar Surface Vehicle Communications [*Aerospace*]
LSVG .... Lifesaving (MSA)
LSVI .... Little Switzerland [*NASDAQ symbol*] (TTSB)
LSVI .... Little Switzerland, Inc. [*NASDAQ symbol*] (SAG)
LSVP .... Landing Ship, Vehicle and Personnel [*Navy symbol*]
LSW .... Detroit, MI [*Location identifier FAA*] (FAAL)
LSW .... Labrador Sea Water [*Oceanography*]
LSW .... Landslide [*Washington*] [*Seismograph station code, US Geological Survey Closed*] (SEIS)
LSW .... LASER Spot Welder
LSW .... Least Significant Word (MCD)
LSW .... Left-Sided Weakness [*Medicine*] (STED)
LSW .... Licensed Shorthand Writer
LSW .... Lifshitz-Slyozov-Wagner Theory of Mineral Recrystallization
LSW .... Light Support Weapon (MCD)
LSW .... Limit Switch [*Electronics*]
LSW .... Line Switch [*Telecommunications*] (IAA)
LSWA .... Large-Amplitude, Slow Wave Activity [*Encephalography*]
LSWA .... Law Society of Western Australia
LSWMA .... Lutheran Society for Worship, Music, and the Arts [*Later, Liturgical Conference*]
LSWP .... Lump-Sum Wage Payments (MCD)
LSWR .... London & South-Western Railway (ROG)
LSWS .... London Society for Women's Service [*British*] (WDAA)
LSWT .... Low-Speed Wind Tunnel (MCD)
LSX .... Landing Ship, Experimental
LSXB .... Balzers/FL [*Switzerland ICAO location identifier*] (ICLI)
LSXD .... Domat-Ems [*Switzerland ICAO location identifier*] (ICLI)
LSXE .... Erstfeld [*Switzerland ICAO location identifier*] (ICLI)
LSXH .... Holziken [*Switzerland ICAO location identifier*] (ICLI)
lsxj-- .... St. Helena [*MARC geographic area code Library of Congress*] (LCCP)
LSXL .... Lauterbrunnen [*Switzerland ICAO location identifier*] (ICLI)
LSXM .... St. Moritz [*Switzerland ICAO location identifier*] (ICLI)
LSXO .... Gossau SG [*Switzerland ICAO location identifier*] (ICLI)
LSXS .... Schindellegi [*Switzerland ICAO location identifier*] (ICLI)
LSXT .... Trogen [*Switzerland ICAO location identifier*] (ICLI)
LSXU .... Untervaz [*Switzerland ICAO location identifier*] (ICLI)
LSXV .... San Vittore [*Switzerland ICAO location identifier*] (ICLI)
LSXW .... Wurenlingen [*Switzerland ICAO location identifier*] (ICLI)
LSY .... Lindsay Aviation, Inc. [*ICAO designator*] (FAAC)
LSY .... Lismore [*Australia Airport symbol*] (OAG)
LSYC .... League of Socialist Youth of Croatia [*Political party*]
LSZA .... Lugano [*Switzerland ICAO location identifier*] (ICLI)
LSZB .... Bern/Belp [*Switzerland ICAO location identifier*] (ICLI)
LSZC .... Bad Ragaz [*Switzerland ICAO location identifier*] (ICLI)
LSZD .... Ascona [*Switzerland ICAO location identifier*] (ICLI)
LSZE .... Bad Ragaz [*Switzerland ICAO location identifier*] (ICLI)
LSZF .... Birrfeld [*Switzerland ICAO location identifier*] (ICLI)
LSZG .... Grenchen [*Switzerland ICAO location identifier*] (ICLI)
LSZH .... Zurich [*Switzerland ICAO location identifier*] (ICLI)
LSZI .... Fricktal-Schupfart [*Switzerland ICAO location identifier*] (ICLI)
LSZJ .... Courtelary [*Switzerland ICAO location identifier*] (ICLI)
LSZK .... Speck-Fehraltorf [*Switzerland ICAO location identifier*] (ICLI)
LSZL .... Locarno [*Switzerland ICAO location identifier*] (ICLI)
LSZM .... Bale [*Switzerland ICAO location identifier*] (ICLI)
LSZN .... Hausen Am Albis [*Switzerland ICAO location identifier*] (ICLI)
LSZP .... Biel/Kappelen [*Switzerland ICAO location identifier*] (ICLI)
LSZR .... Altenrhein [*Switzerland ICAO location identifier*] (ICLI)

LSZS	Samedan [*Switzerland ICAO location identifier*] (ICLI)
LSZT	Lommis [*Switzerland ICAO location identifier*] (ICLI)
LSZU	Buttwil [*Switzerland ICAO location identifier*] (ICLI)
LSZV	Sitterdorf [*Switzerland ICAO location identifier*] (ICLI)
LSZW	Thun [*Switzerland ICAO location identifier*] (ICLI)
LSZX	Schanis [*Switzerland ICAO location identifier*] (ICLI)
LSZY	Porrentruy [*Switzerland ICAO location identifier*] (ICLI)
LSZZ	Collective address for NOTAM and SNOWTAM [*Switzerland ICAO location identifier*] (ICLI)
LT	Fixed Light [*USCG*] (TAG)
LT	Great Sierra [*ICAO designator*] (AD)
LT	Heat-labile Enterotoxin [*Biochemistry*] (DAVI)
LT	Heat-Labile Toxin (STED)
LT	Labile Toxin (DB)
LT	Laboratory Test (IAA)
LT	[*The*] Lake Terminal Railroad Co. [*AAR code*]
LT	Laminar Tomography (STED)
LT	Laminated TEFLON
LT	Landed Terms
LT	Landing Team
LT	Lands Tribunal [*Legal*] [*British*]
LT	Language Translation [*Computer science*]
LT	Laplace Transform [*Mathematics*]
LT	Lapped Transform [*Telecommunications*]
LT	Laptop [*Computer*] (BARN)
LT	Large Tug [*Army*]
LT	Larsen and Toubro Ltd. [*India*] [*Commercial firm*]
LT	LASER Trimming (PDAA)
LT	Last (ROG)
LT	Last Telecast (NTCM)
LT	Lateral Tooth
LT	Lateral Triceps Brachii [*Medicine*]
LT	Latest Time [*Business term*]
LT	Laughter Therapy (EA)
LT	Launch Test [*NASA*] (IAA)
LT	Laundry Tray
LT	Lawn Tennis
LT	Law Times Journal [*A publication*] (DLA)
LT	Law Times Newspaper [*A publication*] (DLA)
LT	Law Times Reports [*British*]
LT	Layout Template (MCD)
L/T	Leading Telegraphist
LT	Leading Torpedoman [*Navy British*]
LT	Lead Time (NG)
LT	League of Tarcisians (EA)
LT	Left
LT	Left Tackle [*Football*]
LT	Left Thigh
LT	Left Triceps [*Anatomy*] (DAVI)
LT	Legal Tender [*Currency*]
LT	Legal Title [*Business term*]
lt	Legal Training [*Navy British*]
Lt	Leptosphaerulina Trifolii [*A fungus*]
LT	Less Than (IBMDP)
LT	Lethal Time (STED)
LT	Letter
LT	Letter of Transmittal (MCD)
LT	Letter Telegram
LT	Leukotriene [*Clinical pharmacology*]
LT	Level Transmitter (NRCH)
LT	Level Trigger
LT	Levin Tube [*Medicine*]
LT	Levothyroxine [*Pharmacy*]
LT	Library Talk [*A publication*] (BRI)
LT	Licentiate in Teaching [*British*]
LT	Licentiate in Theology
LT	Lid Tank
LT	Lieutenant (EY)
Lt	Lieutenant (WA)
LT	Light (AAG)
lt	Light (VRA)
LT	Light Tank
LT	Light Terminal (PDAA)
LT	Light Test (IAA)
LT	Light Trap
LT	Light Truck [*British*]
LT	Limit (DEN)
LT	Limited Term Employee (OICC)
L/T	Line Telecommunications
LT	Line Telegraphy
LT	Line Terminator
LT	Linked Term [*Online database field identifier*]
LT	Link Terminal [*Telecommunications*] (TEL)
LT	Link Testing (NITA)
LT	Link Trainer Instructor
LT	Liquid Toned [*Copier*] [*Reprography*]
LT	Lira Toscana [*Tuscany Pound*] [*Monetary unit*] [*Italian*] (ROG)
LT	Lira Turca [*Turkish Pound*] [*Monetary unit*] [*Italian*] (ROG)
LT	Liter (ECII)
LT	Lithuania [*Internet country code*]
LT	Loader Trainer (MCD)
LT	Loader-Transporter [*British military*] (DMA)
L/T	Load Test (MCD)
LT	Local Time
LT	Locum Tenens [*In the Place Of*] [*Latin*]
LT	Logic Theorist [*or Theory*] [*Computer science*]
LT	Logic Tree
LT	London-Ducretet-Thomson [*Record label*] [*Great Britain, USA, etc.*]
LT	London Transport
LT	Long Term
LT	Long-Term Stay [*in hospital*] [*British*]
LT	Long Throw [*Speaker system*]
LT	Long Ton [*2240 pounds*]
LT	Long Tour [*Military*] (GFGA)
LT	Long Treble [*Crocheting*] (ROG)
LT	Lookthrough (LAIN)
L/T	Loop Test [*Aerospace*] (AAG)
LT	Lot
LT	Lo Ta'aseh [*BJA*]
LT	Lot Time (SAA)
LT	Lower Torso
LT	Low Temperature
LT	Low Tension
LT	Low Torque
LT	Low Transverse [*incision*] [*Obstetrics*] (DAVI)
LT	Lucis Trust (EA)
LT	Lues Test (STED)
LT	Lug Terminal
LT	Lumbar Traction [*Orthopedics*] (DAVI)
LT	Luxury Tax (MHDB)
LT	Lymphocyte Transformation [*Hematology*]
LT	Lymphocyte Transitional [*Medicine*] (STED)
LT	Lymphocytic Thyroiditis [*Medicine*] (STED)
LT	Lymphocytotoxin [*Medicine*] (STED)
LT	Lymphoid Tissue [*Biology*]
LT	Lymphotoxin [*Immunochemistry*]
LT	Turn Left after Takeoff [*Aviation*] (FAAC)
LTA	Land Trust Alliance (EA)
LTA	Large Transport Airplane
LTA	Launch Test Area
LTA	Launch Tube Assembly
LTA	Lawn Tennis Association (EAIO)
LTA	Lead Tetraacetate [*Organic chemistry*]
LTA	Leave Travel Allowance
LTA	Legionarios del Trabajo in America (EA)
LTA	Leisure Time Activity
LTA	LEM Test Article (MCD)
LTA	Less than Adequate (COE)
LTA	Lettera di Transporto Aereo [*Air Waybill*] [*Italian Business term*]
LTA	Lettre de Transport Aerien [*Air Waybill*] [*French Business term*]
LTA	Leucotriene A [*Clinical pharmacology*]
LTA	Leveling Torquer Amplifier
L/T	Library Technical Assistant
LTA	Lighter-than-Air [*Aircraft*]
LTA	Linea Aerea Tama [*Chile*] [*ICAO designator*] (FAAC)
LTA	Linen Trade Association (EA)
LTA	Lipoate Transacetylase [*An enzyme*]
LTA	Lipoteichoic Acid [*Biochemistry*]
LTA	Living Together Arrangement
LTA	LM [*Lunar Module*] Test Article [*NASA*]
LTA	Local Training Area (MCD)
LTA	Logical Transient Area
LTA	Logic Time Analyzer (IAA)
LTA	Long-Term Arrangements [*Department of State*]
LTA	Long-Term Average (CAAL)
LTA	Lower Torso Assembly [*Aerospace*] (MCD)
LTA	Low Temperature Aftercooled [*Automotive engineering*]
LTA	Low-Temperature Ashing [*Analytical chemistry*]
LTA	South Lake Tahoe, CA [*Location identifier FAA*] (FAAL)
LTA	Tzaneen [*South Africa*] [*Airport symbol*] (OAG)
LTAB	Ankara [*Turkey ICAO location identifier*] (ICLI)
LTAB	Guvercinlik [*Turkey ICAO location identifier*] (ICLI)
LTAB	League to Abolish Billionaires [*Fictitious organization mentioned in Donald Duck comic by Carl Barks*]
LTAC	Ankara/Esenboga [*Turkey ICAO location identifier*] (ICLI)
LTAC	Literary Translators Association of Canada (EAIO)
LTACFIRE	Lightweight Tactical Fire Direction System [*Artillery*] [*Army*] (INF)
LTAD	Ankara/Etimesgut [*Turkey ICAO location identifier*] (ICLI)
LTADL	Launcher Tube Azimuth Datum Line
LTAE	Ankara/Murted [*Turkey ICAO location identifier*] (ICLI)
LTAE	Long-Term Agroecosystem Experiment
LTAF	Adana/Sakirpasa [*Turkey ICAO location identifier*] (ICLI)
LTAG	Adana/Incirlik [*Turkey ICAO location identifier*] (ICLI)
LTAH	Afyon [*Turkey ICAO location identifier*] (ICLI)
LTAI	Antalya [*Turkey ICAO location identifier*] (ICLI)
LTAJ	Gaziantep [*Turkey ICAO location identifier*] (ICLI)
LTAK	Iskenderun [*Turkey ICAO location identifier*] (ICLI)
LTAL	Kastamonu [*Turkey ICAO location identifier*] (ICLI)
LTAL	Lower Transition Altitude (SAA)
LTALT	Light Alternating (IAA)
LTAM	Kayseri [*Turkey ICAO location identifier*] (ICLI)
LTaM	Madison Parish Library, Tallulah, LA [*Library symbol Library of Congress*] (LCLS)
LTAN	Konya [*Turkey ICAO location identifier*] (ICLI)
LT & D	Love, Togetherness, and Devotion [*Rock music group*]
LT & S	London, Tilbury & Southend Railway [*British*]
LT & SR	London, Tilbury & Southend Railway [*British*] (ROG)
LTAO	Malatya/Erhac [*Turkey ICAO location identifier*] (ICLI)
LTAP	Merzifon [*Turkey ICAO location identifier*] (ICLI)
LTAQ	Samsun [*Turkey ICAO location identifier*] (ICLI)

LTAR............	Sivas [*Turkey ICAO location identifier*] (ICLI)
LTAS............	Lead Tetraacetate-Schiff (Reaction) [*Clinical chemistry*]
LTAS............	Lighter than Air Society [*An association*] (PDAA)
LTAS............	Zonguldak [*Turkey ICAO location identifier*] (ICLI)
LTAT............	Malatya/Erhac [*Turkey ICAO location identifier*] (ICLI)
LTAU............	Kayseri/Erkilet [*Turkey ICAO location identifier*] (ICLI)
LTAV............	Sivrihisar [*Turkey ICAO location identifier*] (ICLI)
LTAVD	Low-Temperature Arc Vapor Deposition [*Coating technology*]
LTB.............	Acute Laryngotracheobronchitis [*Commonly known as croup*] (PAZ)
Lt B	Bachelor of Literature
LTB.............	Laparoscopic Tubal Banding [*Ligation*] (DAVI)
LTB.............	Laryngo-Tracheal Bronchitis
LTB.............	Last Trunk Busy [*Telecommunications*] (TEL)
LTB.............	Lawrence Traffic Bureau Inc., Kansas City MO [*STAC*]
LTB.............	Law Times Bankruptcy Reports [*United States*] [*A publication*] (DLA)
LTB.............	Leucotriene B [*Clinical pharmacology*]
LTB.............	Light Bay [*Horse racing*]
LTB.............	Limited Test Ban [*Nuclear testing*]
LTB.............	Line Term Buffer [*Computer science*] (AABC)
LTB.............	Local Token-Ring Bridge (CIST)
LTB.............	London Tourist Board [*British*] (DCTA)
LTB.............	London Transport Board [*British*]
LT(B)	Low-Tension (Battery) (DEN)
LTBA............	Die Lexikalischen Tafelserien der Babylonier und Assyrer in den Berliner Museen [*A publication*] (BJA)
LTBA............	Istanbul/Yesilkoy [*Turkey ICAO location identifier*] (ICLI)
LTBA............	Louisiana Thoroughbred Breeders Association (SRA)
LTBB............	Istanbul [*Turkey ICAO location identifier*] (ICLI)
LTBC............	Alasehir [*Turkey ICAO location identifier*] (ICLI)
LTBC............	Lawn Tennis Ball Convention [*British*] (BI)
LTBD............	Aydin [*Turkey ICAO location identifier*] (ICLI)
LTBE............	Bursa [*Turkey ICAO location identifier*] (ICLI)
LTBF............	Balikesir [*Turkey ICAO location identifier*] (ICLI)
LTBG............	Bandirma [*Turkey ICAO location identifier*] (ICLI)
LTBH............	Canakkale [*Turkey ICAO location identifier*] (ICLI)
LTBI.............	Eskisehir [*Turkey ICAO location identifier*] (ICLI)
LTBJ............	Izmir/Cumaovasi [*Turkey ICAO location identifier*] (ICLI)
LTBK............	Izmir/Gaziemir [*Turkey ICAO location identifier*] (ICLI)
LTBL............	Izmir/Cigli [*Turkey ICAO location identifier*] (ICLI)
LtBl	Light Blend [*Horticulture*]
LTBM............	Isparta [*Turkey ICAO location identifier*] (ICLI)
LTBMC........	Long-Term Bone Marrow Culture [*Cell culture*]
LTBN............	Kutahya [*Turkey ICAO location identifier*] (ICLI)
LTBO............	Linear Time Base Oscillator
LTBO............	Usak [*Turkey ICAO location identifier*] (ICLI)
LTBP............	London Tanker Broker Panel
LTBP............	Yalova [*Turkey ICAO location identifier*] (ICLI)
LTBQ............	Topel [*Turkey ICAO location identifier*] (ICLI)
LTBR............	Yenisehir [*Turkey ICAO location identifier*] (ICLI)
LTBS............	Dalaman [*Turkey ICAO location identifier*] (ICLI)
LTBT............	Akhisar [*Turkey ICAO location identifier*] (ICLI)
LTBT............	Limited Test Ban Treaty [*Signed in 1963; prohibits testing of nuclear devices in certain environments*]
LTC.............	Lafferty Transportation [*AAR code*]
LTC.............	Lai [*Chad*] [*Airport symbol*] (AD)
LTC.............	Land Tenure Center [*University of Wisconsin*] [*Research center*]
LTC.............	Land Transport Corps [*British military*] (DMA)
LTC.............	Land Trust Commission (BARN)
LTC.............	Language Testing Center [*University of Melbourne*] [*Australia*]
LTC.............	Large Transformed Cell [*Medicine*] (DMAA)
LTC.............	Last Telecast (WDMC)
LTC.............	Latcharter [*Latvia*] [*FAA designator*] (FAAC)
LTC.............	Lattice (MSA)
LTC.............	Launceston Technical College [*Australia*]
LTC.............	Launch Vehicle Test Conductor [*NASA*] (KSC)
LTC.............	Lawn Tennis Club [*British*]
LTC.............	Lead Telluride Crystal [*Photoconductor*]
LTC.............	Lead to Come [*Publishing*] (WDMC)
LTC.............	Leaseway Transportation Corp. (WDAA)
LTC.............	Left to Count (DAVI)
LTC.............	Lesotho Telecommunications Corp. [*Ministry of Transport and Communications*] [*Lesotho*] (TSSD)
LTC.............	Less than Truckload Cargo (MCD)
LTC.............	Letdown Terrain Clearance (DNAB)
LTC.............	Leukotriene C [*Clinical pharmacology*]
LTC.............	Liberia Telecommunications Corp. (IMH)
LTC.............	Liberty to the Captives [*Later, ACAT*] (EA)
LTC.............	Library Technical Centre [*Polytechnic of Central London*] (NITA)
LTC.............	Lidocaine Tissue Concentration [*Medicine*] (DMAA)
Ltc	Lieutenant Colonel (AABC)
LTC.............	Lieutenant Colonel
LTC.............	Lieutenant Commander (GFGA)
LTC.............	Lightly Treated Coated [*Papermaking*]
LTC.............	Light Terminal Complexes
LTC.............	Linear Transformation Converter (IAA)
LTC.............	Linear Transmission Channel
LTC.............	Line Terminal Control (IAA)
LTC.............	Line Time Clock
LTC.............	Line Traffic Coordinator (CET)
LTC.............	Lithographic Test Chip (AAEL)
LTC.............	Living Tree Center (EA)
LTC.............	Livros Tecnicos e Cientificos Editora Ltda. [*Brazil*]
LTC.............	Load Tap Changing
LTC.............	Local Telephone Circuit [*Telecommunications*] (TEL)
LTC.............	Local Terminal Controller

LTC.............	Lockwood Torday & Carlisle Ltd. [*British*]
LTC.............	Longitudinal Time Code (NTCM)
LTC.............	Longitudinal Time Constant
LTC.............	Long-Term Care [*Medicine*]
LTC.............	Long-Term Contract (ADA)
LTC.............	Long Term Costing [*Military*] (RDA)
LTC.............	Long Time Constant (IEEE)
LTC.............	Loop Test Conference [*Aerospace*] (AAG)
LTC.............	Lotus Cosmetics International Ltd. [*Vancouver Stock Exchange symbol*]
LTC.............	Low-Tar Content [*of cigarettes*]
LTC.............	Low-Temperature Carbonization
LTC.............	Low-Temperature Catalyst
LTC.............	Low-Temperature Coefficient
LTC.............	Low-Temperature Cooling
LTC.............	Low-Tension Current (IAA)
LTC.............	LTC Properties [*NYSE symbol*] (TTSB)
LTC.............	LTC Properties, Inc. [*NYSE symbol*] (SPSG)
LTC.............	Lunar Terrain [*or Topographic*] Camera [*NASA*]
LTC.............	Lynchburg Technology Center (GAAI)
L(TC)	Tax Cases Leaflets [*Legal*] [*British*]
LTCA............	Elazig [*Turkey ICAO location identifier*] (ICLI)
LTCAX........	Thornburg Ltd. Term Muni-Cal. Cl.A [*Mutual fund ticker symbol*] (SG)
LTCB............	Agri [*Turkey ICAO location identifier*] (ICLI)
LTCB............	Long Term Credit Bank [*Japan*] (ECON)
LTCB............	Long-Term Credit Bank of Japan, Ltd. (ECON)
LTCC............	Diyarbakir [*Turkey ICAO location identifier*] (ICLI)
LTCC............	Language Testing and Curriculum Center [*Griffith University*] [*Australia*]
LTCC............	Long-Term Care Campaign (EA)
LTCC............	Low Temperature Co-Fired Ceramic (AAEL)
LTCCM........	Loading Training Captive Carry Missile (MCD)
LTCD............	Erzincan [*Turkey ICAO location identifier*] (ICLI)
LTCDA........	Low Temperature Coal Distillers Association [*British*] (DBA)
LTCDR	Lieutenant Commander
Lt Cdr	Lieutenant Commander (WDAA)
LTCE............	Erzurum [*Turkey ICAO location identifier*] (ICLI)
LTCF............	Kars [*Turkey ICAO location identifier*] (ICLI)
LTCF............	Long-Term Care Facility [*Medicine*]
LTCG............	Long-Term Capital Gain
LTCG............	Trabzon [*Turkey ICAO location identifier*] (ICLI)
LTCH............	Litchfield Financial [*NASDAQ symbol*] (TTSB)
LTCH............	Litchfield Financial Corp. [*NASDAQ symbol*] (SAG)
LTCH............	Urfa [*Turkey ICAO location identifier*] (ICLI)
LTCI............	Van [*Turkey ICAO location identifier*] (ICLI)
LTCJ............	Batman [*Turkey ICAO location identifier*] (ICLI)
LTCL............	Licentiate of Trinity College of Music, London [*British*]
LTCL............	Long-Term Capital Loss
LTCM............	Licentiate of the Toronto Conservatory of Music [*Canada*]
LTCM............	Long-Term Capital Management
LTCMDS	Long-Term Care Minimum Data Set [*Department of Health and Human Services*] (GFGA)
LTCOL........	Lieutenant Colonel
LtCol............	Lieutenant Colonel (ASC)
LTCOM........	Lieutenant Commander (DNAB)
LT COMDR....	Lieutenant Commander (DNAB)
Lt-Comm.....	Lieutenant-Commander [*British military*] (DMA)
LT/COR/WR...	Light Corner Wear [*Deltiology*]
LTC Prp	LTC Properties, Inc. [*Associated Press*] (SAG)
LT/CR..........	Light Crease [*Deltiology*]
LTCS............	Long-Term Contracting Strategy (COE)
LTCS............	Low Transverse Cesarean Section [*Medicine*] (MEDA)
LTCSB........	Long-Term Care Statistics Branch [*Department of Health and Human Services*] (GFGA)
LTCT	Lower Thermal Comfort Threshold [*Environmental heating*]
LTCVD........	Low-Temperature Chemical Vapor Deposition (AAEL)
LTD.............	Ghadames [*Libya*] [*Airport symbol*] (OAG)
LTD.............	Land Titles Division [*South Australia*]
LTD.............	Land Treatment Demonstration [*Environmental science*] (COE)
LTD.............	Language Training Detachment [*Defense Language Institute*] (DNAB)
LTD.............	Laron-Type Dwarfism [*Medicine*]
LTD.............	LASER Target Designator
LTD.............	Launch Test Directive [*NASA*] (KSC)
LTD.............	Letdown [*Nuclear energy*] (NRCH)
LTD.............	Leukotriene D [*Clinical pharmacology*]
LTD.............	Lift-Drag [*Ratio*] (MCD)
LTD.............	Lift-to-Drag [*Aerospace*] (NAKS)
LTD.............	Lightweight Target Designator
Ltd	Limited (EBF)
LTD.............	Limited
ltd	Limited (DAVI)
LTD.............	[*The*] Limited, Inc. [*NYSE symbol*] (SPSG)
LTD.............	Limit to Topographic Development [*Of hillsides*] [*Geology*]
LTD.............	Linear Transport Drive
LTD.............	Linear Tumor Diameter [*Oncology*]
LTD.............	Line Transfer Device
LTD.............	Litchfield, IL [*Location identifier FAA*] (FAAL)
LTD.............	Live Test Demonstration
LTD.............	Local Test Desk [*Telecommunications*] (KSC)
LTD.............	Logistic Technical Data [*Navy*]
LTD.............	Long Tank Delta
LTD.............	Long-Term Depression [*Neurophysiology*]
LTD.............	Long-Term Disability
LTD.............	Low-Temperature Drying
LTD.............	Lumber Transfer and Distribution

LTDA............	Licensed Taxi Drivers' Association [*British*] (DBA)
LTD ED	Limited Edition [*Publishing*]
LTDI............	Learning Technology Dissemination Initiative (AIE)
LTDL............	Life Test Data Logger (CAAL)
LTDM...........	Light Transmittance Difference Meter
LTDP............	Long-Term Defense Program [*NATO*] (MCD)
LTDQ	Limited Quantity [*Refers to a test performed on a scanty specimen*] [*Biochemistry*] (DAVI)
LTD/R..........	LASER Target Designator/Ranger (DWSG)
LTDR...........	LASER Target Designator Receiver
LTDS...........	LASER Target Designator System (MCD)
LTDS...........	Launch Tracking [*or Trajectory*] Data System
LTDSS..........	LASER Target Designator Scoring System (MCD)
LTDSTD	Limited Standard (IAA)
LTDT...........	Langley Transonic Dynamics Tunnel [*NASA*] (KSC)
LTD(U)........	Land Treatment Demonstration [*or Unit*] (GNE)
LTE	Land Trust Exchange [*Later, LTA*] (EA)
LTE	Laplace Transformation Estimator
LTE	Large Table Electroplotter [*Computer science*]
LTE	Large Terminal Repeats [*Genetics*] (DAVI)
LTE	Large Thrust per Element
LTE	Launch to Eject
LTE	Letter to the Editor
LTE	Leucotriene E [*Clinical pharmacology*]
LT(E)..........	Lieutenant (Engineer)
LTE	Limited Technical Evaluation (MCD)
LTE	Limited Test Equipment
LTE	Linear Threshold Element [*Computer science*]
LTE	Line Terminating Equipment (ACRL)
LTE	Line Termination Equipment [*Telecommunications*] (TEL)
LTE	Local Telephone Exchange (NITA)
LTE	Local Thermal Equilibrium [*Physical chemistry*]
LTE	Local Thermodynamic Equilibrium [*or Equivalent*] [*Astronautics, astrophysics*]
LTE	London Transport Executive
LTE	Long-Term Effect
LTE	Long-Term Enhancement [*Neurophysiology*]
LTE	Long-Term Equilibration [*Analytical chemistry*]
LTE	Low-Thrust Engine
LTE	LTE International Airways SA [*Spain*] [*FAA designator*] (FAAC)
LTEA...........	Leaf Tobacco Exporters Association (EA)
LTEC...........	Lincoln Telecmmun [*NASDAQ symbol*] (TTSB)
LTED...........	Long-Term Economic Deterioration [*Department of Commerce*]
LT/ED/WR ...	Light Edge Wear [*Deltiology*]
Ltee.............	Limitee [*Limited*] [*French*]
LTEK...........	Life Technologies [*NASDAQ symbol*] (TTSB)
LTEMP.........	Low Temperature
L T (Eng)	Law Times Journal (England) [*A publication*] (DLA)
LTEP...........	Long-Term Equipment Plan [*Military*] (RDA)
LTER...........	Long Term Ecological Research [*National Science Foundation*]
LTERR.........	Lunar Terrestrial Age
LTF	Landline Telephony [*Aviation*] (DA)
LTF	LASER Terrain Follower
LTF	Latvijas Tautas Fronte [*Popular Front of Latvia*] [*Political party*] (EY)
LTF	Layman Tithing Foundation (EA)
LTF	Leucotriene F [*Clinical pharmacology*]
LTF	Ligand-Responsive Transcription Factor [*Genetics*]
LTF	Light-Float [*Navigation*]
LTF	Lightning Training Flight [*British military*] (DMA)
LTF	Lipotropic Factor [*Choline*] [*Biochemistry*]
LTF	Liquid Thermal Flowmeter
LTF	Lithographic Technical Foundation [*Later, GATF*] (MSA)
LTF	Local Training Flight
LTF	Logical Twin Forward Pointer (MHDI)
LTF	Lymphocyte Transforming Factor [*Immunology*]
LTF	Nicholls State University, Thibodaux, LA [*Library symbol Library of Congress*] (LCLS)
LTFC...........	Landing Traffic [*Aviation*] (FAAC)
LTFC...........	Low-Temperature Fuel Cell [*Energy source*]
LTFCS.........	LASER Tank Fire Control System
LTFD...........	Logic and Test Function Drawer [*Computer science*] (MCD)
LT/FM.........	Long-Term/Frequency Modulation
LTFRD	Lot Tolerance Fraction Reliability Deviation [*Quality control*]
LTFS...........	LASER Terrain Following System
LTFT...........	Low-Temperature Flow Test [*Lubricant technology*]
LTFV...........	Less Than Fair Value [*Business term*]
LTG.............	Catalina Lighting [*NYSE symbol*] (SAG)
LTG.............	Legal Technology Group [*Information service or system*] (IID)
LTG.............	Lettering (ADA)
LTG.............	Lieutenant General (AABC)
LTG.............	Lightening
LTG.............	Lighting
LTG.............	Lightning [*Meteorology*]
LTG.............	Lightning Minerals [*Vancouver Stock Exchange symbol*]
LTG.............	Linear Tangent Guidance (MCD)
LTG.............	Line Trunk Group [*Telecommunications*]
ltg..............	Lithographer [*MARC relator code*] [*Library of Congress*] (LCCP)
LTG.............	Little Theatre Guild [*British*] (DBA)
LTG.............	Local Tactical Grid [*Military*] (NVT)
LTG.............	Long-Term Goals (DAVI)
LTG.............	Lunar Traverse Gravimeter [*Experiment*] [*NASA*]
LTGA...........	Left [*or Levo*] Transposition of the Great Arteries [*Also called corrected transposition*] [*Cardiology*] (DAVI)
LTGC...........	Lieutenant Grand Commander [*Freemasonry*]
LTGCA.........	Lightning Cloud-to-Air [*NWS*] (FAAC)

LTGCC	Lightning Cloud-to-Cloud [*NWS*] (FAAC)
LTGCCCG....	Lightning Cloud-to-Cloud, Cloud-to-Ground [*NWS*] (FAAC)
LTGCG	Lightning Cloud-to-Ground [*NWS*] (FAAC)
LTGCW	Lightning Cloud-to-Water [*NWS*] (FAAC)
LTGE	Lighterage
LTGEN	Lieutenant General
Lt Gen	Lieutenant General (WDAA)
LTGF Newl...	Lawyers' Title Guaranty Funds Newsletter [*A publication*] (DLA)
LTGH	Lightening Hole [*Engineering*]
LTGIC.........	Lightning in Clouds [*NWS*] (FAAC)
LTGL...........	Lee-Tse-Goldberg-Lowe [*Theory*]
LT Gov........	Lieutenant Governor (WGA)
LTH	Enterprise Thesaurus [*Database*]
LTH	Laboratory Test Handbook
LTH	Lactogenic Hormone [*Also, LGH, PR, PRL*] [*Endocrinology*]
L Th	La Themis [*Lower Canada*] [*A publication*] (DLA)
LTH	Leather [*Automotive advertising*]
LTH	Less than Honorable Discharge [*Military*] (VNW)
L Th	Licentiate in Theology
LTH	Light Training Helicopter (WDAA)
LTH	Local Tumor Hyperthermia [*Medicine*] (DB)
LTH	Logical Track Header
LTH	London Teaching Hospitals [*National Health Service*] [*British*] (DI)
LTH	Long-Term Holiday (MHDB)
LTH	Low-Temperature Herschel (OA)
LTH	Low-Temperature Holding
LTH	Low Turret Half
LTH	Luteotrophic Hormone [*Also, PR, PRL*] [*Endocrinology*]
Lth	Martin Luther's German Version of the Bible [*A publication*] (BJA)
LTHA...........	Long-Term Heat Aging
L Theol	Licentiate in Theology [*British*] (WA)
LTHG	Lathing
L Th K	Lexikon fuer Theologie und Kirche [*A publication*] (ODCC)
LTHO	Lighthouse
LTHR...........	Leather (KSC)
LTHV...........	Lucke Tumor Herpesvirus
LTI	Aerotaxis Latinoamericanos SA de CV [*Mexico ICAO designator*] (FAAC)
LTI	Land Training Installations (NATG)
LTI	Lawyers Tile [*NYSE symbol*] (TTSB)
LTI	Lawyers Title Corp. [*NYSE symbol*] (SAG)
LTI	Licentiate of the Textile Institute [*British*] (DBQ)
LTI	Life Technologies, Inc. (HGEN)
LTI	Light Transmission Index
LTI	Limited to Interrogations (MCD)
LTI	Linear Technology, Inc. [*Toronto Stock Exchange symbol*]
LTI	Linear Time Invariant (IAA)
LTI	Lingua Tertii Imperii [*A study of the abuse of language under Nazism by Viktor Klemperer*]
LTI	Long-Term Inmate (WDAA)
LTI	Long-Term Integration (CAAL)
LTI	Lost Time Injury [*Industrial plant safety*]
LTI	Lowell Technological Institute [*Massachusetts*]
LTI	Low-Temperature Isomerization [*Organic chemistry*]
LTI	Low-Temperature Isotope
LTI	Lupus-Type Inclusions [*Medicine*] (DMAA)
LTIB	Lead Technical Information Bureau [*British*] (BI)
LTIC...........	Language Teaching Information Centre [*British*] (CB)
LTID...........	LASER Target Interface Device (RDA)
LTID...........	Light-Intensity Detector (MSA)
Lt Inf..........	Light Infantry [*British military*] (DMA)
LTIOV.........	Latest Time Information of Value [*Military*] (AFM)
LTIP...........	Long-Term Incentive Plan
LTIRF.........	Lowell Technological Institute Research Foundation (MCD)
LTIS...........	LASER Target Interface System
LTIV	Lunar Trajectory Injection Vehicle [*NASA*] (KSC)
LTJ..............	Law Times Journal [*A publication*] (DLA)
LTJ..............	Lutheran Theological Journal [*A publication*] (APTA)
LTJC	Lyons Township Junior College [*Illinois*]
LTJG	Lieutenant Junior Grade [*Navy*]
LT Jo (Eng)...	Law Times Journal (England) [*A publication*] (DLA)
LTK	Latakia [*Syria*] [*Airport symbol*] (OAG)
LTK	Lead To Come [*Copyediting*] (WDMC)
LTK	Leukocyte Tyrosine Kinase [*An enzyme*]
LTK1	Ladies' Touring Kayak, Single Person (ADA)
LTL	Lafourche Parish Library, Thibodaux, LA [*Library symbol Library of Congress*]
LTL	Laparoscopic Tubal Ligation [*Gynecology*] (DAVI)
LTL	Lastourville [*Gabon*] [*Airport symbol*] (OAG)
LTL	Latvian Airlines [*ICAO designator*] (FAAC)
LTL	Learning Through Listening [*Recording for the blind*]
LTL	Learning to Look
LTL	Less than Lethal (INF)
LTL	Less than Truckload [*Under 24,000 pounds*]
LTL	Line-to-Line
LTL	Lintel [*Technical drawings*]
LTL	Listing-Time Limit (MSA)
LTL	Little
LTL	Lot-to-Lot (AAEL)
LTL	Lot-Truck Load
LTL	Lytton Minerals Ltd. [*Toronto Stock Exchange symbol Vancouver Stock Exchange symbol*]
LTLA...........	Launcher Tube Longitudinal Axis
LTLA...........	Louisiana Trial Lawyers Association (SRA)
lt lat...........	Left Lateral [*Medicine*] (MAE)

LTLCG............ Little Change (FAAC)
LTLS .... Lincoln Trail Libraries System [Library network]
LTLS .... Long-Term Lapse Survey [LIMRA]
LTLT .... Long Time Low Temperature [Food processing]
LTM .... Laici per il Terzo Mondo [Italy]
LTM .... LASER Target Marker (RDA)
LTM .... LASER Transfer Module [Telecommunications] (LAIN)
LTM .... Leading Torpedoman [Navy British]
LTM .... Lead Time Matrix (MCD)
LTM .... Leave Trapping Mode (SAA)
LTM .... Lethem [Guyana] [Airport symbol] (OAG)
LTM .... Leverage Transaction Merchant (MHDI)
LTM .... Licentiate in Tropical Medicine [British]
LTM .... Lient Trief Mixed [Cement]
LTM .... Life Test Model
LTM .... Limits-to-Throughput Model [Environmental science]
LTM .... Line Transition Monitoring (NITA)
LTM .... Line Type Modulation [Radio]
LTM .... Little Maria Mountains [California] [Seismograph station code, US Geological Survey] (SEIS)
LTM .... Live Traffic Model [Telecommunications] (TEL)
LTM .... Load Ton Mile (IAA)
LTM .... Logic Theory Machine (SAA)
LTM .... Long-Term Memory
LTM .... Long-Term Monitoring [Environmental science] (BCP)
LTM .... Low Thermal Mass (PDAA)
LTM .... Low-Trajectory Missiles (NRCH)
LTM1 .... Lunar Tele-Operations Model 1 [Mooncolony modeling]
LTMA .... Lithium Trimethoxyaluminium (MEC)
LTMAC .... Lauryltrimethylammonium Chloride [Organic chemistry]
LTMC .... Lymphoid Tissue Mononuclear Cell [Physiology]
LTMED .... Low-Temperature Multieffect Distillation [Chemical engineering]
LTMFM .... Low-Temperature Magnetic Force Microscope
LTMFX .... Thornburg Ltd. Term Munic: Natl. Cl.A [Mutual fund ticker symbol] (SG)
LTMR........... LASER Target Marker Ranger [Aviation] (OA)
LTMR........... Long-Term Multilineage Reconstituting [Cytology]
LTMRSC ...... Long-Term Multilineage Reconstituting Stem Cell [Cytology]
LTMS .... Lubricant Test Monitoring System [Automotive engineering]
LTMS .... Lunar Terrain Measuring System [Aerospace]
LTN .... Aerolineas Latinas CA [Venezuela] [ICAO designator] (FAAC)
LTN .... Alaska Legislative Teleconference Network [Alaska State Legislative Affairs Agency] [Juneau, AK] [Telecommunications service] (TSSD)
LTN .... Liberty Tree Network [An association] (EA)
LTN .... Lightning (ADA)
LTN .... Linear Time-Varying Network
LTN .... Listen (IAA)
LTN .... Long-Term Nephelometer [Instrumentation]
Ltn .... Long Ton (EBF)
LTN .... Luton [England] [Airport symbol] (OAG)
LTNG .... Lightning [Meteorology]
LTNGARR ..... Lightning Arrester (IAA)
LTNGP .... Low-Temperature Noble Gas Process [Nuclear energy] (NRCH)
LTNIF.......... Low-Temperature Neutron Irradiation Facility [Oak Ridge, TN] [Oak Ridge National Laboratory] [Department of Energy] (GRD)
LTNP.......... Long-Term Nonprogressor [Of the human immune deficiency virus]
LT NS .... Law Times. New Series [Pennsylvania] [A publication] (DLA)
LT NS .... Law Times Reports, New Series [England] [A publication] (DLA)
LTNS .... Long Time, No See [Computer science] (DOM)
LT NS (Eng)... Law Times. New Series [England] [A publication] (DLA)
LTNYX .... Rochester Limited Term N.Y. Municipal [Mutual fund ticker symbol] (SG)
LTO .... Landing and Takeoff
LTO .... Leading Torpedoman [Navy British] (DMA)
LTO .... Lead-Tin Overlay [Automotive engineering]
LTO .... Local Tax Office [British]
LTO .... Loreto [Mexico] [Airport symbol] (OAG)
LTO .... Lot Time Order
LTO .... Low-Temperature Orthorhombic [Crystallography]
LTO .... Low Temperature Oxidation [Physical chemistry]
LTO .... Low Temperature Oxide (AAEL)
LTOC.......... Landing-Takeoff Cycle (COE)
LTOC.......... Lowest Total Overall Cost (MHDI)
LTOE.......... Living Table of Organization and Equipment [Army] (INF)
LTOF.......... Low-Temperature Optical Facility
LTOM .... London's Traded Options Market [British] (ECON)
LTON .... Long Ton [2240 pounds]
LTOOR......... Light Truck On-Off Road
LTOP.......... Lease to Ownership Plan
LTOP.......... Lease to Purchase (COE)
LTOS.......... Law Times, Old Series [British]
LT OS .... Law Times Reports, Old Series [England] [A publication] (DLA)
LTOS.......... Long to Short [Computer utility tool] (PCM)
LTOT.......... Latest Time over Target (AFM)
LTP .... Laboratory Test Profile [Medicine] (DB)
LT-P .... Large Transmitter Coated with Paraffin
LTP .... Latpass [Latvia] [FAA designator] (FAAC)
LTP .... Leader Training Program [Army]
LTP .... Lead, Test, Probe (DWSG)
LTP .... LEM [Lunar Excursion Module] Test Procedure [NASA] (KSC)
LTP .... Let's Tax Plutocrats [Humorous interpretation of LTP - Limit on Tax Preferences]
LTP .... Letterpress
LTP .... Leukocyte Thromboplastin (STED)

LTP .... Library Technology Program [Formerly, Library Technology Project] [ALA] [Defunct]
LTP .... Lient Trief Pure [Cement]
LTP .... Limit on Tax Preferences
LTP .... Linear Time Plot (MUGU)
LTP .... Line-Throwing Projectile (NG)
LTP .... Line Type Processor [Radio] (IAA)
LTP .... Lipid Transfer Protein [Biochemistry]
LTP .... Living Together Partner [Lifestyle classification]
LTP .... Local Tourism Plan
LTP .... Local Training Plan [Job Training and Partnership Act] (OICC)
LTP .... Long-Tailed Pair [Electronics] (OA)
LTP .... Long-Term Potentiation [Neurophysiology]
LTP .... Long Term Projections [Townsend-Greenspan & Co., Inc.] [Database]
LTP .... Lower Trip Point
LTP .... Low-Temperature Passivation (PDAA)
LTP .... Low-Temperature Phase (PDAA)
LTP .... Low-Temperature Phosphorimetry [Analytical chemistry]
LTP .... Low-Temperature Physics
LTP .... Low-Temperature Polymer (IAA)
LTP .... L-Tryptophan (STED)
LTP .... Lunar Tidal Perturbation
LTPA .... Louisiana Travel Promotion Association (SRA)
LTPB .... Lactone Terminated Polybutadiene [Organic chemistry] (MCD)
LTPD .... Lot Tolerance Percent Defective [Quality control] (MSA)
LTPE .... Long Term Public Expenditure [British]
LTPHOTORON... Light Photographic Squadron
LTPL .... Long-Term Procedural Language
LTPN .... Long-Term Parenteral Nutrition (PDAA)
LTPO .... LASER Technology Program Office [Navy]
LTPP .... Lipothiamide-Pyrophosphate
LTPP .... Long-Term Pavement Performance [FHWA] (TAG)
LTPR........... Lightproof [Technical drawings] (IAA)
LTPR........... Long Taper
LTPR........... Long-Term Prime Rate [Finance]
LTPS .... Lateral Transitional Phase Shift [Optics]
LTPS .... Lincoln Tube Process Specification (SAA)
LTPT .... Low-Turbulence Pressure Tunnel [NASA]
LTPWG .... LOAD [Low Altitude Defense] Test Planning Working Group
LTPWS......... Low Tire-Pressure Warning System [Automotive engineering]
LTQ .... Le Touquet [France] [Airport symbol] (OAG)
LTQ .... Local Track Quality (NVT)
LTQ .... Low Torque
LTQC.......... Long-Term Quality-Control [Analytical chemistry]
LTR .... AS Lufttransport [Norway ICAO designator] (FAAC)
LTR .... Lander Trajectory Reconstruction [Program] [NASA]
LTR .... Lands Tribunal Rules [Town planning] [British]
LTR .... LASER Tank Range-Finder
LTR .... LASER Target Recognition [Military] (CAAL)
LTR .... Lattice Test Reactor
LTR .... Law Times Reports, New Series [England] [A publication] (DLA)
LTR .... [The] Learning Tree [UTLAS symbol]
LTR .... Left Test Register (IAA)
LTR .... Letter (AFM)
Ltr............ Letter (EBF)
LTR .... Library Technology Reports [American Library Association]
L-TR .... Licensing Technical Review [Nuclear energy] (NRCH)
LTR .... Lighter
LTRS .... Light Tactical Raft
LTR .... Liquid Test Rig [Apollo] [NASA]
LTR .... List Test Resister (PDAA)
LTR .... Living Together Relationship
LTR .... Load Task Register [Computer science] (PCM)
LTR .... Location Transactivating Region [Medicine] (DMAA)
LTR .... Lockheed Training Reactor
LTR .... Loew's Corp. [Formerly, Loew's Theatres, Inc.] [NYSE symbol] (SPSG)
LTR .... Lone Tree Road [California] [Seismograph station code, US Geological Survey] (SEIS)
LTR .... Longitudinal Triangular Ripples [Oceanography]
LTR .... Long Terminal Repeat [or Redundancy] [Genetics]
LTR .... Long-Term Reserve [British military] (DMA)
LTR .... Long-Term Revitalization (OA)
LTR .... Long Treble [Knitting]
LTR .... Long-Tube Recirculation [Evaporator]
LTR .... Lord Treasurer's Remembrancer [British]
LTR .... Low-Temperature Reactor [Chemical engineering]
LTR .... Lymphocyte Transfer Reaction (STED)
LTRA .... Lands Tribunal Rating Appeals [Legal] [British]
LTRA .... Leukotriene Receptor Antagonist [Biochemistry]
L-TRAN .... Lesson Translator (NVT)
L Trans Q .... Law in Transition Quarterly [A publication] (DLA)
LTRB .... Long Term Review Board (WDAA)
LTRC........... Louisiana Transportation Research Center [Louisiana State University] [Research center] (RCD)
LTRCA .... Lawn Tennis Registered Coaches Association [British] (BI)
LTRE .... Learning Tree Intl. [NASDAQ symbol] (TTSB)
LTren .... Left Trendelenburg [Position] [Surgery] (DAVI)
LT Rep .... Law Times Reports, New Series [England] [A publication] (DLA)
LT Rep NS .... Law Times Reports, New Series [England] [A publication] (DLA)
LTRF .... LASER Tank Range-Finder
LTRF .... Low Temperature Research Facility [NASA]
LTRI .... Lightning and Transients Research Institute [St. Paul, MN] (MCD)
LTRN .... Lantern (MSA)

LTRN .... Lantern Slide (VRA)
LTR NS .... Law Times Reports, New Series [England] [A publication] (DLA)
LTRO .... Lateral Tire Run-Out [Automotive engineering]
LTROM .... Linear Transformer Read Only Memory [Computer science] (IAA)
LTRP.......... Long-Term Requirement Plan (NATG)
LTRPRS ...... Letterpress
LTRS........... LASER Target Recognition System
LTRS........... Letters Shift [Teleprinters]
LTRS........... Low Temperature Research Station [British]
LT Rulings... Land Tax Rulings [Australia A publication]
LTS .... Altus, OK [Location identifier FAA] (FAAL)
LTS .... Laboratory Test Set
LTS .... Labor Turnover Statistics (OICC)
LTS .... Landfall Technique School [Navy]
LTS .... Language Teaching System
LTS .... Language Translation System
LTS .... Laparoscopic Tubal Sterilization [Medicine] (STED)
LTS .... LASER Target Simulator (MCD)
LTS .... LASER Test Set (MCD)
LTS .... LASER Time Sharing (PDAA)
LTS .... LASER-Triggered Switch (MCD)
LTS .... Lateral Test Simulator (IAA)
LTS .... Launch Telemetry Station
LTS .... Launch Telemetry System
LTS .... Launch Test Set
LTS .... Launch Tracking Station
LTS .... Launch Tracking System
LTS .... Library Technical Services [Library network]
LTS .... Lifetrends Behavioral Systems, Inc. [Vancouver Stock Exchange symbol]
LTS .... Lift-Off Transmission Subsystem (IAA)
LTS .... Lighting Test Set (KSC)
LTS .... Light Tactile Stimulation [Neurology] (DAVI)
LTS .... Linearity Test Set
LTS .... Line Transient Suppression
LTS .... Link Terminal Simulator
LTS .... Linomatic Tape System [Typography] (DGA)
LTS .... Llantrisant [Welsh depot code]
LTS .... Load Transfer Switch
LTS .... Logistics Test Squadron [Military]
LTS .... Long-Term Stability
LTS .... Long-Term Standard [Lamp for spectrometry]
LTS .... Long-Term Storage [Memory] [Computer science]
LTS .... Long-Term Survival [Medicine] (DMAA)
LTS .... Long-Term Surviving (STED)
LTS .... Long Tract Sign [Neurology] (STED)
LTS .... Love Token Society (EA)
LTS .... Low-Frequency Transmit System (DWSG)
LTS .... Low-Temperature Separation
LTS .... Low-Temperature Smoking (PDAA)
LTS .... Low Threshold Spike [Neurochemistry]
LTS .... LTU [Lufttransport Unternehmen Sud] GmbH [Germany ICAO designator] (FAAC)
LTS .... Lufttransport-Sud [Airline] [Germany]
LTS .... Lunar Touchdown System [NASA] (IAA)
LTS .... Trinity Lutheran Seminary, Columbus, OH [OCLC symbol] (OCLC)
LTSC........... Licentiate in the Technology of Surface Coatings [British] (DBQ)
LTSC........... Licentiate of the Tonic Sol-fa College (WDAA)
LTSC........... Low-Temperature Semiconductor [Electronics]
LTSDE......... Low-Temperature Superconducting Device Electronics (DOMA)
LTSEM........ Low-Temperature Scanning Electron Microscopy
LTSF .... Lid Tank Shielding Facility [Nuclear energy] (NRCH)
LTSG.......... LASER-Triggered Spark Gap
LTSH.......... League of Tarcisians of the Sacred Heart [Later, LT] (EA)
LTSM.......... Long-Range Tactical Strike Missile (MCD)
LT(Sp) .... Lieutenant (Special)
LTSPC......... L'Union Territoriale des Syndicats Professionelles Caledoniens [Territorial Federation of New Caledonian Unions of Private Employees]
LT-SR .... Large Transmitter Coated with Silicon Rubber
LTSR .... Line Trunk Scanner Register [Computer science] (IAA)
LTSS .... Lawrence Timesharing System (CIST)
LTSS .... Long-Term Scientific Study [NATO Defense Research Group] (MCD)
LTSTA......... Light Station [Coast Guard]
LTSV .... Light Savers USA [NASDAQ symbol] (TTSB)
LTSV .... Light Savers USA, Inc. [NASDAQ symbol] (SAG)
LTSV .... Lucerne Transient Streak Virus [Plant pathology]
LTSW.......... Light Switch
LtSwtz........ Little Switzerland, Inc. [Associated Press] (SAG)
LTT .... Lactose Tolerance Test [Medicine] (STED)
LTT .... Landline Teletypewriter [Military]
LTT .... Land Title Trust (DLA)
LTT .... LASER Target Tracker
LTT .... Latakia Type Tobacco [Shipping]
LTT .... Less than Truckload [Under 24,000 pounds] (WGA)
LTT .... Leucine Tolerance Test [Clinical chemistry] (AAMN)
LTT .... Liberty Term Trust-1999 [NYSE symbol] (SPSG)
LT T .... Lieutenant of Treasury [British]
LTT .... Light Tactical Transport (MCD)
LTT .... Light-Travel-Time [Astronomy]
LTT .... Limited Treadmill Test [Medicine] (DMAA)
LTT .... Liquid Toner Transfer [Typography] (DGA)
LTT .... Lithium Thallium Tartrate [Inorganic chemistry]
LTT .... Long-Term Training (MCD)
LTT .... Long-Term Trend [Finance] (MHDI)

LTT .... Louis Trichardt [South Africa] [Seismograph station code, US Geological Survey] (SEIS)
LTT .... Low Temperature Teatment [Materials science]
LTT .... Low-Temperature Test
LTT .... Low-Temperature Tetragonal [Crystallography]
LTT .... Lunar Test Table [Aerospace]
LTT .... Lymphoblastic Transformation Test [Biochemistry] (DAVI)
LTT .... Lymphocyte Transformation Test [Medicine]
LTTA .... Logic Tree Trouble-Shooting Aid (PDAA)
LTTA .... Long Tank Thrust-Augmented (PDAA)
LTTAD......... Long Tank Thrust-Augmented Delta (PDAA)
LTTAS......... Light Tactical Transport Aircraft System [Helicopter] [Military] (RDA)
LTTAT......... Long Tank Thrust-Augmented Thor
LTTB .... Listen to the Band (EA)
LTTBT......... Low-Threshold Test Ban Treaty [Proposed]
LTTC .... Lowry Technical Training Center [Air Force] (AFM)
LTTD .... Letter-Type Technical Directive [Navy] (NG)
LTTE .... Liberation Tigers of Tamil Eelam [Sri Lanka]
LTTL .... Low-Power Transistor-Transistor Logic (IEEE)
LTTMT......... Low-Temperature Thermomechanical Treatment
LTTO .... Lotto World [NASDAQ symbol] (TTSB)
LTTO .... Lotto World, Inc. [NASDAQ symbol] (SAG)
LTTP .... Long-Term Treatment Plan [Environmental science] (COE)
LTTR .... Latter
LTTR .... Long-Term Tape Recorder
LTU .... Land Treatment Unit [Waste disposal]
LTU .... Lawrence Technological University
LTU .... Less Than
LTU .... Lift-Off Time and Update
LTU .... Line Terminating Unit (CET)
LTU .... Line Termination Unit (NITA)
LTU .... Little Mountain [Utah] [Seismograph station code, US Geological Survey] (SEIS)
LTU .... Long-Term Unemployed
LTU .... Long Ton Unit
LTU .... Lufttransport Unternehmen GmbH [Germany ICAO designator] (FAAC)
LTU .... Spencer, IA [Location identifier FAA] (FAAL)
LTUI .... Low Transverse Uterine Incision [Medicine] (STED)
LTUS.......... Garden Fresh Restaurant [NASDAQ symbol] (TTSB)
LTUS.......... Garden Fresh Restaurant Corp. [NASDAQ symbol] (SAG)
LTUSA .... La Trobe University Staff Association [Australia]
LTV .... Land Transport Vehicle (NVT)
LTV .... Large Test Vessel [Nuclear energy] (NRCH)
LTV .... Launch Test Vehicles
LTV .... Life Test Vehicle
LTV .... Light-Vessel [Navigation]
LTV .... Ling-Temco-Vaught (WDAA)
LTV .... Ling-Temco-Vought Co.
LTV .... Load Threshold Value (DA)
LTV .... Loan-to-Value Ratio [Finance]
LTV .... Local Thickness Variation (AAEL)
LTV .... Long-Term Vibration
LTV .... Long Tube Vertical
LTV .... LTV Corp. [Formerly, Ling-Temco-Vought, Inc.] [NYSE symbol] (SPSG)
LTV .... Lucke Tumor Virus [Medicine] (STED)
LTV .... Lunar Excursion Module Test Vehicle [NASA] (IAA)
LTV .... Lung Thermal Volume [Medicine] (STED)
LTVC .... Launcher Tube Vertical Centerline
LTW .... League of Tasmanian Wheelmen [Australia]
LTW .... Leydig-Cell Tumor in Wistar Rat [Medicine] (DMAA)
LTW .... Long-Term Waviness [Metal surface finish]
LTW .... Los Trancos Woods [California] [Seismograph station code, US Geological Survey] (SEIS)
LTW .... Low-Tension Winding (IAA)
LTW .... NV Luchtvaartmaatschappij Twente [Netherlands ICAO designator] (FAAC)
LTWA .... Lawn Tennis Writers' Association of America [Later, USTWA] (EA)
LTWA .... Long Trailing Wire Antenna (MCD)
LTWG .... Launch Test Working Group
LTWT .... Lightweight
LTX .... Lap-Top Expansion [Computer science]
ltx .... Latex (VRA)
LTX .... Leo Taxi Aereo SA de CV [Mexico ICAO designator] (FAAC)
LTX .... Lintronics International Ltd. [Vancouver Stock Exchange symbol]
LTX .... LTX Corp. [Associated Press] (SAG)
LTXRD .... Low-Temperature X-Ray Diffraction [Instrumentation]
LTXW.......... Latex Resources Wrrt [NASDAQ symbol] (TTSB)
LTXX .... LTX Corp. [NASDAQ symbol] (SAG)
LTYR .... Light Year
Lu .... H. Lundbeck [Denmark] [Research code symbol]
LU .... Labor Union (OICC)
LU .... Lamentations over the Destruction of Ur (BJA)
LU .... Laws of Ur Nammu (BJA)
LU .... Left Unity Group [European political movement] (ECON)
LU .... Left Upper [Medicine]
LU .... Liberal-Unionist [British] (ROG)
LU .... Libraries Unlimited [Library network]
LU .... Library Utility [Computer science]
LU .... Lighting Unit (WDAA)
LU .... Ligue Universelle [Esperantiste]
LU .... Line Unit (IAA)
LU .... Line-Up
LU .... List Up

LU	Load Unit
LU	Lock Up (ADA)
LU	Logical Unit [*Computer science*]
LU	Logistical Unit (NATG)
LU	Looking Up [*An association*] (EA)
LU	Loudness Unit
LU	Louisiana State University, Baton Rouge, LA [*Library symbol Library of Congress*] (LCLS)
LU	Lucent Technologies [*NYSE symbol*] (TTSB)
LU	Lucent Technologies, Inc. [*NYSE symbol*] (SAG)
LU	Lues [*Syphilis*] [*Latin*] (WDAA)
Lu	Lumbar [*Anatomy*] (DAVI)
Lu	Lumen [*Anatomy*]
Lu	Lutetium [*Chemical element*]
Lu	Lutheran [*Blood group*]
lu	Luxembourg [*MARC country of publication code Library of Congress*] (LCCP)
LU	Luxembourg [*ANSI two-letter standard code*] (CNC)
LU	Lytic Unit (DB)
LU	St. Luke's Gospel [*New Testament book*] (ROG)
LU	Theron Airways [*ICAO designator*] (AD)
LU	Upper Limen [*Psychology*]
LUA	Launch under Attack [*Nuclear warfare option*]
LUA	Left Upper Arm [*Medicine*]
LUA	Library Users of America (EA)
LUA	Liverpool Underwriters Association (DS)
LUA	Lloyd's Underwriters' Association [*British*] (DBA)
LU-A	Louisiana State University in Alexandria, Alexandria, LA [*Library symbol Library of Congress*] (LCLS)
LUA	Luanda [*Angola*] [*Seismograph station code, US Geological Survey Closed*] (SEIS)
LUA	Luanda Belas [*Angola*] [*Geomagnetic observatory code*]
LUA	Lukla [*Nepal*] [*Airport symbol*] (OAG)
LUA	Luray, VA [*Location identifier FAA*] (FAAL)
LUAC	Life Underwriters Association of Canada
LUAMC	Leading Underwriters' Agreement for Marine Cargo Business (DS)
LUAMH	Leading Underwriters' Agreement for Marine Hull Business (DS)
LUAP	Land Use Adjustment Program
LUAR	Liga de Uniao e Acao Revolucionaria [*Portugal*]
LU-Ar	Louisiana State University, Department of Archives and Manuscripts, Baton Rouge, LA [*Library symbol Library of Congress*] (LCLS)
LUB	Least [*or Lowest*] Upper Bound
LUB	Left Upper Lobe Bronchus [*Anatomy*]
LUB	Logical Unit Block [*Computer science*]
lub	Luba [*MARC language code Library of Congress*] (LCCP)
LUB	Lubbock [*Texas*] [*Seismograph station code, US Geological Survey*] (SEIS)
LUB	Lubricant (WDAA)
LUB	Lubricate [*or Lubrication*] (AAG)
LUB	Luby's Cafeterias [*NYSE symbol*] (TTSB)
LUB	Luby's Cafeterias, Inc. [*NYSE symbol*] (SPSG)
LUB	Lusiana [*Czechoslovakia*] [*ICAO designator*] (FAAC)
LUBA	Limited Underwater Breathing Apparatus (NG)
LUBE	Lubricate (ADA)
LUBEE	Lubrication
Lube Eq	Lube on Equity Pleading [*A publication*] (DLA)
Lube PL	Lube on Equity Pleading [*A publication*] (DLA)
LUBIX	Lutheran Bro. Income [*Mutual fund ticker symbol*] (SG)
LUBO	Lubricating Oil
LUBR	Lubricant
LUBR	Lubricate (ADA)
Lubrizol	[*The*] Lubrizol Corp. [*Associated Press*] (SAG)
LUBS	Large Undisturbed-Bottom Sampler (PDAA)
LUBT	Lubricant (MSA)
Lubys	Luby's Cafeterias, Inc. [*Associated Press*] (SAG)
LUC	Land Use Concurrence [*Acquisition of real estate for the use of US forces on a rent-free basis*] [*Vietnam*]
LUC	Large Unstained Cells [*Cytology*]
LUC	Laucala Island [*Fiji*] [*Airport symbol*] (OAG)
LUC	League of Ukrainian Catholics of America (EA)
LUC	Living under Canvas [*British military*] (DMA)
LU-C	Louisiana State University, Chemistry Library, Baton Rouge, LA [*Library symbol Library of Congress*] (LCLS)
LUC	Louisiana Union Catalog [*Library network*]
Luc	Lucan [*39-65AD*] [*Classical studies*] (OCD)
Luc	Lucas: an Evangelical History Review [*A publication*] (APTA)
Luc	Lucas' Reports [*Modern Reports, Part X*] [*A publication*] (DLA)
LUC	Lucifer (WDAA)
LUC	Luciferase [*An enzyme*]
Luc	Lucullus [*of Plutarch*] [*Classical studies*] (OCD)
Luc	Lucullus or Academica Posteriora [*of Cicero*] [*Classical studies*] (OCD)
LUC	Lukens, Inc. [*NYSE symbol*] (SPSG)
Luc	[*The*] Rape of Lucrece [*Shakespearean work*]
LUCALOX	Translucent Aluminum Oxide [*Ceramic*]
LUCAS	Line Utilization Cable Assignment System (MCD)
Lucas	Lucas' Reports [*Modern Reports, Part X*] [*A publication*] (DLA)
LucasV	Lucasvarity PLC [*Associated Press*] (SAG)
LUCC	Land Use and Cover Change [*Environmental studies*] (ECON)
LUCC	Lehigh University Computing Center [*Pennsylvania*] [*Research center*] (RCD)
Lucent	Lucent Technologies, Inc. [*Associated Press*] (SAG)
LUCF	Load, Unload, Cool, Fracture (PDAA)
LUCHIP	Lutheran Church and Indian People [*An association Defunct*] (EA)
LUCID	Language for Utility Checkout and Instrumentation Development

LUCID	Language Used to Communicate Information System Design
LUCID	Loughborough University Computerized Information and Drawings Project [*British*]
Lucil	Lucilius [*Second century BC*] [*Classical studies*] (OCD)
Lucile	Lucille Farms, Inc. [*Associated Press*] (SAG)
LucileFr	Lucille Farms, Inc. [*Associated Press*] (SAG)
Luck	Indian Law Reports, Lucknow Series [*A publication*] (DLA)
LUCK	Lady Luck Gaming'A' [*NASDAQ symbol*] (TTSB)
LUCK	Lady Luck Gaming Corp. [*NASDAQ symbol*] (SAG)
LUCKN	Logical Unit and Checker (NITA)
LUCKN	Lucknow [*City in India*] (ROG)
Luck Ser	Indian Law Reports, Lucknow Series [*A publication*] (DLA)
LUCO	Lloyd's Underwriters Claims Office (AIA)
LUCOLA	Lutheran Coalition on Latin America (EA)
LUCOLED	Luminescence Conversion Light-Emitting Diode (AAEL)
LUCOM	Lunar Communication [*System*] [*Aerospace*]
Lucor	Lucor, Inc. [*Associated Press*] (SAG)
LUCP	League to Uphold Congregational Principles [*Defunct*] (EA)
LUC PRIM	Luce Primo [*At Daybreak*] [*Pharmacy*]
LUCR	Lucor, Inc. [*NASDAQ symbol*] (SAG)
LUCR	Lucor Inc.`A' [*NASDAQ symbol*] (TTSB)
Lucr	[*The Rape of*] Lucrece [*Shakespearean Work*] (BARN)
LUCR	Lucretius [*Roman poet, 96-55BC*] [*Classical studies*] (ROG)
LUCRE	Lower Unit Costs and Related Earnings (MHDB)
LUCS	London University Computer Services (IAA)
LUCY	Lucille Farms [*NASDAQ symbol*] (TTSB)
LUCY	Lucille Farms, Inc. [*NASDAQ symbol*] (SAG)
LUCYW	Luclle Farm Wrrt [*NASDAQ symbol*] (TTSB)
LUD	Land Use Designation [*US Forest Service*]
LUD	Lift-Up Door [*Technical drawings*]
LUD	Luderitz [*South-West Africa*] [*Airport symbol*] (OAG)
LUD	Lundin Explorations [*Vancouver Stock Exchange symbol*]
LUDA	Land Use Data
Lud & J Tr M	Ludlow and Jenkyns on Trade-Marks [*A publication*] (DLA)
Lud Bolog	Ludovicus Bologninus [*Deceased, 1508*] [*Authority cited in pre-1607 legal work*] (DSA)
Ludd	Ludden's Reports [*43, 44 Maine*] [*A publication*] (DLA)
Ludden	Ludden's Reports [*43, 44 Maine*] [*A publication*] (DLA)
Lud de Ro	Ludovicus Pontanus de Roma [*Deceased, 1439*] [*Authority cited in pre-1607 legal work*] (DSA)
Lud EC	Luder's Election Cases [*England*] [*A publication*] (DLA)
Lud El Cas	Luder's Election Cases [*England*] [*A publication*] (DLA)
Luder Elec Cas	Luder's Election Cases [*England*] [*A publication*] (DLA)
Luders Elec Cas (Eng)	Luder's Election Cases [*England*] [*A publication*] (DLA)
ludes	Quaaludes [*Methaqualone*] [*Pharmacology*] (DAVI)
Lud Gozad	Ludovicus Gozzadini [*Deceased, 1536*] [*Authority cited in pre-1607 legal work*] (DSA)
Ludo	Ludovicus Pontanus de Roma [*Deceased, 1439*] [*Authority cited in pre-1607 legal work*] (DSA)
Ludo Bolog	Ludovicus Bologninus [*Deceased, 1508*] [*Authority cited in pre-1607 legal work*] (DSA)
Ludo Ro	Ludovicus Pontanus de Roma [*Deceased, 1439*] [*Authority cited in pre-1607 legal work*] (DSA)
LUE	Dallas, TX [*Location identifier FAA*] (FAAL)
LUE	Left Upper Entrance [*Theater*]
LUE	Left Upper Extremity [*Anatomy*] (DMAA)
LUE	Linear Unbiased Estimator [*Statistics*]
LUE	Link Utilization Efficiency
LU-E	Louisiana State University in Eunice, Eunice, LA [*Library symbol Library of Congress*] (LCLS)
LU-ECT	Louisiana State at Baton Rouge, Eighteenth Century Short Title Catalogue, Baton Rouge, LA [*Library symbol Library of Congress*] (LCLS)
LUEV	Lucerne Enation Virus [*Plant pathology*]
LUF	Glendale, AZ [*Location identifier FAA*] (FAAL)
LUF	Lift Unit Frame [*Shipping*] (DS)
LUF	Limiting System Utilization Factor (MHDB)
LUF	Local Utah Freight Bureau, Omaha NE [*STAC*]
LUF	Lowest Usable [*or Useful*] Frequency [*Radio*]
LUF	Luteinized Unruptured Follicle [*Medicine*] (DMAA)
LUFK	Lufkin Industries [*NASDAQ symbol*] (TTSB)
LUFK	Lufkin Industries, Inc. [*NASDAQ symbol*] (SAG)
Lufkin	Lufkin Industries, Inc. [*Associated Press*] (SAG)
LUFO	Least Used, First Out [*Computer science*]
LUFS	Luteinized Unruptured Follicle Syndrome [*Medicine*] (DMAA)
LUG	Lesbian Until Graduation
LUG	Lewisburg, TN [*Location identifier FAA*] (FAAL)
LUG	Light Utility Glider
LUG	LOCAS Users Group (NITA)
LUG	Lock-Up Garage
lug	Luganda [*MARC language code Library of Congress*] (LCCP)
LUG	Lugano [*Switzerland*] [*Airport symbol*] (OAG)
LUG	Lugano Resources Ltd. [*Vancouver Stock Exchange symbol*]
LUG	Luganville [*New Hebrides*] [*Seismograph station code, US Geological Survey*] (SEIS)
LUG	Luggage
LUG	Lugger [*Boat*]
LUG BAT	Lugdunum Batavorum [*Leyden*] [*Imprint*] (ROG)
LUGD	Lugdunum [*Lyons*] [*Imprint*] (ROG)
LUGG	Luggage
LUGL	Lumen and Glare Calculations [*Facet Ltd.*] [*Software package*] (NCC)
LUGS	Land Use Game Simulation
LUH	Lumen Hour
LUHF	Lowest Usable [*or Useful*] High-Frequency [*Radio*]

LUI.............	Land Use Intensity (PA)
LUI.............	La Union [Honduras] [Airport symbol Obsolete] (OAG)
LUI.............	Load Upper Immediate [Computer science]
LUI.............	Logical Unit of Information (IAA)
LUI.............	London United Investments [British]
lui..............	Luiseno [MARC language code Library of Congress] (LCCP)
LUIE...........	Leeds University Institute of Education [British] (AIE)
LUIS...........	Library User Information System [Detroit, MI] [Library network]
LUIS...........	Low-Dose Urea in Invert Sugar (AAMN)
LUJ.............	Big Lake, TX [Location identifier FAA] (FAAL)
LUJ.............	Lesotho Union of Journalists (EAIO)
LUJB...........	Left Umbilical Junction Box [Aerospace] (AAG)
LUK.............	Cincinnati, OH [Location identifier FAA] (FAAL)
LUK.............	Leucadia National [NYSE symbol] (TTSB)
LUK.............	Leucadia National Corp. [NYSE symbol] (SPSG)
Lukens.........	Lukens, Inc. [Associated Press] (SAG)
LukMed........	Lukens Medical Corp. [Associated Press] (SAG)
LUKN..........	Lukens Med [NASDAQ symbol] (TTSB)
LUKN..........	Lukens Medical Corp. [NASDAQ symbol] (SAG)
LUL.............	Language, Unseamanlike [Slang Military] (DNAB)
LUL.............	Laurel, MS [Location identifier FAA] (FAAL)
LUL.............	Left Upper Eyelid [Medicine]
LUL.............	Left Upper Limb [Medicine]
LUL.............	Left Upper Lobe [of lung] [Medicine]
LUL.............	London Underground Ltd. [British] (ECON)
LU-L..........	Louisiana State University, Law Library, Baton Rouge, LA [Library symbol Library of Congress] (LCLS)
LULA..........	Loyola University of Los Angeles [Later, Loyola Marymount University]
LULAC	League of United Latin American Citizens (EA)
LULOP........	London Union List of Periodicals
LULS..........	Lunar Logistics System [NASA]
LULU..........	Locally Unwanted Land Use [i.e. garbage incinerators, prisons, roads, etc.]
LULU..........	Logical Unit to Logical Unit
LUM...........	Bellingham, WA [Location identifier FAA] (FAAL)
LUM...........	Launch Utility Mode
LUM...........	Living Utility Module [NASA] (KSC)
LUM...........	Local Urgent Mail [British]
LU-M	Louisiana State University, Medical Center, New Orleans, LA [Library symbol Library of Congress] (LCLS)
LUM...........	Lumbago (WDAA)
LUM...........	Lumbar [Medicine] (WDAA)
LUM...........	Lumber (WDAA)
Lum	Lumen [Record label] [France]
LUM...........	Lumex, Inc. [AMEX symbol] (SPSG)
LUM...........	Luminous (MSA)
LUM...........	Lumonics, Inc. [Toronto Stock Exchange symbol]
LUM...........	Maputo [Mozambique] [Airport symbol]
LUM...........	University of Maryland, School of Law, Baltimore, MD [OCLC symbol] (OCLC)
Lum Ann......	Lumley on the Law of Annuities [A publication] (DLA)
LUMAS	Lunar Mapping System [Aerospace]
lumb	Lumbar [Medicine] (MAE)
Lum Bast.....	Lumley on Bastardy [A publication] (DLA)
Lum BL.......	Lumley on Bye-Laws [A publication] (DLA)
LUMCON......	Louisiana Universities Marine Consortium
LUME.........	Light Utilization More Efficient (MCD)
Lumex	Lumex, Inc. [Associated Press] (SAG)
LUMF.........	Lockheed Underwater Missile Facility (AAG)
LUMI..........	Lumisys, Inc. [NASDAQ symbol] (SAG)
LUMIS	Land Use Management Information System [NASA]
Lumisys......	Lumisys, Inc. [Associated Press] (SAG)
Lumley PLC..	Lumley's Poor Law Cases [1834-42] [A publication] (DLA)
LUMO........	Lowest Unoccupied Molecular Orbital [Atomic physics]
LUMP.........	Last Unattached Male Person
Lum Parl Pr..	Lumley's Parliamentary Practice [A publication] (DLA)
Lumpkin......	Lumpkin's Reports [59-77 Georgia] [A publication] (DLA)
Lum PLC.....	Lumley's Poor Law Cases [1834-42] [A publication] (DLA)
Lum PL Cas..	Lumley's Poor Law Cases [1834-42] [A publication] (DLA)
Lumps	Life-Giving Unselfish Middle-Class Parent Survivors [Facetious term coine d by columnist Erma Bombeck to describe the Yuppies' progenitors] [Lifestyle classification]
Lum Pub H...	Lumley's Public Health Acts [12th ed.] [1950-55 and supplements] [A publication] (DLA)
Lum Sett......	Lumley on the Law of Settlements [A publication] (DLA)
LUN	Logical Unit Number
LUN	Ludington & Northern Railway [AAR code]
LUN	Lunar (KSC)
LUN	Lund [Sweden] [Seismograph station code, US Geological Survey Closed] (SEIS)
LUN	Lunette
lun	Lunette (VRA)
LUN	Lusaka [Zambia] [Airport symbol] (OAG)
LUNA	Language for Users' Needs and Aims (NITA)
Lunar.........	Lunar Corp. [Associated Press] (SAG)
LUNARG	Lunar Gravity Simulator [Aerospace] (MCD)
LUNCO.......	Lloyd's Underwriters Non-Marine Claims Office (AIA)
LUND	Lund International [NASDAQ symbol] (TTSB)
LUND	Lund International Holdings, Inc. [NASDAQ symbol] (SAG)
LundInt.......	Lund International Holdings, Inc. [Associated Press] (SAG)
Lund Pat.....	Lund on Patents [A publication] (DLA)
LUNK	Line/Trunk (MCD)
LUNN	Lunn Industries [NASDAQ symbol] (SAG)
LunnI..........	Lunn Industries, Inc. [Associated Press] (SAG)

LUNR.........	Lunar Corp. [NASDAQ symbol] (SAG)
LUO	Laboratory Unit Operation
LUO	Left Ureteral Orifice [Medicine]
LUO	Luena [Angola] [Airport symbol] (OAG)
LUO	Luogo [As Written] [Music]
LUOQ.........	Left Upper Outer Quadrant [of abdomen] [Medicine]
LUOTC........	London University Officers Training Corps [British military] (DMA)
LUP............	Kalaupapa [Hawaii] [Airport symbol] (OAG)
LUP............	Land Use and Planning [British]
LUP............	Laying-Up Position [British military] (DMA)
LUP............	Liberia Unification Party [Political party]
LUP............	Lupenga Air Charters [Zambia] [ICAO designator] (FAAC)
Lup............	Lupus [Constellation]
LUPAC........	Life Underwriters Political Action Committee
LUPF..........	Linear Utility Prediction Function [Mathematics]
Lupi...........	Lupus [Constellation]
LUPS..........	Logistics Unit Productivity Study [or System] [Army]
LUPUL........	Lupulus [Hops] [Pharmacy] (ROG)
LUPWT.......	Langley Unitary Plan Wind Tunnel [NASA] (KSC)
LUQ..........	Left Upper Quadrant [of abdomen] [Medicine]
LUQ..........	San Luis [Argentina] [Airport symbol] (OAG)
LUR..........	Cape Lisburne [Alaska] [Airport symbol] (OAG)
LUR..........	Land Use Ratio (PA)
LUR..........	Laurasia Resources Ltd. [Toronto Stock Exchange symbol]
LUR..........	Laureate [Numismatics]
LUR..........	Lineas Aereas Latur SA de CV [Mexico ICAO designator] (FAAC)
LUR..........	London Underground Railway
LUR..........	Luria [L.] & Sons, Inc. [NYSE symbol] (SAG)
LUR..........	Luria (L)& Son [NYSE symbol] (TTSB)
LURE	Lunar Ranging Experiment [Aerospace]
Luria	Luria [L.] & Sons, Inc. [Associated Press] (SAG)
LURS	Land Use and Requirements Study (MCD)
LURS	Logistic Unit Productivity System [Army]
LURTx........	Living Unrelated Renal Transplantation [Medicine]
LUS...........	Land Utilization Survey (WDAA)
LUS...........	Laparoscopic Ultrasonography [Medicine]
LUS...........	Large Ultimate Size [Telecommunications] (TEL)
LUS...........	Latch Up Screen
LUS...........	Laws of the United States [A publication] (DLA)
LUS...........	Library of Useful Stories [A publication]
LUS...........	Liquid Upper Stage (NASA)
LUS...........	Load, Update, Subset
LUS...........	Lock-Up Solenoid [Automotive engineering]
LUS...........	Louisiana State University in Shreveport, Library, Shreveport, LA [OCLC symbol] (OCLC)
LU-S	Louisiana State University in Shreveport, Shreveport, LA [Library symbol Library of Congress] (LCLS)
LUS...........	Lusaka [Zambia] [Seismograph station code, US Geological Survey] (SEIS)
LUS...........	Lusitanair-Transportes Aereos Comercials SA [Portugal ICAO designator] (FAAC)
lus	Lustre (VRA)
LUSA	Life USA Holding, Inc. [NASDAQ symbol] (SAG)
LUSA	Life USA Holdings [NASDAQ symbol] (TTSB)
LUSB	Left Upper Sternal Border [Anatomy] (DAVI)
LUSCC	Latymer Upper School Cadet Corps [British military] (DMA)
LUSCS	Lower Uterine Segment Caesarian Section [Medicine] (WDAA)
LUSEX	Lunar Surface Explorer Simulation Program [Aerospace] (MCD)
Lush...........	Lushington's English Admiralty Reports [1859-62] [A publication] (DLA)
Lush Adm	Lushington's English Admiralty Reports [1859-62] [A publication] (DLA)
Lush Pr........	Lush's Common Law Practice [A publication] (DLA)
Lush Pr L.....	Lushington on Prize Law [A publication] (DLA)
LUSI..........	Lunar Surface Inspection [Aerospace]
LUSING........	Lusingando [Coaxingly] [Music]
LUSL..........	Loyola University School of Law (DLA)
LU-SM	Louisiana State University in Shreveport, Medical Center Library, Shreveport, LA [Library symbol Library of Congress] (LCLS)
LUSO	Luso-American Fraternal Federation
LUSOLT	Lakehead University School of Library Technology [Canada]
LUST	Latrine Urinal Shower Toilet [A unit of mobility equipment] [Military]
LUST.........	Leaking Underground Storage Tank [Environmental chemistry]
LUST..........	List Updated Sort and Total (PDAA)
LUST..........	Lustrous (WDAA)
LUST..........	Wanderlust Interactive [NASDAQ symbol] (TTSB)
LUST..........	Wanderlust Interactive, Inc. [NASDAQ symbol] (SAG)
LUSTER	Lunar Dust and Earth Return [NASA] (IAA)
LUSTW	Wanderlust Interactive Wrrt [NASDAQ symbol] (TTSB)
LUSURF.......	Lunar Surface (PDAA)
LUSVC	Logical Unit Services Manager (MHDB)
LUT...........	Launcher-Umbilical Tower [Aerospace] (NAKS)
LUT...........	Launch Umbilical Tower [NASA]
LUT...........	Laura Station [Australia Airport symbol Obsolete] (OAG)
LUT...........	Limited User Test [Military] (RDA)
LUT...........	Line Unit [Computer science] (BUR)
LUT...........	Lining Up Table (DGA)
LUT...........	Local User Terminal
LUT...........	Lookup Table [Computer science] (BYTE)
LUT...........	Loughborough University of Technology [British] (IRUK)
LUT...........	Luteum [Yellow] [Latin]
LUT...........	Miri [Malaysia] [Airport symbol] (AD)
LUTC.........	Life Underwriter Training Council [Washington, DC] (EA)
LUTC.........	Life Underwriter Training Course
LUTCAM	Language Used to Conceal Actual Meaning

LUTE............ Language Understander Translator and Editor (NITA)
Lut Elec Cas... Lutwyche's English Election Cases [*A publication*] (DLA)
Lut Ent........ Lutwyche's Entries [*1704; 1718*] [*A publication*] (DLA)
LUTET......... Lutetia Parisiorum [*Paris*] [*Imprint*] (ROG)
LUTFCSUSTC... Librarians United to Fight Costly, Silly, Unnecessary Serial Title
              Changes [*Defunct*] (EA)
LUTH .... Lutheran
Luth .... Lutheran (WDAA)
LUTH .... Luther Medical Products [*NASDAQ symbol*] (SAG)
LUTH .... Luther Med Products [*NASDAQ symbol*] (TTSB)
LuthMed...... Luther Medical Products, Inc. [*Associated Press*] (SAG)
LUTIRO .... Life and Unit Trust Intermediaries Regulatory Organisation [*British*]
LUTIS.......... Luton Information Service (NITA)
LUTOM .... Land Use Trade Off Model (DICI)
LUTP.......... Land Use and Transport Planning [*British*]
LUT PAR...... Lutetia Parisiorum [*Paris*] [*Imprint*] (ROG)
LUTr........... Lighting Unit Trailer (WDAA)
Lut RC .... Lutwyche's English Registration Appeal Cases [*1843-45*]
              [*A publication*] (DLA)
LUTS........... Light Units, Times Square [*Electronics*]
LUTT........... Launcher Umbilical Tower Transporter [*NASA*] (KSC)
Lutw E .... Lutwyche's English Common Pleas Reports [*A publication*] (DLA)
Lutw Reg Cas... Lutwyche's English Registration Cases [*A publication*] (DLA)
LUU .... Illumination Unit (MCD)
LUU .... Laura [*Australia Airport symbol Obsolete*] (OAG)
LUU .... Louisiana State University, Baton Rouge, LA [*OCLC symbol*] (OCLC)
LUV .... Langgur [*Indonesia*] [*Airport symbol*] (OAG)
LUV............ Large Unilamellar Vesicle [*Pharmacy Biochemistry*]
LUV............ Light Utility Vehicle [*Pickup truck*]
LU-V .... Louisiana State University, School of Veterinary Medicine, Medical
              Library, Baton Rouge, LA [*Library symbol Library of Congress*]
              (LCLS)
LUV............ Southwest Airlines [*NYSE symbol*] (TTSB)
LUV............ Southwest Airlines Co. [*NYSE symbol*] (SPSG)
LUVO .... Lunar Ultraviolet Observatory [*NASA*]
LUW............ Logical Units of Work [*Computer science*] (BYTE)
LUW............ Luwuk [*Indonesia*] [*Airport symbol*] (OAG)
LUX............ Laurens, SC [*Location identifier FAA*] (FAAL)
LUX............ Lincoln Airlines, Inc. [*ICAO designator*] (FAAC)
LUX............ Luxembourg [*Airport symbol*] (OAG)
LUX............ Luxembourg [*ANSI three-letter standard code*] (CNC)
LUX............ Luxembourg [*Seismograph station code, US Geological Survey*]
              (SEIS)
Lux............. Luxembourg (VRA)
LUX............ Luxottica Group ADS [*NYSE symbol*] (SPSG)
LUX............ Luxury [*or Luxurious*] [*Classified advertising*] (ADA)
Luxem .... Luxembourg
LuxLBN........ Bibliotheque Nationale de Luxembourg, Service du Pret,
              Luxembourg, Luxembourg [*Library symbol Library of Congress*]
              (LCLS)
Luxottca...... Luxottica Group [*Associated Press*] (SAG)
Luxtec........ Luxtec Corp. [*Associated Press*] (SAG)
LUXY .... Cinemastar Luxury Theaters [*NASDAQ symbol*] (TTSB)
LUXY .... CinemaStar Luxury Theaters, Inc. [*NASDAQ symbol*] (SAG)
LUXYW .... Cinemastar Luxry Theaters Wrrt [*NASDAQ symbol*] (TTSB)
LUY............. Lushoto [*Tanzania*] [*Airport symbol*] (AD)
LUZED .... Luzon Engineer District [*Army World War II*]
Luzerne Leg Obs (PA)... Luzerne Legal Observer [*Pennsylvania*] [*A publication*]
              (DLA)
Luzerne Leg Reg R (PA)... Luzerne Legal Register Reports [*Pennsylvania*]
              [*A publication*] (DLA)
Luzerne LJ (PA)... Luzerne Law Journal [*Pennsylvania*] [*A publication*] (DLA)
Luz Law T.... Luzerne Law Times [*Pennsylvania*] [*A publication*] (DLA)
Luz Leg Obs... Luzerne Legal Observer [*Pennsylvania*] [*A publication*] (DLA)
Luz Leg Reg Rep... Luzerne Legal Register Reports [*Pennsylvania*]
              [*A publication*] (DLA)
Luz LJ .... Luzerne Law Journal [*Pennsylvania*] [*A publication*] (DLA)
Luz LO .... Luzerne Legal Observer [*Pennsylvania*] [*A publication*] (DLA)
Luz L Reg Rep... Luzerne Legal Register Reports (Continuation of Kulp)
              [*Pennsylvania*] [*A publication*] (DLA)
Luz LT (NS)... Luzerne Law Times. New Series [*Pennsylvania*] [*A publication*]
              (DLA)
Luz LT (OS)... Luzerne Law Times. Old Series [*Pennsylvania*] [*A publication*] (DLA)
LV .... Laboratory Vehicle (MCD)
LV .... Lacrosse Victoria [*Australia An association*]
LV .... Lactobacillus Viridescens [*Biochemistry*] (DAVI)
LV .... Lancastrian Volunteers [*British military*] (DMA)
LV .... Landing Vehicle
LV .... Land Value (ADA)
LV .... Largest Vessel [*British*] (ADA)
LV .... LASER Velocimeter
LV .... LaserVision [*Videodisc system*]
LV .... Last Vehicle [*Railroads*] (ROG)
LV .... Latent Variable [*Data analysis*]
LV .... Lateral Ventricle [*Neuroanatomy*]
LV .... Lateral Vestibular Nucleus [*Neuroanatomy*]
LV .... Latvia [*Internet country code*]
LV .... Launch Vehicle (MCD)
LV .... Launch Verification [*NASA*] (IAA)
LV .... Lava (WGA)
LV .... Laverda SpA [*Italy ICAO aircraft manufacturer identifier*] (ICAO)
LV .... Laws of Virginia [*A publication*] (DLA)
LV .... Leaky Valve [*Nuclear energy*] (NRCH)
LV .... Leave (AFM)
lv .... Leave (STED)

LV .... Lecithovitellin (DB)
LV .... Leeds Volunteers [*British military*] (DMA)
LV .... Left Ventral Fin [*Fish anatomy*]
LV .... Left Ventricle [*Cardiology*]
LV .... Legal Volt
LV .... Lehigh Valley Railroad Co. [*Absorbed into Consolidated Rail Corp.*]
              [*AAR code*]
LV .... Leucovorin (DB)
LV .... Leukemia Virus [*Hematology*] (MAE)
LV .... Lev [*Monetary unit*] [*Bulgaria*]
LV .... Level of Study [*Online database field identifier*]
Lv .... Leviticus [*Old Testament book*]
LV .... Licensed Victualer
LV .... Lift Vector (NASA)
LV .... Light and Variable [*Referring to wind*]
LV .... Light Value [*Photography*] (DICI)
LV .... Light Variegated Maize
LV .... Light Vehicle [*British military*] (DMA)
LV .... Light-Vessel [*Navigation*]
LV .... Limited Visibility Study (MCD)
LV .... Limit Value
LV .... Linear Velocity
LV .... Livery
LV .... Live Vaccine [*Medicine*]
LV .... Live Virus [*Medicine*] (MAE)
LV .... Livre [*Monetary unit*] [*Obsolete French*] (ROG)
LV .... Loading Valve (MCD)
LV .... Load Vertical
L/V .... Local Vertical (KSC)
LV .... Louis Vuitton [*Initials used as a pattern on Vuitton luggage,
              handbags, etc.*]
LV .... Low in Volatiles [*Commercial grading*]
LV .... Low Velocity [*British military*] (DMA)
LV .... Low Voltage
LV .... Low Volume
LV .... Lumbar Vertebra [*Medicine*]
LV .... Luncheon Voucher [*British*]
LV .... Lung Volume (MAE)
LV .... Valda [*France*] [*Research code symbol*]
LVA .... Lancashire Volunteer Artillery [*British military*] (DMA)
LVA .... Landing Vehicle, Airfoil
LVA .... Landing Vehicle, Assault [*Navy symbol*]
LVA .... Large Vertical Aperture Antenna [*Aviation*]
LVA .... Launch Vehicle Availability [*NASA*]
LVA .... Lava Capital Corp. [*Toronto Stock Exchange symbol*]
LVA .... Left Ventricular Aneurysm [*Cardiology*]
LVA .... Left Ventricular Aneurysmectomy [*Medicine*] (STED)
LVA .... Left Ventricular Assistance [*Cardiology*]
LVA .... Left Vertebral Artery [*Medicine*] (STED)
LVA .... Left Visual Acuity [*Medicine*]
LVA .... Literacy Volunteers of America (EA)
LVA .... Local Virtual Address
LVA .... Logarithmic Video Amplifier (IAA)
LVA .... Low-Velocity Anomaly [*Seismology*]
LVA .... Low Vision Aid [*Ophthalmology*]
LVA .... Low-Voltage Activated [*Neurochemistry*]
LVA .... Low-Voltage Avalanche [*Electronics*] (IAA)
LVA .... Lucasvarity PLC [*NYSE symbol*] (SAG)
LV (A) (2).... Landing Vehicle, Tracked (Armored) (Mark II) [*"Water Buffalo,"
              Canopy Type*]
LVAD .... Left Ventricle Assist Device [*Cardiology*]
LVAD .... Low Velocity Air Drop [*Military vehicle specifications*]
LVAIC......... Lehigh Valley Association of Independent College Libraries [*Library
              network*]
L-VAM .... Leuprolide Acetate, Vinblastine, Adriamycin (Doxorubicin), and
              Mitomycin (STED)
L-VAM .... Lupron, Vinblastine, Adriamycin, Mutamycin [*Antineoplastic drug*]
              (CDI)
LVAP........... Launch Vehicle and Propulsion [*NASA*] (IAA)
LVAR .... Launch Vehicle Assessment Report [*or Review*] [*NASA*] (KSC)
LVAR .... Lithuanian Veterans Association Ramove (EA)
LVAS .... Launch Vehicle Alarm System [*NASA*] (IAA)
LVAS .... Left Ventricle Assist System [*Cardiology*]
LVAS .... Left Ventricular Assist System [*Medicine*] (STED)
LVAS .... Light-Vehicle Animation Simulation [*Accident reconstruction*]
              [*Automotive engineering*]
LVAT .... Left Ventricular Activation Time [*Medicine*] (STED)
LVB............ Left Ventricular Bypass [*Cardiology*]
LVB............ Liquid-Vapor Bubble [*Chemical engineering*]
LVB............ Livramento [*Brazil*] [*Airport symbol*] (OAG)
LVB............ Low-Voltage Bias
LVBP.......... Left Ventricle Bypass Pump [*Medicine*] (STED)
LVBR.......... Land Valuation Boards of Review [*Australia*]
LVC............ Decisions of the Lands Tribunal (Rating) [*A publication*] (DLA)
LVC............ Enid, OK [*Location identifier FAA*] (FAAL)
LVC............ Large Vacuum Chamber [*Army*]
LVC............ Lebanon Valley College [*Pennsylvania*]
LVC............ Lebanon Valley College, Annville, PA [*OCLC symbol*] (OCLC)
LVC............ Lillian Vernon [*AMEX symbol*] (TTSB)
LVC............ Lillian Vernon Corp. [*AMEX symbol*] (SPSG)
LVC............ Log Voltmeter Converter
LVC............ Low-Voltage Capacitor
LVC............ Low-Voltage Cutoff [*Battery*]
LVC............ Lutheran Volunteer Corps (EA)
LVCD .... Least Voltage Coincidence Detector

LVCD	Liquid Volume Charge Density [*Automotive fuel systems*]
LVCI	Laser Vision Centers [*NASDAQ symbol*] (TTSB)
LVCI	Laser Vision Centers, Inc. [*NASDAQ symbol*] (SAG)
LVCM	Licentiate of the Victoria College of Music [*London*] (ROG)
LVCP	Laboratory Vehicle Checkout Procedure
LVCS	Low Vertical Caesarean Section [*Medicine*] (STED)
LVCT	Low-Voltage Circuit Tester (MCD)
LVD	Laboratory Vehicle Development
lvd	Leaved
LVD	Left Ventricular Assist Device [*An artificial organ*]
LVD	Left Ventricular Dimension (STED)
LVD	Left Ventricular Dysfunction [*Cardiology*] (DAVI)
LVd	Left Ventricular End-Diastolic Pressure [*Cardiology*] (MAE)
LVD	Level Island, AK [*Location identifier FAA*] (FAAL)
LVD	Light Valve Display
LVD	Liquid Crystal Visual Display [*Electronics*] (EECA)
LVD	Louvered Door (AAG)
LVD	Low-Velocity Detonation [*or Drop*]
LVD	Low-Voltage Drop (CET)
LVD1	Left Ventricular End-Diastolic Pressure [*Medicine*] (STED)
LVDA	Launch Vehicle Data Adapter [*NASA*]
LVDA	Launch Vehicle Deployment Assembly [*NASA*] (MCD)
LVDC	Launch Vehicle Data Center [*NASA*] (KSC)
LVDC	Launch Vehicle Digital Computer [*NASA*]
LVDC	Low-Voltage Direct Current
LVDd	Left Ventricular Dimension in Enddiastole [*Cardiology*] (DMAA)
LVDG	Las Vegas Disc Golf & Tennis [*NASDAQ symbol*] (TTSB)
LVDG	Las Vegas Discount Golf & Tennis [*NASDAQ symbol*] (SAG)
LVDI	Left Ventricular Dimension [*Cardiology*] (DMAA)
LVDIFC	Leroy Van Dyke International Fan Club (EA)
LVDL	Licensed Victuallers' Defence League of England and Wales (BI)
LVDP	Left Ventricular Developed Pressure [*Medicine*] (DMAA)
LVDP	Left Ventricular Diastolic Pressure [*Cardiology*]
LV dp/dt	First Derivation of Left Ventricular Pressure [*Cardiology*] (DAVI)
LVDS	Light-Vehicle Dynamics Simulation [*Accident reconstruction*] [*Automotive engineering*]
LVDS	Liquid, Vee, Diesel-Cycle, Supercharged
LVDS	Low-Voltage Differential Signaling
LVDT	Linear Variable Differential Transformer
LVDT	Linear Variable Displacement Transducer
LVDT	Linear Velocity Displacement Transformer (IEEE)
LVDT	Linear Voltage Differential Transformer (NASA)
LVDT-PRIM	Linear Variable Differential Transformer - Primary
LVDT-SEC	Linear Variable Differential Transformer - Secondary
LVDV	Left Ventricular Diastolic Volume [*Cardiology*] (MAE)
LVE	Launch Vehicle Engine (IAA)
LVE	Leave (WGA)
LVE	Left Ventricular Ejection [*Medicine*] (DMAA)
LVE	Left Ventricular Enlargement [*Cardiology*]
LVE	Linear Vector Equation
LVE	Liquid Vapor Equilibrium
LVED	Left Ventricular End-Diastolic [*Cardiology*]
LVEDC	Left Ventricular End-Diastolic Circumference [*Cardiology*] (MAE)
LVEDD	Left Ventricular End-Diastolic Dimension [*Cardiology*]
LVEDP	Left Ventricular End-Diastolic Pressure [*Cardiology*]
LVEDV	Left Ventricular End-Diastolic Volume [*Cardiology*]
LVEF	Left Ventricular Ejection Fraction [*Time*] [*Cardiology*]
LVEN	Las Vegas Entertainment Network [*NASDAQ symbol*] (SAG)
LVEndo	Las Vegas Entmt Ntwk [*NASDAQ symbol*] (TTSB)
LVEndo	Left Ventricular Endocardial Half [*Cardiology*] (DAVI)
LVENW	Las Vegas Entmt Ntwk Wrrt'A' [*NASDAQ symbol*] (TTSB)
LVENZ	Las Vegas Entmt Ntwk Wrrt'B' [*NASDAQ symbol*] (TTSB)
LVEP	Left Ventricular End-Diastolic Pressure [*Cardiology*] (MAE)
LVEpi	Left Ventricular Epicardial Half [*Cardiology*] (DAVI)
LVER	Liver Fraction Elevated [*Gastroenterology*] (DAVI)
LVER	Local Veterans Employment Representative [*Department of Labor*]
LVES	Low-Voltage Electrical Stimulation [*Meat treatment*]
LVET	Left Ventricular Ejection Time [*Cardiology*]
LVET	Low Volume Eye Test (DMAA)
LVETI	Left Ventricular Ejection Time Index [*Cardiology*]
LVF	Dallas, TX [*Location identifier FAA*] (FAAL)
LVF	Left Ventricular Failure [*Cardiology*]
LVF	Left Visual Field [*Psychometrics*]
LVF	Linear Vector Function
LVF	Low-Voltage Fast [*Electronics*]
LVF	Low-Voltage Foci (MAE)
LVFA	Low Velocity Friction Apparatus (PDAA)
LVFC	Launch Vehicle Flight Control
LVFCS	Launch Vehicle Flight Control System
LVFF	Lloyds Forces Volunteer Fund (WDAA)
LVFP	Left Ventricular Filling Pressure [*Cardiology*]
LVFS	Large Volume Filtration System [*Environmental chemistry*]
LVFT2	Left Ventricular Slow Filling Time [*Medicine*] (STED)
LVG	Lauro/Viceroy/Global Joint Service [*Shipping*] (DS)
LVG	Leaving
LVG	Left Ventral Gluteal [*Injection site*]
LVG	Left Ventriculography [*Medicine*]
LVG	Left Ventrogluteal [*Anatomy*] (DAVI)
LVG	Left Visceral Ganglion [*Medicine*]
LVG	Levengood Oil & Gas, Inc. [*Vancouver Stock Exchange symbol*]
LVGC	Launch Vehicle Guidance Computer [*NASA*]
LVGO	Light Vacuum Gas Oil [*Petroleum technology*]
lvgrm	Living Room (REAL)
LVGSE	Launch Vehicle Ground Support Equipment [*NASA*] (KSC)
LVH	Landing Vehicle, Hydrofoil
LVH	Large Vessel Hematocrit (MAE)
LVH	Left Ventricular Hypertrophy [*Cardiology*]
LVHF	Low Very High Frequency (IAA)
LVHV	Low-Volume High-Velocity (IEEE)
LVHX	Landing Craft, Hydrofoil, Experimental [*Navy symbol*]
LVI	Laus Verbo Incarnato [*Praise to the Incarnate Word*] [*Latin*]
LVI	Lavalin Industries, Inc. [*Toronto Stock Exchange symbol*]
LVI	Left Ventricular Insufficiency [*Cardiology*] (MAE)
LVI	Left Ventricular Ischemia [*Medicine*] (DMAA)
LVI	Lehigh Group, Inc. [*Formerly, LUI Group*] [*NYSE symbol*] (SAG)
LVI	Liquid Vapor Interface
LVI	Livingstone [*Zambia*] [*Airport symbol*] (OAG)
LVI	Local Veterinary Inspector [*British*]
LVI	Low-Viscosity Index (IAA)
LVI	Low-Voltage Inverter [*Electronics*] (AAEL)
LVIA	Lay Volunteers International Association
LVID	Left Ventricle Internal Diameter [*Cardiology*]
LVID	Left Ventricular Internal Diastolic (STED)
LVID	Left Ventricular Internal Dimension [*Cardiology*] (DAVI)
LVIDd	Left Ventricular Internal Dimension Diastole [*Medicine*] (STED)
LVID(ed)	Left Ventricular Internal Diameter, End Diastole [*Medicine*] (STED)
LVID(es)	Left Ventricular Internal Diameter, End Systole [*Medicine*] (STED)
LVIDP	Left Ventricular Initial Diastolic Pressure [*Cardiology*] (AAMN)
LVIDs	Left Ventricular Internal Dimension Systole [*Medicine*] (STED)
L-VIS	LASER Viewdata Information Service (NITA)
LVIS	Launch Vehicle Instrumentation Systems [*NASA*] (KSC)
LVIT	Linear Variable Inductance Transducer
LVIV	Left Ventricular Infarct Volume [*Medicine*] (STED)
LVJ	Cleveland, OH [*Location identifier FAA*] (FAAL)
LVK	Livermore, CA [*Location identifier FAA*] (FAAL)
LVK	Lovelock [*Nevada*] [*Seismograph station code, US Geological Survey Closed*] (SEIS)
LVL	Laminated-Veneer Lumber
LVL	Lawrenceville, VA [*Location identifier FAA*] (FAAL)
LVL	Left Vastus Lateralis [*Anatomy*] (DAVI)
lvl	Level (VRA)
LVL	Level (AAG)
Lvl	Level (TBD)
LVL	Levelland Energy [*Vancouver Stock Exchange symbol*]
LVL	Lex Vehicle Leasing [*British*]
LVL	Long Vertical Left
LVL	Low-Velocity Layer [*Geophysics*] (OA)
LVL	Universite Laval, Bibliotheque [*UTLAS symbol*]
LVLB	Land Valuers' Licensing Board [*Western Australia*]
LVLD	Very Low-Density Lipoproteins [*Chemistry*] (MEC)
LVLG	Left Ventrolateral Gluteal [*Site of injection*] [*Medicine*]
LVLH	Local Vertical/Local Horizontal (NASA)
LVLO	Local Vehicle Licensing Office [*British*]
LVLOF	Level Off [*Aviation*] (FAAC)
LVLP	Large Virus-Like Particle
LVLSH	Level Shifter (NITA)
LVM	LaSallian Volunteer Movement (EA)
LVM	LaSallian Volunteers [*An association*] (EA)
LVM	Launch Vehicle Material (MCD)
LVM	Launch Vehicle Monitor
LVM	Left Ventricular Mass [*Cardiology*]
LVM	Light Vehicle Mine [*Military*]
LVM	Line Voltage Monitor
LVM	Livingston, MT [*Location identifier FAA*] (FAAL)
LVM	Localized Vibrational Mode (PDAA)
LVM	Low-Value Materiel (MCD)
LVMA	Louisiana Veterinary Medical Association (SRA)
LVMC	Low-Variation Medical Condition
LVMF	Left Ventricular Minute Flow [*Medicine*] (DB)
LVMH	Louis Vuitton Moet-Hennessy [*Commercial firm*] [*Belgium*]
LVMH	LVMH Moet Hennessy Louis Vuitton [*Associated Press*] (SAG)
LVMH	LVMH Moet-Hennessy Louis Vuitton [*NASDAQ symbol*] (SAG)
LVMHY	LVMH Most Henn Lou Vttn ADS [*NASDAQ symbol*] (TTSB)
LVMM	Left Ventricular Muscle Mass [*Cardiology*] (DAVI)
LVMP	Launch Vehicle Mission Peculiar
LVMS	LEG [*Liquefied Energy Gas*] Volume Measuring System
LVMS	Limb Volume Measuring System
LVMTAS	Low-Visibility, Moving Target Acquisition and Strike [*Military*]
LVN	Carnegie Public Library, Las Vegas, NM [*OCLC symbol*] (OCLC)
LVN	Lakeville, MN [*Location identifier FAA*] (FAAL)
LVN	Las Vegas [*Nevada*] [*Seismograph station code, US Geological Survey*] (SEIS)
LVN	Lateral Ventricular Nerve [*Medicine*] (DB)
LVN	Lateral Vestibular Nucleus [*Medicine*] (DMAA)
LVN	Levon Resources Ltd. [*Toronto Stock Exchange symbol Vancouver Stock Exchange symbol*]
LVN	Library Video Network [*Video producer*]
LVN	Licensed Visiting Nurse
LVN	Licensed Vocational Nurse
LVN	Light Virgin Naphtha (PDAA)
LVN	Limiting Viscosity Number
LVN	Low-Voltage Neon
LVNAT	Licensed Vocational Nurses Association of Texas (SRA)
LVND	LASER Variable Neutral Density
LVNDL	Licensed Victuallers' National Defence League [*British*] (DI)
LVNG	Living
LVNI	Laser Video Network [*NASDAQ symbol*] (SAG)
LVNIW	Laser Video Network Wrrt'A' [*NASDAQ symbol*] (TTSB)
LVNIZ	Laser Video Network Wrrt'B' [*NASDAQ symbol*] (TTSB)

LVNJ............ Long Valley [New Jersey] [Seismograph station code, US Geological Survey] (SEIS)
LVNTE......... Livent Inc. [NASDAQ symbol] (TTSB)
LVNTF......... Livent, Inc. [NASDAQ symbol] (SAG)
LVO.............. Launch Vehicle Operations
LVO.............. Laverton [Australia Airport symbol] (OAG)
LVO.............. Left Ventricle Outflow [Medicine] (DMAA)
LVO.............. left Ventricular Overactivity [Cardiology] (DAVI)
LVO.............. Lieutenant of the Royal Victorian Order [British] (WDAA)
LVO.............. Lieutenant of the Victorian Order [Canada] (DD)
LVO.............. Lieutenant, Royal Victorian Order [British] (WA)
LVO.............. Lithiated Vanadium Oxide [Battery technology]
LVOA........... Louver Opening
LVOA........... Left Ventricular Overactivity [Cardiology] (DAVI)
LVOD........... Launch Vehicle Operations Division [NASA] (IAA)
LVOP........... Local Vertical and Orbit Plane
LVOR........... Low-Powered, Very-High-Frequency Omnirange
LVOT........... Left Ventricular Outflow Tract [Cardiology] (CPH)
LVP............. Large Volume Parenterals [Medicine]
LVP............. Left Ventricular Pressure [Cardiology]
LVP............. Left Ventricular Pump [Cardiology]
LVP............. Light Valve Projector
LVP............. Low-Value Product
LVP............. Low-Voltage Plate
LVP............. Low-Voltage Protection [Electronics]
LVP............. Lysine Vasopressin [Antidiuretic hormone]
LVPD........... Launch Vehicle Pressure Display [NASA] (KSC)
LVpE.......... Evangeline Parish Library, Ville Platte, LA [Library symbol Library of Congress] (LCLS)
LVPFR........ Left Ventricular Peak Filling Rate [Cardiology] (DMAA)
LVPG.......... Launch Vehicle Planning Group [Aerospace] (AAG)
LVPL........... Liverpool [England]
LVPP........... Launch Vehicle and Propulsion Program [NASA]
LVPS.......... Laboratory Vehicle Procedure Simulator
LVPS.......... Low-Voltage Power Supply
LVPTG........ Lateral Vascularized Patellar Tendon Graft [Orthopedics]
LVPW.......... Left Ventricular Posterior Wall [Cardiology] (DMAA)
LVPWT....... Left Ventricular Posterior Wall Thickness [Cardiology] (DAVI)
LVR............. Laboratory of Virology and Rickettsial Diseases
lvr............... Latvian Soviet Socialist Republic [MARC country of publication code Library of Congress] (LCCP)
LVR............. Lever (MSA)
LVR............. Line Voltage Regulator
LVR............. Liverpool [England] [Seismograph station code, US Geological Survey Closed] (SEIS)
LVR............. London Volunteer Regiment [British military] (DMA)
LVR............. Longitudinal Video Recording
LVR............. Long Vertical Right
LVR............. Louver (MSA)
LVR............. Low-Voltage Rack
LVR............. Low-Voltage Relay
LVR............. Low-Voltage Release [Electronics]
LVR............. Low-Volume Ramjet (MCD)
LVRATS...... Leave Rations [Military] (DNAB)
LVRATS SL.. Leave Rations, Sick Leave [Military] (DNAB)
LVRATS SPEC... Leave Rations, Special Leave [Military] (DNAB)
LVRC.......... Lamoille Valley Railroad Co. [AAR code]
LVR(CE)...... Low-Voltage Release (Continuous Effect) [Electronics] (DNAB)
LVRE.......... Low-Voltage Release Effect [Electronics] (MSA)
LV Rep....... Lehigh Valley Law Reporter [Pennsylvania] [A publication] (DLA)
LVRIS........ Low-Volume Ramjet Inlet System
LVRJ.......... Low-Voltage Ramjet
LVRJ.......... Low-Volume Ramjet
LVRLSE...... Low-Voltage Release [Electronics]
LV-ROM...... LASER Vision Read-Only Memory
LVRR.......... Lehigh Valley Railroad Co. [Absorbed into Consolidated Rail Corp.]
LVRS.......... Launch Vehicle Recovery System [NASA] (IAA)
LVRS.......... Lightweight Video Reconnaissance System [Military] (INF)
LVRT.......... Land and Valuation Review Tribunal [Northern Territory, Australia]
LV/RVV....... Local Vertical/Relative Velocity Vector
LVS............. Las Vegas, NM [Location identifier FAA] (FAAL)
LVS............. Launch Vehicle Simulator [NASA] (IAA)
LVS............. Layout Verification of Schematic (AAEL)
LVS............. Leaves (MSA)
LVS............. Left Ventricular Strain [Cardiology]
LVs............. Left Ventricular Systolic Pressure Mean [Cardiology] (MAE)
LVS............. Light Value System [Photography] (BARN)
LVS............. Logistical Vehicle System
LVS............. Logistics Vehicle System
LVS............. Low-Velocity Scanning
LVSB.......... Lakeview Financial [NASDAQ symbol] (TTSB)
LVSB.......... Lakeview Financial Corp. [NASDAQ symbol] (SAG)
LVSC.......... London Voluntary Service Council [British]
LVSE.......... Launch Vehicle Systems Engineer [NASA] (SAA)
LVSEM....... Low-Voltage Scanning Electron Microscopy (AAEL)
LVSEMI....... Left Ventricular Subendocardia Lischemia [Cardiology] (DMAA)
LVSF.......... Laboratory Vehicle Support Facility
LVSG.......... Launch Vehicle Study Group [NASA] (KSC)
LVS/ITS...... LASER Vibration Sensor Inspection Test System [Army] (RDA)
LVSO.......... Left Ventricular Systolic Output [Medicine] (STED)
LVSP.......... Left Ventricular Systolic Pressure [Cardiology]
LVSS.......... Laboratory Vehicle System Segment
LVSS.......... LASER Vector Scoring System (DWSG)
LVSSTS...... Launch Vehicle Safety System Test Set [NASA] (IAA)
LVST......... Lateral Vestibulospinal Tract [Medicine] (DMAA)

LVST........... Longitudinal Velocity Sorting Tube
LVSTCK....... Livestock
LVSTK......... Livestock
LVSV........... Left Ventricular Stroke Volume [Cardiology]
LVSW.......... Left Ventricular Septal Wall [Cardiology] (DAVI)
LVSW.......... Left Ventricular Stroke Work [Cardiology]
LVSWI........ Left Ventricular Stroke Work Index [Cardiology]
LVT............. Landing Vehicle, Tracked (Unarmored) [Navy symbol]
LVT............. Left Ventricular Tension [Cardiology] (MAE)
LVT............. Lexicon Hebraicum et Aramaicum Veteris Testamenti [Rome] [A publication] (BJA)
LVT............. Licensed Veterinary Technician
LVT............. Linear Velocity Transducer
LVT............. Livingston, TN [Location identifier FAA] (FAAL)
LVT............. Low Voltage Technology (AAEL)
LVT............. Low-Voltage Tubular
LVT............. Lysine Vasotonin [Adrenergic agent]
LVT (1)....... Landing Vehicle, Tracked (Unarmored) (Mark I) ["Alligator"] [Navy symbol]
LVT1........... Left Ventricular Fast Filling Time [Medicine] (STED)
LVT (2)....... Landing Vehicle, Tracked (Unarmored) (Mark II) ["Water Buffalo"] [Navy symbol]
LVT (3)....... Landing Vehicle, Tracked (Unarmored) (Mark III) [Navy symbol]
LVT (4)....... Landing Vehicle, Tracked (Unarmored) (Mark IV)
LVT (A)....... Landing Vehicle, Tracked (Armored) [Turret Type]
LVTA.......... London Vintage Taxi Association - American Section (EA)
LVT (A) (1)... Landing Vehicle, Tracked (Armored) (Mark I) ["Water Buffalo," Turret Type]
LVT (A) (4)... Landing Vehicle, Tracked (Armored) (Mark IV)
LVT (A) (5)... Landing Vehicle, Tracked (Armored) (Mark V)
LVTC.......... Landing Vehicle, Tracked, Command (NVT)
LVTC.......... Launch Vehicle Test Conductor [NASA] (KSC)
LVTCX........ Landing Vehicle, Tracked, Command, Experimental (MCD)
LVTD.......... Las Vegas Mjr League Sports [NASDAQ symbol] (TTSB)
LVTE.......... Landing Vehicle, Tracked, Engineer [Model 1]
LVTH.......... Landing Vehicle, Tracked, Howitzer [Model 6]
LVTL.......... Lexicon in Veteris Testamenti Libros [A publication] (BJA)
LVTP.......... Landing Vehicle, Tracked, Personnel (AABC)
LVTP-CMD ... Landing Vehicle, Tracked Personnel, Command [Marine Corps] (VNW)
LVTPX........ Landing Vehicle, Tracked, Personnel, Experimental (MCD)
LVTR.......... Landing Vehicle, Tracked, Retriever (NVT)
LVT(R)....... Landing Vehicle, Tracked (Rocket) [British military] (DMA)
LVTR.......... Low-VHF [Very-High-Frequency] Transmitter-Receiver
LVTRX........ Landing Vehicle, Tracked, Recovery, Experimental (MCD)
LVTU.......... Landing Vehicle, Tracked (Unarmored)
LVUPK........ Leave and Upkeep Period [Military] (NVT)
LVUSA........ Legion of Valor of the United States of America (EA)
LVV............. Delavan, WI [Location identifier FAA] (FAAL)
LVV............. Left Ventricular Volume [Cardiology]
LVV............. Live Varicella Vaccine [Medicine] (STED)
LVV............. Lvov [Ukraine] [Seismograph station code, US Geological Survey] (SEIS)
LVVC.......... Lincolnshire Vintage Vehicle Club [British] (DCTA)
LVVP.......... Chlorambucil, Vinblastine, Vincristine, Prednisone [Antineoplastic drug regimen] (DAVI)
LVW............ Landing Vehicle, Wheeled
LVW............ Las Vegas [Nevada] [Seismograph station code, US Geological Survey] (SEIS)
LVW............ Lateral Vaginal Wall [Medicine] (STED)
LVW............ Lateral Ventricular Width (STED)
LVW............ Left Ventricular Wall [Anatomy]
LVW............ Left Ventricular Work [Cardiology]
LVW............ Linked Vertical Well [Coal gastification] (DICI)
LVW............ Loaded Vehicle Weight [Automotive engineering]
LVW/HW...... Lateral Ventricular Width to Hemispheric Width (STED)
LVWI.......... Left Ventricular Work Index [Cardiology]
LVWM......... Left Ventricular Wall Motion [Medicine] (STED)
LVWMA....... Left Ventricular Wall Motion Abnormality [Medicine] (STED)
LVWT......... Left Ventricular Wall Thickness [Cardiology] (DMAA)
LVX............. Lily Virus X [Plant pathology]
LVY............. La Verendrye Management Corp. [Toronto Stock Exchange symbol]
LVY............. Levy [Alaska] [Seismograph station code, US Geological Survey] (SEIS)
LVZ............. Low-Viscosity Zone
LW............... Air Nevada [ICAO designator] (AD)
LW............... Griechische und Lateinische Lehnwoerter im Talmud, Midrasch und Targum [A publication] (BJA)
LW............... Lab. Wander [France] [Research code symbol]
LW............... Lacerated Wound
LW............... Landsteiner-Wiener [Serum]
L-W............. Landsverk-Wollan [Radiation survey meter]
LW............... Lane Wood, Inc. (EFIS)
LW............... Langwelle [Long Wave] [German] (MCD)
LW............... Last Word (IAA)
LW............... Lateral Wall [Image on transesophageal echocardiography] [Cardiology] (DAVI)
LW............... Late Warning
LW............... Launch Window [Aerospace] (AAG)
LW............... Lawrence Welk
Lw.............. Lawrencium [Symbol changed, 1963, to Lr] [Chemical element]
LW............... Law Weekly [A publication] (DLA)
LW............... Leave Word [Telecommunications] (TEL)
LW............... Leeway (COE)
LW............... Lee-White Method [Hematology] (MAE)

LW..............	Left Ear, Warm Stimulus [*Medicine*] (MEDA)
LW..............	Left Wing
LW..............	Lethal Weapon [*A motion picture*]
LW..............	Light Wall
LW..............	Light Warning
LW..............	Light Weight [*Technical drawings*]
LW..............	Lightweight RADAR (NATG)
LW..............	Limited War
LW..............	Literatures of the World [*A publication*]
LW..............	Liturgisch Woordenboek [*A publication*] (ODCC)
LW..............	Lives With (ADA)
lw	Loan Word (BJA)
LW..............	Logical Weakness [*Used in correcting manuscripts, etc.*]
LW..............	Logistics Wing [*Military*]
LW..............	Long Wave [*Radio*]
LW..............	Lotus West (EA)
LW..............	Louisville & Wadley Railway Co. [*AAR code*]
LW..............	Low [*Automotive advertising*]
Lw	Lower Hold [*Shipping*] (DS)
LW..............	Low Water [*Tides and currents*]
LW..............	Low Wave (WDAA)
LW..............	Low Wing [*Aviation*] (AIA)
LW..............	Lumens per Watt (ADA)
l/W..............	Lumens per Watt (IDOE)
LW..............	Lung Water
LW..............	United States Law Week [*A publication*] (NTCM)
LWA.............	Last Word Address
LWA.............	Liberian World Airlines, Inc. [*ICAO designator*] (FAAC)
LWA.............	Lightly Wounded in Action
LWA.............	Lightweight Armor
LWA.............	Limited Work Authorizations [*Nuclear energy*]
LWA.............	Local Welfare Authority [*British*]
LWA.............	Long Wire Antenna
LWA.............	University of Southwestern Louisiana, Lafayette, LA [*OCLC symbol*] (OCLC)
LWAAM.......	Light-Weight Air-to-Air Missile (MCD)
LWAR.........	Lightweight Attack and/or Reconnaissance (NATG)
LWASV.......	Lightweight Aircraft-to-Surface Vessel [*Military*]
LW/AW.......	Light Weight / Air Warning
LWAY.........	Lifeway Foods [*NASDAQ symbol*] (SAG)
LWB...........	Greenbrier [*West Virginia*] [*Airport symbol*] (OAG)
LWB...........	Laboratory Workbench
LWB...........	Lewisburg, WV [*Location identifier FAA*] (FAAL)
LWB...........	Light-Water Breeder [*Reactor*]
LWB...........	Lithography Workbench (AAEL)
LWB...........	Long Wheelbase
LWB...........	Lower Bound [*Computer science*]
LWBR.........	Light-Water Breeder Reactor
LWBS.........	Loyal Wheelwrights' and Blacksmiths' Society [*A union*] [*British*]
LWC...........	Lawrence [*Kansas*] [*Airport symbol*] (OAG)
LWC...........	League of Women Composers [*Later, ILWC*] (EA)
LWC...........	Lightweight Coated [*Paper*]
LWC...........	Lightweight Concrete [*Technical drawings*]
LWC...........	Lindsey Wilson College [*Columbia, KY*]
LWcL..........	Liquid Water Content
LWC...........	Lithuanian World Community (EA)
LWC...........	Little Way Circle [*An association*] (EA)
LWC...........	Living with Cancer [*An association*] (EA)
LWC...........	Lost Workday Case (COE)
LWCA.........	Light-Water Critical Assembly [*Nuclear reactor*] [*Japan*]
LWCA.........	Longwave Club of America (EA)
LWCF.........	Land and Water Conservation Fund [*Department of the Interior*]
LWCFA.......	Land and Water Conservation Fund Act of 1965 (COE)
LWCG........	Lightweight Coated Gravure [*Paper*] (DGA)
LWCH........	Lightweight Container Handler (MCD)
LWCHW.....	Light-Water-Cooled, Heavy-Water-Moderated Reactor (NRCH)
LWCMD.....	Licentiate of the Welsh College of Music and Drama [*British*] (DBQ)
LWCMS.....	Lightweight Company Mortar System
LWCO........	Lightweight Coated Offset [*Paper*] (DGA)
LW-COIN....	Limited War - Counterinsurgency
LWCS.........	Limited War Capabilities Study
LWCSS......	Lightweight Camouflage Screen System (MCD)
LWCT........	Lachar-Wrobel Critical Items [*Psychology*] (DAVI)
LWCT........	Lee-White Clotting Time [*Hematology*]
LWD..........	Larger Word [*Computer science*]
LWD..........	Large Woody Debris [*Pisciculture*]
LWD..........	LASER Welder/Driller (PDAA)
LWD..........	Launch Window Display [*Aerospace*] (MCD)
LWD..........	Left Wing Down [*Aviation*]
LWD..........	Long-Working Distance [*Microscopy*]
LWD..........	Loomis-Wood Diagram [*Physics*]
LWD..........	Low-Water Data [*Marine science*] (OSRA)
LWD..........	Low-Water Datum
LWD..........	Worldwide Airline Services, Inc. [*ICAO designator*] (FAAC)
LWDG........	Lightweight Director Group [*Military*] (CAAL)
LWE..........	Allwe [*Former USSR*] [*FAA designator*] (FAAC)
LWE..........	Lawrence Mining [*Vancouver Stock Exchange symbol*]
LWE..........	Liquid Whole Egg
LWECS......	Low-Wind Energy Conversion System (PDAA)
LWeJ..........	Welsh Public Library, Welsh, LA [*Library symbol Library of Congress*] (LCLS)
LWF..........	Lightweight Fighter [*Air Force*]
LWF..........	Local Welfare Authority Full Time [*British*]
LWF..........	Luminous Wall Firing (DICI)

LWF..........	Lutheran World Federation [*See also FLM*] [*Geneva, Switzerland*] (EAIO)
LWF & C...	Low Water Full and Change [*Tides and currents*]
LWFC........	Lloyd Wood Fan Club [*Defunct*] (EA)
LWFCS......	Lightweight Fire Control System [*Military*] (CAAL)
LWFJTF.....	Lightweight Fighter Joint Test Force [*Air Force*]
LWFUSANC...	Lutheran World Federation United States of America National Committee (EA)
LWG..........	Corvallis, OR [*Location identifier FAA*] (FAAL)
LWG..........	Lightweight Gun (NG)
LWG..........	Logistics Working Group (NAKS)
LWG..........	Logistic Work Group [*NATO*] (NATG)
LWG..........	Longwood Gardens Library, Kennett Square, PA [*OCLC symbol*] (OCLC)
LWGCR......	Light-Water Moderated, Gas-Cooled Reactor (IAA)
LWGM	Lightweight Gun Mount [*Military*] (CAAL)
LWGR.......	Light-Water-Cooled, Graphic-Moderated (IAA)
LWH..........	Lawn Hill [*Australia Airport symbol Obsolete*] (OAG)
LWHS........	Lightweight Headset [*Apollo*] [*NASA*]
LWHVR.....	Lightweight High-Velocity Rifle
LWI...........	LASER without Inversion
LWI...........	Load Wear Index
LWI...........	Long Wavelength Infrared (MCD)
LWI...........	Low-Water Interval
LWI...........	Lutheran World Information [*A publication*]
LWI...........	Lwiro [*Zaire*] [*Seismograph station code, US Geological Survey*] (SEIS)
LWIC.........	Lightweight Insulating Concrete [*Technical drawings*]
LWII..........	Long Wavelength Infrared Illuminator
LWinF........	Franklin Parish Library, Winnsboro, LA [*Library symbol Library of Congress*] (LCLS)
LWIR.........	Long-Wave Infrared (MUSM)
LWIR.........	Long Wavelength Infrared
LWIRC.......	Limited Warfare Intelligence Reduction Complex
LWIU.........	Laundry, Dry Cleaning, and Dye House Workers' International Union [*Later, Textile Processors, Service Trades, Health Care, Professional, and Technical Employees International Union*]
LWIU.........	Leather Workers International Union of America (EA)
LWiW.........	Winn Parish Library, Winnfield, LA [*Library symbol Library of Congress*] (LCLS)
LWJ...........	Lucas, William J., Albuquerque NM [*STAC*]
LWK..........	Large White Kidney [*Medicine*] (DMAA)
LWK..........	Lerwick [*Scotland*] Tingwall Airport [*Airport symbol*] (OAG)
LWL..........	Lambair Ltd. [*Canada ICAO designator*] (FAAC)
LWL..........	Land Warfare [*formerly, Limited War*] Laboratory [*Army*]
LWL..........	Length [*of a boat*] at Waterline
LWL..........	Length on the Waterline [*Boating*]
LWL..........	Lightweight Launcher (MCD)
LWL..........	Limited War Laboratory [*Military*] (IIA)
LWL..........	Load Waterline
LWL..........	Low Waterline
LWL..........	Waterline Length [*Navy*]
LWL..........	Wells [*Nevada*] [*Airport symbol Obsolete*] (OAG)
LWLC........	Light-Weight Low-Cost (PDAA)
LWLD........	Lightweight LASER Designator
LWM.........	Larrimore, William M., San Francisco CA [*STAC*]
LWM.........	Lawrence [*Massachusetts*] [*Airport symbol*] (AD)
LWM.........	Lawrence, MA [*Location identifier FAA*] (FAAL)
LWM.........	Leonard Wood Memorial [*American Leprosy Foundation*] (EA)
LWM.........	Liquid Waste Monitor [*Nuclear energy*] (IEEE)
LWM.........	Low Watermark
LWMB.......	Local Works Managing Budget [*British Armed Forces*]
LWMEL......	Leonard Wood Memorial for the Eradication of Leprosy [*Later, LWM*] (EA)
LWML.......	Lutheran Women's Missionary League [*Later, ILWML*] (EA)
LWMS.......	Liquid Waste Management System [*Nuclear energy*] (NRCH)
LWN.........	Loewen Group Capital Ltd. [*NYSE symbol*] (SAG)
LWN.........	Loewen Group, Inc. [*Toronto Stock Exchange symbol*]
LWNA	Lumber [*Timber*], Winter, North Atlantic [*Vessel load line mark*]
LWNGF.....	Loewen Group [*NASDAQ symbol*] (TTSB)
LWNPr.......	Loewen Group Cap Ser'A' 'MIPS' [*NYSE symbol*] (TTSB)
LWO.........	Layout Work Order (MCD)
LWO.........	Limited Warning Operation
LWO.........	Limited War Office [*Air Force*] (MCD)
LWO.........	Long-Wavelength Oscillation [*Astrophysics*]
LWO.........	Lubavitch Women's Organization (EA)
LWO.........	Lwow [*Former USSR Airport symbol*] (OAG)
LWOFC	Lindsay Wagner's Official Fan Club (EA)
LWOP.......	Lease with Option to Purchase (COE)
LWOP.......	Leave without Pay
L-word........	Liberal [*Especially in negative political context*]
LWOS	Low-Water Ordinary Spring [*Tides*]
LWOST	Low-Water Ordinary Spring Tides
LWP..........	Langley Working Paper [*NASA*]
LWP..........	Leave with Pay (KSC)
LWP..........	Limited War Plan
LWP..........	Liquid Waste Processing [*Nuclear energy*] (NRCH)
LWP..........	Liquid-Water Path [*Meteorology*]
LWP..........	Load Water Plane
LWP..........	Low Waterplane (PDAA)
LWPF........	Long-Wave Pass Filter (PDAA)
LWPS........	Liquid Waste Processing System [*Nuclear energy*] (NRCH)
LWQ..........	Low-Water Quadrature
LWQ..........	Walnut Ridge, AR [*Location identifier FAA*] (FAAL)
LWR..........	LASER Warning Receiver (MCD)

LWR.............. Launch Warning Receiver [Electronic countermeasure device] [Military] (VNW)
LWR.............. Lawrence Ins. Group [AMEX symbol] (TTSB)
LWR.............. Lawrence Insurance Group [AMEX symbol] (SPSG)
LWR.............. Light-Water Reactor
LWR.............. Limited War Capability (AAG)
LWR.............. Line Width Reduction (AAEL)
LWR.............. Liquid Waste Release [Nuclear energy] (IEEE)
LWR.............. Local Wage Rate
LWR.............. Long Wavelength Redundant [Camera for spectra]
LWR.............. Long-Wave Radiation
LWR.............. Lower (AAG)
Lwr .... Lower (TBD)
LWR.............. Lutheran World Relief (EA)
LWRECCE .... Lightweight Reconnaissance Aircraft (NATG)
LWRENAM... Leading WREN [Women's Royal Naval Service] Air Mechanic [British military] (DMA)
LWRENCINE... Leading WREN [Women's Royal Naval Service] Cinema Operator [British military] (DMA)
LWRENDHYG... Leading WREN [Women's Royal Naval Service] Dental Hygienist [British military] (DMA)
LWRENDSA... Leading WREN [Women's Royal Naval Service] Dental Surgery Assistant [British military] (DMA)
LWRENEDUC... Leading WREN [Women's Royal Naval Service] Education Assistant [British military] (DMA)
LWRENMET... Leading WREN [Women's Royal Naval Service] Meteorologist [British military] (DMA)
LWRENMT ... Leading WREN [Women's Royal Naval Service] Motor Transport Driver [British military] (DMA)
LWRENPHOT... Leading WREN [Women's Royal Naval Service] Photographer [British military] (DMA)
LWRENQA.... Leading WREN [Women's Royal Naval Service] Quarters Assistant [British military] (DMA)
LWRENREM... Leading WREN [Women's Royal Naval Service] Radio Electrical Mechanic [British military] (DMA)
LWRENRO(M)... Leading WREN [Women's Royal Naval Service] Radio Operator (Morse) [British military] (DMA)
LWRENS(C)... Leading WREN [Women's Royal Naval Service] Stores Assistant (Clothes) [British military] (DMA)
LWRENS(S)... Leading WREN [Women's Royal Naval Service] Stores Assistant (Stores) [British military] (DMA)
LWRENSTD... Leading WREN [Women's Royal Naval Service] Steward [British military] (DMA)
LWRENS(V)... Leading WREN [Women's Royal Naval Service] Stores Assistant (Victualling) [British military] (DMA)
LWRENTEL... Leading WREN [Women's Royal Naval Service] Telephonist [British military] (DMA)
LWRENTSA... Leading WREN [Women's Royal Naval Service] Training Support Assistant [British military] (DMA)
LWRENWA... Leading WREN [Women's Royal Naval Service] Weapon Analyst [British military] (DMA)
LWRENWTR(G)... Leading WREN [Women's Royal Naval Service] Writer (General) [British military] (DMA)
LWRENWTR(P)... Leading WREN [Women's Royal Naval Service] Writer (Pay) [British military] (DMA)
LWRENWTR(S)... Leading WREN [Women's Royal Naval Service] Writer (Shorthand) [British military] (DMA)
LWRM .... Lightweight RADAR Missile (MCD)
LWRO .... Lateral Wheel Run-Out [Automotive engineering]
LWRRI .... Louisiana Water Resources Research Institute [Louisiana State University] [Department of the Interior] [Research center] (RCD)
LWRS .... Lightweight Weather RADAR Set
LWRU .... Lightweight RADAR Unit (NATG)
LWS .... Large Wafer Study (AAEL)
LWS .... LASER Weapon System (MCD)
LWS .... Lewiston [Idaho] [Airport symbol] (OAG)
LWS .... Library Wholesale Services [Information service or system] (IID)
LWS .... Lightning Warning Set [Air Force]
LWS .... Lightning Warning System [NASA] (NASA)
LWS .... Light-Warning RADAR Set (NATG)
LWS .... Lightweight Sight
LWS .... Lightweight Sports [Concept car] [Automotive engineering]
LWS .... Lightweight System
LWS .... Low Water of Spring Tide
LWS .... Low-Water Sensitivity [Brake fluid designation]
LWS .... Lutheran Welfare Services [Australia]
LWSD .... LASER Weapon System Demonstrator [Military]
LWSF .... Lightweight Strike Fighter [NATO Air Forces]
LWSR .... Lightweight Search RADAR (IAA)
LWSR .... Lightweight Strike and Reconnaissance Aircraft (NATG)
LWSR(R) ..... Lightweight Strike and Reconnaissance Aircraft (Reconnaissance Role) (NATG)
LWSR(S)...... Lightweight Strike and Reconnaissance Aircraft (Strike Role) (NATG)
LWSS .... Letter-Writing Support System (PDAA)
LWST .... Light Waste Storage Tank (IEEE)
LWST .... Lowest (MSA)
LW(STA)...... Light Warning (Station)
LWSTC .... Liquid Waste and Sludge Transporter Council (EA)
Lw Stu H .... Law Students' Helper [A publication] (DLA)
LW-SWC ...... Light Weight Sheet Molding Compound
LWT .... Amphibious Warping Tug [Navy symbol]
LWT .... Lamb Weather Type [Meteorology]
LWT .... Lewistown [Montana] [Airport symbol] (OAG)
LWT .... Lightweight Torpedo [Now Mk 50] (DOMA)
LWT .... Lightweight Transponder

LWT .... Lightweight Type [Anchor gear]
LWT .... Liquid Waste Treatment (MCD)
LWT .... Listen While Talk (IAA)
LWT .... Local Winter Time [Astronomy] (IAA)
LWT .... London Weekend Television [England]
LWTA .... LASER Window Test Apparatus [Air Force]
LWTF .... Low-Water-Tolerant Brake Fluid [Automotive engineering]
LWTMA .... Listen While Transmission Multiple Access [Telecommunications] (PDAA)
LWTR .... Leading Writer [British military] (DMA)
LWTS .... Laundry Waste Treatment System [Nuclear energy] (NRCH)
LWTT .... Liquid Waste Test Tank [Nuclear energy] (IEEE)
LWU .... LASER Welder Unit
LWU .... Leather Workers International Union of America
LWUI .... Longshoremen's and Warehousemen's Union International
LWULT......... Least Widely Used and Least Taught Languages (AIE)
LWV .... Lackawanna & Wyoming Valley Railway Co. [Absorbed into Consolidated Rail Corp.] [AAR code]
LWV .... Landwirtschaftsversorgungsamt [German Land Economic Supply Office] [Post-World War II]
LWV .... Lawrenceville [Illinois] [Airport symbol Obsolete] (OAG)
LWV .... League of Women Voters of the United States
LWV .... Light-Weight Van
LWV .... Longitudinal Wave Velocity (AAEL)
LWVEF .... League of Women Voters Education Fund (EA)
LWVUS .... League of Women Voters of the United States (EA)
LWVV .... League of Women Voters of Victoria [Australia]
LWW .... Launch Window Width [Aerospace]
LWW .... Lightweight Weapon
LWWS .... Lightweight Weapons Sight
LWX .... LAN [Linked Access Network]/WAN Exchange [Wide Area Network] [Telecommunications]
LWY .... Lawas [Malaysia] [Airport symbol] (OAG)
LWYACC ..... Lithuanian World Youth Association Communications Center [Defunct] (EA)
LWYR .... Lawyer
LwyrTitl ...... Lawyers Title Corp. [Associated Press] (SAG)
LX .... Crossair [ICAO designator] (AD)
LX .... La Crosse, WI
LX .... Liver Extract [Protein/lipid substance] [Immunology]
LX .... Local Irradiation (MAE)
LX .... Lower Extremity [Anatomy] (DMAA)
LX .... Low Expansion Foam (WDAA)
LX .... Low Index [NWS] (FAAC)
lx .... Lux [Symbol] [SI unit of luminance]
LX .... Lux [Light] [Latin]
LXA .... Lhasa [China] [Airport symbol] (OAG)
LXA .... Lipoxin A [Biochemistry]
LXA .... Load Index from Address
LXAD .... Lexington Army Depot [Kentucky] (AFIT)
LXB .... Lipoxin B [Biochemistry]
LXB .... Pittsburgh, PA [Location identifier FAA] (FAAL)
LXBK .... LSB Bancshares, Inc. North Carolina [NASDAQ symbol] (SAG)
LXBK .... LSB Bancshares(NC) [NASDAQ symbol] (TTSB)
LXC .... Liquid-Ion Exchange Chromatography (PDAA)
LXD .... LASER Transceiver Device
LXD .... Load Index from Decrement
LXE .... LXE, Inc. [Associated Press] (SAG)
LXEI .... LXE, Inc. [NASDAQ symbol] (SAG)
LXFT .... Linear Xenon Flash Tube
LXG .... Luong Namtha [Laos] [Airport symbol] (AD)
LXGB .... Gibraltar/North Front [Gibraltar] [ICAO location identifier] (ICLI)
LXK .... Lexmark International Group [NYSE symbol] (SAG)
LXK .... Lexmark Intl Group'A' [NYSE symbol] (TTSB)
LXL .... Little Falls, MN [Location identifier FAA] (FAAL)
LXM .... Lintex Minerals [Vancouver Stock Exchange symbol]
LXMAR .... Load External Memory Address Register
LXMO .... Lexington B & L Financial Corp. [NASDAQ symbol] (SAG)
LXN .... Lexington, NE [Location identifier FAA] (FAAL)
LXN .... Lexington Resources Ltd. [Vancouver Stock Exchange symbol]
LXP .... Lexington Corporate Prop [NYSE symbol] (TTSB)
LXP .... Lexington Corporate Properties [NYSE symbol] (SAG)
LXP .... Lorain Public Library, Lorain, OH [OCLC symbol] (OCLC)
LXR .... Airluxor Ltda. [Portugal ICAO designator] (FAAC)
LXR .... Luxor [Egypt] [Airport symbol] (OAG)
LXR .... LXR Biotechnology [AMEX symbol] (TTSB)
LXR .... LXR Biotechnology, Inc. [AMEX symbol] (SAG)
LXRBiot ...... LXR Biotechnology, Inc. [Associated Press] (SAG)
LXS .... Lemnos [Greece] [Airport symbol] (OAG)
LX S .... Lux Second
LXT .... Left Exotropia [Ophthalmology]
LXT .... Linear Xenon Tube
LXU .... Lukulu [Zambia] [Airport symbol] (AD)
LXU .... Luxtec Corp. [AMEX symbol] (SAG)
LXV .... Leadville, CO [Location identifier FAA] (FAAL)
LXX .... Septuagint [Version of the Bible]
LXY .... Mexia, TX [Location identifier FAA] (FAAL)
LY .... El Al Israel Airlines [ICAO designator] (AD)
LY .... Lactoalbumin-Yeastolate [Cell growth medium]
LY .... Langley [Unit of sun's heat]
LY .... Last Year's Model [Merchandising slang]
LY .... League for Yiddish [Later, LYI] (EA)
LY .... Leicestershire Yeomanry (Prince Albert's Own) [British military] (DMA)
LY .... Lethal Yellowing [Plant pathology]

ly .... Libya [*MARC country of publication code Library of Congress*] (LCCP)
LY .... Libya [*ANSI two-letter standard code*] (CNC)
LY .... Light Year
ly .... Light Year
LY .... Linear Yard (AFM)
LY .... Lucifer Yellow [*A dye*] [*Organic chemistry*]
Ly .... Lyman [*Spectrography*]
LY .... Lynngold Resources, Inc. [*Toronto Stock Exchange symbol*]
LY .... Queen's Own Lowland Yeomanry [*Military unit*] [*British*]
LYA .... Lynch, Young & Associates [*Newport Beach, CA*] [*Telecommunications*] (TSSD)
LYA .... Lyon Air [*France ICAO designator*] (FAAC)
LYB .... Little Cayman [*West Indies*] [*Airport symbol*] (OAG)
LYBA .... Beograd [*Former Yugoslavia*] [*ICAO location identifier*] (ICLI)
LYBB .... Beograd [*Former Yugoslavia*] [*ICAO location identifier*] (ICLI)
LYBE .... Beograd [*Former Yugoslavia*] [*ICAO location identifier*] (ICLI)
LYBK .... Banja Luka [*Former Yugoslavia*] [*ICAO location identifier*] (ICLI)
LYBNT .... Last Year but Not This [*Fundraising*]
LYC .... Leicestershire Yeomanry Cavalry (Prince Albert's Own) [*British military*] (DMA)
LYC .... Lycoming College, Williamsport, PA [*OCLC symbol*] (OCLC)
Lyc .... Lycurgus [*of Plutarch*] [*Fourth century BC*] [*Classical studies*] (OCD)
LYCD .... Live Yeast Cell Derivative (DB)
Lycoming .... Lycoming Reporter [*Pennsylvania*] [*A publication*] (DLA)
Lycoming R (PA) ... Lycoming Reporter [*Pennsylvania*] [*A publication*] (DLA)
Lycoph .... Lycophron [*Third century BC*] [*Classical studies*] (OCD)
Lycurg .... Lycurgus [*of Plutarch*] [*Fourth century BC*] [*Classical studies*] (OCD)
LYD .... Houston, TX [*Location identifier FAA*] (FAAL)
LYD .... Lydney [*British depot code*]
Lydall .... Lydall, Inc. [*Associated Press*] (SAG)
LYDIEA .... Lymphocyte-Detected Immunoglobulin E Antigen [*Medicine*] (DB)
LYDMA .... Lymphocyte Determined Membrane Antigen [*Immunology*]
Lydnbg .... Lydenburg Platinum Ltd. [*Associated Press*] (SAG)
LYDPY .... Lydenburg Platinum Ltd ADR [*NASDAQ symbol*] (TTSB)
LYDU .... Dubrovnik [*Former Yugoslavia*] [*ICAO location identifier*] (ICLI)
LYE .... Lyneham, FTU [*British*] [*FAA designator*] (FAAC)
LYES .... Liver Yang Exuberance Syndrome [*Medicine*] (DMAA)
LYF .... Lutheran Youth Fellowship (EA)
LYFT .... Low-Yield Fallout Trajectory (DNAB)
LYG .... Lymphomatoid Granulomatosis [*Medicine*]
LYH .... Lynchburg [*Virginia*] [*Airport symbol*] (OAG)
LyHIF .... Lymphoblast Human Interferon (DB)
LYI .... League for Yiddish, Inc. (EA)
LYI .... Libby, MT [*Location identifier FAA*] (FAAL)
LYL .... League of Young Liberals [*British*] (ROG)
LYL .... Lima, OH [*Location identifier FAA*] (FAAL)
LYLJ .... Ljubljana [*Former Yugoslavia*] [*ICAO location identifier*] (ICLI)
LYM .... Last Year's Model [*Marketing*] (WDAA)
LYM .... Lymph [*or Lymphatic*] (WDAA)
LYM .... Lymphocyte
LYM .... Lympne [*England*] [*Airport symbol*] (AD)
LYMB .... Maribor [*Former Yugoslavia*] [*ICAO location identifier*] (ICLI)
LYMBS .... Lodzer Young Men's Benevolent Society (EA)
LYMO .... Mostar [*Former Yugoslavia*] [*ICAO location identifier*] (ICLI)
LYMPH .... Lymphocyte
Lymphos .... Lymphocytes [*Medicine*] (BABM)
LYN .... Atlanta, GA [*Location identifier FAA*] (FAAL)
LYN .... Lamba Youth Network [*An association*] (EA)
LYN .... Lehman Brothers, Inc. [*AMEX symbol*] (SAG)
LYN .... Lynton Aviation [*British ICAO designator*] (FAAC)
Lyn .... Lynx [*Constellation*]
Lynchburg C ... Lynchburg College (GAGS)
LynchC .... Lynch Corp. [*Associated Press*] (SAG)
Lynd .... Lyndwood's Provinciales [*A publication*] (DLA)
Lynd Prov ... Lyndwood's Provinciales [*A publication*] (DLA)
Lyndw Prov ... Lyndwood's Provinciales [*A publication*] (DLA)
Lyne .... Lyne's Irish Chancery Cases (Wallis) [*1766-91*] [*A publication*] (DLA)
LyNeF .... Lytic Nephritic Factor (DB)
Lyne Lea ... Lyne on Leases for Lives [*A publication*] (DLA)
Lyne on Renew ... Lyne on Renewals [*A publication*] (DLA)
Lyne (Wall) ... Wallis' Select Cases, Edited by Lyne [*1766-91*] [*Ireland*] [*A publication*] (DLA)
LYO .... Lubavitch Youth Organization (EA)
LYO .... Lyondell Chemical [*Formerly, Lyondell Petrochem*] [*NYSE symbol*]
LYO .... Lyondell Petrochem [*NYSE symbol*] (TTSB)
LYO .... Lyondell Petrochemical [*NYSE symbol*] (SPSG)
LYO .... Lyons, KS [*Location identifier FAA*] (FAAL)
LYO .... Lyophilized [*Medicine*] (DMAA)
LYOH .... Ohrid [*Former Yugoslavia*] [*ICAO location identifier*] (ICLI)
LYON .... Liquid-Yield Option Note [*Merrill Lynch & Co.*] [*Finance*]
LYON .... Liquid Yield Option Notes (EBF)
Lyon & R BS ... Lyon and Redman on Bills of Sale [*A publication*] (DLA)
Lyondl .... Lyondell Petrochemical Co. [*Associated Press*] (SAG)
Lyon Ind L ... Lyon on the Laws of India [*A publication*] (DLA)
Lyon Just ... Lyon's Institutes of Justinian [*A publication*] (DLA)
LYOS .... Osijek [*Former Yugoslavia*] [*ICAO location identifier*] (ICLI)
Lyot .... Layout (VRA)
LYP .... Faisalabad [*Pakistan*] [*Airport symbol*] (OAG)
LYP .... Lactose, Yeast, and Peptone Agar [*Medicine*] (DMAA)
LYP .... Lower Yield Point [*Medicine*] (DMAA)
LYP .... Lyallpur [*Pakistan*] [*Airport symbol*] (AD)
Lyp .... Lymphosarcoma [*Medicine*] (AAMN)

LYpAS .... Logicheskii Yazyk dlia Predstavleniya Algoritmov Sinteza Releinykh Ustroistv [*A Programming Language for Logic and Coding Algorithm*] [*Book title*]
LYPL .... Pula [*Former Yugoslavia*] [*ICAO location identifier*] (ICLI)
LYPR .... Pristina [*Former Yugoslavia*] [*ICAO location identifier*] (ICLI)
LYPW .... Legion of Young Polish Women (EA)
LYPZ .... Portoroz [*Former Yugoslavia*] [*ICAO location identifier*] (ICLI)
LYR .... Lancashire & Yorkshire Railway [*British*]
LYR .... Layer (MSA)
LYR .... Layer Cloud [*Meteorology*] (DA)
LYR .... Longyear [*Norway*] [*Airport symbol*] (OAG)
Lyr .... Lyra [*Constellation*]
LYR .... Lyric [*or Lyrical*]
Lyr .... Lyrichord [*Record label*]
lyr .... Lyricist [*MARC relator code*] [*Library of Congress*] (LCCP)
LYRI .... Rijeka [*Former Yugoslavia*] [*ICAO location identifier*] (ICLI)
LYRIC .... Language for Your Remote Instruction by Computer [*Computer science*] (MDG)
Lys .... De Lysia [*of Dionysius Halicarnassensis*] [*Classical studies*] (OCD)
LYS .... Light of Yoga Society (EA)
LYS .... Lycksele [*Sweden*] [*Geomagnetic observatory code*]
LYS .... Lyon [*France*] [*Airport symbol*] (OAG)
Lys .... Lysander [*of Plutarch*] [*Classical studies*] (OCD)
LYS .... Lysander Gold [*Vancouver Stock Exchange symbol*]
Lys .... Lysias [*Fifth century BC*] [*Classical studies*] (OCD)
Lys .... Lysine [*Also, K*] [*An amino acid*]
LYS .... Lysine (DMAA)
lys .... Lysine [*An amino acid*] (DOG)
Lys .... Lysistrata [*of Aristophanes*] [*Classical studies*] (OCD)
LYS .... Lysodren (DMAA)
Lys .... Lysosome [*Cytology*]
Lys .... Lysosome (STED)
LYS .... Lysozyme [*Also, LZM*] [*An enzyme*]
LYS .... Lysyl [*Enzymology*]
LYS .... Lytes Electrolytes [*Medicine*] (DMAA)
LYS .... Olean, NY [*Location identifier FAA*] (FAAL)
LYSA .... Sarajevo [*Former Yugoslavia*] [*ICAO location identifier*] (ICLI)
LYSK .... Skopje [*Former Yugoslavia*] [*ICAO location identifier*] (ICLI)
LySLk .... Lymphoma Syndrome Leukemia [*Medicine*] (STED)
Lyso-PC .... Lysophosphatidylcholine [*Also, LPC*] [*Biochemistry*]
LYSP .... Split [*Former Yugoslavia*] [*ICAO location identifier*] (ICLI)
LYSV .... Leek Yellow Stripe Virus [*Plant pathology*]
LYT .... Layout (MSA)
LYTBT .... Low-Yield Test Ban Treaty
Lytes .... Electrolytes [*Medicine*] (BABM)
LYTES .... Electrolytes (STED)
LYTI .... Titograd [*Former Yugoslavia*] [*ICAO location identifier*] (ICLI)
LYTS .... LSI Industries [*NASDAQ symbol*] (TTSB)
LYTS .... LSI Industries, Inc. [*NASDAQ symbol*] (SAG)
LYTT .... Lytta [*A Blistering Fly*] [*Pharmacy*] (ROG)
LYTV .... Tivat [*Former Yugoslavia*] [*ICAO location identifier*] (ICLI)
LYU .... Lehigh University, Bethlehem, PA [*OCLC symbol*] (OCLC)
LYV .... Legume Yellows Virus [*Plant pathology*]
LYVR .... Vrsac [*Former Yugoslavia*] [*ICAO location identifier*] (ICLI)
LYW .... Lyman [*Washington*] [*Seismograph station code, US Geological Survey*] (SEIS)
LYX .... Atlantic Rich 9% Exch Nts'97 [*NYSE symbol*] (TTSB)
LYX .... Atlantic Richfield Co. [*NYSE symbol*] (SAG)
LYX .... Lydd [*England*] [*Airport symbol*]
LYX .... Lynx-Canada Explorations Ltd. [*Toronto Stock Exchange symbol*]
Lyx .... Lyxose [*Also, l*] [*A sugar*]
LYY .... Batesville, AR [*Location identifier FAA*] (FAAL)
LYYY .... Beograd [*Former Yugoslavia*] [*ICAO location identifier*] (ICLI)
LYZ .... Lysozyme [*Medicine*] (DMAA)
LYZA .... Zagreb [*Former Yugoslavia*] [*ICAO location identifier*] (ICLI)
LYZB .... Zagreb [*Former Yugoslavia*] [*ICAO location identifier*] (ICLI)
LYZD .... Zadar [*Former Yugoslavia*] [*ICAO location identifier*] (ICLI)
LZ .... Balkan [*ICAO designator*] (AD)
LZ .... Landing Zone
LZ .... Left Zero (IAA)
LZ .... Lempel Zev [*Computer science*]
LZ .... Leucine Zipper [*Protein structure*]
LZ .... Live Zero (IAA)
LZ .... Loading Zone
LZ .... [*The*] Lubrizol Corp. [*NYSE symbol*] (SPSG)
LZ1 .... Luftschiff Zeppelin 1
LZA .... Labor Zionist Alliance (EA)
LZB .... La-Z Boy Chair [*NYSE symbol*] (TTSB)
LZB .... La-Z Boy Chair Co. [*NYSE symbol*] (SPSG)
LZCC .... Landing Zone Control Center [*Air Force*] (IAA)
LZCO .... Landing Zone Control Officer [*Air Force*] (AFM)
LZD .... Launch Zone Display
LZDF .... Launch Zone Display Flag
LZEEBE .... Long-Term Zonal Earth Energy Budget Experiment [*Spacecraft*] [*NASA*]
LZF .... Launch Zone Flag
LZGF .... Lewis Zero Gravity Facility
LZH .... Lanchow [*Republic of China*] [*Seismograph station code, US Geological Survey*] (SEIS)
LZIF .... Lyudmila Zhivkova International Foundation (EAIO)
LZL .... Landing Zone Locator
LZL .... Launcher, Zero Length [*British military*] (DMA)
LZM .... Lysozyme [*An enzyme*]
lzm .... Lysozyme (STED)
LZO .... Launch Zone Override

LZOA............ Labor Zionist Organization of America - Poale Zion [*Later, LZA*] (EA)
LZOC............ Lincoln Zephyr Owner's Club (EA)
LZP............. Latvian Green Party [*Political party*] (EY)
LZP............. Left Zero Print (IAA)
LZP............. Lorazepam [*Also, L, LOR*] [*Antiepileptic drug*]
LZPC............ Lead-Zinc Producers Committee (EA)
LZR............. Lazurus Distributors [*Vancouver Stock Exchange symbol*]
LZR............. Lizard Island [*Australia Airport symbol*] (OAG)

LZSA............ Landing Zone Support Area (COE)
LZT............. Lead Zirconate Titanate [*Ferroelectric material*]
LZT............. Local Zone Time
LZU............ Lincoln University, Lincoln University, PA [*OCLC symbol*] (OCLC)
LZV............ Lazarev [*Later, NVL*] [*Former USSR Geomagnetic observatory code*]
LZW............ Lempel-Zev-Welch [*Compression*] [*Computer science*] (PCM)
LZW............ Olney-Noble, IL [*Location identifier FAA*] (FAAL)
LZY............ Greensboro, NC [*Location identifier FAA*] (FAAL)
LZZ............. Lampasas, TX [*Location identifier FAA*] (FAAL)

M	Absolute Magnitude [*Astronomy*]
M	All India Reporter, Madras Series [*A publication*] (ILCA)
M	Angular Momentum [*Symbol*] [*Physics*]
M	Bending Moment [*Aerospace*] (AAG)
M	Days before Move Operation [*Usually followed by a number*] [*NASA*] (KSC)
M	Em [*Printing*] (WDMC)
m	Em [*Printing*] (WDMC)
M	Emma [*Phonetic alphabet*] [*In use in 1904 and 1914*] (DSUE)
M	Field Goals Missed [*Football, basketball*]
M	First Sergeant [*Army skill qualification identifier*] (INF)
M	Ground, Mobile [*JETDS nomenclature*]
M	Human Being Movement [*Rorschach*] [*Psychology*]
M	Hungary [*IYRU nationality code*]
M	Imperial Chemical Industries [*Great Britain*] [*Research code symbol*]
M	Indian Law Reports, Madras Series [*A publication*] (DLA)
M	Instrumental Magnitude [*Earthquakes*]
M	Intensity of Magnetization [*Symbol*] (DEN)
m-----	Intercontinental Areas (Eastern Hemisphere) [*MARC geographic area code Library of Congress*] (LCCP)
M	J. F. Macfarlan & Co. [*Scotland*] [*Research code symbol*]
M	Lundi [*French*] (ASC)
M	Macerare [*Macerate*] [*Pharmacy*]
m	Mach (NAKS)
M	Machine
M	Mach Number
M	MacNeil [*Herman A.*] [*Designer's mark, when appearing on US coins*]
M	Macpherson's Scotch Session Cases [*1862-73*] [*A publication*] (DLA)
M	Magenta (WDMC)
m	Magenta (WDMC)
M	Magister [*Master*] [*Latin*]
M	Magistrate
M	Magnaflux
M	Magnetic
M	Magnetic Moment [*Symbol*] (DEN)
M	Magnetic Polarization [*Symbol*] (DEN)
m	Magnetic Quantum Number [*Atomic physics*] [*Symbol*]
M	Magnetron (MDG)
M	Magnification (NTCM)
M	Magnitude
M	Maiden
M	Mail
M	Main
m	Main [*Menu*] [*Computer science*] [*Telecommunications*]
M	Maintainability [*or Maintenance*] (MCD)
m	Maintainability (NAKS)
M	Maintenance and Test Assemblies [*JETDS nomenclature*]
M	Majesty
M	Major [*Cycle*]
m	Major Cycle (NAKS)
M	Make
M	Male [*Electronics*]
m	Male (DD)
M	Malignant [*Medicine*]
M	Maloti [*Plural of Loti*] [*Monetary Unit*] [*Lesotho*] (BARN)
M	Man
M	Mandatory (KSC)
m	Mandatory (NAKS)
M	Mane [*Morning*] [*Pharmacy*]
M	Maneuvering Ship [*In speed triangle of relative movement problems*]
M	Manichaean Middle Persian
M	Manila [*Rope*]
M	Manipulus [*A Handful*] [*Pharmacy*]
M	Mannitol [*Organic chemistry*]
M	Mano [*Hand*] [*Spanish*]
M	Mantissa [*Decimal portion of a logarithm*]
M	Manual
m	Manual (NAKS)
M	Map
M	March
M	Mare [*Thoroughbred racing*]
m	Marginal Propensity to Import [*Economics*]
M	Maria [*Mary*]
M	Marine [*Insurance*]
M	Marine [*FCC*] (NTCM)
M	Marine Corps [*When used as prefix with plane designation*]
M	Marinus de Caramanico [*Flourished, 1269-85*] [*Authority cited in pre-1607 legal work*] (DSA)
M	Maritus [*Bridegroom*] [*Latin*]
M	Mark [*Monetary unit*] [*German*] (GPO)
M	Marker [*Beacon*] (AFM)
M	Markka [*Monetary unit*] [*Finland*]
M	Marksman [*British military*] (DMA)
M	Marquis [*or Marquess*]
M	Married
M	Mars
M	Marshal
M	Martin Co. Division [*Martin-Marietta Corp.*] [*ICAO aircraft manufacturer identifier*] (ICAO)
M	Martinus Gosia [*Authority cited in pre-1607 legal work*] (DSA)
M	Martinus Zamorensis [*Flourished, 13th century*] [*Authority cited in pre-1607 legal work*] (DSA)
M	Martyr
M	Marxist [*Politics*]
M	Masculine
M	Masochism (CDAI)
M	Mason (ROG)
m	Mass [*Symbol*] [*IUPAC*]
M	Massachusetts State Library, Boston, MA [*Library symbol Library of Congress*] (LCLS)
M	Massage
M	Masseur [*Ranking title*] [*British Royal Navy*]
M	Massive [*Agriculture*]
M	Master
M	Mate [*of a ship*]
M	Mater [*Mother*] [*Latin*]
M	Mathematics [*Secondary school course*] [*British*]
M	Matinee
M	Matins [*Early morning prayers*]
M	Matrix
m	Matrix (NAKS)
M	Matron [*British military*] (DMA)
M	Mature
M	Mature Audiences [*Movie rating*] [*Replaced by GP*]
M	Matured Bonds [*Investment term*] (DFIT)
M	Mauthner [*Cell*] [*Neurology*]
M	Maximal [*or Maximum*] [*Medicine*]
M	Maximum Value [*Electronics*]
M	Maxwell [*Electronics*] (DEN)
M	May
M	Mean [*Arithmetic average*]
M	Mean Active Maintenance Downtime [*Computer science*]
M	Meaningfulness [*Psychology*]
M	Mean Square
M	Measure [*Music*]
M	Measured Ceiling [*Aviation*]
M	Mechanical
M	Mechlorethamine [*Also, HN, HN2, MBA, NM*] [*Mustargen, nitrogen mustard*] [*Antineoplastic drug*]
M	Medal (ADA)
M	Media [*Laboratory*] (AAMN)
M	Medial (DAVI)
(M)	Median
M	Mediator
M	Medical
M	Medicinae [*Of Medicine*] [*Latin*]
M	Medicine
M	Medieval
M	Medium [*Size designation for clothing, etc.*]
m	Medium [*Spectral*]
M	Medium [*or 2-engine*] Plane
M	Mega [*A prefix meaning multiplied by one million*] [*Symbol*]
m	Mega (NAKS)
M	Megabyte [*Data storage capacity*] [*Computer science*]
M	Megohm (AAG)
M	Melendus [*Flourished, 1188-1209*] [*Authority cited in pre-1607 legal work*] (DSA)
M	Melittin [*Bee venom*]
M	Melphalan [*Also, A, L-PAM, MPH, MPL*] [*Antineoplastic drug*]
M	Melts At ____ [*Followed by a temperature*]
M	Member

M	Membrana [*Membrane*] [*Anatomy*]
M	Memorandum
M	Memoria [*Memory*] [*Latin*]
M	Memorial; Journal Officiel du Grand Duche de Luxembourg [*A publication*] (ILCA)
M	Memory
M	Mensura [*By Measure*] [*Pharmacy*] (ROG)
M	Mentum [*Chin*]
M	Menzies' Cape Colony Supreme Court Reports [*A publication*] (DLA)
M	Meperidine [*Also, MEP*] [*An analgesic*]
M	Mercaptopurine [*Purinethol*] [*Also, MP, P*] [*Antineoplastic drug*]
M	Mercury [*Chemical symbol is Hg*] (KSC)
m	Mercury (NAKS)
M	Merehurst [*Publisher*] [*British*]
M	Merge [*Computer science*] (IBMDP)
M	Merides [*Latin*] [*Noon*] (WDMC)
m	Meridian (Lower Branch)
M	Meridian (Upper Branch)
M	Meridies [*Noon*] [*Latin*]
M	Meridional Part [*Navigation*]
M	Mesangium [*Anatomy*]
M	Mesh
M	Mesial [*Dentistry*]
M	Mesomeric [*Organic chemistry*]
M	Mesophyll [*Botany*]
m	Meta [*Chemistry*]
M	Metabolite
M	Metacenter
M	Metal
M	Metalsmith [*Navy*]
M	Metamorphosis [*Phylogeny*]
M	Metaproterenol [*Pharmacology*]
M	Metastasis [*Oncology*]
M	Meteorological [*JETDS nomenclature*]
m	Meter [*SI unit of length*]
M	Meter (WDMC)
M	Methionine [*One-letter symbol; see Met*]
M	Method
M	Methodist
M	Methotrexate [*Antineoplastic drug*]
m	Methyl [*As substituent on nucleoside*] [*Biochemistry*]
M	Metoclopramide [*An antiemetic*]
M	Metronome
M	Metropolitan
M	Mews
M	Mezzo [*Moderate*] [*Music*]
M	Michaelmas Term [*British Legal term*] (ILCA)
m	Micro (WGA)
M	Micrococcus [*Genus of bacteria*]
M	Micrometer
M	Microphones [*JETDS nomenclature*] [*Military*] (CET)
M	Microprocessor
M	Microsporum [*Genus of fungi*]
M	Microtubule [*Cytology*]
M	Midazolan [*An anesthetic*]
M	Midday (ADA)
M	Middle
m	Middle (NAKS)
M	Middle School [*British*]
M	Middle Term of a Syllogism [*Logistics*] (WDAA)
M	Midfield [*Men's lacrosse position*]
M	Midline
M	Midnight (ROG)
m	Midship [*Shipping*] (DS)
M	Midwest Stock Exchange [*Chicago, IL*]
m	Mihi [*To Me*] [*Latin*] (EES)
M	Mike [*Phonetic alphabet*] [*International*] [*World War II*] (DSUE)
M	Mil [*Monetary unit*] [*Cyprus*]
m	Mil[*thousand*] (DAVI)
M	Mild (DAVI)
m	mile (WDMC)
M	Mile (WDMC)
M	Miles
M	Miles' Pennsylvania Reports [*A publication*] (DLA)
M	Military
M	Militia
M	Milk (ROG)
M	Mill
M	Mille [*Thousand*] [*Roman numeral*]
m	Milli- [*A prefix meaning divided by 1000*] [*SI symbol*]
M	Milli (DFIT)
M	Millime [*Monetary unit*] [*Tunisia*]
M	Millimicrometer (IAA)
M	Millimicron (IAA)
M	Million
m	Million (NAKS)
M	Mine
M	Minesweeper [*Navy*]
M	Miniature [*Horticulture*]
M	Minim
M	Minimum (ADA)
M	Ministry
M	Minor
M	Mint [*Condition*] [*Numismatics, etc.*]
M	Minus
M	Minute
M	Miotic [*Biology*]
M	Mira [*A star*] [*Astronomy*] (OA)
M	Mired (IAA)
M	Misce [*Mix*] [*Pharmacy*]
M	Miscellaneous
M	Miscible
M	Mishnah [*Basis of the Talmud*] (BJA)
M	Missile [*Air Force*]
M	Missile Carrier Aircraft [*Designation for all US military aircraft*]
m	Missing (NAKS)
M	Missing [*Data*]
M	Missing (Weather Reports Only) [*NWS*] (FAAC)
M	Mission
M	Mist [*Meteorology*]
M	Mistura [*Mixture*] [*Pharmacy*]
M	Mitic Subgroup [*Magnetite, chromite, hematite, ilmenite, titanite, perofskite, rutile*] [*CIPW classification Geology*]
M	Mitochondrion [*Cytology*]
M	Mitomycin [*Also, MC, MT*] [*Antineoplastic drug*]
M	Mitosis [*Cytology*]
M	Mitte [*Send*] [*Latin*]
M	Mix [*or Mixture*]
M	Mixed School [*British*]
M	Mobile [*Missile launch environment symbol*] [*Biology*]
M	Mobilization [*as in M-Day*] [*Military*] (AABC)
M	Modal (Verb) [*Linguistics*]
M	Mode
M	Model [*in military nomenclature*]
M	MODEM [*Computer science*]
M	Moderate
M	Moderate Sea or Swell [*Meteorology*]
M	Modern [*Post-1920*] [*Deltiology*]
M	Modification [*FCC*] (NTCM)
m	Modified [*Regulation or order modified*] [*Used in Shepard's Citations*] [*Legal term*] (DLA)
M	Modulation Coefficient (IDOE)
M	Modulation Depth [*Broadcasting*]
M	Modulator (IAA)
M	Modulus
M	Moisture
M	Mol [*or Mole*] [*Measurement*] (DAVI)
m	Molal [*Solute concentration by weight*] [*Chemistry*]
M	Molar [*Permanent*] [*Dentistry*]
M	Molar [*Solute concentration by volume*] [*Chemistry*]
m	Molar [*Tooth, deciduous*] [*Dentistry*] (DAVI)
M	Molar Mass [*Symbol*] [*IUPAC*]
M	Mole
M	Molecular Weight [*Also, MOL WT, MW*]
M	Moment
M	Moment of Force [*Symbol*] [*IUPAC*]
M	Monastery
M	Monday
M	Money
M	Monitor (MDG)
m	Monitor (NAKS)
M	Monkey [*Phonetic alphabet*] [*Royal Navy World War I Pre-World War II*] (DSUE)
M	Monochrome (IAA)
M	Monoclonal [*Biochemistry*]
M	Monocyte [*Hematology*]
M	Monograph
M	Monophage [*Biology*]
M	Monoplane
M	Monotype (DGA)
M	Monsieur [*Mister*] [*French*]
M	Monsoon
M	Mont [*Monte, etc.*] [*Italy and Sicily only*]
M	Montana (DLA)
M	Montavit Co. [*Austria*] [*Research code symbol*]
M	Month
m	Month (WDMC)
M	Monthly
M	Montmorillonite [*A mineral*]
M	Montreal Stock Exchange
M	Monumentum [*Monument*] [*Latin*]
M	Moon
M	Morgan [*George T.*] [*Designer's mark, when appearing on US coins*]
M	Morison's Dictionary of Decisions, Scotch Court of Session [*1540-1808*] [*A publication*] (DLA)
M	Morning
m	Morning (WDMC)
m	Morpha [*Form*] [*Biology*]
M	Morphine [*Slang*]
M	Morphological Rule [*Linguistics*]
M	Morphometric Analysis [*Botany*]
M	Mort [*Dead*] [*French*] (ROG)
M	Mortar
M	Mortgage
M	Mortis [*Of Death*] [*Latin*]
M	Motel
M	Mother
m	Motile [*Sperm*] (MAE)
M	Motivational Ability
M	Motor

M	Motorship (DS)
M	Motorway [Traffic sign] [British]
M	Moulder [Navy rating British]
M	Mound (MSA)
M	Mountain
M	Mouth
M	Move Being Made [Computer science]
M	Movement [Neurology]
M	[Time in Days Before] Move Operations
M	Mu [Twelfth letter of the Greek alphabet] (DAVI)
M	Mucoid
M	Mucoid Colony [Biochemistry] (DAVI)
M	Mud
M	Muddy [Quality of the bottom] [Nautical charts]
M	Muddy [Track condition] [Thoroughbred racing]
M	Multipara (MAE)
M	Multiplier
M	Municipal Premises [Public-performance tariff class] [British]
M	Murmur [Heart] [Medicine]
M	Muscarinic (DB)
M	Musculus [Muscle] [Anatomy]
M	Music [Films, television, etc.]
M	Mustard Gas [Also, H, HD, HS, HT] [Poison gas US Chemical Corps symbol]
M	Muster
M	Mutitas [Dullness] [Latin]
M	Mutual Companies
M	Mutual Inductance [Symbol] [IUPAC]
M	Mycelium [Biology]
M	Mycobacterium [Genus of microorganisms]
M	Mycoplasma [Medicine] (MAE)
M	Myopia
M	Myosin [Muscle physiology]
M	New York Miscellaneous Reports [A publication] (DLA)
M	Nomina [Names] [Probably a misprint for NN, by some supposed to denote St. Mary, patron saint of girls] [Latin] (ROG)
M	Noon [Meridies]
M	Ohio Miscellaneous Reports [A publication] (DLA)
M	One Thousand [Roman numeral]
M	Ordered Multistate [Botany]
M	Queen Mary (DLA)
M	Radiant Exitance [Symbol] [IUPAC]
M	Reckitt & Sons Ltd. [Great Britain] [Research code symbol]
M	Red Star of Prominent Titanium Oxide Intensity [Astronomy] (BARN)
M	Refractive Modulus (IDOE)
m	Response to Human Being Movement [Rorschach] [Psychology]
M	Strength of Pole [Chemistry] (DAVI)
M	Thioinosine [One-letter symbol; see SIno, Sno]
/M	Thousand
M	Time of Maneuver
M/0/0/S	Minutes Zero Zero Seconds [Aerospace] (AAG)
M/1	Method 1 (NITA)
M_1	Mitral First Sound [Cardiology]
M_1	Money Supply of a Country, Consisting of Currency and Demand Deposits [Economics]
M_1	Sight Dullness [on Auscultation] [Medicine] (DAVI)
M1S	Matte One Side [Aluminum]
M_2	Insular Segment of Middle Cerebral Artery [Cardiology] (DAVI)
M_2	Marked Dullness [on Auscultation] [Medicine] (DAVI)
M2	Masterspec 2 [Production Systems for Architects & Engineers, Inc.] [Information service or system] (IID)
M_2	Mitral Second Heart Sound [Cardiology] (DAVI)
M_2	Money Supply of a Country, Including M_1 and Commercial Time Deposits [Economics]
m2	Square Meter
M2C	Massachusetts Microelectronics Center [Research center] (RCD)
M^2C^2	Multi-Media Communication Control (DOMA)
M^2FCS	Multi-Microprocessor Flight Control System (PDAA)
M2FM	Modified Modified Frequency Modulation
M^{2H2}	Mary Hartman, Mary Hartman [Initialism is shortened form of television program title] [Also, MH2]
M2M	Manager-to-Manager (ACRL)
M2M	May Second Movement [1960s Yale University war protest] (VNW)
M2S	Matte Two Sides [Aluminum]
M^2/S	Square Meters per Second
M_3	Absolute Dullness [on Auscultation] [Medicine] (DAVI)
m3	Cubic Meter
M/3	Middle Third [of long bones] [Orthopedics] (DAVI)
M3	Military Manpower Models
M_3	Money Supply of a Country, Including M_2, Savings and Loan Association Deposits, and Certificates of Deposit [Economics]
M-3 APD	Military Manpower Models Airborne Personnel Detector [Device used to collect and test air samples to identify enemy sites] [Vietnam] (VNW)
M^3/D	Cubic Meters per Day
M^3/J	Cubic Meters per Joule
M^3/KG	Cubic Meters per Kilogram
$M^3/(M A)$	Cubic Meters per Meter Year
$M^3/(M D)$	Cubic Meters per Meter Day
M^3/MIN	Cubic Meters per Minute
M^3/S	Cubic Meters per Second
M-3 TAP	Military Manpower Models Toxicological Agents Protective Suit [Provided protection from chemical agents] (VNW)
M-3V	Movimiento 3V [Nicaragua] [Political party] (EY)
M_4	Cortical Segment of Middle Cerebral Artery [Cardiology] (DAVI)

M4	Message from Multiple Media Maximizes [Communications] (WDMC)
M5	Manual Five Speed [DOE] (TAG)
M/10	Tenth Molar [Solute concentration by volume] [Chemistry] (DAVI)
M12	M12 [Hawaii] [Seismograph station code, US Geological Survey Closed] (SEIS)
M-18-X	Movimiento 18 de Octubre de Accion Revolucionaria Astra [Astra 18th October Movement of Revolutionary Action] [Ecuador] [Political party] (PD)
M-19	Movimiento 19 de Abril [April 19 Movement] [Colombia]
M-20	Movimiento-20 [Panama] [Political party] (EY)
M50	Mean of 1950 [Coordinate system] [NASA] (NASA)
M85	85 Percent/15 Percent Unleaded Gasoline [BTS] (TAG)
M/100	Hundredth Molar [Solute concentration by volume] [Chemistry] (DAVI)
MA	Aircraft Stations [ITU designation] (CET)
MA	Amherst College, Amherst, MA [Library symbol Library of Congress] (LCLS)
ma----	Arab States [MARC geographic area code Library of Congress] (LCCP)
Ma	Ma'arbae (BJA)
Ma	Ma'aserot (BJA)
MA	Machine Accountant [Navy]
Ma	Mach Number [IUPAC]
MA	Macronutrient Additives [Fat substituted for food]
MA	Madras Artillery [British military] (DMA)
MA	Madrid Stock Exchange [Spain]
MA	Magister Artium [Master of Arts] [Latin]
MA	Magma Arizona Railroad Co. [Later, MAA] [AAR code]
MA	Magnesium Association [Later, IMA] (EA)
MA	Magnetic Amplifier
MA	Mahogany Association (EA)
MA	Maids of Athena (EA)
MA	Main Alarm (IAA)
MA	Main Amplifier (OA)
MA	Maintenance
MA	Maintenance Ability (KSC)
MA	Maintenance Actions
M/A	Maintenance Analysis (KSC)
MA	Maintenance Area [Military British]
MA	Maintenance Availability
MA	Major (DSUE)
Ma	Male (DAVI)
M/A	Male, Altered Animal (DMAA)
MA	Maleic Anhydride [Also, MAH] [Organic chemistry]
MA	Malignant Angioendotheliomatosis [Oncology]
MA	Malignant Arrhythmia [Medicine] (DMAA)
MA	Malonaldehyde [Organic chemistry]
MA	Malpractice Association (EA)
MA	Malvalic Acid (PDAA)
MA	Mamma (DSUE)
MA	Mammary Adenocarcinoma [Medicine] (DB)
MA	Management Administration [Department of Labor Statistics] (OICC)
MA	Management Adviser
MA	Manager of Aviation
MA	Manager's Assistant (DCTA)
MA	Mandelic Acid [Organic chemistry] (AAMN)
MA	Manifest Achievement (AAMN)
MA	Manifest Anxiety
MA	Maniilaq Association (EA)
MA	Manpower Administration [Later, Employment and Training Administration] [Department of Labor]
MA	Manual
M/A	Manual or Automatic (NRCH)
MA	Manufacturing Assembly
MA	Manure (ROG)
MA	Manx Airlines Ltd.
MA	Map Analysis
MA	March
Ma	March's Action for Slander and Arbitrament [A publication] (DLA)
MA	Margin Account [Investment term]
MA	Marine Class
MA	Maritime Administration [Also, MARAD, MARITADMIN] [Department of Transportation]
ma	Maritime Antarctic [Air Mass] [Meteorology] (BARN)
MA	Mark [Coin] (ROG)
MA	Market Administration (HCT)
MA	Market Average [Investment term]
MA	Marketing Assistance (MCD)
MA	Marriage Analysis [Psychology]
Ma	Marsh [Maps and charts]
MA	Marshaling Area [Military]
MA	Martin-Albright [Syndrome] [Medicine] (DB)
MA	Martingana [Ship's rigging] (ROG)
Ma	Martinus de Caramanico [Flourished, 1269-85] [Authority cited in pre-1607 legal work] (DSA)
Ma	Martinus Gosia [Authority cited in pre-1607 legal work] (DSA)
MA	Massachusetts [Postal code]
MA	Massachusetts Reports [A publication] (DLA)
MA	Mass Analyzer
Ma_a	Mass Flow of Air [Aviation] (DA)
Ma	Mass of Atom (DMAA)
MA	Mast Aerial (IAA)
MA	Master (MSA)
MA	Master Alarm
MA	Master Assistant [British military] (DMA)

MA	Master-at-Arms [*Navy*]
MA	Master of Arts
MA	Masurium
MA	Matched Angle (OA)
MA	Mater [*Mother*] [*Latin*] (ADA)
MA	Material Authorization (KSC)
MA	Mathematical Association [*British*] (BI)
Ma	Matheus de Mathesillanis [*Flourished, 1381-1402*] [*Authority cited in pre-1607 legal work*] (DSA)
MA	Matrix Antigen [*Biochemistry*]
MA	Matt Art [*Paper*] (DGA)
Ma	Mattes [*Quality of the bottom*] [*Nautical charts*]
MA	Maturational Age [*Also, Development Age*] [*Medical term*] (PAZ)
MA	Mature Adult [*Film and video classification*]
MA	Mature Australia [*An association*]
MA	May
MA	May Department Stores Co. [*NYSE symbol*] (SPSG)
MA	May Dept Stores [*NYSE symbol*] (TTSB)
MA	Mazdaznan Association (EA)
MA	Mean Arterial Blood Pressure [*Medicine*] (MAE)
MA	Measurement Accuracy
MA	Mechanical Accessories (MCD)
MA	Mechanical Advantage
MA	Mechanical Ambush (VNW)
MA	Mechanically Alloyed [*Metallurgy*]
MA	Mechanician Apprentice [*British military*] (DMA)
MA	Mechanoacoustic
MA	Media Alliance (EA)
MA	Medicaid (DLA)
MA	Medical Abbreviation (AAMN)
MA	Medical Assistance [*HEW*]
MA	Medical Assistant (DAVI)
MA	Medical Audit (MAE)
MA	Medical Authority
MA	Medical Authorization (DAVI)
M/A	Mediterranean/Adriatic [*Shipping*] (DS)
MA	Mediterranean Area
MA	Medium Artillery
MA	Mega [*A prefix meaning multiplied by one million*]
Ma	Megaannum (DOG)
MA	Megampere (IEEE)
MA	Melanesian Alliance [*Papua New Guinea*] [*Political party*] (FEA)
MA	Melodious Accord (EA)
MA	Membrane Antigen [*Immunology*]
MA	Memory Address [*Computer science*]
MA	Memory Available [*Computer science*] (IAA)
MA	Menorah Association [*Defunct*] (EA)
MA	Menstrual Age [*Medicine*]
MA	Mental Age [*Psychology*]
MA	Mentum Anterior [*In reference to the chin*]
MA	Mercenary Association (EA)
MA	Mercer Associates (EA)
MA	Mercury Arc (MSA)
MA	Mercury-Atlas [*Spacecraft*] [*NASA*]
MA	Message Assembler
M/A	Mess Attendant
MA	Messies Anonymous [*Commercial firm*] (EA)
MA	Messing Allowance [*British military*] (DMA)
MA	Metabolic Activity
MA	Metabolic Analyzer
MA	Metal Anchor (AAG)
MA	Metallurgistes Unis d'Amerique [*United Steelworkers of America*] (EAIO)
MA	Meteorological Applications [*Branch*] [*Forecast Systems Laboratory*] (USDC)
MA	Meter Amplifier
MA	Meter Angle
M/A	Meters per Year
MA	Methamphetamine [*Pharmacology*]
MA	Methoxylamine [*Organic chemistry*]
MA	Methyl Acrylate [*Organic chemistry*]
MA	Methyl Anthranilate [*Organic chemistry*]
MA	Methylanthranilic Acid
MA	Metric Association [*Later, USMA*] (EA)
MA	Mexican-American
MA	Michigan Amber [*Variety of wheat*]
MA	Microagglutination [*Immunochemistry*] (DAVI)
MA	Microalloy
MA	Microfilm Address (NITA)
MA	Microphone Amplifier
MA	Microscopic Agglutination [*Medicine*] (DMAA)
MA	Microwave Associates, Inc. [*Later, M/A-Com*] (AAG)
MA	Middeck Act
MA	Middeck Aft (MCD)
MA	Middle Ages
MA	Middle Assyrian [*Language, etc.*] (BJA)
MA	Midmarch Associates (EA)
MA	Midwest Academy (EA)
MA	Mike Amplifier (NASA)
MA	Mikes of America (EA)
MA	Mileage Allowance
MA	Miles Laboratories, Inc. [*Research code symbol*]
MA	Military Academy
MA	Military Accountant [*British military*] (DMA)
MA	Military Administration

MA	Military Aircraft
MA	Military Assistance [*or Assistant*]
MA	Military Attache [*Diplomacy*]
MA	Military Aviator
MA	Mill Annealed
MA	Miller-Abbot (Tube) [*Medicine*]
MA	Milliammeter (IAA)
mA	Milliampere [*or Milliamperage*]
MA	Milliampere
MA	Milliangstrom [*Unit of wavelength of light*] (WGA)
Ma	Million Years Ago
MA	Mind Association (EA)
MA	Minimum Aircraft [*Powered hang gliders, replicas of early flying machines, etc.*] [*British*]
MA	Ministry of Aviation [*British*]
MA	Minnesota [*Obsolete*] (ROG)
MA	Miscellaneous at Anchor [*Navy*] (NVT)
MA	Miss Angle
MA	Missed Appointment
MA	Missed Approach
MA	Missile Airframe (AAG)
MA	Missile Away
MA	Mission Accomplished [*Air Force*]
MA	Mission Analysis (MCD)
MA	Missionarius Apostolicus [*Missionary Apostolic*] [*Latin*]
MA	Missouri Appeal Reports [*A publication*] (DLA)
MA	Mistresses Anonymous (EA)
MA	Mitomycin-C and Adriamycin [*Antineoplastic drug regimen*] (DAVI)
MA	Mitotic Apparatus [*Cytology*]
MA	Mitral Annulus [*Cardiology*] (DAVI)
MA	Mobile Airlock (MCD)
MA	Mobilization Augmentee [*Military*] (AFM)
MA	Mobilization for Animals [*Defunct*] (EA)
MA	Moderately Advanced (MAE)
MA	Modern Age [*A publication*] (BRI)
MA	Modified Atmosphere [*Food technology*]
MA	Modify Address (IEEE)
MA	Monarchist Alliance (EA)
MA	Monarticular Arthritis [*Medicine*]
M/A	Monetary Allowance
MA	Monitoring Agency
MA	Monoamine [*Chemistry*]
MA	Monoclonal Antibody [*Medicine*] (DMAA)
MA	Monte Carlo Resources [*Vancouver Stock Exchange symbol*]
MA	Months After
M/A	Mood and/or Affect [*Psychology*] (DAVI)
MA	Moored Alongside [*Navy*] (NVT)
MA	Moral Alternatives [*An association*] (EA)
MA	Moreshet Archives [*Jerusalem*] (BJA)
MA	Morning After (IIA)
MA	Morocco [*IYRU nationality code*] [*ANSI two-letter standard code*] (CNC)
MA	Mortuary Affairs [*Army*] (INF)
MA	Mother's Aide [*Red Cross Nursing Services*]
MA	Mothers of Asthmatics (EA)
MA	Mountain Artillery
MA	Mountaineering Association [*British*] (BI)
MA	Moving Average [*Statistics*]
MA	Multiple Access (NASA)
MA	Multiple Application [*Military*] (AFIT)
MA	Munitionsanstalt [*Ammunition Depot*] [*German military - World War II*]
MA	Munitions Tribunals Appeals, Great Britain High Court of Justice [*A publication*] (DLA)
MA	Muscle Activity (MAE)
MA	Museums' Association (WDAA)
MA	Musical Appreciation [*Record label*]
MA	Music Alliance [*Defunct*] (EA)
MA	Muslim Almanac [*A publication*]
MA	Mutagenic Activity
MA	Mutual Age
MA	My Account [*Business term*]
MA	Myanma Airways (EY)
ma	Myria [*A prefix meaning multiplied by 10⁴*]
MA	United States Military Academy (AAGC)
MA1	Machine Accountant, First Class [*Navy*]
MA2	Machine Accountant, Second Class [*Navy*]
MA3	Machine Accountant, Third Class [*Navy*]
MAA	Aerotransportes Mas de Carga SA de CV [*Mexico ICAO designator*] (FAAC)
MAA	Maastrichtial [*Paleontology*]
MAA	Macroaggregated Albumin [*Medicine*]
MAA	Madras [*India*] [*Airport symbol*] (OAG)
MAA	Magma Arizona Railroad Co. [*AAR code*]
MAA	Major Aircraft Accident (MCD)
MAA	Manantiales [*Argentina*] [*Seismograph station code, US Geological Survey*] (SEIS)
MAA	Mandatory Advertising Association [*Automotive retailing*]
MAA	Manitoba Association of Architects [*1914*] [*Canada*] (NGC)
MAA	Manufacturers' Agents Association of Great Britain and Ireland (BI)
MAA	Manufacturers Aircraft Association [*Supersedes AMA*] [*Defunct*] (EA)
MAA	Marina Association of America [*Defunct*] (EA)
MAA	Marineartillerieabteilung [*Naval Coast Artillery Battalion*] [*German military - World War II*]
MA A	Massachusetts Appeals Court Reports [*A publication*] (DLA)

MAA............	Master Army Aviator
MAA............	Master-at-Arms [Navy]
MAA............	Master of Administrative Arts (GAGS)
MAA............	Master of Aeronautics and Astronautics (GAGS)
MAA............	Master of Applied Art (GAGS)
MAA............	Master of Applied Arts
MAA............	Material Access Area [Nuclear energy] (NRCH)
MAA............	Mathematical Association of America (EA)
MAA............	Mature Age Allowance
MAA............	Maximum Authorized Altitude [Aviation]
MAA............	Mecca Minerals Ltd. [Vancouver Stock Exchange symbol]
MAA............	Mechanical Arm Assembly (NASA)
MAA............	Mediaeval Academy of America (EA)
MAA............	Medical Administrative Assistant (DAVI)
MAA............	Medical Artists Association of Great Britain (PDAA)
MAA............	Medical Assistance for the Aged
MAA............	Medium Antiaircraft Weapon (NATG)
MAA............	Melanoma-Associated Antigen [Oncology]
MAA............	Menthoxyacetic Acid [Organic chemistry]
MAA............	Methacrylic Acid [Organic chemistry]
MAA............	Methanearsonic Acid [Organic chemistry]
MAA............	Methyl Acetoacetate [Organic chemistry]
MAA............	Microlight Aircrafts Association [British] (DI)
MAA............	Mid-Amer Apart Communities [NYSE symbol]
MAA............	[The] Mid-America Apartment Communities [NYSE symbol] (SPSG)
MAA............	Mission Area Analysis (MCD)
MAA............	Mobilization Against AIDS [An association] (EA)
MAA............	Mobilization Automation Appraisal (MCD)
MAA............	Modeling Association of America [Later, MAAI]
MAA............	Moderate Angle of Attack
MAA............	Modified Ames Assay [For toxicology]
MAA............	Monarticular Arthritis [Orthopedics] (DAVI)
MAA............	Moped Association of America [Defunct] (EA)
MAA............	Motel Association of America [Later, National Innkeeping Association]
MAA............	Motor Agents' Association [British]
MAA............	Mouvement Anti-Apartheid [France]
MAA............	Municipal Arborist Association [Later, MAUFS] (EA)
MAAA..........	Master of Arts in Arts Administration (PGP)
MAAA..........	Member of the American Academy of Actuaries
MAAA..........	Metropolitan Area Apparel Association (EA)
MAAAA........	Mid-Am Antique Appraisers Association (EA)
MAAAP........	macroaggregated Albumin Arterial Perfusion [Medicine] (STED)
MAAB..........	Maintenance Air Abort [Air Force] (AFIT)
MAAB..........	Materials Application Advisory Board [NASA] (NASA)
MAABR........	Maintenance Air Abort Rate [Air Force] (AFIT)
MAABS........	Master of Arts in Applied Behavioral Sciences (GAGS)
MAAC..........	Mastic Asphalt Advisory Council [British] (BI)
MAAC..........	Maximum Allowable Actual Charge [Medicare]
MAAC..........	Medical Assistants Advisory Council (DAVI)
MAAC..........	Metro Atlantic Athletic Conference (PSS)
MAAC..........	Mid-Atlantic Area Council [Regional power council]
MAAC..........	Military Assistance Advisory Command (DOMA)
MAAC..........	Milliampere Alternating Current (IAA)
MAAC..........	Mutual Assistance Advisory Committee
MAACBA......	Middle Atlantic Association of Colleges of Business Administration
MAACL........	Multiple Affect Adjective Check List [of Educational and Industrial Testing Service] [Psychology]
MAACP........	Mediterranean Area Airlift Command Post (AFM)
MAACS	Multi Address Asynchronous Communication System
MA ADAM....	Master of Arts in Alcoholism and Drug Abuse Ministry (PGP)
MAADMA.....	Methylaminoacetaldehyde Dimethyl Acetal [Organic chemistry]
MAAE..........	Master of Aeronautical and Astronomical Engineering (GAGS)
MAAE..........	Master of Arts in Applied Economics (GAGS)
MAAF..........	Mediterranean Allied Air Force
MAAF..........	Mediterranean Army Air Forces
MAAF..........	Michael Army Air Field (MCD)
MAAF..........	Museum Association of the American Frontier (EA)
MAA-FDI......	Museum of African Art - Frederick Douglass Institute [Smithsonian Institution] (EA)
MAAG	Military Assistance Advisory Group [Merged with US Military Assistance Command]
MAAGB.......	Medical Artists Association of Great Britain (DAVI)
MAAGI........	Military Assistance Advisory Group, Indochina [Later, MAAGV] (VNW)
MAAGP.......	Member, American Academy of General Practice (CMD)
MAAGV.......	Military Assistance Advisory Group, Vietnam [Formerly, MAAGI] (VNW)
MAAH	Museum of African American History (EA)
MAAH	Museum of Afro-American History (EA)
MAAI..........	Modeling Association of America International (EA)
MAAK	Movement for All-Macedonian Action [Political party]
MAAL.........	Monthly Adjustment Acceptance List [Military] (AFIT)
MAALOX	Magnesium-Aluminum Hydroxide [Commercial antacid]
MAALT........	Multiple Aircraft Approach and Landing Techniques (MCD)
MAAM.........	Medium Antiaircraft Missile
MAAMA.......	Middletown Air Materiel Area (SAA)
MAAmSt	Master of Arts in American Studies (GAGS)
MAAN	Methyleneaminoacetonitrile [Organic chemistry]
MAAN	Mutual Advertising Agency Network [Grand Forks, ND] (EA)
MA & D	Mission Analysis and Design
MA & E.......	Mission Analysis and Engineering [NASA]
MA & P.......	Maintenance Analysis and Planning (NASA)
MA & T.......	Manufacturing Assembly and Test (MCD)
MA and T....	Missile Assembly and Test [Building] (NATG)
MAANPI......	Mutual Aid Association of the New Polish Immigration (EA)
MAAOM.......	Master of Arts in Applied Organizational Management (PGP)
MAAP.........	Maintenance and Administration Panel [Bell System]
MAAP.........	Material Access Authorization Program [Nuclear energy] (NRCH)
MAAP.........	Member, American Association of Physicians (CMD)
MAAP.........	Milan Army Ammunition Plant (AABC)
MAAPA	Massachusetts Aggregates and Asphalt Pavement Association (SRA)
MAAPS	Massachusetts Association of 766 Approved Private Schools (SRA)
MAAR	Mandatory Annual Audit Requirement (AAGC)
MAAR	Monthly Associate Administrator's Review [NASA]
MAARA	Midlands Asthma and Allergy Research Association [British] (DBA)
MAARC	Magnetic Annular Arc (IEEE)
MA Arch	Master of Arts in Architecture
MAARM	Memory-Aided Antiradiation Missile (MCD)
MAARP	Medium Attack Advanced Readiness Program [Navy] (DOMA)
Ma'as.........	Ma'asroth (BJA)
MAAS.........	Manpower Allocation and Accounting Subsystem [Air Force] (AFM)
MAAS.........	Michigan Association of Ambulance Services (SRA)
MAAS.........	Muhammad Ali Amateur Sports
MAAS.........	Multiple Array Avionics Subsystem
MA-ASE......	Multiple Association Application Service Element [Telecommunications] (OSI)
MA(AsianStudies)... Master of Arts (Asian Studies)
MAASL........	Military Assistance Article and Service List (AFIT)
MAASLA	Movimiento Argentino Antiimperialista de Solidaridad Latinoamericana
Ma'asSh	Ma'aser Sheni (BJA)
MAAT.........	MAC [McDonnell Aircraft Corporation] Acquisition and Attack Trainer (MCD)
MAAT.........	Management of Advanced Automation Technology Center [Worcester Polytechnic Institute] [Research center] (RCD)
MAAT.........	Master of Arts in Applied Theology (PGP)
MAAT.........	Master of Arts in Art Therapy (GAGS)
MAAT.........	McCormick Affective Assessment Technique [Teacher evaluation test]
MAAT.........	Member of the Association of Accounting Technicians [British] (DCTA)
MAATAG......	Mission Area Analysis Test Advisory Group [Army]
MAATC.......	Mobile Antiaircraft Training Center
MAAU	Mexican-American Affairs Unit [Office of Education]
MAAW	Medium Antitank Assault Weapon
MAAWS	Middle Atlantic Association of Women Sailors
MAB..........	Macroaddress Bus
MAB..........	Magazine Advertising Bureau [of MPA]
MAB..........	Magnetic Amplifier Bridge
MAB..........	Mainly about Books [A publication]
MAB..........	Malfunction Analysis Branch [NASA]
MAB..........	Man and the Biosphere Program [UNESCO] [Paris, France]
MAB..........	Manganese Alkaline Battery
MAB..........	Manhay [Belgium] [Geomagnetic observatory code]
MAB..........	Manual d'Archeologie Biblique [A publication] (BJA)
MAB..........	Maraba [Brazil] [Airport symbol] (OAG)
MAB..........	Marine Air Base
MAB..........	Marine Amphibious Brigade
MAB..........	Master Acquisition Bus [Computer science] (MCD)
MAB..........	Master of Arts in Business (PGP)
MAB..........	Material Applications Board
MAB..........	Materials Advisory Board [Later, NMAB] [NAS-NRC]
MAB..........	Materials Applications Board (MCD)
MAB..........	Maximum Androgen Blockade [Oncology]
MAB..........	Mechanical Automation Breadboard (KSC)
MAB..........	Medical Advisory Board
MAB..........	Member, Advisory Board
MAB..........	Memorial Advisory Bureau [British] (CB)
MAB..........	Menswear Association of Britain (PDAA)
MAB..........	Methylaminoazobenzene [Organic chemistry]
MAB..........	Metropolitan Asylums Board [British]
MAB..........	Mid-America Bancorp [AMEX symbol] (SPSG)
MAB..........	Millardair Ltd. [Canada ICAO designator] (FAAC)
MAB..........	Missile Activation Building [NWA]
MAB..........	Missile Assembly Building (MCD)
MAB..........	Mission Analysis Branch [Manned Spacecraft Center]
MAB..........	Mobile Assault Bridge [Army]
MAb..........	Monoclonal Antibody [Immunochemistry]
MAB..........	Multibase Arithmetic Block (ADA)
MAB..........	Munitions Assignment Board [Anglo-American] [World War II]
MAB..........	Mutual Air Board [Canada World War II]
MAB..........	Nonclonal Antibody [Medicine] (STED)
MABA.........	Meta-Aminobenzoic Acid [Organic chemistry]
MABA..........	(Methylamino) Benzoic Acid [Organic chemistry]
MABAC	Member of the Association of Business and Administrative Computing [British] (DBQ)
MABAX	Merrill Lynch: Basic Value CL.A [Mutual fund ticker symbol] (SG)
MABB.........	Maximum Achievable Body Burden (PDAA)
MABCGT	Mutual Adjustment Bureau of Cloth and Garment Trades [Defunct] (EA)
MABDG	Marine Aircraft Base Defense Group
MABDW	Marine Air Base Defense Wing
MABE.........	Master of Agricultural Business and Economics (WGA)
MABE.........	Master of Arts in Business Education
MABE.........	Member of the Association of Business Executives (DCTA)
MABE.........	Mobile Assault Bridge Equipment (SAA)
MABF.........	Master of Agricultural Business and Finance
MABF.........	Mobile Assault Bridge/Ferry [Army] (RDA)
MABFEX......	Marine Amphibious Brigade Field Exercise (NVT)
MABI.........	Mother's Assessment of the Behavior of Her Infant (STED)

MABIM	Member, American Board of Internal Medicine (CMD)
MABL	Mass Addition Boundary Layer Program [*NASA*]
MABLE	Miniature Autonetics Baseline Equipment
MABLEX	Marine Amphibious Brigade Landing Exercise (NVT)
MABM	Master of Agribusiness Management (PGP)
MABM	Multilayer Absorbing Bottom Layer
MABNET	Global Network for Monitoring the Biosphere [*Marine science*] (MSC)
MABO	Marianas-Bonins Group
MABOP	Mustargen [*Nitrogen mustard*], Adriamycin, Bleomycin, Oncovin, Prednisone [*Vincristine*] [*Antineoplastic drug regimen*]
MABOPA	Malaysian Book Publishers' Association (EAIO)
MABP	Mean Arterial Blood Pressure [*Medicine*]
MABPD	Military Assistance Basic Planning Document (CINC)
MABR	Member, American Board of Radiologists (CMD)
MABRON	Marine Air Base Squadron
MABS	Maltese-American Benevolent Society (EA)
MABS	Marine Air Base Squadron
MABS	Maritime Application Bridge System (OA)
MABS	Master of Arts in Behavior Science (GAGS)
MABS	Master of Arts in Biblical Studies (PGP)
MABS	Methylmethacrylate-Acrylonitrile-Butadiene-Styrene (EDCT)
MABS	Mixed Air Battle Simulation
MABS	Moored Acoustic Buoy System [*Marine science*] (MSC)
MABU	Maschinengewehr-Eisenbeton-Unterstand [*Machine-Gun-Iron-Reinforced Concrete Emplacement*] [*German "pill box," battlefield redoubts World War I*]
MABUS	Multi-Access Broadcast Unit System (PDAA)
MABX	American Biogenetic Sciences, Inc. [*NASDAQ symbol*] (SAG)
MABXA	Amer Biogenetic Sciences'A' [*NASDAQ symbol*] (TTSB)
MAC	Chief Machine Accountant [*Later, DPC*] [*Navy rating*]
MAC	Macadam (ADA)
MAC	Macalester College, Weyerhaeuser Library, St. Paul, MN [*OCLC symbol*] (OCLC)
MAC	MacAndrew [*Alcoholism scale*]
Mac	Macassey's New Zealand Reports [*A publication*] (DLA)
MAC	Macau [*ANSI three-letter standard code*] (CNC)
Mac	Macbeth [*Shakespearean work*]
MAC	Maccabees [*Old Testament book*] [*Roman Catholic canon*] (ROG)
MAC	MacConkey [*Agar*] [*Microbiology*]
mac	Macedonian [*MARC language code Library of Congress*] (LCCP)
MAC	Macerare [*Macerate*] [*Pharmacy*]
MAC	Macerich Co. [*NYSE symbol*] (SAG)
MAC	Machine-Aided Cognition [*Computer project*] [*Massachusetts Institute of Technology*]
MAC	MacIntosh [*Blade*] (STED)
Mac	Macintosh [*Computer science*] (WDMC)
MAC	Mackerel [*Pimp*] [*Slang*] (DSUE)
MAC	Mackintosh (DSUE)
Mac	Maclean's [*A publication*] (BRI)
Mac	Macnaghten's English Chancery Reports [*A publication*] (DLA)
MAC	Macon, GA [*Location identifier FAA*] (FAAL)
MAC	Macro Authentication Code [*Computer science*]
MAC	Macrocytic Erythrocyte (STED)
MAC	Macule (STED)
MAC	Magistrates' Appeal Cases [*A publication*] (DLA)
MAC	Magnetic Attitude Control
MAC	Magnetic Automatic Calculator (DEN)
MAC	Main Display Console
MAC	Maintenance Advisory Committee [*NSIA*]
MAC	Maintenance Allocation Chart [*Military*]
MAC	Maintenance Analysis Center [*FAA*]
MAC	Maintenance and Construction [*Computer science*] (IAA)
MAC	Major Activity Center
MAC	Major Air Command [*Later, MAJCOM*]
MAC	Major Ambulatory Categories [*Patient classification system*] (DAVI)
MAC	Malignancy-Associated Changes [*Cancer*]
MAC	Malta Air Charter Co. Ltd. [*ICAO designator*] (FAAC)
MAC	Mammary Carcinoma [*Oncology*]
MAC	Management Advisory Committee [*Environmental Protection Agency*] (GFGA)
MAC	Man and Computer (DIT)
MAC	Mandatory Access Control [*Computer science*] (IGQR)
MAC	Maneuver Analysis and Command
MAC	Maneuver Area Command [*Army*]
MAC	Manpower Advisory Committee (OICC)
MAC	Marine Affairs Council [*Marine science*] (MSC)
MAC	Marine Amphibious Corps
MAC	Maritime Advisory Committee [*Terminated, 1968*]
MAC	Maritime Air Command [*Canada NATO*] (NATG)
MAC	Marker and Cell [*Computing technique*] [*NASA*]
MAC	Mark West Springs [*California*] [*Seismograph station code, US Geological Survey*] (SEIS)
MAC	Martial Arts Commission [*British*] (DI)
MAC	Mass Absorption Coefficient
MAC	Massive Algebraic Computation [*Programming language*] [*1958*] [*Computer science*] (CSR)
MAC	Master Acoustical Console [*Army*]
MAC	Master Control (MCD)
M Ac	Master of Accounting
M Ac	Master of Acupuncture (PGP)
MAC	Master of Arts in Communication (GAGS)
MAC	Master of Arts in Counseling (PGP)
MAC	Material Availability Commitment (AAG)
MAC	Materials Analysis Co.
MAC	Materials and Coatings (SSD)

MAC	Maximal Acid Concentration (STED)
MAC	Maximal Allowable Concentration (STED)
MAC	Maximal Allowable Cost (STED)
MAC	Maximum Acceptable Concentration (LDT)
MAC	Maximum Acid Concentration [*Clinical chemistry*]
MAC	Maximum Acquisition Cost (DB)
MAC	Maximum Admissible [*or Allowable*] Concentration
MAC	Maximum Allowable Concentration [*Toxicology*]
MAC	Maximum Allowable Cost [*Medicare, Medicaid*]
MAC	Maximum Atmospheric Concentration
MAC	Maximum Concentration of Organics (NAKS)
MAC	McDonnell Aircraft Co. [*Later, McDonnell Douglas Corp.*] (MCD)
MAC	McLeod Aerating Cardiac
MAC	McMaster University [*Hamilton, ON*] (DSUE)
MAC	Mean Aerodynamic Center
MAC	Mean Aerodynamic Chord
MAC	Measurement and Analysis Center [*Telecommunications*] (TEL)
MAC	Measurement and Control [*A publication*] (IAA)
MAC	Mechanical Advantage Changer
MAC	Mechanical Analog Computer (DEN)
MAC	Media Access Control [*Telecommunications*]
MAC	Media Action Coalition [*Defunct*] (EA)
MAC	Media Assistance Center (DNAB)
MAC	Medical Administrative Corps [*Army World War II*]
MAC	Medical Advisory Committee [*IATA*] (DS)
MAC	Medical Alert Center
MAC	Mediterranean Air Command [*Military*]
MAC	Medium Access Control [*Telecommunications*]
MAC	Membrane Affinity Chromatography
MAC	Membrane Applications Centre [*University of Bath*] [*British*] (CB)
MAC	Membrane Attack Complex [*Biochemistry*]
MAC	Memory Access Command [*Computer science*] (IAA)
MAC	Memory Access Controller
MAC	Memory-Address Counter [*Computer science*] (IAA)
MAC	Men after Christ Band [*R & B recording group*]
MAC	Merchant Aircraft Carrier [*A ship carrying a cargo of oil or grain and provided with a flight deck for the operation of antisubmarine aircraft*] [*British World War II*]
MAC	Message Act Concellation (DA)
MAC	Message Authentication Code
MAC	Message Authenticity Check [*Computer science*]
MAC	Metabolic and Analytical Chemistry
MAC	Metacarpal Ash per Centimeter
MAC	Metal Arc Cutting [*Welding*]
MAC	Methotrexate, Actinomycin D, Cyclophosphamide [*Antineoplastic drug regimen*]
MAC	Methyl Acetamido Cinnamate [*Organic chemistry*]
MAC	Methyl Allyl Chloride [*Organic chemistry*]
MAC	Michigan Apple Committee (EA)
MAC	Microcystic Adnexal Carcinoma [*Oncology*]
MAC	Microfilm Aperture Card
MAC	Microwave-Assisted Curing [*Chemical engineering*]
MAC	Midair Collision (IIA)
MAC	Mid-American Conference [*College football*]
MAC	Midarm Circumference
MAC	Middle Atlantic Conference, East Riverdale MD [*STAC*]
MAC	Midwest Archives Conference (EA)
MAC	Military Aid to the Community [*British military*] (DMA)
Mac	Military Aircraft Command [*Airline call sign*]
MAC	Military Airlift Command [*Formerly, Military Air Transport Service*]
MAC	Military/Allied Commission [*World War II*]
MAC	Military Armistice Commission (KSC)
MAC	Military Assistance Command (CINC)
MAC	Mine Advisory Committee [*NAS-NRC*] (MCD)
MAC	Mineralogical Association of Canada
MAC	Mini-Accommodation Center [*In MAC-1, a low-cost, plastic sleeping module promoted by Texas businessman Charles McLaren*]
MAC	Minimal Alveolar Concentration [*Anesthesiology*]
MAC	Minimal Auditory Capability Test [*Medicine*]
MAC	Minimum Alveolar Concentration [*Physiology*]
MAC	Mining Association of Canada
MAC	Missile Activation Circuit
MAC	Missile Advisory Committee [*Pacific Missile Range*] (MUGU)
MAC	Mission Assignment Code (NATG)
MAC	Mitomycin C, Adriamycin, Cyclophosphamide [*Antineoplastic drug regimen*]
MAC	Mitral Annular Calcification [*Cardiology*]
MAC	MIUW [*Mobile Inshore Undersea Warfare*] Attack Craft [*Navy symbol*]
MAC	Mixed Armistice Commission [*Arab-Israel borders*] (BJA)
MAC	Mobile Inshore Undersea Warfare Attack Craft [*Navy*] (MCD)
MAC	Model Airplane Club
MAC	Model Algorithmic Control [*Chemical engineering*] [*Computer science*]
MAC	Modern Arts Criticism [*A publication*]
MAC	Modern Authors Checklist [*Publication series*]
MAC	Modulator of Adenylate Cyclase (DB)
MAC	Monitor and Control [*Computer science*] (IAA)
MAC	Monitored Anesthesia Care [*Medicine*] (DAVI)
MAC	Monthly Availability Charge (BUR)
MAC	Months after Contract Award
MAC	Morning-After Call [*Sales*]
MAC	Mosaic Resources Ltd. [*Vancouver Stock Exchange symbol*]
MAC	Motion Analysis Camera
MAC	Motor Ambulance Convoy

MAC............	MOUT [*Military Operations on Urbanized Terrain*] Assault Course (INF)
MAC............	Moves, Adds and Changes [*Telecommunications*] (ITD)
MAC............	Movimiento Amplio Colombiano [*Broad-Based Movement of Colombia*] [*Political party*] (PPW)
MAC............	Movimiento Autentico Cristiano [*El Salvador*] [*Political party*] (EY)
MAC............	Movimiento de Autenticidad Colorada [*Paraguay*] [*Political party*] (EY)
MAC............	Mudiad Amdyffyn Cymru [*Welsh Defense Movement*]
MAC............	Multi-Access Computing (NITA)
MAC............	Multiaction Computer
MAC............	Multi-Analyzer Configuration (IAA)
MAC............	Multi-Application Computer (IAA)
MAC............	Multifunctional Automobile Communication System [*Automotive engineering*]
MAC............	Multiple Access Computer
MAC............	Multiple Access Control [*Computer science*] (DIT)
MAC............	Multiple Address Code
MAC............	Multiple Address Computer (IAA)
MAC............	Multiple Analogue Component [*Satellite Television*]
MAC............	Multiple Array Correlation (CAAL)
MAC............	Multiplexed Analog Component [*Satellite television*] [*British*]
MAC............	Multiplexed Analog Components [*Satellite television system*]
MAC............	Multiply and Accumulate [*Computer science*] (PCM)
MAC............	Multipurpose Arthritis Center [*Medical University of South Carolina*] [*Research center*]
MAC............	Municipal Assistance Corp. [*New York*] [*Also known as "Big Mac"*]
MAC............	Munitions Assignments Committee [*World War II*]
MAC............	Museum Association of the Caribbean (EAIO)
MAC............	Museums Association of Canada
MAC............	Musiciens Amateurs du Canada [*Canadian Amateur Musicians*] (EAIO)
MAC............	Mycobacterium Avium Complex
MAC............	Mycobacterium Avium-Intracellulare Complex [*Bacteriology*]
MAc............	Russell Memorial Library, Acuhnet, MA [*Library symbol*] [*Library of Congress*] (LCLS)
MACA.........	Mammoth Cave National Park
MACA.........	Management Assistance Corporation of America (AAGC)
MACA.........	Maritime Air Control Authority [*NATO*] (NATG)
MACA.........	Master of Arts in Communication Arts
MACA.........	Master of Arts in Computer Applications (GAGS)
MAcA.........	Master of the Acupuncture Association [*British*] (DBQ)
MAcA.........	Member of the Acupuncture Association [*British*]
MACA.........	Mental After Care Association [*British*] (EAIO)
MACA.........	Mexican-American Correctional Association (OICC)
MACA.........	Michigan Association of Children's Alliances (SRA)
MACA.........	Military Airlift Clearance Authority (AABC)
MACA.........	Mini-America's Cup Association (EA)
MAC(A).......	Munitions Assignments Committee (Air) [*World War II*]
MACABRE...	Material Ablation with Chemically Active Boundary Layers in Reentry [*NASA*]
MACADS.....	MAC Automated Deployment Reporting System [*Military*] (GFGA)
MACAF.......	Mediterranean Allied Coastal Air Forces
MACAL.......	Military Airlift Command Airlift Operations Report
Macalp Mon L...	Macalpin on Money Lenders [*A publication*] (DLA)
MACAM.......	Military Airlift Command Automated Management
Mac & G......	Macnaghten and Gordon's English Chancery Reports [*A publication*] (DLA)
Mac & H......	Cox, Macrae, and Hertslet's Reports, Crown Cases [*1847-58*] [*England*] [*A publication*] (DLA)
Mac & I......	Macrae and Hertslet's English Insolvency Cases [*1847-52*] [*A publication*] (DLA)
Mac & Rob...	Maclean and Robinson's Scotch Appeal Cases [*1839*] [*A publication*] (DLA)
MACAP.......	Major Appliance Consumer Action Panel (EA)
Mac A Pat Cas...	MacArthur's Patent Cases [*District of Columbia*] [*A publication*] (DLA)
MAC-API......	Mordechai Anielewicz Circle of Americans for Progressive Israel (EA)
MacAr.........	MacArthur's Patent Cases [*A publication*] (DLA)
MacAr.........	MacArthur's Reports [*8-10 District of Columbia*] [*A publication*] (DLA)
MacAr & M...	MacArthur and Mackey's District of Columbia Supreme Court Reports [*A publication*] (DLA)
MacAr & Mackey...	MacArthur and Mackey's District of Columbia Supreme Court Reports [*A publication*] (DLA)
MacAr Pat Cas...	MacArthur's Patent Cases [*District of Columbia*] [*A publication*] (DLA)
MACARS......	Microfilm Aperture Card Automated Retrieval System
MacArth.......	MacArthur's Patent Cases [*A publication*] (DLA)
MacArth.......	MacArthur's Reports [*8-10 District of Columbia*] [*A publication*] (DLA)
MacArth & M...	MacArthur and Mackey's District of Columbia Supreme Court Reports [*A publication*] (DLA)
MacArth & M (Dist Col)...	MacArthur and Mackey's District of Columbia Supreme Court Reports [*A publication*] (DLA)
MacArth Ct Mar...	MacArthur on Courts-Martial [*A publication*] (DLA)
MacArth Pat Cas...	MacArthur's Patent Cases [*United States*] [*A publication*] (DLA)
MacArthur...	MacArthur's Patent Cases [*A publication*] (DLA)
MacArthur...	MacArthur's Reports [*8-10 District of Columbia*] [*A publication*] (DLA)
MacArthur & M...	MacArthur and Mackey's District of Columbia Supreme Court Reports [*A publication*] (DLA)
MacArthur Pat Cas...	MacArthur's Patent Cases [*United States*] [*A publication*] (DLA)
Macas.........	Macassey's New Zealand Reports [*A publication*] (DLA)
MACAS........	Magnetic Capability and Safety System (NVT)
Macask Ex....	Macaskie on Executors, Etc. [*A publication*] (DLA)
MACAT........	Master of Arts in Counseling Psychology: Art Therapy (PGP)
MACAT........	Middle School Alternative Classrooms for the Academically Talented [*Education*]
MA(C)AT......	Motor Accidents (Compensation) Appeal Tribunal [*Northern Territory, Australia*]
Macaulay Hist Eng...	Macaulay's History of England [*A publication*] (DLA)
Macb...........	Macbeth [*Shakespearean work*] (BARN)
MACB.........	Martial Arts Control Board [*Victoria, Australia*]
MACB.........	Michigan Association of Community Bankers (TBD)
MACB.........	Missile Assembly Control Building
MACBAA.....	Maine/Anjou Cattle Breeders' Association of Australia
MACBANK...	Machining Data Bank [*PERA*] [*Software package*] (NCC)
MACBASIC...	Measurement and Control BASIC [*Programming language developed by Analog Devices*]
Macc...........	Maccabees [*Old Testament book*] [*Roman Catholic canon*]
MACC.........	MACC Private Equities [*NASDAQ symbol*] (TTSB)
MACC.........	MACC Private Equities, Inc. [*NASDAQ symbol*] (SAG)
MACC.........	Macro-Ovalocyte [*Biochemistry*] (DAVI)
MACC.........	Madison Academic Computing Center [*University of Wisconsin - Madison*] [*Information service or system Research center*]
MACC.........	Malaysian-American Chamber of Commerce [*Later, AAACC*]
M Acc	Master of Accountancy [*or Accounting*]
MAcc	Master of Accounting (GAGS)
MACC.........	Methotrexate, Adriamycin, Cyclophosphamide, CCNU [*Lomustine*] [*Antineoplastic drug regimen*]
MACC.........	Methotrexate, Adriamycin, Cytoxan, CCNU [*Lomustine*] [*Antineoplastic drug*] (CDI)
MACC.........	Micro Asynchronous Communications Controller (MHDI)
MACC.........	MidAmerican Communications Corp. [*Telecommunications service*] (TSSD)
MACC.........	Military Aid to Civil Community [*British*]
MACC.........	Military Assistant to the Civil Community
MACC.........	Mobility-Affect-Cooperation-Communication [*Psychiatry*]
MACC.........	Modified Air Control Center [*Air Force*] (DOMA)
MACC.........	Modular Alter and Compose Console [*Computer science*]
MACC.........	Multiple Applications Control Center (SSD)
MACC.........	Multiple Architecture Control Console (MCD)
MacCarthy...	MacCarthy's Irish Land Cases [*A publication*] (DLA)
Mac CC	MacGillivray's Copyright Cases [*1901-49*] [*A publication*] (DLA)
Macc Cas.....	Maccala's Breach of Promise Cases [*A publication*] (DLA)
Maccl.........	Maccala's Reports [*Modern Reports, Part X*] [*1710-25*] [*A publication*] (DLA)
Maccl Tr	Macclesfield's Trial (Impeachment) [*1725*] [*London*] [*A publication*] (DLA)
Mac CM	Macomb on Courts-Martial [*A publication*] (DLA)
M Acco	Master of Accounting
M-Accounts...	Merged Accounts (AAGC)
MACCS	Manufacturing and Cost Control System (IAA)
MACCS	Manufacturing Cost Collection System
MACCS	Marine Air Command and Control System (NVT)
M Accs	Master of Accounts
MACCS	Molecular Access System [*Computer program*]
MAccSc.......	Master in Accounting Science (DD)
M Acct	Master of Accountancy (PGP)
M Acct	Master of Accounting (PGP)
MACCT........	Master of Arts in Community College Teaching (GAGS)
MACCT........	Multiple Assembly Cooling Cask Test [*Nuclear energy*] (NRCH)
M ACCUR...	Misce Accuratissime [*Mix Thoroughly*] [*Pharmacy*]
M Accy	Master of Accountancy (PGP)
MACD	MacDermid, Inc. [*NASDAQ symbol*] (NQ)
MacD.........	MacDevitt's Irish Land Commissioner's Reports [*A publication*] (DLA)
MACDAC.....	Machine Communication with Digital Automatic Computer
MACDAC......	Man Communication and Display for an Automatic Computer (PDAA)
MACDAC......	McDonnell Douglas Corp. (KSC)
MACDACsys.	MACDAC system (NITA)
MACDATA...	Materials and Components Development and Testing Association [*Paisley College of Technology*] [*British*] (IRUK)
MACDC	Military Assistance Command Director of Construction
MacDermott Commission...	Commission on the Isle Of Man Constitution. Report [*1959*] [*A publication*] (DLA)
MacDev.......	MacDevitt's Irish Land Cases [*1882-84*] [*A publication*] (DLA)
Macd Jam	Macdougall's Jamaica Reports [*A publication*] (DLA)
MACDP	Metropolitan Atlanta Congenital Defects Program [*Georgia*] (DMAA)
MacDrmd....	MacDermid, Inc. [*Associated Press*] (SAG)
MACDS	Monitor and Control Display System (MCD)
MACE.........	Mace Security International [*NASDAQ symbol*] (SAG)
MACE.........	Mace Security Intl [*NASDAQ symbol*] (TTSB)
MACE.........	Machine-Aided Composition and Editing
MACE.........	Maintenance Analysis Checkout Equipment
MACE.........	Management Applications in a Computer Environment (IEEE)
MACE.........	Managing Company Expansion [*Manpower Services Commission*] [*British*]
MACE.........	Marginal Absolute Certainty Equivalent [*Statistics*]
MACE.........	Master Control Executive (IAA)
MACE.........	Master of Air Conditioning Education (NADA)
MACE.........	Master of Air Conditioning Engineering
MACE.........	Master of Arts in Christian Education (PGP)
MACE.........	Master of Arts in Civil Engineering
MACE.........	Master of Arts in Computer Education (PGP)
MACE.........	Mechanical Antenna Control Electronics (MCD)
MACE.........	Member of the Association of Conference Executives [*British*] (DBQ)
MACE.........	Methylchloroform Chloroacetophenone [*Riot-control gas*]
MACE.........	Metropolitan Architectural Consortium for Education (AIE)
MACE.........	Mid-America Commodity Exchange [*Chicago, IL*]
MACE.........	Military Air Cargo Export [*Subsystem*]
MACE.........	Military Airlift Capability Estimator

MACE........... Military Airlift Center, Europe (MCD)
MACE........... Minority Advisory Committee on Energy [*Terminated, 1982*] (EGAO)
Maced .... Macedonia
MACED .... Macedonian
MACEF........ Mastic Asphalt Council and Employers Federation [*British*] (DBA)
MAC Eng...... Master of Air Conditioning Engineering
MACER .... Macerare [*Macerate*] [*Pharmacy*]
Macerich ...... Macerich Co. [*Associated Press*] (SAG)
MaceSec....... Mace Security International [*Associated Press*] (SAG)
MacF .... MacFarlane's Scotch Jury Court Reports [*1838-39*] [*A publication*] (DLA)
MacF .... MacFarlane's Scotch Jury Trials [*A publication*] (DLA)
MACF.......... Mulitple Association Control Function [*Telecommunications*] (OSI)
MACFA......... Mid-Atlantic Collegiate Fencing Association (PSS)
MacFar .... MacFarlane's Scotch Jury Court Reports [*1838-39*] [*A publication*] (DLA)
MacFarl .... MacFarlane's Scotch Jury Trials [*A publication*] (DLA)
MacFarlane... MacFarlane's Scotch Jury Trials [*A publication*] (DLA)
Macf Cop ...... Macfie on Copyright [*A publication*] (DLA)
Macf Min ..... Macfarland's Digest of Mining Cases [*A publication*] (DLA)
MacF Pr....... MacFarlane's Practice of the Court of Sessions [*A publication*] (DLA)
MacFrug...... MacFrugals Bargains Close Outs [*Associated Press*] (SAG)
MACG .... MacGregor Sports & Fitness [*NASDAQ symbol*] (TTSB)
MACG .... MacGregor Sports & Fitness, Inc. [*NASDAQ symbol*] (SAG)
MacG .... MacGregor Sports & Fitness, Inc. [*Associated Press*] (SAG)
MACG .... Maneuver Analysis and Command Group
MACG .... Marine Air Control Group
MACG .... Marshaling Area Control Group [*Military*] (AABC)
MAC(G)........ Munitions Assignments Committee (Ground) [*World War II*]
MacG CC ..... MacGillivray's Copyright Cases [*1901-49*] [*A publication*] (DLA)
MacGillivray & Parkington... MacGillivray and Parkington's Insurance Law [*6th ed.*] [*1975*] [*A publication*] (DLA)
MacG S........ MacGregor Sports & Fitness, Inc. [*Associated Press*] (SAG)
MacG Sp....... MacGregor Sports & Fitness, Inc. [*Associated Press*] (SAG)
MACGW .... MacGregor Sports&Fitness Wrrt [*NASDAQ symbol*] (TTSB)
MACH .... Machabees [*Old Testament book*] [*Douay version*]
MACH .... Machine [*or Machinery*]
MACH .... Machinist (WDAA)
MACH .... Master of Arts in Church History (PGP)
MACH .... Measure of Achieving Tendency [*Test*] (TMMY)
MACH .... Military Air Command Hunter [*In MACH 3, a video game by Mylstar Electronics*]
MACH .... Modular Automated Container Handling [*Shipping*] (DS)
MACH .... Multilayer Actuator Head [*Epson America, Inc.*] [*Computer science*] (PCM)
MACHA .... Member, American College of Hospital Administration (CMD)
MACHA .... Michigan Automated Clearing House Association
Macha .... Michigan Automated Clearing House Association (TBD)
MACHA .... Mid-Atlantic Clearinghouse Association [*Maryland, Virginia, and Washington, DC*]
MACHA .... Midwest Automated Clearing House Association
MACHA .... Military Armistice Commission Headquarters Area (INF)
MACHALT .... Machinery Alteration
MACH D....... Machine Direction Paper (DGA)
MACHDC..... Machinability Data Center [*Computerized search services*] [*Metcut Research Associates, Inc.*]
Macheez...... Macheezmo Mouse Restaurants, Inc. [*Associated Press*] (SAG)
MA Chem...... Master of Applied Chemistry
MACHG....... Machining
MACHGR...... Machine Group
MACH III...... Maintenance Aided Computer-HAWK-[*Homing All The Way Killer*]-Intelligence/Institutional/Instructor [*Military*]
MA(ChildLit/Reading)... Master of Arts in Children's Literature and Reading
MACHO .... Machismo [*Spanish*] (DSUE)
MACHO .... Massive Compact Halo Object [*Astrophysics*]
MACHO........ Massive Compact Halo Objects [*Astronomy*]
Macho......... Movimiento Anticomunista Hondureno [*Honduran Anti-Communist Movement*] [*Political party*] (PD)
MACHR........ Machiner
MACH R....... Machine Ruling (DGA)
m-AChr........ Muscarinic Acetylcholine Receptor [*Biochemistry*]
MACHST ...... Machinist
MACHY .... Machinery
MACI.......... Member of the American Concrete Institute
MACI.......... Military Adaptation of Command [*or Commercial*] Items [*DoD*] (AABC)
MACI.......... Monitor, Access, and Control Interface (NASA)
MAC II .... Mica and Chessy [*Acronym is name of interior decorating firm and is taken from first names of owners Mica Ertegun and Chessy Rayner*]
MACII.......... Missouri Aptitude and Career Information Inventory [*Vocational guidance test*]
MACIMS ...... Military Airlift Command Integrated Management System
MACIS .... Management and Contracts Information Service
MACJC........ Mississippi Association of Community and Junior Colleges (PSS)
MACK.......... Mackenzie
MAC(K)........ Military Armistice Commission (Korea)
Mack & F Jud A... Mackeson and Forbes' Judicature Acts [*A publication*] (DLA)
Mack BL ...... Mackenzie on Bills of Lading [*A publication*] (DLA)
Mack CL ...... Mackeldey on Modern Civil Law [*A publication*] (DLA)
Mack Crim... Mackenzie's Treatise on Criminal Law [*4 eds.*] [*1678-1758 Scotland*] [*A publication*] (DLA)
Mack Cr L ... Mackenzie's Treatise on Criminal Law [*4th ed.*] [*1678-1758 Scotland*] [*A publication*] (DLA)
Mack Ct Sess... Mackay. Court of Session Practice [*A publication*] (ILCA)

Mackeld....... Mackeldey on Modern Civil Law [*A publication*] (DLA)
Mackeld....... Mackeldey on Roman Law [*A publication*] (DLA)
Mackeld Civil Law... Mackeldey on Modern Civil Law [*A publication*] (DLA)
Mackeld Rom Law... Mackeldey on Roman Law [*A publication*] (DLA)
Mackey....... Mackey's District of Columbia Reports [*12-20 District of Columbia*] [*A publication*] (DLA)
MackFn........ Mackenzie Financial Corp. [*Associated Press*] (SAG)
Mackie........ Mackie Designs, Inc. [*Associated Press*] (SAG)
Mack Inst..... Mackenzie's Institutes of the Law of Scotland [*9 eds.*] [*1684-1758*] [*A publication*] (DLA)
Mack Law of Prop... Mackay's Law of Property [*1882*] [*A publication*] (DLA)
Mack Nat..... Mackintosh's Law of Nature and Nations [*5th ed.*] [*1835*] [*A publication*] (DLA)
Mack Obs..... Mackenzie's Observations on Acts of Parliament [*1675, etc.*] [*Scotland*] [*A publication*] (DLA)
Mack Rom Law... Mackenzie's Studies in Roman Law [*A publication*] (DLA)
Macl .... Maclaren on Wills and Successions [*A publication*] (DLA)
Macl .... Maclaurin's Scotch Criminal Decisions [*A publication*] (DLA)
MACL.......... Master of Arts in Classroom Psychology (PGP)
MACL.......... Maximum Approximate Conditional Likelihood [*Statistics*]
MACL.......... Minimum Acceptable Compliance Level (IAA)
MACL.......... Mood Adjective Check List [*Psychometrics*]
Macl & R..... Maclean and Robinson's Scotch Appeal Cases [*9 English Reprint*] [*A publication*] (DLA)
Macl & Rob... Maclean and Robinson's Scotch Appeal Cases [*9 English Reprint*] [*A publication*] (DLA)
MAC layer ... Media Access Control Layer [*Computer science*] (IGQR)
Macl Bank ... Macleod's Theory and Practice of Banking [*A publication*] (DLA)
Maclean & R... Maclean and Robinson's Scotch Appeal Cases [*9 English Reprint*] [*A publication*] (DLA)
Maclean & R (Sc)... Maclean and Robinson's Scotch Appeal Cases [*9 English Reprint*] [*A publication*] (DLA)
maclib .... Macrolibrary (MHDI)
MAC LLC ..... Media Access Control Logical Link Control [*Computer science*]
Macl Rem Cas... Maclaurin's Remarkable Cases [*1670-1773*] [*Scotland*] [*A publication*] (DLA)
Macl Sh....... Maclachlan on Merchant Shipping [*A publication*] (DLA)
Macl Shipp... Maclachlan on Merchant Shipping [*A publication*] (DLA)
MACM........ Master Chief Machine Accountant [*Later, DPCM*] [*Navy rating*]
MACM........ Master of Arts in Christian Ministries (PGP)
MACM........ Master of Arts in Church Music (PGP)
MACM........ Military Aid to Civil Ministries [*British military*] (DMA)
MA/CM........ Milliamperes per Centimeter
MACM........ Motorized Air Cycle Machine (MCD)
MACMA....... Military and Aerospace Connector Manufacturers Association (EA)
MACMA....... Mutual Aid Centre Managing Agency [*British*] (CB)
MACMH....... Altona Community Memorial Health Centre, Manitoba [*Library symbol National Library of Canada*] (NLC)
MACMIS ..... Maintenance and Construction Management Information System [*Computer science*]
MACMIS ..... Major Army Command Management Information System
MACMO ..... Mobile Acquisition Career Management Office [*Army*]
MACMOL .... Macromolecular
MACMS...... Miniature Arms Collectors/Makers Society (EA)
Macn .... Macnaghten's Hindu Law Cases [*India*] [*A publication*] (DLA)
Macn .... Macnaghten's Nizamut Adalat Cases [*1805-50*] [*Bengal, India*] [*A publication*] (DLA)
Macn .... Macnaghten's Select Cases in Chancery Tempore King [*A publication*] (DLA)
Macn .... Macnaghten's Select Cases, Sadr Diwani Adalat [*1791-1858*] [*Bengal, India*] [*A publication*] (DLA)
MAC(N)....... Munitions Assignments Committee (Navy) [*World War II*]
Macn & G... Macnaghten and Gordon's English Chancery Reports
Macn & G (Eng)... Macnaghten and Gordon's English Chancery Reports [*A publication*] (DLA)
Macn CM ... Macnaghten on Courts-Martial [*A publication*] (DLA)
Macn Cr Ev... Macnaghten's Criminal Evidence [*A publication*] (DLA)
Macn El Hind L... Macnaghten's Elements of Hindu Law [*A publication*] (DLA)
Macn Ev ..... Macnally's Rules of Evidence on Pleas of the Crown [*A publication*] (DLA)
MACNIMAATZ... MacArthur, Nimitz, and Spaatz [*Nickname for World War II command structure of Douglas MacArthur, Chester W. Nimitz, and Carl A. Spaatz*]
Macn NA Beng... Macnaghten's Nizamut Adalat Reports [*Bengal, India*] [*A publication*] (DLA)
Macn Nul..... Macnamara's Nullities and Irregularities in Law [*1842*] [*A publication*] (DLA)
MacNSc....... [*The*] MacNeal-Schwendler Corp. [*Associated Press*] (SAG)
Macn SDA ... Macnaghten's Select Cases, Sadr Diwani Adalat [*1791-1858*] [*Bengal, India*] [*A publication*] (DLA)
Macn Sel Cas... Select Cases in Chancery Tempore King, Edited by Macnaghten [*1724-33*] [*A publication*] (DLA)
MACNYC...... Men's Apparel Club of New York City (EA)
Mac NZ .... Macassey's New Zealand Reports [*A publication*] (DLA)
MACO .... Major Assembly Checkout [*NASA*] (NASA)
MAC(O)....... Management Analysis Course (Class O) [*Navy*] (DNAB)
MACO .... Marshaling Area Control Officer [*Military*] (AABC)
MACO .... Master of Arts in Counseling (PGP)
MACOI .... MACV [*Military Assistance Command, Vietnam*] Office of Information (VNW)
MACOM ...... Maintenance Assembly and Check-Out Model (PDAA)
MACOM ...... Major Army Command (AABC)
M Ac OM .... Master of Arts in Acupuncture and Oriental Medicine (PGP)
Macomb CM... Macomb on Courts-Martial [*A publication*] (DLA)

MA Comm ... Master of Arts in Communication (PGP)
MACOMTELNET... Military Airlift Command Teletype Network (SAA)
MACON .... Maintenance Console (MCD)
MACON .... Matrix Connector Punched Card Programmer [*Computer science*] (IEEE)
MACONS ...... Mid-Atlantic Continental Shelf
MACOP .... Methotrexate, Ara-C, Cyclophosphamide, Oncovin [*Vincristine*], Prednisone [*Antineoplastic drug regimen*]
MACOPS ...... Military Airlift Command Operational Phone System (AFM)
MACOPT ...... Machining Optimisation [*PERA*] [*Software package*] (NCC)
Mac OS .... Macintosh Operating System [*Computer science*] (CDE)
MACOS .... Man - A Course of Study [*Title of social-studies course*] [*National Science Foundation*]
MACOS .... Military Airlift Command Combat Operations Staff
MACOV .... Mechanized and Army Combat Operations Vietnam (AABC)
MACP .... Macro Control Processor [*Computer science*] (IAA)
macp .... Macroprocessor (MHDB)
MACP .... Master of Arts in Community Psychology (PGP)
MACP .... Master of Arts in Counseling Psychology (PGP)
MACP .... Michigan Association of Cherry Producers (EA)
MACP .... Michigan Association of Chiefs of Police (SRA)
MACP .... Military Aid to the Civil Power [*British military*] (DMA)
MACP .... Mission Analysis Computer Program
MACP .... Mortuary Affairs Collection Point [*Army*] (INF)
MACPA .... Maryland Association of Certified Public Accountants (SRA)
MACPA .... Michigan Association of Certified Public Accountants (SRA)
MACPA .... Mid America Crop Protection Association (SRA)
MAC-PAC .... Manufacturing, Planning, and Control [*Arthur Anderson & Co.*] [*Software package*] (NCC)
Mac-Paps .... Mackenzie-Papineau Battalion [*Canada*]
Mac Pat Cas... Macrory's Patent Cases [*England*] [*A publication*] (DLA)
Mac PC .... Macrory's Patent Cases [*England*] [*A publication*] (DLA)
Macph .... Macpherson, Lee, and Bell's Scotch Session Cases [*A publication*] (DLA)
Macph .... Macpherson's Scotch Court of Session Cases [*1862-73*] [*A publication*] (DLA)
Macph Inf .... Macpherson on Infancy [*A publication*] (DLA)
Macph Jud Com... Macpherson's Practice of the Judicial Committee of the Privy Council [*A publication*] (DLA)
Macph L & B... Macpherson, Lee, and Bell [*Scotland*] [*A publication*] (DLA)
Macph Pr C... Macpherson's Practice of the Judicial Committee of the Privy Council [*2nd ed.*] [*1873*] [*A publication*] (DLA)
Macph Priv Counc... Macpherson's Privy Council Practice [*A publication*] (DLA)
Macq .... Macqueen's Scotch Appeal Cases, House of Lords [*A publication*] (DLA)
Macq D .... Macqueen's Debates on Life-Peerage Questions [*A publication*] (DLA)
Macq Div ..... Macqueen's Marriage, Divorce, and Legitmacy [*2nd ed.*] [*1860*] [*A publication*] (DLA)
Macq H & W... Macqueen's Rights and Liabilities of Husband and Wife [*4th ed.*] [*1905*] [*A publication*] (DLA)
Macq HL Cas... Macqueen's Scotch Appeal Cases, House of Lords [*A publication*] (DLA)
Macq Mar .... Macqueen's Marriage, Divorce, and Legitmacy [*2nd ed.*] [*1860*] [*A publication*] (DLA)
Macq Sc App Cas... Macqueen's Scotch Appeal Cases, House of Lords [*A publication*] (DLA)
Mac R .... Macdougall's Jamaica Reports [*A publication*] (DLA)
Mac R .... Maclean and Robinson's Scotch Appeal Cases [*1839*] [*A publication*] (DLA)
Macr .... Macrobii [*of Lucian*] [*Classical studies*] (OCD)
Macr .... MacroChem Corp. [*Associated Press*] (SAG)
MACR .... Macrocytosis [*Hematology*] (DAVI)
MACR .... Macromedia, Inc. [*NASDAQ symbol*] (SAG)
Macr .... Macrory's Patent Cases [*England*] [*A publication*] (DLA)
MACR .... Mean Axillary Count Rate [*Medicine*] (DMAA)
MACR .... Member of the American College of Radiology
MACR .... Methacrolein [*Also, MAL*] [*Organic chemistry*]
MACR .... Minneapolis, Anoka & Cuyuna Range Railroad Co. [*AAR code*]
MACR .... Missing Air Crew Report
MACR .... Multiply, Accumulate, and Round
Macr & H .... Macrae and Hertslet's English Insolvency Cases [*1847-52*] [*A publication*] (DLA)
Macrch .... MacroChem Corp. [*Associated Press*] (SAG)
MACRI .... Mercantile Atlantic Coastal Routing Instructions
MACrimStudies... Master of Arts in Criminological Studies
MACRIT .... Manpower Authorization Criteria [*Army*]
Macrmd .... Macromedia, Inc. [*Associated Press*] (SAG)
MACRO .... Macroassembler (MHDI)
MACRO .... Macrocytosis [*Hematology*] (DAVI)
MACRO .... Macroinstruction (ECII)
MACRO .... Macroprocessor (MHDI)
MACRO .... Massachusetts Association of Community Rehabilitation Organizations (SRA)
MACRO .... Merge and Correlate Recorded Output [*Computer science*] (NASA)
MACRO .... Monopole, Astrophysics and Cosmic Ray Observatory [*Italy*]
Macrob .... Macrobius [*Late fourth and early fifth century AD*] [*Classical studies*] (OCD)
MACROCAL... [*Enhanced*] Macro Version of Common Assembler Language [*Interdata*] (NITA)
MacroCh ...... MacroChem Corp. [*Associated Press*] (SAG)
MACROL ...... Macro-Based Display Oriented Language [*Raytheon Co.*]
Macr Pat Cas... Macrory's Patent Cases [*England*] [*A publication*] (DLA)
Macr P Cas... Macrory's Patent Cases [*England*] [*A publication*] (DLA)
MACRS .... Modified Accelerated Cost Recovery System [*IRS*]

MacS .... MacSweeney on Mines, Quarries, and Minerals [*5 eds.*] [*1884-1922*] [*A publication*] (DLA)
MACS .... Mainline Automated Clearance System [*Interstate trucking*] [*Highway safety*]
MACS .... Management Administration Control System
MACS .... Management & Computer Services, Inc. [*Information service or system*] (IID)
MACS .... Manned Air Combat Simulation (MCD)
MACS .... Marine Air Control Squadron
MACS .... Mass and Charge Spectroscopy
MACS .... Mastoid Air Cell System [*Anatomy*]
MACS .... Maximum Aortic Cusp Separation [*Medicine*] (DMAA)
MACS .... McDonnell Automatic Checkout System [*McDonnell Douglas Corp.*]
MACS .... Media Account Control System (PDAA)
MACS .... Medium-Altitude Communications Satellite
MACS .... Member of the American Chemical Society
MACS .... Merchant Airship Cargo Satellite (PDAA)
MACS .... Metering and Accounting System (NITA)
MACS .... Michigan Association of Christian Schools (SRA)
MACS .... Michigan Association of Convenience Stores (SRA)
MACS .... Micro Anophthalmic Children's Society (WDAA)
MACS .... Microwave Attitude Control Sensor
MACS .... Migrant Advisory Committee
MACS .... Military Aeronautical Communications Service
MACS .... Military Airlift Command Service (NATG)
MACS .... Missile Air-Conditioning System
MACS .... Mississippi Association of Convenience Stores (SRA)
MACS .... Mobile Acoustic Communications System
MACS .... Mobile Air Conditioning Society (EA)
MACS .... Monitoring and Control Station
MACS .... Multi-Access Computer Switch [*Telecommunications*] (TSSD)
MACS .... Multicenter AIDS [*Acquired Immune Deficiency Syndrome*] Cohort Study [*National Institutes of Health*]
MACS .... Multiline Automatic Calling System (HGAA)
MACS .... Multiple Access Communications System [*West German and Dutch*]
MACS .... Multiple Application Connector System
MACS .... Multiple-Technique Analytical Computer System
MACS .... Multiproject Automated Control System
MACS .... Multipurpose Acquisition and Control System (IAA)
MACS .... Multipurpose Arcade Combat Simulator [*Marksmanship training*] [*Army*] (INF)
MACS .... Senior Chief Machine Accountant [*Later, DPCS*] [*Navy rating*]
MACSAT ...... Multiple Access Commercial Satellite (DOMA)
MACSAT ...... Multiple Access Communications Satellite (MED)
MACSCO ...... Metropolitan Academic Consultants Sales Corp.
MACSEA ...... Military Assistance Command, Southeast Asia
MACSIS .... Multi-Agency Community Services Information System
MAC/SM ...... Maintenance Allocation Chart and System Maintenance (MCD)
MACSOG ...... Military Assistance Command Studies and Observation Group (CINC)
MACSQ .... Marine Air Control Squadron
MACSRRPCC... Maxwellian Averaged Cross Section Reactor Physics Computer Code [*Electronics*] (IAA)
MACSS .... Master of Arts in Church Social Services (PGP)
MACSS .... Medium-Altitude Communications Satellite System
MACSV .... Multipurpose Airmobile Combat-Support Vehicle (SAA)
MACSYM ..... Measurement and Control System (MHDB)
MACSYMA ... MAC [*Massive Algebraic Computation*] Symbolic Manipulator [*Programming language*] [*1969*] (CSR)
MACT .... Master of Arts in College Teaching
MACT .... Maximum Achievable [*or Available*] Control Technology [*Environmental chemistry*]
MACT .... Military Assistance Command, Thailand (VNW)
MACT .... Moral Action Choice Test (EDAC)
MACTAR ...... McMaster-Toronto Arthritis and Rehumatism [*Questionnaire*] [*Medicine*] (DMAA)
MACTEC ...... MAC Technical Services Co. (GAAI)
MACTELNET... Military Airlift Command Teletype Network (AFM)
MacTEP .... Mac [*Apple's Mackintosh computer*] Terminal Emulation Program
MACTM .... Master of Applied Communication Theory and Methodology (PGP)
MACTRAC .... Military Airlift Command Traffic Reporting and Control System
MACTU .... Mines and Countermeasures Technical Unit [*Navy*]
MACU .... Monitor and Control Unit [*Aerospace*] (IAA)
MACUL .... Michigan Association for Computer Users in Learning (EDAC)
MACV .... Military Assistance Command, Vietnam
MACV .... Multipurpose Airmobile Combat-Support Vehicle
MACVD .... Microwave-Assisted Chemical Vapor Deposition [*Coating technology*]
MACVNAG .... Military Assistance Command, Vietnam Naval Advisory Group (VNW)
MACVSOG .... Military Assistance Command Vietnam Special Operations Group (INF)
MACV-SOG ... Military Assistance Command, Vietnam Studies and Observations Group (VNW)
MACW .... Midwest Athletic Conference for Women (PSS)
MACW .... Missionary Association of Catholic Women [*Defunct*] (EA)
M Acy .... Master of Accountancy (PGP)
MACY .... Master of Arts in Accountancy (PGP)
Mad .... All India Reporter, Madras [*A publication*] (DLA)
Mad .... Indian Law Reports, Madras Series [*A publication*] (DLA)
Mad .... Indian Rulings, Madras Series [*A publication*] (DLA)
MAD .... Machine Analysis Display
MAD .... Machine ANSI Data
Mad .... Madagascar
MAD .... Madam
MAD .... Madang [*Papua New Guinea*] [*Seismograph station code, US Geological Survey*] (SEIS)

Mad	Maddock's English Chancery Reports [*56 English Reprint*] [*1815-22*] [*A publication*] (DLA)
Mad	Maddock's Reports [*9-18 Montana*] [*A publication*] (DLA)
MAD	Madeco SA [*NYSE symbol*] (SPSG)
MAD	Madeco S.A. ADS [*NYSE symbol*] (TTSB)
MAD	Madison [*Diocesan abbreviation*] [*Wisconsin*] (TOCD)
MAD	Madison, CT [*Location identifier FAA*] (FAAL)
Mad	Madras High Court Reports [*India*] [*A publication*] (DLA)
MAD	Madrid [*Spain*] [*Airport symbol*] (OAG)
MAD	Magnetic Airborne Detector [*Navy*]
MAD	Magnetic Anomaly Detection [*or Detector*]
MAD	Magnetic Azimuth Detector (MCD)
MAD	Main Assembly Drawing
MAD	Maintenance Alert Directive [*Aviation*]
MAD	Maintenance Analysis Data [*or Diagram*] (MCD)
MAD	Maintenance, Assembly, and Disassembly
MAD	Major Affective Disorder [*Medicine*] (DMAA)
MAD	Major Air Disaster (PDAA)
MAD	Management Analysis Division [*NASA*] (MCD)
MAD	Mandibulo-Acral Dysplasia [*Medicine*] (DMAA)
MAD	Manhunter Assignment Device [*Computer science*]
MAD	Manufacturing Assembly Drawing
MAD	Maple Air Services Ltd. [*Canada ICAO designator*] (FAAC)
MAD	Marine Air [*or Aviation*] Detachment
MAD	Marine Air Detection (AFIT)
MAD	Mass Analyzer Detector
MAD	Master Accession Document [*Computer science*] (BUR)
MAD	Master Air Data [*Computer*]
M Ad	Master of Administration (PGP)
MAd	Master of Arts Administration (GAGS)
MAD	Material Analysis Data
MAD	Material Assistance Designated [*Report*] (MCD)
MAD	Material Availability Date (CET)
MAD	Materials for the Assyrian Dictionary (BJA)
MAD	Materiel Acquisition and Delivery [*Military*]
MAD	Mathematical Analysis of Downtime (DNAB)
MAD	Maximum Acceptable Deviation
MAD	Maximum Acid Output [*Biochemistry*] (DAVI)
MAD	Maximum Allowable Dose [*Medicine*] (DB)
MAD	Maximum Applicable Dose [*Environmental chemistry*]
MAD	Mean Absolute Deviation [*Statistics*]
MAD	MeCCNU [*Semustine*], Adriamycin [*Antineoplastic drug regimen*]
MAD	Media Access Device [*Telecommunications*]
MAD	Median Absolute Deviation [*Statistics*]
MAD	Memory Access Director [*Computer science*] (IAA)
MAD	Methylacridone [*Organic chemistry*]
MAD	Methylandrostenediol [*Methandriol*] [*Endocrinology*]
MAD	Michigan Algorithmic Decoder [*IBM Corp.*] [*University of Michigan Programming language 1961*]
MAD	Mileage Accumulation Dynamometer
MAD	Militarischer Abschirmdienst [*Military counterintelligence*] [*Germany*]
MAD	Military Air Distress (LAIN)
MAD	Mind-Altering Drug
MAD	Mine Assembly Depot [*Navy*]
MAD	Mini-Attack Drone
MAD	Minimal Aural Dose
MAD	Minimum Absolute Deviation [*Statistics*]
MAD	Minimum Approach Distance (SAA)
MAD	Minimum Average Dose [*Medicine*] (DMAA)
MAD	Missile Assembly Data
MAD	Mission Analysis Division [*NASA*] (KSC)
MAD	Mission Area Deficiency [*Army*]
MAD	Mitotic Arrest-Deficient [*Cytology*]
MAD	Mixed Analog and Digital [*Telecommunications*] (TEL)
MAD	Model A Drivers (EA)
MAD	More After Dark [*Screen-saver computer program from Berkeley Systems*] (PCM)
MAD	Morse Automatic Decoder (IAA)
MAD	Mortar Air Delivery System [*Military*] (VNW)
MAD	Mosquito Abatement District (DICI)
MAD	Motor Assembly and Disassembly
MAD	Motorsport Advanced Display [*Auto racing*]
MAD	Multiple Access Device
MAD	Multiple Access Drive (NITA)
MAD	Multiple-Aperture Device (MUGU)
MAD	Multiple Audio Distribution [*Communications*]
MAD	Multiple-Wavelength Anomalous Dispersion [*Crystallography*]
MAD	Multiply and Add
MAD	Multiwavelength Anomalous Diffraction [*Physics*]
mAD	Muscle Adenylate Deaminase (DB)
MAD	Music and Dance [*American Dance Festival project*]
MAD	Mutual Ability for Defense [*Pentagon defense policy*]
MAD	Mutual Assured Destruction [*Nuclear warfare*]
MAD	Myoadenylate Deaminase [*An enzyme*]
MADA	Multiple Access Demand Assignment (MCD)
MADA	Multiple Access - Discrete Address [*Navy tactical voice communication*]
MADA	Muscle Adenylate Deaminase (STED)
MADAEC	Military Application Division of the Atomic Energy Commission
MADAG	Madagascar (ROG)
Madag	Madagascar [*Malagasy Republic*] (VRA)
Madag	Malagasy Republic (VRA)
MADAIR	Magnetic Anomaly Detection and Identification Ranging (MCD)
MADALINE	Multi-Adaptive Linear Neuron (PDAA)
MADAM	Maintenance Diagnostic Assistance Module [*Military*] (CAAL)
MADAM	Manchester Automatic Digital Machine [*Manchester University*] [*British*] (DEN)
MADAM	Marine Air-Droppable Area Marker (MCD)
MADAM	Moderately Advanced Data Management [*Computer science*]
MADAM	Multipurpose Automatic Data Analysis Machine
Mad & B	Maddox and Bach's Reports [*19 Montana*] [*A publication*] (DLA)
Mad & Gel	Maddock and Geldart's English Chancery Reports [*A publication*] (DLA)
MADAP	Maastricht Automatic Data Processing and Display System [*Air traffic control*]
MADAR	Malfunction Analysis, Detection, and Recording [*Computer science*]
MADAR	Malfunction and Data Recorder [*Computer science*] (IAA)
MADARS	Maintenance Analysis, Detection, and Reporting System [*Computer science*] (AFM)
MADARS	Malfunction Analysis, Detection, and Recording Subsystem [*Computer science*]
MADARTS	Malfunction Detection Analysis, Recording, and Training System
MADB	Madison Bancshares Group [*NASDAQ symbol*] (TTSB)
Mad Bar	Madox's Barona Anglia [*A publication*] (DLA)
MADC	Machine-Assisted Detection and Classification (NVT)
MADC	Milliampere Direct Current [*Electronics*] (IAA)
MADC	Multiplexer Analog-to-Digital Converter (MCD)
MADCAP	Mammoth Decimal Arithmetic Program [*NASA*] (KSC)
MADCAP	Mobilization and Deployment Capability Assurance Concept [*Military*]
MADCAP	Model of Advection, Diffusion, and Chemistry for Air Pollution [*Environmental Protection Agency*] (GFGA)
MADCAR	Management Data Charting and Review (IAA)
Mad Ch Pr	Maddock's English Chancery Practice [*3rd ed.*] [*1837*] [*A publication*] (DLA)
MADCK	Marine Aide-de-Camp to the King [*British Admiralty*]
Mad Co	Madras Code [*India*] [*A publication*] (DLA)
MAD/CO	Mid-America Dance Company [*St. Louis, MO*]
Madd	Maddock's English Chancery Reports [*A publication*] (DLA)
Madd	Maddox's Reports [*9-18 Montana*] [*A publication*] (DLA)
MADD	Module for Automatic Dock and Detumble [*Orbital rescue*] [*NASA*]
MADD	Mothers Against Drunk Driving (EA)
MADD	Multichannel Analog-to-Digital Data Decoder (IAA)
MADD	Multiple Acyl-CoA Dehydrogenation Deficiency (STED)
MADDAM	Macromodule and Digital Differential Analyzer Machine [*Computer science*]
MADDAM	Multiplexed Analog to Digital, Digital to Analog Multiplexed [*Computer science*]
Madd & B	Maddox and Bach's Reports [*19 Montana*] [*A publication*] (DLA)
Madd & G	Maddock and Geldart's English Chancery Reports [*A publication*] (DLA)
Madd & Gel	Maddock and Geldart's English Chancery Reports [*A publication*] (DLA)
Madd Ch	Maddock's English Chancery Reports [*56 English Reprint*] [*1815-22*] [*A publication*] (DLA)
Madd Ch (Eng)	Maddock's English Chancery Reports [*56 English Reprint*] [*A publication*] (DLA)
Madd Ch Pr	Maddock's English Chancery Practice [*A publication*] (DLA)
MADDDC	Manufacturers of Aerial Devices and Digger-Derricks Council (EA)
Madden	Madden Steven Ltd. [*Associated Press*] (SAG)
MADDIDA	Magnetic Drum Digital Differential Analyzer
MADDWU	Mechanics' Assistants' and Dry Dock Workers' Union [*British*]
MADE	Magnetic Device Evaluator [*Computer science*]
MADE	Manufacturing and Automated Design Engineering
MADE	Master of Agricultural Development Economics
MADE	Microalloy Diffused Electrode
MADE	Minimum Airborne Digital Equipment
MADE	Multichannel Analog-to-Digital Data Encoder
Madeco	Madeco SA [*Associated Press*] (SAG)
M Ad Ed	Master of Adult Education (PGP)
MAdEd	Master of Arts in Adult Education (GAGS)
Ma de Ma	Matheus de Mathesillanis [*Flourished, 1381-1402*] [*Authority cited in pre-1607 legal work*] (DSA)
Ma de Math	Matheus de Mathesillanis [*Flourished, 1381-1402*] [*Authority cited in pre-1607 legal work*] (DSA)
MADEP	Massachusetts Department of Environmental Protection
MADEPSQ	Marine Air Depot Squadron
MADER	Management of Atmospheric Data for Evaluation and Research [*Marine science*] (OSRA)
MADERI	Mexican-American Documentation and Educational Research Institute
MaderSin	Maderas y Sinteticos Sociedad Anonima [*Associated Press*] (SAG)
MADEX	Magnetic Anomaly Detection Exercise (NVT)
Mad Exch	Madox's History of the Exchequer [*A publication*] (DLA)
MADF	Maintenance Action Data Form [*Military*] (CAAL)
Mad Fir Burg	Madox's Firma Burgi [*A publication*] (DLA)
Mad Form	Madox's Formulare Anglicanum [*A publication*] (DLA)
Mad Form Angl	Madox's Formulare Anglicanum [*A publication*] (DLA)
MADG	Madge NV [*NASDAQ symbol*] (SAG)
Madge	Madge NV [*Associated Press*] (SAG)
MadGE	Madison Gas & Electric Co. [*Associated Press*] (SAG)
MADGE	Microwave Aircraft Digital Guidance Equipment [*Helicopters*]
MadgeNt	Madge NV [*Associated Press*] (SAG)
MADGF	Madge Networks N.V. [*NASDAQ symbol*] (TTSB)
MADH	Master of Applied Development and Health (PGP)
MADH	Methylamine Dehydrogenase [*An enzyme*]
Mad HC	Madras High Court Reports [*India*] [*A publication*] (DLA)
Mad Hist Exch	Madox's History of the Exchequer [*A publication*] (DLA)
Madh Pra	All India Reporter, Madhya Pradesh [*A publication*] (DLA)
MADI	Madison Group Assoc [*NASDAQ symbol*] (TTSB)
MADI	Master Data Index

MADICA.......	Massachusetts Acoustical Drywall-Interior Contractors Association (SRA)
MADIS	Burda-MarketingInfoSystem [*Burda GmbH, Marketing Service Department*] [*Information service or system*] (IID)
MADIS	Manual Aircraft Data Input System (MCD)
MADIS	Manual Aircraft Display Information System [*Military*] (CAAL)
MADIS	Millivolt Analog-Digital Instrumentation System
Mad Isls	Madeira Islands
MADIZ	Military Air Defense Identification Zone (MCD)
M/ADJ........	Manual Adjusting [*Automotive engineering*]
Mad Jur......	Madras Jurist [*India*] [*A publication*] (DLA)
MADL........	Microwave Acoustic Delay Line
Mad Law Rep...	Madras Law Reporter [*India*] [*A publication*] (DLA)
MADLR........	Major Assembly Direct Labor Reporting (MCD)
Mad L Rep....	Madras Law Reporter [*India*] [*A publication*] (DLA)
Mad LT........	Madras Law Times [*India*] [*A publication*] (DLA)
Mad LW........	Madras Law Weekly [*India*] [*A publication*] (DLA)
MADM........	Maintenance Automated Data Management
MADM........	Manchester Automatic Digital Machine [*Manchester University*] [*British*]
M Adm........	Master of Administration
MADM........	Medium Atomic Demolition Munition [*Military*] (AABC)
MADMAN.....	Magnetic Anomaly Detector Contact Man (NVT)
MADMAN.....	Master Activity Data Management (DNAB)
M Adm E.....	Master of Administrative Engineering
MAdmin.......	Master of Administration
M Admin......	Master of Administrative Studies
M Adm J.....	Master in Administration of Justice (PGP)
M Adm Mgt...	Master of Administration Management (PGP)
Madn..........	Madden Steven Ltd. [*Associated Press*] (SAG)
MADN........	Metropolitan Area Digital Network (NTCM)
MAD-N........	Mid-America Dance Network [*Kansas City, MO*]
MADN........	Mid-American Dance Network
MADO........	Mulliken Approximation for Differential Overlap [*Physics*]
MADOC........	Medical Analysis of Days of Care [*Report*]
MADOM.......	Magnetic Acoustic Detection of Mines (DOMA)
Madox........	Madox's Formulare Anglicanum [*A publication*] (DLA)
Madox........	Madox's History of the Exchequer [*A publication*] (DLA)
MADP..........	Main Air Display Plot
MADP..........	Major Acquisition Decision Point [*Military*] (MCD)
MADP..........	Material Acquisition Decision Process [*Military*] (MCD)
MADP..........	Mission Area Development Plan [*DoD*]
MADPA........	Medicaid Antidiscriminatory Drug Pricing [*and Patient Benefit Restoration*]Act
MADPAC.......	Materiel Deterioration Prevention and Control [*Program*] [*Army*] (RDA)
Mad Papers...	James Madison's Papers [*A publication*] (DLA)
MADR..........	Madras [*India*] (ROG)
MADR..........	Madritum [*Madrid*] [*Imprint*] [*Latin*] (ROG)
MADR..........	Master of Arts in Dispute Resolution (PGP)
MADR..........	Materiel Acquisition Decision Review [*Army*]
MADR..........	Microprogram Address Register
MAD-R........	Multiapertured Device-Resistance (DNAB)
MA(Drama)...	Master of Arts (Drama)
Madras LJ...	Madras Law Journal and Reports [*India*] [*A publication*] (DLA)
MADRE........	Magnetic Drum RADAR Equipment
MADRE........	Magnetic Drum Receiving Equipment
MADRE........	Manufacturing Data Retrieval System (NASA)
MADRE........	Martin Automatic Data-Reduction Equipment
MADREC.......	Malfunction Detection and Recording [*Checkout system for aircraft*] [*Air Force*]
Mad Reg......	Madden on Registration of Deeds [*A publication*] (DLA)
MADRS........	Montgomery-Asberg Depression Rating Scale (STED)
MADS	Machine-Aided Drafting System (IEEE)
MADS	Maintenance and Diagnosis System [*Military*] (CAAL)
MADS	Mars Atmosphere Density Sensor
MADS	Meteorological Airborne Data System
MADS	Missile Attitude Determination System [*LASER device*] [*Air Force*]
MADS	Mission Area Deficiency Statement [*Army*] (RDA)
MADS	Mobile Airborne Defense Station Concept [*Air Force*]
MADS	Mobile Air Defense System
MADS	Modular Air Defense System (MCD)
MADS	Modular Army Demonstration System (MCD)
MADS	Modular Auxiliary Data System
MADS	Modular Auxiliary Data Systems (NASA)
MADS	Multiple Access Digital System [*Computer science*] (IAA)
MadsBn	Madison Bancshares Group [*Associated Press*] (SAG)
Mad SDAR.,.	Madras Sadr Diwani Adalat Reports [*India*] [*A publication*] (DLA)
Mad Sel Dec...	Madras Select Decrees [*A publication*] (DLA)
Mad Ser	Indian Law Reports, Madras Series [*A publication*] (DLA)
MAD-SMS....	Movement for Autonomous Democracy-Society for Moravia and Silesia [*Former Czechoslovakia*] [*Political party*] (EY)
MADSPM.....	Mobilization Against the Draft and Student Peace Mobilization [*An association*] (EA)
MADT...........	Mean Administrative Delay Time
MADT..........	Micro-Alloy Diffused Base Transistor (NITA)
MADT..........	Microalloy Diffused Transistor (MUGU)
MADU..........	Methylaminodeoxyuridine [*Pharmacology*]
M Ad VE	Master of Administration in Vocational Education (PGP)
MADVEC.......	Magnetic Anomaly Detector Vectoring [*Military*] (CAAL)
MADW........	Military Air Defense Warning Network
Mad WN	Madras Weekly Notes [*A publication*] (DLA)
MADWN.......	Military Air Defense Warning Network (IAA)
Mad WNCC...	Madras Weekly Notes, Criminal Cases [*India*] [*A publication*] (DLA)
MAE.............	Macintosh Application Environment [*Software*] (IGQR)

MAE.............	Madera, CA [*Location identifier FAA*] (FAAL)
MAE.............	Maebashi [*Japan*] [*Seismograph station code, US Geological Survey*] (SEIS)
MAE.............	Maersk Commuter IS [*Netherlands ICAO designator*] (FAAC)
Mae	Maestro [*Record label*] [*Belgium, etc.*]
MAE.............	Maine Association of Engineers (SRA)
MAE.............	Maintenance Engineer
MAE.............	Malignant Angioendotheliomatosis [*Oncology*]
MAE.............	Master Electric (IAA)
MAE.............	Master of Aeronautical Engineering (WDAA)
M Ae	Master of Aeronautics
MAE.............	Master of Aerospace Engineering (PGP)
MAE.............	Master of Agricultural Economics (PGP)
MAE.............	Master of Agricultural Education (PGP)
MAE.............	Master of Agricultural Engineering (GAGS)
MAE.............	Master of Agricultural Extension (GAGS)
MAE.............	Master of Art Education
MAE.............	Master of Arts in Education
MAE.............	Master of Arts in English (PGP)
MAE.............	Master of Automotive Engineering (PGP)
MA E............	Master of Engineering (WDAA)
MAE.............	Material and Equipment [*Nuclear energy*] (IAA)
MAE.............	Matrix Arithmetic Expression
MAE.............	McDonnell Airborne Evaluator [*McDonnell Douglas Corp.*] (MCD)
MAE.............	Mean Absolute Error
MAE.............	Mean Area of Effectiveness (CINC)
MAE.............	Mechanical and Electrical (IAA)
MAE.............	Medical Air Evacuation
MAE.............	Medium Altitude Endurance (RDA)
MAE.............	Memory Address Extension [*Computer science*] (CIST)
MAE.............	Memory Address Register (NITA)
MAE.............	(Methylamino)ethanol [*Organic chemistry*]
MAE.............	Metropolitan Area Exchange [*Telecommunications*] (ACRL)
MAE.............	Micro Aided Engineering (NITA)
MAE.............	Miramar Energy Corp. [*Vancouver Stock Exchange symbol*]
MAE.............	Missile Airborne Equipment (IAA)
MAE.............	Missile Assembly Equipment (IAA)
MAE.............	Mission Accomplishment Estimate [*DoD*]
MAE.............	Mississippi Association of Educators (SRA)
MAE.............	Mobile Ammunition Evaluation
MAE.............	Modified Anglia Engine [*Cosworth racing engines*]
MAE.............	Motion Aftereffect
MAE.............	Movement After-Effect (PDAA)
MAE.............	Moves All Extremities [*Medicine*] (MAE)
MAE.............	Multilingual Aphasia Examination [*Speech and language therapy*] (DAVI)
MAE.............	Mutual Assistance, Executive [*Military appropriation*] (NG)
MAEB...........	Material Application Evaluation Board [*NASA*] (MCD)
MAEBR	Management of Enlisted Bonus Recipients
MAEC..........	Manufacturing Analysis of Engineering Change (MCD)
MAEC..........	Master of Arts in Economics
MAEC..........	Minimum Adverse Effect Concentration [*Pollution technology*]
MAEC..........	Missile Attack Emergency Conference (MCD)
MAECAM.......	Micro-Aided Engineering/Computer Aided Manufacturing [*Micro-Aided Engineering Ltd. and Digital Microsystems Ltd.*] [*Software package*] (NCC)
MAECO	NRA [*National Restaurant Association*] Multi-Unit Architects, Engineers, and Construction Officers (EA)
MA (Econ) ...	Master of Arts in Economic and Social Studies [*University of Manchester*] [*British*]
MA (Econ) ...	Master of Arts in Economic Studies [*Universities of Newcastle and Sheffield*] [*British*]
MAECON.......	Mid-America Electronics Conference
MA(Ed)........	Master of Arts in Education (CMD)
MAED..........	Micro Area Electron Diffraction [*Surface analysis*]
MAEDOS......	Micro-Aided Engineering/Drawing Office System [*Micro-Aided Engineering Ltd.*] [*Software package*] (NCC)
MA EdU	Master of Arts in Education (PGP)
MAEE..........	Marine Aircraft Experimental Establishment
MAeE..........	Master of Aeronautical Engineering [*Canada*] (ASC)
MAEE..........	Mid-Atlantic Electrical Exhibition (ITD)
M Ae Eng...	Master of Aeronautical Engineering
MAEEW........	Moves All Extremities Equally Well [*Neurology*] (DAVI)
MAEF..........	Mastic Asphalt Employers' Federation [*British*] (BI)
MAEI..........	Malaysian-American Electronics Industry
MAEL..........	Marine Aircraft Experimental Laboratory [*British*]
MAELU........	Mutual Atomic Energy Liability Underwriters [*Chicago, IL*] (EA)
MAENF........	Miramar Mining [*NASDAQ symbol*] (TTSB)
MAENF........	Miramar Mining Corp. [*NASDAQ symbol*] (SAG)
MAEO..........	Months after Exercise of Option
MAEP..........	Measure of Adult English Proficiency (EDAC)
MAEP..........	Minimum AUTOLAND [*Automatic Landing*] Entry Point (NASA)
MAEPS........	Model Adoption Exchange Payment System (EDAC)
MAER..........	Maximum Allowable Emission Rate [*Environmental Protection Agency*] (ERG)
MAER..........	Mechanical and Electrical Room (IAA)
MAER..........	Mobile Ammunition and Reconditioning Unit [*Military*]
M Aero E	Master of Aeronautical Engineering
M Aero E	Master of Aerospace Engineering (PGP)
M Aero Eng...	Master of Aeronautical Engineering
MAEROSPOPNSMGT...	Masters Aerospace Operations Management [*Air Force*]
MAERP	Mutual Atomic Energy Reassurance Pool
MAERU	Mobile Ammunition Evaluation and Reconditioning Unit
Maes	Maestoso [*Majestic*] [*Music*]

MAES	Maine Agriculture Experiment Station [*University of Maine at Orono*] [*Research center*] (RCD)
MAES	Manufacturing and Engineering Support (IAA)
M Ae S	Master of Aeronautical Science
MAES	Master of Arts in Environmental Sciences (PGP)
MAES	Medical Aid for El Salvador (EA)
MAES	Mexican-American Engineering Society (EA)
MAES	[*Society of*] Mexican American Engineers and Scientists (NTPA)
MAES	Michigan Agricultural Experiment Station [*Michigan State University*] [*Research center*] (RCD)
MAESA	Measurement for Assessing the Effects of Stratospheric Aircraft [*Marine science*] (OSRA)
MAESA	Measurements for Assessing the Effects of Stratospheric Aircraft (USDC)
M Ae Sc	Master of Aeronautical Science
MAESON	Marxist All-Ethiopian Socialist Movement [*Political party*] (PD)
MAESTO	Maestoso [*Majestic*] [*Music*]
MAESTRO	Machine-Assisted Educational System for Teaching by Remote Operation (IEEE)
MAESTRO	Mission Analysis Evaluation and Space Trajectory Operations [*NASA*]
MAET	Master of Arts in English Teaching (PGP)
MAET	Microwave Amplifier Electron Tube
MAET	Missile Accident Emergency Team (AFM)
MAETS	Medical Air Evacuation Transport Squadron [*Army World War II*]
MAEVIS	Micro-Aided Engineering 3D Visualisation [*Micro-Aided Engineering Ltd. and Micro-Aided Engineering Digital Microsystems Ltd.*] [*Software package*] (NCC)
MAEW	Moves All Extremities Well [*Medicine*] (MEDA)
MAF	Front Militant Autonome [*Autonomous Militant Front*] [*French*] (PD)
MAF	Macrophage Activating Factor [*Biochemistry*]
MAF	Macrophage-Agglutinating Factor (STED)
MAF	Magnetic Anisotropy Field
MAF	Maintenance Action Form
MAF	Major Academic Field
MAF	Manpower Authorization File
MAF	Manual Authority File
MAF	Marine Air Facility
MAF	Marine Amphibious Force (AABC)
MAF	Marriage Adjustment Form [*Psychology*]
MAF	Mass Air Flow [*Automotive engineering*]
MAF	Master Address File [*US Census Bureau*]
MAF	Master Appraisal File [*Real estate*]
MAF	Master Audit File (SSD)
MAF	Master Facility Tool (MCD)
MAF	Master of Arts in Finance (PGP)
MAF	Maximum Amplitude Filter
MAF	Medical Awareness Foundation [*Commercial firm*] (EA)
MAF	Michoud Assembly Facility [*NASA*] (MCD)
MAF	Midland/Odessa [*Texas*] [*Airport symbol*] (OAG)
MAF	Million Acre Feet [*Hydrology*]
MAF	Minimum Audible Field
MAF	Minister of Armed Forces (NATG)
MAF	Ministry of Agriculture and Fisheries [*British*]
MAF	Missile Assembly Facility
MAF	Mission Aviation Fellowship [*Indonesia*] [*ICAO designator*] (FAAC)
MAF	Mixed Amine Fuel
MAF	Mobile Air Force (NATG)
MAF	Mobile Assault Ferry [*Army*]
MAF	Moisture and Ash Free
MAF	Morris Animal Foundation (EA)
MAF	Mouse Amniotic Fluid [*Veterinary science*] (DB)
MAF	Movable Appendage Factor [*IOR*] [*Yacht racing*]
MAF	Movement Aftereffect [*Optics*]
MAF	Multiple Access Facility [*Computer science*]
MAF	Multiple Access Forward (SSD)
MAF	Multiply-Add-Fused [*Computer science*] (CIST)
MAF	Municipal Advantage Fund [*NYSE symbol*] (SAG)
MAFA	Manchester Academy of Fine Arts [*British*]
MAFA	Midarm Fat Area (STED)
MAFA	Middle Atlantic Fencing Association (PSS)
MAFA	Middle Atlantic Fisheries Association (EA)
MAFAC	Marine Fisheries Advisory Committee [*Department of Commerce Washington, DC*] (EGAO)
MAFAP	Minimum Altitude over FAcility on Final Approach Course [*Aviation*] (FAAC)
MAFAS	Marine Automated Flowcharting Analysis System
MAFAs	Movement-Associates Fetal [*Heart rate*] Accelerations [*Obstetrics*] (DAVI)
MAFASA	Marine Amphibious Force Air Support Airfield (MCD)
MAFB	MAF Bancorp [*NASDAQ symbol*] (SPSG)
MAFB	Malmstrom Air Force Base [*Montana*] (KSC)
MAFB	Mitchell Air Force Base
MAF Bcp	MAF Bancorp, Inc. [*Associated Press*] (SAG)
MAFC	MAGTF [*Marine Air Ground Task Force*] All-Source Fusion Center (DOMA)
MAFC	Major Army Field Command (AABC)
MAFC	Master of Arts in Family Counseling (GAGS)
MAFC	Mel Anderson Fan Club [*Defunct*] (EA)
MAFC	Mythadventures Fan Club (EA)
MAFCA	Model A Ford Club of America (EA)
MAFCC	Model A Ford Cabriolet Club (EA)
Mafco	Mafco Consolidated Group [*Associated Press*] (SAG)
MAFCO	Magnetic Field Code
MAFD	Manic Affective Disorder [*Medicine*] (DMAA)
MAFD	Minimum Acquisition Flux Density
MAFE	Maintenance of Air/FMF [*Fleet Marine Force*] Expeditionary Equipment (NG)
MAFES	Mississippi Agricultural and Forestry Experiment Station [*Mississippi State University*] [*Research center*] (RCD)
MAFF	Ministry of Agriculture, Fisheries, and Food [*British*]
MAFF	Ministry of Agriculture, Forestry and Fisheries [*Japan*] (ECON)
MAFFC	Munsters and the Addams Family Fan Club (EA)
MAFFEX	Marine Amphibious Force Field Exercise [*Military*] (NVT)
Maffies	Middle-Aged Affluent Folks [*Lifestyle Classification*]
MAFFS	Modular Airborne Fire Fighting System [*Air Force*]
MAFH	Macroaggregated Ferrous Hydroxide [*Medicine*] (MAE)
MA/FH	Maintenance Actions per Flight Hour (MCD)
MAFH	Multicentric Angiofollicular (Lymph Node) Hyperplasia [*Oncology*]
MAFH	Museum of American Financial History (EA)
MAFI	Medic Alert Foundation International [*Also known as Medic Alert*] (EA)
MAFIA	Marimba and Fife Inspectors Association [*Women's tongue-in-cheek organization*] [*Defunct*]
MAFIA	Morte alla Francia Italia Anelo [*Death to the French is Italy's Cry*] [*When used in reference to the secret society often associated with organized crime, "Mafia" is from the Sicilian word for boldness or lawlessness*]
MAFIA	Multiaccess Executive with Fast Interrupt Acceptance [*Computer science*] (MHDI)
MAFIS	Malaysian Aquatic Sciences and Fisheries Information System [*Marine science*] (OSRA)
MAFIS	Management Farm Information Service (PDAA)
MAFIS	Master of Accountancy and Financial Information Systems (PGP)
MAFIS	Mobile Automated Field Instrumentation System [*TRADOC*] (RDA)
MAFL	Manual of Air Force Law [*British*]
MAFL	Multiaperture Ferrite Logic
MAFLA	Mississippi, Alabama, and Florida [*Oil industry*]
MAFLEX	Marine Amphibious Force Landing Exercise [*Military*] (NVT)
MAFLIR	Modified Advanced Forward-Looking Infrared
MAFLL	Master of Arts in Foreign Language and Literature (PGP)
MAFMIC	Minnesota Association of Farm Mutual Insurance Companies (SRA)
MAFOG	Mediterranean Area Fighter Operations Grid
MAFOR	Marine Forecast [*Pronounced "mayfor"*]
MAFP	Military and Air Force Police [*British military*] (DMA)
MAFPA	Mid-America Food Processors Association (SRA)
MAFR	Merged Accountability and Fund Reporting [*Air Force*] (AFM)
MAfr	Missionaries of Africa (TOCD)
mafr	Missionaries of Africa (TOCD)
MAFR	Modified Anarchy Flood Routing (PDAA)
MAfr	Society of Missionaries of Africa (EAIO)
MAFRC	Middle Atlantic Fisheries Research Center [*National Oceanic and Atmospheric Administration*]
MAFREMO	Malawi Freedom Movement (BUAC)
MAFS	Memoirs. American Folklore Society [*A publication*]
MAFS	Mexico-Albania Friendship Society (EAIO)
MAFS	Mobilization Air Force Specialty
MAFSC	Mobilization Air Force Specialty Code
MAFSI	Manufacturers' Agents for Food Service Industry (NTPA)
MAFSI	Marketing Agents for Food Service Industry (EA)
MAFSS	Multipoint Airfield Fuel Support System
MAFSX	Merrill Lynch: Federal Secs. Trust Cl.A [*Mutual fund ticker symbol*] (SG)
MAFT	Modified-Adopted-Fernald Technique (EDAC)
MAF/TDC	Maintenance Action Form / Technical Directives Compliance [*Military*] (DNAB)
MAFTEP	Method for Analysis of Fleet Tactical Effectiveness Performance [*Navy*] (PDAA)
MAFV	Mean Ambient Flow Vector [*Geology*]
MAFVA	Miniature Armoured Fighting Vehicle Association (EA)
MAG	Air Margarita [*Venezuela*] [*ICAO designator*] (FAAC)
MAG	Macrogenerator [*SEMIS*]
MAG	Madang [*Papua New Guinea*] [*Airport symbol*] (OAG)
MAG	Magadan [*Former USSR Seismograph station code, US Geological Survey*] (SEIS)
mag	Magahi [*MARC language code Library of Congress*] (LCCP)
MAG	Magazine (AFM)
mag	Magazine (VRA)
MAG	Magenta (ROG)
MAG	Maggie Mines [*Vancouver Stock Exchange symbol*]
Mag	[*The*] Magistrate [*London*] [*A publication*] (DLA)
Mag	Magistrate and Municipal and Parochial Lawyer [*London*] [*A publication*] (DLA)
MAG	Magnesium [*Chemical symbol is Mg*]
MAG	MagneTek, Inc. [*NYSE symbol*] (SPSG)
MAG	Magnetic (AFM)
mag	Magnetic (WDMC)
MAG	Magneto (KSC)
MAG	Magnetometer [*or Magnetometry*]
MAG	Magnetron (CET)
MAG	Magnification
MAG	Magnitude (AFM)
MAG	Magnum (WDAA)
MAG	Magnus [*Large*] [*Pharmacy*]
Mag	Magruder's Reports [*1, 2 Maryland*] [*A publication*] (DLA)
MAG	Magyar [*Language, etc.*] (ROG)
MAG	Main Armament Group
MAG	Management Advisory Group [*Environmental Protection Agency*] (GFGA)
MAG	Management Assistance Group [*Washington, DC*] (EA)

MAG............ Marine Aircraft [or Aviation] Group
MAG............ Marine Air Group (VNW)
MAG............ Maritime Action Group [Non-carrier naval task group] (DOMA)
MAG............ Maritime Air Group [Canada]
MAG............ Marker-Adder Generator
MAG............ Marketing Aids Group
M Ag............ Master of Agriculture
MAG............ Master of Applied Geography (PGP)
MAG............ Maximum Available Gain (IAA)
MAG............ Medical Association of Georgia (SRA)
MAg............ Membrane Antigen (DB)
MAG............ Military Advisory Group
MAG............ Military Airlift Group [Air Force]
MAG............ Minnesota Attorney General's Office, St. Paul, MN [OCLC symbol]
                    (OCLC)
MAG............ Mississippi Air National Guard [FAA designator] (FAAC)
MAG............ Mittelassyrisches Gesetz (BJA)
MAG............ Monoammonium Glutamate [Organic chemistry]
MAG............ Motorcycle Action Group [British] (DBA)
MAG............ Mutation Activation Gene [Immunology]
MAG............ Myelin-Associated Glycoprotein [Biochemistry]
MAGA......... Medium-Accuracy Gyro Assembly
MAGA......... Mexican-American Grocers Association (NTPA)
Magal......... Magal Security Systems [Commercial firm Associated Press] (SAG)
Magalog....... Magazine-Catalog [Advertising]
MAGAMP..... Magnetic Amplifier
magamp...... Magnetic Amplifier (IDOE)
Mag & Con.... Magistrate and Constable [A publication] (DLA)
Mag & Const.. Magistrate and Constable [A publication] (DLA)
Mag & E Comp... Magnus and Estrin on Companies [5th ed.] [1978]
                    [A publication] (DLA)
Mag & M & PL... Magistrate and Municipal and Parochial Lawyer [A publication]
                    (DLA)
Mag Antiq.... Magazine Antiques [A publication] (BRI)
Mag Arch..... Magister Architecturae [Master of Architecture] [Latin]
MAGARLM... Military Assistance Advisory Group, Army Branch, Logistics-Medical
                    (CINC)
MAGB......... Maltsters Association [British] (DBA)
MAGB......... Maltsters Association of Great Britain (BUAC)
MAGB......... Masectomy Association of Great Britain
MAGB......... Microfilm Association of Great Britain
MAGB......... Microform Association of Great Britain (BUAC)
Mag Bl........ Magical Blend [A publication]
MAGBNT...... Museums and Art Galleries Board of the Northern Territory
                    [Australia]
MAGBRG...... Magnetic Bearing [Navigation] (DNAB)
MAG BRIT.... Magna Britannia [Great Britain] [Latin] (ROG)
MagC.......... Magma Copper Co. [Associated Press] (SAG)
MAGCAP...... Magazine Capacity [Military]
MAGCARD .. Magnetic Card [Electronics] (ECII)
Mag Cas...... Bittleston, Wise, and Parnell's Magistrates' Cases [England]
                    [A publication] (DLA)
Mag Cas...... Magisterial Cases [England] [A publication] (DLA)
Mag Cas...... Magistrates' Cases [Reprinted from Law Journal Reports]
                    [1892-1910] [A publication] (DLA)
Mag Char.... Magna Charta [or Carta] [Great Charter] [Latin] [A publication] (DLA)
MAGCI........ Magnetic Cast Iron (IAA)
mag cit........ Magnesium Citrate [Pharmacy]
MAGCOM...... Magnetic Contour Matching (MUSM)
MAGCON...... Magnetized Concentration [Lunar]
MagCp......... Magnetech Corp. [Associated Press] (SAG)
MAGCS........ Magnetic Cast Steel (IAA)
Mag Ct....... Magistrates' Court (DLA)
MAGD .... Magdalen College [Oxford University] (ROG)
MAGD .... Magdalene College, Cambridge University [England] (ROG)
MAGDA........ Mobility Aid and Guide Dog Alliance (BUAC)
MAGDARR .. Magnavox Doppler and Ranging RADAR (NG)
MAgDevEc... Master of Agricultural Development Economics (ADA)
Mag Dig ..... Magrath's South Carolina Digest [A publication] (DLA)
Magdl......... Magdalenian (VRA)
MAGE......... Marine Aerosol and Gas Exchange [Marine science] (OSRA)
MAGE.......... Mechanical Aerospace Ground Equipment (TEL)
M Ag Ec...... Master of Agricultural Economics
M Ag Ed ..... Master of Agricultural Education
MagelPt...... Magellan Petroleum Corp. [Associated Press] (SAG)
MagelRst..... Magellan Restauraunt System [Associated Press] (SAG)
MAGEN ...... Matrix Generating and Reporting System [Computer science] (PDAA)
MAGERT ..... Map and Geography Round Table [American Library Association]
MAGES .... Magnitude Estimation Scaling (MCD)
MAgExt....... Master of Agricultural Extension (GAGS)
MAGF......... Male Accessory Gland Fluid [Medicine] (DB)
MAGFET...... Magnetic Metal-Oxide-Semiconductor Field-Effect Transistor (PDAA)
MAGG......... Maggiore [Major] [Music]
MAGG......... Modular Alphanumeric Graphics Generator (IEEE)
MAGGE .... Medium-Altitude Gravity Gradient Experiment
MAggF........ Macrophage Agglutination Factor [Biochemistry] (MAE)
MAGGI........ Million Ampere Generator [British] (DEN)
MagGp........ Magna Group, Inc. [Associated Press] (SAG)
MAGGS .... Modular Advanced Graphics Generation System (IEEE)
Magh .... Maghreb (BJA)
MAGI .... Mackenzie Art Gallery [University of Regina] [Canada Research
                    center] (RCD)
MAGI .... Magna Group, Inc. [NASDAQ symbol] (NQ)

MAGI .... Maryland Automated Geographic Information System [Maryland State
                    Department of State Planning] [Information service or system]
                    (IID)
MAGI .... Master Group Information System [AT & T]
MAGI .... Mathematical Applications Group, Inc. (MCD)
MAGI .... Military Gamma Irradiator
MAGI .... Multiarray Gamma Irradiator
MAGIC .... Machine-Aided Graphics for Illustration and Composition [Bell
                    Telephone]
MAGIC .... Machine for Automatic Graphics Interface to a Computer
MAGIC .... Madison Avenue General Ideas Committee [New York City]
MAGIC .... Magic Foundation for Children's Growth (EA)
MAGIC .... Magnetic and Germanium Integer Calculator (DEN)
MAGIC .... Magnetic Immunochemistry [Laboratory analysis]
MAGIC .... Manual Assisted Gaming of Integrated Combat (PDAA)
MAGIC .... Marine Corps Air-Ground Intelligence Center (MCD)
MAGIC .... Market Analysis Guide - Intercity Communications [AT & T]
MAGIC .... Marketing and Advertising General Information Centre [Datasolve
                    Ltd.] [British Information service or system]
MAGIC .... Matrix Algebra General Interpretive Coding (IEEE)
MAGIC .... Method for Asynchronous Graphics Integral Control [Computer
                    science] (PDAA)
MAGIC .... Michigan Automatic General Integrated Computation (MCD)
MAGIC .... Microprobe Analysis Generalized Intensity Corrections
MAGIC .... Microprocessor Application of Graphic with Interactive
                    Communication
MAGIC .... Modern Analytical Generator of Improved Circuits [Computer science]
MAGIC .... Modified Action Generated Input Control
MAGIC .... Modular Area Graphics Illustrations Composition (DGA)
MAGIC .... Monodisperse Aerosol Generation Interface [Physics]
MAGIC .... Motorola Automatically Generated Integrated Circuits
MAGIC .... Mozambique, Angola, and Guine Information Center [British]
MAGIC .... Multipurpose and Generalized Interface to COBOL [Computer
                    science]
Magic Cap ... Magic Communicating Applications Platform [General Magic]
                    [Computer science]
MAGICS .... Multiphase Model for Air, Groundwater, Immiscible Contaminant and
                    Solute Transport [Computer program for testing water flow]
MAGID .... Magnetic Intrusion Detector (NVT)
MAGIE .... Midwest Agri Industries Expo [Illinois Fertilizer and Chemical
                    Association] (TSPED)
MAGIIC .... Mobile Army Ground Imagery Interpretation Center (MCD)
Mag Ins ...... Magen on Insurance [A publication] (DLA)
MAGIS .... Magistrate
MAGIS .... Marine Air Ground Intelligence System
MAGIS .... Megawatt Air-to-Ground Illumination System (MCD)
MAGIS .... Municipal Automated Geographic Information System [District of
                    Columbia Office of the Mayor] [Information service or system]
                    (IID)
Magis & Const (PA)... Magistrate and Constable [Pennsylvania] [A publication]
                    (DLA)
Magis Ct...... Magistrates' Court (DLA)
MAGL.......... Magna-Lab, Inc. [NASDAQ symbol] (SAG)
MAGL.......... Material Acquisition Guidance Letter (MCD)
MAGLA .... Magna-Lab `A' [NASDAQ symbol] (TTSB)
MAGLAD ..... Marksmanship and Gunnery LASER Device (RDA)
MAGLATCH... Magnetic Latch (MUGU)
MAG-LEV .... Magnetically-Levitated [High-speed ground transportation]
MAGLL........ Magna-Lab Wrrt `E' [NASDAQ symbol] (TTSB)
MAGLOC...... Magnetic Logic Computer
MAGLU .... Magna-Lab Unit [NASDAQ symbol] (TTSB)
MAGLW ...... Magna-Lab Wrrt `A' [NASDAQ symbol] (TTSB)
MAGLZ........ Magna-Lab Wrrt `B' [NASDAQ symbol] (TTSB)
Magmc .... Magma Copper Co. [Associated Press] (SAG)
Mag (MD).... Magruder's Reports [1, 2 Maryland] [A publication] (DLA)
MAGMOD.... Magnetic Modulator
Mag Mor..... Magna Moralia [of Aristotle] [Classical studies] (OCD)
Mag Mun Par Law... Magistrate and Municipal and Parochial Lawyer
                    [A publication] (DLA)
MAGN .... Magainin Pharmaceuticals [NASDAQ symbol] (SPSG)
MAGN .... Magnetic (ROG)
MAGN .... Magnetron [Electricity]
MAGN .... Magnus [Great] [Latin] (ADA)
MAGN .... Monoaminoguanidine Nitrate [Organic chemistry]
Magna .... Magna-Lab, Inc. [Associated Press] (SAG)
MagnaBb ..... Magna Bancorp [Associated Press] (SAG)
Magnal .... Magna International, Inc. [Associated Press] (SAG)
MagnaL .... Magna-Lab, Inc. [Associated Press] (SAG)
Magna Rot Pip... Magnus Rotulus Pipae [Great Roll of the Pipe] [Latin A
                    publication] (DLA)
MAGNA-SID... Magnetic Sensing Intrusion Device [Remote sensor] [Also, M-SID]
                    [Military] (VNW)
MAGNETTOR... Magnetic Modulator (SAA)
magnif........ Magnification
MAGNOLIA... Mississippi Alliance for Gaining New Opportunities through Library
                    Information Access
MAGNOX...... Magnesium Oxide [Magnesium-based alloy]
MagnPet...... Magnum Petroleum [Associated Press] (SAG)
magns .... Magnesium (VRA)
MAGNT....... Museums and Art Galleries of the Northern Territory [Australia]
Magntk .... Magnatek, Inc. [Associated Press] (SAG)
MAGOX....... Magnesium Oxide [Acronym is trademark of Basic Chemicals]
MagP.......... Magnum Petroleum [Associated Press] (SAG)
MAGP .... Master of Arts in Gerontological Psychology (PGP)
MAGP .... Microfibrillar-Associated Glycoprotein [Biochemistry]

MAGp.......... Military Airlift Group [*Air Force*] (AFM)
MagPet....... Magnum Petroleum [*Associated Press*] (SAG)
Mag Pharm... Magister Pharmaciae [*Master of Pharmacy*] [*Latin*]
Mag Phil..... Magister Philosophiae [*Master of Philosophy*] [*Latin*]
Mag Phil Fac Theol... Magister Philosophiae Facultatis Theologicae [*Latin*]
MagPhr....... Magainin Pharmaceuticals [*Associated Press*] (SAG)
MAGPIE...... Machine Automatically Generating Production Inventory Evaluation [*Computer science*] (IEEE)
MAGPIE...... Magazine Page Interactive Editor (DGA)
MAGPIE...... Markov Game Planar Intercept-Evasion Package [*Computer science*]
MAGPIE...... Mega-Ampere Generator for Plasma Implosion Experiments [*Astrophysics*] (ECON)
MagPt......... Magnum Petroleum [*Associated Press*] (SAG)
M Agr .... Master of Agriculture
MAgrDevEc... Master of Agricultural Development Economics
M Agr E....... Master of Agricultural Engineering
MAgrEc....... Master of Agricultural Economics
M Agr Eng... Master of Agricultural Engineering
Mag Rer Nat.. Magister Rerum Naturalium [*Latin*]
Mag Rer Soc Oec... Magister Rerum Socialium Oeconomicarumque [*Latin*]
M Agric....... Master of Agriculture
MAGROCV ... Military Advisory Group, Government of the Republic of China, Vietnam
Mag Rot ..... Magnus Rotulus [*Great Roll of the Exchequer*] [*Latin A publication*] (DLA)
M Agr S....... Master of Agricultural Science
M Agr Sc..... Master of Agricultural Science
MAgrSci....... Master of Agricultural Science
MAgrSt....... Master of Agricultural Studies (ADA)
Magruder..... Magruder's Reports [*1, 2 Maryland*] [*A publication*] (DLA)
MAGS .... Magal Security Systems [*NASDAQ symbol*] (SAG)
MAGS .... Magistrates (ROG)
MAGS .... Medical Action for Global Security (BUAC)
MAGS .... Multiple Aminoglycosides [*Antibacterial agents*]
MAGSAT ..... Magnetic Field Satellite [*NASA*] (MCD)
MAGSAT ..... Magnetometer Satellite (NASA)
MAgSc........ Master of Agricultural Science (ADA)
MAgSci....... Master of Agricultural Science
MAGSF....... Magal Security Systems Ltd [*NASDAQ symbol*] (TTSB)
MagSft........ Magic Software Enterprises [*Associated Press*] (SAG)
MAGSI .... Minimum Altitude at Glide Slope Intersection Inbound [*Aviation*] (FAAC)
MAGSIM ...... Magnetic Shield Simulator (PDAA)
MAgSt......... Master of Agricultural Studies
MAGSTR ...... Magistrate
mag sulf ..... Magnesium Sulfate [*Pharmacology*] (DAVI)
MAGTAF ...... Marine Air-Ground Task Force (AFM)
MAGTC .... Magnetic Tape Controller (NITA)
MagTch....... Magnetics Technology [*Associated Press*] (SAG)
MAGTD .... Magnitude
MAGTF........ Marine Air-Ground Task Force (NVT)
Mag Theol... Magister Theologiae [*Master of Theology*] [*Latin*]
MAG-THOR... Magnesium-Thorium [*Inorganic chemistry*]
MAGTOP ...... Management of Traffic Operations [*Federal Highway Administration*]
MAGTRAC... Magnetic Tracker (MUGU)
MAGUK .... Motorcycle Action Group (BUAC)
MAGW .... Maximum Alternate Gross Weight
Magy .... Magyar Muza [*Record label*] [*Hungary*]
Magz.......... Magazine
MAH............. Collection des Tablettes Cuneiformes du Musee d'Art et d'Histoire de Geneve (BJA)
MAH............. Findlay, OH [*Location identifier FAA*] (FAAL)
MAH............. Hampshire College, Amherst, MA [*Library symbol Library of Congress*] (LCLS)
MAH............. Hanna [*M. A.*] Co. [*NYSE symbol*] (SPSG)
MAH............. Magnesium Aspartate Hydrochloride [*Antihypertensive*]
MAH............. Mahableshwar [*India*] [*Seismograph station code, US Geological Survey Closed*] (SEIS)
MAH............. M.A. Hanna Co. (EFIS)
MAH............. Mahogany (MSA)
mah............. Mahogany (VRA)
MAH............. Mahommedanism (ROG)
MAH............. Mahon [*Spain*] [*Airport symbol*] (OAG)
MAH............. Maleic Anhydride [*Also, MA*] [*Organic chemistry*]
MAH............. Malev-Hungarian Airlines [*ICAO designator*] (FAAC)
MAH............. Malignancy-Associated Hypercalcemia [*Oncology*]
MAH............. Massachusetts Historical Society, Boston, MA [*OCLC symbol*] (OCLC)
MAH............. Master of Arts in Humanities (GAGS)
mAH............. Milliampere Hour
MAH............. Mothers at Home [*An association*] (PAZ)
MAHA .... Metropolitan Association of Handwriting Analysts (EA)
MAHA .... Microangiopathic Hemolytic Anemia [*Medicine*]
Mah & DRT... Mahaffy and Dodson's Road Traffic [*3rd ed.*] [*1961*] [*A publication*] (DLA)
Maharashtra LJ... Maharashtra Law Journal [*India*] [*A publication*] (DLA)
Mahaska...... Mahaska Investment Co. [*Associated Press*] (SAG)
MAHC .... Maximum Allowable Housing Cost [*Army*] (AABC)
MAHCD .... Master of Applied Human and Community Development (PGP)
MAHE .... Master of Arts in Hebrew Education (BJA)
MAHE .... Master of Arts in Human Ecology (GAGS)
MAHE&FE... Master of Arts in Home Economics and Family Ecology (GAGS)
MAHEFE...... Master of Arts in Home Economics and Family Ecology (PGP)
MAHH.......... Malignancy-Associated Humoral Hypercalcemia [*Medicine*] (DMAA)

MAHi .... Amherst Historical Society, Amherst, MA [*Library symbol Library of Congress*] (LCLS)
MAHI .... Monarch Avalon [*NASDAQ symbol*] (TTSB)
MAHI .... Monarch Avalon, Inc. [*NASDAQ symbol*] (NQ)
MAHL.......... Master of Arts in Hebrew Letters (PGP)
MAHL.......... Master of Hebrew Literature (BJA)
Mah LJ........ Maharashtra Law Journal [*India*] [*A publication*] (DLA)
MAHMA .... Midwest Assisted Housing Management Association (SRA)
MAHMO .... Maryland Association of Health Maintenance Organizations (SRA)
MAHN .... Mongolian People's Revolutionary Party [*Political party*] (BUAC)
MAHOC .... Manual for Administration of the Hands-On Component (MCD)
MAHOG .... Mahogany (DSUE)
MA(Hons) .... Master of Arts with Honours (ADA)
MAHP .... Member of the Association of Hypnotists and Physiotherapists [*British*]
MAHRM .... Master of Arts in Human Resource Management (GAGS)
MAHRSI....... Middle Atmosphere High Resolution Spectrograph Investigation
MAHS .... Master of Human Services (GAGS)
MAHSM .... Master of Arts in Human Service Management (GAGS)
MAHT .... Master of Arts in History Teaching (PGP)
MAI .... Air Moravia [*Czechoslovakia*] [*ICAO designator*] (FAAC)
MAI .... Machine-Aided Index (NITA)
MAI .... Machine-Aided Indexing (KSC)
MAI .... Magister in Arte Ingeniaria [*Master of Engineering*]
Mai .... Maine's Reports [*A publication*] (DLA)
mai .... Maithili [*MARC language code Library of Congress*] (LCCP)
MAI .... Maius [*May*] [*Latin*]
MAI .... Maizuru [*Japan*] [*Seismograph station code, US Geological Survey Closed*] (SEIS)
MAI .... Management Assistance, Inc. (EFIS)
MAI .... Mantle Arm Index
MAI .... Manufacturers Association of Israel (BUAC)
MAI .... Mapper Application Interface [*Computer science*]
MAI .... Marianna [*Florida*] [*Airport symbol*] (AD)
MAI .... Marianna, FL [*Location identifier FAA*] (FAAL)
MAI .... Marriage Adjustment Inventory [*Psychology*]
MAI .... Master of Fine Arts International [*British*]
MAI .... Material Annex Item [*Military*]
MAI .... Maximum Allowable Increase [*Environmental Protection Agency*]
MAI .... Mean Annual Increment
MAI .... Media Associates International [*An association*] (EA)
MAI .... Medical Aid for Indochina [*An association*] (EA)
MAI .... Medical Aid for Iraq
MAI .... Medical Assurance [*NYSE symbol*] [*Formerly, MAIC Holdings*] (SG)
MAI .... Member, Appraisal Institute [*American Institute of Real Estate Appraisers of the National Association of Realtors*] [*Designation awarded by*]
MAI .... Member of the Anthropological Institute [*British*]
MAI .... Metropolitan Action Institute [*Formerly, SAI*] (EA)
MAI .... Micanite and Insulators (IAA)
MAI .... Microscopic Aggregation Index (DMAA)
MAI .... Military Assistance Institute [*Air Force*]
MAI .... Minimum Annual Income (WDAA)
MAI .... Ministerium fuer Aussenhandel und Innerdeutschen Handel [*Ministry for Foreign Trade and Domestic German Trade*] [*See also MfAI*]
MAI .... Monash Asia Institute [*Monash University*] [*Australia*]
MAI .... Movement Assessment of Infants [*Pediatrics*] (DMAA)
MAI .... Multilateral Agreement on Investment [*1998*]
MAI .... Multilevel Assessment Instrument [*Medicine*] (DMAA)
MAI .... Multiple Access Interface
MAI .... Multiple Address Instruction
MAI .... Museums Association of India (BUAC)
MAI .... Music Association of Ireland (DBA)
MAI .... Mycobacterium Avium-Intracellulare [*Medicine*]
MAI .... Myobacterium Avium Intercellare (WDAA)
MAIA .... Magnetic Antibody Immunoassay
MAIA .... Master of Arts in Industrial Arts (PGP)
MAIA .... Master of Arts in International Affairs (GAGS)
MAIA .... Member of the American Institute of Appraisers
MAIAA .... Member of the American Institute of Aeronautics and Astronautics [*Formerly, MIAS*]
MAIAA .... Mid-America Intercollegiate Athletics Association (PSS)
MAIAC .... Maine Athletic Conference (PSS)
MAIADA .... Massachusetts Independent Auto Dealers Association (SRA)
Mai Anc L.... Maine's Ancient Law [*A publication*] (DLA)
MAIAW .... Massachusetts Association of Intercollegiate Athletics for Women (PSS)
MAIB .... Marine Accident Investigation Board (BUAC)
MAIB .... Motor Accidents Insurance Board [*Tasmania, Australia*]
MAIBC .... Member of the Architectural Institute of British Columbia [*Canada*] (DD)
MAIBL......... Midland & International Banks Ltd. [*British*]
MAIC .... MAIC Holdings [*NASDAQ symbol*] (TTSB)
MAIC .... MAIC Holdings, Inc. [*NASDAQ symbol*] (SAG)
MAIC .... Maine Aquaculture Innovation Center [*University of Maine*] [*Research center*] (RCD)
MAIC.......... Major Analytical Instrumentation Center [*University of Florida*] [*Research center*] (RCD)
MAIC.......... Michigan Association of Insurance Companies (SRA)
MAIC.......... Mid-America International Agricultural Consortium
MAICE......... Member of the American Institute of Consulting Engineers
MAICh......... Mediterranean Agronomic Institute of Chania (BUAC)
MAIChE........ Member of the American Institute of Chemical Engineers
MAIC Hld .... MAIC Holdings, Inc. [*Associated Press*] (SAG)
MAICS .... Master of Arts in Intercultural Studies (PGP)

MAICYA .... Major Authors and Illustrators for Children and Young Adults [*A publication*]
MAID .... Magnetic Anti-Intrusion Detector (PDAA)
MAID .... Maidstone [*Municipal borough in England*]
MAID .... Maintenance Automatic Integration Director [*Computer science*]
MAID .... Manual Intervention and Display
MAID .... Market Analysis and Information Database [*MAID Systems Ltd.*] [*British Information service or system*] (IID)
MAID .... Master Area Interest Decks (MCD)
MAID .... Master of Arts in Interior Design (GAGS)
MAID .... Master of Arts in International Diplomacy (GAGS)
MAID .... Merger Acquisition Improved Decision [*Computer science*]
MAID .... Monroe Automatic Internal Diagnosis [*Computer science*]
MAID .... Multiple Aircraft Identification Display (PDAA)
MAIDA .... Multi-Attribute Identification and Analysis Program [*Jointly developed by Georgia Tech Research Institute and the US Air Force*]
MAID/MILES... Magnetic Anti-Intrusion Detector/Magnetic Intrusion Line Sensor (MCD)
MAIDS .... Machine-Aided Information and Dissemination Systems
MAIDS .... Management Automated Information Display System (KSC)
MAIDS .... Mouse Acquired Immunodeficiency Syndrome [*Medicine*] (DMAA)
MAIDS .... Multipurpose Automatic Inspection and Diagnostic Systems [*Army*]
MAIDS .... Murine-Acquired Immunodeficiency Syndrome [*Animal pathology*]
MAIDY .... M.A.I.D. ADS [*NASDAQ symbol*] (TTSB)
MAIE .... Member of the British Association of Industrial Editors (DBQ)
MAIEE .... Member of the American Institute of Electrical Engineers
MAIF .... Major Analytical Instruments Facility [*Case Western Reserve University*] [*Research center*] (RCD)
MAIG .... Matsushita Atomic Industrial Group [*Japan*] (BUAC)
MAIIC .... Master of Arts in International Communications (PGP)
Mai Inst ..... Maine's History of Institutions [*A publication*] (DLA)
MAIL .... Mail Boxes Etc. [*NASDAQ symbol*] (NQ)
MAIL .... MILES [*Multiple Integrated LASER Engagement System*] Action Item Log [*Army*]
MailBx .... Mail Boxes Etc. [*Associated Press*] (SAG)
MAILS .... Materiel Acquisition and Integrated Logistics Support
MAILS .... Mid-America Interlibrary Services [*Library network*]
MAILS .... Mississippi Automated Interlibrary Loan System [*Mississippi State Library Commission*] [*Information service or system*] (IID)
MailWell ..... Mail-Well, Inc. [*Associated Press*] (SAG)
Maim .... Moses Maimonides [*Spanish Talmudist, 1135-1204*] (BJA)
MAIME .... Member of the American Institute of Mining and Metallurgical Engineers
MAIME .... Member of the American Institute of Mining Engineers (ASC)
MAIN .... Main St. & Main [*NASDAQ symbol*] (TTSB)
MAIN .... Main St. & Main, Inc. [*NASDAQ symbol*] (SAG)
MAIN .... Maintenance (NASA)
MAIN .... Material Automated Information System
MAIN .... Material Automated Inventory Network (MCD)
MAIN .... Medical Automation Intelligence [*System*]
MAIN .... Mid-America Interconnected Network [*Regional power council*]
MAIN .... Midwest Alliance in Nursing (SRA)
MAIN .... Military Authorization Identification Number
MAIN .... Multiple Access Internal Network [*Computer science*]
MA in Comm... Master of Arts in Communications
MAIND .... Master of Arts in Interior Design (PGP)
MainDta ...... Mainstream Data, Inc. [*Associated Press*] (SAG)
Maine .... Maine Reports [*A publication*] (DLA)
Maine Anc Law... Maine's Ancient Law [*A publication*] (DLA)
Maine PUR.... Maine Public Utilities Commission Reports [*A publication*] (DLA)
Maine R ...... Maine Reports [*A publication*] (DLA)
Maine Rep... Maine Reports [*A publication*] (DLA)
Mainlobe ..... Major Investigation for Low-Frequency Ocean Bottom Loss Experiments [*Marine science*] (MSC)
MAINS .... Marine-Aided Inertial Navigation System (PDAA)
MAINSITE .... Modular Automated Integrated Systems / Interoperability Test and Evaluation (PDAA)
MainSt .... Main St. & Main, Inc. [*Associated Press*] (SAG)
MainStB ...... Main Street BankGroup, Inc. [*Associated Press*] (SAG)
MAINT .... Maintenance (AFM)
maint .... Maintenance (REAL)
Maint .... Maintenance (TBD)
MA/INT .... Maintenance Actions per Interval (MCD)
MAINTBN ...... Maintenance Battalion (DNAB)
MAINTCE ...... Maintenance (ROG)
maintd .... Maintained
MAINTN .... Maintenance [*Automotive advertising*]
MAINTNCE ..... Maintenance [*Freight*]
MAINTRAIN... Maintenance and Training [*in complex equipment*]
MAINTSUPOFC... Maintenance Supply Office (DNAB)
MAINTSUPP... Maintenance and Support (DNAB)
MAINTSUPPORTOFF... Maintenance Support Office [*Navy*]
MA in Urb Pl... Master of Arts in Urban Planning
MAIO .... Mashhad [*Iran*] [*Seismograph station code, US Geological Survey*] (SEIS)
MAIP .... Matrix Algebra Interpretive Program (IEEE)
MAIPP .... Mid-Atlantic Independent Power Producers (SRA)
MAIR .... Manufacturing and Inspection Record (KSC)
MAIR .... Master of Arts in Industrial Relations
MAIR .... Master of Arts in International Relations (GAGS)
MAIR .... Mesaba Holdings [*NASDAQ symbol*] (TTSB)
MAIR .... Mesaba Holdings, Inc. [*NASDAQ symbol*] (SAG)
MAIR .... Modular Airborne Intercept RADAR (IAA)
MAIR .... Molecular Airborne Intercept RADAR
MAIREASTLANT... Maritime Air, Eastern Atlantic (DNAB)

MAIRMAR... Marine Air Depot, Miramar [*California*]
MAIRMED ... Maritime Air Forces Mediterranean [*NATO*] (DNAB)
MAIRS .... Military Air Integrated Reporting System (MCD)
MAIRU .... Mobile Aircraft Instrument Repair Unit
MAIS .... Maintenance Information System [*Military*] (NVT)
MAIS .... Management Audit Information System
MAIS .... Master of Accounting Information Systems (PGP)
MAIS .... Master of Arts in Interdisciplinary Studies (GAGS)
MAIS .... Master of Arts in International Studies (GAGS)
MAIS .... Mechanical Aids for the Individual Soldier [*Army*]
MAIS .... Mediterranean Association of International Schools (EA)
MAIS .... Member, Association of Industrial Surgeons (CMD)
MAIS .... Microfilm Alpha Index System
MAIS .... Minnesota Adaptive Instructional System (EDAC)
MAIS .... Mobile Automated Instrumentation Suite (DWSG)
MAIS .... Mycobacterium Avium-Intracellulare-Scrofulaceum [*Bacteriology*]
MAISA .... Middle Atlantic Intercollegiate Sailing Association
MAISA .... Multiple Analytical Isoelectrofocusing Scanning Apparatus
MAISARC...... Major Automated Information System Review Council [*Army*]
MAISRC....... Major Automated Information Systems Review Council [*Army*]
MAI Sy .... MAI Systems Corp. [*Associated Press*] (SAG)
MAI Sys ...... MAI Systems Corp. [*Associated Press*] (SAG)
MAIT .... Maintenance Assistance and Instruction Team [*Army*] (AABC)
Mait .... Maitland's Select Pleas of the Crown [*A publication*] (DLA)
MAIT .... Matrix Analysis of Insider Threat [*Nuclear energy*] (NRCH)
MAIT .... Methotrexate and Cytosine Arabinoside [*Antineoplastic drug regimen*] (DAVI)
MAIT .... Minimum Autoignition Temperature
MAITA .... Marine and Allied Industries Training Association (AIE)
Mait Gl ...... Maitland's Pleas of the Crown, County of Gloucester [*A publication*] (DLA)
Maitland ..... Maitland's Manuscript Session Cases [*Scotland*] [*A publication*] (DLA)
Maitland ..... Maitland's Pleas of the Crown [*1221*] [*England*] [*A publication*] (DLA)
Maitland ..... Maitland's Select Pleas of the Crown [*A publication*] (DLA)
MAIU .... Marine Accident Investigation Unit (BUAC)
MAIWO .... Member of the Austrlaian Institute of Welfare Officers
MAIZ .... Mediterranean Agronomic Institute of Saragossa (BUAC)
MAJ .... Jones Library, Amherst, MA [*Library symbol Library of Congress*] (LCLS)
MAJ .... Majestic Airlines, Inc. [*ICAO designator*] (FAAC)
MAJ .... Majestic Electronic Stores, Inc. [*Toronto Stock Exchange symbol*]
MAJ .... Majolica [*Ceramics*] (ROG)
maj .... Majolica (VRA)
MAJ .... Major [*Military*] (AABC)
Maj .... Major (WA)
MAJ .... Majority (KSC)
MAJ .... Majuro [*Marshall Islands*] [*Airport symbol*] (OAG)
MAJ .... Maron [*Java*] [*Seismograph station code, US Geological Survey Closed*] (SEIS)
MAJ .... Master of Arts in Journalism (GAGS)
MAJ .... Medical Association of Jamaica (BUAC)
MAJ .... Michael Anthony Jewelers [*AMEX symbol*] (TTSB)
MAJ .... Michael Anthony Jewelers, Inc. [*AMEX symbol*] (SPSG)
MAJ .... Model Air Jet
MAJAC........ Maintenance Antijam Console [*Air Force*]
MAJC......... Master of Arts in Journalism and Communication (PGP)
MAJC......... Mount Aloysius Junior College [*Pennsylvania*]
MAJC......... Mutual Association of Journeymen Coopers [*A union*] [*British*]
MAJCOM.... Major Command [*Formerly, Major Air Command*] [*Military*]
MAJCON ..... Major Air Command Controlled [*Units*]
MAJCS........ Master of Arts in Jewish Communal Service (BJA)
MAJCSSW ... Master of Arts in Jewish Communal Studies and Social Work (BJA)
MAJE .... Master of Arts in Jewish Education (BJA)
MAJ Ed ...... Master of Arts in Jewish Education (PGP)
MAJ GEN .... Major General (AFM)
MAJI .... Magestic Agency for Joint Intelligence
MAJI .... Majority Agency for Joint Intelligence
MAJIC........ Maji Controlled [*A security classification*]
MAJO......... Matsushiro [*Japan*] [*Seismograph station code, US Geological Survey*] (SEIS)
MAJR......... Major Realty [*NASDAQ symbol*] (TTSB)
MAJR......... Major Realty Corp. [*NASDAQ symbol*] (SAG)
MajRty....... Major Realty Corp. [*Associated Press*] (SAG)
MAJS......... Master of Arts in Jewish Studies (PGP)
MAJSR....... Master of Arts in Judaic Studies (BJA)
MAJSR....... Major State Register (MHDB)
MAJY......... Majority (ROG)
MAK.......... Makedonski Aviotrnasport-Macedonian Airline [*FAA designator*] (FAAC)
MAK.......... Makhachkala [*Former USSR Seismograph station code, US Geological Survey*] (SEIS)
MAK.......... Making
MAK.......... Makkoth (BJA)
MAK.......... Malakal [*Sudan*] [*Airport symbol*] (OAG)
MAK.......... Maliair Ltd. [*British ICAO designator*] (FAAC)
MAK.......... Manual Abell-Kendall [*Clinical chemistry*]
mAk.......... Maritime Arctic [*Cold Air*] [*Meteorology*] (BARN)
MAK.......... Markway Resources Ltd. [*Vancouver Stock Exchange symbol*]
MAK.......... Medical Accessories Kit [*Apollo*] [*NASA*]
MAK.......... Methyl Amyl Ketone [*Organic chemistry*]
MAK.......... Methylated Albumin Kieselguhr [*Chromatography*]
MAK.......... Monopulse Antenna Kit
MAKA......... Major Karyotypic Abnormalities [*Medicine*]
MAKETRANS... Make Necessary Transfer [*Military*] (DNAB)

Makhsh........	Makhshirin (BJA)
MAKHU	Moskovsky Akademichesky Khoreografichesky Uchilishche
Makita	Makita Corp. [*Associated Press*] (SAG)
MAKL	Markel Corp. [*NASDAQ symbol*] (NQ)
makm	Makimono (VRA)
MAKO	Mako Marine International, Inc. [*NASDAQ symbol*] (SAG)
MAKO	Mako Marine Intl. [*NASDAQ symbol*] (TTSB)
MakoM	Mako Marine International, Inc. [*Associated Press*] (SAG)
MAKOU	Mako Marine Intl. `Unit' [*NASDAQ symbol*] (TTSB)
MAKRO	Management Analysis of Key Resource Operations [*Military*]
Makromol Chem Symp...	Makromoleculare Chemie Symposia (MEC)
Maks..........	Makhshirin (BJA)
MAKS	Multipurpose Aero-Space Plane [*Russian delta-wing orbiter*]
Maksh.........	Makhshirin (BJA)
MAKSUTSUB...	Make Suitable Substitution
MAL	Macroassembly Language [*Computer science*] (BUR)
MAL	Mad Art Lover
MAL	Magnetic Armature Loudspeaker
MAL	Maintain at Least (Altitude) [*Aviation*] (FAAC)
Mal	Malachi [*Old Testament book*]
MAL	Malachias [*Old testament book*] [*Douay version*]
MAL	Malaga [*Spain*] [*Seismograph station code, US Geological Survey*] (SEIS)
MAL	Malan Realty Investors [*NYSE symbol*] (SAG)
MAL	Malariology Technician [*Navy*]
MAL	Malaspina College Learning Resources Centre [*UTLAS symbol*]
MAL	Malate
MAL	Malay (WDAA)
mal	Malayalam [*MARC language code Library of Congress*] (LCCP)
MAL	Malayan (AABC)
MAL	Malayan Airways Ltd.
MAL	Malaysia (WDAA)
MAL	Malaysian Air Lines
Mal	Maleyl [*Biochemistry*]
MALlon........	Malfunction (KSC)
MAL	Malicious [*FBI standardized term*]
MAL	Malleable (MSA)
mal	Malonate [*Organic chemistry*]
MAL	Malone [*New York*] [*Airport symbol*] (AD)
MAL	Malone College, Canton, OH [*OCLC symbol*] (OCLC)
MAL	Malone, NY [*Location identifier FAA*] (FAAL)
MAL	Malta (WDAA)
mal	Malum [*Ill*] [*Latin*] (MAE)
Mal	Malus [*Constellation*] (WDAA)
MAL	Man and LASER (MCD)
MAL	Marco Resources [*Vancouver Stock Exchange symbol*]
MAL	Master Authorization List
MAL	Materiel Allowance List [*Military*]
MAL	Maximal Acceptable Load (PDAA)
MAL	McAlpine Aviation Ltd. [*British ICAO designator*] (FAAC)
MAL	Medullary Thick Ascending Limb [*Anatomy*]
MAL	Memory Access Logic
MAL	Mercury Arc Lamp
MAL	Meta Assembly Language
MAL	Methacrolein [*Also, MACR*] [*Organic chemistry*]
MAL	Midaxillary Line [*Medicine*]
MAL	Middle Assyrian Laws (BJA)
MAL	Mobile Airlock (MCD)
MAL	Modern American Law [*A publication*] (DLA)
MAL	Multiairline [*Type of British pole line construction*]
MAL	Multiple Address Limit (NOAA)
MALA	Malarial Parasites [*Infectious diseases Laboratory and respiratory*] (DAVI)
MALA	Manpower and Logistics Analysis (MCD)
MALA	Master of Arts in Liberal Arts (PGP)
MALA	Master of Arts in Liturgical Arts (PGP)
MAL-AAACE...	Media and Adult Learning Section of the American Association for Adult and Continuing Education (EA)
MALAC........	Malacology
MALAD	Maladjusted Child [*Social Work*] [*British*] (DSUE)
MALAGOC....	Mutual Assistance of the Latin American Government Oil Companies G2 [*See also ARPEL*] (EA)
Malag Rep...	Malagasy Republic
MalanR........	Malan Realty Investors [*Associated Press*] (SAG)
MALAR	Malaria [*Infectious diseases*] (DAVI)
MALAS........	Master of Arts in Latin American Studies (PGP)
MALAS........	Midwestern Association for Latin American Studies
Malay	Malaysia (VRA)
Malaysa......	Malaysia Fund, Inc. [*Associated Press*] (SAG)
Mal-BSA	Maleated Bovine Serum Albumin [*Medicine*] (DMAA)
MALC	Madison Area Library Council [*Library network*]
MALC	Management of Acquisition Logistics Course (AAGC)
MALCAP	Maryland Academic Library Center for Automated Processing (NITA)
MALCAP	Maryland Library Center for Automated Processing [*Library network*]
MALCD	Matrix-Addressed Liquid Crystal Display
MALCM........	Mercantile Adjuster and the Lawyer and Credit Man [*A publication*] (DLA)
Malcolm Ethics...	Malcolm's Legal and Judicial Ethics [*A publication*] (DLA)
MALCS........	Mujeres Activas en Letras y Cambio Social (EA)
MALD	Master of Arts in Law and Diplomacy
MA(LD)........	Master of Arts (Landscape Design), University of Manchester [*British*] (DBQ)
MALD	Modular Analysis of Learning Difficulties (OICC)
MALDEF.......	Mexican American Legal Defense and Educational Fund (EA)
MALDI	Matrix-Assisted LASER Desorption Ionization [*Spectroscopy*]

Mald Isls	Maldive Islands
MALDMS	Matrix-Assisted LASER Desorption Mass Spectrometry
MALDT........	Mean Administrative and Logistics Downtime [*Quality control*] (MCD)
MALE	Multiaperture Logic Element
MALER	Master of Arts in Labor and Employment Relations (PGP)
Malerei u Zeichn...	Malerei und Zeichnung [*A publication*] (OCD)
Malev	Hungarian Airlines (BUAC)
MALF	Malfunction (KSC)
MALF	Mobile Aerobee Launch Facility
MALG	Minnesota Antilymphoblast Globulin [*Medicine*] (DMAA)
MALI	Material Annex Line Item [*Military*]
MALI	Matrix-Assisted Laser Ionizaion [*Spectrometry*]
MALI	Michigan Accident Location Index [*Michigan State Police*] [*Information service or system*] (IID)
MALIB	Math Analysis Library (MCD)
MA(LibSc) ...	Master of Arts (Library Science)
malig	Malignant [*Medicine*]
MALIMET	Master List of Medical Indexing Terms
Malinc	Mallinckrodt Group [*Formerly, IMCERA Group*] [*Associated Press*] (SAG)
Malinckr	Mallinckrodt Group [*Formerly, IMCERA Group*] [*Associated Press*] (SAG)
MALIPR	Material Annex Line Item Progress Report [*Military*] (NG)
MALIS	Master of Arts in Library and Information Science (PGP)
MALL	Creative Computers [*NASDAQ symbol*] (TTSB)
MALL	Creative Computers, Inc. [*NASDAQ symbol*] (SAG)
MALL	Mall [*Postal Service standard*] (OPSA)
MALL	Malleable
MALL	Master of Arts in Liberal Learning (PGP)
MALL	Minnesota Association of Law Libraries [*Library network*]
MALLAR	Manned Lunar Landing and Return [*NASA*]
Mal Law M...	Malynes' Ancient Law Merchant [*A publication*] (DLA)
Mall Ent......	Mallory's Modern Entries [*A publication*] (DLA)
Mal Lex Merc...	Malynes' Lex Mercatoria [*3 eds.*] [*1622-36*] [*A publication*] (DLA)
Mallon........	Mallon Resources Corp. [*Associated Press*] (SAG)
Mallory	Mallory's Irish Chancery Reports [*A publication*] (DLA)
Mal L Rev ...	Malaya Law Review [*A publication*] (DLA)
MALLS	Multiangle LASER Light-Scattering [*Instrumentation*]
MALM	Maryknoll Associate Lay Missioners (EA)
MALM	Maryknoll Mission Association of the Faithful (EA)
MALMARC	Malaysian MARC (NITA)
MAL MISCH...	Malicious Mischief [*Legal term*] (DLA)
MALN	Minimum Air Low Noise (PDAA)
MALN..........	Mouvement Africain de Liberation Nationale [*African Movement for National Liberation*]
MALODES	Modern Army Logistics Data Exchange System
MALOF........	Minimum Accepted Level of Fill [*Military*]
Malone	Editor, 6, 9, and 10, Heiskell's Tennessee Reports [*A publication*] (DLA)
MALOR	Mortar and Artillery Location RADAR (RDA)
MALOS	Maintenance and Logistics Space [*System*]
MALP	Major Assembly Labor and Performance (MCD)
MALPAS	Malvern Program Analysis System (NITA)
MAL PROS...	Malicious Prosecution [*Legal term*] (DLA)
MALR.........	Mortar/Artillery Locating RADAR (PDAA)
MALRY	Malaysian Leprosy Relief Association (BUAC)
MALS	Master of Arts in Liberal Studies
MALS	Master of Arts in Library Science
MALS	Master of Arts in Library Service (NADA)
MALS	Medium-Intensity Approach Lighting System [*Aviation*]
MALS	Members of an Amalgamated Society [*Slang British*] (DSUE)
MALSCE......	Massachusetts Association of Land Surveyors and Civil Engineers (SRA)
MALSF........	Medium-Intensity Approach Lighting System with Sequenced Flashers [*Aviation*]
MALSF	Medium Intensity Approach Light System with Sequenced Flashing Lights [*FAA*] (TAG)
MALSR	Medium-Intensity Approach Lighting System with Runway Alignment Indicator Lights [*Aviation*]
MALSR	Medium Intensity Approach Light System with Rail [*FAA*] (TAG)
MALS/RAIL...	Minimum-Approach Lighting System with Runway Alignment Indicator Lights [*Aviation*] (DNAB)
MALT..........	Lion Brewery [*NASDAQ symbol*] (TTSB)
MALT..........	Lion Brewery, Inc. (The) [*NASDAQ symbol*] (SAG)
MALT..........	Macosa-Associated Lymphoid Tissue [*Medicine*]
MALT..........	Male, Altered Animal (DMAA)
MALT..........	Maltese (DSUE)
MALT..........	Master of Arts in Language Teaching (GAGS)
MALT..........	Military Adviser's Language Text
MALT..........	Military Assistance Language Training
MALT..........	Mnemonic Assembly Language Translator [*Computer science*] (IEEE)
MALT..........	Monetary Allowance in Lieu of Transportation [*DoD*]
MALT..........	Mucosa-Associated Lymphoid Tissue [*Anatomy*]
MALT..........	Munich Alcoholism Test [*Medicine*] (DMAA)
MALTA........	Middle Atlantic Lawn Tennis Association
Malt CM	Maltby on Courts-Martial [*A publication*] (DLA)
MALU.........	Maine Association of Life Underwriters (SRA)
MALU.........	Massachusetts Association of Life Underwriters (SRA)
MALU.........	Michigan Association of Life Underwriters (SRA)
MALU.........	Minnesota State Association of Life Underwriters (SRA)
MALU.........	Mississippi Association of Life Underwriters (SRA)
MALU.........	Missouri Association of Life Underwriters (SRA)
MALU.........	Mode Annunciator and Logic Unit (PDAA)
MALV.........	Malva [*Mallow*] [*Pharmacy*] (ROG)
MALVINE	Manuscripts and Letters via Integrated Networks in Europe (TELE)

Malynes.......	Malynes' Lex Mercatoria [3 eds.] [1622-36] [A publication] (DLA)
MAm.............	Amesbury Public Library, Amesbury, MA [Library symbol Library of Congress] (LCLS)
M + Am	Compound Myopic Astigmatism [Ophthalmology]
MAM.............	Joint II March-May Study [Coastal Upwelling Ecosystems Analysis] (MSC)
MAM............	Madam (DSUE)
MAM............	Maintenance Assist Module
MAM............	Maintenance Assumes Monitor [Aviation] (FAAC)
MAM............	Mambajao [Philippines] [Seismograph station code, US Geological Survey Closed] (SEIS)
MAM............	Management Analysis Memorandum [DoD] (MCD)
MAM............	Management and Administration Manual (NRCH)
MAM............	Marquis Academic Media [Publisher]
MAM............	Mars Aeronomy Mission (MCD)
MAM............	Master Model (MCD)
MAM............	Master of Agriculture and Management (PGP)
MAM............	Master of Animal Medicine (GAGS)
MAM............	Master of Applied Mechanics (PGP)
MAM............	Master of Arts in Management
MAM............	Master of Arts Management (PGP)
MAM............	Master of Arts - Ministry (PGP)
MAM............	Master of Association Management (PGP)
MAM............	Master of Avian Medicine (PGP)
MAM............	Master of Aviation Management (GAGS)
MAM............	Matamoros [Mexico] [Airport symbol] (OAG)
MAM............	Material Acquisition Manager [Army] (AAGC)
MAM............	Materiel Acquisition Management Program [Army] (RDA)
MAM............	Matter-Anti-Matter (PDAA)
MAM............	Maxxim Medical [NYSE symbol] (TTSB)
MAM............	Maxxim Medical, Inc. [NYSE symbol] (SPSG)
MAM............	Medical Association of Malta (BUAC)
MAM............	Medium-Altitude Missile (MCD)
MAM............	Medium Automotive Maintenance
MAM............	Memory Access Multiplexer (NITA)
MAM............	Memory Allocation Manager
MAM............	Mercury Asset Management [Commercial firm British]
MAM............	Message Access Method [Honeywell, Inc.]
MAM............	Meta Aviotransport-Macedonia [Yugoslavia] [ICAO designator] (FAAC)
MAM............	Methylazoxymethanol (STED)
MAM............	Methylazoxymethanol Acetate [Organic chemistry]
MAM............	Microwave Attenuator Monitor (IAA)
MAM............	Military Air Movement
MAM............	Military Assistance Manual (AFM)
MAM............	Milliammeter
mam............	Milliampere-Minute (STED)
MAM............	Milliampere Minutes
MAM............	Missile Alarm Monitor
MAM............	Missile Assembly and Maintenance [NASA] (IAA)
MAM............	Mission Air Ministries [Defunct] (EA)
MAM............	Mission Area Manager [Army]
MAM............	Monoacetylmorphine [Organic chemistry]
MAM............	Mot a Mot [Word for Word] [French]
MAM............	Multiapplication Monitor
MAM............	Multiple Access to Memory [Computer science] (IEEE)
M+Am............	Myopic Astigmatism [Ophthalmology] (DAVI)
MAM............	Society of Automotive Engineers, Inc. (AAGC)
MAMA.........	Management Accounting Maintenance Advertising, Inc.
MAMA.........	Manual-Automatic Multipoint Apparatus (MCD)
MAMA.........	Material Acquisition Management Application [Suggested name for the Library of Congress computer system]
MAMA.........	Meet-a-Mum Association [British] (DI)
MAMA.........	Midarm Muscle Area (STED)
MAMA.........	Middletown Air Materiel Area [Air Force]
MAMA.........	Mobile Automated Metabolic Analyzer [Aerospace]
MAMA.........	Monoammonium Methanearsonate
MAMA.........	Monoclonal Antimalignant Antibody [Immunochemistry]
MAMA.........	Movement for All-Macedonian Action [Political party]
MAMA.........	Multi-Anode Microchannel Array (PDAA)
MAMAA......	Mothers Against Murder and Aggression [An association] (BUAC)
MAM Ac......	Methylazoxymethanol Acetate [Organic chemistry] (DMAA)
MAMB.........	Master of Applied Molecular Biology (PGP)
MAMB.........	Military Acquisition Management Branch [Army] (RDA)
MAMB.........	Military Advisory Mission, Brazil
MAMB.........	Missile Assembly and Maintenance Building [NASA] (IAA)
MAMBO	Mediterranean Association for Marine Biology and Oceanology [ICSU] (EAIO)
MAMBO	Minuteman Assembly-Maintenance Building, Ogden (SAA)
MAMC........	Altona Medical Centre Library, Manitoba [Library symbol National Library of Canada] (NLC)
MAMC........	Madigan Army Medical Center (AABC)
MAMC........	Master of Arts in Mass Communication (PGP)
MAMC........	Mean Arm Muscle Circumference (STED)
MAMC........	Midarm Muscle Circumference [Myology]
MAMDC	Multipurpose Arthritis and Musculoskeletal Diseases Center [University of Alabama, Birmingham] [Research center] (RCD)
MAME.........	Master of Arts in Missions/Evangelism (PGP)
MAME.........	Missile and Munitions Evaluation (MCD)
MAME.........	Mobile America [NASDAQ symbol] (TTSB)
MAME.........	Mobile America Corp. [NASDAQ symbol] (NQ)
MA Mech	Master of Applied Mechanics
MAMEE.......	Meyer Ammunition Module - Emerson Electric
MAMFC.......	Master of Arts in Marriage and Family Counseling (GAGS)
MAMFCC......	Master of Arts in Marriage, Family, and Child Counseling (PGP)
MAMFT........	Master of Arts in Marriage and Family Therapy (PGP)
MAmg........	Medial Amygdaloid [Nucleus] (STED)
MAMGRAPHY...	Mammography
MA Mgt.......	Master of Arts in Management (PGP)
MAmHi	Amesbury Historical Society, Amesbury, MA [Library symbol Library of Congress] (LCLS)
MAMI...........	Machine-Aided Manufacturing Information [Computer science]
MAMI...........	Modified Alternate Mark Inversion [Telecommunications] (TEL)
MAMI...........	Multiple Association Management Institute [Later, IAMC] (EA)
MAMIE........	Magnetic Amplification of Microwave Integrated Emissions (IEEE)
MAMIE........	Minimum Automatic Machine for Interpolation and Extrapolation
M Am IMME...	Member of the American Institute of Mining and Metallurgical Engineers
MA Min........	Master of Arts in Ministry (PGP)
Ma-Min.......	Milliampere-Minute
MA min.......	Milli-Ampere-Minute (STED)
MAMIS........	Mandatory Modification and Inspection Summary [Aviation] (DA)
MA Missions...	Master of Arts in Missions (PGP)
MAML........	Master of Arts in School Media Librarianship (PGP)
MAMM........	Master of Arts in Ministry Management (PGP)
MAMMA......	Men Against the Maxi-Midi Atrocity [Klosters, Switzerland, group opposing below-the-knee fashions introduced in 1970]
MAMMAX	Machine-Made and Machine-Assisted Index [Computer science] (IAA)
mammo	Mammography [Gynecology] (DAVI)
MAMO	Advanced Mammography Sys [NASDAQ symbol] (TTSB)
MAMO	Advanced Mammography Systems [NASDAQ symbol] (SAG)
MAMOE.......	Medical Administration and Miscellaneous Operating Expenses [Veterans Administration]
MAMOS	Marine Automatic Meteorological Observing Station [Automatic system]
MAMOS	Missouri Associated Migrant Opportunities Services (EA)
MaMP........	Maine State Planning Office, Augusta, ME [Library symbol Library of Congress] (LCLS)
MAMP........	Mainz Army Maintenance Plant (MCD)
MAMP.........	Materiel Acquisition Management Plan
MAMP.........	Michigan Army Missile Plant (MCD)
MAMP.........	Millampere [or Milliamperage] (IAA)
MAMP.........	Mission Area Materiel Plan [Army]
MAMRC	Military Aerospace Maintenance and Regeneration Center (MUSM)
MAMRD	Master of Agricultural Management and Resource Development (GAGS)
MAMRON.....	Marine Aircraft Maintenance Squadron
MAMS.........	Maintenance Activity Management System [Military]
MAMS.........	Maintenance Assist Modules (MCD)
MAMS.........	Marine Meteorological Services [Marine science] (MSC)
MAMS.........	Master of Applied Mathematical Sciences (PGP)
MAMS.........	Master of Associated Medical Sciences (PGP)
MAMS.........	Materiel Acquisition Management System
MAMS.........	Medical Administrative Management System
MAMS.........	Member of the Association of Medical Secretaries, Practice Administrators, and Receptionists [British] (DBQ)
MAMS.........	Military Aircraft Marshaling System
MAMS.........	MIRCOM [Missile Material Readiness Command] Automated Microfilm System [Army] (IID)
MAMS.........	Missile Altitude Measurement System
MAMS.........	Missile Assembly and Maintenance Shop [NASA]
MAMS.........	Missile Assistance Maintenance Structure (IAA)
MAMS.........	Modern Army Maintenance System
MAMS.........	Multiple Access to Memory System [Computer science]
m-AMSA	Acridinyl Ansidide [Antineoplastic drug] (DAVI)
m-AMSA	Amsacrine [Antineoplastic drug] [Also, AMSA] (CDI)
MAMSA.......	Managing and Marketing Sales Association [British] (DBA)
MAM Sc.......	Master of Applied Mathematical Science (PGP)
MAMSER	Mass Mobilisation for Self Reliance, Social Justice, and Economic Recovery [Nigeria] (BUAC)
M Am Soc CE...	Member of the American Society of Civil Engineers
MAMSPAR ...	Member of the Association of Medical Secretaries, Practice Administrators, and Receptionists [British] (DI)
MAMSS.......	Machine Augmented Manual Scheduling System (MCD)
MAMT........	Mean Active Maintenance Time (MCD)
MAMTF.......	Mobile Automated Microwave Test Facility (PDAA)
MAMTR......	Milliammeter
MA (Mus)	Master of Arts in Music
MAMV........	Maclura Mosaic Virus [Plant pathology]
MAmW........	Whittier Home Association, Amesbury, MA [Library symbol Library of Congress] (LCLS)
MAN............	Magnetic Automatic Navigation [System] (RDA)
MAN............	Magnocellular Nucleus [of anterior neostriatum] [Neurology] (DAVI)
MAN............	Mailorder Association of Nurserymen [Defunct] (EA)
MAN............	Mainly about Nature [A publication]
MAN............	Maintenance Alert Network [RCA]
MAN............	Management (WDAA)
MAN............	Manager [or Managing] (EY)
man............	Managing (DD)
Man............	Mancando [Dying Away] [Music]
MAN............	Manchester [England] [Airport symbol] (OAG)
MAN............	Mandato de Accion y Unidad Nacional [Mandate of Action and National Unity] [Bolivia] [Political party] (PPW)
man............	Mandingo [MARC language code Library of Congress] (LCCP)
MAN............	Mane [Morning] [Pharmacy]
MAN............	Manege [Horsemanship] [French]
MAN............	Manhattan
MAN............	Manifest (AABC)

MAN............	Manila [Philippines] [Seismograph station code, US Geological Survey] (SEIS)
Man	Manila (WDAA)
MAN............	Manilla (ADA)
man	Manipulate [Medicine] (MAE)
MAN............	Manipulus [A Handful] [Pharmacy]
MAN............	Manitoba [Canadian province]
Man	Manitoba [Canada] (DD)
Man	Manitoba Law Reports [Canada] [A publication] (DLA)
Man	Manning's Reports [1 Michigan] [A publication] (DLA)
Man	Manning's Reports, English Revision Court [1832-35] [A publication] (DLA)
MAN............	Mannion Air Charter, Inc. [ICAO designator] (FAAC)
MAN............	Mann Oil Resources, Inc. [Vancouver Stock Exchange symbol]
Man	Mannose [A sugar]
MAN............	Mannose (STED)
MAN............	Manpower, Inc. [NYSE symbol] (SPSG)
MAN............	Mansfield State College, Mansfield, PA [OCLC symbol] (OCLC)
Man	Manson's English Bankruptcy Cases [A publication] (DLA)
MAN............	Manual (KSC)
man	Manual [A handbook] (WDMC)
MAN............	Manuel Antonio Noriega [Military commander and de facto ruler of Panama]
MAN............	Manufacture
MAN............	Manufacturer (WDAA)
MAN............	Manufacturers Association of Nigeria (BUAC)
MAN............	Maschinenfabrik Augsburg-Nuernburg [Manufacturer of diesel engines]
MAN............	Meaningful Assistance in the Neighborhood [of Legal Aid Bureau of George Washington University Law School] (EA)
MAN............	Methacrylonitrile (EDCT)
MAN............	Methylammonium Nitrate (EDCT)
MAN............	Metropolitan Area Network [Telecommunications]
MAN............	Microwave Aerospace Navigation
MAN............	Military Aviation Notice [Air Force]
MAN............	Molecular Anatomy
MAN............	Molesters Anonymous (EA)
MAN............	Mouvement pour une Alternative Non-Violente [Movement for a Nonviolent Alternative] [France Political party] (PPE)
MAN............	Movementu Antiyas Nobo [New Antilles Movement] [Netherlands Political party] (EAIO)
MAN............	Movimentu Antiyas Nobo [New Antilles Movement] [Political party] (EY)
MAN............	Movimiento de Accion Nacionalista [National Action Movement] [Uruguay] [Political party] (EY)
MAN............	University of Manitoba Library [UTLAS symbol]
MAN-6-P...	Mannose-6-Phosphate [Chemistry] (DAVI)
MANA	Malawi News Agency (BUAC)
MANA	Manassas National Battlefield Park
MANA	Manatron, Inc. [NASDAQ symbol] (NQ)
MANA	Mannosidase Alpha (DMAA)
MANA	Manufacturers Agents National Association (EA)
MANA	Mexican American Women's National Association (EA)
MANA	Midwives Alliance of North America (EA)
MANA	Music Advisers' National Association [British]
MANA	Musicians Against Nuclear Arms [Defunct] (EA)
MAN-AEDS...	Manitoba Association for Educational Data Systems [Canada] (EDAC)
MANAG.......	Manage
MANAM	Manual Amendment
Man & G......	Manning and Granger's English Common Pleas Reports [A publication] (DLA)
Man & R......	Manning and Ryland's English King's Bench Reports [1827-30] [A publication] (DLA)
Man & R......	Manning and Ryland's English Magistrates' Cases [1827-30] [A publication] (DLA)
Man & Ry....	Manning and Ryland's English King's Bench Reports [1827-30] [A publication] (DLA)
Man & Ry....	Manning and Ryland's English Magistrates' Cases [1827-30] [A publication] (DLA)
Man & Ry KB...	Manning and Ryland's English King's Bench Reports [1827-30] [A publication] (ILCA)
Man & Ry Mag...	Manning and Ryland's English Magistrates' Cases [1827-30] [A publication] (DLA)
Man & Ry Mag Cas...	Manning and Ryland's English Magistrates' Cases [1827-30] [A publication] (DLA)
Man & Ry MC...	Manning and Ryland's English Magistrates' Cases [1827-30] [A publication] (DLA)
Man & S......	Manning and Scott's English Common Bench Reports, Old Series [IX] [A publication] (DLA)
Man & Sask Tax Rep (CCH)...	Manitoba and Saskatchewan Tax Reporter (Commerce Clearing House) [A publication] (DLA)
Man & Sc...	Manning and Scott's English Common Bench Reports, Old Series [IX] [A publication] (DLA)
MANAV	Maneuvering and Navigation System [Military] (IAA)
MANB	Mannosidase Beta (DMAA)
ManBagel....	Manhattan Bagel Co., Inc. [Associated Press] (SAG)
Manb Coke...	Manby's Abridgement of Coke's Reports [A publication] (DLA)
Manb Fines...	Manby on Fines [A publication] (DLA)
Man B News...	Manitoba Bar News [A publication] (ILCA)
MANC	Mancando [Decreasing in Loudness] [Music]
MANCAN......	Man-Carried Automatic Navigator (MCD)
Man Cas	Manumission Cases in New Jersey, by Bloomfield [A publication] (DLA)
MANCH........	Manchester [England]

Manch	Manchuria
MANCO	Mancando [Decreasing in Loudness] [Music]
MANCOVA...	Multivariate Analysis of Covariance
MANCUN......	Mancunium [Signature of the Bishops of Manchester] (ROG)
Mand	Mandaic (BJA)
MAND	Mandamus [We Command] [Latin] (ADA)
MAND	Mandatory (AABC)
Mand	Mandatory (TBD)
mand	Mandibar [Dentistry] (DAVI)
MAND	Mandible
MAND	Mandolin [Music]
mand	Mandolin (WDAA)
MAND	McCarron Assessment of Neuromuscular Development [Psychology] (DHP)
M&A	Maintenance and Administration (CIST)
M & A	Maintenance and Assembly (MCD)
M & A	Management and Administration
M&A	Mergers and Acquisitions (TDOB)
M & A	Mergers & Acquisitions Data Base [MLR Publishing Co.] [Information service or system] (CRD)
M & A	Mississippi & Alabama Railroad (IIA)
M & A	Missouri & Arkansas Railway Co.
M & A	Money and Advice
M & A	Montagu and Ayrton's English Bankruptcy Reports [1833-38] [A publication] (DLA)
M & ABL......	Montagu and Ayrton's Bankrupt Laws [A publication] (DLA)
MANDATE ...	Multiline Automatic Network Diagnostic and Transmission Equipment [Computer science] (CIST)
M & AW	Mountain and Arctic Warfare [British military] (DMA)
M & Ayr......	Montagu and Ayrton's English Bankruptcy Reports [1833-38] [A publication] (DLA)
M & B.........	Marianna & Blountstown [Railroad] (MHDB)
M & B.........	Marianna & Blountstown Railroad Co. (IIA)
M & B.........	Matched and Beaded
M&B	May & Baker (WDAA)
M & B.........	Mild and Bitter [Beer]
M & B.........	Montagu and Bligh's English Bankruptcy Reports [1832-33] [A publication] (DLA)
M & BR.......	Meridian & Bigbee River Railroad Co. (IIA)
M&BU.........	Mother & Baby Unit (WDAA)
M & C.........	Maintenance and Checkout (NASA)
M & C.........	Maintenance and Cure [Legal shorthand] (LWAP)
M & C.........	Manufacturers and Contractors
M&C	Measurement and Control [The Journal of InstMC] (ACII)
M & C.........	Monitor and Control Panel [Computer science] (NASA)
M & C.........	Montagu and Chitty's English Bankruptcy Reports [1838-40] [A publication] (DLA)
M&C	Morphine and Cocaine [Medicine] (DMAA)
M & C.........	Mylne and Craig's English Chancery Reports [A publication] (DLA)
M & C Bills...	Miller and Collier on Bills of Sale [A publication] (DLA)
M & Chit Bankr...	Montagu and Chitty's English Bankruptcy Reports [1838-40] [A publication] (DLA)
M & Cht Bankr...	Montagu and Chitty's English Bankruptcy Reports [1838-40] [A publication] (DLA)
M & C Partidas...	Moreau-Lislet and Carleton's Laws of Las Siete Partidas in Force in Louisiana [A publication] (DLA)
M & CSq...	Mapping and Charting Squadron [Air Force]
M & CU	Monitor and Control Unit [Aerospace] (AAG)
M and CW ...	Maternity and Child Welfare [Medicine British]
M & D	Maidstone & District Motor Services Ltd. [British] (DCTA)
M & D	McCormack & Dodge (NITA)
M & D	Medicine and Duty [Marked on a medical report and implying a suspicion of malingering] [Military British]
M & D	Mergers and Divestures
M & DOD....	Mission and Data Operations Directorate (MCD)
M & DV	Map and Data Viewer [NASA] (KSC)
M & E.........	Maintenance and Equipment (NATG)
M & E.........	Maneuvers and Exercises (NATG)
M & E.........	Material and Equipment [Nuclear energy] (NRCH)
M & E.........	Mechanical and Electrical Room (AAG)
M & E.........	Monitoring and Evaluation (ECON)
M & E.........	Morning and Evening (WDMC)
M & E.........	Music and Effects [Television]
M & E.........	Music and Sound Effects (WDMC)
MANDEC......	Maneuvering Decoy (MCD)
Man Dem....	Mansel on Demurrer [1828] [A publication] (DLA)
M & ER........	Mechanical and Electrical Room (AAG)
M & F.........	Male and Female [Components, as of connecting devices]
M & F.........	Materials and Facilities (MCD)
M & F.........	Mother and Father
MANDFHAB...	Male and Female Homosexual Association of Great Britain
M & G	Macnaghten and Gordon's English Chancery Reports [A publication] (DLA)
M & G	Maddock and Geldart's English Chancery Reports [1815-22] [A publication] (DLA)
M & G	Manning and Granger's English Common Pleas Reports [A publication] (DLA)
M & G	Mapping and Geodesy [Army] (AABC)
M & Gel	Maddock and Geldart's English Chancery Reports [1815-22] [A publication] (DLA)
M & GN	Midland and Great Northern Joint Line [Railway] [British] (ROG)
M & Gord ...	Macnaghten and Gordon's English Chancery Reports [A publication] (DLA)
M&H	Malone & Hyde, Inc. (EFIS)

M & H	Murphy and Hurlstone's English Exchequer Reports [*1836-37*] [*A publication*] (DLA)
M & HDA....	Medical and Hospital Department, Army
M & I	Manpower and Immigration [*Canada*]
M & I	Marine & Industrial
M & I	Marshall & Ilsley Bank
M & I	Minnesota & International Railway
M & I	Modernization and Improvement (AABC)
M & I	Modification and Installation (KSC)
M & I	Moisture and Impurities [*In fats*]
M & I	Movements and Identification [*Military*] (AFM)
M & I	Municipal and Industrial [*Users of water*]
M & IR	Manufacturing and Inspection Record (KSC)
M & K	Mylne and Keen's English Chancery Reports [*A publication*] (DLA)
M and L	Management and Logistics [*NATO*] (NATG)
mandl	Mandorla (VRA)
M&L	Matched and Lost [*Investment term*] (DFIT)
M & LA	Manpower and Logistics Analysis
M & M	Make and Mend
M & M	Manchester & Milford Railway [*Wales*]
M & M	Martha and the Muffins [*Musical group*]
M & M	Materials and Maintenance (NASA)
M & M	Merchants and Manufacturers Association (EA)
M&M	Mess and Maintenance [*Marine Corps*] (MUSM)
M & M	Metals and Minerals Research Services [*British*]
M & M	Milk and Molasses [*Enema*] [*Medicine*]
M&M	Mining & Metallurgy Divisions (ACII)
M & M	Montagu and MacArthur's English Bankruptcy Reports [*A publication*] (DLA)
M & M	Moody and Malkin's English Nisi Prius Reports [*A publication*] (DLA)
M&M	Morbidity and Mortality [*Medicine*] (DMAA)
M & M'A	Montagu and MacArthur's English Bankruptcy Reports [*A publication*] (DLA)
M & McA	Montagu and MacArthur's English Bankruptcy Reports [*A publication*] (DLA)
M & M's	Mass and Meals [*Refers to nuns who appear only at these activities*]
M & N	May and November [*Denotes semiannual payments of interest or dividends in these months*] [*Business term*]
M & N	Medical and Nursing [*Red Cross Disaster Services*]
M & N	Morning and Night [*Medicine*]
M & NA	Missouri & North Arkansas Railroad [*Nickname: May Never Arrive*]
M & NE.......	Manistee & Northeastern Railroad (IIA)
M & NW	Minnesota & Northwestern Railroad
M & O	Machinery and Optics
M & O	Maintenance and Operation (MCD)
M & O	Maintenance and Overhaul
m & o	Maintenance and Overhaul (AD)
M&O	Management and Operations (COE)
M & O	Management and Organization
m & o	Management and Organization (AD)
MANDO	Mancando [*Decreasing in Loudness*] [*Music*] (ROG)
M & O	Manpower and Organization [*Military*]
M & O	Materials and Others
M & O	Mobile & Ohio Railroad
M & O	Muscat and Oran (AD)
M & OB	Maintenance and Operations Branch [*BUPERS*]
M & OC	Monitor and Operations Control System [*Space Flight Operations Facility, NASA*]
M&P	Managerial and Professional (DMAA)
M & P	Maryland & Pennsylvania Railroad Co. (IIA)
M & P	Material and Process
m & p	Materials and Processes (AD)
M & P	Moore and Payne's English Common Pleas Reports [*A publication*] (DLA)
M & PE.......	Materials and Process Engineering (MCD)
M & PP.......	Manitou & Pike's Peak Railway
M & PP.......	Materials and Plant Protection [*Nuclear energy*] (NRCH)
M & P Sh ...	Maude and Pollock's Law of Merchant Shipping [*A publication*] (DLA)
M&Q	Mines and Quarries (AD)
M & R	Maclean and Robinson's Scotch Appeal Cases [*1839*] [*A publication*] (DLA)
m & r	Maintainability and Reliability (AD)
m & r	Maintainability and Repairs (AD)
M & R	Maintenance and Refurbishment (NASA)
M & R	Maintenance and Repair
M & R	Manning and Ryland's English King's Bench Reports [*1827-30*] [*A publication*] (DLA)
M&R	Martini & Rossi
M & R	Measure and Record
M & R	Moody and Robinson's English Nisi Prius Reports [*1830-44*] [*A publication*] (DLA)
M & RA	Manpower and Reserve Affairs
M & RDET ...	Maintenance and Repair Detachment
M & RE.......	Money and Real Estate [*Newspaper section*] (ADA)
M&RF	Maintenance and Refurbishing Facility [*Aerospace*] (NAKS)
M & R I & O...	Measure and Record Intake and Output [*Fluid measurement*] [*Medicine*] (CPH)
M & RMC	Manning and Ryland's English Magistrates' Cases [*1827-30*] [*A publication*] (DLA)
MANDRO	Mechanically-Alterable Nondestructive Read Out [*Computer science*] (IAA)
M & Rob.....	Maclean and Robinson's Scotch Appeal Cases [*1839*] [*A publication*] (DLA)
M & Rob......	Moody and Robinson's English Nisi Prius Reports [*A publication*] (DLA)

M & S.........	Bureau of Medicine and Surgery [*Navy*]
M & S.........	Maintenance and Supply
MANDS.......	Maintenance and Supply
M & S.........	Manning and Scott's English Common Bench Reports [*IX*] [*A publication*] (DLA)
M & S.........	March and September [*Denotes semiannual payments of interest or dividends in these months*] [*Business term*]
M&S	Marketing & Sales Division (ACII)
M & S.........	Marks & Spencer [*English department store chain*]
M & S.........	Marshall and Swift Cost Index (DICI)
M & S.........	Materials and Services [*NASA*] (KSC)
M & S.........	Materials and Structures (SDI)
M&S	Maternity and Surgical (AD)
M & S.........	Maule and Selwyn's English King's Bench Reports [*A publication*] (DLA)
M & S.........	McClelland & Stewart [*Canadian publisher*]
M & S.........	Media and Status [*Code*] [*DoD*]
M&S	Medical and Surgical (AD)
M & S.........	Medicine and Surgery (AD)
M & S.........	Methods and Standards
M & S.........	Microculture and Sensitivity [*Laboratory*] (DAVI)
M & S.........	Milwaukee & Superior Railroad
M & S.........	Model and Series (AAG)
m & s.........	Model and Series (AD)
M & S.........	Modeling and Simulation
M & S.........	Moore and Scott's English Common Pleas Reports [*1831-34*] [*A publication*] (DLA)
m & s.........	Mud and Snow (AD)
M & S.........	Mud and Snow Tire [*Automotive engineering*]
M & SC.......	Missile and Space Council [*Defunct*] (EA)
M & Sc.......	Moore and Scott's English Common Pleas Reports [*1831-34*] [*A publication*] (DLA)
M & Scott...	Moore and Scott's English Common Pleas Reports [*1831-34*] [*A publication*] (DLA)
MANDSD....	Mean and Standard Deviation
M & SS.......	Mapping and Survey System (KSC)
M & SSq......	Maintenance and Supply Squadron [*Air Force*]
M & StP	Milwaukee & St. Paul Railway
M&T	Main and Trim (COE)
M & T	Maintenance and Test (AAG)
M and T	Movements and Transports (NATG)
M & TE.......	Measurement and Test Equipment (KSC)
M & TP.......	Manufacturing and Testing Process (KSC)
M & U	Middletown & Unionville Railroad [*Nickname: Miserable and Useless*]
M and V	Meat-and-Vegetable [*A canned ration*] [*Military*]
M & W.........	Meeson and Welsby's English Exchequer Reports [*A publication*] (DLA)
M&W	Moore & Wright (WDAA)
M&W	Morecambe & Wise [*Comedians*] (WDAA)
M & WAA	Movers' and Warehousemen's Association of America [*Defunct*]
M & W Abr...	Marshall and Wood's Abridgment [*A publication*] (DLA)
M & W Cas...	Mining and Water Cases, Annotated [*United States*] [*A publication*] (DLA)
M & WH	Missile and Warhead Magazines
M & W Law Dic...	Mozley and Whiteley's Law Dictionary [*A publication*] (ILCA)
M & X.........	Microscope and X-Ray Inspection
M & Y.........	Martin and Yerger's Tennessee Reports [*8 Tennessee*] [*1825-28*] [*A publication*] (DLA)
M and Yerger's Rep...	Martin and Yerger's Tennessee Reports [*8 Tennessee*] [*1825-28*] [*A publication*] (DLA)
M & YR	Martin and Yerger's Tennessee Reports [*8 Tennessee*] [*1825-28*] [*A publication*] (DLA)
MAN ED......	Managing Editor (DGA)
Man El Cas...	Manning's English Election Cases (Court of Revision) [*A publication*] (DLA)
M Anesth Ed...	Master of Anesthesiology Education (PGP)
MANEX	Management Experten-Nachweis [*Management Experts Data Base*] [*Society for Business Information*] [*Information service or system*] (IID)
Man Exch Pr...	Manning's English Exchequer Practice [*A publication*] (DLA)
MANF.........	Manifold (KSC)
MANF.........	Manufacturer (WGA)
MANF...........	May, August, November, and February [*Denotes quarterly payments of interest or dividends in these months*] [*Business term*]
MANFG	Manufacturing (ROG)
MANFIST	Maneuver and Fire Support Team (MCD)
Man For......	Management Forum [*A publication*]
MANFOR.....	Manpower Force Packaging [*Military*]
MANFORCE...	Manpower for a Clean Environment [*Water Pollution Control Federation*]
MANFR.......	Manufacturer
MANFRD......	Manufactured
MANFRG......	Manufacturing
MANFST	Manifest
MANG.........	Management
Man G & S...	Manning, Granger, and Scott's English Common Bench Reports, Old Series [*I-VIII*] [*A publication*] (DLA)
Man Gaz	Manitoba Gazette [*A publication*] (DLA)
MANGR........	Manager
Man Gr & S...	Manning, Granger, and Scott's English Common Bench Reports, Old Series [*I-VIII*] [*A publication*] (DLA)
MANGRSS ...	Manageress (ROG)
MANGT	Management (ROG)
Manhattan C...	Manhattan College (GAGS)
Manhattan Sch Music...	Manhattan School of Music (GAGS)

Manhattanville C...	Manhattanville College (GAGS)
MANHC........	Madras Army Native Hospital Corps [British military] (DMA)
MAnHi	Andover Historical Society, Andover, MA [Library symbol Library of Congress] (LCLS)
ManhLfe	Manhattan Life Insurance Co. [Associated Press] (SAG)
MA-NHP.......	Massachusetts Natural Heritage Program [Massachusetts State Division of Fisheries and Wildlife] [Information service or system] (IID)
MANI	Manifold [Automotive engineering]
MANIAC......	Mathematical Analyzer, Numerical Integrator and Computer
MANIAC......	Mechanical and Numerical Integrator and Computer (IEEE)
MANICOM...	Manned Information and Communications Facility (SAA)
MANIF	Manifest
manif...........	Manifesto (VRA)
manifest	Manifestation [Medicine]
MAnimSc....	Master of Animal Science, University of Liverpool [British] (DBQ)
Man Int Law...	Manning's Commentaries on the Law of Nations [A publication] (DLA)
Manip	All India Reporter, Manipur [A publication] (DLA)
manip..........	Manipulation [Medicine]
Manip..........	Manipulus [A Handful] [Pharmacy]
MANIP	Manual Input [Computer science]
MANIS	Modified Atlantic Naval Intelligence Summary
MANIT	Manitoba [Canadian province]
Manitoba	Armour. Queen's Bench and County Court Reports Tempore Wood [Manitoba] [A publication] (DLA)
Manitoba	Manitoba Law Reports [Canada A publication] (DLA)
Manitoba L (Can)...	Manitoba Law Reports [Canada] [A publication] (DLA)
Manitw	[The] Manitowoc Co., Inc. [Associated Press] (SAG)
MANIX	Machine Aids to Nike-X [Army] (AABC)
Mankato St U...	Mankato State University (GAGS)
MANL	Manual (IAA)
MANLA	Malawi National Liberation Army (BUAC)
Man Lim	Mansel on Limitations [1839] [A publication] (DLA)
Man LR	Manitoba Law Reports [Canada A publication] (DLA)
Man LS Chron...	Manchester Law Students' Chronicle [A publication] (DLA)
Man LSJ	Manchester Law Students' Journal [A publication] (DLA)
MANM	Methylated Albumin-Nitrocelluse Membrane [Analytical biochemistry]
MANMAM	Manufacturing Management (PDAA)
MANMAN	Manufacturing Management (MHDI)
MANMED	Manual of the Medical Department [Navy]
MANMEDDEPT...	Manual of the Medical Department [Navy]
MANN	Manna [Pharmacy] (ROG)
Mann	Manning's Digest of the Nisi Prius Reports [England] [A publication] (DLA)
Mann	Manning's English Court of Revision Reports [A publication] (DLA)
Mann	Manning's Reports [1 Michigan] [A publication] (DLA)
MANN	Mannlicher Rifle
ManNac.......	N-Acetylmannosamine [Biochemistry]
Mann & G (Eng)...	Manning and Granger's English Common Pleas Reports [A publication] (DLA)
Mann & R....	Manning and Ryland's English King's Bench Reports [1827-30] [A publication] (DLA)
Mann & R....	Manning and Ryland's English Magistrates' Cases [1827-30] [A publication] (DLA)
Mann & R (Eng)...	Manning and Ryland's English King's Bench Reports [1827-30] [A publication] (DLA)
Mann Bills...	Manning on Bills and Notes [A publication] (DLA)
Mann Com...	Manning's Commentaries on the Law of Nations [A publication] (DLA)
Mann EC......	Manning's Revision Cases [1832-35] [A publication] (DLA)
Mann Ex Pr...	Manning's English Exchequer Practice [A publication] (DLA)
Mann G & S...	Manning, Granger, and Scott's English Common Bench Reports [135-39 English Reprint] [1845-56] [A publication] (DLA)
Mann G & S (Eng)...	Manning, Granger, and Scott's English Common Bench Reports, Old Series [I-VIII] [A publication] (DLA)
Manning	Manning's Reports [1 Michigan] [A publication] (DLA)
Manning	Manning's Unreported Cases [Louisiana] [A publication] (DLA)
Manning LA...	Manning's Unreported Cases [Louisiana] [A publication] (DLA)
Manning's UC...	Manning's Unreported Cases [Louisiana] [A publication] (DLA)
Manning's Unrep Cases...	Manning's Unreported Cases [Louisiana] [A publication] (DLA)
Mann Nat.....	Manning's Commentaries on the Law of Nations [A publication] (DLA)
Mann Unrep Cas...	Manning's Unreported Cases [Louisiana] [A publication] (DLA)
MANO	Manometer
MANOP	Manganese Nodule Program [For sampling on ocean floor]
MANOP	Manual of Operations
MANOR	Manor [Commonly used] (OPSA)
ManorCr	Manor Care, Inc. [Associated Press] (SAG)
MANORS......	Manors [Commonly used] (OPSA)
MANOVA......	Multivariate Analysis of Variance [Statistics]
MANOVA......	Multiway Analysis of Variance (MCD)
MAnP..........	Phillips Academy, Andover, MA [Library symbol Library of Congress] (LCLS)
MANPAD......	Man-Portable Air Defense (AABC)
MANPADS....	Man-Portable Air Defense System (MCD)
MAN PR......	Mane Primo [Early in the Morning] [Pharmacy]
MANPRINT...	Manpower and Personnel Integration [Military] (RDA)
Manpwl........	Manpower, Inc. [Associated Press] (SAG)
MANPWR......	Manpower (KSC)
MANR	Manager (ROG)
Man R	Manitoba Reports [Maritime Law Book Co. Ltd.] [Information service or system A publication A publication] (DLA)
MANR	Ministry of Agriculture and Natural Resources [Nigeria] (BUAC)

Man Ray......	Emmanuel Radnitsky [American artist, 1890-1976]
Man Rev Stat...	Manitoba Revised Statutes [Canada] [A publication] (DLA)
MANRRDC ...	Manpower Resources Research and Development Center [Army] (RDA)
Man RT Wood...	Manitoba Reports Tempore Wood [Canada] [A publication] (DLA)
Mans	Mansfield's Reports [49-52 Arkansas] [A publication] (DLA)
MANS	Mansiones
MANS	Mansions
Mans	Manson's English Bankruptcy and Winding-Up Cases [A publication] (DLA)
MANS	Map Analysis System [Computer science]
MANS	Mathematics Applied to novel Situations Test (EDAC)
MANSA.......	Man-Made Soling Association Ltd. [British] (BI)
MAN/SAFE...	Manual/Automatic Separation and Flotation Equipment (DNAB)
MANSAT	Manned Satellite
Mans Dem...	Mansel on Demurrer [1828] [A publication] (DLA)
Mansf Dig....	Mansfield's Digest of Statutes [Arkansas] [A publication] (DLA)
Mansfield U...	Mansfield University of Pennsylvania (GAGS)
MANSH	Manshead [England]
Mans Lim	Mansel on Limitations [1839] [A publication] (DLA)
Manson........	Manson's English Bankruptcy and Winding-Up Cases [A publication] (DLA)
Manson Bankr Cas...	Manson's English Bankruptcy and Winding-Up Cases [A publication] (DLA)
Mans on C...	Mansel on Costs [A publication] (DLA)
Manson (Eng)...	Manson's English Bankruptcy Cases [A publication] (DLA)
Man Stat......	Manitoba Statutes [Canada] [A publication] (DLA)
MANSWG.....	Manpower Systems Work Group
M Ant	Marcus Antoninus [of Scriptores Historiae Augustae] [Classical studies] (OCD)
MANT	Master of Arts in New Testament (PGP)
MANTAPS....	Maneuver Arms Tactical Protective System [Army] (RDA)
MANTECH....	Manufacturing Technology
MANTIS	Manpack Tactical Intelligence System
MANTRAC....	Manual Angle Tracking Capability
MANTRAP...	Management Training Program [of Center for Research in Business and Economics, University of Houston]
MANTRAPERS...	Manpower, Training, and Personnel (MCD)
Mantrn.........	Manatron, Inc. [Associated Press] (SAG)
Man T Wood...	Manitoba Reports Tempore Wood [Canada] [A publication] (DLA)
manu	Manufacture (DAVI)
MANU	Manugistics Group [NASDAQ symbol] (TTSB)
MANU	Manugistics Group, Inc. [NASDAQ symbol] (SAG)
MANU	Mozambique African National Union [Later, FRELIMO]
MANUF	Manufacturer [or Manufacturing] (ROG)
Manufacturing Mgmt...	Manufacturing and Management [A publication]
MANUFD......	Manufactured (ROG)
MANUFG......	Manufacturing (ADA)
ManufHm.....	Manufactured Home Communities, Inc. [Associated Press] (SAG)
Manugist	Manugistics Group, Inc. [Associated Press] (SAG)
Manum Cas...	Bloomfield's Manumission (or Negro) Cases [New Jersey] [A publication] (DLA)
Manum Cases...	Bloomfield's Manumission (or Negro) Cases [New Jersey] [A publication] (DLA)
Man Unr Cases...	Manning's Unreported Cases [Louisiana] [A publication] (DLA)
Man Unrep Cas...	Manning's Unreported Cases [Louisiana] [A publication] (DLA)
Man Unrep Cas (LA)...	Manning's Unreported Cases [Louisiana] [A publication] (DLA)
MANUPACS...	Manufacturing Planning and Control System (PDAA)
MANUV	Maneuvering (KSC)
Manvl	Manville Corp. [Associated Press] (SAG)
Manvlle	Manville Corp. [Associated Press] (SAG)
MANVOS.....	Manual Visas for Overseas System [Australia]
Manw..........	Manwood's Forest Laws [1592, 1598, 1615] [A publication] (DLA)
Manw For Law...	Manwood's Forest Laws [1592, 1598, 1615] [A publication] (DLA)
Manwood.....	Manwood's Forest Laws [1592, 1598, 1615] [A publication] (DLA)
MANX	Mannion Air Charter, Inc. [Air carrier designation symbol]
MANZ	Medical Association of New Zealand (BUAC)
MANZCP	Member, Australian & New Zealand College of Psychiatry (CMD)
MAO..........	MAC Aviation SL [Spain ICAO designator] (FAAC)
MAO..........	Magnetic Amplifier Output
MAO..........	Mailing Address Only [Military] (AABC)
MAO..........	Maintenance and Operation [Army] (AFIT)
MAO..........	Major Attack Option [Military] (MCD)
MAO..........	Manaus [Brazil] [Airport symbol] (OAG)
MAO..........	Manned Apollo Operations [NASA] (KSC)
mao..........	Maori [MARC language code Library of Congress] (LCCP)
MAO..........	Marion, SC [Location identifier FAA] (FAAL)
MAO..........	Mars Aeronomy Orbiter (MCD)
MAO..........	Massive Attack Option (MCD)
MAO..........	Master of Art of Oratory
MAO..........	Master of the Art of Obstetrics
MAO..........	Matair Ltd. [British ICAO designator] (FAAC)
MAO..........	Material Adjustment Order (MCD)
MAO..........	Maximum [or Minimum] Acid Output [Clinical chemistry]
MAO..........	Mechanization of Algebraic Operations (PDAA)
MAO..........	Medial Ankle Orthosis [Orthopedics] (DAVI)
MAO..........	Medical Assistance Only (GFGA)
MAO..........	Methylaluminoxane [Organic chemistry]
MAO..........	Methyl Aluminoxane Cocatalyst
MAO..........	Military Assistance Officer [Army]
MAO..........	Monoamine Oxidase [An enzyme]
MAO..........	Monoamin Oxidase Inhibitors [An antidepressant]
MAO..........	Movement to Arrest Oppressors (EA)
MAO..........	Muhammadan Anglo-Oriental

MAOA	Meteorological Aspects of Ocean Affairs [*Marine science*] (MSC)
MAOA	Meyers Aircraft Owners Association (EA)
MAOA	Monoamine Oxidase A [*An enzyme*]
MAOA	Panel of Meteorological Aspects of Ocean Affairs [*Marine science*] (OSRA)
MAO-B	Monoamine Oxidase B [*An enzyme*]
MAODP	Medic Alert Organ Donor Program (EA)
MAOE	Master of Adult and Occupational Education (PGP)
MAOF	Mexican-American Opportunity Foundation (EA)
MAOI	Monoamine Oxidase Inhibitor [*Biochemistry*]
MAOM	Master of Aerospace Operations Management (GAGS)
MAOP	Maximum Allowable Operating Pressure [*In pipelines*]
MAOS	Magnetic Amplifier Output Stage
MAOS	Metal Alumina Dielectric Oxide Semiconductor (CIST)
MAOS	Metal-Alumina-Oxide Semiconductor [*Computer science*] (IAA)
MAOS	Metal-Aluminum-Oxide Silicon (MSA)
MAOS	Minimum Airfield Operating Surface [*Military*]
MAOT	Master of Arts in Occupational Therapy
MAOT	Master of Arts in Old Testament (PGP)
MAOT	Maximum Allowable Operating Time (NASA)
MAOT	Medium Aperture Optical Telescope (PDAA)
MAOT	Member, Association of Occupational Therapists [*British*]
MAOT	Military Assistance Observer Team
MAOT	Missile Auxiliary Output Tester
MAOT	Mobile Air Operations Team [*Military*]
MAOU	Member of the American Ornithologists' Union
MAP	Machine Analyzer Package (PDAA)
MAP	Macro Arithmetic Processor [*Computer science*] (MDG)
MAP	Macroassembly Program [*Computer science*]
MAP	Madeira Abyssal Plain [*Geology*]
MAP	Maghreb-Arabe Presse [*Maghreb Arab Press Agency*] [*Morocco*]
MAP	Magnetic-Acoustic-Pressure (NVT)
MAP	Main Arithmetic Processor (IAA)
MAP	Maine Public Service [*AMEX symbol*] (TTSB)
MAP	Maine Public Service Co. [*AMEX symbol*] (SPSG)
MAP	Mainly about People [*A publication*]
MAP	Maintenance Administration Panel (ACRL)
MAP	Maintenance Analysis Procedure [*Computer science*]
MAP	Maintenance Analysis Program [*NASA*] (KSC)
MAP	Maitre en Administration Publique [*Master of Public Administration*]
map	Malayo-Polynesian [*MARC language code Library of Congress*] (LCCP)
MAP	Mamai [*Papua New Guinea*] [*Airport symbol*] (OAG)
MAP	Management Analysis [*or Assessment*] Program
MAP	Management and Planning Committee [*Library of Congress*]
MAP	Management and Programming (IAA)
MAP	Management Application Protocol (ACRL)
MAP	Management Assistance for Profits
MAP	Management Association of the Philippines (BUAC)
MAP	Manifold Absolute Pressure
MAP	Manifold Air Pressure
MAP	Manpower [*A publication*]
MAP	Manpower Absorption Plan [*Department of Labor*]
MAP	Manpower Analysis Paper
MAP	Manpower Assistance Project [*Department of Labor*]
MAP	Manufacturers' Assistance Program [*Michigan State Department of Commerce*] [*Lansing, MI*] [*Information service or system*] (IID)
MAP	Manufacturing Activity Projection
MAP	Manufacturing Automation Protocol [*Data communications standards*]
MAP	MAP [*Medical Assistance Programs*] International (EA)
MAP	Maples, MO [*Location identifier FAA*] (FAAL)
MAP	Mapping (MSA)
MAP	Marine Advisory Program [*Marine science*] (MSC)
MAP	Marketing Action Planner [*National Association of Printers and Lithographers*] [*A publication*]
MAP	Marketing Assistance Program [*Department of Agriculture*]
MAP	Mars Atmosphere Probe
MAP	Master Activity Programming
MAP	Master Air Pilot
MAP	Master Attack Plan [*Military*] (DOMA)
MAP	Master of Applied Psychology (PGP)
MAP	Master of Arts in Planning (PGP)
MAP	Material Acquisition Process [*or Program*] (MCD)
MAP	Materiel Acquisition Plan [*Army*]
MAP	Mathematical Analysis without Programming [*Computer science*]
MAP	Maximal Aerobic Power [*Laboratory*] (DAVI)
MAP	Maximum A Posteriori [*Statistics*]
MAP	Maximum Average Price
MAP	Mean Airway Pressure [*Medicine*] (DMAA)
MAP	Mean Aortic Pressure [*Medicine*]
MAP	Mean Arterial Pressure [*Medicine*]
MAP	Measurement Assurance Program [*National Institute of Standards and Technology*]
MAP	Measure of Academic Progress [*Educational test*]
MAP	Mecury All Position (IAA)
MAP	Media Access Project (EA)
MAP	Media Analysis Project (EA)
MAP	Media and People [*Information service or system*] (IID)
MAP	Medical Aid for the Palestinians (BUAC)
MAP	Medical Aid Post
MAP	Medical Assistace Program [*Public human service program*] (PHSD)
MAP	Medical Audit Program [*Computerized system of abstracted medical record information*]
MAP	Medicare Advocacy Project
MAP	Mediterranean Action Plan (BUAC)
MAP	Megaloblastic Anemia of Pregnancy [*Obstetrics*] (MAE)
MAP	Melphalan, Adriamycin, Prednisone [*Antineoplastic drug regimen*]
MAP	Memory Allocation and Protection
MAP	Memory Allocation Processor (NITA)
MAP	Mercapturic Acid Pathway [*Biochemistry*]
MAP	Mesenterial Arterial Pressure [*Medicine*]
MAP	Message Acceptance Pulse [*Aerospace communications*]
MAP	Meta-Aminophenol [*Organic chemistry*]
MAP	Meta-Aminopyrimethamine [*Biochemistry*]
MAP	Methionyl Aminopeptidase [*An enzyme*]
MAP	Methyl Acceptor Protein [*Biochemistry*] (DAVI)
MAP	Methylacetoxyprogesterone [*Also, MPA*] [*Endocrinology*]
MAP	Methylacetylene Propadiene [*Organic chemistry*]
MAP	Methyl(acetylenyl)putrescine [*Biochemistry*]
MAP	Methyl(amino)propanediol [*Organic chemistry*]
MAP	Methylaminopurine (MAE)
MAP	Microelectronics Application Programme (AIE)
MAP	Microelectronics Application Project [*British*] (DCTA)
MAP	Microlithiasis Alveolarum Pulmonum (DB)
MAP	Microprocessor Application Project [*In manufacturing industry*] [*Department of the Interior*]
MAP	Microprogrammed Array Processor
MAP	Microtubule-Associated Protein [*Cytology*]
MAP	Microwave Anisotropy Probe [*NASA*]
MAP	Microwave Anistropy Probe
MAP	Middle Atmosphere Programme [*International Council of Scientific Unions*]
MAP	Migrant Action Program (OICC)
MAP	Milestone Analysis Procedure
MAP	Military Airport Plan [*FAA*] (TAG)
MAP	Military Assistance Program [*DoD*]
MAP	Military Association of Podiatrists [*Later, FSPMA*] (EA)
MAP	Military Audit Project
MAP	Military Awards Profile [*Information service or system*] (IID)
MAP	Miller Assessment for Preschoolers
MAP	Minimum Acceptable Performance [*Telecommunications*] (TEL)
MAP	Minimum Annual Premium (MHDW)
MAP	Minimum Association Price (WDAA)
MAP	Minimum Attack Parameter [*Military*]
MAP	Minimum Audible Pressure
MAP	Ministry of Aircraft Production [*British*]
MAP	Minorities Advancement Plan
MAP	Missed Approach Point [*Aviation*] (AFM)
MAP	Missed Approach Procedure [*Aviation*]
MAP	Missile and Package Tester
MAP	Missile Application Propulsion
MAP	Missile Assignment Program (SAA)
MAP	Mission Application Program (NASA)
MAP	Mitigation Action Plans (COE)
MAP	Mitogen-Activated Protein [*Biochemistry*]
MAP	Mixed Aniline Point
MAP	Model and Program [*Computer science*]
MAP	Modification Application Plan [*Army*]
MAP	Modified American Plan [*Travel*]
MAP	Modified Atmospheric Packaging [*Food industry*]
MAP	Modular Acoustic Panel
MAP	Modular Analysis Processor [*Applied Data Research, Inc.*]
MAP	Modular Application System [*Computer science*]
MAP	Modular Assembly Prosthesis [*Medicine*]
MAP	Monitoring Attitudes of the Public [*ACLI*]
MAP	Monoammonium Phosphate [*Inorganic chemistry*]
MAP	Monophasic Action Potential [*Electrophysiology*] (AAMN)
MAP	Mothers of AIDS [*Acquired Immune Deficiency Syndrome*] Patients (EA)
MAP	Mouse Antibody Production [*Test for virus*]
MAP	Movement of the Assemblies of People [*Grenada*]
MAP	Multi-Access Pointer (PCM)
MAP	Multibus Accounting Package (PDAA)
MAP	Multichannel Astrometric Photometer [*Astronomy*]
MAP	Multicoverage Account Program [*Insurance*]
MAP	Multicultural Australia Papers [*A publication*]
MAP	Multifunction Adaptive Processor (NITA)
MAP	Multiple Address Processing
MAP	Multiple Aim Point [*ICBM*]
MAP	Multiple Allocation Procedure [*PERT*]
MAP	Multiple Array Processor
MAP	Municipal Airport (MCD)
MAP	Muscle Action Potential
MAP	Museum Assessment Program [*National Foundation on the Arts and the Humanities*]
MAP	Musical Aptitude Profile
MAP	Mutamycin, Adriamycin, Platinol [*Antineoplastic drug*] (CDI)
MAP	Mutual African Press Agency
MAP	Mutual Assistance Pact
MAP	Mutual Assistance Plan (NATG)
MAP	Mutual Assistance Program
MAP	National Oceanic and Atmospheric Administration [*ICAO designator*] (FAAC)
MAP3S	Multistate Atmospheric Power Production Pollution Study [*Department of Energy*]
MAPA	Master of Arts in Public Administration (GAGS)
MAPA	Master of Arts in Public Affairs (GAGS)
MAPA	Mexican-American Political Association
MAPA	Mooney Aircraft Pilots Association (EA)
MAPA	Muscle Adenosine Phosphoric Acid [*Biochemistry*] (DB)

MAPAD	Military Assistance Program Address Directory
MAPAF	Military Assistance Program Address File
MAPAG	Military Assistance Program Advisory Group
MAPAG	Multi-Association Policy Advisory Group [*An association*]
MAPAI	Mifleget Po'alei Eretz-Yisrael (BJA)
MAPAM	Mifleget Po'alim Me'uhedet (BJA)
MAPAR	Materials and Processes Acceptance Requirement
MAPAS	Master of Arts in Public Administration in Spanish (PGP)
MAPBIN	Mauritian Action for Promotion of Breast-Feeding and Infant Nutrition (BUAC)
MAPC	Master of Arts in Pastoral Counseling (PGP)
MAPC	Maximum Allowable Pevailing Charge [*Medicine*]
MAPC	Migrating Action Potential Complex [*Electrophysiology*]
MAPCC	Master of Arts in Pastoral Care and Counseling (PGP)
MAPCC	Military Assistance Program Country Code (AFM)
MAPCHE	Mobile Automatic Programmed Checkout Equipment
MAP/CIO	Military Assistance Program/Common Item Order
MAPCO	Malaysian Association of Private Colleges
MAPCO	MAPCO, Inc. [*Associated Press*] (SAG)
MAPCO	Mid-American Pipeline Co.
MAPCON	Microprocessor Applications Consultancy (NITA)
MAPD	Master Part Dimensioned (MCD)
MAPD	Maximum Allowable Percent Defective (PDAA)
MAPDA	Mid-America Periodical Distributors Association
MAPDFA	Media-Advertising Partnership for a Drug-Free America [*Later, DFA*] (EA)
MAPDU	Management Application Protocol Data Unit [*Telecommunications*] (OSI)
MAPE	Master of Arts in Physical Education (GAGS)
MAPE	Master of Arts in Political Economy (PGP)
MAPE	Maximum Absolute Percentage Error [*Statistics*]
MAPE	Mean Absolute Percentage Error [*Statistics*]
MAPE	Microcomputers and Primary Education
MAPETT	Military Assistance Program Evaluation Team, Thailand (CINC)
MAPEX	Map Exercise [*Military*] (INF)
MAPEX	Mid-America Payment Exchange
MAPEX	Military Articles Pacific Excesses (AFIT)
MAPF	Microatomized Protein Food (MAE)
MAPF	Mobile Aerial Port Flight [*Air Force*]
MAPG	Maximum Available Power Gain (MSA)
MAP-GA	Military Assistance Program - Grant Aid
MAPGEN	Map Generator (MHDI)
MAPHILINDO	Malaya-Philippines-Indonesia
MAPI	Machinery and Allied Products Institute (MHDI)
MAPI	Mail Application Programming Interface [*Computer science*] (PCM)
MAPI	Mail Applications Program Interface [*Microsoft Corp.*]
MAPI	Manufacturers Alliance (NTPA)
MAPI	Manufacturers Alliance for Productivity and Innovation (EA)
MAPI	Messaging API [*Application Programming Interface*] [*Computer science*]
MAPI	Microbial Alkaline Protease Inhibitor (DB)
MAPI	Millon Adolescent Personality Inventory [*Personality development test*] [*Psychology*]
MAPI	Mitsubishi Atomic Power Industries (IAA)
MAPICS	Manufacturing, Accounting and Product Information Central System (NITA)
MAPICS	Manufacturing, Accounting, and Production Information Control System [*IBM Corp.*]
MAPID	Machine-Aided Program for Preparation of Instruction Data
MapInfo	Mapinfo Corp. [*Associated Press*] (SAG)
MAPK	Mitogen Activated Protein Kinase [*An enzyme*]
MAPL	Manufacturing Assembly Parts List
MAPL	Master Allowance Parts List [*Military*] (CAAL)
MAPL	Military Acquisition Position List (RDA)
MAPLA	Military Assistance Program Logistics Agency [*Merged with Defense Supply Agency*]
MAPLE	Marketing and Product Line Evaluation (PDAA)
MAPLE	Minor Atomic Prolonged Life Equipment (PDAA)
MAPLHGN	Maximum Average Planar Linear Heat-Generator [*Nuclear energy*] (IAA)
MAPLHGR	Maximum Average Planar Linear Heat-Generation Rate [*Nuclear energy*] (NRCH)
MAPM	Master of Arts in Pastoral Ministry (PGP)
MAPM	Master of Arts in Pastoral Music (PGP)
M Ap Ma	Master of Applied Mathematics (PGP)
MAP Min	Master of Arts in Pastoral Ministry (PGP)
MAPMIS	Manpower and Personnel Management Information System [*Navy*]
MAPMISMAN	Manpower and Personnel Management Information System Manual [*Navy*] (DNAB)
MAPMOPP	Marine Pollution [*or Petroleum*] Monitoring Pilot Project [*Marine science*] (MSC)
MAPNY	Maritime Association of the Port of New York [*Later, MAPONY/NJ*] (EA)
MAPOLE	Magnetic Dipole Spark Transmitter (NASA)
MAPOM	Military Assistance Program Owned Materiel (AFM)
MAP/One	Manufacturing Automation Protocol/One [*Local area network*] [*Industrial Networking, Inc.*]
MAPONY	Maritime Association of the Port of New York
MAPONY/NJ	Maritime Association of the Port of New York/New Jersey (EA)
MAPORD	Methodology Approach to Planning and Programming Air Force Operational Requirements, Research and Development (IEEE)
MAP/OSP	Military Assistance Program Offshore Procurement (DNAB)
MAPP	Manpower and Personnel Plan [*Army*] (AABC)
MAPP	Manpower and Production Projections [*LIMRA*]
MAPP	Masking Parameter Printout [*Computer science*]
MAPP	MasterCard Automated Point-of-Sale Program
MAPP	Master of Arts in Public Policy (GAGS)
MAPP	Mathematical Analysis of a Perception and Preference
MAPP	Methyl Acetyl Propadrine and Propane (MCD)
MAPP	Mid-Continent Area Power Pool [*Electric power*]
MAPP	Mission Analysis and Performance Program
MAPP	Modern Aids to Planning Program [*Military*] (GFGA)
MApp	Musical Appreciation [*Record label*]
MAppEpidem	Master of Applied Epidemiology
MAPPER	Maintaining, Preparing, and Processing Executive Reports [*Computer science*] (CDE)
MAPPER	Maintaining, Preparing and Producing Executive Reports (NITA)
MAPPEX	Magazine and Periodical Publishers Exhibition (NITA)
MAPPLE	Macro-Associative Processor Programming Language [*Computer science*] (PDAA)
MAppLing	Master of Applied Linguistics
MApplLit	Master of Applied Literature (GAGS)
MApplM	Master of Applied Mathematics (GAGS)
M Appl Stat	Master of Applied Statistics (PGP)
MAppPsych	Master of Applied Psychology
MAPPS	Management Association of Private Photogrammetric Surveyors (EA)
MAppSc	Master of Applied Science
MAppSc-BltEnvir	Master of Applied Science - Built Environment
MAppSci	Master of Applied Science
MAppSc-MedPhys	Master of Applied Science - Medical Physics
MAppSc(SocEcol)	Master of Applied Science in Social Ecology
MAPR	Manufacturing Aids Program Requirements (AAG)
MAPR	Miniature Autonomous Plume Recorder [*Oceanography*]
MAPRAT	Maximum Power Ratio (IEEE)
MAPRC	Mediterranean Allied Photographic Reconnaissance Command
MAPRES	Mini Air Passenger Reservation System
MAPRIAL	Mezhdunarodnaja Assotsiatsija Professorov Russkogo Jazyka i Literatury [*International Association of Teachers of Russian Language and Literature*] (EAIO)
MAPROS	Maintain Production Schedules
MAPRP	Mesoscale Atmospheric Processes Research Program [*National Oceanic and Atmospheric Administration*]
MAPRS	Master of Arts in Pacific Rim Studies (GAGS)
MAPS	Machine Automated Parts System (MCD)
MAPS	Mail Abuse Prevention System
MAPS	Maintenance Analysis and Procedures System [*Computer science*]
MAPS	Major Assembly Performance System (MCD)
MAPS	Make-a-Picture Story [*Psychological testing*]
MAPS	Management Accounting and Payroll System (NITA)
MAPS	Management Accounting and Performance System
MAPS	Management Analysis and Planning System
MAPS	Manifold Air Pressure Sensor [*Automotive engineering*]
MAPS	Manpower Analysis and Planning Society (EA)
MAPS	Manpower and Production Survey [*LIMRA*]
MAPS	Manpower Area Planning System [*Under CAMPS*]
MAPS	Manufacturing and Production System (CIST)
MAPS	Mapinfo Corp. [*NASDAQ symbol*] (SAG)
MAPS	Market-Auction Preferred Stock
MAPS	Marketing, Advertising, and Promotions Solutions Exhibition [*British*] (ITD)
MAPS	Master Activation Phasing Schedule (IAA)
MAPS	Master of Arts in Pastoral Studies (PGP)
MA Ps	Master of Arts in Psychology (PGP)
MAPS	Master of Arts in Public Service
MAPS	McGill Action Planning System
MAPS	Measurement of Air Pollution from Satellites
MAPS	Measurement of Atmospheric Pollution from Satellites (NAKS)
MAPS	Measuring Air Pollution from Space [*Marine science*] (OSRA)
MAPS	Mesoscale Analysis and Prediction System [*Marine science*] (OSRA)
MAPS	Meteorological Applied Problem Solving
MAPS	Methyl(deazaisoalloxazine)propanesulfonic Acid [*Organic chemistry*]
MAPS	Metropolitan Air Post Society (EA)
MAPS	Microprogramable Arithmetic Processor System (PDAA)
MAPS	MidAmerica Automated Payments Systems [*Banking*] (TBD)
MAPS	Middle Atlantic Planetarium Society (EA)
MAPS	Migratory Animal Pathological Survey (PDAA)
MAPS	Military Applications of Photovoltaic Systems
MAPS	Military Aviation Preservation Society (EA)
MAPS	Million Adds per Second
MAPS	Miniature Air Pilot System
MAPIS	Minnesota Analysis and Planning System [*University of Minnesota*] [*Research center*] (RCD)
MAPS	Missile Application Propulsion Study
MAPS	Mission Analysis and Planning System (MCD)
MAPS	Mobile Aerial Port Squadron [*Air Force*]
MAPS	Mobility Analysis Planning System (MCD)
MAPS	Mobilization Asset Planning System [*Army*]
MAPS	Modern Accounts Payable System (MHDW)
MAPS	Modular Acoustic Processing System (MCD)
MAPS	Modular Azimuth Position System [*Army*] (RDA)
MAPS	Monetary and Payments System [*Committee*] [*American Bankers Association*]
MAPS	Monitoring of Air Pollution by Satellites (KSC)
MAPS	Monoclonal Antibody Purification System
MAPS	Monopropellant Accessory Power Supply [*Aerospace*] (AAG)
MAPS	Muhammad Ali Professional Sports [*Commercial firm*]
MAPS	Multicolor Automatic Projection System (IEEE)
MAPS	Multidimensional Affect and Pain Survey [*Medicine*] (DMAA)
MAPS	Multidisciplinary Association for Psychedelic Studies (EA)
MAPS	Multidisciplinary Association for Psychedelic Studies (EA)

MAPS	Multi-jurisdictional Automated Pre-clearance System
MAPS	Multiple Address Processing System
MAPS	Multiple Agency Processing System
MAPS	Multiple Aim-Point System
MAPS	Multiple Application Phototypesetting System (DGA)
MAPS	Multiple Automated Printing Systems (MCD)
MAPS	Multisatellite Attitude Program System [NASA]
MAPS	Multitarget Automatic Plotting System
MAPS	Multivariate Analysis and Prediction of Schedules
MAPS	Multivariate Analysis, Participation, and Structure
MAPSAC	Machine-Aided Planning, Scheduling, and Control
MAPSAD	Military Assistance Property Sales and Disposal (AFM)
MAPS/ALPS	Multiple Aim Point System / Alternate Launch Point System (PDAA)
MAP/SAMSR	Joint Army-Air Force Master Plan for the Satisfaction of Army Meteorological Support Requirements (MCD)
MAPSAS	Member of APSAS [Association of Public Service Administrative Staff] [British]
MApSc	Master of Applied Science (GAGS)
MAPSE	Minimal APSE [Ada Program Support Environment] [Computer science]
MAPSE	Minimum Implementation ADA Programming Support Environment (NITA)
MAPSEP	Mission Analysis Program for Solar Electric Propulsion [Computer science NASA]
MAPSIM	Mesoscale Air Pollution Simulation Model [Environmental Protection Agency] (GFGA)
MAPSq	Mobile Aerial Port Squadron [Air Force]
M Ap Stat	Master of Applied Statistics (PGP)
MAPsych	Master of Arts in Psychology (GAGS)
MAPT	Military Assistance Program Training (AFM)
MAPT	Military Assistance Program Transfer (AFM)
MAPT	Missed Approach Point [Aviation] (FAAC)
MAPT	More Advanced Petrol Tractors [Germany]
MAPT	Mothers Are People Too [Defunct] (EA)
MAPTAC	Methacrylamidopropyltrimethylammonium Chloride [Organic chemistry]
MAPTEL	Maplin Telecommunications (NITA)
MAPTIS	Manpower Personnel and Training Information System [Navy]
MAP-TOE	Management Practices in TOE Units [Military] (GFGA)
MAP/TOP	Manufacturing Automation Protocol / Technical Office Protocol (BTTJ)
MAPU	Memory Allocation and Protection Unit (MSA)
MAPU	Movimiento de Accion Popular Unida [Unified Popular Action Movement] [Chile] [Political party] (PD)
MAPU	Multiple Address Processing Unit [Military] (AABC)
MAPUC	Member of the Association for Promoting the Unity of Christendom [British]
MAPUC	Modified Area Production Urgency Committee [World War II]
MAPW	Master of Arts in Professional Writing (PGP)
MAPW	Medical Association for the Prevention of War [British] (DBA)
MAQ	MAC Aviation, S.L. [Spain] [FAA designator] (FAAC)
maq	Maquette (VRA)
M Aq	Master of Aquaculture (PGP)
MAq	Master of Aquaculture (GAGS)
MAQ	Maximum Acceptance Quantity
MAQ	Measures for Air Quality [Program] [National Institute of Standards and Technology]
MAQ	Monetary Allowance in Lieu of Quarters
MAQ	Sena Maduereira [Brazil] [Airport symbol] (AD)
MAR	Macroaddress Register
MAR	Magnetic Amplifier Relay
MAR	Main Admitting Room (STED)
MAR	Maintainability Action Request (MCD)
MAR	Maintenance Action Request
MAR	Maintenance Analysis Report (MCD)
MAR	Maintenance and Refurbishment (MCD)
MAR	Maintenance and Repair
MAR	Major Aircraft Review [Navy]
MAR	Major Assembly Release [Military] (AABC)
MAR	Malfunction Array RADAR
MAR	Managed Approach Reservoir [FAA] (TAG)
MAR	Management Analysis Report [DoD] (MCD)
MAR	Management Assessment Report (MCD)
MAR	Management Assessment Review (MCD)
MAR	Manistee & Repton R. R. [AAR code]
MAR	Manufacturing Action Request (MCD)
MAR	Manufacturing Assembly Report (IAA)
MAR	Maracaibo [Venezuela] [Airport symbol] (OAG)
MAR	Marasmus (STED)
mar	Marathi [MARC language code Library of Congress] (LCCP)
MAR	March (AFM)
MAR	March Helicopters Ltd. [British ICAO designator] (FAAC)
Mar	March's English King's Bench Reports [1639-42] [A publication] (DLA)
mar	Margin (STED)
MAR	Margin (DAVI)
MAR	Mar-Gold Resources [Vancouver Stock Exchange symbol]
MAR	Marian Minerals [Vancouver Stock Exchange symbol]
MAR	Marimba [Music]
mar	Marimba (WDAA)
MAR	Marine (MSA)
Mar	Marion Laboratories, Inc.
MAR	Maritime
MAR	Maritime Administration Report [Department of Commerce]
MAR	Maritime Central Airways
Mar	Marius [of Plutarch] [Classical studies] (OCD)

mar	Marker [Chromosome] (STED)
MAR	Market
mar	Maroon [Philately]
MAR	Marquette [Diocesan abbreviation] [Michigan] (TOCD)
MAR	Married
MAR	Marriott International [NYSE symbol] (SPSG)
MAR	Marrow (STED)
MAR	Marseilles [France] [Seismograph station code, US Geological Survey Closed] (SEIS)
MAR	Marshal (ROG)
Mar	Marshall and Sevestre's Appeals [1862-64] [Bengal, India] [A publication] (DLA)
Mar	Marshall's Circuit Court Reports [United States] [A publication] (DLA)
Mar	Marshall's Reports [Bengal] [A publication] (DLA)
Mar	Marshall's Reports [Kentucky] [A publication] (DLA)
Mar	Marshall's Reports [Ceylon] [A publication] (DLA)
MAR	Martial [Roman poet of the first century AD] (ROG)
Mar	Martin's Louisiana Reports [A publication] (DLA)
Mar	Martin's North Carolina Reports [1 North Carolina] [A publication] (DLA)
Mar	Marvel's Reports [Delaware] [A publication] (DLA)
Mar	Mary (Queen of England) (DLA)
MAR	Mass Accumulation Rate [Geology]
MAR	Massachusetts College of Art, Boston, MA [OCLC symbol] (OCLC)
M-Ar	Massachusetts Secretary of State, Archives Division, Boston, MA [Library symbol Library of Congress] (LCLS)
MAR	Master Angular Reference (IAA)
M Ar	Master of Architecture
MAR	Master of Arts in Religion
MAR	Master of Arts in Research (GAGS)
MA(R)	Master of Arts (Research) (PGP)
MAR	Material Availability Report [NASA] (KSC)
MAR	Material Availability Request
MAR	Matrix Attachment Region [Genetics]
MAR	Maximal Aggregation Ratio (STED)
MAR	Medication Administration Record [Medicine]
MAR	Memory-Address Register [Computer science]
MAR	Mercury Arc Rectifier (IAA)
MAR	Microanalytical Reagent
MAR	Microprogram Address Register
MAR	Mid-Air Retrieval (MCD)
MAR	Mid-Atlantic Ridge [of sea floor]
MAR	Minimal Angle Resolution
MAR	Minimally Attended RADAR (MCD)
MAR	Minimum Acceptable Rate of Return (MHDW)
MAR	Minimum Acceptable Reliability
MAR	Minimum Angle of Resolution (MCD)
MAR	Miscellaneous Apparatus Rack (IAA)
MAR	Mission Analysis Representative
MAR	Mississippi-Atchafalaya River [System] (USDC)
MAR	Mixed Antiglobulin Reaction (STED)
MAR	Monoclonal Antibody Resistant [Immunochemistry]
MAR	Monoclonal Antibody to Rat (DB)
MAR	Montana Administrative Register [A publication] (AAGC)
MAR	Morocco [ANSI three-letter standard code] (CNC)
MAR	Movimiento di Azione Rivoluzionaria [Revolutionary Action Movement] [Italian] (PD)
MAR	Movimiento de Accion Revolucionaria [Revolutionary Action Movement] [Mexico] (PD)
MAR	Multi-Adversity Resistance [to root rot] [Plant pathology]
MAR	Multifunction Array RADAR
MAR	Multiple Aberration Region [Genetics]
MAR	Multiple Access Relay
MAR	Multiple Access Return (SSD)
MAR	Multiple Array RADAR (IAA)
MAR	Municipal Association Record [A publication]
MAR	Muscarinic Acetylcholine Receptor [Biochemistry]
MaR	Myth and Ritual. Essays on the Myth and Ritual of the Hebrews in Relation to theCulture Pattern of the Ancient East [A publication] (BJA)
MAR	Mythology of All Races [A publication]
MAr	Robbins Public Library, Arlington, MA [Library symbol Library of Congress] (LCLS)
MAR	Tacoma, WA [Location identifier FAA] (FAAL)
MARA	Majority Rule Association (EA)
MARA	Midget Auto Racing Association [Sanctioning organization]
MARAAWEX	Marine Antiair Warfare Exercise (NVT)
MARAC	Marine Athletic Conference (PSS)
MARAD	Maritime Administration [Also, MA, MARITADMIN] [Department of Transportation]
MArAd	Master of Archive Administration, University of Liverpool [British] (DBQ)
MARADVU	Marine Advisory Unit
MARAIRMED	Maritime Air Forces Mediterranean [NATO] (NATG)
MARAIRWING	Marine Aircraft Wing
MARALLWEAFITRARON	Marine All Weather Fighter Training Squadron
Mar & Yer	Martin and Yerger's Tennessee Reports [8 Tennessee] [1825-28] [A publication] (DLA)
MARAS	Middle Airspace RADAR Advisory Service [Military] (DA)
Mar Av	Marvin on General Average [A publication] (DLA)
marb	Marble (VRA)
MARB	Marbled [Edges or sides of cover] [Bookbinding] (ROG)
MARB	Materiel Acquisition Review Board [Army]
MARBA	Mid-America Regional Bargaining Association
MARBARGE	Maritime Maintenance Barge

MARBASSCOL... Marine Corps Basic School
MarbFn........ Marble Financial Corp. [*Associated Press*] (SAG)
MARBI......... Machine-Readable Bibliographic Information (AL)
MARBI......... Machine-Readable Form of Bibliographic Information [*American Library Association*]
Mar Bills ..... Marius on Bills of Exchange [*A publication*] (DLA)
MARBKS....... Marine Barracks
MARBO......... Marianas-Bonins Command
Mar Br......... March's Brooke's New Cases [*1651*] [*England*] [*A publication*] (DLA)
MARBRIG .... Marine Brigade
MARC......... Hruska Meat Animal Research Center [*Department of Agriculture*] (GRD)
MARC......... Maastricht Referendum Campaign [*British*] (ECON) .
MARC......... Machine-Readable Cards
MARC......... Machine-Readable Catalog (NITA)
MARC......... Machine-Readable Cataloging [*Library of Congress*]
MARC......... Machine-Readable Code (IAA)
MARC......... Magnetic Abrasion Resistant Coating (IAA)
MARC......... Manpower Allocation Requirement Criteria [*Military*] (RDA)
MARC......... Manpower Authorization Request for Change [*Air Force*]
MARC......... Manpower Requirements Criteria [*Army*]
MARC......... Manufacturing Resource Control System [*Deritend Computer Bureau Ltd.*] [*Software package*] (NCC)
MARC......... Marcato [*Emphasized*] [*Music*]
Marc.......... Marcellus [*of Plutarch*] [*Classical studies*] (OCD)
MARC......... MARC, Inc. [*NASDAQ symbol*] (SAG)
Marc.......... Marcus [*of Scriptores Historiae Augustae*] [*Classical studies*] (OCD)
M/A/R/C ..... Marketing And Research Counselors Inc. [*Irving, TX*] (WDMC)
MARC......... Maryland Automotive Reclamation Corp. [*Automotive materials recycling project*]
MARC......... Master of Arts in Religious Communication (PGP)
MARC......... Matador Automatic RADAR Command
MARC......... Material Accountability Recoverability Code
MARC......... Materiel Acquisition Resource Committee [*Military*]
MARC......... Media Action Research Center (EA)
MARC......... Methodist Archives and Research Centre [*John Rylands University Library of Manchester*] [*British*] (CB)
MARC......... Methodology for Assessing Radiological Consequences (PDAA)
MARC......... Metropolitan Administration for Review and Comment [*Program using regional councils of government to serve as clearinghouses for Federal grants*]
MARC......... Metropolitan Applied Research Center (BARN)
MARC......... Micronesian Area Research Center [*University of Guam*] [*Research center*] (RCD)
MARC......... Mid-America Regional Council [*Information service or system*] (IID)
MARC......... Mining and Reclamation Council of America (EA)
MARC......... Minority Access to Research Careers [*Program*] [*Public Health Service Bethesda, MD*]
MARC......... Missions Advanced Research and Communication Center (EA)
MARC......... Model ™A∫ Restorers Club (EA)
MARC......... Modified Azimuth RADAR Correlator
MARC......... Monitor and Results Computer (IAA)
MARC......... Monitoring and Assessment Research Centre [*Marine science*] (MSC)
MARC......... Monitoring and Risk Assessment Centre [*British*]
MARC......... Moore Automatic Remote Control
MARC......... Mortgage Account Report Compiler (IAA)
MARC......... Mouvement d'Action pour la Resurrection du Congo [*Action Movement for the Resurrection of the Congo*] [*Zaire*] (PD)
MARC......... Movimiento Agrario Revolucionario del Campesinado Boliviano [*Revolutionary Movement of Bolivian Indian Peasants*] [*Political party*] (PPW)
MARC......... Multiaxial Radial Circuit (IAA)
MARC......... Multifocal and Recurrent Choroidopathy [*Medicine*] (DMAA)
MARC......... Mutliple Access Remote Computing (PDAA)
MA(RCA).... Master of Arts, Royal College of Art (Photography) [*British*] (DBQ)
MARCA .... Mid-Continent Area Reliability Coordination Agreement [*Regional power council*]
MARCAD..... Marine Corps Aviation Cadet
Marcam....... Marcam Corp. [*Associated Press*] (SAG)
MARCAMP... Marine Corps Accrued Military Pay System (NG)
MARCAN..... Maneuvering Reentry Control and Ablation Studies
MarCap....... Marion Capital Holdings, Inc. [*Associated Press*] (SAG)
MARCAS..... Maneuvering Reentry Control and Ablation Studies (MCD)
Mar Cas....... Maritime Cases, by Crockford and Cox [*1860-71*] [*A publication*] (DLA)
MARCCO..... Master Real-Time Circulation Controller (PDAA)
MARCE .... Materiel Asset Redistribution Center Europe [*Military*]
Marcell....... Pro Marcello [*of Cicero*] [*Classical studies*] (OCD)
MARCEP ..... Maintainability and Reliability Cost-Effectiveness Program (IEEE)
MARCH....... Marchioness
March.......... March's English King's Bench and Common Pleas Reports [*A publication*] (DLA)
March.......... March's Translation of Brooke's New Cases, English King's Bench [*82 English Reprint*] [*A publication*] (DLA)
MArch......... Master of Architectural Engineering (GAGS)
M Arch/....... Master of Architecture
MARCH....... Melt-Down Accident Response Characteristics [*Nuclear energy*] (NRCH)
MARCHA...... Methodists Associated Representing the Cause of Hispanic Americans [*An association*]
M Arch Des... Master of Architectural Design
M Arch E ..... Master of Architectural Engineering
M Arch Eng.. Master of Architectural Engineering
MArchH........ Master of Architectural History (GAGS)

M Arch H..... Master of Architectural History (PGP)
M Arch in CP.. Master of Architecture in City Planning
MArchivAdmin... Master of Archives Administration (ADA)
March N ...... March's New Cases, English King's Bench and Common Pleas Reports [*A publication*] (DLA)
March NC .... March's New Cases, English King's Bench [*1639-42*] [*A publication*] (DLA)
March NC .... Translation of Brook's New Cases [*1515-58*] [*A publication*] (DLA)
March NR .... March's New Cases, English King's Bench [*1639-42*] [*A publication*] (DLA)
M Arch Studies... Master of Architectural Studies (PGP)
M Arch UD... Master of Architecture in Urban Design (PGP)
MArchUD ..... Master of Architecture in Urban Design (GAGS)
MARCIA ...... Mathematical Analysis of Requirements for Career Information Appraisal
MARC IS...... MARC Israel (NITA)
MARCIVE ..... MARC Five (NITA)
MARCKS...... Myristoylated Alanine-Rich C-Kinase Substrate [*Biochemistry*]
MARC(LC)... MARC Library of Congress (NITA)
Marc Mant... Marcus Mantua Benavidius [*Deceased, 1582*] [*Authority cited in pre-1607 legal work*] (DSA)
MarcNG....... Marcum Natural Gas Services, Inc. [*Associated Press*] (SAG)
MARCO....... Machine Referenced and Coordinated Outline
MARCO....... Mid-American Research Corp.
MARCOGAZ... Union of the Gas Industries of the Common Market Countries [*Defunct*] (EAIO)
MARCOM..... Maritime Command [*Canada, since 1964*]
MARCOM..... Microwave Airborne Communications Relay (IEEE)
MARCOMM... Maritime Commission (DNAB)
MARCOMMDET... Marine Communications Detachment (DNAB)
MARCOMNAVADGRU... Marine Corps Component Navy Advisory Group (CINC)
MARCON..... Mars Consortium
MARCON..... Micro Archives and Records Online [*Developed by AirS, Inc.*]
MARCONFOR... Maritime Contingency Force [*NATO*] (NATG)
MARCONFORLANT... Maritime Contingency Forces, Atlantic [*NATO*] (NATG)
MARCONP .. Maritime Contingency Plans (NATG)
Mar Conv..... Marcy's Epitome of Conveyancing [*1881*] [*A publication*] (DLA)
Mar Conv St... Marcy's Conveyancing Statutes [*5th ed.*] [*1893*] [*A publication*] (DLA)
MARCOR...... Marine Corps
MARCORABSCOLLUNIT... Marine Corps Absentee Collection Unit (DNAB)
MARCORADMINDET... Marine Corps Administrative Detachment (DNAB)
MARCORASBCOLLUNITDET... Marine Corps Absentee Collection Unit Detachment (DNAB)
MARCORDISBOF... Marine Corps Disbursing Office
MARCOREP... Marine Corps Representative (DNAB)
MARCORESTRACEN... Marine Corps Reserve Training Center
MARCORHISTCEN... Marine Corps Historical Center (DNAB)
MARCORMAN... Marine Corps Manual
MARCORPERSMAN... Marine Corps Personnel Manual
MARCORPS... Marine Corps
MARCORSUPDEP... Marine Corps Supply Depot
MARCORSYSCOM... Marine Corps Systems Command
MARCOT...... Maritime Command Operational Team Training [*Canadian Navy*]
Mar Crp G ... Marine Corps Gazette [*A publication*] (BRI)
MARC-S....... Machine-Readable Cataloguing - Serials (ADA)
MARC(S)...... MARC Serials (NITA)
MARCS........ Marine Computer System (PDAA)
MARCS........ Melcom All Round Adaptive Consolidated Software [*Japan*]
MARC(UK)... MARC (United Kingdom) (NITA)
Marcus....... [*The*] Marcus Corp. [*Associated Press*] (SAG)
Marcus An ... Marcus Antonius Blancus [*Deceased, 1548*] [*Authority cited in pre-1607 legal work*] (DSA)
Marcus Anto... Marcus Antonius Blancus [*Deceased, 1548*] [*Authority cited in pre-1607 legal work*] (DSA)
MARD .... Marine Assessment Research Division [*Now Ocean Environmental Research Division*] (USDC)
MARD .... Marine Assessment Research Division [*Marine science*] (OSRA)
MA-RD........ Maritime Administration Office of Research and Development [*Washington, DC*]
MARD .... Military Aeronautical Research and Development (PDAA)
MARDAC...... Manpower Research and Data Analysis Center [*DoD*] (NVT)
MARDAN...... Marine Differential Analyzer
MARDATA..... Maritime Data Network [*Lloyd's Maritime Data Network Ltd.*] [*Stamford, CT Database*]
MARDB........ Mountain Agricultural Resources Development Bureau [*Taiwan*] (BUAC)
MARDEC...... Malaysian Rubber Development Corp. (BUAC)
Mar de Lau... Martinus Caratti de Laude [*Flourished, 1438-45*] [*Authority cited in pre-1607 legal work*] (DSA)
MARDET...... Marine Detachment
MARDEZ...... Maritime Defense Zone [*Navy*] [*Coast Guard*] (DOMA)
MARDI........ Malaysian Agricultural Research and Development Institute (BUAC)
MARDIS....... Modernized Army Research and Development Information System
MARDIV...... Marine Division
MARDO....... Months after Receipt of Delivery Order (MCD)
MarDrl........ Marine Drilling Co. [*Associated Press*] (SAG)
MARDS....... Medium Artillery Delivered Sensor [*Army*]
MARE......... Major Accident Response Exercise (MCD)
MARE......... Major Account Response Evaluation (MCD)
MARE......... Maritime Engineering [*Canadian Navy*]
MARE......... Master of Arts in Religious Education (PGP)
MARE......... Months after Receipt of Equipment [*Navy*]
MAREA....... Member of the American Railway Engineering Association
MAREA .... Middle Leaf Area [*Botany*]

MARECEBO... Manned Research on Celestial Bodies Committee [*International Academy of Astronautics*]
MARECS ..... Marine Communications Satellites (NITA)
MARECS ..... Maritime Communications Satellite
MARED .... Materiel Acquisition and Readiness Executive Development [*Program*] [*Army*] (RDA)
Ma Reg....... Massachusetts Register [*A publication*] (AAGC)
MAREGSQ.... Marine Air Regulating Squadron
MAREMIC .... Maintenance Repair and Minor Construction [*Program*] [*Air Force*]
Mar Eng....... Marine Engineer (PGP)
MARENTS .... Modified Advanced Research Environmental Test Satellite [*Air Force*]
MAREP .... Marine Environmental Prediction Task Group [*US government*] [*Terminated, 1969*]
MARES .... Marine Corps Automated Readiness Evaluation System
MARES/FORSTAT... Marine Corps Automated Readiness Evaluation System/Status of Forces
MARESTNG... Marine Corps Reserve Training (NVT)
MARF .... Master Area Reference File [*Bureau of the Census*] (GFGA)
MARF.......... Master Availability Reference File [*Army Electronics Command*]
Mar Fa........ Martinus de Fano [*Deceased circa 1275*] [*Authority cited in pre-1607 legal work*] (DSA)
MARFAIR..... Marine Fleet Air
MARFAIRWEST... Marine Fleet Air, West Coast
Mar Fan....... Martinus de Fano [*Deceased circa 1275*] [*Authority cited in pre-1607 legal work*] (DSA)
MARFINCEN... Marine Corps Finance Center (DNAB)
MARFIREX... Marine Firing Exercise (NVT)
MARFOR...... Marine Forces [*Element of a Joint Task Force*]
MARFS .... Multienvironment Active RF [*Radio Frequency*] Seeker
MARG .... Margarine
MARG .... Margin [*or Marginal*]
Marg........... Margin (EBF)
marg........... Margin (WDMC)
MARG .... Marine Amphibious Ready Group (MCD)
MARG .... Market Analysis Report Generator [*Computer science*]
MARG .... Mediterranean Amphibious Ready Group (MCD)
MARGARFOR... Marine Garrison Force
Margate....... Margate Ventures [*Associated Press*] (SAG)
MARGE .... Margarine (ADA)
MARGEN...... Management Report Generator [*Randolph Data Services, Inc.*] [*Software package*] [*Computer science*] (IEEE)
MARGIE .... Memory Analysis, Response Generation, and Interference in English
MARGILSAREA... Marshalls-Gilberts Area
MARGL .... Marginal (ROG)
Margo .... Margo Nursery Farms [*Associated Press*] (SAG)
MARHELILEX... Marine Helicopter Landing Exercise (NVT)
MARI .... Marijuana Cigarette [*Slang*] (DSUE)
Mari............ Marinus de Caramanico [*Flourished, 1269-85*] [*Authority cited in pre-1607 legal work*] (DSA)
MARI .... Medicare Administrative Reform Initiative [*Health Care Financing Administration*]
MARI .... Mercantile Atlantic Routing Instructions
MARI .... Microelectronics Applications Research Institute [*Newcastle-Upon-Tyne, England*]
MARI .... Motivator and Response Indicator
MARIA .... Macroaggregated Radioiodinated Albumin [*Radiology*] [*Pharmacy*] (DAVI)
Maria Soci... Marianus Socinus [*Authority cited in pre-1607 legal work*] (DSA)
MARIC .... Marine Resources Information Center [*Massachusetts Institute of Technology*] (NOAA)
MARID .... Mica-Amphibole-Rutile-Ilmenite-Diopside [*Geology*]
MARIDAS .... Maritime Data System (IAA)
Mariet.......... Marietta Corp. [*Associated Press*] (SAG)
MARIF .... Malang Research Institute for Food Crops [*Indonesia*] (BUAC)
Marijuana Rev... Marijuana Review [*A publication*] (DLA)
MARINCO .... Marketing International Consultants (BUAC)
MARINE....... Management Analysis Reporting Information on the Naval Environment System (NG)
Marine Ct R... Marine Court Reporter (McAdam's) [*New York*] [*A publication*] (DLA)
MarinerH ..... Mariner Health Group, Inc. [*Associated Press*] (SAG)
MARINEX ..... Marine Express (AABC)
Marin Frecc... Marinus Freccia [*Flourished, 16th century*] [*Authority cited in pre-1607 legal work*] (DSA)
MARINTRARON... Marine Instrument Training Squadron
MARIP .... Maintenance And Repair Inspection Program [*Military*] (DNAB)
MARIS .... Materials and Resources Information Service (NITA)
MarisaC .... Marisa Christina, Inc. [*Associated Press*] (SAG)
MARISAT .... Maritime Satellite System [*COMSAT*]
MARISP .... Maritime Strike Plan
MARIT .... Maritime
MARITA .... Maritime Airfield (NATG)
MARITADMIN... Maritime Administration [*Also, MA, MARAD*] [*Department of Transportation*] (MUGU)
MARITCOM... Maritime Commission
Maritimes L Rep (CCH)... Maritimes Law Reporter (Commerce Clearing House) [*A publication*] (DLA)
Maritrn .... Maritrans, Inc. [*Associated Press*] (SAG)
MARITZ........ Maritzburg (ROG)
Marius......... Marius. Concerning Bills of Exchange [*4 eds.*] [*1651-84*] [*A publication*] (DLA)
MARK .... Maintenance and Reliability Kit [*Military*] (NVT)
Mark .... Market
mark........... Market (VRA)

MARK .... Mechanized Assignment and Record Keeping [*Database management system*]
MARK .... Mid-Atlantic Ridge Kane
MARKAR...... Mapping and Reconnaissance Ku-Band Airborne RADAR
MarkCtr....... Mark Centers Trust [*Associated Press*] (SAG)
Mark El........ Markby's Elements of Law [*6th ed.*] [*1905*] [*A publication*] (DLA)
Markel .... Markel Corp. [*Associated Press*] (SAG)
MarkerI .... Marker International [*Associated Press*] (SAG)
MarkIV........ Mark IV Industries, Inc. [*Associated Press*] (SAG)
MARKS .... Modern Army Record Keeping System (INF)
Marks & Sayre... Marks and Sayre's Reports [*108 Alabama*] [*A publication*] (DLA)
Marks & Sayre's... Marks' and Sayre's Reports [*108 Alabama*] [*A publication*] (DLA)
MarksBr....... Marks Bros. Jewelers, Inc. [*Associated Press*] (SAG)
MARKSIM ..... [*A*] Marketing Decision Simulation [*Game*]
MarkSol....... Mark Solutions, Inc. [*Associated Press*] (SAG)
MARKSTRAT... Marketing Strategy [*Simulation package developed by Professors Jean-Claude Larreche and Hubert Gatignon*]
MarkVII....... Mark VII, Inc. [*Associated Press*] (SAG)
MarkWst....... MarkWest Hydrocarbon, Inc. [*Associated Press*] (SAG)
MARL.......... Marlboro [*Vermont*] [*Seismograph station code, US Geological Survey*] (SEIS)
MARL.......... Master of Arts and Letters
MARL.......... Master of Arts in Religious Leadership (PGP)
MARL.......... Mobile Acoustics Research Laboratory (MCD)
Marl........... Statute of Marlborough [*A publication*] (DSA)
Mar LA .... Martin's Louisiana Reports [*A publication*] (DLA)
MARLAB ...... Mobile Air Research Laboratory (PDAA)
MARLAGS.... Marine Life and Geochemical Studies [*Marine science*] (MSC)
MARLB .... Marlborough (ROG)
Mar LC .... Maritime Law Cases, by Crockford [*1860-71*] [*A publication*] (DLA)
Mar L Cas (NS)... Maritime Law Cases (New Series), by Aspinall [*1870-1940*] [*A publication*] (DLA)
Mar LC NS... Maritime Law Cases, New Series, by Aspinall [*1870-1940*] [*England*] [*A publication*] (DLA)
Mar Leg Bib... Marvin's Legal Bibliography [*A publication*] (DLA)
MARLEX .... Marine Corps Reserve Landing Exercise (NVT)
MAR LIC ...... Marriage License (WDAA)
MARLIN .... Middle Atlantic Regional Information Network
MARLIS .... Multi-Agent Relevance Linkage Information System (NITA)
MARLIS .... Multiaspect Relevance Linkage Information System
Mar LJ .... Maryland Law Journal and Real Estate Record [*A publication*] (DLA)
MARLNO...... Marine Liaison Office (DNAB)
MARLO .... Marine Liaison Officer (DOMA)
MARLOG...... Marine Logistical Command (VNW)
Mar LR .... Maritime Law Cases, First Series, by Crockford [*1860-71*] [*A publication*] (DLA)
Mar LR .... Maritime Law Cases, New Series, by Aspinall [*1870-1940*] [*A publication*] (DLA)
Mar L Rec ... Maryland Law Record [*A publication*] (DLA)
MARLSR ...... Manufacturers Association of Robes, Leisurewear, Shirts, and Rainwear [*Defunct*] (EA)
Marlton........ Marlton Technologies, Inc. [*Associated Press*] (SAG)
MarM .... Marine Midland Banks, Inc. [*Associated Press*] (SAG)
MARM .... Mensa Animal Rights Movement (BUAC)
MARM .... Microprocessor Arithmetic Model
MARM .... Middle Atlantic Regional Meeting [*of American Chemical Society*]
MARM .... Moving Average Rating Method [*Insurance*]
Mar Mant..... Marcus Mantua Benavidius [*Deceased, 1582*] [*Authority cited in pre-1607 legal work*] (DSA)
MARMAP ..... Marine Resources Monitoring, Assessment, and Prediction [*National Oceanic and Atmospheric Administration*]
Mar Mech E... Marine Mechanical Engineer
MARMETS ... Marine Meteorological Service
Marm Par .... Marmor Parium [*Classical studies*] (OCD)
MAR/MSR...... Multifunction Array RADAR / Missile Site RADAR (SAA)
MARN .... Marion Capital Holdings [*NASDAQ symbol*] (NQ)
MARNA .... Marine Navigation (NITA)
MARNAF...... Marquardt Navair Fuel [*A boron slurry propellant for spacecraft*]
Mar N & Q... Maritime Notes and Queries [*1873-1900*] [*A publication*] (DLA)
MarNB .... Marine National Bank (California) [*Associated Press*] (SAG)
MarNBk....... Marine National Bank (California) [*Associated Press*] (SAG)
Mar NC .... March's New Cases, English King's Bench [*1639-42*] [*A publication*] (DLA)
Mar NC .... Martin's North Carolina Reports [*1 North Carolina*] [*A publication*] (DLA)
MarnLP........ Marine Ltd. [*Associated Press*] (SAG)
MarnLP........ Marine Ltd. Partnership [*Associated Press*] (SAG)
Mar NR........ March's New Cases [*1639-42*] [*A publication*] (DLA)
Mar NS .... Martin's Louisiana Reports, New Series [*A publication*] (DLA)
MARO .... Maritime Air Radio Organization [*NATO*] (NATG)
MAROPS..... Maritime Operations
MAROTS ..... Maritime Orbital Test Satellite
MARP .... Manpower Allocation/Requirements Plan [*Navy*]
MARP .... Marine Petroleum Trust [*NASDAQ symbol*] (NQ)
MARP .... Maximum Authorized for Repair Parts (DNAB)
MARP .... Mobilization Augmentee Revitalization Program [*Military*]
MARP .... Months after Receipt of Problem [*Navy*] (NG)
MARPAC...... Headquarters, Department of the Pacific [*Marine Corps*]
MARPAC...... Maritime Command [*Canada, since 1964*]
MARPAC/ORT... Maritime Forces Pacific Operational Research Team [*Canada*]
MARPDA...... Mid-America Periodical Distributors Association (EA)
MARPE........ Multi-Atom Resonant Photoemission [*Physics*]
MARPEP...... Marine Physical Environmental Prediction
MarPet......... Marine Petroleum Trust [*Associated Press*] (SAG)

MARPEX ...... Management of Repair Parts Expenditure [*Army*] (PDAA)
MARPIC .... Marine Pollution Information Centre [*Marine Biological Association of the United Kingdom*] (IID)
Marpie......... Middle-Aged Rural Professional [*Lifestyle classification*]
MARPOL ...... International Convention for the Prevention of Pollution from Ships [*1973*]
MARPOL ...... Maritime Pollution Convention [*1978*] (DS)
MARPOLMON... Sub-Group of Experts on Marine Pollution Monitoring [*Marine science*] (MSC)
MARPRO ...... Marine Profile Data Base (GNE)
Mar Prov ..... Maritime Provinces Reports [*Canada*] [*A publication*] (DLA)
MARPS .... Mechanized Accounting Reserve Pay System
marq .... Marquetry (VRA)
MARQ .... Marquette Electronics, Inc. [*NASDAQ symbol*] (SPSG)
MARQ .... Marquette Medical Systems, Inc. [*NASDAQ symbol*] (SAG)
MARQ .... Marquis [*or Marquess*]
MARQA .... Marquette Electronics`A' [*NASDAQ symbol*] (TTSB)
MARQA .... Marquette Medical System [*NASDAQ symbol*] [*Formerly, Marquette Electronics*] (SG)
MarqEl .... Marquette Electronics, Inc. [*Associated Press*] (SAG)
MarqG .... Marquee Group, Inc. (The) [*Associated Press*] (SAG)
MarqGrp ...... Marquee Group, Inc. (The) [*Associated Press*] (SAG)
MarqMed ...... Marquette Medical Systems, Inc. [*Associated Press*] (SAG)
Marqst .... Marquest Medical Products, Inc. [*Associated Press*] (SAG)
Marquette Bus Rev... Marquette Business Review [*A publication*] (DLA)
Marquette U... Marquette University (GAGS)
MARQUIS .... Master Remote Query Interface System [*Computer science*]
Marr............ Hay and Marriott's English Admiralty Reports [*A publication*] (DLA)
MARR........... Marine Accidents Requiring Rescue (OA)
Mar R .... Maritime Law Reports [*A publication*] (DLA)
Marr............. Marrack's European Assurance Cases [*England*] [*A publication*] (DLA)
Marr............. Marriage (DLA)
MARR .... Maximum Annual Rate of Return [*Finance*]
MARR .... Minimum Attractive Rate of Return [*Economics*]
Marr Adm .... Marriott's English Admiralty Reports [*A publication*] (DLA)
MARRC........ Multi-Channel Automatic Remote Recording
MARRCS...... Manpower Requirements and Resources Control System [*Navy*] (NVT)
MARRD........ Married (ROG)
MARRE .... Manual RADAR Reconnaissance Exploitation (MCD)
MARRE .... Marriage (ROG)
Mar Rec B... Martin's Recital Book [*A publication*] (DLA)
Mar Reg ...... Mitchell's Maritime Register [*England*] [*A publication*] (DLA)
MARRES ...... Manual RADAR Reconnaissance Exploitation System [*Air Force*]
Marr Form... Marriott's Formulare Instrumentorum [*Admiralty Court*] [*1802*] [*A publication*] (DLA)
Marriotl .... Marriott International [*Associated Press*] (SAG)
MARRS......... Mechanized Ammunition Recording and Reporting System
MARR SETTL... Marriage Settlement [*Legal term*] (DLA)
MARS .... Machine-Aided Realization System
MARS .... Machine-Assisted Reference Section [*American Library Association*] [*Information service or system*] (IID)
MARS .... Machine-Assisted Reference Service [*St. Paul Public Library*] (OLDSS)
MARS .... Machine Automated Realty Service
MARS .... Machine Retrieval System
MARS .... Magnetic Airborne Recording System
MARS .... Maintenance Activities and Resources Simulation [*Computer science*]
MARS .... Maintenance Analysis and Recording Systems
MARS .... Maintenance Analysis Repair Set
MARS .... Maintenance Assistance and Repair System [*Military*]
MARS .... Major Accident Reporting System [*Engineering*]
MARS .... Management Action Reporting System (MCD)
MARS .... Management Analysis Reporting System [*Computer science*]
MARS .... Management and Administrative Reporting Subsystem [*Department of Health and Human Services*] (GFGA)
MARS .... Management Reports and Statistics
MARS .... Man-Hour Accounting and Reporting System [*Military*] (MCD)
MARS .... Manned Aerodynamic Reusable Spaceship
MARS .... Manned Astronautical Research Station [*Space laboratory*]
MARS .... Marconi Automatic Relay System (IEEE)
MARS .... Marine Account Reconciliation Service
MARS .... Marine Aircraft Repair Squadron
MARS .... Marine Reporting Station [*National Weather Service*]
MARS .... Maritime Surface and Subsurface [*Canadian Navy*]
MARS .... Market Analysis and Reference System [*Vancouver stock exchange computer system*] [*Canada*]
MARS .... Marketing and Advertising Reference Service (NITA)
Mars .... Marsden's Select Pleas in the Court of Admiralty [*Selden Society Publications, Vols. 6, 11*] [*A publication*] (DLA)
MARS .... Marsh Supermarkets, Inc. [*NASDAQ symbol*] (NQ)
MARS .... Martin Automatic Reporting System
MARS .... Master Attitude Reference System
MARS .... Master of Arts in Religious Studies (PGP)
MARS .... Material Action Reporting System (MCD)
MARS .... Material Response Study
MARS .... Materiel Acquisition Resource System [*Military*]
MARS .... Mathematics Anxiety Rating Scale [*Psychology*]
MARS .... Maximum Asset Return Strategy [*Allingham, Anderson, Roll & Ross*] [*British*] (ECON)
MARS .... Measuring Accuracy and Repeatability Study
MARS .... Mechanical Accessory Repair Shop (MCD)
MARS .... Media Alert and Response System [*Public relations project devised by Pharmaceutical Manufacturers Association*]
MARS .... Memory-Address Register Storage [*Computer science*]
MARS .... Meteorological Automatic Reporting Station [*Canada*]
MARS .... Mevinolin Atherosclerosis Regression Study (MEDA)
MARS .... Midair Recovery [*or Retrieval*] System [*Rescue by helicopter*] [*Military*]
MARS .... Migration Agents' Registration Scheme [*Australia*]
MARS .... Military Affiliated Radio System [*or Stations*] [*Amateur-operated radio stations*]
MARS .... Military Airborne RADAR System [*Air Force*] (IAA)
MARS .... Military Amateur Radio System (IAA)
MARS .... Military Amphibious Reconnaissance System (RDA)
MARS .... Millimeter Wave Amplification by Resonance Saturation (IAA)
MARS .... Miniature Attitude Reference System
MARS .... Minimum-Altitude Release and Strafe (MCD)
MARS .... Minolta Automatic Retrieval System (NITA)
MARS .... Mirror Advanced Reactor Study (MCD)
MARS .... Mission Maintenance and Reliability Simulation (MCD)
MARS .... Mobile Atlantic Range Stations [*Tracking stations*] (MUGU)
MARS .... Mobile Automatic Reporting System (MCD)
MARS .... Model Annotation Search and Retrieval System [*Geological program*]
MARS .... Modular Airborne Recorder System (MCD)
MARS .... Modular Attack RADAR System (MCD)
MARS .... Monitor and Replenisher System
MARS .... Monitoring Accounting Reporting and Statistical System [*Aviation*]
MARS .... Monograph Acquisitions and Record System [*Library science*] (TELE)
MARS .... Monthly Aerial Reconnaissance Summary (MCD)
MARS .... Motorola Aerial Remote Sensing [*Flying laboratory*]
MARS .... Mouse Antirat Serum (DB)
MARS .... Multiaperture Reluctance Switch [*Data storage unit*]
MARS .... Multicast Address Resolution Service [*Computer science*]
MARS .... Multiple Access Retrieval System [*Control Data Corp.*]
MARS .... Multiple Action Raid Simulation [*France*]
MARS .... Multiple Aerial Refueling System (PDAA)
MARS .... Multiple Artillery Rocket System [*Army*]
MARS .... Multiuser Archival and Retrieval System [*Computer science*]
MARS .... Multivariate Analysis, Retrieval, and Storage [*System*] [*NASA*]
MARS .... PTS Marketing and Advertising Reference Service [*Predicasts, Inc.*] [*Cleveland, OH*] [*Information service or system*] (IID)
MARSA .... Marsh Supermkts'A' [*NASDAQ symbol*] (TTSB)
MARS-A....... Mathematics Anxiety Rating Scale-Adolescents (STED)
MARSA .... Microfilm Association of the Republic of South Africa (BUAC)
MARSA .... Military Accepts Responsibility for Separation of Aircraft (AFM)
Mars Adm.... Marsden's English Admiralty [*A publication*] (DLA)
Mar Sal .... Marius Salomonius [*Deceased, 1557*] [*Authority cited in pre-1607 legal work*] (DSA)
MARSAM ..... Multiple Airborne Reconnaissance Sensors Assessment Model (MCD)
MARSAS...... Marine Search and Attack System (PDAA)
MARSAT...... Maritime Satellite [*COMSAT*]
MARSATS.... Maritime Satellite System [*COMSAT*]
MARSB .... Marsh Supermkts'B' [*NASDAQ symbol*] (TTSB)
M Ar Sc .... Master of Arts and Sciences
MArSci........ Master of Arts and Sciences (NADA)
Mars Coll..... Marsden's Collisions at Sea [*11th ed.*] [*1961*] [*A publication*] (DLA)
MARSD........ Minimal Attended RADAR Station Display (DWSG)
MARSEN ..... Maritime Remote Sensing (MCD)
Marsh .... Marshall and Sevestre's Appeals [*1862-64*] [*Bengal, India*] [*A publication*] (DLA)
Marsh .... Marshall's Circuit Court Decisions [*United States*] [*A publication*] (DLA)
Marsh .... Marshall's English Common Pleas Reports [*1814-16*] [*A publication*] (DLA)
Marsh .... Marshall's High Court Reports [*Bengal*] [*A publication*] (DLA)
Marsh .... Marshall's Reports [*Ceylon*] [*A publication*] (DLA)
Marsh .... Marshall's Reports [*4 Utah*] [*A publication*] (DLA)
Marsh .... Marshall's Reports [*Kentucky*] [*A publication*] (DLA)
MARSH........ Matching Aid to Restore States Habitat (GNE)
Marshall...... Marshall's Reports [*Bengal*] [*A publication*] (DLA)
Marshall...... Reports of Cases on Appeal [*Calcutta*] [*A publication*] (DLA)
Marshall U... Marshall University (GAGS)
Marsh Beng... Marshall's Reports [*Bengal*] [*A publication*] (DLA)
Marsh Calc... Marshall's Reports [*Calcutta*] [*A publication*] (DLA)
Marsh Car ... Marshall on Railways as Carriers [*A publication*] (DLA)
Marsh Ceylon... Marshall's Ceylon Reports [*A publication*] (DLA)
Marsh Costs... Marshall on the Law of Costs [*A publication*] (DLA)
Marsh CP..... Marshall's English Common Pleas Reports [*A publication*] (DLA)
Marsh Dec.... Marshall on the Federal Constitution [*A publication*] (DLA)
Marsh Dec.... Marshall's Circuit Court Decisions, by Brockenbrough [*United States*] [*A publication*] (DLA)
Marsh (Eng)... Marshall's English Common Pleas Reports [*A publication*] (DLA)
MarshFn ...... Marshalltown Financial Corp. [*Associated Press*] (SAG)
Marshl .... Marshall & Isley Corp. [*Associated Press*] (SAG)
Marshlls ...... Marshall & Isley Corp. [*Associated Press*] (SAG)
Marsh Ins .... Marshall on Marine Insurance [*A publication*] (DLA)
Marsh (KY)... Marshall's Reports [*Kentucky*] [*A publication*] (DLA)
MARSHL...... Marshal (ROG)
Marsh Op..... Marshall's Constitutional Opinions [*A publication*] (DLA)
Marsh Ry..... Marshall on Railways as Carriers [*A publication*] (DLA)
Marsh Ry..... Marshall's Duties and Obligations of Railway Companies [*A publication*] (DLA)
Mar Sill .... Martinus Sillimanus [*Flourished, 13th century*] [*Authority cited in pre-1607 legal work*] (DSA)
MARSIM ...... International Conference on Marine Simulation (PDAA)
MARSL .... Machine-Readable Shelf List [*Carleton University*] [*Canada*] (NITA)
MARSO........ Marine Corps Shipping Order (NG)

MA/RSO...... Mobilization Augmentee/Reserve Supplement Officer [*Air Force*] (AFM)
MARSPTBN... Marine Support Battalion (DNAB)
MARSREPSYS... Military Affiliate Radio System Repeater System (DNAB)
MARSTA...... Marital Status [*Army*] (AABC)
MARSTELSYS... Military Affiliate Radio System Teletypewriter Relay System (DNAB)
MARSTSIC... Marst on Sicca [*England*]
MARSYAS.... Marshall System for Aerospace Simulation [*Programming language*] [*1966-68*] (CSR)
MART.......... Maintenance Analysis Review Technique
Mart............ Martial [*Roman poet, 40-104AD*] [*Classical studies*] (OCD)
MART.......... Martinique [*West Indies*] (WDAA)
Mart............ Martin's Louisiana Term Reports [*1809-30*] [*A publication*] (DLA)
Mart............ Martin's North Carolina Reports [*1 North Carolina*] [*A publication*] (DLA)
Mart............ Martinus Gosia [*Authority cited in pre-1607 legal work*] (DSA)
MART.......... Martius [*March*] [*Latin*]
MART.......... Martyr
MART.......... Master of Arts in Religion and Theology (PGP)
MART.......... Mathematical Modeling and Reliability Transducer (MCD)
MART.......... Mean Active Repair Time (IEEE)
MART.......... Missile Automation Radiation Test (IAA)
MART.......... Mobile Automatic Radiation Tester
MART.......... Multiplicative Algebraic Reconstruction Technique (DMAA)
MARTA...... Metropolitan Atlanta Rapid Transit Authority [*FTA*] (TAG)
MARTAC...... Martin Automatic Rapid Test and Control
Mart & Y.... Martin and Yerger's Tennessee Reports [*8 Tennessee*] [*1825-28*] [*A publication*] (DLA)
Mart & Yer... Martin and Yerger's Tennessee Reports [*8 Tennessee*] [*1825-28*] [*A publication*] (DLA)
Mart & Yerg... Martin and Yerger's Tennessee Reports [*8 Tennessee*] [*1825-28*] [*A publication*] (DLA)
Mart & Y (Tenn)... Martin and Yerger's Tennessee Reports [*8 Tennessee*] [*1825-28*] [*A publication*] (DLA)
Mart Ark...... Martin's Decisions in Equity [*Arkansas*] [*A publication*] (DLA)
MARTC........ Marine Air Reserve Training Command
MartCol...... Martin Color-Fi, Inc. [*Associated Press*] (SAG)
MARTCOM... Marine Air Reserve Training Command
Mart Cond LA... Martin's Condensed Louisiana Reports [*A publication*] (DLA)
Mart Conv... Martin's Practice of Conveyancing [*A publication*] (DLA)
MARTD........ Marine Air Reserve Training Detachment
Mart Dec..... United States Decisions in Martin's North Carolina Reports [*A publication*] (DLA)
MARTEC...... Martin Thin-Film Electronic Circuit
Martek........ Martek Biosciences, Inc. [*Associated Press*] (SAG)
MARTEL...... Missile Antiradiation Television [*Military*] (CAAL)
Marten........ Marten Transport Ltd. [*Associated Press*] (SAG)
Mart Ex....... Martin on Executors [*A publication*] (DLA)
Mart GA...... Martin's Reports [*21-30 Georgia*] [*A publication*] (DLA)
Marth W Ca... Martha Washington Cases [*A publication*] (DLA)
MARTI......... Maneuverable Reentry Technology Investigation
MARTI......... Mobile Advanced Realtime Image (STED)
Martin.......... Martin's Louisiana Reports [*A publication*] (DLA)
Martin.......... Martin's North Carolina Reports [*1 North Carolina*] [*A publication*] (DLA)
Martin.......... Martin's Reports [*21-30, 54-70 Georgia*] [*A publication*] (DLA)
Mart Ind..... Martin's Reports [*54-70 Indiana*] [*A publication*] (DLA)
MARTINI...... Massive Analog Recording Technical Instrument for Nebulous Indications
Martin Index... Martin's Index to Virginia Reports [*A publication*] (DLA)
Martin (Lou) NS... Martin's Louisiana Reports, New Series [*A publication*] (DLA)
Martin's Chy... Martin's Chancery Decisions [*Arkansas*] [*A publication*] (DLA)
Martin's LA Rep... Martin's Louisiana Reports [*A publication*] (DLA)
Martin's LA Rep NS... Martin's Louisiana Reports, New Series [*A publication*] (DLA)
Martin's Louisiana R... Martin's Louisiana Reports [*A publication*] (DLA)
Martin's NS... Martin's Louisiana Reports, New Series [*A publication*] (DLA)
Martin's R NS... Martin's Louisiana Reports, New Series [*A publication*] (DLA)
Martls.......... Martyrdom of Isaiah [*Pseudepigrapha*] (BJA)
Martlsa........ Martyrdom of Isaiah [*Pseudepigrapha*] (BJA)
Mart LA....... Martin's Louisiana Reports, Old and New Series [*A publication*] (DLA)
Mart Laud.... Martinus Caratti de Laude [*Flourished, 1438-45*] [*Authority cited in pre-1607 legal work*] (DSA)
Mart Law Nat... Martens' Law of Nations [*A publication*] (DLA)
Mart MC...... Martin's Mining Cases [*Canada*] [*A publication*] (DLA)
MartMM....... Martin Marietta Materials [*Associated Press*] (SAG)
Mart NC....... Martin's North Carolina Reports [*1 North Carolina*] [*A publication*] (DLA)
Martnln........ Martin Industries, Inc. [*Associated Press*] (SAG)
MartnL......... Martin Lawrence Ltd. [*Associated Press*] (SAG)
Mart NS...... Martin's Louisiana Reports, New Series [*A publication*] (DLA)
Mart NS (LA)... Martin's Louisiana Reports, New Series [*A publication*] (DLA)
MARTOS...... Multiaccess Real-Time Operating System [*AEG Telefunken*] [*Germany*]
Mart OS (LA)... Martin's Louisiana Reports, Old Series [*A publication*] (DLA)
MARTRA & REPLCOMS... Marine Training and Replacement Commands
M Art (RCA)... Master of Art, Royal College of Art
Mart Rep..... Martin's Louisiana Reports [*A publication*] (DLA)
Mart Rep NS... Martin's Louisiana Reports, New Series [*A publication*] (DLA)
MARTS........ Master RADAR Tracking Station
MARTS........ Master RADAR Training System
MARTS........ Mobile Automatic Radio Telephone System (MCD)

MARTS........ Monthly Advance Retail Trade Survey [*Bureau of the Census*] (GFGA)
Mart USCC... Martin's Circuit Court Reports [*1 North Carolina*] [*A publication*] (DLA)
MARU.......... Medical Architecture Research Unit [*Polytechnic of North London*] [*British*] (IRC)
MARU.......... Middle America Research Unit
MARUNET..... Maruzen Online Network [*Maruzen Co. Ltd.*] [*Japan Telecommunications*]
MARUNITNG... Marine Unit Training (NVT)
MARV.......... Maneuverable AntiRADAR Vehicle (MCD)
MARV.......... Maneuverable Reentry Vehicle (AABC)
MARV.......... Marvelous (DSUE)
Marv............ Marvel's Reports [*15-16 Delaware*] [*A publication*] (DLA)
Marv............ Marvetol [*medicine*] (WDAA)
MARV.......... Mobile Acoustic Recording Vehicle (MCD)
MARV.......... Mobile Armored Reconnaissance/Operational Vehicle (MCD)
MARV.......... Multi-Element Articulated Research Vehicle [*Engineering*] (OA)
Marv Av...... Marvin on General Average [*A publication*] (DLA)
Marv (Del)... Marvel's Reports [*15-16 Delaware*] [*A publication*] (DLA)
MARVEL...... Machine-Assisted Realization of the Virtual Electronic Library [*Information service or system Library of Congress*]
Marvel........ Marvel Entertainment Corp. [*Associated Press*] (SAG)
Marvel........ Marvel's Reports [*15-16 Delaware*] [*A publication*] (DLA)
MARVEL...... Mississippi Aerophysics Research Vehicle with Extended Latitude
Marv Leg Bib... Marvin's Legal Bibliography [*A publication*] (DLA)
MARVLS....... MARC Video Disc Library System (NITA)
Marv Wr & S... Marvin on Wreck and Salvage [*A publication*] (DLA)
Mar Wr & S... Marvin on Wreck and Salvage [*A publication*] (DLA)
MARX.......... Mark Aero [*Air carrier designation symbol*]
Mary............ Maryland Reports [*A publication*] (DLA)
MARY.......... Saint Mary Land & Exploration [*NASDAQ symbol*] (SAG)
Marygrove C... Marygrove College (GAGS)
Maryland...... Maryland Reports [*A publication*] (DLA)
Maryland Ch Dec... Maryland Chancery Decisions [*A publication*] (DLA)
Maryville U... Maryville University of St. Louis (GAGS)
Marywood C... Marywood College (GAGS)
MAS............ Lithuanian Catholic Youth Association Ateitis (EA)
MAS............ MacDonald Agricultural Services Ltd. [*British*]
MAS............ Machine Accounting School
MAS............ Macintosh Application System [*Computer science*] (CDE)
MAS............ Macroassembler
MAS............ Madang Air Services [*Australia*]
MAS............ Magic Angle Spinning [*Spectroscopy*]
MAS............ Magnesia-Alumina-Silicate [*Inorganic chemistry*]
MAS............ Maintenance and Services (AFIT)
MAS............ Maintenance and Supply (AFIT)
MAS............ Malaysian Airline System [*ICAO designator*] (FAAC)
MAS............ Management Accounting System
MAS............ Management Advisory Services
MAS............ Management and Administrative Statistics (OICC)
MAS............ Management Appraisal Survey [*Test*]
MAS............ Manchester Astronomical Society [*England*] (BUAC)
MAS............ Maneuvering Attack System (MCD)
MAS............ Manifest Anxiety Scale [*Psychology*]
MAS............ Manned Aerial Surveillance
MAS............ Manual A1 Simplex [*Aviation*]
MAS............ Manufacturing Advisory Service (DCTA)
MAS............ Manufacturing Assembly Specification
MAS............ Manus [*Papua New Guinea*] [*Airport symbol*] (OAG)
MAS............ Manus Island [*Bismarck Archipelago*] [*Airport symbol*] (AD)
MAS............ MAP [*Manufacturing Automation Protocol*]/One Applications Services [*Software*] [*Automotive engineering*]
MAS............ Marine Acoustical Services
MAS............ Marine Advisory Service [*See also NMAS*] [*National Oceanic and Atmospheric Administration Information service or system*] (IID)
MAS............ Maritime Air Superiority (NVT)
MAS............ Market Advisory Service [*British Overseas Trade Board*] (DS)
MAS............ Mars Approach Sensor
mas............ Masai [*MARC language code Library of Congress*] (LCCP)
MAS............ Masco Corp. [*NYSE symbol*] (SPSG)
MAS............ Masculine
MAS............ Mason [*or Masonry*] (ROG)
MAS............ Mason Butte [*Idaho*] [*Seismograph station code, US Geological Survey Closed*] (SEIS)
mas............ Masonry (VRA)
Mas............ Mason's United States Circuit Court Reports [*A publication*] (DLA)
Mas............ Masorah (BJA)
Mas............ Massachusetts Reports [*A publication*] (DLA)
MAS............ Massachusetts State Library, Boston, MA [*OCLC symbol*] (OCLC)
Mas............ Masseketh (BJA)
MAS............ Master (DSUE)
MAS............ Master Activation Schedule (AAG)
MAS............ Master Analysis Scheme [*Monitoring technique*]
MAS............ Master of Accounting Science
MAS............ Master of Actuarial Science
MAS............ Master of Administrative Science (PGP)
MAS............ Master of Administrative Studies (ADA)
MAS............ Master of Aeronautical Science (GAGS)
MAS............ Master of Applied Science
MAS............ Master of Applied Spirituality (PGP)
MAS............ Master of Applied Statistics (GAGS)
MAS............ Master of Archival Studies (GAGS)
MAS............ Material Activity Schedule
MAS............ Material Application Service [*NASA*] (IAA)

MAS............	Material Availability Schedule
MAS............	Mathematics Attitude Scale (EDAC)
MAS............	Mature Age Student (ADA)
MAS............	Maximum Aerobic Speed [*Biology*]
MAS............	McMaster University Library [*UTLAS symbol*]
MAS............	Meconium Aspiration Syndrome [*Medicine*]
MAS............	Media Advisory Service [*British*]
MAS............	Medical Administrative Service (DAVI)
MAS............	Medical Advisory Service [*British*]
MAS............	Medical Audit Statistics (PDAA)
MAS............	Medical Audit Study (HCT)
MAS............	Meiosis-Activating Sterol [*Cytology*]
MAS............	Member of the Arundel Society [*British*]
MAS............	Memory and Auxiliary Storage Subsystem [*Space Flight Operations Facility, NASA*]
MAS............	Mercury Analyzer System [*Perkin-Elmer Co. instrument designation*]
MAS............	Merged Area Schools (OICC)
MAS............	Merseyside Aviation Society [*British*] (DBA)
MAS............	Mesoatrial Shunt [*Medicine*] (DMAA)
MAS............	Metal-Alumina Semiconductor (IAA)
MAS............	Metal-Alumina-Silicon (IEEE)
MAS............	Metal Anchor Slots [*Technical drawings*]
MAS............	Metastable Atomic State
MAS............	Methods and Standards (MCD)
MAS............	Methods of Air Sampling and Analysis [*Air Pollution Control Association*]
MAS............	Mezhdunarodnaya Assotsiatsiya Sudovladeltsev [*International Shipowners' Association*] [*Poland*] (EAIO)
MAS............	Microage Solutions, Inc. (EFIS)
MAS............	Micro-Alloyed Steel [*Metallurgical engineering*]
MAS............	Micro Automation System
MAS............	Microbeam Analysis Society (EA)
MAS............	Microprogram Automation System [*Computer science*] (IAA)
MAS............	Midcourse Active System (MCD)
MAS............	Middle Air Space (PDAA)
MAS............	Military Agency for Standardization [*Brussels, Belgium*] [*NATO*]
MAS............	Military Airlift Squadron [*Air Force*] (CINC)
MAS............	Military Assistance Sales (MCD)
MAS............	Milk-Alkali Syndrome [*Medicine*] (DMAA)
mAs............	Milliampere-Second
MAS............	Ministry of Aviation Supply [*British*]
MAS............	Minnesota Academy of Science
MAS............	Missile Alignment Set
MAS............	Missile Assembly Site (NATG)
MAS............	Missile Assigned Switch
MAS............	Missile Auxiliaries System
MAS............	Mississippi Academy of Sciences (BUAC)
MAS............	MMICS Administration Subsystem (AFIT)
MAS............	Mobile Arm Support [*Orthopedics*] (DAVI)
MAS............	Mobile Atmospheric Spectrometer [*Marine science*] (OSRA)
MAS............	Model Assignment Sheet (MCD)
MAS............	Modern Army Supply
MAS............	Modern Army System
MAS............	Modular Accounting System [*Computer science*] (IAA)
MAS............	Modular Application Systems [*Martin Marietta Data Systems*]
MAS............	Monaco Group, Inc. [*Toronto Stock Exchange symbol*]
MAS............	Monetary Allowance in Lieu of Subsistence
MAS............	Monetary Authority of Singapore (NUMA)
MAS............	Money Advice Scotland (BUAC)
MAS............	Monitor and Alarm System (MCD)
MAS............	Monmouth Antiquarian Society (EA)
MAS............	Monoacetoxylscirpenol [*Organic toxin*]
MAS............	Morgagni-Adam-Stokes (DB)
MasCp............	Mount Angel Seminary [*Oregon*]
MAS............	Movement Alarm System [*Gynecology*]
MAS............	Movimiento al Socialismo [*Movement towards Socialism*] [*Venezuela Political party*] (PPW)
MAS............	Movimiento al Socialismo [*Movement towards Socialism*] [*Argentina Political party*] (PPW)
MAS............	Movimiento de Accion Socialista [*Peru*] [*Political party*] (EY)
MAS............	Movimiento para Accion y Solidaridad [*Guatemala*] [*Political party*] (EY)
MAS............	Muerte a los Secuestradores [*Death to Kidnappers*] [*Colorado*] (PD)
MAS............	Mujeres en Accion Sindical [*Organizes national and international conferences on women in the economy*] [*Mexico*] (CROSS)
MAS............	Multiaspect Signaling (IEEE)
MAS............	Multiple Address System [*Telecommunications*] (CDE)
MAS............	Multiple Aim Structure (MCD)
MAS............	Multiple Award Schedule [*Government contracting*]
MAS............	Municipal Analysis Services, Inc. [*Information service or system*] (IID)
MAS............	Mutually Assured Survival
MASA............	Mail Advertising Service Association International [*Bethesda, MD*]
MASA............	Marine Accessories and Services Association [*Later, NAMPS*] (EA)
MASA............	Master of Advanced Studies in Architecture (PGP)
MASA............	Mathematical Association of South Australia
MASA............	Medical Acronyms, Symbols & Abbreviations [*A publication*]
MASA............	Medical Association of South Africa (DMAA)
MASA............	Men Against Sexual Assault [*Australia*]
MASA............	Mental Retardation-Aphasia-Shuffling Gait-Adducted Thumbs [*Syndrome*] [*Medicine*]
MASA............	Merged Area Schools Administrators Association (OICC)
MASA............	Military Accessories Service Association (EA)
MASA............	Military Automotive Supply Agency
MASA............	Modular Avionics Systems Architecture (MCD)

MASA............	Multiple Anodic Stripping Analyzer (PDAA)
MASA............	Music and Arts Society of America (EA)
MASAAV......	Mid-Atlantic States Association of Avian Veterinarians (EA)
MASAC.......	Master of Arts in Substance Abuse Counseling (PGP)
MASAD.......	Mission Analysis and Systems Acquisition Division (AAGC)
MASAE.......	Member of the American Society of Agricultural Engineering
MASAF.......	Mediterranean Allied Strategic Air Force
MASAI........	Mail Advertising Service Association International (EA)
MASAL.......	Michigan Academy of Science, Arts, and Letters
MASAP.......	Michigan Association of Single Adoptive Parents (EA)
MASAQUE.....	Major Action Significantly Affecting the Quality of the Human Environment (DNAB)
MASAR.......	Management Assurance of Safety, Adequacy, and Reliability (MHDB)
MASAR.......	Microwave Accurate Surface Antenna Reflector (PDAA)
MASAR.......	Multimode Airborne Solid-State Array RADAR System [*Military*] (PDAA)
MASB.........	Main Array Signal Band
MASB.........	MASSBANK Corp. [*NASDAQ symbol*] (NQ)
MA/SB........	Motor Antisubmarine Boat [*Obsolete British*]
MASC.........	Magazine Advertising Sales Club (EA)
MASC.........	Magnetic Attitude Spin Coil
MASC.........	MAGTF [*Marine Air-Ground Task Force*] Automated Services Center (GFGA)
MASC.........	Maintenance Support Concept Model (MCD)
MASC.........	Management Systems Concept (PDAA)
MASC.........	Masculine
masc.........	Mass Concentration [*Medicine*] (MAE)
MASc.........	Master of Agricultural Science (DD)
MA Sc.........	Master of Applied Science
MASC.........	Methylaluminum Sesquichloride [*Organic chemistry*]
MASC.........	Microsoft Access Script Command [*Computer language*]
MASC.........	Middletown Air Service Command [*Air Force*]
MASC.........	Military Automotive Supply Center (MCD)
MASC.........	Model to Evaluate Maintenance Support Concepts (MCD)
MASC.........	Mountain Administrative Support Center [*Marine science*] (OSRA)
MASC.........	Multilayer Aluminium Oxide-Silicon-Dioxide Combination (IAA)
MASC.........	Multiple Award Schedule Contract [*Government contracting*]
MASCA........	Museum Applied Science Center for Archeology [*University of Pennsylvania*]
MASCAC......	Middle Atlantic States Collegiate Athletic Conference (PSS)
MASCDCS.....	Madison Avenue Sports Car Driving and Chowder Society (EA)
MASCE........	Member of the American Society of Civil Engineers
MASCO........	Maintenance Schedule Code (PDAA)
Masco.........	Masco Corp. [*Associated Press*] (SAG)
MASCO........	Mead Access Systems Co.
MASCO........	Microprogrammed and Simulated Computer Organization
MASCOM.....	Master Communications (PDAA)
MASCON.....	Mass Concentration [*of gravitational pull*]
MASCOT.....	Management Advisory System using Computerized Optimization Techniques (PDAA)
MASCOT.....	Manned Shuttle Comprehensive Optimization and Targeting [*NASA*]
Mascot.........	Mascotech [*Commercial firm Associated Press*] (SAG)
MASCOT.....	Meteorological Auxiliary Sea Current Observation Transmitter
MASCOT.....	Military Air-Transportable Satellite Communications Terminal
MASCOT.....	Mobile Air-Transportable Satellite Communications Terminal [*Military*] (IAA)
MASCOT.....	Modern Approach to Software Construction, Operation and Test [*Ministry of Defence*] [*British*]
MASCOT.....	Modular Approach to Software Construction Operation and Test (NITA)
MASCOT.....	Modular Approach to System Construction Operation and Test (MCD)
MASCOT.....	Motorola Automatic Sequential Computer Operated Tester
Mascotch.....	Mascotech [*Commercial firm Associated Press*] (SAG)
MasCp........	MassMutual Corporate Investors, Inc. [*Associated Press*] (SAG)
MASCP........	Multicultural and Cross-Cultural Supplementation Program [*Australia*]
MASCP&T....	Member, American Society for Clinical Pharmacology & Therapeutics (CMD)
MASCS........	Marriage Adjustment Sentence Completion Survey [*Psychology*]
MASCU........	Marine Air Support Control Unit
MASD.........	Mach Aids to Surface-to-Air Missile Development (IAA)
MASD.........	Master of Arts in Spiritual Direction (PGP)
MASD	Mobile Air and Space Defense [*Air Force*]
MASDC.......	Military Aircraft Storage and Disposition Center
MASDR.......	Measurement and Signature Data Requirements (MCD)
MasdSec......	Masada Security Holdings, Inc. [*Associated Press*] (SAG)
MASE.........	McDonnell Airborne Sidewinder Evaluator [*McDonnell Douglas Corp.*]
MASE.........	Medical and Scientific Equipment
MASE.........	Military Assistance Service Fund (AAGC)
MASE.........	Moore School Air Space Simulation Effort (MCD)
MASEA........	Midwest Association of Student Employment Administrators [*Formerly, MAUSED*] (EA)
MASEAN......	Medical Association of South East Asian Nations (BUAC)
MASEC........	Multi-Access Systems Control Terminal (PDAA)
MASEE........	Member of the Association of Supervisory and Executive Engineers [*British*] (DBQ)
MASEFI.......	Mass Air Sequential Electronic Fuel Injection [*Automotive engineering*]
MASER	Microwave [*or Molecular*] Amplification by Stimulated Emission of Radiation
maser.........	Microwave Amplification by Stimulated Emission of Radiation (WDMC)
MASER	Molecular Application by Stimulated Emission of Radiation [*Organic chemistry*] (DAVI)
MASES........	Microcomputer Advice and Selection Expert System (PDAA)

MASEX.........	Maritime Air Superiority Exercise (NVT)
MASF...........	Marconi Advanced Sample Facility (NITA)
MASF...........	Military Assistance Service Funded
MASF...........	Mobile Aeromedical Staging Facility
MASF...........	Multiracial American Scholarship Fund
MASFA........	Middle Atlantic States Fencing Association (PSS)
MASFET.......	Metal-Alumina-Silicon Field Effect Transistor (IAA)
MASFM........	Maintenance and Supply Facility Management (AFIT)
MAS/FS........	Mohawk Aerial Surveillance/Flight Simulator (MCD)
MASG	Marine Air Support Group
MASG	Military Airlift Support Group [Air Force]
MASG	Missile Auxiliary Signal Generator
MASG	Monitor and Alarm Subsystem Group (MCD)
MASGC........	Mississippi-Alabama Sea Grant Consortium [Sea Grant College] [Research center] (RCD)
MASGP........	Military Airlift Support Group [Air Force]
MASH	Manned Antisubmarine Helicopter
MASH	Medical Aid for Sick Hippies [Volunteer medical group]
MASH	Melting-Assimilation-Storage-Homogenization [Geology]
MASH	Michigan Area Serial Holdings Consortium [Library network]
MASH	Micro-Analytic Simulation of Households (PDAA)
MASH	Mobile Army Surgical Hospital [Acronym also used as title of a satirical film, 1970, and a TV series]
MASH	Multiple Accelerated Summary Hearing [Deportation of illegal aliens] [Immigration and Naturalization Service]
MASH	Multiple Automated Sample Harvester [for culture systems]
MASH	Mutual Aid Self-Help Group
MASHONLD..	Mashonaland (ROG)
M/ASI...........	Mach/Airspeed Indicator (GAVI)
MASI...........	Media Association of the Solomon Islands (BUAC)
MASI...........	Multilevel Academic Skills Inventory [Educational test]
MASID	Marine Science Division [Instrument Society of America] (MSC)
MASINT	Measurement and Signature Intelligence (MCD)
MASIS	Management and Scientific Information System [Air Force]
MASIS	Maruzen Scientific Information Service Center [Maruzen Co. Ltd.] [Japan Telecommunications]
MASIS	Mercury Abort Sensing Instrumentation System [NASA] (AAG)
MASK..........	Align-Rite International, Inc. [NASDAQ symbol] (SAG)
MASK..........	Align-Rite Intl. [NASDAQ symbol] (TTSB)
MASK..........	Maneuvering and Seakeeping
MASK..........	Medical Anatomy Segmentation Kit (DMAA)
MASK..........	Mobile Armored Strike Kommand [Game]
MASK..........	Multilevel Amplitude Shift Keying
maskon........	Mass Concentration (BARN)
MAsl	Ashland Public Library, Ashland, MA [Library symbol Library of Congress] (LCLS)
MASL..........	MA [Military Assistance] Articles and Services List [DoD]
masl	Meters above Sea Level
MASL..........	Military Articles and Services List
MASL..........	Military Assistance Article and Service List (MCD)
Masland	Masland Corp. [Associated Press] (SAG)
MASLIG	Association of Management Analysts in State and Local Government (EA)
MASLPI.......	Mexican American State Legislators Policy Institute (CROSS)
MASM..........	Macro Assembler [Computer language] (PCM)
MASM..........	Master of Arts in Sacred Music (BJA)
MASM..........	Meta-Assembler (NITA)
MASM..........	Meta-Assembler Language [Sperry UNIVAC computer language]
MASM..........	Military Assistance and Sales Manual (AFIT)
MASM..........	Motorized Antenna Switching Matrix
MASME.......	Member of the American Society of Mechanical Engineers
MAS/MILS ..	Minerals Availability System/Minerals Industry Location Subsystem [Bureau of Mines] [Database]
MASMOD.....	Mass Model [Computer program]
MASMR	Multidimensional Attitude Scale on Mental Retardation (EDAC)
MASN	Machine Accountant, Seaman [Navy]
masn	Masonite (VRA)
MASN	Maximum Aggregate Student Number [Higher Education Funding Council] (AIE)
MASNC	Minerals Availability System [Bureau of Mines] [Information service or system] (IID)
Mas NE Pr...	Mason's New England Civil Practice [A publication] (DLA)
MASNMR.....	Magic Angle Spinning Nuclear Magnetic Resonance [Spectroscopy]
MASO	Military Assistance Sales Order (CINC)
MASO	Munition Accountable Supply Officer [Air Force] (AFM)
MASOA	Master and Slave Oscillator Array (PDAA)
MA (Social Studies)...	Master of Arts (Social Studies)
MA(SocSci)...	Master of Arts (Social Sciences), University of Glasgow [British] (DBQ)
MASocStud...	Master of Arts in Social Studies (NADA)
MASON	Masonry
Mason	Mason's United States Circuit Court Reports [A publication] (DLA)
Mason CCR..	Mason's United States Circuit Court Reports [A publication] (DLA)
Mason Circt Ct R...	Mason's United States Circuit Court Reports [A publication] (DLA)
MasonDix	Mason-Dixon Bancshares, Inc. [Associated Press] (SAG)
Mason R......	Mason's United States Circuit Court Reports [A publication] (DLA)
Mason's Code...	Mason's United States Code, Annotated [A publication] (DLA)
Mason's R...	Mason's United States Circuit Court Reports [A publication] (DLA)
Mason's Rep...	Mason's United States Circuit Court Reports [A publication] (DLA)
Mason US....	Mason's United States Circuit Court Reports [A publication] (DLA)
Mason US Circ Ct Rep...	Mason's United States Circuit Court Reports [A publication] (DLA)
Mason USR...	Mason's United States Circuit Court Reports [A publication] (DLA)
MASP..........	Microaerophilus Stationary Phase [Biochemistry] (DAVI)

MASP...........	Modular Atmosphere Simulation Program [NASA] (KSC)
MASPAC	Microfilm Advisory Service of the Public Archives of Canada (PDAA)
MAS PIL	Massa Pilularum [A Pill Mass] [Pharmacy]
MasPrt	MassMutual Participation Investors [Associated Press] (SAG)
MASPS	Minimum Aviation System Performance Standards [FAA] (TAG)
MASPSq	Military Airlift Special Squadron [Air Force]
MASPTSq ...	Military Airlift Support Squadron [Air Force]
MASq	Military Airlift Squadron [Air Force] (AFM)
Mas R.........	Massachusetts Reports [A publication] (DLA)
MASR	Memory-Address Select Register [Computer science] (IAA)
MASR	Microwave Atmosphere Sounding Radiometer (PDAA)
MASR	Multiple-Antenna Moving-Target Surveillance RADAR
MASRC	Major Automated System Review Council [Military]
MASRC	Mexican American Studies and Research Center [University of Arizona] [Research center] (RCD)
Mas Rep....	Massachusetts Reports [A publication] (DLA)
MASRT	Marine Air Support RADAR Teams (IEEE)
MASRU	Marine Air Support RADAR Unit [DoD]
MASS	Magic Angle Sample Spinning [Spectroscopy]
MASS	Manned Activity Scheduling System [NASA]
MASS	MARC [Machine-Readable Cataloging] Automated Serials System (PDAA)
MASS..........	MARC-Based Automated Serials System (NITA)
MASS..........	Marine Air Support Squadron
MASS..........	Maritime Anti-Standing SONAR System (DNAB)
MASS..........	Massa [A Mass] [Pharmacy]
MASS..........	Massachusetts (AFM)
MASS..........	Massachusetts Bay (GAAI)
Mass..........	Massachusetts Supreme Judicial Court Reports [A publication] (DLA)
MASS..........	Massage
mass..........	Massage (DMAA)
MA(SS)........	Master of Arts in Social Science (ADA)
MASS..........	Master of Arts in Special Studies (PGP)
M As S	Master of Association Science
MASS..........	Materials Acquisition Sub-System [Computer science]
MASS..........	Matrix Analysis Subsystem (MCD)
MASS..........	Mechanically Accelerated Sabot System [Generation of high-density molecular beams]
MASS..........	Medicine, Angioplasty, or Surgery Study (DMAA)
MASS..........	Membrane Affinity Separation System
MASS..........	Memorandum Accounts Statement System (DCTA)
MASS..........	MICAP [Mission Critical Parts] Asset Sourcing System (DOMA)
MASS..........	Michigan Automatic Scanning System (IEEE)
MAss	Middle Assyrian [Language, etc.] (BJA)
MASS..........	Military Airlift Support Squadron [Air Force]
MASS..........	Missile and Space Summary (MCD)
MASS..........	Missiles/Ammunition System Study
MASS..........	Mobility Analysis Support System [Air Force]
MASS..........	Modern Army Supply System
MASS..........	Modular Adaptive Signal Sorter
MASS..........	Money Advice Support Services (BUAC)
MASS..........	Monitor and Assembly System [or Subsystem] [Computer science] (BUR)
MASS..........	Multiple Access Sequential Selection [Computer science] (BUR)
MASS..........	Multiple Access Switching System (NITA)
Mass Acts....	Acts and Resolves of Massachusetts [A publication] (DLA)
Mass AD	Massachusetts Appellate Decisions [A publication] (DLA)
Mass Admin Code...	Code of Massachusetts Regulations [A publication] (DLA)
Mass Admin Reg...	Massachusetts Register [A publication] (DLA)
Mass ADR....	Massachusetts Appellate Division Reports [A publication] (DLA)
Mass Adv Legis Serv...	Massachusetts Advance Legislative Service [Lawyers Co-Operative Publishing Co.] [A publication] (DLA)
Mass Adv Sh...	Massachusetts Advance Sheets [A publication] (DLA)
Mass Adv Sheets...	Massachusetts Advance Sheets [A publication] (DLA)
Mass Ann Laws...	Annotated Laws of Massachusetts [A publication] (DLA)
Mass App Ct...	Massachusetts Appeals Court Reports [A publication] (DLA)
Mass App Ct Adv Sh...	Massachusetts Appeals Court Advance Sheets [A publication] (DLA)
Mass App Dec...	Massachusetts Appellate Decisions [A publication] (DLA)
Mass App Div...	Massachusetts Appellate Division Reports [A publication] (DLA)
Mass App Rep...	Massachusetts Appeals Court Reports [A publication] (DLA)
MASSAR	Multimode Airborne Solid State Array RADAR
Mass BC & A...	Massachusetts Board of Conciliation and Arbitration Reports [A publication] (DLA)
Massbnk.....	Massbank Corp. [Associated Press] (SAG)
MASSBUS...	Memory Bus [Digital Equipment Corp.]
massc.........	Mass Concentration (DMAA)
M As Sc.......	Master of Association Science
MASSCAL...	Mass Casualties [Military] (AABC)
Mass C Art...	Massachusetts College of Art (GAGS)
Mass Cont Election Cushing S & J...	Massachusetts Controverted Election Cases [A publication] (DLA)
Mass C Pharmacy...	Massachusetts College of Pharmacy (GAGS)
MASSDAR...	Modular Analysis, Speedup, Sampling, and Data Reduction
MASSDATA...	Mark Sense Source Data Automation Test and Analysis (MCD)
MASSDET...	Marine Air Support Squadron Detachment (DNAB)
Mass DIA....	Massachusetts. Department of Industrial Accidents. Bulletin [A publication] (DLA)
Mass Dr Com...	Masse. Le Droit Commercial [A publication] (DLA)
Mass EC L & R...	Loring and Russell's Election Cases in Massachusetts [A publication] (DLA)
Mass Elec Ca...	Massachusetts Election Cases [A publication] (DLA)
Mass Elec Cas...	Massachusetts Election Cases [A publication] (DLA)
Mass Election Cases...	Loring and Russell's Election Cases in Massachusetts [A publication] (DLA)

Mass Election Cases...　Russell's Contested Election Cases [*Massachusetts*] [*A publication*] (DLA)

Mass Gen Laws...　Massachusetts General Laws [*A publication*] (DLA)

Mass Gen Laws Ann (West)...　Massachusetts General Laws, Annotated (West) [*A publication*] (DLA)

MassHe ....　Massachusetts Health & Education Tax Exempt Trust [*Associated Press*] (SAG)

MASS HFD...　Multi-Additional SCSI [*Small Computer System Interface*] Subsystem Hot Fix Device [*Computer science*]

Mass IAB .....　Massachusetts Industrial Accident Board Reports of Cases [*A publication*] (DLA)

MASSIIS ......　Maintenance Analysis and Structural Integration Information System

Mass LRC Dec..　Massachusetts Labor Relations Commission Decisions [*A publication*] (DLA)

MASSOP......　Multi-Automatic System for Simulation and Operational Planning (PDAA)

Mass Pil .....　Massa Pilularum [*A Pill Mass*] [*Pharmacy*]

MASSPO ......　Manned Space Flight Support Project Office [*NASA*] (IAA)

MASSq.........　Military Airlift Support Squadron [*Air Force*] (AFM)

Mass R ....　Massachusetts Reports [*A publication*] (DLA)

Mass Rep ....　Massachusetts Reports [*A publication*] (DLA)

Mass St BC & A...　Massachusetts State Board of Conciliation and Arbitration Reports [*A publication*] (DLA)

Mass Supp...　Massachusetts Reports Supplement [*A publication*] (AAGC)

MASST.........　Major Shipboard SATCOM Terminal (MCD)

MASST.........　Major Ship Satellite Terminal

MASSTER ......　Mobile Army Sensor System Test, Evaluation, and Review

MASSTER ...　Modern Army Selected System Test, Evaluation, and Review

Mass UCC Op...　Massachusetts Unemployment Compensation Commission Opinions [*A publication*] (DLA)

Mass UC Dig...　Massachusetts Division of Unemployment Compensation Digest of Board of Review Decisions [*A publication*] (DLA)

Mass UC Ops...　Massachusetts Division of Unemployment Compensation Opinions [*A publication*] (DLA)

Mass WCC...　Massachusetts Workmen's Compensation Cases [*A publication*] (DLA)

MAST..........　Arousal Seeking Tendency Scale [*Test*] (TMMY)

MAST..........　Machine Automated Speech Transcription (PDAA)

MAST..........　Magnetic Annular Shock Tube

MaST..........　Management and Skills Training (BUAC)

MAST..........　Marine Stable Element

MAST..........　Market Structures and Trends on Italy [*Databank Ltd.*] [*British*] (ECON)

MAST..........　Mastech Corp. [*NASDAQ symbol*] (SAG)

MAST..........　Mastectomy [*Medicine*] (AAMN)

MAST..........　Master (ROG)

Mast ....　Master's Supreme Court Reports [*25-28 Canada*] [*A publication*] (DLA)

MAST..........　Mastoid [*Medicine*]

MAST..........　Measurement and Stimuli System (SSD)

MAST..........　Medical Anti-Shock Trousers [*Military*]

MAST..........　Meteorological Automated Sensor and Transceiver [*Military*]

MAST..........　Michigan Alcoholism Screening Test

MAST..........　Midlevel Positions in Administrative, Staff, and Technical Services [*Civil Service Commission*]

MAST..........　Military Antishock Trousers [*Medicine*]

MAST..........　Military Assistance to Safety and Traffic [*Project*] [*Army*] (RDA)

MAST..........　Minimum Abbreviations of Serial Titles [*A publication*]

MAST..........　Missile Automatic Supply Technique

MAST..........　Mobile Assembly Sterilizer for Testing

MAST..........　Model Assembly Sterilizer for Testing [*NASA*]

MAST..........　Multilevel Academic Survey Test [*Educational test*]

MAST..........　Multiple-Aircraft Simulation Terminal (DA)

MAST..........　Multiple Applications Storage Tube

MAST..........　Munitions Assistance and Standardization Team (MCD)

MASTA.........　Medical Advisory Services for Travellers Abroad [*London School of Hygiene andTropical Medicine*] [*Information service or system*] (IID)

MastAcftCrmnBad...　Master Aircraft Crewman Badge [*Military decoration*] (AABC)

MASTACS ....　Maneuverability Augmentation System for Tactical Air Combat Simulation (PDAA)

MASTAP ......　Master System Tape (IAA)

MASTARAV..　Master Army Aviator (AABC)

Mast AR Av Bad...　Master Army Aviator Badge [*Military decoration*]

MASTARS ....　Mechanical and Structural Testing and Referral Service [*National Institute of Standards and Technology*]

MAStat.........　Master of Applied Statistics

Mast Div Bad...　Master Diver Badge [*Military decoration*]

MAST-E.......　Multicenter Acute Stroke Trial-Europe [*Neurology*]

Mastec.........　Mastec, Inc. [*Associated Press*] (SAG)

Mastech.......　Mastech Corp. [*Associated Press*] (SAG)

Mast El ....　Masterman's Parliamentary Elections [*1880*] [*A publication*] (DLA)

MASTER ......　Manuscript Access through Standards for Electronic Records [*Library science*] (TELE)

MASTER ......　Matching Available Student Time to Educational Resources [*Computer science*]

MASTER ......　Miniaturized Sink-Rate Telemetering RADAR

MASTER ......　Multiple Access Shared Time Executive Routine [*Control Data Corp.*] [*Computer science*]

MASTER KEY...　Managership of Soldier Training, Education, and Readiness with Knowledge and Excellence Year-Round [*Army*] (INF)

MASTICH .....　Mastiche [*Mastic*] [*Pharmacy*] (ROG)

MASTIF........　Multi-Axis Spin Test Inertia Facility [*Training device for astronauts*]

MASTIFF......　Modular Automated System to Identify Friend from Foe [*Military*] (PDAA)

MASTIR ....　Microfilmed Abstract System for Technical Information Retrieval [*Illinois Institute of Technology*] (IID)

MastPrchtBad...　Master Parachutist Badge [*Military decoration*] (AABC)

MASTS.........　Marine Associated Services Technology Systems Exposition [*Canada*] (ITD)

MAStS.........　Member of the Astronomical Society

MASTU ....　Mobile Antisubmarine Training Unit [*British*]

MASU ....　Machined Surface

MASU ....　Mediterranean and African Society of Ultrasound [*France*] (BUAC)

MASU ....　Mesoamerican Archaeology Study Unit [*American Topical Association*] (EA)

MASU ....　Metal Alloy Separation Unit

MASU ....　Mobile Army Surgical Unit

MASU ....　Multiple Acceleration Sensor Unit (PDAA)

MASUA ....　Mid-America State Universities Association [*Defunct*] (EA)

MASURCA....　Marine Surface Contre Avions (SAA)

MASW ....　Master of Arts in Social Work

MASW ....　Master Switch (IAA)

MASW ....　Military Airlift Support Wing [*Air Force*]

MASWEP .....　Medium Active Solid Waste Encapsulation Plant [*Nuclear energy*] (NUCP)

MASWg.........　Military Airlift Support Wing [*Air Force*] (AFM)

MASWSP ....　Manager, Antisubmarine Warfare Systems Project [*Navy*]

MASWSPO....　Manager, Antisubmarine Warfare Systems Project Office [*Navy*]

MASWT.........　Mobile Antisubmarine Warfare Target (MCD)

MASX.........　Mastec, Inc. [*NASDAQ symbol*] (SAG)

MAT ....　Machine-Aided Translation (NITA)

MAT ....　Machine Analysis Table (IAA)

MAT ....　Machine-Assisted Translation

MAT ....　Machine Available Time [*Computer science*]

MAT ....　Maine Aviation Corp. [*ICAO designator*] (FAAC)

MAT ....　Maintainability of Software Analysis Tool (MCD)

MAT ....　Maintenance Access Terminal [*Aviation*]

MAT ....　Maintenance Appraisal Team (MCD)

MAT ....　Mammary Ascites Tumor [*Oncology*]

MAT ....　Management Advisory Team (NRCH)

MAT ....　Manifold Air Temperature [*Automotive engineering*]

MAT ....　Manual Arts Therapist

MAT ....　Marine Air Temperature [*Meteorology*]

MAT ....　Maritime, Aviation, and Transport Insurance (DLA)

MAT ....　Marketing Assistance Test

MAT ....　Master Account Title [*Office of Management and Budget*]

MA(T) ....　Master of Arts in Teaching (PGP)

MAT ....　Master of Arts in Theology (PGP)

MAT ....　Master Operational Recording Tape Address Table (IAA)

MAT ....　Matachewan Consolidated Mines Ltd. [*Toronto Stock Exchange symbol*]

MAT ....　Matadi [*Zaire*] [*Airport symbol Obsolete*] (OAG)

MAT ....　Matching Abacus Test [*Parapsychology*]

MAT ....　Material (AFM)

mat ....　Material (VRA)

MAT ....　Materials Department [*David W. Taylor Naval Ship Research and Development Center*] [*Annapolis, MD*]

MAT ....　Materiel [*Military*] (AFM)

Mat ....　Maternal (STED)

Mat ....　Maternity (STED)

MAT ....　Maternity

MAT ....　Mathematical Automata Theory

MAT ....　Matinee

mat ....　Matinee (WDAA)

MAT ....　Matins (ROG)

MAT ....　Matrix (MSA)

mat ....　Matrix (WDAA)

MAT ....　Matrix Analogies Test [*Intelligence test*]

MAT ....　Matsushiro [*Japan*] [*Seismograph station code, US Geological Survey*] (SEIS)

MAT. ....　Mattel, Inc. [*NYSE symbol*] (SPSG)

Mat ....　Mattheus de Mathesillanis [*Flourished, 1381-1402*] [*Authority cited in pre-1607 legal work*] (DSA)

MAT ....　Matthew [*New Testament book*]

Mat ....　Mature (STED)

MAT ....　Matured

MAT ....　Maturity

Mat ....　Maturity (EBF)

MAT ....　Matutinal (ADA)

MAT ....　Mean Annual Temperature [*Climatology*]

MAT ....　Measurement of Atmospheric Turbulence

MAT ....　Mechanical Aptitude Test

MAT ....　Mechanical Assembly Technique (IAA)

MAT ....　Mechanically Agitated Tank [*Engineering*]

MAT ....　Medial Axes Transformation (MHDI)

MAT ....　Medial Axis Transformation (MHDB)

MAT ....　Medical Assessment Tribunal [*Queensland, Australia*]

MAT ....　Medium Artillery Tractor [*British military*] (DMA)

MAT ....　Medium Assault Transport (MCD)

MAT ....　Memory Access Table [*Computer science*]

MAT ....　Memory-Address Test

MAT ....　Memory Address Translator (NITA)

MAT ....　Mercury Amalgamation Trap [*Analytical chemistry*]

MAT ....　Meridian Administration Tools [*Telecommunications*] (ITD)

MAT ....　Meteorological Atmospheric Turbulence (MCD)

MAT ....　Methionine Adenosyltransferase [*An enzyme*]

MAT ....　Metropolitan Achievement Test

MAT ....　Metropolitan Area Trunk [*Telecommunications*] (TEL)

MAT ....　Microactivity Testing [*Catalysis technology*]

MAT	Microalloy Transistor
MAT	Microtray Agglutination Test [*Clinical chemistry*]
MAT	Microwave Antenna Tower
MAT	Military Aircraft Types
MAT	Military Air Transport
MAT	Miller-Abbott Tube [*Surgery*] [*Medicine*] (DAVI)
MAT	Miller Analogies Test [*Psychology*]
MAT	Mine Assembly Team [*Navy*] (NVT)
MAT	Minimal Aversion Threshold [*to noise*]
MAT	Minimum Allowable Threshold [*Chemistry*]
MAT	Missile Acceptance Team (AAG)
MAT	Missile Acceptance Test
MAT	Missile Acquisition and Track
MAT	Missile Adapter Tester
MAT	Missile Airframe Technology (MCD)
MAT	Missile Antitank
MAT	Mobile Advisor Team [*Vietnamese team trained by US Army advisors*] (VNW)
MAT	Mobile Aerial Target (AAG)
MAT	Mobile Arming Tower (KSC)
MAT	Mobile Assistance Team [*Federal disaster planning*]
MAT	Mobile Mine Assembly Team
MAT	Modular Allocation Technique (PDAA)
MAT	Modular Assembly Technique (IAA)
MAT	Molecular Analysis Team
MAT	Monoamine Transporter [*Biochemistry*]
MAT	Monocyto-Angiotropin [*Biochemistry*]
MAT	Motivation Analysis Test [*Psychology*]
MAT	Motor Ambulance Trolley [*British*]
MAT	Moving Annual Total [*Statistics*] (DCTA)
MAT	Multiallelic Mating-Type Regulatory Gene
MAT	Multifocal Atrial Tachycardia [*Cardiology*]
MAT	Multimedia Access Terminals [*Philips*] [*Electronics*]
MAT	Multiple Access Test
MAT	Multiple Access Time [*Telecommunications*] (ECII)
MAT	Multiple Actuator Test (MCD)
MAT	Multiple Address Telegrams
MAT	Multiple-Agent Chemotherapy [*Medicine*] (DB)
MAT	Multiple Aptitude Test [*Education*] (AEBS)
MATA	Military Assistance Training Advisor
MATA	Motorcycle and Allied Trades Association [*Later, MIC*] (EA)
MATA	Multiple Answering Teaching Aid (PDAA)
MATA	Museums Association of Tropical Africa (BUAC)
MATA	Musical Arena Theatres Association [*Later, PAMI*] (EA)
MATABE	Multiple-Weapon Automatic Target and Battery Evaluator (SAA)
MATAC	Money Advice Trust Advisory Committee (BUAC)
MATACQ	Material Acquisition (NG)
MATADOR	Mobile and Three-Dimensional Air Defense Operations RADAR [*Military*] (PDAA)
MATAF	Mediterranean Allied Tactical Air Force
MATB	Military Air Transport Board
MATB	Missile Auxiliary Test Bench
MATC	Maximum Acceptable Tolerance Concentration (GNE)
MATC	Maximum Acceptable Toxicant Concentration
MATC	Middle Atlantic Conference (PSS)
MATC	Military Air Transport Command (MUGU)
MATC	Milwaukee Area Technical College (PCM)
MATC	Missile Auxiliaries Test Console
MATC	Mobilization Army Training Center
MATC	Mountain Artillery Training Centre [*British military*] (DMA)
MATCALS	Marine Air Traffic Control and Landing System [*Navy*]
MATCALS	Mobile Air Traffic Control and All-Weather Landing System (MCD)
MATCAT	Material Category
MATCH	Manned Attack Torpedo Carrying Helicopter (PDAA)
MATCH	Manpower and Talent Clearinghouse
MATCH	Matching Alcoholism Treatments to Client Heterogeneity
MATCH	Materials and Activities for Teachers and Children
MATCH	Medium-Range Antisubmarine Torpedo Carrying Helicopter (NATG)
MATCH	Mothers Apart from Their Children [*British*] (DI)
MATCH	MTMC [*Military Traffic Management Command*] Automated Transportation Scheduler (GFGA)
MATCH	Multielement Assured Tracking Chopper
MATCM	Master of Acupuncture and Traditional Chinese Medicine (PGP)
MATCO	Materials Analysis, Tracking, and Control [*Johnson Space Center data system*] [*NASA*] (NASA)
MATCO	Military Air Traffic Coordinating Office [*or Officer*] [*Air Force*] (AFM)
MATCOM	Materiel Command [*Army*] (AABC)
MATCOMEUR	Materiel Command, Europe
MATCON	Microwave Aerospace Terminal Control [*Air Force*]
MATCONOFF	Material Control Officer (MCD)
MatCo-Ord(N)	Material Co-Ordination Division (Naval) [*British*]
MATCS	Marine Air Traffic Control Squadron (DNAB)
MATCSDET	Marine Air Traffic Control Squadron Detachment (DNAB)
MATCU	Marine Air Tactical [*later, Traffic*] Control Unit [*Marine Corps*]
MATCU	Military Air Traffic Coordinating Unit [*MTMC*] (TAG)
MATCV	Mobile Air Traffic Control Vehicle [*Military*]
MATD	Mine and Torpedo Detector [*SONAR*] [*Navy*]
MATDA	Methylene-bis-(aminothiadiazole) [*Pesticide*]
MATDEV	Materiel Developer
MATE	Machine-Aided Translation Editing (PDAA)
MATE	Manual Adaptive TMA [*Target Motion Analysis*] Estimator [*Navy*] (ANA)
MATE	Manually Aided Tracking Enhancement (MCD)
MATE	Marital Attitude Evaluation [*Psychology*]
MATE	Married Americans for Tax Equality

MATE	Master of Arts in the Teaching of English
Mat E	Materials Engineer
MATE	Maternal Attitudes Evaluation (STED)
MATE	Matewan BancShares [*NASDAQ symbol*] (TTSB)
MATE	Matewan BancShares, Inc. [*NASDAQ symbol*] (SAG)
MATE	Matrix Automation through EMATS [*Military*] (MCD)
MATE	McDonnell Airborne Trainer and Evaluator [*McDonnell Douglas Corp.*] (MCD)
MATE	Measuring and Test Equipment (IEEE)
MATE	Memory-Assisted Terminal Equipment (PDAA)
MATE	Meteorological Analog Test and Evaluation (PDAA)
MATE	MICOM [*Missile Command*] Automated Test Equipment
MATE	Microprocessor Automatic Testing [*ASMAP Electronics Ltd.*] [*Software package*] (NCC)
MATE	Missile/Aircraft Test Equipment
MATE	Mission Analysis Technique for Experiments
MATE	Mobilization and Training Equipment (MCD)
MATE	Modular Automatic Test Equipment
MATE	Montana Agri-Trade Exposition [*Jerry Hanson and Associates, Inc.*] (TSPED)
MATE	Multiband Automatic Test Equipment
MATE	Multiple-Access Time-Division Experiment (IEEE)
MATE	Multiple Advanced Technique Evaluation [*Military*] (CAAL)
MATE	Multipurpose Automatic Test Equipment
MATE	Multisystem Automatic Test Equipment [*British*]
MATEC	Maintenance Technician (NOAA)
Matec	MATEC Corp. [*Associated Press*] (SAG)
MA (T Ed)	Master of Arts in Teacher Education
MAT-EF	Matrix Analogies Test - Expanded Form [*Intelligence test*]
MATELO	Maritime Air-Radio Telegraph Organization (BUAC)
MATELO	Maritime Air Telecommunications Organization [*NATO*] (NATG)
MATEM	Manual Templating Model (MCD)
MATEP	Matewan Bancshrs 7.5% Cv'A'Pfd [*NASDAQ symbol*] (TTSB)
MATER	Material
MATERN	Maternal (WDAA)
MATERN	Maternity (WDAA)
MATES	Medium Attack Tactical Employment School [*Military*] (CAAL)
MATES	Mobilization and Training Equipment Site [*Military*] (AABC)
MATESL	Master of Arts in Teaching English as a Second Language (PGP)
MA(TESOL)	Master of Arts in Teaching English to Speakers of Other Languages
Matewan	Matewan BancShares, Inc. [*Associated Press*] (SAG)
MATEX	Macrotext Editor (MHDB)
MATEX	Master of Arts in Textiles (PGP)
MATEX	Material Expediting [*Program*] (DNAB)
MATFA	Meat and Allied Trades Federation of Australia (BUAC)
MATFL	Master of Arts in Teaching Foreign Language (PGP)
Math	Adversus Mathematicos [*of Sextus Empiricus*] [*Classical studies*] (OCD)
MA(Th)	Master of Arts in Theology
MATH	Master of Arts in Therapy (PGP)
Math	Mathematics (AL)
MATH	Mathematics (EY)
MATH	Mathematics Abstracts [*Fachinformationszentrum Karlsruhe GmbH*] [*Information service or system*]
Math	Matheus de Mathesillanis [*Flourished, 1381-1402*] [*Authority cited in pre-1607 legal work*] (DSA)
Math	Mathieu's Quebec Reports [*A publication*] (DLA)
MATH	Mathsoft, Inc. [*NASDAQ symbol*] (SAG)
MATH	Mobile, Air-Transportable Hospital [*Military*]
MATH	Modern Approach to Treatment of Hypertension [*Medicine*] (DMAA)
Math D	Doctor of Mathematics
MATHDI	Mathematical Didactics [*Fachinformationszentrum Energie, Physik, Mathematik GmbH*] [*Database*]
Mathe de Afflcti	Matthaeus de Afflictis [*Deceased, 1528*] [*Authority cited in pre-1607 legal work*] (DSA)
MA Theol	Master of Arts in Theology
MATHL	Mathematical
MATHLAB	Mathematical Laboratory [*Programming language*] (CSR)
MATHN	Mathematician (AFM)
Math N	Matthaeus Nerutius [*Flourished, 16th century*] [*Authority cited in pre-1607 legal work*] (DSA)
MATHP	Medium Artillery Terminal Homing Projectile
MATHPAC	Mathematical Package (IAA)
Math Pres Ev	Mathews on Presumptive Evidence [*A publication*] (DLA)
MATHS	Mathematics
Mathsft	Mathsoft, Inc. [*Associated Press*] (SAG)
Math T	Mathematics Teacher [*A publication*] (BRI)
MATI	Maldives Association of the Tourism Industry (EY)
MATIC	Multiple Area Technical Information Center
MATICO	Machine Applications to Technical Information Center Operations
MATIF	Marche a Terme des Instruments Financiere [*French stock exchange*]
MATIF	Marche a Terme des Instruments Financiers [*French Financial Futures Market*]
MATILDA	Microwave Analysis Threat Indication and Launch Direction Apparatus [*Military*]
MATINSP	Material Inspection [*Navy*] (NVT)
MATK	Martek Biosciences, Inc. [*NASDAQ symbol*] (SAG)
MATL	Master of Arts in Teaching of Languages (PGP)
MATL	Material (KSC)
MATL	Materiel
MATL	Middle Atlantic
MATLAB	Matrix Laboratory [*Computer science*]
Matlack	Matlack Systems, Inc. [*Associated Press*] (SAG)
MATLAN	Matrix Language [*Computer science*] (IEEE)

Mat L & T	Mathews on Landlord and Tenant [*A publication*] (DLA)
MATLC	Mid-Atlantic Conference (PSS)
MATL REQ	Material Requisition
MATL RR	Material Receiving Report
MATM	Master of Arts in Teaching of Mathematics (PGP)
MATMO	Medical Advanced Technology Management Office
MATMO	Military Advanced Technology Management Office (RDA)
MATMOP	Materiel Management Optimization Program [*DoD*]
MATMU	Mobile Aircraft Torpedo Maintenance Unit
MATNO	Material Requested Is Not Available
MATO	Military Air Traffic Operations [*British military*] (DMA)
MATP	Masking Template [*Tool*] (AAG)
MATP	Military Assistance Training Program (AABC)
MATP	Missile Auxiliary Test Position
Mat Par	Matthew Paris. Historia Minor [*A publication*] (DLA)
Mat Paris	Matthew Paris. Historia Minor [*A publication*] (DLA)
Mat Part	Mathews on the Law of Partnership [*A publication*] (DLA)
MA-TPM	Maritime Administration Transport Planning Mobilization [*Federal emergency order*]
Mat Por	Mathews on the Law of Portions [*A publication*] (DLA)
MATPS	Machine-Aided Technical Processing System [*Yale University Library*] [*New Haven, CT*] [*Computer science*]
MATR	Management Access to Records
MATR	Matriculate (ROG)
MATR	Matron
MATRAC	Military Air Traffic Control System
MatrCap	Matrix Capital Corp. [*Associated Press*] (SAG)
MATRD	Materiel Release Denial [*Army*] (AABC)
MATRE	Material Requested
MATRED	Material Redistribution [*Program*] (DNAB)
MATRIC	Matriculation
MATRIC	Midwest Agribusiness Trade Research and Information Center [*Iowa State University of Science and Technology*] [*Research center*] (RCD)
MATRIS	Manpower and Training Research Information System [*DoD Information service or system*] (IID)
MATRIS	Medical Manpower and Training Information Service [*British*] (DAVI)
Matritch	Matritech, Inc. [*Associated Press*] (SAG)
MATRIX	Management Trial Exercise [*Career orientation simulation*]
MATRIX	Market Trend Index [*Associated Equipment Distributors program*]
Matrl	Material
MATRL	Matrimonial (ROG)
MATRS	Mattress
MATRS	Military Airlift Training Squadron [*Air Force*]
MATRS	Miniature Airborne Telemetry Receiving Station
Matrtc	Matritech, Inc. [*Associated Press*] (SAG)
MATRW	Military Airlift Training Wing [*Air Force*]
MatrxPh	Matrix Pharmaceutical, Inc. [*Associated Press*] (SAG)
MatrxSv	Matrix Service Co. [*Associated Press*] (SAG)
MATS	Maintenance Analysis Task Sheet
MATS	Maintenance Analysis Test Set
MATS	Manual Versus Automatic Transmission Study (MCD)
MATS	Master of Arts in Teaching of Science (PGP)
MATS	Master of Arts in Theological Studies (PGP)
MATS	Material and Toxicology System
MATS	Material Transport Segment (AAEL)
MATS	Materiel Squadron
MATS	Matrimonial Matters [*Slang*] (DSUE)
Mats	Matson's Reports [*22-24 Connecticut*] [*A publication*] (DLA)
MATS	Mechanical Accounting for Telephone Service (IAA)
MATS	Mechanical Anti-Theft System [*Automotive engineering*]
MATS	Mediterranean Air Transport Service
MATS	Midcourse Airborne Target Signature [*Military*] (PDAA)
MATS	Military Air Transport Service [*Later, Military Airlift Command*]
MATS	Missile Auxiliaries Test Set
MATS	Mission Analysis and Trajectory Simulation (MCD)
MATS	Mobile Automatic Telephone System [*Telecommunications*]
MATS	Mobile Automatic Test Set (MCD)
MATS	Model Aircraft Target System [*British military*] (DMA)
MATS	Monitoring and Test Subsystem
MATS	Multiple-Access Time Sharing [*Computer science*] (IAA)
MATS	Multipurpose Automatic Test System (IAA)
MATSA	Managerial, Administrative, Technical, and Supervisory Association [*British*] (DCTA)
MATSA	Marek-Associated Tumor-Specific Antigen [*Medicine*] (DMAA)
MATSA	Marek Associated Tumor-Specified Antigen [*Medicine*] (STED)
MATSB	Mobile Advance Tactical Support Base [*Navy*] (VNW)
MATSC	Middletown Air Technical Service Command [*Air Force*]
MatSci	Material Sciences Corp. [*Associated Press*] (SAG)
MATSCO	Management and Technical Services Company (AAGC)
MAT-SF	Matrix Analogies Test - Short Form [*Intelligence test*]
MATSG	Marine Aviation Training Support Group (DNAB)
MATSO	Material Requested Being Supplied [*Military*]
Matson	Matson's Reports [*22-24 Connecticut*] [*A publication*] (DLA)
MATSR	Military Air Transport Service [*later, Military Airlift Command*] Regulation
MATSS	Marine Aviation Training Support Squadron (DNAB)
MATSS	Midwest Automated Technical Services Systems [*Information service or system*] (IID)
MATSTAT	Materiel Status [*Military*]
Matsu	Matsushita Electric Industrial Co. Ltd. [*Associated Press*] (SAG)
MAtt	Attleboro Public Library, Attleboro, MA [*Library symbol Library of Congress*] (LCLS)
Matt	Matthew [*New Testament book*]
MATT	Matthews Studio Equipment Group [*NASDAQ symbol*] (NQ)
MATT	Missile ASW [*Antisubmarine Warfare*] Torpedo Target (MCD)
MATT	Mobile Acoustic Torpedo Target (NG)
MATT	Multimission Advanced Tactical Terminal (DWSG)
Mattel	Mattel, Inc. [*Associated Press*] (SAG)
Matth Com	Matthews' Guide to Commissioner in Chancery [*A publication*] (DLA)
Matth Cr L	Matthews' Digest of Criminal Law [*A publication*] (DLA)
Matthe de Affli	Matthaeus de Afflictis [*Deceased, 1528*] [*Authority cited in pre-1607 legal work*] (DSA)
Matthews	Matthews' Reports [*75 Virginia*] [*A publication*] (DLA)
Matthews	Matthews' Reports [*6-9 West Virginia*] [*A publication*] (DLA)
Matth Exe	Matthews' Executors and Administrators [*2nd ed.*] [*1839*] [*A publication*] (DLA)
Matth Gribal	Matthaeus Gribaldus [*Deceased, 1564*] [*Authority cited in pre-1607 legal work*] (DSA)
Matth Part	Matthews on Partnership [*A publication*] (DLA)
Matth Pr Ev	Matthews on Presumptive Evidence [*A publication*] (DLA)
MatthwInt	Matthews International Corp. [*Associated Press*] (SAG)
MatthwSt	Matthews Studio Equipment Group [*Associated Press*] (SAG)
MATTS	Multiple Airborne Target Trajectory System
Mattson	Mattson Technology, Inc. [*Associated Press*] (SAG)
MATU	Marine Air Traffic Unit
MATUT	Matutinus [*In the Morning*] [*Pharmacy*]
matut	Matutinus [*In the Morning*] [*Latin*] (STED)
MATV	Master Antenna Television
MATV	Matav-Cable Systems Media Ltd. [*NASDAQ symbol*] (SAG)
MatvCab	Matav-Cable Systems Media Ltd. [*Associated Press*] (SAG)
MATW	Matthews International Corp. [*NASDAQ symbol*] (SAG)
MATW	Matthews Intl. `A' [*NASDAQ symbol*] (TTSB)
MATW	Metal Awning Type Window
MATWAS	Marine Automatic Telephone Weather Answering Service [*Marine science*] (MSC)
MATWING	Medium Attack Wing (NVT)
MATX	Matrix Pharmaceutical [*NASDAQ symbol*] (TTSB)
MATX	Matrix Pharmaceutical, Inc. [*NASDAQ symbol*] (SAG)
MATZ	Military Aerodrome Traffic Zone
MAU	Air Mauritius Ltd. [*ICAO designator*] (FAAC)
MAU	Maintenance Analysis Unit
MAU	Maintenance Augmenting Unit (NG)
MAU	Marine Advisory Unit [*Marine Corps*]
MAU	Marine Amphibious Unit (NVT)
mau	Massachusetts [*MARC country of publication code Library of Congress*] (LCCP)
MAU	Master Augmentation Unit [*Navy*] (DOMA)
MAU	Mastung [*Pakistan*] [*Airport symbol*] (AD)
MAU	Math Acceleration Unit (NITA)
MAU	Mathematical Advisory Unit [*Ministry of Transport*] [*British*]
MAU	Matua [*Former USSR Seismograph station code, US Geological Survey*] (SEIS)
MAU	Maupiti [*French Polynesia*] [*Airport symbol*] (OAG)
Mau	Mauricius [*Authority cited in pre-1607 legal work*] (DSA)
MAU	Mauritius (ROG)
MAU	Media Access Unit [*Telecommunications*]
MAU	Medical Assistance Unit [*HEW*]
MAU	Medium Access Unit [*Computer science*] (BYTE)
MAU	Medium Attachment Unit [*Computer science*] (TNIG)
MAU	Memory Access Unit
MAU	Meyenburg-Altherr-Uehlinger [*Syndrome*] [*Medicine*] (STED)
mAU	Milliabsorbance Unit [*Spectroscopy*]
MAU	Million Accounting Units (NASA)
MAU	Miscellaneous Armament Unit
MAU	Modern American Usage [*A publication*]
MAU	Mount Allison University [*New Brunswick, Canada*]
MAU	Multiattribute Utility (IEEE)
MAU	Multiple Access Unit
MAU	Multistation Access Unit [*Telecommunications*] (PCM)
MAUA	Master of Arts in Urban Affairs (GAGS)
Mau & Pol Sh	Maude and Pollock's Law of Merchant Shipping [*A publication*] (DLA)
Mau & Sel	Maule and Selwyn's English King's Bench Reports [*A publication*] (DLA)
MAUD	Manually-Assisted Universal Deviator
MAUD	Master of Arts in Urban Design (GAGS)
MAud	Master of Audiology
MAUD	Ministry of Aircraft Uranium Development [*British World War II*]
MAUD	Movimento Academico pela Uniao Democrata [*Academic Movement for Democratic Union*] [*Portugal Political party*] (PPE)
MAUDE	Morse Automatic Decoder
Maude & P	Maude and Pollock's Law of Merchant Shipping [*A publication*] (DLA)
Maude & P Mer Shipp	Maude and Pollock's Law of Merchant Shipping [*A publication*] (DLA)
Maude & P Shipp	Maude and Pollock's Law of Merchant Shipping [*A publication*] (DLA)
MAUDEP	Metropolitan Association of Urban Designers and Environmental Planners (EA)
Maud Ment Res	Maudsley on Mental Responsibility [*A publication*] (DLA)
M Au E	Master of Automobile Engineering
M Au Eng	Master of Automobile Engineering
MAUF	Multiattribute Utility Function
MAUFS	Municipal Arborists and Urban Foresters Society (EA)
MAUG	MicroNet Apple User's Group [*CompuServe*] [*Database*]
Maug Att	Maugham's Attorneys, Solicitors, and Agents [*1825*] [*A publication*] (DLA)
Maug Att	Maugham's Statutes Relating to Attorneys, Etc. [*1839*] [*A publication*] (DLA)

Maug Cr L ... Maugham's Outlines of Criminal Law [*2nd ed.*] [*1842*] [*A publication*] (DLA)

Maugh Lit Pr... Maugham's Literary Property [*1828*] [*A publication*] (DLA)

Maugh RP ... Maugham's Outlines of Real Property Law [*1842*] [*A publication*] (DLA)

Maug Jur ..... Maugham's Outlines of the Jurisdiction [*1838*] [*A publication*] (DLA)

Maug Law ... Maugham's Outlines of Law [*1837*] [*A publication*] (DLA)

MAUK .... Mining Association of the United Kingdom (BUAC)

Maul & Sel... Maule and Selwyn's English King's Bench Reports [*A publication*] (DLA)

Maule & S... Maule and Selwyn's English King's Bench Reports [*A publication*] (DLA)

MAULEX ..... Marine Amphibious Unit Landing Exercise (NVT)

MauLoa ...... Mauna Loa Macadamia Partners Ltd. [*Associated Press*] (SAG)

MAULT........ Manual or Automatic Ultrasonic Laboratory Test

Maur............ Mauritius

Maur............ Mauritius

Maur Dec.... Mauritius Decisions [*A publication*] (DLA)

Maurit.......... Mauritania

MAURP .... Master of Arts in Urban and Regional Planning (GAGS)

Maurti .... Mauritania (VRA)

MAUS .... Mammography Attitudes and Usage Study [*Medicine*] (DMAA)

MAUS .... Mauser Rifle

MAUS .... Messensch Afteliche Autonome Experiment Unter Scheewerelosigkeit

MAUS .... Mobile Automated Scanner

MAUS .... Movimiento de Accion y Unidad Socialista [*Socialist Movement for Action and Unity*] [*Mexico Political party*] (PPW)

MAUSED ...... Midwest Association of University Student Employment Directors [*Later, MASEA*] (EA)

mauso .... Mausoleum (VRA)

MAUTEL ...... Microminiaturized Autonetics Telemetry

MauU .... University of Mauritius, Reduit, Mauritius [*Library symbol Library of Congress*] (LCLS)

MAUV .... Multiple Autonomous Vehicle

MAUW .... Modified Advanced Underwater Weapons (MCD)

MAV............. Macrosiphum avenae Virus

MAV............. Magyar Allamvasutak [*Hungarian State Railways*]

MAV............. Maintenance Assistance Vehicle (MCD)

MAV............. Maloelap [*Marshall Islands*] [*Airport symbol*] (OAG)

MAV............. Manpower Authorization Voucher

MAV............. Mars Ascent Vehicle [*NASA*]

MAV............. Massive Resources Ltd. [*Vancouver Stock Exchange symbol*]

MAV............. Mavesa SA ADS [*NYSE symbol*] (SAG)

MAV............. Max-Aviation [*Canada ICAO designator*] (FAAC)

MAV............. Maximum Allowable Variation [*Net weight labeling*]

MAV............. Mean Absolute Value [*Statistics*]

MAV............. MeCCNU [*Semustine*], Adriamycin, Vincristine [*Antineoplastic drug regimen*]

MAV............. Mechanical Auxiliary Ventricle (PDAA)

MAV............. Micro Air Vehicle [*Remote controlled device*]

MAV............. Military Aerospace Vehicle

mA/V............ Milliamperes per Volt (DEN)

MAV............. Minimal Apparent Viscosity (STED)

MAV............. Minimum Acceptable Value (MCD)

MAV............. Minimum Apparent Viscosity (DB)

MAV............. Minute Alveolar Volume [*Medicine*] (DAVI)

MAV............. Moscavia [*Former USSR*] [*FAA designator*] (FAAC)

MAV............. Motor Ambulance Van [*British*]

MA(V).......... Motorcycling Australia (Victoria) [*Australia An association*]

MAV............. Movement Arm Vector (STED)

MAV............. Multi-Appeal Vehicle

MAV............. Myeloblastosis-Associated Virus

MAV............. Transmembrane Activation Voltage [*Biochemistry*] (DAVI)

MAVA.......... Moored Acoustic Vertical Array

MAVA.......... Multiple Abstract Variance Analysis (STED)

MAVAR .... Microwave Amplification by Variable Reactance (IAA)

MAVAR .... Mixer Amplification by Variable Reactance (IAA)

MAVAR .... Modulating Amplifier Using Variable Resistance

MAVCC .... Mid-America Vocational Curriculum Consortium (OICC)

MAVE........... Model for Articulated Vocational Education (EDAC)

MAVE........... Multiple Aerial Vehicle Expert [*Army*]

MAV Ed....... Master of Administration in Vocational Education (PGP)

MAVERICK ... Manufacturers Assistance in Verifying, Identification in Cataloging

MAVES .... Manned Mars and Venus Exploration Studies

Mavesa........ Mavesa SA ADS [*Associated Press*] (SAG)

MAVI .... Microwave Automatic Vehicle Identification (MCD)

MAVICA ...... Magnetic Video Camera [*Sony Corp.*]

MAVICA ...... Magnetic Video Card (NITA)

MAVIN .... Machine-Assisted Vendor Information Network

MAVIN .... Multiple Angle, Variable Interval, Nonorthogonal [*Magnetic resonance imaging*]

MAVIS .... Master Vision Screener (PDAA)

MAVIS .... McDonnell Douglas Automated Voice Information System (MCD)

MAVIS .... Microprocessor-Based Audio Visual Information System (PDAA)

MAVIS .... Mobile Armored Vehicle Indigo System [*Radio-controlled tank*]

MAVIS .... Mobile Artery and Vein Imaging System [*Medicine*] (STED)

MAVK.......... Maverick Tube [*NASDAQ symbol*] (TTSB)

MAVK.......... Maverick Tube Corp. [*NASDAQ symbol*] (SAG)

MAVPE......... Metal Alkyl Vapor-Phase Epitaxy [*Semiconductor technology*]

MAVR .... Mitral and Aortic Valve Replacement [*Medicine*] (DMAA)

MAVS .... Manned Aerial Vehicle for Surveillance (MCD)

MavTube...... Maverick Tube Corp. [*Associated Press*] (SAG)

MAVU .... Modular Audio Visual Unit (PDAA)

MAVWC .... Military Aircraft Voice Weather Code (NATG)

MAW........... Machinists and Aerospace Workers (DICI)

MAW........... Malden, MO [*Location identifier FAA*] (FAAL)

MAW........... Marine Air Wing

mAw............ Maritime Arctic Warm [*Air Mass*] [*Meteorology*] (BARN)

MAW........... Master of Arts in Worship (PGP)

MAW........... Master of Arts in Writing (GAGS)

MAW........... Mauritius Alliance of Women (BUAC)

MAW........... Mawson [*Antarctica*] [*Seismograph station code, US Geological Survey*] (SEIS)

MAW........... Maximum Allowable Weight [*Military*] (INF)

MAW........... Mechanically Aimed Warhead

MAW........... Medium Active Waste [*Nuclear energy*]

MAW........... Medium Antiarmor Weapon (INF)

MAW........... Medium Antitank Weapon

MAW........... Medium Assault Weapon

MAW........... Microsoft At Work [*Computer software*] (PCM)

MAW........... Mid-American Waste Sys [*NYSE symbol*] (TTSB)

MAW........... Mid-American Waste Systems, Inc. [*NYSE symbol*] (SPSG)

MAW........... Military Airlift Wing [*Air Force*] (MCD)

MAW........... Minor Assist Work

MAW........... Mission Adaptive Wing (MCD)

MAW........... Mustique Airways [*Barbados*] [*ICAO designator*] (FAAC)

MAWA .... Maltese Australian Women's Association

MAWA .... Matehematical Association of Western Australia

MAWA .... Missile Attack Warning and Assessment [*Military*] (PDAA)

MAWB .... Master Air Waybill [*Shipping*] (DS)

MAWC .... Marine Air West Coast

MAWCS .... Mobile Air Weapons Control System [*ESD*]

MAWD .... Mars Atmospheric Water Detection [*NASA*]

MA/WD .... Material Annex/Weapons Dictionary [*Military*]

MAWEC .... Maritime Aircraft Weather Code (NATG)

MAWFA .... Make-a-Wish Foundation of America (EA)

MAWg.......... Military Airlift Wing [*Air Force*] (AFM)

MAWIA .... Mexican American Workers Importation Act

MAWL .... Magnetic Aircraft Weapons Link

MAWLOGS ... Models of the [*US*] Army Worldwide Logistics System (AABC)

MAWP .... Marine Air Wing Pacific

MAWP .... Maximum Allowable Working Pressure (PDAA)

MAWS .... Marine Air Warning Squadron

MAWS .... Minimum Additive Waste Stabilization System [*Department of Energy*]

MAWS .... Missile Approach Warning System (DOMA)

MAWS .... Mobile Aircraft Weighing System (OA)

MAWS .... Modular Automated Weather System

MAWste....... Mid-American Waste Systems, Inc. [*Associated Press*] (SAG)

MAWTS........ Marine Aviation Weapons and Tactics Squadron

MAWTU .... Marine Air Weapons Training Unit (MCD)

MAX............. Cinemax [*Cable television channel*]

MAX............. Madrid, Spain [*Spaceflight Tracking and Data Network*] [*NASA*]

MAX............. Magic Answer Extractor [*Database*]

max .... Manx [*MARC language code Library of Congress*] (LCCP)

MAX............. Matam [*Senegal*] [*Airport symbol*] (OAG)

MAX............. Max-Aviation [*Canada*] [*FAA designator*] (FAAC)

MAX............. Maxilla [*Jawbone*]

MAX............. Maxim (ROG)

MAX............. Maxima (WDAA)

MAX............. Maximilian Numismatic and Historical Society (EA)

Max .... Maximinus [*of Scriptores Historiae Augustae*] [*Classical studies*] (OCD)

MAX............. Maximum

max .... Maximum (WDMC)

MAX............. Maxwell [*Unit of Magnetic Flux*] [*Electronics*] (IAA)

MAX............. Mediterranean Airlines SA [*Greece*] [*ICAO designator*] (FAAC)

MAX............. Mercury Air Group [*AMEX symbol*] (TTSB)

MAX............. Mercury Air Group, Inc. [*AMEX symbol*] (SPSG)

MAX............. Metropolitan Area Express [*Railway*] [*Portland, OR*] (ECON)

MAX............. Mid-Atlantic Crossroads

MAX............. Minerex Resources Ltd. [*Vancouver Stock Exchange symbol Toronto Stock Exchange symbol*]

MAX............. Mobile Automatic Exchange [*Telecommunications*] (NITA)

MAX............. Mobile Automatic X-Ray (PDAA)

MAX............. Modular Applications Executive [*Modular Computer Systems*]

Maxam .... Maxxam Corp. [*Associated Press*] (SAG)

MAXC........... Maxco, Inc. [*NASDAQ symbol*] (NQ)

MAXC........... Multiple Access Xerox Computer (NITA)

MAX CLB ..... Maximum Engine Thrust for Two-Engine Climb (GAVI)

Maxco........... Maxco, Inc. [*Associated Press*] (SAG)

MAXCO .... Maximum Dynamic Pressure (NASA)

MAXCOL ...... Maximum Column [*Computer science*] (PCM)

MAXCOM .... Modular Applications Executive for Communications [*Modular Computer Systems*]

MaxcrHlt ...... Maxicare Health Plans, Inc. [*Associated Press*] (SAG)

MAX CRZ ..... Maximum Engine Thrust for Two-Engine Cruise (GAVI)

Max Dig....... Maxwell's Nebraska Digest [*A publication*] (DLA)

MAXE........... Max & Erma's Restaurants [*NASDAQ symbol*] (TTSB)

MAXE........... Max & Erma's Restaurants, Inc. [*NASDAQ symbol*] (NQ)

Max EP .... Maximal Esophageal Pressure [*Medicine*] (MAE)

MaxEr .... Max & Erma's Restaurants, Inc. [*Associated Press*] (SAG)

MAXG .... Maximum Girth [*Pisciculture*]

MAXI .... Maxicare Health Plans [*NASDAQ symbol*] (TTSB)

MAXI .... Maxicare Health Plans, Inc. [*NASDAQ symbol*] (NQ)

MAXI .... Maximum Potential Licence Period (WDAA)

MAXID .... Maximize Indefinite Delivery Contracts (AFM)

Maxim .... Maxim Integrated Products, Inc. [*Associated Press*] (SAG)

MaximGp..... Maxim Group [*Associated Press*] (SAG)

MaximPh ..... Maxim Pharmaceuticals, Inc. [*Associated Press*] (SAG)

Max Int Stat...	Maxwell on the Interpretation of Statutes [*A publication*] (DLA)
Maxis...........	Maxis, Inc. [*Associated Press*] (SAG)
MAXIT.........	Maximum Interference Threshold [*Telecommunications*] (TEL)
MAX/IT........	Modular, Adaptable, Expandable, Intelligent Terminal [*Link Technologies, Inc.*] (PCM)
Max LD......	Maxwell's Law Dictionary [*A publication*] (DLA)
MAXM.........	Maxim Group [*NASDAQ symbol*] (SAG)
MAXMAR.....	Maximum Mobile Army
Max Mar L...	Maxwell's Marine Law [*A publication*] (DLA)
MAX/MIN	Maximum Disclosure / Minimum Delay (DNAB)
MaxmP........	Maxim Pharmaceuticals, Inc. [*Associated Press*] (SAG) .
MAXNET.....	Modular Application Executive for Computer Networks (PDAA)
MAXNET.....	Modular Applications Executive Network (NITA)
MAXNOR.....	Maximum Number of Runs (MCD)
MAXPAR.....	Maximum Pain Relief [*Medicine*]
MAXPAX	Maxwell House Coffee Package [*Vendor-machine system for Maxwell House coffee*]
MAXPEN	Maximum Penalty
MAXPID	Maximum Pain Intensity Difference [*Medicine*]
MAXS.........	Maxwell Shoe'A' [*NASDAQ symbol*] (TTSB)
MAXS.........	Maxwell Shoe Company, Inc. [*NASDAQ symbol*] (SAG)
MAXSECOM...	Maximum Security Communications (IAA)
MAXSECON..	Maximum Security Communications
Maxserv.......	Maxserv, Inc. [*Associated Press*] (SAG)
MAXTOP......	Maximum Total Duration Penalty
Maxtor........	Maxtor Corp. [*Associated Press*] (SAG)
MAXTTR	Maximum Time to Repair [*Navy*] (CAAL)
MAXTWK	Maximum Total Work Content
Maxu	Maxus Energy Corp. [*Associated Press*] (SAG)
MAXUPO.....	Maximum Undistorted Power Output (IAA)
Maxus.........	Maxus Energy [*Associated Press*] (SAG)
Maxw Cr Proc...	Maxwell's Treatise on Criminal Procedure [*A publication*] (DLA)
Maxwel........	Maxwell Laboratories, Inc. [*Associated Press*] (SAG)
Maxwell.......	Irish Land Purchase Cases [*1904-11*] [*A publication*] (DLA)
Maxwell.......	Maxwell on the Interpretation of Statutes [*A publication*] (DLA)
Maxw Interp St...	Maxwell on the Interpretation of Statutes [*A publication*] (DLA)
MaxwllSh.....	Maxwell Shoe Co., Inc. [*Associated Press*] (SAG)
MaxwllT......	Maxwell Technologies, Inc. [*Associated Press*] (SAG)
Maxxim........	Maxxim Medical, Inc. [*Associated Press*] (SAG)
may............	Malay [*MARC language code Library of Congress*] (LCCP)
MAY............	Malye Karmakuly [*Former USSR Geomagnetic observatory code*]
MAY............	Mangrove Cay [*Bahamas*] [*Airport symbol*] (OAG)
MAY............	Maya Airways Ltd. [*Belize*] [*ICAO designator*] (FAAC)
MAY............	Maybelline, Inc. [*NYSE symbol*] (SPSG)
MAY............	May Department Stores Co., Corporate Information Center, St. Louis, MO [*OCLC symbol*] (OCLC)
MAY............	Mayfield [*Washington*] [*Seismograph station code, US Geological Survey Closed*] (SEIS)
MAY............	Maynard Energy, Inc. [*Toronto Stock Exchange symbol*]
MAY............	Mayor (ROG)
MAYA..........	Most Advanced, Yet Acceptable [*Industrial design*]
MAYA..........	Muslim Arab Youth Association (EA)
May Act......	Mayhew's Action at Law [*1828*] [*A publication*] (DLA)
Maybel	Maybelline, Inc. [*Associated Press*] (SAG)
MAYC..........	Mayflower Conference (PSS)
MAYC..........	Methodist Association of Youth Clubs [*British*] (BI)
May Const Hist...	May's Constitutional History of England [*A publication*] (DLA)
MAYCOR......	Maytag Corp. (EFIS)
May Crim Law...	May's Criminal Law [*A publication*] (DLA)
May Dam	Mayne on the Law of Damages [*A publication*] (DLA)
MayDS.........	May Department Stores Co. [*Associated Press*] (SAG)
MayflCo........	Mayflower Co-Operative Bank [*Associated Press*] (SAG)
May Fr Conv...	May's Fraudulent Conveyances [*3rd ed.*] [*1908*] [*A publication*] (DLA)
May Ins	May on Insurance [*A publication*] (DLA)
May Just......	Mayo's Justice [*A publication*] (DLA)
May LR........	Mayurbhani Law Report [*India*] [*A publication*] (DLA)
May Merg....	Mayhew on Merger [*1861*] [*A publication*] (DLA)
Mayn	Maynard's English Reports, Exchequer Memoranda of Edward I, and Year Books of Edward II [*A publication*] (DLA)
MaynOl........	Maynard Oil Co. [*Associated Press*] (SAG)
Mayo & Moul...	Mayo and Moulton's Pension Laws [*A publication*] (DLA)
Mayo Just....	Mayo's Justice [*A publication*] (DLA)
Mayo Med Sch...	Mayo Medicine School (GAGS)
May Parl......	May's Parliamentary Practice [*A publication*] (ILCA)
May Parl Law...	May's Parliamentary Practice [*A publication*] (DLA)
May Parl Pr...	May's Parliamentary Practice [*A publication*] (DLA)
May PL........	May's Parliamentary Practice [*A publication*] (DLA)
MAYPOLE ...	May Polarization Experiment [*RADAR storm sensing*]
MAYS..........	Mays [*J. W.*], Inc. [*NASDAQ symbol*] (NQ)
MAYS..........	Mays (JW) [*NASDAQ symbol*] (TTSB)
MaysJ..........	Mays [*J. W.*], Inc. [*Associated Press*] (SAG)
MaySpeh	May & Speh, Inc. [*Associated Press*] (SAG)
Maytag	Maytag Corp. [*Associated Press*] (SAG)
MAYW	Maywood & Sugar Creek [*AAR code*]
MAZ............	Mayaguez [*Puerto Rico*] [*Airport symbol*] (OAG)
MAZ............	Mazatlan [*Mexico*] [*Seismograph station code, US Geological Survey*] (SEIS)
MAZ............	Mazzite [*A zeolite*]
MAZ............	Mines Air Service Zambia Ltd. [*ICAO designator*] (FAAC)
MAZ............	Missed Approach Azimuth [*Aviation*]
MAZ............	Mounting Azimuth [*Weaponry*] (INF)
MazelSt	Mazel Stores, Inc. [*Associated Press*] (SAG)
MAZH..........	Missile Azimuth Heading [*Air Force*]

MAZI............	Movement for the Advancement of the Zionist Idea [*Israel*] [*Political party*] (EY)
MAZL...........	Mazel Stores, Inc. [*NASDAQ symbol*] (SAG)
MAZO...........	Missile Azimuth Orientation [*Air Force*] (IAA)
MB............	All India Reporter, Madhya Bharat [*1950-57*] [*A publication*] (DLA)
MB............	Bachelor of Medicine [*Other than from Oxford*]
MB............	Bachelor of Music (WDAA)
mb---.........	Black Sea and Area [*MARC geographic area code Library of Congress*] (LCCP)
Mb............	Body Wave Magnitude (COE)
MB............	Boston Public Library and Eastern Massachusetts Regional Public Library System, Boston, MA [*Library symbol Library of Congress*] (LCLS)
MB............	Countrywide [*ICAO designator*] (AD)
MB............	Machine Batch (AAEL)
MB............	Machine Bolt [*Technical drawings*]
MB............	MacMillan Bloedel Ltd. [*Associated Press*] (SAG)
MB............	Magnetic Bearing [*Navigation*]
MB............	Magnetic Brake [*Industrial control*] (IEEE)
MB............	Magnetron Branch [*Electronics*] (OA)
MB............	Mailbox (AAG)
MB............	Main Ballast
MB............	Main Base [*Air Force*] (AFM)
MB............	Main Battery [*Guns*]
MB............	Main Bus (MCD)
MB............	Maintenance Busy [*Telecommunications*] (TEL)
M-B............	Make-Break
MB............	Mallory Body [*Medicine*]
MB............	Mamillary Body [*Medicine*] (DB)
MB............	Management Baseline (NASA)
MB............	Management Board (ACII)
MB............	Manitoba [*Canadian province*] [*Postal code*]
MB............	March-Bender Factor [*Physiology*]
MB............	Margin Buccal [*Medicine*] (MAE)
MB............	Marie-Bamberger [*Disease*] [*Medicine*] (DB)
MB............	Marine Barracks
MB............	Marine Base
MB............	Marine Board (EA)
MB............	Mark of the Beast [*Disparaging term for 19th century Protestant clerical waistcoats that had Catholic influences*]
MB............	Marks Banco (ROG)
MB............	Marsh-Bender [*Factor*] [*Muscle tissue*]
MB............	Mass Balance
MB............	Material Balance
MB............	May & Baker Ltd. [*Great Britain*] [*Research code symbol*]
MB............	MBB-UV, MBB-UD [*Messerschmitt-Boelkow-Blohm*], und Pneuma-Technik [*Germany ICAO aircraft manufacturer identifier*] (ICAO)
MB............	Measurement Base [*Military*]
MB............	Mechanized Battalion [*Army*]
MB............	Medal of Bravery
MB............	Medial Bilateral (Neuron) [*Neuroanatomy*]
MB............	Median Bundle [*Botany*]
MB............	Medical Board
MB............	Medical Bulletin
MB............	Medicare Bureau [*Health Care Financing Administration - Social Security Administration*] (OICC)
MB............	Medicinae Baccalaureus [*Bachelor of Medicine*] [*Latin*]
MB............	Medium Bomber
MB............	Medium Bronze [*Numismatics*]
MB............	Megabar
Mb............	Megabase [*A unit of molecular size*]
MB............	Megabit [*Binary Digit*] [*Computer science*]
Mb............	Megabit [*Computer science*] (WDMC)
MB............	Megabuck [*Defense industry colloquialism for one million dollars*] (AAG)
MB............	Megabyte [*Data storage capacity*] [*Computer science*]
Mb............	Megabyte
MB............	Melt Back
MB............	Memorandum Book (ROG)
MB............	Memory Bank
MB............	Memory Buffer [*Computer science*]
MB............	Memory Bus
MB............	Mercedes-Benz [*Automobile*]
MB............	Merchant Bank
MB............	Meridian & Bigbee Railroad Co. [*Later, MBRR*] [*AAR code*]
MB............	Mesiobuccal [*Dentistry*]
MB............	Message Buffer (ACRL)
MB............	Message Business
MB............	Messages of the Bible [*A publication*]
MB............	Metabisulfite [*Inorganic chemistry*]
MB............	Metal Box [*Commercial firm British*]
MB............	Methyl Bromide [*Organic chemistry*]
MB............	Methylene Blue [*Organic chemistry*]
MB............	Metrication Board [*British*]
MB............	Metric Board (OICC)
MB............	Microbeam [*Physics*]
MB............	Microbiological Assay [*Biochemistry*] (DAVI)
MB............	Microbody
MB............	Microelectronics Bibliography [*A publication*]
MB............	Midbody
MB............	Middle Babylonian [*Language, etc.*] (BJA)
MB............	Middle Bronze Age (BJA)
MB............	Middle of Bow [*Music*] (ROG)
MB............	Militia Bureau [*Superseded in 1933 by National Guard Bureau*]
mb	Millibar [*Unit of pressure*]

MB............. Millibar
mb............. Millibarn [*Area of nuclear cross-section*]
mb............. Millibyte [*Computer science*]
MB............. Million Bytes [*Computer science*] (BUR)
MB............. Milton Bradley Ltd. [*British*]
MB............. Minimum Bid [*Philately*]
MB............. Misce Bene [*Mix Well*] [*Pharmacy*]
MB............. Miscellaneous Branch, Internal Revenue Bureau [*United States*] (DLA)
MB............. Missed Byte [*Computer science*] (ECII)
MB............. Missile Base [*Military*]
MB............. Missile Body
MB............. Missile Bomber
MB............. Mixed Bed [*Nuclear energy*] (NRCH)
MB............. Mixing Box (OA)
MB............. Mobile Base (DEN)
MB............. Model Block (MSA)
MB............. Module Balance [*Computer science*]
MB............. Mohelbuch (BJA)
MB............. Moisture Balance
MB............. Molecular Biosystems [*NYSE symbol*] (TTSB)
MB............. Molecular Biosystems, Inc. [*NYSE symbol*] (SPSG)
MB............. Molybdenum [*Chemical element*] (ROG)
MB............. Monthly Breakdown [*Used in atmospheric studies*]
MB............. Monthly Bulletin of Decisions of the High Court of Uganda [*A publication*] (DLA)
MB............. Months Before
MB............. Montpelier & Barre Railroad Co. [*AAR code*]
MB............. Mooring Buoy
MB............. Morale Branch [*Military*]
MB............. Morrell's English Bankruptcy Reports [*A publication*] (DLA)
MB............. Mortar Board (EA)
MB............. Motor Barge (ADA)
MB............. Motor Boat
MB............. Mountain Battery [*British military*] (DMA)
MB............. Multiband (DEN)
MB............. Municipal Bond
MB............. Municipal Borough
MB............. Munitions Board [*Abolished 1953, functions transferred to Department of Defense*]
MB............. Museum of Broadcasting
MB............. Mushroom Body [*Nerve center in insects*]
MB............. Musicae Baccalaureus [*Bachelor of Music*]
MB............. Music for the Blind [*Defunct*] (EA)
MB............. Muslim Brotherhood [*Jordan*] (BUAC)
MB............. Must Be [*Sold*] [*Classified advertising*]
MB............. Myocardial Band [*Cardiology*]
Mb............. Myoglobin [*Biochemistry, medicine*]
Mb............. Myoglobin Tritium [*Hematology*] (DAVI)
MB............. Western Airlines [*ICAO designator*] (AD)
MB-2........... Model Boiler-Two [*Nuclear energy*] (GFGA)
MBA............. American Academy of Arts and Sciences, Boston, MA [*Library symbol Library of Congress*] (LCLS)
MBA............. Automobilvertriebs Aktiengesellschaft [*Austria ICAO designator*] (FAAC)
MBA............. Main Battle Area (AABC)
MBA............. Main-Belt Asteroid [*Astronomy*]
MBA............. Make-or-Buy Authorization (AAG)
MBA............. Makers of British Art [*A publication*]
MBA............. Male Bonding Alert [*Screenwriter's lexicon*]
MBA............. Male Bowhunter Aided [*International Bowhunting Organization*] [*Class equipment*]
MBA............. Malta Broadcasting Authority (BUAC)
MBA............. Management Buy-Out Association (BUAC)
MBA............. Mantle Bouguer Anomaly [*Geology*]
MBA............. Manufactured Buildings Association [*Defunct*] (EA)
MBA............. Many-Body Alloy [*Metallurgy*]
MBA............. Marching Bands of America (EA)
MBA............. Marine Biological Association [*British*]
MBA............. Marine Biological Association of the United Kingdom (BUAC)
MBA............. Mass Balance Area (NUCP)
MBA............. Master Bakers' Association [*Australia*]
MBA............. Master Builders' Association [*South Africa*] (BUAC)
MBA............. Master of Business Administration
MBA............. Master of the British Arts Association (DBQ)
MBA............. Material Balance Area [*Nuclear energy*]
MBA............. Maximum Benefit Amount [*Unemployment insurance*]
MBA............. Meier Burnout Assessment [*Psychology*] (DHP)
MBA............. Merion Bluegrass Association [*Defunct*] (EA)
MBA............. Methyl Benzyl Alcohol [*Organic chemistry*]
MBA............. Methylbis(beta-chloroethyl)amine [*Nitrogen mustard*] [*Also, HN, NM Antineoplastic; war-gas base*]
MBA............. Methylbovine Albumin [*Immunology*]
MBA............. Methylenebisacrylamide [*Organic chemistry*]
MBA............. Microbiological Associates, Inc.
MBA............. Migratory Bird Act
MBA............. Military Base Agreement (CINC)
MBA............. Military Benefit Association (EA)
MBA............. Milk Bars Association of Great Britain and Ireland Ltd. (BI)
MBa............. Miniature Ball [*Horticulture*]
MBA............. Minimum Burst Altitude (AABC)
MBA............. Minor Basic Allergens [*Immunology*]
MBA............. Mombasa [*Kenya*] [*Airport symbol*] (OAG)
MBA............. Monument Builders of America [*Later, MBNA*]
MBA............. Mortar Box Assembly

MBA............. Mortgage Bankers Association of America [*Washington, DC*] (EA)
MBA............. Motorized Bicycle Association [*Later, MAA*] (EA)
MBA............. Mount Bingar [*Australia Seismograph station code, US Geological Survey Closed*] (SEIS)
MBA............. Multibeam Antenna
MBA............. Multiple Berthing Adaptor (SSD)
MBA............. Multiple Birth Association [*Australia*]
MBA............. Rural Municipality of Argyle Public Library, Baldur, Manitoba [*Library symbol National Library of Canada*] (NLC)
MBA............. Woodcock-McGrew-Werder Mini-Battery of Achievement [*Test*] (TMMY)
MBAA.......... Master Brewers Association of the Americas (EA)
MBAA.......... Master of Business Administration in Aviation (PGP)
MBAA.......... Messinian Benevolent Association ™Aristomenis∫ (EA)
MBAA.......... Methylene Bisacrylamide (PDAA)
MBAA.......... Mini Bike Association of America (EA)
MBAA.......... Mortgage Bankers of Association of America (NTPA)
MBAA.......... Mortgage Brokers' Association of Australia
MBAA.......... Motel Brokers Association of America [*Later, AHMB*] (EA)
MBAAS........ Master of Business Administration in Actuarial Science
MBab.......... Middle Babylonian [*Language, etc.*] (BJA)
MBABS........ Synod Office, Diocese of Brandon, Anglican Church of Canada, Manitoba [*Library symbol National Library of Canada*] (NLC)
MBAC.......... Assiniboine Community College, Brandon, Manitoba [*Library symbol National Library of Canada*] (NLC)
MBAC.......... Marshall Booster Assembly Contractor (MCD)
MBAC.......... Member of the British Association of Chemists (DAS)
MBACFM...... American Board of Commissioners for Foreign Missions, Boston, MA [*Library symbol Library of Congress*] (LCLS)
M-BACOD .... Methotrexate (High-Dose) (with Citrovorum Factor Rescue), Bleomycin, Adriamycin,Cyclophosphamide, Oncovin [*Vincristine*], Dexamethasone [*Antineoplastic drug regimen*]
M-BACOP.... Myelosuppressive Bleomycin, Adriamycin, Cyclophosphamide, Oncovin [*Vincristine*], Prednisone [*Antineoplastic drug regimen*]
M-BACOS.... Bleomycin, Adriamycin, Cytoxan, Oncovin, Methotrexate with Leucovorin Rescue [*Antineoplastic drug*] (CDI)
MBACT........ Medical Board of the Australian Capital Territory
MBAD .... Medical Badge
MB Adm ...... Master of Business Administration
MBAE.......... Master of Biological and Agricultural Engineering (PGP)
MBAE.......... Master of Biosystems and Agricultural Engineering (PGP)
MBAE.......... Member of the British Association of Electrolysis (DI)
MBA-EP ...... Master of Business Administration - Experienced Professionals (PGP)
MBAG .... Modulated Bayard-Alpert Gauge
MBAG .... Research Station, Agriculture Canada [*Station de Recherches, Agriculture Canada*] Brandon, Manitoba [*Library symbol National Library of Canada*] (NLC)
MBAI.......... Massachusetts Independent Bankers Association, Inc. (TBD)
MBAI.......... Mosquito Biting Activity Index [*Canada*]
MBAIB .... Master of Business Administration in International Business (GAGS)
MBAIT .... Master of Business Administration in International Trade (PGP)
MBAJ.......... Magna Bibliotheca Anglo-Judaica (BJA)
MBAM......... Main Beam Avoidance Maneuver
MBAMT....... Methyl(benzylideneamino)mercaptotriazole [*Reagent*]
MBANSW...... Master Butchers' Association of New South Wales [*Australia*]
MBANSW...... Medical Benevolent Association of New South Wales [*Australia*]
MBAOT........ Member of the British Association of Occupational Therapists (DI)
MBA-PE ...... Master of Business Administration - Physician's Executive (PGP)
mbar.......... Millibar [*Unit of pressure*]
MBAR.......... Multibeam Acquisition RADAR (MCD)
MBAR.......... Myocardial Beta Adrenergic Receptor [*Cardiology*] (DMAA)
MBARI .... Monterey Bay Aquarium Research Institute [*California*]
MBarL......... Barnstable Law Library, Barnstable, MA [*Library symbol*] [*Library of Congress*] (LCLS)
MBAS......... Methylene Blue Active Substance [*Organic chemistry*]
MBAS......... Mutual Benefit and Aid Society [*Later, WBF*] (EA)
MBASA....... Medical Benevolent Association of South Australia
MBASW ...... Member of the British Association of Social Workers
MBAt.......... Boston Athenaeum, Boston, MA [*Library symbol Library of Congress*] (LCLS)
MBATM....... Master of Business in Telecommunication Management (PGP)
MBAUK....... Marine Biological Association of the United Kingdom (ARC)
MBAV......... Main Battle Air Vehicle [*Military*] (PDAA)
MBAWS ...... Marine Base Air Warning System
MBB........... Brandeis University, Waltham, MA [*OCLC symbol*] (OCLC)
MBB........... Make-before-Break
MBB........... Marble Bar [*Australia Airport symbol*] (OAG)
MBB........... Maurer, B. B., Chicago IL [*STAC*]
MBB........... Messerschmitt-Boelkow-Blohm GmbH [*West German aircraft company*]
MBB........... Messerschmitt-Boklow-Blahn (NAKS)
MBB........... Miniature Brushless Blower
MBB........... Modified Barbiturate Buffer (DMAA)
MBB........... Mortgage-Backed Bonds
MBB........... MSB Bancorp, Inc. [*AMEX symbol*] (SAG)
MBBA......... Boston Bar Association, Boston, MA [*Library symbol Library of Congress*] (LCLS)
MBBA......... Methoxybenzylidene Butylaniline [*Organic chemistry*]
MBBA......... (Methozybenzylidene)butylaniline [*Organic chemistry*]
MBBA......... Military Benefit Base Amounts
MBBAQ....... Master Boat Builders' Association of Queensland [*Australia*]
MBBC......... Monterey Bay Bancorp [*NASDAQ symbol*] (TTSB)
MBBC......... Monterey Bay Bancorp, Inc. [*NASDAQ symbol*] (SAG)
MBBI.......... Babson College, Babson Park, MA [*Library symbol Library of Congress*] (LCLS)

MBBI	Multiple-Bit Binary Input
MBBL	Massachusetts Bureau of Library Extension, Boston, MA [*Library symbol Library of Congress*] (LCLS)
MBBL	Thousand Barrels (EG)
MBBLS	Thousands of Barrels (MCD)
MBbM	Massachusetts Maritime Academy, Buzzards Bay, MA [*Library symbol Library of Congress*] (LCLS)
MBBO	Multiple-Bit Binary Output
MBBR	Brokenhead River Regional Library, Beausejour, Manitoba [*Library symbol National Library of Canada*] (NLC)
MBBS	Bostonian Society, Boston, MA [*Library symbol Library of Congress*] (LCLS)
MBBSC	Bachelor of Medicine and Bachelor of Science [*British*] (ROG)
MBC	American Congregational Association, Boston, MA [*Library symbol Library of Congress*] (LCLS)
MBC	Brandon University, Manitoba [*Library symbol National Library of Canada*] (NLC)
MBC	Magnetic Bias Coil (IIA)
MBC	Magnetic Bias Control (DNAB)
MBC	Mailbox Club [*Later, MCI*] (EA)
MBC	Main Beam Clutter
MBC	Male Breast Cancer [*Medicine*] (DB)
MBC	Malwa Bhil Corps [*British military*] (DMA)
MBC	Manhattan Bible College [*Kansas*]
MBC	Manhattan Bowery Corp. (EA)
mbc	Manitoba [*MARC country of publication code Library of Congress*] (LCCP)
MBC	Manual Battery Control (AAG)
MBC	Marine Biomedical Center [*Duke University*] [*Research center*] (RCD)
MBC	Mary Baldwin College [*Virginia*]
MBC	Master Bus Controller [*Computer science*]
MBC	Master of Beauty Culture
MBC	Master of Building Construction (PGP)
MBC	Maximum Bladder Capacity [*Medicine*] (DB)
MBC	Maximum Breathing Capacity
MBC	M'Bigou [*Gabon*] [*Airport symbol*] (OAG)
MBC	McLaughlin-Buick Club of Canada (EAIO)
MBC	Media Briefing Center (COE)
MBC	Mediterranean Bombardment Code
MBC	Mediterrean Burns Club (BUAC)
MBC	Megabar Diamond Cell [*For high-pressure measurements*]
MBC	Memory Bus Controller
MBC	Mercantile Bank of Canada [*Toronto Stock Exchange symbol Vancouver Stock Exchange symbol*]
MBC	Mercantile Bankshares Corp. (EFIS)
MBC	Message Broadcast Controller [*Computer science*] (CIST)
MBC	Metastatic Breast Cancer [*Medicine*]
MBC	Meteor Burst Communications [*Military*]
MBC	Methotrexate, Bleomycin, Cisplatin [*Antineoplastic drug*] (CDI)
MBC	Methyl Benzimidazolecarbamate [*Organic chemistry*]
MBC	Methylthymol Blue Complex (BABM)
MBC	Metropolitan Borough Council [*British*]
MBC	Mewar Bhil Corps [*British military*] (DMA)
MBC	Mickelberry Corp. (EFIS)
MBC	Microcrystalline Bovine Collagen (DB)
MBC	Middle East Broadcasting Centre (BUAC)
MBC	Military Budget Committee [*NATO*] (NATG)
MBC	Miniature Bayonet Cap
MBC	Miniaturized Ballistic Computer
MBC	Minimum Bactericidal Concentration
MBC	Minnesota Bible College [*Rochester*]
MBC	Modified Brequet Cruise [*SST*]
MBC	Monkees Buttonmania Club [*Defunct*] (EA)
MBC	Mononuclear Blood Cell [*Hematology*]
MBC	Morris Brown College [*Atlanta, GA*]
MBC	Morris Brown College, Atlanta, GA [*OCLC symbol*] (OCLC)
MBC	Mortar Ballistic Computer [*Formerly, MFCC*] [*Army*] (INF)
MBC	Mother and Baby Care [*Red Cross Nursing Services*]
MBC	Motorboat Crew [*British military*] (DMA)
MBC	Mould Bay [*Northwest Territories*] [*Seismograph station code, US Geological Survey*] (SEIS)
MBC	Mountain Bike Club [*British*] (DBA)
MBC	Multiple Basic Channel
MBC	Multiple Board Computer (IAA)
MBC	Multiple Burst Correcting
MBC	Munhwa Broadcasting Corp. [*Republic of Korea*] (BUAC)
MBCA	Archives, Brandon University, Manitoba [*Library symbol National Library of Canada*] (BIB)
MBCA	Mechanical Bank Collectors of America (EA)
MBCA	Mercedes-Benz Club of America (EA)
MBCA	Merchant Bank of Central Africa Ltd.
MBCA	Migratory Bird Conservation Act of 1929 (COE)
MBCA	Munitions Board Cataloging Agency
MBCAM	Commonwealth Air Training Plan Museum, Inc., Brandon, Manitoba [*Library symbol National Library of Canada*] (NLC)
MBCC	Massachusetts Bay Community College [*Wellesley*]
MBCC	McLaughlin-Buick Club of Canada (EA)
MBCC	Medical Benefits Consultative Committee
MBCC	Migratory Bird Conservation Commission [*A federal government body*]
MBCD	Modified Binary-Coded Decimal
MBCG	Department of Geography, Brandon University, Manitoba [*Library symbol National Library of Canada*] (NLC)
MBCK	Mallory Body Cytokeratin [*Medicine*]

MBCM	Baccalaureus Medicinae, Chirurgiae Magister [*Bachelor of Medicine, Master of Surgery*]
MBCM	New England Conservatory of Music, Boston, MA [*Library symbol Library of Congress*] (LCLS)
MBCMA	Metal Building Component Manufacturers' Association (EA)
MBCMC	Milk Bottle Crate Manufacturers Council [*Defunct*] (EA)
MBCNt	Multilingual Broadcasting Council of the Northern Territory [*Australia*]
MBCo	Countway Library of Medicine, Boston, MA [*Library symbol Library of Congress*] (LCLS)
MBCO	Member of the British College of Ophthalmic Opticians [*British*] (DBQ)
MbCO	Myoglobin, Carboxy [*Biochemistry, medicine*]
MBCS	Medium Bandwidth Compression System
MBCS	Member of the British Computer Society (DCTA)
MBCS	Meteor Burst Communication System
MBCS	Motion Base Crew Station [*NASA*] (NASA)
MBCU	Mobile Bombardment Communications Unit [*Military*] (IAA)
MBd	Bedford Free Public Library, Bedford, MA [*Library symbol Library of Congress*] (LCLS)
MBD	Episcopal Diocese of Massachusetts, Boston, MA [*Library symbol Library of Congress*] (LCLS)
MBD	Macroblock Design
MBD	Magnetic-Bubble Domain Device [*Computer science*] (IEEE)
MBD	Manual Board [*Telecommunications*] (NITA)
MBD	Manual Burst Disable (AABC)
MBD	Materials-by-Design [*Chemical engineering*]
MBD	Meander Belt Deposit [*Geology*]
MBD	Methotrexate, Bleomycin, Diamminedichloroplatinum [*Cisplatin*] [*Antineoplastic drug regimen*]
MBD	Methoxybenzylaminonitrobenzoxadiazole [*Fluorescent probe*] [*Biochemistry*]
MBD	Methylbutenedial [*Organic chemistry*]
MBD	Methylene Blue Dye [*Organic chemistry*] (MAE)
MBD	Million Barrels Daily
MBD	Minimal Brain Damage [*or Dysfunction*]
MBD	Minimal Brain Dysfunction [*Neurology*] (DAVI)
MBD	Minority Business Development Agency (EBF)
MBD	Mission Baseline Description [*NASA*] (KSC)
MBD	Morquio-Brailsford Disease [*Medicine*] (DMAA)
MBD	Motor Belt Drive (MSA)
MBD	Muzzle Boresight Device [*Army*] (INF)
MBDA	Metal Building Dealers Association [*Later, Systems Builders Association*] (EA)
MBDA	Minority Business Development Agency [*Formerly, OMBE*] [*Department of Commerce*]
MBDAACC	Milling and Baking Division of American Association of Cereal Chemists (EA)
MBdAF	United States Air Force, Cambridge Research Center, Bedford, MA [*Library symbol Library of Congress*] (LCLS)
MBDC	Minority Business Development Center [*Minority Business Development Administration*]
MBdD	Document Research Center, Bedford, MA [*Library symbol Library of Congress*] (LCLS)
MBDET	Mobile Boarding Detachment [*Coast Guard*]
MBDF	Medicare Beneficiaries Defense Fund (EA)
MBDG	Marine Base Defense Group
MBDG	Mesiobuccal Developmental Groove [*Medicine*] (DMAA)
MBDG	Mesiobuccal Development Groove (STED)
MBdgSc	Master of Building Science
MBDI	Major Business Development Initiative
MBDio	Diocesan Library, Boston, MA [*Library symbol Library of Congress*] (LCLS)
MBDL	Missile Battery Data Link (MCD)
MBdM	Middlesex Community College, Bedford, MA [*Library symbol Library of Congress*] (LCLS)
MBdMi	Mitre Corps., Bedford, MA [*Library symbol Library of Congress*] (LCLS)
MBDOE	Million Barrels per Day Oil Equivalent (MHDB)
MBDP	Minority Bank Deposit Program [*Treasury Department*]
MB(DP)AC	Medical Benefits (Dental Practitioners) Advisory Committee
MBDR	Make-or-Buy Data Record (KSC)
MBdR	Raytheon Co., Missile Systems Division Library, Bedford, MA [*Library symbol Library of Congress*] (LCLS)
MBDS	Modular Building Distribution System [*Telecommunications*] (TEL)
MBdV	United States Veterans Administration Hospital, Bedford, MA [*Library symbol Library of Congress*] (LCLS)
MBE	Bethany Lutheran College, Mankato, MN [*OCLC symbol*] (OCLC)
MBE	Emerson College, Boston, MA [*Library symbol Library of Congress*] (LCLS)
MBE	Mail Boxes Etc. USA [*San Diego, CA*] [*Telecommunications*] (TSSD)
MBE	Management by Exception
MBE	Martin-Baker Ltd. [*British ICAO designator*] (FAAC)
MBE	Mary Baker Eddy [*Founder of Christian Science*]
MBE	Master of Bilingual Education (PGP)
MBE	Master of Business Economics
MBE	Master of Business Education (GAGS)
MBE	May Be Elevated [*Medicine*] (DAVI)
MBE	Medium Below-Elbow [*Cast*] (STED)
MBE	Member of the [*Order of the*] British Empire [*Facetious translation: "My Bloody Efforts"*]
MBE	Mennonite Board of Education (EA)
MBE	Metals-Based Engineering
MBE	Minority Business Enterprise (MCD)
MBE	Missile-Borne Equipment
MBE	Molecular Beam Epitaxy [*Crystallography*]

MBE............ Monbetsu [*Japan*] [*Airport symbol*] (OAG)

MBE............ Monumenta Biblica et Ecclesiastica [*Rome*] [*A publication*] (BJA)

MBE............ Mountasia Entertainment Intl., Inc. [*AMEX symbol*] (SAG)

MBE............ Moving Boundary Electrophoresis [*Analytical biochemistry*]

MBE............ Multiple-Beam Experiment [*In MBE-4, a heavy-ion accelerator at the Lawrence Berkeley Laboratory*]

MBE............ Multistate Bar Examination

MBEA.......... Missouri Business Education Association (EDAC)

MBE-ARMS... Multiple Business Entity - Accounts Receivable Management System (MHDB)

MBED.......... Episcopal Diocese of Massachusetts, Diocesan Library and Archives, Boston, MA [*Library symbol*] [*Library of Congress*] (LCLS)

MB Ed......... Master of Business Education

MBehaviouralSc... Master of Behavioural Sciences (ADA)

MBEI........... Member of the Institute of Body Engineers [*British*] (DBQ)

MBEI........... Minnesota Business Educators, Inc (EDAC)

MBELDEF..... Minority Business Enterprise Legal Defense and Education Fund (EA)

MBelm......... Belmont Memorial Library, Belmont, MA [*Library symbol Library of Congress*] (LCLS)

MBelmM...... McLean Hospital, Belmont, MA [*Library symbol Library of Congress*] (LCLS)

MBEmm....... Emmanuel College, Boston, MA [*Library symbol Library of Congress*] (LCLS)

MBEnv........ Master of the Built Environment (ADA)

MBEP.......... Metals-Based Engineering Program

MBEPA........ United States Environmental Protection Agency, Region I Library, Boston, MA [*Library symbol Library of Congress*] (LCLS)

MBER.......... Member

MBER.......... Minority Business Enterprise Representative (COE)

MBER.......... Molecular Beam Electric Resonance [*Physics*]

MBES.......... Member of the Bureau of Engineer Surveyors [*British*] (DBQ)

MBES.......... Mezhdunarodnyi Bank Ekonomicheskovo Sotrudnichestva [*International Bank for Economic Co-Operation - IBEC*] [*Moscow, USSR*] (EAIO)

MBEST........ Modulus Blipped Echo-Planar Single-Pulse Technique (STED)

MBev.......... Beverly Public Library, Beverly, MA [*Library symbol Library of Congress*] (LCLS)

MBev-F....... Beverly Farms Public Library, Beverly, MA [*Library symbol Library of Congress*] (LCLS)

MBevHi....... Beverly Historical Society, Beverly, MA [*Library symbol Library of Congress*] (LCLS)

MBevN........ North Shore Community College, Beverly, MA [*Library symbol Library of Congress*] (LCLS)

MBevT........ Beverly Times, Beverly, MA [*Library symbol Library of Congress*] (LCLS)

MBF........... Main Boundary Fault [*Geophysics*]

MBF........... Master Bibliographic File (ADA)

MBF........... Master Builders Federation [*British*] (BI)

MBF........... Materials Business File [*American Society for Metals, The Institute for Metals*] [*Information service or system*] (IID)

MBF........... MBF USA, Inc. [*Associated Press*] (SAG)

MBF........... Meat Base Formula [*Medicine*] (MEDA)

MBF........... Medullary Blood Flow [*Medicine*] (DMAA)

MBF........... Military Banking Facility

MBF........... Milk Bottlers Federation

MBF........... Missile Beacon Filter

MBF........... Modulator Band Filter (IAA)

MBF........... Molecular Beam Facility [*NASA*]

MBF........... Moving-Bed Filter [*Waste*] (DICI)

MBF........... Multiple Births Foundation (BUAC)

MBF........... Muscle Blood Flow [*Medicine*] (DMAA)

MBF........... Musicians Benevolent Fund [*British*] (BI)

MBF........... Myocardial Blood Flow [*Cardiology*]

MBF........... Thousand Board Feet [*Lumber*]

MBFA.......... Fellows Athenaeum, Boston, MA [*Library symbol Library of Congress*] (LCLS)

MBFA.......... MBF USA, Inc. [*NASDAQ symbol*] (SAG)

MBFC.......... Medial Brachial Fascial Compartment [*Medicine*] (DMAA)

MBFC.......... Moe Bandy Fan Club (EA)

MBFL.......... Mid-Bergen Federation of Public Libraries [*Library network*]

MBFLB........ Monaural Bifrequency Loudness Balance [*Audiology*] (MAE)

MBFM......... Massachusetts Grand Lodge, F & AM, Boston, MA [*Library symbol Library of Congress*] (LCLS)

MBFN.......... Multiple Beam Forming Network [*Military*] (LAIN)

MBFo.......... Forsyth Dental Center, Boston, MA [*Library symbol Library of Congress*] (LCLS)

MBFP.......... Manufacturing, Build, and Flow Plan (NASA)

MBFR.......... Federal Reserve Bank of Boston, Boston, MA [*Library symbol Library of Congress*] (LCLS)

MBFR.......... More Better for Russia [*Facetious translation of MBFR - Mutual and Balanced Force Reduction*]

MBFR.......... Mutual and Balanced Force Reduction [*Proposed reduction of forces in central Europe by NATO and Warsaw Pact nations*]

MBFUSA...... MBF USA, Inc. [*Associated Press*] (SAG)

MBG........... Gardner Museum, Boston, MA [*Library symbol Library of Congress*] (LCLS)

MBG........... Marburg [*Disease*] [*Medicine*] (DMAA)

MBG........... Mean Blood Glucose [*Medicine*] (STED)

MBG........... Missouri Botanical Garden

MBG........... Mobridge, SD [*Location identifier FAA*] (FAAL)

MBG........... Morphine-Benzedrine Group [*Scale*] [*Medicine*] (DMAA)

MBG & H..... Magna Brittannia, Gallia, et Hibernia [*Great Britain, France, and Ireland*] [*Latin*] (ROG)

MBGE.......... Missile-Borne Guidance Equipment (AFM)

MBGH......... Library Services, Brandon General Hospital, Manitoba [*Library symbol National Library of Canada*] (NLC)

MBGi.......... Gillette Co., Boston R and D Laboratory, Boston, MA [*Library symbol Library of Congress*] (LCLS)

MBGil......... Gillette Co., Boston R and D Laboratory, Boston, MA [*Library symbol*] [*Library of Congress*] (LCLS)

MBGS......... Missile-Borne Guidance Set (MCD)

MBGS......... Morphine-Benzedrine Group Scale (STED)

MBGT......... General Theological Library, Boston, MA [*Library symbol Library of Congress*] (LCLS)

MBGT.......... Grand Turk [*Turks and Caicos Islands*] [*ICAO location identifier*] (ICLI)

MBGTS........ Missile-Borne Guidance Test Set (AABC)

MBH........... Manual Bomb Hoist

MBH........... Maryborough [*Australia Airport symbol*] (OAG)

MBH........... Massachusetts Horticultural Society, Boston, MA [*Library symbol Library of Congress*] (LCLS)

MBH........... Massive Black Hole [*Galactic science*]

MBH........... Maximal Benefit from Hospitalization (STED)

MBH........... Medial Basal Hypothalamus [*Medicine*] (STED)

MBH........... Mediobasal Hypothalamus [*Brain anatomy*]

MBH........... Minard, Bryant H., Pennsauken NJ [*STAC*]

mbH........... Mit Beschraenkter Haftung [*With Limited Liability*] [*German*] (EG)

MBH........... Movimiento de Bases Hayistas [*Movement of Hayista Bases*] [*Peru*] [*Political party*] (PPW)

MBH........... Thousands of BTU per Hour

MBH2.......... Reduced Methylene Blue [*Medicine*] (DMAA)

MBHA.......... Member of the British Hypnotherapy Association (DBQ)

MBHC .... Boissevain Health Centre, Manitoba [*Library symbol National Library of Canada*] (NLC)

MBHCM ...... Master of Behavioral Health Care Management (PGP)

MBHE .... Ministries to Blacks in Higher Education (EA)

MBHH .... Handel and Haydn Society, Boston, MA [*Library symbol Library of Congress*] (LCLS)

MBHI .... Member of the British Horological Institute (DBQ)

MBHI .... Millon Behavioral Health Inventory [*Personality development test*] [*Psychology*]

MBHINST..... Member of the British Horological Institute (ROG)

MBHM .... Harvard Musical Association, Boston, MA [*Library symbol Library of Congress*] (LCLS)

MBHO .... Managed Behavioral Healthcare Organization (DMAA)

MBHoM....... Houghton Mifflin Co., Boston, MA [*Library symbol Library of Congress*] (LCLS)

MBHPFC ..... [*The*] Monkees, Boyce and Hart Photo Fan Club (EA)

MBI........... Insurance Library Association of Boston, Boston, MA [*Library symbol Library of Congress*] (LCLS)

MBI........... Major Budget Issue (COE)

MBI........... Management by Initiative [*Management technique*]

MBI........... Marine Biomedical Institute [*University of Texas*] [*Research center*] (RCD)

MBI........... Maritime Bank of Israel (BJA)

MBI........... Maslach Burnout Inventory

MBI........... Master of Biological Illustration (GAGS)

MBI........... May Be Issued

MBI........... Mbeya [*Tanzania*] [*Airport symbol Obsolete*] (OAG)

MBI........... MBIA, Inc. [*NYSE symbol*] (SPSG)

MBI........... Memory Bank Interface

MBI........... Menan Buttes [*Idaho*] [*Seismograph station code, US Geological Survey Closed*] (SEIS)

MBI........... Metal Belt Institute [*Defunct*] (EA)

MBI........... Methylene Blue Installation [*Medicine*] (DAVI)

MBI........... Michigan Biotechnology Institute [*Michigan State University*] [*Research center*] (RCD)

MBI........... Middle Bronze I [*Age*]

MBI........... Military Board Instruction

MBI........... Minimal Baryonic Isocurvature [*Galactic science*]

MBI........... Miscellaneous Babylonian Inscriptions [*A publication*] (BJA)

MBI........... Modular Building Institute (NTPA)

MBI........... Molecular Biosystems, Inc.

MBI........... Multibus Interface [*Computer science*] (MCD)

MBIA.......... Malting Barley Improvement Association (EA)

MBIA.......... MBIA, Inc. [*Associated Press*] (SAG)

MBIA.......... Merchants Bancorp [*NASDAQ symbol*] (SAG)

MBIA.......... Municipal Bond Insurance Association (EA)

MBIAC .... Missouri Basin Inter-Agency Committee

MBIBTC....... Malting and Brewing Industry Barley Technical Committee [*Australia*]

MBIC.......... Michigan Bigfoot Information Center [*Later, MCBIC*] (EA)

MBIC.......... Monmouth Biomedical Information Consortium [*Library network*]

M Bi Ch ...... Master of Biological Chemistry

MBiChem..... Master of Biological Chemistry (NADA)

MBID.......... Member of the British Institute of Interior Design (DBQ)

M Bi E .... Master of Biological Engineering

MBIE.......... Member of the British Institute of Embalmers (DBQ)

MBiEng....... Master of Biological Engineering (NADA)

MBIFCT........ Mgahinga and Bwindi Inpenetrable Forest Conservation Trust (ECON)

MBII.......... Minority Business Information Institute [*Defunct*] (EA)

MBilC.......... Cabot Corp., Technical Information Center, Billerica, MA [*Library symbol Library of Congress*] (LCLS)

MBilHi .... Billerica Historical Society, Billerica, MA [*Library symbol Library of Congress*] (LCLS)

MBIM.......... Member of the British Institute of Management [*Formerly, MIIA*]

MBIO.......... Microprogrammable Block Input/Output

M Bio E ...... Master of Bioengineering (PGP)

MBioEth........ Master of Bioethics

M Biomath...	Master of Biomathematics (PGP)
MBiomedE...	Master of Biomedical Engineering (ADA)
M Biorad...	Master of Bioradiology
MBiotech...	Master of Biotechnology
M Bi Phy	Master of Biological Physics
M Bi S	Master of Biological Sciences
MBIS...........	Master of Business Information Systems
MB (IT).......	Master of Business (Information Technology)
MBIT...........	MegaBIT [Binary Digit] [Computer science] (MDG)
Mbits/sec....	Megabits per Second [Computer science] (IGQR)
MBIU..........	Multiplex Bus Interface Unit (MCD)
MBJ............	Montego Bay [Jamaica] [Airport symbol] (OAG)
MBJ............	Multiple Blinking Jammer (MCD)
MBJI...........	Marks Bros Jewelers [NASDAQ symbol] (TTSB)
MBJI...........	Marks Bros. Jewelers, Inc. [NASDAQ symbol] (SAG)
MBJT..........	Grand Turk [Turks and Caicos Islands] [ICAO location identifier] (ICLI)
MBK...........	Bank of Mitsubishi Ltd. [NYSE symbol] (SAG)
MBK...........	Bank of Tokyo-MitsubishiADS [NYSE symbol] (TTSB)
MBK...........	Madchen-Bibel-Kreise [Bible Reading Circles] [German]
MBK...........	Make-Break Keying (IAA)
MBK...........	Medications and Bandage kit (NAKS)
MBK...........	Methyl Butyl Ketone [Organic chemistry]
MBK...........	Missing, Believed Killed (ADA)
MBK...........	Mitsubishi Bank Ltd. ADS [NYSE symbol] (SPSG)
MBK...........	Multibanc Financial Corp. [Toronto Stock Exchange symbol]
MBK...........	Multiple Beam Klystron
MBL...........	Main Battle Line [Military] (IAA)
MBL...........	Manistee [Michigan] [Airport symbol] (OAG)
MBL...........	Mannan-Binding Lectin [Immunology]
MBL...........	Marble Bar [Australia Seismograph station code, US Geological Survey] (SEIS)
MBL...........	Marine Biological Laboratory
MBL...........	Marine Boundary Layer [Oceanography]
MBL...........	Master Bidders List (NG)
MBL...........	Maximum Benefit Level [Health insurance] (GHCT)
MBL...........	Measured Blood Loss [Physiology]
MBL...........	Mechanical Boundary Layer [Geology]
MBL...........	Medium Brown Loose [Stool] [Gastroenterology] (DAVI)
MBL...........	Menstrual Blood Loss [Medicine]
MBL...........	Miniature Button Light
MBL...........	Minimal Bactericidal Level
MBL...........	Missile Baseline
MBL...........	Mobile (AFM)
MBL...........	Model Breakdown List
MBL...........	Monterey Bay Area Cooperative Library System, Salinas, CA [OCLC symbol] (OCLC)
MBL...........	Movimiento Bolivia Libre [Political party] (EY)
MBL...........	Multiples of Background Level [Of environmental contaminants]
MBL...........	Mutual Benefit Life Insurance Co. (EFIS)
MBLA..........	MBLA Financial Corp. [Associated Press] (SAG)
MBLA..........	Methylbenzyllinoleic Acid [Organic chemistry]
MBLA..........	Mouse Specific Bone-Marrow-Derived Lymphocyte Antigen [Immunology]
MBLA..........	National Mercantile Bancorp [NASDAQ symbol] (NQ)
MBLC..........	Lahey Clinic Foundation, Boston, MA [Library symbol Library of Congress] (LCLS)
MBLC..........	Microbore Liquid Chromatography
MBldg........	Master of Building (ADA)
MBldgSc.....	Master of Building Science (ADA)
MBldSc.......	Master of Building Science
MBLE..........	Mobile Gas Service [NASDAQ symbol] (TTSB)
MBLE..........	Mobile Gas Service Corp. [NASDAQ symbol] (NQ)
MBLF..........	MBLA Financial [NASDAQ symbol] (TTSB)
MBLF..........	MBLA Financial Corp. [NASDAQ symbol] (SAG)
MBLM..........	MobileMedia Corp. [NASDAQ symbol] (SAG)
MBLR..........	Madhya Bharat Law Reports [India] [A publication] (DLA)
MblTel........	Mobile Telecommunications & Technology Corp. [Associated Press] (SAG)
MBLY..........	Mobley Environmental Services [NASDAQ symbol] (SPSG)
MBM..........	Magnetic Bubble Memory [Computer science]
MBM..........	Mambone [Mozambique] [Airport symbol] (AD)
MBM..........	Market Buy Market [Information service or system] (IID)
MBM..........	Market-by-Market Allocation [Business term] (DOAD)
MBM..........	Master of Brand Management (GAGS)
MBM..........	Master of Building Management (ADA)
MBM..........	Master of Business Management
MBM..........	Meat and Bone Meal
MBM..........	Metal-Barrier-Metal (IEEE)
MBM..........	Mineral Basal Medium [Microbiology]
MBM..........	Modern Black Men [Johnson Publishing Co., Inc.] [A publication]
MBM..........	Mother's Breast Milk [Neonatology] (DAVI)
MBM..........	Multibuoy Mooring [Oil platform]
Mbm..........	Thousand Board (Feet) Measure (WPI)
MBM..........	Thousand Feet Board Measure [Lumber] (GPO)
MBM..........	University of Massachusetts, Joseph P. Healy Library, Boston, MA [Library symbol Library of Congress] (LCLS)
MBMA..........	Master Boiler Makers' Association (BUAC)
MBMA..........	Metal Building Manufacturers Association (EA)
MBMA..........	Military Boot Manufacturers Association (EA)
MBMC..........	Middle Caicos [Turks and Caicos Islands] [ICAO location identifier] (ICLI)
MBMCC..........	Mercedes-Benz Model Car Club
MBMetE..........	Metcalf & Eddy, Inc., Boston, MA [Library symbol Library of Congress] (LCLS)
MBMF..........	Multibeam Multifrequency (CAAL)
MBMG..........	Montana Bureau of Mines and Geology [Montana College of Mineral Science and Technology] [Research center] (RCD)
MBMGH-T....	Massachusetts General Hospital, Treadwell Library, Boston, MA [Library symbol Library of Congress] (LCLS)
MBMH..........	Brandon Mental Health Centre, Manitoba [Library symbol National Library of Canada] (NLC)
MBMI..........	Mean Body Mass Index
MBMI..........	Micro Bio-Medics [NASDAQ symbol] (TTSB)
MBMI..........	Micro Bio-Medics, Inc. [NASDAQ symbol] (NQ)
MBMI..........	Mind/Body Medical Institute
MBMS..........	Bachelor of Medicine, Master of Surgery
MBMS..........	Model Base Management Software [Computer science] (IAA)
MBMS..........	Molecular Beam Mass Spectrometry (AAEL)
MBMSA..........	Massachusetts College of Art, Boston, MA [Library symbol Library of Congress] (LCLS)
MBMSE..........	Master of Business Management and Software Engineering (PGP)
MBMU..........	Mobile Base Maintenance Unit
MBMu..........	Museum of Fine Arts, Boston, MA [Library symbol Library of Congress] (LCLS)
MBMU..........	University of Massachusetts, Boston, MA [Library symbol Library of Congress] (LCLS)
MBN..........	Boston Museum of Science, Boston, MA [Library symbol Library of Congress] (LCLS)
MBN..........	Metal Building News [A publication] (APTA)
MBN..........	Methylbenzylnitrosamine [Organic chemistry]
MBN..........	Metrobank NA [AMEX symbol] (SPSG)
MBN..........	Mixed Base Notation
MBN..........	Mombo [Tanzania] [Airport symbol] (AD)
MBN..........	Mutual Black Network (NTCM)
MBNA..........	MBNA Corp. [Associated Press] (SAG)
MBNA..........	Mercedes Benz of North America
MBNA..........	Methyl(butyl)nitrosamine [Organic chemistry]
MBNA..........	Monument Builders of North America (EA)
MBNAD..........	Marine Barracks, Naval Ammunition Depot
MBNAS..........	Marine Barracks, Naval Air Station
MBNC..........	North Caicos [Turks and Caicos Islands] [ICAO location identifier] (ICLI)
MBNECO......	New England College of Optometry, Boston MA [Library symbol Library of Congress] (LCLS)
MBNEH........	New England Historic Genealogical Society, Boston, MA [Library symbol Library of Congress] (LCLS)
MBNEL........	New England School of Law, Boston, MA [Library symbol Library of Congress] (LCLS)
MBNEN........	New England Nuclear Corp., Boston, MA [Library symbol Library of Congress] (LCLS)
MBnet........	[The] Manitoba Network [Canada] [Computer science] (TNIG)
MBNMD........	Marine Barracks, Naval Mine Depot
MBNMHi........	New England Methodist Historical Society, Inc., Boston, MA [Library symbol Library of Congress] (LCLS)
MBNOA........	Member of the British Naturopathic and Osteopathic Association
MBNOB........	Marine Barracks, Naval Operating Base
MBNQA........	Malcolm Baldrige National Quality Award [Department of Commerce]
MBNS........	Marine Barracks, Naval Station
MBNU........	Northeastern University, Boston, MA [Library symbol Library of Congress] (LCLS)
MBNU-L........	Northeastern University, Law School, Boston, MA [Library symbol Library of Congress] (LCLS)
MBNY........	Merchants Bank of New York [NASDAQ symbol] (NQ)
MBNY........	Merchants New York Bancorp [NASDAQ symbol] (SAG)
MBNY........	Merchants NY Bancorp [NASDAQ symbol] (TTSB)
MBNYD........	Marine Barracks, Navy Yard
MBO........	Liberal Bosnian Organization (BUAC)
MBO........	Madison, MS [Location identifier FAA] (FAAL)
MBO........	Mamburao [Philippines] [Airport symbol] (OAG)
MBO........	Management and Budget Office (MCD)
MBO........	Management Buy-Out
MBO........	Management by Objectives [Management technique] [Facetious translations: "Management by Oblivion," and "Management by Others"]
MBO........	M'Bour [Senegal] [Seismograph station code, US Geological Survey] (SEIS)
MBO........	Meacham Bridge Oscillator [Electronics]
MBO........	Mesiobucco-Occlusal [Dentistry]
MBO........	Mobil Oil Ltd. [Canada ICAO designator] (FAAC)
MBO........	Moist Burn Ointment [Medicine]
MBO........	Monostable Blocking Oscillator [Electronics]
MBO........	Motor Burnout (AABC)
MBO........	Moving Base Operator
MBO........	Muslim Bosnian Organization (BUAC)
MbO2........	Myoglobin, Oxy [Biochemistry, medicine]
MBOA........	Methoxybenzoxazolinone [Biochemistry]
MBOA........	Motor Barge Owners Association (BUAC)
MBOC........	Middle Bay Oil [NASDAQ symbol] (TTSB)
MBOC........	Middle Bay Oil Co., Inc. [NASDAQ symbol] (SAG)
MBOC........	Minority Business Opportunity Committee [Federal interagency group]
MBOCA........	Methylenebis(ortho-chloroaniline) [Also, MOCA] [Organic chemistry]
MBOH........	Minimum Break-Off Height
MBOL........	Motor Burnout Locking (AABC)
MBOM........	Boissevain and Morton Regional Library, Boissevain, Manitoba [Library symbol National Library of Canada] (NLC)
Mbone........	Multicast Backbone [Internet terminology] (CDE)
M-bone........	Multicast Backbone [Computer science] (DOM)

MBOR .... Management by Objectives and Results [*Management technique*] (MCD)

MBOS .... Missile Base Operations Supervisor [*Air Force*] (IAA)

MBOS .... Multi-User Business Operating System (NITA)

MBou .... Jonathan Bourne Public Library, Bourne, MA [*Library symbol*] [*Library of Congress*] (LCLS)

MBOU .... Member of the British Ornithologists Union (EY)

MBP.............. Magneto-Dynamic Positioning

MBP.............. Major Basic Protein

MBP.............. Maltose-Binding Protein [*Biochemistry*]

MBP.............. Manhattan Bowery Project (EA)

MBP.............. Manpack Battery Pack

MBP.............. Massachusetts College of Pharmacy, Boston, MA [*Library symbol Library of Congress*] (LCLS)

MBP.............. Master Buy Plan (AAGC)

MBP.............. Maximum Boiling Point

MBP.............. MB Brand Present [*Cardiology*] (DAVI)

MBP.............. Mean Blood Pressure [*Medicine*]

MBP.............. Mean Brachial Artery Pressure [*Medicine*]

MBP.............. Mechanical Balance Package (OA)

MBP.............. Mechanical Booster Pump

MBP.............. Melitensis, Bovine, Porcine [*Antigen*] (AAMN)

MBP.............. Mesiobuccopulpal [*Dentistry*]

MBP.............. Mid-Boiling Point

MBP.............. Monodibutyl Phosphate [*Organic chemistry*] (NUCP)

MBP.............. Myelin Basic Protein [*Neurology*]

MBPA .... Master of Business and Public Administration

MBPA .... Military Blood Program Agency (AABC)

MBPAS .... Monthly Bulk Petroleum Accounting Summary [*Army*] (AABC)

MBP-C .... Mannose-Binding Protein C [*Biochemistry*]

MBPC .... Model-Based Process Control (AAEL)

MBPC .... Munitions Board Petroleum Committee

MBPCX .... Merrill Lynch: Pacific Fund Cl.B [*Mutual fund ticker symbol*] (SG)

MBPD .... Million Barrels per Day

MBPDA .... Metropolitan Bag and Paper Distributors Association (EA)

MBPI .... Pine Cay [*Turks and Caicos Islands*] [*ICAO location identifier*] (ICLI)

MBPKN .... Perry Normal School, Boston, MA [*Library symbol Library of Congress*] (LCLS)

MBPM .... Master of Business and Public Management

MBPM .... Maurice Bishop Patriotic Movement [*Grenada*] (BUAC)

MBPO .... Military Blood Program Office (AABC)

MBPP........... Movimiento Blanco Popular y Progresista [*National Action Movement*] [*Uruguay*] [*Political party*] (EY)

MBPRE .... Multitype Branching Process in a Random Environment [*Computer science*]

MBPS .... Mechanical Booster Pump System

MBPS........... MegaBITS [*Binary Digits*] per Second [*Transmission rate*] [*Computer science*]

Mbps .... Megabits per Second (NAKS)

Mbps .... Megabytes per Second [*Computer science*] (IGQR)

MBPS........... Million BITs [*Binary Digits*] per Second [*Data transmission speed*] [*Computer science*] (NASA)

MBPS........... Multigated Blood Pool Scanning [*Medicine*] (DMAA)

MBPT........... Many-Body Perturbation Theory [*Physics*]

MBPV........... Providenciales [*Turks and Caicos Islands*] [*ICAO location identifier*] (ICLI)

MBPXL......... MBPXL Corp. [*Formerly, Missouri Beef Packers - Kansas Beef Industries*]

MBQ............. Marine Board of Queensland [*Australia*]

MBQ............. Mbarara [*Uganda*] [*Airport symbol*] (OAG)

MBQ............. Medical Board of Queensland [*Australia*]

MBQ............. Modified Biquinary Code [*Computer science*]

MBR............. Maladapted Behavior Record [*Personality development test*] [*Psychology*]

MBR............. Management by Results [*Management technique*]

MBR............. Marker Beacon Receiver

MBR............. Master Bedroom [*Real estate*]

MBR............. Master Beneficiary Record [*Social Security Administration*]

MBR............. Master Boot Record [*Computer science*] (PCM)

MBR............. Material Balance Report [*Nuclear energy*]

MBR............. Maximum Base Rent

MBR............. Mbout [*Mauritania*] [*Airport symbol*] (AD)

MBR............. Mechanical Bag Retriever [*Garbage collector*]

MBR............. Mechanical Buffer Register [*Computer science*]

MBR............. Member (AFM)

mbr............. Member (DD)

Mbr............. Member (AL)

MBR............. Membrane Bioreactor [*Chemical engineering*]

MBR............. Membrane-Bound Ribosomes [*Cytology*]

MBR............. Memory Base Register

MBR............. Memory Buffer Register [*Computer science*]

MBR............. Metal Bulletin Research [*Commercial firm British*] (ECON)

MBR............. Methylene Blue Reduced

MBR............. Microwave Background Radiation [*Physics*]

MBR............. Mini Badge Reader (IAA)

MBR............. Mission Briefing Room [*NASA*] (KSC)

MBR............. Modified Bitumen, Reinforced

MBR............. Montebello Resources Ltd. [*Vancouver Stock Exchange symbol*]

MBR............. Motivation by Rotation

MBR............. Moving Belt Radiator

MBR............. Multibomb Rack

MBr............. Public Library of Brookline, Brookline, MA [*Library symbol Library of Congress*] (LCLS)

MBRA .... Marathon Boat Racers Association

MBRA .... Multibeam Radiometer Antenna

MBradJ........ Bradford Junior College [*Later, BC*], Bradford, MA [*Library symbol Library of Congress*] (LCLS)

MBRC .... Marine Biology Research Centre [*University of Moncton*] [*Canada*] (IRC)

MBRDC .... Medical Bioengineering Research and Development Command [*Army*] (PDAA)

MBRDL .... Medical Bioengineering Research and Development Laboratory [*Army*] (MCD)

MBre........... Brewster Ladies Library, Brewster, MA [*Library symbol*] [*Library of Congress*] (LCLS)

MBRE.......... Memory Buffer Register, Even [*Computer science*]

MBreC .... Cape Cod Museum of Natural History, Brewster, MA [*Library symbol*] [*Library of Congress*] (LCLS)

MBRET......... Middle Breton [*Language, etc.*]

MBRF.......... Midbrain Reticular Formation [*Anatomy*]

MBRG.......... Ropes & Gray, Boston, MA [*Library symbol*] [*Library of Congress*] (LCLS)

MBrH .... Hebrew College, Brookline, MA [*Library symbol*] [*Library of Congress*] (LCLS)

MBrHC .... Hellenic College of Arts and Sciences and Holy Cross Greek Orthodox Theological School, Brookline, MA [*Library symbol Library of Congress*] (LCLS)

MBridT........ Bridgewater State College, Bridgewater, MA [*Library symbol Library of Congress*] (LCLS)

M Brit IRE ... Member of the British Institution of Radio Engineers [*Later, MIERE*]

M/BRK .... Manual Brake [*Automotive engineering*]

MBRK .... Meadowbrook Rehab Grp'A' [*NASDAQ symbol*] (TTSB)

MBRK .... Meadowbrook Rehabilitation Group [*NASDAQ symbol*] (SAG)

MBRL .... Multiple Ballistic Rocket Launcher

MBRM .... Membrane

MBRO .... Memory Buffer Register, Odd [*Computer science*]

MBrock .... Brockton Public Library, Brockton, MA [*Library symbol Library of Congress*] (LCLS)

MBrockV ..... United States Veterans Administration Hospital, Brockton, MA [*Library symbol Library of Congress*] (LCLS)

MBRR .... Meridian & Bigbee Railroad Co. [*Formerly, MB*] [*AAR code*]

MBRS .... MemberWorks, Inc. [*NASDAQ symbol*] (SAG)

MBRS .... Minority Biomedical Research Support Program [*Bethesda, MD*] [*National Institutes of Health*] (GRD)

MBRSHP...... Membership

MBRT.......... Methylene Blue Reduction Time

MBRUU........ May Be Retained until Unserviceable

MBRV .... Maneuverable Ballistic Reentry Vehicle

MBRW .... Minnesota Brewing [*NASDAQ symbol*] (TTSB)

MBRW .... Minnesota Brewing Co. [*NASDAQ symbol*] (SAG)

MBrZ........... Zion Research Library, Brookline, Boston, MA [*Library symbol*] [*Library of Congress*] (LCLS)

MBS .... Bay City-Midland-Saginaw [*Michigan*] [*Airport symbol*] (AD)

MBS .... Bethany Lutheran Theological Seminary, Mankato, MN [*OCLC symbol*] (OCLC)

MBS .... Magnetron Beam Switching

MBS .... Main ™Bang∫ Suppressor

MBS .... Main Buffer Storage (IAA)

MBS .... Maleimidobenzoyl N-Hydroxysuccinimide [*Organic chemistry*]

MBS .... Malta Board of Standards (BUAC)

MBS .... Management by System [*Management technique*] (IAA)

MBS .... Manchester Business School [*England*]

MBS .... Market Basket Survey [*Business term*]

MBS .... Martin-Bell Syndrome [*Medicine*] (DMAA)

MBS .... Master Bibliographic System (ADA)

MBS .... Master of Basic Science

MBS .... Master of Behavioral Science (GAGS)

MBS .... Master of Building Science (GAGS)

MBS .... Medborgerlig Samling [*Citizens Rally*] [*Sweden Political party*] (PPE)

MBS .... Mediterranean Base Section [*Army World War II*]

MBS .... Medium Bomber Strike (NATG)

MBS .... MedQuist, Inc. [*AMEX symbol*] (SAG)

mbs .... Megabits per Second (COE)

Mbs .... Megabits per Second [*Computer science*] (IGQR)

M B/S .... Megabits per Second (NAKS)

MBS .... Megabits Per Second (NITA)

MBS .... Megabytes Per Second (NITA)

MBS .... Member of the Bibliographical Society (ROG)

MBS .... Menorah Book Service (BJA)

MBS .... Methacrylate Butadiene Styrene [*Plastics technology*]

MBS .... Methionyl Bovine Somatotropin [*Biochemistry*]

MBS .... Methodist Boys' School

MBS .... Micro Business Systems (NITA)

MBS .... Miniature Book Society (EA)

MBS .... Minimum Basis Sets [*Chemistry*] (MEC)

MBS .... Mission Budget Statement [*Army*]

MBS .... Mobile-Base Simulator (PDAA)

MBS .... Modular Banking System (PDAA)

MBS .... Monobutyl Sulfate [*Organic chemistry*]

MBS .... Monumental Brass Society (EA)

MBS .... Morpholine-Based Sulfenamide [*Chemistry*]

MBS .... Mortgage-Backed Securities Information Services [*The Bond Buyer, Inc.*] [*New York, NY*] [*Information service or system*] (IID)

MBS .... Mortgage-Backed Security (DFIT)

MBS .... Mortgage-Backed Security Program [*Government National Mortgage Association*]

MBS .... Motion Base Simulator (MCD)

MBS .... Motor Bus Society (EA)

MBS .... Multibit Shifter (IAA)

MBradJ........ Multiblade Slurry Saw [*Semiconductor technology*]

MBS............	Multiblock Synchronization Signal Unit [*Telecommunications*] (TEL)
MBS............	Multicore Bar Solder
MBS............	Multilingual Biblioservice of Alberta, Alberta Culture [*UTLAS symbol*]
MBS............	Multiple Batch Station [*Computer science*]
MBS............	Multiple Business System
MBS............	Music Broadcasting Society (NADA)
MBS............	Mutual Broadcasting System
MBS............	Muzzle Bore Sight [*British military*] (DMA)
MBS............	Saginaw [*Michigan*] [*Airport symbol*] (OAG)
MBS............	Saginaw, MI [*Location identifier FAA*] (FAAL)
MBS............	Social Law Library, Boston, MA [*Library symbol Library of Congress*] (LCLS)
MBSA..........	Main Bus-Switching Assembly (SSD)
MBSA..........	Maleylated Bovine Serum Albumin [*Biochemistry*]
MBSA..........	Manual Business Systems Association [*British*] (DBA)
MBSA..........	Medical Board of South Australia
MBSA..........	Methylated Bovine Serum Albumin
MBSA..........	Model-Based System Analysis (PDAA)
MBSA..........	Modular Building Standards Association (EA)
MBSA..........	Municipal Board Standards Association (NADA)
MBSA..........	Munitions Board Standards Agency
MBSA..........	Museum Board of South Australia
MBSB..........	Marine Barracks, Submarine Base
MBSC..........	Boston State College, Boston, MA [*Library symbol Library of Congress*] (LCLS)
MBSc...........	Master of Behavioural Science
MB Sc..........	Master of Business Science
MBSC..........	Modular Building Systems Council (EA)
MBSC..........	South Caicos [*Turks and Caicos Islands*] [*ICAO location identifier*] (ICLI)
MBSCC........	Mortgage-Backed Securities Clearing Corp. (EMRF)
MBSCSDD....	Master of Back Stabbin', Cork Screwin', and Dirty Dealin' [*Self-conferred degree held by Mordecai Jones in 1967 movie "The Flim-Flam Man"*]
MBSD	Multi-Barrel Smoke Discharger [*Military*] (PDAA)
MBSi...........	Master of Business Information Science (PGP)
MBSI...........	Member of the Boot and Shoe Industry [*British*] (DAS)
MBSI...........	Missile Battery Status Indicator
MBSI...........	Musical Box Society, International (EA)
MBSi...........	Simmons College, Boston, MA [*Library symbol Library of Congress*] (LCLS)
MB-SL.........	British Museum - Sloan Herbarium [*London*]
MBSL..........	Mouse Biochemical Specific Locus [*Test for mutagenesis*]
MBSL..........	Multiple-Bubble Sonoluminescence [*Physics*]
MBSM.........	Maize Bushy Stunt Mycoplasm [*Plant pathology*]
MBSM.........	Mexican Border Service Medal
MBSOGB.....	Musical Box Society of Great Britain
MBSP..........	Main Bang Synchronization Pulse (IAA)
MBSP..........	Mitchell Bancorp, Inc. [*NASDAQ symbol*] (SAG)
MBSpnea.....	Society for the Preservation of New England Antiquities, Boston, MA [*Library symbol Library of Congress*] (LCLS)
MBSP-R.......	Monitoring Basic Skills Progress-Reading (TES)
MBSQ	Music Broadcasting Society of Queensland [*Australia*]
MBSS	Main Beach Signal Station (IAA)
MBSSM.......	Maxfield-Buchholz Scale of Social Maturity [*Psychology*]
MBST..........	Motor Behavior Screening Test [*Physical education*]
MBST..........	Multiple Beam Switching Tube
MBSU	Multi Bus Switching Unit
MBSuf.........	Suffolk University, Boston, MA [*Library symbol Library of Congress*] (LCLS)
MBSufC.......	Suffolk County Court House, Boston, MA [*Library symbol Library of Congress*] (LCLS)
MBSY.........	Salt Cay [*Turks and Caicos Islands*] [*ICAO location identifier*] (ICLI)
MBT...........	Main Ballast Tank
MBT...........	Main Battle Tank
MBT...........	Main Boundary Thrust [*Geology*]
MBT...........	Many-Body Theory [*Physics*] (BARN)
MBT...........	Marble Bar - Town [*Australia Seismograph station code, US Geological Survey Closed*] (SEIS)
MBT...........	Marianna & Blountstown Railroad Co. [*AAR code*]
MBT...........	Masbate [*Philippines*] [*Airport symbol*] (OAG)
MBT...........	Master of Business and Technology
MBT...........	Master of Business Taxation (GAGS)
MBT...........	Mean Body Temperature (WDAA)
MBT...........	Mechanical Bathythermograph
MBT...........	Memory Block Table [*Computer science*] (HGAA)
MBT...........	Mercaptobenzothiazole [*Organic chemistry*]
MBT...........	Mercury Bombardment Thrustor
MBT...........	Metal-Base Transistor [*Electronics*] (IEEE)
MBT...........	Metal Bond Tape
MBT...........	Methylenebisthiocyanate [*Antimicrobial agent*]
MBT...........	Methylene Blue Test [*Analytical chemistry*]
MBT...........	Metropolitan Ballet Theatre [*Detroit*]
MBT...........	Midblastula Stage [*Embryology*]
MBT...........	Mid-Blastula Transition [*Developmental biology*]
MBT...........	Minimum Best Torque
MBT...........	Mixed Bacterial Toxin
MBT...........	Mobile Boarding Team
MBT...........	Modified Boiling Test (PDAA)
MBT...........	Motor Burning Time
MBT...........	Murfreesboro, TN [*Location identifier FAA*] (FAAL)
MBT...........	Vias Aereas Manabitas CIA Ltds. [*Ecuador*] [*FAA designator*] (FAAC)
MBTA..........	Massachusetts Bay Transportation Authority [*Formerly, MTA*]
MBTA..........	Metropolitan Boston Transit Authority (BARN)
MBTA..........	Migratory Bird Treaty Act (GNE)
MBTA..........	Migratory Bird Treaty Act of 1918 (COE)
MBTC..........	Mercedes-Benz Truck Co.
MBTC..........	Model-Based Temperature Control (AAEL)
MBTCA........	Miniature Bull Terrier Club of America (EA)
MBTD/RP.....	Main Battle Tank Distribution/Redistribution Plan (MCD)
MBTFA........	Methylbistrifluoroacetamide [*Organic chemistry*]
MBTH.........	Methylbenzothiazolinone Hydrazone [*Organic chemistry*]
MbThSt.......	Marburger Theologische Studien (BJA)
MBTI..........	Boston Theological Institute, Learning Development Program, Boston, MA [*Library symbol Library of Congress*] (LCLS)
MBTI..........	Manpower Business Training Institute
MBTI..........	Myers-Briggs Type Indicator [*Psychology*]
MBTI:AV......	Myers-Briggs Type Indicator: Abbreviated Version [*Personality development test*] [*Psychology*]
MBTS.........	Mercaptobenzothiazole Disulfide [*Organic chemistry*]
MBTS.........	Meteorological Balloon Tracking System
MBTS.........	Missile Battery Test Set [*Military*] (IAA)
MBtS..........	Saint John's Seminary, Brighton, MA [*Library symbol Library of Congress*] (LCLS)
MBTT.........	Marine Builders Training Trust (AIE)
MBtu..........	Million British Thermal Units
MBTWK.......	Multiple Beam Traveling Wave Klystron
MBU..........	Boston University, Boston, MA [*Library symbol Library of Congress*] (LCLS)
MBU..........	Boston University, School of Medicine, Boston, MA [*OCLC symbol*] (OCLC)
MBU..........	Hayward Map, CA [*Location identifier FAA*] (FAAL)
MBU..........	Magnetic Bubble Unit (NITA)
MBU..........	Mbambanakira [*Solomon Islands*] [*Airport symbol*] (OAG)
MBU..........	Memory Buffer Unit [*Computer science*]
MBU..........	MIRA [*Multifunctional Inertial Reference Assembly*] Basic Unit [*Air Force*] (MCD)
MBU..........	Mission Briefing Unit
MBU-E	Boston University, School of Education, Boston, MA [*Library symbol Library of Congress*] (LCLS)
MBUF.........	United Fruit Co., Boston, MA [*Library symbol Library of Congress*] (LCLS)
MBuild........	Master of Building (ADA)
MBUK	Mercedes-Benz (United Kingdom)
MBU-L	Boston University, School of Law, Boston, MA [*Library symbol Library of Congress*] (LCLS)
MBU-M	Boston University, School of Medicine, Boston, MA [*Library symbol Library of Congress*] (LCLS)
MBUMA	Mean Time between Unscheduled Maintenance Actions
MBUMR	MIRA [*Multifunctional Inertial Reference Assembly*] Basic Unit Mounting Rack [*Air Force*] (MCD)
MBurPRM	P. R. Mallory & Co., Burlington, MA [*Library symbol Library of Congress*] (LCLS)
MBus	Master of Business (ADA)
MBus-Accy...	Master of Business - Accountancy
MBusAd	Master of Business Administration (ADA)
MBus-Comn...	Master of Business - Communication
M Bus Ed....	Master of Business Education
MBus-Mgt....	Master of Business - Management
MBU-T	Boston University, School of Theology, Boston, MA [*Library symbol Library of Congress*] (LCLS)
MBUUC........	Minnesota Business Utility Users Council [*An association*] (TSSD)
MBV..........	Main Base Visit (NASA)
MBV..........	Marine Board of Victoria [*Australia*]
MBV..........	Medical Board of Victoria [*Australia*]
MBV..........	Mexican Border Veterans (EA)
MBV..........	Minimum Breakdown Voltage
MBV..........	United States Veterans Administration Hospital, Boston, MA [*Library symbol Library of Congress*] (LCLS)
MBV-O	United States Veterans Administration, Outpatients Clinic, Boston, MA [*Library symbol Library of Congress*] (LCLS)
MBVP.........	Mechanical Booster Vacuum Pump
MBVPS	Mechanical Booster Vacuum Pump System
MBVT..........	Merchants Banchares, Inc. [*NASDAQ symbol*] (NQ)
MBVT..........	Merchants Bancshares [*NASDAQ symbol*] (SAG)
MBVT..........	Merchants Bancshares (VT) [*NASDAQ symbol*] (TTSB)
MBW.........	Mean Body Weight
MBW.........	Medicine Bow, WY [*Location identifier FAA*] (FAAL)
MBW.........	Medium Black and White [*Film*] (KSC)
MBW.........	Metropolitan Board of Works [*British*]
MBW.........	Microbiological Warfare
MBW.........	Moorabbin [*Airport symbol*]
MBW.........	Mount Baker [*Washington*] [*Seismograph station code, US Geological Survey*] (SEIS)
MBW.........	Movement for a Better World (EA)
MBW.........	Munitions Assignment Board (Washington) [*World War II*]
MBW.........	Western Manitoba Regional Library, Brandon, Manitoba [*Library symbol National Library of Canada*] (NLC)
MBWA	Management by Walking About [*or Wandering Around*] [*Facetious translation of MBO - Management by Objectives*]
MBWI..........	Wentworth Institute of Technical, Boston, MA [*Library symbol Library of Congress*] (LCLS)
MBWO	Microwave Backward Wave Oscillator
MBWS	Wheelock College, Boston, MA [*Library symbol Library of Congress*] (LCLS)
MBX..........	Management by Exception [*Management technique*] (IAA)
MBX..........	Maribor [*Former Yugoslavia*] [*Airport symbol*] (OAG)
MBX..........	Message Bus Exchange (AAEL)
MBY..........	Make Busy (IAA)
MBY..........	Middleby Corp. [*AMEX symbol*] (SPSG)

MBY............	Moberly, MO [*Location identifier FAA*] (FAAL)
MBY & D	Maintenance, Bureau of Yards and Docks [*Budget category*] [*Obsolete; see FEC*] [*Navy*]
Mbyte	Megabyte
Mbyte	Million Bytes [*Computer science*]
MBZ	Magnesia-Buffered Zinc Oxide (PDAA)
MBZ	Mandatory Broadcast Zone [*Telecommunications*] (DA)
MBZ	Maues [*Brazil*] [*Airport symbol*] (AD)
MBZ	Menxel Bouzelfa [*Tunisia*] [*Seismograph station code, US Geological Survey*] (SEIS)
MBZ	Middle Border Zone [*Geology*]
MBZ	Must Be Zero (IAA)
MC	Aermacchi SpA [*Italy ICAO aircraft manufacturer identifier*] (ICAO)
MC	CAA Flying Unit [*British ICAO designator*] (ICDA)
MC	Cambridge Public Library, Cambridge, MA [*Library symbol Library of Congress*] (LCLS)
MC	Chemists' Club [*Formerly, Mining Club*] (EA)
MC	Consolata Missionary Sisters [*Roman Catholic religious order*]
Mc	Maccabees [*Old Testament book*] [*Roman Catholic canon*]
M-C	MacDonald-Cartier Highway [*Canada*]
M/C	Machine (ROG)
MC	Machine Cancellation [*Philately*]
MC	Machine Check [*Computer science*] (IAA)
MC	Machine Code (IAA)
MC	Machine Console
MC	Machine Cycle (IAA)
MC	Machinery Certificate [*Shipping*]
MC	Magic Circle [*An association*] (EA)
MC	Magister Chirurgiae [*Master of Surgery*]
MC	Magistrates Cases [*Legal term British*]
MC	Magnesium Chlorate [*Inorganic chemistry*]
MC	Magnetic Card [*Word processing*]
MC	Magnetic Clutch
MC	Magnetic Core
MC	Magnetic Course [*Navigation*]
M-C	Magovern-Cromie [*Prosthesis*] (AAMN)
MC	Mail Chute (DAC)
MC	Main Cabin
M/C	Main Chamber [*NASA*] (KSC)
MC	Main Channel
MC	Main Chute (KSC)
MC	Main Cock
MC	Main Color [*Crocheting*]
MC	Main Condenser [*Nuclear energy*] (NRCH)
MC	Main Coolant (MSA)
M/C	Maintenance and Calibration
MC	Maintenance Center (MCD)
MC	Maintenance Command [*Obsolete Air Force British*]
MC	Maintenance Console
MC	Maintenance Cycle (MCD)
MC	Major Component
MC	Major Cycle
MC	Makers of Canada [*A publication*]
MC	Making Capacity (IAA)
MC	Malayan Cases [*1908-58*] [*A publication*] (DLA)
M/C	Male, Castrated Animal (DMAA)
MC	Managed Care [*Insurance*] (WYGK)
MC	Managed Competition
MC	Management Committee (IAA)
MC	Management Contents [*Information Access Co.*] [*Information service or system*] (IID)
M/C	Manchester (ROG)
Mc	Mandible Coronoid (STED)
MC	Manganese Centre (EA)
MC	Manhole Cover
MC	Manned Core (SSD)
MC	Manpower Commission (NADA)
MC	Manpower Council [*Northern Ireland*] (BUAC)
MC	Mantle Cavity
MC	Mantle Collar
MC	Manual Code (NITA)
MC	Manual Control
MC	Manufacturing Change (IAA)
MC	Mapping Camera
MC	Maps and Charts [*Interservice*] [*NATO*]
MC	Mare Crisium [*Sea of Crises*] [*Lunar area*]
MC	Marginal Check [*Computer*]
MC	Marginal Checking (NITA)
MC	Marginal Cost [*Business term*]
M/C	Marginal Credit [*Business term*]
MC	Margin Call [*Banking, investments*]
MC	Marine Corps
MC	Marine Craft [*British military*] (DMA)
MC	Maritime Commission [*of Department of Commerce*] [*Merged with Federal Maritime Commission*]
MC	Mark Cross [*Initials often used as pattern on Mark Cross leather goods*]
MC	Marked Capacity [*Freight cars*]
MC	Market Capacity (ADA)
MC	Marketing Center [*Veterans Administration*]
MC	Mark of the Craft [*Freemasonry*]
MC	Marmon Club (EA)
MC	Marque de Commerce [*Trademark*]
MC	Marriage Certificate
MC	Married Couple (ADA)
MC	Martin Co. (MCD)
MC	Maryheart Crusaders (EA)
MC	Mass Communication (NTCM)
MC	Mast Cell
MC	Mast Controller (DNAB)
MC	MasterCard [*Credit card*]
MC	Mastercard International [*New York, NY*] (EA)
MC	Master Change (IAA)
MC	Master Clock (IAA)
MC	Master Commandant
MC	Master Commander [*Navy British*] (ROG)
MC	Master Control
MC	Master of Ceremonies
MC	Master of Chemistry
MC	Master of Classics
MC	Master of Commerce (GAGS)
MC	Master of Communication (GAGS)
MC	Master of Congress [*British*] (DAS)
MC	Master of Counseling (GAGS)
MC	Matara Cases [*Ceylon*] [*A publication*] (DLA)
MC	Material Code (MCD)
MC	Material Control (AAG)
MC	Materials Committee (MCD)
MC	Materiel Change [*Military*]
MC	Materiel Command [*Air Force*]
MC	Materiel Concept [*Army*]
MC	Mathematical Center (IAA)
MC	Matsushita Electric Industrial Co. Ltd. [*NYSE symbol*] (SPSG)
MC	Matsushita El Ind ADR [*NYSE symbol*] (TTSB)
MC	Maury Center for Ocean Science [*Washington, DC*]
MC	Maximum Concentration
MC	Maximum Count Output (IAA)
MC	Mayor's Court (DLA)
MC	Measure Code (NITA)
MC	Mechanical Council (EA)
MC	Media Coalition [*Later, MC/ACF*] (EA)
MC	Medical Care, Civilian Source (DNAB)
MC	Medical Center
MC	Medical Certificate (ADA)
MC	Medical Consultant [*Social Security Administration*] (OICC)
MC	Medical Corps [*Navy*]
MC	Medicine Cabinet [*Technical drawings*] (NFPA)
M-C	Medico-Chirurgical
MC	Medium Capacity [*or Charge*] [*Bomb*]
MC	Medium-Chain [*Triglycerides*] [*Biochemistry*] (MAE)
MC	Medium Curing [*Asphalt grade*]
MC	Medugorje Center (EA)
MC	Medullary Cystic Disease [*Medicine*] (AAMN)
Mc	Megacurie
Mc	Megacycle
mc	Megacycle (IDOE)
MC	Megacycles per Second (IAA)
MC	Melamine Council [*Defunct*] (EA)
MC	Member of Congress
MC	Member of Council
MC	Memorandum Club [*Defunct*] (EA)
MC	Memorandum of Conditions
MC	Memorial Commission [*Federal body*]
MC	Memory Charts
MC	Memory Clear [*Computer science*] (PCM)
MC	Memory Configuration [*Computer science*] (MCD)
mc	Memory Configuration (NAKS)
MC	Memory-Constrained [*Computer science*]
MC	Memory Control [*Unit*] [*Computer science*]
MC	Mercury Club [*Defunct*] (EA)
MC	Mercury Contact (IAA)
MC	Meredith Corp. (EFIS)
MC	Merkel Cell [*Anatomy*]
MC	Mesenteric Collateral [*Cardiology*] (DAVI)
MC	Mesiocervical [*Dentistry*]
MC	Message Center
MC	Message Change (MCD)
MC	Message Check (EA)
MC	Message Composer [*Communications, data processing*]
MC	Mess Call [*Military*]
MC	Metacarpal [*or Metacarpus*] [*Anatomy*]
MC	Metal Carbide
MC	Metal Case [*Bullet*] (DICI)
MC	Metal Clad (IAA)
MC	Metaling Clause [*Marine insurance*]
M/C	Metallic Currency (ROG)
MC	Metatarsocuneiform [*Orthopedics*] (DAVI)
mc	Meter-Candle (IDOE)
MC	Meter-Candle
MC	Methacholine Challenge [*Medicine*]
MC	Methodist Chaplain
MC	Methodist Church (WDAA)
MC	Methyl Carbamate [*Organic chemistry*]
MC	Methylcellulose [*Organic chemistry*]
MC	Methylchloroform [*Organic chemistry*]
MC	Methylcholanthrene [*Also, MCA*] [*Organic chemistry*]
MC	Methylcystyosine [*Biochemistry*]
MC	Methylene Chloride [*Organic chemistry*]
MC	Metric Carat [*200 milligrams*]
MC	Metropolitan Counties [*British*]

MC .... Michigan Central Railroad [*Absorbed into Consolidated Rail Corp.*] [*AAR code*]
MC .... Michigan Chemical Corp.
MC .... Microcarrier [*Cell culture technology*]
MC .... Microcephaly [*Medicine*] (AAMN)
MC .... Microchromatographic
MC .... Microcomputer (IAA)
MC .... Microcontrol
MC .... Microcrystalline Cellulose (DB)
MC .... Microminiature Circuit (IAA)
MC .... Micronesia Coalition [*Defunct*] (EA)
MC .... Midcourse
MC .... Midcourse Correction (SAA)
MC .... Middle Chamber [*Freemasonry*]
MC .... Middle Creek Railroad (IIA)
MC .... Miles on Course
MC .... Military Characteristics
MC .... Military College [*British*] (ROG)
MC .... Military Committee [*NATO*]
MC .... Military Community (COE)
MC .... Military Computer (IEEE)
MC .... Military Construction (AFM)
MC .... Military Coordination [*British*]
MC .... Military Cross [*World War I nickname: Maconochie Cross*] [*British*]
MC .... Mill Cutter [*Tool*] (MCD)
mC .... Millicoulomb (MAE)
mC .... Millicurie [*Also, mCi*]
mc .... Millicurie (IDOE)
MC .... Millicycle [*Also, as millihertz*] (WGA)
MC .... Millipore Corp. [*Bedford, MA*]
MC .... Mine Clearance [*British military*] (DMA)
MC .... Mineralocortcoid (LDT)
M-C .... Mineralo-Corticoid [*Endocrinology*]
m/c .... Minha Carta [*My Respects*] [*Correspondence*] [*Portuguese*]
m/c .... Minha Conta [*My Regards*] [*Correspondence*] [*Portuguese*]
MC .... Minimum Call [*Television studio on standby*]
MC .... Mining Club (EA)
MC .... Minkowski-Chauffard [*Syndrome*] [*Medicine*] (DB)
MC .... Minor Construction (AFIT)
MC .... Minorities in Cable [*Defunct*] (EA)
MC .... Mirror Coil (MCD)
MC .... Miscarriage [*Obstetrics*] (DAVI)
MC .... Misionaras Clarisas [*Poor Clare Missionary Sisters*] [*Roman Catholic religious order*]
MC .... Missile Car (SAA)
MC .... Missile Checkout
MC .... Missile Code (MUGU)
MC .... Missile Command [*Army*]
MC .... Missile Compartment
MC .... Missile Container
MC .... Missile Control
MC .... Missionaries of Charity [*Roman Catholic women's religious order*]
MC .... Missionary Catechists of the Sacred Hearts of Jesus and Mary [*Violetas*] [*Roman Catholic women's religious order*]
MC .... Missionary Church (EA)
MC .... Mission Capability [*NASA*] (NASA)
mc .... Mission Capability [*NASA*] (NAKS)
MC .... Mission Completion (MCD)
mc .... Mission Completion/Continuation [*NASA*] (NAKS)
MC .... Mission Computer (MCD)
MC .... Mission Continuation (MCD)
MC .... Mission Control [*NASA*]
MC .... Mississippi Central [*Railroad*] (MHDB)
MC .... Mississippi Central Railroad (IIA)
MC .... Mitochondrial Complementation
MC .... Mitomycin [*Also, M, MT*] [*Antineoplastic drug*]
MC .... Mitotic Cycle [*Biochemistry*] (DAVI)
MC .... Mitoxantrone, Cytarabine [*Antineoplastic drug*] (CDI)
MC .... Mitral Valve Closure [*Cardiology*]
MC .... Mixed Cell [*Lymphoma classification*]
MC .... Mixed Cellularity [*Biochemistry*] (DAVI)
MC .... Mixed Condition [*Deltiology*]
MC .... Mixed Cryoglobulinemia [*Medicine*]
MC .... Mixing Chamber
M/C .... Mixture Control [*Automobile fuel technology*]
MC .... Mnemonic Code (AAG)
MC .... Mobile Control (DEN)
MC .... Mobile Crane (DCTA)
MC .... Mode Change (CET)
MC .... Mode Code
MC .... Mode Control (IAA)
MC .... Mode Counter
MC .... Model Cities (OICC)
MC .... Modem Controller [*Telecommunications*] (IAA)
MC .... Modular Computer
MC .... Moisture Content
MC .... Molded Components (IEEE)
MC .... Molecular Contamination [*of Clean rooms*]
MC .... Momentary Contact [*Electronics*]
MC .... Monaco [*ANSI two-letter standard code*] (CNC)
mc .... Monaco [*MARC country of publication code Library of Congress*] (LCCP)
MC .... Moneda Corriente [*Current Money*] [*Spanish*]
MC .... Monetary Committee
MC .... Monetary Contact

MC .... Monitor and Control [*Computer science*] (BUR)
MC .... Monitor Call [*Computer science*] (IBMDP)
MC .... Monkey Cells
MC .... Monkey Complement [*Immunology*]
MC .... Monocomponent Highly Purified Port Insulin [*Endocrinology*] [*Pharmacology*] (DAVI)
MC .... Monocoupe Club (EA)
MC .... Mononuclear Cell [*Clinical chemistry*] [*Also, MNC*]
MC .... Monopolies Commission [*British*] (DCTA)
MC .... Monotype Caster (DGA)
MC .... Monte Carlo [*Calculation technique*] [*Nuclear energy*] (NUCP)
MC .... Montessori Center [*Education*]
MC .... Morse Code
MC .... Morse Code - Barry Morse Fan Club (EA)
MC .... Mortar Carrier [*British*]
MC .... Mortgage Constant (DICI)
MC .... Mortgage Credit Condition (EMRF)
MC .... Mothercraft Certificate [*British*] (ADA)
MC .... Motor Car (IAA)
MC .... Motor Carrier
MC .... Motor Chain
MC .... Motor Coaches [*Public-performance tariff class*] [*British*]
MC .... Motor Contact (WGA)
MC .... Motor Converter (IAA)
MC .... Motor Cortex [*Neuroanatomy*]
MC .... Motorcycle
MC .... Motorcycle Driver [*British military*] (DMA)
MC .... Movement Control [*of troops*]
MC .... Moving Coil [*Electronics*] (DEN)
MC .... Muan Chon [*Mass Party*] [*Political party*]
MC .... Mucous Cell
MC .... Multichip [*Circuit*] [*Electronics*]
MC .... Multichromatic
MC .... Multicomputing (IAA)
MC .... Multiconfiguration [*Quantum mechanics*]
MC .... Multipartisan Coalition (EA)
MC .... Multiple Choice
MC .... Multiple Contact
MC .... Multiplex Channel (IAA)
MC .... Munitions Command [*Later, Armaments Command*] [*Army*]
MC .... Mushroom Caucus (EA)
MC .... Mycelial [*of fungi*] (AAMN)
MC .... Myelocytomatosis [*Avian disease*]
MC .... Myocarditis [*Medicine*]
MC .... Myotonia Congenita [*Medicine*]
MC .... Poor Clare Missionary Sisters (TOCD)
MC .... Rapidair [*ICAO designator*] (AD)
MC .... Submarine Chaser [*Navy symbol*]
MC5 .... Motor City Five [*Rock music group*]
MCA .... Arthur D. Little, Inc., Cambridge, MA [*Library symbol Library of Congress*] (LCLS)
MCA .... Macenta [*Guinea*] [*Airport symbol*] (AD)
MCA .... Magic Collectors' Association (EA)
MCA .... Magnetocrystalline Anisotropy [*Physics*]
MCA .... Mail Control Authority (AFM)
MCA .... Main Console Assembly [*NASA*] (KSC)
MCA .... Main Coronary Artery [*Cardiology*] (DAVI)
MCA .... Maintenance Capability Audit [*Military*] (CAAL)
MCA .... Major Coronary Arteries [*Cardiology*]
MCA .... Malaysian Chinese Association [*Political party*] (PPW)
MCA .... Malaysian Commercial Association (BUAC)
MCA .... Management and Command Ashore (NVT)
MCA .... Management Consultants Association [*British*] (DCTA)
MCA .... Management Control Activity
MCA .... Management Control Authority (NVT)
MCA .... Manning Control Authority (MCD)
MCA .... Mannlicher Collectors Association (EA)
MCA .... Manufacturers' Consumer Advertising
MCA .... Manufacturing Change Analysis (MCD)
MCA .... Manufacturing Chemists Association [*Later, CMA*] (EA)
MCA .... Marine Corps Association (EA)
MCA .... Marine Cranking Amperes [*Battery*] [*Automotive engineering*]
MCA .... Maritime Control Area
MCA .... Market Research Corp. of America
MCA .... Marky Cattle Association (EA)
MCA .... Marquee Contractors Association (BUAC)
MCA .... Mars-Crossing Asteroid [*Cosmology*]
MCA .... Master Carvers Association [*British*] (DBA)
MCA .... Master Clock Assembly
MCA .... Master Community Antenna
MCA .... Master Control Assembly [*NASA*] (NASA)
MCA .... Master Craftsmen's Association [*British*] (DBA)
MCA .... Master of Commercial Arts
MCA .... Master of Commercial Aviation (PGP)
MCA .... Master of Communication Arts (PGP)
MCA .... Master of Creative Arts
MCA .... Mastiff Club of America (EA)
MCA .... Material Control Adjustment
MCA .... Material Control and Accountability (NRCH)
MCA .... Material Control Area (AD)
MCA .... Material Coordinating Agency
MCA .... Maternity Center Association (EA)
MCA .... Matrix Case Arrangement (DGA)
MCA .... Maximal Credible Accident [*Nuclear technology*]
MCA .... Maximum Ceiling Absolute [*Aerospace*] (AAG)

MCA	Maximum Credible Accident [*Nuclear energy*] (NRCH)
MCA	Maximum Crossing Altitude (MCD)
MCA	McDonnell Douglas Automation Co., McAuto Campus Library, St. Louis, MO [*OCLC symbol*] (OCLC)
MCA	Measurement Capability Analysis (AAEL)
MCA	Mechanical Contractors Association of America
MCA	Mechanization Control Area (AAG)
MCA	Media Credit Association (EA)
MCA	Medical Care Administration (STED)
MCA	Medical Correctional Association [*Defunct*] (EA)
MCA	Medical Council on Alcoholism [*British*]
MCA	Medicines Control Agency [*British*] (ECON)
MCA	Megestrol, Cyclophosphamide, and Adriamycin (Doxorubicin) (STED)
MCA	Merchandising Corp. of America, Inc. (EFIS)
MCA	Metal Construction Association (EA)
MCA	Methyl Cation Affinity [*Physical chemistry*]
MCA	Methylcholanthrene [*Also, MC*] [*Biochemistry*]
MCA	Methyl Cyanoacrylate [*Organic chemistry*]
MCA	Metropolitan Club of America (EA)
MCA	Microcentrifugal Analyzer [*Instrumentation*]
MCA	Micro Channel [*Computer science*] (CDE)
MCA	Microchannel Analyzer [*Instrumentation*]
MCA	Micro Channel Architecture [*Computer hardware*]
MCA	Microfilm Corporation of America (NITA)
MCA	Microfilming Corp. of America [*Information service or system*] (IID)
McA	Microfilming Corp. of America, Glen Rock, NJ [*Library symbol Library of Congress*] (LCLS)
MCA	Microwave Communications Association (EA)
MCA	Microwave Control Assembly
MCA	Midcontinent Airlines, Inc. [*ICAO designator*] (FAAC)
MCA	Mid-Continental Airlines
MCA	Middle Cerebral Aneurysm [*Cardiology*] [*Neurology*] (DAVI)
MCA	Middle Cerebral Artery [*Anatomy*]
MCA	Mid-West Compensation Association [*Superseded by ACA*] (EA)
MCA	Midwest Curling Association [*Defunct*] (EA)
MCA	Military Chaplains Association of the USA (EA)
MCA	Military Civic Action (DOMA)
MCA	Military Construction Appropriation [*or Authorization*] (AFM)
MCA	Military Construction Army (AFIT)
MCA	Military Coordinating Activity (MCD)
MCA	Millinery Credit Association [*Defunct*] (EA)
MCA	Minimum Crossing Altitude [*Aviation*]
MCA	Ministry of Civil Aviation [*Later, MTCA*] [*British*]
MCA	Missing Children of America (EA)
MCA	Mississippi Code, Annotated [*A publication*] (DLA)
MCA	Mistral Class Association (EA)
MCA	Mitsubishi Clean Air [*Automotive engineering*]
MCA	Model Cities Administration [*HUD*]
MCA	Modified Cost Approach Document [*Department of Housing and Urban Development*]
MCA	Mohair Council of America (EA)
MCA	Monetary Compensation Amount [*European Community*]
MCA	Monitoring and Control Assembly [*NASA*] (NASA)
MCA	Monocarboxylic Acid (STED)
MCA	Monochloroacetic Acid [*Also, MCAA*] [*Organic chemistry*]
MCA	Monoclonal Antibodies [*Microbiology*] (DAVI)
MCA	Montana Code, Annotated [*A publication*] (DLA)
MCA	Motor Carriers Traffic Association Inc., Greensboro NC [*STAC*]
MCA	Motor Control Assembly (MCD)
MCA	Motorcycle Accident (DAVI)
MCA	Motor Cycle Industry Association of Great Britain (EAIO)
MCA	Movement Control Agency [*Army*]
MCA	Movers Conference of America
MCA	Multichannel Analyzer
MCA	Multiple Classification Analysis [*Aviation*]
MCA	Multiple Communications Adapter (DGA)
MCA	Multiple Congenital Abnormalities [*Medicine*] (STED)
MCA	Multiple Congenital Anomaly [*Syndrome*] [*Medicine*]
MCA	Multiplexing Channel Adapter [*Telecommunications*] (IAA)
MCA	Multiprocessor Communications Adapter
MCA	MuniYield CA Insured Fund II [*NYSE symbol*] (TTSB)
MCA	MuniYield California Insured Fund II [*NYSE symbol*] (SPSG)
MCA	Musical Corp. of America (NADA)
MCA	Music Critics Association (EA)
MCA	Musicians Club of America (EA)
MCA	Mustang Club of America (EA)
MCAA	Marine Corps Aviation Association (EA)
MCAA	Mason Contractors Association of America (EA)
MCAA	Measurement, Control, and Automation Association (NTPA)
MCAA	Mechanical Contractors Association of America (EA)
MCAA	Member, Canadian Academy of Allergy (CMD)
MCAA	Messenger Courier Association of America (EA)
MCAA	Military Civil Affairs Administration (NADA)
MCAA	Military Construction Appropriations Act (AAGC)
MCAA	Monochloroacetic Acid [*Also, MCA*] [*Organic chemistry*]
MCAAAC	Medium Caliber Antiarmor Automatic Cannon
MCAAC	Medium Caliber Antiarmor Automatic Cannon (MCD)
MCAAF	Marine Corps Auxiliary Air Facility
MCAAP	McAlester Army Ammunition Plant [*Oklahoma*] (AABC)
MCAAS	Marine Corps Auxiliary Air Station
MCAB	Marine Corps Air Base
MCAB	Monoclonal Antibody [*Immunochemistry*]
MCABM	Manner Common among Business Men
MCAC	Machine Accessory [*Tool*] (AAG)
MCAC	Midlands Collegiate Athletic Conference (PSS)
MCAC	Military Common Area Control
MC/ACF	Media Coalition/Americans for Constitutional Freedom (EA)
MCACS	Marine Centralized Automatic Control System (PDAA)
MCAD	Marine Corps Air Depot
MCAD	Mechanical Computer-Aided Design
MCAD	Medium Chain Acyl-CoA Dehydrogenase (DMAA)
MCAD	Medium Chain Acyl-Coenzyme A Dehydrogenase (DB)
MCAD	Military Contracts Administration Department
MCAD	Minneapolis College of Art and Design
McAdam Landl & T	McAdam on Landlord and Tenant [*A publication*] (DLA)
MCAE	Mechanical Computer-Aided Engineering
MCAE	Mining, Construction, and Agricultural Equipment
MCAF	Macrophage Chemotactic, and Activating Factor (LDT)
MCAF	Marine Corps Air Facility
MCAF	Marine Corps Air Field
MCAF	McAfee Associates [*NASDAQ symbol*] (SAG)
MCAF	Mediterranean Coastal Air Force Headquarters
MCAF	Military Construction, Air Force
MCAFB	McConnell Air Force Base [*Kansas*]
McAfee	McAfee Associates [*Associated Press*] (SAG)
MCA/FYP	Military Construction, Army / Five Year Plan
MCAG	Mapping, Charting, and Geodesy [*Activity*] (MCD)
MCAGCC	Marine Corps Air-Ground Combat Center [*Twenty-nine Palms, Calif.*] (DOMA)
MCAGCTC	Marine Corps Air Ground Combat Training Center (MCD)
MCAG/MGI	Mapping, Charting, and Geodesy/Military Geography Information [*DoD*] (MCD)
MCAI	Maximum Calling Area Indicator (DNAB)
MCAI	Microcomputer-Assisted Instruction (NITA)
MCAIR	McDonnell Aircraft Co. [*Later, McDonnell Douglas Corp.*]
MCAL	Arthur D. Little, Inc., Cambridge, MA [*Library symbol*] [*Library of Congress*] (LCLS)
McAl	McAllister's United States Circuit Court Reports [*A publication*] (DLA)
McA L & Ten	McAdam on Landlord and Tenant [*A publication*] (DLA)
MCALF	Marine Corps Auxiliary Landing Field
McAll	McAllister's United States Circuit Court Reports [*A publication*] (DLA)
McAll (Cal)	McAllister's United States Circuit Court Reports [*California*] [*A publication*] (DLA)
McAllister US Circ Court R	McAllister's United States Circuit Court Reports [*A publication*] (DLA)
MCALS	Minnesota Computer-Aided Library System [*University of Minnesota*]
MCAM	Marcam Corp. [*NASDAQ symbol*]
MCAM	Marine Corps Achievement Medal [*Military decoration*]
MCAM	Member of the Communication, Advertising, and Marketing Education Foundation [*British*] (DBQ)
McA Mar Ct	McAdam's Marine Court Practice [*A publication*] (DLA)
MCA/MR	Multiple Congenital Anomalies/Mental Retardation Syndrome [*Medicine*] (DMAA)
Mcan	J. S. Canner & Co., Boston, MA [*Library symbol Library of Congress*] (LCLS)
MC&A	Material Control and Accountability
MC & A	Material Control and Accounting [*Nuclear energy*] (NRCH)
MC & B	Michigan Contractor & Builder [*A publication*]
MC & C	Measurement, Command, and Control (NASA)
MC & G	Mapping, Charting, and Geodesy [*Air Force*] (AFM)
MC & G/MGI	Mapping, Charting, and Geodesy/Military Geography Information [*DoD*]
MC & R	Manufacturing Controls and Requirements
MC&S	Microscopy Culture & Sensitivity [*Medicine*] (WDAA)
MC & W	Master Caution and Warning [*NASA*] (KSC)
M Can L	Master of Canon Law
MCANSW	Medical Consumers' Association of New South Wales [*Australia*]
MCANW	Medical Campaign against Nuclear Weapons (PDAA)
MCAP	Medical Commission on Accident Prevention (PDAA)
MCAP	[*The*] MicroCap Fund [*NASDAQ symbol*] (SAG)
MCAP	Microwave Circuit Analysis Package (PDAA)
MCAP	Military Construction Authorized Program
MCAP	Minority Contractors Assistance Project [*Jamaica, NY*] (EA)
MCAP	Multiple Channel Analysis Program
MCAPI	Mid-Continent Association of the Pet Industry
MCAR	Machine Check Analysis and Recording (BUR)
MCAR	Machining Arbor [*Tool*] (AAG)
McAr	McArthur's District of Columbia Reports [*A publication*] (DLA)
MCAR	Military Construction, Army Reserve (AABC)
MCAR	Minnesota Code of Agency Rules [*A publication*]
MCAR	Mixed Cell Agglutination Reaction [*Immunology*]
MCAR	Multichannel Acoustic Relay [*Navy*] (ANA)
MCARNG	Military Construction, Army National Guard (AABC)
MCARQUALS	Marine Carrier Qualifications (NVT)
McArth & M	MacArthur and Mackey's District of Columbia Reports [*A publication*] (DLA)
MCAS	Marine Corps Air Station
MCAS	Massachusetts Comprehensive Assessment System [*Education*]
MCAS	Middle Cerebral Artery Syndrome [*Medicine*] (DMAA)
MCAS	Minuteman Configuration Accountability System [*Air Force*] (IAA)
MCASA	Master Cleaners' Association of South Australia [*Australia*]
MCAS(H)	Marine Corps Air Station (Helicopter) (FAAC)
MCASP	Multiple Constraint Alternative Selector Program [*Bell System*]
MCAT	Maritime Central Analysis Team [*NATO*] (NATG)
MCAT	Master of Creative Arts in Therapy (PGP)
MCAT	Medical College Admissions Test (GAGS)
MCAT	Medical College Admission [*or Aptitude*] Test
MCAT	Middle Cerebral Artery Thrombosis [*Medicine*] (DMAA)
MCAT	Midwest Council on Airborne Television

MCATA.........	Management Council of the American Trucking Association [*Defunct*] (EA)
MCATS.........	Marine Corps Automated Test System (DWSG)
M-CATS	Municipal Certificates of Accrual on Tax-Exempt Securities [*Investment term*] (DFIT)
M-cats.........	Municipal Certificates of Accumulation on Tax-Exempt Securities (EBF)
MCAU	Main Carrier Acquisition Unit (MCD)
M CAUTE	Misce Caute [*Mix Cautiously*] [*Pharmacy*]
MCAUTO......	McDonnell Douglas Automation Co. [*Robotics*]
MCAV..........	Modified Constant Angular Velocity (TELE)
MCAWW	Methods for Chemical Analysis of Water and Wastes [*Environmental Protection Agency*]
MCB............	Boyne Regional Library, Carman, Manitoba [*Library symbol National Library of Canada*] (NLC)
MCB............	Machine Coated Board (DGA)
MCB............	Macrochromatin Body [*Genetics*]
MCB............	Main Control Board (NRCH)
MCB............	Malaysian Cocoa Butter
MCB............	Managing Civilians to Budget [*Army*]
MCB............	Marine Construction Battalion
MCB............	Marine Corps Base
MCB............	Markings Center Brief (MCD)
MCB............	Master Car Builder
MCB............	Master Cell Bank [*Cell line*]
MCB............	Master of Clinical Biochemistry
MCB............	Material Classification Board (DNAB)
MCB............	Matheson, Coleman & Bell [*Commercial firm*]
MCB............	MC Beverages [*Vancouver Stock Exchange symbol*]
McB............	McBurney's [*Point*] [*Medicine*]
MCB............	McComb, MS [*Location identifier FAA*] (FAAL)
MCB............	Mechanically Controllable Break [*Junction*] [*In microstructures*]
MCB............	Membranous Cytoplasmic Body
MCB............	Message Control Block [*Computer science*] (CET)
MCB............	Metal Corner Bead [*Technical drawings*]
MCB............	Methodist College, Belfast [*Northern Ireland*]
MCB............	Methylamino(chloro)benzophenone [*Organic chemistry*]
MCB............	Metric Conversion Board (NADA)
MCB............	Metric Conversion Bureau (NADA)
MCB............	Metropolitan Cemeteries Board [*Western Australia*]
MCB............	Miami City Ballet
MCB............	Microcomputer Board
MCB............	Millwork Cost Bureau [*Later, AWI*]
MCB............	Miniature Circuit Breaker
MCB............	Missouri Concert Ballet
MCB............	Mobile Construction Battalion [*Navy*]
MCB............	Modular Controllable Booster (MCD)
MCB............	Module Control Block (KSC)
MCB............	Monochlorinated Biphenyl [*Organic chemistry*]
MCB............	Monochlorobenzene [*Organic chemistry*]
MCB............	Moose Creek [*Alaska*] [*Seismograph station code, US Geological Survey Closed*] (SEIS)
MCB.......∴.	Mortgage Collateralized Bond
MCB............	Moscow Classical Ballet
MCB............	Motor Cargo Boat
MCB............	Motor Carriers Tariff Bureau Inc., Cleveland OH [*STAC*]
MCB............	Multilateral Control Board (SSD)
MCB............	Myocardial Bridging [*Cardiology*]
MCBA..........	Magnesite and Chrome Brickmakers Association [*British*] (DBA)
MCBA..........	Master Car Builders' Association [*Later, CDOA*]
MCBA..........	Mean Cycles Between Assists (AAEL)
MCBA..........	Member of the Certified Bailiffs Association [*British*] (DI)
MCBETH	Military Computer Basic Environment for Test Handling
MCBF..........	Mean Countdown Between Failures
MCBF..........	Mean Cycles between Failures [*Quality control*]
MCBI...........	Mean Cycles Between Interrupts (AAEL)
MCBIC	Michigan/Canadian Bigfoot Information Center (EA)
MCBL..........	Motor Cargo Boat (Large) [*Coast Guard*] (DNAB)
MCBM..........	Marine Corps Brevet Medal
MCBM..........	Muscle Capillary Basement Membrane [*Medicine*]
MCBN..........	Mid-Coast Bancorp [*NASDAQ symbol*] (TTSB)
MCBN	Mid-Coast Bancorp, Inc. [*NASDAQ symbol*] (NQ)
MCBOMF......	Mean Cycles between Operational Mission Failures [*Quality control*]
MCBP..........	Mean Cycles between Premature Removals [*Quality control*] (MCD)
MCBP..........	Melphalan, Cyclophosphamide, BCNU [*Carmustine*], Prednisone [*Antineoplastic drug regimen*]
MCBP..........	Methylchlorobiphenyl [*Organic chemistry*]
MCBP..........	Muscle Calcium Binding Parvalbumin [*Biochemistry*]
McB Pt........	McBurney's Point [*Medicine*] (CPH)
MCBR..........	Master Car Builders' Rules
MCBR..........	Minimum Concentration of Bilirubin [*Medicine*] (MAE)
McBride.......	McBride's Reports [*1 Missouri*] [*A publication*] (DLA)
MCBS..........	Micro Computer Business Services
MCBS..........	Mid Continent Bancshares [*NASDAQ symbol*] (TTSB)
MCBS..........	Mid Continent Bancshares, Inc. [*NASDAQ symbol*] (SAG)
MCBS..........	Mine-Clearing Blade System [*Military*] (INF)
MCBS..........	Missionary Congregation of the Blessed Sacrament (TOCD)
mcbs..........	Missionary Congregation of the Blessed Sacrament (TOCD)
MCBS..........	Multicomponent Boot System [*Army*] (INF)
MCBSE.........	Mean Cycles Between Scrap Event (AAEL)
MCBU..........	Microconfined Bed Unit [*Chemical engineering*]
MCBW	Amalgamated Meat Cutters and Butcher Workmen of North America [*Later, UFCWIU*]
MCC............	MacGillivray's Copyright Cases [*1901-49*] [*A publication*] (DLA)
MCC............	Magdalene College, Cambridge University [*England*] (ROG)
MCC............	Mail Classification Center (DNAB)
MCC............	Main Combustion Chamber (NASA)
mcc............	Main Combustion Chamber [*NASA*] (NAKS)
MCC............	Main Communications Center
MCC............	Main Control Circuit (IAA)
MCC............	Main Control Console [*Diving apparatus*]
MCC............	Maintenance Control Center [*Telecommunications*] (AFM)
MCC............	Maintenance Control Circuit (IAA)
MCC............	Maintenance of Close Contact
MCC............	Major Category Code (MCD)
MCC............	Major City Code [*IRS*]
MCC............	Majority Congress Committee [*Defunct*] (EA)
MCC............	Management Communication Consultants, Inc. [*Cincinnati, OH*] (TSSD)
MCC............	Management Control Center [*Computer science*] (BUR)
MCC............	Mandarin Capital Corp. [*Vancouver Stock Exchange symbol*]
MCC............	Manhattan Chess Club (EA)
MCC............	Manipulative Communications Cover [*Military*] (ADDR)
MCC............	Manned Control Car [*Nuclear energy*]
MCC............	Manual Combat Center [*Air Force*]
MCC............	Manual Control Center [*Air Force*]
MCC............	Map Collectors' Circle [*Defunct*] (EA)
MCC............	Marine Corps Commandant
MCC............	Maritime Coordination Center
MCC............	Marked Cocontraction [*Medicine*]
MCC............	Martin's Mining Cases [*British Columbia*] [*A publication*] (DLA)
MCC............	Maryland Committee for Children (EDAC)
MCC............	Marylebone Cricket Club [*Governing body for cricket*]
MCC............	Master Change Committee
MCC............	Master Control Card [*IRS*]
MCC............	Master Control Center (NATG)
MCC............	Master Control Console
MCC............	Matchbox Collectors Club [*Defunct*] (EA)
MCC............	Material Category Code (MCD)
MCC............	Material Characterization Center [*For nuclear wastes*]
MCC............	Material Control Code
MCC............	Material Control Coordinator (MCD)
MCC............	Maui Community College [*Hawaii*]
MCC............	Maxwell Communication Corp. [*Formerly, BPCC*] [*British*]
McC............	McCarthy [*Panendoscope*] [*Medicine*] (BABM)
McC............	McCoy [*Antibodies*] [*Immunology*]
MCC............	Mean Cell [*or Corpuscular*] Hemoglobin Concentration [*Hematology*]
MCC............	Mechanical Chemical Codes
MCC............	Mechanically Compensated Crystal
MCC............	Media Center for Children (EA)
MCC............	Media Club of Canada [*Formerly, Canadian Women's Press Club*]
MCC............	Media Commentary Council [*Defunct*] (EA)
MCC............	Media Conversion Center [*Space Flight Operations Facility, NASA*]
MCC............	Medical Council of Canada
MCC............	Member of the County Council [*British*]
MCC............	Memory Control Circuit [*Computer science*] (IAA)
MCC............	Mennonite Central Committee (EA)
MCC............	Mercury Control Center
MCC............	Mesoscale Convective Complex [*Meteorology*]
MCC............	Mestek, Inc. [*NYSE symbol*] (SPSG)
MCC............	Metacerebral Cell [*Neurobiology*]
MCC............	Metamorphic Core Complex [*Geology*]
MCC............	Metrology and Calibration Center [*Army*] (MCD)
MCC............	Metropolitan County Council [*British*]
MCC............	Mica Creek [*British Columbia*] [*Seismograph station code, US Geological Survey Closed*] (SEIS)
MCC............	Microclimatic Conditioning
MCC............	Microclimatic Cooling System [*Army*]
MCC............	Microcrystalline Cellulose [*Organic chemistry*]
MCC............	Microcrystalline Chitin
MCC............	Microcrystalline Collagen (DB)
MCC............	Microelectronics and Computer Technology Corp.
McC............	Micro Library Canisianum, Maastricht, Holland [*Library symbol Library of Congress*] (LCLS)
MCC............	Midcourse Correction
MCC............	Middlesex Community College [*Bedford, MA*]
MCC............	Midwest Climate Center [*Marine science*] (OSRA)
MCC............	Midwestern Collegiate Conference (PSS)
MCC............	Migrating Combustion Chamber [*Increases fuel efficiency*]
MCC............	Military Climb Corridor [*Aviation*]
MCC............	Military Code of Conduct (VNW)
MCC............	Military Colonization Company [*British ranch in the Calgary area of Canada*]
MCC............	Military Communications Center, Inc. [*Minneapolis, MN*] (TSSD)
MCC............	Military Comptrollership Course (MCD)
MCC............	Military Cooperation Committee [*US-Canada*]
MCC............	Military Coordinating Committee
MCC............	Mine Countermeasures Command and Support Ship [*Navy*]
MCC............	Miniature Center Cap
MCC............	Miniaturized Cassegranian Concentration [*Instrumentation*]
MCC............	Mini Car Club, USA (EA)
MCC............	Mini-Channel Communications Control (NITA)
MCC............	Minimum Circumscribed Circle [*Manufacturing term*]
MCC............	Minimum Complete-Killing Concentration (MAE)
MCC............	Mining Commissioner's Cases [*Canada*] [*A publication*] (DLA)
MCC............	Ministerial Committee on Military Coordination [*British World War II*]
MCC............	Ministerial Council for Corporations [*Australia*]
MCC............	Minuteman Change Committee [*Air Force*] (IAA)
MCC............	Miscellaneous Common Carrier
MCC............	Missile Capability Console (MCD)

MCC	Missile Change Committed (SAA)
MCC	Missile Checkout Console (SAA)
MCC	Missile Combat Crew (AAG)
MCC	Missile Command Coder (AAG)
MCC	Missile Compensating Control
MCC	Missile Control Center [Air Force]
MCC	Missile Control Console
MCC	Missing in Colon Cancer [Genetics]
MCC	Mission Control Center [NASA] (MCD)
mcc	Mission Control Center [NASA] (NAKS)
MCC	Mission Control Complex [Air Force]
MCC	Mississippi College, Law Library, Clinton, MS [OCLC symbol] (OCLC)
MCC	Mixing Cross-Bar Connector [Telecommunications] (OA)
MCC	Mobile Command Center
MCC	Modern Cereal Chemistry (OA)
MCC	Modified Close Control [Air Force]
MCC	Modified Continuous Cooking [Pulp and paper technology]
MCC	Modulation with Constant Control
MCC	Monitor Control Console (CAAL)
MCC	Monitored Command Code [Marine Corps]
MCC	Moody's English Crown Cases Reserved [1824-44] [A publication] (DLA)
MCC	Morgan Car Club (EA)
MCC	Morrison Commemorative Stamp Committee (EA)
MCC	Mortgage Credit Certificate (EMRF)
MCC	Motor Carrier Cases [ICC]
mcc	Motor Control Center [NASA] (NAKS)
MCC	Motor Control Center [NASA]
MCC	Motor Cycle Club [British]
MCC	Motorcycle Combination [British]
MCC	Movement Control Center [Army]
MCC	Multicell Compound Tire [Automotive engineering]
MCC	Multichannel Communications Controller
MCC	Multicomponent Circuits
MCC	Multiple-Chip Carrier [Computer technology]
MCC	Multiple Communications Control (BUR)
MCC	Multiple Computer Complex
MCC	Municipal Corporation's Chronicle [Privately Printed] [A publication] (DLA)
MCC	Munitions Carriers Conference (EA)
MCC	Muskegon Community College [Michigan]
MCC	Mutated in Colorectal Cancer [Genetics]
MCC	Mutual Capital Certificate
MCC	Ontario Ministry of Culture and Communications (TSSD)
MCC	Royal Military College Certificate (Senior Department) [British] (ROG)
MCC	Sacramento, CA [Location identifier FAA] (FAAL)
MCCA	Conference of the Methodist Church in the Caribbean and the Americas (EAIO)
MCCA	Manufacturers Council on Color and Appearance [Defunct] (EA)
MCCA	Media Conversion Computer Assembly [Space Flight Operations Facility, NASA]
MCCA	Medicare Catastrophic Coverage Act [1988]
MCCA	Minor Counties Cricket Association [British] (DBA)
MCCA	Model Car Collectors Association
MCCA	Motor Car Collectors of America (EA)
MCCAA	Michigan Community College Athletic Association (PSS)
MCCAC	Massachusetts Community College Athletic Conference (PSS)
McCah	McCahon's Kansas Reports [1858-68] [A publication] (DLA)
McCahon	McCahon's Kansas Reports [1858-68] [A publication] (DLA)
McCall Nee	McCall's Needlework [A publication] (BRI)
McCall Pr	McCall's Precedents [A publication] (DLA)
McCanless	McCanless' Tennessee Reports [A publication] (DLA)
McCar	McCarter's New Jersey Equity Reports [A publication] (DLA)
McCart	McCarter's New Jersey Equity Reports [A publication] (DLA)
McCart	McCarty's New York Civil Procedure Reports [A publication] (DLA)
McCarter	McCarter's New Jersey Chancery Reports [A publication] (DLA)
McCartney	McCarty's New York Civil Procedure Reports [A publication] (DLA)
McCarty	McCarty's New York Civil Procedure Reports [A publication] (DLA)
McCarty Civ Proc	McCarty's New York Civil Procedure Reports [A publication] (DLA)
MC Cas	Municipal Corporation Cases, Annotated [11 vols.] [A publication] (DLA)
MCCC	Macomb County Community College [Michigan]
MCCC	Ministerial Consultative Committee on Curriculum [Queensland, Australia]
MCCC	Minnesota Community College Conference (PSS)
MCCC	Missile Combat Crew Commander
MCCC	Mission Control and Computing Center [NASA] (NASA)
mccc	Mission Control and Computing Center [NASA] (NAKS)
MCCCA	Marine Corps Combat Correspondents Association (EA)
McC Cl Ass	McCall's Clerk's Assistant [A publication] (DLA)
MCCD	Marine Corps Clothing Depot
MCCD	Mechanical Compatibility Control Drawing (MCD)
MCCD	Message Cryptographic Check Digits
MCCD	Minimal Cumulative Cardiotoxic Dose [Medicine] (STED)
MCCD	Minimum Cumulative Cardiotoxic Dose [Medicine] (DMAA)
MCCD	Multispectral Close Combat Decoy (DWSG)
MCCDC	Marine Corps Combat Development Command [Quantico, VA] (GRD)
MCC-DoD	Mission Control Center - Department of Defense [NASA] (NASA)
MCCDPA	Marine Corps Central Design and Programming Activity (DNAB)
MCCDS	Modified Central Computer Display Set (DNAB)
MCCE	Montana Council for Computers in Education (EDAC)
MCCEd	Member of the College of Craft Education [British] (DI)
MCCEM	Multi-Chamber Concentration and Exposure Model [Environmental Protection Agency] (AEPA)
MCCES	Marine Corps Communications Electronics School (DNAB)
MCCF	Master Class Code File (MCD)
McC F	McCall's Forms [A publication] (DLA)
MCCF	Michigan Coalition for Clean Forests
M/CCFLS	Manitowoc Calumet Counties Library System [Library network]
MCC-H	Mission Control Center - Houston [NASA] (MCD)
McCl	Micro-Copy, Inc., Rochester, NY [Library symbol] [Library of Congress] (LCLS)
MCCI	MIDCOM Communications [NASDAQ symbol] (TTSB)
MCCI	Midcom Communications, Inc. [NASDAQ symbol] (SAG)
MCCISWG	Military Command, Control, and Information Systems Working Group (NATG)
mccj	Comboni Missionaries of the Heart of Jesus (TOCD)
MCCJ	Comboni Missionaries of the Heart of Jesus (Verona) (TOCD)
McC Just	McCall's New York Justice [A publication] (DLA)
MCC-K	Mission Control Center - Cape Kennedy [NASA] (KSC)
MCCL	Mason City & Clear Lake R. R. [AAR code]
MCCL	McClain Industries [NASDAQ symbol] (TTSB)
MCCL	McClain Industries, Inc. [NASDAQ symbol] (NQ)
McCl	McClelland's English Exchequer Reports [A publication] (DLA)
McClain Cr Law	McClain's Criminal Law [A publication] (DLA)
McClain's Code	McClain's Annotated Code and Statutes [Iowa] [A publication] (DLA)
McCl & Y	McClelland and Younge's English Exchequer Reports [1824-25] [A publication] (DLA)
McClat	McClatchy Newspapers, Inc. [Associated Press] (SAG)
McClatN	McClatchy Newspapers [Associated Press] (SAG)
McCl Dig	McClellan's Florida Digest [A publication] (DLA)
McCle	McClelland's English Exchequer Reports [A publication] (DLA)
McCle & Yo	McClelland and Younge's English Exchequer Reports [1824-25] [A publication] (DLA)
McClel	McClelland's English Exchequer Reports [A publication] (DLA)
McClel Dig	McClellan's Digest of Laws [Florida] [A publication] (DLA)
McClell	McClelland's English Exchequer Reports [A publication] (DLA)
McClell & Y	McClelland and Younge's English Exchequer Reports [1824-25] [A publication] (DLA)
McCl Ex	McClellan's Manual for Executors [A publication] (DLA)
McCl IA Co	McClain's Iowa Code [A publication] (DLA)
McCl Mal	McClelland on Civil Malpractice [A publication] (DLA)
McCln	McClain Industries, Inc. [Associated Press] (SAG)
MCCLPHEI	Mass Conference of Chief Librarians of Public Higher Educational Institutions [Library network]
McCl Pr	McClellan's Probate Practice [A publication] (DLA)
MCCM	Mexican Chamber of Commerce of US
MCCN	Midwest Curriculum Coordination Network (OICC)
MCC-NASA	Mission Control Center - National Aeronautics and Space Administration (NASA)
MCCNSW	Mini Car Club of New South Wales [Australia]
MCCNU	Methylchlorethylcyclakexylinitrosourea (Semustine) [Medicine] (STED)
MCCNU	Methyl-(Chloroethyl)-Cyclohexyl-Nitrosourea [Antineoplastic drug regimen] (DAVI)
MCCO	Monaco Coach [NASDAQ symbol] (TTSB)
MCCO	Monaco Coach Corp. [NASDAQ symbol] (SAG)
MCCOEES	Michigan Community College Occupational Education Evaluation System (EDAC)
McCook	McCook's Reports [1 Ohio] [A publication] (DLA)
MCCOPO	Mennonite Central Committee Overseas Peace Office (EA)
McCor	McCormick & Co., Inc. [Associated Press] (SAG)
MCCOR	Motion Compensation - Coherent on Receive
McCord	McCord's South Carolina Law Reports [1821-28] [A publication] (DLA)
McCord Ch	McCord's South Carolina Equity Reports [1825-27] [A publication] (DLA)
McCord Eq	McCord's South Carolina Chancery Reports [1825-27] [A publication] (DLA)
McCork	McCorkle's Reports [65 North Carolina] [A publication] (DLA)
McCorkle	McCorkle's Reports [65 North Carolina] [A publication] (DLA)
MCCP	Maintenance Console Control Panel
MCCP	Manufacturing Cost Control Program [DoD]
MCCP	Marine Corps Capabilities Plan (DOMA)
MCCP	Meta-Chlorophenylpiperazine [Biochemistry]
MCCP	Microwave Circuit Control Program [Computer science]
MCCP	Mission Control Computer Program [NASA]
MCC/PS	Microclimate Conditioning / Power Subsystem [Army] (RDA)
MCCQE	Medical Council of Canada's Qualifying Examination
MCCR	Master Change Compliance Record
McCr	McCrary's United States Circuit Court Reports [A publication] (DLA)
MCCR	Medical Committee for Civil Rights [Defunct] (EA)
MCCR	Memory Data Capture Cash and Credit Register [Datacap Systems, Inc.]
MCCR	Mission-Critical Computer Resource [Computer science]
MCCR	Molded Case Circuit Breaker
MCCRA	Medicare Catastrophic Coverage Repeal Act of 1989 (WYGK)
McCrary	McCrary's United States Circuit Court Reports [A publication] (DLA)
McCrary Elect	McCrary's American Law of Elections [A publication] (DLA)
McCrary's Rep	McCrary's United States Circuit Court Reports [A publication] (DLA)
McCr Elect	McCrary's American Law of Elections [A publication] (DLA)
MCCRES	Marine Corps Combat Readiness Evaluation System
MCCRK	McCormick & Co. [NASDAQ symbol] (TTSB)
MCCRK	McCormick & Co., Inc. [NASDAQ symbol] (NQ)
MCCRTG	Marine Corps Combat Readiness Training Group
MCCS	Machine Centralized Control System (DWSG)

MCCS............ Master Calendar Control System [*New York City courts' speedup system*]

MCCS............ Mechanized Calling Card Service [*Formerly, ABC*] [*Telecommunications*]

MCCS............ Military Committee in Chiefs of Staff Session [*NATO*] (NATG)

MCCS............ Missile Critical Circuit Simulator

MCCS............ Mission Control Center Simulation [*NASA*] (NASA)

mccs............ Mission Control Center Simulation [*NASA*] (NAKS)

MCCS............ Mission Critical Computer System (DOMA)

MCCS............ Mobile Command and Control System (MCD)

MCCSD........ Charles Stark Draper Laboratory, Inc., Technical Information Center, Cambridge, MA [*Library symbol Library of Congress*] (LCLS)

MCCSL........ Marconi Command and Control Systems Ltd. (NITA)

MCCSP........ Ministerial Council on Common Services Provision [*Australia*]

MCCT............ Multistrip Cesium Contact Thrustor

MCCTA........ Manufacturing Confectioners' Commercial Travellers Association [*British*] (BI)

MCCTP........ Manpower and Community College Counselor Training Program (OICC)

MCCU .... Mobile Coronary Care Unit [*Medicine*]

MCCU .... Multiple Channel Control Unit

MCCU .... Multiple Communications Control Unit [*Computer science*]

McCul Dict.. McCullough's Commercial Dictionary [*A publication*] (DLA)

McCul Pol Econ... McCulloch's Political Economy [*A publication*] (DLA)

MCCUSCUSRPG... Military Coordinating Committee, United States Element, Canada-United States Regional Planning Group (AABC)

MCD............ Air Medical Ltd. [*British ICAO designator*] (FAAC)

MCD............ Doctor of Comparative Medicine

MCD............ Dynatech Research/Development Co., Cambridge, MA [*Library symbol Library of Congress*] (LCLS)

MCD............ Magistrates' Court Decisions [*New Zealand*] [*A publication*] (DLA)

MCD............ Magna Carta Dames, National Society (EA)

MCD............ Magnetic Circular Dichroism

MCD............ Magnetic Crack Definer [*Aviation*]

MCD............ Maintenance Control Department [*Military*] (DNAB)

MCD............ Malaria Control Detachment [*Army World War II*]

MCD............ Manipulative Communications Deception [*Military*] (NVT)

MCD............ Manual Control Device

MCD............ Manufacturing Construction Document (SAA)

MCD............ Marginal Checking and Distribution

MCD............ Margin Crease Distance (STED)

MCD............ Marine Corps District (DNAB)

MCD............ Maritime Commission Decisions

MCD............ Marr, Cahalan & Dunn [*Law firm*]

MCD............ Mast Cell Degranulating [*or Destroying*] Peptide [*Biochemistry*]

MCD............ Mast-Cell Degranulation (STED)

MCD............ Master Clerical Data [*Management system*]

MCD............ Master of Civic Design

MCD............ Master of Communication Disorders (GAGS)

MCD............ Mathematics and Computer Division [*Supreme Headquarters Allied Powers Europe*] (NATG)

MCD............ McDonald's Corp. [*NYSE symbol Toronto Stock Exchange symbol*] (SPSG)

MCD............ McDonnell Douglas Corp.

MCD............ Mean Cell [*or Corpuscular*] Diameter [*Hematology*]

MCD............ Mean Character Difference (EES)

MCD............ Mean of Consecutive Differences (MAE)

MCD............ Median Control Death

MCD............ Medical Care Development, Inc. [*Augusta, ME*] (TSSD)

MCD............ Medical Crew Director

MCD............ Medium Corpuscular Density [*Cardiology*] (DAVI)

MCD............ Medullary Collecting Duct (DB)

MCD............ Medullary Cystic Disease [*Medicine*] (MAE)

MCD............ Megawatt Cassegrain Diplexer

MCD............ Member of the College of Dentists [*British*]

MCD............ Memory Control Data

MCD............ Mercy College of Detroit [*Michigan*]

MCD............ Metabolic Coronary Dilation [*Medicine*] (AAMN)

MCD............ Metacarpal Cortical Density [*Anatomy*]

MCD............ Metal-Covered Door [*Technical drawings*]

MCD............ Metals and Ceramics Division [*Air Force*]

MCD............ Metaphyseal Chondrodysplasia [*Medicine*]

MCD............ Microbial Coal Desulfurization

MCD............ Microelectronic Circuits Division (AAGC)

MCD............ Mid-Central District [*ATSC*]

MCD............ Military Contracts Department

MCD............ Military Coordination Detachment (NATG)

MCD............ Millicandela

mcD............ Millicurie-Destroyed

MCD............ Mines, Countermines, and Demolitions [*Military*] (RDA)

MCD............ Mine Warfare and Clearance Diving [*Navy British*]

MCD............ Minimal Cerebral Dysfunction

MCD............ Minimal Change Disease [*Nephrology*]

MCD............ Minimum Cost Design (MCD)

MCD............ Minor Civil Division [*Bureau of Census*]

MCD............ Missile Countermeasure Device (DWSG)

MCD............ Mission Communication Display (MCD)

MCD............ Mission Control Directorate [*NASA*]

MCD............ Modification of Contract Documents (AAGC)

MCD............ Monitor Criteria Data [*Space Flight Operations Facility, NASA*]

MCD............ Months for Cyclical Dominance [*Economics*]

MCD............ Mouse Cytogenetic Database (HGEN)

MCD............ Movement for Christian Democracy [*Political party*] (WDAA)

MCD............ Movimiento por el Cambio Democratico [*Mexico Political party*] (EY)

MCD............ Multicystic Disease [*Medicine*] (STED)

MCD............ Multiple Carboxylase Deficiency [*Medicine*]

MCD............ Multiple Concrete Duct [*Telecommunications*] (TEL)

MCD............ Municipal Construction Division [*Environmental Protection Agency*] (GFGA)

MCD............ Muscle Carnitine Deficiency [*Medicine*] (STED)

MCDA........ Manpower and Career Development Agency

MCDA........ Micro Channel Developers Association (NTPA)

MCDARS ...... Mechanized Cost Distribution and Reporting System (MCD)

MCDAS .... Metropolitan Cities Drug Association Secretaries (EA)

MC-DAS ...... Multiple Channel Data Acquisition System (NITA)

MCDB .... Master Code Database (MCD)

MCDB .... Minimum Cost Design Booster (KSC)

MCDB .... Molecular Cellular, and Developmental Biology [*A discipline division*]

MCDBSU...... Master Control and Data Buffer Storage Unit

MCDC .... McDonnell Douglas Corp.

MCDC .... Mobilization Concepts Development Center [*Washington, DC DoD*] (MCD)

MCDD .... Monochlorodioxin [*Organic chemistry*]

MCDE........ Microcide Pharmaceuticals [*NASDAQ symbol*] (TTSB)

MCDE........ Microcide Pharmaceuticals, Inc. [*NASDAQ symbol*] (SAG)

MCDE........ Monochlorodimethyl Ether [*Organic chemistry*]

MCDEC .... Marine Corps Development and Education Command

McDerI........ McDermott International, Inc. [*Associated Press*] (SAG)

McDerJ........ McDermott [*J. Ray*] SA [*Associated Press*] (SAG)

McDer Land L... McDermot's Irish Land Laws [*A publication*] (DLA)

McDevitt...... McDevitt's Irish Land Commissioner's Reports [*A publication*] (DLA)

MCDF........ Methyltrichlorodibenzofuran [*Organic chemistry*]

MCDF........ Missile Defense [*or Alert*] System Control and Display Facility [*Air Force*] (IAA)

MCDF........ Mobile Combustion Diagnostic Fixture (MCD)

MCDG .... Monitor Criteria Data Set Generation Processor Assembly [*Space Flight Operations Facility, NASA*]

MCDH .... Master of Community Dental Health, University of Birmingham [*British*] (DBQ)

MCDI .... Minnesota Child Development Inventory [*Child development test*] [*Psychology*]

McDInv ...... McDonald & Co. Investment, Inc. [*Associated Press*] (SAG)

MCDK .... Multicystic Dysplastic Kidney [*Medicine*] (DMAA)

MCDM .... Multiple Criteria Decision Making

MCDN .... Marine Corps Data Network [*Marine Corps*] (CIST)

McDn........ McDonald's Corp. [*Associated Press*] (SAG)

MCDN .... Multi-cellular Data Network [*Metricom*]

McDn25 ...... McDonalds Corp. [*Associated Press*] (SAG)

McDn36 ...... McDonalds Corp. [*Associated Press*] (SAG)

McDnD........ McDonnell Douglas Corp. [*Associated Press*] (SAG)

McDnlds ...... McDonald's Corp. [*Associated Press*] (SAG)

MCDOA........ Minewarfare & Clearance Diving Officers' Association (WDAA)

McDon Jus... McDonald's Justice [*A publication*] (DLA)

McDonnell ... McDonnell's Sierra Leone Reports [*A publication*] (DLA)

McDow Inst... McDowall's Institutes of the Law of Scotland [*A publication*] (DLA)

MCDP .... Microprogrammed Communication Data Processor (MCD)

MCDP .... Missionary Catechists of Divine Providence [*Roman Catholic women's religious order*]

MCDP .... Missionary Catechists of Divine Providence, San Antonio, TX (TOCD)

MCDPrE...... McDonald's Corp. 7.72% Dep Pfd [*NYSE symbol*] (TTSB)

McDr........ McDermott, Inc. [*Associated Press*] (SAG)

MCDR .... Multichannel DIFAR [*Directional Frequency Analysis and Recording System*] Relay (NVT)

MCDS .... Maintenance Control and Display System [*NASA*] (NASA)

MCDS .... Management Communications and Data System (SSD)

MCDS .... Management Control Data System [*Computer science*] (IAA)

MCDS .... Mission-Critical Defense System [*Army*]

MCDS .... Modular Cargo Delivery System [*MARAD*] (TAG)

MCDS .... Multicommand Data System

MCDS .... Multifunction CRT [*Cathode-Ray Tube*] Display System (NASA)

MCDSH ...... Management Communications and Data System Hardware (SSD)

MCD/SLV ...... Minimum Cost Design/Space Launch Vehicle [*NASA*] (KSC)

MCDSP ...... Master Combat Data System Plan [*Military*] (CAAL)

MCDT .... Mast Cell Degranulation Test [*Medicine*] (DAVI)

MCDT .... Mean Corrective Downtime [*Computer science*]

MCDU .... Multifunction CRT [*Cathode-Ray Tube*] Display Unit (NASA)

MCDU .... Multipurpose Control Display Unit (GAVI)

MCDV .... Maize Chlorotic Dwarf Virus [*Plant pathology*]

MCDY .... Microdyne Corp. [*NASDAQ symbol*] (NQ)

MCE............ Episcopal Divinity School, Cambridge, MA [*Library symbol Library of Congress*] (LCLS)

MCE............ MacNeill Industrial, Inc. [*Vancouver Stock Exchange symbol*]

MCE............ Maintenance Cleaning Equipment (MCD)

MCE............ Mandatory Continuing Education

MCE............ Manufacturing Cycle Effectiveness

MCE............ Marginal Cost Efficiency [*Marketing*]

MCE............ Maritime Commission, Emergency Ship

MCE............ Marshall of Cambridge (Engineering) Ltd. [*British ICAO designator*] (FAAC)

MCE............ Master of Chemical Engineering (GAGS)

MCE............ Master of Christian Education

MCE............ Master of Civil Engineering

MCE............ Maximum Capability Envelope

MCE............ MCN Corp. [*NYSE symbol*] (SAG)

MCE............ MCN Corp. 8.75% 'PRIDE' [*NYSE symbol*] (TTSB)

MCE............ Mean Chance Expectation [*Parapsychology*]

MCE............ Media Conversion Equipment [*Space Flight Operations Facility, NASA*]

MCE............ Medical Care Evaluation

MCE............ Medicare Code Editor (MEDA)

MCE	Melbourne Corn Exchange [*Australia*]
MCE	Member of Civil Engineering [*Canada*] (ASC)
MCE	Memphis Cotton Exchange (EA)
MCE	Merced [*California*] [*Airport symbol*] (AD)
MCE	Merced, CA [*Location identifier FAA*] (FAAL)
McE	Microcard Editions, Inc., Englewood, CO [*Library symbol Library of Congress*] (LCLS)
MCE	Microscopically Controlled Excision [*Medicine*]
MCE	Military Characteristics Equipment
MCE	Military Clinical Engineering (DMAA)
MCE	Military Corrective Establishment
MCE	Missile Compensating Equipment
MCE	Mission Control Equipment [*NASA*]
MCE	Mixed Cellulose Esters Membrane Filters
MCE	Mobile Command Element (NATG)
MCE	Modular Control Element (MCD)
MCE	Modular Control Equipment [*DoD*]
MCE	Montgomery Cotton Exchange [*Defunct*] (EA)
MCE	Moscow Commodity Exchange [*Russian Federation*] (EY)
MCE	Multicystic Encephalopathy [*Medicine*] (DMAA)
MCE	Multiple Cartilaginous Exostosis [*Medicine*] (DMAA)
MCE	Myocardial Contrast Echocardiography [*Medicine*] (DMAA)
MCE	National Council of Churches, Ministries in Christian Education (EA)
MCEA	Madison Center for Educational Affairs (EA)
MCEAC	Marine Corps Emergency Actions Center
MCEB	Marine Corps Equipment Board
MCEB	Military Communications-Electronics Board [*DoD Washington, DC*]
MCEC	Marine Corps Education Center
MCED	Episcopal Divinity School, Cambridge, MA [*Library symbol*] [*Library of Congress*] (LCLS)
MC Ed	Master of Commercial Education
MCED	Master of Community Economic Development (PGP)
MC Ed	Master of Continuing Education (PGP)
MC/EDS	Mission Control/Electronic Display System (MCD)
M Ce Eng	Master of Cement Engineering
MCEF	Mixed Cellulose Ester Filter (GNE)
MCEI	Marketing Communications Executives International [*Dallas, TX*] (EA)
MCEL	Machine Check Extended Logout
McEM	Microfilming Executors & Methods Organization Ltd., Dublin, Ireland [*Library symbol Library of Congress*] (LCLS)
MCE(Melb)	Master of Civil Engineering (Melbourne University)
MCEMS	Marine Corps Environmentally Controlled Medical System (MCD)
MCen	Centerville Public Library, Centerville, MA [*Library symbol*] [*Library of Congress*] (LCLS)
MCEN	Modified Current Expendable Launch Vehicle [*NASA*] (KSC)
MCENC	Mid-Central Conference (PSS)
MC Eng	Master of Civil Engineering
MCEP	Maneuver Criteria Evaluation Program [*Army*]
MCEPEN	Midwest Continuing Education Professional Nurses (DHSM)
MCER	Massachusetts Central [*AAR code*]
M Cer E	Master of Ceramic Engineering
MCES	Main Condenser Evacuation System [*Nuclear energy*] (NRCH)
MCES	Major City Earth Stations [*Telecommunications*] (TSSD)
MCES	Medical Care Evaluation Study (HCT)
MCES	Multiple Cholesterol Emboli Syndrome [*Medicine*]
MCESS	Marine Corps Expeditionary Shelter System (MCD)
MCEU	Mobile Civil Emergency Unit
MCEWG	Multinational Communication-Electronics Working Group [*Formerly, SGCEC*] [*NATO*] (NATG)
MCF	Macrophage Chemotactic Factor [*Immunochemistry*] (MAE)
MCF	Magnetic Confinement Fusion [*Physics*]
MCF	Magyar Communion of Friends (EA)
MCF	Maintenance and Checkout Facility [*NASA*] (KSC)
MCF	Maintenance Condemnation Factor (MCD)
MCF	Manual Cervical Fraction [*Medicine*] (DMAA)
MCF	Master Code File
MCF	Master Control File
MCF	Matched Crystal Filters
MCF	Maximal Contraction Force [*Myology*]
MCF	McFinley Red Lake Mines Ltd. [*Toronto Stock Exchange symbol*]
MCF	Mean Carrier Frequency [*Radio*] (IAA)
MCF	Measurement Compensation Factor (PDAA)
MCF	Medical Cybernetics Foundation (EA)
MCF	Medium Corpuscular Fragility [*Hematology*]
MCF	Merced County Free Library, Merced, CA [*OCLC symbol*] (OCLC)
MCF	Meta Content File [*Netscape*] [*Computer science*]
MCF	Meta Content Format [*Computer science*]
MCF	Metroplex Control Facility [*FAA*] (TAG)
MCF	Microcomplement Fixation [*Immunochemistry*]
MCF	Migrant Children's Fund [*Absorbed by NCEMC*]
MCF	Military Computer Family (MCD)
MCF	Milled Carbon Fiber
MCF	Million Cubic Feet
MCF	Mink Cell Focus-Inducing [*Virus*]
MCF	Mission Control Facility (MCD)
MCF	Mission-Critical Function (PDAA)
MCF	Mobile Calibration Facility
MCF	Mode Change Flag
MCF	Modular Combustion Facility (SSD)
MCF	Monolithic Crystal Filter
MCF	Mononuclear Cell Factor [*Cytology*]
MCF	Multichannel Fixed
MCF	Multilateral Clearing Facility [*Caribbean Community and Common Market*] (EY)

MCF	Multiple Cassegrain Feed [*Deep Space Instrumentation Facility, NASA*]
MCF	Multiple Cost Factor
MCF	Museum Communication Format (NITA)
MCF	Mutual Coherence Function
MCF	Myocardial Contractile Force [*Cardiology*]
MCF	Tampa, FL [*Location identifier FAA*] (FAAL)
MCF	Taurus MuniCalif Hldgs [*NYSE symbol*] (TTSB)
MCF	Taurus Municipal California Holdings [*NYSE symbol*] (SPSG)
MCF	Thousand Cubic Feet
MCF-7	Michigan Cancer Foundation - Seventh Sample [*Strain of rapid-growing breast cancer cells used world-wide in cancer research*]
MCFA	Medium-Chain Fatty Acids [*Organic chemistry*]
MCFA	Miniature Centrifugal Fast Analyzer (DMAA)
MCFA	Mitsubishi Caterpillar Forklift America
MCFA	Monosegmented Continuous Flow Analysis [*Analytical chemistry*]
McFar	McFarlane's Jury Court Reports [*Scotland*] [*A publication*] (DLA)
McFarl	McFarland Energy, Inc. [*Associated Press*] (SAG)
MCFC	Mary Jo Cattlett Fan Club (EA)
MCFC	Molten Carbonate Fuel Cell [*Energy source*]
MCFC	Motley Crue Fan Club (EA)
MCFD	Modular Chaff/Flare Dispenser (PDAA)
MCFD	Thousand Cubic Feet per Day
MCFE	McFarland Energy [*NASDAQ symbol*] (TTSB)
MCFE	McFarland Energy, Inc. [*NASDAQ symbol*] (NQ)
MCFF	Moving Call for Fire [*Military*]
MCFH	Thousand Cubic Feet per Hour
MCFIM	Microfilm
MCFIX	Ivy Bond Fund Cl.A [*Mutual fund ticker symbol*] (SG)
MCFL	Master Civilian Facilities Listing [*DoD*]
MCFLM	Microfilm (AAG)
MCFO	Marine Corps Freight Office
MCFP	Mean Circulating Filling Pressure (DMAA)
MCFP	Member of the College of Family Physicians [*British*]
MCFP(EM)	Member, College of Family Physicians (Emergency Medicine) (CMD)
MCFR	Microframe, Inc. [*NASDAQ symbol*] (SAG)
MCFS	Maneuver Control Functional Segment [*Army*] (RDA)
MCFS	Master Container Freight [*MARAD*] (TAG)
MCFSA	Minority Caucus of Family Service America (EA)
MCFSAA	Minorities Caucus of Family Service Association of America [*Later, MCFSA*] (EA)
MCFSHE	Microfische
McFx	Microfax, Universal Information System, Paramus, NJ [*Library symbol*] [*Library of Congress*] (LCLS)
MCG	Magazine Cartoonists Guild [*Later, CG*] (EA)
MCG	Magnetic Compensator Group
MCG	Magnetocardiogram
MCG	Magnetocardiograph (IDOE)
MCG	Magneto Cumulative Generator (MCD)
MCG	Mains Cable Group [*British*] (DBA)
MCG	Man Computer Graphics [*Computer science*] (MCD)
MCG	Marine Corps Gazette [*A publication*] (DOMA)
MCG	Master Control Gauge (IAA)
MCG	Master of Clinical Gerontology (PGP)
MCG	McGill University, Graduate School of Library Science, Montreal, PQ, Canada [*OCLC symbol*] (OCLC)
McG	McGloin's Louisiana Court of Appeal Reports [*A publication*] (DLA)
MCG	McGrath [*Alaska*] [*Airport symbol*] (OAG)
MCG	McGrath, AK [*Location identifier FAA*] (FAAL)
MCG	Medical College of Georgia [*Augusta*]
MCG	Membrane Coating Granule (DB)
MCG	Memory Character Generator
MCG	Memory Controller Group (DWSG)
MCG	Mesangiocapillary Glomerulonephritis (DB)
MCG	Mesencephalic Central Grey (DB)
MCG	Metric Coordinating Group (MCD)
MCG	Microgram [*One millionth of a gram*]
mcg	Microgram (LDT)
MCG	Microwave Command Guidance
MCG	Midbrain Central Gray [*Brain anatomy*]
MCG	Mid-Canada Gold & Copper [*Vancouver Stock Exchange symbol*]
MCG	Midcourse Guidance [*Navy*] (CAAL)
MCG	Millimeter Wave Contrast Guidance [*Munitions*] (MCD)
MCG	Minimally-Cleaned, Coal-Derived Gas
MCG	Minkowski-Chauffard-Gaeusslen [*Syndrome*] [*Medicine*] (DB)
MCG	Mobile Command Guidance
MCG	Mobile Communications Group [*Air Force*] (MCD)
mCG	Monkey Chorionic Gonadotrophin [*Endocrinology*]
MCG	Monoclonal Gammopathy [*Immunochemistry*] (DMAA)
MCG	Moving Coil Galvanometer [*Electronics*]
MCGA	Memory Controller Gate Array [*Computer science*]
MCGA	Multicolor Graphics Adapter [*Computer technology*]
MCGA	Multicolor /Graphics Array [*Computer science*]
MCGC	Metacerebral Giant Cell (DMAA)
MCGC	Michigan Consolidated Gas Co. [*Associated Press*] (SAG)
McGC	Micro Graphic Corp., Garfield, NJ [*Library symbol*] [*Library of Congress*] (LCLS)
MCGCIS	Marine Corps Ground-Controlled Interceptor Squadron (IAA)
MCGCM	Marine Corps Good Conduct Medal
MCGF	Mast Cell Growth Factor (DB)
MCGF	Myeloma Cell Growth Factor [*Biochemistry*]
MCGFP	Maraschino Cherry and Glace Fruit Processors (EA)
MCGH	Marine Corps Gun Howitzer (MCD)
McGill	McGill's Manuscript Decisions, Scotch Court of Session [*A publication*] (DLA)

McGl............ McGloin's Louisiana Courts of Appeal Reports [*A publication*] (DLA)
McGl Al ...... McGlashan. Aliment [*Scotland*] [*A publication*] (DLA)
McGl (LA)... McGloin's Louisiana Courts of Appeal Reports [*A publication*] (DLA)
McGloin........ McGloin's Louisiana Courts of Appeal Reports [*A publication*] (DLA)
McGloin Rep (LA)... McGloin's Louisiana Courts of Appeal Reports
                [*A publication*] (DLA)
McGl Sh ...... McGlashan's Sheriff Court Practice [*Scotland*] [*A publication*] (DLA)
MCGLX .... Ivy Global Fund Cl.A [*Mutual fund ticker symbol*] (SG)
MCGN .... Mesangiocapillary Glomerulonephritis [*Medicine*] (AAMN)
MCGN .... Minimal-Change Glomerular Nephritis [*Minimal-change
                glomerulonephritis*] [*Nephrology*] (DAVI)
MCGN .... Mixed Cryoglobulinemia-Associated Glomerulonephritis [*Medicine*]
MCGP .... Member of the College of General Practitioners [*British*]
MCGp........... Mobile Communications Group [*Air Force*] (AFM)
MCGPPC...... Manual on the Control of Government Property in the Possession of
                Contractors
McGrath....... McGrath's Mandamus Cases [*Michigan*] [*A publication*] (DLA)
McGrH .... McGraw-Hill, Inc. [*Associated Press*] (SAG)
McGrth......... McGrath Rent Corp. [*Associated Press*] (SAG)
MCGS .... Microwave Command Guidance System [*RADC*]
MCGW .... Maximum Certificated Gross Weight [*MCD*]
MCH............. Churchill Public Library, Manitoba [*Library symbol National Library of
                Canada*] (NLC)
MCH............. Machala [*Ecuador*] [*Airport symbol*] (OAG)
MCH............. Machine Channel Handler (ECII)
MCH............. Machine Check Handle (NITA)
MCH............. Machine-Check Handler [*Computer science*] (MCD)
MCH............. Machynlleth [*Welsh depot code*]
M Ch............ Magister Chirurgiae [*Master of Surgery*] [*Latin*]
MCH............. Mail Chute (AAG)
MCH............. March
MCH............. Masachapa [*Nicaragua*] [*Seismograph station code, US Geological
                Survey*] (SEIS)
MCH............. Massachusetts Council for the Humanities [*Defunct*] (EA)
MCH............. Master of Community Health (GAGS)
MCH............. Maternal and Child Health (STED)
MCH............. Maternal and Child Health Services [*Generic term*] (DHSM)
MCH............. McAlpine Helicopters Ltd. [*British ICAO designator*] (FAAC)
MCH............. Mean Cell [*or Corpuscular*] Hemoglobin [*Hematology*]
MCH............. Mean Corpuscular Hemoglobin and Red Cell Indices [*Hematology*]
                (DAVI)
MCH............. Melanin-Concentrating Hormone [*Endocrinology*]
M-Ch............ Memory Channel
MCH............. Methacholine [*A cholinergic*]
MCH............. Methylcyclohexane [*Organic chemistry*]
MCH............. Methylcyclohexanol [*Organic chemistry*]
MCH............. Methylcyclohexenone [*Organic chemistry*]
MCH............. Methylenecyclohexadiene [*Organic chemistry*]
Mch............. Micham Explorations, Inc. [*Vancouver Stock Exchange symbol*]
Mch............. Michigan Reports [*A publication*] (DLA)
McH............. Microeditions Hachette, Paris, France [*Library symbol Library of
                Congress*] (LCLS)
MCH............. Microfibrillar Collagen Hemostat [*Medicine*] (MEDA)
MCH............. Millenium Chemicals, Inc. [*NYSE symbol*] (SAG)
mc-h........... Millicurie-Hour (STED)
MCH............. Mission Chapel [*Church of England*]
MCH............. Mother-Child Health
MCH............. Muscle Contraction Headache [*Medicine*] (CPH)
MCha .... Eldredge Public Library, Chatham, MA [*Library symbol*] [*Library of
                Congress*] (LCLS)
MCHAN .... Multichannel (AABC)
MChB........... Boston College, Chestnut Hill, MA [*Library symbol Library of
                Congress*] (LCLS)
MChB........... Magneto-Chiral Birefringence [*Optics*]
MCHb........... Mean Corpuscular Hemoglobin [*Hematology*] (DAVI)
MCHbC .... Mean Cell Hemoglobin Concentration [*Medicine*] (STED)
MCHbC .... Mean Corpuscular Hemoglobin Concentration [*Hematology*] (DAVI)
MCHbC .... Mean Corpuscular Hemoglobin Count [*Hematology*] (DAVI)
MCHBG .... Maternal and Child Health Block Grant [*Department of Health and
                Human Services*] (GFGA)
MChB-WO.... Boston College, Weston Observatory, Weston, MA [*Library symbol
                Library of Congress*] (LCLS)
MCHC .... Maternal and Child Health Care (STED)
MCHC .... Mean Cell [*or Corpuscular*] Hemoglobin Concentration [*Hematology*]
MCHC .... Mean Corpuscular Hemoglobin Concentration [*Medicine*] (STED)
MCHC .... Mean Corpuscular Hemoglobin Concentration and Red Cell Indices
                [*Hematology*] (DAVI)
MCHC .... Mean Corpuscular Hemoglobin Count [*Hematology*] (DAVI)
MCHC .... Mean Corpusclsar Hemoglobin Concentration [*Physiology*]
MCHC .... Metropolitan Collegiate Hockey Conference (PSS)
MCHC .... Missing Children...Help Center (EA)
MCHCC .... Midwest Christian College Conference (PSS)
MCHCL .... Mechanically Cooled
M Ch D........ Magister Chirurgiae Dentalis [*Master of Dental Surgery*]
MChD.......... Magneto-Chiral Dichroism [*Optics*]
MCHE........... Eskimo Museum, Churchill, Manitoba [*Library symbol National Library
                of Canada*] (NLC)
M Ch E .... Master of Chemical Engineering
MChE........... Member of Chemical Engineering (ASC)
MChelm....... Adams Library (Chelmsford Public Library), Chelmsford, MA [*Library
                symbol Library of Congress*] (LCLS)
MChels .... Chelsea Public Library, Chelsea, MA [*Library symbol Library of
                Congress*] (LCLS)
MChem....... Master of Chemistry (ADA)
MChemA....... Master in Chemical Analysis

M Chem E ... Master of Chemical Engineering
MCHF.......... Marine Corps Historical Foundation (EA)
MCHFR........ Minimum Critical Heat Flux Rates [*Nuclear energy*] (NRCH)
MCHFR........ Minimum Critical Heat Flux Ratio [*Nuclear energy*] (NRCH)
MCHg.......... Mean Corpuscular Hemoglobin [*Hematology*] (DAVI)
MCHgb........ Mean Corpuscular Hemogobin [*Hematology*] (DAVI)
MCHGD .... Mott Center for Human Growth and Development (EA)
MChi........... Chicopee Public Library, Chicopee, MA [*Library symbol Library of
                Congress*] (LCLS)
MCHI .... Mobile Communications Holdings, Inc.
MChiD .... Dow Jones & Co., Inc., Chicopee, MA [*Library symbol Library of
                Congress*] (LCLS)
MChiL .... College of Our Lady of the Elms, Chicopee, MA [*Library symbol
                Library of Congress*] (LCLS)
M Chir .... Magister Chirurgiae [*Master of Surgery*]
MCHL.......... Mayo Clinic Health Letter [*A publication*]
MCHL.......... Mean Corpuscular Hemoglobin [*Count*] [*Hematology*] (DAVI)
MCHM .... MacroChem Corp. [*NASDAQ symbol*] (NQ)
MCHMAS ..... Michaelmas [*Feast of St. Michael the Archangel, September 29*]
                (ROG)
MCHML ...... Macrochem Corp. Wrrt'A' [*NASDAQ symbol*] (TTSB)
MCHMM ...... Macrochem Corp. Wrrt'AA' [*NASDAQ symbol*] (TTSB)
MCHMN ...... Macrochem Corp. Wrrt'X' [*NASDAQ symbol*] (TTSB)
MCHN .... Machine
MCHND........ Machined
M Ch Orth... Master of Orthopaedic Surgery
M Ch Otol ... Master of Oto-Rhino-Laryngological Surgery
MCHP .... (Methylcinnamylhydrazono)propionate [*Biochemistry*]
MCHP .... Microchip Technology [*NASDAQ symbol*] (TTSB)
MCHP .... Microchip Technology, Inc. [*NASDAQ symbol*] (SAG)
MChP........... Pine Manor College, Chestnut Hill, MA [*Library symbol Library of
                Congress*] (LCLS)
M'CHR......... Manchester [*County in England*] (ROG)
MCHR .... Medical Committee for Human Rights [*Defunct*]
mchr .... Millicurie Hour (MAE)
M Chr Ed .... Master of Christian Education
MCHRF......... Mechanically Refrigerated
MChrom....... Master of Chromatics [*British*]
MCHRY........ Machinery (MSA)
MCHS .... Maternal and Child Health Service (EA)
MChS .... Member of the Society of Chiropodists
M chs .... Thousands (10^3) of Characters (NITA)
MCHSM .... Mechanism
MCHST .... Machinist (MSA)
MCHT.......... Merchant
MCHTR......... Maintenance Channel Transmit Receiver Register (MHDI)
M'CHTR........ Manchester [*County in England*] (ROG)
MCHY.......... Machinery (ROG)
Mchy fwd.... Machinery Forward (DS)
MCI............. Kansas City [*Missouri*] [*Airport symbol*] (OAG)
MCI............. Kansas City, MO [*Location identifier FAA*] (FAAL)
MCI............. Machine Check Interrupt (NITA)
MCI............. Machine Check Interruption [*Computer science*] (BUR)
MCI............. Major Capital Improvement [*Justification for rent increase*]
MCI............. Malicious Call Identification [*Telecommunications*] (TEL)
MCI............. Malleable Cast Iron
MCI............. Managed Cost Improvement (NRCH)
MCI............. Management Consultants International, Inc. [*Information service or
                system*] (IID)
MCI............. Manual of Clinical Immunology [*A publication*]
MCI............. Marine Corps Institute
MCI............. Marketing Concepts, Inc. [*New York, NY*] [*Telecommunications*]
                (TSSD)
MCI............. MassMutual Corp. Inv [*NYSE symbol*] (TTSB)
MCI............. MassMutual Corporate Investors [*NYSE symbol*] (SPSG)
MCI............. Master Configuration Index (MCD)
MCI............. Material Concept Investigation (MCD)
MCI............. Materials Cost Index
MCI............. Matsushita Communication Industrial [*Japan*]
MCI............. Maya Carga Internacional SA de CV [*Mexico ICAO designator*]
                (FAAC)
MCI............. MCI Communications Corp. [*Associated Press*] (SAG)
MCI............. Meal, Combat, Individual [*Military*] (AABC)
MCI............. Mean Cardiac Index
MCI............. Media Control Interface
MCI............. Megacurie
MCI............. Member of the Credit Institute
MCI............. Member of the Institute of Commerce [*British*] (DBQ)
MCI............. Meridian Control Integrator
MCI............. Methicillin [*Medicine*] (DMAA)
MCI............. Mexican Coffee Institute (EA)
McI............. Microfilm Center, Incorporated, Dallas, Texas [*Library symbol Library
                of Congress*] (LCLS)
Mcl............. Microplex, Inc., Dallas, TX [*Library symbol*] [*Library of Congress*]
                (LCLS)
MCI............. Microwave Communications Inc. (NITA)
MCI............. Microwave Communications of America, Inc.
MCI............. Milk Can Institute [*Defunct*]
mCi............. Millicurie [*Also, mC*]
MCI............. Ministry of Commerce and Industry [*Korea*]
MCI............. Minnesota Counseling Inventory [*Psychology*]
MCI............. Mission Change Indicator [*Air Force*] (AFIT)
MCI............. Monetary Conditions Index
MCI............. Monte Cassino [*Italy*] [*Seismograph station code, US Geological
                Survey Closed*] (SEIS)

MCI.............. Mother and Child International [Switzerland] (EAIO)
MCI.............. Motor Coach Industries International, Inc. (EFIS)
MCI.............. Motorcycle Industry Association of Great Britain (EAIO)
MCI.............. Mottled Cast Iron
MCI.............. Mucociliary Insufficiency [Medicine] (DMAA)
MCI.............. Multichip Integration [Computer science] (PDAA)
MCI.............. Muscle Contraction Interference [Medicine] (DMAA)
MCIA............ Methyl Chloride Industry Association (EA)
MCIA............ MicroComputer Investors Association [Database producer] (EA)
MCIBS.......... Member of the Chartered Institution of Building Services [British] (DBQ)
MCIC............ Machine Check Interruption Code [Computer science]
MCIC............ Marine Corps Intelligence Center (DOMA)
MCIC............ MCI Communications [NASDAQ symbol] (TTSB)
MCIC............ MCI Communications Corp. [NASDAQ symbol] (NQ)
MCIC............ Medical Care Insurance Commission [Canada]
MCIC............ Member of the Chemical Institute of Canada
MCIC............ Metals and Ceramics Information Center [Battelle Memorial Institute] [DoD Information service or system] (IID)
McIC .... Micro Industrial Corp., Bayville, NJ [Library symbol] [Library of Congress] (LCLS)
MCICU.......... Medical Coronary Intensive Care Unit (DMAA)
MCID .... Malicious Call Identification [Telecommunications] (DOM)
MCID .... Minimum Clinically Important Difference [Medicine] (DMAA)
MCID .... Multipurpose Concealed Intrusion Detector [Army] (RDA)
McIDAS........ Man-Computer Interactive Data Access System
MCIF............ Member of the Canadian Institute of Forestry
mCihr........... Millicurie Hour (MAE)
MCIM.......... Member Canadian Institute of Mining and Metallurgy (DD)
MCIM.......... Member of the Canadian Institute of Mining
MCIMM......... Member of the Canadian Institute of Mining and Metallurgy
McIn & E Jud Pr... McIntyre and Evans' Judicature Practice [A publication] (DLA)
McInc........... MAICO Micrographics, Inc., Wormleysburg, PA [Library symbol] [Library of Congress] (LCLS)
McInc........... Microcomfax, Incorporated, Camp Hill, PA [Library symbol Library of Congress] (LCLS)
MCINS .... Minimal Change Idiopathic Nephrotic Syndrome [Medicine] (DMAA)
MCInstM........ Member of the Canadian Institute of Marketing (ASC)
McInt........... McIntosh Music [Record label]
MCIOB......... Member of the Chartered Institute of Building [British] (DBQ)
MCIP........... Mated Cast Iron Pair
MCIRA .... Microelectronic Replacement Assembly (NG)
MCIS........... Maintenance Control Information System (IEEE)
MCIS........... Map and Chart Information System (MHDB)
MCIS........... Master of Computer and Information Science (PGP)
MCIS........... Master of Computer Information Systems (GAGS)
MCIS........... Materials Compatibility in Sodium [Nuclear energy] (NRCH)
MCIS........... Materials Control Information System (MHDB)
MCIS........... Microsoft Commercial Internet System [Computer science]
MCIS........... Multichannel Initial System (MCD)
MCIS........... Multiple Corridor Identification System [Air Force]
MCISc.......... Master of Clinical Science (CMD)
MCIT........... Institute of Traditional Science, Cambridge, MA [Library symbol Library of Congress] (LCLS)
MCIT........... Member of the Chartered Institute of Transport [British] (DCTA)
MCIU .... Manipulator Controller Interface Unit (NASA)
MCIU .... Master Control and Interface Unit [NASA] (NASA)
MCIU .... Mission Control and Interface Unit [NASA] (NASA)
M Civil E ..... Master of Civil Engineering (PGP)
MCJ............ Maicao [Colombia] [Airport symbol] (OAG)
MCJ............ Master of Comparative Jurisprudence
MCJ............ Master of Criminal Justice (GAGS)
MCJ............ Memory Control J Bus
MCJ............ Michigan Civil Jurisprudence [A publication] (DLA)
MCJ............ Model Car Journal Association [Publishing company] (EA)
MCJA.......... Master of Criminal Justice Administration (GAGS)
MCJC.......... Maryknoll Center for Justice Concerns (EA)
MCJC.......... Mason City Junior College [Iowa]
MCJR.......... Multichannel Jezebel [Sonobuoy System] Relay [Military] (NG)
MCK............ Maintenance Check (FAAC)
MCK............ Manson Creek Resources Ltd. [Vancouver Stock Exchange symbol]
MCK............ Marital Check-Up Kit [Test] (TMMY)
MCK............ Master Cook [Navy]
MCK............ McCook [Nebraska] [Airport symbol] (OAG)
MCK............ McCook, NE [Location identifier FAA] (FAAL)
MCK............ McKesson Corp. [Formerly, SP Ventures] [NYSE symbol] (SPSG)
MCK............ McKinley [Alaska] [Seismograph station code, US Geological Survey] (SEIS)
MCK............ Mission/Communication Keyboard (MCD)
MCK............ Modification Change Kit
MCK............ M-Type Creatine Kinase (DB)
MCK............ Multicystic Kidney [Medicine] (DMAA)
MCK............ Muscle Creatine Kinase [An enzyme]
MCKA.......... Metal Cutting Knife Association (EA)
McK Consol Laws... McKinney's Consolidated Laws of New York [A publication] (DLA)
MCKD.......... Multicystic Kidney Disease [Medicine]
MCKEES....... Marine Corps Key Experiences Evaluation System (MCD)
McKelvey Ev... McKelvey on Evidence [A publication] (DLA)
McKesson...... McKesson Corp. [Associated Press] (SAG)
McKin Jus ... McKinney's Justice [A publication] (DLA)
McKin Phil Ev... McKinnon's Philosophy of Evidence [A publication] (DLA)
MCL............ Intervega - Movement for Compassionate Living the Vegan Way (EAIO)

MCL............ Lesley College, Cambridge, MA [Library symbol Library of Congress] (LCLS)
MCL............ Maintenance Checkoff List
M-CL........... Managment List - Consolidated (IID)
MCL............ Manufacturing Control Language [Computer science] (MCD)
MCL............ Marine Corps League (EA)
MCL............ Mass Change Log (MCD)
MCL............ Master Change Log
MCL............ Master Clear Line (IAA)
MCL............ Master Component List (MCD)
MCL............ Master Configuration List
MCL............ Master Control List
MCL............ Master of Canon Law (PGP)
MCL............ Master of Civil Law
MCL............ Master of Comparative Law
MCL............ Mathematics Computation Laboratory [General Services Administration]
MCL............ Maximum Contaminant Level
MCL............ Maximum Contaminant Levels
MCL............ McClellan Central Laboratory (MCD)
M'CI........... McClelland's English Exchequer Reports [A publication] (DLA)
McL............ McLaren Micropublishing, Toronto, ON, Canada [Library symbol Library of Congress] (LCLS)
Mc L .... McLean's United States Circuit Court Reports [A publication] (DLA)
MCL............ McNeil River [Alaska] [Seismograph station code, US Geological Survey] (SEIS)
MCL............ Medial Collateral Ligament [Anatomy]
MCL............ Medial Cruciate Ligament [Anatomy]
MCL............ Medical Aviation Services Ltd. [British ICAO designator] (FAAC)
MCL............ Medical College of Ohio at Toledo, Toledo, OH [OCLC symbol] (OCLC)
MCL............ Memory Control and Logging [Hewlett-Packard Co.]
MCL............ Message Control Language [Computer science]
MCL............ Metal Crystal Lattice
MCL............ Michigan Compiled Laws (AAGC)
MCL............ Microcomputer Center and Library [Wisconsin State Department of Public Instruction] [Information service or system] (IID)
MCL............ Microcomputer Language [Computer science] (ECII)
MCL............ Microprogram Control Logic [Computer science] (MDG)
MCL............ Microwave Cavity Laboratory (IAA)
MCL............ Mid-Canada Line [RADAR warning chain of fence across Canada; sometimes called the McGill Fence]
MCL............ Midclavicular Line [Medicine]
MCL............ Midcostal Line [Medicine]
MCL............ Mineral Constitution Laboratories [Pennsylvania State University] [Research center] (RCD)
MCL............ Miniature Cartridge Light
MCL............ Mini Circuits Laboratory (IAA)
MCL............ Minimal Computer Load
MCL............ Ministering Children's League [Australia]
MCL............ Minority Carrier Lifetime [Solar cell technology]
MCL............ Missile Continuity Loop (MCD)
MCL............ Modified Chest Lead [Medicine]
MCL............ Molten-Caustic-Leaching [Coal technology]
MCL............ Moore Corp. Ltd. [NYSE symbol Toronto Stock Exchange symbol] (SPSG)
MCL............ Most Comfortable Level [Referring to sound level] [Otorhinolaryngology] (DAVI)
MCL............ Most Comfortable Loudness Test [Audiometry]
MCL............ Moving Coil Loudspeaker [Electronics]
MCL............ Mucocutaneous Leishmaniasis [Medicine]
MCL............ Multicolor LASER
MCL............ Mushroom Canners League (EA)
MCLA.......... Marine Corps League Auxiliary (EA)
MCLA.......... Medical Contact Lens Association [British]
MCLA.......... Michigan Compiled Laws, Annotated [A publication] (DLA)
MCLA.......... Microcoded Communications Line Adapter
MCLA.......... Micro-Coded Communications Link Adaptor (NITA)
MCLAA......... Motor Carrier Lawyers Association (EA)
MCLAA......... Minnesota Computer Literacy and Awareness Assessment (EDAC)
MCLAMS...... Measurement, Control, LEID [Limit of Error of the Inventory Difference], and MUF Inventory Difference Simulation [Material Unaccounted For] [Nuclear energy] (NRCH)
McL & R...... McLean and Robinson's Scotch Appeal Cases [1839] [A publication] (DLA)
M'CI & Y ..... McClelland and Younge's English Exchequer Reports [1824-25] [A publication] (DLA)
M'CI & Yo .... M'Clelland and Younge's English Exchequer Reports [148 English Reprint] [A publication] (DLA)
McLar Tr...... McLaren's Trusts in Scotland [A publication] (DLA)
McLar W...... McLaren's Law of Wills [Scotland] [A publication] (DLA)
M-CLASS..... Mobile CLASS [Cross-Chain Long-Range Navigation Atmospheric Sounding System] (USDC)
MCLB.......... Marine Corps Logistics Base (DOMA)
MCIBiochem... Master of Clinical Biochemistry
MCLC.......... Lesley College, Cambridge, MA [Library symbol] [Library of Congress] (LCLS)
MCLC.......... Mine Clearing Line Charge [Army]
M CI D........ Master of Clinical Dentistry (PGP)
MCLD.......... McLeodUSA, Inc. [NASDAQ symbol] [Formerly, McLeod, Inc.] (SG)
MCLD.......... Multicolor LASER Display
MCLE.......... Mandatory Continuing Legal Education [Australia A publication]
M'Cle.......... M'Clelland's English Exchequer Reports [148 English Reprint] [A publication] (DLA)
McLean........ McLean's United States Circuit Court Reports [A publication] (DLA)

M'Cle & Yo...   M'Clelland and Younge's English Exchequer Reports [*148 English Reprint*] [*A publication*] (DLA)

McLean's CCR...   McLean's United States Circuit Court Reports [*A publication*] (DLA)

McLean's Rep...   McLean's United States Circuit Court Reports [*A publication*] (DLA)

M'Clel.........   M'Clelland's English Exchequer Reports [*148 English Reprint*] [*A publication*] (DLA)

M'Clel & Y...   M'Clelland and Younge's English Exchequer Reports [*148 English Reprint*] [*A publication*] (DLA)

M'Clel & Y (Eng)...   M'Clelland and Younge's English Exchequer Reports [*148 English Reprint*] [*A publication*] (DLA)

M'Clel (Eng)...   McClelland's English Exchequer Reports [*A publication*] (DLA)

MCLFDC ......   Marine Corps Landing Force Development Center

MCLG..........   Major Caliber Lightweight Gun [*Navy*] (MCD)

MCLG..........   Maximum Contaminant Level Goal [*Environmental Protection Agency*]

MCLI...........   Meiklejohn Civil Liberties Institute (EA)

MClinPsych...   Master of Clinical Psychology

MClinPsychol...   Master of Clinical Psychology (ADA)

MClinSc......   Master of Clinical Science (ADA)

MCLJ..........   Mifflin County Legal Journal [*Pennsylvania*] [*A publication*] (DLA)

MCLK..........   Master Clock

MCLL..........   Metrocall, Inc. [*NASDAQ symbol*] (SAG)

MCLL..........   Missile Compartment, Lower Level

MCLL..........   Most Comfortable Loudness Level [*On audiometry*] [*Otorhinolaryngology*] (DAVI)

MCLN..........   Mouvement Centrafricain de Liberation Nationale [*Central African Movement for National Liberation*] (PD)

MCLNS ....   Mucocutaneous Lymph Node Synrome [*Kawasaki's disease*] (DAVI)

MCLO..........   Medical Construction Liaison Office [*or Officer*] [*Air Force*] (AFM)

MCLOF.......   Market Center Limit Order File [*Investment term*] (DICI)

MCLong ......   Longfellow House, Longfellow National Historic Site, Cambridge, MA [*Library symbol Library of Congress*] (LCLS)

MCLORA.....   Marine Corps Level of Repair Analysis

MCLOS ....   Manual Command-to-Line-of-Sight [*Missile guidance system*] (INF)

MCLP..........   Military Committee Representative Liaison Paper to the International Staff [*North Atlantic Council*] (NATG)

MCLR..........   Midwest Center for Labor Research (EA)

MCLR..........   Minimum Critical Leaching Rate

MCLS..........   Maintenance Contractor Logistic Support [*Army*]

MCLS..........   Metropolitan Cooperative Library System [*Library network*]

MCLS..........   Monroe County Library System [*Library network*]

MCLS..........   Mucocutaneous Lymph Node Syndrome [*Medicine*]

MCLSBLANT..   Marine Corps Logistic Support Base, Atlantic (MCD)

MCLSBPAC...   Marine Corps Logistic Support Base, Pacific (MCD)

MClSc........   Master of Clinical Science (ADA)

MClSci........   Master Clinical Science (DAVI)

MCLT..........   Maximum Cruise Level Thrust (MCD)

MCLWG .....   Major Caliber Lightweight Gun [*Navy*] (NG)

MCM..........   Circular Mils, Thousands

MCM..........   Controladora Comercial Mexicana SA de CV [*NYSE symbol*] (SAG)

MCM..........   Cordi-Marian Missionary Sisters [*Roman Catholic religious order*]

MCM..........   Cordi Marian Sisters (TOCD)

MCM..........   Heli-Air-Monaco [*ICAO designator*] (FAAC)

MCM..........   Mac-Am Resources Corp. [*Vancouver Stock Exchange symbol*]

MCM..........   Machine Control Medium (MCD)

MCM..........   Machines for Coordinated Multiprocessing

MCM..........   Macon, MO [*Location identifier FAA*] (FAAL)

MCM..........   Magnetic Card Memory [*Computer science*] (IAA)

MCM..........   Magnetic Core Memory [*Computer science*]

MCM..........   Maintenance Control Manual [*Canadian Airlines International*]

MCM..........   Maintenance Control Module [*Telecommunications*] (TEL)

MCM..........   Manned Circumlunar Mission

MCM..........   Mannes College of Music [*New York, NY*]

MCM..........   Manual Communication Module [*Telecommunication device for the deaf*]

MCM..........   Manual Computer Makeready (DGA)

MCM..........   Manual for Courts-Martial

MCM..........   Manual of Clinical Microbiology [*A publication*]

MCM..........   Manufacturing Cycle Management (AAEL)

MCM..........   Marine Corps Manual

MCM..........   Massachusetts Institute of Technology, Cambridge, MA [*Library symbol Library of Congress*] (LCLS)

MCM..........   Mass Control Module

MCM..........   Master Control Module

MCM..........   Master of Christian Ministry (PGP)

MCM..........   Master of Church Management (PGP)

MCM..........   Master of Church Music

MCM..........   Master of Clinical Microbiology (PGP)

MCM..........   Master of Construction Management (PGP)

MCM..........   Materiel Change Management

MCM..........   McCarthy, Crisanti & Maffei, Inc. [*Information service or system*] (IID)

MCM..........   McMurdo Sound [*Antarctica*] [*Seismograph station code, US Geological Survey Closed*] (SEIS)

MCM..........   Mechanical Current Meter [*Marine science*] (OSRA)

MCM..........   Medical Corps, Merchant Marine [*USNR officer designation*]

MCM..........   Mega Cisterna Magna [*Medicine*]

MCM..........   Megawatt Cassegrain Monopulse

MCM..........   Member of the College of Musicians [*British*]

MCM..........   Memory Control Module

MCM..........   Merged Charge Memory [*Computer science*] (IAA)

MCM..........   Microchip Module

MCM..........   Microcircuit Module

MCM..........   Microcomputer Machine (IAA)

McM ....   Micromedia Ltd., Toronto, ON, Canada [*Library symbol Library of Congress*] (LCLS)

MCM..........   Microwave Circuit Module [*Computer science*] (IAA)

MCM..........   Military Characteristics Motor Vehicles

MCM..........   Military Committee Memorandum [*NATO*] (NATG)

MCM..........   Milli Circular Mil (IAA)

MCM..........   Million Centimeters (MCD)

MCM..........   Mine Countermeasures (NG)

MCM..........   Minichromosome Maintenance [*Cytology*]

MCM..........   Minneapolis College of Music

MCM..........   Miscellaneous Contract Material

MCM..........   Missile Carrying Missile (AAG)

MCM..........   Missile Control Module (NVT)

MCM..........   Mission Communications Manager (SSD)

MCM..........   Mission Control Module

MCM..........   Mississippi College, Clinton, MS [*OCLC symbol*] (OCLC)

MCM..........   Mobile Cinetheodolite Mounts (SAA)

MCM..........   Mode Control Message (MCD)

MCM..........   Modular Auxiliary Data System Control Module [*Aerospace*] (NAKS)

MCM..........   Monolithic Circuit Mask

MCM..........   Monte Carlo [*Monaco*] [*Airport symbol*] (OAG)

MCM..........   Monte Carlo Method [*Computer science*]

MCM..........   Moving Coil Microphone [*Electronics*]

MCM..........   Moving Coil Motor [*Electronics*] (IAA)

MCM..........   Multichip Module [*Computer science*]

MCM..........   Multilayer Ceramic Multichip [*Electronics*]

MCM..........   Multinational Computer Models, Inc. [*Information service or system*] (IID)

MCM..........   Multiple Connected Motor

MCM..........   Multiple Contact Miscible [*Physical chemistry*]

MCM..........   Municipal Court of Montreal (DLA)

MCM..........   Thousand Circular Mils

MCMA.........   Machine Chain Manufacturers Association (EA)

MCMA.........   Marine Corps Mustang Association (EA)

MCMA.........   Metal Cookware Manufacturers Association [*Later, CMA*] (EA)

MCMAI........   Milton Clinical Multi-Axial Inventory [*Psychology*] (DAVI)

McMas RR...   McMaster's New York Railroad Laws [*A publication*] (DLA)

MCMB.........   Multiple Conductor, Marker Buoy (IAA)

MCMC.........   Marine Corps Memorial Commission

MCMC.........   MCM Corp. [*NASDAQ symbol*] (NQ)

MCMC.........   Medicine Cabinet Manufacturers Council (EA)

MCMC.........   Midwest Committee for Military Counseling (EA)

MCMC.........   Military Construction, Marine Corps (DNAB)

MCMCAT.....   Mine Countermeasures Catamaran [*Military*]

MCMCC.......   Marine Corps Movement Coordination Center (DNAB)

McM Com Cas...   McMaster's United States Commercial Cases [*A publication*] (DLA)

McM Com Dec...   McMaster's Commercial Decisions [*A publication*] (DLA)

MCM Cp .....   MCM Corp. [*Associated Press*] (SAG)

McMdL........   Micromedia Ltd., Toronto, ON, Canada [*Library symbol Library of Congress*] (LCLS)

MCMES.......   Member of the Civil and Mechanical Engineering Society

MCM-F........   Massachusetts Institute of Technology, University Film Study Center, Cambridge, MA [*Library symbol Library of Congress*] (LCLS)

MCMFA.......   Meeting of Consultation of Ministers of Foreign Affairs

MCMFE.......   Membrane-Covered Mercury Film Electrode [*Electrochemistry*]

MCMG ....   Man-Carrying Motion Generator [*Space-flight simulation*]

MCMG ....   Marine Corps Meteorological Group (COE)

MCMG ....   Military Committee Meteorological Group [*NATO*] (NATG)

MCM-H ....   Massachusetts Institute of Technology, Francis Russell Hart Nautical Museum, Cambridge, MA [*Library symbol Library of Congress*] (LCLS)

MCMH ....   Mine Counter-Measures Hovercraft [*Military*] (PDAA)

MCMHA ......   Metropolitan College Mental Health Association (EA)

MCMHC ......   Mine Countermeasures Helicopter Controller (MCD)

MCMI..........   Malleable Chain Manufacturers Institute [*Later, American Chain Association*]

MCMI..........   Millon Clinical Multiaxial Inventory [*Psychology*]

MCMI..........   Minneapolis Center for Microbiological Investigations [*Public Health Service*] (GRD)

MCMIS........   Motor Carrier Management Information System [*BTS*] [*MM*] (TAG)

MCM-L........   Massachusetts Institute of Technology, Lincoln Laboratory, Lexington, MA [*Library symbol Library of Congress*] (LCLS)

MCML.........   Missile Compartment, Middle Level

MCMM........   Management Control - Material Management (IEEE)

MCMOPS ....   Mine Countermeasures Operations [*Military*] (NVT)

McMoRn ......   McMoRan Oil and Gas Co. [*Associated Press*] (SAG)

MCMOS ......   Motorola Complementary Metal-Oxide Semi-Conductor [*Electronics*] (IAA)

MCMOV ......   Maize Chlorotic Mottle Virus [*Plant pathology*]

MCMP ....   Multi-Channel Multi-Port [*Telecommunications*]

MCMR ....   Medical Corps, Merchant Marine, General Service [*USNR officer designation*]

MC/MR ....   Minimum Change/Minimum Risk [*Mask design concept*] [*Army*] (INF)

MCMS ....   Medical Corps, Merchant Marine, Special Service [*USNR officer designation*]

MCMS ....   Midwest Center for Mass Spectrometry [*University of Nebraska - Lincoln*] [*Research center*] (RCD)

M-CM-S ......   Mobility, Countermobility, and Survivability

MCMS ....   Multichannel Memory System [*Computer science*] (AAG)

MCMS ....   Multiple Countermeasure System

MCMU ....   Mass Core Memory Unit (MCD)

McMul ....   McMullan's South Carolina Law Reports [*A publication*] (DLA)

McMul Eq ...   McMullan's South Carolina Equity Reports [*A publication*] (DLA)

McMull Eq (SC)...   McMullan's South Carolina Equity Reports [*A publication*] (DLA)

McMull L (SC)...	McMullan's South Carolina Law Reports [A publication] (DLA)
MCMUS	Manual of Courts-Martial, United States
MCMV.........	Maize Chlorotic Mottle Virus [Plant pathology]
MCMV.........	Mine Countermeasures Vessel [or Vehicle] (NATG)
MCMV.........	Mine Counter-Measure Vessel
MCMV.........	Murine Cytomegalovirus
MCMWTC	Marine Corps Mountain Warfare Training Center [Bridgeport, CA]
MCN...........	Mac Dan Aviation Corp. [ICAO designator] (FAAC)
MCN...........	Macon [Georgia] [Airport symbol] (OAG)
MCN...........	Maintenance Communications Net (MCD)
MCN...........	Maintenance Control Number
MCN...........	Management Change Notice (MCD)
MCN...........	Management Control Number [Army] (AABC)
MCN...........	Manual Control Number
MCN...........	Manufacturing Change Notice
MCN...........	Manufacturing Control Number
MCN...........	Mapping Cylinder Neighborhood
MCN...........	Master Change Notice (KSC)
MCN...........	Master Control Number
MCN...........	Master of Clinical Nutrition
MCN...........	Material Change Notice (MCD)
MCN...........	Material Complaint Notice
MCN...........	MCN Corp. [Formerly, Michigan Consolidated Gas Co.] [Associated Press] (SAG)
McN	McNeil Laboratories, Inc. [Research code symbol]
MCN...........	McNeil Mantha, Inc. [Toronto Stock Exchange symbol]
MCN...........	MCN Financing [NYSE symbol] (SAG)
MCN...........	MCN Michigan LP [NYSE symbol] (SAG)
MCN...........	Mercury [Nevada] [Seismograph station code, US Geological Survey Closed] (SEIS)
MCN...........	MichCon (EFIS)
MCN...........	Micro Cellular Network [Computer science]
MCN...........	Micrococcal Nuclease [Also, MN] [An enzyme]
MCN...........	Midcourse Navigation [Navy] (IAA)
MCN...........	Military Construction, Navy
MCN...........	Minimal Change Nephropathy [Medicine] (DMAA)
MCN...........	Missing Children Network [Defunct] (EA)
MC-N........	Mixed Cell Nodular [Lymphoma] [Medicine] (STED)
MCN...........	Molecular and Cellular Neuroscience [A publication]
MCN...........	Mouvement Congolais National [Zaire] [Political party] (EY)
MCN...........	Movimiento de Conciliacion Nacional [National Conciliation Movement] [Dominican Republic] [Political party] (PPW)
MCN...........	Museum Computer Network (NITA)
MCN...........	Museum Computer Network, Inc. [American Association of Museums] [Research center] (RCD)
McNagh	Macnaghten's Select Cases in Chancery Tempore King [A publication] (DLA)
McNal Ev.....	Macnally's Rules of Evidence [A publication] (DLA)
MCNC	Carberry/North Cypress Library, Carberry, Manitoba [Library symbol National Library of Canada] (NLC)
MCNC	Microcomputer Numerical Control (IAA)
MCNC	Microelectronics Center of North Carolina [Research center] (RCD)
McNeese St U..	McNeese State University (GAGS)
MCN F	MCN Financing [Associated Press] (SAG)
MCNG	Military Construction, National Guard
McN-JR.......	McNeil Laboratories, Inc. [Research code symbol]
MCNL.........	Military Committee of National Liberation [Mali] [Political party] (PPW)
MCNMI	MCN Michigan Ltd. [Associated Press] (SAG)
MCNP.........	Monitoring Completed Navigation Projects [Army]
MCNPB	Marine Corps - Navy Publicity Bureau (SAA)
MCNPrT	MCN Mich L.P.9.375% Pfd [NYSE symbol] (TTSB)
MCNR.........	Military Construction, Naval Reserves
MCNRF	Military Construction, Naval Reserve Facilities
MCNRS	Meal Card Number Recording System (MCD)
MCNS	Member, Congress of Neurological Surgeons (CMD)
MCNS	Minimal Change Nephrotic Syndrome [Medicine] (DMAA)
MCNY	Museum of the City of New York
MCO...........	Aerolineas Marcos SA de CV [Mexico ICAO designator] (FAAC)
MCo...........	Concord Free Public Library, Concord, MA [Library symbol Library of Congress] (LCLS)
MCO...........	Magnetron Cutoff
MCO...........	Main Civilian Occupation
MCO...........	Maintenance Checkoff
MCO...........	Manged Care Organization
MCO...........	Manual Change Order (MSA)
MCO...........	Marine Corps Officer
MCO...........	Marine Corps Order
MCO...........	Massachusetts College of Optometry
M Co...........	Master of Cosmology
MCO...........	Medical Care Organization (STED)
MCO...........	Medicare Carve-Out [Insurance] (WYGK)
MCO...........	Merrill Lyn 6.00%'STRYPES' [NYSE symbol] (TTSB)
MCO...........	Merrill Lynch & Co. [NYSE symbol] (SAG)
MCO...........	Metal Catalyzed Oxidation [Chemistry]
MCO...........	Military City Online [Computer program]
MCO...........	Mill Culls Out [Lumber]
MCO...........	Mill Cuts Out [Forest industry] (WPI)
MCO...........	Minneapolis Community College, Minneapolis, MN [OCLC symbol] (OCLC)
MCO...........	Miscellaneous Charges Order [Business term]
MCO...........	Missile Checkout (NG)
MCO...........	Missile Control Officer
MCO...........	Mission Control Operation [NASA]
mco	Mission Control Operations [NASA] (NAKS)
MCO...........	Monaco [ANSI three-letter standard code] (CNC)
MCO...........	Morocco Leather [Bookbinding] (DGA)
MCO...........	Movement Control Officer [Army]
MCO...........	Multi Column Option (DGA)
MCO...........	Multiple Channel Oscilloscope
MCO...........	Orlando, FL [Location identifier FAA] (FAAL)
MCO...........	Orlando [Florida] International [Airport symbol] (OAG)
MCOA	Mastiff Club of America (EA)
MCOA	Music Center Opera Association [Los Angeles]
MCOAG	Marine Corps Operations Analysis Group
MCOAM	Material Control Order Additional Material
MCOA/P.......	Multi-Company Accounts Payable (MHDB)
MCODA.......	Motor Cab Owner Drivers' Association [British] (BI)
M-COFT	Mobile Conduct of Fire Trainer [Combat simulator]
MCOG	Member of the British College of Obstetricians and Gynaecologists (DAS)
MCOGA	Mid-Continent Oil and Gas Association (EA)
MCogSc	Master of Cognitive Science
MCOHM	Military Community Oral Health Managers [Army]
MCOI	Minority Centers of Influence (DNAB)
MCOLF........	Marine Corps Outlying Landing Field
MColIP........	Member of the College of Preceptors [British] (DBQ)
M Com	Master of Commerce
MCOM	Mathematics of Computation (IEEE)
MCOM	Metricom, Inc. [NASDAQ symbol] (SAG)
MCOM	Missile Command [Army] (MCD)
M Com Adm...	Master of Commercial Administration
MComm.......	Master of Commerce (ADA)
M Comm......	Master of Commerce and Administration (ROG)
MCOMM	Minimize Communications
M Comm H....	Master of Community Health
MCommSc....	Master in Commercial Science (DD)
MCommun.....	Master in Communication (DD)
M Comp.......	Master of Computing
M Comp E	Master of Computer Engineering (PGP)
M Comp L	Master of Comparative Law
MCompLaw....	Master of Comparative Law (NADA)
M Com Sc	Master of Commercial Science
MComSc	Master of Computer Science
MCON	EMCON [NASDAQ symbol] (TTSB)
MCON	EMCON Associates [NASDAQ symbol] (NQ)
MCON	Military Construction
MCON	Moment Connections [Computer Services Consultants Ltd.] [Software package] (NCC)
MConsE	Member of the Association of Consulting Engineers [British] (EY)
MCOP	Major Command Orientation Program [Air Force] (AFM)
MCOP	Marine Corps Ordnance Publication
mCOP	Measured Colloidal Osmotic Pressure [Clinical chemistry]
MCOP	Mission Control Operations Panel [NASA] (KSC)
MCOP	Multiple Conductor, Oil-Resistant, Portable [Cable]
MCOPR........	Major Command of Primary Responsibility [Air Force] (AFM)
MCOQ	Multiple Choice Objective Question (DA)
MCOR	Methodist Committee for Overseas Relief [Later, UMCOR] (EA)
MC/ORB	Maritime Command Operational Research Branch [Canada]
MC/ORD......	Maritime Command Operational Research Division [Canada]
M'Cord Eq (SC)...	M'Cord's South Carolina Equity Reports [A publication] (DLA)
M'Cord L (SC)...	M'Cord's South Carolina Law Reports [A publication] (DLA)
MCOS	Microprogrammable Computer Operating System
MCoS..........	Military College of Science [British military] (DMA)
MCot..........	Cotuit Library, Cotuit, MA [Library symbol] [Library of Congress] (LCLS)
MCOT.........	Missile Checkout Trailer
MCOT.........	Missile Control Officer, Trainer (NG)
MCOTEA	Marine Corps Operational Test and Evaluation Activity (CAAL)
Mcoul	Millicoulomb
mcoul	Millicoulomb (STED)
M Coun........	Master of Counseling (PGP)
MCouns(Ed)...	Master of Counselling (Education) (ADA)
MCOV.........	Main Chamber Oxidizer Valve [NASA] (KSC)
MCOV.........	Modified Covariance
MCOW	Medical College of Wisconsin
MCoW.........	Wayside [Minute Man National Historical Park], Concord, MA [Library symbol Library of Congress] (LCLS)
MCOY	Military Citizen of the Year (DNAB)
MCP...........	Bear Stearns Companies, Inc. [AMEX symbol] (SAG)
MCP...........	Bear Sterns 5.50%MRK'CHIPS' [AMEX symbol] (TTSB)
MCP...........	Macapa [Brazil] [Airport symbol] (OAG)
MCP...........	Macrophage-Capping Protein [Biochemistry]
MCP...........	Main Call Process [Telecommunications] (TEL)
MCP...........	Main Condensate Pump [Navy] (CAAL)
MCP...........	Main Coolant Pump (NVT)
MCP...........	Maintenance Control Panel [Navy] (CAAL)
MCP...........	Maintenance Control Point (NG)
MCP...........	Malawi Congress Party [Nyasaland] [Political party] (PPW)
MCP...........	Malayan Communist Party [Political party]
MCP...........	Male Chauvinist Pig [Feminist term]
MCP...........	Management Control Plan
MCP...........	Manual Control Panel
MCP...........	Manufacturing Change Point
MCP...........	Marcana Petroleum Ltd. [Vancouver Stock Exchange symbol]
MCP...........	Marine Corps Capabilities Plan (MCD)
MCP...........	Martinique Communist Party [Political party]
MCP...........	Mary Cheney Library, Manchester, CT [OCLC symbol] (OCLC)
MCP...........	Massachusetts College of Pharmacy [Boston]
MCP...........	Master Change Proposal (KSC)

MCP............ Master Computer Program [*NASA*] (KSC)
MCP............ Master Control Program [*Burroughs Corp.*]
M Cp .... Master of Chiropody
MCP............ Master of City Planning
MCP............ Master of Community Planning (GAGS)
MCP............ Master of Community Psychology (PGP)
MCP............ Master of Counseling Psychology (GAGS)
MCP............ Materials Control Plan (NASA)
MCP............ Materiel Command Procedure [*Military*]
MCP............ Maximal Closure Pressure (STED)
MCP............ Maximal Coverage Problem [*Mathematical modelling*]
MCP............ Maximum Continuous Power
MCP............ Measurements Control Procedure (KSC)
MCP............ Medical College of Pennsylvania
MCP............ Medical Continuation Pay [*Military*] (AABC)
MCP............ MEECN [*Minimum Essential Emergency Communications Network*] Communication Plan (MCD)
MCP............ Melanosis Circumscripta Precancerosa (STED)
MCP............ Melphalan, Cyclophosphamide, Prednisone [*Antineoplastic drug regimen*]
MCP............ Member of the College of Preceptors [*British*]
MCP............ Member of the Colonial Parliament [*British*]
MCP............ Membrane Cofactor Protein [*Biochemistry*]
MCP............ Memory-Centered Processing [*or Processor*] [*System*] [*Computer science*]
MCP............ Message Control Program [*Computer science*]
MCP............ Metacarpal (STED)
MCP............ Metacarpophalangeal [*Anatomy*]
MCP............ Metaclopramide (STED)
MCP............ Meta-Cresol Purple [*Organic chemistry*]
MCP............ Metal Case Profile [*Ammunition*]
MCP............ Metal Casting Pattern (MSA)
MCP............ Meteacarpophalangeal [*Joint*] [*Anatomy*] (DAVI)
MCP............ Methyl-Accepting Chemotaxis Proteins [*Biochemistry*]
MCP............ Methylchlorophenoxyacetic Acid [*Also, MCPA*] [*Herbicide*]
MCP............ Methylcyclopentane [*Organic chemistry*]
MCP............ Microchannel Plate [*Computer science*]
MCP............ Microcrystalline Polymer [*Plastics technology*]
McP............ Micro Photo Division, Bell & Howell Co., Wooster, OH [*Library symbol Library of Congress*] (LCLS)
MCP............ Microwave Coupled Plasma [*Spectroscopy*]
MCP............ Military Construction Plan
MCP............ Military Construction Program (AFIT)
MCP............ Militia Career Program [*DoD*]
MCP............ Missile Control Panel
MCP............ Missile Control Point (NATG)
MCP............ Mission Concept Paper (MCD)
MCP............ Mission Control Programmer [*NASA*] (NAKS)
MCP............ Missioneras Catequestas de los Pobres (TOCD)
MCP............ Mitotic-Control Protein [*Cytology*] (MAE)
MCP............ Moca [*Puerto Rico*] [*Seismograph station code, US Geological Survey*] (SEIS)
MCP............ Mode Control Panel
MCP............ Model Cities Program
MCP............ Monitoring and Control Panel (NASA)
MCP............ Monocalcium Phosphate [*Inorganic chemistry*] [*Food additive*]
MCP............ Monocyte Chemotactic Protein [*Biochemistry*]
MCP............ Monte Capellino [*Italy*] [*Later, ROB*] [*Geomagnetic observatory code*]
MCP............ Mouvement Chretien pour la Paix [*Christian Movement for Peace - CMP*] [*Brussels, Belgium*] (EAIO)
MCP............ Movimiento Civico Popular [*Panama*] [*Political party*] (EY)
MCP............ Mucin Clot-Prevention [*Test*] [*Medicine*] (STED)
MCP............ Multicatalytic Proteinase [*An enzyme*]
MCP............ Multichannel Communications Program (IEEE)
MCP............ Multichip Package (AAEL)
MCP............ Multicomponent Plasma
MCP............ Multiple-Chip Package
MCP............ Multiple Comparison Procedure [*Statistics*]
MCP............ Multiple Control Program [*Computer science*]
MCP............ Municipal Compliance Plan [*Environmental Protection Agency*] (GFGA)
MCP............ Mutation as Cellular Process
MCP............ Polaroid Corp., Cambridge, MA [*Library symbol Library of Congress*] (LCLS)
MCPA.......... Member of the Canadian Psychological Association
MCPA.......... Member of the College of Pathologists Australasia
MCPA.......... Memory Clock Pulse Amplifier
MCPA.......... Methylchlorophenoxyacetic Acid [*Also, MCP*] [*Herbicide*]
MCPA.......... Methylenecyclopropylacetic Acid [*Organic chemistry*]
McPA.......... Microfilm Corp. of Pennsylvania, Pittsburgh, PA [*Library symbol Library of Congress*] (LCLS)
MCPA.......... Midwest College Placement Association
MCPAC .... Military Construction Programs Advisory Committee (AFM)
MCP/AS ...... Master Control Program / Advanced System (HGAA)
MC Path ...... Member of the College of Pathologists [*British*]
MCPBA .... Meta-Chloroperoxybenzoic Acid [*Organic chemistry*]
MCPC.......... Manipulator Combat Power Conditioner (MCD)
MCPC.......... Musee Canadien de la Photographie Contemporaine [*Canadian Museum of Contemporary Photography - CMCP*]
MCPC.......... Parks Canada [*Parcs Canada*] Churchill, Manitoba [*Library symbol National Library of Canada*] (NLC)
MCPC.......... Polaroid Corp. Library, Cambridge, MA [*Library symbol*] [*Library of Congress*] (LCLS)
MCPD .... Marine Corps Procurement District
MCPDM .... Marine Corps Program Decision Meeting (DOMA)

MCPDP........ Meander Channels Plasma Display Panel (IAA)
MCPE.......... Modular Collective Protection Equipment (RDA)
MCPER .... Multiple Critical-Pole Equal-Ripple Rational (MCD)
MCPESCF .... Multiconfiguration Paired Excitation Self-Consistent Field [*Physics*]
MCPF.......... Modular Containerless Processing Facility (SSD)
MCPG .... Multichannel Peak Factor (IAA)
MCPG .... Media Conversion Program Generator
MCPG .... Methycarboxyphenglycine [*Biochemistry*]
MCPH .... Metacarpophalangeal [*Anatomy*]
MCPH .... Ministry of Concern for Public Health (EA)
McPherson... McPherson, Lee, and Bell's Scotch Session Cases [*A publication*] (DLA)
MCPI.......... Medical Consumer Price Index (DHSM)
MCPJ.......... Metacarpal Phalangeal [*Medicine*] (STED)
MCPL.......... Magnetic Circularly Polarized Luminescence [*Spectroscopy*]
MCPL.......... Members of Congress for Peace through Law [*An association*]
MCPL.......... Middle Country Public Library [*New York*]
MCPL.......... Multiple-Cue Probability Learning [*Psychology*]
MCPM......... Marine Corps Personnel Manual (SAA)
MCPM......... Member of the Confederation of Professional Management [*British*] (DBQ)
MCPM......... Moncalcium Phosphate Monohydrate [*Inorganic chemistry*]
MCPO .... Master Chief Petty Officer [*Navy*]
MCPO .... Military Committee Representative Communication to the Private Office of the NATO Secretary General (NATG)
MCPOC .... Master Chief Petty Officer of Command [*Navy*]
MCPOF .... Master Chief Petty Officer of the Fleet [*or Force*] (DNAB)
MCPON .... Master Chief Petty Officer of the Navy
mCPP .... M-Chlorophenylpiperazine [*Organic chemistry*]
MCPP .... Mecoprop [*Herbicide*]
MCPPR .... Marine Corps Program Progress Report
MCPQ .... Municipal Code of the Province of Quebec [*A publication*] (DLA)
MCPR .... Maximum Critical Power Ratio [*Nuclear energy*] (NRCH)
MCPR .... Minimum Critical Power Ratio [*Nuclear energy*] (NRCH)
MC/PRI .... Major Claimant/Priority Rating Indicator (MCD)
MCPS.......... Major Cost Proposal System (MCD)
MCPS.......... Mechanical Copyright Protection Society [*British*]
MCPS.......... Megachips per Second (MCD)
MCPS.......... Megacycles per Second [*Megahertz*] [*See also MC/S, MCS, MH, MHz*]
mcps.......... Megacycles per Second (STED)
MCPS.......... Member of the Cambridge Philosophical Society (ROG)
MCPS.......... Member of the College of Physicians and Surgeons [*British*]
MCPS.......... Military Committee in Permanent Session [*NATO*] (NATG)
MCPS.......... Mini Core Processing Subsystem (TEL)
MCPS.......... Missouri Children's Picture Series [*Child development test*] [*Psychology*]
MCPS.......... Montgomery County Public Schools [*Maryland*]
MCPT.......... Maritime Central Planning Team [*NATO*] (NATG)
MCPTM....... Monte Carlo Particle Trajectory Model [*Physics*]
MCPU......... Master Controller Processor Unit (MCD)
MCPU......... Multiple Central Processing Unit
MCQ.......... Macquarie Island [*Australia Seismograph station code, US Geological Survey*] (SEIS)
Mcq .... Macqueen's Scotch Appeal Cases, House of Lords [*A publication*] (DLA)
MCQ.......... Memory Call Queue [*Computer science*] (IAA)
MCQ.......... Multiple Choice Questions (ADA)
MCQC .... Musicassette Quality Committee (NTCM)
MCQP .... Milk Carton Quality Performing Council (EA)
McQuillin Mun Corp... McQuillin on Municipal Corporations [*A publication*] (DLA)
MCR............ Magistrates' Court Reports [*New Zealand*] [*A publication*] (DLA)
MCR............ Magnetic Card Reader [*Computer science*]
MCR............ Magnetic Character Reader [*Computer science*] (IEEE)
MCR............ Magnetic Character Recognition [*Computer science*] (BUR)
MCR............ Magnetic Confinement Reactor
MCR............ Main Control Room (IEEE)
MCR............ Maintenance Control Report
MCR............ Management Coaching Relations Test
MCR............ Management Control Review (AAGC)
MCR............ Manpower Control Report
MCR............ Manual Change Request (MSA)
MCR............ Manufacturing Change Request
MCR............ Marine Corps Representative (SAA)
MCR............ Marine Corps Reserve
MCR............ Master Change Record
MCR............ Master Clock Receiver
MCR............ Master Control Record System (AABC)
MCR............ Master Control Register
MCR............ Master Control Relay [*Manufacturing term*]
MCR............ Master Control Room (MCD)
MCR............ Master Control Routine
MCR............ Master of Comparative Religion
M Cr .... Master of Criminology
MCR............ Matrimonial Causes Rules [*A publication*] (DLA)
MCR............ Maximum Combat Readiness [*Military*]
MCR............ Maximum Continuous Rating [*Also, MC(S)R*] [*Mechanical engineering*]
MCR............ McCloud River Railroad Co. [*AAR code*]
MCR............ Medical Corps, General Service [*USNR officer designation*]
MCR............ Medical Corps Reserve [*Military*] (DAVI)
MCR............ Mediterranean Communications Region [*Air Force*] (MCD)
MCR............ Melanocortin Receptor [*Biochemistry*]
MCR............ Memory Control Register

MCR............ Mercer [*Alaska*] [*Seismograph station code, US Geological Survey Closed*] (SEIS)
MCR............ Message Competition Ratio (MAE)
MCR............ Metabolic Clearance Rate
MCR............ Methodists for Church Renewal
MCR............ Metronome-Conditioned Relaxation
MCR............ MFS Charter Income Tr [*NYSE symbol*] (TTSB)
MCR............ MFS Charter Income Trust [*NYSE symbol*] (SPSG)
McR............ Micrecord Sales Corp., Chicago, IL [*Library symbol Library of Congress*] (LCLS)
MCR............ Micro
MCR............ Microcarbon Residue [*Petroleum analysis*]
MCR............ Micrographic Catalog Retrieval
MCR............ Micron Industries Ltd. [*Vancouver Stock Exchange symbol*]
MCR............ Military Characteristics Requirement (MCD)
MCR............ Military Command Region (MCD)
MCR............ Military Compact Reactor
MCR............ Mine Clearing Roller [*Military*] (INF)
MCR............ Minimum Cell Rate [*Telecommunications*] (ACRL)
MCR............ Minuteman Change Request [*Air Force*] (IAA)
MCR............ Missed Contact Rate (CAAL)
MCR............ Missile Clock Receiver
MCR............ Missile Computer Room
MCR............ Mission Control Room [*Space Flight Operations Facility, NASA*]
MCR............ Mission Control Routine [*NASA*]
MCR............ Mobile Control Room (DEN)
MCR............ Mobilization Contracting Requirement (AFIT)
MCR............ Modified Community Rating
MCR............ Monacair-Agusta [*Monaco*] [*ICAO designator*] (FAAC)
MCR............ Montreal Condensed Reports [*A publication*] (DLA)
MCR............ Mother-Child Relationship [*Psychology*]
MCR............ Motor Conduction Velocity (DB)
MCR............ Multichannel Receiver
MCR............ Multi-Contact Relay (IAA)
MCR............ Multispectral Cloud Radiometer (MCD)
MCR............ Myotonia Congenita, Recessive Type [*Medicine*] (DMAA)
MCR............ Radcliffe College, Cambridge, MA [*Library symbol Library of Congress*] (LCLS)
MCR............ University of Minnesota Technical College, Crookston, MN [*OCLC symbol*] (OCLC)
MCRA......... Member of the College of Radiologists Australasia
MCRA......... Mitomycin C Resistance Protein A
McRae........ McRae Industries, Inc. [*Associated Press*] (SAG)
MCR-Ar....... Radcliffe College, Archives, Cambridge, MA [*Library symbol Library of Congress*] (LCLS)
MCRB........ Magnetic Compass Record Book
MCRB........ Market Compilation and Research Bureau, Inc. [*North Hollywood, CA*] [*Information service or system*] (IID)
MCRB........ Military Cost Review Board (MCD)
MCRB........ Motor Carrier Rate Bureau
MCRBBS...... Marine Corps Reserve Bulletin Board System (DOMA)
MCRBIO...... Microbiology
MCRBLGY... Microbiology
M Cr C........ Madras Criminal Cases [*A publication*] (DLA)
MCRC........ Marine Corps Recruiting Command
MCRC........ Marketing Communications Research Center [*Later, CMC*]
MCRC........ Master Component Rework Capability (MCD)
McRC........ Microfilm Recording Co., Weston, ON, Canada [*Library symbol Library of Congress*] (LCLS)
MCRD........ Marine Corps Recruit Depot
MCRD........ Marine Corps Requirements Document (MCD)
MCRDAC...... Marine Corps Research, Development, and Acquisition Command [*Quantico, VA*] (GRD)
MCRDEP..... Marine Corps Recruit Depot
MCRDT....... Microdata
McRe......... Micrecord Sales Corp., Lombard, IL [*Library symbol*] [*Library of Congress*] (LCLS)
MCRE......... Mother-Child Relationship Evaluation [*Psychology*]
MCREGIS..... Motor Carrier Regulation Information System [*BTS*] (TAG)
MCREL....... Mid-Continent Regional Educational Laboratory [*Aurora, CO*] [*Department of Education*]
MCRELCTRNC... Microelectronic
MCREP....... Military Committee Representative [*to the North Atlantic Council*] (AABC)
MCRF......... Master Cross-Reference File
MCRFCH...... Microfiche
MCRH........ Main Control Room Habitability [*Nuclear energy*] (NRCH)
MCRHS....... Main Control Room Habitability System [*Nuclear energy*] (NRCH)
MCRHS....... Mid-Continent Railway Historical Society (EA)
MCRI......... Cambridge Research Institute, Inc., Cambridge, MA [*Library symbol Library of Congress*] (LCLS)
MCRI......... Marine Craft Radio Installation
MCRI......... Microcirculation Research Institute [*Texas A & M University*] [*Research center*] (RCD)
MCRI......... Monarch Casino & Resort [*NASDAQ symbol*] (SAG)
MCRI......... Multifactorial Cardiac Risk Index [*Cardiology*] (DMAA)
MCRIB........ Naval Communications Improvement Review Board (DNAB)
MCrim........ Master of Criminology (GAGS)
MCRL......... Mapping and Charting Research Laboratory [*Ohio State University*] (MCD)
MCRL......... Marine Corrosion Research Laboratory [*Navy*] (PDAA)
MCRL......... Master Component Repair List
MCRL......... Master Cross-Reference List
MCRL......... Material Cross-Reference List (MCD)
MCRL......... Micrel, Inc. [*NASDAQ symbol*] (SAG)

MCRML........ Midcontinental Regional Medical Library Program [*University of Nebraska*] [*Library network*] (IID)
MCRMLP ..... Midcontinental Regional Medical Library Program [*McGoogan Library of Medicine*] [*Information service or system*] (IID)
MCRN .... Macaroni
MCRN .... Micronics Computers [*NASDAQ symbol*] (SPSG)
MCRN .... Moscow City Relay Network
MCR (NZ) .... Magistrates' Court Reports (New Zealand) [*A publication*] (ILCA)
MCROA....... Marine Corps Reserve Officers Association (EA)
MCROC....... Marine Corps Recruit Option Center
MCROSCPY... Microscopy
MCRP .... Maritime Coal, Railway & Power Co. Ltd.. [*AAR code*]
MCRP .... Master of City and Regional Planning (GAGS)
MCRR .... Machine Check Recording and Recovery [*Computer science*]
MCRR .... Maine Central Road Railroad (MHDB)
MCRR .... Marine Corps Reserve Ribbon
MCRR .... [*The*] Monongahela Connecting Railroad Co. [*AAR code*]
MCRRCMPTR... Microcomputer
MCRRD .... Marine Corps Reserve/Recruitment District
MCRS .... Maintenance Computing and Recording System
MCRS .... Marine Corps Recruiting Station
MCRS .... Material Condition Reporting System
MCRS .... Micrographic Catalog Retrieval System
MCRS .... Micros Systems, Inc. [*NASDAQ symbol*] (NQ)
MCR-S .... Radcliffe College, Schlesinger Library, Cambridge, MA [*Library symbol Library of Congress*] (LCLS)
MCRSC .... Marine Corps Reserve Support Center
MCRSS .... Marine Corps Recruiting Substation
MCRT......... Mean Cell Retention Time (GNE)
MCRT......... Multichannel Rotary Transformer [*Electronics*]
MCRU .... Medical Care Research Unit [*University of Sheffield*] [*British*] (ECON)
MCRU .... Mobile Control and Reporting Unit (IAA)
MCRV .... Manned Command/Reconnaissance Vehicle
Mcrvsn....... Microvision, Inc. [*Associated Press*] (SAG)
MCRWV ...... Microwave (AAG)
MCS .... Harvard University, Monographic Cataloging Support Service, Cambridge, MA [*OCLC symbol*] (OCLC)
MCS........... MacCartney Clan Society (EA)
MCS........... Machine Cancel Society (EA)
MCS........... Macmillan's Commercial Series [*A publication*]
MCS........... Madras Civil Service [*British*]
MCS........... Magnetic Card Selecting (DNAB)
MCS........... Magnetic Coupling System (MCD)
MCS........... Main Compution System
MCS........... Main Control Station [*Nuclear energy*] (IAA)
MCS........... Maintenance and Checkout Station [*NASA*] (NASA)
mcs........... Maintenance and Checkout Station (NAKS)
MCS........... Maintenance Control Section [*DCE*]
MCS........... Maintenance Control System [*NASA*] (IAA)
MCS........... Maintenance Cost System (MCD)
MCS........... Major Component Schedule (AAG)
MCS........... Malayan Civil Service
MCS........... Management Control System (MCD)
MCS........... Maneuver Control System [*Computer science*]
MCS........... Manpower Consultative Service [*Canada*] (PDAA)
MCS........... Manufacturing and Consulting Services (PCM)
MCS........... Manufacturing Control System
MCS........... Mapping Camera System
MCS........... [*The*] Marcus Corp. [*NYSE symbol*] (SPSG)
MCS........... Marcus Island [*Japan*] [*Seismograph station code, US Geological Survey*] (SEIS)
MCS........... Marine Casualty Statistics (OA)
MCS........... Marine Conservation Society [*British*]
MCS........... Marine Cooks and Stewards Union
MCS........... Marine Corps School [*Quantico, VA*]
MCS........... Marine Corps Station
MCS........... Marine Corps Supply Activity [*Obsolete*]
MCS........... Maritime Communication Subsystem [*INTELSAT/INMARSAT*]
MCS........... Mass Casualty Supplement [*Military*]
MCS........... Mast Check System
MCS........... Mast Connection System (SAA)
MCS........... Master Circuit System
MCS........... Master Composite Specification (MCD)
MCS........... Master Control Set (IAA)
MCS........... Master Control Station (NRCH)
MCS........... Master Control System [*or Subsystem*]
MCS........... Master of Clinical Science (PGP)
MCS........... Master of Commercial Science
MCS........... Master of Communication Studies (PGP)
MCS........... Master of Computer Science (WGA)
MCS........... Material Control System (AAEL)
MCS........... Mathematical Code System
MCS........... Maximal Compatible Set (PDAA)
MCS........... McChip Resources, Inc. [*Toronto Stock Exchange symbol*]
MCS........... Mean Crew Size (MCD)
MCS........... Measurements Calibration System (KSC)
mcs........... Measurements Calibration System (NAKS)
MCS........... Mechanical Control System [*Aviation*]
MCS........... Mechanized Characteristics Screening
MCS........... Medical Computer Services (IEEE)
MCS........... Medical Consultant Staff [*Social Security Administration*] (OICC)
MCS........... Medical Corps, Special Service [*USNR officer designation*]
MCS........... Medium Close Shot [*Photography*] (ADA)
MCS........... Megacycles per Second [*Megahertz*] [*See also MCPS, MH, MHz*]
MCS........... Meridian Control Signal

MCS............ Mesocaval Shunt [*Medicine*] (DMAA)
MCS............ Mesoscale Convective System [*Meteorology*]
MCS............ Message Control Supervisor [*Computer science*] (MHDI)
MCS............ Message Control System [*Burroughs Corp.*] [*Computer science*] (BUR)
MCS............ Meter-Candle Second
MCS............ Method of Constant Stimuli [*Psychophysics*]
MCS............ Methylcholanthrene[*Induced*] Sarcoma [*Medicine*] (DB)
MCS............ Metropolitan Communications Squadron [*British military*] (DMA)
MCS............ Microcirculatory Society (EA)
MCS............ Microcirculatory Society of America (NTPA)
MCS............ Microclimatic Cooling System [*Army*] (DWSG)
MCS............ Microcomputer System
MCS............ Microculture and Sensitivity [*Microbiology*] (DAVI)
McS............. Micromation Systems, Inc., Feasterville, PA [*Library symbol Library of Congress*] (LCLS)
MCS............ Microprocessor Communications System (MCD)
MCS............ Microprogram Certification System (MHDB)
MCS............ Microsoft Consulting Services (CDE)
MCS............ Microwave Carrier Supply
MCS............ Microwave Communication System
MCS............ Milestone Car Society (EA)
MC's........... Military Characteristics [*Technical specification document for nuclear bombs and warheads*]
MCS............ Military Communications Stations
MCS............ Miller Communications Systems Ltd. [*Telecommunications service*] (TSSD)
MCS............ Mine Countermeasures Ship [*Navy symbol*]
MCS............ Mine Countermeasure Support [*Obsolete Military*]
MCS............ Mini-Computer Systems Inc. (NITA)
MCS............ Mini Conference System (PDAA)
MCS............ Minimal Cut Set [*Engineering*]
MCS............ Minimum Chi-Square
MCS............ Missile Calibration Station
MCS............ Missile Checkout Set (AAG)
MCS............ Missile Checkout Station
MCS............ Missile Commit Sequence (AAG)
MCS............ Missile Compensating System
MCS............ Missile Controller Set
MCS............ Missile Control System
MCS............ Missionary Sisters of the Sacred Side (TOCD)
MCS............ Mission Control Segment (SSD)
MCS............ Mitochondrial Capsule Selenoprotein [*Biochemistry*]
MCS............ Mixture Control Solenoid [*Automotive engineering*]
MCS............ Mobile Calibration Station (IAA)
MCS............ Mobile Checkout Station (AAG)
MCS............ Mobile Communications System (MCD)
MCS............ Mobile Computer System
MCS............ Model-Controlled System [*NASA*]
MCS............ Modular Composition System [*Diskettes*]
MCS............ Modular Computer System (IEEE)
MCS............ Modulation-Controlled Synchronization (IAA)
MCS............ Moisture Control System (DB)
MCS............ Monitor and Control Software [*FAA*] (TAG)
MCS............ Monitor and Control Subsystem
MCS............ Monitor and Control System [*Deep Space Instrumentation Facility, NASA*]
MCS............ Monte Carlo Simulation [*Computer science*] (IAA)
MCS............ Monte Caseros [*Argentina*] [*Airport symbol*] (AD)
MCS............ Motor Circuit Switch
MCS............ Movements Control Section [*British military*] (DMA)
MCS............ Multi-Channel Communications Software (NITA)
MCS............ Multichannel Communication System (IAA)
MCS............ Multichannel Scaling [*Mode*]
MCS............ Multichannel Seismology [*Geophysics*]
MCS............ Multichannel Switch (IAA)
MCS............ Multichannel System (IAA)
MCS............ Multi-Console System (NITA)
MCS............ Multidirectional Category System
MCS............ Multimedia Conference Service [*Telecommunications*] (CDE)
MCS............ Multiple Character Set (CMD)
MCS............ Multiple Chemical Sensitivities [*Medicine*]
MCS............ Multiple Column Selector (IAA)
MCS............ Multiple Combined Sclerosis [*Medicine*] (DB)
MCS............ Multiple Compression Shear (OA)
MCS............ Multiple Computer System
MCS............ Multiple Console Support [*Fujitsu Ltd.*] [*Computer science*] (MCD)
MCS............ Multiplexer Computer Systems (MCD)
MCS............ Multiprogrammed Computer System (IEEE)
MCS............ Multipurpose Communications and Signaling
MCS............ Multivendor Customer Service [*Computer science*] (CDE)
MCS............ Music Construction Set [*Computer program designed by Will Harvey and published by Electronic Arts*]
MCS............ Myocardial Contractile State [*Cardiology*] (MAE)
MCS............ Residential Model Conservation Standard [*Pacific Northwest Electric Power and Conservation Planning Council*] [*Portland, OR*] (EGAO)
MCSA.......... Marble Collectors Society of America (EA)
MCSA.......... Marine Corps Supply Activity [*Obsolete*] (NVT)
MCSA.......... Meritorious Civilian Service Award
MCSA.......... Methuen's Commercial Series [*A publication*]
MCSA.......... Metropolitan Church Schoolmasters' Association [*A union*] [*British*]
MCSA.......... Microcomputer Software Association - of ADAPSO [*Association of Data Processing Service Organizations*] (EA)
MCSA.......... Midwest Collegiate Sailing Association

MCSA.......... Military Construction Supply Agency [*Later, Defense Construction Supply Center*]
MCSA.......... Minimal Cross-Sectional Area [*Radiology*] (DAVI)
MCSA.......... Moloney Cell Surface Antigen [*Medicine*] (DMAA)
MCSA.......... Moscow, Camden & San Augustine Railroad [*AAR code*]
MCSA.......... Motor Carrier Safety Act of 1984 [*FHWA*] (TAG)
MCSA.......... Multichannel Spectrum Analyzer [*Instrumentation*]
MCS-A........ Multi-Functional Communications System - Asynchronous (HGAA)
MCSA.......... Smithsonian Institution, Astrophysical Observatory, Cambridge, MA [*Library symbol Library of Congress*] (LCLS)
MCSAP .... Motor Carrier Safety Assistance Program [*Department of Transportation*]
MCSB.......... Motor Carriers Service Bureau
MCSC.......... Magdalen College School Cadets [*British military*] (DMA)
MCSC.......... Marine Corps Supply Center
MC Sc......... Master of Commercial Science
MC Sc......... Master of Computer Science (PGP)
MCSC.......... Materiel Category Structure Code [*Military*]
MCSC.......... Medical College of South Carolina
MCSC.......... Metropolitan Collegiate Swimming Conference (PSS)
MCSC.......... Miami Computer Supply Corp. [*NASDAQ symbol*] (SAG)
MCSC.......... Model Codes Standardization Council [*Defunct*]
MCSC.......... Movement Control Sub-Committee [*IATA*] (DS)
MCSCF........ Multiconfigurational Self-Consistent Field [*Chemical physics*]
MCSCF........ Multiconfiguration Self-Consistent Field [*Physical chemistry*]
MCS/CHS .... Maneuver Control System / Common Hardware System [*Computer science*]
MCSD.......... Marine Corps Supply Depot (MUGU)
MCSDS .... Marlowe-Crowne Social Desirability Scale [*Medicine*] (DMAA)
MC Se .... Master of Commercial Service
MCSE.......... Master of Computer Science and Engineering (GAGS)
MCSE.......... Minimum Critical Size of Ecosystem [*Project*]
MCSEE........ Member of the Canadian Society of Electrical Engineers (DI)
M-CSF .... Macrophage-Colony Stimulating Factor [*Biochemistry*]
MCSF.......... Marine Corps Security Force (DNAB)
MCSF.......... Mobile Cryptologic Support Facility (DOMA)
MCSG.......... Mildly Context-Sensitive Grammar [*Artificial intelligence*]
MCSGX........ Mainstay Government Fund [*Mutual fund ticker symbol*] (SG)
MCSH.......... Maryville College of the Sacred Heart [*Missouri*]
MC Shp........ MC Shipping, Inc. [*Associated Press*] (SAG)
MCSI.......... Mark Solutions [*NASDAQ symbol*] (TTSB)
MCSI.......... Mark Solutions, Inc. [*NASDAQ symbol*] (SAG)
MCSI.......... Member of the Construction Surveyors' Institute [*British*] (DBQ)
MCSJM........ Congregation of Missionary Catechists of the Sacred Heart of Jesus and Mary (TOCD)
MCSL.......... Management Control Systems List [*DoD*]
MCSL.......... Marine Corps Stock [*or Supply*] Lists
MCSM.......... Master of Construction Science/Management (PGP)
MCSMAW .... Marine Corps Shoulder-Launched Multipurpose Assault Weapon (MCD)
MCSO.......... Marine Corps Special Orders (SAA)
MCSOII .... Multiple-Cause, Systems-Oriented Incident Investigation [*Engineering*]
MCSP.......... Maintenance Control and Statistics Process [*Telecommunications*] (TEL)
MCSP.......... Member of the Chartered Society of Physiotherapists [*British*]
MCSP.......... Mission Completion Success Probability (MCD)
MCSP.......... Multiple Conductor, Shielded, Pressure-Resistant [*Cable*]
McSPI......... Multicenter Study of Perioperative Ischemia
MCSR.......... Material Condition Status Report [*Military*]
MC(S)R........ Maximum Continuous (Service) Rating [*Also, MCR*] [*Mechanical engineering*]
MCSR.......... Motor Carrier Safety Regulations [*Department of Transportation*]
MCSRP .... Management Control Systems Research Project (SAA)
MCSS.......... Marine Climatological Summaries Scheme [*World Meteorological Organization*] [*United Nations*] (DUND)
MCSS.......... Mechanical Circulatory Support System
MCSS.......... Microscopic Camera Subsystem (KSC)
MCSS.......... Military Clothing Sales Store
MCSS.......... Military Communications Satellite System
MCSS.......... Mine Countermeasure Support Ship [*Military*] (PDAA)
MCSS.......... Missile Checkout System Selector
MCSS.......... Monitor and Control Subsystem [*Deep Space Instrumentation Facility, NASA*]
MCSSB .... Manufacturers Council of Small School Buses (NTPA)
MCSSCCJM... Missionary Catechists of the Sacred Hearts of Jesus and Mary (TOCD)
MCSSD .... Mobile Combat Service Support Detachment (DOMA)
MCSSG .... Military Committee Special Study Group [*NATO*] (NATG)
MCSSQT ...... Modified Combat System Ship Qualification Trial [*Navy*] (CAAL)
MCSST......... Multichannel Sea Surface Temperature [*Algorithms for oceanography*]
MCSST......... Multi-Channel SST [*Sea Surface Temperature*] (USDC)
MCST.......... Magnetic Card ™Selectric∫ Typewriter [*IBM Corp.*]
MCST.......... Member of the College of Speech Therapists [*British*]
MCST.......... Ministerial Committee on Science and Technology [*South Africa*]
MCSTB......... Motor Carriers Service Tariff Bureau
MCSTSC ...... Military Communications System Technical Standards Committee [*Army*] (AABC)
MCSU.......... Management Consultation Services Unit [*LIMRA*]
MCSU.......... Maximum Card Study Unit (EA)
MCSW .... Mining Club of the Southwest (EA)
MCSW .... Motor Circuit Switch (MSA)
MCSWG .... Multinational Command Systems Working Group (NATG)
MCSX.......... Managed Care Solutions [*NQS*] (TTSB)

MCSX.........	Managed Care Solutions, Inc. [*NASDAQ symbol*] (SAG)
MCSY.........	Medic Computer Systems [*NASDAQ symbol*] (TTSB)
MCSY.........	Medic Computer Systems, Inc. [*NASDAQ symbol*] (SAG)
MCSYSCOM...	Marine Corps System Command (DOMA)
MCT.........	Magnetically-Coupled Transformer (IAA)
MCT.........	Magnetic Card and Tape Unit (IAA)
MCT.........	Magnetic Character Typewriter (PDAA)
MCT.........	Magnetic Compass Table (DNAB)
MCT.........	Magnetic Core Tape
MCT.........	Magnetic Core Tester
MCT.........	Main Central Thrust [*Geophysics*]
MCT.........	Main Control Tank (MSA)
MCT.........	Mainstream Corporation Tax
MCT.........	Managed Change Technique [*Management*]
MCT.........	Manifold Charge Temperature [*Automotive engineering*]
MCT.........	MANPRINT [*Manpower and Personnel Integration*] Coordination Team [*Army*]
MCT.........	Mark Centers Trust [*NYSE symbol*] (SPSG)
MCT.........	Mass Culturing Technique [*Microbiology*]
MCT.........	Master of Christian Training
MCT.........	Mathematical Cuneiform Texts [*A publication*] (BJA)
MCT.........	Maximum Climb Thrust (NASA)
MCT.........	Maximum Continuous Thrust [*Aviation*]
MCT.........	Maxwell Color Triangle
MCT.........	Mean Cell [*or Corpuscular*] Thickness [*Hematology*]
MCT.........	Mean Cell [*or Corpuscular*] Threshold [*Hematology*] (MAE)
MCT.........	Mean Circulation Time [*Medicine*]
MCT.........	Mean Corpuscular Thickness [*Hematology*] (CPH)
MCT.........	Mean Corrective-Maintenance Time (MCD)
MCT.........	Mean Correct Time
MCT.........	Mechanical Comprehension Test
MCT.........	Medial Canthal Tendon [*Medicine*] (DMAA)
MCT.........	Medium-Chain Triglyceride [*Biochemistry*]
MCT.........	Medullary Cancer of the Thyroid [*Medicine*]
MCT.........	Medullary Carcinoma of the Thyroid [*Medicine*] (AAMN)
MCT.........	Medullary Collecting Tubules [*Anatomy*]
MCT.........	Memory Cycle Time [*Computer science*] (MCD)
MCT.........	Mercury Cadmium Telluride [*Photodetector*]
MCT.........	Message Control Task [*Computer science*]
MCT.........	Metabolic Control Theory [*Biochemistry*]
MCT.........	Meta-Chlorotoluene [*Organic chemistry*]
MCT.........	Metal-Oxide-Controlled Thyristor (CIST)
MCT.........	Metric Color Tag [*Computer science*] (PCM)
MCT.........	Metrizamide Computed Tomography
MCT.........	Micro Component Technology Inc. (NITA)
MCT.........	Microstat Development Corp. [*Vancouver Stock Exchange symbol*]
MCT.........	Microtoxicity Test [*Medicine*] (DB)
MCT.........	Microwave Ceramic Triode
MCT.........	Mid-Cycle Test [*Army training*] (INF)
MCT.........	Military Command Technology (AAG)
MCT.........	Minimum Competency Test [*Education*]
MCT.........	Minimum Connecting Time [*Travel industry*]
MCT.........	Minnesota Clerical Test
MCT.........	Missile Compensating Tank
MCT.........	Mission Control Table (MCD)
MCT.........	Mobile Communication Terminal
MCT.........	Mobile Contact Teams [*Military*] (AABC)
MCT.........	Mode Coupling Theory [*Physics*]
MCT.........	Modified Clinical Technique [*Medicine*]
MCT.........	Moment to Change Trim (DS)
MCT.........	Monochlorotriazine [*Organic chemistry*]
MCT.........	Mouse Colon Tumor [*Pathology*]
MCT.........	Movable Core Transformer [*Nuclear energy*]
MCT.........	Movement Control Team [*Air Force*] (AFM)
MCT.........	Mucociliary Transport [*Physiology*]
MCT.........	Multicell Test (MCD)
MCT.........	Multiple Compressed Tablet [*Pharmacy*]
MCT.........	Multistrip Cesium Thrustor
MCT.........	Muscat [*Oman*] [*Airport symbol*] (OAG)
MCT.........	United States Department of Transportation, Technical Information Center, Cambridge, MA [*Library symbol Library of Congress*] (LCLS)
MCTA.........	Metropolitan Commuter Transportation Authority [*Greater New York City*] [*Later, Metropolitan Transportation Authority*]
MCTA.........	Motor Carriers Tariff Association
MCTA.........	Motor Carriers Traffic Association
MCTA.........	Multiple-Cycle Transient Analysis [*Chemistry*]
MCTAS.........	Military/Commercial Transport Aircraft Simulation (PDAA)
MCTB.........	Motor Carriers Tariff Bureau (EA)
MCTC.........	Maritime Cargo Transportation Conference [*of MTRB*]
MCTC.........	Metrizamide Computed Tomography Cisternography [*Medicine*] (DMAA)
MCTC.........	Metropolitan Collegiate Tennis Conference (PSS)
MCTC.........	Movimiento Campesino Tupaj Catari [*Bolivia*] [*Political party*] (PPW)
MCTD.........	Medium Capacity Bomb with Temporary Delay Fuse [*British military*] (DMA)
MCTD.........	Mixed Connective Tissue Disease [*Medicine*]
MCTF.........	Monouclear Cell Tissue Factor [*Medicine*] (DB)
MCTFIST.....	Marine Corps Tank Full-Crew Interactive Simulator Trainer
MCTFL.........	Minnesota Council on the Teaching of Foreign Languages (EDAC)
MCTG.........	Model Change Training Guide
MCTH.........	MedCath, Inc. [*NASDAQ symbol*] (SAG)
MCTI.........	Metal Cutting Tool Institute (EA)
MCTI.........	Micro Component Tech [*NASDAQ symbol*] (TTSB)
MCTI.........	Micro Component Technology, Inc. [*NASDAQ symbol*] (SAG)

MCTL.........	Mediterranean Contingency Target List (MCD)
MCTL.........	Microtel Franchise&Development [*NASDAQ symbol*] (TTSB)
MCTL.........	Microtel Franchise & Development Corp. [*NASDAQ symbol*] (NQ)
MCTL.........	Microtel International, Inc. [*NASDAQ symbol*] (SAG)
MCTL.........	Militarily Critical Technology List [*DoD*]
MCTLA.........	Motor Car Traders' Licensing Authority [*Victoria, Australia*]
MCTNS.........	Manportable Cannon Thermal Night Sight (MCD)
MCTP.........	Missile Control Test Panel
MCTR.........	Mackinac Transportation Co. [*AAR code*]
MCTR.........	Message Center
MCTRAP.........	Mechanized Customer Trouble Report Analysis Plan [*Telecommunications*] (TEL)
MCTS.........	Master Central Timing System [*NASA*]
MCTS.........	Ministerial Correspondence Tracking System [*Australia*]
MCTS.........	Motor Carriers Tariff Service (EA)
MCTSA.........	Military Clothing and Textile Supply Agency [*Merged with Defense Supply Agency*] [*Army*]
MCTSE.........	Marine Corps Test Support Element (MCD)
MCTSSA......	Marine Corps Tactical Systems and Support Activity [*Camp Pendleton, CA*] (GRD)
MCTT.........	Metal-Ceramic Transmitting Tube
MCTV.........	Man-Carrying Test Vehicle (MCD)
MCTV.........	Manhattan Cable TV, Inc. [*New York, NY*] [*Telecommunications*] (TSSD)
MCU.........	Machine Control Unit
MCU.........	Machine Tool Control Unit (IAA)
MCU.........	Magma Copper Co. [*NYSE symbol*] (SPSG)
MCU.........	Magnetic Card Unit [*Computer science*] (IAA)
MCU.........	Main Control Unit (IAA)
MCU.........	Maintenance Communications Unit [*Environmental science*] (COE)
MCU.........	Maintenance Control Unit [*Computer science*]
MCU.........	Major Crime Unit [*Elite police squad on television series "Crime Story"*]
MCU.........	Malaria Control Unit [*Army World War II*]
MCU.........	Management Control Unit (PDAA)
MCU.........	Manual Control Unit
MCU.........	Marble Collectors Unlimited (EA)
MCU.........	Master Clock Unit
MCU.........	Master Control Unit
mcu.........	Master Control Unit [*NASA*] (NAKS)
MCU.........	Maximum Care Unit [*Medicine*]
MCU.........	Measurement Control Unit (IAA)
MCU.........	Median Control Unit (WDAA)
MCU.........	Mediterranean Coordination Unit (GNE)
MCU.........	Medium Close Up [*A photograph or motion picture sequence taken from a relatively short distance*]
MCU.........	Memory Control Unit
MCU.........	Message Construction Unit
MCU.........	Microcomputer Control Unit
MCU.........	Microcontroller Control Unit (CDE)
MCU.........	Micro-Control Unit (NITA)
MCU.........	Microprocessor Control Unit
MCU.........	Microprogram Control Unit (NITA)
MCU.........	Microprogrammed Control Unit [*Navy*]
mcU.........	Microunit
MCU.........	Micturating Cystourethrography [*Medicine*] (DMAA)
MCU.........	Millicurie [*Also, mC, mCI*] (IAA)
MCU.........	Miniature Command Unit
MCU.........	Minicomputer Unit (IAA)
MCU.........	Mission Control Unit (MCD)
mcu.........	Mission Control Unit [*NASA*] (NAKS)
MCU.........	Mobile Calibration Unit (AAEL)
MCU.........	Mobile Care Unit [*Emergency medicine*] (DAVI)
MCU.........	Modern Churchmen's Union [*British*]
MCU.........	Modular Concept Unit (DA)
MCU.........	Monte Cristo Peak [*Utah*] [*Seismograph station code, US Geological Survey*] (SEIS)
MCU.........	Mosquito Conversion Unit [*British military*] (DMA)
MCU.........	Mountain Commando Units (CINC)
MCU.........	Multicoupler Unit [*Antenna*] [*Telecommunications*] (TEL)
MCU.........	Multiplexer Control Unit
MCU.........	Multipoint Control Unit [*Telecommunications*]
MCU.........	Multiprocessor Communications Unit
MCU.........	Multi-System Communications Unit (NITA)
MCU.........	Rochester, NY [*Location identifier FAA*] (FAAL)
MCUAF.......	Multi-Corp. [*NASDAQ symbol*] (TTSB)
MCUAF.......	Multi-Corp, Inc. [*NASDAQ symbol*] (SAG)
MCUB.........	Marine Corps Uniform Board [*Washington, DC*] (EGAO)
MCUG.........	Military Computers Users Group
MCUIS.........	Master Control and User Interface Software Subsystem [*Space Flight Operations Facility, NASA*]
MCUL.........	Missile Compartment, Upper Level
MCUMP.........	Multidisciplinary Center for Urban and Minority Problems [*Florida State University*] [*Research center Defunct*] (RCD)
MCUPA.......	Medical Committee Under the Poisons Act [*Australia*]
MCurrSt.....	Master of Curriculum Studies
MCurrStud.....	Master of Curriculum Studies
MCUSR.........	Memory Control Unit Special Register [*Computer science*] (MHDB)
MCV.........	Magnetic Cushion Vehicle (IEEE)
MCV.........	Manifold Control Valve [*Automotive engineering*]
MCV.........	Manufacturing Council of Victoria [*Australia*]
MCV.........	Maritime Commission, Victory Ship
MCV.........	Mean Cell [*or Corpuscular*] Volume [*Hematology*]
MCV.........	Mean Clinical Value (AAMN)
MCV.........	Mean Corpuscular Volume [*Physiology*]

MCV............	Measles-Containing Vaccine
MCV............	Mechanised Combat Vehicle [*British military*] (DMA)
MCV............	Median Cell Volume (DB)
MCV............	Medical Center of Virginia [*University of Virginia*]
MCV............	Mercury [*Nevada*] [*Seismograph station code, US Geological Survey*] (SEIS)
MCV.........	Mesabi Community College, Virginia, MN [*OCLC symbol*] (OCLC)
MCV.........	Mesoscale Convectively-Generated Vortices [*Marine science*] (OSRA)
MCV............	Method of Composition Velocity [*Physical chemistry*]
MCV............	Microbial Check Valve (PDAA)
MCV............	Molluscum Contagiosum Virus
MCV............	Motor Conduction Velocity (DMAA)
MCV............	Movable Closure Valve (NRCH)
MCV............	Muerto Canyon Virus [*Hantavirus strain*]
MCVD.........	Metal Chemical Vapor Deposition (AAEL)
MCVD.........	Modified Chemical Vapor Deposition [*Telecommunications*]
McVey Dig...	McVey's Ohio Digest [*A publication*] (DLA)
MCVF.........	Multichannel Voice Frequency [*Telecommunications*]
MCVFT........	Multichannel Voice Frequency Telegraphy [*Telecommunications*] (TEL)
MC-V(G)......	Medical Officers (Qualified for General Detail) [*USNR designation*]
MCVG........	Memory Character Vector Generator
MCVP..........	Materials Control and Verification Program [*NASA*] (NASA)
MCVS.........	Management and Cost Visibility System (SSD)
MC-V(S).......	Medical Officers (Qualified for Specialist Duties) [*USNR designation*]
MCW.........	Central Missouri State University, Warrensburg, MO [*OCLC symbol*] (OCLC)
MCW............	Mallinckrodt Chemical Works [*Later, Mallinckrodt, Inc.*]
MCW.........	Mason City [*Iowa*] [*Airport symbol*] (OAG)
MCW.........	Mason City, IA [*Location identifier FAA*] (FAAL)
MCW.........	McDonalds Corp. [*NYSE symbol*] (SAG)
MCW.........	Medical Corps, Women's Reserve [*USNR officer designation*]
MCW.........	Memory Card Writer [*Telecommunications*] (TEL)
MCW.........	Metal Casement Window [*Technical drawings*]
MCW.........	Metro-Cammell Weymaua Ltd. [*British*] (DCTA)
MCW.........	Mills, Clarence W., Laurel MD [*STAC*]
MCW.........	Modified Continuous Wave [*Telecommunications*] (IAA)
MCW.........	Modulated Carrier Wave [*Telecommunications*] (IAA)
MCW.........	Modulated Continuous Wave [*Radio signal transmission*]
mcw............	Modulated Continuous Wave (NAKS)
MCW.........	Mount Constitution [*Washington*] [*Seismograph station code, US Geological Survey*] (SEIS)
MCW.........	Weston School of Theology, Cambridge, MA [*Library symbol Library of Congress*] (LCLS)
MCWA	Malaria Control in War Areas [*Later, Centers for Disease Control*]
MCWA	Mid Continent Wildcatters Association [*Defunct*] (EA)
MCWCS	Ministerial Conference of West and Central African States on Maritime Transportation [*See also CMEAOC*] [*Abidjan, Ivory Coast*] (EAIO)
McWhrtr	McWhorter Technologies, Inc. [*Associated Press*] (SAG)
McWillie.......	McWillie's Reports [*73-76 Mississippi*] [*A publication*] (DLA)
MCWM........	Military Committee Working Memorandum (NATG)
MCWR	Marine Corps Women's Reserve
MCWU	Military Committee of Western European Union (NATG)
MCX............	Marine Corps Exchange
MCX............	MC Shipping [*AMEX symbol*] (TTSB)
MCX............	MC Shipping, Inc. [*AMEX symbol*] (SPSG)
MCX............	Michelin Capital Ltd. [*Toronto Stock Exchange symbol*]
MCX............	Minimum-Cost Expediting
MCX............	Monticello, IN [*Location identifier FAA*] (FAAL)
MCXD..........	Magnetic Circular X-Ray Dichroism [*Light polarization*]
MCXM..........	Marine Corps Exchange Manual (SAA)
MCXO	Microprocessor-Controlled Crystal Oscillator [*Hughes Aircraft Co.*] (ECON)
MCXSERV	Marine Corps Exchange Service Branch (DNAB)
MCY............	Machinery (IAA)
MCY............	Maroochydore [*Australia Airport symbol*] (OAG)
MCY............	Mercury General [*NYSE symbol*] (SAG)
MCY............	Mercury, NV [*Location identifier FAA*] (FAAL)
MCY............	Mount Calvery Resources Ltd. [*Vancouver Stock Exchange symbol*]
M/CYL........	Master Cylinder [*Automotive engineering*]
MCZ............	Maceio [*Brazil*] [*Airport symbol*] (OAG)
MCZ............	Magnetic Czochralski Process [*Crystallization*]
MCZ............	McDonald' Corp. 8.35% `QUIDS' [*NYSE symbol*] (TTSB)
MCZ............	McDonalds Corp. [*NYSE symbol*] (SAG)
MCZ............	Museum of Comparative Zoology [*Harvard University*] [*Research center*]
MCZ............	Williamston, NC [*Location identifier FAA*] (FAAL)
MCZDO	Multicenter Zero Differential Overlap [*Physics*]
MCZNE.........	Minimum When Control Zone Effective (FAAC)
MD...............	Air Madagascar [*ICAO designator*] (AD)
MD...............	Application for Writ of Mandamus Dismissed for Want of Jurisdiction [*Legal term*] (DLA)
MD...............	Biomedical Office [*Kennedy Space Center Directorate*] (NAKS)
MD...............	Delalande [*France*] [*Research code symbol*]
MD...............	Doctor of Medicine (PGP)
MD...............	La Maison-Dieu [*Paris*] [*A publication*] (BJA)
MD...............	Machine Dried Paper (DGA)
MD...............	Macro Data (IAA)
MD...............	Macro Directory [*Computer science*] (IAA)
MD...............	Macular Degeneration [*Ophthalmology*]
Md...............	Madinhae (BJA)
MD...............	Madres de los Desamparados [*Mothers of the Helpless*] [*Roman Catholic religious order*]
MD...............	Magnesium Deficiency [*Medicine*] (DMAA)

MD...............	Magnetic Deflection [*Cathode-ray tube*] (DEN)
MD...............	Magnetic Disk [*Computer science*] (BUR)
MD...............	Magnetic Drum
MD...............	Mail Drop (COE)
MD...............	Main Deck [*Naval engineering*]
MD...............	Main Droite [*With the Right Hand*] [*Music*]
MD...............	Main Drum (CET)
MD...............	Main Duct
MD...............	Maintainability Demonstration (MCD)
M/D.............	Maintenance/Development [*Effort ratio*]
MD...............	Maintenance Documentation [*Bell System*] (IAA)
MD...............	Maintenance Dose [*Medicine*]
M-D.............	Maiz Dulce [*Race of maize*]
MD...............	Make Directory [*Computer science*]
MD...............	Malate Dehydrogenase [*Also, MDH*] [*An enzyme*]
MD...............	Male Treated with DOC [*Deoxycorticosterone*]
MD...............	Malfunction Detection (NASA)
MD...............	Malic Dehydrogenase [*An enzyme*] (MAE)
MD...............	Management Data (MCD)
MD...............	Management Directive
MD...............	Management Division [*Environmental Protection Agency*] (GFGA)
MD...............	Managing Director
MD...............	Managment Domain [*Telecommunications*] (OSI)
M/D.............	Man Day
MD...............	Manic-Depressive
MD...............	Mano Destra [*With the Right Hand*] [*Music*]
MD...............	Mantoux Diameter (MAE)
MD...............	Manual Damper (OA)
MD...............	Manual Data
MD...............	Manual Direct (NASA)
MD...............	Manual Disconnect (MCD)
MD...............	Manu Dextra [*With the Right Hand*] [*Latin*]
MD...............	Map Distance (ADA)
MD...............	Marchand [*Merchant, Trader*] [*French*]
MD...............	Marek's Disease [*Avian pathology*]
MD...............	Marine Detachment
MD...............	Market Day [*British*]
MD...............	Marque Deposee [*Trademark*]
MD...............	Married
MD...............	Maryland [*Postal code*]
MD...............	Maryland Reports [*A publication*] (DLA)
Md...............	Maryland State Library, Annapolis, MD [*Library symbol Library of Congress*] (LCLS)
MD...............	Master Diagram (MCD)
MD...............	Master Dimension (NASA)
MD...............	Master Directory [*NASA Information service or system*] (IID)
MD...............	Master's Decisions (Patents) [*A publication*] (DLA)
MD...............	Match Dissolve [*Cinematography*] (WDMC)
MD...............	Materiel Developer [*Army*]
MD...............	Maternal Deprivation (MAE)
MD...............	Matrimonio Duxit [*Led into Matrimony*] [*Latin*] (ROG)
MD...............	Maturity Date [*Banking*]
MD...............	Maximum Degree Allowed to Fit
MD...............	Maximum Demand (IAA)
MD...............	Maximum Design Meter
MD...............	McDonnell Douglas [*NYSE symbol*] (TTSB)
MD...............	McDonnell Douglas Corp. [*NYSE symbol*] (SPSG)
MD...............	Mean Deviation
MD...............	Measured Depth [*Diamonds*]
MD...............	Measured Discard [*Nuclear energy*] (NRCH)
MD...............	Measured Drilling [*Diamonds*]
MD...............	Mechanical Diode [*Mechanical power transmission*]
Md...............	Median
MD...............	Mediastinal Disease [*Medicine*] (DB)
MD...............	Medical Department [*Army*]
MD...............	Medical Discharge [*from military service*]
MD...............	Medical Doctor
MD...............	Medicinae Doctor [*Doctor of Medicine*] [*Latin*]
M/D.............	Medicines/Drugs
MD...............	Mediodorsal [*Anatomy*]
MD...............	Medium Dosage [*Pharmacology*] (MAE)
MD...............	Medium Duty
MD...............	Megadalton
MD...............	Memorandum of Deposit [*Business term*]
MD...............	Memory Data Register (DNAB)
MD...............	Memory Decrement (MHDB)
Md...............	Mendelevium [*Preferred form, but also see Mv*] [*Chemical element*]
MD...............	Meniere's Disease [*Medicine*] (DMAA)
MD...............	Mentally Deficient
MD...............	Mentally Depressed [*Psychology*] (DB)
MD...............	Mentally Disabled (OICC)
md...............	Mercedarious Descalzos (TOCD)
MD...............	Mesiodistal [*Dentistry*]
Md...............	Mesoderm [*Botany*]
MD...............	Message Data
MD...............	Message Digest (ACRL)
MD...............	Message-Dropping [*Military*]
MD...............	Messages per Day
MD...............	Mess Deck [*Naval*]
MD...............	Metal Deactivator
MD...............	Metal Dome [*Watchmaking*] (ROG)
MD...............	Metals Disintegrating
MD...............	Metaphors Dictionary [*A publication*]
MD...............	Meteorology Department [*Navy*]
M/D.............	Meters per Day

MD	Methyldichloroarsine [*Poison gas*]
MD	Methyldopa [*Also, AMD*] [*Antihypertensive compound*]
MD	Metropolitan District [*British*]
MD	Microalloy Diffused
MD	Microdot (KSC)
MD	Microsoft DoubleSpace [*Computer science*] (PCM)
MD	Microwave Desorber [*Instrumentation*]
MD	Middle Deltoid [*Myology*]
MD	Middle Distillate [*Fuel technology*]
MD	Middle District (DLA)
MD	Middle Door [*Theater*]
MD	Middle Dutch [*Language, etc.*]
MD	Midnight Dumping (MHDW)
MD	Migrant with English Language Difficulty
MD	Mildly Diabetic
MD	Military District [*Former USSR*] (NATG)
mD	Millidarcy
MD	Millwall Dock [*British*]
MD	Mine Depot [*Naval*]
MD	Mine Disposal
MD	Mini Disk [*Audio/video technology*]
MD	Minimum Dosage [*Medicine*]
MD	Minute Difference
MD	Miscellaneous Direct (MCD)
MD	Miscellaneous Document
MD	Miss Distance [*Military*]
MD	Missile Division (AAG)
MD	Missile Driver
MD	Missionary Dentists [*An association*] (EA)
MD	Mission Day
MD	Mission Dependent
MD	Mission Deviation (MCD)
MD	Mission Director [*NASA*] (KSC)
MD	Mitral Disease [*Medicine*]
MD	Mixed Diet (DMAA)
MD	Mobile Depot [*Air Force*] (MCD)
MD	Mode [*Grammar*] (ROG)
MD	Moderate Dose [*Medicine*]
MD	Moderately Differentiated
MD	Modification Document (MCD)
MD	Modified Design [*Cordite*] [*British military*] (DMA)
MD	Modular Design
M-D	Modulation-Demodulation (HGAA)
M/D	Modulator-Demodulator [*Telecommunications*] (CET)
MD	Modulators [*JETDS nomenclature*] [*Military*] (CET)
MD	Moldova [*Internet country code*]
MD	Molecular Diameter
MD	Molecular Dynamics
MD	Money Down
MD	Monitor Displays [*Computer science*] (BUR)
MD	Monocular Deprivation [*Optics*]
MD	Monroe Doctrine
MD	Months after Date [*or Month's Date*] [*Business term*]
md	Months after Date (EBF)
md	Months' Date (EBF)
MD	Mood [*Grammar*] (ROG)
MD	More Dicto [*As Directed*] [*Pharmacy*]
M/D	Mother/Daughter [*Apartment*] (BARN)
MD	Mothers of the Helpless (TOCD)
MD	Motor Direct
MD	Motor Drive
MD	Movement Directive
MD	Movement Disorder (MAE)
MD	Multidimensional
MD	Multidomain [*Grains in rocks*] [*Geophysics*]
MD	Multinomial Distribution [*Statistics*]
MD	Multiple Deficiency [*Syndrome*] [*Medicine*] (DB)
MD	Multiple Dialyzer [*Chemical analysis*]
MD	Multiple Dissemination
MD	Multiply-Divide (IAA)
MD	Multipurpose Display (MCD)
MD	Municipal Docks Railway of the Jacksonville Port Authority [*AAR code*]
MD	Muscular Dystrophy [*Medicine*]
MD	Musicae Doctor [*Doctor of Music*] (ROG)
MD	Musical Director
MD	Music Director (NTCM)
MD	Myocardial Damage [*Cardiology*] (MAE)
MD	Myocardial Disease [*Cardiology*]
MD	Myotonic Dystrophy [*See also MyMD*] [*Medicine*]
MDA	Magen David Adom [*Israel's Red Cross Service*]
MDA	Magic Dealers Association [*Later, IMDA*]
MDA	Magnetic Deflection Amplifier
MDA	Main Distribution Assembly (NASA)
MDA	Maintainability Design Approach
MDA	Maintenance Data Analysis (MCD)
MDA	Maintenance Depot Assistance [*Air Force*] (AFM)
MDA	Maintenance Design Approach
MDA	Malfunction Detector Analyzer (PDAA)
MDA	Malondialdehyde [*Biochemistry*]
MDA	Management Development Adviser (AIE)
MDA	Mandarian Airlines [*ICAO designator*] (FAAC)
MDA	Manic-Depressive Association (EA)
MDA	Manual Dilation of the Anus (AAMN)
MDA	Manufacturing Defect Analyzer [*Automotive engineering*]
MDA	MAPCO, Inc. [*NYSE symbol*] (SPSG)
MDA	Marking Device Association (EA)
MD A	Maryland Appellate Reports [*A publication*] (DLA)
MDA	Master Design Award
MDA	Master Diversion Airfield (AIA)
MDA	Master Drawings Association (EA)
MDA	Master Dyers Association (EA)
MDA	Master of Development Adminstration (PGP)
MDA	Master of Dramatic Art
MDA	Material Data Administrator (DNAB)
MDA	Material Disposal Authority
MDA	Maximum Deficit Amount [*Office of Management and Budget*] (GFGA)
MDA	Maximum Demographic Appeal [*Objective of commercial television programming*]
MDA	Maximum Detachable Activity [*Nuclear energy*] (NUCP)
MDA	McDonnell-Designed Assembly
MDA	McDonnell-Douglas Aerospace (GAVI)
MDA	Measurement, Decision, and Actuation [*Computer science*]
MDA	Mechanically Despun Antenna (KSC)
MDA	Mechanized Directory Assistance [*Telecommunications*] (TEL)
MDA	Media Arts Group [*Stock market symbol*]
MDa	Megadalton (DMAA)
MDA	Menthanediamine [*Organic chemistry*]
MDA	Mento-Dextra Anterior [*A fetal position*] [*Obstetrics*]
MDA	Mentodextroanterior [*Medicine*] (DB)
MDA	Mesocyclone Detection Algorithm [*Marine science*] (OSRA)
MDA	Metal Deactivator [*Fuel technology*]
MDA	Meteoroid Detector-Analyzer
MDA	Methyl Diamphetamine
MDA	Methyldopamine [*Biochemistry*]
MDA	Methylenedianiline [*Also, DAPM, DDM*] [*Organic chemistry*]
MDA	Methylenedioxyamphetamine [*Biochemistry*]
MDA	Microprocessor Development Aid
MDA	Middeck Assembly (MCD)
MDA	Milestone Decision Authority
MDA	Military Damage Assessment
MDA	Millinery Distributors Association [*British*] (BI)
MDA	Minimum Decision Altitude (SAA)
MDA	Minimum Descent Altitude [*Aviation*]
MDA	Minimum Detectable Activity [*Nuclear energy*] (NRCH)
MDA	Minimum Detectable Amount [*of radiation*] [*Analytical chemistry*]
MDA	Minnesota Department of Agriculture, St. Paul, MN [*OCLC symbol*] (OCLC)
MDA	Miscellaneous Defense Activities (AAGC)
MDA	Missilized Driver Assembly (MCD)
MDA	Mission Doctors Association (EA)
MDA	Mixed Distribution Analysis [*Mathematics*]
MDA	Mobile Depot Activities [*Air Force*]
MDA	Modified Diffusion Approximation (PDAA)
MDA	Modulation-Domain Analysis [*Computer science*] (CIST)
MDA	Monoalythic Design Automation (IAA)
MDA	Monochrome Display Adapter [*Computer technology*]
MDA	Monodehydroascorbate [*Biochemistry*]
MDA	Mothers for Decency in Action [*Group opposing sex education in schools*]
MDA	Motorcycling Doctors Association (EA)
MDA	Motor Discriminative Acuity [*Psychology*]
MDA	Motor Drive Amplifier
MDA	Mouvement pour la Democratie en Algerie [*Algeria*] [*Political party*] (MENA)
MDA	Multidimensional Access
MDA	Multidimensional Analysis (IEEE)
MDA	Multidimensional Array
MDA	Multidocking Adapter (IAA)
MDA	Multiple Digit Absorbing [*Telecommunications*] (TEL)
MDA	Multiple Discriminant Analysis [*Statistics*]
MDA	Multiple Docking Adapter [*Apollo*] [*NASA*]
MDA	Multivariant Discriminant Analysis [*Medicine*] (DMAA)
MDA	Muscular Dystrophy Association (EA)
MDA	Museum Documentation Association [*British*] (DBA)
MDA	Music Distributors Association (EA)
MDA	Mutual Defense Agency (NADA)
MDA	Mutual Defense Assistance
MDA	San Antonio, TX [*Location identifier FAA*] (FAAL)
MdAA	Hall of Records Commission, Annapolis, MD [*Library symbol Library of Congress*] (LCLS)
MDAA	Mon-Dak Athletic Association (PSS)
MDAA	Muscular Dystrophy Associations of America (EA)
MDAA	Mutual Defense Assistance Act
MdAAC	Public Library of Annapolis and Anne Arundel County, Annapolis, MD [*Library symbol Library of Congress*] (LCLS)
MDaAr	Danvers Archival Center, Peabody Institute, Danvers, MA [*Library symbol Library of Congress*] (LCLS)
MDAC	McDonnell Douglas Aircraft Corp.
MDAC	McDonnell Douglas Astronautics Co. (NAKS)
MDAC	Medical Data Acquisition System
MDAC	Methyl(ciethylamino)coumarin [*Organic chemistry*]
MDAC	Multi-Channel Digital Audio Codec [*Intraplex, Inc.*]
MDAC	Multiplying Digital-to-Analog Converter [*Computer science*] (IEEE)
MDAC	Muscular Dystrophy Association of Canada
MDACad	Mutual Defense Assistance, General Area of China
MdaCad	ModaCad, Inc. [*Associated Press*] (SAG)
MDACC	Management of Defense Acquisition Contracts Course [*DoD*] (RDA)
MdaCd	ModaCad, Inc. [*Associated Press*] (SAG)

MDAD .... Mineral Dust Airway Disease [*Medicine*] (DMAA)

MDAD .... Monitoring and Data Analysis Division [*Environmental Protection Agency*] (GFGA)

MD Admin Code... Code of Maryland Regulations [*A publication*] (DLA)

MdAEPA.......... United States Environmental Protection Agency, Annapolis Field Office, AnnapolisScience Center, Annapolis, MD [*Library symbol Library of Congress*] (LCLS)

MDAERP ...... Medical Devices Adverse Experience Reporting Project

MDAF .... Memoires. Delegation Archeologique Francaise [*A publication*] (BJA)

MDAFWP ..... Motor-Driven Auxiliary Feedwater Pump (IEEE)

MDAGT .... Mutual Defense Assistance, Greece and Turkey

MDAH .... M. D. Anderson Hospital and Tumor Institute [*Houston, TX*]

MDAI .... Marking Device Association International (NTPA)

MDAI .... Multidisciplinary Accident Investigation [*National Accident Sampling System*]

MDAIKP ...... Mutual Defense Assistance, Iran, Republic of Korea, and Philippines

MDAIS .... McDonnell Douglas Aerospace Information Services [*Formerly, MCATO*] (MCD)

MD Ala .... United States District Court for the Middle District of Alabama (DLA)

MDAN .... Angelina, Cotui [*Dominican Republic*] [*ICAO location identifier*] (ICLI)

MdAN........... United States Naval Academy, Annapolis, MD [*Library symbol Library of Congress*] (LCLS)

MDANAA...... Mutual Defense Assistance, North Atlantic Area

MD & D ...... Montagu, Deacon, and De Gex's English Bankruptcy Reports [*1840-44*] [*A publication*] (DLA)

MD & DeG... Montagu, Deacon, and De Gex's English Bankruptcy Reports [*1840-44*] [*A publication*] (DLA)

MD & S .... Macon, Dublin & Savannah Railroad (IIA)

MdANE........ United States Navy, Naval Ship Research and Development Laboratory, Annapolis, MD [*Library symbol Library of Congress*] (LCLS)

MD Ann Code... Annotated Code of Maryland [*A publication*] (DLA)

MDANSW.... Muscular Dystrophy Association of New South Wales [*Australia*]

MDAO .... Mutual Defense Assistance Office (DOMA)

MDAP .... Machover Draw-A-Person Test [*Psychology*]

MDAP .... Major Defense Acquisition Program (AAGC)

MDAP .... Materiel Deployment/Acceptance Plan (MCD)

MDAP .... Morphological Dictionary Adaptor Program (PDAA)

MDAP .... Mutual Defense Assistance Pact [*or Program*]

MDaP........... Peabody Institute, Danvers, MA [*Library symbol Library of Congress*] (LCLS)

MdApg .... United States Army, Technical Library, Aberdeen Proving Ground, Aberdeen, MD [*Library symbol Library of Congress*] (LCLS)

MdApgC ...... United States Army, Chemical Systems Laboratory, Aberdeen Proving Ground, Aberdeen, MD [*Library symbol Library of Congress*] (LCLS)

MdApgO...... United States Army, Ordnance School, Aberdeen Proving Ground, Aberdeen, MD [*Library symbol Library of Congress*] (LCLS)

MdApgOB .... United States Army, Ordnance Board, Aberdeen Proving Ground, Aberdeen, MD [*Library symbol Library of Congress*] (LCLS)

MdApgP ...... United States Army, Post Library, Aberdeen Proving Ground, Aberdeen, MD [*Library symbol Library of Congress*] (LCLS)

MD App .... Maryland Appellate Reports [*A publication*] (DLA)

MDAR .... Malfunction Detection Analysis and Recording [*NASA*] (KSC)

MDAR .... Minimum Daily Adult Requirement

MDAR .... Mobile Detection Assessment Response System [*USA*]

MDar 1 .... Dartmouth Public Library, Darmouth, MA [*Library symbol*] [*Library of Congress*] (LCLS)

MDarHi........ Old Dartmouth Historical Society, Dartmouth, MA [*Library symbol Library of Congress*] (LCLS)

MDARS .... Military Damage Assessment Reporting System (MCD)

MDARS .... Mobile Detection, Assessment, and Response System

MDAS .... Manpower Data Automated System (DNAB)

MDAS .... Medical Data Acquisition System (KSC)

MDAS .... Meteorological Data Acquisition System [*NASA*] (KSC)

MDAS .... Miniature Data Acquisition System

MDAS .... Mission Data Acquisition System [*NASA*] (NASA)

MDAS .... Modular Data Acquisition System (NITA)

MdAS........... Saint John's College, Annapolis, MD [*Library symbol Library of Congress*] (LCLS)

MDASA .... Muscular Dystrophy Association of South Australia

MDAVG .... Mission Duration, Average (MCD)

M (Day) ...... Mobilization Day [*Military*] (AFM)

M (Days) ..... Metrication Days [*Sponsored by the Metrication Board to educate merchants and public on metric system*] [*British*]

MDB............. Bren Del Win Centennial Library, Deloraine, Manitoba [*Library symbol National Library of Canada*] (NLC)

MDB............. Enoch Pratt Free Library, Baltimore, MD [*OCLC symbol*] (OCLC)

MDB............. Maintenance Data Bank

MDB............. Management Database (ACRL)

MDB............. Master Database

MDB............. Master Distribution Box [*Missile system*] [*Army*]

MDB............. Material Distribution Board (DNAB)

MDB............. MDI Mobile Data International, Inc. [*Toronto Stock Exchange symbol Vancouver Stock Exchange symbol*]

MDB............. Medulloblastoma [*Medicine*] (DMAA)

MDB............. Memory-Data Bank

MDB............. Mersey Dock Board [*British*] (DAS)

MDB............. Message Database (MCD)

MDB............. Methylenedioxybenzene [*Organic chemistry*]

MDB............. Metrology Data Bank [*GIDEP*]

MDB............. Minimally Distinct Border [*Color perception*]

MDB............. Mission Data Book [*NASA*] (NASA)

MDB............. Mission Display Board Assembly [*Space Flight Operations Facility, NASA*]

MDB............. Mitglied des Deutschen Bundestages [*Member of the German Federal Parliament*]

MDB............. Mojave Desert Block [*Geology*]

MDB............. Movimento Democratico Brasileiro [*Brazilian Democratic Movement*] [*Political party*] (PPW)

MDB............. Multilateral Development Bank

MDB............. Multiple Drive Block

MDB............. Multiplex Data Bus [*Computer science*] (MCD)

MDB............. Mutual Defense Board [*US-Philippines*] (CINC)

MDB............. Professional Bancorp [*AMEX symbol*] (SPSG)

MdBAE......... United States Army, Corps of Engineers, Baltimore, MD [*Library symbol Library of Congress*] (LCLS)

MdBaH......... Harford Community College, Bel Air, MD [*Library symbol Library of Congress*] (LCLS)

MdBaHC....... Harford County Library, Bel Air, MD [*Library symbol Library of Congress*] (LCLS)

MdBAS......... Armco, Inc., Advanced Materials Division, Research Library, Baltimore, MD [*Library symbol Library of Congress*] (LCLS)

MdBASI........ Allied Signal, Inc., Baltimore, MD [*Library symbol*] [*Library of Congress*] (LCLS)

MdBASI-C..... Allied Signal, Inc., Communications Diviaion, Baltimore, MD [*Library symbol*] [*Library of Congress*] (LCLS)

MdBB........... Baltimore Bar Library, Baltimore, MD [*Library symbol Library of Congress*] (LCLS)

MdBb........... United States Naval Training Center, Bainbridge, MD [*Library symbol Library of Congress*] (LCLS)

MdBBC......... Baltimore Conference, Inc., United Methodist Historical Society, Baltimore, MD [*Library symbol Library of Congress*] (LCLS)

MdBBJC........ Community College of Baltimore, Baltimore, MD [*Library symbol Library of Congress*] (LCLS)

MdBbN......... US Naval Training Center, Bainbridge, MD [*Library symbol*] [*Library of Congress*] (LCLS)

MdBBO......... [*The*] Baltimore & Ohio Railroad Co., Employees' Library, Baltimore, MD [*Library symbol Library of Congress Obsolete*] (LCLS)

MdBBR .... Bendix Corp., Baltimore, MD [*Library symbol Library of Congress*] (LCLS)

MdBBS......... Bon Secours Medical Library, Baltimore, MD [*Library symbol Library of Congress*] (LCLS)

MdBCC......... Catonsville Community College, Learning Resources Division, Baltimore, MD [*Library symbol Library of Congress*] (LCLS)

MdBCH .... Baltimore City Court House, Baltimore, MD [*Library symbol Library of Congress*] (LCLS)

MdBCIC........ Counter Intelligence Center Corps School, Fort Holabird, Baltimore, MD [*Library symbol Library of Congress*] (LCLS)

MdBCP......... Baltimore County Public Library, Towson, MD [*Library symbol Library of Congress*] (LCLS)

MdBCPM....... Chemical Pigment Co., Metals Division, Baltimore, MD [*Library symbol Library of Congress*] (LCLS)

MdBCS......... Coppin State College, Baltimore, MD [*Library symbol Library of Congress*] (LCLS)

MDBDF .... March of Dimes Birth Defects Foundation (EA)

MdBDH .... United States Department of Health and Human Services, Health Care Financing Administration, Office of Research Demonstrations and Statistics, Baltimore, MD [*Library symbol Library of Congress*] (LCLS)

MdBE........... Enoch Pratt Free Library, Baltimore, MD [*Library symbol Library of Congress*] (LCLS)

MdBeCA........ Concepts Analysis Agency, Bethesda, MD [*Library symbol Library of Congress*] (LCLS)

MdBeCI......... Congressional Information Service, Bethesda, MD [*Library symbol Library of Congress*] (LCLS)

MdBEs .... Essex Community College, Baltimore, MD [*Library symbol Library of Congress*] (LCLS)

MdBeU.......... Uniform Services University of the Health Sciences, Bethesda, MD [*Library symbol Library of Congress*] (LCLS)

MDBF........... Mean Distance between Failures [*Quality control*] (MCD)

MdBFamP...... Family Planning Training Institute, Baltimore, MD [*Library symbol Library of Congress*] (LCLS)

MdBFH.......... Fort Holabird Post Library, Baltimore, MD [*Library symbol Library of Congress*] (LCLS)

MdBFM......... Grand Lodge of Ancient Free and Accepted Masons of Maryland, Masonic Library, Baltimore, MD [*Library symbol Library of Congress*] (LCLS)

MdBFr.......... Friends Meeting, Stony Run, Baltimore, MD [*Library symbol Library of Congress*] (LCLS)

MdBG........... Goucher College, Baltimore, MD [*Library symbol Library of Congress*] (LCLS)

MdBGM-E .... Martin Marietta Corp., Science and Technology Library, Baltimore, MD [*Library symbol Library of Congress*] (LCLS)

MdBGM-N.... Martin Marietta Corp., RIAS Library, Baltimore, MD [*Library symbol Library of Congress*] (LCLS)

MdBH........... Baltimore City Hospitals, Doctors' Library, Baltimore, MD [*Library symbol Library of Congress*] (LCLS)

MDBH .... Barahona [*Dominican Republic*] [*ICAO location identifier*] (ICLI)

MdBHC .... Baltimore Hebrew College, Baltimore, MD [*Library symbol Library of Congress*] (LCLS)

MDBI .... Mean Days between Injuries

MDBI .... Murray Darling Basin Initiative [*Australia*]

MdBJ .... Johns Hopkins University, Baltimore, MD [*Library symbol Library of Congress*] (LCLS)

MdBJ-A......... Johns Hopkins University, Applied Physics Laboratory, Silver Spring, MD [*Library symbol Library of Congress*] (LCLS)

MdBJ-AIS...... Johns Hopkins University, School of Advanced International Studies, Washington, DC [*Library symbol Library of Congress*] (LCLS)

MdBJ-C........ Johns Hopkins university, Alan Chesney Medical Archives, Baltimore, MD [*Library symbol*] [*Library of Congress*] (LCLS)

MdBJ-G........ Johns Hopkins University, John Work Garrett Library, Baltimore, MD [*Library symbol Library of Congress*] (LCLS)

MdBJ-H........ Johns Hopkins University, School of Hygiene and Public Health, Maternal and Child Health-Population Dynamics Library, Baltimore, MD [*Library symbol Library of Congress*] (LCLS)

MdBJ-P........ Johns Hopkins University, George Peabody Library, Baltimore, MD [*Library symbol Library of Congress*] (LCLS)

MdBJ-W........ Johns Hopkins University, William H. Welch Medical Library, Baltimore, MD [*Library symbol Library of Congress*] (LCLS)

MDBK .... Madin-Darby Bovine Kidney [*Cell line*]

MDBK .... Medford Bancorp [*NASDAQ symbol*] [*Formerly, Medford Savings Bank*] (SG)

MDBK .... Medford Savings Bank [*NASDAQ symbol*] (SAG)

MdbkIns....... Meadowbrook Insurance Group [*Associated Press*] (SAG)

MDBL........ Maintainability Data Baseline (MCD)

MDBL........ Maintainability Design Baseline (MCD)

MdBLH......... Lutheran Hospital of Maryland, Baltimore, MD [*Library symbol Library of Congress*] (LCLS)

MdBLN........ Loyola - Notre Dame Library, Inc., Baltimore, MD [*Library symbol Library of Congress*] (LCLS)

MdBM......... Medical and Chirurgical Faculty of the State of Maryland, Baltimore, MD [*Library symbol Library of Congress*] (LCLS)

MDBM........ MULTICS Data Base Manager

MdBMA........ Baltimore Museum of Art, Baltimore, MD [*Library symbol Library of Congress*] (LCLS)

MdBMC....... Morgan State College [*Later, Morgan State University*] Baltimore, MD [*Library symbol Library of Congress*] (LCLS)

MDBMC ...... Murray-Darling Basin Ministerial Council [*Australia*]

MdBMH....... Mercy Hospital, McGlannan Memorial Library, Baltimore, MD [*Library symbol Library of Congress*] (LCLS)

MdBMH-N.... Mercy Hospital, School of Nursing, Baltimore, MD [*Library symbol Library of Congress*] (LCLS)

MdBMI........ Maryland Institute, School of Fine and Applied Arts, Baltimore, MD [*Library symbol Library of Congress*] (LCLS)

MDBMS ...... Medical Data Base Management System (SSD)

MdBMStA ... Mount Saint Agnes College, Baltimore, MD [*Library symbol Library of Congress*] (LCLS)

MdBNA .... National Institute on Aging, Gerontology Research Center, Baltimore, MD [*Library symbol Library of Congress*] (LCLS)

MdBo .... Bowie State College, Bowie, MD [*Library symbol Library of Congress*] (LCLS)

MdBOAS ...... United States Social Security Administration, Baltimore, MD [*Library symbol Library of Congress*] (LCLS)

MdBP......... Enoch Pratt Free Library, George Peabody Branch, Baltimore, MD [*Library symbol Library of Congress*] (LCLS)

MDBP........ Mechanically Deboned Broiler Product [*Food technology*]

MDBPB .... Microsoft DoubleSpace BIOS [*Basic Input-Output System*] Parameter Block [*Computer science*] (PCM)

MdBPC......... Peabody Conservatory of Music, Baltimore, MD [*Library symbol Library of Congress*] (LCLS)

MdBPH .... United States Public Health Service Hospital, Baltimore, MD [*Library symbol Library of Congress*] (LCLS)

MdBPM .... Peale Museum, Baltimore, MD [*Library symbol Library of Congress*] (LCLS)

MdBR.......... Research Institute for Advanced Study, Baltimore, MD [*Library symbol Library of Congress*] (LCLS)

MdBREC ...... Engineering Society of Baltimore, Baltimore, MD [*Library symbol Library of Congress*] (LCLS)

MdbrkRe...... Meadowbrook Rehabilitation Group [*Associated Press*] (SAG)

MDBS .... Micro Data Base Systems (NITA)

MDBS .... Mobile Database Station [*Telecommunications*] (ACRL)

MdBS.......... Saint Mary's Seminary and University, Baltimore, MD [*Library symbol Library of Congress*] (LCLS)

MdBSAr .... Sulpician Archives Baltimore, Baltimore, MD [*Library symbol Library of Congress*] (LCLS)

MdBSet........ Seton Psychiatric Institute, Baltimore, MD [*Library symbol Library of Congress*] (LCLS)

MdBSH........ Sinai Hospital, Staff Library, Baltimore, MD [*Library symbol Library of Congress*] (LCLS)

MdBS-P .... Saint Mary's Seminary and University, Philosophy Library, Baltimore, MD [*Library symbol Library of Congress*] (LCLS)

MdBSP......... Sheppard-Pratt Hospital, Baltimore, MD [*Library symbol Library of Congress*] (LCLS)

MdBSp......... Sunpapers Library, Baltimore, MD [*Library symbol Library of Congress*] (LCLS)

MDBSS .... Mischell-Dutton Balanced Salt Solution (STED)

MdBSt......... Saint Agnes Hospital, Baltimore, MD [*Library symbol Library of Congress*] (LCLS)

MdBSTS....... Space Telescope Science Institute, Baltimore, MD [*Library symbol*] [*Library of Congress*] (LCLS)

MdBSup....... Sunpapers Library, Baltimore, MD [*Library symbol*] [*Library of Congress*] (LCLS)

MdBT.......... Towson State University, Baltimore, MD [*Library symbol Library of Congress*] (LCLS)

MdBU......... University of Baltimore, Baltimore, MD [*Library symbol Library of Congress*] (LCLS)

MdBU-L .... University of Baltimore, Law Library, Baltimore, MD [*Library symbol Library of Congress*] (LCLS)

MdBUM........ Union Memorial Hospital, Finney Medical Library, Baltimore, MD [*Library symbol Library of Congress*] (LCLS)

MdBV.......... United States Veterans Administration Hospital, Baltimore, MD [*Library symbol Library of Congress*] (LCLS)

MdBWA........ Walters Art Gallery, Baltimore, MD [*Library symbol Library of Congress*] (LCLS)

MdBWe........ Westinghouse Defense and Space Center, Baltimore, MD [*Library symbol Library of Congress*] (LCLS)

MdBWesE .... Western Electric Co., Inc., Baltimore, MD [*Library symbol Library of Congress*] (LCLS)

MdBwiNA..... National Aeronautics and Space Administration, Scientific and Technical Information Facility, Baltimore/Washington International Airport, MD [*Library symbol*] [*Library of Congress*] (LCLS)

MDC............ Atlantic Aero, Inc. [*ICAO designator*] (FAAC)

MDC............ Boston, MA [*Location identifier FAA*] (FAAL)

MDC............ Dow Chemical Co., Library, Midland, MI [*OCLC symbol*] (OCLC)

MDC............ Machinability Data Center [*Computerized search service*] [*Metcut Research Associates, Inc.*] (IID)

MDC............ Machinery Diagnostic Consultant [*Software program*]

MDC............ Macrophage-Derived Chemokine [*Immunology*]

MDC............ Main Display Console

MDC............ Maintenance Data Center (MCD)

MDC............ Maintenance Data Collection [*Military*] (AFM)

MDC............ Maintenance Dependency Chart (IEEE)

MDC............ Major Diagnostic Categories [*Medicine*]

MDC............ Management Development Course (MCD)

MDC............ Manhattan Drug Co.

MDC............ Manual Direction Center [*Air Force*] (AFM)

MDC............ Mason-Dixon Conference (PSS)

MDC............ Master Data Center, Inc. [*Information service or system*] (IID)

MDC............ Master Direction Center [*Air Force*]

MDC............ Materials Dissemination Center [*Institute for Development of Educational Activities*]

MDC............ Maximum Deductible Contribution [*Superannuation*]

MDC............ Maximum Dependable Capacity [*Nuclear energy*] (NRCH)

MDC............ Maximum Depth of Colonization [*Botany*]

MDC............ McDonnell Douglas Corp. (MCD)

MDC............ MDC Corp. [*Associated Press*] (SAG)

MDC............ M.D.C Hldgs [*NYSE symbol*] (TTSB)

MDC............ MDC Holdings, Inc. [*NYSE symbol*] (SPSG)

MDC............ Mead Data Central, Inc. [*Dayton, OH*]

MDC............ Mead Data Control (NITA)

MDC............ Mechanically Deboned Chicken [*Food technology*]

MDC............ Medial Dorsal Cutaneous [*Nerve*] [*Medicine*] (STED)

MDC............ Medullary Collecting Duct [*Medicine*] (STED)

MDC............ Memory Disk Controller

MDC............ Menado [*Indonesia*] [*Airport symbol*] (OAG)

MDC............ Message Display Console (MCD)

MDC............ Message Distribution Center (NATG)

MDC............ Meteorological Data Collection

MDC............ Metropolitan District Commission

MDC............ Metropolitan District Council [*British*]

MDC............ Microprocessor Development Center [*American Microsystems Inc. US*] (NITA)

MDC............ Mild Detonating Cord (MCD)

MDC............ Military District Commander

MDC............ Million Dollar Contract [*File*] [*Military*]

MDC............ Milwaukee-Downer College [*Later, Lawrence University*] [*Wisconsin*]

MDC............ Mine Dispatch Control

MDC............ Miniature Detonating Cord (MCD)

MDC............ Minimal Detectable Concentration (STED)

MDC............ Minimobile Data Center [*Military*]

MDC............ Minimum Detectable Concentration [*Analytical chemistry*]

MDC............ Ministere des Communications [*Department of Communications*] [*Canada*]

MDC............ Missile Development Center [*Air Force*]

MDC............ Missile Direction Center

MDC............ Mission Director Center [*NASA*] (KSC)

MDC............ Mission Duty Cycle [*NASA*] (KSC)

MDC............ Mobile Defence Corps [*British military*] (DMA)

MDC............ Mobile Distress Call

MDC............ Modification Detection Code (HGAA)

MDC............ Mongoloid Development Council [*Later, NADS*] (EA)

MDC............ Montreal Diocesan College [*Quebec*]

MDC............ Montreux Development [*Vancouver Stock Exchange symbol*]

MDC............ More Developed Country

MDC............ Mother's Day Council (EA)

MDC............ Motor Dealers' Council [*New South Wales, Australia*]

MDC............ Motor Direct-Connected

MDC............ Mount Diablo [*California*] [*Seismograph station code, US Geological Survey*] (SEIS)

MDC............ Movement Designator Code

MDC............ Muller Data Corp. [*Information service or system*] (IID)

MDC............ Multidimensional Concept [*Combines robotic combat vehicles with other unmanned systems*] [*Army*] (RDA)

MDC............ Multilayer Dielectric Coating

MDC............ Multiple Delay Code (AFIT)

MDC............ Multiple Device Controller

MDC............ Multiple Drone Control (MCD)

MDC............ Multistage Depressed Collector (IAA)

MDCA .... Main Distribution Control Assembly (MCD)

MDCA .... Manufacturing Design Change Analysis

MDCA .... Mind Development and Control Association (EA)

MDCAC........ Manufacturing Department Change Analysis Commitment (SAA)

MdCam....... Dorchester County Public Library, Cambridge, MD [*Library symbol Library of Congress*] (LCLS)

MdCatSG .... Spring Grove State Hospital, Catonsville, MD [*Library symbol Library of Congress*] (LCLS)

MDCB .... Moisture Detector Control Box

MDCC .... Master Data Control Console
MDCC .... Molecular Devices [*NASDAQ symbol*] (TTSB)
MDCC .... Molecular Devices Corp. [*NASDAQ symbol*] (SAG)
MDCC .... Monaural Detection with Contralateral Cue (PDAA)
MDCD .... Meridian Data [*NASDAQ symbol*] (TTSB)
MDCD .... Meridian Data, Inc. [*NASDAQ symbol*] (SAG)
MdCe .... Queen Anne's County Free Library, Centreville, MD [*Library symbol Library of Congress*] (LCLS)
MDCEF ...... Medical-Dental Committee on Evaluation of Fluoridation [*Defunct*] (EA)
MDCGC ...... Multidimensional Capillary Gas Chromatography
MD Ch .... Maryland Chancery Reports, by Johnson [*4 vols.*] [*A publication*] (DLA)
MDCH .... MDC Holdings, Inc. (MCD)
MDCH .... Middlesex, Duke of Cambridge's Hussars [*Military unit*] [*British*]
MD Chan .... Maryland Chancery Decisions [*A publication*] (DLA)
MD Chan Dec... Maryland Chancery Decisions [*A publication*] (DLA)
MD Ch D...... Maryland Chancery Decisions [*A publication*] (DLA)
MD Ch Dec... Maryland Chancery Decisions [*A publication*] (DLA)
MdChW...... Washington College, Chestertown, MD [*Library symbol Library of Congress*] (LCLS)
MDCI .... Medical Action Industries [*NASDAQ symbol*] (TTSB)
MDCI .... Medical Action Industries, Inc. [*NASDAQ symbol*] (NQ)
MDCI .... Multidisciplinary Counterintelligence (MCD)
MDCK .... Madin-Darby Canine Kidney [*Cell line*]
MDCL .... Medical Control [*NASDAQ symbol*] (SAG)
MDCL .... MedicalControl Inc [*NASDAQ symbol*] (TTSB)
MDCLW...... MedicalControl Wrrt [*NASDAQ symbol*] (TTSB)
MDCM .... Doctor of Medicine and Master of Surgery (DD)
MDCM .... Medicinae Doctor Chirurgia Magister [*Doctor of Medicine and Master of Surgery*]
MDCMA...... Melvil Dui Chowder and Marching Association [*Later, MDMCA*] (EA)
MDCO .... Consuelo, San Pedro De Macoris [*Dominican Republic*] [*ICAO location identifier*] (ICLI)
MDCO .... Marine Drilling [*NASDAQ symbol*] (TTSB)
MDCO .... Marine Drilling Co. [*NASDAQ symbol*] (NQ)
MdCoA........ Arctec, Inc., Columbia, MD [*Library symbol Library of Congress*] (LCLS)
MD Code Ann... Annotated Code of Maryland [*A publication*] (DLA)
MdCoG........ W. R. Grace & Co., Research Library, Columbia, MD [*Library symbol Library of Congress*] (LCLS)
MdCoH........ Hittman Associates, Inc., Columbia, MD [*Library symbol Library of Congress*] (LCLS)
MdConn .... Mid-Conn Bank [*Associated Press*] (SAG)
MD Const..... Maryland Constitution [*A publication*] (DLA)
Mdcore .... Medicore, Inc. [*Associated Press*] (SAG)
MdCpM........ United States Bureau of Mines, College Park Research Center, College Park, MD [*Library symbol Library of Congress*] (LCLS)
MDCPZ........ Monodesmethylchlorpromazine [*Biochemistry*]
MDCR.......... Cabo Rojo [*Dominican Republic*] [*ICAO location identifier*] (ICLI)
MDCR.......... Maintenance Data Collection Report (MCD)
MDCR.......... Medcross, Inc. [*NASDAQ symbol*] (NQ)
MDCR.......... Miller-Dieker Chromosomal Region [*Genetics*]
MDCRS........ Meteorological Data Collection and Reporting System [*FAA*] (TAG)
MDCS .... Maintenance Data Collection System [*or Subsystem*] [*Navy*]
MDCS .... Malfunction Display and Control System (MCD)
MDCS .... Manufacturing and Distribution Control System
MDCS .... Master Data Control System [*Computer science*] (IAA)
MDCS .... Master Digital Command System
MDCS .... Material Data Collection System [*NASA*] (KSC)
MDCS .... Metering and Directional Control System
MDCS .... Mission Data Collection Sheets (CINC)
MDCS .... Mutual Defense Control Staff [*Department of State*]
MDCS .... Santo Domingo [*Dominican Republic*] [*ICAO location identifier*] (ICLI)
MDCSC ...... McDonnell Douglas Computer Systems Co. [*Formerly, MICRODATA*] (MCD)
MDC/SS ...... Multiple Drone Control Strike System (MCD)
MD/CSU .... Motor Drive Cassette Support Unit
MDCT.......... Mechanical Draft Cooling Tower [*Nuclear energy*] (NRCH)
MDCT.......... Median Corrective Maintenance Time (MCD)
MDCT.......... Multidimensional Compensatory Task
MdCtr.......... Medical Control [*Associated Press*] (SAG)
MdCu .... Allegany County Library, Cumberland, MD [*Library symbol Library of Congress*] (LCLS)
MDCU .... Magnetic Disk Control Unit
MDCU .... Mobile Dynamic Checkout Unit (AAG)
MdCuAC...... Allegany Community College, Cumberland, MD [*Library symbol Library of Congress*] (LCLS)
MdCvH........ Crownsville State Hospital, Crownsville, MD [*Library symbol Library of Congress*] (LCLS)
MDCZ.......... Constanza [*Dominican Republic*] [*ICAO location identifier*] (ICLI)
MdD............ Caroline County Public Library, Denton, MD [*Library symbol Library of Congress*] (LCLS)
MDD .... Doctor of Dental Medicine
MDD .... Machine Dependent Data (OA)
MDD .... Madrid [*Spain*] [*Seismograph station code, US Geological Survey Closed*] (SEIS)
MDD .... Magnetic Disk Drive
MDD .... Maintenance Design Disclosure
MDD .... Maintenance Due Date (NVT)
MDD .... Major Depressive Disorder [*Psychiatry*]
MdD............ Mandaic Dictionary [*Oxford*] [*A publication*] (BJA)
MDD .... Manic-Depressive Disorder [*Medicine*] (STED)
MDD .... Marijuana Detection Dog (DNAB)
MDD .... Mate/Demate Device [*Aerospace*] (NAKS)

MDD .... McDonald & Co. Invest [*NYSE symbol*] (TTSB)
MDD .... McDonald & Co. Investments, Inc. [*NYSE symbol*] (SPSG)
MDD .... Mean Daily Difference [*Medicine*]
MDD .... Mean Daily Dose
MdD........... Median Deviation [*Statistics*]
MDD .... Median Droplet Diameter
MDD .... Meteorological Data Distribution
MDD .... Midland, TX [*Location identifier FAA*] (FAAL)
MDD .... Milligrams per Square Decimeter per Day
MDD .... Million-Dollar Deal
MDD .... Million Dollar Directory [*Dun's Marketing Services*] [*Parsippany, NJ Database*]
MDD .... Mission Data Display
MDD .... Mission Description Document (SSD)
MDD .... Mouvement Democratique Dahomeen [*Dahomean Democratic Movement*] [*Political party*]
MDD .... Multichannel Demultiplexer and Distributor
MDD .... Multidimensional Database
MDD .... Puerto Maldonado [*Peru*] [*Airport symbol*] (AD)
MDDA .... Manic Depressive and Depressive Association [*Later, NDMDA*] (EA)
MDDA .... Mechanicsburg Defense Depot Activity [*AEC*]
MDDA .... Minnesota Differential Diagnosis of Aphasia (STED)
MDDC .... Management Decisions Development Corporation [*Canada*] (NITA)
MDDC .... Manhattan District Declassified Code [*AEC*]
MDDC .... Motor Dealers' Disputes Council [*Australia*]
MDDCS .... Memorial Dose Distribution Computation Service [*Memorial Sloan-Kettering Cancer Center*] [*Information service or system*] (IID)
MDDD .... Merrill-Demos DD Scale [*Drug abuse and delinquent behavior test*]
MDDE .... Maryland & Delaware Railroad Co. [*AAR code*]
MDDF .... Minimum Delay Data Format (MCD)
MDDI .... Medical Devices, Diagnostics, & Instrumentation [*Center for Devices and Radiological Health*] [*Also known as The Gray Sheet*] [*A publication*]
MDDJ......... Dajabon [*Dominican Republic*] [*ICAO location identifier*] (ICLI)
MDDPC....... Methyl Dimethyldihydropyrancarboxylate [*Organic chemistry*]
MDDPM ..... Magnetic Drum Data Processing Machine (IAA)
MDDR .... Mimimum Distance Decoding Rule (IAA)
MDDS .... Maintainability Design Data Sheets (MCD)
MDDS .... Material Directory Data Sheet (MCD)
MDDT .... Master Digital Data Tape (PDAA)
MDDX .... Middlesex [*Region of London*]
MDE .... Cincinnati, OH [*Location identifier FAA*] (FAAL)
MDE .... Madame (ROG)
MDE .... Magnetic Decision Element [*Computer science*] (BUR)
MDE .... Main Distribution Equipment (IAA)
MDE .... Major Defense Equipment (MCD)
MDE .... Major Depressive Episode [*Medicine*] (DMAA)
MDE .... Master of Developmental Economics (PGP)
MDE .... Master of Distance Education (PGP)
MDE .... Master of Domestic Economy (NADA)
MDE .... Matrix Difference Equation
MDE .... McDermott, Inc. [*Formerly, Offshore Pipelines*] [*NYSE symbol*] (SAG)
MDE .... Mechanical Design Environment
MDE .... Medeea Ltd. [*Romania*] [*FAA designator*] (FAAC)
MDE .... Medellin [*Colombia*] [*Airport symbol*] (OAG)
MDE .... Meteoroid Detection Experiment (KSC)
MDE .... Metina Development [*Vancouver Stock Exchange symbol*]
MDE .... Military Damage Expectancy
MDE .... Mindy Explorations Ltd. [*Vancouver Stock Exchange symbol*]
MDE .... Minnesota State Department of Education, Professional Library, St. Paul, MN [*OCLC symbol*] (OCLC)
MDE .... Missile Display Equipment
MDE .... Mission Defendent Experiment
MDE .... Mission Dependent Elements [*NASA*] (KSC)
MDE .... Mission Dependent Equipment [*NASA*] (KSC)
MDE .... Mission Dependent Experiment [*NASA*] (NASA)
MDE .... Mission Display Equipment
MDE .... Mobile District Engineer (AAG)
MDE .... Mobile Telemetering Station [*ITU designation*] (DEN)
MDE .... Modern Drug Encyclopedia [*A publication*]
MDE .... Modular Design of Electronics (MCD)
MDE .... Modular Display Electronics (MCD)
MDE .... Mooring Dynamics Experiment [*Marine science*] (MSC)
MdE .... Mount St. Mary's College, Emmitsburg, MD [*Library symbol Library of Congress*] (LCLS)
MDE .... National Library of Medicine [*Source file*] [*UTLAS symbol*]
MDEA......... Marketing and Distributive Education Association [*Later, MEA*] (EA)
MDEA......... Methyldiethanolamine [*Organic chemistry*]
MDEA......... Methylenedioxyethamphetamine [*Biochemistry*]
MdEa .... Talbot County Free Library, Easton, MD [*Library symbol Library of Congress*] (LCLS)
MDEBP .... Mean Daily Erect Blood Pressure (STED)
M Dec S ..... Master of Decision Sciences (PGP)
MdEdgA...... United States Army, Technical Library, Army Chemical Center, Edgewood, MD [*Library symbol Library of Congress*] (LCLS)
MDedHi ...... Dedham Historical Society, Dedham, MA [*Library symbol Library of Congress*] (LCLS)
MDee.......... Dickinson Library, Deerfield, MA [*Library symbol Library of Congress*] (LCLS)
MDeeD .... Deerfield Academy, Deerfield, MA [*Library symbol Library of Congress*] (LCLS)
MDeeH .... Historic Deerfield, Inc., Deerfield, MA [*Library symbol Library of Congress*] (LCLS)
MDeeP......... Pocumtuck Valley Memorial Association, Deerfield, MA [*Library symbol Library of Congress*] (LCLS)

MDefStudies... Master of Defence Studies
MDEFWP ..... Motor-Driven Emergency Feedwater Pump [*Nuclear energy*] (NRCH)
MDEL........... Major Defense Equipment List
M-DEMO...... Maintenance Demonstration [*DoD*]
MDEN .... Enriquillo [*Dominican Republic*] [*ICAO location identifier*] (ICLI)
MDEN .... Males, Density Of [*Ecology*]
MDENDET.... Mobile Dental Detachment [*Coast Guard*]
M Dent Sc ... Master of Dental Science [*British*]
MDEP.......... Maine Department of Environmental Protection
MDEP.......... Management Decision Package [*DoD*]
MDEPrA ...... McDermott Inc $2.20 cm Cv A Pfd [*NYSE symbol*] (TTSB)
MDEPrB ...... McDermott Inc. $2.60 cm Pfd [*NYSE symbol*] (TTSB)
MDERDA...... Maximum Degree of Emissions Reduction Deemed Achievable [*Environmental Protection Agency*]
M Des .... Master of Design
MDes........... Mercedarios Descalzos (TOCD)
MDES.......... Multiple Data Entry System
M Des (RCA)... Master of Design, Royal College of Art
MDesS......... Master of Design Studies (GAGS)
MDesSt........ Master of Design Studies
MDET.......... Militarized Digital Element Tester (MCD)
MDEU.......... Material Delivery Expeditor Unit (DNAB)
MDEX.......... Medex, Inc. [*NASDAQ symbol*] (NQ)
MDF............. Macrodefect Free [*Materials science*]
MDF............. Magnetic Direction Finding [*Meteorology*]
MDF............. Magyar Demokrata Forum [*Hungarian Democratic Forum*] [*Political party*] (EY)
MDF............. Main Distributing Frame [*Bell System*]
MDF............. Main Distribution Frame (NITA)
MDF............. Maintenance Depot Fabrication
MDF............. Manipulator Deployment Facility (MCD)
MDF............. Manipulator Development Facility [*NASA*] (NASA)
MDF............. Manual Direction Finder [*Radio*]
MDF............. Manufacturer's Designated Fuel [*Automotive engineering*]
MDF............. Market Development Funds [*Business term*]
MDF............. Master Data File (AFIT)
MDF............. Master Directory File [*Computer science*]
MDF............. Master Distribution Frame [*Electronics*] (ECII)
MDF............. Master Document File [*Computer science*]
MDF............. Mate/Demate Facility [*NASA*] (NASA)
MDF............. Mean Dominant Frequency (MAE)
MDF............. Median Demagnetizing Field [*Geophysics*]
MDF............. Medium Density Fiberboard
MDF............. Medium-Frequency Direction Finder [*or Finding*]
MDF............. Metals Datafile [*Materials Information*] [*Information service or system*] (IID)
MDF............. Metric Data Facility (MCD)
MDF............. Microcomputer Development Facilities (IEEE)
MDF............. Micro Defect Free
MDF............. Micro-Dose-Focusing [*Electron microscopy*]
MDF............. Midland Doherty Financial Corp. [*Toronto Stock Exchange symbol*]
MDF............. Midfly Aps [*Denmark ICAO designator*] (FAAC)
MDF............. Mild Detonating Fuse
MDF............. Mixed Dipterocarp Forest
MDF............. Modify
MDF............. Mooreland, OK [*Location identifier FAA*] (FAAL)
MDF............. Multiband Direction Finder
MDF............. Myocardial Depressant Factor
MDF/1......... Metals Data File/1 (NITA)
MDFA.......... Magnet Distributors and Fabricators Association (NTPA)
MDFAT........ Microsoft DoubleSpace File Allocation Table (PCM)
MDFC.......... Mason Dixon International Fan Club (EA)
MDFC.......... Matt Dillon Fan Club (EA)
MDFC.......... McDonnell Douglas Finance Corp. Ltd. [*British*]
MDFD.......... Map-Dot-Fingerprint Dystrophy [*Medicine*] (DMAA)
MdFdBc .... Maryland Federal Bancorp, Inc. [*Associated Press*] (SAG)
MdFdM........ United States Army Medical Intelligence and Information Agency, Fort Detrick, MD [*Library symbol Library of Congress*] (LCLS)
MdFhV .... United States Veterans Administration Hospital, Fort Howard, MD [*Library symbol Library of Congress*] (LCLS)
MD Fla .... United States District Court for the Middle District of Florida (DLA)
MDFLT........ Multi-Directional Forklift Truck (MCD)
MdFmA........ United States Army, Fort George G. Meade Post Recreation Services Library, Fort George G. Meade, MD [*Library symbol Library of Congress*] (LCLS)
MdFmN........ National Security Agency, Fort George G. Meade, MD [*Library symbol Library of Congress*] (LCLS)
MDFMR ...... M-Day Force Materiel Requirement
MDFNA........ Maximum Density Fuming Nitric Acid
MDFP.......... Mission Data Formats Project [*NASA*] (SSD)
MDFR.......... Make Descent From [*Aviation*] (FAAC)
MdFre.......... Frederick County Public Library, Frederick, MD [*Library symbol*] [*Library of Congress*] (LCLS)
MdFreCR ..... Frederick Cancer Research Center, Frederick, MD [*Library symbol Library of Congress*] (LCLS)
MdFreD........ Fort Detrick Technical Library, Frederick, MD [*Library symbol Library of Congress*] (LCLS)
MdFreFC...... Frederick Community College, Frederick, MD [*Library symbol Library of Congress*] (LCLS)
MdFreH........ Hood College, Frederick, MD [*Library symbol Library of Congress*] (LCLS)
MdFreHi ...... [*The*] Historical Society of Frederick County, Inc., Frederick, MD [*Library symbol Library of Congress*] (LCLS)
MdFreSD ..... Maryland School for the Deaf, Frederick, MD [*Library symbol*] [*Library of Congress*] (LCLS)

MdFroS........ Frostburg State College, Frostburg, MD [*Library symbol Library of Congress*] (LCLS)
MDFRR........ Mission Directors Flight Readiness Review [*NASA*] (KSC)
MDG .... Air Madagascar, Societe Nationale Malgache de Transports Aeriens [*ICAO designator*] (FAAC)
MDG .... Machinery Defective, Government-Furnished (DNAB)
MDG .... Machining-Intensive Durable Goods [*Manufacturing*]
MDG .... Madagascar [*ANSI three-letter standard code*] (CNC)
MDG .... Madang [*Papua New Guinea*] [*Seismograph station code, US Geological Survey*] (SEIS)
MDG .... Marina Development Group [*Commercial firm*] [*British*]
MDG .... Mean Diastolic Gradient [*Medicine*] (DMAA)
MDG .... Medical Director-General [*Navy British*]
MDG .... Meridian Gold [*NYSE symbol*] [*Formerly, FMC Gold*] (SG)
MDG .... Metal Density Gauge
MDG .... Metasystems Design Group, Inc. [*Arlington, VA*] [*Telecommunications service*] (TSSD)
MDG .... Methyladenine Deoxyribonucleic Acid Glycosylase [*Medicine*] (DMAA)
MDG .... Molecular Drag Gauge [*Instrumentation*]
MDG .... Mono/Diglycerides
MDG .... Multimedia Development Group (DDC)
MDG .... Multiplier Decoder Gate [*Computer science*]
MDG .... Multipurpose Display Group (MCD)
MDG .... Valdosta, GA [*Location identifier FAA*] (FAAL)
MDGA .... Guerra [*Dominican Republic*] [*ICAO location identifier*] (ICLI)
MD GA .... United States District Court for the Middle District of Georgia (DLA)
MDGC .... Multidimensional Gas Chromatography
MDGD .... Mercury Doped Germanium Detector
MDGF .... Macrophage Derived Growth Factor [*Biochemistry*]
MDG(N) ...... Medical Director-General (Navy) [*British*]
MDGP .... Medgroup Inc. Calif [*NASDAQ symbol*] (TTSB)
MDGR .... Multi-Differential GPS Receiver
MDGT .... Midget (MSA)
MDH............ Carbondale [*Illinois*] [*Airport symbol*] (OAG)
MDH............ Carbondale/Murphysboro, IL [*Location identifier FAA*] (FAAL)
MDH............ Madison Holdings Ltd. [*Vancouver Stock Exchange symbol*]
MDH............ Magnetic Drum Head
MDH............ Malate Dehydrogenase [*Also, MD*] [*An enzyme*]
MDH............ Maneuver Director Headquarters [*Military*]
MDH............ Maximum Diameter Heat [*Nuclear science*] (OA)
MDH............ Mean Dominant Height
MDH............ Medullary Dorsal Horn [*Anatomy*]
MDH............ Minimum Descent Height [*Aviation*] (FAAC)
MDH............ Month-Day-Hour [*Automotive manufacturing*]
MDH............ Multidirectional Harassment (PDAA)
MDHA .... Masters Deerhounds Association [*British*] (DBA)
MdHag......... Washington County Free Library, Hagerstown, MD [*Library symbol Library of Congress*] (LCLS)
MDHBA....... Medical-Dental-Hospital Bureaus of America (EA)
MDHC .... McDonnell Douglas Helicopter Co. [*Formerly, HHI*] (MCD)
MDHC .... Mersey Docks and Harbour Co. [*British*]
MDHE .... Herrera [*Dominican Republic*] [*ICAO location identifier*] (ICLI)
MdHeH .... Henryton State Hospital, Henryton, MD [*Library symbol Library of Congress*] (LCLS)
MdHi........... Maryland Historical Society, Baltimore, MD [*Library symbol Library of Congress*] (LCLS)
MDHJ.......... Methyl Dihydrojasmonate [*Organic chemistry*]
MDHL.......... Modified Hodges-Lehmann Estimator [*Statistics*]
MDHR......... Maximum Determined Heart Rate (STED)
MDHR......... Methyl Dihydroretinoate [*Biochemistry*]
MDHR......... Mini-Decay Heat Removal [*Nuclear energy*] (NRCH)
MDHS .... Malate Dehydrogenase, Soluble (STED)
MDHS .... McDonnell Douglas Helicopter Systems
MDHTSNAGEJTR... Movement of Dependents and Household Goods to Temporary Station[*s*] Not Authorized at Government Expense, Except as Prescribed in Joint Travel Regulations [*Army*] (AABC)
MDHV .... Marek's Disease Herpesvirus [*Medicine*] (DMAA)
MDHY .... Higuey [*Dominican Republic*] [*ICAO location identifier*] (ICLI)
MdHyD........ De Sales Hall School of Theology, Hyattsville, MD [*Library symbol Library of Congress*] (LCLS)
MdHyP........ Prince George's County Memorial Library, Hyattsville, MD [*Library symbol Library of Congress*] (LCLS)
MDI............. Bemidji, MN [*Location identifier FAA*] (FAAL)
MDI............. Magnetic Detection Indicator (IAA)
MDI............. Magnetic Direction Indicator
MDI............. Makurdi [*Nigeria*] [*Airport symbol*] (OAG)
MDI............. Management Development Institute (MCD)
MDI............. Manic Depression Interval [*Course*]
MDI............. Manic Depressive Illness
MDI............. Manual Data Input [*SAGE*]
MDI............. Market Decisions, Inc. [*Information service or system*] (IID)
MDI............. Market Development Index [*Business term*] (DOAD)
MDI............. Master Dimension Information
MDI............. Master Direction Indicator
MDI............. Master of Didactics
MDI............. Material Departmental Instruction
MDI............. Mechanical Dynamics Inc. (NITA)
MDI............. Media Directions, Inc.
MDI............. Medium Dependent Interface [*Computer science*] (CDE)
MDI............. Memotec Data, Inc. [*Toronto Stock Exchange symbol*]
MDI............. Mental Development Index [*Bayley Scales of Infant Development*] [*Psychometrics*]
MDI............. Meridian Diagnostics, Inc.
MDI............. Metered Dose Inhaler [*Medicine*]
MDI............. Methylenebis (Phenylisocyanate) (GNE)

MDI	Methylene Diisocyanate [*Organic chemistry*]
MDI	Methylene Diphenyl Diisocyanate [*Organic chemistry*]
MDI	Methylenediphenyl Isocyanate [*Organic chemistry*]
MDI	Michelson Doppler Imager [*Instrumentation*]
MDI	Michigan Disposal, Inc. (EFIS)
MDI	Micro Design International
MDI	Microdosimetric Instrumentation
MDI	Mid America Realty, Inc. [*Formerly, Dial REIT*] [*NYSE symbol*] (SAG)
MDI	Mid-America Realty Inv [*NYSE symbol*] (TTSB)
MDI	Military Decision Items (AFIT)
MDI	Mineral Deposit Inventory Database [*Ontario Geological Survey*] [*Information service or system Canada*] (CRD)
MDI	Minimum Discrimination Information [*Statistics*]
MDI	Miss-Distance Indicator [*Missiles*] (MUGU)
MDI	Mission Dependent Interface
MDI	Mission to the Deaf, International (EA)
MDI	Mobilization Day Increment [*Military*]
MDI	Mobilization Day Index [*Military*] (NG)
MDI	Monopulse Display Improvement (IAA)
MDI	Monthly Debit Industrial [*Insurance*]
MDI	Mouvement pour la Democratie et l'Independance [*Movement for Democracy and Independence*] [*Central Africa*] (PD)
MDI	Multiple Daily Injection [*Medicine*] (STED)
MDI	Multiple Design Interface
MDI	Multiple Display Indicator
MDI	Multiple Document Interface [*Computer science*] (PCM)
MDI	Multiple Dosage Insulin [*Medicine*] (STED)
MDI	Multiscore Depression Inventory [*Medicine*] (STED)
MDIA	Mental Development Index, Adjusted (STED)
MDIA	Multidimensional Intraction Analysis (DMAA)
MDIB	Minimum Distribution Incidental Benefit [*Finance*]
MDIBL	Mount Desert Island Biological Laboratory [*Salsbury Cove, ME*] [*Research center*]
MDIC	Microwave Dielectric Integrated Circuit (IEEE)
MDIC	Multi-Disciplinary Counter Intelligence
MDIC	Multilateral Disarmament Information Centre [*British*]
MDICP	McDonnell Douglas Industrial Control Products (MCD)
M DICT	More Dicto [*As Directed*] [*Pharmacy*]
M Dict	Morison's Dictionary of Decisions, Scotch Court of Session [*1540-1808*] [*A publication*] (DLA)
M Dict	Morrison's Dictionary of Decisions, Scotch Court of Session [*A publication*] (DLA)
M Did	Master of Didactics
M Di E	Master of Diesel Engineering
MDIE	Mother-Daughter Ionosphere Experiment
M Di Eng	Master of Diesel Engineering
MDIF	Manual Data Input Function [*Computer science*]
MDIF & W	Maine Department of Inland Fisheries and Wildlife, Fishery Research Management Division [*Research center*] (RCD)
MDII	Mechanical Dynamics [*NASDAQ symbol*] (TTSB)
MDII	Mechanical Dynamics, Inc. [*NASDAQ symbol*] (SAG)
MDII	Multiple Daily Insulin Injection (STED)
MDIN	Medalist Indus [*NASDAQ symbol*] (TTSB)
MDIN	Medalist Industries, Inc. [*NASDAQ symbol*] (NQ)
Md Inst C Art	Maryland Institute College of Art (GAGS)
MDIO	Maine Debris Information Office [*National Oceanic and Atmospheric Administration*]
M Dip	Master of Diplomacy
M-DIRT	Miss-Distance-Indicator Radioactive Tests [*Missiles*] (MUGU)
MDIS	Manual Data Input Section [*Computer science*]
MDIS	Manual Data Input System [*Computer science*]
M Dis	Marriage Dissolved
MDIS	McDonnell Douglas Information Services
MDIS	Medical Digital Imaging Support (RDA)
MDIS	Metadata Interchange Specification [*Computer science*]
MDISC	McDonnell Douglas International Sales Corp. (MCD)
MDISE	Merchandise
MDIT	Mean Disintegration Time (STED)
MDIU	Manned Data Insertion Unit (KSC)
MDIU	Manual Data Input Unit [*Computer science*]
M Div	Master of Divinity
MDJ	Jaro International SA [*Romania*] [*ICAO designator*] (FAAC)
MdJC	Maryland House of Corrections, Jessup, MD [*Library symbol Library of Congress*] (LCLS)
MDJCS	Memorandum by the Director, Joint Staff for the Joint Chiefs of Staff (MCD)
Md J Int'l L & Trade	Maryland Journal of International Law and Trade [*A publication*] (DLA)
MDJM	Jainamosa [*Dominican Republic*] [*ICAO location identifier*] (ICLI)
MDK	Mbandaka [*Zaire*] [*Airport symbol*] (OAG)
MDK	Mechanical Disconnect Kit
MDK	Medicore, Inc. [*AMEX symbol*] (SPSG)
MDK	Multimedia Development Kit [*Microsoft Corp.*] [*Computer science*]
MDL	Macro Description Language [*Computer science*] (BUR)
MDL	Madill [*S.*] Ltd. [*Vancouver Stock Exchange symbol*]
MDL	Magnetic Delay Line
MDL	Magnetic Double Layer
MDL	Main Defense Line (IAA)
MDL	Maintenance and Diagnostic Logic Display [*Burroughs*] (NITA)
MDL	Maintenance Diagnostic Logic [*Computer science*] (BUR)
MDL	Management Data List (AABC)
MDL	Manager's Discretionary Limit (DCTA)
MDL	Mandala Airlines PT [*Indonesia*] [*ICAO designator*] (FAAC)
MDL	Mandalay [*Myanmar*] [*Airport symbol*] (OAG)
MDL	Mandalay [*Burma*] [*Airport symbol*] (AD)

MDL	Man Days Lost (NUCP)
MDL	Master Data Library [*NASA*]
MDL	Master Deliverables List (AAEL)
MDL	Master Drawing List
MDL	Master Drug List (STED)
MDL	Master of Divine Literature
MDL	Material Deviation List [*Military*]
MDL	Medulloblastoma [*A type of brain cancer*] (CDI)
MDL	Mercury Delay Line
MDL	Method Detection Limit [*Analytical chemistry*]
MDL	Microprocessor Development Lab (MHDI)
MDL	MicroStation Development Language [*Intergraph Corp.*] (PCM)
MDL	Microwave Delay Line
MDL	Microwave Development Laboratories
MDL	Middle (MSA)
MDL	Military Demarcation Line (CINC)
MDL	Mine Defense Laboratory [*Panama City, Florida*] [*Navy*]
MDL	Miniature Display Light
MDL	Minimum Detection Limit [*Chemistry*]
MDL	Model (ADA)
MDL	Modular Design Language [*Computer science*] (CSR)
MDL	Modular Dummy Load
MDL	Module (MSA)
MDL	Morris Dam Laboratory
MDL	Motor Distal Latency [*Medicine*]
MDL	Muddle [*A computer language*]
MDL	Multipurpose Data Link (GAVI)
MDL	S Madill Ltd. [*Vancouver Stock Exchange symbol*]
MDL	University of Baltimore, Law Library, Baltimore, MD [*OCLC symbol*] (OCLC)
MD LA	United States District Court for the Middle District of Louisiana (DLA)
MdLaD	Divine Saviour Seminary, Lanham, MD [*Library symbol Library of Congress*] (LCLS)
MdLapC	Charles County Community College, La Plata, MD [*Library symbol Library of Congress*] (LCLS)
MD Laws	Laws of Maryland [*A publication*] (DLA)
MDLB	Municipal Development and Loan Board [*Canada*]
MDLC	Materiel Development and Logistic Command [*Army - replaced Ordnance, Engineer, Signal, Chemical and Quartermaster Overall Commands*]
MDLC	Mutliple Data Link Controller
MDLD	Midland Financial Group [*NASDAQ symbol*] (SAG)
MDLF	Mobile Drydock Launch Facility
MDLI	MDL Information Sys [*NASDAQ symbol*] (TTSB)
MDLI	MDL Information Systems, Inc. [*NASDAQ symbol*] (SAG)
MDL Info	MDL Information Systems, Inc. [*Associated Press*] (SAG)
Md-LL	Maryland State Law Library, Annapolis, MD [*Library symbol Library of Congress*] (LCLS)
MDLLE	Mademoiselle
MDLLS	Mediastinal Diffuse Large-Cell Lymphoma with Sclerosis [*Oncology*]
MDLND	Midland
MDLP	Mobile Dryer Loan Program
MdLP	United States Department of the Interior, Patuxent Wildlife Research Center, Laurel, MD [*Library symbol Library of Congress*] (LCLS)
MDLR	La Romana [*Dominican Republic*] [*ICAO location identifier*] (ICLI)
Md-LR	Maryland Department of Legislative Reference, Baltimore, MD [*Library symbol Library of Congress*] (LCLS)
MDLRC	Mental Disability Legal Resource Center [*Later, MPDLRSDB*] (EA)
MD L Rec	Maryland Law Record [*Baltimore*] [*A publication*] (DLA)
MD L Rep	Maryland Law Reporter [*Baltimore*] [*A publication*] (DLA)
MDLS	Marine Data Logger System
MdLuW	Maryland College for Women, Lutherville, MD [*Library symbol Library of Congress*] (LCLS)
MDLX	Military Demarcation Line Extended (MCD)
MdLxp	Lexington Park Library, Lexington Park, MD [*Library symbol Library of Congress*] (LCLS)
Mdm	Madam (WGA)
MDM	Magnetic Disc Memory
MDM	Magnetic Drum Memorex [*Computer science*] (IAA)
MDM	Magneto-Optical Display Memory
MDM	Maintenance Depot Material Control
MDM	Maize Dwarf Mosaic Virus [*Plant pathology*]
MDM	Manipulator Deployment Mechanism (MCD)
MDM	Manpower Determination Model [*Military*]
MDM	Marking Diagram Master (MCD)
MDM	Marshall Drummond McCall, Inc. [*Toronto Stock Exchange symbol*]
MDM	Mass Democratic Movement [*Political coalition*] [*South Africa*]
MDM	Master of Development Management
MDM	Maternal Diabetes Mellitus [*Medicine*]
MDM	Maximum Design Meter (MSA)
MDM	Mechanically Deboned Meat [*Food technology*]
MDM	Medical Decision Making (DMAA)
MDM	Medical Monitor (MCD)
MDM	Medium (AABC)
MDM	Medium-Depth Mine (MCD)
MDM	MedPartners/Mullikin [*NYSE symbol*] (TTSB)
MDM	Metal-Dielectric-Metal [*Filter*]
MDM	Metal Disintegration Machining [*Nuclear energy*] (NRCH)
MDM	Methylenedioxymethamphetamine [*A hallucinogenic drug, also known as "Ecstasy," banned in 1985*] [*Also, MDMA*]
MDM	Michigan-Dartmouth-Massachusetts Institute of Technology [*Observatory*]
MDM	Microdensitometer (IAA)
MDM	Midas Minerals, Inc. [*Toronto Stock Exchange symbol*]
MDM	Mid-Diastolic Murmur [*Medicine*]

MDM............ Minor Determinant Mix [*Penicillin*] [*Medicine*] (STED)
MDM............ Minor Determinant Mixture [*Medicine*]
MDM............ Mixed Dark Matter [*Cosmology*]
MDM............ Mobile Depot Maintenance [*Air Force*] (AFM)
MDM............ Modified Diffusion Method (NRCH)
MDM............ Modular Data Module (HGAA)
MDM............ Monolithic Diode Matrix
MDM............ Movement for a Democratic Military (EA)
MDM............ Movimento Democratico de Mocambique [*Democratic Movement of Mozambique*] (AF)
MDM............ Multiplexer/Demultiplexer (NASA)
MDM............ Multiprocessor Diagnostic Monitor (IAA)
MDMA .... M-Day Materiel Assets (AFIT)
MDMA .... Medical Device Manufacturers Association (NTPA)
MDMA .... Methylenedioxymethamphetamine [*A hallucinogenic drug, also known as "Ecstasy," banned in 1985*] [*Also, MDM*]
MDMAA ...... Mess Deck Master-at-Arms (DNAB)
MDMAF....... Mekong Delta Mobile Afloat Force [*Vietnam*]
Mdmarco ..... Medmarco, Inc. [*Associated Press*] (SAG)
MDMC .... Medmarco, Inc. [*NASDAQ symbol*]
MDMC .... Monte Cristy [*Dominican Republic*] [*ICAO location identifier*] (ICLI)
MDMCA ...... Melvil Dui Marching and Chowder Association (EA)
MdMC-G ..... Montgomery College, Germantown Campus, Germantown, MD [*Library symbol Library of Congress*] (LCLS)
MdMC-R ...... Montgomery College, Rockville Campus, Rockville, MD [*Library symbol Library of Congress*] (LCLS)
MdMC-T....... Montgomery College, Takoma Park Campus, Takoma Park, MD [*Library symbol Library of Congress*] (LCLS)
MDMCW ...... Medmarco Inc. Wrrt'A' [*NASDAQ symbol*] (TTSB)
MDMCZ ...... Medmarco Inc. Wrrt'B' [*NASDAQ symbol*] (TTSB)
mDMD .... Mouse Duchenne Muscular Dystrophy [*Medicine*]
MDME.......... Madame
Md-MH .... Maryland Department of Mental Hygiene, Baltimore, MD [*Library symbol Library of Congress*] (LCLS)
MDMH .... Methylol Dimethylhydantoin [*Organic chemistry*]
MDML .... Modified Maximum Likelihood [*Statistics*]
MDMN .... Modified Posterior Mean [*Statistics*]
MD-MOS ..... Multi-Drain Metal-Oxide Semiconductor (AAEL)
MDMR .... M-Day Materiel Requirement (AFIT)
MDMR .... M-Day Mobilization Requirement
MDMS .... Maintenance Data Management Schedule
MDMS .... Marketing Data Management System [*British*]
MDMS .... Microbiology Data Management System
MDMS .... Miss-Distance Measuring System
MDMS .... Moore Data Management Services [*Information service or system*] (IID)
MDMS .... Multiple Database Management System (NITA)
MDMV .... Maize Dwarf Mosaic Virus [*Plant pathology*]
MdMwH ...... Mount Wilson State Hospital, Mount Wilson, MD [*Library symbol Library of Congress*] (LCLS)
MDN .... Madison, IN [*Location identifier FAA*] (FAAL)
MDN .... Maiden Race [*Horse racing*]
MDN .... Managed Data Network
MdN .... Mandibular Nerve [*Anatomy*]
MDN .... Manufacturing Day Number (MCD)
MDN .... Mark der Deutschen Notenbank [*Mark of the German Bank of Issue*] [*Later, M*] (EG)
MDN .... Median (STED)
MDN .... Meridian Industrial Trust [*NYSE symbol*] (TTSB)
MDN .... Meridian Industrial Trust, Inc. [*AMEX symbol*] (SAG)
MDN .... Ministere de la Defense Nationale [*Department of National Defense*] [*Canada*]
MDN .... Mobilisation pour le Developpement National [*Haiti*] [*Political party*] (EY)
MDN .... Movimiento Democratico Nacionalista [*Nationalist Democratic Movement*] [*Guatemala*] [*Political party*]
MDN .... Movimiento Democratico Nicaraguense [*Nicaraguan Democratic Movement*] [*Political party*] (PPW)
MDN .... Universair [*Spain ICAO designator*] (FAAC)
MDNA .... Machinery Dealers National Association (EA)
MDNA .... Maximum Density Nitric Acid
MDNA .... Mobilehome Dealers National Association (EA)
MDNB .... Mean Daily Nitrogen Balance [*Medicine*]
MDNB .... Meta-Dinitrobenzene [*Organic chemistry*]
MD/NC .... Mechanical Drafting/Numerical Control (IEEE)
MDNC .... United States District Court for the Middle District of North Carolina (DLA)
MDNF .... Minimal Disjunctive Normal Form (MHDB)
MDNIS .... Machinery Dealers' National Information System
MDNMNA.... Moorish Divine and National Movement in North America (EA)
MDNP .... Methyl Dinitropentanoate [*An explosive*]
Md-NR .... Maryland State Department of Natural Resources, Annapolis, MD [*Library symbol Library of Congress*] (LCLS)
MDNR .... Michigan Department of Natural Resources
MDNR .... Minnesota Department of Natural Resources
MDNR .... Missouri Department of Natural Resources (DOGT)
MDNS .... Managed Data Network Services (NITA)
MDNT .... Midnight
MDN.WS..... Meridian Indl Tr Wrrt [*AMEX symbol*] (TTSB)
MDNX .... Modern Air Transport [*Air carrier designation symbol*]
MDO .... Macedonia AS [*Yugoslavia*] [*ICAO designator*] (FAAC)
MDO .... Maintenance Development Officer (MCD)
MDO .... MARC Development Office (NITA)
MDO .... Marine Diesel Oil
MdO .... Masoreten des Ostens (BJA)

MDO .... Massive Dark Object [*Galactic science*]
MDO .... Mechanized Desert Operations [*Military*] (MCD)
MDO .... Medium Density Overlay [*Plywood*]
MDO .... Membrane-Derived Oligosaccharide [*Biochemistry*]
MDO .... Methylenedioxyphenyl [*Organic chemistry*]
MDO .... Middleton Island, AK [*Location identifier FAA*] (FAAL)
MDO .... Mobile District Office [*Army Corps of Engineers*]
MDO .... Monthly Debit Ordinary [*Insurance*]
MdO .... Ruth Enlow Library of Garrett County, Oakland, MD [*Library symbol Library of Congress*] (LCLS)
MDOA .... Material Date of Arrival (DNAB)
MDOC .... Missouri Department of Conservation
MdOdN .... National Plastics Products Co., Odenton, MD [*Library symbol Library of Congress Obsolete*] (LCLS)
MdOdS........ Saran Yarn Co., Odenton, MD [*Library symbol Library of Congress Obsolete*] (LCLS)
MDOF .... Multiple Degree of Freedom [*Acoustics*]
MdOmR ...... Rosewood Center, Owing Mills, MD [*Library symbol Library of Congress*] (LCLS)
MDOP .... Malicious Destruction of Property
MDOP .... Maximum Design Operating Pressure [*NASA*]
MDOPA....... Methyldopamine [*Biochemistry*]
MDOS .... Motorola Disk Operating System
MDOSIS ..... Management Data Online Status/Inquiry System (MCD)
MDOT .... Michigan Department of Transportation
MDOT .... Modular Digital Output Timer
MDovC .... Chickering House, Dover, MA [*Library symbol Library of Congress*] (LCLS)
MDovS........ Saint Stephen's College, Dover, MA [*Library symbol Library of Congress*] (LCLS)
MDP .... Coppin State College, Parlett L. Moore Library, Baltimore, MD [*OCLC symbol*] (OCLC)
MDP .... Ferrocarril Mexicano del Pacifico [*Mexican Pacific Railroad Co., Inc.*] [*AAR code*]
MDP .... Magyar Dolgozok Partja [*Hungarian Workers' Party*] [*Political party*] (PPE)
MDP .... Main Data Path
MDP .... Main Display Panel (SAA)
MDP .... Maintainability Demonstration Plan (MCD)
MDP .... Maintenance Data Program (MCD)
MDP .... Maintenance Depot Production
MDP .... Maintenance Diagnostic Processor (NITA)
MDP .... Maintenance Diagnostic Program [*Computer science*] (IAA)
MDP .... Maintenance Display Panel (MCD)
MDP .... Malfunction Detection Package
MDP .... Malicious Destruction of Property
MDP .... Management Development Programme [*British*] (DCTA)
MDP .... Managing Director Posts [*British*] (DCTA)
MDP .... Mandibular Dysostosis and Peromelia (DB)
MDP .... Manic Depressive Psychosis
MDP .... Manpower Development Program [*Department of Labor*]
MDP .... Master Decommissioning Plan [*Nuclear energy*] (NRCH)
MDP .... Master Design Plan (MCD)
MDP .... Master Display Panel (KSC)
MDP .... Maximum Diastolic Potential [*Physiology*]
MDP .... Mean Datum Plane
MDP .... Mean Designation Point (CAAL)
MDP .... Mechanically Deboned Poultry [*Food technology*]
MDP .... Menthyldiphenyphosphine [*Organic chemistry*]
MDP .... Mento-Dextra Posterior [*A fetal position*] [*Obstetrics*]
MDP .... Meredith Corp. [*NYSE symbol*] (SPSG)
MDP .... Message Discrimination Process [*Telecommunications*] (TEL)
MDP .... Meteorological Datum Plane
MDP .... Methyldichlorophosphine [*Organic chemistry*]
MDP .... Methylene Diphosphonate [*Organic chemistry*]
MDP .... Methylenediphosphonic Acid [*Organic chemistry*]
MDP .... Microprocessor Debugging Program [*Computer science*] (IAA)
MDP .... Milliyetci Demokrasi Partisi [*Nationalist Democracy Party*] [*Turkey Political party*] (EY)
MDP .... Mindiptana [*Indonesia*] [*Airport symbol*] (OAG)
MDP .... Minimum Discernible Pulse (MCD)
MDP .... Missile Data Processor (OA)
MDP .... Mode Products, Inc. [*Vancouver Stock Exchange symbol*]
MDP .... Moslem Democratic Party [*Philippines*] [*Political party*] (PPW)
MDP .... Most Dispensable Program [*Television*]
MDP .... Motorola Data Processor [*Computer science*] (IAA)
MDP .... Mouvement Democratique et Populaire [*Popular Democratic Movement*] [*Senegal*] [*Political party*] (PPW)
MDP .... Mouvement Democratique Populaire [*Popular Democratic Party*] [*The Comoros*] [*Political party*] (PPW)
MDP .... Mouvement des Democrates Progressistes [*Burkina Faso*] [*Political party*] (EY)
MDP .... Movimento Democratico Portugues [*Portuguese Democratic Movement*] [*Political party*] (PPE)
MDP .... Movimiento Democratico del Pueblo [*Paraguay*] [*Political party*] (EY)
MDP .... Movimiento Democratico Peruano [*Peruvian Democratic Movement*] [*Political party*]
MDP .... Movimiento Democratico Popular [*Popular Democratic Movement*] [*Ecuador*] [*Political party*] (PPW)
MDP .... Movimiento Democratico Popular [*Popular Democratic Movement*] [*Chile*] [*Political party*] (PPW)
MDP .... Moving Deformable Barrier [*NHTSA*] (TAG)
MDP .... Multi-Disciplinary Practice
MDP .... Multidomain Polymer [*Biology*]
MDP .... Muramyl Dipeptide [*Immunochemistry*]

MDP .... Parkland Regional Library, Dauphin, Manitoba [*Library symbol National Library of Canada*] (NLC)
MD PA .... United States District Court for the Middle District of Pennsylvania (DLA)
MdPa .... United States Naval Air Station, Patuxent River, MD [*Library symbol Library of Congress*] (LCLS)
MDPC .... Mount Diablo Peace Center (EA)
MDPC .... Punta Cana [*Dominican Republic*] [*ICAO location identifier*] (ICLI)
MDPD .... Medical Director
MDPE .... Medium-Density Polyethylene (EDCT)
MDPF .... Methoxy(diphenyl)furanone [*Organic chemistry*]
MDPG .... Magnetic Digital-Pulse Generator
MDPHI .... Media Development Project for the Hearing Impaired (NITA)
MDPI .... Mathematics Diagnostic/Prescriptive Inventory (EDAC)
MDPM .... Maintenance Douglas Process Manual
MDPM .... Mechanically Deboned Poultry Meat [*Food technology*]
MdPM .... University of Maryland, Eastern Shore, Princess Anne, MD [*Library symbol Library of Congress*] (LCLS)
MDPN .... Midshipman
MDPP .... Puerto Plata/La Union [*Dominican Republic*] [*ICAO location identifier*] (ICLI)
MDPPQ .... Mouvement pour la Defense des Prisonniers Politiques du Quebec [*Movement for the Defense of Political Prisoners of Quebec*]
MdPpV .... United States Veterans Administration Hospital, Perry Point, MD [*Library symbol Library of Congress*] (LCLS)
MDPR .... Madrid Predict [*Orbit identification*]
MDPR .... Manufacturing Development and Process Request (AAG)
MDPS .... Metric Data Processing System [*Air Force*]
MDPS .... Mission Data Preparation System [*Military*] (CAAL)
MDPS .... Mobilization and Deployment Planning System [*Army*]
MDPS .... Mouvement pour la Democratie et le Progres Social [*Benin*] [*Political party*] (EY)
MDPSK .... Multilevel Differential Phase Shift Keying [*Computer science*] (CIST)
MDPT .... Median Preventive Maintenance Time (MCD)
MDPVM ...... Missionary Daughters of the Most Pure Virgin Mary (TOCD)
MDQ .... Mar Del Plata [*Argentina*] [*Airport symbol*] (OAG)
MDQ .... Market Driven Quality (AAEL)
MDQ .... MDC Communication CI [*AMEX symbol*] [*Formerly, MDC Corp. CI*] (SG)
MDQ .... MDC Communication CI'A' [*AMEX symbol*] (TTSB)
MDQ .... MDC Corp. [*AMEX symbol*] (SAG)
MDQ .... MDE Explorations [*Vancouver Stock Exchange symbol*]
MDQ .... Memory Deviation Quotient (DMAA)
MDQ .... Menstrual Distress Questionnaire [*Medicine*] (DMAA)
MDQ .... Minimum Detectable Quantity
MDQL .... Multidimensional Query Language [*Computer science*]
MDQS .... Management Data Query System [*Computer science*]
MDQW .... Modulation Dope Quantum Well (AAEL)
MDR .... Compania Mexicana de Aeroplanos SA [*Mexico ICAO designator*] (FAAC)
MDR .... Madras [*India*] [*Seismograph station code, US Geological Survey*] (SEIS)
MDR .... Magnetic Dipole Radiation
MDR .... Magnetic Disc Recorder (NTCM)
MDR .... Magnetic Document Reader (IAA)
MDR .... Magnetic Drum Recorder
MDR .... Magnetic Field Dependent Resistor (IAA)
MDR .... Maintainability Demonstration Report (MCD)
MDR .... Maintenance Data Report [*Army*] (AABC)
MDR .... Maintenance Demand Rate (NASA)
MDR .... Maintenance Design Requirement
MDR .... Major Design Review (KSC)
MDR .... Mandatory Device Reporting [*Program*]
MDR .... Manual Data Room
MDR .... Mark Document Reader [*Trademark*] [*Bell & Howell*]
MDR .... Market Data Retrieval [*Westport, CT*] [*Information service or system*] (IID)
MD R .... Maryland Reports [*A publication*] (DLA)
MDR .... Master Data Record (NG)
MDR .... Master Discrepancy Report (AAG)
MDR .... Master of Dispute Resolution (PGP)
MDR .... Material Deficiency Reports [*Program*]
MDR .... McDermott International, Inc. [*NYSE symbol*] (SPSG)
MDR .... McDermott Intl. [*NYSE symbol*] (TTSB)
MDR .... MD Review [*Social Security Administration*] (OICC)
MDR .... Mechanical Development Report (MCD)
MDR .... Medfra, AK [*Location identifier FAA*] (FAAL)
MDR .... Median Detection Range (NVT)
MDR .... Medical Device Register, Inc. (IID)
MDR .... Medical Device Reporting System
MDR .... Medium Data Rate (DOMA)
MDR .... Medium Deep Recess [*Automotive engineering*]
MDR .... Memory-Data Register
MDR .... Message Detail Recording [*Later, SMDR*] [*Telecommunications*]
MDR .... Metropolitan District Railway [*London*]
MDR .... MicroDesign Resources
MDR .... Microwave Device Reliability (MCD)
MDR .... Milestone Decision Review (MCD)
MDR .... Military Defense Readiness (SAA)
MDR .... Minimum Daily Requirement [*of a vitamin, etc.*] [*Later, Recommended Daily Requirement FDA*]
MDR .... Minor Discrepancy Repair [*NASA*] (KSC)
MDR .... Minor Discrepancy Review [*NASA*] (GFGA)
MDR .... Missile Deviation Report (AAG)
MDR .... Missing Data Report (NASA)

MDR .... Mission Data Reduction
MDR .... Mock-Up Discrepancy Report [*Aerospace*] (AAG)
MDR .... Monthly Director's Review [*NASA*] (NASA)
MDR .... Morphine-Dependent Rate
MDR .... Morphology Dependent Resonance [*Physics*]
MDR .... Motion Detection Radar [*Hughes Electronics*]
MDR .... Motor-Driven Relay [*or Roter*]
MDR .... Multichannel Data Recorder
MDR .... Multi Disc Reader [*Computer science*] (DGA)
MDR .... Multidrug Resistance [*Medicine*]
MDR .... Munition Data Requirement
MDRA .... Multidrug-Resistance Associated [*Genetics*]
MDRAF .... Mekong Delta Riverine Assault Force [*Vietnam*]
MDRAM .... Multibank DRAM [*Computer science*]
MDRAM .... Multibank Dynamic Random Access Memory [*Computer science*]
MDRC .... Manual Data Relay Center (MCD)
MDRC .... Materiel Development and Readiness Command [*Formerly, AMC*] [*See also DARCOM*] [*Army*]
MDRD .... Mission Data Requirements Document [*NASA*] (KSC)
MDRE .... Mass Driver Reaction Engine [*Aerospace*]
MD Rep .... Maryland Reports [*A publication*] (DLA)
MdRFD .... United States Food and Drug Administration, Rockville, MD [*Library symbol Library of Congress*] (LCLS)
MDRL .... Mandrel [*Mechanical engineering*]
MDRM .... Mouvement Democratique de Renovation Malgache [*Democratic Movement Malagasy Restoration*]
MdRMC .... Montgomery County Department of Public Libraries, Rockville, MD [*Library symbol Library of Congress*] (LCLS)
MdRNIO .... National Institute for Occupational Safety and Health, Rockville, MD [*Library symbol Library of Congress*] (LCLS)
MDRO .... Mission Disaster Relief Officer
MDROC .... Mission Design Requirements, Objectives, and Constraints
MDROF .... Managing Director of Royal Ordnance Factories [*British*] (RDA)
MDRP .... Migrant Dropout Reconnection Program [*Board of Cooperative Educational Services Geneseo Migrant Center*] (EA)
MDRP .... Movimiento Democratico Reformista Peruano [*Peruvian Democratic Reformist Movement*] [*Political party*] (PPW)
MDRS .... Management Data Reporting System (MCD)
MDRS .... Manpower Data Relay Station (IAA)
MDRS .... Manufacturing Data Retrieval System (NASA)
MDRS .... Mattis Dementia Rating Scale [*Medicine*] (DMAA)
MDRS .... Mission Data Retrieval System [*NASA*]
MDRS .... Mobilization Designation Reserve Section
MDRS .... Mylar Diaphragm Rupture System
MDRSF .... Multi-Dimensional Random Sea Facility [*Hydraulics Research Station*] (PDAA)
MDRSV .... Maize Dwarf Ringspot Virus [*Plant pathology*]
MDRT .... Million Dollar Round Table [*Des Plaines, IL*] (EA)
MDRTB .... Multidrug-Resistant Tuberculosis [*Medicine*]
MDRTC .... Diabetes Research and Training Center [*University of Michigan*] [*Research center*] (RCD)
MDRUS .... Miniature Donkey Registry of the United States (EA)
MDRX .... Medicis Pharmaceutical `A' [*NASDAQ symbol*] (TTSB)
MDRX .... Medicis Pharmaceutical Corp. [*NASDAQ symbol*] (SAG)
MDRY .... Madison Railway Co., Inc. [*AAR code*]
MDS .... Macintosh Development System [*Computer science*]
MDS .... Madison [*Wisconsin*] [*Seismograph station code, US Geological Survey Closed*] (SEIS)
MDS .... Madison, SD [*Location identifier FAA*] (FAAL)
Mds .... Madrepores [*Quality of the bottom*] [*Nautical charts*]
MDS .... Madrona Resources, Inc. [*Vancouver Stock Exchange symbol*]
MDS .... Magnetic Detection of Submarines [*British military*] (DMA)
MDS .... Magnetic Disk Storage [*Computer science*] (IAA)
MDS .... Magnetic Drum Storage [*Computer science*] (IAA)
MDS .... Magnetic Drum System
MDS .... Mail Distribution Schedule [*Air Force*] (AFM)
MDS .... Mail Distribution Scheme [*Army*]
MDS .... Main Device Scheduler (IAA)
MDS .... Main Dressing Station
MDS .... Maintenance Data System (MCD)
MDS .... Maintenance Diagnostic System (MCD)
MDS .... Maintenance Distribution Services Ltd. (EFIS)
MDS .... Maintenance Documentation System [*Bell System*]
MDS .... Malfunction Detection System [*Gemini*] [*NASA*]
MDS .... Management Data System (NASA)
MDS .... Manual Data Supervisor [*Computer science*] (IAA)
MDS .... Marine Distress Signal (IAA)
MDS .... Market Data System [*NYSE*]
MDS .... Market Decision System (HGAA)
MDS .... Mass Digital Storage
MDS .... Master Delivery Schedule (AAG)
MDS .... Master Development Schedule (KSC)
MDS .... Master Dimension Specification (MSA)
MDS .... Master Drum Sender
MDS .... Master of Decision Sciences (GAGS)
MDS .... Master of Dental Science (GAGS)
MDS .... Master of Dental Surgery
MDS .... Materiel Deployment Schedule
MDS .... Maternal Deprivation Syndrome [*Medicine*] (DMAA)
MDS .... Mccarron-Dial System (TES)
MDS .... Mechanized Documentation System
MDS .... Medical Documentation Service [*College of Physicians of Philadelphia*] [*Information service or system*] (IID)
MDS .... Medical Dressing Station
MDS .... Megawatt Demand Setter (NRCH)

MDS............	Memory Disk System [*Computer science*] (IEEE)
MDS............	Mennonite Disaster Service (EA)
MDS............	Message Distribution Systems
MDS............	Message-Dropping Station [*Military*] (IAA)
MDS............	Metal-Dielectric Semiconductor [*Electronics*] (PDAA)
MDS............	Metastable-Atom De-excitation Spectroscopy
MDS............	Meteoroid Detection Satellite [*NASA*]
MDS............	Meteorological Data System
MDS............	Methods Development Survey [*Bureau of the Census*] (GFGA)
MDS............	Metrofiber Multi-Megabit Data Service [*Metropolitan Fiber Systems, Inc.*]
MDS............	Metropolitan Dairymen's Society [*British*] (BI)
MDS............	Metropolitan Disposal Services, Inc. (EFIS)
MDS............	™Micky the D∫ Show [*Later, MDS/MMFC*] [*An association*] (EA)
MDS............	Microcomputer Development System (IAA)
MDS............	Microprocessor Development System [*Motorola, Inc.*]
MDS............	Microsurgery Drill System (DAVI)
MDS............	Microwave Doppler Speed [*Electronic engineering*]
MDS............	Microwave Multipoint Distribution Systems (EDAC)
MDS............	Middle Caicos [*British West Indies*] [*Airport symbol*] (OAG)
MDS............	Middle Distance Swimmer
MDS............	Milford Docks Air Services Ltd. [*British ICAO designator*] (FAAC)
MDS............	Milk Drinker's Syndrome [*Medicine*] (DMAA)
MDS............	Miller-Dieker Lissencephaly Syndrome [*Medicine*]
MDS............	Miller-Dieker Syndrome [*Medicine*] (DMAA)
MDS............	Mine Detection Set
MDS............	Minerals Data System [*Database*]
MDS............	Minimum Data Set [*Computer science*]
MDS............	Minimum Detectable Signal
MDS............	Minimum Discernable System
MDS............	Minimum Discernible Signal [*Radio*]
MDS............	Minimum Discernible System (NASA)
MDS............	Minuteman Defense Study [*DoD*]
MDS............	Minuteman Defense System [*DoD*]
MDS............	Mission Design and Series [*Military*] (AFM)
MDS............	Mission Development Simulator [*NASA*] (NASA)
MDS............	Mission Display System [*Navy*] (DOMA)
MDS............	Mobile Data Service (DA)
MDS............	Mobile Dental Services
MDS............	Mobile Distribution System (AFM)
MDS............	Model Designation and Series [*Military*] (AFIT)
MDS............	Modern Data Systems (IEEE)
MDS............	Modify Device Status (AAEL)
MDS............	Modular Data System
MDS............	Modular Decontamination System (DWSG)
MDS............	Modular Disc Storage (NITA)
MDS............	Modular Distribution System
MDS............	Modulate-Demodulate Subsystem
MDS............	Mohawk Data Sciences [*Computer science*] (IAA)
MDS............	Mohawk Data Systems Corporation (NITA)
MDS............	Molybdenum Disulfide [*Inorganic chemistry*]
MDS............	Monitor Distribution System [*Television*]
MDS............	Montant de Soutien [*Amount of Support*] [*A trade negotiating plan EC*]
MDS............	Mouvement Democrate Socialiste [*Democratic Socialist Movement*] [*France Political party*] (PPW)
MDS............	Mouvement des Democrates Socialistes [*Movement of Socialist Democrats*] [*Tunisia*] [*Political party*] (PPW)
MDS............	Mouvement pour la Democratie Sociale [*Burkina Faso*] [*Political party*] (EY)
MDS............	Movement for a Democratic Slovakia [*Former Czechoslovakia*] [*Political party*] (EY)
MDS............	Multidimensional Scaling [*Statistics*]
MDS............	Multiple Dataset System
MDS............	Multiple Deficiency Syndrome [*Medicine*] (DB)
MDS............	Multiple Deployment System [*Military*] (IAA)
MDS............	Multipoint Distribution Service [*Educational television*]
MDS............	Multipoint Distribution Services (ACRL)
MDS............	Multipoint Distribution System [*Line-of-sight relay system for electronic signals*]
MDS............	Multipoint Microwave Distribution System (WDAA)
MDS............	Multiprocessor Distributed System [*Raytheon*] (NITA)
MDS............	Municipal Data Service [*International City Management Association*] [*Information service or system*] (IID)
MDS............	Myelodysplasia [*Medicine*]
MDS............	Myelodysplastic Syndrome [*Medicine*]
MDS............	Myocardial Depressant Substance [*Cardiology*] (DAVI)
MDS............	St. Mary's College of Maryland, St. Mary's City, MD [*OCLC symbol*] (OCLC)
MdSalS.......	Salisbury State College, Salisbury, MD [*Library symbol Library of Congress*] (LCLS)
MdSalW......	Wicomico County Free Library, Salisbury, MD [*Library symbol Library of Congress*] (LCLS)
MDSB	Message Digest Signature Block (HGAA)
MDSC	Management Data Service Center
MD Sc	Master of Dental Science [*British*]
MDSC	Modular Digital Scan Converter (MCD)
MDSCB	Model Data Set Control Block (NITA)
MDSCC	Madrid Deep Space Communications Complex
MDSD	Magnetic Disk Storage Device [*Computer science*]
MDSD	Mate/Demate Stiff Leg Derrick (MCD)
MDSD	Monitoring and Data Support Division [*Environmental Protection Agency*] (GFGA)
MDSD	Santo Domingo/De las Americas Internacional [*Dominican Republic*] [*ICAO location identifier*] (ICLI)
MDSE	Merchandise (AFM)
Mdse	Merchandise (EBF)
mdse	Merchandise (WDAA)
MDSF	Mass Data Storage Facility
MDSF	Mission for Deep Sea Fishermen [*British*] (DI)
MDSF	Mouvement Democrate Socialiste de France [*Democratic Socialist Movement of France*] [*Political party*] (PPE)
MDSG	Merchandising
mdsg	Merchandising (DD)
MDSHPMN...	Midshipman
MDSI	Manufacturing Data Systems Inc. (NITA)
MDSI	San Isidro [*Dominican Republic*] [*ICAO location identifier*] (ICLI)
MDSIA	MDS [*Multipoint Distribution System*] Industry Association [*Telecommunications*] (EA)
MDSIC	Metal-Dielectric-Semiconductor Integrated Circuit [*Electronics*] (PDAA)
MdSim........	Howard County Library, Simpsonville, MD [*Library symbol Library of Congress*] (LCLS)
MDSJ	San Juan [*Dominican Republic*] [*ICAO location identifier*] (ICLI)
MDSL	Medis E Ltd. [*NASDAQ symbol*] (SAG)
MDSL	Moderate Speed Digital Subscriber Line [*Telecommunications*] (ACRL)
MDSLD	Mate/Demate Stiff Leg Derrick
MDSLF	Medis El Ltd [*NASDAQ symbol*] (TTSB)
MDS/MMFC...	™Micky the D∫ Show/Metal Micky Fan Club (EA)
MDS-MPOLL...	Mail Distribution Scheme / Military Post Office Location List (DNAB)
MDSN	Madisn Gas & Elec [*NASDAQ symbol*] (TTSB)
MDSN	Madison Gas & Electric Co. [*NASDAQ symbol*] (NQ)
MDSN	Maximum Dissolved Solids Nebulizer [*Product of Applied Research Laboratories*]
MDSNG........	Merchandising
MdSnW........	Worcester County Public Library, Snow Hill, MD [*Library symbol*] [*Library of Congress*] (LCLS)
MDSO	Medical and Dental Supply Office [*Military*]
MDSO	Mentally Disordered Sex Offender
MDSOR........	Monthly Depot Space and Operating Report
Md-SP	Maryland State Planning Commission, Baltimore, MD [*Library symbol Library of Congress*] (LCLS)
MDSP	San Pedro De Macoris [*Dominican Republic*] [*ICAO location identifier*] (ICLI)
MDSPR	Mode Suppressor (KSC)
MDSS	Magnetic Drum Storage System
MDSS	MAGTF [*Marine Air-Ground Task Force*] Decision-Support System (DOMA)
MDSS	Maintenance Decision Support System
MDSS	Mass Digital Storage System
MDSS	McDonnell Douglas Support Services (MCD)
MDSS	Medical Decision Support System (DMAA)
MDSS	Meteorological Data Sounding System (IEEE)
MDSS	Microprocessor Development Support System
MDSS	Mission Data Support System [*NASA*] (KSC)
MDSS	Multidimensional Switching System [*Instrumentation*]
MdSsD........	Library of Dianetics and Scientology, Silver Spring, MD [*Library symbol Library of Congress*] (LCLS)
MdSsFD	United States Food and Drug Administration, Bureau of Medical Services, Silver Spring, MD [*Library symbol Library of Congress*] (LCLS)
MdSsGS.......	Church of Jesus Christ of Latter-Day Saints, Genealogical Society Library, Silver Spring Branch, Silver Spring, MD [*Library symbol Library of Congress*] (LCLS)
MDSS-PCT...	Multidimensional Switching System - Packed Column Trap [*Instrumentation*]
MdSsV........	Vitro Laboratories, Silver Spring Laboratory Library, Silver Spring, MD [*Library symbol Library of Congress*] (LCLS)
MdSsW.......	Washington Theological Coalition, Silver Spring, MD [*Library symbol Library of Congress*] (LCLS)
MdSsX........	Xaverian College, Silver Spring, MD [*Library symbol Library of Congress*] (LCLS)
MDST..........	Mountain Daylight Saving Time (SSD)
MDST..........	Santiago [*Dominican Republic*] [*ICAO location identifier*] (ICLI)
MdStm.........	St. Mary's College of Maryland, St. Mary's City, MD [*Library symbol Library of Congress*] (LCLS)
MDSU	Mobile Diving and Salvage Unit (COE)
MdSuFR.......	Washington National Records Center, General Services Administration, Suitland, MD [*Library symbol Library of Congress*] (LCLS)
MDSV	Manned Deep Space Vehicle
MdsxWat	Middlesex Water Co. [*Associated Press*] (SAG)
MdSyH........	Springfield State Hospital, Sykesville, MD [*Library symbol Library of Congress*] (LCLS)
MDT............	Compagnie Air Mediterrannee [*France ICAO designator*] (FAAC)
MDT............	Harrisburg [*Pennsylvania*] [*Airport symbol*] (OAG)
MDT............	Maintenance Demand Time (MCD)
MDT............	Maintenance Downtime (MCD)
MDT............	Mandatory Date of Transportation [*Military*]
MDT............	Mandatory Drugs Testing (WDAA)
MDT............	Manual Data Technician [*Computer science*] (IAA)
MDT............	Manufacturers Delegated Testing (NITA)
MDT............	Mass Cell Degeneration Test [*Medicine*] (DB)
MDT............	Maximum Dive Time
MDT............	Mean Death Time
MDT............	Mean Delay Time
MDT............	Mean Detonating Time (CAAL)
MDT............	Mean Downtime (NASA)
MDT............	Mean Downtime [*Computer science*]
MDT............	Measurement Descriptor Table (NASA)

MDT............	Mechanically Deboned Turkey [Food technology]
MDT............	Median Detection Threshold (MAE)
MDT............	Median Dorsal Tract [Anatomy]
MDT............	Medium Data Technique [Computer science] (IAA)
MDT............	Med-Tech Systems, Inc. [Vancouver Stock Exchange symbol]
MDT............	Medtronic, Inc. [NYSE symbol] (SPSG)
MDT............	Mento-Dextra Transversa [A fetal position] [Obstetrics]
MDT............	Merchant Deposit Transmittal
MDT............	Mercury Dynamic Test
MDT............	Message Direction Table (MCD)
MDT............	Message Display Terminal (MCD)
MDT............	Middletown, PA [Location identifier FAA] (FAAL)
MDT............	Mini Disc Terminal [Computer science] (DGA)
MDT............	Minnesota Dance Theatre
MDT............	Mobile Data Terminal (MCD)
MDT............	Mobile Display Terminal [Vehicle navigation systems]
MDT............	Moderate (AFM)
MDT............	Modified Data Tag [Computer science] (IAA)
MDT............	Modular Display Tactical
MDT............	Most Demands to Be Traded [Baseball]
MDT............	Mountain Daylight Time
MDT............	Moviment de Defensa de la Terra [Spain Political party] (EY)
MDT............	Multidimensional Tasking [Honeywell, Inc.]
MDT............	Multidisciplinary Team
MDT............	Munitions Disposal Technician (SAA)
MDT............	Mutual Defense Treaty
MDT2..........	Martin Marietta, Diehl, Thorn-EMI, Thomson [Army]
MDTA..........	Manpower Development and Training Act [1962] [Later, CETA Department of Labor]
MDTA..........	McDonald Deep Test of Articulation [Speech and language therapy] (DAVI)
MDTA..........	Modulation, Demodulation, Terminal, and Associated Equipment
MDTB..........	Milk Distribution Trade Board [British] (DAS)
MDTC..........	MDT Corp. [NASDAQ symbol] (NQ)
MDT Cp	MDT Corp. [Associated Press] (SAG)
MD Tenn......	United States District Court for the Middle District of Tennessee (DLA)
MDTF..........	Macular Degeneration Task Force [Medicine]
MDTI...........	Missile Director Train Indicator
MDTI...........	Multiple Director Train Indicator (MCD)
MDTL..........	Modified Diode Transistor Logic [Electronics] (IAA)
MDTM.........	Mechanically Deboned Turkey Meat [Food technology]
MDTP..........	Materiel Developer's Test Program [Military]
MDTP..........	Multidisciplinary Treatment Plan [Medicine] (DAVI)
MDTR.........	Mean Diameter-Thickness Ratio (MAE)
MDTS.........	MegaBIT [Binary Digit] Digital Troposcatter Subsystem [Communications] (MCD)
MDTS.........	Mobile Doppler Tracking Station
MDTS.........	Modular Data Transaction System
MDTSCO......	Multiple Dealer Trading System [Investment term] (DICI)
MDTSCO......	McDonnell Douglas Technical Services Co. (NAKS)
MDTU.........	Mobile Dockside Transfer Unit
MdTW.........	Washington Missionary College, Tacoma Park, MD [Library symbol Library of Congress Obsolete] (LCLS)
MDTWN	Midtown
MDU	Maintenance Data Unit (MCD)
MDU	Maintenance Diagnostic Unit
mdu	Maryland [MARC country of publication code Library of Congress] (LCCP)
MDU	Master Driver Unit
MDU	MDU Resources Group [NYSE symbol] (TTSB)
MDU	MDU Resources Group, Inc. [NYSE symbol] (SPSG)
MDU	Medical Defence Union Ltd. [British] (BI)
MDU	Mendi [Papua New Guinea] [Airport symbol] (OAG)
MDU	Message Decoder Unit
MDU	Middle Dutch [Language, etc.]
MDU	Mid-North Resources [Vancouver Stock Exchange symbol]
MDU	Mine Disposal Unit
MDU	Missile Design Unit (SAA)
MDU	Mobile Demonstration Unit
MDU	Mobile Development Unit [Military] (GFGA)
MDU	Mobile Dynamic Unit (AAG)
MDU	Modular Dispensing Unit (AAEL)
MDU	Moral Development Unit [Prisoner reform program]
mdu	More Dicto Utendus [To Be Used as Directed] [Latin] (WDAA)
MDU	Motion Detection Unit [Nuclear energy] (NRCH)
MDU	Multidimensional Unfolding [Model] [Statistics]
MDU	University of Maryland, Baltimore, Health Sciences Library, Baltimore, MD [OCLC symbol] (OCLC)
MdU	University of Maryland, College Park, MD [Library symbol Library of Congress] (LCLS)
MdU-A	University of Maryland, Art Library, College Park, MD [Library symbol Library of Congress] (LCLS)
MdU-Ar.......	University of Maryland, Architecture Library, College Park, MD [Library symbol Library of Congress] (LCLS)
MdU-BC......	University of Maryland, Baltimore County Campus, Baltimore, MD [Library symbol Library of Congress] (LCLS)
MdU-C	University of Maryland, Chemistry Library, College Park, MD [Library symbol Library of Congress] (LCLS)
MdU-E	University of Maryland, Engineering and Physical Sciences Library, College Park,MD [Library symbol Library of Congress] (LCLS)
MdU-H	University of Maryland, Health Sciences Library, Baltimore, MD [Library symbol Library of Congress] (LCLS)
MDuHi........	Duxbury Rural and Historical Society, Duxbury, MA [Library symbol Library of Congress] (LCLS)
MdU-I	International Piano Archives at Maryland, University of Maryland, College Park, MD [Library symbol Library of Congress] (LCLS)
MdU-L	University of Maryland, School of Law, Baltimore, MD [Library symbol Library of Congress] (LCLS)
MDUO........	Myocardial Disease of Unknown Origin [Cardiology]
MdU-U	University of Maryland, Undergraduate Library, College Park, MD [Library symbol Library of Congress] (LCLS)
MDV............	Baltimore, MD [Location identifier FAA] (FAAL)
MDV............	Doctor of Veterinary Medicine
MDV............	Maldives [ANSI three-letter standard code] (CNC)
MDV............	Map and Data Viewer [NASA] (KSC)
MDV............	Marek's Disease Virus [Avian pathology]
MDV............	Master of Veterinary Medicine
MDV............	Maxim Development Ltd. [Vancouver Stock Exchange symbol]
MDV............	Medeva [AMEX symbol] (SPSG)
MDV............	Medeva ADR [AMEX symbol] (TTSB)
MDV............	Medium-Dollar Value
MDV............	Medouneu [Gabon] [Airport symbol] (OAG)
MDV............	Middlebury [Vermont] [Seismograph station code, US Geological Survey] (SEIS)
MDV............	Midivariant [Genetics]
MDV............	Mine-Dispensing Vehicle [Army]
MDV............	Minimum Detectable Velocity [Physics]
MDV............	Minimum Domian Velocity (IAA)
MDV............	Moldavian Airlines [Macedonia] [FAA designator] (FAAC)
MDV............	Mouvement Democratique Voltaique [Upper Volta Democratic Movement]
MDV............	Mucosal Disease Virus
MDV............	Multiple Dose Vial [Pharmacy]
M-DVD........	Magnetic Digital Versatile Disc
MDVL..........	Medeva plc [LO, exchange symbol] (TTSB)
mdvl	Medieval (VRA)
MDW	Chicago [Illinois] Midway [Airport symbol] (OAG)
MDW	Delta Waterfowl Research Station, Manitoba [Library symbol National Library of Canada] (NLC)
MDW	Fort Myer Library System and Fort McNair Post Library, Fort Myer, VA [OCLC symbol] (OCLC)
MDW	Mars Departure Window [Aerospace]
MdW	Masoreten des Westens (BJA)
MDW	Mass Destruction Weapons
MDW	Meadow [Postal Service standard] (OPSA)
MDW	Meadow Mountain [Vancouver Stock Exchange symbol]
MDW	Measured Daywork [Payment system]
MDW	Midway [Washington] [Seismograph station code, US Geological Survey] (SEIS)
MDW	Midway Airlines, Inc. [FAA designator] (FAAC)
MDW	Midway Aviation, Inc. [ICAO designator] (FAAC)
MDW	Military Defence Works [British]
MDW	Military District of Washington [DC]
MDW	Mine Disposal Weapon (NATG)
MDW	Minnesota, Dakota & Western Railway Co. [AAR code]
MDW	Multidimensional Warfare [Military] (CAAL)
MDW	Multipair Distribution Wire
MDW	Multiple Drop Wire [Telecommunications] (TEL)
MDWAC	Midwest Athletic Conference (PSS)
MD WCC.....	Maryland Workmen's Compensation Cases [A publication] (DLA)
MdWem......	Carroll County Public Library, Westminster, MD [Library symbol Library of Congress] (LCLS)
MdWemC....	Western Maryland College, Westminster, MD [Library symbol Library of Congress] (LCLS)
MdWemHi ...	Carroll County Historical Society, Westminister, MD [Library symbol] [Library of Congress] (LCLS)
MdwEx........	Midwest Exprss Holding [Associated Press] (SAG)
MDWF	Midwife
MdwFdl.......	Midwest Federal Financial [Associated Press] (SAG)
MDWFY	Midwifery
MDWS........	Meadows (MCD)
MdWst........	Med Waste [Associated Press] (SAG)
MDWST	Midwest
MDWSTRN...	Midwestern
MDWV........	Medwave, Inc. [NASDAQ symbol] (SAG)
MDWY........	Midway
MDX............	Medical Data Exchange [Los Altos, CA] [Commercial firm]
MDX............	Mercedes [Argentina] [Airport symbol] (OAG)
MDX............	Merritech Development [Vancouver Stock Exchange symbol]
MDX............	Middlesex [County in England]
MDX............	Multi-Indexing [Computer science] (CIST)
MDX............	University of Maryland, College of Library and Information Services, College Park, MD [OCLC symbol] (OCLC)
MDXDCR.....	Mode Transducer (KSC)
MDXR.........	Medar, Inc. [NASDAQ symbol] (NQ)
MDY............	Magnetic Deflection Yoke
MDY............	Middlebury College, Middlebury, VT [OCLC symbol] (OCLC)
MDY............	Midland Gold Corp. [Formerly, Midland Energy Corp.] [Vancouver Stock Exchange symbol]
MDY............	Midway [Midway Islands] [Seismograph station code, US Geological Survey Closed] (SEIS)
MDY............	Month, Date, Year
MDY............	Standard & Poor's MidCap 400 Depository Receipts [AMEX symbol] (SAG)
MDY............	Standard & Poor's MidCap Dep Rc [AMEX symbol] (TTSB)
MDYN.........	Molecular Dynamics, Inc. [NASDAQ symbol] (SAG)
MDZ............	Maritime Defense Zone [Program for drug interdiction]
MDZ............	MDC Corp. [Toronto Stock Exchange symbol]
MDZ............	Medford, WI [Location identifier FAA] (FAAL)

MDZ .... Mendoza [*Argentina*] [*Seismograph station code, US Geological Survey*] (SEIS)
MDZ .... Middle Zero (IAA)
MDZ .... Missile Danger Zone (NVT)
Me .... C. H. Boehringer Sohn, Ingelheim [*Germany*] [*Research code symbol*]
me---- .... Eurasia [*MARC geographic area code Library of Congress*] (LCCP)
ME .... Mache Einkeit (STED)
M/E .... Machine (ROG)
M/E .... Macrocytic/Normochromic [*Anemia*] [*Hematology*] (DAVI)
ME .... Macular Edema [*Ophthalmology*] (DAVI)
ME .... Magic Eye (DEN)
ME .... Magnetic Estimation (OA)
ME .... Magnetoelastic
ME .... Magneto-Electronic (PDAA)
ME .... Magnitude Estimation
ME .... Maine [*Postal code*]
ME .... Main Engine (KSC)
ME .... Main Entry [*Library Science*] [*Online database field identifier*]
Me .... Maine Reports (AAGC)
Me .... Maine State Library, Augusta, ME [*Library symbol Library of Congress*] (LCLS)
ME .... Maine Supreme Judicial Court Reports [*A publication*] (DLA)
ME .... Maintenance Equipment
ME .... Maintenance Evaluation (MCD)
ME .... Maitre [*Barrister, Advocate*] [*French*] (ROG)
ME .... Majestic Eagles (EA)
ME .... Male Equivalents [*Entomology*]
ME .... ™Malic∫ Enzyme
ME .... Malt Extract [*Microbiology*]
ME .... Management Engineering (KSC)
ME .... Management Evaluation [*Food Stamp Program*] [*Department of Agriculture*] (GFGA)
ME .... Managing Editor
ME .... Man-Hours Earned
ME .... Manic Episode (STED)
ME .... Manpower Estimate (AAG)
ME .... Manson Evaluation [*Psychology*]
ME .... Manufacturing Engineering (MCD)
ME .... Marbled Edges [*Bookbinding*]
ME .... Marche de l'Europe [*March of Europe*] (EAIO)
ME .... Marine Engine
ME .... Marine Engineer
ME .... Marriage Encounter
ME .... Marriage Evaluation [*Marital relations test*]
M-E .... Martini-Enfield [*Rifle*]
ME .... Master Equatorial
ME .... Master of Education
ME .... Master of Elements
ME .... Master of Engineering
ME .... Master of Mechanical Engineering [*Canada*] (ASC)
ME .... Materials Evaluation (PDAA)
ME .... Math Error [*IRS*]
ME .... Mature Equivalent (OA)
ME .... Maximum Effort
ME .... Maximum Energy
ME .... Meal
ME .... Measurement Engine (IAA)
ME .... Measuring Element
ME .... Mechanical Efficiency
M/E .... Mechanical/Electrical (AAG)
ME .... Mechanical Engineer [*or Engineering*]
ME .... Mechanical Equipment
ME .... Medial Eminence (DB)
ME .... Medial Epicondyle [*Medicine*]
Me .... Median
ME .... Median Eminence [*of hypothalamus*] [*Anatomy*]
ME .... Medical Education (MAE)
ME .... Medical Examiner
ME .... Medication Evaluation (DHP)
ME .... Medium Electroendosmosis [*Analytical biochemistry*]
ME .... Medium Energy
ME .... Megacycle (IAA)
Me .... Me'ilah (BJA)
Me .... Melendus [*Flourished, 1188-1209*] [*Authority cited in pre-1607 legal work*] (DSA)
ME .... Memory Element [*Computer science*]
ME .... Memory Error (WDAA)
ME .... Meningoencephalitis [*Medicine*] (DB)
ME .... Mercaptoethanol [*Biochemistry*]
ME .... Message Element [*Telecommunications*] (TEL)
ME .... Messerschmitt AG [*Germany ICAO aircraft manufacturer identifier*] (ICAO)
ME .... Metabolic and Electrolyte Disorders [*Medicine*] (MEDA)
ME .... Metabolism (STED)
ME .... Metabolizable Energy
ME .... Metal Evaporated [*Videotape*]
ME .... Metalsmith [*Navy*]
ME .... Metamyelocyte (STED)
ME .... Meters [*JETDS nomenclature*] [*Military*] (CET)
ME .... Methionine Enkephalin [*Biochemistry*]
ME .... Methodist
ME .... Methodist Episcopal
ME .... Methods Engineering (NG)
ME .... Methoxyethanol [*Organic chemistry*]

Me .... Methyl [*Organic chemistry*]
ME .... Methyleugenol (STED)
ME .... Mexican Stock Exchange
ME .... Microelectronic
ME .... Microembolization (STED)
M-E .... Microencapsulated
ME .... Micrometeoroid Explorer [*Satellite*]
ME .... Microsoft Editor [*Computer program*] (PCM)
ME .... Middle Ear
ME .... Middle East [*or Middle Eastern*]
ME .... Middle East Airlines [*ICAO designator*] (AD)
ME .... Middle English [*Language, etc.*]
ME .... Mid-Engine [*Automotive engineering*]
ME .... Military Electronics (MCD)
ME .... Military Engineer
ME .... Mill Edge (ADA)
ME .... Milliequivalent [*or Milligram Equivalent*] [*Also, MEQ*]
ME .... Mining Engineer
ME .... Minneapolis Eastern Railway
ME .... Miscellaneous Equipment (KSC)
ME .... Missile Electrician
ME .... Missionary Ecumenical (Rome) (TOCD)
ME .... Mission Capital Ltd. [*NYSE symbol*] (SAG)
ME .... Mission Envelope (AAG)
ME .... Mistress of English
ME .... Miter End [*Technical drawings*]
ME .... Mobility Equipment [*Military*] (AFM)
ME .... Modular Electronics (IAA)
ME .... Modulation Efficiency
ME .... Moessbauer Effect (OA)
ME .... Molecular Electronics
ME .... Moment Estimator (PDAA)
ME .... Moneta Porcupine Mines, Inc. [*Toronto Stock Exchange symbol*]
ME .... Montreal Exchange [*Canada*] (NUMA)
ME .... Morristown & Erie Railroad Co. [*AAR code*]
ME .... Most Eminent [*Freemasonry*] (ROG)
ME .... Most Excellent [*In titles*]
ME .... Mottled Edges [*Bookbinding*] (DGA)
ME .... Mouse Embryo [*Medicine*] (DMAA)
ME .... Mouse Encephalitis
ME .... Mouse Epithelial [*Cells*] [*Hematology*] (DAVI)
ME .... Mouvement Europeen [*European Movement*]
ME .... Movie Editor
ME .... Muhammadan Era
ME .... Multiengine
ME .... Municipal Engineering and Environmental Technology [*A publication British*]
ME .... Munitions Effectiveness
ME .... Muscle Examination (STED)
ME .... Muzzle Energy
ME .... Myalgic Encephalomyelitis [*Medicine*]
ME .... Mycobacterial Extracts [*Biochemistry*]
M:E .... Myeloid:Erythroid [*Ratio*] [*Hematology*]
ME .... Myoepithelium [*Cytology*]
ME3 .... Minority Engineering Education Effort [*Later, NACME*]
MEa .... Eastham Public Library, Eastham, MA [*Library symbol*] [*Library of Congress*] (LCLS)
MEA .... Macae [*Brazil*] [*Airport symbol*] (OAG)
MEA .... Magnetic Engineering Associates, Inc.
MEA .... Main Electronics Assembly (MCD)
MEA .... Maine State Library, Augusta, ME [*OCLC symbol*] (OCLC)
MEA .... Maintenance Engineering Analysis
MEA .... Male-Enhanced Antigen [*Medicine*] (DMAA)
MEA .... Malic Enzyme A (DB)
MEA .... Malt Extract Agar [*Culture media*]
MEA .... Manufacturing Engineering Analysis
MEA .... Marine Engineering Artificer [*Navy rating British*]
MEA .... Marine Engineers' Association [*A union*] [*British*]
MEA .... Marine Environmental Activities [*Marine science*] (MSC)
MEA .... Maritime Employers Association (NADA)
MEA .... Marketing Education Association (EA)
MEA .... Master of Engineering Administration
MEA .... Master of Engineering Architecture (GAGS)
MEA .... Material Experiment Analysis
MEA .... Materials Experiment Assembly
MEA .... [*The*] Mead Corp. [*NYSE symbol*] (SPSG)
MEA .... Meanook [*Canada*] [*Geomagnetic observatory code*]
MEA .... Measurements (NATG)
MEA .... Meat Extract Agar [*Microbiology*]
MEA .... Meath [*County in Ireland*] (ROG)
MEA .... Medical Equestrian Association [*British*] (DBA)
MEA .... Medical Exhibitors Association [*Later, HCEA*] (EA)
MEA .... Memory Inspection Ending Address (MHDB)
MEA .... Mercaptoethylamine [*Pharmacology*]
MEA .... Metal Edge Amplifier (MCD)
MEA .... Metopon Ethnikis Adadimiourgias [*National Regeneration Front*] [*Greece*] [*Political party*] (PPE)
MEA .... Metropolitan Economic Area
MEA .... Metropolitan Entertainers' Association [*British*] (BI)
MEA .... Middle East Airlines - Air Liban [*Lebanon*]
MEA .... Middle East Association [*British*] (EAIO)
MEA .... Minimum Energy Absorbed
MEA .... Minimum Enroute Altitude
MEA .... Minimum en Route IFR Altitude [*FAA*] (TAG)
MEA .... Minister, External Affairs (CINC)

MEA .... Ministry of External Affairs, Library Services Division [*UTLAS symbol*]
MEA .... Missionary Evangelical Alliance [*See also AME*] [*Switzerland*] (EAIO)
MEA .... Modular Engine Analyzer [*Automotive engineering*]
MEA .... Moisture Evaluation Analysis (PDAA)
MEA .... Monoethanolamine [*Organic chemistry*]
MEA .... Monoethylamine [*Organic chemistry*]
MEA .... Monteagle [*Australia Seismograph station code, US Geological Survey Closed*] (SEIS)
MEA .... Multimode Error Analysis
MEA .... Multiple Endocrine Abnormalities [*Medicine*]
MEA .... Multiple Endocrine Adenomas [*Oncology*]
MEA .... Multiple Endocrine Adenomatosis [*Medicine*] (DMAA)
MEA .... Multiple Endocrine Adenopathy [*Endocrinology*] (DAVI)
MEA .... Municipal Employees Association (NADA)
MEA .... Munitions Effectiveness Assessment (DOMA)
MEA .... Musical Educators Association (NADA)
MEA .... Music Editors Association (EA)
MEA .... Myalgic Encephalomyelitis Association [*British*] (DBA)
MEAB .... Maintenance Engineering Analysis Board
MEAC .... Manufacturing Engineering Applications Center [*Worchester Polytechnic Institute*] [*Research center*] (RCD)
MEAC .... Mid-Eastern Athletic Conference
MEACE .... Military Engineering Applications of Commercial Explosives [*Army*] (PDAA)
MEACN .... Maintenance Engineering Analyses Control Number [*DoD*]
MEACON ..... Masking Beacon (IAA)
MEACONING... Measuring and Confusing (DNAB)
ME Acts ...... Acts, Resolves, and Constitutional Resolutions of the State of Maine [*A publication*] (DLA)
MEAD .... Maintenance Engineering Analysis Data
Mead .... [*The*] Mead Corp. [*Associated Press*] (SAG)
MEAD .... Memphis Army Depot (AABC)
MEAD .... Microbial Evaluation Analysis Device (PDAA)
Mead-J .... Mead Johnson [*Commercial firm*] [*Pharmacology*] (DAVI)
MEADOW ..... Meadow [*Commonly used*] (OPSA)
MEADOWS... Meadows [*Commonly used*] (OPSA)
MEADS .... Maintenance Engineering Analysis Data System
MEADS .... Medium [*Range*] Extended Air Defense System [*USA-Europe*]
MEAF .... Middle East Air Force [*British*]
MEAFSA ...... Middle East/Southern Asia and Africa South of the Sahara [*Military*]
MeAIB .... (Methylamino)isobutyric Acid [*Biochemistry*]
MEAL .... Master Equipment Allowance [*or Authorization*] List [*Military*]
MEAL .... Media Expenditure Analysis Ltd. [*Database producer*]
MEA(L) .... Mission of Economic Affairs in London [*World War II*]
MEAL .... Mobile Equipment Allowance List (MCD)
MEAM .... Advisory Committee for Mechanical Engineering and Applied Mechanics [*Washington, DC*] [*Terminated, 1985*] [*National Science Foundation*] (EGAO)
MeAM .... Augusta Mental Health Institute, Augusta, ME [*Library symbol Library of Congress*] (LCLS)
MeAMH .... Maine State Department of Human Services, Augusta, ME [*Library symbol Library of Congress*] (LCLS)
MeAMM .... Maine State Museum, Augusta, ME [*Library symbol Library of Congress*] (LCLS)
MeAMP .... Maine State Planning Office, Augusta, ME [*Library symbol*] [*Library of Congress*] (LCLS)
MEAN .... Manganese-Enhanced Austenitic Nitrogen Steel
MEAN .... Microcomputer Education Application Network [*Commercial firm*] (EA)
MEANINGEX... Meaning Extraction [*Programming language*] [*1971*] (CSR)
Means .... Mean's Kansas Reports [*A publication*] (DLA)
MEANT .... Meat Exporters' Association of the Northern Territory [*Australia*]
MEAP .... Maintenance Engineering Analysis Program
MEAP .... Michigan Educational Assessment Program
MEAP .... Military Economic Advisory Panel (MCD)
MEAP .... Multiphasic Environmental Assessment Procedure (DMAA)
MEAPL .... Manufacturing and Engineering Assembly Parts List [*File*]
MEAPS .... Method of Ensemble Average of Periodic Systems
MEAR .... Maintenance Engineering Analysis Record [*or Report*]
MEAR .... Maintenance Engineering Analysis Request [*NASA*] (NASA)
MEARS .... Multi-User Engineering Change Proposal Automated Review System (RDA)
Mears Just... Mears' Edition of Justinian and Gaius [*A publication*] (DLA)
MEAS .... Measure (AABC)
MEAS .... Measurement (ROG)
meas .... Measurement (REAL)
MEAS .... Measuring
MEASAT ...... Malaysia East Asia Satellite
MEASCAL .... Measure Calibrate (IAA)
Meas Control (1962-64)... Measurement and Control (1962-64) [*A publication*]
Meas Spcl ... Measurement Specialities, Inc. [*Associated Press*] (SAG)
MEASURE ... Metrology Automated System for Uniform Recall and Reporting [*Navy*]
MEAT .... Manpower Employment Assistance Training [*Act*] [*Pennsylvania*]
MEAT .... Meat Exporters' Association of Tasmania [*Australia*]
MEAT .... Multiedge Adaptive Tracker (MCD)
MEATR .... Materials, Engineering, and Advanced Test Reactor (SAA)
MeAu .... Auburn Public Library, Auburn, ME [*Library symbol Library of Congress*] (LCLS)
MeAU .... University of Maine at Augusta, Augusta, ME [*Library symbol Library of Congress*] (LCLS)
MeAub .... Auburn Public Library, Auburn, ME [*Library symbol*] [*Library of Congress*] (LCLS)
MEAV .... Meat Exporters' Association of Victoria [*Australia*]
MeaVlly .... Meadow Valley Corp. [*Associated Press*] (SAG)

MeaVly .... Meadow Valley Corp. [*Associated Press*] (SAG)
MEAWS .... Maintenance Engineering Analysis Work Sheet (DNAB)
Me B .... Bachelor of Metaphysics
MEB .... Bangor Mental Health Institute, Bangor, ME [*OCLC symbol*] (OCLC)
MeB .... Bowdoin College, Brunswick, ME [*Library symbol Library of Congress*] (LCLS)
MEB .... Main Electronics Box (NASA)
MEB .... Maine Motor Rate Bureau, Portland ME [*STAC*]
MEB .... Malic Enzyme B (DB)
MEB .... Manufacturing Evaluation Board (MCD)
MEB .... Marine Expeditionary Brigade
MEB .... Master Electronics Board
MEB .... Maxton, NC [*Location identifier FAA*] (FAAL)
MEB .... Mechanical Engineering Bulletin [*A publication*] (GFGA)
MEB .... Medial Efferent Bundle [*Neuroanatomy*]
MEB .... Medical Board
MEB .... Medical Evaluation Board [*Military*] (DAVI)
MEB .... Melbourne [*Australia Airport symbol*] (OAG)
MEB .... Mercury Electron Bombardment
MeB .... Methylene Blue [*Organic chemistry*]
MEB .... Midlands Electricity Board [*British*]
MEB .... Military Early Bird
MEB .... Modem Evaluation Board (NITA)
MEB .... Moderate Environment Buoy [*Marine science*] (MSC)
MEB .... Muscle-Eye-Brain [*Disease*] [*Medicine*] (DMAA)
MeBa .... Bangor Public Library, Bangor, ME [*Library symbol Library of Congress*] (LCLS)
MEBA .... Marine Engineers' Beneficial Association
MeBaH .... Husson College, Bangor, ME [*Library symbol Library of Congress*] (LCLS)
MeBaHi .... Bangor Historical Society, Bangor, ME [*Library symbol Library of Congress*] (LCLS)
MeBarhJ ...... Jackson Laboratory, Bar Harbor, ME [*Library symbol Library of Congress*] (LCLS)
MeBaT .... Bangor Theological Seminary, Bangor, ME [*Library symbol Library of Congress*] (LCLS)
MeBath .... Patten Free Library, Bath, ME [*Library symbol Library of Congress*] (LCLS)
MeBathM ..... Maine Maritime Museum, Bath, ME [*Library symbol*] [*Library of Congress*] (LCLS)
MEBBAS ...... Mission Essential Bare Base Augmentation Sets [*Air Force*]
MeBC .... Captain John Curtis Memorial Library, Brunswick, ME [*Library symbol*] [*Library of Congress*] (LCLS)
MEBD .... Medical Evaluation Board [*Military*] (GFGA)
MEBE .... Middle East Basic Encyclopedia [*A publication*] (MCD)
MEBES .... Manufacturing Electron Beam Exposure System (IAA)
MEBFEX ...... Marine Expeditionary Brigade Field Exercise (NVT)
ME-BH .... Medial Eminence-Basal Hypothalamus (DB)
MEBLEX ...... Marine Expeditionary Brigade Landing Exercise
MEBO .... Main Engine Burnout (NASA)
MeBP .... Pejepscot Historical Society, Brunswick, ME [*Library symbol Library of Congress*] (LCLS)
Me-BPH ...... Maine State Library Service for the Blind and Physically Handicapped, Augusta, ME [*Library symbol Library of Congress*] (LCLS)
MEBS .... Marketing, Engineering, and Business Services [*Telecommunications*] (TEL)
MEBS .... Medium Energy Backscattering Spectrometry (AAEL)
MEBS .... Multicore Extruded Bar Solder
MeBSA .... Methylated Bovine Serum Albumin [*Biochemistry*]
MEBU .... Maschinengewehr-Eisenbeton-Unterstand [*Machine-Gun-Iron-Concrete-Emplacement*] [*German "pill box," battlefield redoubts World War I*]
MEBU .... Mission Essential Backup (MCD)
MEC .... Maine Central Railroad Co. [*AAR code*]
MEC .... Main Engine Console (AAG)
MEC .... Main Engine Controller [*NASA*] (NASA)
MEC .... Main Engine Cutoff [*Aerospace*] (AAG)
MEC .... Main Evaluation Center (NVT)
MEC .... Major Events Committee [*Victoria, Australia*]
MEC .... Manta [*Ecuador*] [*Airport symbol*] (OAG)
MEC .... Manual Emergency Controls [*Aerospace*] (KSC)
MEC .... Manufacturing Engineering Council (EA)
MEC .... Map Editing Console
MEC .... Marginal Efficiency of Capital [*Economics*]
MEC .... Marine Expeditionary Corps (NVT)
MEC .... Maritime Electric Co. Ltd. [*Toronto Stock Exchange symbol*]
MEC .... Market Economy Country
MEC .... Master Evaluation Center (MCD)
MEC .... Master Event Controller [*NASA*] (NASA)
M Ec .... Master of Economics
MEC .... Master of Engineering Chemistry
MEC .... Materials Engineering Code
MEC .... Maximum Endurable Concentration (NATG)
MEC .... Mechernich [*Federal Republic of Germany*] [*Seismograph station code, US Geological Survey Closed*] (SEIS)
MEC .... Meconium [*Gynecology*]
MEC .... Median Effective Concentration (DMAA)
MEC .... Medical Examination Centre [*British World War II*]
MEC .... Medicines Evaluation Committee [*Australia*]
MEC .... Member of Executive Council [*British*]
MEC .... Mercado Comune Europeo [*European Common Market*] [*Spanish*] (DLA)
MEC .... Mercury Aircourier Service [*ICAO designator*] (FAAC)

MEC	Merrimack Education Center [*Chelmsford, MA*] [*Information service or system*]
MEC	Meteorological Equipment Change (MCD)
MEC	Meteorology Engineering Center [*Navy*] (MCD)
MEC	Methodist Episcopal Church
MEC	Metrolina Educational Consortium [*North Carolina*] (EDAC)
MEC	Microelectronics Center
MEC	Microencapsulation [*Chemical engineering*]
MEC	Microwave Electronics Corp.
MEC	MidAmerican Energy [*NYSE symbol*] (TTSB)
MEC	Mid American Energy Co. [*NYSE symbol*] (SAG)
MEC	Middle Ear Canal (DMAA)
MEC	Middle Ear Cell (BABM)
MEC	Middle East Centre [*University of Cambridge*] [*British*] (CB)
MEC	Middle East Command [*Military*]
MEC	Military Equipment Code (DNAB)
MEC	Military Essentiality Class [*or Code*]
MEC	Minimum Effective Concentration [*Medicine*]
MEC	Minimum Energy Curve (IAA)
MEC	Minimum Essential Criteria (MCD)
MEC	Minimum Explosive Concentration [*Safety*]
MEC	Missile Engagement Console [*Military*] (CAAL)
MEC	Missile Engagement Controller [*Military*] (CAAL)
MEC	Missile Equipment Code
MEC	Mission Events Controller [*NASA*] (MCD)
MEC	Mitchell Energy Corp. (EFIS)
MEC	Mobile Examination Center [*Department of Health and Human Services*] (GFGA)
MEC	Mobility Equipment Command [*Later, TROSCOM*] [*Army*]
MEC	Molecular Exclusion Chromatography
MEC	Monetary and Economic Council (NADA)
MEC	Monethylcholine [*Biochemistry*]
MEC	Most Excellent Companion [*Freemasonry*] (ROG)
MEC	Movimiento Emergente de Concordia [*Emerging Movement for Harmony*] [*Guatemala*] [*Political party*] (PPW)
MEC	Multimedia European Center
MECA	Macedonian Educational and Cultural Association [*Australia*]
MECA	Main Engine Controller Assembly [*NASA*] (NASA)
MECA	Maintainable Electronics Component Assembly
MECA	Malfunctioned Equipment Corrective Action
MECA	Manufacturers of Emission Controls Association (EA)
MECA	Map Exercise Computer Assistance (MCD)
MECA	Mars: Evolution of Its Climate and Atmosphere [*Planetary science project*]
MECA	Matsushita Electric Corp. of America (IAA)
MECA	Measure of Elementary Communication Apprehension (EDAC)
MECA	Medical Emergency Calling Aid (MCD)
MECA	Mercury Evaporation and Condensation Analysis [*NASA*]
MECA	Micro Education Corp. of America
MECA	Military Educators and Counselors Association (EA)
MECA	Missile Electronics and Computer Assembly [*Military*] (PDAA)
MECA	Molecular Emission Cavity Analysis [*Flame spectrophotometry*]
MECA	Multielement Centrifugal Aerowindow
MECA	Multielement Component Array
MECA	Multivalue Electronic Circuit Analysis (IAA)
MECAB	Regional Bureau of the Middle East Committee for the Affairs of the Blind [*Saudi Arabia*] (EAIO)
MECACON	Middle East Civil Aviation Conference (PDAA)
Mecano	Mechanotherapy [*Physical therapy*] (DAVI)
MECAP	Medical Examiners and Coroners Alert Program [*Consumer Product Safety Commission*]
MECAR	Metropolitan Engineers Council on Air Resources
MECAS	Middle East Center for Arab Studies
MECAS	Multienergy Californium Assay System [*Nuclear energy*] (NRCH)
MeCasM	Maine Maritime Academy, Castine, ME [*Library symbol Library of Congress*] (LCLS)
MECAssn	Medical Eye Centre Association [*British*] (DBA)
MECC	Micellar Electrokinetic Capillary Chromatography
MECC	Middle East Council of Churches (EA)
MECC	Minnesota Educational Computing Corp. [*NASDAQ symbol*] (SAG)
MECC	Muslim Education Co-Ordinating Council (AIE)
MECCA	Manufacturing Engineering and Cost Control Applications (NITA)
MECCA	Master Electrical Common Connector Assembly (MCD)
MECCA	Mechanized Catalog (IEEE)
MECCA	Milwaukee Exposition and Convention Center and Arena
MECCA	Missile Environment Computer Control Analysis (MCD)
MECCA	Missionary and Ecumenical Council of the Church Assembly [*Church of England*]
MECCA	Modular Electron Column Control and Automation
MECCAS	Microbial Exchanges and Coupling in Coastal Atlantic Systems
MeCCNU	Methyl(chloroethyl)cyclohexylnitrosourea [*Semustine*] [*Antineoplastic drug*]
MECD	Military Equipment Characteristics Document (RDA)
MEcDev	Master of Economics of Development
MECE	Master of Electrical and Computer Engineering (PGP)
MECE	Master of Electrochemical Engineering
MECE	Micellar Electrokinetic Capillary Electrophoresis [*Analytical chemistry*]
MECE	Movement, Ethyl Chloride, and Elevation [*Medicine*]
MECEA	Mutual Educational and Cultural Exchange Act of 1961
MEC-ECR	Management Engineering Steering Committee for Embedded Computer Resources (MCD)
MECEd	Master of Early Childhood Education
MECEP	Marine Corps Enlisted Commissioning Education Program (DNAB)
MECF	Main Engine Computational Facilities [*NASA*] (NASA)
MECF	Micks External Compression Fixator [*Instrumentation*]
MECG	Material Electrocardiogram (MCD)
MECG	Maternal Electrocardiogram [*Cardiology*] [*Obstetrics*] (DAVI)
MECH	Mechanic [*or Mechanics*] (AFM)
Mech	Mechanica [*of Aristotle*] [*Classical studies*] (OCD)
MECH	Mechanical (NAKS)
mech	Mechanical (DD)
Mech	Mechanical (AL)
MECH	Mechanics Savings Bank [*NASDAQ symbol*] (SAG)
MECH	Mechanism [*Automotive engineering*]
Mech	Mechanized (VNW)
MECH	Mechanized (DOMA)
MECH	Methodist Episcopal Church
MECHBAD	Mechanic Badge
MECHBAT	Mechanized Battalion [*Army*]
MechDy	Mechanical Dynamics, Inc. [*Associated Press*] (SAG)
ME Ch E	Master of Electrochemical Engineering
Mech E	Mechanical Engineer (PGP)
ME(Chem)	Master of Engineering (Chemical) (ADA)
Mechem	Mechem on Agency [*A publication*] (DLA)
Mechem	Mechem on Partnership [*A publication*] (DLA)
Mechem Ag	Mechem on Agency [*A publication*] (DLA)
Mechem Pub Off	Mechem on Public Offices and Officers [*A publication*] (DLA)
MECHEN	Mechanical Engineering (NITA)
Mech Eng	Mechanical Engineer
MECHENGR	Mechanical Engineer
MECH/HYD	Mechanical/Hydraulic
MECH I/C	Mechanic in Charge (DCTA)
MECHINF	Mechanized Infantry [*Army*]
MECHL	Mechanical
MECH L	Mechanic's Lien [*Legal term*] (DLA)
MECHN	Mechanician [*Navy British*]
MECHNL	Mechanical
MECHSFIL	Mechanized Sandbag Filler and Sealer (MCD)
MECHSIM	Mechanical Simulation [*of a computer-based directory assistance system*]
MECHSM	Mechanism
MechSv	Mechanics Savings Bank [*Associated Press*] (SAG)
MECHTRAM	Mechanization of Selected Transportation Movement
MECI	Member of the Institute of Employment Consultants [*British*] (DBQ)
MECI	Mission Essential Contingency Item [*Military*]
MECIF	Monocyte-Derived Endothelial Cell Inhibitory Factor (DB)
MECK	Mecklermedia Corp. [*NASDAQ symbol*] (SAG)
Mecklm	Mecklermedia Corp. [*Associated Press*] (SAG)
MECL	Motorola Emitter-Coupled Logic (IEEE)
MECL	Multiemitter-Coupled Logic (IAA)
MECM	Meridional Elementary Circulation Mechanism
MECN	Mecon Inc. [*NASDAQ symbol*] (TTSB)
MECO	Main Engine Cutoff [*Aerospace*]
MECO	Manual Equipment Checkout (NG)
MECOBO	Military Export Cargo Offering and Booking Office
MECOM	Marine Engine Condition Monitor (PDAA)
MECOM	Middle East Command [*Military*]
MECOM	Middle East Electronic Communications Show and Conference [*Arabian Exhibition Management WLL*] [*Manama, Bahrain*]
MECOM	Mobility Equipment Command [*Later, TROSCOM*] [*Army*]
MECOMSAG	Mobility Equipment Command Scientific Advisory Group (MCD)
M Econ	Master of Economics (PGP)
MEconS	Master of Economic Science (ADA)
MEconSt	Master of Economic Studies (ADA)
MeCP	Methyl-CCNU, Cytoxan, Prednisone [*Antineoplastic drug*] (CDI)
MECP	Multielliptical Cavity Pump
MECPr	MidAmer Energy $1.7375 Pfd [*NYSE symbol*] (TTSB)
MECR	Maintenance Engineering Change Request (MCD)
MEc(Reg Plan)	Master of Economics in Regional Planning (ADA)
MECS	Manufacturing Energy Consumption Survey [*Department of Energy*] (GFGA)
MECS	Maximal Electroconvulsive Seizure [*Neurophysiology*]
MECS	Medicus Systems Corp. [*NASDAQ symbol*] (SAG)
MECS	Medicus Systems Softwr [*NASDAQ symbol*] (TTSB)
MECT	Mission Endurance Cycle Test
MECU	Master Engine Control Unit
MECU	Member of the English Church Union
MECU	Municipal Employees Credit Union (NADA)
MECWB	Middle East Committee for the Welfare of the Blind (EA)
MECY	Methotrexate, Cyclophosphamide [*Antineoplastic drug regimen*]
MECZ	Mechanize (AAG)
MED	Chicago, IL [*Location identifier FAA*] (FAAL)
MED	Macro Editor/Debugger [*Personics Corp.*] [*Computer science*] (PCM)
MED	Maine Department of Transportation, Augusta, ME [*OCLC symbol*] (OCLC)
MED	Manhattan Engineer District [*Developed atomic bomb; dissolved, 1946*]
MED	Manipulative Electronics Deception (MCD)
MED	Manual Electron Device
MED	Manual Entry Device
MED	Manufacturing Engineering Document (SAA)
M Ed	Master of Education
MEd	Master of Education [*British*] (DET)
MED	Master of Education of the Deaf (GAGS)
MED	Master of Elementary Didactics
MED	Master of English Divinity
MED	Master of Environmental Design (GAGS)
MED	Mechanical Equipment Design
MED	Meckeren-Ehlers-Danlos [*Syndrome*] [*Medicine*] (DB)
MED	Medal [*Numismatics*]

med .... Medal (VRA)
MED .... Medallion Explorations Ltd. [Vancouver Stock Exchange symbol]
MED .... Medallist [British] (ROG)
MED .... Medan [Sumatra] [Seismograph station code, US Geological Survey Closed] (SEIS)
Med .... Medea [of Euripides] [Classical studies] (OCD)
MED .... Media
med .... Medial [Medicine]
MED .... Median (AFM)
med .... Median (DMAA)
MED .... Median Effective Dose [Medicine]
MED .... Median Erythrocyte Diameter [Medicine]
Med .... Mediator [Legal term] (DLA)
MED .... Medical (AFM)
Med .... Medical (PHSD)
MED .... Medical Engineering Development (IIA)
MED .... Medicamenta [Medicaments] [Pharmacy] (ROG)
MED .... Medication
med .... Medication (DMAA)
Med .... Medicine (AL)
MED .... Medicine (AABC)
med .... Medicine (WDAA)
MED .... Medieval
MED .... Medina [Saudi Arabia] [Airport symbol] (OAG)
MED .... MEDIQ, Inc. [AMEX symbol] (SPSG)
MED .... Meditation (ROG)
MED .... Mediterranean (AFM)
MED .... Mediterranean Engineer Division [Army Engineers]
MED .... Medium (AFM)
med .... Medium (DMAA)
MED .... Message Entry Device
MED .... Microelectronic Device
MED .... Microwave Emission Detector [Instrumentation]
MED .... Mid-Continent Ecology Division [Duluth] [Environmental Protection Agency] (AEPA)
MED .... Military Energy Depot (SAA)
MED .... Minimal Effective Dose [Medicine]
MED .... Minimal Erythema Dose [Medicine]
MED .... Minimum Effective Dose [Medicine] (LDT)
MED .... Minimum Engineering Development (MCD)
MED .... Minority Enterprise Development
MED .... Mobile Energy Depot
MED .... Modeling for Equipment Design (AAEL)
MED .... Modem Equivalent Device (ACRL)
MED .... Modular Evolutionary Development (MCD)
MED .... Molecular Electronic Device
MED .... Monitor Execution Dump [Computer science]
MED .... Multieffect Distillation [Chemical engineering]
MED .... Multiformat Electroluminescent Display (PDAA)
MED .... Multiple Epiphyseal Dysplasia [Medicine] (CPH)
MED .... Municipal Electricity Department [New Zealand] (WDAA)
MEDA .... Medaphis Corp. [NASDAQ symbol] (SPSG)
MEDA .... Mennonite Economic Development Associates (EA)
MEDA .... (Mercaptoethyl)dimethylammonium Chloride [Organic chemistry]
MEDA .... Military Emergency Diversion Aerodrome (DA)
MEDA .... Multiplex Electronic Doppler Analyzer
MEDAB .... Middle East Database (IID)
MEDAC .... Medical Accounting [and Billing Process]
MEDAC .... Medical Electronic Data Aquisition and Control
MEDAC .... Medical Equipment Display and Conference (IAA)
MEDAC .... Military Electronic Data Advisory Committee [NATO] (NATG)
MEDAC .... Mouvement de l'Evolution Democratique de l'Afrique Centrale [Central African Democratic Evolution Movement]
MEDAC .... Multiple, Endocrine Deficiency - Addison's Disease - Candidiasis [Syndrome] [Endocrinology] (DAVI)
MEDAC .... Multiple Endocrine Deficiency, Autoimmune-Candidiasis [Syndrome] [Medicine]
MEDACS ..... Medical Administrative Control System (IAA)
MedAct .... Medical Action Industries, Inc. [Associated Press] (SAG)
MEdAd .... Master of Educational Administration (ADA)
MEdAdm ..... Master of Educational Administration (ADA)
Med Adm C .. Medical Administrative Corps [Army World War II]
MEdAdmin ... Master of Educational Administration
MEDAL .... Medallion [Automotive engineering]
MEDAL .... Micromechanized Engineering Data for Automated Logistics
MEDALS ...... Modular Engineering Drafting and Library System (IAA)
MEDALSA .... Mediterranean Algeria-Sahara Zone [NATO] (NATG)
Medalst .... Medalist Industries, Inc. [Associated Press] (SAG)
Medamic ..... Medamicus, Inc. [Associated Press] (SAG)
Medaph ...... Medaphis Corp. [Associated Press] (SAG)
Medar .... Medar, Inc. [Associated Press] (SAG)
Medarex ...... Medarex, Inc. [Associated Press] (SAG)
MED-ART ..... Medical Automated Records Technology (STED)
Medarx .... Medarex, Inc. [Associated Press] (SAG)
MEDAS .... Medical Emergency Decisions Assistance System (MCD)
MEDAS .... Meteorological Data Acquisition System [NASA] (KSC)
MEDAS .... Microfilm Enhanced Data System (PDAA)
MEDAUG ..... Medical Augmentation (MCD)
MEDAX .... Message Data Exchange Terminal (MCD)
MEDBAD ...... Medical Badge
MEDBN .... Medical Battalion [Marine Corps]
MEDBO .... Mediterranean Shipping Board [World War II]
MEDBR .... Medical Branch
MEDC .... [The] Med-Design Corp. [NASDAQ symbol] (SAG)

MEDC .... Microelectronics Educational Development Centre [Paisley College] [British] (CB)
MEDC .... Moessbauer Effect Data Center [University of North Carolina] [Information service or system] (IID)
MEdCA .... Master of Education in Creative Arts
MEDCAP ...... Patrol [or Assistance] [or Program] [Military]
MEDCASE .... Medical Care Support Equipment (AABC)
MEDCAT ...... Medical Civic Action Teams
MEDCAT ...... Medium Altitude Clear-Air Turbulence (MCD)
MEDCAT ...... Medium-Altitude Critical Atmospheric Turbulence (MCD)
MedCath ..... MedCath, Inc. [Associated Press] (SAG)
MEDCEN ...... Medical Center [Army] (AABC)
MEDCENT .... Central Mediterranean Area [NATO]
Med C Georgia... Medical College of Georgia (GAGS)
MEDCL .... Medical
MEDCMNT ... Medicament
MedCmp ...... Medic Computer Systems, Inc. [Associated Press] (SAG)
MEDCN .... Medicine
Med C Ohio... Medical College of Ohio at Toledo (GAGS)
MEDCOM ..... Medical Command (MCD)
MEDCOM ..... Mediterranean Communications [Military] (AFM)
MEDCOMP ... Medical Early Direct Commissioning Program (MCD)
MEDCOMPLAN... Mediterranean Communications Plans [NATO] (NATG)
MEDCON ...... Medical Contingency Report [Air Force]
MEDCOOP .... Medical Continuity of Operations Plan [Army] (AABC)
MEDCORE .... Medical Resources Consortium of Central New Jersey [Library network]
MEDCORPS... Medical Corps [Air Force]
MEDCOS ...... Mediterranean Chiefs of Staff [British World War II]
Med C Penn... Medicine College of Pennsylvania (GAGS)
MedcR .... Medco Research, Inc. [Associated Press] (SAG)
Medcross..... Medcross, Inc. [Associated Press] (SAG)
MedCtrl....... Medical Contol [Associated Press] (SAG)
Med C Wis... Medicine College of Wisconsin (GAGS)
Medd .... Meddaugh's Reports [13 Michigan] [A publication] (DLA)
MEDD .... Medical Device Technol [NASDAQ symbol] (TTSB)
MEDD .... Medical Device Technologies, Inc. [NASDAQ symbol] (SAG)
MEDDA .... Mechanized Defense Decision Anticipation [AFSC]
MEDDAC ..... Medical Department Activity [Army] (AABC)
MEDDARS .... Medical Display Analysis and Recording System
Meddaugh ... Meddaugh's Reports [13 Michigan] [A publication] (DLA)
MED-DENT... Medical Dental Division [Air Force]
Med Devices Rep (CCH)... Medical Devices Reports (Commerce Clearing House) [A publication] (DLA)
MedDevT ..... Medical Device Technologies, Inc. [Associated Press] (SAG)
MEDDF .... Master Engineering Drawing Data File System
MEdDHi .... Dukes County Historical Society, Edgartown, MA [Library symbol Library of Congress] (LCLS)
MEDDIC .... Medical Evidence Disaggregated Direct Input of Costs Database [Social Security Administration] (GFGA)
MEDDOC ...... Medical Documentation Systems [Eli Lilly & Co.] [Information service or system] (IID)
MEDDPERSA... Medical Department Personnel Support Agency [Army] (MCD)
MEDDS .... Medical Data Specialist (AABC)
MedDsg ...... [The] Med-Design Corp. [Associated Press] (SAG)
MedDv .... Medical Device Technologies, Inc. [Associated Press] (SAG)
MedDvt .... Medical Device Technologies, Inc. [Associated Press] (SAG)
MEDDY .... Mediterranean Eddy [Oceanography]
MedDyn ...... Medical Dynamics, Inc. [Associated Press] (SAG)
MEDEA........ Masters Degree in Energy and Environmental Management and Economics (ECON)
MEDEA........ Measurements of Earth Data for Environmental Analysis [Marine science] (OSRA)
MEDEA........ Multidiscipline Engineering Design, Evaluation, and Analysis (RDA)
MEDEAST .... Eastern Mediterranean Area [NATO] (NATG)
MEd(Ed/Psych)... Master of Education (Educational Psychology), University of Birmingham [British] (DBQ)
MEDEMG ..... Medical Emergencies [Computerized management course]
MEDes .... Master of Environmental Design (DD)
Medeva........ Medeva Ltd. [Associated Press] (SAG)
MEDEVAC .... Medical Evacuation Team [Army]
MEDEVAL .... Medical Evaluation [Military] (AABC)
MEDEX........ Medecin Extension [Doctors' Aides, or Medics] [French]
Medex .... Medex, Inc. [Associated Press] (SAG)
MEDF.......... Maximum Energy Distribution Function
MEDF.......... Midexpiratory Dynamic Flow Rate [Medicine] (DAVI)
MedfdSv ..... Medford Savings Bank [Associated Press] (SAG)
MEDFLY...... Mediterranean Fruit Fly
MEDGP .... Medical Group [Air Force]
MedGr .... Medical Graphics Corp. [Associated Press] (SAG)
MEd(Guid&Coun)... Master of Education in Guidance and Counselling
MEDH .... Maintainability Engineering Design Handbook
MEDI........... Marine Environmental Data Information Referral System [UNESCO] [Paris, France]
medi .... Media (VRA)
MEDI........... Medicine (DSUE)
MEDI........... MedImmune, Inc. [NASDAQ symbol] (SPSG)
MEDI........... Missile Error Data Integration [Military] (IAA)
MEDI........... Moessbauer Effect Data Index
MEDIA .... Magnavox Electronic Data Image Apparatus
MEDIA .... Man's Environments - Display Implication and Applications (PDAA)
MEDIA .... Manufacturers Educational Drug Information Association
MEDIA .... Measures for Encouraging the Development of the Audiovisual Production Industry [EC] (ECED)
Media .... Media General, Inc. [Associated Press] (SAG)

MEDIA .... Missile Era Data Integration Analysis
MEDIA .... Modular Electronic Digital Instrumentation Assemblies (PDAA)
MEDIA .... Move to End Deception in Advertising [*Student legal action organization*]
MediaArt...... Media Arts Group, Inc. [*Associated Press*] (SAG)
Media L & P... Media Law and Practice [*A publication*] (DLA)
MediaLog .... Media Logic, Inc. [*Associated Press*] (SAG)
Media M...... Media and Methods [*A publication*] (BRI)
MEDIA/M ..... Media/Medicine (NITA)
MEDIC .... Mechanized Design and Integrated Control
MEDIC .... Medical Electronic Data Interpretation and Correlation (IAA)
Medic .... Medicamina Faciei [*of Ovid*] [*Classical studies*] (OCD)
MEDICAID.... Medical Aid [*Federal program providing financial assistance for medical expenses of individual needy citizens*]
MEDICARE... Medical Care [*Federal program providing financial assistance for medical expenses of individual senior citizens*]
MEDICI .... Melodic Dictation Computerized Instruction (EDAC)
Medicinal Chem... Medicinal Chemistry (MEC)
Medicis........ Medicis Pharmaceutical Corp. [*Associated Press*] (SAG)
MEDICO .... Medical Information Cooperation (DAVI)
MEDICO .... Medical International Cooperation
MEDICO .... Model Experiment in Drug Indexing by Computer [*Rutgers University*]
MEDICOM.... Medical Communications
MEDICOR..... Centre for Offshore and Remote Medicine [*Memorial University of Newfoundland*] [*Research center*] (RCD)
MEDICOS..... Mediterranean Instructions to Convoys [*World War II*]
MEDICS .... Majors Electronic Data Interchange Communications System [*Computer science*]
MEDICS .... Medical Information and Career Service [*British*] (DAVI)
MEDICS .... Medical Information and Communications System (NITA)
MEDICS .... Medical Information Computer System (NASA)
MEDICS .... Michael E. DeBakey International Cardiovascular Society [*Later, MEDISS*] (EA)
Medicus....... Medicus Systems Corp. [*Associated Press*] (SAG)
MEDIEV........ Medieval
MEDIF.......... Medical Information Form [*British*]
Medigap ...... Medicare Supplement Insurance
medi gen..... Media Generated (VRA)
MEDIHC .... Military Experience Directed into Health Careers [*DoD/HEW project*]
MedImun ..... MedImmune, Inc. [*Associated Press*] (SAG)
MedInd .... Medical Industries of America [*Associated Press*] (SAG)
MedIndA...... Medical Industries of America [*Associated Press*] (SAG)
MEDINET ..... Medical Information Network [*GTE Telenet Communications Corp.*] [*Telecommunications*]
MEDINFO..... Medical Informatics
MedInn........ Medical Innovations, Inc. [*Associated Press*] (SAG)
MEDINSP..... Medical Inspection [*Military*] (NVT)
MEDINT........ Medical Intelligence (MCD)
MEDIOC .... Mediocris [*Middling*] [*Pharmacy*] (ROG)
MEDIOL .... Mediolanum [*Milan*] [*Imprint*] (ROG)
MEDIPHOR... Monitoring and Evaluation of Drug Interactions in a Pharmacy-Oriented Reporting System [*National Center for Health Services Research*] (DHSM)
MEDIPP .... Medical District Initiated Program Planning [*Veterans Administration*]
MEDIPRO..... Medical District Initiated Peer Review Organization [*Veterans Administration*] (GFGA)
Mediq .... Mediq, Inc. [*Associated Press*] (SAG)
MEDIS .... Message Diversion Relay System (IAA)
MedisE .... Medis E Ltd. [*Associated Press*] (SAG)
MediSens .... MediSense, Inc. [*Associated Press*] (SAG)
MEDI-SOTA LIBR... Medi-Sota Library Consortium [*Library network*]
MEDISS .... Michael E. DeBakey International Surgical Society (EA)
MEDISTAT ... Banque de Donnees Socio-Economiques des Pays Mediterraneens [*Socioeconomic Data Bank on the Mediterranean Countries*] [*International Center for Advanced Mediterranean Agronomic Studies*] [*Information service or system*] (IID)
MEDIT.......... Mediterranean
MEDITEC...... Dodumentation Medizinische Technik [*Medical Technology Documentation*] [*TechnicalInformation Center*] [*Germany*] [*Information service or system*] (IID)
Meditr.......... Meditrust [*Associated Press*] (SAG)
MEDIUM ...... Missile Era Data Integration - Ultimate Method
Mediwre ...... Mediware Information Systems, Inc. [*Associated Press*] (SAG)
M Ed J......... Music Educators Journal [*A publication*] (BRI)
MED JUR..... Medical Jurisprudence (ADA)
MEDL........... Marconi Electronic Devices Ltd. [*British*] (IRUK)
MEDL........... Materials Evaluation and Development Laboratory [*General Services Administration*]
MEDL........... Medical
MEDLA......... Molecular Electron Density Lego Assembler [*Modeling technique*] [*Organic chemistry*]
Med L & P... Media Law and Practice [*1980*] [*A publication*] (DLA)
Med L & Pub Pol... Medicine, Law, and Public Policy [*A publication*] (DLA)
MEDLARS.... Medical Literature Analysis and Retrieval System [*National Library of Medicine*] [*Bethesda, MD Database*]
Med Lat....... Medieval Latin [*Language*]
Med-Legal J... Medico-Legal Journal [*A publication*] (DLA)
Med-Legal Soc'y Trans... Medico-Legal Society. Transactions [*A publication*] (DLA)
Med Leg Pap... Medico-Legal Papers [*A publication*] (DLA)
Med Leg Soc Trans... Transactions. Medico-Legal Society [*A publication*] (ILCA)
Med Leg Vic Proc... Medico-Legal Society of Victoria. Proceedings [*A publication*]
MEDLI.......... Motoring Experience for the Disabled by Lions International [*British*]
MEDLINE ..... Medical Information Online (NITA)
MEDLINE ..... MEDLARS [*Medical Literature Analysis and Retrieval System*] On-Line [*National Library of Medicine*] [*Bibliographic database*]
MEDList....... Master Enumeration District List [*Bureau of Census*]
medln.......... Medallion (VRA)
Med LN........ Medico-Legal News [*A publication*] (DLA)
MEDLOC ...... Mediterranean Lines of Communication [*Military*] (IAA)
MEDLOC ...... Mediterranean Location [*Navy*]
Med LP........ Medico-Legal Papers [*A publication*] (DLA)
Med L Rptr... Media Law Reporter [*A publication*] (NTCM)
M Ed LS ...... Master of Education in Library Science
M ED L SC... Master of Education in Library Science (WDAA)
MEDM.......... Medamicus, Inc. [*NASDAQ symbol*] (SAG)
MEDM.......... Medium
Medm .... Medmarco, Inc. [*Associated Press*] (SAG)
MEDMAF...... Mekong Delta Mobile Afloat Force [*Vietnam*] [*Military*] (VNW)
MEDMAILCOORD... Mediterranean Mail Coordinating Office (DNAB)
MEDMAL...... Medical Malpractice Lawsuit Filings [*Medical Malpractice Verdicts, Settlements & Experts*] [*Information service or system*] (CRD)
MEd(Maths)... Master of Education (Mathematics)
MEDMATS ... Medical Materiel Management System [*Army*]
med men..... Medial Meniscectomy [*orthopedics*] (DAVI)
med men..... Medial Meniscus [*Orthopedics*] (DAVI)
MEDMER ..... Medical Emergency Report [*Air Force*]
MedMgt....... Medical Management, Inc. [*Associated Press*] (SAG)
MEDMIS ...... Medical Management Information System [*Army*]
Med Moor.... Mediterranean Moor (MUSM)
Mednet .... Mednet MPC Corp. [*Associated Press*] (SAG)
MEDNOREAST... Northeast Mediterranean Area [*NATO*] (NATG)
MEDNTPS.... Mediterranean Near-Term Prepositioned Ship
MEDO .... Middle East Defense Organization (NATG)
MEDO .... Multipole Expansion of Diatomic Overlap [*Physics*]
MEDOC .... Medical Documents [*Eccles Health Sciences Library - University of Utah*] [*Salt Lake City, UT Bibliographic database*]
MEDOC .... Mediterranean Oceanographic Project [*1969*]
MEDOC .... Western Mediterranean Area [*NATO*] (NATG)
MEDOCHAN... Mary Ellen, Dorothy, Chuck, Ann [*Famous Canadian resort, named for the owners' children*]
MEDOFCOM... Medical Officer-in-Command [*Military*]
MEDOL .... Medically Oriented Language
MEDOWS..... Meadows [*Commonly used*] (OPSA)
MEDP.......... Medium Port
MEDP........... MedPlus, Inc. [*NASDAQ symbol*] (SAG)
MedPAC....... Medicare Payment Advisory Commission
MEDPAR...... Medicare Provider Analysis and Review (GFGA)
MedPart...... MedPartners, Inc. [*Associated Press*] (SAG)
MEDPES ...... Medical Planning and Execution System (COE)
MedPlus ...... MedPlus, Inc. [*Associated Press*] (SAG)
MEDPr......... MEDIQ Inc. Cv Pfd [*AMEX symbol*] (TTSB)
MEDPRO...... Medical Education Resources Program (MEDA)
MEdPsych.... Master of Educational Psychology (ADA)
MEDQ .... MedQuist Inc. [*NASDAQ symbol*] (TTSB)
MedQst........ MedQuist, Inc. [*Associated Press*] (SAG)
MedRA......... Medical Resource Companies of America [*Associated Press*] (SAG)
MEDRAMS... Medical Readiness Assemblage Medical System [*Air Force*] (GFGA)
MEDRC .... Medical Reserve Corps [*Military*] (WDAA)
MEDRED ...... Medical Unit Readiness Report [*Air Force*]
MEDREGREP... Medical Regulating Report (COE)
MedResc ..... Medical Resources, Inc. [*Associated Press*] (SAG)
MEDRESCO... Medical Research Council (NADA)
MEDRETES... Medical Readiness Training Exercises [*Army*]
MEDREX ...... Medical Readiness Exercise (MCD)
medRNA ...... Ribonucleic Acid, Mini-Exon-Derived [*Biochemistry, genetics*]
MEd(RuralEd)... Master of Education in Rural Education
MEDS........... Marine Ecological Database System [*Marine science*] (OSRA)
MEDS........... Marine Environmental Data Service [*Canada*] (NOAA)
MEDS........... Master of Environmental Design Studies [*Canada*] (ASC)
MEDS........... Mechanized Embarkation Data System [*Military*] (NVT)
MEDS........... Medical Electronics and Data Society [*Later, MES*] (EA)
MEDS........... Medical Evaluation Data System (IEEE)
Meds .... Medications [*or Medicines*]
MEDS........... Medstone International, Inc. [*NASDAQ symbol*] (SAG)
MEDS........... Medstone Intl. [*NASDAQ symbol*] (TTSB)
MEDS........... Meteorological and Environmental Data Services (USDC)
MEDS........... Meteorological Environmental Data Services [*Marine science*] (OSRA)
MEDS........... Multifunction Electronic Display System [*NASA*]
MEDSAC ...... Medical Service Activity [*Army*] (AABC)
MEDSARS.... Maintenance Engineering Data Storage and Retrieval System (NG)
Med Sc D .... Doctor of Medical Science [*or the Science of Medicine*]
MEDSCH ...... Medical School (ADA)
MedSch(N)... Institute of Naval Medicine [*British*]
Med Sci Sports and Exercise... Medicine and Science in Sports and Exercise (MEC)
MEDSERV.... Medical Service Corps [*Military*] (MCD)
MEDSERVC... Medical Service Corps [*Military*]
MEDSERWRNT... Medical Service Warrant
MEDSOM ..... Medical Supply, Optical, and Maintenance [*Army*] (RDA)
MEDSOUEAST... Southeast Mediterranean Area [*NATO*] (NATG)
MEDSPECC... Medical Specialist Corps [*Military*]
MEd(SpecEd)... Master of Education (Special Education)
MEd(SpEd)... Master of Education in Special Education (ADA)
MEDSS .... Multiple Echelon Direct Support System (MCD)
MEdSt.......... Master of Educational Studies (ADA)
MEDSTAR .... Medical Staffing and Training to Augment Readiness (MCD)
MEDSTAT .... Medicaid Statistical Reporting and Analysis System (GFGA)
MEDSTATS... Medical Statistics Expert System (DMAA)
med stern.... Median Sternotomy (CPH)

MEDSTOC.... Medical Stock Control System [*Army*]
Medstone ... Medstone International, Inc. [*Associated Press*] (SAG)
MEdStud..... Master of Educational Studies
MEDSUPDEP... Medical Supply Depot
Medsupp...... Medicare Supplement Insurance
MedSurg...... Medicine and Surgery (DAVI)
M Ed T........ Master of Education in Teaching (PGP)
MEDT.......... Mean Elapsed Downtime [*Computer science*] (MCD)
MedT.......... Medical Technology Systems, Inc. [*Associated Press*] (SAG)
MEDT.......... Military Equipment Delivery Team
MEDTC........ Military Equipment Delivery Team Cambodia (VNW)
med tech .... Medical Technician [*or Technologist*] (AAMN)
Med Tech .... Medical Technology (DAVI)
MedTech...... Medical Technology Systems, Inc. [*Associated Press*] (SAG)
Med Tox ..... Medical Toxicology and Adverse Drug Experience (MEC)
MEDTRAIN... Medical Literature Training File (NITA)
Medtrnc...... Medtronic, Inc. [*Associated Press*] (SAG)
Medusa....... Medusa Corp. [*Associated Press*] (SAG)
MEDUSA...... Multiple Element Directional Universally Steerable Antenna
Med U So Car... Medical University of South Carolina (GAGS)
MedVat........ MediVators, Inc. [*Associated Press*] (SAG)
MEDW .... Mediware Information Sys [*NASDAQ symbol*] (TTSB)
MEDW .... Mediware Information Systems, Inc. [*NASDAQ symbol*] (SAG)
Medwve...... Medwave, Inc. [*Associated Press*] (SAG)
MEDX .... Medarex, Inc. [*NASDAQ symbol*] (SPSG)
MEDXW ...... Medarex Inc. Wrrt [*NASDAQ symbol*] (TTSB)
MEDY......... Medial Dynamics [*NASDAQ symbol*] (TTSB)
MEDYN .... Medical Dynamics, Inc. [*NASDAQ symbol*] (NQ)
MEE .... Maine Office of Energy Resources Library, Augusta, ME [*OCLC symbol*] (OCLC)
MEE .... Maintenance Engineering Evaluation (MCD)
MEE .... Mare [*Loyalty Islands*] [*Airport symbol*] (OAG)
MEE .... Mass Energy Equivalent
MEE .... Master of Electrical Engineering
MEE .... Measured Energy Expenditure (DMAA)
MEE .... Mechanical, Electrical, and Electronic (MCD)
MEE .... Mechanical Evaluation Equipment
MEE .... Meerut [*India*] [*Seismograph station code, US Geological Survey Closed*] (SEIS)
MEE .... Merrill Lynch & Co., Inc. [*NYSE symbol*] (SAG)
MEE .... Methyl Ethyl Ether [*Organic chemistry*]
MEE .... Middle Ear Effusion [*Medicine*]
MEE .... Migration Enhanced Epitaxy (AAEL)
MEE .... Military Essential Equipment (CINC)
MEE .... Minimum Essential Equipment
MEE .... Mission Essential Equipment [*NASA*] (KSC)
MEE .... Multilocus Enzyme Electrophoresis (DMAA)
MEE .... Muskogee, OK [*Location identifier FAA*] (FAAL)
MEECN........ Minimum Essential Emergency Communications Network [*Military*]
MEED .... Medium-Energy Electron Diffraction
MEED .... Microbial Ecology Evaluation Device [*NASA*] (KSC)
MEED .... Middle East Economic Digest [*A publication*]
ME-EE......... Mechanical Engineer and Electrical Engineer [*Academic degree*]
MEEF .... Manufacturing Engineering Education Foundation
MEEF .... Mobile Equipment Employment File [*Air Force*] (AFM)
MEEL .... Mission Equipment Essentiality List
MeEl .... William Fogg Memorial Library, Eliot, ME [*Library symbol Library of Congress*] (LCLS)
ME(Elec)...... Master of Engineering (Electrical) (ADA)
MEEM .... Master of Environmental Engineering and Management (PGP)
MEEM .... Metastable Electron Emission Microscopy
ME Eng........ Master of Electrical Engineering
MEEP .... Management and Equipment Evaluation Program
MEER .... Mechanical/Electrical Equipment Room (MCD)
MEERS........ Maximum Effective Echo Ranging Speed (NVT)
MEES.......... Marine-Estuarine-Environmental Sciences (PDAA)
MEES.......... Medical Element Engineering and Simulation (DMAA)
MEES.......... Middle East Economic Survey [*A publication*]
MEES.......... Multipurpose Electromagnetic Environment Simulator (MCD)
Mees & Ros... Meeson and Roscoe's English Exchequer Reports [*A publication*] (DLA)
Mees & W... Meeson and Welsby's English Exchequer Reports [*A publication*] (DLA)
Mees & Wels... Meeson and Welsby's English Exchequer Reports [*A publication*] (DLA)
MEET .... Minimum Essential Equipment for Training
MEETA........ Maximum Improvement in Electronics Effectiveness through Advanced Techniques
MEETAT .... Maximum Improvement in Electronics Effectiveness through Advanced Techniques
MEEV.......... Maintenance and Electricity Equipment Vault (MCD)
MEF .... Emerging Mexico Fund [*NYSE symbol*] (SPSG)
MEF .... Maintenance Efficiency Factor
MEF .... Major Emitting Facility [*Environmental Protection Agency*]
MEF .... Major Equipment File (MCD)
MEF .... Management Engineering Flight [*Air Force*]
MEF .... Marine Expeditionary Force
MEF .... Maximal Expiratory Flow [*Medicine*]
MEF .... Mechanized Engineering File
MEF .... Median Energy of Fission (NRCH)
MEF .... Mediterranean Expeditionary Force [*World War I*] [*British*]
MEF .... Melfi [*Chad*] [*Airport symbol*] (AD)
MEF .... Mesopotamian Expeditionary Force [*British*]
MEF .... Middle Ear Fluid
MEF .... Middle East Forces [*British*]

MEF .... Middle East Forum [*Lebanon*] (BJA)
MEF .... Mideast File [*Tel-Aviv University*] [*Israel*] [*Information service or system*] (IID)
MEF .... Midexpiratory Flow [*Medicine*] (DMAA)
MEF .... Migration Enhancement Factor [*Biochemistry*]
MEF .... Minimum Essential Force (CINC)
MEF .... Ministry for Environment and Forests [*India*]
MEF .... Mission Equipment Facility (MCD)
MEF .... Mortality Enhancing Factors [*Chemical and biological warfare*]
MEF .... Mouse Embryo Fibroblast
MEF .... Multiple Effect Flash [*Evaporator*] [*Seawater conversion system*]
MEF .... Multi-Purpose Electric Furnace (PDAA)
MEF .... Muscle Enhancer Factor [*Genetics*]
MEF .... Musicians Emergency Fund (EA)
MEF .... Myocyte Enhancing Factor [*Genetics*]
MEFA .... Metal Etching and Fabricating Association [*Later, National Association of Name Plate Manufacturers*] (EA)
MEFA .... Methyl-CCNU 5-Fluorouracil, Adriamycin [*Antineoplastic drug regimen*] (DAVI)
MeFarGS .... Church of Jesus Christ of Latter-Day Saints, Genealogical Society Library, Augusta Branch, Farmingdale, ME [*Library symbol Library of Congress*] (LCLS)
MeFarU....... University of Maine at Farmington, Farmington, ME [*Library symbol Library of Congress*] (LCLS)
MEFC .... Maximum Economic Finding Cost
MEFC .... Mister Ed Fan Club (EA)
MEFEX .... Middle East Food and Equipment Exhibition [*Arabian Exhibition Management*]
M-EFF .... Myocardial Efficiency [*Cardiology*]
MEFFEX ...... Marine Expeditionary Force Field Exercise (NVT)
MEFLEX ...... Marine Expeditionary Force Landing Exercise (NVT)
MEFPAK ...... Manpower and Equipment Force Packaging [*Military*]
MEFR .... Maximum Expiratory Flow Rate [*Medicine*]
MEFR .... Maximum Midexpiratory Flow Rate [*Medicine*] (DAVI)
MEFS .... Midterm Energy Forecasting System [*Department of Energy*] (GFGA)
ME/FS .... Missing/Embryo Fetus Syndrome
MEFSR........ Maximal Expiratory Flow Static Recoil Curve [*Medicine*] (MAE)
MeFtkU .... University of Maine at Fort Kent, Fort Kent, ME [*Library symbol Library of Congress*] (LCLS)
MEFTL .... Middle East Force Target List (MCD)
MEFV .... Maintenance Equipment Floor Valve (NRCH)
MEFV .... Maximal Expiratory Flow Volume [*Medicine*] (AAMN)
MEG .... Madly Enthusiastic about Grapes
MEG .... Magnetoencephalogram [*Medicine*]
MEG .... Magnetoencephalography [*Medicine*] (ECON)
MEG .... Malange [*Angola*] [*Airport symbol*] (OAG)
MEG .... Management Evaluation Group [*Department of State*]
MEG .... Media General, Inc. [*AMEX symbol*] (SPSG)
MEG .... Mega [*A prefix meaning multiplied by one million*] (AAG)
Meg .... Megabyte (COE)
MEG .... Megabyte [*Computer science*] (DDC)
meg .... Megabyte
MEG .... Megacycle (NTCM)
Meg .... Megakaryocyte [*Hematology*]
meg .... Megaloblastic [*Cytology*] (AAMN)
meg .... Megaron (VRA)
MEG .... Megaton (WDAA)
MEG .... Megawatt (WDAA)
Meg .... Megiddo (BJA)
MEG .... Megillah (BJA)
MEG .... Megohm (AAG)
meg .... Megohm (IDOE)
Meg .... Megone's Companies Acts Cases [*1888-90*] [*England*] [*A publication*] (DLA)
MEG .... Mercaptoethylguanidine [*Biochemistry*] (AAMN)
MEG .... Message Entry Generator (NVT)
MEG .... Message Expediting Group (IEEE)
MEG .... Methyl(ethyl)glycine [*Biochemistry*]
MEG .... Midlands Examining Group [*British*] (AIE)
MEG .... Miniature Electrostatic Gyro
MEG .... Monoethylene Glycol [*Chemicals*]
MEG .... Multifocal Eosinophilic Granuloma [*Medicine*] (DMAA)
MEG .... Multimedia Environmental Goals [*Environmental Protection Agency*]
MEG .... NRA [*National Restaurant Association*] Marketing Executives Group [*Chicago, IL*] (EA)
MEGA.......... Megaampere (IAA)
MEGA.......... Megakaryocyte [*Hematology*] (DAVI)
MEGA.......... Military Evaluation of Geographic Areas
mega-......... Millions (10⁶) (IDOE)
MEGA.......... Molecular Evolutionary Genetics Analysis [*Computer software*]
MEGACE ...... Megestrol Acetate [*Antineoplastic drug*]
MEGAFLOPS... Millions of Floating Point Operations per Second (PDAA)
Me-GAG ...... Methylglyoxalbis(guanylhydrazone) [*Mitoguazone*] [*Also, MGBG*] [*Antineoplastic drug*]
MeGar .... Gardiner Public Library, Gardiner, ME [*Library symbol Library of Congress*] (LCLS)
Megarry...... Megarry's The Rent Acts [*A publication*] (DLA)
MEGAS .... Multienergy Gamma Assay System [*Nuclear energy*] (NRCH)
MEGASTAR... Meaning of Energy Growth: An Assessment of Systems, Technologies, and Requirements [*NASA*]
Megatest ..... Megatest Corp. [*Associated Press*] (SAG)
MEGC.......... Megacycle (IAA)
MEGC.......... Megacycle per Second [*Megahertz*] (IAA)
mEGF .... Mouse Epidermal Growth Factor
mEGF-URO... Mouse Epidermal Growth Factor - Urogastrone [*Endocrinology*]

MEGG	Merging (FAAC)
Megg Ass	Meggison's Assets in Equity [1832] [A publication] (DLA)
Meg-GPA	Megakaryocyte Growth-Promoting Activity [Hematology]
MEGHP	Most Excellent Grand High Priest [Freemasonry]
MEGI	Missile Exhaust Gas Ingestion (MCD)
MEGLUMINE...	N-Methylglucamine [USAN] [Organic chemistry]
MEGM	Most Eminent Grand Master [Freemasonry] (ROG)
MEGO	Mego Financial [NASDAQ symbol] (TTSB)
MEGO	Mego Financial Corp. [NASDAQ symbol] (SAG)
MEGO	Megohm (MSA)
MEGO	My Eyes Glaze Over [An article, written about an important subject, that resists reader interest and has a soporific effect] [Journalistic slang]
MegoFin	Mego Financial Corp. [Associated Press] (SAG)
MegoFinl	Mego Financial [Associated Press] (SAG)
MegoMrt	Mego Mortgage Corp. [Associated Press] (SAG)
Megone	Megone's Companies Acts Cases [1888-90] [England] [A publication] (DLA)
Me Gov't Reg...	Maine Government Register [A publication] (AAGC)
MEGS	Male Electronic Genital Stimulator [Developed by Biosonics, Inc.]
MEGS	Market Entry Guarantee Scheme [Board of Trade] [British] (DI)
MEGS	Megasecond (AAG)
MEGS	Missile End-Game Scoring System (DWSG)
MEGSSS	Mathematics Education for Gifted Secondary School Students Project (EDAC)
MEGT	Megatest Corp. [NASDAQ symbol] (SAG)
MEGT	Megaton [Nuclear equivalent of one million tons of high explosive] (AAG)
MegTa'an	Megillat Ta'anit (BJA)
MEGV	Megavolt (AAG)
MEGW	Megawatt [Also, MW]
MEGWH	Megawatt-Hour
MEGX	Megacards Inc. [NASDAQ symbol] (TTSB)
MEGX	Monoethylglycine Xylidide [Biochemistry]
MEH	Maine State Department of Human Services, Augusta, ME [OCLC symbol] (OCLC)
MEH	Meacham, OR [Location identifier FAA] (FAAL)
MEH	Mehamn [Norway] [Airport symbol] (OAG)
MEH	Midwest Express Holdings [NYSE symbol] (SAG)
MEH	Multi-Engined Helicopter (MCD)
Meharry Med C...	Meharry Medicine College (GAGS)
MEHDHQ......	Medical Embarkment and Hospital Distribution Headquarters [World War II]
MeHi	Maine Historical Society, Portland, ME [Library symbol Library of Congress] (LCLS)
MEHL	Mehl Biophile International Corp. [NASDAQ symbol] (SAG)
MehlBio	Mehl Biophile International Corp. [Associated Press] (SAG)
MEHP	Mean Effective Horsepower (IAA)
MEHP	Monoethylhexyl Phthalate [Organic chemistry]
MEHQ	Monomethyl Ether of Hydroquinone [Organic chemistry]
MEHT	Minimum Eye Height over Threshold [Aviation] (FAAC)
MEI	Main Economic Indicators (NITA)
MEI	Main Engine Ignition [Aerospace]
MEI	Maintenance and Engineering Inspection
MEI	Maintenance Effectiveness Inspection (MCD)
MEI	Maintenance Engineering Investigation [DoD]
MEI	Maintenance Evaluation Inspection (MCD)
MEI	Major End Item
MEI	Management Education Institute [Arthur D. Little, Inc.]
MEI	Management Effectiveness Inspection
MEI	Manpower Education Institute (EA)
MEI	Manual of Engineering Instructions
MEI	Marginal Efficiency of Investment
MEI	Marketing Economics Institute Ltd. [New York, NY]
MEI	Master Inspection Item [NASA] (NAKS)
MEI	Maximally Exposed Individual
MEI	Maximum Exposed Individual [Health risk assessment] [Environmental Protection Agency]
Mel	Meconium Ileus [Medicine]
MEI	Medicare Economic Index
Mei	Meiji Seika Kaisha Ltd. [Japan]
MEI	Meres et Enfants Internationale [Switzerland] (EAIO)
MEI	Meridian [Mississippi] [Airport symbol] (OAG)
MEI	Meridian, MS [Location identifier FAA] (FAAL)
MEI	Metals Engineering Institute (EA)
MEI	Middle East Information Service (BJA)
MEI	Middle East Institute (EA)
MEI	Military Engineering Item (MCD)
MEI	Military Environment Inventory [Rudolf H. Moos] (TES)
MEI	Military Environment Inventory [Psychology] (DHP)
MEI	[The] Ministry of Electronics Industry [China]
MEI	Minnesota Enterprises, Inc. (EFIS)
MEI	Minority Educational Institution
MEI	Mission Essential Item [Army]
MEI	Morpholinoethylisocyanide [Organic chemistry]
MEI	Most Exposed Individual [Environmental science] (FFDE)
MEI	Myocardial Efficiency Index [Cardiology]
MEIA	Member of the Institution of Engineers Australia
MEIA	Microparticle Enzyme Immunoassay
MEIAW........	Marine Athletic Intercollegiate Association for Women (PSS)
MEIC	Member of the Engineering Institute of Canada
MEIC	Middle East Intelligence Center [World War II]
Meid	Against Meidias [of Demosthenes] [Classical studies] (OCD)
MEIDL..........	Manually Entered Identification Library (CAAL)
MEIDS	Military [or Miniaturized] Electronic Information Delivery System (MCD)
MEIE	Microcomputer Electronic Information Exchange [Institute for Computer Science and Technology]
MEIEA........	Music and Entertainment Industry Educators Association (NTPA)
MEIF	Mobile Equipment Information File [Air Force] (AFM)
MEIG..........	Main Engine Ignition [Aerospace] (KSC)
MEIGN	Main Engine Ignition [Aerospace]
Meigs	Meigs' Tennessee Supreme Court Reports [1838-39] [A publication] (DLA)
Meigs Dig ..	Meigs' Digest of Decisions of the Courts of Tennessee [A publication] (DLA)
Meigs' R....	Meigs' Tennessee Reports [A publication] (DLA)
Me'il	Me'ilah (BJA)
MEIM	Minuteman Engineering Instruction Manual (SAA)
MEIMN.......	Multiend Item Modification Notice [NASA] (KSC)
MEIN	Medium-Energy Intense Neutron
MEIP	Mean Effective Injection Pressure [Diesel engines]
MEIR	Mideast Information Resource (BJA)
MEIR	Ministere Federal de l'Expansion Industrielle Regionale [Department of Regional Industrial Expansion - DRIE] [Canada]
MEIS	Medium Energy Ion Scattering (MCD)
MEIS	Middle East Information Service (BJA)
MEIS	Military Entomology Information Service
MEISONE....	All Ethiopia Socialist Union
MEISR	Minimum Essential Improvement in System Reliability (MCD)
MEIT	Momentum/Energy Integral Technique (MCD)
MEITS	Mission Effective Information Transmission System
MEIU	Main Engine Interface Unit (MCD)
MEIU	Middle East Interpretation Unit [British]
MEIU	Mobile Explosives Investigation Unit
MEIVA........	Men's Intercollegiate Volleyball Association (PSS)
MEJ	Maine Criminal Justice Academy, Waterville, ME [OCLC symbol] (OCLC)
MEJ	Marman Expansion Joint
MEJ	Maximum Economic Justification
MEJ	Meade, KS [Location identifier FAA] (FAAL)
MEJ	Medjet International, Inc. [ICAO designator] (FAAC)
MEJ	Middle East Journal [A publication] (BRI)
MEJ	Movement for Economic Justice (EA)
MEJC	Miniature Excitatory Junction Potential [Neurophysiology]
MEK	Maine State Library, Bookmobiles, Augusta, ME [OCLC symbol] (OCLC)
MEK	Med-Trans of Florida, Inc. [ICAO designator] (FAAC)
MEK	Meekatharra [Australia Seismograph station code, US Geological Survey] (SEIS)
Mek	Mekhilta (BJA)
MEK	Meknes [Morocco] [Airport symbol] (AD)
MEK	Methyl Ethyl Ketone [Organic chemistry]
MEK	Salomon, Inc. [AMEX symbol] (SPSG)
MEK	Salomon Inc. 5% MSFI'ELKA' [AMEX symbol] (TTSB)
MEKC	Micellar Electrokinetic Chromatography
MeKh	Mekhilta (BJA)
MEKO	Methyl Ethyl Ketoxime [Organic chemistry]
MEKP	Methyl Ethyl Ketone Peroxide [Organic chemistry]
MEKTS........	Modular Electronic Kay Telephone System (IAA)
MeL	Lewiston Public Library, Lewiston, ME [Library symbol Library of Congress] (LCLS)
MEL	Magnesium Elektron Ltd. [British] (IRUK)
MEL	Maintenance Expenditure Limit (MCD)
MEL	Maneuvering Element [Military] (AABC)
MEL	Many-Element LASER
MEL	Marchwood Engineering Laboratories [Research center British] (IRUK)
MEL	Marine Engineering Laboratory [Navy]
MEL	Master Equipment List [Military] (NG)
M EI	Master of Elements
MEL	Master of English Language (PGP)
MEL	Master of English Literature
MEL	Material Engineering Laboratory
MEL	Materials Evaluation Laboratory (MCD)
MEL	Maximum Engagement Line [Military] (INF)
MEL	Maximum Excess Loss
MEL	Maximum Expenditure Limit (MCD)
MEL	Maximum Exposure Limit [Hazardous material control]
MEL	Mean Ear Location [Automotive engineering]
MEL	Melamine
MEL	Melanoma [Oncology]
MEL	Melbourne [Australia Seismograph station code, US Geological Survey] (SEIS)
MEL	Melbourne [Australia Airport symbol] (OAG)
MEL	Melbourne [Later, TOO] [Australia Geomagnetic observatory code]
mel	Melena [Gastroenterology] (DAVI)
Mel	Melendus [Flourished, 1188-1209] [Authority cited in pre-1607 legal work] (DSA)
MEL	Mellis [Of Honey] [Pharmacy] (ROG)
MEL	Mellon Bank Corp. [NYSE symbol] (SPSG)
MEL	Melody
Mel	Melphalan [Antineoplastic drug] (DAVI)
MEL	Melrose Resources Ltd. [Vancouver Stock Exchange symbol]
MEL	Metabolic Equivalent Level [Medicine]
MEL	Microenergy Logic (IAA)
MEL	Military Education Level (INF)
MEL	Minimum Earnings Level
MEL	Minimum Equipment List

MEL	Mistress of English Literature
MEL	Mobile Erector Launcher [*Military*]
MEL	Moslem Electoral Lobby [*Australia*]
MEL	Mouse Erythroleukemia
MEL	Multiengine Land [*Pilot rating*] (AIA)
MEL	Murine Erythroleukemia [*Oncology*]
MEL	Music Education League [*Defunct*] (EA)
MEL	Muzika Esperanto Ligo [*Esperantist Music League*] (EAIO)
ME L	University of Maine. Law Review [*A publication*] (DLA)
MEL-A	Marine Engineering Laboratory - Annapolis [*Navy*] (DNAB)
MELA	Middle East Librarians' Association (EA)
MELAB	Mechanical Engineering Laboratory [*NASA*] (KSC)
MELAB	Michigan English Language Assessment Battery (GAGS)
MELABS	Microwave Engineering Laboratories, Inc. (MCD)
Melami	Melamine Chemicals, Inc. [*Associated Press*] (SAG)
MELAN	Melanesia (ROG)
MELAN	Melanin [*Pigmentation*] (DAVI)
Melanges d'Arch...	Melanges d'Archeologie et d'Histoire. Ecole Francaise de Rome [*A publication*] (OCD)
MELAS	Mitochondrial Myopathy, Encephalopathy, Lactic Acidosis, and Stroke-Like Episod es [*Medicine*]
MeLB	Bates College, Lewiston, ME [*Library symbol Library of Congress*] (LCLS)
MELB	Mission Enhancement-Little Bird [*Military*] (RDA)
MELBA	Multipurpose Extended Lift Blanket Assembly (IEEE)
Melb Rpt	Melbourne Report [*A publication*]
Melb Stud Ed...	Melbourne Studies in Education [*A publication*]
MELC	Melcombe [*England*]
MELC	Mouse Erythroleukemia Cell
MELC	Murine Erythroleukemia Cell [*Medicine*] (DB)
MELC	Murine Erythroleukemia Cell [*Medicine*] (STED)
MELCO	Melville Shoe Corp. (EFIS)
MELCO	Mitsubishi Electric Corp. [*Japan*]
MELCOM	Middle East Libraries Committee
MELCU	Multiple External Line Control Unit
MeLDL	Methylated Low-Density Lipoprotein [*Biochemistry*]
MELDOS	Melioidosis [*Dermatology*] (DAVI)
MELEC	Microelectronics (IEEE)
M Elec E	Master of Electrical Engineering (PGP)
ME Legis Serv...	Maine Legislative Service [*A publication*] (DLA)
MELEM	Microelement (IEEE)
MELF	Metal Electrode Face Bonding (IAA)
MELF	Middle East Land Forces [*British*] (NATG)
MELG	Middle East Liaison Group [*Military*] (AABC)
MELH	Missile Elevation Heading (IAA)
MELI	Master Equipment List Identification [*Military*] (IAA)
MELI	Master Equipment List Index [*Military*] (KSC)
MELI	Met-Enkaphalin-Like Immunoreactivity [*Medicine*] (STED)
MELI	Minimum Equipment List Index (NASA)
MELIOS	Miniature Eyesafe LASER Infrared Observation Set [*A rangefinder*]
MELISS	Mitsubishi Electric Corp. Literature and Information Search Service
MELKONG	Mechanical Electric Kong [*Robot*]
MELL	Mellis [*Of Honey*] [*Pharmacy*] (ROG)
MellonBk	Mellon Bank Corp. [*Associated Press*] (SAG)
MellonP	Mellon Participating Mortgage Trust Commercial Property Series [*Associated Press*] (SAG)
Mell Parl Pr...	Mell's Parliamentary Practice [*A publication*] (DLA)
MELM	Middle East Lutheran Ministry [*Lebanon*] (EAIO)
MELM	Minimum Equipment List Manual
Mel Maspo	Melanges Maspero [*A publication*] (OCD)
Meln	Mellon Bank Corp. [*Associated Press*] (SAG)
M Elo	Master of Elocution
MELO	Minimum Expected Loss [*Statistics*]
Melon	Mellon Bank Corp. [*Associated Press*] (SAG)
MELP	Measure of Language Proficiency (EDAC)
MELP	Mid-European Law Project
MELPrJ	Mellon Bk 8.50% `J'Pfd [*NYSE symbol*] (TTSB)
MELPrK	Mellon Bk 8.20% `K' Pfd [*NYSE symbol*] (TTSB)
MELPrI	Mellon Bk 9.60% `I' Pfd [*NYSE symbol*] (TTSB)
Me-LR	Law and Legislative Reference Library, Augusta, ME [*Library symbol Library of Congress*] (LCLS)
MELS	Microwave and Electronic System (IAA)
MELS	Molecularly Engineered Layered Structure
MELSA	Metropolitan Library Service Agency [*Library network*]
MELSOR	Marx, Engels, Lenin, Stalin, October Revolution [*Given name popular in Russia after the Bolshevik Revolution*]
MELT	Mantle Electromagnetic and Tomography [*Geology*]
MELT	Minimum Equipment Level for Training (MCD)
MELUS	Society for the Study of Multi-Ethnic Literature of the United States (BARN)
MELV	Melilotus Latent Virus [*Plant pathology*]
MELVA	Military Electronic Light Valve
Melvile	Melville Corp. [*Formerly, Melville Shoe Corp.*] [*Associated Press*] (SAG)
Melv Tr	Melvill's Trial (Impeachment) [*London*] [*A publication*] (DLA)
MELVYL	Melvil Dewey [*Public access online catalog, University of California*] (NITA)
Mem	De Memoria [*of Aristotle*] [*Classical studies*] (OCD)
MEM	Macrophage Electrophoretic Migration [*Clinical chemistry*] (AAMN)
MEM	Macrophage Electrophoretic Mobility (STED)
MEM	Macrophage Electrophoretic Mobility Test (MAE)
MEM	Magnetic Electron Multiplier (PDAA)
MEM	Magyar Elet Mozgalma [*Movement of Hungarian Life*] [*Political party*] (PPE)
MEM	Maine State Museum, Augusta, ME [*OCLC symbol*] (OCLC)
MEM	Malic Enzyme, Mitochondrial (STED)
MEM	Marine Engineering Mechanic [*Navy rating British*]
MEM	Mars Excursion Mission [*NASA*] (IAA)
MEM	Mars Excursion Module
MEM	Master of Ecosystem Management (PGP)
MEM	Master of Educational Ministry (PGP)
MEM	Master of Engineering Management
MEM	Master of Environmental Management (PGP)
Me M	Master of Metaphysics
MEM	Maximum Entropy Method [*Geomagnetism*] [*Computer science*]
MEM	Mediterranean Air Ambulance, SL [*Spain*] [*FAA designator*] (FAAC)
MEM	Membach [*Belgium*] [*Seismograph station code, US Geological Survey*] (SEIS)
MEM	Member (EY)
mem	Member (WDMC)
MEM	MEM Co. [*AMEX symbol*] (TTSB)
MEM	MEM Co., Inc. [*AMEX symbol*] (SPSG)
MEM	Memento
MEM	Memoir
mem	Memoir (WDMC)
Mem	Memorabilia [*of Xenophon*] [*Classical studies*] (OCD)
MEM	Memorandum
mem	Memorandum (WDMC)
mem	Memorial (WDMC)
MEM	Memorial
MEM	Memory (MSA)
MEM	Memphis [*Tennessee*] [*Airport symbol*] (OAG)
MEM	Meteoroid Exposure Module (MCD)
MEM	Methoxyethoxymethyl [*Organic chemistry*]
MEM	Micro Electro Mechanical (AAEL)
MEM	Middle-Ear Muscle [*Anatomy*]
MEM	Minimal Essential Medium (STED)
MEM	Minimum Essential Medium [*Culture medium*]
MEM	Mirror Electron Microscope (PDAA)
MEM	Missile Engagement Mechanism (MCD)
MEM	Model Emission Model [*Environmental Protection Agency*] (GFGA)
MEM	Module Exchange Mechanism [*NASA*] (NASA)
MEM	Molecular Exciton Microscopy
MEM	Mondpaca Esperantista Movado [*Esperantist Movement for World Peace - EMWP*] [*Tours, France*] (EAIO)
MEM	Most Efficient/Effective Method [*DoD*]
MEM	Most Excellent Master [*Freemasonry*]
MEM	Mount Emily Exploration Ltd. [*Vancouver Stock Exchange symbol*]
MEM	Multienvironmental Electron Microscope
MEMA	Marine Engine Manufacturers Association [*Formerly, OMMA*] (EA)
MEMA	Methyl Methacrylate (STED)
MEMA	Microelectronic Modular Assembly
MEMA	Middle-Ear Muscle Activity
MEMA	Motor and Equipment Manufacturers Association (EA)
MEMAC	Middle East Medical Advisory Committee [*World War II*]
MeMacU	University of Maine at Machias, Machias, ME [*Library symbol Library of Congress*] (LCLS)
MEMA/TTC...	Motor and Equipment Manufacturers Association's Technical Training Council
MEMB	Member
Memb	Member (TBD)
Memb	Membership (AL)
MEMB	Membranaceous Vellum [*Manuscripts*] (ROG)
MEMB	Membrane (MSA)
memb	Membrane (STED)
MEMBERS ...	Microprogrammed Experimental Machine with a Basic Executive for Real-Time Systems (PDAA)
MEMBIS ...	Member Budget Information System [*for House of Representatives*]
MEMBLE	Memorable (ROG)
MEMC	MEMC Electronic Materials, Inc. [*Associated Press*] (SAG)
MEMC	Memco Software Ltd. [*NASDAQ symbol*] (SAG)
MEMC	Methoxyethylmercuric Chloride
Mem Comm Solar Observ Aust...	Memoirs. Commonwealth Solar Observatory. Australia [*A publication*]
MEMCON ...	Memorandum of Conversation
MemcoSf	Memco Software Ltd. [*Associated Press*] (SAG)
MEMDA ...	Memoranda (ROG)
MEMDB	Medieval and Early Modern Data Bank [*Information service or system*] (IID)
MEMDUM	Memorandum (ROG)
MEME	Magnetic Environment Measuring Equipment (CAAL)
MEME	Multiple Entry Multiple Exit
MEME	Multitasking Extensible Messaging Environment
MEMEC	Memory and Electronic Components [*Commercial firm British*]
ME(Mech)	Master of Engineering (Mechanical) (ADA)
MEM ERR	Memory Error [*Information retrieval*]
Mem Geol Survey Vic...	Memoirs. Geological Survey of Victoria [*Australia A publication*]
MEMI	Master Equipment Management Index [*Air Force*] (AFM)
MeMi	Millinocket Memorial Library, Millinocket, ME [*Library symbol Library of Congress*] (LCLS)
MEMIC	Medical Microbiology Interdisciplinary Committee [*International Council of Scientific Unions*]
MEMIC	Mobile Eletromagnetic Incompatibility (PDAA)
MEMISTOR...	Memory Resistor (DEN)
MEML	Master Equipment Management List [*Air Force*] (AFM)
MEML	Memorial
MEML	Molecular Engineering and Materials Laboratory [*MIT*] (MCD)
MEMLACTV..	Memorial Activities [*Military*] (AABC)
Mem LJ	Memphis Law Journal [*Tennessee*] [*A publication*] (DLA)

MEMLZ	Memorialize (ABBR)
MEMLZD	Memorialized (ABBR)
MEMLZG	Memorializing (ABBR)
MEMLZN	Memorialization (ABBR)
MEMLZR	Memorializer (ABBR)
MEMMA	Mining Electromechanical Maintenance Association (IAA)
MEMMDLE...	Memory Module (IAA)
MEMO.......	Marine Environmental Management Office [*Marine science*] (MSC)
MEMO.......	Medical Equipment Management Office [*Air Force*] (AFM)
MEMO.......	Memorandum
memo.........	Memorandum (WDMC)
MEMO.......	Middle East Money [*London-Beirut*] (BJA)
MEMO.......	Minnesota Educational Media Organization (EDAC)
MEMO.......	Mission Essential Maintenance Only (MCD)
MEMO.......	Mission Essential Maintenance Operation (MCD)
MEMO.......	Model for Evaluating Maximum Missile Observation
MEMO.......	More Education - More Opportunities (DNAB)
MEMO.......	Voice It Worldwide [*NASDAQ symbol*] (TTSB)
MEMO.......	Voice It Worldwide, Inc. [*NASDAQ symbol*] (SAG)
MEMOCS......	Mitsubishi Electric Corp. Multiterm Out-of-Context System
Memo Mgmt...	Memo to Management [*Australian Institute of Management, Queensland Division*] [*A publication*]
Memorex	Memorex Telex NV [*Associated Press*] (SAG)
MEMOREX ...	Memory Excellence [*Brand name*]
MEMOS.......	Manufacturing Engineering Management Operations System (MCD)
MEMP........	Maximization of Expected Maximum Profit [*Econometrics*]
Memphis LJ..	Memphis Law Journal [*Tennessee*] [*A publication*] (DLA)
Memphis St U...	Memphis State University (GAGS)
Memp LJ	Memphis Law Journal [*Tennessee*] [*A publication*] (DLA)
MEMPP.......	Morpholinoethylmethylphenylpyridazone [*An analgesic*]
MEMPT.......	Memory Point
MEMQ........	Married Enlisted Men's Quarters
ME (MR).....	Medical Evidence (Medical Report or Record) (OICC)
MEMR........	Memory Read [*Computer science*] (MHDI)
MEMR........	Multiple Exostoses-Mental Retardation Syndrome [*Medicine*] (DMAA)
MEMRA.......	Mechanical Equipment Manufacturers Representatives Association (EA)
MEMRAC	Mission Essential Material Readiness and Condition (MCD)
memrl.......	Memorial (VRA)
MEMS........	Master of Emergency Medical Service (PGP)
MEMS........	Master of Engineering in Manufacturing Systems (GAGS)
MEMS........	Microbial Ecological Monitoring System [*Apollo*] [*NASA*]
MEMS........	Microelectromechanical System [*Materials science and technology*]
MEMS........	Micro Electro Mechanical Systems
MEMS........	Mineral Economics and Management Society
MEMS........	Missile Equipment Maintenance Sets (MUGU)
MEMS........	Modular Engine Management System [*Automotive engineering*]
MEMSEL......	Multieffect, Multistage
MEMSEL......	Memory Select [*Computer science*] (MHDI)
Mem St UL Rev...	Memphis State University. Law Review [*A publication*] (DLA)
Memtec.......	Memtec Ltd. [*Associated Press*] (SAG)
MEMU........	Manned Extravehicular Manipulating Unit (MCD)
MEMW........	Memory Write [*Computer science*] (MHDB)
MemWks	MemberWorks, Inc. [*Associated Press*] (SAG)
MEMX........	Memorex Telex NV [*NASDAQ symbol*] (SAG)
MEMXY.......	Memorex Telex ADS [*NASDAQ symbol*] (TTSB)
MEMY........	Memory (ROG)
MEN..........	Master Equipment Number [*Military*] (NG)
M En.........	Master of English
Men..........	Menaechmi [*of Plautus*] [*Classical studies*] (OCD)
Men..........	Menahot (BJA)
Men..........	Menander [*Fourth century BC*] [*Classical studies*] (OCD)
men..........	Mende [*MARC language code Library of Congress*] (LCCP)
MEN..........	Mendoza [*Argentina*] [*Seismograph station code, US Geological Survey Closed*] (SEIS)
men..........	Meningeal (STED)
MEN..........	Mennonite (ABBR)
MEN..........	Meno [*Slower*] [*Music*]
MEN..........	Menology
Men..........	Menorah: Australian Journal of Jewish Studies [*A publication*] (APTA)
Men..........	Mensa [*Constellation*]
MEN..........	Mense [*or Menses*] (ABBR)
MEN..........	Men's Equality Now International (EA)
MEN..........	Menstruation (ABBR)
MEN..........	Mensuration (ABBR)
MEN..........	Mention
Men..........	Menzies' Cape Of Good Hope Reports [*1828-49*] [*A publication*] (DLA)
MEN..........	Methylethylnitrosamine (STED)
MEN..........	Mistozen Electronic Nebulizer
MEN..........	Multiple Earthed Neutral (IAA)
MEN..........	Multiple Endocrine Neoplasia [*Medicine*]
MEN..........	Multiple Endocrine Neoplasia/Neoplasms (STED)
MEN..........	Multiple Event Network
MEN..........	MuniEnhanced Fund [*NYSE symbol*] (SPSG)
MENA........	Middle East and North Africa [*A publication*]
MENA........	Middle East News Agency
MENA........	Mission Element Need Analysis (MCD)
MENA........	Mitsubishi Engine North America
MENA........	Mitsubishi Engine North America, Inc.
MENC........	Music Educators National Conference (EA)
MENCAP	Royal Society for Mentally Handicapped Children & Adults [*England*]
Mence Lib...	Mence's Law of Libel [*1824*] [*A publication*] (DLA)
MEND	Massive Economic Neighborhood Development [*New York City*]
MEND	Maximum Entropy Noise Deconvolution [*Statistics*]
MEND	Medical Education for National Defense
MEND	Mendelism
MEND	Mothers Embracing Nuclear Disarmament [*An association*] (EA)
MENEV.......	Menevensis [*Signature of the Bishops of St. David's*] [*British*] (ROG)
MENEX.......	Maintenance Engineering Exchange
Menex	Menexemus [*of Plato*] [*Classical studies*] (OCD)
M Eng........	Master of Engineering
M Eng........	Master of English
MENG	Meaning (ABBR)
M Eng........	Mechanical Engineer
MEng.........	Member of Environmental Sciences/Studies [*Canada*] (ASC)
M-ENG........	Multiengined
M Eng & PA..	Master in Engineering and Public Administration
MENGF	Meaningful (ABBR)
MENGFY	Meaningfully (ABBR)
MENGLS	Meaningless (ABBR)
MENGLSY ...	Meaninglessly (ABBR)
M Eng Mgt..	Master of Engineering Management (PGP)
MEngPA......	Master of Engineering and Public Administration (NADA)
M Engr........	Master of Engineering (PGP)
MEngS	Master of Engineering Science
M Eng Sc.....	Master of Engineering Science
MEngSt.......	Master of Engineering Studies (ADA)
ME(NI)........	Ministry of Education (Northern Ireland)
MENI..........	Multiple Endocrine Neoplasia Type I [*Medicine*] (DMAA)
MENIT........	Mennonite
MENJ.........	Menley & James, Inc. [*NASDAQ symbol*] (SPSG)
Menken.......	Menken's Civil Procedure Reports [*30 New York*] [*A publication*] (DLA)
MenleyJ.......	Menley & James, Inc. [*Associated Press*] (SAG)
Menn	Menninger [*Karl Augustus*] [*American psychiatrist*] (DAVI)
MENNON.....	Mennonite (ABBR)
MENNS	Meanness (ABBR)
MENO	Menopause (DSUE)
MENO	Menorrhoea (ABBR)
MENP.........	Menopause (ABBR)
MENPL........	Menopausal (ABBR)
Men Rel	Menandri Reliquiae [*A publication*] (OCD)
MENS........	K&G Men's Center [*NQS*] (TTSB)
MENS........	K & G Mens Center, Inc. [*NASDAQ symbol*] (SAG)
M En S	Master of Environmental Science (PGP)
Mens	Mensa [*Constellation*]
MENS........	Mensis [*Month*] [*Latin*]
MENS........	Mensura [*By Measure*] [*Pharmacy*]
MENS........	Middle East Neurosurgical Society (EAIO)
MENS........	Missile Element Need Statement
MENS........	Mission Element Needs Statement (MCD)
Men's J	Men's Journal [*A publication*] (BRI)
menst	Menstrual [*or Menstruate*] (AAMN)
MENSTD	Menstruated (ABBR)
MENSTG	Menstruating (ABBR)
MENSTL......	Menstrual (ABBR)
MENSTN	Menstruation (ABBR)
MENSUR.....	Mensuration (ROG)
M Ent.........	Master of Entomology
MENT........	Mental
MENT........	Mentalis (ABBR)
MENT........	Mentioned
MENT........	Mentor Graphics [*NASDAQ symbol*] (TTSB)
MENT........	Mentor Graphics Corp. [*NASDAQ symbol*] (NQ)
Mental & Physical Disab L Rep...	Mental and Physical Disability Law Reporter [*A publication*] (DLA)
MENTD.......	Mentioned
MentGr	Mentor Graphics Corp. [*Associated Press*] (SAG)
MENTH	Mentha [*Mint*] [*Pharmacy*] (ROG)
Ment Hlth Aust...	Mental Health in Australia [*A publication*]
MentInc	Mentor Income Fund [*Associated Press*] (SAG)
MENTL........	Mental
MentlHlt	Mental Health Management, Inc. [*Associated Press*] (SAG)
MENTLY	Mentally (ABBR)
MENTN	Mention (ROG)
MENTNB	Mentionable (ABBR)
MENTND	Mentioned (ABBR)
MENTNG	Mentioning (ABBR)
MENTNR	Mentioner (ABBR)
Mentor........	Mentor Corp. [*Associated Press*] (SAG)
MENTOR	Mobile Electrical Network Testing, Observation, and Recording (PDAA)
MENTOR......	[*A*] Programming Language [*1963*] (CSR)
MENTT........	Mentality (ABBR)
MENTY........	Mentally (ABBR)
M Env	Master of Environment (PGP)
MEnv.........	Master of Environmental Studies (DD)
M Env Des...	Master of Environmental Design (PGP)
M Env E......	Master of Environmental Engineering (PGP)
MENVEGR....	Master of Environmental Engineering (PGP)
M Envir E.....	Master of Environmental Engineering (PGP)
MEnvPlan....	Master of Environmental Planning
MEnvS	Master of Environmental Science (GAGS)
MEnvS	Master of Environmental Studies
MEnvSc........	Master of Environmental Science (ADA)
M Env Sc.....	Master of Environmental Science (PGP)
MEnvSt........	Master of Environmental Studies (ADA)
MEnvStud	Master of Environmental Studies (ADA)
MEnvStudies...	Master of Environmental Studies

MenWre.......	Mens Warehouse [*Associated Press*] (SAG)
MeNwS	Saint Joseph's College, North Windham, ME [*Library symbol Library of Congress*] (LCLS)
Menz...........	Menzies' Cape Of Good Hope Reports [*1828-49*] [*A publication*] (DLA)
Menz Conv...	Menzies' Conveyancing [*A publication*] (DLA)
Menzies.......	Menzies' Cape Of Good Hope Reports [*1828-49*] [*A publication*] (DLA)
MEO............	Jefferson City, MO [*Location identifier FAA*] (FAAL)
MEO............	Maintenance Engineering Order [*NASA*] (KSC)
MEO............	Major Engine Overhaul
MEO............	Manned Earth Orbit
MEO............	Manned Extravehicular Operation
MEO............	Marine Engineer Officer [*British*]
MEO............	Mass in Earth Orbit [*NASA*]
MEO............	Medical Emergency Officer (DAVI)
MEO............	Medium Earth Orbit (SSD)
MEO............	Military Equal Opportunity (MCD)
MEO............	Mining Engineering Officer [*British military*] (DMA)
MEO............	Montello Resources Ltd. [*Vancouver Stock Exchange symbol*]
MEO............	Most Efficient/Effective Organization [*DoD*]
MEO............	Scandinavian Aviation Center AS [*Denmark ICAO designator*] (FAAC)
MEOC.........	Marine Emergency Operations Center [*Western Australia*]
MEOC.........	Marine Environmental Quality Committee [*Marine science*] (OSRA)
MEOER	Member of the European Osteopathic Register
MEOF.........	Marine Environmental Observation and Forecasting (NOAA)
MEOH	Methanex Corp. [*NASDAQ symbol*] (SAG)
MEOH	Methyl Alcohol
MEOHF	Methanex Corp. [*NASDAQ symbol*] (TTSB)
MEOL.........	Manned Earth Orbit Laboratory (IAA)
MEOM.........	Manned Earth Orbit Mission
MEOOW.......	Marine Engineer Officer of the Watch [*British*]
MEOP.........	Maximum Engine Operating Pressure
MEOP.........	Maximum Expected Operating Pressure
MEOR.........	Microbial Enhanced Oil Recovery [*Petroleum technology*]
MEOS.........	Medium Earth Orbit Satellites (ACRL)
MEOS.........	Microsomal Ethanol-Oxidizing System [*Biochemistry*]
MEOS.........	Mode/Energy Offset
MEOSAB	Missile Explosive Ordnance Safety Advisory Board [*Pacific Missile Range*] (MUGU)
MEOTBF.......	Mean Engine Operating Time between Failures [*Quality control*]
MEOV.........	Maximum Expected Operating Value [*FCC*]
MEOW	Marine Engineer Officer's Writer [*British military*] (DMA)
MEOW	[*The*] Moral Equivalent of War [*Phrase used by President Jimmy Carter to describe his energy bill*]
MEOWS	Multimode Electro-Optical Weapon System
MEP............	Magnetic Energy Product
MEP............	Magyar Elet Partja [*Party of Hungarian Life*] [*Political party*] (PPE)
MEP............	Mahajana Eksath Peramuna [*People's United Front*] [*Sri Lanka*] [*Political party*] (PPW)
MEP............	Main Engine Propellant (MCD)
MEP............	Main Entry Point (NASA)
MEP............	Maintainability Evaluation Process (MCD)
MEP............	Major Electronics Procurement
MEP............	Major Extinction Position [*Polarizer-Analyzer*]
MEP............	Management Engineering Program [*Air Force*] (AFM)
MEP............	Management Evaluation Program (AAG)
MEP............	Manual Entry Panel [*Military*] (CAAL)
MEPA.........	Manuals of Engineering Practice [*ASCE*]
MEP............	Manufacturing Engineering Plan
MEP............	Manufacturing Extension Partnership [*National Institute for Science and Technology*]
MEP............	Mars Entry Probe
MEP............	Master Environmental Plan (BCP)
MEP............	Master Evaluation Plan [*Army*]
MEP............	Master of Engineering Physics
MEP............	Master of Environmental Planning (GAGS)
MEP............	Maximal Expiratory Pressure [*Medicine*] (DB)
MEP............	Maximum Economic Potential
MEP............	Maximum Entropy Principle (PDAA)
MEP............	Maximum Escape Performance [*Ejection seat*] (MCD)
MEP............	Maximum Expiratory Pressure [*Medicine*] (DMAA)
MEP............	Maxwell Electronic Publishing [*Information service or system*] (IID)
MEP............	Mean Effective Pressure
MEP............	Medical Education Program [*Air Force*]
MEP............	Member of the European Parliament
MEP............	Meperidine [*Also, M*] [*An analgesic*]
MEP............	Mersing [*Malaysia*] [*Airport symbol*] (OAG)
MEP............	Methanol Environmental Performance [*Automotive engineering*]
MEP............	Methods Engineering Program [*Navy*] (NVT)
MEP............	Methyl(ethyl)pyridine [*Organic chemistry*]
MEP............	Methyl Parathion [*Also, MP, MPN*] [*Pesticide*]
MEP............	Microcircuit Emulation Program
MEP............	Micro-Electronics Education Programme (NITA)
MEP............	Microelectronics Programme [*British*]
MEP............	Microfile Enlarger Printer (NITA)
MEP............	Middle East Policy [*A publication*] (BRI)
MEP............	Midwest Express Airlines, Inc. [*ICAO designator*] (FAAC)
MEP............	Minimum Energy Path [*Physical chemistry*]
MEP............	Minimum Entry Point (MCD)
MEP............	Minority Entrepreneurship Program [*Small Business Administration*]
MEP............	Minuteman Education Program [*Air Force*] (AFM)
MEP............	Mission Effects Projector [*Lunar exploration*]
MEP............	Mission Equipment Package
MEP............	Mitochondrial Encephalopathy [*Medicine*] (DMAA)
MEP............	Mobile Electric Power (NG)
MEP............	Mobil Exploration & Producing Services, Inc., Dallas, TX [*OCLC symbol*] (OCLC)
MEP............	Mogul End Prong [*Lamp base*] (NTCM)
MEP............	Molecular Electrostatic Potentials [*Physical chemistry*]
MEP............	Moon-Earth-Plane (SAA)
MEP............	Motor End Plate
MEP............	Motor-Evoked Potential (OA)
MEP............	Mouvement d'Ecologie Politique [*Ecology Political Movement*] [*France Political party*] (PPW)
MEP............	Movimiento Electoral del Pueblo [*People's Electoral Movement*] [*Netherlands Antilles*] [*Political party*] (PPW)
MEP............	Movimiento Electoral del Pueblo [*People's Electoral Movement*] [*Venezuela*] [*Political party*] (PPW)
MEP............	Mucoid Exopolysaccharide [*Biochemistry*]
MEP............	Multielliptical Pump
MEP............	Multimodality Evoked Potential [*Neurophysiology*]
MEP............	Multiple-Exposure Photography
MEP............	Multiple Extraction Procedure (GNE)
MEP............	Paris Foreign Mission Society (TOCD)
mep............	Paris Foreign Mission Society (TOCD)
MeP............	Portland Public Library, Portland, ME [*Library symbol Library of Congress*] (LCLS)
MEP............	Societas Parisiensis Missionum ad Exteros [*Paris Foreign Missions Society*] [*Roman Catholic men's religious order*]
MEP-91........	Mesoscale Evolution Project-1991 [*Marine science*] (OSRA)
MEPA.........	Marine and Estuarine Protected Area
MEPA.........	Master in Engineering and Public Administration
MEPARC	Middle East Policy and Research Center (EA)
MEPC.........	Marine Environment Protection Committee [*IMCO*] (MSC)
MEPC.........	Maritime Environment Protection Committee (NADA)
MEPC.........	Master of Environmental Pollution Control (GAGS)
MEPC.........	MEPC International Capital LP [*Associated Press*] (SAG)
MEPC.........	Miniature End Plate Current
MEPCOM	Military Enlistment Processing Command [*DoD*]
MEPD.........	Master of Education - Professional Development (PGP)
MEPDP	Meander Electrodes Plasma Display Panel (IAA)
MEPED.......	Medium-Energy Proton and Electron Detector
MEPES.......	Medical Planning and Execution System (DOMA)
MEPES.......	Medical Planning and Execution System (Model)
MEPF.........	Multiple Experiment Processing Furnace
MEPGS	Mobile Electric Power Generator Set (MCD)
MEPH.........	Master of Public Health Engineering (NADA)
MEPH.........	Mephobarital [*A sedative and anticonvulsant*] [*Pharmacology*] (DAVI)
MEPHISTO ...	Mephistopheles [*Foreman*] [*Slang British*] (DSUE)
ME Phy	Master of Engineering Physics
MePM.........	Maine Charitable Mechanic Association, Portland, ME [*Library symbol Library of Congress*] (LCLS)
MEPM.........	Medium-Term Energy Policy Model
MePMC.......	Maine Medical Center, Portland, ME [*Library symbol Library of Congress*] (LCLS)
MEPOL.......	Metropolitan Police Officers [*British*]
MePosS	United Society of Shakers, Shaker Library, Poland Spring, ME [*Library symbol Library of Congress*] (LCLS)
MEPP.........	Marine Electric Power Plant (PDAA)
MEPP.........	Middle East Peace Project (EA)
MEPP.........	Miniature End Plate Potential
MEPP.........	Mobile Electric Power Plant (NG)
MEPrA........	Mission Capital 9.875%`MIPS' [*NYSE symbol*] (TTSB)
MEPrB........	Mission Capital 8.50% `MIPS' [*NYSE symbol*] (TTSB)
MePriU	University of Maine at Presque Isle, Presque Isle, ME [*Library symbol Library of Congress*] (LCLS)
MEPROB	Meprobamate [*Mythyl propyltrimethylene carbamate*] [*Tranquilizer*] (DAVI)
MEPROBAMATE...	Methyl Propyltrimethylene Carbamate [*Tranquilizer*]
MEPRS	Military Entrant-Processing and Reporting System (GFGA)
MEPRS/DDS...	Medical Expense and Performance Reporting System/Dental Data System [*Air Force*] (GFGA)
MePS...........	Maine Public Service Co. [*Associated Press*] (SAG)
MEPS.........	Means-End Problem-Solving Procedure [*or Test*] [*Psychology*]
MEPS.........	Medium-Energy Particle Spectrometer (MCD)
MEPS.........	Members of the European Parliament (ECON)
MEPS.........	Message Editing and Processing System (MCD)
MEPS.........	Military Entrance and Processing Station
MEPS.........	Modular Electrical Power Station
MEPS.........	Monochrome Electronic Prepress Systems (DGA)
MEPS.........	Multimedia Environmental Pollutant Assessment System (COE)
MEPSA........	Middle East Peace and Stability Act [*1957*]
mEPSC........	Miniature Excitory Postsynaptic Currents [*Neurobiology*]
MEPSCAT ...	Military Entrance Physical Strength Capacity Test (INF)
MEPSDU	Module Experimental Process System Development Unit [*Photovoltaic energy systems*]
MEPSI........	Mexico-Elmhurst Philatelic Society, International (EA)
MEPSP........	Miniature Excitatory Postsynaptic Potential [*Neurophysiology*]
MEPU..........	Monofuel Emergency Power Unit
MEQ...........	Marine Environmental Quality [*Marine science*] (MSC)
MEQ...........	Married Enlisted Quarters
MEQ...........	Middle East Quarterly [*A publication*] (BRI)
meq...........	Milliequivalent [*Gram equivalent weight*] (DOG)
MEQ...........	Milliequivalent [*or Milligram Equivalent*] [*Also, ME*]
MEQA.........	Mechanized Equipment Assignment [*AT & T*]
MEQC.........	Medicaid Eligibility Quality Control (GFGA)
MEQ/L.......	Milliequivalent per Liter
MEQPT........	Major Equipment (COE)

MER	Ethamoxytriphetol [*An antiestrogen*] (DAVI)
MER	Madras European Regiment [*British military*] (DMA)
MER	Magneto-Elastic Resonance (PDAA)
MER	Main Engine Room [*Navy*] (CAAL)
MER	Maine State Department of Environmental Protection and Department of Conservation, Augusta, ME [*OCLC symbol*] (OCLC)
MER	Maintenance Engineering Report (MCD)
MER	Management Expense Ratio
MER	Mandatory Experience Regulation (DB)
MER	Manned Earth Reconnaissance [*Naval Air Electronic Systems Command project*]
MER	Manpower Estimate Report (AAGC)
MER	Manpower Estimating Relationships (MCD)
MER	Manpower Evaluation Report [*Military*]
MER	Marine Environmental Response [*USCG*] (TAG)
MER	Market Exchange Rates [*Monetary conversion rate*] (ECON)
MER	Mass Energy Relationship
MER	Master Employee Record [*DoD*]
MER	Master of Energy Resources (GAGS)
MER	Maximum Effective Range
MER	Maximum Efficient Rate [*Oil*]
MER	Maximum Energy Recovery [*Chemical engineering*]
MER	Mean Ejection Rate [*Medicine*]
MER	Mechanical Equipment Room (DAC)
MER	Mechanics, Electrical, and Radio (MCD)
MER	Medical Emergency Room (DMAA)
MER	Medication Errors Reporting
MER	Mercantile
MER	Merced, CA [*Location identifier FAA*] (FAAL)
MER	Merchandise (ADA)
MER	Merchant (AFM)
MER	Mercurial (WDAA)
MER	Mercury (ADA)
Mer	Mercury [*Record label*]
MER	Merida [*Mexico*] [*Seismograph station code, US Geological Survey*] (SEIS)
MER	Meridian (KSC)
MER	Meridional [*Geology*]
Mer	Merivale's English Chancery Reports [*A publication*] (DLA)
MER	Merlinoite [*A zeolite*]
MER	Merrell-National Laboratories [*Research code symbol*]
MER	Merrill Lynch [*NYSE symbol*] (TTSB)
MER	Merrill Lynch & Co. [*NYSE symbol*] (SAG)
MER	Merrill Lynch & Co. Preferred Capital Trust I [*NYSE symbol*] (SAG)
MER	Metal Etch Resist
MER	Metal Evaporated Resistor
MER	Methanol Extraction [*or Extruded*] Residue [*Immunology*]
MER	Methow Aviation, Inc. [*ICAO designator*] (FAAC)
MER	Middle East Record [*A publication*] (BJA)
MER	Minimum Energy Requirements
MER	Mission Evaluation Room [*NASA*] (NASA)
MER	Mitteleuropaeisches Reisebuero [*Middle European Travel Bureau*] [*German*]
MER	Monthly Energy Review [*Department of Energy*] [*Database*]
MER	Most Economical Rating
MER	Multielement RADAR
MER	Multiple Ejector Rack (NG)
MER	Murmur/Energy Ratio (DMAA)
MER	Museum Education Roundtable (EA)
MER	Myeloid-Erythrocyte [*or Erythroid*] [*Hematology*] (DAVI)
MER-29	Triparanol [*Pharmacology*] [*A cholesterol biosynthesis inhibitor removed from market due to side effects*] (DAVI)
MERA	Maeventec Employers Rated Almanac [*Maeventec*] [*Information service or system*] (CRD)
MERA	Microelectronics for RADAR Application (MCD)
MERA	Molecular Electronics for RADAR Applications (IEEE)
MERA	Mormons for ERA (EA)
MERADCOM	Mobility Equipment Research and Development Command [*Army*]
MERADO	Mechanical Engineering Research and Development Organisation
MERALCO	Manila Electric Railroad & Light Company [*Still known by acronym, although official name now Manila Electric Company*]
MERALT	Meridian Altitude [*Navigation*]
Mer & St Corp	Merewether and Stephen's Municipal Corporations [*A publication*] (DLA)
MERB	Medical Examination and Review Board [*DoD*] (DAVI)
MerBkNY	Merchants New York Bancorp [*Associated Press*] (SAG)
MerBNY	Merchants New York Bancorp [*Associated Press*] (SAG)
MERC	Chicago Mercantile Exchange (EBF)
MERC	Meat Export Research Center [*Iowa State University*] [*Research center*] (RCD)
MERC	Mercantile (ROG)
Merc	Mercator [*of Plautus*] [*Classical studies*] (OCD)
MERC	Mercedes [*Automobile*] (DSUE)
MERC	[*A*] Mercenary
MERC	Mercurial (ABBR)
MERC	Mercury
MERC	Mercury Project [*NASA*] (KSC)
MERC	Middle-Atlantic Educational and Research Center
MERC	Middle East Regional Cooperation [*U.S. Agency for International Development*]
MERC	Middle East Resource Center [*Defunct*] (EA)
MERC	Minimum Electrical Resistance Condition (PDAA)
MERC	Minority Economic Resource Center [*Howard University, Washington, DC*]
MERC	Mobile Equipment Replacement Cask [*Nuclear energy*] (NUCP)

MERC	Multi-Racial Education Resources Centre [*British*] (AIE)
MERC	Music Education Research Council (EA)
Merc Ad & Law & Credit Man	Mercantile Adjuster and Lawyer and Credit Man [*A publication*] (DLA)
MercAir	Mercury Air Group, Inc. [*Associated Press*] (SAG)
MERCASREP	Merchant Ship Casualty Report [*Navy*] (NVT)
MERCAST	Merchant Ship Broadcast [*Navy*]
MERCASUM	Merchant Ship Casualty Summary [*Navy*] (NVT)
MercBcp	Mercantile Bancorp [*Associated Press*] (SAG)
Merc Cas	Mercantile Cases [*A publication*] (DLA)
MERCE	Mercedes [*Automobile*] (DSUE)
Mercer	Mercer County Law Journal [*Pennsylvania*] [*A publication*] (DLA)
Mercer	Mercer International [*Associated Press*] (SAG)
Mercer Beasley L Rev	Mercer Beasley Law Review [*A publication*] (DLA)
Mercer BL Rev	Mercer Beasley Law Review [*A publication*] (DLA)
Mercer U	Mercer University (GAGS)
MercFn	Mercury Finance Co. [*Associated Press*] (SAG)
MercGn	Mercury General Corp. [*Associated Press*] (SAG)
Merch	Merchant (TBD)
MERCH	Merchantable
Merch Dict	Merchants' Dictionary [*A publication*] (DLA)
Merc (Hob)	Mercury (Hobart) [*A publication*]
MERCHT	Merchant
Merch V	[*The*] Merchant of Venice [*Shakespearean work*] (BARN)
MercInt	Mercury Interactive Corp. [*Associated Press*] (SAG)
Merck	Merck & Co., Inc. [*Associated Press*] (SAG)
Merc LJ	Mercantile Law Journal [*New York or Madras*] [*A publication*] (DLA)
MERCM	Mercantilism (ABBR)
MERCO	Mercantile Communications [*Shipping*]
MERCO	Merchant Ship Control [*Navy*]
MERCOFORM	Merchant Ship Communications Formatted (MCD)
MERCOMMS	Merchant Marine Communications System (DNAB)
MERCON	Universal Transversal Mercator Converter [*Computer program*]
MERCOS	Merchant Codes [*Shipping*]
MERCOSUR	Common Market of the South
MERCPAC	Mercury Enthusiast Restorer Custom Performance Auto Club (EA)
MERCRy	Mercury [*Chemistry*] (DAVI)
MERCS	Mercer International SBI [*NASDAQ symbol*] (SPSG)
MERCS	Mercer Intl. SBI [*NASDAQ symbol*] (TTSB)
MercSt	Mercantile Stores Co., Inc. [*Associated Press*] (SAG)
MERCT	Mercantilist (ABBR)
MERCTL	Mercantile
MerctlBk	Mercantile Bankshares Corp. [*Associated Press*] (SAG)
MERCY	Medical Emergency Relief Care for Youth
MERDC	Mobility Equipment Research and Development Center [*Army*] (MCD)
MERDI	Montana Energy and Magneto-Hydrodynamics Research Institute [*Later, Montana Energy Research and Development Institute*] [*Research center*]
MERDIFF	Meridian Difference
MerdIns	Meridian Insurance Group, Inc. [*Associated Press*] (SAG)
MERDL	Medical Equipment Research and Development Laboratory [*Army*]
MerdrNt	Meridian National Corp. [*Associated Press*] (SAG)
Merdth	Meredith Corp. [*Associated Press*] (SAG)
MEREA	Member of the American Electrical Railway Engineering Association
MERECEN	Movimiento Estable Republicano Centrista [*El Salvador*] [*Political party*] (EY)
MEREP	Merchant Ship Arrival and/or Departure Report (NATG)
MEREP	Merchant Ship Report [*Navy*]
ME(Res)	Master of Engineering (Research)
MERES	Matrix of Environmental Residuals for Energy Systems [*Computerized information system*]
ME Rev Stat	Maine Revised Statutes [*A publication*] (DLA)
ME Rev Stat Ann	Maine Revised Statutes, Annotated [*A publication*] (DLA)
MERF	Medical Education Research Foundation [*San Diego*]
MERG	Macular Electroretinogram (DB)
MERGE	Mechanized Retrieval for Greater Efficiency [*Computer science*]
MERGV	Martian Exploratory Rocket Glide Vehicle
MERI	Medical Education Research and Information Database
MERI	Meritrust Federal Savings Bank [*NASDAQ symbol*] (SAG)
MERI	Meritrust Fed Svg Bk Morgan [*NASDAQ symbol*] (TTSB)
MERI	Mineral Exploration Research Institute [*See also IREM*] [*Canada Research center*] (RCD)
MERI	Mining and Excavation Research Institute [*Research center*] (RCD)
MERIC	Michigan Education Resources Information Center [*Michigan State Library*] [*Information service or system Defunct*] (IID)
MERID	Meridian (ABBR)
MeridDia	Meridian Diagnostics, Inc. [*Associated Press*] (SAG)
MeridDta	Meridian Data, Inc. [*Associated Press*] (SAG)
MeridI	Meridian Industrial Trust, Inc. [*Associated Press*] (SAG)
Meridn	Meridian [*A publication*]
MeridSpt	Meridian Sports, Inc. [*Associated Press*] (SAG)
MERIE	Magnetically Enhanced Reactive Ion Etching [*By plasmas*]
MeriFdl	Meritrust Federal Savings Bank [*Associated Press*] (SAG)
MerilCp	Merrill Corp. [*Associated Press*] (SAG)
MERINT	Merchant Intelligence Report [*Navy*]
MERINT	Merchant Ship Intelligence (NVT)
MERINTREP	Merchant Ship Arrival and/or Departure Intermediate Report (NATG)
MERIONS	Merionethshire [*County in Wales*]
MERIP	Middle East Research and Information Project (EA)
MERIS	Medium Resolution Imaging Spectrometer (SSD)
Merisel	Merisel, Inc. [*Associated Press*] (SAG)
MerisL	Meris Laboratories, Inc. [*Associated Press*] (SAG)
MERIT	Maastricht Economic Research Institute on Innovation and Technology
MERIT	Medicl Relief International (NADA)

MERIT..........	Method to Extend Research in Time [*National Institutes of Health*]
MERIT..........	Michigan Educational Research Information Triad, Inc.
MERIT..........	Monitor the Earth Rotation and Intercompare Techniques [*by means of radio telescope measurements*]
MERIT..........	Multiple RADAR-Integrated Tracking [*Military*] (PDAA)
MERIT..........	[*The*] The Michigan Educational Research Network [*Computer science*] (TNIG)
MeritH..........	Merit Holding Corp. [*Associated Press*] (SAG)
MERITOC.....	Meritocracy (ABBR)
MERITOC.....	Meritocrat (ABBR)
Meriv..........	Merivale's English Chancery Reports [*A publication*] (DLA)
Meriv (Eng)..	Merivale's English Chancery Reports [*A publication*] (DLA)
Merix Cp......	Merix Corp. [*Associated Press*] (SAG)
MERL..........	Marine Ecosystem Research Laboratory [*University of Rhode Island*] [*Research center*]
MERL..........	Materials Engineering Research Laboratory [*NASA*] (NASA)
MERL..........	Materials Engineering Research Laboratory Ltd. [*British*] (IRC)
MERL..........	Materials Equipment Requirements List (NASA)
MerL..........	Merrill Lynch & Co., Inc. [*Associated Press*] (SAG)
MerL..........	Merrill Lynch & Co. Preferred Capital Trust I [*Associated Press*] (SAG)
MERL..........	Municipal Environmental Research Laboratory [*Environmental Protection Agency*] (GRD)
MerLEur.......	Merrill Lynch & Co., Inc. [*Associated Press*] (SAG)
MERLIN	Machine Readable Library Information [*British Library*] [*Information service or system*] (IID)
MERLIN	Management of Expenditure and Resident-Linked Information Network [*Computer science*]
MERLIN	Medium-Energy Reactor Light-Water Industrial Neutron [*British*] (DEN)
MERLIN	Multielement Radio-Linked Interferometer Network [*Astronomy*]
Mer LJ........	Mercantile Law Journal [*Madras, India*] [*A publication*] (DLA)
MERM..........	Masters of Earth Resources Management (PGP)
MERM..........	Material Evaluation Rocket Motor
MERM..........	Multilateral Exchange Rate Model (ADA)
Mermic.......	Merrimac Industries, Inc. [*Associated Press*] (SAG)
MERMLS.......	Mid-Eastern Regional Medical Library Service [*Library network*]
MERMUT	Mobile Electronic Robot Manipulator and Underwater Television (IEEE)
MERP..........	Maximum Effective Radiated Power [*Telecommunications*] (OTD)
MERP..........	Miniature Electronic Repair Program (DNAB)
MerP6..........	Meridian Point Realty Trust VI Co. [*Associated Press*] (SAG)
MERPASS ...	Meridian Passage [*Navigation*]
MERPL.........	Mission Essential Repair Parts List (MCD)
MerPnt 8.....	Meridian Point Realty Trust VIII [*Associated Press*] (SAG)
MERPrA.......	Merrill Lynch 9% Sr'A'Dep Pfd [*NYSE symbol*] (TTSB)
MERPS........	Multiple Event Record and Playback System (NTCM)
MerPt4........	Meridian Point Realty Trust IV [*Associated Press*] (SAG)
MerPt6........	Meridian Point Realty Trust VI [*Associated Press*] (SAG)
MerPt7........	Meridian Point Realty Trust VII [*Associated Press*] (SAG)
MerPt 8........	Meridian Point Realty Trust VIII Co. [*Associated Press*] (SAG)
MerPt83.......	Meridian Point Realty Trust 1983 [*Associated Press*] (SAG)
MERQ..........	Mercury Interactive [*NASDAQ symbol*] (TTSB)
MERQ..........	Mercury Interactive Corp. [*NASDAQ symbol*] (SAG)
MerR	Mercuric Ion Receptor [*Biochemistry*]
MERR	Minor Equipment Relocations, Replacements (DNAB)
MERRA	Middle East Relief and Rehabilitation Administration [*World War II*]
Merr Att.....	Merrifield on Attorneys [*1830*] [*A publication*] (DLA)
MERRC........	Middle Eastern Regional Radioisotope Centre for the Arab Countries [*Cairo, Egypt*] (WND)
Merr Costs...	Merrifield's Law of Costs [*A publication*] (DLA)
MERRECT	Mercury Rectifier (IAA)
MERRF........	Myoclonic Epilepsy Associated with Ragged Red Fibres [*Medicine*]
Merrimack...	Smith's New Hampshire Reports [*A publication*] (DLA)
MerrLyn.......	Merrill Lynch & Co., Inc. [*Associated Press*] (SAG)
Merry W	[*The*] The Merry Wives of Windsor [*Shakespearean work*] (BARN)
MERS..........	Medical Equipment Reporting System [*Veterans Administration*]
MERS..........	Meris Laboratories [*NASDAQ symbol*] (SPSG)
MERS..........	Mobile Emergency Response Support
MERS..........	Mobility Environmental Research Studies
MERS..........	Most Economical Route Selection [*Also, ARS*] [*Bell System*] [*Telecommunications*]
MERS..........	Movimiento de Estudiantes Revolucionarios Salvadorenos [*Revolutionary Movement of Salvadoran Students*] (PD)
MERS..........	Multielement Radiometer System
MERSAP	Merchant Ship Auxiliary Program (DNAB)
MERSAR	Merchant Ship Search and Rescue (PDAA)
MERSAT	Meteorology and Earth Observation Satellite (NASA)
MERSEX	Merchant Ship Code Systems [*NATO*] (NATG)
Mersey........	Merseyside [*County in England*] (WGA)
MERSHIP.....	Merchant Ship [*Navy*] (NVT)
MERSIGS.....	Merchant Signals [*Shipping*]
MERT..........	Maintenance Engineering Review Team [*Navy*] (NG)
Mert..........	Merten's Law of Federal Income Taxation [*A publication*] (DLA)
MERT..........	Merton College [*Oxford University*] (ROG)
MERT..........	Milwaukee Electric Railway & Transport Co. [*AAR code*]
MERT..........	Modified Effective-Range Theory (PDAA)
MER/TER	Multiple Ejection Rack/Triple Ejection Rack (MCD)
MertMd........	Merit Medical Systems, Inc. [*Associated Press*] (SAG)
MERTS........	Micropound Extended Range Thrust Stand [*NASA*]
MERU..........	Milliearth Rate Unit [*NASA*] (KSC)
MERX..........	Mercer Enterprises [*Air carrier designation symbol*]
MERX..........	Merix Corp. [*NASDAQ symbol*] (SAG)
MeryL..........	Merry Land & Investment Co., Inc. [*Associated Press*] (SAG)
MeryLd	Merry Land & Investment Co., Inc. [*Associated Press*] (SAG)
MERZONE....	Merchant Shipping Control Zone [*NATO*] (NATG)
MES..........	Maharashtra Ekikaran Samithi [*India*] [*Political party*] (PPW)
MES..........	Main Engine Start [*NASA*] (KSC)
MES..........	Main Equipment Supplier (NATG)
MES..........	Maine State Planning Office, Augusta, ME [*OCLC symbol*] (OCLC)
MES..........	Mainly English-Speaking
MES..........	Maintenance Electrolyte Solution [*Physiology*]
MES..........	Management Engineering Squadron [*Air Force*]
MES..........	Manned Exploration Site (MCD)
MES..........	Manual Entry System [*or Subsystem*] (IEEE)
MES..........	Manuals of Elementary Science [*A publication*]
MES..........	Manufaturing Execution System [*Engineering*]
MES..........	Marketable Equity Securities [*Investment term*] (DICI)
MES..........	Mass Expulsion System (MCD)
MES..........	Master, Environmental Studies (CMD)
MES..........	Master Erection Schedule (DNAB)
MES..........	Master of Engineering Sciences
MES..........	Master of Engineering Studies
MES..........	Master of Environmental Science (DD)
MES..........	Master of Environmental Studies (PGP)
MES..........	Master of Special Education (PGP)
MES..........	Mated Elements [*or Events*] Simulator [*NASA*] (MCD)
MES..........	Mated Events Simulator
MES..........	Maximal Electroshock [*Physiology*]
MES..........	Maximum Electroshock Seizure [*Medicine*]
MES..........	Medan [*Indonesia*] [*Airport symbol*] (OAG)
MES..........	Medical Electronics Society [*Defunct*] (EA)
MES..........	Medium Energy Source Program [*Air Force*]
MES..........	Medsource Systems, Inc. [*Vancouver Stock Exchange symbol*]
MES..........	Melville Corp. [*Formerly, Melville Shoe Corp.*] [*NYSE symbol*] (SPSG)
MES..........	Mesaba Aviation [*ICAO designator*] (FAAC)
Mes..........	Mesencephalic (DB)
MES..........	Mesozoic [*Period, era, or system*] [*Geology*]
MES..........	Message Entry System (MCD)
MES..........	Messina [*Italy*] [*Seismograph station code, US Geological Survey*] (SEIS)
MES..........	Mesylate [*Organic chemistry*]
ME(S)	Methodist Episcopal, South
MES..........	Mexican Epigraphic Society (EA)
MES..........	Military Engineer Services [*British*]
MES..........	Minerals Engineering Society [*British*]
MES..........	Miniature Edison Screw
MES..........	Minimum Efficiency Scale
MES..........	Miscellaneous Equipment Specification (HGAA)
MES..........	Missile Electrical Simulator
MES..........	Missile Engineering Station
MES..........	Mission Events Sequence (MCD)
MES..........	Mobile Earth Station (DA)
M-ES..........	Mobile End System (ACRL)
M-ES..........	Moessbauer Emission Spectroscopy
MES..........	MOL [*Manned Orbiting Laboratory*] Environmental Shelter
MES..........	Monitoring Energy Systems
MES..........	More Effective Schools [*Program*] [*Defunct*]
MES..........	Morpholinoethanesulfonic Acid [*A buffer*]
MES..........	Motor End Support
MES..........	Movimento de Esquerda Socialista [*Movement of the Socialist Left*] [*Portugal Political party*] (PPE)
MES..........	Moving Earth Simulator (MCD)
MES..........	Multiengine Sea [*Pilot rating*] (AIA)
MES..........	Multilinear Events Sequencing [*Engineering*]
MES..........	Multiple Earning Statement [*Banking*] (MHDW)
MES..........	Multiple Endocrine Syndrome [*Endocrinology*]
MES..........	Myoelectric Signal
MESA..........	Maintenance Engineering Support Analysis [*Military*] (CAAL)
MesA	Maitre es Arts [*Master of Arts*] [*French*]
MESA..........	Malaria Eradication Special Account
MESA..........	Manned Environmental Systems Assessment [*NASA*]
MESA..........	Marine Ecosystems Analysis [*Pollution-monitoring project*]
MESA..........	Maximum Entropy Spectrum Analysis
MESA..........	Mechanics Educational Society of America (EA)
MESA..........	Medium Power-Switching Application (IAA)
MESA..........	Men to End Spouse Abuse (EA)
MESA..........	Mesa Air Group [*NASDAQ symbol*] (TTSB)
MESA..........	Mesa Air Group, Inc. [*NASDAQ symbol*] (SAG)
MESA..........	Mesa Airlines, Inc. [*NASDAQ symbol*] (NQ)
MESA..........	Meta Email Search Agent [*Computer science*]
MESA..........	Microsurgical Epididymal Sperm Aspiration
ME/SA..........	Middle East/Southern Asia
MESA..........	Middle East Studies Association of North America (EA)
M ESA..........	Miniature Electrostatic Accelerometer (NAKS)
MESA..........	Miniature Electrostatically Suspended Accelerometer (MCD)
MESA..........	Minimum Essential Support Analysis (MCD)
MESA..........	Mining Enforcement and Safety Administration [*Terminated, 1978; functions transferred to Mine Safety and Health Administration, Department of Labor*]
MESA..........	Mobile Entertainments, Southern Area [*British military*] (DMA)
MESA..........	Model Experimental Systems Analysis [*In-depth study of sewage outfall in the New York Bight*] [*Inactive*] (OSRA)
M ESA..........	Modular Equipment Stowage Assembly [*Aerospace*] (NAKS)
MESA..........	Modularized Equipment Storage [*or Stowage*] Area [*or Assembly*] [*Apollo*] [*NASA*]
MESA..........	Multiple Engagement Simulation Analyzer [*Military*]
MESA..........	Music Editor, Scorer, and Arranger [*Computer program*] (PCM)
MESA..........	Myoepithelial Sialadenitis [*Medicine*] (DMAA)

MesaAir.......	Mesa Air Group, Inc. [*Associated Press*] (SAG)
MesaAr........	Mesa Airlines, Inc. [*Associated Press*] (SAG)
MESAB.......	Medical Education for South African Blacks [*An association*] (EA)
Mesab........	Mesabi Trust [*Associated Press*] (SAG)
Mesaba........	Mesaba Holdings, Inc. [*Associated Press*] (SAG)
MesabaH......	Mesaba Holdings, Inc. [*Associated Press*] (SAG)
MeSaco.......	Dyer Library, Saco, ME [*Library symbol Library of Congress*] (LCLS)
MeSacoT	Thornton Academy, Saco, ME [*Library symbol Library of Congress*] (LCLS)
MesaInc.......	Mesa, Inc. [*Associated Press*] (SAG)
MesaLb.......	Mesa Laboratories, Inc. [*Associated Press*] (SAG)
MESAN	Mouvement de l'Evolution Sociale de l'Afrique Noire [*Black African Social Evolution Movement*]
MesaR........	Mesa Royalty Trust [*Associated Press*] (SAG)
MESAR.......	Minimum-Essential Security Assistance Requirements (COE)
MESAR.......	Multifunction Electric Scan Adaptive RADAR [*Military British*]
MESB.........	Michigan Environmental Science Board
MESBIC......	Minority Enterprise Small Business Investment Company
MESC.........	Marine Environmental Sciences Consortium [*Library network*]
MESC.........	Master Event Sequence Controller (KSC)
ME Sc.........	Master of Engineering Science
MESC.........	Mescaline
MESC.........	Middle East Service Command [*Army World War II*]
MESC.........	Middle East Supercomputer Centre [*Bahrain Centre for Studies and Research*] (ECON)
MESC.........	Middle East Supply Center [*World War II*]
MESC.........	Middle East Supply Council [*World War II*]
MESC.........	Miniature Excitatory Synaptic Current [*Neurophysiology*]
MESC.........	Mission Events Sequence Controller [*NASA*] (KSC)
MESC.........	Modular Equipment Standards Committee (AAEL)
MESCH.......	Multi-Environment Scheme [*Medicine*] (DMAA)
MESCO	Message Electronic Switching Computer (IAA)
MESCPL......	Mess Corporal [*Marine Corps*]
MESC(W).....	Middle East Supply Committee (Washington) [*World War II*]
MESD.........	Mesdames [*Plural of Mrs.*] [*France*]
MeSepPM...	Penobscot Marine Museum, Searsport, ME [*Library symbol Library of Congress*] (LCLS)
MESF.........	Minimum Engineered Safety Features (NRCH)
MESF.........	Mobile Earth Station Facility
MESFET......	Metal-Semiconductor Field-Effect Transistor
MESG.........	Maximum Experimental Safe Gap (IEEE)
MESG.........	Mediterranean Shipping Group [*NATO*] (NATG)
MESG.........	Microelectrostatic Gyro
MESGA.......	Microelectrostatic Gyro-Accelerometer
MESGE.......	Message (ABBR)
MESGER......	Messenger (ABBR)
MESH........	Marine Aspects of Earth System History [*Research programs*]
MESH........	Medical Subject Headings (NITA)
MeSH........	Medical Subject Headings Vocabulary File [*National Library of Medicine*] [*Information service or system*] (CRD)
MESH........	Multiple Electronically Synopsing Hierarchy (RDA)
MESH........	Museum Exchange for System's Help [*National Museum of Natural History*] (IID)
MESI.........	Modified, Exclusive, Shared, and Invalid Data (PCM)
MESIM.......	Mission Essential Subsystem Inoperative Maintenance
MeSk	Skowhegan Free Public Library, Skowhegan, ME [*Library symbol Library of Congress*] (LCLS)
MeSkS.......	Margaret Chase Smith Library Center, Skowhegan, ME [*Library symbol Library of Congress*] (LCLS)
MESL........	Marine Environment Studies Laboratory [*Marine science*] (OSRA)
MESL........	Membrane-Enveloped Soil Layer
MESL........	Merchants' Exchange of St. Louis (EA)
MESL........	Microwave Electronic Systems Ltd.
MESL........	Mission Essential Subsystems List (NVT)
MESM........	Master of Environmental Science (PGP)
MESM........	Mission Essential Subsystem Matrix [*Navy*] (ANA)
MESM........	Multiechelon Supply Model (AABC)
MesoAm......	Meso American (VRA)
Mesol........	Mesolithic (VRA)
Mesop........	Mesopotamia (VRA)
MESOP.......	Mesopotamia
MESOPAC...	Mesoscale Meteorological Preprocessor Program (COE)
MESP........	Minuteman Extended Survivable Power (DWSG)
MesPGN.....	Mesangial Proliferative Glomerulonephritis [*Nephrology*] (DMAA)
MESPOT	Mesopotamia (DSUE)
MeSprN......	Nasson College, Springvale, ME [*Library symbol Library of Congress*] (LCLS)
MESq	Management Engineering Squadron [*Air Force*]
MESRF.......	Middle East Special Requirement Fund
MESROM.....	Materials-Evaluation Subcaliber Rocket Motor (SAA)
Mesrx........	Measurex Corp. [*Associated Press*] (SAG)
MESS........	Magnetic Emulsion Spectrometer
MESS........	Master of Exercise and Sport Sciences (PGP)
MESS........	Maximum Effective SONAR Speed (NVT)
MESS........	Maximum Efficiency Structural System (IAA)
MESS........	Mechanical Electronic Subassembly Simulator
MESS........	Messenger (MSA)
MESS........	Messerschmitt [*German fighter aircraft*] (DSUE)
MESS........	Misalignment Estimation Software System (MCD)
MESS........	Mixed Evolutionarily Stable Strategy [*Breeding selection*]
MESS........	Model Evaluation Support System (COE)
MESS........	Monitor Event Simulation System (IEEE)
MESSAGE...	Modular Electronic Solid-State Aerospace Ground Equipment
MESSCPL...	Mess Corporal [*Marine Corps*]
MESSE........	Messuage (ROG)
MESSER	Messerschmitt [*German fighter aircraft*] (DSUE)
MESSR	Multispectrum Electronic Self-Scanning Radiometer (MCD)
MESSRS	Messieurs [*Plural of Mister*] [*French*]
MESSSGT ...	Mess Sergeant [*Marine Corps*]
MESST	Eucharistic Missionaries of the Most Holy Trinity (TOCD)
MEST.........	Eucharistic Missionaries of St. Theresa (Mexico) (TOCD)
MEST.........	Maintenance Engineering Support Team (MCD)
MEST.........	Mestizo (ABBR)
MEST.........	Ministere d'Etat, Sciences et Technologie [*Ministry of State for Science and Technology - MOSST*] [*Canada*]
MEST.........	Missile Electrical System Test (NG)
MEST.........	Mouse Ear Swelling Test [*Analytical biochemistry*]
MESTA.......	Marine Ecosystem Study in Tropical Areas [*Marine science*] (MSC)
Mestek.......	Mestek, Inc. [*Associated Press*] (SAG)
MESTS.......	Missile Electric System Test Set [*Military*] (PDAA)
MESU.........	Microelectronics Support Unit [*for the Microelectronics Education Programme*] [*British*]
MESUCORA..	Measurement, Control, Regulation, and Automation (IEEE)
MESUR	Mars Environmental Survey [*NASA*]
MESW........	Meta-Software [*NASDAQ symbol*] (TTSB)
MESW........	Meta-Software, Inc. [*NASDAQ symbol*] (SAG)
MET..........	East Tennessee State University, Medical Library, Johnson City, TN [*OCLC symbol*] (OCLC)
MET..........	Magic Eye Tube
MET..........	Maintenance Engineering Technique
MET..........	Maintenance Evaluation Team
MET..........	Management Engineering Team [*Air Force*] (AFM)
MET..........	Manufacturer's Excise Tax
MET..........	Master Events Timer (MCD)
MET..........	Master of Education in Teaching (GAGS)
MET..........	Maximal Exercise Test (DMAA)
MET..........	Mean Elapsed Time (MCD)
met..........	Measurement (DS)
MET..........	Mechanical Engineering Technician
MET..........	Medium Equipment Transporter (MCD)
MET..........	Memphis [*Tennessee*] [*Seismograph station code, US Geological Survey*] (SEIS)
MET..........	Metabolic Equivalent [*Medicine*]
MET..........	Metabolic Equivalent of the Task (DMAA)
MET..........	Metal [*or Metallic*] (AAG)
MET..........	Metallic [*Automotive advertising*]
met..........	Metallic [*Referring to breath sounds*] [*Medicine*] (DAVI)
MET..........	Metallurgical
MET..........	Metalore Resources Ltd. [*Toronto Stock Exchange symbol*]
Met..........	Metamorphoses [*of Ovid*] [*Classical studies*] (OCD)
Met..........	Metamorphoses [*of Apuleius*] [*Classical studies*] (OCD)
MET..........	Metaphor
MET..........	Metaphysics
MET..........	Metastasis [*Medicine*]
MET..........	Metatarsus [*Flamenco dance term*]
Met..........	Metcalfe's Reports [*58-61 Kentucky*] [*A publication*] (DLA)
Met..........	Metcalf's Reports [*Massachusetts*] [*A publication*] (DLA)
Met..........	Metcalf's Reports [*Rhode Island*] [*A publication*] (DLA)
MET..........	Meteorological (NAKS)
MET..........	Meteorological Broadcast (IAA)
MET..........	Meteorological Office [*British*] (DSUE)
MET..........	Meteorological Research Flight [*British ICAO designator*] (FAAC)
MET..........	Meteorology (AFM)
Met..........	Methionine [*Also, M*] [*An amino acid*]
MET..........	Methionine (DB)
met..........	Methionine [*An amino acid*] (DOG)
MET..........	Metronome [*Music*]
MET..........	Metropolis (ROG)
MET..........	Metropolitan (AAG)
MET..........	Metropolitan Electric Tramways [*British*] (ROG)
MET..........	Metropolitan Music Hall [*London*] [*British*] (DSUE)
Met..........	[*New York*] Metropolitan Opera House
Met..........	Metropolitan Police [*British*] (WDAA)
MET..........	[*The*] Metropolitan Railway [*British*] (ROG)
MET..........	Metropolitan Realty [*AMEX symbol*] (TTSB)
MET..........	Metropolitan Realty Corp. [*AMEX symbol*] (CTT)
MET..........	Metuchen [*Diocesan abbreviation*] [*New Jersey*] (TOCD)
MET..........	Micro-Electronic Technology (ADA)
MET..........	Midexpiratory Time [*Medicine*]
MET..........	Midshipman Embarkation Team [*Navy*]
MET..........	Minimum Energy Trajectory
MET..........	Minimum Essentials Test [*Educational test*]
MET..........	Minimum Exposure Time
MET..........	Minor Expendable Tool (MCD)
MET..........	Missile Electrical Technician [*Aerospace*] (IAA)
MET..........	Missile Escort Team [*Air Force*] (AFM)
MET..........	Mission Elapsed Time [*NASA*] (NAKS)
MET..........	Mission Entry Time
MET..........	Mission Environment Tape
MET..........	Mission Event Timer [*NASA*] (KSC)
MET..........	Mobile Engineering Team [*Navy*]
MET..........	Mobile Equipment Transporter [*NASA*]
MET..........	Modality Examination Terminal (DMAA)
MET..........	Modesto & Empire Traction Co. [*Formerly, METC*] [*AAR code*]
MET..........	Modified Expansion Tube (IEEE)
MET..........	Modular Equipment Transporter [*NASA*]
MET..........	Molecular Electronic Technique
MET..........	Mond Excavation at Thebes [*London*] [*A publication*] (BJA)
MET..........	Motorola Environmental Telemetry
MET..........	Multibutton Electronic Telephone (NITA)

MET .... Multiemitter Transistor
MET .... Multi-Environment Trainer (MCD)
MET .... Multiple Employer Trust [*Insurance*]
MET .... Multistage Exercise Test (DMAA)
MET .... Multistage Exercise Testing (DB)
META .... Computer series [*Digital Scientific*]
META .... Maritime Education and Training Act of 1980
META .... Megachannel Extraterrestrial Array [*For receiving possible radio signals from non-earth civilizations*]
meta .... Metacarpal [*Anatomy*] (DAVI)
META .... metamyelocyte [*Hematology*] (DAVI)
meta .... Metatarsal [*Anatomy*] (DAVI)
META .... Metatec Corp. [*NASDAQ symbol*] (SAG)
META .... Methods of Extracting Text Automatically [*Programming language*] [*General Electric Co.*] [*Computer science*] (IEEE)
META .... Metropolitan Educational Television Association [*Canada*]
META .... Model Engineering Trade Association [*British*] (BI)
META 1 ...... Metabolic Profile 1 [*Biochemistry*] (DAVI)
METAB .... Metabolism
METABC ...... Metabolic (ABBR)
Metabol ...... Metabolism: Clinical and Experimental (MEC)
METABZ ...... Metabolize (ABBR)
METABZD .... Metabolized (ABBR)
METABZG .... Metabolizing (ABBR)
METAC .... Medium Tactical Transport Aircraft [*Military*]
METAC .... Methacryloyloxyethyltrimethylammonium Chloride [*Organic chemistry*]
METADEX .... Metal Abstracts Index Data Base [*Bibliographic database*] [*British*] (IID)
METADEX .... Metals Abstracts Inex (NITA)
METADS ...... Meteorological Acquisition and Display System (PDAA)
METAF .... Meteorological Terminal Aviation Weather Forecast [*FAA*] (TAG)
METAG .... Meteorological Advisory Group [*ICAO*] (DA)
MetaGp ...... Meta Group, Inc. [*Associated Press*] (SAG)
METAL .... Metallurgy
METAL .... Militarily Significant Emergent Technologies Awareness List [*Proposed*] [*DoD*]
MetalcId ...... Metaclad Corp. [*Associated Press*] (SAG)
MetalcId ...... Metalclad Corp. [*Associated Press*] (SAG)
METALL ...... Metallurgy
METALLOG .. Metallography (DGA)
MetalR .... Metallica Resources, Inc. [*Associated Press*] (SAG)
META M...... Metaphysical Magazine [*A publication*] (ROG)
MET & E...... Medical Equipment Test and Evaluation [*Army Medical Material Agency*] (PDAA)
METAPH ...... Metaphorical (ROG)
Metaph .... Metaphysica [*of Aristotle*] [*Classical studies*] (OCD)
METAPH ...... Metaphysical [*or Metaphysics*] (ROG)
METAPH ...... Metaphysician (ABBR)
metaph .... Metaphysics [*Parapsychology*] (DAVI)
METAPHYS.. Metaphysic (ABBR)
METAPLAN... Methods of Extracting Text Automatically Programming - Language [*General Electric Co.*] [*Computer science*] (IEEE)
METAR........ Aviation Routine Weather Report [*ICAO*] (FAAC)
METAR........ Meteorological Terminal Aviation Routine Weather Report [*FAA*] (TAG)
METAS........ Metastasize [*Medicine*]
MetaSft....... Meta-Software, Inc. [*Associated Press*] (SAG)
METASYMBOL... Metalanguage Symbol
Metatec ...... Metatec Corp. [*Associated Press*] (SAG)
METATH...... Metathesis
METB .... Metal Base
METB .... MetroBanCorp [*NASDAQ symbol*] (SAG)
METB .... Metropolitan Borough
METBX........ Mgn. Stanley D. Witter Precious Metals & Min. [*Mutual fund ticker symbol*] (SG)
METC .... Medesto & Empire Traction Co. (MHDB)
METC .... Metal Curb (AAG)
Metc .... Metcalfe's Reports [*58-61 Kentucky*] [*A publication*] (DLA)
Metc .... Metcalf's Reports [*Rhode Island*] [*A publication*] (DLA)
Metc .... Metcalf's Reports [*Massachusetts*] [*A publication*] (DLA)
METC .... Metropolitan Conference (PSS)
METC .... Military Equipment Test Center (CAAL)
METC .... Modesto & Empire Traction Co. [*Later, MET*] [*AAR code*]
METC .... Monthly Estimate to Completion (MCD)
METC .... Morgantown Energy Technology Center [*Morgantown, WV*] [*Department of Energy*] (GRD)
METC .... Mouse Embryo Tissue Culture
METCA........ Merchant Token Collectors Association (EA)
METCAL...... Metrology and Calibration [*Air Force*] (AFIT)
METCAN...... Metal Matrix Composite Analyzer [*Organic chemistry*]
MET-CAR .... Metallo-Carbohedrene [*Organic chemistry*]
Metc Cont.... Metcalf on the Law of Contracts [*A publication*] (DLA)
Metc KY...... Metcalfe's Reports [*58-61 Kentucky*] [*A publication*] (DLA)
Metc Mass... Metcalf's Reports [*Massachusetts*] [*A publication*] (DLA)
METCO........ Meteorological Coordination Officer (MUGU)
METCO........ Metropolitan Council for Educational Opportunity (EA)
METCO........ Mobile Engine Tester, Computer-Operated (DNAB)
MetCoil .... Met Coil Systems Corp. [*Associated Press*] (SAG)
METCON ...... Metropolitan Consortium for Minorities in Science and Engineering (USDC)
Metc Yelv .... Metcalf's Edition of Yelverton [*A publication*] (DLA)
METD.......... Management Education Training and Development (AIE)
METD.......... Mean Effective Temperature Difference [*Refrigeration*]
METD.......... Metal Door
METD.......... Metastatic Disease [*Oncology*]

METDLGY.... Methodology
Met E .... Metallurgical Engineer
Mete .... Meteorologica [*of Aristotle*] [*Classical studies*] (OCD)
METE .... Multiple ECM [*Electronic Countermeasures*] Threat Environment [*Military*] (CAAL)
METE .... Multiple Engagement Test Environment [*Military*] (PDAA)
METE .... Multiple Environment Threat Emitter (MCD)
METEC .... Meteoroid Technology [*Satellite*] [*NASA*]
METEC .... Meteorologist Technician (NOAA)
MetEC .... Metropolitan Edison Capital Ltd. [*Associated Press*] (SAG)
MetEng ...... Metallurgical Engineering (DD)
METEOR ...... Manned Earth-Satellite Terminal Evolving from Earth-to-Orbit Ferry Rockets (SAA)
METEOR ...... Marine Environmental Testing and Electro-Optical Radiation (MCD)
METEOR ...... Meteorological Satellite [*Former USSR*]
METEOR ...... Meteorology
METEORIT .... Meteoritical
METEOROL... Meteorology
METEOROLO... Meteorology (ABBR)
METEOSAT... Meteorological Satellite [*European Space Agency*]
METEPA...... Tris(methylethylene)phosphoric Triamide [*Organic chemistry*]
METER........ Machine Examination Teaching, Evaluation, and Re-education (PDAA)
METF .... Metal Flashing
MetFACS...... Metropolitan Life Insurance Co. Financial and Administrative Customer Services System (HGAA)
METG .... META Group [*NASDAQ symbol*] (TTSB)
METG .... Meta Group, Inc. [*NASDAQ symbol*] (SAG)
METG .... Metal Grill
METG .... Middle East Task Group (DNAB)
METGL........ Meteorological (WGA)
MetGlob...... Metro Global Media, Inc. [*Associated Press*] (SAG)
Meth .... Mercaptoethanol [*Organic chemistry*]
METH .... Methadone (ABBR)
METH .... Methamphetamine (ABBR)
METH .... Methane (AAG)
Meth .... Methaphetamine Hydrochloride [*An amphetamine, commonly known as speed*] (VNW)
Meth .... Methedrine [*Stimulant*]
METH .... Methicillin [*An antibiotic*]
METH .... Method (ROG)
METH .... Methode Electronics, Inc. [*NASDAQ symbol*] (NQ)
METH .... Methodist
Meth .... Methodist (WDAA)
meth .... Methyl [*Organic chemistry*] (DAVI)
METH .... Methylated (ADA)
METH .... Methylated Spirit (DSUE)
METH .... Methylmeth (ABBR)
METH .... Methyprylon (ABBR)
METHA........ Methode Electronics'A' [*NASDAQ symbol*] (TTSB)
Methanx ...... Methanex Corp. [*Associated Press*] (SAG)
MetHb......... Methemoglobin [*Biochemistry, medicine*]
METHB........ Methode Electronics'B' [*NASDAQ symbol*] (TTSB)
METHC........ Methodic (ABBR)
MethCh....... Methodist Chaplain [*Navy British*]
MeThCh....... Methylthiocholine [*Biochemistry*]
Meth Ch Ca... Report of Methodist Church Cases [*A publication*] (DLA)
Methd......... Methode Electronics, Inc. [*Associated Press*] (SAG)
METHDST .... Methodist
MeTHF........ Methyltetrahydrofolic Acid [*Biochemistry*]
met hgb...... Methemoglobin [*Biochemistry*] (DAVI)
METHIMAZOLE... Methylmercaptoimidazole [*Also, MMI*] [*Thyroid inhibitor*]
METHO .... Methodology (ABBR)
METHOG ...... Methodology (ABBR)
METHOGL.... Methodological (ABBR)
METHS........ Methylated Spirits (ADA)
methyl-CCNU... Methyl-1-(2-chloroethyl)-3-cyclohexyl-1 Nitrosourea [*Antineoplastic drug regimen*] (DAVI)
Methyl-GAG... Methylglyoxal-bis-guanylhydrazone [*Antineoplastic drug*] (CDI)
METHZ........ Methodize (ABBR)
METHZD...... Methodized (ABBR)
METI .... Major Engineering Test Item (AAG)
METI .... Medical Education Technologies, Inc.
METIC .... Meticulous (ABBR)
METIMP...... Meteorological Equipment Improvement Program (NG)
METJ .... Metal Jalousie
METJET........ Meteorological Sounding Rocket, Ramjet-Powered [*NASA*] (SAA)
METL .... Materials and Ecological Testing Laboratory [*Research center*] (RCD)
METL .... Metal
METL .... Metallica Resources, Inc. [*NASDAQ symbol*] (SAG)
METL .... Mission Essential Task List [*Army*] (INF)
METL .... Multielement Two-Layer (AAEL)
Met Lab ...... Metabolic Laboratory [*Colorado State University*] (RCD)
METLC .... Metallic
METLLRGCL... Metallurgical
METLLRGST... Metallurgist
METLO .... Metrological Equipment and Technical Liaison Officer [*Navy*] (NG)
METM .... Master of Engineering and Technology Management (PGP)
METM .... Metal Mold
MET/M........ Missile Engine Technician/Mechanic (AAG)
Metmail ...... Metromail Corp. [*Associated Press*] (SAG)
metMb........ Metmyoglobin [*Medicine*] (MEDA)
M et N .... Mane et Nocte [*Morning and Night*] [*Pharmacy*]
m et n .... Mane et Nocte [*Morning and night*] [*Latin*] [*Pharmacy*] (DAVI)
METO .... Maximum Engine Takeoff [*Power*] [*Air Force*]

METO..........	Maximum Except during Takeoff
METO..........	Meteorological Office [or Officer] [Air Force]
METO..........	Metro Capital Corp. [NASDAQ symbol] (SAG)
METO..........	Middle East Treaty Organization
METOB........	Meteorologist Observation (NOAA)
METOF........	Meteorological Office
Met Off.......	Meteorological Office [British] (AIA)
METOFOR	Methodology for Total Force Concept [Military]
METON........	Measured Tons Discharged or Loaded [Shipping]
METON........	Metonymy
METOP.........	Maximum Expected Takeoff Power (AFM)
Metopera.....	Metropolitan Opera Association (EA)
MeToV.........	United States Veterans Administration Center, Togus, ME [Library symbol Library of Congress] (LCLS)
METOXI.......	Military Effectiveness in a Toxin Environment (AABC)
METP..........	Metal Partition
METP..........	Metal Portion
MetPro........	Met-Pro Corp. [Associated Press] (SAG)
metpt.........	Metalpoint (VRA)
METR..........	Metal Roof
METR..........	Meteorology (NG)
METR..........	Metropolitan
MetR..........	Metropolitan Railway [British]
METR..........	Minimum Essential Training Requirements
METRA........	Metal RADAR
METRA........	Multiple-Event Time Recording Apparatus (PDAA)
MetraB........	Metra Biosystems [Associated Press] (SAG)
MetrBcp.......	MetroBancorp [Associated Press] (SAG)
Metrbk.......	Metrobank North America [Associated Press] (SAG)
MetrCap.......	Metro Capital Corp. [Associated Press] (SAG)
Metrcm.......	Metricom, Inc. [Associated Press] (SAG)
METREX.......	Metropolitan Centrex [Telephone network]
METRI.........	Military Essentiality through Readiness Indices
METRIA.......	Metropolitan Tree Improvement Alliance (EA)
METRIC.......	Multiechelon Technique for Recoverable Item Control (MCD)
MetrisCo......	Metris Companies, Inc. [Associated Press] (SAG)
METRL........	Meteorology (NG)
METRL........	Metrology Requirements List [DoD]
METRLGST...	Meteorologist
MetRlt........	Metropolitan Realty Corp. [Associated Press] (SAG)
MetrNet	Metro Networks, Inc. [Associated Press] (SAG)
METRO	Materiel Essential to Reconstitution Operations [Air Force] (AFM)
METRO	Messenger Transport Organizer [Developmental biology]
METRO	Meteorological Equipment Terminal and Representative Observation (MCD)
METRO	Meteorology
METRO	Metering and Traffic Recording with Offline Processing (PDAA)
Metro..........	Metro-Goldwyn-Mayer (WDMC)
METRO	Metropolitan
Metro..........	Metropolitan (AL)
METRO	Metropolitan Collegiate Athletic Conference (EA)
METRO	Michigan Effectuation, Training, and Research Organization [Computer-programmed simulation game]
METRO	New York Metropolitan Reference and Research Library Agency [Brooklyn, NY] [Library network]
MetroBcp.....	Metropolitan Bancorp [Associated Press] (SAG)
METROC......	Meteorological Rocket
Metrocall.....	Metrocall, Inc. [Associated Press] (SAG)
MetroFn.......	Metro Financial Corp. [Associated Press] (SAG)
Metrogs......	Metrogas SA [Associated Press] (SAG)
METROL	Metrology
Metrolog......	Metrologic Instruments, Inc. [Associated Press] (SAG)
Metromda.....	Metromedia International Group [Associated Press] (SAG)
METROMEX..	Metropolitan Meteorological Experiment
METROP	Metropol (WDAA)
METROP	Metropolis (ADA)
METROP	Metropolitan
METROPOL...	Metropolis [or Metropolitan] (ABBR)
Metrotrn......	Metrotrans Corp. [Associated Press] (SAG)
MetroV........	MetroVision of North America, Inc. [Associated Press] (SAG)
METRRA	Metal Re-Radiation RADAR [Mine detection system] [Army] (RDA)
MetRS........	Methionyl-Transfer Ribonucleic Acid Synthetase [An enzyme]
MetrTl........	Metro-Tel Corp. [Associated Press] (SAG)
MetrV.........	MetroVision of North America, Inc. [Associated Press] (SAG)
METS..........	Maintainability Evaluation and Tracking System (MCD)
METS..........	Materials and Equipment Trading Service (AAEL)
METS..........	Mechanized Export Traffic System [Army] (AABC)
METS..........	Metabolic Equivalents [Medicine] (DMAA)
METS..........	Metal Strip
Mets..........	Metastasis [Oncology] (MAE)
METS..........	Met-Coil Systems [NASDAQ symbol] (TTSB)
METS..........	Met-Coil Systems Corp. [NASDAQ symbol] (NQ)
METS..........	Metropolitan Emergency Telephone System (COE)
MET/S........	Missile Electrical Technician/Specialist (AAG)
METS..........	Missile Environmental Testing Study
METS..........	Mobile Electronic Test Set (MCD)
METS..........	Mobile Engine Test Stand
METS..........	Modified Engineered Time Standards
METS..........	Modular Engine Test System (MCD)
METS..........	Modularized Equipment Transport System [NASA]
METS..........	Multiple Exposure Testing System [Advertising analysis]
METSAAT.....	Meteorological Satellite (USDC)
MET/SAT.....	Meteorological Satellite
METSATT.....	Meteorological Satellite [Marine science] (OSRA)
m et sig.......	Misce et Signa [Mix and write a label] [Latin] [Pharmacy] (DAVI)

M et Sig	Misce et Signa [Mix and Label] [Pharmacy]
m et sign....	Misce et Signa [Mix and Label] [Latin] (WDAA)
METT..........	Manned, Evasive Target Tank [Army]
METT..........	Maximum Exercise Tolerance Test (DMAA)
METT..........	Microwave Energy Transmission Test (SSD)
METT..........	Mission, Enemy, Terrain and Weather, Troops and Firepower Available
METTM........	Mission, Enemy, Terrain and Weather, Troops and Firepower Available, and Maneuver Space (MCD)
Met Tr J	Metal Trades Journal [A publication]
METT-T.......	Mission, Enemy, Terrain and Weather, Troops and Firepower Available and Time (INF)
METTW........	Mission, Enemy, Terrain, Tactics, Weather [Criteria for establishing military strategy] [Army] (VNW)
METU..........	Marine Electronic Technical Unit (MUGU)
METU..........	Mobile Electronics Technical Unit
METU..........	Mobile Electronics Training Unit
METVC........	Main Engine Thrust Vector [Aerospace] (NAKS)
METVC........	Main Engine Thrust Vector Control (MCD)
METW..........	Military Emergency Travel Warrant [MTMC] (TAG)
METW..........	Municipality of East Troy, Wisconsin [AAR code]
metwk........	Metalwork (VRA)
Metz..........	Metzenbaum [Instruments] [Surgery] (DAVI)
meu	Maine [MARC country of publication code Library of Congress] (LCCP)
MEU	Main Electronic Unit (INF)
MEU	Marine Expeditionary Unit
MEU	Marromeu [Mozambique] [Airport symbol] (AD)
MEU	Maximum Expected Utility (DMAA)
MEU	Memory Expansion Unit
MEU	Message Encoder Unit
MEU	Methylumbelliferone [Biochemistry]
MEU	Mind Extension University [Cable television channel]
MEU	Modern English Usage (WDAA)
MEU	Multiplexer Encoder Unit
MEU	Municipal Electricity Undertaking
MeU	University of Maine, Orono, ME [Library symbol Library of Congress] (LCLS)
MEUA..........	Million European Units of Account (PDAA)
MEUF..........	Micellar-Enhanced Ultrafiltration [Chemical engineering]
MEUG..........	Major Energy Users' Group [British]
MeU-G........	University of Maine at Portland/Gorham, Gorham, ME [Library symbol Library of Congress] (LCLS)
MeU-L	University of Maine, Law Library, Portland, ME [Library symbol Library of Congress] (LCLS)
MEULEX......	Marine Expeditionary Unit Landing Exercise (NVT)
MeUmb.......	Methylumbelliferyl [Biochemistry]
MeU-P	University of Maine at Portland/Gorham, Portland, ME [Library symbol Library of Congress] (LCLS)
MEU/SOC....	Marine Expeditionary Unit/Special Opperations Capable (MUSM)
MEV	Manned Entry Vehicle
MEV	Medical Evacuation Vehicle (MCD)
MeV	Mega-Electronvolt (ODBW)
MEV	Mega [or Million] Electron Volts
MEV	Million Electron Volts (MCD)
MeV	Million Electronvolts (COE)
MEV	Minden, NV [Location identifier FAA] (FAAL)
MEV	Murine Erythroblastosis Virus [Medicine] (DB)
MEvA	Avco-Everett Research Laboratory, Everett, MA [Library symbol Library of Congress] (LCLS)
MEVE........	Mesa Verde National Park
MeVEMsJ.....	Mercury, Venus, Earth, Mars, Jupiter (PDAA)
MEvP	Parlin Memorial Library, Everett, MA [Library symbol Library of Congress] (LCLS)
MEW..........	Manitoba Department of Environment, Workplace Safety, and Health [UTLAS symbol]
MEW..........	Manufactures Empty Weight (MCD)
MEW..........	Marine Early Warning
MEW..........	Mean Equivalent Wind [Meteorology] (DA)
MEW..........	Measure of Economic Welfare
MEW..........	Microwave Early Warning [Radio] [Air Force]
MEW..........	Middle East Watch [An association] (EA)
MEW..........	Minimum Envelope Weight (MCD)
MEW..........	Ministry of Economic Warfare [British]
MEW..........	Missionaries of the Eternal Word [Formerly, CFMA] (EA)
MEW..........	Mobile Early Warning
MEW..........	Modern English Writers [A publication]
MeW..........	Waterville Public Library, Waterville, ME [Library symbol Library of Congress] (LCLS)
MEWA........	Ministry of Education, Western Australia
MEWA........	Motor and Equipment Wholesalers Association [Later, ASIA]
MEWA........	Multiple Employer Welfare Arrangement
MEWA........	Multiple-Employer Welfare Association (WYGK)
MeWC........	Colby College, Waterville, ME [Library symbol Library of Congress] (LCLS)
MEWC........	Middle East Section of the War Cabinet [British World War II]
MEWC........	Middle East War Council [British military] (DMA)
MEWD	Missile Electronic Warfare Division [White Sands Missile Range] (AAG)
MeWe........	Wells Public Library, Wells, ME [Library symbol Library of Congress] (LCLS)
MeWebr.......	Walker Memorial Library, Westbrook, ME [Library symbol Library of Congress] (LCLS)
MEWG	Maintenance Engineering Working Group [NASA] (NASA)
MEWO	Manufacturing Engineering Work Order (MCD)

MEWS.........	Mews [*Postal Service standard*] (OPSA)
Mews..........	Mews' Digest of English Case Law [*A publication*] (DLA)
MEWS.........	Microwave Electronic Warfare System
MEWS.........	Missile Early Warning Station (AFM)
MEWS.........	Missile Electronic Warfare System [*Army*]
MEWS.........	Mission Essential Weapon System [*Military*] (CAAL)
MEWS.........	Mobile Electronic Warfare Simulator (MCD)
MEWS.........	Modular Electronic Warfare Simulator [*Navy*]
Mews..........	[*The*] Reports [*1893-95*] [*England*] [*A publication*] (DLA)
Mews Dig	Mews' Digest of English Case Law [*A publication*] (DLA)
MEWSG	Multiservice Electronic Warfare Support Group [*Originally Maritime Electronic Warfare Support Group*] [*NATO*] (DOMA)
MEWSS.......	Mobile Electronic Warfare Support System [*Military*] (LAIN)
MEWT........	Matrix Electrostatic Writing Technique
MEWT........	Microelectronic Weld Tester
MEWTA.......	Missile Electronic Warfare Technical Area [*White Sands Missile Range*] (AABC)
MEX...........	Mariner Explorations [*Vancouver Stock Exchange symbol*]
M Ex	Master of Expression
MEx...........	Mekhilta Exodus (BJA)
MEX...........	Memorex Corp., Memorex Technical Information Library, Santa Clara, CA [*OCLC symbol*] (OCLC)
MEX...........	Metro Express II, Inc. [*ICAO designator*] (FAAC)
MEX...........	Mexican (ROG)
MEX...........	Mexico [*ANSI three-letter standard code*] (CNC)
Mex	Mexico · (VRA)
MEX...........	Mexico City [*Mexico*] [*Airport symbol*] (OAG)
MEX...........	Military Engineering Experimental Establishment [*British*]
MEX...........	Military Exchange
MEX...........	Mississippi Export Railroad (IIA)
MEX...........	Mobile Exercise
MEX...........	MODEM Executive [*Computer telecommunications program*]
MEX...........	Temporary Rank [*Army slang*]
MExB.........	Motor Explosive Boat [*British military*] (DMA)
MEXE.........	Military Engineering Experimental Establishment [*British*]
MexEqt	Mexico Equity & Income Fund [*Associated Press*] (SAG)
MexFd	[*The*] Mexico Fund, Inc. [*Associated Press*] (SAG)
MEXH.........	Multi-Energy X-Ray Holography [*Physics*]
MexP	Mexican Pharmacopoeia [*A publication*]
MExSt	Master of Experimental Statistics (GAGS)
MEXT........	Maximal Exercise Testing
MExtEd	Master of Extension Education (GAGS)
MEY	Mapleton, IA [*Location identifier FAA*] (FAAL)
MEY	Maximum Economic Yield [*Fishery management*] (MSC)
MEY	Meghauli [*Nepal*] [*Airport symbol*] (OAG)
Meyer Des Inst Judiciares...	Meyer's Des Institutiones Judiciares [*A publication*] (DLA)
MeYoO........	Old York Historical Society, York, ME [*Library symbol*] [*Library of Congress*] (LCLS)
MEZ	Augusta Mental Health Institute, Augusta, ME [*OCLC symbol*] (OCLC)
MEZ	Mena, AR [*Location identifier FAA*] (FAAL)
MEZ	Merces [*Brazil*] [*Airport symbol*] (AD)
Mez	Mezuzah (BJA)
MEZ	Mezzo [*Moderate*] [*Music*]
mez............	Mezzotint (VRA)
MEZ	Mezzotinto [*Medium Tint, Half Tone*] [*Engraving*] (ROG)
MEZ	Missile Engagement Zone (NVT)
MEZ	Mittel Europaeische Zeit [*Central European Time*] [*German*]
MEZN.........	Mezzanine (ABBR)
mezn.........	Mezzanine (VRA)
MEZT	Mezzotint [*Printing*] (ABBR)
MEZZ	Mezzanine (KSC)
MEZZ	Mezzotint [*Printing*] (ABBR)
MEZZO.......	Mezzosoprano (ABBR)
MEZZO.......	Mezzotint [*Printing*] (ROG)
MF............	5-Methyltetrahydrofolate [*Biochemistry*] (DAVI)
MF............	Fall River Public Library, Fall River, MA [*Library symbol Library of Congress*] (LCLS)
MF............	Le Maitre Phonetique [*A publication*] (BJA)
MF............	Machine Finish [*Paper*]
mf............	Machine-Finish Paper (WDMC)
MF............	Magazines for Friendship [*An association*] (EA)
MF............	Magnetic Field
MF............	Magnetic Fluid [*Physics*]
MF............	Magnetic Focus [*of cathode-ray tube*] (DEN)
MF............	Magneto [*or Magnetic*] Field Generators [*JETDS Nomenclature*] [*Military*] (CET)
MF............	Magnetomotive Force (KSC)
MF............	Main Feed [*Technical drawings*]
MF............	Main Force [*Military*]
M/F............	Mainframe (NITA)
MF............	Maintenance Factor
MF............	Maintenance Float [*Military*]
MF............	Maintenance Fuel
M/F............	Maintenance to Flight [*Ratio*]
MF............	Major Facilitator [*Biochemistry*]
MF............	Major Function (MCD)
M/F............	Make From (SAA)
MF............	Malaysia Fund [*NYSE symbol*] (TTSB)
MF............	Malaysia Fund, Inc. [*NYSE symbol*] (SPSG)
MF............	Male to Female [*Ratio*]
MF............	Mali Franc [*Monetary unit*]
MF............	MAM Aviation Ltd. [*British ICAO designator*] (ICDA)
MF............	Mandatory Frequency (DA)

MF..............	Mantle Floor
MF..............	Manufacture (WGA)
MF..............	Mare Feccunditatis [*Sea of Fertility*] [*Lunar area*]
M/F..............	Marked For
MF..............	Mark Forward [*Papers*] [*British*]
MF..............	Martinus de Fano [*Deceased circa 1275*] [*Authority cited in pre-1607 legal work*] (DSA)
MF..............	Masculinity-Femininity (AEBS)
MF..............	Massey-Ferguson, Inc. (EFIS)
M$_f$..............	Mass Flow of Fuel [*Aviation*] (DA)
MF..............	Massora Finalis (BJA)
M/F..............	Master File
MF..............	Master Frame
MF..............	Master of Finance
MF..............	Master of Forestry
MF..............	Mastic Floor [*Technical drawings*]
MF..............	Matching Funds (OICC)
MF..............	Mate and Ferry [*NASA*] (NASA)
MF..............	Material Factor
MF..............	Maurice-Farman [*British military*] (DMA)
mf..............	Mauritius [*MARC country of publication code Library of Congress*] (LCCP)
MF..............	Maximum Flowering Day [*Botany*]
MF..............	Measurement Facility [*Computer science*] (IBMDP)
MF..............	Meat Free [*Diet*]
MF..............	Mechanical Flap [*Aviation*]
MF..............	Meclofenamate [*Organic chemistry*]
MF..............	Medal of Freedom [*Military decoration*]
MF..............	Media Filter (ACRL)
MF..............	Media Forum (EA)
MF..............	Medical Foundation [*Australia*]
MF..............	Medium Frequency [*Radio electronics*]
mf..............	Medium Frequency (WDMC)
MF..............	Melamine-Formaldehyde [*Plastics technology*]
MF..............	Melomanes Francais [*Record label*] [*France*]
MF..............	Membrane Filter
MF..............	Merck Frosst Laboratories [*Canada*]
MF..............	Merthiolate-Formaldehyde [*Solution*]
MF..............	Message Format (ECII)
MF..............	Metal Factor [*Geophysical measurement*]
MF..............	Metallic Film
MF..............	Methotrexate, Fluorourcil, Calcium Leucovorin Rescue [*Antineoplastic drug*] (CDI)
MF..............	Methyl Farnesoate [*Organic chemistry*]
MF..............	Methyl Formate [*Organic chemistry*]
MF..............	Methylfuran [*Organic chemistry*]
MF..............	Mezzo Forte [*Moderately Loud*] [*Music*] (ROG)
MF..............	Microfarad
MF..............	Microfiche [*Sheet microfilm*]
mf..............	Microfilaria (STED)
Mf..............	Microfilariae
MF..............	Microfilm
MF..............	Microfiltration
MF..............	Microflocculation [*Biochemistry*] (DAVI)
MF..............	Microform
MF..............	Microscopic Factor
MF..............	Midcavity Forcep [*Medicine*] (DMAA)
MF..............	Middeck Forward (MCD)
MF..............	Middle Fork [*AAR code*]
MF..............	Middle French [*Language, etc.*]
MF..............	Middling Fair (IAA)
mf..............	Mid-Frequency (IDOE)
MF..............	Mid Fuselage
MF..............	Mi Favor [*My Favor*] [*Spanish*]
MF..............	Mike Force [*Indigenous personnel trained and commanded jointly by US and Vietnamese forces, and used as a reaction and/or reinforcing unit*]
MF..............	Milk Foundation [*National Dairy Council*] (EA)
MF..............	Millard Filmore [*US president, 1800-1874*]
MF..............	Miller-Fischer [*Syndrome*] [*Medicine*] (DB)
MF..............	Mill Finish
MF..............	Mill Fixture (MCD)
MF..............	Millifarad (GPO)
mF..............	Millifarad (IDOE)
MF..............	Millipore Filter [*Intravenous therapy*] (CPH)
MF..............	Mind Freedom
MF..............	Minister [*or Ministry*] of Food [*British*]
M/F..............	Minorities/Females
MF..............	Missile Failure (AAG)
MF..............	Mitogenic Factor [*Cytology*]
MF..............	Mitomycin, Fluorouracil [*Antineoplastic drug regimen*]
MF..............	Mitotic Figure [*Genetics*]
MF..............	Mixed Flow (AAG)
MF..............	Mobile Facility (MCD)
MF..............	Modern Fiction
MF..............	Modifying Factor [*Toxicology*]
MF..............	Modulation Factor
MF..............	Molecular Formula (NITA)
MF..............	Mole Fraction [*Chemistry*]
M-F..............	Monday through Friday (CDAI)
MF..............	More Follows [*Newspaper copy*] (DGA)
mf..............	More Follows [*Copyediting*] (WDMC)
MF..............	More Fragments (ACRL)
MF..............	Morningstar Foundation (EA)
MF..............	Morphogenetic Furrow [*Cell differentiation*]

MF	Morris Foundation [British] (DBA)
MF	Mossy Fiber [Neuroanatomy]
MF	Mother Fooler [Bowdlerized version]
MF	Motor Field
MF	Motor Freight
MF	Mucosal Fluid (DB)
MF	Multifamily (PA)
MF	Multifrequency [Telecommunications]
MF	Multifunctional (MCD)
MF	Multiple Feedback (MED)
MF	Multiplying Factor [Microscopy]
MF	Muscle Fiber
MF	Musicians Foundation (EA)
MF	Mutation Frequency [Medicine] (DMAA)
MF	Mutual Fund [Business term]
MF	Mycosis Fungoides [Dermatology]
MF	Myelinated Fiber [Neuroanatomy]
MF	Myelin Figure [Medicine]
MF	Myelofibrosis [Medicine] (DB)
M/F	My Favor (ADA)
MF	Myocardial Fibrosis [Cardiology]
MF	Myofibrillar [Anatomy]
MF	Red Carpet Flying Service [ICAO designator] (AD)
MF	Royal Munster Fusiliers [Military unit] (DMA)
MF	SAAB-Scania AB [Sweden ICAO aircraft manufacturer identifier] (ICAO)
MF	Spofa Ltd. [Czechoslovakia] [Research code symbol]
MF/1	Measurement Frequency/1 [IBM] (NITA)
MF²K	Medical Force 2000 [Army] (DOMA)
MFA	Mafia Islands [Tanzania] [Airport symbol] (OAG)
MFA	Malfunction Alert [Computer science] (BUR)
MFA	Malicious False Alarm [Firefighting]
MFA	Malta Fencible Artillery [British]
MFA	Managed Futures Association (NTPA)
MFA	Manned Flight Awareness [NASA] (NASA)
MFA	Marconi-Franklin Antenna
MFA	Marine Fabricators Association (NTPA)
M Fa	Martinus de Fano [Deceased circa 1275] [Authority cited in pre-1607 legal work] (DSA)
MFA	Master Fencers Association (NADA)
MFA	Master File Activities [Computer science]
MFA	Master of Fine Arts
MFA	Material Fielding Agreement [Army]
MFA	Mauritius Freeport Authority
MFA	McAlpin(e) Family Association (EA)
MFA	Menningar- og Fraedslusamband Althydu [Workers' Educational Association] [Iceland] (EY)
MFA	Men's Fashion Association of America (EA)
MFA	Mercantile Fleet Auxiliary [British]
MFA	Metal Finishing Association [British] (DBA)
MFA	Methyl Fluoracetate [Organic chemistry]
MFA	Miami, FL [Location identifier FAA] (FAAL)
MFA	Microelectronics for All Kit (NITA)
MFA	Military Flying Area [Canadian]
MFA	Military Functions Appropriation (AABC)
MFA	Minimum Flight Altitude [Aviation] (DA)
MFA	Minister for Foreign Affairs [British]
MFA	Mississippi Forestry Association (WPI)
MFA	Missouri Farmers Association (EFIS)
MFA	Mitchell Field [Alaska] [Seismograph station code, US Geological Survey Closed] (SEIS)
MFA	Mobilization for Animals (EA)
MFA	Monofluoroacetate [Organic chemistry]
MFA	Motor Factors Association [British] (BI)
MFA	Movement for Federation of the Americas (EA)
MFA	Movimento das Forcas Armadas [Armed Forces Movement] [Portugal Political party] (PPE)
MFA	Multi-Fiber Arrangement [International trade]
MFA	Multifocal Functional Autonomy [Medicine] (DMAA)
MFA	Multifunctional Acrylate [Organic chemistry]
MFA	Multifunction Antenna
MFA	Multiple Factor Analysis (DB)
MFA	Multiple Filer Audit Program
MFA	Mumpower Family Association (EA)
MFA	Museum of Fine Arts [Boston] (BJA)
MFAA	Masters of Foxhounds Association of America [Later, American Master of Foxhounds Association] (EA)
MFA & A	Monuments, Fine Arts, and Archives [SHAEF] [World War II]
MFAB	Museum of Fine Arts, Boston
MFAB-F	Mobile Floating Assault Bridge-Ferry [Military]
MFAC	Magnetic Fusion Advisory Committee [Department of Energy] [Washington, DC]
MFAC	Market Facts [NASDAQ symbol] (TTSB)
MFAC	Market Facts, Inc. [NASDAQ symbol] (NQ)
MFAD	Maneuver Force Air Defense
MFai	Millicent Library, Fairhaven, MA [Library symbol Library of Congress] (LCLS)
MFAIRWEST	Marine Fleet Air, West Coast
MFal	Falmouth Public Library, Falmouth, MA [Library symbol Library of Congress] (LCLS)
MFalHi	Falmouth Historical Society, Falmouth, MA [Library symbol Library of Congress] (LCLS)
MFAMUS	Master of Fine Arts in Music (WDAA)
MFAMW	Modern Free and Accepted Masons of the World (EA)
MF & P	Materials Finishes and Processes (MCD)

MF & R	Manpower Forces and Readiness [Military]
MF & S	Magazine Flooding and Sprinkling
MFANSW	Master Farriers' Association of New South Wales [Australia]
MFAP	Manned Flight Awareness Program [NASA] (KSC)
MFAR	Modernized Fleet Accounting and Reporting
MFAR	Multi-Function Array RADAR (MCD)
MFARS	Defense Mapping Agency Federal Acquisition Regulation Supplement [A publication] (AAGC)
MFAS	Master of Fisheries and Aquatic Science (PGP)
MFAT	Multifocal Atrial Tachycardia [Cardiology] (DAVI)
MFAW	Master of Fine Arts in Writing (PGP)
MFB	Bristol Community College, Fall River, MA [Library symbol Library of Congress] (LCLS)
MFB	Mammal Fibroblast (DB)
MFB	Mass Fraction Burn [Automotive engine combustion analysis]
MFB	Master of Finance and Banking (PGP)
MFB	Medial Forebrain Bundle [Medicine]
MFB	Message from Base
MFB	Metallic Foreign Body
MFB	Metropolitan Fire Brigade [British]
MFB	MFB Mutual Insurance Co. [from Manufacturers Mutual Fire Insurance Co., Firemen's Mutual Insurance Co., Blackstone Mutual Insurance Co.]
MFB	Mill Fixture Base (MCD)
MFB	Mixed Functional Block (IEEE)
MFB	Moisture Free Basis
MFB	Motional Feedback
MFB	Motor Freight Tariff Bureau, Springfield IL [STAC]
MFBAR	Multifunction Band Airborne Radio
MFBB	Mexican Food and Beverage Board (EA)
MFBC	MFB Corp. [NASDAQ symbol] (SAG)
MFB Cp	MFB Corp. [Associated Press] (SAG)
MFBF	Mean Flights between Failures [Military] (CAAL)
MFBF	Minimum Film Boiling Flux
MFBI	Major Fuel Burning Installation (GFGA)
MFBM	Thousand Feet Board Measure [Lumber]
MFBMP	Project Manager, Fleet Ballistic Missile [Navy]
MFBP	Main Feed Booster Pump (NVT)
MFBP	Manufacturing Flow and Building Plan (NASA)
MFBS	Marine and Freshwater Biomedical Science (GNE)
MFC	Magnesium Flat Cell
MFC	Magnetic Film Counter
MFC	Magnetic Tape Field Scan [Computer science]
MFC	Main Fuel Control (MCD)
MFC	Manual Frequency Control
MFC	Maritime Fruit Carriers [Steamship] (MHDW)
MFC	Mass Flow Controller [Engineering]
MFC	Master File Copy [Computer science] (KSC)
MFC	Master Flow Controller [Nuclear energy] (NRCH)
MFC	Master of Forest Conservation (PGP)
MFC	Mastership in Food Control [British] (DBQ)
MFC	Mean Frequency of Compensation (STED)
MFC	Median Femoral Condyle [Anatomy]
MFC	Medicated Face Conditioner [Brand manufactured by Mennen]
MFC	Membrane Fecal Coliform (PDAA)
m-FC	Membrane Focal Coli [Broth] (STED)
MFC	Merrell's Fan Club (EA)
MFC	Metal-Finishing Category (GNE)
MFC	Meteorological and Oceanographic Forecast Center (COE)
MFC	Microfibrillated Cellulose (DB)
MFC	Microfilm Frame Card
MFC	Microfunctional Circuit
MFC	Microsoft Foundation Classes [Computer science] (PCM)
MFC	Microsoft Foundation Class Library [Computer science] (PCM)
MFC	Military Frequency Changer
MFC	Minimal Flight Forecasting Charts [Air Force]
MFC	Minimal Fungicidal Concentration [Medicine] (DMAA)
MFC	Mirinda's Friendship Club (EA)
MFC	Missile Fire Control (MCD)
MFC	Mission Football Conference (PSS)
MFC	Mississippi Flyway Council
MFC	Modern Foods Council [Defunct] (EA)
MFC	Moncton Flying Club [Canada ICAO designator] (FAAC)
MFC	Morrison Fresh Cooking [NYSE symbol] (TTSB)
MFC	Morrison Fresh Cooking, Inc. [NYSE symbol] (SAG)
MFC	Mortar Fire Controller [British]
MFC	Mortgage Funding Corp. [British]
MFC	Most-Favored Customer (AAGC)
MFC	Motor Freight Controller [National Accounting and Finance Council] [A publication]
MFC	Motorized Flow Control
MFC	Movimiento Familiar Cristiano (EA)
MFC	Multi-Frequency Code [Telecommunications] (DA)
MFC	Multifrequency Signaling, Compelled [Telecommunications] (TEL)
MFC	Multifunctional Concentrate (EDCT)
MFC	Multiple File Concept (DNAB)
MFC	Multiple Flight Computer (NASA)
MFC	Multiple Flight Controller (NASA)
MFC	Municipal Financial Corp. [Toronto Stock Exchange symbol]
MFCA	Master File Change Activity [Computer science] (MCD)
MFCA	Miniature Figure Collectors of America (EA)
MFCA	Multi-Function Communications Adaptor (NITA)
MFCA	Multifunction Communications Adapter
MFCAE	Masters of Foxhounds Club of America and England [Defunct] (EA)
MFCB	Michigan Financial Corp. [NASDAQ symbol] (SAG)

MFCB............	Michigan Finl Corp. [*NASDAQ symbol*] (TTSB)
MFCC............	Marriage and Family Counseling Certificate (PGP)
MFCC............	Marriage, Family, and Child Counseling (PGP)
MFCC............	Marriage, Family, and Child Counselor [*Psychology*] (DAVI)
MFCC............	Maximum Free Carrier Concentration (AAEL)
MFCC............	Minimum Functional Combat Capability
MFCC............	Missile Fire Control Computer [*Military*] (CAAL)
MFCC............	Missile Flight Caution Corridor (AFM)
MFCC............	Mortar Fire Control Calculator [*Later, MBC*] [*Military*] (INF)
MFCC............	Mortar Fire Direction Center Data Calculator [*Army*]
MFCD............	Modular Flare Chaff Dispenser [*Military*] (PDAA)
MFCF............	Multinational Fuel Cycle Facility
MFCI............	Molten Fuel Coolant Interaction [*Nuclear energy*] (NRCH)
MFCL............	Master Fund Control List [*Air Force*] (AFM)
MFC/LB........	Multi-Frequency / Local Battery [*Telecommunications*] (DA)
MFCM..........	Member of the Faculty of Community Medicine [*British*]
MFCM..........	Multifunction Card Machine (BUR)
MFCMA........	Magnuson Fishery Conservation and Management Act [*1976*] [*Also, FCMA*]
MFCO............	Manual Fuel Cutoff (AAG)
MFCO............	Microwave Filter [*NASDAQ symbol*] (TTSB)
MFCO............	Microwave Filter Co., Inc. [*NASDAQ symbol*] (NQ)
MFCP............	Multifunction Control/Panel (MCD)
MFCS............	Magnetic Field Calibration System
MFCS............	Manual Flight Control System [*NASA*]
MFCS............	Master of Family and Consumer Sciences (PGP)
MFCS............	Mathematical Foundation of Computer Science (PDAA)
MFCS............	Maximum Flat Control System
MFCS............	Medical Function Control System (PDAA)
MFCS............	Microprocessor Flight Control System (DOMA)
MFCS............	Missile Fire Control System (NG)
MFCS............	Mortar Fire Control System [*Military*] (INF)
MFCT............	Major Fraction Thereof
MFCU............	Multifunction Card Unit
MFCV............	Modulating Flow Control Valve (MCD)
MFCV............	Muscle Fibre Conduction Velocity (DMAA)
MFCX............	Marshalltown Financial [*NASDAQ symbol*] (TTSB)
MFCX............	Marshalltown Financial Corp. [*NASDAQ symbol*] (SAG)
MFD............	Canadian Department of Fisheries and Oceans, Marine Fish Division [*Research center*] (RCD)
MFD............	Magic Foods, Inc. [*Vancouver Stock Exchange symbol*]
MFD............	Magnetic Frequency Detector
MFD............	Magnetofluiddynamic
MFD............	Main Feed (MCD)
MFD............	Malfunction Detection (NASA)
MFD............	Malfunctioning Display (DA)
MFD............	Mandibulofacial Dysostosis (STED)
MFD............	Manifold [*Paper*] (DGA)
MFD............	Mansfield [*Ohio*] [*Airport symbol*] (OAG)
MFD............	Mansfield, OH [*Location identifier FAA*] (FAAL)
MFD............	Manufactured
mfd............	Manufactured (WDAA)
MFD............	Master File Directory [*Computer science*]
MFD............	Maximum Frequency Difference [*Statistics*]
MFD............	Mechanical-Front-Drive [*Tractor*]
MFD............	Memory-for-Designs [*Test*] [*Psychology*]
MFD............	Message Format Designator
MFD............	Metal Floor Deck [*Technical drawings*]
MFD............	Microfarad
MFD............	Midforceps Delivery [*Obstetrics*]
MFD............	Military Forwarding Depot [*British military*] (DMA)
MFD............	Milk-Free Diet (STED)
MFD............	Millifarad (MCD)
MFD............	Minimal Fatal Dose [*Medicine*] (STED)
MFD............	Minimum Fatal Dose
MFD............	Minimum Focusing Distance [*Optics*]
MFD............	Multifunction Display (MCD)
MFD............	Multiple Family Dwelling [*Real estate*]
MFD............	Multistage Flash Distillation (PDAA)
MFD............	Multivariable Frequency Domain
MFD............	Municipal Facilities Division [*Environmental Protection Agency*] (GFGA)
MFDC............	Main Facility Device Controller [*Telecommunications*] (CIST)
MFDC............	Morzen Mortar Fire Data Computer [*Military British*] (INF)
MFDC............	Mouvement des Forces Democratiques de la Casamance [*Senegal*] [*Political party*]
MFDCC.........	Marine Fire Detection Control Center
MF/DF..........	Medium-Frequency Direction Finder [*or Finding*] (NVT)
MFDO	Member of the Faculty of Dispensing Opticians [*British*] (DBQ)
MFDP............	Maintenance Float Distribution Point [*Computer science*] (NATG)
MFDP............	Mississippi Freedom Democratic Party
MFDS............	Modular Fuel Delivery Station [*Shipboard installation*] [*Navy*] (DOMA)
MFDSG..........	Multifunction Display Symbol Generator (MCD)
MFDSUL	Multifunction Data Set Utility Language
MFDT............	Memory-for-Designs Test [*Psychology*]
MFDU	Multifunction Display Unit [*Aviation*]
MFE	Machinery and Fixed Equipment [*British*]
MFE	Magnetic Field Energy
MFE	Magnetic Field Explorer [*NASA*]
MFE	Magnetic Fusion Energy
MFE	Maison de la Fondation Europeenne (EAIO)
MFE	Major Fleet Escort
MFE	Manual of Field Engineering [*British military*] (DMA)
MFE	Master of Financial Economics (PGP)
MFE	Master of Forest Engineering

MFE	McAllen [*Texas*] [*Airport symbol*] (OAG)
MFE	McAllen, TX [*Location identifier FAA*] (FAAL)
MFE	Mean Fibre Extent (PDAA)
MFE	Mercury Film Electrode [*Electrochemistry*]
MFE	Microabrasion Foil Experiment [*For cosmic dust retrieval*]
MFE	Mid-Frequency Execution
MFE	Mid-Frequency Executive (NASA)
MFE	Mischief Enterprises Ltd. [*Vancouver Stock Exchange symbol*]
MFE	Moire Fringe Effect (PDAA)
MFE	Mouvement Federaliste Europeen [*European Federalist Movement*] [*France*]
MFEA	Magnetic Fusion Engineering Act
MFEA	Mutual Fund Education Alliance (NTPA)
MFED	Manned Flight Engineering Division [*NASA*]
MFED	Maximum Flat Envelope Delay
MFed	Miners' Federation of Great Britain (DAS)
MFEIP	Ministry of Food Education and Information Practice [*British*]
MFEL	Medical Free Electron LASER
MFEM	Maximal Forced Expiratory Maneuver [*Medicine*] (DAVI)
MFENET......	Magnetic Fusion Energy Research Network [*Department of Energy*]
MF Eng	Master of Forest Engineering
MFEQ	Mechanical Facilities and Equipment (SAA)
MFES	Main Fixed Earth Station [*NASA*] (PDAA)
MFES	Major Fleet Escort Study [*Navy*] (CAAL)
MFF	Flin Flon Public Library, Manitoba [*Library symbol National Library of Canada*] (NLC)
MFF	Magnetic Flip-Flop [*Computer science*]
MFF	Mariposa Folk Foundation (EAIO)
MFF	Master Freight File
MFF	Match Flip Flop [*Computer science*] (MHDI)
MFF	Matching Familiar Figures [*Psychology*]
MFF	MDM [*Manipulator Deployment Mechanism*] Flight Forward [*NASA*] (GFGA)
MFF	Melbourne Film Festival [*Australia*]
MFF	Mezzo Fortissimo [*Rather Loud*] [*Music*] (ADA)
MFF	Military Free Fall [*Parachute jump*] (MCD)
MFF	Moanda [*Gabon*] [*Airport symbol*] (OAG)
MFF	Munitions Filling Factory (ADA)
MFF	St. Martin Du Fouilloux [*France*] [*Seismograph station code, US Geological Survey*] (SEIS)
MFFC	Milton Federal Financial [*NASDAQ symbol*] (TTSB)
MFFC	Milton Federal Financial Corp. [*NASDAQ symbol*] (SAG)
MFFGH	Flin Flon General Hospital, Manitoba [*Library symbol National Library of Canada*] (NLC)
MFF/HALO ...	Military Free Fall / High Altitude Low Opening Parachute
MFFHB........	Hudson Bay Mining & Smelting Co. Ltd., Flin Flon, Manitoba [*Library symbol National Library of Canada*] (NLC)
MFFLR.........	Muffler [*Automotive advertising*]
MFFR..........	Modified Field Fire Range (MCD)
MFFT..........	Matching Familiar Figures Test [*Education*]
MFFT	Minimum Film Formation Temperature [*Coating technology*]
MFG	Major Functional Group [*NASA*] (KSC)
MFG	Manufacturing (AFM)
mfg	Manufacturing (DD)
MFG	Message Flow Graph
MFG	Milk Fat Globule
MFG	Modified Heat-Degraded Gelatin [*Medicine*] (MEDA)
MFG	Molded Fiberglass
MFG	Multi-Function Generator (NITA)
MFG	Munitions Family Group
MFGA	Master Furriers Guild of America (EA)
MFGM..........	Milk Fat Globule Membrane
MFGR..........	Manufacturer
MFH..........	Magnetic Film Handler (CMD)
MFH..........	Malignant Fibrous Histiocytoma [*Oncology*]
MFH..........	Markel Financial Holdings Ltd. [*Toronto Stock Exchange symbol*]
MFH..........	Master of Fox Hounds
MFH..........	Master of the Fox Hunt (DD)
MFH..........	Membrane-Free Hemolystate [*Hematology*] (DAVI)
MFH..........	Military Family Housing (AFM)
MFH..........	Mobile Field Hospital
MFHA..........	Masters of Foxhounds Association [*British*] (BI)
MFHA..........	Medal for Humane Action [*Berlin Airlift, 1948-9*] [*Military decoration*]
MFHBF	Mean Flight Hours between Failures [*Quality control*]
MFHBMA......	Mean Flight Hours between Maintenance Actions [*Quality control*] (NVT)
MFHBUMA......	Mean Flight Hour between Unscheduled Maintenance Actions [*Quality control*] (MCD)
MFHC..........	Missile Flight Hazard Corridor (AFM)
MFHD..........	My First Hard Drive [*Computer science*]
MFHFS..........	Multifunction High-Frequency SONAR (MCD)
MF Hom	Member of the Faculty of Homoeopathy [*British*]
MFHR..........	Media Fund for Human Rights (EA)
m/f/h/v......	Male, Female, Handicapped, Veteran (BARN)
MFi..........	Fitchburg Public Library and Regional Center for Central Massachusetts, RegionalLibrary System, Fitchburg, MA [*Library symbol Library of Congress*] (LCLS)
MFI..........	MacFrugal's Bargains [*Formerly, Pic'n'Save Corp.*] [*NYSE symbol*] (SPSG)
MFI..........	MacFrugals Bargains Closeouts [*NYSE symbol*] (TTSB)
MFI..........	Magazines for Industry [*An association*]
MFI..........	Magnetic Field Indicator
MFI..........	Magnetic Field Intensity
MFI..........	Major Force Issues [*Army*] (AABC)
MFI..........	Marketfax Infoservices Ltd. [*Vancouver Stock Exchange symbol*]

MFI .... Marketing Freedom Index [*OPEC*] [*Business term*]
MFI .... Marshfield [*Wisconsin*] [*Airport symbol*] (OAG)
MFI .... Marshfield, WI [*Location identifier FAA*] (FAAL)
MFI .... Master Facility Inventory [*Department of Health and Human Services*] (GFGA)
MFI .... Mean Flourescence Intensity [*Biochemistry*]
MFI .... Melt-Flow Index [*of plastics*]
MFI .... Metal Fabricating Institute (EA)
MFI .... Metal-Finishing Industy
MFI .... Military Financial Instruction
MFI .... Mobile Fuel Irradiator (IEEE)
MFI .... Multi-point Fuel Injection
MFI .... Multiport Fuel Injection [*Automotive technology*]
MFI .... Myofibril Fragmentation Index [*Food technology*]
MFIA .... Member, Fundraising Institute-Australia, Inc. (NFD)
MFIA .... Municipal Finance Industry Association (NTPA)
MFIC .... Microfluidics International [*NASDAQ symbol*] (TTSB)
MFIC .... Microfluidics International Corp. [*NASDAQ symbol*] (SAG)
MFIC .... Military Flight Information Center
MFIC .... Mutual Federation of Independent Cooperatives [*Later, Northeast Dairy Cooperative Federation*] (EA)
MFID .... Multiple-Electrode Flame Ionization Detector
MFIE .... Magnetic Field Integral Equation (PDAA)
MF-IFGR ...... Michael Fund (International Foundation for Genetic Research) (EA)
MFin .... Master of Finance
MFIN .... Metro Financial Corp. [*NASDAQ symbol*] (SAG)
MFinStud ...... Master of Financial Studies
MFIP .... Microforms in Print [*Database*]
MFIS .... Magnetic Field-Induced Superconductivity
MFisc .... Maitrise en Fiscalite (DD)
MFISH .... Multiplex Fluorescence in Situ Hybridization
MFiT .... Fitchburg State College, Fitchburg, MA [*Library symbol Library of Congress*] (LCLS)
MFIT .... Manual Fault Isolation Test
MFIT .... Modified Flight Intersection Tape (SAA)
MFIV .... Mainwater Feed Isolation Valve [*Nuclear energy*] (NRCH)
MFJ .... Moala [*Fiji*] [*Airport symbol*] (OAG)
MFJ .... Modified Final Judgment [*Telecommunications*]
MFJ .... Movement for Freedom and Justice [*Ghana*] [*Political party*] (EY)
MFJC .... Memorial Foundation for Jewish Culture (EA)
MFJSA .... Mass Finishing Job Shops Association (EA)
MFK .... Mafeking [*South Africa*] [*Airport symbol*] (OAG)
MFK .... Mill Fixture Key [*Tool*]
MFKP .... Multifrequency Key Pulsing
MFKT .... Mobile Field Kitchen Trailer (MCD)
MFKY .... Maxey Flats, Kentucky [*Commercial waste site*] (GAAI)
MFL .... Magnetic Field Line
MFL .... Main Feedwater Line [*Nuclear energy*] (NRCH)
MFL .... Maintain Flight Level [*Aviation*]
MFL .... Maintenance-Free Lifetime (PDAA)
MFL .... Master Force List [*DoD*]
MFL .... Master of Family Life
MFL .... Matrimonial and Family Law [*New York, NY A publication*]
MFL .... Matrimonial and Family Life [*A publication*]
MFL .... Maximum Foreseeable Loss [*Insurance*]
MFL .... Methodists for Life [*Defunct*] (EA)
MfL .... Microfile (Pty.) Ltd., Johannesburg, South Africa [*Library symbol Library of Congress*] (LCLS)
MFL .... Missile Firing Laboratory (KSC)
MFL .... Mobile Field Laboratory
MFL .... Mobile Field Laundry [*Military*]
MFL .... Modern Foreign Language
MFL .... Motor Freight Line
MFL .... Multiple Fragment Laceration [*Shrapnel wound*] [*Military*] (VNW)
MFLA .... Midwest Federation of Library Associations
m flac .... Membrana Flaccida [*Flaccid Membrane*] [*Latin Medicine*] (MAE)
MFLB .... Motor Fuel Licensing Board [*Australia*]
MFLC .... Mid-Florida Conference (PSS)
MFLD .... Male-Female Longevity Difference
MFLD .... Manifold (KSC)
MFLD .... Message Field [*Computer science*]
MFlem .... Middle Flemish [*Language*] (BARN)
MFLFd .... MuniVest Florida Fund [*Associated Press*] (SAG)
MFLIC .... Modified Fluid in Cell [*Automotive engine combustion analysis*]
MFLOP .... Mega-Floating Point Operation
MFLOP .... Mega Floating-Point Operations per Second [*Computer science*]
MFLOPS ...... Million Floating Point Instructions per Second (AAEL)
MFLOPS ...... Million Floating-Point Operations per Second [*Processing power units*] [*Computer science*]
Mflops .... Million Floating-Point Operations per Second [*Computer science*] (ODBW)
MFLOPS ...... Millions of Floating Point Operations Per Second [*Telecommunications*] (ACRL)
MFLP .... Mattel Family Learning Program
MFLP .... Multifile Linear Programming
MFLR .... Mayflower Co-Operative Bank [*NASDAQ symbol*] (NQ)
MFLT .... Mathematics Functional Literacy Test (EDAC)
MFLT .... Mean Fault Location Time (DNAB)
MFLT .... Mean First Lesions Time [*Immunochemistry*]
MFLZ .... Mejdunarodna Fondatzia Lyudmila Zhivkova [*Lyudmila Zhivkova International Foundation*] (EAIO)
MFm .... Framingham Town Library, Framingham, MA [*Library symbol Library of Congress*] (LCLS)
MFM .... Glenair [*British*] [*FAA designator*] (FAAC)
MFM .... Magnetic-Field Modulation [*Computer science*] (PCM)

MFM .... Magnetic Field Monitor [*NASA*]
MFM .... Magnetic Force Microscope
MFM .... Magnetic Forming Machine
MFM .... Magnetofluid Mechanic
MFM .... Mass Flow Meter (AAEL)
MFM .... Master File Maintenance [*Computer science*]
MFM .... Master of Financial Management (ADA)
MFM .... Materials Flow Management [*Manufacturing*]
MFM .... Maximally Flat Magnitude
MFM .... Meals for Millions Foundation [*Later, MFM/FFH*] (EA)
MFM .... MFC Mining Finance Corp. [*Toronto Stock Exchange symbol Vancouver Stock Exchange symbol*]
MFM .... MFS Municipal Income Trust [*NYSE symbol*] (SPSG)
MFM .... MFS Municipal Inc. Tr [*NYSE symbol*] (TTSB)
MFM .... Micrometer Frequency Meter
MFM .... Minced Fish Meat [*Food technology*]
MFM .... Mine Firing Mechanism
MFM .... Miniature Fluxgate Magnetometer
MFM .... Minneapolis-St. Paul [*Minnesota*] [*Seismograph station code, US Geological Survey*] (SEIS)
MFM .... Missile Farm Monitor [*Army*] (AABC)
MFM .... Missile Fatigue Monitor
MFM .... Mississippi State University, Mississippi State, MS [*OCLC symbol*] (OCLC)
MFM .... Modified Frequency Modulation [*Electronics*]
MFM .... Morrissey, Fernie & Michel Railway [*AAR code*]
MFM .... Mouvement pour le Pouvoir Proletarien [*or aux Petits*] [*Movement for Proletarian Power Malagasy*] [*Political party*] (PPW)
MFM .... Movable Fine Mesh
MFM .... Multi-Faith Meal [*Army*] (INF)
MFM .... Multifunctional Monomer [*Organic chemistry*]
MFM .... Multistage Frequency Multiplexer
MFMA .... Maple Flooring Manufacturers Association (EA)
MFMA .... Metal Findings Manufacturers Association (EA)
MFMA .... Metal Framing Manufacturers Association (EA)
MFMA .... Midwest Feed Manufacturers Association [*Later, AFMA*] (EA)
MFMA .... Monolithic Ferrite Memory Array
MFMANSW ... Master Fish Merchants' Association of New South Wales [*Australia*]
MFMBARS ... Multi-Function, Multi-Band Airborne Radio System (PDAA)
MFmcM .... Marist College and Seminary, Framingham Center, MA [*Library symbol Library of Congress*] (LCLS)
MFMD .... MonofluoromethylDOPA (DB)
MFM/FFH ..... Meals for Millions/Freedom from Hunger Foundation (EA)
MFMH .... Monofluoromethylhistidine [*Antineoplastic drug*]
MFmHi .... Framingham Historical society, Framingham, MA [*Library symbol*] [*Library of Congress*] (LCLS)
MFMI .... Men for Missions International (EA)
MFMM .... Microwave Frequency Measurement Module
MFMR .... Multifrequency Microwave Radiometer (MCD)
MFmT .... Framingham State College, Framingham, MA [*Library symbol Library of Congress*] (LCLS)
MFMT .... Maryland Functional Mathematics Test (EDAC)
MFMT .... Microwave Frequency Modulation Transmitter
MF/MWS ...... Male/Female - Married/Widow [*or Widower*]/Single
MFN .... MDC Financial, Inc. [*Vancouver Stock Exchange symbol*]
MFN .... Mercury Finance [*NYSE symbol*] (TTSB)
MFN .... Mercury Finance Co. [*NYSE symbol*] (SPSG)
MFN .... Metabolic Fecal Nitrogen (PDAA)
MFN .... Milford Sound [*New Zealand*] [*Airport symbol*] (OAG)
MFN .... Most-Favored-Nation [*Trading status*]
MFN .... Muffin (ABBR)
MFNG .... Motion for a Finding of Not Guilty
MFNS .... Millard Fillmore National Society [*Defunct*] (EA)
MFO .... Mafco Consolidated Group [*NYSE symbol*] (SAG)
MFO .... Major Function Overlay (MCD)
MFO .... Marine Fuel Oil
MFO .... Master Frequency Oscillator (NG)
MFO .... Material Fielding Operations (MCD)
MFO .... Medium Frequency Oscillator (DMAA)
MFO .... Military Forwarding Officer
MFO .... Military Forwarding Organization
MFO .... Missile Field Office (AAG)
MFO .... Missile Firing Order
MFO .... Mixed-Function Oxidase [*Biochemistry*]
MFO .... Multinational Force and Observers [*Eleven-nation peace-keeping force for the Sinai*]
MFO .... Multiple Facility Organization
MFOA .... Municipal Finance Officers Association of US and Canada [*Later, GFOA*] (EA)
MFOC .... Military and Government Fiber Optics and Communications [*Conference*] (TSSD)
MFOD .... Manned Flight Operations Directive [*NASA*] (KSC)
MFOE .... Mixed-Function Oxidase Enzyme System
MFOI .... Major Force Oriented Issue [*Military*] (AFM)
MFOM .... Master, Faculty of Occupational Medicine (DAVI)
MFOM .... Member, Faculty of Occupational Medicine (CMD)
MFON .... Missile Firing Order Normal [*Military*] (CAAL)
MFOPP .... Missile Firing Order Patch Panel
MFor .... Master of Forestry
MForSc .... Master of Forest Science (ADA)
MFOT .... Mean Forced Outage Time (PDAA)
MFOW .... Pacific Coast Marine Firemen, Oilers, Watertenders, and Wipers Association
MFP .... Franciscan Missionaries Our Lady of Peace (TOCD)
MFP .... Magnetic Field Perturbation

MFP............	Main Feed Power [*Nuclear energy*] (NRCH)
MFP............	Main Feed Pump (NVT)
MFP............	Main Feedwater Pump [*Nuclear energy*] (NRCH)
MFP............	Main Force Patrol [*In movie "Mad Max"*]
MFP............	Major Force Program [*Air Force*] (AFIT)
MFP............	Management Framework Plan
MFP............	Master File Program [*Computer science*]
MFP............	Matched Filter Performance
MFP............	Materiel Fielding Plan
MFP............	Maximum Fluoride Protection [*Colgate-Palmolive Co.*]
MFP............	Maximum Freezing Point
MFP............	Mean Free Path
MFP............	Meat, Fish and Poultry
MFP............	Melphalan, Fluorouracil, Farlutal (Medroxyprogesterone acetate) [*Antineoplastic drug regimen*]
MF(P)........	Microfiche (Positive)
MFP............	Middle Free Path
MFP.........	Minimal Flight Path
MFP.........	Ministry of Fuel and Power [*British*]
MFP.........	Mixed Fission Products [*Nuclear energy*]
MFP............	Mobile Flux Platform (USDC)
MFP............	Moca [*Fernando Poo*] [*Equatorial Guinea*] [*Seismograph station code, US Geological Survey*] (SEIS)
MFP............	Molecular Free Path
MFP............	Monofluorophosphate [*Inorganic chemistry*]
MFP............	Movement for a Free Philippines (EA)
MFP............	Multi-Factor Productivity
MFP............	Multiform Printer
MFP............	Multifrequency Pulsing (MSA)
MFP............	Multifunction Peripheral [*Chip*] [*Computer science*]
MFP............	Multifunction Polis
MFP............	Multifunction Printers (PS)
MFP............	Myofascial Pain [*Medicine*]
MFPA........	Monolithic Focal Plane Array (PDAA)
MFPB........	Mineral Fiber Products Bureau
MFPC........	Man-Made Fibres Producers Committee [*British*] (DBA)
MFPC........	Multifunction Protocol Converter
MFPD........	Modern Federal Practice Digest [*A publication*] (DLA)
MFPE........	Minimum Final Prediction Error (MHDI)
MFPF........	Minefield Planning Folder [*Navy*] (DOMA)
MFPG........	Mechanical Failures Prevention Group
MFPG........	Mixed Fission Products Generator [*Nuclear energy*]
MFPh........	Member of the Faculty of Physiotherapists [*British*]
MFPHM...	Member, Faculty of Public Health Medicine (CMD)
MFPhys......	Member of the Faculty of Physiatrists [*British*]
MFPK........	Multifunction Program Keyboard (MCD)
MFP/MTP...	Materiel Fielding Plan/Materiel Transfer Plan [*Army*] (RDA)
MFPS........	Member of the Faculty of Physicians and Surgeons [*Glasgow*]
MFPS........	Mobile Field Photographic Section (NATG)
MFPS........	Modular Force Planning System (MCD)
MFPT........	Machinery Failure Prevention Technology (RDA)
MFPT........	Main Feedwater Pump Turbine [*Nuclear energy*] (NRCH)
MFPT........	Mean First-Passage Time [*Biochemistry*]
MFPTC......	Main Feed Pump Turbine Condenser [*Nuclear energy*] (NRCH)
MFP-UK......	Mothers for Peace - UK (EAIO)
MFPUL.......	Mississippi Forest Products Utilization Laboratory [*Mississippi State University*] [*Research center*] (RCD)
MFPVC......	Multifocal Premature Ventricular Contractions [*Medicine*] (MEDA)
MFQ............	Maradi [*Niger*] [*Airport symbol*] (OAG)
M'F R........	MacFarlane's Scotch Jury Court Reports [*1838-39*] [*A publication*] (DLA)
MFR............	Macfie Resources [*Vancouver Stock Exchange symbol*]
MFR............	Mail File Requirement [*Code*] [*Computer science*]
MFR............	Malfunctional Review
MFR............	Malfunction Rate
MFR............	Malfunction Receiver
MFR............	Manipulator Foot Restraint (NASA)
MFR............	Manufacture [*or Manufacturer*] (AFM)
mfr............	Manufacture (DD)
MFr............	Mare Frigoris [*Sea of Cold*] [*Lunar area*]
MFR............	Marine Fishery Reserve
MFR............	Master Facility Register [*Nuclear energy*]
MFR............	Master Frame Recognize (MCD)
MFR............	Master Frequency Record [*FCC list*] (NTCM)
MFR............	Master of Forest Resources (GAGS)
M Fr............	Master of French (PGP)
MFR............	Maximum Flight Rate (NASA)
MFR............	Mean Firing Rate [*Neurophysiology*]
MFR............	Mean Flow Rate (DB)
MFR............	Medford [*Oregon*] [*Airport symbol*] (OAG)
MFR............	Medford, OR [*Location identifier FAA*] (FAAL)
MFr............	Melomanes Francais [*Record label*] [*France*]
MFR............	Melt-Flow Rate [*of plastics*]
MFR............	Memorandum for Record [*Military*]
MfR............	Microform Review, Inc., Weston, CT [*Library symbol Library of Congress*] (LCLS)
MFR............	Middle French [*Language, etc.*]
MFR............	Mid-Forceps Rotation [*Obstetrics*] (DAVI)
MFR............	Military Field Representative (SAA)
MFR............	Missile Firing Range (AAG)
MFR............	Model Form and Record
MFR............	Mucus Flow Rate (MAE)
MFR............	Multifrequency Receiver [*Telecommunications*]
MFR............	Multifunctional Receiver
MFR............	Multifunctional Review (NASA)

MFR............	Multifunction RADAR
MFR............	Mutual Force Reductions
MFran........	Ray Memorial Library, Franklin, MA [*Library symbol Library of Congress*] (LCLS)
MFRC........	Maritimes Forest Research Centre [*Research center*] (RCD)
MFRC........	Master of Forest Resources and Conservation (PGP)
MFRD........	Manufactured (ABBR)
MFRE........	Manufacture (ADA)
MFREA......	Multiple Food Retailers Employers' Association [*British*]
MFRF........	Mean-Family Replacement Factor
MFRG........	Manufacturing
MFRG........	Medical Functional Requirements Group (MCD)
MFRI........	MFRI, Inc. [*NASDAQ symbol*] (SPSG)
MFRI........	Migratory Fish Research Institute [*University of Maine*] [*Research center*] (RCD)
MFRN........	Manufacturers Number
MFRP........	Midwest Fuel Recovery Plant [*AEC*]
MFRP........	Multigrade Functional Rehabilitation Platform [*Medicine*]
MFRPA......	Maxey Flats Radioactive Protective Association (EA)
MFRR........	Manufacturer (ABBR)
MFRS........	Master File Replacement System [*Computer science*]
MFRS........	Multifunction Receiver System
MFRT........	Maryland Functional Reading Test (EDAC)
MFRT........	Modulated Frequency Radio Telephone (PDAA)
MFRY........	Manufactory (ABBR)
MFS............	Fleet Minesweeper (Steel-Hulled) [*Navy symbol*]
MFS............	Frostburg State College, Library, Frostburg, MD [*OCLC symbol*] (OCLC)
MFS............	Macintosh File Structure [*Apple Computer, Inc.*] [*Computer science*] (CIST)
MFS............	Macintosh File System [*Computer science*]
MFS............	Magnetic Field Strength
MFS............	Magnetic Tape Field Search [*Computer science*]
MFS............	Malleable Founders' Society [*Later, Iron Castings Society - ICS*]
MFS............	Maltese Falcon Society [*Defunct*] (EA)
MFS............	Manned Flying System (MCD)
MFS............	Manufactures
MFS............	Marble Falls, TX [*Location identifier FAA*] (FAAL)
MFS............	Marfan Syndrome [*Medicine*]
MFS............	Marine-Finish Slate (MSA)
MFS............	Massachusetts Financial Services
MFS............	Master Fabrication Schedule (DNAB)
MFS............	Master of Family Studies (GAGS)
MFS............	Master of Food Science
MFS............	Master of Foreign Service
MFS............	Master of Foreign Study
MFS............	Master of Forensic Science (GAGS)
MFS............	Master of Forest Science (GAGS)
MFS............	Master of Forest Studies (PGP)
MFS............	Master of French Studies (PGP)
MFS............	Material False Statement [*Nuclear energy*] (NUCP)
MFS............	Maxillofacial Surgery [*Medical specialty*] (DHSM)
MFS............	McCloud Flat South [*California*] [*Seismograph station code, US Geological Survey*] (SEIS)
MFS............	Medal Field Service [*Canada*]
MFS............	Medicare Fee Schedule
MFS............	Mercury Feed System
MFS............	Message Format Service
MFS............	Metropolitan Fiber Systems, Inc.
MfS............	Microfilm Systems, Colorado Springs, CO [*Library symbol Library of Congress*] (LCLS)
MFS............	Microfuel Systems [*Vancouver Stock Exchange symbol*]
MFS............	Military Flight Service
MFS............	Miller Flying Services, Inc. [*ICAO designator*] (FAAC)
MfS............	Ministerium fuer Staatssicherheit [*Ministry for State Security*] [*See also MISTAI, MSS*] [*Germany*] (EG)
MFS............	Minnesota Follow-Up Study Rehabilitation Rating Scale
MFS............	Miraflores [*Colombia*] [*Airport symbol*] (OAG)
MFS............	Missile Firing Simulator (NATG)
MFS............	Missile Firing Station [*Army*]
MFS............	Missile Fuse Set Servo
MFS............	Missing from Shelf (ADA)
MFS............	Missouri Followback Survey [*Department of Health and Human Services*] (GFGA)
MFS............	Mitral First Sound [*Cardiology*] (CPH)
MFS............	Modern Fiction Studies [*A publication*] (BRI)
MFS............	Modified Filing System [*Computer science*] (PCM)
MFS............	Modified Full Spray
MFS............	Modular Flexible Scheduling [*Education*]
MFS............	Multi-Frequency Signalling [*Telecommunications*] (NITA)
MFS............	Multifunction Sensor (MCD)
MFS............	Multi-Function Switch [*Automotive engineering*]
MFS............	Multiple-Frequency Synthesizer
MFS............	Multiple Sclerosis Foundation (EA)
MFS............	Municipal Ferrous Scrap
MFS............	National Mobilization for Survival (EA)
MFSA........	Master Floor Sanders Association (NADA)
MFSA........	Metal Finishing Suppliers' Association (EA)
MFSA........	Methodist Federation for Social Action (EA)
MFSB........	Mother, Father, Sister, Brother [*Musical group*]
MFSB........	Mutual Bancompany [*NASDAQ symbol*] (TTSB)
MFSB........	Mutual Bancompany, Inc. [*NASDAQ symbol*] (SAG)
MFSc........	Master of Fisheries Science
MFS C........	MFS Communication Co. [*Associated Press*] (SAG)
MFSC........	Missile Flight Safety Center [*Pacific Missile Range*] (MUGU)

MFS Cm ...... MFS Communication Co. [*Associated Press*] (SAG)
MFSE .... Main Fire Support Element (AABC)
MFSF .... Magazine of Fantasy and Science Fiction [*A publication*] (BRI)
MFSFU .... Matt-Finish Structural Facing Units [*Technical drawings*]
MFSG .... Missile Firing Safety Group (MUGU)
MFSK .... Multiple-Frequency Shift Keying
MFSL .... Maryland Fed Bancorp [*NASDAQ symbol*] (TTSB)
MFSL .... Maryland Federal Bancorp, Inc. [*NASDAQ symbol*] (NQ)
MFSL .... Mathematical and Functional Subroutine Library (MHDB)
MFSO .... Missile Flight Safety Officer
MFSOA .... Missile Flight Safety Officer Assistant (MUGU)
MFSOC .... Missile Flight Safety Officer Console (MUGU)
MF SOL ...... Merthiolate-Formaldehyde [*Stock*] Solution (BABM)
MFSOP .... Missile Flight Safety Operations Plan
MFSR .... Magnetic Film Strip Recorder
MFSS .... Medical Field Service School [*Army*]
MFSS .... Missile Flight Safety System (AAG)
MFSS .... Multi-Frequency Signalling System [*Telecommunications*] (EECA)
MFST .... Manifest
Mfst .... Manifest (EBF)
MFST .... Medical Field Service Technician (BABM)
MFST .... MFS Communiations [*NASDAQ symbol*] (TTSB)
MFST .... MFS Communication Co. [*NASDAQ symbol*] (SAG)
MFST .... Mobile Fire Safety Team
MFSTB .... Manifestable (ABBR)
MFSTD .... Manifested (ABBR)
MFSTG .... Manifesting (ABBR)
MFSTN .... Manifestation (ABBR)
MFSTO .... Manifesto (ABBR)
MFSTP .... MFS Commun 8% Cv Dep'A'Pfd [*NASDAQ symbol*] (TTSB)
MFSU .... Mobile Field Service Unit
MFSW .... Membrane-Filtered Sea Water
MFT .... Drury Military Extension, Springfield, MO [*OCLC symbol*] (OCLC)
MFT .... Magnetic Flow Transmitter
MFT .... Mail for Tots (EA)
MFT .... Mainframe Termination [*Telecommunications*] (TEL)
MFT .... Major Fraction Thereof
MFT .... Manufacturing Fit Test
MFT .... Marconi Fast Tuning (MCD)
MFT .... Marriage and Family Therapist [*Psychology*]
MFT .... Master File Tax [*Code*] [*IRS*]
MFT .... Master Fitness Trainer [*Army*] (INF)
MFT .... Master of Family Therapy (GAGS)
MFT .... Master of Foreign Trade
MFT .... Materiel Fielding Team [*Army*] (RDA)
MFT .... Materiel Field Test (MCD)
MFT .... Mean Flight Time (KSC)
MFT .... Mean Free Time
MFT .... Mechanized Flame Thrower
MFT .... Medical Field Service Technician [*Navy*]
MFT .... Meson Field Theory
MFT .... Metal Film Resistor
MFT .... Metallic Facility Terminal [*Telecommunications*] (TEL)
MFT .... Meter Fix Time/Slot Time [*FAA*] (TAG)
MFT .... Mine Fuse Train
MFT .... Minimum Film-Forming Temperature [*Wax polishes*]
MFT .... Missile Flight Time
MFT .... Mission Flight Trainer [*Navy*]
M FT .... Mistura Fiat [*Let a Mixture Be Made*] [*Pharmacy*]
MFT .... Mobile Foot Restraint (SSD)
MFT .... Molecular Field Theory [*Physical chemistry*]
MFT .... Monolayer Formation Time [*Physical chemistry*] (OA)
MFT .... Morgan Financial Corp. [*Toronto Stock Exchange symbol*]
MFT .... Most-Favorable Term (MHDW)
MFT .... Motor Freight Tariff [*Business term*] (ADA)
MFT .... Motor Freight Terminal
MFT .... Multifocal Atrial Tachycardia [*Cardiology*] (DMAA)
MFT .... Multilingual Forestry Terminology
MFT .... Multiple Family Therapy (DHP)
MFT .... Multiposition Frequency Telegraphy [*Telecommunications*] (OA)
MFT .... Multiprogramming (NITA)
MFT .... Multiprogramming with a Finite Amount of Trouble [*Computer science*]
MFT .... Multiprogramming with Fixed Number of Tasks [*Computer science*] (BUR)
MFT .... MuniYield FL Insured Fund [*NYSE symbol*] (TTSB)
MFT .... MuniYield Florida Insured Fund [*NYSE symbol*] (SPSG)
MFT .... Muscle Function Test
MFTA .... Managed Futures Trade Association (EA)
MFTA .... Multiduct Fuel Test Assembly [*Nuclear energy*] (NRCH)
MFTAD .... Master Flight Test Assignment Document [*NASA*]
MFTAD .... Master Flight Test Assignments Document [*NASA*]
MFTB .... Motor Freight Tariff Bureau
MFTC .... Metalworking Fair Trade Coalition [*Later, MTC*] (EA)
MFTCom ...... Member of the Faculty of Teachers in Commerce [*British*] (DBQ)
MFTD .... Mobile Field Training Detachment [*Military*] (AFM)
MF-TDA .... Multiple-Feedback, Time-Division Multiple Access (MED)
MFTDMA ...... Multiple Frequency Time Division Multiple Access (LAIN)
MFTF .... Mirror Fusion Test Facility [*For study of new energy source*]
MFTF .... Missionary Flight Training Foundation [*Defunct*]
MFTGS .... Midcourse Fix and Terminal Guidance System (MCD)
MFTHBA .... Missouri Fox Trotting Horse Breed Association (EA)
MFT L .... Millifoot Lamberts (DEN)
MFTL .... My Favorite Toy Language [*Computer hacker terminology*] (NHD)
M FT M .... Misce Fiat Mistura [*Mix to Make a Mixture*] [*Pharmacy*]

m ft mist ..... Misce Flat Mistura [*Mix and Let a Mixture be Made*] [*Latin*] (WDAA)
MFTP .... Modified Federal Test Procedure [*EPA engine test*]
MFTRS .... Magnetic Flight Test Recording System
MFTS .... Medial Femorotibial Space [*Anatomy*]
MFT/S .... Missile Facilities Technician/Specialist (AAG)
MFTU .... Macao Federation of Trade Unions
MFTV .... Mechanical Fit Test Vehicle
MFTVP .... Motor-Free Test of Visual Perception [*Psychology*] (DAVI)
MFU .... Magnetic Force Upset [*Metals*]
MFU .... Marine Forecast Unit [*National Weather Service*]
MFU .... Mfuwe [*Zambia*] [*Airport symbol*] (OAG)
MFU .... Military Foul-Up [*Bowdlerized version*] (DSUE)
MFU .... MIRA [*Multifunctional Inertial Reference Assembly*] Fighter Unit [*Air Force*] (MCD)
MFU .... Myoclonus Families United (EA)
MFU .... Pacific Coast Marine Firemen, Oilers, Watertenders, and Wipers Association [*Also known as Marine Firemen's Union*] (EA)
MFUA .... Medical Follow-Up Agency [*National Research Council*]
MFUI .... Mechanics Friendly Union Institution [*British*]
MFUMR .... MIRA [*Multifunctional Inertial Reference Assembly*] Fighter Unit Mounting Rack [*Air Force*] (MCD)
MFUN .... Morgan Funshares [*NASDAQ symbol*] (TTSB)
MFUN .... Morgan Funshares, Inc. [*NASDAQ symbol*] (SAG)
Mfurers Mon ... Manufacturers' Monthly [*A publication*]
MFUSYS .... Microfiche File Update System [*Computer science*] (PDAA)
MFUW .... Magnetic Force Upset Welding [*Metals*]
MFV .... Forward Visibility More than ___ Miles [*Aviation*] (FAAC)
MFV .... Magnetic Field Vector
MFV .... Main Feedwater Valve [*Nuclear energy*] (NRCH)
MFV .... Main Fuel Valve [*Aerospace*] (NAKS)
MFV .... Maintenance Floor Valve (NRCH)
MFV .... Mars Flyby Vehicle [*Aerospace*]
MFV .... Melfa, VA [*Location identifier FAA*] (FAAL)
MFV .... Methanol-Fueled Vehicle [*Automotive engineering*]
MFV .... MFS Special Value Trust [*NYSE symbol*] (SPSG)
MFV .... Microfilm Viewer
MFV .... Military Flight Vehicles
MFV .... Motor Fishing Vessel [*British military*] (DMA)
MFVD .... Maximum Forward Voltage Drop
MFVP .... Mauler Feasibility Validation Program
MFVPT .... Motor-Free Visual Perception Test
mfVSG .... Membrane Form of Variant Surface Glycoprotein [*Biochemistry*]
MFW .... Main Feedwater [*Nuclear energy*] (NRCH)
MFW .... Maritime Federation of the World (NADA)
MFW .... Metres of Fresh Water
MFW .... Migrant Farm Worker (OICC)
MFW .... Milton-Freewater [*Oregon*] [*Seismograph station code, US Geological Survey*] (SEIS)
MFW .... Ms. Foundation for Women (EA)
MFW .... Multiple Fragment Wound (MAE)
MFWC .... Marine Fleet Air, West Coast
MFWCS .... Main Feedwater and Condensate System [*Environmental science*] (COE)
MFWD .... Mechanical Front Wheel Drive [*Off-highway equipment*]
MFWLB .... Main Feedwater Line Break [*Nuclear energy*] (NRCH)
MFWP .... Maryland Functional Writing Program (EDAC)
MFWV .... Main Feedwater Valve [*Nuclear energy*] (NRCH)
MFX .... Mirror Fusion Experiment [*Nuclear energy*]
MFXT .... Meter Fix Time [*Aviation*] (FAAC)
MFY .... Manufactory (ABBR)
MFY .... Mobilization for Youth
MFY .... Music for Youth
MFZ .... Mezzo Forzando [*Music*]
MFZ .... Missile Firing Zone
MFZ .... Mofaz Air [*Malawi*] [*FAA designator*] (FAAC)
MG .... Geometric Mean [*Psychology*]
MG .... Groundswell, Inc. of Minnesota (EA)
mg .... Guadalupe Missioners (TOCD)
MG .... Gudalupe Missioners (TOCD)
MG .... Machine-Glazed [*Poster paper*]
MG .... Machine Gun (MUGU)
MG .... Machine Gunner [*British military*] (DMA)
MG .... Machinery of Government [*British*]
MG .... Madagascar [*ANSI two-letter standard code*] (CNC)
mg .... Mafic Granulite [*Geology*]
MG .... Magenta (ROG)
MG .... Maggioni & C. [*Italy*] [*Research code symbol*]
Mg .... Maghemite [*A mineral*]
MG .... Magna International, Inc. [*Toronto Stock Exchange symbol*]
Mg .... Magnesium [*Chemical element*]
MG .... Magnetic Armature (MSA)
MG .... Maharashtrawadi Gomantak [*India*] [*Political party*] (PPW)
MG .... Main Gauche [*With the Left Hand*] [*Music*]
MG .... Main Generator (IAA)
MG .... Major General
Mg .... Major General
MG .... Make Good
MG .... Malachite Green [*A dye*]
mg .... Malagasy Republic [*Madagascar*] [*MARC country of publication code Library of Congress*] (LCCP)
MG .... Mammary Gland [*Anatomy*]
MG .... Managerial Grid
MG .... Manager's Guide
Mg .... Mangrove [*Maps and charts*]
MG .... Manual Group (NRCH)

MG	Manufactured Goods (AAEL)
MG	Manufacturing
MG	Maof Airlines [Israel] [ICAO designator] (ICDA)
MG	Marcus Gunn (Pupil) [Ophthalmology]
MG	Margin (DAVI)
MG	Marginal (AAG)
MG	Marine Gunner
MG	Martinus Gosia [Authority cited in pre-1607 legal work] (DSA)
MG	Master-General [Military British]
MG	Master Generator [Telecommunications] (OA)
MG	Matrix Glass [Geology]
MG	Meaning (ROG)
MG	Medal for Gallantry
MG	Media General Financial Services [Information retrieval]
MG	Medial Gastrocnemius [Anatomy]
MG	Medium Grain [Lumber]
MG	Megagram
Mg	Megagram (COE)
MG	Membranous Glomerulopathy [Nephrology]
MG	Menopausal Gonadotropin [Endocrinology]
MG	Mesiogingival [Dentistry]
MG	Message Generator
MG	Metal Glass (IAA)
MG	Metal Goods [Department of Employment] [British]
MG	Metallgesellschaft [German commodities and futures contractor] (ECON)
MG	Metallurgical Grade
MG	Meteorological Group [Range Commanders Council] [White Sands Missile Range, NM]
MG	Methylene Glutamine
MG	Methylglucoside [Organic chemistry]
MG	Methylglyoxal [Also, MGLY] [Organic chemistry]
MG	Methyl Green [A dye]
MG	MG Car Club (EA)
MG	MGM Grand Air [ICAO designator] (AD)
MG	Michaelis-Gutmann Bodies (MAE)
mg	Microgram (DAVI)
MG	Microwave Generator
MG	Middle Gimbal [Yaw]
M/G	Miles per Gallon
MG	Military Government [or Governor]
MG	Millard-Gubler [Syndrome] [Medicine] (DB)
MG	Millennium Guild (EA)
MG	Mill Glazed [Paper]
MG	Milligauss (ABBR)
mg	Milligram
MG	Millwright Group (EA)
MG	Minnesota Groundswell (EA)
MG	Minority Group
MG	Miracle of Grace [Pseudonym used by William Smith]
MG	Misioneros de Guadalupe [Missionaries of Guadalupe] [Mexico] (EAIO)
MG	Missile Gas
MG	Missile Guidance
MG	Mixed Grain
MG	[The] Mobile & Gulf Railroad Co. [Formerly, MGU] [AAR code]
MGS	Mobile Generator (KSC)
MG	Modified Guaranteed [Securities trading]
MG	Moeso-Gothic [Language, etc.] (ROG)
MG	Monoglyceride [An enzyme] (MAE)
MG	Morgan Group [AMEX symbol] (TTSB)
MG	[The] Morgan Group, Inc. [AMEX symbol] (SAG)
MG	Morning
MG	Morris Garages [British automobile manufacturer; initialism used as name of sports car it produces]
MG	Motion for Mandamus Granted [Legal term] (ILCA)
MG	Motor Generator
MG	Mug (ABBR)
MG	Multigauge
MG	Muncie-Getrag [Refers to an automotive transmission designed by Getrag, a West German company, and built by General Motors in Muncie, IN]
MG	Muscle Group (MAE)
MG	Myasthenia Gravis [Medicine]
MG	Myasthenia Gravis Foundation (EA)
MG	Mycoplasma Gallisepticum (DB)
MG	Myoglobin [Medicine] (DMAA)
MG	Myriagram [Ten Thousand Grams] (ROG)
MG	Pompano Airways [ICAO designator] (AD)
Mg/₁	Milligrams per Liter (GNE)
MGA	Magna International, Inc. [NYSE symbol] (SPSG)
MGA	Major-General in Charge of Administration [British]
MGA	Managing General Agency [Insurance]
MGA	Managing General Agent [Insurance]
MGA	Managua [Nicaragua] [Airport symbol] (OAG)
MGA	Marble and Granite Association [British] (BI)
MGA	Martin Goffman Associates (IID)
MGA	Master Gemology Association (EA)
MGA	Master of General Administration (DMAA)
MGA	Master of Government Administration (GAGS)
MGA	Matrox Graphics Architecture [Matrox Eletronics Systems Ltd.] (PCM)
MGA	Medium-Gain Antenna
MGA	Megaline Resources [Vancouver Stock Exchange symbol]
MGA	Melengestrol Acetate [Endocrinology]
MGA	Mercantile Gold [Vancouver Stock Exchange symbol]
MGA	Middle Gimbal Angle (NASA)
MGA	Middle Gimbal Assembly (KSC)
MGA	Middle Gimbal Axis (KSC)
MGA	Milagra Ridge [California] [Seismograph station code, US Geological Survey] (SEIS)
MGA	Military Government Association
MGA	Module Generator Assembly (DWSG)
MGA	Monochrome Graphics Adapter [Hercules] [Computer science] (PCM)
MGA	[The] Monongahela Railway Co. [AAR code]
MGA	Mother Guardian Allowance
MGA	Multimedia Graphics Architecture [Computer science] (PCM)
MGA	Multiple Gas Analyzer
MGA	Mushroom Growers Association [Commercial firm] (EA)
MGA	Mushroom Growers Cooperative Association [Defunct] (EA)
MGAA	Medium-Gain Autotrack Antenna
MGAA	Miniature Golf Association of America (EA)
MGAB	Maintenance Ground Abort [Air Force] (AFIT)
MGABR	Maintenance Ground Abort Rate [Air Force] (AFIT)
MGAD	Machine-Gun Artillery Division [Former USSR]
mgal	Milligal [Unit of acceleration]
MGAL	Thousand Gallons (EG)
MGAL/D	Million Gallons per Day
mgallon	Million Gallons (COE)
MGALS	Milligals (ABBR)
MGAM	Member Get a Member [Prodigy Services Co.]
MGAM	Morgan Grenfell Asset Management [Investment management firm] [British]
MGAM	Multimedia Games [NASDAQ symbol] (TTSB)
MGAM	Multimedia Games, Inc. [NASDAQ symbol] (SAG)
MGaMW	Mount Wachusett Community College, Gardner, MA [Library symbol Library of Congress] (LCLS)
MG&E	Madison Gas & Electric Co. (EFIS)
MG & L	Measurement of Gains and Losses (DICI)
MG & S	Manning, Granger, and Scott's English Common Pleas Reports [1845-56] [A publication] (DLA)
MGAO	Minority Graphic Arts Organization (EA)
MGAP	Magnetic Attitude Prediction
MGAP	Micro-Grain Array Processor [Electronics]
MGAS	Marcum Natural Gas Service, Inc. [NASDAQ symbol] (SAG)
MGAS	Marcum Natural Gas Svcs [NASDAQ symbol] (TTSB)
MGAS	Motor Gasoline [Military]
MGAT	Manchester General Ability Test [Education] (AEBS)
MGAWA	Market Gardeners' Association of Western Australia
MGAWD	Make Good All Works Distributed [Legal term] (BARN)
MGB	Main Gear Box (MCD)
MGB	Manageable (ABBR)
MGB	Medium-Girder Bridge (RDA)
MGB	Ministerstvo Gosudarstvennoy Bezopasnosti [Ministry of State Security] [Former USSR] (LAIN)
MGB	Mobile Garbage Bin
MGB	Morgan Stan Global Opt Bd Fd [NYSE symbol] (TTSB)
MGB	Morgan Stanley Global Opportunities Bond Fund, Inc. [NYSE symbol] (SAG)
MGB	Motor Gunboat [British]
MGB	Mount Gambier [Australia Airport symbol] (OAG)
MGBC	Maranatha Gospel Bottle Crusade [Later, CEM] (EA)
MGBCS	Murray Grey Beef Cattle Society [Australia]
MGBG	Methylglyoxal-Bis[guanylhydrazone] (DB)
MGBG	Methylglyoxalbis(guanylhydrazone) [Mitoguazone] [Also, Me-GAG] [Antineoplastic drug]
MGBN	Bananera [Guatemala] [ICAO location identifier] (ICLI)
MGBT	Manageability (ABBR)
MGBY	Manageably (ABBR)
MGC	Machine-Gun Car [or Carrier] [British]
MGC	Machine-Gun Co. [or Corps]
MGC	Machine-Gun Combination [British]
MGC	Magec Aviation Ltd. [British ICAO designator] (FAAC)
MGC	Magic (ABBR)
MgC	Magnocellular Neuroendocrine Cell [Medicine] (DMAA)
MGC	Major Gain Control
MGC	Major General Commandant [Marine Corps]
MGC	Management Group Codes (MCD)
MGC	Manual Gain Control
MGC	Manufactured Goods Collection (AAEL)
MGC	Marriage Guidance Council [British]
MGC	Metacerebral Giant Cell [Cytology]
MGC	Metallized Glass Coil
MGC	Michigan City [Indiana] [Airport symbol] (OAG)
MGC	Michigan City, IN [Location identifier FAA] (FAAL)
MGC	Midcourse Guidance and Control
MGC	Middle Georgia College [Cochran]
MGC	Minimal Glomerular Change [Nephrology]
MGC	Minimum Gelling Concentration [Hematology]
MGC	Missile Guidance and Control
MGC	Missile Guidance Computer (MCD)
MGC	Montgomery County Community College, Blue Bell, PA [OCLC symbol] (OCLC)
MGC	Morgan Grenfell Smallcap [NYSE symbol] (TTSB)
MGC	Morgan Grenfell Smallcap Fund, Inc. [NYSE symbol] (SPSG)
MGC	Mouse Genome Conference (HGEN)
MGC	Movers Association of Greater Chicago, Chicago, IL [STAC]
MGC	Museums and Galleries Commission [Government body] [British]
MGCA	Men's Garden Clubs of America (EA)
MGCA	Mobile Ground-Controlled Approach [Aviation]
MGCA	Mushroom Growers Cooperative Association [Defunct]

MGCB	Coban [*Guatemala*] [*ICAO location identifier*] (ICLI)
MGCC	Medical Graphics [*NASDAQ symbol*] (TTSB)
MGCC	Medical Graphics Corp. [*NASDAQ symbol*] (NQ)
MGCC	MG [*Morris Garage*]Car Club
MGCC	Missile Guidance and Control Computer
MGCD	Maximum Gapless Coverage Distance (NG)
MGCI	Master Ground-Controller Interception RADAR (NATG)
MGCL	Magical (ABBR)
MGCLY	Magically (ABBR)
mg/cm	Milligram per Centimeter (COE)
MGCN	Magician (ABBR)
MGCO	Mars Geoscience/Climatology Orbiter
MGCOA	National Golf Course Owners Association (NTPA)
MGCR	Carmelita [*Guatemala*] [*ICAO location identifier*] (ICLI)
MGCR	Maritime Gas-Cooled Reactor
MGCRB	Medicare Geographic Classification Review Board
MGCR-CX	Maritime Gas-Cooled Reactor Critical Experiment
MGCS	Meteosat Ground Computer System [*Aviation*] (DA)
MGCS	Missile Guidance and Control System (MCD)
MGCS	Missile Guidance Cooling System (DWSG)
MGCT	Coatepeque [*Guatemala*] [*ICAO location identifier*] (ICLI)
MGCYL	Megacycle (ABBR)
MGD	Machine Gaming Division [*Queensland, Australia*]
MGD	Magadan [*Later, FUR*] [*Former USSR Geomagnetic observatory code*]
MGD	Magadan 1 [*Former USSR Seismograph station code, US Geological Survey*] (SEIS)
MGD	Magnetogasdynamic
MGD	Managed
MGD	Master of Graphic Design (PGP)
MGD	Maximal Glucose Disposal [*Medicine*] (DMAA)
MGD	Mean Gain Deviation (IEEE)
MG/D	Megagrams per Day
MGD	Mercury Germanium Detector
MGD	Miehle-Goss-Dexter [*Rockwell International Corp.*]
MGD	Military Geographic Documentation (AABC)
mg/d	Milligrams per Deciliter
MGD	Million Gallons per Day
MGD	Millions of Gallons per Day (COE)
MGD	Minority Group Designator [*Office of Personnel Management*] (GFGA)
MGD	Mixed Gonadal Dysgenesis [*Medicine*]
MGD	Molybdopterin Guanine Dinucleotide [*Biochemistry*]
MGD	Mouse Genome Database
MGD	Mugged (ABBR)
MGD	Murgold Resources, Inc. [*Toronto Stock Exchange symbol*]
MGD	North-East Cargo Airlines [*Russian Federation*] [*ICAO designator*] (FAAC)
MGDC	Morgan Grenfell Development Capital (WDAA)
MgdCare	Managed Care Solutions, Inc. [*Associated Press*] (SAG)
MGDF	Megakaryocyte Growth and Development Factor [*Cytology*]
MGDF	Modified Granular Diffusion Flame [*Propellant*]
MgdHi	Managed High-Income Income Portfolio [*Associated Press*] (SAG)
MgdMun	Managed Municipals Portfolio [*Associated Press*] (SAG)
MgdMun2	Managed Municipals Portfolio II [*Associated Press*] (SAG)
MGDS	Member in General Dental Surgery (DMAA)
MGDSRCS Eng	Membership in General Dental Surgery, Royal College of Surgeons of England [*British*] (DBQ)
MGE	Evergreen Regional Library, Gimli, Manitoba [*Library symbol National Library of Canada*] (NLC)
MGE	Maintenance Ground Equipment [*Formerly, GSF*]
MGE	Manage (ABBR)
MGE	Marge Enterprises [*Vancouver Stock Exchange symbol*]
MGE	Marietta, GA [*Location identifier FAA*] (FAAL)
MGE	Master of Geological Engineering (NADA)
MGE	Message (ADA)
MGE	Milwaukee Grain Exchange [*Defunct*]
MGE	Minneapolis Grain Exchange (EA)
MGE	Missile Guidance Element
MGE	Modular Geographic Environment
MGEB	Manageable (ABBR)
MGEBT	Manageability (ABBR)
MGEBY	Manageably (ABBR)
MGED	Managed (ABBR)
M Ge E	Master of Geological Engineering
M Ge Eng	Master of Geological Engineering
MGEG	Managing (ABBR)
mg-el	Milligram-Element (MAE)
MGEM	Modern Gun Effectiveness Model (MCD)
M GEN	Major General
MGEN	Micro General [*NASDAQ symbol*] (TTSB)
MGEN	Micro General Corp. [*NASDAQ symbol*] (NQ)
M Gen E	Master of General Engineering (PGP)
MGenStud	Master of General Studies (ADA)
MGENT	Management (ABBR)
M Geo E	Master of Geological Engineering (PGP)
M Geol E	Master of Geological Engineering
MGeolEng	Master of Geological Engineering (NADA)
MGER	Manager (ABBR)
MGERL	Managerial (ABBR)
MGES	Esquipulas [*Guatemala*] [*ICAO location identifier*] (ICLI)
MGES	Maintenance Ground Equipment Section
MGES	Multiple-Gated Equilibrium Scintigraphy (DB)
MGEUS	Maintenance Ground Equipment Utilization Sheets
Mgf	Free Magnesium

MGF	Macrophage Growth Factor (PDAA)
MGF	Magnify (MSA)
MGF	Maringa [*Brazil*] [*Airport symbol*] (OAG)
MGF	Mast-Cell Growth Factor [*Cytology*]
MGF	Maternal Grandfather (AAMN)
MGF	MFS Government Markets Income Trust [*NYSE symbol*] (SPSG)
MGF	MFS Gvt Mkts Income Tr [*NYSE symbol*] (TTSB)
MGF	Missionary Gospel Fellowship (EA)
MGF	Mobile Guerrilla Force [*Vietnam*]
MGF	Moment-Generating Function [*Mathematics*]
MGF	Motor-Generator Flywheel (MCD)
MGF	Myasthenia Gravis Foundation
MGF	Myoblast Growth Factor [*Biochemistry*]
MGF	Myxoma Growth Factor [*Biochemistry*]
MGFC	Mickey Gilley Fan Club [*Defunct*] (EA)
MGFE	Moment-Generating Function Estimator
MGFEL	Master Government-Furnished Equipment List (NVT)
MGFG	Magnifying
MGFL	Flores [*Guatemala*] [*ICAO location identifier*] (ICLI)
MGFS	Media General Financial Services, Inc. [*Information service or system*] (IID)
MGFZB	Mein Gott, Fueg Es zum Besten [*My God, Order It for the Best*] [*Motto of Sophie, consort of Georg Friedrich, Margrave of Brandenburg-Anspach (1563-1639)*] [*German*]
MGG	Machine Gun Guards [*British military*] (DMA)
MGG	Managing (ABBR)
MGG	May-Gruenwald-Giemsa [*A stain*] [*Hematology*]
MGG	Mega Gold Resources Ltd. [*Vancouver Stock Exchange symbol*]
MGG	Memory Gate Generator [*Computer science*]
MGG	MGM Grand [*NYSE symbol*] (TTSB)
MGG	MGM Grand, Inc. [*NYSE symbol*] (SPSG)
MGG	Missile Guidance Group
MGG	Monopropellant Gas Generator (PDAA)
MGG	Mouse Gamma-Globulin
MGG	Mugging (ABBR)
MGG	Musik in Geschichte und Gegenwart [*A publication*]
MGGB	Modular Guided Glide Bomb (MCD)
MGGH	Methylglyoxal Guanylhydrazone [*Antineoplastic drug*] (MAE)
MGGM	Mars General Circulation Model [*For planetary weather study*]
MGGS	Major General, General Staff
MGGT	Guatemala/La Aurora [*Guatemala*] [*ICAO location identifier*] (ICLI)
MGH	Margate [*South Africa*] [*Airport symbol*] (OAG)
MGH	Massachusetts General Hospital (DAVI)
MGH	Massachusetts General Hospital, Treadwell Library, Boston, MA [*OCLC symbol*] (OCLC)
mgh	Milligram Hour [*Pharmacy*]
MGH	Monoglyceride Hydrolase [*An enzyme*] (MAE)
MGH	Monumenta Germaniae Historica [*A publication*] (ODCC)
MGH	Morden & Helwig Group, Inc. [*Toronto Stock Exchange symbol*]
MGH	Museum of Garden History [*British*]
MgHiYld	Managed High Yield Fund [*Associated Press*] (SAG)
MGHT	Huehuetenango [*Guatemala*] [*ICAO location identifier*] (ICLI)
MGI	Gillam Municipal Library, Manitoba [*Library symbol National Library of Canada*] (NLC)
MGI	Macrophage and Granulocyte Inducer [*Biochemistry*]
MGI	Magnetics International Ltd. [*Toronto Stock Exchange symbol*]
MGI	Management Games Institute [*Raytheon Co.*]
MGI	Marine Geological Institute [*Indonesia*] [*Marine science*] (OSRA)
MGI	Matagorda Island, TX [*Location identifier FAA*] (FAAL)
MGI	Mavtech Holdings, Inc. [*Toronto Stock Exchange symbol*]
MGI	Medial Giant Interneuron [*Neurobiology*]
MGI	Member of the Gas Institute [*British*]
MGI	Member of the Institute of Certificated Grocers [*British*]
MGI	Metal Grating Institute [*Defunct*]
MGI	MGI Properties [*NYSE symbol*] (SPSG)
MGI	Microbial Genome Initiative (HGEN)
MGI	Military Geographic Information [*or Intelligence*] (MCD)
MGI	Mobile Gamma Irradiator [*Nuclear energy*]
MGI	Multigraphic Interface [*XOR Systems*]
MGIB	Management and Graduate Item Bank [*Reasoning skills test*]
MGIB	Montgomery GI Bill (INF)
MGIC	Magic Software Enterprises, Inc. [*NASDAQ symbol*] (SAG)
MGIC	MGIC Investment Co. [*Associated Press*] (SAG)
MGIC	Mortgage Guaranty Insurance Corp. [*Subsidiary of MGIC Investment Corp.*]
MGICF	Magic Software Enterprises [*NASDAQ symbol*] (TTSB)
MGID	Military Geographic Information and Documentation (AABC)
MGIKQ	Magic Restaurants [*NASDAQ symbol*] (TTSB)
MGIN	Margin (ROG)
MGINS	Mugginess (ABBR)
MGI Phr	MGI PHARMA, Inc. [*Associated Press*] (SAG)
MGI Prp	MGI Properties [*Associated Press*] (SAG)
MGIR	Motor Glider Instructor Rating [*Aviation*] (DA)
MGIWQ	Magic Restaurants Wrrt [*NASDAQ symbol*] (TTSB)
MGJ	Montgomery, NY [*Location identifier FAA*] (FAAL)
MGK	Michele Gold Mountain Ltd. [*Vancouver Stock Exchange symbol*]
MGk	Middle Greek [*Language*] (BARN)
MGK	Modern Greek [*Language, etc.*]
mg/kg	Milligrams per Kilogram (AAMN)
MGl	Gloucester Lyceum and Sawyer Free Public Library, Gloucester, MA [*Library symbol Library of Congress*] (LCLS)
MGL	Machine Gun LASER (MCD)
MGL	Magalia [*California*] [*Seismograph station code, US Geological Survey*] (SEIS)
MGL	Magellan Health Svcs [*AMEX symbol*] (TTSB)

MGL............. Magnanimous Green Leprechaun
MGL............. Malachite Green Leucocyanite (OA)
MGL............. Marginal (MSA)
MGL............. Matrix Generator Language [*Computer science*] (BUR)
mg/l............ Milligram per Liter (COE)
MG/L............ Milligrams per Liter
mg/L............ Milligrams per Liter (MEC)
MGL............. Mingle (ABBR)
MGL............. Missouri Gravity Low [*Geology*]
MGL............. Mogul
MGL............. Mongolian Airlines [*ICAO designator*] (FAAC)
MGL............. Mongrel (ABBR)
MGL............. Mono Gold Mines, Inc. [*Vancouver Stock Exchange symbol*]
MGL............. Monteagle, TN [*Location identifier FAA*] (FAAL)
MGL............. Move-Grow-Learn [*Program for visual perception development*]
MGLA........... Massachusetts General Laws Annotated [*A publication*]
M GLAM...... Mid Glamorgan [*County in Wales*]
MGLC........... Misty Mountain Gold Ltd. [*NASDAQ symbol*] (SAG)
MGLD.......... Mild General Learning Disability
MGLD.......... Mingled (ABBR)
MGLG.......... Mingling (ABBR)
MGIHi.......... Cape Ann Historical Association, Gloucester, MA [*Library symbol Library of Congress*] (LCLS)
MGLL........... La Libertad [*Guatemala*] [*ICAO location identifier*] (ICLI)
MGLMNA..... Megalomania (ABBR)
MGLMNAC... Megalomaniac (ABBR)
MGLP.......... Methylglucose Lipopolysaccharide [*Biochemistry*]
MGLPS........ Megalopolis (ABBR)
MGLY.......... Methylglyoxal [*Also, MG*] [*Organic chemistry*]
MGM........... Mailgram
MGM........... Master Group Multiplexer
MGM........... Maternal Grandmother (AAMN)
MGM........... Mayer's Ganz Mispocheh [*Mayer's Whole Family*] [*A Yiddish nickname for Metro-Goldwyn-Mayer, it reflects the tendency of early studio chiefs to hire their relatives and friends*]
MGM........... Mechanics of Granular Materials
MGM........... Medical Group Missions of the Christian Medical and Dental Society (EA)
MGM........... Member-Get-a-Member [*Marketing*] (WDMC)
MGM........... Metro-Goldwyn-Mayer [*Record label*] [*USA, Great Britain, etc.*]
MGM........... MGM Grand Air, Inc. [*ICAO designator*] (FAAC)
mgm........... Milligram
MGM........... Milligram (DFIT)
MGM........... Mobile-Launched Ground-Attack Missile
MGM........... Molecular and Genetic Medicine
MGM........... Montgomery [*Alabama*] [*Airport symbol*] (OAG)
MGM........... Morgain Minerals, Inc. [*Vancouver Stock Exchange symbol*]
MGM........... Mother's Grandmother (MAE)
MG/M²........ Megagrams per Square Meter
MG/M³........ Megagrams per Cubic Meter
mg/m₃........ Milligrams of Material per Cubic Meter of Air (GNE)
MGMA........ Magma (ABBR)
MGMA........ Medical Group Management Association (EA)
MGMA........ Metro Global Media [*NASDAQ symbol*] (TTSB)
MGMA........ Metro Global Media, Inc. [*NASDAQ symbol*] (SAG)
MG-MA....... Motor Generator-Motor Alternator (COE)
MGMC........ Multiple Gun Motor Carriage
MGMD........ Ministerial Group on the Misuse of Drugs [*British*]
MGMG........ MGM Grand, Inc. [*Associated Press*] (SAG)
MGMGMG.... Milwaukee and Greatlakes MG [*Morris Garage*] Motorcar Group
MGMI.......... Metallgezellschaft Metals Index [*British*] (NUMA)
MGMIS........ Medical Group Management Information Service [*Medical Group Management Association*] (DHSM)
MGML.......... Malacatan [*Guatemala*] [*ICAO location identifier*] (ICLI)
MGMM........ Melchor De Mencos [*Guatemala*] [*ICAO location identifier*] (ICLI)
MGMNT....... Management
MGMR......... Ministry of Geology and Mineral Resources [*China*]
MGMT......... Make Good a Magnetic Track of (Degrees) [*Aviation*] (FAAC)
MGMT......... Management
mgmt.......... Management (DD)
Mgmt......... Management (TBD)
Mgmt Forum... Management Forum [*A publication*]
MGN........... Magangue [*Colombia*] [*Airport symbol*] (AD)
MGN........... Magazine (ABBR)
MGN........... Magneto [*Generator*]
MGN........... Margin [*Accounting*]
MGN........... Medial Geniculate Nucleus [*Medicine*]
MGN........... Membranous Glomerulonephritis [*Nephrology*]
MGN........... Mendial Geniculate Nucleus (PDAA)
MGN........... Mengen [*Turkey*] [*Seismograph station code, US Geological Survey*] (SEIS)
MGN........... Micrograin (ABBR)
MGN........... Mirror Group Newspapers [*British*]
MGN........... Morgan Aviation Services Ltd. [*Nigeria*] [*ICAO designator*] (FAAC)
MGN........... Morgan Products Ltd. [*NYSE symbol*] (SPSG)
MGN........... Multigrounded Neutral [*Telecommunications*] (TEL)
Mgna.......... Magna-Lab, Inc. [*Associated Press*] (SAG)
MGNAN....... Margination (ABBR)
MGNES....... Metal Goods Not Elsewhere Specified [*Department of Employment*] [*British*]
MGNETC..... Magnetic (ABBR)
MGNETCY... Magnetically (ABBR)
MGNETMTR... Magnetometer (ABBR)
MGNETSM... Magnetism (ABBR)
MGNETZ...... Magnetization (ABBR)

MGNETZ...... Magnetize [*or Magnetized*] (ABBR)
MGNFI........ Magnify (ABBR)
MGNFIB...... Magnifiable (ABBR)
MGNFID...... Magnified (ABBR)
MGNFIG...... Magnifying (ABBR)
MGNFIN...... Magnification (ABBR)
MGNFIR...... Magnifier (ABBR)
MGNFNC..... Magnificence (ABBR)
MGNFNT..... Magnificent (ABBR)
MGNFTY..... Magnificently (ABBR)
MGNIA........ Marginalia (ABBR)
MGNL......... Magna Bancorp [*NASDAQ symbol*] (SAG)
MGNLT........ Marginality (ABBR)
MGNLY........ Marginally (ABBR)
MGNMT....... Magnanimity (ABBR)
MGNMU...... Magnanimous (ABBR)
MGNSM....... Magnesium [*Chemical symbol is Mg*]
MGNT......... Magnate (ABBR)
MGNT......... Magnet (ABBR)
MGNTC....... Magnetic
MGNTO....... Magneto
MGNTUD..... Magnitude (ABBR)
MGNTZD..... Magnetized
MGO........... Machine Gun Officer [*British military*] (DMA)
MGO........... Management by Goals and Objectives (MCD)
MGO........... Master General of the Ordnance [*Army British*]
MGO........... Master of Gynaecology and Obstetrics (ADA)
MGO........... Mato Grosso [*Brazil*] [*Airport symbol*] (AD)
MGO........... Megagauss-Oersted [*Magnetic field strength*]
MGO........... Military Government Officer
MGO........... Million Gauss Oersted [*Unit of energy density*]
MGO........... Mortgage Insurance Co. of Canada [*Toronto Stock Exchange symbol*]
MGOCC....... Morris Garage Octagon Car Club [*British*] (EAIO)
MGOe......... Megagauss-Oersted [*Also, MGO*] [*Magnetic field strength*]
MGOS......... Metal-Glass-Oxide-Silicon (PDAA)
MGOT......... Maggot (ABBR)
M GOTH..... Moeso-Gothic [*Language, etc.*] (ROG)
MGP........... Application for Mandamus Granted in Part [*Legal term*] (DLA)
MGP........... Macarthur Gruen Party [*Political party Australia*]
MG(P)........ Machinery of Government, Parliamentary Procedure [*British*]
MGP........... Maguayo [*Puerto Rico*] [*Seismograph station code, US Geological Survey*] (SEIS)
MGP........... Maintenance Ground Point
MGP........... Manga [*Papua New Guinea*] [*Airport symbol*] (OAG)
MGP........... Manufactured Gas Plant [*Environmental biotechnology*]
MGP........... Marginal Granulocyte Pool [*Hematology*]
MGP........... Mary Glawgow Publications [*Publisher*] [*British*]
MGP........... Membranous Glomerulopathy [*Medicine*] (DB)
MGP........... Merchants Group [*AMEX symbol*] (TTSB)
MGP........... Merchants Group, Inc. [*AMEX symbol*] (SPSG)
MGP........... Methylglucose Polysaccharide [*Biochemistry*]
MGP........... Methyl Green Pyronine [*A stain*]
MGP........... Micro-G Physics and Chemistry Experiments Group [*NASA*] (SSD)
MGP........... Monochrome Graphics Printer [*Computer science*] (CDE)
MGP........... Morrison-Grey Enterprises [*Vancouver Stock Exchange symbol*]
MGP........... Mountain Gorilla Project (EA)
MGP........... Mouvement Gaulliste Populaire [*Popular Gaullist Movement*] [*France Political party*] (PPW)
MGP........... Mucous Glycoproteins [*Biochemistry*]
MGP........... Multiple Goal Programming
MGP........... Museum of the Great Plains [*Lawton, OK*]
MGPB......... Puerto Barrios [*Guatemala*] [*ICAO location identifier*] (ICLI)
MGPC......... Grandview Personal Care Home, Manitoba [*Library symbol National Library of Canada*] (NLC)
MGPCU....... Missile Ground Power Control Unit (AAG)
M-GPD........ Million US Gallons per Day [*AEC, OSW*]
MGPF......... Multiprogram General-Purpose Facilities [*Oak Ridge National Laboratory*]
MGPGP...... Master of Group Process and Group Psychotherapy (PGP)
MGPHN...... Megaphone (ABBR)
MGPL......... Marine Gene Probe Laboratory [*Dalhousie University*] [*Canada*]
MGPP......... Poptun [*Guatemala*] [*ICAO location identifier*] (ICLI)
MGPPL....... Motor Glider Private Pilot's Licence [*British*] (AIA)
MGPR......... M.G. Products [*NASDAQ symbol*] (TTSB)
MGPR......... MG Products, Inc. [*NASDAQ symbol*] (SAG)
MG Prod..... MG Products, Inc. [*Associated Press*] (SAG)
MGQ........... Mogadishu [*Somalia*] [*Airport symbol*] (OAG)
MGQC......... Quiche [*Guatemala*] [*ICAO location identifier*] (ICLI)
MGQZ......... Quezaltenango [*Guatemala*] [*ICAO location identifier*] (ICLI)
MGR........... Machine Gun Regiment [*British military*] (DMA)
mgr............ Magister [*Master*] [*Latin*]
MGR........... Manager (AFM)
Mgr............ Manager (ODBW)
mgr............ Manager (DD)
MGR........... Marrow Granulocyte Reserves [*Hematology*]
MGR........... Medieval Greek [*Language, etc.*]
MGR........... Merry-Go-Round Entertainment (EFIS)
MGR........... Metal Glaze Resistor
MGR........... Method of Generated Responses [*Psychology*]
MGR........... Micro-Graphic Reporting (PDAA)
MGR........... Middlegate Resources, Inc. [*Vancouver Stock Exchange symbol*]
M GR.......... Middle Greek [*Language, etc.*] (ROG)
MGR........... Mixed Gas Rebreather
MGR........... Mobile-Launched Ground-Attack Rocket

MGR	Modified Gain Ratio [*Medicine*] (MAE)
MGR	Modular Gas-Cooled Reactor [*Developed by MIT*] [*Nuclear energy*]
MGR	Monsignor
Mgr	Monsignor (ODBW)
MGR	Moraga Resources Ltd. [*Vancouver Stock Exchange symbol*]
MGR	Moultrie, GA [*Location identifier FAA*] (FAAL)
MGR	Moultrie/Thomasville [*Georgia*] [*Airport symbol*] (OAG)
MGR	Mouvement de la Gauche Reformatrice [*Movement of the Reformist Left*] [*France Political party*] (PPW)
MGR	Mugger (ABBR)
MGR	Multiple Gas Rebreathing [*Medicine*] (DMAA)
MGR	Murmurs, Gallops, or Rubs [*Cardiology*] (DAVI)
MGRA	Major-General, Royal Artillery [*Army British*]
MGRA	Migrate (ABBR)
MGRAD	Migrated (ABBR)
MGRAG	Migrating (ABBR)
MGRAN	Migration (ABBR)
MGranbyS...	Saint Hyacinth College and Seminary, Granby, MA [*Library symbol Library of Congress*] (LCLS)
MGRATR	Migrator (ABBR)
MGRATRY	Migratory (ABBR)
MGRC	McGrath RentCorp [*NASDAQ symbol*] (NQ)
MGRC	Melbourne Greyhound Racing Club [*Australia*]
mgrd	Middleground (VRA)
MGREC	Magnetic Recorder [*or Recording*] (IAA)
MGrefC	Greenfield Community College, Greenfield, MA [*Library symbol Library of Congress*] (LCLS)
MGRESS	Manageress (ROG)
MGRGT	Modular Gas-Cooled Reactor Gas Turbine [*Developed by MIT*] [*Nuclear energy*]
MGRHS	May God Rest His Soul
MGRI	Mobile Ground Radio Installation
MGRL	Managerial (ABBR)
MGRM	Major-General, Royal Marines [*British military*] (DMA)
MGRM	Metallgesellschaft Refining & Marketing [*American subsidiary of the German commodities and futures contractor*] (ECON)
MGRM	Milligram (ROG)
MGRN	Migration (ABBR)
MGRNL	Migrational (ABBR)
MGRP	Minimum-Gradient Reaction Path [*Chemical kinetics*]
MGRS	Ferrocarriles Nacionales de Mexico [*AAR code*]
MGrS	Groton School, Groton, MA [*Library symbol Library of Congress*] (LCLS)
MGRS	Meter Gauge Rolling-Stock [*British*]
MGRS	Military Grid Reference System (AABC)
MGRT	Migrant (ABBR)
MGRT	Retalhuleu [*Guatemala*] [*ICAO location identifier*] (ICLI)
MGRTY	Migratory (ABBR)
MGRW	Matrix Generator and Report Writer [*Computer science*]
MGRY	Milgray Electronics [*NASDAQ symbol*] (TTSB)
MGRY	Milgray Electronics, Inc. [*NASDAQ symbol*] (NQ)
MGS	Machine Gun School [*British military*] (DMA)
MGS	Magellan Resources Corp. [*Vancouver Stock Exchange symbol*]
MGS	Mangaia [*Cook Islands*] [*Airport symbol*] (OAG)
MGS	Marine Geophysical Survey [*NOO*]
MGS	Mars Global Surveyor [*NASA*]
MGS	Master Gemology Society [*Defunct*] (EA)
MGS	Master of General Studies (GAGS)
MGS	Master of Gerontological Studies (GAGS)
MG's	Memphis Group [*In name of singing group "Booker T and the MG's"*]
MGS	Metal Gravel Stop
MGS	Metre-Gram-Second
MGS	Metrogas SA [*NYSE symbol*] (SAG)
MGS	MetroGas S.A. CI'B'ADS [*NYSE symbol*] (TTSB)
MGS	Microcomputer Graphic System
MGS	Middleton Gardens [*South Carolina*] [*Seismograph station code, US Geological Survey*] (SEIS)
MGS	Midwestern Gilbert and Sullivan Society (EA)
MGS	Military Government Section [*World War II*]
MGS	Missile Guidance Section [*or Set, or System*]
MGS	Mission Ground Station (MCD)
MGS	Mobile Gas Service Corp. (EFIS)
MGS	Mobile Ground System
MGS	Moment Gyro System
MGS	Motor Generator Set (CAAL)
MGSA	Marriage Guidance South Australia
MGSA	Melanoma Growth Stimulatory Activity [*Biochemistry*]
MGSA	Military General Supply Agency [*Merged with Defense General Supply Center*]
MGSA	Modern Greek Studies Association (EA)
MGSC	Missile Guidance Set Control
MGSCD	Martha Graham School of Contemporary Dance [*New York, NY*]
MGSE	Maintenance Ground Support Equipment
MGSE	Mechanical Ground Support Equipment
MGSE	Missile Ground Support Equipment
MGSE	Mobile Ground Support Equipment
MGSE-ECM...	Maintenance Ground Support Equipment-Environmental Controls and Mechanisms (SAA)
MGSGT	Master Gunnery Sergeant [*Marine Corps*] (DNAB)
MGSIUF	Marquis Giuseppe Sciclunal International University Foundation (EA)
MGSJ	San Jose [*Guatemala*] [*ICAO location identifier*] (ICLI)
MGSM	San Marcos [*Guatemala*] [*ICAO location identifier*] (ICLI)
MGSpS	Guadalupan Missionaries of the Holy Spirit (TOCD)
MGSS	Manned Geosynchronous Spacecraft Servicer (SSD)

MGST	Miles [*Multiple Integrated Laser Engagement System*] Gunnery Skills Test [*USA*]
MGST	Military Geography Specialist Team
MGSTL	Magisterial (ABBR)
MGSTRA	Magistrate (ABBR)
MGT	Magenta Development Corp. [*Vancouver Stock Exchange symbol*]
MGT	Major Ground Test (NASA)
MGT	Management (AFM)
Mgt	Management (AL)
MGT	Margate Air Services [*South Africa ICAO designator*] (FAAC)
MGT	Master-Group Translator [*Telecommunications*] (TEL)
MGT	Master of Gas Technology (GAGS)
MGT	Megaton [*Nuclear equivalent of one million tons of high explosive*] (AAG)
MGT	Meteorological and Geoastrophysical Titles
MGT	Millingimbi [*Airport symbol*]
MGT	Mobile [*Truck-Mounted*] Ground Terminal
MGT	Movie Going Time
MGTANALYSO...	Management Analysis Officer [*Air Force*]
MGTAV	Modern Greek Teachers' Association of Victoria [*Australia*]
MGTENGR....	Management Engineer [*Air Force*]
MGTI	Member of the Gymnastic Teachers' Institute [*British*] (ROG)
MGTIR	Mightier (ABBR)
mgtis	Meningitis [*Medicine*] (MAE)
MGTIST	Mightiest (ABBR)
MGTMTR	Magnetometer
MGTNS	Mightiness (ABBR)
MGTO	Mexican Government Tourism Office (EA)
MgtTch	Management Technologies, Inc. [*Associated Press*] (SAG)
MGTY	Mighty (ABBR)
MGU	Main-Group Ureilite [*Meteorite component*]
MGU	MGM Resources Corp. [*Vancouver Stock Exchange symbol*]
MGU	Midcourse Guidance Unit [*Navy*] (CAAL)
MGU	Military Government Unit
MGU	[*The*] Mobile & Gulf Railroad Co. [*Later, MG*] [*AAR code*]
MGU	Moskovskiy Gosudarstvenniy Universitet [*Moscow State University*] [*Former USSR*] (MSC)
MGUN	Marine Gunner
MGUS	Monoclonal Gammopathies of Undetermined Significance [*Medicine*] (DMAA)
MGV	Mechanically-Guided Vehicle
MGV	Miniature Gate Valve
MGV	Monogram Oil & Gas, Inc. [*Vancouver Stock Exchange symbol*]
MGVC	Manual Governing Valve Control [*Nuclear energy*] (NRCH)
MGVT	Mated Ground Vibration Test (NASA)
MGVT	Montgomery [*Vermont*] [*Seismograph station code, US Geological Survey*] (SEIS)
MGW	Magnesium Sulfate, Glycerine, and Water (Enema) [*Medicine*]
MGW	Maximum Gross Weight (WDAA)
MGW	Mission Gross Weight
MGW	Morgantown [*West Virginia*] [*Airport symbol*] (OAG)
MGW	Morgantown, WV [*Location identifier FAA*] (FAAL)
MGWA	Marriage Guidance Western Australia
MGWR	Midland Great Western Railway [*British*] (ROG)
MGWS	Modular Guided Weapon System (MCD)
MGX	Moabi [*Gabon*] [*Airport symbol*] (OAG)
MGX	Mossimo, Inc. [*NYSE symbol*] (SAG)
MGXI	Micrografx, Inc. [*NASDAQ symbol*] (SAG)
M-GXT	Multistage Graded Exercise Test [*Cardiology*] (DAVI)
MGY	Dayton, OH [*Location identifier FAA*] (FAAL)
MGY	Mega-Dyne Industrial Corp. [*Vancouver Stock Exchange symbol*]
MGY	Muggy (ABBR)
MGYSGT	Master Gunnery Sergeant [*Marine Corps*]
MGZ	Maschinengewehr-Zieleinrichtung [*Machine-Gun Sighting Mechanism*] [*German military - World War II*]
MGZ	Mayaguez [*Diocesan abbreviation*] [*Puerto Rico*] (TOCD)
MGZ	Mergui [*Myanmar*] [*Airport symbol*] (OAG)
MGZF	Maschinengewehr-Zielfernrohr [*Machine-Gun Telescopic Sight*] [*German military - World War II*]
MH	Air-Cushion Vehicle built by Mitsubishi [*Japan*] [*Usually used in combination with numerals*]
MH	[*A*] Grammar of Masoretic Hebrew [*A publication*] (BJA)
MH	Ha-Mo'atsah ha-Hakla'it (BJA)
MH	Harvard University, Cambridge, MA [*Library symbol Library of Congress*] (LCLS)
mh	Macao [*MARC country of publication code Library of Congress*] (LCCP)
MH	Magnetic Head [*or Heading*]
MH	Magnetite-Hematite [*Geology*]
MH	Mail Handler [*Computer science*]
MH	Main Hatch
MH	Maintenance Handbook
MH	Maintenance Hemodialysis [*Nephrology*] (CPH)
MH	Makkabi Hazair (BJA)
MH	Malaysia Airlines [*Airline flight code*] (ODBW)
MH	Malaysian Airline System [*ICAO designator*] (AD)
MH	Malden Hospital [*Malden, MA*]
MH	Maleic Hydrazide [*Plant growth regulator*]
MH	Malignant Histiocytosis [*Medicine*]
MH	Malignant Hyperpyrexia [*Medicine*]
MH	Malignant Hypertension [*Medicine*] (DMAA)
MH	Malignant Hyperthermia [*Medicine*]
MH	Malt House
MH	Mammotropic Hormone [*Endocrinology*]
MH	Manhole (AAG)

MH	Man-Hour (MCD)
MH	Mannoheptulose (DB)
MH	Manual Hold [*Telecommunications*]
MH	Manufactured Housing (PA)
MH	Manufacturers Hanover Corp. (EFIS)
MH	Mare Humorum [*Sea of Moisture*] [*Lunar area*]
MH	Marital History
MH	Marshall Islands [*ANSI two-letter standard code*] (CNC)
M-H	Martini-Henry [*Rifle*]
MH	Masonic Hall (ROG)
MH	Master Herbalist
MH	Master Hosts [*An association Defunct*] (EA)
MH	Master of Hamburgerology [*McDonald's Corp. Hamburger University*]
MH	Master of Harriers [*British*] (WDAA)
MH	Master of Health (GAGS)
MH	Master of Horticulture
MH	Master of Hounds [*British*]
MH	Master of Humanics
MH	Master of Humanities (GAGS)
MH	Master of Hygiene
MH	Master of the Horse [*British*] (ROG)
MH	Master of the Hunt
MH	Materials Handling (NATG)
MH	Maximum Height [*Ballistics*]
M-H	McGraw-Hill (NITA)
MH	Mechanical Handling [*Describes type of produce; for example, MH-1 refers to a kind of tomato*]
MH	Medal of Honor [*Often erroneously called Congressional Medal of Honor*] [*Military decoration*]
MH	Medial Hypothalamus [*Medicine*] (DMAA)
MH	Medical History
MH	Megahertz [*Megacycles per second*] [*See also MCPS, MCS, MC/S, MHZ*] (NATG)
Mh	Mehri (BJA)
MH	Melanophore Hormone [*Also, MSH*] [*Endocrinology*]
MH	Melanophore-Stimulating Hormone [*Medicine*] (DMAA)
MH	Mended Hearts (EA)
MH	Menstrual History [*Medicine*]
MH	Mental Health
MH	Mental Hygiene (DMAA)
MH	Mentally Handicapped (AIE)
MH	Merchants Haulage (DS)
MH	Mercurihematoporphyrin [*Pharmacology*]
MH	Meristem Height [*Botany*]
MH	MeSH Heading [*Online database field identifier*]
MH	Message Handler [*Computer science*]
MH	Metal Halide (MCD)
M/H	Meters per Hour
M/H	Microcytic/Hypochromic [*Anemia*] [*Hematology*] (DAVI)
MH	Microhematuria [*Medicine*]
MH	Middlesex Hussars (Duke of Cambridge's) [*British military*] (DMA)
M/H	Miles per Hour [*Also, MPH*]
MH	Military History (AABC)
MH	Military Hospital (ADA)
mH	Millihenry (GPO)
mH	Millihour [*One-thousandth of an hour*] (AAG)
MH	Ministry of Health [*British*]
M-H	Minneapolis-Honeywell Regulator Co. [*Later, HON*]
MH	Miscellaneous Hardware
MH	Mishnaic Hebrew [*Language, etc.*] (BJA)
MH	Mitsubishi Heavy Industries Ltd. [*Japan ICAO aircraft manufacturer identifier*] (ICAO)
MH	Mobile High-Power [*Reactor*] [*Proposed*] (NRCH)
MH	Mobile Home (WGA)
MH	Mobility Haiti (EA)
MH	Moist Heat (STED)
MH	Molting Hormone [*Endocrinology, entomology*]
MH	Monosymptomatic Hypochondriasis [*Medicine*] (DMAA)
MH	Most High [*Freemasonry*]
MH	Most Honorable
MH	Mount Hood Railway Co. [*AAR code*]
M-H	Mueller-Hinton [*Agar*] [*Microbiology*]
MH	Mulberry Heart (OA)
MH	Multihandicapped
MH	Multiple Handicapped (STED)
MH	Murine Hepatitis
MH	Music Hall [*Record label*]
MH	Mutant Hybrid [*Medicine*] (DMAA)
MH	Muzzle Hatch
MH	Myohyoid [*Medicine*] (DMAA)
MH2	Mary Hartman, Mary Hartman [*Initialism is shortened form of television program title*] [*Also, M²H²*]
MHA	Hamline University, St. Paul, MN [*OCLC symbol*] (OCLC)
MH-A	Harvard University, Arnold Arboretum, Cambridge, MA [*Library symbol Library of Congress*] (LCLS)
MHa	Haverhill Public Library, Haverhill, MA [*Library symbol Library of Congress*] (LCLS)
MHA	Machinery Haulers Association Agent, Saint Paul MN [*STAC*]
MHA	Madonna House Apostolate [*Combermere, ON*] (EAIO)
MHA	Mahdia [*Guyana*] [*Airport symbol*] (OAG)
MHA	Maintenance Hazard Analysis (MCD)
MHA	Man-Hour Accounting (NVT)
MHA	Manila Hemp Association [*British*] (DBA)
MHA	Mansion House Association on Transport, Inc. [*British*] (BI)
MHA	Marine Historical Association [*Later, MSM*] (EA)

MHA	Masonry Heather Association of North America (NTPA)
MHA	Master of Health Administration
MHA	Master of Hospital Administration
MHA	Material Handling Area
MHA	Maximum Hypothetical Accident [*Nuclear energy*] (IEEE)
MHA	Mean Horizontal Acceleration
MHA	Meat Hygiene Authority [*Australia*]
MHA	Medal for Humane Action [*Berlin Airlift, 1948-9*] [*Military decoration*]
MHA	Member of House of Assembly [*British*]
MHA	Mennonite Health Association (EA)
MHA	Mental Health Abstracts [*Database*] [*IFI/Plenum Data Co.*] [*Information service or system*] (CRD)
MHA	Mental Health Administration [*Later, ADAMHA*]
MHA	Mental Health Analysis [*Psychology*] (AEBS)
MHA	Mental Health Association [*Later, NMHA*] (EA)
MHA	Mental Health Authority (NADA)
MHA	Methemalbumin [*Medicine*] (MAE)
MHA	Methionine Hydroxy Analog [*Poultry feed*]
MHA	Methodist Homes for the Aged [*British*] (BI)
MHA	Microangiopathic Hemolytic Anemia [*Medicine*]
MHA	Microhemagglutination [*Test for Syphilis*] [*Immunochemistry*] (DAVI)
MHA	Military Health Affairs (DOMA)
MHA	Minehunter, Auxiliary [*Navy symbol Obsolete*]
MHA	Minimum Holding Altitude [*Aviation*]
MHA	Mixed Hemadsorption Assay [*Clinical chemistry*]
MHA	Modified Handling Authorized [*Air Force*]
MHA	Mormon History Association (EA)
MHA	Mountain High Aviation [*ICAO designator*] (FAAC)
MHA	Mueller Hinton Agar [*Microbiology*] (OA)
MHA	Multiple Handicapped Association (NADA)
MHA	Multiple Headset Adapter [*Aerospace*] (NAKS)
MHA	Mutual Households Associations Ltd. [*British*] (BI)
MH-AA	Harvard University, Afro-American Studies, Lamont Undergraduate Library, Cambridge, MA [*Library symbol Library of Congress*] (LCLS)
MHAC	Man-Hour Accounting Card
MHAC	Multifrequency High-Gain Antenna Configuration (SSD)
MHadP	Porter-Phelps-Hunting Foundation, Hadley, MA [*Library symbol*] [*Library of Congress*] (LCLS)
MH-AH	Harvard University, Andover-Harvard Theological Library, Cambridge, MA [*Library symbol Library of Congress*] (LCLS)
MHAM	Amapala [*Honduras*] [*ICAO location identifier*] (ICLI)
MHAM	Multiple Hamartoma [*Medicine*] (DMAA)
MHAMS	Master of Historical Administration and Museum Studies (GAGS)
MHaNE	Northern Essex Community College, Haverhill, MA [*Library symbol Library of Congress*] (LCLS)
MHansAF	United States Air Force Research Library, Hanscom Air Force Base, Hanscom, MA [*Library symbol Library of Congress*] (LCLS)
MH-AO	Harvard University, Oakes Ames Orchid Library, Cambridge, MA [*Library symbol Library of Congress*] (LCLS)
MHAQ	Material Handling Association of Quebec (AC)
MHar	Brooks Free Library, Harwich, MA [*Library symbol*] [*Library of Congress*] (LCLS)
MH-Ar	Harvard University Archives, Cambridge, MA [*Library symbol Library of Congress*] (LCLS)
MH-AS	Harvard University, George R. Agassiz Station, Cambridge, MA [*Library symbol Library of Congress*] (LCLS)
MHAS	Man-Hour Accounting System (DNAB)
MHathD	Danvers State Hospital, Hathorne, MA [*Library symbol Library of Congress*] (LCLS)
MHA-TP	Microhemagglutination Assay Treponema Pallidum [*Immunochemistry*]
MHAUS	Malignant Hyperthermia Association of the United States (EA)
MHAWA	Master Hairdressers' Association of Western Australia
MHB	Maintenance Handbook
MHB	Mary Hardin-Baylor College, Belton, TX [*OCLC symbol*] (OCLC)
MHB	Master Horizontal Bomber
MHB	Maximum Hospital Benefit [*Medicine*] (DMAA)
MHb	Medial Habenular [*Neuroanatomy*]
MHb	Methemoglobin [*Biochemistry, medicine*]
MHb	Methemoglobin [*Immunochemistry*] (DAVI)
MHB	Military History Branch [*USMACV*]
MHB	Mine-Hauling Bogie [*Mining engineering*]
MHB	Mueller-Hinton Base (DMAA)
MHB	Mueller-Hinton Broth [*Cell growth medium*]
MHb	Myohemoglobin [*Hematology*]
MH-BA	Harvard University, Graduate School of Business Administration, Boston, MA [*Library symbol Library of Congress*] (LCLS)
MHBA	Morgan Horse Breeders Association [*Defunct*] (EA)
MH-BH	Harvard University, Blue Hill Meteorological Observatory, Cambridge, MA [*Library symbol Library of Congress*] (LCLS)
MH-BL	Harvard University, Biological Laboratories, Cambridge, MA [*Library symbol Library of Congress*] (LCLS)
MH-BM	Harvard University, George David Birkhoff Mathematics Library, Cambridge, MA [*Library symbol Library of Congress*] (LCLS)
MHBM	Modern Heavy Ballistic Missile (ADA)
MHBN	Mothers' Home Business Network (EA)
MH-BR	Harvard University, Busch-Reisinger Museum of Germanic Culture, Cambridge, MA [*Library symbol Library of Congress*] (LCLS)
MH-BS	Harvard University, Biochemical Sciences Tutorial Library, Cambridge, MA [*Library symbol Library of Congress*] (LCLS)
MHBSS	Modified Hank's Balanced Salt Solution [*Cell culture*]
MH-C	Harvard University, Chemistry Library, Cambridge, MA [*Library symbol Library of Congress*] (LCLS)
MHC	Historical Committee of the Mennonite Church (EA)

MHC............	MAD [*Magnetic Anomaly Detector*] Hunting Circle (NVT)
MHC............	Madras High Court Reports [*India*] [*A publication*] (DLA)
MHC............	Major Histocompatibility Complex [*Immunology*]
MHC............	Manipulator Hand Controller [*Aerospace*] (NAKS)
MHC............	Manipulator Handset Controller (MCD)
MHC............	Manufactured Home Communities [*NYSE symbol*] (SPSG)
MHC............	Manufacturers Hanover Corp. (EFIS)
MHC............	Mars Hill College [*North Carolina*]
MHC............	Mary Holmes College, West Point, MS [*OCLC symbol*] (OCLC)
MHC............	Material Handling Crane [*Autocrane*] (MCD)
MHC............	Mean Horizontal Candle [*Aerospace*]
MHC............	Mechanical-Hydraulic Control [*Nuclear energy*] (NRCH)
MHC............	Mental Health Care [*British*] (DAVI)
MHC............	Mental Health Center (MEDA)
MHC............	Mental Health Clinic (DAVI)
MHC............	Mental Health Course [*British*]
MHC............	Mild Hydrocracking [*Petroleum technology*]
MHC............	Minehunter, Coastal [*Navy symbol*]
MHC............	Mobile Housing Carriers Conference Inc., Arlington VA [*STAC*]
MHC............	Modified Huffman Coding (NITA)
MHC............	Moisture Holding Capacity
MHC............	Morgan Horse Club [*Later, American Morgan Horse Association*] (EA)
MHC............	Morris Harvey College [*West Virginia*]
MHC............	Mount Hamilton [*Lick Observatory*] [*California*] [*Seismograph station code, US Geological Survey*] (SEIS)
MHC............	Mount Holyoke College [*South Hadley, MA*]
MHC............	Multiphasic Health Checkup [*Medicine*] (AAMN)
MHC............	Myosin Heavy Chain [*Muscle biology*]
MHCA.........	Catacamas [*Honduras*] [*ICAO location identifier*] (ICLI)
MHCA.........	Master of Health Care Administration (GAGS)
MHC & W....	Mississippi, Hill City & Western Railroad
MHCAT........	Minehunter Catamaran [*Military*]
MHCC.........	Mobile Housing Carriers Conference [*Defunct*] (EA)
MHCC.........	Multipak Heliax Coaxial Cable
MH/CD........	Mental Health/Chemical Dependency
MH-CE........	Harvard University, Commission on Extension Courses, Cambridge, MA [*Library symbol Library of Congress*] (LCLS)
MH-CE........	Materials Handling and Construction Equipment (DNAB)
MHCG.........	Comayagua [*Honduras*] [*ICAO location identifier*] (ICLI)
MHCH.........	Choluteca [*Honduras*] [*ICAO location identifier*] (ICLI)
MH-CI.........	Harvard University, Center for International Affairs, Semitic Museum, Cambridge,MA [*Library symbol Library of Congress*] (LCLS)
MHCI..........	Master of Human-Computer Interaction (PGP)
MHCIMA......	Member of the Hotel, Catering, and Institutional Management Association [*British*] (DBQ)
MH-CL........	Harvard University, Career Reference Library, Cambridge, MA [*Library symbol Library of Congress*] (LCLS)
MH-CM.......	Harvard University, Child Memorial and English Tutorial Library, Cambridge, MA [*Library symbol Library of Congress*] (LCLS)
MHCO.........	Marquette & Huron Mountain Railroad Co., Inc. [*AAR code*]
MHCO.........	Mine-Hunting Control Officer (NATG)
MHCO.........	Moore-Handley, Inc. [*Birmingham, AL*] [*NASDAQ symbol*] (NQ)
MHCOA......	Motor, Hearse, and Car Owners Association (EA)
MH-CP........	Harvard University, Center for Population Studies, Boston, MA [*Library symbol Library of Congress*] (LCLS)
MHCP.........	Mean Horizontal Candlepower
MHCR.........	Madras High Court Reports [*India*] [*A publication*] (DLA)
MH-CS........	Harvard University, Godfrey Lowell Cabot Science Library, Cambridge, MA [*Library symbol Library of Congress*] (LCLS)
MHCS.........	Mental Hygiene Consultation Service
M/hct.........	Microhematocrit [*Clinical chemistry*]
MHCT.........	Modified Human Calcitonin (DB)
MHCT.........	Puerto Castilla [*Honduras*] [*ICAO location identifier*] (ICLI)
MHCU.........	Mental Health Care Unit [*Medicine*]
MHD..........	Magnetohydrodynamic [*Simulation*] [*Marine science*] (OSRA)
MHD..........	Magnetohydrodynamics [*Electric power*]
MHD..........	Maintenance Hemodialysis [*Medicine*] (DMAA)
MHD..........	Mashhad [*Iran*] [*Airport symbol*] (OAG)
MHD..........	Master of Human Development (PGP)
MHD..........	Masthead (MSA)
MHD..........	Mean Hemolytic Dose [*Pharmacology*] (MAE)
MHD..........	Mechanized Hebrew Dictionary [*A publication*] (BJA)
MHD..........	Medical Holding Detachment
MHD..........	Medium Hard Drawn (MSA)
MHD..........	Mental Health Department [*Medicine*]
MHD..........	Mental Health Digest
MHD..........	Meshed [*Iran*] [*Airport symbol*] (AD)
MHD..........	Meter Heading Differential
MHD..........	Military History Detachment
MHD..........	Minimal Hemolytic Dose [*Medicine*] (LDT)
MHD..........	Minimum Hamming Distance [*Computer science*]
MHD..........	Minimum Hemolytic Dilution [*Medicine*] (DMAA)
MHD..........	Minimum Hemolytic Dose
MHD..........	Movable Head Disc (NITA)
MHD..........	Moving Head Disk [*Computer science*] (TEL)
MHD..........	Multihead Disk (NASA)
MHD..........	Multiple Head Disc (NITA)
MHDA.........	Modified High-Density Acid (MCD)
MHDC.........	Magnetohydrodynamic Conversion [*Nuclear energy*] (NRCH)
MHDDE......	Medium Heavy-Duty Diesel Engine [*Motor vehicle specifications*]
MHDF.........	Medium- and High-Frequency Direction-Finding Station
MHDG.........	Magnetohydrodynamic Generator (PDAA)
MHDI..........	Morgan Horse Development Institute [*Defunct*] (EA)

MH-DJ.........	Harvard University, Documentation Center on Contemporary Japan, Cambridge, MA [*Library symbol*] [*Library of Congress*] (LCLS)
MHDL.........	Magnetohydrodynamic LASER (PDAA)
MHDNA......	Mobile Home Dealers National Association [*Defunct*]
MH-DO.......	Harvard University, Harvard University Development Office, Cambridge, MA [*Library symbol*] [*Library of Congress*] (LCLS)
MHDPA......	Monohexadecylphosphoric Acid [*Organic chemistry*]
MHDSRIP ...	May His Departed Soul Rest in Peace (BJA)
MHDU........	Medical Hemodialysis Unit [*Nephrology*] (DAVI)
MHE..........	Maintenance and Handling Equipment
MHE..........	Manufactured Home Estates
MHE..........	Mass Health & Education Tax-Exempt [*AMEX symbol*] (SPSG)
MHE..........	Mass Hlth & Edu Tax-Exempt Tr [*AMEX symbol*] (TTSB)
MHE..........	Master of Health Education (GAGS)
MHE..........	Master of Higher Education (GAGS)
MHE..........	Master of Highway Engineering (NADA)
MHE..........	Master of Home Economics (GAGS)
MHE..........	Master of Home Economics Engineering (NADA)
MHE..........	Master of Human Ecology (PGP)
MHE..........	Materials Handling Equipment [*Military*] (AFM)
MHE..........	Materiel Handling Equipment [*Army*] (INF)
MHE..........	Mean Hook Extent (PDAA)
MHE..........	Mechanical Handling Equipment (MCD)
MHE..........	Mental Health Enquiry [*Medical/computing registers*] [*British*]
MHE..........	Missile Handling Equipment
MHE..........	Mitchell [*South Dakota*] [*Airport symbol*] (OAG)
MHE..........	Mitchell, SD [*Location identifier FAA*] (FAAL)
MHE..........	Multiple Headspace Extraction [*Analytical chemistry*]
MHE..........	Munitions Handling Equipment (MCD)
MHE..........	Muzzle Hatch Electrical
MH-EA........	Harvard University, East Asian Research Center, Cambridge, MA [*Library symbol Library of Congress*] (LCLS)
MHEA.........	Mechanical Handling Engineers' Association [*British*] (BI)
MHealthAdmin...	Master of Health Administration (ADA)
MHEANA.....	Masonic Homes Executives' Association of North America (EA)
MH-EB........	Harvard University, Oakes Ames Library of Economic Botany, Cambridge, MA [*Library symbol Library of Congress*] (LCLS)
MHeb..........	Middle Hebrew [*Language, etc.*] (BJA)
MH Ec........	Master of Home Economics (PGP)
MHEC.........	Muzzle Hatch Electrical Control
MH-Ed	Harvard University, Graduate School of Education, Cambridge, MA [*Library symbol Library of Congress*] (LCLS)
MHEd..........	Master of Health Education (GAGS)
MHEd..........	Master of Higher Education
MHEDA......	Material Handling Equipment Distributors Association (EA)
MHEE.........	Master of Home Economics Education (NADA)
MHEEd.......	Master of Home Economics Education (NADA)
MHEF.........	Milton H. Erickson Foundation (EA)
MHEG.........	Multimedia and Hypermedia Expert Group (TELE)
MHEO........	Migrant Health Education Officer [*Australia*]
MH-ER........	Harvard University, East Asian Studies Reading Room, Cambridge, MA [*Library symbol Library of Congress*] (LCLS)
MH-ES	Harvard University, Center for European Studies, Cambridge, MA [*Library symbol Library of Congress*] (LCLS)
MHET.........	Monolithic Hot Electron Transistor (NITA)
MHEX........	Methohexital [*An anesthetic*]
MH-F	Harvard University, Farlow Reference Library, Cambridge, MA [*Library symbol Library of Congress*] (LCLS)
MHF..........	Master History File
MHF..........	Medium-High Frequency
MHF..........	Meridian House Foundation [*Later, MHI*]
MHF..........	Microsillon et Haute-Fidelite [*Record label*] [*France*]
MHF..........	Mixed Hydrazine Fuel
MHF..........	Municipal High Care [*NYSE symbol*] (TTSB)
MHF..........	Municipal High Income Fund, Inc. [*NYSE symbol*] (CTT)
MHF..........	Muni High Income Fund (EFIS)
MHF..........	Myosin Head Fragment [*Biochemistry*]
MHF..........	Smith Point, TX [*Location identifier FAA*] (FAAL)
MH-FA........	Harvard University, Fine Arts Library, Cambridge, MA [*Library symbol Library of Congress*] (LCLS)
MHFA.........	Multiple Conductor, Heat and Flame Resistant, Armor [*Cable*]
MHFB.........	Mental Health Film Board (EA)
MHFC.........	Merle Haggard Fan Club (EA)
MH/FH	Man-Hours per Flying Hour [*Air Force*] (DNAB)
MHFPR......	Maximum Hypothetical Fission Product Release [*Nuclear energy*] (NRCH)
MHFR........	Maximum Hypothetical Fission Product Release [*Nuclear energy*] (NRCH)
MHF(V)......	Mental Health Foundation (Victoria) [*Australia*]
MHFWPR...	Mental Health Fieldwork Performance Report [*Occupational therapy*]
MH-G	Harvard University, Gray Herbarium, Cambridge, MA [*Library symbol Library of Congress*] (LCLS)
MHG	Mahogany (WGA)
MHG	Malartic Hygrade Gold Mines Ltd. (MHDW)
MHG	Mannheim [*Germany Airport symbol*] (OAG)
MHG	MDS Health Group Ltd. [*Toronto Stock Exchange symbol*]
MHG	Message Header Generator (PDAA)
MHG	Metropolitan Health Group (DMAA)
MHG	Middle High German [*Language, etc.*]
MHG	Midrash ha-Gadol (BJA)
mHg	Millimeters of Mercury [*A measurement of pressure*] (MAE)
MHG	Miniature Hydrogen Generator
MHG	Modern High German [*Language, etc.*] (ROG)

MH-GG......... Harvard University, Committee on Experimental Geology and Geophysics, Hoffman Laboratory, Cambridge, MA [*Library symbol Library of Congress*] (LCLS)

MH-GI......... Harvard University, Hamilton A. R. Gibb Islamic Seminar, Cambridge, MA [*Library symbol Library of Congress*] (LCLS)

MH-GM....... Harvard University, Gordon McKay Library, Cambridge, MA [*Library symbol Library of Congress*] (LCLS)

MH-GS........ Harvard University, Geological Sciences Library, Cambridge, MA [*Library symbol Library of Congress*] (LCLS)

MH-H.......... Harvard University, Houghton Library, Cambridge, MA [*Library symbol Library of Congress*] (LCLS)

MHH .... Mandala Holistic Health [*Defunct*] (EA)

MH-H........... Mare Humorum-Helmet [*Lunar area*]

MHH .... Marsh Harbour [*Bahamas*] [*Airport symbol*] (OAG)

MH-HD........ Harvard University, History Department Library, Cambridge, MA [*Library symbol Library of Congress*] (LCLS)

MH-HF........ Harvard University, Harvard Forest Library, Petersham, MA [*Library symbol Library of Congress*] (LCLS)

MHHFC ...... Machine and Hull History File Card (DNAB)

MH-Hi......... Harvard University, Hilles Library of Radcliffe College, Cambridge, MA [*Library symbol Library of Congress*] (LCLS)

MHHI .... Multihandicapped Hearing-Impaired

MH-HJ .... Harvard University, Arnold Arboretum, Horticultural Library, Jamaica Plain, MA [*Library symbol Library of Congress*] (LCLS)

MH-HO........ Harvard University, Lucien Howe Library of Ophthalmology, Boston, MA [*Library symbol Library of Congress*] (LCLS)

MH-HP........ Harvard University, Center for Analysis of Health Practices, Cambridge, MA [*Library symbol Library of Congress*] (LCLS)

MHHPA ...... Methylhexahydrophthalic Anhydride [*Organic chemistry*]

MH-HS........ Harvard University, History of Science Library, Cambridge, MA [*Library symbol Library of Congress*] (LCLS)

MHHS .... Medal of Honor Historical Society (EA)

MHHW .... Mean Higher High Water [*Tides and currents*]

MHHWS...... Mean Higher High-Water Springs [*Tides and currents*]

MH-HY........ Harvard University, Harvard-Yenching Library, Cambridge, MA [*Library symbol Library of Congress*] (LCLS)

MHI .... Malignant Histiocytosis of Intestine [*Medicine*] (DMAA)

MHI .... Manufactured Housing Insitute (WPI)

MHI .... Manufactured Housing Institute (EA)

MHI .... Marine Hydrophysical Institute

MHI .... Mashhad [*Iran*] [*Seismograph station code, US Geological Survey*] (SEIS)

MHi .... Massachusetts Historical Society, Boston, MA [*Library symbol Library of Congress*] (LCLS)

MHI .... Material Handling Institute (EA)

MHI .... Material Hazard Index (AAEL)

MHI .... Materials Handling Institute, Inc.

MHI .... Mental Health Index (DMAA)

MHI .... Mental Health Institute (OICC)

MHI .... Mental Health Inventory (DMAA)

MHI .... Meridian House International (EA)

MHI .... Meridian International Center [*Washington, D.C.*] (EA)

MHI .... Military Health Institute

MHI .... Military History Institute [*Army*] (MCD)

MHI .... Mitsubishi Heavy Industries

MHI .... Mitsubishi Heavy Industries Ltd.

MHI .... Morgan Hydrocarbons, Inc. [*Toronto Stock Exchange symbol*]

MHI .... Morrison Health Care, Inc. [*NYSE symbol*] (SAG)

MHIA .... Material Handling Industry Association (NTPA)

MHIA .... Mitsubishi Heavy Industries America, Inc.

MHIBL .... Mile High Intercollegiate Baseball League (PSS)

MH-IC......... Harvard University, Collection of Historic Scientific Instruments Collection, Cambridge, MA [*Library symbol*] [*Library of Congress*] (LCLS)

MHIC .... Islas Del Cisne O Santanilla [*Honduras*] [*ICAO location identifier*] (ICLI)

MH-ID......... Harvard University, Harvard Institute for International Development, Cambridge, MA [*Library symbol*] [*Library of Congress*] (LCLS)

MHID .... Medical and Health Information Directory [*A publication*]

MHIDAS...... Major Hazard Incident Data Service [*Atomic Energy Authority*] [*British Information service or system*] (IID)

M Hi E .... Master of Highway Engineering

M Hi Eng .... Master of Highway Engineering

MHIFC .... Michael Harding International Fan Club (EA)

MHIFM........ Milton Helpern Institute of Forensic Medicine (EA)

MHILC .... Hampshire Inter-Library Center, Inc., Amherst, MA [*Library symbol Library of Congress Obsolete*] (LCLS)

MHingM...... Hingham Marine Museum, Hingham, MA [*Library symbol Library of Congress*] (LCLS)

MHIP .... Missile Homing Improvement Program (DWSG)

MHISL .... Mile High Intercollegiate Softball League (PSS)

MHJ .... Microwave Hybrid Junction

MHJU.......... Juticalpa [*Honduras*] [*ICAO location identifier*] (ICLI)

MHK .... Manhattan [*Kansas*] [*Airport symbol*] (OAG)

MHK .... Manhattan, KS [*Location identifier FAA*] (FAAL)

MHK .... Master of Human Kinetics (GAGS)

MHK .... Member of the House of Keys [*Isle Of Man*] [*British*]

MHK .... Military History of Korea

MHK .... Morgan Stanley Group, Inc. [*AMEX symbol*] (SAG)

MH-KG........ Harvard University, Kennedy School of Government, Cambridge, MA [*Library symbol Library of Congress*] (LCLS)

MH-KM .... Harvard University, Kennedy Inter-Faculty Program in Medical Ethics, Cambridge, MA [*Library symbol Library of Congress*] (LCLS)

MHKVLY ...... Mohawk Valley (FAAC)

MHL............. Hamline University, School of Law, St. Paul, MN [*OCLC symbol*] (OCLC)

MH-L .... Harvard University, Law School, Cambridge, MA [*Library symbol Library of Congress*] (LCLS)

M (HL)........ House of Lords' Appeals, in Macpherson's Court of Sessions Cases, Third Series [*1862-73*] [*Scotland*] [*A publication*] (DLA)

MHL............. March Resources [*Vancouver Stock Exchange symbol*]

MHL............. Marshall Islands [*ANSI three-letter standard code*] (CNC)

MHL............. Marshall, MO [*Location identifier FAA*] (FAAL)

MHL............. Master of Hebrew Letters (BJA)

MHL............. Master of Hebrew Literature

MHL............. Master of Humane Letters

MHL............. Mast Hull Loop

MHL............. Metastable Helium Level

MHL............. Microprocessor Host Loader [*Electronics*]

MHL............. Minimum Helium Loss [*System*]

MHI............. Morrison Health Care [*NYSE symbol*] (TTSB)

MHLA.......... McGraw-Hill Learning Architecture

MHLC.......... La Ceiba/Goloson Internacional [*Honduras*] [*ICAO location identifier*] (ICLI)

MHLC.......... Multidimensional Health Locus of Control [*Diagnostic scale*]

MHLE.......... La Esperanza [*Honduras*] [*ICAO location identifier*] (ICLI)

MHLH.......... Myogenic Helix-Loop-Helix [*Genetics*]

MH-Li .... Harvard University, Linguistics Library, Cambridge, MA [*Library symbol Library of Congress*] (LCLS)

MHLLDA ...... Mobile Home Landscapers and Landscape Designers Association (EA)

MH-Lm .... Harvard University, Lamont Undergraduate Library, Cambridge, MA [*Library symbol Library of Congress*] (LCLS)

MHLM.......... San Pedro Sula/La Mesa Internacional [*Honduras*] [*ICAO location identifier*] (ICLI)

MHLP.......... Mental Health Law Project (EA)

MHLS .... Metabolic Heat Load Simulator

MHLS .... Mid-Hudson Library System [*Library network*]

MHLTA......... Men's Hat Linings and Trimmings Association [*Defunct*] (EA)

MHLW......... Mean Higher Low Water [*Tides and currents*]

MHM .... Master of Hotel Management (PGP)

MHM .... Mental Health Management [*AMEX symbol*] (SPSG)

MHM .... Metal-Hydrogen-Metal [*Chemical bond*]

MHM .... MHM Services [*AMEX symbol*] (SAG)

mhm .... Mill Hill Missionaries (TOCD)

MHM .... Mill Hill Missionaries [*Roman Catholic men's religious order*]

MHM .... Minchumina, AK [*Location identifier FAA*] (FAAL)

MHM .... Minimum Hardware Modification [*Aircraft landing*]

MHM .... Mount Hope Mineral Railroad Co. [*Absorbed into Consolidated Rail Corp.*] [*AAR code*]

MHM .... Muzzle Hatch Mechanical

MHMA .... Marcala [*Honduras*] [*ICAO location identifier*] (ICLI)

MHMA .... Master House Movers' Association [*Australia*]

MHMA .... Mobile Home Manufacturers Association [*Later, Manufactured Housing Institute*]

MHMC .... Mental Health Materials Center (EA)

MH-ME .... Harvard University, Center for Middle Eastern Studies, Cambridge, MA [*Library symbol Library of Congress*] (LCLS)

MHME......... More Heart More Edge [*Screenwriter's lexicon*]

MHMey....... Meyerson [*M.H.*] & Co. [*Associated Press*] (SAG)

MHMeyer.... Meyerson [*M.H.*] & Co. [*Associated Press*] (SAG)

MH-MH .... Harvard University, John Peabody Monks Library, Cambridge, MA [*Library symbol Library of Congress*] (LCLS)

MH-ML .... Harvard University, Ticknor Library of Modern Languages, Cambridge, MA [*Library symbol Library of Congress*] (LCLS)

MH/MR .... Mental Health and Mental Retardation (DAVI)

MHMS .... Master of Health Management Systems (PGP)

MHMS .... Master of Human Movement Studies (ADA)

MHMS .... Material Handling and Management Society (EAIO)

MHMS .... Modular Hydrologic Modeling System [*Marine science*] (OSRA)

MHM Serv ... MHM Services [*Associated Press*] (SAG)

MH-Mu .... Harvard University, Music Library, Cambridge, MA [*Library symbol Library of Congress*] (LCLS)

MHMY .... Meyerson [*M.H.*] & Co. [*NASDAQ symbol*] (SAG)

MHMY .... M.H. Meyerson & Co. [*NASDAQ symbol*] (TTSB)

MHMYW ...... M H Meyerson & Co. Wrtt [*NASDAQ symbol*] (TTSB)

MHN .... Manhattan Mineral [*Vancouver Stock Exchange symbol*]

MHN .... Mannitol Hexanitrate [*Organic chemistry*]

MHN .... Massive Hepatic Necrosis [*Medicine*] (MAE)

MHN .... McGraw-Hill News [*Database*] (IT)

MHN .... Mullen, NE [*Location identifier FAA*] (FAAL)

MHNAMT ..... Methyl(hydroxylnaphthalamino)mercaptotriazole [*Organic chemistry*]

MH-NE .... Harvard University, Near Eastern Languages and Literatures Library, Cambridge, MA [*Library symbol Library of Congress*] (LCLS)

MHNGS....... Marble Hill Nuclear Generating Station (NRCH)

MHNJ.......... Guanaja [*Honduras*] [*ICAO location identifier*] (ICLI)

MH-NJ .... Harvard University, Nieman Collection of Contemporary Journalism, Cambridge, MA [*Library symbol Library of Congress*] (LCLS)

MHNPS....... Marble Hill Nuclear Power Station (NRCH)

MHNV .... Nuevo Ocotepeque [*Honduras*] [*ICAO location identifier*] (ICLI)

MH-O .... Harvard University, Harvard College Observatory, Cambridge, MA [*Library symbol Library of Congress*] (LCLS)

MHO .... Manchester Resources Corp. [*Vancouver Stock Exchange symbol*]

MHO .... Microsomal Heme Oxygenase (DB)

MHO .... Millhouse Developments Ltd. [*British ICAO designator*] (FAAC)

MHO .... Minehunter Ocean [*Navy*] (ANA)

MHO .... M/I Schottenstein Homes, Inc. [*NYSE symbol*] (SPSG)

MHO .... Mohanbari [*India*] [*Airport symbol*] (AD)

MHO .... Mount Hopkins Observatory [*Later, FLWO*] [*Smithsonian Institution*] (GRD)

mho .... Reciprocal Ohm [*Unit of conductance*]

MHOA .... Mutual Help and Occupancy Agreement [*Department of Housing and Urban Development*] (GFGA)

MHOA .... Olanchito [*Honduras*] [*ICAO location identifier*] (ICLI)

M Ho Ec ...... Master of Household Economy

MHOF .... Mobile Home Owners Federation [*NFMHO*] [*Superseded by*] (EA)

MH/OH .... Man Hours per Operating Hour [*Maintenance*] (RDA)

MHoly .... Holyoke Public Library, Holyoke, MA [*Library symbol Library of Congress*] (LCLS)

MHolyC .... Holyoke Community College, Holyoke, MA [*Library symbol Library of Congress*] (LCLS)

M Hor .... Master of Horticulture

MHort(RHS)... National Diploma in Horticulture (Royal Horticultural Society) [*British*] (DBQ)

MHortSc ...... Master of Horticultural Science

M Ho Sc .... Master of Household Science

MH-P .... Harvard University, Peabody Museum, Cambridge, MA [*Library symbol Library of Congress*] (LCLS)

MHp .... Harwich Port Library Association, Harwich Port, MA [*Library symbol*] [*Library of Congress*] (LCLS)

MHP............ Maclean Hunter Ltd. [*Toronto Stock Exchange symbol*]

MHP............ Master of Health Planning (ADA)

MHP............ Master of Health Professions (PGP)

MHP............ Master of Heritage Preservation (GAGS)

MHP............ Master of Historical Preservation (GAGS)

MHP............ Master of Humanities in Philosophy (PGP)

MHP............ McGraw-Hill Companies [*NYSE symbol*] (TTSB)

MHP............ McGraw-Hill, Inc. [*NYSE symbol*] (SPSG)

MHP............ Medium-High Pressure (MSA)

MHP............ Mental Health Project

MHP............ Mercurihydroxypropane [*Clinical chemistry*]

MHP............ Message Handling Processor

MHP............ Metabolic Heat Production [*Physiology*]

MHP............ Military Health Plan [*DoD*]

MHP............ Milli Hedef Partisi [*National Goal Party*] [*Turkish Cyprus*] [*Political party*] (PPE)

MH-PA .... Harvard University, Littauer Library of the Kennedy School of Government, Cambridge, MA [*Library symbol Library of Congress*] (LCLS)

MHPA .... Palmerola [*Honduras*] [*ICAO location identifier*] (ICLI)

MH-PC .... Harvard University, Palaeography Library, Cambridge, MA [*Library symbol Library of Congress*] (LCLS)

MHPD .... Masonite Hydropress Die (MSA)

MHPE.......... Master of Health Professions Education (PGP)

MHPE.......... Methoxy-Hydroxyphenylethanol [*Organic chemistry*] (MAH)

MHPE.......... Progreso [*Honduras*] [*ICAO location identifier*] (ICLI)

MH PE & R... Master of Health, Physical Education, and Recreation

MHPE Conj.. Methoxy-Hydroxyphenylethanol Conjugate [*Organic chemistry*] (DAVI)

MHPEd........ Master of Health Personnel Education (ADA)

MHPG .... (Methoxyhydroxyphenyl)ethyleneglycol [*Also, MOPEG*] [*Organic chemistry*]

MHPG Conj.. Methoxyhydropheny Gylcol Conjugate [*Organic chemistry*] (DAVI)

MHPH .... Man-Hours per Flying Hour [*Air Force*] (AFIT)

MH-PL .... Harvard University, Milman Parry Collection of Oral Literature, Cambridge, MA [*Library symbol Library of Congress*] (LCLS)

MHPL.......... Puerto Lempira [*Honduras*] [*ICAO location identifier*] (ICLI)

MH-PO .... Harvard University, Personnel Office Library, Cambridge, MA [*Library symbol Library of Congress*] (LCLS)

MH-PP .... Harvard University, Public Policy Program, Cambridge, MA [*Library symbol Library of Congress*] (LCLS)

MH-PR .... Harvard University, Physics Research Library, Cambridge, MA [*Library symbol Library of Congress*] (LCLS)

MH-Ps .... Harvard University, Psychology Research Library, Cambridge, MA [*Library symbol Library of Congress*] (LCLS)

MHPU .... Puerto Cortes [*Honduras*] [*ICAO location identifier*] (ICLI)

MH-Pv .... Harvard University, Preservation Center, Cambridge, MA [*Library symbol*] [*Library of Congress*] (LCLS)

MHQ .... Mariehamn [*Finland*] [*Airport symbol*] (OAG)

MHQ .... Maritime Headquarters (NVT)

MH-R .... Harvard University, Russian Research Center, Cambridge, MA [*Library symbol Library of Congress*] (LCLS)

MHR .... Major Histocompatibility Region [*Immunology*]

MHR .... Major Homology Region [*Biochemistry*]

MHR .... Malignant Hyperthermia Resistance [*Medicine*] (DMAA)

MHR .... Man-Hour

MHR .... Master of Human Resources (GAGS)

MHR .... Maximum Heart Rate

MHR .... McGraw-Hill Ryerson Ltd. [*Toronto Stock Exchange symbol*]

MHR .... Measurement Handicap Rule [*Sailing*]

MHR .... Medical Humanities Review [*A publication*] (BRI)

MHR .... Member of the House of Representatives

MHR .... Methemoglobin Reductase [*Hematology and laboratory*] (DAVI)

MHR .... Microwave Hologram RADAR

MHR .... Miniature Helium Refrigerator

MHR .... Missile Hazard Report (AFM)

MHR .... Mount Hamilton Road [*California*] [*Seismograph station code, US Geological Survey*] (SEIS)

MHr .... Myohemerythrin [*Biochemistry*]

MHR .... Sacramento, CA [*Location identifier FAA*] (FAAL)

MHR .... United States Army Military History Institute, Carlisle Barracks, PA [*OCLC symbol*] (OCLC)

MH-RA........ Harvard University, Harvard Radio Astronomy Center, Fort Davis, TX [*Library symbol Library of Congress*] (LCLS)

MHRA .... Modern Humanities Research Association, American Branch [*Defunct*] (EA)

MHRA .... Morab Horse Registry of America (EA)

MHRAC .... Mine Health Research Advisory Committee [*National Institute for Occupational Safety and Health*] [*Morgantown, WV*] (EGAO)

MH-RB .... Harvard University, Rubel Asiatic Research Bureau, Fogg Art Museum, Cambridge, MA [*Library symbol Library of Congress Obsolete*] (LCLS)

MHRB .... Mental Health Review Board [*Victoria, Australia*]

MH-RC .... Harvard University, Fred N. Robinson Celtic Seminar, Cambridge, MA [*Library symbol Library of Congress*] (LCLS)

MHRD .... Master in Human Resource Department (PGP)

MH-RI .... Harvard University, RISM-US Project Center, Cambridge, MA [*Library symbol*] [*Library of Congress*] (LCLS)

MHRI .... Mental Health Research Institute [*University of Michigan*] [*Research center*]

MHRIM .... Master of Hotel, Restaurant, and Institutional Management (PGP)

MHRIR........ Master of Human Resources and Industrial Relations (PGP)

MHRM .... Master of Human Resources Management (PGP)

MHRM .... Microcomputers in Human Resource Management [*Advanced Personnel Systems*] [*Information service or system*] (CRD)

MHROD....... Master of Human Resources and Organization Development (PGP)

MH-RP .... Harvard University, Robbins Library of Philosophy, Cambridge, MA [*Library symbol Library of Congress*] (LCLS)

MHRS .... Magnetic Heading Reference System

MHRST........ Medical and Health Related Sciences Thesaurus [*A publication*] (IEEE)

MHRT .... Mental Health Review Tribunal [*British*]

MHRTA .... Masters in Hotel, Restaurant, Tourism, and Administration (PGP)

MHRU .... Ruinas De Copan [*Honduras*] [*ICAO location identifier*] (ICLI)

MHRV .... Movement for Human Rights in Vietnam [*Defunct*] (EA)

MH-S .... Harvard University, Statistics Library, Cambridge, MA [*Library symbol Library of Congress*] (LCLS)

MHS .... Machined Hemispherical Shell

MHS .... Magnetic Heading System (AAG)

MHS .... Magnetomotive Hammer System

MHS .... Maher, Inc. [*Toronto Stock Exchange symbol*]

MHS .... Mail Handling System [*Computer science*]

MHS .... Major Histocompatibility System [*Immunology*]

MHS .... Malignant Hyperthermia Susceptible [*Medicine*]

MHS .... Malignant Hypothermia Susceptible [*Patients*] [*Emergency medicine*] (DAVI)

MHS .... Mammoth Hot Springs [*Wyoming*] [*Seismograph station code, US Geological Survey*] (SEIS)

MHS .... Man-Hours per Sortie [*Air Force*] (AFIT)

MHS .... Marine Hospital Service [*Public Health Service*]

MHS .... Master Hotel Supplier [*Educational Institute of the American Hotel and M otel Association*] [*Designation awarded by*]

MHS .... Master of Health Sciences (PGP)

MHS .... Master of Health Services (GAGS)

MHS .... Master of Hispanic Studies (PGP)

MHS .... Master of Humane Studies (PGP)

MHS .... Master of Human Services (GAGS)

MHS .... Maximum Histalog Stimulation [*Gastroenterology*] (DAVI)

MHS .... McMaster University Health Sciences Library [*UTLAS symbol*]

MHS .... Measurement Handicapping System [*Yacht racing*]

MHS .... Mechanical Handling System

MHS .... Member of the Historical Society

MHS .... Message Handling Service [*Telecommunications*] (PCM)

MHS .... Message Handling System [*Computer science*]

MHS .... Methylhydrazine Sulfate [*Organic chemistry*]

M/H/S .... Miles per Hour per Second

MHS .... Military Historical Society [*Defunct*] (EA)

MHS .... Ministry of Home Security [*British*]

MHS .... Minnesota Historical Society, St. Paul, MN [*OCLC symbol*] (OCLC)

MHS .... Missile Hazard Space (AFM)

MHS .... Moravian Historical Society (EA)

MHS .... Mount Shasta, CA [*Location identifier FAA*] (FAAL)

MHS .... Multiple Hospital System

MHS .... Multiple Host Support

MHS .... Musical Heritage Society [*Commercial firm*] (EA)

MHS .... Sisters of the Most Holy Sacrament [*Roman Catholic religious order*]

MHSA .... Master of Health Services Administration (GAGS)

MHSA .... Master of Human Services Administration (PGP)

MH/SA .... Mental Health/Substance Abuse

MH-SC .... Harvard University, Herbert Weir Smyth Classical Library, Cambridge, MA [*Library symbol Library of Congress*] (LCLS)

MHSC .... Manipulator Handset Controller (MCD)

MHSc .... Master of Health Sciences (CMD)

MHSC .... Mental Health Study Center [*National Institute of Mental Health*] (GRD)

MHSCP .... Mean Hemispherical Candlepower

MH-SD........ Harvard University, Graduate School of Design, Cambridge, MA [*Library symbol Library of Congress*] (LCLS)

MHSDC .... Multiple High-Speed Data Channel

MHSE.......... Master of Health Science Education (PGP)

MH-SF .... Harvard University, Schering Foundation Library, Boston, MA [*Library symbol Library of Congress*] (LCLS)

MHSH .... Mental Health Services for the Homeless [*Department of Health and Human Services*] (GFGA)

MHSH .... Mission Helpers of the Sacred Heart [*Roman Catholic women's religious order*]

MH-SI .... Harvard University, Program for Science and International Affairs Library, Cambridge, MA [*Library symbol Library of Congress*] (LCLS)
MHSIP .... Mental Health Statistics Improvement Program [*Department of Health and Human Services*] (GFGA)
MH-SL .... Harvard University, Sanskrit Library, Cambridge, MA [*Library symbol Library of Congress*] (LCLS)
MHSLN .... Midwest Health Science Library Network [*Library network*]
MHSM .... Mason & Hanger-Silas Mason Co., Inc. (RDA)
MHSO .... Masada, the Holocaust Survivors Organization (EA)
MHSO .... Minehunter Sweeper Ocean [*Navy*] (ANA)
MH-SP .... Harvard University, Science and Public Police Program Library, Cambridge, MA [*Library symbol Library of Congress*] (LCLS)
MHSP .... Municipal Health Services Program [*Department of Health and Human Services*] (GFGA)
MHSP .... San Pedro Sula [*Honduras*] [*ICAO location identifier*] (ICLI)
MH-SR .... Harvard University, Social Relations Library, Cambridge, MA [*Library symbol Library of Congress*] (LCLS)
MHSR .... Santa Rosa De Copan [*Honduras*] [*ICAO location identifier*] (ICLI)
MHSS .... Materials Handling Support System [*Military*] (AFM)
MHSS .... Mental Health Special Interest Section [*American Occupational Therapy Association*]
MHSS .... Message Handling System Service (NITA)
MHSS .... Military Health Service System
MHSS(NI) ..... Ministry of Health and Social Services (Northern Ireland)
MHSSRI .... Michigan Health and Social Security Research Institute [*Detroit, MI*] [*Research center*] (RCD)
MHST .... Multiphasic Health Screen Test (DAVI)
MHSTB .... Mental Handicap Staff Training Board [*British*]
MHSV .... Multipurpose High-Speed Vehicle (MCD)
MHSZ .... Santa Barbara [*Honduras*] [*ICAO location identifier*] (ICLI)
MHT .... Maghemite, Inc. [*Vancouver Stock Exchange symbol*]
MHT .... Main Himalayan Thrust [*Geology*]
MHT .... Manchester [*New Hampshire*] [*Airport symbol*] (OAG)
MHT .... Manchester, NH [*Location identifier FAA*] (FAAL)
MHT .... Manhattan [*Kansas*] [*Seismograph station code, US Geological Survey Closed*] (SEIS)
MHT .... Manufacturers Hanover Trust Co. [*of Manufacturers Hanover Corp.*] [*Nickname: "Manny Hanny"*]
MHT .... Mean High Tide [*Tides and currents*]
MHT .... Methyl(hydroxyethyl)thiazole [*Organic chemistry*]
MHT .... Meyer Hydraulic Theory
MHT .... Mild Heat Treatment (IEEE)
MHT .... Missile Handling Trailer (AAG)
MHT .... Museum of History and Technology [*Smithsonian Institution*]
MHTA .... Molten High-Temperature Alloy
MHTE .... Tela [*Honduras*] [*ICAO location identifier*] (ICLI)
MHTF .... Manufactured Housing Task Force [*Defunct*] (EA)
MHTG .... Marine Helicopter Training Group (NVT)
MHTG .... Tegucigalpa/Toncontin Internacional [*Honduras*] [*ICAO location identifier*] (ICLI)
MHTGR .... Modular High-Temperature Gas Reactor [*Nuclear energy*]
MHTJ .... Trujillo [*Honduras*] [*ICAO location identifier*] (ICLI)
MHTL .... Motorola High-Threshold Logic
MHTS .... Main Heat Transport System [*Nuclear energy*] (NRCH)
MHTS .... Multiphasic Health Testing Services (DMAA)
MHTTA .... Member of the Highway and Traffic Technicians Association [*British*] (DBQ)
MHTV .... Manned Hypersonic Test Vehicle (MCD)
M Hu .... Master of Humanities
MHU .... Material Handling Unit (AFIT)
MHUC .... Mid-Hudson Conference (PSS)
MHUD .... Monocular Heads-Up Display [*Aviation*]
MHuGH .... John H. Glenn High School, Huntington, NY [*Library symbol Library of Congress*] (LCLS)
M Hum .... Master of Humanities
M Hum Svcs... Master of Human Services (PGP)
MH-UR .... Harvard University, Ukrainian Research Institute Reference Library, Cambridge, MA [*Library symbol Library of Congress*] (LCLS)
MHV .... Magnetic Heart Vector [*Cardiology*]
MHV .... Manned Hypersonic Vehicle
MHV .... Mean Horizontal Velocity
MHV .... Mill Hill Virus [*Medicine*] (DB)
MHV .... Mill Hill Vocabulary Scale [*Test*] (TMMY)
MHV .... Miniature Homing Vehicle [*Missile*]
MHV .... Mojave, CA [*Location identifier FAA*] (FAAL)
MHV .... Mouse Hepatitis Virus
MHV .... Murine Hepatitis Virus
MHVD .... Marek's Herpesvirus Disease [*Avian pathology*] (MAE)
MHVDF .... Medium-, High-, and Very-High-Frequency Direction-Finding Station
MHVPS .... Manual High-Voltage Power Supply
MHW .... Mean High Water [*Tides and currents*]
MHW .... Medial Heel Wedge [*Orthopedics*] (DAVI)
MHW .... Merrill Lynch & Co. [*AMEX symbol*] (SAG)
MHW .... Ministry of Health and Welfare [*Japan*] (ECON)
MHW .... Morgan, H. W., Los Angeles CA [*STAC*]
MHW .... Multihundred Watt
MH-WA .... Harvard University, Charles Warren Center for Studies in American History, Cambridge, MA [*Library symbol Library of Congress*] (LCLS)
MHWI .... Mean High-Water Lunitidal Interval [*Tides and currents*]
MHWLR .... Mobile Hostile Weapon Locating RADAR (NATG)
MHWN .... Mean High-Water Neap [*Tides and currents*]
MHW-RTG .... Multi-Hundred-Watt Radioisotope Thermoelectric Generator (PDAA)
MHWS .... Mean High-Water Springs [*Tides and currents*]

M Hx .... Medical History (MAE)
MHX .... MeriStar Hospitality [*Formerly, CapStar Hotel*] [*NYSE symbol*]
MHX .... Mine Hunter Experimental
MHy .... Hyannis Public Library, Hyannis, MA [*Library symbol Library of Congress*] (LCLS)
MHY .... Managed High Income Portfolio [*NYSE symbol*] (SPSG)
MHY .... Managed High Inc. Portfolio [*NYSE symbol*] (TTSB)
M Hy .... Master of Hygiene
MHY .... Morehead [*Papua New Guinea*] [*Airport symbol*] (OAG)
M Hyg .... Master of Hygiene
MHyT .... State Teachers' College, Hyannis, MA [*Library symbol Library of Congress Obsolete*] (LCLS)
MH-Z .... Harvard University, Museum of Comparative Zoology, Cambridge, MA [*Library symbol Library of Congress*] (LCLS)
MHz .... Megahertz [*Megacycles per Second*] [*See also MCPS, MCS, MC/S, MH*]
MHZ .... Millihertz (WDAA)
MI .... Lab. Miquel [*Spain*] [*Research code symbol*]
MI .... Mach Indicated
MI .... Machine Independent
MI .... Machine Intelligence (RDA)
MI .... Mackey International Airlines [*ICAO designator*] (AD)
MI .... Mackey International, Inc. [*USA*] [*ICAO designator*] (OAG)
MI .... Madras Infantry [*British*]
MI .... Magazine Index [*Information Access Corp.*] [*Information service or system*] (IID)
MI .... Maintenance Instruction (AAG)
MI .... Major Issue (MCD)
MI .... Major Item [*Military*]
MI .... Malachi [*Old Testament book*] (BJA)
MI .... Malleable Iron
MI .... Management Information (CAAL)
mi .... Management Information (NAKS)
MI .... Management Intern
MI .... Manhattan Industries, Inc. (EFIS)
MI .... Manual Individual [*Nuclear energy*] (NRCH)
MI .... Manual Input [*Computer science*]
MI .... Manufacturing Index (MCD)
MI .... Manufacturing Industries [*Department of Employment*] [*British*]
MI .... Manufacturing Inspector (FAAC)
MI .... Manufacturing Instruction (MSA)
MI .... Marconi Industries [*General Electric Co.*] [*British*]
MI .... Mare Imbrium [*Sea of Showers*] [*Lunar area*]
MI .... Mare Island, California [*Site of naval base*]
MI .... Marginal Income [*Economics*]
MI .... Marine Insurance
MI .... Marine Investigation (LAIN)
MI .... Market Identifiers [*Dun's Marketing Services*] [*Database*]
MI .... Market Investigation [*Army*]
MI .... Marshall Indus [*NYSE symbol*] (TTSB)
MI .... Marshall Industries [*NYSE symbol*] (SPSG)
MI .... Marshall Islands
MI .... Massa Intermedia (DB)
MI .... Master Index
MI .... Master Item (MSA)
MI .... Master of Instruction (PGP)
MI .... Master of Insurance (GAGS)
MI .... Match Institute [*Defunct*] (EA)
MI .... Material Inspection [*Navy*]
MI .... Maturation Index (MAE)
MI .... Meat Inspection Division [*of ARS, Department of Agriculture*]
MI .... Mechanical Impedance
M/I .... Mechanical Impulse (KSC)
MI .... Meconium Ileus [*Medicine*]
MI .... Medical Illustrator
MI .... Medical Improvement [*Social Security Administration*]
MI .... Medical Inspection
MI .... Medium Intensity (MSA)
MI .... Melanophore Index [*Biology*]
MI .... Mellon Institute [*Carnegie-Mellon University*] [*Research center*] (RCD)
MI .... Meloidogyne incognita [*A nematode*]
MI .... Melt Inclusions [*Geology*]
MI .... Memorial Inscription
MI .... Memory Interface
MI .... Mensa International [*British*] (EAIO)
MI .... Menstrual Induction [*Medicine*]
MI .... Mental Illness
MI .... (Mercaptoethyl)trimethylammonium Iodide [*Pharmacology*]
MI .... Mercaptoimidazole [*Organic chemistry*] (MAE)
MI .... Merit Increase (MHDW)
MI .... Merritt Island [*Florida*] [*NASA*] (KSC)
MI .... Mesha Inscription (BJA)
MI .... Mesioincisal [*Dentistry*]
MI .... Meso-Inositol [*or Myoinositol*] [*Organic chemistry*]
MI .... Metabolic Index
MI .... Metal-to-Insulator [*Transition*]
MI .... Metastases below the Head and Neck [*Oncology*]
MI .... Method Index [*British police term*]
MI .... Methods Instruction (DNAB)
MI .... Methylindole [*Organic chemistry*]
M-I .... Metro-International Program Services of New York (EA)
Mi .... Mica [*A mineral*]
Mi .... Micah [*Old Testament book*]
MI .... Michelson Interferometer (PDAA)

MI	Michigan [*Postal code*]
MI	Michigan Reports [*A publication*] (DLA)
Mi	Michigan State Library, Lansing, MI [*Library symbol Library of Congress*] (LCLS)
MI	Microbiological Inputs [*Canning*] (DICI)
MI	Microinch (IAA)
MI	Microinstruction [*Computer science*]
MI	Micru International (EA)
MI	Middle Initial
MI	Middle Iron Age (BJA)
MI	Migration Index [*Immunology*]
MI	Migration Inhibition [*Cytology*]
MI	Mil [*Former USSR ICAO aircraft manufacturer identifier*] (ICAO)
MI	Mile
mi	Mile
MI	Military Institute
MI	Military Intelligence [*Army*]
MI	Military Internee
MI	Military Item
MI	Militia Mariae Immaculatae [*Militia of the Immaculate*] (EAIO)
MI	Mill
MI	Miller Integrator
MI	Mineral Insulated [*Cable*] (NRCH)
MI	Miniaturized Instrumentation (MCD)
M/I	Minimum Impulse (KSC)
MI	Ministry of Information [*British World War II*]
MI	Minor (ROG)
MI	Minority Institution
MI	Minority Interest [*Business term*]
MI	Minute (ADA)
MI	Miscellaneous Income (MHDW)
MI	Mishnah [*Basis of the Talmud*] (BJA)
MI	Missed Interception [*Military*]
MI	Missile (CINC)
MI	Missile Industry (AAG)
MI	Missionary Internship [*An association*] (EA)
MI	Mission Independent [*NASA*]
MI	Mississippi [*Obsolete*] (ROG)
MI	Missouri-Illinois Railroad Co. [*AAR code*]
MI	Mitomycin C [*Also, MMC, MTC*] [*Antineoplastic drug*]
MI	Mitotic Indices [*Cytology*]
MI	Mitral Incompetence [*Cardiology*]
MI	Mitral Insufficiency [*Cardiology*]
MI	Mixed Income
MI	Mobility Impairment (NVT)
MI	Mobility International (EA)
MI	Mode Indicator (HGAA)
MI	Moderately Included [*Colored gemstone grade*]
MI	Modification Instructions (KSC)
MI	Moment of Inertia
MI	Monetary Incentive
MI	Money Stock [*British*] (DCTA)
MI	Monitoring Information (NITA)
MI	Monitor Inspection (AFM)
MI	Monitor International (ASF)
MI	Mononucleosis Infectiosa [*Medicine*] (DB)
MI	Monument Inscription [*Genealogy*]
MI	Mooseheart, International
MI	Moose, International (EAIO)
MI	Morphologic Index [*Volume of trunk divided by length of limbs*]
MI	[*The*] Mortgage Index [*Hale Systems, Inc.*] [*Information service or system*] (CRD)
MI	Mortgage Insurance (EMRF)
MI	Motility Index [*Of intestine*] [*Gastroenterology*]
MI	Motorola Interconnect [*Electronics*]
MI	Mounted Infantry
MI	Move In (WDMC)
MI	Movement Instruction [*British military*] (DMA)
MI	Multi-Industry Interest
MI	Multiple Instruction (HGAA)
MI	Murphy International Transport [*Commercial firm British*]
MI	Muskies, Inc. (EA)
MI	Mutual Inductance
MI	Mutual Interference
MI	Myocardial Infarction [*Cardiology*]
MI	Myo-Inositol [*Chemistry*] [*Dietetics*] (DAVI)
MI	Writ of Mandamus Will Issue [*Legal term*] (DLA)
mi²	Square Mile (CDAI)
MI³MS	Minolta Integrated Information and Image Management System [*Optical disc*] (IT)
MI5	Military Intelligence [*State security*] [*British*] (ODBW)
MI6	Military Intelligence [*Espionage*] [*British*] (ODBW)
MiA	Alma Public Library, Alma, MI [*Library symbol Library of Congress*] (LCLS)
MIA	AMI (Air Mercury International) [*Belgium ICAO designator*] (FAAC)
MIA	[*An*] Introduction to the Apocrypha [*B. Metzger*] [*A publication*] (BJA)
MIA	Manchester International Airport [*British*] (DS)
MIA	Manila International Airport
MIA	Marble Institute of America (EA)
MIA	Maritime Information Association [*British*] (EAIO)
MIA	Master of Industrial Arts
MIA	Master of Intercultural Administration (PGP)
MIA	Master of Internal Affairs (NADA)
MIA	Master of International Administration (PGP)
MIA	Master of International Affairs
MIA	Medical Indemnity of America, Inc. (DHSM)
MIA	Medically Indigent Adult (MEDA)
MIA	Member of the Institute of Arbitrators [*British*]
MIA	Metal Interface Amplifier
MIA	Methylisatoic Anhydride [*Organic chemistry*]
MIA	Metropolitan Intercollegiate Association (PSS)
MIA	Miami [*Florida*] [*Seismograph station code, US Geological Survey Closed*] (SEIS)
MIA	Miami University, Oxford, OH [*OCLC symbol*] (OCLC)
MIA	Mica Industry Association [*Defunct*] (EA)
MIA	Military Inspection Agency (NATG)
MIA	Military Intelligence Agency (MCD)
MIA	Millinery Institute of America [*Later, MIB*] (EA)
MIA	Minimum IFR Altitude [*FAA*] (TAG)
MIA	Minimum Instrument Altitude [*Aviation*] (AFM)
MIA	Missile Intelligence Agency (AABC)
MIA	Missing in Action [*Military*]
MIA	Mission-Independent Area [*NASA*]
MIA	Monoiodoacetic Acid [*Organic chemistry*]
MIA	Moore's Indian Appeals [*A publication*] (DLA)
MIA	™Mouse in Able∫ Program
MIA	Multiflex Interface Adapter
MIA	Multiplexer Interface Adapter (NASA)
MIA	Multiplex Interface Adapter (NASA)
MIA	Murrumbidgee Irrigation Area [*Australia*] (BARN)
MIA	Music Industries Association [*British*] (DBA)
MIA	Mutual Improvement Association [*Mormon Youth Movement*] (BARN)
MIA	Mythmaking in America [*A publication*]
MiAa	Ann Arbor Public Library, Ann Arbor, MI [*Library symbol Library of Congress*] (LCLS)
MIAA	Medical Industry Association of Australia
MIAA	Meetings Industry Association of Australia
MIAA	Member of the Incorporated Association of Architects and Surveyors [*British*] (DBQ)
MIAA	Member of the Institute of Affiliate Accountants (ADA)
MIAA	Member of the Institute of Automobile Assessors [*British*]
MIAA	Michigan Intercollegiate Athletics Association (PSS)
MIAA	Miniatures Industry Association of America (EA)
MIAA	Mutual Insurance Advisory Association [*Defunct*] (EA)
MiAaC	Concordia Lutheran College, Ann Arbor, MI [*Library symbol Library of Congress*] (LCLS)
MiAaE	Environmental Research Institute of Michigan, Ann Arbor, MI [*Library symbol Library of Congress*] (LCLS)
MiAaF	Gerald R. Ford Library, Ann Arbor, MI [*Library symbol*] [*Library of Congress*] (LCLS)
MiAaFL	Great Lakes Fisheries Laboratory, Ann Arbor, MI [*Library symbol Library of Congress*] (LCLS)
MiAaI	Inter-University Consortium for Political and Social Research, Ann Arbor, MI [*Library symbol*] [*Library of Congress*] (LCLS)
MiAaK	KMS Fusion, Inc., Ann Arbor, MI [*Library symbol Library of Congress*] (LCLS)
MiAaP	Parke, Davis & Co., Research Library, Ann Arbor, MI [*Library symbol Library of Congress*] (LCLS)
MIA(APS)	Meat Inspectors' Association (Australian Public Service)
MIAASM	Member, International Academy of Aviation & Space Medicine (CMD)
MiAaW	Washtenaw County Library, Ann Arbor, MI [*Library symbol Library of Congress*] (LCLS)
MiAaWC	Washtenaw Community College, Ann Arbor, MI [*Library symbol Library of Congress*] (LCLS)
MIAB	Magnetically Impelled Arc Butt [*Welding*] (MCD)
MIAB	Modular Interchangeable Ambulance Body [*Military British*]
MiAC	Alma College, Alma, MI [*Library symbol Library of Congress*] (LCLS)
MIAC	Maintenance Information and Control [*Environmental science*] (COE)
MIAC	Manufacturing Industries Advisory Council (NADA)
MIAC	Material Identification Accounting Code
MIAC	Metals Information Analysis Center (IID)
MIAC	Minimum Automatic Computer (IEEE)
MIAC	Minnesota Intercollegiate Athletic Conference (PSS)
MIACF	Multipoint Interactive Audio-Visual Communication (NITA)
MIACF	Meander Inverted Autocorrelated Function
MIACS	Manufacturing Information and Control System
MiAd	Adrian Public Library, Adrian, MI [*Library symbol Library of Congress*] (LCLS)
MiAdC	Adrian College, Adrian, MI [*Library symbol Library of Congress*] (LCLS)
MiAdL	Lenawee County Library, Adrian, MI [*Library symbol Library of Congress*] (LCLS)
MIADS	Map Information Assembly and Display System
MIADS	Minot Air Defense Sector [*ADC*]
MiAdS	Siena Heights College, Adrian, MI [*Library symbol Library of Congress*] (LCLS)
MIAE	Member of the Institution of Automobile Engineers [*British*]
MIAEA	Member of the Institute of Automotive Engineer Assessors [*British*] (DBQ)
MI Ae E	Member of the Institute of Aeronautical Engineers [*British*]
MIAEF	Missed Interception Due to Airborne Equipment Failure [*Air Force*]
MIAeS	Member of the Institute of Aeronautical Sciences
MIAESR	Melbourne Institute of Applied Economic and Social Research [*Australia*]
MIAFTR	Motor Insurance Anti-Fraud and Theft Register [*Database*] [*British*]
MIAG	Management Information and Analysis Group (MCD)
MIAgrE	Member of the Institution of Agricultural Engineers [*British*]
MiAhO	Oakland Community College, Auburn Heights, MI [*Library symbol Library of Congress*] (LCLS)
MIAIF	Meteorological Information for Aircraft in Flight

MIAK............ Methyl Isoamyl Ketone [*Organic chemistry*]
MiAlb........... Albion Public Library, Albion, MI [*Library symbol Library of Congress*] (LCLS)
MiAlbC......... Albion College, Albion, MI [*Library symbol Library of Congress*] (LCLS)
MiAlbW........ Woodlands Library Cooperative, Albion, MI [*Library symbol Library of Congress*] (LCLS)
MiAld........... Helena Township Public Library, Alden, MI [*Library symbol Library of Congress*] (LCLS)
MiAll........... Allendale Township Library, Allendale, MI [*Library symbol Library of Congress*] (LCLS)
MiAlle.......... Allegan Public Library, Allegan, MI [*Library symbol Library of Congress*] (LCLS)
MiAllG .... Grand Valley State College, Allendale, MI [*Library symbol Library of Congress*] (LCLS)
MiAlmo....... Henry Stephens Memorial Library, Almont, MI [*Library symbol Library of Congress*] (LCLS)
MiAln.......... Alanson Public Library, Alanson, MI [*Library symbol Library of Congress*] (LCLS)
MiAlp.......... Alpena County Library, Alpena, MI [*Library symbol Library of Congress*] (LCLS)
MiAlpC........ Alpena Community College, Alpena, MI [*Library symbol Library of Congress*] (LCLS)
MIALS......... Medium Intensity Approach Light System [*Aviation*] (DA)
MIAM.......... Major Items Automated Management (AAGC)
MIAM.......... Mid-Am, Inc. [*NASDAQ symbol*] (NQ)
MIAMA........ Member of the Incorporated Advertising Managers' Association [*British*] (DAS)
MIAME........ Member of the Institute of Automotive Mechanical Engineers (ADA)
MIAMI......... Metoprolol in Acute Myocardial Infarction [*Cardiology study*]
MIAMI......... Microwave Ice Accretion Measurement Instrument (MCD)
MiamiCm...... Miami Computer Supply Corp. [*Associated Press*] (SAG)
Miami LQ .... Miami Law Quarterly [*A publication*] (DLA)
Miami L Rev... Miami Law Review [*Florida*] [*A publication*] (DLA)
Miami U (Ohio)... Miami University (Ohio) (GAGS)
MIAMP........ Mid Am $1.8125 Cv'A'Pfd [*NASDAQ symbol*] (TTSB)
MiamSb....... Miami Subs Corp. [*Associated Press*] (SAG)
MIAMSI....... Mouvement International d'Apostolat des Milieux Sociaux Independants [*International Movement of Apostolate in the Independent Social Milieux*] [*Vatican City*] (EAIO)
MI & RR ...... Material Inspection and Receiving Report [*Military*] (KSC)
MIANG........ Michigan Air National Guard (MUSM)
MIAO .... Master Index Assembly Outline [*Paper*]
MiAp........... Allen Park Public Library, Allen Park, MI [*Library symbol Library of Congress*] (LCLS)
MIAP........... Member of the Institution of Analysts and Programmers [*British*] (DBQ)
MIAP........... Military Incentive Analysis Program (MCD)
MIAPD .... Mid-Central Air Procurement District
MiApDB ...... Detroit Baptist Divinity School, Allen Park, MI [*Library symbol Library of Congress*] (LCLS)
MIAPL........ Master Index of Allowable Parts Lists [*Navy*]
MiApV......... United States Veterans Administration Hospital, Allen Park, MI [*Library symbol Library of Congress*] (LCLS)
MIAQ .... Music Industry Association of Queensland [*Australia*]
MIAR .... Microaddress Register [*Computer science*] (MHDI)
MI Arch....... Master of Interior Architecture (PGP)
M I Arch Eng... Master of Interior Architectural Engineering
MiArm .... Armada Free Public Library, Armada, MI [*Library symbol Library of Congress*] (LCLS)
MIARS........ Maintenance Information Automated Retrieval System [*DoD*]
MIARS .... Microfilm Information and Retrieval System (DNAB)
MIAS.......... Maintenance Information Authorizing System (MCD)
MIAS.......... Major Item Automated System [*Army Materiel Command*] (AABC)
MIAS.......... Marine Information and Advisory Service [*Institute of Oceanographic Sciences*] [*Databank*] [*British*] (IID)
MIAS.......... Member of the Incorporated Association of Architects and Surveyors [*British*] (DBQ)
MIAS.......... Member of the Institute of Aeronautical Science [*Later, MAIAA*]
MIAS.......... Monroe Institute of Applied Sciences [*Later, TMI*] (EA)
MIAS.......... Muhyiddin Ibn Arabi Society
MIASA .... Motorcycle Industry Association of South Australia
MIAT.......... Mean Interarrival Time (MHDB)
MIAT.......... Member of the Institute of Asphalt Technology [*British*] (DBQ)
MiAt........... Montmorency County Public Library, Atlanta, MI [*Library symbol Library of Congress*] (LCLS)
MIAT.......... Music Industry Association of Tasmania [*Australia*]
MIATA........ Murrumbidgee Irrigation Area Tourist Association [*Australia*]
MIATCO ...... Mid-America International Agri-Trade Council
MiAth.......... Athens Township Library, Athens, MI [*Library symbol Library of Congress*] (LCLS)
MiAu.......... Augusta-Ross Township District Library (McKay Library), Augusta, MI [*Library symbol Library of Congress*] (LCLS)
MIAX.......... McCulloch International Airlines [*Air carrier designation symbol*]
MIB........... Management Improvement Board (AAG)
MIB........... Management Information Base
MIB........... Management Information Block [*Computer science*]
MIB........... Manual Input Buffer [*Computer science*]
MIB........... Marine Index Bureau
MIB........... Maritime Information Bureau (NADA)
MIB........... Marketing of Investments Board [*Finance British*]
MIB........... Master Instruction Book
MIB........... Master Interconnect Board (MCD)
MIB........... Master of International Business (GAGS)
MIB........... Mechanized Infantry Battalion (MCD)

MIB............ Medical Impairment Bureau [*Insurance*]
MIB............ Medical Information Bureau [*Databank*]
MIBC........... Medium Industry Bank [*South Korea*] (IMH)
MIB............ Men in Black [*UFO mythology*]
MIB............ Men in Black [*UFO mythology*]
MIB............ Mexican Investment Board [*Public relations and investor assistance*] [*Mexico*] (CROSS)
MIB............ Mezhdunarodnyi Investitsionnyi Bank [*International Investment Bank - IIB*] [*Moscow, USSR*] (EAIO)
MIB............ Michigan Intra-State Motor Tariff Bureau Inc., Lansing MI [*STAC*]
MIB............ Microinstruction Bus [*Computer science*]
MIB............ Midland Bancorp [*NYSE symbol*] (SPSG)
MIB............ Midland Bank PLC [*NYSE symbol*] (SAG)
MIB............ Military Intelligence Battalion (MCD)
MIB............ Military Intelligence Board (MCD)
MIB............ Millinery Information Bureau (EA)
MIB............ Minimum Impulse BIT [*Binary Digit*] [*Computer science*] (MCD)
MIB............ Minot, ND [*Location identifier FAA*] (FAAL)
MIB............ Mint in the Box [*Doll collecting*]
MIB............ Missionary Information Bureau
MIB............ Montana Independent Bankers (TBD)
MIB............ Motor Inspection Building
MIB............ Motor Insurers' Bureau Ltd. [*British*] (ILCA)
MIB............ Mouvement d'Insoumission Bretonne [*Breton Insubordination Movement*] [*France*] (PD)
MIB............ Multibanc NT Financial Corp. [*Toronto Stock Exchange symbol*]
MIB............ Multilayer Interconnection Board
MIB............ Mustard Information Bureau (EA)
MIB............ Mutual Inductance Bridge
MiBa.......... Bad Axe Public Library, Bad Axe, MI [*Library symbol Library of Congress*] (LCLS)
MIBA.......... Malta International Business Authority (EY)
MIBA.......... Master of International Business Administration (GAGS)
MIBA.......... Member of the Institute of British Architects (ROG)
MIBA.......... Metropolitan Intercollegiate Basketball Association (EA)
MIBA.......... Miniere de Bakwanga [*Zaire*]
MIBA.......... Missouri Independent Bankers Association (TBD)
MiBal.......... Pathfinder Community Library, Baldwin, MI [*Library symbol Library of Congress*] (LCLS)
MiBar.......... Barryton Public Library, Barryton, MI [*Library symbol Library of Congress*] (LCLS)
MiBar.......... Burr Oak Township Library, Burr Oak, MI [*Library symbol Library of Congress*] (LCLS)
MIBAR .... Multi-Channel In-Band Airborne Relay (PDAA)
MIBARS .... Military Intelligence Battalion Aerial Reconnaissance and Support [*Army*] (AFM)
MiBat.......... Battle Creek Public School, Battle Creek, MI [*Library symbol Library of Congress*] (LCLS)
MiBatC........ Battle Creek College, Battle Creek, MI [*Library symbol Library of Congress Obsolete*] (LCLS)
MiBatK........ Kellogg Community College, Battle Creek, MI [*Library symbol Library of Congress*] (LCLS)
MiBatV........ United States Veterans Administration Hospital, Battle Creek, MI [*Library symbol Library of Congress*] (LCLS)
MiBatW........ Willard Public Library, Battle Creek, MI [*Library symbol Library of Congress*] (LCLS)
MiBay.......... Bay City Public Library, Bay City, MI [*Library symbol Library of Congress*] (LCLS)
MiBayM....... Bay Medical Center, Bay City, MI [*Library symbol Library of Congress*] (LCLS)
MiBayS........ Bay County Library System, Bay City, MI [*Library symbol Library of Congress*] (LCLS)
MiBayS-A .... Bay County Library System, Auburn Branch Library, Auburn, MI [*Library symbol Library of Congress*] (LCLS)
MiBayS-B .... Bay County Library System, Broadway Branch Library, Bay City, MI [*Library symbol Library of Congress*] (LCLS)
MiBayS-L .... Bay County Library System, Linwood Branch Library, Linwood, MI [*Library symbol Library of Congress*] (LCLS)
MiBayS-P .... Bay County Library System, Pinconning Branch Library, Pinconning, MI [*Library symbol Library of Congress*] (LCLS)
MiBayS-S .... Bay County Library System, Sage Branch Library, Bay City, MI [*Library symbol Library of Congress*] (LCLS)
MIBB.......... Missouri & Illinois Bridge & Belt Railroad [*AAR code Terminated*]
MIBC.......... Methyl Cap. Isobutyl Carbinol [*Also, MIC*] [*Organic chemistry*]
MIBCO .... Member of the Institution of Building Control Officers [*British*] (DBQ)
MiBeiM....... Beaver Island Mormon Colony Library, St. James, Beaver Island, MI [*Library symbol Library of Congress Obsolete*] (LCLS)
MiBel.......... Bellevue Township Library, Bellevue, MI [*Library symbol Library of Congress*] (LCLS)
MiBela........ Bellaire Public Library, Bellaire, MI [*Library symbol Library of Congress*] (LCLS)
MiBen.......... Benzonia Public Library, Benzonia, MI [*Library symbol Library of Congress*] (LCLS)
MiBes.......... Bessemer Public Library, Bessemer, MI [*Library symbol Library of Congress*] (LCLS)
MiBeu.......... Beulah Public Library, Beulah, MI [*Library symbol Library of Congress*] (LCLS)
MIBF.......... Member of the Institute of British Foundrymen
MIBF.......... Montreal International Book Fair
MIBG.......... Meta-Iodobenzylguanidine [*Biochemistry*]
MiBh.......... Benton Harbor Public Library, Benton Harbor, MI [*Library symbol*] [*Library of Congress*] (LCLS)
MiBhL.......... Lake Michigan College, Benton Harbor, MI [*Library symbol Library of Congress*] (LCLS)

MiBhW.........	Whirlpool Corp., Technical Information Center, Benton Harbor, MI [*Library symbol Library of Congress*] (LCLS)
MiBicr..........	Thomas Fleschner Memorial Library, Birch Run, MI [*Library symbol Library of Congress*] (LCLS)
Mibid	Madrid Interbank Bid Rate [*Spain*] (NUMA)
MI Biol	Member of the Institute of Biology [*British*] (EY)
MiBir	Baldwin Public Library, Birmingham, MI [*Library symbol Library of Congress*] (LCLS)
MIBK..........	Methyl Isobutyl Ketone [*Also, MIK*] [*Organic chemistry*]
MiBla..........	Rolland Township Library, Blanchard, MI [*Library symbol Library of Congress*] (LCLS)
MiBloA........	Cranbrook Academy of Art, Bloomfield Hills, MI [*Library symbol Library of Congress*] (LCLS)
MiBloC........	Cranbrook Institute of Science, Bloomfield Hills, MI [*Library symbol Library of Congress*] (LCLS)
MiBloCAr.....	Cranbrook Eductional Community, Archives and Historical Collections, Bloomfield Hills, MI [*Library symbol*] [*Library of Congress*] (LCLS)
MiBloGS......	Church of Jesus Christ of Latter-Day Saints, Genealogical Society Library, Bloomfield Hills Branch, Bloomfield Hills, MI [*Library symbol Library of Congress*] (LCLS)
MIBOC........	Marketing of Investments Board Organising Committee [*British*]
MIBOR........	Madrid Interbank Offered Rate (MHDW)
MIBOS	Measurement of Ingratiatory Behaviours in Organisational Settings (WDAA)
MiBoy..........	Boyne City Public Library, Boyne City, MI [*Library symbol Library of Congress*] (LCLS)
MiBoyf	Boyne Falls Public Library, Boyne Falls, MI [*Library symbol Library of Congress*] (LCLS)
MIBPA	Methyliminobispropylamine [*Organic chemistry*]
Mi-BPH	Michigan Department of Education, State Library Services, Blind and Physically Handicapped Library, Lansing, MI [*Library symbol Library of Congress*] (LCLS)
MIBPrA	Midland Bank A1/A2 Unit ADS [*NYSE symbol*] (TTSB)
MIBPrB	Midland Bank B1/B2 Unit ADS (TTSB)
MIBPrC	Midland Bank C1/C2 Unit ADS [*NYSE symbol*] (TTSB)
MiBr..........	Big Rapids Community Library, Big Rapids, MI [*Library symbol Library of Congress*] (LCLS)
MIBRAG......	Mitteldeutschen Brunkohle (ECON)
MiBrc..........	Brown City Public Library, Brown City, MI [*Library symbol Library of Congress*] (LCLS)
MiBre..........	Howe Memorial Library, Breckenridge, MI [*Library symbol Library of Congress*] (LCLS)
MiBrF..........	Ferris State College, Big Rapids, MI [*Library symbol Library of Congress*] (LCLS)
MiBrid	Bridgeport Public Library, Bridgeport, MI [*Library symbol Library of Congress*] (LCLS)
MiBridm	Bridgman Public Library, Bridgman, MI [*Library symbol Library of Congress*] (LCLS)
MiBrig	Brighton City Library, Brighton, MI [*Library symbol Library of Congress*] (LCLS)
MIBritE	Member of the Institute of British Engineers (EY)
MIBritishE....	Member of the Institute of British Engineers
MIBs..........	Management Information Bases [*Compaq*] [*Computer science*]
MIBS..........	Master of International Business Studies
MIBS..........	Miami International Boat Show and Sailboat Show (ITD)
MiBs..........	Sparks Memorial Library, Berrien Springs, MI [*Library symbol Library of Congress*] (LCLS)
MiBsA..........	Andrews University, Berrien Springs, MI [*Library symbol Library of Congress*] (LCLS)
MIBT..........	Methyl Isatin-beta-thiosemicarbazone
MiBu..........	Taymouth Township Library, Burt, MI [*Library symbol Library of Congress*] (LCLS)
MiBur..........	Burr Oak Township Library, Burr Oak, MI [*Library symbol*] [*Library of Congress*] (LCLS)
MiBurl	Burlington Township Library, Burlington, MI [*Library symbol Library of Congress*] (LCLS)
MIBURN......	Mississippi Burning [*Code name of FBI investigation*]
MIBWG	Military Intelligence Board Working Group
MIC..........	Aerolineas de Michoacan [*Mexico ICAO designator*] (FAAC)
MIC..........	Congregatio Clericorum Regularium Marianorum sub titulo Immaculatae ConceptionisBeatae Mariae Virginis [*Marian Fathers*] [*Roman Catholic religious order*]
mic..........	Congregation of Marians of the Immaculate Conception (TOCD)
MIC..........	Congregation of Marians of the Immaculate Conception (TOCD)
MIC..........	IEEE Medical Imaging Committee (EA)
MIC..........	Itasca Community College, Grand Rapids, MN [*OCLC symbol*] (OCLC)
MIC..........	Machinery Installation Certificate
MIC..........	Made in Canada [*Business term*]
MIC..........	Magnesium Industry Council [*British*] (BI)
MIC..........	Magnetic Ink Character [*Computer science*] (HGAA)
MIC..........	Maintenance Identification Code [*Military*] (CAAL)
MIC..........	Maintenance Index Code (DNAB)
MIC..........	Maintenance Information Center [*Navy*] (NG)
MIC..........	Maintenance Information Chart [*DoD*]
MIC..........	Maintenance Inventory Center [*Air Force*] (AFIT)
MIC..........	Major Immunogene Complex [*Genetics*] (DOG)
MIC..........	Malaysian Indian Congress [*Political party*] (PPW)
MIC..........	Management & Industrial Consultants
MIC..........	Management Indicator Code (MCD)
MIC..........	Management Information Center
mic..........	Management Information Center (NAKS)
MIC..........	Management Information Corp. [*Cherry Hill, NJ*] [*Information service or system*] (IID)
MIC..........	Management Integration Consortium
MIC..........	Marine Information Centre [*Information service or system*] (IID)
MIC..........	Market Impact Clearance
MIC..........	Marketing Intelligence Corp. [*Information service or system*] (IID)
MIC..........	Marketing International Corp. [*Washington, DC*] (TSSD)
MIC..........	Maruman Integrated Circuits (NITA)
MIC..........	Maruzen International Co., Inc. [*Information service or system*] (IID)
MIC..........	Masonry Industry Committee (EA)
MIC..........	Master Interrupt Control [*Computer science*] (OA)
MIC..........	Match Indicator Code (MCD)
MIC..........	Material Identification and Control (DNAB)
MIC..........	Material Inventory Control
MIC..........	Materials Irradiation Chamber
MIC..........	Maternal and Infant Care [*Medicine*]
MIC..........	Maximum Inscribed Circle [*Manufacturing term*]
MIC..........	Meat Importers' Council [*Later, MICA*] (EA)
MIC..........	Meat Industry Council [*Australia*]
MIC..........	Mechanized Information Center [*Information service or system*]
MIC..........	Medical Imaging Committee (NTPA)
MIC..........	Medical Industrial Complex
MIC..........	Medical Information Centre (NITA)
MIC..........	Medical Intensive Care
MIC..........	Medical Interfraternity Conference (EA)
MIC..........	Medium-Intensity Conflict [*Military*]
MIC..........	Medium Interface Connector [*Optics*] (CDE)
MIC..........	Medugorje Information Center (EA)
MIC..........	Mellonics Information Center [*Information service or system*] (IID)
MIC..........	Mellon InvestData Corp. [*New York, NY Information service or system*] (IID)
MIC..........	Memory in Cassette
MIC..........	Memory Interface Connection [*Computer science*]
MIC..........	Merseyside Innovation Centre Ltd. [*Research center British*] (CB)
MIC..........	Message Identification Code [*Computer science*] (BUR)
MIC..........	Meteorological Information Committee [*NATO*] (NATG)
MIC..........	Meteorologist-In-Charge [*Marine science*] (OSRA)
MIC..........	Methylisobutyl Carbinol [*Also, MIBC*] [*Organic chemistry*]
MIC..........	Methyl Isocyanate [*Organic chemistry*]
MIC..........	Metro Industrial [*Vancouver Stock Exchange symbol*]
Mic..........	Micah [*Old Testament book*]
MIC..........	Michigan Information Center [*Michigan State Department of Management and Budget*] [*Information service or system*] (IID)
MIC..........	Michigan Instructional Computer
MIC..........	Michilla [*Chile*] [*Seismograph station code, US Geological Survey*] (SEIS)
mic..........	Micmac [*MARC language code Library of Congress*] (LCCP)
MIC..........	Microbiologically-Influenced Corrosion [*Metallurgical engineering*]
MIC..........	Microcomputer Index [*Information service or system*] (IID)
MIC..........	Microcytosis [*Biochemistry*] (DAVI)
MIC..........	Microelectronic Integrated Circuit (MCD)
MIC..........	Micrometer [*A "mike"*]
mic..........	Micrometer (WDMC)
mic..........	Microphone (WDMC)
MIC..........	Microphone (AABC)
MIC..........	Microscopic (DAVI)
MIC..........	Microscopic Findings in Centrifugal Urinary Sediment [*Biochemistry*] (DAVI)
Mic..........	Microscopium [*Constellation*]
MIC..........	Microscopy
MIC..........	Microwave Integrated Circuitry
MIC..........	Microwave Integrated Circuits (NITA)
MIC..........	Microwave Interference Coordination
MIC..........	Middle Income Country [*Category of developing country*]
MIC..........	Mid-Intensity Conflict [*Military*] (INF)
MIC..........	Midwest Intercollegiate Conference (PSS)
MIC..........	Military Indoctrination Center
M-IC..........	Military-Industrial Complex
MIC..........	Military Information Center [*Defunct*] (EA)
MIC..........	Military Introductory Letter
MIC..........	Millicm International Cellular S.A. [*Commercial firm*] [*Luxembourg*]
MIC..........	Mineral Industries Census
MIC..........	Minimal [*or Minimum*] Inhibitory Concentration
MIC..........	Minimal Isorrheic Concentration [*Medicine*]
MIC..........	Minimum Ignition Current (IEEE)
MIC..........	Minimum Inhibitory Concentration [*Bactericidal characteristic*]
MIC..........	Minneapolis, MN [*Location identifier FAA*] (FAAL)
MIC..........	Minocycline [*Antibiotic compound*] (AAMN)
MIC..........	Minor Care Clinic [*Medicine*]
MIC..........	Missile Identification Code [*Military*] (CAAL)
MIC..........	Missing Interruption Character (NITA)
MIC..........	Missing Interruption Checker (MCD)
MIC..........	Missionary Sisters of the Immaculate Conception [*Roman Catholic religious order*]
MIC..........	Missionary Sisters of the Immaculate Conception (Canada) (TOCD)
MIC..........	Mississippi Industrial College [*Holly Springs*]
MIC..........	Mobile Incident Center (WDAA)
MIC..........	Mobile Information Center [*An association*]
MIC..........	Mobile Intensive Care [*Medicine*] (DHSM)
MIC..........	Model Immune Complex [*Medicine*] (DMAA)
MIC..........	Monitoring, Identification, and Correlation
MIC..........	Monolithic Integrated Circuit
MIC..........	Mononuclear Inflammatory Cell (DMAA)
MIC..........	Morphology-Immunology-Cytogenetics [*Classification of Leukemias*]
MIC..........	Mortgage Insurance Certificate (EMRF)
MIC..........	Mortgage Insurance Co.
MIC..........	Motorcycle Industry Council (EA)

MIC .... Mountain Instructor's Certificate [British] (DI)
MIC .... Movimiento de Integracion Colorada [Paraguay] [Political party] (EY)
MIC .... Multichip Integrated Circuit (NITA)
MIC .... Multimedia Interactive Control
MIC .... Multinational Intelligence Cell (MCD)
MIC .... Multiperil Insurance Conference
MIC .... MuniYield CA Insured Fund [NYSE symbol] (TTSB)
MIC .... MuniYield California Insured Fund [NYSE symbol] (SPSG)
MIC .... Music Industry Conference (EA)
MIC .... Music Industry Council [Later, Music Industry Conference] (EA)
MIC .... Music Information Center (TELE)
MIC .... Mutual Improvement Class [British railroad term]
MIC .... Mutual Interference Chart (IEEE)
MiCa .... Indianfields Public Library, Caro, MI [Library symbol Library of Congress] (LCLS)
MICA .... Macroinstruction Compiler Assembler [Computer science]
MICA .... Major Incidents Computer Application (PDAA)
MICA .... Meat Importers' Council of America (EA)
MICA .... Mentally Ill Chemical Abuser
MICA .... MicroAge, Inc. [NASDAQ symbol] (SAG)
MICA .... Mobile Industrial Caterers' Association (EA)
MICA .... Mortgage Insurance Companies of America (EA)
MiCac .... Rawson Memorial Library, Cass City, MI [Library symbol Library of Congress] (LCLS)
MiCad .... Cadillac-Wexford Public Library, Cadillac, MI [Library symbol Library of Congress] (LCLS)
MICAD .... Multipurpose Integrated Chemical Agent Alarm [Army] (DOMA)
MiCadCS .... Cadillac Public School, Cadillac, MI [Library symbol] [Library of Congress] (LCLS)
MiCadM .... Mid-Michigan Library League, Cadillac, MI [Library symbol Library of Congress] (LCLS)
MiCadPS .... Wexford Public Schools, Cadillac, MI [Library symbol Library of Congress] (LCLS)
MICAF .... Measuring Improved Capability of Army Forces
MiCal .... Calumet Public-School Library, Calumet, MI [Library symbol Library of Congress] (LCLS)
MICALL .... Microprocedure Call [Computer science] (MHDB)
MiCam .... Camden Township Library, Camden, MI [Library symbol Library of Congress] (LCLS)
MICAM .... Microammeter [Electronics]
MICAM .... Micro Camera (NITA)
MICAM .... Micro-Connection Assembly Method
MICAM .... Mid-Function Integral Control Alarm Module [Electronics systems] [Automotive engineering]
MICAP .... Measuring Improved Capability [Army]
MICAP .... Mission Capability
MICAP .... Mission Incapable, Awaiting Parts (MCD)
MICAPS .... Mine/Countermine Casualty Assessment Producing System (MCD)
MICAS .... Military Intelligence Co., Aerial Surveillance (MCD)
MiCassC .... Cass County Library, Cassopolis, MI [Library symbol Library of Congress] (LCLS)
MICB .... Meck Island Control Building [Army] (AABC)
MICBM .... Mobile Intercontinental Ballistic Missile
MiCc .... Carson City Public Library, Carson City, MI [Library symbol Library of Congress] (LCLS)
MICC .... Metal Interconnect Cascade Cell [Photovoltaic energy systems]
MICC .... Military Information Control Committee (CINC)
MICC .... Millicom International Cellular [NASDAQ symbol] (SAG)
MICC .... Mineral Insulated, Copper Covered [Cable]
MICC .... Mitogen-Induced Cellular Cytotoxicity [Medicine] (DB)
MICC .... Mortgage Insurance Co. of Canada
MICCF .... Millicom Intl Cellular S.A. [NASDAQ symbol] (TTSB)
MICCI .... Malaysia International Chamber of Commerce and Industry (EAIO)
MICCLE .... Michigan Interorganizational Committee on Continuing Library Education (EDAC)
MICCO .... Model Inner City Community Organization [Washington, DC]
MICCS .... Minuteman Integrated Command and Control System [Missiles]
Mic D .... Doctor of Microbiology
MICD .... Mechanical, Thermal, and Optical Interface Control Document (MCD)
MICDS .... Movable In-Core Detector System [Nuclear energy] (NRCH)
MICE .... Management Information Capability for Enforcement [Environmental Protection Agency] (GFGA)
MICE .... Man's Impact on Coastal and Estuarine Ecosystems [Marine science] [United Nations] (OSRA)
MICE .... Material Transfer, Information Transfer, Control Transfer, Energy Transfer
MICE .... Member of the Institution of Civil Engineers [Formerly, AMICE] [British]
MICE .... Methods Information Communication Exchange Service (AEPA)
MICE .... Microelectronic Integrated Checkout Equipment
MICE .... Money, Ideology, Compromise, Ego [CIA acronym for possible explanations for spy defections]
MICE .... Mutual Insurance Council of Editors [Later, PICA] (EA)
MiCe .... Nottawa Township Library, Centerville, MI [Library symbol Library of Congress] (LCLS)
MiCeG .... Glen Oaks Community College, Centreville, MI [Library symbol Library of Congress] (LCLS)
MICEI .... Member of the Institution of Civil Engineers of Ireland
MICELEM .... Microphone Element (IEEE)
MiCen .... Leslie R. Foss Public Library, Center Line, MI [Library symbol Library of Congress] (LCLS)
MiCenl .... Central Lake Township Library, Central Lake, MI [Library symbol Library of Congress] (LCLS)
MiCES .... Microcomputer-Controlled Electroanalysis System [Interactive Microwave]

MiCf .... Crystal Falls Community Library, Crystal Falls, MI [Library symbol Library of Congress] (LCLS)
MicFocu .... Micro Focus Group PLC [Associated Press] (SAG)
Micfrm .... Microframe, Inc. [Associated Press] (SAG)
MICG .... Macromolecular Insoluble Cold Globulin (DMAA)
MICG .... Management Information Coordinating Group [Navy]
MICG .... Mercury Iodide Crystal Growth
MICG .... Microfield Graphics [NASDAQ symbol] (TTSB)
MICG .... Microfield Graphics, Inc. [NASDAQ symbol] (SAG)
MICH .... Michaelmas [Feast of St. Michael the Archangel, September 29]
Mich .... Michaelmas Term [British Legal term] (DLA)
MICH .... Michaels [J.], Inc. [NASDAQ symbol] (NQ)
MICH .... Michaels J [NASDAQ symbol] (TTSB)
MICH .... Micheas [Old Testament book] [Douay version]
MICH .... Michigan
Mich .... Michigan (ODBW)
Mich .... Michigan Supreme Court Reports [A publication] (DLA)
MiCha .... Chase Public Library, Chase, MI [Library symbol Library of Congress] (LCLS)
Mich Admin Code ... Michigan Administrative Code [A publication] (DLA)
Mich Adv .... Michigan Reports Advanced Sheets [A publication] (DLA)
MichAnt .... Michael Anthony Jewelers, Inc. [Associated Press] (SAG)
Mich App .... Michigan Court of Appeals Reports [A publication] (DLA)
MiChar .... Charlotte Public Library, Charlotte, MI [Library symbol Library of Congress] (LCLS)
Mich Att'y Gen Biennial Rep ... Biennial Report of the Attorney General of the State of Michigan [A publication] (DLA)
MichBr .... Michigan Brewery, Inc. [Associated Press] (SAG)
MichBrw .... Michigan Brewery, Inc. [Associated Press] (SAG)
Mich Calidon ... Michael Calidonius [Flourished, 16th century] [Authority cited in pre-1607 legal work] (DSA)
Mich CCR .... Michigan Circuit Court Reporter [A publication] (DLA)
Mich Comp L Ann ... Michigan Compiled Laws, Annotated [A publication] (DLA)
Mich Comp Laws ... Michigan Compiled Laws [A publication] (DLA)
Mich Comp Laws ... Michigan Compiled Laws Annotated [West] [A publication] (AAGC)
Mich Comp Laws Ann ... Michigan Compiled Laws, Annotated [A publication] (DLA)
Mich Cr Ct Rep ... Michigan Circuit Court Reporter [A publication] (DLA)
Mich Ct Cl ... Michigan Court of Claims (AAGC)
Mich Ct Cl ... Michigan Court of Claims Reports [A publication] (DLA)
MiChe .... Cheboygan Area Public Library, Cheboygan, MI [Library symbol Library of Congress] (LCLS)
MiChel .... McKune Memorial Library, Chelsea, MI [Library symbol Library of Congress] (LCLS)
MIChemE .... Member of the Institution of Chemical Engineers [British] (EY)
MiChes .... Chesaning Public Library, Chesaning, MI [Library symbol Library of Congress] (LCLS)
MichFncl .... Michigan Financial Corp. [Associated Press] (SAG)
Michie's GA Repts Ann ... Georgia Reports, Annotated [A publication] (DLA)
Michie's Jur ... Michie's Jurisprudence of Virginia and West Virginia [A publication] (DLA)
MichJ .... Michaels [J.], Inc. [Associated Press] (SAG)
Mich Jur .... Michigan Jurisprudence [A publication] (DLA)
Mich L .... Michigan Lawyer [A publication] (DLA)
Mich Legis Serv ... Michigan Legislative Service [A publication] (DLA)
Mich Leg News ... Michigan Legal News [A publication] (DLA)
MichIF .... Michael Foods, Inc. [Associated Press] (SAG)
Mich LJ .... Michigan Law Journal [A publication] (DLA)
Mich Nisi Prius ... Brown's Michigan Nisi Prius Reports [A publication] (DLA)
Mich NP .... Brown's Michigan Nisi Prius Reports [A publication] (DLA)
Mich Pub Acts ... Public and Local Acts of the Legislature of the State of Michigan [A publication] (DLA)
Mich PUC Ops ... Michigan Public Utilities Commission Orders and Opinions [A publication] (DLA)
Mich R .... Michigan Reports [A publication] (DLA)
Mich RC Dec ... Michigan Railroad Commission Decisions [A publication] (DLA)
MICHS .... Michaelmas [Feast of St. Michael the Archangel, September 29]
Mich SBA Jo ... Michigan State Bar Association. Journal [A publication] (DLA)
Mich Stat Ann ... Michigan Statutes, Annotated [A publication] (DLA)
MichStr .... Michael Stores [Associated Press] (SAG)
Mich St U .... Michigan State University (GAGS)
Mich Supr Ct Rep ... Michigan Reports [A publication] (DLA)
Mich T .... Michaelmas Term [British Legal term] (DLA)
Mich Tech U ... Michigan Technological University (GAGS)
MiChv .... Charlevoix Public Library, Charlevoix, MI [Library symbol Library of Congress] (LCLS)
Mich Vac .... Michaelmas Vacation [British Legal term] (DLA)
Mich WCC ... Michigan Industrial Accident Board, Workmen's Compensation Cases [A publication] (DLA)
MICIS .... Material Information Control and Information System (MCD)
MiCiS .... Material Information Control and Information System (NAKS)
MICIS .... Material Inventory Control and Inventory System (NASA)
MICIS .... Microbial Culture Information Service [Department of Trade and Industry] [British Information service or system]
MICIS .... Midwestern Climate Information System [Marine science] (OSRA)
MICK .... Manufacturers Item Correlation Key
MICL .... Missile In-Commission Level
MiCla .... Garfield Memorial Public Library, Clare, MI [Library symbol Library of Congress] (LCLS)
MICLE .... Institute of Continuing Legal Education, University of Michigan (DLA)
MICLIC .... Mine Clearing Line Charge [Army] (INF)
MiClin .... Clinton Public Library, Clinton, MI [Library symbol Library of Congress] (LCLS)
MICLO .... Management Information Control Liaison Officers (MCD)

MICM......... Associate Member of the Institute of Credit Management [*British*] (DBQ)
MICM........... MICOM Communications [*NASDAQ symbol*] (TTSB)
MICM........... Micom Communications Corp. [*NASDAQ symbol*] (SAG)
MICM........... Monolithic Integrated Circuit Mask
MICMD........ Milwaukee Contract Management District (SAA)
MICMPTR .... Microcomputer (MSA)
MICN........... Medical Intensive Care Nurse (DAVI)
MICN........... Micrion Corp. [*NASDAQ symbol*] (SAG)
MICN........... Mobile Intensive Care Nurse [*Emergency Medicine*] (DAVI)
MICNS.......... Modular Integrated Communications and Navigation System (RDA)
MICO .... Management Information Systems Control Officer (MCD)
MICO .... Mankato Industrial Corp. [*Automotive industry supplier*]
MICO .... Member of the Institute of Careers Officers [*British*] (DBQ)
MICO .... Midland Continental R. R. [*AAR code Obsolete*]
MICO .... MLV Integration and Checkout (MCD)
MICOFT........ Mutual Insurance Committee on Federal Taxation (EA)
MiCol.......... Coloma Public Library, Coloma, MI [*Library symbol Library of Congress*] (LCLS)
MiCole......... Coleman Area Library, Coleman, MI [*Library symbol Library of Congress*] (LCLS)
MiColo......... Colon Township Library, Colon, MI [*Library symbol Library of Congress*] (LCLS)
MiCom......... Comstock Township Library, Comstock, MI [*Library symbol Library of Congress*] (LCLS)
MICOM .... Missile Command [*Redstone Arsenal, AL*] [*Army*]
MICOM .... US Army Missile Command (AAGC)
MicomC ...... Micom Communications Corp. [*Associated Press*] (SAG)
MICOM-RDEC... Missile Command Research, Development, and Engineering Center [*Army*] (RDA)
MICOMS ...... Maintenance Information Concerning [*the repair and operation of*] Missile Systems
MiCon.......... Constatine Township Library, Constatine, MI [*Library symbol Library of Congress*] (LCLS)
MICON.......... Military Construction Program (MUGU)
micon.......... Motion Icon [*Computer science*] (WDMC)
MICONEX..... Multinational Instrumentation Conference and Exposition [*China Instrument Society*]
MiCoop........ Coopersville District Library, Coopersville, MI [*Library symbol Library of Congress*] (LCLS)
MI-COPICS... Management Information for COPICS [*Communications Oriented Production Information and Control System*] Users [*IBM Corp.*]
MICorrST ..... Member of the Institute of Corrosion Science and Technology [*British*] (DBQ)
MICOS .... Mini Computer Systems (NITA)
MICP............ Management and Investment Companies Program
MICP............ Military Inventory Control Point (MCD)
MICPAC .... Microelectronic Integrated Circuit Package (MCD)
MICPAK .... Modular Integrated Circuit Package
MIC PAN ...... Mica Panis [*Crumb of Bread*] [*Pharmacy*]
MicPwr .... Microwave Power Devices, Inc. [*Associated Press*] (SAG)
MICR .... Magnetic Ink Character Recognition [*Banking*] [*Computer science*]
MICR .... Management Improvement and Cost Reduction Project Reporting System
MICR .... Microenergy, Inc. [*NASDAQ symbol*] (SAG)
MICR .... Microscope (MSA)
Micr .... Microscopium [*Constellation*]
MICRA .... Medical Injury Compensation Reform Act
MICRA .... Miniature Insulated Contact Range (PDAA)
MICRAD .... Microwave Radiometry (MCD)
MICRADS..... Microwave Radiation System (PDAA)
MICRAM ...... Microminiature Individual Components Reliable Assembled Modules
MicrBi........ Micro Bio-Medics, Inc. [*Associated Press*] (SAG)
Micrdy........ Microdyne Corp. [*Associated Press*] (SAG)
Micrel.......... Micrel, Inc. [*Associated Press*] (SAG)
Micrenr........ Microenergy, Inc. [*Associated Press*] (SAG)
MicrFlt........ Microwave Filter Co., Inc. [*Associated Press*] (SAG)
Micrgfx........ Micrografx, Inc. [*Associated Press*] (SAG)
MicrGn........ Micro General Corp. [*Associated Press*] (SAG)
Micrion........ Micrion Corp. [*Associated Press*] (SAG)
Micrl.......... Microleague Multimedia, Inc. [*Associated Press*] (SAG)
Micrleag...... Microleague Multimedia, Inc. [*Associated Press*] (SAG)
MICR/MIMR... Magnetic Ink Character Recognition / Magnetic Ink Mark Recognition (BTTJ)
MIC-RN........ Mobile Intensive Care Registered Nurse [*Emergency medicine*] (DAVI)
Micrnics ...... Micronics Computers, Inc. [*Associated Press*] (SAG)
MicrnT........ Micron Technology [*Associated Press*] (SAG)
micro.......... Extremely Small (IDOE)
MICRO......... Microcomputer
MICRO......... Microelectronics Innovation and Computer Science Research Program [*University of California*] [*Research center*] (RCD)
MICRO......... Microprocessor
micro.......... Microscopic
MICRO......... Multiple Indexing and Console Retrieval Operations (NITA)
MICRO......... Multiple Indexing and Console Retrieval Options [*Information retrieval Computer science*]
MICROACE... Microminiature Automatic Checkout Equipment
MicroAge..... MicroAge, Inc., [*Associated Press*] (SAG)
MICROBIOL.. Microbiological [*or Microbiology*]
MicroCap..... [*The*] MicroCap Fund [*Associated Press*] (SAG)
MICROCAT... Micro-Catalogue (NITA)
Microchip..... Microchip Technology, Inc. [*Associated Press*] (SAG)
Microcm...... Microcom, Inc. [*Associated Press*] (SAG)
MICROCON... Microcomputer Based Services for Retrospective Conversions (NITA)

microcryst ... Microcrystalline (BARN)
MicroCSI..... MicroStation Customer Support Library [*Intergraph Corp.*] (PCM)
MicroCT...... Micro Component Technology, Inc. [*Associated Press*] (SAG)
MICRODIS ... Microform Document of Information System (MCD)
MICRO-DISC... Microcomputer-Videodisc
MICRODOC... Council for Microphotography and Document Reproduction [*British*]
Microfd....... Microfield Graphics, Inc. [*Associated Press*] (SAG)
MicrofdG..... Microfield Graphics, Inc. [*Associated Press*] (SAG)
Microflu....... Microfluidics International Corp. [*Associated Press*] (SAG)
MICROG....... Microgram [*One millionth of a gram*]
MicroIntg .... Micro-Integration Corp. [*Associated Press*] (SAG)
MICROLAB... Microfabrication Laboratory [*University of California, Berkeley*] [*Research center*] (RCD)
Microlg....... Microlog Corp. [*Associated Press*] (SAG)
MicroLin..... Micro Linear Corp. [*Associated Press*] (SAG)
MICROM...... Microinstruction Read-Only Memory [*Computer science*]
MICROMIN... Microminiature (IEEE)
MICRON....... Micronavigator [*Air Force*]
MicronEl...... Micron Electronics, Inc. [*Associated Press*] (SAG)
MICRONET... Microcomputer Network (NITA)
Micront ...... Micronetics, Inc. [*Associated Press*] (SAG)
Microp .... Micropolis Corp. [*Associated Press*] (SAG)
MICROPAC... Micromodule Data Processor and Computer (IEEE)
MicroPh...... Microcide Pharmaceuticals, Inc. [*Associated Press*] (SAG)
MICROPSI.... Microcomputer Printed Subject Indexes (NITA)
MICROS....... Microscopy
Micros....... Micros Systems, Inc. [*Associated Press*] (SAG)
MICROSECS.. Microfilm Sequential Coding System [*Bell System*]
Microsft...... Microsoft Corp. [*Associated Press*] (SAG)
MICROSID.... Small Seismic Intrusion Detector (PDAA)
MicroSIFT.... Microcomputer Software and Information for Teachers [*Northwest Regional Educational Laboratory*] [*Information service or system*] (IID)
MICROSIM... Microinstruction Simulator [*Computer science*] (MHDI)
Microsoft.... Microsoft Corp. [*Associated Press*] (SAG)
MicrosTo ..... Micros-To Mainframe, Inc. [*Associated Press*] (SAG)
Microtel...... Microtel International, Inc. [*Associated Press*] (SAG)
Microtl....... Microtel Franchise & Development Corp. [*Associated Press*] (SAG)
MicroTo ...... Micros-To Mainframe, Inc. [*Associated Press*] (SAG)
MICRO TR ... Microwave Tower [*Nautical charts*]
MICRO-VERS.. Microcomputer Vocational Education Reporting System (EDAC)
MicroWre..... Micro Warehouse, Inc. [*Associated Press*] (SAG)
MicrPck...... Microelectronic Packaging, Inc. [*Associated Press*] (SAG)
MICRS .... Main Instrument Console and Readout Stations (NATG)
MicrtcRs ..... Microtec Research, Inc. [*Associated Press*] (SAG)
Micrtek....... Microtek Medical, Inc. [*Associated Press*] (SAG)
Micrtest...... Microtest, Inc. [*Associated Press*] (SAG)
MICRU .... MICRU International (EA)
Micrvisn...... Microvision, Inc. [*Associated Press*] (SAG)
MICS .... Maintenance Inventory Control System [*Bell System*]
MICS .... Management Information and Control System [*Navy*]
MICS .... Management Integrated Control System
MICS .... Manned Interactive Control Stations (MCD)
MICS .... Manufacturing Information and Control System (OA)
MICS .... Material Inventory Control System [*NASA*] (SSD)
MICS .... Medical Instrument Calibration System (PDAA)
MICS .... Microprocessor Inertia and Communication System
MICS .... Military Integrated Communications System (CINC)
MICS .... Mineral-Insulated Copper-Sheathed [*Cable*] (IEEE)
MICS .... Missile Inspection Completion Sheet (MCD)
MICS .... Mitsubishi Intelligent Cockpit System [*Automotive engineering*]
MICS .... Multiplex Interior Communications (NG)
MICS .... Museum of the International College of Surgeons (NADA)
MICS .... MVS Integrated Control System (NITA)
MICSA .... Maine Indian Claims Settlement Act [*1980*]
MicSem ...... Microsemi Corp. [*Associated Press*] (SAG)
Micsft........ Microsoft Corp. [*Associated Press*] (SAG)
MICTAR ...... Minnesota Center for Twin and Adoption Research (ECON)
MictchS ...... Microtouch Systems, Inc. [*Associated Press*] (SAG)
MictchSy..... Microtouch Systems, Inc. [*Associated Press*] (SAG)
MICU .... Medical Intensive Care Unit [*Medicine*]
MICU .... Mobile Intensive Care Unit [*Medicine*]
MICU(N) ...... Mobile Intensive Care Unit [*or Nurse*] (GNE)
MICV.......... Mechanized Infantry Combat Vehicle [*Army*]
MICV-FPW ... Mechanized Infantry Combat Vehicle - Firing Port Weapon (MCD)
MICVS .... Mechanized Infantry Combat Vehicle Systems [*Army*] (RDA)
MiCw .... Coldwater Public Library, Coldwater, MI [*Library symbol Library of Congress*] (LCLS)
MICW.......... Member of the Institute of Clerks of Works of Great Britain, Inc. (DBQ)
Micware ..... Microware Systems Corp. [*Associated Press*] (SAG)
MiCwB........ Branch County Library, Coldwater, MI [*Library symbol Library of Congress*] (LCLS)
MiD........... Detroit Public Library, Detroit, MI [*Library symbol Library of Congress*] (LCLS)
MID........... Magnetically Insulated Diode [*Physics*]
MID........... Maintenace Index Page (DNAB)
MID........... Manpower Information Division [*Navy*]
MID........... Mare Island Division [*San Francisco Bay Naval Shipyard, Vallejo, CA*]
MID........... Marginally Indigent Defendant
MID........... Master of Industrial Design
MID........... Master of Interior Design (GAGS)
MID........... Material Identification (AAEL)
MID........... Maximum Inhibiting Dilution [*Medicine*] (MAE)

MID............. Maximum Inhibiting Duration [*Medicine*] (DAVI)
MID............. Measure of Intellectual Development (EDAC)
MID............. Meat Inspection Division [*of ARS, Department of Agriculture*]
MID............. Median Infective Dose [*Bacteriology*]
MID............. Mentioned in Dispatches (ADA)
MID............. Merida [*Mexico*] [*Airport symbol*] (OAG)
MID............. Mesioincisodistal [*Dentistry*]
MID............. Message Identification [*Computer science*]
MID............. Message Identifier (ACRL)
MID............. Message Input Description
MID............. Message Input Device (AABC)
MID............. Mid Airways [*France*] [*FAA designator*] (FAAC)
MID............. Midbody
MID............. Midcon Oil & Gas Ltd. [*Toronto Stock Exchange symbol*]
MID............. Middle (AFM)
mid............. Middle (VRA)
MID............. Middleton Island [*Alaska*] [*Seismograph station code, US Geological Survey*] (SEIS)
MID............. Middling Space [*Typesetting*] (DGA)
Mid............. Middoth (BJA)
MID............. Midland [*Topography*] (ROG)
MID............. MIDLNET [*Midwest Regional Library Network*], St. Louis, MO [*OCLC symbol*] (OCLC)
MID............. Midnight
Mid............. Midrash [*Interpretation of Old Testament writings*] (BJA)
MID............. Midshipman [*Navy*]
Mid............. Midshipman (WDAA)
MID............. Midway Railroad Co. [*AAR code*]
MID............. Midwest Stock Exchange [*Chicago, IL*] (CDAI)
MID............. Midwifery (ROG)
MID............. Military Intelligence Detachment (AABC)
MID............. Military Intelligence Division [*War Department*] [*World War II*]
MID............. Minimal Inhibiting Dose [*Medicine*]
MID............. Minimum Infective Dose [*Bacteriology*]
MID............. Ministerstvo Inostrannykh Del [*Ministry of Foreign Affairs*] [*Former USSR*]
MID............. Missile Intelligence Directorate [*Army*] (AABC)
MID............. Missile Intelligence Directory
MID............. Modified Ionization Detector (MCD)
MID............. Mortgage Interest Differential
MID............. Movimiento de Integracion Democratica [*Democratic Integration Movement*] [*Dominican Republic*] [*Political party*] (PPW)
MID............. Movimiento Independiente Democratico [*Independent Democratic Movement*] [*Panama*] [*Political party*] (PPW)
MID............. Multi-Information Display [*Automotive engineering*]
MID............. Multiple Infant Dementia [*Neurology*] (CPH)
MID............. Multiple Infarct Dementia [*Neurology*]
MID............. Multiple Ion Detection
MID............. Multiplexing Identifier [*Telecommunications*] (ACRL)
MID............. Munitions Inventions Department [*British military*] (DMA)
MID............. Musically Intelligent Device [*Electronic musical instruments*]
MiDA............ Detroit Institute of Arts, Detroit, MI [*Library symbol Library of Congress*] (LCLS)
MIDA............ Major Items Data Agency [*Military*]
MIDA............ Message Interchange Distributed Application [*Telecommunications*] (OSI)
MIDA............ Mid-American International Development Association [*Nigeria*]
MIDA............ Moviemiento de Integracion Democratica [*The Dominican Republic*] [*Political party*] (EY)
MIDA............ Myocardial Ischemia Dynamic Analysis [*Medicine*] (DMAA)
MiDAA........... Catholic Archdiocese of Detroit, Archives, Detroit, MI [*Library symbol Library of Congress*] (LCLS)
MidAApt........ Mid America Apartment Communities, Inc. [*Associated Press*] (SAG)
MidABc......... Mid-America Bancorp [*Associated Press*] (SAG)
MIDAC.......... Management Information for Decision and Control
MIDAC.......... Michigan [*University of*] Digital Automatic Computer
MiDACI......... American Concrete Institute, Detroit, MI [*Library symbol Library of Congress*] (LCLS)
MIDADE........ Mouvement International d'Apostolat des Enfants [*International Movement of Apostolate of Children*] [*France*]
MidAE.......... Mid American Energy Co. [*Associated Press*] (SAG)
MidAg.......... Midrash Aggadah (BJA)
Mid-Am......... Mid-America: An Historical Review [*A publication*] (BRI)
MIDAM......... Midamerica Commodity Exchange (EA)
MidAm.......... Mid-Am, Inc. [*Associated Press*] (SAG)
MiDAMA........ Automobile Manufacturers' Association, Inc., Detroit, MI [*Library symbol Library of Congress*] (LCLS)
MidAmEn....... Mid American Energy Co. [*Associated Press*] (SAG)
MidAmIn........ Mid-Am, Inc. [*Associated Press*] (SAG)
MidAmR........ Mid America Realty, Inc. [*Formerly, Dial REIT*] [*Associated Press*] (SAG)
MIDAN......... Microprocessor Data Analyzer [*Instrumentation*]
MIDANET....... Mortgage Information Direct Access Network [*FHLMC*] (EMRF)
MidAp.......... Mid America Apartment Communities [*Associated Press*] (SAG)
MIDAR......... Microwave Detection and Ranging
MIDAR......... Motion Indicating RADAR (MCD)
MID-ARK....... Mid-Arkansas Regional Library [*Library network*]
MIDARM........ Microdynamic Angle and Rate Monitoring System
MIDAS......... Mainline Information Display and Automation System [*Salford Electrical Instruments*] (NITA)
MIDAS......... Maintenance Integrated Data Access System (MCD)
MIDAS......... Management Information and Development Aids System (SSD)
MIDAS......... Management Integrated Data Accumulating System
MIDAS......... Management Interactive Data Accounting System [*Computer science*] (CIST)

MIDAS......... Man-Machine Integration Design and Analysis System (GAVI)
MIDAS......... Maritime Industrial Development Area [*Navy*]
MIDAS......... Materiel Inventory Data Acquisition System
MIDAS......... Measurement Information Data Analysis System [*or Subsystem*] (IEEE)
MIDAS......... Mechanism Integration Design and Analysis System [*Computer-assisted engineering*]
MIDAS......... Medical Information Dissemination Using ASSASSIN (NITA)
MIDAS......... Memory Implemented Data Acquisition Systems
MIDAS......... Meteorological Information and Dose Acquisition System [*Nuclear energy*] (NRCH)
MIDAS......... Meteorological Integrating Data Acquisition System [*Marine science*] (MSC)
MIDAS......... Microcomputer-Interfaced Data Acquisition System [*Computer science*]
MIDAS......... Micro-Diagnostics for Analysis and Repair (NITA)
MIDAS......... Microimaged Data Addition System [*CAPS Equipment Ltd.*]
MIDAS......... Microprogrammable Integrated Data Acquisition System
MIDAS......... Microprogramming Design Aided System [*RCA*]
MIDAS......... Microscopic Image Digital Acquisition System (PDAA)
MIDAS......... Mine Detection and Avoidance System (MCD)
MIDAS......... Miniature Data Acquisition System
MIDAS......... Missile Defense Alarm [*or Alert*] System [*Air Force*]
MIDAS......... Missile Detection and Alarm System [*Army*] (AABC)
MIDAS......... Missile Detection and Surveillance (CAAL)
MIDAS......... Missile Intercept Data Acquisition System
MIDAS......... Model for Interheater Deployment by Air and Sea [*DoD*]
MIDAS......... Modified Integration Digital Analog Simulator [*Computer science*] (MCD)
MIDAS......... Modular Integrated Design Automated System
MIDAS......... Modular Interactive Data Acquisition System [*National Institute of Standards and Technology*]
MIDAS......... Modular International Dealing and Accounting System (NITA)
MIDAS......... Modulator Isolation Diagnostic Analysis System (IEEE)
MIDAS......... Monopoly Information and Data Analysis System
MIDAS......... Multicenter Isradipine Diuretic Atherosclerosis Study
MIDAS......... Multi-Discipline Data Analysis System (GAVI)
MIDAS......... Multi-Mode International Data Acquisition Service (NITA)
MIDAS......... Multioptional Interactive Display and Analytic System (MCD)
MIDAS......... Multiple Index Data Access System [*Prime Computer, Inc.*]
MIDAS......... Multiple Input Data Acquisition System [*Bell System*]
MIDAS......... Multiple Integrated Document Assembly System [*Computer science*] (BYTE)
MIDAS......... Multitier Distributed Application Services [*Computer science*]
MID/ASIA..... Middle East/Asia Region [*USTTA*] (TAG)
MIDATA....... Marconi Integrated Design and Test Automation [*Marconi Industries*] [*Telecommunications British*]
MIDATL........ Mid-Atlantic (DNAB)
MidAtlan....... Mid-Atlantic Medical Services, Inc. [*Associated Press*] (SAG)
MidatRty....... Midatlantic Realty Trust [*Associated Press*] (SAG)
MiDb.......... Dearborn Public [*Henry Ford Centennial*] Library, Dearborn, MI [*Library symbol Library of Congress*] (LCLS)
MiDB.......... Detroit Bar Association, Detroit, MI [*Library symbol Library of Congress*] (LCLS)
MiD-B......... Detroit Public Library, Burton Historical Collection, Detroit, MI [*Library symbol Library of Congress*] (LCLS)
MIDB.......... Misr Iran Development Bank
MiDBA......... Detroit Bar Association, Detroit, MI [*Library symbol*] [*Library of Congress*] (LCLS)
MidBay........ Middle Bay Oil Co., Inc. [*Associated Press*] (SAG)
MiDbEI........ Edison Institute [*Henry Ford Museum and Greenfield Village*] Library, Dearborn, MI [*Library symbol Library of Congress*] (LCLS)
MiDbF......... Ford Motor Co., Dearborn, MI [*Library symbol Library of Congress*] (LCLS)
MiDbGS....... Church of Jesus Christ of Latter-Day Saints, Genealogical Society Library, Dearborn Stake Branch, LDS Chapel, Dearborn, MI [*Library symbol Library of Congress*] (LCLS)
MiDbHi........ Dearborn Historical Museum, Dearborn, MI [*Library symbol Library of Congress*] (LCLS)
MidBk......... Midland Bank PLC [*Associated Press*] (SAG)
MiDbME....... Society of Manufacturing Engineers, Dearborn, MI [*Library symbol*] [*Library of Congress*] (LCLS)
MidbO........ Oakwood Hospital, Dearborn, MI [*Library symbol*] [*Library of Congress*] (LCLS)
MiDbU........ University of Michigan, Dearborn Campus, Dearborn, MI [*Library symbol Library of Congress*] (LCLS)
MIDBX........ Mgn. Stanley D. Witter Mid-Cap Growth Cl.B [*Mutual fund ticker symbol*] (SG)
MiDC.......... Detroit Chancery [*Catholic Church*] Archives, Detroit, MI [*Library symbol Library of Congress*] (LCLS)
MIDC.......... MidConn Bank [*NASDAQ symbol*] (NQ)
MIDC.......... Movement for an Independent and Democratic Cuba (EA)
MiDCh......... Children's Hospital of Michigan, Detroit, MI [*Library symbol Library of Congress*] (LCLS)
MiDChryE..... Chrysler Corp., Engineering Division, Detroit, MI [*Library symbol Library of Congress*] (LCLS)
MiDCL......... Detroit College of Law, Detroit, ME [*Library symbol*] [*Library of Congress*] (LCLS)
Midcom....... Midcom Communications, Inc. [*Associated Press*] (SAG)
MidContB...... Mid Continent Bancshares, Inc. [*Associated Press*] (SAG)
MIDCRU....... Midshipman Cruise [*Navy*] (NVT)
MidCst........ Mid-Coast Bancorp, Inc. [*Associated Press*] (SAG)
MidcstE....... Midcoast Energy Resources, Inc. [*Associated Press*] (SAG)
MIDD.......... Middleby Corp. [*NASDAQ symbol*] (TTSB)

MIDDLE .... Microprogram Design Description Language [*1977*] [*Computer science*] (CSR)
Middlebury C. ... Middlebury College (GAGS)
MiDDS .... Duns Scotus College, Detroit, MI [*Library symbol Library of Congress*] (LCLS)
MIDDX .... Middlesex [*County in England*]
Middx .... Middlesex [*County in England*] (ODBW)
Middx Sit..... Sittings for Middlesex at Nisi Prius [*A publication*] (DLA)
MIDEASTFOR... Middle East Force [*Military*] (AABC)
Mid East L Rev... Middle East Law Review [*A publication*] (DLA)
MIDEAST MI LIB... Mideastern Michigan Library Cooperative [*Library network*]
MiDec .... Van Buren County Library, Decatur, MI [*Library symbol Library of Congress*] (LCLS)
MiDecD .... Decatur Township Library, Webster Memorial Library Building, Decatur, MI [*Library symbol Library of Congress*] (LCLS)
MiDeck .... Deckerville Public Library, Deckerville, MI [*Library symbol Library of Congress*] (LCLS)
MiDecV .... Van Buren County Library, Webster Memorial Library Building, Decatur, MI [*Library symbol Library of Congress*] (LCLS)
MiDEd .... Detroit Edison Co., Detroit, MI [*Library symbol Library of Congress*] (LCLS)
MIDEF .... Microprocedure Definition
MIDEFO .... Mission Debrief Forms (CINC)
MiDelD .... Delton District Library, Delton, MI [*Library symbol Library of Congress*] (LCLS)
MIDES .... Missile Detection System
MiDet .... De Tour Area School and Public Library, De Tour Village, MI [*Library symbol Library of Congress*] (LCLS)
MiDew .... De Witt Public Library, De Witt, MI [*Library symbol Library of Congress*] (LCLS)
MiDex .... Dexter District Library, Dexter, MI [*Library symbol Library of Congress*] (LCLS)
MIDF .... Major Item Data File (AABC)
MIDF .... Multiple Input Describing Function (PDAA)
MiDG .... Gale Research Co., Detroit, MI [*Library symbol Library of Congress*] (LCLS)
Mid G .... Graduate Midwife
MiDGH .... Detroit General Hospital, Medical Library, Detroit, MI [*Library symbol Library of Congress*] (LCLS)
MiDGM-L ..... General Motors World Headquarters, General Motors Law Library, Detroit, MI [*Library symbol Library of Congress*] (LCLS)
MiDGrH .... Grace Hospital, Detroit, MI [*Library symbol Library of Congress*] (LCLS)
MIDH .... Middletown & Hummelstown Railroad Co. [*AAR code*]
MIDH .... Mouvement pour l'Instauration de la Democratie en Haiti [*Political party*] (EY)
MidHag .... Midrash ha-Gadol (BJA)
MiDHF .... Henry Ford Hospital, Detroit, MI [*Library symbol Library of Congress*] (LCLS)
MiDHH .... Harper Hospital, Department of Libraries, Detroit, MI [*Library symbol Library of Congress*] (LCLS)
MiDHi .... Detroit Historical Society, Detroit, MI [*Library symbol Library of Congress*] (LCLS)
MIDI .... Midisoft Corp. [*NASDAQ symbol*] (SAG)
MIDI .... Minnesota Infant Development Inventory [*Child development test*] [*Psychology*]
MIDI .... Miss Distance Indicator (MCD)
MIDI .... Musical Instrument Digital Interface [*Port*] [*Socket on an electronic synthesizer that permits a direct computer connection*]
MiDi .... Windsor Township Library, Dimondale, MI [*Library symbol Library of Congress*] (LCLS)
MIDIRS .... Midwives Information and Resource Service [*British*] (EAIO)
Midisoft ...... Midisoft Corp. [*Associated Press*] (SAG)
MIDIST .... Mission Interministerielle de l'Information Scientifique et Technique [*Interministerial Mission for Scientific and Technical Information*] [*France Information service or system*] (IID)
MiDIT .... Detroit Institute of Technology, Detroit, MI [*Library symbol Library of Congress*] (LCLS)
MidIwa .... Mid Iowa Financial Corp. [*Associated Press*] (SAG)
MIDIZ .... Mid-Canada Identification Zone
MidJob .... Midrash Job (BJA)
MidJonah .... Midrash Jonah (BJA)
MiDL .... Michigan Library Consortium, Wayne State University, Detroit, MI [*Library symbol Library of Congress*] (LCLS)
MIDL .... Midland [*English dialect*] (ROG)
MIDL .... Midlantic Corp. [*NASDAQ symbol*] (NQ)
MIDLAT .... Middle Latitude [*Navigation*]
MidlBk .... Midland Bank PLC [*Associated Press*] (SAG)
Midlby .... Middleby Corp. [*Associated Press*] (SAG)
MidlCp .... Midlantic Corp. [*Associated Press*] (SAG)
MidLekTov ... Midrash Lekah Tov (BJA)
MidlFn .... Midland Financial Group [*Associated Press*] (SAG)
MIDLIS .... Multifamily Insurance and Direct Loan Information System [*Department of Housing and Urban Development*] (GFGA)
Midlnd .... Midland Co. [*Associated Press*] (SAG)
MIDLNET .... Midwest Regional Library Network
MidlRs .... Midland Resources, Inc. [*Associated Press*] (SAG)
MiDM .... Marygrove College, Detroit, MI [*Library symbol Library of Congress*] (LCLS)
MiDMC .... Mercy College of Detroit, Detroit, MI [*Library symbol Library of Congress*] (LCLS)
MiDMch .... Mariners' Church, Detroit, MI [*Library symbol Library of Congress*] (LCLS)
MID-MO .... Mid-Month [*Amount of pay to be received by payee on the 15th day of the month*] (AABC)

MiDMP .... Merrill-Palmer Institute, Detroit, MI [*Library symbol Library of Congress*] (LCLS)
MIDMS .... Machine Independent Data Management System [*Defense Intelligence Agency*] (MCD)
MiDMtC .... Mount Carmel Mercy Hospital, Medical Library, Detroit, MI [*Library symbol Library of Congress*] (LCLS)
MIDN .... Midshipman [*Navy*]
MIDNET .... Midland Network (NITA)
MIDnet .... [*The*] Midwest Network [*Computer science*] (TNIG)
midnoc .... Midnight (DAVI)
MiDo .... Dorr Township Library, Dorr, MI [*Library symbol Library of Congress*] (LCLS)
MIDOC .... Mildew-Induced Defacement of Organic Coatings
MidOcn .... Mid Ocean Ltd. [*Associated Press*] (SAG)
MiDolb .... Osceola Township Public and School Library, Dollar Bay, MI [*Library symbol Library of Congress*] (LCLS)
MIDOP .... Missile Doppler
MIDOR .... Miss Distance Optical Recorder [*Military*] (PDAA)
MIDOT .... Multiple Interferometer Determination of Trajectories
MiDow .... Dowagiac Public Library, Dowagiac, MI [*Library symbol Library of Congress*] (LCLS)
MIDP .... Major Item Distribution Plan (AABC)
MIDP .... Microbiology and Infectious Diseases Program [*Bethesda, MD*] [*National Institute of Allergy and Infectious Diseases*] [*Department of Health and Human Services*] (GRD)
MIDP .... Microwave Induced Delayed Phosphorescence (AAEL)
MIDP .... Motor Industry Development Program
MiDP .... Providence Hospital, School of Nursing, Detroit, MI [*Library symbol Library of Congress*] (LCLS)
MIDPAC ...... Mid-Pacific
MIDPAC ...... US Army Forces, Middle Pacific [*Name commonly used for AFMIDPAC*] [*World War II*]
MiDPD .... Parke, Davis & Co., Detroit, MI [*Library symbol Library of Congress*] (LCLS)
MIDPM .... Member of the Institute of Data Processing Management [*British*] (DCTA)
MidProv .... Midrash Proverbs (BJA)
MidPs .... Midrash Tehillim [*or The Midrash on Psalms*] (BJA)
MIDPT .... Midpoint (FAAC)
MIDR .... Mandatory Incident and Defect Reporting (NATG)
MidR .... Midland Resources, Inc. [*Associated Press*] (SAG)
Midr .... Midrash [*Interpretation of Old Testament writings*] (BJA)
MID-RATS... Midnight Rations [*Navy*]
MiDRI .... Rehabilitiation Institute, Detroit, MI [*Library symbol*] [*Library of Congress*] (LCLS)
MidrR .... Midrash Rabbah (BJA)
MidrSong... Midrash to the Song of Songs (BJA)
MiDry .... Dryden Township Library, Dryden, MI [*Library symbol Library of Congress*] (LCLS)
MIDS .... Management Information and Data Systems (NVT)
MIDS .... Management Information Decision Support [*Computer science*] (CIST)
MIDS .... Management Information Decision System [*Computer science*] (CIST)
MIDS .... Management Information Display System (MCD)
MIDS .... Marketing Information Data Systems, Inc. [*Information service or system*] (IID)
MIDS .... Matrix Information and Directory Services
MIDS .... Matrix Information and Directory Services, Inc.
MIDS .... Mid-South Insurance Co. [*NASDAQ symbol*] (NQ)
MIDS .... Miniature Integrated Data System (MCD)
MIDS .... Miscarriage Infant Death Stillbirth Support Group
MIDS .... Missile Ignition and Destruct Simulator
MIDS .... Movable Instrument Drive System [*Nuclear energy*] (NRCH)
MIDS .... Movement Information Distribution Station
MIDS .... Multifunctional Information Distribution System [*NATO*] (MCD)
MIDS .... Multimode Information Distribution System
Midsag .... Midsagittal [*Medicine*]
MidSam .... Midrash Samuel (BJA)
MIDSD .... Management Information and Data Systems Division [*Environmental Protection Agency*] (GFGA)
MiDSH .... Sacred Heart Seminary, Detroit, MI [*Library symbol Library of Congress*] (LCLS)
MIDSIM .... Maxwell International Development Simulation
MiDSn .... Sinai Hospital, Detroit, MI [*Library symbol Library of Congress*] (LCLS)
Mids ND ...... [*A*] Midsummer Night's Dream [*Shakespearean work*] (BARN)
MidSou .... Mid-South Insurance Co. [*Associated Press*] (SAG)
MIDSR .... Midsummer (ROG)
MidStat .... Mid-States PLC [*Associated Press*] (SAG)
Midsth .... Midsouth Bancorp, Inc. [*Associated Press*] (SAG)
MidsthB .... Midsouth Bancorp, Inc. [*Associated Press*] (SAG)
MIDTA .... Member of the International Dance Teachers' Association [*British*] (DBQ)
MidTan .... Midrash Tanna'im on Deuteronomy (BJA)
Mid'Tehil..... Midrash Tehillim [*or The Midrash on Psalms*] (BJA)
Mid Tenn St U... Middle Tennessee State University (GAGS)
MIDTRARON... Midshipman Training Squadron [*Navy*] (NVT)
MIDU .... Malfunction Insertion and Display Unit [*Aviation*]
MiDU .... University of Detroit, Detroit, MI [*Library symbol Library of Congress*] (LCLS)
MiDU-C .... University of Detroit, Colombiere Campus, Clarkston, MI [*Library symbol Library of Congress*] (LCLS)
MiDU-D .... University of Detroit, Dental Library, Detroit, MI [*Library symbol Library of Congress*] (LCLS)

MiDU-L........ University of Detroit, Law Library, Detroit, MI [*Library symbol Library of Congress*] (LCLS)

MIDW.......... Midwestern (AFM)

MiDW.......... Wayne State University, Detroit, MI [*Library symbol Library of Congress*] (LCLS)

MiDW-AL..... Wayne State University, Walter P. Reuther Library of Labor and Urban Affairs, Archivesof Labor History and Urban Affairs, Detroit, MI [*Library symbol*] [*Library of Congress*] (LCLS)

MidwBn....... Midwest Bancshares [*Associated Press*] (SAG)

MiDWc........ Wayne County Records, Court House, Wayne County, Detroit, MI [*Library symbol Library of Congress*] (LCLS)

MiDWcC...... Wayne County Community College, Detroit, MI [*Library symbol Library of Congress*] (LCLS)

MIDWEEK ... Manager Integrated Dictionary Week [*Manager Software Products*] (EA)

MIDWEST .... Midwest Automated Clearing House Association (TBD)

MIDWESTNAVFACENGCOM... Midwest Division Naval Facilities Engineering Command

Midwest S U... Midwestern State University (GAGS)

MidwGm...... Midway Games, Inc. [*Associated Press*] (SAG)

MidwGr........ Midwest Grain Products, Inc. [*Associated Press*] (SAG)

MiDW-L........ Wayne State University, Law Library, Detroit, MI [*Library symbol Library of Congress*] (LCLS)

MiDW-M...... Wayne State University, Medical Library, Detroit, MI [*Library symbol Library of Congress*] (LCLS)

MiDW-Mi..... Wayne State University, Miles Manuscript Collection, Detroit, MI [*Library symbol Library of Congress Obsolete*] (LCLS)

MiDW-P....... Wayne State University, School of Pharmacy, Detroit, MI [*Library symbol Library of Congress*] (LCLS)

MidwRE...... Midwest Real Estate Shopping Centers Ltd. [*Associated Press*] (SAG)

MiDW-S....... Wayne State University, Kresge-Hooker Science Library, Detroit, MI [*Library symbol Library of Congress*] (LCLS)

MIE............. Aero Premier de Mexico, SA de CV [*Mexico*] [*FAA designator*] (FAAC)

MiE............. East Lansing Public Library, East Lansing, MI [*Library symbol Library of Congress*] (LCLS)

MIE............. European Federation for Medical Informatics [*Sweden*] (EAIO)

MIE............. Magnetic Isotope Effect [*Physics*]

MIE............. Magnetron Ion Etching [*Semiconductor technology*]

MIE............. Major Items of Equipment

MIE............. Management Improvement and Evaluation

MIE............. Management Information Element [*Telecommunications*] (OSI)

MIE............. Maserati Information Exchange (EA)

MIE............. Mass Inertia Excitation

MIE............. Master of Industrial Engineering

MIE............. Master of Irrigation Engineering

MIE............. Merrill Lynch & Co. ™MITTS∫98 [*NYSE symbol*] (SPSG)

MIE............. Meteor Ionizing Efficiency

Mi-E............. Michigan State Library, Escanaba Branch, Escanaba, MI [*Library symbol Library of Congress*] (LCLS)

MiE............. Minimum Effect [*Pharmacology*]

MIE............. Minimum Ignition Energy

MIE............. Mission-Independent Equipment [*NASA*]

MIE............. Mobile Inspection Equipment (SAA)

MIE............. Muncie [*Indiana*] [*Airport symbol*] (OAG)

MIE............. Muncie, IN [*Location identifier FAA*] (FAAL)

MIEA.......... Music Industry Educators Association (EA)

MiEad......... East Detroit Memorial Library, East Detroit, MI [*Library symbol Library of Congress*] (LCLS)

MiEat......... Eaton Rapids Public Library, Eaton Rapids, MI [*Library symbol Library of Congress*] (LCLS)

MIEAWA ...... Meat Industries Employers' Association of Western Australia

MIEC.......... Branche Africaine du Mouvement International des Etudiants Catholiques [*African International Movement of Catholic Students - AIMCS*] (EAIO)

MiEc .... Eau Claire District Library, Eau Claire, MI [*Library symbol Library of Congress*] (LCLS)

MIEC.......... Meteorological Information Extraction Center

MIEC.......... Military Intelligence Exchange Center (CINC)

MIEC.......... Mixed Ionic and Electronic Conducting [*Polymers*]

MIEC.......... [*Meteorological Information Extraction Center*] Operator Guide

MIEC.......... Pax Romana, Mouvement International des Etudiants Catholiques [*Pax Romana, International Movement of Catholic Students - IMCS*] [*Paris, France*] (EAIO)

MIED.......... Member of the Institution of Engineering Designers [*British*] (DBQ)

MIEE.......... Mechanical, Instrument, and Electrical Engineering [*Department of Employment*] [*British*]

MIEE.......... Member of the Institution of Electrical Engineers [*Formerly, AMIEE*] [*British*] (EY)

MIEEE........ Member of the Institute of Electrical and Electronic Engineers

MIEETAT...... Major Improvements in Electronic Effectiveness through Advanced Technology (MCD)

MIEF.......... Master Imagery Exchange Format (MCD)

MIEI........... Member of the Institution of Engineering Inspection [*British*]

MIE(Ind) ...... Member of the Institution of Engineers, India

MiEIb......... Elberta Public Library, Elberta, MI [*Library symbol Library of Congress*] (LCLS)

MIEIecIE...... Corporate Member of the Institution of Electrical and Electronics Incorporated Engineers [*British*] (DBQ)

MiEIk .... Elk Rapids District Library, Elk Rapids, MI [*Library symbol Library of Congress*] (LCLS)

MiEm.......... Glen Lake Community Library, Empire, MI [*Library symbol Library of Congress*] (LCLS)

MIEM.......... Master in International Economics and Management (ECON)

MIEM.......... Master Member of the Institute of Executives and Managers [*British*] (DBQ)

MIEM.......... Masters Degree in International Economics and Management (ECON)

MiEM.......... Michigan State University, East Lansing, MI [*Library symbol Library of Congress*] (LCLS)

MIE Mgmt.... Master of Industrial Engineering Management (PGP)

MiEmp........ Glen Lake Community Library, Empire, MI [*Library symbol*] [*Library of Congress*] (LCLS)

MI Eng........ Master of Industrial Engineering

MIER.......... Management-Initiated Early Retirement (ADA)

MIERE........ Member of the Institution of Electronic and Radio Engineers [*Formerly, M Brit IRE*] [*British*]

MIERS .... Modernized Imagery Exploitation and Reporting System (MCD)

MIES........... Member of the Institution of Engineers and Shipbuilders, Scotland

MiEsc.......... Escanaba Public Library, Escanaba, MI [*Library symbol Library of Congress*] (LCLS)

MiEscB .... Bay De Noc Community College, Escanaba, MI [*Library symbol Library of Congress*] (LCLS)

MIESR .... Matrix Isolation and Electron Spin Resonance [*Analytical chemistry*]

MiEv.......... Evart Public Library, Evart, MI [*Library symbol Library of Congress*] (LCLS)

MiEw.......... McMillan Township Library, Ewen, MI [*Library symbol Library of Congress*] (LCLS)

MI Ex .... Member of the Institute of Export [*British*]

MIExE.......... Member of the Institute of Executive Engineers and Officers [*British*] (DBQ)

MIEx(Grad)... Member of the Institute of Export [*British*] (DBQ)

MIExpE .... Member of the Institute of Explosives Engineers [*British*] (DBQ)

MIF............. Macrophage Inhibitory Factor [*Immunology*]

MIF............. Maker Interchange Format [*Computer science*] (CDE)

MIF............. Malfunction Investigations File (MCD)

MIF............. Management Information File [*Computer science*] (PCM)

MIF............. Management Information Format [*Computer science*]

MIF............. Manual Intervention Facility

MIF............. MARC [*Machine-Readable Cataloging*] International Format

MIF............. Maritime Interception Force (DOMA)

MIF............. Mass-Independent Fractionation [*Chemistry*]

MIF............. Master Index File

MIF............. Master Inventory File (AFIT)

MIF............. Master Item File (MCD)

MIF............. Maximal Inspiratory Flow [*Medicine*]

MIF............. Medina, OH [*Location identifier FAA*] (FAAL)

MIF............. Melanocyte-Inhibiting Factor [*Endocrinology*]

MIF............. Melanocyte-Stimulating-Hormone Release Inhibiting Factor [*Also, MRIF*] [*Endocrinology*]

MIF............. Melanotropin Inhibiting Factor [*Biochemistry*]

MIF............. Melbourne International Festival [*Australia*]

MIF............. Membrane Immunofluorescence [*Analytical biochemistry*]

MIF............. Merthiolate-Iodine-Formaldehyde [*Technique*]

MIF............. Mesoderm-Inducing Factor [*Embryology*]

MIF............. Midinspiratory Flow [*Medicine*] (DMAA)

MIF............. Migration Inhibition [*or Inhibitory*] Factor [*Cytology*]

MIF............. Milk Industry Foundation (EA)

MIF............. Milk in First [*Tea-pouring procedure*]

MIF............. Miners' International Federation [*See also FIM*] [*Brussels, Belgium*] (EAIO)

MIF............. Missile-in-Flight

MIF............. Mixed Immunofluorescence [*Medicine*] (MAE)

MIF............. Mobile Instrument Facility

MIF............. Module Integration Facility (SSD)

MIF............. Monopulse Interference Filter

MIF............. Mortgage Indemnity Fund [*Veterans Administration*]

MIF............. Multisource Intelligence File (MCD)

MIF............. MuniInsured Fund Inc. [*AMEX symbol*] (SPSG)

MIF............. MuniInsred Fund [*AMEX symbol*] (TTSB)

MIF............. Myocardial Infarction [*Cardiology*] (DHSM)

MIFA.......... Mitomycin C, Fluorouracil, Adriamycin [*Antineoplastic drug regimen*]

MIFACS....... Medical Institutions' Financial Accounting System

MI-FA-MI ..... Misery, Famine, Misery [*Said to be "earth's song," in theory that all planets emit musical sounds governed by their paths around the sun*]

MIFAS.......... Mechanized Integrated Financial Accounting System [*Department of State*]

MIFASS....... Marine Integrated Fire and Air Support System

MiFaw .... Farwell Public Library, Farwell, MI [*Library symbol Library of Congress*] (LCLS)

MIFC.......... Madonna International Fan Club [*Defunct*] (EA)

MIFC.......... Merthiolate-Iodine Formalin Concentration

MIFC.......... Mid Iowa Financial Corp. [*NASDAQ symbol*] (SAG)

MIFC.......... Mid-Iowa FinI [*NASDAQ symbol*] (TTSB)

MIFD.......... Material Information Flow Device [*Military*] (AFM)

MIFE.......... Manila International Futures Exchange [*Philippines*] (NUMA)

MIFE.......... Minimum Independent Failure Element

MIFF.......... Management Information Format File [*Computer science*]

MIFF.......... Member of the Institute of Freight Forwarders [*British*] (ODBW)

MiFg .... Fairgrove Township Library, Fairgrove, MI [*Library symbol Library of Congress*] (LCLS)

MIFG.......... Micro Focus Group Ltd. [*NASDAQ symbol*] (SAG)

MIFG.......... Patches of Shallow Fog not Deeper Than Two Meters [*NWS*] (FAAC)

MIFGY .... Micro Focus Grp ADS [*NASDAQ symbol*] (TTSB)

MIFI........... Missile In-Flight Indicator

MiFil........... Fife Lake Public Library, Fife Lake, MI [*Library symbol Library of Congress*] (LCLS)

MIFIR.......... Microwave Instantaneous Frequency Indication Receiver (MCD)

MIFirE......... Member of the Institution of Fire Engineers [*British*] (DCTA)

MIFireE	Member of the Institution of Fire Engineers [*British*] (EY)
MIFL	Master International Frequency List
MiFli	Flint Public Library, Flint, MI [*Library symbol Library of Congress*] (LCLS)
MiFliACS	AC Spark Plug Co., General Motors Corp., Flint, MI [*Library symbol Library of Congress*] (LCLS)
MiFliC	University of Michigan at Flint, and Charles Stewart Mott Community College, Flint, MI [*Library symbol Library of Congress*] (LCLS)
MiFliG	GMI Engineering and Management Institute, Flint, MI [*Library symbol Library of Congress*] (LCLS)
MiFos	Watertown Township Library, Fostoria, MI [*Library symbol Library of Congress*] (LCLS)
MiFow	Fowlerville Public Library, Fowlerville, MI [*Library symbol Library of Congress*] (LCLS)
MIFR	Master International Frequency Register
MIFR	Maximal Inspiratory Flow Rate [*Medicine*]
MIFR	Monitored International Frequency Register (NITA)
MIFR	Multiband Infrared Filter Radiometer
MiFra	Frankfort City Library, Frankfort, MI [*Library symbol Library of Congress*] (LCLS)
MiFram	James E. Wickson Memorial Library, Frankenmuth, MI [*Library symbol Library of Congress*] (LCLS)
MiFras	Fraser Public Library, Fraser, MI [*Library symbol Library of Congress*] (LCLS)
MiFrem	Fremont Public Library, Fremont, MI [*Library symbol Library of Congress*] (LCLS)
MIFS	Material Information Flow System [*Military*] (AFM)
MIFS	Multiplex Interferometric Fourier Spectroscopy
MIFSA	Missile In-Flight Safety Approval (MUGU)
MIFT	Manchester International Freight Terminal [*British*] (DS)
Mig	De Migratione Abrahami [*Philo*] (BJA)
MIG	Magnetic Injection Gun (IEEE)
MIG	Magnetized Ionized Gas
MIG	Malaria Immune Globulin
MIG	Management Information Guide [*Reference series*]
MIG	Mars Investigation Group [*Defunct*] (EA)
MIG	Meadowbrook Insurance Group [*NYSE symbol*] (SAG)
MIG	Meadowbrook Insurance Grp [*NYSE symbol*] (TTSB)
MIG	Measles Immune Globulin [*Immunology*]
MIG	Meat Innovation Grant
MIG	Medial Inferior Geniculate Artery [*Anatomy*]
MIG	Medicare Insured Group (HCT)
M-Ig	Membrane Immunoglobulin [*Immunology*]
MIG	Metal-Inert-Gas [*Underwater welding*]
MIG	Methane Inert Gas (MCD)
Mig	Mignon [*Horticulture*]
MIG	Mikoyan and Gurevich [*Acronym used as designation for a Russian aircraft and is formed from the names of the aircraft's designers*]
MIG	Military Intelligence Group (MCD)
MIG	Military Intelligence Guide (MCD)
MIG	Millington, TN [*Location identifier FAA*] (FAAL)
MIG	Ming Mines Ltd. [*Vancouver Stock Exchange symbol*]
MIG	Miniature Integrating Gyroscope
MIG	Minimum Income Guarantee
MIG	Moody's Investment Grade
MIG	Mortgage Indemnity Guarantee (WDAA)
MIG	Multilevel Interconnect Generator
MIG-1	Moody's Investment Grade (DFIT)
MIGA	Multilateral Investment Guarantee Agency [*World Bank*]
MiGal	Galesburg Memorial Library, Galesburg, MI [*Library symbol Library of Congress*] (LCLS)
MI/GAL	Miles per Gallon (WDAA)
MiGali	Galien Township Public Library, Galien, MI [*Library symbol Library of Congress*] (LCLS)
MIGasE	Member of the Institution of Gas Engineers [*British*]
MiGay	Gaylord-Otsego County Public Library, Gaylord, MI [*Library symbol Library of Congress*] (LCLS)
MIGB	Millinery Institute of Great Britain (BI)
MiGc	Garden City Public Library, Garden City, MI [*Library symbol Library of Congress*] (LCLS)
MIGCAP	MIG [*Mikoyan and Gurevich*] Combat Air Patrol (DNAB)
MIGD	Member of the Institute of Grocery Distribution [*British*] (DBQ)
MIGeol	Member of the Institution of Geologists [*British*] (DBQ)
MIGET	Miniature Interface General-Purpose Economy Terminal [*Computer science*] (MHDB)
MIgG	Monkey Immunoglobulin G [*Immunology*]
MiGh	Loutit Library, Grand Haven, MI [*Library symbol Library of Congress*] (LCLS)
MIGI	Meridian Insrance Gp [*NASDAQ symbol*] (TTSB)
MIGI	Meridian Insurance Group, Inc. [*NASDAQ symbol*] (NQ)
MiGl	Gladstone Public Library, Gladstone, MI [*Library symbol Library of Congress*] (LCLS)
MiGlad	Gladwin County Library, Gladwin, MI [*Library symbol Library of Congress*] (LCLS)
MiGlad-B	Gladwin County Library, Beaverton Branch Library, Beaverton, MI [*Library symbol Library of Congress*] (LCLS)
MIGN	Michigan Northern Railway Co., Inc. [*AAR code*]
MiGp	Grosse Pointe Public Library, Grosse Pointe, MI [*Library symbol Library of Congress*] (LCLS)
MiGr	Grand Rapids Public Library, Grand Rapids, MI [*Library symbol Library of Congress*] (LCLS)
MiGrA	Aquinas College, Grand Rapids, MI [*Library symbol Library of Congress*] (LCLS)
MiGran	Grant Public Library, Grant, MI [*Library symbol Library of Congress*] (LCLS)
MiGray	Crawford County Library, Grayling, MI [*Library symbol Library of Congress*] (LCLS)
MiGrB	Grand Rapids Baptist College, Grand Rapids, MI [*Library symbol Library of Congress*] (LCLS)
MiGrC	Calvin College and Seminary, Grand Rapids, MI [*Library symbol Library of Congress*] (LCLS)
MiGre	Greenville Public Library, Greenville, MI [*Library symbol*] [*Library of Congress*] (LCLS)
MiGrJC	Grand Rapids Junior College, Grand Rapids, MI [*Library symbol Library of Congress*] (LCLS)
MiGrl	Grand Ledge Public Library, Grand Ledge, MI [*Library symbol Library of Congress*] (LCLS)
MiGrL	Grand Rapids Law Library, Grand Rapids, MI [*Library symbol Library of Congress*] (LCLS)
MiGrlP	Grand Ledge Public Library, Grand Ledge, MI [*Library symbol*] [*Library of Congress*] (LCLS)
MiGrMtM	Mount Mercy Academy, Grand Rapids, MI [*Library symbol Library of Congress*] (LCLS)
MiGrW	Western Michigan Genealogical Society, Grand Rapids, MI [*Library symbol Library of Congress*] (LCLS)
MIGS	Metal-Induced Gap States (AAEL)
MIGS	Miniature Infrared Guidance Sensor
MIGS	Music Industries Golfing Society [*British*] (BI)
MiGw	Forsythe Township Public Library, Gwinn, MI [*Library symbol Library of Congress*] (LCLS)
MIH	Brownsville, TX [*Location identifier FAA*] (FAAL)
MIH	Master of Industrial Health
MIH	Melanocyte-Stimulating Hormone-Inhibitory Hormone [*Endocrinology*] (DAVI)
MIH	Member of the Institute of Housing [*British*] (DBQ)
MIH	Member of the Institute of Hygiene [*British*]
MIH	Migraine with Interparoxysmal Headache [*Neurology*] (DAVI)
MIH	Miles in the Hour [*Rate of military march*]
MIH	Minimal Intermittent [*Dosage of*] Heparin [*Pharmacology*] (DAVI)
MIH	Missing Interruption Handler [*Computer science*] (IBMDP)
MIH	Molecule-Induced Homolysis [*Chemistry*]
MIH	Molt Inhibitory Hormone
MIH	Multiplex Interface Handler
MiHa	Hart Public Library, Hart, MI [*Library symbol Library of Congress*] (LCLS)
MIHA	Move-In Housing Allowance
MiHaf	Hartford Public Library, Hartford, MI [*Library symbol Library of Congress*] (LCLS)
MiHal	Cromaine Library, Hartland, MI [*Library symbol Library of Congress*] (LCLS)
MiHam	Hamtramck Public Library, Hamtramck, MI [*Library symbol Library of Congress*] (LCLS)
MiHamb	Hamburg Township Library, Hamburg, MI [*Library symbol Library of Congress*] (LCLS)
MiHan	Hancock Public-School Library, Hancock, MI [*Library symbol Library of Congress*] (LCLS)
MiHanS	Suomi College, Hancock, MI [*Library symbol Library of Congress*] (LCLS)
MiHars	Harrison Public Library, Harrison, MI [*Library symbol Library of Congress*] (LCLS)
MiHarsM	Mid-Michigan Community College, Harrison, MI [*Library symbol Library of Congress*] (LCLS)
MiHarv	Alcona County Library, Harrisville, MI [*Library symbol Library of Congress*] (LCLS)
MiHas	Hastings Public Library, Hastings, MI [*Library symbol Library of Congress*] (LCLS)
MiHb	Harbor Beach Public Library, Harbor Beach, MI [*Library symbol Library of Congress*] (LCLS)
Mi-HC	Michigan Historical Commission, State Archives Library, Lansing, MI [*Library symbol Library of Congress*] (LCLS)
MIHC	M. I. Hummel Club (EA)
MiHe	Hesperia Public Library, Hesperia, MI [*Library symbol Library of Congress*] (LCLS)
MIHE	Member of the Institute of Health Education [*British*]
MIHEc	Member of the Institute of Home Economics [*British*] (DBQ)
MiHem	Mary C. Rauchholz Memorial Library, Hemlock, MI [*Library symbol Library of Congress*] (LCLS)
MIHIC	Mile High Conference (PSS)
MiHil	Mitchell Public Library, Hillsdale, MI [*Library symbol Library of Congress*] (LCLS)
MiHilC	Hillsdale College, Hillsdale, MI [*Library symbol Library of Congress*] (LCLS)
MiHilm	Hillman Public Library, Hillman, MI [*Library symbol Library of Congress*] (LCLS)
MiHl	Houghton Lake Public Library, Houghton Lake, MI [*Library symbol Library of Congress*] (LCLS)
MIHM	Master of International Health Management (PGP)
MiHM	Michigan Technological University, Houghton, MI [*Library symbol Library of Congress*] (LCLS)
MIHO	Miles Homes [*NASDAQ symbol*] (TTSB)
MIHO	Miles Homes, Inc. [*NASDAQ symbol*] (SAG)
MiHol	Herrick Public Library, Holland, MI [*Library symbol Library of Congress*] (LCLS)
MiHolH	Hope College, Holland, MI [*Library symbol Library of Congress*] (LCLS)
MiHolW	Western Theological Seminary, Holland, MI [*Library symbol Library of Congress*] (LCLS)
MiHom	Homer Public Library, Homer, MI [*Library symbol Library of Congress*] (LCLS)

MiHow......... Howell Carnegie Library, Howell, MI [*Library symbol Library of Congress*] (LCLS)

MiHp............ McGregor Public Library, Highland Park, MI [*Library symbol Library of Congress*] (LCLS)

MiHP .... Portage Lake District Library, Houghton, MI [*Library symbol Library of Congress*] (LCLS)

MiHpDH...... Detroit Osteopathic Hospital, Highland Park, MI [*Library symbol Library of Congress*] (LCLS)

MIHPED...... Microwave-Induced Helium Plasma Emission Detection (NATG)

MiHPL .... Portage Lake District Library, Houghton, MI [*Library symbol*] [*Library of Congress*] (LCLS)

MIHT............ Member of the Institution of Highways and Transportation [*British*] (DBQ)

MiHu............ Hudson Public Library, Hudson, MI [*Library symbol Library of Congress*] (LCLS)

MiHudv........ Hudsonville Public Library, Hudsonville, MI [*Library symbol Library of Congress*] (LCLS)

MIHVE .... Member of the Institution of Heating and Ventilating Engineers [*British*]

MII.............. Caddo Mills, TX [*Location identifier FAA*] (FAAL)

MII.............. Management Interest Inventory [*Test*]

MII.............. Manufacturing Impact Item (MCD)

MII.............. Marilia [*Brazil*] [*Airport symbol*] (OAG)

MI/I............ Microinches per Inch (KSC)

MII.............. Military Intelligence Interpreter

MII.............. Military Intelligence Interrogation

MII.............. Mineral Information Institute (EA)

MII.............. Minnesota Interlibrary Telecommunications Exchange, Minneapolis, MN [*OCLC symbol*] (OCLC)

MII.............. Morton International [*NYSE symbol*] (TTSB)

MII.............. Morton International, Inc. [*NYSE symbol*] (SPSG)

MII.............. Motorists Information, Inc. [*Defunct*] (EA)

MIIA............ Medical Intelligence and Information Agency [*Formerly, MIO*] [*DoD*]

MIIA............ Member of the Institute of Industrial Administration [*Later, MBIM*] [*British*]

MIIA............ Merritt Island Industrial Area [*NASA*] (KSC)

MIIA............ Mine Inspectors' Institute of America (EA)

MIIC............ Pax Romana, Mouvement International des Intellectuels Catholiques [*Pax Romana, International Catholic Movement for Intellectual and Cultural Affairs - ICMICA*] [*Geneva, Switzerland*] (EAIO)

MIICS.......... Master Item Identification Control System

MiId............ Idlewild Public Library, Idlewild, MI [*Library symbol*] [*Library of Congress*] (LCLS)

MIID............ Media Institutes for Institute Directors

MIIDS .... Missile Interior Intrusion Detection System (DWSG)

MIIF............ Master Item Intelligence File

MIIFC.......... Michigan Intercollegiate Football Conference (PSS)

MIIL............ Master Item Identification List

MIIM............ Master of International and Intercultural Management (PGP)

MIIM............ Member of the Institution of Industrial Managers [*British*] (DCTA)

MI Inf Sc .. Member of the Institute of Information Scientists [*British*]

MiInr........... Indian River Public Library, Indian River, MI [*Library symbol Library of Congress*] (LCLS)

MI insuf...... Mitral Insufficiency [*Cardiology*] (DAVI)

MiInt........... Interlovhen Public Library, Interlochen, MI [*Library symbol*] [*Library of Congress*] (LCLS)

MilrmD........ Dickinson County Library, Iron Mountain, MI [*Library symbol Library of Congress*] (LCLS)

MilrmD-N ... Dickinson County Library, Norway Branch, Norway, MI [*Library symbol Library of Congress*] (LCLS)

MilrmM....... Mid-Peninsula Library Federation Headquarters, Iron Mountain, MI [*Library symbol Library of Congress*] (LCLS)

MilrmV .... United States Veterans Administration Hospital, Iron Mountain, MI [*Library symbol Library of Congress*] (LCLS)

MiIrr .... West Iron District Library, Iron River, MI [*Library symbol Library of Congress*] (LCLS)

MiIrw.......... Ironwood Carnegie Library, Ironwood, MI [*Library symbol Library of Congress*] (LCLS)

MiIs .... Ishpeming Carnegie Library, Ishpeming, MI [*Library symbol Library of Congress*] (LCLS)

MIIS............ Miscellaneous Inputs Information Subsystem [*Computer science*]

MIIS............ Monterey Institute of International Studies (ECON)

MIISA.......... Management Information and Instructional Systems Activity (DNAB)

MIISADET ... Management Information and Instructional Systems Activity Detachment (DNAB)

MIISAU....... Management Information and Instructional Systems Activity Unit (DNAB)

MIISE.......... Member of the International Institute of Social Economics [*British*] (DBQ)

MIISec........ Member of the Institute of Industrial Security [*British*] (DBQ)

MIIT............ Manned Interceptor Integration Team (SAA)

MiIt............. Thompson Home Library, Ithaca, MI [*Library symbol Library of Congress*] (LCLS)

MIJ............. Dugway/Tooele, UT [*Location identifier FAA*] (FAAL)

MIJ............. Maatschappij [*Joint Stock Company*] [*Netherlands*]

MIJ............. Master of International Journalism (PGP)

MIJ............. Member of the Institution of Journalists

MIJ............. Metal Insulator Junction

MIJ............. Mili [*Marshall Islands*] [*Airport symbol*] (OAG)

MiJa .... Jackson Public Library, Jackson, MI [*Library symbol Library of Congress*] (LCLS)

MiJaC .... Jackson County Library, Jackson, MI [*Library symbol Library of Congress*] (LCLS)

MiJaCc .... Jackson Community College, Jackson, MI [*Library symbol Library of Congress*] (LCLS)

MiJaCP........ Consumers Power Co., Parnall Technical Library, Jackson, MI [*Library symbol*] [*Library of Congress*] (LCLS)

MiJam .... Jamestown Township Library, Jamestown, MI [*Library symbol Library of Congress*] (LCLS)

MIJARC...... Mouvement International de la Jeunesse Agricole et Rurale Catholique [*International Movement of Catholic Agricultural and Rural Youth - IMCARY*] [*Louvain, Belgium*] (EAIO)

MIJC .... Mouvement International des Juristes Catholiques, Pax Romana [*France*]

MiJen .... Georgetown Township Library, Jenison, MI [*Library symbol Library of Congress*] (LCLS)

MIJI .... Meaconing, Intrusion, Jamming, Interference [*Military*] (NVT)

MIJO .... Missile Joint Optimization

MiK............. Kalamazoo Public Library, Kalamazoo, MI [*Library symbol Library of Congress*] (LCLS)

MIK .... Meerblick, SA [*Spain*] [*FAA designator*] (FAAC)

MIK .... Methyl Isobutyl Ketone [*Also, MIBK*] [*Organic chemistry*]

MIK .... Mikkeli [*Finland*] [*Airport symbol*] (OAG)

Mik .... Mikva'ot (BJA)

MIK .... Minitrack [*Alaska*] [*Seismograph station code, US Geological Survey Closed*] (SEIS)

MIK .... More in the Kitchen [*Family dinner-table expression*]

MiKa .... Kalkaska County Library, Kalkaska, MI [*Library symbol Library of Congress*] (LCLS)

MIKA .... Medical Imaging Centers of America (EFIS)

MIKA .... Minor Karyotypic Abnormalities [*Medicine*]

MIKADOS... Mini Instant Keyboard Assembler, Debug, and Operating System [*Computer science*] (MHDI)

Mikasa........ Mikasa, Inc. [*Associated Press*] (SAG)

MiKB........... Borgess Hospital, Medical Library, Kalamazoo, MI [*Library symbol Library of Congress*] (LCLS)

MiKC........... Kalamazoo College, Kalamazoo, MI [*Library symbol Library of Congress*] (LCLS)

MiKCS .... Institute of Cistercian Studies, Western Michigan University, Kalamazoo, MI [*Library symbol Library of Congress*] (LCLS)

MIKE .... Manipulator Interactive Kinematics Evaluator (SSD)

MIKE .... Mass-Analyzed Ion Kinetic Energy

MIKE .... Measurement of Instantaneous Kinetic Energy (IEEE)

MIKE .... Michael Stores [*NASDAQ symbol*] (SAG)

MIKE .... Micro Interpreter for Knowledge Engineering [*Computer science*]

MIKE .... Microphone (CET)

mike .... Microphone (IDOE)

MIKE .... Multiwave Italian Key System (NITA)

MIKER .... Microbalance Inverted Knudsen Effusion Recoil

MIKES .... Mass-Analyzed Ion Kinetic Energy Spectrometry

MikGed....... Mikra'ot Gedolot (BJA)

MiKin.......... Kingston Community Public Library, Kingston, MI [*Library symbol Library of Congress*] (LCLS)

MiKins........ Kingsley Public Library, Kingsley, MI [*Library symbol Library of Congress*] (LCLS)

MIKK .... Medjunarodni Institut za Kucnu Knjizevnost [*International Institute for Home Literature - IIHL*] [*Belgrade, Yugoslavia*] (EAIO)

MiKL........... Kalamazoo Library System, Kalamazoo, MI [*Library symbol Library of Congress*] (LCLS)

MIKL .... Michael Foods [*NASDAQ symbol*] (TTSB)

MIKL .... Michael Foods, Inc. [*NASDAQ symbol*] (NQ)

MIKN .... Mikohn Gaming [*NASDAQ symbol*] (TTSB)

MIKN .... Mikohn Gaming Corp. [*NASDAQ symbol*] (SAG)

Mikohn .... Mikohn Gaming Corp. [*Associated Press*] (SAG)

MiKPSc....... Kalamazoo Public School District, Kalamazoo, MI [*Library symbol Library of Congress*] (LCLS)

MIKR .... Mikron Instr [*NASDAQ symbol*] (TTSB)

MIKR .... Mikron Instrument Co., Inc. [*NASDAQ symbol*] (NQ)

Mikron........ Mikron Instrument Co., Inc. [*Associated Press*] (SAG)

MiKUp .... Upjohn Co., Kalamazoo, MI [*Library symbol Library of Congress*] (LCLS)

MiKUp_B .... Upjohn Co., Business Library, Kalamazoo, MI [*Library symbol*] [*Library of Congress*] (LCLS)

MiKV........... Kalamazoo Valley Community College, Kalamazoo, MI [*Library symbol Library of Congress*] (LCLS)

Mikv........... Mikva'ot (BJA)

MiKW.......... Western Michigan University, Kalamazoo, MI [*Library symbol Library of Congress*] (LCLS)

MiKWUp ..... W. E. Upjohn Institute for Employment Research, Kalamazoo, MI [*Library symbol Library of Congress*] (LCLS)

miky............ Milky [*Philately*]

MiL............. Lansing Public Library, Lansing, MI [*Library symbol Library of Congress*] (LCLS)

MIL............. Magnetic Indicator Loop (NVT)

MIL............. Malfunction Indicator Light [*Automotive engineering*]

MIL............. Malfunction Investigation Laboratory

MIL............. Marine Instrumentation Laboratory [*Marine science*] (OSRA)

MIL............. Master Index List (MCD)

MIL............. Master Instrumentation List

MIL............. Master Item Identification List (AABC)

MIL............. Material

MIL............. Member of the Institute of Linguists [*British*]

MIL............. Mensa International [*British*] (EAIO)

MIL............. Merritt Island Tracking Station [*Florida*]

MIL............. Microimplementation Language [*Burroughs Corp.*]

MIL............. Milan [*Italy*] [*Seismograph station code, US Geological Survey Closed*] (SEIS)

MIL............. Mileage

Mil............. Miles' Pennsylvania Reports [*A publication*] (DLA)

MIL............. Military (EY)

Mil............	Military (CMD)
MIL............	Military Instrumentation List
MIL............	Military Specification [*Followed by a single capital letter and numbers*] (IEEE)
MIL............	Militia
mil.............	Militia (WDAA)
Mil............	Miller's Reports [*3-18 Maryland*] [*A publication*] (DLA)
Mil............	Miller's Reports [*1-5 Louisiana*] [*A publication*] (DLA)
MIL............	Millieme [*Monetary unit*] [*Egypt, Sudan*]
mil.............	Milli-Inch
MIL............	Milliliter
MIL............	Milling
MIL............	Million
MIL............	Millipore Corp. [*NYSE symbol*] (SPSG)
Mil............	Mills' New York Surrogate's Court Reports [*A publication*] (DLA)
Mil............	Mill's South Carolina Constitutional Reports [*A publication*] (DLA)
MIL............	Milwaukee [*Wisconsin*]
MIL............	Minnesota Instructional Language [*Computer science*] (CSR)
MIL............	Missile Industry Liaison (SAA)
MIL............	Module Interconnection Language
MIL............	Mothers-in-Law Club International (EA)
MIL............	Movimiento Iberico Libertario [*Spain Political party*]
MIL............	Moving Inspection Lot
MIL............	Office of Public Library and Interlibrary Cooperation, St. Paul, MN [*OCLC symbol*] (OCLC)
Mil............	Pro Milone [*of Cicero*] [*Classical studies*] (OCD)
MILA...........	Merritt Island Launch Area [*NASA*]
Mila...........	Militia [*British military*] (DMA)
MILAA.........	Milastar Corp. [*NASDAQ symbol*] (NQ)
MiLac.........	Missaukee County Library, Lake City, MI [*Library symbol Library of Congress*] (LCLS)
MiLacES......	Lake City Elementary School, Lake City, MI [*Library symbol*] [*Library of Congress*] (LCLS)
MiLacHS......	Lake City High School, Lake City, MI [*Library symbol*] [*Library of Congress*] (LCLS)
MILAD........	Military Advisor [*SEATO or ANZUS Council*] (CINC)
MILADGOVT..	Military Advisory Government
MILADGRU...	Military Advisory Group
MILADREP...	Military Advisors Representative (CINC)
MiLai.........	Laingsburg Public Library, Laingsburg, MI [*Library symbol Library of Congress*] (LCLS)
MiLakv........	Cato Township Public Library, Lakeview, MI [*Library symbol of Congress*] (LCLS)
MiLal.........	Lake Linden-Hubbell Public School Library, Lake Linden, MI [*Library symbol Library of Congress*] (LCLS)
MiLan.........	L'Anse Township School and Public Library, L'Anse, MI [*Library symbol Library of Congress*] (LCLS)
MILAN........	Missile d'Infanterie Leger Antichar
MILAN........	Missile, Infantry Light Antiarmor [*Antitank system*] (INF)
Mil & Vet C...	Military and Veterans Code [*A publication*] (DLA)
MILAS........	Micrometer Low-Approach System
Mil Av........	Military Aviator [*Army*]
MiLaw........	Lawton Public Library, Lawton, MI [*Library symbol Library of Congress*] (LCLS)
MILBA........	Military Base Agreement (CINC)
MiLC..........	Lansing Community College, Lansing, MI [*Library symbol Library of Congress*] (LCLS)
MILC..........	Metal Ion Liquid Chromatography
MILC..........	Midwest Interlibrary Center [*Later, CRL*]
MILC..........	Military Characteristics
MILCAP.......	Military Civic Action Program
MILCAP.......	Military Standard Contract Administration Procedures [*DoD*]
MILCEST......	Military Communications Electronic Systems Technology (MCD)
MilcmIn.......	Millicom International Cellular [*Associated Press*] (SAG)
MILCOM......	Military Command (DNAB)
MILCOM......	Military Committee Communication [*NATO*]
MILCOMP.....	Military Computer
MILCOMSAT..	Military Communications Satellite
MILCON.......	Military Construction
MILCON-DA...	Military Construction, Defense Agencies
MILCONF.....	Military Confinement
MILCS.........	Metropolitan Interlibrary Cooperative System [*New York Public Library*] [*Information service or system*]
MILDAT.......	Military Damage Assessment Team (AABC)
MILDDU......	Military-Industry Logistics Data Development Unit
MILDEC.......	Military Decision (NATG)
MILDEP.......	Military Department (COE)
MILDEPS.....	Military Departments (AABC)
MILDEPT.....	Military Department
MILDET.......	Military Detachment
MILDIP.......	Military-Industry Logistics Data Interchange Procedures
MILDIS.......	Military-Industry Logistics Data Interchange System
MILDOC......	Military Document (AAGC)
MiLe..........	Leland Township Public Library, Leland, MI [*Library symbol Library of Congress*] (LCLS)
MILE..........	Minuteman Integrated Life Extension [*Telecommunications*] (LAIN)
MIL-E-CON...	Military Electronic Conference
MileH.........	Miles Homes, Inc. [*Associated Press*] (SAG)
MileHme.....	Miles Homes, Inc. [*Associated Press*] (SAG)
MilePr........	Milestone Properties [*Associated Press*] (SAG)
MiLer.........	LeRoy Public Library, LeRoy, MI [*Library symbol Library of Congress*] (LCLS)
MILES........	Magnetic Intrusion Line Sensor (PDAA)
Miles.........	Miles' District Court Reports [*1825-41*] [*Philadelphia, PA*] [*A publication*] (DLA)

MILES........	Military Implications of LASER Employment by the Soviets
MILES........	Multiple Integrated LASER Engagement Simulation [*or System*] [*Army*]
MILES........	Multiple Integrated LASER Engagement System (COE)
MILES/AGES..	Multiple-Integrated LASER Engagement Simulation / Air Ground Engagement Simulator
Miles (PA)...	Miles' Pennsylvania Reports [*A publication*] (DLA)
Miles R.......	Miles' Pennsylvania Reports [*A publication*] (DLA)
Miles R & O...	Miles' Rules and Orders [*A publication*] (DLA)
Miles Rep....	Miles' Pennsylvania Reports [*A publication*] (DLA)
MilestnSci....	Milestone Scientific, Inc. [*Associated Press*] (SAG)
MiLew.........	Lewiston Public Library, Lewiston, MI [*Library symbol Library of Congress*] (LCLS)
MiLex.........	Moore Public Library, Lexington, MI [*Library symbol Library of Congress*] (LCLS)
MILF..........	Moro Islamic Liberation Front [*Philippines*] [*Political party*]
MiLG..........	Great Lakes Bible College, Lansing, MI [*Library symbol Library of Congress*] (LCLS)
MILGA........	Member of the Institute of Local Government Administrators [*British*] (ODBW)
MiLGH........	Lansing General Hospital Library, Lansing, MI [*Library symbol*] [*Library of Congress*] (LCLS)
MILGP........	Military Group
Milgray.......	Milgray Electronics, Inc. [*Associated Press*] (SAG)
MILGRP......	Military Group (DNAB)
MILGRU......	Military Group (DNAB)
MiLGS........	Church of Jesus Christ of Latter-Day Saints, Genealogical Society Library, Lansing Branch, Stake Center, Lansing, MI [*Library symbol Library of Congress*] (LCLS)
MIL-HDBK....	Military Handbook
MIL-I.........	Military Instruction (AAGC)
MIL-I.........	Military Specification on Interference (IEEE)
MILI..........	Multilevel Informal Language Inventory [*Test*]
MILIC........	Microwave Insular Line Integrated Circuit (IEEE)
MILIC........	Millimeter Insular Line Integrated Circuit (PDAA)
MILIC........	Ministerial Libraries and Information Centers
MiLIM........	Ingham Medical Center, John W. Chi Memorial Library, Lansing, MI [*Library symbol*] [*Library of Congress*] (LCLS)
MILINREP....	Military Incident Report (MCD)
MILIRAD......	Millimeter RADAR (MCD)
MILIRAD......	Millimeter Wave RADAR Fuze (MCD)
MILIS........	Multicenter Investigation of the Limitation of Infarct Size (MEDA)
MiLit..........	Litchfield District Library, Litchfield, MI [*Library symbol Library of Congress*] (LCLS)
MILIT.........	Military
milit..........	Military (WDAA)
Military LJ...	Military Law Journal [*A publication*] (DLA)
MILITRAN.....	Military in Transition Database [*Information service or system*] (IID)
MiLivM.......	Madonna College, Livonia, MI [*Library symbol Library of Congress*] (LCLS)
MiLivPS......	Livonia Public Schools, Livonia, MI [*Library symbol Library of Congress*] (LCLS)
Mil Jur Cas & Mat...	Military Jurisprudence, Cases and Materials [*A publication*] (DLA)
MILJUSDOCFILE...	Military Justice Docket File (DNAB)
MILL..........	Mill [*Commonly used*] (OPSA)
MILL..........	Miller Industries, Inc. [*NASDAQ symbol*] (SAG)
Mill..........	Miller's Reports [*1-5 Louisiana*] [*A publication*] (DLA)
Mill..........	Miller's Reports [*3-18 Maryland*] [*A publication*] (DLA)
MILL..........	Million
Mill..........	Mills' New York Surrogate's Court Reports [*A publication*] (DLA)
Mill..........	Mill's South Carolina Constitutional Reports [*A publication*] (DLA)
Mill & C Bills...	Miller and Collier on Bills of Sale [*A publication*] (DLA)
Mill & F Pr...	Miller and Field's Federal Practice [*A publication*] (DLA)
Mill & V Code...	Milliken and Vertrees' Tennessee Code [*A publication*] (DLA)
Mill Civ L....	Miller's Civil Law of England [*1825*] [*A publication*] (DLA)
Mill Code....	Miller's Iowa Code [*A publication*] (DLA)
Mill Const....	Mill's South Carolina Constitutional Reports [*A publication*] (DLA)
Mill Const (SC)...	Mill's South Carolina Constitutional Reports [*A publication*] (DLA)
Mill Dec......	Miller's Circuit Court Decisions (Woolworth) [*United States*] [*A publication*] (DLA)
Mill Dec......	Miller's United States Supreme Court Decisions [*Condensed, Continuation of Curtis*] [*A publication*] (DLA)
Mill El........	Miller's Elements of the Law of Insurances [*A publication*] (DLA)
MillenCh.....	Millenium Chemicals, Inc. [*Associated Press*] (SAG)
Millenia......	Millenia, Inc. [*Associated Press*] (SAG)
Mill Eq M	Miller's Equitable Mortgages [*1844*] [*A publication*] (DLA)
Miller........	Miller's Reports [*3-18 Maryland*] [*A publication*] (DLA)
Miller........	Miller's Reports [*1-5 Louisiana*] [*A publication*] (DLA)
Miller Const...	Miller on the Constitution of the United States [*A publication*] (DLA)
MillerIn......	Miller Indusries, Inc. [*Associated Press*] (SAG)
Miller's Code...	Miller's Revised and Annotated Code [*Iowa*] [*A publication*] (DLA)
Millersville U...	Millersville University of Pennsylvania (GAGS)
MILLIE........	Maximum Interchange of the Latest Logistic Information Is Essential
milli IU/ml...	Milli-International Unit per Milliliter (DAVI)
Millin........	Petty Sessions Cases [*1875-98*] [*Ireland*] [*A publication*] (DLA)
Mill Ins......	Miller's Elements of the Law of Insurances [*A publication*] (DLA)
Millipore.....	Millipore Corp. [*Associated Press*] (SAG)
Millipore.....	Millipore Corp. [*Associated Press*] (SAG)
millisec......	Millisecond
Mill LA	Miller's Reports [*1-5 Louisiana*] [*A publication*] (DLA)
Mill Log......	Mill's Logic [*A publication*] (DLA)
Mill MD......	Miller's Reports [*3-18 Maryland*] [*A publication*] (DLA)
Mill Op	Miller's Circuit Court Decisions (Woolworth) [*United States*] [*A publication*] (DLA)

Mill Part...... Miller on Partition [*A publication*] (DLA)
MillPhar ...... Millennium Pharmaceuticals, Inc. [*Associated Press*] (SAG)
Mill Pl & Pr... Miller's Iowa Pleading and Practice [*A publication*] (DLA)
MillrHr........ Miller [*Herman*], Inc. [*Associated Press*] (SAG)
MILLS.......... Mills [*Commonly used*] (OPSA)
Mills........... Mills' New York Surrogate's Court Reports [*A publication*] (DLA)
Mills Ann St... Mills' Annotated Statutes [*Colorado*] [*A publication*] (DLA)
Mills C........ Mills College (GAGS)
MillsCp........ Mills Corp. [*Associated Press*] (SAG)
Mills Em D.... Mills on Eminent Domain [*A publication*] (DLA)
Mills Em Dom... Mills on Eminent Domain [*A publication*] (DLA)
Mills (NY).... Mills' New York Surrogate's Court Reports [*A publication*] (DLA)
Mills' Surr Ct... Mills' New York Surrogate's Court Reports [*A publication*] (DLA)
MIL-M.......... Military Manual (MCD)
MILMO......... Military Motorcycle [*Army*] (INF)
MILNET........ Military Network
MILNRY....... Millinery
MILO........... Mainframe Interface to Libraries Online [*Illinois Library Computer Systems Office online union catalog*]
MILO........... Maryland Interlibrary Loan (NITA)
MILO........... Maryland Interlibrary Organization [*Information service or system*] (IID)
MILO........... Miami Valley Library Organization [*Library network*]
MILO........... Most Input for the Least Output [*Business term*]
MILOC......... Military Oceanography (PDAA)
MILocoE ..... Member of the Institution of Locomotive Engineers [*British*] (EY)
MIL OPS ..... Military Operations [*USCG*] (TAG)
MIL/OS .... Military/Ordnance Specification (MCD)
Mil P .... Military Post
MILP........... Mixed Integer Linear Program [*Statistics*]
MILPAC....... Military Personnel Accounting Activity [*Army*] (AABC)
MILPAS........ Miscellaneous Information Listing Program Apollo Spacecraft [*NASA*] (KSC)
MILPERCEN... Military Personnel Center [*Alexandria, VA*] [*Army*] (AABC)
MILPERS ..... Military Personnel
MILPERSINS... Military Personnel Information System
MILPERSINST... Military Personnel Instructions (MCD)
MILPERSIS... Military Personnel Information Subsystem (MCD)
MILPHAP.... Military Provincial Health Assistance Program (AABC)
MILPINS ..... Military Police Information System (DNAB)
MILPO........ Military Personnel Office (AABC)
MILPOD...... Mixed Integer and Linear Programming Open Deck (PDAA)
MilPr .... Milestone Properties [*Associated Press*] (SAG)
MILR.......... Maintenance Incident Log Report [*Navy*] (CAAL)
MILR.......... Master of Industrial and Labor Relations
MilrBld .... Miller Building Systems, Inc. [*Associated Press*] (SAG)
MILREP....... Military Representative (NATG)
Mil Rep ...... Militia Reporter [*Boston*] [*A publication*] (DLA)
Mil Rev...... Military Review [*A publication*] (BRI)
MILRIS .... Military Routing Identifier System
MILS.......... Marine Integrated Logistics System
MILS.......... Master of Information and Library Science (GAGS)
MILS.......... Medication Information Leaflet for Seniors [*Medicine*] (DMAA)
MILS.......... Member of the Incorporated Law Society [*British*]
MILS.......... Microcomputer Integrated Library System
MILS.......... Microwave Instrument Landing System
MILS.......... Military Standard Logistics System (MCD)
MILS.......... Milliradians (KSC)
MILS Part..... Mineral Industry Location System [*Bureau of Mines*] [*Information service or system*] (IID)
MILS.......... Missile Impact Locating [*or Location*] System
MiLS........... Sparrow (E.W.) Hospital Library, Lansing, MI [*Library symbol*] [*Library of Congress*] (LCLS)
MILSAT....... Military Satellite
MILSATCOM... Military Satellite Communications [*Systems*]
MILSBILLS... Military Standard Billing System
MILSCAP ..... Military Standard Contract Administration Procedures [*DoD*]
MILSICCS ... Military Standard Item Characteristics Coding Structure (SAA)
MILSIMDS ... Military Standard Item Management Data System
MILSIMS..... Military Standard Inventory Management System
MILSO .... Military Standard Logistics Systems Office [*DoD*] (MCD)
MILS/PAC .... Missile Impact Location System, Pacific (SAA)
MILSPEC..... Military Specification
MILSPEC..... Military Specifications (GAVI)
Mil-Specs.... Military Specifications (WDAA)
MILSPETS... Military Standard Petroleum System (MCD)
MIL SPOT .... Military Standard Procurement Operations Technique
MILSPOT ..... Military Standard Purchase Operating Technique
MILSPRED... Military Standard for Providing Research and Exploratory Development Data
MILSTAAD .... Military Standard Activity Address Directory
MILSTAC.... Military Staff Communication (NATG)
MILSTAG.... Military Standardization Agreement (CINC)
MILSTAM.... International Military Staff Memorandum [*NATO*] (NATG)
MILSTAMP... Military Standard Transportation and Movement Procedure
MILSTAN .... Military Agency for Standardization [*NATO*]
MILSTAR..... Military Strategic and Tactical Relay System [*Satellite communications*]
MILSTARAP... Military Standard Transportation Action Report and Accounting Procedures (MCD)
MILSTD....... Military Standard
MILSTEP..... Military Standard Evaluation Procedure
MILSTEP..... Military Supply and Transportation Evaluation Procedures (AFM)
MILSTICC ... Military Standard Item Characteristics Coding
MILSTICCS... Military Standard Item Characteristics Coding Structure

MILSTIICS ... Military Standard Item Identification Coding System
MiLStL........ Saint Lawrence Hospital Medical Library, Lansing, MI [*Library symbol*] [*Library of Congress*] (LCLS)
MILSTRAMP... Military Standard Transportation and Movement Procedure
MILSTRAP .. Military Standard Requisition and Accounting Procedures (MCD)
MILSTRAP .. Military Standard Transaction Reporting and Accounting Procedures
MILSTRIP .. Military Standard Requisitioning and Issue Procedure
MILSVC....... Military Services
MILT.......... Military Language Tutor
MILT.......... Milton [*England*]
MILT.......... Miltope Group [*NASDAQ symbol*] (TTSB)
MILT.......... Miltope Group, Inc. [*NASDAQ symbol*] (NQ)
MILTAG...... Military Technical Assistance Group
MILTAM...... Misrad Isre'eli Li-tevi'ot Mi-Germanyah (BJA)
MiLTC........ Thomas M. Cooley Law School, Lansing, MI [*Library symbol Library of Congress*] (LCLS)
MILTELCOMM... Military Telecommunications
MiltonF....... Milton Federal Financial Corp. [*Associated Press*] (SAG)
MILTOP...... Man-in-the-Loop Trajectory Optimization Program [*NASA*]
Miltope....... Miltope Group, Inc. [*Associated Press*] (SAG)
MILTOSS ... Military Transportation of Small Shipments (NVT)
MIL TRA ... Military Training [*USCG*] (TAG)
MiLud .... Ludington Public Library, Ludington, MI [*Library symbol Library of Congress*] (LCLS)
MiLut .... Luther Public Library, Luther, MI [*Library symbol*] [*Library of Congress*] (LCLS)
MiLv .... Mink Endogenous Virus (DB)
MILVAN ...... Military Van (MCD)
MILW......... Chicago, Milwaukee, St. Paul & Pacific Railroad Co. [*AAR code*]
Milw .... Milward's Irish Ecclesiastical Reports [*1819-43*] [*A publication*] (DLA)
Milw .... Milwaukee [*Wisconsin*]
Milwaukee Law... Milwaukee Lawyer [*A publication*] (DLA)
Milwau Sch Eng... Milwaukee School of Engineering (GAGS)
Milw Ir Ecc Rep... Milward's Irish Ecclesiastical Reports [*1819-43*] [*A publication*] (DLA)
MilwLnd ...... Milwaukee Land Co. [*Associated Press*] (SAG)
MiLy .... Lyons Public Library, Lyons, MI [*Library symbol Library of Congress*] (LCLS)
MIM .... Magnetic Interaction Mechanism
MIM .... Maintenance Instructions Manual [*DoD*]
MIM .... Maintenance Interface Machine (NITA)
MIM .... Manufacturing Information Memorandum
MIM .... Marine Information Management [*Marine science*] (MSC)
MIM .... Master of Industrial Management
MIM .... Master of International Management
MIM .... Member of the Institute of Management (DD)
MIM .... Member of the Institution of Metallurgists [*British*] (DBQ)
MIM .... Mendelian Inheritance in Man [*Genetics*]
MIM .... Merimbula [*Australia Airport symbol*] (OAG)
MIM .... Message Input Module [*Telecommunications*] (TEL)
MIM .... Metal Injection Molding [*Metal fabrication*]
MIM .... Metal Insulator Metal [*Light detector*]
MIM .... Microion Mill
MIM .... Microwave Interface Module
MIM .... Mid Mountain Mining [*Vancouver Stock Exchange symbol*]
MIM .... Military Iranian Mission [*World War II*]
MIM .... Milo [*Maine*] [*Seismograph station code, US Geological Survey*] (SEIS)
Mim .... Mimeograph (AAGC)
MIM .... Mimeographed (ADA)
MIM .... Mimino [*Former USSR*] [*FAA designator*] (FAAC)
MIM .... Mindanao Independence Movement [*Philippines*] [*Political party*]
MIM .... Minimum (DA)
MIM .... Minorities in Media (EA)
MIM .... Minorities in Medicine [*Eastern Michigan University Macy Scholarship*]
MIM .... Misappropriation, Interference and Misrepresentation
MIM .... Missile Identification Module [*Military*] (CAAL)
MIM .... Mobile-Launched Interceptor Missile
MIM .... MODEM Interface Modules [*Computer science*]
MIM .... Modified Index Method (IEEE)
MIM .... Montagu Investments Management [*Commercial firm British*]
MIM .... Morality in Media (EA)
MIM .... Mouvement Independantiste Martiniquais [*Martinique Independence Movement*] [*Political party*] (PD)
MIM .... Multilateral Initiative in Malaria
MIM .... Multilateral Initiative on Malaria [*International coordination effort*]
MIM .... Multilayer Interference Mirror [*Optical instrumentation*]
MIM .... Multiple Ion Monitoring [*Mass spectrometry*]
Mim .... United States Internal Revenue Bureau, Commissioner's Mimeographed Published Opinions [*A publication*] (DLA)
MIMA .... Member, Industrial Medical Association (CMD)
MIMA .... Metal Injection Molding Association (NTPA)
MIMA .... Mineral Insulation Manufacturers Association (EA)
MIMA .... Minor Machine Accessory (MCD)
MIMA .... Minute Man National Historical Park
MIMA .... Music Industry Manufacturers Association [*Defunct*] (EA)
MIMAA........ Motor Inn, Motel and Accommodation Association [*Australia*]
MiMaci .... Mackinac Island Public Library, Mackinac Island, MI [*Library symbol Library of Congress*] (LCLS)
MiMack....... Mackinaw City Public Library, Mackinaw City, MI [*Library symbol Library of Congress*] (LCLS)
MIMAF........ Musicians International Mutual Aid Fund
MiMan .... Manchester Township Library, Manchester, MI [*Library symbol Library of Congress*] (LCLS)

MiManc .... Mancelona Township Library, Mancelona, MI [*Library symbol Library of Congress*] (LCLS)

MiManf .... Member of the Institute of Manufacturing [*British*] (DBQ)

MiMani .... Manistee County Library, Manistee, MI [*Library symbol Library of Congress*] (LCLS)

MiMant .... Manton Public Library, Manton, MI [*Library symbol Library of Congress*] (LCLS)

MiMar .... M. Alice Chapin Memorial Library, Marion, MI [*Library symbol Library of Congress*] (LCLS)

MiMarc .... Marcellus Township Library, Marcellus, MI [*Library symbol Library of Congress*] (LCLS)

MIMarE .... Member of the Institute of Marine Engineers [*British*] (EY)

MiMarl .... Marlette Township Library, Marlette, MI [*Library symbol Library of Congress*] (LCLS)

MiMaRP ...... Maple Rapids Public Library, Maple Rapids, MI [*Library symbol*] [*Library of Congress*] (LCLS)

MiMarq .... Peter White Public Library, Marquette, MI [*Library symbol Library of Congress*] (LCLS)

MiMarqAS ... Marquette-Alger Intermediate School District, Learning Materials Center, Marquette, MI [*Library symbol Library of Congress*] (LCLS)

MiMarqHi .... Marquette County Historical Society, John M. Longyear Memorial Library, Marquette, MI [*Library symbol Library of Congress*] (LCLS)

MiMarqN ..... Northern Michigan University, Marquette, MI [*Library symbol Library of Congress*] (LCLS)

MiMarqNA ... Northern Michigan University, University Archives and Historical Collections, Marquette, MI [*Library symbol*] [*Library of Congress*] (LCLS)

MiMarqS ..... Superiorland Library Cooperative System, Marquette, MI [*Library symbol Library of Congress*] (LCLS)

MiMars .... Marshall Public Library, Marshall, MI [*Library symbol Library of Congress*] (LCLS)

MiMary .... Marysville Public Library, Marysville, MI [*Library symbol Library of Congress*] (LCLS)

MiMas .... Ingham County Library, Mason, MI [*Library symbol Library of Congress*] (LCLS)

MIMAS .... Magnetically Insulated Macroparticle Accelerator System

MiMay .... Mayville District Public Library, Mayville, MI [*Library symbol Library of Congress*] (LCLS)

MIMBM .... Member of the Institute of Municipal Building Management [*British*] (DBQ)

MIMC .... Management Inventory on Managing Change [*Test*]

MIMC .... Massachusetts Interactive Media Council

MimC .... Maxwell International Microforms Corporation, Fairview Park, Elmsford, NY [*Library symbol Library of Congress*] (LCLS)

MIMC .... Member of the Institute of Management Consultants

MIMC .... Microforms International Marketing Corp. [*Pergamon*]

MIMC .... Multivariable Internal Model Control [*Control engineering*]

MIMCO .... McGraw-Hill Information Management Co. [*Database producer*] (IID)

MiMD .... Dorsch Memorial Public Library, Monroe, MI [*Library symbol Library of Congress*] (LCLS)

MIMD .... Management Information of Metrology Data (AAEL)

MIMD .... Multiple Instruction/Multiple Data (NITA)

MIMD .... Multiple Instruction, Multiple Data Processor [*Computer science*] (CIST)

MIMD .... Multiple Instruction Stream, Multiple Data Stream (MCD)

MIME .... Member of the Institute of Mining Engineers

MIME .... Member of the Institution of Mechanical Engineers [*Formerly, AMIMechE*] [*British*]

MIME .... Microcomputers in Mathematics Education (AIE)

MIME .... Ministry of Information Middle East [*British World War II*]

MIME .... Minor Machine Equipment (MCD)

MIME .... Multipurpose Internet Mail Extension [*Computer science*]

MIME .... Multipurpose Internet Mail Extensions [*Computer science*] (ACRL)

MiMe .... Spies Public Library, Menominee, MI [*Library symbol Library of Congress*] (LCLS)

MiMec .... Morton Township Library, Mecosta, MI [*Library symbol Library of Congress*] (LCLS)

MIMechE ..... Member of the Institution of Mechanical Engineers [*Formerly, AMIMechE*] [*British*] (EY)

MiMen .... Mendon Township Library, Mendon, MI [*Library symbol Library of Congress*] (LCLS)

MIMEO .... Mimeographed (ADA)

MIMEO .... Multiple Input Memo Engineering Order (MCD)

MiMer .... Merrill District Library, Merrill, MI [*Library symbol Library of Congress*] (LCLS)

MiMes .... Mesick Public Library, Mesick, MI [*Library symbol Library of Congress*] (LCLS)

MIMEX .... Major Item Material Excess [*Air Force*] (AFIT)

MIMF .... Member of the Institute of Metal Finishing [*British*] (DBQ)

MIMGTechE... Member of the Institution of Mechanical Engineers and General Technician Engineers [*British*] (DBQ)

MIMH .... Member of the Institute of Materials Handling [*British*] (DBQ)

MIMI .... Member of the Institute of Motor Industry [*British*]

MIMI .... Micro Miniature Compact Harness (MCD)

MIMIC .... Measure and Inspection Masks for Integrated Circuits (MCD)

MIMIC .... Method of Micromolding in Capillaries [*Materials science*]

MIMIC .... Microfilm Information Master Image Converter (PDAA)

MIMIC .... Micromoulding in Capillaries [*Plastics technology*]

MIMIC .... Microwave and Millimeter-Wave Monolithic Integrated Circuits Project [*DoD*]

MIMIC .... Microwave Monolithic Integrated Circuit [*Used in wireless communication*]

MIMIC/CUS... Michigan Metropolitan Information Center/Center for Urban Studies [*Wayne State University*] [*Information service or system*] (IID)

MIMICS .... Micromodule Microprogrammed Computer System (PDAA)

MiMid .... Grace A. Dow Memorial [*Public*] Library, Midland, MI [*Library symbol Library of Congress*] (LCLS)

MiMidD .... Dow Chemical Co., Midland, MI [*Library symbol Library of Congress*] (LCLS)

MiMidDC ...... Dow Corning Corp., Midland, MI [*Library symbol Library of Congress*] (LCLS)

MiMidDG ..... Dow Gardens, Midland, MI [*Library symbol*] [*Library of Congress*] (LCLS)

MiMidGS ..... Church of Jesus Christ of Latter-Day Saints, Genealogical Society Library, Midland Stake Branch, Midland, MI [*Library symbol Library of Congress*] (LCLS)

MiMidN .... Northwood Institute, Midland, MI [*Library symbol Library of Congress*] (LCLS)

MiMil .... Milan Public Library, Milan, MI [*Library symbol Library of Congress*] (LCLS)

MiMill .... Millington Township Library, Millington, MI [*Library symbol Library of Congress*] (LCLS)

MI MIN .... Miles per Minute (WDAA)

MIMinE .... Member of the Institution of Mining Engineers [*British*] (EY)

MiMio .... Oscoda County Public Library, Mio, MI [*Library symbol Library of Congress*] (LCLS)

MIMIT .... Member of the Institute of Musical Instrument Technology [*British*] (DBQ)

MIMJ .... Metal Insulator - Metal Junction

MIMM .... Management Inventory on Modern Management [*Test*]

MIMM .... Master of Mining and Metallurgy (DD)

MIMM .... Member of the Institute of Mining and Metallurgy [*British*] (EY)

MIMMIS .... Marine Corps Integrated Manpower Management Information System

MIMMS .... Marine Corps Integrated Maintenance Management System

MIMO .... Man In, Machine Out [*Computer science*]

MIMO .... Modified Input - Modified Output [*Computer science*]

MiMo .... Monroe County Library System, Monroe, MI [*Library symbol Library of Congress*] (LCLS)

MIMO .... Multi-Input, Multi-Output [*Electronics*] (AAEL)

MIMO .... Multiple-Input/Multiple-Output [*Computer science*]

MiMoHi .... Monroe County Historical Museum, Archives, Monroe, MI [*Library symbol*] [*Library of Congress*] (LCLS)

MIMOLA ...... Machine Independent Microprogramming Language

MiMor .... Stair Public Library, Morenci, MI [*Library symbol Library of Congress*] (LCLS)

MiMory .... Morley-Stanwood Community Library, Morley, MI [*Library symbol Library of Congress*] (LCLS)

MIMOSA ...... Mission Modes and Space Analysis (NASA)

MIMOT .... Master of International Management of Technology (PGP)

MIMP .... Magazine Industry Market Place [*A publication*]

MIMR .... Magnetic Ink Mark Recognition

MIMR .... May Institute of Medical Research

MIMR .... Minimal Inhibitor Mole Ratio [*Biochemistry*]

MIMS .... Major Item Management System (AABC)

MIMS .... Manifest Information Management System (GAAI)

MIMS .... Master of Integrated Manufacturing Systems (PGP)

MIMS .... Material Information Management System (MCD)

MIMS .... Medical Information Management System [*NASA*]

MIMS .... Medical Information Management System (NAKS)

MIMS .... Medical Inventory Management System

MIMS .... Member of the Institute of Management Specialists [*British*] (DBQ)

MIMS .... Metal Impact Monitoring System [*Nuclear energy*] (NRCH)

MIMS .... Mineral Insulated, Metal Sheathed [*Cable*]

MIMS .... Missile Maintenance Squadron [*Air Force*]

MIMS .... Mitrol Industrial Management System [*Mitrol, Inc.*] [*Information service or system*] (IID)

MIMS .... Modular Isodrive Memory Series

MIMS .... Monthly Index of Medical Specialties [*A publication*] (DB)

MIMS .... Multi-Item Multisource (IEEE)

MIMS .... Multiple Independently Maneuvering Submunitions (MCD)

MIMSq .... Missile Maintenance Squadron [*Air Force*] (AFM)

MIMT .... Member of the Institute of Music Teachers (ADA)

MiMtc .... Mount Clemens Public Library, Mount Clemens, MI [*Library symbol Library of Congress*] (LCLS)

MiMtcM .... Macomb County Library, Mount Clemens, MI [*Library symbol Library of Congress*] (LCLS)

MiMtp .... Mount Pleasant Public Library, Mount Pleasant, MI [*Library symbol Library of Congress*] (LCLS)

MiMtpC .... Chippewa Library League, Mt. Pleasant, MI [*Library symbol Library of Congress*] (LCLS)

MiMtpT .... Central Michigan University, Mount Pleasant, MI [*Library symbol Library of Congress*] (LCLS)

MiMu .... Hackley Public Library, Muskegon, MI [*Library symbol Library of Congress*] (LCLS)

MiMuB .... Muskegon Business College, Muskegon, MI [*Library symbol Library of Congress*] (LCLS)

MIMUG .... Meetings Industry Microcomputer Users Group [*Defunct*] (EA)

MiMul .... Mulliken District Library, Mulliken, MI [*Library symbol Library of Congress*] (LCLS)

MiMuM .... Muskegon County Library, Muskegon, MI [*Library symbol Library of Congress*] (LCLS)

MiMun .... Munising Public Library, Munising, MI [*Library symbol Library of Congress*] (LCLS)

MiMunE .... Member of the Institute of Municipal Engineers [*British*] (EY)

MIMUSA ...... Matrix Iteration Method of Unfolding Spectra [*Computer science*]

MIMV .... Mirabilis Mosaic Virus [*Plant pathology*]

MIN .... Business European Airways Ltd. [*British*] [*FAA designator*] (FAAC)

MIN............. Marketing Information Network [*Information service or system*] (IID)
MIN............. Master of Insurance
MIN............. Media Industry Newsletter [*A publication*]
MIN............. Medial Interlaminar Nucleus (DMAA)
MIN............. Meeting Individual Needs [*Educational publishing*]
MIN............. Member Information Network [*for House of Representatives*]
MIN............. Member of the Institute of Navigation [*British*]
MIN............. MFS Intermediate Income SBI [*NYSE symbol*] (SPSG)
MIN............. MFS Intermediate Income Trust [*Associated Press*] (SAG)
MIN............. MFS Interm Incme SBI [*NYSE symbol*] (TTSB)
min............. Microinch (BARN)
Min............. Minaean [*or Minean*] (BJA)
MIN............. Mine [*or Minecraft*] [*Navy*]
MIN............. Mine Identification and Neutralization (PDAA)
MIN............. Mineral [*California*] [*Seismograph station code, US Geological Survey*] (SEIS)
MIN............. Mineralogy
MIN............. Miniature
MIN............. Minim
MIN............. Minimum (AFM)
min............. Minimum [*A minim measurement*] (DAVI)
Min............. Minimum (DFIT)
min............. Mining (DD)
MIN............. Mining
MIN............. Minion [*Typography*] (DGA)
MIN............. Minister [*or Ministry*]
Min............. Minister [*or Ministry*] (ODBW)
Min............. Minnesota Reports [*A publication*] (DLA)
MIN............. Minor
MIN............. Minority
Min............. Minor's Alabama Reports [*A publication*] (DLA)
MIN............. Minto Resources [*Vancouver Stock Exchange symbol*]
MIN............. Minute (AFM)
min............. Minute (IDOE)
MIN............. Mobile Identification Number (ACRL)
MIN............. Mobilization Identification Number [*Military*]
MIN............. Molasses Information Network (EA)
MIN............. Most in Need Population
MIN............. Movimiento de Integracion Nacional [*National Integration Movement*] [*Ecuador*] [*Political party*] (PPW)
MIN............. Movimiento de Integracion Nacional [*National Integration Movement*] [*Venezuela*] [*Political party*] (PPW)
MIN............. Movimiento de Izquierda Nacional [*National Left-Wing Movement*] [*Bolivia*] [*Political party*] (PPW)
MINA .... Member of the Institution of Naval Architects [*British*]
MINA .... Monoisonitrosoacetone [*Biochemistry*]
MINA .... Multiplexed Input NHRE [*National Hail Research Experiment*] Averager
MINABB ...... Minimum Abbreviations [*of MAST*]
MINAC .... Miniature Navigation Airborne Computer
MINAC .... Minuteman Action Committee (SAA)
MINAGE ...... Minimum Seed-Bearing Age [*Botany*]
MiNas .... Putnam Public Library, Nashville, MI [*Library symbol Library of Congress*] (LCLS)
MINAT .... Miniature
minat .... Miniature (VRA)
MiNazC .... Nazareth College, Nazareth, MI [*Library symbol Library of Congress*] (LCLS)
MiNb........... New Buffalo Public Library, New Buffalo, MI [*Library symbol Library of Congress*] (LCLS)
MINBATFOR... Minecraft Battle Force, Pacific Fleet
Min B/L .... Minimum Bill of Lading (DS)
M-in-C .... Matron-in-Chief [*Navy British*]
MINC .... Minicomputer
MINCOM ...... Miniaturized Communications [*Navy*] (DNAB)
MINCOMS.... Multiple Interior Communications System (MCD)
MINCONMAR... Ministerial Conference of West and Central African States on Maritime Transport [*Ivory Coast*] (EAIO)
MIND .... Magnetic Integrator Neuron Duplicator
MIND .... Management Institute for National Development
MIND .... Method in Natural Development [*Mental diet plan*]
MIND .... Methods of Intellectual Development [*National Association of Manufacturers*]
MIND .... Mining Item Name Directory [*A publication*]
MIND .... Mitcham Indus [*NASDAQ symbol*] (TTSB)
MIND .... Mitcham Industries [*NASDAQ symbol*] (SAG)
MIND .... Modular Interactive Network Designer
MIND .... Multidisciplinary Institute for Neuropsychological Development (EA)
MINDAC ...... Marine Inertial Navigation Data Assimilation Computer (IEEE)
MIndAdm..... Master of Industrial Administration (GAGS)
MINDAP ...... Microwave-Induced Nitrogen Discharge at Atmospheric Pressure [*Spectrometry*]
MINDAT ...... Minerals Data Base [*of the Law of the Sea*] (GNE)
MINDD........ Minimum Due Date per Order
MIndEd....... Master of Industrial Education
MIN-DEF..... Ministry of Defence [*British*]
Min Dig .... Minot's Digest [*Massachusetts*] [*A publication*] (DLA)
MINDIV....... Mine Division [*Navy*]
MINDO........ Modified Intermediate Neglect of Diatomic Overlap (AAEL)
MINDO........ Modified Intermediate Neglect of Differential Overlap [*Quantum mechanics*]
MINDS........ Mental Illness Nervous Disorders Society [*Australia*]
MindSpr....... MindSpring Enterprises, Inc. [*Associated Press*] (SAG)
MINE........... Medical Improvement not Expected (DHP)

MINE........... Mesna, Ifosfamide, Mitoxantrone, Etoposide [*Antineoplastic drug*] (CDI)
MINE........... Microbial Information Network Europe [*EEC*]
Min E........... Mineral Engineer
Min E........... Mining Engineer
MINE........... Minneapolis Eastern Railway Co. [*AAR code*]
MINE........... Montana Information Network Exchange [*Library network*]
MINE........... Multi-Indenture NORS [*Not Operationally Ready Status*] Evaluator (MCD)
MINEAC ...... Miniature Electronic Auto-Collimator
MINEASYFAC... Mine Assembly Facilities
MINEC .... Military Necessity
MINECTRMEASSTA... Mine Countermeasure Station [*Military*]
MINECTRMEASTA... Mine Countermeasures Station [*Military*] (DNAB)
M In Ed........ Master of Industrial Education (PGP)
MINEDEFLAB... Mine Defense Laboratory [*Navy*]
MiNeg......... Negaunee Public Library, Negaunee, MI [*Library symbol Library of Congress*] (LCLS)
MINELCO ..... Miniature Electronic Component (WDAA)
MINEPACSUPPGRU... Mine Force, Pacific Fleet, Support Group Unit (DNAB)
miner.......... Minerology (DD)
MINERAL ..... Mineralogy
MINERALOG... Mineralogical
MINERVA..... Minimization of Earthworks for Vertical Alignment (PDAA)
MineSf......... Mine Safety Appliances Co. [*Associated Press*] (SAG)
MINET......... Medical Information Network [*GTE Telenet Communications Corp.*] [*Reston, VA*] [*Telecommunications*]
MINET......... Metropolitan Information Network
MIN EV .... Minutes of Evidence [*Legal term*] (DLA)
MINEVDET.... Mine Warfare Evaluation Detachment
MiNew........ Newaygo Carnegie Public Library, Newaygo, MI [*Library symbol Library of Congress*] (LCLS)
MINEWARCOM... Mine Warfare Command [*Navy*]
MiNew-C...... Croton Public Library, Newaygo, MI [*Library symbol Library of Congress*] (LCLS)
MINEX .... Minelaying, Minesweeping, and Mine-Hunting Exercise [*NATO*] (NATG)
MINEX .... Mine Warfare Exercise (NVT)
MINFLOT ..... Mine Flotilla [*Navy*]
MInfoTech ... Master of Information Technology and Communication
MInfSys ...... Master of Information Systems
MING .... Magnetic Induction Nuclear Gyroscope
MIng........... Maitre en Ingenierie [*Master of Engineering*] [*French*]
MIng........... Maitrise en Ingenierie [*Master of Engineering*] (DD)
MING .... Middle Class, Intelligent, Nice Girl [*Lifestyle classification*]
MINGSE ...... Minimum Ground Support Equipment Concept (MCD)
MiNhL......... Lenox Township Library, New Haven, MI [*Library symbol Library of Congress*] (LCLS)
MINI .... Method of Implicit Nonstationary Iteration (PDAA)
MINI .... Miniature (KSC)
MINI .... Minicomputer Industry National Interchange [*An association*] (EA)
MINI .... Minimize Individually Negotiated Instruments (AFM)
MINI .... Minimum (DSUE)
MINI .... Mobile Mini [*NASDAQ symbol*] (TTSB)
MINI .... Mobile Mini, Inc. [*NASDAQ symbol*] (SAG)
MiNi........... Niles Community Library, Niles, MI [*Library symbol Library of Congress*] (LCLS)
MINIA .... Monkey Intranuclear Inclusion Agent (MAE)
MINIACT ...... Minimum Acquisition Tracking System (MUGU)
MINIAPS ..... Miniature Accessory Power Supply
MINICATS .... Miniaturization of Federal Catalog System Publications
MINICOM .... Minimum Communications
MINI COMP.. Miniature Compact (MCD)
MINICS .... Minimal-Input Cataloguing System [*Loughborough University of Technology*]
MINICS/PDS.. MINICS Periodicals Data System (NITA)
MINIDOS..... Mini Disk Operating System (IDOE)
MINI-ELS .... Mini-Emitter Location System (MCD)
Miniluv .... Ministry of Love [*From George Orwell's novel, "1984"*]
MiniMd .... MiniMed, Inc. [*Associated Press*] (SAG)
MINI MUX.... Miniaturized Multiplexes (MCD)
MiNiN .... National Standard Information Resources, Niles, MI [*Library symbol*] [*Library of Congress*] (LCLS)
Mining Chem Engng Rev... Mining and Chemical Engineering Review [*A publication*]
Mining Engng Rev... Mining and Engineering Review [*A publication*]
MiningS....... Mining Services International Corp. [*Associated Press*] (SAG)
Min Inst....... Minor's Institutes of Common and Statute Law [*A publication*] (DLA)
MIN INVEST... Minimum Investment [*Finance*]
Minipax ...... Ministry of Peace [*From George Orwell's novel, "1984"*]
Miniplenty ... Ministry of Plenty [*From George Orwell's novel, "1984"*]
MINIRAD..... Minimum Radiation (CAAL)
MINIRAR..... Minimum Radiation Requirements [*Missiles*] (IEEE)
MINISID...... Miniature Seismic Intrusion Detector [*DoD*]
MINISINS..... Miniature Ship Inertial Navigation System (MCD)
MINI-SUBLAB... Miniature Submarine Laboratory
MINIT......... Minimum Interference Threshold [*Telecommunications*] (TEL)
MINITAS ..... Miniature True Airspeed Computer
MINITEX ..... Minnesota Interlibrary Telecommunications Exchange [*Library cooperative*] [*Minnesota Higher Education Coordinating Board Minneapolis, MN*]
MINITRACK... Minimum-Weight Tracking [*System*] (MUGU)
Minitrue..... Ministry of Truth [*From George Orwell's novel, "1984"*]
MINIVAR..... Minimum Variance Orbit Determination (MCD)
MINIW .... Mobile Mini Wrrt [*NASDAQ symbol*] (TTSB)

MINK .... Missouri-Iowa-Nebraska-Kansas League [*Old baseball league*]
MINL.......... Minimum Licence Period (WDAA)
MINLANT ..... Mine Warfare Forces, Atlantic [*Navy*]
MinI E.......... Mineral Engineer (PGP)
MINLP .... Mixed-Integer Nonlinear Program [*Computer science*]
MINMAC-PC... Mini-Macroeconomic Personal Computer Model [*Department of Energy*] (GFGA)
MIN MC .... Minimum Material Condition [*Computer science*]
MINN .... Minnesota (AFM)
Minn .... Minnesota (ODBW)
Minn .... Minnesota Supreme Court Reports [*A publication*] (DLA)
Minn Admin Reg... Minnesota State Register [*A publication*] (DLA)
MinnBrw ...... Minnesota Brewing Co. [*Associated Press*] (SAG)
Minn Code Agency... Minnesota Code of Agency Rules [*A publication*] (DLA)
Minn Code Ann... Minnesota Code, Annotated [*A publication*] (DLA)
Minn Ct Rep... Minnesota Court Reporter [*A publication*] (DLA)
Minn DL & I Comp... Minnesota Department of Labor and Industries. Compilation of Court Decisions [*A publication*] (DLA)
MINN DPW LIB... Minnesota Department of Public Welfare Library Consortium [*Library network*]
MinnEd .... Minnesota Educational Computing Corp. [*Associated Press*] (SAG)
MINNEMAST... Minnesota School Mathematics and Science Teaching Project [*University of Minnesota*] (AEE)
Minn Gen Laws... Minnesota General Laws [*A publication*] (DLA)
Minn (Gil).... Minnesota Reports (Gilfillan Edition) [*A publication*] (DLA)
Minn (Gill)... Minnesota Reports (Gilfillan Edition) [*A publication*] (DLA)
Minn Law J... Minnesota Law Journal [*A publication*] (DLA)
Minn Laws... Laws of Minnesota [*A publication*] (DLA)
Minn LJ ...... Minnesota Law Journal [*St. Paul*] [*A publication*] (DLA)
MinnMul ...... Minnesota Municipal Income Trust [*Associated Press*] (SAG)
MinnMuT ...... Minnesota Municipal Term Trust [*Associated Press*] (SAG)
MinnPL .... Minnesota Power & Light Co. [*Associated Press*] (SAG)
Minn R & WCAT Div... Minnesota Railroad and Warehouse Commission. Auto Transportation Co. Division Reports [*A publication*] (DLA)
Minn Reg..... Minnesota Register [*A publication*] (AAGC)
Minn Rep..... Minnesota Reports [*A publication*] (DLA)
Minn Reps... Minnesota Reports [*A publication*] (DLA)
Minn Sess Law Serv (West)... Minnesota Session Law Service (West) [*A publication*] (DLA)
Minn Stat..... Minnesota Statutes [*A publication*] (AAGC)
Minn Stat Ann... Minnesota Statutes, Annotated [*A publication*] (DLA)
Minn Stat Ann (West)... West's Minnesota Statutes, Annotated [*A publication*] (DLA)
Minntc .... Minntech Corp. [*Associated Press*] (SAG)
MinnTr2 ...... Minnesota Term Trust, Inc. II [*Associated Press*] (SAG)
Minn WCD ... Minnesota Workmen's Compensation Decisions [*A publication*] (DLA)
MiNop.......... Leelanau Township Library, Northport, MI [*Library symbol Library of Congress*] (LCLS)
Minor........... Minor's Alabama Supreme Court Reports [*1820-26*] [*A publication*] (DLA)
Minor........... Minor's Institutes [*A publication*] (DLA)
Minor (Ala)... Minor's Alabama Reports [*A publication*] (DLA)
Minor (Ala)... Minor's Institutes [*Alabama*] [*A publication*] (DLA)
Minorc .... Minorco [*Formerly, Minerals & Resources Corp. Ltd.*] [*Associated Press*] (SAG)
Minor Inst.... Minor's Institutes of Common and Statute Law [*A publication*] (DLA)
Minor's Alabama Rep... Minor's Alabama Reports [*A publication*] (DLA)
Minor's Ala R... Minor's Alabama Reports [*A publication*] (DLA)
Minor's Ala Rep... Minor's Alabama Reports [*A publication*] (DLA)
Minor's R ... Minor's Alabama Reports [*A publication*] (DLA)
Minor's Rep... Minor's Alabama Reports [*A publication*] (DLA)
MINOS .... Main Injector Neutrino Oscillation Search [*Particle Physics*]
MINOS .... Manual Intervention and Observation Simulator (AAG)
MINOS .... Mine Operating System (PDAA)
MINOS .... Mixed Integer Operational Scheduling (PDAA)
MINOS .... Modular Input/Output System
Minot St U... Minot State University (GAGS)
MINOX .... Minimum Oxidizer (KSC)
MinP........... Minnesota Power & Light Co. [*Associated Press*] (SAG)
MINPAC ...... Mine Warfare Forces, Pacific [*Navy*]
MIN PLEN .... Minister Plenipotentiary (WDAA)
MINPOREN... National Association of Commercial Broadcasters in Japan (EY)
MINPROC .... Mineral Processing Technology [*Canada Department of Energy, Mines, and Resources*] [*Information service or system*] (CRD)
MINPRT ...... Minimum Processing Time per Operation
MINQU........ Minimum Norm Quadratic Unbiased [*Statistics*]
MINQUE...... Minimum Norm Quadratic Unbiased Estimation [*Statistics*] (PDAA)
MINR .... Minimum R Factor [*Spectrometry*]
Min R .... Minnesota Reports [*A publication*] (DLA)
MINRA .... Miniature International Racing Association
MINRAD...... Minimum Radiation (MCD)
Min Rep ...... Minnesota Reports [*A publication*] (DLA)
MINRL .... Mineral
MINRON ...... Mine Squadron [*Navy*]
MINRTY .... Minority
MINS .... Mare Island Naval Shipyard [*Also, MINSY*] [*Later, MID*]
MINS .... Miniature Inertial Navigation System
MINS .... Minors in Need of Supervision [*Classification for delinquent children*]
MINSAT ...... Minimum Safe Air Travel (SAA)
MINSD .... Minimum Planned Start Date per Operation
MINSK .... [*A*] Russian digital computer [*Moscow University*]
MINSOP ...... Minimum Slack Time per Operation
MINSQ .... Minimum Squares [*Mathematical statistics*]
MInstAEA.... Member of the Institute of Automotive Engineer Assessors [*British*] (DBQ)

M Inst AM ... Member of the Institute of Administrative Management [*British*] (DCTA)
MInstBB....... Member of the Institute of British Bakers (DBQ)
MInstBCA.... Member of the Institute of Burial and Cremation Administration [*British*] (DBQ)
MInstBE....... Member of the Institution of British Engineers
MInstBRM.... Member of the Institute of Baths and Recreation Management [*British*] (DBQ)
MInstBRMDip... Diploma Member of the Institute of Baths and Recreation Management [*British*] (DBQ)
MInstBTM .... Member of the Institute of Business and Technical Management [*British*] (DBQ)
MInstCE .... Member of the Institution of Civil Engineers [*Later, MICE*] [*British*] (EY)
M Inst CM ... Member of the Institute of Commercial Management [*British*] (DCTA)
MInstD .... Member of the Institute of Directors [*British*] (DI)
MInstE .... Member of the Institute of Energy [*British*] (DBQ)
MInstE .... Member of the Institution of Engineers [*British*] (EY)
MInstF .... Member of the Institute of Fuel [*British*]
MInstFF .... Member of the Institute of Freight Forwarders [*British*] (DBQ)
MInstGasE .. Member of the Institution of Gas Engineers [*British*] (EY)
MInstHE ...... Member of the Institution of Highway Engineers [*British*]
M INST J ..... Member of the Institute of Journalists [*British*] (DGA)
M Inst Jour... Member of the Institute of Journalists [*British*] (ROG)
MInstM .... Member of the Institute of Marketing [*British*]
MInstMC...... Member of the Institute of Measurement and Control [*British*] (DBQ)
MInstME ...... Member of the Institution of Mining Engineers [*British*]
MInstMet ..... Member of the Institute of Metals [*British*]
MInstMM ..... Member of the Institution of Mining and Metallurgy [*British*]
MInstMO...... Member of the Institute of Market Officers [*British*] (DI)
MInstNA...... Member of the Institution of Naval Architects [*British*] (EY)
MInstNDT .... Member of the British Institute of Non-Destructive Testing (DBQ)
MInstP......... Member of the Institute of Physics (ADA)
MInstPE ...... Member of the Institute of Petroleum Engineers (ADA)
MInstPet ..... Member of the Institute of Petroleum [*British*] (EY)
MInstPI........ Member of the Institute of Patentees and Inventors [*British*] (EY)
MInstPkg ..... Member of the Institute of Packaging [*British*] (DI)
M Inst PS .... Member of the Institute of Purchasing and Supply [*British*] (DCTA)
MInstR......... Member of the Institute of Refrigeration [*British*] (DBQ)
MINSTR .... Minister
MInstRA....... Member of the Institute of Registered Architects [*British*]
MInstSMM ... Member of the Institute of Sales and Marketing Management [*British*] (DBQ)
MInstSP ...... Member Institution of Sewage Purification [*Ecology*] (DAVI)
MInstStructE... Member of the Institution of Structural Engineers (ADA)
MInstSWM ... Member of the Institute of Solid Waste Management [*British*] (DI)
MInstT .... Member of the Institute of Technology [*British*] (EY)
MInstT .... Member of the Institute of Transport [*British*]
M Inst TA .... Member of the Institute of Transport Administration [*British*] (DCTA)
MInstTM ...... Member of the Institute of Travel Managers in Industry and Commerce [*British*] (ODBW)
MInstW........ Member of the Institute of Welding [*British*]
MInstWE...... Member of the Institution of Water Engineers [*British*]
MInstWHS ... Member of the Institute of Works and Highways Superintendents [*British*] (DI)
MInstWPC.... Member of the Institution of Water Pollution Control [*British*] (DI)
MINSY .... Mare Island Naval Shipyard [*Also, MINS*] [*Later, MID*]
MINT........... Bank of Montreal, Canadian Imperial Bank of Commerce, Bank of Nova Scotia, and Toronto-Dominion Bank
MINT........... Major International Narcotics Traffickers [*Register*] [*Drug Enforcement Administration*]
MINT........... Materiel Identification and New Item Control Technique [*AFLC*]
MINT........... Media Integration [*Computer science*]
MINT........... Micro-Integration [*NASDAQ symbol*] (TTSB)
MINT........... Micro-Integration Corp. [*NASDAQ symbol*] (SAG)
MINT........... Minorities International Network for Trade (EA)
MINT........... Municipal Insured National Trust
MinTch .... Minerals Technologies, Inc. [*Associated Press*] (SAG)
MINTEC ...... Mining Technology Abstracts [*Canada Centre for Mineral and Energy Technology*] [*Information service or system*] (CRD)
MINTECH ..... Ministry of Technology [*British*]
MINTEL........ Market Intelligence Report
MINTER .... Ministerio do Interior [*Ministry of the Interior*] [*Information service or system*] (IID)
MINTIE........ Minimum Test Instrumentation Equipment
MIntLaw ...... Master of International Law
MIntMed...... Master of International Medicine (NADA)
MINTR .... Miniature (MSA)
MINTS .... Mutual Institutions National Transfer System, Inc. [*Banking*]
MINTS .... Mutual Insurance National Transfer System, Inc.
MINTWK ..... Minimum Total Work Content
MINU .... Mobile Instrument Investigation Unit
MINucE........ Member of the Institution of Nuclear Engineers [*British*]
MI Nucl E ... Member of the Institution of Nuclear Engineers [*British*]
MINUET ...... Minimum Energy Trajectory Model [*Army*] (AABC)
MiNun......... Crockery Township Library, Nunica, MI [*Library symbol Library of Congress*] (LCLS)
MINUS .... Modular Integrated Utility Systems (MCD)
MinutInt....... Minuteman International [*Associated Press*] (SAG)
MINW .... Master Interface Network (MCD)
MINWARTECH... Mine Warfare Technician [*Navy*] (DNAB)
MINWR .... Minimum Weapon Radius (SAA)
MIN WT ...... Minimum Weight (WDAA)
MINX .... Multimedia Information Network Exchange [*Computer science*]
MINY .... Mineralogy (ROG)

MINY	Minority (ROG)
MIO	Management Improvement and Operating Plan [*Department of Housing and Urban Development*] (GFGA)
MIO	Management Information Office [*or Officer*] [*Air Force*] (AFM)
MIO	Management Integration Office [*NASA*] (NASA)
mio	Management Integration Office (NAKS)
MIO	Map Information Office [*US Geological Survey*]
MIO	Marine Inspection Office [*Coast Guard*]
MIO	Marine Inspection Operations [*USCG*] (TAG)
MIO	Maritime Interception Operations [*Coast Guard*] (DOMA)
MIO	Medical Intelligence Office [*Later, MIIA*] [*DoD*]
MIO	Meteoritic Impact Origin (AAG)
MIO	Metric Information Office [*National Institute of Standards and Technology*]
MIO	Miami, OK [*Location identifier FAA*] (FAAL)
MIO	Midas Commuter Airlines CA [*Venezuela*] [*ICAO designator*] (FAAC)
MIO	Military Intelligence Officer [*British military*] (DMA)
MIO	Minimal Identifiable Odor
MIO	Mobile Ionospheric Observatory [*Boston University*]
MIO	Mobile Issuing Office [*Navy*]
MIO	Modular Input/Output [*Telecommunications*]
MIO	Motility Indol Ornithine [*Medium*] [*Medicine*] (BABM)
MIO	Motility Indol Ornithine [*Medium*] [*Microbiology*] (DAVI)
MIO	Movements Identification Officer [*Air Force*]
MIO	Movements Integration Office
MIO	Multi-Institutional Organization [*Generic term*] (DHSM)
MIO	Multiple Input/Output (NITA)
MIO	Multiple Input/Output Stream [*Computer science*]
MIOA	Medical Industries of America [*NASDAQ symbol*] (SAG)
MIOAC	Military Intelligence Officer Advanced Course (DOMA)
MIOB	Member of the Institute of Building [*British*]
MiOC	Olivet College, Olivet, MI [*Library symbol Library of Congress*] (LCLS)
MIOD	Message Input-Output Devices (MCD)
MIOG	Manual of Investigative and Operational Guidelines [*FBI*]
MIOK	Magyar Izraelitak Orszagos Kepviselete (BJA)
MiOIA	Alumni Memorial Library, Orchard Lake, MI [*Library symbol Library of Congress*] (LCLS)
MIONP	Microwave-Induced Optical Nuclear Polarization [*Physics*]
MiOnt	Ontonagon Township Library, Ontonagon, MI [*Library symbol Library of Congress*] (LCLS)
MIOP	Magnetic Iron Oxide Particle (DMAA)
MIOP	Master Input/Output Processor (NITA)
MIOP	Member of the Institute of Osteopathy and Physiotherapy [*British*]
MIOP	Member of the Institute of Printing [*British*] (DBQ)
MIOP	Multiplexing Input-Output Processor [*Computer science*] (BUR)
MIOS	Modular Input-Output System [*Telecommunications*] (TEL)
MIOS	Multi-IMU [*Internal Measuring Unit*] Operation System [*NASA*]
MIOSH	Member of the Institution of Occupational Safety and Health [*British*] (DCTA)
MIOT	Member of the Institute of Operating Theatre Technicians [*British*]
MIOT	Municipal Income Opportunities Trust [*Associated Press*] (SAG)
MiOt	Otsego District Public Library, Otsego, MI [*Library symbol Library of Congress*] (LCLS)
MIOT2	Municipal Income Opportunities Trust II [*Associated Press*] (SAG)
MIOT3	Municipal Income Opportunities Trust III [*Associated Press*] (SAG)
MiOv	Ovid Public Library, Ovid, MI [*Library symbol Library of Congress*] (LCLS)
MiOw	Owosso Public Library, Owosso, MI [*Library symbol Library of Congress*] (LCLS)
MiOwJW	John Wesley College, Owosso, MI [*Library symbol Library of Congress*] (LCLS)
MIP	Machine Independent Package (DGA)
MIP	Machine Instruction Processor [*Computer science*] (BUR)
MIP	Macrophage-Induced Protein [*Biochemistry*]
MIP	Macrophage Inflammatory Protein [*Biochemistry*]
MIP	Main Instrument Panel (MCD)
MIP	Maintainer Instructional Package (MCD)
MIP	Maintenance Implementation Plan [*FAA*] (TAG)
MIP	Maintenance Improvement Program
MIP	Maintenance Index Page
MIP	Major Intrinsic Protein [*Biochemistry*]
MIP	Malleable Iron Pipe
MIP	Management Implementation Plan (MCD)
MIP	Management Improvement Plan
MIP	Management Improvement Program [*Military*]
MIP	Management Incentive Program
MIP	Management Information Protocol [*Telecommunications*] (OSI)
MIP	Management Intern Program
MIP	Mandatory Inspection Point (KSC)
MIP	Manual Index Page [*SNMMMS*]
MIP	Manual Input Processing [*or Program*] [*Computer science*]
MIP	Manufacturers of Illumination Products (EA)
MIP	Marche International des Programmes de Television International [*International Marketplace for Buyers and Sellers of Television Programs*] (NTCM)
MIP	Marine Insurance Policy
MIP	Master Improvement Program (AFIT)
MIP	Master Information Paper [*Military*] (CAAL)
MIP	Master Insurance Program
MIP	Master of Intellectual Property (PGP)
MIP	Material Improvement Plan [*or Program*] [*Aviation*]
MIP	Material in Process [*Computer science*] (CIST)
MIP	Materiel Improvement Project [*Military*]
MIP	Matrix Inversion Program [*Computer science*] (BUR)

MIP	Maximum Inspiratory Pressure [*Medicine*]
MIP	Maximum Investment Plan (WDAA)
MIP	Mean Indicated Pressure
MIP	Mean Intravascular Pressure [*Cardiology*] (MAE)
MIP	Mechanized Infantry Program [*United States Army, Europe*] (MCD)
MIP	Medicaid Interim Payments
MIP	Member of the Institute of Plumbing [*British*] (DBQ)
MIP	Membrane-Intercalated Particles [*Cytology*]
MIP	Membrane Isolation Process [*Food technology*]
MIP	Merfin Hygienic [*Vancouver Stock Exchange symbol*]
MIP	Message Input Processor
MIP	Methodology Investigation Proposal (MCD)
MIP	Methods Improvement Program [*IBM Corp.*]
MIP	Microelectronic Integrated Processing [*Symposium*]
MIP	Microwave-Induced Plasma [*Spectrometry*]
MIP	Microwave Interference Protection
MIP	Middle Interphalangeal Joint [*Anatomy*] (DAVI)
MIP	Military Improvement Program
MIP	Military Information Program
MIP	Military Interdepartmental Purchase
MIP	Million Instructions per Second
MIP	Milton, PA [*Location identifier FAA*] (FAAL)
MIP	Minimal Inspiratory Pressure [*Medicine*] (DB)
MIP	Minimum Import Prices [*Economics*]
MIP	Minimum Impulse Pulse
MIP	Mint in Package [*Doll collecting*]
MIP	Missile Impact Predictor [*Air Force*]
MIP	Missile Instrumentation Package [*Military*] (CAAL)
MIP	Mission Integration Panel [*NASA*] (SSD)
MIP	Missouri Institute of Psychiatry Library, St. Louis, MO [*OCLC symbol*] (OCLC)
MIP	Mixed Integer Programming [*Computer science*]
MIP	MMU [*Manned Maneuvering Unit*] Integration Plan [*NASA*] (GFGA)
MIP	Mobilization Improvement Program [*MTMC*] (TAG)
MIP	Model Implementation Plan
MIP	Model Improvements Program [*TRADOC*] (MCD)
MIP	Model Installation Program (AAGC)
MIP	Modern Irish Printer [*A publication British*] (DGA)
MIP	Modest Improvement Program [*Military*] (NVT)
MIP	Modification Instruction Package (KSC)
MIP	Modulated Interframe Plan
MIP	Molecularly Imprinted Polymer [*Biotechnology*]
MIP	Monthly Intelligence Production (MCD)
MIP	Monthly Investment Plan [*Stock exchange term*] (SPSG)
MIP	Mortgage Insurance Premium
MIP	Mortgage Investments Plus, Inc. (MHDW)
MIP	Most Important Person
MIP	Motivation Indoctrination Program [*Military*]
MIP	Mouvement Independent Populaire [*Popular Independent Movement*] [*Luxembourg*] [*Political party*] (PPE)
MIP	Mouvement Islamique Progressiste [*Islamic Progressive Movement*] [*Tunisia*] [*Political party*] (PD)
MIP	Movimiento Independiente Peruano [*Peruvian Independent Movement*] [*Political party*]
MIP	Multipurpose Information Processor [*Computer science*] (MHDB)
MIP	Mycorrhiza Inoculum Potential [*Soil science*]
MIP	Myo-inositolphosphate [*Biochemistry*]
MIPA	Macrophage Inflammatory Protein Alpha (DMAA)
MIPA	Master of International Public Administration (GAGS)
MIPA	Member of the Institute of Practitioners in Advertising [*British*]
MIPA	Member of the Institute of Public Administration (ADA)
MIPA	Methylisopropylaniline [*Organic chemistry*]
MIPA	Missile Procurement, Army (AABC)
MIPA	Monoisopropylamine [*Organic chemistry*]
MiPa	Port Austin Township Library, Port Austin, MI [*Library symbol Library of Congress*] (LCLS)
MIP-AES	Microwave-Induced Plasma-Atomic Emission Spectroscopy
MiPal	Richmond Township Public Library, Palmer, MI [*Library symbol Library of Congress*] (LCLS)
MiPar	Parchment Community Library, Parchment, MI [*Library symbol Library of Congress*] (LCLS)
MIPAS	Management Information Planning and Accountancy Service (MHDI)
MiPaw	Paw Paw Public Library, Paw Paw, MI [*Library symbol Library of Congress*] (LCLS)
MIPB	Macrophage Inflammatory Protein Beta (DMAA)
MIPB	Monoisopropylbiphenyl (PDAA)
MIPC	Manifold Ignition Primary Charge
MIPC	Member of the Institute of Production Control [*British*] (DBQ)
MIPC	Metropolitan Information Processing Conference (MCD)
MIPD	Manpower Intelligence and Planning Division (AIE)
MIPD	Manufacturing Industry Products Division (MCD)
MIPE	Magnetic Induction Plasma Engine
MIPE	Member of the Institution of Production Engineers [*British*] (DAS)
MIPE	Men's International Peace Exchange (EA)
MIPE	Mobile Intelligence Processing Element (DOMA)
MIPE	Modular Information Processing Equipment
MiPec	Elk Township Library, Peck, MI [*Library symbol Library of Congress*] (LCLS)
MiPel	Pellston Public Library, Pellston, MI [*Library symbol Library of Congress*] (LCLS)
MiPen	Pentwater Township Library, Pentwater, MI [*Library symbol Library of Congress*] (LCLS)
MiPet	Petoskey Public Library, Petoskey, MI [*Library symbol Library of Congress*] (LCLS)

MiPetN .... North Central Michigan College, Petoskey, MI [*Library symbol Library of Congress*] (LCLS)
MIPEX........ Model Improvement Experiment (MCD)
MIPG .... Master Index Pulse Generator
MiPh............ Saint Clair County Library System, Port Huron, MI [*Library symbol Library of Congress*] (LCLS)
MIPHE .... Member of the Institute of Public Health Engineers [*British*] (DBQ)
MiPhM......... Saint Clair County Community Mental Health Services, Port Huron, MI [*Library symbol*] [*Library of Congress*] (LCLS)
MiPhS.......... Saint Clair County Community College, Port Huron, MI [*Library symbol Library of Congress*] (LCLS)
MIPI............ Medicine in the Public Interest (EA)
MIPI............ Member of the Institute of Professional Investigators [*British*] (DBQ)
MiPi............ Pigeon District Library, Pigeon, MI [*Library symbol Library of Congress*] (LCLS)
MIPIE.......... Michigan Products Information Exchange [*Interchange Plus, Inc.*] [*Information service or system*] (IID)
MiPin........... Pinckney Community Public Library, Pinckney, MI [*Library symbol Library of Congress*] (LCLS)
MIPIR .... Missile Precision Instrumentation RADAR
MIPIR .... Multimission Imagery Photographic Interpretation Report (MCD)
MiPit............ Pittsford Township Library, Pittsford, MI [*Library symbol Library of Congress*] (LCLS)
MIPK............ Methyl Isopropyl Ketone [*Organic chemistry*]
MiPl............. Charles A. Ransom Public Library, Plainwell, MI [*Library symbol Library of Congress*] (LCLS)
MIPL............ Master Indentured Parts List
MIPL............ Monthly Intelligence Production Listing (MCD)
MIPlantE...... Member of the Institution of Plant Engineers [*British*]
MIPLOGS..... Marine Integrated Personnel and Logistics Subsystem
MiPlS........... State Technical Institute and Rehabilitation Center, Plainwell, MI [*Library symbol Library of Congress*] (LCLS)
MiPlySJ .... Saint John's Provincial Seminary, Plymouth, MI [*Library symbol Library of Congress*] (LCLS)
MIPM........... Member of the Institute of Personnel Management [*British*]
MIP/MA....... Missile in Place/Missile Away
MIPMS......... Microwave-Induced Plasma Mass Spectrometry
MIPO .... Multiple Item Purchase Order (AAG)
MiPon.......... Pontiac Public Libraries, Pontiac, MI [*Library symbol Library of Congress*] (LCLS)
MiPonO........ Oakland County Law Library, Clark J. Adams-Philip Pratt Library, Pontiac, MI [*Library symbol Library of Congress*] (LCLS)
MiPonSJ ...... Saint Joseph Mercy Hospital, General Medical Library, Pontiac, MI [*Library symbol Library of Congress*] (LCLS)
MiPor........... Portage Public Library, Portage, MI [*Library symbol Library of Congress*] (LCLS)
MIPORN....... Miami Pornography [*FBI undercover investigation, 1977-80*]
MiPorPS ...... Portage Public Schools, Portage, MI [*Library symbol Library of Congress*] (LCLS)
MiPorS .... Seventh Day Adventists Junior Academy, Portage, MI [*Library symbol*] [*Library of Congress*] (LCLS)
MiPot........... Benton Township - Potterville District Library, Potterville, MI [*Library symbol Library of Congress*] (LCLS)
MIPP............ Maintainability Index Prediction Procedure
MIPP............ Master of International Public Policy (GAGS)
MIPP............ Milk Indemnity Payment Program
MiPPT.......... McMaster Institute for Polymer Production Technology [*McMaster University*] [*Canada*] (IRC)
MIPR .... Manhattan Institute for Policy Research (EA)
MIPR .... Medical Intelligence Production Requirements (MCD)
MIPR .... Member of the Institute of Public Relations [*British*]
MIPR .... Military Interdepartmental Procurement [*or Purchase*] Request
MIPR .... Military Intergovernmental Purchase Request (NASA)
MIPR .... Monthly Interim Progress Report
MIPRCS .... Microprocessor (MSA)
MIProdE....... Member of the Institution of Production Engineers [*British*] (EY)
MIPS............ Management Information Progress Sheets (MCD)
MIPS............ Marine Integrated Personnel System (MCD)
MIPS............ Martinsried Institute for Protein Sequences [*Database producer*]
MIPS............ Member of the Phonographic Society [*British*] (ROG)
MIPS............ Membership Information Processing System [*AARP*]
MIPS............ Merritt Island Press Site [*NASA*] (NASA)
MIPS............ Microprocessor Without Interlocked Pipeline Stages (NITA)
MIPS............ Microwave-Induced Plasma Spectroscopy (MEC)
MIPS............ Microwave Pulse Storage System [*or Subsystem*] (MCD)
MIPS............ Military Information Processing System
mips .... Million Instructions Per Second [*Computer science*] (WDMC)
MIPS............ Millions of Instructions per Second [*Facetious translations: "Meaningless Indication of Performance"; "Meaningless Instructions per Second"; "Meaningless Indicator of Processor Speed"*] [*Computer science*]
MIPS............ Millon Index of Personality Styles [*Test*] (TMMY)
MIPS............ Miniature Implantable Power System
MIPS............ Missile Impact Prediction System
MIPS............ Missile Information Processing System (MCD)
MIPS............ Modular Instrumentation Package System (MCD)
MIPS............ Modular Integrated Pallet System [*Tank monitoring*] [*Army*] (RDA)
MIPS............ Multiple Index Processing System (MCD)
MIPS............ Myocardial Isotopic Perfusion Scan [*Cardiology*] (DAVI)
MiPs............ Sanilac Township Library, Port Sanilac, MI [*Library symbol Library of Congress*] (LCLS)
MIPsiMed.... Member of the Institute of Psionic Medicine [*British*]
MIPSM......... Member of the Institute of Purchasing and Supply Management (ADA)
MIPSNY....... Metro-International Program Services of New York (EA)
MIPTC.......... Men's International Professional Tennis Council [*Defunct*] (EA)
MI PTG M.... Member of the Institute of Printing Management [*British*] (DGA)
MiPtl............ Portland District Library, Portland, MI [*Library symbol Library of Congress*] (LCLS)
MIPTV.......... Marche International des Programmes de Television [*Cannes Film Festival*] [*France*]
MIPVCE........ Multiple-Input Phase-Variable Canonical Form (PDAA)
MIQ............. Maiquetia [*Venezuela*] [*Airport symbol*] (AD)
MIQ............. Maniwaki [*Quebec*] [*Seismograph station code, US Geological Survey*] (SEIS)
MIQ............. Member of the Institute of Quarrying [*British*] (DBQ)
MIQ............. Minimum Identifiable Quantity [*Analytical chemistry*]
MIQ............. Minnesota Importance Questionnaire [*Vocational test*]
Miq .... Miqva'ot [*or Miqwa'ot*] (BJA)
MIQA .... Member of the Institute of Quality Assurance [*British*] (DBQ)
MIQPS .... Member of the Institute of Qualified Private Secretaries [*British*] (DI)
Mir............. Horne's Mirror of Justice [*A publication*] (DLA)
MIR............. Magnetic Ink Read
MIR............. Main Immunogenic Region [*Immunology*]
MIR............. Maintenance Infusion Rate [*Medicine*]
MIR............. Maintenance Inspection Report
MIR............. Malfunction Investigation Report [*NASA*] (KSC)
MIR............. Management Information Report
MIR............. Management Information Repository [*Computer science*] (CIST)
MIR............. Mandatory Inspection Report (MCD)
MIR............. Manual Input Room (SAA)
MIR............. Master Index of Repairables (MCD)
MIR............. Master Inventory Record
MIR............. Master of Industrial Relations
MIR............. Material Inspection Report [*Navy*]
MIR............. Material Investigators Reactor [*NASA*]
MIR............. Maverick Interim Report
MIR............. Maximum Incremental Reactivity [*Exhaust emissions*] [*Automotive engineering*]
MIR............. Maximum Individual Risk [*Environmental science*] (FFDE)
MIR............. Medical Incident Report
MIR............. Member of the Institute of Population Registration [*British*] (DBQ)
MIR............. Memory-Information Register [*Computer science*]
MIR............. Memory Input Register [*Computer science*]
MIR............. Method Improvement Request (MCD)
MIR............. Method of Integral Relations
MIR............. Microinstruction Register
MIR............. Micropower Impulse RADAR [*For fluid level sensing*]
MIR............. Middle Irish [*Language, etc.*]
MIR............. Mid-Infrared Spectrum [*Spectroscopy*]
MIR............. Military Intelligence, Research [*World War II*]
MIR............. Mineta Resources Ltd. [*Vancouver Stock Exchange symbol*]
MIR............. Minimum Income Requirements (OICC)
MIR............. Minneapolis Industrial Railway Co. [*AAR code*]
MIR............. Mirage Resorts [*NYSE symbol*] (SPSG)
MIR............. Miramichi Air Services Ltd. [*Canada ICAO designator*] (FAAC)
MIR............. MIRLYN [*Michigan Research Library Network*]
MIR............. Mirny [*Antarctica*] [*Seismograph station code, US Geological Survey*] (SEIS)
MIR............. Mirror (KSC)
MIR............. Mishap Investigation Report (MCD)
MIR............. Missile Identification Record
MIR............. Missile Intelligence Report
MIR............. Mission Inherent Reliability
MIR............. Mitochondrial Import Receptor [*Biochemistry*]
MIR............. Model Incident Report [*Telecommunications*] (TEL)
MIR............. Modular Integrated Rack (MCD)
MIR............. Moisture Insulation Resistance [*Electronics*] (AAEL)
MIR............. Monastir [*Tunisia*] [*Airport symbol*] (OAG)
MIR............. Mouvement International de la Reconciliation [*International Fellowship of Reconciliation*]
MIR............. Mouvement pour l'Independance de la Reunion [*Movement for the Independence of Reunion*] [*Political party*] (PD)
MIR............. Movimiento de Izquierda Revolucionario [*Movement of the Revolutionary Left*] [*Bolivia*] [*Political party*] (PPW)
MIR............. Movimiento de Izquierda Revolucionario [*Movement of the Revolutionary Left*] [*Venezuela Political party*]
MIR............. Movimiento de Izquierda Revolucionario [*Movement of the Revolutionary Left*] [*Chile*] [*Political party*]
MIR............. Multiband Infrared Radiometer
MIR............. Multiple Instrumentation RADAR (MCD)
MIR............. Multiple Internal Reflectance (EDCT)
MIR............. Multiple Internal Reflection [*Spectroscopy*]
MIR............. Multiple Isomorphous Replacement [*Crystallography*]
MIR............. Multiplex Intensity Rules
MIR............. Multitarget Instrumentation RADAR [*Military*] (CAAL)
MIR............. Music Information Retrieval [*Computer science*]
MIR............. Mutual Interference Report (MCD)
MIRA .... Merchants Instant Response Authorization (SAA)
MIRA .... Miniature Infrared Alarm
MIRA .... Monterey Institute for Research in Astronomy
MIRA .... Monthly Index of Russian Accessions [*Library of Congress*]
MIRA .... Motor Industry Research Association [*British*] (DCTA)
MIRA .... Movimiento de Independencia Revolutionaria en Armas [*Puerto Rican independence group*] [*Political party*]
MIRA .... Movimiento Independentista Armado [*Armed Pro-Independence Movement*] [*Puerto Rico*] [*Political party*] (PD)
MIRA .... Multifunctional Inertial Reference Assembly [*Air Force*] (MCD)
MIRAC .... Management Information Research Assistance Center (AABC)
MIRAC .... Master Index Remote Access Capability (MHDI)

MIRAC	Microfilmed Reports and Accounts (PDAA)
MIRACL	Management Information Report Access without Computer Languages [Computer science] (IEEE)
MIRACL	Mid-Infrared Advanced Chemical LASER
MIRACLE	Mokum Industrial Research Automatic Calculator for Laboratory and Engineering
MIRACLE	Multidisciplinary Integrated Research Activities in Complex Laboratory Environments [National Science Foundation]
MIRACLE	Music and Image Resources Assisted Computer Library Exchange (TELE)
MIRACODE	Microfilm Information Retrieval Access Code
MIRAD	Monostatic Infrared Intrusion Detector (WDAA)
MIRADCOM	Missile Research and Development Command [Army]
MIRADOR	Minefield Reconnaissance and Detector System [Army]
MIRADS	Management Information and Display System [NASA]
MIRADS	Marshall [Space Flight Center] Information Retrieval and Display System [NASA] (PDAA)
MIRAGE	Microelectronic Indicator for RADAR Ground Equipment (MCD)
MIRAGE	Moessbauer Isotopic Resonant Absorption of Gamma Emission [Physics]
MIRAID	Maintenance Information Retrieval Aid
MIRAID	Maritime Institute for Research and Industrial Development [Washington, DC] (EA)
Miramr	Miramar Mining Corp. [Associated Press] (SAG)
MIRAN	Miniature Infrared Analyzer [Spectrometer]
MIRAN	Missile Ranging
MIRAS	Mortgage Interest Relief at Source [British] (DCTA)
MIRAS	Multiple Isomorphous Replacement with Anomalous Scattering [Crystallography]
MIRAT	MILPERCEN Initial Recruiting and Training Plan (MCD)
MIRB	Mutual Insurance Rating Bureau [Defunct] (EA)
MIRBM	Medium Intermediate-Range Ballistic Missile (MCD)
MIRC	Market Intelligence Research Co. [Palo Alto, CA] (TSSD)
MIRC	Michael-Initiated Ring Closure [Organic chemistry]
MIRC	Microtubuloreticular Complex (DMAA)
MIRC	Missile-in-Range Computer (MCD)
MiRc	Reed City Public Library, Reed City, MI [Library symbol Library of Congress] (LCLS)
MIRCEN	Microbiological Resource Center [UNESCO]
Mirch D & S	Mirchall's Doctor and Student [A publication] (DLA)
MIRCOM	Missile Materiel Readiness Command [Army]
MIRCS	Mechanical Instrument Repair and Calibration Shop (DNAB)
MIRD	Medical Internal Radiation Dose [Committee] [Society of Nuclear Medicine]
MIRD	Medium Internal Radiation Dose (WDAA)
MIRD	Minor Irregularities and Deficiencies
MiRd	Seville Township Library, Riverdale, MI [Library symbol Library of Congress] (LCLS)
MIRE	Member of the Institution of Radio Engineers [British] (EY)
MiRea	Reading Community Library, Reading, MI [Library symbol] [Library of Congress] (LCLS)
MIRECC	Mental Illness Research, Education, and Clinical Center [Department of Veterans Affairs]
MIRED	Microreciprocal Degrees
Mireh Advow	Mirehouse on Advowsons [1824] [A publication] (DLA)
Mireh Ti	Mirehouse on Tithes [2nd ed.] [1822] [A publication] (DLA)
MiRem	Wheatland Township Library, Remus, MI [Library symbol Library of Congress] (LCLS)
MiRep	Republic-Michigamme Public Library, Republic, MI [Library symbol Library of Congress] (LCLS)
MIREQ	Minimum Requirements Specified
MiRes	Reading Community Library, Reading, MI [Library symbol Library of Congress] (LCLS)
MIRF	Major Item Removal Frequency [Army Aviation Systems Command]
MIRF	Multiple Instantaneous Response File
MIRF	Myopia International Research Foundation (EA)
MIRFAC	Mathematics in Recognizable Form Automatically Compiled [Computer science]
MIRIAM	Major Incident Room Index and Action Management [Police computer] [British]
MiRic	Richmond Public Library, Richmond, MI [Library symbol Library of Congress] (LCLS)
MiRicl	Richland Community Library, Richland, MI [Library symbol Library of Congress] (LCLS)
MIRICLE	Mirrored Ions Closed-Loop Electrons (MCD)
MIRID	Miniature RADAR Illumination Detector (MCD)
MIRID	Monostatic Infrared Intrusion Detector (PDAA)
MIRINZ	Meat Industry Research Institute of New Zealand
MIR-IR	Multiple Internal Reflectance Infrared Spectroscopy (MCD)
MIRIS	Modified Infrared Interferometer Spectrometer
Mir Just	Horne's Mirror of Justice [A publication] (DLA)
MIRL	Medium Intensity Runway Edge Lights [Aviation] (FAAC)
MIRL	Mineral Industry Research Laboratory
MIRN	Movimento Independente da Reconstrucao Nacional [Independent Movement of National Reconstruction] [Portugal] (PPE)
MIRN-PDP	Movimento Independente de Reconstrucao Nacional - Partido da Derecha Portuguesa [Independent Movement for National Reconstruction - Party of the Portuguese Right] [Political party] (PPW)
MIRO	Mineral Industry Research Organisation [British] (DBA)
MIRO	Mining Industry Research Organisation [British]
MiRochOU	Oakland University, Rochester, MI [Library symbol Library of Congress] (LCLS)
MiRog	Presque Isle County Library, Rogers City, MI [Library symbol Library of Congress] (LCLS)
MiRom	Romeo District Library, Romeo, MI [Library symbol Library of Congress] (LCLS)
MIROS	Modulation Inducing Retrodirective Optical System [NASA]
MiRos	Roseville Public Library, Roseville, MI [Library symbol Library of Congress] (LCLS)
MiRosc	Gerrish-Higgins School District Public Library, Roscommon, MI [Library symbol Library of Congress] (LCLS)
MiRoscK	Kirtland Community College, Roscommon, MI [Library symbol Library of Congress] (LCLS)
MiRoy	Royal Oak Public Library, Royal Oak, MI [Library symbol Library of Congress] (LCLS)
MiRoyWB	William Beaumont Hospital, Royal Oak, MI [Library symbol Library of Congress] (LCLS)
MIRP	Manipulated Information Rate Processor
MIRP	Myocardial Infarction Rehabilitation Program [Cardiology] (DAVI)
Mir Parl	Mirror of Parliament, London [A publication] (DLA)
Mir Pat Off	Mirror of the Patent Office [Washington, DC] [A publication] (DLA)
MIR-Peru	Movimiento de Izquierda Revolucionaria [Movement of the Revolutionary Left of Peru] [Political party] (PPW)
MIRPF	Micro Image Relative Position Formula [Computer science]
MIRPL	Major Item Repair Parts List (NATG)
MIRPS	Multiple Information Retrieval by Parallel Selection
Mirr	Horne's Mirror of Justice [A publication] (DLA)
MIRR	Material Inspection and Receiving Report [Military]
mirr	Mirror (VRA)
MIRR	Mitsubishi Research Reactor [Japan]
MIRRC	Motor Insurance Repair Research Centre [British] (CB)
MIRRER	Microwave Identification Railroad Encoding Reflector (DNAB)
MIRROR	Management Information Reporting and Review of Operational Resources System
MIRROS	Modulation Inducing Reactive Retrodirective Optical System [NASA]
MirRsrt	Mirage Resorts [Associated Press] (SAG)
MIRS	Manpower Information Retrieval System (IEEE)
MIRS	Medical Information Retrieval Service (NITA)
MIRS	Micro-Interactive Retrieval System (DNAB)
MIRS	Military Intelligence Research Section [Navy]
MIRS	MOTS [Module Test Set] Information Retrieval System
MIRS	Multiple Internal Reflection Spectroscopy
MIRS	Multi-purpose Infrared Sight (PDAA)
MIRS	Musical Information Retrieval System (TELE)
MiRsc	Ogemaw District Library, Rose City, MI [Library symbol Library of Congress] (LCLS)
MIRSE	Member of the Institution of Railway Signal Engineers [British] (DBQ)
MIRSE	Multipurpose Imaging Radiometer Spectrometer Equipment
MIRSI	Monthly Inventory Report of Special Items
MIRSIM	Mineral Resource Simulation Model (PDAA)
MIRST	Multiple Infrared Scattered Light Recorder
MIRT	Molecular Infrared Track (IEEE)
MIRTAK	Martin Infrared Tracker
MIRTE	Member of the Institute of Road Transport Engineering [British] (DBQ)
MIRTOS	Minimum Real Time Operating System (NITA)
MIRTRAC	Missile Infrared Tracking System (DNAB)
MIRTRAK	Martin Infrared Tracker (SAA)
MIRU	Myocardial Infarction Research Unit [Cardiology] (DAVI)
MiRud	Rudyard School Public Library, Rudyard, MI [Library symbol Library of Congress] (LCLS)
MIRV	Multiple Independently-Guided Re-entry Vehicle [NASA] (PDAA)
MIRV	Multiple Independently-Targetable Reentry Vehicle [Military]
MIS	Maintenance Indicator System [TACOM] [Army] (RDA)
MIS	Managed Internet Service [Computer science]
MIS	Management Information Science
MIS	Management Information Service
MIS	Management Information Specialist
MIS	Management Information Strategy
MIS	Management Information System [Generic term]
mis	Management Information System [NASA] (NAKS)
MIS	Management Information Systems [Corporation for Public Broadcasting] [Information service or system] (IID)
MIS	Management Integrated System (TEL)
MIS	Manifold Interest Schedule
MIS	Man in Space
MIS	Manpower Information System (MCD)
MIS	Manson Impact Structure [Iowa] [Geology]
MIS	Manufacturing Information System [Computer science] (BUR)
MIS	Marine Information System (NITA)
MIS	Marine Isotope Stage [Climatology]
MIS	Market Impact Study
MIS	Marketing Information System
MIS	Mary Immaculate Seminary [Pennsylvania]
MIS	Master Implementation Schedule [NATO Air Defense Ground Environment] (NATG)
MIS	Master Integrated Schedule (AAG)
MIS	Master of Individualized Studies (GAGS)
MIS	Master of Information Science (PGP)
MIS	Master of Information Services (GAGS)
MIS	Master of Information Systems (PGP)
MIS	Master of Interdisciplinary Studies (GAGS)
MIS	Master of International Service
MIS	Master of International Studies (PGP)
MIS	Material Inspection Service [Navy]
MIS	Maturation-Inducing Substance [Endocrinology]
MIS	Mechanical Impact System [Aerospace]
MIS	Mechanical Insulation Services, Inc. (EFIS)
MIS	Mechanical Interruption Summary [FAA]

MIS	Mechanically Induced Stress [*Agriculture*]
MIS	Media and Information Services [*Queensland, Australia*]
MIS	Median Iris Society (EA)
MIS	Medical Information Science
MIS	Medical Information System (COE)
MIS	Meiosis-Inducing Substance (DB)
MIS	Member of the Institute of Statisticians [*Formerly, AIS*] [*British*]
MIS	Member of the Institute of Surveyors (ADA)
MIS	Merchandise Information System (PDAA)
MIS	Metal Insulated Structure
MIS	Metal-Insulator-Semiconductor (MCD)
MIS	Metal Insulator Silicon (AAEL)
MIS	Meteorological Impact Statement [*FAA*] (TAG)
MIS	Metering Information System [*Telecommunications*] (OA)
MIS	Metrology Information Service [*GIDEP*]
MIS	MICOM [*Missile Command*] Specification [*Army*]
MIS	MicroServe Information Systems
MIS	Midstate Airlines, Inc. [*ICAO designator*] (FAAC)
MIS	Milieu Information Service (EA)
MIS	Military Intelligence Section [*South Africa*]
MIS	Military Intelligence Services [*Army*]
MIS	Military Intelligence Summary [*Defense Intelligence Agency*]
MIS	Military Interim Specification [*Army*] (MCD)
MIS	Mine Issuing Ship
MIS	Mineral Industry Survey [*Department of Commerce*] (GFGA)
MIS	Mineral Information Section [*Natural Environment Research Council*] (IID)
MIS	Minicube System, Inc., Carlisle PA [*STAC*]
MIS	Minority Institutions (COE)
MIS	Minstrel Instruction Service (NADA)
MIS	Miscarriage (DSUE)
mis	Miscellaneous [*MARC language code Library of Congress*] (LCCP)
MIS	Miscellaneous (NATG)
MIS	Miserable (DSUE)
MIS	Mishima [*Japan*] [*Seismograph station code, US Geological Survey*] (SEIS)
MIS	Misima [*Papua New Guinea*] [*Airport symbol*] (OAG)
Mis	Misopogon [*of Julian*] [*Classical studies*] (OCD)
MIS	Missile
MIS	Missile Interim Specification [*Army*]
MIS	Missile Specification
MIS	Missing (AABC)
MIS	Mission College, Santa Clara, CA [*OCLC symbol*] (OCLC)
mis	Mission Information Subsystem [*NASA*] (NAKS)
MIS	Mission Information System [*or Subsystem*]
Mis	Mississippi Reports [*A publication*] (DLA)
MIS	Missouri
Mis	Missouri Reports [*A publication*] (DLA)
MIS	Mistico [*Ship's rigging*] (ROG)
MIS	Mobility Information Service [*British*]
MIS	Modified in Situ [*Experimental technique for converting shale into oil*]
MIS	Monte-Carlo Inelastic Scattering [*Code*] [*Computer science*] (NRCH)
MIS	Month-in-Sample [*Bureau of the Census*] (GFGA)
MIS	Months in Service
MIS	Moody Institute of Science (EA)
MIS	Moody's Investor Service [*A publication*] (MHDW)
MIS	Motor Inert Storage
MIS	Muellerian Inhibiting Substance [*Embryology*] [*Biochemistry*]
MIS	Multicultural Information Strategy
Mis	New York Miscellaneous Reports [*A publication*] (DLA)
MIS	NRA [*National Restaurant Association*] Management Information Services [*Defunct*] (EA)
MiS	Saginaw Public Libraries, Saginaw, MI [*Library symbol Library of Congress*] (LCLS)
MISA	Maxwell International Subscription Agency
MISA	Meat Industry Suppliers Association (EA)
MISA	Military Impacted Schools Association (NTPA)
MISA	Military-Industrial Supply Agency
MISA	Motorists Information Services Association (EA)
MISA	Municipal and Industry Strategy for Abatement
MISAA	Middle Income Student Assistance Act [*1978*]
MISAC	Member of the Incorporated Society of Advertisement Consultants [*British*] (DAS)
MiSal	Saline Public Library, Saline, MI [*Library symbol Library of Congress*] (LCLS)
MISAM	Multiple Index Sequential Access Method
MiSan	Sandusky Public Library, Sandusky, MI [*Library symbol Library of Congress*] (LCLS)
MISAR	Microfilm Information Storage and Retrieval (MCD)
MISAR	Microprocessed Sensing and Automatic Regulation [*Engine control system*] [*Automotive industry*]
MISAR	Miniature Information Storage and Retrieval (PDAA)
MiSaS	Spring Arbor College, Spring Arbor, MI [*Library symbol Library of Congress*] (LCLS)
Mis Astig	Mixed Astigmatism [*Ophthalmology*] (DAVI)
MiSb	Bingham Township Library, Suttons Bay, MI [*Library symbol Library of Congress*] (LCLS)
MiS-B	Saginaw Public Libraries, Butman-Fish Library, Saginaw, MI [*Library symbol Library of Congress*] (LCLS)
MISC	Malaysian International Shipping Corp. (DS)
MiSc	Mason County Library, Scottville, MI [*Library symbol Library of Congress*] (LCLS)
MISC	Minimum Instruction Set Computer (CIST)
MISC	Miscarriage [*Medicine*]
MISC	Miscellaneous (AFM)
Misc	Miscellaneous (DFIT)
misc	Miscellaneous (WDMC)
MISC	Miscellaneous and Other Operations [*USCG*] (TAG)
Misc	Miscellaneous Reports [*New York*] [*A publication*] (DLA)
MISC	Movement for an Independent Socialist Canada
MiS-C	Saginaw Public Libraries, Claytor Branch Library, Saginaw, MI [*Library symbol Library of Congress*] (LCLS)
Misc 2d	Miscellaneous Reports, Second Series [*New York*] [*A publication*] (DLA)
MisCa	Mission Capital Ltd. [*Associated Press*] (SAG)
MISCAP	Mission Capability (COE)
MISCAP	Mission Capability Statement (MCD)
Misc Dec	Ohio Miscellaneous Decisions (Gottschall) [*1865-73*] [*A publication*] (DLA)
Misc Doc	Miscellaneous Document [*US. House of Representatives of Senate*] (BARN)
Miscel	Miscellaneous Reports [*New York*] [*A publication*] (DLA)
MISCEND	Miscendus [*To Be Mixed*] [*Pharmacy*]
MISCEX	Miscellaneous Exercise [*Military*] (NVT)
MISchott	Schottenstein [*M. I.*] Homes, Inc. [*Associated Press*] (SAG)
MISCL	Miscellaneous
Misc New York	Miscellaneous New York Reports [*A publication*] (AAGC)
Misc (NY)	Miscellaneous Reports [*New York*] [*A publication*] (DLA)
MISCO	McCall Information Systems Co.
MISCON	Misconduct
Misc Rep	Miscellaneous Reports [*New York*] [*A publication*] (DLA)
Misc Reports	New York Miscellaneous Reports [*A publication*] (DLA)
Misc Repts	New York Miscellaneous Reports [*A publication*] (DLA)
MiScW	West Shore Community College, Scottville, MI [*Library symbol Library of Congress*] (LCLS)
MISD	Management Information Systems Directorate [*Army Missile Command*] [*Redstone Arsenal, AL*]
MISD	Misdemeanor [*FBI standardized term*]
MISD	Multiple Instruction, Single Data [*Processor configuration*] (IEEE)
MISDAS	Mechanical Impact System Design for Advanced Spacecraft (IEEE)
MISDM	Misdemeanor [*Legal shorthand*] (LWAP)
MISDM	Misdemeanor and Cure [*Legal shorthand*] (LWAP)
MISDMR	Misdemeanor (ROG)
MISDO	Management Information System Development Office (DNAB)
MISE	Mechanized Infantry in a Smoke Environment (MCD)
MISE	Miniature Sample (AAG)
MiSe	Sebewaing Township Library, Sebewaing, MI [*Library symbol Library of Congress*] (LCLS)
MISEA	Management Information Systems Economic Analysis
MISEA	Meat Industry Supply and Equipment Association [*Later, MISA*] (EA)
MISED	Machine Independent Systems Effectiveness Data System (MCD)
MISEG	Management Information System Executive Group (DNAB)
MISEP	Mutual Information System on Employment Policies in Europe (IID)
MISER	Management Information System for Expenditure Reporting (PDAA)
MISER	Manned Interceptor SAGE Evaluation Routine (MCD)
MISER	Mean Integral Square Error (PDAA)
MISER	Media Insertion Schedule Evaluation Report [*Advertising*]
MISER	Microwave Space Electronics Relay
MISER	Militant Society for the Eradication of Rounds [*British*] (DI)
MISER	Miniature, Indicating and Sampling Electronic Respirometer (PDAA)
MISER	Minimum Size Executive Routines
MISES	Merchandises (ROG)
MiSf	Southfield Public Library, Southfield, MI [*Library symbol Library of Congress*] (LCLS)
MiSfB	Bendix Corp., Engineering Development Center, Bendix Center, Southfield, MI [*Library symbol Library of Congress*] (LCLS)
MiSfE	Eaton Corp. Engineering Research Center, Southfield, MI [*Library symbol*] [*Library of Congress*] (LCLS)
MISFET	Metal-Insulator-Semiconductor Field-Effect Transistor
MiSfL	Lawrence Institute of Technology, Southfield, MI [*Library symbol Library of Congress*] (LCLS)
MiSfM	Midrasha College of Jewish Studies, Southfield, MI [*Library symbol Library of Congress*] (LCLS)
MiSfP	Providence Hospital Library, Southfield, MI [*Library symbol*] [*Library of Congress*] (LCLS)
MISFROR	Multiple Investment Sinking Fund Rate of Return (ADA)
MISG-C	Maintenance Interservice Support Group Center (MCD)
Mish	Mishnah [*Basis of the Talmud*] (BJA)
MiSh	Shelby Public Library, Shelby, MI [*Library symbol Library of Congress*] (LCLS)
MISHAP	Missiles High-Speed Assembly Program
MISHAP	Much Increased Salary, Hardly Any Pension [*Lifestyle classification*]
MiShep	Coe Township Library, Shepherd, MI [*Library symbol Library of Congress*] (LCLS)
MiSHS	Saginaw Health Sciences Library, Saginaw, MI [*Library symbol Library of Congress*] (LCLS)
MISI	Member of the Iron and Steel Institute [*British*]
MISI	Metro Information Services [*Stock market symbol*]
MISI	Multipath Intersymbol Interference (PDAA)
MISIAS	Management Information Systems Inventory and Analysis System [*Navy*]
MIS/IL	Metal-Insulator-Semiconductor Inversion Layer [*Photovoltaic energy systems*]
MISIM	Metal-Insulator-Semiconductor Insulator Metal (MCD)
MIS(India)	Member of the Institution of Surveyors of India
MISIP	Management Information System Improvement Plan
MISIP	Merck Infrared Spectral Interpretation Package [*For minicomputers*] [*Analytical chemistry*]
MISIP	Minority Institutions Science Improvement Program [*National Science Foundation*]

MISIS.......... Micro Integrated Storm Information System [*Marine science*] (OSRA)
MISL........... Major Indoor Soccer League [*Defunct*] (EA)
MISL........... Malfunction Investigation Support Laboratory [*NASA*] (KSC)
MISL........... Management Information System Laboratory
MISL........... Missile
MiSl........... South Lyon Public Library, South Lyon, MI [*Library symbol Library of Congress*] (LCLS)
MIS LABS .... Midwest Integrated Systems Laboratories, Inc. [*Watertown, WI*] (TSSD)
MISLIC........ Mid- and South Staffordshire Libraries in Cooperation (NITA)
MISLPA........ Major Indoor Soccer League Players Association (EA)
MISM......... Member of the Institute of Supervisory Management [*British*] (DBQ)
MISM......... Metal-Insulator-Semiconductor Metal (MCD)
MiSM......... Michigan Lutheran Seminary, Saginaw, MI [*Library symbol Library of Congress*] (LCLS)
MISMA........ Major Item Supply Management Agency
MISMA........ Member of the Incorporated Sales Managers Association [*British*] (DAS)
MISMA........ Model Improvement and Study Management [*Army*]
MISMAC ...... Missile and Munitions Materiel Center (MCD)
MISMD .... Medical Illustration Service for Museum Design [*Armed Forces Institute of Pathology*] (RDA)
MISMDS ...... Multiple Instruction Streams Multiple Data Steams
MISMO .... Maintenance Interservice [*or Intersupport*] Management Office [*DARCOM*] (AFIT)
Mis Mus ...... Mistress of Music
MISN .... Misnumbered (WGA)
MISO........... Maintenance Interservice Office [*Air Force*] (AFIT)
MISO........... Management Information Systems Office (AABC)
MISO........... Military Intelligence Service Organization (NADA)
MISO........... Misonidazole [*Azomycin*] [*Oncology, Radiosensitizer*]
MiSod.......... Sodus Township Library, Sodus, MI [*Library symbol Library of Congress*] (LCLS)
Misonix....... Misonix, Inc. [*Associated Press*] (SAG)
Misonx........ Misonix, Inc. [*Associated Press*] (SAG)
MISP........... Management Information System Plan
MISP........... Manned Interceptor Simulation Program
MISP........... Mathematics in Society Project (AIE)
MISP........... Medical Information Systems Program [*Computer science*] (BUR)
MISP........... Member of the Institute of Sales Promotion [*British*] (DI)
MISP........... Microelectronics Industry Support Programme (NITA)
MISP........... Microprocessor Industry Support Programme [*British*] (DCTA)
MISPC .... Mechanized Infantry Squad Proficiency Course [*Army*]
MiSpl.......... Warner Baird Library, Spring Lake, MI [*Library symbol Library of Congress*] (LCLS)
MIS-Q .... Maintenance Information System for Quality (MCD)
MISR .... Major Item Status Report
MISR .... Mars In-situ-utilization Sample Return [*Computer science*]
MISR .... Matrix Ion Species Ratio [*Spectroscopy*]
MISR .... Minimum Industrial Sustaining Role (NG)
Mis R .... Missouri Reports [*A publication*] (DLA)
MISR .... Modular Industrial Solar Retrofit Program [*Department of Energy*]
MISR .... Mosler Information Storage and Retrieval System (MCD)
MISR .... Multi-Angle Imaging Spectrometer [*Marine science*] (OSRA)
MISR .... Multi-Impact Signature Register (PDAA)
MISR .... Multiple Input Signal Register (NITA)
MISRAN....... Missile Range
MISRC .... Management Information Systems Research Center [*University of Minnesota*] [*Research center*] (RCD)
MISRE .... Microwave Space Relay [*Electronics*]
MISREP ...... Misrepresentation [*Legal shorthand*] (LWAP)
MISREP ...... Mission Report [*Air Force*] (AFM)
Mis Rep....... Missouri Reports [*A publication*] (DLA)
MISS .... Major Item Special Study [*Army Aviation Systems Command*]
MISS .... Management and Information System Staff [*United Nations Development Program*]
MISS........... Man in Space Simulator
MISS........... Man in Space Soonest
MISS........... Mechanical Interruption Statistical Summary (IEEE)
MISS........... Medical Information Science Section [*National Institutes of Health*] [*Information service or system*] (IID)
MISS........... Microwave Imager Sensor Study (MCD)
MISS........... Mid-Course Surveillance System (MCD)
MISS........... Miniature SOFAR [*Sound Fixing and Ranging*] System
MISS........... Minicomputer Interfacing Support System [*Computer science*]
MISS........... Missile Intercept Simulation System
MISS........... Mission
miss........... Missionary
MISS........... Mississippi (AFM)
Miss........... Mississippi (ODBW)
MISS........... Mississippian [*Railway*] [*AAR code*]
MISS........... Mississippian [*Period, era, or system*] [*Geology*]
MISS........... Mississippi Chemical [*NASDAQ symbol*] (TTSB)
MISS........... Mississippi Chemical Corp. [*NASDAQ symbol*] (SAG)
Miss........... Mississippi Supreme Court Reports [*A publication*] (DLA)
MISS........... Mobile Instrumentation Support System
MISS........... Mobile Integrated Support System (MCD)
MISS........... Multiband Image Scanning System
MISS........... Multi-Input-Safety-Shutdown (PDAA)
MISS........... Multi-Item Single Source (IEEE)
MiS-S .... Saginaw Public Libraries, South Jefferson Branch, Saginaw, MI [*Library symbol Library of Congress*] (LCLS)
MiSs .... Sault Ste. Marie Carnegie Public Library, Sault Ste. Marie, MI [*Library symbol Library of Congress*] (LCLS)

MiSsB.......... Baylis Public Library, Sault Ste. Marie, MI [*Library symbol Library of Congress*] (LCLS)
Miss C .... Mississippi College (GAGS)
MissChm ..... Mississippi Chemical Corp. [*Associated Press*] (SAG)
Miss Code Ann... Mississippi Code, Annotated [*A publication*] (DLA)
MISS-D........ Minuteman Integrated Schedules Status and Data Systems [*Missiles*]
Miss Dec ..... Mississippi Decisions [*A publication*] (DLA)
MIS-SDS...... Multiple Instruction Streams - Single Data Streams [*Computer science*] (MHDB)
MISSIL........ Management Information System Symbolic Interpretive Language [*Computer science*] (MCD)
MISSILEX .... Missile Firing Exercise (NVT)
MISSIO .... Internationales Katholisches Missionswerk [*Pontifical Mission Society*] [*Aachen, Federal Republic of Germany*] (EAIO)
MISSION..... Manufacturing Information System Support Integrated Online [*Computer science*] (MHDI)
MISSION..... Mission [*Commonly used*] (OPSA)
MISSIS .... Mississippi Student Information System (EDAC)
MiSsL......... Lake Superior State College, Sault Ste. Marie, MI [*Library symbol Library of Congress*] (LCLS)
Miss Law..... Mississippi Lawyer [*A publication*] (DLA)
Miss Law Rev... Mississippi Law Review [*A publication*] (DLA)
Miss Laws ... General Laws of Mississippi [*A publication*] (DLA)
Miss Lawyer... Mississippi Lawyer [*A publication*] (DLA)
Miss L Rev... Mississippi Law Review [*A publication*] (DLA)
MISSN .... Mission [*Commonly used*] (OPSA)
MissnW .... Mission West Properties [*Associated Press*] (SAG)
Misso......... Missouri Reports [*A publication*] (DLA)
MISSOPH..... Man in Space Sophisticated (MUGU)
Misso R....... Missouri Reports [*A publication*] (DLA)
Misso Rep .... Missouri Reports [*A publication*] (DLA)
Missouri ..... Missouri Reports [*A publication*] (DLA)
Missouri R.... Missouri Reports [*A publication*] (DLA)
Missouri Rep... Missouri Reports [*A publication*] (DLA)
Missour Rep... Missouri Reports [*A publication*] (DLA)
MissPw....... Mississippi Power Co. [*Associated Press*] (SAG)
MISSR .... Missioner (ROG)
Miss R .... Mississippi Reports [*A publication*] (DLA)
Miss RC ...... Mississippi Railroad Commission Reports [*A publication*] (DLA)
Miss Reg..... Mississippi Register [*A publication*] (AAGC)
Miss Rep..... Mississippi Reports [*A publication*] (DLA)
Miss Serv W... Missionary Service With
Miss St Ca ... Morris' Mississippi State Cases [*1818-72*] [*A publication*] (DLA)
Miss St Cas... Morris' Mississippi State Cases [*1818-72*] [*A publication*] (DLA)
Miss St U .... Mississippi State University (GAGS)
Miss St U Women... Mississippi State University for Women (GAGS)
MISST........ Missile-Supersonic Transport
MissVly....... Mississippi Valley Bancshares, Inc. [*Associated Press*] (SAG)
MissVw....... Mississippi View Holding Co. [*Associated Press*] (SAG)
MISSY .... Missionary
MIST.......... Avalon Capital [*NASDAQ symbol*] (TTSB)
MIST.......... Avalon Capital, Inc. [*NASDAQ symbol*] (SAG)
MI St .... Master of Information Studies (PGP)
MIST.......... Maximum Isothermal System Temperature [*Nuclear energy*] (NRCH)
MIST.......... Medical Information System via Telephone [*University of Alabama*]
MIST.......... Member of the Institute of Science Technology [*British*] (DBQ)
MIST.......... Metal Insulator Silicon Field-Effect Transistor [*Also, MISFET*] (EECA)
MIST.......... Microbursts in Severe Thunderstorms
MIST+........ Microcomputer Information Support Tools [*2B Enterprises*] [*Washington, DC*] (TSSD)
MIST.......... Minimum Structure Module
MIST.......... Minor Isotopes Safeguards Techniques [*Nuclear energy*]
MIST.......... Mistura [*Mixture*] [*Pharmacy*]
MIST.......... MIUS [*Modular Integrated Utility Systems*] Integration and Subsystems Test (MCD)
MIST.......... Multi-Input Standard Tape
MIST.......... Multiloop Integral System Test [*Nuclear energy*] (NRCH)
MIST.......... Multipurpose In-Space Throttleable Engine (MCD)
MIST......... Music Information System for Theorists (PDAA)
MISTAF....... Management Information Systems Task Force (SAA)
MiStan........ Stanton Public Library, Stanton, MI [*Library symbol Library of Congress*] (LCLS)
MISTC........ Member of the Institute of Scientific and Technical Communicators [*British*] (DBQ)
MISTC........ Men's International Squash Tournament Council [*Cardiff, Wales*] (EAIO)
MiStc......... Saint Clair Shores Public Library, Saint Clair Shores, MI [*Library symbol Library of Congress*] (LCLS)
MiStch........ Saint Charles Public Library, Saint Charles, MI [*Library symbol Library of Congress*] (LCLS)
MiSte......... Lincoln Township Public Library, Stevensville, MI [*Library symbol Library of Congress*] (LCLS)
MISTE .... Military Intelligence Special Training Element (DOMA)
MiStep........ Menominee County Library, Stephenson, MI [*Library symbol Library of Congress*] (LCLS)
MISTER....... Mobile Integrated System Trainer, Evaluator, and Recorder [*Navy*]
MIST-FOAL... Multi-Stage Force Allocation (SAA)
MiSth......... Sterling Heights Public Library, Sterling Heights, MI [*Library symbol Library of Congress*] (LCLS)
MiSthe........ Richfield Township Public Library, St. Helen, MI [*Library symbol Library of Congress*] (LCLS)
MISTI.......... Multipurpose International Securities Trading Information (MHDW)
MiSti.......... St. Ignace Public Library, St. Ignace, MI [*Library symbol Library of Congress*] (LCLS)
MISTIC........ Michigan State Integral Computer

MISTIC......... Missile System Target Illuminator Controlled (MCD)
MISTIC......... Model Interstate Scientific and Technical Information Clearinghouse
MISTIR......... Multifunction Imaging Search/Track Infrared
MiStjo......... Bement Public Library, St. Johns, MI [*Library symbol Library of Congress*] (LCLS)
MiStjW......... Whirlpool Corp., Research Library, St. Joseph, MI [*Library symbol Library of Congress*] (LCLS)
MiStlo......... Theodore Austin Cutler Memorial Library, St. Louis, MI [*Library symbol Library of Congress*] (LCLS)
MISTM......... Member of the Institute of Sales Technology and Management [*British*] (DBQ)
MISTR......... Management of Items Subject to Repair [*Air Force*] (AFM)
MISTRA......... Minnesota Study of Twins Reared Apart
MISTRAM.... Missile Trajectory Measurement [*Air Force*]
MISTRANS... Mistranslation (ADA)
MISTRAULANT... Missile Weapons System Training Unit, Atlantic (DNAB)
MISTRAUPAC... Missile Weapons System Training Unit, Pacific (DNAB)
MistrJay...... Mister Jay Fashions International, Inc. [*Associated Press*] (SAG)
MIStructE..... Member of the Institution of Structural Engineers [*British*] (EY)
MISTT......... Midwest Interstate Sulfur Transformation and Transport [*Meteorology*]
MiStu......... Sturgis Public Library, Sturgis, MI [*Library symbol Library of Congress*] (LCLS)
MistyM......... Misty Mountain Gold Ltd. [*Associated Press*] (SAG)
MiSun......... Sunfield District Library, Sunfield, MI [*Library symbol Library of Congress*] (LCLS)
MISURA......... Miskito, Sumo, and Rama [*Nicaraguan Indian coalition*]
MISURASATA... Miskito, Sumo, and Rama [*Nicaraguan Indian coalition*]
MiSV......... United States Veterans Administration Hospital, Saginaw, MI [*Library symbol Library of Congress*] (LCLS)
MISVE......... Management Information Systems for Vocational Education (OICC)
MISW......... Member of the Institute of Social Welfare [*British*] (DBQ)
MiSW......... White Pine Library System, Saginaw, MI [*Library symbol Library of Congress*] (LCLS)
MiS-Z......... Saginaw Public Libraries, Zauel Memorial Library, Saginaw, MI [*Library symbol Library of Congress*] (LCLS)
MIT......... Machine Interface Terminal [*Tangram Computer Aided Engineering*] [*Software package*] (NCC)
MIT......... Macrotrends International [*Vancouver Stock Exchange symbol*]
MIT......... Makari Intradermal Test [*Medicine*] (DB)
MIT......... Male Impotence Test [*Medicine*] (DMAA)
MIT......... Management Information Tree [*Telecommunications*] (OSI)
MIT......... Mandatory Independent Taxation [*British*] (DI)
MIT......... Manual Inputs-Tracks (SAA)
MIT......... Market if Touched [*Stock exchange term*]
MIT......... Marrow Iron Turnover [*Medicine*] (DMAA)
MIT......... Massachusetts Institute of Technology (GAGS)
MIT......... Massachusetts Investors Trust
MIT......... Master Instruction Tape [*Computer science*]
MIT......... Master in Teaching (PGP)
MIT......... Master of Industrial Technology (PGP)
MIT......... Master of Initial Teaching (PGP)
MIT......... Material Improvement Team (MCD)
MIT......... Material in Transit (MCD)
MIT......... Material Introduction Team
MIT......... Medium Intertheater Transport (MCD)
MIT......... Melodic Intonation Therapy (DMAA)
MIT......... Mercury Integrated Test
MIT......... Mercury Ion Thruster
MIT......... Merrill Lynch & Co., Inc. [*NYSE symbol*] (SPSG)
MIT......... Merrill Lynch & Co'MITTS' 2001 [*NASDAQ symbol*] (TTSB)
MIT......... Metabolism Inhibition Test [*Medicine*] (DMAA)
MIT......... Metal Insulator Transition [*Electronics*] (AAEL)
MIT......... Middle Italian [*Language, etc.*]
MIT......... Miles in-Trail [*FAA*] (TAG)
MIT......... Military Intelligence Translator
MIT......... Milled in Transit [*Commodities*]
MIT......... Miller Air Transporters [*ICAO designator*] (FAAC)
MIT......... Milwaukee Institute of Technology [*Wisconsin*]
MIT......... Minimum Individual Training
MIT......... Ministry of Industry and Trade [*Israel*]
MIT......... Miracidal Immobilization Test [*Parasitology*]
MIT......... Miscellaneous Tool (SAA)
MIT......... Missouri-Illinois Traffic Service, East Saint Louis IL [*STAC*]
Mit......... Mitannian (BJA)
MIT......... Miter
MIT......... Mitigate
MIT......... Mito [*Japan*] [*Seismograph station code, US Geological Survey*] (SEIS)
MIT......... Mitomycin [*Medicine*] (DMAA)
MIT......... Mitsubishi Electric Corporation (NITA)
MIT......... Mitte [*Send*] [*Latin*]
MIT......... Mobile Instructor Team (MCD)
MIT......... Mobile Instructor Training [*Army*]
MIT......... Modern Investment Theory [*Finance*] (MHDB)
MIT......... Modular Industrial Terminal
MIT......... Modular Intelligent Terminal
MIT......... Monoiodotyrosine [*Biochemistry*]
MIT......... Motorist Inclusive Tour [*British*] (DCTA)
MIT......... Movements Identification Technican (SAA)
MIT......... Multiple Incidence Technique [*Structure testing*]
MIT......... Municipal Investment Trust
MIT......... Shafter, CA [*Location identifier FAA*] (FAAL)
MIT......... Society of Management Information Technology [*British*]
MiT......... Traverse City Public Library, Traverse City, MI [*Library symbol Library of Congress*] (LCLS)
MITA......... Maine Island Trail Association
MITA......... Member of the Industrial Transport Association [*British*]
MITA......... Microcomputer Industry Trade Association
MITA......... Minority Information Trade Annual [*A publication*]
MITAG......... Minority Affairs Task Group (DNAB)
MITAN......... Microwave Technology as Applied to Air Navigation (ADA)
MITASK......... Mission Tasking (COE)
MITB......... Missile Interface Test Bench
MiTc......... Iosco-Arenac Regional Library, Tawas City, MI [*Library symbol Library of Congress*] (LCLS)
MITC......... Methylisothiocyanate [*Pesticide*]
MITC......... Microfilm and Information Technology Center
MiTc-A......... Iosco-Arenac Regional Library, AuGres Branch Library, AuGres, MI [*Library symbol Library of Congress*] (LCLS)
MiTc-E......... Iosco-Arenac Regional Library, East Tawas Branch Library, East Tawas, MI [*Library symbol Library of Congress*] (LCLS)
Mitch......... Mitcham Industries [*Associated Press*] (SAG)
Mitcham...... Mitcham Industries [*Associated Press*] (SAG)
Mitch B & N... Mitchell on Bills, Notes, Etc. [*1829*] [*A publication*] (DLA)
Mitchell's Mar Reg... Mitchell's Maritime Register [*England*] [*A publication*] (DLA)
Mitch Mod Geog... Mitchell's Modern Geography [*A publication*] (DLA)
Mitch MR..... Mitchell's Maritime Register [*England*] [*A publication*] (DLA)
Mit Ch Pl..... Mitford on Equity Pleading [*A publication*] (DLA)
MiTc-O......... Iosco-Arenac Regional Library, Oscoda Township Branch Library, Oscoda, MI [*Library symbol Library of Congress*] (LCLS)
MiTc-P......... Iosco-Arenac Regional Library, Plainfield Township Branch Library, Hale, MI [*Library symbol Library of Congress*] (LCLS)
MiTc-S......... Iosco-Arenac Regional Library, Standish Branch Library, Standish, MI [*Library symbol Library of Congress*] (LCLS)
MiTc-T......... Iosco-Arenac Regional Library, Tawas City Branch Library, Tawas City, MI [*Library symbol Library of Congress*] (LCLS)
MiTc-W......... Iosco-Arenac Regional Library, Whittemore Branch Library, Whittemore, MI [*Library symbol Library of Congress*] (LCLS)
MITD......... Member of the Institute of Training and Development [*British*] (DBQ)
MITDA......... Maryland Independent Truckers and Drivers Association [*Later, ITDA*] (EA)
Mit Drunk.... Mittermaier's Effect of Drunkenness on Criminal Responsibilty [*A publication*] (DLA)
MITE......... Magnetic Insulation Test Experiment
MITE......... Master Instrumentation Timing Equipment (CET)
MITE......... Meetings and Incentive Travel Exposition [*Trade show*]
MITE......... Microelectronic Integrated Test Equipment
MITE......... Microelectronics Test and Evaluation [*Raytheon Co.*]
MITE......... Microprocessor Industrial Terminal [*Computer science*] (MHDB)
MITE......... Miniaturized Integrated Telephone Equipment
MITE......... Missile Integration Terminal Equipment [*Computer science*]
MITE......... Multiple Input Terminal Equipment
MiTe......... Tecumseh Public Library, Tecumseh, MI [*Library symbol Library of Congress*] (LCLS)
MITECS......... Multi-International Teacher Education Cooperatives (EDAC)
MiTek......... Tekonsha Public Library, Tekonsha, MI [*Library symbol Library of Congress*] (LCLS)
MitekS......... Mitek Systems, Inc. [*Associated Press*] (SAG)
MITEL......... Mike and Terry's Lawnmowers [*Commercial firm*] [*canada*]
Mitel......... Mitel Corp. [*Associated Press*] (SAG)
MITER......... Modular Installation of Telecommunications Equipment Racks (TEL)
MITF......... Municipal Investment Trust Fund
MITF......... Musser International Turfgrass Foundation (EA)
MITFA......... Metropolitan Intercollegiate Track & Field Association (PSS)
Mitf & Ty Eq Pl... Tyler's Edition of Mitford's Equity Pleading [*A publication*] (DLA)
Mitf Eq Pl.... Mitford on Equity Pleading [*A publication*] (DLA)
MITGS......... Marine Institute of Technology and Graduate Studies [*Baltimore*]
MITH......... Marble-in-the-Hole [*Game used in psychometrics*]
MITH......... Mithracin [*Antineoplastic drug*] (CDI)
Mith......... Mithramycin [*Antineoplastic drug*] (DAVI)
MiTho......... Betsie Valley District Library, Thompsonville, MI [*Library symbol Library of Congress*] (LCLS)
MiThr......... Three Rivers Public Library, Three Rivers, MI [*Library symbol Library of Congress*] (LCLS)
MITI......... Ministry of International Trade and Industry [*Japan*]
MITI......... Moms in Touch International (EA)
MITI......... Myocardial Infarction, Triage, and Intervention Project [*or Trial*] [*Cardiology study*]
MITIC......... Myanmar International Trust and Investment Co. (ECON)
MITIL......... Massachusetts Institute of Technology Instrumentation Laboratory (SAA)
MITILAC......... Massachusetts Institute of Technology Information Laboratory Automatic Coding
Mit Insuf...... Mitral Insufficiency [*Cardiology*]
MITJ......... Member of the Institute of Technical Journalists [*British*] (DGA)
MITK......... Mitek Systems [*NASDAQ symbol*] (TTSB)
MITK......... Mitek Systems Inc. [*NASDAQ symbol*] (SAG)
MITKA......... Movimiento Indio Tupaj Katari [*Tupaj Katari Indian Movement*] [*Bolivia*] [*Political party*] (PPW)
MITL......... Man-in-the-Loop [*Army*]
MITLA......... Microcircuit Technology in Logistics Applications [*Defense Logistics Agency*]
MIT/LL......... Massachusetts Institute of Technology/Lincoln Laboratory (AAG)
MITLS......... Man-in-the-Loop Simulator [*Military*]
MITM......... Management Inventory on Time Management [*Test*]
MITM......... Military-Industry Technical Manual
MITMA......... Member of the Institute of Trade Mark Agents [*British*]
MITMA......... Military Traffic Management Agency [*Later, DTMS*]
Mit MR......... Mitchell's Maritime Register [*England*] [*A publication*] (ILCA)
MITMS......... Military-Industry Technical Manual Specifications

MITN	Michigan Information Technology Network
MiTN	Northwestern Michigan College, Traverse City, MI [*Library symbol Library of Congress*] (LCLS)
MIT/NSL	Massachusetts Institute of Technology/Naval Supersonic Laboratory (AAG)
MITO	Meat Industry Training Organisation (AIE)
MITO	Member of the Institute of Training Officers [*International Institute of Social Economics*] [*British*] (DI)
MITO	Minimum Interval Takeoff
Mito	Mitomycin-C [*Antineoplastic drug*] (DAVI)
MITO-C	Mitomycin-C [*Antineoplastic drug*] (DAVI)
MITOC	Multiple Intercommunications Technical Operations Communications [*NASA*] (KSC)
MITOCS	Missile Technical Operations Communications System (MCD)
MITOL	Machine-Independent Telemetry-Oriented Language [*Computer science*] (IEEE)
MiTop	Topinabee Public Library, Topinabee, MI [*Library symbol Library of Congress*] (LCLS)
MITP	Master Intern Training Plan [*Military*]
MITP	Measurement and Instrumentation Technology Panel (ACII)
MITP	Miniature Template [*Tool*]
MiTP	Peninsula Community Library, Traverse City, MI [*Library symbol Library of Congress*] (LCLS)
MITR	Massachusetts Institute of Technology Reactor
MITR	Mortgage Interest Tax Relief [*British*]
MiTr	Troy Public Library, Troy, MI [*Library symbol Library of Congress*] (LCLS)
MitrArd	Mitropolia Ardealului [*Sibiu, Rumania*] (BJA)
MitrBan	Mitropolia Banatului [*Timisoara, Rumania*] (BJA)
MITRE	Massachusetts Institute of Technology Research Establishment (NATG)
MITRE	Miniature Individual Transmitter-Receiver Equipment (MCD)
MitrMoldSuc	Mitropolia Moldovei si Sucevei [*Jassy, Rumania*] (BJA)
MiTrWB	William Beaumont Hospital, Troy, MI [*Library symbol Library of Congress*] (LCLS)
MITS	Management Information and Text System
MITS	Management Information Tracking System (COE)
MITS	Man-in-the-Sea Program [*Navy*]
MITS	Man in the Street [*The average man*] [*Usually "Mr. Mits" See also T C MITS*]
MITS	Master's Intelligent Terminal System [*Software package*] [*Nippon Kokan*]
MITS	Michigan Information Transfer Source [*University of Michigan*] (IID)
MITS	Michigan Travel System
MITS	Microfiche Image Transmission System (MCD)
MITS	Micro Instrumentation and Telemetry Systems (NITA)
MITS	Missile Ignition Test Simulator
MITS	Missile Interface Test Set
MITS	Missouri-Illinois Traffic Service
MITS	Mitsui & Co. Ltd. [*NASDAQ symbol*] (NQ)
MITS	Mobile Independent Target System (INF)
MITS	Monthly International Terrorist Summary (MCD)
MITS	Multiple Inward-Turning Scoop (MCD)
MITS	Multiplex Information Transfer System (PDAA)
MITSA	Member of the Institute of Trading Standards Administration [*British*] (DBQ)
mit sang	Mitte Sanguinem [*Take Away Blood*] [*Latin*] (MAE)
MitsbBk	Mitsubishi Bank Ltd. [*Associated Press*] (SAG)
MITSG	Massachusetts Institute of Technology Sea Grant Program (NOAA)
MIT/SL	Massachusetts Institute of Technology/Sloan Laboratory (AAG)
MIT/SmL	Massachusetts Institute of Technology/Servomechanisms Laboratory (AAG)
MIT/SpL	Massachusetts Institute of Technology/Spectroscopy Laboratory (AAG)
Mitsui	Mitsui & Co. Ltd. [*Associated Press*] (SAG)
MITSY	Mitsui & Co ADR [*NASDAQ symbol*] (TTSB)
MITT	Member of the Institute of Travel and Tourism [*British*] (ODBW)
MITT	Mitte [*Send*] [*Latin*]
MITT	Mobile Imagery Transmission Terminal (DOMA)
MITT	Mobile Integrated Tactical Terminal (DOMA)
MITTAT	Mittatur [*Let Be Sent*] [*Pharmacy*] (ROG)
Mitte Sang	Mitte Sanguinem [*Bleed*] [*Pharmacy*] (BABM)
mitte sang	Mitte Sanguineum [*Bleed*] [*Latin*] (DAVI)
MITTINS	Michigan Travel Trade Information Service
MITTS	Minutes of Telecommunications Traffic [*Measure of voice, fax, and data transmission*]
MITTS	Mobile IGOR [*Intercept Ground Optical Recorder*] Tracking Telescope System [*Air Force*]
MITT SANG ad UNC SALTEM	Mitte Sanguinem ad Uncias ___ Saltem [*Take Away ___ Ounces of Blood at Least*] [*Pharmacy*] (ROG)
MITT TAL	Mitte Tales [*Send Such*] [*Pharmacy*]
MiTu	Tustin Public Library, Tustin, MI [*Library symbol Library of Congress*] (LCLS)
MITY	Mity Lite, Inc. [*NASDAQ symbol*] (SAG)
MityLite	Mity Lite, Inc. [*Associated Press*] (SAG)
MIU	Machine Interface Unit (HGAA)
MIU	Maharishi International University [*Fairfield, IA*]
MIU	Maharishi International University, Fairfield, IA [*OCLC symbol*] (OCLC)
MIU	Maiduguri [*Nigeria*] [*Airport symbol*] (OAG)
MIU	Malfunction Insertion Unit [*Aviation*]
MIU	Message Interface Unit (CAAL)
MIU	Methylisourea [*Organic chemistry*]
miu	Michigan [*MARC country of publication code Library of Congress*] (LCCP)

MIU	Microalgae International Union (EA)
mIU	Milli-International Unit
MIU	Missile Interface Unit
MIU	Mobile Inspection Unit [*Military*] (AFM)
MIU	Model Interface Unit (NITA)
MIU	Moisture, Insolubles, and Unsaponifiables [*Fat analysis*]
MIU	Motor Impeller Unit
MIU	Multiplex Interface Unit (NASA)
miu	Multiplex Interface Unit (NAKS)
MIU	Multistation Interface Unit [*Computer science*]
MiU	University of Michigan, Ann Arbor, MI [*Library symbol Library of Congress*] (LCLS)
MiU-A	University of Michigan, Asia Library, Ann Arbor, MI [*Library symbol Library of Congress*] (LCLS)
MiUb	Sleeper Public Library, Ubly, MI [*Library symbol Library of Congress*] (LCLS)
MiU-BA	University of Michigan, Graduate School of Business Administration, Ann Arbor, MI [*Library symbol Library of Congress*] (LCLS)
MiU-C	University of Michigan, William L. Clements Library, Ann Arbor, MI [*Library symbol Library of Congress*] (LCLS)
MiUcD	Delta College, University Center, MI [*Library symbol Library of Congress*] (LCLS)
MiUcS	Saginaw Valley College, University Center, MI [*Library symbol Library of Congress*] (LCLS)
MIU/FCO	Mobile Inspection Unit / Functional Checkout (SAA)
MiU-G	University of Michigan, Bureau of Government Library, Ann Arbor, MI [*Library symbol Library of Congress*] (LCLS)
MiU-H	University of Michigan, Michigan Historical Collection, Ann Arbor, MI [*Library symbol Library of Congress*] (LCLS)
MiU-Ho	University of Michigan, Avery and Julie Hopwood Room, Ann Arbor, MI [*Library symbol Library of Congress*] (LCLS)
MiU-L	University of Michigan, Law Library, Ann Arbor, MI [*Library symbol Library of Congress*] (LCLS)
MiU-M	University of Michigan, Medical Center, Ann Arbor, MI [*Library symbol Library of Congress*] (LCLS)
MiUnv	Columbia Township Library, Unionville, MI [*Library symbol Library of Congress*] (LCLS)
MiU-RE	University of Michigan, Center for Research on Economic Development, Ann Arbor, MI [*Library symbol Library of Congress*] (LCLS)
MIUS	Modular Integrated Utility System [*HUD*]
MIUSA	Mobility International USA (EA)
MiU-T	University of Michigan, Transportation Library, Ann Arbor, MI [*Library symbol Library of Congress*] (LCLS)
MiUt	Utica Public Library, Utica, MI [*Library symbol Library of Congress*] (LCLS)
MIUTC	Military Intelligence Unit Training Center (AABC)
MiUtS	Shelby Township Library, Utica, MI [*Library symbol Library of Congress*] (LCLS)
MIUU	Meteorological Institute of the University of Uppsala [*Sweden*] (USDC)
MIUU	Meterorological Institute of the University of Uppsala, Sweden [*Marine science*] (OSRA)
MIUW	Mobile Inshore Undersea Warfare [*Navy*] (NG)
MIUWG	Mobile Inshore Undersea War Group [*Navy*] (VNW)
MIUWS	Mobile Inshore Undersea Warfare Surveillance [*Navy*] (NVT)
MIUWSU	Mobile Inshore Undersea Warfare Surveillance Unit [*Navy*] (CINC)
MIV	Main Instrumentation Van [*NASA*]
MIV	Mi-Avia [*Russian Federation*] [*ICAO designator*] (FAAC)
MIV	MICC Investments Ltd. [*Toronto Stock Exchange symbol*]
MIV	Millville, NJ [*Location identifier FAA*] (FAAL)
MIV	Mobile Instrumentation Van (KSC)
MIV	Moving Ion Voltmeter
MiVa	Bullard-Sanford Public Library, Vassar, MI [*Library symbol Library of Congress*] (LCLS)
MIVA	Midwestern Intercollegiate Volleyball Association (PSS)
MIVA	Missionary Vehicle Association (EA)
MIVA-America	Missionary Vehicle Association of America (EA)
MIVAC	Microwave Vacuum [*Dryer*] (MCD)
MIVC	Magnetically Induced Velocity Charge [*Southwest Research Institute*]
MIVEC	Mitsubishi Innovative Valve Timing and Lift Electronic Control System [*Automotive engineering*] (PS)
MiVer	Vermontville Public Library, Vermontville, MI [*Library symbol Library of Congress*] (LCLS)
MiVes	Vestaburg Public Library, Vestaburg, MI [*Library symbol Library of Congress*] (LCLS)
MIVH	Mississippi View Holding [*NASDAQ symbol*] (TTSB)
MIVI	Mississippi View Holding Co. [*NASDAQ symbol*] (SAG)
MiVi	Vicksburg Community Library, Vicksburg, MI [*Library symbol Library of Congress*] (LCLS)
MIVPO	Modified Inside Vapor Phase Oxidation (EECA)
MIW	Airborne of Sweden AB [*ICAO designator*] (FAAC)
MIW	Marshalltown, IA [*Location identifier FAA*] (FAAL)
MIW	Microinstruction Word
MIW	Milk Ingredient Water (OA)
MIW	Mine Warfare (NVT)
MiWaC	Wayne County Federated Library System, Wayne, MI [*Library symbol Library of Congress*] (LCLS)
MiWaC-B	Wayne County Federated Library System, Department for the Blind and Physically Handicapped, Wayne, MI [*Library symbol Library of Congress*] (LCLS)
MiWak	Wakefield Public Library, Wakefield, MI [*Library symbol Library of Congress*] (LCLS)
MiWal	Melrose Township Public Library, Walloon Lake, MI [*Library symbol Library of Congress*] (LCLS)

MiWald........	Waldron District Library, Waldron, MI [*Library symbol Library of Congress*] (LCLS)
MiWalv........	Walkerville Public Library, Walkerville, MI [*Library symbol Library of Congress*] (LCLS)
MiWar	Warren Public Library, Warren, MI [*Library symbol Library of Congress*] (LCLS)
MiWarBH....	Bi-County Community Hospital, Warren, MI [*Library symbol Library of Congress*] (LCLS)
MiWarGME...	General Motors Corp., Engineering Library and Information Services, Warren, MI [*Library symbol*] [*Library of Congress*] (LCLS)
MiWarGMR...	General Motors Corp., Research Laboratories Division, Warren, MI [*Library symbol Library of Congress*] (LCLS)
MiWarGMR-E..	General Motors Corp., Engineering Staff Library, Warren, MI [*Library symbol Library of Congress*] (LCLS)
MiWarM	Macomb County Community College, Warren, MI [*Library symbol Library of Congress*] (LCLS)
MiWatv........	Watervliet Public Library, Watervliet, MI [*Library symbol Library of Congress*] (LCLS)
MiWbH	Holocaust Memorial Center, West Bloomfield, MI [*Library symbol*] [*Library of Congress*] (LCLS)
MIWE..........	Member of the Institution of Water Engineers [*British*] (EY)
MiWe..........	West Branch Public Library, West Branch, MI [*Library symbol Library of Congress*] (LCLS)
MiWeld........	Gladys MacArthur Memorial Library, Weidman, MI [*Library symbol Library of Congress*] (LCLS)
MIWES.........	Member of the Institution of Water Engineers and Scientists [*British*] (DI)
MiWh..........	White Pigeon Township Library, White Pigeon, MI [*Library symbol Library of Congress*] (LCLS)
MiWhc	E. Jack Sharpe Public Library, White Cloud, MI [*Library symbol Library of Congress*] (LCLS)
MIWHR........	Melpomene Institute for Women's Health Research (EA)
MIWHTE	Member of the Institution of Works and Highways Technician Engineers [*British*] (DBQ)
MiWin..........	Fremont Township Library, Winn, MI [*Library symbol Library of Congress*] (LCLS)
MIWM..........	Member of the Institution of Works Managers [*British*]
MIWMA........	Member of the Institute of Weights and Measures Administration [*British*]
MiWol..........	Wolverine Community Library, Wolverine, MI [*Library symbol Library of Congress*] (LCLS)
MiWp...........	Carp Lake Township Library, White Pine, MI [*Library symbol Library of Congress*] (LCLS)
MIWPC	Member of the Institute of Water Pollution Control [*British*]
MIWS..........	Multipurpose Individual Weapon System (MCD)
MIWSP	Member of the Institute of Work Study Practitioners [*British*]
MIWT..........	Member of the Institute of Wireless Technology [*British*]
MiWy...........	Bacon Memorial Public Library, Wyandotte, MI [*Library symbol Library of Congress*] (LCLS)
MIX.............	Magnetic Ionization Experiment
MIX.............	McGraw-Hill Information Exchange for Educators
MIX.............	Member Information Exchange [*American Society for Training and Development - ASTD*] [*Alexandria, VA*] [*Information service or system*] (IID)
MIX.............	Merrill Lynch & Co. [*NYSE symbol*] (SAG)
MIX.............	Merrill Lynch & Co'MITTS' 2001 [*NYSE symbol*] (TTSB)
MIX.............	Methylisobutylxanthine [*Also, IBMX*] [*Biochemistry*]
MIX.............	Metropolis, IL [*Location identifier FAA*] (FAAL)
MIX.............	Microprogram Index Register [*Computer science*] (CIST)
MIX.............	Mix Canyon Road [*California*] [*Seismograph station code, US Geological Survey*] (SEIS)
MIX.............	Mixing
MIX.............	Mixture (KSC)
mix.............	Mixture (MEC)
MIX.............	Mores Island [*Bahamas*] [*Airport symbol*] (AD)
mix mon	Mixed Monitor [*Obstetrics*] (DAVI)
MIXT..........	Mixtura [*Mixture*] [*Pharmacy*]
MIXX...........	Medical Innovations [*NASDAQ symbol*] (TTSB)
MIXX...........	Medical Innovations, Inc. [*NASDAQ symbol*] (NQ)
MIY.............	Miyako [*Japan*] [*Seismograph station code, US Geological Survey*] (SEIS)
MIY.............	Montgomeryshire Imperial Yeomanry [*British military*] (DMA)
MIY.............	MuniYield Michigan Insured Fund [*NYSE symbol*] (SPSG)
MIY.............	MuniYield MI Insured Fund [*NYSE symbol*] (TTSB)
MiY.............	Ypsilanti Area Public Library, Ypsilanti, MI [*Library symbol Library of Congress*] (LCLS)
MiYCC	Cleary College, Ypsilanti, MI [*Library symbol Library of Congress*] (LCLS)
MiYEM........	Eastern Michigan University, Ypsilanti, MI [*Library symbol Library of Congress*] (LCLS)
MIZ.............	Marginal Ice Zone [*Oceanography*]
MIZ.............	Missile Interception Zone [*Military*]
Miz.............	Mizrachi [*or Mizrahi*] (BJA)
MIZ.............	Mizusawa [*Japan*] [*Seismograph station code, US Geological Survey*] (SEIS)
MiZ.............	Zeeland Public Library, Zeeland, MI [*Library symbol Library of Congress*] (LCLS)
Mizar	Mizar, Inc. [*Associated Press*] (SAG)
MIZEX.........	Marginal Ice Zone Experiment [*Oceanography*]
MIZPAC........	Marginal Sea Ice Zone Pacific [*Marine science*] (MSC)
MIZR..........	Mizar, Inc. [*NASDAQ symbol*] (SAG)
MJ	Lineas Aereas Privadas Argentinas [*ICAO designator*] (AD)
MJ	Madras Jurist [*India*] [*A publication*] (DLA)
MJ	Main Jet [*Automotive engineering*]
MJ	Major Subject Descriptor [*Online database field identifier*]
MJ	Manufacturers' Junction Railway Co. [*AAR code*]
MJ	Marijuana
MJ	Marine Jet
MJ	Master of Journalism
MJ	Master of Jurisprudence
MJ	Mastic Joint [*Technical drawings*]
MJ	Mead Johnson & Co. [*Research code symbol*]
MJ	Mechanical Joint (NASA)
MJ	Megajoule
MJ	Michael Joseph [*Commercial firm British*]
MJ	Microturbo [*France ICAO aircraft manufacturer identifier*] (ICAO)
MJ	Military Judge (AFM)
MJ	Military Justice Reporter (West) [*A publication*] (DLA)
MJ	Milwaukee Journal [*A newspaper*]
mj	Missionaries of St. Joseph (TOCD)
MJ	Missionaries of St. Joseph (Mexico) (TOCD)
MJ	Missionary Sisters of Jesus (TOCD)
mj	Montserrat [*MARC country of publication code Library of Congress*] (LCCP)
MJA	Manja [*Madagascar*] [*Airport symbol*] (OAG)
MJA	Master of Justice Administration (PGP)
MJA	Medical Journalists Association [*British*] (DBA)
MJA	Merchant Jewellers' Association Ltd. [*British*] (BI)
MJA	Midstates Jeepster Association (EA)
MJAA	Messianic Jewish Alliance of America (EA)
MJAJ	Maanpuolustuksen ja Turvallisuuden Ammattijaerjestoet [*Defence and Security Employees Union*] [*Finalnd*] (EY)
MJAO	Mediterranean Joint Air Orders
MJB	Master Jet Base [*Navy*] (NVT)
MJB	Mejit [*Marshall Islands*] [*Airport symbol*] (OAG)
MJB	Missile Junction Box
MJB	Moore Jig Borer
MJC	Junior College District, Kansas City, MO [*OCLC symbol*] (OCLC)
MJC	Majestic Contractors Ltd. [*Toronto Stock Exchange symbol*]
MJC	Man [*Ivory Coast*] [*Airport symbol*] (OAG)
MJC	Manitoba Journal of Counselling [*A publication*]
MJC	Marshalltown Junior College [*Iowa*]
MJC	Medieval Jewish Chronicles [*A publication*] (BJA)
MJC	Mercy Junior College [*Missouri*] [*Closed, 1971*]
MJC	Miami-Jacobs College [*Ohio*]
MJC	Midway Junior College [*Kentucky*]
MJC	Military Junior College (AABC)
MJC	Moberly Junior College [*Missouri*]
MJC	Modesto Junior College [*California*]
MJC	Montgomery Junior College [*Maryland*]
MJC	Morse Junior College [*Connecticut*]
MJC	Morton Junior College [*Later, Morton College*] [*Cicero, IL*]
MJC	Muscatine Junior College [*Iowa*]
MJCA	Midbody Jettison Control Assembly (NASA)
MJCAA	Mississippi Junior College Athletic Association (PSS)
MJCAC	Midwest Junior College Athletic Conference (PSS)
MJCC	Maryland Junior College Athletic Conference (PSS)
MJCC	Melbourne Junior Chamber of Commerce [*Australia*]
MJCS	Memorandum for the Joint Chiefs of Staff (MCD)
MJD	Doctor of Medical Jurisprudence
MJD	Management Job Description (PDAA)
MJD	Modified Julian Date [*Astronomy*] (TEL)
MJD	Mohenjo Daro [*Pakistan*] [*Airport symbol*] (OAG)
MJD	Mouvement de la Jeunesse Djiboutienne [*Political party*] (EY)
MJDQ	Minnesota Job Description Questionnaire [*Research test*]
MJ Ed	Master of Jewish Education (PGP)
MJF	Greenville, TX [*Location identifier FAA*] (FAAL)
MJF	Multiple Juxtapositional Fixedness [*Tongue-in-cheek description of unusually strong bonding between metal ions and some ligands*]
MJG	Mayajigua [*Cuba*] [*Airport symbol*] (AD)
MJG	Moore Jig Grinder
MJGA	Manufacturing Jewelers Golf Association (EA)
MJGA	Midwest Job Galvanizers Association [*Defunct*] (EA)
MJH	Majma [*Saudi Arabia*] [*Airport symbol*] (AD)
MJI	Maji [*Ethiopia*] [*Airport symbol*] (AD)
MJI	Masters and Johnson Institute [*St. Louis, MO*] [*Formerly, Reproductive Biology Research Foundation*] [*Research center*]
MJI	Member of the Journalists Institute
MJI	MuniYield New Jersey Insured Fund [*NYSE symbol*] (SPSG)
MJI	MuniYield NJ Insured Fund [*NYSE symbol*] (TTSB)
MJIE	Member of the Junior Institute of Engineers [*British*]
MJL	Medial Joint Line [*Orthopedics*] (DAVI)
MJL	Meyer, Jr., L. Agnew, Washington DC [*STAC*]
MJL	Mouila [*Gabon*] [*Airport symbol*] (OAG)
MJL	Murray's Jat Lancers [*British military*] (DMA)
MJM	Man-Job Match [*Military*]
MJM	Mbuji-Mayi [*Zaire*] [*Airport symbol*] (OAG)
MJMA	Mechanical Jack Manufacturers Association [*Defunct*] (EA)
MJMI	Messianic Jewish Movement International (EA)
MJMJ	Missionaries of Jesus, Mary, and Joseph [*Roman Catholic women's religious order*]
MJMT	Mean Job Mill Time [*Quality control*] (MHDB)
MJN	Majunga [*Madagascar*] [*Airport symbol*] (OAG)
MJN	Royal Air Force of Oman (Air Transport) [*ICAO designator*] (FAAC)
MJNMM.......	Master of Journalism in New Media Management (GAGS)
MJO	Mariner Jupiter Orbit [*NASA*]
MJO	Owens Technical College, Learning Resource Media Center, Toledo, OH [*OCLC symbol*] (OCLC)
MJP	Jackson Metropolitan Library System, Jackson, MS [*OCLC symbol*] (OCLC)

MJP .... Master of Jewish Pedagogy
MJP .... Mastuj [*Pakistan*] [*Airport symbol*] (AD)
MJP .... Mount John Pukaki [*New Zealand*] [*Seismograph station code, US Geological Survey*] (SEIS)
MJPM .... Master of Justice Policy and Management (PGP)
MJPS .... Mouvement des Jeunesses Progressistes Soudanaises [*Sudanese Progressive Youth Movement*] [*Mali*]
MJQ .... Jackson, MN [*Location identifier FAA*] (FAAL)
MJQ .... Modern Jazz Quartet [*Musical group*]
MJR .... Maintenance Job Request
Mjr .... Major [*Record label*]
MJR .... Major
MJR .... Management Job Review [*LIMRA*]
MJS .... Maintenance Jettison System [*NASA*]
MJS .... Manipulator Jettison System [*or Subsystem*] (MCD)
MJS .... Mariner Jupiter-Saturn [*NASA*]
MJS .... Master of Japanese Studies (ADA)
MJS .... Master of Judaic Studies (PGP)
MJS .... Master of Juridical Science (DLA)
MJS .... Member of the Japan Society
MJS .... Movimiento Juvenil Salesiano [*Salesian Youth Movement - SYM*] (EAIO)
MJSA .... Manufacturing Jewelers and Silversmiths of America (EA)
MJSA .... Manufacturing Jewelers Sales Association
MJSA .... Mouvement des Jeunesses Socialistes Africaines [*African Socialist Youth Movement*]
MJSD .... March, June, September, and December [*Denotes quarterly payments of interest or dividends in these months*] [*Business term*]
MJSG .... Medem Jewish Socialist Group [*Defunct*] (EA)
MJSTC .... Majestic
MJT .... Magic Johnson Theaters
MJT .... Majorteck Industries [*Vancouver Stock Exchange symbol*]
MJT .... Materials Joining Tool
MJT .... Mead Johnson Tube [*Medicine*] (DMAA)
MJT .... Multijet Transport
MJT .... Museum of Jurassic Technology
MJT .... Mytilene [*Greece*] [*Airport symbol*] (OAG)
MJU .... Jackson State University, Jackson, MS [*OCLC symbol*] (OCLC)
MJU .... Mamuju [*Indonesia*] [*Airport symbol*] (OAG)
MJU .... Mariner Jupiter-Uranus [*Mission*] [*NASA*]
MJu .... Medica Judaica [*A publication*] (BJA)
MJU .... Multijunction Unit [*Computer science*] (BUR)
MJUO .... Mount John University Observatory [*New Zealand*]
MJUPG .... Movimiento da Juventude da Uniao Popular da Guine [*Youth Movement of Guinean People's Union*]
MJUPS .... Mouvement des Jeunes de l'Union Progressiste Senegalaise [*Youth Movement of the Senegalese Progressive Movement*]
MJur .... Master of Jurisprudence
MJV .... Murcia [*Spain*] [*Airport symbol*] (OAG)
MJW .... Madison Junction [*Wyoming*] [*Seismograph station code, US Geological Survey Closed*] (SEIS)
MJWG .... MANPRINT [*Manpower and Personnel Integration*] Joint Working Group [*Army*]
MJX .... Masjed Soleyman [*Iran*] [*Airport symbol*] (AD)
MJX .... Toms River, NJ [*Location identifier FAA*] (FAAL)
MJY .... Majesty Resources [*Vancouver Stock Exchange symbol*]
MJZ .... Mahfid [*South Arabia*] [*Airport symbol*] (AD)
MJZ .... Mount John [*New Zealand*] [*Seismograph station code, US Geological Survey*] (SEIS)
MK .... Air Mauritius [*ICAO designator*] (AD)
MK .... Macedonia [*Internet country code*]
MK .... Magic Kingdom [*Walt Disney World*]
MK .... Malawi Kwacha [*Monetary unit*]
MK .... Manual Clock [*Computer science*] (MDG)
MK .... Mark [*Ammunition*] (NATG)
Mk .... Mark [*New Testament book*]
mk .... Mark (WDMC)
MK .... Markka [*Monetary unit*] [*Finland*] (GPO)
MK .... Marschkolonne [*March Column*] [*German military - World War II*]
MK .... Mask [*Computer science*]
MK .... Master Key [*Locks*] (ADA)
MK .... Mebyon Kernow [*Sons of Cornwall*] [*National liberation party*] [*Political party*]
MK .... Megakaryocyte (DMAA)
MK .... Member of Knesset (BJA)
MK .... Menaquinone [*Vitamin K*] [*Also, MQ*] [*Biochemistry*]
MK .... Merck & Co., Inc. [*Research code symbol*]
MK .... Metarrithmistikon Komma [*Reformist Party*] [*Greece*] [*Political party*] (PPE)
MK .... Microphone (MDG)
MK .... Middle Kingdom [*Egyptology*] (ROG)
mK .... Millikelvin
MK .... Milton Keynes [*Russian city*]
MK .... Miscellaneous Kits [*JETDS nomenclature*] [*Military*] (CET)
MK .... Mit Kappe [*With Cap*] [*German military - World War II*]
MK .... Mit Kern [*With Core*] [*German military - World War II*]
MK .... Modification Kit (AAG)
MK .... Mo'ed Katan (BJA)
MK .... Monk
MK .... Monkey Kidney
MK .... More-Kraepelin [*Disease*] [*Medicine*] (DB)
MK .... Morgan Keenan [*System*] [*Astronomy*]
M-K .... Morrison-Knudsen Co., Inc. [*Boise, ID*] (TSSD)
MK .... Morse Key (DEN)

MK .... Mounier-Kuhn [*Syndrome*] [*Medicine*] (DB)
MK .... Multiple Kill [*Aerospace*]
mk .... Muscat and Oman [*Oman*] [*MARC country of publication code Library of Congress*] (LCCP)
MK .... Myokinase (DMAA)
MKA .... Machine Knife Association (EA)
MKA .... Makaopuhi [*Hawaii*] [*Seismograph station code, US Geological Survey*] (SEIS)
MKA .... Marine-Kuestenartillerie [*Naval Coast Artillery*] [*German military - World War II*]
MKA .... Master Kennel Association [*Commercial firm*] (EA)
MKA .... Miller, SD [*Location identifier FAA*] (FAAL)
MKA .... MK Aircargo [*British ICAO designator*] (FAAC)
MKAS .... Meyer-Kendall Assessment Survey [*Interpersonal skills and attitudes test*]
MKAU .... MK Gold [*NASDAQ symbol*] (TTSB)
MKAU .... MK Gold Co. [*NASDAQ symbol*] (SAG)
MKB .... Megakaryoblast [*Hematology*]
MKB .... Mekambo [*Gabon*] [*Airport symbol*] (OAG)
MKBF .... Mean Kilometers between Failures
MKBWU ...... Machine Knife and Bayonet Workers' Union [*British*]
MKC .... Kansas City [*Missouri*] [*Airport symbol*] (OAG)
MKC .... Magic Kingdom Club [*Walt Disney Productions*]
MKC .... Mammal Kidney Cell (DB)
MKC .... Mark Resources, Inc. [*Toronto Stock Exchange symbol*]
MKC .... McKeesport Connecting Railroad Co. [*AAR code*]
MKC .... Moncks Corner [*South Carolina*] [*Seismograph station code, US Geological Survey Closed*] (SEIS)
MKC .... Monkey Kidney Cell (DMAA)
MKC .... University of Health Sciences, Kansas City, MO [*OCLC symbol*] (OCLC)
MKD .... Marked (MSA)
MKDIR .... Make Directory [*Computer science*]
MKE .... General Mitchell International Airport [*FAA*] (TAG)
MKE .... Milwaukee [*Wisconsin*] [*Airport symbol*] (OAG)
MKE .... Molecular Kinetic Energy
MKF .... Mackenzie Financial Corp. [*Toronto Stock Exchange symbol*]
MKFC .... Mackenzie Financial Corp. [*NASDAQ symbol*] (SAG)
MKFCF .... Mackenzie Financial [*NASDAQ symbol*] (TTSB)
MKG .... Magnetocardiogram
MKG .... Making
MKG .... Mallinckrodt Group [*Formerly, IMCERA Group*] [*NYSE symbol*] (SAG)
MKG .... Marking
MKG .... Maurer Kunst Geselle [*Fellowcraft*] [*Freemasonry*] [*German*]
M-KG .... Meteor-Kilogram
M-KG .... Meter-Kilogram (KSC)
MKG .... Munson, K. G., Weyers Cave VA [*STAC*]
MKG .... Muskegon [*Michigan*] [*Airport symbol*] (OAG)
MKG .... Muskegon, MI [*Location identifier FAA*] (FAAL)
MK Gold ...... MK Gold Co. [*Associated Press*] (SAG)
MKgP .... Posse School, Inc., Kendal Green, MA [*Library symbol Library of Congress Obsolete*] (LCLS)
MKGPr .... Mallincrodt Group 4% Pfd [*NYSE symbol*] (TTSB)
MKGS .... Markings
MKH .... Mauna Kea [*Hawaii*] [*Seismograph station code, US Geological Survey*] (SEIS)
MKH .... Million of Kilowatt Hours (MCD)
MKH .... Mokhotlong [*Lesotho*] [*Airport symbol*] (OAG)
MKH .... Multiple Key Hashing
MKHS .... Menkes' Kinky Hair Syndrome [*Medicine*] (DMAA)
MKI .... M-Corp Inc. [*Formerly, Mike's Submarines*] [*Toronto Stock Exchange symbol*]
MKIE .... Mackie Designs [*NASDAQ symbol*] (TTSB)
MKIE .... Mackie Designs, Inc. [*NASDAQ symbol*] (SAG)
M Kin .... Master of Kinesiology (PGP)
MkIS .... Marketing Information System
MKJ .... Makoua [*Congo*] [*Airport symbol*] (OAG)
MKJK .... Kingston [*Jamaica*] [*ICAO location identifier*] (ICLI)
MKJM .... Montego Bay [*Jamaica*] [*ICAO location identifier*] (ICLI)
MKJP .... Kingston/Norman Manley International [*Jamaica*] [*ICAO location identifier*] (ICLI)
MKJS .... Montego Bay/Sangster International [*Jamaica*] [*ICAO location identifier*] (ICLI)
MKK .... Kaunakakai, HI [*Location identifier FAA*] (FAAL)
Mkk .... Markka [*Monetary unit*] [*Finland*]
MKK .... Molokai/Kaunakakai [*Hawaii*] [*Airport symbol*] (OAG)
MkK .... Monkey Kidney [*Medicine*] (DMAA)
MKK .... Morgan, Keenan, Kellman [*System*] [*Astronomy*]
MKL .... Jackson [*Tennessee*] [*Airport symbol*] (OAG)
MKL .... Jackson, TN [*Location identifier FAA*] (FAAL)
MKL .... Lakeland Regional Library, Killarney, Manitoba [*Library symbol National Library of Canada*] (NLC)
MKL .... Maskali [*Djibouti*] [*Seismograph station code, US Geological Survey*] (SEIS)
MKLP .... Megakaryocytic Leukemia [*Hematology*]
MKLP .... Mitotic Kinesin-Like Protein [*Biochemistry*]
MKM .... Kansas City, MO [*Location identifier FAA*] (FAAL)
MKM .... Marksman [*Marine Corps*]
MKM .... Mink Minerals Resources, Inc. [*Vancouver Stock Exchange symbol*]
MKM .... Mukah [*Malaysia*] [*Airport symbol*] (OAG)
MKM .... Myopic Keratomileusis [*Ophthalmology*]
MKMA .... Machine Knife Manufacturers Association (EA)
MkmQualBad... Marksman Qualification Badge [*Military decoration*] (AABC)
MKN .... Malekolon [*Papua New Guinea*] [*Airport symbol*] (OAG)

MKN............	Mouvement Cooperatif National [Haiti] [Political party] (EY)
MKN............	Northeast Missouri State University, Kirksville, MO [OCLC symbol] (OCLC)
MKO............	Makung Airlines [Taiwan] [ICAO designator] (FAAC)
MKO............	Mauna Kea Observatory [Hawaii] (BARN)
MKO............	Mikado Resources Ltd. [Vancouver Stock Exchange symbol]
MKO............	Modification Kit Order
MKO............	Muskogee, OK [Location identifier FAA] (FAAL)
MKP............	Magyar Kommunista Part [Hungarian Communist Party] [Political party] (PPE)
MKP............	Makemo [French Polynesia] [Airport symbol] (OAG)
MKP............	McKeesport, PA [Location identifier FAA] (FAAL)
MkP	Mikropress GmbH, Bonn, Germany [Library symbol Library of Congress] (LCLS)
MKP............	Myokinetic Psychodiagnosis [Psychology] (AEBS)
MKPL............	Computer Marketplace [NASDAQ symbol] (TTSB)
MKPL............	Computer Marketplace, Inc. [NASDAQ symbol] (SAG)
MKPLW........	Computer Marketplace Wrrt'A' [NASDAQ symbol] (TTSB)
MKPLZ.........	Computer Marketplace Wrrt'B' [NASDAQ symbol] (TTSB)
MKQ............	Merauke [Indonesia] [Airport symbol] (OAG)
MKQCP	Member of the King's and Queen's College of Physicians [Ireland]
MKR............	Glasgow, MT [Location identifier FAA] (FAAL)
MKR............	Maker
mkr............	Maker (VRA)
MKR............	Marker [Beacon]
MKR............	Meekatharra [Australia Airport symbol] (OAG)
MK Rail	MK Rail Corp. [Associated Press] (SAG)
mKRB	Modified Krebs-Ringer Bicarbonate [Solution]
MKRL............	MK Rail [NASDAQ symbol] (TTSB)
MKRL...........	MK Rail Corp. [NASDAQ symbol] (SAG)
MKS............	Makassar [Celebes] [Seismograph station code, US Geological Survey] (SEIS)
MKS............	Marks & Spencer Canada, Inc. [Toronto Stock Exchange symbol]
MKS............	Marksman [Marine Corps]
MKS............	Mekane [Ethiopia] [Airport symbol] (OAG)
MKS............	Meter-Kilogram-Second [System of units]
mks............	Meter-Kilogram-Second (IDOE)
MKS............	Microwave Keying Switch
MKS............	Mikasa, Inc. [NYSE symbol] (SAG)
MKS............	Moncks Corner, SC [Location identifier FAA] (FAAL)
MKS............	Mortice Kern Systems, Inc. [Waterloo, ON Canada] [Commercial firm] (CDE)
MKS............	Pimichikamac Air Ltd. [Canada] [FAA designator] (FAAC)
MKSA...........	Meter-Kilogram-Second-Ampere [System of units]
MKSS...........	Microwave Keying Switching Station
MKSTNG......	Marksmanship Training (NVT)
MKT............	Mankato [Minnesota] [Airport symbol] (OAG)
MKT............	Mankato, MN [Location identifier FAA] (FAAL)
MKT............	Market
Mkt............	Market (EBF)
mkt	Market (WDMC)
MKT............	Missouri-Kansas-Texas Railroad Co. [AAR code]
MKT............	Mobile Kitchen Trailer [Military] (INF)
MKT............	Mu Kappa Tau (EA)
MKTA..........	Makita Corp. [NASDAQ symbol] (SAG)
MKTAY........	Makita Corp. [NASDAQ symbol] (TTSB)
MKTC..........	Monkey Kidney Tissue Culture (DB)
MktFct	Market Facts, Inc. [Associated Press] (SAG)
MKTG..........	Marketing
Mktg	Marketing (TBD)
mktg	Marketing (WDMC)
MKTI..........	Mission Kit Technical Instruction
MKTI..........	Morrison-Knudsen Technologies, Inc. [Boise, ID] [Telecommunications] (TSSD)
MKTL..........	MarketLink, Inc. [NASDAQ symbol] (SAG)
MKTLH........	Tri-Lake Health Centre, Killarney, Manitoba [Library symbol National Library of Canada] (NLC)
MktLink........	MarketLink, Inc. [Associated Press] (SAG)
MKTNG	Marketing
MKTP..........	Mark Template [Tool]
MKTT..........	Missouri-Kansas-Texas Railroad Co. (of Texas) [AAR code]
MKTU..........	Marksmanship Training Unit (AABC)
MkTwain......	Mark Twain Bancshares, Inc. [Associated Press] (SAG)
MKU............	Makokou [Gabon] [Airport symbol] (OAG)
MKU............	Mock-Up
MKUP	Makeup
MKV............	Killed-Measles Vaccine [Immunology] (MAE)
MKV............	Marksville, LA [Location identifier FAA] (FAAL)
MKV............	Miniature Kill Vehicle [Military] (SDI)
MKV............	Multiple Kill Vehicle
MKVNV	Muskmelon Vein Necrosis Virus [Plant pathology]
MKW............	Magnetokinetic Wave
MKW............	Manokwari [Indonesia] [Airport symbol] (OAG)
MKW............	Mikawa [Japan] [Seismograph station code, US Geological Survey] (SEIS)
MKW............	Military Knight of Windsor [British]
MKW............	Munitionskraftwagen [Ammunition Truck] [German military - World War II]
MKX............	Mukalla [South Arabia] [Airport symbol] (AD)
MKY............	Mackay [Australia Airport symbol] (OAG)
MKY............	Makeyevka [Former USSR Seismograph station code, US Geological Survey Closed] (SEIS)
MKY............	Marco Island, FL [Location identifier FAA] (FAAL)
MKY............	Monky Aerotaxis SA [Mexico ICAO designator] (FAAC)
MKYFC........	Mike and Kathy Yager Fan Club [Later, MYFC] (EA)
MKZ............	Los Angeles, CA [Location identifier FAA] (FAAL)
MKZ............	Malacca [Malaysia] [Airport symbol] (OAG)
ML	Aviation Services [ICAO designator] (AD)
ML	Land Mobile Station [ITU designation] (NATG)
ML	Licentiate in Medicine
ML	Licentiate in Midwifery
ML	Machine Language [Computer science]
ML	Madras Lancers [British military] (DMA)
ML	Magic Lantern Society of the United States and Canada (EA)
ML	Magnetic Latching [Electronics] (OA)
ML	Magnetogasdynamics Laboratory [MIT] (MCD)
ML	Magnitude Local (COE)
ML	Mail
ML	Mainland (MUGU)
ML	Main Line [Business term]
ML	Main Lobe
ML	Maintained Load (WDAA)
ML	Maintenance Laboratory (MUGU)
M/L	Maintenance Loop (MCD)
ML	Major League [Baseball]
ML	Major Lobe (MSA)
ML	Malachi [Old Testament book]
ML	Mali [ANSI two-letter standard code] (CNC)
ml	Mali [MARC country of publication code Library of Congress] (LCCP)
ML	Malignant Lymphoma [Oncology]
M:L	maltase-to-Lactase [Ratio] [Biochemistry] (DAVI)
ML	Management Level
ML	Management List
ML	Mandibular Line [Jaw anatomy]
ML	Manipulation Language (NITA)
ML	Manipulator Language [Computer science]
ML	Mantle Length
ML	Mantle Lip
ML	Manual Loader (AAG)
ML	Manual Local (IAA)
ML	Manufacturing License (NRCH)
ML	Maple Leaf Gardens Ltd. [Toronto Stock Exchange symbol]
ML	March for Life (EA)
ML	Marie-Leri [Syndrome] [Medicine] (DB)
ML	Mark-Up Language [Computer science]
MI	Marl [Quality of the bottom] [Nautical charts]
M-L	Martin-Lewis [Medium] [Microbiology]
M/L	Mass to Luminosity [Ratio] [Astronomy]
ML	Master of Laws
ML	Master of Letters
ML	Master of Librarianship (GAGS)
ML	Master of Literature
ML	Material List (MSA)
ML	Mater Lectionis (BJA)
ML	Maule Aircraft Corp. [ICAO aircraft manufacturer identifier] (ICAO)
ML	Maximum Likelihood [Statistics]
ML	Mean Level
ML	Medial Lemniscus [Neuroanatomy]
ML	Medical Letter (EA)
ML	Medieval Latin [Language, etc.]
ML	Medium Lorry [British]
ML	Megaliter
ML	Member Library [OCLC or RLIN]
ML	Member's Liability [Health insurance] (GHCT)
ML	Memory Location [Computer science]
ML	Merrill Lynch & Co., Inc. (EFIS)
ML	Mesiolingual [Dentistry]
ML	Metabolic Loss [Physiology]
M-L	Metallic-Longitudinal (IEEE)
ML	Meteorological Devices [JETDS nomenclature] [Military] (CET)
ML	Meteorology Laboratory (GNE)
ML	Methods of Limits (IEEE)
ML	Metromail Corp. [NYSE symbol] (SAG)
ML	Mexican League [Baseball]
ML	Microprogramming Language
ML	Microwave Laboratory [Stanford University] (MCD)
ML	Middeck Left (MCD)
ML	Middle Latin [Language, etc.]
ML	Middle Left (WDAA)
ML	Middle Lobe [Of lung]
ML	Midlife (DAVI)
ML	Midline
ML	Migne Series [Latina] [A publication] (BJA)
ML	Milan Stock Exchange [Italy]
ml	Mile (IDOE)
ML	Milieu
ML	Military Law
ML	Military Leave (GFGA)
ML	Military Liaison
ML	Military Payroll Money List
ML	Mill
ml	Millilambert
mL	Milliliter
ml	Milliliter (IDOE)
ML	Mine Layer (WDAA)
ML	Mineral Lease (ADA)
ML	Minerva Library [A publication]
ML	Minilab
ML	Mining and Logging [Tires]
ML	Missile Launcher

ML	Missile Layout
ML	Missile Lethality [*Military*]
M/L	Missile-Lift [*Aerospace*] (AAG)
ML	Missile Liner
ML	Mission Life [*Aerospace*]
ML	Mission Load (AABC)
ML	Mixed Lengths
ML	Mobile Launcher [*NASA*] (KSC)
ML	Mobile Low-Power [*Reactor*] (NRCH)
ML	Mode-Locked [*Laser technology*]
ML	Moderate Load service [*Automotive engineering*]
ML	Moderately Long [*Botany*]
ML	Modern Languages (AIE)
ML	Modern Lithographer [*A publication*] (DGA)
ML	Modified License [*FCC*] (NTCM)
ML	Molder [*Navy rating*]
ML	Mold Line [*Technical drawings*]
ML	Molecular Layer [*of the hippocampus*] [*Neurology*]
ML	Monarchist League [*Defunct*] (EA)
ML	Moneda Legal [*Legal Tender*] [*Spanish Business term*]
ML	Money List
M/L	Monocyte-Lymphocyte [*Ratio*] [*Clinical chemistry*]
ML	Monolayer [*Physical chemistry*]
ML	Monolithic
ML	Morocco Lined [*Covers*] [*Bookbinding*] (ROG)
ML	Motherwell [*Postcode*] (ODBW)
ML	Motor Launch
ML	Mountain Leader [*British military*] (DMA)
ML	Mouse Laminin
ML	Mouse Lysozyme [*Biochemistry*]
ML	Mucolipidosis [*Medicine*]
ML	Mucrones Length [*Of Crustacea*]
ML	Multilayer [*Pharmacy*]
ML	Multiple-Line [*Insurance*]
ML	Multiple Location [*Insurance*]
ML	Multiple-Locus [*Light flashes*]
ML	Munitions List
ML	Music Library Records [*Record label*]
ML	Muslim League [*Bangladesh*] [*Political party*] (FEA)
ML	Mutual Inductance [*Symbol*] (DEN)
ML	Muzzle-Loading
ML	Myelogenous Leukemia [*Oncology*]
ML	Myeloid Leukemia [*Medicine*] (DB)
ML	Myrialiter [*Unit of measurement*] (ROG)
ML	Small Minesweeper [*Navy symbol*]
ML1	Molder, First Class [*Navy rating*]
ML2	Molder, Second Class [*Navy rating*]
ML3	Molder, Third Class [*Navy rating*]
MLA	Auxiliary Motor Launches (NATG)
MLA	Forty-Mile Air [*ICAO designator*] (FAAC)
MLA	Macedonian Literary Association [*Australia*]
MLA	Magnetic Lens Assembly
MLA	Maine Lobstermen's Association (EA)
mla	Malagasy [*MARC language code Library of Congress*] (LCCP)
MLA	Malaspina [*Alaska*] [*Seismograph station code, US Geological Survey*] (SEIS)
MLA	Malta [*Airport symbol*] (OAG)
MLA	Mandatory Liquid Assets [*Finance*]
MLA	Maneuver Limited Altitude (GAVI)
MLA	Maneuver Load Alleviation [*Aviation*]
MLA	Manpack Loop Antenna
MLA	Manufacturing License Agreement
MLA	Marine Librarians Association (EA)
MLA	Maritime Law Association of the US (EA)
MLA	Marker-Labelled Antigen (DB)
MLA	Marlat Resources Ltd. [*Vancouver Stock Exchange symbol*]
MLA	Martin Landau Aficionados [*An association*]
MLA	Master Locksmiths Association [*British*] (BI)
MLA	Master of Landscape Architecture
MLA	Master of Liberal Arts (GAGS)
MLA	Matching Logic and Adder
MLA	MDM [*Manipulator Deployment Mechanism*] Launch Aft [*NASA*]
MLA	Mean Line of Advance [*Military*] (NVT)
MLA	Mechanical Lubricator Association
MLA	Medial Left Abdomen [*Injection site*]
MLA	Medical Library Association (EA)
MLA	Member of the Legislative Assembly
MLA	Member of the Library Association [*British*] (ROG)
MLA	Mento-Laeval Anterior [*A fetal position*] [*Obstetrics*]
MLA	Merritt Island Tracking Station [*Florida*]
MLA	Mesiolabial [*Dentistry*]
MLa	Mesiolabial (DB)
MLA	Metal Lath Association [*Later, ML/SFA*] (EA)
MLA	Metrolina Library Association [*Library network*]
MLA	Microprocessor Language Assembler [*Computer science*]
MLA	Microwave Linear Accelerator
MLA	Midland Co. [*AMEX symbol*] (SPSG)
MLA	Midwest Lacrosse Association (PSS)
MLA	Military Liaison Assistant (DOMA)
MLA	Minimal Lactose-Arabinose [*Culture medium*]
MLA	Mining Lease Application
MLA	Mistress of Liberal Arts
MLA	Mixed Lead Alkalis (EDCT)
MLA	Mixed Lead Alkyl [*Organic chemistry*]
MLA	Modern Language Association (NADA)

MLA	Modern Language Association of America (EA)
MLA	Monochrome Lens Assembly (MCD)
MLA	Monocytic Leukemia, Acute (MAE)
MLA	Motor Launch, Auxiliary [*NATO*]
MLA	Multi-Housing Laundry Association (EA)
MLA	Multilinear Array [*In earth scanning*]
MLA	MultiLink Advanced [*Local area network*] [*The Software Link, Inc.*]
MLA	Multiple Line Adaptor (NITA)
MLA	Multiplex Line Adapter
MLA	Multispectral Linear Array (SSD)
MLA	Music Library Association (EA)
MLA	Muzzle Loaders' Association of Great Britain
MLA	Valetta [*Malta*] [*Airport symbol*] (AD)
MLAA	Medical Library Assistance Act [*1965*]
MLAB	Mesa Laboratories [*NASDAQ symbol*] (TTSB)
MLAB	Mesa Laboratories, Inc. [*NASDAQ symbol*] (SAG)
MLAB	Modeling Laboratory [*Programming language*] [*1970*] (CSR)
MLAB	Multilingual Aphasia Battery [*Medicine*] (DMAA)
M Lab R	Monthly Labor Review [*A publication*] (BRI)
MLAF	Missile Loading Alignment Fixture
MLAGB	Muzzle Loaders Association of Great Britain (BI)
MLAI	Mesiolabioincisal [*Dentistry*]
M La L	Master of Latin Letters
MLal	Mesiolabioincisal [*Medicine*] (MEDA)
MLAMH	Mona Lisas and Mad Hatters [*Defunct*] (EA)
MLANA	Melkite Laymen's Association of North America (EA)
MLanc	Lancaster Town Library, Lancaster, MA [*Library symbol Library of Congress*] (LCLS)
MLandArch	Master of Landscape Architecture [*Canada*] (DD)
MLandEc	Master in Land Economy
ML&T	Master of Law and Taxation (GAGS)
MLAP	Mean Left Atrial Pressure [*Cardiology*]
MLaP	Mesiolabiopulpal [*Dentistry*]
MLAP	Migrant Legal Action Program (EA)
MLAP	Muslim League Assembly Party [*Pakistan*] [*Political party*] (FEA)
MLAPU	Marxist-Leninist Armed Propaganda Unit [*Turkey*]
MLAR	Mill Arbor
MLAR	Multilayer Antireflection [*Coating*]
ML Arch	Master of Landscape Architecture
MLAS	Master of Laboratory Animal Science (PGP)
MLASES	Molasses [*Freight*]
MLA-SMHL	Medical Library Association, Section on Mental Health Libraries (EA)
MLAT	Mean Latitude
MLAT	Modern Language Aptitude Test [*Military*] (AFM)
MLAUD	Master of Landscape Architecture in Urban Development (GAGS)
MLAUK	Member of the Library Association, United Kingdom (ROG)
M'Laur	M'Laurin's Scotch Judiciary Cases [*1774*] [*A publication*] (DLA)
MLaw	Lawrence Free Public Library, Lawrence, MA [*Library symbol Library of Congress*] (LCLS)
MLb	Macrolymphoblast (DB)
MLB	Magnetic Linear Birefringence (MCD)
MLB	Major League Baseball
MLB	Malabar [*Java*] [*Seismograph station code, US Geological Survey Closed*] (SEIS)
MLB	Manufacturing Load Boards (MCD)
MLB	Maritime Labor Board [*Terminated, 1942*]
MLB	Maritime Law Book Key Number Data Base [*Maritime Law Book Co. Ltd.*] [*Canada Information service or system*] (CRD)
MLB	Medallion Books Ltd. [*Vancouver Stock Exchange symbol*]
MLB	Melbourne [*Florida*] [*Airport symbol*] (OAG)
MLB	Merrill Lynch & Co. [*NYSE symbol*] (SAG)
MLB	Metallic Link Belt (AABC)
MLB	Metropolitan Toronto Library Board, Systems Unit [*UTLAS symbol*]
MLB	Micro-Laryngobronchoscopy [*Medicine*] (DMAA)
MLB	Middle Linebacker [*Football*]
MLB	Mini Landbridge [*MARAD*] (TAG)
MLB	Mobile Logistics Support Base (NVT)
MLB	Monaural Loudness Balance [*Audiology*]
MLB	Motor Lifeboat
MLB	Multilayer Board
MLB	Multiple Listing Board (BARN)
MLBC	ML Bancorp. [*NASDAQ symbol*] [*Formerly, MLF Bancorp.*] (SG)
MLBC	ML Bancorp, Inc. [*NASDAQ symbol*] (SAG)
MLBM	Modern Large Ballistic Missile
ML Bncp	ML Bancorp, Inc. [*Associated Press*] (SAG)
MLBPA	Mailing List Brokers Professional Association [*Defunct*] (EA)
MLBPA	Major League Baseball Players Association (EA)
MLBR	Medium Low-BIT [*Binary Digit*] Rate [*Computer science*]
MLBU	Mobile Laundry and Bath Unit [*Military British*]
MLC	Machine Level Control [*Computer science*]
MLC	Madras Light Cavalry [*British military*] (DMA)
MLC	Magnetic Ledger Card (CMD)
MLC	Main Lobe Clutter
MLC	Major Landing Craft
MLC	Major Legislation of Congress [*Data processing system*] [*Congressional Research Service*]
MLC	Major Line Component [*of NOAA*] (NOAA)
MLC	Management Level Chart [*Military*] (AFIT)
MLC	Management Level Code [*Military*] (AFIT)
ML-C	Management List - Consolidated
MLC	Maneuver Load Control [*Aviation*]
MLC	Manhattan National Corp. [*NYSE symbol*] (SPSG)
MLC	Manufacturers Life Capital Corp., Inc. [*Toronto Stock Exchange symbol*]

MLC............	Manzanita Lake [*California*] [*Seismograph station code, US Geological Survey*] (SEIS)
MLC............	Maple Leaf Club (EA)
MLC............	Master Labor Contract (AABC)
MLC............	McAlester [*Oklahoma*] [*Airport symbol*] (OAG)
MLC............	McAlester, OK [*Location identifier FAA*] (FAAL)
MLC............	Meat and Livestock Commission [*British*] (ARC)
MLC............	Median Lethal Concentration [*Toxiclogy*] (LDT)
MLC............	Medical Liability Commission [*Defunct*] (EA)
MLC............	Medical Library Center (DIT)
MLC............	Member of the Legislative Council
MLC............	Memphis Library Council [*Library network*]
MLC............	Merrill Lynch & Co., Inc. [*NYSE symbol*] (SAG)
MLC............	Merrill Lyn GI' MITTS'98 [*NYSE symbol*] (TTSB)
MLC............	Mesh Level Control
MLC............	Metropolitan Toronto Library Board, Cataloguing Department [*UTLAS symbol*]
MLC............	Micellar Liquid Chromatography
MLC............	Michigan Library Consortium [*Lansing, MI*] [*Library network*]
MLC............	Microelectric Logic Circuit
MLC............	Microprogram Location Counter
MLC............	Midlife Conversion
MLC............	Miles College, Birmingham, AL [*OCLC symbol*] (OCLC)
MLC............	Military Landing Craft
MLC............	Military Liaison Committee [*Energy Research and Development Administration*]
MLC............	Military Load Class (RDA)
MLC............	Military Load Classification [*BTS*] (TAG)
MLC............	Minimum Lethal Concentration
MLC............	Missile Logistics Center [*Army*]
MLC............	Mississippi-Louisiana Conference (PSS)
MLC............	Mississippi State Library Commission [*Information service or system*] (IID)
MLC............	Mixed Leukocyte Culture [*Hematology*]
MLC............	Mixed Ligand Chelate (DB)
MLC............	Mixed Lymphocyte Culture [*Hematology*]
MLC............	Mobile Launch Center
MLC............	Mobile Launcher Computer [*NASA*] (NASA)
MLC............	Modern Language Caucus [*of New University Conference*]
MLC............	Modern Language Centre [*Ontario Institute for Studies in Education*] [*Canada*] (IRC)
MLC............	Molder, Chief [*Navy rating*]
MLC............	MOL [*Manned Orbiting Laboratory*] Launch Complex (MCD)
MLC............	Monarchist League of Canada (EAIO)
MLC............	Morphine-Like Compound [*Immunology*]
MLC............	Motor Launch, Cabin
MLC............	Motor Load Control
MLC............	Mountain Leadership Certificate [*British*] (DI)
MLC............	Multilamellar Cytosome [*Biochemistry*] (MAE)
MLC............	Multilayer Capacitor [*Electronics*]
MLC............	Multilayer Ceramic [*Materials technology*]
MLC............	Multilayer Ceramic Capacitor (NITA)
MLC............	Multilayer Circuit
MLC............	Multilens Camera
MLC............	Multi-Level Cell (AAEL)
MLC............	Multiline Control (BUR)
MLC............	Multilink Control Field [*Telecommunications*] (ACRL)
MLC............	Multiplanar Link Chain
MLC............	Municipal Leasing Corp.
MLC............	Myelomonocytic Leukemia, Chronic (MAE)
MLC............	Myosin Light Chain [*Muscle biology*]
MLC............	Myth, Legend, Custom in the Old Testament [*A publication*] (BJA)
MLCAEC......	Military Liaison Committee to the Atomic Energy Commission (IEEE)
MLCB..........	Missile Launch Control Blockhouse
MLCB..........	Moored Limited Capability Buoy [*Marine science*] (MSC)
MLCB..........	Multilayer Circuit Board
ML/CB-CC..	Malignant Lymphoma/Centroblastic-Centrocytic [*Oncology*]
ML/CC........	Malignant Lymphoma/Centrocytic [*Oncology*]
MLCC..........	Mined Land Conservation Conference [*Later, BCR*]
MLCC..........	Multilayer Ceramic Capacitor [*Electronics*]
MLCG..........	Missile Launcher Control Group
MLCH..........	Major Logistical Control Headquarters (MCD)
MLCH..........	MLC Holdings, Inc. [*NASDAQ symbol*] (SAG)
MLC Hld	MLC Holdings, Inc. [*Associated Press*] (SAG)
MLCIM........	Marquette League for Catholic Indian Missions [*Defunct*] (EA)
MLCK..........	Myosin Light Chain Kinase [*An enzyme*]
MLCM..........	Molder, Master Chief [*Navy rating*]
MLCN..........	Multilocular Cystic Nephroma (DMAA)
MLCNY	Medical Library Center of New York [*Information service or system*] (IID)
MLCO..........	Member of the London College of Osteopathy [*British*] (DI)
MLCOM........	Member of the London College of Osteopathic Medicine [*British*] (DBQ)
MLCox99n ...	Merrill Lynch & Co. [*Associated Press*] (SAG)
MLCP..........	Mobile Land Command Post (AABC)
MLCP..........	Multilayer Ceramic Package [*Electronics*]
MLCP..........	Multiline Communications Processor
MLCP..........	Myosin Light-Chain Phosphatase (DB)
MLCPX........	Merrill Lynch: Capital Fund Cl.A [*Mutual fund ticker symbol*] (SG)
MLCR..........	Medical Laboratories Army Chemical Center [*Maryland*]
MLCR..........	Medical Laboratory Contract Reports [*Army*] (MCD)
MLCR..........	Mixed Lymphocyte Culture Reaction [*Hematology*] (AAMN)
MLCS..........	Molder, Senior Chief [*Navy rating*]
MLCS..........	Multilayer Ceramic Substrates [*Electronic circuit boards*]
MLCT..........	Metal-to-Ligand Charge Transfer [*Physical chemistry*]
MLCU..........	Magnetic Ledger Card Unit [*Computer science*] (MHDB)
MLCU..........	Mill Cutter [*Tool*]
MLCur.........	Merrill Lynch & Co. [*Associated Press*] (SAG)
MLD............	Air Moldova [*ICAO designator*] (FAAC)
MLD............	Legislative Reference Library - Minnesota Document Collection, St. Paul, MN [*OCLC symbol*] (OCLC)
MLD............	Machine Language Debugger [*National Computer Sharing Service*]
MLD............	Main Line of Defense
MLD............	Malad City, ID [*Location identifier FAA*] (FAAL)
MLD............	Malden [*Missouri*] [*Seismograph station code, US Geological Survey Closed*] (SEIS)
MLD............	Marginally Learning Disabled
MLD............	Masking Level Difference [*Hearing*]
MLD............	Master Layout Duplicate (MSA)
MLD............	Master of Landscape Design
MLD............	Maximum Lateral Damage (PDAA)
MLD............	Maximum Likelihood Detection (MCD)
MLD............	Mean Low-Water Datum [*Nuclear energy*] (NRCH)
MLD............	Medial Lethal Dose [*Genetics*] (DOG)
MLD............	Median Lethal Dose [*Also, LD_{50}*] [*Lethal for 50%*] [*Medicine*]
MLD............	Mesencephalicus Lateralis Dorsalis (DB)
MLD............	Metachromatic Leukodystrophy [*Medicine*]
MLD............	Middle Landing
MLD............	Midland [*AAR code*]
MLD............	Mild (WGA)
MLD............	Minimal Lesion Disease
MLD............	Minimum Lethal Dose
MLD............	Minimum Line of Detection [*Air Force*]
MLD............	Missile Launch Detector (MCD)
MLD............	Mixed Layer Depth (MCD)
MLD............	Moderate Learning Difficulties (AIE)
mld............	Mold (VRA)
MLD............	Molded (KSC)
MLD............	Molding [*Technical drawings*]
MLD............	Mouvement pour la Liberation de Djibouti [*Movement for the Liberation of Djibouti*] (PD)
MLDAS	Meteorological and Lighting Data Acquisition System [*NASA*] (KSC)
MLDB..........	Regional Library, Lac Du Bonnet, Manitoba [*Library symbol National Library of Canada*] (NLC)
MLDC..........	Miner's Legal Defense Committee [*Defunct*] (EA)
MLDD	Moderately Lightly Doped Drains (NITA)
MLDD	Mooring Leg Deployment Device (PDAA)
ML Des.......	Master of Landscape Design
MLDG..........	Molding (KSC)
MLDI..........	Meter List Display Interval [*FAA*] (TAG)
ML Dig & R...	Monthly Law Digest and Reporter [*Canada*] [*A publication*] (DLA)
ML Direct	ML Direct, Inc. [*Associated Press*] (SAG)
MLDL..........	Mooring Line Data Line [*Environmental buoy cable*]
MLDLP........	Mailing Label and Directory Lookup Package (PDAA)
MLDNG.......	Moulding
MLDR	ML Direct, Inc. [*NASDAQ symbol*] (SAG)
MLDR	Molder (ADA)
MLDS..........	Motor Launch, Double Shelter
MLD/S	Multi-Legend Display Switch (MCD)
MLDT..........	Mean Logistic Delay Time [*Military*] (CAAL)
MLDT..........	Mean Logistic Down Time
MLDU.........	Marriage Law Defence Union [*British*]
MLE	Magazine Lee-Enfield [*British military*] (DMA)
MLE	Male [*Maldives*] [*Airport symbol*] (OAG)
MLE	Manned Lunar Exploration [*NASA*] (AAG)
MLE	Mariner-Like Elements [*Genetics*]
MLE	Martin Lawrence Limited Editions [*NYSE symbol*] (SAG)
MLE	Martin Lawrence Ltd Editions [*NYSE symbol*] (TTSB)
MLE	Maryland Law Encyclopedia [*A publication*] (DLA)
MLE	Master of Applied Linguistics and Exegesis (PGP)
MLE	Master of Land Economy
MLE	Maximum Likelihood Estimate [*or Estimator*] [*Statistics*]
MLE	Maximum Loss Expectancy [*Insurance*]
MLE	Medium Local Exchange [*Telecommunications*] (TEL)
MLE	Merrill Lynch Economics (NITA)
MLE	Microprocessor Language Editor [*Computer science*]
MLE	Midline Episiotomy [*Obstetrics*] (DAVI)
MLE	Mile
MLE	Mileto [*Italy*] [*Seismograph station code, US Geological Survey Closed*] (SEIS)
MLE	Missile Launch Envelope
MLE	Mobile Launcher Equipment [*NASA*] (SAA)
MLE	Module Resources, Inc. [*Vancouver Stock Exchange symbol*]
MLE	Molecular Layer Epitaxy [*Coating technology*]
MLE	Muconate Lactonizing Enzyme
MLE	Myocardial Lactate Extraction [*Clinical chemistry*]
MLEA	Omaha, NE [*Location identifier FAA*] (FAAL)
MLEA	Multiple-Line Exclusive Agent [*Insurance*]
M'Lean's R...	McLean's United States Circuit Court Reports [*A publication*] (DLA)
MLED	Maximum Likelihood Estimator Deconvolution [*Statistics*]
MLegS	Master of Legal Studies
MLEL	Malignant Lymphoepithelial Lesion [*Medicine*] (DMAA)
MLenB	Berkshire Christian College, Lenox, MA [*Library symbol Library of Congress*] (LCLS)
ML Eng	Master of Landscape Engineering
MLeo	Leominster Public Library, Leominster, MA [*Library symbol Library of Congress*] (LCLS)
MLeoHi.......	Leominster Historical Society, Inc., Leominster, MA [*Library symbol*] [*Library of Congress*] (LCLS)
MLEP..........	Manned Lunar Exploration Program [*NASA*] (KSC)

MLEP	Minority Legislative Education Program
MLEP	Multipurpose Long Endurance Plane
MLES	Multiple-Line Encryption System (AABC)
MLEV	Manned Lifting Entry Vehicle (MCD)
MLex	Cary Memorial Library, Lexington, MA [Library symbol Library of Congress] (LCLS)
MLexHi	Lexington Historical Society, Lexington, MA [Library symbol Library of Congress] (LCLS)
MLexK	Kennecott Copper Corp., Ledgemont Laboratory, Lexington, MA [Library symbol Library of Congress] (LCLS)
MLexM	Museum of Our National Heritage, Lexington, MA [Library symbol Library of Congress] (LCLS)
MLexSC	Scottish Rite of Freemasonry, Northern Jurisdiction USA, Supreme Council Library, Lexington, MA [Library symbol Library of Congress] (LCLS)
MLF	Fast Motor Launches (NATG)
MLF	Maintenance Level Function
MLF	Male Liberation Foundation (EA)
MLF	Malolactic Fermentation
MLF	Maple Leaf Foods [Toronto Stock Exchange symbol] (SPSG)
MLF	Maximum Load Factor
MLF	MDM [Manipulator Deployment Mechanism] Launch Forward [NASA]
MLF	Media Language and Format (CET)
MLF	Medial Longitudinal Fasciculus [Medicine]
MLF	Medical Liberation Front (EA)
M/LF	Medium/Low Frequency (NATG)
MLF	Milford [Ohio] [Seismograph station code, US Geological Survey] (SEIS)
MLF	Milford, UT [Location identifier FAA] (FAAL)
MLF	Mobile Land Force (NATG)
MLF	Mobile Launcher Facility [NASA] (KSC)
MLF	MOL [Manned Orbiting Laboratory] Launch Facilities (MCD)
MLF	Morphine-Like Factor [Medicine] (DB)
MLF	Motor Launch, Fast [NATO]
MLF	Multilateral Force [NATO]
MLFA	Fireman Apprentice, Molder, Striker [Navy rating]
MLFA	Maine Lobster Fishermen's Association (EA)
MLFA	Merrill Lynch Financial Advantage
MLFAT	MOL [Manned Orbiting Laboratory] Launch Facilities Acceptance Team (MCD)
MLFB	MLF Bancorp [NASDAQ symbol] (TTSB)
MLFB	MLF Bancorp, Inc. [NASDAQ symbol] (SAG)
MLF Bc	MLF Bancorp, Inc. [Associated Press] (SAG)
MLFC	Michele Lee Fan Club (EA)
MLFC	Michigan Library Film Circuit [Library network]
MLFC	Mike Lunsford Fan Club (EA)
MLFC	Moses Lake Flight Center [Washington] (SAA)
MLFN	Fireman, Molder, Striker [Navy rating]
MLFS	Magic Lantern Film Society [An association]
MLFX	Mill Fixture [Tool]
MLG	Mailing
MLG	Main Landing Gear [Aerospace] (NAKS)
MLG	Malang [Indonesia] [Airport symbol] (OAG)
MLG	Metalgesellschaft Canada Investment [Toronto Stock Exchange symbol]
MLG	Middle Low German [Language, etc.]
MLG	Milling [Freight]
MLG	Mission Liaison Group [Military]
MLG	Mitochondria Lipid Glucogen [Cytology] (AAMN)
MLG	Moulage
MLG	Multiple Line Group [Radiation]
MLG	Musicland Stores [NYSE symbol] (SAG)
MLGCV	Movement for the Liberation of Portuguese Guinea and the Cape Verde Islands
MLGN	Minimal Lesion Glomerulonephritis [Medicine] (DMAA)
MLGP	Movimento de Libertacao da Guine Portuguesa [Movement for the Liberation of Portuguese Guinea]
MLGS	Microwave Landing Guidance System [FAA]
MLGT98	Merrill Lynch & Co., Inc. [Associated Press] (SAG)
MLGW	Maximum Landing Gross Weight
ML-H	Malignant Lymphoma, Histiocytic [Medicine] (DB)
MLH	Mauna Loa [Hawaii] [Seismograph station code, US Geological Survey] (SEIS)
MLH	Medium Lift Helicopter (MCD)
MLH	Merlin Resources Ltd. [Vancouver Stock Exchange symbol]
MLH	Minimum List Heading [Standard Industrial Classification] (PDAA)
MLH	Mulhouse/Basel [France] [Airport symbol] (OAG)
MLHCP	Mean Lower Hemispherical Candlepower (IAA)
MLHGR	Maximum Linear Heat Generation Ratio (NRCH)
MLHIX	Merrill Lynch: Corp. Bond: Hi Inc. CL.A [Mutual fund ticker symbol] (SG)
MLHK	Merrill Lynch & Co. [Associated Press] (SAG)
MLHR	Master of Labor and Human Resources (PGP)
MLHR	Miller (Herman) [NASDAQ symbol] (TTSB)
MLHR	Miller [Herman], Inc. [NASDAQ symbol] (NQ)
MLHW	Mean Lower High Water [Tides and currents]
MLHYX	Merrill Lynch: Muni Bond National Cl.A [Mutual fund ticker symbol] (SG)
MLI	Machine Language Instruction
MLI	Magnetic Level Indicator
MLI	Maislin Industries Ltd. [Toronto Stock Exchange symbol]
MLI	Malad Range [Idaho] [Seismograph station code, US Geological Survey] (SEIS)
MLI	Mali [ANSI three-letter standard code] (CNC)
MLI	Maltese Light Infantry [British military] (DMA)

MLI	Marine Light Infantry [Navy British] (ROG)
MLI	Marker Light Indicator
MLI	Master Listing Index
MLI	Master of Literary Interpretation
MLI	Mean Linear Intercept
MLI	Mesiolinguoincisal [Dentistry]
MLI	Message Level Interface (NITA)
MLI	Minimum Line of Interception [Air Force]
MLI	Mixed Lymphocyte Interaction [Immunology]
MLI	Moline [Illinois] [Airport symbol] (OAG)
MLI	Moline, IL [Location identifier FAA] (FAAL)
MLI	Mollie Gibson Mines [Vancouver Stock Exchange symbol]
MLI	Mueller Industries [NYSE symbol] (SPSG)
MLI	Muller Industries [NYSE symbol] (SAG)
MLI	Multilayer Insulation
MLI	Multiple Link Interface [Computer science]
MLI	Munitions List Item (MCD)
MLIA	Multiplex Loop Interface Adapter
MLib	Master of Librarianship
M Libr	Master of Librarianship (PGP)
M Lib Sc	Master of Library Science (BARN)
MLibSci	Master of Library Science (NADA)
MLIC	Manhattan Life Insurance [NASDAQ symbol] (TTSB)
MLIC	Manhattan Life Insurance Co. [NASDAQ symbol] (SAG)
MLID	Multiple Link Interface Drive [Telecommunications] (PCM)
MLID	Multiple Link Interface Driver [Telecommunications] (ACRL)
MLIFC	Mark Lindsay International Fan Club [Defunct] (EA)
MLIFC	Michelle Lynn International Fan Club (EA)
MLIGL01	Merrill Lynch & Co. [Associated Press] (SAG)
MLIM	Matrix Log-In Memory
MLIN	Micro Linear [NASDAQ symbol] (TTSB)
MLIN	Micro Linear Corp. [NASDAQ symbol] (SAG)
MLing	Master of Languages [British] (DBQ)
MLIP	Message Level Interface Port (NITA)
MLIR	Master of Labor and Industrial Relations (GAGS)
MLIRB	Multi-Line Insurance Rating Bureau [Later, ISO]
MLIS	Master of Library and Information Science
MLIS	Measurement Laboratory Information Service [Battelle Memorial Institute]
MLIS	Metal-Liquid-Insulator Semiconductor [Electronics] (PDAA)
MLIS	Micropolis Corp. [NASDAQ symbol] (NQ)
MLIS	Molecular LASER Isotope Separation
MLIS	Multiple Level Indexing Scheme [Computer science]
MLISP	Meta LISP [List Processor] [Programming language] [Computer science] (CSR)
M Lit	Master of Letters
M Lit	Master of Literature
MLitl	Inforonics Inc., Littleton, MA [Library symbol Library of Congress] (LCLS)
MLitM	Master of Liturgical Music (GAGS)
MLitSt	Master of Literary Studies (ADA)
M Litt	Master of Letters
MLitt	Master of Literature
ML IV	Mucolipidosis IV [A genetic disease]
MLJ	Memphis Law Journal [A publication] (DLA)
MLJ	Milledgeville, GA [Location identifier FAA] (FAAL)
MLJ	Modern Language Journal [A publication] (BRI)
MLK	Malta, MT [Location identifier FAA] (FAAL)
MLK	Martin Luther King, Jr.
MLK	Matlack Systems [NYSE symbol] (TTSB)
MLK	Matlack Systems, Inc. [NYSE symbol] (CTT)
MLK	Milford [Kansas] [Seismograph station code, US Geological Survey] (SEIS)
MLKCNSC	Martin Luther King, Jr., Center for Nonviolent Social Change (EA)
MLKCSC	Martin Luther King, Jr., Center for Social Change [Later, MLKCNSC] (EA)
MLKIII	Martin Luther King III
MLL	Mandella Resources Ltd. [Vancouver Stock Exchange symbol]
MLL	Manned Lunar Landing [NASA]
MLL	Marshall [Alaska] [Airport symbol] (OAG)
MLL	Marshall, AK [Location identifier FAA] (FAAL)
MLL	Master Lines Layout (MSA)
MLL	Master of Latin Literature
MLL	Master of Law Librarianship (ILCA)
MLL	Maynard Listener Library [Defunct] (EA)
MLL	MDM [Manipulator Deployment Mechanism] Launch Left [NASA]
MLL	Mean Lesion Length [Pathology]
ML/L	Milliliters per Liter (EG)
MLL	Mistress of Liberal Learning
MLL	Mixed Lineage Leukemia [Medicine] (DMAA)
MLL	Modify Lot Location (AAEL)
MLL	Music Lovers League (NADA)
MLL	University of Minnesota, Law Library, Minneapolis, MN [OCLC symbol] (OCLC)
MLLA	Mineral Lands Leasing Act of 1920 (COE)
MLLAA	Modern Language Association of America (NADA)
ML/LB	Malignant Lymphoma/Lymphoblastic [Oncology]
MLLE	Mademoiselle [Miss] [French] (EY)
Mlle	Mademoiselle [Miss] [French] (WA)
MLLE	Medium Large Local Exchange [Telecommunications] (TEL)
Mlles	Mesdemoiselles [Misses] [French]
MLLFT	Modified Lensless Fourier Transform (PDAA)
ML Libr	Master of Law Librarianship
MLLP	Manned Lunar Landing Program [NASA]
ML/LPC	Malignant Lymphoma/Lymphoplasmacytoid [Oncology]

MLLW	Mean Lower Low Water [*Tides and currents*]
MLLW	Medium Level Liquid Waste [*Nuclear energy*] (NUCP)
MLLW	Mixed Low-Level Waste (GAAI)
MLLWK	Millwork
MLLWL	Mean Lower Low Water Line [*Tides and currents*] (PDAA)
MLLWS	Mean Lower Low-Water Springs [*Tides and currents*]
MLM	Magazine Lee-Metford [*British military*] (DMA)
MLM	Mailing-List Manager [*Type of database*]
MLM	Martin Marietta Materials [*NYSE symbol*] (SAG)
MLM	Massive Liver Metastasis [*Oncology*]
MLM	Master of Landscape Management
MLM	Master of Library Media (PGP)
MLM	Maximum Likelihood Method [*Statistics*]
MLM	Membrane Light Modulator (PDAA)
MLM	Mesa Lucera [*New Mexico*] [*Seismograph station code, US Geological Survey*] (SEIS)
MLM	Metall Mining Corp. [*Toronto Stock Exchange symbol*]
MLM	Microbial Load Monitor (MCD)
MLM	Military Liaison Mission [*Germany*]
MLM	Minesweeper, River [*Navy symbol*] (VNW)
MLM	Mixed Level Matrix
MLM	Moody Literature Ministries (EA)
MLM	Morelia [*Mexico*] [*Airport symbol*] (OAG)
MLM	Mound Laboratory, Miamisburg [*AEC*] (MCD)
MLM	Multilayer Metalization (IEEE)
MLM	Multilevel Marketing
MLM	Multilevel Metal (AAEL)
MLM	Multi-Longitudinal Mode (ACRL)
MLM	Multipurpose Lightweight Missile
MLM	Multnomah Literature Ministries [*Publisher*] [*Portland, OR*]
MLMA	Metal Ladder Manufacturers Association (EA)
MLMA	Metal Lath Manufacturers Association [*Later, ML/SFA*]
MLMA	Miners' Lamp Manufacturers' Association [*British*] (BI)
MLMA	Multilevel Multiaccess
MLMBX	Merrill Lynch: Muni Bond: Insured Cl.A [*Mutual fund ticker symbol*] (SG)
MLMGIC98	Merrill Lynch & Co. [*Associated Press*] (SAG)
MLMI	Microleague Multimedia [*NASDAQ symbol*] (TTSB)
MLMI	Microleague Multimedia, Inc. [*NASDAQ symbol*] (SAG)
MLMIA	Multi-Level Marketing International Association [*Irvine, CA*] (EA)
ml/min/m²	Milliliters per Minute per Square Meter (CPH)
MLMIW	Microleague Multimedia Wrrt [*NASDAQ symbol*] (TTSB)
MLML	Moss Landing Marine Laboratories [*San Jose State University*] [*Research center*] (RCD)
MLMS	Member of the London Mathematical Society
MLMS	Multipurpose Lightweight Missile System
MLMTT	Marxism-Leninism-Mao Tse-Tung Thought [*Ideologies guiding the New People's Army, a guerrilla movement in the Philippines*]
MLN	Management List - Navy (NVT)
MLN	Melilla [*Spain*] [*Airport symbol*] (OAG)
MLN	Membranous Lupus Nephropathy [*Medicine*] (STED)
MLN	Mesenteric Lymph Node [*Medicine*] (STED)
MLN	Metropolitan Library Network [*Library network*]
MLN	Mid-Lateral Nerve
MLN	Milan Resources & Development [*Vancouver Stock Exchange symbol*]
MLN	Minuteman Library Network [*Information service or system*] (IT)
MLN	MLN (Modern Language Notes) [*A publication*] (BRI)
MLN	Mouvement de Liberation Nationale [*National Liberation Movement*] [*Burkina Faso Banned, 1974*] [*Political party*]
MLN	Movimiento de Liberacion Nacional [*National Liberation Movement*] [*Guatemala*] [*Political party*] (PPW)
MLN	Movimiento de Liberacion Nacional [*National Liberation Movement*] [*Uruguay*] [*Political party*]
MLN	Multiple Length Number
MLN	Mulungwishi [*Zaire*] [*Seismograph station code, US Geological Survey*] (SEIS)
MLN	Museum Loan Network
MLNC	Missouri Library Network Corp. [*Information service or system*] (IID)
MlndW	Maximum Landing Weight [*Aviation*] (DA)
MLNG	Melange
MLNik 97	Merrill Lynch & Co. [*Associated Press*] (SAG)
MLNIS	Modified Atlantic Naval Intelligence Summary (MCD)
MLNM	Millennium Pharmaceuticals [*NASDAQ symbol*] (TTSB)
MLNM	Millennium Pharmaceuticals, Inc. [*NASDAQ symbol*] (SAG)
MLNR	Milliner (WGA)
mLNRc	Mouse Lymph Node Homing Receptor
MLNS	Ministry of Labour and National Service [*British World War II*]
MLNS	Mucocutaneous Lymph Node Syndrome [*Medicine*] (STED)
MLNYX	Merrill Lynch: N.Y. Muni Bond Cl.B [*Mutual fund ticker symbol*] (SG)
MLO	Main Lube Oil [*System*] (NRCH)
MLO	Manipulative Learning Operation [*in laboratory work*]
MLO	Manned Lunar Orbiter [*NASA*]
MLO	Marxisten-Leninisten Oesterreichs [*Marxists-Leninists of Austria*] [*Political party*] (PPE)
MLO	Master Layout Original (MSA)
MLO	Mauna Loa Observatory [*Hawaii*] [*National Weather Service*]
MLO	Mechanized Letter Office (DCTA)
MLO	Media Liaison Officer
MLO	Mesiolinguo-Occlusal [*Dentistry*]
MLO	Military Landing Officer
MLO	Military Liaison Officer [*British*]
MLO	Milos [*Greece*] [*Airport symbol*] (OAG)
MLO	Missile Launch Officer (AAG)
MLO	Missile Lift-Off (AAG)
MLO	M. L. Cass Petroleum [*Vancouver Stock Exchange symbol*]
MLO	Mortgage Loan Officer [*Banking*] (TBD)
MLO	Movement Liaison Officer (NATG)
MLO	Mycoplasma-Like Organisms [*Microbiology*]
MLOG	Microlog Corp. [*NASDAQ symbol*] (NQ)
MLOI	Master List of Outstanding Items [*Military*] (DNAB)
MLon	Richard Salter Storrs Library, Longmeadow, MA [*Library symbol Library of Congress*] (LCLS)
MLonHi	Longmeadow Historical Society, Longmeadow, MA [*Library symbol Library of Congress*] (LCLS)
MLOR	Maintenance/Logistics Observer Report
MLow	Lowell City Library, Lowell, MA [*Library symbol Library of Congress*] (LCLS)
MLowT	Lowell Technological Institute, Lowell, MA [*Library symbol Library of Congress Obsolete*] (LCLS)
MLowTC	Lowell State College, Lowell, MA [*Library symbol Library of Congress Obsolete*] (LCLS)
MLowU	University of Lowell, Lowell, MA [*Library symbol Library of Congress*] (LCLS)
MLowU-N	University of Lowell - North Campus, Alumni/Lydon Memorial Library, Lowell, MA [*Library symbol Library of Congress*] (LCLS)
MLP	Machine Language Program [*Computer science*]
MLP	Major Late Promoter [*Genetics*]
MLP	Major Late Promotor [*Biochemistry*]
MLP	Malabang [*Philippines*] [*Airport symbol*] (OAG)
MLP	Malaspina [*Alaska*] [*Seismograph station code, US Geological Survey*] (SEIS)
MLP	Malfunction-Linked People
MLP	Malta Labor Party [*Political party*] (PPW)
MLP	Master Limited Partnership
MLP	Master Logistics Plan (AABC)
MLP	Mauritius Labor Party [*Political party*] (PPW)
MLP	Maximum Likelihood Program
MLP	Mentoleva Posterior [*A fetal position*] [*Obstetrics*]
MLP	Mesa Limited Partnership (EFIS)
MLP	Mesiolinguopulpal [*Dentistry*]
MLP	Metal Lath and Plaster [*Technical drawings*]
MLP	Michigan Law and Practice [*A publication*] (DLA)
MLP	Microsomal Lipoprotein [*Immunochemistry*]
MLP	Millipore Corp., Bedford, MA [*OCLC symbol*] (OCLC)
MLP	Minimum Latency Programming
MLP	Mirror Landing Procedures (MCD)
MLP	Mobile Launcher Platform [*NASA*] (NASA)
MLP	Modified Longest Path
MLP	Mortgage Loan Partnership [*Investment term*]
MLP	Movimiento de Liberacion del Pueblo [*People's Liberation Movement*] [*El Salvador*] [*Political party*] (PD)
MLP	Movimiento de Liberacion Proletaria [*Proletarian Liberation Movement*] [*Mexico Political party*]
MLP	Mullan Pass, ID [*Location identifier FAA*] (FAAL)
MLP	Multi-Layered Packaging (PDAA)
MLP	Multi-Layer Perceptron (AAEL)
MLP	Multilevel Precedence
MLP	Multilevel Procedure (MCD)
MLP	Multilevel Programmer
MLP	Multilink Procedure [*Computer science*] (TNIG)
MLP	Multilink Protocol [*Telecommunications*] (ACRL)
MLP	Multiple Line Printing (CMD)
MLP	Multi-Step Products [*Toronto Stock Exchange symbol*]
MLPA	Modified Link Pack Area (MCD)
MLPC	Management-Labor Policy Committee
MLPC	Mouvement de Liberation du Peuple Centrafricain [*Movement for the Liberation of the Central African People*] (PD)
MLPC	Multilayer Printed Circuit
MLPCB	Machine Language Printed Circuit Boards [*Computer science*] (IEEE)
MLPD	Maximum Likelihood Predictive Density [*Statistics*]
ML-PDL	Malignant Lymphoma, Poorly Differentiated Lymphocytic [*Medicine*] (STED)
MLPED	Mobile Launcher Pedestal [*NASA*] (NASA)
MLPF	Miniature Low Pass Filter
MLPFS	Merrill Lynch, Pierce, Fenner & Smith [*of Merrill Lynch & Co., Inc.*] [*Stockbrokers Wall Street slang name: "Thundering Herd"*]
MLPNPP	Mobile Low-Power Nuclear Power Plant
MLPP	Multilevel Precedence and Preemption [*Telecommunications*] (TEL)
ML-PPP	Multilink Point-to-Point Protocol [*Telecommunications*] (ACRL)
MLPS	Multilingual Publishing Software
MLPS	Myxoid Liposarcoma [*Genetics*]
MLP USA	Marxist-Leninist Party of the USA (EA)
MLPWB	Multilayer Printed-Wiring Board (IEEE)
MLQ	Malabar Law Quarterly [*A publication*] (DLA)
MLQ	Malalaua [*Papua New Guinea*] [*Airport symbol*] (OAG)
MLR	Leaf Rapids Public Library, Manitoba [*Library symbol National Library of Canada*] (NLC)
MLR	Magnetic Latching Relay (MCD)
MLR	Mailer
MLR	Main Line of Resistance
M/LR	Maintenance Loop Recorder (MCD)
MLR	Malayan Law Reports [*1950-54*] [*A publication*] (DLA)
MLR	Manitoba Law Reports [*Canada*] [*A publication*] (DLA)
MLR	Marginal Lending Rate [*Finance*]
MLR	Marine Life Resources [*Program*]
MLR	Maryland Law Record [*A publication*] (DLA)
MLR	Master-Locating RADAR (AABC)
MLR	Matched Logistic Regression [*Statistics*]
MLR	Mauritius Law Reporter [*A publication*] (DLA)

MLR............	MDM [*Manipulator Deployment Mechanism*] Launch Right [*NASA*]
MLR............	Mean Length Response (DMAA)
MLR............	Mean Lethal Radius
MLR............	Mechanized Line Records [*Later, LMOS*] [*Bell System*]
MLR............	Medium-Lift Requirement [*Helicopter/VSTOL*] [*Marine Corps*] (DOMA)
MLR............	Memory Lockout Register [*Computer science*]
MLR............	Message Log Report (AAEL)
MLR............	Meston Lake Resources, Inc. [*Toronto Stock Exchange symbol Vancouver Stock Exchange symbol*]
MLR............	Middle Latency Response [*Medicine*]
MLR............	Miller Industries [*NYSE symbol*] (TTSB)
MLR............	Millersburg, OH [*Location identifier FAA*] (FAAL)
MLR............	Minimum Latency Routine
MLR............	Minimum Lending Rate
MLR............	Minnesota Legislative Reference Library, St. Paul, MN [*OCLC symbol*] (OCLC)
MLR............	Missile Launch Response [*Navy*] (CAAL)
MLR............	Mixed Leukocyte Reaction [*Analytical biochemistry*]
MLR............	Mixed Lymphocyte [*or Leukocyte*] Reaction [*or Response*] [*Immunology*]
MLR............	Modern Language Review [*A publication*] (BRI)
MLR............	Monodisperse Latex Reactor
MLR............	Monotone Likelihood Ratio [*Statistics*]
MLR............	Monthly Letter Report
MLR............	Montreal Law Reports [*A publication*] (DLA)
MLR............	Mortar Locating RADAR (MCD)
MLR............	MPM Launch Right (MCD)
MLR............	Multi-Disperse Latex Reactor
MLR............	Multilayer Resist [*Lithography*]
MLR............	Multilevel Resist [*For microlithography*]
MLR............	Multiple Linear Regression [*Mathematics*]
MLR............	Multiple Location Risk [*Insurance*]
MLR............	Multiply and Round
MLR............	Muntele Rosu [*Romania*] [*Seismograph station code, US Geological Survey*] (SEIS)
MLR............	Muzzle-Loading Rifle
MLRA...........	Major Land Resource Area [*USDA topographic characterization*]
MLRA...........	Marriage Law Reform Association [*British*]
MLRA...........	Multivariate Linear Regression Analysis [*Advertising marketing*]
MLRB...........	Master Logistics Review Board (AAG)
MLRB...........	Mutual Loss Research Bureau [*Later, Property Loss Research Bureau*] (EA)
MLRC...........	Mallon Resources [*NASDAQ symbol*] (TTSB)
MLRC...........	Mallon Resources Corp. [*NASDAQ symbol*] (CTT)
MLRC...........	Master Logistics Review Committee (AAG)
MLRC...........	Mickey Leland National Urban Air Toxics Research Center (COE)
MLRC...........	Minor League Research Committee (EA)
MLRC...........	Multilevel Rail Car
MLRCA	Mini Lop Rabbit Club of America (EA)
MLR CS	Montreal Law Reports, Superior Court [*Canada*] [*A publication*] (DLA)
MLRG	Marine Life Research Group [*Scripps Institution of Oceanography*]
MLRG	Muzzle-Loading Rifled Gun
MLRHR........	Master of Labor Relations and Human Resources (PGP)
MLRP..........	Marine Corps Long-Range Plans
MLRP..........	Marine Life Research Program
MLRP..........	Minuteman Long Range Plan [*Telecommunications*] (LAIN)
MLRQB........	Montreal Law Reports, Queen's Bench [*A publication*] (DLA)
MLRS..........	Manual Launch - RADAR Search
MLRS..........	McDonald Laser Ranging System [*For observations*]
MLRS..........	Monodisperse Latex Reactor System
MLRS..........	Multiple Launch Rocket System [*DoD*] (MCD)
MLRSC	Montreal Law Reports, Superior Court [*Canada*] [*A publication*] (DLA)
MLRS ER	Multiple Launch Rocket System Extended Range Rocket [*Military*]
MLRS-PGM...	Multiple Launch Rocket System Precision Guided Munitions (RDA)
MLRS-TGW...	Multiple Launch Rocket System Terminally Guided Warhead
MLRTP........	Multileaving Remote Terminal Processor [*Computer science*] (MHDI)
MLRus98	Merrill Lynch & Co. [*Associated Press*] (SAG)
MLRV..........	Manned Lunar Roving Vehicle [*NASA*] (PDAA)
MLRV..........	Myrobalan Latent Ringspot Virus [*Plant pathology*]
MLS............	Machine Literature Searching [*Computer science*] (DIT)
MLS............	Mac Library System [*Computer Advanced Software Products - CASPR*] [*Cupertino, CA*] [*Information service or system*] (IID)
MLS............	Macrolide/Lincosamide/Streptogramine (DB)
MLS............	Magnetically-Linked Solenoid (MCD)
MLS............	Maintenance Loading Sheet (MCD)
MLS............	Major League Soccer
MLS............	Mall Airways, Inc. [*ICAO designator*] (FAAC)
MLS............	Manistique & Lake Superior R. R. [*AAR code*]
MLS............	Manned Lunar Surface [*NASA*]
MLS............	Master Laboratory Station
MLS............	Master of Legal Studies (GAGS)
MLS............	Master of Liberal Studies (GAGS)
MLS............	Master of Librarianship
MLS............	Master of Library Science
MLS............	Master of Library Services (PGP)
MLS............	Master of Library Studies
MLS............	Master of Life Science (GAGS)
MLS............	Maximized LOD [*Logarithm of the Odds*] Score [*Statistics*]
MLS............	Maximum Life-Span
MLS............	Maxwell Library Systems [*Information service or system*] (IID)
MLS............	Mean Lifespan (AAMN)
MLS............	Mechanical Limit Stop
MLS............	Mechanical Limit Switch
MLS............	Median Life Span [*Oncology*] (DAVI)
MLS............	Median Longitudinal Section
MLS............	Medium Life Span
MLS............	Medium Long Shot [*A photograph or motion picture sequence taken from a relatively great distance*]
MLS............	Metal Slitting
MLS............	Metropolitan Libraries Section [*Public Library Association*]
MLS............	Microwave Landing System [*Aviation*]
MLS............	Microwave Limb Sounder
MLS............	Microwave Line Stretcher
MLS............	Middle Lobe Syndrome [*Medicine*] (STED)
MLS............	Miles City [*Montana*] [*Airport symbol*] (OAG)
MLS............	Miles City, MT [*Location identifier FAA*] (FAAL)
MLS............	Military Labor Service
MLS............	Military Sealift Command
ML/S...........	Milliliters per Second
MLS............	Mills (MCD)
MLS............	Mills Corp. [*NYSE symbol*] (SAG)
MLS............	Miniature Linguistic Systems
MLS............	Minimum Launch Speed [*British military*] (DMA)
MLS............	Minimum Legal Size [*Pisciculture*]
MLS............	Minor Lymphocyte Stimulating [*Genetics*]
MLS............	Missile-Launching System (NG)
MLS............	Missile Lift System (AAG)
MLS............	Missile Location System (IEEE)
MLS............	Mississippi County Library System, Blytheville, AR [*Inactive*] [*OCLC symbol*] (OCLC)
MLS............	Mixed Language System (PDAA)
MLS............	Mobile Library Service [*British*]
MLS............	Mobile Logistic Support (CINC)
MLS............	MOL [*Manned Orbiting Laboratory*] Launch Site (MCD)
MLS............	Moulis [*France*] [*Seismograph station code, US Geological Survey*] (SEIS)
MLS............	Movimento per le Liberta Statuarie [*Movement for Statutory Liberty*] [*Sanmarinese*] (PPE)
MLS............	Movimiento de Liberacion Sebta [*Ceuta Liberation Movement*] [*Spain*] (PD)
MLS............	Multifrequency LASER Sounding (MCD)
MLS............	Multilanguage System [*Computer science*] (IEEE)
MLS............	Multilayered Structure [*Botany*]
MLS............	Multi-Layer Steel [*Engine gaskets*] [*Automotive engineering*]
MLS............	Multilevel Security (MCD)
MLS............	Multiline Selection [*Asahi Glass of Japan*]
MLS............	Multiparameter Light Scattering [*Physics*]
MLS............	Multiple Listing Service [*Real estate*]
MLS............	Music Learning System [*Trademark*]
MLS............	Myelomonocytic Leukemia, Subacute (MAE)
MLSA...........	Ministry of Labour Staff Association [*British*]
ML SAI99....	Merrill Lynch & Co. [*Associated Press*] (SAG)
MLSB...........	Major League Scouting Bureau [*Baseball*]
MLSB...........	Member of the London School Board
MLSB...........	Migrating Long Spike Burst (DMAA)
ML Sc..........	Master of Library Science
MLSC..........	Member of the London Society of Compositors
MLSC..........	Micronesian Legal Services Corp. (EA)
MLS/CP.......	Microwave Landing System / Curved Path [*Aviation*]
MLSE..........	Mechanical Launch Support Equipment [*NASA*] (KSC)
MLSF..........	Mobile Logistic Support Forces (MCD)
ML/SFA.......	Metal Lath/Steel Framing Association Division of National Association of Architectural Metal Manufactureres (EA)
MLSG..........	Mobile Logistics Support Group (NVT)
MLSI...........	Mulitple Line Scan Imaging (DMAA)
MLSI...........	Multilevel Large-Scale Integration
MLSIT.........	Master of Library Science and International Technology (PGP)
MLSJ..........	Macquarie Law Students Journal [*A publication*]
MLSK..........	Master Lock, Skeleton Key
MLSO..........	Mode-Locked Surface-Acoustic Wave Oscillator [*Telecommunications*] (TEL)
MLSOP	Movement for the Liberation of Soa Tome and Principe [*Political party*]
MLSP..........	Master of Law and Social Policy (GAGS)
MLSP..........	Multiple-Link Satellite Program
MLSP97.......	Merrill Lynch & Co., Inc. [*Associated Press*] (SAG)
MLSP98.......	Merrill Lynch & Co., Inc. [*Associated Press*] (SAG)
M-L-S-R......	Missing, Lost, Stolen, or Recovered [*Government property*] (DNAB)
MLSR..........	Molder, Ship Repair [*Navy rating*]
MLSRC........	Molder, Ship Repair, Cupola Tender [*Navy rating*]
MLSRF........	Molder, Ship Repair, Foundryman [*Navy rating*]
MLSRM........	Molder, Ship Repair, Molder [*Navy rating*]
MLSS..........	Mechanized Letter Sorting System [*Hong Kong Post Office*]
MLSS..........	Military and Federal Specifications and Standards [*Information Handling Services*] [*Information service or system*] (CRD)
MLSS..........	Mixed-Liquor Suspended Solid [*Water pollution*]
MLST..........	Medico-Legal Society of Tasmania [*Australia*]
MLST..........	Merrill Language Screening Test [*Educational test*]
MLST..........	Milstead [*AAR code*]
MLSTP.........	Movimento de Libertacao de Sao Tome e Principe [*Movement for the Liberation of Sao Tome and Principe*] [*Portugal*] (PPW)
ML SYP98 ...	Merrill Lynch & Co. [*Associated Press*] (SAG)
MLT............	Madras Law Times [*India*] [*A publication*] (DLA)
MLT............	Magnetic Levitation Transportation
MLT............	Magnetic Local Time
MLT............	Malta [*ANSI three-letter standard code*] (CNC)
mlt.............	Maltese [*MARC language code Library of Congress*] (LCCP)
MLT............	Manned Lunar Test [*NASA*] (KSC)

MLT	Manufacturing Lead Time
MLT	Mass Loaded Transducer
MLT	Master Library Tape [*Computer science*]
MLT	Master of Law and Taxation
MLT	Maximum Lethal Time [*of radiation exposure*] (DEN)
MLT	Mean Latency Time (DB)
MLT	Mean Length per Turn
MLT	Mean Life Time (NATG)
MLT	Mean Logistical Time (IEEE)
MLT	Mean Low Tide [*Tides and currents*]
MLT	Mechanized Line Testing [*Telecommunications*] (TEL)
MLT	Mechanized Loop Testing (MCD)
MLT	Median Lethal Time (DB)
MLT	Medical Laboratory Technician [*or Technologist*]
MLT	Medium Level Tripod [*British military*] (DMA)
MLT	Melatonin
MLT	Mentolaeva Transverse [*A fetal position*] [*Obstetrics*] (AAMN)
MLT	Microlayer Transistor
MLT	Millinocket, ME [*Location identifier FAA*] (FAAL)
MLT	Misallat [*Egypt*] [*Geomagnetic observatory code*]
MLT	Mitel Corp. [*NYSE symbol Toronto Stock Exchange symbol*] (SPSG)
MLT	Mixing-Length Theory [*Physics of convection*] [*Chemical engineering*]
MLT	Mobile Laboratory Table
MLT	Mobile Launch Tower
MLT	Modulated Lapped Transform [*Telecommunications*]
MLT	Muexins-Length Theory
MLTA	Multiple Line Terminal Adapter [*Computer science*] (BUR)
MLT-AD	Medical Laboratory Technology-Associate Degree
MLT (AMT)	Medical Laboratory Technician (American Medical Technologists) (DAVI)
MLT(ASCP)	Medical Laboratory Technician (American Society of Clinical Pathologists) (DMAA)
MLTC	Mixed Lymphocyte-Tumor Culture [*Immunology*]
MltcPrt	Multicanal Participacoes [*Associated Press*] (SAG)
ML Tech01	Merrill Lynch & Co. [*Associated Press*] (SAG)
MLTF	Major Late Transcription Factor [*Genetics*]
MLTF	Military Law Task Force (EA)
MLTG	Melting
MLTG	Missile Launch Tube Group
MLTI	Mixed Lymphocyte Target Interaction (DMAA)
MLTI	Mixed Lymphocyte-Tumor [*Cell*] Interaction [*Immunology*]
ML/TL	Mucrones Length to Total Body Length Ratio [*Of Crustacea*]
MLTLVL	Melting Level [*NWS*] (FAAC)
MltmdG	Multimedia Games, Inc. [*Associated Press*] (SAG)
MLTMS	Multileg Tanker Mooring System (MCD)
MLTN	Molten Metal Technology [*NASDAQ symbol*] (TTSB)
MLTN	Molten Metal Technology, Inc. [*NASDAQ symbol*] (SAG)
MLTP	Ministers Leadership Training Program [*Defunct*] (EA)
MLTPL	Multiplane
MLTRY	Military
MLTSL	Multiple Sail [*Navy*] (NVT)
MLTU	Missile Loop Test Unit
MLTY	Military (MDG)
MLU	Major League Umpires Association
MLU	Malka Resources Ltd. [*Vancouver Stock Exchange symbol*]
MLU	Mean Length of Utterance [*Linguistics*]
MLU	Memory Loading Unit [*of FADAC*] [*Military*]
MLU	Memory Logic Unit [*Computer science*]
MLU	Mid-Life Update
MLU	Miscellaneous Live Unit [*Military*] (AFM)
MLU	Mobile Laundry Unit
MLU	Mobile Living Unit [*Mobile home*]
MLU	Monroe [*Louisiana*] [*Airport symbol*] (OAG)
MLU	Monroe, LA [*Location identifier FAA*] (FAAL)
MLU	Montlucon Air Service [*France ICAO designator*] (FAAC)
MLU	Multiple Logical Unit
MLUA	Major League Umpires Association (EA)
MLURI	Macaulay Land Use Research Institute, Aberdeen [*British*] (IRUK)
MLUS	Merrill Lynch & Co. [*Associated Press*] (SAG)
ML/USA	Mailing List User and Supplier Association [*Defunct*] (EA)
MLV	Air Moldova International, SA [*FAA designator*] (FAAC)
MLV	Magnetic Levitation Vehicle (BARN)
MLV	Main LOX [*Liquid Oxygen*] Valve [*NASA*] (KSC)
MLV	Malvaux [*France*] [*Seismograph station code, US Geological Survey*] (SEIS)
MLV	Matrix Light Valve
MLV	Maximum Lung Volume [*Physiology*]
MLV	McDonnell Launch Vehicle [*McDonnell Douglas Corp.*] (MCD)
MLV	Medium Launch Vehicle
MLV	Membrane Light Valve [*Optics*]
MLV	Memory Loader Verifier (DWSG)
MLV	Mobile Launch Vehicle [*Air Force*]
MLV	Modify Logging Versions (AAEL)
MLV	Moloney Leukemia Virus [*Medicine*] (DMAA)
MLV	Mouse Leukemia Virus (MAE)
MLV	Mulberry Latent Virus [*Plant pathology*]
MLV	Multilamellar Large Vesicle [*Pharmacy Biochemistry*]
MLV	Multilamellar Lipid Vesicle (DB)
MLV	Multilaminar Phospholipid Vesicle [*Immunology*]
MLV	Multilaminar Vesicle [*Medicine*] (DMAA)
MLV	Murine Leukemia Virus [*Also, MuLV*]
MLV(A)	Murine Leukemia Virus (Abelson)
MLVDP	Maximum Left Ventricular Developed Pressure [*Cardiology*] (DMAA)
MLV(M)	Murine Leukemia Virus (Moloney)
MLVP	Manned Lunar Vehicle Program [*NASA*] (AAG)
MLVPS	Manual Low-Voltage Power Supply
MLV(R)	Murine Leukemia Virus (Rauscher)
MLVS	Mill Vise
MLVS	Multilevel Voltage Select (MCD)
MLVSS	Mixed-Liquor Volatile Suspended Solids [*Chemical engineering*]
MLVT	Mobile Launch Vehicle Transporter [*Air Force*]
MLW	Madras Law Weekly [*India*] [*A publication*] (DLA)
MLW	Master Warning Light (IAA)
MLW	Maximum Landing Weight [*Aviation*]
MLW	Mean Low Water [*Tides and currents*]
MLW	Medium-Level Radioactive Waste (NUCP)
MLW	Milwaukee [*Wisconsin*] [*Seismograph station code, US Geological Survey Closed*] (SEIS)
MLW	Monrovia [*Liberia*] [*Airport symbol*] (OAG)
MLW	Multiple Logical Windowing [*Computer science*]
MLWA	Maximum Landing Weight Authorized [*Aviation*] (DA)
MLWG	Modern Languages Working Group (AIE)
MLWI	Mean Low-Water Lunitidal Interval [*Tides and currents*]
MLWL	Mail-Well, Inc. [*NASDAQ symbol*] (SAG)
MLWMS	Miscellaneous Liquid Waste Management System (NRCH)
MLWN	Mean Low-Water Neap [*Tides and currents*]
MLWS	Mean Low-Water Spring [*Tides and currents*]
MLWS	Miniature LASER Weapon Simulator (MCD)
MLWS	Minimum Level Water Stand (NATG)
MLX	Malatya [*Turkey*] [*Airport symbol*] (OAG)
MLX	Mauna Loa 2 [*Hawaii*] [*Seismograph station code, US Geological Survey*] (SEIS)
MLX	Merritt Island, Florida [*Spaceflight Tracking and Data Network*] [*NASA*]
MLX	MLX Corp. [*Associated Press*] (SAG)
MLX01	Magnetically-levitated Linear Motor Vehicle
MLXR	MLX Corp. [*NASDAQ symbol*] (SAG)
MLy	Lynn Public Library, Lynn, MA [*Library symbol Library of Congress*] (LCLS)
MLY	Manley Hot Springs [*Alaska*] [*Airport symbol*] (OAG)
MLY	Manley Hot Springs, AK [*Location identifier FAA*] (FAAL)
MLY	Moly Mite Resources [*Vancouver Stock Exchange symbol*]
MLY	Multiply (MDG)
Mly	National Library of Malaysia, Kuala Lumpur, Malaysia [*Library symbol*] [*Library of Congress*] (LCLS)
MlyKA	Arkib Negara [*National Archives of Malaysia*], Federal Government Building, Kuala Lumpur, Malaysia [*Library symbol Library of Congress*] (LCLS)
MlyKgM	Sarawak Museum, Kuching, Malaysia [*Library symbol*] [*Library of Congress*] (LCLS)
MlyKU	University of Malaya, Kuala Lumpur, Malaysia [*Library symbol Library of Congress*] (LCLS)
MlyL	Lynn Public Library, Lynn, MA [*Library symbol*] [*Library of Congress*] (LCLS)
MlyPS	Universiti Sains Malaysia (University of Science, Malaysia), Minden, Penang, Malaysia [*Library symbol Library of Congress*] (LCLS)
MLZ	Melo [*Uruguay*] [*Airport symbol*] (OAG)
MM	Machine Made Paper (DGA)
MM	Machine-Made Snow [*Skiing*]
MM	Machinery
MM	Machinist's Mate [*Navy rating*]
M/m	Made Merchandise (EBF)
MM	Made Merchantable
MM	Maelzel's Metronome [*Music*]
MM	Magister Melendus [*Flourished, 1188-1209*] [*Authority cited in pre-1607 legal work*] (DSA)
MM	Main Memory
mm	Main Memory (NAKS)
MM	Main Module (NAKS)
MM	Main Module (NASA)
MM	Maintenance Manual
MM	Maintenance Monitor
MM	Majesties
MM	Major Medical [*Insurance*]
MM	Major Mode (KSC)
mm	Major Mode (NAKS)
MM	Malignant Melanoma [*Oncology*]
mm	Malta [*MARC country of publication code Library of Congress*] (LCCP)
MM	Management Manual (KSC)
M/M	Man/Machine
MM	Manmade [*Diamonds*]
MM	Man-Month (AFM)
mm	Man-Month (NAKS)
MM	Manual Maximal Displacement [*Sports medicine*]
MM	Manual Morse (MCD)
MM	Manufacturing Management
MM	Manufacturing Manual (AAG)
MM	Manufacturing Methods (AAEL)
MM	Marilyn Monroe [*American motion picture star, 1926-1962*]
MM	Mariner Mars Project [*NASA*]
MM	Maritime Mobile
MM	Mark Mason (ROG)
MM	Mark Master [*Freemasonry*]
MM	Marshall Manual (SSD)
MM	Marshall-Marchetti Procedure [*Medicine*] (MAE)
MM	Martha Movement (EA)
M-M	Martin Marietta Corp.
MM	Martyres [*Martyrs*]

mm	Maryknoll Fathers, Catholic Foreign Mission Society of America (TOCD)
MM	Maryknoll Missioners [*Catholic Foreign Mission Society*] [*Roman Catholic religious order*]
MM	Maryknoll Sisters of St. Dominic (TOCD)
MM	Mass Memory (NASA)
mm	Mass Memory (NAKS)
MM	Massorah Magna [*or Massora Magna*] (BJA)
MM	Master Mason [*Freemasonry*]
MM	Master Mechanic
MM	Master Monitor
MM	Master of Management
MM	Master of Mathematics (GAGS)
MM	Master of Medicine
MM	Master of Ministry (PGP)
MM	Master of Modern Studies (PGP)
MM	Master of Music (GAGS)
MM	Masters
MM	Materials Management [*Nuclear energy*]
MM	Materials Measurement (IEEE)
MM	Materia Medica (ROG)
MM	Mathematics Model
MM	Math Model (KSC)
mm	Math Model (NAKS)
MM	Matrimonium [*Matrimony*] [*Latin*]
M/M	Maximum and Minimum (KSC)
MM	Measure for Measure [*Shakespearean work*]
MM	Mechanical Maintenance
MM	Medal for Merit [*Military decoration*]
MM	Medial Malleolus [*Anatomy*] (AAMN)
MM	Medial Meniscus [*Anatomy*]
MM	Median Method [*Mathematics*]
MM	Medical Man (ROG)
mm----	Mediterranean Sea and Area [*MARC geographic area code Library of Congress*] (LCCP)
MM	Medium Maintenance
MM	Med Mera [*And So Forth*] [*Latin*] (ILCA)
MM	Megamega [*A prefix meaning multiplied by one trillion*] (DEN)
MM	Megameter
MM	Melanotic Melanoma [*Medicine*] (DB)
MM	Melaveh Malka (BJA)
MM	Melbourne Marathon [*Australia*]
MM	Melody Maker [*A publication*] (WDAA)
MM	Membranes [*Leaves of parchment*] (ROG)
MM	Memory Module (MCD)
MM	Memory Multiplexer [*Computer science*] (MDG)
MM	Mercantile Marine
MM	Merchant Marine
MM	Mesoscale Model [*Marine science*] (OSRA)
MM	Messageries Maritimes [*Forwarding agents*] [*French*]
MM	Messieurs [*Plural of Mister*] [*French*]
MM	Metal Manufacture [*Department of Employment*] [*British*]
MM	Metered Market Service [*A. C. Nielsen Co.*] (NTCM)
MM	Methadone Maintenance [*Medicine*] (DHP)
MM	Methylmalonyl-CoA Mutase [*An enzyme*]
MM	Methyl Mercaptan [*Organic chemistry*]
MM	Methyl Methacrylate [*Also, MMA*] [*Organic chemistry*]
MM	Metronome Mark (ROG)
MM	Microfilm
MM	Micromanipulator [*Instrumentation*]
MM	Micromodule (AAG)
MM	Midcourse Mode [*Navy*] (CAAL)
MM	Middle Manager
MM	Middle Marker [*in an instrument landing system*]
MM	Middle Minoan [*Archaeology*] (BJA)
MM	Military Medal [*World War I nickname: Maconochie Medal*] [*British*]
MM	Military Medicine
MM	Milla Wa-Milla (BJA)
mm	Millimeter [*Metric*]
MM	Millimeter (DFIT)
mM	Millimole [*Mass*]
mm	Million (WDMC)
MM	Minelayer Fleet [*Navy symbol Obsolete*]
MM	Minimal Medium [*Microbiology*]
M/M	Minimum/Maximum
MM	Minister of Munitions [*British World War II*]
MM	Ministry of Mines [*British*] (DAS)
MM	Mint Mark [*Numismatics*]
MM	Minuteman [*Missile*] (AABC)
Mm	Misch Metal [*A commercial mixture of rare earth metals*]
MM	Mismated [*Merchandising slang*]
MM	Missile Master [*Fire direction and coordination system*]
MM	Missile Minder (MCD)
MM	Missile Motion
mm	Mission Manager [*NASA*] (NAKS)
MM	Mission Manager [*NASA/USAF*]
MM	Mission Module
MM	Mission Monitor (MCD)
M/M	Mister or Mrs. [*In addresses*] [*Correspondence*]
MM	Mistress of Music
MM	Mitochondrial Myopathy [*Medicine*]
mm	Mixed Media (VRA)
MM	Mixed Monitor [*External Tocotransducer and internal scalp exectrode*] [*Neonatology*] [*Obstetrics*] (DAVI)
MM	Moderation Management
MM	Modern Motor [*A publication*]
MM	Modification or Maintenance [*Aircraft*]
MM	Modified Mercalli [*Scale measuring earthquake intensity*] [*Seismology*]
MM	Modigliani-Miller Propositions [*Corporate finance*] (ECON)
MM	Mois Maconnique [*Masonic Month*] [*Freemasonry*] [*French*]
MM	Molecular Mechanics [*Physical chemistry*]
MM	Money Market [*Investment term*]
MM	Mononeuritis Multiplex [*Inflammation of nerves*] [*Medicine*] (TAD)
MM	Monostable Multivibrator [*Electronics*] (OA)
MM	Monthly Meetings [*Quakers*]
MM	Morality in Media (EA)
MM	Moral Majority [*An association*] (EA)
MM	Morbidity and Mortality [*Medicine*] (DMAA)
MM	Morel-Morgagni [*Syndrome*] [*Medicine*] (DB)
MM	More Moderate Service [*Automotive engineering*]
MM	Morrison-Maierle, Inc. (EFIS)
MM	Moslem Mosque (EA)
MM	Mothers Matter [*Commercial firm*] (EA)
MM	Motor Magnet
MM	Motor Maintenance [*Army*]
MM	Motor Maintenance Aptitude Area [*Army*]
MM	Motor Meal [*Medicine*] (MEDA)
MM	Motor Mechanic [*British military*] (DMA)
MM	Mould Made Paper (DGA)
MM	Mouse Myoblast [*Cell line*]
MM	Moving Magnet [*Stereo equipment*]
MM	Mozambique Metical [*Monetary unit*] (IMH)
M/M	Mr. & Mrs. (VRA)
MM	Much Married [*Slang*]
MM	Mucous Membrane
MM	Multi-Media (OICC)
MM	Multimeter
MM	Multimode
MM	Multiple Master [*Computer science*] (CDE)
MM	Multiple Myeloma [*Medicine*]
MM	Multipolar Magnetic [*Sun*] (DICI)
MM	Munitions Maintenance (MCD)
mm	Murmur [*Cardiology*] (DAVI)
MM	Muscles [*Medicine*]
MM	Muscularis Mucosa [*Medicine*] (MAE)
MM	Museum Media [*A publication*]
MM	Musical Majority [*Defunct*] (EA)
MM	Mutatis Mutandis [*With the Necessary Changes*] [*Latin*]
MM	Mutual Risk Management [*NYSE symbol*] (SPSG)
MM	Myanmar [*Internet country code*]
MM	Myeloid Metaplasia [*Medicine*]
MM	Myelomeningocele [*Medicine*]
MM	Myriameters [*Metric system*] (ROG)
MM	SAM Colombia [*Airline flight code*] (ODBW)
MM	Sociedad Aeronautica Medellin [*ICAO designator*] (AD)
MM	Xaverian Missionary Society of Mary, Inc. [*Roman Catholic women's religious order*]
MM1	Machinist's Mate, First Class [*Navy rating*]
MM2	Machinist's Mate, Second Class [*Navy rating*]
MM²	Square Millimeter
MM³	Cubic Millimeter
MM3	Machinist's Mate, Third Class [*Navy rating*]
MM4	Mesoscale Meteorological Model-Version 4 [*Marine science*] (OSRA)
MM5	Mesoscale Model Version 5 [*Marine science*] [*Pennsylvania State University*] (OSRA)
MMA	Average Male Mass
MMA	MacRobertson Miller Airline Services [*Australia*]
MMA	Magnetotactic Multicellular Aggregate [*Microbiology*]
MMA	Major Machine Accessory (MCD)
MMA	Major Maintenance Availability (MHDB)
MMA	Malmo [*Sweden*] [*Airport symbol*] (OAG)
MMA	Management and Marketing Abstracts [*PIRA*] [*Bibliographic database*] [*British*]
MMA	Maneuver Motor Array (MCD)
MMA	Manual Metal Arc [*Welding*]
MMA	Maria Mitchell Association (EA)
MMA	Marine Mammal Act [*1972*] (MSC)
MMA	Marine Maritime Academy
MMA	Marine Motor Association (ROG)
MMA	Married Man's Allowance [*Taxes*] [*British*]
MMA	Massachusetts Maritime Academy [*Buzzards Bay*]
MMA	Massachusetts Maritime Academy, Captain C. H. Hurley Library, Buzzards Bay, MA [*OCLC symbol*] (OCLC)
MMA	Massachusetts Military Academy
MMA	Master of Management and Administration, Cranfield Institute of Technology [*British*] (DBQ)
MMA	Master of Manpower Administration (GAGS)
MMA	Master of Marine Affairs (GAGS)
MMA	Master of Media Arts (PGP)
MMA	Master of Medical Art (GAGS)
MMA	Master of Municipal Administration
MMA	Master of Musical Art (GAGS)
MMA	Master of Musical Arts
MMA	Masters of Medicine [*A publication*]
MMA	Mastitis-Metritis-Agalactia Syndrome [*Medicine*] (DMAA)
MMA	Material Manufacturing Authorization (AAG)
MMA	Materials Marketing Associates [*Hartford, CT*] (EA)
MMA	Maymac Petroleum Corp. [*Vancouver Stock Exchange symbol*]
MMA	Mazda Motors of America

MMA............ Medical Management Analysis System (HCT)
MMA............ Medical Marketing Association (NTPA)
MMA............ Medical Materiel Account [*Military*] (AABC)
MMA............ Medical Mutual Aid (GNE)
MMA............ Memory-to-Memory Adapter [*Computer science*]
MMA............ Merchandise Marks Act (ROG)
MMA............ Merchants and Manufacturers Association
MMA............ Mercy Medical Airlift (EA)
MMA............ Merrill's Marauders Association (EA)
MMA............ Meter Manufacturers' Association (IAA)
MMA............ Methylmalonic Acid [*Organic chemistry*]
MMA............ Methylmalonic Acidemia [*Medicine*]
MMA............ Methyl Methacrylate [*Also, MM*] [*Organic chemistry*]
MMA............ Metro Manila Airways International, Inc. [*Philippines*] [*ICAO designator*] (FAAC)
MMA............ Metropolitan Magazine Association [*Later, Magazine Publishers Association*] (EA)
MMA............ Metropolitan Museum of Art [*New York*] (BJA)
MMA............ Microcomputer Managers Association (HGAA)
MMA............ Microminiature Mixer Amplifier
MMA............ Microtome Manufacturers Association [*British*] (DBA)
MMA............ Middle Meningeal Artery [*Neuroanatomy*]
MMA............ Military Medical Academy [*Armed forces medical college*]
MMA............ Millimeter Array [*Astronomy*]
MMA............ Minelayer Auxiliary Ship [*Navy symbol Obsolete*]
MMA............ Mirror Manufacturers Association
MMA............ Missile Maintenance Area (AAG)
MMA............ Mitomycin A [*Antineoplastic drug*]
MMA............ Modified Motorcycle Association
MMA............ Monomethylamine [*Organic chemistry*]
MMA............ Monomethyl Arsonic Acid [*Organic chemistry*]
MMA............ Monorail Manufacturers Association (EA)
MMA............ Monovalent Metal Azide [*Inorganic chemistry*]
MMA............ Mothers and Midwives Action [*Australia An association*]
MMA............ Motoring in Miniature Association (EA)
MMA............ Motorsports Marketing Association [*Langhorne, PA*] [*Defunct*] (EA)
MMA............ Multifunction Microwave Aperture
MMA............ Multiple Module Access
MMA............ Multiplexed Matrix Array
MMA............ Mummy Mountain [*Arizona*] [*Seismograph station code, US Geological Survey Closed*] (SEIS)
MMA............ Municipal Mortgage & Equity LLC [*AMEX symbol*] (SAG)
MMA............ Music Masters' Association [*British*]
MMA............ Music of Modern Art (NADA)
MMAA.......... Acapulco/General Juan N. Alvarez Internacional [*Mexico ICAO location identifier*] (ICLI)
MMAA.......... Man/Machine Assembly Analysis (MCD)
MMAA.......... Merchandise Mart Apparel Association [*Defunct*]
MMAA.......... Mini-Microaggregates of Albumin (DMAA)
MMAA.......... Monomethylarsonic Acid [*Organic chemistry*]
MMAA.......... Mono-N-methylacetoacetamide [*Organic chemistry*]
MMAC.......... Material Management Aggregation Code (MCD)
MMAC.......... Medical Materiel Advice Code [*Military*] (AFM)
MMAC.......... Multi-Media Access Center [*Cabletron Systems, Inc.*]
MMAC.......... Multiple Model Adaptive Control [*Flight control*]
MMAC-FNB.. Multi-Media Access Center with Flexible Network Bus [*Cabletron Systems, Inc.*]
MMACS........ Maintenance Management and Control System (MCD)
MMACS........ Medicaid/Medicare Automated Certification System (GFGA)
MMAD.......... Mass-Median Aerodynamic Diameter [*of particles*]
MM Adm...... Master of Municipal Administration
M Ma E........ Master of Marine Engineering
MMAE.......... Master of Mechanical and Aerospace Engineering (PGP)
M Ma Eng.... Master of Marine Engineering
MMal.......... Malden Public Library, Malden, MA [*Library symbol Library of Congress*] (LCLS)
M-MALS ..... Multimode Aircraft Landing System (MCD)
MMam.......... Marstons Mills Public Library, Marstons Mills, MA [*Library symbol Library of Congress*] (LCLS)
MMAN .... Aeropuerto del Norte [*Mexico ICAO location identifier*] (ICLI)
MMAN .... Minuteman International [*NASDAQ symbol*] (SAG)
MMAN .... Minuteman Int'l [*NASDAQ symbol*] (TTSB)
MM & F....... Merchant Marine and Fisheries Committee [*Congressional committee*] (MSC)
MM & M....... Material Manual and Memorandum (AAG)
MM & M....... Minerals, Mining, and Metallurgy
MM & M Soc of Am... Member of the Mining and Metallurgical Society of America
MM & SC..... Major Mission and Support Category
MM & T....... Manufacturing Methods and Technology [*Program*] [*Army Materiel Command*] (RDA)
MManHi...... Manchester Historical Society, Manchester, MA [*Library symbol Library of Congress*] (LCLS)
MMAO .... Monomethylamine Oxidase (DB)
MMAP.......... Microwave Multi-Application Payload [*NASA*] (PDAA)
MMAR .... Main Memory Address Register
MMar.......... Marlborough Public Library, Marlborough, MA [*Library symbol Library of Congress*] (LCLS)
MMAR .... Money Management Analytical Research Group
M-MARP...... Mobilization Manpower Allocations/Requirements Plan [*Military*]
MMarsW...... Historic Winslow House, Marshfield, MA [*Library symbol Library of Congress*] (LCLS)
MMART........ Mobile Medical Augmentation Readiness Team (DNAB)
MMAS.......... Aguascalientes [*Mexico ICAO location identifier*] (ICLI)
MMAS.......... Manufacturing Management Accounting System (PDAA)
MMAS.......... Manufacturing Management Accounting Systems (MHDI)

MMAS.......... Master of Military Art and Science (MCD)
MMAS.......... Material Management Accountability System (NASA)
MMAS.......... Material Management and Accounting System (AAGC)
MMAS.......... Minerva Mikrofilm A/S, Hellerup, Denmark [*Library symbol Library of Congress*] (LCLS)
MMAS.......... Mini-Manned Aircraft System (PDAA)
MMASC....... Major Mission and Support Category
MMat.......... Free Public Library, Mattapoisett, MA [*Library symbol Library of Congress*] (LCLS)
MMAT.......... Mobile Mine Assembly Team (NG)
MMath.......... Master of Mathematics
MMATP........ Methadone Maintenance and Aftercare Treatment Program [*Medicine*] (DMAA)
M Mat SE ... Master of Material Science and Engineering (PGP)
MMAU.......... Master Multiattribute Utility (IEEE)
MMAU .... Millimass Unit (IAA)
MMB........... Marine Midland Banks, Inc. [*NYSE symbol*] (SPSG)
MMB........... Master Menu Board [*Military*]
MMB........... Master of Medical Biochemistry (GAGS)
MMB........... Memanbetsu [*Japan*] [*Geomagnetic observatory code*]
MMB........... Membrane [*Medicine*]
MMB........... Mercedarian Missionaries of Berriz [*Also, OMerc*] [*Roman Catholic women's religious order*]
MMB .... Method of Mass Balance [*Physical chemistry*]
MMB .... Methylmercury Bromide [*Organic chemistry*]
MMB .... Metropolitan Milk Board [*South Australia*]
MMB .... Midwest Motor Carriers Bureau, Inc., Oklahoma City OK [*STAC*]
MMB .... Milk Marketing Board (NADA)
MMB .... Milk Marketing Board for England and Wales
MMB .... Million Barrels
MMB .... Minimum Monthly Balance [*Finance*]
MMB .... Mixer Manufacturers Bureau [*Defunct*] (EA)
MMB .... Multiport Memory Bank [*Computer science*] (MHDB)
MMBA.......... Money Market Deposit Account (EBF)
MMBAT....... Main Missile Battery
MMBB......... Molecular Marine Biology and Biotechnology [*A publication*]
MMB/D .... Million Barrels per Day
MMBEMD ... Mean Miles between Essential Maintenance Demand [*Quality control*]
MMBF......... Mean Miles between Failures [*Quality control*]
MMBF......... Million Board Feet (WPI)
MMBL.......... MacMillan Bloedel Ltd. [*NASDAQ symbol*] (NQ)
MMBLF........ MacMillan-Bloedel [*NASDAQ symbol*] (TTSB)
MMBMF....... Mean Miles between Mission Failures [*Quality control*] (MCD)
MMBOMF ... Mean Miles between Operational Mission Failures [*Quality control*] (MCD)
MMBP.......... Military Medical Benefits Property (AABC)
MMBR.......... Mean Miles between Removals [*Quality control*] (MCD)
MMBR.......... Microbiology and Molecular Biology Reviews [*A publication*]
MMBSF....... Mean Miles between System Failures [*Quality control*] (MCD)
MMBTU....... Million British Thermal Units (MENA)
MMBUMA .... Mean Miles between Unscheduled Maintenance Actions [*Quality control*] (MCD)
MMC........... Ciudad Mante [*Mexico*] [*Airport symbol*] (AD)
MMC........... Machinist's Mate, Chief [*Navy rating*]
MMC........... Magnesium Methyl Carbonate [*Organic chemistry*]
MMC........... Main Memory Controller [*Computer science*] (CIST)
MMC........... Maintenance Management Center
MMC........... Maintenance Management Course [*Army*]
MMC........... Man-Machine Communication [*Computer science*]
MMC........... Man Marketing Council [*New York City*]
MMC........... Manufacturing Methods Committee
MMC........... Manufacturing Methods Council (AAEL)
MMC........... Marine Mammal Commission [*Marine science*] (MSC)
MMC........... Marsh & McLennan [*NYSE symbol*] (TTSB)
MMC........... Marsh & McLennan Companies, Inc. [*NYSE symbol*] (SPSG)
MMC........... Martin Marietta Corp. (KSC)
mmc........... Martin Marietta Corp. (NAKS)
MMC........... Martin's Reports of Mining Cases [*Canada*] [*A publication*] (DLA)
MMC........... Mary Morstan's Companions [*An association*]
MMC........... Marymount Manhattan College [*New York, NY*]
MMC........... Massachusetts Microelectronics Center [*Research center*] (RCD)
MMC........... Master of Mass Communication (GAGS)
MMC........... Matched Memory Cycle [*Computer science*]
MMC........... Materiel Management Center [*Military*] (AABC)
MMC........... Materiel Management Code [*Military*] (AFM)
MMC........... Maximum Material Condition
MMC........... Maximum Metal Concept
MMC........... Maximum Metal Condition (IEEE)
MMC........... Maximum Miscibility Composition [*Physical chemistry*]
MMC........... Mazda Motor Corp.
MMC........... Mean Meridional Circulation [*Climatology*]
MMC........... Meet Me Conference [*Telecommunications*] (DOM)
MMC........... Melbourne Magistrates Court [*Australia*]
MMC........... Memory Management Controller (IEEE)
MMC........... Merchant Marine Council [*Coast Guard*]
MMC........... Metabolic Measurement Cart [*Beckman Instruments, Inc.*]
MMC........... Metal-Matrix Composite
MMC........... Metropolitan Motor Carriers Conference Inc., Dover NJ [*STAC*]
MMC........... Microcomputer Marketing Council [*Direct Marketing Association*] (PCM)
MMC........... Micrometeoroid Capsule (OA)
MMC........... Micronesian Minerals [*Vancouver Stock Exchange symbol*]
MMC........... Microsoft Management Control
MMC........... Midcourse Measurement Correction

Acronyms, Initialisms & Abbreviations Dictionary • 27th Edition

MMC .... Middle Cape [*Alaska*] [*Seismograph station code, US Geological Survey*] (SEIS)
MMC .... Mid Motor Controller [*Aerospace*] (NAKS)
MMC .... Migrating Myoelectric Complexes [*Electrophysiology*]
MMC .... Millsaps College, Jackson, MS [*OCLC symbol*] (OCLC)
MMC .... Minelayer, Coastal [*Navy symbol Obsolete*]
MMC .... Minicar and Microcar Club (EA)
MMC .... Minimal Medullary Concentration [*Medicine*] (MAE)
MMC .... Missile Maintenance Crew (AFM)
MMC .... Missile Measurements Center
MMC .... Missile Motion Computer
MMC .... Mission Management Center [*NASA*] (NASA)
mmc .... Mission Management Center [*NASA*] (NAKS)
MMC .... Mission Monitoring Center [*Army*]
MMC .... Mitomycin C [*Mutamycin*] [*Also, Mi, MTC*] [*Antineoplastic drug*]
MMC .... Mitsubishi Motors Corp.
MMC .... Money Management Council [*British*]
MMC .... Money Market Certificate [*Investment term*]
MMC .... Monopolies and Mergers Commission [*British*]
MMC .... Mortar Motor Carrier
MMC .... Mount Marty College [*South Dakota*]
MMC .... Mount Mary College [*Wisconsin*]
MMC .... Mount Mercy College [*Iowa; Pennsylvania*]
MMC .... Mucosal Mast Cell [*Medicine*]
MMC .... Multimedia Marketing Council (DOM)
MMC .... Multipart Memory Controller (NITA)
MMC .... Multiport Memory Controller
MMCA .... Cananea [*Mexico ICAO location identifier*] (ICLI)
MMCA .... Methyl Monochloroacetate [*Organic chemistry*]
MMCA .... Midbody Motor Control Assembly (NASA)
MMCA .... Mid Motor Controller Assembly [*Aerospace*] (NAKS)
MMCA .... Minor Military Construction, Army
M McA .... Montague and McArthur's English Bankruptcy Reports [*A publication*] (DLA)
MM Cas ...... Martin's Reports of Mining Cases [*Canada*] [*A publication*] (DLA)
MMCB .... Cuernavaca [*Mexico ICAO location identifier*] (ICLI)
MMCB .... Methods in Molecular and Cellular Biology [*A publication*]
MMCB .... Midwest Motor Carriers Bureau, Inc.
MMCBE .... Machinist's Mate, Construction Battalion, Equipment Operator [*Navy rating*]
MMCC .... Ciudad Acuna [*Mexico ICAO location identifier*] (ICLI)
MMCC .... Manhattan Miniature Camera Club (EA)
MMCC .... Mid-Century Mercury Car Club (EA)
MMCC .... Military Manpower Claimant Code (DNAB)
MMCC .... Multimini Computer Compiler (MHDI)
MMCCS .... MILSTAR [*Military Strategic and Tactical Relay System*] Mobile Consolidation and Control Station (DWSG)
MMCD .... Master Monitor Criteria Data File
MMCD .... Multimedia CD [*Computer science*]
MMCD .... Multimedia Compact Disc
MMCE .... Ciudad Del Carmen [*Mexico ICAO location identifier*] (ICLI)
MMCF .... Million Cubic Feet
MMCF .... Multimedia Communications Forum (DDC)
MMCFD .... Million Cubic Feet a Day
MMCG .... Mid-Murray Citrus Growers [*Australia*]
MMCG .... Nuevo Casas Grandes [*Mexico ICAO location identifier*] (ICLI)
MMCH .... Chilpancingo [*Mexico ICAO location identifier*] (ICLI)
MMCI .... Mopar Muscle Club International (EA)
MMCI .... MultiMedia Concepts International, Inc. [*NASDAQ symbol*] (SAG)
MMCI .... MultiMedia Concepts Intl. [*NASDAQ symbol*] (TTSB)
MMCIAC ...... Metal Matrix Composites Information Analysis Center [*DoD Information service or system*] (IID)
MMCIW .... MultiMedia Concepts Intl-Wrrt [*NASDAQ symbol*] (TTSB)
MMCIW .... MultiMedia Concepts International, Inc. [*NASDAQ symbol*] (SAG)
MMCL .... Culiacan [*Mexico ICAO location identifier*] (ICLI)
MMCL .... Major Missile Component List
MMCL .... Master Measurement and Control List (MCD)
MMCM .... Chetumal [*Mexico ICAO location identifier*] (ICLI)
MMCM .... Machinist's Mate, Master Chief [*Navy rating*]
MMCM .... Master of Music in Church Music (PGP)
MMCMP ...... Mobilization, Military and Civilian Manpower Program (AABC)
MMCN .... Ciudad Obregon [*Mexico ICAO location identifier*] (ICLI)
MMCNA ...... Moto Morini Club of North America (EA)
MMCO .... Maintenance Material Control Officer (DNAB)
MMCP .... Campeche [*Mexico ICAO location identifier*] (ICLI)
MMCP .... Micro-Master Control Processor (NITA)
M/MCRP ..... AUTODIN Memory/Memory Control Replacement Program (MCD)
MMCS .... Ciudad Juarez/Abraham Gonzalez Internacional [*Mexico ICAO location identifier*] (ICLI)
MMCS .... Machinist's Mate, Senior Chief [*Navy rating*]
MMCS .... Mass Memory Control Subsystem (TEL)
MMCS .... McCullough/McCulloch Clan Society (EA)
MMCS .... Minimum Modified Chi-Squared [*Statistics*]
MMCS .... Missile and Munitions Center and School [*Army*] (RDA)
MMCS .... Mitsubishi Multi-Communication System [*Driver information system*]
MMCS .... Modernization Management and Control System [*Social Security Administration*]
MMCS .... Multidimensional-Multiattributional Causality Scale (EDAC)
MMCS .... Multiple-Mission Command System [*NASA*]
MMCSA .... Microwave Microminiature Communications System for Aircraft (DNAB)
MMCSEER ... Marjorie Mayrock Center for CIS [*Commonwealth of Independent States*] and East European Research [*Israel*] (EAIO)
MMCT .... Maritime Mobile Coastal Telegraphy
MMCT .... Metal-to-Metal Charge Transfer [*Physical chemistry*]

MMCT .... Microcell-Mediated Chromosome Transfer [*Genetics*]
MMCT .... Mobile Maintenance Contact Team (MCD)
MMCTS .... Material Management Center Theater Supply [*Army*]
MMCU .... Chihuahua/Internacional [*Mexico ICAO location identifier*] (ICLI)
MMCV .... Ciudad Victoria [*Mexico ICAO location identifier*] (ICLI)
MMCY .... Celaya [*Mexico ICAO location identifier*] (ICLI)
MMCZ .... Cozumel/Internacional [*Mexico ICAO location identifier*] (ICLI)
MMD .... Magical Mystery Disease (WDAA)
MMD .... Magnetic Mirror Device
MMD .... Maintenance Management Division [*Army*] (INF)
MMD .... Manual of the Medical Department [*Navy*]
MMD .... Mass Median Diameter
MMD .... Master Makeup and Display
MMD .... Master Monitor Display
MMD .... Material, Maintenance, and Distribution (MCD)
MMD .... Materiel Management Decision [*Military*]
MMD .... Materiel Management Division [*Army*]
MMD .... Maximum Mixing Depths [*Meteorology*]
MMD .... Mean Mass Density
MMD .... Mean Mass Diameter
MMD .... Mean Measure of Divergence [*Statistics*]
MMD .... Mean Missile [*or Mission*] Duration (KSC)
MMD .... Merchang Mariner's Document [*Navy*]
MMD .... Merchant Marine Detail
MMD .... Microlithographic Mask Development [*Program*] (AAEL)
MMD .... Microwave Mixer Diode
MMD .... Middle Management Development
MMD .... Minami Daito Jima [*Volcano Islands*] [*Airport symbol*] (OAG)
MMD .... Minelayer, Fast [*Navy symbol*]
MMD .... Minimal Morbidostatic Dose [*Medicine*] (MAE)
MMD .... Mini-Module Drive (PDAA)
MMD .... Missile Miss Distance [*Military*] (CAAL)
MMD .... Mission Management and Dissemination (MCD)
MMD .... Mobile Servicing Center, Maintenance Department [*Canada*]
MMD .... Molecular Mass Distribution [*Organic chemistry*]
MMD .... Money Market Directories, Inc. [*Also, an information service or system*] (IID)
MMD .... Moore Medical Corp. [*AMEX symbol*] (SPSG)
MMD .... Movement for Multi-Party Democracy [*Zambia*] [*Political party*]
MMD .... Moving Map Display
MMD .... Moyamoya Disease [*Medicine*] (DMAA)
MMD .... MSC [*Mobile Servicing Center*] Maintenance Depot (SSD)
MMD .... MSFC [*Marshall Space Flight Center*] Management Directive [*NASA*]
MMD .... Multi-Effect Multistage Distillation (PDAA)
MMD .... Multimode Display
MMD .... Myotonic Muscular Dystrophy [*Medicine Medicine*] (DMAA)
MMD .... Servite Missionary Sisters of the Sorrowful Mother (TOCD)
MMDA .... Mass Merchandising Distributors' Association (EA)
MMDA .... (Methoxy)methylenedioxyamphetamine [*A hallucinogen*]
MMDA .... Money Market Deposit Account [*Investment term*]
MMDA .... Myristicin [*or glyceryl trimyristate*] [*Chemical dependency*] (DAVI)
MMDB .... Mass Memory Database (NASA)
MMDB .... Master Measurement Database (NASA)
MMDC .... Manual Master Direction Center
MMDC .... Master Message Display Console (MCD)
MMDC .... Mount Misalignment Data Collection Routine
MMDDS ...... Mucous Membrane Drug Delivery System [*Medicine*] (DB)
mmddyy ...... Month, Day, Year (HGAA)
MMDF .... Mission Mode Data File
MMDF .... Mission Model Data File [*NASA*] (NASA)
MMDG .... Mark Morris Dance Group
MMDI .... Middle Management Development Initiative
MMDI .... Momentum Distribution (EFIS)
MMDL .... Microminiature Delay Line
MMDM .... Ciudad Mante [*Mexico ICAO location identifier*] (ICLI)
MMDM .... Mobile Mixed Deployment Minuteman (SAA)
MMDO .... Durango [*Mexico ICAO location identifier*] (ICLI)
MMDOC ...... Merchant Mariners Documentation [*BTS*] (TAG)
MMDP .... Middle Management Development Program
MMDR .... Microcircuit Module, Driver/Receiver
MMDS .... Maintenance Management Data System [*Military*] (CAAL)
MMDS .... Martin Marietta Data Systems
MMDS .... Multichannel Multipoint Distribution Service [*Broadcasting term*]
MMDS .... Multichannel, Multipoint Distribution System [*Telecommunications*] (ACRL)
MMDS .... Multipoint Microwave Distribution System (WDAA)
MME .... Machinist's Mate, Engineman [*Navy rating*]
Mme .... Madame (WA)
MME .... Major Machine Equipment (MCD)
MME .... Major Movable Equipment (MEDA)
MME .... Master of Manufacturing Engineering (PGP)
MME .... Master of Material Engineering (GAGS)
MME .... Master of Mathematics for Educators (PGP)
MME .... Master of Mechanical Engineering (GAGS)
M Me .... Master of Metaphysics
MME .... Master of Mineral Engineering (GAGS)
MME .... Master of Mining Engineering
MME .... Master of Music Education
MME .... Material Military Establishment [*Formerly, OSRD*] (MCD)
MME .... Maximum Maintenance Effort [*Military*] (AFM)
MMe .... Medford Public Library, Medford, MA [*Library symbol Library of Congress*] (LCLS)
MME .... Mediterranean Medical Entente (EAIO)
MME .... Methylmethacrylate [*Organic chemistry*]
MME .... Micrometeoric Erosion (AAG)

MME	Mid-Atlantic Medical Services, Inc. [*NYSE symbol*] (SAG)
MME	Mid Atlantic Medical Svcs [*NYSE symbol*] (TTSB)
MME	Middlesborough [*England*] [*Airport symbol*] (AD)
MME	Million Market Edition [*US News and World Report*]
MME	Minimum Mean Estimate
MME	Missile Maintenance Equipment (AABC)
MME	M-Mode Echocardiography [*Medicine*] (DB)
MME	Montessori Method of Education (WDAA)
MME	Tees-Side [*England*] [*Airport symbol*] (OAG)
MMEC	Machinery Maintenance Engineering Center (AFIT)
MMEC	Machinery-Metals Export Club [*Later, International Industrial Marketing Club*] (EA)
MMEC	Migrating Myoelectric Complex [*Physiology*]
M Mech E	Master of Mechanical Engineering
MMechEng	Master of Mechanical Engineering (NADA)
MMECT	Multiple-Monitored Electroconvulsive Therapy [*Schizophrenia*]
MMED	Mass Median Equivalent Diameter [*of airborne particles*]
M Med	Master of Medicine
MM Ed	Master of Music Education
MMed	Moore Medical Corp. [*Associated Press*] (SAG)
MMED	Multimedia, Inc. [*NASDAQ symbol*] (SAG)
MMedAnaes	Master of Medicine (Anaesthesia)
MMEDC	Multimedia, Inc. (MHDW)
MMedCardiol	Master of Medicine (Cardiology)
MMed(CM)	Master of Medicine (Community Medicine)
MMedEd	Master of Medical Education
MMedPaed	Master of Medicine (Paediatrics)
MMedPath	Master of Medicine (Pathology)
MMedRadD	Master of Medicine (Diagnostic Radiology)
M Med Sc	Master of Medical Science
MMedVen	Master of Medicine (Venereology)
MMEE	Medicare, Medicaid, Education and the Environment [*President Clinton political agenda*]
MMEF	Maximal Midexpiratory Flow [*Also, MMF*] [*Medicine*]
MMEFR	Maximal Midexpiratory Flow Rate [*Medicine*]
MMEI	Military Medicine Education Institute [*DoD*] (DOMA)
MMEL	Master Minimum Equipment List (DA)
MMel	Melrose Public Library, Melrose, MA [*Library symbol Library of Congress*] (LCLS)
MM Eng	Master of Mechanical Engineering
MMEP	Marine Mammal Events Program (EA)
MMEP	Minuteman Education Program [*Air Force*] (AFM)
MMEP	Missouri Mathematics Effectiveness Project (EDAC)
MMEP	Multiple Modality Evoked Potential [*Neurophysiology*]
MMEP	Tepic [*Mexico ICAO location identifier*] (ICLI)
MMES	Ensenada [*Mexico ICAO location identifier*] (ICLI)
MMES	Master Material Erection Schedule [*Shipbuilding*] (NG)
Mmes	Mesdames [*Ladies*] [*French*]
MMES	MSFC [*Marshall Space Flight Center*] Mated Element Systems [*NASA*] (NASA)
MMES	Southwestern Manitoba Regional Library, Melita, Manitoba [*Library symbol National Library of Canada*] (NLC)
MMET	Maintenance Management Engineering Team [*Military*]
M Met	Master of Metallurgy
MMeT	Tufts University, Medford, MA [*Library symbol Library of Congress*] (LCLS)
M Met E	Master of Metallurgical Engineering
MMetEng	Master of Metallurgy and Engineering, University of Sheffield [*British*] (DBQ)
MMeT-EP	Tufts University, Eliot Pearson Department of Child Study, Medford, MA [*Library symbol Library of Congress*] (LCLS)
MMeT-F	Tufts University, Fletcher School of Law and Diplomacy, Medford, MA [*Library symbol Library of Congress*] (LCLS)
MMeT-Hi	Tufts University, Universalist Historical Society, Medford, MA [*Library symbol Library of Congress*] (LCLS)
MMeT-M	Tufts University, Medical and Dental School, Boston, MA [*Library symbol Library of Congress*] (LCLS)
MMEX	Map Maneuver Exercise (MCD)
MMEX	Mexico [*Mexico ICAO location identifier*] (ICLI)
MMF	Fleet Minelayer [*Navy symbol*]
mmf	Magnetomotive Force
MMF	Mamfe [*Cameroon*] [*Airport symbol*] (OAG)
MMF	Maritime Life Assurance Co. [*Toronto Stock Exchange symbol*]
MMF	Maximum Midexpiratory Flow [*Also, MMEF*] [*Medicine*]
MMF	Mean Maximum Flow [*Medicine*]
MMF	Mechanical Machine-Finished Paper (DGA)
MMF	Member of the Medical Faculty
MMF	Microelectronics Manufacturing Facility [*Philco-Ford Corp.*] (MCD)
MMF	Micromation Microfilm
MMF	Micromembrane Filter
MMF	Micromicrofarad (MUGU)
mmf	Micromicrofarad (IDOE)
MMF	Minelayer, Fleet [*Navy symbol Obsolete*]
MMF	Mobile Magnetic Field
MMF	Mobile Missile Facility (MCD)
MMF	Mobility Maintenance Facility (NVT)
MMF	Module Maintenance Facility
MMF	Money Market Fund [*Investment term*]
MMF	Moravian Music Foundation (EA)
MMF	Moving Magnetic Feature [*Astronomy*] (OA)
MMF	Multimode Fiber (ACRL)
MMF	MultiMode Fiberoptic Cable [*Telecommunications*] (DDC)
MMF	Mutual Musicians Foundation (EA)
MMF	National Association of Master Mechanics and Foremen of Naval Shore Establishments
MMFA	Fireman Apprentice, Machinist's Mate, Striker [*Navy rating*]
MMFC	Michael Murphy Fan Club (EA)
MMFCC	Master of Marriage, Family and Child Counseling (GAGS)
MMFCG	Maintenance Management Functional Coordinating Group [*Army*]
MMFC-MF	Marilyn Monroe Fan Club - Marilyn Forever (EA)
MMFCS	Multi-Missile Fire Control System [*Military*]
MMFD	Micromicrofarad (GPO)
MMFITB	Man-Made Fibres Producing Industry Training Board [*British*] (BI)
MMFM	Modified Modified Frequency Modulation (NITA)
MMFN	Fireman, Machinist's Mate, Striker [*Navy rating*]
MMFO	Maintenance Management Field Office [*Military*] (MCD)
MMFO	Material Management Field Office
MMFPA	Man-Made Fiber Producers Association [*Later, MMFPAI*] (EA)
MMFPAI	Man-Made Fiber Producers Association, Inc. (EA)
MMFPB	Mill Mutual Fire Prevention Bureau [*Defunct*] (EA)
MMFR	Maximal Midflow Rate [*Medicine*] (MAE)
MMFR	Maximum Midexpiratory Flow Rate [*Physiology*]
MMFS	Manufacturing Message Format Service (NITA)
MMFS	Manufacturing Messaging Format Standards [*Automotive engineering*]
MMFT	Master of Marriage and Family Therapy (GAGS)
MMFV	Manned Mars Flyby Vehicle [*Aerospace*]
MMG	Machinist's Mate, Industrial Gas Generating Mechanic [*Navy rating*]
MMG	MacMillan Gold [*Vancouver Stock Exchange symbol*]
MMG	Magdalena Milpas Altas [*Guatemala*] [*Seismograph station code, US Geological Survey*] (SEIS)
MMG	Mean Maternal Glucose [*Clinical chemistry*]
MMG	Mechanomyography [*Medicine*]
MMG	Medium Machine Gun
MMG	Metromedia International Group [*AMEX symbol*] (SAG)
MMG	Metromedia Intl Grp [*AMEX symbol*] (TTSB)
MMG	Motor Machine Gun Corps [*British military*] (DMA)
MMG	Motor-Motor Generator [*Nuclear energy*] (NRCH)
MMG	Mount Magnet [*Australia Airport symbol*] (OAG)
MMG	Movie Makers Guild (EA)
MMG	Multimode Guidance (MCD)
MMGA	Mannequin and Models' Guild of Australia
MMGB	Motor Machine Gun Battalion [*British military*] (DMA)
MMGC	Mego Mortgage Corp. [*NASDAQ symbol*] (SAG)
MMGI	Medical Marketing Group (EFIS)
MMGI	Member of the Mining, Geological, and Metallurgical Institute of India
MMGL	Guadalajara/Miguel Hidalgo Y Costilla Internacional [*Mexico ICAO location identifier*] (ICLI)
MMGM	Guaymas/General Jose Maria Yanez Internacional [*Mexico ICAO location identifier*] (ICLI)
M Mgmt	Master of Management (PGP)
MMGS	Motor Machine Gun Service [*British military*] (DMA)
MMGT	Guanajuato [*Mexico ICAO location identifier*] (ICLI)
MMgt	Master of Management
MMGT	Medical Management, Inc. [*NASDAQ symbol*] (SAG)
MMgtEng	Master of Management Engineering (NADA)
MMh	Abbot Public Library Marblehead, Ma [*Library symbol*] [*Library of Congress*] (LCLS)
MMH	Macromicromodular Hyperplasia [*Medicine*]
MMH	Maintenance Man-Hours (NG)
MMH	Mammoth Lakes [*California*] [*Airport symbol*] (OAG)
MMH	Mammoth Lakes, CA [*Location identifier FAA*] (FAAL)
MMH	Maplex Management & Holdings Ltd. [*Toronto Stock Exchange symbol*]
MMH	Master of Management in Hospitality (PGP)
MMH	Master of Medical Humanities (PGP)
MMH	Methylmercuric Hydroxide [*Organic chemistry*]
MMH	Mikromatika Air Cargo Ltd. [*Hungary ICAO designator*] (FAAC)
MM/H	Millimeters per Hour
MMH	Monomethylhydrazine [*Organic chemistry*]
MMH	Multimode Hydrophone [*Military*] (CAAL)
MMHA	Metropolitan Mutual Housing Association [*Defunct*] (EA)
MMHC	Tehuacan [*Mexico ICAO location identifier*] (ICLI)
MMH/FH	Maintenance Man-Hours per Flight Hours
mmHg	Millimeters of Mercury [*A measurement of pressure*] (KSC)
MMhHi	Marblehead Historical Society, Marblehead, MA [*Library symbol Library of Congress*] (LCLS)
MMHi	Milton Historical Society, Milton, MA [*Library symbol Library of Congress*] (LCLS)
MMHIO	Midwest Migrant Health Information Office (EA)
MMH/MA	Mean Manhours per Maintenance Action
MMHO	Hermosillo/Internacional [*Mexico ICAO location identifier*] (ICLI)
MMH/OH	Maintenance Man-Hours per Operating Hours (MCD)
MMHQ	Meta-Methoxyhydroquinone [*Organic chemistry*]
MMHR	Maintenance Man-Hours
MMHR/FH	Maintenance Man-Hours per Flight Hours (MCD)
MMH/S	Maintenance Man-Hours per Sortie [*Aerospace*] (MCD)
MMHS	Mechanized Materials Handling System [*Air Force*]
MMHSRA	Marine Mammal Health and Stranding Response Act
MMI	Athens, TN [*Location identifier FAA*] (FAAL)
MMI	Macrophage Migration Inhibition [*Cytology*]
MMI	Main Memory Interface (NITA)
MMI	Major Market Index
MMI	Management and Maintenance Inspection (NVT)
MMI	Management of Motives Index [*Test*]
MMI	Man-Machine Interaction (NITA)
MMI	Man-Machine Interface
MMI	Manpower Management Information
MMI	Manufacturing Message Interface [*Data communications standards*]
MMI	Martin Marietta International

MMI............ Materials Management Institute
MMI............ Mature Market Institute [*An association Defunct*] (EA)
MMI............ Mean Motility Index [*For intestine*]
MMI............ Mechanized Manufacturing Information
MMI............ Medicus Mundi Internationalis [*International Organization for Cooperation in Health Care - IOCHC*] [*Nijmegen, Netherlands*] (EAIO)
MMI............ Methylmercaptoimidazole [*Also, METHIMAZOLE*] [*Thyroid inhibitor*]
MMI............ Michigan Molecular Institute, Inc. [*Formerly, Midland Macromolecular Institute*] [*Research center*] (RCD)
MMI............ Micromagnetic Industries
MMI............ Middle Management Institute [*Special Libraries Association*]
MMI............ Midland Macromolecular Institute [*Midland, MI*]
MMI............ Mild [*or Minimal*] Memory Impairment [*Medicine*]
MMI............ Minnesota Mining & Manufacturing Co., St. Paul, MN [*OCLC symbol*] (OCLC)
MMI............ MMI Companies [*NYSE symbol*] (SPSG)
MMI............ Mode-Media Interaction (MCD)
MMI............ Modified Mercalli Intensity [*Earthquake magnitude*] [*Seismology*]
MMI............ Money Management Institute [*Commercial firm*] (EA)
MMI............ Monolithic Memories, Inc. [*Computer science*]
MMI............ Montana Myotis Leukoencephalitis [*Virus*]
MMI............ MSFC [*Marshall Space Flight Center*] Management Instruction [*NASA*]
MMI............ Multi-Message Interface (NITA)
MMI............ Multiport Memory Interface [*Computer science*] (MHDB)
MMI............ Mutual Mortgage Insurance Fund [*FHA*] (EMRF)
MMIA......... Colima [*Mexico ICAO location identifier*] (ICLI)
MMIA......... Medical Malpractice Insurance Association
MMIA......... Military Mission to the Italian Army [*World War II*]
MMIB......... Man-Machine Integration Branch [*Ames Research Center*] [*NASA*]
MMIC......... Maintenance Management Information and Control (MCD)
M Mic......... Master of Microbiology
MMIC......... Millimeter/Microwave Integrated Circuit
MMIC......... Miniature Microwave Integrated Circuit
MMIC CoS... Monolithic Microwave Integrated Circuit
MMI CoS..... MMI Companies [*Associated Press*] (SAG)
MMICRO-LANGUAGE ARTS... Microcomputer Managed Information for Criterion Referenced Objectives-Language Arts [*Educational Development Corp.*] (TES)
MMICRO-MATH... Microcomputer Managed Information for Criterion Referenced Objectives-Math [*R. Hambleton*] (TES)
MMICS........ Maintenance Management Information and Control System
MMID......... Merida [*Mexico ICAO location identifier*] (ICLI)
MMidwif..... Master of Midwifery
M Mi E....... Master of Mining Engineering
MMiEng...... Master of Mining Engineering (NADA)
MMIF......... Macrophage Migration Inhibitory Factor (DMAA)
MMIF......... Mutual Mortgage Insurance Fund [*Federal Housing Administration*]
MMIFC....... Marilyn Monroe International Fan Club (EA)
MMIHS....... Megacystis-Microcolon-Intestinal Hypoperistalsis Syndrome [*Medicine*] (DMAA)
MMII.......... Mass Marketing Insurance Institute (EA)
MMII.......... Multimedia Individualized Instruction [*Army*]
MMIIL........ Multi-Input Multi-Output Integrated Injection Logic (IAA)
MMIIP........ Multimedia Individualized Instructional Package [*Army*]
MMIJ.......... Mining and Materials Processing Institute of Japan
MMIlt......... Milton Public Library, Milton, MA [*Library symbol Library of Congress*] (LCLS)
MMIltC........ Curry College, Milton, MA [*Library symbol Library of Congress*] (LCLS)
MMIM......... Isla Mujeres [*Mexico ICAO location identifier*] (ICLI)
M Min......... Master of Ministries (PGP)
MMinMgt.... Master of Mining Management
MMIO......... Saltillo [*Mexico ICAO location identifier*] (ICLI)
MMIP......... Maintenance Management Improvement Program (MCD)
MMIP......... Manual of Meat Inspection Procedures [*of the USDA*]
MMIPS....... Man-Machine Interactive Processing System (PDAA)
MMIPS....... Multiple Mode Integrated Propulsion System (PDAA)
MMIRC....... Mind-Machine Interaction Research Center [*University of Florida*] [*Research center*] (RCD)
MMIS......... Maintenance Management Information System [*Military*] (AFM)
MMIS......... Master of Management Information Systems (GAGS)
MMIS......... Medicaid Management Information System [*HEW*]
MMIS......... Multinational Meetings Information Services BV [*Netherlands Information service or system*] (IID)
MMIS......... Municipal Management Information System [*Civil Defense*]
M Miss....... Master of Missiology (PGP)
MMIT......... Iztepec [*Mexico ICAO location identifier*] (ICLI)
MMIT......... Man-Machine Interrogation Technique
MMIU......... Multi-Part Memory Interface Unit (NITA)
MMIU......... Multiport Memory Interface Unit
MMJ.......... Main Metering Jet [*Automotive engineering*]
MMJ.......... Matsumoto [*Japan*] [*Airport symbol*] (OAG)
MMJ.......... Pittsburgh, PA [*Location identifier FAA*] (FAAL)
MMJA......... Jalapa [*Mexico ICAO location identifier*] (ICLI)
MMJC......... Meridian Municipal Junior College [*Mississippi*]
MMJP......... Main Metering Jet-Primary [*Automotive engineering*]
MMJS......... Main Metering Jet-Secondary [*Automotive engineering*]
MMK.......... Loparskaya [*Formerly, Murmansk*] [*Former USSR Geomagnetic observatory code*]
MMK.......... Maison Master Keyed [*Locks*] (ADA)
MMK.......... Marshall-Marchetti-Krantz [*Procedure*] [*Medicine*] (MEDA)
MMK.......... Material Mark
MMK.......... Meriden, CT [*Location identifier FAA*] (FAAL)

MMK.......... Murmansk [*Former USSR Airport symbol*] (OAG)
MMKR........ Middle Marker [*in an instrument landing system*]
MML.......... Maintenance Management Level [*Military*]
MML.......... Managing the Modern Laboratory [*A publication*]
MML.......... Man-Machine Language [*Computer science*] (TEL)
MML.......... Manual of Military Law [*British*]
MML.......... Marshall [*Minnesota*] [*Airport symbol*] (OAG)
MML.......... Marshall, MN [*Location identifier FAA*] (FAAL)
MML.......... Massachusetts Mutual Life Insurance Co. (EFIS)
MML.......... Master Measurements List (NASA)
MML.......... Master of Modern Languages
MML.......... McKinley Memorial Library, Niles, OH [*OCLC symbol*] (OCLC)
MML.......... Menika Mining Ltd. [*Vancouver Stock Exchange symbol*]
MML.......... Merrill Lyn 6.50%'STRYPES' [*NYSE symbol*] (TTSB)
MML.......... Merrill Lynch & Co. [*NYSE symbol*] (SAG)
MML.......... Metal-Metal Laminate
MML.......... Micromedia Ltd. [*ACCORD*] [*UTLAS symbol*]
mM/L......... Millimole/Liter [*Chemistry*]
MML.......... Moloney Murine Leukemia [*Medicine*] (DMAA)
MML.......... Monomethyllysine (DB)
MML.......... Mote Marine Laboratory (NOAA)
MML.......... Motor Movement Latency
MML.......... Multimaterial Laminate
MML.......... Myelomonocytic Leukemia [*Medicine*] (DMAA)
MMLA........ Midwest Modern Language Association (BARN)
MMLA........ Military Mission of Liaison Administration [*World War II*]
MMLC........ Lazaro Cardenas [*Mexico ICAO location identifier*] (ICLI)
MMLD........ Merchant Mariners Licensing and Documentation [*BTS*] (TAG)
MMLE........ Modified Maximum Likelihood Estimates [*Statistics*]
MMLEC...... Munitions Management and Labour Efficiency Committee [*British World War II*]
MMLES....... Map-Matching Location - Estimation System [*Aviation*]
MMLL........ Michigan Regional Libraries Film Program at Cadillac [*Library network*]
MMLM........ Los Mochis [*Mexico ICAO location identifier*] (ICLI)
MMLME...... Mediterranean, Mediterranean Littoral, and/or Middle East
MMLO........ Leon [*Mexico ICAO location identifier*] (ICLI)
MMLP........ La Paz/General Manuel Marquez de Leon Internacional [*Mexico ICAO location identifier*] (ICLI)
MMLS........ Military Microwave Landing System (MCD)
M-M-L-S..... Model-Modes-Loads-Stresses [*Aerospace*] (NAKS)
MMLSA....... Military Microwave Landing System, Avionics (DWSG)
MMLT........ Loreto [*Mexico ICAO location identifier*] (ICLI)
MMLV........ Moloney Murine Leukaemia Virus [*Medicine*] (BABM)
MMLV........ Moloney Murine Leukemia Virus [*of mice*] [*Veterinary medicine*] (DAVI)
MMM......... Aviation Co. Meridian [*Former USSR*] [*FAA designator*] (FAAC)
MMM......... Maine Maritime Academy, Castine, ME [*OCLC symbol*] (OCLC)
MMM......... Maintenance and Material Management [*Navy*]
MMM......... Maintenance Management Manual
MMM......... Maintenance Man-Minute
MMM......... Manned Maneuvering Module [*Aerospace*] (IIA)
MMM......... Manned Mars Mission [*NASA*]
MMM......... Margaret Morris Movement [*British*] (BI)
MMM......... Marine & Aviation Management International [*British ICAO designator*] (FAAC)
MMM......... Marine Multipurpose Missile (DNAB)
MMM......... Mark Master Mason [*Freemasonry*]
MMM......... Mars Mission Module
MMM......... Mass Media Ministries [*An association*]
MMM......... Master in Media Management
MMM......... Master of Management in Manufacturing (PGP)
MMM......... Master of Medical Management (PGP)
MMM......... Master of Ministry Management (PGP)
MMM......... Material Maintenance Management (MCD)
MMM......... Material Movement Management (AAEL)
MMM......... McAdam Resources, Inc. [*Toronto Stock Exchange symbol*]
MMM......... Measuring Monitoring Module (KSC)
MMM......... Medical Materiel Manager [*Military*] (AABC)
MMM......... Medical Missionaries of Mary [*Roman Catholic women's religious order*]
MMM......... Member of the Order of Military Merit [*Canada*] (DD)
MMM......... Mesocale and Microscale Meteorology (GNE)
mmm......... Micromillimeter (WGA)
MMM......... Microsome-Mediated Mutagenesis (DB)
MMM......... Middle Management Module
MMM......... Middlemount [*Australia Airport symbol*] (OAG)
MMM......... Militia Mea Multiplex [*Pseudonym used by William Tooke*]
mmm......... Millimicron [*Microscopy*] (CPH)
MMM......... Minnesota Min'g/Mfg [*NYSE symbol*] (TTSB)
MMM......... Minnesota Mining & Manufacturing Co. [*Also known as 3M Co.*] [*Associated Press*] (SAG)
MMM......... Modern Music Masters Society
MMM......... Money Market Monitor [*Financial Products Group*] [*Information service or system*] (IID)
MMM......... Monomethylmetoxuron [*Organic chemistry*]
MMM......... Montana Myotis Meningoencephalitis [*Medicine*] (DB)
MMM......... Mormon Mesa, NV [*Location identifier FAA*] (FAAL)
MMM......... Mouvement Militant Mauricien [*Mauritian Militant Movement*] [*Political party*] (PPW)
MMM......... Mouvement Mondial des Meres [*World Movement of Mothers - WMM*] [*Paris, France*] (EAIO)
MMM......... Multigrid Modulator Multiplier
MMM......... Multimission Module [*Aerospace*]
MMM......... Multimode Mode Matrix (MCD)

MMM .... Myelofibrosis and Myeloid Metaplasia [*Hematology*]
MMM .... Myelosclerosis with Myeloid Metaplasia [*Medicine*] (MAE)
MMMA........ Matamoros Internacional [*Mexico ICAO location identifier*] (ICLI)
MMMA........ Metalforming Machinery Makers Association [*British*] (DBA)
MMMA........ Milking Machine Manufacturers Association [*British*] (DBA)
MMMA........ Music Masters and Mistresses Association (AIE)
MMMC........ Machine Material Movement Component (AAEL)
MMMC........ Medical Materiel Management Center [*Military*] (AABC)
MMMC........ Milking Machine Manufacturers Council (EA)
MMMC........ Minimum Monthly Maintenance Charge (MHDW)
MMMD........ Merida/Lic. Manuel Crecencio Rejon Internacional [*Mexico ICAO location identifier*] (ICLI)
MMME........ Martin Marietta Missile Electronics Division [*Military*]
MMME........ Master of Metallurgical and Materials Engineering (PGP)
MMMEP...... Military Manpower Management Evaluation Project (NG)
MMMF........ Man-Made Mineral Fiber
MMMF........ Money Market Mutual Fund [*Investment term*]
MMMF........ Multinational Mixed Manned Force (NATG)
MMMFS...... Money Market Mutual Fund Shares [*Investment term*]
MMMFTP...... Matched Maturity Marginal Fund Transfer Pricing (EBF)
MMMI........ Meat Machinery Manufacturers Institute (EA)
MMMIS........ Maintenance and Material Management Information System
MMML........ Mexicali/General Rodolfo Sanchez Taboada Internacional [*Mexico ICAO location identifier*] (ICLI)
MMMM........ Man, Material, Machinery, Methods [*Statistical process control*]
MMMM........ Morelia [*Mexico ICAO location identifier*] (ICLI)
MMMN........ [*The*] Memorial of Moses on Mount Nebo [*A publication*] (BJA)
MMMOS ...... Mobile Micrometeorological Observation System
MMMPC...... Maintenance and Material Management Project Center [*Navy*]
MMMR........ Medical Material Mission Reserve [*Military*] (AABC)
MMMS........ Maintenance and Material Management System (KSC)
MMMS........ Martin Marietta Missile System [*Military*]
MMMS........ Material Movement Management Standard (AAEL)
MMMS........ Merck Molecular Modelling System (DB)
MMMS........ Minerals, Metals, and Materials Society (EA)
MMMS-OL.... Medical Materiel Management System-On Line [*Air Force*] (GFGA)
MMMSP...... Mouvement Militant Mauricien Socialiste Progressiste [*Mauritius Militant Socialist Progressive Movement*] (PPW)
MMMT........ Malignant Mixed Muellerian Tumor [*Oncology*]
MMMT........ Minatitlan [*Mexico ICAO location identifier*] (ICLI)
MMMTF........ Mobilization Materiel Management Task Force
MMMV........ Monclova [*Mexico ICAO location identifier*] (ICLI)
MMMX........ Mexico/Lic. Benito Juarez Internacional [*Mexico ICAO location identifier*] (ICLI)
MMMY........ Monterrey/General Mariano Escobedo Internacional [*Mexico ICAO location identifier*] (ICLI)
MMMZ........ Mazatlan/General Rafael Buelna [*Mexico ICAO location identifier*] (ICLI)
MMn .... Elizabth Taber Library, Marion, MA [*Library symbol*] [*Library of Congress*] (LCLS)
MMN........... Marathon Minerals [*Vancouver Stock Exchange symbol*]
MMN........... Medial Muscle Motoneuron [*Neuroanatomy*]
MMN........... Miami, FL [*Location identifier FAA*] (FAAL)
MMN........... Mismatch Negativity [*Neurophysiology*]
MMN........... Modified Melin-Norkram's Agar [*Microbiology*]
MMN........... Morbus Maculosus Neonatorum [*Medicine*] (DMAA)
MMNA .... Moto Morini Club of North America (EA)
MMNAFWB... Master's Men of the National Association of Free Will Baptists (EA)
MMNC .... Marrow Mononuclear Cell (DMAA)
MMNG .... Nogales/Internacional [*Mexico ICAO location identifier*] (ICLI)
MMNIC .... Main Mediterranean Naval Intelligence Center [*Navy*]
MMNL .... Nuevo Laredo [*Mexico ICAO location identifier*] (ICLI)
MMNOM ...... Monmouths Nominal [*Software engineering cost model*]
MM(NSW).... Milk Marketing (New South Wales) [*Australia*]
MMNU .... Nautla [*Mexico ICAO location identifier*] (ICLI)
MMO .... Intel Mobile Module [*Computer science*]
MMO .... Mach Max Operating (GAVI)
MMO .... Main Meteorological Office
MMO .... Maio [*Cape Verde Islands*] [*Airport symbol*] (OAG)
MMO .... Marseilles, IL [*Location identifier FAA*] (FAAL)
M_mo .... Maximum Operating Mach Number [*Aviation*] (DA)
MMO .... Medio Mundo [*Nicaragua*] [*Seismograph station code, US Geological Survey*] (SEIS)
MMO .... Medium Machine Oil (BARN)
MMO .... Mercantile Marine Office [*or Officer*] [*British*]
MMO .... Methane Monooxygenase [*An enzyme*]
MMO .... Micrographics Management Officer (MCD)
MMO .... Minuteman Ordnance (SAA)
MMO........... MIPR [*Military Interdepartmental Purchase Request*] Management Office (AFIT)
MMO........... MMT Resources [*Vancouver Stock Exchange symbol*]
MMO........... Mobile Module [*Computer science*]
MMO........... Monarch Machine Tool Co. [*NYSE symbol*] (SPSG)
MMO........... Monarch Mach Tool [*NYSE symbol*] (TTSB)
MMO........... Multimodel Optimization (AAEL)
MMO........... Music Minus One [*Recording label*]
MMOA .... Maxillary Mandibular Odentectomy Alveolectomy [*Dentistry*] (DAVI)
MMOA .... Mobile Modular Office Association (EA)
MMOAG ...... Research Station, Agriculture Canada [*Station de Recherches, Agriculture Canada*] Morden, Manitoba [*Library symbol National Library of Canada*] (NLC)
MMOB .... Military Money Order Branch (AFM)
MMOBCD.... Millions of Octane-Barrels per Calendar Day [*Petroleum industry*]
MMOC .... Modified Method of Characteristics [*Environmental Protection Agency*] (AEPA)

MMOD .... Micromodule (IEEE)
MMODE....... Mirror Mode (MCD)
MMODS ...... Master Material Ordering and Delivery Schedule (DNAB)
MMOECB .... Maintenance Mode Operational Equipment Checkout Box (MCD)
MMOG .... Merchant Marine Officers Guild [*Defunct*] (EA)
mmol .... Millimole [*Mass*]
MMoL .... Myelomonoblastic Leukemia [*Medicine*] (DMAA)
mmol/l........ Millimole per Liter [*Measurement*] (DAVI)
MMONS ...... Methyl-methoxy-nitrostilbene [*Organic chemistry*]
MMOS .... Message Multiplexer Operating System
MMOS .... Mobile Micrometeorological Observation System (KSC)
MMOS .... Modified Metal-Oxide Semiconductor (AAEL)
MMOS .... Multicomputing Multitasking Operating System (NITA)
MMOS .... Multimode Optical Sensor (NASA)
mmos .... Multimode Optical Sensor (NAKS)
MMOU .... Multilateral Memorandum of Understanding
MMOW .... Morden-Winkler Regional Library, Morden, Manitoba [*Library symbol National Library of Canada*] (NLC)
MMOW .... South Central Regional Library, Morden, Manitoba [*Library symbol National Library of Canada*] (NLC)
MMOX .... Oaxaca [*Mexico ICAO location identifier*] (ICLI)
MMP .... AMP, Inc. [*FAA designator*] (FAAC)
MMP .... International Organization of Masters, Mates, and Pilots (EA)
MMP .... Machined Metal Part
MMP .... Magnetospheric Multiprobe (SSD)
MMP .... Magnetotactic, Many-Celled Prokaryote [*Biology*]
MMP .... Magyar Megujulas Partja [*Party of Hungarian Renewal*] [*Political party*] (PPE)
MMP .... Maintenance Management Plan
MMP .... Maintenance Message Process [*Telecommunications*] (TEL)
MMP .... Maintenance Monitor Panel (MCD)
MMP .... M & M Porcupine Gold Mines [*Vancouver Stock Exchange symbol*]
MMP .... Manufacturing Methods Procedure (MCD)
MMP .... Marian Movement of Priests (EA)
MMP .... Maritime Mobile Phone
MMP .... Mashonaland Mounted Police [*British military*] (DMA)
MMP .... Master Mobilization Plan [*DoD*]
MMP .... Master Music Printers and Engravers Association (DGA)
MMP .... Master of Marine Policy (GAGS)
MMP .... Master of Museum Practice (GAGS)
MMP .... Master of Music Performance (PGP)
MMP .... Matabeleland Mounted Police [*British military*] (DMA)
MMP .... Matrix Metalloproteinase [*An enzyme*]
MMP .... Maxim Pharmaceuticals, Inc. [*AMEX symbol*] (SAG)
MMP .... Merchant Marine Personnel Division [*Coast Guard*]
MMP .... Methadone Maintenance Program
MMP .... Methyl-D-Mannopyranoside [*Organic chemistry*]
MMP .... Microprogrammable Multiprocessor (MCD)
MMP .... Microsatelite Mutator Phenotype [*Oncology*]
MMP .... Microsatellite Mutator Phenotype [*Cytology*]
MMP .... Military Mounted Police
MMP .... Minimum Miscibility Pressure [*Physical chemistry*]
MMP .... Missile Mode Panel (MCD)
mmp .... Mixed Melting Point [*Chemistry*]
MMP .... Modernization Management Plan
MMP .... Modes in Math Project [*National Science Foundation*]
MMP .... Modular Midcourse Package [*DoD*]
MMP .... Momentum Management Program [*NASA*] (KSC)
MMP .... Mompos [*Colombia*] [*Airport symbol*] (OAG)
MMP .... Money Market Preferred Stock [*Investment term*]
MMP .... Monitoring/Metering Panel [*Telecommunications*] (OA)
MMP .... Mortar Master Plan [*Military*] (INF)
MMP .... Mount Mary [*New Zealand*] [*Seismograph station code, US Geological Survey*] (SEIS)
MMPL .... Multiplexed Message Processor
MMPA .... Magnetic Materials Producers Association (EA)
MMPA .... Magnetic Materials Products Association (AAGC)
MMPA .... Marine Mammals Protection Act [*1972*]
MMPA .... Mining and Mineral Policy Act of 1970 (COE)
MMPA .... Poza Rica [*Mexico ICAO location identifier*] (ICLI)
MMPAS ...... Mobilization Manpower Policy Analysis [*Military*]
MMPB .... Manpower Management Planning Board
MMPB .... Puebla [*Mexico ICAO location identifier*] (ICLI)
MMPC .... Maritime Mobile Phone Coastal
MMPC .... Market Milk Producers' Council [*Australia*]
MMPC .... Mobilization Material Procurement Capability
MMPC .... Pachuca [*Mexico ICAO location identifier*] (ICLI)
MMPD .... Material Movement Priority Designator (DNAB)
MMPD .... Methoxy-Meta-Phenylenediamine [*Organic chemistry*]
MMPD .... Money Manager Profile Diskettes [*Investment Management Institute*] [*Information service or system*] (IID)
MMPDABC ... Medical Materiel Program for Defense Against Biological and Chemical Agents [*Army*] (AABC)
MMPDC ...... Maritime Mobile Phone Distress and Calling
MMPDS ...... Methoxy-Meta-Phenylenediamine Sulfate [*Organic chemistry*]
MMPE .... Punta Penasco [*Mexico ICAO location identifier*] (ICLI)
MMPF .... Master Military Pay File (AABC)
MMPF .... Microgravity and Materials Processing Facility
MMPG .... Piedras Negras [*Mexico ICAO location identifier*] (ICLI)
MMPI .... Marquest Medical Products, Inc. [*NASDAQ symbol*] (NQ)
MMPI .... McGill-Melzack Pain Index [*Questionnaire and Home Life Change Index*] (DAVI)
MMPI .... Minnesota Multiphasic Personality Inventory [*Psychology*]
MMPI .... Montgomery Medical and Psychological Institute (EA)
MMPI .... Marquest Medical Products [*NASDAQ symbol*] (TTSB)

MMPM.........	Multimedia Presentation Manager [*IBM Corp.*] (PCM)
MMPN	Uruapan [*Mexico ICAO location identifier*] (ICLI)
MMPNC	Medical Materiel Program for Nuclear Casualties [*Army*] (AABC)
MMPP.........	Mechanized Market Programming Procedures [*Computer science*] (TEL)
mmpp	Millimeters Partial Pressure
MMPPPA	Medicare and Medicaid Patient and Program Protection Act
MMPR	Methylmercaptopurine Ribose [*Biochemistry*]
MMPR	Missile Manufacturer's Planning Report
MMPR	Puerto Vallarta/Lic. Gustavo Dias Ordaz Internacional [*Mexico ICAO location identifier*] (ICLI)
MMPS.........	Manufacturing Material Planning System (MHDB)
MMPS.........	Manufacturing Message Format System
MMPS.........	Medical Media Production Service [*Commercial firm*] (DAVI)
MMPS.........	MEECN Message Processing System [*Military*]
MMPS.........	Money Market Preferred Stock (EBF)
MMPS.........	Puerto Escondido [*Mexico ICAO location identifier*] (ICLI)
MMPSE........	Multiuse Mission Payload Support Equipment (MCD)
MMPT.........	Man-Machine Partnership Translation [*Telecommunications*] (IEEE)
MMPT.........	Monitored and Modulated Periodontal Therapeutics [*Dentistry*]
mm-PTH	Mid-Molecule Parathyroid Hormone [*Endocrinology*] (DAVI)
MMPU	Memory Manager and Protect Unit (IEEE)
MMPVS........	Modified Military Pay Voucher System (AABC)
MMQ	Minimum Manufacturing Quality
MMQT.........	Queretaro [*Mexico ICAO location identifier*] (ICLI)
MMR	Austin, TX [*Location identifier FAA*] (FAAL)
MMR	Machinist's Mate, Refrigeration [*Navy rating*]
MMR	Mach Meter Reading (MCD)
MMR	Magnetically-Modulated Microwave Reflection [*Spectrometer*]
MMR	Magnetic Memory Record (NITA)
MMR	Maine State Department of Marine Resources, West Boothbay Harbor, ME [*OCLC symbol*] (OCLC)
MMR	Main Memory Register
MMR	Maintenance Management Review (MCD)
MMR	Management Milestone Records [*Navy*] (NG)
MMR	Mass Miniature Radiography
MMR	Master Microfiche Record
MMR	Master of Marketing Research (GAGS)
MMR	Materiel Management Review [*DoD*]
MMR	Maternal Mortality Rate [*Gynecology*]
MMR	Mean Motion Resonance [*Astrophysics*]
MMR	Measles-Mumps-Rubella [*Immunology*]
MMR	Merchant Marine Reserve (DNAB)
MMR	Method of Mixed Ranges (PDAA)
MMR	Midline Malignant Reticulosis [*Hematology*] (DAVI)
MMR	Military Media Review [*A publication*] (DNAB)
MMR	Miniature Micropower Resistor
MMR	Minimum Marginal Return
MMR	Minnedosa Regional Library, Minnedosa, Manitoba [*Library symbol National Library of Canada*] (NLC)
MMR	Mismatch Repair [*Genetics*]
MMR	Missed Message Rate (CAAL)
MMR	Mitchell's Maritime Register [*England*] [*A publication*] (DLA)
MMR	Mixed Municipal Refuse
MMR	Mobile Mass X-Ray (MAE)
MMR	Mobilization Materiel Requirement [*Military*]
MMR	Modular Multiband Radiometer
MMR	Monomethylolrutin [*Organic chemistry*]
MMR	Monroe Mendelsohn Research, Inc. [*Information service or system*] (IID)
MMR	Monthly Meteorological Records (DNAB)
MMR	Monumental Maintenance Requirements (MCD)
MMR	Morris Minor Registry (EA)
MMR	Motorized Microfilm Reader
MMR	Multi-Market Radio
MMR	Multimode RADAR
MMR	Multimode Radiometer (MCD)
MMR	Multi-Mode Receiver [*Navigation systems*]
MMR	Multiple Match Resolver
MMR	Mumps-Measles-Rubella Vaccine (ECON)
MMR	Mustang Motorcycle Registry [*Defunct*] (EA)
MMR	Myocardial Metabolic Rate [*Cardiology*] (MAE)
MMRA	Maritime Marshland Rehabilitation [*Canada*] (BUAC)
MMRA	Mobilization Materiel Requirement Adjustment [*Military*] (NG)
MMR & S	Military Medical Research and Services Program (CINC)
MMRB	Maintenance Management Review Board (MCD)
MMRB	Master Material Review Board (NADA)
MMRB	Materiel Management Review Board (AFIT)
MMRB	MOS [*Military Occupational Specialty*] Medical Retention Board [*Army*]
MMRBM	Mobile Medium-Range Ballistic Missile [*Air Force*]
MMRC	Materials and Mechanics Research Center [*Army*] (MCD)
MMRC	Mature Market Resource Center (EA)
MMRC	Mental Retardation Research Center
MMRC	Mountain Meadow Research Center [*Colorado State University*] [*Research center*] (RCD)
M-MRCP	Multi-Management Resolution Control Processor
MMRD	Materials and Molecular Research Division [*Lawrence Berkeley Laboratory*] [*Research center*] (RCD)
MMRD	Miniature Multipurpose RADIAC Device (MCD)
MMRE	Materials Methods Research and Engineering (MCD)
MMRF	Marshfield Medical Research Foundation (HGEN)
MMRI	Macheezmo Mouse Restaurants, Inc. [*NASDAQ symbol*] (SAG)
MMRI	Metallurgy and Materials Science Research Institute [*Thailand*] (BUAC)
MMRI	Mississippi Mineral Resources Institute [*University of Mississippi*] [*Research center*] (RCD)
MMRIM	Mat Molding Reaction Injection Molding [*Plastics technology*]
MMRI	Macheezmo Mouse Restaurants [*NASDAQ symbol*] (TTSB)
MMRP	Marine Corps Midrange Objectives Plan (MCD)
MMRP	Minerals and Materials Research Programs [*North Carolina State University*] [*Research center*] (RCD)
MMRP	Missile Master Replacement Program
MMRR	Military Manpower Requirements Report (MCD)
MMRRI	Utah Mining and Minerals Resources Research Institute [*University of Utah*] [*Research center*] (RCD)
MMRS	Manned Military Recovery System (SAA)
MMRS	Metal and Minerals Research Service (BUAC)
MMRX	Mecdet MPC Corp. [*NASDAQ symbol*] (SAG)
MMRX	Mednet MPC [*NASDAQ symbol*] (TTSB)
MMRX	Mednet MPC Corp. [*NASDAQ symbol*] (SAG)
MMRX	Reynosa/General Lucio Blanco Internacional [*Mexico ICAO location identifier*] (ICLI)
MMS	Macbride Museum Society (EA)
MMS	Machinist's Mate, Shop Mechanic [*Navy rating*]
MMS	Macmillan's Manuals for Students [*A publication*]
MMS	Magnetic Minesweeping (MSA)
MMS	Maintenance Management Software
MMS	Maintenance Management System
MMS	Man-Machine System (MCD)
MMS	Manpower Management Staff [*NATO*] (NATG)
MMS	Manpower Management System [*Marine Corps*]
MMS	Manufacturing Message [*or Messaging*] Specification [*or Standard*] [*Computer science*]
MMS	Manufacturing Monitoring System [*Computer science*] (IBMDP)
MMS	Marist Missionary Sisters (BUAC)
MMS	Marks, MS [*Location identifier FAA*] (FAAL)
MMS	Massachusetts Medical Society (BUAC)
MMS	Mass Mammographic Screening [*Medicine*] (DMAA)
MMS	Mass Memory Store [*Computer science*] (IEEE)
MMS	Mass Memory Subsystem [*Aviation*]
MMS	Master of Management Science (GAGS)
MMS	Master of Management Studies
MMS	Master of Marine Science (GAGS)
MMS	Master of Marketing Science (PGP)
MMS	Master of Materials Science (GAGS)
MMS	Master of Mechanical Science
MMS	Master of Medical Science
MMS	Master of Modern Studies (PGP)
MMS	Mast Mounted Sight
MMS	Mast Mounted Signal (MCD)
MMS	Matam [*Senegal*] [*Seismograph station code, US Geological Survey Closed*] (SEIS)
MMS	Maternity and Maternity Services [*British*]
MMS	Medical Mission Sisters (EA)
MMS	Meetings Management Society (NTPA)
MMS	Member of the Institute of Management Services [*British*] (DBQ)
MMS	Memory Management System
MMS	Merchant Management System [*Forman Interactive*] [*Computer science*]
MMS	Merchant Marine Safety
MMS	Message Management System [*Computer science*] (CIST)
MMS	Metabolic Monitoring System
MMS	Metacaine Methanesulfonate [*Local anesthetic*]
MMS	Metastable Metal Surface [*Catalyst science*]
MMS	Meteorological Measuring System
MMS	Methodist Missionary Society [*British*]
MMS	Methyl Methanesulfonate [*Experimental mutagen*]
MMS	Metropolitan Map Series [*Bureau of the Census*] (GFGA)
MMS	Mexican Mathematical Society (BUAC)
MMS	Mexican Meteorological Service
MMS	Michigan Multispectral Scanner
MMS	Microfiche Management System
MMS	Micro Measurement System [*3D Digital Design & Development Ltd.*] [*Software package*] (NCC)
MMS	Micromembrane Suppressor [*Ion chromatography*]
MMS	Micro Memory Systems (NITA)
MMS	Middle Meningeal System [*Neuroanatomy*]
MMS	Military Message Service [*British military*] (DMA)
MM/S	Millimeters per Second
MMS	Minerals Management Service [*Department of the Interior Washington, DC*]
MMS	Mini-Mental State [*Psychometric testing*]
MMS	Minimum Mean Square (PDAA)
MMS	Missile Maintenance Squadron (SAA)
MMS	Missile Mix Study [*NAVAIR*] (NG)
MMS	Missile Monitor System [*Army*]
MMS	Mission Modular Spacecraft (MCD)
mms	Mission Modular Spacecraft [*NASA*] (NAKS)
MMS	Mississippi County Community College Library, Blytheville, AR [*OCLC symbol*] (OCLC)
MMS	Mobile Monitoring Station
MMS	Modular Measuring System
MMS	Modular Modeling System
MMS	Modular Multiband Scanner (MCD)
mms	Modular Multiband Scanner (NAKS)
MMS	Modular Multimission Spacecraft [*NASA*]
MMS	Modular Multispectral Scanner
MMS	Module Management System [*Computer science*] (CIST)
MMS	Mohs' Micrographic Surgery

MMS............ Momentum Management System [*NASA*] (SSD)
MMS............ Money Management System
MMS............ Money Market Services, Inc. [*Belmont, CA*] [*Database producer*]
MMS............ Moravian Missionary Society
MMS............ Motor Minesweeper
MMS............ Multimedia System
MMS............ Multimission Modular Spacecraft [*NASA*] (NASA)
mms............ Multimission Modular Spacecraft [*NASA*] (NAKS)
MMS............ Multimission Ship [*DoD*]
MMS............ Multimode Seeker (MCD)
MMS............ Multi-Part Memory System [*Perkin-Elmer*] (NITA)
MMS............ Multiplex Modulation System
MMS............ Municipal Management System (HGAA)
MMS............ Munitions Maintenance and Storage
MMS............ Munitions Maintenance Squadron [*Air Force*]
MMS............ Musical Masterpiece Society [*Record label*] [*USA, Europe*]
MMS............ Myeloma Morphology Score [*Oncology*]
MMSA......... Man-Machine System Analysis [*Engineering*]
MMSA......... Manual Molder Shielded Arc
MMSA......... Master of Midwifery, Society of Apothecaries
MMSA......... Materials and Methods Standards Association (EA)
MMSA......... Medical Mycological Society of the Americas (EA)
MMSA......... Member, Medical Specialists' Association (CMD)
MMSA......... Mercantile Marine Service Association [*British*]
MMSA......... Methods and Materials Standards Association (EA)
MMSA......... Military Medical Supply Agency [*Later, Defense Medical Supply Center*]
MMSA......... Mining and Metallurgical Society of America (EA)
MMSA......... Mitsubishi Motor Sales of America, Inc.
MMSA......... Multiple-Mission Support Area [*Space Flight Operations Facility, NASA*]
MMSAA....... Metals and Minerals Shippers Association of Australia
MMSB........ Methyl(methionine)sulfonium Bromide [*Organic chemistry*]
MMSBC...... Master, Medical Science in Biomedical Communication (CMD)
MMSc......... Master of Management Science (GAGS)
MMSc......... Master of Marine Science (GAGS)
MM Sc......... Master of Mechanical Science
MMSc......... Master of Medical Science (GAGS)
MMSC........ Mediterranean Marine Sorting Center
MMSC........ Minnesota Metropolitan State College
MMSC........ Multimode SONAR Console
MMSCFD .... Million Standard Cubic Feet per Day
MMSCV...... Manned Military System Capability Vehicle
MMSD .... Mass Memory Storage Device (DWSG)
MMSD .... Mixed Motor and Sensory Deficits [*Neurology*]
MMSD .... Multimode Seeker Deduction (DWSG)
MMSD .... Multiple Minor Symptoms Day [*Environmental medicine*]
MMSD .... San Jose Del Cabo [*Mexico ICAO location identifier*] (ICLI)
MMSE........ Master of Manufacturing Systems Engineering (PGP)
MMSE........ Mini-Mental State Examination [*Psychometrics*]
MMSE........ Minimum Mean Squared Error
MMSE........ Minimum Mean Square Error
MMSE........ Mission Module Simulation Equipment (MCD)
MMSE........ Multiple-Mission Support Equipment [*NASA*]
MMSE........ Multiuse Mission Support Equipment [*NASA*] (NAKS)
MMSG........ Molecular Manufacturing Shortcut Group (BUAC)
MMSI......... Merit Medical Systems, Inc. [*NASDAQ symbol*] (SAG)
MMSI......... Multi-Medium Scale Integration (SAA)
MMSIP........ Maintenance Management Systems Improvement Project [*Air Force*] (DOMA)
MMSJ......... Medical Mobilization for Soviet Jewry (EA)
MMSI......... Merit Medical Systems [*NASDAQ symbol*] (TTSB)
MMSL........ Microgravity Materials Science Laboratory [*NASA*]
MMSM........ Santa Lucia [*Mexico ICAO location identifier*] (ICLI)
MMSP......... Malignant Melanoma of Soft Parts [*Medicine*] (DMAA)
MMSP......... San Luis Potosi [*Mexico ICAO location identifier*] (ICLI)
MMSQ........ Munitions Maintenance Squadron [*Air Force*]
MMSR........ Machinist's Mate, Ship Repair [*Navy rating*]
MMSR........ Master Materiel Support Record
MMSR........ Monthly Materiel Status Report
MMSR........ Multiple-Mission Support Recording [*NASA*]
MMSRC...... Mediterranean Maritime Surveillance and Reconnaissance Center (DNAB)
MMSRE....... Machinist's Mate, Ship Repair, Engine Operator [*Navy rating*]
MMSRI .... Machinist's Mate, Ship Repair, Instrument Maker [*Navy rating*]
MMSRO....... Machinist's Mate, Ship Repair, Outside Machinist [*Navy rating*]
MMSRS....... Machinist's Mate, Ship Repair, Inside Machinist [*Navy rating*]
MMSS......... Manned Maneuverable Space System
MMSS......... Manual Mode Space Simulator
MMSS......... Marine Meteorological Services System [*WMO*] (MSC)
MMSS......... Massachusettensis Medicinae Societatis Socius [*Fellow of the Massachusetts Medical Society*]
MMSS......... Mast Mounted Sight System (MCD)
M/MSS........ Medicare and Medicaid Statistical Systems (GFGA)
MMSS......... Missile Motion Subsystem
MMSS......... Multimodule Space Station [*NASA*] (KSC)
MM St......... Master of Museum Studies (PGP)
MMST......... Microelectronics Manufacturing Science and Technology (AAEL)
MMST......... Multimode Storage Tube
MM ST......... Muscle Strength (BABM)
mm st.......... Muscle Strength [*Neurology*] (DAVI)
MMSTP........ Master Missile System Training Program (SAA)
MMSV......... Mouse Moloney Sarcoma and Leukemia Virus [*Medicine*] (DB)
MMSW......... International Union of Mine, Mill, and Smelter Workers [*Later, USWA*]
MMT............ Alpha-Methyl-m-tyrosine [*Pharmacology*]

MMT............ Columbia, SC [*Location identifier FAA*] (FAAL)
MMT .... Macmillan's Manuals for Teachers [*A publication*]
MMT .... Main Mantle Thrust [*Geology*]
MMT .... Manportable MILSTAR [*Military Strategic and Tactical Relay*] Terminal [*Army*]
MMT .... Manual Muscle Test
MMT .... Manufacturing Methods Technology (AAGC)
MMT .... Marine Minerals Technology [*National Oceanic and Atmospheric Administration*]
MMT .... Maritime Mobile Telegraph
MMT .... Mass Memory Test (NASA)
MMT .... Master of Medical Technology
MMT .... Master of Movement Therapy (GAGS)
MMT .... Master of Music Teaching (GAGS)
MMT .... Math Model Test (MCD)
MMT .... Merchant Marine Technical Division [*Coast Guard*]
MMT .... Metal Mount
MMT .... Methylcyclopentadienyl Manganese Tricarbonyl [*Organic chemistry*]
MMT .... MFS Multimarket Income [*NYSE symbol*] (SPSG)
MMT .... MFS Multimarket Income Trust [*Associated Press*] (SAG)
MMT .... MFS Multimkt Income [*NYSE symbol*] (TTSB)
MMT .... Military Mail Terminal (AFM)
MMT .... Military Maintenance Technician
MMT .... Million Metric Tons (IMH)
MMT .... Miniature Moving Target (MCD)
MMT .... Mini Mobile Target [*Military*] (CAAL)
MMT .... Missile Maintenance Technician (AABC)
MMT .... Missile Mate Test
MMT .... Mobile Maintenance Team (MCD)
MMT .... Modernization Management Team [*Military*] (CAAL)
MMT .... Molten Metal Technology [*Waste management*] (ECON)
MMT .... Monolithic Mirror Telescope
mmt .... Monomethoxytrityl [*As substituent on nucleoside*] [*Biochemistry*]
MMT .... Monthly Mean Temperature [*Meteorology*]
MMT .... Monument Resources [*Vancouver Stock Exchange symbol*]
MMT .... Morse Mission Trainer
mMT .... Mouse Metallothionein [*Biochemistry*]
MMT .... Muenchner Mode-Tage [*Germany*]
MMT .... Multimode Tonotron
MMT .... Multiple-Mirror Telescope [*Mount Hopkins, AZ*] [*Jointly operated by Smithsonian Institution and the University of Arizona Astronomy*]
MMT .... Multiple-Mission Telemetry [*NASA*]
MMT .... Murine Metallothionein [*Biochemistry*]
MMTA......... Mercantile Marine Trawlermen's Association [*A union*] [*British*]
MMTA......... Methylmetatyramine (DB)
MMTA......... Minor Metals Traders' Association [*British*]
MMTA......... MultiMedia Telecommunications Association (DDC)
MMTA......... Tlaxcala [*Mexico ICAO location identifier*] (ICLI)
MMTB......... Tuxtla Gutierrez [*Mexico ICAO location identifier*] (ICLI)
MMTC......... Marine Minerals Technology Center [*National Oceanic and Atmospheric Administration*]
MMTC......... Maritime Mobile Telegraphy Calling
MMTC......... Materiel Management Training Center [*Military*]
MMTC......... Memtec Ltd. [*NASDAQ symbol*] (SAG)
MMTC......... Minerals and Metals Trading Corp. (BUAC)
MMTC......... Mouvement Mondial des Travailleurs Chretiens [*World Movement of Christian Workers - WMCW*] [*Brussels, Belgium*] (EAIO)
MMTC......... Torreon [*Mexico ICAO location identifier*] (ICLI)
MMTCY....... Memtec Ltd ADS [*NASDAQ symbol*] (TTSB)
MMTD......... Multimode Tonotron Display
MMTDC....... Maritime Mobile Telegraph Distress and Calling
MMTF......... Military Manpower Task Force
MMTG......... Tuxtla Gutierrez [*Mexico ICAO location identifier*] (ICLI)
MMTIC........ Murphy-Meisgeier Type Indicator for Children [*Test*] (TES)
MMTJ .... Tijuana/General Abelardo L. Rodriguez Internacional [*Mexico ICAO location identifier*] (ICLI)
MMTL......... Tulancingo [*Mexico ICAO location identifier*] (ICLI)
M Mtl E ...... Master of Materials Engineering (PGP)
M Mtl E ...... Master of Metal Engineering (PGP)
MMTLN....... Map Margin Top Line (SAA)
MMT/M....... Missile Maintenance Technician/Mechanic (AAG)
MMTM........ Multimedia Training Material
MMTM........ Tampico/General Francisco Javier Mina Internacional [*Mexico ICAO location identifier*] (ICLI)
MMTN......... Tamuin [*Mexico ICAO location identifier*] (ICLI)
MMTO......... Missiles Made to Order [*Military*] (RDA)
MMTO......... Multiple Mirror Telescope Observatory [*Research center*] (RCD)
MMTO......... Toluca [*Mexico ICAO location identifier*] (ICLI)
MMTP......... Methadone Maintenance Treatment Program (AAMN)
MMTP......... Methyl(methylthio)phenol [*Organic chemistry*]
MMTP......... Tapachula [*Mexico ICAO location identifier*] (ICLI)
MMTQ......... Tequesquitengo [*Mexico ICAO location identifier*] (ICLI)
MMTR......... Mean-Maintenance-Man-Hours to Repair (MCD)
MMTR......... Military Manpower Training Report (MCD)
M/MTRG..... Main Metering [*Automotive engineering*]
MMTS......... Maximum Minimum Temperature System
MMTS......... Methyl Methanethiolsulfonate [*Organic chemistry*]
MMTS......... Multi-Media Tutorial [*NASDAQ symbol*] (TTSB)
MMTS......... Multi-Media Tutorial Services, Inc. [*NASDAQ symbol*] (SAG)
MMTS......... Multiple-Mission Telemetry System [*NASA*]
MMTSF....... Million Metric Tons of Standard Fuel
MMTSW...... Multi-Media Tutorial Wrrt [*NASDAQ symbol*] (TTSB)
MMTT......... Mobile Minuteman Train Test (SAA)
MMTT......... Multimechanical Thermal Treatment
MMTTU........ Modular Magnetic Tape Transport Units (MCD)

MMTV	Mouse Mammary Tumor Virus
MMTX	Tuxpan [*Mexico ICAO location identifier*] (ICLI)
MMTY	Monterrey [*Mexico ICAO location identifier*] (ICLI)
MMU	Main Memory Unit
MMU	Managed Municipal Portfolio [*NYSE symbol*] (SPSG)
MMU	Managed Muni Portfolio [*NYSE symbol*] (TTSB)
MMU	Manchester Metropolitan University [*British*] (AIE)
MMU	Manned Maneuvering Unit [*Aerospace*]
mmu	Manned Maneuvering Unit [*NASA*] (NAKS)
mmu	Mass Memory Unit (NAKS)
MMU	Mass Memory Unit
MMu	Master of Music (GAGS)
MMu	Medical Maintenance Unit [*Army World War II*]
MMU	Memory Management Unit [*Computer chip*]
MMU	Memory Mapping Unit (NITA)
MMU	Mercaptomethyl Uracil [*Pharmacology*] (MAE)
MMU	Metered Message Unit [*Telecommunications*] (TEL)
MMU	Midcourse Maneuvering Unit [*Aerospace*] (MCD)
MMU	Midcourse Measurement Unit [*Aerospace*] (KSC)
MMU	Millimass Unit (DEN)
MMU	Million Monetary Units (PDAA)
MMU	Missile Motion Unit
MMU	Mobile Monitoring Unit
MMU	Modular Maneuvering Unit [*Aerospace*]
MMU	Monolithic Memory Unit
MMU	Morristown, NJ [*Location identifier FAA*] (FAAL)
MMU	Multimessage Unit [*Telecommunications*] (TEL)
MMU	University of Missouri, Columbia, Health Sciences Library, Columbia, MO [*OCLC symbol*] (OCLC)
MMUA	Major Mail Users of Australia
MMUC	Mazda Motor Manufacturing USA Corp.
MMUC	Midwest Medical Union Catalog
MMUD	Monolithic Memory Unit Diagnostic
M Mu Ed	Master of Music Education (PGP)
M'Mul Ch SC	M'Mullan's South Carolina Equity Reports [*1840-42*] [*A publication*] (DLA)
M'Mul LSC	M'Mullan's South Carolina Law Reports [*1840-42*] [*A publication*] (DLA)
MMuLV	Moloney Murine Leukemia Virus [*Medicine*] (DMAA)
MMuLv	Moloney Murine Leukemia Virus [*Medicine*] (DB)
MMUN	Cancun [*Mexico ICAO location identifier*] (ICLI)
MMus	Master of Music (GAGS)
M Mus Ed	Master of Music Education
M Mus (Mus Ed)	Master of Music in Music Education
M Mus (Mus Lit)	Master of Music in Music Literature
M Mus (PSM)	Master of Music in Public School Music
M Mus (RCM)	Master of Music, Royal College of Music
M Mus (W Inst)	Master of Music in Wind Instruments
MMV	Maize Mosaic Virus [*Plant pathology*]
MMV	Mandatory Minute Ventilation (DMAA)
MMV	Mandatory Minute Volume (DMAA)
MMV	Mast Mount Visionics (MCD)
MMV	Maubois, Mocquot, and Vassal [*Cheesemaking*]
MMV	McMinnville, OR [*Location identifier FAA*] (FAAL)
MMV	Monostable Multivibrator
mmv	Monostable Multivibrator (IDOE)
MMVA	Villahermosa [*Mexico ICAO location identifier*] (ICLI)
MMVD	Mixed Mitral Valve Disease [*Medicine*] (DMAA)
MMVF	Multimedia Video File [*Computer science*]
MMVR	Veracruz/General Heriberto Jara [*Mexico ICAO location identifier*] (ICLI)
MMVS	Mast Mount Visionics System (MCD)
MMW	Main Magnetization Winding [*Telecommunications*] (OA)
MMW	Mean Maximum Weight
MMW	Miami, OK [*Location identifier FAA*] (FAAL)
MMW	Millimeter Wave
MMW	Multimegawatt (SDI)
mmwave	Millimeter Wave (AAEL)
MMWCS	Multimission Weapons Control System
MMWE	Millimeter Wave Experiment
MMWG	Military Mobilization Working Group
MMWR	Morbidity and Mortality Weekly Report [*A publication*] (DMAA)
MMWW	Metamor Worldwide [*NASDAQ symbol*] [*Formerly, COREstaff, Inc.*]
MMX	Mastergroup Multiplex [*AT & T*]
MMX	Matrix Math Extensions (PCM)
MMX	Memory Multiplexer [*Computer science*]
MMX	Micron's Millenia XKU [*Computer science*]
MMX	Miracema do Norte [*Brazil*] [*Airport symbol*] (AD)
MMX	Multimedia Extensions (PCM)
MMY	Many, LA [*Location identifier FAA*] (FAAL)
MMY	Mental Measurements Yearbook [*Psychology A publication*]
MMY	Military Man-Years (AABC)
MMY	Miyakojima [*Japan*] [*Airport symbol*] (OAG)
MMYD	Mental Measurements Yearbook Database [*University of Nebraska, Lincoln*] [*Database*]
MMZ	Maimana [*Afghanistan*] [*Airport symbol Obsolete*] (OAG)
MMZC	Zacatecas [*Mexico ICAO location identifier*] (ICLI)
MMZH	Zihuatanejo [*Mexico ICAO location identifier*] (ICLI)
MMZM	Zamora [*Mexico ICAO location identifier*] (ICLI)
MMZO	Manzanillo [*Mexico ICAO location identifier*] (ICLI)
MMZP	Zapopan [*Mexico ICAO location identifier*] (ICLI)
MMZT	Mazatlan [*Mexico ICAO location identifier*] (ICLI)
MN	Machinery Numeral [*Marine insurance*] (DS)
MN	Madeleine Mines Ltd. [*Toronto Stock Exchange symbol*]
MN	Magnetic North
MN	Main (AAG)
MN	Main Network [*Telecommunications*] (TEL)
MN	Making of the Nations [*A publication*]
MN	Malignant Nephrosclerosis [*Medicine*] (DB)
MN	Management Network (MCD)
Mn	Manganese [*Chemical element*]
MN	Mantle Nerve
MN	Manual
MN	Manufacturer's Name (NITA)
MN	Manx Airlines Ltd.
MN	Mare Nectaris [*Sea of Nectar*] [*Lunar area*]
MN	Marketspan Corp. [*NYSE symbol*] [*Formerly, Long Island Lighting*]
MN	Master Navigator [*Air Force*]
MN	Master of Nursing
MN	Material Number
MN	Materiel Needs [*Army*]
MN	Maxim Nordenfelt Gun
Mn	Mean Range [*Difference in height between mean high water and mean low water*] [*Tides and currents*]
MN	Measurement Name (NITA)
MN	Mecanorma [*Graphic artist products*] [*British*]
MN	Medial Interlaminar Nucleus [*Neurology*] (DAVI)
MN	Media Network (EA)
MN	Median Nerve [*Anatomy*]
MN	Meeting Number (NITA)
MN	Meetings Name (NITA)
MN	Meganewton
MN	Melena Neonatorum (DB)
MN	Meniere's Network [*An association*] (EA)
MN	Meningopneumonitis [*Medicine*]
MN	Merchant Navy
Mn	Merchant Navy (WDAA)
M-N	Merrell-National [*Commercial firm*] (DAVI)
MN	Metanephrine [*Medicine*] (DMAA)
m-N	Meter-Newton
MN	Michigan [*Obsolete*] (ROG)
MN	Micrococcal Nuclease [*Also, MCN*] [*An enzyme*]
M/N	Microcytic/Normochromic [*Anemia*] [*Hematology*] (DAVI)
MN	Microneutralization [*Chemistry*]
MN	Midnight
MUN	Migrating Neuron [*Neuroanatomy*]
mN	Millinormal [*One one-thousandth of normal*]
MN	Mineman [*Navy rating*]
MN	Minnesota [*Postal code*]
Mn	Minnesota State Law Library, St. Paul, MN [*Library symbol Library of Congress*] (LCLS)
MN	Minor Subject Descriptor [*Online database field identifier*]
MN	Mission Need
MN	Mnemonic
Mn	Modern [*Linguistics*]
M/N	Moneda Nacional [*National Money*] [*Spanish*]
MN	Mongolia [*ANSI two-letter standard code*] (CNC)
MN	Mononuclear [*Hematology*]
MN	Month Name (BJA)
MN	Moon (ROG)
MN	Moreh Nebukhim [*Maimonides*] (BJA)
M-N	Motility Nitrate [*Medium*] [*Microbiology*] (DAVI)
MN	Moto Nave [*Motor ship*] [*Latin*] (IIA)
MN	Motor Neuron [*Anatomy*]
MN	Mouvement National [*Morocco*] [*Political party*] (EY)
MN	Movimiento Nacional [*Costa Rica*] [*Political party*] (EY)
MN	Multinodular [*or Multinodulate*] [*Medicine*]
MN	Mutato Nomine [*The Name Being Changed*] [*Latin*]
MN	Myoneural [*Medicine*]
MN1	Mineman, First Class [*Navy rating*]
MN2	Mineman, Second Class [*Navy rating*]
MN3	Mineman, Third Class [*Navy rating*]
MnA	Aitken Public Library, Aitken, MN [*Library symbol*] [*Library of Congress*] (LCLS)
MNA	Augsburg College, Minneapolis, MN [*OCLC symbol*] (OCLC)
MNA	Master Negative Assembly [*Monophoto*] (DGA)
M Na	Master of Navigation
MNA	Master of Nonprofit Administration (GAGS)
MNA	Master of Nurse Anesthesia (PGP)
MNA	Master of Nursing Administration
MN(A)	Material Need (Abbreviated) (MCD)
MNA	Maximum Noise Area
MNA	Melanguane [*Indonesia*] [*Airport symbol*] (OAG)
MNA	Melinga Resources Ltd. [*Vancouver Stock Exchange symbol*]
MNA	Member of the National Assembly [*British*]
MNA	Merpati Nusantara Airlines PT [*Indonesia*] [*ICAO designator*] (FAAC)
MNA	Meta-Nitroaniline [*Organic chemistry*]
MNA	Methoxynaphthylamine [*Organic chemistry*]
MNA	Methylnadic Anhydride [*Organic chemistry*]
MNA	Methylnitroaniline [*Organic chemistry*]
MNA	Mina [*Nevada*] [*Seismograph station code, US Geological Survey*] (SEIS)
MNA	Minnesota Municipal Term Trust [*NYSE symbol*] (SPSG)
MNA	Minnesota Muni Term Trust [*NYSE symbol*] (TTSB)
MNA	Missing, Not Enemy Action
MNA	Mouvement d'Action Politique et Sociale [*Political and Social Action Movement*] [*Switzerland Political party*] (PPW)
MNA	Mouvement National Algerien [*National Algerian Movement*]
MNA	Multinetwork Area [*Term used in TV ratings*]
MNA	Multiple Newsagents Association [*British*] (DBA)

MNA............ Multishare Network Architecture [*Mitsubishi Corp.*] (BUR)

MNA............ Myanmar News Agency (EY)

MNAA .... Molecular Neutron Activation Analysis

MNA,B,C..... Main Bus A,B, or C (NASA)

MnAbnE...... Alborn Elementary School, Alborn, MN [*Library symbol*] [*Library of Congress*] (LCLS)

MnAd .... Annandale Public Library, Annandale, MN [*Library symbol*] [*Library of Congress*] (LCLS)

Mn-Ad.......... Minnesota State Department of Administration, Budget Library, St. Paul, MN [*Library symbol Library of Congress*] (LCLS)

MnAda .... Ada Public Library, Ada, MN [*Library symbol*] [*Library of Congress*] (LCLS)

MNAdaE....... Ada Elementary School, Ada, MN [*Library symbol*] [*Library of Congress*] (LCLS)

MnAdaH........ Ada High School, Ada, MN [*Library symbol*] [*Library of Congress*] (LCLS)

MnAdBE....... Bendix Elementary School Annandale, MN [*Library symbol*] [*Library of Congress*] (LCLS)

MnAdH......... Annandale High School, Annandale, MN [*Library symbol*] [*Library of Congress*] (LCLS)

MnADM....... Depot Museum, Aitken, MN [*Library symbol*] [*Library of Congress*] (LCLS)

MnAdMS..... Annandale Middle School, Annandale, MN [*Library symbol*] [*Library of Congress*] (LCLS)

MNAEA .... Member of the National Association of Estate Agents [*British*] (DBQ)

Mn-Ag.......... Minnesota Department of Agriculture, St. Paul, MN [*Library symbol Library of Congress*] (LCLS)

MnAJ .... Aitken Jr.-Sr. High School Media Center, Aitken, MN [*Library symbol*] [*Library of Congress*] (LCLS)

MnAkE .... Akeley Elementary School, Akeley, MN [*Library symbol*] [*Library of Congress*] (LCLS)

MnAkH......... Akeley High School, Akeley, MN [*Library symbol*] [*Library of Congress*] (LCLS)

MnAl .... Albany Public Library, Alabany, MN [*Library symbol*] [*Library of Congress*] (LCLS)

MnAlb.......... Albert Lea Public Library, Albert Lea, MN [*Library symbol Library of Congress*] (LCLS)

MnAlbeCH ... Chokio-Alberta High School, Alberta, MN [*Library symbol*] [*Library of Congress*] (LCLS)

MnAle.......... Alexandria Public Library, Alexandria, MN [*Library symbol*] [*Library of Congress*] (LCLS)

MnAleCJ...... Central Junior High School, Alexandria, MN [*Library symbol*] [*Library of Congress*] (LCLS)

MnAleDH ..... Douglas County Hospital, Health Science Library, Alexandria, MN [*Library symbol*] [*Library of Congress*] (LCLS)

MnAleJH...... Jefferson High School, Alexandria, MN [*Library symbol*] [*Library of Congress*] (LCLS)

MnAleLE...... Lincoln Elementary School, Alexandria, MN [*Library symbol*] [*Library of Congress*] (LCLS)

MnAleR........ Alexandria Runestone Museum, Alexandria, MN [*Library symbol*] [*Library of Congress*] (LCLS)

MnAleSM..... St. Mary's School, Alexandria, MN [*Library symbol*] [*Library of Congress*] (LCLS)

MnAleTI...... Alexandria Technical Institute, Alexandria, MN [*Library symbol*] [*Library of Congress*] (LCLS)

MnAleWE..... Washington Elementary School, Alexandria, MN [*Library symbol*] [*Library of Congress*] (LCLS)

MnAlFE........ Farming Elementary School, Albany, MN [*Library symbol*] [*Library of Congress*] (LCLS)

MnAlH .... Holy Family School, Albany, MN [*Library symbol*] [*Library of Congress*] (LCLS)

MnAlJ .... Albany Jr. H.S./Elementary Library, Albany, MN [*Library symbol*] [*Library of Congress*] (LCLS)

MnAlmA....... Amador Heritage Center, Almelund, MN [*Library symbol*] [*Library of Congress*] (LCLS)

MnAlS.......... Albany Senior High School, Albany, MN [*Library symbol*] [*Library of Congress*] (LCLS)

MnAlSP........ St. Pius V School, Albany, MN [*Library symbol*] [*Library of Congress*] (LCLS)

MnAlvE........ Albertville Elementary School, Albertville, MN [*Library symbol*] [*Library of Congress*] (LCLS)

MNAM .... Military North African Mission [*World War II*]

MNam........ Nantucket Athenaeum, Nantucket, MA [*Library symbol Library of Congress*] (LCLS)

MnAnA......... Anoka-Ramsey Community College, Anoka, MN [*Library symbol Library of Congress*] (LCLS)

MN & ALOA... Merchant Navy and Air Line Officers' Association [*A union*] [*British*] (DS)

MNANG....... Minnesota Air National Guard (MUSM)

MnAnGS ...... Anoka County Genealogical Society, Anoka, MN [*Library symbol Library of Congress*] (LCLS)

MnAnHi........ Anoka County Historical Society, Anoka, MN [*Library symbol Library of Congress*] (LCLS)

MNanHi .... Nantucket Historical Association, Nantucket, MA [*Library symbol Library of Congress*] (LCLS)

MNanMM..... Nantucket Maria Mitchell Association, Nantucket, MA [*Library symbol Library of Congress*] (LCLS)

MnAnVT....... Anoka Area Vocational Technical Institute, Anoka, MN [*Library symbol Library of Congress*] (LCLS)

MNanW........ Nantucket Whaling Museum, Nantucket, MA [*Library symbol Library of Congress*] (LCLS)

MNAO .... Mobile Naval Airfield Organization

MNAOA........ Merchant Navy and Air Line Officers' Association [*A union*] [*British*] (DCTA)

MnAp .... Appleton Public Library, Appleton, MN [*Library symbol*] [*Library of Congress*] (LCLS)

MNAP .... Mixed Nerve Action Potential [*Medicine*] (DMAA)

MnApH........ Appleton Municipal Hospital, Appleton, MN [*Library symbol*] [*Library of Congress*] (LCLS)

MnApPS...... Appleton Public Schools, Appleton, MN [*Library symbol*] [*Library of Congress*] (LCLS)

MN Arch ..... Master of Naval Architecture

MnARE........ Rippleside Elementary School, Rippleside Elementary IMC, Aitken, Mn [*Library symbol*] [*Library of Congress*] (LCLS)

MnArS......... Argyle School, Argyle, MN [*Library symbol*] [*Library of Congress*] (LCLS)

MNAS........ Member of the National Academy of Sciences

MnAsHi........ Pine County Historical Reference Library, Askov, MN [*Library symbol*] [*Library of Congress*] (LCLS)

MnAshS .... Ashby Public School, Ashby, MN [*Library symbol*] [*Library of Congress*] (LCLS)

MNASSA ..... Monthly Notes. Astronomical Society of Southern Africa [*A publication*]

MNASTD ..... Multicultural Network of the American Society for Training and Development (EA)

MnAt........... Atwater Public Library, Atwater, MN [*Library symbol*] [*Library of Congress*] (LCLS)

MnAtPS....... Atwater-Grove City Public Schools, Atwater, MN [*Library symbol*] [*Library of Congress*] (LCLS)

MNatQ........ United States Quartermaster Research and Development Center, Natick, MA [*Library symbol Library of Congress*] (LCLS)

MNatRes...... Master of Natural Resources (ADA)

MNatSci....... Master of Natural Science (GAGS)

MnAtSJS...... St. John's Lutheran School, Atwater, MN [*Library symbol*] [*Library of Congress*] (LCLS)

MnAu .... Austin Public Library, Austin, MN [*Library symbol Library of Congress*] (LCLS)

MNAU .... Mobile Naval Airfield Unit

MnAudS....... Audubon Public School, Audubon, MN [*Library symbol*] [*Library of Congress*] (LCLS)

MnAuH........ Hormel Institute, University of Minnesota, Austin, MN [*Library symbol Library of Congress*] (LCLS)

MnAuPS...... Austin Public Schools Media, Austin, MN [*Library symbol Library of Congress*] (LCLS)

MnAur......... Aurora Public Library, Aurora, MN [*Library symbol*] [*Library of Congress*] (LCLS)

MnAurH....... Mesabi East High School, Aurora,MN [*Library symbol*] [*Library of Congress*] (LCLS)

MnAuS......... Austin State Junior College, Austin, MN [*Library symbol Library of Congress*] (LCLS)

MnAuV......... Austin Vocational Technical Institute, Austin, MN [*Library symbol Library of Congress*] (LCLS)

MnAvoE .... Avon Elementary School, Avon, MN [*Library symbol*] [*Library of Congress*] (LCLS)

MnAvZ........ Minnesota Zoological Garden, Apple Valley, MN [*Library symbol Library of Congress*] (LCLS)

MnB............ Becker Public Library, Becker Elementary School, Becker, MN [*Library symbol*] [*Library of Congress*] (LCLS)

MNB............ Bemidji State University, Bemidji, MN [*OCLC symbol*] (OCLC)

MNB............ Maldives News Bureau (EY)

MNB............ Mannosidase Beta (DMAA)

MNB............ Maverick Naturalite Beef Corp. [*Vancouver Stock Exchange symbol*]

MNB............ Median Neuroblast [*Cytology*]

MNB............ Medical Negligence Board (WDAA)

MNB............ Minnesota Muni Term Tr-II [*AMEX symbol*] (TTSB)

MNB............ Minnesota Term Trust, Inc. II [*AMEX symbol*] (SAG)

MNB............ Mint No Box [*Doll collecting*]

MNB............ Moanda [*Zaire*] [*Airport symbol*] (OAG)

MNB............ Mobile Naval Base [*British military*] (DMA)

MNB............ Moscow Narodny Bank Ltd. [*Former USSR*]

MNB............ Multinozzle Base

MNB............ Murine Neuroblastoma (DB)

MNB............ Texte de Louvre [*Paris*]: Monuments de Ninive et de Babylone [*A publication*] (BJA)

MnBa .... Balaton Public Library, Balaton, MN [*Library symbol*] [*Library of Congress*] (LCLS)

MNBA .... Minimum Normal Burst Altitude

MNBA .... Mono-normal-butylamine [*Organic chemistry*]

MNBA .... Multinational Business Association (BUAC)

MnBab........ Babbitt Public Library, Babbitt, MN [*Library symbol*] [*Library of Congress*] (LCLS)

MnBabE....... J.F. Kennedy Elementary School, Babbit, MN [*Library symbol*] [*Library of Congress*] (LCLS)

MnBabH....... J.F. Kennedy High School, Babbitt, MN [*Library symbol*] [*Library of Congress*] (LCLS)

MnBacS....... Backus School, Backus, MN [*Library symbol*] [*Library of Congress*] (LCLS)

MnBadS....... Badger School, Badger, MN [*Library symbol*] [*Library of Congress*] (LCLS)

MnBag .... Bagley Public Library, Bagley, MN [*Library symbol*] [*Library of Congress*] (LCLS)

MnBagE....... Bagley Elementary School, Bagley, MN [*Library symbol*] [*Library of Congress*] (LCLS)

MnBaPS...... Balaton Public Schools, Balaton, MN [*Library symbol*] [*Library of Congress*] (LCLS)

MnBar......... Barnesville Public Library, Barnesville, MN [*Library symbol*] [*Library of Congress*] (LCLS)

MnBarFe...... Florence Atkinson Elementary School, Barnesville, MN [*Library symbol*] [*Library of Congress*] (LCLS)

MnBarH .... Barnesville High School, Barnesville, MN [*Library symbol*] [*Library of Congress*] (LCLS)

MnBaSPL ..... St. Peter's Lutheran School, Balaton, MN [*Library symbol*] [*Library of Congress*] (LCLS)

MnBatS .... Battle Lake Public School, Battle Lake, MN [*Library of Congress*] (LCLS)

MnBau .... Baudette Public Library, Baudette, MN [*Library symbol*] [*Library of Congress*] (LCLS)

MnBauLH .... Lake of the Woods High School, Baudette, MN [*Library symbol*] [*Library of Congress*] (LCLS)

MnBaxE .... Baxter Elementary School, Baxter, MN [*Library symbol*] [*Library of Congress*] (LCLS)

MNBB .... MNB Bancshares [*NASDAQ symbol*] (SAG)

MNB Bn ...... MNB Bancshares [*Associated Press*] (SAG)

MNBDF .... Meta-Nitrobenzenediazonium Tetrafluoroborate [*Organic chemistry*]

MNBDO .... Mobile Naval Base Defence Organization [*British World War II*]

MnBE .... Becker Elementary School, Becker, MN [*Library symbol*] [*Library of Congress*] (LCLS)

MnBeaPS ..... Beardlsey-Brown Valley Public Schools, Beardlsey, MN [*Library symbol*] [*Library of Congress*] (LCLS)

MnBeB .... Bertha-Hweitt School, Bertha, MN [*Library symbol*] [*Library of Congress*] (LCLS)

MNBedf .... New Bedford Free Public Library, New Bedford, MA [*Library symbol Library of Congress*] (LCLS)

MNBedfHi .... Old Dartmouth Historical Society, New Bedford Whaling Museum, New Bedford, MA [*Library symbol Library of Congress*] (LCLS)

MnBelPS ...... Bellingham Public Schools, Bellingham, MN [*Library symbol*] [*Library of Congress*] (LCLS)

MnBem .... Bemidji Public Library, Bemidji, MN [*Library symbol*] [*Library of Congress*] (LCLS)

MnBemCE .... Central Elementary School, Bemidji, MN [*Library symbol*] [*Library of Congress*] (LCLS)

MnBemDE .... Deer Lake Elementary School, Bemidji, MN [*Library symbol*] [*Library of Congress*] (LCLS)

MnBemH ...... Bemidji High School, Bemidji, MN [*Library symbol*] [*Library of Congress*] (LCLS)

MnBemHE .... Horace May Elementary School, Bemidji, MN [*Library symbol*] [*Library of Congress*] (LCLS)

MnBemJE ..... J.W. Smith Elementary School, Bemidji, MN [*Library symbol*] [*Library of Congress*] (LCLS)

MnBemLE ..... Lincoln Elementary School, Bemidji, MN [*Library symbol*] [*Library of Congress*] (LCLS)

MnBemMS ... Benidji Middle School, Bemidji, MN [*Library symbol*] [*Library of Congress*] (LCLS)

MnBemNE ..... Northern Elementary School, Bemidji, MN [*Library symbol*] [*Library of Congress*] (LCLS)

MnBemOH ... Oak Hills Bible College, Bemidji, MN [*Library symbol*] [*Library of Congress*] (LCLS)

MnBemPE ..... Paul Bunyan Elementary School, Bemidji, MN [*Library symbol*] [*Library of Congress*] (LCLS)

MnBemS ...... Bemidji State College [*Later, Bemidji State University*], Bemidji, MN [*Library symbol Library of Congress*] (LCLS)

MnBemSE .... Solway Elementary School, Bemidji, MN [*Library symbol*] [*Library of Congress*] (LCLS)

MnBemSP .... St. Philips School, Bemidji, MN [*Library symbol*] [*Library of Congress*] (LCLS)

MnBenPS ..... Benson Public Schools, Benson, MN [*Library symbol*] [*Library of Congress*] (LCLS)

MnBenSF ..... St. Francis Xavier School, Benson, MN [*Library symbol*] [*Library of Congress*] (LCLS)

MnBevPS ..... Belview Public School, Bleview, MN [*Library symbol*] [*Library of Congress*] (LCLS)

MnBf .... Buffalo Public Library, Buffalo, MN [*Library symbol*] [*Library of Congress*] (LCLS)

MnBfaE .... Big Falls Elementary School, Big Falls, MN [*Library symbol*] [*Library of Congress*] (LCLS)

MnBfH .... Buffalo Memorial Hospital, Medical Library, Buffalo, MN [*Library symbol*] [*Library of Congress*] (LCLS)

MnBfHi .... Wright County Historical Society, Buffalo, MN [*Library symbol*] [*Library of Congress*] (LCLS)

MnBfI .... Buffalo Intermediate School, Buffalo, MN [*Library symbol*] [*Library of Congress*] (LCLS)

MnBfJ .... Buffalo Junior High School, Buffalo, MN [*Library symbol*] [*Library of Congress*] (LCLS)

MnBfoS .... Bigfork School, Bigford, MN [*Library symbol*] [*Library of Congress*] (LCLS)

MnBfP .... Buffalo Primary Library, Buffalo, MN [*Library symbol*] [*Library of Congress*] (LCLS)

MnBfS .... Buffalo Senior High School, Buffalo, MN [*Library symbol*] [*Library of Congress*] (LCLS)

MnBfSF .... St. Francis Xavier School, Buffalo, MN [*Library symbol*] [*Library of Congress*] (LCLS)

MnBfW .... Wright Vocational Coop Center, Buffalo, MN [*Library symbol*] [*Library of Congress*] (LCLS)

MnBg .... Myrtle Mabee Library, Belgrade, MN [*Library symbol*] [*Library of Congress*] (LCLS)

MnBgE .... Belgrade Elementary School, Belgrade, MN [*Library symbol*] [*Library of Congress*] (LCLS)

MnBgH .... Belgrade High School, Media Center, Belgrade, MN [*Library symbol*] [*Library of Congress*] (LCLS)

MnBH .... Becker High School, Becker, MN [*Library symbol*] [*Library of Congress*] (LCLS)

MnBHi .... Sherbourne County Historical Society, Becker, MN [*Library symbol*] [*Library of Congress*] (LCLS)

MnBhM .... Braham Middle School, Braham, MN [*Library symbol*] [*Library of Congress*] (LCLS)

MnBhSE .... Southview Elementary School, Braham, MN [*Library symbol*] [*Library of Congress*] (LCLS)

MnBhWH .... Westview High School, Media Center, Braham, MN [*Library symbol*] [*Library of Congress*] (LCLS)

MnBi .... Bird Island Public Library, Bird Island, MN [*Library symbol*] [*Library of Congress*] (LCLS)

MnBirlS .... Indus School, Birchdale, MN [*Library symbol*] [*Library of Congress*] (LCLS)

MnBiSM ...... St. Mary's School, Bird Island, MN [*Library symbol*] [*Library of Congress*] (LCLS)

MnBiwE .... Bray Elementary School, Biwabik, MN [*Library symbol*] [*Library of Congress*] (LCLS)

MnBiwH ...... V.L. Reishus High School, Biwabik, MN [*Library symbol*] [*Library of Congress*] (LCLS)

MNBK .... Marine National Bank (California) [*NASDAQ symbol*] (SAG)

MNBK .... Marine Nat'l Bank [*NASDAQ symbol*] (TTSB)

MnBkES ...... Blomkest Elementary School, Blomkest, MN [*Library symbol*] [*Library of Congress*] (LCLS)

MNBKW ...... Marine Natl Bk Irvine CA Wrrt [*NASDAQ symbol*] (TTSB)

MnBl .... Big Lake Public Library, Big Lake, MN [*Library symbol*] [*Library of Congress*] (LCLS)

MNBL .... Bluefields [*Nicaragua*] [*ICAO location identifier*] (ICLI)

MnBla .... Blackduck Public Library, Blackduck, MN [*Library symbol*] [*Library of Congress*] (LCLS)

MnBlaE .... Blackduck Elementary School, Blackduck, MN [*Library symbol*] [*Library of Congress*] (LCLS)

MnBlaH .... Blackduck High School, Blackduck, MN [*Library symbol*] [*Library of Congress*] (LCLS)

MnBlE .... Big Lake Elementary School, Big Lake, MN [*Library symbol*] [*Library of Congress*] (LCLS)

MNBLE .... Modified Nearly Best Linear Estimator [*Statistics*]

MnBlH .... Big Lake High School, Big Lake, MN [*Library symbol*] [*Library of Congress*] (LCLS)

MnBloPS ...... Bloomington Public Schools, Bloomington, MN [*Library symbol*] [*Library of Congress*] (LCLS)

MnBmE .... Barnum Elementary School, Barnum, MN [*Library symbol*] [*Library of Congress*] (LCLS)

MnBmH .... Barnum High School, Barnum, MN [*Library symbol*] [*Library of Congress*] (LCLS)

MNBO .... Management Buy-Out

MnBov .... Bovey Public Library, Bovey, MN [*Library symbol*] [*Library of Congress*] (LCLS)

MnBovM ...... Connor-Jasper Middle School, Bovey, MN [*Library symbol*] [*Library of Congress*] (LCLS)

MnBovS .... Balsam School, Bovey, MN [*Library symbol*] [*Library of Congress*] (LCLS)

MnBr .... Brainerd Public Library, Brainerd, MN [*Library symbol*] [*Library of Congress*] (LCLS)

MNBR .... Los Brasiles/Carlos Ulloa [*Nicaragua*] [*ICAO location identifier*] (ICLI)

MnBraS .... Brandon Public School, Brandon, MN [*Library symbol*] [*Library of Congress*] (LCLS)

MnBrC .... Brainerd Community College, Brainerd, MN [*Library symbol Library of Congress*] (LCLS)

MnBre .... Breckenridge Public Library, Breckenridge, MN [*Library symbol*] [*Library of Congress*] (LCLS)

MnBreE .... Breckenridge Elementary School, Breckenridge, MN [*Library symbol*] [*Library of Congress*] (LCLS)

MnBreH .... Breckenridge High School, Breckenridge, MN [*Library symbol*] [*Library of Congress*] (LCLS)

MnBrFJ .... Franklin Junior High School, Brainerd, MN [*Library symbol*] [*Library of Congress*] (LCLS)

MnBrGE .... Garfield Elementary School, Brainerd, MN [*Library symbol*] [*Library of Congress*] (LCLS)

MnBrHE .... Harrison Elementary School, Brainerd, MN [*Library symbol*] [*Library of Congress*] (LCLS)

MnBrHS .... Brainerd High School, Brainerd, MN [*Library symbol*] [*Library of Congress*] (LCLS)

MnBrLE .... Lincoln Elementary School, Brainerd, MN [*Library symbol*] [*Library of Congress*] (LCLS)

MnBrLoE ...... Lowell Elementary School, Brainerd, MN [*Library symbol*] [*Library of Congress*] (LCLS)

MnBro .... Browntown Public Library, Browntown, MN [*Library symbol*] [*Library of Congress*] (LCLS)

MnBroPS ...... Brownton Public Schools, Brownton, MN [*Library symbol*] [*Library of Congress*] (LCLS)

MnBrRE .... Riverside Elementary School, Brainerd, MN [*Library symbol*] [*Library of Congress*] (LCLS)

MnBruE .... Bruno Elementary School, Bruno, MN [*Library symbol*] [*Library of Congress*] (LCLS)

MnBrv .... Carnegie Public Library, Browns Valley, MN [*Library symbol*] [*Library of Congress*] (LCLS)

MnBrvPS ...... Beardsley-Browns Valley Public Schools, Browns Valley, MN [*Library symbol*] [*Library of Congress*] (LCLS)

MnBrWE ...... Whittier Elementary School, Brainerd, MN [*Library symbol*] [*Library of Congress*] (LCLS)

MnBrwES ..... Brewster Elementary School, Brewster, MN [*Library symbol*] [*Library of Congress*] (LCLS)

MnBrWM .... Washington Middle School, Brainerd, MN [*Library symbol*] [*Library of Congress*] (LCLS)

MnBtH .... Brooten High School, Brooten, MN [*Library symbol*] [*Library of Congress*] (LCLS)

MnBul .... Buhl Public Library, Buhl, MN [*Library symbol*] [*Library of Congress*] (LCLS)

MnBulR........ Range Geneaological Society, Buhl, MN [*Library symbol Library of Congress*] (LCLS)

MnBuS......... St. Michael School, Buckman, MN [*Library symbol*] [*Library of Congress*] (LCLS)

MnBvC......... Christ the King School, Browerville, MN [*Library symbol*] [*Library of Congress*] (LCLS)

MnBvP.......... Browerville Public School, Browerville, MN [*Library symbol*] [*Library of Congress*] (LCLS)

MNBWS....... Miami Nature Biotechnology Winter Symposium (HGEN)

MNBZ........... Bonanza [*Nicaragua*] [*ICAO location identifier*] (ICLI)

MNC............. Concordia College, St. Paul, MN [*OCLC symbol*] (OCLC)

MNC............. Magnocellular Neurosecretory Cells

MNC............. Major NATO Command [*or Commander*] (NATG)

MNC............. Mental Nurses' Cooperation (ROG)

MNC............. Microcomputer Numerical Control (MCD)

MNC............. Mineman, Chief [*Navy rating*]

MNC............. Ministerial Nomination Committee [*Australia*]

Mn-C............ Minnesota State Department of Corrections, St. Paul, MN [*Library symbol Library of Congress*] (LCLS)

MNC............. MIT Airlines Ltd. [*ICAO designator*] (FAAC)

MNC............. Moncalieri [*Italy*] [*Seismograph station code, US Geological Survey Closed*] (SEIS)

MNC............. Monica Resources [*Vancouver Stock Exchange symbol*]

MNC............. Mononuclear Cell (DB)

MNC............. Mononucleated Cell [*Clinical chemistry*] [*Also, MC*]

MNC............. Mouvement National Congolais [*Congolese National Movement*]

MNC............. Mouvement National du Congo-Lumumba [*Congo National Movement-Lumumba*] [*Zaire*] (PD)

MNC............. Movimiento Nacional Conservador [*National Conservative Movement*] [*Colorado Political party*] (EY)

MNC............. Multinational Company [*Business term*]

MNC............. Multinational Corp.

MNC............. Multiplicative Noise Compensator [*Telecommunications*] (TEL)

MNC............. Nacala [*Mozambique*] [*Airport symbol*] (AD)

MNC............. Shelton, WA [*Location identifier FAA*] (FAAL)

MnCaCC....... Cambridge Community College, Cambridge, MN [*Library symbol*] [*Library of Congress*] (LCLS)

MnCaE......... East Central Regional Library, Cambridge, MN [*Library symbol Library of Congress*] (LCLS)

MnCaES....... Cambridge Elementary School, Media Center, Cambridge, MN [*Library symbol*] [*Library of Congress*] (LCLS)

MnCaH......... Cambridge Memorial Hospital, Health Sciences Library, Cambridge, MN [*Library symbol*] [*Library of Congress*] (LCLS)

MnCaHi........ Isanti County Historical Society, Cambridge, MN [*Library symbol*] [*Library of Congress*] (LCLS)

MnCaHS...... Cambridge High School, Media Center, Cambridge, MN [*Library symbol*] [*Library of Congress*] (LCLS)

MnCalE........ Callaway Elementary School, Callaway, MN [*Library symbol*] [*Library of Congress*] (LCLS)

MnCaM........ Cambridge Middle School, Media Center, Cambridge, MN [*Library symbol*] [*Library of Congress*] (LCLS)

MnCamE....... Campbell-Tintah Elementary School, Campbell, MN [*Library symbol*] [*Library of Congress*] (LCLS)

MnCamH...... Campbell-Tintah High School, Campbell, MN [*Library symbol*] [*Library of Congress*] (LCLS)

MnCan.......... Canby Public Library, Canby, MN [*Library symbol*] [*Library of Congress*] (LCLS)

MnCanH....... Canby Community Hospital, Canby, MN [*Library symbol*] [*Library of Congress*] (LCLS)

MnCanHS.... Canby High School, Canby, MN [*Library symbol*] [*Library of Congress*] (LCLS)

MnCarE........ Carlos Elementary School, Carlos, MN [*Library symbol*] [*Library of Congress*] (LCLS)

MnCas......... Cass Lake Community Library, Lake, MN [*Library symbol*] [*Library of Congress*] (LCLS)

MnCasCB...... Chief Bug-O-Nay-Ge-Shig Library, Cass Lake, MN [*Library symbol*] [*Library of Congress*] (LCLS)

MnCaSD...... Cambridge Seventh Day Adventist Library, Cambridge, MN [*Library symbol*] [*Library of Congress*] (LCLS)

MnCasE....... Cass Lake Elementary School, Cass Lake, MN [*Library symbol*] [*Library of Congress*] (LCLS)

MnCaSH...... Cambridge State Hospital, Staff Library, Cambridge, MN [*Library symbol*] [*Library of Congress*] (LCLS)

MnCasHS..... Cass Lake High School, Cass Lake, MN [*Library symbol*] [*Library of Congress*] (LCLS)

MNCC......... Multinational Coordination Center [*NATO*]

MnCcH......... Hazelden Foundation, Staff library, Center City, MN [*Library symbol*] [*Library of Congress*] (LCLS)

MnCgL.......... Lakeside Intermediate Media Center, Chisago City, MN [*Library symbol*] [*Library of Congress*] (LCLS)

MnCgP......... Chisago Lakes Primary School, Chisago City, MN [*Library symbol*] [*Library of Congress*] (LCLS)

MnCh............ Carver County Library, Chaska, MN [*Library symbol Library of Congress*] (LCLS)

MNCH.......... Chinandega/German Pomares [*Nicaragua*] [*ICAO location identifier*] (ICLI)

MnChaHS.... Chandler-Lake Wilson High School, Chandler, MN [*Library symbol*] [*Library of Congress*] (LCLS)

MnChi.......... Chisholm Public Library, Chisholm, MN [*Library symbol*] [*Library of Congress*] (LCLS)

MnChiE......... Vaughan-Steffensrud Elementary School, Chisholm, MN [*Library symbol*] [*Library of Congress*] (LCLS)

MnChiJ......... Chisholm Junior High School, Chisholm, MN [*Library symbol*] [*Library of Congress*] (LCLS)

MnChil.......... Iron Range Research Library, Chisholm, MN [*Library symbol Library of Congress*] (LCLS)

MnChiSH..... Chisholm Senior High School, Chisholm, MN [*Library symbol*] [*Library of Congress*] (LCLS)

MnChoE........ Chokio-Alberta Elementary School, Chokio, MN [*Library symbol*] [*Library of Congress*] (LCLS)

MNCI........... Corn Island [*Nicaragua*] [*ICAO location identifier*] (ICLI)

MNCI........... Neepawa Collegiate Institute, Manitoba [*Library symbol National Library of Canada*] (NLC)

MNCIS......... Management Numerical Control Information System (MCD)

MNC-K......... Mouvement National Congolais - Kalonji [*Congolese National Movement*] [*Kalonji Wing*]

MnCl............ Cloquet Public Library, Cloquet, MN [*Library symbol Library of Congress*] (LCLS)

MNCL.......... Monoclonal Gammopathy Identified [*Immunology*] (DAVI)

MNC-L......... Mouvement National Congolais - Lumumba [*Congolese National Movement*] [*Lumumba Wing*]

MnClaE........ Clarissa Elementary School, Clarissa, MN [*Library symbol*] [*Library of Congress*] (LCLS)

MnCLaH....... Clarissa High School, Clarissa, MN [*Library symbol*] [*Library of Congress*] (LCLS)

MnClc.......... Clara City Public Library, Clara City, MN [*Library symbol*] [*Library of Congress*] (LCLS)

MnCICE........ Churchill Elementary School, Cloquet, MN [*Library symbol*] [*Library of Congress*] (LCLS)

MnClcPS...... Clara City Public Schools, Clara City, MN [*Library symbol*] [*Library of Congress*] (LCLS)

MnCleS........ Clearbrook Public School, Clearbrook, MN [*Library symbol*] [*Library of Congress*] (LCLS)

MnClHi......... Carlton County Historical Society, Cloquet, MN [*Library symbol*] [*Library of Congress*] (LCLS)

MnClim......... Climax Public Library, Climax, MN [*Library symbol*] [*Library of Congress*] (LCLS)

MnClimS....... Climax-Shelly School, Climax, MN [*Library symbol*] [*Library of Congress*] (LCLS)

MnClkE......... Clearview Elementary School, Clear lake, MN [*Library symbol*] [*Library of Congress*] (LCLS)

MnClM......... Cloquet Middle School, Cloquet, MN [*Library symbol*] [*Library of Congress*] (LCLS)

MnClOS........ Fond du Lac Ojibway School, Cloquet, MN [*Library symbol*] [*Library of Congress*] (LCLS)

MnCls.......... Cold Spring Community Library, Cold Spring, MN [*Library symbol*] [*Library of Congress*] (LCLS)

MnClsE......... Cold Spring Elementary/Rocori Junior School, Cold Spring, MN [*Library symbol*] [*Library of Congress*] (LCLS)

MnCISH....... Cloquet Senior High School, Cloquet, MN [*Library symbol*] [*Library of Congress*] (LCLS)

MnClsR........ Rocori High School, Cold Spring, MN [*Library symbol*] [*Library of Congress*] (LCLS)

MnClsS........ St. Boniface Elementary School, Cold Spring, MN [*Library symbol*] [*Library of Congress*] (LCLS)

MnClWE....... Washington Elementary School, Cloquet, MN [*Library symbol*] [*Library of Congress*] (LCLS)

MnCm.......... Calumet Public Library, Calumet, MN [*Library symbol*] [*Library of Congress*] (LCLS)

MNCM........ Mineman, Master Chief [*Navy rating*]

MNCMPTR... Minicomputer (MSA)

MnCo............ Cokato Public Library, Cokato, MN [*Library symbol*] [*Library of Congress*] (LCLS)

MnCoD......... Dassel-Cokato Jr./Sr. High School, Cakoto, MN [*Library symbol*] [*Library of Congress*] (LCLS)

MnCoE......... Cokato Elementary School, Media Center, Cokato, MN [*Library symbol*] [*Library of Congress*] (LCLS)

MnCohS....... Cohasset School, Cohasset, MN [*Library symbol*] [*Library of Congress*] (LCLS)

MnCol.......... Coleraine Public Library, Coleraine, MN [*Library symbol*] [*Library of Congress*] (LCLS)

MnColH........ Greenway High School, Coleraine, MN [*Library symbol*] [*Library of Congress*] (LCLS)

MnCoM........ Cokato Museum, Cokato, MN [*Library symbol*] [*Library of Congress*] (LCLS)

MnCoo......... Cook Public Library, Cook, MN [*Library symbol*] [*Library of Congress*] (LCLS)

MnCooS........ Cook Public School, Cook, MN [*Library symbol*] [*Library of Congress*] (LCLS)

MnCosPS..... Cosmos Public School, Cosmos, MN [*Library symbol*] [*Library of Congress*] (LCLS)

MnCotS........ Cotton Public School, Cotton, MN [*Library symbol*] [*Library of Congress*] (LCLS)

MNCP.......... Math Network Curriculum Project (EDAC)

MNCP.......... Mbandzeni National Convention Party [*Swaziland*] (BUAC)

MNCPL........ Municipal

MNCPPC...... Maryland-National Capital Park and Planning Commission

MNCPPLTY... Municipality

MnCr............ Crookston Public Library, Crookston, MN [*Library symbol*] [*Library of Congress*] (LCLS)

MNCR.......... Material Nonconformance Report (COE)

MnCr............ Polk County Library, Crookston, MN [*Library symbol Library of Congress*] (LCLS)

MnCrCH....... Central High School, Crookston,MN [*Library symbol*] [*Library of Congress*] (LCLS)

MnCrHE........ Highland Elementary School, Crookston, MN [*Library symbol*] [*Library of Congress*] (LCLS)

MnCrLE........ Lincoln Elementary School, Crookston, MN [*Library symbol*] [*Library of Congress*] (LCLS)

MnCrMS ...... Mount St. Benedict, Crookston, MN [*Library symbol*] [*Library of Congress*] (LCLS)

MnCroE....... Crosby-Ironton Elementary School, Crosby, MN [*Library symbol*] [*Library of Congress*] (LCLS)

MnCroH ...... Crosby-Ironton High School, Crosby, MN [*Library symbol*] [*Library of Congress*] (LCLS)

MnCrpM....... Mercy Medical Center, Coon Rapids, MN [*Library symbol Library of Congress*] (LCLS)

MnCrU .... University of Minnesota Technical College, Crookston, MN [*Library symbol Library of Congress*] (LCLS)

MnCrWE ...... Washington Elementary School, Crookston, MN [*Library symbol*] [*Library of Congress*] (LCLS)

MnCrwHS .... Cromwell High School, Cromwell, MN [*Library symbol*] [*Library of Congress*] (LCLS)

MNCS .... Mineman, Senior Chief [*Navy rating*]

MNCS .... Multipoint Network-Control System

MnCS........... St. John's University, Collegeville, MN [*Library symbol Library of Congress*] (LCLS)

MnCt........... Carlton Public Library, Carlton, MN [*Library symbol*] [*Library of Congress*] (LCLS)

MnCtE......... South Terrace Elementary School, Carlton, MN [*Library symbol*] [*Library of Congress*] (LCLS)

MnCtH .... Carlotn High School, Carlton, MN [*Library symbol*] [*Library of Congress*] (LCLS)

MnCtwPS ..... Cottonwood Public School, Cottonwood, MN [*Library symbol*] [*Library of Congress*] (LCLS)

MNCV .... Motor Nerve Conduction Velocity [*Medicine*]

MnCyS .... Cyrus Public School, Cyrus, MN [*Library symbol*] [*Library of Congress*] (LCLS)

MND .... Mandalay [*Burma*] [*Seismograph station code, US Geological Survey Closed*] (SEIS)

MND .... Marlin Developments [*Vancouver Stock Exchange symbol*]

MND .... Martin Nuclear Division [*AEC*] (MCD)

MND .... Material Need Document [*DoD*]

MND .... Mean Narrow Dose [*Radiation therapy*] (DAVI)

MND .... Medial Nuclear Division [*Cytology*]

MND .... Mendenhall, AK [*Location identifier FAA*] (FAAL)

MND .... Midsummer Night's Dream [*Shakespearean work*]

MND .... Minimum Necrosing Dose

MND .... Minister of National Defence [*Canada*]

MND .... Ministry of National Defence [*British*] (MCD)

MND .... Minor Neurological Dysfunction

MND .... Mission Need Determination (DOMA)

MND .... Mission Need Document [*DoD*]

MND .... Mission Non-Delivery (MCD)

MND .... Mitchell Energy & Development Corp. [*NYSE symbol*] (SAG)

MND .... Modified Neck Dissection [*Medicine*] (DMAA)

MND .... Motor Neuron Disease [*Medicine*]

MND .... Mound

MND .... Movimento Nacional Democratico [*National Democratic Movement*] [*Portugal Political party*] (PPE)

MND .... University of Minnesota-Duluth, Duluth, MN [*OCLC symbol*] (OCLC)

MNDA .... Missionary Sisters of Notre Dame des Anges [*Roman Catholic religious order*]

MNDA .... Missionary Sisters of Our Lady of the Angels (BUAC)

MND A......... Mitchell Energy/Dev'A' [*NYSE symbol*] (TTSB)

MNDA.......... Motor Neurone Disease Association [*British*] (DBA)

MnDaw .... Carnegie Library, Dawson, MN [*Library symbol*] [*Library of Congress*] (LCLS)

MNDAWA..... Motor Neurone Disease Association of Western Australia

MnDawJH .... Johnson Memorial Hospital and Nursing School, Dawson, MN [*Library symbol*] [*Library of Congress*] (LCLS)

MnDawPS.... Dawson-Boyd Public Library, Dawson, MN [*Library symbol*] [*Library of Congress*] (LCLS)

MND B........ Mitchell Energy/Dev'B' [*NYSE symbol*] (TTSB)

MNDD.......... Mouvement National pour la Democratie et le Developpement [*Benin*] [*Political party*] (EY)

MnDe .... Delano Public Llbbrary, Delano, MN [*Library symbol*] [*Library of Congress*] (LCLS)

MnDeE......... Delano Elementary School, Delano, MN [*Library symbol*] [*Library of Congress*] (LCLS)

MnDeH .... Delano High School, Delano, MN [*Library symbol*] [*Library of Congress*] (LCLS)

MnDeM........ Delano Middle School, Delano, MN [*Library symbol*] [*Library of Congress*] (LCLS)

MnDerE........ King Elementary School, Deer River, MN [*Library symbol*] [*Library of Congress*] (LCLS)

MnDerH .... Deer River High School, Deer River, MN [*Library symbol*] [*Library of Congress*] (LCLS)

MnDES........ Dassel Elementary School, Media Center, Dassel, MN [*Library symbol*] [*Library of Congress*] (LCLS)

MnDeSP ...... St. Peter's School, Delano, MN [*Library symbol*] [*Library of Congress*] (LCLS)

MnDI........... Detroit Lakes Public Library, Detroit Lakes, MN [*Library of Congress*] (LCLS)

MnDIH .... Community High School, Detroit Lakes, MN [*Library symbol*] [*Library of Congress*] (LCLS)

MnDIHi .... Becker County Historical Society, Detroit Lakes, MN [*Library symbol*] [*Library of Congress*] (LCLS)

MnDIJ.......... Community Junior High School, Detroit Lakes, MN [*Library symbol*] [*Library of Congress*] (LCLS)

MnDILe........ Lincoln Elementary School, Detroit Lakes, MN [*Library symbol*] [*Library of Congress*] (LCLS)

MnDIRE .... Rossman Elementary School, Detroit Lakes, MN [*Library symbol*] [*Library of Congress*] (LCLS)

MnDITI......... Detroit Lakes Technical Institute, Detroit Lakes, MN [*Library symbol*] [*Library of Congress*] (LCLS)

MnDIWE ...... Washington Elementary School, Detroit Lakes, MN [*Library symbol*] [*Library of Congress*] (LCLS)

MNDO......... Merchant Navy Discipline Organisation [*British*] (DS)

MNDO......... Modified Neglect of Diatomic Overlap (AAEL)

MNDO......... Modified Neglect of Differential Overlap [*Quantum mechanics*]

MNDP......... Bibliotheque Pere Champagne [*Pere Champagne Library*], Notre-Dame-De-Lourdes, Manitoba [*Library symbol National Library of Canada*] (BIB)

MNDP......... Multinational Data Processing (MHDB)

MNDTH....... Minimum Depth (NOAA)

MNDTS .... Member of the Non-Destructive Testing Society of Great Britain

MnDu.......... Duluth Public Library, Duluth, MN [*Library symbol Library of Congress*] (LCLS)

MnDuBE...... Birchwood Elementary School, Duluth, MN [*Library symbol*] [*Library of Congress*] (LCLS)

MnDuBVE .... Bay View Elementary School, Duluth, MN [*Library symbol*] [*Library of Congress*] (LCLS)

MnDuCE...... Cobb Elementary Library, Duluth, MN [*Library symbol*] [*Library of Congress*] (LCLS)

MnDuCH ..... Central High School, Duluth, MN [*Library symbol*] [*Library of Congress*] (LCLS)

MnDuCOE.... Congdon Park Elementary School, Duluth, MN [*Library symbol*] [*Library of Congress*] (LCLS)

MnDuCPE.... Chester Park Elementary School, Duluth, MN [*Library symbol*] [*Library of Congress*] (LCLS)

MnDuDH ..... Denfeld High School, Duluth, MN [*Library symbol*] [*Library of Congress*] (LCLS)

MnDuEH ..... East High School, Duluth, MN [*Library symbol*] [*Library of Congress*] (LCLS)

MnDuEPA .... United States Environmental Protection Agency, National Water Quality Laboratory, Duluth, MN [*Library symbol Library of Congress*] (LCLS)

MnDuGE...... Grant Elementary School, Duluth, MN [*Library symbol*] [*Library of Congress*] (LCLS)

MnDuHE...... Homcroft Elementary School, Duluth, MN [*Library symbol*] [*Library of Congress*] (LCLS)

MnDuHi .... Northeast Minnesota Historical Center Library, Duluth, MN [*Library symbol*] [*Library of Congress*] (LCLS)

MnDuHS ..... Hermantown High School, Duluth, MN [*Library symbol*] [*Library of Congress*] (LCLS)

MnDuLE...... Lincoln Elementary School, Duluth, MN [*Library symbol*] [*Library of Congress*] (LCLS)

MnDuLOE.... Lowell Elementary School, Duluth, MN [*Library symbol*] [*Library of Congress*] (LCLS)

MnDuLPE.... Lester Park Elementary School, Duluth, MN [*Library symbol*] [*Library of Congress*] (LCLS)

MnDuLWE.... Lakewood Elementary School, Duluth, MN [*Library symbol*] [*Library of Congress*] (LCLS)

MnDuM....... Miller-Dawn Hospital and Medical Center, Duluth, MN [*Library symbol Library of Congress*] (LCLS)

MnDuME...... Merritt Elementary School, Duluth, MN [*Library symbol*] [*Library of Congress*] (LCLS)

MnDuMPJ.... Morgan Park Junior High School, Duluth, MN [*Library symbol*] [*Library of Congress*] (LCLS)

MnDuMS..... Marshall School, Duluth, MN [*Library symbol*] [*Library of Congress*] (LCLS)

MnDuMWE.... MacArthue/West Elementary School, Duluth MN [*Library symbol*] [*Library of Congress*] (LCLS)

MnDuNE...... Nettleton Elementary School, Duluth, MN [*Library symbol*] [*Library of Congress*] (LCLS)

MnDuNR...... Natural Resources Research Institute, Duluth, MN [*Library symbol*] [*Library of Congress*] (LCLS)

MnDuNSE.... North Shore Elementary School, Duluth, MN [*Library symbol*] [*Library of Congress*] (LCLS)

MnDuOJ....... Ordean Junior High School, Duluth, MN [*Library symbol*] [*Library of Congress*] (LCLS)

MnDuPC...... Duluth Prison Camp, Duluth, MN [*Library symbol*] [*Library of Congress*] (LCLS)

MnDuPE....... Piedmont Elementary School, Duluth, MN [*Library symbol*] [*Library of Congress*] (LCLS)

MnDuSE...... Stowe Elementary School, Duluth, MN [*Library symbol*] [*Library of Congress*] (LCLS)

MnDuSLH ... St. Louis County Helth Dept., Duluth, MN [*Library symbol*] [*Library of Congress*] (LCLS)

MnDuStL..... Saint Luke's Hospital, Duluth, MN [*Library symbol Library of Congress*] (LCLS)

MnDuStM .... Saint Mary's Hospital, Duluth, MN [*Library symbol Library of Congress*] (LCLS)

MnDuStS ..... College of Saint Scholastica, Duluth, MN [*Library symbol Library of Congress*] (LCLS)

MnDuTI........ Duluth Technical Institute, Duluth, MN [*Library symbol*] [*Library of Congress*] (LCLS)

MnDuTRC .... Teachers' Resource Center, Duluth, MN [*Library symbol*] [*Library of Congress*] (LCLS)

MnDuU .... University of Minnesota, Duluth, MN [*Library symbol Library of Congress*] (LCLS)

MnDuWE...... Washburn Elementary School, Duluth, MN [*Library symbol*] [*Library of Congress*] (LCLS)

MnDuWJ..... Washington Junior High School, Duluth, MN [*Library symbol*] [*Library of Congress*] (LCLS)

MnDuWJH ... Woodland Junior High School, Duluth, MN [*Library symbol*] [*Library of Congress*] (LCLS)

MNDX......... Mobile Non-Director Exchange [*Telecommunications*] (NITA)

MNE	College of St. Catherine, St. Paul, MN [*OCLC symbol*] (OCLC)
Mne	Marine [*British military*] (DMA)
MNE	Master of Naval Engineering
MNE	Master of Nuclear Engineering
MNE	Mentone [*France*] [*Airport symbol*] (AD)
MNE	Merchant Navy Establishment [*British*] (DS)
MNE	Methylallyl Nitrophenyl Ether [*Organic chemistry*]
MNE	Methylnorepinephrine [*Also, Normetanephrine*] [*Biochemistry*]
MNE	Minden, LA [*Location identifier FAA*] (FAAL)
MNE	Mineo [*Sicily*] [*Seismograph station code, US Geological Survey Closed*] (SEIS)
MNE	Minimum Number of Elements
Mn-E	Minnesota State Department of Education, St. Paul, MN [*Library symbol Library of Congress*] (LCLS)
MNE	Modern English [*Language, etc.*]
MNE	Moneygram Payment Systems [*NYSE symbol*] (SAG)
MNE	Multinational Enterprise
MNe	Newburyport Public Library, Newburyport, MA [*Library symbol Library of Congress*] (LCLS)
MNEA	Merchant Navy Establishment Administration [*British*] (DS)
MnEb	Eagle Bend Public Library, Eagle Bend, MN [*Library symbol*] [*Library of Congress*] (LCLS)
MnEbS	Eagle Bend School, Eagle Bend, MN [*Library symbol*] [*Library of Congress*] (LCLS)
MnEcES	Echo-Wood Lake Elementary School, Echo, MN [*Library symbol*] [*Library of Congress*] (LCLS)
MNECP	Mobile National Emergency Command Post [*Air Force*]
MN Ed	Master of Nursing Education
MN ED	Material Need Engineering Development (MCD)
MnEdS	Southdale-Hennepin Area Library, Edina, MN [*Library symbol Library of Congress*] (LCLS)
MNEE	Mission Nonessential Equipment [*NASA*] (KSC)
MNeeS	GTE-Sylvania, Electric Systems Group, Needham, MA [*Library symbol Library of Congress*] (LCLS)
MnEfAE	Adams Elementary School, Fergus Falls, MN [*Library symbol*] [*Library of Congress*] (LCLS)
MnEfS	Effie School, Effie, MN [*Library symbol*] [*Library of Congress*] (LCLS)
MnEgfCE	Crestwood Elementary School, East Grand Forks, MN [*Library symbol*] [*Library of Congress*] (LCLS)
MnEgfH	East Grand Forks High School, East Grand Forks, MN [*Library symbol*] [*Library of Congress*] (LCLS)
MnEgfJ	Central Junior High School, Grand Forks, MN [*Library symbol*] [*Library of Congress*] (LCLS)
MnEgfRE	River Heights Elementary School, East Grand Forks, MN [*Library symbol*] [*Library of Congress*] (LCLS)
MnEgfTI	East Grand Forks Technical Institute, East Grand Forks, MN [*Library symbol*] [*Library of Congress*] (LCLS)
MnEgfVE	Valley Elementary School, East Grand Forks, MN [*Library symbol*] [*Library of Congress*] (LCLS)
MNeHi	Newburyport Historical Society, Newburyport, MA [*Library symbol Library of Congress*] (LCLS)
MnElb	Thorsen Memorial Public Library, Elbow Lake, MN [*Library symbol*] [*Library of Congress*] (LCLS)
MnElbE	West Central Elementary School, Elbow Lake, MN [*Library symbol*] [*Library of Congress*] (LCLS)
MnElbH	West Central High School, Elbow Lake, MN [*Library symbol*] [*Library of Congress*] (LCLS)
MnEly	Ely Public Library, Ely, MN [*Library symbol*] [*Library of Congress*] (LCLS)
MnElyJS	Memorial Junior/Senior High School, Ely, MN [*Library symbol*] [*Library of Congress*] (LCLS)
MnElyV	Vermillion Community College, Ely, MN [*Library symbol Library of Congress*] (LCLS)
MnElyWE	Washington Elementary School, Ely, MN [*Library symbol*] [*Library of Congress*] (LCLS)
Mnemos	Mnemosyne [*A publication*] (OCD)
MN Eng	Master of Naval Engineering
MnEr	Elk River Public Library, Elk River, MN [*Library symbol*] [*Library of Congress*] (LCLS)
MNERAM	Members of New England Regional Art Museum
MnErHE	Handke Elementary School, Elk River, MN [*Library symbol*] [*Library of Congress*] (LCLS)
MnErPE	K.G. Parker Elementary School, Elk River, MN [*Library symbol*] [*Library of Congress*] (LCLS)
MnErS	Elk River Senior High School, Elk River, MN [*Library symbol*] [*Library of Congress*] (LCLS)
MnErSA	St. Andrew's School, Elk River, MN [*Library symbol*] [*Library of Congress*] (LCLS)
MnErSJ	Salk Junior High School, Elk River, MN [*Library symbol*] [*Library of Congress*] (LCLS)
MnErSJL	St. John's Lutheran School, Elk River, MN [*Library symbol*] [*Library of Congress*] (LCLS)
MnErsS	Erksine Public School, Erkskine, MN [*Library symbol*] [*Library of Congress*] (LCLS)
MnErVJ	Vandenberge Junior High School, Elk River, MN [*Library symbol*] [*Library of Congress*] (LCLS)
MNES	Mine Safety Appl [*NASDAQ symbol*] (TTSB)
MNES	Mine Safety Appliances Co. [*NASDAQ symbol*] (NQ)
MnEskH	Esko High School, Esko, MN [*Library symbol*] [*Library of Congress*] (LCLS)
MnEskWE	Winterquist Elementary School, Esko, MN [*Library symbol*] [*Library of Congress*] (LCLS)
MNET	Mission and Data Operations Directorate Network (MCD)
MNET	Multicom Publishing [*NASDAQ symbol*] (SAG)
MNEV	Musica Nostra et Vostra, National Corp. of America (EA)
MnEvaE	Evansville Elementary School, Evansville, MN [*Library symbol*] [*Library of Congress*] (LCLS)
MnEvaH	Evansville High School, Evansville, MN [*Library symbol*] [*Library of Congress*] (LCLS)
MnEvH	Eden Valley-Watkins High School, Eden Valley, MN [*Library symbol*] [*Library of Congress*] (LCLS)
MnEvl	Eveleth Public Library, Eveleth, MN [*Library symbol*] [*Library of Congress*] (LCLS)
MnEvlFE	Franklin Elementary School, Eveleth, MN [*Library symbol*] [*Library of Congress*] (LCLS)
MnEvlSH	Eveleth-Gilbert Senior High School, Eveleth, MN [*Library symbol*] [*Library of Congress*] (LCLS)
MnF	Buckham Memorial Library, Faribault, MN [*Library symbol Library of Congress*] (LCLS)
MNF	College of St. Benedict, St. Joseph, MN [*OCLC symbol*] (OCLC)
MNF	Forbes Library, Northampton, MA [*Library symbol Library of Congress*] (LCLS)
MNF	Mana [*Fiji*] [*Airport symbol*] (OAG)
MNF	Manitou Reef Resources [*Vancouver Stock Exchange symbol*]
MNF	Millers' National Federation (EA)
MNF	Miso National Front [*India*] [*Political party*] (BUAC)
MNF	Mizo National Front [*India*] (PD)
MNF	Morehead & North Fork R. R. [*AAR code*]
MNF	Mountain View, MO [*Location identifier FAA*] (FAAL)
MNF	Multilateral Nuclear Force
MNF	Multinational Force [*Eleven-nation peace-keeping force for the Sinai*]
MNF	Multisystem Networking Facility
MnFa	Martin County Library, Fairmont, MN [*Library symbol Library of Congress*] (LCLS)
MNFD	Manifold (ECII)
MNFE	Missile Not Fully Equipped (AAG)
MnFer	Fertile Public Library, Fertile, MN [*Library symbol*] [*Library of Congress*] (LCLS)
MnFerS	Fertile-Betrami School, Fertile, MN [*Library symbol*] [*Library of Congress*] (LCLS)
MnFf	Fergus Falls Public Library, Fergus Falls, MN [*Library symbol Library of Congress*] (LCLS)
MNFF	Magyar Nemzeti Fueggetlensegi Front [*Hungarian National Independence Front*] [*Political party*]
MnFfC	Fergus Falls Community College, Fergus Falls, MN [*Library symbol Library of Congress*] (LCLS)
MnFfCE	Cleveland Elementary School, Fergus Falls, MN [*Library symbol*] [*Library of Congress*] (LCLS)
MnFfEC	West Central Educational Cooperative Service Unit, Fergus Falls, MN [*Library symbol*] [*Library of Congress*] (LCLS)
MnFfH	Lake Region Hospital, Fergus Falls, MN [*Library symbol Library of Congress*] (LCLS)
MnFfHA	Hillcrest Academy, Fergus Falls, MN [*Library symbol*] [*Library of Congress*] (LCLS)
MnFfHi	Otter Tail County Historical Society, Fergus Falls, MN [*Library symbol*] [*Library of Congress*] (LCLS)
MnFfL	Lutheran Brethren Schools, Fergus Falls, MN [*Library symbol Library of Congress*] (LCLS)
MnFfM	Fergus Falls Middle School, Fergus Falls, MN [*Library symbol*] [*Library of Congress*] (LCLS)
MnFfME	McKinley Elementary School, Fergus Falls, MN [*Library symbol*] [*Library of Congress*] (LCLS)
MnFfO	Otter Tail Power Co., Fergus Falls, MN [*Library symbol*] [*Library of Congress*] (LCLS)
MnFfRT	Fergus Falls Regional Treatment Center, Fergus Falls, MN [*Library symbol*] [*Library of Congress*] (LCLS)
MnFfSH	Fergus Falls Senior High School, Fergus Falls, MN [*Library symbol*] [*Library of Congress*] (LCLS)
MnFfV	Viking Library System, Fergus Falls, MN [*Library symbol*] [*Library of Congress*] (LCLS)
MNFI	Michigan Natural Features Inventory [*Michigan State Department of Natural Resources*] [*Information service or system*] (IID)
MnFiE	Finlayson Elementary School, Finlayson, MN [*Library symbol*] [*Library of Congress*] (LCLS)
MnFiH	Finlayson High School, Finlayson, MN [*Library symbol*] [*Library of Congress*] (LCLS)
MnFisS	Fisher Public School, Fisher, MN [*Library symbol*] [*Library of Congress*] (LCLS)
MNFLD	Manifold (KSC)
MnFILS	Lincoln School, Floodwood, MN [*Library symbol*] [*Library of Congress*] (LCLS)
MnFo	Foley Community Library, Foley, MN [*Library symbol*] [*Library of Congress*] (LCLS)
MnFoE	Foley Elementary School, Foley, MN [*Library symbol*] [*Library of Congress*] (LCLS)
MnFoH	Foley High School, Foley, MN [*Library symbol*] [*Library of Congress*] (LCLS)
MnFoS	St. John's School, Foley, MN [*Library symbol*] [*Library of Congress*] (LCLS)
MNFP	Magyar Nemzeti Fueggetlensegi Part [*Hungarian National Independence Party*] [*Political party*] (PPE)
MNFP	Multinational Fighter Program [*Air Force*]
MNFP	Multiple Number of Faults per Pass (PDAA)
MnFpS	Sacred Heart School, Freeport MN [*Library symbol*] [*Library of Congress*] (LCLS)
MnFraE	Frazee Elementary School, Frazee, MN [*Library symbol*] [*Library of Congress*] (LCLS)
MnFraHS	Frazee-Vergas High School, Frazee, MN [*Library symbol*] [*Library of Congress*] (LCLS)
MNFRM	Main Frame

MnFrnCES.... Cedar Mt. Elementary School, Franklin, MN [*Library symbol*] [*Library of Congress*] (LCLS)

MnFrUH....... Unity Hospital, Fridley, MN [*Library symbol Library of Congress*] (LCLS)

MnFS........... Seabury Divinity School, Faribault, MN [*Library symbol Library of Congress*] (LCLS)

MnFt............ Fosston Public Library, Fosston,MN [*Library symbol*] [*Library of Congress*] (LCLS)

MnFtH.......... Fosston High School, Fosston, MN [*Library symbol*] [*Library of Congress*] (LCLS)

MnFtME....... Magelssen Elementary School, Fosston, MN [*Library symbol*] [*Library of Congress*] (LCLS)

MnFu .... Fulda Public Library, Fulda, MN [*Library symbol*] [*Library of Congress*] (LCLS)

MNFU .... Manx National Farmers Union [*British*] (DBA)

MnFuES...... Fulda Elementary School, Fulda, MN [*Library symbol*] [*Library of Congress*] (LCLS)

MnFuJSH.... Fulda Junior-Senior High School, Fulda, MN [*Library symbol*] [*Library of Congress*] (LCLS)

MnFuStP.... St. Paul's Lutheran School, Fulda, MN [*Library symbol*] [*Library of Congress*] (LCLS)

MNG .... Gustavus Adolphus College, St. Peter, MN [*OCLC symbol*] (OCLC)

MNG .... Managing (MSA)

Mng .... Managing (TBD)

MNG .... Mangahao [*New Zealand*] [*Seismograph station code, US Geological Survey*] (SEIS)

MNG .... Maningrida [*Australia Airport symbol Obsolete*] (OAG)

mng .... Meaning

MNG .... Microwave Negative Grid

MNG .... Modulated Noise Generator (PDAA)

MNG .... Mongolia [*ANSI three-letter standard code*] (CNC)

MNG .... Morning

MNG .... Mourning (ROG)

MNG .... Multinodular Goiter [*Endocrinology*] (DAVI)

MnGarE....... Garfield Elementary School, Garfield, MN [*Library symbol*] [*Library of Congress*] (LCLS)

MnGBES ..... Helen Baker Elementary School, Glencoe, MN [*Library symbol*] [*Library of Congress*] (LCLS)

MnGc.......... Grove City Public Library, Grove City, MN [*Library symbol*] [*Library of Congress*] (LCLS)

MnGcJH....... Atwater-Grove City Junior High School, Grove City, MN [*Library symbol*] [*Library of Congress*] (LCLS)

MnGeH .... Grey Eagle High School, Grey Eagle, MN [*Library symbol*] [*Library of Congress*] (LCLS)

MnGf........... Granite Falls Public Library, Granite Falls, MN [*Library symbol*] [*Library of Congress*] (LCLS)

MnGfH .... Granite Falls Municipal Hospital, Granite Falls, MN [*Library symbol*] [*Library of Congress*] (LCLS)

MnGfODS..... Open Door Bible School, Granite Falls, MN [*Library symbol*] [*Library of Congress*] (LCLS)

MnGfPS .... Granite Falls Public School, Granite Falls, MN [*Library symbol*] [*Library of Congress*] (LCLS)

MnGfTC........ Southwest Technical College, Granite Falls, MN [*Library symbol*] [*Library of Congress*] (LCLS)

MnGGH .... Glencoe Hospital, Glencoe, MN [*Library symbol*] [*Library of Congress*] (LCLS)

MnGHS .... Glencoe Public High School, Glencoe, MN [*Library symbol*] [*Library of Congress*] (LCLS)

MnGi........... Gilbert Public Library, Gilbert, MN [*Library symbol*] [*Library of Congress*] (LCLS)

MnGiHi .... Iron Range Historical Society, Gilbert MN [*Library symbol*] [*Library of Congress*] (LCLS)

MnGiJH........ Gilbert-Eveleth Junior High School, Gilbert, MN [*Library symbol*] [*Library of Congress*] (LCLS)

MnGiNSE ..... Nelle Shean Elementary School, Gilbert, MN [*Library symbol*] [*Library of Congress*] (LCLS)

MnGle.......... Glenwood Public Library, Glenwood, MN [*Library symbol*] [*Library of Congress*] (LCLS)

MnGLES....... Lincoln Elementary School, Glencoe, MN [*Library symbol*] [*Library of Congress*] (LCLS)

MnGleSH .... Glenwood Senior High School, Glenwood, MN [*Library symbol*] [*Library of Congress*] (LCLS)

MNGLX .... Montgomery Global Long-Short Fund [*Investment term*]

MnGlyE........ Glyndon Elementary School, Glyndon, MN [*Library symbol*] [*Library of Congress*] (LCLS)

MnGlyHS ..... Glyndon-Felton High School, Glyndon, MN [*Library symbol*] [*Library of Congress*] (LCLS)

MnGm.......... Grand Marais Public Library, Grand Marais, MN [*Library symbol*] [*Library of Congress*] (LCLS)

MnGmFT....... United States National Park Service, Grand Portage Northern Minnesota Fur Trade Library, Grand Marais, MN [*Library symbol*] [*Library of Congress*] (LCLS)

MnGmH .... Cook County High School, Grand Marais, MN [*Library symbol*] [*Library of Congress*] (LCLS)

MnGMS........ Glencoe Middle School, Glencoe, MN [*Library symbol*] [*Library of Congress*] (LCLS)

MnGmSE...... Sawtooth Elementary School, Grand Marais, MN [*Library symbol*] [*Library of Congress*] (LCLS)

MNGMT .... Management (ADA)

MNGNG....... Managing

MnGonS....... Gonvick-Trail Community School, Gonvick, MN [*Library symbol*] [*Library of Congress*] (LCLS)

MnGoos .... Goodridge Public School, Goodridge, MN [*Library symbol*] [*Library of Congress*] (LCLS)

MNGP .... Monticello Nuclear Generating Plant (NRCH)

MnGpE......... Grand Portage Elementary School, Grand Portage, MN [*Library symbol*] [*Library of Congress*] (LCLS)

MnGr .... Grand Rapids Public Library, Grand Rapids, MN [*Library symbol*] [*Library of Congress*] (LCLS)

MNGR.......... Manager

MNGR.......... Monsignor

MnGra .... Graceville Public Library, Graceville, MN [*Library symbol*] [*Library of Congress*] (LCLS)

MnGraBS ..... Big Stone Hutterite Colony School, Graceville, MN [*Library symbol*] [*Library of Congress*] (LCLS)

MnGraCHS... Clinton-Graceville High School, Graceville, MN [*Library symbol*] [*Library of Congress*] (LCLS)

MnGraH .... Holy Trinity Hospital, Graceville, MN [*Library symbol*] [*Library of Congress*] (LCLS)

MnGre .... Greenbush Public Library, Greenbush, MN [*Library symbol*] [*Library of Congress*] (LCLS)

MnGrEMS .... Edna I. Murphy School, Grand Rapids, MN [*Library symbol*] [*Library of Congress*] (LCLS)

MnGreS .... Greenbush Public School, Greenbush, MN [*Library symbol*] [*Library of Congress*] (LCLS)

MnGrFLS ..... Forrest Lake School, Grand Rapids, MN [*Library symbol*] [*Library of Congress*] (LCLS)

MnGrFW ...... Forest Wildlife Population and Research Group, Grand Rapids, MN [*Library symbol*] [*Library of Congress*] (LCLS)

MnGrI .... Itasca Community College, Grand Rapids, MN [*Library symbol Library of Congress*] (LCLS)

MnGrM .... Grand Rapids Middle School, Grand Rapids, MN [*Library symbol*] [*Library of Congress*] (LCLS)

MNGRM....... Monogram

MnGrRS....... Riverview School, Grand Rapids, MN [*Library symbol*] [*Library of Congress*] (LCLS)

MnGrSH....... Grand Rapids Senior HighSchool, Grand Rapids, MN [*Library symbol*] [*Library of Congress*] (LCLS)

MnGrSS .... Southwest School, Grand Rapids, MN [*Library symbol*] [*Library of Congress*] (LCLS)

MnGryS........ Grygla Public School, Grygla, MN [*Library symbol*] [*Library of Congress*] (LCLS)

Mngt .... Management

MnGvH......... Golden Valley Health Center, Golden Valley, MN [*Library symbol Library of Congress*] (LCLS)

MNH .... Magnum Resources [*Vancouver Stock Exchange symbol*]

MNH .... Makers of National History [*A publication*]

Mn-H .... Minnesota State Department of Health, St. Paul, MN [*Library symbol Library of Congress*] (LCLS)

MNH .... Mint Never Hinged [*Philately*]

MNH .... Monarch Airlines [*ICAO designator*] (FAAC)

MNH .... Munich [*Germany*] [*Seismograph station code, US Geological Survey Closed*] (SEIS)

MNH .... Museum of Natural History [*Smithsonian Institution*]

MNH .... University of Minnesota-Duluth, Health Science Library, Duluth, MN [*OCLC symbol*] (OCLC)

MnHaH .... Norman County West High School, Halstad, MN [*Library symbol*] [*Library of Congress*] (LCLS)

MnHal.......... Hallock Public Library, Hallock, MN [*Library symbol*] [*Library of Congress*] (LCLS)

MnHalH .... Hallock High School, Hallock, MN [*Library symbol*] [*Library of Congress*] (LCLS)

MnHan......... Hancock Community Library, Hancock, MN [*Library symbol*] [*Library of Congress*]. (LCLS)

MnHanE....... Hancock Elementary School, Hancock, MN [*Library symbol*] [*Library of Congress*] (LCLS)

MnHanH....... Hancock High School, Hancock, MN [*Library symbol*] [*Library of Congress*] (LCLS)

MnHaw .... Hawley Public Library, Hawley, MN [*Library symbol*] [*Library of Congress*] (LCLS)

MnHawE....... Hawley Elementary School, Hawley, MN [*Library symbol*] [*Library of Congress*] (LCLS)

MnHawH....... Hawley High School, Hawley, MN [*Library symbol*] [*Library of Congress*] (LCLS)

MnHcS......... Hill City School, Hill City, MN [*Library symbol*] [*Library of Congress*] (LCLS)

MnHe .... Hector Public Library, Hector, MN [*Library symbol*] [*Library of Congress*] (LCLS)

MnHE .... Hinckley Elementary School, Hinckley, MN [*Library symbol*] [*Library of Congress*] (LCLS)

MnHel.......... Heron Lake Public Library, Heron Lake, MN [*Library symbol*] [*Library of Congress*] (LCLS)

MnHelES...... Heron Lake Elementary School, Heron Lake, MN [*Library symbol*] [*Library of Congress*] (LCLS)

MnHendH..... Hendricks Community Hospital, Hendricks, MN [*Library symbol*] [*Library of Congress*] (LCLS)

MnHendPS... Hendircks Public School, Hendricks, MN [*Library symbol*] [*Library of Congress*] (LCLS)

MnHenE....... West Elementary School, Hendrum, MN [*Library symbol*] [*Library of Congress*] (LCLS)

MnHennS..... Henning Public School, Henning, MN [*Library symbol*] [*Library of Congress*] (LCLS)

MnHePS....... Hector Public School, Hector, MN [*Library symbol*] [*Library of Congress*] (LCLS)

MnHH .... Hinckley High School, Hinckley, MN [*Library symbol*] [*Library of Congress*] (LCLS)

MnHi............ Minnesota Historical Society, St. Paul, MN [*Library symbol Library of Congress*] (LCLS)

MnHi-Ar....... minnesota Historical Society, Division of Archives and Manuscripts, St. Paul, MN [*Library symbol*] [*Library of Congress*] (LCLS)

MnHib .... Hibbing Public Library, Hibbing, MN [*Library symbol Library of Congress*] (LCLS)

MnHibC .... Hibbing Community College, Hibbing, MN [*Library symbol Library of Congress*] (LCLS)

MnHibM .... Central Mesabi Medical Center, Hibbing, MN [*Library symbol*] [*Library of Congress*] (LCLS)

MnHilCS ...... Hills Christian School, Hills, MN [*Library symbol*] [*Library of Congress*] (LCLS)

MnHilES ...... Hills-Beaver Creek Elementary School, Hills, MN [*Library symbol*] [*Library of Congress*] (LCLS)

MnHilHS ...... Hills-Beaver Creek High School, Hills, MN [*Library symbol*] [*Library of Congress*] (LCLS)

MnHitE .... Ulen-Hitterdal Elementary School, Hitterdal, MN [*Library symbol*] [*Library of Congress*] (LCLS)

MnHl .... Howard Lake Public Library, Howard Lake, MN [*Library symbol*] [*Library of Congress*] (LCLS)

MNHLA .... Musicians National Hot Line Association (EA)

MnHldSDS ... Seventh Day Adventist School, Holland, MN [*Library symbol*] [*Library of Congress*] (LCLS)

MnHlE .... Howard Lake-Waverly Elementary School, Howard Lake, MN [*Library symbol*] [*Library of Congress*] (LCLS)

MnHlH .... Howard Lake-Waverly High School, Howard Lake, MN [*Library symbol*] [*Library of Congress*] (LCLS)

MnHlS .... St. James Lutheran School, Howard Lake, MN [*Library symbol*] [*Library of Congress*] (LCLS)

MnHoE .... Holdingford Elementary School, Holdingford, MN [*Library symbol*] [*Library of Congress*] (LCLS)

MnHofS .... Hoffman Public School, Hoffman, MN [*Library symbol*] [*Library of Congress*] (LCLS)

MnHoH .... Holdingford Jr./Sr. High School, Holdingford, MN [*Library symbol*] [*Library of Congress*] (LCLS)

MnHol .... Hoyt Lakes Public Library, Hoyt Lakes, MN [*Library symbol*] [*Library of Congress*] (LCLS)

M-NHSS .... Modified New Haven Schizophrenic Scale

MnHu .... Hutchinson Public Library, Hutchinson, MN [*Library symbol*] [*Library of Congress*] (LCLS)

MnHuHMS ... Hutchinson Middle School, Hutchinson, MN [*Library symbol*] [*Library of Congress*] (LCLS)

MnHumS ...... Humbolt School, Humbolt, MN [*Library symbol*] [*Library of Congress*] (LCLS)

MnHuPES .... Park Elementary School, Hutchinson, MN [*Library symbol*] [*Library of Congress*] (LCLS)

MnHuSH ...... Hutchinson Senior High School, Hutchinson, MN [*Library symbol*] [*Library of Congress*] (LCLS)

MnHuStA ..... St. Anastasis School, Hutchinson, MN [*Library symbol*] [*Library of Congress*] (LCLS)

Mn-Hw .... Minnesota State Department of Transportation, St. Paul, MN [*Library symbol Library of Congress*] (LCLS)

MNI .... Mach Number Indicated (MCD)

MNI .... Madras Native Infantry [*British*]

MNI .... Maina Air Ltd. [*Nigeria*] [*FAA designator*] (FAAC)

MNI .... Manado [*Celebes*] [*Seismograph station code, US Geological Survey*] (SEIS)

MNI .... Manning, SC [*Location identifier FAA*] (FAAL)

MNI .... Many [*Amanteur radio shorthand*] (WDAA)

MNI .... McClatchy Newspapers, Inc. [*NYSE symbol*] (SPSG)

MNI .... Member of the Nautical Institute [*British*]

MNI .... Meridian Technologies [*TS, exchange symbol*] (TTSB)

MNI .... Meridian Technologies, Inc. [*Toronto Stock Exchange symbol*]

MnI .... Mille lacs Lake Community Library, Isle, MN [*Library symbol*] [*Library of Congress*] (LCLS)

MNI .... Minimum Number of Individuals [*Statistics*]

MNI .... Ministry of National Insurance [*British*]

MNI .... Montserrat [*West Indies*] [*Airport symbol*] (OAG)

MNI .... Movimiento Nacionalista de Izquierda [*Bolivia*] (PPW)

MNI .... Winona State University, Winona, MN [*OCLC symbol*] (OCLC)

MNIA .... Member of the National Institute of Accountants [*Australia*]

MnIf .... International Falls Public Library, International Falls, MN [*Library symbol Library of Congress*] (LCLS)

MnIfBC .... Boise Cascade Corp., Research Library, International Falls, MN [*Library symbol Library of Congress*] (LCLS)

MnIfE .... International Falls Elementary School, International Falls, MN [*Library symbol*] [*Library of Congress*] (LCLS)

MnIfH .... International Falls High School, International Falls, MN [*Library symbol*] [*Library of Congress*] (LCLS)

MnIfM .... A.B. Middle School, International Falls, MN [*Library symbol*] [*Library of Congress*] (LCLS)

MnIfRC .... Rainy River Community College, International Falls, MN [*Library symbol Library of Congress*] (LCLS)

MnIgS .... Inver Hills State Junior College, Inver Grove Heights, MN [*Library symbol Library of Congress*] (LCLS)

MnIH .... Isle High School/Elementary School, Isle, MN [*Library symbol*] [*Library of Congress*] (LCLS)

MNIH .... Member of the National Institute of Hardware [*British*] (DBQ)

MNIMH .... Member of the National Institute of Medical Herbalists [*British*]

MnIrCS .... Cherry Public School, Iron, MN [*Library symbol*] [*Library of Congress*] (LCLS)

MNIS .... Manning & Napier Information Services

MnIsE .... Isanti Elementary School, Isanti, MN [*Library symbol*] [*Library of Congress*] (LCLS)

MnIsM .... Isnati Middle School, Isanti, MN [*Library symbol*] [*Library of Congress*] (LCLS)

MnIv .... Ivanhoe Public Library, Ivanhoe, MN [*Library symbol*] [*Library of Congress*] (LCLS)

MnIvEHS ...... Lincoln Elementary-High School, Ivanhoe, MN [*Library symbol*] [*Library of Congress*] (LCLS)

MnJ .... Jackson County Library System, Jackson, MN [*Library symbol*] [*Library of Congress*] (LCLS)

MNJ .... Mananjary [*Madagascar*] [*Airport symbol*] (OAG)

MNJ .... Microelectronic Noise Jammer

MNJ .... Middletown & New Jersey Railway Co., Inc. [*AAR code*]

MNJ .... Movimiento Nacionalista Justicialista [*Justicialist Nationalist Movement - JNM*] [*Argentina*] (PPW)

MNJ .... Myoneural Junction [*Medicine*]

MNJ .... St. John's University, Collegeville, MN [*OCLC symbol*] (OCLC)

MnJaPS .... Jasper Public Schools, Jasper, MN [*Library symbol*] [*Library of Congress*] (LCLS)

MnJeJSH ...... Storden-Jeffers Junior Senior High School, Jeffers, MN [*Library symbol*] [*Library of Congress*] (LCLS)

MnJES .... Jackson Elementary School, Jackson, MN [*Library symbol*] [*Library of Congress*] (LCLS)

MnJoTS .... Trinity Lutheran School, Johnson, MN [*Library symbol*] [*Library of Congress*] (LCLS)

MnJPS .... Jackson Public Schools, Jackson, MN [*Library symbol*] [*Library of Congress*] (LCLS)

MNJTS .... Mouvement National des Jeunes Travailleurs du Senegal [*National Movement of Young Workers of Senegal*]

MNK .... Bethel College, Learning Resources Center, St. Paul, MN [*OCLC symbol*] (OCLC)

MnK .... Kimball Public Library, Kimball, MN [*Library symbol*] [*Library of Congress*] (LCLS)

MNK .... Maiana [*Kiribati*] [*Airport symbol*] (OAG)

MNK .... Mankoya [*Zambia*] [*Airport symbol*] (AD)

MNK .... Pleshenitzi [*Formerly, Minsk*] [*Former USSR Geomagnetic observatory code*]

MNK .... Rochester, MN [*Location identifier FAA*] (FAAL)

MNKA .... Minimum Number of Animals Known Alive [*Ecology*]

MnKaES .... Kandiyohi Elementary School, Kandiyohi, MN [*Library symbol*] [*Library of Congress*] (LCLS)

MnKarE .... Karlstad Elementary School, Karlstad, MN [*Library symbol*] [*Library of Congress*] (LCLS)

MnKarH .... Tri-County High School, Karlstad, MN [*Library symbol*] [*Library of Congress*] (LCLS)

MnKE .... Kimball Elementary School, Kimball, MN [*Library symbol*] [*Library of Congress*] (LCLS)

MnKee .... Keewatin Public Library, Keewatin, MN [*Library symbol*] [*Library of Congress*] (LCLS)

MnKeEs .... Kerkhoven-Murdoch-Sunberg Elementary School, Kerkhoven, MN [*Library symbol*] [*Library of Congress*] (LCLS)

MnKeHS ...... Kerkhoven-Murdoch-Sunberg High School, Kerkhoven, MN [*Library symbol*] [*Library of Congress*] (LCLS)

MnKenS .... Kensington Public School, Kensington, MN [*Library symbol*] [*Library of Congress*] (LCLS)

MnKeP .... Kerkoven Public Library, Kerkoven, MN [*Library symbol*] [*Library of Congress*] (LCLS)

MnKH .... Kimball High School, Kimball, MN [*Library symbol*] [*Library of Congress*] (LCLS)

MnKHC .... Holy Cross School, Kimball, MN [*Library symbol*] [*Library of Congress*]. (LCLS)

MnKin .... Kinney Public Library, City Hall, Kinney, MN [*Library symbol*] [*Library of Congress*] (LCLS)

MNL .... Mangla [*New Mirpur*] [*Pakistan*] [*Seismograph station code, US Geological Survey*] (SEIS)

MNL .... Manila [*Philippines*] [*Airport symbol*] (OAG)

MNL .... Manual (MSA)

MNL .... Marine Navigating Light

MNL .... Marked Neutrophilic Leukocytosis [*Medicine*] (DMAA)

MNL .... Maximum Number of Lamellae (DMAA)

MNl .... McClatchy Newspapers'A' [*NYSE symbol*] (TTSB)

MNL .... McConnell Peel Resources [*Vancouver Stock Exchange symbol*]

MNL .... Medical Nutrition Laboratory [*Army*]

MNL .... Mesenteric Node Lymphocyte

MNL .... Minerals Officer [*Foreign service*]

MNL .... Miniliner SRL [*Italy ICAO designator*] (FAAC)

MNL .... Minnesota National Laboratory

MNL .... Molecular Neurobiology Laboratory [*Salk Institute for Biological Studies*]

MNL .... Mononuclear Leukocyte [*Hematology*]

MNL .... Montgomery County-Norristown Public Library, Norristown, PA [*OCLC symbol*] (OCLC)

MNL .... Movement for National Liberation [*Barbados*] [*Political party*] (PPW)

MNL .... Multinomial Logit [*Statistics*]

MNL .... National Liberation Movement [*Guatemala*] [*Political party*] (PD)

MNL .... Valdez, AK [*Location identifier FAA*] (FAAL)

MNLA .... Mon National Liberation Army [*Myanmar*] [*Political party*] (EY)

MnLaiL .... Lake Itasca Forestry and Biological Station, Lake Itasca, MN [*Library symbol Library of Congress*] (LCLS)

MnLam .... Lamberton Public Library, Lamberton, MN [*Library symbol*] [*Library of Congress*] (LCLS)

MnLamS .... Lamberton School, Lamberton, MN [*Library symbol*] [*Library of Congress*] (LCLS)

MnLanS .... Lancaster Public School, Lancaster, MN [*Library symbol*] [*Library of Congress*] (LCLS)

MnLapS .... Laporte Public School, Laporte, MN [*Library symbol*] [*Library of Congress*] (LCLS)

MnLb .... Lake Benton Public Library, Lake Benton, MN [*Library symbol*] [*Library of Congress*] (LCLS)

MnLbBa .... Buffalo Ridge Baptist Academy, Lake Benton, MN [*Library symbol*] [*Library of Congress*] (LCLS)

MnLbPS....... Lake Benton Public Schools, Lake Benton, MN [*Library symbol*] [*Library of Congress*] (LCLS)

MNLCA .... Methylnorlaudanosolinecarboxylic Acid [*Biochemistry*]

MNLD .... Mainland (FAAC)

Mn-Leg........ Minnesota State Legislative Library, St. Paul, MN [*Library symbol Library of Congress*] (LCLS)

MnLeoCS..... Leota Christian School, Leota, MN [*Library symbol*] [*Library of Congress*] (LCLS)

MnLepPS..... Lester Prairie Public School, Lester Prairie, MN [*Library symbol*] [*Library of Congress*] (LCLS)

MnLeW .... Washington County Library, Lake Elmo, MN [*Library symbol Library of Congress*] (LCLS)

MnLf............ Carnegie City Library, Little Falls, MN [*Library symbol*] [*Library of Congress*] (LCLS)

MNLF........... Malayan National Liberation Front [*Singapore*] [*Political party*] (PD)

MNLF........... Moro National Liberation Front [*Philippines*] [*Political party*] (PD)

MnLfCL........ Charles Lindbergh Elementary School, Little Falls, MN [*Library symbol*] [*Library of Congress*] (LCLS)

MnLfH.......... Little Falls Community High School, Little Falls, MN [*Library symbol*] [*Library of Congress*] (LCLS)

MnLfLE........ Lincoln Elementary School, Little Falls, MN [*Library symbol*] [*Library of Congress*] (LCLS)

MnLfM......... Little Falls Community Middle School, Little Falls, MN [*Library symbol*] [*Library of Congress*] (LCLS)

MnLfMS....... Mid-State Educational Cooperative, Little Falls, MN [*Library symbol*] [*Library of Congress*] (LCLS)

MnLfN.......... North Star Christian Academy, Little Falls, MN [*Library symbol*] [*Library of Congress*] (LCLS)

MnLfO.......... Our Lady of Lourdes School, Little Falls, MN [*Library symbol*] [*Library of Congress*] (LCLS)

MnLfoE........ Littlefork Elementary School, Littlefork, MN [*Library symbol*] [*Library of Congress*] (LCLS)

MnLfoH........ Littlefork High School, Littlefork, MN [*Library symbol*] [*Library of Congress*] (LCLS)

MnLfS.......... St. Francis Convent, Little Falls, MN [*Library symbol*] [*Library of Congress*] (LCLS)

MnLfSG........ St. Gabriel's Hospital, Little Falls, MN [*Library symbol*] [*Library of Congress*] (LCLS)

MnLfSM....... St. Mary's School, Little Falls, MN [*Library symbol*] [*Library of Congress*] (LCLS)

MnLfW......... Weyerhauser Memorial Museum, Little Falls, MN [*Library symbol*] [*Library of Congress*] (LCLS)

MnLi............ Lindstrom Public Library, Lindstrom, MN [*Library symbol*] [*Library of Congress*] (LCLS)

MnLiJ .... Chisago Lakes Area Junior High School, Lindstrom, MN [*Library symbol*] [*Library of Congress*] (LCLS)

MnLiS........... Chisago Lakes Senior High School, Lindstrom, MN [*Library symbol*] [*Library of Congress*] (LCLS)

MnLit........... Litchfield Public Library, Litchfield, MN [*Library symbol*] [*Library of Congress*] (LCLS)

MnLitSH ...... Litchfield Senior High School, Litchfield, MN [*Library symbol*] [*Library of Congress*] (LCLS)

MnLitSP....... St. Philip's School, Litchfield, MN [*Library symbol*] [*Library of Congress*] (LCLS)

MnLitWES.... Wagner Elementary School, Litchfield, MN [*Library symbol*] [*Library of Congress*] (LCLS)

MnLkpE........ Lake Park Elementary School, Lake Park, MN [*Library symbol*] [*Library of Congress*] (LCLS)

MnLkpH........ Lake Park High School, Lake Park, MN [*Library symbol*] [*Library of Congress*] (LCLS)

MnLl............ Lake Lillian Public Library, Lake Lillian, MN [*Library symbol*] [*Library of Congress*] (LCLS)

MNLL........... Malaysian National Liberation League (NADA)

MNLN .... Leon/Fanor Urroz [*Nicaragua*] [*ICAO location identifier*] (ICLI)

MnLon.......... Margaret Welch Memorial Library, Longville, MN [*Library of Congress*] (LCLS)

MnLp .... Long Prairie Public Library, Long Prairie, MN [*Library symbol*] [*Library of Congress*] (LCLS)

MnLpCHi....... Christie Home Historical Society, Long Prairie, MN [*Library symbol*] [*Library of Congress*] (LCLS)

MnLpE .... Long Prairie Elementary School, Long Prairie, MN [*Library symbol*] [*Library of Congress*] (LCLS)

MnLpH......... Long Prairie High School, Long Prairie, MN [*Library symbol*] [*Library of Congress*] (LCLS)

MnLpHi......... Todd County Historical Society, Long Prairie, MN [*Library symbol*] [*Library of Congress*] (LCLS)

MnLpM .... Meadowview School, Long Prairie, MN [*Library symbol*] [*Library of Congress*] (LCLS)

MnLpS......... St. Mary of Mt. Carmel, Long Prairie, MN [*Library symbol*] [*Library of Congress*] (LCLS)

MnLpT .... Trinity Lutheran School, Long Prairie, MN [*Library symbol*] [*Library of Congress*] (LCLS)

MNLS........... Marine Navigating Light System

MNLS........... Modified New Least Square (PDAA)

MnLS........... St. John Nepomuk School, Lastrup, MN [*Library symbol*] [*Library of Congress*] (LCLS)

MnLsG .... Green Giant Corp., Le Sueur, MN [*Library symbol Library of Congress*] (LCLS)

MnLucOLS ... Our Lady of Victory School, Lucan, MN [*Library symbol*] [*Library of Congress*] (LCLS)

MNLY........... Mainly (FAAC)

MnLyPS .... Lynd Public Library, Lynd, MN [*Library symbol*] [*Library of Congress*] (LCLS)

MNM............ Mankato State University, Mankato, MN [*OCLC symbol*] (OCLC)

MNM............ Master of Nonprofit Management (PGP)

MNM............ Menominee [*Michigan*] [*Airport symbol*] (OAG)

MNM............ Metal Nonmetal [*Materials science*]

MNM............ Military Necessity Modification

MNM............ Minimum

mnm .... Minimum (AD)

MNM............ Minneapolis [*Minnesota*] [*Seismograph station code, US Geological Survey*] (SEIS)

MnM .... Minneapolis Public Library and Information Center, Minneapolis, MN [*Library symbol Library of Congress*] (LCLS)

mnm .... Mnemonic (AD)

MNM............ Museum of New Mexico [*Research center*] (RCD)

MnMA .... Augsburg College and Seminary, Minneapolis, MN [*Library symbol Library of Congress*] (LCLS)

MnMAb........ Abbott-Northwestern Hospitals, Inc., Minneapolis, MN [*Library symbol Library of Congress*] (LCLS)

MnMAC........ Anoka County Library, Minneapolis, MN [*Library symbol Library of Congress*] (LCLS)

MnMaE .... Mahnomen Elementary School, Mahnomen, MN [*Library symbol*] [*Library of Congress*] (LCLS)

MnMah .... Mahnomen High School, Mahnomen, MN [*Library symbol*] [*Library of Congress*] (LCLS)

MnMAM........ American Medical Systems, Inc., Minneapolis, MN [*Library symbol Library of Congress*] (LCLS)

MnManBC..... Bethany Lutheran College, Mankato, MN [*Library symbol Library of Congress*] (LCLS)

MnManBS..... Bethany Lutheran Theological Seminary, Mankato, MN [*Library symbol Library of Congress*] (LCLS)

MnManM ..... Minnesota Valley Regional Library, Mankato, MN [*Library symbol Library of Congress*] (LCLS)

MnManS....... Mankato State College [*Later, Mankato State University*], Mankato, MN [*Library symbol Library of Congress*] (LCLS)

MnManTD...... Traverse des Sioux Library System, Mankato, MN [*Library symbol Library of Congress*] (LCLS)

MNMANY...... Men's Neckwear Manufacturers Association of New York [*Defunct*] (EA)

MnMAR........ American Rehabilitation Foundation Minneapolis, MN [*Library symbol Library of Congress*] (LCLS)

MnMar......... Marshall-Lyon County Library, Marshall, MN [*Library symbol Library of Congress*] (LCLS)

MnMarb........ Marble Public Library, Marble, MN [*Library symbol*] [*Library of Congress*] (LCLS)

MnMarC....... Marshall-Lyon County Library, Marshall, MN [*Library of Congress*] (LCLS)

MnMarH ...... Weiner Memorial Hospital, Marshall, MN [*Library symbol*] [*Library of Congress*] (LCLS)

MnMarLS..... Samuel Lutheran School, Marshall, MN [*Library symbol*] [*Library of Congress*] (LCLS)

MnMarPE...... Parkside Elementary School, Marshall, MN [*Library symbol*] [*Library of Congress*] (LCLS)

MnMarS....... Southwest Minnesota State College, Marshall, MN [*Library symbol Library of Congress*] (LCLS)

MnMarWES... West Side Elementary School, Marshall, MN [*Library symbol*] [*Library of Congress*] (LCLS)

MnMay .... Maynard Public Library, Maynard, MN [*Library symbol*] [*Library of Congress*] (LCLS)

MnMayPS .... Maynard Public Schools, Maynard, MN [*Library symbol*] [*Library of Congress*] (LCLS)

MnMBL........ Bakken Library of Electricity in Life, Minneapolis, MN [*Library symbol Library of Congress*] (LCLS)

MNMC........... Medical Network for Missing Children (EA)

MnMc .... Monticello Public Library, Monticello, MN [*Library symbol*] [*Library of Congress*] (LCLS)

MnMCA........ Minneapolis College of Art and Design, Minneapolis, MN [*Library symbol Library of Congress*] (LCLS)

MnMCC........ Minneapolis Community College, Minneapolis, MN [*Library symbol Library of Congress*] (LCLS)

MnMcgE ...... McGrath Elementary School, McGrath, MN [*Library symbol*] [*Library of Congress*] (LCLS)

MnMcgr .... McGregor Public Library, McGregor, MN [*Library symbol*] [*Library of Congress*] (LCLS)

MnMcgrS...... McGregor School, McGregor, MN [*Library symbol*] [*Library of Congress*] (LCLS)

MnMcgrSL ... Sandy Lake Visitor Center, McGregor, MN [*Library symbol*] [*Library of Congress*] (LCLS)

MnMcH .... Monticello-Big Lake Community Hospital Library, Monticello, MN [*Library symbol*] [*Library of Congress*] (LCLS)

MnMci .... McInotosh Public Library, McIntosh, MN [*Library symbol*] [*Library of Congress*] (LCLS)

MnMciE .... McIntosh Elementary School, McIntosh, MN [*Library symbol*] [*Library of Congress*] (LCLS)

MnMciH .... McIntosh-Winger High School, McIntosh, MN [*Library symbol*] [*Library of Congress*] (LCLS)

MnMcJ......... Monticello Junior High School, Monticello, MN [*Library symbol*] [*Library of Congress*] (LCLS)

MnMck......... McKinley Public Library, McKinley, MN [*Library symbol*] [*Library of Congress*] (LCLS)

MnMcPE ...... Pinewood East Elementary School, Monticello, MN [*Library symbol*] [*Library of Congress*] (LCLS)

MnMcPW...... Pinewood West Elementary School, Monticello, MN [*Library symbol*] [*Library of Congress*] (LCLS)

MnMcR .... Rivercrest Christian School, Monticello, MN [*Library symbol*] [*Library of Congress*] (LCLS)

MnMcS .... Monticello Senior High School, Monticello, MN [*Library symbol*] [*Library of Congress*] (LCLS)

MnMcSR...... St. Henry Catholic Church, School of Religion Library, Monticello, MN [*Library symbol*] [*Library of Congress*] (LCLS)

MNMD......... MiniMed, Inc. [*NASDAQ symbol*] (SAG)

MnMe.......... Melrose Public Library, Melrose, MN [*Library symbol*] [*Library of Congress*] (LCLS)

MnMeaS...... Toivola-Meadowlands School, Meadowlands, MN [*Library symbol*] [*Library of Congress*] (LCLS)

MnMeE........ Melrose, New Munich, Spring Hill Elementary School, Melrose, MN [*Library symbol*] [*Library of Congress*] (LCLS)

MnMeH........ Melrose High School, Melrose, MN [*Library symbol*] [*Library of Congress*] (LCLS)

MnMeJ........ Melrose Junior High School, Melrose, MN [*Library symbol*] [*Library of Congress*] (LCLS)

MnMenE...... Menahga Elementary School, Menagha, MN [*Library symbol*] [*Library of Congress*] (LCLS)

MnMenH...... Menagha High School, Menagha, MN [*Library symbol*] [*Library of Congress*] (LCLS)

MnMeS........ St. John-St. Andrew School, Melrose, MN [*Library symbol*] [*Library of Congress*] (LCLS)

MnMeSM...... St. Mary's Elementary School, Melrose, MN [*Library symbol*] [*Library of Congress*] (LCLS)

MnMF......... Fairview Hospital, Minneapolis, MN [*Library symbol Library of Congress*] (LCLS)

MnMFL........ Association of Free Lutheran Congregation and Seminary Headquarters, Minneapolis, MN [*Library symbol Library of Congress*] (LCLS)

MnMFR........ Federation Reserve Bank of Minneapolis, Minneapolis, MN [*Library symbol*] [*Library of Congress*] (LCLS)

MnMG......... Golden Valley Lutheran College, Minneapolis, MN [*Library symbol Library of Congress*] (LCLS)

MNMG......... Managua/Augusto Cesar Sandino [*Nicaragua*] [*ICAO location identifier*] (ICLI)

MnMGM....... General Mills, Inc., Minneapolis, MN [*Library symbol Library of Congress*] (LCLS)

MnMGS........ Church of Jesus Christ of Latter-Day Saints, Genealogical Society Library, Minneapolis Branch, Minneapolis, MN [*Library symbol Library of Congress*] (LCLS)

MnMH......... Hennepin County Medical Society, Minneapolis, MN [*Library symbol Library of Congress*] (LCLS)

MnMHCL...... Hennepin County Library, Minneapolis, MN [*Library symbol Library of Congress*] (LCLS)

MnMHen...... Henkel Corp., Minneapolis, MN [*Library symbol Library of Congress*] (LCLS)

MnMHH....... Hennepin County General Hospital, Minneapolis, MN [*Library symbol Library of Congress*] (LCLS)

MnMHLL...... Hennepin County Law Library, Minneapolis, MN [*Library symbol Library of Congress*] (LCLS)

MnMI.......... Interlutheran Theological Seminary and Bible School, Minneapolis, MN [*Library symbol Library of Congress*] (LCLS)

MNMIA........ Men's Neckwear Manufacturers Institute of America (EA)

MNMIC........ Modernized National Military Intelligence Center

MNMIC........ Modernized NMIC [*National Military Intelligence Center*] (MCD)

MnMiE........ Milaca Elementary School, Milaca, MN [*Library symbol*] [*Library of Congress*] (LCLS)

MnMiH........ Milaca High School, Milaca, MN [*Library symbol*] [*Library of Congress*] (LCLS)

MnMilE........ Miltona Elementary School, Miltona, MN [*Library symbol*] [*Library of Congress*] (LCLS)

MnMiM........ Milaca Middle School, Milaca, MN [*Library symbol*] [*Library of Congress*] (LCLS)

MnMIn........ Interstudy, Minneapolis, MN [*Library symbol Library of Congress*] (LCLS)

MnMinPS..... Minneota Public Schools, Minneota, MN [*Library symbol*] [*Library of Congress*] (LCLS)

MnMinSE..... St. Edward School, Minneota, MN [*Library symbol*] [*Library of Congress*] (LCLS)

MnMirS........ Middle River School, Middle River, MN [*Library symbol*] [*Library of Congress*] (LCLS)

MnMK......... Kenny Rehabilitation Institute, Minneapolis, MN [*Library symbol*] (LCLS)

MNMKT....... Money Market (NITA)

MNMLD....... Lutheran Deaconess Hospital, Minneapolis, MN [*Library symbol Library of Congress*] (LCLS)

MNMIE......... Maple Lake Elementary School, Maple Lake, MN [*Library symbol*] [*Library of Congress*] (LCLS)

MnMIH......... Maple Lake High, Maple Lake, MN [*Library symbol*] [*Library of Congress*] (LCLS)

MnMIn .... Milan Public Library, Milan, MN [*Library symbol*] [*Library of Congress*] (LCLS)

MnMInES..... Milan Elementary School, Milan, MN [*Library symbol*] [*Library of Congress*] (LCLS)

MnMIS........ St. Timothy School, Maple Lake, MN [*Library symbol*] [*Library of Congress*] (LCLS)

MnMlyPS.... Milroy Public Schools, Milan, MN [*Library symbol*] [*Library of Congress*] (LCLS)

MnMMC....... Metropolitan State Community College, Minneapolis, MN [*Library symbol Library of Congress*] (LCLS)

MnMMe .... Medtronic, Inc., Minneapolis, MN [*Library symbol Library of Congress*] (LCLS)

MnMMeH...... Methodist Hospital, Minneapolis, MN [*Library symbol Library of Congress*] (LCLS)

MnMMet...... Metropolitan Medical Center, Medical Library, Minneapolis, MN [*Library symbol Library of Congress*] (LCLS)

MnMMet-H... Metropolitan Medical Center, Hospital Services Library, Minneapolis, MN [*Library symbol Library of Congress*] (LCLS)

MnMMetS.... Metropolitan State Junior College, Minneapolis, MN [*Library symbol Library of Congress*] (LCLS)

MnMMH....... Minneapolis-Honeywell Regulator Co., Minneapolis, MN [*Library symbol Library of Congress*] (LCLS)

MnMMSC..... MTS Systems Corporation, Minneapolis, MN [*Library symbol Library of Congress*] (LCLS)

MnMMSP..... Minnesota School of Professional Psychology, Minneapolis, MN [*Library symbol*] [*Library of Congress*] (LCLS)

MnMMtS...... Mount Sinai Hospital, Minneapolis, MN [*Library symbol Library of Congress*] (LCLS)

MnMN......... Normandale Community College, Minneapolis, MN [*Library symbol Library of Congress*] (LCLS)

MnMNC....... North Central Bible College, Minneapolis, MN [*Library symbol Library of Congress*] (LCLS)

MnMnCMS... Cedar Mountain School, Morgan, MN [*Library of Congress*] (LCLS)

MnMNH .... North Memorial Hospital, Minneapolis, MN [*Library symbol Library of Congress*] (LCLS)

MnMNHe ..... North Hennepin Community College, Minneapolis, MN [*Library symbol Library of Congress*] (LCLS)

MnMnI .... Mountain Lake Public Library, Mountain Lake, MN [*Library symbol*] [*Library of Congress*] (LCLS)

MnMnICS.... Mountain Lake Christian School, Mountain Lake, MN [*Library symbol*] [*Library of Congress*] (LCLS)

MnMnIHS ... Mountain Lake Public High School, Mountain Lake, MN [*Library symbol*] [*Library of Congress*] (LCLS)

MnMnIMB ... Mt. Bethany Christian School, Mountain Lake, MN [*Library symbol*] [*Library of Congress*] (LCLS)

MnMnP .... Morgan Pubic Library, Morgan, MN [*Library symbol*] [*Library of Congress*] (LCLS)

MnMo .... Morris Public Library, Morris, MN [*Library symbol*] [*Library of Congress*] (LCLS)

MnMoE .... Morris Elementary School, Morris, MN [*Library symbol*] [*Library of Congress*] (LCLS)

MnMoh .... Moorhead Public Library, Moorhead, MN [*Library symbol*] [*Library of Congress*] (LCLS)

MnMohC...... Concordia College, Moorhead, MN [*Library symbol Library of Congress*] (LCLS)

MnMohEE.... Edison Elementary School, Moorhead, MN [*Library symbol*] [*Library of Congress*] (LCLS)

MnMohHi..... Clay County Historical Society, Library and Archives, Moorhead, MN [*Library symbol*] [*Library of Congress*] (LCLS)

MnMohJ ...... Moorhead Junior High School, Moorhead, MN [*Library symbol*] [*Library of Congress*] (LCLS)

MnMohL ...... Lake Agassiz Regional Library, Moorhead, MN [*Library symbol Library of Congress*] (LCLS)

MnMohPS.... Moorhead Public Schools System, Moorhead, MN [*Library symbol Library of Congress*] (LCLS)

MnMohS...... Moorhead State College, Moorhead, MN [*Library symbol Library of Congress*] (LCLS)

MnMohSA.... St. Ansgar Hospital, Health Science Library, Moorhead, MN [*Library symbol*] [*Library of Congress*] (LCLS)

MnMohSH.... Moorhead Senior High School, Moorhead, MN [*Library symbol*] [*Library of Congress*] (LCLS)

MnMohSJ .... St. Joseph School, Moorhead, MN [*Library symbol*] [*Library of Congress*] (LCLS)

MnMohWE... Washington Elementary School, Moorhead, MN [*Library symbol*] [*Library of Congress*] (LCLS)

MnMol .... Moose Lake Public Library, Moose Lake, MN [*Library symbol*] [*Library of Congress*] (LCLS)

MnMolS....... Moose Lake Public School, Moose Lake, MN [*Library symbol*] [*Library of Congress*] (LCLS)

MnMoM ...... Morris Middle School, Morris, MN [*Library symbol*] [*Library of Congress*] (LCLS)

MnMoMHS... Morris High School, Morris, MN [*Library symbol*] [*Library of Congress*] (LCLS)

MnMotS...... Motley School, Motley, MN [*Library symbol*] [*Library of Congress*] (LCLS)

MnMoU........ University of Minnesota, Morris, MN [*Library symbol Library of Congress*] (LCLS)

MnMov .... Chippewa County Library System, Montevideo, MN [*Library symbol Library of Congress*] (LCLS)

MnMovCH... Chippewa County-Montevideo Hospital, Montevideo, MN [*Library symbol*] [*Library of Congress*] (LCLS)

MnMovMS... Montevideo Middle School, Montevideo, MN [*Library symbol*] [*Library of Congress*] (LCLS)

MnMovRE.... Ramsey Elementary School, Montevideo, MN [*Library symbol*] [*Library of Congress*] (LCLS)

MnMovSE.... Sanford Elementary School, Montevideo, MN [*Library symbol*] [*Library of Congress*] (LCLS)

MnMovSEC... Southwest-West Central Educational Cooperative Service Unit, Montevideo, MN [*Library symbol*] [*Library of Congress*] (LCLS)

MnMovSH.... Montevideo Senior High School, Montevideo, MN [*Library symbol*] [*Library of Congress*] (LCLS)

MnMP.......... Pillsbury Co., Minneapolis, MN [*Library symbol*] [*Library of Congress*] (LCLS)

MnMrFE...... Fairview Elementary Library, Mora, MN [*Library symbol*] [*Library of Congress*] (LCLS)

MnMrH .... Mora High School, Mora, MN [*Library symbol*] [*Library of Congress*] (LCLS)

MnMrHi ...... Kanabec County Historical Society, Mora, MN [*Library symbol*] [*Library of Congress*] (LCLS)

MnMrMS...... Mora Fairview Central Middle School, Mora, MN [*Library symbol*] [*Library of Congress*] (LCLS)

MnMrR .... Rum River Vocational Center, Mora, MN [*Library symbol*] [*Library of Congress*] (LCLS)

MnMS .... Saint Louis Park Medical Center, Minneapolis, MN [*Library symbol Library of Congress*] (LCLS)

MnMSMC ..... Saint Mary's Junior College, Minneapolis, MN [*Library symbol Library of Congress*] (LCLS)

MnMSMH ... Saint Mary's Hospital, Minneapolis, MN [*Library symbol Library of Congress*] (LCLS)

MNMT .... Monument

MnMtE .... Montrose Elementary School, Montrose, MN [*Library symbol*] [*Library of Congress*] (LCLS)

MnMti .... Mountain Iron Public Library, Mt. Iron, MN [*Library symbol*] [*Library of Congress*] (LCLS)

MnMtiE .... Merritt Elementary School, Mt. Iron, MN [*Library symbol*] [*Library of Congress*] (LCLS)

MnMtiHS ..... Mt. Iron High School, Mt. Iron, MN [*Library symbol*] [*Library of Congress*] (LCLS)

MnMuKS ..... Kerkhover-Murdock-Sunberg School, Murdock, MN [*Library symbol*] [*Library of Congress*] (LCLS)

MnMULS ..... University of Minnesota Union List of Serials, Minneapolis, MN [*Library symbol Library of Congress*] (LCLS)

MnMVA .... United States Veterans Administration Hospital, Minneapolis, MN [*Library symbol Library of Congress*] (LCLS)

MnMW .... Walker Art Center, Minneapolis, MN [*Library symbol*] [*Library of Congress*] (LCLS)

MNN .... Carleton College, Northfield, MN [*OCLC symbol*] (OCLC)

MNN .... Madness Network News (EA)

MNN .... Main Network Node [*Computer science*] (CIST)

MNN .... Marion, OH [*Location identifier FAA*] (FAAL)

MNN .... Minneapolis [*Minnesota*] [*Seismograph station code, US Geological Survey*] (SEIS)

Mn-N .... Minnesota State Department of Natural Resources, St. Paul, MN [*Library symbol Library of Congress*] (LCLS)

MNN .... Monenco Ltd. [*Toronto Stock Exchange symbol*]

MnNaSH ...... Nashwauk-Keewatin Senior High School, Nashwauk, MN [*Library symbol*] [*Library of Congress*] (LCLS)

MnNbU .... United Theological Seminary of the Twin Cities, New Brighton, MN [*Library symbol Library of Congress*] (LCLS)

MnNC .... Carleton College, Northfield, MN [*Library symbol Library of Congress*] (LCLS)

MnNeS .... Nevis Public School, Nevis, MN [*Library symbol*] [*Library of Congress*] (LCLS)

MnNeuL ...... Doctor Martin Luther College, New Ulm, MN [*Library symbol Library of Congress*] (LCLS)

MNNG .... Methylnitronitrosoguanidine [*Biochemistry*]

MnNHi .... Norwegian-American Historical Association, Northfield, MN [*Library symbol Library of Congress*] (LCLS)

MnNisE .... Nisswa Elementary School, Nisswa, MN [*Library symbol*] [*Library of Congress*] (LCLS)

MnNl .... New London Public Library, New London, MN [*Library symbol*] [*Library of Congress*] (LCLS)

MnNIES .... New London Elementary School, New London, MN [*Library symbol*] [*Library of Congress*] (LCLS)

MnNIJSH ..... New London-Spicer Junior Senior High School, New London, MN [*Library symbol*] [*Library of Congress*] (LCLS)

MnNIPES ..... Prairie Woods Elementary School, New London, MN [*Library symbol*] [*Library of Congress*] (LCLS)

MnNmT .... Mankato Area Vocational-Technical Institute, North Mankato, MN [*Library symbol Library of Congress*] (LCLS)

MnNob .... North Branch Area Library, North Branch, MN [*Library symbol*] [*Library of Congress*] (LCLS)

MnNobH ...... North Branch High School, North Branch, MN [*Library symbol*] [*Library of Congress*] (LCLS)

MnNobM ...... North Branch Middle School, North Branch, MN [*Library symbol*] [*Library of Congress*] (LCLS)

MnNoS .... Northome School, Northome, MN [*Library symbol*] [*Library of Congress*] (LCLS)

MNNP .... Malawi Nyika National Park (AD)

MnNS .... Saint Olaf College, Northfield, MN [*Library symbol Library of Congress*] (LCLS)

MnNS-K .... Saint Olaf College, Kierkegaard Library, Northfield, MN [*Library symbol*] [*Library of Congress*] (LCLS)

MnNym .... New York Mills Public Library, New York Mills, MN [*Library symbol*] [*Library of Congress*] (LCLS)

MnNymH ..... New York Mills High School, New York Mills, MN [*Library symbol*] [*Library of Congress*] (LCLS)

MNO .... Maddona Resources Corp. [*Vancouver Stock Exchange symbol*]

mno .... Manobo [*MARC language code Library of Congress*] (LCCP)

MNO .... Manono [*Zaire*] [*Airport symbol*] (OAG)

MNO .... Master of Nonprofit Organization (PGP)

MNO .... Mauritanian Nationalist Organisation (BUAC)

MnO .... Owatonna Free Public Library, Owatonna, MN [*Library symbol Library of Congress*] (LCLS)

MNO .... Refugio, TX [*Location identifier FAA*] (FAAL)

MNO .... Saint Olaf College, Northfield, MN [*OCLC symbol*] (OCLC)

MNoadT ...... North Adams State College, North Adams, MA [*Library symbol Library of Congress*] (LCLS)

MNoanM ..... Merrimack College, North Andover, MA [*Library symbol Library of Congress*] (LCLS)

MNoanMV .... Merrimack Valley Textile Museum, North Andover, MA [*Library symbol Library of Congress*] (LCLS)

MNodS .... Southeastern Massachusetts University, North Dartmouth, MA [*Library symbol Library of Congress*] (LCLS)

MNoeS .... Stonehill College, North Easton, MA [*Library symbol Library of Congress*] (LCLS)

MnOgS .... Ogilvie Public School, Ogilvie, MN [*Library symbol*] [*Library of Congress*] (LCLS)

MnOkaHJH .. Huron Lake-Okabena-Lakefield Junior High School, Okabena, MN [*Library symbol*] [*Library of Congress*] (LCLS)

MnOkS .... Oklee Public School, Oklee, MN [*Library symbol*] [*Library of Congress*] (LCLS)

MnOl .... Olivia Public Library, Olivia, MN [*Library symbol*] [*Library of Congress*] (LCLS)

MnOlES .... Olivia Elementary School, Olivia, MN [*Library symbol*] [*Library of Congress*] (LCLS)

MnOlStA ..... St. Aloysious School, Olivia, MN [*Library symbol*] [*Library of Congress*] (LCLS)

MNOMU ...... Mobile Nuclear Ordnance Maintenance Unit (MCD)

MnOnC .... Crosier Seminary Library, Onamia, MN [*Library symbol*] [*Library of Congress*] (LCLS)

MnOnE .... Onamia Elementary School, Onamia, MN [*Library symbol*] [*Library of Congress*] (LCLS)

MnOnG .... Galloway Boy's Ranch School, Onamia, MN [*Library symbol*] [*Library of Congress*] (LCLS)

MnOnH .... Onamia High School, Onamia, MN [*Library symbol*] [*Library of Congress*] (LCLS)

MNOPF .... Merchant Navy Officers' Pension Fund [*British*] (DS)

MNOR .... Missile Not Operationally Ready [*Air Force*] (SAA)

MNORM .... Missile Not Operationally Ready - Maintenance [*Air Force*]

MNORP .... Missile Not Operationally Ready - Parts [*Air Force*]

MnOrS .... Orr Public School, Orr, MN [*Library symbol*] [*Library of Congress*] (LCLS)

MnOrv .... Ortonville Public Library, Ortonville, MN [*Library symbol*] [*Library of Congress*] (LCLS)

MnOrvH ...... Ortonville Hospital, Ortonville, MN [*Library symbol*] [*Library of Congress*] (LCLS)

MnOrvPS ..... Ortonville Public School, Ortonville, MN [*Library symbol*] [*Library of Congress*] (LCLS)

mnos .... Metallic Nitrogen-Oxide Semiconductor (AD)

MNOS .... Metal-Nitride-Oxide Silicon [*or Semiconductor*]

MNOSFET .... Metal-Nitride-Oxide-Semiconductor Field-Effect Transistor

MnOsS .... Osakis School, Osakis, MN [*Library symbol*] [*Library of Congress*] (LCLS)

MNOS/SOS... Metal-Nitride Oxide Semiconductor / Silicon-on-Sapphire

MNot .... Cobb Memorial Library, North Truro, MA [*Library symbol*] [*Library of Congress*] (LCLS)

MNoW .... Wheaton College, Norton, MA [*Library symbol Library of Congress*] (LCLS)

MNP .... Malay National Party [*Political party*] (AD)

MNP .... Marsabit National Park [*Kenya*] (AD)

MNP .... Maximum Negative Pressure [*Nuclear energy*] (NRCH)

MNP .... Meru National Park [*Equatorial Kenya*] (AD)

MNP .... Meta-Nitrophenol [*Organic chemistry*]

MNP .... Microcom Networking Protocol [*Telecommunications*] (ACRL)

MNP .... Microcomputer Networking Protocol

MNP .... Microcone Networking Protocol

MNP .... Midnapore (1979) Resources, Inc. [*Vancouver Stock Exchange symbol*]

MNP .... Mikumi National Park [*Tanzania*] (AD)

Mn-P .... Minnesota State Department of Planning, St. Paul, MN [*Library symbol Library of Congress*] (LCLS)

MNP .... Mononuclear Phagocyte (DMAA)

MNP .... Moravian National Party [*Czech Republic*] [*Political party*] (BUAC)

MNP .... More Nearly Perfect [*Microsoft Corp.*] [*Computer science*]

MNP .... Mouvement Nationale Patriotique [*Haiti*] [*Political party*] (EY)

MNP .... Movimiento Nacionalista Popular [*Popular Nationalist Movement*] [*Chile*] [*Political party*] (PD)

MNP .... Movimiento Nacional y Popular [*Paraguay*] [*Political party*] (EY)

MNP .... Movimiento No Partidarizado [*Peru*] [*Political party*] (EY)

MNP .... Multinomial Probit [*Statistics*]

MNP .... Municipal Partners Fund [*NYSE symbol*] (SPSG)

MNP .... Mushandike National Park [*Rhodesia*] (AD)

MNP .... Northern Mariana Islands [*ANSI three-letter standard code*] (CNC)

MnP .... Princeton Community Library, Princeton, MN [*Library symbol*] [*Library of Congress*] (LCLS)

MNP .... University of Minnesota, St. Paul, MN [*OCLC symbol*] (OCLC)

MNP-4 .... Microcon Network Protocol-4 [*Computer science*] (DDC)

MNP5 .... Microcom Networking Protocol, Class Five [*Computer science*]

MNP-5 .... Microcom Network Protocol-5 [*Computer science*] (DDC)

MNPA .... Malaysian Newspaper Publishers Association (EAIO)

MNPA .... Mono-normal-propylamine [*Organic chemistry*]

MnPapH ...... Parkers Prairie High School, Parkers Prairie, MN [*Library symbol*] [*Library of Congress*] (LCLS)

MnParFE ..... Frank White Elementary School, Park Rapids, MN [*Library symbol*] [*Library of Congress*] (LCLS)

MnParH .... Park Rapids Area High School, Park Rapids, MN [*Library symbol*] [*Library of Congress*] (LCLS)

MnParM .... Park Rapids Middle School, Park Rapids, MN [*Library symbol*] [*Library of Congress*] (LCLS)

MnPc .... Pine City Pubic Library, Pine City, MN [*Library symbol*] [*Library of Congress*] (LCLS)

MNPC .... Puerto Cabezas [*Nicaragua*] [*ICAO location identifier*] (ICLI)

MnPcE .... Pine City Elementary School, Pine City, MN [*Library symbol*] [*Library of Congress*] (LCLS)

MnPcH .... Pine City High School, Pine City, MN [*Library symbol*] [*Library of Congress*] (LCLS)

MnPcS .... St. Mary's School, Pine City, MN [*Library symbol*] [*Library of Congress*] (LCLS)

MnPcT .... Pine Technical Institute Learning Resource Center, Pine City, MN [*Library symbol*] [*Library of Congress*] (LCLS)

MNPD	Missile and Nuclear Programming Data (AABC)
MnPeC	Pease Community Christian School, Pease, MN [_Library symbol_] [_Library of Congress_] (LCLS)
MnPelE	Pequot Lakes Elementary School, Pequot Lakes, MN [_Library symbol_] [_Library of Congress_] (LCLS)
MnPelH	Pequot Lakes High School, Pequot Lakes MN [_Library symbol_] [_Library of Congress_] (LCLS)
MnPerH	Pelican Rapids High School, Pelican Rapids, MN [_Library symbol_] [_Library of Congress_] (LCLS)
MnPerVE	Viking Elementary School, Pelican Rapids, MN [_Library symbol_] [_Library of Congress_] (LCLS)
MnPH	Princeton High School, Princeton, MN [_Library symbol_] [_Library of Congress_] (LCLS)
MnPhE	Perham Elementary School, Perham, MN [_Library symbol_] [_Library of Congress_] (LCLS)
MnPhP	Perham Public Library, Perham, MN [_Library symbol_] [_Library of Congress_] (LCLS)
MNPI	Microcom, Inc. [_NASDAQ symbol_] (NQ)
MnPi	Pierz Public Library, Pierz, MN [_Library symbol_] [_Library of Congress_] (LCLS)
MnPiH	Healy High School, Pierz, MN [_Library symbol_] [_Library of Congress_] (LCLS)
MnPiHE	Harding Elementary School, Pierz, MN [_Library symbol_] [_Library of Congress_] (LCLS)
MnPiIS	Pillager Public School, Pillager, MN [_Library symbol_] [_Library of Congress_] (LCLS)
MnPiS	St. Joseph's Elementary School, Pierz, MN [_Library symbol_] [_Library of Congress_] (LCLS)
MnPJ	Princeton Junior High School, Princeton, MN [_Library symbol_] [_Library of Congress_] (LCLS)
MNPL	Machinists Non-Partisan Political League (EA)
MnPluS	Pershing Public School, Plummer, MN [_Library symbol_] [_Library of Congress_] (LCLS)
MnPNE	Princeton North Elementary School, Princeton, MN [_Library symbol_] [_Library of Congress_] (LCLS)
mnpo	Main Port (AD)
MNPO	Median Preoptic Area [_Brain anatomy_]
MnPO	Median Preoptic Area (DB)
MNPO	Mobile Navy Post Office
MNPP	Midland Nuclear Power Plant (NRCH)
MnPpBES	Dr. Brown Elementary School, Pipestone, MN [_Library symbol_] [_Library of Congress_] (LCLS)
MnPpHES	Hill Elementary School, Pipestone, MN [_Library symbol_] [_Library of Congress_] (LCLS)
MnPpHS	Pipestone Cental High School, Pipestone, MN [_Library symbol_] [_Library of Congress_] (LCLS)
MN-PPL	Machinists Non-Partisan Political League (EA)
MnPpTC	Southwest Technical College, Pipestone, MN [_Library symbol_] [_Library of Congress_] (LCLS)
MnPr	Kitchigami Regional Library, Pine River, MN [_Library symbol Library of Congress_] (LCLS)
MnPrbMCS	Central Minnesota Christian School, Prinsburg, MN [_Library symbol_] [_Library of Congress_] (LCLS)
MnPrbPS	Prinsburg Public Schools, Prinsburg, MN [_Library symbol_] [_Library of Congress_] (LCLS)
MnPrE	Pine River Elementary School, Pine River, MN [_Library symbol_] [_Library of Congress_] (LCLS)
MnPrH	Pine River High School, Pine River, MN [_Library symbol_] [_Library of Congress_] (LCLS)
MnProJ	Jedlicka Junior High School, Proctor, MN [_Library symbol_] [_Library of Congress_] (LCLS)
MnProSH	Proctor Senior High School, Proctor, MN [_Library symbol_] [_Library of Congress_] (LCLS)
MnPrP	Pine River Public Library, Pine River, MN [_Library symbol_] [_Library of Congress_] (LCLS)
MNPS	Millstone Nuclear Power Station (NRCH)
MNPS	Minimum Navigation Performance Specification [_Aviation_] (FAAC)
MNPS	Movimiento Nazionale Pan-Somalo [_Pan-Somali National Movement_] [_Political party_]
MNPSA	Minimum Navigation Performance Specification Airspace [_Aviation_] (FAAC)
MnPSE	Princeton South Elementary School, Princeton, MN [_Library symbol_] [_Library of Congress_] (LCLS)
MNPT	Meta-Nitro-para-toluidine [_Organic chemistry_]
MnPv	Paynesville Public Library, Paynesville, MN [_Library symbol_] [_Library of Congress_] (LCLS)
MnPvEM	Paynesville Elementary & Middle School, Paynesville, MN [_Library symbol_] [_Library of Congress_] (LCLS)
MnPvH	Paynesville Hospital, Medical Staff Library, Paynesville, MN [_Library symbol_] [_Library of Congress_] (LCLS)
MnPvHi	Paynesville Historical Society, Paynesville, MN [_Library symbol_] [_Library of Congress_] (LCLS)
MnPvHS	Paynesville, High School, Paynesville, MN [_Library symbol_] [_Library of Congress_] (LCLS)
MNPWR	Manpower (AFM)
MNPZ	Mononitrosopiperazine [_Biochemistry_]
mnpz	Monopolize (AD)
mnpzd	Monopolized (AD)
mnpzg	Monopolizing (AD)
mnpzn	Monopolization (AD)
MNQ	Manicouagan [_Quebec_] [_Seismograph station code, US Geological Survey_] (SEIS)
MNQ	Manifest Needs Questionnaire (EDAC)
MNQ	Methylnaphthoquinone [_Organic chemistry_]
MNQ	Monto [_Australia Airport symbol_] (OAG)

MNQ	Montoro Resources [_Vancouver Stock Exchange symbol_]
MNQ	University of Minnesota, Waseca, Waseca, MN [_OCLC symbol_] (OCLC)
MNR	James J. Hill Reference Library, St. Paul, MN [_OCLC symbol_] (OCLC)
MNR	Maintenance/Nonconformance Record (MCD)
MNR	Manor (MCD)
MNR	Manor Care [_NYSE symbol_] (TTSB)
MNR	Manor Care, Inc. [_NYSE symbol_] (SPSG)
MNR	Marrow Neutrophil Reserve [_Medicine_]
MNR	Massive Nuclear Retaliation (AAG)
mnr	Massive Nuclear Retaliation (AD)
MNR	Maximum Number of Records (MHDB)
MNR	McMaster Nuclear Reactor [_Canada_]
MNR	McNellen Resources, Inc. [_Vancouver Stock Exchange symbol Toronto Stock Exchange symbol_]
MNR	Mean Neap [_Tide_] Rise [_Tides and currents_]
mnr	Mean Neap Rise (AD)
Mnr	Mijnheer [_Mr._] [_Dutch_] (AD)
MNR	Mines Road [_California_] [_Seismograph station code, US Geological Survey_] (SEIS)
MNR	Minimum Noise Routes
MNR	Monair SA [_Switzerland ICAO designator_] (FAAC)
MNR	Mongu [_Zambia_] [_Airport symbol_] (OAG)
MNR	Morphine-Naive Rats
MNr	Morrill Memorial Library, Norwood, MA [_Library symbol Library of Congress_] (LCLS)
MNR	Mouvement Nationaliste Revolutionnaire [_Revolutionary Nationalist Movement_] [_France Political party_] (PD)
MNR	Movimiento Nacionalista Revolucionario [_National Revolutionary Movement_] [_Bolivia_] [_Political party_] (PPW)
MNR	Movimiento Nacional Reformista [_National Reformist Movement_] [_Honduras_] [_Political party_]
MNR	Movimiento Nacional Revolucionario [_National Revolutionary Movement_] [_El Salvador_] [_Political party_] (PPW)
MNR	Mozambique National Resistance [_Political party_] (AD)
MNR	Mozambique National Resistance Movement
MnR	Rochester Public Library, Rochester, MN [_Library symbol Library of Congress_] (LCLS)
MnRa	Raymond Public Library, Raymond, MN [_Library symbol_] [_Library of Congress_] (LCLS)
MnRaKE	Knight Elementary School, Randall, MN [_Library symbol_] [_Library of Congress_] (LCLS)
MNRC	Minorco [_Formerly, Minerals & Resources Corp. Ltd._] [_NASDAQ symbol_] (NQ)
MnRc	Rush City Public Library, Rush City, MN [_Library of Congress_] (LCLS)
MnRcE	Rush City Elementary School, Rush City, MN [_Library symbol_] [_Library of Congress_] (LCLS)
MnRcH	Rush City High School, Rush City, MN [_Library symbol_] [_Library of Congress_] (LCLS)
MNRCS	Median Normalized RADAR Cross Section
MNRCY	Minorco ADR [_NASDAQ symbol_] (TTSB)
MnRelE	Redlake Elementary School, Redlake, MN [_Library symbol_] [_Library of Congress_] (LCLS)
MnRelH	Redlake High School, Redlake, MN [_Library symbol_] [_Library of Congress_] (LCLS)
MnRemE	Remer Elementary School, Remer, MN [_Library symbol_] [_Library of Congress_] (LCLS)
MnRemH	Northland High School, Remer, MN [_Library symbol_] [_Library of Congress_] (LCLS)
MnRen	Renville City Library, Renville, MN [_Library symbol_] [_Library of Congress_] (LCLS)
MnRenBPS	Bird Island-Danube-Renville-Sacred Heart (BDRSH) Public Schools, Renville, MN [_Library symbol_] [_Library of Congress_] (LCLS)
MNRF	Moonroof [_Automotive advertising_]
MnRfE	Rockford Elementary School, Rockford, MN [_Library symbol_] [_Library of Congress_] (LCLS)
MnRfH	Rockford High School, Rockford, MN [_Library symbol_] [_Library of Congress_] (LCLS)
MnRfM	Rockford Middle School, Rockford, MN [_Library symbol_] [_Library of Congress_] (LCLS)
MnRgE	Rogers Elementary School, Rogers, MN [_Library symbol_] [_Library of Congress_] (LCLS)
MnRgS	St. Martin's School, Rogers, MN [_Library symbol_] [_Library of Congress_] (LCLS)
MNRH	Movimiento Nacionalista Revolucionario Historico [_Historic Revolutionary Nationalist Movement_] [_Bolivia_] [_Political party_] (PPW)
MnRiE	Rice Elementary School, Rice, MN [_Library symbol_] [_Library of Congress_] (LCLS)
MNRJ	Museo Nacional de Rio de Janeiro [_National Museum of Rio de Janeiro_] [_Portugal_] (AD)
mnrl	Mineral (VRA)
MNRL	Mineral (MSA)
MNrL	Morrill Memorial Library, Norwood, MA [_Library symbol_] [_Library of Congress_] (LCLS)
MnRlF	Red Lake Falls Public Library, Red Lake Falls, MN [_Library symbol_] (LCLS)
MnRlfHE	J.A. Hughes Elementary School, Red Lake Falls, MN [_Library symbol_] [_Library of Congress_] (LCLS)
MnRlPS	Sioux Valley-Round Lake-Brewster Public School, Round Lake, MN [_Library symbol_] [_Library of Congress_] (LCLS)
MNRM	Master of Natural Resource Management (PGP)

MnRM.......... Mayo Clinic, Rochester, MN [*Library symbol Library of Congress*] (LCLS)

MnRmE........ Richmond Elementary School, Richmond, MN [*Library symbol*] [*Library of Congress*] (LCLS)

MnRMeH ..... Rochester Methodist Hospital, Rochester, MN [*Library symbol Library of Congress*] (LCLS)

MnRmP....... Richmond Public Library, Richmond, MN [*Library symbol*] [*Library of Congress*] (LCLS)

MnRmS....... Sts. Peter and Paul Elementary School Library, Richmond, MN [*Library symbol*] [*Library of Congress*] (LCLS)

MNRO.......... Monroe Muffler Brake [*NASDAQ symbol*] (SPSG)

MNRO.......... Monro Muffler Brake, Inc. [*NASDAQ symbol*] (SAG)

MnRoN .... Northwestern College, Roseville, MN [*Library symbol Library of Congress*] (LCLS)

MnRoP........ Minnesota State Pollution Control Agency, Roseville, MN [*Library symbol Library of Congress*] (LCLS)

MnRos......... Roseau Public Library, Roseau, MN [*Library symbol*] [*Library of Congress*] (LCLS)

MnRosE....... Roseau Elementary School, Roseau, MN [*Library symbol*] [*Library of Congress*] (LCLS)

MnRosH...... Roseau High School, Roseau, MN [*Library symbol*] [*Library of Congress*] (LCLS)

MnRosMS.... Malung School, Roseau, MN [*Library symbol*] [*Library of Congress*] (LCLS)

MnRothS..... Rothsay Public School, Rothsay, MN [*Library symbol*] [*Library of Congress*] (LCLS)

MnRoy......... Royalton Public Library, Royalton, MN [*Library symbol*] [*Library of Congress*] (LCLS)

MnRoyS....... Royalton School, Royalton, MN [*Library symbol*] [*Library of Congress*] (LCLS)

MNRP.......... Movimiento Nacionalista Revolucionario del Pueblo [*Nationalist Revolutionary People's Movement*] [*Bolivia*] [*Political party*] (PPW)

MNRPM....... Malay Nationalist Revolutionary Party of Malaya [*Partai Kebangsaan Melayu Revolusioner Malaya*] [*Political party*] (PPW)

MnRPS........ Rochester Public Schools, Rochester, MN [*Library symbol Library of Congress*] (LCLS)

MnRR .... Rochester State Junior College, Rochester, MN [*Library symbol Library of Congress*] (LCLS)

MNRS.......... Manors [*Postal Service standard*] (OPSA)

MNRS.......... Mobile Neutron Radiographic System

MnRS........... Southeastern Libraries Cooperating [*SELCO*], Rochester Public Library, Rochester, MN [*Library symbol Library of Congress*] (LCLS)

Mnrsm......... Mannerism (VRA)

MnRStM ...... Saint Mary's Hospital, Rochester, MN [*Library symbol Library of Congress*] (LCLS)

mnrt............. Minaret (VRA)

MNRT .... Monmouth Real Estate Investment Trust [*NASDAQ symbol*] (NQ)

MNRTA........ Monmouth R.E. Inv CL'A' [*NASDAQ symbol*] (TTSB)

MNRU.......... Medical Neuropsychiatric Research Unit

MNRU.......... Modulated Noise Reference Unit [*Telecommunications*] (TEL)

MnRuPS ...... Ruthton Public Schools, Ruthton, MN [*Library symbol*] [*Library of Congress*] (LCLS)

MnRusPS.... Russell Public Schools, Russell, MN [*Library symbol*] [*Library of Congress*] (LCLS)

MNRV .... Movimiento Nacionalista Revolucionario - Vanguardia Revolucionaria 9 de Abril [*Bolivia*] [*Political party*] (EY)

MnRvJ .... John Clark Elementary School, Rockville, MN [*Library symbol*] [*Library of Congress*] (LCLS)

MnRw .... Red Wing Public Library, Red Wing, MN [*Library symbol Library of Congress*] (LCLS)

MnRwf......... Redwood Falls Public Library, Redwood Falls, MN [*Library symbol*] [*Library of Congress*] (LCLS)

MnRwfGES... Reede Gray Elementary School, Redwood Falls, MN [*Library symbol*] [*Library of Congress*] (LCLS)

MnRwfH....... Redwood Falls Hospital, Redwood Falls, MN [*Library symbol*] [*Library of Congress*] (LCLS)

MnRwfJSH... Redwood Falls-Morton Junior Senior High School, Redwood Falls, MN [*Library symbol*] [*Library of Congress*] (LCLS)

MnRwfSJL... St. John's Lutheran School, Redwood Falls, MN [*Library symbol*] [*Library of Congress*] (LCLS)

MNS............. College of Saint Scholastica Library, Duluth, MN [*OCLC symbol*] (OCLC)

MNS............. MacNeal-Schwendler [*AMEX symbol*] (TTSB)

MNS............. [*The*] MacNeal-Schwendler Corp. [*AMEX symbol*] (SPSG)

MNS............. Malayan Nature Society (BUAC)

MNS............. Management Need Statement (AAGC)

Mns............. Manaus (AD)

MNS............. Manitoba Naturalists Society [*Canada*] (BUAC)

MNS............. Mansa [*Zambia*] [*Airport symbol*] (OAG)

MNS............. Martin's Louisiana Reports, New Series [*A publication*] (DLA)

MNS............. Master of Natural Sciences (GAGS)

MNS............. Master of Nuclear Science (GAGS)

MNS............. Master of Nursing Science

MNS............. Master of Nutritional Science

MNS............. Master of Nutritional Sciences (GAGS)

MNS............. Materiel Need Statement [*Army*]

MNS............. Maturity News Service

MNS............. McGuire Nuclear Station (NRCH)

MNS............. Mechanical Neutral Start [*Automotive engineering*]

MNS............. Medial Nuclear Stratum (DB)

MNS............. Member of the Numismatical Society [*British*]

mns............. Metal-Nitride-Semiconductor (AD)

MNS............. Meta-Nitride Semiconductor (MCD)

MNS............. Microband National System, Inc. [*New York, NY*] [*Telecommunications*] (TSSD)

MNS............. Microneurography Society (EA)

MNS............. Mine Neutralization System [*Military*] (CAAL)

MNS............. Mines

Mns............. Mines (AD)

MNS............. Ministic Air [*Canada ICAO designator*] (FAAC)

MNS............. Ministry of National Service [*World War I*] [*British*]

MNS............. Minneapolis, Northfield & Southern Railway [*AAR code*]

MNS............. Minutes [*International telex abbreviation*] (WDMC)

MNS............. Mission Needs Statement [*Army*] (RDA)

MNS............. Molded Nylon Screw

MNS............. Moravian National Party [*Political party*] (BUAC)

MNS............. Movement for a New Society [*Defunct*] (EA)

MNS............. Movimiento Nacional de Salvacion [*National Movement of Salvation*] [*Dominican Republic*] [*Political party*] (PPW)

MNS............. Smith College, Northampton, MA [*Library symbol Library of Congress*] (LCLS)

MnS............. St. Paul Public Library, St. Paul, MN [*Library symbol Library of Congress*] (LCLS)

MnSa........... Sandstone Public Library, Sandstone, MN [*Library symbol*] [*Library of Congress*] (LCLS)

MNSA .... Seaman Apprentice, Mineman, Striker [*Navy rating*]

MnSaE........ Sandstone Elementary School, Sandstone, MN [*Library symbol*] [*Library of Congress*] (LCLS)

MnSaF........ Federal Correctional Institute Library, Sandstone, MN [*Library symbol*] [*Library of Congress*] (LCLS)

MnSAG .... Minnesota Attorney General's Office, St. Paul, MN [*Library symbol Library of Congress*] (LCLS)

MnSagHS .... Albrook High School, Saginaw, MN [*Library symbol*] [*Library of Congress*] (LCLS)

MnSaH........ Sandstone Area Hospital/Nursing Home, Sandstone, MN [*Library symbol*] [*Library of Congress*] (LCLS)

MnSaJS....... Sandstone Junior/Senior High School, Sandstone, MN [*Library symbol*] [*Library of Congress*] (LCLS)

MnSanLS..... Zion Lutheran School, Sanborn, MN [*Library symbol*] [*Library of Congress*] (LCLS)

MnSanPS.... Sanborn Public School, Sanborn, MN [*Library symbol*] [*Library of Congress*] (LCLS)

MnSarH....... Sartell High School, Sartell, MN [*Library symbol*] [*Library of Congress*] (LCLS)

MnSarM....... Sartell Middle School, Sartell, MN [*Library symbol*] [*Library of Congress*] (LCLS)

MnSarS........ St. Francis Xavier School, Sartell, MN [*Library symbol*] [*Library of Congress*] (LCLS)

MNSaS .... Swift River Valley Historical Society, New Salem, MA [*Library symbol Library of Congress*] (LCLS)

MnSB........... Bethel College, St. Paul, MN [*Library symbol Library of Congress*] (LCLS)

MNSBC .... Minnesota North Stars Booster Club (EA)

MnSBH .... Bethesda Lutheran Hospital, St. Paul, MN [*Library symbol Library of Congress*] (LCLS)

MNSC .... Main Network Switching Center [*Telecommunications*] (TEL)

MN Sc .... Master of Nursing Science

MNSC .... San Carlos/San Juan [*Nicaragua*] [*ICAO location identifier*] (ICLI)

MnSc........... Sauk Centre Public Library, Sauk Centre, MN [*Library symbol Library of Congress*] (LCLS)

MnSCC........ Concordia College, St. Paul, MN [*Library symbol Library of Congress*] (LCLS)

MnSCH .... Children's Hospital, St. Paul, MN [*Library symbol Library of Congress*] (LCLS)

MnScHF....... Holy Family School, Sauk Center, MN [*Library symbol*] [*Library of Congress*] (LCLS)

MNSCL .... Miniscule

MnScL .... Sinclair Lewis Foundation, Sauk Centre, MN [*Library symbol Library of Congress*] (LCLS)

MnScM .... Meadow View School, Sauk Centre, MN [*Library symbol*] [*Library of Congress*] (LCLS)

MnScML ...... Mary Lyon School, Minnesota Correctional Facility, Sauk Centre, MN [*Library symbol*] [*Library of Congress*] (LCLS)

MnScP .... Sauk Centre Public Schools, Sauk Centre, MN [*Library symbol*] [*Library of Congress*] (LCLS)

MnScSM ...... St. Michael's Hospital and Convalescent and Nursing Center, Sauk Centre, MN [*Library symbol*] [*Library of Congress*] (LCLS)

MNSD .... Mouvement National pour une Societe de Developpement [*Niger*] [*Political party*] (EY)

MnSEA........ Minnesota Energy Agency, St. Paul, MN [*Library symbol Library of Congress*] (LCLS)

MnSebS....... Sebeka School, Sebeka, MN [*Library symbol*] [*Library of Congress*] (LCLS)

MNSER .... Mean Normalized Systolic Ejection Rate [*Cardiology*]

MNSF........... Monoclonal-Nonspecific Suppressor Factor [*Immunology*]

MnSG........... Gillette State Hospital for Crippled Children, St. Paul, MN [*Library symbol Library of Congress*] (LCLS)

MnSGC .... Minnesota Governor's Commission on Crime Prevention and Control, St. Paul, MN [*Library symbol Library of Congress*] (LCLS)

MnSGH .... Group Health, Inc., St. Paul, MN [*Library symbol Library of Congress*] (LCLS)

MnSH.......... Hamline University, St. Paul, MN [*Library symbol Library of Congress*] (LCLS)

MnSheS .... Shelly School, Shelly, MN [*Library symbol*] [*Library of Congress*] (LCLS)

MnSH-L .... Hamline University, School of Law, St. Paul, MN [*Library symbol Library of Congress*] (LCLS)

MnShS......... Scott County Library, Shakopee, MN [*Library symbol Library of Congress*] (LCLS)

MNSI.......... Siuna [*Nicaragua*] [*ICAO location identifier*] (ICLI)

MnSib.......... Silver Bay Public Library, Silver Bay, MN [*Library symbol*] [*Library of Congress*] (LCLS)

MnSibHS..... Wm. Kelley High School, Silver Bay, MN [*Library symbol*] [*Library of Congress*] (LCLS)

MnSibME..... Mary MacDonald Elementary School, Silver Bay, MN [*Library symbol*] [*Library of Congress*] (LCLS)

MnSifE......... Holler Elementary School, South International Falls, MN [*Library symbol*] [*Library of Congress*] (LCLS)

MnSJ........... James J. Hill Reference Library, St. Paul, MN [*Library symbol Library of Congress*] (LCLS)

MnSL........... Luther Theological Seminary, St. Paul, MN [*Library symbol Library of Congress Obsolete*] (LCLS)

MNSL........... Mainsail

MnSLBF....... Lutheran Brotherhood Foundation Reformation Library, St. Paul, MN [*Library symbol*] [*Library of Congress*] (LCLS)

MnSLN......... Luther-Northwestern Seminary, St. Paul, MN [*Library symbol Library of Congress*] (LCLS)

MnSly.......... Slayton Public Library, Slayton, MN [*Library symbol*] [*Library of Congress*] (LCLS)

MnSlyES....... Slayton Elementary School, Slayton, MN [*Library symbol*] [*Library of Congress*] (LCLS)

MnSlyJSH.... Slayton Junior-Senior High School, Slayton, MN [*Library symbol*] [*Library of Congress*] (LCLS)

MnSM.......... Macalester College, St. Paul, MN [*Library symbol Library of Congress*] (LCLS)

MnSmH........ St. Michael-Albertville High School, St. Michael, MN [*Library symbol*] [*Library of Congress*] (LCLS)

MnSmM........ St. Michael-Albertville Middle School, St. Michael, MN [*Library symbol*] [*Library of Congress*] (LCLS)

MnSMMfg..... Minnesota Mining & Manufacturing Co., Technical Library, St. Paul, MN [*Library symbol Library of Congress Obsolete*] (LCLS)

MnSMN......... Mounds-Midway School of Nursing, St. Paul, MN [*Library symbol Library of Congress*] (LCLS)

MnSmP........ St. Michael Parish School, St. Michael, MN [*Library symbol*] [*Library of Congress*] (LCLS)

MnSN........... Northwestern Lutheran Theological Seminary, St. Paul, MN [*Library symbol Library of Congress Obsolete*] (LCLS)

MNSN........... Seaman, Mineman, Striker [*Navy rating*]

MnSOD........ Manganese Superoxide Dismutase

MnSOEO...... Minnesota Office of Economic Opportunity, St. Paul, MN [*Library symbol Library of Congress*] (LCLS)

MnSP........... Saint Paul Public Library, St. Paul, MN [*Library symbol*] [*Library of Congress*] (LCLS)

MnSpES....... Spicer Elementary School, Spicer, MN [*Library symbol*] [*Library of Congress*] (LCLS)

MnSpP......... Spicer Public Library, Spicer, MN [*Library symbol*] [*Library of Congress*] (LCLS)

MNSQ.......... Motor Neurone Society of Queensland [*Australia*]

MnSqlS........ Squaw Lake School, Squaw Lake, MN [*Library symbol*] [*Library of Congress*] (LCLS)

MnSrB......... Benton County Historical Museum, Sauk Rapids, MN [*Library symbol*] [*Library of Congress*] (LCLS)

MnSRC........ Ramsey County Public Library, St. Paul, MN [*Library symbol Library of Congress*] (LCLS)

MnSrH......... Sauk Rapids High School, Sauk Rapids, MN [*Library symbol*] [*Library of Congress*] (LCLS)

MnSrHJ........ Hillside Junior High School, Sauk Rapids, MN [*Library symbol*] [*Library of Congress*] (LCLS)

MnSRM........ Ramsey County Medical Society, St. Paul, MN [*Library symbol Library of Congress*] (LCLS)

MnSrPE........ Pleasantview Elementary School, Sauk Rapids, MN [*Library symbol*] [*Library of Congress*] (LCLS)

MnSrS......... Sacred Heart School, Sauk Rapids, MN [*Library symbol*] [*Library of Congress*] (LCLS)

MnSrT.......... Trinity Lutheran School, Sauk Rapids, MN [*Library symbol*] [*Library of Congress*] (LCLS)

MNSS.......... Modified Need Satisfaction Schedule

MNS-S.......... Smith College, Sophia Smith Collection, Northampton, MA [*Library symbol Library of Congress*] (LCLS)

MnSS........... St. Paul Seminary, St. Paul, MN [*Library symbol Library of Congress*] (LCLS)

MNSSA........ Motor Neurone Society of South Australia

MnSSC......... College of St. Catherine, St. Paul, MN [*Library symbol Library of Congress*] (LCLS)

MnSSEP....... Median Nerve Somatosensory Evoked Potential [*Neurology*] (DAVI)

MnSSJ......... St. John's Hospital, St. Paul, MN [*Library symbol Library of Congress*] (LCLS)

MnSSJos..... St. Joseph's Hospital, St. Paul, MN [*Library symbol Library of Congress*] (LCLS)

MnSSM........ Science Museum of Minnesota, Louis S. Headley Memorial Library, St. Paul, MN [*Library symbol*] [*Library of Congress*] (LCLS)

MnSSP......... St. Paul Ramsey Hospital, St. Paul, MN [*Library symbol Library of Congress*] (LCLS)

MnSSpU...... Sperry UNIVAC, St. Paul, MN [*Library symbol Library of Congress*] (LCLS)

MnSST......... College of St. Thomas, St. Paul, MN [*Library symbol Library of Congress*] (LCLS)

MNST........... Motor Neurone Society of Tasmania [*Australia*]

MnSt........... Staples Public Library, Staples, MN [*Library symbol*] [*Library of Congress*] (LCLS)

MNSTB........ Monostable (MSA)

MNSTBMV... Monostable Multivibrator (MSA)

MnStbSP...... Saint Paul Bible College, Saint Bonifacius, MN [*Library symbol Library of Congress*] (LCLS)

MnStcIA....... Appollo High School, St. Cloud, MN [*Library symbol*] [*Library of Congress*] (LCLS)

MnStcIBS..... Benton/Stearns Special Education Professional Library, St. Cloud, MN [*Library symbol*] [*Library of Congress*] (LCLS)

MnStcICF..... Minnesota Corrections Facility Library, St. Cloud, MN [*Library symbol*] [*Library of Congress*] (LCLS)

MnStcICH.... St. Cloud Cathedral High School, St. Cloud, MN [*Library symbol*] [*Library of Congress*] (LCLS)

MnStcID...... Diocese of St. Cloud, St. Cloud, MN [*Library symbol*] [*Library of Congress*] (LCLS)

MnStcIEC..... Central Minnesota Educational Cooperative Service Unit, St. Cloud, MN [*Library symbol*] [*Library of Congress*] (LCLS)

MnStcIER..... Central Minnesota Educational Research and Development Council, Film Library, St. Cloud, MN [*Library symbol*] [*Library of Congress*] (LCLS)

MnStcIG....... Great River Regional Library, St. Cloud, MN [*Library symbol Library of Congress*] (LCLS)

MnStcIGP.... Green Pastures Christian School, St. Cloud, MN [*Library symbol*] [*Library of Congress*] (LCLS)

MnStcIH....... St. Cloud Hospital, Health Sciences Library, St. Cloud, MN [*Library symbol*] [*Library of Congress*] (LCLS)

MnStcIHi...... Stearns County Historical Society, St. Cloud, MN [*Library symbol*] [*Library of Congress*] (LCLS)

MnStcIHS.... Holy Spirit School, St. Cloud, MN [*Library symbol*] [*Library of Congress*] (LCLS)

MnStcIJ....... Jefferson Elementary School, St. Cloud, MN [*Library symbol*] [*Library of Congress*] (LCLS)

MnStcIL....... Lincoln Elementary School, St. Cloud, MN [*Library symbol*] [*Library of Congress*] (LCLS)

MnStcIM...... Madison Elementary School, St. Cloud, MN [*Library symbol*] [*Library of Congress*] (LCLS)

MnStcIMc.... McKinley Elementary School, St. Cloud, MN [*Library symbol*] [*Library of Congress*] (LCLS)

MnStcIMS.... St. Cloud Media Services, St. Cloud, MN [*Library symbol*] [*Library of Congress*] (LCLS)

MnStcIN...... St. Cloud School of Nursing Library, St. Cloud, MN [*Library symbol*] [*Library of Congress*] (LCLS)

MnStcIP....... Sts. Peter & Paul Primary School, St. Cloud, MN [*Library symbol*] [*Library of Congress*] (LCLS)

MnStcIR....... Roosevelt Elementary School, St. Cloud, MN [*Library symbol*] [*Library of Congress*] (LCLS)

MnStcIS....... St. Cloud State University, St. Cloud, MN [*Library symbol Library of Congress*] (LCLS)

MnStcISA..... St. Anthony School, St. Cloud, MN [*Library symbol*] [*Library of Congress*] (LCLS)

MnStcISC..... Stearns/Benton Counties Law Library, St. Cloud, MN [*Library symbol*] [*Library of Congress*] (LCLS)

MnStcISE..... St. Cloud South Elementary School, St. Cloud, MN [*Library symbol*] [*Library of Congress*] (LCLS)

MnStcISM.... St. Mary Help of Christians School, St. Cloud, MN [*Library symbol*] [*Library of Congress*] (LCLS)

MnStcISP..... Sts. Peter & Paul Middle Schol, St. Cloud, MN [*Library symbol*] [*Library of Congress*] (LCLS)

MnStcISt...... St. Augustine School, St. Cloud, MN [*Library symbol*] [*Library of Congress*] (LCLS)

MnStcIV....... United States Veterans Administration Hospital, St. Cloud, MN [*Library symbol Library of Congress*] (LCLS)

MnStcIVT..... St. Cloud Area Vo-Tech Institute, St. Cloud, MN [*Library symbol*] [*Library of Congress*] (LCLS)

MnStcIW...... Westwood Elementary School, St. Cloud, MN [*Library symbol*] [*Library of Congress*] (LCLS)

MnSteE........ Stephen Elementary School, Stpehen, MN [*Library symbol*] [*Library of Congress*] (LCLS)

MnSteH........ Stephen High School, Stephen, MN [*Library symbol*] [*Library of Congress*] (LCLS)

MnStH......... United District Hospital, Staples, MN [*Library symbol*] [*Library of Congress*] (LCLS)

MnStHS....... Staples High School, Staples, MN [*Library symbol*] [*Library of Congress*] (LCLS)

MnStj.......... Watonwan County Library, St. James, MN [*Library symbol Library of Congress*] (LCLS)

MnStjoKE..... Kennedy Elementary School, St. Joseph, MN [*Library symbol*] [*Library of Congress*] (LCLS)

MnStjoL....... St. Joseph Lab School, St. Joseph, MN [*Library symbol*] [*Library of Congress*] (LCLS)

MnStjoS....... College of St. Benedict, St. Joseph, MN [*Library symbol Library of Congress*] (LCLS)

MnStLE....... Lincoln Model Elementary School, Staples, MN [*Library symbol*] [*Library of Congress*] (LCLS)

MnSTM........ Three M (3M) Co., St. Paul, MN [*Library symbol*] [*Library of Congress*] (LCLS)

MnSTM-A.... Three M (3M) Co., St. Paul, MN [*Library symbol*] [*Library of Congress*] (LCLS)

MnSTM-B.... Three M (3M) Co., Business Information Service, St. Paul, MN [*Library symbol*] [*Library of Congress*] (LCLS)

MnSTM-E.... Three M (3M) Co., Engineering Information Services, St. Paul, MN [*Library symbol Library of Congress*] (LCLS)

MnSTM-G.... Three M (3M) Co., St. Paul, MN [*Library symbol*] [*Library of Congress*] (LCLS)

MnSTM-H.... Three M (3M) Co., Health Care Library, St. Paul, MN [*Library symbol*] [*Library of Congress*] (LCLS)

MnSTM-M.... Three M (3M) Co., St. Paul, MN [*Library symbol*] [*Library of Congress*] (LCLS)

MnSTM-P .... Three M (3M) Co., St. Paul, MN [*Library symbol*] [*Library of Congress*] (LCLS)

MnSTM-T..... Three M (3M) Co., St. Paul, MN [*Library symbol*] [*Library of Congress*] (LCLS)

MnStNE........ North Elementary School, Staples, MN [*Library symbol*] [*Library of Congress*] (LCLS)

MnStoES...... Storden-Jeffers Elementary School, Storden, MN [*Library symbol*] [*Library of Congress*] (LCLS)

MnStpeG...... Gustavus Adolphus College, St. Peter, MN [*Library symbol Library of Congress*] (LCLS)

Mnstr .... Munster (AD)

MNSTRY ...... Ministry

MnStS.......... Sacred Heart School, Staples, MN [*Library symbol*] [*Library of Congress*] (LCLS)

MnStT.......... Staples Technical Institute, Staples, MN [*Library symbol*] [*Library of Congress*] (LCLS)

MnStwPS..... Stewart Public Schools, Stewart, MN [*Library symbol*] [*Library of Congress*] (LCLS)

MnSU........... University of Minnesota, St. Paul, MN [*Library symbol Library of Congress*] (LCLS)

MnSU-Bc ..... University of Minnesota, Biochemistry Library, St. Paul, MN [*Library symbol Library of Congress*] (LCLS)

MnSuES....... Sunberg Elementary School, Sunberg, MN [*Library symbol*] [*Library of Congress*] (LCLS)

MnSU-Et ...... University of Minnesota, Entomology Library, St. Paul, MN [*Library symbol Library of Congress*] (LCLS)

MnSU-F .... University of Minnesota, Forestry Library, St. Paul, MN [*Library symbol Library of Congress*] (LCLS)

MnSUH .... United Hospitals, Inc., St. Paul, MN [*Library symbol Library of Congress*] (LCLS)

MnSU-PP .... University of Minnesota, Plant Pathology Library, St. Paul, MN [*Library symbol Library of Congress*] (LCLS)

MnSUSF ...... United States Forest Service, North Central Forest Experiment Station, St. Paul,MN [*Library symbol Library of Congress*] (LCLS)

MnSU-V .... University of Minnesota, Veterinary Medicine Library, St. Paul, MN [*Library symbol Library of Congress*] (LCLS)

MNSV .... Motor Neurone Society of Victoria [*Australia*]

MnSw .... Swanville Public Library, Swanville, MN [*Library symbol*] [*Library of Congress*] (LCLS)

MnSwE .... Swanville Elementary School, Swanville, MN [*Library symbol*] [*Library of Congress*] (LCLS)

MnSwH .... Swanville High School, Swanville, MN [*Library symbol*] [*Library of Congress*] (LCLS)

MnSWM...... William Mitchell College of Law, St. Paul, MN [*Library symbol Library of Congress*] (LCLS)

MNT............. College of St. Thomas, St. Paul, MN [*OCLC symbol*] (OCLC)

M/N/T........... Main/Satellite/Tributary Network [*Telecommunications*] (ACRL)

MNT............. Maintained [*Automotive advertising*]

mnt .... Mean Neap Tide (AD)

MNT............. Minnesota and Ontario Paper [*Stock exchange symbol*] (AD)

Mn-T............ Minnesota State Department of Taxation, St. Paul, MN [*Library symbol Library of Congress*] (LCLS)

MNT............. Minto [*Alaska*] [*Airport symbol*] (OAG)

MNT............. Minute [*Angle*]

MNT............. Modern Network Theory [*Electrical engineering computer*]

MNT............. Moffatt New Testament Commentary [*A publication*] (BJA)

MNT............. Monitor

MNT............. Mononitrotoluene [*Organic chemistry*]

MNT............. Montedison SpA [*NYSE symbol*] (SPSG)

MNT............. Montedison S p AADS [*NYSE symbol*] (TTSB)

MNT............. Montoro Gold, Inc. [*Vancouver Stock Exchange symbol*]

MNT............. Montreal [*Quebec*] [*Seismograph station code, US Geological Survey*] (SEIS)

MNT............. Montserrat Airways Ltd. [*Antigua and Barbuda*] [*ICAO designator*] (FAAC)

MNT............. Mount (KSC)

MNT............. Mountain

MNt............. Newton Free Library, Newton, MA [*Library symbol Library of Congress*] (LCLS)

MNTAIN .... Mountain [*Commonly used*] (OPSA)

MnTalE .... North Elementary School, Talmoon, MN [*Library symbol*] [*Library of Congress*] (LCLS)

MntasiaE ..... Mountasia Entertainment International, Inc. [*Associated Press*] (SAG)

MNTB.......... Medial Nucleus of Trapezoid Body [*Neuroanatomy*]

MNTB.......... Merchant Navy Training Board [*British*] (DS)

MNTC.......... Mexican National Tourist Council (EA)

MNTC.......... Moffatt New Testament Commentary [*A publication*] (BJA)

MNtcA......... Andover Newton Theological School, Newton Center, MA [*Library symbol Library of Congress*] (LCLS)

MnTcFW ..... United States Fish and Wildlife Service, Science Reference Library, Twin Cities,MN [*Library symbol Library of Congress*] (LCLS)

MnTcM .... United States Bureau of Mines, Twin Cities, MN [*Library symbol Library of Congress*] (LCLS)

MNTD .... Maximum Non-Toxic Dose [*Toxicology*] (LDT)

MnTEC .... Northwest Education Cooperative Service Unit, Thief River Falls, MN [*Library symbol*] [*Library of Congress*] (LCLS)

MnTf .... Taylor Falls Public Library, Taylor Falls, MN [*Library symbol*] [*Library of Congress*] (LCLS)

MnTFM .... Franklin Middle School, Thief River Falls, MN [*Library symbol*] [*Library of Congress*] (LCLS)

MnTfS .... Taylor Falls School, Taylor Falls, MN [*Library symbol*] [*Library of Congress*] (LCLS)

MNTG .... Mounting

MnTh .... Two Harbors Public Library, Two Harbors, MN [*Library symbol*] [*Library of Congress*] (LCLS)

MnThE .... John A. Johnson Elementary School, Two Harbors, MN [*Library symbol*] [*Library of Congress*] (LCLS)

MnThHS...... Two Harbors High School, Two Harbors, MN [*Library symbol*] [*Library of Congress*] (LCLS)

MNTHLY ..... Monthly

MnThM .... Minnehaha Middle School, Two Harbors, MN [*Library symbol*] [*Library of Congress*] (LCLS)

MNTHZ .... Methylnitrosothiazolidine [*Organic chemistry*]

MNTK.......... Mezhotraslevoi Naucho-Tekhni-Cheskii Kompleks [*Interdisciplinary Scientific-Technological Complex*] [*Russian*]

MNTK.......... Movimiento Nacional Tupaj Katari [*Bolivia*] [*Political party*] (PPW)

MnTKS......... Knox School, Thief River Falls, MN [*Library symbol*] [*Library of Congress*] (LCLS)

MNTL .... Manufacturers National (EFIS)

MNTL .... Mental

MnTLH......... Lincoln High School, Thief River Falls, MN [*Library symbol*] [*Library of Congress*] (LCLS)

mntmp .... Minimum Temperature (AD)

MNTMP....... Minimum Temperature (NOAA)

MnTMT .... Mark Twain School, Thief River Falls, MN [*Library symbol*] [*Library of Congress*] (LCLS)

mntn .... Maintain (AD)

MNTN .... Maintain

MNTN .... Mountain

MnTN .... Northland State Junior College, Thief River Falls, MN [*Library symbol Library of Congress*] (LCLS)

mntnc .... Maintenance (AD)

MNTNC .... Maintenance

mntnd .... Maintained (AD)

mntng .... Maintaining (AD)

MnTNo........ Northrop Resource Room, Thief River Falls, MN [*Library symbol*] [*Library of Congress*] (LCLS)

MnTNR .... Northwest Regional Library, Thief River Falls, MN [*Library symbol Library of Congress*] (LCLS)

MNTNS .... Mountains [*Commonly used*] (OPSA)

MNTO .... Moroccan National Tourist Office (AD)

MnToS .... Togo School, Togo, MN [*Library symbol*] [*Library of Congress*] (LCLS)

MnTP .... Thief River Falls Public Library, Thief River Falls, MN [*Library symbol*] [*Library of Congress*] (LCLS)

MnTPC........ Pennington County Extension Office, Thief River Falls, MN [*Library symbol*] [*Library of Congress*] (LCLS)

MnTPPS....... Manganese Tetraphenylporphine Sulfonate [*Organic chemistry*]

MNTPr .... Montedison Bearer Svg Pfd ADS [*NYSE symbol*] (TTSB)

MNTR .... Mentor Corp. [*NASDAQ symbol*] (NQ)

MNTR .... Monitor (MDG)

mntr .... Monitor (AD)

MnTrES........ Tracy Elementary School, Tracy, MN [*Library symbol*] [*Library of Congress*] (LCLS)

MnTrJSH...... Trace Junior-Senior High School, Tracy, MN [*Library symbol*] [*Library of Congress*] (LCLS)

MNTRNG...... Monitoring

MnTrStM....... St. Mary's School, Tracy, MN [*Library symbol*] [*Library of Congress*] (LCLS)

MNTS.......... Medial Nucleus Tractus Solitarius [*Neuroanatomy*]

MNTS.......... Methyl(Nitroso) Toluenesulphonamide [*Organic chemistry*]

MNTS.......... Mountains

MNtS .... Swedenborg School of Religion, Newton, MA [*Library symbol Library of Congress*] (LCLS)

MnTSB......... St. Bernard's School, Thief River Falls, MN [*Library symbol*] [*Library of Congress*] (LCLS)

MNtSH .... Newton College of the Sacred Heart [*Later, Newton College*], Newton, MA [*Library symbol Library of Congress*] (LCLS)

MNTV.......... Mercury Network Test Vehicle (MUGU)

MnTW .... Washington School, Thief River Falls, MN [*Library symbol*] [*Library of Congress*] (LCLS)

MnTwvE....... Twin Valley Elementary School, Twin Valley, MN [*Library symbol*] [*Library of Congress*] (LCLS)

MnTwvH ...... Twin Valley High School, Twin Valley, MN [*Library symbol*] [*Library of Congress*] (LCLS)

MNTX.......... Minntech Corp. [*NASDAQ symbol*] (NQ)

MnTy .... Tyler Public Library, Tyler, MN [*Library symbol*] [*Library of Congress*] (LCLS)

MnTyHS....... Russell-Tyler-Ruthon High School, Tyler, MN [*Library symbol*] [*Library of Congress*] (LCLS)

MNU .... Maniti Sugar [*Stock exchange symbol*] (AD)

MNu .... Mare Nubium [*Sea of Clouds*] [*Lunar area*]

MNU .... Methylnitrosourea [*Also, NMU*] [*Organic chemistry*]

MNU .... Middle Name Unknown (MCD)

MNU .... Milford North [*Utah*] [*Seismograph station code, US Geological Survey*] (SEIS)

MNU .... Minimum Number of Units [*Chemical engineering*]

mnu .... Minnesota [*MARC country of publication code Library of Congress*] (LCCP)

MNU .... Moulmein [*Myanmar*] [*Airport symbol*] (OAG)

MNU .... Movement for National Unity [*St. Vincent*] (BUAC)

MNU .... Mundee Mines Ltd. [*Vancouver Stock Exchange symbol*]

MnU............ University of Minnesota, Minneapolis, MN [*Library symbol Library of Congress*] (LCLS)

MNU .... University of Minnesota, Minneapolis, MN [*OCLC symbol*] (OCLC)

MnU-Ar........ University of Minnesota, Archives, Minneapolis, MN [*Library symbol Library of Congress*] (LCLS)

MnU-B .... University of Minnesota, Biomedical Library, Minneapolis, MN [*Library symbol Library of Congress*] (LCLS)

MNucSc .... Master of Nuclear Science (GAGS)

MnU-Fb........ University of Minnesota, Freshwater Biological Institute, Navarre, MN [*Library symbol Library of Congress*] (LCLS)

MnU-IA .... University of Minnesota, Immigration History Research Center, St. Paul, MN [*Library symbol Library of Congress*] (LCLS)

MnU-K .... University of Minnesota, Kerlan Children's Books Collection, Minneapolis, MN [*Library symbol Library of Congress*] (LCLS)

MnU-L .... University of Minnesota, Law Library, Minneapolis, MN [*Library symbol Library of Congress*] (LCLS)

MnUIH .... Ulen-Hitteral High School, Ulen, MN [*Library symbol*] [*Library of Congress*] (LCLS)

MnU-MS ...... University of Minnesota, Manuscript Collection, Minneapolis, MN [*Library symbol Library of Congress*] (LCLS)

MnUnS........ Underwood Public School, Underwood, MN [*Library symbol*] [*Library of Congress*] (LCLS)

MnUpE .... Upsala Elementary School, Upsala, MN [*Library symbol*] [*Library of Congress*] (LCLS)

MnU-Ph .... University of Minnesota, Pharmacy Library, Minneapolis, MN [*Library symbol Library of Congress*] (LCLS)

MnUpH .... Upsala High School, Upsala, MN [*Library symbol*] [*Library of Congress*] (LCLS)

MNUR.......... Mouvement National pour l'Union et la Reconciliation au Zaire [*National Movement for Union and Reconciliation in Zaire*] [*Political party*] (PD)

MnU-Rb .... University of Minnesota, Rare Book Division, Minneapolis, MN [*Library symbol Library of Congress*] (LCLS)

MNurs.......... Master of Nursing (NADA)

MNursing..... Master of Nursing

MnU-SW ...... University of Minnesota, Social Welfare History Archives Center, St. Paul, MN [*Library symbol Library of Congress*] (LCLS)

MNUT .... Methylnitrosourethane [*Organic chemistry*]

MNutrSc ...... Master of Nutritional Science

MNV............. Madisonville, TN [*Location identifier FAA*] (FAAL)

MNV............. Marginal Net Value

MNV............. Marion Power Shovel [*Stock exchange symbol*] (AD)

MNV............. Mina [*Nevada*] [*Seismograph station code, US Geological Survey*] (SEIS)

MNV............. Mine-Neutralization Vehicle [*Military*] (MCD)

Mn-V............ Minnesota State Vocational Rehabilitation Library, St. Paul, MN [*Library symbol Library of Congress*] (LCLS)

MNV............. Modular Nuclear Vehicle

MNV............. Southwest State University, Marshall, MN [*OCLC symbol*] (OCLC)

MNV............. United States Veterans Administration Hospital, Northampton, MA [*Library symbol Library of Congress*] (LCLS)

MnV .... Virginia Public Library, Virginia, MN [*Library symbol Library of Congress*] (LCLS)

MnVA........... Arrowhead Library System, Virginia, MN [*Library symbol Library of Congress*] (LCLS)

MnVePS....... Verdi Public School, Verdi, MN [*Library symbol*] [*Library of Congress*] (LCLS)

MnVerS........ Verndale Public School, Verndale, MN [*Library symbol*] [*Library of Congress*] (LCLS)

MnVHS .... Virginia Junior-Senior High School, Virginia, MN [*Library symbol*] [*Library of Congress*] (LCLS)

MnViilS........ Villard Public School, Villard, MN [*Library symbol*] [*Library of Congress*] (LCLS)

MnVM........... Mesabi Community College, Virginia, MN [*Library symbol Library of Congress*] (LCLS)

MNVM .... Million Nighttime Vehicle Mile

MnVME........ James Madison Elementary School, Virginia, MN [*Library symbol*] [*Library of Congress*] (LCLS)

MNVR .... Maneuver

MnVRE......... Roosevelt Elementary School, Virginia, MN [*Library symbol*] [*Library of Congress*] (LCLS)

MnVRM........ Virginia Regional Medical Center, Virginia, MN [*Library symbol*] [*Library of Congress*] (LCLS)

Mn-W .... Minnesota State Department of Public Welfare, St. Paul, MN [*Library symbol Library of Congress*] (LCLS)

MNW .... Moneywise Resources [*Vancouver Stock Exchange symbol*]

MNW .... Monowai [*New Zealand*] [*Seismograph station code, US Geological Survey*] (SEIS)

MNW .... Northwest Missouri State University, Maryville, MO [*OCLC symbol*] (OCLC)

MnWa........... Wabasso Public Library, Wabasso, MN [*Library symbol*] [*Library of Congress*] (LCLS)

MnWad........ Wadena City Library, Wadena, MN [*Library symbol*] [*Library of Congress*] (LCLS)

MnWadE...... Wadena Elementary School, Wadena, MN [*Library symbol*] [*Library of Congress*] (LCLS)

MnWadH...... Wadena High School, Wadena, MN [*Library symbol*] [*Library of Congress*] (LCLS)

MnWadJ ...... Wadena Junior High School, Wadena, MN [*Library symbol*] [*Library of Congress*] (LCLS)

MnWaES...... Wabasso Elementary School, Wabasso, MN [*Library symbol*] [*Library of Congress*] (LCLS)

MnWaHS ..... Wabasso High School, Wabasso, MN [*Library symbol*] [*Library of Congress*] (LCLS)

MnWal.......... Walker Public Library, Walker, MN [*Library symbol*] [*Library of Congress*] (LCLS)

MnWalC........ Cass County Extension Office, Walker, MN [*Library symbol*] [*Library of Congress*] (LCLS)

MnWalH ...... Walker-Hackensack High School, Walker, MN [*Library symbol*] [*Library of Congress*] (LCLS)

MnWalHi ..... Cass County Historical Society, Walker, MN [*Library symbol*] [*Library of Congress*] (LCLS)

MnWanS...... Wannaska School, Wannaska, MN [*Library symbol*] [*Library of Congress*] (LCLS)

MnWar......... Godell Memorial Library, Warren, MN [*Library symbol*] [*Library of Congress*] (LCLS)

MnWarE....... Warren Elementary School, Warren, MN [*Library symbol*] [*Library of Congress*] (LCLS)

MnWarJS...... Warren Junior/Senior High School, Warren, MN [*Library symbol*] [*Library of Congress*] (LCLS)

MnWarr........ Warroad Public Library, Warroad, MN [*Library symbol*] [*Library of Congress*] (LCLS)

MnWarrE...... Warroad Elementary School, Warroad, MN [*Library symbol*] [*Library of Congress*] (LCLS)

MnWarrH..... Warroad High School, Warroad, MN [*Library symbol*] [*Library of Congress*] (LCLS)

MnWas......... Le Sueur-Waseca Regional Library, Waseca, MN [*Library symbol Library of Congress*] (LCLS)

MnWaStA..... St. Anne School, Wabasso, MN [*Library symbol*] [*Library of Congress*] (LCLS)

MnWasU...... University of Minnesota Technical College, Waseca, MN [*Library symbol Library of Congress*] (LCLS)

MnWatSA..... St. Anthony School, Watkins, MN [*Library symbol*] [*Library of Congress*] (LCLS)

MnWauWE... Waubon-Ogema-White Earth School, Waubon, MN [*Library symbol*] [*Library of Congress*] (LCLS)

MnWayC....... Cargill Instructional Center, Wayzata, MN [*Library symbol Library of Congress*] (LCLS)

MnWbIL........ Lakewood Community College, White Bear Lake, MN [*Library symbol Library of Congress*] (LCLS)

MnWbS........ Warba School, Warba, MN [*Library symbol*] [*Library of Congress*] (LCLS)

MnWE.......... Isle-Wahkon Elementary School, Wahkon, MN [*Library symbol*] [*Library of Congress*] (LCLS)

MNWEB .... Merseyside and North Wales Electricity Board [*British*] (AD)

MnWeCS...... Westbrook Christian School, Westbrook, MN [*Library symbol*] [*Library of Congress*] (LCLS)

MnWeP........ Westbrook Public Library, Westbrook, MN [*Library symbol*] [*Library of Congress*] (LCLS)

MnWePS...... Westbrook Public School, Westbrook, MN [*Library symbol*] [*Library of Congress*] (LCLS)

MnWgMS...... Westbrook-Walnut Grove Middle School, Walnut Grove, MN [*Library symbol*] [*Library of Congress*] (LCLS)

MNWH......... Mojo Nixon World Headquarters (EA)

MnWhe........ Wheaton Community Library, Wheaton, MN [*Library symbol*] [*Library of Congress*] (LCLS)

MnWheH...... Wheaton Community Hospital, Wheaton, MN [*Library symbol*] [*Library of Congress*] (LCLS)

MnWheHS ... Wheaton-Dumont High School, Wheaton, MN [*Library symbol*] [*Library of Congress*] (LCLS)

MnWhePE... J.E. Pearson Elementary School, Wheaton, MN [*Library symbol*] [*Library of Congress*] (LCLS)

MnWil.......... Lawson Memorial Library, Willmar, MN [*Library symbol*] [*Library of Congress*] (LCLS)

MnWilCS...... Christian Community School, Willmar, MN [*Library symbol*] [*Library of Congress*] (LCLS)

MNWiLES..... Lafayette Elementary School, Willmar, MN [*Library symbol*] [*Library of Congress*] (LCLS)

MnWilGES... Garfield Elementary School, Willmar, MN [*Library symbol*] [*Library of Congress*] (LCLS)

MnWilH .... Rice Memorial Hospital, Willmar, MN [*Library symbol*] [*Library of Congress*] (LCLS)

MnWilIL........ Immanuel Lutheran School, Willmar, MN [*Library symbol*] [*Library of Congress*] (LCLS)

MnWilJES..... Jefferson Elementary School, Willmar, MN [*Library symbol*] [*Library of Congress*] (LCLS)

MnWilJS....... Willmar Junior High School, Willmar, MN [*Library symbol*] [*Library of Congress*] (LCLS)

MnWilLiS...... Lincoln Elementary School, Willmar, MN [*Library symbol*] [*Library of Congress*] (LCLS)

MnWilPS ..... Willmar Public Schools, Willmar, MN [*Library symbol*] [*Library of Congress*] (LCLS)

MnWilRC...... Willmar Regional Treatment Center, Staff Library, Willmar, MN [*Library symbol*] [*Library of Congress*] (LCLS)

MnWilRE...... Roosevelt Elementary School, Willmar, MN [*Library symbol*] [*Library of Congress*] (LCLS)

MnWilRL....... Crow River Regional Library, Willmar, MN [*Library symbol Library of Congress*] (LCLS)

MnWilS......... Willmar State Junior College, Willmar, MN [*Library symbol Library of Congress*] (LCLS)

MnWilSH ..... Willmar Senior High School, Willmar, MN [*Library symbol*] [*Library of Congress*] (LCLS)

MnWilTC...... Willmar Technical Center, Willmar, MN [*Library symbol*] [*Library of Congress*] (LCLS)

MnWilWES... Washington Elementary School, Willmar, MN [*Library symbol*] [*Library of Congress*] (LCLS)

MnWin......... Windom Public Library, Windom, MN [*Library symbol*] [*Library of Congress*] (LCLS)

MnWinH....... Windom Area Hospital, Windom, MN [*Library symbol*] [*Library of Congress*] (LCLS)

MnWinHS..... Windom Area High School, Windom, MN [*Library symbol*] [*Library of Congress*] (LCLS)

MnWino....... Winona Public Library, Winona, MN [*Library symbol Library of Congress*] (LCLS)

MnWinoCT... College of Saint Teresa, Winona, MN [*Library symbol Library of Congress*] (LCLS)

MnWinoS.... Winona State College [*Later, Winona State University*], Winona, MN [*Library symbol Library of Congress*] (LCLS)

MnWinoSM... Saint Mary's College, Winona, MN [*Library symbol Library of Congress*] (LCLS)

MnWinWES... Winfair Elementary School, Windom, MN [*Library symbol*] [*Library of Congress*] (LCLS)

MnWlHS...... Echo-Wood Lake High School, Wood Lake, MN [*Library symbol*] [*Library of Congress*] (LCLS)

MnWISJ....... St. John's School, Wood Lake, MN [*Library symbol*] [*Library of Congress*] (LCLS)

MnWnSJL.... St. John's Lutheran School, Winsted, MN [*Library symbol*] [*Library of Congress*] (LCLS)

MnWoCCS ... Calvary Christian School, Worthington, MN [*Library symbol*] [*Library of Congress*] (LCLS)

MnWoCES.... Central Elementary School, Worthington, MN [*Library symbol*] [*Library of Congress*] (LCLS)

MnWoH....... Worthington Regional Hospital, Worthington, MN [*Library symbol*] [*Library of Congress*] (LCLS)

MnWoJH...... Worthington Junior High, Worthington, MN [*Library symbol*] [*Library of Congress*] (LCLS)

MnWoLS...... Lakeview School, Worthington, MN [*Library symbol*] [*Library of Congress*] (LCLS)

MnWoN....... Nobles County Library, Worthington, MN [*Library symbol Library of Congress*] (LCLS)

MnWoP....... Plum Creek Library System, Worthington, MN [*Library symbol Library of Congress*] (LCLS)

MnWoS....... Worthington State Junior College [*Later, Worthington Community College*], Worthington, MN [*Library symbol Library of Congress*] (LCLS)

MnWoSH ..... Worthington Senior High School, Worthington, MN [*Library symbol*] [*Library of Congress*] (LCLS)

MnWoSMS... St. Mary's School, Worthington, MN [*Library symbol*] [*Library of Congress*] (LCLS)

MnWoWCS... Worthington Christian School, Worthington, MN [*Library symbol*] [*Library of Congress*] (LCLS)

MnWoWES... West Elementary School, Worthington, MN [*Library symbol*] [*Library of Congress*] (LCLS)

MnWp......... Waite Park Public Library, Waite Park, MN [*Library symbol*] [*Library of Congress*] (LCLS)

MnWpS........ St. Joseph's School, Waite Park, MN [*Library symbol*] [*Library of Congress*] (LCLS)

MNWR........ Malheur National Wildlife Refuge [*Oregon*] (AD)

MNWR........ Mattamuskeet National Wildlife Refuge [*North Carolina*] (AD)

MNWR........ Merced National Wildlife Refuge [*California*] (AD)

MNWR........ Mingo National Wildlife Refuge [*Missouri*] (AD)

MNWR........ Minidoka National Wildlife Refuge [*Idaho*] (AD)

MNWR........ Mississiquoi National Wildlife Refuge [*Vermont*] (AD)

MNWR........ Modoc National Wildlife Refuge [*California*] (AD)

MNWR........ Montezuma National Wildlife Refuge [*New York*] (AD)

MNWR........ Moosehorn National Wildlife Refuge [*Maine*] (AD)

MnWrC....... Willow River Camp Library, Willow River, MN [*Library symbol*] [*Library of Congress*] (LCLS)

MnWreS ...... Wrenshall Public School, Wrenshall, MN [*Library symbol*] [*Library of Congress*] (LCLS)

MnWriLE..... Lincoln Elementary School, Wright, MN [*Library symbol*] [*Library of Congress*] (LCLS)

MnWrS .... Willow River School, Willow River, MN [*Library symbol*] [*Library of Congress*] (LCLS)

MnWs......... Winsted Public Library, Winsted, MN [*Library symbol*] [*Library of Congress*] (LCLS)

MnWsHT...... Holy Trinity School, Winsted, MN [*Library symbol*] [*Library of Congress*] (LCLS)

MNWSL....... Merchant Navy War Service League [*Australia*]

MnWspD...... Dakota County Library, West St. Paul, MN [*Library symbol Library of Congress*] (LCLS)

MnWsPS...... Winsted Public School, Winsted, MN [*Library symbol*] [*Library of Congress*] (LCLS)

MNX........... Manx Airlines Ltd. [*British ICAO designator*] (FAAC)

Mnx .... Manx Gaelic (AD)

MNX........... University of Minnesota, Morris, Morris, MN [*OCLC symbol*] (OCLC)

MNY........... Money

MNY........... Mono Island [*Solomon Islands*] [*Airport symbol*] (OAG)

MNY........... Monteynard [*France*] [*Seismograph station code, US Geological Survey*] (SEIS)

MNY........... Saint Mary's College, Winona, MN [*OCLC symbol*] (OCLC)

MNY........... Taurus Municipal New York Holdings [*NYSE symbol*] (SPSG)

MNY........... Taurus MuniNewYork Hldgs [*NYSE symbol*] (TTSB)

MNYRC....... Metropolitan New York Rugby Conference (PSS)

MNZ........... College of Saint Teresa, Winona, MN [*OCLC symbol*] (OCLC)

MNZ........... Manassas [*Virginia*] [*Airport symbol*] (OAG)

MNZ........... Manzanillo [*Mexico*] [*Seismograph station code, US Geological Survey*] (SEIS)

MnZE .... Zimmerman Elementary School, Zimmerman, MN [*Library symbol*] [*Library of Congress*] (LCLS)

Mnzlo......... Manzanillo (AD)

MO............. Abbott Laboratories [*Research code symbol*]

MO............. Calm Air International [*ICAO designator*] (AD)

MO............. Macau [*ANSI two-letter standard code*] (CNC)

MO............. Machine Operation (AFM)

Mo .... Maestro GG1MasterGG2 [*Italian*] (AD)

MO............. Magneto-Optic [*Computer science*]

MO............. Magneto-Optical [*Physics*]

mo .... Mail Order (AD)

MO............. Mail Order [*Business term*]

MO............. Maintenance and Operating [*Factor*] (NG)

MO............. Maintenance Officer (MCD)

M/O............ Maintenance/Organization (MCD)

M/O............ Maintenance to Operation [*Ratio*]

m/o............ Maintenance-to-Operation (AD)

MO............. Maize Oil (PDAA)

MO............. Major Objective (KSC)

mo .... Major Objective (NAKS)

MO............. Make Offer

MO............. Making Objects [*Research test*] [*Psychology*]

MO............. Malaoxon (LDT)

m/o............ Male Oriental (AD)

MO............. Managed Object [*Telecommunications*] (OSI)

MO............. Management Office

MO............. Management Order (NOAA)

M/O............ Manned and Operational (MUGU)

MO............. Manned Orbiter (MCD)

mo .... Manned Orbiter [*NASA*] (NAKS)

MO............. Manually Operated

mo .... Manual Operation (AD)

MO............. Manual Orientation (MCD)

mo .... Manual Orientation (NAKS)

MO............. Manual Output

MO............. Manufacturer's Output

MO............. Manufacturing Order (NASA)

mo .... Manufacturing Order (NAKS)

MO............. Manufacturing Outline

MO............. March Order [*Military*]

MO............. Marketing Organization (AD)

MO............. Mark Off

MO............. Mars Observer Mission (MCD)

MO............. Mars Orbiter [*NASA*] (KSC)

MO............. Masonry Opening [*Technical drawings*]

mo .... Masonry Opening (AD)

mo .... Mass Observation (AD)

MO............. Mass Observation

MO............. Master of Obstetrics

MO............. Master of Oratory

MO............. Master of Osteopathy

MO............. Master Oscillator [*Radio*]

mo .... Master Oscillator (AD)

MO............. Mature Outlook (EA)

MO............. Medial Oblique [*View*] [*Radiology*] (DAVI)

MO............. Medical Officer [*Military*]

MO............. Medical Orderly (WDAA)

MO............. Medium Oocyte

MO............. Member Organisation (ACII)

MO............. Memory Operation

MO............. Memory Output [*Computer science*]

MO............. Mesio-Occlusal [*Dentistry*]

MO............. Mesityl Oxide [*Also, MSO*] [*Organic chemistry*]

MO............. Metal-Organic (AAEL)

MO............. Meteorological Office [*British*]

MO............. Meteorology Officer (MUGU)

MO............. Method of Operation

mo .... Method of Operation (AD)

MO............. Methoxime [*Organic chemistry*]

MO............. Methyl Orange [*Organic chemistry*]

MO............. Micro-Opaque

mo .... Microoperation (MHDB)

MO............. Micro-Osmometer

MO............. Microwave Oven (PDAA)

MO............. Middeck Overhead (MCD)

mo .... Middeck Overhead (NAKS)

mo .... Mid-Oxygen [*Beta-alumina crystallography*]

MO............. Military Observer (WDAA)

MO............. Military Operations [*British military*] (DMA)

MO............. Military Orders Issued by the President as Commander in Chief of the Armed Forces [*A publication*] (DLA)

MO............. Military Services [*Diocesan abbreviation*] [*Maryland*] (TOCD)

MO............. Mineral Oil

Mo .... Mineral Oil (DB)

MO............. Mineral Order [*Defense Minerals Exploration Administration*] [*Department of the Interior A publication*] (DLA)

MO............. Ministerstvo Oborony [*Ministry of Defense*] [*Former USSR*]

MO............. Minor-Oppenheim [*Syndrome*] [*Medicine*] (DB)

MO............. Minute Output [*Of heart*]

m/o............ Mi Orden [*My Order*] [*Spanish*] (AD)

MO............. Miscellaneous Operation (MUGU)

MO............. Missile Officer (AAG)

MO............. Mission Operations [*NASA*]

mo .... Mission Operations [*NASA*] (NAKS)

MO............. Mission Oriented

MO............. Missouri [*Postal code*] (AFM)

mo .... Missourian (AD)

Mo .... Missouri Reports [*A publication*] (AAGC)

Mo .... Missouri State Library, Jefferson City, MO [*Library symbol Library of Congress*] (LCLS)

MO............. Missouri Supreme Court Reports [*1821-1956*] [*A publication*] (DLA)

MO............. Mitral Valve Opening [*Cardiology*]

MO............. Mixed Oxide (NRCH)

MO............. Mobile Object [*Telecommunications*] (OA)

MO............. Mobile Station [*Air Force*]

Mo .... Mode [*Statistics*]

MO............. Moderato [*Moderate Speed*] [*Music*] (ADA)

MO............. Moderator

MO	Modern Orthodox (BJA)
Mo	Modern Reports [England] [A publication] (DLA)
MO	Modification Order (AFIT)
MO	Modulate Open [Nuclear energy] (NRCH)
MO	Modus Operandi [Police term for distinctive techniques used by criminals]
MO	Mohawk Airlines, Inc. [Obsolete]
MO	Molded [Construction]
MO	Molecular Orbital [Atomic physics]
mo	Molecular Orbital (AD)
Mo	Moloney [Strain] [Medicine] (DB)
Mo	Molybdenum [Chemical element]
MO	Moment (DSUE)
mo	Moment (AD)
MO	Monaco [IYRU nationality code] (IYR)
Mo	Monaldus [Flourished, 13th century] [Authority cited in pre-1607 legal work] (DSA)
Mo	Monday (CDAI)
MO	Money Order
MO	Monitor Output
MO	Monooxygenase [An enzyme]
MO	Month (AFM)
mo	Month (WDMC)
MO	Monthly Order [Navy]
MO	Months Old (MEDA)
m-o	Months Old (AD)
Mo	Montreal Stock Exchange [Canada]
MO	Mooney Aircraft, Inc. [ICAO aircraft manufacturer identifier] (ICAO)
Mo	Moore's English Privy Council Reports [1836-62] [A publication] (DLA)
Mo	Moore's Indian Appeals [A publication] (DLA)
MO	Moral Obligation (MHDW)
MO	Moravian
MO	Morning
Mo	Morphine [Medicine] (WDAA)
M-O	Morris-Oxford (AD)
MO	Morse Code Light [or Fog Signal] [Navigation signal]
mo	Moth Eaten (AD)
MO	Mother
MO	Motion for Mandamus Overruled [Legal term] (DLA)
MO	Motor Operated (MSA)
mo	Motor Operated (AD)
MO	Moustache (DSUE)
MO	Mouth
MO	Move (NASA)
mo	Move (NAKS)
MO	Movement Orders
MO	Move Out (WDMC)
MO	Multi-Option (MCD)
MO	Municipal Offices (ROG)
MO	Murphy Oil Co. Ltd. [Toronto Stock Exchange symbol]
MO	Mustered Out [of military service]
mo	Mustered Out (AD)
MO	No Evidence of Distal Metastasis [Oncology] (DAVI)
MO	Philip Morris Companies, Inc. [NYSE symbol] (SPSG)
MO	Philip Morris Cos. [NYSE symbol] (TTSB)
MO$_2$	Mixed Oxides
MO$_2$	Myocardial Oxygen Consumption [Cardiology] (MAE)
MO7	Magneto-Optic 7 (IGQR)
MOA	Made on Assembly
MOA	Magnetic Optical Activity
MOA	Mail Order Association of America (NTPA)
MOA	Make on Arrival (NASA)
MOA	Management Operations Audit [Navy] (NG)
MOA	Manual-Off-Automatic (KSC)
MOA	Marine Office of America (AD)
MOA	Marine Officer's Attendant [British military] (DMA)
MOA	Matrix Output Amplifier
MOA	McDonald's Operators' Association (EA)
MOA	Mechanism of Action [Medicine] (DAVI)
MOA	Medical Outreach for Armenians (EA)
MOA	Medium Observation Aircraft
moa	Medium Observation Aircraft (AD)
M o A	Memorandum of Agreement (AD)
MOA	Memorandum of Agreement
MOA	Memorandum of Assistance
MoA	Memorandum of Association (WDAA)
MOA	Method of Accomplishment (AFIT)
MOA	Method of Adjustment [Aviation]
MOA	Methods of Administration [Department of Education] (OICC)
MOA	Metropolitan Opera Association (AD)
MOA	Metropolitan Opera Auditions (AD)
MOA	Microwave Oven Association (BUAC)
MOA	Military Assistance Program Order Amendment (AFM)
MOA	Military Operations Area [FAA] (TAG)
MoA	Ministry of Agriculture [British] (AD)
MoA	Ministry of Aviation [British]
MOA	Minnesota Orchestral Association (AD)
moa	Minute of Angle (AD)
MOA	Minute of Angle
MOA	Misr Overseas Airways [Egypt]
MOA	Missile Optical Alignment
moa	Missile Optical Alignment (AD)
MOA	Missouri Botanical Garden, St. Louis, MO [OCLC symbol] (OCLC)
MOA	Moa [Cuba] [Airport symbol] (OAG)

MOA	Modern Operating Agreement [Labor negotiations]
MOA	Molln [Austria] [Seismograph station code, US Geological Survey] (SEIS)
MOA	Mountain Lake Resources, Inc. [Vancouver Stock Exchange symbol]
moa	Mud on Airstrip (AD)
MOA	Municipal Officers' Association (ROG)
MoA	Museum of Australia (BUAC)
MOA	Music Operators of America [Later, AMOA] (EA)
MOAA	Mail Order Association of America (EA)
MOAA	Marina Operators Association of America (NTPA)
MOAA	Municipal Officers' Association of Australia
MoAB	Monoclonal Antibody [Immunochemistry]
MOABWEPO	Members of Anything Bill [Clinton] Was Ever Part Of [Pronounced "Mo-ab-wee-po"]
MOAC	Ministry of Agriculture and Cooperatives [Thailand] (BUAC)
MOAD	Methotrexate, Oncovin [Vincristine] L-asparaginase, Dexamethasone [Antineoplastic drug regimen] (DAVI)
MO Admin Code	Missouri Code of State Regulations [A publication] (DLA)
MO Admin Reg	Missouri Register [A publication] (DLA)
MOADS	Montgomery Air Defense Sector [of SAGE] (MUGU)
MOAE	Mitigation of Adverse Effect [Environmental science] (COE)
MOAF	Meteorological and Oceanographic Analyst/Forecaster [Course] (DNAB)
MOAF	Ministry of Agriculture and Forests [Republic of Korea] (BUAC)
Moak	Moak's English Reports [A publication] (DLA)
Moak (Eng)	Moak's English Reports [A publication] (DLA)
Moak Eng Rep	Moak's English Reports [A publication] (DLA)
Moak Und	Moak's Edition of Underhill on Torts [A publication] (DLA)
Moak Underh Torts	Moak's Edition of Underhill on Torts [A publication] (DLA)
Moak Van S Pl	Moak's Edition of Van Santvoord's Equity Pleading [A publication] (DLA)
MOAL	Mail-Order Action Line [Direct marketing association] (WDMC)
MOALC	Mobile Air Logistics Center [Air Force]
MOAMA	Mobile Air Materiel Area
MO & DSD	Mission Operations and Data Systems Directorate (SSD)
MO & G	Master of Obstetrics and Gynaecology
MO & O	Memorandum Opinion and Order (NTCM)
Mo & P	Moore and Payne's English Common Pleas Reports [A publication] (DLA)
Mo & R	Moody and Robinson's English Nisi Prius Reports [A publication] (DLA)
Mo & S	Moore and Scott's English Common Pleas Reports [1831-34] [A publication] (DLA)
Mo & Sc	Moore and Scott's English Common Pleas Reports [1831-34] [A publication] (DLA)
MOANG	Missouri Air National Guard (MUSM)
MO Ann Stat (Vernon)	Vernon's Annotated Missouri Statutes [A publication] (DLA)
MO Ap	Missouri Appeal Reports [A publication] (DLA)
MO App	Missouri Appeal Reports [A publication] (DLA)
MO Appeals	Missouri Appeal Reports [A publication] (DLA)
MO App (KC)	Missouri Appeal Reports [Kansas City] [A publication] (DLA)
MO App Rep	Missouri Appeal Reports [A publication] (DLA)
MO Apps	Missouri Appeal Reports [A publication] (DLA)
MO App (St L)	Missouri Appeal Reports [St. Louis] [A publication] (DLA)
MO AR	Missouri Appellate Reporter [A publication] (DLA)
MOARS	Mobilization Assignment Reserve Section [Military]
moAt	Mainstream of American Thought (AD)
MOAT	Methods of Appraisal and Test (MHDB)
MOAT	Missile on Aircraft Test
moat	Missile-on-Aircraft Testing [Military] (AD)
MOATL	Modal Acoustic Transmission Loss (MCD)
MOB	Mail Order Buyer (WDMC)
MOB	Main Olfactory Bulb [Anatomy]
MOB	Main Operating Base
MOB	Make or Buy [Economics]
mob	Make or Buy (AD)
MOB	Man-Overboard
MOB	Master of Organizational Behavior (GAGS)
MOB	Medical Office Building (DAVI)
MOB	Menlo Park [California] [Seismograph station code, US Geological Survey] (SEIS)
MOB	Methane-Oxidizing Bacteria
MOB	Missile Order of Battle (AFM)
MOB	Mobil Corp. [NYSE symbol Toronto Stock Exchange symbol] (SPSG)
MOB	Mobile [Alabama] [Airport symbol]
mob	Mobile (AD)
Mob	Mobile, Alabama [Maritime abbreviation] (AD)
mob	Mobile Vulgus [Disorderly Group of People] [Latin] (AD)
MOB	Mobility [MTMC] (TAG)
MOB	Mobilization [or Mobilize] (AFM)
Mob	Mobley's Contested Election Cases, United States House of Representatives [1882-89] [A publication] (DLA)
MOB	Mock-Up Board [Navy] (AFIT)
MOB	Modification of Benefits [Health insurance] (GHCT)
MOB	Money-Order Business
MOB	Montreux-Oberland-Bernois [Railway] [Canada] (AD)
MOB	Municipals over Bonds [Investment term]
MOB	Mustargen [Nitrogen mustard], Oncovin , Bleomycin [Vincristine] [Antineoplastic drug regimen]
MOB	Southwest Baptist College, Bolivar, MO [OCLC symbol] (OCLC)
MOBA	Military Operations in Built-Up Areas
MOBAC	Monterey Bay Area Cooperative Library System [Library network]
MOBAS	Model Basin
MOBAT	Mobile Battalion Antitank Gun [British military] (DMA)

Mo' Bay	Mobile Bay, Alabama [*Montego Bay, Jamaica*] (AD)
MOBCOM	Mobile Command [*Canada*] (AD)
mobcom	Mobile Communications (AD)
MOBCOM	Mobile Communications
Mob Con	Mobilising Control (WDAA)
MOBCON	Mobilization Construction Plan [*Military*] (NVT)
MOBCON	Mobilization Movement Control [*MTMC*] (TAG)
MOBCONBAT	Mobile Construction Battalion [*Navy*] (DNAB)
MOBCTR	Mobilization Center (DNAB)
MOBDES	Mobilization Designation [*or Designee*]
MOBDIC	Mobile Digital Computer
MOBED	Mobile Education Demonstration
MoBeHi	Scott County Historical Society, Benton, MO [*Library symbol*] [*Library of Congress*] (LCLS)
MOBERS	Mobilization Equipment Redistribution System
MOBEU	Mobile Emergency Unit (NOAA)
mobeu	Mobile Emergency Unit (AD)
MOBEX	Mobile Excursion (MCD)
MOBEX	Mobile Exploration [*NASA*]
MOBEX	Mobility Test Exercise [*Military*]
MOBIDA	Mobile Data Acquisition System (MCD)
MOBIDAC	Mobile Data Acquisition System
MOBIDACS	Mobile Data Acquisition System (AD)
mobidic	Mobile Digital Computer (AD)
MOBIDIC	Mobile Digital Computer [*Sylvania Electric Products Co.*]
MOB-III	Methotrexate, Oncovin [*Vineristine*], Bleomycin [*Antineoplastic drug regimen*] (DAVI)
MOB-III	Mitomycin C, Oncovin [*Vincristine*], Bleomycin, Cisplatin [*Antineoplastic drug regimen*]
Mobil	Mobil Corp. [*Associated Press*] (SAG)
MOBIL	Mobility
mobil	Mobility (AD)
Mobilarian	Mobile Branch Librarian (AD)
mobilary	Mobile Library (AD)
MOBILESAT	Mobile Satellite Corp. [*King Of Prussia, PA*] [*Telecommunications*] (TSSD)
MOBIS	Management-Oriented Budget Information System
MOBL	Macro-Oriented Business Language [*Computer science*]
mobl	Macro-Oriented Business Language [*Computer science*] (AD)
MOBL	Main Operating Base LASER
Mobl	Mobley's Contested Election Cases, United States House of Representatives [*1882-89*] [*A publication*] (DLA)
mobl	Mopliert [*Furnished*] [*German*] (AD)
MoblAm	Mobile America Corp. [*Associated Press*] (SAG)
moblas	Mobile LASER Satellite Tracking Station (AD)
Mobley	Mobley Environmental Services [*Associated Press*] (SAG)
MoblGs	Mobile Gas Service Corp. [*Associated Press*] (SAG)
mob lib	Mobile Librarian (AD)
MoblM	Mobile Mini, Inc. [*Associated Press*] (SAG)
MoblMin	Mobile Mini, Inc. [*Associated Press*] (SAG)
mob lt	Man Overboard and Breakdown Light (AD)
MOBMAN	Mobilization Manpower Planning System [*DoD*]
MobMda	MobileMedia Corp. [*Associated Press*] (SAG)
MOBMDR	Mobilization Master Data Record [*Army*]
Mob O	Mobilising Officer (WDAA)
MOBOL	Mohawk Business-Oriented Language [*Mohawk Data Systems*]
MoBoIS	Southwest Baptist College, Bolivar, MO [*Library symbol Library of Congress*] (LCLS)
MOBOT	Mobile Remote-Controlled Robot
mobot	Mobile Robot (AD)
MOBOT	Modular Robot
MOBPERSACS	Mobilization Personnel Structure and Composition System [*DoD*]
MoBr	Brentwood Public Library, Brentwood, MO [*Library symbol Library of Congress*] (LCLS)
MOBRASOP	Mobilization Requirements in Support of the Army Strategic Objectives Plan
MOBS	Mobile Hospitals [*Military slang*]
MOBS	Mobile Ocean Basing System (PDAA)
MOBS	Moebius Syndrome [*Medicine*] (DMAA)
MOBS	Multiple-Orbit Bombardment System
MOBSCOPE	Mobilization Shipments Configured for Operation Planning and Execution [*MTMC*] (TAG)
MOBSF	Mobility Support Flight [*Military*]
MOBSS	Mobility Support Squadron [*Air Force*]
MOBSS	Mobilization Support System [*MTMC*] (TAG)
MOBSSL-UAF	Merritt and Miller's Own Block Structured Simulation Language, Unpronounceable Acronym For [*1969*] [*Computer science*] (CSR)
MOBSSq	Mobility Support Squadron [*Air Force*]
MOBSUPPGRU	Mobile Support Group [*Military*] (DNAB)
MOBTA	Mobilization Table of Distribution and Allowances (AD)
MOBTB	Mobilization Troop Basis [*Army*] (AABC)
MOBTDA	Mobilization Table of Distribution and Allowances [*Military*] (AABC)
MOBTR	Mobile Trainer
MOBU	Mobilization Base Units
MOBULA	Model Building Language [*Programming language*] (IEEE)
mobula	Model-Building Language (AD)
MOBYC	My Own Bloody Yacht Club [*Founded in England; registered with Lloyds of London*]
MOC	Magnetic Optic Converter
MOC	Maintenance Operational Check
MOC	Maintenance Operations Center [*Military*]
MOC	Maintenance Operations Control [*Canadian Airlines International*]
MOC	Makapuu Oceanic Center [*Hawaii*] (AD)
MOC	Management and Operating Contractor (ODBW)
MOC	Management of Change
MOC	Management-Oriented Computing (MHDB)
MOC	Manual Operations Control
moc	Manufacturing Other Charges (AD)
MOC	Manufacturing Outreach Center
MOC	Marcos Owners Club [*Formerly, Marcos Club*] (EA)
MOC	Margin of Control [*Environmental science*] (COE)
MOC	Margin of Criticality [*Environmental science*] (COE)
MOC	Marine Operation Center [*NASA*] (NASA)
moc	Marine Operation Center (NAKS)
MOC	Market on Close [*Investment term*] (NUMA)
MOC	Marlin Owners' Club (EA)
MOC	Mars Orbiter Camera
MOC	Master Operational Computer [*or Controller*]
moc	Master Operation Control (AD)
MOC	Master Operations Center
MOC	Master Operations Console
MOC	Master Operations Control
MOC	Master Ordnance Configuration File [*Navy*]
MOC	Mathematical Operations Computer
MOC	Mauna Olu College [*Maui*] (AD)
MOC	Maximum Operational Capacity [*Chemical engineering*]
MOC	Maximum Oxygen Consumption
MOC	Mechanical Off-Machine Coated Paper (DGA)
MOC	Memorandum of Conditions
MOC	Memory Operating Characteristic [*Computer science*] (IEEE)
MOC	Merland Explorations Ltd. [*Toronto Stock Exchange symbol*]
MOC	Messerschmitt Owners Club (EA)
MOC	Method of Characteristics [*Equilibrium flow*]
MOC	Metropolitan Owners' Club [*Woking, Surrey, England*] (EAIO)
MOC	Mid Ocean Limited [*NYSE symbol*] (SAG)
MOC	Mid Ocean Ltd [*NYSE symbol*] (TTSB)
MOC	Mid-Ohio Conference (PSS)
MOC	Military Occupation Code (MCD)
MOC	Military Order of the Carabao (EA)
MOC	Minimal Oxygen Consumption
MOC	Minimum Obstacle Clearance [*Aviation*] (FAAC)
MOC	Minimum Operational Characteristics
MOC	Ministry of Communications (CINC)
MOC	Ministry of Construction [*Republic of Korea*] (BUAC)
MOC	Missile Operation Center [*Air Force*]
MOC	Missionaries of Charity [*Australia*]
MOC	Mission Operation Computer
MOC	Mission Operations Complex [*NASA*] (KSC)
moc	Mission Operations Computer (AD)
MOC	Mobile Oil Cooler
MOC	Mobile Operations Center [*Air Force*] (DOMA)
moc	Mocassin (AD)
MOC	Moccasin
MOC	Modern Operating Contract [*Autombile industry labor relations*]
MOC	Modular Organization Charting (PDAA)
MOC	Montes Claros [*Brazil*] [*Airport symbol*] (OAG)
MOC	Morris College, Sumter, SC [*Inactive*] [*OCLC symbol*] (OCLC)
MOC	Mother of the Chapel [*Unions*] [*British*] (DI)
MOC	Multiple Ocular Coloboma [*Medicine*] (DMAA)
MOC	Mustang Owners Club (EA)
MOC	Supreme Pup Tent, Military Order of the Cootie (EA)
MOCA	Methotrexate, Oncovin [*Vincristine*], Cyclophosphamide, Adriamycin [*Antineoplastic drug regimen*]
MOCA	Methylenebis(ortho-chloroaniline) [*Also, MBOCA*] [*Organic chemistry*]
MOCA	Minimum Obstruction Clearance Altitude [*Aviation*]
moca	Minimum Obstruction Clearance Altitude (AD)
MOCA	Mitsubishi Owner's Club of America
MOCA	Mixed Object Document Content Architecture [*Computer science*] (CIST)
MOCA	Montezuma Castle National Monument
MOCA	Museum of Contemporary Art [*Los Angeles*]
MOCAM	Mobile Checkout and Maintenance (AAG)
mocamp	Motor Camp (AD)
MOCAN	Motor Can
MoCanC	Culver-Stockton College, Canton, MO [*Library symbol Library of Congress*] (LCLS)
MOCAPT	Missouri Center for Agricultural Products Technology (BUAC)
MOCAS	Mechanization of Contract Administration Service (MCD)
MOCC	Master Operations Control Center (SAA)
MOCC	Metal-Oxygen Cluster Compounds [*Chemistry*]
MOCC	MG Octagon Car Club [*Formerly, Octagon Car Club*] (EA)
MOCC	Mission Operations Control Center (SSD)
MOCC	Mobile Operations Command Center (DOMA)
MOCCA	, Cyclophosphamide, Alkeran [*Lomustine*] [*Melphalan*] [*Antineoplastic drug regimen*]
MOCCA	Mobile Computing & Communication Appliance [*Digital Equipment Corp.*]
MoCCA	Mobile Computing and Communication Appliance [*Digital Equipment Corp.*]
MOCCAC	Missouri Community College Athletic Conference (PSS)
MOCCC	Massachusetts Organized Crime Control Council (AD)
MOccThy	Master of Occupational Therapy (ADA)
MOcE	Master of Oceanographic Engineering (GAGS)
MOCEM	Meteorological and Oceanographic Equipment Maintenance Course (DNAB)
MOCF	Maintenance Operations Control File (MCD)
MOCF	Manchester Open College Federation [*British*] (AIE)
MOCF	Mission Operations Computational Facilities [*NASA*] (NASA)
MoCg	Cape Girardeau Public Library, Cape Girardeau, MO [*Library symbol Library of Congress*] (LCLS)

MoCgS......... Southeast Missouri State University, Cape Girardeau, MO [*Library symbol Library of Congress*] (LCLS)

MoCheL....... Logan College of Chiropractic, Chesterfield, MO [*Library symbol*] [*Library of Congress*] (LCLS)

mochwr....... Mochaware (VRA)

MOCI.......... Ministry of Commerce and Industry [*British*] (AD)

MOCI.......... Ministry of Commerce and Industry [*Republic of Korea*] (BUAC)

MOCI.......... Mound City Group National Monument

MOCI.......... Mustang Owners Club International (EA)

MOCIC........ Molecular Orbital Constraint of Interaction Coordinates [*Atomic physics*]

MOCL.......... Metz Owners Club Library (EA)

MoCli.......... Henry County Library, Clinton, MO [*Library symbol*] [*Library of Congress*] (LCLS)

MoClS......... Saint Louis Junior College, Clayton, MO [*Library symbol Library of Congress Obsolete*] (LCLS)

MOCM......... Missile Out of Commission for Maintenance (MUGU)

MOCN......... Mid Ocean Ltd. [*NASDAQ symbol*] (SAG)

MOCN......... Modern Controls, Inc. [*Associated Press*] (SAG)

MOCNA....... Maserati Owners Club of North America (EAIO)

MOCNA....... Metropolitan Owners Club of North America (EA)

MOCNESS... Multiple Opening-Closing Net and Environmental Sensing System [*For collecting marine samples*]

MOCNESS... Multiple Opening-Closing Net Environmental Sampling System (USDC)

MOCO.......... Machinery Overhaul Co.

MOCO.......... Missile Operations Control Officer (AAG)

MOCO.......... Modern Controls [*NASDAQ symbol*] (TTSB)

MOCO.......... Modern Controls, Inc. [*NASDAQ symbol*] (NQ)

MoCoC......... Christian College, Columbia, MO [*Library symbol Library of Congress*] (LCLS)

Mo Code Regs... State of Missouri Code of State Regulations Annotated [*A publication*] (AAGC)

MOCODES.... Mobile Coastal Defense System (MCD)

MoCoGS ...... Church of Jesus Christ of Latter-Day Saints, Genealogical Society Library, Columbia Missouri Branch, Columbia, MO [*Library symbol Library of Congress*] (LCLS)

MoCoJ .... Joint Collection, Western Historical Manuscript Collection and State Historical,Columbia, MO [*Library symbol*] [*Library of Congress*] (LCLS)

MoCom........ Mobile Command (AD)

MOCOM .... Mobility Command [*AMC*]

MOCON........ Mobile Repair Parts Container

MoConA....... Conception Abbey and Seminary, Conception, MO [*Library symbol Library of Congress*] (LCLS)

MoCoS......... Stephens College, Columbia, MO [*Library symbol Library of Congress*] (LCLS)

MoCoV......... Harry S Truman Memorial Veterans Hospital, Columbia, MO [*Library symbol Library of Congress*] (LCLS)

MOCP.......... Missile Out of Commission for Parts (AFM)

mocp.......... Missile Out of Commission for Parts [*Military*] (AD)

MOCR.......... Metz Owners Club Register (EA)

mocr.......... Mission Operation Control Room (AD)

MOCR.......... Mission Operations Control Room

MOCR.......... Moores Creek National Military Park

MOCS.......... Managed Object Conformance Statement [*Telecommunications*] (OSI)

MOCS.......... Master Operations Control System (KSC)

MOCS.......... Military Order of Columbia's Shield (EA)

MOCS.......... Multichannel Ocean Color Sensor [*NASA*]

mocs.......... Multichannel Ocean Color Sensor (NAKS)

MOCS.......... Multiple Output Control System (ECII)

MoCStP....... Saint Paul's College, Concordia, MO [*Library symbol Library of Congress*] (LCLS)

MOCSW........ Monitor and Operations Control Software Subsystem [*Space Flight Operations Facility, NASA*]

MOCT.......... Mean Overhaul Cycle Time [*Quality control*] (MCD)

MOCV .... Manual Oxygen Control Valve (NASA)

MO-CVD....... Metal-Organic Chemical Vapor Deposition [*Also, MO-VPE, OM-CVD, OM-VPE*] [*Semiconductor technology*]

MOD .... Drury College, Springfield, MO [*OCLC symbol*] (OCLC)

Mod .... Made Over Democrat [*Facetious translation referring to Mods - Moderate Republicans*]

MOD .... Magnetic Optical Display

MOD .... Magneto-Optical Disc [*Digital audio technology*]

mod .... Magneto-Optical Disc (AD)

MOD .... Magneto-Optic Disk [*Computer science*] (CIST)

MOD .... Mail-Order Delivery

MOD .... Mail Order Department [*Business term*]

MOD .... Maintenance of Deception

MOD .... Management and Organization Division [*Environmental Protection Agency*] (GFGA)

MOD .... Manager on Duty

MOD .... Manned Orbital Development Station [*See also MODS, MOSS, MTSS*] [*Air Force/NASA*]

MOD .... Manpower and Organization Division [*Air Force*]

MOD .... Manual Overdrive [*Automotive engineering*]

MOD .... Manufacturers Operations Division [*Environmental Protection Agency*] (GFGA)

MOD .... Mapping of Disease

MOD .... March of Dimes (HGEN)

MOD .... March on Drugs [*An association*]

MOD .... Marine Operations Division [*Environmental Protection Agency*] (GFGA)

Mod .... Marxist on Drugs [*Mods - Facetious translation referring to Moderate Republicans*]

MOD .... Master of Organizational Development (GAGS)

MOD .... Masters of Disaster [*Computer hacker gang*]

MOD .... Maturity Onset Diabetes [*Medicine*]

MOD .... Medical Officer of the Day [*Military*]

MOD .... Medical Officer on Duty (DAVI)

MOD .... Medicine, Osteopathy, and Dentistry [*HEW program*]

MOD .... Memorandum of Decision (COE)

MOD .... Mesial, Occlusal, and Distal [*Describes location of openings in a carious tooth*] [*Dentistry*]

m-o-d .... Mesial-Occlusal-Distal [*Dentistry*] (AD)

MOD .... Message Output Description [*Computer science*]

MOD .... Message Output Descriptor [*Computer science*] (CIST)

MOD .... Metallo-Organic Deposition [*Materials technology*]

MOD .... Method of Delivery

MOD .... Microfilm-Output Device

MOD .... Microsoft Office 2000 Developer [*Microsoft*]

MOD .... Microwave Oscillating Diode (MCD)

MOD .... Military Obligation Designator

MOD .... Military Orbital Development System [*See also MODS, MOSS, MTSS*] [*Air Force/NASA*]

Mod .... Mindless Operative of the Devil [*Mods - Facetious translation referring to Moderate Republicans*]

M o D .... Ministry of Defence [*British*] (AD)

MOD .... Ministry of Defence [*British*]

MOD .... Ministry of Overseas Development [*British*] (ILCA)

MOD .... Minuteman Operating Directive (SAA)

MOD .... Miscellaneous Obligation Document

MOD .... Mission Objectives Document (MCD)

MOD .... Mission Operations Director [*NASA*] (KSC)

MOD .... Mobile Obstacle Detachment (MCD)

MOD .... Mobility Opportunity and Development

mod .... modality [*Physical therapy*] (DAVI)

MOD .... Modal (Verb) [*Linguistics*]

MOD .... Modatech Systems, Inc. [*Vancouver Stock Exchange symbol*]

MOD .... Model (KSC)

mod .... Model (AD)

mod .... Moderate (AD)

MOD .... Moderate [*or Moderator*] (AABC)

MOD .... Moderato [*Moderate Speed*] [*Music*]

MOD .... Modern

Mod .... Modern (AD)

mod .... Modern (AD)

Mod .... Modern Reports [*England*] [*A publication*] (DLA)

MOD .... Modesto [*California*] [*Airport symbol*] (OAG)

MOD .... Modification [*or Modify*] (AFM)

mod .... Modification (AD)

MOD .... Modifier [*Linguistics*]

MOD .... Modiim [*Israel*] [*Later, AMT*] [*Geomagnetic observatory code*]

mod .... Modular (AD)

MOD .... Modular Observation Device (RDA)

MOD .... Modulation [*Telecommunications*] (KSC)

MOD .... Modulator (CET)

mod .... Modulator (IDOE)

MOD .... Modulator-Demodulator [*Telecommunications*] (MCD)

MOD .... Module [*or Modular or Modulation*] (KSC)

mod .... Modulo [*Mathematics*] (CDE)

mod .... Modulus (IDOE)

MOD .... Modulus

MOD .... Money-Order Department

MOD .... Month of Detachment

MOD .... Motor-Operated Disconnect [*Nuclear energy*] (NRCH)

MOD .... Moving Domain Memories [*Computer science*] (MDG)

Mod .... Style's English King's Bench Reports [*1646-55*] [*A publication*] (DLA)

MOD .... Supreme Industries [*AMEX symbol*] (SAG)

MOD10 .... Modulus 10 Check Digit [*Computer science*]

MODA .... Ministry of Defense and Aviation (MCD)

MODA .... ModaCad, Inc. [*NASDAQ symbol*] (SAG)

MODA .... Motion Detector and Alarm [*Army*]

MODABUND... Mosquito Data Bank of the University of Notre Dame

MODAC........ Mountain System Digital Automatic Computer

MODACS...... Modular Data Acquisition and Control System [*or Subsystem*] [*Modular Computing Systems, Inc.*]

MOD(AD) .... Ministry of Defence (Army Department) [*British*]

Mod Am Law... Modern American Law [*A publication*] (DLA)

MODAP........ Modified Apollo [*NASA*] (MCD)

MODAP........ Multiple Operational Data Acquisition Program [*Computer science*]

MODAPS...... Maintenance and Operational Data Presentation Study (AAG)

MODAPS...... Modal Data Acquisition and Processing System

MODAPTS.... Modular Arrangement of Predetermined Time Standards

MODARI...... Methods of Defeating Advanced RADAR Threats [*NASA*] (NAKS)

MODART...... Methods of Defeating Advanced RADAR Threats (NASA)

MODAS........ Multidirectional Osmotic Drug Absorption System [*Medicine*]

MODASM...... Modular Air-to-Surface Missile (MCD)

modasm....... Modular Air-to-Surface Missile [*Military*] (AD)

MODATS...... Mohawk Data Transmission System (MCD)

MODAW....... ModaCAD Inc. Wrrt [*NASDAQ symbol*] (TTSB)

m-o-d-b .... Mesial-Occlusal-Distal-Buccal [*Dentistry*] (AD)

MODB .... Military Occupational Data Bank [*Later, AOSP*] (AABC)

MODCA........ Mixed Object Document Content Architecture [*Computer science*] (BTTJ)

MO:DCA....... Mixed Object: Document Content Architecure [*Computer science*] (CDE)

MODCAR...... Modified Owners and Drivers Corp. for the Advancement of Racing (EA)
Mod Cas ...... Modern Cases [*6 Modern Reports*] [*1702-45*] [*A publication*] (DLA)
Mod Cas L & Eq... Modern Cases at Law and Equity [*8, 9 Modern Reports*] [*1721-55*] [*A publication*] (DLA)
Mod Cas per Far... Modern Cases Tempore Holt, by Farresley [*7 Modern Reports*] [*A publication*] (DLA)
Mod Cas T Holt... Modern Cases Tempore Holt, by Farresley [*7 Modern Reports*] [*A publication*] (DLA)
modcom ...... Modernity Commercialized (AD)
MODCOM...... Modular Computer System
MODCOMP... Modular Computer Systems Inc. (NITA)
MODCON ..... Man Machine System for the Optimum Design and Construction of Buildings (PDAA)
MOD CON ... Modern Convenience (DSUE)
mod-cons..... Modern-Construction Houses (AD)
mod cons..... Modern Conveniences (AD)
MODCPS...... Multiple Output Direct Current Power Supply
MODD .... Military Order of Devil Dogs (EA)
Modd .... Modern Medical Modalities Corp. [*Associated Press*] (SAG)
moddem...... Modulator-Demodulator (AD)
mod/demod... Modulate-Demodulate (AD)
MODDF .... Military Order, Devil Dog Fleas (EA)
MOD DICT ... In the Manner Directed [*Abbreviation from the Latin*] [*Pharmacy*] (ROG)
MODE .... Management of Objectives with Dollars through Employees [*Department of Agriculture*]
MODE .... Merchant Oriented Data Entry
MODE .... Methoxy(O-desmethyl)encainide [*Biochemistry*]
MODE .... Mid-Ocean Dynamics Experiment [*National Science Foundation*]
ModE .... Modern English (AD)
MODE .... Monitor Data Equipment
MODE .... Monitoring Overseas Direct Employment (DNAB)
MODE C ...... Music on Demand (TELE)
MODE C ...... Altitude Reporting Mode of Secondary Radar [*FAA*] (TAG)
MO Dec ...... Missouri Decisions [*A publication*] (DLA)
MODEC........ Motor Optimization Design Evaluation Code (MCD)
Model Bus Corp Act Anno 2d... American Bar Association Model Business Corporation Act, Annotated, Second Series [*A publication*] (DLA)
Model Business Corp Act... American Bar Association Model Business Corporation Act, Annotated [*A publication*] (DLA)
MODELH/PRDH... Mouvement pour la Liberation d'Haiti/Parti Revolutionnaire d'Haiti [*Political party*] (EY)
ModelImp .... Model Imperial, Inc. [*Associated Press*] (SAG)
Model Land Dev Code... American Law Institute Model Land Development Code [*A publication*] (DLA)
Model R ...... Model Railroader [*A publication*]
MODEM .... Modulate/Demodulate [*or Modulation/Demodulation or Modulator-Demodulator*] [*Computer science*]
modem .... Modulating-Demodulating (AD)
modem .... Modulator/Demodulator [*Computer science*] (WDMC)
Mod (Eng) ... English King's Bench Modern Reports [*86-88 English Reprint*] [*A publication*] (DLA)
MOD ENT..... Modern Entries [*Legal term*] (DLA)
Modern Lib... Modern Library (AD)
MODEST ...... Missile Optical Destruction Technique
Modest Pistor... Modestinus Pistoris [*Deceased, 1565*] [*Authority cited in pre-1607 legal work*] (DSA)
MODET .... Mortar Detection
MODEX .... Mobilization Deployment Exercise (MCD)
modf............ Modification (AD)
MODF .... Modify (AAG)
MODFET ...... Modulation-Doped Field-Effect Transistor [*Solid-state physics*]
MODFLIR...... Modular Forward-Looking Infrared Seeker
MODFN .... Modification (AAG)
MODFR........ Modifier (AAG)
Mod'g .... Modifying [*Legal term*] (DLA)
ModGr .... Modern Greek [*Language*]
MODHATR ... Modified Hatrack [*Cyclone forecasting*] [*Navy*]
ModHeb....... Modern Hebrew (AD)
MODI .... Major Oversea Depot and Installation Method [*Army*]
MODI .... Modified Distribution
MODI .... Modine Manufacturing Co. [*NASDAQ symbol*] (NQ)
MODI .... Modine Mfg [*NASDAQ symbol*] (TTSB)
MODI .... Modular Optical Digital Interface
MODIA........ Method of Designing Instructional Alternatives (PDAA)
MODICON .... Modular-Dispersed-Control
MODIF .... Modification (KSC)
MODIG .... Modular Digital Image Generation [*Computer science*]
MODIGSI..... Modular Digital Simulation (MCD)
MODIL .... Manufacturing Operations Development and Integration Laboratory
MODILS ...... Modular Instrument Landing System
MODIM .... MOTS [*Module Test Set*] Design Information Memorandum
Modine .... Modine Manufacturing Co. [*Associated Press*] (SAG)
Mod Int ...... Brown's Modus Intrandi [*A publication*] (DLA)
Modio .... MODEM and Radio [*Telecommunications*]
MOD/IRAN ... Modification/Inspection and Repair as Necessary
mod/iran..... Modification, Inspection, and Repair as Necessary (AD)
MODIS .... Moderate-Resolution Imaging Spectrometer (MCD)
MODIS .... Mode Shape Display [*Module*]
MODISCO .... Mechanization of Defense Industrial Security Clearance Office [*DoD*]
MODL .... Model Imperial, Inc. [*NASDAQ symbol*] (SAG)
ModL .... Modern Latin [*Language*]
ModLA........ Modern Language Association, New York, NY [*Library symbol Library of Congress*] (LCLS)

Mod L & Soc'y... Modern Law and Society [*A publication*] (DLA)
ModLA-R ..... Modern Language Association Research in Progress Program, New York NY [*Library symbol*] [*Library of Congress*] (LCLS)
MOD LITH... Modern Lithographer [*A publication*] (DGA)
MODLOC...... Modified Location
MODLOG 77... Modernization of Logistics 1977 [*Army*]
MODM .... Magneto-Optical Display Memory
MODM .... Major Oversea Depot Method [*Army*]
MODM .... Manned One-Day Mission [*NASA*]
MODM .... Mature-Onset Diabetes Mellitus (MAE)
MODM .... Modern Medical Modalities Corp. [*NASDAQ symbol*] (SAG)
MODM .... Modern Medl Modalities [*NASDAQ symbol*] (TTSB)
ModMd .... Modern Medical Modalities Corp. [*Associated Press*] (SAG)
ModMed ...... Modern Medical Modalities Corp. [*Associated Press*] (SAG)
Mod Med Aust... Modern Medicine of Australia [*A publication*]
MODMW ...... Modern Med Modalities Wrrt'A' [*NASDAQ symbol*] (TTSB)
MODMZ .... Modern Med Modalities Wrr'B' [*NASDAQ symbol*] (TTSB)
MOD(N)....... Ministry of Defence (Navy) [*British*]
MoDNM .... Morpholinodaunomycin [*Also, MRD*] [*Antineoplastic drug*]
MODO .... Moderato [*Moderate Speed*] [*Music*] (ROG)
modo .... Moderato [*Moderately*] [*Italian*] (AD)
Mod Off Dat Man... Modern Office and Data Management [*A publication*]
Mod Office Data Mgmt... Modern Office and Data Management [*A publication*]
MOD/OP...... Maintenance of Deception/Operation
MODOP........ Mobil Oil Direct Oxidation Process [*Gas desulfurization process*]
MODOR........ Molecularized Doppler RADAR
MODP......... Modern Programming Practice
MODPAC...... Modular Restraint, Recovery, and Survival Package
MOD(PE)..... Ministry of Defence (Procurement Executive) [*British*]
MODPOT...... Model Potential [*Physics*]
Mod Pract Comm... Modern Practice Commentator [*A publication*] (DLA)
mod praes... Modo Praescripto [*In the manner prescribed*] [*Latin*] [*Pharmacy*] (BARN)
MOD PRAESC... Modo Praescripto [*In the Manner Prescribed*] [*Latin Pharmacy*] (MAH)
MOD PRAESCRIPT... Modo Praescripto [*In the Manner Prescribed*] [*Pharmacy*]
mod pres..... Modo Prescripto [*In the Manner Prescribed*] [*Latin*] (AD)
MOD PRESCR... Modo Praescripto [*In the Manner Prescribed*] [*Pharmacy*] (ROG)
mod pst ...... Modeling Paste (VRA)
MODR......... Microwave Optical Double Resonance (PDAA)
modr........... Moderate Room Rate Desired (AD)
MODR......... Monodetail Drawing (MSA)
MODREFTRA... Modified Refresher Training [*Navy*] (NVT)
Mod Rep...... Modern Reports [*England*] [*A publication*] (DLA)
Mod Rep...... Style's English King's Bench Reports [*1646-55*] [*A publication*] (DLA)
MODS .... Major Operations Data System (NVT)
MODS .... Manned Orbital Development Station [*See also MOD, MOSS, MTSS*] [*Air Force/NASA*]
MODS .... Manpower Operations Data System [*Employment and Training Administration*] [*Department of Labor*]
MODS .... Material Ordering and Delivery Schedule (DNAB)
MODS .... Medically Oriented Data System (MCD)
MODS .... Medium Ocean Data Station
mods .... Mesial-Occlusal-Distal [*Dentistry*] (AD)
MODS .... Military Orbital Development System [*See also MOD, MOSS, MTSS*] [*Air Force/NASA*]
MODS .... Missile Offense/Defense System
MODS .... Mission Operations Design Support
MODS .... Mobility-Planning Data System [*Military*] (GFGA)
MODS .... Models (MCD)
MODS .... Models for Organizational Design and Staffing (DNAB)
Mods .... Moderates [*Reference to political philosophy of some members of the Republican party*]
MODS .... Moderations [*First public Oxford examination*] (ROG)
MODS .... Modifications
MODS .... Modular Oriented Direct Support (MCD)
MODS .... Multiple Organ Dysfunction Syndrome [*Medicine*]
MODSA........ Ministry of Defence Staff Association (BUAC)
MODSAF...... Modular Semi-Automatic Forces
MODSC........ Magnetooptically Detected Spin Conversion [*Physics*]
MODT .... Mean Operational Delay Time
MODT .... Modtech, Inc. [*NASDAQ symbol*] (SAG)
Modtec .... Modtech, Inc. [*Associated Press*] (SAG)
MODTEPS.... Modular Toxic Environment Protective Suit [*NASA*]
MODTLE ...... Mobilization on Development, Trade, Labor, and Environment [*An association*]
MODTO .... Moderato [*Moderate Speed*] [*Music*]
modto .... Moderato [*Moderately*] [*Italian*] (AD)
MODU .... Mobile Offshore Drilling Unit
MODULA...... Modular Programming Language (CSR)
Modula-2 ..... Modular Language-2 [*Computer science*]
MODULAB.... Modular Clinical Laboratory [*Military*] (CAAL)
MOD/UM...... Modulated/Unmodulated (SSD)
Mod Un........ Modern Unionist [*A publication*]
Mod Unionist... Modern Unionist [*A publication*]
MODUS........ Modular One Dynamic User System [*Computer science*] (MHDI)
MODUSSE.... Manufacturers of Domestic Unvented Supply Systems Equipment [*British*] (DBA)
MODWORS... Modification Work Order Report Status
MODY .... Maturity Onset Diabetes of the Young [*Medicine*] (DMAA)
MOE........... Evangel College, Springfield, MO [*OCLC symbol*] (OCLC)
MOE........... MAD Operational Effectiveness (DNAB)
MOE........... Maintenance of Effort [*Medicare Act*]
MOE........... Major Organizational Entity (MCD)
MOE............ Margin of Exposure [*Toxicology*]

MOE	Mars Orbit Ejection (MCD)
MOE	Master of Ocean Engineering (GAGS)
MOE	Master of Oral English
MOE	Maximum Output Entropy (PDAA)
MOE	Measure of Effectiveness
moe	Measure of Effectiveness (AD)
MoE	Ministry of Education [British] (AD)
MOE	Ministry of Education [British] (DAS)
M o E	Ministry of Energy [British] (AD)
MOE	Ministry of Environment [Canada]
MOE	Ministry of the Environment [Bulgaria] (BUAC)
MOE	Mission-Oriented Equipment
MOE	Model Operational Environment (SAA)
MOE	Modulus of Elasticity [Mechanics]
MOE	Moli Energy Ltd. [Toronto Stock Exchange symbol Vancouver Stock Exchange symbol]
MOE	Momeik [Myanmar] [Airport symbol] (OAG)
MOE	Mu Phi Epsilon [An association] (NTPA)
MOE	Mythical Operational Environment (SAA)
MOE	Ontario Ministry of Education, Information Centre, Research Branch [UTLAS symbol]
MOE	Telemetering Mobile Station [ITU designation]
MOEA	Ministry of Economic Affairs [British] (AD)
MOED	Molecular Orbital Energy Diagram
MOED	Morristown-Edison National Park Service Group
MOEDA	Measures of Effectiveness, Development, and Application (MCD)
MOEH	Medical Officer for Environmental Health (WDAA)
MOEP	Meteorological and Oceanographic Equipment Program (NG)
MOER	MACOM [Major Command] Outstanding Excess Report
MOERO	Medium Orbiting Earth Resources Observatory (IEEE)
MOES	Mathematics Olympiads for Elementary Schools (EDAC)
MOETLO	Meteorological and Oceanographic Equipment Technical Liaison Officer
MoExGS	Excelsior Springs Genealogical Society, Excelsior Springs, MO [Library symbol Library of Congress] (LCLS)
MOF	Fontbonne College, St. Louis, MO [OCLC symbol] (OCLC)
MOF	Manned Orbital Flight [NASA] (NASA)
MOF	Marine Oxidation/Fermentation
MOF	Maumere [Indonesia] [Airport symbol] (OAG)
MOF	Maximum Observed Frequency [Radio]
mof	Maximum Observed Frequency (AD)
MOF	Maximum Operating Frequency
MOF	MeCCNU [Semustine], Oncovin , Fluorouracil [Vincristine] [Antineoplastic drug regimen]
MOF	Member of the Force (LAIN)
mof	Member of the Police Force (AD)
mof	Metal Oxide Film (AD)
MOF	Metal-Oxide Film
MOF	Methotrexate, Oncovin [Vincristine] 5-Fluorouracil [Antineoplastic drug regimen] (DAVI)
MOF	Methoxyflurane [Anesthetic] (AAMN)
MOF	Methylo-CCNU, Vineristine, Fluorouracil [Antineoplastic drug regimen] (DAVI)
MOF	Michoud Operations Facility [NASA] (AAG)
MOF	Ministry of Finance [Japan] (ECON)
MoF	Ministry of Finance [British] (AD)
MOF	Ministry of Food [British]
MOF	Mission Operations Facility [NASA] (KSC)
MOF	Moffat Communications Ltd. [Toronto Stock Exchange symbol]
MOF	Months of Operational Flying (DNAB)
MOF	Multi-Option Facility
MOF	Multioption Fuze (MCD)
MOF	Multiple Organ Failure [Medicine]
MOFA	Multi-Option Fuze, Artillery
MOFAB	Mobile Floating Assault Bridge-Ferry [Military] (MCD)
MOFACS	Multiorder Feedback and Compensation Synthesis
MOFAP	Ministry of Fuel and Power [British]
M of Arch	Master of Architecture
MOFARS	Maintenance Overload Factor Reporting System
MOFAST	Mechanization of Freight and Shipping Terminal [DoD]
MoFC	Central Methodist College, Fayette, MO [Library symbol Library of Congress] (LCLS)
M of C	Master of Commerce
MOFC	Michael O'Leary Fan Club [Defunct] (EA)
M of D	Ministry of Defence [British]
M of E	Ministry of Education [British]
M of E	Minutes of Evidence
MOFERT	Ministry of Foreign Economic Relations and Trade [China]
Mofert	Ministry of Foreign Economic Relations and Trade [China] (BUAC)
MOFF	Multiple Options Funding Facility [Euronotes]
M of HA	Matrons of Hospitals Association (ROG)
M of Hist	Magazine of History [A publication] (BRI)
M of I	Moment of Inertia
MoFIM	Mark Twain Shrine, Mark Twain State Park, Florida, MO [Library symbol Library of Congress] (LCLS)
MoFloSS	Saint Stanislaus Seminary, Florissant, MO [Library symbol Library of Congress] (LCLS)
M of M	Maintenance of Membership [Labor unions]
MOFN	MovieFone Cl'A' [NASDAQ symbol] (TTSB)
MOFN	MovieFone, Inc. [NASDAQ symbol] (SAG)
M of R	Minister of Reconstruction [British] (AD)
MOFS	Multiple Organ Failure Syndrome [Medicine] (DMAA)
MOF-STREP	MeCCNU [Semustine], Oncovin , Fluorouracil, Streptozotocin [Vincristine] [Antineoplastic drug regimen]

Moftec	Ministry of Foreign Trade and Economic Co-Operation [China] (BUAC)
MOFTEC	Ministry of Foreign Trade & Economic Cooperation [China]
MOFTU	MIG Operational Fighter Training Unit [India] [Air Force]
MoFuWC	Westminster College, Fulton, MO [Library symbol Library of Congress] (LCLS)
M of V	[The] Merchant of Venice [Shakespearean work]
M of W	Maintenance of Way [Railroading]
MOFW	Military Order of Foreign Wars of the United States (EA)
MOG	Assemblies of God Graduate School, Springfield, MO [OCLC symbol] (OCLC)
MOG	Machinery of Government
MOG	Mannville Oil & Gas Ltd. [Toronto Stock Exchange symbol]
Mog	Margaret (AD)
MOG	Master of Obstetrics and Gynecology (AD)
MOG	Material Ordering Guide [Shipbuilding]
MOG	Material Other than Grape [Wine making]
MOG	Medical Oncology Group
MOG	Metropolitan Opera Guild (EA)
MOG	Micro-Optic Gyroscope
MOG	Milicias Obreras Guatemaltecas [Guatemalan Workers' Militia] (PD)
MOG	Mogadishu [Somalia] [Seismograph station code, US Geological Survey Closed] (SEIS)
MOG	Monghsat [Myanmar] [Airport symbol] (OAG)
MOG	Montague, CA [Location identifier FAA] (FAAL)
MOG	Moog, Inc. [AMEX symbol] (SPSG)
MOG	Morgan [Automobile]
MOG	Municipal Officers' Guild (ROG)
MOG	Myelin Oligodendrocyte Glycoprotein [Biochemistry]
MOGA	Management of Officer Grade Authorization (MCD)
MOGA	Microwave and Optical Generation and Amplification (MCD)
MOGA	Montana Outfitters and Guides Association (EA)
MOGAS	Motor Gasoline [Military]
mogas	Motor Gasoline (AD)
MOGN	MGI PHARMA, Inc. [NASDAQ symbol] (NQ)
MOGN	Molecular Genetics, Inc. (MHDW)
MOGUNTIA	Model of the Global Universal Tracer Transport in the Atmosphere [Marine science] (OSRA)
Moguyde	Mouvement Guyanais de Decolonisation [Guiana Decolonization Movement] [France Political party] (PPW)
MoGvS	Grain Valley Associated School District, Grain Valley, MO [Library symbol] [Library of Congress] (LCLS)
MoH	Hannibal Free Public Library, Hannibal, MO [Library symbol Library of Congress] (LCLS)
MOH	Hydrological and Meteorological Mobile Station [ITU designation]
MOH	Master, Occupational Health (CMD)
MOH	Master of Occupational Health (PGP)
MOH	Master of Otter Hounds
moh	Material Overhead (AD)
moh	Maximum Operating Hours (AD)
MOH	Maximum Operating Hours (MCD)
MOH	Medal of Honor [Often erroneously called Congressional Medal of Honor] [Military decoration]
MOH	Medical Officer of Health [British]
MOH	Ministry of Health [British]
M o H	Ministry of Health [British] (AD)
MOH	Moche Resources, Inc. [Vancouver Stock Exchange symbol]
moh	Mohawk [MARC language code Library of Congress] (LCCP)
MOH	Mohawk Airlines, Inc. [Obsolete]
MOH	Museum of Holography [New York City]
MOH	Music on Hold (ITD)
MOH	New York, NY [Location identifier FAA] (FAAL)
MOH	St. Louis Priory School, St. Louis, MO [OCLC symbol] (OCLC)
MOH	Tigerfly [British ICAO designator] (FAAC)
MoHam	Hamilton Public Library, Hamilton, MO [Library symbol] [Library of Congress] (LCLS)
Moham	Mohammedan (AD)
MOHAM	Mohammedan (ROG)
MoHarC	Cass County Public Library, Harrisonville, MO [Library symbol Library of Congress] (LCLS)
MOHAT	Modular Handling and Transport
MOHATS	Mobile Overland Hauling and Transport System [Air Force]
MOHAVE	Measurement of Haze and Visual Effects [Study] [Marine science] (OSRA)
MOHAVE	Measurement of Haze and Visual Effects [Study] (USDC)
Mohawk	Mohawk Industries, Inc. [Associated Press] (SAG)
MOHEC	Maintenance of Hercules Capability (SAA)
MoHi	Missouri State Historical Society, Columbia, MO [Library symbol Library of Congress] (LCLS)
MoHig	Robertson Memorial Library, Higginsville, MO [Library symbol] [Library of Congress] (LCLS)
MoHigH	Habilitation Center, Higginsville, MO [Library symbol] [Library of Congress] (LCLS)
MOHILL	Machine-Oriented High-Level Language [Computer science] (HGAA)
MOHK	Mohawk Industries [NASDAQ symbol] (SAG)
MOHLG	Ministry of Housing and Local Government [British] (AD)
MOH(LHA)	Medical Officer of Health (Local Health Authority) [British]
MoHM	Mark Twain Museum, Hannibal, MO [Library symbol Library of Congress] (LCLS)
MOHMS	Milliohms (WDAA)
mohms	Milliohms (AD)
moho	Mohorovicic Discontinuity [Geology] (AD)
MOHO	Mohorovicic Discontinuity [Geology]
MOHOL	Machine-Oriented Higher Order Language [Computer science] (MHDI)

MOHS	Master of Occupational Health and Safety
mohs	Mud, Oil, Hooks, Slings [*Insurance*] (AD)
MOHSLG	Health Sciences Library [*Library network*]
MoHu	Huntsville Public Library, Huntsville, MO [*Library symbol Library of Congress*] (LCLS)
MOI	Main-d'Oeuvre Indigene [*Indigenous Manpower*] [*Congo - Leopoldville*]
MOI	Maintenance Operating Instruction [*Air Force Logistics Command*]
MOI	Make on Installation (SAA)
MOI	Marine Officer Instructor (DOMA)
MOI	Mars Orbit [*or Orbital*] Insertion [*Aerospace*]
MOI	Maximum Obtainable Irradiance
moi	Maximum Obtainable Irradiance (AD)
MOI	Maximum Oxygen Intake [*Medicine*] (DB)
MOI	Memorandum of Instruction (INF)
MOI	Memorandum of Intent (COE)
MOI	Memorandum of Interest (MCD)
MOI	Message of Operational Intent (NVT)
MOI	Methods of Instruction
MOI	Military Occupational Information (AABC)
moi	Military Occupational Information (AD)
MOI	Military Operations and Intelligence
MOI	Minimum Operating Inventory [*Business term*]
MOI	Ministry of Information [*British World War II*]
MoI	Ministry of the Interior [*British*] (AD)
MOI	Mitiaro [*Cook Islands*] [*Airport symbol*] (OAG)
MOI	Molco Industries [*Vancouver Stock Exchange symbol*]
MOI	Moment of Inertia
MOI	Monaco Oceanographic Institute
MOI	Mouvement Ouvrier International (BJA)
MOI	Multiplicity of Infection
moi	Multiplicity of Infection (AD)
MOI	William Jewell College, Liberty, MO [*OCLC symbol*] (OCLC)
Mo IA	Moore's Indian Appeals [*A publication*] (DLA)
MOIAA	Missouri Intercollegiate Athletic Association (PSS)
MOIC	Medical Officer-in-Charge [*Military*]
MOIC	Medical Officer in Command (AD)
MOIC	Military Oceanographic Information Center (NATG)
MOIDE	Military Occupational Information Data Bank
MOIG	Master of Occupational Information and Guidance
MOIL	Marine Operations and Instrumentation Laboratory [*Marine science*] (OSRA)
MOIL	Maynard Oil [*NASDAQ symbol*] (TTSB)
MOIL	Maynard Oil Co. [*NASDAQ symbol*] (NQ)
MOIL	Motor Oil
MoIM	Mid-Continent Public Library Service, Independence, MO [*Library symbol Library of Congress*] (LCLS)
MoIMC	Independence Medical Center, Independence, MO [*Library symbol Library of Congress*] (LCLS)
MOIP	Mandatory Oil Import Program
MOIP	Missile on Internal Power
moip	Missile on Internal Power [*Military*] (AD)
MOIPI	Multi-Purpose Offshore Industrial Port Islands (NOAA)
MoIPS	Independence Public School District, Independence, MO [*Library symbol*] [*Library of Congress*] (LCLS)
MOIR	Maximum Ozone Incremental Reactivity [*Environmental science*]
MOIR	Movimiento Obrero Independiente Revolucionario [*Independent Revolutionary Workers' Movement*] [*Colorado Political party*] (PPW)
MOIR	Movimiento Obrero Izquierdista Revolucionario [*Colorado Political party*] (PPW)
MOIRA	Model of International Relations in Agriculture (PDAA)
MoIRC	Reorganized Church of Jesus Christ of Latter-Day Saints, Independence, MO [*Library symbol Library of Congress*] (LCLS)
Moir Cap Pun	Moir on Capital Punishment [*A publication*] (DLA)
MoIS	Independence Sanitarium and Hospital, Independence, MO [*Library symbol Library of Congress*] (LCLS)
MOIS	Maritime Operational Intelligence Summary
MOIS	Michigan Occupational Information System [*Michigan State Department of Education*] [*Lansing*] [*Information service or system*] (IID)
MOIS	Minnesota Occupational Information System (AD)
MOIS	Mission Operations Intercommunication System [*NASA*]
Moish	Moishe (AD)
MOIST	Macro Output System [*NASA*] (KSC)
MOISTR	Moisture
MoIT	Harry S Truman Library, Independence, MO [*Library symbol Library of Congress*] (LCLS)
MOIV	Mechanically Operated Inlet Valve (ADA)
moiv	Mechanically Operated Inlet Valve (AD)
MOJ	Material on Job Date [*Telecommunications*] (TEL)
MOJ	Metering over Junction [*Network administration*] [*Telecommunications*] (TEL)
MOJ	Ministry of Jute [*Bangladesh*]
MOJ	Muong Sing [*Laos*] [*Airport symbol*] (AD)
MOJA	Movement for Justice in Africa [*Liberia*] [*Political party*] (PPW)
MOJAC	Mood, Orientation, Judgment, Affect, Content (AAMN)
MOJA-G	Movement for Justice in Africa-Gambia [*Political party*]
MoJc	Thomas Jefferson Library System, Jefferson City, MO [*Library symbol Library of Congress*] (LCLS)
MoJcL	Lincoln University, Jefferson City, MO [*Library symbol Library of Congress*] (LCLS)
MOJMRP	Meteorological Office Joint Meteorological Radio Propagation (IAA)
MOJMRP	Meteorological Office, Joint Meteorological Radio Propagation Sub-Committee (BUAC)

MoJo	Joplin Public Library, Joplin, MO [*Library symbol Library of Congress*] (LCLS)
MoJoM	Missouri Southern State College, Joplin, MO [*Library symbol Library of Congress*] (LCLS)
MOJT	Managed On-the-Job Training (DNAB)
Mo Jur	Monthly Jurist [*A publication*] (DLA)
MoK	Kansas City Public Library, Kansas City, MO [*Library symbol Library of Congress*] (LCLS)
MOK	Mohawk Carpet Mills [*Stock exchange symbol*] (AD)
MOK	Mokapu [*Hawaii*] [*Seismograph station code, US Geological Survey*] (SEIS)
Mok	Mokpo (AD)
MoKA	American Nurses' Association, Kansas City, MO [*Library symbol Library of Congress*] (LCLS)
MOKA	Coffee People, Inc. [*NASDAQ symbol*] (SAG)
MoKAI	Kansas City Arts Institute, Kansas City, MO [*Library symbol Library of Congress*] (LCLS)
MoKAv	Avila College, Kansas City, MO [*Library symbol Library of Congress*] (LCLS)
MoKB	Bar Library Association of Kansas City, Kansas City, MO [*Library symbol Library of Congress*] (LCLS)
MoKBa	Barstow School, Kansas City, MO [*Library symbol Library of Congress*] (LCLS)
MoKBen	Bendix Corp., Technical Information Center, Kansas City, MO [*Library symbol Library of Congress*] (LCLS)
MoKBH	Baptist Memorial Hospital, Kansas City, MO [*Library symbol Library of Congress*] (LCLS)
MoKBM	Burns and McDonnell Engineering Co., Kansas City, MO [*Library symbol Library of Congress*] (LCLS)
MoKBV	Black & Veatch Consulting Engineers, Central Library, Kansas City, MO [*Library symbol Library of Congress*] (LCLS)
MoKCH	Children's Mercy Hospital, Kansas City, MO [*Library symbol Library of Congress*] (LCLS)
MoKChe	Chemagro, Kansas City, MO [*Library symbol Library of Congress*] (LCLS)
MoKCO	Kansas City College of Osteopathic Medicine, Kansas City, MO [*Library symbol Library of Congress*] (LCLS)
MoKCoH	Jackson County Public Hospital, Kansas City, MO [*Library symbol Library of Congress*] (LCLS)
MOKE	Magneto-Optic Kerr Effect
MoKEP	United States Environmental Protection Agency, Kansas City, MO [*Library symbol Library of Congress*] (LCLS)
MoKF	Farmland Industries Inc., Communications Services, Kansas City, MO [*Library symbol Library of Congress*] (LCLS)
MoKFR	Federal Reserve Bank of Kansas City, Kansas City, MO [*Library symbol Library of Congress*] (LCLS)
MoKGH	Kansas City General Hospital, Kansas City, MO [*Library symbol Library of Congress*] (LCLS)
MoKGS	Church of Jesus Christ of Latter-Day Saints, Genealogical Society Library, Kansas City Branch, Kansas City, MO [*Library symbol Library of Congress*] (LCLS)
MoKHA	Kansas City Area Hospital Association, Kansas City, MO [*Library symbol Library of Congress*] (LCLS)
MoKHC	Hallmark Cards, Inc., Kansas City, MO [*Library symbol*] [*Library of Congress*] (LCLS)
MoKiCO	Kirksville College of Osteopathy and Surgery, Kirksville, MO [*Library symbol Library of Congress*] (LCLS)
MoKiU	Northeast Missouri State University, Kirksville, MO [*Library symbol Library of Congress*] (LCLS)
MoKJ	Jackson County Medical Society, Kansas City, MO [*Library symbol Library of Congress*] (LCLS)
MoKKM	Martin Luther King Memorial Hospital, Kansas City, MO [*Library symbol Library of Congress*] (LCLS)
MoKL	Linda Hall Library, Kansas City, MO [*Library symbol Library of Congress*] (LCLS)
MoKLH	Lakeside Hospital, Kansas City, MO [*Library symbol Library of Congress*] (LCLS)
MoKLo	Loretto in Kansas City, Kansas City, MO [*Library symbol Library of Congress*] (LCLS)
MoKMB	Midwestern Baptist Theological Seminary, Kansas City, MO [*Library symbol Library of Congress*] (LCLS)
MoKMC	Midwest College of Medical Assistants, Kansas City, MO [*Library symbol Library of Congress*] (LCLS)
MoKMI	Missouri Institute of Technology, Kansas City, MO [*Library symbol Library of Congress*] (LCLS)
MoKML	Marion Laboratories, Inc., Kansas City, MO [*Library symbol Library of Congress*] (LCLS)
MoKMM	Menorah Medical Center, Kansas City, MO [*Library symbol Library of Congress*] (LCLS)
MoKMoC	Mobay Chemical Corp., Kansas City, MO [*Library symbol*] [*Library of Congress*] (LCLS)
MoKMR	Midwest Research Institute, Kansas City, MO [*Library symbol Library of Congress*] (LCLS)
MoKMW	Maple Woods Community College, Kansas City, MO [*Library symbol Library of Congress*] (LCLS)
MoKN	Nazarene Theological Seminary, Kansas City, MO [*Library symbol Library of Congress*] (LCLS)
MoKNA	Nelson-Atkins Museum of Art, Spencer Art Reference Library, Kansas City, MO [*Library symbol*] [*Library of Congress*] (LCLS)
MoKNE	Newman Ecumenical Seminary, Kansas City, MO [*Library symbol Library of Congress*] (LCLS)
MoKNG	Nelson Art Gallery, Art Reference Library, Kansas City, MO [*Library symbol Library of Congress*] (LCLS)
MoKNT	Saint Paul School of Theology, Kansas City, MO [*Library symbol Library of Congress*] (LCLS)

MoKP	Penn Valley Junior College, Kansas City, MO [*Library symbol Library of Congress*] (LCLS)
MoKPC	Pembroke County Day School, Kansas City, MO [*Library symbol Library of Congress*] (LCLS)
MoKPh	Park Hill North Junior High School, Kansas City, MO [*Library symbol Library of Congress*] (LCLS)
MoKPhJH	Park Hill North Junior High School, Kansas City, MO [*Library symbol*] [*Library of Congress*] (LCLS)
MoKPHS	Pembroke Hill School, Kansas City, MO [*Library symbol*] [*Library of Congress*] (LCLS)
MoKPhSD	Park Hill School District, Kansas City, MO [*Library symbol*] [*Library of Congress*] (LCLS)
MoKPi	Pioneer Community College Library, Kansas City, MO [*Library symbol*] [*Library of Congress*] (LCLS)
MoKR	Rockhurst College, Kansas City, MO [*Library symbol Library of Congress*] (LCLS)
MoKRes	Research Hospital and Medical Center, Kansas City, MO [*Library symbol Library of Congress*] (LCLS)
MoKRh	Rockhurst High School, Kansas City, MO [*Library symbol Library of Congress*] (LCLS)
MoKSH	Sunset Hill School, Kansas City, MO [*Library symbol Library of Congress*] (LCLS)
MoKStJ	Saint Joseph's Hospital, Kansas City, MO [*Library symbol Library of Congress*] (LCLS)
MoKStL	Saint Luke's Hospital of Kansas City, Kansas City, MO [*Library symbol Library of Congress*] (LCLS)
MoKStM	Saint Mary's Hospital, Kansas City, MO [*Library symbol Library of Congress*] (LCLS)
MoKStP	Saint Paul Theological Seminary, Kansas City, MO [*Library symbol*] [*Library of Congress*] (LCLS)
MoKStT	Saint Theresa's Academy, Kansas City, MO [*Library symbol Library of Congress*] (LCLS)
MoKT	Teachers College of Kansas City, Kansas City, MO [*Library symbol Library of Congress Obsolete*] (LCLS)
MoKTrL	Trinity Lutheran Hospital, Kansas City, MO [*Library symbol Library of Congress*] (LCLS)
MoKU	University of Missouri at Kansas City, Kansas City, MO [*Library symbol Library of Congress*] (LCLS)
MoKU-D	University of Missouri at Kansas City, Dental School, Kansas City, MO [*Library symbol Library of Congress*] (LCLS)
MoKU-I	University of Missouri at Kansas City, Instructional Materials Center, Kansas City, MO [*Library symbol Library of Congress*] (LCLS)
MoKu-L	University of Missouri at Kansas City, Law Library, Kansas City, MO [*Library symbol*] [*Library of Congress*] (LCLS)
MoKU-M	University of Missouri at Kansas City, Medical Library, Kansas City, MO [*Library symbol Library of Congress*] (LCLS)
MoKU-Mus	University of Missouri at Kansas City, Music Conservatory, Kansas City, MO [*Library symbol Library of Congress*] (LCLS)
MoKVA	United States Veterans Administration Hospital, Kansas City, MO [*Library symbol Library of Congress*] (LCLS)
MoKW	Western Missouri Mental Health Center, Kansas City, MO [*Library symbol Library of Congress*] (LCLS)
MOL	Machine-Oriented Language [*Programming language*]
mol	Machine-Oriented Language (AD)
MOL	Manned Orbiting Laboratory [*NASA*]
MOL	Master of Organizational Leadership (PGP)
MOL	Master of Oriental Languages
MOL	Master of Oriental Learning
MOL	Maximum Operating Level
MOL	Maximum Order Limitation (AAGC)
mol	Maximum Output Level (AD)
MOL	Maximum Output Level
MOL	Maximum Overall Length (DAC)
MOL	Metallo-Organic LASER
MOL	Method of Lines [*Mathematics*]
MOL	Microtel International, Inc. [*AMEX symbol*] (SAG)
MOL	Microtel Intl [*AMEX symbol*] (TTSB)
MOL	Minimum Oxygen Concentration [*at which ignition occurs*]
M o L	Minister of Labour [*British*] (AD)
MOL	Ministry of Labour [*Later, DE*] [*British*]
MOL	Missouri State Library, Jefferson City, MO [*OCLC symbol*] (OCLC)
mol	Moldavian [*MARC language code Library of Congress*] (LCCP)
MOL	Molde [*Norway*] [*Airport symbol*] (OAG)
mol	Mole [*Amount of substance*] [*SI unit*]
mol	Molecular (AD)
MOL	Molecular (DMAA)
MOL	Molecular Layer
MOL	Molecule [*or Molecular*] (AAG)
MOL	Molesting [*FBI standardized term*]
MOL	Moliere [*Pseudonym of French actor and dramatist Jean Baptiste Poquelin, 1622-1673*] (ROG)
Mol	Mollendo (AD)
mol	Mollis [*Soft*] [*Latin*] (AD)
Mol	Molloy's De Jure Maritimo [*A publication*] (DLA)
Mol	Molloy's Irish Chancery Reports [*1827-31*] [*A publication*] (DLA)
MOL	Molodezhnaya [*Former USSR Geomagnetic observatory code*]
MOL	Molson Companies Ltd. [*Toronto Stock Exchange symbol Vancouver Stock Exchange symbol*]
MOL	Montebello, VA [*Location identifier FAA*] (FAAL)
MOL	Multiple On-Line Programming [*Computer science*] (EECA)
M-O-L	My Old Lady [*Wife*] [*Slang*]
MOL	Universite de Moncton, Law Library [*UTLAS symbol*]
MOLA	Mars Orbiter LASER Alitmeter
MOLA	Mars Orbiter LASER Altimeter
MOLA	Midwest Open Land Association (EA)
MOLAB	Mobile Laboratory [*NASA*]
molab	Mobile Laboratory (AD)
MOLAB	Mobile Lunar Laboratory (AD)
MOL/ACTS	Manned Orbiting Laboratory / Altitude Control and Transmission System (DNAB)
MOLARA	Motoring Organisations Land Access and Rights Association [*British*] (DBA)
MOLARS	Meteorological Office Library Accessions and Retrieval System (NITA)
Mo Law Rep	Monthly Law Reporter [*A publication*] (DLA)
MO Laws	Laws of Missouri [*A publication*] (DLA)
MOLB	Majestic Circle, Military Order of Lady Bugs of USA (EA)
MolBio	Molecular Biosystems, Inc. [*Associated Press*] (SAG)
molc	Molar Concentration [*Chemistry*] (MAE)
MOLC	Multiple Operational Launch Complex (MUGU)
MOLCAB	Mobile Landing Craft Advanced Base
Mol Crys Liq Crys	Molecular Crystals and Liquid Crystals (AD)
MOLD	Model of Light Diode
Mol De Jure Mar	Molloy's De Jure Maritimo et Navali [*A publication*] (DLA)
MOLDS	Management On-Line Data System [*University of Syracuse*]
MOLDS	Modernization of Land Data Systems [*North American Institute for the Modernization of Land Data Systems*] [*Falls Church, VA*]
MOLDS	Multiple Online Debugging System [*Computer science*] (IEEE)
Moldv	Moldavia (AD)
MOLE	Market Odd-Lot Execution (PDAA)
MOLE	Market Odd-Lot Execution System [*Computer science*] (MHDI)
mole	Molecular (AD)
MOLE	Molecular Optics LASER Examiner [*Spectrometry*]
MOLEC.	Molecular
MolecDev	Molecular Devices Corp. [*Associated Press*] (SAG)
MolecDy	Molecular Dynamics, Inc. [*Associated Press*] (SAG)
molecom	Molecularized Computer (AD)
MOLECOM	Molecularized Digital Computer
MoLeeH	Lee's Summit Hospital, Lee's Summit, MO [*Library symbol Library of Congress*] (LCLS)
MoLeeL	Longview Community College, Lee's Summit, MO [*Library symbol Library of Congress*] (LCLS)
MoLeeS	Lees Summit Public School District, Lees Summit, MO [*Library symbol*] [*Library of Congress*] (LCLS)
MoLeeU	Unity School Library, Lee's Summit, MO [*Library symbol Library of Congress*] (LCLS)
Mo Leg Exam	Monthly Legal Examiner [*New York*] [*A publication*] (DLA)
MO Legis Serv (Vernon)	Missouri Legislative Service (Vernon) [*A publication*] (DLA)
MOLEM	Mobile Lunar Excursion Module [*NASA*] (PDAA)
MOLETRONICS	Molecular Electronics
MOLEVATOR	Motor Elevator [*Mechanical lifting stand for arc lamps*]
MOLEX	Molecular Executive [*Graphic substructure chemical search system*]
Molex	Molex, Inc. [*Associated Press*] (SAG)
molfr	Mole Fraction [*Chemistry*] (DMAA)
MOLGEN	Molecular Genetics [*Program*] [*Computer science*]
MOLIDER	Movimiento Liberal Democratico Revolucionario [*Revolutionary Democratic Liberal Movement*] [*Honduras*] [*Political party*]
Molink	Moscow Link (AD)
MOLINK	Moscow/Washington Emergency Communications Link (MCD)
MoLiPS	Liberty Public Schools District, Liberty, MO [*Library symbol*] [*Library of Congress*] (LCLS)
Molirena	Movimiento Liberal Republicano Nacionalista [*Nationalist Liberal Republican Movement*] [*Panama*] [*Political party*] (PPW)
MOLISV	Movement for Liberation and Development [*Italy Political party*] (EAIO)
MoLiWJ	William Jewell College, Liberty, MO [*Library symbol Library of Congress*] (LCLS)
Mol JM	Molloy's De Jure Maritimo et Navali [*A publication*] (DLA)
MOLL	Metallo-Organic Liquid LASER
moll	Metallo-Organic Liquid LASER (AD)
mol/l	Molecules per Liter [*Measurement*] (DAVI)
Moll	Moller Organ Co. [*Record label*]
MOLL	Mollis [*Soft*] [*Pharmacy*]
Moll	Molloy's De Jure Maritimo [*A publication*] (DLA)
Moll	Molloy's Irish Chancery Reports [*1827-31*] [*A publication*] (DLA)
MOLLE	Modular Light-Weight Load-Carrying Equipment [*Army*]
MOLLI	Micro OnLine Library Information [*Nichols Advanced Technologies, Inc.*]
mollie	Mollienisia (AD)
MOLLUS	Military Order of the Loyal Legion of the United States (EA)
Mollus	Mollusca (AD)
MOLLUSA	Military Order of the Loyal Legion of the USA (AD)
MOL/M³	Moles per Cubic Meter
Mo L Mag	Monthly Law Magazine [*London*] [*A publication*] (DLA)
MOLNS	Ministry of Labour and National Service [*World War II British*] (DAS)
MOLO	Mideastern Ohio Library Organization [*Library network*]
MOLOC	Ministry of Labour Occupational Classification [*Later, CODOT*] [*British*]
MOLP	Multiple Objective Linear Programming [*Computer science*] (PDAA)
Mol Pharmacol	Molecular Pharmacology (MEC)
Mol Phys	Molecular Physics (AD)
MOLS	Magnetic-Operated Limit Switch
MOLS	Mirror Optional Landing System [*Aviation*] (NG)
MOLS	Mobile Object Location System
MOLS	Multiple Object Location System [*Army*]
MOLS	Mutually Orthogonal Latin Square
MOLSINK	Molecular Sink of Outer Space [*Vacuum testing chamber for spacecraft systems*]
MOLT	Manually-Operated Lift Truck (DWSG)

MOLT.......... Molten

molt............ Molten (AD)

MoltenM...... Molten Metal Technology, Inc. [Associated Press] (SAG)

MOLTOL ...... Manned Orbiting Laboratory Test-Oriented Language [NASA] (MCD)

MOL WT ...... Molecular Weight [Also, M, MW]

Mol wt .... Molecular Weight (DB)

mol wt .... Molecular Weight (AD)

MOLX.......... Molex, Inc. [NASDAQ symbol] (NQ)

MOLXA .... Molex Inc'A' [NASDAQ symbol] (TTSB)

MOLY.......... Molecular Analysis [by a computer graphics system] [Chemistry]

moly .... Molybdenum (AD)

Moly .... Molyneaux's Reports. English Courts, Tempore Car. I [A publication] (DLA)

MOLY.......... Mouse Lymphoma Cells [Oncology]

MOM............ Macro Observation Module [Microscopy]

MOM............ Maintenance Operations Management (MCD)

MOM............ Management of Migration [of wastewaters]

MOM............ Manned Orbiting Mission [NASA]

MOM............ Man-on-the-Move [Military slang] (DNAB)

MOM............ Man Overboard Module [Boating]

MOM............ Mark XII Output and Monitoring System (SAA)

m/ o m/ ...... Mas o Menos [More or Less] [Spanish] (AD)

MOM............ Master of Manufacturing (PGP)

MOM............ Measure of Merit (MCD)

MOM............ Message-Oriented Middleware [Computer science]

MOM............ Message Output Module [Telecommunications] (TEL)

MOM............ Metal-Oxide Metal (MCD)

MOM............ Methods of Moderation [An association] (EA)

MOM............ Methoxymethyl [Organic chemistry]

MOM............ Micromation Online Microfilmer

mom .... Micromation Online Microfilmer [Computer science] (AD)

MOM............ Microsoft Office Manager [Microsoft Corp. computer program] (PCM)

m-o-m .... Middle of Month (AD)

MOM............ Middle of the Month

MOM............ Military Official Mail (AABC)

MOM............ Military Ordinary Mail (AABC)

mom .... Military Ordinary Mail (AD)

MOM............ Military Overseas Mail [An association] (EA)

MOM............ Milk of Magnesia

mom .... Milk of Magnesia (AD)

MOM............ Minutes of Meeting

MOM............ Missile Operations Manager (MUGU)

MOM............ Missionary Sisters of Our Lady of Mercy [Roman Catholic religious order]

MOM............ Mitochondrial Outer-Membrane [Biochemistry]

MOM............ Modified Operational Missile

MOM............ Modular Ocean Model (USDC)

MOM............ Moment

mom .... Moment (NAKS)

MOM............ Momentary (MSA)

MOM............ Momentum

Mom .... Momma (AD)

MOM............ Momote [Admiralty Islands] [Seismograph station code, US Geological Survey] (SEIS)

MOM............ Mother's Restaurants Ltd. [Toronto Stock Exchange symbol]

MOM............ Mucoid Otitis Media [Medicine] (DMAA)

MOM............ Musee Oceanographique Monaco [Monaco Oceanographic Museum] [France] (AD)

M-O-M .... My Old Man [Husband] [Slang]

MOMA .... Madagasikara Otronin'ny Malagasy [Formerly, MONIMA] [Madagascar Led by Malagasy]

MOMA .... Methoxyhydroxymandelic Acid [Organic chemistry]

MOMA .... Museum of Modern Art [New York]

MoMA .... Museum of Modern Art [New York] (AD)

MOMAC .... Monkey Mountain Advisory Center [Military] (CINC)

MOMAG ...... Mobile Mine Assembly Group [Military] (CAAL)

MOMAGDET.. Mobile Mine Assembly Group Detachment (DNAB)

MOMAGU..... Mobile Mine Assembly Group Unit (DNAB)

MoManW...... Laura Ingalls Wilder - Rose Wilder Lane Home and Museum, Mansfield, MO [Library symbol Library of Congress] (LCLS)

MOMAR .... Modern Mobile Army [Military]

momar......... Modern Mobile Army (AD)

MoMaryU..... Northwest Missouri State University, Maryville, MO [Library symbol Library of Congress] (LCLS)

MOMAT........ Mobile Mine Assembly Team

MOMATLANT.. Mobile Mine Assembly Team, Atlantic (DNAB)

MOMATPAC... Mobile Mine Assembly Team, Pacific (DNAB)

MOMAU .... Mobile Mine Assembly Unit (NVT)

momau .... Mobile Mine Assembly Unit (AD)

MOMAULANT.. Mobile Mine Assembly Unit, Atlantic (DNAB)

MOMAULANTDETKEF.. Mobile Mine Assembly Unit, Atlantic, Keflavik Detachment (DNAB)

MOMAUPAC.. Mobile Mine Assembly Unit, Pacific (DNAB)

MOMB .... Mombasa [Island near Kenya] (ROG)

MOMBE........ Metallo-Organic Molecular Beam Epitaxy [Solid state physics]

MOMC .... Mount McKinley National Park

MOMCOMS... Man-on-the-Move Communications

MOMCOMS... Mobile Mine Countermeasures Command (DNAB)

MoMex .... Mexico-Audrain County Library, Mexico, MO [Library symbol Library of Congress] (LCLS)

MOMI.......... Museum of the Moving Image [London] (ECON)

MOMIMTS ... Military and Orchestral Musical Instrument Makers' Trade Society [A union] [British] (DCTA)

m-o-m in am if no bm by pm... Milk-of-Magnesia in the Morning if No Bowel Movement by Evening [Medicine] (AD)

MOMISMAINTU... Mobile, Missile Maintenance Unit (DNAB)

MOML .... Moslem Meal [Airline notation] (ADA)

Moml .... Moslem Meal (AD)

MoMLV........ Moloney Murine Luekemia Virus [Used for gene transfer protocols] (DOG)

MoMM .... Missouri Valley College, Marshall, MO [Library symbol Library of Congress] (LCLS)

MOMM .... Motor Machinist's Mate [Navy rating]

MOMMSR .... Motor Machinist's Mate, Ship Repair [Navy rating]

MOMO .... Macrosomia-Obesity-Macrocephaly-Ocular Abnormalities [Syndrome] [Medicine] (DMAA)

MOMP .... Major Outer Membrane Protein [Biochemistry]

MOMP .... Michigan Ordnance Missile Plant [Army]

MOMP .... Mid-Ocean Meeting Place

MOMP .... Mustargen [Nitrogen mustard], Oncovin , Methotrexate, Prednisone [Vincristine] [Antineoplastic drug regimen]

MOMR .... Mayor's Office of Manpower Resources (AD)

MOMS .... Manganese Oxide Mesoporous Structure [Inorganic Chemistry]

MOMS .... Measure of Mission Success [Military] (CAAL)

MOMS .... Member of the Organisation and Methods Society [British] (DI)

moms .... Mervaerdiomsaetningsskat [Value-Added Tax] [Danish] (AD)

MOMS .... Meteorological and Oceanographic Measurements System [Chevron Oil Co.]

MOMS .... Meteorological Optic Measuring System (MCD)

MOMS .... Micro-Opto-Mechanical Systems

moms .... Missile Operate Mode Simulator (AD)

MOMS .... Missile Operate Mode Simulator

MOMS .... Modified Operational Missile System (DNAB)

MOMS .... Modular Optoelectronic Multispectral Scanner (MCD)

MOMS .... Mothers for Moral Stability [Group opposing sex education in schools]

MOMS .... Mothers of Men in Service [World War II]

MOMS .... Multimegabit Operation Multiplexer System

MOMS .... Multiple Orbit - Multiple Satellite

MOMS .... Multiple Organ Malrotation Syndrome [Medicine] (DMAA)

MOM's........ Multiples over the Median [Statistics]

MoMSV....... Moloney Mouse Sarcoma Virus

MoMuLV...... Moloney Murine Leukemia Virus [Also, MLV]

MOM/WOW... Men Our Masters/Women Our Wonders [Antifeminist group] (EA)

MON .... Above Mountains [ICAO] (FAAC)

mon .... Maison [House] [French] (AD)

MON .... Member of the Order of the Niger [Nigeria]

MON .... Memorandum of Need

MON .... Memorandum of Negotiation (MCD)

MON .... Missouri Valley College, Marshall, MO [Inactive] [OCLC symbol] (OCLC)

MON .... Mixed Oxides of Nitrogen

MON .... Monaco [Monaco] [Seismograph station code, US Geological Survey] (SEIS)

Mon .... Monaco (AD)

MON .... Monaghan [County in Republic of Ireland] (ROG)

Mon .... Monaghan's Unreported Cases (Pennsylvania Superior Court) [A publication] (DLA)

MON .... Monarch [Record label] [British]

MON .... Monarch Airlines Ltd. [British ICAO designator] (FAAC)

MON .... Monarch Investments Ltd. [Toronto Stock Exchange symbol]

MON .... Monastery

MON .... Monday (AFM)

Mon .... Monday (AD)

MON .... Monegasque (AD)

mon .... Monetary (AD)

MON .... Monetary (AFM)

mon .... Mongol [MARC language code Library of Congress] (LCCP)

Mon .... Mongol (AD)

Mon .... Mongol [One affected with Down's syndrome] [Medicine] (DAVI)

MON .... Mongolian (AABC)

Mon .... Moniteur Belge [A publication] (ILCA)

MON .... Monitor [Navy ship symbol]

Mon .... Monitor (AD)

mon .... Monitor (WDMC)

mon .... Monitor/Contractor [MARC relator code] [Library of Congress] (LCCP)

MON .... Monmouthshire [County in Wales]

Mon .... Monmouthshire (AD)

Mon .... Monoceros [Constellation]

MON .... Monoclinic [Crystallography]

Mon .... Monoclonal Antibodies, Inc.

MON .... Monocyte [Hematology]

MON .... Monogram [Numismatics]

mon .... Monograph (BJA)

MON .... Monomoy Surfboat [Coast Guard] (DNAB)

MON .... Monon [Railroad] (MHDW)

Mon .... Monongahela (AD)

Mon .... Monsieur [Mister] [French]

Mon .... Monsignor (WGA)

mon .... Monsoon (AD)

Mon .... Montag [Monday] [German] (AD)

MON .... Montana

Mon .... Montana Reports [A publication] (DLA)

Mon .... Montana Supreme Court Reports [A publication] (DLA)

MON .... Month

MON .... Monticello, AR [Location identifier FAA] (FAAL)

MON .... Monument (AAG)

Mon .... Monument (AD)

mon .... Monument (AD)

MON .... Monument Still Exists [*Genealogy*] (ROG)
MON .... Motor Octane Number [*Fuel technology*]
mon .... Motor Octane Number (AD)
MoN............ Mountain Name (BJA)
MON .... Mount Cook [*New Zealand*] [*Airport symbol*] (OAG)
MoN............ North Kansas City Public Library, North Kansas City, MO [*Library symbol Library of Congress*] (LCLS)
MON .... Universite de Moncton, Bibliotheque [*UTLAS symbol*]
Mona .... Madonna [*Our Lady*] [*Italian*] (AD)
MONA .... Marche des Options Negociables sur Actions [*Options exchange*] [*France*] (EY)
MONA .... Modular Navigation [*Aviation*]
Mona .... Monaco (VRA)
Mona .... Monaghan's Reports [*147-165 Pennsylvania*] [*A publication*] (DLA)
MONA .... Monitor Assembly [*Ground Communications Facility, NASA*]
MONAB .... Mobile Naval Advanced Base [*British military*] (DMA)
MONAB .... Mobile Noise Analysis Barge
MONAB .... Mobile Operating Naval Air Base
Monac .... Monaco Finance [*Associated Press*] (SAG)
MonacoC ..... Monaco Coach Corp. [*Associated Press*] (SAG)
MonacoF ..... Monaco Finance [*Associated Press*] (SAG)
Monag .... Monaghan (AD)
Monag .... Monaghan's Reports [*147-165 Pennsylvania*] [*A publication*] (DLA)
MONAGH ..... Monaghan [*County in Republic of Ireland*] (ROG)
Monaghan ... Monaghan's Reports [*147-165 Pennsylvania*] [*A publication*] (DLA)
Monaghan (PA)... Monaghan's Reports [*147-165 Pennsylvania*] [*A publication*] (DLA)
MONAGN ..... Monaghan [*County in Republic of Ireland*]
MONAL .... Mobile Nondestructive Assay Laboratory [*AEC*]
Mon Anc ..... Monumentum Ancyranum [*Classical studies*] (OCD)
Mon Angl..... Monasticon Anglicanum [*A publication*] (DLA)
Monas .... Monastic (AD)
Monash Univ Law Rev... Monash University. Law Review [*A publication*]
MonAvl .... Monarch Avalon, Inc. [*Associated Press*] (SAG)
monbas....... Monobasic (AD)
MONC .... Metropolitan Opera National Council
MonCap ...... Monmouth Capital Corp. [*Associated Press*] (SAG)
MonCasn ..... Monarch Casino & Resort [*Associated Press*] (SAG)
monch .... Monochrome (VRA)
Monc Inn .... Moncrieff's Liability of Innkeepers [*1874*] [*A publication*] (DLA)
MOND .... Mondavi [*Robert*] [*NASDAQ symbol*] (SAG)
MOND .... Monday (ROG)
MOND .... Robert Mondavi `A' [*NASDAQ symbol*] (TTSB)
Mondavi ...... Mondavi [*Robert*] [*Associated Press*] (SAG)
MON/DIR ..... Mission Monitoring Direction
mon/dir ...... Monitoring Direction (AD)
MONE .... Money Store [*NASDAQ symbol*] (TTSB)
MONE .... [*The*] Money Store, Inc. [*NASDAQ symbol*] (SAG)
MONECA...... Motor Network Calculator
MONEP .... Marche des Options Negotiables de Paris [*French Traded Options Market*] (ODBW)
MONES .... Molecular Nonthermal Excitation Spectrometry
MONET .... Mobile Networks Integration [*Telecommunications*]
MONET .... Monetary
MONET .... Multi-Wavelength Optical Network (AAEL)
MONEVAL .... Monthly Evaluation Report [*Military*]
MONEX .... Monsoon Experiment [*Also, MONSOONEX*]
monex .... Monsoon Experiment (AD)
Moneygr ...... Moneygram Payment Systems [*Associated Press*] (SAG)
MoneySt ..... [*The*] Money Store, Inc. [*Associated Press*] (SAG)
MONF .... Monaco Finance [*NASDAQ symbol*] (SAG)
MONFA .... Monaco Finance'A' [*NASDAQ symbol*] (TTSB)
Mong .... Mongol (AD)
MONG .... Mongolian [*Language, etc.*]
mong .... Mongolisch [*Mongolian*] [*German*] (AD)
MONG .... Mongrel (DSUE)
MONG .... Moning [*Tea trade*] (ROG)
Mongo .... Mongolia (VRA)
mon-H .... Monohydrogen (AD)
MoNHI .... Missouri Natural Heritage Inventory [*Missouri State Department of Conservation*] [*Information service or system*] (IID)
MONICA...... Monitoring of Trends and Determinants in Cardiovascular Disease
monik .... Moniker (AD)
MONIL .... Mobile Non-Destructive Inspection Laboratory (DNAB)
MONIMA...... Mouvement National pour l'Independance de Madagascar [*National Movement for the Independence of Madagascar*] [*Political party*] (PPW)
Mon Law Mag... Monthly Law Magazine [*London*] [*A publication*] (DLA)
Mon Law Rep... Monthly Law Reporter [*A publication*] (DLA)
Mon Leg R (PA)... Monroe Legal Reporter [*Pennsylvania*] [*A publication*] (DLA)
MONM .... Monmouth Capital [*NASDAQ symbol*] (TTSB)
MONM .... Monmouth Capital Corp. [*NASDAQ symbol*] (SAG)
Mon Meth.... Monahan's Method of the Law [*1878*] [*A publication*] (DLA)
MoNMH .... North Kansas City Memorial Hospital, North Kansas City, MO [*Library symbol Library of Congress*] (LCLS)
Monmouth C... Monmouth College (GAGS)
MONMS ...... Monmouthshire [*County in Wales*]
Mon Not Roy Soc Tas... Monthly Notices. Royal Society of Tasmania [*A publication*]
MONO .... Monaural (KSC)
Mono .... Monoceros [*Constellation*]
MONO .... Monochrome (DSUE)
mono .... Monocyte [*Hematology*]
Mono .... Monogram [*Record label*]
MONO .... Mononucleosis [*Medicine*]

mono .... Mononucleosis [*Medicine*] (AD)
mono .... Monophonic (AD)
MONO......... Monophonic
mono .... Monopoly (AD)
mono .... Monopropellant (AD)
mono .... Monorail (AD)
MONO......... Monorail (WDAA)
MONO......... Monotone (DOAD)
MONO......... Monotype (ADA)
mono .... Monotype (AD)
monob........ Mobile Noise Barge (AD)
MONOB....... Mobile Noise Barge
MONOC....... Monocoque (MSA)
MONOCL...... Monoclinic
monocl .... Monoclinic (AD)
monocot ..... Monocotyledon [*Biology*] (BARN)
Monod .... Monon Railroad (AD)
monog .... Monogram (AD)
monog .... Monograph (AD)
MONOG....... Monograph
MONOK....... Monitor Resumed Normal Operation [*Aviation communications*]
MONOP .... Monopoly [*Legal shorthand*] (LWAP)
monos .... Monitor Out of Service (AD)
MONOS .... Monitor Out of Service [*Aviation communications*]
monot .... Monotonous (AD)
monot .... Monotype (AD)
MonP .... Monongahela Power Co. [*Associated Press*] (SAG)
MonP25 ...... Monongahela Power Co. [*Associated Press*] (SAG)
monpl .... Monopoly (AD)
monpr......... Monoprint (VRA)
MonPw .... Montana Power Co. [*Associated Press*] (SAG)
Monrch .... Monarch Machine Tool Co. [*Associated Press*] (SAG)
MoNRDEP.... Ministry of Natural Resources Development and Environmental Protection [*Ethiopia*] (ECON)
MonRE .... Monmouth Real Estate Investment Corp. [*Associated Press*] (SAG)
Mon River ... Monongahela River (AD)
Monro......... Acta Cancellariae [*England*] [*A publication*] (DLA)
Monro AC .... Monro's Acta Cancellariae [*1545-1625*] [*A publication*] (DLA)
Monroc....... Monroc, Inc. [*Associated Press*] (SAG)
Monroe .... Monroe Legal Reporter [*Pennsylvania*] [*A publication*] (DLA)
Monroe LR... Monroe Legal Reporter [*Pennsylvania*] [*A publication*] (DLA)
MonroM....... Monro Muffler Brake, Inc. [*Associated Press*] (SAG)
MONS .... Monastery
MONS .... Monmouthshire [*County in Wales*]
MONS .... Monsieur [*In France this form is considered contemptuous*] [*Preferred form is M*]
Mons .... Monsieur [*Mister*] [*French*] (AD)
Monsan....... Monsanto Co. [*Associated Press*] (SAG)
Mons Cur .... Monsoon Current (AD)
MONSEE ..... Monitoring of the Sun Earth Environment [*International Council of Scientific Unions*] (MCD)
Monsig .... Monseigneur [*My Lord*] [*French*] (AD)
MONSIG...... Monsignor [*Lord, Sir*] [*French*]
MONSOONEX... Monsoon Experiment [*Also, MONEX*]
MonSt......... Montgomery Street Income Securities, Inc. [*Associated Press*] (SAG)
monstro .... Monstrosity (AD)
MONSTRY.... Monastery
Mont .... Montagu's English Bankruptcy Reports [*A publication*] (DLA)
MONT .... Montana (AFM)
Mont .... Montana (AD)
Mont .... Montana Supreme Court Reports [*A publication*] (DLA)
Mont .... Monterrey (AD)
Mont .... Montevideo (AD)
Mont .... Montgomery (AD)
MONT .... Montgomeryshire [*County in Wales*]
Mont .... Montilla [*Record label*] [*USA, Spain, etc.*]
MONT .... Montmorillonite [*Mineralogy*]
Mont .... Montpelier (AD)
Mont .... Montreal (AD)
Mont .... Montriou's Bengal Reports [*A publication*] (DLA)
mont .... Monument (VRA)
Mont Admin R... Administrative Rules of Montana [*A publication*] (DLA)
Mont Admin Reg... Montana Administrative Register [*A publication*] (DLA)
MonTal .... Monumenta Talmudica (BJA)
Mont & A..... Montagu and Ayrton's English Bankruptcy Reports [*1833-38*] [*A publication*] (DLA)
Mont & Ayr... Montagu and Ayrton's English Bankruptcy Reports [*1833-38*] [*A publication*] (DLA)
Mont & Ayr Bankr... Montagu and Ayrton's English Bankruptcy Reports [*1833-38*] [*A publication*] (DLA)
Mont & Ayr Bankr (Eng)... Montagu and Ayrton's English Bankruptcy Reports [*1833-38*] [*A publication*] (DLA)
Mont & Ayr BL... Montagu and Ayrton's Bankrupt Laws [*A publication*] (DLA)
Mont & B..... Montagu and Bligh's English Bankruptcy Reports [*1832-33*] [*A publication*] (DLA)
Mont & B Bankr... Montagu and Bligh's English Bankruptcy Reports [*1832-33*] [*A publication*] (DLA)
Mont & B Bankr (Eng)... Montagu and Bligh's English Bankruptcy Reports [*1832-33*] [*A publication*] (DLA)
Mont & Bl.... Montagu and Bligh's English Bankruptcy Reports [*1832-33*] [*A publication*] (DLA)
Mont & C..... Montagu and Chitty's English Bankruptcy Reports [*1838-40*] [*A publication*] (DLA)
Mont & C Bankr... Montagu and Chitty's English Bankruptcy Reports [*1838-40*] [*A publication*] (DLA)

Mont & C Bankr (Eng)... Montagu and Chitty's English Bankruptcy Reports [*1838-40*] [*A publication*] (DLA)
Mont & Ch... Montagu and Chitty's English Bankruptcy Reports [*1838-40*] [*A publication*] (DLA)
Mont & Chitt... Montagu and Chitty's English Bankruptcy Reports [*1838-40*] [*A publication*] (DLA)
Mont & M... Montagu and MacArthur's English Bankruptcy Reports [*A publication*] (DLA)
Mont & MacA... Montagu and MacArthur's English Bankruptcy Reports [*A publication*] (DLA)
Mont & M Bankr (Eng)... Mantagu and MacArthur's English Bankruptcy Reports [*1826-30*] [*A publication*] (DLA)
Mon T B ...... T. B. Monroe's Kentucky Reports [*17-23 Kentucky*] [*A publication*] (DLA)
Mont Bankr (Eng)... Montagu's English Bankruptcy Reports [*A publication*] (DLA)
Mont Bank Rep... Montagu's English Bankruptcy Reports [*A publication*] (DLA)
MontBB....... Monterey Bay Bancorp, Inc. [*Associated Press*] (SAG)
Mont BC ...... Montagu's English Bankruptcy Reports [*A publication*] (DLA)
Mont Bk L... Montagu's Bankrupt Law [*4th ed.*] [*1827*] [*A publication*] (DLA)
Mont Cas..... Montriou's Cases in Hindoo Law [*A publication*] (DLA)
Montclair St C.. Montclair State College (GAGS)
Mont CMS&T... Montana College of Mineral Science and Technology (GAGS)
Mont Code Ann... Montana Code, Annotated [*A publication*] (DLA)
Mont Comp... Montagu on Composition [*1823*] [*A publication*] (DLA)
Mont Cond Rep... Montreal Condensed Reports [*A publication*] (DLA)
Mont D & DeG... Montagu, Deacon, and De Gex's English Bankruptcy Reports [*1840-44*] [*A publication*] (DLA)
Mont Dig ..... Montagu's Digest of Pleadings in Equity [*A publication*] (DLA)
Monte .... Montebianco (AD)
Monte .... Monte Carlo (AD)
Monte .... Montefiore (AD)
Monte .... Montevideo (AD)
Monte .... Montgomery (AD)
Monted .... Montedison SpA [*Associated Press*] (SAG)
Monten .... Montenegro
Mont Eq Pl... Montagu's Digest of Pleadings in Equity [*A publication*] (DLA)
Monterey Inst... Monterey Institute of Foreign Studies (GAGS)
montg .... Montage (VRA)
MONTG....... Montgomeryshire [*County in Wales*]
MONTGOM... Montgomeryshire [*County in Wales*]
Montgom ..... Montgomeryshire [*England*] (AD)
Month Dig Tax Articles... Monthly Digest of Tax Articles [*A publication*] (DLA)
Month JL ..... Monthly Journal of Law [*A publication*] (DLA)
Month Jur..... Monthly Jurist [*Bloomington, IL*] [*A publication*] (DLA)
Month Law Bul... Monthly Law Bulletin [*New York*] [*A publication*] (DLA)
Month Law Rep... Law Reporter [*Boston*] [*A publication*] (DLA)
Month L Bull (NY)... Monthly Law Bulletin (New York) [*A publication*] (DLA)
Month Leg Ex... Monthly Legal Examiner [*New York*] [*A publication*] (DLA)
Month Leg Exam... Monthly Legal Examiner [*New York*] [*A publication*] (DLA)
Month Leg Exam (NY)... Monthly Legal Examiner (New York) [*A publication*] (DLA)
Month LJ..... Monthly Journal of Law [*Washington*] [*A publication*] (DLA)
Month LM..... Monthly Law Magazine [*London*] [*A publication*] (DLA)
Month L Rep.. Monthly Law Reporter [*Boston*] [*A publication*] (DLA)
Month L Rep.. Monthly Law Reports [*Canada*] [*A publication*] (DLA)
Month L Rev.. Monthly Law Review [*A publication*] (DLA)
Monthly Lab Rev... Monthly Labor Review [*A publication*] (DLA)
Monthly L Bul... New York Monthly Law Bulletin [*A publication*] (DLA)
Month West Jur... Monthly Western Jurist [*A publication*] (DLA)
Mont Ind...... Monthly Index to Reporters [*A publication*] (DLA)
Mont Inst..... Montriou's Institutes of Jurisprudence [*A publication*] (DLA)
Mont Law ..... Montana Lawyer [*A publication*] (DLA)
Mont Laws... Laws of Montana [*A publication*] (DLA)
Mont Leg News... Montreal Legal News [*A publication*] (DLA)
Mont Liens... Montagu on Liens [*A publication*] (DLA)
Mont LR...... Montreal Law Reports, Queen's Bench [*A publication*] (DLA)
Mont LR ...... Montreal Law Reports, Superior Court [*A publication*] (DLA)
Mont LRQB.. Montreal Law Reports, Queen's Bench [*A publication*] (DLA)
Mont LRSC.. Montreal Law Reports, Superior Court [*A publication*] (DLA)
Mont Merc Law... Montefiore's Synopsis of Mercantile Law [*A publication*] (DLA)
montp .... Monotype (VRA)
Montparno... Montparnasse (AD)
Mont Part ... Montagu's Digest of the Law of Partnership [*A publication*] (DLA)
MontPas ...... Monterey Pasta [*Associated Press*] (SAG)
MONTR........ Montreal [*Canada*]
Montr........... Montreal [*Canada*] (AD)
Montr........... Montriou's Bengal Reports [*A publication*] (DLA)
Montr........... Montriou's Supplement to Morton's Reports [*A publication*] (DLA)
Montr Cond Rep... Montreal Condensed Reports [*A publication*] (DLA)
Montreal LQB (Can)... Montreal Law Reports, Queen's Bench [*Canada*] [*A publication*] (DLA)
Montreal LRQB... Montreal Law Reports, Queen's Bench [*Canada*] [*A publication*] (DLA)
Montreal LRSC... Montreal Law Reports, Superior Court [*Canada*] [*A publication*] (DLA)
Montreal LSC (Can)... Montreal Law Reports, Superior Court [*Canada*] [*A publication*] (DLA)
Mont Rep..... Montriou's Reports, Supreme Court [*1846*] [*Bengal, India*] [*A publication*] (DLA)
Mont Rev Code Ann... Montana Revised Code, Annotated [*A publication*] (DLA)
MONTRG...... Monitoring (AABC)
montrg......... Monitoring (AABC)
Montr Leg N... Montreal Legal News [*A publication*] (DLA)
Montr QB..... Montreal Law Reports, Queen's Bench [*A publication*] (DLA)
Montr Super... Montreal Law Reports, Superior Court [*A publication*] (DLA)
MontryH....... Monterey Homes Corp. [*Associated Press*] (SAG)

MontryR....... Monterey Resources, Inc. [*Associated Press*] (SAG)
Mont S......... Montreal Star [*A publication*] (AD)
MONTSAME... Mongolyn Tsahilgaan Medeeniy Agentlag [*Press agency*] [*Mongolia*]
Mont SO ..... Montagu. Set-Off [*2nd ed.*] [*1828*] [*A publication*] (DLA)
Mont Sp L ... Montesquieu's Spirit of Laws [*A publication*] (DLA)
Mont St U... Montana State University (GAGS)
Mont Super... Montreal Law Reports, Superior Court [*A publication*] (DLA)
MONT TER... Montana Territory
Monty .... Montgomery (AD)
Monty .... Montmorency (AD)
Mon ULR ..... Monash University. Law Review [*A publication*]
MoNvC......... Cottey College, Nevada, MO [*Library symbol Library of Congress*] (LCLS)
Mon WJ....... Monthly Western Jurist [*A publication*] (DLA)
Mony .... Monastery (AD)
MONY .... Music Operators of New York (AD)
MONY .... Mutual of New York [*Insurance company*]
MOO .... Management Operations Officer [*Social Security Administration*]
MOO .... Milkbottles Only Organization (EA)
MOO .... Missile Operations Officer [*NASA*] (KSC)
MOO .... Money-Order Office
Moo .... Moody's English Crown Cases [*168, 169 English Reprint*] [*A publication*] (DLA)
MOO .... Moomba [*Australia Airport symbol Obsolete*] (OAG)
MOO .... Moongold Resources [*Vancouver Stock Exchange symbol*]
MOO .... Moorlands [*Tasmania*] [*Seismograph station code, US Geological Survey*] (SEIS)
MOO .... MUD [*Multi-User Dungeon*] Object-Oriented [*Computer science*] (DOM)
MOO .... Multiple-User Dimension Object Oriented [*Computer technology*]
MOO .... School of the Ozarks, Point Lookout, MO [*OCLC symbol*] (OCLC)
Moo A.......... Moore's Reports [*Bosanquet and Puller*] [*England*] [*A publication*]
Moo & M.... Moody and Malkin's English Nisi Prius Reports [*A publication*] (DLA)
Moo & Mal... Moody and Malkin's English Nisi Prius Reports [*A publication*] (DLA)
Moo & P...... Moore and Payne's English Common Pleas Reports [*A publication*]
Moo & Pay... Moore and Payne's English Common Pleas Reports [*A publication*] (DLA)
Moo & R...... Moody and Robinson's English Nisi Prius Reports [*A publication*] (DLA)
Moo & Rob... Moody and Robinson's English Nisi Prius Reports [*A publication*] (DLA)
Moo & S...... Moore and Scott's English Common Pleas Reports [*1831-34*] [*A publication*] (DLA)
Moo & Sc.... Moore and Scott's English Common Pleas Reports [*1831-34*] [*A publication*] (DLA)
Moo CC....... Moody's English Crown Cases Reserved [*1824-44*] [*A publication*] (DLA)
MOO C of S... Management Office, Office, Chief of Staff
Moo CP....... Moore's English Common Pleas Reports [*A publication*] (DLA)
Moo Cr C..... Moody's English Crown Cases Reserved [*1824-44*] [*A publication*] (DLA)
Mood.......... Moody's English Crown Cases Reserved [*1824-44*] [*A publication*] (DLA)
Mood & M... Moody and Malkin's English Nisi Prius Reports [*A publication*] (DLA)
Mood & Malk... Moody and Malkin's English Nisi Prius Reports [*A publication*] (DLA)
Mood & R.... Moody and Robinson's English Nisi Prius Reports [*A publication*] (DLA)
Mood & Rob... Moody and Robinson's English Nisi Prius Reports [*A publication*] (DLA)
Mood CC...... Moody's English Crown Cases Reserved [*1824-44*] [*A publication*] (DLA)
Moody .... Moody's English Crown Cases [*168, 169 English Reprint*] [*A publication*] (DLA)
Moody & M... Moody and Malkin's English Nisi Prius Reports [*A publication*] (DLA)
Moody & M (Eng)... Moody and Malkin's English Nisi Prius Reports [*A publication*] (DLA)
Moody & R... Moody and Robinson's English Nisi Prius Reports [*A publication*] (DLA)
Moody & R (Eng)... Moody and Robinson's English Nisi Prius Reports [*A publication*] (DLA)
Moody CC (Eng)... Moody's English Crown Cases [*168, 169 English Reprint*] [*A publication*] (DLA)
Moody Cr C... Moody's English Crown Cases [*168, 169 English Reprint*] [*A publication*] (DLA)
Moody Cr Cas... Moody's English Crown Cases [*168, 169 English Reprint*] [*A publication*] (DLA)
Moog .... Moog, Inc. [*Associated Press*] (SAG)
Moo GC....... Moore's Gorham Case, English Privy Council [*A publication*] (DLA)
Moo Ind App... Moore's Reports, Privy Council, Indian Appeals [*1836-72*] [*A publication*] (DLA)
MOON .... Meeting Our Operational Needs
Moon .... Moon's Reports [*133-144 Indiana*] [*6-14 Indiana Appeals*] [*A publication*] (DLA)
moop .... Mechlorethamine, Vincristine, Procarbazine, Prednisone [*Medicine*] (AD)
MOOP .... Ministerstvo Okhrany Obshchestvennogo Poryadka [*Ministry for Maintenance of Public Order*] [*Former USSR*] (LAIN)
MOOP .... Missile Out of Order for Parts (MCD)
Moo PC....... Moore's English Privy Council Cases, Old and New Series [*A publication*] (DLA)
Moo PCC ..... Moore's English Privy Council Cases [*A publication*] (DLA)

Moo PC Cas NS...	Moore's English Privy Council Cases, New Series [*A publication*] (DLA)
Moo PCC NS...	Moore's English Privy Council Cases, New Series [*A publication*] (DLA)
Moo PC (NS)...	Moore's English Privy Council Cases, New Series [*A publication*] (DLA)
Moor...........	Dartmoor Prison [*Devon, England*] (AD)
Moor...........	English King's Bench Reports, by Sir Francis Moore [*1512-1621*] [*A publication*] (DLA)
Moore.........	Moore Corp. Ltd. [*Associated Press*] (SAG)
Moore.........	Moore's English Common Pleas Reports [*A publication*] (DLA)
Moore.........	Moore's English Privy Council Reports [*A publication*] (DLA)
Moore.........	Moore's Reports [*Arkansas*] [*A publication*] (DLA)
Moore.........	Moore's Reports [*Texas*] [*A publication*] (DLA)
Moore.........	Moore's Reports [*Alabama*] [*A publication*] (DLA)
Moore A	Moore's Reports [*Bosanquet and Puller*] [*England*] [*A publication*] (DLA)
Moore Abs...	Moore's Abstracts of Title [*6th ed.*] [*1925*] [*A publication*] (DLA)
Moore & P...	Moore and Payne's English Common Pleas Reports [*A publication*] (DLA)
Moore & P (Eng)...	Moore and Payne's English Common Pleas Reports [*A publication*] (DLA)
Moore & S...	Moore and Scott's English Common Pleas Reports [*1831-34*] [*A publication*] (DLA)
Moore & S (Eng)...	Moore and Scott's English Common Pleas Reports [*1831-34*] [*A publication*] (DLA)
Moore & W...	Moore and Walker's Reports [*22-24 Texas*] [*A publication*] (DLA)
Moore & Walker...	Moore and Walker's Reports [*22-24 Texas*] [*A publication*] (DLA)
Moore CP	Moore's English Common Pleas Reports [*A publication*] (DLA)
Moore Cr Law...	Moore's Criminal Law and Procedure [*A publication*] (DLA)
Moore EI...	Moore's East Indian Appeals [*A publication*] (DLA)
Moore Fed Practice...	Moore's Federal Practice [*A publication*] (DLA)
Moore GC	Moore's Gorham Case, English Privy Council [*A publication*] (DLA)
MooreHd......	Moore-Handley, Inc. [*Associated Press*] (SAG)
Moore Ind App...	Moore's Indian Appeals [*A publication*] (DLA)
Moore Ind App (Eng)...	Moore's Indian Appeals [*England*] [*A publication*] (DLA)
Moore Indian App...	Moore's Indian Appeals [*England*] [*A publication*] (DLA)
Moore Int L...	Moore's Digest of International Law [*A publication*] (DLA)
MooreP........	Moore Products Corp. [*Associated Press*] (SAG)
Moore PC	Moore's English Privy Council Reports [*A publication*] (DLA)
Moore PCC...	Moore's English Privy Council Cases [*A publication*] (DLA)
Moore PCC (Eng)...	Moore's English Privy Council Cases [*A publication*] (DLA)
Moore PCC NS...	Moore's English Privy Council Cases, New Series [*A publication*] (DLA)
Moore PCC NS (Eng)...	Moore's English Privy Council Cases, New Series [*A publication*] (DLA)
Moore PC NS...	Moore's English Privy Council Reports, New Series [*A publication*] (DLA)
Moore Presby Dig...	Moore's Presbyterian Digest [*A publication*] (DLA)
Moore QB	Moore's English Queen's Bench Reports [*A publication*] (DLA)
Moore's Adj...	Moore's International Adjudications [*Legal term*] (AD)
Moore's Arb...	Moore's International Arbitrations [*Legal term*] (AD)
Moore's Dig...	Moore's Digest [*Legal term*] (AD)
Moorhead St U...	Moorhead State University (GAGS)
MOORNG	Mooring [*Freight*]
MOOS..........	Modular Ocean Observation System [*Marine science*] (MSC)
MoOs..........	Saint Clair County Library, Osceola, MO [*Library symbol Library of Congress*] (LCLS)
MOOSE	Man [*or Manual*] Orbital Operations Safety Equipment [*Space life raft*] [*NASA*]
MOOSE	Man Out of Space Easiest
MOOSE	Move Out of Saigon Expeditiously [*or Earliest*] [*Army project, Vietnam*]
MOOSEMUSS...	Maneuver, Objective, Offensive, Surprise, Economy of Force, Mass, Unity of Command, Simplicity, Security [*Basic principles of war*] [*See also MOSS MOUSE*]
Moo Sep Rep...	Moore's Separate Report of Westerton Versus Liddell [*A publication*] (DLA)
MOOSSE......	Manned Orbital Oceanographic Survey System Experiment
moot............	Moved Out of Town (AD)
MOOT	Move Out of Town [*Reduction of troop concentrations in cities*] [*Military*]
Moot Ct Bull...	University of Illinois. Moot Court Bulletin [*A publication*] (DLA)
Moo Tr........	Moore's Divorce Trials [*A publication*] (DLA)
MOOTW	Military Operations Other than War (RDA)
MOOV	Moovies, Inc. [*NASDAQ symbol*] (SAG)
Moovie.........	Moovies, Inc. [*Associated Press*] (SAG)
MOOW	Medical Officer of the Watch
MOP...........	Magnetized Orange Pipe [*Minesweeping device*] [*Navy*]
MOP...........	Maintenance of Property
MOP...........	Maintenance Operating Procedure (MCD)
MOP...........	Maintenance Operations Protocol (ACRL)
MOP...........	Maintenance Outline Procedure [*Nuclear energy*] (NRCH)
MOP...........	Major Organ Profile [*Medicine*] (DMAA)
MOP...........	Major Overhaul Program [*Navy*]
MOP...........	Manned Orbital Platform
MOP...........	Manner of Performance [*Officer rating*]
MOP...........	Manual of Practice (GNE)
MOP...........	Manual Operations Panel
MOP...........	Manual Override Panel (AAG)
MOP...........	Manufacturers Output Policy [*Insurance*]
MOP...........	Manuscript on Paper
MOP...........	Margin of Profit [*Accounting*]
MOP...........	Master Operating Panel (CAAL)

MOP...........	Matrix Operations Programming
MOP...........	Measures of Performance (MCD)
MOP...........	Medical Outpatient
mop...........	Medical Outpatient (AD)
M o P	Member of Parliament [*British*] (AD)
MOP...........	Member of Parliament [*British*]
MOP...........	Memorandum of Policy
MOP...........	Memory Organization Packet [*Artificial intelligence*]
MOP...........	Message Output Processing
MOP...........	Methallyloxyphenol
MOP...........	Method of Procedure [*Telecommunications*] (ITD)
MOP...........	Methoxypsoralen [*Also, MP*] [*Pharmacology*]
MOP...........	Migrant Opportunity Program [*Department of Labor*]
MOP...........	Military Operation (GFGA)
MOP...........	Minimum Ordered Partition
MOP...........	Ministerio de Obras Publicas [*Ministry of Public Works*] [*Spanish*] (AD)
M o P	Minister of Pensions [*British*] (AD)
M o P	Minister of Power [*British*] (AD)
M o P	Minister of Production [*British*] (AD)
MOP...........	Ministry of Pensions [*British*]
MOP...........	Ministry of Power [*British*]
MOP...........	Ministry of Production [*British*]
MOP...........	Minute of Program [*Broadcasting*] (NTCM)
MOP...........	Mission Operations Plan (MCD)
MOP...........	Mobility Operating Procedure [*Military*] (AFM)
MOP...........	Model Office Project
MOP...........	Model Operational Plan
MOP...........	Mode of Operation
MOP...........	Modify Operating Procedures (AAEL)
MOP...........	Modular Operating Procedure (MUGU)
MOP...........	Modulation on the Pulse (NG)
MOP...........	Monarch Peak [*California*] [*Seismograph station code, US Geological Survey*] (SEIS)
MOP...........	Mother-of-Pearl
mop...........	Mother of Pearl (AD)
MOP...........	Mount Pleasant, MI [*Location identifier FAA*] (FAAL)
MOP...........	Mouvement d'Organisation du Pays [*Haiti*] [*Political party*] (EY)
MOP...........	Mouvement Ouvriers-Paysans [*Workers' and Peasants' Movement*] [*Haiti*] (PD)
MOP...........	Mouvement pour l'Ordre et la Paix [*Movement for Order and Peace*] [*New Caledonia*] [*Political party*] (PD)
MOP...........	Multiple Online Processing (NITA)
MOP...........	Multiple Online Programming [*Computer science*] (DIT)
MOP...........	Multiple Output Program (MCD)
MOP...........	Muriate of Potash [*Fertilizer*]
MOP...........	Mustard, Onions, Pickles [*Restaurant slang*]
MOP...........	Mustargen [*Nitrogen mustard*], Oncovin , Prednisone [*Vincristine*] [*Antineoplastic drug regimen*]
MOP...........	Mustering-Out Pay [*Military*]
mop...........	Mustering-Out Pay (AD)
MOP...........	, Procarbazine [*Vincristine*] [*Antineoplastic drug regimen*]
MOP...........	St. Louis College of Pharmacy, St. Louis, MO [*OCLC symbol*] (OCLC)
MOPA	Mail Order Publisher Authority (PDAA)
mopa	Master Oscillator Power Amplifier (AD)
MOPA	Master Oscillator Power Amplifier [*Radio*]
MOPA	Method of Physical Action [*Acting technique*] (WDAA)
MOPA	Methoxyphenylacetic Acid [*Herbicide*]
MOPA	Methoxypropylamine [*Organic chemistry*]
MOPA	Modus Operandi - Personal Appearance [*FBI computer procedure*]
MOPA	Museum of Photographic Arts [*San Diego*] (AD)
MOPAC	Methoxyhydroxyphenylacetic Acid [*Organic chemistry*]
MOPAC	Missouri Pacific Railroad Co.
MoPac	Missouri Pacific - Texas & Pacific (AD)
MOPAC	Mixed Oligonucleotide Primed Amplification of cDNA [*Biochemistry*]
MOPALI	Movimiento Paraguayo de Liberacion [*Political party*] (EY)
MOPAR	Master Oscillator Power Amplifier RADAR
mopar	Master Oscillator-Power Amplifier RADAR (AD)
MOPAR	Motor Parts [*Chrysler Corp.*]
MoParkC	Park College, Parkville, MO [*Library symbol Library of Congress*] (LCLS)
MOPB	Manually Operated Plotting Board
mopb	Manually Operated Plotting Board (AD)
MOPB	Metallo-Organic Petroleum-Based Coating [*Materials science*]
MOP-BAP....	Mustargen [*Nitrogen mustard*], Oncovin , Procarbazine, Bleomycin, Adriamycin, Prednisone [*Vincristine*] [*Antineoplastic drug regimen*]
Mo PC	Moore's English Privy Council Reports [*A publication*] (DLA)
MOPC........	Mouse Plasmocytoma [*Cell line*]
MOPCOM....	Matrix Operations Programming Combination of Estimates
MOPD	Maximum Operating Pressure Differential (ECII)
MOPE..........	Method of Personnel Evaluation
MOPE..........	Multiple Object Parameter Estimation
MOPED	Ministry of Planning and Economic Development [*Ethiopia*] (ECON)
MOPED	Motor/Pedal [*Motorized bicycle*]
mopeds........	Motorized Pedals (AD)
MOPEG	(Methoxyhydroxyphenyl)ethyleneglycol [*Also, MHPG*] [*Organic chemistry*]
MoPeS........	Saint Mary's Seminary, Perryville, MO [*Library symbol Library of Congress*] (LCLS)
MOPET........	Methoxyhydroxyphenylethanol [*Organic chemistry*]
MOPF	Missile Onloading Prism Fixture
mopf	Missile Onloading Prism Fixture (AD)
MOPF	Mobile Optical Propagation Facility

MOPH	Military Order of the Purple Heart of the United States of America (EA)
MOPI	Maximum [*Rate*] Output Initiator
MOPI	Maximum Rate Output Initiator (NASA)
MOPIC	Motion Picture [*Army*] (AABC)
mopic	Motion Picture [*Military*] (WDMC)
MOPIMS	Mathematical, Optical, and Philosophical Instrument Makers' Society [*A union*] [*British*]
MOPITT	Measurements of Pollution in the Troposphere
MOPIX	Motion Pictures
MoPIS	School of the Ozarks, Point Lookout, MO [*Library symbol Library of Congress*] (LCLS)
MOPMS	Modular Pack Mine System (RDA)
MOPN	Methoxypropionitrile [*Organic chemistry*]
MoPobT	Three Rivers Community College, Poplar Bluff, MO [*Library symbol Library of Congress*] (LCLS)
MoPobV	United States Veterans Administration Hospital, Medical Library, Poplar Bluff, MO [*Library symbol Library of Congress*] (LCLS)
MOPOCO	Movimiento Popular Colorado [*Colorado Popular Movement*] [*Paraguay*] [*Political party*] (PD)
MOPP	Mechlorethamine, Oncovin, Procarbazine, Prednisone [*Medicine*] (MEDA)
MOPP	Methotrexate, Oncomycin, Prednisone, Procarbazine [*Antineoplastic drug regimen*] (DAVI)
MOPP	Military Operational Protective Posture [*Chemical warfare*] (RDA)
MOPP	Mission-Oriented Protection Posture [*Army*] (AABC)
MOPP	Mission Oriented Protective Posture [*Gear*] [*USA*]
MOPP	Modular Operating Procedure (MUGU)
MOPP	Mustargen hydrochloride, Oncovin [*Vincristine*], Procarbazine, Prednisone [*Antineoplastic drug regimen*]
MOPP	Mustargen [*Nitrogen mustard*], Oncovin , Procarbazine, Prednisone [*Vincristine*] [*Antineoplastic drug regimen*]
MOPP	Mustine, Oncovin [*Vincristine*] Procarbazine, Prednisone [*Antineoplastic drug regimen*] (DAVI)
MOPP/ABV	Mustargen [*Nitrogen mustard*], Oncovin , Procarbazine, Prednisone, Adriamycin, Bleomycin, Vinblastine [*Vincristine*] [*Antineoplastic drug regimen*]
MOPP/ABVD	Mechlorethamine, Oncovin [*Vincristine*] Procarbazine, Prednisone, Doxo rubicin, Bleomycin, Vinblastine, Dacarbazine [*Antineoplastic drug regimen*] (DAVI)
MOPP-BLEO	Mustargen [*Nitrogen mustard*], Oncovin , Procarbazine, Prednisone, Bleomycin [*Vincristine*] [*Antineoplastic drug regimen*]
MOPPCPF	Mustargen [*Nitrogen mustard*], Oncovin , Procarbazine, Prednisone (for Patients with Compromised Pulmonary Function) [*Vincristine*] [*Antineoplastic drug regimen*]
MOPPE	Modified Operational Propulsion Plan Examination [*Navy*] (NVT)
MOPPHDB	Mustargen [*Nitrogen mustard*], Oncovin , Procarbazine, Prednisone, High-Dose Bleomycin [*Vincristine*] [*Antineoplastic drug regimen*]
MOPPLDB	Mustargen [*Nitrogen mustard*], Oncovin , Procarbazine, Prednisone, Low-DoseBleomycin [*Vincristine*] [*Antineoplastic drug regimen*]
MOPP-LO BLEO	Mechlorethamine [*Vincristine*] Procarbazine, Prednisone, Bleomycin [*Antineoplastic drug regimen*] (DAVI)
mopr	Manner of Performance Rating (AD)
MOPR	Manner of Performing Rating
MOPR	Mission Operations Planning Review [*NASA*] (NASA)
MOPR	Mission Operations Planning Room (MCD)
MOPR	Mop Rack
mopr	Mop Rack (AD)
MOPr	Mustargen [*Nitrogen mustard*], Oncovin , Procarbazine [*Vincristine*] [*Antineoplastic drug regimen*]
MOPr	, Prednisone [*Vincristine*] [*Antineoplastic drug regimen*]
Mo Prec	Moile's Precedents [*A publication*] (DLA)
moprl	Mother-of-Pearl (VRA)
MOPS	Mail-Order Protection Scheme [*British*]
MOPS	Maneuver Operations Program System [*NASA*]
MOPS	Man-Operated Propulsion System
MOPS	Marine Oil Pickup Service [*Marine science*] (MSC)
MOPS	Maritime Officer Production Study [*Canadian Navy*]
MOPS	Mechanization Outside Plant Scheduling System (MHDB)
MOPS	Mechanized Outdoor Planning System
MOPS	Merchandise Ordering Processing System (AD)
MOPS	Microwave Optical-Photoselection Microscopy
MOPS	Military Operation Phone System
MOPS	Million Operations per Second [*Processing power units*] [*Computer science*]
MOPS	Minimum Operational Performance Standard [*Aviation*] (DA)
MOPS	Missile Operations
MOPS	Missile Operations Paging [*or Phone*] System [*NASA*]
MOPS	Missile Operations System (AD)
MOPS	Mission Operations Planning System [*NASA*] (KSC)
MOPS	Morpholinopropanesulfonic Acid [*A buffer*]
MOPS	Mothers of Preschoolers International (PAZ)
MOPS	Multispectral Opium Poppy Sensor System
MO PSC	Missouri Public Service Commission Reports [*A publication*] (DLA)
MO PSC (NS)	Missouri Public Service Commission Reports (New Series) [*A publication*] (DLA)
MO PSCR	Missouri Public Service Commission Reports [*A publication*] (DLA)
MOPSS	Management & Operation of Public Services Section [*Reference and User Services Association*] [*American Library Association*]
MOPSS	Multispectral Opium Poppy Sensor System (AD)
MOPSY	Multi-Programming Operating System [*Computer science*] (PDAA)
MOpt	Master of Optometry (GAGS)
MOPT	Mean One Way Propagation Time [*Telecommunications*] (TEL)
MOPTAR	Multiobject Phase Tracking and Ranging [*FAA*]
MOPTARS	Multi-Object Phase-Tracking and Ranging System [*FAA*] (PDAA)
MOPTE	Measure of Potential Training Effectiveness [*Army*]
MOptom	Master of Optometry (ADA)
MOPTS	Mobile Photographic Tracking Station (IEEE)
MO PUR	Missouri Public Utility Reports [*A publication*] (DLA)
MOPV	Monovalent Oral Polio Vaccine [*Immunology*]
MOPW	Ministry of Population Welfare [*Pakistan*] (ECON)
MOQ	Fort Stewart (Hinesville), GA [*Location identifier FAA*] (FAAL)
MOQ	Lindenwood College, St. Charles, MO [*OCLC symbol*] (OCLC)
MOQ	Married Officer Quarters
MOQ	Minimum Order Quantity (MCD)
MOQ	Morocco Explorations [*Vancouver Stock Exchange symbol*]
MOQ	Morondava [*Madagascar*] [*Airport symbol*] (OAG)
MOR	AS Morefly [*Norway ICAO designator*] (FAAC)
MOR	Magneto-Optical Rotation
MOR	Management Operating Ratios (NG)
MOR	Mandatory Occurrence Reporting
MOR	Manufacturing Operation Record (NASA)
MOR	Market Opinion Research, Inc. [*Information service or system*] (IID)
MOR	Mars Orbital Rendezvous
MOR	Master of Operations Research (PGP)
M Or	Master of Oratory
MOR	Maximum Ozone Reactivity [*Exhaust emissions*] [*Automotive engineering*]
MOR	Medical Officer Report [*Navy*] (NG)
MOR	Memorandum of Record (COE)
MOR	Memory Output Register [*Computer science*]
MOR	Merchandising and Operating Results
MOR	Meteorological Optical Range (PDAA)
MOR	Middle of the Road [*Broadcasting*]
mor	Middle of the Road (AD)
MOR	Mid-Oceanic Ridge
MOR	Military Operations Research
M o R	Ministry of Reconstruction [*British*] (AD)
MOR	Missile Operationally Ready [*Air Force*]
MOR	Mission Operations Room (MCD)
MOR	Missions Operations Report [*NASA*] (KSC)
MO R	Missouri Reports [*A publication*] (DLA)
MOR	Modulus of Rupture [*Mechanics*]
MOR	Monthly Operating Report (IEEE)
MOR	Monthly Operating Review (USDC)
MOR	Moral (ROG)
Mor	Moralia [*of Plutarch*] [*Classical studies*] (OCD)
MOR	Moravian College, Bethlehem, PA [*OCLC symbol*] (OCLC)
MOR	Moray [*County in Scotland*] (ROG)
MOR	Mordenite [*A zeolite*]
Mor	Morelia (AD)
Mor	Morelos (AD)
mor	Morendo [*Dying Away*] [*Italian*] (AD)
MOR	Morendo [*Gradually Softer*] [*Music*]
MOR	Morgan Keegan & Co., Inc. [*NYSE symbol*] (SPSG)
MOR	Morgan Keegan Inc. [*NYSE symbol*] (TTSB)
MOR	Morgan, M. B., Glen Burnie MD [*STAC*]
MOR	Morgan Owners Register (EA)
MOR	Mori [*Japan*] [*Seismograph station code, US Geological Survey Closed*] (SEIS)
Mor	Morisco (AD)
Mor	Morison's Dictionary of Decisions, Scotch Court of Session [*1540-1808*] [*A publication*] (DLA)
MOR	Morning Star Resources [*Vancouver Stock Exchange symbol*]
Mor	Moroccan (AD)
mor	Morocco (AD)
MOR	Morocco
MOR	Morocco Leather [*Bookbinding*] (ROG)
MOR	Morphine [*A narcotic*]
MOR	Morpholine [*Organic chemistry*]
Mor	Morris' Reports [*Jamaica*] [*A publication*] (ILCA)
MOR	Morristown, TN [*Location identifier FAA*] (FAAL)
MOR	Mortality Odds Ratio
MOR	Mortar
mor	Mortar (AD)
MOR	Movimiento Obrero Revolucionario Salvado Cayetano Carpio [*El Salvador*] [*Political party*] (EY)
MOR	Museum of the Rockies [*Montana, USA*]
MORA	Mandibular Orthopedic Repositioning Appliance [*Dentistry*]
MORA	Mimimum Off-Route Altitude [*Aviation*] (DA)
MORA	Mount Rainier National Park
MORAB	Morgan and Arabian [*Type of horse developed from these two breeds*] [*Acronym is also said to stand for "Muscular, Outstanding, Refined, Athletic, Beautiful," the horse's distinguishing characteristics*]
MORAL	Massachusetts Organization for the Repeal of Abortion Laws
Mor & Carl	Moreau-Lislet and Carleton's Laws of Las Siete Partidas in Force in Louisiana [*A publication*] (DLA)
MORASS	Modern Ramjet System Synthesis (MCD)
Morav	Moravia (AD)
MORB	Mid-Ocean Ridge Basalt [*Geology*]
Morb	Morbihan (AD)
MORBREPT	Morbidity Report
MORBTGREPT	Morbidity Telegraphic Report
MORC	Medical Officers' Reserve Corps
MORC	Midget Ocean Racing Class [*or Club*]
Mor Chy Acts	Morgan's Chancery Acts and Orders [*6th ed.*] [*1885*] [*A publication*] (DLA)
MORCO	Morrison, Inc. (EFIS)
Mor Comp	Morris on Compensations [*A publication*] (DLA)

Mor Corp ..... Morawetz on Private Corporations [*A publication*] (DLA)
MORD .... Magneto-Optic Rotary Dispersion (PDAA)
MORD .... Medical Operations Requirements Document (MCD)
MORD .... Military Operations Research Department
MORD .... Ministry of Revolutionary Development [*Vietnam*]
MORD .... Mission Operations Requirements Document [*NASA*] (NASA)
Mord .... Mordehai (AD)
Mordhy .... Mordehai (AD)
Mor Dic .... Morison's Dictionary of Decisions, Scotch Court of Session [*1540-1808*] [*A publication*] (DLA)
mor dict .... More Dicto [*As Directed*] [*Latin*] (AD)
Mor Dict ...... Morison's Dictionary of Decisions, Scotch Court of Session [*1540-1808*] [*A publication*] (DLA)
MOR DICT ... Moro Dicto [*As Directed*] [*Pharmacy*]
Mor Dig .... Morley's Digest of the Indian Reports [*A publication*] (DLA)
Mor Dig .... Morrison's New Hampshire Digest [*A publication*] (DLA)
Mor Dil .... Morris on Dilapidations [*2nd ed.*] [*1871*] [*A publication*] (DLA)
MORDS .... Manned Orbital Research and Development System
MORDT .... Mobilization Operational Readiness Deployment Test [*DoD*]
Mordy .... Mordechai (AD)
MORE .... Management of Radiographic Environments [*Radiology*] (DAVI)
MORE .... Meal, Ordered Ready-to-Eat [*Army*] (RDA)
MORE .... Microbial Oil Recovery Enhancement [*Petroleum technology*]
MORE .... Midwest Organization for Research in Education (AEBS)
MORE .... Military Officer Record Examination
MORE .... Minority Officer Recruitment Effort
MORE .... Mission for Outreach, Renewal, and Evangelism (AD)
MORE .... Money, Opportunity, Responsibility, and Equality [*Of organization "MORE for Women"*]
MORE .... Multioptical Reconnaissance Equipment [*Military*] (CAAL)
Mor E & RD Law... Morice's English and Roman Dutch Law [*A publication*] (DLA)
Mor Eas .... Morris on the Law of Easements [*A publication*] (DLA)
Moreau & Carleton's Partidas... Moreau-Lislet and Carleton's Laws of Las Siete Partidas in Force in Louisiana [*A publication*] (DLA)
MORE DICT... More Dicto [*As Directed*] [*Pharmacy*] (ROG)
Morehead St U... Morehead State University (GAGS)
Morehouse Sch of Med... Morehouse School of Medicine (GAGS)
MOREL .... Michigan-Ohio Regional Educational Laboratory
More Lect .... More's Lectures on the Law of Scotland [*A publication*] (DLA)
MORENA ...... Mouvement de Redressement National [*Gabon*] [*Political party*] (EY)
MORENA ...... Movimiento de Renovacion Nacional [*National Renewal Movement*] [*Venezuela Political party*] (PPW)
MORENA ...... Movimiento de Restauracion Nacional [*National Restoration Movement*] [*Colorado Political party*] (EY)
MORENET .... Missouri Research and Education Network
MO Rep .... Missouri Reports [*A publication*] (DLA)
MOREP .... Monthly Report
MOREPS ...... Monitor Station Reports
moreps .... Monitor Station Reports (AD)
MORES .... Minerals, Oils, and Resources Shares Fund [*British*]
MORE SOL... More Solito [*In the Usual Way*] [*Pharmacy*] (ROG)
MOREST ...... Mobile Arresting Gear [*Navy*]
More St .... More's Notes on Stair's Institutes of Scotland [*A publication*] (DLA)
MORET .... Moreton [*England*]
MO Rev Stat... Missouri Revised Statutes [*A publication*] (DLA)
Morey Out Rom Law... Morey's Outlines of Roman Law [*A publication*] (DLA)
MORF .... Male or Female (NHD)
MorF .... Male or Female
MORF .... Manned Orbital Research Facility [*NASA*] (MCD)
mor fib .... Moral Fiber (AD)
MORG .... Morgan Financial Corp. [*NASDAQ symbol*] (SAG)
MORG .... Morgan Finl (Del) [*NASDAQ symbol*] (TTSB)
Morg .... Morgan's Chancery Acts and Orders [*6th ed.*] [*1885*] [*A publication*] (DLA)
MORG .... Movements Reports Generator (DNAB)
MORG .... Museo Oceanografico de Rio Grande [*Oceanographic Museum of Rio Grande*] [*Brazil*] (AD)
MORGA .... Municipal Organization Act (DICI)
Morgan .... Morgan [*J. P.*] & Co., Inc. [*Associated Press*] (SAG)
Morgan .... Morgan's Digest [*Ceylon*] [*A publication*] (DLA)
Morg & Ch Jud Acts... Morgan and Chute on the Judicature Acts [*A publication*] (DLA)
Morg & WLJ... Morgan and Williams' Law Journal [*London*] [*A publication*] (DLA)
Morgan LM... Morgan's Legal Miscellany [*Ceylon*] [*A publication*] (DLA)
Morgan St U... Morgan State University (GAGS)
Morg Ch ...... Morgan's Chancery Acts and Orders [*6th ed.*] [*1885*] [*A publication*] (DLA)
MorgFn .... Morgan Financial Corp. [*Associated Press*] (SAG)
MorgFun ...... Morgan Funshares, Inc. [*Associated Press*] (SAG)
MorgGr .... Morgan Grenfell Smallcap Fund, Inc. [*Associated Press*] (SAG)
MorgK .... Morgan Keegan [*Associated Press*] (SAG)
MorgKeg .... Morgan Keegan & Co., Inc. [*Associated Press*] (SAG)
Morg Lit .... Morgan on the Law of Literature [*A publication*] (DLA)
morg mar .... Morganatic Marriage (AD)
Morgn .... Morgan [*J. P.*] & Co., Inc. [*Associated Press*] (SAG)
MorgnF .... Morgan's Foods, Inc. [*Associated Press*] (SAG)
MorgnP .... Morgan Products Ltd. [*Associated Press*] (SAG)
MorgSt .... Morgan Stanley Group, Inc. [*Associated Press*] (SAG)
Morg Tar ..... Morgan on the United States Tariff [*A publication*] (DLA)
Mor Hors ..... Morrell on the Law of Horses [*A publication*] (DLA)
MORI .... Market and Opinion Research International [*Polling organization*]
Mori .... Market and Opinion Research International [*Polling organization*] (ODBW)
Mor IA .... Morris' Iowa Reports [*1839-46*] [*A publication*] (DLA)
MORIE .... Metalorganic Reactive Ion Etching (AAEL)
MORIF .... Microprogram Optimization Technique Considering Resource Occupancy and Instruction Formats (MHDB)
MoRih .... Richmond Heights Memorial Library, Richmond Heights, MO [*Library symbol Library of Congress*] (LCLS)
MORITZER... Mortar Howitzer (NATG)
moritzer .... Mortar Howitzer (AD)
MorKnd .... Morrison-Knudsen Co., Inc. [*Associated Press*] (SAG)
MORL .... Manned Orbital [*or Orbiting*] Research Laboratory [*NASA*]
MORL .... Medium-Sized Orbital Research Laboratory (SAA)
Morl Dig ...... Morley's East Indian Digest [*A publication*] (DLA)
Mor Lib .... Morgan Library (AD)
Mor M .... Master Mortician
MORM .... Mormon (WDAA)
Morm .... Mormon (AD)
MoRM .... University of Missouri at Rolla, Rolla, MO [*Library symbol Library of Congress*] (LCLS)
Mor Maj ...... Moral Majority (AD)
Mor Min Rep... Morrison's Mining Reports [*A publication*] (DLA)
Mor Miss ..... Morris' Reports [*Mississippi*] [*A publication*] (DLA)
MORN .... Morning
morn .... Morning (AD)
MornGp .... Morningstar Group [*Associated Press*] (SAG)
Morningside C... Morningside College (GAGS)
Moro .... Book of Moroni (AD)
Moro .... Morocco (VRA)
MORO .... Morocco Leather [*Bookbinding*] (ROG)
Moroc .... Moroccan (AD)
MORP .... Medical and Occupational Radiation Program [*HEW*]
MORP .... Meteorite Observation and Recovery Project [*Canada*]
MORP .... Mid-Ocean Ridge Peridotite [*Geology*]
MORP .... Moore Products [*NASDAQ symbol*] (TTSB)
MORP .... Moore Products Co. [*NASDAQ symbol*] (NQ)
MORPH .... Morphine (WDAA)
morph .... Morphine (AD)
morph .... Morphology (AD)
MORPH .... Morphology
Morphing ..... Metamorphosizing [*Video technology*]
MORPHOL ... Morphology
morphophysio... Morphophysiological (AD)
MORPHS ...... Minicomputer-Operated Retrieval (Partially Heuristic) System [*Computer science*]
Mor Pr .... Morehead's Practice [*A publication*] (DLA)
Mor Priv Corp... Morawetz on Private Corporations [*A publication*] (DLA)
MORPS .... Maritime Other Ranks Production Study [*Canadian Navy*]
MorR .... Bibliotheque Generale et Archives, Rabat, Morocco [*Library symbol Library of Congress*] (LCLS)
Morr .... Morrell's English Bankruptcy Reports [*A publication*] (DLA)
Morr .... Morris' Iowa Reports [*1839-46*] [*A publication*] (DLA)
Morr .... Morris' Jamaica Reports [*A publication*] (DLA)
Morr .... Morris' Reports [*California*] [*A publication*] (DLA)
Morr .... Morris' Reports [*Bombay, India*] [*A publication*] (DLA)
Morr .... Morris' Reports [*Oregon*] [*A publication*] (DLA)
MORR .... Morristown National Historical Park
Morr Bankr Cas... Morrell's English Bankruptcy Cases [*A publication*] (DLA)
Morr BC .... Morrell's English Bankruptcy Reports [*A publication*] (DLA)
Morr Bomb... Morris' Reports [*Bombay, India*] [*A publication*] (DLA)
Morr Cal ...... Morris' Reports [*California*] [*A publication*] (DLA)
Morr Dict ..... Morrison's Dictionary of Decisions, Scotch Court of Session [*A publication*] (DLA)
Morr Dig ...... Morrison's Digest of Mining Decisions [*A publication*] (DLA)
Morr Dig ...... Morrison's New Hampshire Digest [*A publication*] (DLA)
Morrell Bankr Cas... Morrell's English Bankruptcy Cases [*A publication*] (DLA)
Morrell BC... Morrell's English Bankruptcy Cases [*A publication*] (DLA)
Morrell (Eng)... Morrell's English Bankruptcy Cases [*A publication*] (DLA)
Mor Rep ...... Morris' Law of Replevin [*A publication*] (DLA)
Morris .... Morris' Iowa Reports [*1839-46*] [*A publication*] (DLA)
Morris .... Morris' Jamaica Reports [*A publication*] (DLA)
Morris .... Morris' Reports [*Mississippi*] [*A publication*] (DLA)
Morris .... Morris' Reports [*Oregon*] [*A publication*] (DLA)
Morris .... Morris' Reports [*Bombay, India*] [*A publication*] (DLA)
Morris .... Morris' Reports [*California*] [*A publication*] (DLA)
Morris .... Morrissett's Reports [*80, 98 Alabama*] [*A publication*] (DLA)
Morris & Har... Morris and Harrington's Reports [*Bombay, India*] [*A publication*] (DLA)
Morris (IA)... Morris' Iowa Reports [*1839-46*] [*A publication*] (DLA)
Morris (Iowa)... Morris' Iowa Reports [*1839-46*] [*A publication*] (DLA)
Morrison ...... Morrison Restaurants, Inc. [*Associated Press*] (SAG)
Morrison Min Rep... Morrison's Mining Reports [*United States*] [*A publication*] (DLA)
Morris R ...... Morris' Jamaica Reports [*A publication*] (DLA)
Morris Repl... Morris on Replevin [*A publication*] (DLA)
Morris St Cas... Morris' Mississippi State Cases [*1818-72*] [*A publication*] (DLA)
Morr Jam ..... Morris' Jamaica Reports [*A publication*] (DLA)
MorrKn .... Morrison Knudsen Corp. [*Associated Press*] (SAG)
MorrKnud .... Morrison Knudsen Corp. [*Associated Press*] (SAG)
Morr Mines... Morrison's Digest of Mining Decisions [*A publication*] (DLA)
Morr Min R... Morrison's Mining Reports [*United States*] [*A publication*] (DLA)
Morr Min Rep... Morrison's Mining Reports [*A publication*] (DLA)
Morr Miss .... Morris' Reports [*Mississippi*] [*A publication*] (DLA)
Morr MR ...... Morrison's Mining Reports [*United States*] [*A publication*] (DLA)
MorrowSn .... Morrow Snowboards, Inc. [*Associated Press*] (SAG)
Morr Repl .... Morris' Law of Replevin [*A publication*] (DLA)
Morr St Cas... Morris' Mississippi State Cases [*1818-72*] [*A publication*] (DLA)
Morr Trans... Morrison's Transcript of United States Supreme Court Decisions [*A publication*] (DLA)

Mor Ry Com...   Morris on Railway Compensations [*A publication*] (DLA)
MORS.........   Midland Operational Research Society (AD)
MORS.........   Military Operations Research Society (EA)
MORS.........   Military Operations Research Symposia (MCD)
MORS.........   Multi-Outlet Reservoir Study [*Department of the Interior*] (GRD)
mor sal........   More Solito [*In the Usual Manner*] [*Latin*] (AD)
M Or Sc...   Master of the Science of Oratory
MORSEAFRON...   Moroccan Sea Frontier [*Navy World War II*]
Morse Arb ...   Morse on the Law of Arbitration and Award [*A publication*] (DLA)
Morse Banks...   Morse on the Law of Banks and Banking [*A publication*] (DLA)
Morse Bk.....   Morse on the Law of Banks and Banking [*A publication*] (DLA)
Morse Exch Rep...   Morse's Exchequer Reports [*Canada*] [*A publication*] (DLA)
MorSEm.......   Morgan Stanley Emerging Markets [*Associated Press*] (SAG)
Morse Tr......   Morse's Famous Trials [*A publication*] (DLA)
MORSL........   Mobilization Reserve Stockage List [*Army*] (AABC)
MorsnFr.......   Morrison Fresh Cooking, Inc. [*Associated Press*] (SAG)
MorsnHl......   Morrison Health Care, Inc. [*Associated Press*] (SAG)
mor sol........   More Solito [*In the usual manner*] [*Latin*] [*Pharmacy*] (DAVI)
MOR SOL.....   More Solito [*In the Usual Way*] [*Pharmacy*]
Mor St Ca ...   Morris' Mississippi State Cases [*1818-72*] [*A publication*] (DLA)
Mor St Cas...   Morris' Mississippi State Cases [*1818-72*] [*A publication*] (DLA)
Mor Supp....   Morison's Dictionary of Decisions, Scotch Court of Session, Supplement [*1620-1768*] [*A publication*] (DLA)
Mor Syn.......   Morison's Synopsis, Scotch Session Cases [*1808-16*] [*A publication*] (DLA)
moRt..........   Mainstream of Republican Thought (AD)
MORT ....   Management Oversight and Risk Tree (NASA)
MORT ....   Master Operational Recording Tape [*SAGE*]
MORT ....   Missile Operation [*or Ordnance*] Readiness Test [*or Testing*]
MORT ....   Morse Taper
mor t ....   Morse Taper (AD)
mort...........   Mortal (AD)
mort...........   Mortality
MORT ....   Mortar (AABC)
mort...........   Mortar (AD)
Mort..........   Mortemart (AD)
mort..........   Mortgage (AD)
MORT ....   Mortgage (ADA)
mort..........   Mortician (AD)
MORT ....   Mortician
Mort..........   Mortimer (AD)
Mort..........   Morton (AD)
MORT ....   Mortuary (ADA)
MORTAL ......   Mortality (BABM)
mortal........   Mortality [*Statistics*] (DAVI)
MORTG........   Mortgage
MortnRst.....   Mortons Restaurant Group [*Associated Press*] (SAG)
Morton..........   Morton's Reports, Calcutta Superior Court [*India*] [*A publication*] (DLA)
Morton Int ...   Morton International, Inc. [*Associated Press*] (SAG)
Mor Tran .....   Morrison's Transcript of United States Supreme Court Decisions [*A publication*] (DLA)
MORTREP....   Mortar Bombing Report
Mort Vend ...   Morton's Vendors and Purchasers [*1837*] [*A publication*] (DLA)
MORU..........   Mount Rushmore National Memorial
MORV ....   Mobile Overpass Roadway-Repair Vehicle
Mor Wills ....   Morrell on the Law of Wills [*A publication*] (DLA)
Mos ....   Book of Mosiah (AD)
Mos ....   De Vita Mosis [*Philo*] (BJA)
MOS...........   Machinery and Occupational Safety Act [*Environmental science*]
MOS...........   Magneto-Optical System (AD)
MOS...........   Mail-Order Sales (WDAA)
MOS...........   Maintenance Operations Section [*Marine Corps*] (DOMA)
MOS...........   Major Operating System [*Army*] (AABC)
MOS...........   Management Operating System
MOS...........   Management Operations Staff [*Environmental Protection Agency*] (GFGA)
MOS...........   Management Orientation School [*LIMRA*]
MOS...........   Manned Orbital Station (AAG)
MOS...........   Man on the Street (WDMC)
MOS...........   Man-on-the-Street Interview [*Journalism*]
MOS...........   Manual Override Switch
MOS...........   Manufacturing Operating System [*IBM Corp.*]
MOS...........   Manufacturing Operations Survey (MCD)
MOS...........   Margin of Safety [*Business term*]
MOS...........   Marine Observation Satellite [*Japan*]
MOS...........   Marine Occupational Standard (DNAB)
MOS...........   Maritime Operational Intelligence Summary (MCD)
MOS...........   Marking of Overseas Shipments
MOS...........   Master Operating System [*Sperry UNIVAC*]
MOS...........   Material Ordering Schedule
MOS...........   Mathematical Off-Print Service [*American Mathematical Society*]
MOS...........   Mean Opinion Score
MOS...........   Measurement of Skill (AEBS)
MOS...........   Measure of Suitability (CAAL)
MOS...........   Mechanical Oblique Sketcher
MOS...........   Medial Orbital Sulcus (DB)
MOS...........   Medical Outcomes Study (DMAA)
MOS...........   Memory Operating Software [*Computer science*]
MOS...........   Memory-Oriented System
MOS...........   Mercantile Open Stock
MOS...........   Mesa Offshore Trust (EFIS)
MOS...........   Metal Oxide on a Substrate (MCD)
MOS...........   Metal-Oxide Semiconductor
mos ....   Metal-Oxide Semiconductor (AD)

mos ....   Metal-Oxide Silicon (AD)
MOS...........   Metal-Oxide-Silicon [*Integrated circuit*] [*Electronics*]
MOS...........   Microprogram Operating System
MOS...........   Microsomal Ethanol-Oxidizing System (DMAA)
mos ....   Military Occupational Specialty (AD)
MOS...........   Military Occupational Specialty [*Army*]
MOS...........   Military Occupational Specification Serial Number [*British World War II*]
MOS...........   Military Oceanography Subcommittee [*National Security Industrial Association*] (USDC)
MOS...........   Military Overseas Supply [*British*]
mOs...........   Milliosmole [*or Milliosmolar*] (AAMN)
MOS...........   Minimum Operating System [*Sperry Univac*] (NITA)
MOS...........   Ministry of State [*British*]
MOS...........   Ministry of Supply [*Also, MS*] [*British*]
MOS...........   Minus Optical Sound [*Film industry*]
MOS...........   MISR Overseas Airways [*Egypt*] [*ICAO designator*] (FAAC)
MOS...........   Missile on Stand
mos ....   Missile On Stand (AD)
MOS...........   Missile Operations Station
MOS...........   Mission Operations Strategy [*NASA*]
MOS...........   Mission Operations System [*NASA*]
MOS...........   Mit Out Sound [*i.e., "without sound"*] [*Film industry*]
mos ....   Mit-Out Sound (AD)
MOS...........   Mitral Opening Sound [*Cardiology*]
MOS...........   Model Output Statistics [*Meteorology*]
MOS...........   Modular Operating System (BUR)
MOS...........   Moloney Murine Sarcoma [*Medicine*] (DMAA)
mos ....   Months (AD)
MOS...........   Months
MOS...........   Morton Air Services Ltd.
MOS...........   Mosaic
mos ....   Mosaic (VRA)
Mos ....   Mosca [*Moscow*] [*Italian*] (AD)
Mos ....   Moscou [*Moscow*] [*French*] (AD)
Mos ....   Moscow (AD)
MOS...........   Moscow [*Russia*] [*Seismograph station code, US Geological Survey*] (SEIS)
Mos ....   Moscu [*Moscow*] [*Spanish*] (AD)
Mos ....   Moseley's English Chancery Reports [*25 English Reprint*] [*A publication*] (DLA)
Mos ....   Mosella [*of Ausonius*] [*Classical studies*] (OCD)
MOS...........   Moses Point, AK [*Location identifier FAA*] (FAAL)
Mos ....   Moshe (AD)
Mos ....   Moskau [*Moscow*] [*German*] (AD)
Mos ....   Moskou [*Moscow*] [*Dutch*] (AD)
Mos ....   Moslem (AD)
MOS...........   Mosport Park Corp. [*Vancouver Stock Exchange symbol*]
mos ....   Mossi [*MARC language code Library of Congress*] (LCCP)
MOS...........   Multiple Object Spectroscopy (PDAA)
MOS...........   Multiprogramming Operating System
MoS...........   Museum of Sydney [*Australia*]
MOS...........   Myelofibrosis Osteosclerosis [*Medicine*] (DMAA)
MOS...........   Springfield-Greene County Library, Springfield, MO [*OCLC symbol*] (OCLC)
MoS...........   St. Louis Public Library, St. Louis, MO [*Library symbol Library of Congress*] (LCLS)
MOSA ....   Medical Officers of Schools Associations [*British*]
MOSA ....   Method of Standard Addition [*Statistics*]
MOSA ....   Minimum Operational Safe Altitude (DOMA)
MOSA ....   Ministry of Science and Arts [*US and Israel*]
MoSAB........   Anheuser-Busch, Inc., St. Louis, MO [*Library symbol Library of Congress*] (LCLS)
MOSAIC ......   Macro Operation Symbolic Assembler and Information Compiler [*Computer science*] (IEEE)
MOSAIC ......   Metal-Oxide-Semiconductor Advanced Integrated Circuit [*Electronics*] (IEEE)
MOSAIC ......   Method of Scenic Alternative Impacts by Computer (PDAA)
MOSAIC ......   Ministry of Supply Automatic Integrator and Computer [*British*] (DEN)
MOSAIC ......   Mobile System for Accurate ICBM Control (MCD)
MOSAICS .....   Melcom Optical Software Applications for Integrated Commercial Systems (PDAA)
MOSAR........   Modulation Scan Array RADAR [*or Receiver*]
MOSASR......   Metal Oxide Semiconductor Analogue Shift Register [*Electronics*] (PDAA)
MoSavHi......   Andrew County Historical Society, Savannah, MO [*Library symbol Library of Congress*] (LCLS)
MOSAW ....   Medium Operating Speed Automatic Weapon [*Military*]
MOSB ....   Military Order of the Stars and Bars (EA)
MoSB..........   Missouri Botanical Garden, St. Louis, MO [*Library symbol Library of Congress*] (LCLS)
Mosbas.......   Moscow Basin (AD)
MOSC ....   Management Orientation Study Course [*LIMRA*]
mosc..........   Manned Orbital Systems Concept (AD)
MOSC ....   Manned Orbital Systems Concepts [*NASA*]
MOS-C ....   Metal-Oxide Semiconductor Capacitor (AAEL)
MOSC ....   Midland-Odessa Symphony and Chorale (AD)
MOSC ....   Military Occupational Specialty Code (AABC)
MOSC ....   Military Oil Subcommittee [*of North African Economic Board*] [*World War II*]
MOSC ....   Mosaic
MOSCA ....   McNamara-O'Hara Service Contract Act of 1965 (WYGK)
MOSCAP......   Modified Service Contract and Procedures [*DoD*]

MoSCC......... St. Louis Community College, Instructional Resource Technical Services, St. Louis, MO [*Library symbol Library of Congress*] (LCLS)

MoSCEx....... Christ Seminary-Seminex, St. Louis, MO [*Library symbol Library of Congress*] (LCLS)

MoSCH........ Concordia Historical Institute, St. Louis, MO [*Library symbol Library of Congress*] (LCLS)

MOSCH........ Moschus [*Musk*] [*Pharmacology*] (ROG)

MoSCo......... St. Louis County Library, St. Louis, MO [*Library symbol Library of Congress*] (LCLS)

Moscom....... Moscom Corp. [*Associated Press*] (SAG)

Mos Cont..... Moseley's Contraband of War [*1861*] [*A publication*] (DLA)

MOSCOW.... Museum of Soviet Calculators on the Web [*Computer science*]

MoSCP........ St. Louis College of Pharmacy, St. Louis, MO [*Library symbol Library of Congress*] (LCLS)

MoSCRR...... Center for Reformation Research, St. Louis, MO [*Library symbol Library of Congress*] (LCLS)

MoSCS........ Concordia Seminary, St. Louis, MO [*Library symbol Library of Congress*] (LCLS)

MoSCT........ Covenant Theological Seminary, St. Louis, MO [*Library symbol Library of Congress*] (LCLS)

MoSDM........ United States Air Force, Defense Mapping Agency Aerospace Center, St. Louis, MO [*Library symbol Library of Congress*] (LCLS)

Mose .... Moises (AD)

Mose .... Moseley (AD)

Mose .... Mosen (AD)

Mose .... Moses (AD)

MoSe .... Sedalia Public Library, Sedalia, MO [*Library symbol Library of Congress*] (LCLS)

MoSE .... United States Army, Corps of Engineers, District Library St. Louis, St. Louis, MO [*Library symbol Library of Congress*] (LCLS)

MoSed .... Sedalia Public Library, Sedalia, MO [*Library symbol*] [*Library of Congress*] (LCLS)

MOSEL........ Molten-Salt Epithermal Reactor

Moseley....... Moseley's English Chancery Reports [*25 English Reprint*] [*A publication*] (DLA)

Mos El L...... Moseley's Elementary Law [*2nd ed.*] [*1878*] [*A publication*] (DLA)

Mosely (Eng)... Moseley's English Chancery Reports [*25 English Reprint*] [*A publication*] (DLA)

MOSES .... Manned Open Sea Experiment Station (NOAA)

MOSES .... Manufacturing Operations Short Event Scheduling

MOSES .... Massive Open Systems Environment Standard [*Computer science*]

MOSES .... Molecular Orbital Self-Consistent Energy System (PDAA)

MOSES .... Motor-Operated Sled Ejection System (MCD)

MOSES .... Movable Search System (MCD)

MOSES .... Multioccupant Sealed Environment Simulator

MoSF .... Fontbonne College, St. Louis, MO [*Library symbol Library of Congress*] (LCLS)

MOSFET...... Metal Oxide Semiconductor Field Effect Transformer (NITA)

mosfet .... Metal-Oxide Semiconductor Field-Effect Transistor (AD)

MOSFET...... Metal-Oxide-Semiconductor [*or Silicon*] Field-Effect Transistor

MOSFET...... Metal-Oxide-Silicon Field-Effect Transistor (IDOE)

MOSFETS ... Metal Oxide Substrate Field Effect Transistor

MoSFi .... Eugene Field House, St. Louis, MO [*Library symbol Library of Congress*] (LCLS)

MoSFRR ...... Foundation for Reformation Research, St. Louis, MO [*Library symbol Library of Congress Obsolete*] (LCLS)

MoSGS .... Church of Jesus Christ of Latter-Day Saints, Genealogical Society Library, St. Louis Branch, St. Louis, MO [*Library symbol Library of Congress*] (LCLS)

Mosh .... Moshav [*or Moshava*] (BJA)

MoSHi .... Missouri Historical Society, St. Louis, MO [*Library symbol Library of Congress*] (LCLS)

MoSHS .... Harris-Stowe State College Library, St. Louis, MO [*Library symbol*] [*Library of Congress*] (LCLS)

MoSHT......... Harris Teachers College, St. Louis, MO [*Library symbol Library of Congress*] (LCLS)

MOSI .... Mosinee Paper [*NASDAQ symbol*] (TTSB)

MOSI .... Mosinee Paper Corp. [*NASDAQ symbol*] (NQ)

mosic.......... Metal-Oxide-Semiconductor Integrated Circuit (AD)

MOSID .... Ministry of Supply Inspection Department [*British*] (AD)

MoSIG .... International Graduate School, St. Louis, MO [*Library symbol Library of Congress*] (LCLS)

Mosine .... Mosinee Paper Co. [*Associated Press*] (SAG)

MoSIO .... International Library, Archives, and Museum of Optometry, St. Louis, MO [*Library symbol Library of Congress*] (LCLS)

MoSIP.......... Missouri Institute of Psychiatry, St. Louis, MO [*Library symbol Library of Congress*] (LCLS)

MOSIS .... MOS Implementation Service (NITA)

Mosk........... Moscovici (AD)

Mosk........... Moscowitz (AD)

Mosk........... Moskowitz (AD)

MoSL .... Law Library Association of St. Louis, St. Louis, MO [*Library symbol Library of Congress*] (LCLS)

MOSLS .... Military Occupational Specialty Level System

MOS/LSI ..... Metal Oxide Silicon/Large Scale Integration [*Electronics*]

MOSM .... Metal-Oxide Semimetal (IEEE)

mOsm.......... Milliosmol [*or Milliosmole*] [*Chemistry*]

mosm .... Milliosmol (AD)

MOSM .... Mission Operations System Manager [*NASA*]

MoSM .... St. Louis Mercantile Library Association, St. Louis, MO [*Library symbol Library of Congress*] (LCLS)

MoSMa .... Maryville College, St. Louis, MO [*Library symbol Library of Congress*] (LCLS)

MoSMal....... Mallinckrodt Chemical Works [*Later, Mallinckrodt, Inc.*], St. Louis, MO [*Library symbol Library of Congress*] (LCLS)

Mos Man ..... Moses on the Law of Mandamus [*A publication*] (DLA)

MoSMc .... McDonnell Douglas Corp., Corporate Library, St. Louis, MO [*Library symbol Library of Congress*] (LCLS)

MoSMcA...... McDonnell Douglas Automation Co., St. Louis, MO [*Library symbol Library of Congress*] (LCLS)

MoSMed ...... St. Louis Medical Society, St. Louis, MO [*Library symbol Library of Congress*] (LCLS)

mOsmol....... Milliosmole [*Measurement*] (DAVI)

MoSMon....... Monsanto Chemical Co., St. Louis, MO [*Library symbol Library of Congress*] (LCLS)

MOSNAG..... Mossine Nagant Rifle

MOSOP....... Missouri Sexual Offender Program (AD)

MOSOP....... Movement for the Survival of Ogoni People

MOSOP....... Movement for the Survival of the Ogoni People

MOSP .... Master Ordnance Systems Pattern File [*Navy*]

MOSP .... Medical and Osteopathic Scholarship Program (DNAB)

MoSp .... Public Libraries of Springfield and Greene County, Springfield, MO [*Library symbol Library of Congress*] (LCLS)

MoSpA........ Assemblies of God Graduate School, Springfield, MO [*Library symbol Library of Congress*] (LCLS)

MoSpBB...... Baptist Bible College, Springfield, MO [*Library symbol Library of Congress*] (LCLS)

MoSpCB...... Central Bible College, Springfield, MO [*Library symbol Library of Congress*] (LCLS)

MoSpD........ Drury College, Springfield, MO [*Library symbol Library of Congress*] (LCLS)

MoSPD .... St. Louis Post-Dispatch, St. Louis, MO [*Library symbol Library of Congress*] (LCLS)

MoSpDC ..... Drury College, Springfield, MO [*Library symbol*] [*Library of Congress*] (LCLS)

MoSpE .... Evangel College, Springfield, MO [*Library symbol Library of Congress*] (LCLS)

MoSPI......... Pet, Inc., St. Louis, MO [*Library symbol*] [*Library of Congress*] (LCLS)

MOSPO .... Mobile Satellite Photometric Observatory [*NASA*] (NASA)

MOS Poland... Ministerstwo Opieki Spotecznes [*Ministry of Social Welfare*] [*Poland*] (AD)

MOSPOR...... Movement for the Struggle for Political Rights [*Uganda*] (PD)

MoSpS......... Southwest Missouri State College, Springfield, MO [*Library symbol Library of Congress*] (LCLS)

MoSPS........ St. Louis Priory School, St. Louis, MO [*Library symbol Library of Congress*] (LCLS)

MoSPSc ...... Saint Louis Priory School, St. Louis, MO [*Library symbol*] [*Library of Congress*] (LCLS)

MoSR.......... City Art Museum of St. Louis, St. Louis, MO [*Library symbol Library of Congress*] (LCLS)

MoSR.......... Saint Louis Art Museum, Richardson Memorial Library, St. Louis, MO [*Library symbol*] [*Library of Congress*] (LCLS)

MOSRAM..... Metal-Oxide Semiconductor Random-Access Memory (EECA)

MOSRD....... Motor Machinist's Mate, Ship Repair, Diesel Engineering Mechanic [*Navy rating*]

MOSRG....... Motor Machinist's Mate, Ship Repair, Gasoline Engine Mechanic [*Navy rating*]

MOSROM..... Metal-Oxide Semiconductor Read-Only Memory [*Computer science*] (CIST)

MOSROM..... Metal-Oxide-Silicon Read-Only Memory (IDOE)

moss........... Maintenance-Operations Support Set (AD)

MOSS .... Maintenance-Operations Support Set (AFM)

MOSS .... Management and Organisation in Secondary Schools (AIE)

MOSS .... Manned Orbital Space Station [*or System*] [*See also MOD, MODS, MTSS Air Force/NASA*]

MOSS .... Market Opening Sector Specific (AD)

MOSS .... Market-Oriented, Sector-Selective [*or Specific*] [*Trade negotiations between United States and Japan*]

MOSS .... Market Oversight Surveillance System

MOSS .... Middle-Aged, Overstressed, Semiaffluent Suburbanite [*Lifestyle classification*]

MOSS .... Military Orbital Space System [*See also MOD, MODS, MTSS*] [*Air Force/NASA*]

MOSS .... Military Overseas Shelter Survey [*Civil Defense*]

MOSS .... Mobile Submarine Simulator (NVT)

MOSS .... Mobility Support Set [*or System*] [*for aircraft*] (MCD)

MOSS .... Modelling Systems [*Moss Systems Ltd.*] [*Software package*] (NCC)

MOSS .... Monitor Output Signal Strength

MOSS .... Mothers of Sons in Service [*World War II*]

MOSS .... Mutually Owned Society for Songwriters

MOSSA........ Northern Rhodesia Mine Officials and Salaried Staff Association

Mossies....... Middle-Aged, Overstressed Semiaffluent Suburbanites [*Lifestyle Classification*]

Mossimo...... Mossimo, Inc. [*Associated Press*] (SAG)

MoSSJ......... St. John Cantius Seminary, St. Louis, MO [*Library symbol Library of Congress*] (LCLS)

MOSS MOUSE... Maneuver, Objective, Security, Surprise, Mass, Offensive, Unity of Command, Simplicity, Economy of Force [*Basic principles of war*] [*See also MOOSEMUSS*] (MCD)

MOSSRS...... Management Order Ship Status Reporting System (MCD)

MOSST .... Ministry of State for Science and Technology [*Canada*]

MOST .... Management Operation System Technique

MOST .... Manned Orbital Solar Telescope

MOST.......... Mass Optical Storage Technologies [*Computer science*]

MOST.......... Metal-Oxide-Semiconductor Transistor

most........... Metal-Oxide Semiconductor Transistor (AD)

MOST.......... Metal-Oxide-Silicon Transistor (IDOE)

MOST...........	Michigan Opportunities and Skills Training (AD)
MOST...........	Mission Oriented System Tape [*Military*] (CAAL)
MOST...........	Mobile Optical Surveillance Tracker
MOST...........	Mobile Oversnow Transport
MOST...........	Mobile SONAR Technology [*Marine science*] (MSC)
MOST...........	Modified OECD [*Organization for Economic Cooperation and Development*] Screening Test [*Biodegradability Test*]
MOST...........	Molonglo Observatory Synthesis Telescope
MOST...........	Mothers of Super Twins [*Military*]
MOST...........	Motorcycle Operator Skill Test
MOST...........	Multipulse Observation Sizing Technique [*Southwest Research Institute*]
MOSTA	Midwest Old Settlers and Threshers Association (EA)
MOSTAB	Modular Stability [*Derivative program*]
MO St Ann...	Missouri Statutes, Annotated [*A publication*] (DLA)
MoStc	St. Charles City-County Library, St. Charles, MO [*Library symbol Library of Congress*] (LCLS)
MoStcL	Lindenwood College, St. Charles, MO [*Library symbol Library of Congress*] (LCLS)
Mostell	Mostellaria [*of Plautus*] [*Classical studies*] (OCD)
MoStgA........	Sainte Genevieve Archives, Sainte Genevieve County Court, Ste. Genevieve, MO [*Library symbol Library of Congress*] (LCLS)
MoStj	St. Joseph Public Library, St. Joseph, MO [*Library symbol Library of Congress*] (LCLS)
MoStjM........	Methodist Medical Center, St. Joseph, MO [*Library symbol Library of Congress*] (LCLS)
MoStjMW ...	Missouri Western State College, St. Joseph, MO [*Library symbol Library of Congress*] (LCLS)
MoStjS.........	St. Joseph State Hospital, St. Joseph, MO [*Library symbol Library of Congress*] (LCLS)
MOSTL.........	Metal-Oxide-Semiconductor Transistor Logic (CET)
mostl	Metal-Oxide Semiconductor Transistor Logic (AD)
MOST/TDIS...	Mobile SONAR Technology/Technical Document Information System [*Marine science*] (MSC)
MOSU	Mobile Ordnance Service Unit
MoSU...........	St. Louis University, St. Louis, MO [*Library symbol Library of Congress*] (LCLS)
MoSU-C	St. Louis University, School of Commerce and Finance, St. Louis, MO [*Library symbol Library of Congress*] (LCLS)
MoSU-D.......	St. Louis University, School of Divinity, St. Louis, MO [*Library symbol Library of Congress*] (LCLS)
MoSUE.........	Union Electric Co., St. Louis, MO [*Library symbol Library of Congress*] (LCLS)
MoSU-L	St. Louis University, School of Law, St. Louis, MO [*Library symbol Library of Congress*] (LCLS)
MoSU-M	St. Louis University, School of Medicine, St. Louis, MO [*Library symbol Library of Congress*] (LCLS)
MoSU-P.......	St. Louis University, School of Philosophy, St. Louis, MO [*Library symbol Library of Congress*] (LCLS)
MOSUPPU ...	Mobile Support Unit (DNAB)
MoSV...........	Catholic Central Union of America, St. Louis, MO [*Library symbol Library of Congress*] (LCLS)
MoSVA........	United States Veterans Administration Hospital, St. Louis, MO [*Library symbol Library of Congress*] (LCLS)
MoSW..........	Washington University, St. Louis, MO [*Library symbol Library of Congress*] (LCLS)
MoSW-D	Washington University, School of Dentistry, St. Louis, MO [*Library symbol Library of Congress*] (LCLS)
MoSW-F	Washington University, School of Fine Arts, St. Louis, MO [*Library symbol Library of Congress*] (LCLS)
MoSW-L	Washington University, School of Law, St. Louis, MO [*Library symbol Library of Congress*] (LCLS)
MoSW-M	Washington University, Medical School, St. Louis, MO [*Library symbol Library of Congress*] (LCLS)
MOSZ..........	Massive Offshore Surf Zone
MOT.............	Aeromonterrey SA [*Mexico ICAO designator*] (FAAC)
MOT.............	Magneto-Optical Trap [*Physics*]
MOT.............	Management of Technology
MOT.............	Manned Orbital Telescope [*NASA*]
MOT.............	Manufacturing Operation and Tooling
MOT.............	[*The*] March of Time [*Radio and motion picture series*]
MOT.............	Marine Oil Transportation [*AAR code*]
MOT.............	Mark on Top (NVT)
MOT.............	Master of Occupational Therapy (GAGS)
MOT.............	Master Operability Test (CAAL)
MOT.............	Maximum Operating Time (NG)
MOT.............	McDonald Observatory [*Texas*] [*Seismograph station code, US Geological Survey*] (SEIS)
MOT.............	Mean Operating Time
mot..............	Mean Operating Time (AD)
MOT.............	Means of Testing [*Telecommunications*] (OSI)
MOT.............	Mechanical Operability Test
mot..............	Mechanical Operability Test (AD)
MOT.............	Medial Olfactory Tract [*Anatomy*]
MOT.............	Member of Our Tribe [*Jewish slang*]
mot..............	Member of Our Tribe (AD)
MOT.............	Men of the Trees [*Australia An association*]
MOT.............	Method of Testing (MCD)
mot..............	Middle of Target (AD)
MOT.............	Military Ocean Terminal (AABC)
MOT.............	Mineral-Oil Tolerance [*of resin solutions*]
M o T...........	Minister of Transport [*British*] (AD)
MOT.............	Ministry of Tourism [*Philippines*] (DS)
MOT.............	Ministry of Transport [*British or Canadian*]
MOT.............	Minot [*North Dakota*] [*Airport symbol*] (OAG)
MOT.............	Missile Operability Test (MCD)
MOT.............	Molecular-Orbital Theory [*Physical chemistry*]
MOT.............	Monalta Resources, Inc. [*Vancouver Stock Exchange symbol*]
MOT.............	Month of Travel [*Military*]
MOT.............	Motion
MOT.............	Motor (AAG)
mot.............	Motor (AD)
MOT.............	Motorized
MOT.............	Motorola, Inc. [*NYSE symbol*] (SPSG)
MOT.............	Motor Operating Time
MOT.............	Mouse Operating Table [*Research instrumentation*]
MOT.............	Mouse Ovarian Tumor [*Veterinary science*] (DB)
MOT.............	Murine Ovarian Teratocarcinoma [*Animal pathology*]
MOT.............	Tarkio College, Tarkio, MO [*OCLC symbol*] (OCLC)
MOTA...........	Mail Order Traders Association (MHDB)
MOTA...........	Manitoba Oculo-Tricho-Anal [*Syndrome*] [*Medicine*] (DMAA)
MOTA...........	Materials Open-Test Assembly [*Nuclear energy*] (NRCH)
MOTA...........	Michigan Ohio Telecommunications Association (TSSD)
MOTA...........	Mid-Ocean Target Array (AAG)
MOTA...........	Museum of Temporary Art [*Washington, DC*]
MoTaC	Tarkio College, Tarkio, MO [*Library symbol Library of Congress*] (LCLS)
MOTACC	Manufacturers of Telescoping and Articulating Cranes Council (EA)
MOT & E......	Multinational Operational Test and Evaluation
MOTAR	Modular Thermal Analyzer Routine [*Computer science*]
MOTARDES...	Moving Target Detection System (IEEE)
MOTARDIV...	Mobile Target Division [*Mine Force*] [*Navy*]
MOTARDS.....	Moving Target Detection System
MOTAS........	Member of the Appropriate Sex (NHD)
MOTAT.........	Museum of Transport and Technology (AD)
MOTBA	Military Ocean Terminal, Bay Area [*Oakland, CA*] (AABC)
MOTBY	Military Ocean Terminal, Bayonne (AABC)
MOTC...........	Ministry of Transit and Communications [*Philippines*] (AD)
MOTC...........	Montreal Tramways [*AAR code*]
MotClb	Motor Club of America [*Associated Press*] (SAG)
M o TCP	Ministry of Town and Country Planning [*British*] (AD)
MOTE...........	Measure of Training Effectiveness [*Military*]
MOTECS	Mobile Tactical Exercise Control System (DNAB)
MOTEL.........	Motor Hotel
MOTESZ.......	Magyar Orvostudomanyi Tarsasagok Szovetsege [*Federation of Hungarian Medical Societies*] (EAIO)
MOTET.........	Mother Tongue and English Teaching (AIE)
MOTF..........	Manganese Oxide Thin Film
MOTG..........	Marine Operational Training Group
MOTG..........	Morally Obliged to Go [*British Slang*]
moth	Mother (AD)
moth-in-law...	Mother-in-Law (AD)
Moth Jones...	Mother Jones [*A publication*] (BRI)
MothrWk......	Mothers Work, Inc. [*Associated Press*] (SAG)
MOTI..........	Message Oriented Text Interchange [*Telecommunications*] (OSI)
MOTIF.........	Maui Optical Tracking and Identification Facility [*Hawaii*] [*Air Force*]
MOTIS	Message Oriented Text Interchange System [*Telecommunications*] (OSI)
MOTIS	Missile on Stand Timing Simulator (MCD)
MOTIS	MOS Timing Simulator Software (NITA)
MOTKI	Military Ocean Terminal, King's Bay (AABC)
MOTN	Motion
MOTNAC......	Manual of Tumor Nomenclature [*Medicine*] (DHSM)
MOTNE	Meteorological Operational Telecommunications Network Europe
MOTNEG	Meteorological Operational Telecommunication Network in Europe, Regional Planning Group [*ICAO*] (PDAA)
MOTO	Moto Photo [*NQS*] (TTSB)
MOTO	Moto Photo, Inc. [*NASDAQ symbol*] (NQ)
motoboard...	Motorized Skateboard (AD)
motocross...	Motorcycle Cross Country Race (AD)
MOTOGAS....	Motor Gasoline [*Military*]
mot op	Motor Operated (AD)
MotoPh........	Moto Photo, Inc. [*Associated Press*] (SAG)
MOTOR........	Mobile Oriented Triangulation of Reentry
MOTOR........	Monthly Throughput Observation Report (DNAB)
motorcade ...	Motorized-Vehicle Parade (AD)
motorcross ...	Motorcycle Cross (AD)
MOTOREDE...	Movement to Restore Decency [*Group opposing sex education in schools*]
Motorola......	Motorola, Inc. [*Associated Press*] (SAG)
MOTORWAY...	Motorway [*Commonly used*] (OPSA)
MOTOS	Member of the Opposite Sex [*Electronic mail language*]
MOTP..........	Manufacturing or Testing Process (KSC)
MOTP..........	Medical Officer Training Plan [*Canada*]
MOTPICT	Motion Picture
MoTr............	Grundy County-Jewett Norris Library, Trenton, MO [*Library symbol Library of Congress*] (LCLS)
MOTR	Moto Club of Amer [*NASDAQ symbol*] (TTSB)
MOTR	Motor Club of America [*NASDAQ symbol*] (NQ)
MOTR	Multiple Object-Tracking RADAR (MCD)
MotrPrt........	Motorcar Parts & Accessories, Inc. [*Associated Press*] (SAG)
MOTS..........	Mend Our Tongues Society (EA)
MOTS..........	Metal Oxide Threshold Switches (MCD)
MOTS..........	Minitrack Optical Tracking Station [*or System*] [*NASA*]
mots	Minitrack Optical Tracking System (AD)
MOTS..........	Missile Operability Test Station (MCD)
MOTS..........	Mobile Optical Tracking System
MOTS..........	Module Test Set
MOTSS	Member of the Same Sex [*Electronic mail language*]
MOTSU	Military Ocean Terminal, Sunny Point (AABC)

MOTT	Mycobacteria Other Than Tubercle Bacilli	
MOTU	Mobile Operational Training Unit	(MCD)
MOTU	Mobile Optical Tracking Unit	(MCD)
MOTU	Mobile Ordnance Technical Unit [*Military*]	(CAAL)
MOTU	Mobile Technical Unit	(NG)
MOTUDET	Mobile Ordnance Technical Unit Detachment	(DNAB)
MOTV	Manned Orbit Transfer Vehicle	(MCD)
MotV	Motor Nucleus of the Trigeminal Nerve [*Medicine*]	(DB)
MOU	Maximum Oxygen Uptake	
MoU	Memorandum of Understanding	(AD)
mou	Memorandum of Understanding	(AD)
mou	Missouri [*MARC country of publication code Library of Congress*]	(LCCP)
MOU	Mountain Village [*Alaska*] [*Airport symbol*]	(OAG)
Mou	Mouse [*Computer science*]	(PCM)
MOU	Southwest Missouri State University, Springfield, MO [*OCLC symbol*]	(OCLC)
MoU	University of Missouri, Columbia, MO [*Library symbol Library of Congress*]	(LCLS)
MoU-D	University of Missouri, School of Dentistry, Kansas City, MO [*Library symbol Library of Congress*]	(LCLS)
MOUG	Map Online Users Group	(EA)
MOUG	Maryland Online User Group	(NITA)
Moult Ch	Moulton's New York Chancery Practice [*A publication*]	(DLA)
Moult Ch P	Moulton's New York Chancery Practice [*A publication*]	(DLA)
MoU-M	University of Missouri, Medical Library, Kansas City, MO [*Library symbol Library of Congress*]	(LCLS)
MOUND	Mound Plant [*Department of Energy*] [*Miamisburg, OH*]	(GAAI)
MOUNT	Mount [*Commonly used*]	(OPSA)
MOUNTAIN	Mountain [*Commonly used*]	(OPSA)
MOUNTAINS	Mountains [*Commonly used*]	(OPSA)
Mountbtn	Mountbatten, Inc. [*Associated Press*]	(SAG)
MOUNTIN	Mountain [*Commonly used*]	(OPSA)
MountPr	Mountain Province Mining, Inc. [*Associated Press*]	(SAG)
MOURAD	Mouvement pour la Renovation et l'Action Democratique [*The Comoros*] [*Political party*]	(EY)
MOUS	Multiple Occurrences of Unexplained Symptoms [*Medicine*]	
MOUSE	Manager Owner User Systems Engineer	(OA)
MOUSE	Minimum Orbital Unmanned Satellite	(AD)
MOUSE	Minimum Orbital Unmanned Satellite of the Earth	
MOUSS	Management and Operation of User Services Section	
MOUSS	Management and Operations of User Services Section [*American Library Association*]	
MoU-St	University of Missouri at St. Louis, St. Louis, MO [*Library symbol Library of Congress*]	(LCLS)
MOUT	Military Operations on Urbanized Terrain	(MCD)
MOUTH	Modular Output Unit for Talking to Humans	
MOUTRE	Mission Oriented Unit Training by Echelon [*Military*]	(INF)
MoU-V	University of Missouri, Veterinary Medicine Library, Columbia, MO [*Library symbol Library of Congress*]	(LCLS)
mov	Apple QuickTime [*Computer science*]	
MOV	Main Oxidizer Valve	(KSC)
mov	Main Oxidizer Valve	(NAKS)
MOV	Manned Orbiting Vehicle [*NASA*]	
MOV	Manuscript on Vellum	
MOV	Mass of Vehicle	
MOV	Materiel Obligation Validation	(AFIT)
MOV	Metal-Oxide Varistor	
MOV	Method of Validation	
MOV	Military-Owned Vehicle	
MOV	Minimal Occlusive Volume	(DMAA)
MOV	Monclova, MX [*Location identifier FAA*]	(FAAL)
MOV	Monument Valley, UT [*Location identifier FAA*]	(FAAL)
MOV	Moranbah [*Australia Airport symbol*]	(OAG)
MOV	Morovis [*Puerto Rico*] [*Seismograph station code, US Geological Survey*]	(SEIS)
MOV	Moshassuck Valley Railroad Co. [*AAR code*]	
MOV	Motor-Operated Valve	(NRCH)
MOV	Movable [*Technical drawings*]	
mov	Movable	(AD)
MOV	Movement	(AABC)
MOV	Movie	
mov	Movimento [*Movement*] [*Italian*]	(AD)
mov	Multiple-Orifice Valve	(AD)
MOV	Stephens College, Columbia, MO [*OCLC symbol*]	(OCLC)
MOVA	Microprocessor Optimized Vehicle Actuation	
MOVA	Movado Group [*NASDAQ symbol*]	(TTSB)
MOVA	Movado Group, Inc. [*NASDAQ symbol*]	(SAG)
Movado	Movado Group, Inc. [*Associated Press*]	(SAG)
M-OVAL	Macrovalocytes [*Microbiology*]	(DAVI)
MOVCO	Movement Control Organisation [*British military*]	(DMA)
MOVCORD	Movement Coordinator	
MOVDHHG	Movement of Dependents and Household Goods in Advance of Permanent Change of Station Orders is Authorized [*Army*]	(AABC)
MOVE	Cinema Ride [*NASDAQ symbol*]	(SAG)
MOVE	Cinema Ride Inc. [*NASDAQ symbol*]	(TTSB)
MOVE	Management of Value Engineering	
MOVE	Manage Old Vehicles Easily [*Performance Data Services, Inc.*] [*Software*]	
move	Movement	(WDAA)
MOVE	Moving	
MOVE	Multiple Occupancy Vehicles	(DICI)
MOVECAP	Movement Capabilities [*Military*]	(CINC)
MOVEM	Movement Overseas Verification of Enlisted Members [*Army*]	(AABC)
movem	Movement Overseas Verification of Enlisted Members	(AD)
moverep	Movement Report	(AD)
MOVEREP	Movement Report [*Military*]	(NATG)
Move Short Soc	Movement Shorthand Society	(AD)
MOVEW	Cinema Ride Wrrt [*NASDAQ symbol*]	(TTSB)
movi	Movie	(AD)
MOVI	Movie Gallery [*NASDAQ symbol*]	(TTSB)
MOVI	Movie Gallery, Inc. [*NASDAQ symbol*]	(SAG)
MovieFn	MovieFone, Inc. [*Associated Press*]	(SAG)
MovieGal	Move Gallery, Inc. [*Associated Press*]	(SAG)
MovieGal	Movie Gallery, Inc. [*Associated Press*]	(SAG)
MovieStr	Movie Star, Inc. [*Associated Press*]	(SAG)
MOVIMS	Motor Vehicle Information Management System [*Bell System*]	
MOVLAS	Manually Operated Visual Landing Aid System	(NG)
MOVMT	Movement	
MOVORD	Movement Order [*Military*]	(NVT)
movord	Movement Order	(AD)
MOVP	Military-Owned Vehicle Plan	(AFM)
MO-VPE	Metal-Organic Vapor Phase Epitaxy [*Also, MO-CVD, OM-CVD, OM-VPE*] [*Semiconductor technology*]	
MOVPER	Supreme Council, Mystic Order Veiled Prophets of Enchanted Realm	(EA)
MOVREP	Movement Report [*Military*]	(NVT)
MOVS	Manual Overseas Visa System	
MOVS	Military-Owned Vehicle Service	(AABC)
MOVT	Movement [*Music*]	(ROG)
MOW	Catskill Airways, Inc. [*FAA designator*]	(FAAC)
MOW	Meals on Wheels	
M o W	Minister of Works [*British*]	(AD)
MOW	Ministry of Works [*British*]	(MCD)
mow	Mission Operations Wing [*NASA*]	(NAKS)
MOW	Mission Operation Wing [*NASA*]	(KSC)
MOW	Mohawk Airlines [*ICAO designator*]	(FAAC)
MOW	Montana Western Railway [*AAR code*]	
MOW	Moscow [*Former USSR Airport symbol*]	(OAG)
MOW	Movement for the Ordination of Women [*British lobbying group*]	(ECON)
MOW	Movie of the Week [*Television programming*]	
MOW	Westminster College, Fulton, MO [*OCLC symbol*]	(OCLC)
MOWA	Meals-on-Wheels America [*An association*]	
MOWA	Michigan Outdoor Writers Association	
MOWAM	Mobile Water Mine	(MCD)
MoWarbT	Central Missouri State University, Warrensburg, MO [*Library symbol Library of Congress*]	(LCLS)
MoWarbTR	Trails Regional Library, Johnson County-Lafayette County Library, Warrensburg, MO [*Library symbol Library of Congress*]	(LCLS)
MOWASP	Mechanization of Warehousing and Shipment Procedures [*or Processing*] [*Defense Supply Agency*]	
mowasp	Mechanization of Warehousing and Shipment Processing	(AD)
MOWB	Ministry of Works and Buildings [*British*]	
MOWBC	Winnipeg Bible College, Otterburne, Manitoba [*Library symbol National Library of Canada*]	(NLC)
MoWD	Ministry of Works and Development [*British*]	(AD)
MoWgK	Saint Louis Roman Catholic Theological [*Kenrick*] Seminary, Webster Groves, MO [*Library symbol Library of Congress*]	(LCLS)
MoWgT	Eden Theological Seminary, Webster Groves, MO [*Library symbol Library of Congress*]	(LCLS)
MoWgW	Webster College, Webster Groves, MO [*Library symbol Library of Congress*]	(LCLS)
MoWhAF	United States Air Force, Whiteman Air Force Base Library, Whiteman AFB, MO [*Library symbol*] [*Library of Congress*]	(LCLS)
MoWitt	Mobile Window Thermal Test Facility [*Berkeley, CA*] [*Lawrence Berkeley Laboratory*] [*Department of Energy*]	(GRD)
Mo W Jur	Monthly Western Jurist [*A publication*]	
MOWOG	Morris Wolseley Group [*Automobile manufacturing organization*]	
MOWOS	Meteorological Office Weather Observing System	(PDAA)
MOWS	Manned Orbital Weapon Station [*or System*]	
Mow St	Mowbray's Styles of Deeds [*A publication*]	(DLA)
M o WT	Minister of War Transport [*British*]	(AD)
MOWT	Ministry of War Transport [*Terminated, 1956*] [*British*]	
MOWW	Military Order of the World Wars	(EA)
MOX	Manually-Operated Changeover [*Computer science*]	
MOX	Mars Oxident Experiment [*NASA*]	
MOX	Mixed Oxide [*Fuel*]	
mox	Mixed Oxides	(AD)
MOX	Morris, MN [*Location identifier FAA*]	(FAAL)
MOX	Moxa [*German Democratic Republic*] [*Seismograph station code, US Geological Survey*]	(SEIS)
MOX	Moxalactam [*An antibiotic*]	
mox	Oxidized Metal Explosive	(AD)
MOXB	Moxham Bank [*NASDAQ symbol*]	(TTSB)
MOXB	Moxham Bank Corp. [*NASDAQ symbol*]	(SAG)
Moxham	Moxham Bank Corp. [*Associated Press*]	(SAG)
MOXIE	Men Organized to X-press Indignant Exasperation [*Seattle group opposing below-the-knee fashions introduced in 1970*]	
MOXY	McMoRan Oil & Gas [*NASDAQ symbol*]	(TTSB)
MOXY	McMoRan Oil and Gas Co. [*NASDAQ symbol*]	(SAG)
MOXY	Model X-Y [*AEC computer code*]	
MOY	Mahogany Minerals [*Vancouver Stock Exchange symbol*]	
MOY	Mondy [*Former USSR Seismograph station code, US Geological Survey*]	(SEIS)
MOY	Money	
moy	Money	(AD)
MOY	Monterrey [*Colombia*] [*Airport symbol*]	(AD)
MOY	Salt Lake City, UT [*Location identifier FAA*]	(FAAL)

MOYC	Moyco Technologies [*NASDAQ symbol*] (TTSB)
MOYC	Moyco Technologies, Inc. [*NASDAQ symbol*] (SAG)
MoycoT	Moyco Technologies, Inc. [*Associated Press*] (SAG)
Moyle	Moyle's Criminal Circulars [*India*] [*A publication*] (DLA)
Moyle	Moyle's Entries [*1658*] [*England*] [*A publication*] (DLA)
MOZ	Aerocharter GmbH [*Austria ICAO designator*] (FAAC)
MOZ	Mezhdunarodnaya Organizacia Zhurnalistov [*International Organization of Journalists*] [*Russian*] (AD)
MOZ	Missouri Southern State College, Library, Joplin, MO [*OCLC symbol*] (OCLC)
MOZ	Moorea Island [*French Polynesia*] [*Airport symbol*] (OAG)
MOZ	Mozambique [*ANSI three-letter standard code*] (CNC)
Moz	Mozambique (AD)
MOZAIC	Measurement of Ozone by Airbus-in-Service Aircraft
Mozam	Mozambique (AD)
Moz & W	Mozley and Whiteley's Law Dictionary [*A publication*] (DLA)
Moz Cur	Mozambique Current (AD)
MOZL	Military Order of the Zouave Legion of the United States (EA)
Mozley & W	Mozley and Whiteley's Law Dictionary [*A publication*] (DLA)
Mozley & Whiteley	Mozley and Whiteley's Law Dictionary [*A publication*] (DLA)
MOZLUS	Military Order of the Zouave Legion of the US (EA)
MOZMVUS	Military Order of Zouaves, Militia and Volunteers of the United States (EA)
mozza	Mozzarella (AD)
MP	All India Reporter, Madhya Pradesh [*A publication*] (DLA)
MP	Atlantis Airlines [*ICAO designator*] (AD)
Mp	Import [*Economics*]
MP	Machine Pistol [*Military*] (IIA)
MP	Machine Pressed
MP	Macroprocessor
MP	Madonna Plan (EA)
MP	Magnetic Particle
MP	Magnetic Pressure (NVT)
MP	Magnetopause [*In a magnetic field*]
MP	Magnifying Power (IIA)
MP	Mail Payment (EBF)
mp	Mail Payment (AD)
M/P	Main Parachute (MCD)
MP	Main Phase (IEEE)
MP	Main Propulsion (DNAB)
MP	Mains Propres [*Personal Delivery*] [*French*]
MP	Maintainability Plan
MP	Maintenance Panel (AAG)
mp	Maintenance Part (AD)
MP	Maintenance Period
MP	Maintenance Plan
MP	Maintenance Point
MP	Maintenance Prints
MP	Maintenance Procedure (MCD)
MP	Maintenance Program
MP	Major Program (CAAL)
MP	Mallinckrodt, Inc. [*Research code symbol*]
MP	Management Package (NASA)
MP	Management Plan
MP	Managing Printer [*A publication*] (DGA)
MP	Manifold Pressure
mp	Manifold Pressure (AD)
MP	Manpower
MP	Manpower and Personnel (MCD)
MP	Mansfield Park [*Novel by Jane Austen*]
MP	Manual Proportional [*Attitude control system of Mercury spacecraft*]
MP	Manual Pulser
MP	Manufacturing Process
MP	Manu Propria [*In documents, after king's signature*] [*Italian*]
MP	Marbled Paper (DGA)
MP	Marching Pack (DNAB)
MP	Marginal Physical Product [*Economics*]
MP	Marginal Product
MP	Marine Police
MP	Marine Pollution
MP	Marine Provost [*British military*] (DMA)
MP	Maritime Patrol (NATG)
MP	Maritime Polar Air Mass
MP	Maritime Policy [*British*] (ROG)
MP	Market Price [*Business term*]
MP	Marshall's Posse (EA)
MP	Maschinenpistole [*Submachine Gun*] [*German*] (AD)
MP	Massa Pilularum [*A Pill Mass*] [*Pharmacy*] (ROG)
MP	Massively Parallel (AAEL)
MP	Massorah Parva [*or Massora Parva*] (BJA)
MP	Mass Properties (MCD)
MP	Master of Painting
MP	Master of Pharmacy (GAGS)
MP	Master of Planning (GAGS)
MP	Master Pointer [*Computer science*] (BYTE)
MP	Master Printer (DGA)
MP	Master Printers Annual [*A publication*] (DGA)
MP	Match Problems [*Research test*] [*Psychology*]
MP	Material Pass (AAG)
MP	Material Professional [*Army*]
MP	Mathematical Programming [*Computer science*]
MP	Matrix Protein (DB)
MP	Matthew Pelosi [*Designer's mark when appearing on US coins*]
MP	Maturity Phase
MP	Maxillary Process
MP	Maximum Flowering Period [*Botany*]
M/P	Maximum Performance [*Automotive engineering*]
MP	Mean Pressure (MAE)
MP	Measurement Pipette
MP	Measurement Pragmatic [*Computer science*] (OA)
MP	Measuring Point (NASA)
MP	Mechanical Paper
MP	Mechanical Part
MP	Mechanical Printer
MP	Medial Pallium [*Neuroanatomy*]
MP	Media Processor [*Computer science*] (BUR)
MP	Media Project (EA)
MP	Medical Payment [*Insurance*]
MP	Medium Pressure
mp	Medium Pressure (AD)
mp	Meeting Point (AD)
MP	Meeting Point [*Military*]
MP	Melchor Developments Ltd. [*Toronto Stock Exchange symbol*]
MP	Melphalan, Prednisone [*Antineoplastic drug regimen*]
MP	Melting Point
mp	Melting Point (AD)
MP	Melting Pot
MP	Member of Parliament [*British*]
MP	Member of Police
MP	Membrane Production (SSD)
M/P	Memorandum of Partnership [*Business term*]
MP	Menstrual Period [*Medicine*]
MP	Mental Process [*Work-factor system*]
MP	Mentum Posterior [*In reference to the chin*]
MP	Mercaptopurine [*Purinethol*] [*Also, M, P Antineoplastic drug*]
MP	Mercator's Projection (BARN)
MP	Meridional Part [*Navigation*]
MP	Merzbacher-Pelizaeus [*Disease*] [*Medicine*] (DB)
MP	Mesiopulpal [*Dentistry*]
MP	Message Processor
MP	Metacarpophalangeal [*Anatomy*]
M-P	Metal or Plastic (AAG)
m-p	Metal-Point (AD)
MP	Metal-Powder [*Videotape*]
MP	Metatarsophalangeal [*Anatomy*]
MP	Meteorology Panel (MCD)
MP	Methodist Protestant
MP	Methoxypsoralen [*Also, MOP*] [*Pharmacology*]
MP	Methyl Palmoxirate [*Organic chemistry*]
MP	Methyl Parathion [*Also, MEP, MPN*] [*Pesticide*]
MP	Methylphenidate [*Central Nervous system stimulant*]
MP	Methylprednisolone [*Endocrinology*]
MP	Methylprednisolone Sodium Succinate [*Medicine*] (DAVI)
MP	Methylpurine [*Organic chemistry*]
MP	Metra Potential (NITA)
MP	Metropolitan Police
MP	Mexican Peso [*Monetary unit*]
MP	Mezzo Piano [*Moderately Soft*] [*Music*]
mp	Mezzo-Piano [*Moderately Soft*] [*Italian*] (AD)
MP	Michoud Plant [*NASA*] (MCD)
M(P)	Microfilm (Positive)
MP	Micronized Progesterone
MP	Microprint
MP	Microprocessor [*Instrumentation*]
MP	Microprogram
M/P	Middle phalanx [*Anatomy*] (DAVI)
MP	Middle Point
MP	Midland Plant [*Nuclear energy*] (NRCH)
MP	Midline Precursor [*Cytology*]
MP	Mid-Phase
MP	Mile-Post
mp	Milepost (AD)
MP	Military Pay (AFM)
MP	Military Police [*Army*]
MP	Military Prohibitionist [*Slang*]
MP	Military Property (MCD)
M/P	Milk/Plasma [*Ratio*] [*Physiology*]
m/p	Milk Powder (AD)
mp	Mille Pasuum [*Thousand Paces*] [*Latin*] (AD)
MP	Millia Passuum [*1,000 Paces; the Roman mile*]
MP	Minimum Phase (IEEE)
MP	Minimum Premium [*Insurance*]
MP	Mining Permit (AD)
MP	[*The*] Mini Page [*A newspaper supplement*]
MP	Minister Plenipotentiary
MP	Minister Provincial (AD)
MP	Minuteman Platform
MP	Minutes Played [*Hockey*]
MP	Miscellaneous Paper [*or Publication*]
MP	Miscellaneous Proposal (AD)
MP	Missile Platform
MP	Missile Positioning
MP	Missile Possessed (SAA)
MP	Missing Perforation [*Philately*]
MP	Missing Person
MP	Mission Payload (MCD)
MP	Mission Planner (MCD)
MP	Mission Profile (MCD)
MP	Mississippi Power Co. [*NYSE symbol*] (SPSG)
MP	Missouri Pacific Railroad Co. [*AAR code*]

MP	Mistress of Philosophy	MPA	Mechanical Packing Association [*Later, Fluid Sealing Association*] (EA)
MP	Mitsubishi Plastics [*Japan*] (PDAA)	MPA	Medical Procurement Agency
MP	Mixed Pattern	MPA	Medroxyprogesterone [*Medicine*] (AD)
MP	Mixed Population	MPA	Medroxyprogesterone Acetate [*Also, MAP*] [*Endocrinology*]
MP	Mobilization Plan	MPa	Megapascal
MP	Modern Philology [*A publication*] (BRI)	mpa	Megapascal (AD)
MP	Modification Package	MPA	Mercaptopropionic Acid [*Organic chemistry*]
MP	Modified Construction Permit [*FCC*] (NTCM)	MPA	Metal Powder Association [*Later, MPIF*]
MP	Modo Praescripto [*In the Manner Prescribed*] [*Pharmacy*]	MPA	Methacrylate Producers Association (EA)
MP	Modus Ponens [*Rule of inference*] [*Logic*] [*Latin*]	MPA	Methoxypropylamine [*Organic chemistry*]
MP	Molecular Pair [*Physical Chemistry*]	MPA	Methylphosphoric Acid [*Organic chemistry*]
MP	Monetary Policy	MPA	Methylprednisolone Acetate [*A glucocorticoid*] (MAE)
mp	Mongolia [*MARC country of publication code Library of Congress*] (LCCP)	MPA	Metropolitan Pensions Associations (AD)
MP	Monitor Panel	MPA	Micropattern Analyzer (DB)
MP	Monitor Printer (CET)	MPA	Microwave Power Absorption (AAEL)
MP	Monophosphate [*Chemistry*] (MAE)	MPA	Microwave Power Amplifier
MP	[*The*] Month in Parliament [*A publication British*]	MPA	Mid Pacific Air Corp. [*ICAO designator*] (FAAC)
MP	Months after Payment (EBF)	MPA	Midwestern Psychological Association (MCD)
MP	Monumentum Posuit [*Erected a Monument*] [*Latin*]	MPA	Military Pay Account
MP	Mooring Pipe [*or Post*] (ADA)	MPA	Military Pay and Allowance
M/P	Morjumiid-Pterocephalid Boundary [*Paleogeologic boundary*]	MPA	Military Pay Area (AFM)
MP	Morning Prayer (WGA)	MPA	Military Personnel Appropriation (AFM)
MP	Mortgage-Participation Certificate [*Investment term*]	MPA	Military Personnel, Army
MP	Mortgage Payment in Full	MPA	Military Police Association [*Defunct*] (EA)
MP	Motherland Party [*Anatavan Partisi*] [*Turkey Political party*] (PPW)	MPA	Military Proposal and Analysis
MP	Motion Picture (NTCM)	mPa	Millipascal [*Unit of pressure*]
mp	Motion Picture (AD)	MPA	Miniature Pendulum Accelerometer (SAA)
MP	Motion Picture Production [*Navy*]	MPA	Miniature Photocell Activator
MP	Motor Potential	MPA	Miniature Piston Actuator (MCD)
MP	Mounted Police	MPA	Missile Procurement, Army (AABC)
MP	Mouth Pressure [*Dentistry*] (DAVI)	MPA	Missionary Pilots Association [*Defunct*] (EA)
MP	Mouvement Populaire [*Popular Movement*] [*Morocco*] [*Political party*] (PPW)	MPA	Mission Payload Assessment [*Air Force*] (DOMA)
MP	Mouvement Progressif [*Cameroon*] [*Political party*] (EY)	MPA	Mission Performance Assessment [*NASA*] (KSC)
MP	Movement Protein [*Cytology*]	MPA	Mission Phase Analysis
MP	Mucopeptide [*Biochemistry*]	MPA	Mission Profile Analysis
MP	Mucopolysaccharide [*Also, MPS*] [*Clinical chemistry*]	MPA	Mixer/Power Amplifier [*Telecommunications*]
MP	Mucopurulent [*Biochemistry*] (DAVI)	MPA	Mobile Press Association (EA)
MP	Multilink PPP [*Point-to-Point Protocol*] (PCM)	MPA	Models and Photographers of America (EA)
MP	Multiparous [*Obstetrics*]	MPA	Modern Poetry Association (EA)
MP	Multiperil [*Insurance*]	MPA	Modification Proposal and Analysis (MCD)
MP	Multiphase [*Physics*]	MPA	Modulated Pulse Amplifier [*Telecommunications*] (IAA)
MP	Multi Phonon (AAEL)	MPA	Molybdeophosphoric Acid [*Inorganic chemistry*]
MP	Multiple Processor [*or Multiprocessing*] [*Computer science*] (BUR)	MPA	Monthly Product Announcement [*Bureau of the Census*] (GFGA)
MP	Multiple Punch (DNAB)	MPA	Moose Pass [*Alaska*] [*Seismograph station code, US Geological Survey*] (SEIS)
MP	Multiplier Phototube	MPA	Mortar Package Assembly
MP	Multipole	MPA	Mortar Producers Association [*British*] (DBA)
mp	Multipole (AD)	MPA	Motion Picture Alliance
MP	Multiprocessing [*Computer science*] (CDE)	MPA	Motion Picture Association (NTPA)
mp	Multipurpose (AD)	MPA	Motoring Press Association
MP	Multipurpose	MPA	Multiplant Action [*Nuclear energy*] (NRCH)
MP	Municipal Police	MPA	Multiple Parameter Analysis
M/P	Muscle Plasma [*Ratio*]	MPA	Multiple Peptide Analysis [*Biochemistry*]
MP	Mycoplasma Pneumonia [*Medicine*]	MPA	Multiple-Period Average (IEEE)
MP	Mycoplasma Pulmonis [*A bacterium*]	MPA	Multiple Peripheral Adapter
mp	Myeloma Protein [*Oncology*] (DAVI)	MPA	Multiple Product Announcement (NTCM)
MP	My Pal [*Slang*]	mpa	Multiple Product Announcement (AD)
MP	Northern Mariana Islands [*ANSI two-letter standard code*] (CNC)	MPA	Multiple Protocol Architecture [*Computer science*] (PCM)
MP	Pinawa Public Library, Manitoba [*Library symbol National Library of Canada*] (NLC)	MPA	Multiple-Use Planning Area
MP2D	Multipart, Two Dimensional	MPA	Multi-Point Asynchronous (NITA)
MPA	Magazine Publisher's Association (NTCM)	MPA	Multiprecision Arithmetic
MPA	Magazine Publishers of America [*New York, NY Database producer*] (IID)	MPA	Multipurpose Additive (EDCT)
MPA	Main Political Administration [*of the Army and Navy*] [*Russian*] (DOMA)	MPA	MuniYield Pennsylvania Fund [*NYSE symbol*] (SPSG)
MPA	Main Propulsion Assistant	MPA	Museum Publications of America
MPA	Main Pulmonary Artery [*Anatomy*]	MPA	Music Publishers Association (NADA)
MPA	Maintenance Planning Analysis (MCD)	MPA	Music Publishers' Association of the United States (EA)
MPA	Major Projects Association [*British*] (DBA)	MPA	Mycophenolic Acid [*Biochemistry*]
MPA	Management Professionals Association [*Madras, India*] (EA)	MPA	Nampa, ID [*Location identifier FAA*] (FAAL)
MPA	Maneuver Propulsion Assembly (MCD)	MPA	Premenstrual Asthma [*Medicine*] (DAVI)
MPA	Manpower and Personnel Administration [*Military British*]	MPAA	Motion Picture Association of America (EA)
MPA	Man-Powered Aircraft	MPAA	Motorcar Parts & Accesories, Inc. [*NASDAQ symbol*] (SAG)
MPA	Marine Physician Assistant (AD)	MPAA	Motorcar Parts & Accessories [*NASDAQ symbol*] (TTSB)
MPA	Marine Preservation Association	MPAA	Musical Performing Arts Association (NTCM)
MPA	Maritime Patrol Aircraft (NATG)	MPAB	Military Petroleum Advisory Board
mpa	Maritime Patrol Aircraft (AD)	MPAC	Impact Systems [*NASDAQ symbol*] (TTSB)
MPA	Marketing and Promotion Association [*British*]	MPAC	Impact Systems, Inc. [*NASDAQ symbol*] (NQ)
MPA	Maryland & Pennsylvania Railroad Co. [*AAR code*]	MPAC	Master Plan for Academic Computing (AD)
mpa	Maryland Port Authority (AD)	MPAC	Military Pay and Allowance Committee (AFM)
M Pa	Master of Painting	MPAC	Multipurpose Application Console (SSD)
MPA	Master of Physician Assistant (PGP)	MP Acc	Master of Professional Accountancy (PGP)
MPA	Master of Professional Accountancy [*or Accounting*]	MP Acc	Master of Professional Accounting (PGP)
MPA	Master of Professional Accounting (NADA)	MPAcc	Master of Public Accounting (GAGS)
MPA	Master of Professional Arts	MP Acct	Master of Professional Accounting (PGP)
MPA	Master of Public Administration	MPACS	Management Planning and Control System [*IBM Corp.*]
MPA	Master of Public Affairs	MPACT	Microprocessor Application to Control-Firmware Translator [*Computer science*] (MHDI)
MPA	Master Pastrycooks' Association [*Australia*]	MPAD	Manpower Personnel Assignment Document (AFM)
MPA	Master Personnel Administration	MPAD	Maximum Permissible Accumulated Dose [*of radiation*] (ADA)
MPA	Master Photographers Association (AD)	mpad	Maximum Permissible Annual Dose (AD)
MPA	Master Photographers Association of Great Britain (BI)	MPAD	Menlo Park Applications Development [*IBM Corp.*]
MPA	Master Printers of America (EA)	MPAD	Mission Planning and Analysis Division [*NASA*]
MPA	Master Project Assignment (MCD)	MP Adm	Master of Public Administration
		MPAE	Max-Planck-Institut fur Aeronomie [*An association*]
		MPAEA	Mountain Plains Adult Education Association (AEBS)

MPaed	Master of Paediatrics
MPAFD	Multiple Pulse Arm Fire Device (MCD)
MP Aff	Master of Public Affairs (PGP)
MPAG	Maxwell Pensioners' Action Group (WDAA)
MPAGB	Modern Pentathlon Association of Great Britain (DBA)
mpai	Maximum Permissible Annual Intake (AD)
MPAI	Maximum Permissible Annual Intake [*Radiation*] (NRCH)
MPAIAC	Movimiento para la Autodeterminacion y Independencia del Archipielago Canario [*Movement for the Self-Determination and Independence of the Canary Archipelago*] [*Canary Islands*] [*Spanish*] (PD)
MPAJA	Malayan People's Anti-Japanese Army [*World War II*]
MPAJU	Malayan People's Anti-Japanese Union [*World War II*]
MPAM	Maritime Polar Air Mass (MSA)
mpam	Maritime Polar Air Mass (AD)
MPAMA	Milk Products Advertising-Merchandising Association (EA)
MP&C	Maintenance Planning and Control
MP & CS	Management Planning and Control System
MP & IS	Material Process and Inspection Specification (AAG)
MP & MAC	Marine Petroleum and Minerals Advisory Committee [*Terminated, 1976*] [*National Oceanic and Atmospheric Administration*] (NOAA)
mp & rs	Motive Power and Rolling Stock (AD)
MP & TF	Motion Picture and Television Fund
MPANSW	Master Patternmakers' Association of New South Wales [*Australia*]
MPANSW	Master Poulterers' Association of New South Wales [*Australia*]
MPAP	Mean Pulmonary Artery Pressure [*Cardiology*]
MPAPS	Motivation and Potential for Adoptive Parenthood Scale [*Psychology*]
MPAR	Maintenance Program Analysis Report
MPAR	Microprogram Address Register
MPAR	Multicanal Participacoes [*NASDAQ symbol*] (SAG)
m part	Movable Partition (AD)
MPAS	Maritime Patrol Airship Study
MPAS	Maryland Parent Attitude Survey [*Psychology*]
MPAS	Master of Physical Activity Studies (PGP)
MPAS	Master of Physician Assistant Studies (PGP)
MPAS	Mild Perioxic Acid Schiff [*Reaction*] [*Medicine*] (DMAA)
mpas	Millipascal Second (AD)
MPASK	Multi-Phase and Amplitude-Shift-Keying [*Computer science*] (PDAA)
MPASS	Modular Processing and Support System
MPast	Master in Pastoral Studies
MPAT	Management Postition Analysis Test [*William J. Reddin*] (TES)
MPAT	Multipurpose All-Terrain Vehicle
MPATI	Midwest Program for Airborne Television Instruction [*Defunct*]
MPA-URP	Master of Public Affairs and Urban and Regional Planning (PGP)
MPAUS	Music Publishers' Association of the United States (DGA)
m payl	Maximum Payload (AD)
MPB	Berkshire Athenaeum, Pittsfield, MA [*Library symbol Library of Congress*] (LCLS)
MPB	Machine-Pressed Bales
MPB	Magnetic Particle Brake
MPB	Maine Potato Board (EA)
MPB	Maintenance Parts Breakdown (KSC)
MPB	Male-Pattern Baldness
mpb	Male Pattern Baldness (AD)
MPB	Master of Physical Biology
MPB	Material Performance Branch [*Air Force*]
MPB	Materials Properties Branch [*Army*] (RDA)
MPB	Matrix Program Board
MPB	Maximum Participation Base (IIA)
MPB	Mechanically Processed Beef [*Food technology*]
MPB	Mephobarbital [*Antiepileptic drug*]
MPB	Meprobamate (DMAA)
MPB	Merit Promotion Bulletin [*Military*]
MPB	Miami [*Florida*] Public Seaplane Base [*Airport symbol*] (OAG)
MPB	Miniature Precision Bearing, Inc.
MPB	Miniature Precision Bearings (AD)
MPB	Missing Persons Bureau
MPB	Montpelier & Barre Railroad Co. [*Later, MB*] [*AAR code*]
MPB	Motorized Pontoon Bridge (MCD)
MPB	Mouvement Progressiste de Burundi [*Progressive Movement of Burundi*]
MPB	Multilayer Printed Board
MPB	Munitions Packaging Branch [*Picatinny Arsenal*] [*Army*] (RDA)
MPB	Musica Popular Brasileira [*Pop music*]
MPBA	Machine Printers' Beneficial Association [*Later, MPEA*]
MPBA	Model Power Boat Association [*British*] (DBA)
mpbb	Maximum Permissible Body Burden [*of Radiation*] (AD)
MPBB	Maximum Permissible Body Burden [*Radiation*]
MPBB	Methyl(phenyl)(butyl)barbituric (Acid) [*Biochemistry*]
MPBC	Berkshire Community College, Pittsfield, MA [*Library symbol Library of Congress*] (LCLS)
MPBC	Memphis Power Boat Club [*Tennessee*] (AD)
MPBDS	Material Properties Bibliographic Data System [*Purdue University*] [*Database*]
MPBE	Molten Plutonium Burn-Up Experiment [*Nuclear energy*] (IEEE)
MPBEA	Mountain Plains Business Education Association (AEBS)
MPBL	Berkshire Law Library Association, Pittsfield, MA [*Library symbol Library of Congress*] (LCLS)
MPBME	Munitions Production Base Modernization, Expansion (RDA)
MPBN	Military Police Battalion
MPBO	Bocas Del Toro [*Panama*] [*ICAO location identifier*] (ICLI)
MPBP	Mechanically Processed Beef Product [*Food technology*]
MPBP	Metal Polishers, Buffers, Platers, and Allied Workers International Union (EA)
MPBR	Multipunch Bar
mp br	Multipunch Bar (AD)
MPBS	Medical Pocket-Book Series [*A publication*]
MPBS	Multipurpose Bayonet System [*Army*] (INF)
MPBS	Mutual Permanent Building Society (AD)
MPBW	Ministry of Public Building and Works [*Later, DOE*] [*British*]
MPC	Machine Punch Card
MPC	Magellan Petroleum [*Exchange Symbol*] (TTSB)
MPC	Magnetic Particle Clutch
MPC	Maharashtra Prajatantra Congress [*India*] [*Political party*] (PPW)
MPC	Maharashtra Progressive Congress [*India*] [*Political party*] (PPW)
MPC	Maidstone Paper Converters [*Commercial firm British*]
MPC	Maine Potato Council [*Later, MPB*] (EA)
MPC	Maintenance Parts Catalog
MPC	Maintenance Policy Council [*DoD Washington, DC*]
MPC	Maintenance Priority Code
MPC	Maintenance Procedure Chart
MPC	Mandatory Product Control
MPC	Manpower and Personnel Council [*DoD*]
MPC	Manpower Planning Council
MPC	Manpower Priorities Committee
MPC	Manual Pointing Controller (MCD)
MPC	Manufacturing Plan Change
MPC	Manufacturing, Planning, and Control
MPC	Marco Polo Club (EA)
MPC	Marginal Producers Cost [*Engineering economics*]
MPC	Marginal Propensity to Consume [*Economics*]
mpc	Marginal Propensity to Consume (AD)
MPC	Marine Policy Center (GNE)
MPC	Marine Pollution Control, Inc. (EFIS)
MPC	Marine Protein Concentrate [*See also FPC*] (MSC)
mpc	Marine Protein Concentrate (AD)
MPC	Marker Pulse Conversion [*Telecommunications*] (TEL)
MPC	Market Performance Committee [*of NYSE*]
MPC	Master Control Program [*Computer science*] (ECII)
MPC	Master of Pastoral Counseling (PGP)
MPC	Master of Personnel Counseling (GAGS)
MPC	Master of Professional Counseling (PGP)
MPC	Master of Public Communication (PGP)
MPC	Master Parts Card
MPC	Master Phasing Chart (MCD)
MPC	Master Program Chart (MCD)
MPC	Materials Preparation Center [*Ames, IA*] [*Ames Laboratory*] [*Department of Energy*] (GRD)
MPC	Materials Processing Center [*Massachusetts Institute of Technology*] [*Research center*] (RCD)
mpc	Materials Program Code (AD)
MPC	Materials Properties Council (EA)
MPC	Materiel Program Code [*Air Force*] (AFM)
mpc	Mathematics, Physics, Chemistry (AD)
mpc	Maximum Permissible Concentration (AD)
MPC	Maximum Permissible Concentration [*Later, RCG*] [*Radiation*]
MPC	Mechanical Positioning Control
MPC	Mechanized Production Control
MPC	Medical Practices' Committee (WDAA)
MPC	Medium Processing Channel [*Carbon*] (DICI)
MPC	Megaparsec
MPC	Member of Parliament of Canada
MPC	Member Pickwick Club [*From "The Pickwick Papers" by Charles Dickens*]
MPC	Membrane Protein Complex [*Cytology*]
MPC	Memory Protection Check (MCD)
MPC	Meperidine, Promethazine, and Chlorpromazine [*Drug regime*]
MPC	Merleau-Ponty Circle (EA)
MPC	Message Processing Center
MPc	Metallophthalocyanine [*Organic chemistry*]
MPC	Meteorological Prediction Center (KSC)
MPC	Metromedia Producers Corp.
MPC	Metropolitan Police College (AD)
MPC	Metropolitan Police Commissioner (AD)
MPC	Microcircuit Power Converter
MPC	Microparticle Concentration [*Analytical chemistry*]
MPC	Microprocessor [*Computer science*] [*Unit*] (ECII)
MPC	Microprogram Control
MPC	Micropurulent Cervicitis [*Medicine*]
MPC	Midbody Pyro Controller (NASA)
MPC	Mid Power Controller [*Aerospace*] (NAKS)
MPC	Midwest Parentcraft Center (EA)
MPC	Military Payment Certificate
mpc	Military Payment Certificate (AD)
MPC	Military Personnel Center (AFM)
MPC	Military Pioneer Corps [*British*]
MPC	Military Police Corps
MPC	Military Police Force (AD)
MPC	Military Postal Clerk (AFM)
MPC	Military Property Custodian (AFIT)
Mpc	Million Parsecs [*Interstellar space measure*]
MPC	Mineral Policy Center (EA)
MPC	Miniature Protector Connector [*Telecommunications*] (TEL)
MPC	Minimal Flight Planning Charts [*Air Force*]
MPC	Minimum Mycoplasmacidal Concentration [*Medicine*] (MAE)
mpc	Minimum Planning Chart (AD)
MPC	Minimum Protozoacidal Concentration
MPC	Minor Planet Center [*Smithsonian Institution*]
MPC	Mission Planning Center (MCD)

MPC............ Mission Profile Course (MCD)
MPC............ Mississippi Library Commission, Jackson, MS [*OCLC symbol*] (OCLC)
MPC............ Mobile Processing Center (MCD)
MPC............ Mode and Power Control [*Aviation*]
MPC............ Model Penal Code (AD)
MPC............ Model Predictive Control [*Chemical engineering*]
MPC............ Model Procurement Code [*for State and Local Governments*] (AAGC)
MPC............ Modular Peripheral Interface Converter
MPC............ Monagas Pipeline Crude [*Petrochemical engineering*]
MPC............ Monetary Policy Committee [*France*] (ECON)
MPC............ Monetary Policy Committee [*Bank of England*]
MPC............ Monitor Proportional Counter (MCD)
MPC............ Monolayer-Protected Metal Cluster [*Materials science*]
MPC............ Monterey Peninsula College [*California*]
MPC............ Montreal Presbyterian College
MPC............ Moore's English Privy Council Cases [*A publication*] (DLA)
MPC............ Morphine Positive Control [*Epidemiology*]
MPC............ Mortgage-Participation Certificate [*Investment term*] (GFGA)
MPC............ Most Probable Cost (AAGC)
MPC............ Mother-of-Pearl Clouds [*Meteorology*] (PDAA)
MPC............ Motion Picture Camera (MCD)
MPC............ Motion Picture Control Panel (MSA)
MPC............ Mountain Pacific Air Ltd. [*Canada ICAO designator*] (FAAC)
MPC............ Mouse Myeloma Cell [*Cell biology*]
MPC............ Mouvement Patriotique Congolais [*Congo Patriotic Movement*] [*Political party*]
MPC............ Movable Platform Configuration
MPC............ Multicultural Psychiatric Center [*Australia*]
MPC............ Multielectron Photoactive Center [*Physical chemistry*]
MPC............ Multimedia Personal Computer
MPC............ Multimedia Personal Computer Group [*Subsidiary of Software Publishers Association*] (IGQR)
MPC............ Multi-Party Conference [*Namibia*] [*Political party*] (PPW)
MPC............ Multipath Core
MPC............ Multiple Payload Carrier (SSD)
MPC............ Multiple Process Chart
MPC............ Multiple-Profile Configuration (MCD)
MPC............ Multiple-Purpose Communications (NG)
MPC............ Multiprocessor Computer
MPC............ Multiprogram Control [*Computer science*]
mpc .... Multipurpose Carrier (AD)
MPC............ Multipurpose Center
MPC............ Multipurpose Computer (CMD)
MPC............ Multispectral Photographic Camera (KSC)
MPC............ Myeloblastpromyelocyte Compartment [*Hematology*] (DAVI)
MPC............ Thousand Pieces (EG)
MPCA.......... Magnetic Powder Core Association (EA)
MPCA.......... Marine and Ports Council of Australia (AD)
MPCA.......... Markham Prayer Card Apostolate (EA)
MPCA.......... Master Pastry Cooks Association (AD)
MPCA.......... Melanin-Producing Cell Autoantibody [*Endocrinology*]
MPCA.......... Mid Power Controller Assembly [*Aerospace*] (NAKS)
MPCA.......... Miniature Pinscher Club of America (EA)
MPCA.......... Multiway Principal Components Analysis [*Mathematics*]
MPCABS ..... Michigan Project for Computer-Assisted Biblical Studies [*University of Michigan*] [*Information service or system*] (IID)
MPCAG .... Military Parts Control Advisory Group [*DoD*]
MPCB.......... Manufacturing Plan Control Board (AD)
MPCB.......... Minuteman Parts Control Board [*Missiles*]
MPCB.......... Multilayer Printed Circuit Board
MPCblack .... Medium Processing Channel Black (EDCT)
mpc black.... Medium-Processing Channel Black (AD)
MPCC.......... Manufacturing Planning Change Coordination (MCD)
MPCC.......... Material Purchase Contracts Control
MPCC.......... Microprogrammable Communications Controller [*Computer science*] (MHDI)
MPCC.......... Minnesota Private College Council (AD)
MPCC.......... Multiprocessor Computer Complex
MPCC.......... Multiprotocol Communications Controller
MPCCC........ Metropolitan Post Card Collectors Club (EA)
MPCD .... Manufacturing Process Control Document (KSC)
MPCD .... Minimum Perceptible Color Difference
MPCD .... Mouvement Populaire Constitutionnel Democratique [*Popular Democratic Constitutional Movement*] [*Morocco*] [*Political party*] (PPW)
MPCD .... Multipurpose Color Display
MPCE.......... Music Publishers Contact Employees
MPCF.......... Campo De Francia/Enrique A. Jimenez [*Panama*] [*ICAO location identifier*] (ICLI)
MPCF.......... Millions of Particles per Cubic Foot (PDAA)
MPCFP........ Canadian Food Products Development Center, Portage La Prairie, Manitoba [*Library symbol National Library of Canada*] (NLC)
MPCH .... Changuinola/Cap. Manuel Nino [*Panama*] [*ICAO location identifier*] (ICLI)
MPCH .... Methodist Protestant Church
MPCI.......... Mandatory Product Control Items (MCD)
MPCI.......... Microsoft Press Computer Dictionary
MPCI.......... Military Police Criminal Investigation
MPCI.......... Multiport Programmable Communications Interface
MPCID......... Military Police Criminal Investigation Detachment
MPCL.......... Monolithical Peltier Cooled LASER (MCD)
MPCL.......... Mooney Problem Check List [*Psychology*]
MPCL.......... Movimiento Patriotico Cuba Libre [*Free Cuba Patriotic Movement*] [*Political party*] (AD)

MPCL(G)...... Maximum Permissible Contaminent Level (Goal) (GNE)
MPCLP........ Mental Patient Civil Liberties Project (EA)
MPCM......... Microprogram Control Memory
MPCM......... Multi-Purpose Central Mount/Module [*Military*] (LAIN)
MPCO .... Colon [*Panama*] [*ICAO location identifier*] (ICLI)
MPCO .... Micropolycystic Ovary [*Syndrome*] [*Medicine*] (DMAA)
MPCO .... Military Police Commanding Officer (MCD)
MPCO .... Military Police Company
MPCP.......... Mid-Peninsula Conversion Project [*Later, CEC*] (EA)
MP/CP........ Military Personnel/Civilian Personnel
MPCP.......... Missile Power Control Panel (AAG)
mpcp .... Missile Power Control Panel (AD)
MPCPA....... Music Publishers Contact Personnel Association [*British*] (DBA)
MPCR .... Memorandum Program Change Request [*Military*] (CAAL)
MPCR .... Microprogram Count Register [*Computer science*] (MHDB)
MPCRI........ Mercantile Pacific Coastal Routing Instructions
MPCS......... Machinery, Plant Control System [*Navy*]
MPCS......... Manual Propositional Control System (AAG)
MPCS......... Master Plan for Computing Services (AD)
MPCS......... Multiparty Connection Subsystem [*Telecommunications*] (TEL)
MPCS......... Multiprocessing Control System [*Computer science*]
MPCSOT...... Machinery, Plant Control System Operator Trainer [*Navy*]
MPCSW....... Multipurpose Close Support Weapon [*Military*] (AABC)
MPCU .... Marine Pollution Control Unit [*Department of Transportation*]
MPCU .... Maximum Permissible Concentration of Unidentified Radionuclides in Water
mpcur .... Maximum Permissible Concentration of Unidentified Radionuclides (AD)
MPD............ Disability Ministries [*Formerly, Ministry with Persons with Disabilities*] (EA)
MPD............ Magnetoplasmadynamic
mpd............ Magnetoplasmadynamics (AD)
MPD............ Magnetospheric Particle Detector (MCD)
MPD............ Main DC [*Direct Current*] Power Distributor Assembly (MCD)
MPD............ Main Pancreatic Duct [*Anatomy*]
MPD............ Maintenance Policy Document [*Deep Space Instrumentation Facility, NASA*]
MPD............ Make per Drawing (SAA)
MPD............ Management Policy and Directives
MPD............ Map Pictorial Display
MPD............ Marlborough Productions Ltd. [*Vancouver Stock Exchange symbol*]
M Pd............ Master of Pedagogy
MPD............ Master of Product Design (GAGS)
MPD............ Master Planned Community (PA)
MPD............ Material Property Damage (DNAB)
MPD............ Materials Physics Division [*Air Force*]
MPD............ Materials Proximity Detector
MPD............ Maximum Packing Depth (NG)
MPD............ Maximum Permissible Dose [*Radiation*]
mpd............ Maximum Permissible Dose (AD)
MPD............ Maximum Possible Dose [*Medicine*] (WDAA)
MPD............ Mean Phenetic Distance
MPD............ Mean Photon Flux Density
MPD............ Mean Population Doubling [*Cytology*]
MPD............ Medical Pay Date
MPD............ Membrane Polarographic Detector [*Instrumentation*]
MPD............ Membrane Potential Difference [*Medicine*] (DMAA)
MPD............ Meridian Point Realty IV [*AMEX symbol*] (SPSG)
MPD............ Meta-Phenylenediamine [*Organic chemistry*]
MPD............ Methane Phophonyl Dichloride [*Nerve gas intermediate*] [*Organic chemistry*]
MPD............ Methylpentanediol [*Organic chemistry*]
MPD............ Methylphosphonic Diamide [*Flame retardant*] [*Organic chemistry*]
MPD............ Metropolitan Park District (AD)
MPD............ Metropolitan Police Department (AD)
MPD............ Metropolitan Police District [*London*]
MPD............ Microprocessor Developments (NITA)
MPD............ Microwave Plasma Detector [*Instrumentation*]
MPD............ Midwest Presenters Directory [*Information service or system*] (IID)
MPD............ Military Pay Division (AD)
MPD............ Military Pay Division, Finance Center, US Army
MPD............ Military Position Description
MPD............ Military Priority Date
MPD............ Military Prisons Department [*British military*] (DMA)
MPD............ Minimal Perceptible Difference (DMAA)
MPD............ Minimal Phototoxic Dose [*Medicine*] (DMAA)
MPD............ Minimum Permissible Dose
MPD............ Minimum Premarket [*Health and Safety*] Data [*OEEC*]
MPD............ Minnesota Percepto-Diagnostic Test
MPD............ Missile Purchase Description [*Army*]
mpd............ Missile Purchase Description (AD)
MPD............ Missing Pulse Detector (MHDI)
MPD............ Mode-Power Distribution [*Electronics*]
MPD............ Modification Program Directive (AFIT)
MPD............ Movement for Democratic Process [*Zambia*] [*Political party*] (EY)
MPD............ Movement Priority Designator (DNAB)
MPD............ Movimiento para Democracia [*Cape Verde*] [*Political party*] (EY)
MPD............ Movimiento Popular Democratico [*Popular Democratic Movement*] [*Ecuador*] [*Political party*] (PPW)
MPD............ Movimiento Popular Dominicano [*Dominican Popular Movement*] [*Dominican Republic*] [*Political party*] (PPW)
MPD............ Mpanda [*Tanzania*] [*Airport symbol*] (AD)
MPD............ m-Phenylenediamine [*Also, MPDA*] [*Organic chemistry*]
MPD............ Multiperson Prisoner's Dilemma [*Statistics*]
MPD............ Multiphoton Dissociation [*Physical chemistry*]

MPD............	Multiple Personality Disorder
mpd	Multiple Personality Disorder (AD)
MPD............	Multipurpose Diffractometer
MPD............	Multipurpose Display (MCD)
MPD............	Myeloproliferative Disease [*Medicine*] (DMAA)
MPD............	Myofascial Pain Dysfunction [*Neurology*]
MPDA	David/Enrique Malek [*Panama*] [*ICAO location identifier*] (ICLI)
MPDA	Monitor-Printer-Diskette Adapter
MPDA	Motion Picture Distributors Association (AD)
MPDA	m-Phenylenediamine [*Also, MPD*] [*Organic chemistry*]
MPDAA	Motion Picture Distributors' Association of Australia
MPDB	Main Power Distribution Box (SSD)
MPD-C	Manpack Personnel Detector-Chemical [*Officially the Olfractronic Personnel Detector*] [*Military*] (VNW)
MPDC	Mechanical Properties Data Center [*Defense Logistics Agency*] [*Information service or system*]
MPDC	Missile Prelaunch Data Computer (MCD)
MPDD	Meteorological Penetration Detection Development
MPDE	Maximum Permissible Dose Equivalent (ERG)
MPDES	Microprocessor Data Extraction System [*Military*] (CAAL)
MPDFA	Master Photo Dealers' and Finishers' Association [*Later, PMA*] (EA)
MPDI	Marine Products Development Irradiator
MPDI	Microwave Power Devices [*NASDAQ symbol*] (TTSB)
MPDI	Microwave Power Devices, Inc. [*NASDAQ symbol*] (SAG)
MPDI	Multipunch Die
mp di	Multipunch Die (AD)
MPDL	Mission Profile Development List
MPDL	Movimiento Pro-Democracia y Libertad [*Panama*] [*Political party*] (EY)
MPDLRSDB...	Commission on the Mentally Disabled [*Formerly, Mental and Physical Disability Legal Research Services and Data Bases*] (EA)
MPDM	Maintenance Planning Data Manual (MUGU)
MPDP	Manpower Development Program [*Department of Labor*]
MPDPIS	Master Plan for Data Processing and Information Systems (AD)
MPDS	Mandibular Pain Dysfunction Syndrome [*Medicine*] (DMAA)
MPDS	Mechanical Provisioning Data System
MPDS	Message Processing and Distributing System [*Navy*] (NVT)
MPDS	Missile Piercing Discarding Sabot (PDAA)
MPDS	Mission Planning Debriefing Station (MCD)
MPDS	Monitored Professional Development Scheme (WDAA)
MPDS	Multi-Purpose Display System (DA)
MPDS	Myofascial Pain Dysfunction Syndrome [*Neurology*] (DAVI)
MPDSA	Master Painters, Decorators, and Signwriters Association (AD)
MPDSANSW..	Master Painters, Decorators and Signwriters' Association of New South Wales [*Australia*]
MPDT	Magnetoplasmadynamic Thruster [*Electric thruster type*]
MPDT	Mean Preventive Downtime [*Computer science*]
MPDT	Minnesota Perception Diagnostic Test (AD)
MPDT	Minnesota Percepto-Diagnostic Test [*Psychology*]
MPDTL	Medium-Power Diode-Transistor Logic (ECII)
MPDU	Message Protocol Data Unit [*Telecommunications*] (OSI)
MPDU	Mobile Power Distribution Unit (DWSG)
MP-DV	Multiply-Divide (NITA)
MPE	Management Program for Executives (ECON)
MPE	Manual Plot Entry (MCD)
MPE	Master of Physical Education
MPE	Mathematical and Physical Sciences and Engineering (IEEE)
MPE	Maximum Permissible Exposure [*Radiation*]
mpe	Maximum Permissible Exposure [*to Radiation*] (AD)
MPE	Maximum Possible Error
MPE	Max-Planck-Institut fur Extraterrestrische Physik [*Germany*]
MPE	Meat Promotion Executive [*British*]
MPE	Mechanized Production of Electronics
MPE	Meeting Planners Expo (ITD)
MPE	Memory Parity Error
MPE	Metaphenoxylene [*Analytical chemistry*]
MPE	Methidiumpropyl Ethylenediaminetetraacetic Acid [*Analytical biochemistry*]
MPE	Minimum Perceptible Erythema [*Dermatology*]
MPE	Minimum Performance Envelope (MCD)
MPE	Minimum Potential Energy [*Fission*]
MPE	Missile Positioning Equipment (KSC)
MPE	Mission and Performance Envelope
MPE	Mission-Peculiar Equipment
MPE	Mission to Planet Earth (USDC)
MPE	Monthly Project Evaluation
MPE	Moving Paper Electrophoresis
MPE	Multiphoton Excitation [*Physics*]
MPE	Multipion Exchange
MPE	Multiple Phase Ejector
MPE	Multiple Protective Earthing (IAA)
MPE	Multiprogramming Executive [*Hewlett-Packard Co.*]
MPEA	Machine Printers and Engravers Association of the United States (EA)
MPEA	Meat and Poultry Export Association
MPEA	Motion Picture Exhibitors Association (AD)
MPEA	Mouvement Populaire d'Evolution Africaine [*African People's Evolution Movement*]
MPEAA	Motion Picture Export Association of America (EA)
MPeaHi........	Peabody Historical Society, Peabody, MA [*Library symbol Library of Congress*] (LCLS)
MPeal	Peabody Institute, Peabody, MA [*Library symbol Library of Congress*] (LCLS)
MPEAUS	Machine Printers and Engravers Association of the United States (DGA)
MPEAUS	Master Printers and Engravers Association of the United States (AD)
MPEC	Miniature Piano Enthusiast Club (EA)
MPEC	Multicultural Publishing and Education Council (NTPA)
MPECC........	Multiprocessor Experimental Computer Complex
MPEd	Master of Physical Education
M Pe E	Master of Petroleum Engineering
M Pe Eng....	Master of Petroleum Engineering
MPEG	Methoxypolyethylene Glycol [*Organic chemistry*]
MPEG	Military Police Escort Guard
MPEG	Motion Picture Experts Group
mpeg	Motion Picture Experts Group [*Computer science*]
MPEG	Moving [*or Motion*] Pictures Experts Group [*Motion video standard*] (PCM)
MPEH	Methylphenylethylhydantoin [*Organic chemistry*] (MAE)
MPE/iX	Multiprogramming Executive / POSIX [*Portable Operating System Interface for Unix*] [*Computer science*] (CDE)
MPEL	Maximum Permissible Exposure Levels [*Radiation*]
M Pen	Minister of Pensions [*British*] (AD)
M Pen	Ministry of Pensions [*British*] (AD)
MPEP	Manual of Patent Examining Procedures
MPEP	Metalworking Processes and Equipment Program
MPEP	Model Performance Evaluation Program [*Centers for Disease Control*]
MPER	Master of Personnel and Employee Relations (GAGS)
MPER	Material-in-Process Engineering Request
MP-ER	Multiple Punch, Error Release (DNAB)
M Perf A	Master of Performing Arts (PGP)
MPERR	Master Personnel Record
MPers	Middle Persian (AD)
MPES	Management Planning and Evaluation Staff [*Environmental Protection Agency*] (GFGA)
MPE/S	Maritime Prepositioned Equipment and Supplies [*Navy*] (ANA)
MPES	Mass Properties Engineering Section
MPES	Mathematical, Physical, and Engineering Science (AD)
MPES	Maximum Performance Ejection Seat [*Navy*]
MPES	Medical Planning and Execution System (DOMA)
MPESS........	Mission Peculiar Experiment Support Structure
MPET	Magellan Petroleum Corp. [*NASDAQ symbol*] (NQ)
MPetE	Master of Petroleum Engineering (GAGS)
MP Ex	Modern Practice of the Exchequer [*A publication*] (DLA)
MPF	Machine Parts Fabrication
MPF	Major Project Funding
MPF	Malaysian Peasants Front [*Political party*] (AD)
MPF	Mapping Field (ACRL)
MPF	Maritime Patrol Force (MCD)
MPF	Maritime Prepositioning Force (DOMA)
MPF	Master Parts File (MCD)
MPF	Materials Processing Facility [*NASA*] (KSC)
MPF	Maturation-Promoting Factor [*Cytology*]
MPF	Mean Power Frequency [*of myoelectric signals*]
MPF	Median and Paired Fins [*Ichthyology*]
MPF	Medical Passport Foundation [*Defunct*] (EA)
MPF	Melamine-Phenol-Formaldehyde (EDCT)
MPF	Meridian Point Realty VI [*AMEX symbol*] (SPSG)
MPF	Metallurgical Plantmakers Federation (AD)
MPF	Metal Parts Furnace (MCD)
MPF	Methodist Peace Fellowship [*Defunct*] (EA)
MPF	Metropolitan Police Force [*Scotland Yard*] [*London, England*]
MPF	Mexico Pilgrims Foundation (EA)
MPF	Micellar Polymer Flooding [*Petroleum technology*]
MPF	Micro Professor (NITA)
MPF	Million Pair Feet [*Telecommunications*] (TEL)
MPF	Missile Pressure Fuel (AAG)
MPF	Missile Procurement Fund (AAGC)
MPF	Mission Planning Forecast
MPF	Mitosis-Promoting Factor [*Cytology*]
MPF	Mizrachi Palestine Fund (EA)
MPF	Modern Polar Front [*Climatology*]
mpf	Motion-Picture Film (AD)
MPF	M-Phase Promoting Factor [*Cytology*]
MPF	Multiple Primary Feed [*Deep Space Instrumentation Facility, NASA*]
MPF	Multipurpose Facility (DOMA)
mpf	Multi-Purpose Food (AD)
MPF	Multipurpose Food [*Refers to a specific combination of ingredients used in a food relief program*]
MPF	Multispectral Photographic Facility
MPF	Murine Pathogen Free [*Rats or mice*]
MPF	Religious Teachers, Filippini [*Roman Catholic women's religious order*]
MPFASAF	Military Police Functional Automation System for the Army in the Field (MCD)
MPFC..........	Mamas and the Papas Fan Club (EA)
MPFC..........	Mobile Petrol Filling Centre [*British military*] (DMA)
MPFC..........	Morgan Plus Four Club (EA)
MPFC..........	Mountain Parks Financial Corp. [*NASDAQ symbol*] (SAG)
MPFC..........	Mountain Parks Fin'l [*NASDAQ symbol*] (TTSB)
MPFC..........	Multipurpose Fire Control System
MPFE..........	Motion Picture Film Editors [*Defunct*] (EA)
MPFI..........	Multi-Point Fuel Injection [*Automotive engineering*]
MPFP..........	Melt-Processable Fluoropolymers [*Plastics technology*]
MPFS..........	Fuerte Sherman [*Panama*] [*ICAO location identifier*] (ICLI)
MPFS..........	MACRIT [*Manpower Authorization Criteria*] Planning Factors Study [*Army*]

MPFS.......... Microwave Position-Fixing System (NOAA)
MPFS.......... Multiple Primary Feed System [*Deep Space Instrumentation Facility, NASA*]
MPFW.......... Multishot Portable Flame Weapon (MCD)
MPG............ General Electric Co., Pittsfield, MA [*Library symbol Library of Congress*] (LCLS)
MPG............ Georgetown University, Medical Library Processing Center, Washington, DC [*OCLC symbol*] (OCLC)
MPG............ Magazine Promotion Group [*Defunct*] (EA)
MPG............ Magnetic Porous Glass [*Materials science*]
MPG............ Magnetopneumogram [*Medicine*]
MPG............ Main Professional Grade (WDAA)
MPG............ Manhattan Publishing Group (EA)
MPG............ Maritime Patrol Group
MPG............ Matched Power Gain
MPG............ Max-Planck-Gesellschaft [*West German research organization*]
MPG............ McArthur, OH [*Location identifier FAA*] (FAAL)
MPG............ Meridian Point Realty VII [*AMEX symbol*] (SPSG)
MPG............ Micrograms per Gram
MPG............ Microwave Pulse Generator
MPG............ Mid Plate Gyre [*Nuclear energy*] (NUCP)
MPG............ Miles per Gallon
MPG............ Military Products Group
MPG............ Milk Protein Hydrolysate [*Biochemistry*] (DAVI)
MPG............ Miniature Precision Gyrocompass (IEEE)
MPG............ Mobile Protected Gun [*Army*] (RDA)
MPG............ Molecular Presentation Graphics [*Software program*]
MPG............ Monopropylene Glycol [*Chemicals*]
MPG............ MPG Investment Corp. Ltd. [*Toronto Stock Exchange symbol Vancouver Stock Exchange symbol*]
MPG............ Multimedia Publishers Group (EA)
MPG............ Multiple Point Ground (NAKS)
MPG............ Multipoint Grounding (NASA)
MPG............ Patrologia Graeca [*J. P. Migne*] [*Paris*] [*A publication*] (BJA)
MPGA......... Maine Personnel and Guidance Association (AD)
MPGA......... Maryland Personnel and Guidance Association (AD)
MPGA......... Metropolitan Public Gardens Association [*British*] (BI)
MPGA......... Michigan Personnel and Guidance Association (AD)
MPGA......... Minnesota Personnel and Guidance Association (AD)
MPGA......... Missouri Personnel and Guidance Association (AD)
MPGF......... Male Pronucleus Growth Factor [*Biochemistry*]
MPGHM...... Mobile Payload Ground Handling Mechanism (MCD)
MPGI......... Mouvement Populaire pour la Guadeloupe Independante [*Popular Movement for Independent Guadeloupe*] (PD)
MPGM........ Monophosphoglycerate Mutase [*Biochemistry*] (DAVI)
mpgn......... Membrano Proliferative Glomerulonephritis [*Medicine*] (AD)
MPGN........ Membranoproliferative Glomerulonephritis [*Nephrology*]
MPGN........ Mesangioproliferative Glomerulonephritis [*Nephrology*] (DAVI)
MPGR........ Mana Pools Game Reserve [*Rhodesia*] (AD)
MPGS........ Microprogram Generating System
MPGS........ Microprogramming Generating System (NITA)
MPGS........ Mobile Protected Gun System [*Army*] (MCD)
MPGS........ Multi-Purpose Graphic System [*Computer science*]
MPH.......... Maintenance Parts Handbook
MPH.......... Male Pseudohermaphroditism [*Medicine*] (DB)
MPH.......... Martinair Holland NV [*Netherlands ICAO designator*] (FAAC)
M Ph......... Master of Philosophy
MPh.......... Master of Philosophy [*Canada*] (ASC)
MPH.......... Master of Physical Education and Health
MPH.......... Master of Public Health
MPH.......... McGregor Point, HI [*Location identifier FAA*] (FAAL)
MPH.......... Meat Packing House (AD)
MPH.......... Melphalan [*Also, A, L-PAM, M, MPL*] [*Antineoplastic drug*]
MPH.......... Mentally and Physically Handicapped (OICC)
MPH.......... Meridian Point Realty [*AMEX symbol*] (SPSG)
MPH.......... Meridian Point Rlty VIII [*AMEX symbol*] (TTSB)
MPH.......... Methodist Publishing House (DGA)
MPH.......... Methylphenidate [*Pharmacology*] (DAVI)
MPH.......... Micro-Phonics Technology International Corp. [*Vancouver Stock Exchange symbol*]
MPH.......... Miles per Hour [*Also, M/H*]
mph.......... Miles per Hour (IDOE)
MPH.......... Milk Protein Hydrolysate (BABM)
MPH.......... Missionary Sisters of Our Lady of Perpetual Help (TOCD)
M Ph......... Mistress of Philosophy
MPH.......... Multiple Probe Head [*Laboratory technology*]
MPH&TM..... Master of Public Health and Tropical Medicine (GAGS)
M Phar....... Master of Pharmacy
M Phar C.... Master of Pharmaceutical Chemistry
M Pharm.... Master of Pharmacy
M Ph C....... Master of Pharmaceutical Chemistry
MPHC........ Metal-Skinned, Paper-Honeycomb Cored (PDAA)
MPHE........ Master of Public Health Education (PGP)
MPHE........ Master of Public Health Engineering
MPHE........ Material and Personnel Handling Equipment (NASA)
MPHEC....... Maritime Provinces Higher Education Commission (AD)
MPH Ed...... Master of Public Health Education
MPH Eng.... Master of Public Health Engineering
M Phil....... Master of Philosophy
M Phil F..... Master of Philosophical Foundations (PGP)
MPHN........ Master of Public Health Nursing
MPHO........ Howard Air Force Base [*Panama*] [*ICAO location identifier*] (ICLI)
M Pho........ Master of Photography
MPHP........ Multiple-Pass Heuristic Procedure (PDAA)
MPHPr........ Meridian Point Rlty VIII Pfd [*AMEX symbol*] (TTSB)

mphps........ Miles Per Hour Per Second (AD)
MPHPS....... Miles per Hour per Second
MPHR........ Maximum Predicted Heart Rate [*Cardiology*]
M Ph S...... Master of Physical Science
M Ph Sc.... Master of Physical Science
MPHTM...... Master of Public Health and Tropical Medicine
MPhty......... Master of Physiotherapy [*British*] (ADA)
M Phy........ Master of Physics
M Phys A.... Member of the Physiotherapists' Association [*British*]
MPhysics..... Master of Physics (DD)
mpi............ Magnetic Particle Inspection (AD)
MPI............ Magnetic Particle Inspection
MPI............ Magnetic Peripherals Inc. (NITA)
MPI............ Magnetic Press, Inc. [*Information service or system*] (IID)
MPI............ Malaria Philatelists International (EA)
MPI............ Mamitupo [*Panama*] [*Airport symbol*] (OAG)
MPI............ Management Partnerships International, Inc. (IID)
MPI............ Mandsley Personality Inventory [*Psychology*] (DB)
MPI............ Manitoba Properties, Inc. [*Toronto Stock Exchange symbol Vancouver Stock Exchange symbol*]
MPI............ Mannosephosphate Isomerase [*An enzyme*]
MPI............ Man-Portable Illuminator
MPI............ Manufacturing Process Instructions
MPI............ Marginal Propensity to Invest [*Economics*]
mpi............ Marginal Propensity to Invest
MPI............ Marine Pollution Incident [*Marine science*] (OSRA)
MPI............ Marriage-Personality Inventory [*Psychology*]
MPI............ Mass Psychogenic Illness
MPI............ Master Patient Index (MEDA)
MPI............ Masterpiece Theatre [*Public television*]
MPI............ Material Process Instruction (AD)
MPI............ Matter of Public Importance (ADA)
MPI............ Maudsley Personality Inventory [*Psychology*]
MPI............ Maximal Permitted Intake [*Medicine*]
MPI............ Maximum Point of Impulse
mpi............ Maximum Point of Impulse (AD)
MPI............ Maximum Potential Intensity
MPI............ Maximum Precipitation Intensity [*Meteorology*] (PDAA)
MPI............ Max-Planck-Institut
MPI............ Max Planck Institute (AD)
MPI............ Max-Planck Institute for Meteorology [*Marine science*] [*Germany*] (OSRA)
MPI............ Max-Planck-Institut fuer Astronomie [*Max Planck Institute for Astronomy*] [*Germany*]
MPI............ Mean Point of Impact [*Air Force*]
mpi............ Mean Point of Impact (AD)
MPI............ Medicine in the Public Interest (AD)
MPI............ Medi-Physica, Inc. (DAVI)
MPI............ Meeting Planners International (EA)
MPI............ Meeting Professionals International (NTPA)
MPI............ Message Passing Interface [*Software program conducted at Mississippi State University*]
MPI............ Message Pattern Indicator
MPI............ Message Processing Interactive (MCD)
MPI............ Metal Powder Industries Federation
MPI............ Michelson Polarizing Interferometer [*Instrumentation*]
MPI............ Microprocessor Interface
MPI............ Milestone Properties [*NYSE symbol*] (SPSG)
MPI............ Military Police Investigator [*or Investigation*] (AABC)
MPI............ Military Procurement Instruction
MPI............ Miltarpsykologiska Institutet [*Military Psychology Institute*] [*Sweden*] (PDAA)
MPI............ Minneapolis Public Library and Information Center, Minneapolis, MN [*OCLC symbol*] (OCLC)
MPI............ Minnesota Prekindergarten Inventory [*Ireton and Thwing*] (TES)
MPI............ Minnesota Preschool Inventory [*Child development test*]
MPI............ Missile Periodic Inspection (AAG)
MPI............ Missing Persons International (EA)
MPI............ Mission Payload Integration (MCD)
MPI............ Mitsui Petrochemical Industries (AD)
MPI............ Molded Plastic Insulation
MPI............ Molecular Parameter Index
MPI............ Monographs of the Peshitta Institute [*A publication*] (BJA)
MPI............ Monsoon Pollen Index [*Paleoceanography*]
MPI............ Morris Pratt Institute Association (EA)
MPI............ Movimiento Patriotico Institucional [*Panama*] [*Political party*] (EY)
MPI............ Movimiento pro Independencia de Puerto Rico (EA)
MPI............ Multibus Peripheral Interface [*Intel Corp.*] [*Computer science*] (CIST)
MPI............ Multiphase Ionization [*Chemical physics*]
MPI............ Multiphasic Personality Inventory
mpi............ Multiphasic Personality Inventory (AD)
mpi............ Multiphoton Ionization (AD)
MPI............ Multiphoton Ionization [*Spectrometry*]
MPI............ Multiple Power Input (RDA)
MPI............ Multiple Protocol Interface [*Computer science*]
MPI............ Multipoint-Electronic Fuel Injection [*Automotive engineering*]
MPI............ Museum of the Plains Indians (AD)
MPI............ Mutagenic Potency Index [*For toxicology*]
MPI............ Myocardial Perfusion Imaging [*Cardiology*]
MPIA.......... Master in Political and Institutional Administration
MPIA.......... Master of Pacific International Affairs (GAGS)
MPIA.......... Master of Public and International Affairs (GAGS)
MPIA.......... Max-Planck-Institut fuer Astronomie [*Max Planck Institute for Astronomy*] [*Germany*]

MPIAD	MOD [*Maintenance of Deception*] Personnel Interceptor Assembly/Disassembly
MPIC	Message Processing Interrupt Count
MPIC	Mobile Phase Ion Chromatography
MPIC	Motion Picture Industry Controllers (EA)
MPIC	Motion Picture Industry Council (EA)
MPIC	Motion Picture Institute of Canada
MPIF	Message Passing Interface Forum (USDC)
MPIF	Metal Powder Industries Federation (EA)
MPIIN	Modification Procurement Instrument Identification Number [*NASA*] (NASA)
M-pill	Menstruation Pill [*Medicine*] (AD)
MPIM	Max-Planck-Institute fuer Meteorologie [*Marine science*] [*Germany*] (OSRA)
MPIM	Max-Planck-Institut fur Meteorologie (USDC)
MPIM	Multipurpose Individual Munition [*Weapon*]
MPIM/SRAW	Multi-Purpose Individual Munition/Short Range Assault Weapon [*Military*] (RDA)
MPIO	Mission and Payload Integration Office [*NASA*]
MPIP	Machine Parts Inspection Plans (MCD)
MPIP	Maintenance Posture Improvement Program (MCD)
MPIP	Meat and Poultry Inspection Program [*Department of Agriculture*]
MPIP	Miniature Precision Inertial Platform (OA)
MPIPrA	Milestone Properties Cv $0.78Pfd [*NYSE symbol*] (TTSB)
MPIR	Missile Precision Instrumentation RADAR (MSA)
MPIRO	Multiple Peril Insurance Rating Organization [*Later, Multiperil Insurance Conference*]
MPIX	Microelectronic Packaging [*NASDAQ symbol*] (TTSB)
MPIX	Microelectronic Packaging, Inc. [*NASDAQ symbol*] (SAG)
MPJ	Member of the Profession of Journalism [*British*] (DGA)
MPJ	Metacarpophalangeal Joint [*Anatomy*]
MPJ	Morrilton, AR [*Location identifier FAA*] (FAAL)
MPJ	Mouvement Panafricain de la Jeunesse [*Pan-African Youth Movement - PYAM*] [*Algeria*]
MPJE	Jaque [*Panama*] [*ICAO location identifier*] (ICLI)
MP-JFI	Managerial and Professional Job Functions Inventory [*Test*]
mPK	Cold Maritime Polar Air Mass [*Meteorology*] (BARN)
MPK	Maintenance Parts Kit (MSA)
mpk	Manpack
MPK	Martis Peak [*California*] [*Seismograph station code, US Geological Survey*] (SEIS)
MPK	McKinley Park [*Alaska*] [*Airport symbol*] (AD)
MPK	Methyl Propyl Ketone (EDCT)
MPK	Microphone Probe Kit
mPk	Polar Maritime Air Colder than Underlying Surface (AD)
MPKC	Management Problem-Knowledge Coupler
MPL	Macro Programming Language [*Computer application*] (PCM)
MPL	Magnesium Pemoline [*Pharmacology*]
MPL	Maintenance Parts Lists
MPL	Mandatory Parts List [*DoD*]
MPL	Manipulation Positioning Latches [*Aerospace*] (NAKS)
MPL	Manipulator Positioning Latches (MCD)
MPL	Man Position Locator
MPL	Manufacturing Parts List (AAG)
mpl	Maple (DAC)
MPL	Maple
MPL	Maple Technology Ltd. [*Vancouver Stock Exchange symbol*]
MPL	Marine Physical Laboratory [*Research center*] (RCD)
MPL	Marine Physics Laboratory [*Scripps*]
MPL	Mars Probe Lander [*Aerospace*]
MPL	Master of Patent Law
MPl	Master of Planning
MPL	Master of Polite Literature
MPL	Master of Public Law
MPL	Master Parts List
MPL	Master Planner, Inc. [*ICAO designator*] (FAAC)
MPL	Material Processing Laboratory (SSD)
MPL	Mathematical Programming Language [*Computer science*] (PDAA)
mpl	Mathematical Programming Language [*Computer science*] (AD)
MPL	Mavis, Paul A., South Bend IN [*STAC*]
MPL	Maxillofacial Prosthesis Laboratory [*WRAMC*] (RDA)
mpl	Maximum Payload (AD)
MPL	Maximum Penalized-Likelihood [*Statistics*]
mpl	Maximum Permissible Language (AD)
mpl	Maximum Permissible Level (AD)
MPL	Maximum Permissible Level [*Radiation*] (DEN)
MPL	Maximum Possible Loss (COE)
MPL	Maximum Probable Loss [*Insurance*]
MPL	Maximum Procurement Level (AFIT)
MPL	Mechanical Parts List (NASA)
MPL	Mechanical Properties Loop [*Nuclear energy*] (NRCH)
MPL	Megneto Photo Luminescence (AAEL)
MPL	Melphalan [*Also, A, L-PAM, M, MPH*] [*Antineoplastic drug*]
MPL	Memphis Public Library (AD)
MPL	Mesiopulpolingual [*Dentistry*] (MAE)
MPL	Message Processing Language [*Burroughs Corp.*]
mpl	Message Processing Language [*Computer science*] (AD)
MPL	Metals Processing Laboratory [*MIT*] (MCD)
MPL	Metering Pumps Limited
MPL	Metropolitan Police Laboratory (AD)
MPL	Metropolitan Property & Liability Insurance Co. (EFIS)
MPL	Miami Public Library (AD)
MPL	Micro Power Light [*Automotive lighting*]
MPL	Microprocessor [*or Motorola's*] Programming Language [*1975*] [*Computer science*] (CSR)

MPL	Microprogramming Language (NITA)
MPL	Milwaukee Public Library (AD)
MPL	Mine Planter (NATG)
MPL	Minimum Power Level [*Aerospace*] (NAKS)
MPL	Minnesota Power [*NYSE symbol*] [*Formerly, Minnesota Power & Light*]
MPL	Minnesota Power & Light Co. [*AMEX symbol*] (SAG)
MPL	Minnesota Power & Light Co. [*NYSE symbol*] (SPSG)
MPL	Minnesota Pwr & Lt [*NYSE symbol*] (TTSB)
MPL	Mission Planning Laboratory [*NASA*] (KSC)
MPL	Missouri Pacific Lines (AD)
MPL	Mistress of Polite Literature
MP/L	Modified Construction Permit and License [*FCC*] (NTCM)
MPL	Monessen Public Library, Monessen, PA [*OCLC symbol*] (OCLC)
MPL	Monkey Placental Lactogen
MPL	Monophosphoryl Lipid [*Biochemistry*]
MPL	Montoneros Patria Libre [*Guerrilla group*] [*Ecuador*] (EY)
MPL	Montpellier [*France*] [*Airport symbol*] (OAG)
MPL	Montreal Public Library [*Canada*] (AD)
MPL	Motion Picture Laboratories [*Commercial firm*]
MPL	Motivated Productivity Level [*Quality control*]
MPL	Mouvement Politique Lulua [*Lulua Political Movement*] [*Political party*]
MPL	Movimento Politica dei Lavoratori [*Workers' Political Movement*] [*Italy Political party*] (PPE)
MPL	Movimiento Popular de Liberacion ™Cinchoneros∫ [*"Cinchoneros" Popular Liberation Movement*] [*Honduras*] [*Political party*]
MPL	Multiple Payload Launcher
mpl	Multiple-Position Lock (AD)
MPL	Multipurpose Limousine
MPL	Multischedule Private Line
MPL	Multi-Services, Inc. [*FAA designator*] (FAAC)
MPL	Patrologia Latina [*J. P. Migne*] [*Paris*] [*A publication*] (BJA)
MPI	Plymouth Public Library, Plymouth, MA [*Library symbol Library of Congress*] (LCLS)
MPIA	Antiquarian House, Plymouth, MA [*Library symbol Library of Congress*] (LCLS)
MPLA	Malayan People's Liberation Army
MPLA	Mask Programmable Logic Array (NITA)
MPLa	Mesiopulpolabial [*Dentistry*] (MAE)
MPLA	Metropolitan Public Libraries Association [*New South Wales, Australia*]
MPLA	Monophosphoryl Lipid A [*Biochemistry*]
MPLA	Mountain Plains Library Association (AEBS)
MPLA	Movimento Popular de Libertacao de Angola [*Popular Movement for the Liberation of Angola*] [*Political party*]
MPlan	Master of Planning
MPlanStud	Master of Planning Studies
MPlanStudies	Master of Planning Studies
MPLA-PT	Movimento Popular de Libertacao de Angola - Partido do Trabalho [*Popular Movement for the Liberation of Angola - Party of Labor*] [*Political party*] (PPW)
MPLAW	Melamine Paper Laminate (PDAA)
MPLAW	Modified Programmers Language [*Computer science*] (PDAA)
MPLAW	Moving Part Logic (PDAA)
MPLAW	Multipulse Scaling-Law Code using Data Base Interpolation (PDAA)
MPLB	Balboa/Albrook [*Panama*] [*ICAO location identifier*] (ICLI)
MPLB	Maximum Permissible Lung Burden [*Industrial hygiene*]
MPLC	Medium-Pressure Liquid Chromatography
MPLC	Mid-Peninsula Library Cooperative [*Library network*]
MPLC	Movimento Popular de Libertacao de Cabinda [*Popular Movement for the Liberation of Cabinda*] [*Angola*] [*Political party*] (PD)
MPLC	Movimiento Popular de Liberacion Cinchonero [*Guerrilla forces*] [*Honduras*] (EY)
MPLD	Mouvement Populaire pour la Liberation de Djibouti [*Political party*] (EY)
MPLE	Multipurpose Long Endurance [*Aircraft*]
MPLG	Multi-Purpose Lithium Grease
MPLH	Multipurpose Light Helicopter (DOMA)
MPLI	Michigan Picture Language Inventory (EDAC)
MPLL	Malayan People's Liberation League
MPLM	Mini-Pressurized Logistic Modules [*Space technology*]
MPLN	Maintenance Planning [*Database*] (NASA)
MPLO	Military Postal Liaison Office
MPLP	La Palma [*Panama*] [*ICAO location identifier*] (ICLI)
MPLP	Marxist Progressive Labor Party [*Political party*] (AD)
MPLP	Mental Patients Liberation Projects
MPIP	Plimoth Plantation, Inc., Plymouth, MA [*Library symbol Library of Congress*] (LCLS)
MPLP	Portage Plains Regional Library, Portage La Prairie, Manitoba [*Library symbol National Library of Canada*] (NLC)
MPLPC	Multipulse Linear Productive Coding (PDAA)
MPLPDC	MDC Library, Manitoba Developmental Centre, Portage La Prairie [*Library symbol National Library of Canada*] (BIB)
MPLPM	Manitoba School, Portage La Prairie, Manitoba [*Library symbol National Library of Canada*] (NLC)
MPLPr	MP&L Cap l 8.05% 'QUIPS' [*NYSE symbol*] (TTSB)
MPLPrA	Minn Pwr & Lt 5% cm Pfd [*AMEX symbol*] (TTSB)
MPL + PRED	Melphalan and Prednisone [*Antineoplastic drug regimen*] (DAVI)
MPL + PRED(MP)	Melphalan and Prednisone [*Antineoplastic drug regimen*] (DAVI)
MPIPS	Pilgrim Society, Plymouth, MA [*Library symbol Library of Congress*] (LCLS)
MPLR	Medium Power Loop Range
MPLS	Maximal Principle Least Squares

Mpls .... Minneapolis (AD)
MPLSM .... Multiple Position Letter Sorting Machine (PDAA)
MPLSM .... Multiple Position Letter Sort Machine
MPLSS .... Marketing of Public Library Services Section [*Public Library Association*]
MPLU .... Most Probable Library User
MPLX .... Multiplexer
MPLXR .... Multiplexer
MPM .... Magnetic Phase Modulator
MPM .... Magnum Petroleum [*AMEX symbol*] (SAG)
MPM .... Main Propulsion Motor
MPM .... Maintenance Planning Manual (NG)
MPM .... Maintenance Program Management [*Military*] (AABC)
MPM .... Major Program Memorandum [*Military*]
MPM .... Major Project Manager
MPM .... Malignant Papillary Mesothelioma [*Medicine*]
MPM .... Manipulator Positioning Mechanism [*Aerospace*] (NAKS)
MPM .... Manpower Planning Model
MPM .... Manufacture Procedure Manual (KSC)
MPM .... Maputo [*Mozambique*] [*Airport symbol*] (OAG)
MPM .... Marginal Propensity to Import [*Economics*]
MPM .... Marshall Plan of the Mind [*BBC radio program*] (ECON)
MPM .... Master of Personnel Management (GAGS)
MPM .... Master of Pest Management (DD)
MPM .... Master of Professional Management (PGP)
MPM .... Master of Project Management (PGP)
MPM .... Master of Psychological Management
MPM .... Master of Psychological Medicine (ADA)
MPM .... Master of Public Management
MPM .... Maximum Permitted Mileage [*Airlines*]
MPM .... Maximum Pionization Method (OA)
MPM .... Medical Planning Module (DOMA)
MPM .... Message Processing Modules (MCD)
MPM .... Metal-Plastic Metal [*Automotive engineering*]
MPM .... Meters per Minute
mpm .... Meters Per Minute (AD)
MPM .... Metra-Potential Method [*Graph theory*]
MPM .... Microprogram Memory
MPM .... Microscope-Photometer
MPM .... Microwave Power Meter
MPM .... Mid-Pacific Mountains [*Geology*]
MPM .... Miles per Minute
MPM .... Milestone Planning Meeting (MCD)
MPM .... Milwaukee Public Museum (AD)
MPM .... Miniaturized Pointing Mount [*Spacelab*] [*NASA*]
MPM .... Missile Power Monitor (AAG)
mpm .... Missile Power Monitor (AD)
MPM .... Modest Petrovich Mussorgsky [*1839-1881*] (AD)
mpm .... Mole-Percent Metal (AD)
MPM .... Monoclonal Paratopic Molecule (DB)
MPM .... Monocycle Position Modulation
MPM .... Mortality Probability Models [*Medicine*]
MPM .... Mouse Peritoneal Macrophages
MPM .... Mouvement Populaire Mahorais [*Mayotte People's Movement*] [*Comoros*] [*Political party*] (PPW)
MPM .... Moving Presentation Mode
MP/M .... Multiprocessing Monitor Control Program [*Computer science*]
MP/M .... Multiprogramming Control Program for Microcomputers
MP/M .... Multiprogramming Control Program for Microprocessors (NITA)
MPM .... Multiprogramming Monitor
MPM .... Multipurpose Meal
mpm .... Multipurpose Meal (AD)
MPM .... Multipurpose Missile (MCD)
MP-M .... Museum Plantin Moretus [*Belgium*] (AD)
MPMA .... Master of Public Management and Administration
MPMA .... Metal Packaging Manufacturers Association [*British*] (DBA)
MPMA .... Methylphorbol Myristate Acetate [*Organic chemistry*]
MPMA .... Montford Point Marine Association (EA)
MPMA .... Motion Picture Museum Association [*British*] (BI)
MPM&PH .... Master of Preventive Medicine and Public Health (GAGS)
MPMC .... Microprogram Memory Control (NITA)
MPMC .... Military Personnel, Marine Corps
MPMCANSW... Master Plumbers and Mechanical Contractors Association of New South Wales [*Australia*]
MPMCAV ..... Master Plumbers and Mechanical Contractors' Association of Victoria [*Australia*]
MPMCAWA.. Master Plumbers and Mechanical Contractors' Association of Western Australia
MPMG .... Marine Pollution Management Group [*British*]
MPMG .... Melt-Powder Melt-Growth [*Materials Science*]
MPMG .... Multi-Purpose Molybdenum Grease
MPMG .... Panama/Paitilla, Marco A. Gelabert [*Panama*] [*ICAO location identifier*] (ICLI)
MPMH .... Mean Preventive Maintenance Hours
MPMI .... Magazine and Paperback Marketing Institute (EA)
MPMIC .... Mechanical Properties of Materials Information Center (MCD)
MPMIS .... Military Police Management Information System
MPML .... Mid-Pacific Marine Laboratory (MSC)
MP/ML .... Modified Construction Permit and Modified License [*FCC*] (NTCM)
MPML .... MPM Technologies, Inc. [*NASDAQ symbol*] (SAG)
MPMLE .... MPM Technologies [*NASDAQ symbol*] (TTSB)
MPMMG ..... Marine Pollution Monitoring Management Group (ASF)
MPMO .... Motion Picture Machine Operator [*A union*] (NTCM)
MPMP .... Mass Properties Management Plan (NASA)
MPMP .... (Methylpiperidyl)methylphenothiazine [*Sedative*]

MPMP .... Modification Program Management Plan (MCD)
MPMPR ...... Metropolitan Police Missing Persons Register [*British*]
MPMPrEC ... Magnum Pete $1.10 Cv'C'Pfd [*AMEX symbol*] (TTSB)
MPMR .... Movimiento Patriotica Manuel Rodriguez [*Manuel Rodriguez Patriotic Movement*] [*Chile*] [*Political party*] (EY)
MPMRP .... Master Petroleum Material Requirements Plan (MCD)
MPMS .... Mattress and Palliasse Makers' Society [*A union*] [*British*]
MPMS .... Missile Performance Measuring System (MCD)
MPMS .... Multiple-Pressure Measuring System
MPMSE ...... Multiuse Payload and Mission Support Equipment (MCD)
MPMT .... Mean Preventive Maintenance Time (MCD)
MPMT .... Mellon Participating Mortgage Trust Commercial Properties Series [*NASDAQ symbol*] (NQ)
MPMT .... Multiple Primary Malignant Tumor [*Oncology*]
MPM Tch .... MPM Technologies, Inc. [*Associated Press*] (SAG)
MPMUL .... Military Production Master Urgency List
MPMV .... Mason-Pfizer Monkey Virus
MPN .... Manpower Personnel, Navy (DOMA)
MPN .... Manufacturers Part Number (MCD)
MPN .... Manufacturer's Productivity Network [*Hewlett-Packard Co.*]
MPN .... Mariner Post-Acute Network [*Formerly, Paragon Health Network*] [*NYSE symbol*]
MPN .... Master in Psychiatric Nursing (GAGS)
MPN .... Master Part Number (MCD)
MPN .... Mean Probable Number (MCD)
MPN .... Medial Preoptic Nucleus [*Brain anatomy*]
MPN .... Methyl Parathion [*Also, MEP, MP*] [*Pesticide*]
MPN .... Military Pay, Navy [*An appropriation*]
MPN .... Military Personnel, Navy
MPN .... Military Procurement, Navy (MCD)
MPN .... Monongahela Power Co. [*AMEX symbol*] (SPSG)
MPN .... Most Probable Number
mpn .... Most Probable Number (AD)
MPNA .... Midwest Professional Needlework Association [*Later, APNRA*] (EA)
MPNC .... Mouvement pour le Progres National Congolais [*Movement for National Congolese Progress*]
MPNDS .... Material Properties Numerical Data System [*Purdue University*] [*Database*]
MPNE .... Manpower Needs [*Military*]
MPNF .... Manpower-Needs Forecasting (MCD)
MPNI .... Ministry of Pensions and National Insurance [*Later, MSS*] [*British*]
MPNPrA ...... Monogahela Pwr 4.4% Pfd [*AMEX symbol*] (TTSB)
MPNPrC ...... Monongah Power 4/50%cm C Pfd [*AMEX symbol*] (TTSB)
MPNST .... Malignant Peripheral Nerve Sheath Tumor
MPO .... Macedonian Patriotic Organization of US and Canada (EA)
MPO .... Major Program Objective (MCD)
MPO .... Management and Personnel Office (ODBW)
MPO .... Managerial & Professional Officers (WDAA)
MPO .... Managers, Proprietors, and Officials
MPO .... Manufacturing Production Order (NRCH)
MPO .... Maputo [*Mozambique*] [*Geomagnetic observatory code*]
MPO .... Maximum Power Output
MPO .... Medial Preoptic [*Brain anatomy*]
MPO .... Member of the Post Office [*British*]
MPO .... Memorandum Purchase Order (AD)
mpo .... Memory Printout (AD)
MPO .... Memory Printout [*Computer science*]
MPO .... Memory Protect Override
MPO .... Mercury Project Office [*NASA*] (SAA)
MPO .... Metropolitan Planning Organization
MPO .... Metropolitan Police Office [*Familiarly called "Scotland Yard" from its site at New Scotland Yard*] [*British*]
MPO .... Miami Philharmonic Orchestra (AD)
MPO .... Military Pay Order
MPO .... Military Permit Office [*or Officer*]
MPO .... Military Personnel Office
MPO .... Military Planning Office [*SEATO*] (CINC)
MPO .... Military Post Office
MPO .... Misconduct Policy Officer [*National Institutes of Health*]
MPO .... Missile Processing Operation (MCD)
MPO .... Mobile Post Office
MPO .... Mobile Printing Office (AD)
MPO .... Modular Personnel Office (SSD)
MPO .... Motion Picture Operator
MPO .... Mount Pocono, PA [*Location identifier FAA*] (FAAL)
MPO .... Mustering Petty Officer
MPO .... Myeloperoxidase [*An enzyme*]
MPOA .... Medial Preoptic Area [*Medicine*]
MPOA .... Multiprotocol over Asynchronous Transfer Mode [*Computer science*] (IGQR)
MPOA .... Puerto Obaldia [*Panama*] [*ICAO location identifier*] (ICLI)
MPOAH .... Medial Preoptic-Anterior Hypothalamic [*Brain anatomy*]
MPOD .... Mean Planned Outage Duration [*Electronics*] (IEEE)
MP-OES ...... Multi-Point Optical Emission Spectroscopy (AAEL)
MPOI .... Master Program of Instruction [*Army*] (AABC)
MPOIS .... Military Police Operations and Information System [*Army*] (MCD)
MPol .... Master of Policy
M Pol .... Master of Political Science (PGP)
MPolAdmin.. Master of Policy and Administration
MPolEcon ... Master of Political Economy [*British*] (ADA)
MPOLL .... Military Post Office Location List (AFM)
MPolLaw .... Master of Policy and Law
M Pol Sc .... Master of Political Science
MPOM .... Maintenance Program Operations Management [*Military*] (AABC)
MPOR .... Maintenance Plant at Ober Ramstadt [*Army*] (MCD)

MPOS	Manportable Office System [*Army*] (RDA)
MPOS	Military Plans and Operations Staff
MPOS	Mobile Post Office Society (EA)
MPOS	Movie Projector Operator's School (DNAB)
MPOS	Multipurpose Optimization System [*Computer science*]
MPOSC	Master of Polar and Ocean Science
MPOT	Master in Psychiatric Occupational Therapy (GAGS)
M-POTS	Mobile Psychological Operations Transmitter (DOMA)
MPP	Mailer's Postmark Permit
MPP	Maintainability Program Plan
MPP	Major Program Proposal (AAG)
MPP	Manipur People's Party [*India*] [*Political party*] (PPW)
MPP	Marginal Physical Product [*Agriculture*]
mpp	Marginal Physical Product (AD)
MPP	Marine Power Plant (PDAA)
MPP	Market Promotion Program (WPI)
MPP	Martens Polarization Photometer [*Physics*]
MPP	Massively Parallel Processor [*Image processing*]
MPP	Massive Periretinal Proliferation [*Ophthalmology*] (DAVI)
MPP	Master in Public Policy [*National University of Singapore*]
MPP	Master of Physical Planning (NADA)
MPP	Master of Public Policy
MPP	Master Patch Panel [*Air Force*] (MCD)
MPP	Master Program Plan (NG)
MPP	Material Processing Procedure (NASA)
MPP	Materials Preparation Program (SAA)
MPP	Materiel Performance Package [*Military*] (AFM)
MPP	Matrix Processing Peptidase [*An enzyme*]
MPP	Maximum Perfusion Pressure [*Cardiology*] (DAVI)
MPP	Maximum Positive Pressure [*Nuclear energy*] (NRCH)
MPP	Medical Personnel Pool
MPP	Medical Properties (EFIS)
MPP	Melanesian Progressive Parti [*Vanuatu*] [*Political party*] (EY)
MPP	Melphalan, Prednisone, Procarbazine [*Antineoplastic drug regimen*]
MPP	Member of Provincial Parliament [*British*]
MPP	Memory Parity and Protect (NITA)
MPP	Mercaptopyrazidopyrimidine [*Antineoplastic drug*] (MAE)
MPP	Merit Promotion Plan [*or Program*] [*NASA*] (NASA)
MPP	Message Processing Program [*Computer science*]
MPP	Meta Postprocessor [*Software program*] [*Symbolic Control, Inc.*]
MPP	Methyl(phenyl)pyridine [*Biochemistry*]
MPP	Methylpiperazine [*Organic chemistry*]
MPP	Microfilm Printer/Plotter
MPP	Microprogrammable Processor (MCD)
MPP	Miles per Pound [*NASA*] (KSC)
MPP	Military Pay Procedures
MPP	Minimum Premium Plans [*Insurance*]
MPP	Minority Procurement Policy (AAGC)
MPP	Miscellaneous Personal Property [*Legal term*] (DLA)
MPP	Missile Power Panel (AAG)
MPP	Mission-Planning Program [*Gerospace*] (BARN)
MPP	Mitochondrial Processing Peptidase [*Biochemistry*]
MPP	Modern Programming Practice
MPP	Molypermalloy Powder [*Metallurgy*] (EECA)
MPP	Mongol People's Party [*Mongolia*] [*Political party*] (FEA)
MPP	Monodisperse Polymer Particle
MPP	Mono Power Pack (HGAA)
MPP	Most Probable Position [*Navigation*]
mpp	Most Probable Position (AD)
MPP	Mothers in Prison Projects (EA)
MPP	Motion Picture Pioneers (EA)
MPP	Motion Picture Projector (MSA)
MPP	Mount Pasian [*Philippines*] [*Seismograph station code, US Geological Survey*] (SEIS)
MPP	Mulatupo [*Panama*] [*Airport symbol*] (OAG)
MPP	Multiphase Printing (AAEL)
MPP	Multiple Particle Plasma
MPP	Multiple Payload Program [*Military*]
MPP	Multiple-Product Pricing [*Business term*] (MHDB)
MPP	Programme of Mass Privatisation [*Poland*] (ECON)
MPPA	Master of Public Policy Administration (GAGS)
MPPA	Metal Powder Producers Association (EA)
MPPA	Music Publishers' Protective Association [*Later, NMPA*] (EA)
MPPAA	Multiemployer Pension Plan Amendments Act [*1980*] (GFGA)
MPPAR	Mouse Peroxisome Proliferator-Activated Receptor [*Biochemistry*]
MPPAV	Master Poultry Processors' Association of Victoria [*Australia*]
MPPB	Methyl(phenyl)(propyl)barbituric (Acid) [*Biochemistry*]
MPPC	Mailer's Postmark Permit Club (EA)
MPPC	Master Program Phasing Chart (MCD)
MPPC	Medical Personnel (Priority) Committee [*World War II*]
MPPC	Microsoft Point to Point Compression [*Microsoft Corp.*] [*Computer science*] (PCM)
MPPC	Military Pay Procedure Committee
MPPC	Multipotent Hematopoietic Progenitor Cell [*Biochemistry*]
MPPC	Panama [*Panama*] [*ICAO location identifier*] (ICLI)
MPPCA	Maryland Probation, Patrol and Corrections Association (AD)
MPPCF	Million Particles per Cubic Foot [*in air*]
mppcf	Millions of Particles per Cubic Foot of Air (AD)
MPPD	Maximum Probable Property Damage [*Hazard analysis*]
MPPEC	Mean Peak Plasma Ethanol Concentration [*Medicine*] (DMAA)
MPPG	Magnesium Pyridoxal Phosphate Glutamate [*Biochemistry*]
MPPH	(Methylphenyl)phenylhydantoin [*Organic chemistry*]
MPPH	Motion Picture Phonographic Unit
MPPHA	Multiparameter Pulse Height Analyzer
MPPhS	Member of the Royal Pharmaceutical Society [*Canada*] (DD)
mp pl	Multipunch Plate (AD)
MPPL	Multipunch Plate
MPPL	Multipurpose Processing Language [*Computer science*] (IEEE)
MPPL	Multipurpose Programming Language
MPPLT	Military Police Platoon (DNAB)
MPPM	Master of Public and Private Management
MPPM	Materials-Process-Product Model (PDAA)
MPPM	Military Personnel Procurement Manual
MPPM	Mission Prediction and Performance Module [*Aerospace*]
MPPN	Malignant Persistent Positional Nystagmus [*Medicine*] (DMAA)
MPPO	Modified Polyphenylene Oxide [*Plastics technology*]
MPPP	Mechanically Processed Pork Product [*Food technology*]
MPPP	Methyl(phenyl)(propionoxy)piperidine [*Organic chemistry*]
MPPP	Money-Purchase Pension Plan [*Human resources*] (WYGK)
MPPPM	Master of Plant Protection and Pest Management (GAGS)
MPPR	Mobilization Production Planning Requirements [*Military*]
MPPR	Modification Program Progress Report (AFIT)
MPPR	Monthly Production Progress Reports (MCD)
MPPrA	Mississippi Pwr 7.25% Dep Pfd [*NYSE symbol*] (TTSB)
MPPRB	Materiel Procurement Priorities Review Board [*Army*] (AABC)
MPPrB	Mississippi Pwr 6.65% Dep Pfd [*NYSE symbol*] (TTSB)
MPPRC	Materiel Procurement Priorities Review Committee [*Army*] (RDA)
MPPrC	Mississippi Pwr 6.32% Dep Pfd [*NYSE symbol*] (TTSB)
MPPRCA	Marine Plastic Pollution Research and Control Act
MPPS	Master Production Planning Schedule [*Air Force*] (AFIT)
MPPS	Master Program Planning Schedule
MPPS	Medicare Prospective Payment System
mpps	Million Pulses per Second (AD)
MPPS	Moroccan Party of Progress and Socialism [*Political party*]
MPPS	Multipurpose (AABC)
MPPSE	Multipurpose Payload Support Equipment (NASA)
MPPT	Maximum Power Point Tracking [*Power system*]
MPPT	Methylprednisolone Pulse Therapy [*Medicine*]
MPPT	Moller-Plesset Perturbation Theory [*Physical chemistry*]
MPPUP	Master of Public Policy and Urban Planning (PGP)
MPPWCOM...	Military Police Prisoner of War Command (AABC)
MPQ	Manchester Personality Questionnaire [*Test*] (TMMY)
MPQ	Manpower Planning Quota (PDAA)
mpq	Manpower-Planning Quota (AD)
MPQ	McGill Pain Questionnaire [*Dentistry*]
MPQ	Morgan Stanley Group [*AMEX symbol*] (SAG)
MPQ	Multidimensional Personality Questionnaire [*Personality development test*] [*Psychology*]
MPQA	Minuteman Production Quality Assurance (MCD)
MPQ/T	Mean Personnel Quantity per Task (MCD)
MPR	Machined Part Requisition (MCD)
MPR	Maculopapular Rash [*Medicine*]
MPR	Madjelis Permusiawaratan Rakat [*People's Deliberative Assembly*] [*Indonesia*] (AD)
MPR	Maintainability Problem Report (NASA)
MPR	Maintainability Program Requirements (AD)
MPR	Maintenance Personnel Roster
MPR	Management Program Review [*NASA*] (NASA)
MPR	Manager Profile Record [*Test*] [*Richardson, Bellows, Henry, and Co. Inc.*] (TES)
MPR	Mane Primo [*Early in the Morning*] [*Pharmacy*] (ROG)
MPR	Mannose Phosphate Receptor [*Biochemistry*]
MPR	Manpower (AABC)
MPR	Manpower Policy and Requirements Branch [*Department of Defence*] [*Australia*]
MPR	Manufacturing Parts Record (KSC)
MPR	Manufacturing Planning Review (MCD)
MPR	Mariposa Resources, Inc. [*Vancouver Stock Exchange symbol*]
MPR	Maritime Provinces Reports [*Canada*] [*A publication*] (DLA)
MPR	Marrow Production Rate [*Hematology*]
MPR	Master Power Regulator
MPR	Material Purchase Requisition
MPR	Materials and Process Requirement [*Navy*]
MPR	Mauritanian Party for Renewal [*Political party*] (EY)
MPR	Maximum Potential Representation (MUGU)
MPR	Maximum Practical Rate [*Aviation*]
MPR	Mayaguez [*Puerto Rico*] [*Seismograph station code, US Geological Survey*] (SEIS)
MPR	McPherson, KS [*Location identifier FAA*] (FAAL)
MPR	Mechanical Pressure Regulator (NRCH)
MPR	Medium Power RADAR (NATG)
mpr	Medium-Power RADAR (AD)
MPR	Mercaptopurine Ribonucleoside [*Antineoplastic drug*]
MPR	Mercury Plunger Relay
MPR	Message Processing Region [*IBM Corp.*]
MPR	Met-Pro Corp. [*AMEX symbol*] (SPSG)
MPR	Microprogram Register (MHDI)
MPR	Military Pay Record
MPR	Military Personnel Record (AFM)
MPR	Military Photo-Reconnaissance (PDAA)
MPR	Mine Production Report
MPR	Minimum Processing Requirement
MPR	Mock-Up Purchase Request [*NASA*] (NASA)
MPR	Mongolian Peoples Republic
MPR	Monoclonal Antibody Production Rate
MPR	Monopulse RADAR (MSA)
MPR	Monthly Program Review (USDC)
MPR	Monthly Progress Report
MPR	Monthly Project Report

MPR............	Mouvement Populaire de la Revolution [*Popular Revolutionary Movement*] [*Zaire*] [*Political party*] (PD)
MPR............	Mouvement Populaire Revolutionnaire [*Popular Revolutionary Movement*] [*Tunisia*] [*Political party*] (PD)
MPR............	Movimento Popolare Rivoluzionario [*Popular Revolutionary Movement*] [*Italy Political party*] (PD)
MPR............	Multiple Provider Router [*Computer science*] (ACRL)
MPR............	Multi-Port Repeater [*Computer science*] (CIST)
MPR............	MultiProtocol Router [*Novell, Inc.*] (PCM)
MPR............	Multipurpose Recorder
MPR............	Music Power Rating
M Pr A........	Master of Professional Accountancy (PGP)
MPRA..........	Military Police Regimental Association (EA)
MPRC..........	Maryland Psychiatric Research Center [*University of Maryland*] [*Research center*] (RCD)
MPRC	Medical Program Review Committee [*DoD Washington, DC*] (EGAO)
MPRC..........	Military Personnel Records Center (MCD)
MPRC..........	Motion Picture Research Council
MPRC..........	Multipurpose Range Complex [*Army*] (INF)
MPRC-H.......	Multipurpose Range Complex - Heavy [*Army*]
MPRC-L.......	Multipurpose Range Complex - Light [*Army*]
MPRE..........	Medium Power Reactor Experiment
MPRE..........	Minimum Pure Radium Equivalent (MCD)
MPRES........	Modular Plasma Reactor Simulator (AAEL)
MPRESS	Medium Pressure
mpress........	Medium Pressure (AD)
mPRF..........	Median Pontine Reticular Formation [*Neurophysiology*]
MPRF..........	Medium Pulse Recurrence Frequency (MCD)
MPRF..........	Motion Picture Relief Fund [*Later, MPTF*] (EA)
M Pr Gph.....	Master in Professional Geophysics
MPRH..........	Rio Hato [*Panama*] [*ICAO location identifier*] (ICLI)
MPRI..........	Member of the Plastics and Rubber Institute [*British*] (DBQ)
MPRI	Merchant Pacific Routing Instructions [*Shipping*]
MPRI	Mount Prat [*Italy*] [*Seismograph station code, US Geological Survey*] (SEIS)
MPRI	Multiphoton Resonance Ionization [*Spectrometry*]
MPRJ..........	Military Personnel Records Jacket [*Army*] (AABC)
MPRL..........	Manpower and Personnel Research Laboratory [*Army Research Institute for the Behavioral and Social Sciences*] (RDA)
MPRL..........	Master Parts Reference List
MPRL..........	Military Physics Research Laboratory [*University of Texas*] (MCD)
M Pr M.......	Master of Preventive Medicine
MPrMet.......	Master of Professional Meteorology (GAGS)
MPRO	Machine Processing Section [*National Security Agency*]
M Prob S.....	Master of Probability and Statistics (PGP)
MProcEng	Master of Process Engineering, University of Sheffield [*British*] (DBQ)
M Prof Acc...	Master of Professional Accountancy
MProfAcc....	Master of Professional Accounting (GAGS)
M Prof Past..	Master of Professional Pastoral (PGP)
MPROM	Mask Programmed Read-Only Memory [*Computer science*]
MPRP	Mercaptopurine Ribonucleotide [*Antineoplastic drug*]
MPRP	Mongolian People's Revolutionary Party [*Mongol Ardyn Khuv'sgalt Nam*] [*Political party*] (PPW)
MPRP	Moslem People's Republican Party [*Iran*] [*Political party*] (PPW)
MPRP	Muslim Peoples Republican Party [*Political party*] (AD)
MPRR	Management Program Review Report [*NASA*] (MCD)
MPRS	Management Planning and Reporting System (COE)
MPRS	Marine Pollution Retrieval System [*BTS*] (TAG)
MPRS	Microform Personnel Records System (NVT)
MPRSA	Marine Protection, Research, and Sanctuaries Act [*1972*]
MPRST	Maximum Probability Ratio Sequential Test (PDAA)
MPRT..........	Multipurpose Rail Transport (NRCH)
MPRTM........	Master of Park, Recreation, and Tourism Management (GAGS)
MPRT/R	Missile Pneudraulic Repair Technician/Repairman (AAG)
MPS............	Individual Style Survey [*Test*] (TMMY)
MPS............	Magazine Printers Section (EA)
MPS............	Magnetic Pole Strength
MPS............	Mail Preference Service [*Direct Mail Advertising Association*]
MPS............	Main Power Switch
MPS............	Main Propulsion System [*or Subsystem*] [*NASA*] (KSC)
MPS............	Maintenance Performance System [*DoD*]
MPS............	Maintenance Problem Summary
MPS............	Management Policy Statement
MPS............	Managerial Philosophies Scale [*Test*]
MPS............	Manpower System (NRCH)
MPS............	Manual Phase Shifter
MPS............	Manufacturing Process Specification (AAG)
MPS............	Marbled Paper Sides [*Bookbinding*]
mps	Marbled Paper Sides (AD)
MPS............	Marginal Propensity to Save [*Economics*]
MPS............	Marine Polymetalic Sulfide
MPS............	Marine Prepositioned Ships Program
MPS............	Maritime Postmark Society [*Later, USCS*] (EA)
MPS............	Maritime Prepositioning Ship (MCD)
MPS............	Maritime Prepositioning Squadron (DOMA)
MPS............	Marriage Prediction Schedule [*Psychology*]
MPS............	Master of Pastoral Studies (PGP)
MPS............	Master of Personnel Service (GAGS)
MPS............	Master of Personnel Services
MPS............	Master of Policy Sciences (PGP)
MPS............	Master of Political Science (GAGS)
MPS............	Master of Professional Studies (PGP)
MPS............	Master of Professional Studies in Human Relations
M Ps............	Master of Psychology
MPS............	Master of Public Service (GAGS)
MPS............	Master Performance System
MPS............	Master Planning Schedule (MCD)
MPS............	Master Production Schedule
MPS............	Master Program Schedule (NASA)
MPS............	Master Project Summary [*Civil Defense*]
MPS............	Material Planning Study
MPS............	Material Planning System [*Manufacturing management*]
MPS............	Material Processing Specification (NASA)
MPS............	Material Processing System
MPS............	Materials Processing in Space [*NASA*]
MPS............	Materiel Planning Study [*Army*]
MPS............	Mathematical Programming Society [*Voorburg, Netherlands*] (EAIO)
MPS............	Mathematical Programming System [*Computer science*]
MPS............	Maximum Performance Escape System (MCD)
MPS............	Max Planck Society [*Germany*]
MPS............	Mechanical Phase Shifter
MPS............	Mechanical Power Systems
MPS............	Median Period of Survival
MPS............	Medical Polymers Tech [*VS, exchange symbol*] (TTSB)
MPS............	Medical Practice Study
MPS............	Medical Protection Society [*British*] (DBA)
MPS............	Medical Provider Survey [*Department of Health and Human Services*] (GFGA)
MPS............	Medical Publishing Standard (DB)
MPS............	MegaBITS [*Binary Digits*] per Second [*Transmission rate*] [*Computer science*] (MCD)
mps	Megacycles per Second (AD)
MPS............	Megacyles [*Also, MCPS*] (WDAA)
MPS............	Meiosis-Preventing Substance [*Cyctology*]
MPS............	Member of the Pharmaceutical Society [*British*]
MPS............	Member of the Philological Society [*British*]
MPS............	Member of the Physical Society [*British*]
MPS............	Memory Processor Switch
MPS............	Mercury Procedures Simulator [*NASA*]
MPS............	Merit Pay System (MCD)
MPS............	Mervyn Peake Society (EA)
MPS............	Message Processing System (NVT)
MPS............	Meters per Second
mps	Meters per Second (AD)
MPS............	Methodist Philatelic Society (EA)
MPS............	Methyl Phenyl Sulfide [*Organic chemistry*]
MPS............	Michigan Picture Stories [*Psychology*] (DAVI)
MPS............	Microbial Profile System [*Microbiology*]
MPS............	Microphone Power Supply
MPS............	Microprocessor Series [*or System*] (MDG)
MPS............	Microwave Phase Shifter
MPS............	Microwave Pressure Sounder (MCD)
MPS............	Microwave Pulse Source
MPS............	Miles per Second
mps	Miles per Second (IDOE)
MPS............	Military Planning Staff (CINC)
MPS............	Military Postal Service (AFM)
MPS............	Military Production Specifications
MPS............	Milwaukee Public Museum (AD)
MPS............	Minimum Performance Specification (DA)
MPS............	Minimum Piecework Standard [*British*]
MPS............	Minimum Property Standards [*FHA*]
MPS............	Minister of Public Security [*British*]
MPS............	Misioneras del Perpetual Socorro (TOCD)
MPS............	Missionary Sisters of Our Lady of Perpetual Help (TOCD)
MPS............	Mission Parcels Society [*British*]
MPS............	Mission Preparation Sheet
MPS............	Mission-Processing Subsystem (MCD)
MPS............	Mission Profile Simulator [*NASA*]
MPS............	Miss Porter's School [*Farmington, CT*]
MPS............	Mixed Potential System (PDAA)
MPS............	Mobile Positioning Ship (DNAB)
MPS............	Modular Power System (MCD)
MPS............	Modular Processor System [*Computer science*] (PCM)
MPS............	Molecular Photoemission Spectroscopy
MPS............	Mononuclear Phagocyte System [*Hematology*]
MPS............	Mont Pelerin Society (EA)
MPS............	Montreal Platelet Syndrome [*Medicine*] (DMAA)
MPS............	Motion Picture Service [*Department of Agriculture*]
mps	Motor Parts Stock (AD)
MPS............	Motor Pump System (MCD)
MPS............	Mount Pleasant [*Texas*] [*Airport symbol Obsolete*] (OAG)
MPS............	Mouvement Patriotique du Salut [*Chad*] [*Political party*] (EY)
MPS............	Mouvement Populaire Senegalais [*Senegalese Popular Movement*] [*Political party*]
MPS............	Movement-Produced Stimuli
MPS............	Movimiento de Patria Socialista [*Venezuela Political party*] (EY)
MPS............	MPS [*Mucopolysaccharidoses*] Society (EA)
MPS............	Mucopolysaccharide [*Also, MP*] [*Clinical chemistry*]
MPS............	Mucopolysaccharidosis [*Medicine*]
MPS............	Multi-Format Photointerpretation System (SAA)
MPS............	Multiparticle Spectrometer [*Brookhaven National Laboratory*]
MPS............	Multiphasic Screening [*Medicine*]
MPS............	Multi-Plane Programming System (NITA)
MPS............	Multiple Peptide Synthesis [*Biochemistry*]
MPS............	Multiple Protective Structure [*Missile bases*]
MPS............	Multiple Vertical Protective Shelter [*for missiles*]
MPS............	Multiprocessing System [*Computer science*]
MPS............	Multiprogramming Periodic Tasking System (NITA)
MPS............	Multiprogramming System [*Computer science*]

MPS............ Multipurpose Ship (AABC)
MPS............ Muzzle Position Sensor (MCD)
MPS............ Myeloma Progression Score [Oncology]
MPS............ Myocardial Perfusion Scintigraphy [Medicine] (DB)
MPS............ Society for Mucopolysaccharide Diseases (EA)
MPSA.......... Master of Public School Art
MPSA.......... Metropolitan Pharmaceutical Secretaries Association (EA)
MPSA.......... Military Petroleum Supply Agency [Later, Defense Petroleum Supply Center]
MPSA.......... Military Postal Service Agency
MPSA.......... Santiago [Panama] [ICAO location identifier] (ICLI)
MPSC.......... Marianas Political Status Commission
MPSC.......... Material Planning Schedule and Control [Division of Inspection Offices, Navy]
MPSC.......... Military Personnel Security Committee
MPSC.......... Military Provost Staff Corps [British]
MPSC.......... Movimiento Popular Socialcristiano [Christian Social Popular Movement] [El Salvador] [Political party] (PD)
MPSCL........ Mathematical Programming System Control Language [1974] [Computer science] (CSR)
MP/SCM ...... Multiport Semiconductor Memory (MHDI)
MPSE.......... Motion Picture Sound Editors (EA)
MPSE.......... Multipurpose Payload Support Equipment (MCD)
MPSF.......... Mountain Pacific Sports Federation (PSS)
MPSF.......... Multi-Purpose Special Fund [Asian Development Bank] [United Nations] (EY)
MPSG .... Marketing Programs and Services Group, Inc. [Gaithersburg, MD] [Information service or system Telecommunications] (TSSD)
MPSG .... Multi-Band Portable Signal Generator (PDAA)
MPSH .... Mean Pressure Suction Head (AAG)
mpsh .... Mean Pressure Suction Head (AD)
MPS-HHSA... Master of Professional Studies-Hospital and Health Services Administration
MPSI........... Message Processing Systems, Inc. [Charlotte, NC] [Telecommunications service] (TSSD)
MPSI........... MPSI Systems, Inc. [NASDAQ symbol] (SAG)
MPS I .... Mucopolysaccharidoses [Hurler Syndrome] [Also, Scheie Syndrome and Hurler/Scheie Syndrome] (PAZ)
MPSIG .... Monty Python Special Interest Group (EA)
MPS II .... Mucopolysaccharidoses [Hunter Syndrome] (PAZ)
MPS IV .... Mucopolysaccharidoses [Morquio Syndrome] (PAZ)
MPSK......... Multiple Phase Shift Keying [Computer science] (TEL)
MPSM......... Master of Public School Music
MPSM......... Master Problem Status Manual
MPSM......... MODEM Pooling Service Module [Telecommunications]
MPSM......... Multipurpose Submunition (RDA)
MPSMT....... Merrill-Palmer Scale of Mental Tests [Psychology] (DAVI)
MPSN......... Microwave Pulse Shaping Network
MPSNY .... Montserrat Progressive Society of New York (EA)
MPsO.......... Master of Psychology Orientation (NADA)
MP SOV GR COM... Most Puissant Sovereign Grand Commander [United States] [Freemasonry] (ROG)
MPSP.......... Mathematical Problem-Solving Project [National Science Foundation]
MP(S)P........ Mechanically Processed (Species) Product (DICI)
MPSP.......... Military Personnel Security Program
MPSR......... Mission Profile Storage and Retrieval [NASA] (NASA)
MPSR......... Multipurpose Support Room (MCD)
MPSRE....... Master of Professional Studies in Real Estate (PGP)
MPSRON..... Maritime Prepositioning Ship Squadron (DOMA)
MPSRT....... Matched-Pairs Signed-Rank Test [Statistics]
MPSS.......... Main Parachute Support Structure (NASA)
MPSS.......... Maryland Preschool Self-Concept Scale (EDAC)
MPSS.......... Mission Payload System Segment
MPSS.......... Multiple Protective Structure System (AD)
MPSS.......... Multipurpose Sampling System
M Ps Sc...... Master of Physic Sciences
MPsSc........ Master of Psychological Science (GAGS)
MPST......... Minimum Performance Standard Test [Military] (CAAL)
MPST......... Multipurpose Support Team [NASA] (NAKS)
M Ps Th...... Master of Psycho-Therapy
MPSTWG.... Mission Planning System Test Working Group [Military] (CAAL)
MPSU .... Missile Pressure Status Unit (AAG)
MPSV.......... Myeloproliferative Sarcoma Virus
MPSW......... Master of Psychiatric Social Work (NADA)
MP SWAT ... Military Police Special Weapons and Tactics Team (VNW)
MPSX.......... Mathematical Programming System Extended [IBM Corp.] [Computer science]
MPsych........ Master of Psychology
MPsychApp... Master of Applied Psychology (ADA)
MPsych(Clin)... Master of Psychology (Clinical)
MPsych(Ed)... Master of Psychology (Education)
MPsychMed... Master of Psychological Medicine, University of Liverpool [British] (DBQ)
MPsychol..... Master of Psychology
MPsychTh.... Master of Psychotherapy
M Psy Med... Master of Psychological Medicine
MPT............ Alpha-Methyl-p-tyrosine [Also, AMPT] [Pharmacology]
MPT............ Magnetic Particle Testing [Nuclear energy] (NRCH)
MPT............ Main Propulsion Test [NASA] (NASA)
MPT............ Male Pipe Thread (MSA)
mpt............ Male Pipe Thread (AD)
MPT............ Maneuver Planning Table [NASA]
MPT............ Manpower and Training (DOMA)
MPT............ Manpower, Personnel, and Training
MPT............ Marginal Propensity to Tax [Economics]

MPT............ Maryland Public Television [Owings Mills] [Information service or system Telecommunications] (TSSD)
Mpt............ Maryport (AD)
MPT............ Master of Pastoral Theology (PGP)
MPT............ Master of Physical Therapy (GAGS)
MPT............ Matupit Island [New Britain] [Seismograph station code, US Geological Survey] (SEIS)
MPT............ Maximum Power Transfer (IDOE)
MPT............ Mean Preventive Maintenance Time (MCD)
MPT............ Mean Pulse Time
MPT............ Mechanical Power Transmission
M PT.......... Melting Point (ROG)
mpt............ Melting Point (AD)
MPT............ Memory Processing Time
MPT............ Mercury Procedures Trainer
MPT............ Message Processing Task [Computer science] (ECII)
MPT............ Metal-Phthalocyanine Tetramine [Organic chemistry]
MPT............ Methyl-para-Tyrosine [Biochemistry]
MPT............ Michigan Picture Test [Psychology]
mpt............ Microprocessing Programmable Terminal [Computer science] (AD)
MPT............ Microprogramming Technique
mpt............ Midpoint (AD)
MPT............ Miles per Tankful (AD)
mpt............ Miles per Tankful (AD)
MPT............ Military Potential Test (AABC)
MPT............ Milk Pasteurization Tribunal [Australia]
MPT............ Minimum Pressurization Temperature [Nuclear energy] (NRCH)
MPT............ Minimum Process Time
MPT............ Ministry of Posts and Telecommunications [People's Republic of China] (ECON)
MPT............ Ministry of Posts and Telecommunictions [China] (ECON)
MPT............ Missile Preflight Tester
MPT............ Missile Procedure Trainer
MPT............ Mission Planning Table [NASA] (KSC)
MPT............ Mission Planning Terminal (MCD)
MPT............ Mixed Parotid Gland Tumor [Oncology]
MPT............ Modern Poetry in Translation [A publication] (WDAA)
MPT............ Modern Portfolio Theory [Finance]
MPT............ Molydopterin [Biochemistry]
MPT............ Morphine Provocative Test [Gastroenterology] (DAVI)
MPT............ MOS [Military Occupational Specialty] Proficiency Training [DoD]
MPT............ Motional Pickup Transducer (MCD)
MPT............ Mouvement Populaire Tchadien [Chadian Popular Movement] [Political party]
MPT............ Mouvement Populaire Togolais [Togolese Popular Movement] [Political party]
MPT............ Mouvement pour le Progres et la Tolerance [Burkina Faso] [Political party] (EY)
MPT............ Multilateral Preparatory Talks (NATG)
MPT............ Multiple Pure Tone [Sound]
mpt............ Multiple Pure Tone (AD)
MPT............ Multiple-Purpose Telescope
mpt............ Multipower Transmission (AD)
MPT............ Municipal Partners Fund [NYSE symbol] (SPSG)
MPT............ Municipal Partners Fund II [NYSE symbol] (TTSB)
MPTA.......... Machine Power Transmission Association (AD)
mpta .... Main Propulsion Test Article (AD)
MPTA.......... Main Propulsion Test Article [Aerospace] (NAKS)
MPTA.......... Manpower, Personnel, and Training Analysis
MPTA.......... Mechanical Power Transmission Association (EA)
MPTA.......... Municipal Passenger Transport Association, Inc. [British] (BI)
MPTAO........ Military Personnel and Transportation Assistance Office (MCD)
MPTB.......... Meridian Point Realty Trust [NASDAQ symbol] (SAG)
MPTB.......... Monophosphate Tungsten Bronze [Metallurgy]
MPTB.......... Multisolid Pneumatic Transport Bed [Chemical engineering]
MPTBS........ Meridian Point Rity Tr 83 [NASDAQ symbol] (TTSB)
MPTCA........ Motion Picture and Television Credit Association (EA)
MPTCC....... Most Probable Total Contract Cost (AAGC)
MPTCMA...... Motion Picture and Television Credit Managers Association [Later, MPTCA] (EA)
MPTDS .... MPTER [Multiple Point Source Model with Terrain] Model with Deposition andSettling of Pollutants [Environmental Protection Agency] (GFGA)
MPTE.......... Multipurpose Test Equipment
MPTEDA...... Mechanical Power Transmission Equipment Distributors Association [Later, Power Transmission Distributors Association] (EA)
MPTER........ Multiple Point Source Model with Terrain [Environmental Protection Agency] (GFGA)
MPTF.......... Main Propulsion Test Facility [NASA] (NASA)
MPTF.......... Mission Planning Task Force (KSC)
MPTF.......... Motion Picture and Television Fund (EA)
MPTF.......... Music Performance Trust Funds (EA)
MPTH.......... Methylphenothiazine [Organic chemistry]
MPTL.......... Materials Processing Technology Laboratory (SSD)
MPTMH....... Major Peace Treaties of Modern History, 1648-1967 [A publication] (DLA)
MPTN.......... Multiprotocol Transport Network [Telecommunications] (ACRL)
MPTO.......... Methods and Procedures Technical Orders
MPTO.......... Tocumen/General Omar Torrijos H. [Panama] [ICAO location identifier] (ICLI)
MPTP.......... Main Propulsion Test Program (MCD)
MPTP.......... Methyl(phenyl)tetrahydropyridine [Organic chemistry]
MPTP.......... Music Preference Test of Personality [Psychology]
MPTR.......... MedPartners, Inc. [NASDAQ symbol] (SAG)
MPTR.......... Mobile Position Tracking RADAR

MPTR...........	Motor, Pain, Touch, Reflex [_Neurology_] (DAVI)
MPTR...........	Multipurpose Training Range [_Army_]
MPTS...........	Manpower, Personnel, and Training Support [_Military_] (CAAL)
MPTS...........	Manpower, Personnel, Training, and Safety [_Army_]
MPTS...........	Metal Parts (AABC)
MPTS...........	Mobile Photographic Tracking Station
MPTS...........	Multi-Protocol Transport Service [_Telecommunications_]
MPTS...........	Multipurpose Test Set (DWSG)
MPTS...........	Multipurpose Tool Set (MCD)
MPT-SD........	Multipurpose, Tracer, Self-Destruct [_Army_]
MP(TSWG)...	Military Police Tripartite Standing Working Group (AABC)
MPTT...........	Maintenance Part Task Trainer [_Army_]
MPTUS........	Marble Polishers' Trade Union Society [_British_]
MPTV...........	MPTV, Inc. [_NASDAQ symbol_] (SAG)
MPTWT.......	Medium Power Traveling Wave Tube
MPU...........	Magnetic Pickup [_Electronics_]
MPU...........	Main Power Unit
MPU...........	Main Propulsion Unit
MPU...........	Malayan Planning Unit [_World War II_]
MPU...........	Manpack Unit (MCD)
MPU...........	Mapua [_Papua New Guinea_] [_Airport symbol Obsolete_] (OAG)
MPU...........	Medical Practitioners' Union [_Later, Medical Practitioners' Section - MPS_] [_British_] (DCTA)
MPU...........	Memory Protection Unit
MPU...........	Mental Parents Union (AD)
MPU...........	Message Picking-Up
MPU...........	Microprocessor Unit [_CPU of microcomputer_] [_Computer science_]
mpu...........	Microprocessor Unit (AD)
MPU...........	MIDI [_Musical Instrument Digital Interface_] Processing Unit [_Computer technology_]
MPU...........	Miniature Portable Unit
MPU...........	Minutes per Unit
MPU...........	Missile Power Unit (DNAB)
MPU...........	Missing Persons Unit (AD)
MPU...........	Mixing and Pumping Unit [_Bulk explosives_] (MCD)
MPU...........	Mobile Production Unit [_On-site television recording_] (NTCM)
MPU...........	Monitor Printing Unit [_Computer science_]
mpu...........	Monitor Printing Unit (AD)
MPU...........	Motorola Processor Unit
MPU...........	Motor Pressurization Unit
M Pub........	Master of Publishing (PGP)
M Pub Adm...	Master of Public Administration
MPubAdmin...	Master of Public Administration
MPubLaw....	Master of Public Law
MPubPol......	Master of Public Policy
MPUL........	Military Production Urgencies List (NG)
MPUS........	Military Production Urgencies System
MPV...........	Magistrae Piae Venerini [_Religious Venerini Sisters_] [_Roman Catholic religious order_]
MPV...........	Magnetic Polarization Vector
MPV...........	Main Portal Vein [_Medicine_] (DMAA)
MPV...........	Man-Powered Vehicle
M-P v.........	Mason-Pfizer Virus [_Medicine_] (AD)
MPV...........	Mass Mutual Participating Investors [_NYSE symbol_] (CTT)
MPV...........	MassMutual Participation Investors [_NYSE symbol_] (SAG)
MPV...........	MassMutual Part'n Inv [_NYSE symbol_] (TTSB)
MPV...........	Mean Platelet Volume [_Hematology_]
MPV...........	Meerwein-Ponndorf-Verley [_Organic chemistry_]
MPV...........	Metatarsus Primus Varus [_Orthopedics_] (DAVI)
MPV...........	Methane-Powered Vehicle
MPV...........	Military Pay Voucher
MPV...........	Mitral Valve Prolapse [_Medicine_] (DMAA)
MPV...........	Montpelier [_Vermont_] [_Airport symbol_] (OAG)
MPV...........	Mountain Province [_Vancouver Stock Exchange symbol_]
MPV...........	Multipurpose Passenger Vehicle
MPV...........	Multipurpose Vehicle [_Automotive engineering_]
mpv...........	Multipurpose Vehicle (AD)
MPV...........	Religious Venerini Sisters (TOCD)
MPVA........	Main Propellant Valve Actuator (MCD)
MP/VAP......	Maritime Patrol/Reconnaissance Attack Aircraft (NATG)
MPVI........	Mountain Province Mining, Inc. [_NASDAQ symbol_] (SAG)
MPVIF.......	Mountain Province Mining [_NASDAQ symbol_] (TTSB)
MPVM........	Master of Preventive Veterinary Medicine (GAGS)
MPVP........	Mean Pulmonary Venous Pressure [_Cardiology_]
MPVR........	El Porvenir [_Panama_] [_ICAO location identifier_] (ICLI)
MPVSCS......	Military Pay Voucher Summary and Certification Sheet
MPVT........	Montpelier [_Vermont_] [_Seismograph station code, US Geological Survey_] (SEIS)
MPW........	Macintosh Programmer's Workshop [_Computer science_] (BTTJ)
mPw.........	Maritime Polar [_Air Mass_] Warm [_Meteorology_] (BARN)
MPW........	Master of Public Works (PGP)
MPW........	Minneapolis-Moline [_Stock exchange symbol_] (AD)
MPW........	Modified Plane Wave (IEEE)
MPW........	Multi-Product Wafer (AAEL)
MPW........	Whiteshell Nuclear Research Establishment, Atomic Energy of Canada [_Etablissement de Recherche Nucleaire Whiteshell, L'Energie Atomique du Canada_] Pinawa,Manitoba [_Library symbol National Library of Canada_] (NLC)
MPWB........	Multilayer Printed-Wiring Board
MPWBS.......	Master Plan Works Breakdown Structure (AD)
MPWC........	Michigan Pure Water Council (EA)
MPWD........	Machine-Prepared Wiring Data [_Telecommunications_] (TEL)
MPWG........	Minuteman Parts Working Group [_Missiles_]
MPWS........	Mobile Protected Weapon System (RDA)

MPWU........	Movement for Political World Union [_Blommenslyst, Fyn, Denmark_] (EA)
MPX...........	Aeromexpress, SA de CV [_Mexico_] [_FAA designator_] (FAAC)
MPX...........	Magazine Page Exposure [_Publishing_] (WDMC)
MPX...........	Mapped Programming Executive [_Systems Engineering Laboratories U.S._] (NITA)
MPX...........	Microprocessor Exchange [_Computer science_]
MPX...........	Mid-America Payment Exchange [_Banking_] (TBD)
MPX...........	Multiplex [_or Multiplexer_] [_Telecommunications_]
mpx...........	Multiplex (AD)
MPX...........	Multiprocessor Extension (PCM)
MPX...........	Multiprogramming Executive [_Computer science_]
MPXR........	Multiplexer
mpxr........	Multiplexor (AD)
Mpy...........	Maatschappij [_Company_] [_Dutch_] (AD)
MPY...........	Milli-Inches per Year [_Corrosion technology_]
MPY...........	Multiple Problem Youth
MPY...........	Multiply (MDG)
mpy...........	Multiply (AD)
MPZ...........	Mid-Continent Petroleum [_Stock exchange symbol_] (AD)
MPZ...........	Modified Protamine Zinc [_Insulin_]
MPZ...........	Mount Pleasant, IA [_Location identifier FAA_] (FAAL)
MPZ...........	Myelin Protein, Zero (DMAA)
MPZL........	Panama [_Panama_] [_ICAO location identifier_] (ICLI)
MQ...........	Magnum Airlines [_ICAO designator_] (AD)
MQ...........	Management Quarterly Magazine [_A publication_] (EAAP)
MQ...........	MARC [_Machine-Readable Cataloging_] Quebecois [_Source file_] [_UTLAS symbol_]
MQ...........	Marketing Quota
mq...........	Martinique [_MARC country of publication code Library of Congress_] (LCCP)
MQ...........	Martinique [_ANSI two-letter standard code_] (CNC)
MQ...........	Memory Quotient
mq...........	Memory Quotient (AD)
MQ...........	Menaquinone [_Vitamin K_] [_Also, MK_] [_Biochemistry_]
MQ...........	Merit Quotient
MQ...........	Metol-Quinol [_Developer_] [_Photography_] (ROG)
mq...........	Metol-Quinol [_Medicine_] (AD)
mq...........	Metol-Quinone [_Medicine_] (AD)
MQ...........	Metol-Quinone [_Medicine_] (AD)
MQ...........	Mining and Quarrying [_Department of Employment_] [_British_]
MQ...........	Mo'ed Qatan [_or Qattan_] (BJA)
Mq...........	Mosque (AD)
mq...........	Mosque (BARN)
MQ...........	Mothering Quotient
mq...........	Multiple Quotient (AD)
MQ...........	Multiplier Quotient [_Computer science_]
MQ...........	Musical Quarterly [_A publication_] (BRI)
MQ...........	Simmons Airlines [_ICAO designator_] (AD)
MQ...........	Thomas Crane Public Library, Quincy, MA [_Library symbol Library of Congress_] (LCLS)
MQA...........	Adams Mansion, Quincy, MA [_Library symbol Library of Congress_] (LCLS)
MQA...........	Manual of Qualification for Advancement
MQA...........	Manufacturing Quality Assurance
MQA...........	Medical Quality Assurance (AD)
MQA...........	Multiple Queue Assignment [_Computer science_] (ITD)
MQA...........	Murrayaquinone-A [_Biochemistry_]
MQAB........	Medical Quality Assurance Board (AD)
MQAD........	Materials Quality Assurance Directorate [_Ministry of Defence_] [_British_]
MQB........	Macomb, IL [_Location identifier FAA_] (FAAL)
MQB........	Mining Qualifications Board [_British_] (BI)
MQC........	Macroscopic Quantum Coherence [_Physics_]
MQC........	Mammography Quality Control
MQC........	Manufacturing Quality Control (MCD)
MQC........	Microbiologic Quality Control (DMAA)
MQCL........	Master Quality Characteristic List (MCD)
MQD........	Manhattan, KS [_Location identifier FAA_] (FAAL)
MQD........	Metallurgical Quenching Dilatometry
MQD........	Milner. Questions de Droit [_A publication_] (DLA)
MQD........	Monolithic Quad Device
MQDT........	Multichannel Quantum Defect Theory [_Physics_]
MQE........	Martinique [_West Indies_] (WDAA)
Mqe........	Martinique (AD)
MQE........	Message Queue Element [_Computer science_]
MQEM........	Michigan Quarterly Economic Model (NITA)
mqf........	Mobile Quarantine Facility (AD)
MQf........	Mobile Quarantine Facility [_NASA_]
MQG........	General Dynamics, Quincy Shipbuilding Division, Quincy, MA [_Library symbol Library of Congress_] (LCLS)
MQG........	Milgarra [_Queensland_] [_Airport symbol_] (AD)
MQHi........	Quincy Historical Society, Quincy, MA [_Library symbol Library of Congress_] (LCLS)
MQI........	Macquarie Island [_Australia Seismograph station code, US Geological Survey Closed_] (SEIS)
MQI........	Maiquetia [_Venezuelan airport_] (AD)
MQI........	Manteo, NC [_Location identifier FAA_] (FAAL)
MQIFX........	Mutual Qualified Fund [_Mutual fund ticker symbol_] (SG)
MQIL........	Miniature Quartz Incandescent Lamp
mqil........	Miniature Quartz Incandescent Lamp (AD)
MQJ........	Indianapolis, IN [_Location identifier FAA_] (FAAL)
MQK........	Youngstown, OH [_Location identifier FAA_] (FAAL)
MQL........	Method Quantification Limits (COE)
MQL........	Mildura [_Australia Airport symbol_] (OAG)
MQL........	Miniature Quartz Lamp

mql	Miniature Quartz Lamp (AD)
MQM	Master of Quality Management (PGP)
MQM	Master of the Queen's Music [*British*] (AD)
MQM	Message Queue Manager [*Computer science*] (MCD)
MQM	Mohajir Qami Movement [*Pakistan*] [*Political party*]
MQM	Monida, MT [*Location identifier FAA*] (FAAL)
MQM	Muhajir Qaumi Movement [*Pakistan*] [*Political party*] (ECON)
MQM	University of New Mexico, Medical Center Library, Albuquerque, NM [*OCLC symbol*] (OCLC)
MQN	Magnetic Quantum Number [*Atomic physics*]
MQ-NMR	Multiple Quantum Nuclear Magnetic Resonance (AAEL)
MQO	Marksmanship Qualification Order [*Marine Corps*]
MQO	Mosquito Creek Gold Mining [*Vancouver Stock Exchange symbol*]
MQP	Mandatory Quote Period (NUMA)
MQP	Military Qualification Program (NG)
MQP	Mineral Wells, TX [*Location identifier FAA*] (FAAL)
MQP	Motor Qualification Program (NG)
MQQ	Moundou [*Chad*] [*Airport symbol*] (AD)
MQR	Michigan Quarterly Review [*A publication*] (BRI)
MQR	Miscellaneous Quote Request (MCD)
MQR	Multiplier Quotient Register [*Computer science*]
MQRNS	Modified Quadratic Residue Number System (MCD)
MQS	Coatesville, PA [*Location identifier FAA*] (FAAL)
MQS	Maintenance Quality Specialist (MCD)
MQS	Master of Quantitative Systems
MQS	Military Qualification Standard
MQS	Mobile Quality Services (AD)
MQS	Motion to Quash Subpoena (NRCH)
MQS	Multiprogrammed Queued Tasking System (NITA)
MQS	Mustique [*Windward Islands*] [*Airport symbol*] (OAG)
MQSA	Mammography Quality Standards Act of 1992
MQSS	Mary Queen of Scots Society (EAIO)
MQT	Macquest Resources Ltd. [*Toronto Stock Exchange symbol*]
MQT	Macroscopic Quantum Tunneling [*Quantum mechanics*]
MQT	Marquette [*Michigan*] [*Airport symbol*] (OAG)
MQT	Military Qualification Test (NG)
MQT	Mission Qualification Training
MQT	Model Qualification Test
MQT	Motor Qualification Test (NG)
MQT	MuniYield Quality Fund II [*NYSE symbol*] (SPSG)
MQU	Beckley, WV [*Location identifier FAA*] (FAAL)
MQU	Makus Resources, Inc. [*Vancouver Stock Exchange symbol*]
MQU	Mariquita [*Colombia*] [*Airport symbol*] (OAG)
MQU	Media Quality Unit [*Communications*]
MQU	Multiplier Quotient Unit [*Computer science*]
MQUAD	Metal Quad
MQV	Ministere de la Qualite de la Vie [*Ministry of the Quality of Life*] [*France*] (AD)
MQW	McRae, GA [*Location identifier FAA*] (FAAL)
MQW	Multiple Quantum Well [*Switch for an optical computer*]
MQW	Multiquantum Well (NITA)
MQWL	Multiquantum Well Lasers (NITA)
MQX	Makale [*Ethiopia*] [*Airport symbol*] (OAG)
MQY	MuniYield Quality Fund [*NYSE symbol*] (SPSG)
MQY	Smyrna, TN [*Location identifier FAA*] (FAAL)
mqyco	Minimum Quantity Yards per Color (AD)
mqyds	Minimum Quantity Yards per Design (AD)
MR	Air Mauritanie [*Mauritania*] [*ICAO designator*] (ICDA)
MR	Application for Writ of Mandamus Refused [*Legal term*] (DLA)
M/R	Machine Receipt
mr	Machine Record (AD)
MR	Machine Records
MR	Machine Rifle
mr	Machine Rifle (AD)
MR	Machinery Repairman [*Navy rating*]
MR	Macrophage Rich
MR	Magister [*Master*] [*Latin*] (ROG)
MR	Magnetic Recorder (DEN)
MR	Magnetic Resonance
MR	Magnetic Resonating (AD)
MR	Magnetoresistive
MR	Magnitude of Rotation
MR	Maintainability Report
M+R	Maintenance and Refurbishment
M+R	Maintenance and Repair
MR	Maintenance Ratio (MCD)
MR	Maintenance Review
MR	Management Requirements (MCD)
MR	Management Reserve (MCD)
MR	Mandelate Racemase [*An enzyme*]
MR	Manitoba Law Reports [*Canada*] [*A publication*] (DLA)
MR	Mannose Resistant [*Biochemistry*]
MR	Manpower Requirements
MR	Manual Removal [*Medicine*]
MR	Manufacturer's Representative
MR	Manufacturing Requisition
MR	Map Reading
m/r	Map Reading (AD)
mr	Map Reference (AD)
MR	Map Reference
MR	Marble (AAG)
MR	Marca Registrada [*Registered Trademark*] [*Spanish*]
MR	March
MR	Marginal Return [*Army*] (AABC)
MR	Marginal Revenue [*Economics*]
mr	Marginal Revenue (AD)
MR	Marianist Sisters (TOCD)
MR	Maritime Reconnaissance (NATG)
MR	Maritime Regiment
MR	Marketing Research Division [*of AMS, Department of Agriculture*]
MR	Mark Russell (AD)
MR	Mask Register
MR	Master [*British military*] (DMA)
Mr.	Master (AD)
MR	Master of the Rolls
MR	Master Relay [*Electrical*] (DICI)
MR	Master Reset (MCD)
MR	Master Routing (SAA)
MR	Material Request [*or Requisition*] (MCD)
MR	Material Review [*Aviation*] (AAG)
MR	Materiel Readiness [*Army*]
MR	Mate's Receipt
MR	Mauritania [*ANSI two-letter standard code*] (CNC)
MR	Mauritius Decisions [*A publication*] (DLA)
MR	Mauritius Reports [*A publication*] (DLA)
MR	Maximal Response
MR	Maximum Range (IAA)
MR	May Repeat [*Medicine*]
MR	McCloud River [*Railroad*] (MHDW)
MR	Mean Radius (MCD)
MR	Measles, Rubella [*Immunology*]
MR	Measured Rating [*IOR*] [*Yacht racing*]
MR	Mechanical Restraint [*for mental patients*] [*British*]
MR	Medial Rectus [*Eye anatomy*]
MR	[*The*] Media Report [*A publication*] (NTCM)
MR	Medical Record
MR	Medical Rectus [*Muscle*] [*Anatomy*]
MR	Medical Report
MR	Medium Range
mr	Medium Range (AD)
MR	Medium-Range Planes [*Navy*]
MR	Medium Reduction (NITA)
MR	Medium Release (WDAA)
MR	Medium Resolution
MR	Medullary Ray [*Botany*] (BARN)
mr	Meester [*Master*] [*Dutch*] (AD)
MR	Megarayleigh [*Optics*]
MR	Melkersson-Rosenthal [*Syndrome*] [*Medicine*] (DB)
MR	Memorandum for Record [*Military*] (AFM)
MR	Memorandum Receipt [*Military*] (MUGU)
MR	Memorandum Report
MR	Memory Read [*Computer science*]
MR	Memory Recall [*Computer science*] (PCM)
MR	Memory Reclaimer
MR	Memory Register [*Computer science*]
mr	Mentally Retarded (AD)
MR	Mental Retardation
MR	Mental Retardation Program [*Public human service program*] (PHSD)
MR	Mercury-Redstone [*NASA*]
MR	Message Register (AAG)
MR	Message Repeat
MR	Metabolic Rate
mr	Metabolic Rate (AD)
MR	Meter
MR	Methacholine Response [*Medicine*]
MR	Methyl Red [*A dye*]
mr	Methyl Red (AD)
MR	Methyl Reductase [*An enzyme*]
MR	Metropolitan Railway [*British*]
MR	Michael Resources Ltd. [*Vancouver Stock Exchange symbol*]
MR	Michigan Reformatory (AD)
MR	Microminiature Relay
MR	Microplate Reader [*Computer science*]
MR	Middle Repetitive [*Genetics*]
m/r	Middle Right (AD)
MR	[*The*] Middlesex Regiment [*British*]
MR	Mid-Engine, Rear-Drive [*Automotive engineering*]
MR	Midland Railway [*British*]
MR	Midrib [*Botany*]
MR	Migration Ratio (DNAB)
MR	Military Railroad (AD)
MR	Military Readiness
MR	Military Region [*Viet Cong term*]
MR	Military Regulation
MR	Military Representative (NATG)
MR	Military Requirement
M/R	Military Reserve (CINC)
MR	Military Review (MCD)
MR	Militia Reserve [*British military*] (DMA)
MR	Milk-Ring [*Test*] [*Medicine*] (MEDA)
MR	Milliradian (DEN)
MR	Millirem (DEN)
mr	Milliroentgen
mR	Milliroentgen (AD)
MR	Mill Run (AD)
MR	Mill Run [*Unselected lot of a manufactured product*]
MR	Milrinone [*Biochemistry*]
MR	Mine Rake (DWSG)
MR	Mineralo-Corticoid Receptor [*Endocrinology*]
MR	Mineral Range Railroad (IIA)

MR.............	Mineral Rubber
mr..............	Mineral Rubber (AD)
mr..............	Mine Run (AD)
MR.............	Mine-Run
MR.............	Minimum Required
MR.............	Mining Reports, Edited by R. S. Morrison [Chicago] [A publication] (DLA)
MR.............	Mining Review [A publication]
MR.............	Mini Registry (EA)
MR.............	Minister-Residentiary [Diplomacy]
MR.............	Ministry of Reconstruction [World War I] [British]
MR.............	Minnesota Review [A publication] (BRI)
MR.............	Minor Repair (MCD)
MR.............	Mi Remesa [My Remittance] [Spanish Business term]
MR.............	Miscellaneous Report
MR.............	Missed Recognition (SAA)
MR.............	Missile RADAR [Military] (CAAL)
MR.............	Missile Receiver
MR.............	Missile Reference
MR.............	Missile Rounds (MCD)
M/R............	Missiles and Rockets [A publication]
MR.............	Missionarius Rector [Missionary Rector] [Latin]
MR.............	Mission Radius (MCD)
MR.............	Mission Ready [Aircraft]
MR.............	Mission Reliability
MR.............	Mission Report [NASA]
MR.............	Mister
Mr..............	Mister (WDAA)
MR.............	Mistura [Mixture] [Pharmacy] (ROG)
MR.............	Mitochondriarich [Cytology]
MR.............	Mitral Reflux [Cardiology] (MAE)
MR.............	Mitral Regurgitation [Cardiology]
MR.............	Mittleres Reich in Aegypten [A publication] (BJA)
MR.............	Mixture Ratio (KSC)
Mr..............	Mobile Revertant [Bacteriology]
MR.............	Mobility Required [Civil Service]
MR.............	Mobilizacion Republicana [Republican Mobilization] [Nicaragua] [Political party] (AD)
MR.............	Mobilization Regulation [Army]
MR.............	MODEM Ready [Computer science]
MR.............	Moderately Resistant [Plant pathology]
MR.............	[The] Modern Reader's Bible (1907) [A publication] (BJA)
M-R............	Modification and Restriction [of DNA] [Biochemistry, genetics]
MR.............	Modification Request [or Requirement]
MR.............	Modular Redundancy
MR.............	Modulation Rate (DB)
MR.............	Modulation Response
MR.............	Moisture Resistant (IEEE)
MR.............	Molar Refraction
MR.............	Molecular Replacement [Crystallography]
MR.............	Moment of Resistance
MR.............	Mondcivitan Republic [Defunct] (EAIO)
MR.............	Monitor Recorder
MR.............	Monon Railroad (AD)
MR.............	Monthly Report
MR.............	Monthly Review
MR.............	Moon Rise (DNAB)
MR.............	Morgan's Food [AMEX symbol] (TTSB)
MR.............	Morgan's Foods, Inc. [AMEX symbol] (SPSG)
MR.............	Morning Report [Army]
mr..............	Morocco [MARC country of publication code Library of Congress] (LCCP)
MR.............	Morris Register [An association] (EAIO)
MR.............	Mortality Rates
MR.............	Mortality Ratio (MAE)
Mr..............	Mother (AD)
mr..............	Motivational Research (AD)
MR.............	Motivation Research
MR.............	Motormannes Riksforbund [Motorists' Association] [Swedish] (AD)
MR.............	Motor Reduction
MR.............	Mounted Route (TBD)
MR.............	Multifamily Residential Zone (AD)
MR.............	Multi-Mirror Reflector [Lamp]
MR.............	Multiple Requesting [IBM Corp.]
MR.............	Multiplier Register
MR.............	Multi-Reflecton [Lighting]
MR.............	Municipal Reform [or Reformer]
MR.............	Muscle Receptor [Medicine] (DMAA)
MR.............	Muscle Relaxant [Medicine] (DMAA)
MR.............	Music Records [Record label]
MR.............	Muster Report
MR.............	Mutual Recognition
MR.............	Mutual Responsibility [Movement within Anglican Communion to make its mission more efficacious]
MR.............	Mycorrhizal Roots [Botany]
MR.............	Radiolocation Mobile Station [ITU designation]
MR.............	Reading Public Library, Reading, MA [Library symbol Library of Congress] (LCLS)
mr----	Red Sea and Area [MARC geographic area code Library of Congress] (LCCP)
Mr..............	Relative Molecular Mass (DOG)
MR1............	Machinery Repairman, First Class [Navy rating]
MR2............	Machinery Repairman, Second Class [Navy rating]
MR3............	Machinery Repairman, Third Class [Navy rating]
MR-13	Movimiento Revolucionario 13 de Noviembre [November 13 Revolutionary Movement] [Guatemala]
MR-13 Movement of 13 NoGuatemala...	Movimiento Revolucionario de 13 de Noviembre [Revolutionary Movement of 13 November] [Guatemala] [Political party] (AD)
MRA............	Golden Myra Resources, Inc. [Toronto Stock Exchange symbol]
MRA............	Machine Readable Archives Division [Public Archives of Canada] [Information service or system] (IID)
MRA............	Machine Records Activity
MRA............	Magnetic Reaction Analyzer (PDAA)
MRA............	Magnetic Resonance Angiography [Medicine] (DMAA)
MRA............	Main Renal Artery [Medicine] (DB)
MRA............	Maneuver Right Area [Army]
MRA............	Manufacturers Representatives of America (EA)
MRA............	Maritime Royal Artillery [British military] (DMA)
MRA............	Marketing Research Association [Chicago, IL] (EA)
MRA............	Marrow Repopulating Activity [Medicine] (DB)
MRA............	Marrow Repopulation Activity [Medicine] (DMAA)
MRA............	Martinaire [ICAO designator] (FAAC)
MRA............	Masonic Relief Association of USA and Canada (EA)
MRA............	Master of Recreation Administration (GAGS)
MRA............	Master of Rehabilitation Administration (GAGS)
MRA............	Master of Resource Administration (GAGS)
MRA............	Master Retailers Association (AD)
MRA............	Masters Retailers Association (NADA)
MRA............	Material Review Activity
MRA............	Materials Requirement Analysis (PDAA)
MRA............	Materials Review Area (AAG)
MRA............	Matrix Reducibility Algorithm (PDAA)
MRA............	Maximum Rendezvous Altitude
MRA............	Mazda Research & Development of North America
MRA............	Mean Reference Axis (MCD)
MRA............	Mean Right Atrial [Cardiology]
MRA............	Mechanical Readiness Assessment (NASA)
MRA............	Medial Right Abdomen [Injection site]
MRA............	Medical Record Administrator
MRA............	Medical Record Analyst (HCT)
MRA............	Medical Resource Co. of America [AMEX symbol] (SPSG)
mra............	Medium-Powered Radio Range (AD)
MRA............	Medium-Powered Radio Range (Adcock)
MRA............	Men's Rights Association
MRA............	Menswear Retailers of America (EA)
MRA............	Messtechnik, Regelungstechnik, Automatik [Hoppenstedt Wirtschaftsdatenbank GmbH] [Germany Information service or system] (CRD)
MRA............	Metro Rating Area [Arbitron television ratings] (NTCM)
mra............	Metro Rating Area (AD)
MRA............	Microgravity Research Associates
MRA............	Midwest Resources Association [Defunct]
MRA............	Minimum Reception Altitude [Aviation]
mra............	Minimum Reception Altitude (AD)
MRA............	Minimum Reserve Authorization
MRA............	Minimum Resolvable Angle
MRA............	Minimum Retirement Age (GFGA)
MRA............	Ministry for Rural Affairs [British] (WDAA)
MRA............	Missile RADAR Altimeter (MCD)
MRA............	Misurata [Libya] [Airport symbol] (OAG)
MRA............	Mixed Refrigerant Autocascade [Cryogenic system]
MRA............	Model Reporting Area [for Blindness Statistics] [HEW]
MRA............	Module Rack Assembly
MRA............	Moral Re-Armament (EA)
MRA............	Motorcycle Retailers of America [Later, NMRA] (EA)
MRA............	Mountain Rescue Association (EA)
MRA............	Multiple Recording Accelerometer
MRA............	Multiple Regression Analysis
MRA............	Multiple Resource Area Nomination [National Register of Historic Places]
MRA............	Multivariate Regression Analysis [Medicine] (DMAA)
MRA............	Mycelium Radius Atrovirens [A fungus]
MRA............	Rapid City Regional Library, Manitoba [Library symbol National Library of Canada] (NLC)
MRAA	Marine Retailers Association of America (EA)
MRAAA	Mental Retardation Association of America (EA)
MRAALS	Marine Corps Remote Area Approach and Landing System (MCD)
MRAAM	Medium-Range Air-to-Air Missile (MCD)
mraam	Medium-Range Air-to-Air Missile [Military] (AD)
MRA & L	Manpower, Reserve Affairs and Logistics (MCD)
MRAC	Manifold-Regulator Accumulator Charging [Formerly, NCP] (AAG)
mrac	Manifold-Regulator Accumulator Charging (AD)
MRAC	Member of the Royal Agricultural College [British]
MRAC	Meter-Reading Access Circuit [Bell Laboratories]
MRACGP.....	Member of the Royal Australasian College of General Practice (BABM)
MRACO	Member of the Royal Australasian College of Ophthalmologists [British] (BABM)
MRACP	Member of Royal Australasian College of Physicians
MRACR	Member of the Royal Australasian College of Radiologists [British] (BABM)
MRAD	Mass Random Access Disk [Computer science]
M Rad	Master of Radiology
mrad	Megarad (AD)
mrad	Millirad (AD)
mrad	Milliradian (IDOE)
MRAD	Milliradians (KSC)
MRAD	Minor Restricted Activity Day [Environmental medicine]

MRAD	Multiple Range Alignment Device [*Army*] (INF)
MRadA	Member of the Radionic Association [*British*]
M Rad (D)	Master of Radiology (Radiodiagnosis)
MRAD/IN	Milliradians per Inch
MRADS	Mass Random Access Data Storage [*Computer science*]
M Rad (T)	Master of Radiology (Radiotherapy)
M Ra E	Master of Radio Engineering
M Ra Eng	Master of Radio Engineering
MRAeS	Member of the Royal Aeronautical Society [*British*] (ADA)
MRAF	Marshal of the Royal Air Force [*British*]
MRAF	Missile Round Assembly Facility
M-RAG	Moderately Repressive Authoritarian Government
MRAIC	Member of the Royal Architectural Institute of Canada
MRAJ	Aranjuez [*Costa Rica*] [*ICAO location identifier*] (ICLI)
MRaK	Myth, Ritual, and Kingship. Essays on the Theory and Practice of Kingship in theAncient Near East and in Israel [*A publication*] (BJA)
MRAL	Alajuela [*Costa Rica*] [*ICAO location identifier*] (ICLI)
MRAL	Mandatory Retirement Age Law of 1978 (WYGK)
MRAL	Materiel Readiness Authorization List [*Military*]
MRAM	Amubri [*Costa Rica*] [*ICAO location identifier*] (ICLI)
MRAM	Magnetic Random-Access Memory [*Computer science*] (PS)
MRAM	Member of the Royal Academy of Music [*British*]
MRAM	Multi-Mission Redeye Air-Launched Missile [*Military*] (PDAA)
MRAN	Medical Resident Admitting Note (MEDA)
MR & A	Market Research and Analysis
MR & D	Material Redistribution and Disposal
MR & DA	Material Redistribution and Disposal Administration
MR & DC	Medical Research and Development Command [*Army*] (AD)
MR&DF	Malleable Research and Development Foundation (AD)
MR & S	Materials Research and Standards (AD)
MR & T	Mississippi River and Tributaries [*Flood-control project*]
MRANZCP	Member of the Royal Australian and New Zealand College of Psychiatrists [*British*] (BABM)
MRAO	Mobilization Reserve Acquisition Objective [*Military*]
MRAO	Mullard Radio Astronomy Observatory (USDC)
MRAP	Management Review and Analysis Program (AD)
MRAP	Marginal Revenue/Average Physical Product [*Economics*]
MRAP	Mean Right Atrial Pressure [*Cardiology*]
MRAP	Mortgage and Rental Assistance Program [*Australia*]
MRAP	Mouvement Contre le Racisme et pour l'Amitie Entre les Peuples [*Movement Against Racism and for Friendship between People*] (EAIO)
MRAP	Movimiento de Resistencia Armada Puertorriquena [*Puerto Rican Armed Resistance Movement*] [*Political party*] (PD)
MRAPCON	Mobile RADAR Approach Control (AFM)
MRAPM	Materials Research and Protection Methods (SAA)
MRAR	Atirro [*Costa Rica*] [*ICAO location identifier*] (ICLI)
MRAR	Manpower Requirements Analysis Report [*Military*]
MRAS	Main Renal Artery Stenosis [*Medicine*] (DMAA)
MRAS	Management Resources Accounting System
MRAS	Manpower Resources Accounting System [*Air Force*]
MRAS	Member of the Royal Academy of Science [*British*]
MRAS	Member of the Royal Asiatic Society [*British*]
MRAS	Member of the Royal Astronomical Society [*British*] (DI)
MRAS	Model Reference Adaptive System (PDAA)
MRASB	Member of the Royal Asiatic Society of Bengal
MRASE	Member of the Royal Agricultural Society of England
MRASM	Medium-Range Air-to-Surface Missile (MCD)
mrasm	Medium-Range Air-to-Surface Missile [*Military*] (AD)
MRASTU	Marine Reserve Aviation Supply Training Unit (DNAB)
MRAT	Altamira De San Carlos [*Costa Rica*] [*ICAO location identifier*] (ICLI)
mrat	Medium-Range Applied Technology (AD)
MRAT	Mobile Radiation Tester (IAA)
MRATE	Money Market Rates [*I. P. Sharp Associates*] [*Canada Information service or system*] (CRD)
MR ATOMIC	Multiple Rapid Automatic Test of Monolithic Integrated Circuits (PDAA)
MRAUSCAN	Masonic Relief Association of the United States and Canada (AD)
MRB	Magnetic Recording Boresight [*or Borescope*]
MRB	Magnetospheric Radio Burst
MRB	Maintenance Review Board (MCD)
MRB	Malaysian Rubber Bureau (EA)
MRB	Marble [*Technical drawings*]
MRB	Marble Base (AAG)
mrb	Marble Base (AD)
MRB	Martinsburg, WV [*Location identifier FAA*] (FAAL)
MRB	Master Reference Buoy [*Navy*] (NVT)
MRB	Material Review Board [*Aviation*] (MCD)
MRB	Metals Reserve Board [*of the Reconstruction Finance Corp.*]
MRB	Microcircuit Reliability Bibliography (NITA)
MRB	Mileage Rationing Board [*World War II*]
MRB	Mission Review Board [*NASA*]
MRB	Mister Build Industry, Inc. [*Vancouver Stock Exchange symbol*]
MRB	Mobile Riverine Base [*Navy*]
MRB	Modification Requirements Board [*NASA*] (KSC)
MRB	Modification Review Board (AFM)
MRB	Mortgage Revenue Bond
MRB	Motorized Rifle Battalion [*Former USSR*]
MRB	Motor Rescue Boat
MRB	Motor Surfboat [*Coast Guard*] (DNAB)
MRB	Motor Truck Rate Bureau Inc., Columbia SC [*STAC*]
MRB	Multi-Role Bomber [*Program*] [*DoD*]
MRB	Mutual Reinsurance Bureau (EA)
MRBA	Buenos Aires [*Costa Rica*] [*ICAO location identifier*] (ICLI)

MRBA	Mississippi River Bridge Authority (AD)
MRBB	Babilonia [*Costa Rica*] [*ICAO location identifier*] (ICLI)
MRBC	Barra Del Colorado [*Costa Rica*] [*ICAO location identifier*] (ICLI)
MRBC	Missouri River Basin Commission
MRBC	Molded Rubber Blended Cover
MRBC	Monkey Red Blood Cells
MRBC	Mouse Red Blood Cell [*Medicine*] (DMAA)
MRBCMA	Mean Rounds between Corrective Maintenance Actions [*Quality control*] (MCD)
MR-BD	Mercury-Redstone Booster Development [*Spacecraft*] [*NASA*]
MRBF	Mean Renal Blood Flow [*Nephrology*]
MRBF	Mean Rounds between Failures [*Military*] (CAAL)
MRBIR	Municipal Registered Bond Interest Record [*Standard & Poor's Corp.*] [*Information service or system*] (CRD)
MRBK	Mercantile Bankshares [*NASDAQ symbol*] (TTSB)
MRBK	Mercantile Bankshares Corp. [*NASDAQ symbol*] (NQ)
MRBL	Marble
MRBL	Marble Financial Corp. [*NASDAQ symbol*] (NQ)
MRBM	Bremen [*Costa Rica*] [*ICAO location identifier*] (ICLI)
MRBM	Medium [*or Mid*]-Range Ballistic Missile
mrbm	Medium-Range Ballistic Missile [*Military*] (AD)
MRBN	Bataan [*Costa Rica*] [*ICAO location identifier*] (ICLI)
MRBNA	Member of the Royal British Nursing Association (ROG)
MRBO	Boca Naranjo [*Costa Rica*] [*ICAO location identifier*] (ICLI)
MRBOMF	Mean Rounds between Operational Mission Failures [*Quality control*] (MCD)
MRBP	Barra De Parismina [*Costa Rica*] [*ICAO location identifier*] (ICLI)
MRBP	Missouri River Basin Project
MRBS	Mean Rounds between Stoppages [*Quality control*] (MCD)
MRBS	Modified Road Brigade Slice (MCD)
MRBT	Barra De Tortuguero [*Costa Rica*] [*ICAO location identifier*] (ICLI)
MRBT	Multirod Burst Test [*Nuclear energy*] (NRCH)
MRC	Columbia/Mt. Pleasant, TN [*Location identifier FAA*] (FAAL)
MRC	Graduate Center for Materials Research [*University of Missouri - Rolla*] [*Research center*] (RCD)
MRC	Interdepartmental Committee on Manpower Requirements [*British World War II*]
MRC	Machine-Readable Code
MRC	Machinery Repairman, Chief [*Navy rating*]
MRC	Magnetic Rectifier Control
mrc	Magnetic Rectifier Control (AD)
MRC	Magnetic Research Corp. (MCD)
MRC	Maintenance and Repair Craft [*Military*]
MRC	Maintenance and Repair Cycle
MRC	Maintenance Requirement Card
MRC	Major Readiness Command (MCD)
MRC	Major Reality Corp. (EFIS)
MRC	Major Regional Contingency (DOMA)
MRC	Major Retail Center
MRC	Malaria Research Centre [*India*]
MRC	Management Research Center [*University of Wisconsin - Milwaukee*] [*Research center*] (RCD)
MRC	Management Research Corp. [*Shelbyville, IN*] [*Information service or system*] (IID)
MRC	Manitoba Research Council [*Research center*] (RCD)
MRC	Manpower Requirements Change [*Military*] (GFGA)
MRC	Manufacturing Resource Control [*Kongsberg Vaapenfabrikk*] [*Software package*] (NCC)
MRC	Marietta College, Marietta, OH [*OCLC symbol*] (OCLC)
MRC	Marine Research Committee
MRC	Marine Research Corp. [*Marine science*] (OSRA)
MRC	Marine Research Corporation (USDC)
MRC	Marine Resources Council
MRC	Marketing Research Council (NTPA)
MRC	Market Research Council
MRC	Marlin-Rockwell Corp. (AD)
MRC	Master of Rehabilitation Counseling
MRC	Master Requirements Code
MRC	Master Routing Control (SAA)
MRC	Material Redistribution Center
MRC	Materials Research Center [*Northwestern University*] (RCD)
MRC	Materials Research Center [*Lehigh University*] (RCD)
MRC	Materials Research Corp.
MRC	Materials Review Crib (AAG)
MRC	Materiel Readiness Command [*Military*]
MRC	Materiel Release Confirmation [*Army*] (AABC)
MRC	Mathematics Research Center (MCD)
Mrc	Mauricio [*Mauritius*] [*Spanish*] (AD)
MRC	Maximum Recycling Capacity (DMAA)
MRC	Maximum Reverse Current
MRC	Measurement Requirements Committee [*NASA*] (NASA)
MRC	Measurement Research Center [*University of Iowa*]
MRC	Media Resource Center [*Adelaide, Australia*]
MRC	Medical Registration Council [*British*] (DAVI)
MRC	Medical Research Committee
MRC	Medical Research Council [*Research center British*] (IRC)
MRC	Medical Reserve Corps
MRC	Mekong River Commission [*Thailand*]
MRC	Memorial Research Center [*University of Tennessee*] [*Research center*] (RCD)
MRC	Memory Request Controller
MRC	Men's Republican Club (NADA)
MRC	Men's Resource Center (EA)
MRC	Men's Resource Connection [*An association*] (EA)
MRC	Metabolic Clearance Rate (DB)

MRC............	Metals Reserve Co. [*World War II*]
MRC............	Meteorological Research Committee [*British*]
MRC............	Methods Research Corp. (AD)
MRC............	Methylrosaniline Chloride [*Also, GV*] [*A dye*]
MRC............	Metrics Research Corp. [*Information service or system*] (IID)
MRC............	Mid-Roll Interchange [*Advanced photo system*]
MRC............	Midwestern Relay Co. [*Milwaukee, WI*] [*Telecommunications*] (TSSD)
MRC............	Military Reform Caucus (EA)
MRC............	Military Region Command (MCD)
MRC............	Military Representatives Committee [*NATO*] (NATG)
MRC............	Military Reunions Council (EA)
MRC............	Military Revolutionary Council (CINC)
MRC............	Minnesota Restitution Center (AD)
MRC............	Minorco Canada Ltd. [*Toronto Stock Exchange symbol*]
MRC............	Missile Research Corp.
MRC............	Mission Requirements Change [*NASA*] (KSC)
MRC............	Mission Resources Center [*Sydney, Australia*]
MRC............	Mississippi River Commission [*Vicksburg, MS*] [*Army*]
MRC............	Mobile Radio Communications
MRC............	Model Railway Club [*British*]
MRC............	Modern Railroad Club (AD)
MRC............	Monterey Resources, Inc. [*NYSE symbol*] (SAG)
MRC............	Montrose [*Colorado*] [*Seismograph station code, US Geological Survey Closed*] (SEIS)
MRC............	Moon's RADAR Coordinates
MRC............	Morning Readiness Check
MRC............	Motorized Rifle Co. (INF)
MRC............	Motor Racing Club (AD)
MRC............	Mouvement des Renovateurs Communistes [*France Political party*] (EY)
MRC............	Movement Report Center [*Military*]
MRC............	Mueller-Ribbing-Clement [*Syndrome*] [*Medicine*] (DB)
MRC............	Multiple Register Counter (IEEE)
MRC............	Multiple Regression/Correlation [*Statistical analysis*]
MRCA.........	Canas [*Costa Rica*] [*ICAO location identifier*] (ICLI)
MRCA.........	Market Research Corp. of America (AD)
MRCA.........	Most Recent Common Ancestor
MRCA.........	Multirole Combat Aircraft
mrca.........	Multirole Combat Aircraft (AD)
MRCAS......	Monetary Ration Credit Allowance System [*Military*] (AFM)
MRCAT.......	Miniature Radio-Controlled Aerial Target (MCD)
MrcBnc......	Merchants Bancshares [*Associated Press*] (SAG)
MRCC........	Coto 47 [*Costa Rica*] [*ICAO location identifier*] (ICLI)
MRCC........	Maritime Rescue Coordination Center [*Australia*]
MRCC........	Material Review Central Control [*Aviation*] (MCD)
MRCC........	Medical Research Council of Canada (BARN)
MRCC........	Member of the Royal College of Chemistry [*British*]
MRCC........	Mercury Recovery Control Center
MRCC........	Molded Rubber Coupling Cushion
MRCC........	Movement Report Control Center [*Military*]
MRCCC......	Medical Research Council, Collaborative Centre [*British*] (CB)
MRCD........	Caledonia [*Costa Rica*] [*ICAO location identifier*] (ICLI)
MRCD........	Memory Raster Colour Display (PDAA)
MRCE........	Carate [*Costa Rica*] [*ICAO location identifier*] (ICLI)
MRCE........	Marginal Relative Certainty Effect [*Statistics*]
MRCF........	Martin Color-Fi, Inc. [*NASDAQ symbol*] (SAG)
MRCF........	Martin Color-Fl [*NASDAQ symbol*] (TTSB)
MRCF........	Mayo Biotechnology Research Computer Facility [*Mayo Clinic*] [*Research center*] (RCD)
MRCF........	Microsoft Real-Time Compression Format [*Microsoft Corp.*] (PCM)
MRCF........	Missile Recycle Facility (SAA)
MRCF........	Module Repair Calibration Facility
MRCGP......	Member of the Royal College of General Practitioners [*British*]
MRCGP......	Member, Royal College of General Practice [*British*] (CMD)
MRCH........	Chacarita [*Costa Rica*] [*ICAO location identifier*] (ICLI)
MrchBcp......	Merchants Bcp. [*Associated Press*] (SAG)
MrchBnc......	Merchants Bancshares, Inc. [*Associated Press*] (SAG)
MrchGp.......	Merchants Group, Inc. [*Associated Press*] (SAG)
MRCHNT.....	Merchant
MRCI.........	Ciruelas [*Costa Rica*] [*ICAO location identifier*] (ICLI)
MRCI.........	Maximum Rescue Coverage Intercept [*Environmental science*] (COE)
MRCI.........	Medical Registration Council of Ireland (AD)
MRCI.........	Medical Research Council of Ireland (SLS)
MRCI.........	Microsoft Real-Time Compression Interface [*Microsoft Corp.*] (PCM)
MRCI.........	Mine Readiness/Certification Inspection (MCD)
MRCI.........	Multireference Configuration Interaction [*Quantum chemistry*] (MCD)
MRCL.........	Master Cross-Reference List
MRCL.........	Mercurial
MRCM........	Machinery Repairman, Master Chief [*Navy rating*]
MRCN........	Minuteman Requirement Control Number (SAA)
MRCo.........	Malaysian Refrigerator Co. (AD)
MRCO........	Manufacturing Research Corp. of Ontario [*Research center Canada*] (RCD)
MRCO........	Member of the Royal College of Organists [*British*]
MRCO........	Meridan Natl [*NASDAQ symbol*] (TTSB)
MRCO........	Meridian National Corp. [*NASDAQ symbol*] (NQ)
MRCOA......	Medical Research Council Trial in Older Adults
MRCOG......	Member of the Royal College of Obstetricians and Gynaecologists [*British*]
MRCOL......	Meridian Natl Wrrt'A' [*NASDAQ symbol*] (TTSB)
MRCOP......	Meridan Natl $3.75 Cv'B'Pfd [*NASDAQ symbol*] (TTSB)
MRCOZ......	Meridian Natl Wrrt [*NASDAQ symbol*] (TTSB)
MRCP........	Maoist Revolutionary Communist Party [*Political party*] (AD)
MRCP........	Master of Regional and City Planning (PGP)
MRCP........	Master of Regional and Community Planning (GAGS)
MRCP.........	Member of the Royal College of Physicians [*British*]
MRCP.........	Member of the Royal College of Preceptors [*British*]
MRCP.........	Microfilm Research Centers Project [*Defunct*] (EA)
MRCP.........	Mobile RADAR Control Post
MRCPA......	Mobilization Reserve Components Program of the Army (AABC)
MRC Path...	Member of the Royal College of Pathologists [*British*]
MRCPE......	Member of the Royal College of Physicians, Edinburgh
MRCPEd.....	Member of the Royal College of Physicians of Edinburgh
MRCP Edin...	Member of the Royal College of Physicians of Edinburgh
MRCPGlas...	Member of the Royal College of Physicians of Glasgow
MRCP (Glasg)...	Member of the Royal College of Physicians and Surgeons of Glasgow (AAMN)
MRCP Glasg...	Member of the Royal College of Physicians of Glasgow
MRCPI......	Member of the Royal College of Physicians of Ireland
MRCP Irel...	Member of the Royal College of Physicians of Ireland
MRC Psych...	Member of the Royal College of Psychiatrists [*British*]
MRCPUK.....	Member of the Royal College of Physicians of the United Kingdom [*British*] (AD)
MRCP UK....	Member of the Royal Colleges of Physicians of the United Kingdom
MRCR........	Carrillo [*Costa Rica*] [*ICAO location identifier*] (ICLI)
MRCR........	Measurement Requirement Change Request [*NASA*] (KSC)
MRCRR........	Machine-Readable Collections Reading Room [*Library of Congress*] (IT)
MRCS.........	Machinery Repairman, Senior Chief [*Navy rating*]
MRCS.........	Mechanoreceptor Cueing Subsystem (MCD)
MRCS.........	Medium Resolution Camera System (MCD)
MRCS.........	Member of the Royal College of Surgeons [*British*]
MRCS.........	Missile Range Calibration Satellite
MRCS.........	Multiple Report Creation System
MRCS.........	Multiple RPV [*Remotely Piloted Vehicle*] Control System (PDAA)
MRCSA......	Migrant Resource Center of South Australia
MRCSE......	Member of the Royal College of Surgeons, Edinburgh
MRCSI......	Member of the Royal College of Surgeons, Ireland (ROG)
MRCTS......	Missile Round Cable Test System
MRCU........	Mini-Remote Control Unit (MHDI)
MRCV........	Cabo Velas [*Costa Rica*] [*ICAO location identifier*] (ICLI)
MRCV........	Mixture Ratio Control Valve (KSC)
MRCVS......	Member of the Royal College of Veterinary Surgeons [*British*] (EY)
MRCWA......	Midland Railway Company of Western Australia (AD)
MRCY........	Mercury General [*NASDAQ symbol*] (TTSB)
MRCY........	Mercury General Corp. [*NASDAQ symbol*] (NQ)
MRCZ........	Carrizal [*Costa Rica*] [*ICAO location identifier*] (ICLI)
MRD..........	Mandatory Retirement Date [*Army*] (AABC)
MRD..........	Manual Ringdown [*Telecommunications*] (TEL)
MRD..........	Maritime Research Department [*An association Inactive*] (EA)
MRD..........	Marketing Requirement Document
MRD..........	Master Requirements Directory [*Military*] (AFM)
MRD..........	Material Required Date
MRD..........	Material Requirements Deck (AAG)
MRD..........	Material Requirements Drawing (MCD)
MRD..........	Material Review Disposition [*Aviation*]
MRD..........	Materiel Redistribution Division [*Army*] (AFIT)
MRD..........	Materiel Release Denial [*Military*] (AABC)
MRD..........	Materiel Requirements Document [*Army*]
MRD..........	Medical Records Department (DAVI)
MRD..........	Medical Reference Department (AD)
MRD..........	Medical Research Division
MRD..........	Melcor Developments Ltd. [*Toronto Stock Exchange symbol*]
MRD..........	Memorandum for Regional Directors (AAGC)
MRD..........	Memory Raster Display [*Computer science*]
MRD..........	Memory Read [*Computer science*] (MHDI)
MRD..........	Merida [*Venezuela*] [*Airport symbol*] (OAG)
MRD..........	Meridian Air Cargo, Inc. [*ICAO designator*] (FAAC)
MRD..........	Mesoscale Research Division [*National Severe Storms Laboratory*] (USDC)
mrd..........	Metal Rolling Door (AD)
MRD..........	Metal Rolling Door [*Technical drawings*]
MRD..........	Metal Roof Deck [*Technical drawings*]
mrd..........	Metal Roof Deck (AD)
MRD..........	Microbiological Research Department (AD)
MRD..........	Milestone Review Documentation [*Army*]
MRD..........	Military Reference Data
MRD..........	Military Requirements Determination
mrd..........	Millirutherford
MRD..........	Minimal Residual Disease [*Medicine*]
MRD..........	Minimum Reacting Dose
mrd..........	Minimum Reacting Dose (AD)
MRD..........	Mission Requirements Document [*NASA*] (KSC)
MRD..........	Mississippi River Division [*Army Corps of Engineers*]
MRD..........	Missouri River Division [*Army Corps of Engineers*]
MRD..........	Mobil Research & Development Corp., Engineering Information Center, Princeton, NJ [*OCLC symbol*] (OCLC)
MRD..........	Monostable Relay Driver
MRD..........	Morpholinodaunorubicin [*Also, MoDNM*] [*Antineoplastic drug*]
MRD..........	Mortality Rate to Double
MRD..........	Motorized Rifle Division [*Military*] (AD)
MRD..........	Motor Racing Developments
MRD..........	Motor Receiving Dolly
MRD..........	Movement for the Restoration of Democracy [*Nepal*] [*Political party*]
MRD..........	Movement for the Restoration of Democracy [*Pakistan*] [*Political party*] (PD)
MRD..........	Multireference Double Excitation [*Physics*]
MRD..........	Russell and District Regional Library, Russell, Manitoba [*Library symbol National Library of Canada*] (NLC)
MRDA.........	Maintenance Requirement Development Activity [*Military*] (CAAL)

MRDA	Media Research Directors Association (EA)
MRDAC	Manpower Research and Data Analysis Center [*DoD*] (DNAB)
MRDB	Mission Requirements Data Base [*NASA*] (SSD)
MRDC	Medical Research and Development Command [*Frederick, MD*] [*Army*]
MRDC	Military Requirement and Development Committee (NATG)
MRDC	Military Research and Development Center [*US-Thailand*]
MRDC	Missile Research and Development Command [*Army*] (MCD)
MRDC	Module RADAR Display Console
MRDCC	Metropolitan Refuse Disposal Consultative Committee [*Melbourne, Australia*]
MRDD	Don Diego [*Costa Rica*] [*ICAO location identifier*] (ICLI)
MR/DD	Mentally Retarded and Developmentally Disabled
MRDD	Mental Retardation and Developmental Disabilities [*National Institutes of Health*]
MRDE	Mining Research and Development Establishment [*National Coal Board*] [*British*]
MRDEC	Missile Research Development and Engineering Center [*Formerly, Army Missile Laboratory*] (RDA)
MRDF	Machine-Readable Data Files
mrdf	Machine-Readable Data Files [*Computer science*] (AD)
MRDF	Marine Resources Development Foundation
MRDF	Maritime Radio Direction Finding
MRDF	Metals Research and Development Foundation [*Defunct*] (EA)
MRDFS	Man-Portable Radio Direction-Finding System
MRDG	Manufacturing Research and Design Group [*McMaster University*] [*Canada Research center*] (RCD)
mrdhd	Maximum Recommended Daily Human Dose (AD)
MRDIS	Message Reproduction and Distribution System [*Military*] (CAAL)
MRDL	Mean Reciprocal Detection Latency
MRDL	Mineral Respurces Development Laboratory [*Australia*]
MRDL	Missouri River Division Laboratory [*Army Corps of Engineers*]
MRDN	Material Receipt Discrepancy Notice (AD)
MRDN	Meridian Bancorp, Inc. [*NASDAQ symbol*] (NQ)
MrdN	Meridian National Corp. [*Associated Press*] (SAG)
MRDN	Mouvement Revolutionnaire pour la Democratie Nouvelle [*Revolutionary Movement for New Democracy*] [*Senegal*] (PD)
MrdN 99	Meridian National Corp. [*Associated Press*] (SAG)
MrdnBc	Meridian Bancorp, Inc. [*Associated Press*] (SAG)
MRDNL	Meridional
MRDO	Dieciocho [*Costa Rica*] [*ICAO location identifier*] (ICLI)
MRDOS	Mapped Real-Time Disk Operating System [*Computer science*] (MDG)
MRDR	Material Receipt Discrepancy Record
MRDR	Material Review Disposition Record (NASA)
MRDS	Malfunction Rate Detection System (DNAB)
MRDS	MARC [*Machine-Readable Cataloging*] Records Distribution Service [*National Library of Canada*] (IID)
MRDS	Member of the Royal Drawing Society [*British*] (ROG)
MRDS	Message Reproduction and Distribution System [*Military*] (MCD)
MRDS	Mineral Resources Data System [*US Geological Survey*] [*Information service or system*] (IID)
MRDS	Mission Recorder Display Set (MCD)
MRDS	Modular Responsive Defense System
MRDS	Molded Rubber Duct System
MRDT	Mortality Rate Doubling Time
MRDTI	Metal Roof Deck Technical Institute [*Later, Steel Deck Institute*] (EA)
MRDV	Maize Rough Dwarf Virus [*Plant pathology*]
MRDY	Message Ready [*Computer science*] (MHDI)
MRE	Major Research Equipment
MRE	Manicore [*Brazil*] [*Airport symbol*] (AD)
MRE	Mara Lodges [*Kenya*] [*Airport symbol*] (OAG)
MRE	Maritime Radio Executive [*British*]
M Re	Master of Religion
MRE	Master of Religious Education
MRE	Materiel Readiness Expediter [*Army*]
MRE	Matter (ROG)
MRE	Maximal Relative Error [*Mathematical statistics*]
MRE	Maximal Resistive Exercise (DMAA)
MRE	Maximal Respiratory Effectiveness (DMAA)
MRE	Mazda Research of Europe [*Automobile manufacturer operations*]
MRE	Meal, Ready-to-Eat [*Army rations designation, replaces C-rations*]
mre	Meal Ready to Eat (AD)
MRE	Meals Rejected by Everyone
mre	Mean Radial Error (AD)
MRE	Mean Radial Error
MRE	Medco Research [*AMEX symbol*] (TTSB)
MRE	Medco Research, Inc. [*AMEX symbol*] (SAG)
MRE	Melissa Resources, Inc. [*Vancouver Stock Exchange symbol*]
MRE	Memory Register Exponent [*Computer science*] (MHDI)
MRE	Metal Regulatory Element [*Genetics*]
MRE	Metal-Responsive Element [*Genetics*]
MR-E	Methemoglobin Reductase [*An enzyme*] (MAE)
MRE	Microbiological Research Establishment [*British*]
MRE	Microrocket Engine
MRE	Mid-Range Estimate
MRE	Militia Royal Engineers [*British military*] (DMA)
MRE	Missile Recertification Equipment
MRE	Missile Recycle Equipment (SAA)
MRE	Mobil Research & Development Corp., Paulsboro, NJ [*OCLC symbol*] (OCLC)
MRE	Modern Ramjet Engine (MCD)
MRE	Morally Repugnant Elite [*Lifestyle classification*] (ECON)
MRE	Movimiento Revolucionario Espartaco [*Bolivia*] [*Political party*] (PPW)
MRE	Movimiento Revolucionario Estudantil [*Colorado Political party*] (EY)
MRE	Multiple-Response Enable (IEEE)
MREA	Estero Azul [*Costa Rica*] [*ICAO location identifier*] (ICLI)
MREAC	Mon Repos Est au Ciel [*My Rest Is in Heaven*] [*Motto of Ludwig Philipp, Count of the Palatinate of Simmern (1602-1654)*] [*French*]
MREC	El Carmen [*Costa Rica*] [*ICAO location identifier*] (ICLI)
MREC	Medical Research Ethics Committee
MRECM	Master of Real Estate and Construction Management (GAGS)
MRED	Master of Real Estate Development (GAGS)
MREd	Master of Recreation Education (GAGS)
MR Ed	Master of Religious Education
MREDA	Marine Resources and Engineering Development Act [*1966*] (MSC)
M Re E	Master of Refrigeration Engineering
M Re Eng	Master of Refrigeration Engineering
MREF	Medical Research Endowment Fund
MRefEng	Master of Refrigeration Engineering (NADA)
MREGAD	Multiplexer Regenerator Address [*Computer science*] (MHDI)
MRegSc	Master of Regional Science (ADA)
MReh	Blanding Free Public Library, Rehoboth, MA [*Library symbol Library of Congress*] (LCLS)
MREHIS	Member of the Royal Environmental Health Institute of Scotland (DBQ)
MREI	Marriage Role Expectation Inventory [*Psychology*]
M-REIT	Mutual Real Estate Investment Trust
M Rel	Master of Religion (PGP)
MRELB	Malaysian Rubber Exchange and Licensing Board (AD)
MRelEd	Master of Religious Education (GAGS)
mrem	Millirem
MREM	Milliroentgen Equivalent Man [*Radiation measurement*]
mrem	Milliroentgen Equivalent Man (AD)
mrem/h	Millirem per Hour (DS)
MREmpS	Member of the Royal Empire Society [*British*]
MREP	Maneuvering Room Equipment Panel (DNAB)
MREP	Medical Remedial Enlistment Program (DNAB)
mrep	Milliroentgen Equivalent Physical (MAE)
MRER	El Ron Ron [*Costa Rica*] [*ICAO location identifier*] (ICLI)
MRERF	Manufacturers Representatives Educational Research Foundation [*Rolling Meadows, IL*] (EA)
MRES	Material Requirements Estimation System [*Navy*]
MRES	Member of the Royal Entomological Society [*British*] (ROG)
MRES	Military Requirements Estimation System
MResEnvS	Master of Resource and Environmental Studies
MResEnvSt	Master of Resource and Environmental Studies
MRESS	Marine Recreational Fishing Statistics Survey [*Marine science*] (OSRA)
MResSc	Master of Resource Science
MRET	Esterillos [*Costa Rica*] [*ICAO location identifier*] (ICLI)
M Ret	Master of Retailing
MRET	Merit Holding [*NASDAQ symbol*] (TTSB)
MRET	Merit Holding Corp. [*NASDAQ symbol*] (SAG)
M REV	Most Reverend
MRev	Revere Public Library, Revere, MA [*Library symbol Library of Congress*] (LCLS)
MRF	Magnetorheological Finishing [*Optics manufacturing*] (RDA)
MRF	Maintenance and Refurbishment Facility [*NASA*] (KSC)
MRF	Maintenance Repair Facility
MRF	Maintenance Repair Frequency
MRF	Maintenance Replacement Factor (NG)
mrf	Maintenance Replacement Factor (AD)
MRF	Maintenance Responsibility File (MCD)
MRF	Mankind Research Foundation (EA)
MRF	Marble Floor (AAG)
mrf	Marble Floor (AD)
MRF	Marfa, TX [*Location identifier FAA*] (FAAL)
MRF	MariFarms, Inc. [*Later, Marine Harvest International*] [*AMEX symbol*] (SPSG)
MRF	Marine Recreational Fishing [*Marine science*] (MSC)
MRF	Markov Random Field [*Mathematics*]
MRF	Materials Recovery Facility [*for recycling of glass, plastics, etc.*]
MRF	Maternal Resistance Factor (BARN)
MRF	Maximum Retarding Force (NASA)
MRF	Mayo Research Foundation (AD)
MRF	Measurements/Stimuli Request Form [*NASA*] (NASA)
MRF	Medical Record File (DMAA)
MRF	Medium-Range Forecast [*Model*] [*Marine science*] (OSRA)
MRF	Megawatt Receiver Filter
MRF	Melanocyte-Stimulating Hormone Releasing Factor [*Endocrinology*]
MRF	Melanotropin Releasing Factor [*Biochemistry*]
MRF	Mental Retardation Facility
MRF	Mentor Income Fund [*Formerly, RAC Income Fund*] [*NYSE symbol*] (SPSG)
MRF	Merfin Resources Ltd. [*Vancouver Stock Exchange symbol*]
MRF	Mesencephalic [*or Midbrain*] Reticular Formation [*Anatomy*]
MRF	Message Refusal [*Telecommunications*] (TEL)
MRF	Metal Regulatory Factor [*Genetics*]
MRF	Meteorological Rocket Facility
MRF	Metering Research Facility [*Research center*] (RCD)
MRF	Methodist Relief Fund [*British*]
MRF	Midbrain Reticular Formation [*Brain anatomy*]
MRF	Milestone Reference File [*Military*] (CAAL)
MRF	Military Reconnaissance Force [*British military*] (DMA)
MRF	Miraflores [*Peru*] [*Seismograph station code, US Geological Survey*] (SEIS)
MRF	Missile Reconstitution Force [*Air Force*] (DOMA)
MRF	Mission Readiness Flying

MRF............	Mission Reliability Factor [Military] (AABC)
MRF............	Mitral Regurgitant Flow [Medicine]
MRF............	Mobile Riverine Force [Navy] (NVT)
MRF............	Moderate Renal Failure [Medicine] (DMAA)
MRF............	Modular Rigid Frame (PDAA)
MRF............	Module Repair Facility (DNAB)
MRF............	Monoclonal Rheumatoid Factor [Medicine] (DB)
MRF............	Movement for Rights and Freedoms [Bulgaria] [Political party]
MRF............	MSH [Melanophore-Stimulating Hormone] Releasing Factor [Medicine] (DAVI)
MRF............	Muellerian Regression Factor [Embryology] (DAVI)
MRF............	Muellerian Repressor Factor [Embryology]
MRF............	Multipath Reduction Factor [Electronics]
MRF............	Multirole Fighter [Replacement for the F-16] [Air Force] (DOMA)
MRF............	Muscle Regulatory Factor [Physiology]
MRF............	Music Research Foundation
MRF............	Myopia Research Foundation [Later, MIRF]
MRFA........	Fireman Apprentice, Machinery Repairman, Striker [Navy rating]
MRFAC	Manufacturers Radio Frequency Advisory Committee (EA)
MRFB........	Malayan Rubber Fund Board (AD)
MRFC........	Malawi Rural Finance Co. Ltd.
MRFC........	Mouse Rosette-Forming Cell (DMAA)
MRFCA......	Mental Residual Functional Capacity Assessment [Social Security Administration]
MRFD........	Finca Delicias [Costa Rica] [ICAO location identifier] (ICLI)
MRFDK......	Mechanical Remote Fuze Disassembly Kit [Military] (CAAL)
MRFI..........	Finca 10 (Nuevo Palmar Sur) [Costa Rica] [ICAO location identifier] (ICLI)
MRFI..........	Mutually Responsible Facilitation Inventory [Personality development test] [Psychology]
MRFIT........	Multiple Risk Factor Intervention Trial [Cardiology]
MRFL.........	Flamengo [Costa Rica] [ICAO location identifier] (ICLI)
MRFL.........	Master Radio Frequency List (NATG)
mr flight	Meteorological Research Flight (AD)
MRFN	Fireman, Machinery Repairman, Striker [Navy rating]
MRFP.........	Finca La Promesa [Costa Rica] [ICAO location identifier] (ICLI)
MRFR.........	Mobilization Reserve for Retention [Military]
MRFS.........	Finca 63 [Costa Rica] [ICAO location identifier] (ICLI)
MRFS.........	Mid-Range Force Study [DoD]
MRFSS	Marine Recreational Fishing Statistics Survey (USDC)
MRFT.........	Missile Ready for Test (MCD)
MRFT.........	Modified Rapid Fermentation Test
MRFU.........	Multiple Rocket Firing Unit
MRFV.........	Maize Rayado Fino Virus [Plant pathology]
MRG	Magnetic Radiation Generator
mrg............	Magnetic Radiation Generator (AD)
MRG	Magnetic Resonance Gyro (MCD)
MRG	Main Repair Group [British military] (DMA)
MRG	Maintainability Requirements Group (AD)
MRG	Maintenance Requirements General (MCD)
MRG	Management Research Groups [British]
MRG	Mandatory Resource Group (MCD)
MRG	Manridge Explorations Ltd. [Toronto Stock Exchange symbol]
mrg............	Margin (AD)
mrg............	Marginalia (AD)
MRG	Master of Religious Guidance
MRG	Master Reference Gyro (PDAA)
MRG	Material Review Group [Aviation]
MRG	Medium Range
MRG	Merge [Computer science]
MRG	Mesters Vig [Greenland] [Airport symbol] (AD)
mrg............	Methane-Rich Gas (AD)
MRG	Methane Rich Gas
MRG	Minorities Research Group (AD)
MRG	Minority Rights Group (EAIO)
MRG	Mission Rules Guidelines [NASA] (KSC)
MRG	Mobile River Group [Navy] (VNW)
MRG	Modelling Research Group [University of Southern California] [Research center] (RCD)
MRG	Modern Rythmic Gynmastics (EDAC)
MRG	Mooring (MSA)
MRG	Morgantown [West Virginia] [Seismograph station code, US Geological Survey] (SEIS)
MRG	Mortons Restaurant Group [NYSE symbol] (SAG)
MRG	Mouvement des Radicaux de Gauche [Left Radical Movement] [Wallis and Futuna Islands] [Political party] (EY)
MRG	Mouvement des Radicaux de Gauche [Left Radical Movement] [France Political party] (PPE)
MRG	Movement Requirements Generator
MRG	Municipal Reform Group [Tasmania, Australia]
MRG	Murmurs, Rubs, and Gallops [Cardiology] (DAVI)
MRGA........	Garza [Costa Rica] [ICAO location identifier] (ICLI)
MRGA........	Manhattan Ryegrass Growers Association (EA)
MRGF........	Golfito [Costa Rica] [ICAO location identifier] (ICLI)
MRGI.........	Minority Rights Group International [British] (EAIO)
MRGITF.....	Machine-Readable Government Information Task Force [Government Documents Round Table] [American Library Association]
MRGO........	Margo Nursery Farms [NASDAQ symbol] (TTSB)
MRGO........	Margo Nursery Farms, Inc. [NASDAQ symbol] (NQ)
MRGO........	Mississippi River Gulf Outflow (AD)
MR-GO.......	Mississippi River-Gulf Outlet
MRGP........	Guapiles [Costa Rica] [ICAO location identifier] (ICLI)
MRGR........	Mean Relative Growth Rate [Physiology]
MRGS	Member of the Royal Geographical Society [British]
MrgS...........	Morgan Stanley Group, Inc. [Associated Press] (SAG)
MrgSHY	MorgaN Stanley High Yield Fund [Associated Press] (SAG)
MRGT	Guatuso [Costa Rica] [ICAO location identifier] (ICLI)
MRGU	Guanacaste [Costa Rica] [ICAO location identifier] (ICLI)
MRGV	Marine Research Group of Victoria [Australia]
MRH	Beaufort, NC [Location identifier FAA] (FAAL)
MRH	Hinds Junior College, Raymond, MS [OCLC symbol] (OCLC)
MRH	Magnetic Recording Head
MRH	Mango Resources [Vancouver Stock Exchange symbol]
MRH	Master of Russian History
MRH	Mechanical Recording Head
MRH	Melanocyte-Releasing Hormone [Endocrinology]
MRH	Member of the Royal Household [British] (AD)
mr/h	Microroentgon per Hour (COE)
MRH	Mild Resid Hydrocracking [M. W. Kellogg Co. process]
mr/h	Milliroentgens per Hour (DS)
MRH	Mission-Related Hardware
MRH	Mobile Remote Handler
MRH	MSH [Melanophore-Stimulating Hormone] Releasing Hormone [Laboratory Science] (DAVI)
MRH	Rossburn District Hospital, Rossburn, Manitoba [Library symbol National Library of Canada] (NLC)
MRHA.........	Mannose-Resistant Hemagglutination
MRHD........	Mounted Ration Heating Device [Army] (INF)
MR head.....	Magneto-Resistive Head [Computer science] (DDC)
MRHG........	Hacienda Rancho Grande [Costa Rica] [ICAO location identifier] (ICLI)
MRHIB	Multiantimicrobial Resistant Hemophilus Influenza B
MRHJ.........	Hacienda Jaco (Harbor Land) [Costa Rica] [ICAO location identifier] (ICLI)
mrhm.........	Milliroentgens per Hour at One Meter
MRHMC	Michael Reese Hospital and Medical Center (AD)
MRHO........	Hacienda Rio Cuarto [Costa Rica] [ICAO location identifier] (ICLI)
MRHP........	Hacienda Platanar [Costa Rica] [ICAO location identifier] (ICLI)
mr/hr	Milliroentgens per Hour
MRHS	Hacienda La Suerte [Costa Rica] [ICAO location identifier] (ICLI)
MRHS	Materiel Request History and Status
MRHS	Member of the Royal Historical Society [British] (ROG)
MRHS	Midwest Railway Historical Society (EA)
MRHSF.......	Materiel Request History and Storage File
MRI............	Anchorage, AK [Location identifier FAA] (FAAL)
MRI............	Information Dynamics Corp., Reading, MA [Library symbol Library of Congress] (LCLS)
MRI............	Machine Records Installation [Military]
MRI............	Magazine Research, Inc. (AD)
mri.............	Magnetic-Resonance Imager (AD)
MRI............	Magnetic Resonance Imaginery (AAEL)
MRI............	Magnetic Resonance Imaging [Medicine]
mri.............	Magnetic Rubber Inspection (AD)
MRI............	Malt Research Institute [Later, NMRI]
MRI............	Management Recruiters International (HGAA)
MRI............	Manufacturing Run-In
MRI............	Marine Research Institute
MRI............	Marital Roles Inventory [Psychology]
MRI............	Mass Retailing Institute [Formerly, Mass Merchandising Research Institute] [Later, NMRI]
MRI............	Material Receiving Instruction [Bechtel] [Nuclear energy] (NRCH)
MRI............	Material Review Item [Aviation]
MRI............	Mauritius Island [Mascarene Islands] [Seismograph station code, US Geological Survey Closed] (SEIS)
MRI............	McRae Industries, Inc. [AMEX symbol] (SPSG)
MRI............	Mean Rise Interval [Tides and currents]
mri.............	Mean Rise Interval (AD)
MRI............	Measurement Requirements and Interface (MCD)
MRI............	Meat Research Institute [British]
MRI............	Mediamark Research, Inc. [Database producer and database] [Information service or system] (IID)
MRI............	Mediator Release Inhibitor [Biochemistry]
MRI............	Medical Records Index (AD)
MRI............	Medical Records Institute (NTPA)
MRI............	Medical Research Institute [Florida Institute of Technology] [Research center] (RCD)
MRI............	Medium-Range Interceptor
mri.............	Medium-Range Interceptor (AD)
MRI............	Member of the Royal Institution [British]
MRI............	Memory Reference Instruction
MRI............	Mental Research Institute (EA)
MRI............	Message Routing Indicator (COE)
MRI............	Meteorological Research Institute (AD)
MRI............	Microwave Research Institute [Polytechnic Institute of Brooklyn] (MCD)
MRI............	Midwest Research Institute
MRI............	Military Reform Institute (AD)
mri.............	Milstrip Routing Identifier (AD)
MRI............	Mineral Resources Institute [University of Alabama] [Research center] (RCD)
MRI............	Mineral Resources International Ltd. [Toronto Stock Exchange symbol]
MRI............	Minimum Release Interval (DNAB)
MRI............	Minority Research Institution [Program] [National Science Foundation]
MRI............	Miscellaneous RADAR Input
MRI............	Missile Range Index
MRI............	Moderate Renal Insufficiency [Medicine]
MRI............	Monopulse Resolution Improvement
mri.............	Monopulse Resolution Improvement (AD)

MRI............	Motor Repair Insurance (AD)
MRI............	Multiple RADAR Interrogator (MUGU)
MRIA	Magnetic Recording Industry Association [*Later, Electronic Industries Association*] (EA)
MRI.A	McRae Indus'A' [*AMEX symbol*] (TTSB)
MRIA	Member of the Royal Irish Academy (EY)
MRIA	Model Railroad Industry Association (EA)
MRIAI	Member of the Royal Institute of the Architects of Ireland
MRI.B	McRae Indus Cv 'B' [*AMEX symbol*] (TTSB)
MRIBA	Member of the Royal Institute of British Architects (ROG)
MRIC	Mandatory Recovery Items Code (MCD)
M-RIC	Manpower Resource Identification Code [*Military*]
MRIC	Member of the Royal Institute of Chemistry [*British*]
MRIC	Morning Report Indicator Code (AABC)
MRIC	Revolutionary Movement of the Christian Left [*Ecuador*] [*Political party*] (PPW)
MRICC	Missile and Rockets Inventory Control Center [*Army*]
MRICD	Medical Research Institute of Chemical Defense (RDA)
MRICS	Member of the Royal Institution of Chartered Surveyors [*British*]
MRIF	Maintenance Ratio Intermediate Forward
MRIF	Melanocyte-Stimulating-Hormone Release Inhibiting Factor [*Also, MIF*] [*Endocrinology*]
MRIF	MSH [*Melanophore-Stimulating Hormone*] Release Inhibiting Factor [*Laboratory science*] (DAVI)
MRIH	Melanocyte-Stimulating Hormone-Release-Inhibiting Hormone [*Endocrinology*] (MAE)
MRII...........	Medical Resources [*NASDAQ symbol*] (TTSB)
MRII...........	Medical Resources, Inc. [*NASDAQ symbol*] (SAG)
MRIID	Medical Research Institute of Infectious Diseases [*Army*] (RDA)
MRIL	Mandatory Recovery Items List (MCD)
MRIL	Master Repairable Item List
MRIN	Member of the Royal Institute of Navigation [*British*] (DBQ)
MRINA	Member of the Royal Institution of Naval Architects [*British*]
MR INC	Men's Rights, Inc. (EA)
MRINDO	Modified Rydberg Intermediate Neglect of Differential Overlap [*Physics*]
MRINZ	Meat Research Institute of New Zealand (AD)
MRIO	Multiregional Input-Output
MRIP	Imperio [*Costa Rica*] [*ICAO location identifier*] (ICLI)
MRIP	Management Review and Improvement Program [*Department of Labor*]
MRIP	Prairie Crocus Regional Library, Rivers, Manitoba [*Library symbol National Library of Canada*] (NLC)
MRIPA	Member of the Royal Institute of Public Administration (ADA)
MRIPHH.......	Member of the Royal Institute of Public Health and Hygiene [*British*]
MRIPWC	Member of the Royal Institute of Painters in Water Colours [*British*] (ROG)
mrir	Medium Resolution Infrared (AD)
MRIR	Medium-Resolution Infrared Radiometer [*NASA*]
MRIRBM.......	Medium-Range and Intermediate-Range Ballistic Missile (MCD)
MRIS	Maritime Research Information Service [*National Academy of Sciences*]
MRIS	Market Research Information System [*Bell System*]
MRIS	Marshall & Ilsley [*NASDAQ symbol*] (TTSB)
MRIS	Marshall & Isley Corp. [*NASDAQ symbol*] (NQ)
MRIS	Material Readiness Index System [*Military*]
MRIS	Medical Research Information System [*Veterans Administration*]
MRIS	Mobile Range Instrumentation System
MRIS	Modernization Resource Information Submission [*Army*] (RDA)
MRISAN.......	Maintenance Requirement Interim Support Asset Notice (MCD)
MRIT..........	Marine RADAR Interrogator-Transponder (PDAA)
MRIT..........	Mean Re-Initialization Time
MRIT..........	Merit Software, Inc. [*NASDAQ symbol*] (SAG)
MRITC	Methylrhodamine Isothiocyanate [*Organic chemistry*]
MRIU	Missile Round Interface Unit
MRIX	Midland Resources [*NASDAQ symbol*] (SPSG)
MRIXZ	Midland Res Inc. Wrrt [*NASDAQ symbol*] (TTSB)
MRJ...........	Microwave Rotary Joint
MRJ...........	Mineral Point, WI [*Location identifier FAA*] (FAAL)
MRJ...........	Miniature Revolving Joint
MRJE	Multileaving Remote Job Entry [*IBM Corp.*]
MRJE	Multiple Remote Job Entry (NITA)
MRJY	Mister Jay Fashions International, Inc. [*NASDAQ symbol*] (SAG)
MRJY	Mr Jay Fashions Intl [*NASDAQ symbol*] (TTSB)
MRK..........	Marco Island [*Florida*] [*Airport symbol*] (OAG)
MRK..........	Mark
mrk...........	Mark (VRA)
MRK..........	Markair, Inc. [*ICAO designator*] (FAAC)
MRK..........	Merck & Co. [*NYSE symbol*] (TTSB)
MRK..........	Merck & Co., Inc. [*NYSE symbol*] (SPSG)
MRK..........	Merrimack College, McQuade Library, North Andover, MA [*OCLC symbol*] (OCLC)
MRK..........	Millrock Development Corp. [*Vancouver Stock Exchange symbol*]
MRK..........	Modified Redlich-Kwong [*Chemical equation*]
MRK..........	Morioka [*Japan*] [*Seismograph station code, US Geological Survey*] (SEIS)
MRK..........	Myth, Ritual, and Kingship [*A publication*] (BJA)
MRK..........	Rayville, LA [*Location identifier FAA*] (FAAL)
MRKD	Marked [*Computer science*] (MDG)
mrkd	Marked (AD)
mrkg	Marking (AD)
mrkr..........	Marker (AD)
MRKR	Marker (WGA)
MRKR	Marker International [*NASDAQ symbol*] (SAG)
MRKR	Marker Intl. [*NASDAQ symbol*] (TTSB)

MRKTPLC	Marketplace
MRKTR	Marketer
Mrkts	Markets (AD)
MRL............	Aeromorelos SA de CV [*Mexico ICAO designator*] (FAAC)
MRL............	Machine Representation Language
MRL............	Main Rail Launcher (DWSG)
MRL............	Maintenance Repair Level (MCD)
MRL............	Maintenance Requirements List (MCD)
MRL............	Manipulator Retention Latch [*or Lock*] (NASA)
MRL............	Manufacturing Reference Line
MRL............	Manufacturing Research Laboratory
MRL............	Marine Drilling [*NYSE symbol*]
MRL............	Maritime Rear Link (MCD)
MRL............	Marketing Research Library
MRL............	Martel Oil & Gas [*Vancouver Stock Exchange symbol*]
MRL............	Master Repair List (AFIT)
MRL............	Master Report List
MRL............	Material Requirements Lists
MRL............	Materials Research Laboratories [*National Science Foundation*] [*Research center*]
MRL............	Materiel Requirements List [*Military*]
MRL............	Maximized Relative Likelihood (PDAA)
MRL............	Maximum Recording Level
MRL............	Maximum Residue Limit (PDAA)
MRL............	Meaning-Representation Language [*Computer science*]
MRL............	Medical Record Librarian
MRL............	Medical Records Library (AD)
MRL............	Medical Research Laboratory [*Navy and Air Force*] (MCD)
MRL............	Medium-Powered Radio Range [*Loop radiators*]
mrl............	Medium-Powered Radio Range (AD)
MRL............	Merrell-National Laboratories [*Research code symbol*]
MRL............	Minerals Research Laboratory (MCD)
MRL............	Minimal Response Level [*Audiometry*]
MRL............	Minimum Residue Level
MRL............	Minimum-Risk Level [*Environmental science*] (COE)
MRL............	Missionary Research Library (EA)
MRL............	Mobile Replenishment List (AFIT)
MRL............	Motor Refrigeration Lighter (ADA)
mrl............	Motor Refrigerator Lighter (AD)
mrl............	Multiple Rocket Launcher (AD)
MRL............	Multiple Rocket Launcher
MRL............	Multiple Ruby LASER
MRL............	Multipoint Recorder/Logger
MRLA.........	La Paquita [*Costa Rica*] [*ICAO location identifier*] (ICLI)
MRLA.........	Malayan Races Liberation Army
MRLB.........	Liberia/Tomas Guardia Internacional [*Costa Rica*] [*ICAO location identifier*] (ICLI)
MRLC.........	Los Chiles [*Costa Rica*] [*ICAO location identifier*] (ICLI)
MRLE.........	Laurel [*Costa Rica*] [*ICAO location identifier*] (ICLI)
MRLF.........	La Flor [*Costa Rica*] [*ICAO location identifier*] (ICLI)
MRLF.........	Monthly Report on the Labor Force (OICC)
MRLG	La Garroba [*Costa Rica*] [*ICAO location identifier*] (ICLI)
MRLI	La Ligia [*Costa Rica*] [*ICAO location identifier*] (ICLI)
MRLL.........	Las Lomas [*Costa Rica*] [*ICAO location identifier*] (ICLI)
MRLL.........	Merrill Corp. [*NASDAQ symbol*] (NQ)
MRLM.........	Limon/Limon Internacional [*Costa Rica*] [*ICAO location identifier*] (ICLI)
MRLOGAEUR...	Minimum Required Logistics Augmentation Europe (MCD)
MRLP.........	Monster Raving Loony Party (WDAA)
MRLPC	Mouvement de Regroupement et de Liberation du Peuple Congolais [*Movement for the Regroupment and Liberation of the Congolese People*]
MRLR	La Roca [*Costa Rica*] [*ICAO location identifier*] (ICLI)
MRLT.........	Las Trancas [*Costa Rica*] [*ICAO location identifier*] (ICLI)
MRLU.........	La Maruca [*Costa Rica*] [*ICAO location identifier*] (ICLI)
MRLV.........	La Cueva [*Costa Rica*] [*ICAO location identifier*] (ICLI)
MRLY.........	La Yolanda [*Costa Rica*] [*ICAO location identifier*] (ICLI)
MRM..........	Aerocharter, Inc. [*Canada ICAO designator*] (FAAC)
MRM..........	Magnetic Resonance Microscopy
mrm..........	Mail Readership Measurement (AD)
MRM..........	Mail Readership Measurement
MRM..........	Maintenance, Reporting, and Management [*Military*] (MCD)
MRM..........	Management Responsibility Matrix
MRM..........	Management Review Meeting (AFIT)
MRM..........	Manari [*Papua New Guinea*] [*Airport symbol*] (OAG)
MRM..........	Master of Resource Management (GAGS)
mrm..........	Mechanically Recovered Meat (AD)
MRM..........	Mechanically Removed Meat
MRM..........	Medical Record Manager
MRM..........	Medical Repair Technician [*Navy*]
MRM..........	Medium-Range Missile (MCD)
MRM..........	Merrimac Industries [*AMEX symbol*] (TTSB)
MRM..........	Merrimac Industries, Inc. [*AMEX symbol*] (SPSG)
MRM..........	Metabolic Rate Monitor [*Trademark*]
MRM..........	Metastable Reaction Monitoring [*Analytical chemistry*]
MRM..........	Michelson Rotating Mirror
MRM..........	Miles of Relative Movement [*Navigation*]
mrm..........	Miles of Relative Movement (AD)
MRM..........	Miscellaneous Radioactive Material (GAAI)
MRM..........	Most Recently Used Master [*Computer science*]
MRM..........	Movement for the Redemption of Liberian Muslims [*Political party*] (EY)
MRM..........	Movimento da Resistencia de Mozambique [*Mozambique Resistance Movement*]
MRM..........	Multiple Reaction Monitoring [*Chemistry*]

MRM............	Music for the Rights of Man (EA)
MRMA	Montealto [*Costa Rica*] [*ICAO location identifier*] (ICLI)
MRMC	Medical Research Modernization Committee (EA)
MRMC	Murcielago [*Costa Rica*] [*ICAO location identifier*] (ICLI)
MRMJ........	Mojica [*Costa Rica*] [*ICAO location identifier*] (ICLI)
MRML	Medium-Range Missile Launcher
MRML........	Montelimar O Los Sitios [*Costa Rica*] [*ICAO location identifier*] (ICLI)
MRMO	Mobilization Reserve Materiel Objective [*Army*]
MRMO-A.....	Mobilization Reserve Materiel Objective - Acquisition [*Army*] (AFIT)
MRMP	Marginal Revenue/Marginal Physical Product [*Economics*]
MRMPO	Mobilization Reserve Materiel Procurement Objective [*Army*]
MRMR	Mining Rock-Mass Rating [*Mining technology*]
MRMR	Mobilization Reserve Materiel Requirement [*Army*]
MRMS	MARC [*Machine-Readable Cataloging*] Record Management System
MRMS	Metabolic Rate Measuring System
MRMS	Mobile Remote Manipulator System (MCD)
MRMS	Mobile/Tracked Remote Manipulator System (SSD)
MRMS	Monetary Ration Management System [*Military*] (AFM)
MRMS	Mount Rushmore Memorial Society (EA)
MRMU	Mobile Radiological Measuring Unit
MRMU	Mobile Remote Manipulating Unit [*Air Force*]
MRMVA	Master Retail Milk Vendors Association (AD)
MRMW	Memory Write [*Computer science*] (MHDI)
MRN	Marion [*South Africa*] [*Geomagnetic observatory code*]
MRN	Maritime Radionavigation
MRN	Material Recorder Notice (AD)
MRN	Median Raphe Nucleus [*Medicine*]
MRN	Medium-Round Nose [*Diamond drilling*]
MRN	Meteorological Rocket Network [*NASA*]
MRN	Minimum Rejection Number
MRN	Missions Gouvernementales Francaises [*France ICAO designator*] (FAAC)
MRN	Modified Random Network [*Crystallography*]
MRN	Moran Resources Corp. [*Vancouver Stock Exchange symbol*]
MRN	Morganton, NC [*Location identifier FAA*] (FAAL)
MRN	Morning (ROG)
MRN	Morrison Knudsen [*NYSE symbol*] (TTSB)
MRN	Morrison-Knudsen Co., Inc. [*NYSE symbol*] (SPSG)
MRN	Motor Racing Network
MRN	Mouvement pour la Reconstruction Nationale [*Haiti*] [*Political party*] (EY)
MRN	Movimiento de Renovacion Nacional [*Movement for National Renovation*] [*Colorado Political party*] (PPW)
MRNA	Marina
mRNA	Ribonucleic Acid, Messenger [*Biochemistry, genetics*]
MRNC	Marine Ltd. Partnership [*NASDAQ symbol*] (SAG)
MRNC	Meteorological Rocket Network Committee [*NASA*] (SAA)
MRNC	Nicoya [*Costa Rica*] [*ICAO location identifier*] (ICLI)
MRNCZ	Marina Ltd Partnership [*NASDAQ symbol*] (TTSB)
MRND	Maintenance Required Not Developed (MSA)
MRND	Mouvement Revolutionnaire National pour le Developpement [*National Revolutionary Movement for Development*] [*Rwanda*] [*Political party*] (PPW)
MRNE	Marine
MRNet	[*The*] Minnesota Regional Network [*Computer science*] (TNIG)
mrng...........	Mooring (AD)
mrng...........	Morning (AD)
MRNG.........	Morning
MRNJ.........	Naranjo (Seveers) [*Costa Rica*] [*ICAO location identifier*] (ICLI)
MRNL	Medical Research and Nutrition Laboratory [*Army*] (MCD)
MRNP.........	Mount Rainier National Park [*Washington*] (AD)
MRNP.........	Mount Revelstoke National Park [*British Columbia*] (AD)
mRNP.........	Ribonucleoprotein, Messenger [*Biochemistry*]
MRNPF	Member, Royal Nurses Pension Fund [*British*] (ROG)
MRNR	Mariner Health Group [*NASDAQ symbol*] (TTSB)
MRNR	Mariner Health Group, Inc. [*NASDAQ symbol*] (SAG)
MRNS	Modular Reusable Nuclear Shuttle
MRNS	Nosara [*Costa Rica*] [*ICAO location identifier*] (ICLI)
Mro.............	Maestro (AD)
mro.............	Maintenance, Repair, and Operating (AD)
MRO	Maintenance, Repair, and Operating Supplies (AAGC)
MRO	Maintenance, Repair, and Operation
MRO	Maintenance, Repair, and Overhaul
MRO	Maintenance Report Order (SAA)
MRO	Management Review Officer
MRO	Manufacturing Rework Order
MRO	Master Reference Oscillator (DMAA)
MRO	Masterton [*New Zealand*] [*Airport symbol*] (OAG)
MRO	Materiel Readiness Officer (MCD)
MRO	Materiel Release Order [*Air Force*]
MRO	Mechanized RADAR Observer
MRO	Media Resources Officer (AIE)
MRO	Medical Regulating Office [*or Officer*] [*Army*] (AABC)
MRO	Medical Research Organization [*Generic term*]
MRO	Medical Review Officer (GFGA)
MRO	Member of the Register of Osteopaths [*British*]
MRO	Meridor Resources Ltd. [*Vancouver Stock Exchange symbol*]
MRO	Message Releasing Officer
MRO	Message Review Officer (MCD)
MRO	Mid-Range Objectives
MRO	Military Release Orders
MRO	Mine Radiographic Outfit [*Military*] (PDAA)
MRO	Minimal Recognizable Odor [*Medicine*] (DMAA)
MRO	Minority Recruiting Officer (DNAB)
MRO	Morrison Flying Service, Inc. [*ICAO designator*] (FAAC)
MRO	Motor Routing Order
MRO	Movement Report Office [*Military*]
MRO	Multi-Region Option (HGAA)
MRO	Muscle Receptor Organ [*Neurophysiology*]
MRO	Rossburn Regional Library, Manitoba [*Library symbol National Library of Canada*] (NLC)
MRO	USX-Marathon Group [*NYSE symbol*] (SPSG)
MRO	USX-Marathon Grp [*NYSE symbol*] (TTSB)
MROA	Magnetic Raman Optical Activity [*Spectrometry*]
MROAR	Modification and Repair Order and Acceptance Record (AD)
MROC	Mobile Range Operation Center (NVT)
MROC	Monroc, Inc. [*NASDAQ symbol*] (SAG)
MROC	San Jose/Juan Santamaria Internacional [*Costa Rica*] [*ICAO location identifier*] (ICLI)
MROD	Medical Research and Operations Directorate [*NASA*] (KSC)
MROF	Maintenance, Repair, and Operation of Facility (KSC)
MROL	Minimum Resolvable Object Length
MROM	Macro Read-Only Memory [*Computer science*]
MROM	Masked Read-Only Memory [*Computer science*]
mrov...........	Moreover (AD)
MRoxH........	Hebrew Teachers College, Roxbury, MA [*Library symbol Library of Congress*] (LCLS)
MRP............	Application for Writ of Mandamus Refused in Part [*Legal term*] (DLA)
MRp............	Carnegie Library, Rockport, MA [*Library symbol Library of Congress*] (LCLS)
MRP............	Machine-Readable Passport (DA)
mrp............	Machine-Readable Passport (AD)
MRP............	Magnum Rifle Powder (DICI)
MRP............	Maintenance Rally Point [*Military*] (INF)
MRP............	Maintenance Real Property (NVT)
MRP............	Malfunction Reporting Program [*Navy*]
MRP............	Management Readiness Profile [*London House, Inc.*] (TES)
MRP............	Manned Reusable Payload
mrp............	Manned Reusable Payload (AD)
mrp............	Manned Reusable Product (AD)
MRP............	Manned Rotating Platform
MRP............	Manual Reporting Post (NATG)
MRP............	Manufacturer's Recommended Price (ODBW)
MRP............	Manufacturing Requirements Planning [*Purchasing computer program*] (PCM)
MRP............	Manufacturing Resource Planning [*Computer science*]
MRP............	Marginal Revenue Product [*Economics*]
mrp............	Marginal Revenue Product (AD)
MRP............	Markov Renewal Program
MRP............	Marla [*Australia Airport symbol*] (OAG)
MRP............	Mass Resolving Power [*Physics*]
MRP............	Master in Regional Planning (DD)
MRP............	Master of Regional Planning
MRP............	Master Restationing Plan [*DoD*]
MRP............	Material Reliability Program [*Military*] (AFIT)
MRP............	Material Requirements Planning [*Pronounced "merp"*]
MRP............	Material Reserve Planning
MRP............	Material Resource Planning (ACII)
MRP............	Materiel Returns Program [*Military*] (AFIT)
MRP............	Mathematics Resources Project [*National Science Foundation*]
MRP............	Maximum Rated Power
MRP............	Maximum Resolving Power
mrp............	Maximum Resolving Power (AD)
mrp............	Maximum Retail Price (AD)
MRP............	Maximum Retail Price [*British*]
MRP............	Medical Record Practitioner [*Medicare*] (DHSM)
MRP............	Medical Reimbursement Plan
MRP............	Members Retirement Plan [*of the American Medical Association*] (DAVI)
MRP............	Merapi [*Java*] [*Seismograph station code, US Geological Survey Closed*] (SEIS)
MRP............	Message Routing Process [*Telecommunications*] (TEL)
MRP............	Mid-Range Plan [*1969-70*] [*Military*]
MRP............	Militarism Resource Project (EA)
MRP............	Military Rated Power (NG)
MRP............	Military Representatives of Associated Pacific Powers [*World War II*]
MRP............	Military Requirements Plan (NATG)
MRP............	Minimum Reaction Posture (NVT)
MRP............	Miscellaneous Relay Panel (MCD)
MRP............	Mississippi River Plume [*Marine science*] (OSRA)
MRP............	Mitochondrial RNA [*Ribonucleic Acid*] Processing [*Cytology*]
MRP............	Mobile RADAR Post
MRP............	Mobile Repair Party (MCD)
MRP............	Modern Religious Problems [*A publication*]
MRP............	Molybdate-Reactive Phosphorus [*Analytical chemistry*]
MRP............	Monthly Report of Progress
MRP............	Morley Library, Painesville, OH [*OCLC symbol*] (OCLC)
MRP............	Morrison Petroleums Ltd. [*Toronto Stock Exchange symbol*]
MRP............	Motor Racing Publications [*Publisher*] [*British*]
MRP............	Mouvement Republicain Populaire [*Popular Republican Movement*] [*France Political party*] (PPE)
MRP............	Mouvement Revolutionnaire du Peuple [*Chad*] [*Political party*] (EY)
MRP............	Movimiento Republicano Progresista [*Progressive Republican Movement*] [*Venezuela Political party*] (EY)
MRP............	Movimiento Revolucionario del Pueblo - Ixim [*People's Revolutionary Movement - Ixim*] [*Guatemala*] [*Political party*] (PD)
MRP............	Movimiento Revolucionario Popular [*Venezuela Political party*] (EY)
MRP............	Multiplex Recording Photography
MRP............	Multi-Racial Party [*Zambia*] [*Political party*] (EY)

MRP............ Reston and District Regional Library, Reston, Manitoba [*Library symbol National Library of Canada*] (NLC)
MR/PA......... Make Ready / Put Away (DNAB)
MRPA.......... Master of Recreation and Parks Administration (GAGS)
MRPA.......... Metropolitan Region Planning Authority (AD)
MRPA.......... Modified Random Phase Approximation
MRPA.......... Punta Burica [*Costa Rica*] [*ICAO location identifier*] (ICLI)
MRPARABAD... Master Parachutist Badge [*Military decoration*]
MRPB.......... Playa Blanca [*Costa Rica*] [*ICAO location identifier*] (ICLI)
MRPC.......... Mercury Rankine Power Conversion [*Nuclear energy*]
MRPC.......... Mouvement de Regroupement des Populations Congolaises [*Movement for the Regroupment of the Congolese People*] [*Political party*]
MRPC.......... Paso Canoas [*Costa Rica*] [*ICAO location identifier*] (ICLI)
MRPD.......... Pandora [*Costa Rica*] [*ICAO location identifier*] (ICLI)
MRPE.......... Palo Verde [*Costa Rica*] [*ICAO location identifier*] (ICLI)
MRPF.......... Maintenance of Real Property Facilities (AABC)
MRPG.......... Potrero Grande [*Costa Rica*] [*ICAO location identifier*] (ICLI)
MRPhS........ Member of the Royal Pharmaceutical Society [*Canada*] (DD)
MRPI.......... Paissa [*Costa Rica*] [*ICAO location identifier*] (ICLI)
MRPJ.......... Puerto Jimenez [*Costa Rica*] [*ICAO location identifier*] (ICLI)
MRPL.......... Material Requirements Planning List [*Navy*]
MRPL.......... Portalon [*Costa Rica*] [*ICAO location identifier*] (ICLI)
MRPM.......... Material Research and Production Methods (MCD)
MRPM.......... Palmar Sur [*Costa Rica*] [*ICAO location identifier*] (ICLI)
MRPN.......... Pelon Nuevo [*Costa Rica*] [*ICAO location identifier*] (ICLI)
MRPP.......... Maoist Reorganization Movement of the Party of the Proletariat [*Political party*] (AD)
MRPP.......... Mortgage Rate Protection Program [*Canada*]
MRPR.......... Parrita [*Costa Rica*] [*ICAO location identifier*] (ICLI)
MRPRA........ Malaysian Rubber Producers' Research Association [*Research center British*] (IRC)
MRPS.......... Manufacturing and Resource Planning System [*Cincom Systems Ltd.*] [*Software package*] (NCC)
MRPS.......... Marine Petrol Tr [*NASDAQ symbol*] (TTSB)
MRPS.......... Materials Requirement Planning System (HGAA)
M rps.......... Mauritius Rupee [*Monetary unit*] (AD)
MRPS.......... Paissa [*Costa Rica*] [*ICAO location identifier*] (ICLI)
MRPV.......... Mini-Remotely Piloted Vehicle (PDAA)
MRPV.......... San Jose/Tobias Bolanos Internacional [*Costa Rica*] [*ICAO location identifier*] (ICLI)
MRQ........... Marinduque [*Philippines*] [*Airport symbol*] (OAG)
MRQ........... Marquardt Corp. [*Stock exchange symbol*] (AD)
MRQ........... Maximum Release Quantity [*DoD*]
MRQE.......... Marquee Group, Inc. (The) [*NASDAQ symbol*] (SAG)
MRQP.......... Quepos (La Managua) [*Costa Rica*] [*ICAO location identifier*] (ICLI)
MRR........... Macara [*Ecuador*] [*Airport symbol*] (OAG)
MRR........... Machine-Readable Record (MCD)
MRR........... [*The*] Magistrates of the Roman Republic [*A publication*] (OCD)
MRR........... Maintenance, Repairs, and Replacements [*Military*]
MRR........... Maintenance, Replacement, Removal (AFIT)
MRR........... Mandatory Removal Roster [*Army*]
MRR........... Manistee Railroad
MRR........... Marrow Release Rate [*Hematology*]
MRR........... Master Record Repository (MCD)
MRR........... Material Readiness Report (MCD)
MRR........... Material Receiving [*Inspection*] Report [*Nuclear energy*] (NRCH)
MRR........... Material Rejection Report
MRR........... Material Reliability Report (MCD)
MRR........... Material Removal Rate (MCD)
MRR........... Material Review Record [*or Reports*] [*Aviation*] (MCD)
MRR........... Material Review Request
MRR........... Materiel Readiness Report [*Army*] (AABC)
MRR........... Maximal Relaxation Rate [*Medicine*]
MRR........... Maximum Rate of Rise [*Biometrics*]
MRR........... Mechanical Reliability Report [*FAA*]
MRR........... Mechanical Research Report
MRR........... Medical Research Reactor
mrr............. Medical Research Reactor (AD)
MRR........... Medium-Range RADAR (NG)
MRR........... Medium-Range Recovery
MRR........... Metal Removal Rate
MRR........... Microelectronic Radio Receiver
MRR........... Microfilm Reader Recorder
MRR........... Mid-Atlantic Realty Trust [*AMEX symbol*] (SPSG)
MRR........... Milestone Readiness Review [*NASA*] (KSC)
MRR........... Military Renegotiation Regulation
MRR........... Miniature Reed Relay
MRR........... Minimum Rediscount Rate
MRR........... Minimum Reporting Requirement [*NASA*] (KSC)
MRR........... Minimum Risk Route (MCD)
MRR........... Missile Restraint Release
MRR........... Mission Reconfiguration Request (MCD)
MRR........... Molecular Rotational Resonance
MRR........... Monomer Reactivity Ratio (PDAA)
MRR........... Monthly Review Report
MRR........... Motorized Rifle Regiment [*Former USSR*]
MRR........... Multiple Response Resolver
MRR........... Multirole RADAR
MRR........... Muroran [*Japan*] [*Seismograph station code, US Geological Survey*] (SEIS)
MRRA.......... Master of Recreation Resources (F6) Administration (PGP)
MRRA.......... Military Retirement Reform Act
MRRAS........ Murder Release Risk Assessment Scale (AD)
MRRB.......... Maintenance Requirements Review Board [*Military*] (AFIT)

MRRB.......... Materiel Release Review Board [*Military*]
MRRB.......... Materiel Requirements Review Board [*Military*] (AFIT)
MRRC.......... Materiel Requirements Review Committee [*Military*]
MRRC.......... Mechanical Reliability Research Center
MRRC.......... Mental Retardation Research Center [*University of California, Los Angeles*] [*Research center*] (RCD)
MRRC.......... Ralph L. Smith Mental Retardation Research Center [*University of Kansas*] [*Research center*] (RCD)
MRRD.......... Marine Resources Research Division [*Now Ocean Environment Research Division*] (USDC)
MRRDB........ Malaysian Rubber Research and Development Board (AD)
MRRF.......... Monitor Research and Recovery Foundation
MRRF.......... Rio Frio O Progreso [*Costa Rica*] [*ICAO location identifier*] (ICLI)
MRRI.......... Marine Resources Research Institute [*South Carolina Wildlife and Marine Resources Department*] [*Research center*] (RCD)
MRRL.......... Materiel Repair Requirement List [*Military*] (AFIT)
MRRL.......... Metabolism and Radiation Research Laboratory [*North Dakota State University*] [*Research center*] (RCD)
MRRM.......... Rancho Del Mar [*Costa Rica*] [*ICAO location identifier*] (ICLI)
MRRN.......... Rancho Nuevo [*Costa Rica*] [*ICAO location identifier*] (ICLI)
MRRP.......... Maintenance and Repair of Real Property [*Military*]
MRRP.......... Motorways, Roads, and Road Programmes [*British*]
MRRS.......... Magnetic Reed Rotary Switch
MRRS.......... Materiel Readiness Reporting System [*Army*]
MRRS.......... Mobile Rail Repair Shop (MCD)
MRRS.......... Multiple Railroad System
MRRS.......... Multi-Rail Rocket System (PDAA)
MRRT.......... Maintenance Requirements Review Team (MUGU)
MRRW......... Morrow Snowboards [*NASDAQ symbol*] (TTSB)
MRRW......... Morrow Snowboards, Inc. [*NASDAQ symbol*] (SAG)
MRRX.......... Roxana Farms [*Costa Rica*] [*ICAO location identifier*] (ICLI)
MRS........... Airline of the Marshall Islands [*ICAO designator*] (FAAC)
MRS........... Maars [*Alaska*] [*Seismograph station code, US Geological Survey*] (SEIS)
MRS........... Mado Robin Society [*Defunct*] (EA)
MRS........... Magnetic Reed Switch
MRS........... Magnetic-Resonance Spectroscopy [*Biochemistry*] (ECON)
MRS........... Magnetic Resonance Spectrum
MRS........... Maintenance, Repair, and Service
MRS........... Maintenance Reporting System [*Army*]
MRS........... Maintenance Requirement Substantiated (MSA)
MRS........... Malfunction Reporting System [*Boeing*]
MRS........... Management Relations Survey [*Test*]
MRS........... Management Reporting System
MRS........... Management Review System (NASA)
MRS........... Manipulator Repair Shop (NRCH)
MRS........... Manned Reconnaissance Satellite [*Air Force*]
MRS........... Manned Repeater Station [*Telecommunications*] (OA)
MRS........... Manufacturers Railway Co. [*AAR code*]
MRS........... Marches (ROG)
MRS........... Marginal Rate of Substitution [*Economics*]
mrs............ Marginal Rate of Substitution (AD)
MRS........... Mariah Resources Ltd. [*Vancouver Stock Exchange symbol*]
MRS........... Market Research Society [*British*]
MRS........... Marseille [*France*] [*Airport symbol*] (OAG)
MRS........... Master Repair Schedule [*Air Force*] (AFM)
MRS........... Material Request [*or Requirement*] Summary
MRS........... Material Returned to Store [*NASA*] (KSC)
MRS........... Material Routing Slip
MRS........... Materials Research Society (EA)
MRS........... Materiel Repair System [*Air Force*] (AFM)
MRS........... Media Recognition System [*Computer science*] (PCM)
MRS........... Media Report Service (NITA)
MRS........... Media Resource Service [*Scientists' Institute for Public Information*] [*Information service or system*] (IID)
MRS........... Medical Receiving Station
MRS........... Medical Reception Station [*Military*]
MRS........... Medical Research Society [*British*]
MRS........... Medium Range Search
MRS........... Medium-Range SONAR (NVT)
MRS........... Melkersson-Rosenthal Syndrome [*Medicine*] (DMAA)
MRS........... Memo Routing Slip
MRS........... Metals Removal System [*Petroleum refining*]
MRS........... Methicillin-Resistant Staphylococcus [*Qureus*] [*Medicine*] (DAVI)
MRS........... Methicillin-Resistant Staphylococcus Aureus [*Antimicrobial therapy*] (MEDA)
MRS........... Metro Recovery Systems (EFIS)
MrS............ Microfilm Records System, Inc., Mamaroneck, NY [*Library symbol*] [*Library of Congress*] (LCLS)
MRS........... Microfilm Replacement System [*Computer science*]
MRS........... Micro Reflective Structure [*Computer science*]
MRS........... Midcoast Energy Resources, Inc. [*AMEX symbol*] (SAG)
MRS........... Midlands Research Station [*British Gas*] (WDAA)
MRS........... Migration and Refugee Services (EA)
MRS........... Military Railway Service [*Army*]
MRS........... Military Requirements Study (AAGC)
MRS........... Military Retirement System
MRS........... Minimum Radial Separation [*Manufacturing term*]
MRS........... Minimum Reporting Standard [*Broadcasting*] (NTCM)
MRS........... Mini-Reconstruction System (MCD)
MRS........... Ministry of Recreation and Sport [*British*] (AD)
MRS........... Missile Reentry Systems (AFIT)
MRS........... Missile Round Simulator
MRS........... Mission de Ras Shamra [*A publication*] (BJA)
MRS........... Mission-Related Software

Mrs	Missus (AD)
Mrs	Mistress (AD)
MRS.	Mistress (DAVI)
MRS.	Mixed Reproductive Strategy [Avian biology]
MRS.	Mobile Radio Service (DA)
MRS.	Mobile Remote Servicer (SSD)
MRS.	Mobility Requirements Study [DoD]
MRS.	Mobilization Requirement Study
MRS.	Mobilization Reserve Stocks [Army]
MRS.	Moderator Recovery System (COE)
MRS.	Modification Record Sheet [NASA] (KSC)
MRS.	Monitored Retrievable Storage [of nuclear waste]
MRS.	Monitored Retrievable Storage Facility [Environmental science] (COE)
MRS.	Monorail System
MRS.	Moore-Rott-Sears [Theory]
MRS.	Mortgage-Related Security (EMRF)
MRS.	Mothers Return to School
MRS.	Motor Rotation Stand
MRS.	Mountain Rescue Service (AD)
MRS.	Mouvement Republicain Senegalais [Senegalese Republican Movement] [Political party] (PPW)
MRS.	Movement and Reinforcement Study (MCD)
MRS.	Movement Report Sheet [Military]
MRS.	Movement Report System [Military]
MRS.	Multilateral RADAR Strike System [Air Force] (MCD)
MRS.	Multilateral RADAR Surveillance System [Air Force] (MCD)
MRS.	Multiple Representative Sections [Pathology] (DAVI)
MRS.	Multipurpose Research System
MRS.	Multipurpose Reusable Spacecraft (IIA)
MRS.	Music Reading Software (PCM)
MRS.	Muzzle Reference System (MCD)
MRS3.	Multilateral RADAR Surveillance/Strike System [Air Force]
MRSA	Machinery Repairman, Seaman Apprentice [Navy rating]
MRSA	Maine Revised Statutes, Annotated [A publication] (DLA)
MRSA	Mandatory RADAR Service Area
MRSA	Marisa Christina [NASDAQ symbol] (TTSB)
MRSA	Marisa Christina, Inc. [NASDAQ symbol] (SAG)
MRSA	Materiel Readiness Support Activity [Army] (RDA)
MRSA	Materiel Readiness Support Agency [Navy]
MRSA	Medium Range Surveillance Aircraft [Military] (PDAA)
mrsa	Medium-Range Surveillance Aircraft (AD)
MRSA	Member of the Royal Society of Arts [British]
MRSA	Merrimack River Study Act of 1990 (COE)
MRSA	Metal Roofing Systems Association (NTPA)
MRSA	Methicillin-Resistant Staphylococcus Aureus [Antimicrobial therapy]
MRSA	Microwave Radiometer, Scatterometer, and Altimeter (MCD)
MRSA	Military RADAR Service Area [Aviation] (AIA)
MRSA	San Alberto [Costa Rica] [ICAO location identifier] (ICLI)
MR San A	Member of the Royal Sanitary Association of Scotland
MR San Asn	Member of the Royal Sanitary Association [British] (AD)
MRSB	Material Requirements for Stock Balance
MRSB	San Cristobal [Costa Rica] [ICAO location identifier] (ICLI)
Mr SBA	Maryland State Bar Association, Report [A publication] (DLA)
MRSC	Maritime Rescue Sub-Center [Canada]
MRSc	Master of Rural Science [British] (ADA)
MRSC	Member of the Royal Society of Canada
MRSC	Member of the Royal Society of Chemistry [British] (DBQ)
MRSC	Mississippi Remote Sensing Center [Mississippi State University] [Research center] (RCD)
MRSC	Santa Cruz [Costa Rica] [ICAO location identifier] (ICLI)
MRSD	Maximum Rated Standard Deviation [Statistics]
MRSD	Mission Requirements on System Design [NASA]
MRSG	Santa Clara De Guapiles [Costa Rica] [ICAO location identifier] (ICLI)
MRSH	Marsh (ADA)
MRSH	Member of the Royal Society of Health [British]
MRSH	Shiroles [Costa Rica] [ICAO location identifier] (ICLI)
MRSHLL	Marshall
MrshlInd	Marshall Industries [Associated Press] (SAG)
MrshMc	Marsh & McLennan Companies, Inc. [Associated Press] (SAG)
MrshS	Marsh Supermarkets, Inc. [Associated Press] (SAG)
MrshSu	Marsh Supermarkets, Inc. [Associated Press] (SAG)
MRSI	Maintenance and Repair Support Items
MRSI	Maintenance Repair Spares Instruction (MCD)
MRSI	Medium-Range SOF [Special Operations Forces] Insertion (DOMA)
MRSI	Member of the Royal Sanitary Institute [British] (ROG)
MRSI	Michigan Recovery Systems, Inc. (EFIS)
MRSI	Mobilization Requirements, Secondary Items
MRSI	MRS Technology [NASDAQ symbol] (TTSB)
MRSI	MRS Technology, Inc. [NASDAQ symbol] (SAG)
MRSI	San Isidro De El General [Costa Rica] [ICAO location identifier] (ICLI)
MRSJ	Commission for Racial Justice (EA)
MRSJ	San Jose [Costa Rica] [ICAO location identifier] (ICLI)
MRSJ	United Church of Christ Ministers for Racial and Social Justice (EA)
MRSL	Member of the Royal Society of Literature [British]
MRSM	Maintenance and Reliability Simulation Model (PDAA)
MRSM	Member of the Royal Society of Medicine [British] (DI)
MRSM	Member of the Royal Society of Musicians [British] (DI)
MRSM	Mississippi River Suspended Matter
MRSM	Santa Marta [Costa Rica] [ICAO location identifier] (ICLI)
MRSMA	Member of the Royal Society of Marine Artists [British] (DI)
MRSMGB	Member of the Royal Society of Musicians of Great Britian (AD)
MRSMP	Member of the Royal Society of Miniature Painters [British] (DI)
MRSN	Machinery Repairman, Seaman [Navy rating]
MRSN	Sirena [Costa Rica] [ICAO location identifier] (ICLI)
MRSO	Mobilization Reserve Stockage Objective [Army]
MRSO	Santa Maria De Guacimo [Costa Rica] [ICAO location identifier] (ICLI)
MRSP	Multifunction RADAR Signal Processor (MCD)
MRSP	Myakka River State Park [Florida]
MRSP	San Pedro [Costa Rica] [ICAO location identifier] (ICLI)
MRSPE	Member of the Royal Society of Painters and Etchers [British] (DI)
MRSPWC	Member of the Royal Society of Painters in Water Colours [British]
MR-SR	Material Review - Ships Record (MCD)
MRSR	Multi-Role Survivable Radar [Army] (DOMA)
MRSR	Samara [Costa Rica] [ICAO location identifier] (ICLI)
MRSS	Main and Reheat Steam System [Nuclear energy] (NRCH)
MRSS	Manned Rovolving Simulated Space Station (SAA)
MRSS	Master Remote Slave Station (MCD)
MRSS	Missile Response Simulation Software
MRSS	San Joaquin de Abangares [Costa Rica] [ICAO location identifier] (ICLI)
mrsss	Manned Revolving Space Systems Simulator (AD)
MRST	Member of the Royal Society of Teachers [British]
MRST	Minimum Remaining Slack Time (PDAA)
MRST	San Agustin [Costa Rica] [ICAO location identifier] (ICLI)
MRS Tch	MRS Technology, Inc. [Associated Press] (SAG)
MRSV	Maneuverable Recoverable Space Vehicle
MRSV	Military Railway Service Veterans (EA)
MRSV	San Vito De Jaba [Costa Rica] [ICAO location identifier] (ICLI)
MRSW	Member of the Royal Society of Scottish Painters and Watercolours [British] (DAS)
MRSX	Sixaola [Costa Rica] [ICAO location identifier] (ICLI)
MRT	Air Mauritanie [Mauritania] [ICAO designator] (FAAC)
Mrt	Maart [March] [Dutch] (AD)
MRT	Machine-Readable Tapes [Computer science]
MRT	Maintainability Review Team [Navy] (NG)
MRT	Maintenance Readiness Training (DNAB)
MRT	Major Role Therapy [Schizophrenia]
MRT	Malignant Rhabdoid Tumor [Oncology]
MRT	Marble Threshold (AAG)
MRT	Marietta Resources [Vancouver Stock Exchange symbol]
Mrt	Martinique (AD)
MRT	Marysville, OH [Location identifier FAA] (FAAL)
MRT	Mass Rapid Transit (AD)
MRT	Mass Rapid Transport [British]
MRT	Material Review Tag [Aviation] (MCD)
MRT	Mauritania [ANSI three-letter standard code] (CNC)
MRT	Maximum Rated Thrust (MCD)
MRT	Maximum Repair Time (PDAA)
MRT	Maze-Running Time [Psychology]
MRT	MBB [Messerschmidt, Boelkow, Blohm] Raytheon-Thompson
MRT	Mean Radiant Temperature
mrt	Mean Radiant Temperature (AD)
MRT	Mean Radiative-Transfer [Meteorology]
MRT	Mean Ready Time (MCD)
MRT	Mean Repair Time
MRT	Mean Residence Time [Kinetics]
MRT	Mean Retention Time [Physiology]
MRT	Measured Rate of Time (PDAA)
MRT	Median Recognition Threshold (MAE)
MRT	Medical Records Technician (DAVI)
MRT	Medical Record Technician (HCT)
MRT	Medium Range Truck [Military]
MRT	Medium-Range Typhon [Missile] (NG)
MRT	Meridional Ray Trace
Mrt	Merit [Record label]
MRT	Metropolitan Readiness Test
mrt	Mid-Range Trajectory (AD)
mrt	Mildew-Resistant Thread (AD)
MRT	Mildew-Resistant Thread
MRT	Milestones Reporting Techniques
MRT	Military Rated Thrust (NG)
mrt	Military-Rated Thrust (AD)
MRT	Military Reserve Technician (GFGA)
MRT	Military Review Team (AD)
MRT	Milk Ring Test (PDAA)
MRT	Miniature Receiver Terminal
MRT	Minimum Resolvable Temperature (MCD)
MRT	Ministere de la Recherche et de la Technologie (USDC)
MRT	Missile Round Trainer (MCD)
MRT	Missile Round Transporter (MCD)
mrt	Mission Readiness Tester (AD)
MRT	Mobile RADAR Target
MRT	Modified Rhyme Test
MRT	Modulus of Rupture Test (AD)
MRT	Mortgage & Realty Trust (EFIS)
MRT	Movimento Revolucionario Tiradentes [Revolutionary Tiradentes Movement] [Brazil Political party] (PD)
MRT	Multiple Requests Terminal [Computer science] (HGAA)
MRT	Murotomisaki [Japan] [Seismograph station code, US Geological Survey] (SEIS)
MRT	Muscle Response Test
MRT	Reformed Theological Seminary, Jackson, MS [OCLC symbol] (OCLC)
MRTA	Maintenance Requirements Task Analysis (AD)
MRTA	Marietta Corp. [NASDAQ symbol] (NQ)
MRTA	Marketing Research Trade Association [Later, MRA] (EA)

MRTA............	Mechanical Response Tissue Analyzer [*For measuring bone strength*]
MRTA............	Movimiento Revolucionario Tupac Amaru [*Peru*] [*Political party*] (EY)
MRTA............	Tamarindo de Bagaces [*Costa Rica*] [*ICAO location identifier*] (ICLI)
MRTB............	Ticaban [*Costa Rica*] [*ICAO location identifier*] (ICLI)
MRTC............	Marine Corps Reserve Training Center
MRTC............	Military Real-Time Computer (AAG)
MRTC............	Multiple Real-Time Commands (NASA)
MRTD............	Minimum Resolvable Temperature Difference (PDAA)
MRTE............	Master of Radio and Television Engineering
MRTE............	Missile Round Test Equipment
MRT Eng........	Master of Radio and Television Engineering
MRTFB.........	Major Range and Test Facility Base [*Military*] (CAAL)
MRTFM........	Mean Rounds to First Maintenance [*Army*]
MRTG...........	Mortgage
MRTG...........	Taboga [*Costa Rica*] [*ICAO location identifier*] (ICLI)
MRTHN........	Marathon
MRTI............	Multirole Thermal Imager [*Defense electronics*]
MRTK...........	Movimiento Revolucionario Tupaj Katari [*Tupaj Katari Revolutionary Movement*] [*Bolivia*] [*Political party*] (PPW)
MRTM..........	Maritime
mrtm...........	Maritime (AD)
MRTM..........	Tamarindo de Santa Cruz [*Costa Rica*] [*ICAO location identifier*] (ICLI)
MRTN	Marten Transport [*NASDAQ symbol*] (TTSB)
MRTN	Marten Transport Ltd. [*NASDAQ symbol*] (NQ)
Mrtnz..........	Martinez (AD)
mrto...........	Miscellaneous Reference Tool (AD)
MRTP..........	Master of Regional and Town Planning
MRTP..........	Master of Rural and Town Planning (GAGS)
MRTP..........	Military Reliable Tube Program
MRTPI.........	Member of the Royal Town Planning Institute [*British*]
MRTR..........	Mortar [*Technical drawings*] (DAC)
MRTR..........	Tambor [*Costa Rica*] [*ICAO location identifier*] (ICLI)
MRTRY........	Mortuary
mrts...........	Marginal Rate of Technical Substitution (AD)
MRTS..........	Marginal Rate of Technical Substitution [*Ecology*]
MRTS..........	Mass Rapid Transit System (AD)
MRTS..........	Master RADAR Tracking Station
Mrts...........	Mauritius (AD)
MRTS..........	Meteorological Real-Time System [*Computer science*] (KSC)
MRTS..........	Microwave Repeater Test Set (DA)
MRTS..........	Missile Round Test Set
MRTS..........	Multi-Media Remote Teaching System [*AT & T Co., Illinois Institute of Technology*]
MRTT..........	Modular Record Traffic Terminal [*Formerly, COED*] [*Army*] (MCD)
MRTU..........	Multiplex Remote Terminal Unit (MCD)
MRU	Machine Records Unit [*Computer science*]
MRU	Main Resource Unit
MRU	Maintenance Replaceable Unit (MCD)
MRU	Mano River Union [*See also UFM*] (EAIO)
MRU	Maritime Reconnaissance Unit [*British military*] (DMA)
MRU	Mass Radiography Unit
mru	Mass Radiography Unit (AD)
MRU	Material Recovery Unit
MRU	Mauritius [*Airport symbol*] (OAG)
MRU	Medical Rehabilitation Unit (AD)
MRU	Message Retransmission Unit
MRU	Microfilm Recording Unit
MRU	Microwave Relay Unit
MRU	Military RADAR Unit [*Aviation*] (FAAC)
mru	Minimal Reproductive Unit (AD)
MRU	Minimal Reproductive Units [*Bacteriology*]
MRU	Minimum Replacement Unit
MRU	Mobile Radio Unit [*Air Force*]
mru	Mobile Radio Unit (AD)
MRU	Mobile Refrigeration Unit (KSC)
MRU	Mobile Remote Unit [*From computer game "Hacker II"*]
MRU	Most Recently Used [*Computer science*]
MRU	Most Recently Used Data [*Computer science*] (PCM)
MRU	Motion Reference Unit (MCD)
MRU	Mountain Rescue Unit (COE)
MRU	Movement Release Unit [*MTMC*] (TAG)
MRU	Much Regret, I Am Unable
MRU	Multifunction Reference Unit (MCD)
MRUA..........	Mobile Radio Users' Association (IAA)
MRUASTAS...	Medium-Range Unmanned Aerial Surveillance and Target Acquisition System (NATG)
M Ru E	Master of Rural Engineering
M Ru Eng ...	Master of Rural Engineering
MRUP..........	Upala [*Costa Rica*] [*ICAO location identifier*] (ICLI)
MRurSc........	Master of Rural Science [*British*] (ADA)
MRUSI.........	Member of the Royal United Service Institution [*British*]
MRV............	Maneuvering Reentry Vehicle
MRV............	Mark V Petroleums & Mines [*Vancouver Stock Exchange symbol*]
MRV............	Mars Roving Vehicle [*NASA*] (PDAA)
MRV............	Marvel Entertainment Group [*NYSE symbol*] (SPSG)
MRV............	Marvel Entertainment Grp [*NYS*] (TTSB)
mrv............	Material Receipt Voucher (AD)
MRV............	Middlesex Rifle Volunteers [*Military British*] (ROG)
MRV............	Mineral Nyye Vody [*Former USSR Airport symbol*] (OAG)
MRV............	Mini-Rotary Viscometer [*Mechanical engineering*]
MRV............	Minute Respiratory Volume
MRV............	Miravia Ltd. [*Romania*] [*FAA designator*] (FAAC)
MRV............	Missile Recovery Vessel (AD)
mrv	Missile Re-Entry Vehicle (AD)
mrv	Mixed Respiratory Vaccine [*Medicine*] (AD)
MRV	Mixed Respiratory Vaccine
MRV	Mouvement de Regroupement Voltaique [*Upper Volta Regroupment Movement*] [*Political party*]
MRV	Mulberry Ringspot Virus [*Plant pathology*]
MRV	Multiple Reentry Vehicle [*Military*]
MRVA	Member of the Rating and Valuation Association [*British*] (DI)
MRVC	Member of the Royal Veterinary College [*British*]
MRVC	MRV Communications, Inc. [*NASDAQ symbol*] (SAG)
MRVC	MRV Communicatons [*NASDAQ symbol*] (TTSB)
MRV Cm	MRV Communications, Inc. [*Associated Press*] (SAG)
MRVI	Monte Reale Valcellina [*Italy*] [*Seismograph station code, US Geological Survey*] (SEIS)
MRVLP	Maneuvering Reentry Vehicle for Low-Level Penetration (MCD)
MRVP	Mean Right Ventricular Pressure [*Cardiology*]
MRVP	Methyl-Red, Voges-Proskauer [*Medium*] [*Bacteriology*]
mrV-P	Methyl Red Voges-Proskauer [*Bacteriology*] (AD)
MRVT..........	Miravant [*NASDAQ symbol*]
MRVT..........	Miravant Medical Technologies
MRVT..........	Multiple Rate Voice Terminal [*Telecommunications*] (LAIN)
MRVTB	Maximally Restrictive Verifiable Test Ban [*For nuclear bombs*]
MRW	Morale, Recreation, and Welfare [*Military*] (AFM)
mrw	Morale, Recreation, and Welfare (AD)
MRW	Morioka [*Japan*] [*Airport symbol*] (OAG)
mr/w	Multiple Read/Write (AD)
MRWA	Midland Railway of Western Australia (AD)
mrwc	Multiple Reading, Writing, Compiling (AD)
MRWC	Multiple Read-Write Compute
MRWS	Mobile RADAR Weather System (DNAB)
MRX	Hermens/Markair Express [*ICAO designator*] (FAAC)
MRX	Magnetoresistive Extended [*Computer science*]
MRX	Medicis Pharmaceutical ™A∫[*NYSE symbol*]
MRX	Memorex (NITA)
MRX	Memorex Corp. (IAA)
MRX	Mineiros [*Brazil*] [*Airport symbol*] (AD)
MRX	Mobil Oil Corp., Toxicology Division, Information Center, Princeton, NJ [*OCLC symbol*] (OCLC)
MRX	Movement Research Exchange
MRX	Riverside, CA [*Location identifier FAA*] (FAAL)
MRXS	Mental Retardation, X-Linked, Syndrome [*Medicine*] (DMAA)
MRY	Marilyn Resources [*Vancouver Stock Exchange symbol*]
MRY	Mary [*Former USSR Seismograph station code, US Geological Survey Closed*] (SEIS)
MRY	Merry Land & Invest [*NYSE symbol*] (TTSB)
MRY	Merry Land & Investment [*NYSE symbol*] (SAG)
MRY	Monterey [*California*] [*Airport symbol*] (OAG)
MRYPr........	Merry Land & Inv Sr'A'Cv Pfd [*NYSE symbol*] (TTSB)
MRYPrC......	Merry Land & Inv Sr'C'Cv Pfd [*NYSE symbol*] (TTSB)
mrytm..........	Must Have Reply Here by Tomorrow Morning (AD)
mrz	Marzo [*March*] [*Spanish*] (AD)
MRZ	Moree [*Australia Airport symbol*] (OAG)
MRZ	Syracuse, NY [*Location identifier FAA*] (FAAL)
MRZP...........	Zapotal De Guanacaste [*Costa Rica*] [*ICAO location identifier*] (ICLI)
MS............	Egyptair [*ICAO designator*] (AD)
MS............	IEEE Magnetics Society (EA)
MS............	Ma'aser Sheni (BJA)
MS............	Machinery Survey [*Shipping*]
MS............	Machine Screw
ms............	Machine Screw (AD)
MS............	Machine Selection (IEEE)
MS............	Machine Steel
ms............	Machine Steel (AD)
MS............	Machining System (IAA)
MS............	Macromodular System [*Computer science*] (IEEE)
MS............	Macro Society (EA)
MS............	Magnetic South
MS............	Magnetic Stirrer [*Biotechnology*]
MS............	Magnetic Storage [*Computer science*]
MS............	Magnetic Strip (IAA)
MS............	Magnetic Synchron (IAA)
MS............	Magnetostatic [*Telecommunications*] (IAA)
MS............	Magnetostriction
MS............	Mail Steamer
M/S............	Mail Stop
MS............	Main Sequence [*Astronomy*]
M/S............	Mainstage [*NASA*] (KSC)
MS............	Main Steam (NRCH)
MS............	Main Storage
MS............	Main Switch
ms............	Main Switch (AD)
ms............	Maintenance and Service (AD)
MS............	Maintenance and Service
MS............	Maintenance Schedule (DA)
MS............	Maintenance Squadron
MS............	Maintenance Standard
MS............	Maintenance Superintendent [*Military*] (AFIT)
MS +............	Maintenance Support Positive
MS............	Maintenance System (ACII)
MS............	Majority Stockholder
MS............	Major Subject [*Military*]
ms............	Major Subject (AD)
MS............	Maladjustment Score [*Psychology*]
MS............	Male Servant
MS............	Malone Society (EA)

MS	Mammal Society (EAIO)
MS	Management Science [Computer science] (BUR)
MS	Management Services (KSC)
MS	Management Staff [Environmental Protection Agency] (GFGA)
MS	Management System (OICC)
MS	Manic State [Medicine] (DB)
MS	Manned Station (IAA)
M/S	Mannlicher-Schoenauer (AD)
MS	Mannose Sensitive [Biochemistry]
MS	Mano Sinistra [With the Left Hand] [Music]
M/S	Manslaughter
MS	Man Station [Military]
MS	Manual Sequential (NRCH)
MS	Manual Supplement
MS	Manual System (DCTA)
MS	Manufacturing in Space
MS	Manufacturing Specification (AAG)
MS	Manufacturing Standard
MS	Manufacturing Status (AAG)
MS	Manufacturing Support
MS	Manuscript (WDAA)
ms	Manuscript (VRA)
Ms	Manuscript (AL)
MS	Manuscript Reports [A publication] (DLA)
MS	Manuscript Society (EA)
MS	Manuscriptum [Manuscript] [Latin]
MS	Mare Serenitatis [Sea of Serenity] [Lunar area]
MS	Margin of Safety [Engineering]
ms	Margin of Safety (AD)
MS	Marian Sisters of the Diocese of Lincoln (TOCD)
MS	Marie-See [Syndrome] [Medicine] (DB)
MS	Marie-Struempell [Disease] [Medicine] (DB)
MS	Marijuana Smoke
Ms	Mariners [Seattle Baseball Team] (AD)
MS	Marital Status
MS	Marker Switch (IAA)
m/s	Marking and Stenciling (AD)
MS	Mark Sense (NITA)
MS	Mark Sensing (MSA)
MS	Marquandia Society (EA)
MS	Marshall Steel Ltd. [Toronto Stock Exchange symbol]
MS	Mass Spectrography
Ms	Mass Spectrometer (NAKS)
MS	Mass Spectrometer (AAEL)
ms	Mass Spectrometric (AD)
MS	Mass Spectrometry
MS	Mass Storage [Computer science]
MS	Master of Science (GAGS)
MS	Master of Sociology
MS	Master of Surgery
MS	Master Scene [Major script sequence] (NTCM)
MS	Master Scheduler (CMD)
MS	Master Sequencer (AAG)
MS	Master Sergeant
M-S	Master-Servant [Legal shorthand] (LWAP)
MS	Master Shot [Film production] (NTCM)
MS	Master-Slave [Computer science] (MHDI)
MS	Master Switch
ms	Master Switch (AD)
MS	Master Synchronizer (CET)
MS	Mast Section (IAA)
MS	Matched Set [Philately]
ms	Matched Set (AD)
Ms	Material Specification (NAKS)
MS	Material Specifications
MS	Materials Science
MS	Material Standard (AD)
MS	Material Support
MS	Mathis Society [Defunct] (EA)
MS	Mating Sequence and Control (NASA)
Ms	Mating Sequence and Control [NASA] (NAKS)
MS	Matrix Spike
Ms	Mature Motion Pictures (AD)
MS	Mauritius
MS	Maximum Stress
ms	Maximum Stress (AD)
ms	Mean Square (AD)
MS	Mean Square
MS	Measured Service Pricing [Telecommunications] (TEL)
M/S	Measurement Stimuli (NASA)
MS	Measuring Set
MS	Measuring System
MS	Mechanical Seal
MS	Mechanical Stimulation (DB)
MS	Mechanized Scheduling [Telecommunications] (TEL)
MS	Meckel Syndrome [Medicine] (DMAA)
MS	Medial Septum [Anatomy]
MS	Media-Service GmbH [Database producer] (IID)
MS	Media Society [British] (DBA)
MS	Medical Science (DAVI)
MS	Medical Services [Navy British]
MS	Medical Staff [British military] (DMA)
MS	Medical Student (DAVI)
MS	Medical Supplies [Military]
MS	Medical Survey [Navy]

MS	Medicine and Surgery [Navy] (IEEE)
MS	Medium-Scale (IAA)
MS	Medium Setting [Asphalt grade]
MS	Medium Shot [Refers to distance from which a photograph or motion picture sequence is taken]
ms	Medium Shot (AD)
MS	Medium Soft (IAA)
MS	Medium-Speed (IAA)
MS	Medium Steel
ms	Medium Steel (AD)
MS	Meeting of Signatories [INTELSAT]
MS	Meeting Series [Online database field identifier]
MS	Megasecond (IAA)
MS	Mega Society (EA)
MS	Megasporocyte [Botany]
M/S	Melville Society (EA)
M/S	Member State (DCTA)
M/S	Memorandum Slip [for informal interoffice communications]
MS	Memoriae Sacrum [Sacred to the Memory Of] [Latin]
MS	Memory Store [Computer science] (PCM)
MS	Memory System
MS	Mencken Society (EA)
Ms	Mendes (AD)
MS	Men of the Stones (EA)
MS	Mental Status [Psychology]
MS	Merchant Shipping
MS	Mercury-Scout [Spacecraft] [NASA]
MS	Merit System (OICC)
MS	Mesa [Type of transistor] (MDG)
Ms	Mesothorium (AD)
MS	Message Store [Telecommunications] (OSI)
MS	Message Switching [Telecommunications] (IAA)
MS	Mess Management Specialist [Military] (MUSM)
MS	Mestome Sheath [Botany]
Ms	Mesyl [Organic chemistry]
MS	Metallurgical Society (NADA)
m/s	Metal Shank (AD)
MS	Metals Society [Later, IOM] (EAIO)
MS	Metal Stamping
MS	Meteoritical Society (EA)
MS	Meteoroid Shield (KSC)
MS	Meteor Scatter (PDAA)
M/S	Meters per Second
ms	Meters per Second (AD)
MS	Methionine Synthase [An enzyme]
MS	Method of Sale
MS	Methyl Salicylate [Organic chemistry]
MS	Metric Size (IAA)
MS	Metric System
ms	Metric System (AD)
MS	Mezzo Soprano [Music] (ROG)
MS	Michigan State University of Agriculture and Applied Sciences (AD)
MS	Microbial Susceptibility [Medicine] (DB)
MS	Microcirculatory Society (EA)
MS	Microprogram Storage [Computer science] (MDG)
MS	Microscope Slide (DMAA)
MS	Microscopic System
ms	Microseismic (AD)
MS	Microsoft [Software manufacturer]
MS	Microsoft Corporation (WDMC)
MS	Microsphere
MS	Microwave Scanner [Marine science] (OSRA)
MS	Microwave Spectrum
MS	Mid-Shot
MS	Mild Steel
ms	Mild Steel (AD)
m/s	Milestone (AD)
MS	Milestone (KSC)
Ms	Milestone (NAKS)
MS	Military Science (AABC)
MS	Military Secretary [British]
MS	Military Service
MS	Military Service Act [British]
MS	Military Specification (AAG)
MS	Military Staff [British military] (DMA)
Ms	Military Standard (NAKS)
MS	Military Standard [Parts designation]
MS	Military Survivors (EA)
MS	Millennium Society (EA)
ms	Millisecond
Ms	Millisecond (NAKS)
mS	Millisiemens
MS	Minesweeper [or Minesweeping]
MS	Miniature Screw [Lamp base] (NTCM)
m/s	Miniature Sheet of Stamps (AD)
MS	Minimal Support (DAVI)
ms	Minimum Stress (AD)
MS	Minister of State [British]
MS	Ministry of Shipping [British]
MS	Ministry of Supply [Also, MOS] [British]
MS	Minority Stockholder
M/S	Minor Support (KSC)
MS	Mint State
ms	Mint State (AD)
MS	Minus

MS	Minutes (AAG)
MS	Miscellaneous
MS	Miscellaneous Services [Department of Employment] [British]
MS	Missile Station (AAG)
MS	Missile System
ms	[The] Missionaries of Our Lady La Salette (TOCD)
MS	Missionaries of Our Lady of LaSalette [Roman Catholic religious order]
MS	Missionary Sisters of Our Lady of Africa [White Sisters] [Roman Catholic religious order]
MS	Missionary Society [British]
MS	Mission Sequencer (SAA)
MS	Mission Simulator
MS	Mission Specialist (MCD)
Ms	Mission Specialist [NASA] (NAKS)
Ms	Mission Station [NASA] (NAKS)
MS	Mission Station (MCD)
MS	Missions to Seamen (EA)
MS	Mission Support
MS	Mississippi [Postal code]
Ms	Mississippi State Library, Jackson, MS [Library symbol Library of Congress] (LCLS)
MS	Miss or Mrs. [Pronounced "Miz"]
Ms	Mistress (DAVI)
ms	Mitral Stenosis (AD)
MS	Mitral Stenosis [Cardiology]
MS	Mittelsatz [Middle Movement] [Music]
M-S	Mitte-Seite [Stereo] (IEEE)
MS	Mobile Searchlight [British]
MS	Mobile Service [Telecommunications] (TEL)
MS	Mobile Surgery [British]
MS	Mobilization Station [DoD]
MS	Modal Sensation [Psychology]
MS	Modal Sensitivity [Medicine]
MS	Model Station
MS	Moderately Susceptible [Plant pathology]
MS	Modern Science [A publication]
MS	Modulation Sensitivity
MS	Moessbauer Spectroscopy
MS	Molar Degree of Substitution [Organic chemistry]
MS	Molar Solution [Dentistry]
MS	Molar Substitution (DB)
MS	Molecular Sieve (MCD)
MS	Molecular Staffing [Optics] (EECA)
MS	Molecular Substitution
M-S	Monday through Saturday (AD)
MS	Money Supply
MS	Mongolian Spot [Medicine]
MS	Monitor Station
MS	Monorail Society (EA)
m/s	Month after Sight (AD)
ms	Months after Sight (AD)
MS	Months after Sight [or Month's Sight] [Business term]
MS	Montserrat [ANSI two-letter standard code] (CNC)
MS	More Significant [Statistics]
MS	Morgan Stanley Group [NYSE symbol] (TTSB)
MS	Morgan Stanley Group, Inc. [NYSE symbol] (SPSG)
MS	Morphine Sulfate [Narcotic]
MS	Morquio-Silverkioeld [Syndrome] [Medicine] (DB)
MS	Morse Tape (IAA)
MS	Most Severe [Automotive engineering]
MS	Most Significant
MS	Motile Sperm
MS	Motion Sensitivity (KSC)
MS	Motor Ship
m/s	Motorskib [Motorship] [Norwegian] (AD)
MS	Motor Starting (IAA)
MS	Motor Supports
MS	Mucosubstance (MAE)
MS	Multilateral Staff [Environmental Protection Agency] (GFGA)
MS	Multiple Sclerosis [Medicine]
ms	Multiple Sclerosis (AD)
MS	Multiple Section (MSA)
ms	Multiple Starters (AD)
MS	Multiplexer Storage (IAA)
MS	Multistart [Optimization method]
MS	Multistring (NASA)
Ms	Multistring (NAKS)
MS	Murashige-Skoog [Medium] [Botany]
Ms	Murmurs [Medicine] (DMAA)
MS	Murphy-Sturm [Lymphosarcoma] [Medicine] (DB)
MS	Muscle Shortening [Medicine]
MS	Muscle Strength
ms	Muscle Strength (AD)
MS	Musculactive Substance [Medicine]
MS	Musculoskeletal [Medicine]
Ms	Mussels [Quality of the bottom] [Nautical charts]
MS	Mustard Seed (EA)
MS	Mycoplasma Synoviae [A pathogen]
MS	Mythopoeic Society (EA)
MS	Ship Station [ITU designation] (CET)
MS	Somerset Library [Bibliotheque Somerset], Manitoba [Library symbol National Library of Canada] (BIB)
MS	Springfield City Library, Springfield, MA [Library symbol Library of Congress] (LCLS)
MS1	Mess Management Specialist, First Class [Navy rating] (DNAB)
MS-2	Mare Serenitatis [Sea of Serenity] [Lunar area]
MS2	Mess Management Specialist, Second Class [Navy rating] (DNAB)
M/S^2	Meters per Second Squared
MS2	Micro-Set System 2 (NITA)
MS3	Mess Management Specialist, Third Class [Navy rating] (DNAB)
MS-3	Military Staffing Standards System
MS3	Munitions Support Structure Study [Army]
MS3-X	Munitions System Support Structure
MS3-X	Munitions System Support Structure - Extended [Army]
mS-222	Tricaine Methane Sulphonate [Chemistry] (DAVI)
MSA	Magazine Shippers Association
MSA	Mahri, Suqutri, and Shahri (BJA)
MSA	Main Store Allocator
MSA	Maintenance Support Activity
MSA	Major System Acquisition (COE)
MSA	Malaysia-Singapore Airlines
MSA	Male Specific Antigen (PDAA)
MSA	Management Science Associates, Inc. [Information service or system] (IID)
MSA	Management Science of America (HGAA)
MSA	Management System Analysis
MSA	Mandusa Resources Ltd. [Vancouver Stock Exchange symbol]
MSA	Manitoba Society of Artists [1925] [Canada] (NGC)
MSA	Mannitol Salt Agar (MAE)
MSA	Marigold Society of America (EA)
MSA	Marine Safety Agency (WDAA)
MSA	Marine Science Activities [Program] [Coast Guard]
MSA	Marine Stewards' Association [Australia]
MSA	Mariological Society of America (EA)
MSA	Maritime Safety Agency (NADA)
MSA	Marker Signal Attenuation
MSA	Market Science Associates, Inc. [Information service or system] (IID)
MSA	Marlowe Society of America (EA)
MSA	Marquetry Society of America (EA)
MSA	Marshal Sprayable Ablative [NASA]
MSA	Masonic Service Association of the United States (EA)
MSA	Massachusetts School of Art
MSA	Mass-Separating Agent [Chemical engineering]
MSA	Mass Storage Adapter
MSA	Master of School Administration (PGP)
MSA	Master of Science Administration (PGP)
MSA	Master of Science and Arts
MSA	Master of Science in Accountancy
MSA	Master of Science in Accounting (GAGS)
MSA	Master of Science in Administration (GAGS)
MSA	Master of Science in Agriculture
MSA	Master of Science in Anesthesia (PGP)
MSA	Master of Science in Anthropology (PGP)
MSA	Master of Scientific Agriculture
MSA	Master of Sport Administration (GAGS)
MSA	Material Service Area
MSA	Material Stores Area (KSC)
MSA	Material Surveillance Assembly [Nuclear energy] (NRCH)
MSA	Matrix Scheme for Algorithms (PDAA)
MSA	Mature Students' Association [British] (BI)
MSA	Mean Spherical Approximation [Physical chemistry]
MSA	Measure of Sampling Adequacy Index (EDAC)
MSA	Mechanical Signature Analysis
MSA	Media Studies Association [British]
MSA	Medical Savings Account
MSA	Medical Scientists' Association [Australia]
MSA	Medical Service Agency (WYGK)
MSA	Medical Services Account
MSA	Medical Services Administration [HEW]
MSA	Medusa Corp. [NYSE symbol] (CTT)
MSA	Member of the Society of Apothecaries [British]
MSA	Member of the Society of Architects [British] (DAS)
MSA	Member of the Society of Arts [British]
MSA	Membrane-Stabilizing Activity [Cardiology]
MSA	Membrane Surface Area [Cytology]
MSA	Merchant Shipping Act
MSA	Mercury Singapore Airlines
MSA	Mermaid Series [A publication]
MSA	Mesa Public Library, Mesa, AZ [OCLC symbol] (OCLC)
MSA	Metaphysical Society of America (EA)
MSA	Meteorological Satellite Activity (IAA)
MSA	Meteorological Support Activity [Army Electronics Command]
MSA	Methacrylate Structural Adhesive
MSA	Methanesulfonic Acid [Organic chemistry]
MSA	Method of Standard Additions
MSA	Methyltrimethylsilylacetamide [Organic chemistry]
MSA	Metropolitan Service Area [Telecommunications] (TSSD)
MSA	Metropolitan Statistical Area [Census Bureau]
MSA	Metropolitan Statistical Area Standard
MSA	Michigan Statutes Annotated [A publication] (AAGC)
MSA	Microcomputer Software Association (EA)
MSA	Microgravity Science and Applications
MSA	Microscopy Society of America (NTPA)
MSA	Microsomal Antibody
MSA	Middle States Association (NADA)
MSA	Middle States Association of Colleges and Schools (EA)
MSA	Middle Stone Age [Anthropology]
MSA	Midsystolic Click [Medicine] (DB)
MSA	Military Service Act [British] (DMA)

MSA	Military Subsistence Agency [*Merged with Defense Supply Agency*]
MSA	Milton Society of America (EA)
MSA	Mineralogical Society of America (EA)
MSA	Mine Safety Appliance
MSA	Minesweeper, Auxiliary [*Navy symbol Obsolete*]
MSA	Minimum Safe Altitude [*Aviation*]
MSA	Minimum Surface Area (KSC)
MSA	Minnesota Statutes, Annotated [*A publication*] (DLA)
MSA	Misce Secundum Artem [*Mix Pharmaceutically*] [*Latin*]
MSA	Missile Support Activity (MCD)
MSA	Missile System Analyst (SAA)
MSA	Missile System Availability (MCD)
MSA	Missionary Sisters of the Assumption [*Roman Catholic religious order*]
MSA	Mission Services Association (EA)
MSA	Mission Support Area [*NASA*]
MSA	Mistral Air SRL [*Italy ICAO designator*] (FAAC)
MSA	Mobile Subscriber Access (MCD)
MSA	Modern Studies Association [*British*] (DBA)
MSA	Monitor and Switching Assembly
MSA	Morale Support Activities [*Military*] (AABC)
MSA	Most Seriously Affected [*Food-deficient nations*]
MSA	Motor Schools' Association of Great Britain (BI)
MSA	Mount Pleasant, TX [*Location identifier FAA*] (FAAL)
MSA	Mount San Antonio [*New Mexico*] [*Seismograph station code, US Geological Survey*] (SEIS)
MSA	Mouse Serum Albumin [*Clinical chemistry*]
MSA	Mouvement Socialiste Africain [*African Socialist Movement*] [*Political party*]
MSA	Mouvement Souverainete Association [*Canada*] (PPW)
MSA	Multichannel Signal Averager [*Computer science*]
MSA	Multiple System Atrophy [*Medicine*]
MSA	Multiplication Stimulating Activity [*Cytochemistry*]
MSA	Multisubsystem Adapter [*Sperry UNIVAC*]
MSA	Multivariate Survival Analysis [*Statistics*]
MSA	Municipal Saleyards Association [*Victoria, Australia*]
MSA	Muscle Sympathetic Activity [*Medicine*] (DMAA)
MSA	Museum Store Association (EA)
MSA	Muslim Students' Association of the US and Canada (EA)
MSA	Mutual Security Act [*1954*]
MSA	Mutual Security Agency [*Functions transferred to Foreign Operations Administration, 1953*]
MSA	Mutual Society of Arts (NADA)
MSA	Mycological Society of America (EA)
MSa	Salem Public Library, Salem, MA [*Library symbol Library of Congress*] (LCLS)
MSAA	Master of Science in Astronautics and Aeronautics (PGP)
MSAA	Membrane Structures Association of Australasia
MSAA	Microsoft Active Accessibility [*Computer science*]
MSAA	Moderately Severe Aplastic Anemia [*Hematology*]
MSAA	Multiple-Sclerosis-Associated Agent [*A virus*]
MSAA	Multiple Sclerosis Association of America
MSAAB	Military Services Ammunition Allocation Board (AABC)
MSAAC	Mower Specialists' Association of Australia Cooperative
MSAAE	Master of Science in Aeronautical and Astronautical Engineering (GAGS)
MSAAP	Mississippi Army Ammunition Plant (AABC)
MSAAT	Member of the Society of Architectural and Allied Technicians [*British*] (DI)
MsAb	Evans Memorial Library, Aberdeen, MS [*Library symbol Library of Congress*] (LCLS)
MS/AB	Massenet Society/American Branch (EA)
MSAc	Master of Science in Accounting
MSAC	Mid-State Athletic Conference (PSS)
MSAC	Missile System Analyst Console (AAG)
MSAC	Moore School of Automatic Computers [*University of Pennsylvania*]
MSAC	Mount Saint Agnes College [*Maryland*] [*Merged with Loyola College*]
MSAC	Murray State Agricultural College [*Oklahoma*]
MSAC	Sonsonate/Acajutla [*El Salvador*] [*ICAO location identifier*] (ICLI)
MSACC	Master of Science in Accounting (PGP)
MS Acct	Master of Science in Accounting (PGP)
MS/Accy	Master of Science in Accountancy
MSACHA	Mid-South Automated Clearing House Association
MSACM	Master of Science in Acquisition and Contract Management (PGP)
MSACS	Middle States Association of Colleges and Schools (DHP)
MSAD	Materials Summary Acceptance Document (MCD)
MSAD	Motor Safe and Arm Device
MSAD	Multisatellite Attitude Determination [*NASA*]
MS Admin	Master of Science in Administration (PGP)
MSADY	Mid-States plc ADS [*NASDAQ symbol*] (TTSB)
MSaE	Essex Institute, Salem, MA [*Library symbol Library of Congress*] (LCLS)
MSAE	Master of Science in Aeronautical Engineering
MSAE	Master of Science in Aerospace Engineering (GAGS)
MSAE	Master of Science in Agricultural Engineering (PGP)
MSAE	Master of Science in Architectural Engineering (PGP)
MSAE	Master of Science in Art Education (PGP)
MSAE	Member of the Society of Automotive Engineers
MSAER	Master of Science in Aerospace Engineering (PGP)
MSAF	Meconium Stained Amniotic Fluid [*Neonatology*] (DAVI)
MSafetySc	Master of Safety Science
MSAFP	Maternal Serum Alpha Fetoprotein [*Clinical chemistry*]
MSAfrica	Morgan Stanley Africa Investment Fund [*Associated Press*] (SAG)
MSafSc	Master of Safety Science
MS (Ag)	Master of Science in Agriculture
MS (Ag E)	Master of Science in Agricultural Engineering
MS Agr	Master of Science in Agriculture
MSAgrEng	Master of Science in Agricultural Engineering (NADA)
MSAI	American International College, Springfield, MA [*Library symbol Library of Congress*] (LCLS)
MSAI	Master of Science in Artificial Intelligence (GAGS)
MSAICE	Member of the South African Institution of Civil Engineers
MSAInstMM	Member of the South African Institute of Mining and Metallugy
MSAL	Mammal Serum Albumin (DB)
MSALAS	Medical Sickness Annuity & Life Assurance Society (WDAA)
MsAM	Alcorn Agricultural and Mechanical College, Lorman, MS [*Library symbol Library of Congress*] (LCLS)
MSAM	Master of Science in Applied Mechanics
M-SAM	Medium Surface-to-Air Missile [*Army*]
MSAM	Mobile Surface-to-Air Missile
MSAM	Morgan Stanley Asset Management [*Commercial firm*]
MSAM	Morpholinomethyl Salicyclamide [*Analgesic compound*]
MSAM	Multi-Indexed Sequential Access Method [*Computer science*]
MSAM	Multiple Sequential Access Method (NITA)
MSAMP	Master Ship Acquisition Milestone Plan
MSAMS	Mobile Surface-to-Air Missile System (MCD)
M San	Master of Sanitation
MS & C	Marley, Scrooge, and Cratchit [*Accounting agency*]
MS & E	Materials Science and Engineering
MS & FR	Missile Stability and Frequency Response
MS & LR	Manchester, Sheffield & Lincolnshire Railway [*Later, Great Central*] [*British*] (ROG)
MS & NI	Michigan Southern & Northern Indiana Railroad
MS & P	Materials Synthesis and Processing [*National Science Foundation*]
MS & R	Merchant Shipbuilding and Repairs
MS & W	Maintenance Shop and Warehouse (NRCH)
MSanHi	Sandwich Historical Society, Sandwich, MA [*Library symbol Library of Congress*] (LCLS)
MSANS	Multiple Small-Angle Neutron Scattering [*Surface analysis*]
M San Sc	Master of Sanitary Science
MSanSc&PH	Master of Sanitary Science and Public Health (GAGS)
MSAO	Medical Services Accountable Officer
MSAO	Morale Support Activities Office
MSAP	Master of Science in Applied Physics (PGP)
MSAP	Master of Science in Applied Psychology (PGP)
MSAP	Master Space Allocation Plan (MCD)
MSAP	Mean Systemic Arterial Pressure [*Cardiology*]
MSAP	Military Security Assistance Projection [*Military*]
MSAP	Multisatellite Attitude Prediction [*NASA*]
MSaP	Peabody Museum of Salem, Salem, MA [*Library symbol Library of Congress*] (LCLS)
MSApSc	Master of Science in Applied Science (GAGS)
MSAR	Mines Safety Appliance Research (IEEE)
Ms-Ar	Mississippi Department of Archives and History, Jackson, MS [*Library symbol Library of Congress*] (LCLS)
MSARC	Marine Systems Acquisition Review Council (MCD)
MS Arch	Master of Science in Architecture
MS Arch St	Master of Architectural Studies (PGP)
MSAS	Malaysia Singapore Australia Society
MSAS	Mandel Social Adjustment Scale [*Psychology*]
MSAS	Marine Sciences Affairs Staff [*A publication*]
MSAS	Master of Science in Architectural Studies (GAGS)
MSa/s	MegaSamples per Second (CDE)
MSAS	Microwave Signature Acquisition System (MCD)
MSAS	Minnesota School Attitude Survey [*Educational test*]
MSAS	Modal Suppression Augmentation System [*Aerospace*]
M Sa Sc	Master of Sacred Sciences
MSAsia	Morgan Stanley Asia Pacific Fund [*Associated Press*] (SAG)
MSAT	Master of Science in Advanced Technology (PGP)
MSAT	Minnesota Scholastic Aptitude Test
MSAT	Missile System Analyst Technician (SAA)
MSaT	Salem State College, Salem, MA [*Library symbol Library of Congress*] (LCLS)
MSATA	Motorcycle, Scooter, and Allied Trades Association [*Later, MIC*]
MSAT-A	Multisensor Aided Targeting-Air [*Army*] (DOMA)
MSATF	Missile Site Activation Task Force (SAA)
MSATT	Martian Surface and Atmosphere through Time [*NASA*]
MSAT-X	Mobile Satellite Experiment (MCD)
MSAU	Multistation Access Unit [*Telecommunications*] (TSSD)
MSAUSC	Muslim Students' Association of the United States and Canada (EA)
MSAutE	Member of the Society of Automobile Engineers [*British*]
MSAV	Medical Scientists' Association of Victoria [*Australia*]
MSAV	Microsoft Anti-Virus [*Microsoft Corp.*] [*Computer science*] (PCM)
MSAW	Minimum Safe Altitude Warning [*Aviation*]
MSAWA	Migrant and Seasonal Agricultural Worker Act of 1983 (WYGK)
MSAWS	Mobile Surface-to-Air Weapon System (MCD)
MsB	Biloxi Public Library, Biloxi, MS [*Library symbol Library of Congress*] (LCLS)
MSB	Iola, KS [*Location identifier FAA*] (FAAL)
MSB	Magnetic Susceptibility Bridge
MSB	Main Steamline Break [*Nuclear energy*] (NRCH)
MSB	Main Support Base [*Air Force*] (AFM)
MSB	Main Support Battalion [*Army*] (DOMA)
MSB	Main Switchboard
MSB	Maintenance Standard Book
MSB	Maintenance Support Base [*Military*]
MSB	Male Sexual Biomass [*Botany*]
MSB	Manpower Services Branch [*Military*] (MCD)
MSB	Maritime Subsidy Board [*Maritime Administration*] [*Department of Commerce*]

MSB............ Martin's Scarlet Blue [Histologic stain]
MSB............ Mass Spectrometry Bulletin [Mass Spectrometry Data Centre] [Bibliographic database] [British]
Ms B........... Master of Bacteriology
MSB............ Master of Science in Business
MSB............ Material Support Branch [NASA] (KSC)
MSB............ Mediterranean Shipping Board [World War II]
MSB............ Member of the School Board [British] (ROG)
MSB............ Memory Storage Buffer [Computer science] (CAAL)
MSB............ Mesabi Tr Ctfs SBI [NYSE symbol] (TTSB)
MSB............ Mesabi Trust [NYSE symbol] (SAG)
MSB............ Methylstyrylbenzene [Fluorescent compound]
MSB............ Metropolitan Separate School Board [UTLAS symbol]
MSB............ Michael Stanley Band [Musical group]
MSB............ Mid-Small Bowel [Gastroenterology] (DAVI)
MSB............ Military Security Board
MSB............ Military Service Branch [World War I] [Canada]
MSB............ Mine Subsidence Board [New South Wales, Australia]
MSB............ Minesweeping Boat [Navy symbol]
MSB............ Minority Small Business (BARN)
MSB............ Missile Storage Building (NATG)
MSB............ Missile Support Base (SAA)
MSB............ Mission Simulator Building (MCD)
MSB............ Mobile Support Base (DNAB)
MSB............ Montadale Sheep Breeders Association (EA)
MSB............ Most Significant BIT [Binary Digit] [Computer science]
MSB............ Motor Surfboat
MSB............ Multi-Step Industries [Vancouver Stock Exchange symbol]
MSB............ Multnomah School of the Bible [Oregon]
MSB............ Municipal Securities Board [Approved by Congress May 22, 1975] [Securities and Exchange Commission]
MSB............ Museum of Southwestern Biology [University of New Mexico] [Research center] (RCD)
MSB............ Music Sound Books [Record label]
MSB............ Mutual Savings Bank
MSBA......... Malaysia, Singapore, and Brunei Association [British] (DBA)
MSBA......... Master of Science in Business Administration
MSBA......... Military School Band Association (EA)
MSBAE....... Master of Science in Biological and Agricultural Engineering (PGP)
MSBAE....... Master of Science in Biosystems and Agricultural Engineering (PGP)
MsBB......... Beauvoir, the Jefferson Davis Shrine, Biloxi, MS [Library symbol Library of Congress] (LCLS)
MSBB......... MSB Bancorp [NASDAQ symbol] (TTSB)
MSBB......... MSB Bancorp, Inc. [NASDAQ symbol] (SAG)
MSB Bcp...... MSB Bancorp, Inc. [Associated Press] (SAG)
MSBC......... MainStreet BankGroup [NASDAQ symbol] (TTSB)
MSBC......... MainStreet BankGroup, Inc. [NASDAQ symbol] (SAG)
MSBC......... Master of Science in Building Construction
MSBC......... Steinbach Bible College, Manitoba [Library symbol National Library of Canada] (BIB)
MSBCA .... Maryland State Board of Contract Appeals (AAGC)
MSB-COD .... Minority Small Business-Capital Ownership Development Program [Small Business Administration]
MSBE......... Master of Science in Biomedical Engineering (GAGS)
MSBE......... Master of Science in Business Education (PGP)
MSBEl......... Molten-Salt Breeder Experiment [Nuclear energy]
MsBel......... Humphreys County Library, Belzoni, MS [Library symbol Library of Congress] (LCLS)
MSBENG ...... Master of Science in Bioengineering (PGP)
MSBF......... Mean Sorties between Flights (MCD)
MSBF......... MSB Financial [NASDAQ symbol] (TTSB)
MSBF......... MSB Financial, Inc. [NASDAQ symbol] (SAG)
MSB Fn........ MSB Financial, Inc. [Associated Press] (SAG)
MSBIC .... Minority Small Business Investment Company (AAGC)
MSBK......... Mutual Savings Bank [NASDAQ symbol] (TTSB)
MSBK......... Mutual Savings Bank FSB [NASDAQ symbol] (SAG)
MSBL......... Member of the School Board, London [Defunct British] (ROG)
MSBLA........ Mouse Specific B Lymphocyte Antigen [Immunology]
MSBLK....... Mild Steel, Black Finish (IAA)
MSBLMS...... Multi Station Boundary Layer Model System (PDAA)
MSBLS........ Microwave Scanning Beam Landing Station [or System] [NASA] (NASA)
MSBLS........ Microwave Scanning Beam Land Station [NASA]
MSBLS-GS... Microwave Scanning Beam Landing System Ground Station [NASA]
MsBm .... Blue Mountain College, Blue Mountain, MS [Library symbol Library of Congress] (LCLS)
MSBM......... Master of Science in Business Management (PGP)
MSBME....... Master of Science in Biomedical Engineering (PGP)
MSBMS....... Master of Science in Basic Medical Science (PGP)
MSBNSW..... Maritime Services Board of New South Wales [Australia]
MSBO......... Mooring and Salvage Boat [Navy British]
MSBP......... Munchausen Syndrome by Proxy [Medicine]
Ms-BPH .... Mississippi Library Commission, Services for the Handicapped, Jackson, MS [Library symbol Library of Congress] (LCLS)
MsBr........... Lincoln-Lawrence-Franklin Regional Library, Brookhaven, MS [Library symbol Library of Congress] (LCLS)
MSBR .... Maximum Storage Bus Rate
MSBR .... Military Strength Balance Report (AFM)
MSBR .... Molten-Salt Breeder Reactor
MSbrA .... American Optical Corp., Southbridge, MA [Library symbol Library of Congress] (LCLS)
MSBRT .... Mild Steel, Bright Finish (IAA)
MsBs .... City-County Memorial Library, Bay St. Louis, MS [Library symbol Library of Congress] (LCLS)
MSBS......... Minimum Social Behavior Scale [Psychology]

MsBsNA....... National Aeronautics and Space Administration, NASA/NSTL Research Library, NSTL Station, Bay St. Louis, MS [Library symbol Library of Congress] (LCLS)
MsBsNO....... United States Naval Oceanographic Office NSTL Station, Bay St. Louis, MS [Library symbol] [Library of Congress] (LCLS)
MsBsS .... Divine Word Seminary, Bay St. Louis, MS [Library symbol Library of Congress] (LCLS)
MSBT.......... Missionary Servants of the Most Blessed Trinity [Roman Catholic women's religious order]
MSBTh......... Member of the Society of Health and Beauty Therapists [British] (DBQ)
MSBu......... Thousand Standard Bushels (EG)
MS Bus........ Master of Science in Business
MSBV......... Mooring Salvage and Boom Vessel (PDAA)
MSBVW....... Magnetostatic Backward Volume Wave [Telecommunications] (TEL)
MSBY......... Most Significant Byte [Computer science]
MSC.......... Chief Mess Management Specialist [Formerly, CSC, CST, SDC] [Navy rating]
MSC.......... College de St.-Boniface, Manitoba [Library symbol National Library of Canada] (NLC)
MSC.......... Congregation of the Marianites of the Holy Cross (TOCD)
MSC.......... Congregation of the Sisters Marianites of Holy Cross [Roman Catholic religious order]
MSC.......... [The] MacNeal-Schwendler Corp.
MSC.......... Macro Selection Compiler [Computer science] (BUR)
MSC.......... Madras Staff Corps [British]
MSC.......... Magnetically Settable Counter
MSC.......... Magnetic Surface Current
MSC.......... Magnitude Square of the Complex Coherence (PDAA)
MSC.......... Maharashtra Socialist Congress [India] [Political party] (PPW)
MSC.......... Mailstop Code
MSC.......... Maine Sardine Council (EA)
MSC.......... Main Storage Control [Computer science] (BUR)
MSC.......... Main Switching Centre [Telecommunications] (NITA)
MSC.......... Maintenance Support Center (MCD)
MSC.......... Maisach [Federal Republic of Germany] [Geomagnetic observatory code]
MSC.......... Major Subcontract (MCD)
MSC.......... Major Subordinate Command [Military]
MSC.......... Malaysian Multimedia Super Corridor
MSC.......... Management Service Center [Marine science] (OSRA)
MSC.......... Management Services Contractor [INTELSAT]
MSC.......... Manchester Ship Canal
MSC.......... Mandatory Settlement Conference [Insurance]
MSC.......... Mandatum sine Clausula [Authority without Restriction] [Latin]
MSC.......... Mankato State College [Later, Mankato State University] [Minnesota]
MSC.......... Manned Spacecraft Center [Later, Johnson Space Center] [NASA]
msc.......... Manned Spacecraft Center [NASA] (NAKS)
MSC.......... Manpower Services Commission [British]
MSC.......... Maple Syrup Council (EA)
MSC.......... Marine Safety Council [Coast Guard]
MSC.......... Marine Science Center [Oregon State University] [Research center] (RCD)
MSC.......... Marine Science Council [Marine science] (MSC)
MSC.......... Marine Stewardship Council
MSC.......... Marital Status Code [IRS]
MSC.......... Maritime Safety Committee [Advisory Committee on Pollution of the Sea]
MSC.......... Maritime Service Committee [New York, NY] (EA)
MSC.......... Marketing Services Conference [LIMRA]
MSC.......... Marquise [Marchioness] [French] (ROG)
MSC.......... Marrow Stromal Cell [Biochemistry]
MSC.......... Maryland State College [Merged with University of Maryland]
MSC.......... Mass Storage Control [Computer science] (BUR)
MSC.......... Mass Storage Controller (NITA)
MSc.......... Master of Science [Academic degree] (AIE)
MSC.......... Master of Science in Commerce (DD)
MSC.......... Master of Science in Communication (PGP)
MSC.......... Master of Science in Counseling (GAGS)
MSc.......... Master of Science in Epidemiology & Biostatistics (CMD)
MSC.......... Master of Speech Communication (GAGS)
MSC.......... Master Sequence Controller (NASA)
msc.......... Master Sequence Controller (NAKS)
MSC.......... Master Status Chart
MSC.......... Material Sciences [NYSE symbol] (TTSB)
MSC.......... Material Sciences Corp. [NYSE symbol] (SPSG)
MSC.......... Material Source Code
MSC.......... Materials Science Center [Cornell University]
MSC.......... Materials Service Center [NASA] (NASA)
msc.......... Materials Service Center (NAKS)
MSC.......... Materiel Screening Code [DoD] (AFIT)
MSC.......... Materiel Status Committee [Military] (AABC)
MSC.......... Materiel Support Center (MCD)
MSC.......... Materiel Support Command (MCD)
MSC.......... Mathematics, Science, and Computer [Education]
MSC.......... Mathematics/Science/Computer
MSC.......... Mean Spherical Candlepower [Computer science] (IAA)
MSC.......... Mechanical Super-Calendered Paper (DGA)
MSC.......... Medical Service Commission [Canada]
MSC.......... Medical Service Corps [Military]
MSC.......... Medical Social Coordinator
MSC.......... Medical Specialist Corps [Military]
MSC.......... Medical Staff Corps [British]
MSC.......... Mediterranean Society of Chemotherapy (EAIO)
MSC.......... Mediterranean Sub-Commission [Silva Mediterranea] [FAO]

MSC............	Medium-Scale Computer (IAA)
MSC............	Memory Storage Control [*Computer science*]
MSC............	Memphis Service Center [*IRS*]
MSC............	Mesa [*Arizona*] [*Airport symbol Obsolete*] (OAG)
MSC............	Mesitylenesulfonyl Chloride [*Biochemistry*]
MSC............	Message Sequence Chart [*Telecommunications*] (TEL)
MSC............	Message Switching Center [*Telecommunications*]
MSC............	Message Switching Computer [*Telecommunications*] (TEL)
MSC............	Message Switching Concentration
MSC............	Metal Shielded Cabinet
MSC............	Meteorological Satellite Center [*Aerospace*] (IAA)
MSC............	Methane Sulfonyl Chloride [*Organic chemistry*]
MSC............	Metric System - Conversion (NATG)
MSC............	Metropolitan State College [*Denver, CO*]
MSC............	Micronesia Support Committee [*Later, MC*] (EA)
MSC............	Microscale Cloud [*Module*] [*Air Force*]
MSC............	Microsystems Centre (NITA)
MSC............	Microwave Stripline-Circuit (PDAA)
MSC............	Mid-South Conference (PSS)
MSC............	Midwestern Simulation Council
MSC............	Migent Software [*Vancouver Stock Exchange symbol*]
MSC............	Mile of Standard Cable
MSC............	Milestone Schedule Charts (MCD)
MSC............	Military Scout Car [*British*]
MSC............	Military Sealift Command [*Formerly, MSTS, NTS*] [*Navy*] (NOAA)
msc............	Military Sealift Command (NAKS)
MSC............	Military Staff Committee [*United Nations*] (DLA)
MSC............	Military Studies Center (EA)
msc............	Millisecond (WGA)
MSC............	Milliwatts per Square Centimeter
MSC............	Minesweeper, Coastal [*Nonmagnetic*] [*Navy symbol*]
MSC............	Minor Suma Corp. [*Kansas City, MO*] (TSSD)
MSC............	Mirror Sign Convention
MSC............	Mirror Streak Camera
MSC............	Miscellaneous (ADA)
MSC............	Missile and Space Council [*Defunct*] (AAG)
MSC............	Missile Sequence Charts (AAG)
MSC............	Missile Support Co. [*Army*]
MSC............	Missile System Checkout (AAG)
MSC............	Missionaries of the Sacred Heart (TOCD)
msc............	Missionaries of the Sacred Heart (TOCD)
MSC............	Missionarii Sacratissimi Cordis [*Missionaries of the Most Sacred Heart*] [*Roman Catholic men's religious order*]
MSC............	Missionarii Sancti Caroli [*Missionaries of St. Charles*] [*Roman Catholic men's religious order*]
msc............	Missionary Servants of Christ (TOCD)
MSC............	Missionary Sisters of the Most Sacred Heart of Jesus [*Roman Catholic religious order*]
MSC............	Missionary Sisters of the Most Sacred Heart of Jesus of Hiltrup (TOCD)
MSC............	Missionary Sisters of the Sacred Heart [*Cabrini Sisters*] [*Roman Catholic religious order*]
MSC............	Mississippi Central R. R. [*AAR code*]
Ms-C............	Mississippi Library Commission, Jackson, MS [*Library symbol Library of Congress*] (LCLS)
MSC............	Mississippi Southern College
MSC............	Mixing Smoke Chamber (MCD)
MSC............	Mobile Servicing Center [*Canada*]
MSC............	Mobile Switching Center (ACRL)
MSC............	Mode Selector Controller (MCD)
MSC............	Moding Sequencing and Control (MCD)
msc............	Moding Sequencing and Control (NAKS)
MSC............	Mono-Stereo Compatible (PDAA)
MSC............	Montana State College (MCD)
MSC............	Moorhead State College [*Minnesota*]
MSC............	Morgan State College [*Later, Morgan State University*] [*Baltimore, MD*]
MSC............	Moscow Airways [*Russian Federation*] [*ICAO designator*] (FAAC)
MSC............	Most Significant Character [*Computer science*] (MDG)
MSC............	Motor Speed Changer (IAA)
MSC............	Motor Speed Control
MSC............	Motor Starting Contractor
MSC............	Motor Submersible Canoe [*British Marines' Special Forces*] [*World War II*]
MSC............	Moved, Seconded, and Carried
MSC............	Multimedia Super Corridor [*Proposed, Malaysia*]
MSC............	Multiple Scan Correlator
MSC............	Multiple Spindle Chucker
MSC............	Multiple Systems Coupling [*Computer science*]
MSC............	Multipotential Stem Cells [*Hematology*]
MSC............	Multisensor Correlator (CAAL)
MSC............	Multiservice Center
MSC............	Multistrip Coupler [*Telecommunications*] (TEL)
MSC............	Multisystem Coupling [*Computer science*]
MSC............	Murray State College [*Later, MSU*] [*Kentucky*]
MSC............	Museum Support Center [*Smithsonian Institution*]
MSC............	Muskingum College, New Concord, OH [*OCLC symbol*] (OCLC)
Msc............	New York Miscellaneous Reports [*A publication*] (DLA)
MSC............	Springfield College, Springfield, MA [*Library symbol Library of Congress*] (LCLS)
Msc 2d	New York Miscellaneous Reports. Second Series [*A publication*] (DLA)
MsCa	Canton Public Library, Canton, MS [*Library symbol Library of Congress*] (LCLS)
MScA...........	Maitre es Sciences Appliquees [*Master of Applied Science*] [*French*]
MSCA...........	Make or Subcontract Authorization (AAG)
MScA...........	Master of Applied Science (DD)
M Sc A	Master of Science (Applied) (PGP)
MScA...........	Master of Social Administration (GAGS)
MSCA...........	McCarthy Scales of Children's Abilities [*Education*]
MSCA...........	Mechanical Service Contractors of America (NTPA)
MSCA...........	Microwave Switch Control Assembly
MSCA...........	Military Support to Civil Authorities (AABC)
MSCA...........	Missile Site Construction Agency [*Army*]
msca...........	Missing Cargo (DS)
MSCA...........	Mixed Spectrum Critical Assembly [*Nuclear energy*]
MSCA...........	M.S Carriers [*NASDAQ symbol*] (TTSB)
MSCA...........	MS Carriers, Inc. [*NASDAQ symbol*] (NQ)
MSCA...........	Multi-Site Cooperative Agreement (COE)
MSCAC........	Massachusetts State Collegiate Athletic Conference (PSS)
MSc(Acoustics)...	Master of Science (Acoustics) (ADA)
MSc(AeroMed)...	Master of Science (Aeromedicine)
MSc(Ag)	Master of Science (Agriculture)
MScAgri.......	Master of Science in Agriculture
MSc(Agric)....	Master of Science in Agriculture
MSc(AgricE)...	Master of Science (Agricultural Economics) (ADA)
MSc(AgricEc)...	Master of Science (Agricultural Economics) (ADA)
MSCAJC.......	Martin Steinberg Center of the American Jewish Congress (EA)
MsCaM	Madison County Library, Canton, MS [*Library symbol Library of Congress*] (LCLS)
MSc(Appl) ...	Master of Science (Applied) (ADA)
MsCar..........	Leake County Library, Carthage, MS [*Library symbol Library of Congress*] (LCLS)
MSc(Arch) ...	Master of Science (Architecture)
MSc(Arch)(Cons)...	Master of Science (Architectural) (Conservation)
M Sc (Architecture)...	Master of Science in Architecture
MS Carr	MS Carriers, Inc. [*Associated Press*] (SAG)
MSCAT........	Minesweeper Catamaran [*Military*]
MSCB...........	Missile Site Control Building (AABC)
MsCba	Shelby Memorial Library, Columbia, MS [*Library symbol Library of Congress*] (LCLS)
MSc(Biochem)...	Master of Science (Biochemistry)
MSc(Biotech)...	Master of Science (Biotechnology) (ADA)
M Sc BMC ...	Master of Science in Biomedical Communications (PGP)
MSc(BuildServ)...	Master of Science (Building Services) (ADA)
MSCC...........	Major Subcontract Change Coordination (MCD)
MSCC...........	Manned Space Flight Control Center [*Air Force*]
MSCC...........	Master of Science in Christian Counseling (PGP)
MScC...........	Master of Science in Commerce (DD)
MSCC...........	Master Simulator Control Console (MCD)
MSCC...........	Microsemi Corp. [*NASDAQ symbol*] (NQ)
MSCC...........	Midstream Clean Catch [*Urine Sample*] (DAVI)
MSCC...........	Military Space Surveillance Control Center (IAA)
MSCC...........	Missile Site Control Center (MCD)
MSCC...........	Morgan Sports Car Club (EA)
MSCCC........	Minimum Shuffle Control Cell Core [*Nuclear energy*] (NUCP)
M Sc CE	Master of Science in Chromo-Electronic Science
MScCE........	Master of Science in Civil Engineering [*British*] (ADA)
MSc(Cer)	Master of Science in Ceramics (ADA)
MScChemTech...	Master of Science in Chemical Technology [*British*] (ADA)
MScCom	Master in Commercial Sciences
MScComm...	Master in Commercial Science (DD)
MSc(CommMed)...	Master of Science (Community Medicine)
M Sc CS	Master of Science in Computer Science (PGP)
MScD..........	Doctor of Medical Science (DAVI)
MScD..........	Doctor of Science in Medicine (DAVI)
M Sc D	Doctor of the Science of Medicine
MScD..........	Magister Scientia Dentalis [*Master of Dental Science*] [*British*]
MScD..........	Master of Dental Science
MScD..........	Master of Science in Communication Disorders (PGP)
MScD..........	Master of Science in Dentistry (GAGS)
MSCD	Military Support of Civil Defense (AABC)
MSCD	Mobile Source Control Division
MSCDC........	Missouri State Census Data Center [*Information service or system*] (IID)
MSc(Dent) ...	Master of Science in Dentistry
MSCDEX	Microsoft Compact Disc Extension [*Computer science*] (DOM)
MSCDEX	MicroSoft Compact Disc Read Only Memory Extensions [*Computer science*] (IGQR)
MSCDEX	MS-DOS, CD-ROM Extension [*Computer science*]
MSCDIS	Master of Science in Communication Disorders (PGP)
MSCDR	Mohawk Synchronous Communication Data Recorder [*Military*] (PDAA)
MSCE..........	Main Storage Control Element [*Computer science*] (IEEE)
MSCE..........	Master of Science in Civil Engineering
MSCE..........	Master of Science in Clinical Engineering (PGP)
MSCE..........	Master of Science in Clinical Epidemiology (PGP)
MSCE..........	Master of Science in Computer Engineering (GAGS)
MScE..........	Master of Science in Engineering (DD)
M Sc (Econ)...	Master of Science in Economics
MSCEd........	Master of Science in Continuing Education (GAGS)
M Sc Ed.......	Master of Science in Education
MSc(EdPsych)...	Master of Science in Educational Psychology (CMD)
MSCEE........	Master of Science in Civil and Environmental Engineering (PGP)
M Sc EE......	Master of Science in Electrical Engineering
MSc(Elec)...	Master of Science in Electronics [*British*] (ADA)
M Sc (Elec Eng)...	Master of Science in Electrical Engineering
MSCELM.....	Military Sealift Command, Eastern Atlantic and Mediterranean (DNAB)
MSCEM........	Master of Science in Civil Engineering Management (PGP)

M Sc (Eng)... Master of Science (Engineering)
MSc(Engg).. Master of Science (Engineering)
M Sc Engr .. Master of Science in Engineering (PGP)
MSc(Epid)... Master of Science (Epidemiology)
MS (Cer E).. Master of Science in Ceramic Engineering
MSCF .... Master of Science in Computational Finance (PGP)
M Sc F........ Master of Science in Forestry (PGP)
MScF .... Master of the Science of Forestry [or Master of Science in Forestry]
MSCF .... Millions of Standard Cubic Feet (AAG)
MSCF .... Multisource Correlation Facility (MCD)
MSCFAM...... Royal Canadian Army Museum, Canadian Forces Base, Shilo, Manitoba [Library symbol National Library of Canada] (NLC)
M Sc FE...... Master of Science in Forest Engineering (PGP)
MSCFE........ Military Sealift Command, Far East (DNAB)
M Sc (For)... Master of Science in Forestry
MSCGpe ...... Missionaries of the Sacred Heart of Jesus and of Our Lady of Guadalupe (TOCD)
msch.......... Microscheduler (MHDI)
MSCH .... Mode Switch Chassis
MsCh .... Tallahatchie County Library, Charleston, MS [Library symbol Library of Congress] (LCLS)
MSChE........ Master of Science in Chemical Engineering
M Sch Mus... Master of School Music
MSc(HomeScience)... Master of Science (Home Science)
MSc(Hort)... Master of Science in Horticulture [British] (ADA)
MSCI.......... Madrid Stock-Exchange Index [Spain] (ECON)
MSCI.......... Master Ships Configuration Index (MCD)
MSCI.......... Mediterranean Secret Convoy Instructions [World War II]
MSCI.......... Missile Status Control Indicator [Military] (CAAL)
M/SCI......... Mission/Safety Critical Item [NASA] (NASA)
MSCI.......... Molten Steel Coolant Interaction (NRCH)
MSCI.......... Morgan Stanley Capital Index (NUMA)
MSCI.......... Morgan Stanley Capital International
MSCI-EAFE... Morgan-Stanley Capital International - Europe, Australia, Far East [Free] [Index - Financial]
M Sci Mil ... Master of Military Science
M Sc in Agr Eng... Master of Science in Agricultural Engineering
M Sc in Agr Ex... Master of Science in Agricultural Extension
MSC(IndDes)... Master of Science (Industrial Design) (ADA)
M Sc in ME... Master of Science in Mechanical Engineering
MSCIS .... Master of Science in Computer Information Science (PGP)
MSCIS .... Master of Science in Computer Information Systems
MScitHi........ Scituate Historical Society, Scituate, MA [Library symbol Library of Congress] (LCLS)
MSCJ.......... Master of Science in Criminal Justice (WGA)
MSCJA......... Master of Science in Criminal Justice Administration (PGP)
MSCJA-AJC... Martin Steinberg Center for Jewish Artists - American Jewish Congress [Defunct] (EA)
MSCK.......... Missionary Sisters of Christ the King (TOCD)
MSCKC .... Measurement of Self Concept in Kindergarten Children [Psychology]
M Sc L........ Master of the Science of Law
MSCL.......... Master Ships Configuration List (MCD)
MSCL.......... Mississippi State Chemical Laboratory [Mississippi State University] [Research center] (RCD)
MSCL.......... Springfled City Library, Springfield, MA [Library symbol] [Library of Congress] (LCLS)
MSCLANT .... Military Sealift Command, Atlantic (DNAB)
MSCLANTDET... Military Sealift Command, Atlantic Detachment (DNAB)
MsCld .... Carnegie Public Library, Clarksdale, MS [Library symbol Library of Congress] (LCLS)
MsCle .... Bolivar County Library, Cleveland, MS [Library symbol Library of Congress] (LCLS)
MSCLE........ Maximum Space Charge Limited Emission (IAA)
MsCleD........ Delta State College, Cleveland, MS [Library symbol Library of Congress] (LCLS)
MsCleP........ Presbyterian Church Library, Cleveland, MS [Library symbol Library of Congress] (LCLS)
MsCliBHi ..... Mississippi Baptist Historical Society, Clinton, MS [Library symbol Library of Congress] (LCLS)
MsCliM........ Mississippi College, Clinton, MS [Library symbol Library of Congress] (LCLS)
MSC LNO..... Major Subordinate Command Liaison Officer
M Sc (Lond)... Master of Science, London
MSCLS........ Master of Science in Clinical Laboratory Science (PGP)
MSCLS........ Master of Science in Clinical Laboratory Studies (PGP)
MSCM.......... Master Chief Mess Management Specialist [Formerly, SDCM] [Navy rating]
M Sc M........ Master of the Science of Medicine
MSCM.......... Mobile Surface Contamination Monitor
MSCM.......... MOSCOM Corp. [NASDAQ symbol] (NQ)
M Sc (Mech Eng)... Master of Science in Mechanical Engineering
M Sc Med.... Master of Medical Science
MScMed ..... Master of Science in Medicine [British] (ADA)
MSc(Med)... Master of Science (Medical)
M Sc Met.... Master of Science in Metallurgy
MSc(Min) ... Master of Science in Mining [British] (ADA)
MScN.......... Master of Science in Nursing
MSc(NatResMgt)... Master of Science in Natural Resources Management
MSc(NeuChem)... Master of Science (Neurochemistry)
MSCNU........ Master of Science in Clinical Nutrition (PGP)
MSc(Nut)... Master of Science (Nutrition)
MSc(Nutr)... Master of Science in Nutrition [British] (ADA)
MSCNY .... Marine Society of the City of New York (EA)
MSCO .... Manned Spacecraft Operations [NASA] (KSC)
MSCO .... Manual Sustainer Cutoff [NASA] (KSC)

M Sc O .... Master of the Science of Oratory
MSC(O)........ Minesweeper, Coastal (Old) [Navy symbol]
MSc(OccMed)... Master of Science (Occupational Medicine)
MsCol .... Lowndes County Library System, Columbus, MS [Library symbol Library of Congress] (LCLS)
MsColS........ Mississippi State College for Women, Columbus, MS [Library symbol Library of Congress] (LCLS)
MS Cons...... Master of Science in Conservation
MSCOP .... Missile Systems Checkout Program [Aerospace] (IAA)
MSc(Ophth)... Master of Science (Ophthalmology)
MScOptom... Master of Science in Optometry (ADA)
MsCor......... Northeast Regional Library, Corinth, MS [Library symbol Library of Congress] (LCLS)
M Sc (Ost)... Master of Science in Osteopathy
MSCOTSG .... Medical Service Corps, Office of the Surgeon General
MS Coun...... Master of Science in Counseling (PGP)
MSCP.......... Mass Storage Control Protocol (NITA)
MSCP.......... Master of Science in Community Planning
MSCP.......... Master of Science in Counseling Psychology (PGP)
M Sc P .... Master of Science in Planning (PGP)
MSCP.......... Mean Spherical Candlepower
MSCP.......... Member of the Society of Certified Professionals [British] (DBQ)
MSCP.......... Missile Systems Checkout Programmer [Aerospace] (IAA)
MSCP.......... Motor Short-Circuit Protector (IAA)
MSCPAC ...... Military Sealift Command, Pacific (DNAB)
MS Cp E ..... Master of Science in Computer Engineering (PGP)
MScPhm ..... Master of Science in Pharmacy (ADA)
M Sc Pl .... Master of Science in Planning (PGP)
M/S/CPO..... Master/Senior/Chief Petty Officer of the Command (DNAB)
MSCPR .... Mixed-Suspension, Classified-Product Removal [Crystallizer] [Chemical engineering]
M Sc PT ..... Master of Science in Physical Therapy (PGP)
MSCR .... Machine Screw
MSCR .... Measurement/Stimuli Change Request (MCD)
MSCR .... Multilayer Side-Cladded Ridge Waveguide (PDAA)
MSCR/A .... Major Subcontract Change Request/Approval (MCD)
MSc(Rehab)... Master of Science (Rehabilitation Medicine)
MSCREP .... Military Sealift Command Representative (DNAB)
MSCRP .... Master of Science in City and Regional Planning (PGP)
MSCRP .... Master of Science in Community and Regional Planning (PGP)
MsCs .... Crystal Springs Library, Crystal Springs, MS [Library symbol Library of Congress] (LCLS)
MSCS.......... Management Scheduling and Control System [Telecommunications] (TEL)
MSCS.......... Manual SHORAD [Short Range Air Defense] Control System (RDA)
MSCS.......... Mass Storage Control System [Computer science] (IAA)
MSCS.......... Master of Science in Computer Science
MSCS.......... Merchant Ship Control Service [Navy]
MSCS.......... Microsoft Clustering Server [Computer science]
MSCS.......... Miner Sentence Completion Scale [Psychology]
MSCS.......... Multiservice Communications Systems (RDA)
MSCS.......... Senior Chief Mess Management Specialist [Formerly, CSCS, SDCS] [Navy rating]
MS CSCO.... Morgan Stanley Group, Inc. [Associated Press] (SAG)
MSCSD........ Master of Science in Communication Sciences and Disorders (PGP)
MSCSE........ Master of Science in Computer and Systems Engineering (PGP)
MSCSE........ Master of Science in Computer Science and Engineering (PGP)
M Sc (Social Sciences)... Master of Science in the Social Sciences
M Sc (Soc Sci)... Master of Science (Social Science)
MSCSO-M & R... Military Sealift Command Service Office - Maintenance and Repair (DNAB)
MSCSO-OCPO... Military Sealift Command Service Office - Operations Cargo Passenger Office (DNAB)
MSCSO-SA... Military Sealift Command Service Office - Supply Assistant (DNAB)
MScSt.......... Master of Scientific Studies (ADA)
MSCT.......... Malignant Small Cell Tumor [Oncology]
MScT .... Master of Science in Teaching (GAGS)
MScT .... Master of Science Teaching (GAGS)
MSCT.......... Member of the Society of Cardiological Technicians [British]
MSCT.......... Miniature Synaptic Calcium Transient [Neurophysiology]
MSCTC........ Mass Storage Control Table Create [Computer science] (MHDI)
M Sc Tech .. Master of Science in Technology
M Sc Tech .. Master of Technical Science
MSCTRANSU... Military Sealift Command Transportation Unit (DNAB)
MSCU .... Medical Special Care Unit (DMAA)
MSCU .... Military Sealift Command Unit (DNAB)
MSCU .... Modular Store Control Unit
MSCU .... Multistation Control Unit [Telecommunications] (IAA)
MSC(UN) .... Military Staff Committee of the United Nations
MSCV.......... Connecticut Valley Historical Museum, Springfield, MA [Library symbol Library of Congress] (LCLS)
MSCVAN...... [An] MSC [Military Sealift Command] Leased/Controlled Seavan or Milvan
MSCW .... Marked Stack Control Word
MSCW .... Mississippi State College for Women [Columbus]
MSD.......... Doctor of Medical Science
Ms D.......... Doctor of Metaphysics
MsD.......... Holmes County Library, Durant, MS [Library symbol Library of Congress] (LCLS)
MSD.......... Magnetic Storage Drum [Computer science]
MSD.......... Major Seismic Disturbance
MSD.......... Management Services Department [British] (DCTA)
MSD.......... Management Services Division (NITA)
MSD.......... Management Systems Division [Environmental Protection Agency] (EPA)

MSD............ Mansfield, LA [*Location identifier FAA*] (FAAL)
MSD............ Manual SHORAD [*Short Range Air Defense*] Control System [*Army*]
MsD............ Manuscript Decisions [*Comptroller General*] [*United States*] [*A publication*] (DLA)
MSD............ Marginal Support Date (COE)
MSD............ Marine Sanitation Device
MSD............ Marine Sciences Directorate [*Canada*] (MSC)
MSD............ Marine Signal Detachment (SAA)
MSD............ Maritime-Self-Defense
MSD............ MARS [*Modular Airborne Recorder System*] Supplemental Data (GFGA)
MSD............ Mass Selector Detector [*Gas chromatography*]
MSD............ Mass Sensor Demonstration
MSD............ Mass Storage Device [*Computer science*]
MSD............ Master of Dietetics (GAGS)
MSD............ Master of Science in Dentistry
MSD............ Master of Science in Design (PGP)
MSD............ Master of Science in Dietetics (PGP)
MSD............ Master of Scientific Didactics
MSD............ Master Resources & Developments Ltd. [*Vancouver Stock Exchange symbol*]
MSD............ Master Standard Data
MSD............ Master Surgeon Dentist
MSD............ Material Safety Data
MSD............ Materials and Structures Division [*NASA*]
MSD............ Material Support Data (MCD)
MSD............ Material Support Date (DOMA)
MSD............ Matrix Spike Duplicate
MSD............ McNaney Spectroelectric Device
MSD............ Mean Solar Day
MSD............ Mean Squared Distance [*Data analysis*]
MSD............ Mean Square Deviation [*or Difference*]
MSD............ Mean-Square Displacement [*Statistical graphing*]
MSD............ Mechanical Setting Device
MSD............ Medical Stores Department [*Tanzania*]
MSD............ Merck, Sharp & Dohme [*Later, Merck & Co., Inc.*]
MSD............ Merck, Sharp & Dohme [*Later, Merck & Co., Inc.*] Research Laboratory, West Point, PA [*OCLC symbol*] (OCLC)
MSD............ Metal Sensor Detection
MSD............ Metering Suction Differential (NG)
MSD............ Method of Steepest Descent
MSD............ Metropolitan Sewer District (GNE)
MSD............ Microdata Software Development (MCD)
MSD............ Microsoft Diagnostics [*Microsoft Corp.*] [*Computer science*] (PCM)
MSD............ Mild Sickle Cell Disease (AAMN)
MSD............ Military Sales Department
MSD............ Military Store Department [*British military*] (DMA)
MSD............ Military Support Division [*of Materiel Testing Directorate*] (RDA)
MSD............ Minesweeper, Drone [*Navy symbol*]
MSD............ Minimal Steric Difference [*Organic chemistry*]
MSD............ Minimum Safe Distance (AABC)
MSD............ Misce, Signa, Da [*Mix, Write (the Directions), and Give (to the Patient)*] [*Pharmacy*] (ROG)
MSD............ Missiles and Space Division [*NASA*] (KSC)
MSD............ Missile Support Days (AAG)
MSD............ Missile Systems Development (AAG)
MSD............ Mission Systems Data (SAA)
MSD............ MODEM Sharing Device
MSD............ Molecular Size Distribution [*Chemistry*]
MSD............ Molecular Structures and Dimensions [*A publication*]
MSD............ Molten Salt Destruction [*Incineration process*]
MSD............ Monorail and Suspension Device [*British*]
MSD............ Morale Support Detachment [*Army*]
MSD............ Morgan Stanley Emerging Markets Debt Fund, Inc. [*NYSE symbol*] (SAG)
MSD............ Morgan Stanley Emer'g Mkt Debt [*NYSE symbol*] (TTSB)
MSD............ Mossoro [*Brazil*] [*Airport symbol*] (AD)
MSD............ Most Significant Decade (IAA)
MSD............ Most Significant Digit [*Computer science*]
MSD............ Motor Storage Dolly
MSD............ Mount Pleasant [*Utah*] [*Airport symbol*] (OAG)
MSD............ Movimento Social Democrata [*Social Democrat Movement*] [*Portugal Political party*] (PPE)
MSD............ Moving Scene Display
MSD............ Multifrequency Signal Detector [*Telecommunications*]
MSD............ Multiple Spark Discharge [*Autotronic Controls Corp.*] [*Automotive engineering*]
MSD............ Multiple Sulfatase Deficiency [*Medicine*] (AAMN)
MSD............ Multisatellite Dispenser (MCD)
MSD............ Multisensor Display
MSD............ Multisensory Disorder
MSDA.......... Masada Security Holdings, Inc. [*NASDAQ symbol*] (SAG)
MSDAC........ Minnesota State Drafting Advisory Committee (EDAC)
MSDB.......... Main Storage Database
MSDBP........ Mean Squared Distance Between Pairs [*Statistics*] (PDAA)
MSDC.......... Maintenance Signal Data Cassette (MCD)
MSDC.......... Maintenance Signal Data Converter (MCD)
MSDC.......... Manual Slave Direction Center [*RADAR site*]
MSDC.......... Mass Spectrometry Data Centre [*Royal Society of Chemistry*] (IID)
MSDC.......... Microwave Spectra Data Center [*National Institute of Standards and Technology*]
MSDC.......... Molten Salts Data Center [*Rensselaer Polytechnic Institute*] [*National Institute of Standards and Technology Research center*] (IID)
MSDD.......... Master of Science in Design and Development (PGP)
MSDD.......... Milli-Second Delay Detonator [*Military*] (PDAA)

MSde.......... Tilton Library, South Deerfield, MA [*Library symbol Library of Congress*] (LCLS)
MSDEF........ Missile System Development and Evaluation Facility (MCD)
MS Dent...... Master of Science in Dentistry
MSDEQ........ Mothers' Sensory Developmental Expectation Questionnaire [*Occupational therapy*]
MSDerm....... Master of Science in Dermatology (NADA)
MS Des....... Master of Science in Design
MSDF.......... Maritime Self-Defense Force [*Japan*]
MSDF.......... Maritime Staff Defense Force (CINC)
MSDFF........ Master Slave D Flip Flop (NITA)
MSDG.......... Multiple Sensor Display Group (MCD)
MSDI.......... Mainstream Data, Inc. [*NASDAQ symbol*] (SAG)
MS Di......... Master of Scientific Didactics
MSDI.......... Mayonnaise and Salad Dressings Institute [*Later, Association for Dressings and Sauces*] (EA)
MSDIG........ McGuire Safe Driver Interview Guide (AEBS)
MSDL.......... Magnetostrictive Delay Line
MSD licence... Music, Singing & Dancing Licence (WDAA)
MSDM........ Medium-Speed DynaBIT [*Binary Digit*] Memory [*Computer science*]
MSDM........ Morgan Stanley Group, Inc. [*Associated Press*] (SAG)
MSDN........ Microbial Strain Data Network [*Information service or system*] (IID)
MSDN........ Microsoft Developer Network [*Computer software*] (PCM)
MSDN........ Microsoft Developer's Network [*Computer science*] (PCM)
MSDNA....... Multicopy Single-Stranded Deoxyribonucleic Acid [*Biochemistry, genetics*]
MSDO.......... Management Systems Development Office
MS-DOS...... Microsoft Disk Operating System [*IBM Corp.*] [*Computer science*]
MSDP.......... Missile Site Data Processor (AABC)
MSDPS........ Missile Site Data Processing System (AABC)
MSDPSS...... Missile Site Data Processing Subsystem (AABC)
MSDR.......... Main Storage Data Register [*Computer science*] (IAA)
MSDR.......... Maintenance Signal Data Recorder (MCD)
MSDR.......... Master Sensor Data Record [*For spacecraft*]
MSDR.......... Materials Science Double Rack
MSDR.......... Multiplexer Storage Data Register [*Computer science*] (IAA)
MSDRS........ Maintenance Signal Data Recording Set [*or System*] (MCD)
MSDS.......... Magnetic Storage Drum System [*Computer science*]
MSDS.......... Maintenance Safety Data Sheets (MCD)
MSDS.......... Manufacturer's Safety Data Sheet (WDAA)
MSDS.......... Marconi Space and Defence Systems (MUSM)
MSDS.......... Master Simulation Data System (Model) [*Army*]
MSDS.......... Material Safety Data Sheet (GNE)
MSDS.......... Material Safety Data Sheets [*Occupational Health Services, Inc.*] [*Information service or system*]
MSDS.......... McGuire Safe Driver Scale (AEBS)
MSDS.......... Message Switching Data Service
MSDS.......... Missile Static Development Site (AAG)
MSDS.......... Missile System Development Stand (AAG)
MSDS.......... Multisolvent Delivery System
MSDS.......... Multispectral Scanner and Data System
MSDT.......... Maintenance Strategy Diagraming Technique (IEEE)
MSDT.......... Mean Supply Downtime (CAAL)
MSDT.......... Meshless Storage Display Tube
MSDX......... Mason-Dixon Bancshares [*NASDAQ symbol*] (TTSB)
MSDX......... Mason-Dixon Bancshares, Inc. [*NASDAQ symbol*] (SAG)
MSE........... Magnetic Strain Energy
MSE........... Maintenance Support Equipment [*Deep Space Instrumentation Facility, NASA*]
MSE........... Major Source of Employment
MSE........... Major Support Element (DOMA)
MSE........... Manned Spacecraft Engineer (MCD)
MSE........... Manston [*England*] [*Airport symbol*] (AD)
MSE........... Manufacturing Systems Engineering
MSE........... Marshall Energy Ltd. [*Vancouver Stock Exchange symbol*]
MSE........... Mask Superposition Error [*Computer science*] (IAA)
MSE........... Mass Storage Editor [*Computer science*] (MCD)
MSE........... Master of Sanitary Engineering
MSE........... Master of Science in Chemical Engineering
MSE........... Master of Science in Education
MSE........... Master of Science in Engineering
MSE........... Master of Software Engineering (GAGS)
MSE........... Master of Systems Engineering
MSE........... Materiel Status Evaluation [*Army*] (AABC)
MSE........... Mean Square Error [*Statistics*]
MSE........... Measuring and Stimuli Equipment (NASA)
MSE........... Mechanical Support Equipment (KSC)
MSE........... Medical Support Equipment (NASA)
MSE........... Member of the Society of Engineers [*British*]
MSE........... Mental Status Examination [*Neurology*] (DAVI)
MSE........... Merck, Sharp & Dohme [*Later, Merck & Co., Inc.*] Research Laboratory, Rahway , NJ [*OCLC symbol*] (OCLC)
MSE........... Merit Students Encyclopedia [*A publication*]
MSE........... Metaphloem Sieve Element [*Botany*]
MSE........... Mexican Stock Exchange (MHDW)
MSE........... Mid-Song Element [*Ornithology*]
MSE........... Midwest Stock Exchange [*Chicago, IL*] (EA)
MSE........... Military Specification Exception (RDA)
MSE........... Military Standard Engines
MSE........... Milk-Sensitive Enteropathy [*Medicine*]
MSE........... Milwaukee School of Engineering [*Wisconsin*]
MSE........... Minus Sense (SAA)
MSE........... Missile Support Element (AABC)
MSE........... Missile Support Equipment
MSE........... Mission Staff Engineer (MCD)

MSE............	Mission Support Element (MCD)
MSE............	Mississippi Export Railroad Co. [*AAR code*]
MSE............	Mobile Subscriber Equipment [*Military*]
MSE............	Modern Ship Equivalent
MSE............	Montreal Stock Exchange (CDAI)
MSE............	Moose
MSE............	Morgan Stan Fin 8.40% Cp Uts [*NYSE symbol*] (TTSB)
MSE............	Morgan Stanley Finance PLC Capital Unit [*NYSE symbol*] (SAG)
MSE............	Motorsteuerelectronik
MSE............	Multiple Simultaneous Engagement (MCD)
MSE............	Multi-Position Small Engine [*Automotive engineering*]
MSE............	Muscle-Specific Enhancer [*Genetics*]
MSE............	Muscle-Specific Enolase [*Medicine*] (DMAA)
MSEA........	M & S [*Modeling and Simulation*] Executive Agent [*Army*]
M Se A........	Master of Secretarial Arts
MSEA........	Medical Society Executives Association [*Later, AAMSE*] (EA)
MSEA........	Metropolitan Bancorp [*NASDAQ symbol*] (TTSB)
MSEA........	Metropolitan Bancorp Seattle [*NASDAQ symbol*] (SAG)
MSEC........	Maintenance Support Equipment Center
MSEC........	Master of Science in the Economic Aspects of Chemistry
MSEC........	Master Separation Events Controller (MCD)
MSEC........	Materials Science and Engineering Commission [*British*]
msec...........	Millisecond
MSECE........	Master of Science in Electrical and Computer Engineering (PGP)
MS Eco......	Master of Science in Economics (PGP)
MS Econ.....	Master of Science in Economics (PGP)
MSecSchSci...	Master of Secondary School Science (GAGS)
MS Ed.........	Master of Sanitary Education
MSEd.........	Master of Science Education (GAGS)
MS Ed.........	Master of Science in Education
MSED.........	Minimum Signal Element Duration [*Telecommunications*] (TEL)
MSED.........	Ministry of State for Economic Development [*Canada*]
MSED.........	Mobile Source Enforcement Division [*Environmental Protection Agency*]
MS EdU	Master of Science in Education (PGP)
MSEE.........	Major Source Enforcement Effort [*Environmental Protection Agency*] (GFGA)
MSEE.........	Master of Science in Electrical Engineering
MSEE.........	Master of Science in Environmental Engineering (GAGS)
MSEE.........	Mean Square Error Efficiency [*Statistics*]
MSE (Elec)..	Master of Science in Engineering - Electrical
MSEF.........	Missile System Evaluation Flight (MUGU)
MSEG.........	Medical Service Group [*Military*]
MSEG.........	Memory-Segment [*Computer science*]
MSEG.........	Missile Systems Evaluation Group (CINC)
MSEH.........	Master of Science in Environmental Health (PGP)
MSEI.........	Mean Square Error Inefficiency [*Statistics*]
MSEL.........	Lord Selkirk Regional School, Selkirk, Manitoba [*Library symbol National Library of Canada*] (NLC)
MSEL.........	Master of Science and English Literature
MSEL.........	Master of Science in Environmental Law (PGP)
MSEL.........	Master Scenario Events List (MCD)
MSEL.........	Merisel, Inc. [*NASDAQ symbol*] (SPSG)
MSEL.........	Mullen Scales of Early Learning [*Child development test*] [*Psychology*]
MSEL.........	Selkirk Community Library, Manitoba [*Library symbol National Library of Canada*] (NLC)
MS Elect E..	Master of Science in Electrical Engineering
MSEM.........	Mainstreamed Special Educator Model (EDAC)
MSEM.........	Master of Science in Engineering and Mining (GAGS)
MSEM.........	Master of Science in Engineering Management (PGP)
MSEM.........	Master of Science in Engineering Mechanics
MSEM.........	Master of Science in Engineering of Mines (PGP)
MSEM.........	Master of Science in Environmental Management (PGP)
MSEM.........	Metrology Specific Equipment Model (AAEL)
MSEM.........	Mission Status and Evaluation Module
MS EMD	Morgan Stanley Emerging Markets Debt Fund, Inc. [*Associated Press*] (SAG)
MSEMech	Master of Science in Engineering Mechanics (GAGS)
MSEMgt......	Master of Science in Engineering Management (GAGS)
MSEMH........	Selkirk Mental Health Centre, Manitoba [*Library symbol National Library of Canada*] (NLC)
MS/EMI.......	Mission Sequence/Electromagnetic Interference
MSEMPR......	Missile Support Equipment Manufacturers Planning Reports (MCD)
MS En E	Master of Science in Environmental Engineering (PGP)
MS Eng.......	Master of Sanitary Engineering
MS Eng.......	Master of Science in Engineering
MS Engr	Master of Science in Engineering (PGP)
MS Engr Sci...	Master of Science in Engineering Science (PGP)
MS Ent........	Master of Science in Entomology
MS Env E....	Master of Science in Environmental Engineering (PGP)
MSEnvrE.....	Master of Science in Environmental Engineering (GAGS)
MSEO.........	Marine Services Engineer Officer [*Navy British*]
MSEP.........	Maintenance Standardization Evaluation Program [*Air Force*] (AFM)
MSEP.........	Mean Square Error of Prediction [*Statistics*] (PDAA)
MSEP.........	Mercury Scientific Experiment Panel
MSEP.........	Military Standard Evaluation Program
MSEPN	School of Psychiatric Nursing, Selkirk, Manitoba [*Library symbol National Library of Canada*] (NLC)
MSEPS........	Modular Space Electrical Power Station
M/SEQ	Master Sequencer
MSER.........	Management System Evaluation Review (NG)
MSER.........	Master of Science in Energy Resources (GAGS)
MSER.........	Mean Systolic Ejection Rate [*Cardiology*]
MSER.........	Multiple Stores Ejection Rack [*For munitions*] (MCD)

MSERD........	Ministry of State for Economic and Regional Development [*Canada*]
MSERT........	Member of the Society of Electronic and Radio Technicians [*British*] (DBQ)
MSES..........	Marine Scientific Equipment Service [*British*]
MSES..........	Master of Science in Engineering Science (PGP)
MSES..........	Master of Science in Environmental Studies (PGP)
MSES..........	Medical School Environmental Stress
MSES..........	Medical Service Squadron [*Military*]
MSES Sc.....	Mobile Status Entry System
M Se Sc	Master of Secretarial Science
MSESM........	Master of Science in Engineering Science and Mechanics (PGP)
MSESS........	Master of Science in Exercise and Sport Studies (GAGS)
M Se St	Master of Secretarial Studies
MSET..........	Maintenance Standardization and Evaluation Team (MCD)
MSET..........	Multistage Exercise Test [*Medicine*] (CPH)
MSETM........	Master of Science in Environmental Technology Management (PGP)
MSE TPN	Mobile Subscriber Equipment Tactical Packet Network [*Computer science Military*] (RDA)
MSEUE........	Mouvement Socialiste pour les Etats Unis d'Europe
MSEuro........	Morgan Stanley European Emerging Markets Ltd. [*Associated Press*] (SAG)
MSEVM........	Master of Science in Environmental Management (PGP)
MSEW..........	Medical Service Wing [*Military*]
MSEX..........	Middlesex Water [*NASDAQ symbol*] (TTSB)
MSEX..........	Middlesex Water Co. [*NASDAQ symbol*] (NQ)
MS Exp Surg...	Master of Science in Experimental Surgery (PGP)
MSF............	Congregatio Missionariorum a Sancta Familia [*Congregation of the Missionaries of the Holy Family*] [*Roman Catholic men's religious order*]
MSF............	Congregation of the Missionaries of the Holy Family (TOCD)
msf............	Congregation of the Missionaries of the Holy Family (TOCD)
MSF............	Construction Education Foundation [*Formerly, Merit Shop Foundation*] (EA)
MSF............	Macrophage Spreading Factor [*Hematology*]
MSF............	Magnetic Silencing Facility [*Kingsburg, GA*] (DWSG)
MSF............	Maintenance Source File (MCD)
MSF............	Manned Space Flight [*NASA*] (KSC)
MSF............	Manufacturing, Science, and Finance Union [*British*] (WA)
MSF............	Manufacturing Science Finance [*A union*] [*British*]
MSF............	Mark Sense Form (MCD)
MSF............	Mass Storage Facility [*Computer science*] (IBMDP)
MSF............	Master of Science in Finance
MSF............	Master of the Science of Forestry
MSF............	Master Source File [*Computer science*] (BUR)
MSF............	Matched Spatial Filter [*Optics*]
MSF............	Maximum Shear Force
MSF............	Max Sea Food SA de CV [*El Salvador*] [*ICAO designator*] (FAAC)
MSF............	Medecins sans Frontieres [*Doctors without Borders - DWB*] [*France*] (EAIO)
MSF............	Medium Standard Frequency (DEN)
MSF............	Member of the Society of Floristry [*British*] (DI)
MSF............	Merit Shop Foundation [*Washington, DC*] (EA)
MSF............	Metal Space-Frame (MCD)
MSF............	MetaScience Foundation (EA)
MSF............	Metastasis-Stimulating Factor [*Immunosuppressant*]
MSF............	Methanesulfonyl Fluoride [*Organic chemistry*]
MSF............	Migration Stimulating Factor [*Cytology*]
MSF............	Military Support Fund (MCD)
MSF............	Mind Science Foundation (EA)
MSF............	Minesweeper, Fleet [*Steel hull*] [*Navy symbol*]
MSF............	Minimum Sustaining Field [*Atomic reactor*]
MSF............	Missionary Sisters of the Holy Family (TOCD)
MSF............	Mission Simulator Facility
MSF............	Mobile Striking Force [*Military*]
MSF............	Mobility Support Forces [*Military*]
MSF............	Moisture Seekers Foundation [*Later, Sjogren's Syndrome Foundation - SSF*] (EA)
MSF............	Monoecious Sex Form
MSF............	Month-Second-Foot [*Measurement*]
MSF............	Morale Support Funds (MCD)
MSF............	Morgan Stanley Emerging Market [*NYSE symbol*] (SPSG)
MSF............	Morgan Stanley Emerging Mkt [*NYSE symbol*] (TTSB)
MSF............	Moroccan Sea Frontier [*Navy World War II*]
MSF............	Motorcycle Safety Foundation (EA)
MSF............	Mott Scattering Formula [*Physics*]
MSF............	Multiaxial Stress Field
MSF............	Multistage Flash [*Desalination method*]
MSF............	Muscle Shock Factor
MsFa	Jefferson County Library, Fayette, MS [*Library symbol Library of Congress*] (LCLS)
MSFA..........	Mid-States Football Association (PSS)
MSFAM........	Master of Science in Family Studies (PGP)
MSFB..........	Multi-Solids Fluidized Bed [*Chemical engineering*]
MSFC..........	Mark Slade Fan Club (EA)
MSFC..........	Marshall Space Flight Center [*Also known as GCMSC*] [*NASA*]
MSFC..........	McCarver Sisters Fan Club (EA)
MSFC..........	Medical Students for Choice
MSFC..........	Mid-South Football Conference (PSS)
MSFC..........	Mobile Strike Force Command [*Military*] (VNW)
MSFC..........	Morale Support Fund Council [*Military*] (AABC)
MSFC..........	Mutual Society of the French Community (EA)
MSFCV........	Main Stream Flow Control Valve [*Nuclear energy*] (NUCP)
MSFD..........	Millimeter Wave Seeker Feasibility Demonstration
MSFDC........	Microsoft and First Data Corp.
MSFDPS	Manned Space Flight Data Processing System [*NASA*]

MSFEB.........	Manned Space Flight Experiments Board [*NASA*] (KSC)
MSFET.........	Metal-on-Silicon Field-Effect Transistor [*Electronics*] (IAA)
MSFET.........	Metal Schottky Gate Field Effect Transistor [*Electronics*] (IAA)
MSFF...........	Master Slave Flipflop [*Nuclear energy*] (IAA)
MSFH...........	Manned Space Flight Headquarters [*NASA*]
MSFI............	MS Financial [*NASDAQ symbol*] (TTSB)
MSFI............	MS Financial Corp. [*NASDAQ symbol*] (SAG)
MS Fin.........	Morgan Stanley Finance PLC Capital Unit [*Associated Press*] (SAG)
MSFL...........	Manned Space Flight Laboratory [*NASA*] (IAA)
MSFLV.........	Manned Space Flight and Launch Vehicles [*Panel*]
MSFM..........	Master of Financial Management (PGP)
MSFM..........	Master of Science in Forest Management
MSFN..........	Manned Space Flight Network [*NASA*]
MSFn...........	Morgan Stanley Finance PLC Capital Unit [*Associated Press*] (SAG)
MS Fncl.......	MS Financial, Inc. [*Associated Press*] (SAG)
MSFNOC......	Manned Space Flight Network Operations Center [*NASA*] (KSC)
MSFO..........	Manned Space Flight Operations [*NASA*] (KSC)
MS For........	Master of Science in Forestry
MSFOR........	Master of Science in Forestry (PGP)
MSFP..........	Manned Space Flight Program [*NASA*] (KSC)
MSFP..........	Migrant and Seasonal Farmworkers Program [*Title III*] (OICC)
MSFRSP......	Male Sterile-Facilitated Recurrent Selection Population [*Plant breeding*]
MSFS..........	Main Steam and Feed Water System (IEEE)
MSFS..........	Manned Space Flight Subcommittee [*NASA*] (AAG)
MSFS..........	Manned Space Flight System [*NASA*] (IAA)
MSFS..........	Master of Science in Family Studies (PGP)
MSFS..........	Master of Science in Financial Services (PGP)
MSFS..........	Master of Science in Foreign Service (GAGS)
MSFS..........	Master of Science in Forensic Science (GAGS)
MSFS..........	Missionaries of St. Francis of Sales [*Roman Catholic religious order*]
MSFSG........	Manned Space Flight Support Group (MCD)
MSFSRD......	Manned Space Flight Support Requirements Documentation [*NASA*]
MSFT..........	Microsoft Corp. [*NASDAQ symbol*] (NQ)
MSFU..........	Merchant Service Fighter Unit [*Air Force British*]
MSFVW.......	Magnetostatic Forward Volume Wave [*Telecommunications*] (TEL)
MSFW.........	Migrant and Seasonal Farmworkers
MSFX..........	Master Fixture
MSG............	[*The*] Imperial Merchant Service Guild [*British*]
MSG............	Madison Square Garden [*New York, NY*] (NADA)
MSG............	Madison Square Garden Network [*Cable-television system*]
MSG............	Maintenance Steering Group (MCD)
MSG............	Management Steering Group (AAEL)
MSG............	Manufacturers Standard Gauge
MSG............	Mapper Sweep Generator
MSG............	Mapping Supervisor Gap Filler (SAA)
MSG............	Marine Security Guard
MSG............	Maritime Studies Group [*Military*] (VNW)
MSG............	Mascot Gold Mines Ltd. [*Toronto Stock Exchange symbol Vancouver Stock Exchange symbol*]
MSG............	Massage (DAVI)
MSG............	Master of Science in Gerontology (GAGS)
MSG............	Master Sergeant [*Army*] (AABC)
MSG............	Maximum Stable Gain (IAA)
MSG............	Mechanical Subsystem Group [*NASA*] (NASA)
MSG............	Message (AFM)
msg............	Message (IDOE)
MSG............	Methysergide [*A serotonin antagonist*] [*Pharmacology*] (DAVI)
MSG............	Microcomputer Support Group
MSG............	Microwave Signal Generator
MSG............	Miners' Support Group (WDAA)
MSG............	Ministry of Solicitor General [*Canada*]
MSG............	Ministry of the Solicitor General Library [*UTLAS symbol*]
MSG............	Miscellaneous Simulation Generator
MSG............	Missile Systems Group [*of General Motors Corp.*]
MSG............	Missing [*Military*]
MSG............	Mission Support Groups (MCD)
MSG............	Mobile Support Group [*Military*] (NVT)
MSG............	Modular Steam Generator (NRCH)
MSG............	Modulation Signal Generator (NITA)
MSG............	Moessingen [*Federal Republic of Germany*] [*Seismograph station code, US Geological Survey*] (SEIS)
MSG............	Monosodium Glutamate [*Food additive*] [*Pharmacology*]
MSG............	Multiplicand Select Gate (IAA)
MsG............	William Alexander Percy Memorial Library, Greenville, MS [*Library symbol Library of Congress*] (LCLS)
MSGA..........	Master Gauge
MSGA..........	Merchant Service Guild of Australia
MSGB..........	Manorial Society of Great Britain (EAIO)
MSGB..........	Muslim Society in Great Britain
MSGBI.........	Mineralogical Society of Great Britain and Ireland (EAIO)
MSGC..........	Master of Science in Genetic Counseling (PGP)
MSGC..........	Multinucleated Stromal Giant Cell
MSGCEN......	Message Center
MSGCTR......	Message Center [*Aviation*] (FAAC)
MSGDPU......	Message-Drop and Pick-Up [*Military*] (IAA)
MSGE..........	Master of Science in Geological Engineering (NADA)
MS Geo E	Master of Science in Geological Engineering (PGP)
MSGFLG......	Message Flag [*Computer science*] (MHDI)
MSGFM.......	Message Form (MUGU)
MS-GFW......	Memory for Sequence Subtest of the Goldman-Fristoe-Woodcock Auditory Skills TestBattery (EDAC)
MSGG.........	Message Generator (MSA)
MSGI..........	Marketing Services Group
MSGID........	Message Identifier
MSGL..........	Multishot Grenade Launcher (RDA)
MSGL..........	Thousand Square Feet of Single Glueline (WPI)
MSGlobl	Morgan Stanley Global Opportunities Bond Fund, Inc. [*Associated Press*] (SAG)
MSGM.........	Master of Science in Government Management
MSG Mgt	Master of Science in Game Management
MSGO	Mediterranean Secret General Orders
MSGO	Miskimins Self-Goal-Other Discrepancy Scale [*Psychology*] (DHP)
MsGoH........	Holmes Junior College, Goodman, MS [*Library symbol Library of Congress*] (LCLS)
MSGP	Mobile Support Group [*Military*]
MSGR	Messenger (AFM)
MSGR	Mobile Support Group [*Military*]
MSGR	Monseigneur
MSGR	Monsignor
MsGren........	Grenada County Library, Grenada, MS [*Library symbol Library of Congress*] (LCLS)
MSGT	Master Sergeant
MsGu	Gulfport-Carnegie-Harrison County Library, Gulfport, MS [*Library symbol Library of Congress*] (LCLS)
MSGV	Mouse Salivary Gland Virus [*Medicine*] (DMAA)
MsGW.........	Washington County Library System, Greenville, MS [*Library symbol Library of Congress*] (LCLS)
MSGWA	Military and Sporting Gun Workers' Association [*A union*] [*British*]
MsGwL........	Greenwood-Leflore Public Library, Greenwood, MS [*Library symbol Library of Congress*] (LCLS)
MSG/WTG....	Message Waiting (MDG)
MSh............	Ma'aser Sheni (BJA)
MSH............	Magnetoelastic Static Hysteresis (MCD)
MSH............	Mashhad [*Iran*] [*Seismograph station code, US Geological Survey Closed*] (SEIS)
MSH............	Master of Science in Horticulture (NADA)
MSH............	Master of Science in Hospice (PGP)
MSH............	Master of Science in Hygiene (NADA)
MSH............	Master of Staghounds
MSH............	Mauler Seeker Head
MSH............	Medical Self-Help [*Defunct*]
MSH............	Melanocyte-Stimulating Hormone [*Also, MH*] [*Endocrinology*]
MSH............	Melanophore-Stimulating Hormone [*Endocrinology*] (AAMN)
MSH............	Men of the Sacred Hearts (EA)
MSH............	Metastable Helium (MCD)
MSH............	Metropolitan Cooperative Library System, Pasadena, CA [*OCLC symbol*] (OCLC)
MSH............	Minesweeper Hunter Vessel
MSH............	Mishibishu Resources [*Vancouver Stock Exchange symbol*]
MSH............	Missionaries of the Sacred Heart [*Roman Catholic men's religious order*]
Ms-H	Mississippi State Board of Health, Jackson, MS [*Library symbol Library of Congress*] (LCLS)
MSH............	Mount St. Helens [*Washington*] [*Geology*]
MSH............	US Marshal Service [*Department of Justice*] [*ICAO designator*] (FAAC)
MsHa	Hattiesburg Public Library, Hattiesburg, MS [*Library symbol Library of Congress*] (LCLS)
MSHA	Mannose-Sensitive Hemagglutination [*Medicine*] (DMAA)
MSHA	Master of Science in Health Administration (PGP)
MSHA	Master of Science in Hospital Administration
MSHA	Mine Safety and Health Administration [*Department of Labor*]
MSha	Sharon Public Library, Sharon, MA [*Library symbol Library of Congress*] (LCLS)
MSHAA	Member of the Society of Hearing Aid Audiologists [*British*] (DBQ)
MSHAA	Morocco Spotted Horse Association of America [*Defunct*] (EA)
MShaK........	Kendall Whaling Museum, Sharon, MA [*Library symbol Library of Congress*] (LCLS)
MSH & Ph Ed...	Master of Science in Health and Physical Education
MsHaP........	The Library-Hattisburg, Petal Forrest County, Hattiesburg, MS [*Library symbol*] [*Library of Congress*] (LCLS)
MsHaU........	University of Southern Mississippi, Hattiesburg, MS [*Library symbol Library of Congress*] (LCLS)
MsHaW.......	William Carey College, Hattiesburg, MS [*Library symbol Library of Congress*] (LCLS)
MSHB	Minimum Safe Height of Burst [*Military*]
MSHCS	Master of Science in Human and Consumer Science (PGP)
MsHe	First Regional Library, Hernando, MS [*Library symbol Library of Congress*] (LCLS)
MSHE	Master of Science in Home Economics
MSHE	Master of Science in Hydraulic Engineering
MSH Ec.......	Master of Science in Home Economics
MSH Ed	Master of Science in Health Education (PGP)
MSHES	Master of Science in Human Environmental Sciences (PGP)
MSHG	Meshing
MSHI	Medium Scale Hybrid Integration [*Computer science*] (IAA)
MSH-IF	Melanocyte-Stimulating Hormone-Inhibiting Factor [*Endocrinology*] (MAE)
MSH-IF	Melanophore-Stimulating Hormone [*Intermedin*] Inhibiting Factor [*Laboratory science*] (DAVI)
MSHJ	Medical Staff Hospital Joint Venture
MSHK	Megadata Corp. (MHDW)
MSHK	Morgan Stanley Group, Inc. [*Associated Press*] (SAG)
Mshl	Marshal (BARN)
MShM.........	Mount Holyoke College, South Hadley, MA [*Library symbol Library of Congress*] (LCLS)
MS Hort.......	Master of Science in Horticulture
MsHos	Marshall County Library, Holly Springs, MS [*Library symbol Library of Congress*] (LCLS)

MsHosR......	Rust College, Holly Springs, MS [*Library symbol Library of Congress*] (LCLS)
MsHou.........	Houston Carnegie Public Library, Houston, MS [*Library symbol Library of Congress*] (LCLS)
Mshp	Machine Shop (MHDB)
MSHP	Maintain System History Program [*IBM Corp.*]
MSHP	Master of Science in Health Professions (PGP)
MSHP	Missionary Sisters of the Holy Family (Poland) (TOCD)
MSHR	Master of Science in Human Resources (PGP)
MSHR	Melanocyte Stimulating Hormone Receptor [*Medicine*] (DMAA)
MSHR	Missionary Sisters of Our Lady of the Holy Rosary [*Blackrock, County Dublin, Republic of Ireland*] (EAIO)
MSHRF	Melanocyte-Stimulating Hormone Releasing Factor (DB)
MSHRM	Master of Science in Human Resources Management (PGP)
MSHS	Master of Science in Health and Safety (GAGS)
MSHS	Master of Science in Health Science (PGP)
MSHS	Master of Science in Health Systems (GAGS)
MSHS	Medical Sciences History Society [*British*] (DBA)
MSHSA	Master of Science in Human Service Administration (PGP)
MSHSE	Master of Science in Health Science Education (PGP)
MSHy	Master of Science in Hygiene (DAVI)
MS Hyg.......	Master of Science in Hygiene
MsHz	Copiah-Jefferson Regional Library, Hazelhurst, MS [*Library symbol Library of Congress*] (LCLS)
MSI	Magnetic Source Imaging [*Neuroscience*]
msi	Maintenance Significant Item (NAKS)
MSI	Maintenance Significant Items (NASA)
MSI	Maintenance Supply Item
MSI	Maintenance Support Index
MSI	Management Style Inventory [*Test*] (TMMY)
MSI	Manned Satellite Inspector
MSI	Man System Integration (IAA)
MSI	Marine Science Institute [*University of California, Santa Barbara*] [*Research center*] (RCD).
MSI	Marine Science Institute [*Philippines*]
MSI	Marital Satisfaction Inventory [*Psychology*]
MSI	Marketing Science Institute [*Cambridge, MA*] (EA)
MSI	Master of Science in Instruction (PGP)
MSI	Master of Science in Insurance
MSI	Mathematical Sciences Institute [*Cornell University*] [*Research center*] (RCD)
MSI	Maximum Speed Indicator
MSI	Maxwell Scientific International [*Inc.*]
MSI	Mean Spleen Index
MSI	Medical Seminars International (EA)
MSI	Medium-Scale Integration [*Circuit packaging*]
msi	Medium Scale Integration (NAKS)
MSI	Megapounds per Square Inch
MSI	Member of the Sanitary Institute [*British*] (ROG)
MSI	Member of the Surveyors' Institution [*British*] (ROG)
MSI	Mentoring Style Indicator [*Test*] (TMMY)
MSI	Messina ING [*Istituto Nazionale Geodetico*] [*Sicily*] [*Seismograph station code, US Geological Survey*] (SEIS)
MSI	Metal Support Interaction [*Catalysis*]
MSI	Microbiological Safety Index (DB)
MSI	Microwave Services International, Inc. [*Denville, NJ*] [*Telecommunications*] (TSSD)
MSI	Middle-Scale Integration [*Computer science*] (IAA)
MSI	Military Service Indicator (MCD)
MSI	Military Standard Item (MCD)
MSI	Military Static Inverter
MSI	Mill Service, Inc. (EFIS)
MSI	Minesweeper, Inshore [*Navy symbol*]
MSI	Missile Status Indicator
MSI	Missile Subsystem Integration (SAA)
MSI	Mission Success Indicator (MCD)
MSI	Moderate Scale Integration [*Electronics*]
MSI	Molecular Sciences Institute
MSI	Molecular Surface Ionization
MSI	Money Store (EFIS)
MSI	Moon Sphere of Influence (KSC)
MSI	Moshi [*Tanzania*] [*Airport symbol*] (AD)
MSI	Mother Symptom Inventory [*Psychology*]
MSI	Motor Sich [*Ukraine*] [*FAA designator*] (FAAC)
MSI	Motor Skills Inventory [*Sensorimotor skills test*]
MSI	Movie Star, Inc. (SPSG)
MSI	Movimento Sociale Italiano [*Italian Social Movement*] [*Political party*] (PPE)
MSI	Multicomm Sciences International, Inc. [*Denville, NJ*] (TSSD)
MSI	Multiple Spark Igniter
MSI	Multiple Subcutaneous Insulin [*Medicine*]
MSI	Multisensor Imagery
MSI	Multispectral Imagery (DOMA)
MSI	Multisystem Involvement [*Medicine*]
MSI	Museum of Science and Industry [*Chicago, IL*]
MSI	Museum Services Institute [*Department of Education*] (OICC)
MSI	Mustang Software International [*California*] [*Bulletin board system*]
MSI	Second Independence Movement [*Ecuador*] [*Political party*] (PPW)
MSIA	Church of the Movement for Spiritual Inner Awareness (ECON)
MSIA	Mass Spectrometric Immunoassay
MSIA	Master of Institutional Administration (GAGS)
MSIA	Master of Science in Industrial Administration
MSIA	Master of Science in International Adminstration (PGP)
MSIA	Master of Science in International Affairs (GAGS)
MSIA	Member of the Society of Industrial Artists [*British*]

MSIA	Multispectral Image Analyzer (MCD)
MSIAD	Member of the Society of Industrial Artists and Designers [*British*] (DBQ)
MSIB	Master of Science in International Business (PGP)
MSIB	Modular Systems Interface Bus (NITA)
MSIBK	Master of Science in International Banking (PGP)
MsIbM	Mississippi Valley State College, Itta Bena, MS [*Library symbol Library of Congress*] (LCLS)
MSIC	Mid-South Independent Conference (PSS)
MSIC	Missile and Space Intelligence Center [*DoD*]
MSIC	Mixed-Signal Integrated Circuit [*Electronics*]
M-SID	Magnetic Sensing Intrusion Device [*Remote sensor*] [*Also, MAGNA-SID*] [*Military*] (VNW)
MSID	Mass Spectrometric Isotope Dilution
MSID	Measurement Stimulation Identification (MCD)
MSID	Medium-Scale Integration Device [*Circuit packaging*]
MSI-DN.......	Movimento Sociale Italiano-Destra Nazionale [*Italian Social Movement-National Right*] [*Political party*] (EY)
MSIE	Master of Science in Industrial Engineering
MSIE	Master of Science in International Economics (PGP)
MSIEOR	Master of Science in Industrial Engineering and Operations Research (GAGS)
MSIF	Multi-Systems Integration Facility (SSD)
MSIG	Most Significant (IAA)
MSIGM	Macintosh Special Interest Group of Mensa (EA)
MS IGT	Morgan Stanley Group, Inc. [*Associated Press*] (SAG)
MSIGX	Oppenheimer Main Street Inc. & Growth [*Mutual fund ticker symbol*] (SG)
MSIIP	Missile System Installation Interrupted for Parts (NVT)
MSIL	Master of Science in International Logistics (PGP)
MSIM	Master of Science in Industrial Management
MSIM	Master of Science in Information Management (GAGS)
MSIMC	Master of Science in Information Management and Communication (PGP)
MSIMD	Multiple Single Instruction, Multiple Data (MCD)
MsIn	Henry M. Seymour Library, Indianola, MS [*Library symbol Library of Congress*] (LCLS)
MS in Aero E...	Master of Science in Aeronautical Engineering
MS in Ag	Master of Science in Agriculture
MS in Ag E..	Master of Science in Agricultural Education
MS in Ag Ec...	Master of Science in Agricultural Economics
MS in Agr...	Master of Science in Agriculture
MS in Agr Ed...	Master of Science in Agricultural Education
MS in AN....	Master of Science in Agricultural Engineering
MS in Aud & Sp...	Master of Science in Audiology and Speech
MS in BA....	Master of Science in Business Administration
MS in Bl Sc...	Master of Science in Biological Sciences
MS in C	Master of Science in Commerce
MS in C & BA...	Master of Science in Commercial and Business Administration
MS in CE....	Master of Science in Civil Engineering
MS in Cer....	Master of Science in Ceramics
MS in Cer E...	Master of Science in Ceramic Engineering
MS in Cer Tech...	Master of Science in Ceramic Technology
MS in Ch	Master of Science in Chemistry
MS in Ch E...	Master of Science in Chemical Engineering
MS in Ch Eng...	Master of Science in Chemical Engineering
MS in Con ...	Master of Science in Conservation
MS in CRP...	Master of Science in City and Regional Planning
MS Ind E ...	Master of Science in Industrial Engineering
MSIndEng....	Master of Science in Industrial Engineering (NADA)
MS in Derm...	Master of Science in Dermatology
MS India...	Morgan Stanley India Investment Fund [*Associated Press*] (SAG)
MS in Dt.....	Master of Science in Dietetics
MS in E	Master of Science in Education
MS in E	Master of Science in Engineering
MS in Ed	Master of Science in Education
MS in EE	Master of Science in Electrical Engineering
MS in EM	Master of Science in Engineering Mechanics
MS in EM	Master of Science in Engineering of Mines
MS in E Mgt..	Master of Science in Engineering Management
MS in EP	Master of Science in Engineering Physics
MS in ES	Master of Science in Engineering Science [*or Sciences*]
MS in For....	Master of Science in Forestry
MS in GE....	Master of Science in General Engineering
MS in Gp Engr...	Master of Science in Geophysical Engineering
MS in GSM...	Master of Science in General Science and Mathematics
MS in HE....	Master of Science in Home Economics
MS in H Ec...	Master of Science in Home Economics
MS in HR....	Master of Science in Human Relations
MS in ID.....	Master of Science in Industrial Design
MS in IE	Master of Science in Industrial Engineering
MS in IM	Master of Science in Industrial Management
MS in Ind Ed...	Master of Science in Industrial Education
MS in LS	Master of Science in Library Science
MS in ME	Master of Science in Mechanical Engineering
MS in Mech..	Master of Science in Engineering Mechanics
MS in Med...	Master of Science in Medicine
MS in Met ...	Master of Science in Metallurgy
MS in Met E...	Master of Science in Metallurgical Engineering
MS in Mus...	Master of Science in Music
MS in Mus Ed...	Master of Science in Music Education
MS in N.....	Master of Science in Nursing
MS in NE....	Master of Science in Nursing Education
MS in N Ed...	Master of Science in Nursing Education
MS in Nr Ed...	Master of Science in Nursing Education

MS in NT....	Master of Science in Nuclear Technology
MS in Nucl E..	Master of Science in Nuclear Engineering
MS in PA....	Master of Science in Public Administration
MS in PE....	Master of Science in Petroleum Engineering
MS in PE....	Master of Science in Physical Education
MS in P Ed...	Master of Science in Physical Education
MS in Pet E...	Master of Science in Petroleum Engineering
MS in PH....	Master of Science in Public Health
MS in Phar...	Master of Science in Pharmacy
MS in Phy...	Master of Science in Physics
MS in PRE...	Master of Science in Petroleum Refining Engineering
MS in PSM...	Master of Science in Public School Music
MS in Py Sc...	Master of Science in Poultry Science
MS in Rad...	Master of Science in Radiology
MS in Rec...	Master of Science in Recreation
MS in Ret....	Master of Science in Retailing
MS in Sp....	Master of Science in Speech
MS in SS....	Master of Science in Sanitary Science
MS in SS....	Master of Science in Social Service
MS in SW....	Master of Science in Social Work
MS in T & I...	Master of Science in Trade and Industrial Education
MS in Trans E...	Master of Science in Transportation Engineering
MSINZ	Member of the Surveyors' Institute of New Zealand
MSIO	Mass Storage Input-Output [*Computer science*] (IEEE)
MSIO	Medical Systems Integration Office [*Army*] (RDA)
MSIP..........	Mechanical Stress Improvement Process [*Nuclear energy*] (NUCP)
MSIP..........	Minority Science Improvement Program [*Department of Education*] (GFGA)
MSIP..........	Modeling and Simulation Investment Plan [*Army*]
MSIP..........	Multinational Staged Improvement Program (MCD)
MSIP..........	Multistage Improvement Program (DOMA)
MSIPC	Master of Science in Information Processing and Communications (PGP)
MSIR	Machine Survey and Installation Report
MSIR	Master of Science in Industrial Relations (GAGS)
MSIR	Master of Social and Industrial Relations
MSIR	Master Stock Item Record
MSIS..........	Main Steam Isolation Signal [*Nuclear energy*] (NRCH)
MSIS..........	Manned Satellite Inspection System
MSIS..........	Man-Systems Integration Standard (SSD)
MSIS..........	Marine Safety Information System [*Coast Guard*] (MSC)
MSIS..........	Mask Shop Information System [*Bell Laboratories*]
MSIS..........	Mass Spectral Information System
MSIS..........	Master of Science in Computer-Based Information Systems
MSIS..........	Master of Science in Information Science (GAGS)
MSIS..........	Master of Science in Information Systems (PGP)
MSIS..........	Master of Science in Interdisciplinary Studies (PGP)
MSIS..........	Model State Information System [*Environmental Protection Agency*] (GFGA)
MSIS..........	Multisensor Stabilized Integrated System
MSIS..........	Multistate Information System [*Patient records*]
MSISL........	Moore School Information Systems Laboratory
Ms IT	Manuscript, Inner Temple [*A publication*] (DLA)
MSIT..........	Master of Science in Industrial Technology (PGP)
MSIT..........	Member of the Society of Instrument Technology [*British*]
MSITTL.......	Medium Scale Integration Transistor-Transistor Logic (CIST)
MSIV..........	Main Steam Isolation Valve [*Nuclear energy*] (NRCH)
MSIVLCS	Main Steam Isolation Valve Leakage Control System [*Nuclear energy*] (NRCH)
MS/IWS	Master of Science/Industry Work Study
MSIX	Mining Services International Corp. [*NASDAQ symbol*] (NQ)
MSIX..........	Mining Svcs Intl [*NASDAQ symbol*] (TTSB)
MsJ.............	Jackson Municipal Library, Jackson, MS [*Library symbol Library of Congress*] (LCLS)
MSJ	Machine Screw Jack
MSJ	Master of Science in Journalism
MSJ	Medical Sisters of St. Joseph (TOCD)
MSJ	Misawa [*Japan*] [*Airport symbol*] (OAG)
MSJ	Mission San Jose [*California*] [*Seismograph station code, US Geological Survey*] (SEIS)
MSJ	Multiple Subsonic Jet
MSJ96	Morgan Stanley Group, Inc. [*Associated Press*] (SAG)
MSJA..........	Master of Science in Judicial Administration (GAGS)
MsJB	Belhaven College, Jackson, MS [*Library symbol Library of Congress*] (LCLS)
MSJBS........	Master of Science in Japanese Business Studies (PGP)
MsJG	Mississippi Bureau of Geology, Jackson, MS [*Library symbol*] [*Library of Congress*] (LCLS)
MsJMC	Millsaps College, Jackson, MS [*Library symbol Library of Congress*] (LCLS)
MsJPED	Episcopal Diocese of Mississippi, Jackson, MS [*Library symbol Library of Congress*] (LCLS)
MSJPS........	Master of Science in Justice and Public Safety (PGP)
MSJPS........	Master of Science in Justice and Public Service (GAGS)
MsJRD	Research and Development Center Library, Jackson, MS [*Library symbol Library of Congress*] (LCLS)
MsJRT	Reformed Theological Seminary, Jackson, MS [*Library symbol Library of Congress*] (LCLS)
MsJS	Jackson State College [*Later, Jackson State University*], Jackson, MS [*Library symbol Library of Congress*] (LCLS)
MSJS	Master of Science in Jewish Studies (PGP)
MsJV	United States Veterans Administration Hospital, Jackson, MS [*Library symbol Library of Congress*] (LCLS)
MsJW	Wesley Biblical Seminary, Jackson, MS [*Library symbol Library of Congress*] (LCLS)

MSK...........	Grupo Indl Maseca ADS [*NYSE symbol*] (TTSB)
MSK...........	Grupo Industrial Maseca SA de CV [*NYSE symbol*] (SAG)
MSK...........	Magyar Statisztikai Kozlemenyek [*Hungary*]
MSK...........	Major Subcontractor
MSK...........	Manual Select Keyboard [*Computer science*] (KSC)
MSK...........	Mask [*Computer science*] (IAA)
MSK...........	Master of Science in Kinesiology (GAGS)
MSK...........	Mastic Point [*Andros Islands, Bahamas*] [*Airport symbol*] (AD)
MSK...........	Medullary Sponge Kidney [*Anatomy*] (MAE)
MSK...........	Medvedev, Sponheuer, Karnick [*Earthquake intensity scale*]
MsK...........	Mid-Mississippi Regional Library, Kosciusko, MS [*Library symbol Library of Congress*] (LCLS)
MSK...........	Minimal Shift Keying (NITA)
MSK...........	Minimum Shift Keying
MSK...........	Misaki [*Japan*] [*Seismograph station code, US Geological Survey Closed*] (SEIS)
MSK...........	Mission Support Kit
MSK...........	Mobility Support Kit
MSK...........	Mostek Corporation (NITA)
MSKB..........	Musculoskeletal [*Orthopedics*] (DAVI)
MSKB..........	Microsoft Knowledge Base [*Computer science*] (PCM)
MSKC.........	Memorial Sloan-Kettering Cancer Center [*Research center*] (RCD)
MSKCC	Memorial Sloan-Kettering Cancer Center [*New York*]
MSKCP	Missionary Sisters of Christ the King of Polonia (TOCD)
MSKM.........	Minimum Shift Keyed Modulation (NITA)
MSKP.........	Management Skills - Knowledge Profile [*Business term*]
MSKP.........	Medical Sciences Knowledge Profile (DAVI)
MsL...........	Laurel Library Association, Laurel, MS [*Library symbol Library of Congress*] (LCLS)
MSL..........	Machine Specification Language
MSL..........	Magnetic Surfaces Laboratory
MSL..........	Main Sea Level (AAG)
MSL..........	Main Steam Line [*Nuclear energy*] (NRCH)
MSL..........	Maintenance Supply Liaison [*Air Force*] (AFM)
MSL..........	Major Soccer League (BARN)
MSL..........	Management Selection Ltd.
MSL..........	Management Systems Laboratories [*Virginia Polytechnic Institute and State University*] [*Research center*] (RCD)
MSL..........	Manned Space Laboratory [*NASA*] (IAA)
MSL..........	Manpower Source Listing (MCD)
MSL..........	Marine Systems Laboratory [*Smithsonian Institution*]
MSL..........	Master of Sacred Literature
MSL..........	Master of Science in Language
MSL..........	Master of Science in Librarianship (PGP)
MSL..........	Master of Science in Limnology (PGP)
MSL..........	Master of Science in Linguistics
MSL..........	Master of Studies in Law (PGP)
MSL..........	Master Save List [*Military*] (AFIT)
MSL..........	Master Scheduling Letter
MSL..........	Masterseal [*Record label*]
MSL..........	Master Support List (MCD)
MSL..........	Materialien zum Sumerischen Lexikon. B. Landsberger. Patrologiae Cursus Completus. Series Latina [*A publication*] (BJA)
MSL..........	Materials and Structures Laboratory [*Texas A & M University*] [*Research center*] (RCD)
MSL..........	Maximum Service Life [*or Limit*] (AAG)
MSL..........	Maximum Stillwater Level [*Nuclear energy*] (NRCH)
MSL..........	Mean Sea Level
MSL..........	Measurement Standards Laboratory
MSL..........	Measurement System Laboratory (MCD)
MSL..........	Mechanical Systems Laboratory [*NASA*] (NASA)
MSL..........	Message Switched Line (MCD)
MSL..........	Meteorological Satellite Laboratory
MSL..........	Methuen's Standard Library [*A publication*]
MSL..........	Microcomputer Sales and Leasing, Inc.
MSL..........	Microgravity Science Laboratory [*NASA*]
MSL..........	Microstar Software Ltd. [*Nepean, ON*] [*Telecommunications*] (TSSD)
MSL..........	MidSouth Bancorp [*AMEX symbol*] (TTSB)
MSL..........	Midsouth Bancorp, Inc. [*AMEX symbol*] (SAG)
MSL..........	Midsternal Line
MSL..........	Military Shipping Label
MSL..........	Military Side Loader [*Air transport*] [*British*]
MSL..........	Military Support List (MCD)
MSL..........	Minesweeping Launch [*Navy ship symbol*]
MSL..........	Minimum Size Limit [*Pisciculture*]
MSL..........	Minneapolis & St. Louis [*Railroad*] (MHDB)
MSL..........	Minnesota State Law Library, St. Paul, MN [*OCLC symbol*] (OCLC)
MSL..........	Missile (AFM)
MSL..........	Missile Sea Level
MSL..........	Missile Site Load (MCD)
MSL..........	Modify System Logging (AAEL)
MSL..........	Molecular Spectroscopy Laboratory [*Fisk University*] [*Research center*] (RCD)
MSL..........	Mouvement des Sociaux-Liberaux [*Movement of Social Liberals*] [*France Political party*] (PPW)
MSL..........	Multiple Stinger Launcher
MSL..........	Multiple Symmetric Lipomatosis [*Medicine*] (DMAA)
MSL..........	Municipal Savings & Loan Corp. [*Toronto Stock Exchange symbol*]
MSL..........	Muscle Shoals [*Alabama*] [*Airport symbol*] (OAG)
MSL..........	Snow Lake Community Library, Manitoba [*Library symbol National Library of Canada*] (NLC)
MSIA.........	Atlantic Union College, South Lancaster, MA [*Library symbol Library of Congress*] (LCLS)
MSLA.........	Main Steam Line Accident [*Nuclear energy*] (NRCH)
MSLA.........	Master of Science in Legal Administration (PGP)

MSLA............ Missionary Sisters of Our Lady of the Angels [*Lennoxville, PQ*] (EAIO)

MSLA............ Mouse Specific Lymphocyte Antigen [*Immunology*]

MSLA............ Multisample Luer Adapter [*Medicine*] (MEDA)

MSLAET........ Member of the Society of Licensed Aircraft Engineers and Technologists [*British*] (DBQ)

MsLb .... Long Beach Public Library, Long Beach, MS [*Library symbol Library of Congress*] (LCLS)

MSLB............ Main Steam Line Break [*Nuclear energy*] (NRCH)

MsLbU .... University of Southern Mississippi, Gulf Park, Richard G. Cox Library, Long Beach, MS [*Library symbol Library of Congress*] (LCLS)

MSLC............ Minnesota Short Lines Co. [*AAR code*]

MSLC............ Missile Sites Labor Commission [*A federal government body*] [*Abolished 1967; functions transferred to Federal Mediation and Conciliation Service*]

MSLCOMD ... Missile Command [*Army*]

MSLD............ Masland Corp. [*NASDAQ symbol*] (SAG)

MSLD............ Mass Spectrometer Leak Detector (NRCH)

MsLE .... Lauren Rogers Library and Museum of Art, Laurel, MS [*Library symbol Library of Congress*] (LCLS)

MSLEX........ Missile Exercise (DOMA)

MSLF............ Mountain States Legal Foundation (EA)

MSLFM........ Massenet Society and Lovers of French Music [*Later, MSAB*] (EA)

MSLG............ Maintenance Support Logistics Group [*Military*] (CAAL)

Ms LI .... Manuscript, Lincoln's Inn [*A publication*] (DLA)

MsLi .... Microfilm Services Ltd., Auckland, New Zealand [*Library symbol Library of Congress*] (LCLS)

MSLIR .... Master of Science in Labor and Industrial Relations

MS Litt .... Master of Sacred Letters

MSLIVSS ..... Main Steam Line Isolation Valve Sealings System [*Nuclear energy*] (NRCH)

MSLM............ Microchannel Spatial Light Modulator [*Electronics*]

MSLMAINTSq.. Missile Maintenance Squadron [*Air Force*]

MSLN............ Mari Sandoz Library Network [*Library network*]

MSLO............ Master Layout

MSLO............ Medical Service Liaison Officer [*Air Force*]

MSLOUG...... Medium-Sized Libraries/OCLC [*Online Computer Library Center*] Users Group

MSLP............ Malawi Socialist Labour Party [*Political party*] (EY)

MSLP............ Master of Speech-Language Pathology (PGP)

MSLP............ San Salvador/El Salvador Internacional [*El Salvador*] [*ICAO location identifier*] (ICLI)

MSLPr .... MidSouth Bancorp Sr'A'Cv Pfd [*AMEX symbol*] (TTSB)

MSLQ............ Motivated Strategies for Learning Questionnaire [*Test*] (TMMY)

MSLR............ Mixed Skin Cell-Leukocyte Reaction [*Medicine*] (DMAA)

MSLS............ Maneuverable Satellite Landing System (MUGU)

MSLS............ Master of Science in Law and Society (DLA)

MSLS............ Master of Science in Library Science

MSLS............ Master of Science in Logistics Systems (PGP)

MSLS............ Missile Site Location System (MCD)

MSLS............ Multi-Slice Least Squares [*Software for crystallography*]

MSLSc .... Master of Science in Library Science

MSLT............ Military Solid Logic Technology (IAA)

MSLT............ Multiple Sleep Latency Test

MSLWARNINGSq... Missile Warning Squadron [*Air Force*]

MSLY............ Mostly (MSA)

MSM............ Maastricht School of Management [*Netherlands*]

MSM............ Major System Mode (CAAL)

MSM............ Manhattan School of Music

MSM............ Manned Support Module [*NASA*] (NASA)

msm .... Manned Support Module [*NASA*] (NAKS)

MSM............ Manufacturing Shop Manual (SAA)

MSM............ Manufacturing Standards Manual

MSM............ Marine Safety Manual [*Coast Guard*] [*A publication*] (DLA)

MSM............ Mars Surface Module (MCD)

MSM............ Mass Scatterable Mine (RDA)

MSM............ Master of Medical Science

MSM............ Master of Sacred Ministry (PGP)

MSM............ Master of Sacred Music

MSM............ Master of Science in Management

MSM............ Master of Science in Music

MSM............ Master of Service Management (PGP)

MSM............ Master Scheduling Manager

MSM............ Master Slave Manipulator [*Nuclear energy*]

MSM............ Mauritian Socialist Movement [*Political party*]

MSM............ Meal Semiconductor Metal (IAA)

MSM............ Mechanically Separated Meat [*Food technology*]

MSM............ Medium Minesweeper (NATG)

MSM............ Memory Storage Module

MSM............ Men Who Have Sex with Men [*Australia An association*]

MSM............ Mercury Specialist Management [*Commercial firm British*]

MsM............ Meridian Public Library, Meridian, MS [*Library symbol Library of Congress*] (LCLS)

MSM............ Meritorious Service Medal [*Military decoration*]

MSM............ Messman

MSM............ Metal-Semiconductor-Metal (IEEE)

MSM............ Methyl Sulfonylmethane [*Biochemistry*]

MSM............ Micro Surface Mapping [*Software package*] (NCC)

MSM............ Microwave Switch Matrix (LAIN)

MSM............ Millimeter and Submillimeter Conference (MCD)

MSM............ Mineral Salts Medium [*Medicine*] (DMAA)

MSM............ Minesweeper, River [*Navy symbol Obsolete*]

MSM............ Missile Standards Manual [*Military*] (IAA)

MSM............ Mission Simulation Model

MSM............ Missouri School of Mines

MSM............ Modified Source Multiplication (NRCH)

MSM............ Montana School of Mines

MSM............ Morehouse School of Medicine [*Atlanta, GA*]

MSM............ Motorized Switching Matrix

MSM............ Motorsteuermonolith

MSM............ Mount St. Mary's College, Emmitsburg, MD [*OCLC symbol*] (OCLC)

MSM............ Mouvement Social Mohutu [*Mohutu Social Movement*]

MSM............ Mouvement Solidaire Muluba [*Muluba Solidarity Movement*] [*Political party*]

MSM............ MSC Industrial Direct'A' [*NYSE symbol*] (TTSB)

MSM............ Mystic Seaport Museum (EA)

MSM............ Thousand Feet Surface Measure [*Lumber*]

MSMA............ Mail Systems Management Association [*New York, NY*] (EA)

MSMA............ Major Symphony Managers Association (EA)

MSMA............ Margarine and Shortening Manufacturers Association (EAIO)

MSMA............ Master Sign Makers' Association (NADA)

MSMA............ Medical-Surgical Manufacturers Association [*Later, HIMA*]

MSMA............ Metal Sink Manufacturers Association [*British*] (DBA)

MSMA............ Meteorological Services to Marine Activities [*WMO*] (MSC)

MSMA............ Metropolitan Symphony Managers Association (EA)

MSMA............ Monosodium Methyl Arsonate [*Herbicide*]

MSMA............ Monosodium Salt of Methylarsonic Acid [*Agriculture*]

MsMac............ Noxubee County Library, Macon, MS [*Library symbol Library of Congress*] (LCLS)

MSMAE .... Master of Science in Materials Engineering (PGP)

MSMAN .... Master Sign Makers' Association [*British*] (BI)

MsMar .... Quitman County Library, Marks, MS [*Library symbol Library of Congress*] (LCLS)

MSMAS........ Master of Science in Media Arts and Sciences (PGP)

MS Mat........ Master of Science in Materials Engineering (PGP)

MS Mat E .... Master of Science in Materials Engineering (PGP)

MS Mat SE ... Master of Science in Material Science and Engineering (PGP)

MSMatSE..... Master of Science in Materials Science Engineering (GAGS)

MSMAV........ Master Stone Masons' Association of Victoria [*Australia*]

MSMB............ Mortgage Secondary Market Board [*Australia*]

MSMC............ Master of Science in Marketing Communication (GAGS)

MSMC............ Master of Science in Mass Communication (GAGS)

MSMC............ Master Schedule and Milestone Chart (MCD)

MSMC............ Member of the Spectacle Makers Co. [*British*] (ROG)

MSMC............ Migrant Studies and Media Center [*Australia*]

MSMC............ Military Subsistence Market Center (MUGU)

MsMc............ Pike-Amite Library System, McComb, MS [*Library symbol Library of Congress*] (LCLS)

MSMCS........ Master of Science in Management and Computer Science (PGP)

MSMD............ Madras Subordinate Medical Department [*British military*] (DMA)

MSMDA .... Mutual Sewing Machine Dealers Association (EA)

MSME .... Master of Science in Mathematics Education (PGP)

MSME .... Master of Science in Mechanical Engineering

MSMEA........ Multiwall Sack Manufacturers Employers Association [*British*] (DBA)

MS Mech E ... Master of Science in Mechanical Engineering

MSMed........ Master of Medical Science (NADA)

MS Met E .... Master of Science in Metallurgical Engineering

MS Metr ...... Master of Science in Meteorology (PGP)

MSMF............ Maintenance Support Management File (MCD)

MSMFE........ Master of Science in Manufacturing Engineering (PGP)

MS Mfg E .... Master of Science in Manufacturing Engineering (PGP)

MsMFM........ Masonic Library, Meridian, MS [*Library symbol Library of Congress*] (LCLS)

MS Mf SE .... Master of Science in Manufacturing Systems Engineering (PGP)

MSMG .... Missionary Sisters of the Mother of God [*Roman Catholic religious order*]

MSMgt........ Master of Science in Management (GAGS)

MS Mgt E ... Master of Science in Management Engineering

MSMI............ Master of Science in Medical Illustration (GAGS)

MSMIA......... Medical and Sports Music Institute of America (EA)

MS Min........ Master of Science in Mining (PGP)

MS Min E .... Master of Science in Mining Engineering (PGP)

MSMIS........ Master of Science in Management Information Systems (PGP)

MS/MIS........ Master of Science/Management Information Systems

MSML............ Minesweeping Motorlaunch [*Navy*]

MSMLCS....... Mass Service Mainline Cable Systems

MSMM............ Master of Science in Manufacturing Management (PGP)

MsMM .... Meridian Junior College, Meridian, MS [*Library symbol Library of Congress*] (LCLS)

MsMo .... Lawrence County Public Library, Monticello, MS [*Library symbol Library of Congress*] (LCLS)

MS Mot........ Master of Science in Management of Technology (PGP)

MSMP............ Master Sensitized Material Print (MSA)

MSMP............ Modeling and Simulation Master Plan [*Army*]

MSMP............ Multispectral Measurements Program (MCD)

MSMPR........ Mixed-Suspension, Mixed-Product Removal [*Crystallizer*] [*Chemical engineering*]

MSMQ .... Microsoft Message Queue Server [*Computer science*]

MSMR............ Missouri School of Mines Reactor

MSMS............ Machine Strap Makers' Society [*A union*] [*British*]

MSMS............ Marine Safety Management System [*BTS*] (TAG)

MS/MS............ Mass Spectrometry/Mass Spectrometry

MSMS............ Master of Science in Management Science (PGP)

MSMS............ Master of Science in Medical Sciences (PGP)

MS/MS............ Materials Science and Manufacturing in Space [*Program*] [*NASA*]

MSMS............ Max Steiner Memorial Society (EA)

MSMS............ Membership Section for Multihospital Systems [*Later, HCS*] (EA)

MSMS............ Meteorological Systems Management Section

MSMS............ Mutual Security Military Sales

MS-MS .... Tandem Mass Spectroscopy

MSMSA.......	Master of Science in Management Systems Analysis (PGP)
MSMSE.......	Master of Science in Manufacturing Systems Engineering (PGP)
MSMSE.......	Master of Science in Material Science Engineering (PGP)
MSMSEd......	Master of Science in Mathematics and Science Education (GAGS)
MSMSP.......	Project Manager, Surface Missile Systems [Navy]
MsMStA.......	Saint Aloysius Academy, Meridian, MS [Library symbol Library of Congress] (LCLS)
MS MT........	Manuscript, Middle Temple [A publication] (DLA)
MSMT........	Master of Science in Medical Technology (GAGS)
MSMT.........	Measurement (KSC)
MS Mt E.......	Master of Science in Materials Engineering (PGP)
MSMTH.......	Metalsmith [Navy]
MsMU.........	Mississippi State University, Meridian Branch, Meridian, MS [Library symbol Library of Congress] (LCLS)
MSMU.......	Mobile Spectrum Monitoring Unit
MSMus.......	Master of Science in Music (NADA)
MSMusEd....	Master of Science in Music Education (NADA)
MSMV.........	Monk Seal Morbillivirus
MSMV.........	Monostable Multivibrator
MSMW........	Magnetically Suspended Momentum Wheel
MSN..........	Dane County Regional-Truax Field [FAA] (TAG)
MSN..........	Emerson Radio [AMEX symbol] (TTSB)
MSN..........	Emerson Radio Corp. [AMEX symbol] (SAG)
MSN..........	Madison [Wisconsin] [Airport symbol] (OAG)
MSN..........	Main-Stem Node [Botany]
MSN..........	Maintenance and Support Network
MSN..........	Manned Space Network [NASA] (MCD)
MSN..........	Mason
MSN..........	Master of Science in Nursing
MSN..........	Master Serial Number (AAG)
MSN..........	Material Supply Notice (AAG)
MSN..........	Median Sample Number (PDAA)
MSN..........	Message Sequence Number (CAAL)
MSN..........	Microsoft Network [Microsoft Corp.]
MSN..........	Mildly Subnormal [Medicine] (MAE)
MSN..........	Military Serial Number
MSN..........	Military Service Number
MSN..........	Mission (AFM)
MSN..........	Mobil Showcase Network [Television]
MSN..........	Modern Satellite Network [Cable-television system]
MSN..........	Morrison Minerals Ltd. [Toronto Stock Exchange symbol]
MSN..........	Movimiento de Salvacion Nacional [National Salvation Movement] [Colorado Political party] (EY)
MSN..........	Mozambique Support Network (EA)
MSN..........	Multiple Subscriber Number [Telecommunications] (DOM)
MSN..........	Music, Sport, News [Radio broadcasting format]
MsN..........	Public Library of Natchez and Adams County, Natchez, MS [Library symbol Library of Congress] (LCLS)
MsNa..........	Jennie Belle Stephens Smith Library, New Albany, MS [Library symbol Library of Congress] (LCLS)
MSNA.........	Master of Science in Nurse Anesthesia (GAGS)
MSNA.........	Master of Science in Nursing Administration (GAGS)
MSNA.........	Mission Accomplished [Military] (AABC)
MSNAP.......	Merchant Ship Naval Augmentation Program [Navy]
MSNAP.......	Microwave Steerable Null Antenna Processor (MCD)
MSNBC.......	Microsoft Corp. National Broadcasting Co. [Cable news channel]
MSNC.........	Masonic
MSNCDRFAIRECONRON...	Mission Commander, Fleet Air Reconnaissance Squadron (DNAB)
MSND.........	Mercury Substitution and Nucleonic Detection (PDAA)
MSND.........	Mouvement Social pour la Nouvelle Democratie [Cameroon] [Political party] (EY)
MSNE..........	Master of Science in Nuclear Engineering (GAGS)
MsNe..........	Newton Public Library, Newton, MS [Library symbol Library of Congress] (LCLS)
MSNeC.......	Clarke Memorial College, Newton, MS [Library symbol Library of Congress] (LCLS)
MSNEd.......	Master of Science in Nursing Education (NADA)
MS-Net.......	Microsoft Network [Computer science] [Also, MSN] (CDE)
MSNET.......	Microsoft Network [Computer science] (HGAA)
MSNF.........	Milk Solids - Not Fat [Food industry]
MSNF.........	Multisystem Networking Facility [Computer science]
MSNGR.......	Messenger (ADA)
MSNHP.......	Mississippi Natural Heritage Program [Mississippi State Department of Wildlife Conservation] [Jackson, MS] [Information service or system] (IID)
MSNI.........	(Mesitylenesulfonyl)nitroimidazole [Organic chemistry]
MSNik 97.....	Morgan Stanley Group, Inc. [Associated Press] (SAG)
MSN(R).......	Master of Science in Nursing (Research) (PGP)
MSNRY.......	Masonry (MSA)
MSNS.........	Master of Science in Natural Science (PGP)
MSNS.........	MediSense, Inc. [NASDAQ symbol] (SAG)
MSN/SSN.....	Military Service Number / Social Security Number (DNAB)
MS Nsurg.....	Master of Science in Neurosurgery (PGP)
MSNT.........	(Mesitylenesulfonyl)nitrotriazolide [Biochemistry]
MSNuclEng...	Master of Science in Nuclear Engineering (NADA)
MSNY........	Massena [New York] [Seismograph station code, US Geological Survey] (SEIS)
MSNY........	Mattachine Society of New York [Defunct] (EA)
MSO..........	Main Signal Office [British]
MSO..........	Maintenance Standard Order
MSO..........	Maintenance Support Office [Navy]
MSO..........	Malaysian Students' Organization [Australia]
MSO..........	Managed Service Organization [Health Insurance]
MSO..........	Management Science Office
MSO..........	Management Service Organization
MSO..........	Management Systems Office [NASA]
MSO..........	Mandatory Second Surgical Opinion [Health insurance] (GHCT)
MSO..........	Manned Solar Observatory (MCD)
MSO..........	Manned Spacecraft Operations [NASA] (KSC)
MSO..........	Manufacturer's Statement of Origin
MSO..........	Manufacturing Sequence Outline (MCD)
MSO..........	Marginally Stable Orbit [Physics]
MSO..........	Marine Safety Office (MCD)
MSO..........	Marine Staff Officers (EA)
MSO..........	Marketing Services Officer [Insurance]
MSO..........	Mars Surface Operation
MSO..........	Mass Spectrometer Outgasing (KSC)
MSO..........	Master of Science in Orthodontics (GAGS)
M So.........	Master of Sociology
MSO..........	Master of the Science of Oratory
MSO..........	Material Sales Order
MSO..........	Materiel Status Office (MCD)
MSO..........	Medial Superior Olive [Brain anatomy]
MSO..........	Medical Staff Organization (HCT)
MSO..........	Medisave-cum-Subsidized Outpatient Scheme [Medical benefit program] [Singapore]
MSO..........	Member of the Society of Osteopaths [British]
MSO..........	Mesityl Oxide [Also, MO] [Organic chemistry]
MSO..........	Methionine Sulfoxime [Biochemistry]
MSO..........	Military Satellite Organization
MSO..........	Military Service Obligation (AFM)
MSO..........	Military Supply Officer (AFM)
MSO..........	Minesweeper, Ocean [Nonmagnetic] [Navy symbol]
MSO..........	Missabe Southern Railroad
MSO..........	Missile Safety Officer (AFM)
MSO..........	Missoula [Montana] [Seismograph station code, US Geological Survey] (SEIS)
MSO..........	Mixed Services Organisation [British Armed Services]
MSO..........	Mobile Switching Office [Bell System]
MSO..........	Model for Spare Optimization (MCD)
MSO..........	Morale Support Officer [Military] (AABC)
MSO..........	Moss Resources Ltd. [Vancouver Stock Exchange symbol]
MSO..........	Mouvement Socialiste Occitan [Occitanian Socialist Movement] [France Political party] (PPE)
MSO..........	Mozambique Solidarity Office (EA)
MSO..........	Multiple System Operator [Cable television]
MSO..........	Multiple Systems Operator (ACRL)
MSO..........	Multistage Operation (MHDI)
MSo..........	Public Library of the City of Somerville, Somerville, MA [Library symbol Library of Congress] (LCLS)
MSOA........	Military Studies and Operational Analysis (ADA)
MSOB........	Manned Spacecraft Operations Building [NASA] (KSC)
MSOB........	Master of Science in Organizational Behavior
MSobPR......	New England Regional Primate Research Center, Harvard University, Southborough, MA [Library symbol] [Library of Congress] (LCLS)
MSOC........	MANPRINT [Manpower and Personnel Integration] Staff Officer Course [Military] (RDA)
MSOC........	Marine Systems Operational Compiler
MSOC........	Maritime Sector Operations Center [NATO] (NATG)
MSoc.........	Master of Sociology (ADA)
MSocAdmin...	Master of Social Administration
MSOCC.......	Multisatellite Operations Control Center [NASA]
msocc.......	Multisatellite Operations Control Center [NASA] (NAKS)
M Soc E......	Member of the Society of Engineers [British]
MSocPol......	Master of Social Policy
M Soc Sc.....	Master of Social Science (PGP)
MSocSc......	Master of Social Sciences
MSocSci......	Master of Social Sciences
MSocSt......	Master of Social Studies
MSocStud....	Master of Social Studies (ADA)
MSocWk.....	Master of Social Work
MSOD........	Master of Science in Organizational Development (GAGS)
MSOD........	Military Service Obligation Date (AFM)
MSOD........	Mobile Source Operations Division
MSOE........	Master of Science in Ocean Engineering (PGP)
MSOE........	Milwaukee School of Engineering [Wisconsin]
MSOE........	Multiband Spectral Observation Equipment
MSOF........	Multisystem Organ Failure [Medicine] (CPH)
MSOG........	Glenwood and Souris Regional Library, Souris, Manitoba [Library symbol National Library of Canada] (NLC)
MSOG........	Molecular Sieve Oxygen Generating (PDAA)
MSohG.......	Gordon-Conwell Theological Seminary Library, South Hamilton, MA [Library symbol Library of Congress] (LCLS)
MSOIN.......	Minor Subcontractor or IDWA [Interdivisional Work Authorization] Notification [NASA] (NASA)
MSOIN.......	Minor Subcontractor Or Iowa [Interdivisional Work Authorization] Notification
MSOINST....	Maintenance Support Office Instructions [Navy]
MSOL........	Manned Scientific Orbital Laboratory [NASA] (IAA)
MSOLA......	Missionary Sisters of Our Lady of Africa (TOCD)
MSOM........	Master of Science in Organization and Management (PGP)
MSOM........	Modernized Systems Operations Manual [Computer science]
MSom........	Somerset Public Library, Somerset, MA [Library symbol] [Library of Congress] (LCLS)
MSON........	Misonix, Inc. [NASDAQ symbol] (SAG)
MSonHi.......	South Natick Historical, Natural History, and Library Society, South Natick, MA [Library symbol Library of Congress] (LCLS)
MSONW......	Misonix Inc. Wrrt [NASDAQ symbol] (TTSB)
MSOP........	Measurement System Operating Procedure (NG)

MSOP .... Medical School Objectives Project (DMAA)
MSOP .... Mezzo Soprano [*Music*]
MSOP .... Mutual Security Objectives Plan (CINC)
MSOphthal... Master of Ophthalmological Surgery (NADA)
M Sopr .... Mezzo Soprano [*Music*]
MSOR .... Master of Science in Operations Research (GAGS)
MSOR .... Maximum System Operational Range
MSOR .... Missile Systems Operational Report [*Military*] (IAA)
MS Orn Hort... Master of Science in Ornamental Horticulture
MSORS .... Mechanized Sales Office Record System [*Telecommunications*]
            (TEL)
MS(Orth) ...... Master of Surgery (Orthopedic)
MSOS .... Mass Storage Operating System [*Control Data Corp.*] [*Computer
            science*] (NVT)
M So Sc ...... Master of Social Science
M So Se ...... Master of Social Service
MSOT.......... Master of Science in Occupational Technology (PGP)
MSOT.......... Master of Science in Occupational Therapy (GAGS)
MS Otol ...... Master of Science in Otolaryngology (PGP)
M So W .... Master of Social Work
MSOW .... Modular Standoff Weapon [*Ballistic missile*]
MsP .... Jackson County - Pascagoula City Library, Pascagoula, MS [*Library
            symbol Library of Congress*] (LCLS)
MSP............ Macrophage Stimulating Protein [*Biochemistry*]
MSP............ Magnetic Scalar Potential
MSP............ Maintenance Service Plan
MSP............ Maintenance Support Plan [*or Program*] [*Army*]
MSP............ Maintenance Surveillance Procedure (IEEE)
MSP............ Management System Programmers Ltd. (NITA)
MSP............ Manager Software Products Ltd. (NITA)
MSP............ Manager Support Programs (MCD)
MSP............ Manual Switching Position (IAA)
MSP............ Marine Security Program [*FHWA*] (TAG)
MSP............ Marine Shale Processors, Inc. (EFIS)
MSP............ Maritime Shore Patrol
MSP............ Market Stabilization Price [*Department of Agriculture*]
MSP............ Mass Storage Processor [*Honeywell, Inc.*]
MSP............ Master of School Psychology (PGP)
MSP............ Master of Science in Pharmacy
MSP............ Master of Science in Planning (PGP)
MSP............ Master of Social Psychology (PGP)
M Sp .... Master of Speech
MSP............ Master of Speech Pathology (PGP)
MSP............ Master Shuttle Verification Plan (MCD)
MSP............ Master Simulator Program (NVT)
MSP............ Matched Sale-Purchase Agreement [*Business term*]
MSP............ Material Support Plan [*or Program*]
MSP............ Maximum Silo Price [*Farming terminology*]
MSP............ Maximum Sound Pressure
MSP............ Measurement Sensitive Products (DICI)
MSP............ Mededelingen Spinozahuis [*A publication*] (BJA)
MSP............ Media Suite Pro [*Computer software*] (CDE)
MSP............ Medical Specialist
MSP............ Medium Side Prong [*Lamp base type*] (NTCM)
MSP............ Medium-Speed Printer (AABC)
MSP............ Medium Stressed Platform
MSP............ Merozoite Surface Protein [*Of protozoa*]
MSP............ Metal Splash Pan (AAG)
MSP............ Microsoft Paint [*Computer science*] (CDE)
MSP............ Microsoft Solution Provider [*Computer science*] (CDE)
MSP............ Microspectrophotometry
MSP............ Microsuspension Seeded Polymerization (DICI)
MSP............ Military Space Program (AAG)
MSP............ Millisecond Pulsar [*Astronomy*]
MSP............ Minesweeper, Patrol [*Navy*] (DNAB)
MSP............ Miniature Series of Painters [*A publication*]
MSP............ Minimum Sustaining Power
MSP............ Minneapolis-St. Paul [*Minnesota*] [*Airport symbol*]
MSP............ Miscellaneous Small Parts
MSP............ Missile Setting Panel [*Military*] (CAAL)
MSP............ Missile Simulator Plug
MSP............ Missile Support Plan
MSP............ Missionaries of St. Paul (TOCD)
msp .... Missionaries of St. Paul (TOCD)
MSP............ Mission Scientifique en Perse (BJA)
MSP............ Mission Support Plan (MCD)
MSP............ Mobile Support Package (MCD)
MSP............ Moderata Samlingspartiet [*Moderate Unity Party*] [*Sweden Political
            party*] (PPE)
MSP............ Mode Select Panel (IAA)
MSP............ Modular System Programs [*IBM Corp.*]
MSP............ Monosodium Orthophosphate [*Inorganic chemistry*]
MSP............ Monosodium Phosphate (EDCT)
MSP............ Morgan Stan Fin 8.20% Cp Uts [*NYSE symbol*] (TTSB)
MSP............ Morgan Stanley Finance PLC Capital Unit [*NYSE symbol*] (SAG)
msp .... Mortuus sine Prole [*Dead without Issue*] [*Latin*] (WGA)
MSP............ Mosaic Sensor Program (MCD)
MSP............ Most Significant Position (CMD)
MSP............ Motorized Set Point (IAA)
MSP............ Mount St. Thomas [*Philippines*] [*Seismograph station code, US
            Geological Survey*] (SEIS)
MSP............ Mouse Serum Protein [*Biochemistry*] (DAVI)
MSP............ Movimento Socialista Popular [*Popular Socialist Movement*] [*Portugal
            Political party*] (PPE)
MSP............ Multiprocessing Server Pack [*Computer science*] (CDE)

MSP............ Multipurpose Semi-Submersible Platform (DNAB)
MSP............ Multisensor Processor (CAAL)
MSP............ Multi-Tech Supervisory Protocol [*Telecommunications*] (PCM)
MSP............ Mutual Security Program
MSP............ Mutual Support Program
MSP............ Servicio de Vigilancia Aerea del Ministerio de Seguridad Publica
            [*Costa Rica*] [*ICAO designator*] (FAAC)
MSPA......... Maine Sardine Packers Association (EA)
MSPA......... Marin Self-Publishers Association (EA)
MSPA......... Master of Science in Professional Accountancy (PGP)
MSPA......... Master of Science in Public Administration (GAGS)
MSPA......... Master of Speech Pathology and Audiology (PGP)
MSPA......... Member, Society of Pension Actuaries [*American Society of Pension
            Actuari es*] [*Designation awarded by*]
MSPA......... Migrant and Seasonal Worker Protection Act (WPI)
MSPA......... Modified Sodium Polyacrylate [*Organic chemistry*]
MSP & SSM... Minneapolis, St. Paul & Sault Ste. Marie Railway Co. (IIA)
MSPAW ...... Miedzynarodowe Stowarzyszenie Przyjaciele Angkor Wat
            [*International Association of Friends of Angkor Wat*] [*Multinational
            association based in Poland*] (EAIO)
MSPB......... Medical Specialist Preference Blank
MSPB......... Merit Systems Protection Board [*Formerly, Civil Service Commission*]
MSPC......... Manufacturer Standard Paint Color [*Motor vehicle specification*]
MSPC......... Medical Specialist Corps [*Military*]
MSPC......... MOPAR Scat Pack Club (EA)
MSPC......... Multivariate Statistical Process Control
MSPCL....... Lower Fort Garry National Historic Park, Parks Canada [*Parc
            Historique National Lower Fort Garry, Parcs Canada*] Selkirk,
            Manitoba [*Library symbol National Library of Canada*] (NLC)
MSPCP...... Mobile Source Pollution Control Program [*Environmental Protection
            Agency*]
MSPD........ Master of Social Planning and Development (ADA)
MSPD........ Matrix Solid-Phase Dispersion [*Analytical chemistry*]
MSPD........ Maximum Speed
MSPD........ Mulheres Portuguesas Social-Domocratas [*An association*] (EAIO)
MSPE........ Maintenance Safety and Protection Equipment (AFIT)
MSPE........ Master of Science in Petroleum Engineering (PGP)
MSPE........ Master of Science in Physical Education
MSPE........ Master Plate [*Tool*] (AAG)
MSpecEd .... Master of Special Education
MSpEd .... Master of Special Education
MsPeM .... Mississippi Gulf Coast Junior College, Perkinston, MS [*Library
            symbol Library of Congress*] (LCLS)
MSPEQ .... Morgan Stanley Group [*Associated Press*] (SAG)
MSpeSJ....... Saint Joseph's Abbey, Spencer, MA [*Library symbol Library of
            Congress*] (LCLS)
MSPetE...... Master of Science in Petroleum Engineering (GAGS)
MSPetEng... Master of Science in Petroleum Engineering (NADA)
MSP Ex...... Master of Science in Exercise Physiology (PGP)
MSPEx....... Master of Science in Physiology of Exercise (GAGS)
MSPF........ Maritime Special Purpose Force (COE)
MSPF........ Multispectral Photographic Facility
MSPFW....... Multishot Portable Flame Weapon (DNAB)
MSPG....... Magnetic Shock Pulse Generator (IAA)
MSPG....... Master of Science in Psychology (PGP)
MSPG....... Materiel Support Planning Guidance [*Military*] (AABC)
MSPG....... Measure Specific Performance Guarantee [*Calculation*] (AAGC)
MSPG....... MindSpring Enterprises [*NASDAQ symbol*] (TTSB)
MSPG....... MindSpring Enterprises, Inc. [*NASDAQ symbol*] (SAG)
MSPGN...... Mesangial Proliferative Glomerulonephritis [*Nephrology*]
MSPH....... Master of Science in Poultry Husbandry
MSPH....... Master of Science in Public Health
MsPh .... Neshoba County Library, Philadelphia, MS [*Library symbol Library of
            Congress*] (LCLS)
MSPharm .... Master of Science in Pharmacy (NADA)
MSPHE....... Master of Science in Public Health Engineering
MSPH Ed ... Master of Science in Public Health Education
MS Phr .... Master of Science in Pharmacy (PGP)
MS Phys Op... Master of Science in Physiological Optics (PGP)
MsPi .... Crosby Memorial Library, Picayune, MS [*Library symbol Library of
            Congress*] (LCLS)
MSPI.......... Modified Ship Plan Index
MSPIR....... Master of Science in Personnel and Industrial Relations
MSPLT....... Master Source Program Library Tape [*Computer science*] (BUR)
MsPMF .... United States Department of Commerce, National Marine Fisheries
            Service, Pascagoula, MS [*Library symbol Library of Congress*]
            (LCLS)
MSPM Rehab... Master of Science in Physical Medicine and Rehabilitation (PGP)
MSPN........ Medical Student's Progress Note (DMAA)
MSPNGE..... Master of Science in Petroleum and Natural Gas Engineering (PGP)
MSPO .... Mercury Support Planning Office (MUGU)
MSPO .... Meridian Sports [*NASDAQ symbol*] (TTSB)
MSPO .... Meridian Sports, Inc. [*NASDAQ symbol*] (SAG)
MSPO .... Military Support Planning Officer [*Civil Defense*]
MSPO .... Mission System Project Office [*Military*] (CAAL)
MsPog .... Harriette Person Memorial Library, Port Gibson, MS [*Library symbol
            Library of Congress*] (LCLS)
MSPoly .... Master of Science in Polymers (GAGS)
MsPon .... Dixie Regional Library, Pontotoc, MS [*Library symbol Library of
            Congress*] (LCLS)
MsPop .... Poplarville Public Library, Poplarville, MS [*Library symbol Library of
            Congress*] (LCLS)
MSPP.......... Merit System Protection Plan
MSPP.......... Michigan Screening Profile of Parenting [*Psychology*]

MsPr .... Jefferson Davis County Library, Prentiss, MS [*Library symbol Library of Congress*] (LCLS)
MSPR .... Master Spares Positioning Resolver [*Data processing*]
MSPR .... Medical System Program Review [*Army*] (RDA)
MSPR .... Model State Packaging Regulation [*National Institute of Standards and Technology*]
MSPr .... Morgan Stanley 9.36% Pfd [*NYSE symbol*] (TTSB)
MSPRB .... Meteorological Satellite Program Review Board [*NOAA and NASA*]
MSPrB .... Morgan Stanley 8.88% Dep Pfd [*NYSE symbol*] (TTSB)
MSPrC .... Morgan Stanley 8.75% Dep Pfd [*NYSE symbol*] (TTSB)
MSPrD .... Morgan Stanly 7.375% Dep Pfd [*NYSE symbol*] (TTSB)
MSPRS .... Multispectral Photographic Reconnaissance (MCD)
MSPS .... Maneuvering Satellite Propulsion System (MCD)
MSPS .... Master of Science in Planning Studies (PGP)
MSPS .... Master of Science in Psychological Services (GAGS)
MSPS .... Megasample per Second (IAA)
MSPS .... Mega Symbols per Second (MCD)
MSpS .... Misioneros del Espiritu Santo [*Missionaries of the Holy Spirit*] [*Mexico*] (EAIO)
msps .... Missionaries of the Holy Spirit (TOCD)
MSpS .... Missionaries of the Holy Spirit (TOCD)
MSPS .... Mobilization Station Planning System [*MTMC*] (TAG)
MSPS .... Modular Space Power Station
MSPS .... Multisource Processing System (MCD)
MSPS .... Myocardial Stress Perfusion Scintigram [*Medicine*]
MSPT .... Master of Science in Physical Therapy (GAGS)
MSpThy ...... Master of Speech Therapy (ADA)
MS Pw .... Mississippi Power Co. [*Associated Press*] (SAG)
Msq .... Masque [*Record label*]
MSQ .... Minnesota Satisfaction Questionnaire
MSQ .... Minsk [*Former USSR Airport symbol*] (OAG)
MSQ .... Mosquito Construction Gold [*Vancouver Stock Exchange symbol*]
MSQT .... Missile Ship Qualification Test [*Navy*] (NVT)
MSQT .... Modified Ship Qualification Test
MsR .... Capital Area Regional Library, Raymond, MS [*Library symbol Library of Congress*] (LCLS)
MSR .... Egypt Air [*ICAO designator*] (FAAC)
MSR .... Machine Status Register [*Computer science*] (OA)
MSR .... Machine Stress Rated
MSR .... Macrophage Scavenger Receptor [*Immunology*]
MSR .... Magnetic Shift Register
MSR .... Magnetic Silencing Range [*Navy*] (DOMA)
MSR .... Magnetic Silencing Ranger (DWSG)
MSR .... Magnetic Storage Ring [*Computer science*]
MSR .... Magnetic Stripe Reader (IAA)
MSR .... Magnetic Superresolution
MSR .... Main Supply Road [*or Route*]
MSR .... Makassar [*Sulawesi, Indonesia*] [*Airport symbol*] (AD)
MSR .... Male Seniors [*International Bowhunting Organization*] [*Class equipment*]
MSR .... Mammalian Selectivity Ratio (FFDE)
MSR .... Management Systems Representative (MCD)
MSR .... Manual Sliding Roof [*Automotive accessory*]
MSR .... Manufacturing Service Request (MCD)
MSR .... Manufacturing Specification Request (AAG)
MSR .... Marketing Service Representative
MSR .... Marketing Support Representative
MSR .... Market Share Reporter [*A publication*]
MSR .... Mark Sense Reading
MSR .... Mark Sheet Reader [*Computer science*] (BUR)
MSR .... Mass Storage Resident [*Computer science*] (IEEE)
MS (R) .... Master of Science in Research
MSR .... Master Stock Record (DNAB)
MSR .... Material Status Report [*AEC*]
MSR .... Maximum Steam Rate [*Nuclear energy*] (NRCH)
MSR .... McDonnell Simulator Recorder [*McDonnell Douglas Corp.*] (MCD)
MSR .... Mean Spring Rise [*Tides and currents*]
MSR .... Mean Square Residual
MSR .... Mean Square Root (IAA)
MSR .... Mechanized Storage and Retrieval [*Computer science*]
MSR .... Medium Stocking Rate [*Agriculture*] (OA)
MSR .... Member of the Society of Radiographers [*British*]
MSR .... Membrane-Spanning Region [*Cytology*]
MSR .... Memory Select Register (NITA)
MSR .... Merchant Ship Reactor [*Navy*]
MSR .... Message Has Been Misrouted [*Communications*]
MSR .... Metal Seal Ring
MSR .... Metalsmith, Ship Repair [*Navy*]
MSR .... Meteorological Sounding Rocket
MSR .... Microsoft Research Center
MSR .... Micro Support Resource Corp. [*Atlanta, GA*]
MSR .... Midwest Sunbeam Registry (EA)
MSR .... Milestone Status Report [*Military*] (AFIT)
MSR .... Mineral-Surface Roof [*Technical drawings*]
MSR .... Mine Smelter and Refinery Databank [*Commodities Research Unit Ltd.*] [*Information service or system*] (CRD)
MSR .... Minesweeper, Patrol [*Navy symbol Obsolete*]
MSR .... Minesweeper River [*Navy symbol*] (VNW)
MSR .... Minimum Sales Responsibility [*Automotive sales quotas*]
MSR .... Minimum Security Requirement
MSR .... Minimum Sustaining Rate (MCD)
MSR .... Missile Scoring Reliability (MCD)
MSR .... Missile Site RADAR [*Army*] (MCD)
MSR .... Missile Site Range
MSR .... Missile Surface RADAR (MCD)

MSR .... Mission Success Ratio [*Military*] (CAAL)
MSR .... Mission Support Recording [*Deep Space Instrumentation Facility, NASA*]
MSR .... Mission Support Room [*NASA*] (KSC)
MSR .... Mobile Sea Range (NVT)
MSR .... Mode Status Register (IAA)
MSR .... Modification Status Report (KSC)
MSR .... Module Support Rack (NASA)
MSR .... Moisture Separator Reheater (NRCH)
MSR .... Molten-Salt Reactor
MSR .... Monthly Status Report [*Navy*]
MSR .... Montserrat [*ANSI three-letter standard code*] (CNC)
MSR .... Movimiento Socialista Revolucionario [*Revolutionary Socialist Movement*] [*Panama*] [*Political party*] (PPW)
MSR .... MSR Exploration [*AMEX symbol*] (TTSB)
MSR .... MSR Exploration Ltd. [*Associated Press*] (SAG)
MSR .... Multi-Carrier Station Radio [*or Remote*] Control Equipment (PDAA)
MSR .... Multicomet Sample Return [*Space science*]
MSR .... Multijunction Semiconductor Rectifier
MSR .... Multispeed Repeater
MSR .... Munster [*Germany Airport symbol*] (OAG)
MSR .... Muscle Stretch Reflexes [*Medicine*] (DAVI)
MSR .... Musicians for Social Responsibility (EA)
MSR .... St. Louis Art Museum, St. Louis, MO [*OCLC symbol*] (OCLC)
MSRA .... Master of Science in Recreation Administration (PGP)
MSRA .... Middle States Regatta Association (EA)
MSRA .... Midwest Ski Representatives Association (EA)
MSRA .... Multiple Shoe Retailers' Association [*British*] (BI)
MSRadSc .... Master of Science in Radiation Science (GAGS)
MSR/ASR .... Main Supply Route/Alternative Supply Route (MCD)
MSRB .... Margaret Sanger Research Bureau [*Defunct*] (EA)
MSRB .... Metalsmith, Ship Repair, Blacksmith [*Navy*]
MSRB .... Metrology Standards Requirements Board (ACII)
MSRB .... Municipal Securities Rulemaking Board [*Securities and Exchange Commission*]
MSRC .... Marine Sciences Research Center [*State University of New York at Stony Brook*] [*Research center*] (RCD)
MSRC .... Marine Spill Response Corp. [*An association*]
MSRC .... Master of Science in Resource Conservation (PGP)
MSRC .... Materiel Studies Review Committee [*Army*]
MSRC .... Medical and Surgical Relief Committee [*Defunct*] (EA)
MSRC .... Metalsmith, Ship Repair, Coppersmith [*Navy*]
MSRD .... Marine Sciences Research Division [*Now Coastal and Arctic Research Division*] (USDC)
MSRD .... Mean Square Relative Displacement [*Spectra*]
MSRD .... Mobile Servicing and Repair Detachment [*Military British*]
MSRE .... Master of Science in Real Estate and Urban Affairs
MSRE .... Master of Science in Religious Education (PGP)
MSRE .... Molten Salt Reactor Experiment
MSRE .... Moon Signal Rejection Equipment (AFM)
MSRec .... Master of Science in Recreation (NADA)
MSRet .... Master of Science in Retailing (NADA)
MSRF .... Metalsmith, Ship Repair, Forger-Anglesmith [*Navy*]
MSRF .... Microwave Space Research Facility
MSRFT .... Minesweeper Refresher Training [*Navy*] (NVT)
MSRG .... Medieval Settlement Research Group [*British*] (DBA)
MSRG .... Member of the Society of Remedial Gymnasts [*British*]
MSRG .... Moated Sites Research Group (EA)
MSRG .... Modular Shift Register Generator
MsRH .... Hinds Junior College, Raymond, MS [*Library symbol Library of Congress*] (LCLS)
MSRI .... Mathematical Sciences Research Institute [*University of California, Berkeley*] (PDAA)
MSRI .... Mathematical Sciences Research Institute [*University of Minnesota*] (PDAA)
MsRi .... Pine Forest Regional Library, Richton, MS [*Library symbol Library of Congress*] (LCLS)
MSRIS .... Molten-Salt Reactor Information System
MSRK .... Mathias-Soave-Redlich-Kwong [*Equation of state*]
MSRL .... Marine Sciences Research Laboratory [*Canada*] (MSC)
MSRL .... Mobile Secondary Reference Laboratory
MSRM .... Main Steam Radiation Monitor (IEEE)
MSRMNT .... Measurement
MSRMP .... Master of Science in Radiological Medical Physics (PGP)
MSRNW .... North-West Regional Library, Swan River, Manitoba [*Library symbol National Library of Canada*] (NLC)
MSRO .... Missile System Requirements Outline (MCD)
MSRP .... Management Sciences Research Project [*University of California*] (MCD)
MSRP .... Manufacturer's Suggested Retail Price
MSRP .... Massive Selective Retaliatory Power (NATG)
MSRP .... Meteorological Sounding Rocket Program [*NASA*]
MSRP .... Missile, Space and Range Pioneers (EA)
MSRP .... Mission Support Real Property [*NASA*] (KSC)
MSRPP .... Multidimensional Scale for Rating Psychiatric Patients
MS(R)PT ..... Master of Science (Research) in Physical Therapy (PGP)
MSR (R) ...... Member of the Society of Radiographers (Radiography) [*British*]
MSRR .... Mission and System Requirements Review [*NASA*]
MSRS .... Main Steam Radiation System (IEEE)
MSRS .... Master of Science in Recreational Studies (PGP)
MSRS .... Materiel System Requirements Specification [*Military*]
MSRS .... Metalsmith, Ship Repair, Sheet Metal Worker [*Navy*]
MSRS .... Meteoroid Shield Release System (MCD)
MSRS .... Military Spending Research Services, Inc. [*Information service or system*] (IID)

MSRS	Missile Strike Reporting System
MSRS	Multiple Stylus Recording System (OA)
MSRSIM	Missile Site RADAR Simulation [*Missile system evaluation*] (RDA)
MSRT	Mean Supply Response Time
MSR (T)	Member of the Society of Radiographers (Radiotherapy) [*British*]
MSRT	Missile System Readiness Test (IEEE)
MSRT	Mobile Subscriber Radio Terminal [*Army*]
MSRTE	Misroute
MS-RTP	Micelle-Stabilized Room-Temperature Phosphorescence
MSRTS	Migrant Student Records Transfer System (GFGA)
MS Russ	Morgan Stanley Russia & New Europe Fund, Inc. [*Associated Press*] (SAG)
MSRV	Main Steam Relief Valve [*Nuclear energy*] (NRCH)
MSRY	Masonry
mss	Illuminated Manuscript (VRA)
MSS	Magnetic Spark Spectrometer (PDAA)
MSS	Magnetic Stereotaxis System [*Surgery*]
MSS	Magnetic Storm Satellite [*Air Force/NASA*]
MSS	Main Steam System [*Nuclear energy*] (NRCH)
MSS	Main Support Structure (NRCH)
MSS	Maintenance Standards Study (MCD)
MSS	Maintenance Status System (MCD)
mss	Maintenance Status System (NAKS)
MSS	Maintenance Support Schedule [*Air Force*] (AFM)
MSS	Major Stationary Source [*Environmental Protection Agency*]
MSS	Make Suitable Substitution
MSS	Managed Security Services
MSS	Management Science Systems (IEEE)
MSS	Management Statistics Subsystem (TEL)
MSS	Management Summary Sheets (MCD)
MSS	Management Supplier Selection (AAG)
MSS	Management Support Staff [*Social Security Administration*]
MSS	Management Support System (USDC)
MSS	Management Systems Study (MCD)
MSS	Manned Space Station [*NASA*]
MSS	Manual Safety Switch
mss	Manufacturers Standardization Society (NAKS)
mss	Manufacturers Standardization Society (AAGC)
MSS	Manufacturers Standardization Society of the Valve and Fittings Industry (EA)
MSS	Manuscripta [*Manuscripts*] [*Latin*]
MSS	Manuscript, Signed
MSS	MAP [*Manufacturing Automation Protocol*]/One System Software [*Industrial Networking, Inc.*]
MSS	Marine Safety Services [*British*] (DCTA)
MSS	Marital Satisfaction Scale [*Psychology*] (DAVI)
MSS	Maritime Support Service
MSS	Mary Stuart Society of America (EA)
MSS	Massage
MSS	Massena [*New York*] [*Airport symbol*] (OAG)
MSS	Mass Storage Service [*Computer science*]
MSS	Mass Storage System [*Computer science*]
MSS	Mastergroup Surveillance System [*AT & T*]
MSS	Master of Sanitary Science
MSS	Master of Science in Safety (GAGS)
MSS	Master of Selected Studies (PGP)
MSS	Master of Social Science
MSS	Master of Social Service
MSS	Master of Social Studies
MSS	Master of Sport Science (GAGS)
MSS	Master Station Subsystem
MSS	Master Surveillance Station [*Air Force*]
MSS	Master Switching Station (MCD)
MSS	Master System Schedule (MCD)
MSS	Mayo Smith Society (EA)
MSS	Mean Solar Second (IAA)
MSS	Measurement Specialities, Inc. [*AMEX symbol*] (SAG)
MSS	Measurement Specialties [*AMEX symbol*] (TTSB)
MSS	Measurement Standard Sensitivity (DICI)
MSS	Mechanical and Structural Subsystems (MCD)
MSS	Mechanically Separated Spleen [*Food technology*]
MSS	Mechanical Speed Switch
MSS	Mechanical Support System (MCD)
mss	Mechanical Support Systems (NAKS)
MSS	Medical Service School [*Air Force*] (AFM)
MSS	Medical Social Services
MSS	Medical Superintendents' Society (DAVI)
MSS	Medium Survey Ship [*Marine science*] (MSC)
MSS	Megasample per Second (IAA)
MSS	Member of the Statistical Society [*British*] (ROG)
MSS	Memory System Security [*Computer science*] (ECII)
MSS	Men's Social Services [*Salvation Army*]
MSS	Mental Status Schedule [*Psychology*]
MSS	Message Support Subsystem (MCD)
MSS	Message Switching Station [*Telecommunications*] (CET)
MSS	Message Switching System
MSS	Messtetten [*Federal Republic of Germany*] [*Seismograph station code, US Geological Survey*] (SEIS)
MSS	Metal Spring Seal
MSS	Metastable State (IAA)
MSS	Meteorological Satellite Section
MSS	Meter Stamp Society (EA)
MSS	Methylprednisolone Sodium Succinate [*Antirheumatoid compound*]
MSS	Metropolitan Speleological Society [*Australia*]
MSS	Mexican-Spanish Speaking (OICC)

MSS	Microwave Switching Station
MSS	Midcourse Surveillance System (MCD)
MSS	Midwest Sociological Society (AEBS)
MSS	Military Security Service [*RVNAF*]
MSS	Military Supply Standards [*DoD*] (MCD)
MSS	Mine Search System [*Navy*] (DOMA)
MSS	Minesweeper, Special [*Device*] [*Navy symbol*]
MSS	Miniature Signaling System [*Railway term*] (DCTA)
MSS	Miniature Stepping Switch
MSS	Ministry of Social Security [*British*]
MSS	Minnesota Satisfactoriness Scale [*Job performance test*]
MSS	Minor Surgery Suite [*Medicine*] (DAVI)
MSS	Missile Safety Set (IAA)
MSS	Missile Security Squadron
MSS	Missile Select Switch
MSS	Missile Sight System [*Army*]
MSS	Missile Stabilization System
MSS	Missile Station Select
MSS	Missile Subsystem
MSS	Missile Support Stand (MCD)
MSS	Mission Simulator System
MSS	Mission Specialist Station [*NASA*] (NASA)
mss	Mission Specialist Station [*NASA*] (NAKS)
mss	Mission Status Summary [*NASA*] (NAKS)
MSS	Mission Status Summary (MCD)
MSS	Mission Support Site [*Army*]
MSS	Mission System Simulator (MCD)
MSS	Mississauga Public Library [*UTLAS symbol*]
MSS	Mixed Spectrum Superheater [*Nuclear energy*]
MSS	Mobile Satellite Service
MSS	Mobile Satellite System (DA)
MSS	Mobile Service Structure (KSC)
mss	Mobile Service Structure (NAKS)
MSS	Mobile Servicing System [*For space station*]
MSS	Mobility Subsystem (KSC)
MSS	Modelling and Simulation Studies [*Marine science*] (MSC)
MSS	Model Skin Surface [*Artificial skin*]
MSS	Modern Satellite Systems, Inc. [*Whitehouse Station, NJ*] [*Telecommunications*] (TSSD)
MSS	Mode Selection Switch (KSC)
MSS	Mode Sickness Susceptibility (KSC)
MSS	Modified Scram System [*Nuclear energy*] (NRCH)
MSS	Modify System State (AAEL)
MSS	Modular Space Station
MSS	Moored Sonobuoy System (MCD)
MSS	Moored Surveillance System [*To detect and destroy enemy submarines*] [*Navy*]
MSS	Morris Air Service [*ICAO designator*] (FAAC)
MSS	Motion Sickness Susceptibility (MCD)
MSS	Motor Surveillance Service [*MTMC*] (TAG)
MSS	Movement Shorthand Society [*Later, Center for Sutton Movement Writing*] (EA)
MSS	Mucus-Stimulating Substance
MSS	Multibeam Steering System
MSS	Multi-LAN Storage System [*Computer science*] (HGAA)
MSS	Multiple Sclerosis Society [*British*]
MSS	Multiple Selling Service (OA)
MSS	Multiple Steady States [*Chemical engineering*]
MSS	Multispectral Scanner [*or Sensor*]
mss	Multispectral Scanner System (NAKS)
MSS	Multispectral Scanner System
MSS	Multitask Single Stream System (NITA)
MSS	Muscular Subaortic Stenosis [*Cardiology*]
MSS	Music Story Series [*A publication*]
MSS	Special Minesweeper [*Navy symbol*]
MSs	Swansea Free Public Library, Swansea, MA [*Library symbol*] [*Library of Congress*] (LCLS)
MSSA	Maintenance Supply Services Agency (NATG)
MSSA	Manchester Scales of Social Adaptation [*Psychology*]
MSSA	Master of Science in Social Administration (GAGS)
MSSA	Master Safeguards and Security Agreements (DOMA)
MSSA	Midland Steel Stockholders Association [*British*] (DBA)
MSSA	Military Selective Service Act (OICC)
MSSA	Military Subsistence Supply Agency [*Later, Defense Subsistence Supply Center*]
MSsA	Missionaries of the Holy Apostles [*Roman Catholic men's religious order*]
mssa	Missionaries of the Holy Apostles (TOCD)
MSSA	Missionary Servants of St. Anthony [*Roman Catholic women's religious order*]
MSSA	Modification of Special Service Authorization [*FCC*] (NTCM)
MSS & H	Master of Science in Speech and Hearing
MSSanE	Master of Science in Sanitary Engineering
MSS AS	Multistatic Sonar System Acoustic Source (DOMA)
MSSB	Mid-State Federal Savings Bank (EFIS)
MSSB	Missile Servicing and Storage Building [*Military*] (IAA)
MSSC	Main Storage Stock Control [*Computer science*] (IAA)
MSSC	Management System for Support Contracts [*Social Security Administration*]
MSSC	Mass Storage System Communications (NITA)
MSSC	Mass Storage System Communicator [*Computer science*] (IBMDP)
MSSc	Mass Storage System Control [*Computer science*] (BUR)
MS Sc	Master of Sanitary Science
MS Sc	Master of Social Science
MSSc	Master of Surgical Science, University of Dundee [*British*] (DBQ)

MSSC.......... Medium SEAL [*Sea, Air, and Land*] Support Craft [*Navy symbol*]
MSSC.......... Metropolitan School Study Council [*Columbia University*] (AEE)
MSSC.......... Military Standard and Specification Committee
MSSC.......... Military Store Staff Corps [*British military*] (DMA)
MSSC.......... Missile System Software Center
MSSC.......... Missionary Society of St. Columban (EAIO)
MSSC.......... Mobile Service Switching Center
MSSCB........ Missionary Sisters of St. Charles Borromeo (TOCD)
MSSCC........ Military Space Surveillance Control Center (MUGU)
MSSCC........ Missionaries of the Sacred Hearts of Jesus and Mary (TOCD)
msscc......... Missionaries of the Sacred Hearts of Jesus and Mary (TOCD)
MSSCC........ Missionarii a Sacris Cordibus Jesu et Mariae [*Missionaries of the Sacred Hearts of Jesus and Mary*] [*Roman Catholic men's religious order*]
MSSCC........ Multicolor Spin-Scan Cloudcover Camera
MSSCE........ Mixed Spectrum Superheater Critical Experiment [*Nuclear energy*]
MSSCS........ Manned Space Station Communications System [*NASA*]
MSSD.......... Model Secondary School for the Deaf (EA)
MSSE.......... Master of Science in Sanitary Engineering
MSSE.......... Master of Science in Secondary Education of Students (who are Deaf or Hard of Hearing)
MSSE.......... Missile System Support Equipment
MSS/EC....... Missile System Supervisor/Engagement Controller [*Military*] (CAAL)
MSSEng....... Master of Science in Sanitary Engineering (NADA)
MSSG......... Marine Expeditionary Unit Service Support Group (DOMA)
MSSG......... Message
MSSG......... Multiple Sclerosis Susceptibility Gene [*Medicine*] (DB)
MSSH.......... Master of Science in Speech and Hearing (PGP)
MSSH.......... Springfield Hospital, Medical Center Library, Springfield, MA [*Library symbol Library of Congress*] (LCLS)
MSSI........... Master of Science in Strategic Intelligence (PGP)
MSSJ.......... Missionary Servants of St. Joseph [*Roman Catholic women's religious order*]
MSSJ.......... Multiple Subsonic Jet
MSSL.......... Management Systems Summary List
MSSL.......... Master of Science in Speech and Language (PGP)
MSSL.......... Missile System Stockage List (AFIT)
MSSL.......... Mullard Space Science Laboratory [*University of London*] (PDAA)
MSSM......... Mars Spinning Support Module [*NASA*] (KSC)
MSSM......... Master of Science in Science Management (PGP)
MSSM......... Master of Science in Systems Management (PGP)
MSSM......... Missionary Sisters of the Society of Mary [*Italy*] (EAIO)
MsSM......... Mississippi State University, State College, MS [*Library symbol Library of Congress*] (LCLS)
MSSM......... Mount Sinai School of Medicine [*New York*] (PDAA)
MSSM......... Multiple-Sine-Slit Microdensitometer (PDAA)
MSSMS........ Munitions Section of Strategic Missile Squadron (AAG)
MSSN......... Mean Square Signal-to-Noise (IAA)
MSSN......... Mission
MSSNRY...... Missionary
MSSNSW..... Multiple Sclerosis Society of New South Wales [*Australia*]
MSSP.......... International Association of Marble, Slate and Stone Polishers, Rubbers and Sawyers, Tile and Marble Setters' Helpers, and Marble Mosaic and Terrazzo Workers' Helpers [*Later, Tile, Marble, Terrazzo Finishers, Shopworkers, and Granite Cutters International Union*] (EA)
MSSP.......... Miscellaneous Small Special Projects (AAG)
MSSP.......... Missionary Society of Saint Paul [*Australia*]
MSSp.......... Mission Sisters of the Holy Spirit [*Roman Catholic religious order*]
MSSP.......... Model Seafood Surveillance Project [*National Marine Fisheries Service*]
MSSPA........ Master of Speech Pathology and Audiology (GAGS)
MSSPA........ Missionary Society of St. Paul the Apostle (EA)
MSSPC........ Missionary Sisters of St. Peter Claver (EA)
MS Sp Ed .... Master of Science in Special Education (PGP)
MS-SPRING... Multiplex-Section, Shared-Protection Rings
MSSQ......... Mission Support Squadron
MSSQ......... Multiple Sclerosis Society of Queensland [*Australia*]
MSSR......... Mars Soil [*or Surface*] Sample Return
MSSR......... Medical Society for the Study of Radiesthesia (EA)
MSSR......... Mixed Spectrum Superheat Reactor
MSSR......... Mobility, Survivability, Sizing Recommendations (MCD)
MSSR......... Monopulse Secondary Surveillance RADAR (DA)
MSSS.......... Main Steam Supply System [*Nuclear energy*] (NRCH)
MSSS.......... Maintenance and Service Subsystem (IAA)
MSSS.......... Maintenance Supply Services System (NATG)
MSSS.......... Manned Space Station Simulator [*NASA*] (MUGU)
MSSS.......... Manned Static Space Simulator
MSSS.......... Manuscripts, Signed
MSSS.......... Mass Spectral Search System [*National Bureau of Standards, Environmental Protection Agency, and National Institutes of Health*] [*Database*]
MSSS.......... Master of Science in Social Science
MSSS.......... Missionary Sisters of the Most Blessed Sacrament [*Roman Catholic religious order*]
MSSS.......... Mobile Spectrum Search System
MSSS.......... Mobile Submarine Simulator System (DWSG)
MSSS.......... Multiple-Start Systematic Sampling [*Statistics*]
MSSS.......... San Salvador/Ilopango Internacional [*El Salvador*] [*ICAO location identifier*] (ICLI)
MSSSM-MMS... Missionary Sisters of the Society of Saint Mary - Marist Missionary Sisters (EA)
MSSST......... Meeting Street School Screening Test [*Used to detect learning disabilities*]
MSSSW........ Mass Spectral Search System-Wiley [*Cornell University*] [*Database*]

MSST.......... Manufacturing Standards and Specifications for Textbooks
MSST.......... Master of Science in Science Teaching
MSST.......... Mean Sea Surface Temperature
MSST.......... Meldesammelstelle [*Message Center*] [*German military - World War II*]
MSST.......... Member of the Society of Surveying Technicians [*British*] (DBQ)
MSST.......... Ministry of State for Science and Technology [*Canada*]
MSST.......... Missionary Servants of the Most Holy Trinity [*Roman Catholic men's religious order*]
MSST.......... Multiple Sclerosis Society of Tasmania [*Australia*]
MsSt.......... Oktibbeha County Library System, Starkville, MS [*Library symbol Library of Congress*] (LCLS)
MSST.......... Springfield Technical Community College, Springfield, MA [*Library symbol Library of Congress*] (LCLS)
MSStat........ Master of Science in Statistics (GAGS)
MSSTC......... Mobile Service Structure Test Conductor (KSC)
MSStEng...... Master of Science in Structural Engineering (NADA)
MsStL......... Oktibbeha County Library System, Starkville, MS [*Library symbol*] [*Library of Congress*] (LCLS)
MSSTM....... Military Space Systems Technology Model (MCD)
MSSU......... Meteorology on Stamps Study Unit [*American Topical Association*] (EA)
MSSU......... Midstream Specimen of Urine [*Medicine*]
MSSU......... Mississippi State University (PDAA)
MsSu.......... Sunflower County Library, Sunflower, MS [*Library symbol Library of Congress*] (LCLS)
MS Surg ..... Master of Science in Surgery (PGP)
MSSV......... Maize Sterile Stunt Virus [*Plant pathology*]
MSSV......... Maximum Safe Sampling Volume [*Analytical chemistry*]
MSSV......... Multiple Sclerosis Society of Victoria [*Australia*]
MSSVD....... Medical Society for the Study of Venereal Diseases [*Leeds, England*] (EAIO)
MSSVFI....... Manufacturers Standardization Society of the Valve and Fittings Industry (EA)
MSSW .... Magnetostatic Surface Wave [*Telecommunications*] (TEL)
MSSW .... Master of Science in Social Work
MSSWA...... Multiple Sclerosis Society of Western Australia
MS Sy Sc.... Master of Science in Systems Science (PGP)
MST........... Aeroamistad SA de CV [*Mexico ICAO designator*] (FAAC)
MST........... Association of Maximum Service Telecasters (EA)
MsT .... Lee-Itawamba Regional Library, Tupelo, MS [*Library symbol Library of Congress*] (LCLS)
MST............ Maastricht [*Netherlands*] [*Airport symbol*] (OAG)
MST............ Machinery Safety Tag
MST............ Machine Shock Test
MST............ Machine Steel
MST............ Magnetostrictive Transducer
MST............ Maintenance Standard Tests [*Military*]
MST............ Maintenance Support Team (MCD)
MST............ Management Survey Team (AAG)
MST............ Manifold Surface Temperature [*Automotive engineering*]
MST............ Marconi Self-Tuning (IAA)
MST............ Marine Science Technician [*Coast Guard*] (MUSM)
MST............ Mass Spectrometer Tube
MST............ Mass Storage Task [*Computer science*] (NOAA)
MST............ Master (MCD)
MST............ Master of Sacred Theology
MST............ Master of Science in Taxation (GAGS)
MST............ Master of Science in Teaching
MST............ Master of Science in Tourism (GAGS)
MST............ Master of Science Teaching (GAGS)
MST............ Master of Science Technology (PGP)
MST............ Master of Secondary Teaching (GAGS)
MST............ Master of Speech Therapy (GAGS)
M St............ Master of Statistics
MSt............ Master of Studies, University of Oxford [*British*] (DBQ)
MST............ Master of Systems Technology (PGP)
MST............ Master of Teaching
MST............ Maximal Stimulation Test (DMAA)
MST............ Maximum Service Telecasters
MST............ Maximum Summer Temperature [*Climatology*]
MST............ Mean Selected Temperature
MST............ Mean Service Time (CIST)
MST............ Mean Solar Time
MST............ Mean Survival Time
MST............ Mean Swell Time [*Botulism test*] [*Food analysis*]
MST............ Measurement
MST............ Measurement Status Table (NASA)
MST............ Mechanics Support Team [*Military*] (GFGA)
MST............ Medial Superior Temporal [*Brain Anatomy*]
MST............ Median Survival Time
MST............ Media Systems Technology (HGAA)
MST............ Medium-Scale Technology
MST............ Medium STOL [*Short Takeoff and Landing*] Transport [*Aircraft*]
MST............ Memotron Storage Tube
MST............ Mercantile Stores [*NYSE symbol*] (TTSB)
MST............ Mercantile Stores Co., Inc. [*NYSE symbol*] (SPSG)
MST............ Mercury System Test [*NASA*]
MST............ Mesosphere-Stratosphere-Troposphere (USDC)
MST............ Mesosphere-Stratosphere-Troposphere [*Marine science*] (OSRA)
MST............ Message Status Table (MCD)
MST............ Microsecond Trip
MST........... Micro System Technology (AAEL)
MST............ Microwave Satellite Technologies, Inc. [*Wellington, NJ*] (TSSD)
MST............ Midsummer Time

MST	Military Science Training
MST	Military Shipping Tag
MST	Miniature Situations Test (EDAC)
MST	Minimal Spanning Tree [*Computer science*]
MST	Minimum Spawning Time [*Pisciculture*]
MST	Ministry, Society, and Theology [*A publication*] (APTA)
MST	Missile Surveillance Technology (MCD)
MST	Missile System Test
MST	Mission Simulator Test (MCD)
MST	Mission Support Team (MCD)
MST	Mistral Resources Ltd. [*Vancouver Stock Exchange symbol*]
MST	Mobile Service Tower [*Aerospace*]
MST	Mobile Strike Team
MST	Mobile Support Team (NVT)
MST	Modal Survey Test (MCD)
MST	Module Service Tool (NASA)
MST	Moisture-Proof Heat-Sealing Transparent [*Flexography*] (DGA)
MST	Monolithic Systems Technology
M St	More's Notes on Stair's Institutes of Scotland [*A publication*] (ILCA)
MST	Morphine Sulphate [*Medicine*] (WDAA)
MST	Mostar [*Yugoslavia*] [*Seismograph station code, US Geological Survey Closed*] (SEIS)
MST	Mountain Standard Time
MST	Movimento Sem Terra [*Political party*] [*Brazil*]
MST	Multimode Storage Tube
MST	Multisystem Test [*Military*]
MST	Mutual Security Treaty (MCD)
MST	St. Cloud State University, St. Cloud, MN [*OCLC symbol*] (OCLC)
MST3K	Mystery Science Theater 3000 [*Cable television program*]
MSTA	Manufacturers Surgical Trade Association [*Later, HIMA*] (EA)
MSTA	Master of Science in Statistics (PGP)
MSTA	Master Tape (AAG)
MSTA	Member of the Swimming Teachers' Association [*British*] (DBQ)
MSTA	Mumps Skin Test Antigen [*Clinical chemistry*]
MSTAB	Manufacturing Systems Technical Advisory Board (AAEL)
MSTACCMB	Master Aircraft Crewman Badge [*Military decoration*] (GFGA)
MSTAN	Modal Stamen Number per Flower [*Botany*]
MST & E	Multiservice Test and Evaluation [*Military*]
MSTAR	MLRS [*Multiple Launch Rocket System*] Smart Tactical Rocket [*USA*]
MSTARAVB	Master Army Aviator Badge [*Military decoration*] (GFGA)
MSTAT	Marine Safety Training and Assistance Team [*RSPA*] (TAG)
M Stat	Master of Statistics (PGP)
MStat	Master of Statistics
mstb	Mastaba (VRA)
MSTB	Mission Simulator and Training Building
MS TBR	Morgan Stanley Group [*Associated Press*] (SAG)
MSTC	Management Systems Training Council [*British*]
MSTC	Manned Spacecraft Test Center [*NASA*] (KSC)
MSTC	Manufacturing Systems and Technology Center [*Baltimore, MD*] [*Westinghouse Electric Corp.*]
MSTC	Maryland State Teachers College
MSTC	Massachusetts State Teachers College
MSTC	Master of Science in Telecommunications (PGP)
MSTC	Mastic
MSTC	Microwave Sensitivity Time Control [*Circuit*]
MSTC	Midwest Securities Trust Co.
MSTCS(GB)	Member of the Society of Thoracic and Cardiovascular Surgeons (Great Britain)
MSTD	Master Steward [*Marine Corps*]
MSTD	Member of the Society of Typographic Designers (DGA)
MSTDIVB	Master Diver Badge [*Military decoration*] (GFGA)
MSTE	Master of Science in Technical Education (GAGS)
MSTE	Master of Science in Transportation Engineering (GAGS)
M St E	Master of Structural Engineering
MSTE	Steinbach Public Library, Manitoba [*Library symbol National Library of Canada*] (NLC)
MS (T Ed)	Master of Science in Teacher Education
MSTEd	Master of Science in Technical Education (GAGS)
MSTEL	Member of the Society of Telegraph Engineers, London [*British*] (ROG)
M St Eng	Master of Structural Engineering
MSTEODBAD	Master Explosive Ordnance Disposal Badge [*Military decoration*] (GFGA)
M-STEP	Multi-State Teacher Education Project
MSText	Master of Science in Textiles (GAGS)
MS Text Chem	Master of Science in Textile Chemistry (PGP)
MSTFA	(Methyl)trimethylsilyltrifluoroacetamide [*Organic chemistry*]
MSTFLSB	Master Flight Surgeon Badge [*Military decoration*] (GFGA)
MSTG	Mass Storage Task Group [*CODASYL*]
MstG	Master Glaziers Karate International [*Associated Press*] (SAG)
MSTG	Material Safety Task Group [*Air Force*] (AFM)
MSTG	Melbourne Screen and Theatre Guild [*Australia*]
MSTG	Mustang Software [*NASDAQ symbol*] (TTSB)
MSTG	Mustang Software, Inc. [*NASDAQ symbol*] (SAG)
MSTGA	Library Allard, St. Georges, Manitoba [*Library symbol National Library of Canada*] (BIB)
MstGlaz	Master Glaziers Karate International [*Associated Press*] (SAG)
MSTGP	Material Safety Task Group [*Air Force*]
MSTh	Mesothorium [*Radioelement*]
MsTI	Itawamba Junior College, Tupelo Campus, Tupelo, MS [*Library symbol Library of Congress*] (LCLS)
MSTI	Miniature Sensor Technology Integration [*Orbital satellites*]
MSTI	Multiple Soft Tissue Injuries [*Medicine*] (DMAA)
M ST J	Ordinary Member of the Order of St. John of Jerusalem

MSTJ	Public Library, St. James-Assiniboia, Manitoba [*Library symbol National Library of Canada*] (NLC)
MSTL	Military Subvention Type Lorry [*British*]
MSTL	Minneapolis & St. Louis Railway Co. [*Later, MSL Industries, Inc.*] [*AAR code*]
MSTLAB	Materials and Science Toxicology Laboratory [*University of Tennessee*] [*Research center*] (RCD)
MSTLY	Mostly [*NWS*] (FAAC)
MSTM	Master of Science in Teaching Mathematics (PGP)
MSTM	Master of Science in Technology Management (GAGS)
MSTM	Master of Science in Tropical Medicine (GAGS)
MSTM	Mennonite Village Museum, Steinbach, Manitoba [*Library symbol National Library of Canada*] (NLC)
MSTM	Missile Service Test Model [*Military*] (IAA)
MS TMX	Morgan Stanley Group, Inc. [*Associated Press*] (SAG)
MSTO	Main-Sequence Turnoff [*Stellar physics*]
MSTO	Military System Training Organization (SAA)
MStoc	Stockbridge Library Association, Stockbridge, MA [*Library symbol Library of Congress*] (LCLS)
MStocA	Austen Riggs Center, Inc., Stockbridge, MA [*Library symbol Library of Congress*] (LCLS)
MSTOL	Medium-Slow Takeoff and Landing
MSTOS	South Interlake Regional Library, Stonewall, Manitoba [*Library symbol National Library of Canada*] (NLC)
MsToT	Tougaloo College, Tougaloo, MS [*Library symbol Library of Congress*] (LCLS)
MSTP	Maintenance Support Test Package [*Military*]
MStp	Maize Stripe [*Plant pathology*]
MSTP	Manual System Training Program (SAA)
MSTP	Master Template
MSTP	Medical Scientist Training Program [*National Institutes of Health*]
MStP & A	Minneapolis, St. Paul & Ashland Railway
MSTP & SSM	Minneapolis, St. Paul & Sault Ste. Marie Railway Co.
MSTPHC	Multistop Time-to-Pulse Height Converter [*NASA*]
MSTPJ	Jolys Regional Library, St. Pierre, Manitoba [*Library symbol National Library of Canada*] (NLC)
MSTPRCHT	Master Parachutist Badge [*Military decoration*] (GFGA)
MStpV	Maize Stripe Virus [*Plant pathology*]
MSTR	[*The*] Massena Terminal Railroad Co. [*AAR code*]
mstr	Master (VRA)
MSTR	Master
MSTR	Moisture [*NWS*] (FAAC)
MSTR	Morningstar Group [*NASDAQ symbol*] (SAG)
MSTR	Multivariable Self-Tuning Regulator [*Control technology*]
MSTR	Ste-Rose Regional Library, Manitoba [*Library symbol National Library of Canada*] (NLC)
MSTrans	Master of Science in Transportation (NADA)
MSTransE	Master of Science in Transportation Engineering (NADA)
MSTRE	Moisture (MSA)
MSTS	Manifold Surface Temperature Sensor [*Automotive engineering*]
MSTS	McDonnell Scrap Tool System [*McDonnell Douglas Corp.*] (MCD)
MSTS	Mean Standard Toxicity Score (MCD)
MSTS	Microprocessor Spark Timing System
MSTS	Military Sea Transportation Service [*Later, MSC*] [*Navy*]
MSTS	Missile Simulator Test Set (MCD)
MSTS	Missile Static Test Site [*Air Force*]
MSTS	Missile Station Test Set (MCD)
MSTS	Missile Subsystem Test Set [*Military*] (CAAL)
MSTS	Multisubscriber Time-Sharing Systems [*Computer system*]
MSTS	Multisystem Training System
MSTSFE	Military Sea Transport Service, Far East
MSTSL	Master of Science in Teaching a Second Language (GAGS)
MSTSO	Military Sea Transportation Service Office [*Obsolete*]
MSTU	Military Sea Transport Union
MStuO	Old Sturbridge Village Library, Sturbridge, MA [*Library symbol Library of Congress*] (LCLS)
MSTV	Maize Stripe Virus [*Plant pathology*]
MSTV	Manned Supersonic Test Vehicle (MCD)
MSTV	Master-Scale Television
MsTy	Walthall County Library, Tylertown, MS [*Library symbol Library of Congress*] (LCLS)
MSu	Goodnow Library, Sudbury, MA [*Library symbol Library of Congress*] (LCLS)
MSU	Main Storage Unit [*Computer science*]
MSU	Main Switching Unit [*Telecommunications*] (NITA)
MSU	Maintenance and Status Unit [*Telecommunications*] (TEL)
MSU	Maintenance Service Unit (IAA)
MSU	Maintenance Signal Unit [*Telecommunications*] (TEL)
MSU	Malaria Survey Unit [*Army World War II*]
MSU	Management Signal Unit [*Telecommunications*] (TEL)
MSU	Management Support Unit
MSU	Management Systems Unit
MSU	Maple Sugar [*or Syrup*] Urine [*Medicine*] (DMAA)
MSU	Marysvale [*Utah*] [*Seismograph station code, US Geological Survey*] (SEIS)
MSU	Maseru [*Lesotho*] [*Airport symbol*] (OAG)
MSU	Masonic Study Unit [*American Topical Association*] (EA)
MSU	Mass Storage Unit [*Computer science*] (NASA)
msu	Mass Storage Unit (NAKS)
MSU	Material Salvage Unit
MSU	Mathematical Study Unit [*American Topical Association*] (EA)
msu	Measuring Stimuli Unit (NAKS)
MSU	Measuring Stimuli Units (NASA)
MSU	Medical Service Unit [*Air Force*] (AFM)
MSU	Medical Studies Unit (DAVI)

MSU............ Medical Subjects Unit [*American Topical Association*] (EA)
MSU............ Memory Service Unit [*Computer science*]
MSU............ Memphis State University [*Tennessee*]
MSU............ Message Switching Unit
MSU............ Meteorology on Stamps Study Unit [*American Topical Association*] (EA)
MSU............ Michigan State University [*East Lansing*]
MSU............ Microelectronics Support Unit [*Department of Education and Science*] (NITA)
MSU............ Microwave Sounding Unit [*Telecommunications*] (TEL)
MSU............ Midstream Specimen of Urine [*Medicine*]
MSU............ Mid-Stream Urine [*Medicine*] (DMAA)
MSU............ Mill Sawyers' Union [*British*]
msu .... Mississippi [*MARC country of publication code Library of Congress*] (LCCP)
MSU............ Mobile Signals Unit [*British military*] (DMA)
MSU............ MODEM-Sharing Unit [*Telecommunications*] (TSSD)
MSU............ Modern Sharing Unit [*Computer science*] (OA)
MSU............ Mode Selector Unit
MSU............ Monosodium Urate [*Organic chemistry*]
MSU............ Montana State University [*Bozeman*]
MSU............ Morgan Stan Fin 7.82% Cp Uts [*NYSE symbol*] (TTSB)
MSU............ Morgan Stanley Financial [*NYSE symbol*] (SPSG)
MSU............ Morgan State University, Baltimore, MD [*OCLC symbol*] (OCLC)
MSU............ Motor-Switching Unit (MCD)
MSU............ Multiblock Synchronization Signal Unit [*Telecommunications*] (TEL)
MSU............ Multiple Signal Unit [*Telecommunications*] (TEL)
MSU............ Murray State University [*Kentucky*]
MSU............ Myocardial Substrate Uptake [*Medicine*] (DMAA)
MsU............ University of Mississippi, University, MS [*Library symbol Library of Congress*] (LCLS)
MSUAG........ Michigan State University Advisory Group [*Contracted with the Government of South Vietnam to provide-civilian training*] (VNW)
MSU Business Topics... Michigan State University Business Topics [*A publication*] (DLA)
MSUCLE ...... Missouri State University Continuing Legal Education (DLA)
MSUD........ Maple Sugar [*or Syrup*] Urine Disease [*Medicine*]
MSUD........ Master of Science in Urban Design (GAGS)
MSUDC........ Michigan State University Discrete Computer
MSUDFSG... MSUD [*Maple Syrup Urine Disease*] Family Support Group (EA)
MSUESM ..... Master of Science in Urban Environmental Systems Management (PGP)
MSuL........ Goodnow Library, Sudbury, MA [*Library symbol*] [*Library of Congress*] (LCLS)
MSUL........ Medical Schools of the University of London (DAS)
MsU-L.......... University of Mississippi, Law School, University, MS [*Library symbol Library of Congress*] (LCLS)
MSUM .... Mission Society for United Methodists (EA)
MSUM .... Monosodium Urate Monohydrate [*Organic chemistry*]
MsU-M........ University of Mississippi, Medical Center, Jackson, MS [*Library symbol Library of Congress*] (LCLS)
MSUP .... Mouvement pour la Solidarite, l'Union et le Progres [*Benin*] [*Political party*] (EY)
MsU-P .... University of Mississippi, School of Pharmacy, University, MS [*Library symbol Library of Congress*] (LCLS)
M Sur .... Master of Surgery
MSurg......... Master of Surgery (BABM)
MSurgery..... Master of Surgery (NADA)
MSurv......... Master of Surveying
MSurvMap .. Master of Surveying and Mapping
MSurvSc...... Master of Surveying Science
MSUS .... Mouvement Socialiste d'Union Senegalaise [*Senegalese Socialist Movement*] [*Political party*]
MSUSM .... Medical Society of the United States and Mexico (EA)
MSUS/PALS... Minnesota State Universities System Project for Automated Library Systems [*Mankato State University Library*] [*Mankato, MN*] [*Information service or system*]
MSuSR .... Sperry Rand Research Center, Sudbury, MA [*Library symbol Library of Congress*] (LCLS)
MSV............ Catskills/Sullivan County [*New York*] [*Airport symbol Obsolete*] (OAG)
MSV............ Magnetically Supported Vehicle
MSV............ Maintenance Support Vessel
MSV............ Maize Streak Virus [*Plant pathology*]
MSV............ Manned Space Vehicle [*NASA*] (AAG)
MSV............ Martian Surface Vehicle
MSV............ Mass Stimulated Vehicles (MCD)
MSV............ Mass Storage Volume
MSV............ Maximal Sustained Level of Ventilation [*Medicine*]
MSV............ Mean Square Velocity
MSV............ Mean Square Voltage (NRCH)
MSV............ Meteor Simulation Vehicle (SAA)
mSv............ Millisievert [*Radiation dose*]
MSV............ Miniature Solenoid Valve
MSV............ Missionary Sisters of Verona [*Roman Catholic religious order*]
MSV............ Mississippi & Skuna Valley Railroad Co. [*AAR code*]
MSV............ Mobile Surface Vehicle (AAG)
MSV............ Molecular Solution Volume
MSV............ Molinia Streak Virus
MSV............ Moloney Sarcoma Virus (AAMN)
MSV............ Monitored Sine Vibration [*Test*] (MCD)
msv............ Monitored Sine Vibration (NAKS)
MSV............ Monticello, NY [*Location identifier FAA*] (FAAL)
MSV............ Morgan Stan Fin 9% Cp Uts [*NYSE symbol*] (TTSB)

MSV............ Morgan Stanley Finance Markets Ltd. Capital Units [*NYSE symbol*] (SAG)
MSV............ Mouse Sarcoma Virus
MSV............ Multifunctional Service Vessel [*Off-shore drilling technology*]
MSV............ Multipurpose Support Vessel [*Offshore drilling*]
MSV............ Murine Sarcoma Virus
MSV............ Musica sul Velluto (EAIO)
MsV............ Vicksburg Public Library, Vicksburg, MS [*Library symbol Library of Congress*] (LCLS)
MSVA........ Magnetic Speed Variable Assist [*General Motors*] [*Power steering*]
MSVC........ Mass Storage Volume Control [*Computer science*] (BUR)
MSVC........ Master of Vocational Counseling (GAGS)
MSVC........ Maximal Sustained Ventilatory Capacity [*Medicine*] (DMAA)
MSVC........ Mount St. Vincent College [*New York*]
MSVCS........ Missile Sight Video Camera Systems (MCD)
MSVD .... Missile and Space Vehicle Department [*NASA*] (KSC)
MsVE .... United States Army, Corps of Engineers, Waterways Experiment Station, Vicksburg,MS [*Library symbol Library of Congress*] (LCLS)
MSVI .... Mass Storage Volume Inventory [*Computer science*] (IAA)
MSV(M)....... Murine Sarcoma Virus (Moloney)
MSVO .... Missile and Space Vehicle Office [*NASA*] (IAA)
MsVO .... Old Court House Museum Library, Vicksburg, MS [*Library symbol Library of Congress*] (LCLS)
MSVP .... Master Shuttle Verification Plan (MCD)
MSVR .... Mandatory Securities Valuation Reserve [*National Association of Insurance Commissioners*]
MSW........... Machine Status Word [*Computer science*]
MSW........... Macht Sich Wichtig (BJA)
MSW........... Magnetostatic Waves [*Telecommunications*] (TEL)
MSW........... Massawa [*Ethiopia*] [*Airport symbol*] (OAG)
MSW........... Master of Social Welfare
MSW........... Master of Social Work
MSW........... Master Switch
MSW........... Maximum Shipping Weight [*MTMC*] (TAG)
MSW........... Mean Sea Water
MSW........... Mean Shallow Water
MSW........... Medical Social Worker [*British*]
MSW........... Meters of Seawater [*Deep-sea diving*]
MSW........... Metres of Salt Water
MSW........... Microswitch
MSW........... Microwave Spectrometer (TEL)
MSW........... Mikheyev-Smirnov-Wolfenstein Theory [*Oscillation effect*] [*Particle physics*]
MSW........... MI Software Co. [*Vancouver Stock Exchange symbol*]
MSW........... Mission West Prop [*AMEX symbol*] (TTSB)
MSW........... Mission West Properties [*AMEX symbol*] (SPSG)
MSW........... Multiple Shrapnel Wounds
MSW........... Multiple Stab Wounds [*Emergency medicine*] (DAVI)
MSW........... Municipal Solid Waste
MSW........... Western Massachusetts Regional Public Library System, Springfield, MA [*Library symbol Library of Congress*] (LCLS)
MSWAP ...... Master of Social Welfare and Administration Planning
MSWD .... Mean Square Weighted Deviation [*Statistics*]
MSWD .... Multisystem Weapon Delivery [*Air Force*]
M Sw En...... Master of Software Engineering (PGP)
MSWG .... Manpower Systems Work Group
MSWG .... Modeling and Simulation Working Group
MsWJ .... Jefferson College, Washington, MS [*Library symbol Library of Congress Obsolete*] (LCLS)
MSWJ .... Midland and South Western Junction Railway [*British*]
MSWL......... Municipal Solid Waste Landfill
MSWLF....... Municipal Solid Waste Landfill
MSWLFS...... Municipal Solid Wast Landfills (BCP)
MSWM........ Men Who Have Sex With Men [*AIDS transmission group*]
MsWov .... Wilkinson County Library System, Woodville, MS [*Library symbol Library of Congress*] (LCLS)
MsWp .... Tombigbee Regional Library, West Point, MS [*Library symbol Library of Congress*] (LCLS)
MsWpCt...... Court House Library, West Point, MS [*Library symbol Library of Congress*] (LCLS)
MsWpMH.... Mary Holmes College, West Point, MS [*Library symbol Library of Congress*] (LCLS)
MSWREE ..... Master of Science in Water Resources and Environmental Engineering (PGP)
MSWT......... Minimum-Speed Wind Tunnel (MCD)
MsWv .... Water Valley Public Library, Water Valley, MS [*Library symbol Library of Congress*] (LCLS)
MSWYE........ Modified Seawater Yeast Extract [*Agar*] [*Microbiology*] (DAVI)
MSX........ Mascota [*Mexico*] [*Airport symbol*] (AD)
MSX........ MascoTech, Inc. [*NYSE symbol*] (SPSG)
MSX........ Microsoft Extended Basic (NITA)
MSX........ Midcourse Space Experiment (MCD)
MSX........ Minesweeper, Experimental [*Navy symbol*]
MSX........ Mossendjo [*Congo*] [*Airport symbol*] (OAG)
MSX........ Multinucleate Nature, Spherical Shape, Unknown History
MSXPr........ Masco Tech Inc. Cv Pfd [*NYSE symbol*] (TTSB)
MSY........ Massey University School of Aviation [*New Zealand*] [*ICAO designator*] (FAAC)
MSY........ Maximum Sustainable Yield
MSY........ Minimum Sustainable Yield [*Pisciculture*]
MSY........ Morgan Stanley High Yield Fund [*NYSE symbol*] (SPSG)
MSY........ Morgan Stanley Hi Yld Fd [*NYSE symbol*] (TTSB)
MSY........ New Orleans [*Louisiana*] [*Airport symbol*]

MsY	Yazoo-Sharkey Library System, Yazoo City, MS [*Library symbol Library of Congress*] (LCLS)
MSYNC	Master Synchronization [*Telecommunications*] (TEL)
MSYNC	Master Synchronizer (MSA)
MSYS	Medical Technology Systems, Inc. [*NASDAQ symbol*] (NQ)
M-SysFD	M-Systems Flash Disk Pioneers Ltd. [*Associated Press*] (SAG)
M Sy Th	Master of Systematic Theology
MSZ	Massive Surf Zone
MSZ	Milford Sound [*New Zealand*] [*Seismograph station code, US Geological Survey*] (SEIS)
MSZ	Moga Stan Fin 7.80% Cp Uts [*NYSE symbol*] (TTSB)
MSZ	Morgan Stanley Finance Markets Ltd. Capital Unit [*NYSE symbol*] (SAG)
MSZ	Mossamedes [*Angola*] [*Airport symbol*] (OAG)
MSZDP	Magyar Szocial Demokrata Part [*Hungarian Social Democratic Party*] [*Political party*] (PPE)
MSZMP	Magyar Szocialista Munkaspart [*Hungarian Socialist Workers' Party*] [*Political party*] (PPE)
MSzP	Magyar Szocialista Part [*Hungarian Socialist Party*] [*Political party*] (EY)
MT	Core Melt Through [*Nuclear energy*] (IEEE)
MT	Empty [*Slang*]
MT	Flame Tight
MT	Internacia Asocio Monda Turismo [*International Association for World Tourism*] (EAIO)
MT	Internal Revenue Bureau Miscellaneous Tax Ruling [*United States*] [*A publication*] (DLA)
MT	Machine Tool
MT	Machine Tool Technology Program [*Association of Independent Colleges and Schools specialization code*]
MT	Machine Translation [*Computer science*]
M-T	Mac Knight Airlines [*ICAO designator*] (AD)
M-T	Macroglobulin-Trypsin [*Complex*] (DAVI)
M-T	Macroglobulin-Trypsin Complex [*Medicine*] (BABM)
MT	Magic Tee (IAA)
MT	Magnetic
MT	Magnetic Particle Testing [*Nuclear energy*] (IEEE)
MT	Magnetic Tape
MT	Magnetic Tube
mt	Magnetite [*CIPW classification*] [*Geology*]
MT	Magnetotelluric [*Geological surveying*]
MT	Mail Transfer
MT	Mail Tray (AAG)
MT	Main Telescope
MT	Maintenance Technician (MUGU)
MT	Maintenance Time
MT	Maintenance Trailer
MT	Maintenance Trainer (MCD)
MT	Malaria Therapy [*British*]
MT	Malignant Teratoma [*Oncology*]
MT	Malta [*IYRU nationality code*] [*ANSI two-letter standard code*] (CNC)
MT	Mammary Tumor [*Medicine*]
MT	Mammilothalamic Tract [*Anatomy*]
MT	Management Team
MT	Mandated Territory
MT	Mannesman Tally (NITA)
MT	Mantle Tentacle
MT	Manual Test
M/T	Manual Transmission [*Automotive engineering*]
MT	Manufacturing Technology (RDA)
MT	Mare Tranquillitatis [*Sea of Tranquility*] [*Lunar area*]
MT	Maritime Tropical Air Mass
MT	Market Town [*Geographical division*] [*British*]
MT	Mark Trunk (IAA)
MT	Masking Template (MCD)
MT	Masoretic Text [*of the Bible*] [*Hebrew tradition*]
M/T	Masses or Tumors [*Medicine*] (CPH)
MT	Mast (IAA)
MT	Master of Taxation (GAGS)
MT	Master of Teaching (GAGS)
MT	Master of Technology (GAGS)
MT	Master of Textiles (PGP)
MT	Master Teacher (ADA)
MT	Master Timer
MT	Master Tool (NASA)
MT	Mat
MT	Materials Test (IEEE)
MT	Material Test (IAA)
MT	Material Transfer (NRCH)
Mt	Matthew [*New Testament book*]
MT	Maximal Therapy [*Medicine*]
MT	Maximum Torque
MT	Mean Tide [*Tides and currents*]
MT	Mean Time
MT	Measured Time
MT	Measurement (IAA)
MT	Measurement Ton (MUGU)
M/T	Measurement Tons (COE)
MT	Measuring Transformer (IAA)
MT	Mechanical Technician (KSC)
M-T	Mechanical Test (MCD)
MT	Mechanical Time [*Fuse*] (AABC)
MT	Mechanical Traction [*British military*] (DMA)
MT	Mechanical Translation [*Computer science*]
MT	Mechanical Transport
MT	Mediaeval Towns [*A publication*]
MT	Medial Triceps Brachii [*Medicine*]
MT	MediaTel [*Database*] [*British*]
MT	Medical Technician [*British military*] (DMA)
MT	Medical Technologist
MT	Medical Transcriptionist (DAVI)
MT	Medical Transfer (WDAA)
MT	Meditrust Corp. [*NYSE symbol*] [*Formerly, Meditrust SBI*] (SG)
MT	Meditrust SBI [*NYSE symbol*] (SPSG)
MT	Medium Truck [*British*]
MT	Megaton [*Nuclear equivalent of one million tons of high explosive*] (AFM)
MT	Megatron (CET)
Mt	Meitnerium [*Proposed name and symbol for recently-discovered element*]
MT	Melt Through [*Nuclear energy*] (NRCH)
MT	Membrana Tympani [*Anatomy*]
MT	Mesenteric Traction [*Medicine*]
MT	Mesotocin [*Endocrinology*]
MT	Message Table [*Computer science*] (OA)
MT	Metallothionein [*Biochemistry*]
MT	Metal Threshold (AAG)
MT	Metatarsal [*Anatomy*]
MT	Meteor Construzioni Aeronautiche & Elettroniche SpA [*Italy ICAO aircraft manufacturer identifier*] (ICAO)
MT	Meter (MCD)
MT	Methoxytryptamine [*Biochemistry*]
MT	Methoxytyramine [*Biochemistry*]
MT	Methyltryptophan [*Biochemistry*]
MT	Methyltyrosine [*Biochemistry*]
Mt	Metical (ODBW)
MT	Metric Ton [*1,000 kilograms*]
MT	Michaelmas Term [*British Legal term*] (ROG)
MT	Microptic Theodolite
MT	Microsyn Torquer (SAA)
MT	Microthrombus [*Hematology*]
MT	Microtome [*Instrumentation*]
MT	Microtubule [*Cytology*]
MT	Microwave Thermograph [*Medical instrumentation*]
MT	Middle Temple [*London*] [*One of the Inns of Court*]
MT	Middle Temporal [*Anatomy*]
MT	Middle Temporal Lobe [*of the brain*]
MT	Middle Turbinate [*Otorhinolaryngology*] (DAVI)
MT	Midland Terminal Railroad (IIA)
MT	Midrash Tanna'im (BJA)
MT	Midship Deep Tank
MT	Might
MT	Migratory Trout
MT	Military Tanker [*British*]
MT	Military Technician
MT	Military Tractor [*British*]
MT	Military Train [*British military*] (DMA)
MT	Military Training
MT	Military Transport
mT	Millitesla
MT	Miniature Tube (NTCM)
MT	Minimum Temperature (DS)
MT	Minimum Threshold [*Medicine*] (DB)
MT	Minimum Transfer (DCTA)
MT	Ministry of Transport [*Later, DOE*] [*British*]
MT	Mishneh Torah [*Maimonides*] (BJA)
MT	Missile Technician [*Navy rating*]
MT	Missile Test
MT	Missile Tilt
MT	Mission Time (MCD)
MT	Mission Trajectory (MCD)
MT	Mitomycin [*Also, M, MC*] [*Antineoplastic drug*]
MT	Mitotic Time (DB)
MT	Mitral [*Valve*] [*Cardiology*]
MT	Mobile Team
MT	Mobile Terminal (DA)
MT	Mobile Traveler [*Recreational vehicle*]
MT	Mode Transducer
MT	Modified Tape Armor [*Telecommunications*] (TEL)
MT	Modus Tolens [*Rule of inference*] [*Logic*] [*Latin*]
MT	Monroe Tidal Drainage [*Medicine*] (DMAA)
MT	Montana [*Postal code*]
MT	Montana Reports [*A publication*] (DLA)
Mt	Montana State Library, Helena, MT [*Library symbol Library of Congress*] (LCLS)
MT	More Than
MT	Morse Taper (IAA)
MT	Most (WGA)
MT	Motilin [*Biochemistry*]
MT	Mo Time [*An association*] (EA)
MT	Motor Driver [*British military*] (DMA)
MT	Motor Tanker
MT	Motor Terminal (IAA)
MT	Motor Threshold [*Medicine*]
MT	Motor Transport [*Military*]
MT	Motor Trend Magazine [*A publication*]
MT	Mount [*Maps and charts*] (KSC)
Mt	Mount (ODBW)
mt	Mountain (VRA)
MT	Mountain [*Board on Geographic Names*]

MT	Mountain Time
MT	Mounted [*Technical drawings*]
MT	Mountings [*JETDS nomenclature*] [*Military*] (CET)
MT	Mounting Tray
MT	Movement Time [*Physical education*]
MT	Moxalactam/Ticarcillin (DB)
MT	MTC Electronic [*Vancouver Stock Exchange symbol*]
MT	Muertos Trough [*Geology*]
MT	Multiple Transfer
MT	Multiple Twin (IAA)
MT	Multitasking
MT	Muscle and Tendon [*Medicine*] (MAE)
MT	Music Therapist [*or Therapy*]
MT	MUX [*Multiplex*] Terminal (MCD)
Mt	Mycobacterium Tuberculosis [*Bacteriology*]
MT	Myelotomography [*Medicine*]
MT	Transcona Public Library, Manitoba [*Library symbol National Library of Canada*] (NLC)
MT1	Missile Technician, First Class [*Navy rating*]
MT2	Missile Technician, Second Class [*Navy rating*]
MT3	Missile Technician, Third Class [*Navy rating*]
MT6	Mercaptomerin [*Pharmacology*] (DAVI)
MTA	MAC [*Military Airlift Command*] Transportation Authorization (AFM)
MTA	Magnetic Tape Accessory [*General Electric Co.*]
MTA	Mail Transfer Agent [*Computer science*]
MTA	Maintenance Task Analysis
MTA	Major Test Article (NASA)
MTA	Major Training Area [*Army*]
MTA	Malignant Teratoma, Anaplastic [*Medicine*] (DMAA)
MTA	Mammary Tumor Agent (DOG)
MTA	Managed Thermactor Air [*Automotive engineering*]
MTA	Management by Talking Around [*Business term*]
MTA	Management Transactions Audit [*Test*]
MTA	Manpower Training Association (AEBS)
MTA	Man-Tended Approach (SSD)
MTA	Manual Target Acquisition (MCD)
MTA	Marine Trades Association [*British*] (DBA)
MTA	Maritime Training Association (EA)
MTA	Market Technicians Association (NADA)
MTA	Mark Twain Association (EA)
MTA	Mass Thermal Analysis (MCD)
MTA	Master of Tax Accounting (GAGS)
MTA	Master of Teaching Arts (GAGS)
MTA	Master of Theater Arts (GAGS)
MTA	Master Timer Assembly
MTA	Materials Testing Activity (MCD)
MTA	Materiel Transfer Agreement [*DoD*]
MTA	Mean Tryptic Activity (PDAA)
MTA	Media Technology Associates Ltd. [*Bethesda, MD*] [*Telecommunications service*] (TSSD)
MTA	Medical and Technical Assistant
MTA	Medical Technical Assistant (DMAA)
MTA	Medical Technology Assessment (DMAA)
MTA	Melamine Tableware Association (EA)
MTA	Message Terminal Area (MCD)
MTA	Message Transfer Agent [*Telecommunications*] (PCM)
MTA	Message Transfer Architecture [*Computer science*]
MTA	Message Transport Agent [*Telecommunications*] (PCM)
MTA	Meta Communications Group, Inc. [*Toronto Stock Exchange symbol*]
MTA	Metatarsus Adductus [*Anatomy*] (DAVI)
MTA	MetaTechnologies Associates [*Oakland, CA*] [*Telecommunications service*] (TSSD)
MTA	Methods-Time Analysis [*Industrial engineering*]
MTA	Methylthionadenosine [*Biochemistry*]
MTA	Metric Tons per Annum
MTA	Metropolitan Transit Authority [*Later, MBTA*] [*Initialism also title of folk song about Boston's transit system*]
MTA	Metropolitan Transportation Authority [*Greater New York City*]
MTA	Metropolitan Travel Agents [*Inactive*] (EA)
MTA	Midterm Availability
MTA	Mid-West Truckers Association (EA)
MTA	Military Technical Advisor (DNAB)
MTA	Military Testing Association (MCD)
MTA	Military Training Airspace (NATG)
MTA	Military Training Area (DA)
MTA	Military Transportation Authorization [*Air Force*]
MTA	Miniature Truck Association [*Defunct*] (EA)
MTA	Minimum Terms Agreement
MTA	Minimum Terrain-Clearance Altitude [*Aviation*]
MTA	Minor Task Authorization [*Navy*]
MTA	Missile Transfer Area (IAA)
MTA	Missile Tube Air
MTA	Mississippi Test Area [*Aerospace*] (AAG)
MTA	Mitchell Aero, Inc. [*ICAO designator*] (FAAC)
MTA	Mobile Training Assistance (CINC)
MTA	Mobility Test Article [*Lunar-surface rover*] [*NASA*]
MTA	Modified Tape Armor [*Telecommunications*] (IAA)
MTA	Monopulse Tracking Antenna
MTA	Motion-Time Analysis
MTA	Motorhome Travelers Association [*Defunct*] (EA)
MTA	Motor Trade Association (NADA)
MTA	Mount Allison University Library [*UTLAS symbol*]
MTA	Mount Auburn Hospital, Cambridge, MA [*OCLC symbol*] (OCLC)
MTA	Movimiento Teresiano de Apostolado [*Teresian Apostolic Movement - TAM*] [*Italy*] (EAIO)

MTA	M Technology Association
MTA	Multilateral Trade Agreement (AAGC)
MTA	Multiple Tailors Association [*British*] (BI)
MTA	Multiple-Terminal Access [*Computer science*] (IBMDP)
MTA	Multiterminal Adapter (IEEE)
MTA	Multitumor Antibody [*Clinical chemistry*]
MTA	Municipal Treasurers Association of the United States and Canada
MTA	Museum Trustee Association (EA)
MTA	Musical Theatres Association
MTA	Music Teachers' Association [*British*] (BI)
MTA	Music Trades' Association [*British*] (BI)
MTA	Muslim Teachers' Association (AIE)
MTA	Myoclonic Twitch Activity [*Neurology*] (DAVI)
MTA	Reference My Talk Address [*Military*] (IAA)
MTa	Taunton Public Library, Taunton, MA [*Library symbol Library of Congress*] (LCLS)
MTA 4	Medical Technician, Acting, 4th Class [*British military*] (DMA)
MTAA	Mopar Trans-Am Association [*Commercial firm*] (EA)
MTaB	Bristol County Law Library, Taunton, MA [*Library symbol Library of Congress*] (LCLS)
MTAB	Marginal Terrain Assault Bridge [*Military*] (RDA)
MTAB	Military Technical Acceptance Board (MCD)
MTAC	Mailers Technical Advisory Committee (EA)
MTAC	Mathematical Tables and Other Aids to Computation
MTAC	Michigan Test of Aural Comprehension [*J. Upshur*] (TES)
MTAC	Mid-Atlantic Technology Applications Center [*University of Pittsburgh*] [*Research center*] (RCD)
MTAC	Multiple Acceptance Test Criteria [*Lubricant testing*]
MTAC	Multiple Test Acceptance Code [*Lubricants testing*] [*Automotive engineering*]
MTAC	Multiple Test Acceptance Criteria
MTACC	Multiple Time Around Clutter
MTACCS	Marine Tactical Command and Control System (MCD)
MTACLS	Marine Tactical Air Control and Landing System
MTACP	Magnetic Tape Ancillary Control Process [*Computer science*] (CIST)
MTAD	N-methyl-triazolinedione
MTADS	Marine Corps Tactical Data System (AFIT)
MTAE	Message Transfer Agent Entity [*Telecommunications*] (OSI)
MTAF	Mediterranean Tactical Air Force Headquarters
MTAG	Manufacturing Technology Advisory Group [*DoD*] (RDA)
MTAG	Mission Theological Advisory Group (WDAA)
MTaHi	Old Colony Historical Society, Taunton, MA [*Library symbol Library of Congress*] (LCLS)
MtAHS	Alberton High School, Alberton, MT [*Library symbol*] [*Library of Congress*] (LCLS)
MTAI	Meal Tickets Authorized and Issued [*Army*] (AABC)
MTAI	Member of the Institute of Travel Agents [*British*]
MTAI	Minnesota Teacher Attitude Inventory
MTAIF	Member of the Australasian Institute for Fundraising (NFD)
MTAK	Magyar Tudomanyos Akademia Konyvtara [*Hungarian Academy of Sciences Library*] (IID)
mTAL	Medullary Thick Ascending Limb [*Anatomy*]
MTAM	Maritime Tropical Air Mass (MSA)
MT(AMT)	Medical Technologist (American Medical Technologists) (DAVI)
MT & AETF	Missile Tilt and Azimuth Error Test Fixture
MT & CE	Missile Test and Checkout Equipment
MT&RC	Marine Training and Replacement Command (SAA)
MT & SE	Maintenance Test and Support Equipment
MTANSW	Motor Trades Association of New South Wales [*Australia*]
MTANSW	Music Teachers' Association of South Australia
MTAP	Management Technical Applications Plan (MCD)
MTAP	Methylthioadenosine Phosphorylase [*An enzyme*]
MTAR	Manual Terrain Avoidance RADAR
MTAR	Moving Target Acquisition RADAR (MCD)
MTAS	Membrana Tympana Auris Sinistrae [*Medicine*] (DMAA)
MTAS	Multisensor Target Acquisition System [*Military*] (RDA)
MTASA	Motor Trade Association of South Australia
MT(ASCP)	Registered Medical Technologist (American Society of Clinical Pathologists)
MT(ASCP)SBB	Medical Technologist (American Society of Clinical Pathologists) Specialist in Blood Bank [*Technology*] (DAVI)
MTase	Methyltransferase [*An enzyme*]
MTA/SME	Machining Technology Association of the Society of Manufacturing Engineers (EA)
MTAT	Mean Turn-Around Time [*Quality control*]
MTA US & C	Municipal Treasurers Association of the US and Canada (EA)
MTAWA	Motor Trade Association of Western Australia
M Tax	Master of Taxation (PGP)
MtB	Bozeman Pubic Library, Bozeman, MT [*Library symbol*] [*Library of Congress*] (LCLS)
MTB	Maintenance of True Bearing
MTB	Maintenance Time Budget
MTB	Main Terminal Board
MTB	Main Time Base [*Electronics*]
MTB	Malaysian Tin Bureau [*Defunct*] (EA)
MTB	M&T Bank [*NYSE symbol*] [*Formerly, First Empire State*]
MTB	Marcaptan Terminated Polybutadiene (PDAA)
MTB	Marine Test Boat
MTB	Mark Twain Bancshares, Inc. [*NYSE symbol*] (SAG)
MTB	Materials Testing Branch [*NASA*]
MTB	Materials Transportation Bureau [*Department of Transportation*]
MTB	Maximum Theoretical Bandwidth (MHDI)
MTB	Mechanical Time Base
MTB	Medium Tank Battalion
MTB	Message to Base

MTB............	Methantheline [or Methanthine] Bromide [Pharmacology]
MTB............	Methoxy(trifluoromethyl)butyrophenone [Biochemistry]
MTB............	Methylthymol Blue [An indicator] [Chemistry]
MTB............	Modified Tyrode's Buffer [Clinical chemistry]
MTB............	Module Test Bed [Military] (CAAL)
MTB............	Monte Libano [Colombia] [Airport symbol] (OAG)
MTB............	Monterey, CA [Location identifier FAA] (FAAL)
MTB............	(Morpholinylthio)benzothiazole [Organic chemistry]
MTB............	Motor Tariff Bureau, Charleston WV [STAC]
MTB............	Motor Torpedo Boat
MTB............	Multichannel Triple Bridge
MTB............	Seaplane Bomber [Russian symbol]
MTBA..........	Machine Tool Builders' Association
MTBA..........	Mean Time Between Assists (AAEL)
MTBA..........	Melbourne Tenpin Bowling Association [Australia]
MTBA..........	Methyl-tert-butylaniline [Organic chemistry]
MTBA..........	Multi-Threat Body Armor [Army]
MtBaF.........	Fallon County Library, Baker MT [Library symbol] [Library of Congress] (LCLS)
MtBaHS	Baker High School, Baker, MT [Library symbol] [Library of Congress] (LCLS)
MTBAMA......	Mean Time between Any Maintenance Actions [Quality control] (MCD)
MTBASIC	Multitasking BASIC [Computer science]
MtBC..........	Montana State University at Bozeman, Bozeman, MT [Library symbol Library of Congress] (LCLS)
MTBCA........	Mean Time between Corrective Action (MCD)
MTBCD........	Mean Time Between Confirmed Defects [Quality control] (MHDI)
MTBCF........	Mean Time between Confirmed Failures [Quality control]
MTBCF........	Mission Time between Critical Failures
MTBCME.....	Mean Time between Corrective Maintenance Events [Quality control] (CAAL)
MTBCMI......	Mean Time between Corrective Maintenance Interrupts [Quality control] (CAAL)
MTBD..........	Mean Time between Defects [Quality control] (PDAA)
MTBD..........	Mean Time between Degradations [Quality control] [Telecommunications] (TEL)
MTBD..........	Mean Time between Demands [Quality control] (MCD)
MTBD..........	Mean Time between Discrepancies [Quality control]
MTBD..........	Methyl(triazabicyclo)decene [Organic chemistry]
MTBDE........	Mean Time between Downing Events [Quality control]
MTBDR........	Mean Time between Depot Repair [Quality control] (PDAA)
MTBE..........	Mean Time between Errors [Quality control]
MTBE..........	Mean Time between Events [Quality control]
MTBE..........	Meningeal Tick-Borne Encephalitis [Medicine] (DMAA)
MTBE..........	Methyl Tertiary Butyl Ether [Fuel additive]
MtBeHS	Rocky Boy Tribal High School, Box Elder, MT [Library symbol] [Library of Congress] (LCLS)
MTBEMA......	Mean Time between Essential Maintenance Actions [Quality control]
MTBER........	Mean Time between Engine Removal [Quality control] (DNAB)
MTBERA	Mean Time between Essential Replacement Actions [Quality control]
MtBeS........	Stone Child Community College, Box Elder, MT [Library symbol] [Library of Congress] (LCLS)
MTBETF	Methyl Tertiary Butyl Ether Task Force (EA)
MTBF..........	Mean Time Between Failures [DMAA]
MTBFA........	Mean Time between False Alarms [Quality control] (AABC)
MTBFC........	Mean Time between Failures, Critical [Military]
MTBFC........	Mean Time between Flight Cancellations [Quality control]
MTBFEC.......	Motor Truck, Bus, and Fire Engine Club [Defunct] (EA)
MTBFL........	Mean Time between Function Loss [Quality control]
MTBFRO	Mean Time between Failures Requiring Overhaul [Quality control]
MTBHA........	Mark Twain Boyhood Home Associates (EA)
MTBHMF......	Maintenance between Hardware Mission Failures [Quality control]
MTBHQ........	Mono-Tertiarybutylhydroquinone [Also, TBHQ] [Organic chemistry]
MTBI..........	Mean Time between Interrupts [Quality control]
MtBil...........	Billings Public Library, Billings, MT [Library symbol Library of Congress] (LCLS)
MtBilB	Bureau of Land Management, Billings, MT [Library symbol Library of Congress] (LCLS)
MtBilBH	Big Sky Hospice, Billings, MT [Library symbol] [Library of Congress] (LCLS)
MtBilC	Billings Clinic, Billings, MT [Library symbol] [Library of Congress] (LCLS)
MtBilD	Deaconess Medical Center, Billings, MT [Library symbol] [Library of Congress] (LCLS)
MtBilE	Eastern Montana College, Billings, MT [Library symbol Library of Congress] (LCLS)
MtBilFW	United States Fish and Wildlife, Billings, MT [Library symbol Library of Congress] (LCLS)
MtBilGS	Church of Jesus Christ of Latter-Day Saints, Genealogical Society Library, Billings Branch, Billings, MT [Library symbol Library of Congress] (LCLS)
MtBilMH	Billings Mental Health Center, Billings, MT [Library symbol] [Library of Congress] (LCLS)
MtBilNC	Northern Rockies Cancer Center, Billings, MT [Library symbol] [Library of Congress] (LCLS)
MtBilPP	Planned Parenthood of Billings, Billings, MT [Library symbol] [Library of Congress] (LCLS)
MtBilR	Rocky Mountain College, Billings, MT [Library symbol Library of Congress] (LCLS)
MtBilRF	Rimrock Foundation Library, Billings, MT [Library symbol] [Library of Congress] (LCLS)
MtBils..........	Billings Public Schools, Billings, MT [Library symbol] [Library of Congress] (LCLS)
MtBilSV	Saint Vincents Hospital, Billings, MT [Library symbol Library of Congress] (LCLS)
MtBilY	Yellowstone Treatment Center, Billings, MT [Library symbol] [Library of Congress] (LCLS)
MtBilYH	Yellowstone City-County Helth Department, Billings, MT [Library symbol] [Library of Congress] (LCLS)
MTblack......	Medium Thermal Black (EDCT)
MTBM.........	Mean Time between Maintenance [Quality control] (AFM)
MTBM.........	Mean Time between Malfunctions [Quality control]
MTBM.........	Microtunneling Boring Machine (RDA)
MTBMA.......	Mean Time between Maintenance Actions [Quality control]
MTBMAF......	Mean Time between Mission Affecting Failures [Quality control]
MTBMCF.....	Mean Time between Mission Critical Failure [Quality control]
MTBME.......	Mean Time between Malfunction Events [Quality control] (CAAL)
MTBN.........	Motor Transportation Battalion [Military]
MTBN.........	Mountbatten, Inc. [NASDAQ symbol] (SAG)
MTBO.........	Mean Time Before Obsolescence [Navy] (DOMA)
MTBO.........	Mean Time between Outages [Quality control] [Telecommunications] (TEL)
MTBO.........	Mean Time between Overhauls [Quality control] (MCD)
MTBO.........	Minimum Time before Overhaul [Quality control]
MTBOF........	Mean Time between Operational Failures [Quality control]
MTBOMF.....	Mean Time between Operational Mission Failures [Quality control] (MCD)
MTBPER......	Mean Time between Permanent Engine Removal [Quality control] (DNAB)
MTBPM.......	Mean Time Between Planned Maintenance [Engineering]
MtBr..........	Broadus Public Library, Broadus, MT [Library symbol] [Library of Congress] (LCLS)
MTBR.........	Mean Time between Removal [or Repair or Replacement] [Quality control]
MTBR.........	Mean Time Between Replacement
MTBRDR......	Mean Time between Removal for Depot Repair [Quality control] (MCD)
MTBRON	Motor Torpedo Boat Squadron [Navy]
MTBS.........	Mean Time between Service [Quality control] (MCD)
MTBS.........	Mean Time Between Stops [Quality control] (IAA)
MTBS.........	Methuen's Text-Books of Science [A publication]
MTBSD........	Mean Time between Supply Demands [Quality control] (MCD)
MTBSE........	Mean Time Between Software Errors [Quality control] (MHDI)
MTBSF........	Mean Time between Software Failures [Quality control] (CAAL)
MTBSF........	Mean Time between System Failures [Quality control]
MTBSHF	Mean Time between System Hardware Failures [Quality control] (MCD)
MTBSOF.....	Mean Time between System Operational Failures [Quality control] (MCD)
MTBSP........	Mobilization Troop Basic Stationing Plan (MCD)
MTBSTC.....	Motor Torpedo Boat Squadrons Training Center [Melville, RI] [Navy]
MTBT.........	Miniature Thermal Bar Torch [Army] (RDA)
MTBTF........	Mean Time between Testable Failures [Quality control]
MtBu..........	Butte Free Public Library, Butte, MT [Library symbol Library of Congress] (LCLS)
MtBuE........	Montana Energy Research and Development Institute, Butte, MT [Library symbol Library of Congress] (LCLS)
MTBUF........	Mean Time Between Undetected Failures [Quality control] (IAA)
MtBULM.....	Union List of Montana Serials, Bozeman, MT [Library symbol Library of Congress] (LCLS)
MTBUM.......	Mean Time Between Unscheduled Maintenance [Quality control] (MHDI)
MtBuM........	Montana College of Mineral Science and Technology, Butte, MT [Library symbol Library of Congress] (LCLS)
MTBUMA	Mean Time between Unscheduled Maintenance Actions [Quality control]
MTBUR........	Mean Time between Unscheduled Removals [or Replacements] [Quality control]
MtBwB........	Blackfeet Community College Library, Browning, MT [Library symbol] [Library of Congress] (LCLS)
MTC............	Carroll College, Library, Helena, MT [OCLC symbol] (OCLC)
MTC............	Machine Tool Control
MTC............	Machine Trim Compensator (AAG)
MTC............	Magnetic Tape Cassette [Computer science]
MTC............	Magnetic Tape Channel [Computer science]
MTC............	Magnetic Tape Command [Computer science] (IAA)
MTC............	Magnetic Tape Control [Computer science]
MTC............	Magnetic Tape Controller (NITA)
MTC............	Magnetization Transfer Contrast [Imaging technique]
MTC............	Maintenance Task Cycle
MTC............	Maintenance Time Constraint (IEEE)
MTC............	Main Trunk Circuit [World Meteorological Organization] [Telecommunications] (TEL)
MTC............	Majestic Resources [Vancouver Stock Exchange symbol]
MTC............	Make Today Count (EA)
MTC............	Maneuver Training Command [Army] (AABC)
MTC............	Manhattan Theater Club
MTC............	Man-Tended Capability (SSD)
MTC............	Man-Tended Committee (SSD)
MTC............	Manual Traffic Control (MCD)
MTC............	Manufacturing Technology Center
MTC............	Manufacturing Technology Centre of New Brunswick [Research center] (RCD)
MTC............	Marcus Tullius Cicero [Roman orator and author, 106-43 BC]
MTC............	Maritime Transport Committee [OECD] (DS)
MTC............	Mass Transfer Coefficient
MTC............	Master of Textile Chemistry
MTC............	Master Table of Contents (IAA)

MTC	Master Tape Control
MTC	Master Thrust Control [*or Controller*] [*NASA*] (NASA)
MTC	Master Training Concept [*Problem solving*]
MTC	Material Testing Center
MTC	Materiel Testing Command [*Merged with Weapons and Mobility Command*] [*Army*]
MTC	Maximum Tolerable Concentration [*Toxicology*]
MTC	Maximum Toxic Concentration [*Medicine*]
MTC	Maximum Track Capacity
MTC	Mechanical Torpedo Countermeasure [*Military*] (CAAL)
MTC	Mechanical Transport Corps
MTC	Medical Test Cabinet
MTC	Medical Training Center [*Later, Academy of Health Sciences*] [*Army*]
MTC	Medium Terminal Complexes (MCD)
MTC	Medullary Thyroid Carcinoma [*Medicine*]
MTC	Meet the Composer (EA)
MTC	Member of Technical College [*British*] (DI)
MTC	Memory Test Computer [*SAGE*]
MTC	Message Table of Contents (MCD)
MTC	Message Transmission Controller
MTC	Meteorological Training Center
Mtc	Methylthiocarbamoyl [*Biochemistry*]
MTC	Metocurine [*A muscle relaxant*]
MTC	MIDI [*Musical Instrument Digital Interface*] Time Code
MTC	Military Tactical Computer (MCD)
MTC	Military Training Cadets [*A boys' World War II organization*]
MTC	Military Transportation Command
MTC	Military Transportation Committee [*NATO*] (NATG)
mtC	Million Tonnes Carbon (EES)
MTC	Missile Technician, Chief [*Navy rating*]
MTC	Missile Test Center
MTC	Missile Transfer Car
MTC	Missile Tube Control
MTC	Mission and Test Computer
MTC	Mission and Traffic Control
MTC	Mitomycin C [*Mutamycin*] [*Also, Mi, MMC*] [*Antineoplastic drug*]
MTC	Mitsui Toatsu Chemicals, Inc. [*Japan*]
MTC	Mobile Tactical Computer (PDAA)
MTC	Mobile Target Carrier
MTC	Moderator Temperature Coefficient (NRCH)
MTC	Modulation Transfer Curve (OA)
MTC	Monsanto Co. [*NYSE symbol*] (SPSG)
MTC	Morgan Territory [*California*] [*Seismograph station code, US Geological Survey*] (SEIS)
MTC	Morse Telegraph Club (EA)
MTC	Motor Transport Corps [*Military*]
MTC	Mount Clemens, MI [*Location identifier FAA*] (FAAL)
MTC	MOUT [*Military Operations on Urbanized Terrain*] Training Complex [*Army*] (INF)
MTC	Mouvement Traditionaliste Congolais [*Congolese Traditionalist Movement*]
MTC	Moving Target Carrier (MCD)
MTC	Multicomm Telecommunications Corp. [*Formerly, Mutual Satellite Services*]
MTC	Multiple Tube Counts
MTC	Multistate Tax Commission (EA)
MTC	Music Teacher's Certificate [*British*] (DI)
MTC	Mutating Transformation Converter (IAA)
MTC	Mystic Terminal Co. [*AAR code*]
MTC	Ontario Ministry of Transportation and Communications [*Canada*] (TSSD)
MTCA	Cayes [*Haiti*] [*ICAO location identifier*] (ICLI)
MTCA	Methyltetrahydrocarbolinecarboxylic Acid [*Organic chemistry*]
MTCA	Methylthiazolidinecarboxylic Acid [*Organic chemistry*]
MTCA	Military Terminal Control Area
MTCA	Minimum Terrain-Clearance Altitude [*Aviation*]
MTCA	Ministry of Transport and Civil Aviation [*Later, MT*] [*British*] (MCD)
MTCA	Monitor and Test Control Area [*NASA*] (NASA)
MTCA	Multiple-Terminal Communication Adapter [*Computer science*]
MtCaC	Little Big Horn College, Crow Agency, MT [*Library symbol*] [*Library of Congress*] (LCLS)
MTCACS	Marine Corps Tactical Command and Control System (MCD)
MTCB	Metropolitan Taxicab Board (NADA)
MTCC	Magnetics Technology [*NASDAQ symbol*] (SAG)
MTCC	Magnetic Technologies [*NASDAQ symbol*] (TTSB)
MTCC	Master Timing and Control Circuit
MTCC	Military Air Transport Service [*later, Military Airlift Command*] TransportControl Center
MTCC	Modular Tactical Communications Center
MTCD	Microvolume Thermal Conductivity Detector [*Instrumentation*]
MTCE	Maintenance [*Telecommunications*] (TEL)
MTCE	Million Tons of Coal Equivalent [*A comparative unit of energy content widely used in the oil industry*]
MTCF	Mean Time to Catastrophic Failure [*Quality control*]
MTCF	Missile Tube Comparator Fixture
MtCG	Glacier County Library, Cut Bank, MT [*Library symbol*] [*Library of Congress*] (LCLS)
MtCh	Blaine County library, Chinook, MT [*Library symbol*] [*Library of Congress*] (LCLS)
MTCH	Cap Haitien Internacional [*Haiti*] [*ICAO location identifier*] (ICLI)
MTCH	Magnetic Tape Channel (NITA)
MT Ch	Master of Textile Chemistry
MTCH	Mining Technology Clearing House [*British Information service or system*] (IID)
MtchBnc	Mitchell Bancorp, Inc. [*Associated Press*] (SAG)

MtChe	Liberty County Library, Chester, MT [*Library symbol*] [*Library of Congress*] (LCLS)
MtchIE	Mitchell Energy & Development Corp. [*Associated Press*] (SAG)
MtCi	George McCone Memorial County Library, Circle, MT [*Library symbol*] [*Library of Congress*] (LCLS)
MTCI	Magnetic Tape Control Interface (MCD)
MTCI	Management Technologies [*NASDAQ symbol*] (TTSB)
MTCI	Management Technologies, Inc. [*NASDAQ symbol*] (NQ)
MTCI	Member of the Trust Companies Institute (DD)
MTCL	Motorcycle
MTCM	Master of Traditional Chinese Medicine (PGP)
MTCM	Missile Technician, Master Chief [*Navy rating*]
MTCNOLD	Minimum Tax Credit Net Operating Loss Deduction [*Business term*]
MTCO	Macon Terminal Co. [*AAR code*]
MTCOECD	Maritime Transport Committee of the Organization for Economic Cooperation and Development [*France*] (EAIO)
MtCoHS	Columbus High School, Columbus, MT [*Library symbol*] [*Library of Congress*] (LCLS)
MtCol	Colstrip Bicentennial Library, Colstrip, MT [*Library symbol*] [*Library of Congress*] (LCLS)
MtCon	Conrad Public Library, Conrad, MT [*Library symbol*] [*Library of Congress*] (LCLS)
MTCON	Microwave Aeropace Terminal Control [*Air Force*] (IAA)
MTCP	Master of Town and Country Planning (ADA)
MTCP	Ministry of Town and Country Planning [*British*]
MTCR	Missile Technology Control Regime [*US, Canada, Britain, France, West Germany, Japan*]
MTCS	Madelian Thomas Completion Stories [*Psychology*] (DAVI)
MTCS	Melbourne Theatre Cooperative Society [*Australia*]
MTCS	Meteor Trail Communications System
MTCS	Minimal Terminal Communications System (NVT)
MTCS	Minimum Teleprocessing Commmunications System
MTCS	Missile Technician, Senior Chief [*Navy rating*]
MTCT	Manipulator/Teleoperator Control Technology (SSD)
MTCU	Magnetic Tape Control Unit [*Computer science*]
MTCV	Main Turbine Control Valve (IEEE)
MTCW	Major 20th-Century Writers [*A publication*]
MTD	Macknight Airlines [*Australia ICAO designator*] (FAAC)
MTD	Magnetic Tape Disk (MCD)
MTD	Main Technical Directorate (RDA)
MTD	Maintenance Task Demand File (MCD)
MTD	Maintenance Tasks Distribution
MTD	Maintenance Technical Directive (SAA)
MTD	Maintenance Technology Development
MTD	Maintenance Training Department
MTD	Manager, Traffic Department
MTD	Manager, Transportation Department
MTD	Manufacturing Technology Development (RDA)
MTD	Manufacturing Technology Directorate [*Army*] (RDA)
MTD	Manufacturing Technology Division [*Air Force*]
MTD	Marine Technology Directorate [*British*]
MTD	Maritime Trades Department, AFL-CIO [*American Federation of Labor and Congress of Industrial Organizations*] (EA)
MTD	Mass Tape Duplicator/Verifier [*Computer science*] (MCD)
MTD	Master of Textile Dyeing
MTD	Master of Transport Design
MTD	Master Tape Data
MTD	Master Time Display
MTD	Master Tracking Data [*NASA*]
MTD	Materiel Testing Directorate [*Army*] (RDA)
MTD	Maximum Tolerated Dose [*Medicine*]
MTD	Mean Temperature Difference
MTD	Mean Therapeutic Dose [*Medicine*]
MTD	Mean Tolerated Dose [*Medicine*]
MTD	Mean Total Dose [*Medicine*] (DMAA)
MTD	Mean Tubular Diameter
MTD	Mechanical Road Transport Driver [*British military*] (DMA)
MTD	Metacarpal Total Density [*Anatomy*]
MTD	Metal Trades Department, AFL-CIO [*American Federation of Labor and Congress of Industrial Organizations*] (EA)
MTD	Metastatic Trophoblastic Disease [*Medicine*] (AAMN)
MTD	Meta-Toluenediamine [*Organic chemistry*]
MTD	Methyltriazolinedione [*Organic chemistry*]
MTD	Microwave Target Designator
MTD	Midwife Teacher's Diploma [*British*]
MTD	Military Test Directorate [*Program*] [*Army*] (RDA)
MTD	Minimal Toxic Dose (IEEE)
MTD	Mintel International Development Corp. [*Vancouver Stock Exchange symbol*]
MTD	Mitte Tales Doses [*Send Such Doses*] [*Pharmacy*]
MTD	Mobile Target Division [*Mine Force*] [*Navy*]
MTD	Mobile Training Detachment
MTD	Mobilization Table of Distribution [*Military*]
MTD	Monroe Tidal Drainage [*Urology*] (DAVI)
MTD	Mount Darwin [*Zimbabwe*] [*Seismograph station code, US Geological Survey*] (SEIS)
MTD	Mounted
mtd	Mounted (VRA)
MTD	Moving Target Detector [*RADAR*]
MTD	Multiple Target Deception (MCD)
MTD	Multiple Target Discrimination (MCD)
MTD	Multiple Tile Duct [*Telecommunications*] (TEL)
MTDA	Marine Tactical Data
MTDA	Methyl Trimethylsilyl Dimethylketene Acetal [*Organic chemistry*]
MTDA	Modification Table of Distribution and Allowances [*Army*] (AABC)

MTDB	Metropolitan Transit Development Board (NADA)	**MTEM**	Mechanical Maintenance Test Equipment (NASA)
MTDC	Modified Total Direct Costs [*Economics*]	**MT Eng**	Master of Textile Engineering
MTDDA	Minnesota Test for Differential Diagnosis of Aphasia [*Psychology*]	**MTEO**	Maintenance Test Equipment, Optical (NASA)
MTDDIS	Mesoscale Transport Diffusion and Deposition Model for Industrial Sources [*Environmental Protection Agency*] (GFGA)	**M'TER**	Manchester [*City in England*] (ROG)
MTDE	Maritime Tactical Data Exchange (NATG)	**MTER**	Multitest Evaluation Report [*Nuclear energy*] (NRCH)
MTDE	Modern Technology Demonstration Engine	**MTES**	Metastable Transfer Emission Spectroscopy
MT Des	Master of Textile Design	**MTES**	Methyltriethoxysilane [*Organic chemistry*]
MtDeSP	Montana State Prison, Conley Lake, Deer Lodge, MT [*Library symbol*] [*Library of Congress*] (LCLS)	**MTESL**	Master in Teaching English as a Second Language (PGP)
MTDF	Master Tracking Data File [*NASA*]	**MTET**	Maximal Treadmill Exercise Test
MTDF	Mobile Tank Depermer Facility (DWSG)	**Mtewan**	Matewan BancShares [*Associated Press*] (SAG)
MtDi	Dillon City Library, Dillon, MT [*Library symbol*] [*Library of Congress*] (LCLS)	**MTEWS/AD**	Mobile Tactical Early Warning System for Air Defense [*NATO*]
MtDiGS	Church of Jesus Christ of Latter-Day Saints, Genealogical Society Library, ButteStake Branch, Dillon Chapel, Dillon, MT [*Library symbol Library of Congress*] (LCLS)	**MTEX**	Mission Template Expert (SSD)
		MText	Master of Textiles (NADA)
MtDiW	Western Montana College, Dillon, MT [*Library symbol Library of Congress*] (LCLS)	**MTF**	Fairbanks, AK [*Location identifier FAA*] (FAAL)
MTDL	Multiple Tap Delay Line	**MTF**	Machine Tool Forum
mtDNA	Deoxyribonucleic Acid, Mitochondrial [*Biochemistry, genetics*]	**MTF**	Maintenance Test Facility [*Telecommunications*] (OTD)
mtDNA	Mitochondrial DNA [*Deoxyribonucleic acid*] (USDC)	**MTF**	Maintenance Test Flight (MCD)
MTDP	Medium Term Defense Plan (NATG)	**MTF**	Maintenance Training Flight [*Military*]
MTDP	Medium Term Development Plan [*Economics*] (FEA)	**MTF**	Manufacturing Technology Facility [*US Army Communications-Electronics Command*] [*Fort Monmouth, NJ*] (RDA)
MTDS	Manufacturing Test Data System (IEEE)		
MTDS	Marine Tactical Data System	**MTF**	Matrix Test Facility (MCD)
MTDS	Marine Toebreak Data System (NG)	**MTF**	Maximum Terminal Flow (MAE)
MTDS	Metallurgical and Thermochemical Data Service [*Department of Trade and Industry*] [*Information service or system*] (IID)	**MTF**	Mean Time to Failure [*Quality control*]
		MTF	Mechanical Time Fuze
MTDS	Missile Trajectory Data System (MUGU)	**MTF**	Medical Treatment Facility (AABC)
MTDSK	Magnetic Tape Disk [*Computer science*] (NASA)	**MTF**	Medical Treatment Faculty (DAVI)
MTDT	Modified Tone Decay Test (MAE)	**MTF**	Megawatt Transmitter Filter
MTE	AirTran Airways, Inc. [*FAA designator*] (FAAC)	**MTF**	Men's Tie Foundation [*Later, NAA*] (EA)
MtE	Ekalaka Public Library, Ekalaka, MT [*Library symbol*] [*Library of Congress*] (LCLS)	**MTF**	Message Text Formatting
		MTF	Message Transfer Facility [*Telecommunications*] (OSI)
MTE	Magnetic Tape Encoder [*Computer science*] (IAA)	**MTF**	Metal Trades Federation (NADA)
MTE	Magnetosphere-Thermosphere Explorer [*NASA*]	**MTF**	Metastable Time of Flight
MTE	Maintenance Test Equipment (MCD)	**MTF**	Meteorological Task Force (MCD)
MTE	Maintenance Training Equipment (MCD)	**MTF**	Microsoft Tape Format [*Microsoft Corp.*] [*Computer science*] (PCM)
MTE	Manteigas [*Portugal*] [*Seismograph station code, US Geological Survey*] (SEIS)	**MTF**	Microwave Test Facility
		MTF	Military Treatment Facility [*DoD*]
MTE	Master of Teacher Education (PGP)	**MTF**	Mississippi Test Facility [*Later, NSTL*] [*NASA*]
MTE	Master of Textile Engineering	**MTF**	Mizan Teferi [*Ethiopia*] [*Airport symbol Obsolete*] (OAG)
MTE	Maximum Temperature Engine	**MTF**	Mock-Up Test Facility (MCD)
MTE	Maximum Tracking Error	**MTF**	Modulation Transfer Function [*Resolution measure*]
MTE	Measurement and Test Equipment [*Environmental science*] (COE)	**mtf**	More to Follow [*Copyediting*] (WDMC)
MTE	Member of the Telegraph Engineers [*British*] (ROG)	**MTF**	Motif
MTE	Merit Technologies Ltd. [*Vancouver Stock Exchange symbol*]	**MTF**	Moulded Fiber Technology
mte	Metal-Engraver [*MARC relator code*] [*Library of Congress*] (LCCP)	**MTF**	Multiple Tube Fermentation
MtE	Metropolitan Edison Co. [*Associated Press*] (SAG)	**MTF**	Multitarget Frequency
MTE	Microwave Test Equipment	**MTFA**	Medium-Term Financial Assistance
MTE	Missile Test Engineer (MUGU)	**MTFA**	Modulation Transfer Function Analyzer
MTE	Mitre Corp., Bedford Operations Library, Bedford, MA [*OCLC symbol*] (OCLC)	**MtFb**	Chouteau County Free Library, Fort Benton, MT [*Library symbol*] [*Library of Congress*] (LCLS)
MTE	Mobile Telephone Exchange [*Nordic Mobile Telephone*]	**MTFC**	Masters Track and Field Committee (EA)
MTE	Modern Technology Engine	**MTFCA**	Model ™T∫ Ford Club of America (EA)
MTE	Modular Threat Emitter (DWSG)	**MTFCI**	Model T Ford Club International (EA)
MTE	Module Table Entry [*Computer science*] (BYTE)	**MTFD**	Minimum Tracking Flux Density
MTE	Monte Alegre [*Brazil*] [*Airport symbol*] (AD)	**MTFE**	Mercury Thin Film Electrode [*Electrochemistry*]
MTE	Multiple Terminal Emulator	**MTFEX**	Mountain Field Exercise [*Military*] (NVT)
MTE	Multiple Terminator Emulator (NITA)	**MTFF**	Man-Tended Free Flyer (MCD)
MTE	Multipurpose Test Equipment	**MTFF**	Mean Time to First Failure [*Quality control*] (AAG)
MTE	Multisystem Test Equipment [*Military*]	**MtFhV**	United States Veterans Administration Center, Fort Harrison, MT [*Library symbol Library of Congress*] (LCLS)
MTE	Multithreshold Element (IAA)		
MTE-5	Multielectrolyte Concentrate [*Pharmacology*] (DAVI)	**MTFL**	Mean Time to Fault Locate [*Quality control*] (CAAL)
MTEA	Maintenance Training Effectiveness Analysis [*Army*]	**MTFMPP**	Meta-Trifluoromethylphenylpiperazine [*Biochemistry*]
MTEA	Metal Trades Employers Association (NADA)	**MTFO**	Modular Training Field Option (NASA)
MTEA	Minimum Target Elevation Angle (MCD)	**MTFP**	Marema Tlou Freedom Party [*Lesotho*]
MTEAA	(Methylthio)ethyl Acetoacetate [*Organic chemistry*]	**MTFR**	Mean Time for Repair [*Quality control*] (IAA)
MTEC	Maintenance Test Equipment Catalog (MCD)	**MTFR**	Message Text Formatting Reporting
MTec	Metric Tons Energy Consumption	**MTFR**	Metal Furring [*Technical drawings*]
MTEC	Microtec Research, Inc. [*NASDAQ symbol*] (SAG)	**MTFR**	[*The*] Minnesota Transfer Railway Co. [*AAR code*]
MTEC	Monash Timber Engineering Center [*Australia*]	**MtFR**	Rosebud County Library, Forsyth, MT [*Library symbol*] [*Library of Congress*] (LCLS)
M Tech	Master of Technology		
MTECP	Maintenance Test Equipment Certification Procedure (SAA)	**MtFrHS**	Frenchtown High School, Frenchtown, MT [*Library symbol*] [*Library of Congress*] (LCLS)
MTECR	Maintenance Test Equipment Certification Requirement (SAA)	**MTFS**	Marine Terminal Fuel Separator (MCD)
MTEE	Electrical Maintenance Test Equipment	**MTFS**	Medium-Term Financial Strategy
MTEE	Maintenance Test Equipment, Electrical (NASA)	**MTFSC**	Ministerial Task Force on Soil Conservation [*Australia*]
MTEE	Mean Transverse Emmission Energy (PDAA)	**MTFTS**	Marine Terminal Fuel Tankage System (MCD)
MTEE	Mission Time Extreme Environment [*NASA*] (KSC)	**MTG**	Aviation Co. Mostransgas [*Former USSR*] [*FAA designator*] (FAAC)
MTEEC	Maintenance Test Equipment, Electronic (NASA)	**MtG**	Glendive Public Library, Glendive, MT [*Library symbol Library of Congress*] (LCLS)
MTEF	Maintenance Test Equipment, Fluid (NASA)		
MTEG	Mickey Thompson Entertainment Group [*Auto racing*]	**MTG**	Main Tank Gun [*Army*]
MTEG	Port-Au-Prince [*Haiti*] [*ICAO location identifier*] (ICLI)	**MTG**	Main Traffic Group [*Telecommunications*] (TEL)
MTEL	Manning Table and Equipment List	**MTG**	Main Turbogenerator
MTEL	Maximum Tolerable Exposure Level [*Toxicology*]	**MTG**	Media Task Group [*Environmental Protection Agency*] (GFGA)
MTEL	Methyltriethyllead [*Organic chemistry*]	**MTG**	Meeting (AFM)
MTEL	Mobile Telecommunications & Technology Corp. [*NASDAQ symbol*] (SAG)	**MTG**	Melt-Textured Growth [*Chemistry*]
		MTG	Methanol-to-Gasoline [*Process*] [*Mobil Oil Corp.*]
MTEL	Mobile Telecommun Tech [*NASDAQ symbol*] (TTSB)	**MTG**	Methoxytriglycol [*Organic chemistry*]
MTelEng	Master of Telecommunications Engineering (NADA)	**MTG**	Methyl Tetradecylglycidate [*Biochemistry*]
MtELH	Lincoln County Senior High School, Eureka, MT [*Library symbol*] [*Library of Congress*] (LCLS)	**MTG**	(Methyl)thiogalactoside [*Biochemistry*]
		MTG	MGIC Investment [*NYSE symbol*] (TTSB)
		MTG	MGIC Investment Co. [*NYSE symbol*] (SPSG)
MTELP	Michigan Test of English Language Proficiency [*J. Upshur*] (TES)	**MTG**	Microsyn Torque Generator (SAA)
MTEM	Maintenance Test Equipment Module (MCD)	**MTG**	Montague Island [*Alaska*] [*Seismograph station code, US Geological Survey*] (SEIS)
		MTG	Mortgage [*Finance*] (SPSG)
		Mtg	Mortgage (EBF)

MTG.............	Motorsports Technology Group [*General Motors Corp.*]
MTG.............	Motor-Torque Generator
MTG.............	Mounting
MTG.............	Multiple-Trigger Generator
MTG.............	Multipurpose Target Generator
MTGAS........	Mechanical Transport Gasoline [*Military British*]
MTGBKT	Mounting Bracket (IAA)
MTGC..........	Mounting Center (MSA)
MTGCF........	Mobile Transportation Ground Command Facility (MCD)
MtGD	Dawson College, Glendive, MT [*Library symbol Library of Congress*] (LCLS)
MTGD	Mortgaged (ROG)
MtGDH.........	Dawson County High School, Glendive, MT [*Library symbol*] [*Library of Congress*] (LCLS)
mtge	Mortgage (DD)
MTGE..........	Mortgage
Mtge	Mortgage (TBD)
MTGEE........	Mortgagee
MTGF..........	Mouse Transforming Growth Factor [*Biochemistry*]
MTGHS	Magnetic, True, and Grid Heading Select (MCD)
MtGl.............	Glasgow City-County Library, Glasgow, MT [*Library symbol Library of Congress*] (LCLS)
MTGOR........	Mortgagor
MTGP..........	Monitor Table Generator Program (MCD)
MtGr............	Great Falls Public Library, Great Falls, MT [*Library symbol Library of Congress*] (LCLS)
MtGrCE	College of Great Falls, Great Falls, MT [*Library symbol Library of Congress*] (LCLS)
MtGrCH........	Columbus Hospital, Health Sciences Library, Great Falls, MT [*Library symbol Library of Congress*] (LCLS)
MtGrGS	Church of Jesus Christ of Latter-Day Saints, Genealogical Society Library, GreatFalls Branch, Great Falls, MT [*Library symbol Library of Congress*] (LCLS)
MtGrPS	Great Falls Public Schools, Great Falls, MT [*Library symbol*] [*Library of Congress*] (LCLS)
MTGS...........	Metal-to-Glass Seal
MTGS...........	Midcourse and Terminal Guidance System [*NASA*]
MTGU	Australian Master Tax Guide Updater [*A publication*]
MTGU	Main Turbine / Gearing Unit (PDAA)
MTGW	Maximum Total Gross Weight (MCD)
MTG/WESS...	Main Tank Gunfire/Weapon Effects Signature Simulator (MCD)
MtH..............	Helena Public Library, Helena, MT [*Library symbol Library of Congress*] (LCLS)
MTH.............	Magnetic Tape Handler [*Computer science*]
MTH.............	Marathon [*Florida*] [*Airport symbol*] (OAG)
MTH.............	Massachusetts Institute of Technology [*ICAO designator*] (FAAC)
M Th............	Master of Theology
MTH.............	Master of Tropical Health
MTH.............	Meath [*County in Ireland*] (ROG)
MTH.............	Meritage Corp. [*Formerly, Monterey Homes Corp.*] [*NYSE symbol*]
MTH.............	Metharbital [*An anticonvulsant*] [*Pharmacology*] (DAVI)
MTH.............	Methylthiohydantoin [*Organic chemistry*]
MTH.............	Microptic Theodolite
MTH.............	Mithramycin [*Medicine*] (DMAA)
MTH.............	Mithramycin (Aureolic acid, mithracin) [*Antineoplastic drug*]
MTH.............	Monterey Homes Corp. [*NYSE symbol*] (SAG)
MTH.............	Month
MTH.............	Mount Holyoke College, South Hadley, MA [*OCLC symbol*] (OCLC)
MTH.............	Mount Hood Railway Co. [*Later, MH*] [*AAR code*]
Mth..............	Mouth [*Maps and charts*]
MTH.............	Thompson Public Library, Manitoba [*Library symbol National Library of Canada*] (NLC)
MtHa............	Havre Hill County Library, Havre, MT [*Library symbol*] [*Library of Congress*] (LCLS)
MThA...........	Master of Theatre Arts
MtHam.........	Bitter Root Public Library, Hamilton, MT [*Library symbol*] [*Library of Congress*] (LCLS)
MtHamRL	United States National Institute of Health, Rocky Mountain Laboratory Library, Hamilton, MT [*Library symbol Library of Congress*] (LCLS)
MtHaN	Northern Montana College, Havre, MT [*Library symbol*] [*Library of Congress*] (LCLS)
MtHar	Big Horn County Public Library, Hardin, MT [*Library symbol Library of Congress*] (LCLS)
MtHarC	Fort Belknap College, Harlem, MT [*Library symbol*] [*Library of Congress*] (LCLS)
MtHarlF	Fort Belknap Community College, Harlem, MT [*Library symbol*] [*Library of Congress*] (LCLS)
MTHB..........	Mark Twain Home Board (EA)
MTHBD	Motherboard (MSA)
MtHC	Carroll College, Helena, MT [*Library symbol Library of Congress*] (LCLS)
MtHCE	Montana Census and Economic Information Center, Helena, MT [*Library symbol*] [*Library of Congress*] (LCLS)
MTHD..........	Method (MSA)
MtHe...........	Laurie Hill Library, Heron, MT [*Library symbol*] [*Library of Congress*] (LCLS)
M Theol.......	Master of Theology
MTHF..........	Methyltetrahydrofolate [*or Methyltetrahydrofolic*] [*Biochemistry*]
MTHF..........	Methyltetrahydrofuran [*Organic chemistry*]
MTHFR........	Methylene Tetrahydrofolate Reductase [*An enzyme*]
MtHG	United States Geological Survey, Water Resources Division, Helena, MT [*Library symbol*] [*Library of Congress*] (LCLS)
MThGH	Metallothionein-Human Growth Hormone [*Endocrinology*]
MtHGS	Church of Jesus Christ of Latter-Day Saints, Genealogical Society Library, Helena Branch, Helena, MT [*Library symbol Library of Congress*] (LCLS)
MTHHF	Methyltetrahydrohomofolate [*Biochemistry*]
MtHHS	Helena High School, Helena, MT [*Library symbol*] [*Library of Congress*] (LCLS)
MtHi............	Montana Historical Society, Helena, MT [*Library symbol Library of Congress*] (LCLS)
Mthly	Monthly (DLA)
MTHM..........	Metric Ton of Heavy Metal (NUCP)
MTHM..........	Million Tons Heavy Metal
MtHMv.........	Mountain View School, Helena, MT [*Library symbol*] [*Library of Congress*] (LCLS)
Mt Holyoke C...	Mount Holyoke College (GAGS)
MTHPA	Methyltetrahydrophthalic Anhydride [*Organic chemistry*]
MThPast	Maitre en Theologie Pastorale [*Master in Pastoral Theology*] [*French*]
M Th Past....	Master of Pastoral Theology (PGP)
MtHPI	Montana Office of Public Instruction, Resource Center, Helena, MT [*Library symbol*] [*Library of Congress*] (LCLS)
MTHR	Merthyr [*Cardiff*] [*Welsh depot code*]
MTHR	Mother
MTHRD	Male Threaded
MtHs............	Hot Springs Public Library, Hot Springs, MT [*Library symbol*] [*Library of Congress*] (LCLS)
MtHS	Shodair Children's Hospital, Helena, MT [*Library symbol Library of Congress*] (LCLS)
MtHSH........	Shodair Hospital, Helena, MT [*Library symbol*] [*Library of Congress*] (LCLS)
MtHsHS	Hot Springs High School, Hot Springs, MT [*Library symbol*] [*Library of Congress*] (LCLS)
MtHSP	Saint Peter's Community Hospital, Helena, MT [*Library symbol Library of Congress*] (LCLS)
MTHWL........	Motherwell [*Scotland*]
mthy	Monthly [*Publishing*] (WDMC)
MTI.............	Arturo Rodriguez Martinez [*Mexico*] [*FAA designator*] (FAAC)
MTI.............	Machine Tools Industry (MCD)
MTI.............	Maeventec Travel Information [*Maeventec*] [*Information service or system*] (CRD)
MTI.............	Magyar Tavviati Iroda [*Hungarian News Agency*] (BARN)
MTI.............	Main Tank Injection
MTI.............	Maintenance Team Inspection [*Environmental science*] (COE)
MTI.............	Malignant Teratoma Intermediate [*Oncology*] (MAE)
MTI.............	Manitoba Technical Institute [*Canada*]
MTI.............	Manpower Training Institute
MTI.............	Marked Temperature Inversion [*Aviation*] (DA)
MTI.............	Marketing and Training Institute (EA)
MTI.............	Materials Technology Institute of the Chemical Process Industries (EA)
MTI.............	Material Thickness Indicator
MTI.............	Maximum Therapeutic Index (EDCT)
MTI.............	Mechanical Technology, Inc.
MTI.............	Mechanical Tolerance Index [*Food technology*]
MTI.............	Media Technology International [*British*]
MTI.............	Member of the Trust Institute (DD)
MTI.............	Metal Treating Institute (EA)
MTI.............	Methylthioinosine [*Biochemistry*]
MTI.............	Methyltransferase I [*An enzyme*]
MTI.............	Military Training Instructor (AFM)
MTI.............	Minimum Time Interval [*Medicine*]
MTI.............	Ministry of Trade and Industry [*Canada*]
MTI.............	Missile Training Installation (NATG)
MTI.............	Mission Training International (EA)
MTI.............	Mobile Training Institute [*Klamath Falls, OR*] [*Telecommunications service*] (TSSD)
MTI.............	Modern Telecommunications, Inc. [*New York, NY*] (TSSD)
MTI.............	Mosteiros [*Cape Verde Islands*] [*Airport symbol*] (OAG)
MTI.............	Mouvement de la Tendance Islamique [*Islamic Trend Movement*] [*Tunisia*] (PD)
MTI.............	Moving Target Indicator
MTI.............	Multi-Spectral Thermal Imager Spacecraft [*Department of Energy*]
MTI.............	MuniYield Insured Fund II [*NYSE symbol*] (SPSG)
MTIA...........	Metal Trades Industry Association (NADA)
MTIAA.........	Metal Trades Industry Association of Australia
MTIAC.........	Manufacturing Technology Information Analysis Center [*DoD Information service or system*] (IID)
MTIC...........	Malaysia Tourist Information Center (EA)
MTIC...........	Moving Target Indicator Coherent (IEEE)
MTICFAR.....	Moving Target Indicator Constant False Alarm Rate (CET)
MTID...........	Master of Technology for International Development (PGP)
MTIE...........	Microthrust Ion Engine
MTIF...........	Maritime Technical Information Facility [*Maritime Administration*] [*Database producer*] (IID)
MTIF...........	Master Tailored Interest File [*Navy*] (NG)
MTIG...........	MTI Technology [*NASDAQ symbol*] (TTSB)
MTIHM.........	Metric Tons Initial Heavy Metal (GAAI)
MTIK...........	Miller Building Sys [*NASDAQ symbol*] (TTSB)
MTIK...........	Miller Building Systems, Inc. [*NASDAQ symbol*] (NQ)
MTIK...........	Missile Test Installation Kit
MTIK...........	Moving Target Indicator Kit
MTIL...........	Maximum Tolerable Insecurity Level (OA)
MTIM...........	Manual Trim in Motion [*Aviation*]
MTIN...........	Martin Industries [*NASDAQ symbol*] (TTSB)
MTIN...........	Martin Industries, Inc. [*NASDAQ symbol*] (SAG)
MTIN...........	Mountain [*Commonly used*] (OPSA)

MTIRA .... Machine Tool Industry Research Association [*Research center British*]

MTIRI .... Multispectral Thermal Infrared Imager (SSD)

MTIS .... Maintenance Task Information System (NG)

MTIS .... Material Turned into Stores

MTIS .... Mean Time in Shop [*Quality control*] (MCD)

MTIS .... Multimodal Traveler Information Systems [*FTA*] (TAG)

MTIS .... Multiplex Transmitter Input Signals (PDAA)

MTI Tch .... MTI Technology Corp. [*Associated Press*] (SAG)

MTIX .... Mechanical Technology (EFIS)

MTJ .... Mesifta Tifereth Jerusalem (BJA)

MTJ .... Midtarsal Joint [*Anatomy*] (DAVI)

MTJ .... Missile Track Jamming [*Military*] (CAAL)

MTJ .... Montrose [*Colorado*] [*Airport symbol*] (OAG)

MTJ .... Mount Tsukuba [*Japan*] [*Seismograph station code, US Geological Survey*] (SEIS)

MTJA .... Jacmel [*Haiti*] [*ICAO location identifier*] (ICLI)

MTJE .... Jeremie [*Haiti*] [*ICAO location identifier*] (ICLI)

MtJG .... Garfield County Library, Jordan, MT [*Library symbol*] [*Library of Congress*] (LCLS)

MTK .... Camp Ripley/Little Falls, MN [*Location identifier FAA*] (FAAL)

MtK .... Flathead County Free Library, Kalispell, MT [*Library symbol Library of Congress*] (LCLS)

MTK .... Makin [*Kiribati*] [*Airport symbol*] (OAG)

MTK .... Mechanical Time Keeping (NASA)

MTK .... Medium Tank

MTK .... Mintek Resources [*Vancouver Stock Exchange symbol*]

MTK .... Mitaka [*Japan*] [*Seismograph station code, US Geological Survey Closed*] (SEIS)

mtk .... Tropical Maritime Cold Air Mass [*Meteorology*] (BARN)

MtKF .... Flathead Valley Community College, Kalispell, MT [*Library symbol Library of Congress*] (LCLS)

MtKFH .... Flathead Senior High School, Kalispell, MT [*Library symbol*] [*Library of Congress*] (LCLS)

MtKGS .... Church of Jesus Christ of Latter-Day Saints, Genealogical Society Library, Kalispell Branch, Kalispell, MT [*Library symbol Library of Congress*] (LCLS)

MtKH .... Kalispell Regional Hospital, Kalispell, MT [*Library symbol Library of Congress*] (LCLS)

MTL .... Magnetic Tape Loader

MTL .... Main Transfer Line (MCD)

MTL .... Maitland [*Australia Airport symbol*] (OAG)

MTL .... Mantle Zone Lymphoma [*Medicine*] (DMAA)

MTL .... Manufacturing and Technology Laboratory

MTL .... Mass-Transport-Limited [*Chemical engineering*]

MTL .... Master Tape Loading

MTL .... Matched Transmission Line

MTL .... Material (KSC)

MTL .... Materials Technology Laboratory [*Watertown, MA*] [*Army*] (RDA)

MTL .... Materials Test Loop [*Nuclear energy*] (NRCH)

MTL .... Mean Tide Level [*Tides and currents*]

MTL .... Mean Time Level

MTL .... Medial Temporal Lobe [*Brain anatomy*]

MTL .... Median Tolerance Limit [*Toxicity*]

MTL .... Medium Term Loan (DCTA)

MTL .... Mercantile Bancorp [*NYSE symbol*] (TTSB)

MTL .... Mercantile Bancorp, Inc. [*NYSE symbol*] (SPSG)

MTL .... Merged-Transistor Logic

MTL .... Message Transfer Layer [*Telecommunications*] (OSI)

MTL .... Metal (AAG)

MTL .... Microelectronic Test Laboratory (IAA)

MTL .... Minimum Time Limit

MTL .... Minimum Triggering Level [*Aviation*] (DA)

MTL .... Mobilization Training Loss [*Military*]

MTL .... Mobiltherm Light (NRCH)

Mt-L .... Montana State Law Library, Helena, MT [*Library symbol Library of Congress*] (LCLS)

MTL .... Motel

MTL .... Motivation and Training Laboratory [*Army*] (RDA)

MTL .... Mount Taylor [*New Mexico*] [*Seismograph station code, US Geological Survey*] (SEIS)

MTL .... Multiple Conductor Transmission Line (PDAA)

MTL .... Raf-Avia [*Latvia*] [*ICAO designator*]

MTLA .... Micropublishers' Trade List Annual [*A publication*]

MTLC .... Mass Transfer Limiting Current (PDAA)

MTLC .... Metalclad Corp. [*NASDAQ symbol*] (SAG)

MTLC .... Metallic (MSA)

MTLD .... Mouvement pour le Triomphe des Libertes Democratiques [*Movement for the Triumph of Democratic Liberties*] [*Algeria*]

MtLdD .... Dull Knife Memorial College Library, Lame Deer, MT [*Library symbol*] [*Library of Congress*] (LCLS)

MtLe .... Lewistown City Library, Lewistown, MT [*Library symbol Library of Congress*] (LCLS)

MTLG .... Metrologic Instruments [*NASDAQ symbol*] (TTSB)

MTLG .... Metrologic Instruments, Inc. [*NASDAQ symbol*] (SAG)

Mtlg .... Mitteilung [*Report*] [*German*] (BJA)

MTLGY .... Metallurgy

MTLI .... MTL, Inc. [*NASDAQ symbol*] (SAG)

MtLib .... Lincoln County Free Library, Libby, MT [*Library symbol*] [*Library of Congress*] (LCLS)

MtLibH .... Libby High School, Libby, MT [*Library symbol*] [*Library of Congress*] (LCLS)

MtLibJ .... Libby Junior High School, Libby, MT [*Library symbol*] [*Library of Congress*] (LCLS)

MTL Inc .... MTL, Inc. [*Associated Press*] (SAG)

MTLM .... Metal Management [*NASDAQ symbol*] (TTSB)

MTLNG .... Metallizing

MTLP .... Master Tape Loading Program

MTLP .... Metabolic Toxemia of Late Pregnancy [*Medicine*]

MTLP .... Monitor Table Listing Program (NASA)

MTLR .... Moving Target Locating RADAR (AABC)

MTLS .... Mesial Temporal Lobe Seizure [*Medicine*]

MTLS .... MetaTools Inc. [*NASDAQ symbol*] (TTSB)

MTLS .... Munitions Transfer [*or Transporter*] and Loading System (MCD)

MtLv .... Livingston Public Library, Livingston, MT [*Library symbol*] [*Library of Congress*] (LCLS)

MtLvHS .... Park High School, Livingston, MT [*Library symbol*] [*Library of Congress*] (LCLS)

MtLvMS .... Livingston Middle School, Livingston, MT [*Library symbol*] [*Library of Congress*] (LCLS)

MtLvSD .... Livingston Elementary Schools, Livingston, MT [*Library symbol*] [*Library of Congress*] (LCLS)

M-TLX .... Mitsubishi Transfer-Line Heat Exchanger

MTLZ .... Metallize (MSA)

MTM .... Magnetic Tape Message

MTM .... Maintenance Task Monitor (MCD)

MTM .... Maintenance Test Module

MTM .... Manpower Tradeoff Methodology [*Military*]

MTM .... Mark-to-Market [*Securities*]

MTM .... Mark Twain Memorial (EA)

MTM .... Marlborough Technical Management [*British*]

MTM .... Mary Tyler Moore [*Actress after whom film studio MTM Enterprises is named*]

MTM .... Masked Terrain Map [*Military*]

MTM .... Master in the Teaching of Mathematics (PGP)

MTM .... Master of Theology and Ministry (PGP)

MTM .... Master of Transport Management

MTM .... Master of Tropical Medicine

MTM .... Matsumoto [*Japan*] [*Seismograph station code, US Geological Survey*] (SEIS)

MTM .... Mean Time Measurement

MTM .... Mechanical Road Transport Mechanic [*British military*] (DMA)

MTM .... Mechanical Test Model

MTM .... Methods-Time Measurement [*Industrial engineering*]

MTM .... Method-Times Measurement (DICI)

MTM .... Methylthiomethyl [*Organic chemistry*]

MTM .... Metlakatla [*Alaska*] [*Airport symbol*] (OAG)

MTM .... Metlakatla, AK [*Location identifier FAA*] (FAAL)

MTM .... Michelin Tire Monitor [*System*] [*Automotive engineering*]

MTM .... Million Ton Miles

MTM .... Million Train Miles

MTM .... Mission Test Module (IAA)

MTM .... Mobile Transfer Method (AAG)

MTM .... Modified Thayer-Martin [*Medium*] [*Microbiology*]

MTM .... Modular Torque Motor

MTM .... Moving Terrain Model

MTM .... Mt. Grant Mines Ltd. [*Vancouver Stock Exchange symbol*]

MTM .... MTM [*Methods-Time Measurement*] Association for Standards and Research (EA)

MTM .... MTM Aviation GMBH Munchen [*Federal Republic of Germany*] [*FAA designator*] (FAAC)

MTM .... MTM Productions, Inc. [*Named for actress Mary Tyler Moore*]

MTM .... Multiple Terminal Manager (NITA)

MTM .... Multiple Threat Modulation [*Military*] (CAAL)

MTM .... Multi-Taper Method [*Spectroscopy*]

MTM .... Multi-Tasking Monitor (NITA)

MTM .... Multi-Terminal Monitor (NITA)

MTM .... Myotubular Myopathy [*Medicine*] (DMAA)

MTM .... Thayer-Martin, Modified [*Agar*] (DMAA)

MTMA .... Methods Time-Measurement Association (IAA)

MTMA .... Military Terminal Major Aerodromes (NATG)

MTMA .... Military Traffic Management Agency [*Later, DTMS*]

MtMa .... Phillips County Library, Malta, MT [*Library symbol*] [*Library of Congress*] (LCLS)

MTMAINTCO... Motor Maintenance Company (DNAB)

MTMASR ..... MTM [*Methods-Time Measurement*] Association for Standards and Research [*Later, MTM*] (EA)

MTMB .... Military Traffic Management Bulletin (SAA)

MTMC .... (Methylthio)-meta-Cresol [*Organic chemistry*]

MTMC .... Micros-To Mainframe, Inc. [*NASDAQ symbol*] (SAG)

MTMC .... Micros To Mainframes [*NASDAQ symbol*] (TTSB)

MtMc .... Miles City Public Library, Miles City, MT [*Library symbol Library of Congress*] (LCLS)

MTMC .... Military Traffic Management Command [*DoD*]

MtMcC .... Miles Community College, Miles City, MT [*Library symbol Library of Congress*] (LCLS)

MTMCEA ...... Military Traffic Management Command, Eastern Area [*Bayonne, NJ*]

MTMC-OA ..... Military Traffic Management Command Operations Analysis Division [*Newport News, VA*]

MtMcPh .... Pine Hill School, Miles City, MT [*Library symbol*] [*Library of Congress*] (LCLS)

MTMCTEA ..... Military Traffic Management Command Transportation Engineering Agency (AABC)

MTMCTTC ..... Military Traffic Management Command Transportation Terminal Command; Europe [*MTMC*] (TAG)

MTMCTTU ..... Military Traffic Management Command Transportation Terminal Unit (AABC)

MTMCWA ..... Military Traffic Management Command, Western Area [*Oakland, CA*]

MTM/D .... Million Ton Miles/Day (MCD)

MT/MF .... Magnetic Tape to Microfilm

MTMF	Multiple Task Management Feature (NITA)
MTM-GPD	Methods Time Measurement and General Purpose Data (PDAA)
MTMH	Master of Tropical Medicine and Hygiene (GAGS)
MTMI	Microtek Medical [*NASDAQ symbol*] (TTSB)
MTMI	Microtek Medical, Inc. [*NASDAQ symbol*] (SAG)
MtMis	Missoula Public and Missoula County Free Library, Missoula, MT [*Library symbol Library of Congress*] (LCLS)
MtMisGS	Church of Jesus Christ of Latter-Day Saints, Genealogical Society Library, Missoula Branch, Missoula, MT [*Library symbol Library of Congress*] (LCLS)
MtMisSP	Saint Patrick Hospital, Missoula, MT [*Library symbol Library of Congress*] (LCLS)
MtMisW	Western Montana Clinic, Missoula, MT [*Library symbol Library of Congress*] (LCLS)
MTMOD	Magnetic Tape Module (IAA)
MTMP	MACOM [*Major Command*] Telephone Modernizations Program
MTMR	Military Traffic Management Regulation
mt mRNA	Mitochondrial Messenger RNA[*Ribonucleic Acid*] [*Genetics*] (DOG)
MTM's	Magnetic Tape Transmissions (CET)
MTMS	Memorex Tape Management System [*Computer science*] (IAA)
MTMS	Metal-to-Metal Seal
MTMS	Methyltrimethoxysilane [*Organic chemistry*]
MTMS	Military Traffic Management Service (MCD)
MTMS	Mobilization Training Management System [*DoD*]
MTMS	Multi-Terminal Modular System (DGA)
MTMTS	Military Traffic Management and Terminal Service [*Later, MTMC*] [*Army*]
MTMTS-TSP	Military Traffic Management and Terminal Service Transportation Strike Plan (DNAB)
MTN	Baltimore, MD [*Location identifier FAA*] (FAAL)
MTN	Main Telecommunication Network [*United Nations*] (EY)
MTN	Manton [*Australia Seismograph station code, US Geological Survey*] (SEIS)
MTN	Medical Television Network (BARN)
MTN	Medium-Term Note [*Finance*]
MTN	Metatolylnitrile [*Organic chemistry*]
MTN	Mirtone International, Inc. [*Toronto Stock Exchange symbol*]
MTN	Mizlou Television Network
MTN	Mobil Producing TX & NM, Inc., Houston, TX [*OCLC symbol*] (OCLC)
MTN	Motion (MSA)
MTN	Mountain
Mtn	Mountain (TBD)
MTN	Mountain Air Cargo, Inc. [*FAA designator*] (FAAC)
MTN	Multilateral Trade Negotiations
MTN	Multinational Trade Negotiations (IAA)
MTNA	Music Teachers National Association (EA)
MTND	Mercury Tube Nutation Damper
MTNFC	Mel Tillis National Fan Club (EA)
MTNHP	Montana Natural Heritage Program [*Helena, MT*] [*Information service or system*] (IID)
MT-NMR	Magnetic Transfer Nuclear Magnetic Resonance (DB)
MtnPkFn	Mountain Parks Financial Corp. [*Associated Press*] (SAG)
MTNS	Metal-Thick Nitride Semiconductor (IAA)
MTNS	Metal-Thick Nitride-Silicon (IAA)
MTNS	Metal-Thick Oxide-Nitride-Silicon
MTNS	Mountains [*Postal Service standard*] (OPSA)
MTNT	Metro Networks, Inc. [*NASDAQ symbol*] (SAG)
MtNxPS	Noxon Public School, Noxon, MT [*Library symbol*] [*Library of Congress*] (LCLS)
MTO	Made to Order (ODBW)
MTO	Magnetic Tape Operator (MCD)
MTO	Maintenance Technology Office [*Air Force Logistics Command*]
MTO	Manitoulin Air Services Ltd. [*Canada ICAO designator*] (FAAC)
MTO	Man-Tended Operation (SSD)
MTO	Manufacturing Technical Order (SAA)
MTO	Manufacturing Technology Objective
MTO	Master Terminal Operator (IAA)
MTO	Master Timing Oscillator (MCD)
MTO	Mattoon [*Illinois*] [*Airport symbol*] (OAG)
MTO	Maximum Time Out (MCD)
MTO	Medical Transport Officer [*Navy*]
MTO	Mediterranean Theater of Operations, United States Army [*Shortened form of MTOUSA*] [*World War II*]
MTO	Message Terminal Operation [*Military*] (CAAL)
MTO	Methanol-to-Olefin [*Process*]
MTO	Missile Test Operator (SAA)
MTO	Mission, Task, Objective
MTO	Mission Type Order (DOMA)
MTO	Mississippi Test Operations [*NASA*]
MTO	Modification Task Outline (KSC)
MTO	Motor Transport Officer [*Military*]
MTO	Mouvement Togolais pour la Democratie [*Togolese Movement for Democracy*] [*Political party*] (PD)
MTO	Movement Transfer Order (MCD)
MTO	Muffin-Tin Orbital [*Physics*]
MTO	Multilateral Trading Organization (ECON)
MTO	Multimodal Transport Operator
MTOAL	Mobilization Table of Allowance Listing [*Military*] (DNAB)
MTOB	Manned Test Operations Board [*NASA*]
MTOC	Microtubular Organizing Complex [*Physiology*]
MTOC	Microtubule Organizing Center [*Cytology*]
MTOC	Mitotic Organizing Center [*Cytology*]
MTOC	Monitoring Transport of Ocean Currents [*Project*] [*Marine science*] (OSRA)
MTOCs	Microtubule Organizing Centers (DOG)

MTOE	Million Tons of Oil Equivalent
MTOE	Modification Table of Organization and Equipment [*Army*] (AABC)
MTOGW	Maximum Takeoff Gross Weight [*Aviation*] (MCD)
MTOL	Mean Time off Line (AAEL)
MTOL	Mean Time on Line (AAEL)
MTOM	Master of Traditional Oriental Medicine (PGP)
MTON	Measurement Ton
MTON	Metro One Telecommunications, Inc. [*NASDAQ symbol*] (SAG)
MTONS	Metal-Thick Oxide-Nitride-Silicon (MSA)
MTOP	Molecular Total Overlap Population (IEEE)
MTOPS	Million Theoretical Operations per Second [*Computer science*]
MTORQ	Maximum Torque
MTOS	Magnetic Tape Operating System (NITA)
MTOS	Magnetic Tape Operations System [*Computer science*] (NRCH)
MTOS	Major Trauma Outcome Study [*American College of Surgeons Committee on Trauma*]
MTOS	Metal-Thick Oxide Semiconductor (IAA)
MTOS	Metal-Thick Oxide-Silicon
MTOS	Multi-Tasking Operating System (NITA)
MTOSFET	Metal-Thick Oxide Semiconductor Field Effect Transistor (IAA)
MTOUSA	Mediterranean Theater of Operations, United States Army [*Sometimes shortened to MTO*] [*World War II*]
MTOW	Maximum Takeoff Weight [*Aviation*] (MCD)
MTox	Master of Toxicology (GAGS)
MTP	Island Helicopters, Inc. [*ICAO designator*] (FAAC)
MTP	Magnetic Tape Processor (NITA)
MTP	Maintenance Test Package (MCD)
MTP	Manual Troubleshooting Procedures [*Army*]
MTP	Manufacturing Technical Procedure [*NASA*] (NASA)
MTP	Manufacturing Technology Program [*Aviation Systems Command*] (RDA)
MTP	Manufacturing Technology Projects [*Manufacturing Technology Information Analysis Center*] [*Information service or system*] (CRD)
MTP	Manufacturing Test Procedure
MTP	Master of Town and Country Planning
MTP	Master of Town Planning
MTP	Master of Transpersonal Psychology (PGP)
MTP	Master Test Plan (KSC)
MTP	Master Training Plan [*Navy*] (ANA)
MTP	Master Transportation Plan (AAG)
MTP	Master Typography Program (DNAB)
MTP	Materiel Test Procedure [*Army*]
MTP	Materiel Transfer Plan [*Army*]
MTP	Maximum Tire Pressure (ADA)
MTP	Maximum Total Trihalomethane Potential (EG)
MTP	Mechanical Thermal Pulse (IEEE)
MTP	Message Transfer Protocol [*Telecommunications*] (OSI)
MTP	Message Transmission Part [*Telecommunications*] (TEL)
MTP	Metatarsophalangeal [*Anatomy*]
MTP	Methods Test Panel [*Bureau of the Census*] (GFGA)
MTP	(Methylthio)phenol [*Organic chemistry*]
MTP	Microsomal Triglyceride Transfer Protein [*Biochemistry*]
MTP	Microtubule Protein [*Cytology*]
MTP	Military Type Property
MTP	Miniature Trimmer Potentiometer
MTP	Minimum Time Path (OA)
MTP	Missile Transfer Panel (AAG)
MTP	Missile Tube Pressurization
MTP	Mission Tailored Product
MTP	Mission Tasking Package (COE)
MTP	Mission Test Plan (KSC)
MTP	Mission Training Plan [*Military*] (INF)
MTP	Mobilization Training Program [*Military*]
MTP	Mobilization Troop Program [*Army*]
MTP	Modular Terminal Processor (NITA)
MTP	Montana Power [*NYSE symbol*] (TTSB)
MTP	Montana Power Co. [*NYSE symbol*] (SPSG)
MTP	Montauk Point [*New York*] [*Airport symbol Obsolete*] (OAG)
MTP	Monte Pirata [*Puerto Rico*] [*Seismograph station code, US Geological Survey*] (SEIS)
MTP	MOS [*Military Occupation Specialty*] Training Plan
MTP	Mother Tongue Project (AIE)
MTP	Movimiento Todos par la Patria [*Argentina Political party*] (EY)
MTP	Multiple-Task Performance
MTP	Multiply Twinned Particles (DICI)
MTP	Multipoint (DNAB)
MTP	Muramyl Tripeptide (DB)
MtP	Plains Public Library, Plains, MT [*Library symbol*] [*Library of Congress*] (LCLS)
MTP	The Pas Public Library, Manitoba [*Library symbol National Library of Canada*] (NLC)
MTPA	Master Textile Printers Association (EA)
MTPA	(Methoxy)trifluoromethylphenylacetic Acid [*Organic chemistry*]
MTPA	Mobile Transponder Performance Analyzer [*Aviation*] (DA)
MtPaS	Salish Kootenai College Library, Pablo, MT [*Library symbol*] [*Library of Congress*] (LCLS)
MtPaTS	Two Eagle School, Pablo, MT [*Library symbol*] [*Library of Congress*] (LCLS)
MTPC	Metal Tube Packaging Council of North America [*Later, TCNA*] (EA)
MTPC	Minimal Total Processing Time (NITA)
MTPCNA	Metal Tube Packaging Council of North America [*Later, TCNA*]
MTPE	Mission to Planet Earth [*Proposed NASA satellite*]
MTPF	Maximum Total Peaking Factor [*Nuclear energy*] (NRCH)
MTP FET	Metal/Tunnelling-Nitride Polysilicon Gate FET (NITA)

MTPH............ Maximum Temperature of Previous Heating [*Archaeology*]
MTPI............ Member of the Town Planning Institute [*British*]
MTPJ............ Metatarsophalangeal Joint [*Medicine*] (DMAA)
MTPK............ Keewatin Community College, The Pas, Manitoba [*Library symbol National Library of Canada*] (NLC)
MTPM............ Mean Time to Provide Manpower (DNAB)
MtPoF............ Fort Peck Community College, Poplar, MT [*Library symbol*] [*Library of Congress*] (LCLS)
MtPol............ Polson City Library, Polson, MT [*Library symbol*] [*Library of Congress*] (LCLS)
MTPP............ Material Test Procedure Pamphlet
MTPP............ Missile-to-Target Patch Panel
MTPP............ Port-Au-Prince/Internacional [*Haiti*] [*ICAO location identifier*] (ICLI)
MTP-PE............ Muramyl Tripeptide Phosphatidylethanolamine [*Antineoplastic drug*] (CDI)
MtPPS............ Plains Public School Library, Plains, MT [*Library symbol*] [*Library of Congress*] (LCLS)
MTPR............ Miniature Temperature Pressure Recorder [*Marine science*] (OSRA)
MTPS............ Magnetic Tape Programming System [*Computer science*] (IEEE)
MTPS............ Modern Talking Picture Service, Inc. [*Funded by U.S. Department of Education*] (PAZ)
MTPT............ Minimal Total Processing Time (IEEE)
MTPU............ Missile Tank Pressurization Unit (AAG)
MTPUG............ Pascal/MT Users Group [*Defunct*] (EA)
MTPW............ Master of Technical and Professional Writing (GAGS)
MtPw............ Sheridan County Free Library, Plentywood, MT [*Library symbol*] [*Library of Congress*] (LCLS)
MTPX............ Port-De-Paix [*Haiti*] [*ICAO location identifier*] (ICLI)
MTPY............ Millions of Tons per Year [*of solids, e.g., coal*]
MTQ............ CAAA Air Martinique [*France ICAO designator*] (FAAC)
MTQ............ Greenville, MS [*Location identifier FAA*] (FAAL)
MTQ............ Martinique [*ANSI three-letter standard code*] (CNC)
MTQ............ Methaqualone [*or Methyltolylquinazolone, or Metolquizolone*] [*Sedative*]
MTQ............ Mitchell [*Australia Airport symbol*] (OAG)
MTQ............ Mount Allard Resources [*Vancouver Stock Exchange symbol*]
MTQAS............ Methadone Treatment Quality Assurance System [*National Institute on Drug Abuse*]
MTQM............ Master of Total Quality Management (PGP)
MTR............ Magic-Tone Records [*Record label*]
MTR............ Magnetic Core Transistor Relay (IAA)
MTR............ Magnetic Tape Reader (NITA)
MTR............ Magnetic Tape Recorder
MTR............ Main Timing Register
MTR............ Major Trouble Report (MCD)
MTR............ Mass, Tenderness, Rebound [*On abdominal examination*] [*Gastroenterology*] (DAVI)
MTR............ Mass-Transfer Rate [*Chemical engineering*]
MTR............ Mass Transit Railway (DS)
MTR............ Master Tool Record (SAA)
MTR............ Materials Testing Reactor
MTR............ Materials Testing Report
MTR............ Material Transfer Recorder [*LASER*] [*Army*]
MTR............ Maximum Tracking Range
MTR............ Mean Time to Removal [*Quality control*]
MTR............ Mean Time to Restore [*Quality control*] (IAA)
MTR............ Measa Royalty Trust [*NYSE symbol*] (SAG)
MTR............ Meinicke Turbidity Reaction [*Obsolete test for syphilis*]
MTR............ Mental Treatment Rules [*British*]
MTR............ Mesa Royalty Tr UBI [*NYSE symbol*] (TTSB)
mtr............ Meter (IDOE)
MTR............ Meter [*or Metering*] (AAG)
MTR............ Methylthioribose [*Biochemistry*]
MTR............ Metroflight, Inc. [*ICAO designator*] (FAAC)
Mtr............ Metronome [*Record label*] [*Scandinavia, Germany, etc.*]
MTR............ Mid-Term Review
MTR............ Migration Traffic Rate (OA)
MTR............ Military Technical Revolution (DOMA)
MTR............ Military Temperature Range
MTR............ Military Training Route [*Aviation*] (FAAC)
MTR............ Military Training Routes [*FAA*] (TAG)
MTR............ Milliammeter (IAA)
MTR............ Miniature Temperature Recorder (USDC)
MTR............ Minimum Technological Requirement
MTR............ Minimum Time Rate
MTR............ Miscellaneous Tax Ruling [*IRS*] (AAGC)
MTR............ Missile Track [*or Tracking*] RADAR [*Air Force*]
MTR............ MITRE Corp., Library Department, McLean, VA [*OCLC symbol*] (OCLC)
MTR............ Mobile Tracking Range [*Military*] (CAAL)
MTR............ Modification Traceability Record (MCD)
MTR............ Modular Tree Representation (MHDI)
MTR............ Monitor [*Computer science*] (BUR)
MTR............ Monopulse Tracking Receiver
MTR............ Monteria [*Colombia*] [*Airport symbol*] (OAG)
MTR............ Monterrey [*California*] [*Seismograph station code, US Geological Survey*] (SEIS)
MTR............ Montour Railroad Co. [*AAR code*]
MTR............ Motor (AABC)
MTR............ Moving Target Reactor
MTR............ Moving Target Resolver (MCD)
MTR............ Multiple Thermocouple Reference
MTR............ Multiple Token Ring [*Telecommunications*] (OSI)
MTR............ Multiple Tracking Range
MTR............ Multiple Track RADAR

MTR............ Museum of Television and Radio [*New York*]
MTR............ Mutual Resources [*Vancouver Stock Exchange symbol*]
MTR............ Universite de Montreal, Bibliotheque [*UTLAS symbol*]
MTRA............ Machine Tools Research Association (WDAA)
MTRA............ Meta Biosystems [*NASDAQ symbol*] (SAG)
MTRA............ Metra Biosystems [*NASDAQ symbol*] (SAG)
M/TRANS............ Manual Transmission [*Automotive engineering*]
MTransEc............ Master of Transport Economics
MTRB............ Man-Tended Review Board (SSD)
MTRB............ Maritime Transportation Research Board [*National Research Council*]
MTRB............ Motor Truck Rate Bureau
MTRC............ Man-Tended Reference Configuration (SSD)
MTRC............ Metric
MTRCL............ Motorcycle (AABC)
Mtrclt............ Motorcyclist [*Army*]
MTRCYL............ Motorcycle
MtRd............ Community Library, Roundup, MT [*Library symbol*] [*Library of Congress*] (LCLS)
MtRd-E............ Roundup Central Elementary School Library, Roundup, MT [*Library symbol*] [*Library of Congress*] (LCLS)
MTRDN............ Motor-Driven
MTRE............ Magnetic Tape Recorder End
MTRE............ Missile Test and Readiness Equipment
MTRE............ Missile Test and Readiness Evaluation [*Military*] (IAA)
MT REVD............ Most Reverend (ROG)
MTRF............ Mark Twain Research Foundation (EA)
MTRF............ Master Training File [*Computer science*]
MTRG............ Metering (MSA)
MTRI............ Missile Test Range Instrumentation
MTRK............ Minitrack (KSC)
MTRL............ Material
MTRM............ Modulated Throat-Rocket Motor (MCD)
MTRN............ Metrotrans Corp. [*NASDAQ symbol*] (SAG)
mtRNA............ Ribonucleic Acid, Mitochondrial [*Biochemistry, genetics*]
MTRNTY............ Maternity
MTRO............ Metro-Tel Corp. [*NASDAQ symbol*] (NQ)
MtRo............ Ronan City Library, Ronan, MT [*Library symbol*] [*Library of Congress*] (LCLS)
MtroOne............ Metro One Telecommunications, Inc. [*Associated Press*] (SAG)
MTR OP............ Motor Operated [*Freight*]
MTRP............ Machine Tool Retrofit Program
MTRP............ Master of Town and Regional Planning [*British*] (ADA)
mtrRNA............ Mitochondrial Ribosomal RNA[*Ribonucleic Acid*] [*Genetics*] (DOG)
MTRS............ Magnetic Tape Recorder Set
MTRS............ Magnetic Tape Recorder Start
MTRS............ Magnetic Tape Reformatting System [*Hewlett-Packard Co.*]
MTRS............ Mattress (MSA)
MTRS............ Metris Companies, Inc. [*NASDAQ symbol*] (SAG)
MT Rulings... Miscellaneous Tax Rulings [*Australia A publication*]
MTRUW............ Mixed Transuranic Waste (GAAI)
MtrVac............ MotorVac Technologies, Inc. [*Associated Press*] (SAG)
MTRX............ Matrix Service [*NASDAQ symbol*] (TTSB)
MTRX............ Matrix Service Corp. [*NASDAQ symbol*] (NQ)
MTRY............ Momentary (FAAC)
MTS............ Machine-Tractor Stations
MTS............ Magnetic Tape Station [*Computer science*] (CET)
MTS............ Magnetic Tape Storage [*Computer science*] (IAA)
MTS............ Magnetic Tape System [*Computer science*]
MTS............ Magnetic Type System [*Computer science*] (IAA)
MTS............ Mainsborne Telecontrol System (NITA)
MTS............ Maintenance Training Set (MCD)
MTS............ Maintenance Transmittal Sheet
MTS............ Main Trunk System [*Telecommunications*] (TEL)
MTS............ Management Tracing System (COE)
MTS............ Management Tracking System [*Environmental Protection Agency*] (EPA)
MTS............ Manitoba Telephone System [*Telecommunications service*] (TSSD)
MTS............ Manned Teller System
MTS............ Manpower Training Services
MTS............ Mantrust Asahi Airways PT [*Indonesia*] [*ICAO designator*] (FAAC)
MTS............ Manual Testing System [*Sports medicine*]
MTS............ Manufacturing Technology Section [*Navy*]
MTS............ Manzini [*Swaziland*] [*Airport symbol*] (OAG)
MTS............ Mardan Test Set
MTS............ Marine Technology Society (EA)
MTS............ Maritime Tactical Schools (MCD)
MTS............ Marketing and Transportation Situation [*Series*] [*A publication*]
MTS............ Marketing Technical Services
MTS............ Mark Twain Society [*Defunct*] (EA)
MTS............ MARS [*Military Affiliate Radio System*] Technical Service (CET)
MTS............ Mass Target Sensor
MTS............ Mass Termination System [*Computer science*] (IEEE)
MTS............ Master of Teaching of Science (GAGS)
MTS............ Master of Theological Studies (WGA)
MTS............ Master Test Station
MTS............ Master Timing Schedule
MTS............ Master Timing System
MTS............ Material Test Specification (MSA)
MTS............ Material Tracking Standard (AAEL)
MTS............ Matsue [*Japan*] [*Seismograph station code, US Geological Survey*] (SEIS)
MTS............ Medical Testing Systems [*Commercial firm*]
MTS............ Medicare Transaction System (DMAA)
MTS............ Member of the Technical Staff [*A generic term*]
MTS............ Memory Test System

MTS............	Meridian Telecommunication Services [*Indianapolis, IN*] (TSSD)
MTS............	Message Telecommunications Service
MTS............	Message Telephone Service (NITA)
MTS............	Message Toll Service [*Communications*]
MTS............	Message Traffic Study
MTS............	Message Transfer Service
MTS............	Message Transfer System [*Telecommunications*] (OSI)
MTS............	Message Transmission Subsystem [*Telecommunications*] (TEL)
MTS............	Meteoroid Technology Satellite [*NASA*]
MTS............	Methods-Time Study [*Industrial engineering*]
MTS............	Methyltrichlorosilane [*Organic chemistry*]
MTS............	Metric Time System (NASA)
MTS............	Metropolitan Transportation System (PA)
MTS............	Michigan Terminal System [*Computer science*]
MTS............	Microprocessor Training System [*Integrated Computer Systems*] (NITA)
MTS............	Microsoft Transaction Server [*Computer science*]
MTS............	Microtubule-Stabilizing Solution [*Cytology*]
MTS............	Microwave Test Set (MCD)
MTS............	Military Test Satellite
MTS............	Military Training Standard (AFM)
MTS............	Million (10^6) Transitions Per Second [*Of magnetic storage*] (NITA)
MTS............	Missile Test Set
MTS............	Missile Test Stand
MTS............	Missile Test Station
MTS............	Missile Tracking Station [*DoD*]
MTS............	Missile Tracking System (IEEE)
MTS............	Missile Training Squadron
MTS............	Missile Tube Supply
MTS............	Missions to Seamen [*British*]
MTS............	Mississippi Test Site [*Aerospace*] (AAG)
MTS............	Mobile Telephone Service
MTS............	Mobile Terminal System [*IBM Corp.*]
MTS............	Mobile Tracking Station [*NASA*]
MTS............	Mobile Training Set (AFM)
MTS............	Mobil-Trac System [*MTMC*] (TAG)
MTS............	Modem Test Set (NITA)
MTS............	Moderate Tactile Stimulus [*Neurology*] (DAVI)
MTS............	Modernization through Spares [*Army program*]
MTS............	Modular Television System [*Telecommunications*] (CDE)
MTS............	Modular Terminal System (NITA)
MTS............	Module Test Set (MCD)
MTS............	Module Test System (IAA)
MTS............	Module Tracking System (NRCH)
MTS............	Money Transfer System (IAA)
MTS............	Monosyllable, Trochee, Spondee Test [*Of speech discrimination*] (DAVI)
MTS............	Montgomery St Inc. Sec [*NYSE symbol*] (TTSB)
MTS............	Montgomery Street Income Securities, Inc. [*NYSE symbol*] (SPSG)
MTS............	Monthly Treasury Statement [*Government*] (AFM)
MTS............	Morale Tendency Score (AEE)
MTS............	Motion-Time Standards [*Industrial engineering*]
MTS............	Motor-Operated Transfer Switch
MTS............	Motor Tariff Service
MTS............	Motor Turbine Ship (IIA)
MTS............	Mountains [*Board on Geographic Names*]
MTS............	Moving Target Screen (MCD)
MTS............	Moving Target Simulator (RDA)
MTS............	Moving Time Series
MTS............	MTS Systems Corp. [*Associated Press*] (SAG)
MTS............	Multicellular Tumor Spheroid [*Medicine*] (DB)
MTS............	Multichannel Television Sound [*or Stereo*]
MTS............	Multichannel TV Sound (WDMC)
MTS............	Multichannel TV Stereo (WDMC)
MTS............	Multiple Target Screen
MTS............	Multiple Terminal System (NITA)
MTS............	Multiple Time Scale
MTS............	Multiple Tumor Suppressor [*Oncology*]
MTS............	Muscle Testing System [*Myology*]
MTS............	Musculotendinous Structure (DMAA)
MTS............	State Law Library of Montana, Helena, MT [*OCLC symbol*] (OCLC)
MTS1..........	Multiple Tumour Suppressor 1 [*Genetics*] (ECON)
MTSA..........	Seaman Apprentice, Missile Technician, Striker [*Navy rating*]
MTSAA........	Multidiscipline Technical Safety Assurance Appraisal [*Environmental science*] (COE)
MTSAT........	Multi-functional Transport Satellite
MtSc...........	Daniels County Free Library, Scobey, MT [*Library symbol*] [*Library of Congress*] (LCLS)
MTSC..........	Magnetic Tape Selectric Composer [*IBM Corp.*]
MTSC..........	Master of Teaching Speech Communication (GAGS)
MTSC..........	Master of Technical and Scientific Communication (GAGS)
MTSC..........	Master of Theological Studies Counseling (PGP)
MTSC..........	MTS Systems [*NASDAQ symbol*] (TTSB)
MTSC..........	MTS Systems Corp. [*NASDAQ symbol*] (NQ)
MTSD..........	Military Transmission Systems Department [*NORAD*]
MTSE..........	Magnetic Trap Stability Experiment (IEEE)
MTSF..........	Mean Time to System Failure [*Quality control*] (PDAA)
MTS/GMS.....	Module Test Set / Guided Missile System (DWSG)
MTSGT........	Master Technical Sergeant [*Marine Corps*]
MTSGT(C)....	Master Technical Sergeant (Commissary) [*Marine Corps*]
MtSh...........	Toole County Free Library, Shelby, MT [*Library symbol*] [*Library of Congress*] (LCLS)
MTSI...........	Micro Touch Systems [*NASDAQ symbol*] (TTSB)
MTSI...........	Microtouch Systems, Inc. [*NASDAQ symbol*] (SAG)

MtSid..........	Sidney Public Library, Sidney, MT [*Library symbol*] [*Library of Congress*] (LCLS)
Mt Sinai Sch Med...	Mount Sinai School of Medicine of The City University of New York (GAGS)
MTSL..........	Message Transfer Sublayer [*Telecommunications*] (OSI)
MTSL..........	Monitoring and Technical Support Laboratory [*Environmental Protection Agency*] (GFGA)
MTSN..........	Mattson Technology [*NASDAQ symbol*] (TTSB)
MTSN..........	Mattson Technology, Inc. [*NASDAQ symbol*] (SAG)
MTSN..........	Seaman, Missile Technician, Striker [*Navy rating*]
MTSO..........	Mobile Telephone Switching Office [*Telecommunications*]
MTSP..........	Maintenance Test Support Package [*Army*]
MTSPS........	Multiple Transducer Seismic Profiling System
MTSQ..........	Mechanical Time, Superquick [*Fuse*] [*Weaponry*]
MTSQF........	Mechanical Time, Superquick Fuze [*Weaponry*] (MCD)
MTSR..........	Maximal Temperature of the Synthesis Reaction [*Chemical engineering*]
MTSR..........	Mean Time to Service Restoral [*Quality control*] [*Telecommunications*] (TEL)
MTSR..........	Mid-Term Status Reports
MTSS..........	Magnetic Tape Storage System
MTSS..........	Manned Test Space System [*See also MOD, MODS, MOSS*] [*Air Force/NASA*]
MTSS..........	Military Test Space Station [*See also MOD, MODS, MOSS*] [*Air Force/NASA*]
MTSSL........	Methanethiosulphonate Spin Label [*Analytical chemistry*]
MTST..........	Magnetic Tape Selectric Typewriter [*IBM Corp.*]
MTST..........	Maximal Treadmill Stress Test [*Medicine*] (DMAA)
MTST..........	Microtest, Inc. [*NASDAQ symbol*] (SAG)
Mt St Mary's C...	Mount St. Mary's College (GAGS)
MtStrS.........	St. Regis School, St. Regis, MT [*Library symbol*] [*Library of Congress*] (LCLS)
MTSU..........	Magnetic Tape Search Unit [*Computer science*]
MTSU..........	Middle Tennessee State University
MtSu...........	Mineral County Public Library, Superior, MT [*Library symbol*] [*Library of Congress*] (LCLS)
MTS/VO......	Motor Transportation Supervisor/Vehicle Operator (AAG)
MTT............	Magnetic Tape Terminal [*Computer science*]
MTT............	Magnetic Tape Transport [*Computer science*] (IEEE)
MTT............	Maintenance Training Team
MTT............	Malignant Trophoblastic Teratoma [*Oncology*] (MAE)
MTT............	Mammillothalamic Tract [*Neuroanatomy*]
MTT............	Maritime Telegraph & Telephone Co. Ltd. [*Toronto Stock Exchange symbol*]
MTT	Masked Terrain Trainer [*Military*]
MTT............	Master of Textile Technology
MTT............	Material Testing Technology (MCD)
MTT............	Maximal Treadmill Test (CPH)
MTT............	Maximum Touch Temperature (MCD)
MTT............	Mean Transit Time
MTT............	Mediterranean Tours and Travel [*Egypt*]
MTT............	Medium Tactical Transport [*Army*]
MTT............	Medium Tactical Truck [*Army*] (RDA)
MTT............	Message Transfer Time (NITA)
MTT............	Methyl(thio)tetrazole [*Biochemistry*]
MTT............	Metropolitan Edison Co. [*NYSE symbol*] (SPSG)
MTT............	Microwave Theory and Technique (MCD)
MTT............	Military Training Team (MCD)
MTT............	Minatitlan [*Mexico*] [*Airport symbol*] (OAG)
MTT............	Missionary Tech Team (EA)
MTT............	Mi-Tsiyon Tetse Torah [*Tel Aviv*] (BJA)
MTT............	Mobile Training Team
MTT............	Mobile Travel Team (MCD)
MTT............	Monetta Fire Tower [*South Carolina*] [*Seismograph station code, US Geological Survey*] (SEIS)
MTT............	Monotetrazolium [*Medicine*] (MAE)
MTT............	Multiple Target Tracker
MTT............	Munitions Transfer Truck (MCD)
MTT............	Orion SpA [*Italy ICAO designator*] (FAAC)
MtT.............	Prairie County Library, Terry, MT [*Library symbol*] [*Library of Congress*] (LCLS)
MTTA..........	Machine Tool Technologies Association [*British*] (EAIO)
MTTA..........	Machine Tool Trades Association (ACII)
MTTA..........	Mean Time to Accomplish [*Quality control*] (NASA)
MTTA..........	Mean Time to Assist (AAEL)
MTTA..........	Multi-Tenant Telecommunications Association (EA)
MTTB..........	Mean Time to Bench [*Repair*] [*Quality control*]
MTTC..........	Manufacturing Technology Technical Council
MTTC..........	Mean Time to Change Parts [*Quality control*] (MCD)
MTTC..........	Mean Time to Correct (AAEL)
MTTC..........	Mechanised Transport Training Corps [*British military*] (DMA)
MtTcES.......	Trout Creek Elementary School, Trout Creek, MT [*Library symbol*] [*Library of Congress*] (LCLS)
MTTD..........	Mean Time to Detect [*Quality control*] (MCD)
MTTD..........	Mean Time to Diagnosis [*Quality control*] (BUR)
MTTE..........	Magnetic Tape Terminal Equipment [*Computer science*] (CET)
MTTE..........	Mean Time to Exchange [*Quality control*] (MCD)
MTTEA........	Marine Towing and Transportation Employers Association [*Defunct*] (EA)
MTTF..........	Mean Time to Failure [*Quality control*]
MtTf...........	Thompson Falls Public Library, Thompson Falls, MT [*Library symbol*] [*Library of Congress*] (LCLS)
MTTFF........	Mean Time to First Failure [*Quality control*]
MtTfS.........	Thompson Falls Schools, Thompson Falls, MT [*Library symbol*] [*Library of Congress*] (LCLS)

MTTFSF......	Mean Time to First System Failure [*Quality control*] (PDAA)
MTTFSR......	Mean Time to First System Repair [*Quality control*] (PDAA)
MTTHS........	Modern Transport Technical and Historical Society [*Later, SFCH*] (EA)
MTTI..........	Magnetic Tape Transport Interface [*Computer science*] (MCD)
MTTI..........	Mean Time to Inspect [*Quality control*] (CAAL)
MTTI..........	Modified Tension Time Index [*Cardiology*]
MTTL..........	Motorola Transistor-Transistor Logic (IAA)
MTTM........	Magnetic Tape and Telemetry (MCD)
MTTM........	Mean Time to Maintain [*Quality control*] (CMD)
MTTN........	Multi-Tranche Tap Note [*Finance*] [*British*]
MTTO.........	Minuetto [*Slow Air*] [*Music*] (ROG)
MTTOP.......	Machine Tool Trigger Order Program (MHDB)
MTTP.........	Materials Testing and Technology Program
MTTP.........	Maximum Total Trihalomethane Potential (FFDE)
MTTPO.......	Mean Time to Planned Outage (IEEE)
MTTPrC......	Metropol Ed 3.90% cm Pfd [*NYSE symbol*] (TTSB)
MTTPrZ......	Met-Ed Capital L.P.'MIPS' [*NYSE symbol*] (TTSB)
MTTR.........	Magnetic Tape Transport Replacement (DWSG)
MTTR.........	Maximum Time to Repair (MCD)
MTTR.........	Maximum Time to Replace [*Navy*] (IAA)
MTTR.........	Mean Time to Removal [*Quality control*]
MTTR.........	Mean Time to Repair [*Quality control*] (CAAL)
MTTR.........	Mean Time to Replacement [*Quality control*]
MTTR.........	Mean Time to Restore [*Quality control*] (IEEE)
MTTR.........	Missile Target Tracking RADAR (MCD)
MTTRF........	Mission Time to Restore Function
mttRNA......	Mitochondrial Transfer RNA[*Ribonucleic Acid*] [*Genetics*] (DOG)
MTTRS.......	Mean Time to Restore Software [*Quality control*] (CAAL)
MTTRS.......	Mean Time to Restore System [*Quality control*]
MTTS..........	IEEE Microwave Theory and Techniques Society (EA)
MTTS..........	Marine Terminal Tankage System (MCD)
MTTS..........	Mean Time to Service [*Quality control*]
MTTS..........	Mobile Target Tracking System
MTTS..........	Multiple Target Tracking System
MTTS..........	Multitask Terminal System
MTTSF........	Mean Time to System Failure [*Quality control*] (PDAA)
MTTT..........	Mean Time to Test (MCD)
MTTU.........	Modular Timing Terminal Unit
MTTUO.......	Mean Time to Unplanned Outage (IEEE)
MTTV.........	Maneuvering Target Test Vechicle
MTTW........	Mean Time to Wait for Parts [*Quality control*] (MCD)
MtTyrSH	Troy Senior High School, Troy, MT [*Library symbol*] [*Library of Congress*] (LCLS)
MTU..........	Magnetic Tape Unit [*Computer science*]
MTU..........	Maintenance Training Unit
MTU..........	malignant Teratoma Undifferentiated [*Oncology*] (DAVI)
MTU..........	Managed Municipal Portfolio II [*NYSE symbol*] (SPSG)
MTU..........	Managed Muni Portfolio II [*NYSE symbol*] (TTSB)
MTU..........	Manchester Terminal Unit (NITA)
MTU..........	Master Terminal Unit [*Instrumentation*]
MTU..........	Master Time Unit
MTU..........	Master Timing Unit [*Aerospace*] (NAKS)
MTU..........	Master Trigger Unit (IAA)
MTU..........	Maximum Transmission Unit [*Computer science*] (IGQR)
MTU..........	Medical Therapy Unit (DMAA)
MTU..........	Memory Transfer Unit (NITA)
MTU..........	Methylthiouracil [*Pharmacology*]
MTU..........	Metric Tons of Uranium
MTU..........	Metric Ton Unit
MTU..........	Metric Units (DFIT)
MTU..........	Michigan Technological University [*Houghton*]
MTU..........	MIRA [*Multifunctional Inertial Reference Assembly*] Transport Unit [*Air Force*] (MCD)
MTU..........	Missile Tracking Unit (MCD)
MTU..........	Missile Training Unit [*Air Force*]
MTU..........	Mist Therapy Unit [*Medicine*]
MTU..........	Mobile Technical Unit (MCD)
MTU..........	Mobile Test Unit [*Army*] (RDA)
MTU..........	Mobile Training Unit
MTU..........	Mobile Treatment Unit [*Environmental Protection Agency*] (GFGA)
MTU..........	Module Test Unit [*Nuclear energy*] (NRCH)
mtu	Montana [*MARC country of publication code Library of Congress*] (LCCP)
MTU..........	Montreal Trustco, Inc. [*Toronto Stock Exchange symbol*]
MTU..........	Mosquito Training Unit [*British military*] (DMA)
MTU..........	Motorinen Turbo-Union [*Germany*]
MTU..........	Multiplexer and Terminal Unit
MTU..........	Multiterminal Unit (TEL)
MTU..........	Myton, UT [*Location identifier FAA*] (FAAL)
MtU..........	University of Montana at Missoula, Missoula, MT [*Library symbol Library of Congress*] (LCLS)
M TUBERC...	Mycobacterium Tuberculosis [*Bacteriology*] (CPH)
MtU-L	University of Montana at Missoula, Law School, Missoula, MT [*Library symbol Library of Congress*] (LCLS)
MTUMR	MIRA [*Multifunctional Inertial Reference Assembly*] Transport Unit MountingRack [*Air Force*] (MCD)
MTUOP.......	Mobile Training Units Out for Parts
MTUR	Mean Time between Unscheduled Removals [*or Replacements*] [*Quality control*] (IIA)
MTUR	Mean Time to Unscheduled Replacement [*Quality control*] (PDAA)
MTV..........	Conference des Ministres Europeens du Travail [*Conference of European Ministers of Labour*] (EAIO)
MTV..........	Mammary Tumor Virus
MTV..........	Management Television [*Air Force*] (AFM)

MTV..........	Maneuvering Technology Vehicle
MTV..........	Marginal Terrain Vehicle
MTV..........	Martinsville, VA [*Location identifier FAA*] (FAAL)
M TV..........	Master of Television
MTV..........	Mean Transformed Value
MTV..........	Media Transforming Virus [*Alleged virus causing immunodeficiency disease*]
MTV..........	Medium Tactical Vehicle [*Army*] (RDA)
MTV..........	Metatarsus Varus [*Anatomy*] (DAVI)
MTV..........	Missile Test Vehicle
MTV..........	Missile Training Vehicle
MTV..........	Modulated Throttle Valve [*Automotive engineering*]
MTV..........	Mota Lava [*Vanuatu*] [*Airport symbol*] (OAG)
MTV..........	Motor Test Vehicle (IAA)
MTV..........	Motor Torpedo Vessel [*British*]
MTV..........	Motor Transport Volunteers [*Military unit*] [*British*]
MTV..........	Mountain Valley Air Service, Inc. [*ICAO designator*] (FAAC)
MTV..........	Mount Tassie [*Australia Seismograph station code, US Geological Survey Closed*] (SEIS)
MTV..........	Mouse Mammary Tumor Virus (DMAA)
MTV..........	Multicultural Television (ADA)
MTV..........	Munitions Tow Vehicle (MCD)
MTV..........	Munition Test Vehicle
MTV..........	Music Television [*Warner Amex Satellite Entertainment Co.*] [*Cable-television system*]
MTV..........	Mutatur Terminatio Versiculi [*The Termination of the Little Verse Is Changed*]
MTVAL.......	Master Tape Validation
MTVC........	Manned [*or Manual*] Thrust Vector Control (MCD)
MTVP........	Moving Target Video Processor
MTVS........	Mission Test and Video System
MTVU........	Module Thruster Valve Unit
MTW.........	Machine Tool Wire
MTW.........	Main Trawl Winch
MTW.........	Manitowoc [*Wisconsin*] [*Airport symbol*] (OAG)
MTW.........	Manitowoc Co. [*NYSE symbol*] (SPSG)
MTW.........	Marinette, Tomahawk & Western Railroad Co. [*AAR code*]
MTW.........	Maximum Taxi Weight [*Aviation*]
MTW.........	Mean Tumor Weight [*Medicine*] (DB)
MTW.........	Military Transport Wagon [*British*]
MTW.........	Mission to the World (EA)
MTW.........	Mobile Training Wing [*Air Force*]
MTW.........	Music Treasures of the World [*Record label*]
mtw	Tropical Maritime Warm Air Mass [*Meteorology*] (BARN)
MtW..........	Wibaux Public Library, Wibaux, MT [*Library symbol*] [*Library of Congress*] (LCLS)
MTWA........	Maximum Total Weight Authorized [*Aviation*] (AIA)
MTWC........	Morgan Three-Wheeler Club (EA)
MTWF........	Metal Thru-Wall Flashing [*Technical drawings*]
MtWfSH	Whitefish Senior High School, Whitefish, MT [*Library symbol*] [*Library of Congress*] (LCLS)
MTWN	Mark Twain Bancshares, Inc. [*NASDAQ symbol*] (NQ)
MTWN	Mark Twain Bancshrs [*NASDAQ symbol*] (TTSB)
MTWO........	Material Test Work Order (SAA)
MTWO........	Melamine Chemicals [*NASDAQ symbol*] (TTSB)
MTWO........	Melamine Chemicals, Inc. [*NASDAQ symbol*] (NQ)
MTWP........	Multiplier Traveling Wave Phototube (IAA)
MtWp........	Roosevelt County Library, Wolf Point, MT [*Library symbol*] [*Library of Congress*] (LCLS)
MTWS........	MAGTF [*Marine Air-Ground Task Force*] Tactical Warfare Simulation [*DoD*]
MTWS........	Manual Track While Scan
MtWs........	Montana State Hospital, Patient Library, Warm Springs, MT [*Library symbol*] [*Library of Congress*] (LCLS)
MTWX........	Mechanized Teletypewriter Exchange (TEL)
MTWY........	Motorway [*Postal Service standard*] (OPSA)
MTX..........	Fairbanks [*Alaska*] Metro Field [*Airport symbol Obsolete*] (OAG)
MTX..........	Manual Transaxle
MTX..........	Master of Taxation
MTX..........	Matrix (IAA)
MTX..........	Message Text Format (COE)
MTX..........	Methotrexate [*Antineoplastic drug*]
MTX..........	Microwave TOKAMAK [*Toroidal Kamera Magnetic*] Experiment [*Plasma physics*]
MTX..........	Military Traffic Expediting Service (AABC)
MTX..........	Minerals Technologies [*NYSE symbol*] (SPSG)
MTX..........	Morrell Tank Line [*AAR code*]
MTXC........	Matrix Capital Corp. [*NASDAQ symbol*] (SAG)
MTX-CF......	Methotrexate with Citrovorum Factor Rescue [*Antineoplastic drug regimen*]
MTX + MP ...	Methotrexate and Mercaptopurine [*Antineoplastic drug regimen*] (DAVI)
MTX + MP + CTX...	Methotrexate, Mercaptopurine, and Cytoxan [*Cyclophosphamide*] [*Antineoplastic drug regimen*] (DAVI)
MTY..........	Empty
MTY..........	Marlton Technologies [*AMEX symbol*] (TTSB)
MTY..........	Marlton Technologies, Inc. [*AMEX symbol*] (SPSG)
MTY..........	Matsuyama [*Japan*] [*Seismograph station code, US Geological Survey*] (SEIS)
MTY..........	Maturity [*Business term*]
Mty..........	Maturity (EBF)
MTY..........	Mekhon ha-Tekanim ha-Yisre'eli (BJA)
MTY..........	Million Tons per Year
MTY..........	Monterrey [*Mexico*] [*Airport symbol*] (OAG)
mtydm	Martyrdom (VRA)

MTZ .... Mass Transfer Zone [Chemical engineering]
MTZ .... Montezuma [Chile] [Seismograph station code, US Geological Survey Closed] (SEIS)
MTZ .... Motorized (AAG)
MTZ .... Tuskegee, AL [Location identifier FAA] (FAAL)
MU .... Akaflieg Muenchen Mitsubishi Heavy Industries [Germany Japan ICAO aircraft manufacturer identifier] (ICAO)
MU .... China Eastern Airlines [ICAO designator] (AD)
Mu .... Mache Unit [Measure of radium emanation from solutions] (AAMN)
MU .... Machine Unit
MU .... Mail Unit (KSC)
MU .... Maintenance Unit [Military]
MU .... Makeup (NRCH)
MU .... Management Unit [Aviation]
MU .... Maneuvering Unit (KSC)
mu .... Map Unit (DOG)
MU .... Marginal Utility [Economics]
MU .... Markup
MU .... Mass Units
MU .... Master Unit (NASA)
mu .... Master Unit (NAKS)
mu .... Mauritania [MARC country of publication code Library of Congress] (LCCP)
MU .... Mauritius [ANSI two-letter standard code] (CNC)
MU .... Measurement Unit
MU .... Memory Unit [Computer science] (MCD)
MU .... Mental Units of Growth [Psychology]
MU .... Mescaline Unit (DB)
MU .... Message Unit [Telecommunications]
MU .... Methylene Unit
MU .... Methylumbelliferone [Biochemistry]
MU .... Methylurea [Organic chemistry]
MU .... Micro [One millionth] (WDAA)
mu .... Micron [Micrometer] (AAMN)
MU .... Micron Technology [NYSE symbol] (TTSB)
MU .... Micron Technology, Inc. [NYSE symbol] (SPSG)
mu .... Millimicro- [Now nano] (IDOE)
mu .... Millimicron [Nanometer] (IDOE)
Mu .... Millimicron (AAG)
MU .... Million Units
mU .... Milliunit (AAMN)
MU .... Misrair [ICAO designator] (AD)
MU .... Mobile Unit
mu .... Mobile Unit (NAKS)
mu .... Mockup (NAKS)
MU .... Mock-Up (AAG)
MU .... Modular Unit (IAA)
MU .... Monetary Unit (ADA)
M/U .... Monitor Unit [Telecommunications] (TEL)
MU .... Montevideo Units [Of uterine activity]
MU .... Mothers' Union [Episcopalian]
MU .... Motor Union
MU .... Motor Unit
MU .... Mouse Unit [Medicine] (DMAA)
mu .... Mouse Unit (LDT)
MU .... Mueller Cell [Eye anatomy]
MU .... Mulching [Environmental science] (COE)
MU .... Multidestination [Carrier]
MU .... Multiple Unit
mu .... Multiple Unit (NAKS)
MU .... Multiple Use (IAA)
MU .... Multiplexing Unit
MU .... Munitions Command [Later, Armaments Command] [Army] (MCD)
Mu .... Muscle [Anatomy] (DAVI)
MU .... Musical Union [Oberlin College] [Ohio]
MU .... Musician [Navy rating]
MU .... Musicians' Union [British] (DCTA)
MU .... Music Program [Association of Independent Colleges and Schools specialization code]
MU .... Muster [Business term] (DCTA)
Mu .... Mutator [A bacteriophage]
MU .... University of Massachusetts, Amherst, MA [Library symbol Library of Congress] (LCLS)
MU1 .... Musician, First Class [Navy rating]
MU2 .... Musician, Second Class [Navy rating]
MU3 .... Musician, Third Class [Navy rating]
MUA .... Machinery Users' Association [British] (BI)
MUA .... Mail Users' Association [British]
MUA .... Manipulation Under Anesthesia [Medicine] (DMAA)
MUA .... Manned Undersea [or Underwater] Activity [Marine science]
MUA .... Maritime Union of Australia
MUA .... Master of Urban Affairs (GAGS)
MUA .... Master of Urban Architecture (GAGS)
MUA .... Materials Usage Agreement (NASA)
MUA .... Maximum Usable Altitude [Aviation]
MUA .... Memorandum of Understanding and Agreement
MUA .... Metallurgistes Unis d'Amerique [United Steelworkers of America - USWA]
MU A .... Microampere (WDAA)
MUA .... Middle Uterine Artery [Medicine] (DMAA)
MUA .... Ministry of State for Urban Affairs [Canada]
MUA .... Mixed Underachievers [Education]
MUA .... Monotype Users' Association (NADA)
MUA .... Mothers' Union in Australia
MUA .... Motor Unit Activity (DMAA)

MUA .... Multiple Unit Activity [Neurophysiology]
MUA .... Munda [Solomon Islands] [Airport symbol] (OAG)
MUA .... Muniassets Fund [NYSE symbol] (SPSG)
MUA .... Murray Aviation, Inc. [ICAO designator] (FAAC)
MUAA .... Major Unit Assembly Area (MCD)
MUAC .... Mid Upper Arm Circumference [Anatomy]
MUACS .... Manpower Utilization and Control System
MUADEE ...... [The] Mars Upper Atmosphere Dynamics, Energetics and Evolution Spacecraft [NASA] (ECON)
MUAG .... Central Agramonte [Cuba ICAO location identifier] (ICLI)
MU/AG .... Mid-Upper [Turret] Air Gunner [British military] (DMA)
MU & P .... Makeup and Purification [Nuclear energy] (NRCH)
MUAP .... Motor Unit Action Potential [Physiology]
MUARC .... Monash University Accident Research Center [Australia]
MUART .... Microprocessor Universal Asynchronous Receiver Transmitter (IAA)
MUAT .... Antilla [Cuba ICAO location identifier] (ICLI)
MUAT .... Mobile Underwater Acoustic Unit (NATG)
MUB .... Maun [Botswana] [Airport symbol] (OAG)
MUB .... University of Maryland, Baltimore County Campus, Catonsville, MD [OCLC symbol] (OCLC)
MUBA .... Baracoa/Oriente [Cuba ICAO location identifier] (ICLI)
MU BAR ...... Microbar (WDAA)
MUBE .... El Caribe [Cuba ICAO location identifier] (ICLI)
MUBI .... Cayo Mambi [Cuba ICAO location identifier] (ICLI)
MUBIS .... Multiple Beam Interval Scanner
MUBO .... Batabano [Cuba ICAO location identifier] (ICLI)
MUBR .... Mean Units between Replacement [Quality control]
MUBY .... Bayamo [Cuba ICAO location identifier] (ICLI)
MUC .... Maximum Urinary Concentration [Medicine]
MUC .... Meritorious Unit Citation [Military decoration]
MUC .... Meritorious Unit Commendation [Military decoration] (AFM)
MUC .... Missionary Union of the Clergy [British] (BI)
MUC .... Mount Union College [Alliance, OH]
MUC .... Mucilaginous (ROG)
MUC .... Mucosal Ulcerative Colitis [Medicine]
MUC .... Multicoupler
MUC .... Multiple Use Counter (IAA)
MUC .... Munich [Germany Airport symbol] (OAG)
MUC .... Musician, Chief [Navy rating]
MUCA .... Ciego De Avila [Cuba ICAO location identifier] (ICLI)
MuCA2 .... Muniyield California Insured Fund II [Associated Press] (SAG)
MuCAIns ...... MuniYield California Insured Fund [Associated Press] (SAG)
MUCB .... Caibarien [Cuba ICAO location identifier] (ICLI)
MUCC .... Cunagua [Cuba ICAO location identifier] (ICLI)
MUCC .... Michigan United Conservation Clubs
MUCF .... Cienfuegos [Cuba ICAO location identifier] (ICLI)
MUCG .... Macquarie University Caving Group [Australia]
MUCG .... Management/Union Consultative Group [Australia]
Much D & S... Muchall's Doctor and Student [A publication] (DLA)
MUCHFET .... Multichannel Field Effect Transistor (IAA)
MUCIA .... Midwest Universities Consortium for International Activities [University of Indiana]
MUCILAG..... Mucilaginous (ROG)
MUCL .... Cayo Largo Del Sur [Cuba ICAO location identifier] (ICLI)
MUCM .... Camaguey/Ignacio Agramonte [Cuba ICAO location identifier] (ICLI)
MUCM .... Musician, Master Chief [Navy rating]
MUCN .... Ciego De Avila Norte [Cuba ICAO location identifier] (ICLI)
MUCO .... Colon [Cuba ICAO location identifier] (ICLI)
MUCO .... Materiel Utilization Control Office (AFIT)
MUCOM .... Munitions Command [Later, Armaments Command] [Army]
Mu Corp Ca.. Municipal Corporation Cases [United States] [A publication] (DLA)
Mu Corp Cir.. Municipal Corporation Circular [England] [A publication] (DLA)
MUCROMAF... Multiple Critical Root Maximally Flat (PDAA)
MUCS .... Central Noel Fernandez [Cuba ICAO location identifier] (ICLI)
MUCS .... Musician, Senior Chief [Navy rating]
MUCU .... Santiago De Cuba/Antonio Maceo [Cuba ICAO location identifier] (ICLI)
MUCUSA...... Missionary Union of the Clergy in the United States of America [Later, PMUPR] (EA)
MUCV .... Las Clavellinas [Cuba ICAO location identifier] (ICLI)
MUCY .... Cayajabo [Cuba ICAO location identifier] (ICLI)
MUD .... Macromind Utility Disk
MUD .... Master of Urban Design (GAGS)
MUD .... Master User Directory (MHDI)
MUD .... Memory Unit Drum [Computer science]
MUD .... Mercaptoundecanol [Organic chemistry]
MUD .... Middle, Up, Down [in game of bridge]
MUD .... Minimum Urticarial Dose [Medicine] (DMAA)
MUD .... Mouvement pour l'Unite et la Democratie [Djibouti] [Political party] (EY)
MUD .... Mouvement Union Democratique [Democratic Union Movement] [Monaco] [Political party] (PPE)
MUD .... Multiple User Dimension [Computer science]
MUD .... Multiple User Dungeon [Computer science]
MUD .... Multiuser Dialogue [Computer science] (IGQR)
MUD .... Multi-User Domain [Computer science]
MUD .... Multi-User Dungeon [Computer game]
MUD .... Municipal Utility District [Investment term] (DFIT)
MUD .... Murchison Falls [Uganda] [Airport symbol] (AD)
MUDAID ...... Multivariate, Univariate, and Discriminant Analysis of Irregular Data [Statistics] (IAA)
MUDAR........ Mulheres por um Desenvolvimento Alternativo [Development Alternatives with women for a New Era - DAWN] [Brazil] (EAIO)
MUDD .... Multisource Unified Data Distribution (PDAA)
MUDDC........ Multiunit Direct Digital Control (IAA)

MUDET	Militarized Universal Digital Element Tester (MCD)
MUDL	Microwave Ultrasonic Delay Line
MUDPIE	Museum and University Data Processing Information Exchange (IAA)
MUDR	Multidetail Drawing (MSA)
MUDS	Multiple Usage Data Sheet (MCD)
MUDSS	Mobile Underwater Debris Survey System
Mudst	Mudstone Soil [Agronomy]
MUDWNT	Makeup Demineralizer Waste Neutralizer Tank (IEEE)
MUE	Kamuela [Hawaii] [Airport symbol] (OAG)
MUE	Meritorious Unit Emblem [Military decoration]
MUE	Microcomputer Users in Education (AIE)
MUE	Motor Unit Estimate (DB)
MUE	Motor Unit Estimated (DMAA)
MUEI	Micron Electronics, Inc. [NASDAQ symbol] (SAG)
MUEI	Micron Electronics [NASDAQ symbol] (TTSB)
MUEL	Mueller [Paul] Co. [NASDAQ symbol] (NQ)
Mueller	Mueller Industries [Associated Press] (SAG)
MuellerInd	Muller Industries [Associated Press] (SAG)
MuellerP	Mueller [Paul] Co. [Associated Press] (SAG)
MUERI	Murdoch University Energy Research Institute [Australia]
MUF	Makeup Feed [Boiler]
MUF	Material Unaccounted For [Nuclear energy]
MUF	Maximum Usable Frequency [Signal transmission]
MU F	Microfarad (WDAA)
MUF	Muffler
MUF	Muting [Indonesia] [Airport symbol] (OAG)
MUFC	Central Amancio Rodriguez [Cuba ICAO location identifier] (ICLI)
MUFD	Makeup Feed [Boiler]
MUFFIN	Multi-Use Interagency News [FSS database] (AAGC)
MUFL	Florida [Cuba ICAO location identifier] (ICLI)
MuFLIn	MuniYield Florida Insured Fund [Associated Press] (SAG)
MUFLNG	Mouvement pour l'Unification des Forces de Liberation de la Guadeloupe [Movement for the Unification of National Liberation Forces of Guadeloupe] [Political party] (PD)
MUFLR	Muffler
MUFM	Mouvement Universal pour une Federation Mondiale [World Association of World Federalists - WAWF] [Netherlands]
MUFON	Mutual UFO [Unidentified Flying Object] Network (EA)
MUFT	Multigroup Fourier Transform [Code] [Nuclear energy] (NRCH)
MUFTI	Minimum Use of Force Tactical Intervention [British police]
MUG	Macintosh User Group [Computer science] (WDMC)
MUG	Make-Up Gas [Chemical engineering]
MUG	Manning Unit Group [Air Force] (AFM)
MUG	Marcive Users Group [Library network]
MUG	MARC Users Group (NITA)
MUG	Maximum Unilateral Gain (IAA)
MUG	Maximum Usable Gain [Bell System]
MUG	Methylumbelliferylglucuronide [Biochemistry]
MU G	Microgram (WDAA)
MUG	Ministry of Useless Gestures [Organization to increase number of voters] [British]
MUG	Mitosis with Unreplicated Genome [Cytology]
MUG	Mulege [Mexico] [Airport symbol Obsolete] (OAG)
MUG	Multiset Users Group (EA)
MUG	MUMPS [Massachusetts General Hospital Utility Multiprogramming System] Users' Group (EA)
MUG	Murgor Resources, Inc. [Vancouver Stock Exchange symbol]
MUGA	Multigated Angiogram [Cardiology] (DAVI)
MUGA	Multiple Gate Acquisition Analysis [Scan] (DAVI)
MUGA	Multiple-Gated Acquisition [Nuclear medicine]
MU-GAL	Methylumbelliferyl-B-Galactosidase [Biochemistry] (MAE)
MUGA scan	Multiple-Gated Arteriography Scan [Medicine] (WDAA)
MUGB	Methylumbelliferyl Guanidinobenzoate [Biochemistry]
MUGEx	Multigated Blood Pool Image during Exercise [Hematology] (DMAA)
MUGM	Guantanamo, US Naval Air Base [Cuba ICAO location identifier] (ICLI)
MUGN	Giron [Cuba ICAO location identifier] (ICLI)
MUGR	Multigated Blood Pool Image at Rest [Medicine] (DMAA)
MUGSE	Multimission-Unique Ground Support Equipment (MCD)
MUGT	Guantanamo [Cuba ICAO location identifier] (ICLI)
MUGX	Multiple Gated Acquisition Exercise [Scan] [Cardiology] (DAVI)
MUH	Memorial University of Newfoundland, Health Sciences Library [UTLAS symbol]
MUH	Mersa Matruh [Egypt] [Airport symbol] (AD)
MU H	Microhenry (WDAA)
MUHA	Habana/Jose Marti [Cuba ICAO location identifier] (ICLI)
MUHG	Holguin [Cuba ICAO location identifier] (ICLI)
MUI	Fort Indiantown Gap (Annville), PA [Location identifier FAA] (FAAL)
MUI	Machine Utilization Index [Computer science]
MUI	Mashhad University [Iran] [Seismograph station code, US Geological Survey] (SEIS)
MUI	Mass Unbalance Input [Computer science]
MUI	Mode-Independent Unnumbered Information
MUI	Monsoonal Upwelling Index [Paleoceanography]
MUI	Movement for the Unity of the Left [Ecuador] [Political party] (PPW)
MUI	Trans Air [FAA designator] (FAAC)
MUIFX	Nationwide Fund [Mutual fund ticker symbol] (SG)
MUIG	Minicomputer Users Interest Group [Later, Mini/Micro Special Interest Group] (EA)
MU IN	Microinch (WDAA)
MuInII	Muniyield Insured Fund [Associated Press] (SAG)
MUIR	Microinstruction Register (MHDI)
Muir Gai	Muirhea's Institutes of Gaius [A publication] (DLA)
MUIS	Isabella [Cuba ICAO location identifier] (ICLI)
MulT	Municipal Income Trust [Associated Press] (SAG)
MulT2	Municipal Income Trust II [Associated Press] (SAG)
MulT3	Municipal Income Trust III [Associated Press] (SAG)
MUJ	Mui [Ethiopia] [Airport symbol] (OAG)
MUJA	Majana [Cuba ICAO location identifier] (ICLI)
MUK	Alamogordo, NM [Location identifier FAA] (FAAL)
MUK	Mauke [Cook Islands] [Airport symbol] (OAG)
MUK	MEPC International Capital LP [NYSE symbol] (SAG)
MUK	Muk Air Taxi [Denmark ICAO designator] (FAAC)
MUK	Mukerian [India] [Seismograph station code, US Geological Survey Closed] (SEIS)
MUKPrA	MEPC Intl Cap 9.125%'QUIPS' [NYSE symbol] (TTSB)
MUL	Manned Underwater Laboratories [Marine science] (MSC)
MUL	Manufacturing under Licence [British] (DS)
MUL	Master Urgency List [Navy]
MUL	Mobile-Moored Undersea Laboratory
MUL	Modify User Login (AAEL)
MUL	Moultrie, GA [Location identifier FAA] (FAAL)
MUL	Mullan [Idaho] [Seismograph station code, US Geological Survey] (SEIS)
MUL	MULS [Minnesota Union List of Serials], Minneapolis, MN [OCLC symbol] (OCLC)
MUL	Multicae Companies [NYSE symbol] (SAG)
MUL	Multicare Cos. [NYSE symbol] (TTSB)
mul	Multilingual [MARC language code Library of Congress] (LCCP)
MUL	Multiplexer
MUL	Multiply (MDG)
MULASSS	Multiple LASER Source Signature Simulator (MCD)
MULB	Habana [Cuba ICAO location identifier] (ICLI)
MULDEM	Multiplexer/Demultiplexer [Bell Laboratories]
MULDEX	Multiplexer/Demultiplexer
MULDEX	Multipoint Cross-Reference Index
MULE	Manned-Unmanned Lunar Explorer
MULE	Modular Universal LASER Equipment (MCD)
MULE	Multiple-Use Linear Engergizer [Automotive engineering]
MULH	Habana [Cuba ICAO location identifier] (ICLI)
MULL	Modern Uses of Logic in Law
MULL	Mullion [Technical drawings]
MULM	La Coloma [Cuba ICAO location identifier] (ICLI)
MulMR	Multi-Market Radio, Inc. [Associated Press] (SAG)
MulMRad	Multi-Market Radio, Inc. [Associated Press] (SAG)
MULO	Multipurpose Lightweight Overboot [Army]
MULQUAL	Multiple Goal Water Quality Model (PDAA)
MULR	Malayan Union Law Reports [1946-47] [A publication] (ILCA)
MULR	Muller
MULS	Mobile Unit Launch Site (IAA)
MULS	Signed Multiplication [Computer science]
MULSF	Macquarie University Law School Foundation [Australia]
MULSP	Missouri Union List of Serial Publications [St. Louis Public Library] [Missouri] [Information service or system] (IID)
MULT	Multiple
MULT	Multiply (NASA)
MULTA	Multiple-Use Land Alliance (EA)
MultClr	Multi-Color Corp. [Associated Press] (SAG)
MULTEWS	Multiple Electronics Warfare Surveillance [DoD]
MULTEWS	Multitarget Electronic Warfare System
MULTH	Multilith
multi	Multicolored [Philately]
MULTI	Multiple (DAVI)
MULTI	Multiplexer
Multicne	Multicare Companies [Associated Press] (SAG)
MULTICOR	Multinational Finance Corp. [Indonesia] (EY)
MultiCp	Multi-Corp, Inc. [Associated Press] (SAG)
Multicre	Multicare Companies [Associated Press] (SAG)
MULTICS	Multiplexed Information and Computing Service [Honeywell, Inc.]
MultiCul R	MultiCultural Review [A publication] (BRI)
Multilink PPP	Multichannel Connection Protocol Based on the Point-to-Point Protocol [Computer science]
Multilink PPP	Multilink Point-to-Point Protocol [Computer science]
MultiMC	MultiMedia Concepts International, Inc. [Associated Press] (SAG)
MultiMed	MultiMedia Concepts International, Inc. [Associated Press] (SAG)
MULTIMED	Multimedia Exposure Assessment Model [Environmental Protection Agency] (AEPA)
multip	Multiparous [Obstetrics]
MULTIPAC	Multiple Pool Processor and Computer (PDAA)
MULTIPLE	Multipurpose Program that Learns [Computer science] (PDAA)
MULTIV	Multivibrator (IAA)
multivits	Multivitamins [Pharmacy]
MultM	Multi-Market Radio, Inc. [Associated Press] (SAG)
MultMC	MultiMedia Concepts International, Inc. [Associated Press] (SAG)
Multmd	Multimedia Concepts International, Inc. [Associated Press] (SAG)
MultMT	Multi-Media Tutorial Services, Inc. [Associated Press] (SAG)
MULTOTS	Multiple Units Link 11 Test and Operational Training System [Navy] (NVT)
MULTP	Multiplier (NITA)
MultPb	Multicom Publishing [Associated Press] (SAG)
MULTR	Multimeter (AAG)
MULTR	Multiplier
MultZns	Multiple Zones International, Inc. [Associated Press] (SAG)
MULU	Unsigned Multiplication [Computer science]
MuLV	Murine Leukemia Virus [Also, MLV]
MuLv	Murine Leukemia Virus [Medicine] (DB)
Mum	Chrysanthemum [Horticulture]
MUM	Maximum Useful Magnification (MCD)
MUM	Method of Unweighted Means [Statistics]

MUM.......... Methodology for Unmanned Manufacture [*Robotics project*] [*Japan*]
MUM.......... Multiple Unit Message [*Telecommunications*] (IEEE)
MUM.......... Multiuse Manuscript
MUM.......... Multiuse Mnemonics (IAA)
MUM.......... Multi-User Message (NITA)
MUM.......... Multiuser Monitor
MUM.......... Mumias [*Kenya*] [*Airport symbol Obsolete*] (OAG)
MUM.......... University of Mississippi, University, MS [*OCLC symbol*] (OCLC)
MU M².......... Square Micrometer (WDAA)
MU M³.......... Cubic Micrometer (WDAA)
MUMA.......... Punta De Maisi [*Cuba ICAO location identifier*] (ICLI)
MUMAD.......... Museum Angkatan Darat [*Indonesia*]
Mumf.......... Mumford's Jamaica Reports [*A publication*] (DLA)
MUMG.......... Managua [*Cuba ICAO location identifier*] (ICLI)
MUMH.......... Matahambre [*Cuba ICAO location identifier*] (ICLI)
MUMI.......... Manzanillo [*Cuba ICAO location identifier*] (ICLI)
MUMJ.......... Mayajigua [*Cuba ICAO location identifier*] (ICLI)
Mum Jam.......... Mumford's Jamaica Reports [*A publication*] (DLA)
MUMLIB.......... Multimedia Technology in Libraries (TELE)
MUMMERS... Manned-Unmanned Environmental Research Station (MSC)
MUMMS.......... Marine Corps Unified Materiel Management System
Mummy.......... Mature Upwardly Mobile Mommy [*Lifestyle classification*]
MUMO.......... Moa [*Cuba ICAO location identifier*] (ICLI)
MUMP.......... Marshall - University of Michigan Probe [*Rocket flight*]
MUMPS.......... Massachusetts General Hospital Utility Multiprogramming System [*Programming language*]
MUMPS.......... Multiple-Unit, Moving-Projectile System (MCD)
MUMS.......... Mobile Utility Module System (IEEE)
MUMS.......... Mothers United for Moral Support
MUMS.......... Multiple Unguided Mine System (MCD)
MUMS.......... Multiple-Use MARC [*Machine-Readable Cataloging*] System [*Online retrieval system*] [*Information service or system Library of Congress*]
MUMS.......... MUMS National Parent-to-Parent Network [*Formerly, Mothers United for Moral Support*] (EA)
MUMSU.......... Monash University Malaysian Students' Union [*Australia*]
MUMT.......... Matanzas [*Cuba ICAO location identifier*] (ICLI)
MuMTV.......... Murine Mammary Tumor Virus
MUMZ.......... Manzanillo [*Cuba ICAO location identifier*] (ICLI)
MUN.......... Aeromundo Ejecutivo, SA de CV [*Mexico*] [*FAA designator*] (FAAC)
MUN.......... Maturin [*Venezuela*] [*Airport symbol*] (OAG)
MUN.......... Memorial University of Newfoundland [*Marine science*] (MSC)
MUN.......... Memorial University of Newfoundland Library [*UTLAS symbol*]
MUN.......... Mundaring [*Australia Seismograph station code, US Geological Survey*] (SEIS)
Mun.......... Munford's Reports [*15-20 Virginia*] [*A publication*] (DLA)
MUN.......... Municipal
Mun.......... Municipal (TBD)
Mun.......... Municipal Law Reporter [*A publication*] (DLA)
MUN.......... Munitions (AFM)
Mun.......... Munitions Appeals Reports [*England*] [*A publication*] (DLA)
MUN.......... Munsingwear, Inc. [*NYSE symbol*] (SPSG)
MUNA.......... La Cubana [*Cuba ICAO location identifier*] (ICLI)
MUNA.......... United Nations Association of Mauritius (EAIO)
MunAdv.......... Municipal Advantage Fund [*Associated Press*] (SAG)
MUNAF.......... Movimento de Unidade Nacional Antifacista [*National United Antifascist Movement*] [*Portugal Political party*] (PPE)
Mun & El Cas... Municipal and Election Cases [*India*] [*A publication*] (DLA)
Mun App.......... Munitions Appeals Reports [*England*] [*A publication*] (DLA)
Mun App Rep... Munitions Appeals Reports [*England*] [*A publication*] (DLA)
Mun App Sc... Munitions of War Acts, Appeal Reports [*1916-20*] [*Scotland*] [*A publication*] (DLA)
MUNB.......... San Nicolas De Bari [*Cuba ICAO location identifier*] (ICLI)
MUNBG.......... Munitions Building [*Washington, DC*] [*Obsolete*]
MUNBLDG... Munitions Building [*Obsolete Washington, DC*] (DNAB)
MUNC.......... Munitions Command [*Later, Armaments Command*] [*Army*]
MUNC.......... Nicaro [*Cuba ICAO location identifier*] (ICLI)
MunCA.......... MuniYield California Fund [*Associated Press*] (SAG)
Mun Corp Cas... Municipal Corporation Cases [*A publication*] (DLA)
Mun Ct.......... Municipal Court (DLA)
Mun Ct App Dist Col... Municipal Court of Appeals for the District of Columbia (DLA)
Mund.......... De Mundo [*of Aristotle*] [*Classical studies*] (OCD)
MUND.......... Model Urban Neighborhood Demonstration
Mundy.......... Abstracts of Star Chamber Proceedings [*1550-58*] [*A publication*] (DLA)
MUNE.......... Multiple Negative [*Circuit*] (AAG)
Munf.......... Munford's Reports [*15-20 Virginia*] [*A publication*] (DLA)
MunFL.......... MuniYield Florida Fund [*Associated Press*] (SAG)
MUNFLA.......... Memorial University of Newfoundland Folklore and Language Archive [*Research center Canada*] (RCD)
Munf (VA).... Munford's Reports [*15-20 Virginia*] [*A publication*] (DLA)
MUNG.......... Mush until No Good [*Describes destruction of computer software*]
MUNG.......... Nueva Gerona [*Cuba ICAO location identifier*] (ICLI)
MUNGE.......... Movimiento para la Unificacion Nacional de Guinea Ecuatorial [*Movement for National Unification of Equatorial Guinea*] [*Political party*] (EY)
Mung Pay.... Munger on Application of Payments [*A publication*] (DLA)
MunHi.......... Municipal High Income Fund, Inc. [*Associated Press*] (SAG)
MUNI.......... Municipal (AFM)
Muni.......... Municipal (EBF)
Muniast.......... Muniassets Fund, Inc. [*Associated Press*] (SAG)
MUNIC.......... Municipal
Munic & PL... Municipal and Parish Law Cases [*England*] [*A publication*] (DLA)
Munic LR (PA)... Municipal Law Reporter [*Pennsylvania*] [*A publication*] (DLA)
MUNIDB.......... Municipal Bonds Databank (NITA)
MuniFd.......... MuniEnhanced Fund [*Associated Press*] (SAG)
MuniIn.......... Muni Insured Fund, Inc. [*Associated Press*] (SAG)
MUNIMT.......... Muniment (ROG)
MuniMtg.......... Municipal Mortgage & Equity LLC [*Associated Press*] (SAG)
MunIns.......... MuniYield Insured Fund [*Associated Press*] (SAG)
MUNIREP.......... Munitions Report [*Worldwide report of location and status of air munitions*] [*Military*]
MUniv.......... Master of the University
Muniv2.......... Munivest Fund II [*Associated Press*] (SAG)
Muniyld.......... MuniYield Fund, Inc. [*Associated Press*] (SAG)
MuNJIn.......... MuniYield New Jersey Insured Fund [*Associated Press*] (SAG)
Munk Emp Liab... Munkman's Employer's Liability at Common Law [*8th ed.*] [*1975*] [*A publication*] (DLA)
Mun LJ.......... Municipal Law Journal [*A publication*] (DLA)
Mun LR.......... Municipal Law Reporter [*Pennsylvania*] [*A publication*] (DLA)
Mun LR.......... Municipal Law Reports [*1903-13*] [*Scotland*] [*A publication*] (DLA)
Mun L Rep... Chrostwaite's Pennsylvania Municipal Law Reporter [*A publication*] (DLA)
MunMI.......... MuniYield Michigan Fund [*Associated Press*] (SAG)
MunMIIn.......... MuniYield Michigan Insured Fund [*Associated Press*] (SAG)
MunNJ.......... MuniYield New Jersey Fund [*Associated Press*] (SAG)
MunNY.......... MuniYield New York Insured Fund [*Associated Press*] (SAG)
MunPA.......... MuniYield Pennsylvania Fund [*Associated Press*] (SAG)
MunPrt.......... Municipal Partners Fund [*Associated Press*] (SAG)
MunPrt2.......... Municipal Partners Fund 2 [*Associated Press*] (SAG)
MunQ12.......... Muniyield Quality Fund II, Inc. [*Associated Press*] (SAG)
MunQlty.......... MuniYield Quality Fund, Inc. [*Associated Press*] (SAG)
Mun Rep.......... Municipal Reports [*Canada*] [*A publication*] (DLA)
Munsng.......... Munsingwear, Inc. [*Associated Press*] (SAG)
MUNSS.......... Munition Support Squadron
Mun Tort Lib... Municipal, School, and State Tort Liability [*A publication*] (DLA)
MUNU.......... Central Brasil [*Cuba ICAO location identifier*] (ICLI)
Munvst.......... MuniVest Fund, Inc. [*Associated Press*] (SAG)
MuNY2.......... Muniyield New York Insured Fund II [*Associated Press*] (SAG)
MuNY3.......... Muniyield New York Insured Fund III [*Associated Press*] (SAG)
MunyAZ.......... Muniyield Arizona Fund II [*Associated Press*] (SAG)
MunyIAZ.......... Muniyield Arizona Fund [*Associated Press*] (SAG)
MUO.......... Maximum Undistorted Output
MUO.......... Mountain Home, ID [*Location identifier FAA*] (FAAL)
MUO.......... Municipal University of Omaha [*Later, University of Nebraska at Omaha*]
MUO.......... Myocardiopathy of Unknown Origin [*Cardiology*]
MUO.......... Pioneer Interest Shares [*Formerly, Mutual of Omaha Interest Shares, Inc.*] [*NYSE symbol*] (SPSG)
MUO.......... Pioneer Interest Shs [*NYSE symbol*] (TTSB)
MUOD.......... Mean Unplanned Outage Duration (IEEE)
MUON.......... Mu-Meson [*An elementary particle*]
MUP.......... Major Urinary Protein (DB)
MUP.......... Make-Up Pay (MHDB)
MUP.......... Manchester University Press [*Manchester, England*]
MUP.......... Master of Urban Planning
MUP.......... Metalworking under Pressure (PDAA)
MUP.......... Modify User Password (AAEL)
MUP.......... Molded Urea Plastics
MUP.......... Motor Unit Potential
MUP.......... Mouse Urine Protein [*Biochemistry*] (DAVI)
MUP.......... Mouvement de l'Unite Populaire [*Popular Unity Movement*] [*Tunisia*] [*Political party*] (PD)
MUP.......... Movimiento da Unidade Progressiva [*Brazil Political party*] (EY)
MUP.......... Multiple Utility Peripheral (NITA)
MUPA.......... Punta Alegre [*Cuba ICAO location identifier*] (ICLI)
MuPAIns.......... MuniVest Pennsylvania Insured Fund [*Associated Press*] (SAG)
MUPB.......... Baracoa Playa/Habana [*Cuba ICAO location identifier*] (ICLI)
MUPDD.......... Master of Urban Planning, Design, and Development (PGP)
MUPEJARS... Multiple Peanut-Butter Jars [*Unconventional musical instrument used in performance by the "Music for Homemade Instruments" ensemble*]
MUPF.......... Modified Ultrapherical Polynominal Filter (IAA)
MUPID.......... Multiple Universally Programmable Intelligent Decoder [*Telecommunications*] (TSSD)
MUPID.......... Multi-Purpose Universal Programmable Intelligent Decoder (NITA)
MuPIT.......... Municipal Premier Income Trust [*Associated Press*] (SAG)
MUPL.......... Military Urgency Planning List (NG)
MUPL.......... Mock-Up Planning
MUPL.......... Pilon [*Cuba ICAO location identifier*] (ICLI)
MUPO.......... Maximum Undistorted Power Output
MUPO.......... Multiple Positive [*Circuit*] (AAG)
MUPP.......... Master of Urban Planning and Policy (GAGS)
MUPPATS.... Multiparticle Position- and Time- Sensitive Detector
MUPPET.......... Marionette and Puppet
Muppie.......... Mennonite Urban Professional [*Lifestyle classification*]
Muppie.......... Middle-Aged Urban Pinhead [*Lifestyle classification*]
Muppie.......... Middle-Aged Urban Professional [*Lifestyle classification*]
Muppy.......... Male Urban Professional [*Lifestyle classification*]
MUPR.......... Pinar Del Rio [*Cuba ICAO location identifier*] (ICLI)
MUPROF.......... Multiple Projected Fibonacci [*Microwave circuit*]
MUPS.......... Central Guatemala [*Cuba ICAO location identifier*] (ICLI)
MUPS.......... Manpower Utilisation and Payment Structure [*Imperial Chemical Industries*] [*British*]
MUPS.......... Mechanized Unit Property System [*Telecommunications*] (TEL)
MUPS.......... Minimum Universal Pension System [*Proposed to reform pension coverage*]
MUPS.......... Multiple Utility Peripheral System [*Computer science*]
MUPT.......... Patria [*Cuba ICAO location identifier*] (ICLI)

MuPV .... Murine Polyomavirus [*Medicine*]
MUR .... Aerolinea Muri [*Mexico ICAO designator*] (FAAC)
MUR .... Management Update and Retrieval System (NRCH)
MUR .... Manpower Utilization Report (MCD)
MUR .... Marudi [*Malaysia*] [*Airport symbol*] (OAG)
MUR .... Mock-Up Reactor [*NASA*]
MUR .... Montana Utilities Reports [*A publication*] (DLA)
MUR .... Movimiento de Unidad Revolucionaria [*Guerrilla forces*] [*Honduras*] (EY)
mur .... Mural (VRA)
Mur .... Muramic Acid [*Also, MurA*] [*Biochemistry*]
MUR .... Murder [*FBI standardized term*]
MUR .... Murgab [*Former USSR Seismograph station code, US Geological Survey Closed*] (SEIS)
Mur .... Murlyn [*Record label*]
Mur .... Murphey's Reports [*5-7 North Carolina*] [*A publication*] (DLA)
MUR .... Murphy Oil [*NYSE symbol*] (TTSB)
MUR .... Murphy Oil Corp. [*NYSE symbol*] (SPSG)
Mur .... Murray's Ceylon Reports [*A publication*] (DLA)
Mur .... Murray's Jury Court Cases [*1815-30*] [*Scotland*] [*A publication*] (DLA)
MUR .... Mustang Resources, Inc. [*Vancouver Stock Exchange symbol*]
Mur .... Pro Murena [*of Cicero*] [*Classical studies*] (OCD)
MUR .... Radio Relay Message Unit [*Telecommunications*] (TEL)
MURA .... Midwestern Universities Research Association
MurA .... Muramic Acid [*Also, Mur*] [*Biochemistry*]
Mur & H ...... Murphy and Hurlstone's English Exchequer Reports [*1836-37*] [*A publication*] (DLA)
Mur & Hurl... Murphy and Hurlstone's English Exchequer Reports [*1836-37*] [*A publication*] (DLA)
Murat Antiq Med Aevi... Muratori's Antiquitates Medii Aevi [*A publication*] (DLA)
MURATREC... Multi-RADAR Track Reconstitution [*Aviation*] (DA)
MURB .... Multiple Unit Residential Building [*Canada*]
MUrbDes(Arch)... Master of Urban Design
MUrbRegPlg... Master of Urban and Regional Planning
MURC .... Measurable Undesirable Respiratory Contaminants [*Pollution index*] [*Superseded by PSI*]
MURC .... Murdock Communications Corp. [*NASDAQ symbol*] (SAG)
MURCO .... Murphy Oil Corp. (EFIS)
MURD .... Murder (ROG)
Murdck .... Murdock Communications Corp. [*Associated Press*] (SAG)
Murd Epit..... Murdoch's Epitome Canada [*A publication*] (DLA)
Murdock .... Murdock Communications Corp. [*Associated Press*] (SAG)
MURF .... Material Utilization Reference File [*Military*]
MURFAAM ... Mutual Reduction of Forces and Armaments and Associated Measures
MURFAAMCE... Mutual Reduction of Forces and Armaments and Associated Measures in Central Europe
Murfree Off Bonds... Murfree on Official Bonds [*A publication*] (DLA)
MURG .... Machine Utilization Report Generator
MURI .... Mild Upper Respiratory Illness [*Virus*] [*Obsolete usage*]
MURIEL ...... Multimedia Remote Interactive Electronic Documents (TELE)
MURL .... Major Urban Resource Library [*Department of Education*] (GFGA)
MURL .... Mock-Up Release
MurNAc........ N-Acetylmuramate [*Laboratory science*] (DAVI)
MURP .... Manned Upperstage Reusable Payload
MURP .... Master of Urban and Regional Planning
MURP .... Master of Urban and Rural Planning (GAGS)
Murp & H .... Murphy and Hurlstone's English Exchequer Reports [*1836-37*] [*A publication*] (ILCA)
Murph.......... Murphey's Reports [*5-7 North Carolina*] [*A publication*] (DLA)
Murph & H... Murphy and Hurlstone's English Exchequer Reports [*1836-37*] [*A publication*] (DLA)
Murph (NC)... Murphey's Reports [*5-7 North Carolina*] [*A publication*] (DLA)
MURPL .... Master of Urban and Regional Planning (PGP)
MurpO .... Murphy Oil Corp. [*Associated Press*] (SAG)
Murr............ Murray's Ceylon Reports [*A publication*] (DLA)
Murr............ Murray's Jury Court Cases [*1815-30*] [*Scotland*] [*A publication*] (DLA)
Murr............ Murray's Laws and Acts of Parliament [*Scotland*] [*A publication*] (DLA)
MURR .... University of Missouri Research Reactor
Murray......... Murray's Scotch Jury Court Reports [*A publication*] (DLA)
Murray (Ceylon)... Murray's Ceylon Reports [*A publication*] (DLA)
Murray (Scot)... Murray's Scotch Jury Trials [*A publication*] (DLA)
Murray's Eng Dict... Murray's English Dictionary [*A publication*] (DLA)
Murray St U... Murray State University (GAGS)
Murr Over Cas... Murray's Overruled Cases [*A publication*] (DLA)
MURS .... Machine Utilization Reporting System (PDAA)
MURS .... Machine Utilization Report System [*Computer science*] (IAA)
MURS .... Minority Undergraduate Research Support
MURS .... Mouvement Universel de la Responsabilite Scientifique [*Universal Movement for Scientific Responsibility - UMSR*] (EAIO)
MURS .... Mursley [*England*]
Mur Tab Cas... Murray's Table of United States Cases [*A publication*] (DLA)
MURTF .... Nur Advanced Technologies [*NASDAQ symbol*] (TTSB)
MURTS .... Multiple User Remote Terminal Supervisor (MHDI)
Mur Us .... Murray's History of Usury [*A publication*] (DLA)
Mur US Ct ... Murray's Proceedings in the United States Courts [*A publication*] (DLA)
MURXF .... International Murex Technologies [*NASDAQ symbol*] (SAG)
MURXF .... Intl Murex Technologies [*NASDAQ symbol*] (TTSB)
MUS............ Magnetic Unloading System
MUS............ Maintenance Utilization Sheet
MUS............ Manned Underwater Station

MUS............ Manual Update Service (NITA)
MUS............ Mass Unbalance Spin
MUS............ Master of Urban Studies (ADA)
MUS............ Mauritius [*ANSI three-letter standard code*] (CNC)
MUS............ Methylumbelliferone Sulfate [*Biochemistry*]
MU S............ Microsecond (WDAA)
MUS............ Monetary Unit Sampling (ADA)
MUS............ Mouse Urologic Syndrome (DMAA)
MUS............ Multiprogramming Utility System [*Regnecentralen*] [*Denmark*]
MUS............ Multiutility System (MCD)
Mus............ Musca [*Constellation*]
MUS............ Muschocho Explorations Ltd. [*Toronto Stock Exchange symbol*]
MUS............ Muscimol [*Biochemistry*]
mus............ Musee (VRA)
mus............ Museen (VRA)
mus............ Museo (VRA)
mus............ Museum (VRA)
Mus............ Museum (AL)
MUS............ Museum
MUS............ Music
MUS............ Muskinabad [*Former USSR Seismograph station code, US Geological Survey Closed*] (SEIS)
mus............ Muskogee [*MARC language code Library of Congress*] (LCCP)
Mus............ Muslim
MUS............ University of Southern Mississippi, Hattiesburg, MS [*OCLC symbol*] (OCLC)
MUSA .... Manufacturing USA [*A publication*]
MUSA .... Multiple Unit Steerable Antenna [*Electronics*]
MUSA .... Multiple Unit Steerable Array (NITA)
MUSA .... San Antonio De Los Banos [*Cuba ICAO location identifier*] (ICLI)
MUSA .... Seaman Apprentice, Musician, Striker [*Navy rating*]
Mus AD........ Doctor of Musical Arts
MUS & T ...... Manned Undersea Science and Technology [*Marine science*] (MSC)
MUSAP .... Multisatellite Augmentation Program [*NASA*]
MUSARC....... Major United States Army Reserve Command (AABC)
MUSAT .... Multiple Station Analytical Triangulation (PDAA)
MUSAT .... Multipurpose UHF [*Ultra High Frequency*] Satellite (IAA)
MUSB .... Mobile Unit Support Base (AAG)
Mus B.......... Musicae Baccalaureus [*Bachelor of Music*] [*Latin*]
Mus Bac ...... Musicae Baccalaureus [*Bachelor of Music*] [*Latin*]
Mus Bach ..... Musicae Baccalaureus [*Bachelor of Music*] [*Latin*]
Mus Belge ... Musee Belge [*A publication*] (OCD)
MUSC .... Medical University of South Carolina
MUSC .... Memphis Union Station Co. [*AAR code*]
MUSC .... Multiunit Supervisory Control (IAA)
Musc........... Musca [*Constellation*]
MUSC .... Muscarine [*Alkaloid*]
MUSC .... Muscles [*or Muscular*]
MUSC .... Music
MUSC .... Santa Clara [*Cuba ICAO location identifier*] (ICLI)
MUSCL .... Musical
MUSCLE ...... Millions of Unusual Small Creatures Lurking Everywhere [*Toy by Mattel, Inc.*]
MUSCM .... Missile Unit Simulated Combat Mission (SAA)
MUSCO........ Muhoroni Sugar Co. Ltd.
Mus D.......... Musicae Doctor [*Doctor of Music*] [*Latin*]
Mus Doc ...... Musicae Doctor [*Doctor of Music*] [*Latin*]
MUSE .... Mace Utilities Sector Editor [*Computer science*]
MUSE .... Machine User Symbiotic Environment (PDAA)
MUSE .... Machine User Symbolic Environment (IAA)
MUSE .... Medical Urethral System for Erection
MUSE .... Medical Use of Simulation Electronics
MUSE .... Microcomputer Users in Education
MUSE .... MIDI [*Musical Instrument Digital Interface*] Users Sequencer/Editor [*Roland International Corp.*]
MUSE .... Mobile Utilities Support Equipment [*Navy*] (NG)
MUSE .... Model to Understand Simple English (PDAA)
MUSE .... Modular Utilities for Systems Education (IAA)
MUSE .... Monitor of Ultraviolet Solar Energy
MUSE .... Multimedia User Environment [*Computer science*]
MUSE .... Multiple Sub-Nyquist Subsampling Encoding [*Digital recording system introduced 1984*]
MUSE .... Multiuser Shared Environment [*Computer science*] (IGQR)
MUSE .... Multi-User-Simulated Environment (PS)
MUSE .... Musicians United for Safe Energy (EA)
MUSE .... Musicians United to Stop Exclusion [*Defunct*] (EA)
Mus Ed B ..... Bachelor of Music Education
Mus Ed D..... Doctor of Music Education
MUSEDET ..... Mobile Utilities Support Equipment Detachment [*Navy*] (DNAB)
Mus Ed M..... Master of Music Education
MUSF .... Habana/Santa Fe [*Cuba ICAO location identifier*] (ICLI)
MUSG .... Sagua La Grande [*Cuba ICAO location identifier*] (ICLI)
Mus G Paed... Musicae Graduatus Paedagogus [*Graduate Teacher in Music*]
MUSH .... Multiuser Shared Hallucination [*Computer science*] (IGQR)
MusH........... Music Hall [*Record label*] [*Argentina*]
MUSHes .... Multiuser Shared Hallucinations [*Computer game players*]
MUSI .... Mexico-United States Institute (EA)
musi .... Musical (VRA)
MUSIC .... Machine Utilization Statistical Information Collection (IAA)
MUSIC .... Mass Unity Sounding in Concert [*Duke Ellington definition of music*]
MUSIC .... McGill University System for Interactive Computing
MUSIC .... Multiple System Intelligent Controller [*Computer science*]
MUSIC .... Multisensor Intelligence Correlator (IAA)
MUSICAM .... Masking Pattern Universal Sub-Band Integrated Coding and Multiplexing [*Broadcasting*]

MusicLd.......	Musicland Stores [*Associated Press*] (SAG)
MUSICOL.....	Musical Instruction Composition Oriented Language (NITA)
MUSICOMP...	Music Composition
MUSIL.........	Multiprogramming Utility System Interpretive Language [*Regnecentralen*] [*Denmark*]
MUSJ..........	San Julian (Escuela de Aviacion) [*Cuba ICAO location identifier*] (ICLI)
MUSL..........	Marconi Underwater Systems Ltd. [*British*]
MUSL..........	Multiple Stinger Launcher
MUSL..........	Musician's Library [*A publication*]
MUSL..........	Muslin (ROG)
musl...........	Muslin (VRA)
MUSL..........	Santa Lucia [*Cuba ICAO location identifier*] (ICLI)
MUSLE.........	Modified Universal Soil Loss Equation [*Agricultural Research Service*]
MUSLO........	Morocco-United States Liaison Office (AFM)
Mus M........	Musicae Magister [*Master of Music*] [*Latin*]
MusMComp...	Master of Music Composition, University of Manchester [*British*] (DBQ)
MusMPerf....	Master of Music Performance, University of Manchester [*British*] (DBQ)
Musn	Musician [*British military*] (DMA)
MUSN.........	Seaman, Musician, Striker [*Navy rating*]
MUSN.........	Siguanea, Isla De La Juventud [*Cuba ICAO location identifier*] (ICLI)
MUSR.........	Simon Reyes [*Cuba ICAO location identifier*] (ICLI)
MUSRP.......	McGill University Savanna Research Project (MCD)
MUSS.........	Manchester University Software System (NITA)
MUSS.........	Missile Unit Support System
MUSS.........	Mobile Unit Support System (IAA)
MUSS.........	Module Utility Support Structure (NASA)
muss.........	Module Utility Support Structure (NAKS)
MUSS.........	Musical Series [*A publication*]
MUSS.........	Sancti Spiritus [*Cuba ICAO location identifier*] (ICLI)
MUST..........	Machine Utilization Report Generator (DNAB)
MUST..........	Malaysian University of Science and Technology
MUST..........	Manned Undersea Science and Technology [*Marine science*] (OSRA)
MUST..........	Manned Undersea Station
MUST..........	Manpower Utilization System and Techniques [*Department of State*]
MUST..........	Maximum Utilization of Skills and Training [*Civil Service Commission*]
MUST..........	Medical Unit Self-Contained Transportable [*Field hospital*] [*Army*]
MUST..........	Meeting Updates in Skill Training [*International Labor Organization*] [*Information service or system United Nations*] (DUND)
MUST..........	Message User Service Transcriber (IAA)
MUST..........	Mobile Underwater Surveillance Team (MCD)
MUST..........	Mobile Unit Sanitation Trailer
MUST..........	Multi-Mission UHF [*Ultra High Frequency*] SATCOM [*Satellite Command*] Terminal
MUST..........	Multiple Source Technique
MUST..........	Multipurpose User-Oriented Software Technology (MHDI)
MUSTA........	Mock-Up Spallation Target Assembly (PDAA)
MUSTARD....	Multi-Racial Union of Squatters to Alleviate Racial Discrimination [*British*] (DI)
MUSTARD....	Multiunit Space Transport and Recovery Device (MCD)
MUSTARD....	Museum and University Storage and Retrieval of Data (NITA)
MUSTPAC-1...	Medical Ultrasound, Three-Dimensional and Portabel with Advanced Communications [*An imaging device*] (INF)
MUSTRAC....	Multiple-Simultaneous-Target Steerable Telemetry Tracking System [*Navy*]
MUSTRAN....	Music Translation (NITA)
MustSft.......	Mustang Software, Inc. [*Associated Press*] (SAG)
MUSYA........	Multiple-Use Sustained-Yield Act of 1960
MU Sys E....	Master of Urban Systems Engineering (PGP)
Mut.............	De Mutatione Nominum [*Philo*] (BJA)
MUT...........	Makeup Tank [*Nuclear energy*] (NRCH)
MUT...........	Mean Up Time [*NASA*] (KSC)
MUT...........	Mercury Unit Test
MUT...........	Mock-Up Template
MUT...........	Modular Universal Terminal (IAA)
MUT...........	Module under Test
MUT...........	Multinational Resources [*Vancouver Stock Exchange symbol*]
MUT...........	Multiservicios Aeronauticos SA de CV [*Mexico ICAO designator*] (FAAC)
MUT...........	Muntinlupa [*Philippines*] [*Geomagnetic observatory code*]
MUT...........	Muscatine, IA [*Location identifier FAA*] (FAAL)
MUT...........	Mutagen (DMAA)
MUT...........	Mutilated
MUT...........	Mutual (ADA)
Mut.............	Mutual (TBD)
Mut.............	Mutukisna's Ceylon Reports [*A publication*] (DLA)
MUTA..........	Made-Up Textiles Association [*British*] (DBA)
MUTA..........	Military Upper Traffic Control Area (DA)
MUTA..........	Multiple Unit Training Assembly [*Army*] (AABC)
MUTACI.......	Mutuelle des Autochtones de la Cote d'Ivoire [*Mutual Association of the Natives of the Ivory Coast*]
MUTCD........	Manual on Uniform Traffic Control Devices [*Highway engineering*] [*A publication*]
MUTCD........	Manual on Uniform Traffic Control Traffic Control Devices [*Federal Housing Adminstration*]
MUTD	Trinidad [*Cuba ICAO location identifier*] (ICLI)
MUTE..........	Mobile Universal Test Equipment (PDAA)
MUTE..........	Multiple Unit for Transmission Elimination [*Military*] (CAAL)
MUTES........	Multiple Threat Emitter System [*Air Force*]
MUTEX........	Multiuser Terminal Executive (MHDI)
MUTEX........	Multi-User Transaction Executive (NITA)
MUTHX........	Mutual Shares Fund [*Mutual fund ticker symbol*] (SG)
MUTI..........	Manati [*Cuba ICAO location identifier*] (ICLI)
MUTL..........	Mutual (ROG)
MUTR	Makai Undersea Test Range (DNAB)
MutRisk	Mutual Risk Management Ltd. [*Associated Press*] (SAG)
MUTS..........	Manual Unit Test Set
MUTS..........	Multiple Target Simulation (MCD)
MutSvg........	Mutual Savings Bank FSB [*Associated Press*] (SAG)
MUTT..........	Military Utility Tactical Transport
MUTT..........	Military Utility Tactical Truck
MUTT..........	Mobile Utility Transfer Tank [*To collect used oils*]
MUTT..........	Multiuse Terminal Translator (MHDI)
mutt............	Mutton [*An em space*] [*Typesetting*] (WDMC)
MUTTS........	Multiple Unit Terminal Test Set (MCD)
MutualB.......	Mutual Bancompany, Inc. [*Associated Press*] (SAG)
Mutukisna....	Mutukisna's Ceylon Reports [*A publication*] (DLA)
MUU..........	Mount Union, PA [*Location identifier FAA*] (FAAL)
MUU..........	Mouse Uterine Unit [*Gynecology*] (MAE)
MUU..........	University of Missouri, Columbia, Columbia, MO [*OCLC symbol*] (OCLC)
MUV..........	Marine Unit Vietnam (VNW)
MUV..........	Mechanized Utility Vehicle (MCD)
MU V..........	Microvolt (WDAA)
MUV..........	Middle Ultraviolet
MUV..........	Mobile Underwater Vehicle
MUV..........	Philadelphia, PA [*Location identifier FAA*] (FAAL)
MUVA..........	Central Primero De Enero [*Cuba ICAO location identifier*] (ICLI)
MuvCAIn......	Munivest California Insured Fund [*Associated Press*] (SAG)
MuvMIIn......	MuniVest Michigan Insured Fund [*Associated Press*] (SAG)
MuvNJfd	MuniVest New Jersey Fund [*Associated Press*] (SAG)
MuvNYIn......	MuniVest New York Insured Fund [*Associated Press*] (SAG)
MUVR..........	Varadero [*Cuba ICAO location identifier*] (ICLI)
MUVT..........	Las Tunas [*Cuba ICAO location identifier*] (ICLI)
MUW..........	Mascara [*Algeria*] [*Airport symbol*] (OAG)
MU W..........	Microwatt (WDAA)
MUW..........	Music Wire
MUW..........	Mutarara [*Mozambique*] [*Airport symbol*] (AD)
MUW..........	University of Mississippi, School of Law Library, University, MS [*OCLC symbol*] (OCLC)
MUWO	Muir Woods National Monument
MUWS	Manned Underwater Station
MUWU	Mouse Uterine Weight Unit [*Gynecology*]
MUX...........	Multan [*Pakistan*] [*Airport symbol*] (OAG)
MUX...........	Multiplex [*or Multiplexer*] [*Telecommunications*]
mux	Multiplex (NAKS)
Mux	Multiplexer (AAEL)
MUX...........	Musto Explorations Ltd. [*Toronto Stock Exchange symbol*]
MUXARC......	Multiplexing Automatic Error Correction (IAA)
MUXART......	Multiplexed Asynchronous Receiver/Transmitter (MCD)
MUX/DEMUX...	Multiplexer and Demultiplexer
MUXER	Multiplexer
MUXES	Multiplexes [*or Multiplexers*] [*Telecommunications*]
MUXIC	Multiplex/Multiple Voice Interior Communications (DNAB)
MUXMOD.....	Multiplex Modulation
MUX/PRI/SEC...	Multiplexer/Priority/Second
MUY...........	Lehman Br Micron`YEELD"97 [*AMEX symbol*] (TTSB)
MUY...........	Lehman Brothers, Inc. [*AMEX symbol*] (SAG)
MUY...........	Toolik, AK [*Location identifier FAA*] (FAAL)
MUZ...........	Musoma [*Tanzania*] [*Airport symbol*] (OAG)
Muza..........	Muza and Other Labels [*Record label*] [*Poland*]
MUZAK	Music and Kodak [*Terms combined to coin brand name for canned music*]
MUZG	Zaragoza [*Cuba ICAO location identifier*] (ICLI)
MUZH	Muzzle Hatch
MUZM	Makerere-University Zoology Museum [*Uganda*]
MV.............	Airlines of Western Australia [*Australia ICAO designator*] (ICDA)
MV.............	MacRobertson-Miller Airline Service [*ICAO designator*] (AD)
M/V.............	Magnetic Variation (MCD)
MV.............	Mahzor Vitry [*A publication*] (BJA)
MV.............	Maintenance Version (IAA)
MV.............	Main Verb [*Linguistics*]
MV.............	Majority-Vote Technique [*Parapsychology*]
MV.............	Maldives [*ANSI two-letter standard code*] (CNC)
MV.............	Manifold Vacuum [*Automotive engineering*]
MV.............	Manned Vehicle
MV.............	Manpower Voucher [*Army*] (AABC)
MV.............	Mantle Vessel
MV.............	Manual Valve (MCD)
mv.............	Manual Valve (NAKS)
mv.............	Manufacturing Verification (NAKS)
mv.............	Manufacturing Verification (NASA)
MV.............	Mare Vaporum [*Sea of Vapor*] [*Lunar area*]
MV.............	Mariner Venus Project [*NASA*]
MV.............	Market Value
MV.............	Mauve [*Philately*] (ROG)
MV.............	Mean Value
MV.............	Mean Variation
MV.............	Mean Voltage (IAA)
MV.............	Measles Virus
MV.............	Measured Value
MV.............	Mechanical Ventilation [*Medicine*]
MV.............	Medial Vestibular Nucleus [*Neuroanatomy*]
MV.............	Medicus Veterinarius [*Veterinary Physician*]
MV.............	Medium Voltage
MV.............	Medium Volume
MV.............	Megavolt
Mv	Mendelevium [*Symbol is Md*] [*Chemical element*]

MV	Mentor Exploration & Development Co. Ltd. [Toronto Stock Exchange symbol]
MV	Merchant Vessel
MV	Mercury Vapor
MV	Methyl Violet [A dye]
MV	Methyl Viologen [Organic chemistry]
MV	Mezza Voce [Half the Power of the Voice] [Music]
MV	Microvilli [Cytology]
MV	Microwave [Physics] (DAVI)
MV	Midland Valley R. R. [AAR code]
MV	Military Vehicle
MV	Military Vigilance (NATG)
MV	Million Volts
mV	Millivolt
mv	Millivolt (NAKS)
MV	Miniature Vehicle (MCD)
MV	Minimal Variant (IAA)
MV	Minimum Viscosity
MV	Minute Ventilation [Medicine]
MV	Minute Volume [Medicine]
MV	Mitoxantrone, VePesid [Antineoplastic drug] (CDI)
MV	Mitral Valve [Cardiology]
MV	Mixed Venous [Blood]
MV	Modern Varieties [Agriculture]
MV	Modus Vivendi [Way of Living] [Latin]
MV	Molar Volume [Chemistry]
MV	Money Velocity [Economics]
MV	Monochromatic Vision (WDAA)
MV	Montevideo [City in Uruguay] (ROG)
MV	Mostly Verbatim [FAR clauses] (AAGC)
MV	Motorized Valve (KSC)
MV	Motor Vehicle (CDAI)
MV	Motor Vehicle Mishap (DNAB)
MV	Motor Vessel
mv	Motor Vessel (ODBW)
MV	Motor Volunteers [British military] (DMA)
MV	Move [Telecommunications] (TEL)
MV	Multiconverter Vector [Computer science] (IAA)
MV	Multivessel [Medicine] (DB)
MV	Multivibrator
MV	Multivitamins [Nutrition]
MV	Musica Viva (ADA)
MV	Muzzle Velocity [Ballistics]
MV	Mycoplasmatales Virus
MVA	Machine Vision Association [Later, MVA/SME] (EA)
MVA	Machining Variation Analysis
MVA	Machinists Vise Association [Later, HTI] (EA)
MVA	Main Valve Actuator (NASA)
MVA	Malignant Ventricular Arrhythmias [Cardiology] (DAVI)
MVA	Manufacturing Value Added
MVA	Marginal Value Analysis (MCD)
MVA	Market-Value Accounting [Banking] (ECON)
MVA	Market Value Added
MVA	Market Value Appraiser (DD)
MVA	Master of Visual Arts (GAGS)
MVA	Mean Vertical Acceleration
MVA	Mechanical Ventricular Assistance [Medicine] (DMAA)
MVA	Megavolt-Ampere
MVA	Mercury Volatilizing Activity
MVA	Merrimack Valley College Library, Manchester, NH [OCLC symbol] (OCLC)
MVA	Mevalonic Acid [Organic chemistry]
MVA	Million Volt Amperes
MVA	Millivolt Ampere [Nuclear energy] (IAA)
MVA	Mina, NV [Location identifier FAA] (FAAL)
MVA	Minimum Vectoring Altitude [FAA] (TAG)
MVA	Minnova, Inc. [Toronto Stock Exchange symbol] (SPSG)
MVA	Mississippi Valley Airlines, Inc. [ICAO designator] (FAAC)
MVA	Missouri Valley Authority
MVA	Mitral Valve Area [Cardiology]
MVA	Modern Volunteer Army
MVA	Monovinylacetylene [Organic chemistry]
MVA	Motor Vehicle Accident [Medicine] (AFM)
MVA	Motor Vehicle Allowance
MVA	Motor Vehicle Assembly [Military World War II]
MVA	Multivariate Analysis (GFGA)
MVA	Music Video Association (EA)
MVA	Myvatn [Iceland] [Airport symbol Obsolete] (OAG)
M-VAC	Methotrexate, Vinblastine, Adriamiacin [Doxorubicin] Cisplatin [Antineoplastic drug regimen] (DAVI)
MVAC	Methotrexate, Vinblastine, Adriamycin, Cisplatin [Antineoplastic drug] (CDI)
MVAC	MotorVac Technologies [NASDAQ symbol] (TTSB)
MVAC	MotorVac Technologies, Inc. [NASDAQ symbol] (SAG)
MVACS	Mars Volatiles and Climate Survey [NASA]
MVal	Market Value [Insurance]
MV & P	Morton's Vendors and Purchasers [1837] [A publication] (DLA)
MVAP	Modern Volunteer Army Program (AABC)
MVAPCA	Motor Vehicle Air Pollution Control Act (GFGA)
MVAR	Megavar
MVAR	Megavolt-Ampere Reactive [Nuclear energy] (IAA)
MVARH	Megavar-Hour
MVAS	Multipurpose Ventricular Actuating System (NASA)
MVAS	Murray Valley Air Service [Australia]
MVA/SME	Machine Vision Association [Society of Manufacturing Engineers] (EA)
MVAT	MediVators, Inc. [NASDAQ symbol] (SAG)
MVAT	Metacyclic Variant Antigen Type [Immunology]
MVAU	Maximum Volt-Ampere Utilization [Electronics]
MVB	Martin Van Buren [US president, 1782-1862]
MVB	Mechanical Vacuum Booster
MVB	Mississippi Valley Motor Freight Bureau, Saint Louis MO [STAC]
MVB	Mixed Venous Blood [Medicine] (DAVI)
MVB	Motor V-Belt
MVB	Motor Vessel Boat
MVB	Multivesicular Body
MVB	Multivibrator
MVB	Mvengue [Gabon] [Airport symbol] (OAG)
MVBD	Multiple V-Belt Drive
MVBF	Motor Vehicle Brake Fluid [Automotive engineering]
MVBFC	Martin Van Buren Fan Club (EA)
MVBI	Mississippi Valley Bancshares [NASDAQ symbol] (TTSB)
MVBI	Mississippi Valley Bancshares, Inc. [NASDAQ symbol] (SAG)
MVBL	Movable (MSA)
MVBR	Multivibrator
MVC	Management Verification Consortium (AIE)
MVC	Manual Volume Control
mvc	Manual Volume Control (NAKS)
MVC	Maryville College, St. Louis, MO [OCLC symbol] (OCLC)
MVC	Master Vellum Center [Jet Propulsion Laboratory; NASA]
MVC	Master Volume Control (NASA)
mvc	Master Volume Control (NAKS)
MVC	Maui Volcanic Complex [Geology]
MVC	Maximal Voluntary Contraction
MVC	Maximum Vital Capacity [Medicine] (DAVI)
MVC	Mechanical Vapor Compressor [Engineering]
MVC	Micro Ventures Ltd. [Vancouver Stock Exchange symbol]
MVC	Mississippi Vocational College
MVC	Missouri Valley College
MVC	Missouri Valley Conference [Sports]
MVC	Model-View-Controller [Computer science]
MVC	Monroeville, AL [Location identifier FAA] (FAAL)
MVC	Motor Volunteer Corps [British military] (DMA)
MVC	Multiple Variate Counter (IEEE)
MVC	MuniVest CA Insured Fund [NYSE symbol] (TTSB)
MVC	MuniVest California Insured Fund [NYSE symbol] (SPSG)
MVC	Myocardial Vascular Capacity [Cardiology] (MAE)
MVCC	Military Vehicle Collectors Club [Later, MVPA] (EA)
MVCC	Mountain Valley Collegiate Conference (PSS)
MVCM	Millivolt per Centimeter [Nuclear energy] (IAA)
MVCMB	Murray Valley Citrus Marketing Board [Australia]
MVCO	Meadow Valley [NASDAQ symbol] (TTSB)
MVCO	Meadow Valley Corp. [NASDAQ symbol] (SAG)
MVCOW	Meadow Valley Wrrt [NASDAQ symbol] (TTSB)
MVCS	Marine Vapor Control System
MVCS	Motor Vehicle Certification System
MVCU	Multivariable Control Unit [Computer science]
MVD	Doctor of Veterinary Medicine
MVD	Map and Visual Display
MVD	Metal Vapor Deposition (EDCT)
MVD	Mineralny Vody Department of Cibil Aviation [Former USSR] [FAA designator] (FAAC)
MVD	Minimum-Variance Deconvolution (MCD)
MVD	Mission Variation Drawing (MCD)
MVD	Mitral Valve Disease [Cardiology]
MVD	Montevideo [Uruguay] [Airport symbol] (OAG)
MVD	Motor Vehicle Department (DLA)
MVD	Motor Vehicle Distributing [Military]
MVD	Motor Vehicle Driver Selection Battery [Army]
MVD	Motor Voltage Drop (IAA)
MVDA	Motor Vehicle Dealers Act
MVDA	Motor Vehicles Dismantlers Association [British] (BI)
MVDA	Multivariate Variance and Discriminant Analysis [Mathematics]
MVDC	Megavolt Direct Current [Nuclear energy] (IAA)
MVDC	Millivolt Direct Current [Nuclear energy] (IAA)
MVDF	Medium- and Very-High-Frequency Direction-Finding Station
MVDFC	Mamie Van Doren Fan Club (EA)
MVDI	Microfield Virtual Device Interface [Computer science] (HGAA)
MVDLB	Motor Vehicle Dealers' Licensing Board [Western Australia]
MVDM	Multiple Virtual DOS [Disk Operating System] Machine [Computer science] (PCM)
MVD-MGB	Ministerstvo Vnutrennikh Del-Ministerstvo Gosudarstvennoe Bezopasnosti [Later, KGB]
MVDr	Medicus Veterinarius Doctor [Doctor of Veterinary Medicine]
MVDS	Modular Vault Dry Store [Nuclear energy] (NUCP)
MVDS	Modular Video Data System [Sperry UNIVAC]
MVDS	Multipoint Video Distribution Service (AAEL)
MVE	Maple Valley Explorations Ltd. [Vancouver Stock Exchange symbol]
MVE	Master of Vocational Education (NADA)
MVE	Mauve [Philately] (ROG)
MVE	Methyl Vinyl Ether [Organic chemistry]
MVE	Mitral Valve Echogram [Cardiology]
MVE	Mobile Vocational Evaluation [Vocational guidance test]
MVE	Montevideo, MN [Location identifier FAA] (FAAL)
MVE	Multivariate Exponential Distribution [Statistics]
MVE	Murray Valley Encephalitis [Virus]
MVE	Virden-Elkhorn Regional Library, Virden, Manitoba [Library symbol National Library of Canada] (NLC)
MV Ed	Master of Vocational Education

MVEE.......... Military Vehicles and Engineering Establishment [*Research center British*]

MVEFS........ Motor Vehicle Emission and Fuel Standards (COE)

MVEL.......... Motor Vehicle Emission Laboratory [*Environmental Protection Agency*]

MVEMJSUNP... My Very Excellent Mother Just Served Us Nine Pies [*Mnemonic guide to the nine planets: Mercury, Venus, Earth, Mars, Jupiter, Saturn, Uranus, Neptune, Pluto*]

MVetClinStud... Master of Veterinary Clinical Studies

MVetMed..... Master of Veterinary Medicine (NADA)

M Vet Sc ..... Master of Veterinary Science (PGP)

MVetSc........ Master of Veterinary Science [*British*] (ADA)

MVetSci....... Master of Veterinary Science (NADA)

MVetSt........ Master of Veterinary Studies

MVF.......... Manned Vertical Flight (MCD)

MVF.......... Missile Verification Firing

MVF.......... Mitral Valve Flow [*Medicine*] (DMAA)

MVF.......... Moisture Volume Fraction (PDAA)

MVF.......... MuniVest Fund [*AMEX symbol*] (TTSB)

MVF.......... MuniVest Fund, Inc. [*AMEX symbol*] (SPSG)

MVFC......... Mack Vickery Fan Club (EA)

MVFC......... Mr. V Fan Club [*Defunct*] (EA)

MVFC......... Municipal Valuation Fees Committee [*Victoria, Australia*]

MVFV......... Manned Venus Flyby Vehicle

MVG.......... Mengenverbrauchsguttern [*Mass Consumption Goods*] [*German*]

MVG.......... Minven Gold Corp. [*Toronto Stock Exchange symbol*]

MVG.......... Most Valuable Girl

MVG.......... Moving

MVG.......... Mycoplasmatales Virus [*from*] Goat

MVGA......... Monochrome Video Graphics Array [*Computer science*] (CDE)

MVGF......... Myxoma Virus Growth Factor [*Biochemistry*]

MV Grad..... Mitral Valve Gradient [*Cardiology*] (MAE)

MVGVT .... Mated Vertical Ground Vibration Test [*NASA*] (NASA)

MVH.......... Massive Vitreous Hemorrhage [*Medicine*] (DMAA)

MVH.......... Methotrexate, VP-16 Hyxamethylmelamine [*Antineoplastic drug regimen*] (DAVI)

MVH.......... Mohave Gold, Inc. [*Vancouver Stock Exchange symbol*]

MVH.......... Mountain View [*Hawaii*] [*Seismograph station code, US Geological Survey*] (SEIS)

MVh.......... Vineyard Haven Public Library, Vineyard Haven, MA [*Library symbol Library of Congress*] (LCLS)

MVHD .... Hospital District Number 10, Virden, Manitoba [*Library symbol National Library of Canada*] (NLC)

MVI.......... Macrotrends Ventures, Inc. [*Vancouver Stock Exchange symbol*]

Mvl .... Marcive, Inc., San Antonio, TX [*Library symbol*] [*Library of Congress*] (LCLS)

MVI.......... Maximum Visual Impact (DNAB)

MVI.......... Medium Value Item (NATG)

MVI.......... Medium Viscosity Index (PDAA)

MVI.......... Melt Volume Index [*Materials science*]

MVI.......... Merchant Vessel Inspection Division [*Coast Guard*]

MVI.......... Mercury Vapor Isolator

MVI.......... Metal Ventilator Institute (EA)

MV/I.......... Millivolt to Current [*Converter*] [*Nuclear energy*] (NRCH)

MVI.......... Minami Daito Jima [*Volcano Islands*] [*Seismograph station code, US Geological Survey*] (SEIS)

MVI.......... Miniature Variable Inductor

MVI.......... Motor Vehicle Inspection

MVI.......... Multiple Vitamin Infusion [*Pharmacology*] (DAVI)

MVI.......... Multivalvular Involvement [*Medicine*] (DMAA)

MVI.......... Multivitamins Intravenously [*Pharmacology*] (DAVI)

MVIC......... Mitsubishi Variable Intake System [*Automotive engine design*]

MVICSA ...... Motor Vehicle Information and Cost Saving Act

MVICSA ...... Motor Vehicle Information and Cost Savings Act (EG)

MVII.......... Mark VII [*NASDAQ symbol*] (TTSB)

MVII.......... Mark VII, Inc. [*NASDAQ symbol*] (SAG)

MVII.......... Minnesota Vocational Interest Inventory

MVIJC........ Motor Vehicle Industry Joint Council [*British*] (DCTA)

MVI/M........ Motor Vehicle Inspection/Maintenance (GFGA)

MVIN .... Medium Viscosity Index-Naphthenic (PDAA)

MVIP .... Medium Viscosity Index-Paraffinic (PDAA)

MVIP .... Multi-Vendor Integration Protocol [*Computer science*]

MVIS.......... Maximum Voluntary Isometric Strength

MVIS.......... Microvision, Inc. [*NASDAQ symbol*] (SAG)

MVIS.......... Murrumbidgee Irrigation Area Vine Improvement Society [*Australia*]

MVJ.......... Mandeville [*Jamaica*] [*Airport symbol Obsolete*] (OAG)

MVJ.......... MuniVest New Jersey Fund [*NYSE symbol*] (SPSG)

MVJ.......... MuniVest NJ Fund [*NYSE symbol*] (TTSB)

MVJC......... Mount Vernon Junior College [*Washington, DC*]

MVK.......... Methyl Vinyl Ketone [*Organic chemistry*]

MVK.......... Mulka [*Australia Airport symbol Obsolete*] (OAG)

MVL.......... Magadan Airlines [*Russian Federation*] [*ICAO designator*] (FAAC)

MVL.......... Man-Vehicle Laboratory [*Massachusetts Institute of Technology*] [*Research center*] (RCD)

MVL.......... Manville Corp. [*NYSE symbol*] (CTT)

MVL.......... Marley Vehicle Leasing [*Commercial firm British*]

MVL.......... Mercury Vapor Lamp

MVL.......... Metal Vapor LASER

MVL.......... Mitral Valve Leaflet (DMAA)

MVL.......... Morrisville, VT [*Location identifier FAA*] (FAAL)

MVL.......... Mountain Valley Library System, Sacramento, CA [*OCLC symbol*] (OCLC)

MVL.......... Multiple-Valued Logic [*Computer science*]

MVL.......... Murray Valley League [*Australia*]

MVL.......... Mycoplasmatales Virus [*from*] Acholeplasma laidlawii

MVL .... Mylan Ventures Ltd. [*Vancouver Stock Exchange symbol*]

MVL.......... Naval

MVLA......... Mount Vernon Ladies' Association of the Union (EA)

MVLDC .... Murray Valley League for Development and Conservation [*Australia*]

MVLS......... Magic Valley Regional Library System [*Library network*]

MVLS......... Mandibular Vestibulolingual Sulcoplasty [*Surgery*]

MVLS......... Meecham Verbal Language Scale (DAVI)

MVLU........ Minimum Variance Linear Unbiased [*Statistics*]

MVLUE....... Minimum Variance Linear Unbiased Estimator [*Statistics*] (OA)

MVM.......... Air Cargo America, Inc. [*ICAO designator*] (FAAC)

MVM.......... Manager Virtual Machine [*Computer science*] (CIST)

mvm.......... Mariner Venus/Mercury (NAKS)

MVM.......... Mariner Venus-Mercury Project [*NASA*]

MVM.......... Massachusetts Volunteer Militia (HGAA)

MVM.......... Master of Veterinary Medicine

MVM.......... Medium-Voltage Mode

MVM.......... Microvillous Membrane [*Cytology*] (MAE)

MVM.......... Million Vehicle Miles

mV/m........ Millivolts per Meter (DEN)

MVM.......... Minimum Virtual Memory

MVM.......... Minute Virus of Mice

MVM.......... Multiple Virtual Modem [*Computer science*] (CIST)

MVM.......... Multivolume Monographs

MVM.......... MuniVest Michigan Insured Fund [*NYSE symbol*] (SPSG)

MVMA........ Motor Vehicle Manufacturers Association (NADA)

MVMA........ Motor Vehicle Manufacturers Association of the United States (EA)

MVMC........ Motor Vehicle Maintenance Course

MVMF........ Ministerstvo Voenno-Morskogo Flota [*Ministry of the Navy*] [*1950-53; merged into the MO*] [*Former USSR*]

MVMFB....... Mississippi Valley Motor Freight Bureau

MVMNT....... Movement

MVMT....... Movement (AFM)

MVN.......... Magna Ventures Ltd. [*Vancouver Stock Exchange symbol*]

MVN.......... Marvin Ltd. [*British ICAO designator*] (FAAC)

MVN.......... Medial Ventromedial Nucleus [*Medicine*] (DMAA)

MVN.......... Median Ventricular Nerve [*Medicine*]

MVN.......... Mount Vernon [*Illinois*] [*Airport symbol*] (OAG)

MVO.......... Maximum Venous Outflow [*Medicine*]

MVO.......... Member of the Royal Victorian Order [*British*]

MVO.......... Military Vehicles Operation [*of General Motors Corp.*]

MVO.......... Mitral Valve Opening [*Medicine*] (DMAA)

MVO.......... MMC Video One Canada Ltd. [*Toronto Stock Exchange symbol Vancouver Stock Exchange symbol*]

MVO.......... Money Value Only (AFIT)

MVO.......... Mongo [*Chad*] [*Airport symbol*] (AD)

MVO₂........ Myocardial Oxygen Consumption [*Cardiology*] (DAVI)

MVo₂........ Myocardial Oxygen Ventilation Rate [*Cardiology*] (MAE)

MVOA........ Mitral Valve Orifice Area [*Cardiology*] (DMAA)

MVP.......... Magnetic Vector Potential

MVP.......... Maintenance Verification Plan

MVP.......... Manpower Validation Program

MVP.......... Marginal Value of Product [*Agriculture*]

MVP.......... Master Verification Plan (MCD)

MVP.......... Mechanical Vacuum Pump

MVP.......... Methylvinylpyridine [*Organic chemistry*]

MVP.......... Methyl-Violet Paper (MSA)

MVP.......... Microvascular Pressure [*Medicine*] (DMAA)

MVP.......... Millivolt Potentiometer (IDOE)

MVP.......... Minimum Viable Population [*Demographics*]

MVP.......... Minority Vendors Program

MVP.......... Mitral Valve Prolapse [*Cardiology*]

MVP.......... Mitu [*Colombia*] [*Airport symbol*] (OAG)

MVP.......... Most Valuable Player [*Athletics*] [*Facetious translation: "Most Volatile Player"*]

MVP.......... Most Valuable Princess [*Princess Diana*] [*British Slang*]

MVP.......... Most Valuable Product (PCM)

MVP.......... Mountain View Public Library, Mountain View, CA [*OCLC symbol*] (OCLC)

MVP.......... Multimedia Video Processor [*Texas Instruments*] (PS)

MVP.......... Multiple Virtual Processing (NITA)

MVP.......... Multivalue Program [*Computer science*]

MVP.......... Multivariable Program [*Computer science*] (IAA)

MVP.......... MuniVest Pennsylvania Insured Fund [*NYSE symbol*] (SPSG)

MVP.......... MVP Capital Corp. [*Toronto Stock Exchange symbol*]

MVPA......... Military Vehicle Preservation Association (EA)

MVPA......... Motor Vehicle Plan Administration

MVPCB....... Motor Vehicle Pollution Control Board (NADA)

MVPCCS ..... Motor Vehicle Post Crash Communications System (PDAA)

MVPD-26 .... metrotrexate, Citrovorum Factor, VM-26, Procarbazine, Dexamethasone [*Antineoplastic drug regimen*] (DAVI)

MVPP......... Mechlorethamine/Vinblastine/Procarbazine/Prednisone (DB)

MVPP......... Mustargen [*Nitrogen mustard*], Vinblastine, Procarbazine, Prednisone [*Antineoplastic drug regimen*]

MVPp......... Mustine, Vinblastine, Procarbazine, prednisone [*Antineoplastic drug regimen*] (DAVI)

MVPR......... Master Verification Process Requirement (SSD)

MVPS......... Manually Variable Phase Shifter

MVPS......... Mechanical Vacuum Pump System

MVPS......... Medicare Volume Performance Standard

MVPS......... Medium-Voltage Power Supply (IAA)

MVPS......... Mitral Valve Prolapse Syndrome [*Cardiology*]

MVPS......... Multiple Vertical Protective Shelter [*for missiles*] (MCD)

MVPT......... Motor-Free Visual Perception Test

MVPTG .... Medial Vascularized Patellar Tendon Graft [*Sports medicine*]

MVQ........... Malvern, AR [*Location identifier FAA*] (FAAL)

MVR............ Malabar Volunteer Rifles [British military] (DMA)
MVR............ Maneuver (AABC)
MVR............ Maroua [Cameroon] [Airport symbol] (OAG)
MVR............ Massive Vitreous Retraction (MAE)
MVR............ Massive Vitreous Retractor [Blade] [Ophthalmology] (DAVI)
MVR............ Master Verification Requirement (SSD)
MVR............ Maverick Airways Corp. [FAA designator] (FAAC)
MVR............ Maximum Ventilation Rate [Medicine] (DAVI)
MVR............ Mean Value Reference [Mathematics]
MVR............ Mechanical Vapor Recompression [For evaporators]
MVR............ Microvitreoretinal (DMAA)
MVR............ Minimal Vascular Resistance [Medicine] (DMAA)
MVR............ Minisatellite Variant Repeat [Genetics]
MVR............ Missing Volume Report
MVR............ Mitral Valve Regurgitation [Cardiology] (DAVI)
MVR............ Mitral Valve Replacement [Cardiology]
mvr............ Moldavian Soviet Socialist Republic [MARC country of publication code Library of Congress] (LCCP)
MVR............ Mondavi Resources Ltd. [Vancouver Stock Exchange symbol]
MVR............ Motor Vehicle Report
MVR............ Mover
MVR............ Mussoorie Volunteer Rifles [British military] (DMA)
MVRA.......... Metropolitan Visiting and Relief Association [British]
MVRDC........ Motor Vehicle Repair Disputes Committee [New South Wales, Australia]
MVRG.......... Medieval Village Research Group (EA)
MVRI............ Mixed Vaccine, Respiratory Infection [Medicine]
MVRIAG....... Murray Valley Rural Industry Assistance Group [Australia]
MVRIC......... Motor Vehicle Repair Industry Council [New South Wales, Australia]
MVRO.......... Minimum-Variance Reduced-Order [Statistics] (PDAA)
MVRS........... Marine Vapor Recovery System (GNE)
MVRS........... Mechanical Vapor Recovery System [Engineering]
MVRS........... Mystic Valley Railway Society (EA)
MVS............ Magnetic Voltage Stabilizer
MVS............ Manifold Vacuum Sensor [Automotive engineering]
MVS............ Master of Valuation Sciences (GAGS)
MVS............ Master of Veterinary Studies
MVS............ Master of Veterinary Surgery
MVS............ Mechanical Vibration System
MVS............ Megastar Ventures [Vancouver Stock Exchange symbol]
MVS............ Mennonite Voluntary Service
MVS............ Metal Vapour Synthesis [Chemistry]
MVS............ Metering Valve Sensor [Automotive engineering]
mvs............ Middle Value Select (NAKS)
MVS............ Middle Valve Select (MCD)
MVS............ Millersville State College, Millersville, PA [OCLC symbol] (OCLC)
MVS............ Mine Ventilation System [Engineering]
MVS............ Minimum Visual Signal
MVS............ Ministerstvo Vooruzhennykh Sil [Ministry of the Armed Forces] [1946-50; superseded by VM, MVMF] [Former USSR]
MVS............ Missile Velocity Servo
MVS............ Mission Video System [NASA]
MVS............ Mitral Valve Stenosis [Cardiology] (DAVI)
MVS............ Mobile Video Services Ltd. [Washington, DC] [Telecommunications] (TSSD)
MVS............ Modular 8mm Video System [Eastman Kodak Co.]
MVS............ Modularized Vehicle Stimulation [Program]
MVS............ Most Valued Supplier [Mazda Motor Corp.]
MVS............ Multiple Vibration System
MVS............ Multiple Virtual Storage [IBM Corp.] [Computer science]
mvs............ Multiple Virtual Storage (NAKS)
MVS............ Multiple Virtual System [Computer science]
MVS............ Multiprogramming with Virtual Storage [Computer science] (ECII)
MVS............ Multivariable Storage [Computer science]
MVS............ Multivendor Service (DMAA)
MVS............ MuniVest Florida Fund [NYSE symbol] (SPSG)
MVSB.......... Motor Vehicle Storage Building
MV Sc.......... Master of Veterinary Science
MVSc........... Master of Veterinary Science [Canada] (ASC)
MVSI........... MVSI, Inc. [NASDAQ symbol] (SAG)
MVSL.......... Mouse Visible Specific Locus [Test for mutagenesis]
MVSMA....... Mechanical Vibrating Screen Manufacturers Association [Later, Vibrating Screen Manufacturers Association] (EA)
MVSN .... Milizia Volontaria per la Sicurezza Nazionale [Italian Voluntary Militia for National Security] (WDAA)
MVSP.......... Maintain Visual Separation [Aviation]
MVSR.......... Monthly Vital Statistics Report [A publication] (DHSM)
MVSS.......... Motor Vehicle Safety Standard
MVSS.......... Motor Vehicle Storage Shed [Army] (AABC)
MVSSE........ Multiple Virtual Storage System Extension
MVS/SE....... MVS/System Extension (NITA)
MVS/SP....... MVS/System Product (NITA)
MVSt.......... Master of Veterinary Studies (ADA)
MVS/XA....... MVS/Extended Architecture (NITA)
MVSZGA ...... Mein Vertrauen Steht zu Gott Allein [My Trust Is in God Alone] [Motto of Johann Adolf II, Duke of Saxony-Weissenfels (1649-97)] [German]
MVT............ Malfunction Verification Test (MCD)
MVT............ Marginal Value Theorem [Mathematical model developed by Dr. Eric Charnov]
MVT............ Market-Value Transmission [Pricing concept]
MVT............ Mataiva [French Polynesia] [Airport symbol] (OAG)
MVT............ Maximal Ventilation Time [Medicine] (DAVI)
MVT............ Miscellaneous Vector Table
MVT............ Mission Verification Test [NASA] (NASA)

MVT............ Mississippi Valley Type [Ore deposits] [Geology]
MVT............ Moisture Vapor Transmission (EDCT)
MVT............ Moisture Vapor Transmission Rate
MVT............ Monte Vettore [Italy] [Seismograph station code, US Geological Survey] (SEIS)
MVT............ Motor Vehicle Title
MVT............ Mount Vernon Terminal [AAR code]
MVT............ Movement (MSA)
MVT............ Multinational Volunteer Teams
MVT............ Multiprogramming with a Variable Number of Tasks [IBM Corp.] [Control program] [Computer science]
MVT............ Multivariable Task (MCD)
MVT............ Munivest Fund II [NYSE symbol] (SAG)
MVT............ MuniVest Fund, Inc. [NYSE symbol] (SPSG)
MVTE.......... Master of Vocational Technical Education (GAGS)
MVT Ed........ Master of Vocational and Technical Education (PGP)
MVTL.......... Modified Variable-Threshold Logic [Computer science]
MVTLEA....... Motor Vehicle Theft Law Enforcement Act [1984]
MVTR.......... Moisture Vapor Transmission Rate
MVTS.......... Motor Vehicle Test Station (COE)
MVT/TSO ..... MVT/Time Sharing Option (NITA)
MVTV.......... MetroVision of North America, Inc. [NASDAQ symbol] (SAG)
MVU............ Minimum Variance Unbiased [Statistics]
MVU............ Mulege [Mexico] [Airport symbol] (AD)
MVU............ Musgrave [Australia Airport symbol Obsolete] (OAG)
MVUE.......... Man/Vehicular User Equipment
MVUE.......... Minimum Variance Unbiased Estimate [Statistics]
MVULE........ Minimum Variance Unbiased Linear Estimator [Statistics]
MVV............ Mannheimer Versorgungs und Verkehrsgesellschaft [Germany]
MVV............ Maximum Voluntary Ventilation
MVV............ Maximum Voluntary Volume [Medicine] (DAVI)
MVV............ Mean Vertical Velocity
MVV............ Mitsubishi Vertical Vortex [Automotive engineering]
MVV............ Mixed Vespid Venom [Pharmacology] (DAVI)
MVV₁.......... Maximal Ventilatory Volume (MAE)
MVVPP .... Mustargen [Nitrogen mustard], Vincristine, Vinblastine, Procarbazine, Prednisone [Antineoplastic drug regimen]
MVW........... Minot-Von Willebrand [Syndrome] [Medicine] (DB)
MVW........... Missile Viewing Window
MVW........... Mount Vernon [Washington] [Airport symbol] (OAG)
MVW........... Mud Volcano [Wyoming] [Seismograph station code, US Geological Survey] (SEIS)
MVWDU....... Missile Viewing Window Deicing Unit
MVWGS....... Multi-Vintage Wine Growers Society [British] (DBA)
MVX........... Media Videotex [Vancouver Stock Exchange symbol]
MVX........... Minvoul [Gabon] [Airport symbol] (OAG)
MVX........... Multiplex
MVY........... Martha's Vineyard [Massachusetts] [Airport symbol] (OAG)
MVY........... MuniVest New York Insured Fund [NYSE symbol] (SPSG)
MVY........... MuniVest NY Insured Fund [NYSE symbol] (TTSB)
MVZ........... Museum of Vertebrate Zoology [University of California, Berkeley]
MVZG.......... Mein Verlangen zu Gott [My Desires (I Give) to God] [Motto of Anna Marie, Margravine of Brandenburg (1609-80)] [German]
MVZS.......... Manifold Vacuum Zone Switch [Automotive engineering]
MW............ Machine Word (IAA)
MW............ Magnesiowustite [Mineralogy]
mw............ Malawi [MARC country of publication code Library of Congress] (LCCP)
MW............ Malawi [ANSI two-letter standard code] (CNC)
M-W........... Mallory-Weiss Syndrome [Medicine] (MEDA)
MW............ Management World [Administrative Management Society] [A publication]
MW............ Manual Word
MW............ Manufacturing Week (MCD)
MW............ Man Watchers (EA)
MW............ Man-Week (NASA)
mw............ Man Week (NAKS)
MW............ Marginal Wage [Economics]
MW............ Marginal Wings [Botany]
MW............ Master of Wine [Bestowed by the Worshipful Company of Vintners, one of the ancient guilds in the City of London]
M/W........... Mate With (MCD)
MW............ Maya Airways [ICAO designator] (AD)
MW............ Media Watch [An association] (EA)
MW............ Medium Wall
MW............ Medium Wave (WA)
MW............ Medium Wave Band
MW............ Meetings Word (NITA)
MW............ Megawatt [Also, MEGW]
MW............ Memory Write [Computer science]
M-W........... Merriam-Webster [Publisher]
MW............ Message Waiting
MW............ Metachrondral Wave [Physiology]
MW............ Metalworker [British military] (DMA)
M/W........... Methanol/Water
MW............ Microwave
mw............ Microwave (NAKS)
MW............ Middle Welsh [Language, etc.]
MW............ Midwing [Aviation] (AIA)
MW............ Migratory Worker (OICC)
MW............ Million (10^6) Words (NITA)
mW............ Milliwatt
mw............ Milliwatt (NAKS)
MW............ Mine Warfare
MW............ Mine Warning (NATG)

MW............. Ministry of Works [British]
MW............. Minnesota Western Railroad (IIA)
MW............. Mixed Wastes [Environmental science] (COE)
MW............. Mixed Widths
mw............. Mixed Widths [Forest industry] (WPI)
MW............. Mobile Workshop [British]
MW............. Modulated Wave (IAA)
MW............. Moewe Flugzeugbau, Heini Dittmar [Germany ICAO aircraft manufacturer identifier] (ICAO)
MW............. Molecular Weight [Also, M, MOL WT]
MW............. Money Wages [Economics]
MW............. Monier-Williams Method (RDA)
MW............. Montana Western Railway (IIA)
MW............. Most Worshipful [Freemasonry]
MW............. Most Worthy
MW............. Motor Wagon [British]
MW............. Mud Weight [Well drilling technology]
MW............. Multiple Wounds
MW............. Multipurpose Weapon (MCD)
MW............. Multiwire (IAA)
MW............. Music of the World [American Forces Radio and Television Service] (DNAB)
MW............. Music Wire
Mw............. Weighted Mean [Psychology]
MW............. Winnipeg Centennial Library, Manitoba [Library symbol National Library of Canada] (NLC)
MW............. Worcester Public Library and Central Massachusetts Regional Library System Headquarters, Worcester, MA [Library symbol Library of Congress] (LCLS)
MWA............ American Antiquarian Society, Worcester, MA [Library symbol Library of Congress] (LCLS)
MWA............ Major World Authors [A publication]
MWA............ Management by Walking Around
MWA............ Manitoba Department of Agriculture, Winnipeg, Manitoba [Library symbol National Library of Canada] (NLC)
MWA............ Manufacturing Work Authority
MWA............ Marion [Illinois] [Airport symbol] (OAG)
MWA............ Married Women's Association [British] (DBA)
MWA............ Mayflower Warehousemen's Association (EA)
MWA............ Media Women's Association
MWA............ Meteorological Watch Advisory
MWA............ Mid-West Abrasive Co. (EFIS)
MWA............ Mineral Workings Act [Town planning] [British]
MWA............ Modern Woodmen of America (EA)
MWA............ Momentum-Wheel Assembly
MWA............ Movers' & Warehousemen's Association of America Inc., Washington DC [STAC]
MWA............ Munitions of War Act [British]
MWA............ Mystery Writers of America (NADA)
MW/AA........ Missile Warning/Attack Assessment (MCD)
MWAA.......... Movers' and Warehousemen's Association of America [Defunct] (EA)
MWAC......... Air Command Headquarters, Canadian Forces Base, Westwin, Manitoba [Library symbol National Library of Canada] (NLC)
MWAC......... Assumption College, Worcester, MA [Library symbol Library of Congress] (LCLS)
MWAC......... Midwest Archeological Center [National Park Service] (GRD)
MWAD......... Alcohol and Drug Education Service, Winnipeg, Manitoba [Library symbol National Library of Canada] (NLC)
MWAE.......... Minimum-Weighted-Absolute Error [Statistics] (PDAA)
MWAF.......... Alcoholism Foundation of Manitoba, Winnipeg, Manitoba [Library symbol National Library of Canada] (NLC)
MWAG......... Research Station, Agriculture Canada [Station de Recherches, Agriculture Canada] Winnipeg, Manitoba [Library symbol National Library of Canada] (NLC)
MWAI........... Mystery Writers of America Inc. (NADA)
MWal........... Waltham Public Library, Waltham MA [Library symbol Library of Congress] (LCLS)
MWalA......... American Jewish Historical Society, Waltham, MA [Library symbol Library of Congress] (LCLS)
MWalAF....... African Studies Association, Brandeis University, Waltham, MA [Library symbol Library of Congress] (LCLS)
MWalB........ Brandeis University, Waltham, MA [Library symbol Library of Congress] (LCLS)
MWalBe........ Bentley College, Waltham, MA [Library symbol Library of Congress] (LCLS)
MWalFAR .... Federal Archives and Records Center, General Services Administration, Waltham, MA [Library symbol Library of Congress] (LCLS)
MWalG .... General Telephone & Electronics Laboratories, Inc., Waltham Research Center Library, Waltham, MA [Library symbol Library of Congress] (LCLS)
MWalK........ John F. Kennedy Library, Waltham, MA [Library symbol Library of Congress] (LCLS)
MWalMT...... Mobil Tyco Solar Energy Corp., Waltham, MA [Library symbol Library of Congress] (LCLS)
MWAMA ..... Administration Branch, Manitoba Department of Municipal Affairs, Winnipeg, Manitoba [Library symbol National Library of Canada] (NLC)
MWAMT...... Aikins, MacAulay, and Thorvaldson Law Firm, Winnipeg, Manitoba [Library symbol National Library of Canada] (NLC)
MWAR .... Microware Systems Corp. [NASDAQ symbol] (SAG)
MWAR .... Microwave Systems [NASDAQ symbol] (TTSB)
MWar......... Wareham Free Library, Wareham, MA [Library symbol] [Library of Congress] (LCLS)
MWARA....... Major World Air Route Area

MWARN...... Manitoba Association of Registered Nurses, Winnipeg, Manitoba [Library symbol National Library of Canada] (NLC)
MWARS...... Major Command Worldwide Ammunition Reporting System [Army]
MWARS ...... Synod Office, Diocese of Rupert's Land, Anglican Church of Canada, Winnipeg, Manitoba [Library symbol National Library of Canada] (NLC)
MWAS .... Arthritis Society, Winnipeg, Manitoba [Library symbol National Library of Canada] (NLC)
MWASD...... Assiniboine South School Division No. 3, Winnipeg, Manitoba [Library symbol National Library of Canada] (NLC)
MWat......... Watertown Free Public Library, Watertown, MA [Library symbol Library of Congress] (LCLS)
MWatM....... Massachusetts Bay Community College, Watertown, MA [Library symbol Library of Congress] (LCLS)
MWatP....... Perkins School for the Blind, Watertown, MA [Library symbol Library of Congress] (LCLS)
MWatP-BP ... Massachusetts Regional Library for the Blind and Physically Handicapped, PerkinsSchool for the Blind, Watertown, MA [Library symbol] [Library of Congress] (LCLS)
MWatP-BPH... Regional Library for the Blind and Physically Handicapped, Perkins School for the Blind, Watertown, MA [Library symbol Library of Congress] (LCLS)
MWAV .... M-Wave, Inc. [NASDAQ symbol] (SAG)
MWAVE....... Microwave
M-Wave...... M-Wave, Inc. [Associated Press] (SAG)
MWAX .... Mountain West Airline [Air carrier designation symbol]
M-Way........ Motorway [British]
MWayR........ Raytheon Co., Wayland, MA [Library symbol Library of Congress] (LCLS)
MWB............ Master Work Book (NASA)
MWB............ Maxwell-Wien Bridge [Electronics]
MWB............ Metropolitan Water Board [British]
MWB............ Middlewest Motor Freight Bureau, Kansas City MO [STAC]
MWB............ Ministry of Works and Buildings [British]
MWB............ Motor Whale Boat
MWB............ Multilayer Wiring Board
MWBA.......... Bristol Aerospace Ltd., Winnipeg, Manitoba [Library symbol National Library of Canada] (NLC)
MWBAS ...... Mail Will Be Addressed to Show
MWBC .... Mean Wafers Between Cleans (AAEL)
MWBC .... Technical Library, Boeing of Canada Ltd., Winnipeg, Manitoba [Library symbol National Library of Canada] (NLC)
MWBe........ Becker Junior College, Worcester, MA [Library symbol Library of Congress] (LCLS)
MWBH .... Bethel Hospital, Winkler, Manitoba [Library symbol National Library of Canada] (NLC)
MWBI........... Midwest Bacshares Del [NASDAQ symbol] (TTSB)
MWBI........... Midwest Bancshares [NASDAQ symbol] (SAG)
MWBL........ Mounted Warfighting Battlespace Laborarory [Army] (RDA)
MWBM........ Bethania Mennonite Personal Care Home, Winnipeg, Manitoba [Library symbol National Library of Canada] (NLC)
MWBP .... Missile Warning Bypass (DWSG)
MWbriM....... Massasoit Community College, West Bridgewater, MA [Library symbol Library of Congress] (LCLS)
MWC........... Clark University, Worcester, MA [Library symbol Library of Congress] (LCLS)
MWC........... Mad World Campaign [An association Defunct] (EA)
MWC........... Magnetoionic Wave Component
MWC........... Major Wingfield Club (EA)
MWC........... Mary Washington College [University of Virginia]
MWC........... Maxwell Communication Corp. [Toronto Stock Exchange symbol]
MWC........... Medium Weight Coated Paper (DGA)
MWC........... Melbourne Walking Club [Australia]
MWC........... Midwest Conference (PSS)
MWC........... Miltonvale Wesleyan College [Kansas]
MWC........... Milwaukee, WI [Location identifier FAA] (FAAL)
MWC........... Minister for [or Ministry of] War Communications [British World War II]
MWC........... Missile Weapons Control (MCD)
MWC........... Monod-Wyman-Changeux [Model] [Enzymology]
MWC........... Mount Wilson [California] [Seismograph station code, US Geological Survey] (SEIS)
MWC........... Moving-Withdrawal Chromatography
MWC........... Multiple Water Connector (KSC)
MWC........... Municipal Waste Combustor (GFGA)
MWC........... Music and Record Library, Canadian Broadcasting Corp. [Musicotheque et Discotheque, Societe Radio-Canada] Winnipeg, Manitoba [Library symbol National Library of Canada] (NLC)
MWCA .... Monetary Working Capital Adjustment [British]
MWCA .... Monterey Wine Country Association (EA)
MWCAC ...... Midwest Collegiate Athletic Conference (PSS)
MWCB .... Cayman Brac/Gerrard Smith [Cayman Islands] [ICAO location identifier] (ICLI)
MWCB .... Manufacturer's Working Cell Bank [Cell line]
MWCC .... Metropolitan Wrestling Coach's Conference (PSS)
MWCC .... Mineral Water Co. of Canada (ECON)
MWCCA ...... Manitoba Department of Consumer and Corporate Affairs, Winnipeg, Manitoba [Library symbol Obsolete National Library of Canada] (NLC)
MWCCAC .... Midwest Community College Athletic Conference (PSS)
MWCCI .... Manitoba Consumer's Bureau, Winnipeg, Manitoba [Library symbol National Library of Canada] (NLC)

MWCCIR ...... Central Region Information Resources Center, Canada Department of Communications[*Centre de Documentation Region du Centre, Ministere des Communications*] Winnipeg, Manitoba [*Library symbol National Library of Canada*] (NLC)

MWC/CS ...... Mechanized Wire Centering/Cross Section [*AT & T*] [*Telecommunications*] (TEL)

MWCE .... Controlled Environments Ltd., Winnipeg, Manitoba [*Library symbol National Library of Canada*] (NLC)

MWCE .... Millimeter Wave Communications Experiment

MWCF .... Canadian Forces Aerospace and Navigation School, Canadian Forces Base Winnipeg, Westwin, Manitoba [*Library symbol National Library of Canada*] (NLC)

MWCG .... Grand Cayman [*Cayman Islands*] [*ICAO location identifier*] (ICLI)

MWCH .... Concordia Hospital, Winnipeg, Manitoba [*Library symbol National Library of Canada*] (NLC)

MWCHA .... Charles Howard & Associates, Winnipeg, Manitoba [*Library symbol National Library of Canada*] (NLC)

MWCHD .... Charleswood Public Library, Winnipeg, Manitoba [*Library symbol National Library of Canada*] (NLC)

MWCI .... Canertech, Inc., Winnipeg, Manitoba [*Library symbol National Library of Canada*] (NLC)

MWCL .... Little Cayman/Boddenfield [*Cayman Islands*] [*ICAO location identifier*] (ICLI)

MWCL .... Worcester County Law Library Association, Worcester, MA [*Library symbol Library of Congress*] (LCLS)

MWCLC .... Midwest Classic Conference (PSS)

MWCM .... Canadian Mennonite Bible College, Winnipeg, Manitoba [*Library symbol National Library of Canada*] (NLC)

MWCM .... Milliwatt per Square Centimeter (IAA)

MWCMS ...... Centre for Mennonite Brethren Studies in Canada, Winnipeg, Manitoba [*Library symbol National Library of Canada*] (NLC)

MWCO .... Medium Weight Coated Offset Paper (DGA)

MWCO .... Molecular Weight Cutoff [*Chemistry*]

MWCR .... Georgetown/Owen Roberts International [*Cayman Islands*] [*ICAO location identifier*] (ICLI)

MWCR .... Mercury-Wetted Contact Relay

MWCS .... Marine Wing Communication Squadron

MWCS .... Mental Welfare Commission for Scotland

MWCS .... Midwest Cable & Satellite, Inc. [*Minneapolis, MN*] [*Telecommunications*] (TSSD)

MWCS .... Millimeter Wave Contrast Seeker (MCD)

MWCS .... Missile Weapons Control System (MCD)

MWCS .... Mobile Weapons Control System

MWCSC .... Midwest Collegiate Ski Conference (PSS)

MWCSCC ..... Midwest Council of Sports Car Clubs

MWCSJ .... Minimum Wage Coalition to Save Jobs [*Defunct*] (EA)

MWCT .... Manitoba Cancer Treatment and Research Foundation, Winnipeg, Manitoba [*Library symbol National Library of Canada*] (NLC)

MWCU .... Credit Union Central of Manitoba, Winnipeg, Manitoba [*Library symbol National Library of Canada*] (NLC)

MWCU .... Molecular Weight Cut-Off [*Metallurgy*]

MWCWB ...... Canadian Wheat Board [*Commission Canadienne du Ble*] Winnipeg, Manitoba [*Library symbol National Library of Canada*] (NLC)

MWD .... Measurement-While Drilling [*Drilling technology*]

MWD .... Megawatt-Day

MWD .... Megaword

MWD .... Metering Water Dispenser [*Apollo*] [*NASA*]

MWD .... Meters Water Depth

MWD .... Metropolitan Water District

MWD .... Microwave Diathermy [*Physical therapy*] (DAVI)

MWD .... Military Working Dog (DOMA)

MWD .... Millimeter Wave Device

MWD .... Molecular Weight Distribution

MWD .... Morgan Stanley Dean Witter [*NYSE symbol*] [*Formerly, Dean Witter Discover & Co.*] (SG)

MWD .... Moving Window Display (MCD)

MWD .... Rochester, NY [*Location identifier FAA*] (FAAL)

MWDAC .... Mountain West Desegregation Assistance Centers (EDAC)

MWDCA .... Midwest Decoy Collectors Association (EA)

MWDDEA ..... Mutual Weapons Development Data Exchange Agreement [*NATO*]

MWDDEP ..... Mutual Weapons Development Data Exchange Procedures [*NATO*]

MWDI .... Master Water Data Index [*US Geological Survey*] [*Information service or system*] (CRD)

MWDL .... Deer Lodge Hospital, Winnipeg, Manitoba [*Library symbol National Library of Canada*] (NLC)

MWD/MTU ... Megawatt-Days per Metric Ton of Uranium

MWDP .... Mutual Weapons Development Program [*NATO*]

MWDRR .... Manitoba Department of Renewable Resources, Winnipeg, Manitoba [*Library symbol National Library of Canada*] (NLC)

MWDS .... Med Waste [*NASDAQ symbol*] (SAG)

MWDS .... Med/Waste Inc. [*NASDAQ symbol*] (TTSB)

MWDS .... Missile Warning and Display System [*or Subsystem*] (MCD)

MWDSW ...... Med/Waste Inc. Wrrt'A' [*NASDAQ symbol*] (TTSB)

MWD/T .... Megawatt-Days per Ton

MWDT .... Mutual Weapons Development Team [*Military*]

MWDU .... Ducks Unlimited, Winnipeg, Manitoba [*Library symbol National Library of Canada*] (NLC)

MWE .... Manitoba Department of Education, Winnipeg, Manitoba [*Library symbol National Library of Canada*] (NLC)

MWE .... Manufacturer's Weight Empty (DA)

MWE .... Megawatt Electric (IAA)

MWe .... Megawatts of Electric Power

MWE .... Merowe [*Sudan*] [*Airport symbol*] (OAG)

MWE .... Meters of Water Equivalent

MWE .... Millimeter Wave Experiment

MWeA .... Westfield Athenaeum, Westfield, MA [*Library symbol Library of Congress*] (LCLS)

MWEAE .... Central Region Headquarters, Atmospheric Environment Service, Environment Canada[*Quartier-General de la Region Centrale, Service de l'Environnement Atmosphe rique, Environnement Canada*] Winnipeg, Manitoba [*Library symbol National Library of Canada*] (NLC)

MWeba .... Whelden Memorial Library, West Barnstable, MA [*Library symbol*] [*Library of Congress*] (LCLS)

MWebaC .... Cape Cod Community College, West Barnstable, MA [*Library symbol Library of Congress*] (LCLS)

MWECW ...... Canadian Wildlife Service, Environment Canada [*Service Canadien de la Faune, Environnement Canada*] Winnipeg, Manitoba [*Library symbol National Library of Canada*] (NLC)

MWEE .... Mechanised Warfare Experimental Establishment [*British military*] (DMA)

MWEEP .... Environmental Protection Service, Environment Canada [*Service de la Protection de l'Environnement, Environnement Canada*] Winnipeg, Manitoba [*Library symbol National Library of Canada*] (NLC)

MWEIA .... Montessori World Educational Institute Australia

MWeIC .... Wellesley College, Wellesley, MA [*Library symbol Library of Congress*] (LCLS)

MWeID .... Dana Hall School Library, Wellesley, MA [*Library symbol Library of Congress*] (LCLS)

MWeldI .... Member of the Welding Institute [*British*] (DBQ)

MWEM .... Manitoba Environmental Management Division, Winnipeg, Manitoba [*Library symbol National Library of Canada*] (NLC)

MWEM .... Mine Warfare Evaluation Model

MWEMM .... Manitoba Energy and Mines, Winnipeg, Manitoba [*Library symbol National Library of Canada*] (NLC)

MWenhG .... Gordon College, Wenham, MA [*Library symbol Library of Congress*] (LCLS)

MWenhHi .... Wenham Historical Society and Museum, Wenham, MA [*Library symbol Library of Congress*] (LCLS)

MWES .... Member of the Women's Engineering Society [*British*] (DBQ)

MWESM .... Special Materials Services, Manitoba Department of Education, Winnipeg, Manitoba [*Library symbol National Library of Canada*] (NLC)

MWesR .... Regis College, Weston, MA [*Library symbol*] [*Library of Congress*] (LCLS)

MWestonGS... Church of Jesus Christ of Latter-Day Saints, Genealogical Society Library, Boston Branch, Weston, MA [*Library symbol Library of Congress*] (LCLS)

MWestonR ... Regis College, Weston, MA [*Library symbol Library of Congress*] (LCLS)

MWeT .... Westfield State College, Westfield, MA [*Library symbol Library of Congress*] (LCLS)

MWEWSH .... Manitoba Department of Environment, Workplace Safety and Health, Winnipeg, Manitoba [*Library symbol National Library of Canada*] (NLC)

MWeyAA .... Abigail Adams Historical Society, Weymouth, MA [*Library symbol Library of Congress*] (LCLS)

MWF .... Make-a-Wish Foundation [*Later, MWFA*] (EA)

MWF .... Marine General Workers' Federation

MWF .... Medical Women's Federation [*British*] (DAS)

MWF .... Medical Working File (DOMA)

MWF .... Monday, Wednesday, Friday (BARN)

MWFA .... Make-a-Wish Foundation of America (EA)

MWFC .... Mary Wilson Fan Club (EA)

MWFC .... Midwest Football Conference (PSS)

MWFCA .... Motor Wheel and Flyer Club of America [*Defunct*] (EA)

MWFCS .... Multiweapons Fire Control System (DNAB)

MWFD .... Fred Douglas Lodge Nursing Home, Winnipeg, Manitoba [*Library symbol National Library of Canada*] (NLC)

MWFD .... Midwest Federal Financial [*NASDAQ symbol*] (SAG)

MWFD .... Midwest Fed Finl [*NASDAQ symbol*] (TTSB)

MWFG .... Fort Garry Public Library, Winnipeg, Manitoba [*Library symbol National Library of Canada*] (NLC)

MWFI .... Manitoba Department of Finance, Winnipeg, Manitoba [*Library symbol National Library of Canada*] (NLC)

MWFM .... Microwave Window Failure Mechanism

MWfo .... J. V. Fletcher Library, Westford, MA [*Library symbol Library of Congress*] (LCLS)

MWFOPS ..... Mine Warfare Operations (NVT)

MWFP .... Winnipeg Free Press Co. Ltd., Manitoba [*Library symbol National Library of Canada*] (NLC)

MWFRS .... Manitoba Department of Fitness, Recreation and Sport, Winnipeg, Manitoba [*Library symbol National Library of Canada*] (NLC)

MWFS .... Marine Wing Facilities Squadron

MWFS .... Maritime Warfare School [*Canadian Navy*]

MWFSD .... Frontier School Division, Winnipeg, Manitoba [*Library symbol National Library of Canada*] (NLC)

MWFW .... Freshwater Institute, Fisheries and Oceans Canada [*Institut des Eaux Douces, Peches et Oceans Canada*] Winnipeg, Manitoba [*Library symbol National Library of Canada*] (NLC)

MWG .... Maintenance Analyzer Working Group (MCD)

MWG .... Management Working Group [*Army*] (RDA)

MWG .... Meteorological Working Group

MWG .... Missile-Warning Group [*Military*]

MWG .... Model Work Group [*Environmental Protection Agency*] (GFGA)

MWG .... Muenster-Westfalen [*Federal Republic of Germany*] [*Seismograph station code, US Geological Survey*] (SEIS)

MWG .... Music Wire Gauge

MWGBP .... Guertin Brothers Paint Library, Winnipeg, Manitoba [*Library symbol National Library of Canada*] (NLC)

MWGC .... Midwestern Governors Conference

MWGCP .... Most Worthy Grand Chief Patriarch

MWGH .... Grace Hospital, Winnipeg, Manitoba [*Library symbol National Library of Canada*] (NLC)

MWGHA .... Gunn Hoffer & Associates Law Firm, Winnipeg, Manitoba [*Library symbol National Library of Canada*] (NLC)

MWGM .... Most Worshipful [*or Worthy*] Grand Master [*Freemasonry*]

MWGP .... Midwest Grain Products [*NASDAQ symbol*] (TTSB)

MWGP .... Midwest Grain Products, Inc. [*NASDAQ symbol*] (CTT)

MWGR .... Canadian Grain Commission, Agriculture Canada [*Commission Canadienne des Grains, Agriculture Canada*] Winnipeg, Manitoba [*Library symbol National Library of Canada*] (NLC)

MWGW .... Great West Life Assurance Co., Winnipeg, Manitoba [*Library symbol National Library of Canada*] (NLC)

MWH .... College of the Holy Cross, Worcester, MA [*Library symbol Library of Congress*] (LCLS)

MWH .... Manitoba Hydro, Winnipeg, Manitoba [*Library symbol National Library of Canada*] (NLC)

MWh .... Megawatt-Hour (MCD)

Mwh .... Megawatt Hour

MW(H) .... Megawatts (Heat) (IEEE)

MWH .... Milliwatt Hour

MWH .... Model Wave Height

MWH .... Mokuaweoweo [*Hawaii*] [*Seismograph station code, US Geological Survey*] (SEIS)

MWH .... Moses Lake [*Washington*] [*Airport symbol*] (OAG)

MWHB .... Hudson's Bay House, Winnipeg, Manitoba [*Library symbol National Library of Canada*] (NLC)

MWhB .... Marine Biological Laboratory, Woods Hole, MA [*Library symbol Library of Congress*] (LCLS)

MWHF .... Michigan Wildlife Habitat Foundation

MWHG .... Marine Wing Headquarters Group

MWHGL .... Multiple Wheel Heavy Gear Loading [*Aviation*]

MWHi .... Worcester Historical Society, Worcester, MA [*Library symbol Library of Congress*] (LCLS)

MWhN .... United States National Marine Fisheries Service, Northeast Fisheries Center, Woods Hole, MA [*Library symbol Library of Congress*] (LCLS)

MWHO .... Manitoba Health Organizations, Winnipeg, Manitoba [*Library symbol National Library of Canada*] (NLC)

MWHP .... Information Resources Center, Manitoba Health, Winnipeg, Manitoba [*Library symbol National Library of Canada*] (NLC)

MWHR .... Henderson Regional Library, Winnipeg, Manitoba [*Library symbol National Library of Canada*] (NLC)

MWHS .... Library Services, Health Sciences Centre, Winnipeg, Manitoba [*Library symbol National Library of Canada*] (NLC)

MWHS .... Marine Wing Headquarters Squadron (NVT)

MWHS .... Micro Warehouse [*NASDAQ symbol*] (TTSB)

MWHS .... Micro Warehouse, Inc. [*NASDAQ symbol*] (SAG)

MWHS .... Modified Warhead Section (MCD)

MWHSC .... Manitoba Health Services Commission, Winnipeg, Manitoba [*Library symbol National Library of Canada*] (NLC)

MWHSDET ... Marine Wing Headquarters Squadron Detachment (DNAB)

MWHT .... Miscellaneous Waste Holdup Tank [*Nuclear energy*] (NRCH)

MWHX .... MarkWest Hydrocarbon, Inc. [*NASDAQ symbol*] (SAG)

MWI .... Insurance Institute of Winnipeg, Manitoba [*Library symbol National Library of Canada*] (NLC)

MWI .... Malawi [*ANSI three-letter standard code*] (CNC)

MWI .... Mantle Width Index

MWI .... Many Worlds Interpretation [*Term coined by authors John Barrow and Frank Tipler in their book, "The Anthropic Cosmological Principle"*]

MWI .... Master Weavers Institute (EA)

MWI .... Measured Workload Index [*Aviation*]

MWI .... Message-Waiting Indicator

MWI .... Missionary Women International (EA)

MWI .... Montserrat [*West Indies*] [*Seismograph station code, US Geological Survey*] (SEIS)

MWI .... Motor-Ways Inc., Des Moines IA [*STAC*]

MWIA .... Medical Women's International Association [*See also AIFM*] [*Cologne, Federal Republic of Germany*] (EAIO)

MWIAP .... Prairie Regional Office, Parks Canada [*Bureau Regional des Pres, Parcs Canada*] Winnipeg, Manitoba [*Library symbol National Library of Canada*] (NLC)

MWIC .... Manitoba Department of Economic Development, Winnipeg, Manitoba [*Library symbol National Library of Canada*] (NLC)

MWiCA .... Sterling and Francine Clark Art Institute, Williamstown, MA [*Library symbol Library of Congress*] (LCLS)

MWIDE .... IDE Engineering Co., Winnipeg, Manitoba [*Library symbol National Library of Canada*] (NLC)

MWIE .... Indus Electronic, Winnipeg, Manitoba [*Library symbol National Library of Canada*] (NLC)

MWIF .... Ivan Franko Museum & Library, Winnipeg, Manitoba [*Library symbol National Library of Canada*] (NLC)

MWIFC .... Midwest Intercollegiate Football Conference (PSS)

MWIN .... Indian and Northern Affairs Canada [*Affaires Indiennes et du Nord Canada*],Winnipeg, Manitoba [*Library symbol National Library of Canada*] (BIB)

MWIP .... Mixed Waste Integrated Program [*Department of Energy*]

MWIR .... Medium-Wavelength Infrared

MWIR .... Midwave Infrared Sensor (MCD)

MWIR .... Mixed Waste Inventory Report [*Department of Energy*]

MWIS .... National Network of Minority Women in Science (EA)

MWIV .... Mean Wildlife Index Value [*Statistics*] (PDAA)

MWIVA .... Midwest Intercollegiate Volleyball Association (PSS)

MWiW .... Williams College, Williamstown, MA [*Library symbol Library of Congress*] (LCLS)

MWiW-C ...... Williams College, Chapin Library, Williamstown, MA [*Library symbol Library of Congress*] (LCLS)

MWJ .... Canada Department of Justice [*Ministere de la Justice*] Winnipeg, Manitoba [*Library symbol National Library of Canada*] (NLC)

MWJ .... Matthews Ridge [*Guyana*] [*Airport symbol*] (OAG)

MWJC .... Marjorie Webster Junior College [*Washington, DC*]

MWJCAC ...... Midwestern Junior College Athletic Conference (PSS)

MWJHS .... Jewish Historical Society of Western Canada, Winnipeg, Manitoba [*Library symbol National Library of Canada*] (NLC)

MWJP .... Jewish Public Library, Winnipeg, Manitoba [*Library symbol National Library of Canada*] (NLC)

MWK .... Kelvin High School, Winnipeg, Manitoba [*Library symbol National Library of Canada*] (NLC)

MWK .... Mill Work [*Technical drawings*]

MWK .... Milwaukee Land [*AMEX symbol*] (TTSB)

MWK .... Milwaukee Land Co. [*AMEX symbol*] (SPSG)

MWK .... Mount Airy, NC [*Location identifier FAA*] (FAAL)

MWL .... Law Society of Manitoba, Winnipeg, Manitoba [*Library symbol National Library of Canada*] (NLC)

MWL .... Malawi Women's League

MWL .... Mean Water Level

MWL .... Meteoric Water Line [*Geology*]

MWL .... Milled-Wood Lignin

mWL .... Milliwatt Logic

MWL .... Mineral Wells [*Texas*] [*Airport symbol*] (AD)

MWL .... Mineral Wells, TX [*Location identifier FAA*] (FAAL)

MWL .... Minimum Wage Laws (OICC)

MWL .... Motor Water Lighter (ADA)

MWL .... Municipal Waste Leachate (GNE)

MWL .... Muslim World League (BJA)

MWL .... Mutual Welfare League (NADA)

MWLAE .... Millimeter Wave Large Antenna Experiment [*NASA*] (PDAA)

MWLCC .... Lutheran Council in Canada, Winnipeg, Manitoba [*Library symbol National Library of Canada*] (NLC)

MWLD .... Man Worn LASER Detector [*Assembly*] (MCD)

MWLD .... Man-Worn LASER Device [*Army*]

MWLDA .... Maine Wholesale Lobster Dealers Association [*Defunct*] (EA)

MWLG .... Midwest Women's Legal Group (EA)

MWLMV .... Maize White Line Mosaic Virus [*Plant pathology*]

MWLR .... Labour Research Library, Manitoba Department of Labour and Manpower, Winnipeg, Manitoba [*Library symbol National Library of Canada*] (NLC)

MWLS .... Faculty of Law, University of Manitoba, Winnipeg, Manitoba [*Library symbol National Library of Canada*] (NLC)

MWM .... Maxwell-Wagner Mechanism [*Physics*]

MWM .... Medical Library, University of Manitoba, Winnipeg, Manitoba [*Library symbol National Library of Canada*] (NLC)

MWM .... Millimeter Wave Mixer

MWM .... Minskoff, Wiseman, Minskoff [*Program for the development of language abilities*]

MWM .... Mode-Woche-Muenchen [*Munich Fashion Week - International Fashion Fair*] [*Germany*] (TSPED)

MWM .... Moments with Meredith - Meredith Baxter-Birney Fan Club [*Defunct*] (EA)

MWM .... Morfee Wheel Manufacturing [*Vancouver Stock Exchange symbol*]

MWM .... Windom, MN [*Location identifier FAA*] (FAAL)

MWM .... Worcester Art Museum, Worcester, MA [*Library symbol Library of Congress*] (LCLS)

MWMA .... Manitoba Department of Municipal Affairs, Winnipeg, Manitoba [*Library symbol National Library of Canada*] (NLC)

MWMA .... Multiple Wine Merchants Association [*British*] (BI)

MWMA .... Municipal Waste Management Association (NTPA)

MWM & R .... Metal-Working Machine and Robot

MWMBC ...... Mennonite Brethren Bible College, Winnipeg, Manitoba [*Library symbol National Library of Canada*] (NLC)

MWMC .... Metropolitan Waste Management Council [*Melbourne, Australia*]

MWmC .... Midwest Microfilm Service, Co., Springfield, IL [*Library symbol*] [*Library of Congress*] (LCLS)

MWMCA ...... Michigan Women for Medical Control of Abortion (EA)

MWME .... Maclaren Engineering, Winnipeg, Manitoba [*Library symbol National Library of Canada*] (NLC)

MWMF .... Mixed Waste Management Facility [*Environmental science*] (COE)

MWMFB ...... Middlewest Motor Freight Bureau

MWMG .... Misericordia General Hospital, Winnipeg, Manitoba [*Library symbol National Library of Canada*] (NLC)

MWMH .... Winnipeg Municipal Hospital, Manitoba [*Library symbol National Library of Canada*] (NLC)

MWMHC ...... Mennonite Heritage Centre, Winnipeg, Manitoba [*Library symbol National Library of Canada*] (NLC)

MWMM .... Manitoba Museum of Man & Nature, Winnipeg, Manitoba [*Library symbol National Library of Canada*] (NLC)

MWMMP ...... Meadowood Manor Personal Care Home, Winnipeg, Manitoba [*Library symbol National Library of Canada*] (NLC)

MWMP .... City of Winnipeg Metro Planning Division, Manitoba [*Library symbol National Library of Canada*] (NLC)

MWMPE ...... Manitoba Pool Elevators Library, Winnipeg, Manitoba [*Library symbol National Library of Canada*] (NLC)

MWMRC ...... Manitoba Research Council, Winnipeg, Manitoba [*Library symbol National Library of Canada*] (NLC)

MWMRTL .... Milliwatt Motorola Resistor Transistor Logic (IAA)

MWMSE ...... Minimum-Weighted Mean Square Error (IAA)

MWMT .... Metal-Working Machine Tool
MWMTC .... Manitoba Theater Center, Winnipeg, Manitoba [*Library symbol National Library of Canada*] (NLC)
MWMTS .... Manitoba Teachers Socity, Winnipeg, Manitoba [*Library symbol National Library of Canada*] (NLC)
MWMU .... University of Massachusetts, Medical Center, Worcester, MA [*Library symbol Library of Congress*] (LCLS)
MWn............ GAR Memorial Library, West Newbury, MA [*Library symbol Library of Congress*] (LCLS)
MWN .... Gordon College, Wenham, MA [*Inactive*] [*OCLC symbol*] (OCLC)
MWN .... Madras Weekly Notes [*India*] [*A publication*] (DLA)
MWN .... Mount Washington, NH [*Location identifier FAA*] (FAAL)
MWNCC .... Madras Weekly Notes, Criminal Cases [*India*] [*A publication*] (DLA)
MWNT .... Multiwalled Nanotube [*Materials science*]
MWNT .... Multiwall Nanotube [*Materials science*]
MWO .... Maintenance Work Order
MWO .... Manufacturing Work Order
MWO .... Master Warrant Officer [*Canadian Forces, since 1964*]
MWO .... Master Work Order (AAG)
MWO .... Mental Welfare Officer [*British*]
MWO .... Middletown, OH [*Location identifier FAA*] (FAAL)
MWO .... Millimeter Wavelength Oscillator
MWO .... Millimeter Wave Observatory [*University of Texas at Austin*] [*Research center*] (RCD)
MWO .... Modification Work Order
MWO .... Mount Wilson Observatory (NADA)
MWO .... Rev. Peres Oblats, Winnipeg, Manitoba [*Library symbol National Library of Canada*] (NLC)
MWo............ Woburn Public Library, Woburn, MA [*Library symbol Library of Congress*] (LCLS)
MWOA .... Mizrachi Women's Organization of America [*Later, AMW*] (EA)
MWOC .... Mothers without Custody (EA)
MWOFP .... Modification Work Order Fielding Plan
MWolIE .... Eastern Nazarene College, Wollaston, MA [*Library symbol Library of Congress*] (LCLS)
MWOP .... Mixed Waste Office Paper [*Pulp and paper technology*]
MWOT .... Master Warrant Officer Training [*DoD*]
MWP............ Legislative Library of Manitoba, Winnipeg, Manitoba [*Library symbol National Library of Canada*] (NLC)
MWP............ Malta Workers Party [*Political party*] (PPE)
MWP............ Maneuvering Work Platform [*NASA*]
MWP............ Mangla [*Pakistan*] [*Airport symbol*] (AD)
MWP............ Master of Welfare Policy
MWP............ Maximum Working Pressure
MWP............ Mean Wedge Pressure (DMAA)
MWP............ Mechanical Wood Pulp [*Paper*]
MWP............ Medieval Warm Period [*Geoscience*]
MWP............ Membrane Waterproofing
MWP............ Metabolic Waste Production
MWP............ Meteorological Weather Processor (GAVI)
MWP............ Meteorologist Weather Processor [*FAA*] (TAG)
MWP............ Mexican Water Plan [*Land use*]
MWP............ Millimeter Wave Propagation
MWP............ Ministry of Works and Planning [*British*]
MWP............ Missile Warning Position (MCD)
MWP............ Most Worthy Patriarch
MWP............ Worcester Polytechnic Institute, Worcester, MA [*Library symbol Library of Congress*] (LCLS)
MWPA .... Married Women's Property Act [*1882*] [*British*] (AIA)
MWPA .... Provincial Archives of Manitoba, Winnipeg, Manitoba [*Library symbol National Library of Canada*] (NLC)
MWPC .... Moorepark Whey Protein Concentrate (OA)
MWPC .... Multiple Wire Proportional Counter
MWPC .... Multiwire Proportional Chamber (IAA)
MWPCPA ..... Archaeology Subsection Office, Prairie Region Library, Parks Canada [*Recherches Archeologiques, Bibliotheque de la Region des Pres, Parcs Canada*] Winnipeg, Manitoba [*Library symbol National Library of Canada*] (NLC)
MWPCPH ..... Historic Resources Conservation Subsection Office, Prairie Region Library, ParksCanada [*Ressources et Conservation Historiques, Bibliotheque de la Region de s Pres, Parcs Canada*] Winnipeg, Manitoba [*Library symbol National Library of Canada*] (NLC)
MWPCR .... Riding Mountain National Park, Parks Canada [*Parc National Riding Mountain, Parcs Canada*] Wasagaming, Manitoba [*Library symbol National Library of Canada*] (NLC)
MWPF .... Marine Wildlife Preservation Fund
MWPI........... Munson-Williams-Proctor Institute [*Utica, NY*]
MWPL.......... Public Library Services, Manitoba Department of Culture, Heritage and Recreation, Winnipeg, Manitoba [*Library symbol National Library of Canada*] (NLC)
MWPNR .... Park Management Library, Manitoba Department of Natural Resources, Winnipeg, Manitoba [*Library symbol National Library of Canada*] (NLC)
MWPO .... Mine Warfare Project Office [*Naval Material Command*]
MWpP.......... Westport Free Public Library, Westport, MA [*Library symbol*] [*Library of Congress*] (LCLS)
MWPPH .... Provincial Public Health Nursing Services, Winnipeg, Manitoba [*Library symbol National Library of Canada*] (NLC)
MWPR .... Monthly Work Package Report [*NASA*] (NASA)
MWPS .... Manitoba Probation Services, Winnipeg, Manitoba [*Library symbol National Library of Canada*] (NLC)
MWPS .... Master of Wood and Paper Science (GAGS)
MWPS .... Multimeter Wave Power Source
MWQ .... Magwe [*Myanmar*] [*Airport symbol*] (OAG)

MWQ .... Quinsigamond Community College, Worcester, MA [*Library symbol Library of Congress*] (LCLS)
MWQCG .... Media and Information Services, Quadraplegic Communications Group, Inc., Winnipeg, Manitoba [*Library symbol National Library of Canada*] (NLC)
MWR .... Maintenance Work Request [*or Requirement*]
MWR .... Man-Worn Receiver (MCD)
mwr .... Marwari [*MARC language code Library of Congress*] (LCCP)
MWR .... Mean Width Ratio
MWR .... Metal Whisker Reinforcement
MWR .... Method of Weighted Residual
MWR .... Millimeter-Wave Radar (DOMA)
MWR .... Mine Watching RADAR (NATG)
MWR .... Mini Web Reel (DGA)
MWR .... Missile-Warning Receiver (MCD)
MWR .... Morale, Welfare, and Recreation [*DoD*]
MWR .... Mountain-West Resources [*Vancouver Stock Exchange symbol*]
MWR .... Mower
MWR .... Muncie & Western Railroad Co. [*AAR code*]
MWR .... Royal Winnipeg Ballet, Manitoba [*Library symbol National Library of Canada*] (NLC)
MWRA .... Master of Water Resources Administration (PGP)
MWRA .... Morale, Welfare, and Recreation Activity [*DoD*] (AFIT)
MWRAILS ..... Microwave Remote Area Instrument Landing System (IAA)
MWRC .... Maintain Well to Right of Course [*Aviation*] (FAAC)
MWRC .... Melbourne Western Region Commission [*Australia*]
MWRC .... Mount Washington Railway Co. [*AAR code*]
MWRC .... RCMP [*Royal Canadian Mounted Police*] Crime Laboratory, Winnipeg, Manitoba [*Library symbol National Library of Canada*] (NLC)
MWRCC .... Roman Catholic Chancery Office, Winnipeg, Manitoba [*Library symbol National Library of Canada*] (NLC)
MWRK .... Mothers Work [*NASDAQ symbol*] (TTSB)
MWRK .... Mothers Work, Inc. [*NASDAQ symbol*] (SAG)
MWroxV .... United States Veterans Administration Hospital, West Roxbury, MA [*Library symbol Library of Congress*] (LCLS)
MWRR .... Learning Resources Centre, Red River Community College, Winnipeg, Manitoba [*Library symbol National Library of Canada*] (NLC)
MWRRC .... Montana Water Resources Research Center [*Montana State University, University ofMontana, and Montana College of Mineral Science and Technology*] [*Research center*] (RCD)
MWRRL........ Library Technician Program, Red River Community College, Winnipeg, Manitoba, LS [*National Library of Canada*] (NLC)
MWRS .... Millimeter Wave Radio System (MCD)
MWRS .... Richardson Securities of Canada, Winnipeg, Manitoba [*Library symbol National Library of Canada*] (NLC)
MWRT .... Mobile Wing Reconnaissance Technical [*Squadron*]
mWRTL........ Milliwatt Resistor-Transistor Logic (IDOE)
MWS .... Major Weapon System [*Manager*] (MCD)
MWS .... Management Work Station (BUR)
MWS .... Marden-Walker Syndrome [*Medicine*] (DMAA)
MWS .... Marine Weather Service (NOAA)
MWS .... Master of Women's Studies (PGP)
MWS .... Mawashi [*Ryukyu Islands*] [*Seismograph station code, US Geological Survey Closed*] (SEIS)
MWS .... Maximum Wind Speed
MWS .... Medium Wide Shot [*Photography*]
MWS .... Megawatt Waveguide Switch
MWS .... Member of the Wernerian Society [*British*] (ROG)
MWS .... Microwave Scatterometer [*Telecommunications*] (TEL)
MWS .... Microwave Station
MWS .... Microwave Wind Spectrometer
MWS .... Mikity-Wilson Syndrome [*Neonatology*] (DAVI)
MWS .... Mini Workstation (SSD)
MWS .... Missile Warning Squadron
MWS .... Missile Weapon System [*Military*] (CAAL)
MWS .... Missouri Western State College, St. Joseph, MO [*OCLC symbol*] (OCLC)
MWS .... Mobile Weapon System
MWS............ Modular Weapons System (MCD)
MWS............ Moersch-Woltman Syndrome [*Medicine*] (DMAA)
MWS............ Most Wise Sovereign [*Freemasonry*]
MWS............ Most Worshipful Scribe [*Freemasonry*] (ROG)
MWS............ Mount Wilson, CA [*Location identifier FAA*] (FAAL)
MWS............ Multiwork Station
MWSA .... St. Andrew's College, Winnipeg, Manitoba [*Library symbol National Library of Canada*] (NLC)
MWSAC .... St. Amant Center, Winnipeg, Manitoba [*Library symbol National Library of Canada*] (NLC)
MWSACB ..... Salvation Army Catherine Booth Bible College, Winnipeg, Manitoba [*Library symbol National Library of Canada*] (BIB)
MWSB .... Saint Boniface Public Library, Winnipeg, Manitoba [*Library symbol National Library of Canada*] (NLC)
MWSBM .... Saint Boniface General Hospital Medical Library, Winnipeg, Manitoba [*Library symbol National Library of Canada*] (NLC)
MWSBN .... Saint Boniface General Hospital School of Nursing Library, Winnipeg, Manitoba [*Library symbol National Library of Canada*] (NLC)
MWSC .... American Men and Women of Science [*Database*] [*R. R. Bowker Co.*] [*Information service or system*] (CRD)
MWSC .... Midwestern Simulation Council
MWSC .... Society for Manitobans with Disabilities, Inc., Winnipeg, Manitoba [*Library symbol National Library of Canada*] (NLC)
MWSCS .... Midwestern Signal Corps School
MWSD .... Missile and Weapons Systems Division [*Military*] (IAA)

MWSD	Teachers' Library and Resource Centre, Winnipeg School Division No. 1, Manitoba [*Library symbol National Library of Canada*] (NLC)
MWSE	Midwest Stock Exchange, Inc. (HGAA)
MWSG	Marine Wing Support Group (NVT)
MWSGDET...	Marine Wing Support Group Detachment (DNAB)
MWSGR	Marine Wing Staff Ground (MCD)
MWSH	Worcester State Hospital, Worcester, MA [*Library symbol Library of Congress*] (LCLS)
MWSJ	St. John's College, Winnipeg, Manitoba [*Library symbol National Library of Canada*] (NLC)
MWSM	Stony Mountain Institution Library, Winnipeg, Manitoba [*Library symbol National Library of Canada*] (NLC)
MWSOGH	Educational Services, Seven Oaks General Hospital, Winnipeg, Manitoba [*Library symbol National Library of Canada*] (NLC)
MWSP	St. Paul's College, Winnipeg, Manitoba [*Library symbol National Library of Canada*] (NLC)
MWSPA	Spiece Associates, Winnipeg, Manitoba [*Library symbol National Library of Canada*] (NLC)
MWSPC	Social Planning Council of Winnipeg, Manitoba [*Library symbol National Library of Canada*] (NLC)
MW Sprg	Mid-West Spring Manufacturing Co. [*Associated Press*] (SAG)
MWSR	Magnetic Wire Shift Register
MWSR	Microwave Water Substance Radiometer [*Marine science*] (OSRA)
MWSS	Manitoba Regional Library, Secretary of State Canada [*Bibliotheque Regionale du Manitoba, Secretariat d'Etat*], Winnipeg, Manitoba [*Library symbol National Library of Canada*] (NLC)
MWSS	Marine Wing Support Squadron [*Navy*] (ANA)
MWSS	Metropolitan Waterworks and Sewerage System [*Philippines*]
MWSS	Metwork Six [*NASDAQ symbol*] (TTSB)
MWSS	Mid-West Spring Manufacturing Co. [*NASDAQ symbol*] (SAG)
MWSSE........	Mid-West Spring Mfg [*NASDAQ symbol*] (TTSB)
MWST	Mean Weighted Skin Temperature
MWST	Miscellaneous Waste Storage Tank [*Nuclear energy*] (NRCH)
MWST..........	Missile Warning System Test (MCD)
MWSV	St. Vital Public Library, Winnipeg, Manitoba [*Library symbol National Library of Canada*] (NLC)
MWT	Makeup Water Treatment (IEEE)
MWT	Marconi Wireless Telegraph [*Telecommunications*] (IAA)
MWT	Master of Wood Technology
MWT	McWhorter Technologies, Inc. [*NYSE symbol*] (SAG)
MWT	Mean Water Temperature
MWT	Megawatt Thermal [*Nuclear energy*] (NRCH)
MWT	Michigan Walleye Tour
MWT	Midwest Aviation [*Southwest Aviation, Inc.*] [*ICAO designator*] (FAAC)
MWT	Millimeter Wave Tube
MWT	Ministry of War Transport [*Terminated, 1956*] [*British*]
MWT	M McWhorter Technologies [*NYSE symbol*] (TTSB)
MWt............	Molecular Weight [*Also, M, MOL WT, MW*] (AAMN)
MWT	Monitor Wafer Turner (AAEL)
MWT	Moolawatana [*Australia Airport symbol Obsolete*] (OAG)
MWT	Mountain War Time
MWT	Myocardial Wall Thickness [*Cardiology*] (DMAA)
Mwt	Thermal Megawatt [*Also, TMW*]
MWT	Winnipeg Tribune, Manitoba [*Library symbol National Library of Canada*] (NLC)
MWTA..........	Airworthiness Library, Central Region, Transport Canada [*Bibliotheque de la Navigabilite Aerienne, Region Centrale, Transports Canada*], Winnipeg, Manitoba [*Library symbol National Library of Canada*] (NLC)
MWTA..........	Medical Waste Tracking Act [*1988*] (FFDE)
MWTA..........	Medical Waste Treatment Act
MWTC..........	Ministry of War Time Communications [*British World War II*]
MWTC..........	Teshmount Consultants, Winnipeg, Manitoba [*Library symbol National Library of Canada*] (NLC)
MWTCR	Central Regional Library, Transport Canada [*Bibliotheque Regionale du Centre, Transports Canada*], Winnipeg, Manitoba [*Library symbol National Library of Canada*] (NLC)
MWTCS........	Modernized Weather Teletypewriter Communications System (FAAC)
MWTE..........	Interdisciplinary Engineering, Winnipeg, Manitoba [*Library symbol National Library of Canada*] (NLC)
MWTE..........	Modern Weapons Training Exercises (MCD)
MW(th)	Megawatts (Thermal)
MWTHA	Michigan Wild Turkey Hunters Association
MWTP..........	Mixed Waste Treatment Project
MWTR	Mean Waiting Time for Supply Replacement (DNAB)
MWTR	Monthly Wholesale Trade Report [*A publication*]
MWTS..........	Manitoba Telephone System, Winnipeg, Manitoba [*Library symbol National Library of Canada*] (NLC)
MWTU	Marble Workers' Trade Union [*British*]
MWU	Maccabi World Union [*Ramat Gan, Israel*] (EAIO)
MWU	Mercer University, Southern School of Pharmacy, Atlanta, GA [*OCLC symbol*] (OCLC)
MWU	Mine Workers Union [*South Africa*] (IMH)
MWU	Modified Wohlgemuth Unit [*Of hydrolytic enzyme activity*]
MWU	Mussau [*Papua New Guinea*] [*Airport symbol*] (OAG)
MWU	University of Manitoba, Winnipeg, Manitoba [*Library symbol National Library of Canada*] (NLC)
MWUA	Ukrainian Academy of Arts and Science, Winnipeg, Manitoba [*Library symbol National Library of Canada*] (NLC)
MWUAF	Architecture and Fine Arts Library, University of Manitoba, Winnipeg, Manitoba [*Library symbol National Library of Canada*] (NLC)
MWUC	University of Winnipeg, Manitoba [*Library symbol National Library of Canada*] (NLC)
MWUCE	Ukrainian Cultural and Educational Centre, Winnipeg, Manitoba [*Library symbol National Library of Canada*] (NLC)
MWUD	Dental Library, University of Manitoba, Winnipeg, Manitoba [*Library symbol National Library of Canada*] (NLC)
MWUG	Department of Geography, University of Manitoba, Winnipeg, Manitoba [*Library symbol National Library of Canada*] (NLC)
MWUGG......	United Grain Growers, Winnipeg, Manitoba [*Library symbol National Library of Canada*] (NLC)
MWUM	Map and Atlas Collection, University of Manitoba, Winnipeg, Manitoba [*Library symbol National Library of Canada*] (NLC)
MWUML	Underwood McLellan Ltd., Winnipeg, Manitoba [*Library symbol National Library of Canada*] (NLC)
MWUSA	Minute Women of the United States of America (EA)
MWV...........	Maximum Working Voltage [*Electronics*]
MWV...........	Mexican War Veteran
MWV...........	Milkweed Virus
MWV...........	Modulated Wavy Vortex [*Fluid mechanics*]
MWV...........	Motor Tariff Bureau of West Virginia, Charleston WV [*STAC*]
MWVGH	Victoria General Hospital, Winnipeg, Manitoba [*Library symbol National Library of Canada*] (NLC)
MWVS	Branch Library, Manitoba Veterinarian Services, Winnipeg, Manitoba [*Library symbol National Library of Canada*] (NLC)
MWW..........	Majestic Wine Warehouses [*Commercial firm*] [*British*]
MWW..........	Manual Wire Wrap
MWW..........	Mark's Work Wearhouse Ltd. [*Toronto Stock Exchange symbol*]
MWW..........	Marquis Who's Who [*Marquis Who's Who, Inc.*] [*Information service or system A publication*]
MWW..........	[*The*] Merry Wives of Windsor [*Shakespearean work*] (BARN)
MWW..........	Municipal Wastewater
MWW..........	William Ave. Branch, Winnipeg Public Library, Manitoba [*Library symbol National Library of Canada*] (NLC)
MWW..........	Worcester State College, Worcester, MA [*Library symbol Library of Congress*] (LCLS)
MWWA	Winnipeg Art Gallery, Manitoba [*Library symbol National Library of Canada*] (NLC)
MWWC	Military Weather Warning Center (NOAA)
MWWC	Winnipeg Clinic, Manitoba [*Library symbol National Library of Canada*] (NLC)
MWWF	Manual Wire Wrap Fixture
MWWII	Mothers of World War II
MWWK	West Kildonan Public Library, Winnipeg, Manitoba [*Library symbol National Library of Canada*] (NLC)
MWWLW	W. L. Wardrop & Associates, Winnipeg, Manitoba [*Library symbol National Library of Canada*] (NLC)
MWWR	Water Resources Division, Manitoba Department of Natural Resources, Winnipeg, Manitoba [*Library symbol National Library of Canada*] (NLC)
MWWSH......	Manitoba Workplace Safety and Health Division, Winnipeg, Manitoba [*Library symbol National Library of Canada*] (NLC)
MWWU	Marine Wing Weapon Unit
MWWV	Movement of Working Women and Volunteers [*Tel Aviv, Israel*] (EAIO)
MWX...........	Montpelier, VT [*Location identifier FAA*] (FAAL)
MWY...........	Midway Games, Inc. [*NYSE symbol*] (SAG)
MWY...........	Miranda Downs [*Australia Airport symbol Obsolete*] (OAG)
MWYE.........	Megawatt Year of Electricity (IAA)
MWZ...........	Mwanza [*Tanzania*] [*Airport symbol*] (OAG)
MX	Compania Mexicana de Aviacion [*ICAO designator*] (OAG)
MX	Mail Exchange [*Computer science*]
mx	Management (DAVI)
MX	Master Agility Excellent
MX	Matrix (BUR)
Mx	Maxwell [*Unit of magnetic flux*] [*Also, abWb*]
MX	Measurex Corp. [*NYSE symbol*] (SPSG)
MX	Metaxylene
MX	Mexicana [*Airline*] (DS)
MX	Mexicana de Aviacion [*ICAO designator*] (AD)
MX	Mexican L & P Co. Ltd. [*Toronto Stock Exchange symbol*]
MX	Mexico [*ANSI two-letter standard code*] (CNC)
mx	Mexico [*IYRU nationality code*] [*MARC country of publication code Library of Congress*] (LCCP)
MX	Middlesex [*Region of London*]
MX	Missile, Experimental
MX	Mix
MX	Motocross (WGA)
MX	Multiple Address
MX	Multiplex [*or Multiplexer*]
mx	Multiplex (NAKS)
MX	Murexide [*An indicator*] [*Chemistry*]
MXA...........	Compania Mexicana de Aviacion SA [*Mexico ICAO designator*] (FAAC)
MXA...........	Manila, AR [*Location identifier FAA*] (FAAL)
MXA...........	Minnesota Municipal Income Portfolio [*AMEX symbol*] (SPSG)
MXA...........	Minnesota Muni Inc. Portfolio [*AMEX symbol*] (TTSB)
MXA...........	Mobile Exercise Area [*Military*] (NVT)
MXAL.........	Mercury Xenon Arc Lamp
MXB...........	Masamba [*Indonesia*] [*Airport symbol*] (OAG)
MXC...........	MATEC Corp. [*AMEX symbol*] (SPSG)
MXC...........	Maxon Computer Systems, Inc. [*Toronto Stock Exchange symbol*]
MXC...........	Mexair SA [*Switzerland ICAO designator*] (FAAC)
MXC...........	Monticello [*Utah*] [*Airport symbol*] (OAG)
MXC...........	Multiplexer Channel [*Computer science*]
MXC...........	University of Cincinnati, Medical Center, Cincinnati, OH [*OCLC symbol*] (OCLC)

MxChGS......	Church of Jesus Christ of Latter-Day Saints, Genealogical Society Library, Colonia Juarez Branch, Chihuahua, Mexico [*Library symbol Library of Congress*] (LCLS)
MXD............	Marion Downs [*Queensland*] [*Airport symbol*] (AD)
MXD............	Mixed
MXD............	Mixed Artillery [*Military*] (VNW)
MXD............	Mixed Use Development (PA)
MXD............	Multiple Transmitter Duplicator
MXDA..........	Meta-Xylenediamine [*Organic chemistry*]
MXD CL.......	Mixed Carload [*Freight*]
MXDCR........	Mode Transducer (MSA)
MXDTH........	Maximum Depth (NOAA)
MXE............	Manx Airlines (Europe) Ltd. [*British ICAO designator*] (FAAC)
MXE............	Mexico Eqty & Income Fd [*NYSE symbol*] (TTSB)
MXE............	Mexico Equity & Income Fund [*NYSE symbol*] (SPSG)
MXE............	Modena, PA [*Location identifier FAA*] (FAAL)
MXF............	Mexico Fund [*NYSE symbol*] (TTSB)
MXF............	[*The*] Mexico Fund, Inc. [*NYSE symbol*] (SPSG)
MXF............	Montgomery, AL [*Location identifier FAA*] (FAAL)
MXFL..........	Mixed Flow
MXG............	Mixing (MSA)
MxGuBF......	Biblioteca Benjamin Franklin, Guadalajara, Mexico [*Library symbol Library of Congress*] (LCLS)
MXIC..........	MX Information Center [*Defunct*] (EA)
MXICY........	Macronix Intl ADR [*NASDAQ symbol*] (TTSB)
MXIM..........	Maxim Integrated Prod [*NASDAQ symbol*] (TTSB)
MXIM..........	Maxim Integrated Products, Inc. [*NASDAQ symbol*] (NQ)
MXIS..........	Maxis, Inc. [*NASDAQ symbol*] (SAG)
MXK............	Camp Springs, MD [*Location identifier FAA*] (FAAL)
MXK............	Metekel [*Ethiopia*] [*Airport symbol*] (AD)
MXK............	Multiple-Frequency X- and K-Band
MXL............	Mexicali [*Mexico*] [*Airport symbol*] (OAG)
MXL............	Mixed Workload [*Computer science*] (PCM)
MXLU..........	Malcolm X Liberation University
MXM............	Matrix Memory (MHDI)
MXM............	Maximum (ADA)
MXM............	MAXXAM, Inc. [*AMEX symbol*] (SPSG)
MXM............	Morombe [*Madagascar*] [*Airport symbol*] (OAG)
MxMBF.......	Biblioteca Benjamin Franklin, Mexico City, Mexico [*Library symbol Library of Congress*] (LCLS)
MxMBN.......	Biblioteca Nacional de Mexico, Mexico City, Mexico [*Library symbol Library of Congress*] (LCLS)
MxMC..........	Centro de Investigacion y de Estudios Avanzados, Instituto Politecnico Nacional,Mexico City, Mexico [*Library symbol Library of Congress*] (LCLS)
MxMCM.......	Colegio de Mexico, Mexico, Mexico City, Mexico [*Library symbol Library of Congress*] (LCLS)
MxMGS........	Church of Jesus Christ of Latter-Day Saints, Genealogical Society Library, Mexico City Branch, Mexico City, Mexico [*Library symbol Library of Congress*] (LCLS)
MxMI..........	Universidad Iberoamericana, Mexico [*Library symbol Library of Congress*] (LCLS)
MX/MM........	Missile X/Minuteman Missile
MxMoT........	Instituto Tecnologico y de Estudios Superiores de Monterrey, Monterrey, Mexico [*Library symbol Library of Congress*] (LCLS)
MX/MPS	Missile X [*Deploy In*] Multiple Protective Shelters
MxN............	Maxillary Nerve [*Neuroanatomy*]
MXN............	Morlaix [*France*] [*Airport symbol*] (OAG)
MX-NM........	Matrix - National Module
MXO............	Monticello, IA [*Location identifier FAA*] (FAAL)
MXP............	May Air Xpress, Inc. [*ICAO designator*] (FAAC)
MXP............	Mesa, Inc. [*NYSE symbol*] (SAG)
MXP............	Milan [*Italy*] Malpensa Airport [*Airport symbol*] (OAG)
MXPST........	Maximum Possible Storm (NOAA)
MXQ............	Modular X-Ray Quantometer
MXQ............	Wilmington, OH [*Location identifier FAA*] (FAAL)
MXR............	Mask Index Register
MXR............	Mass X-Ray
MXR............	Merrix Air Ltd. [*British ICAO designator*] (FAAC)
MXR............	Mixer (MSA)
MXR............	Moussoro [*Chad*] [*Airport symbol*] (AD)
MXR............	Raton, NM [*Location identifier FAA*] (FAAL)
MXRAN........	Maximum Rainfall (NOAA)
M-X/RES......	M-X [*Missile*] Renewable Energy System
MXRV..........	Middlesex Rifle Volunteers [*Military British*] (DMA)
MXS............	Max Minerals, Inc. [*Vancouver Stock Exchange symbol*]
MXS............	Maxus Energy Corp. [*NYSE symbol*] (SPSG)
MXSBP........	Maxus Energy [*NASDAQ symbol*] (SAG)
MXSBP........	Maxus Energy $4 Cv Pfd [*NASDAQ symbol*] (TTSB)
MXSPrA.......	Maxus Energy $2.50 Pfd [*NYSE symbol*] (TTSB)
MXSV..........	Maxserv, Inc. [*NASDAQ symbol*] (SAG)
MXT............	Chicago, IL [*Location identifier FAA*] (FAAL)
MXT............	Maintirano [*Madagascar*] [*Airport symbol*] (OAG)
MXT............	Message Exchange Terminal
MXT............	Mixture
MXT............	Morgan StanGp 6.00% Tele'PERQS' [*AMEX symbol*] (TTSB)
MXT............	Morgan Stanley Group, Inc. [*AMEX symbol*] (SAG)
MXTMP........	Maximum Temperature (NOAA)
MXTR..........	Maxtor Corp. [*NASDAQ symbol*] (NQ)
MXU............	Mobile Exhibition Unit (NITA)
MXU............	Mullewa [*Australia Airport symbol Obsolete*] (OAG)
MXU............	Multiplexer Unit [*Telecommunications*]
MxU............	Universidad Nacional Autonoma de Mexico, Mexico City, Mexico [*Library symbol Library of Congress*] (LCLS)
MXVRC	Middlesex Volunteer Rifle Corps [*British military*] (DMA)

MXW............	Maxwell, CA [*Location identifier FAA*] (FAAL)
MXWL..........	Maxwell Laboratories, Inc. [*NASDAQ symbol*] (NQ)
MXWL..........	Maxwell Labs [*NASDAQ symbol*] (TTSB)
MXWL..........	Maxwell Technologies, Inc. [*NASDAQ symbol*] (SAG)
MXWND.......	Maximum Wind (NOAA)
MXX............	Merchant Express Aviation [*Nigeria*] [*ICAO designator*] (FAAC)
MXX............	Mora [*Sweden*] [*Airport symbol*] (OAG)
MXY............	McCarthy [*Alaska*] [*Airport symbol*] (OAG)
MXY............	McCarthy, AK [*Location identifier FAA*] (FAAL)
MXY............	[*The*] Yarumal Foreign Mission Institute (Colombia) (TOCD)
MY...............	Air Mali [*ICAO designator*] (AD)
My..............	All India Reporter, Mysore Series [*A publication*] (ILCA)
MY..............	Machine Yield [*Agriculture*] (OA)
MY..............	Mahzor Yanai (BJA)
MY..............	Malaysia [*IYRU nationality code*] [*ANSI two-letter standard code*] (CNC)
my	Malaysia [*MARC country of publication code Library of Congress*] (LCCP)
MY..............	Man-Year (AFM)
M/Y.............	Marshaling Yards [*Military*]
MY..............	May
my..............	Mayer [*A unit of heat capacity*]
MY..............	Mean Year (IAA)
MY..............	Mean Yield [*Agriculture*]
MY..............	Miller-Yoder Language Comprehension Test
MY..............	Million Years
MY..............	Model Year [*Automotive industry*]
MY..............	Montgomeryshire Yeomanry [*British military*] (DMA)
MY..............	Motor Yacht
MY..............	Muddy [*Track condition*] [*Thoroughbred racing*]
MY..............	Myopia
MY..............	Myria [*A prefix meaning multiplied by 10⁴*]
MY..............	Myxedematous [*Endocrinology*] (DAVI)
MYA............	Million Years Ago
MYA............	Model Yachting Association [*British*] (DBA)
MYA............	Moruya [*Australia Airport symbol*] (OAG)
MYA............	Myasishchev [*Aircraft*] [*Commonwealth of Independent States*]
MYA............	Myflug HF [*Iceland*] [*ICAO designator*] (FAAC)
mya............	Myiare (BARN)
MYAB..........	Clarence Bain, Andros Island [*Bahamas*] [*ICAO location identifier*] (ICLI)
MYAF..........	Andros Town, Andros Island [*Bahamas*] [*ICAO location identifier*] (ICLI)
MYAG	Gorda Cay, Abaco Island [*Bahamas*] [*ICAO location identifier*] (ICLI)
MYAK..........	Congo Town, Andros Island [*Bahamas*] [*ICAO location identifier*] (ICLI)
MYAM..........	Marsh Harbour, Abaco Island [*Bahamas*] [*ICAO location identifier*] (ICLI)
MYAN..........	San Andros, Andros Island [*Bahamas*] [*ICAO location identifier*] (ICLI)
My & C	Mylne and Craig's English Chancery Reports [*A publication*] (DLA)
My & Cr.......	Mylne and Craig's English Chancery Reports [*A publication*] (DLA)
My & K	Mylne and Keen's English Chancery Reports [*A publication*] (DLA)
MYAO..........	Moores Island, Abaco Island [*Bahamas*] [*ICAO location identifier*] (ICLI)
MYAP..........	Spring Point [*Bahamas*] [*ICAO location identifier*] (ICLI)
MYAPP........	Main Yankee Atomic Power Plant (NRCH)
MYAS..........	Sandy Point, Abaco Island [*Bahamas*] [*ICAO location identifier*] (ICLI)
MYAT..........	Treasure Cay, Abaco Island [*Bahamas*] [*ICAO location identifier*] (ICLI)
MYAW	Walker Cay, Abaco Island [*Bahamas*] [*ICAO location identifier*] (ICLI)
MYB............	Aerolineas Del Mayab, SA de CV [*Mexico*] [*FAA designator*] (FAAC)
MYB............	Mayoumba [*Gabon*] [*Airport symbol*] (OAG)
MYBC..........	Chub Cay, Berry Island [*Bahamas*] [*ICAO location identifier*] (ICLI)
MYBC..........	Myosin-Binding Protein C (DMAA)
MYBG	Bullocks Harbour/Great Harbour Cay, Berry Island [*Bahamas*] [*ICAO location identifier*] (ICLI)
MYBO	Ocean Cay, Bimini Island [*Bahamas*] [*ICAO location identifier*] (ICLI)
MYBP..........	Million Years before Present [*Geology*]
MYBS..........	Alice Town/South Bimini, Bimini Island [*Bahamas*] [*ICAO location identifier*] (ICLI)
MYBT..........	Cistern Cay, Berry Island [*Bahamas*] [*ICAO location identifier*] (ICLI)
MYBW	Big Whale Cay, Berry Island [*Bahamas*] [*ICAO location identifier*] (ICLI)
MYBX..........	Little Whale Cay, Berry Island [*Bahamas*] [*ICAO location identifier*] (ICLI)
MYC............	Malartic Hygrade Gold Mines Ltd. [*Vancouver Stock Exchange symbol*]
MYC............	Maracay [*Venezuela*] [*Airport symbol*] (OAG)
MYC............	Massenya [*Chad*] [*Airport symbol*] (AD)
MYC............	Middlesex Yeomanry Cavalry [*British military*] (DMA)
MYC............	Montgomeryshire Yeomanry Cavalry [*British military*] (DMA)
MYC............	Multiyear Contract
MYC............	MuniYield California Fund [*NYSE symbol*] (SPSG)
MYC............	Mycology (WGA)
MYCA..........	Arthur's Town, Eleuthera Island [*Bahamas*] [*ICAO location identifier*] (ICLI)
MYCB..........	New Bight, Cat Island [*Bahamas*] [*ICAO location identifier*] (ICLI)
MYCH..........	Hawks Nest Creek/Hawks Nest, Cat Island [*Bahamas*] [*ICAO location identifier*] (ICLI)
MYCI...........	Colonel Hill, Crooked Island [*Bahamas*] [*ICAO location identifier*] (ICLI)
MYCI...........	Mirrer Yeshiva Central Institute (EA)
MYCO	Mycobacterium

MYCO	Mycogen Corp. [*NASDAQ symbol*] (NQ)
Myco	Mycoplasma [*A bacterium*] (DAVI)
Mycogn	Mycogen Corp. [*Associated Press*] (SAG)
MYCOL	Mycology
MYCOS	My Compact Operating System [*Toshiba*]
MYCOS/SS	MYCOS Support System (NITA)
MYCP	Pittsdown, Crooked Island [*Bahamas*] [*ICAO location identifier*] (ICLI)
MYCS	Cay Sal [*Bahamas*] [*ICAO location identifier*] (ICLI)
MYCX	Cutlass Bay, Cat Island [*Bahamas*] [*ICAO location identifier*] (ICLI)
MYD	Malindi [*Kenya*] [*Airport symbol*] (OAG)
MYD	Miyadu [*Japan*] [*Seismograph station code, US Geological Survey Closed*] (SEIS)
MYD	MuniYield Fund [*NYSE symbol*] (SPSG)
MYD	Myotonic Muscular Dystrophy [*Medicine*] (DB)
MYDP	Multi-Year Development Plan [*Environmental Protection Agency*] (ERG)
MYDW	Multiple Yield Defense Weapon
MYE	Mary Ellen Resources Ltd. [*Vancouver Stock Exchange symbol*]
MYE	Miyake Jima [*Japan*] [*Airport symbol*] (OAG)
MYE	Myers Indus [*AMEX symbol*] (TTSB)
MYE	Myers Industries, Inc. [*AMEX symbol*] (SPSG)
MYEC	Cape Eleuthera, Eleuthera Island [*Bahamas*] [*ICAO location identifier*] (ICLI)
MYEG	George Town, Exuma Island [*Bahamas*] [*ICAO location identifier*] (ICLI)
MYEH	North Eleuthera, Eleuthera Island [*Bahamas*] [*ICAO location identifier*] (ICLI)
MYEL	Mulitple Myeloma [*Hematology*] (DAVI)
MYEL	Myelin [*or Myelinated*] [*Medicine*]
MYEL	Myelocyte [*Hematology*]
MYEL	Myelogram [*Medicine*] (AAMN)
MYEL	Staniel Cay, Exuma Island [*Bahamas*] [*ICAO location identifier*] (ICLI)
myelo	Myelocyte [*Hematology*]
MYEM	Governor's Harbour, Eleuthera Island [*Bahamas*] [*ICAO location identifier*] (ICLI)
MYEN	Norman's Cay, Exuma Island [*Bahamas*] [*ICAO location identifier*] (ICLI)
MYER	Rock Sound/International, Eleuthera Island [*Bahamas*] [*ICAO location identifier*] (ICLI)
Myer Dig	Myer's Texas Digest [*A publication*] (DLA)
Myer Fed Dec	Myer's Federal Decisions [*A publication*] (DLA)
MyerL	[*The*] Myers [*L. E.*] Co. Group [*Associated Press*] (SAG)
Myer's Fed Dec	Myer's Federal Decisions [*United States*] [*A publication*] (DLA)
MyersInd	Myers Industries, Inc. [*Associated Press*] (SAG)
MYES	Lee Stocking Island, Exuma Island [*Bahamas*] [*ICAO location identifier*] (ICLI)
MYEY	Hog Cay, Exuma Island [*Bahamas*] [*ICAO location identifier*] (ICLI)
MYF	Methodist Youth Fellowship
MYF	MuniYield Florida Fund [*NYSE symbol*] (SPSG)
MYF	Myogenic Factor (DMAA)
MYF	San Diego [*California*] Montgomery Field [*Airport symbol Obsolete*] (OAG)
MYFV	Melandrium Yellow Fleck Virus [*Plant pathology*]
MYG	Massachusetts Institute of Technology, Cambridge, MA [*OCLC symbol*] (OCLC)
MYG	Matka [*Yugoslavia*] [*Seismograph station code, US Geological Survey*] (SEIS)
MYG	Mayaguana [*Bahamas*] [*Airport symbol*] (OAG)
MYG	Maytag [*NYSE symbol*] (SAG)
MYG	Maytag Corp. [*NYSE symbol*] (TTSB)
MYG	Myasthenia Gravis [*Medicine*]
MYG	Myriagram [*Ten Thousand Grams*]
MYGD	Deep Water Cay, Grand Bahama Island [*Bahamas*] [*ICAO location identifier*] (ICLI)
MYGF	Freeport/International, Grand Bahama Island [*Bahamas*] [*ICAO location identifier*] (ICLI)
MYGM	Grand Bahama Auxiliary Air Force Base, Grand Bahama Island [*Bahamas*] [*ICAO location identifier*] (ICLI)
MYGN	Myriad Genetics [*NASDAQ symbol*] (TTSB)
MYGN	Myriad Genetics, Inc. [*NASDAQ symbol*] (SAG)
MYGW	West End, Grand Bahama Island [*Bahamas*] [*ICAO location identifier*] (ICLI)
MYH	Rosh-Pina [*Israel*] [*Airport symbol*] (AD)
MYHEC	Michigan Youth Hunter Education Challenge
MY I	First Multiyear Contract [*Military*] (RDA)
MYI	Magical Youths International (EA)
MYI	Metallic Yarns Institute [*Defunct*]
MYI	MuniYield Insured Fund [*NYSE symbol*] (SPSG)
MYIG	Matthew Town, Great Inagua Island [*Bahamas*] [*ICAO location identifier*] (ICLI)
MY II	Second Multiyear Contract [*Military*] (RDA)
MYIM	Mylar Insulation Material
MYJ	Matsuyama [*Japan*] [*Airport symbol*] (OAG)
MYJ	MuniYield New Jersey Fund [*NYSE symbol*] (SPSG)
MYK	May Creek [*Alaska*] [*Airport symbol*] (OAG)
MYK	May Creek, AK [*Location identifier FAA*] (FAAL)
MYK	Miyakojima [*Ryukyu Islands*] [*Seismograph station code, US Geological Survey*] (SEIS)
MYL	Aeromyl SA de CV [*Mexico ICAO designator*] (FAAC)
MYL	McCall, ID [*Location identifier FAA*] (FAAL)
MYL	Mylan Laboratories, Inc. [*NYSE symbol*] (SPSG)
MYL	Mylan Labs [*NYSE symbol*] (TTSB)
MYL	Myrialiter [*Unit of measurement*]
Mylan	Mylan Laboratories, Inc. [*Associated Press*] (SAG)

Myl & C	Mylne and Craig's English Chancery Reports [*A publication*] (DLA)
Myl & C (Eng)	Mylne and Craig's English Chancery Reports [*A publication*] (DLA)
Myl & Cr	Mylne and Craig's English Chancery Reports [*A publication*] (DLA)
Myl & K	Mylne and Keen's English Chancery Reports [*A publication*] (DLA)
Myl & K (Eng)	Mylne and Keen's English Chancery Reports [*A publication*] (DLA)
MYLD	Deadman's Cay, Long Island [*Bahamas*] [*ICAO location identifier*] (ICLI)
Mylex	Mylex Corp. [*Associated Press*] (SAG)
My LJ	Mysore Law Journal [*India*] [*A publication*] (DLA)
Mylne & K	Mylne and Keen's English Chancery Reports [*A publication*] (DLA)
MYLR	Diamond Roads, Long Island [*Bahamas*] [*ICAO location identifier*] (ICLI)
MYLS	Mid-York Library System [*Library network*]
MYLS	Stella Maris, Long Island [*Bahamas*] [*ICAO location identifier*] (ICLI)
MYLX	Mylex Corp. [*NASDAQ symbol*] (NQ)
MYM	Managing Your Money [*MECA Software, Inc.*] (PCM)
MYM	Marley Mines Ltd. [*Vancouver Stock Exchange symbol*]
MYM	Monkey Mountain [*Guyana*] [*Airport symbol*] (OAG)
MYM	Muniyield Michigan Fund [*NYSE symbol*] (SAG)
MYM	Myriameter
MyMD	Myotonic Muscular Dystrophy [*See also MD*] [*Medicine*]
MYMM	Mayaguana Auxiliary Air Force Base, Mayaguana Island [*Bahamas*] [*ICAO location identifier*] (ICLI)
MYMS	Mothers of Young Mongoloids [*Later, PODSC*] (EA)
MYMV	Mungbean Yellow Mosaic Virus [*Plant pathology*]
MYN	Mareb [*Yemen*] [*Airport symbol Obsolete*] (OAG)
myn	Mayan [*MARC language code Library of Congress*] (LCCP)
MYN	Mayan Energy, Inc. [*Vancouver Stock Exchange symbol*]
MYN	MuniYield New York Insured Fund [*NYSE symbol*] (SPSG)
MYN	MuniYield NY Insured Fund [*NYSE symbol*] (TTSB)
MYNA	Nassau [*Bahamas*] [*ICAO location identifier*] (ICLI)
MYNN	Nassau/International, New Providence Island [*Bahamas*] [*ICAO location identifier*] (ICLI)
MYO	Myocardial [*or Myocardium*] [*Cardiology*] (AAMN)
MYO	Myoglobin (DB)
MYOB	Mind Your Own Business [*Slang*]
MYOBB	Mind Your Own Business, Buster [*Slang*]
MYOC-A	Myocarditis, Pericarditis [*Cardiology*] (DAVI)
MYOGLB	Myoglobin [*hematology*] (DAVI)
MYOP	Multiyear Operational Plan [*Long-range forecast produced by the Canadian government*]
myop	Myopia [*Ophthalmology*] (DAVI)
MYP	Mannito-Egg Yolk Polymyxin (OA)
MY/P	Mean Yield/Plants [*Agriculture*]
MYP	Montgomery [*Pakistan*] [*Airport symbol*] (AD)
MYP	Multiyear Procurement [*DoD*]
MYPO	Multiyear Procurement Objective [*DoD*]
MYQ	Windsor Locks, CT [*Location identifier FAA*] (FAAL)
MYR	Maximum Yield Research [*Agricultural technology*]
m/yr	Milli-Inches per Year [*Corrosion technology*]
MYR	Million Years [*Also, MY*]
MYR	Miriadair [*France ICAO designator*] (FAAC)
MYR	[*The*] Myers [*L. E.*] Co. Group [*NYSE symbol*] (SPSG)
MYR	MYR Group [*NYSE symbol*] (TTSB)
Myr	Myrick's California Probate Court Reports [*1872-79*] [*A publication*] (DLA)
myr	Myrtle [*Philately*]
MYR	Myrtle Beach [*South Carolina*] Myrtle Air Force Base [*Airport symbol*] (OAG)
MYRA	Multiyear Rescheduling Agreement [*Banking*]
MYRAA	Model Yacht Racing Association of America (EA)
Myr Cal Prob	Myrick's California Probate Court Reports [*1872-79*] [*A publication*] (DLA)
MYRD	Duncan Town, Exuma Island [*Bahamas*] [*ICAO location identifier*] (ICLI)
Myriad	Myriad Genetics, Inc. [*Associated Press*] (SAG)
Myrick (Cal)	Myrick's California Probate Court Reports [*1872-79*] [*A publication*] (DLA)
Myrick Prob (Cal)	Myrick's California Probate Court Reports [*1872-79*] [*A publication*] (DLA)
Myrick's Prob Rep	Myrick's California Probate Court Reports [*1872-79*] [*A publication*] (DLA)
MYRP	Port Nelson, Exuma Island [*Bahamas*] [*ICAO location identifier*] (ICLI)
Myr Prob	Myrick's California Probate Court Reports [*1872-79*] [*A publication*] (DLA)
Myr Prob Rep	Myrick's California Probate Court Reports [*1872-79*] [*A publication*] (DLA)
Mys	All India Reporter, Mysore [*A publication*] (DLA)
MYS	Maderas y Sinteticos [*NYSE symbol*] (SPSG)
MYS	Maderas y Sinteticos ADS [*NYSE symbol*] (TTSB)
MYS	Malaysia [*ANSI three-letter standard code*] (CNC)
MYS	Man-Year-Space [*Army*] (AABC)
MYS	Masisa S.A. ADS [*Formerly, Maderas y Sinteticos ADS*] [*NYSE symbol*]
MYS	Myasthenic Syndrome [*Neurology*]
MYS	Mystery Mountain Minerals [*Vancouver Stock Exchange symbol*]
MYS	Mystic, KY [*Location identifier FAA*] (FAAL)
MYS	Mystic Marinelife Aquarium, New London, CT [*OCLC symbol*] (OCLC)
Mys Ch Ct	Mysore Chief Court Reports [*India*] [*A publication*] (DLA)
Mys HCR	Mysore High Court Reports [*India*] [*A publication*] (DLA)
Mys LJ	Mysore Law Journal [*India*] [*A publication*] (DLA)

Mys LR........ Mysore Law Reports [*India*] [*A publication*] (DLA)

MYSM......... Cockburn Town, San Salvador Island [*Bahamas*] [*ICAO location identifier*] (ICLI)

MySoft........ MySoftware Co. [*Associated Press*] (SAG)

MYSOLN...... Mysoline [*An anticonvulsant*] [*Wyeth-Ayerst Laboratorie*] (DAVI)

Mysore .... Mysore Law Reports [*India*] [*A publication*] (DLA)

Mysore LJ ... Mysore Law Journal [*India*] [*A publication*] (DLA)

Mys R (R).... Mysore Reports (Reprint) [*1878-1923*] [*India*] [*A publication*] (DLA)

MYST......... Mystery

MYSTIC....... Mystic

MYSW......... MySoftware Co. [*NASDAQ symbol*] (SAG)

Mys WN...... Mysore Weekly Notes [*1891-92*] [*India*] [*A publication*] (DLA)

MYT............ MuniYield New York Insured Fund II [*NYSE symbol*] (SPSG)

MYT............ MuniYield NY Insured Fund II [*NYSE symbol*] (TTSB)

MYT............ Myitkyina [*Myanmar*] [*Airport symbol*] (OAG)

MYT............ Mytec Technology, Inc. [*Vancouver Stock Exchange symbol*]

MYT............ Mythology

MYTA.......... Maintainability Task Analyses (NASA)

MYTAB........ Myristyltrimethylammonium Bromide [*Organic chemistry*]

MYTD.......... Model Year to Date

MYTGC....... Miller-Yoder Test of Grammatical Comprehension [*Speech and lanaguage therapy*] (DAVI)

MYTH.......... Mythology

MYTHOL ..... Mythology (WGA)

Myth Vat..... Mythographi Vaticani [*A publication*] (OCD)

MYTK.......... Mitek Surgical Products (EFIS)

MYU............ Mekoryuk [*Alaska*] [*Airport symbol*] (OAG)

MYV............ Malva Yellows Virus [*Plant pathology*]

MYV............ Marysville [*California*] [*Airport symbol*] (AD)

MYV............ Marysville, CA [*Location identifier FAA*] (FAAL)

MYVAL........ Maintainability Evaluation (NASA)

MYW........... Mtwara [*Tanzania*] [*Airport symbol*] (OAG)

MYW........... Multiple Yield Weapon

MYWF........ Masonic Youth Welfare Fund [*Australia*]

MYX........... Marion, VA [*Location identifier FAA*] (FAAL)

MYX........... Menyamya [*Papua New Guinea*] [*Airport symbol*] (OAG)

MYX........... Methotrexate [*Antineoplastic drug*] (CDI)

MYXO......... Myxomatosis (DSUE)

MYY............ Miri [*Malaysia*] [*Airport symbol*] (OAG)

MYY............ MuniYield MY Insured Fund III [*NYSE symbol*] (TTSB)

MYY............ MuniYield New York Insured Fund III [*NYSE symbol*] (SPSG)

MYY............ Philadelphia, PA [*Location identifier FAA*] (FAAL)

MYZ............ Marysville, KS [*Location identifier FAA*] (FAAL)

MYZ............ Mayoko [*Gabon*] [*Airport symbol*] (AD)

MYZ............ Miyazaki [*Japan*] [*Seismograph station code, US Geological Survey*] (SEIS)

MZ .... Mantle Zone

MZ .... Marginal Zone [*Neurology*]

m-z .... Mass to Charge Ratio

MZ .... Merpati Nusantara Airlines [*ICAO designator*] (AD)

Mz.............. Methoxyphenylazobenzyloxycarbonyl [*Biochemistry*]

MZ .... Mezzo [*Moderate*] [*Music*] (ROG)

MZ .... Midzone Phenomenon [*Immunology*]

MZ .... Miesiecznik Zydowski (BJA)

MZ .... Minus Zero (IAA)

MZ .... Monozygotic [*Genetics*]

MZ .... Mozambique [*ANSI two-letter standard code*] (CNC)

mz.............. Mozambique [*MARC country of publication code Library of Congress*] (LCCP)

MZ .... Museum of Zoology (NADA)

MZA............ Air Zory [*Bulgaria*] [*FAA designator*] (FAAC)

MZA............ Mariazell [*Austria*] [*Seismograph station code, US Geological Survey*] (SEIS)

MZA............ Monozygotic Twins Reared Apart [*Genetics*]

MZA............ MuniYield Arizona Fund [*AMEX symbol*] (TTSB)

MZA............ MuniYield Arizona Fund, Inc. [*AMEX symbol*] (SPSG)

MZAD.......... Mains Army Depot [*Germany*]

MZB............ Mocimboa da Praia [*Mozambique*] [*Airport symbol*] (AD)

MZB............ San Diego, CA [*Location identifier FAA*] (FAAL)

MZBZ.......... Belize/International [*Belize*] [*ICAO location identifier*] (ICLI)

MZC............ Mitzic [*Gabon*] [*Airport symbol*] (OAG)

MZCP.......... Mean Zonal Candlepower (IAA)

MZF............ Manganese Zinc Ferrite

MZF............ Mazirat [*France*] [*Seismograph station code, US Geological Survey*] (SEIS)

MZFR.......... Mehrzweck Forschungs [*Reactor*] [*Germany*] (NRCH)

MZFW......... Maximum Zero Fuel Weight [*Aviation*] (MCD)

MZG............ Makung [*Taiwan*] [*Airport symbol*] (OAG)

MZI............. Mopti [*Mali*] [*Airport symbol*] (OAG)

MZJ............ Marana, AZ [*Location identifier FAA*] (FAAL)

MZK............ Marakei [*Kiribati*] [*Airport symbol*] (OAG)

MZL............ Aerovias Montes Azules, SA de CV [*Mexico*] [*FAA designator*] (FAAC)

MZL............ Manizales [*Colombia*] [*Airport symbol*] (OAG)

MZL............ Muzzle (MSA)

MZM........... Metz [*France*] [*Airport symbol*] (OAG)

MZN........... Maruzen Co. Ltd. [*UTLAS symbol*]

MZN........... Minj [*New Guinea*] [*Airport symbol*] (AD)

MZN........... Mount Vernon Nazarene College, Mount Vernon, OH [*OCLC symbol*] (OCLC)

MZO........... Manzanillo [*Cuba*] [*Airport symbol*] (OAG)

MZO........... Mazie Landing [*Oklahoma*] [*Seismograph station code, US Geological Survey*] (SEIS)

MZOA.......... Masada of the Zionist Organization of America (EA)

MZON .... Multiple Zones International, Inc. [*NASDAQ symbol*] (SAG)

M-ZONE....... Manufacturing Zone (MHDB)

MZP............ Meta-Azidopyrimethamine [*Biochemistry*]

MZP............ Modulated Zone Plate (PDAA)

MZPI........... Microwave Zone Position Indicator (IAA)

MZQ........... Mozambique [*Mozambique*] [*Airport symbol*] (AD)

MZR........... Mazar-I-Sharif [*Afghanistan*] [*Airport symbol*] (OAG)

MZR........... Monroe, LA [*Location identifier FAA*] (FAAL)

MZR........... Multi-Zone Recording (CIST)

MZS........... Mahfooz Aviation [*Gambia*] [*FAA designator*] (FAAC)

MZS........... Master of Zoology Science (GAGS)

MZS........... Spokane, WA [*Location identifier FAA*] (FAAL)

MZ Sc........ Master of Zoological Science

MZSCS........ Martinek-Zaichkowsky Self-Concept Scale for Children [*Child development test*]

MZSH.......... Missionary Zelatrices of the Sacred Heart [*Roman Catholic women's religious order*]

MZsL .... Magyar Zsido Lexikon [*A publication*] (BJA)

MZT............ Mazatlan [*Mexico*] [*Airport symbol*] (OAG)

MZT............ Monozygotic Twins Reared Together [*Genetics*]

MZU........... Muzaffarpur [*India*] [*Airport symbol*] (AD)

MZV........... Magyar Zsidok Vilagszovetsege [*World Federation of Hungarian Jews*] (EAIO)

MZV........... Moline, IL [*Location identifier FAA*] (FAAL)

MZX........... Augusta, GA [*Location identifier FAA*] (FAAL)

MZX........... Massio [*Ethiopia*] [*Airport symbol*] (AD)

MZY........... Mzimba [*Malawi*] [*Airport symbol*] (AD)

MZZ........... Marion [*Indiana*] [*Airport symbol*] (AD)

MZZ........... Marion, IN [*Location identifier FAA*] (FAAL)

N
By Acronym

N	All India Reporter, Nagpur Series [*A publication*] (ILCA)
n	Amino [*As substituent on nucleoside*] [*Biochemistry*]
n	Amount of Substance [*Molecular quantity*] [*Symbol IUPAC*]
N	Asparagine [*Biochemistry*] (DAVI)
N	Avogadro Number [*Number of molecules in one gram-molecular weight of a substance*]
N	Carbon Star [*Astronomy*] (BARN)
N	Cementex [*Research code symbol*]
N	Digestum Novum [*A publication Authority cited in pre-1607 legal work*] (DSA)
N	Dr. Karl Thomae GmbH [*Germany*] [*Research code symbol*]
N	Dumb [*Auxiliary craft suffix*] [*British Navy*]
N	Educational Premises [*Public-performance tariff class*] [*British*]
N	Efficiency [*Physics*] (BARN)
N	Electron N-Type Semiconductor Material
N	Employment [*Economics*]
N	En [*Typography*] (WDAA)
n	En [*Printing measurement*] (WDMC)
N	Flying Boat [*Russian aircraft symbol*]
n	Footnote (DLA)
N	Haploid Chromosome Number (DOG)
N	Haploid Number [*Genetics*]
N	H. Lundbeck [*Denmark*] [*Research code symbol*]
N	INCO Ltd. [*Formerly, International Nickel Co. of Canada Ltd.*] [*NYSE symbol Toronto Stock Exchange symbol*] (SPSG)
n	[*An*] Indefinite Quantity [*Mathematics*] (ROG)
N	Knight [*Chess*]
N	Magnetic Flux [*Symbol*] (ROG)
N	Nail
N	Name
N	Nan [*Phonetic alphabet*] [*World War II*] (DSUE)
n	Nano [*A prefix meaning divided by one billion*] [*SI symbol*]
N	Naringenin [*Organic chemistry*]
N	Naris [*Nostril*] [*Pharmacy*]
N	Narrow
N	Nasal
N	National [*Screw threads*]
N	Nationalist (ROG)
N	Nationalist Party [*British Political party*]
N	National League [*Baseball*]
N	Native [*Ecology*]
N	Natural Division [*Geography*]
N	Naturalization (DNAB)
N	Natural Number (IDOE)
N	Natus [*Birth*] [*Latin*]
N	Nautical
N	Naval [*British military*] (DMA)
N	Navigation
N	Navigational Aids [*JETDS nomenclature*]
N	Navy
N	Nay [*Vote*]
N	Near [*Optics*] (WDAA)
N	Near the Nut (or Heel) of the Bow [*Music*] (ROG)
N	Necrotic
N	Need [*Psychology*]
n	Negative [*Crystal*]
N	Negro
N	Neisseria [*Medicine*]
N	Nematic Phase [*Physical chemistry*]
N	Nematocyst [*Zoology*]
N	Neper [*A unit on a natural logarithmic scale*] (DEN)
N	Nephew
N	Nepos [*Grandson*] [*Latin*]
N	Nervus [*Nerve*] [*Anatomy*]
N	Nested [*Freight*]
N	Nesting [*Ornithology*]
N	Net
N	Network [*FCC program source designation*] (NTCM)
n	Network (WDMC)
N	Neuraminidase [*An enzyme*]
N	Neurogenic Element
N	Neurology
N	Neuropathy [*Medicine*] (DAVI)
N	Neuter
N	Neutral
n	Neutral (MEC)
n	Neutron [*A nuclear particle*]
N	Neutron (NAKS)
N	Neutron Number [*Physics*] (DAVI)
N	Neutrophil [*Hematology*]
N	New [*Stock exchange term*] (SPSG)
N	New Issue [*Investment term*] (DFIT)
N	New Persian
N	News
n	News (WDMC)
N	Newspaper
N	News Program (NTCM)
N	Newton [*Symbol*] [*SI unit of force*]
N	New York State Library, Albany, NY [*Library symbol Library of Congress*] (LCLS)
N	New York Stock Exchange [*New York, NY*]
n	Next [*Computer science*] [*Telecommunications*]
N	Ngultrum [*Monetary unit*] [*Bhutan*] (BARN)
N	Nichrome (IAA)
N	Nicolaus Furiosus [*Flourished, 12th century*] [*Authority cited in pre-1607 legal work*] (DSA)
N	Nicotinamide [*Also, NAA*] [*Vitamin*]
N	Niece (ADA)
N	Nifedipine [*Pharmacology*]
N	Night [*Approach and landing charts*] [*Aviation*]
N	Night [*Broadcasting term*]
N	Night (WDMC)
N	Night Fighter [*When suffix to plane designation*] [*Navy*]
N	Night Game [*Baseball*]
N	Nighttime (NTCM)
N	Nitrogen [*Chemical element*]
N	No
N	Nocardia [*Genus of bacteria*] (MAE)
N	Nocte [*At Night*] [*Pharmacy*]
N	Nodal [*Oncology*]
N	Node [*Lymphatic*] [*Anatomy*]
N	Noise [*Broadcasting*]
N	Nomen [*Name*] [*Latin*]
N	Nominal [*Stock exchange term*] (SPSG)
N	Nominally Labeled [*Compound, with radioisotope*]
N	Nominative
N	None
N	Nonmalignant [*Of tumors*] [*Medicine*]
N	Nonne [*Globulin test*]
N	Nontactical [*Military*]
N	Noon
n	Noon (WDMC)
N	Norein [*Geology*]
N	Norland Potato
N	Norm (WDAA)
n	Normal [*Molecular structure*] [*Chemistry*]
N	Normal [*Solute concentration*] [*Chemistry*]
N	Normal Depth [*Earthquakes*]
N	Normal Horsepower
N	Normal Solution (DOG)
N	Norse [*Language, etc.*]
N	Norske Veritas [*Norwegian ship classification society*] (ROG)
N	North [*or Northern*]
n-----	North America [*MARC geographic area code Library of Congress*] (LCCP)
N	Northeastern Reporter [*Commonly cited NE*] [*A publication*] (DLA)
N	Northern Ireland Law Reports [*A publication*] (DLA)
N	Northgate Exploration Ltd. [*Gold producer*] [*Canada*]
N	North London [*Postcode*] (ODBW)
N	Northwestern Reporter [*Commonly cited NW*] [*A publication*] (DLA)
N	Norway [*IYRU nationality code*]
N	Noster [*Our*] [*Latin*]
N	Nostril (AAMN)
N	Not (DAVI)
N	Notative Speed (WDAA)
N	Note
n	Note (WDMC)
n	Noun (WDMC)
N	Noun
N	No Uniform [*For schoolgirls*] [*British*]
N	Novellae [*Novels*] [*New Constitutions of Justinian*] [*A publication*] (DLA)

N................. Novelty [*Insulation*]
N................. November [*Phonetic alphabet*] [*International*] (DSUE)
N................. Novice Slope [*Skiing*]
N................. Nu [*Thirteenth letter of the Greek alphabet*] (DAVI)
N................. Nuclear
N................. Nuclear Propelled [*When following vessel classification, as CAG(N)*] [*Navy*]
N................. [*A*] Nucleoside [*One-letter symbol; see Nuc*]
N................. Nucleus [*of a cell*] [*Biology*]
n................. Nucleus [*Psychology*]
N................. Nucleus (of Syllable) [*Linguistics*]
N................. Nullity [*Divorce cases*] [*British*] (ROG)
N................. Number
n................. Number [*Usually integer*] (IDOE)
N................. Number (of Bits) [*Computer science*] (ECII)
N................. Number of Molecules [*Symbol*] [*IUPAC*]
n................. Number of Observations [*Statistics*] (DAVI)
N................. Number (of Turns) [*Electronics*] (ECII)
N................. Numeric
N................. Nun [*Buoy*]
N................. Nunnery
N................. Nupta [*Married*] [*Latin*]
N................. Nurse (ADA)
N................. Nuts [*Phonetic alphabet*] [*Royal Navy World War I Pre-World War II*] (DSUE)
N................. Nylon (AAG)
N................. Nymph [*Entomology*]
N................. Nystatin [*Antifungal antibiotic*]
N................. Population Size [*Symbol*] (MAE)
n................. Principal Quantum Number [*Atomic physics*] (DEN)
n................. Probe [*Missile vehicle type symbol*]
n................. Refractive Index [*Symbol*] [*Physics*]
N................. Rockwell International Corp. [*ICAO aircraft manufacturer identifier*] (ICAO)
N................. Size of Sample [*Statistics*] (DAVI)
N................. Sound in Air [*JETDS nomenclature*]
N................. South African Law Reports, Natal Province Division [*1910-46*] [*A publication*] (DLA)
N................. Special Test, Permanent [*Aircraft classification letter*]
N................. Stauffer Chemical Co. [*Research code symbol*]
N................. Tilt Correction
N1E............. Nosed One Edge [*Lumber*] (DAC)
N₂................. Molecular Nitrogen [*Chemistry*] (DAVI)
N2............... Nitrogen
N2E............. Nosed Two Edges [*Lumber*] (DAC)
N2H4 .... Hydrazine (NAKS)
N2H04......... Nitrogen Peroxide (NAKS)
N2N .... Neighbor to Neighbor [*An association*] (EA)
N2N .... Project Neighbor to Neighbor (EA)
N₂0............. Nitrous Oxide [*An Anesthetic*] (DAVI)
N₂0:0₂........ Nitrous Oxide to Oxygen Ratio [*Anesthesiology*] (DAVI)
N3............... Cyclophosphamide, Vincristine, Triflurothymidine, Papaverine [*Antineoplastic drug regimen*] (DAVI)
N3F............. National Fantasy Fan Federation (EA)
N4A............. National Academic Athletic Advisors' Association (NTPA)
N4A............. National Association of Academic Advisors for Athletics (EA)
N4A............. National Association of Area Agencies on Aging [*Also, NAAAA*] (EA)
N4-HC......... National 4-H Council (EA)
N4WDA....... National 4 Wheel Drive Association (EA)
N/30........... Net in Thirty Days
N204........... Nitrogen Tetroxide (NAKS)
NA.............. Academician of the National Academy of Design, New York [*1825*] (NGC)
Na.............. Avogadro's Number [*Chemistry*] (DAVI)
NA.............. De Natura Animalium [*of Aelianus*] [*Classical studies*] (OCD)
Na.............. Exchangeable Body Sodium (AD)
NA.............. Nabisco Holdings'A' [*NYSE symbol*] (TTSB)
NA.............. Nabisco Holdings Corp. [*NYSE symbol*] (SAG)
NA.............. Nachrichtenabteilung [*Signal battalion*] [*German military - World War II*]
NA.............. Nachrichten-Aufklaerung [*Signal intelligence*] [*German military - World War II*]
NA.............. Nadir (WGA)
Na.............. Nahum [*Old Testament book*]
NA.............. Nailable [*Technical drawings*]
Na.............. Naira [*Monetary unit*] [*Nigeria*]
N/A............. Name and Address
NA.............. Namibia [*ANSI two-letter standard code*] (CNC)
nA.............. Nanoampere [*One billionth of an ampere*]
NA.............. Naphthalene Dicarboxylic Acid
NA.............. Naphthylacetamide [*Organic chemistry*]
NA.............. Naphthylamine [*Organic chemistry*]
NA.............. Napoleonic Association [*Enfield, Middlesex, England*] (EAIO)
NA.............. Narcolepsy Association [*British*] (DBA)
NA.............. Narcotics Anonymous (EA)
NA.............. Narrow Angle
NA.............. Nash Papyrus (BJA)
NA.............. National Academician
NA.............. National Academy (ROG)
NA.............. National Acme [*Thread*]
NA.............. National Action [*Australia*]
NA.............. National Aerospace Standards Committee (AAGC)
NA.............. National Airlines, Inc. [*ICAO designator*]
NA.............. National Airport [*Under control of BAA*] [*British*]
NA.............. National Alliance (EA)

NA.............. National Ambucs (EA)
NA.............. [*The*] National Archives [*of the United States*]
NA.............. National Army
NA.............. National Assistance [*British*]
NA.............. National Association [*National Bank*]
NA.............. National Bank of Canada [*Toronto Stock Exchange symbol Vancouver Stock Exchange symbol*]
NA.............. Nationale Aktion fuer Volk und Heimat [*National Action for People and Homeland*] [*Switzerland Political party*] (PPE)
NA.............. Natl Bk of Canada [*MS, exchange symbol*] (TTSB)
Na.............. Natrium [*Sodium*] [*Chemical element*]
NA.............. Natural Axis
NA.............. Naturally Aspirated [*Diesel engines*]
NA.............. Nautical Almanac
NA.............. Nautical Archaeology [*Oceanography*]
NA.............. Naval Academy
NA.............. Naval Accounts [*British*]
NA.............. Naval Aircraft
NA.............. Naval Airman [*Navy rating British*]
NA.............. Naval Air Systems Command Manual
NA.............. Naval Architect
NA.............. Naval Assistant [*Navy rating British*]
NA.............. Naval Attache [*Diplomacy*]
NA.............. Naval Auxiliary
NA.............. Naval Aviator
NA.............. Navigation Aid (IAA)
NA.............. Navion Aircraft Co. [*ICAO aircraft manufacturer identifier*] (ICAO)
NA.............. Navy Aircraft (IAA)
NA.............. Needle Aspiration [*Surgery*]
NA.............. Needs Assessment (OICC)
NA.............. Nelson Associates [*Also, an information service or system*] (IID)
NA.............. Neo-Assyrian [*or New Assyrian*] [*Language, etc.*] (BJA)
NA.............. Net Assessment Organization [*Navy*]
NA.............. Net Assets [*Banking*]
na.............. Netherlands Antilles [*MARC country of publication code Library of Congress*] (LCCP)
NA.............. Network Adapter (MCD)
NA.............. Network Administrator (DMAA)
NA.............. Neuraminidase (DMAA)
NA.............. Neuraminidase Activity [*An enzyme*]
NA.............. Neurologic Age (DMAA)
NA.............. Neuropathology [*Medicine*] (DHSM)
NA.............. Neurotics Anonymous (NADA)
NA.............. Neutral Axis
NA.............. Neutralizing Antibody [*Immunochemistry*]
NA.............. Neutrophil Antibody [*Immunology*] (DAVI)
NA.............. New Account
NA.............. New African [*A publication*]
NA.............. New Age [*Later, LR*] [*An association*] (EA)
NA.............. New Alternative Party [*Venezuela Political party*]
NA.............. New Associations [*Later, NAP*] [*A publication*]
NA.............. Newsletter Association (EA)
NA.............. Newton Abbot [*British depot code*]
NA.............. Next Action (NASA)
NA.............. Next Assembly
NA.............. Ney-Allen [*Astronomy*]
NA.............. Nicotinic Acid [*Biochemistry*]
NA.............. Night Alarm [*Telecommunications*] (TEL)
NA.............. Night Answer (WDMC)
NA.............. Nitrobenzene Association [*Defunct*] (EA)
NA.............. Nizamut Adalat Reports [*India*] [*A publication*] (DLA)
NA.............. No Abnormality [*Medicine*] (MAE)
NA.............. No Access [*Telecommunications*] (TEL)
NA.............. No Account [*Banking*]
N/A............. No Action
N/A............. No Advice [*Business term*]
N/A............. No Alternative (DAVI)
NA.............. No Answer (WDMC)
NA.............. No Approval Required (MHDW)
NA.............. No Assets (AFIT)
NA.............. Noctes Atticae [*of Gellius*] [*Classical studies*] (OCD)
NA.............. Nomina Anatomica [*System of anatomical terminology*]
N/A............. Nonacceptance [*Business term*]
NA.............. Nonacquiescence [*Legal term*] (DLA)
NA.............. Nonactivated
NA.............. Nonalcoholic
NA.............. Non Allocatur [*Legal*] [*Latin*] (ROG)
NA.............. Non-Attached [*European political movement*] (ECON)
NA.............. Nonattainment (COE)
NA.............. Nonattendance
NA.............. Nora Alice [*DoD satellite*]
NA.............. Noradrenaline [*Also known as NE: Norepinephrine*] [*Biochemistry*]
NA.............. Normal Adult
NA.............. Normal Alarm (SAA)
NA.............. Normally Aspirated [*Automotive engineering*]
NA.............. North Africa
NA.............. North America
NA.............. Northanger Abbey [*Novel by Jane Austen*]
NA.............. North Atlantic Industries
NA.............. Northern Alberta Railways Co. (IIA)
NA.............. Nostra Aetate [*Declaration on the Relationship of the Church to the Non-Christian Religions*] [*Vatican II document*]
NA.............. Nostro Account [*Our Account*] [*An account maintained by a bank with a bank in a foreign country*]
N/A............. Not Above

NA	Not Accurate (CIST)
NA	Not Admitted [Medicine] (MAE)
N/A	Not Affected (AAG)
NA	Not Allowed
NA	Not And [Logical operator] [Computer science]
NA	Not Applicable
n/a	Not Applicable (WA)
NA	Not Appropriated
NA	Not Assigned
NA	Not Authorized
NA	Not Available
n/a	Not Available (WA)
NA	Noticias Argentinas SA [News agency] [Argentina] (EY)
NA	Novice Agility
NA	Nozzle Assembly
NA	Nuclear Antibody (DMAA)
NA	Nucleic Acid [Biochemistry]
NA	Nucleus Accumbens [Neuroanatomy]
NA	Nucleus Ambiguus [Neuroanatomy]
NA	Nueva Alternativa [Venezuela Political party] (EY)
NA	Number of Aimpoints [Military]
NA	Numerical Analysis [Computer science] (BUR)
NA	Numerical Aperture [Microscopy]
NA	Nurse Anesthetist (AAMN)
NA	Nurse's Aide
NA	Nurses Almanac
NA	Nursing Assistant
NA	Nursing Auxiliary [British]
NA	Nurturant-Authoritative [Psychotherapy]
NA	Nutrient Agar [Microbiology]
NA	Organon, Inc. [Research code symbol]
Na	Sodium [Chemical element] (AAMN)
nA	Transitional Antarctic Coastal Air Mass [Meteorology] (BARN)
NA 1SL	Naval Assistant to the First Sea Lord [British military] (DMA)
NAA	1-Naphthaleneacetic Acid (LDT)
NAA	Naalehu [Hawaii] [Seismograph station code, US Geological Survey Closed] (SEIS)
NAA	Nanny Academy of America [Defunct] (EA)
NAA	Naphthaleneacetic Acid [Biochemistry] (DAVI)
NAA	Naphthylacetic [or Napthaleneacetic] Acid [Organic chemistry]
NAA	Narrabri [Australia Airport symbol] (OAG)
NAA	Narrow-Angle Acquisition
NAA	National Academy of Arbitrators (EA)
NAA	National Academy of Astrology [Defunct] (EA)
NAA	National Aeronautic Association (NADA)
NAA	National Aeronautic Association of the USA (EA)
NAA	National Aeronautics and Space Administration, Washington, DC [OCLC symbol] (OCLC)
NAA	National Aerosol Association (EA)
NAA	National Aftermarket Audit Co.
NAA	National Aggregates Association (NTPA)
NAA	National Airspace Analysis [FAA] (TAG)
NAA	National Aldrich Association (EA)
NAA	National Alumni Association (EA)
NAA	National Apartment Association (EA)
NAA	National Arborist Association (EA)
NAA	National Archery Association of the United States (EA)
NAA	National Ash Association (EA)
NAA	National Association of Accountants [Montvale, NJ] (EA)
NAA	National Auctioneers Association (EA)
NAA	National Automobile Association (NADA)
NAA	National Oceanic and Atmospheric Administration [Department of Commerce ICAO designator] (FAAC)
NAA	Natural Areas Association (EA)
NAA	Naval Air Arm [British]
NAA	Naval Airship Association (EA)
NAA	Naval Attache for Air
NAA	Neckwear Association of America (EA)
NAA	Network Analysis Area [Space Flight Operations Facility, NASA]
NAA	Neuron Activation Analysis [Neurology] (DAVI)
NAA	Neutral Amino Acid [Biochemistry]
NAA	Neutron Activation Analysis
NAA	New Art Association (EA)
NAA	Newsletter Association of America (EA)
NAA	Newspaper Association of America [Reston, VA] (WDMC)
NAA	Nicotinic Acid Amide [Also, N]
NAA	Nigerian-American Alliance (EA)
NAA	Nitroanthranilic Acid [Organic chemistry]
NAA	No Apparent Abnormalities [Medicine]
NAA	Nocturnal Acid Accumulation [Botany]
NAA	Nonattainment Area [Environmental Protection Agency] (EPA)
NAA	Nord Africa Aviazione
NAA	North American Aviation, Inc. [Later, Rockwell International Corp.]
NAA	North Atlantic Alliance
NAA	North Atlantic Assembly
NAA	Northern Attack Area
NAA	Norway-America Association (EA)
NAA	Notable Asian Americans [A publication]
NAA	Not Always Afloat [Shipping]
naa	Not Always Afloat [Shipping] (ODBW)
NAA	Nuclear Activation Analysis (PDAA)
NAAA	National Agricultural Aviation Association (EA)
NAAA	National Alarm Association of America (EA)
NAAA	National Alliance of Athletic Associations [Defunct] (EA)
NAAA	National Association of American Academicians (NADA)
NAAA	National Association of Arab Americans (EA)
NAAA	National Auto Auction Association [Lincoln, NE] (EA)
NAAAA	National Association for the Advancement of Aardvarks in America [Defunct] (EA)
NAAAA	National Association of Area Agencies on Aging [Also, N4A] (EA)
NAAACC	National Association of Antique Automobile Clubs of Canada
NAAACPA	National Association of Asian American Certified Public Accountants (EA)
NAAAID	National Association of Americans of Asian Indian Descent (EA)
NAAAP	National Association of Asian-American Professionals (EA)
NAAAP	North American Association of Alcoholism Programs [Later, ADPA] (EA)
NAAAS	National Association for Applied Arts and Sciences (EA)
NAAAS	National Association of African American Studies (NTPA)
NAAASL	National Association of African American Students of Law (EA)
NAAB	National Architectural Accrediting Board (EA)
NAAB	National Archival Appraisal Board [Canada]
NAAB	National Association of Animal Breeders (EA)
NAABA	National Association for the Advancement of the Black Aged (EA)
NAABAVE	National Association for the Advancement of Black Americans in Vocational Education (EA)
NAABC	National Association American Business Clubs [High Point, NC]
NAABCV	National Association American Balloon Corps Veterans (EA)
NAABI	National Association of Alcoholic Beverage Importers [Later, NABI] (EA)
NAABSA	Not Always Afloat but Safe Aground [Shipping]
NAAC	National Adoption Assistance Center (EA)
NAAC	National Agricultural Advisory Commission (NADA)
NAAC	National Air Access Council (NTPA)
NAAC	National Association for Ambulatory Care (EA)
NAAC	National Association of Agricultural Contractors [British] (BI)
NAAC	National Association of Avon Collectors
NAAC	Navy Aeroballistics Advisory Committee (MCD)
NAAC	North American Adoption Congress (EA)
NAACC	National Association for American Composers and Conductors (EA)
NAACC	National Association of Angling and Casting Clubs [Later, ACA]
NAACC	Northwest Athletic Association of Community Colleges (PSS)
NAACE	National Association of Advisers in Computer Education (AIE)
NAACLS	National Accrediting Agency for Clinical Laboratory Sciences (EA)
NAACO	National Association of American Community Organizations (EA)
NAACOG	NAACOG: the Organization for Obstetric, Gynecologic, and Neonatal Nurses [Formerly, Nurses Association of the American College of Obstetricians and Gynecologists] (EA)
NAACP	National Association for the Advancement of Colored People (EA)
NAACP	Neoplasia, Allergy, Addison's Disease, Collagen Disease, and Parasites [Medicine]
NAACPA	National Association of Asian American Certified Public Accountants (MHDB)
NAACS	National Association of Accredited Cosmetology Schools (EA)
NAACS	National Association of Adult College Students (EA)
NAACS	National Association of Aircraft and Communications Suppliers [Defunct] (EA)
NAACSS	National Association for the Accreditation of Colleges and Secondary Schools (EA)
NAACSW	North American Association of Christians in Social Work [Later, NACSW] (EA)
NAACT	National Association of Assessors and Collectors of Taxes [A union] [British]
NAAD	National Association of Aluminum Distributors (EA)
NAAD	Navajo Army Depot [Arizona] (AABC)
NAAD	Nicotinic Acid Adenine Dinucleotide [Biochemistry]
NAAD	North American Association for the Diaconate (EA)
NAADAA	National Antique and Art Dealers Association of America (EA)
NAADAC	National Association of Alcoholism and Drug Abuse Counselors (EA)
NAADC	National Association of Art and Design Companies (EA)
NAADC	North American Air Defense Command (AAG)
NAADD	National Association of Athletic Development Directors
NAADI	National Association of Approved Driving Instructors [British] (DBA)
NAADS	New Army Authorization Documents System (AABC)
NAADS	New Army Automatic Data System
NAAE	National Association of Aeronautical Examiners (EA)
NAAE	National Association of Afro-American Educators
NAAE	National Association of Agriculture Employees (EA)
NAAE	Nordic Association for Adult Education (EAIO)
NAAE	North American Academy of Ecumenists (EA)
NAAEE	North American Association of Environmental Educators (EA)
NAAF	National Alopecia Areata Foundation (EA)
NAAF	Naval Auxiliary Air Facility
NAAF	New Amino Acid Formula [Nutrition]
NAAF	North African Air Force [World War II]
NAAFA	National Association of Agricultural Fair Agencies (NTPA)
NAAFA	National Association to Advance Fat Acceptance (EA)
Naafi	Navy, Army & Air Force Institute (WDAA)
NAAFI	Navy, Army, and Air Force Institutes [Responsible for clubs, canteens, and provision of some items for messing of British armed forces]
NAAFW	National Association of Air Forces Women
NAAG	N-Acetylaspartylglutamic Acid [Biochemistry]
NAAG	National Association of Attorneys General (EA)
NAAG	NATO Army Advisory Group (NATG)
NAAG	NATO Army Armaments Group (AABC)
NAAG	Nordic Association of Applied Geophysics (EA)
NAAG	North African Adjutant General [World War II]
NAAGA	North African Adjutant General, Analysis and Control Division [World War II]

NAAGC.........	North African Adjutant General, Casualty Branch [*World War II*]
NAAGE.........	North African Adjutant General, Personnel Division [*World War II*]
NAAGG.........	North African Adjutant General, Executive Division [*World War II*]
NAAGO.........	North African Adjutant General, Operations Division [*World War II*]
NAAGP.........	North African Adjutant General, Postal Division [*World War II*]
NAAGS.........	North African Adjutant General, Statistical Division [*World War II*]
NAAHE.........	National Association for the Advancement of Humane Education [*LA NAHEE*] (EA)
NAAHL.........	National Association of Affordable Housing Lenders (NTPA)
NAAHP.........	National Association of Advisors for the Health Professions (EA)
NAAHSC......	North American Association of Hunter Safety Coordinators
NAAI...........	National Alliance of Arts and Industry
NAAI...........	National Association of Accountants in Insolvencies (EA)
NAA-ICIF.....	North American Association of the ICIF [*International Cooperative Insurance Federation*] [*Detroit, MI*] (EA)
NAAIS........	National Aircraft Accident Investigation School [*FAA*]
NAAIS.........	North American Association of Inventory Services [*Greensboro, NC*] (EA)
NAAJ..........	National Association of Agricultural Journalists (NTPA)
NAAJHHA....	North American Association of Jewish Homes and Housing for the Aging (EA)
NAAJS	National Academy for Adult Jewish Studies (EA)
NAAK	Nerve Agent Antidote Kit [*Military*] (RDA)
NAAL..........	National Alliance for Animal Legislation [*Defunct*] (EA)
NAAL..........	North American Academy of Liturgy (EA)
NAAL..........	North American Aerodynamic Laboratory [*Wind tunnel*] (NASA)
NAALBWV...	National Association for the Advancement of Leboyer's Birth Without Violence (EA)
NAALC........	National Afro-American Labor Council [*Later, NALC*]
NAALS	Navigational Aids and Landing Systems (MCD)
NAAM	National Association of Anvil Makers [*A union*] [*British*]
NAAM	National Association of Architectural Metal Manufacturers (IAA)
NAAM	North American Aliyah Movement (EA)
NAAMA	National Agricultural Advertising and Marketing Association [*Later, NAMA*]
NAAMACC...	National Association for the Accreditation of Martial Arts Colleges and Curriculum (EA)
NAAMIC.......	National Association of Automotive Mutual Insurance Companies [*Later, American Insurers Highway Safety Alliance*] (EA)
NAAMM	National Association of Architectural Metal Manufacturers (EA)
NAAMM	North American Academy of Musculoskeletal Medicine (EA)
NAAMO	National Association Agricultural Marketing Officials (NTPA)
NAAN..........	National Advertising Agency Network [*New York, NY*] (EA)
NAAN..........	North American Advertising Agency Network (NTPA)
NAAN..........	Nuclear Arms Alert Network [*Defunct*] (EA)
NAANACM...	National Association for the Advancement of Native American Composers and Musicians
NAANAD	National Association of Anorexia Nervosa and Associated Disorders (DHP)
NAANBW......	National Amalgamated Association of Nut and Bolt Workers [*A union*] [*British*]
NAAND.........	North American Association for the Diaconate (EA)
NA & D C & O...	Selection of Cases Decided in the Native Appeal and Divorce Court, Cape and Orange Free State [*A publication*] (DLA)
NA & DT & N...	Transvaal and Natal Native Appeal and Divorce Court Decisions [*A publication*] (DLA)
NA & G........	Norgulf Lines (North Atlantic & Gulf) (AD)
NA & G........	North Atlantic & Gulf Steamship Co. (MHDW)
Na & K	Sodium and Potassium [*Urine test*] [*Biochemistry*] (DAVI)
Na & KSP.....	Sodium and Potassium Spot [*Urine Test*] (DAVI)
NAANGHT	National Association of Air National Guard Health Technicians (EA)
NAANP........	National Alliance for the Advancement of Nodnarbian Philosophy (EA)
NAAO	National Association of Amateur Oarsmen [*Later, USRA*] (EA)
NAAO	National Association of Artists' Organizations (EA)
NAAO	National Association of Assessing Officers [*Later, IAAO*]
NAAO	Navy Area Audit Office [*London*]
NAAO	North American Automotive Operations [*Ford Motor Co.*]
NAAOJ	National Association for the Advancement of Orthodox Judaism (EA)
NAAOP	National Association for the Advancement of Older People (EA)
NAAOSE.......	National Association of Advisory Officers Special Education [*British*] (DBA)
NAAP..........	N-Acetylaminophenazone [*Organic chemistry*]
NAAP..........	National Association for Accreditation in Psychoanalysis (EA)
NAAP..........	National Association fot the Advancement of Psychoanalysis (NTPA)
NAAP..........	National Association of Activity Professionals (EA)
NAAP..........	National Association of Advertising Publishers [*Later, AFCP*] (EA)
NAAP..........	National Association of Apnea Professionals (EA)
NAAP..........	Newport Army Ammunition Plant (AABC)
NAAPABAC...	National Association for the Advancement of Psychoanalysis and the American Boards for Accreditation and Certification (EA)
NAAPABAP...	National Association for the Advancement of Psychoanalysis and the American Board for Accreditation in Psychoanalysis (EA)
NAAPAE.......	National Association for Asian and Pacific American Education (EA)
NAAPHE.......	National Association for the Advancement of Private Higher Education [*Later, United Student Association*] (EA)
NAAPI.........	National Association of Accountants for the Public Interest [*Later, API*] (EA)
NAAPM	National Association for the Advancement of Perry Mason (EA)
NAAPPB.......	National Association of Amusement Parks, Pools, and Beaches [*Later, IAAPA*]
NAAPS........	Nozzle Actuator Auxiliary Power Supply (SAA)
NAAQS........	National Ambient Air Quality Standards [*Environmental Protection Agency*]
NAAR..........	National Association of Advertising Representatives (DGA)
NAARD.........	North American Aviation Rocketdyne Division (SAA)
Naar Elec.....	Naar on Suffrage and Elections [*A publication*] (DLA)
NAARFC.......	National Association of Auto Racing Fan Clubs
NAARMC.......	National Association of Auto Racing Memorabilia Collectors (EA)
NAARPR	National Alliance Against Racist and Political Repression (EA)
NAARS........	National Automated Accounting Research System [*American Institute of Certified Public Accountants*] [*Database*] [*Information service or system*] (IID)
NAAS	National Academy of American Scholars (EA)
NAAS	National Agricultural Advisory Service [*Later, ADAS*] [*British*]
NAAS	National Air Audit System [*Environmental Protection Agency*] (GFGA)
NAAS	National Anorexic Aid Society (EA)
NAAS	National Association of Academies of Science (EA)
NAAS	National Association of Art Services [*Later, NAADC*] (EA)
NAAS	National Aviation Assistance
NAAS	Naval Area Audit Service
NAAS	Naval Auxiliary Air Station
NAAS	Navy Aircraft Accounting System
NAAS	Navy Area Audit Service (DNAB)
NAAS	NORAD Attack Alert System (MCD)
NAAS	Nordic Association for American Studies (EAIO)
NAAS	North American Apiotherapy Society (EA)
NAASC........	North American Aviation Science Center (SAA)
NAASC........	Northwest African Air Service Command [*World War II*]
NAASD........	North American Aviation Space Division (SAA)
NAASER.......	National Association of American School Employees and Retirees (EA)
NAASERLDC...	National Association of American School Employees and Retirees Legal Defense Counsel (EA)
NAASFEP	National Association of Administrators of State and Federal Education Programs (EA)
NAASL	North American Academy of the Spanish Language (EA)
NAASLANT...	Navy Auxiliary Air Stations, Atlantic
NAASLN	National Association for Adults with Special Learning Needs (EA)
NAASMWB..	National Amalgamated Association of Sheet Metal Workers and Blaziers [*A union*] [*British*]
NAASPAC.....	Navy Auxiliary Air Stations, Pacific
NAASPL	North American Association of State and Provincial Lotteries (EA)
NAASR........	National Association for Armenian Studies and Research (EA)
NAASR........	North American Association for the Study of Jean-Jacques Rousseau (EA)
NAASS	North American Association of Summer Sessions (EA)
NAASW	Nonacoustic Antisubmarine Warfare [*Military*]
NAAT	National Association of Agricultural Teachers [*Australia*]
NAAT	Naval Air Advance Training (SAA)
NAATA	National Asian American Telecommunications Association (EA)
NAATC	Naval Air Advanced Training Command
NAATD	North-American Association of Telecommunications Dealers (NTPA)
NAATP	National Association of Addiction Treatment Providers (EA)
NAATP	National Association of Alcoholism Treatment Programs (EA)
NAATPWB...	National Amalgamated Association of Tin Plate Workers and Blaziers [*A union*] [*British*]
NAATS......	National Association of Air Traffic Specialists (EA)
NAATS......	National Association of Auto Trim Shops (EA)
NAATTFO	National Association of Alcohol and Tobacco Tax Field Officers
NAAUS........	National Archery Association of the United States (NADA)
NAAUSA......	National Association of Assistant United States Attorneys (NTPA)
NAAUTC	National Amateur Athletic Union Taekwondo Committee [*Later, NAAUTUUSA*] (EA)
NAAUTUUSA...	National AAU [*Amateur Athletic Union*] Taekwondo Union of the United Statesof America [*Formerly, NAAUTC*] (EA)
NAAV	National Alliance Against Violence (EA)
NAAV	National Association of Atomic Veterans (EA)
NAAV	North American Association of Ventriloquists (EA)
NAAW	National Association of Accordion Wholesalers [*Defunct*] (EA)
NAAWER......	National Association of Arc Welding Equipment Repairers [*British*] (DBA)
NAAWFS......	Naval Air All Weather Flight Squadron
NAAWP.......	National Association for the Advancement of White People [*Defunct*] (EA)
NAAWS........	NATO Anti-Air Warfare System (DOMA)
NAAWS........	NORAD Automatic Attack Warning System (TEL)
NAAWS........	North American Association of Wardens and Superintendents (EAIO)
NAAWUL......	National Agricultural and Allied Workers' Union of Liberia (IMH)
NAB............	Mina Airline Company [*Egypt*] [*FAA designator*] (FAAC)
Nab.............	Nabatean (BJA)
NAB............	National Acoustics Board (MUGU)
NAB............	National Advisory Board (ACII)
NAB............	National Advisory Body [*British*]
NAB............	National Aircraft Beacon
NAB............	National Alliance of Business [*Washington, DC*] (EA)
NAB............	National Alliance of Businessmen (NADA)
NAB............	National Apex Body [*India*] (BUAC)
NAB............	National Associated Businessmen [*Defunct*] (EA)
NAB............	National Association of Bioengineers [*Defunct*] (EA)
NAB............	National Association of Boards of Examiners for Nursing Home Administrators (EA)
NAB............	National Association of Bookmakers Ltd. [*British*] (BI)
NAB............	National Association of Broadcasters (EA)
NAB............	National Audience Board [*An association*] (NTCM)
NAB............	National Australia Bank ADS [*NYSE symbol*] (SPSG)
NAB............	Natl Australia Bk ADR [*NYSE symbol*] (TTSB)
NAB............	Naval Advanced Base
NAB............	Naval Air Base
NAB............	Naval Amphibious Base

NAB	Navigational Aid to Bombing [*Air Force*]
NAB	Needle Aspiration Biopsy [*Surgery*]
NAB	Net Asset Backing
NAB	New American Bible
NAB	News Agency of Burma
NAB	Newspaper Advertising Bureau [*New York, NY*] (EA)
NAB	Nickel Alkaline Battery
NAB	Nigeria-Arab Bank Ltd.
NAB	Nitrosoanabasine [*Organic chemistry*]
NAB	Non-A, Non-B [*Hepatitis*] [*Infectious diseases*] (DAVI)
NAB	None of the Above
NAB	North American Biologicals, Inc.
NAB	Not Above [*Aviation*]
NAB	Novarsenobenzene (DMAA)
NAB	Nuclear Air Burst
NAB	Nuclear Assembly Building
NAB	Nut and Bolt
NAB$2CC	National Association of Bicentennial $2 Cancellation Collectors (EA)
NAB A	NAB Asset Corp. [*Associated Press*] (SAG)
NABA	National Alliance of Black Americans
NABA	National Amateur Basketball Association (EA)
NABA	National Association of Black Accountants [*Washington, DC*] (EA)
NABA	National Association of Breweriana Advertising (EA)
NABA	Naval Amphibious Base Annex
NABA	Nitro-(amino)butyric Acid
NABA	North American Ballet Association [*Defunct*] (EA)
NABA	North American Benefit Association [*Port Huron, MI*] (EA)
NABA	North American Bungee Association
NABA	North American Butterfly Association
NABA	Woman's Life Insurance Society
NABAC	National Association for Bank Auditors and Comptrollers [*Later, BAI*] (EA)
NABARD	National Bank for Agricultural and Rural Development [*India*] (BUAC)
NABAS	National Association of Ballon Suppliers (BUAC)
NABAS	National Association of Balloon Artists and Suppliers [*Great Britain*]
NABATRA	Naval Air Basic Training Center
NABB	National Association for Better Broadcasting (EA)
NABB	National Association of Barber Boards (EA)
NABB	National Association of Business Brokers (EA)
NABBA	National Amateur Body Building Association [*British*] (BI)
NABBA	North American Brass Band Association (EA)
NABBEA	National Association of Boards of Barbers Examiners of America [*Later, NABB*] (EA)
NABBS	National Association of Bench and Bar Spouses (EA)
NABC	NAB Asset Corp. [*NASDAQ symbol*] (SAG)
NABC	National Association of Basketball Coaches of the United States (EA)
NABC	National Association of Bingo Clubs [*British*] (BI)
NABC	National Association of Boys' Clubs [*British*]
NABC	Normative Adaptive Behavior Checklist (TES)
NABC	North American Blueberry Council (EA)
NABCA	National Alcoholic Beverage Control Association (EA)
NABCA	National Association for Bank Cost Analysis (EA)
NABCA	National Association for Bank Cost and Management Accounting (EA)
NABCA	National Association of Black Catholic Administrators (EA)
NABCE	National Association of Black Consulting Engineers (EA)
NABCJ	National Association of Blacks in Criminal Justice (EA)
NABCM	National Association of Baby Carriage Manufacturers (EA)
NABCM	National Association of Brattice Cloth Manufacturers (EA)
NABCO	National Alliance of Breast Cancer Organizations (EA)
NABCO	National Association of Black County Officials (EA)
NABCO	National Association of Building Cooperatives [*Ireland*] (BUAC)
NABCO	Nippon Air Brake Co. Ltd. [*Tokyo, Japan*]
NAB curve	National Association of Broadcasters Curve (MED)
NABD	National Association of Bank Directors [*Later, ASBD*] (EA)
NABD	National Association of Blood Donors (BUAC)
NABD	National Association of Brick Distributors (EA)
NABD	Naval Advanced Base Depot
NABDC	National Association of Blueprint and Diazotype Coaters [*Later, ARMM*]
NABDCC	North American Band Directors Coordinating Committee (EA)
NABE	National Association for Bilingual Education (EA)
NABE	National Association of Bar Executives (EA)
NABE	National Association of Biological Engineering
NABE	National Association of Boards of Education (EA)
NABE	National Association of Book Editors [*Defunct*] (EA)
NABE	National Association of Business Economists (EA)
NABE	National Association of Business Education (IAA)
NABE	Nuclear Air Burst Effect
NABEA	North American Bicycle Exhibitor Association [*Defunct*] (EA)
NABER	National Association of Business and Educational Radio (EA)
NABESS	National Association of Business Education State Supervisors [*Stillwater, OK*] (EA)
NABET	National Association Broadcast Employees and Technicians (EA)
NABF	National Alliance of Black Feminists (EA)
NABF	National Amateur Baseball Federation (EA)
NABF	North American Baptist Fellowship (EA)
NABF	North American Boxing Federation (EA)
NABG	National Association of Blacks within Government (EA)
NABGG	National Association of Black Geologists and Geophysicists (EA)
NABHP	National Association of Black Hospitality Professionals (EA)
NABI	NABI, Inc. [*NASDAQ symbol*] (SAG)
NABI	National Association of Beverage Importers (EA)
NABI	National Association of Biblical Instructors [*Later, American Academy of Religion*] (EA)

NABI	National Association of Bunco Investigators
NABI	North American Biologicals, Inc. (EFIS)
NABIL	Nepal Arab Bank Ltd. (BUAC)
NABIM	National Association of Band Instrument Manufacturers (EA)
NABIM	National Association of British and Irish Millers [*Incorporated*] (DBA)
NABio	North American Biologicals, Inc. [*Associated Press*] (SAG)
NABIR	Natural and Accelerated Bioremediation Research [*Department of Energy*]
NABIS	National Association of Business and Industrial Saleswomen [*Denver, CO*] (EA)
NABIS	National Biological Survey
NABISCO	National Biscuit Co. [*Acronym now used as company name*]
NabisH	Nabisco Holdings Corp. [*Associated Press*] (SAG)
NABJ	National Association of Black Journalists (EA)
NAB-JOBS	National Alliance of Business - Job Opportunities in the Business Sector (OICC)
NABL	National Association of Bond Lawyers (EA)
NABL	National Association of Builders' Labourers [*A union*] [*British*]
NABLOC	Brussels Tariff Nomenclature for the Latin American Free Trade Association (BARN)
NABLT	National Association of Business Law Teachers [*Later, NBLC*] (EA)
NABM	National Association of Bedding Manufacturers [*Later, ISPA*] (EA)
NABM	National Association of Biscuit Manufacturers (BUAC)
NABM	National Association of Black Manufacturers (EA)
NABM	National Association of Blouse Manufacturers (EA)
NABM	National Association of Boating Magazines [*Defunct*] (EA)
NABM	National Association of Boat Manufacturers (EA)
NABM	National Association of Book Manufacturers [*Defunct*] (EA)
NABM	National Association of British Manufacturers
NABM	National Association of Building Manufacturers [*Later, HMC*] (EA)
NABMA	National Association of British Market Authorities
NABMCC	National Association of Black and Minority Chambers of Commerce [*Later, NBCC*] (EA)
NABMO	NATO Bullpup Management Office [*Missiles*] (NATG)
NABMP	National Association of Black Media Producers
NABO	National Alliance of Black Organizations (EA)
NABO	National Association of Boat Owners (BUAC)
NABO	North Atlantic Biocultural Organization [*A research cooperative*]
NABOB	National Association of Black Owned Broadcasters (EA)
NABOM	National Association of Building Owners and Managers [*Later, BOMA*] (EA)
NABOR	National Association of Bank Club Organization
Nabors	Nabors Industries, Inc. [*Associated Press*] (SAG)
NABP	National Association of Black Professors (EA)
NABP	National Association of Boards of Pharmacy (EA)
NABP	National Association of Book Publishers (NADA)
NABPAC	National Association of Business Political Action Committees (EA)
NABPARS	Navy Automatic Broadcasting, Processing, and Routing System (NG)
NABPLEX	National Association of Boards of Pharmacy Licensure Examination
NABPO	NATO Bullpup Production Organization [*Missiles*] (NATG)
NABPP	National Association of Black Procurement Professionals (NTPA)
NABPR	National Association of Baptist Professors of Religion (EA)
NABPS	National Association of Business and Industrial Saleswomen (NTPA)
NABPULP	National Book Pulping Centre (BUAC)
NABR	National Association for BioMedical Research (EA)
NABR	National Association of Baby Sitter Registries [*Later, NASR*] (EA)
NABR	National Association of Basketball Referees (NTPA)
NABR	National Association of Beverage Retailers (NTPA)
NABR	Natural Bridges National Monument
NaBr	Sodium Bromide [*Pharmacology*] (DAVI)
NABREP	National Association of Black Real Estate Professionals (EA)
NABRT	National Association for Better Radio and Television (NADA)
NABRTI	National Association of Bar-Related Title Insurers [*San Diego, CA*] (EA)
NABS	National Advertising Benevolent Society [*British*]
NABS	National AIDS Behavioral Survey
NABS	National Alliance of Blind Students (EA)
NABS	National Association of Bank Servicers (EA)
NABS	National Association of Barber Schools [*Later, NABSS*] (EA)
NABS	National Association of Bereavement Services (BUAC)
NABS	National Association of Black Students
NABS	National Association of Breeders Services (DBA)
NABS	National Association of Business Services [*Baldwin, NY*] (EA)
NABS	National Association of Buying Services (EA)
NABS	NATO Airborne SATCOM (MCD)
NABS	Nordic Association for British Studies (BUAC)
NABS	Normal Abdominal Bowel Sound [*Medicine*] (CPH)
NABS	Normoactive Bowel Sounds [*Gastroenterology*] (DAVI)
NABS	North American Benthological Society (EA)
NABS	North American Blue-Bird Society (EA)
NABS	Nuclear-Armed Bombardment Satellite [*Study*] [*Air Force*] (AAG)
NABSC	National Association of Building Service Contractors [*Later, BSCA*]
NABSCAN	National Advertised Brands Scanning Reports [*Research project*]
NABSE	National Alliance of Black School Educators (EA)
NABS/GMF	NATO Airbase Satellite/Ground Mobile Force (MCD)
NABSMSW	National Alliance of Black Salesmen and Saleswomen (NTPA)
NABSP	National Association of Blue Shield Plans [*Later, BCBSA*] (EA)
NABSS	National Alliance of Black School Superintendents (AEE)
NABSS	National Association of Barber Styling Schools (EA)
NABST	National Advisory Board on Science and Technology [*Canada*]
NABSTP	Navy Adult Basic Skills Training Program (NVT)
NABSW	National Association of Black Social Workers (EA)
NABT	National Association of Bankruptcy Trustees (EA)
NABT	National Association of Biology Teachers (EA)
NABT	National Association of Black Professors (BUAC)

NABT	National Association of Blind Teachers (EA)
NABTA	National Association of Business Travel Agents (EA)
NABTC	National Associated Building Trades Council [*A union*] [*British*]
NABTC	Naval Air Base Training Command
NABTE	National Association for Business Teacher Education [*Reston, VA*] (EA)
NABTFP	National Association of Black Television and Film Producers (NTCM)
NABTO	National Association of Bar and Tavern Owners (NTPA)
NABTRACOM	Naval Air Basic Training Command (DNAB)
NABTS	National Alliance Building Trades Society [*A union*] [*British*]
NABTS	National Association of Broadcast Transmission Standards (PCM)
NABTS	North American Basic Teletext Specification (WDMC)
NABTS	North American Braodcast Teletext Standard (OSI)
NABTS	North American Broadcast Teletext Standard (NTCM)
NABTTI	National Association of Business Teacher-Training Institutions
NABU	Naval Advanced Base Unit
NABU	Nonadjusting Ball-Up [*A hopeless state of confusion*] [*Military slang*]
NABUG	National Association of Broadcast Unions and Guilds (EA)
NABV	National Association for Black Veterans (EA)
NABVICU	National Association of Blind and Visually Impaired Computer Users [*Defunct*] (EA)
NABW	National Association of Bank Women [*Chicago, IL*] (EA)
NABWA	National Association of Black Women Attorneys (EA)
NABWE	National Association of Black Women Entrepreneurs [*Detroit, MI*] (EA)
NABWMT	National Association of Black and White Men Together: A Gay Multiracial Organiz ation for All People (EA)
NABWS	National Amalgamated Brass Workers' Society [*A union*] [*British*]
NABWU	North American Baptist Women's Union (BUAC)
NAC	Association of Chiropodists (NADA)
NAC	CDC National AIDS Clearinghouse (EA)
NAC	Nacelle [*Aviation*]
NAC	N-Acetyl-L-Cysteine [*Biochemistry*]
NAC	Naples Alcofuel Club [*Defunct*] (EA)
NAC	National Abortion Campaign [*British*] (DBA)
NAC	National Academy of Conciliators (EA)
NAC	National Accelerator Center [*South Africa*] [*Research center*]
NAC	National Access Center [*Defunct*] (EA)
NAC	National Accreditation Council for Agencies Serving the Blind and Visually Handicapped (EA)
NAC	National Achievement Clubs (EA)
NAC	National Action Committee on the Status of Women [*Canada*] (CROSS)
NAC	National Adoption Center [*Information service or system*] (IID)
NAC	National Advertising Campaign [*Army*]
NAC	National Advisory Committee
NAC	National Advisory Council
NAC	National Aero Club (EA)
NAC	National Aeronautical Corp.
NAC	National Agency Check [*Security clearance*]
NAC	National Agricultural Centre [*British*] (CB)
NAC	National Agricultural Council (BUAC)
NAC	National Air Carrier Association (MCD)
NAC	National Air Charters [*Zambia*] (BUAC)
NAC	National Air Communications [*British*]
NAC	National Alumni Council of the United Negro College Fund (EA)
NAC	National Amusements Council (BUAC)
NAC	National Anglers' Council [*British*]
NAC	National Anxiety Center (EA)
NAC	National Aquaculture Council (EA)
NAC	National Archives Council (BUAC)
NAC	National Arts Centre [*Canada*]
NAC	National Arts Club (EA)
NAC	National Asbestos Council (EA)
NAC	National Association for the Childless [*British*] (DBA)
NAC	National Association of Cemeteries [*Later, ACA*] (EA)
NAC	National Association of Choirs [*British*] (BI)
NAC	National Association of Composers, USA (EA)
NAC	National Association of Concessionaires (EA)
NAC	National Association of Conveyancers [*British*] (DBA)
NAC	National Association of Coopers [*A union*] [*British*]
NAC	National Association of Coroners (EA)
NAC	National Association of Counselors (EA)
NAC	National Association of Counties
NAC	National Asthma Campaign (BUAC)
NAC	National Asthma Center [*Later, NJCIRM*]
NAC	National Audience Composition [*Nielsen Television Index*] (NTCM)
NAC	National Audiovisual Center [*General Services Administration*]
NAC	National Automotive Center [*Army*] (RDA)
NAC	National Aviation Club (EA)
NAC	National Aviation Corp.
NAC	Native American Church (ECON)
NAC	Native Appeal Courts [*South Africa*] [*A publication*] (DLA)
NAC	Natural Area Council (EA)
NAC	Naval Academy
NAC	Naval Air Center
NAC	Naval Air Command [*British*]
NAC	Naval Aircraftman [*British*]
NAC	Naval Amyloid Component [*Medicine*]
NAC	Naval Avionics Center (MCD)
NAC	Navy Acquisition Circular (AAGC)
NAC	Navy Activity Control (DNAB)
NAC	Navy Advanced Concept (CAAL)
NAC	Nebraska Administrative (Code) Rules and Regulations [*A publication*] (AAGC)
NAC	Negative Air Cushion [*Aviation Air Force*]
NAC	Neighbourhood Advice Council
NAC	Neo-American Church (EA)
NAC	Net Advertising Circulation (DOAD)
NAC	Network Access Center [*Telecommunications*]
NAC	Network Access Controller
NAC	Network Advisory Committee [*to Library of Congress and Council on Library Resources*]
NAC	Network Analysis Center [*Contel, Inc.*] [*Telecommunications service*] (TSSD)
NAC	Network Appliance Corp. [*Commercial firm*]
NAC	New American Community (MHDB)
NAC	New Apostolic Church
NAC	New Assembly of Churches (BUAC)
NAC	Nielson Audience Composition
NAC	Nipple Areolar Complex [*Oncology*]
NAC	Nitric Acid Concentrator (MCD)
NAC	Nitrogen Mustard [*Mustargen*], Adriamycin, CCNU [*Lomustine*] [*Antineoplastic drug regimen*]
NAC	NMCS [*Nuclear Material Control System*] Automatic Control
NAC	No Additional Charge
NAC	No Apparent Change (MCD)
NAC	Noise Advisory Council [*British*]
NAC	Nonairline Carrier [*Aerospace*]
NAC	Nordic Academic Council [*Defunct*] (EA)
NAC	Nordic Actors' Council (EAIO)
NAC	Nordic Association for Campanology (EA)
NAC	Normal Approach Course [*Navy*] (NVT)
NAC	North America Mtge [*NYSE symbol*] (TTSB)
NAC	North American Collectors (EA)
NAC	North American Committee [*An association*] (EA)
NAC	North American Mortgage Co. [*NYSE symbol*] (SPSG)
NAC	North Atlantic Coast
NAC	North Atlantic Conference (PSS)
NAC	North Atlantic Council
NAC	North Atlantic Current [*Oceanography*]
NAC	North Atlantic Shipping Conference (DS)
NAC	Northeast Air Command
NAC	Northern Air Cargo, Inc. [*ICAO designator*] (FAAC)
NAC	Nozzle Area Control
NAC	Nuclear Assurance Corp.
NAC	Nursing Audit Committee (MEDA)
NAC	US Catholic Bishops' National Advisory Council (EA)
NACA	National Academy of Code Administration (EA)
NACA	National Acoustical Contractors Association [*Later, CISCA*] (EA)
NACA	National Advisory Committee for Aeronautics [*Functions transferred to NASA, 1958*]
NACA	National Advisory Committee on Aeronautics [*OST*] (TAG)
NACA	National Agricultural Chemicals Association (EA)
NACA	National Air Carrier Association (EA)
NACA	National Animal Control Association (EA)
NACA	National Armored Car Association (EA)
NACA	National Association for Campus Activities (EA)
NACA	National Association for Children of Alcoholics (DHP)
NACA	National Association for Clean Air [*South Africa*] (BUAC)
NACA	National Association for Court Administration (EA)
NACA	National Association of Catastrophe Adjusters [*Comfort, TX*] (EA)
NACA	National Association of Cellular Agents (EA)
NACA	Negative Association of Child Advocates (EA)
NACA	National Association of Childbirth Assistants (EA)
NACA	National Association of Christians in the Arts (EA)
NACA	National Association of Consumer Advocates (EA)
NACA	National Association of Cost Accountants [*Later, NAA*]
NACA	National Association of County Administrators (EA)
NACA	National Association of Cuban Architects (in Exile) [*Defunct*] (EA)
NACA	National Athletic and Cultural Association [*Ireland*] (EAIO)
NACA	National Athletic and Cycling Association (BUAC)
NACA	National Autosound Challenge Association [*Later, IASCA*] (EA)
NACA	Naval Aviation Cadet Act of 1942
NACA	Netherlands-America Community Association (EA)
NACA	Network of Aquaculture Centres in Asia (BUAC)
NACA	North American Center on Adoption [*Defunct*] (EA)
NACA	North American College of Acupuncture
NACA	North American Corriente Association (EA)
NACA	North American Currach Association (EA)
NACA	North Australian Canine Association
NACAA	National Assembly of Community Arts Agencies (EA)
NACAA	National Association of Community Action Agencies (EA)
NACAA	National Association of Computer-Assisted Analysis (IAA)
NACAA	National Association of Consumer Agency Administrators (EA)
NACAA	National Association of County Agricultural Agents (EA)
NACAB	National Accreditation Council for Agencies Serving the Blind and Visually Handicapped [*New York, NY*]
NACAB	National Agricultural Centre Advisory Board (BUAC)
NACAB	National Association of Citizens Advice Bureaus [*British*] (DBA)
NACA BCA	Nationalo Advisory Commission for Aeronautics Board of Contract Appeals (AAGC)
NACAC	National Association of Catholic Alumni Clubs [*Later, CACI*] (EA)
NACAC	National Association of College Admission Counselors (EA)
NACAC	North African Antiaircraft Section [*World War II*]
NACAC	North American Council on Adoptable Children (EA)
NACACP	National Cash Register Applied COBOL [*Common Business-Oriented Language*] Package (IAA)
NACADA	National Academic Advising Association (EA)
NACAE	National Advisory Council on Adult Education [*Washington, DC*]

NACAE .... National Advisory Council on Art Education (BUAC)
NACAF .... Northwest African Coastal Air Force [*World War II*]
NACAL .... Navy Air Cooperation and Liaison Committee
NACAM ...... National Association of Corn and Agricultural Merchants (BUAC)
NAC & O ...... Cape and Orange Free State Native Appeal Court, Selected Decisions [*A publication*] (DLA)
NACAO .... National Association of County Arts Officers (BUAC)
NACAP .... National Association of Claims Assistance Professionals (EA)
NACAP .... National Association of Co-Op Advertising Professionals [*Defunct*] (EA)
NACAR .... National Advisory Committee on Aeronautical Research [*South Africa*] (BUAC)
NACARM ...... Northwest America Civil Air Routes Manual
NACAS .... National Advisory Committee on Agricultural Services [*Canada*] (BUAC)
NACAS .... National Association of College Auxiliary Services (EA)
NACAT .... National Association of College Automotive Teachers (DBA)
NACAT .... North American Council of Automotive Teachers (NTPA)
NACATS ...... North American Clear Air Turbulence Tracking System [*Aviation*]
NACAWM-USA... National Association of Cuban Women and Men of the United States (EA)
NACAW-USA... National Association of Cuban-American Women of the USA (EA)
NACB .... National Academy of Clinical Biochemistry (NTPA)
NACB .... National Association of Catering Butchers [*British*] (DBA)
NACB .... National Association of College Broadcasters (EA)
NACB .... National Association of Convention Bureaus (NADA)
NACB .... Native American Community Board (EA)
NACB .... Navy and Army Canteen Board [*British military*] (DMA)
NACBA .... National Association of Church Business Administration (EA)
NACBC .... Natinal Advisory Centre on the Battered Child (BUAC)
NACBFAA ..... National Association of Customs Brokers and Forwarders Association of America
NACBO .... National Association of Cosmetic Boutique Owners (EA)
NACBP .... No-Adjust Car Building Process [*Ford Motor Co.*] [*Automotive engineering*]
NACBS .... National Affiliation of Concerned Business Students [*Defunct*] (EA)
NACBS .... National Association and Council of Business Schools
NACBS .... North American Conference on British Studies (EA)
NACC .... National Aboriginal Consultative Committee [*Australia*] (BUAC)
NACC .... National Advisory Cancer Council
NACC .... National Agency Check Center (AFM)
NACC .... National Air Conservation Commission (EA)
NACC .... National Alliance of Czech Catholics (EA)
NACC .... National Association for Colitis and Crohn's Disease (BUAC)
NACC .... National Association for Core Curriculum (EA)
NACC .... National Association of Catholic Chaplains (EA)
NACC .... National Association of Childbearing Centers (EA)
NACC .... National Association of Collegiate Commissioners [*Later, CCA*] (EA)
NACC .... National Association of Counsel for Children (EA)
NACC .... National Automatic Controls Conference
NACC .... Naval Academy Computer Center
NACC .... Nigerian-American Chamber of Commerce (NTPA)
NACC .... North American-Chilean Chamber of Commerce (EA)
NACC .... North Atlantic Christian Conference (PSS)
NACC .... North Atlantic Cooperation Council
NACC .... Norwegian American Chamber of Commerce
NACC .... Novel Architectures Computing Committee [*British*]
NAC (C) ...... Selected Decisions of the Native Appeal Court (Central Division) [*1948-51*] [*South Africa*] [*A publication*] (DLA)
NACCA .... National Association for Creative Children and Adults (EA)
NACCA .... National Association of Claimants' Counsel of America [*Also known as NACCA Bar Association*] [*Later, ATLA*]
NACCA .... National Association of Consumer Credit Administrators (EA)
NACCA .... National Association of County 4-H Club Agents [*Later, NAE4-HA*] (EA)
NACCA .... National Association of County Civil Attorneys (EA)
NACCAC ...... National Community College Athletic Conference (PSS)
NACCALJ .... National Association of Claimants' Compensation Attorneys. Law Journal [*A publication*] (DLA)
NACCAM ...... National Coordinating Committee for Aviation Meteorology
NACCAN ...... National Association of Christian Councils and Networks (BUAC)
NAC (C & O)... Reports of the Decisions of the Native Appeal Courts, Cape Province and the Orange Free State [*South Africa*] [*A publication*] (ILCA)
NACCAS ...... National Accrediting Commission of Cosmetology Arts and Sciences (EA)
NACCB .... National Accreditation Council for Certification Bodies (AIE)
NACCB .... National Association of Computer Consultant Businesses (EA)
NACCC .... National Association of Citizens Crime Commissions (EA)
NACCC .... National Association of Congregational Christian Churches [*Later, CCCNA*] (EA)
NACCC .... Network of Access and Child Contact Centres (BUAC)
NACCC .... North American-Chilean Chamber of Commerce (NTPA)
NACCCA ...... National Association of Civilian Conservation Corps Alumni (EA)
NACCCAN .... National Centre for Christian Communities and Networks [*Westhill College*] [*British*] (CB)
NACCD .... National Advisory Commission on Civil Disorders (NADA)
NACCDD ...... National Association of County Community Development Directors (EA)
NACCE .... National Advisory Council on Continuing Education (OICC)
NACCE .... North American Conference on Christianity and Ecology (EA)
NACCED ...... National Association for County Community and Economic Development (NTPA)
NACCES ...... Naval Air Crew Combat Ejection Seat (DWSG)

NACCG .... National Association of Crankshaft and Cylinder Grinders [*British*] (BI)
NACCHO ...... National Aboriginal Community-Controlled Health Organization [*Australia*]
NACCHO ...... National Association of County and City Health Officials (NTPA)
NACCIC .... National Association of County Intergovernmental Relations Officials (NTPA)
NACCM .... National Association for Child Care Management [*Defunct*] (EA)
NACCMHC... National Academy of Certified Clinical Mental Health Counselors (DHP)
NACCO .... NACCO Industries, Inc. [*Associated Press*] (SAG)
NACCO .... North American Coal Corp. (EFIS)
NACCRRA ... National Association of Child Care Resource and Referral Agencies (EA)
NACCRT .... North America Coordinating Center for Responsible Tourism (EA)
NACCS .... National Association for Chicana and Chicano Studies (NTPA)
NACCSMA... NATO Command and Control Systems Management Agency (PDAA)
NACCSS .... National Association of Commodity Cargo Superintendents and Suveyors [*British*] (DBA)
NACCU .... National Association of Canadian Credit Unions (BUAC)
NACCW .... National Advisory Centre on Careers for Women [*British*] (CB)
NACCWO...... National Association of Civil Court Welfare Officers (BUAC)
NACD .... National Alliance of Cleaning Distributors [*Commercial firm*] (EA)
NACD .... National Association for Cave Diving [*Inactive*]
NACD .... National Association for Community Development [*Defunct*] (EA)
NACD .... National Association of Chemical Distributors (EA)
NACD .... National Association of Conservation Districts
NACD .... National Association of Container Distributors (EA)
NACD .... National Association of Corporate Directors [*Washington, DC*] (EA)
NACD .... Not Acidified [*Biochemistry*] (DAVI)
NACDA .... National Archive for Computerized Data on Aging [*Department of Health and Human Services*] (GFGA)
NACDA .... National Arts and Cultural Development Act of 1964
NACDA .... National Association of Collegiate Directors of Athletics (EA)
NACDAC ...... National Association for City Drug and Alcohol Coordination [*Defunct*] (EA)
NACDAP .... National Advisory Council for Drug Abuse Prevention [*Terminated, 1975*] (EGAO)
NACDC .... National Association of Career Development Consultants (EA)
NACDD .... National Advisory Council on Services and Facilities for the Developmentally Disabled [*Terminated, 1978*] [*HEW*] (EGAO)
NACDE .... National Association for Child Development and Education [*Later, NACCM*] (EA)
NACDET .... National Association of Colleges in Distributive Education and Training (BUAC)
NACDFB ...... National Association of Canada Dry Franchise Bottlers (EA)
NACDFLM ... National Association of Catholic Diocesan Family Life Ministers [*Later, NACFLM*] (EA)
NACDL .... National Association of Criminal Defense Lawyers (EA)
NACDLF .... National Association of Community Development Loan Funds (EA)
NACDPA....... National Association of County Data Processing Administrators (EA)
NACDR .... National Association of College Deans and Registrars [*Later, NACDRAO*] (EA)
NACDRAO .... National Association of College Deans, Registrars, and Admissions Officers (EA)
NACDS........ National Association of Chain Drug Stores (EA)
NACDS........ North American Clinical Dermatologic Society (EA)
NACE .... National Advisory Committee for Electronics
NACE .... National Advisory Committee on Electronics [*India*] (BUAC)
NACE .... National Association for Career Education (EA)
NACE .... National Association for Curriculum Enrichment and Extension [*British*] (EAIO)
NACE .... National Association of Catering Executives (EA)
NACE .... National Association of Childbirth Education [*Defunct*] (EA)
NACE .... National Association of Corrosion Engineers (EA)
NACE .... National Association of Counsellors in Education (AIE)
NACE .... National Association of County Engineers (EA)
NACE .... National Autobody Congress and Exposition [*Precision Planning and Sales, Inc.*] (TSPED)
NACE .... Native Americans for a Clean Environment (EA)
NACE .... Neutral Atmospheric Composition Experiment [*Geophysics*]
NACE .... NMCSSC [*National Military Command System Support Center*] Automated ControlExecutive
NACE .... North American Commission on the Environment
NACE .... North American Cycle Exhibitor Association (EA)
NACEBE ...... National Association of Classroom Educators in Business Education [*Cambridge City, IN*] (EA)
NACEC .... National Association of Charitable Estate Counselors (EA)
NACEC .... North American Center for Emergency Communications (EA)
NACEC .... North American Committee of Enamel Creators (EA)
NACECE ...... National Advisory Council on Extension and Continuing Education
NACED .... National Advisory Committee on the Education of the Deaf [*Terminated, 1973*] [*HEW*] (EGAO)
NACED .... National Advisory Council on the Employment of Disabled People (BUAC)
NACED .... National Advisory Council on the Employment of the Disabled [*British*]
NACEDC ...... National Advisory Council on Education of Disadvantaged Children (OICC)
NAC/EDP ...... National Advisory Council on Education Professions Development [*HEW*] (EGAO)
NAC-EDTA ... N-Acetyl-L-Cysteine Ethylenediaminetetra-Acetic Acid [*Biochemistry*] (MAE)
NACEEO .... National Advisory Council on Equality of Educational Opportunity [*Termina ted, 1979*] [*HEW*] (EGAO)

NACEHC....... National Accreditation Council for Environmental Health Curricula (EA)

NACEIC........ National Advisory Council on Education for Industry and Commerce (MCD)

NACEL........ Navy Air Crew Equipment Laboratory [*Philadelphia, PA*]

NACEO........ National Advisory Council on Economic Opportunity (EA)

NACEPD........ National Advisory Council on Education Professions Development [*Terminate d, 1976*] [*HEW*] (OICC)

NACEPE....... National Association of Creamery Proprietors and Wholesale Dairymen (BUAC)

NACEPT .... National Advisory Committee for Environmental Policy and Technology [*Environmental Protection Agency*]

NACERI....... National Advisory Council for Educational Research and Improvement [*Washington, DC Department of Education*] (GRD)

NACES........ National Association of Credential Evaluation Services (EA)

NACES .... Navy Aircrew Common Ejection Seat [*British*]

NACESW........ National Association of Chief Education Social Workers (AIE)

NACETA .... National Association of County Employment and Training Administrators [*Later, NACTEP*] (EA)

NACEW....... National Advisory Council on the Employment of Women [*New Zealand*] (BUAC)

NACF .... National Agricultural Cooperative Federation [*Republic of Korea*] (BUAC)

NACF .... National Art-Collectors' Fund [*British*]

NACF .... National Association of Church Furnishers [*British*] (BI)

NACF .... Navy Air Combat Fighter (MCD)

NACFA .... North American Clun Forest Association (EA)

NACFE .... National Association of Certified Fraud Examiners (EA)

NACFFA .... National Advisory Committee for the Flammable Fabrics Act

NACFL .... National Advisory Committee on Farm Labor [*Defunct*] (EA)

NACFLM .... National Association of Catholic Family Life Ministers (EA)

NACFR .... National Association of Casual Furniture Retailers (EA)

NACFRC....... North Atlantic Coastal Fisheries Research Centre (BUAC)

NACFT .... National Academy of Counselors and Family Therapists (EA)

NACG .... National Association of Conservative Graduates (AIE)

NACG .... National Association of County Governments (OICC)

NACG .... North African Commanding General [*World War II*]

NACGC .... National Association of Collegiate Gymnastics Coaches (Men) (EA)

NACGC .... National Association of Colored Girls Clubs [*Later, NAGC*] (EA)

NACGG........ North American Commercial Gladiolus Growers [*Later, CGD-NAGC*] (EA)

NACGM .... National Association of Chewing Gum Manufacturers (EA)

NACGT .... National Association of Careers and Guidance Teachers [*British*] (DBA)

NACH .... National Academy of Clinicians and Holistic Health (EA)

NACH .... National Advisory Committee on the Handicapped

NACH .... National Advisory Council for the Handicapped (NADA)

NACH .... National Association for the Craniofacially Handicapped (EA)

NACH .... National Association of Clergy Hypnotherapists (EA)

NACH .... National Association of Coal Haulers [*Defunct*] (EA)

nAch .... Need for Achievement

NACHA .... National Automated Clearing House Association [*Washington, DC*] (EA)

NACHA .... National Collegiate Hockey Association (PSS)

NACHC .... National Advisory Committee on Handicapped Children [*Terminated, 1973*] [*HEW*] (EGAO)

NACHC .... National Association of Christian Colleges (PSS)

NACHC .... National Association of Community Health Centers (EA)

Nach Chem Tech... Nachrichten aus Chemie, Technik und Laboratorium (MEC)

NACHES........ Association of Jewish Family, Children's Agency Professionals (EA)

NACHFA .... National Association of County Health Facility Administrators (EA)

NACHGR ...... National Advisory Council for Human Genome Research (HGEN)

NACHM .... Nachmittags [*Afternoon*] [*German*]

NACHO .... National Association of County Health Officials (EA)

NACHP........ National Association of Counsellors, Hypnotherapists and Psychotherapists (BUAC)

NACHP........ North African Chaplain's Section [*World War II*]

NAChR .... Nicotinic Acetylcholine Receptor [*Immunology*]

NACHRI........ National Association of Children's Hospitals and Related Institutions (EA)

NACHRK ...... North American Coalition for Human Rights in Korea (EA)

NACHSA....... National Association of County Human Services Administrators (EA)

NACHVRO .... National Air Conditioning, Heating, Ventilating, and Refrigeration Officials (EA)

NACI .... Naphthenic Acid Corrosion Index

NACI .... National Agency Check and Written Inquiries

NACI .... National Association for the Cottage Industry (EA)

NACIA .... National Association of Crop Insurance Agents [*Anoka, MN*] (EA)

NACIE .... National Advisory Council on Indian Education (OICC)

NACIFO .... National Association of Church and Institutional Financing Organizations [*Atlanta, GA*] (EA)

NACIME ...... North American Committee for IME [*Institut Medical Evangelique*] [*Defunct*] (EA)

NACIO .... National Association of County Information Officers (EA)

NACIO .... Naval Air Combat Information Office [*or Officer*]

NACIP .... Navy Assessment and Control of Installation Pollutants

NACIS .... National Credit Information Service [*TRW, Inc.*] [*Long Beach, CA Credit-information databank*] (IID)

NACIS .... Naval Air Combat Information School

NACIS .... Navy Air Control and Identification System

NACIS .... Networking Analytical and Computing Information Systems [*National Aeronautics and Space Administration*]

NACIS .... North American Cartographic Information Society (EA)

NACISA .... North Atlantic Communications and Information Systems Agency [*NATO*]

NACISO .... NATO Communications and Information Systems Organization (EAIO)

NACITA .... National Association of County Information Technology Administrators (NTPA)

NACJ.......... National Association of Costume Jewelers [*Defunct*] (EA)

NACJP .... National Association of Criminal Justice Planners [*Defunct*] (EA)

NACK .... National Advisory Committee on Kangaroos (BUAC)

NACK .... Negative Acknowledgment [*Telecommunications*]

NACK .... Nonacknowledgment Character [*Computer science*]

NACL .... National Advisory Commission on Libraries

NACL .... National Association for Community Leadership (EA)

NACL .... Navy/ARPA [*Advanced Research Projects Agency*] Chemical LASER (MCD)

NACL .... Nippon Aviatronics Corp. Ltd. [*Japan*]

NaCl .... Sodium Chloride [*Salt*] [*Chemistry*] (DAVI)

NACLA .... North American Congress on Latin America (EA)

NACLC .... National Association of Community Legal Centers [*Australia*]

NACLE .... National Association of Chimney Lining Engineers [*British*] (DBA)

NACLEO .... National Association of Coin Laundry Equipment Operators (EA)

NACLIS .... National Commission on Libraries and Information Science [*Washington, DC*]

NACLM .... North African Claims Section [*World War II*]

NACLO .... National Association of Canoe Liveries and Outfitters (EA)

NACLO .... National Association of Community Leadership Organizations [*Later, National Association for Community Leadership*] (EA)

NACLS .... National Association of Commission Lumber Salesmen

NACLS .... North Alabama Cooperative Library System [*Library network*]

NACLS .... North American Canon Law Society (EA)

NACLSO .... National Assembly of Chief Livestock Sanitary Officials [*Later, United States Animal Health Association*] (EA)

NACM .... National Association for Court Management (EA)

NACM .... National Association of Chain Manufacturers (EA)

NACM .... National Association of Charcoal Manufacturers [*British*] (DBA)

NACM .... National Association of Cider Makers [*British*] (BI)

NACM .... National Association of Colliery Managers [*British*] (DBA)

NACM .... National Association of Cotton Manufacturers (BUAC)

NACM .... National Association of Credit Management

NACMA .... National Armored Cable Manufacturers Association (EA)

NACMA .... National Association of Collegiate Marketing Administrators

NACMB .... National Association of Certified Mortgage Bankers [*Later, NSREF*] (EA)

NACMC .... National Association for Church Management Consultants (EA)

NACMC .... National Association of Christian Marriage Counselors [*Defunct*] (EA)

NACMCF .... National Advisory Committee on Microbiological Criteria for Foods

NACME .... National Action Council for Minorities in Engineering (EA)

NACMEMS ... National Association of Continuing Medical Education Meetings and Seminars [*Defunct*] (EA)

NACMHD....... National Association of County Mental Health Directors (NTPA)

NACMIS .... Navy Automated Civilian Management Information System

NACMO .... National Association of Cigarette Machine Operators [*British*] (DBA)

NACMO .... National Association of Competitive Mounted Orienteering (EA)

NACMW .... North American Council for Muslim Women

NACN .... Newspaper Advertising Co-Op Network (EA)

NAC (N & T)... Decisions of the Native Appeal and Divorce Court (Transvaal and Natal) [*South Africa*] [*A publication*] (ILCA)

NAC (NE) ..... Decisions of the Native Appeal Court (North Eastern Division) [*South Africa*] [*A publication*] (ILCA)

NACNE .... National Advisory Council on Nutrition Education [*British*]

NACNS........ National Association of Clinical Nurse Specialists (NTPA)

NACO .... Name Authority Co-Operative (NITA)

NACO .... National Advisory Committee on Oceanography [*Marine science*] (MSC)

NACO .... National Agricultural Co. [*St. Christopher and Nevis*] (BUAC)

NACO .... National Agricultural Credit Office [*Vietnam*] (BUAC)

NACO .... National Association of Charterboat Operators (EA)

NACO .... National Association of Condominium Owners

NACO .... National Association of Consumer Organizations

NACO .... National Association of Cooperative Officials [*A union*] [*British*] (DCTA)

NACo .... National Association of Counties (EA)

NACO .... National Coordinated Cataloging Operations [*Library science*]

NACO .... Navy Acquisition-Contracting Officer (MCD)

NACO .... Navy Coolant [*Gunpowder*]

NACO .... Night Alarm Cutoff (AAG)

NACOA .... If Not Available Your Command, Obtain Accounting Data from Administrative Command [*Army*] (AABC)

NACOA .... National Advisory Committee on Oceans and Atmosphere [*Marine science*] (MSC)

NACOA .... National Association for Children of Alcholics (BUAC)

NACoA .... National Association for Children of Alcoholics (EA)

NACOA .... National Association for Children of Alcoholism and Other Addictions (EA)

NACOA .... National Association of Cruise Only Agencies (NTPA)

NACODS .... National Association of Colliery Overmen, Deputies, and Shotfirers [*A union*] [*British*] (DCTA)

NACOEJ .... North American Conference on Ethiopian Jewry (EAIO)

NACOI .... National Association of Canadians of Origins in India

NACOL .... National Advisory Commission on Libraries

NACOLADS... National Council on Libraries, Archives and Documentation Services [*Jamaica*] (BUAC)

NACOM .... National Communications [*System*]

NACOM .... Northern Area Command

NACOMEX... National Computer Exchange

NACON........ Newspaper Advertising Co-Op Network (EA)

NACOP........ National Association of Chiefs of Police (NTPA)

NACOPRW ... National Conference of Puerto Rican Women (EA)
NACOR ... National Advisory Committee on Radiation
NaCOR ... National Center on Occupational Readjustment [*Defunct*] (EA)
NACORE ... National Association of Corporate Real Estate Executives (EA)
NACORF ... National Association of Counties Research Foundation
NACOS ... National Communications Schedule
NACOS ... NATO Courier Service (NATG)
NACOS ... North African Chief of Staff [*World War II*]
NACOSH ... National Advisory Committee on Occupational Safety and Health
NACOSH ... National Advisory Committee on Scouting for the Handicapped (EA)
NACOSS ... National Approval Council for Security Systems (BUAC)
NACP ... National Academy of Cable Programming (NTCM)
NACP ... National Accounts Capability Programme [*United Nations*] (EY)
NACP ... National Association of Chiefs of Police (AD)
NACP ... National Association of County Planners (EA)
NACP ... Navy Acoustical Communication Program (MCD)
NACP ... Network Against Coercive Psychiatry (EA)
NACP ... NORAD/CONAD Airborne Command Post
NACP ... North Atlantic Consultive Process (OSI)
NACPA ... National Association of Church Personnel Administrators (EA)
NACPA ... National Association of County and Prosecuting Attorneys [*Later, NDAA*]
NACPA ... North American Concert Promoters Association (NTPA)
NACPC ... North American Christian Peace Conference (EA)
NACPCC ... National Advisory Committee for Pig Carcase Competitions (BUAC)
NACPD ... National Association of County Planning Directors [*Later, NACP*] (EA)
NACPDCG ... National Association of Catholic Publishers and Dealers in Church Goods (EA)
NACPDE ... National Advice Centre for Postgraduate Dental Education (BUAC)
NACPR ... National Association of Corporate and Professional Recruiters (EA)
NACPRO ... National Association of County Park and Recreation Officials (EA)
NACPU ... National Amalgamated Coal Porters' Union [*British*]
NACPUISCW ... National Amalgamated Coal Porters' Union of Inland and Seaborne Coal Workers [*British*]
NACR ... National Advisory Committee on Radiation
NACRC ... National Association of Community Relations Council (BUAC)
NACRC ... National Association of County Recorders and Clerks (EA)
NACRCD ... National Advisory Council on Rural Civil Defense
NAC Re ... NAC RE Corp. [*Associated Press*] (SAG)
NACRE ... North American Coalition on Religion and Ecology (EA)
NACRF ... National Association of Counties Research Foundation (OICC)
NACRMR ... National Advisory Committee on Rhesus Monkey Requirements
NACRO ... National Association for the Care and Resettlement of Offenders [*British*]
nacro ... Night-Alarm Cutoff (AD)
NACRS ... National Asbestos-Contractor Registration System (COE)
NACRS ... North African Censorship Section, US [*World War II*]
NACR (SR) ... Native Appeal Court Reports (Southern Rhodesia) [*A publication*] (ILCA)
NACRT ... National Association of Canadian Race Tracks
NACRU ... North American Committee for Reconciliation in Ulster (EA)
NACS ... National Advisory Committee on Semiconductors
NACS ... National Association for Check Safekeeping [*Washington, DC*] (EA)
NACS ... National Association for Chicano Studies (EA)
NACS ... National Association of Carpet Specialists [*Defunct*]
NACS ... National Association of Chimney Sweeps [*British*] (DBA)
NACS ... National Association of Christian Schools [*Defunct*] (EA)
NACS ... National Association of Christian Singles (EA)
NACS ... National Association of Civic Secretaries (EA)
NACS ... National Association of Collection Sites (EA)
NACS ... National Association of College Stores (EA)
NACS ... National Association of Computer Stores [*Later, IVCI*] [*Defunct*] (EA)
NACS ... National Association of Concession Services (EA)
NACS ... National Association of Consumer Shows (NTPA)
NACS ... National Association of Convenience Stores (EA)
NACS ... National Association of Cosmetology Schools (EA)
NACS ... National Association of County Surveyors (NTPA)
NACS ... Natural Areas of Canadian Significance [*NPPAC*]
NACS ... NetWare Asynchronous Communication Service [*Novell, Inc.*]
NACS ... Neurologic and Adaptive Capacity Scoring [*System*]
NACS ... Nordic Association for Clinical Sexology (BUAC)
NACS ... North American Catalysis Society (NTPA)
NACS ... North Atlantic Current System [*Oceanography*]
NACS ... Northern Area Communications System (MCD)
NACS ... Nucleic Acid Chromatography System
NAC (S) ... Selected Decisions of the Native Appeal Court (Southern Division) [*South Africa*] [*A publication*] (ILCA)
NACSA ... National Advisory Committee on Safety in Agriculture
NACSA ... National Association for Corporate Speaker Activities (EA)
NACSA ... National Association of Casualty and Surety Agents [*Bethesda, MD*] (EA)
NACSA ... North American Computer Service Association (EA)
NACSAA ... National Advisory Council for South Asian Affairs (EA)
NACSAP ... National Alliance Concerned with School-Age Parents [*Defunct*] (EA)
NACSARS ... National Association of Companion Sitter Agencies and Referral Services [*Later, PCA*] (EA)
NACSB ... Naval Aviation Cadet Selection Board
NACSC ... National Association of Cold Storage Contractors (EA)
NACSCAOM ... National Accreditation Commission for Schools and Colleges of Acupuncture and Oriental Medicine (EA)
NACSCC ... National Association of Community Schools, Colleges, and Centres [*British*] (DBA)
NACSCS ... National Advisory Council on Supplementary Centers and Services
NACSDA ... National Association of Commissioners, Secretaries, and Directors of Agriculture[*Later, NASDA*] (EA)
NACSDC ... North American Conference of Separated and Divorced Catholics (EA)
NACSE ... National Association of Casualty and Surety Executives [*New York, NY*] (EA)
NACSE ... National Association of Civil Service Employees (EA)
NACSE ... Non-Avionics Common Support Equipment (MCD)
NACSI ... National Communications Security Instruction (COE)
NACSIC ... National Association of Cold Storage Insulation Contractors (EA)
NACSIM ... NATO Communications Security Information (NATG)
NACSIS ... National Center for Science Information Systems [*Japan*]
NACSM ... National Association of Catalog Showroom Merchandisers (EA)
NACSPMR ... National Association of Coordinators of State Programs for the Mentally Retarded[*Later, National Association of State Mental Retardation Program Directors*] (EA)
NACSS ... National Approved Council for Security Systems (WDAA)
NACSS ... National Association of Clerical and Supervisory Staffs (BUAC)
NACST ... National Association of Catholic School Teachers (EA)
NACSW ... National Action Committee on the Status of Women [*Canada*] (AD)
NACSW ... North American Association of Christians in Social Work (EA)
NACT ... NASA Activities [*A publication*]
NACT ... National Alliance of Cardiovascular Technologists (EA)
NACT ... National Association of Careers Teachers (AD)
NACT ... National Association of Chapter 13 Trustees (MHDB)
NACT ... National Association of Clinical Tutors [*British*] (DBA)
NACT ... National Association of Consumers and Travelers (EA)
NACT ... National Association of Corporate Treasurers [*Washington, DC*] (EA)
NACT ... National Association of Craftsman Tailors [*British*] (BI)
NACT ... National Association of Cycle Traders [*British*] (BI)
NACT ... National Association of Cycle Trades (AD)
NACT ... National Automatic Controller for Testing (MUGU)
NACTA ... National Association of Colleges and Teachers of Agriculture (EA)
NACTAC ... Navy Antenna Computer Tracking and Command
NAC (T & N) ... Reports of the Decisions of the Native Appeal Courts (Transvaal and Natal) [*South Africa*] [*A publication*] (ILCA)
NACTEFL ... National Advisory Council on the Teaching of English as a Foreign Language (EA)
NACTEP ... National Association of County Training and Employment Professionals [*Washington, DC*] (EA)
NACTFO ... National Association of County Treasurers and Finance Officers (EA)
NACTP ... National Association of Computerized Tax Processors (EA)
NACTST ... National Advisory Council on the Training and Supply of Teachers (AD)
NACTU ... National Affiliation of Carpet Trade Unions (BUAC)
NACTU ... National Council of Trade Unions [*South Africa*] (BUAC)
NACTU ... Night Attack Combat Training Unit [*Navy*]
NACU ... National Association of Colleges and Universities
NACUA ... National Association of College and University Administrators [*Superseded by NEA Higher Education Council*] (EA)
NACUA ... National Association of College and University Attorneys (EA)
NACUBO ... National Association of College and University Business Office Associations (AD)
NACUBO ... National Association of College and University Business Officers [*Washington, DC*] (EA)
NACUC ... National Association of College and University Chaplains and Directors of Religious Life (EA)
NACUC ... National Association of Credit Union Chairmen (NTPA)
NACUFS ... National Association of College and University Food Services (EA)
NACUP ... National Association of Credit Union Presidents (EA)
NACUSA ... National Association of Composers, USA (EA)
NACUSIP ... National Congress of Union in the Sugar Industry of the Philippines (BUAC)
NACUSO ... National Association of Credit Union Service Organizations (NTPA)
NACUSS ... National Association of College and University Summer Sessions [*Later, NAASS*]
NACUTCD ... National Advisory Committee on Uniform Traffic Control Devices [*Terminated, 1979*] [*Department of Transportation*] (EGAO)
NACUTSO ... National Association of College and University Traffic and Security Officers (EA)
NACV ... National Association of Concerned Veterans (EA)
NACVA ... National Association of Certified Valuation Analysts (NTPA)
NACVCB ... National Association of Crime Victim Compensation Boards (EA)
NACVE ... National Advisory Council on Vocational Education
NA-CVR ... National Association for Crime Victims Rights (EA)
NACVS ... National Association of Councils for Voluntary Service (BUAC)
NACW ... National Advisory Committee on Women (AD)
NACW ... National Association of College Women [*Later, NAUW*] (EA)
NACW ... National Association of Commissions for Women (EA)
NACWAA ... National Association of Collegiate Women Athletic Administrators (NTPA)
NACWC ... National Association of Colored Women's Clubs (EA)
NACWD ... National Association of County Welfare Directors [*Later, NACHSA*] (EA)
NACWEP ... National Advisory Council on Women's Educational Programs (OICC)
NACWIS ... Navy Controlled Waste Information System
NACWPI ... National Association of College Wind and Percussion Instructors (EA)
NACWPI ... National Association of College Wind and Percussion Instruments (AD)
NACWRR ... National Advisory Committee on Water Resources Research [*Canada*]
NACWS ... North African Chemical Warfare Section [*World War II*]
NACX ... Northern Air Cargo, Inc. [*Air carrier designation symbol*]
NACYS ... National Advisory Council for Youth Services (AIE)

NAd.............. Addison Public Library, Addison, NY [*Library symbol Library of Congress*] (LCLS)
NAD .... Nadir (WDAA)
nad .... Nadir (AD)
NAD .... Naphthaleneacetamide [*Herbicide*]
NAD .... National Academy of Design (EA)
NAD .... National Advertising Division [*of the Council of Better Business Bureaus*]
NAD .... National Alliance for Democracy [*Political party*] (AD)
NAD .... National Armaments Director (NATG)
NAD .... National Association of the Deaf (EA)
NAD .... National Audience Demographics Report [*Nielsen Television Index*] (NTCM)
NAD .... NATO Air Doctrine (NATG)
NAd.............. Naval Adviser [*British*]
NAD .... Naval Air Defense (NATG)
NAD .... Naval Air Depot
NAD .... Naval Air Detachment (MCD)
NAD .... Naval Air Detail
NAD .... Naval Air Development Center
NAD .... Naval Air Development Center, Warminster, PA [*OCLC symbol*] (OCLC)
NAD .... Naval Air Division [*British*]
NAD .... Naval Ammunition Depot [*Charleston, SC*]
NAD .... Naval Armament Depot [*British*]
NAD .... Naval Aviation Depot (AAGC)
Nad.............. Nedezhda (AD)
NAD .... Network Access Device
nad .... Networking Addressing Device [*Computer science*] (AD)
NAD .... New Antigenic Determinant [*Immunochemistry*]
NAD .... Nicotinamide-Adenine Dinucleotide [*Preferred form, but also see ARPPRN, DPN, NADH*] [*Biochemistry*]
NAD .... Nicotinamide Adenine Dinucleotide Oxidized (EDCT)
NAD .... Nicotinic Acid Dehydrogenase [*An enzyme*] (AAMN)
NAD .... Nielson Audience Demographic Report [*A publication*] (DOAD)
NAD .... Night Air Defence [*British World War II*]
NAD .... Nitric Acid Dihydrate [*Inorganic chemistry*]
Nad.............. Nitrosamide [*Biochemistry*]
NAD .... No Abnormal Discovery [*Medicine*] (DB)
NAD .... No Abnormality Detected [*Medicine*]
NAD .... No-Acid Descaling (IEEE)
NAD .... No Active Disease (DAVI)
NAD .... No Acute Distress [*Medicine*]
NAD .... No Apparent Defect [*Shipping*]
nad .... No Apparent Defect (AD)
NAD .... No Apparent Distress [*Medicine*]
nad .... No Appreciable Difference (AD)
nad .... No Appreciable Disease (AD)
NAD .... No Appreciable Disease [*Medicine*]
NAD .... Nobelair [*Turkey*] [*ICAO designator*] (FAAC)
NAD .... Node Administration (NITA)
NAD .... Noise Amplitude Distribution
NAD .... Nordiska Namden for Alkohol- och Drogforskning [*Nordic Council for Alcohol and Drug Research - NCADR*] (EAIO)
NAD .... Normal Axis Deviation [*Medicine*]
NAD .... North American Aero Dynasty [*Vancouver Stock Exchange symbol*]
NAD .... North American Datum
NAD .... North Atlantic Division [*Army Engineers*]
NAD .... Nothing Abnormal Detected [*or Discovered*] [*Medicine*]
nad .... Nothing Abnormal Detected (AD)
nad .... Not on Active Duty [*Military*] (AD)
NAD .... Not on Active Duty
NAD .... Nuclear Accident Dosimetry
NAD83 .... North American Datum of 1983 (USDC)
NADA .... N-Acetyldopamine [*Biochemistry*]
NADA .... National Art Dealers Association [*Later, ADA*] (EA)
NADA .... National Association for Disabled Athletes (EA)
NADA .... National Association of Dealers in Antiques (EA)
NADA .... National Association of Dental Assistants (EA)
NADA .... National Association of Drama Advisers [*British*]
NADA .... National Association of Drug Addiction (AD)
NADA .... National Automobile Dealers Association [*McLean, VA*] (EA)
NADA .... National Democratic Alliance [*Zambia*] [*Political party*] (EY)
NADA .... Navajo Army Depot Activity [*Arizona*] [*Army*]
NADA .... New Animal Drug Application [*Food and Drug Administration*]
NADABA .... N-Adenosyldiaminobutyric Acid [*Biochemistry*] (DB)
NADABB....... National Alzheimer's Disease Autopsy and Brain Bank (AD)
NADAC .... National Air Duct Cleaners Association
NADAC......... National Anti-Drug Abuse Campaign (AD)
NADAC......... National Damage Assessment Center
NADAC......... Naval ASW [*Antisubmarine Warfare*] Data Center (NVT)
NADAC......... Navigation Data Assimilation Computer (IAA)
NADAC......... Pacific Command, North Vietnam Air Defense Analysis and Coordinating Group (CINC)
NADAF......... National Association of Decorative Architectural Finishes (EA)
NADAG......... National Association of Diocesan Altar Guilds of the Protestant Episcopal Church (EA)
NADAP......... National Association on Drug Abuse Problems (EA)
NADAPI....... National Alcoholism and Drug Abuse Program Inventory [*Department of Health and Human Services*] (GFGA)
NADAR........ No After Duty Action Required [*Military*]
NADAR........ North American Data Airborne Recorder
NADase....... Nicotinamide-Adenine Dinucleotide Glycohydrolase [*Also, DPNase*] [*An enzyme*]

NADASO ...... National Association Drug and Allied Sales Organizations [*Wyncote, PA*] (EA)
NADASO ...... National Association of Design and Art Service Organizations (EA)
NADB.......... National Aerometric Data Bank [*Office of Air and Radiation*] (COE)
NADB.......... National Air Data Branch [*Environmental Protection Agency Information service or system*] (IID)
NADB.......... National Atmospheric Data Bank (GNE)
NADB.......... National Audience Data Bank [*Newspaper Marketing Bureau*] [*Information service or system*] (CRD)
NADB.......... North American Development Bank
NADBR........ National Association for the Deaf, Blind, and Rubella [*British*]
NADBRH...... National Association for Deaf-Blind and Rubella Handicapped (BUAC)
NADC.......... National Advisory Drug Committee [*HEW*]
NADC.......... National Animal Data Centre (BUAC)
NADC.......... National Animal Disease Center [*Ames, IA*] [*Department of Agriculture*] [*Research center*] (GRD)
NADC.......... National Anti-Drug Coalition [*Defunct*] (EA)
NADC.......... National Anti-Dumping Committee (AD)
NADC.......... National Association of Demolition Contractors (EA)
NADC.......... National Association of Demonstration Companies (NTPA)
NADC.......... National Association of Dredging Contractors (EA)
NADC.......... NATO Air Defense Committee
NADC.......... NATO Defense College [*Also, NADEFCOL, NDC*]
NADC.......... Naval Aide-de-Camp [*British military*] (DMA)
NADC.......... Naval Air Development Center [*Also, NADEVCEN, NAVAIRDEVCEN*] [*Warminster, PA*]
NADC.......... Naval Ammunition Depot, Concord [*California*]
NADC.......... Northern Agricultural Development Corp. (AD)
NADC.......... Northern Region Agricultural Development Centre [*Thailand*] (BUAC)
NADCA........ National Air Duct Cleaners Association
NADCA........ National Animal Damage Control Association (EA)
NADCA........ North American Draft Cross Association (EA)
NADC-AC .... Naval Air Development Center - Aerospace Crew Equipment Department
NADC-ACL ... Naval Air Development Center - Aeronautical Computer Laboratory (DNAB)
NADC-AE...... Naval Air Development Center - Aero-Electronic Technology Department
NADC-AI ..... Naval Air Development Center - Aeronautical Instruments Laboratory
NADC-AM .... Naval Air Development Center - Aero-Mechanics Department
NADC-AML... Naval Air Development Center - Aeronautical Materials Laboratory (DNAB)
NADCAP....... National Aerospace and Defense Contractors Accreditation Program [*DoD*]
NADC-AP ..... Naval Air Development Center - Aeronautical Photographic Experimental Laboratory
NADC-AR .... Naval Air Development Center - Aviation Armament Laboratory
NADC-ASL ... Naval Air Development Center - Aeronautical Structures Laboratory (DNAB)
NADC-ASW... Naval Air Development Center - Antisubmarine Warfare Laboratory
NADC-AW ... Naval Air Development Center - Air Warfare Research Department
NADC-AWG... Naval Air Development Center - Acoustical Working Group
NADC-CS .... Naval Air Development Center - Crew Systems Department
NADC-ED ..... Naval Air Development Center - Engineering Development Laboratory
NADC-EL...... Naval Air Development Center - Aeronautical Electronic and Electrical Laboratory
NADC-LS...... Naval Air Development Center - Life Sciences and Bio-Equipment Group
NADC-ML.... Naval Air Development Center - Aviation Medical Acceleration Laboratory
NADC-MR ... Naval Air Development Center - Aerospace Medical Research Department
NADCO........ National Agricultural Development Co. [*Saudi Arabia*] (BUAC)
NADCO........ National Association of Development Companies (EA)
NAD-CO ...... Naval Ammunition Depot, Concord [*California*]
NADCORP.... National Development Corp. [*Ireland*] (BUAC)
NAD-CR ...... Naval Ammunition Depot, Crane [*Indiana*]
NADC-SD ..... Naval Air Development Center - Systems Analysis and Engineering Department
NADC-ST..... Naval Air Development Center - Aero Structures Department
NADC-SY..... Naval Air Development Center - Systems Project Department
NADC-WR ... Naval Air Development Center - Air Warfare Research Department
NADD.......... National Association for the Dually Diagnosed (PAZ)
NADD.......... National Association of Deputising Doctors [*British*] (DBA)
NADD.......... National Association of Diemakers and Diecutters [*Formerly, DDA*] (EA)
NADD.......... National Association of Disco Disc Jockeys [*Defunct*] (EA)
NADD.......... National Association of Distributors and Dealers of Structural Clay Products [*Later, NABD*] (EA)
NADD.......... NNational Association of Diaconante Directors (NTPA)
NADDC........ National Association of Developmental Disabilities Councils (EA)
NADDIS....... Narcotics and Dangerous Drugs Intelligence File (AD)
NADDM........ National Association of Daytime Dress Manufacturers [*Defunct*]
NADDMI/MR.. National Association for the Dually Diagnosed Mental Illness/Mental Retardation (NTPA)
NADDRG...... North American Deep Drawing Research Group [*Automotive metal stampings*]
NADE.......... National Association for Design Education [*British*]
NADE.......... National Association for Developmental Education (EA)
NADE.......... National Association for Drama in Education [*Australia*]
NADE.......... National Association of Disability Examiners (EA)
NADE.......... National Association of Document Examiners (EA)
NADEC........ National Agricultural Development Co. [*Saudi Arabia*] (BUAC)

NADEC........	National Association of Development Education Centres [British] (DBA)
NADEC........	Navy Decision Center
NADEC........	Navy Development Center (CAAL)
NADECO......	National Development Co. [Ghana] (BUAC)
NADECT.......	National Association for Drama in Education and Children's Theatre (BUAC)
NADEE........	National Association of Divisional Executives for Education [British]
NADEEC.......	NATO Air Defense Electronic Environment Committee
NADeFA.......	North American Deer Farmers Association (NTPA)
NaDefCo.......	NATO [North Atlantic Treaty Organization] Defense College (AD)
NADEFCOL...	NATO Defense College [Also, NADC, NDC] [Rome, Italy]
NADEM........	National Association of Dairy Equipment Manufacturers [Later, DFISA] (EA)
NADEO........	National Association of Diocesan Ecumenical Officers (EA)
NADEP........	National Association of Disability Evaluating Professionals (NTPA)
NADEP........	Naval Aviation Depot (MCD)
NADEPA.......	National Democratic Party [Solomon Islands] [Political party] (PPW)
NADET........	National Association of Distributive Education Teachers
NADE(V)......	National Association for Drama in Education (Victoria) [Australia]
NADEVCEN...	Naval Air Development Center [Also, NADC, NAVAIRDEVCEN]
NaDevCen......	Naval Air Development Center (AD)
NADEX........	NATO Data Exchange (NATG)
NADF..........	National Addison's Disease Foundation (EA)
NADF..........	National Adrenal Diseases Foundation (EA)
NADF..........	National Alzheimer's Disease Foundation (AD)
NADF..........	National Arbor Day Foundation (EA)
NADF..........	North American Directory Forum
NADFA........	North American Deer Farmers Association (EA)
NADFAS.......	[The] National Association of Decorative and Fine Arts Societies [British]
NADFAS.......	National Association of Design and Fine Art Societies (AD)
NADFD........	National Association of Decorative Fabric Distributors (EA)
NADFPM......	National Association of Domestic and Farm Pump Manufacturers [Later, WSC]
NADFS........	National Association of Drop Forgers and Stampers (AD)
NADG..........	Nicotinamide Adenine Dinucleotide Glycohydrolase [An enzyme] (DMAA)
NADGE........	NATO Air Defense Ground Environment
NADGE........	NATO Air Defense Ground Equipment
NADGECO......	NATO Air Defense Ground Environment Consortium
NADGEMO ...	NADGE [NATO Air Defense Ground Environment] Management Office [Belgium]
NADGEMO ...	NATO Air Defense Ground Environment Management Organization (NATG)
NADH..........	Dihydronicotinamide Adenine Dinucleotide (AD)
NADH..........	Naval Ammunition Depot, Hawaii
NADH..........	Nicotinamide-Adenine Dinucleotide (Reduced) [See also NAD] [Biochemistry]
NADHCI.......	North American District Heating and Cooling Institute [Defunct] (EA)
NADHPRS	Naval Ammunition Depot Hawthorne Police Records System (DNAB)
NADI...........	National Association of Display Industries [New York, NY] (EA)
NADI...........	Naval Ammunition Depot, Indiana
NADIB.........	North American Defense Industrial Base
NADIBO........	North American Defense Industrial Base Organization
NADIN.........	National Airspace Data Interchange Network [FAA] (TAG)
NADIN II	National Airspace Data Interchange Network II [National digital message switching network for aeronautical data] (GAVI)
NADIP.........	Navy Display Improvement Program
NADIS.........	National Aerometric Data Information System [Environmental Protection Agency]
NADJ	National Association of Disk Jockeys (BUAC)
NADL..........	National Animal Disease Laboratory [Iowa]
NADL..........	National Association of Dental Laboratories (EA)
NADL..........	Navy Authorized Data List (NG)
NADLCC.......	National Association of Defense Lawyers in Criminal Cases [Later, NACDL] (EA)
NAD-LLL......	Naval Ammunition Depot - Lwalualei [Hawaii] (DNAB)
NADM	National Association of Discount Merchants [Defunct] (EA)
NADM	National Association of Doll Manufacturers [Later, NADSTM] (EA)
NADM	Naval Administration
NADMC........	Naval Air Development and Material Center
NADME........	Noise Amplitude Distribution Measuring Equipment (PDAA)
NADMR........	National Association of Diversified Manufacturers Representatives [Later, NAGMR] (EA)
NADMW.......	National Association of Direct Mail Writers
NAD/NADH...	Nicotinamide Adenine Dinucleotide (AD)
NADO..........	National Association of Development Organizations (EA)
NADO..........	Navy Accounts Disbursing Office
NADOA........	National Association of Division Order Analysts (EA)
NADOC........	Naval Aviation Depot Operations Center (DOMA)
NADOI........	National Association of Dog Obedience Instructors (EA)
NADONA/LTC...	National Association of Directors of Nursing Administration in Long Term Care (EA)
NADOP........	North American Defense Operation Plan [NORAD]
NADORF	National Association of Development Organization Research Fund
NADORF	National Association of Development Organizations Research Foundation (EA)
NADOT........	North Atlantic Deepwater Oil Terminal (PDAA)
NADOW.......	National Association for Training the Disabled in Office Work (AD)
NADP..........	National Acid Deposition Program [Air pollution]
NADP..........	National Association of Deafened People (BUAC)
NADP..........	National Association of Dental Plans (NTPA)
NADP..........	National Association of Desktop Publishers (EA)
NADP..........	National Association of Doctors in Practice [British] (DI)

NADP	National Atmospheric Deposition Program [Department of Agriculture]
NADP	NAVAIR Advanced Development Plan (MCD)
NADP	Nicotinamide-Adenine Dinucleotide Phosphate [Preferred form, but see also TPN] [Biochemistry]
nadp	Nicotinamide Adenine Dinucleotide Phosphate (AD)
NADPAS.......	National Association of Discharged Prisoners' Aid Societies [British] (DI)
NADPB	North Atlantic Defense Production Board (NATG)
NADPH........	Dihydronicotinamide Adenine Dinucleotide Phosphate (AD)
nadph	Dihydronicotinamide Adenine Dinucleotide Phosphate (AD)
NADPH........	Nicotinamide-Adenine Dinucleotide Phosphate (Reduced) [Preferred form, but see also TPNH] [Biochemistry]
NADREG	National Alliance for Democratic Restoration in Equatorial Guinea [Switzerland] (EAIO)
NADREPS	National Armaments Directors Representatives
NADS	National Advanced Driver Simulator [NHTSA] (TAG)
NADS	National Armament Directors [NATO]
NADS	National Association Diaper Services (EA)
NADS	National Association for Down Syndrome (EA)
NADS	Naval Air Development Station
NADS	North American Dostoevsky Society (EA)
NADS	North Atlantic Defense System
NADSA........	National Agricultural Diversification and Settlement Authority [Sri Lanka] (BUAC)
NADSA........	National Association of Dramatic and Speech Arts (EA)
NADSA........	North American Dairy Sheep Association (NTPA)
NADSC........	National Association of Direct Selling Companies [Later, DSA] (EA)
NADSP........	National Association of Dental Service Plans [Insurance] (DHSM)
NADSTM.....	National Association of Doll and Stuffed Toy Manufacturers (EA)
NADT	National Association for Drama Therapy (EA)
NADTP	National Association of Desktop Publishers (NTPA)
NADU.........	Naval Aircraft Delivery Unit
NADU.........	Naval Air Development Unit (MUGU)
NADUG.......	North American Datamanager Users Group (EA)
NADUS.......	National Association of Doctors in the United States (EA)
NADUSM.....	National Association of Deputy United States Marshals (EA)
NADVH.......	National Association of Drama with the Visually Handicapped (BUAC)
NADW........	National Association of Disabled Writers (BUAC)
NADW........	North Atlantic Deep Water [Oceanography]
NADWAGNS...	National Association of Deans of Women and Advisors to Girls in Negro Schools [Defunct] (EA)
NADWARN ...	National Disaster Warning System (AD)
NADWARN ...	Natural Disaster Warning
NADWARN ...	Natural Disaster Warning System (IAA)
NADWAS......	Natural Disaster Warning Survey (NOAA)
NADWAS......	North American Dr. Who Appreciation Society (EA)
NADX.........	National Dentex Corp. [NASDAQ symbol] (SAG)
NADX.........	Natl Dentex [NASDAQ symbol] (TTSB)
Nae...........	Exchangeable Body Sodium (MAE)
NAE...........	N-Acylethanolamine [Organic chemistry]
NAE...........	Nake [Tuamotu Archipelago] [Seismograph station code, US Geological Survey] (SEIS)
NAE...........	National Academy of Education
NAE...........	National Academy of Engineering [Washington, DC] (GRD)
NAE...........	National Administrative Expenses (NATG)
nae...........	National Administrative Expenses (AD)
NAE...........	National Adoption Exchange (EA)
NAE...........	National Aeronautical Establishment [Research center Canada] (IRC)
NAE...........	National Association of Entrepreneurs
NAE...........	National Association of Evangelicals (EA)
NAE...........	Nations Air Express, Inc. [FAA designator] (FAAC)
NAE...........	Naval Aeronautical Establishment [Canada] (AD)
NAE...........	Naval Aircraft Establishment (AD)
NAE...........	Navy Acquisition Executive (MCD)
NAE...........	Net Acid Excretion (DMAA)
NAE...........	Netware Application Engine [Networth, Inc.]
NAE...........	New Age Encyclopedia [A publication]
NAE...........	No American Equivalent [Language]
nAe...........	No American Equivalent (AD)
NAE...........	Noise Acoustic Emitter [Military] (CAAL)
NAE...........	Noram Energy Corp. [Formerly, Arkla, Inc.] [NYSE symbol] (SAG)
NAE...........	Noram Financing I [NYSE symbol] (SAG)
nae...........	Not Always Excused (AD)
NAE...........	Nursery Association Executives [Later, NAENA] (EA)
NAE4-HA.....	National Association of Extension 4-H Agents (EA)
NAEA	National Aerospace Education Association [Formerly, NAEC] [Defunct]
NAEA	National Art Education Archive (AIE)
NAEA	National Art Education Association (EA)
NAEA	National Artists Equity Association (EA)
NAEA	National Association of Enrolled Agents (EA)
NAEA	National Association of Estate Agents [British] (EAIO)
NAEA	National Association of Extension 4-H Agents (EA)
NAEA	Newspaper Advertising Executives Association [Later, INAME] (EA)
NAEA	Newspaper Advertising Executives Association of Canada (BUAC)
NAEA	Newspaper Advertising Executives' Association (DOAD)
NAE-ASEB ...	National Academy of Engineering Aeronautics and Space Engineering Board
NAEB	National Association of Educational Broadcasters [Formerly, Association of Collegeand University Broadcasting Stations (1934)] (EA)
NAEB	National Association of Educational Buyers [Woodbury, NY] (EA)
NAEB	Naval Aviation Evaluation Board
NAEB	North African Economic Board [World War II]

NAEBM .... National Association of Engine and Boat Manufacturers [*Later, NMMA*] (EA)
NAEC .... National Aboriginal Education Committee (BUAC)
NAEC .... National Advisory Eye Council
NAEC .... National Aeronautical Establishment, Canada (BUAC)
NAEC .... National Aerospace Education Council [*Later, NAEA*] (EA)
NAEC .... National Agricultural Engineering Corp. [*China*] (BUAC)
NAEC .... National Association Executives Club (EA)
NAEC .... National Association for Educational Computing (EA)
NAEC .... National Association of Electric Companies [*Later, EEI*] (EA)
NAEC .... National Association of Elevator Contractors (EA)
NAEC .... National Association of Engineering Companies (EA)
NAEC .... National Association of Exhibition Contractors [*British*] (BI)
NAEC .... National Aviation Education Council [*Later, National Aerospace Education Council*] (AEBS)
NAEC .... Naval Air Engineering Center [*Closed*]
NAEC .... Northern Agricultural Energy Center
NAECA .... National Appliance Energy Conservation Act [*1987*]
NAEC-ACEL... Naval Air Engineering Center Aerospace Crew Equipment Laboratory [*Lakehurst, NJ*]
NAEC-AEL .... Naval Air Engineering Center Aeronautical Engine Laboratory [*Lakehurst, NJ*]
NAEC-AML... Naval Air Engineering Center Aeronautical Materials Laboratory [*Lakehurst, NJ*]
NAEC-ASL.... Naval Air Engineering Center Aeronautical Structures Laboratory [*Lakehurst, NJ*]
NAEC-ENG ... Naval Air Engineering Center Engineering Department [*Lakehurst, NJ*]
NAECFO .... Naval Air Engineering Center Field Office (DNAB)
NAEC-GSED... Naval Air Engineering Center Ground Support Equipment Department [*Lakehurst, NJ*]
NAECOE .... National Academy of Engineering Committee on Ocean Engineering
NAECON........ National Aerospace Electronics Conference [*IEEE*] (MCD)
NAEd........... National Academy of Education (EA)
NAED .... National Association of Electrical Distributors (EA)
NAED .... National Association of Engravers and Diestampers (BUAC)
NAEDA......... National American Eskimo Dog Association (EA)
NAEDA......... North American Equipment Dealers Association (EA)
NAEDS......... National Association of Educational Data Systems (IAA)
NAEDS......... National Association of Engravers and Die-Stampers [*British*] (BI)
NAEE........... National Association of Environmental Education [*British*] (DBA)
NAEE........... North American Association for Environmental Education (EA)
NAEEO .... National Association for Equal Educational Opportunities (EA)
NAEF........... Naval Air Engineering Facility (MCD)
NAEFA.......... North American Economics and Finance Association (EA)
NAEF-ENG.... Naval Air Engineering Facility Ship Installations Engineering Department [*Philadelphia, PA*]
NAEFR .... North American English Ford Registry (EA)
NAEFTA........ National Association of Enrolled Federal Tax Accountants (EA)
NAEGA......... North American Export Grain Association (EA)
NAEGS......... National Association of Educational Guidance Services for Adults [*British*] (DBA)
NAEH .... National Alliance to End Homelessness (EA)
NAEHCA....... National Association of Employers on Health Care Action
NAEHCA....... National Association of Employers on Health Care Alternatives (EA)
NAEHE .... National Association of Extension Home Economists (EA)
NAEHMO...... National Association of Employers on Health Maintenance Organizations [*Later, NAEHCA*] (EA)
NAEIAC .... National Association of Educational Inspectors, Advisers, and Consultants (AIE)
NAEIC .... Nevada Applied Ecology Information Center [*Department of Energy*] (IID)
NAEIR .... National Association for the Exchange of Industrial Resources (EA)
NAEKM .... National Association of Electronic Keyboard Manufacturers (EA)
NAEL............ Naval Air Engineering Laboratory (MCD)
NAEL............ No-Adverse-Effect Level [*Toxicology*] (LDT)
NAELA .... National Academy of Elder Law Attorneys (EA)
NAELB .... National Association of Equipment Leasing Brokers (NTPA)
NAELC .... National Architect-Engineer Liaison Commission [*Defunct*] (EA)
NAEL-ENG.... Naval Air Engineering Laboratory Ship Installations Engineering Department [*Philadelphia, PA*]
NAELSI .... Naval Air Electronics Shipboard Installation
NAEM........... National Association for Environmental Management
NAEM........... National Association of Exposition Managers (EA)
NAEM........... Naval Air Effect Model (PDAA)
NAEMB .... National Academy of Engineering Marine Board
NAEMSP .... National Association of Emergency Medical Service Physicians (EA)
NAEMT......... National Association of Emergency Medical Technicians (EA)
NAEN .... National Association of Educational Negotiators (EA)
NAENA......... Nursery Association Executives of North America (EA)
NAE-NEPP.... National Academy of Engineering Navy Environmental Protection Program Study Group
NAENG......... North African Engineer Section [*World War II*]
NAEO .... National Activity Education Organization (EA)
NAEO .... National Association of Extradition Officials (EA)
NAEOM .... National Association of Electronic Organ Manufacturers
NAEOP......... National Association of Educational Office Personnel (EA)
NAEP .... National Assessment of Educational Progress (AD)
NAEP .... National Assessment of Educational Progress, The Nation's Report Card (EA)
NAEP .... National Association of Educational Programs [*Carnegie Foundation*] (AD)
NAEP .... National Association of Environmental Professionals (EA)
NAEP .... National Asthma Education Program (DMAA)
NAEPC .... National Association of Estate Planning Councils (EA)
NAEPDC....... National Adult Education Professional Development Consortium (NTPA)
NAEPIRS...... National Assessment of Educational Progress Information Retrieval System [*National Institute of Education*] [*Database*]
NAEPIS .... North America Engineering Parts Inquiry System
NAEPrA........ Noram Energy $3 Cv Ex A Pfd [*NYSE symbol*] (TTSB)
NAEPS .... National Academy of Economics and Political Science (EA)
NAER .... National Association of Executive Recruiters (EA)
NAERC .... North American Electric Reliability Council (EA)
NAES .... National Association for Ethnic Studies (EA)
NAES .... National Association of Ecumenical Staff (EA)
NAES .... National Association of Educational Secretaries [*Later, NAEOP*] (EA)
NAES .... National Association of Episcopal Schools (EA)
NAES .... National Association of Executive Secretaries (EA)
NAES .... Native American Educational Service [*Later, NAESC*] (EA)
NAES .... Naval Air Experimental Station
NAES .... Nevada Agricultural Experiment Station [*University of Nevada - Reno*] [*Research center*] (RCD)
NAES .... North African Army Exchange Service [*World War II*]
NAESA......... National Association of Elevator Safety Authorities (EA)
NAESA......... North American Economic Studies Association (EA)
NAESC .... National Association of Energy Service Companies (EA)
NAESC .... Native American Educational Services College (EA)
NAESCO....... National Association of Energy Service Companies (EA)
NAESP .... National Association of Elementary School Principals (EA)
NAEST .... National Archives for Electrical Science and Technology (PDAA)
NAESU .... Naval Aviation Electronic Service Unit (MCD)
NAESU .... Naval Aviation Engineering Service Unit [*Philadelphia, PA*]
NAESUDET... Naval Aviation Engineering Service Unit Detachment (DNAB)
NAET........... National Association for Educational Television (NTCM)
NAET........... National Association of Educational Technicians [*British*]
NAETS .... Naval Air Emission-Tracking System
NAETV .... National Association for Educational Television [*Defunct*]
NAEUSA....... National Academy of Engineering of the United States of America (NTPA)
NAEW .... NATO Airborne Early Warning
NAEWS .... NATO Airborne Early Warning System
NAEWTF ...... NATO Aircrew Electronic Warfare Tactics Facility (NATG)
NAEYC .... National Association for the Education of Young Children (EA)
NAF............. Guilder [*Florin*] [*Monetary unit Netherlands Antilles*]
NAF............. Nafimidone [*Biochemistry*]
NAF............. Name and Address File [*IRS*]
NAF............. National Abortion Federation (EA)
NAF............. National Abortion Foundation (AD)
NAF............. National Aging Foundation (EA)
NAF............. National Amputation Foundation (EA)
NAF............. National Analytical Facility [*National Oceanic and Atmospheric Administration*]
NAF............. National Angling Federation [*British*]
NAF............. National Arts Foundation (EA)
NAF............. National Ataxia Foundation (EA)
NAF............. National Aviation Forum
NAF............. Naval Aircraft Factory
NAF............. Naval Air Facility
NAF............. Naval Air Force
NAF............. Naval Avionics Facility [*Later, NAC*] [*Indianapolis, IN*]
NAF............. Nernst Approximation Formula [*Physics*]
NAF............. Net Acid Flux [*Medicine*] (DMAA)
NAF............. Netherland-America Foundation [*Later, Netherlands-America Community Association*] (EA)
NAF............. Network Access Facility
NAF............. New Age Federation (EA)
NAF............. New Age Media Fund [*NYSE symbol*] (SPSG)
NAF............. No Abnormal Findings [*Medicine*]
NAF............. Nonappropriated Fund [*or Funds*]
naf.............. Nonappropriated Funds (AD)
NAF............. Non-urea Adducting Fatty Acid [*Food science*]
NAF............. Nordisk Anaestesiologisk Forening [*Scandinavian Society of Anaesthesiologists - SSA*] (EA)
NAF............. Norges Automobil Fornund [*Norway Automobile Association*] (AD)
NAF............. North American Federation of Third Order Franciscans (EA)
NAF............. North American Fire [*Vancouver Stock Exchange symbol*]
NAF............. Northern Attack Force [*Navy*]
NAF............. North West Atlantic Fisheries, Memorial University [*UTLAS symbol*]
NAF............. Notice of Adverse Finding [*Food and Drug Administration*]
NAF............. Nouvelle Action Francaise [*New French Action*] [*Political party*] (PPE)
NAF............. Numbered Air Force (AFM)
NAF............. Royal Netherlands Air Force [*ICAO designator*] (FAAC)
NaF............. Sodium Fluoride [*Chemistry*] (DAVI)
NAFA .... National Academy of Foreign Affairs (AD)
NAFA .... National Aerobic Fitness Award (AD)
NAFA .... National Aircraft Finance Association (EA)
NAFA .... National Air Filtration Association (EA)
NAFA .... National American Farmers Association [*Defunct*] (EA)
NAFA .... National Association of Fine Arts [*Defunct*] (EA)
NAFA .... National Association of Fleet Administrators [*Iselin, NJ*] (EA)
NAFA .... National Association of Furniture Agents [*Australia*]
NAFA .... National Association to Aid Fat Americans [*Bellrose, NY*]
NAFA .... Net Acquisition of Financial Assets (ADA)
NAFA .... Nonappropriated Fund Activity (CINC)
NAFA .... North American Falconers Association (EA)
NAFA .... North American Farm Alliance (EA)
NAFA .... Northwest Atlantic Fisheries Act of 1950
NAFAC .... National Association for Ambulatory Care [*Formerly, NAFEC*] (EA)

NAFAD	National Association of Fashion and Accessory Designers (EA)
NAFAG	NATO Air Force Advisory Group (NATG)
NAFAG	NATO Air Force Armaments Group
NAFAPAC	National Association for Association Political Action Committees (EA)
NAFARE	National Association for Families and Addiction Research and Education (PAZ)
NAFAS	National Association of Flower Arrangement Societies (AD)
NAFAS	National Association of Flower Arrangement Societies of Great Britain (BI)
NAFAS	Nonappropriated Fund Accounting System [*Military*] (DNAB)
NAFAX	National Facsimile Network [*National Weather Service*]
NAFB	National Association of Farm Broadcasters (EA)
NAFB	National Association of Franchised Businessmen [*Defunct*] (EA)
NAFB	Norton Air Force Base [*California*]
NAFB & AE	National Association of Farriers, Blacksmiths, and Agricultural Engineers [*British*] (DBA)
NAFBO	National Association for Business Organizations [*Baltimore, MD*] (EA)
NAFBRAT	National Association for Better Radio and Television [*Later, NABB*] (EA)
NAFC	Nash Finch Co. [*NASDAQ symbol*] (TTSB)
NAFC	National Accounting and Finance Council [*Alexandria, VA*] (EA)
NAFC	National Anthropological Film Center [*Smithsonian Institution*] (GRD)
NAFC	National Anti-Fluoridation Campaign [*British*] (DBA)
NAFC	National Association of Fan Clubs (EA)
NAFC	National Association of Financial Consultants (EA)
NAFC	National Association of Food Chains (NADA)
NAFC	National Association of Formwork Contractors [*British*] (DBA)
NAFC	National Association of Friendship Centres [*Canada*]
NAFC	National Average Fuel Consumption
NAFC	Naval Air Ferry Command [*World War II*]
NAFC	Navy Accounting and Finance Center
NAFC	North American Fishing Club (EA)
NAFC	North American Forestry Commission [*UN Food and Agriculture Organization*]
NAFC	North American Forum on the Catechumenate (EA)
NAFC	Northern Attack Force Commander [*Navy*]
NAFCA	North American Family Campers Association (EA)
NAFCC	National Association for Family Child Care (NTPA)
NAFCD	National Association of Floor Covering Distributors (EA)
NAFCE	National Association of Federal Career Employees [*Defunct*] (EA)
NAFCI	National Association of Floor Covering Installers [*Later, AIDS International*] (EA)
NAFCM	National Association for Community Mediation (NTPA)
NAFCO	National Association of Franchise Companies (EA)
NAFCO	National Floor Products Co., Inc.
NAFCR	National Association of Foster Care Reviewers (EA)
NAFCU	National Association of Federal Credit Unions (EA)
NAFD	National Air Forwarding Division [*Institute of Freight Forwarders*] (AD)
NAFD	National Association of Farm Directors (NTCM)
NAFD	National Association of Flour Distributors (EA)
NAFD	National Association of Funeral Directors [*British*] (BI)
NAFDC	National Association for Family Day Care (EA)
NAFDI	National Foundation for Depressive Illness (EA)
NAFE	National Association for Female Executives [*New York, NY*] (EA)
NAFE	National Association for Film in Education [*British*]
NAFE	National Association for Free Enterprise [*Defunct*] (EA)
NAFE	National Association of Forensic Economists (EA)
NAFE	Non-Advanced Further Education [*British*]
NAFEA	National Association for the Education and Advancement of Cambodian, Laotian, and Vietnamese Americans
NAFEC	National Association of Farmer Elected Committeemen (EA)
NAFEC	National Association of Freestanding Emergency Centers [*Later, NAAC*] (EA)
NAFEC	National Aviation Facilities Experimental Center [*of FAA*] [*Atlantic City, NJ*]
NAFED	National Association of Fire Equipment Distributors (EA)
NAFEM	National Association of Food Equipment Manufacturers (EA)
NAFEMS	National Agency for Finite Element Methods and Standards [*British*] (IRUK)
NAFEO	National Association for Equal Opportunity in Higher Education (EA)
NAFEPA	National Association of Federal Education Program Administrators (NTPA)
NAFEX	North American Fruit Explorers (EA)
NAFF	National Association for Freedom [*British*]
nAff	Need for Affection
NAFF	Need for Affiliation (MHDB)
naff	Need for Affiliation (AD)
NAFFP	National Association of Frozen Food Packers [*Later, AFFI*] (EA)
NAFFP	National Association of Frozen Food Producers (AD)
NAFFS	National Association of Fruits, Flavors, and Syrups (EA)
NAFFW	National Association of Full Figured Women (EA)
NAFGDA	National Auto and Flat Glass Dealers Association [*Later, NGA*]
NAFGPD	National Association of Foster Grandparent Program Directors (EA)
NAFI	National Association of Fire Investigators (EA)
NAFI	National Association of Flight Instructors (EA)
NAFI	Naval Air Fighting Instructions
NAFI	Naval Avionics Facility (AD)
NAFI	Naval Avionics Facility, Indianapolis [*Later, NAC*]
NAFI	Nonappropriated Fund Instrumentalities [*DoD*] (MCD)
NAFIC	National Association of Fraternal Insurance Counsellors [*Sheboygan, WI*] (EA)
NAFIN	North African Finance Section [*World War II*]
NAFINSA	Nacional Financiera [*National Finance Coro.*] [*Spanish*] (AD)
NAFIP	National Foreign Intelligence Program [*DoD*] (MCD)
NAFIPS	North American Fuzzy Information Processing Society (EA)
NAFIS	National Association of Federally Impacted Schools (EA)
NAFIS	Naval Forces Intelligence Study (MCD)
NAFIS	Navigational Aid Flight Inspection System (AFM)
NAFISS	Nonappropriated Funds Information Standard System [*Army*]
NAFL	National Alliance for Family Life [*Later, NACFT*] (EA)
NAFLAC	Navy Department Fuel and Lubricants Advisory Committee [*Ministry of Defense*] [*British*] (PDAA)
NAFLANT	Naval Air Facilities, Atlantic
NAFLFD	National Association of Federally Licensed Firearms Dealers (EA)
NAFLI	Natural Flight Indication (MCD)
NAFLI	Natural Flight Instrument System
NAFM	National Armed Forces Museum (AD)
NAFM	National Association of Fan Manufacturers [*Later, AMCA*]
NAFM	National Association of Flag Manufacturers
NAFM	National Association of Furniture Manufacturers [*Later, AFMA*] (EA)
NAFMA	NATO European Fighter Management Agency
NAFMAB	National Armed Forces Museum Advisory Board [*Smithsonian Institution*]
NAFMB	National Association of FM [*Frequency Modulation*] Broadcasters [*Later, NRBA*] (EA)
NAFMC	Nonappropriated Funds, Marine Corps (DNAB)
NAFMDA	North American Folk Music and Dance Alliance (NTPA)
NAFMG	National Association of Foreign Medical Graduates [*Later, ACIP*]
NAFMIS	Nonappropriated Funds Management Information System
NAFMOW	National Action Forum for Midlife and Older Women (EA)
NAFMW	National Action for Former Military Wives (EA)
NAFN	Norton Administrator for Networks [*Symantec Corp.*] [*Telecommunications*] (PCM)
NAFO	National Association of Farmworker Organizations [*Defunct*] (EA)
NAFO	National Association of Fire Officers [*British*] (DI)
NAFO	Northwest Atlantic Fisheries Organization (EA)
NAFOW	National Action Forum for Midlife and Older Women (EA)
NAFOW	National Action Forum for Older Women [*Later, NAFMOW*] (EA)
NAFP	National Association of Factoring Professionals (NTPA)
NAFP	National Association of Food Processors (ECON)
NAFP	Naval Air Force, Pacific Fleet (DNAB)
NAFP	New Armed Forces of the Philippines (AD)
NAFPA	National Alcohol Fuels Producers Association [*Defunct*] (EA)
NAFPA	National Association of Federal Education Program Administrators (EA)
NAFPAC	Naval Air Facilities, Pacific
NAFPB	National Association of Freight Payment Banks [*Pittsburgh, PA*] (EA)
NAFPC	National Academy for Fire Prevention and Control [*of FEMA*]
NAFPD	National Association of Family Planning Doctors [*British*] (DBA)
NAFPP	National Accelerated Food Production Project [*Agency for International Development*]
NAFPP	National Association of Fresh Produce Processors (EA)
NAFPU	North American Friends of Palestinian Universities [*Defunct*] (EA)
NAFR	National Association of First Responders (NTPA)
N Afr	North Africa
NAFRC	National Association of Fiscally Responsible Cities [*Defunct*] (EA)
NAFRC	North Atlantic Fisheries Research Center (PDAA)
NAFRD	National Association of Fleet Resale Dealers [*Los Angeles, CA*] (EA)
NAFRF	Navy Alternate Fuel Reference File [*Battelle Memorial Institute*] [*Information service or system Defunct*] (IID)
NAFRLG	National Alliance of Financially-Responsible Local Governments (AD)
NAFRTM	National Association of Farm and Ranch Trailer Manufacturers [*Defunct*] (EA)
NAFS	National Association of Fastener Stockholders [*British*] (DBA)
NAFS	National Association of Foot Specialists (AD)
NAFS	National Association of Forensic Sciences (AD)
NAFS	Naval Air Fighter School
NA/FS	Naval Aviator/Flight Surgeon (MCD)
NAFS	Newark Air Force Station [*Ohio*]
NAFSA	National Association for Foreign Student Affairs (EA)
NAFSA	National Association of Fire Science and Administration [*Defunct*] (EA)
NAFSA	National Association of Foreign Student Advisors (AD)
NAFSA	No American Flag Shipping Available
NAFSC	North American Farm Show Council (NTPA)
NAFSLAC	National Association of Federations of Syrian and Lebanese American Clubs (EA)
NAFSMA	National Association of Flood and Stormwater Management Agencies (NTPA)
NAFSO	National Association of Field Studies Officers [*British*] (DBA)
NAFSONW	Nonappropriated Fund Statement of Operations and Net Worth
NAFSWMA	National Association of Flood and Storm Water Management Agencies (EA)
NAFT	National Alternative Fuel Test (AD)
NAFT	Natural Adjuvant Factor Toxoid [*Medicine*]
NAFT	Network for Analysis of Fireball Trajectories (EA)
NAFTA	National Amalgamated Furnishing Trades Association [*A union*] [*British*]
NAFTA	National Association of Futures Trading Advisors [*Defunct*] (EA)
NAFTA	National Association of Future Teachers of America [*Later, Student National Education Association*] (AEBS)
NAFTA	New Zealand-Australia Free Trade Agreement (AD)
NAFTA	North American Free Trade Agreement [*Passed in 1993*]
NAFTA	North American Free-Trade Area (ECON)
NAFTA	North Atlantic Free Trade Area
NAFTAT	National Association for the Advancement of Time (EA)
NAFTC	National Association of Freight Transportation Consultants (EA)

NAFTF.......... National Association of Finishers of Textile Fabrics [*Later, ATMI*] (EA)
NAFTM....... National Association of Fund Raising Ticket Manufacturers (NTPA)
NAFTOC...... NORAD Automated Forward Tell Output to Canada (MCD)
NAFTRAC..... National Foreign Trade Council (EA)
NAFTZ......... National Association of Foreign-Trade Zones [*Washington, DC*] (EA)
NAFV .... National Association of Federal Veterinarians (EA)
NAFW .... National Association of Future Women [*Later, NAFWIC*] (EA)
NAFWA....... North American Flowerbulb Wholesalers Association (EA)
NAFWIC....... National Association for Women in Careers (EA)
NAFWR....... National Association of Furniture Warehousemen and Removers (AD)
Nag............. All India Reporter, Nagpur [*A publication*] (DLA)
NAG .... Goddard Space Flight Center, Greenbelt, MD [*OCLC symbol*] (OCLC)
Nag............. Indian Law Reports, Nagpur Series [*A publication*] (DLA)
Nag............. Indian Rulings, Nagpur Series [*A publication*] (DLA)
NAG .... N-Acetylglucosamine [*Biochemistry*]
NAG .... N-Acetylglucosaminidase [*An enzyme*]
NAG .... Nachrichten der Akademie der Wissenschaften in Goettingen. Philologisch-Historische Klasse [*A publication*] (BJA)
Nag............. Nagasaki [*Japan*] (AD)
Nag............. Nagoya [*Japan*] (AD)
NAG .... Nagoya [*Japan*] [*Seismograph station code, US Geological Survey*] (SEIS)
NAG .... Nagpur [*India*] [*Airport symbol*] (OAG)
NAG .... Narrow Angle Glaucoma [*Medicine*]
NAG .... National Academy of Geosciences (EA)
NAG .... National Acquisitions Group [*Libraries*] [*British*]
NAG .... National Action Group [*Antibusing organization*]
NAG .... National Advisory Group, Convenience Stores/Petroleum Companies (EA)
NAG .... National Air-Racing Group (EA)
NAG .... National Association of Gagwriters (EA)
NAG .... National Association of Gardeners [*Later, PGMS*] (EA)
NAG .... National Association of Goldsmiths [*British*]
NAG .... National Association of Grooms [*British*] (DI)
NAG .... National Association of Groundsmen [*British*] (DI)
NAG .... Naval Advisory Group
NAG .... Naval Analysis Group (MCD)
NAG .... Naval Applications Group
NAG .... Navy Astronautics Group (MUGU)
NAG .... Negro Actors Guild (NADA)
NAG .... Negro Actors Guild of America (EA)
NAG .... Neighborhood Action Group (AD)
NAG .... NERVA [*Nuclear Engine for Rocket Vehicle Application*] Advisory Group [*NASA*] (KSC)
NAG .... Net Annual Gain [*Business term*] (PDAA)
nag .... Net Annual Gain (AD)
NAG .... Networking Advisory Group [*Library of Congress*]
N-Ag .... Neutralization Antigenic Site [*Immunogenetics*]
Nag............. No-Acronym Sort of Guy [*Term coined by William F. Doescher, publisher of "D & B Reports"*] [*Lifestyle classification*]
NAG .... Nonagglutinable [*or Nonagglutinating*] [*Immunochemistry*]
NAG .... Nor-Acme Gold Mines Ltd. [*Toronto Stock Exchange symbol*]
NAG .... Northern Army Group (NATG)
NAG .... Nova Scotia Agricultural College Library [*UTLAS symbol*]
NAG .... Numerical Algorithms Group (CIST)
NAG .... Nystagmus Action Group [*British*] (DBA)
NAGA .... National Advertising Golf Association (EA)
NAGA .... National Amputee Golf Association (EA)
NAGA .... North American Gamebird Association (EA)
NAGA .... North American Ginseng Association [*Defunct*] (EA)
NAGAP........ National Association of Gay Alcoholism Professionals [*Later, NALGAP*] (EA)
NAGAP........ National Association of Graduate Admissions Professionals (NTPA)
NAGARA ...... National Association of Government Archives and Records Administrators (EA)
NAGARD ...... NATO Advisory Group for Aeronautical Research and Development
Nagas.......... Nagasaki [*Japan*] (AD)
NAGASA...... North American Graphic Arts Suppliers Association (NTPA)
NAGB & SPA... North American Game Breeders and Shooting Preserve Association [*Later, NAGA*] (EA)
NAGBM....... National Association of Golf Ball Manufacturers (EA)
NAGC.......... National Association for Gifted Children (EA)
NAGC.......... National Association of Girls Clubs (EA)
NAGC.......... National Association of Government Communicators (EA)
NAGC.......... National Gaming Corp. [*NASDAQ symbol*] (SAG)
NAGC.......... Naval Armed Guard Center
NAGC.......... Navy Astronautics Group Conference [*Navy*]
NAGC.......... North American Gladiolus Council (EA)
NAGCD........ National Association of Glass Container Distributors [*Later, NACD*] (EA)
NAGCM........ National Association of Golf Club Manufacturers (EA)
NAGCO........ Naval Air Ground Center
NAGCP........ National Association of Greeting Card Publishers [*Later, GCA*] (EA)
NAGCR........ North American Guild of Change Ringers (EA)
NAGDCA ...... National Association of Government Deferred Compensation Administrators (EA)
NAGDM....... National Association of Garage Door Manufacturers (EA)
NAGE .... National Association of Government Employees (EA)
NAGE .... NATO Air Defense Group Environment (AABC)
N-age.......... Nuclear Age (AD)
NAGGL........ National Association of Government Guaranteed Lenders (NTPA)
NagHammSt... Nag Hammadi Studies [*A publication*] (BJA)

NAGHSR ...... National Association of Governors' Highway Safety Representatives (EA)
NAGI .... National Association of Government Inspectors [*Later, National Association of Government Inspectors and Quality Assurance Personnel*] (EA)
NAGIM........ North American Gunnery Instruction Monitor
NAGI/QAP ... National Association of Government Inspectors and Quality Assurance Personnel (EA)
NAGIS......... National Airport Grant Information System [*FAA*] (TAG)
Nag LJ .... Nagpur Law Journal [*India*] [*A publication*] (DLA)
Nag LN .... Nagpur Law Notes [*India*] [*A publication*] (DLA)
NAGLO........ National Association of Governmental Labor Officials (EA)
Nag LR .... Nagpur Law Reports [*India*] [*A publication*] (DLA)
NAGM .... National Association of Glove Manufacturers (EA)
NAGM .... National Association of Glue Manufacturers [*Defunct*] (EA)
NAGM .... National Association of Governors and Managers [*British*] (DBA)
NAGMR........ National Association of General Merchandise Representatives [*Chicago, IL*] (EA)
Nagp........... Nagpur, India (AD)
NAGPFS....... National Association of Governors' Councils on Physical Fitness and Sports (NTPA)
NAGPIPM..... National Association of Graphic and Product Identification Manufacturers (NTPA)
NAGPM....... National Association of Grained Plate Makers (AD)
NAGP/NCP ... North American Great Plains/North China Plain Project [*Agriculture*]
NAGPRA...... Native American Graves Protection and Repatriation Act [*Enacted 1990*]
NAGPTDU..... National Action Group for the Prevention and Treatment of Decubitus Ulcers (EA)
NAGRA........ National Association of Gambling Regulatory Agencies (EA)
NAGRA........ Nationalen Genossenschaft fuer die Lagerung Radioaktiver Abfaelle [*National Cooperative Society for the Storage of Radioactive Wastes*] [*Germany*] (AD)
NAGRA........ Nation Association of Govenment Archives and Records Administration (TELE)
NAGS .... National Allotments and Gardens Society Ltd. [*British*] (BI)
NAGS .... National Association of Government Secretaries [*Defunct*]
NAGS .... Naval Air Gunners School
NAGSC........ National Association of Government Service Contractors [*Defunct*] (EA)
NAGSCT....... National Association of Guidance Supervisors and Counselor Trainers
NAGT .... National Association of Geology Teachers (EA)
NAGT .... National Association of Geoscience Teachers (NTPA)
NAGTADD..... National Association of Government Training and Development Directors (NTPA)
NAGTC........ North American Gasoline Tax Conference (EA)
Nag UCL Mag... Nagpur University. College of Law. Magazine [*1933-34*] [*India*] [*A publication*] (DLA)
NAGVG........ National Association Greenhouse Vegetable Growers (EA)
NAGWS........ National Association for Girls and Women in Sport (EA)
NAH .... Autism Services Center [*Formerly, National Autism Hotline*] (EA)
NAH .... Naha [*Ryukyu Islands*] [*Airport symbol*] (OAG)
NAH .... Nahanni Air Services Ltd. [*Canada ICAO designator*] (FAAC)
nah .... Nahuatlan [*MARC language code Library of Congress*] (LCCP)
Nah............ Nahum [*Old Testament book*]
NAH .... National Association of Homebuilders (AD)
NAH .... National Autism Hotline (EA)
NAH .... Night Adoration in the Home (EA)
NAH .... No-Antihalation Film
NAH .... Nordic Association for Hydrology (EA)
NAH .... Nordic Association for the Handicapped (EA)
NAH .... Nordic Association of Hairdressers [*Sweden*] (EAIO)
NAH .... Not at Home
NAHA .... National Association for Holistic Aromatherapy (NTPA)
NAHA .... National Association of Handwriting Analysts
NAHA .... National Association of Health Authorities [*British*] (EAIO)
NAHA .... National Association of Health Authorities in England and Wales (AIE)
NAHA .... National Association of Hotel Accountants [*Later, International Association of Hospitality Accountants*] (EA)
NAHA .... North American Highway Association
NAHA .... Norwegian-American Historical Association (EA)
NAHAD........ National Association of Hose and Accessories Distributors (EA)
Nahal.......... Na'or Halutsi Lohem [*Fighting Pioneer Youth*] [*Israel*] (AD)
NAHAL .... Noar Halutzi Lohem [*Pioneering Fighting Youth*] [*Israel*]
NAHAM .... National Association of Healthcare Access Management (EA)
NAHAM .... National Association of Hospital Admitting Managers (EA)
NAHAT .... National Association of Health Authorities and Trusts [*British*] (EAIO)
NAHAWA...... North American Heating and Airconditioning Wholesalers Association
NAHB .... National Alliance of Homebased Businesswomen [*Defunct*] (EA)
NAHB .... National Association of Home Builders (NADA)
NAHB .... National Association of Home Builders of the United States (EA)
NAHB .... National Association of Homes for Boys [*Later, NFCCE*]
NAHBB........ National Association of Home Based Businesses [*Baltimore, MD*] (EA)
NAHBE........ Naval Academy Heat Balanced Engine [*Pronounced "knobby"*]
NAHBO........ National Association of Hospital Broadcasting Organizations [*British*] (DBA)
NAHB/RC ..... NAHB Remodelers Council (EA)
NAHC.......... National Advisory Health Council
NAHC.......... National Anti-Hunger Coalition (EA)
NAHC.......... National Association for Home Care (EA)
NAHC.......... National Association of Holiday Centres [*British*] (DBA)
NAHC.......... National Association of Homes for Children (EA)

NAHC .... National Association of Housing Cooperatives (EA)
NAHC .... North American Hunting Club (EA)
NAHCAC...... National Ad Hoc Committee Against Censorship (AD)
NAHCO .... National Association of Hispanic County Officials (NTPA)
NAHCR .... National Association of Healthcare Recruitment (EA)
NAHCS .... National Association of Health Career Schools (EA)
NAHCS .... National Association of Health Center Schools (DMAA)
NAHCSP....... National Association of Hospital Central Service Personnel [*Later, IAHCSM*] (EA)
NAHD .... National Association for Hospital Development (EA)
NAHD .... National Association for Human Development (EA)
NAHD .... National Association of Hillel Directors [*Later, IAHD*] (EA)
NAHDDM ..... National Association of House and Daytime Dress Manufacturers (EA)
NAHDO .... National Association of Health Data Organizations (EA)
NAHDSA ...... National Association of Hebrew Day School Administrators (EA)
NAHE .... National Alliance for Hydroelectric Energy (EA)
NAHE .... National Association for Holocaust Education (EA)
NAHE .... National Association for Humanities Education (EA)
NAHEE .... National Association for Humane and Environmental Education (EA)
NAHEM .... National Association of Health Estates Managers [*British*] (DBA)
NAHES .... National Association of Home Economics Supervisors [*Later, NASSVHE*] (EA)
NAHFAGIF.... National Archives and Historical Foundation of the American GI Forum (EA)
NAHFE .... National Association of Hispanic Federal Executives (EA)
NAHFO .... National Association of Hospital Fire Officers [*British*] (DBA)
NAHG .... National Association of Homoeopathic Groups [*British*] (DBA)
NAHG .... National Association of Humanistic Gerontology (EA)
NAHGT .... National Aboriginal Health Goals and Targets [*Australia*]
NAHHA .... National Association of Home Health Agencies [*Later, NAHC*] (EA)
NAHHH .... National Association of Hospital Hospitality Houses (EA)
NAHHIC........ National Association of House to House Installment Companies [*Later, NAIC*] (EA)
NAHI .... National Association of Home Inspectors (NTPA)
NAHI .... National Athletic Health Institute (EA)
NAHICUS ..... Nuclear Attack Hazards in the Continental United States
NAHIM .... National Association of Housing Information Managers (NTPA)
NAHIS .... National Arts and Handicapped Information Service (EA)
NAHJ .... National Association of Hispanic Journalists (EA)
NAHL .... North American Hockey League
NAHLS .... National Association of Hispanic and Latino Studies (NTPA)
NAHM .... National Association of Home Manufacturers [*Later, HMC*] (EA)
NAHM .... National Association of Hosiery Manufacturers (EA)
NAHMA .... National Affordable Housing Management Association (NTPA)
NAHMA .... National Assisted Housing Management Association (NTPA)
NAHMA .... National Association of Hotel and Motel Accountants [*Later, International Association of Hospitality Accountants*]
NAHMOR ..... National Association of HMO [*Health Maintenance Organization*] Regulators
NAHN .... National Association of Hispanic Nurses (EA)
NAHNS........ National Association of the Holy Name Society (EA)
NAHO .... National Association of Hearing Officials (NTPA)
NAHO .... National Association of Homeowners [*British*] (DBA)
NAHOD .... N-Acetylhexosamine Oxidase (DB)
NAHP .... National Association of Hispanic Publications (EA)
NAHP .... National Association of Horseradish Packers [*Defunct*] (EA)
NAHP .... National Association of Hypnotists and Psychotherapists [*British*] (DBA)
NAHPA .... National Association of Hospital Purchasing Agents [*Later, NAHPMM*] (EA)
NAHPM .... National Association of Hospital Purchasing Management [*Later, NAHP MM*] (EA)
NAHPMM ..... National Association of Hospital Purchasing Materials Management (EA)
NAHPS......... North American Habitat Preservation Society (EA)
NAHQ .... National Association for Healthcare Quality (EA)
NAHRMP...... National Association of Hotel and Restaurant Meat Purveyors [*Later, NAMP*] (EA)
NAHRO .... National Association of Housing and Redevelopment Officials (EA)
NAHRW........ National Association of Human Rights Workers (EA)
NAHS .... National Aboriginal Health Strategy [*Australia*]
NAHS .... National Association of Health Stores [*British*] (DBA)
NAHS .... National Association of Horological Schools (EA)
NAHS .... New American High Schools [*Initiative*]
NAHS .... North American Heather Society (EA)
NAHS .... North American Hernia Society (NTPA)
NAHSA .... National Association for Hearing and Speech Action (EA)
NAHSA .... National Association of Hearing and Speech Agencies (AEBS)
NAHSA .... North American Horticultural Supply Association (EA)
NAHSC .... National Association of Homes and Services for Children (EA)
NAHSC .... National Automated Highway System Consortium
NAHSE .... National Association of Health Services Executives (EA)
NAHSL .... North Atlantic Health Sciences Libraries
NAHSO .... National Association of Hospital Supplies Officers [*British*] (BI)
NAHSPO ..... National Association of Health Service Personnel Officers [*British*] (DBA)
NAHSQCD ... National Association of Human Service Quality Control Directors (NTPA)
NAHSSO ..... National Association of Health Service Security Officers [*British*] (DBA)
NAHST .... National Association of Human Services Technologies [*Defunct*] (EA)
NAHSTA ...... National Hiking and Ski Touring Association (EA)
NAHSWP...... National Aboriginal Health Strategy Working Party [*Australia*]
NAHT .... National Association of Head Teachers [*British*]

NAHU .... NAHU, an Association of Bull Users [*Formerly, North American Honeywell Users Association*] (EA)
NAHU .... National Association of Health Underwriters [*Washington, DC*] (EA)
NAHUC .... National Association of Health Unit Clerks-Coordinators (EA)
NAHUC .... National Association of Health Unit Coordinators [*Formerly, National Association of Health Unit Clerks-Coordinators*] (EA)
NAHW .... National Association of Hardwood Wholesalers [*Defunct*]
NAHWMUMC... National Association of Health and Welfare Ministries of the United Methodist Church [*Later, United Methodist Association of Health and Welfare Ministries - UMA*] (EA)
NAHWW ...... National Association of Home and Workshop Writers (EA)
NAI.............. Annai [*Guyana*] [*Airport symbol*] (OAG)
NAI.............. N-Acetylimidazole [*Organic chemistry*]
NAI.............. Nairobi [*Kenya*] [*Seismograph station code, US Geological Survey*] (SEIS)
NAI.............. Named Areas of Interest [*Army intelligence matrix*] (INF)
NAI.............. Nanjing Aeronautical Institute [*China*] (BUAC)
NAI.............. National Agricultural Institute [*Later, ACA*] (EA)
NAI.............. National Apple Institute [*Later, IAI*] (EA)
NAI.............. National Association of Independent Insurance Auditors and Engineers (NTPA)
NAI.............. National Association of Instructors (BUAC)
NAI.............. National Association of Interpretation (EA)
NAI.............. Natural Alternatives International [*AMEX symbol*] (SPSG)
NAI.............. Natural Alternatives Intl [*AMEX symbol*] (TTSB)
NAI.............. Negro Airmen International (EA)
NAI.............. Net Acid Input [*Medicine*] (DB)
NAI.............. Net Annual Inflow [*Pensions*]
NAI.............. Netherlands Arbitration Institute (ILCA)
NAI.............. Network Associates, Inc. [*Computer science*]
NAI.............. New Acronyms and Initialisms [*Later, NAIA*] [*A publication*]
NAI.............. New Alchemy Institute [*Defunct*] (EA)
NAI.............. No Accidental Injury (DMAA)
nai .... No Action Indicated (AD)
NAI.............. No Action Indicated
NAI.............. No Acute Inflammation [*Medicine*] (DMAA)
nai .... No Address Instruction (AD)
NAI.............. No-Address Instruction (AAG)
NAI.............. No Airborne Intercept [*Fighter aircraft lacking airborne intercept RADAR*]
NAI.............. Nonaccidental Injury
NAI.............. Nonadherence Index (DMAA)
nai .... North American Indian [*MARC language code Library of Congress*] (LCCP)
NAI.............. North American Internet Co.
NAI.............. Northern Alberta Institute of Technology [*UTLAS symbol*]
NAI.............. Northrop Aeronautical Institute [*Later, Northrop University*]
NAI.............. Northrop Aircraft, Inc. (MCD)
NAI.............. N'shei Agudath Israel (BJA)
NAI.............. Nurse Attitudes Inventory (TES)
NAIA .... National Agricultural and Industrial Association [*Australia*]
NAIA .... National Association of Industrial Artists [*Later, IG*]
NAIA .... National Association of Insurance Agents [*Later, IIAA*] (EA)
NAIA .... National Association of Intercollegiate Athletics (EA)
NAIA .... New Acronyms, Initialisms, and Abbreviations [*Formerly, NAI*] [*A publication*]
NAIA .... North American Indian Association (EA)
NAIAD .... Nerve Agent Immobilised Enzyme Alarm and Detector (PDAA)
NAIB .... National Association of Independent Business [*Defunct*]
NAIB .... National Association of Insurance Brokers [*Washington, DC*] (EA)
NAIBD .... National Association of Industries for the Blind and Disabled [*British*] (DBA)
NAIC .... National Adoption Information Clearinghouse (EA)
NAIC .... National Advice and Information Centre for Outdoor Education [*Doncaster Metropolitan Institute of Higher Education*] [*British*] (CB)
NAIC .... National AIDS [*Acquired Immune Deficiency Syndrome*] Information Clearinghouse [*Information service or system*] (IID)
NAIC .... National Art Industry Council [*Australia*]
NAIC .... National Association of Installment Companies [*New York, NY*] (EA)
NAIC .... National Association of Insurance Commissioners [*Kansas City, MO*] (EA)
NAIC .... National Association of Intercollegiate Commissioners (EA)
NAIC .... National Association of Investment Clubs [*British*] (DBA)
NAIC .... National Association of Investment Companies
NAIC .... National Association of Investors Corp. (EA)
NAIC .... National Astronomy and Ionosphere Center [*Ithaca, NY*] [*National Science Foundation*]
NAIC .... Naval Aircraft Investigation Center (AD)
NAIC .... Nuclear Accident and Incident Control [*Army*] (AABC)
NAICA .... National American Indian Cattlemen's Association (EA)
NAICC .... National Alliance of Independent Crop Consultants (EA)
NAICC .... National Association of Independent Computer Companies
NAICC .... Nuclear Accident and Incident Control Center [*Army*] (AABC)
NAICCA ...... National American Indian Court Clerks Association (EA)
NAICJA ...... National American Indian Court Judges Association (EA)
NAICO .... Nuclear Accident and Incident Control Officer [*Army*] (AABC)
NAICOM/MIS... Navy Integrated Command Management Information System
NAICP .... Nuclear Accident and Incident Control Plan [*Army*]
NAICPS .... National Association of Independent Colleges and Private Schools (EA)
NAICS .... North American Industry Classification System (AAGC)
NAICU .... National Association of Independent Colleges and Universities (EA)
NAICV .... National Association of Ice Cream Vendors [*Defunct*] (EA)
NAID .... National Associates for Informed Depressives [*Defunct*] (EA)

NAID .... National Association of Industrial Distributors [*British*] (DBA)
NAID .... National Association of Installation Developers (EA)
NAID .... National Association of Interior Designers [*Defunct*] (EA)
NAIDA .... National Agricultural and Industrial Development Association [*Republic of Ireland*] (BI)
NAIDM .... National Association of Insecticide and Disinfectant Manufacturers (BUAC)
NAIDS .... North Atlantic Institute for Defense Studies [*NATO*] (AD)
NAIDST .... National AIDS Trust [*British*]
NAIEA .... National Association of Inspectors and Educational Advisers [*British*]
NAIEC .... National Association for Industry-Education Cooperation [*Buffalo, NY*] (EA)
NAIEHS .... National Association of Importers and Exporters of Hides and Skins [*Later, USHSLA*] (EA)
NAIEM .... National Association of Insect Electrocutor Manufacturers (EA)
NAIEO .... National Association of Inspectors of Schools and Educational Organisers [*British*] (BI)
NAIES .... National Adoption Information Exchange System [*Formerly, ARENA*] (EA)
NAIES .... National Association of Interdisciplinary Ethnic Studies (EA)
NAIF .... National Association for Irish Freedom (EA)
NAIF .... Nordiska Akademiska Idrottsforbund [*Scandinavian Federation for University Sport*] (EA)
NAIFA .... National Association of Independent Fee Appraisers (EA)
NAIFR .... National Association of Independent Food Retailers [*Defunct*] (EA)
NAIG .... National Insurance Group [*NASDAQ symbol*] (NQ)
NAIG .... Natl Insurance Group [*NASDAQ symbol*] (TTSB)
NAIG .... Nippon Atomic Industry Group [*Japan*]
NAIHC .... National American Indian Housing Council (EA)
NAII .... National Association of Ice Industries [*Later, PIA*]
NAII .... National Association of Independent Insurers [*Des Plaines, IL*] (EA)
NAII .... Natural Alternatives International [*NASDAQ symbol*] (SAG)
NAIIA .... National Association of Independent Insurance Adjusters [*Chicago, IL*] (EA)
NAIIU .... Not Authorized If Issued Under [*Army*]
NAIJ .... National Association for Irish Justice [*Superseded by National Association for Irish Freedom*] (EA)
NAIL .... National Argo Industries Ltd. [*Seychelles*] (BUAC)
NAIL .... National Association for Independent Living (EA)
NAIL .... National Association of Independent Lubes (EA)
NAIL .... National Association of Independent Lumbermen [*Defunct*] (EA)
NAIL .... Naval Aircraft Inventory Log (AD)
NAIL .... Neurotics Anonymous International Liaison (EA)
NAIL .... North American Indian Landmarks [*A publication*]
NAILBA .... National Association of Independent Life Brokerage Agencies [*Washington, DC*] (EA)
NAILD .... National Association of Independent Lighting Distributors (EA)
NAILDD .... North American Interlibrary Loan and Document Delivery [*Project*] (TELE)
NAILG .... National Awards for Innovation in Local Government [*Australia*]
NAILM .... National Association of Institutional Laundry Managers [*Later, National Association of Institutional Linen Management*] (EA)
NAILM .... National Association of Institutional Linen Management (EA)
NAILS .... National Airspace Integrated Logistics Support [*FAA*] (TAG)
NAILS .... National Automated Immigration Lookout System [*Immigration and Naturalization Service*]
NAILS .... Naval Aviation Integrated Logistic Support Task Force (NG)
NAILSC .... Naval Aviation Integrated Logistic Support Center (MCD)
NAILTE .... National Association of Instructional Leaders in Technical Education (EA)
NAIM .... NAIM [*North American Indian Mission*] Ministries (EA)
NAIM .... Number Allocation and Inspection Module (PDAA)
NAIMA .... North American Indian Museums Association (EA)
NAIMA .... North American Insulation Manufacturers Association (NTPA)
NAIMD .... National Association of Independent Music Dealers [*Defunct*] (EA)
NAIME .... National Association of Independent Maritime Educators (EA)
NAIMIS .... NAVAIRSYSCOM [*Naval Air Systems Command*] Integrated Management InformationSystem (DNAB)
NAIMS .... National Airspace Information System [*BTS*] (TAG)
NAIMSAL .... National Anti-Imperialist Movement in Solidarity with African Liberation (EA)
NAION .... Nonarteritic Anterior Ischemic Optic Neuropathy
NAIOP .... National Association of Industrial and Office Parks (EA)
NAIOP .... Navigational Aid Inoperative for Parts
naiop .... Navigational Aids Inoperative for Parts (AD)
NAIP .... National Assault on Illiteracy Program (EA)
NAIP .... National Association of Independent Publishers (EA)
NAIP .... National Association of Industrial Parks [*Later, NAIOP*]
NAIP .... National Association of Insured Persons [*Defunct*] (EA)
NAIP .... Neuronal Apoptosis Inhibitory Protein [*Genetics*]
NAIP .... Neuronal Apoptpsos Inhibitory Protein [*Cytology*]
NAIPFA .... National Association of Independent Public Finance Advisors
NAIPR .... National Association of Independent Publishers Representatives (NTPA)
NAIPRC .... Netherlands Automated Information Processing Research Centre (NITA)
NAIPTS .... National Amalgamated Iron Plate Trade Society [*A union*] [*British*]
NAIR .... Narrow Absorption Infrared
NAIR .... National Arrangements for Incidents Involving Radioactivity [*Nuclear energy*] (NUCP)
NAIR .... National Association of Independent Resurfacers (EA)
NAIR .... National Association of Independent Retailers [*Ireland*] (BUAC)
NAIR .... Network Action Item Report (MCD)
NAIR .... Nonadrenergic Inhibitory Response (DB)
NAIRA .... Northamerican Industrial Representatives Association (NTPA)
NAIRD .... National Association of Independent Record Distributors and Manufacturers (EA)
NAIRDM .... National Association of Independent Record Distributors and Manufacturers (EA)
NAIRE .... National Association of Internal Revenue Employees [*Later, NTEU*] (EA)
NAIREC .... Nimbus Arctic Ice Reconnaissance [*Canadian project*]
Nairns .... Nairnshire, Scotland (AD)
NAIRO .... National Association of Intergroup Relations Officials [*Later, NAHRW*] (EA)
NAIRS .... National Athletic Injury/Illness Reporting System [*Pennsylvania State University*] [*Defunct*]
NAIRS .... Navy Aircraft and Readiness System
NAIRU .... Naval Air Intelligence Reserve Units
NAIRU .... Non-Accelerating-Inflation Rate of Unemployment
NAIS .... National Administrative Information System [*Computer science*] (IID)
NAIS .... National Aquaculture Information System (NOAA)
NAIS .... National Association for Information Services (EA)
NAIS .... National Association of Independent Schools (EA)
NAIS .... National Association of Investigative Specialists (EA)
NAIS .... Navy Attitudinal Information System (NVT)
NAIS .... Neutral Administrative Inspection Scheme (COE)
NAIS .... Night Attack Interdiction System
NAISC .... National American Indian Safety Council (EA)
NAISEO .... National Association of Inspectors of Schools and Educational Organisers [*British*]
NAISS .... National Association of Iron and Steel Stockholders (AD)
NAIT .... National Alliance for Infusion Therapy [*An association*]
NAIT .... National Association of Industrial Technology (EA)
NAIT .... Naval Air Intermediate Training
NAIT .... North American Islamic Trust (EA)
NAIT .... Northern Alberta Institute of Technology [*Edmonton, AB*]
NAITA .... National Association of Independent Travel Agents (BUAC)
NAI Tc .... NAI Technologies [*Associated Press*] (SAG)
NAIT(C) .... Naval Air Intermediate Training (Command)
NAITE .... National Association of Industrial Teacher Educators [*Later, NAITTE*] (EA)
NAI Tech .... NAI Technologies [*Associated Press*] (SAG)
NAITF .... Naval Air Intercept Training Facility (MUGU)
NAITP .... National Association of Income Tax Preparers [*Defunct*] (EA)
NAITPD .... National Association of Independent Television Producers and Distributors [*Defunct*] (EA)
NAITTE .... National Association of Industrial and Technical Teacher Educators (EA)
NAIW .... National Association of Insurance Women (International) [*Tulsa, OK*] (EA)
NAIWA .... North American Indian Women's Association (EA)
NAIWC .... National Association of Inland Water Carriers [*British*] (BI)
NAIWC .... National Association of Inland Waterway Carriers [*British*] (DBA)
NAIY .... National Association of Indian Youth (BUAC)
NAJ .... Napierville Junction Railway Co. [*Later, NJ*] [*AAR code*]
NAJ .... National Academy of Jazz (EA)
NAJ .... National Aeronautics and Space Administration, Johnson Space Center, Houston, TX [*OCLC symbol*] (OCLC)
NAJ .... National Association for Justice
NAJA .... National Association of Jewelry Appraisers (EA)
NAJA .... National Association of Junior Auxiliaries (EA)
NAJA .... North American Judges Association [*Later, AJA*]
NAJAE .... National Association of Jai Alai Frontons (NTPA)
NAJAFRA .... National Jazz Fraternity
NAJAG .... North African Judge Advocate General's Section [*World War II*]
NAJAKS .... Nordic Association for Japanese and Korean Studies (BUAC)
NAJAS .... National Association of Japan-America Societies
NAJC .... National Assessment of Juvenile Correction [*University of Michigan*] (AD)
NAJC .... Northern Australia Jockey Club (AD)
NAJC .... Northwest Alabama Junior College (AD)
NAJCA .... National Association of Juvenile Correctional Agencies (EA)
NAJCW .... National Association of Jewish Center Workers [*Later, AJCW*] (EA)
NAJD .... National Association of Journalism Directors [*Later, JEA*] (EA)
NAJD/MBAP ...... National Association of JD/MBA [*Juris Doctor/Master of Business Administration*] Professionals [*Defunct*] (EA)
NAJE .... National Association of Jazz Education (AD)
NAJE .... National Association of Jazz Educators [*Later, IAJE*] (EA)
NAJEM .... North African Joint Economic Mission [*World War II*]
NAJF .... National Association of Jai Alai Frontons (EA)
NAJFCHP .... National Association of Jewish Family, Children's, and Health Professionals (EA)
NAJHA .... National Association of Jewish Homes for the Aged [*Later, NAAJHHA*] (EA)
NAJHHA .... North American Association of Jewish Homes and Housing for the Aging (EA)
NAJIT .... National Association of Judiciary Interpreters and Translators (NTPA)
NAJLA .... North American Junior Limousin Association (EA)
NAJRC .... North African Joint Rearmament Committee [*World War II*]
NAJSA .... North American Jewish Students Appeal (EA)
NAJSN .... North American Jewish Students' Network (EA)
NAJU .... Nordic Association of Journalists' Unions (EA)
NAJVS .... National Association of Jewish Vocational Services (EA)
NAJYC .... North American Jewish Youth Council [*Defunct*] (EA)
NAK .... Nakhichevan [*Former USSR Seismograph station code, US Geological Survey Closed*] (SEIS)
NAK .... National Auto Credit, Inc. [*NYSE symbol*] (SAG)
NAK .... Natl Auto Credit [*NYSE symbol*] (TTSB)
NAK .... Negative Acknowledge [*or Acknowledgment*] [*Data communication*]

nak............	Negative Acknowledge Character [*Computer science*] (AD)
NAK	Negative Acknowledge Character (ECII)
NAK	Negative Acknowledgment (DOM)
nak............	Negative Knowledge (AD)
NAK	Network Acknowledgment
NAK	Nothing Adverse Known (ADA)
nak............	Nothing Adverse Known (AD)
Na K-ATPase...	Adenosine Triphosphatase (Na, K-Activated) [*An enzyme*]
NAKBA	National Association to Keep and Bear Arms (EA)
nakl	Naklad [*Edition*] [*Polish*] (AD)
nakl	Nakladatel [*Edition*] [*Czech*] (AD)
NAKMAS	National Association of Karate & Martial Arts Schools (BUAC)
NAKN	National Anti-Klan Network (EA)
NAKOSTA.....	Natural Convection in the Stationary Condition [*Computer program*]
NAKS	North American Kant Society (EA)
NAI	Albany Public Library, Albany, NY [*Library symbol Library of Congress*] (LCLS)
NAL..............	N-Acetyllactopamine [*Biochemistry*]
NAL..............	Naloxone [*A drug*]
NAL..............	Name, Address, and Legal File [*Real estate*]
NAL..............	National Accelerator Laboratory [*AEC*]
NAL..............	National Acoustics Laboratory [*Australia*] (ECON)
NAL..............	National Aeronautical Laboratory (MCD)
NAL..............	National Aerospace Laboratory (AD)
NAL..............	National Agricultural Library [*Department of Agriculture*] [*Beltsville, MD*]
NAL..............	National Airlines (AD)
NAL..............	National Assistance League (EA)
NAL..............	National Association of Laity (EA)
NAL..............	National Association of Landowners (EA)
NAL..............	National Astronomical League
NAL..............	Naval Aeronautical Laboratory
NAL..............	New Aalesund [*Norway*] [*Geomagnetic observatory code*]
NAL..............	Newalta Corp. [*Toronto Stock Exchange symbol*]
NAL..............	New American Library [*Publisher*]
NAL..............	New Assembly Language
NAL..............	Nigeria America Line (AD)
NAL..............	Niue Airways Ltd. (EY)
NAL..............	No Activity Log (MCD)
NAL..............	Nonadherent Leukocyte (DB)
NAL..............	Non-Associated Labor (WDAA)
NAL..............	North American Lighting [*Automotive industry supplier*]
NAL..............	Northway Aviation Ltd. [*Canada ICAO designator*] (FAAC)
NAL..............	Norwegian America Line
NAL..............	Novell Application Launcher [*Computer science*]
NAL..............	Numerical Analysis Laboratory (MCD)
nal	Sodium Iodide [*Pharmacology*] (DAVI)
NAIA	Albany Medical College, Albany, NY [*Library symbol Library of Congress*] (LCLS)
NALA	National Academy of Literary Arts (EA)
NALA	National Adult Literacy Agency [*Ireland*] (BUAC)
NALA	National Affiliation for Literacy Advance (EA)
NALA	National Agricultural Limestone Association [*Later, National Limestone Institute*]
NALA	National Association of Language Advisers [*British*]
NALA	National Association of Legal Assistants (EA)
NALAA	National Assembly of Local Arts Agencies (EA)
NALAC	National Association of Local Arts Councils (BUAC)
NALAM	National Association of Livestock Auction Markets
NAIb.............	Shelter Rock Public Library, Albertson, NY [*Library symbol Library of Congress*] (LCLS)
NALBA	North American Log Builders Association (EA)
NAIBC	Albany Business College, Albany, NY [*Library symbol Library of Congress*] (LCLS)
NAIbH	Human Resources Center, Albertson, NY [*Library symbol Library of Congress*] (LCLS)
NAIbHM	Herricks Middle School, Albertson, NY [*Library symbol*] [*Library of Congress*] (LCLS)
NAIbi	Swan Library, Albion, NY [*Library symbol Library of Congress*] (LCLS)
NAIbiH	Arnold Gregory Memorial Hospital, Albion, NY [*Library symbol Library of Congress*] (LCLS)
NAIbME........	Meadow Drive Elementary School, Albertson, NY [*Library symbol*] [*Library of Congress*] (LCLS)
NALBOH......	National Association of Local Boards of Health
NAIbSE........	Searington Elementary School, Albertson, NY [*Library symbol*] [*Library of Congress*] (LCLS)
NALC	National Afro-American Labor Council (EA)
NALC	National Association of Ladies Circles [*British*] (DBA)
NALC	National Association of Ladies Circles of Great Britain and Ireland (BUAC)
NALC	National Association of Laryngectomee Clubs [*British*] (DBA)
NALC	National Association of Lawyers for Children (BUAC)
NALC	National Association of Letter Carriers (NADA)
NALC	National Association of Letter Carriers of the USA (EA)
NALC	National Association of Life Companies [*Washington, DC*] (EA)
NALC	National Association of Litho Clubs (EA)
NALC	National Association of Local Councils [*British*]
NALC	National Association of Louisiana Catahoulas (EA)
NALC	Natl Lodging [*NASDAQ symbol*] (TTSB)
NALC	Naval Aviation Logistics Center (NVT)
NALC	Navy Ammunition Logistics Code
NALC	New Age Learning Center [*Defunct*] (EA)
NALCC	National Automatic Laundry and Cleaning Council (EA)
NALCD	National Agricultural Library and Centre for Documentation [*Hungary*] (BUAC)
NALCDVE.....	National Association of Large City Directors of Vocational Education (EA)
NAICI	Center for International Studies, Albany, NY [*Library symbol Library of Congress*] (LCLS)
NAICJ...........	New York State Division of Criminal Justice Services, Albany, NY [*Library symbol*] [*Library of Congress*] (LCLS)
NALCM	National Association of Lace Curtain Manufacturers [*Defunct*]
Nalco	Nalco Chemical Co. [*Associated Press*] (SAG)
NALCO	Naval Air Logistics Control Office
NALCO	Newfoundland & Labrador Corp.
NALCOEASTPAC...	Naval Air Logistics Control Office Eastern Pacific (DNAB)
NALCOEURREP...	Naval Air Logistics Control Office European Representative
NALCOLANT...	Naval Air Logistics Control Office Atlantic
NALCOMIS...	Naval Aviation Logistics Command Management Information System (MCD)
NALCOMIS-OS...	Naval Air Logistics Command Management Information System for Operating and Support (DNAB)
NALCON.......	Navy Laboratory Computer Network
NALCOPAC...	Naval Air Logistics Control Office Pacific
NALCOPACREP...	Naval Air Logistics Control Office Pacific Representative
NALCOREP...	Naval Air Logistics Control Office Representative
NALCOWESTPAC...	Naval Air Logistics Control Office Western Pacific (DNAB)
NALCOWESTPACREP...	Naval Air Logistics Control Office Western Pacific Representative (DNAB)
NAICSR........	College of Saint Rose, Albany, NY [*Library symbol Library of Congress*] (LCLS)
NAID	Dudley Observatory, Albany, NY [*Library symbol Library of Congress*] (LCLS)
NALD	National Association of Limbless and Disabled [*British*] (DBA)
NALD	National Association of Limbless Disabled (BUAC)
NALD	Nonattainment Areas Lacking Demonstrations [*Environmental science*] (COE)
NALDA	Naval Aviation Logistics Data Analysis (NVT)
NaLDAP	National Learning Disabilities Assistance Project
NALDEF	Native American Legal Defense and Education Foundation (EA)
NAIDH.........	New York State Department of Health, Division of Laboratories and Research, Albany, NY [*Library symbol Library of Congress*] (LCLS)
NAIDS..........	New York State Department of State, Community Affairs Library, Albany, NY [*Library symbol Library of Congress*] (LCLS)
NALEAO	National Association of Latino Elected and Appointed Officials (AD)
NALECOM	National Law Enforcement Telecommunications System
NALED	National Association of Limited Edition Dealers (EA)
NAIeNH.......	E. J. Noble Hospital, Medical Library, Alexandria Bay, NY [*Library symbol Library of Congress*] (LCLS)
NALEO	National Association of Latino Elected and Appointed Officials (EA)
NAIf	Alfred University, Alfred, NY [*Library symbol Library of Congress*] (LCLS)
NALF............	NAL Financial Group [*NASDAQ symbol*] (TTSB)
NALF............	NAL Financial Group, Inc. [*NASDAQ symbol*] (SAG)
NALF............	National Agricultural Legal Fund [*Defunct*] (EA)
NALF............	Naval Auxiliary Landing Field (NG)
NALF............	North American Limousin Foundation (EA)
NALF............	North American Loon Fund (EA)
NAIfC	State University of New York, College of Ceramics at Alfred University, Alfred, NY [*Library symbol Library of Congress*] (LCLS)
NALFMA	National Association of Law Firm Marketing Administrators (EA)
NAL Fn	NAL Financial Group, Inc. [*Associated Press*] (SAG)
NAIf-ST........	Alfred University, School of Theology, Alfred, NY [*Library symbol Library of Congress Obsolete*] (LCLS)
NAIfUA........	State University of New York, Agricultural and Technical College at Alfred, Alfred, NY [*Library symbol Library of Congress*] (LCLS)
NALG	National Association for Loss and Grief [*Australia*]
NALG	National Association of Left-Handed Golfers (EA)
NALGA	National Association of Local Government Auditors (NTPA)
NALGAP	National Association of Lesbian/Gay Alcoholism Professionals (EA)
NALGG........	National Association for Lesbian and Gay Gerontology (AD)
NALGHW......	National Association of Local Governments on Hazardous Wastes (EA)
NALGM	National Association of Lawn and Garden Manufacturers [*Defunct*] (EA)
NALGM	National Association of Leather Glove Manufacturers [*Later, NAGM*]
NALGO........	National and Local Government Officers' Association [*British*]
NALGO........	National Association of Local Government Officers (AIE)
NAIGS..........	United States Geological Survey, Water Resources Services, New York District, Albany, NY [*Library symbol Library of Congress*] (LCLS)
NALGWC......	National Association of Local Government Women's Committees (BUAC)
NAIH	Hospital Educational and Research Fund, Inc., Albany, NY [*Library symbol Library of Congress*] (LCLS)
NALHC........	National Acoustic Laboratories Hearing Center [*Australia*]
NALHC........	North American Log Homes Council (EA)
NALHF........	National Association of Leagues of Hospital Friends [*British*] (DI)
NALHI.........	National Authority for the Ladies Handbag Industry (EA)
NALHM.......	National Association of Licensed House Managers [*Pronounced "nalem"*] [*A union*] [*British*] (DCTA)
NAII	Albany Institute of History of Art, Albany, NY [*Library symbol Library of Congress*] (LCLS)
NALI...........	National Agricultural Limestone Institute [*Later, National Limestone Institute*]
NALI...........	National Association of Legal Investigators (EA)

NALI............ National Association of the Launderette Industry [*British*] (DBA)
NALI............ North Atlantic Lobster Institute (EA)
NALIC......... National Association of Loft Insulation Contractors [*British*] (DI)
NALIN......... National Library Information Network (TELE)
NALIJ.......... Junior College of Albany, Albany, NY [*Library symbol Library of Congress*] (LCLS)
NALJS......... Nordic Atomic Libraries Joint Secretariat [*Information service or system*] (IID)
NALLA .... National Long-Lines Agency (NATG)
NALLD .... National Association of Learning Laboratory Directors [*Later, IALL*]
NAILL.......... New York State Department of Law Library, Albany, NY [*Library symbol*] [*Library of Congress*] (LCLS)
NALLO......... National Association of License Law Officials [*Later, NARELLO*] (EA)
NAILS .... Albany Law School, Albany, NY [*Library symbol Library of Congress*] (LCLS)
NALLS .... National Aboriginal Literacy and Language Strategy [*Australia*]
NAIM .... Maria College, Albany, NY [*Library symbol Library of Congress*] (LCLS)
NALM.......... National Association for Lay Ministry (EA)
NALM.......... National Association of Lift Makers [*British*] (BI)
NALMA .... North American Land Mammal Age [*Geological epoch*]
NALMC .... National Association of Labor-Management Committees (EA)
NALMCO...... International Association of Lighting Management Companies (EA)
NALMCO...... National Association of Lighting Maintenance Contractors (EA)
NAIMem ...... Memorial Hospital, Medical Library, Albany, NY [*Library symbol Library of Congress*] (LCLS)
NAIMH .... New York State Department of Mental Hygiene, Mental Hygiene Research Library, Albany, NY [*Library symbol Library of Congress*] (LCLS)
NALMS .... North American Lake Management Society (EA)
NAIMV .... New York State Department of Motor Vehicles, Research Library, Albany, NY [*Library symbol Library of Congress*] (LCLS)
NALN .... National Agricultural Libraries Network [*National Agricultural Library*]
NALN .... Native Authority Legal Notice [*Northern Nigeria*] [*A publication*] (DLA)
NALN .... North African Liaison Section [*World War II*]
NALNET .... NASA Library Network [*NASA Washington, DC Library network*] (MCD)
NALO .... National Association of Launderette Owners (BUAC)
NALO .... National Association of Launderette Owners Ltd. [*British*] (BI)
NALO .... Naval Air Liaison Officer
NALO .... Naval Air Logistics Office (DOMA)
NALOG......... Natural Logarithm (IAA)
NALOH......... National Association Legions of Honor (EA)
NALOP......... NATO Letter of Promulgation
NALOXONE... N-Allylnoroxymorphone [*Narcotic antagonist*]
NAIP .... Albany College of Pharmacy, Albany, NY [*Library symbol Library of Congress*] (LCLS)
NALP .... National Association for Law Placement (EA)
NALPA .... National American Legion Press Association (EA)
NALPM .... National Association of Lithographic Plate Manufacturers [*Defunct*] (EA)
NALPN .... National Association of Licensed Practical Nurses (EA)
NALR .... National Acid Lakes Registry [*Environmental Protection Agency*]
NALR .... National Association of Lighting Representatives (EA)
NALR .... North American Liturgy Resources (BUAC)
NALRET .... National Association for Learning Resources Educational Technology (BUAC)
NALS .... National Advisory Logistics Staff (NATG)
NALS .... National Association of Laboratory Suppliers [*Defunct*] (EA)
NALS .... National Association of Labor Students [*British*] (DI)
NALS .... National Association of Legal Secretaries (International) [*Tulsa, OK*] (EA)
NALS .... National Association of Lumber Salesmen (EA)
NALS .... North American Lily Society (EA)
NAIS .... Saint Peter's Hospital, Albany, NY [*Library symbol Library of Congress*] (LCLS)
NALSA .... Native American Law Students Association (EA)
NALSA .... North American Land Sailing Association (AD)
NALSAP ...... National Association of Leadership for Student Assistance Programs (NTPA)
NALSAS ...... National Association for Legal Support of Alternative Schools (EA)
NALSAT .... National Association of Land Settlement Association Tenants (AD)
NALSC .... National Association of Legal Search Consultants (NTPA)
NALSF .... National ALS [*Amyotrophic Lateral Sclerosis*] Foundation (EA)
NALSI .... National Association of Life Science Industries [*Defunct*] (EA)
NALSO......... National Association of Labour Student Organisations [*British*] (BI)
NAISS......... New York State Department of Social Sciences, Social Services and Statistics Library, Albany, NY [*Library symbol Library of Congress*] (LCLS)
Nal St P....... Nalton's Collection of State Papers [*A publication*] (DLA)
NAISU......... State University of New York, Union List of Serials, Albany, NY [*Library symbol Library of Congress*] (LCLS)
NALSVHE..... National Association of Local Supervisors of Vocational Home Economics (EA)
NALT........... Naltrexone [*A drug*]
NALT........... National Association of the Legitimate Theatre [*Defunct*] (EA)
NaI (TI)........ Thallium-Activated Sodium Iodide [*Scintillation detector*] [*Medicine*] (MEDA)
NAItL .... La Salette Seminary, Altamont, NY [*Library symbol Library of Congress*] (LCLS)
NALTOACS... Navy Laboratory Technical Office for ADP and Communication Systems (GFGA)
NALTS .... National Advertising Lead Tracking System [*Navy*] (NVT)
NALU .... National Association of Life Underwriters [*Washington, DC*] (EA)

NAIU .... State University of New York at Albany, Albany, NY [*Library symbol Library of Congress*] (LCLS)
NALUAS....... North American Life Union Assurance Society (EA)
NAIU-F........ State University of New York at Albany, Filmdex, Albany, NY [*Library symbol Library of Congress*] (LCLS)
NAIUHL....... Upper Hudson Library Federation, Albany, NY [*Library symbol Library of Congress*] (LCLS)
NAIU-L........ State University of New York at Albany Library School, Albany, NY [*Library symbol Library of Congress*] (LCLS)
NAIULS........ New York State Union List of Serials, Albany, NY [*Library symbol Library of Congress*] (LCLS)
NAIU-PA ...... State University of New York at Albany, Graduate School of Public Affairs, Albany, NY [*Library symbol Library of Congress*] (LCLS)
NALUS .... National Association of Leagues, Umpires, and Scorers (EA)
NALV .... National Association of Legal Vendors (NTPA)
NAIVA......... United States Veterans Administration Hospital, Albany, NY [*Library symbol Library of Congress*] (LCLS)
NALW .... Not an A-List Writer [*Screenwriter's lexicon*]
NAM........... N-Acetylmethionine [*Organic chemistry*]
NAM........... N-(Acridinyl)maleimide [*Organic chemistry*]
NAM........... Namangan [*Former USSR Seismograph station code, US Geological Survey Closed*] (SEIS)
NAM........... NAM Corp. [*Associated Press*] (SAG)
NAM........... Named
NAM........... Namibia [*ANSI three-letter standard code*] (CNC)
NAM........... Namlea [*Indonesia*] [*Airport symbol*] (OAG)
NAM........... National Account Management [*Bell System*]
NAM........... National Aero Manufacturing (AD)
NAM........... National Air Museum [*of the Smithsonian Institution*] [*Later, NASM*]
NAM........... National Apple Month (EA)
NAM........... National Army Museum [*British military*] (DMA)
NAM........... National Association of Manufacturers (NTCM)
NAM........... Natural Actomyosins [*Biochemistry*]
NAM........... Nautical Air Miles
NAM........... Naval Aircraft Modification
NAM........... Naval Air Material (SAA)
NAM........... Naval Air Mechanic [*British military*] (DMA)
NAM........... Naval Aviation Museum [*Pensacola, FL*]
NAM........... Navy Achievement Medal [*Military decoration*]
NAM........... Nederlandsche Aluminium Maatschappij [*Netherlands Aluminum Co.*] (AD)
nam........... Network Access Machine [*Computer science*] (AD)
NAM........... Network Access Machine [*National Institute of Standards and Technology Computer science*]
NAM........... Network Access Method [*Control Data Corp.*] [*Telecommunications*] (TEL)
NAM........... Network Analysis Model
NAM........... New America Movement (EA)
NAM........... New American Man [*Lifestyle classification coined by Robert Bly*] (ECON)
NAM........... New Architectural Movement [*British*] (DI)
NAM........... Newspaper Association Managers (EA)
NAM........... NOAA [*National Oceanic and Atmospheric Administration*] Accounting Manual (NOAA)
NAM........... Nonadditive Mixing (DICI)
NAM........... Nonaligned Movement
nam........... Non-Aligned Movement (AD)
N Am .... North America (AD)
NAM........... North America
NAM........... North American Metals Corp. [*Vancouver Stock Exchange symbol*]
NAM........... North American Movement (AD)
NAM........... North American Region [*USTTA*] (TAG)
NAM........... Nortland Air Manitoba [*Canada ICAO designator*] (FAAC)
NAM........... Norwegian American Museum Corp. (EA)
NAM........... Numerical Assignment Number [*Computer science*]
NAM........... Nurses Against Misrepresentation (EA)
NAM........... State University of New York at Albany, Albany, NY [*OCLC symbol*] (OCLC)
Nam............ Vietnam
NAma.......... Amagansett Free Library, Amagansett, NY [*Library symbol Library of Congress*] (LCLS)
NAMA .... National Account Marketing Association (EA)
NAMA .... National Agenda for a Multicultural Australia
NAMA .... National Agri-Marketing Association (EA)
NAMA .... National Air-Monitoring Audit [*Environmental Protection Agency*] (GFGA)
NAMA .... National Assistance Management Association [*Washington, DC*] (EA)
NAMA .... National Association of Master Appraisers (EA)
NAMA .... National Association of Mathematics Advisers [*British*] (DBA)
NAMA .... National Automatic Merchandising Association [*Chicago, IL*] (EA)
NAMA .... National Automotive Muffler Association [*Defunct*] (EA)
NAMA .... Naval Aeronautical Material Area (NG)
NAMA .... New Amsterdam Musical Association (AD)
NAMA .... North American Manx Association (EA)
NAMA .... North American Maritime Agencies (AD)
NAMA .... North American Mycological Association (EA)
NAMAB .... National Air Museum Advisory Board (MUGU)
NAMAC .... National Alliance for Media Arts and Culture (NTPA)
NAMAC .... National Alliance of Media Arts Centers (EA)
NAMAC .... National Amateur Missile Analysis Center
NAMAC .... National Association of Men's Apparel Clubs [*Later, NAMBAC, Bureau of WholesaleSales Representatives*]
NAMAC .... National Association of Merger and Acquisition Consultants (EA)
NAMAD .... National Association of Minority Automobile Dealers [*Detroit, MI*] (EA)

NAMAE .... Northern Air Materiel Area, Europe [*Army*]
NAmaHi .... Amagansett Historical Association, Amagansett, NY [*Library symbol Library of Congress*] (LCLS)
NAMAINTRADET... Naval Air Maintenance Training Detachment (DNAB)
NAMAINTRAGRU... Naval Air Maintenance Training Group (DNAB)
NAMAP .... Northern Air Materiel Area, Pacific [*Army*]
NAMAPUS.... Naval Assistant to the Military Aide to the President of the United States
NAMAR .... North American Mustang Association and Registry (EA)
NAMARA...... Navy and Marine Corps Appellate Review Activity (DNAB)
NAMARCO ... National Marketing Corp [*Philippines*] (BUAC)
NAMAS .... National Measurement Accreditation Service [*Research center British*] (IRC)
NAMAST ...... System of National Accounts and System of Material Product Balances [*United Nations Statistical Office*] [*Information service or system*] (CRD)
NAMATCEN... Naval Air Material Center [*Also, NAMC, NAVAIRMATCEN*]
NAMATE ...... Naval Air Material Command
NAMB .... National Agricultural Marketing Board [*Canada*] (BUAC)
NAMB .... National Association of Master Bakers [*British*] (DI)
NAMB .... National Association of Master Bakers, Confectioners, and Caterers [*British*] (DBA)
NAMB .... National Association of Media Brokers (EA)
NAMB .... National Association of Minority Businesses (AAGC)
NAMB .... National Association of Mortgage Brokers [*Washington, DC*] (EA)
NAMB .... Naval Academy Midshipmen Branch
NAMB .... Naval Amphibious Base
NAMBAC...... National Association of Men's and Boys' Apparel Clubs [*Later, Bureau of Wholesale Sales Representatives*] (EA)
NAMBC .... National Association of Milk Bottle Collectors (EA)
NAMBLA ...... North American Man-Boy Love Association
NAMBLA ...... North American Men-Boy Love Association (BUAC)
NAMBO .... National Association of Motor Bus Operators (AD)
NAMBO .... National Association of Motor Bus Owners [*Later, ABA*] (EA)
NAMC .... NAM Corp. [*NASDAQ symbol*] (SAG)
NAMC .... National Air Material Center (KSC)
NAMC .... National Association of Management Consultants (EA)
NAMC .... National Association of Minority Contractors (EA)
NAMC .... National Association of Mothers' Centers (EA)
NAMC .... Naval Aerospace Medical Center
NAMC .... Naval Air Material Center [*Also, NAMATCEN, NAVAIRMATCEN*]
NAMC .... Naval Air Materiel Command
NAMC .... Nihon Aeroplane Manufacturing Co. (AD)
NAMC .... North Atlantic Military Committee
NAMCA .... National Association for Middle Class Americans (EA)
NAMC-AEL... Naval Air Material Center - Aeronautical Engine Laboratory
NAMC-AIL.... Naval Air Material Center - Aeronautical Instruments Laboratory [*Philadelphia, PA*]
NAMC-AML... Naval Air Material Center - Aeronautical Materials Laboratory
NAMC-APEL... Naval Air Material Center - Aeronautical Photographic Experimental Laboratory
NAMCAR...... North America/Caribbean
NAMC-ARRL... Naval Air Material Center - Aeronautical Radio and RADAR Laboratory
NAMC-ASL... Naval Air Material Center - Aeronautical Structures Laboratory
NAMCC .... National Association of Mutual Casualty Companies (EA)
NAM-CDH .... Non Absorbing Mirror Constricted Double Heterostructure (NITA)
NAMCF .... National Association of Minority CPA [*Certified Public Accounting*] Firms
NAMCO........ Air-Cushion Vehicle built by Nakamura Seisakusho [*Usually used in com bination with numerals*] [*Japan*]
NAMCO........ Naval and Mechanical Co. (AD)
NAMCO........ North American Management Council (BUAC)
NAMCO........ North Atlantic Marine Cooperative Commission (BUAC)
NAM Cp ...... NAM Corp. [*Associated Press*] (SAG)
NAMCP .... National Association of Managed Care Physicians (EA)
NAMCPAF .... National Association of Minority Certified Public Accounting Firms (EA)
NAMCS .... National Ambulatory Medical Care Survey [*National Center for Health Statistics*]
NAMCU .... National Association of Minority Consultants and Urbanologists [*Defunct*] (EA)
NAMCW .... National Association of Maternal and Child Welfare [*British*]
NAMD .... National Association for Membership Development (NTPA)
NAMD .... National Association of Marble Dealers [*Later, MIA*] (EA)
NAMD .... National Association of Marine Dealers
NAMD .... National Association of Market Developers [*New York, NY*] (EA)
NAMD .... National Association of Membership Directors of Chambers of Commerce [*Defunct*] (EA)
NAMD .... Naval Ammunition Depot [*Charleston, SC*]
NAMD .... Newsletter of the Army Medical Department
NAMDA........ North American Medical/Dental Association (EA)
NAMDAR...... North American Data Airborne Recorder (IAA)
NAMDB........ National Association of Medical-Dental Bureaus [*Later, MDHBA*]
NAMDDU ..... Naval Air Mine Defense Development Unit (MUGU)
NAMDEX...... Name Index
NAMDI .... National Marine Data Inventory
NAMDRA...... National American Motors Drivers and Racers Association (EA)
NAMDRC...... National Association for Medical Direction of Respiratory Care (NTPA)
NAMDRC...... National Association of Medical Directors for Respiratory Care (EA)
NAMDRP...... Naval Aviation Maintenance Discrepancy Reporting Program (DNAB)
NAMDT .... National Association of Milliners, Dressmakers, and Tailors (EA)
NAME........... National Anti-Racist Movement in Education [*British*] (DBA)
NAME........... National Association for Mediation in Education (EA)
NAME........... National Association for Minority Education
NAME........... National Association for Multiracial Education [*British*]
NAME........... National Association of Management/Marketing Educators [*Defunct*] (EA)
NAME........... National Association of Marine Enginebuilders [*British*] (BI)
NAME........... National Association of Marine Engineers (AD)
NAME........... National Association of Marine Engineers of Canada (BUAC)
NAME........... National Association of Maritime Educators (NTPA)
NAME........... National Association of Media Educators (EA)
NAME........... National Association of Medical Examiners (EA)
NAME........... National Association of Metal Name Plate Manufacturers (AD)
NAME........... National Association of Miniature Enthusiasts (EA)
NAME........... National Association of Minority Entrepreneurs (EA)
NAME........... National Association of Modeling and Entertainment (EA)
NAME........... New American Music in Europe [*An association*] (BUAC)
NAME........... Nitroarginine Methyl Ester [*Organic chemistry*]
NAME........... North American Monogrammers and Embroiderers [*Defunct*] (EA)
NAMEB .... National Association of Marine Engine Builders (AD)
NAMEC .... National Association of Marine Engineers of Canada
NAMED .... North African Medical Section [*World War II*]
NAMEDCEN... Naval Aviation Medical Center (DNAB)
NAMEPA ...... National Association of Minority Engineering Program Administrators (EA)
NAMES .... National Association of Medical Equipment Suppliers (EA)
NAMES .... NAVDAC [*Naval Data Automation Command*] Assembly, Monitor, Executive System (PDAA)
NAMESAKES... Naval Aviators Must Energetically Sell Aviation to Keep Effective Strength
NAMESU ...... National Association of Music Executives in State Universities (EA)
NAMET......... Naval Mathematics and English Test [*British military*] (DMA)
NAMF........... National Association of Metal Finishers (EA)
NAMF........... Naval Aviation Museum Foundation (DNAB)
NAMFAX ...... National and Aviation Meteorological Facsimile Network [*National Weather Service*]
NAMFC .... North Atlantic Mediterranean Freight Conference (EA)
NAMFI .... NATO Missile Firing Installation
NAMFREL .... National Citizens' Movement for Free Elections [*Philippines*] [*Political party*]
NAMFSM ..... National Association of Meat and Food Seasoning Manufacturers [*Later, NSMA*] (EA)
NAMG .... Narrow-Angle Mars Gate [*NASA*]
NAMG .... National Association of Mining Groups (EA)
NAMG .... National Association of Multiple Grocers [*British*] (BI)
NAMGAR...... North American MGA [*Morris Garage Automobile*] Register (EA)
NAMH .... National Association for Mental Health (EA)
NAMHA .... North American Morab Horse Association (EA)
NAMHH........ National Association of Methodist Hospitals and Homes
NAMHI.......... National Association for the Mentally Handicapped of Ireland (EAIO)
NAMHO......... National Association of Mining History Organizations [*British*] (DBA)
NAmi .... Amityville Public Library, Amityville, NY [*Library symbol Library of Congress*] (LCLS)
NAMI .... National Alliance for the Mentally Ill (EA)
NAMI .... National Association of Malleable Ironfounders [*British*] (BI)
NAMI .... Naval Aerospace Medical Institute
NAMIA .... National Association of Mutual Insurance Agents [*Later, PIA*] (EA)
Namib........... Namibia (AD)
NAMIC .... National Association of Mutual Insurance Companies [*Indianapolis, IN*] (EA)
NAMID .... National Moving Image Database [*American Film Institute*] [*Information service or system*] (IID)
NAmiGH....... Brunswick General Hospital, Amityville, NY [*Library symbol Library of Congress*] (LCLS)
NAmiHS....... Amityville Memorial High School, Amityville, NY [*Library symbol*] [*Library of Congress*] (LCLS)
NAmiJH .... Amityville Junior High School, Amityville, NY [*Library symbol*] [*Library of Congress*] (LCLS)
NAMilCom ... North Atlantic Military Committee (AD)
NAMILCOM... North Atlantic Military Committee
NAMILPO..... NATO Military Posture (AABC)
NAMIM .... National Association of Musical Instrument Mechanics (EA)
NAMIS .... Nitride-Barrier Avalanche Injection Missile (MCD)
NAmiSH....... South Oaks Hospital, Amityville, NY [*Library symbol Library of Congress*] (LCLS)
NAMISTESTCEN... Naval Air Missile Test Center
naml .... Namligen [*Namely*] [*Swedish*] (AD)
NAML........... National Applied Mathematics Laboratory [*National Institute of Standards and Technology*] (MCD)
NAML........... National Association of Marine Laboratories (BUAC)
NAML........... Naval Aircraft Materials Laboratory (MCD)
NAML Dig.... National Association of Manufacturers Law Digest [*A publication*] (DLA)
NAMLM........ National Association for Multi-Level Marketing (EA)
NAMLNC...... National Association of Medical Legal Nurse Consultants (EA)
NAMM .... National Association of Margarine Manufacturers (EA)
NAMM .... National Association of Mass Merchandisers (EA)
NAMM .... National Association of Master Masons [*British*] (DBA)
NAMM .... National Association of Mirror Manufacturers (EA)
NAMM .... National Association of Music Merchandisers (AD)
NAMM .... National Association of Music Merchants (EA)
NAMM .... North African Military Mission [*World War II*]
NAMMA .... NATO Multi-Role Combat Aircraft Development and Production Management Agency
NAMMA .... North American Maritime Ministry Association (EA)
NAMMC .... Natural Asphalt Mineowners' and Manufacturers' Council (AD)
NAMMC .... North Atlantic Marine Mammal Commission (BUAC)

NAMMD .... National Association of Marinas and Marine Dealers (EA)
NAMME .... National Association of Medical Minority Educators (EA)
NAMME .... National Association of Minority Media Executives (NTPA)
NAMMIS ...... Navy Aviation Maintenance and Material Support System (NG)
NAMMM ...... National Association of Musical Merchandise Manufacturers [*Later, GAMA*] (EA)
NAMMO .... NATO Multi-Role Combat Aircraft Management Organization (PDAA)
NAMMO .... North Atlantic Treaty Organization [*NATO*] Multi-Role Combat Aircraft Development and Production Management Organization (AAGC)
NAMMO Development a... NATO [*North Atlantic Treaty Organization*] Multi-Role Combat Aircraft Development a (AD)
NAMMOS ..... Navy Manpower Mobilization System
NAMMR .... National Association for Milk Marketing Reform [*Later, NIDA*] (EA)
NAMMR .... North American Mini Moke Registry (EA)
NAMMS .... Navy Aviation Maintenance and Material Support System
NAMMW ...... National Association of Musical Merchandise Wholesalers [*Later, MDA*] (EA)
NAMN .... Nicotinic Acid Mononucleotide (DMAA)
NAMNPM ..... National Association of Metal Name Plate Manufacturers
NAMO .... National Agricultural Marketing Officials [*Richmond, VA*] (EA)
NAMO .... National Association of Manufacturing Opticians (EA)
NAMO .... National Association of Multifamily Owners
NAMO .... Naval Aircraft Maintenance Orders
NAMOA .... National Association of Miscellaneous Ornamental and Architectural Products Contractors (EA)
NAMORB ...... North Atlantic Mid-Ocean-Ridge Basalt [*Geology*]
NAMOS .... National Art Museum of Sport (EA)
NAMP .... National Alliance of Mental Patients [*Later, NAPS*] (EA)
NAMP .... National Antibiotic Minimization Program [*Australia*]
NAMP .... National Association of Magazine Publishers [*Later, Magazine Publishers Association*]
NAMP .... National Association of Marble Producers (EA)
NAMP .... National Association of Married Priests (AD)
NAMP .... National Association of Mature People (EA)
NAMP .... National Association of Meal Programs (EA)
NAMP .... National Association of Meat Purveyors (EA)
NAMP .... National Association of Midwifery Practitioners [*Defunct*] (EA)
NAMP .... NATO Annual Manpower Plan (NATG)
NAMP .... Naval Aviation Maintenance Program (MCD)
NAMP .... Nonaccounting Majors Program
NAMP .... North American Meat Processors Association (NTPA)
NAMPA .... NATO Maritime Patrol Aircraft Agency (NATG)
NAMPBG ..... National Association of Manufacturers of Pressed and Blown Glassware [*Defunct*] (EA)
nampg .... Nautical Air Miles per Gallon (AD)
NAMPI .... National Association of Missing Persons Investigators [*Defunct*] (EA)
NAMPMW ... Vietnam Prisoners of War [*An association*] (AD)
namppf .... Nautical Air Miles per Pound of Fuel (AD)
NAMPPF ...... Nautical Air Miles per Pound of Fuel (AAG)
NAMPS .... National Association of Marine Products and Services (EA)
NAMPS .... Navy Manpower Planning System (NVT)
NAMPUS ..... National Association of Master-Plumbers of the United States (BUAC)
NAMPW ...... National Association of Meat Processors and Wholesalers (EA)
NAMPW ...... National Association of Minority Political Women (EA)
NAMRA .... North American Mini-Champ Racing Association (EA)
NAMRAD..... Non-Atomic Military Research and Development [*Subcommittee*]
NAMRC .... North American Marten Rabbit Club (EA)
NAMRI .... Naval Aerospace Medical Research Institute (DNAB)
NAMRI/SME... North American Manufacturing Research Institution of SME [*Society of Manufacturing Engineers*] (EA)
NAMRL .... Naval Aerospace Medical Research Laboratory
NAMRP .... National Apostolate with Mentally Retarded Persons (EA)
NAMRU....... Navy Medical Research Unit [*World War II*]
NAMRU....... Navy Medical Reserve Unit (DAVI)
NAms .... Amsterdam Free Library, Amsterdam, NY [*Library symbol Library of Congress*] (LCLS)
NAMS .... National Account Management Society (NTPA)
NAMS .... National Air Monitoring [*Environmental Protection Agency*] (GNE)
NAMS .... National Air Monitoring Station [*Environmental Protection Agency*] (ERG)
NAMS .... National Ambient Air Monitoring Station [*or System*] [*Environmental Protection Agency*]
NAMS .... National Association of Marine Services (EA)
NAMS .... National Association of Marine Surveyors (EA)
NAMS .... National Association of Military Spouses (EA)
NAMS .... National Association of Municipal Securities Dealers
NAMS .... North American Membrane Society (EA)
NAMS .... North American Menopause Society (EA)
NAMS .... Nurses and Army Medical Specialists
NAMSA .... NATO Maintenance and Supply Agency
NAMSA .... North American Multihull Sailing Association (EA)
NAMSB .... National Association of Men's Sportswear Buyers (EA)
NAMSB .... National Association of Mutual Savings Banks (EA)
NAMSC .... North American Maple Syrup Council (EA)
NAMSCO...... National Association of MDS [*Multipoint Distribution System*] Service Companies [*Later, MDSIA*] (EA)
NAMSDIC..... National Arthritis and Musculoskeletal and Skin Diseases Information Clearinghouse [*Later, NAMSIC*] (EA)
NAMSE .... National Association of Minority Students and Educators in Higher Education (EA)
NAMSIC ...... National Arthritis and Musculoskeletal and Skin Diseases Information Clearinghouse (EA)
NAmsM........ Mohasco Corp., Corporate Planning Library, Amsterdam, NY [*Library symbol Library of Congress*] (LCLS)

NAMSO....... NATO Maintenance and Supply Organization [*Formerly, NATO Maintenance Supply Service Agency*] [*Luxembourg*]
NAMSO........ Navy Maintenance Support Office
NAMSOINST... Navy Maintenance Support Office Instruction (MCD)
NAMSP .... National Association of Mail Service Pharmacies [*Later, AMCPA*] (EA)
NAMSR .... National Association of Multiple Shoe Repairers [*British*] (DBA)
NAMSRC..... National AM Stereophonic Radio Committee
NAMSS .... National Association Medical Staff Services (EA)
NAmSv......... North American Savings Bank [*Associated Press*] (SAG)
NAMT .... National Association for Music Therapy (EA)
NAMT .... Naval Aircraft Mobile Trainer
NAMT .... Naval Air Maintenance Trainer (MUGU)
NAMT .... Norwegian Association of Microbiological Technologists (BUAC)
NAMTA .... National Art Materials Trade Association (EA)
NAMTAC ..... National Association of Management and Technical Assistance Centers [*Washington, DC*] (EA)
NamTai....... Nam Tai Electronics, Inc. [*Associated Press*] (SAG)
NAMTC .... Naval Air Missile Test Center
NAmTch ...... North American Technologies Corp. [*Associated Press*] (SAG)
NAMTD .... Naval Air Maintenance Training Detachment
NAMTD .... Naval Air Maintenance Training Devices
NAMTG .... Naval Air Maintenance Training Group (MCD)
NAMTGD..... Naval Air Maintenance Training Group Detachment (DNAB)
NAMtge....... North American Mortgage Co. [*Associated Press*] (SAG)
NAMTM ...... Naval Air Mobile Training Maintenance
NAMTRA..... Naval Air Maintenance Training
NAMTRADET... Naval Air Maintenance Training Detachment (MCD)
NAMTRAGRU... Naval Air Maintenance Training Group (MCD)
NAMTRAGRUDET... Naval Air Maintenance Training Group Detachment (DNAB)
NAMTRAGRUP... Naval Air Maintenance Training Group (SAA)
NAMTRATCLOFLT... Naval Air Maintenance Training Type Commander Liaison Office, Fleet (DNAB)
NAMTRATCLOLANT... Naval Air Maintenance Training Type Commander Liaison Officer, Atlantic (DNAB)
NAMTRATCLOPAC... Naval Air Maintenance Training Type Commander Liaison Office, Pacific (DNAB)
NAMU .... Naval Aircraft Material Utility
NAMU .... Naval Aircraft Modification Unit
NAMV .... Narcissus Mosaic Virus [*Plant pathology*]
NAMW .... National Association of Media Women (EA)
NAMW .... National Association of Military Widows (EA)
NAMW .... National Association of Ministers' Wives [*Later, NAMWMW*] (EA)
NAMWB .... National Association of Minority Women in Business [*Kansas City, MO*] (EA)
NAMWMW ... National Association of Ministers' Wives and Ministers' Widows (EA)
NAMZ......... Neue Allgemeine Missions-Zeitschrift [*A publication*] (BJA)
NAN .... N-Acetylneuraminic Acid [*Also, AcNeu, NANA*] [*Biochemistry*]
NAN .... Nadi [*Fiji*] [*Airport symbol*] (OAG)
Nan .... Nancy (AD)
Nan .... Nanette (AD)
Nan .... Nanking [*China*] (AD)
NAN .... Nanking [*Republic of China*] [*Seismograph station code, US Geological Survey*] (SEIS)
NAN .... Nantucket Indus [*AMEX symbol*] (TTSB)
NAN .... Nantucket Industries, Inc. [*AMEX symbol*] (SPSG)
NAN .... National Academy of Needlearts (EA)
NAN .... National Academy of Neuropsychology (EA)
NAN .... National AIDS [*Acquired Immune Deficiency Syndrome*] Network [*Defunct*] (EA)
NAN .... National Airlines, Inc. [*ICAO designator*] (FAAC)
NAN .... National Association of Neighborhoods (EA)
NAN .... Network Application Node
NAN .... News Agency of Nigeria (EY)
NAN .... Nisi Aliter Notetur [*Unless Otherwise Noted*] [*Latin*]
nan .... Nisi Aliter Notetur [*Unless It is Otherwise Noted*] [*Latin*] (AD)
Nan .... Nitrosamine [*Biochemistry*]
NAN .... No Action Necessary [*Military*] (CINC)
NAN .... Non-Ammonia-Nitrogen (PDAA)
NAN .... North American Nippon Technologies Corp. [*Vancouver Stock Exchange symbol*]
NAN .... North Atlantic Network (EA)
NAN .... Norton Administrator for Networks [*Computer software*] [*Symantec Corp.*] (PCM)
NaN .... Not a Number [*Computer programming*] (BYTE)
NANA .... N-Acetylneuraminic Acid [*Also, AcNeu, NAN*] [*Biochemistry*]
nana .... N-Acetylneuraminic Acid (AD)
NANA .... National Advertising News Association (AD)
NANA .... National Advertising Newspaper Association [*Later, SNA*] (EA)
NANA .... National Association of Nail Artists [*Later, NANAA*] (EA)
NANA .... Newsagents' Association of New South Wales and the Australian Capital Territory,Inc.
NANA .... North American Newspaper Alliance
NANA .... North American Normande Association (EA)
NANA .... Northwest Alaska Native Association [*Later, MA*]
NANAA .... National Aesthetician and Nail Artist Association [*Formerly, NANA*] [*WINBA*] [*Absorbed by*] (EA)
NANAC .... National Aircraft Noise Abatement Council [*Defunct*] (EA)
NANAC .... National Aviation Noise Abatement Council (AD)
NANACA....... National Association for Native American Children of Alcoholics (EA)
NANACOA...... National Association for Native American Children of Alcoholics (EA)
NANAI......... Dutch Actiongroup for Indians of North America
NANAP........ Non-Aligned News Agency Pool (BUAC)
NANASP...... National Association of Nutrition and Aging Services Programs (EA)
NANAWO ..... Namibia National Women's Organzation (BUAC)

NAnB .... Bard College, Annandale-On-Hudson, NY [*Library symbol Library of Congress*] (LCLS)
NANB .... Non-A, Non-B [*Virology*]
NANBA .... North American National Broadcasters Association (EA)
NANBH .... Non-A, Non-B Hepatitis [*Medicine*]
NANBPWC ... National Association of Negro Business and Professional Women's Clubs [*Washington, DC*] (EA)
NANBV .... Non-A, Non-B Hepatic Virus
NANC .... National Association of New Careerists (EA)
NANC .... Non-Adrenergic, Non-Cholinergic [*Neurology*]
NANCA .... North American Natural Casing Association (EA)
NANCB .... National Association of Negotiated Commissioned Brokers [*Defunct*] (EA)
NANCF .... North Atlantic Naval Coastal Frontier
NANCI .... New Aeronautical and Nautical Chart Investigations (NOAA)
NANCO .... National Association of Noise Control Officials (EA)
NANCRFUG... North American NCR [*National Cash Register Co.*] Financial Users Group (EA)
NAND .... Naval Ammunition and Net Depot
NAND .... Not And [*Logical operator*] [*Computer science*]
NAND .... `Not' and `And' (NITA)
N & A .... Nautical & Aviation Publishing Co.
NANDA .... North American Nursing Diagnosis Association (EA)
N&CR .... [*The*] Nash and Cibinic Report [*A publication*] (AAGC)
N & D .... Nodular and Diffuse Lymphoma [*Oncology*]
N&G .... Navigation and Guidance
N & GS .... Navigation and Guidance Subsystem [*NASA*] (KSC)
N & H .... Nott and Hopkins' Reports [*United States Court of Claims*] [*A publication*] (DLA)
N & H .... Nott and Huntington's Reports [*1-7 United States Court of Claims*] [*A publication*] (DLA)
N & Hop ...... Nott and Hopkins' Reports [*United States Court of Claims*] [*A publication*] (DLA)
N & Hunt ..... Nott and Huntington's Reports [*1-7 United States Court of Claims*] [*A publication*] (DLA)
N&M .... Nerves and Muscles (DMAA)
N & M .... Nevile and Manning's English King's Bench Reports [*A publication*] (DLA)
N&M .... Night and Morning (DMAA)
N & M .... November and May [*Denotes semiannual payments of interest or dividends in these months*] [*Business term*]
N & Macn .... Neville and Macnamara's Railway and Canal Cases [*1855-1950*] [*A publication*]
N & MC .... Navy and Marine Corps [*Medal*]
N & Mc .... Nott and McCord's South Carolina Reports [*A publication*] (DLA)
N & McC ...... Nott and McCord's South Carolina Reports [*A publication*] (DLA)
N & MCM ..... Navy and Marine Corps Medal [*Military decoration*]
N & McN ...... Neville and Macnamara's Railway and Canal Cases [*1855-1950*] [*A publication*] (DLA)
N & M Mag... Nevile and Manning's English Magistrates' Cases [*A publication*] (DLA)
N & MMC .... Nevile and Manning's English Magistrates' Cases [*A publication*] (DLA)
N & P .... Nevile and Perry's English King's Bench Reports [*1836-38*] [*A publication*] (DLA)
N & P Mag... Nevile and Perry's English Magistrates' Cases [*1836-37*] [*A publication*] (DLA)
N & PMC ..... Nevile and Perry's English Magistrates' Cases [*1836-37*] [*A publication*] (DLA)
N & S .... Nicholls and Stops' Reports [*1897-1904*] [*Tasmania*] [*A publication*] (DLA)
N & SDCP.... Neurological and Sensory Disease Control Program
N & SE .... Nacogdoches & Southeastern Railroad (IIA)
N & T .... Navigation and Timing
N & T .... Nose and Throat [*Medicine*]
N & V .... Nausea and Vomiting
N & W .... Norfolk & Western Railway Co.
NANE .... National Association for Nursery Education [*Later, NAEYC*] (EA)
NANEAP ...... North Africa, Near East, Asia, and Pacific Region [*Program of ACTION, an independent government agency*]
NANEP .... Navy Air Navigation Electronic Project
NANEWS...... Naval Aviation News
NANFA .... North American Native Fishes Association (EA)
NANFAC ...... Naval Air Navigation Facility Advisory Committee
NANFM .... National Association of Non-Ferrous Scrap Metal Merchants (BUAC)
NANFORMS... Naval Aviator/Naval Flight Officer Reporting Management System (DNAB)
NANFPT ...... National Association of Natural Family Planning Teachers (BUAC)
NAng .... Angelica Free Library, Angelica, NY [*Library symbol Library of Congress*] (LCLS)
NANHC........ National Association of Neighborhood Health Centers [*Later, NACHC*] (EA)
NANHPH ...... National Association of Nursing Homes and Private Hospitals [*Australia*]
NANI .... National Academy of Nannies, Inc. (EA)
NA/NLP........ National Association of Neuro-Linguistic Programming (EA)
NANM .... N-Allylnormetazocine [*Biochemistry*]
NANM .... N-Allylnormorphine [*Narcotic antagonist*]
NANM .... National Association of Negro Musicians (EA)
NANMT .... National Association of Nurse Massage Therapists
NANMV .... Nandina Mosaic Virus [*Plant pathology*]
NANN .... National Association of Neonatal Nurses (EA)
NANN .... National Association of Nursery Nurses (BUAC)
NANNP........ Nordic Association of Non-Commercial Phonogram Producers (EA)
nano- .... Billionth (IDOE)

NANO .... Nanometrics, Inc. [*NASDAQ symbol*] (NQ)
nano .... One billionth [*From the Latin nanus*] (WDMC)
NanomtR ...... Nanometrics, Inc. [*Associated Press*] (SAG)
NANOVA ...... Nonorthogonal Analysis of Variance (ADA)
nanova .... Non-Orthogonal Analysis of Variance (AD)
NANP .... National Alliance of Nurse Practitioners (EA)
NANP .... National Association of Naturopathic Physicians [*Defunct*] (EA)
NANPA .... North American Nature Photography Association
NANPE .... National Association of Newspaper Purchasing Executives [*Later, NPMA*] (EA)
NANPMA...... North American Nutrition and Preventive Medicine Association (EA)
NANPRH ..... National Association of Nurse Practitioners in Reproductive Health (EA)
NANR .... National Association of Nurse Recruiters [*Later, NAHCR*] (EA)
NANS .... National Association for Neighborhood Schools (EA)
NANS .... National Association of Nigerian Students (BUAC)
NANS .... National Association of Non-Smokers (EA)
NANS .... National Catholic News Service (EA)
NANS .... Naval Air Navigation School
NANS .... North American Nietzsche Society (EA)
NANS .... North Atlantic and Neighboring Seas
NANT .... National Association of Nephrology Technologists (EA)
NANT .... National Associaton of Nephrology Technicians/Technologists (EA)
Nantck .... Nantucket Industries, Inc. [*Associated Press*] (SAG)
NANTDDDC... National Association of Negro Tailors, Designers, Dressmakers, and Dry Cleaners (EA)
NANTIS .... Nottingham and Nottinghamshire Technical Information Service [*British*] (AD)
NANTS .... National Association of Naval Technical Supervisors (EA)
NANU .... National Association of NIDS [*National Investor Data Service*] Users (EA)
NANU .... National Association of Non-Unionists (BUAC)
NANVH&SWO... National Assembly of National Voluntary Health and Social Welfare Organizations (AD)
NANWEP ...... Navy Numerical Weather Prediction [*Computer system*] [*Control Data Corp.*]
NANWEP...... Navy Numerical Weather Problems [*Group*]
NANWR .... North American Network of Women Runners (EA)
NAO .... Charleston, SC [*Location identifier FAA*] (FAAL)
NAO .... Her Majesty's Nautical Almanac Office [*British*] (PDAA)
NAO .... National Academy of Opticianry (EA)
NAO .... National Accordion Organisation of the United Kingdom (BUAC)
NAO .... National Accordion Organization [*British*] (DBA)
NAO .... National Adhering Organization
NAO .... National Association of Outfitters (AD)
NAO .... National Astronomical Observatory [*Japan*]
NAO .... National Audit Office [*British*] (ECON)
NAO .... Nautical Almanac Office (BUAC)
NAO .... Naval Audit Office (DNAB)
NAO .... Naval Aviation Observer [*Obsolete*]
NAO .... NOAA [*National Oceanic and Atmospheric Administration*] Administrative Order (USDC)
NAO .... Noise Abatement Office (AD)
NAO .... Non-Asbestos Organic [*Friction materials*]
NAO .... Norsar Array Site 01A00 [*Norway*] [*Seismograph station code, US Geological Survey*] (SEIS)
NAO .... North American Airlines, Inc. [*ICAO designator*] (FAAC)
NAO .... North Atlantic Oscillation [*Climatology*]
NAO .... Nurse Aide/Orderly (OICC)
NAOA .... National Apartment Owners Association [*Later, NAA*] (EA)
NAOA .... National Association of Older Americans [*Later, Heartline/National Association of Older Americans*] (EA)
NAOA .... Naval Aviation Observer Aerology (SAA)
NAOA .... Navy Officers Accounts Office (AD)
NAOB .... Naval Aviation Observer Bombardier (MUGU)
NAOBMISB... National Association of Operative Boiler Makers and Iron Ship Builders [*A union*] [*British*]
NAOC .... National Antique Oldsmobile Club (EA)
NAOC .... Naval Aviation Observer Controller (MUGU)
NAOC .... Naval Aviation Officer Candidate
NAOC .... Nigerian Agip Oil Co. (AD)
NAOC .... North Absheron Operating Co.
NAOCJ .... National Association of Operative Carpenters and Joiners [*A union*] [*British*]
NAOCP .... Novice Amateur Operator's Certificate of Proficiency [*Radio*]
NAOE .... National Association for Outdoor Education [*British*]
NAOEJ .... National Association of Oil Equipment Jobbers [*Later, PEI*] (EA)
NAOFD .... National Association of Office Furniture Dealers (NTPA)
NAOGE .... National Association of Government Engineers [*Defunct*] (EA)
NAOGTC....... North American Opel GT [*Gran Turismo*] Club (EA)
NAOH .... National Alliance for Oral Health (NTPA)
NaOH .... Sodium Hydroxide
NAOHSM...... National Association of Oil Heating Service Managers (EA)
NAOI .... Naval Aviation Observer Intercept (MUGU)
NAOIG .... North African Inspector General's Section [*World War II*]
NAOJ .... National Astronomical Observatory of Japan
NAOL .... National Association of Orchestra Leaders (EA)
NAOMI......... National Association of Ovulation Method Instructors [*British*] (DBA)
NAON .... National Association of Orthopaedic Nurses (EA)
NAON .... Naval Aviation Observer Navigator (MUGU)
NAOO .... National Association of Optometrists and Opticians (EA)
NAOODA ...... North American Offshore One-Design Association (EA)
NAOP .... National Alliance for Optional Parenthood (DAVI)
NAOP .... National Association for Olmsted Parks (EA)
NAOP .... National Association of Operative Plasterers

NAOP	National Association of Operative Plumbers [*A union*] [*British*]
NAOP	Nonadditive Operational Project [*Military*]
NAOPL	National Association of Operative Plasterers' Labourers [*A union*] [*British*]
NAOR	Naval Aviation Observer RADAR (MUGU)
NAORD	North African Ordnance Section [*World War II*]
NAORPB	North Atlantic Ocean Regional Planning Board [*NATO*]
NAORPG	North Atlantic Ocean Regional Planning Group [*NATO*] (NATG)
NAORTS	Naval Aviation Ordnance Test Station
NAOS	NASA Aircrew Oxygen System
NAOS	North Atlantic Ocean Station [*WMO*]
NAOSH	Naitonal Authority for Occupational Safety and Health [*Ireland*] (BUAC)
NAOSMM	National Association of Scientific Material Managers (EA)
NAOSOF	National Association of Soap Opera Fans
NAOSP	North Atlantic Ocean Stations Program (MUGU)
NAOSW	National Association of Oncology Social Workers (EA)
NAOT	National Association of Organ Teachers [*Later, IAOT*]
NAOT	National Association of Orthopaedic Technologists (EA)
NAOT	Naval Air Operational Training
NAOT	Naval Aviation Observer Tactical (SAA)
NAOTB	National Association of Off-Track Betting (EA)
NAOTC	National Association of OTC [*Over-the-Counter*] Companies [*Later, APTC*] (EA)
NAOTC	National Association of Timetable Collectors (EA)
NAOTC	Naval Air Operational Training Command
NAOTS	Naval Aviation Ordnance Test Station
NAOWES	National Association of Older Worker Employment Services [*Washington, DC*] (EA)
NAP	Armed Proletarian Nuclei [*Italy*]
NAP	Bangladesh National Awami Party [*Political party*] (PPW)
nap	Knapsack (AD)
nap	Napalm (AD)
NAP	Napa Resources, Inc. [*Vancouver Stock Exchange symbol*]
NAP	Napay [*Former USSR Seismograph station code, US Geological Survey Closed*] (SEIS)
nap	Naphtha (AD)
NAP	Napier Air Service, Inc. [*ICAO designator*] (FAAC)
NAP	Naples [*Italy*] [*Airport symbol*] (OAG)
Nap	Naples (AD)
Nap	Napoleon (AD)
Nap	Napoleon [*or Napoleonic*]
NAP	Napoleonic Age Philatelists (EA)
NAP	[*The*] Narragansett Pier Railroad Co., Inc. [*AAR code*]
NAP	Nasion Pogonion [*Anatomy*] (MAE)
NAP	National Academies of Practice (NTPA)
NAP	National Action Party [*Sierra Leone*] [*Political party*] (EY)
NAP	National Action Party [*Turkey Political party*] (PD)
NAP	National Advertising Program
NAP	National Aerospace Plane (AD)
NAP	National Afforestation Program (BUAC)
NAP	National Agency for Privatisation [*Romania*] (BUAC)
NAP	National Alliance Party [*Sierra Leone*] [*Political party*] (BUAC)
NAP	National Apprenticeship Program [*Bureau of Apprenticeship and Training*] [*Department of Labor*]
NAP	National Archives Publication
NAP	National Association for the Paralysed (AD)
NAP	National Association of Parliamentarians (EA)
NAP	National Association of Planners [*Defunct*] (EA)
NAP	National Association of Postmasters (NADA)
NAP	National Association of Postmasters of the United States
NAP	National Association of Publishers [*Defunct*] (EA)
NAP	National Association of the Professions (EA)
NAP	National Audit Plan
NAP	National Awami Party [*Pakistan*] [*Political party*] (PD)
NAP	National Awami Party-Bashani [*Bangladesh*] [*Political party*] (FEA)
NAP	National Awareness Partner (TELE)
NAP	National Processing, Inc. [*NYSE symbol*] (SAG)
NAP	Native American Program (OICC)
NAP	Native Americans in Philanthropy
NAP	Naval Academy Prepatory Student (DNAB)
NAP	Naval Air Plan (CAAL)
NAP	Naval Airplane Pusher [*Slang*] (DNAB)
NAP	Naval Air Priorities
NAP	Naval Auxiliary Patrol [*British military*] (DMA)
NAP	Naval Aviation Pilot
nap	Naval Aviation Pilot (AD)
NAP	Naval Aviation Plan (NVT)
NAP	Navigation Analysis Program [*NASA*] (NASA)
NAP	Neighborhood Action Program [*New York City*] (EA)
NAP	Neighborhood Awareness Program (AD)
NAP	Network Access Point [*Telecommunications*]
NAP	Network Access Pricing [*Telecommunications*] (TEL)
NAP	Network Access Program [*Computer science*] (CIST)
NAP	Network Access Protocol
NAP	Network Applications Platform [*Computer science*] (CIST)
NAP	Neutrophil Activating Protein
NAP	Neutrophil Alkaline Phosphatase [*An enzyme*]
NAP	New Age Patriot [*An association*] (EA)
NAP	New Aspiration Party [*Thailand*]
NAP	New Associations and Projects [*Formerly, NA*] [*A publication*]
NAP	Niger Agricultural Project [*Nigeria*] (BUAC)
NAP	Night Attack Program [*Military*]
NAP	Nitroaminophenol [*Organic chemistry*]
NAP	Noise Abatement Procedure (AAG)
NAP	Noise Analysis Program
NAP	Nomina Anatomica Parisiensia [*Medicine*]
NAP	Nonacquisition Project [*Military*] (CAAL)
NAP	Nonadvertising Promotion [*Public relations*] (WDMC)
nap	Non-Agency Purchase (AD)
NAP	Nonagency Purchase
NAP	Nonaggression Pact
NAP	Nonnuclear Armament Plan (MCD)
NAP	Normal Administrative Practice
NAP	Normalized Abundance Pattern [*Geochemistry*]
NAP	North American Philips Corp. (IAA)
NAP	North Australia Program
NAP	Northern Agricultural Producers (BUAC)
NAP	Not a Priori
NAP	Not at Present
nap	Not at Present (AD)
NAP	Nuclear Action Project (EA)
NAP	Nuclear-Active Particles [*Astrophysics*]
NAP	Nuclear Auxiliary Power
NAP	Nuclei Armati Proletari [*Armed Proletarian Nuclei*] [*Italian*] (PD)
NAP	Nucleic Acid Phosphorus [*Biochemistry*]
NAP	Nucleoacidic Protein [*Cytochemistry*]
NAPA	N-Acetyl-p-aminophenol [*Organic chemistry*]
NAPA	N-Acetylprocainamide [*Cardiac depressant*]
NAPA	National Academy of Public Administration (EA)
NAPA	National Agricultural Plastics Association [*Later, ASP*] (EA)
NAPA	National Agricultural Press Association (EA)
NAPA	National Alcohol Producers' (BUAC)
NAPA	National Amateur Press Association (EA)
NAPA	National Asphalt Pavement Association (EA)
NAPA	National Association for Photographic Art [*Canada*] (EAIO)
NAPA	National Association for the Practice of Anthropology (EA)
NAPA	National Association of Park Administrators [*British*] (BI)
NAPA	National Association of Performing Artists
NAPA	National Association of Polish Americans
NAPA	National Association of Press Agencies (BUAC)
NAPA	National Association of Pro America (EA)
NAPA	National Association of Purchasing Agents [*Later, NAPM*] (EA)
NAPA	National Association of the Partners of the Alliance [*Later, Partners of the Americas*] (EA)
NAPA	National Automotive Parts Association (EA)
NAPA	National Police Officers Association of America
NAPA	Native American Press Association (EA)
NAPA	Network Against Psychiatric Assault (EA)
NAPA	North American Photonics Association [*Defunct*] (EA)
NAPA	North American Pizza Association [*Defunct*]
NAPA	North Atlantic Ports Association (EA)
NAPAA	National Association for Promotional and Advertising Allowances, Inc. (NTPA)
NAPAAW	National Association of Professional Asian-American Women (EA)
NAPAC	National Arson Prevention and Action Coalition (EA)
NAPAC	National Association for Professional Associations and Corporations (EA)
NAPAC	National Association of Paper and Advertising Collectors (EA)
NAPAC	National Program for Acquisitions and Cataloging [*Library of Congress*]
NAPAEO	National Association of Principal Agricultural Education Officers [*British*]
NAPAF	National Association of Private Art Foundations [*Defunct*] (EA)
NAPAG	National Academies Policy Advisory Group
NAPall	North American Palladium [*Associated Press*] (SAG)
napalm	Naphthene Palmitate (AD)
NAPALM	Naphthenic and Palmitic Acids [*Major constituents of flame thrower*]
NAPALM	National ADP [*Automatic Data Processing*] Program for AMC Logistics Management [*Army Materiel Command*]
NAPALM	National Automatic Data Processing Program for Army Material Command Logistics Management (IAA)
NAPALSA	National Asian Pacific American Law Student Association (EA)
NAPAMA	National Association of Performing Arts Managers and Agents (EA)
NAPAMS	Navy Automated Pilot Aptitude Measurement System
NAPAN	National Association for the Prevention of Addiction to Narcotics [*Later, NADAP*]
NAPAP	National Acidic Precipitation Assessment Program (BUAC)
NAPAP	National Acid Precipitation Assessment Program [*Council on Environmental Quality*] [*Washington, DC*]
NAPAP	Noyaux Armes pour l'Autonomie Populaire [*Armed Cells for Popular Autonomy*] [*France*] (PD)
NAPARE	National Association for Perinatal Addiction Research and Education (EA)
NAPAS	National Association of Protection and Advocacy Systems (EA)
NAPATMO	NATO Patriot Management Office
NAPAVHEE	National Association of Postsecondary and Adult Vocational Home Economics Educators (EA)
NAPB	National Agricultural Products Boards [*Tanzania*] (BUAC)
NAPB	National Association for the Preservation of Baseball (EA)
NAPB	National Association of Professional Bureaucrats [*Later, INATAPROBU*]
NAPBC	National Action Plan on Breast Cancer
NAPBC	Native American Public Broadcasting Consortium (EA)
NAPBFC	National Association of Pat Boone Fan Clubs (EA)
NAPBIRT	National Association of Professional Band Instrument Repair Technicians (EA)
NAPBL	National Association of Professional Baseball Leagues (EA)
NAPBN	National Air Pollution Background Network [*Environmental Protection Agency*] (GFGA)

NAPBTA	National American Pit Bull Terrier Association (EA)
NAPC	National Air Pollution Control (KSC)
NAPC	National Alliance of Preservation Commissions (EA)
NAPC	National Assault Prevention Center (EA)
NAPC	National Association of Parish Councils [British] (BI)
NAPC	National Association of Pastoral Counselors [Defunct] (EA)
NAPC	National Association of Personnel Consultants [Defunct] (EA)
NAPC	National Association of Pet Cemeteries [Later, IAPC]
NAPC	National Association of Plumbing Contractors [Later, NAPHCC]
NAPC	National Association of Precancel Collectors (EA)
NAPC	Naval Air Photographic Center (DNAB)
NAPC	Naval Air Priorities Center (DNAB)
NAPC	Naval Air Propulsion Center [Trenton, NJ]
NAPC	Non-Adherent Peritoneal Cell (PDAA)
napc	Non-Adherent Peritoneal Cells (AD)
NAPC	North American Paleontological Convention
NAPCA	National Air Pollution Control Administration (AAGC)
NAPCA	National Asian Pacific Center on Aging (EA)
NAPCA	National Association of Pension Consultants and Administrators [Atlanta, GA] (EA)
NAPCA	National Association of Pipe Coating Applicators (EA)
NAPCA	National Association of Professional Contracts Administrators (AAGC)
NAPCA	National Automatic Pistol Collectors Association (EA)
NAPCA	North American Poultry Cooperative Association [Defunct] (EA)
NAPCAE	National Association for Public Continuing and Adult Education (EA)
NAPCE	National Association of Pastoral Care in Education [British] (DBA)
NAPCE	National Association of Professors of Christian Education (EA)
NAPCMM-ELCA	Native American Program Commission for Multicultural Ministries of ELCA [Evangelical Lutheran Church in America] (EA)
NAPC/MS	Naval Air Propulsion Center Measurement and Information Systems Department [Trenton, NJ]
Napco	Napco Security Systems, Inc. [Associated Press] (SAG)
NAPCOR	National Association for Plastic Container Recovery (EA)
NAPC-PE	Naval Air Propulsion Center Propulsion Engineering Department [Trenton, NJ]
NAPCR	National Association for Puerto Rican Civil Rights
NAPCRG	North American Primary Care Research Group (EA)
NAPCRO	National Association of Police Community Relations Officers (EA)
NAPCS	National Association of Postpartum Care Services (PAZ)
NAPCTAC	National Air Pollution Control Techniques Advisory Committee [Environmental Protection Agency] (GFGA)
NAPCU	Northwest Association of Private Colleges and Universities [Library network] (EA)
NAPCWA	National Association of Public Child Welfare Administrators (EA)
NAPD	National Association of Pharmaceutical Distributors [British] (BI)
NAPD	National Association of Plastics Distributors (EA)
NAPD	National Association of Police Driving (AD)
NAPD	National Association of Precollege Directors (EA)
NAPDA	North American Professional Driver's Association [Defunct] (EA)
NAPDD	Non-Acquisition Program Definition Document [Navy] (DOMA)
NAPDEA	North American Professional Driver Education Association (EA)
NAPDP	National Association of Prepaid Dental Plans (DMAA)
NAPE	Naphthenic-Palmitic Acid [Mixture used in flame-throwing weapons and bombs] [Also, NAPALM] (VNW)
NAPE	National Alliance of Postal Employees [Later, NAPFE]
NAPE	National Association of Partners in Education
NAPE	National Association of Physicians for the Environment (EA)
NAPE	National Association of Port Employers [British]
NAPE	National Association of Power Engineers (EA)
NAPE	National Association of Primary Education [British] (DBA)
NAPE	National Association of Private Enterprise [Fort Worth, TX] (EA)
NAPE	National Association of Professional Educators (EA)
NAPE	National Association of Professional Engravers (EA)
NAPE	Nuclear Attack Preparedness Evaluation
NAPEC	National Association of Professional Environmental Communicators (NTPA)
NAPEC	Naval Ammunition Production Engineering Center
NAPECW	National Association for Physical Education of College Women [Later, NAPEHE] (EA)
NAPEDNC	National Association of Political Ex-Deportees of the Nazi Camps [Italy Political party] (EAIO)
NAPEGG	Association of Professional Engineers, Geologists & Geophysicists of the Northwest Territories (AC)
NAPEHE	National Association for Physical Education in Higher Education (EA)
NAPEM	National Association of Public Exposition Managers [Later, HGSEI] (EA)
NAPENA	National Association of Public Employer Negotiators and Administrators [Later, NAPPENA] (EA)
Na Pent	Sodium Pentothal [Thiopental Sodium] [A brand name] [Pharmacology] (DAVI)
NAPEO	National Association of Professional Employer Organizations (NTPA)
NAPEP	National Association of Planners, Estimators, and Progressmen (EA)
NAPET	National Association of Photo Equipment Technicians (EA)
NAPEX	National Philatelic Exhibition
NAPF	National Association of Pension Funds [British] (DI)
NAPF	National Association of Petroleum Funds [British]
NAPF	National Association of Plastic Fabricators (EA)
NAPF	Naval Aviation Publication Facility
NAPF	Nonappropriated Funds (DNAB)
NAPF	Nuclear Age Peace Foundation (EA)
NAPFA	National Association of Personal Financial Advisors (EA)
NAPFE	National Alliance of Postal and Federal Employees (EA)
NAPFM	National Association of Packaged Fuel Manufacturers [Defunct] (EA)
NAPFR	National Association of Professional Fund Raisers (EA)
NAPFSC	National Association of Professional Forestry Schools and Colleges (WPI)
NAPG	National Association of Professional Gardeners [Later, PGMS]
NAP(G)	Naval Aviation Pilot (Glider)
NAPG	News America Publishing Group
NaPG	Sodium Pregnanediol Glucuronide [Medicine] (DMAA)
NAPGC	National Association of Public Golf Courses [British] (BI)
NAPGCM	National Association of Private Geriatric Care Managers (EA)
NAPGCW	National Association of Plasters, Granolithic, and Cement Workers [A union] [British]
NAPH	Naphtha (ADA)
naph	Naphtha (AD)
naph	Naphthyl (AD)
NAPH	Naphthyl [Organic chemistry] (MAE)
NAPH	National Association of Professors of Hebrew (EA)
NAPH	National Association of Public Hospitals (EA)
NAPH	National Association of the Physically Handicapped (EA)
NAPH	Nicotinamide Adenine Dinucleotide Phosphate [An enzyme] (DMAA)
NAPHA	National Amusement Park Historical Association (EA)
NAPhA	North American Photonics Association (EA)
NAPH & MSC	National Association of Plumbing, Heating, and Mechanical Service Contractors [British] (DBA)
NAPHC	National Association of Plumbing/Heating/Cooling Contractors (AD)
NAPHCC	National Association of Plumbing-Heating-Cooling Contractors [Formerly, NAPC] (EA)
NAPHS	National Association of Psychiatric Health Systems (NTPA)
NAPHT	National Association of Patients on Hemodialysis and Transplantation [Later, AAKP] (EA)
NAPI	National Appaloosa Pony (EA)
NAPI	National Association of Property Inspectors (NTPA)
NAPI	National Association of the Pet Industry [Defunct] (EA)
NAPI	Naval Aeronautical Publications Index (EA)
NAPI	Neurobehavioral Assessment of the Preterm Infant [Test] (TMMY)
NAPIA	National Affiliate of Printing Industries of America (AD)
NAPIA	National Association of Public Insurance Adjusters [Baltimore, MD] (EA)
NAPIAP	National Agricultural Pesticide Impact Assessment Program [Department of Agriculture]
NAPIC	National Association of Private Industry Councils [Washington, DC] (EA)
NAPIL	National Association for Public Interest Law (EA)
NAPIM	National Association of Printing Ink Manufacturers (EA)
NAPJPO	National Aerospace Plane Joint Programs Office
NAPL	National Air Photo Library [Canada] (PDAA)
NAPL	National Association of Photolithographers (IAA)
NAPL	National Association of Police Laboratories (EA)
NAPL	National Association of Printers and Lithographers (EA)
NAPL	Nonaqueous Phase Liquid [Chemistry]
NAPLIB	National Association Aerial of Photographic Libraries [British] (DBA)
NAPLO	National Association of Power Loom Overlookers [British] (DBA)
NAPLP	National Association of Para-Legal Personnel (AD)
NAP-LP	National Association of Para-Legals Personnel (EA)
NAPLPS	North American Presentation Level Protocol Standard (DOM)
NAPLPS	North American Presentation Level Protocol Syntax [Computer display system] [Pronounced "naplips"]
NAPM	National Association of Paper Merchants [British]
NAPM	National Association of Pastoral Musicians (BUAC)
NAPM	National Association of Pattern Manufacturers [LA PPTBA] (EA)
NAPM	National Association of Perry Makers [British] (DBA)
NAPM	National Association of Pharmaceutical Manufacturers (EA)
NAPM	National Association of Photographic Manufacturers (EA)
NAPM	National Association of Punch Manufacturers (EA)
NAPM	National Association of Purchasing Management (EA)
NAP-M	National Awami Party-Muzaffar [Bangladesh] [Political party] (FEA)
NAPMA	NATO AEWC [Airborne Early Warning and Control] Program Management Agency
NAPMA	North American Punch Manufacturers Association (NTPA)
NAPMDAC	National Air Pollution Manpower Development Advisory Committee [Terminate d, 1976] [HEW] (EGAO)
NAPMECA	National Association of Postgraduate Medical Education Centre Administrators (BUAC)
NAPMG	North African Provost Marshal General [World War II]
NAPMM	National Association of Produce Market Managers [Hartford, CT] (EA)
NAPMO	NATO Airborne Early Warning and Control Programme Management Organization [Brunssum, Netherlands]
NAPMR	National Apostolate with People with Mental Retardation (EA)
NAPMW	National Association of Professional Mortgage Women
NAPN	National Association of Physician Nurses (EA)
NAPN	Native American Policy Network (EA)
NAPN	Native Authority Public Notice [Nigeria] [A publication] (ILCA)
NAPN	North American Poetry Network (EA)
NAPNAP	National Association of Pediatric Nurse Associates and Practitioners (EA)
NAPNE	National Association for Practical Nurse Education (DAVI)
NAPNES	National Association for Practical Nurse Education and Service (EA)
NAPNM	National Association of Pipe Nipple Manufacturers [Defunct] (EA)
NAPNOC	Neighborhood Arts Program National Organizing Committee (EA)
NAPNSC	National Association of Private, Nontraditional Schools and Colleges (EA)
NAPNW	Nurses Alliance for the Prevention of Nuclear War [Defunct] (EA)
NAPO	NASA Pasadena Office
NAPO	National Association of Performing Artists (AD)
NAPO	National Association of Pizza Operators [Commercial firm] (EA)
NAPO	National Association of Police Organizations (EA)

NAPO .... National Association of Pool Owners
NAPO .... National Association of Prison Officers [*British*] (DI)
NAPO .... National Association of Probation Officers [*British*] (DI)
NAPO .... National Association of Professional Organizers (EA)
NAPO .... National Association of Property Owners (EA)
NAPO .... National Association of Purchasing Agents (AD)
NAPO .... NATO Airborne Early Warning Program Office (NATG)
NAPO .... Naval Air Priorities Office
NAPO .... New Afrikan People's Organization (EA)
NAPO .... United National Association of Post Office Craftsmen [*Later, APWU*]
NAPOG .... Naval Airborne Project Press Operations Group [*Hickam AFB, HI*]
NAPOLI .... National Politics [*Behavioral science game*]
NAPOMHWMGL ... National Association of Post Office Mail Handlers, Watchmen, Messengers, and Group Leaders [*Later, NPOMHWMGL*] (EA)
NAPOTS .... National Aboriginal Project Officer Training Scheme [*Australia*]
NAPP .... National Association for the Protection of Punters (BUAC)
NAPP .... National Association of Paralegal Personnel (NTPA)
NAPP .... National Association of Patient Participation [*British*] (DBA)
NAPP .... National Association of Play Publishers
NAPP .... National Association of Poultry Packers Ltd. [*British*] (BI)
NAPP .... National Association of Priest Pilots (EA)
NAPP .... National Association of Printing Purchasers [*Defunct*] (EA)
NAPP .... National Association of Private Process Servers (EA)
NAPP .... Native American Publishing Program [*of Harper & Row, Publishers, Inc.*]
NAPP .... Naval Aviation Preparatory Program
NAPP .... Neighborhood Adult Participation Project
NAPP .... Net Aerial Primary Productivity [*Forestry*]
NAPP .... Nonattainment Plan Provision [*Environmental Protection Agency*]
NAPPA .... National Association of Physical Plant Administrators of Universities and Colleges [*Later, Association of Physical Plant Administrators of Universities and Colleges*] (EA)
NAPPA .... National Association of Prevention Professionals and Advocates (NTPA)
NAPPA .... National Association of Pupil Personnel Administrators [*Later, NAPSA*] (EA)
NAPPB .... National Association of Professional Print Buyers (EA)
NAPPC .... National Association of Party Plan Companies [*Defunct*] (EA)
NAPPC .... North American Plant Preservation Council (NTPA)
NAPPENA .... National Association of Public and Private Employer Negotiators and Administrators (EA)
NAPPH .... National Association of Private Psychiatric Hospitals (EA)
Nappie .... Neuilly, Auteil, and Passy [*Elegant Paris neighborhoods; the term, Nappie, is used as a nickname for French Yuppies*]
Nappies .... New Age Professional People in Esoteric Studies [*Lifestyle classification*]
NAPPO .... National Association of Plant Patent Owners (EA)
NAPPO .... North American Plant Protection Organization [*Canada*] (BUAC)
Nap Pres .... Napier. Prescription [*A publication*] (ILCA)
NAPPS .... National Association for the Preservation and Perpetuation of Storytelling (EA)
NAPPS .... National Association of Private Placement Syndicators [*Later, California Investment Real Estate Forum*] (EA)
NAPPS .... National Association of Private Process Servers (NTPA)
NAPPS .... National Association of Professional Pet Sitters (NTPA)
NAPPS .... National Association of Professional Process Servers (EA)
NAPPS .... North American Pediatric Pseudo-Obstruction Society (EA)
na pr .... Na Priklad [*For Example*] [*Czech*] (AD)
NAPR .... NASA Procurement Regulation
NAPR .... National Association for Pastoral Renewal [*Defunct*] (EA)
NAPR .... National Association of Park Rangers (EA)
NAPR .... National Association of Physician Recruiters (EA)
NAPR .... National Association of Pram Retailers (BUAC)
NAPR .... National Association of Publishers' Representatives (EA)
NAPR .... NATO Armaments Planning Review (NATG)
NAPRA .... National Association of Progressive Radio Announcers (EA)
NAPRA .... New Age Publishing and Retailing Alliance (EA)
NAPRA Int'l ... New Age Publishing and Retailing Alliance International (NTPA)
NAPRALERT ... Natural Products Alert [*University of Illinois at Chicago*] [*Information service or system*] (IID)
NAPRC .... National Association for the Prevention of Rape by Castration (AD)
NAPRCR .... National Association for Puerto Rican Civil Rights (EA)
NAPRE .... National Association Practical Refrigerating Engineers [*Later, RETA*] (EA)
NAPRECA .... Natural Products Research Network for Eastern and Central Africa [*UNESCO*] [*Ethiopia*] (BUAC)
NAPRFMR .... National Association of Private Residential Facilities for the Mentally Retarded (EA)
NAPRI .... National Animal Production Research Institute [*Nigeria*] (BUAC)
NaPro .... NaPro BioTherapeutics, Inc. [*Associated Press*] (SAG)
NaProBio .... NaPro BioTherapeutics, Inc. [*Associated Press*] (SAG)
NAPRS .... National Airspace Performance Reporting System [*Aviation*] (FAAC)
NAPRW .... Northwest African Photographic Reconnaissance Wing [*World War II*]
NAPS .... National Alliance of Postal Supervisors (AD)
NAPS .... National Association for Premenstrual Syndrome (BUAC)
NAPS .... National Association for Professional Saleswomen (EA)
NAPS .... National Association of Personal Secretaries (BUAC)
NAPS .... National Association of Personnel Services (NTPA)
NAPS .... National Association of Pet Sitters (EA)
NAPS .... National Association of Postal Supervisors (EA)
NAPS .... National Association of Premenstrual Syndrome [*British*] (DBA)
NAPS .... National Association of Presbyterian Scouters (EA)
NAPS .... National Association of Private Secretaries [*British*] (BI)
NAPS .... National Association of Psychiatric Survivors (EA)
NAPS .... National Auricula and Primula Society (BUAC)
NAPS .... National Auxiliary Publications Service [*American Society for Information Science*]
NAPS .... Nationwide Association of Preserving Specialists [*British*] (DBA)
NAPS .... Naval Academy Preparatory School
NAPS .... Navy Acquisition Procedures Supplement [*A publication*] (AAGC)
NAPS .... Nerve Agent Pre-Treatment Set [*A cholinergic drug*] [*Used for protective immunization by the military*]
NAPS .... Night Aerial Photographic System
NAPS .... Nimbus Automatic Programming System (IEEE)
NAPS .... Nissan Air Pollution System (AD)
NAPS .... Nonspecific Air Pollution Syndrome
NAPS .... North American Patristic Society (EA)
NAPS .... North American Precis Syndicate
NAPS .... North American Pro Series [*Auto racing*]
NAPS .... North Anna Power Station [*Virginia*] [*Nuclear energy*] (NRCH)
NAPSA .... National Appliance Parts Suppliers Association (EA)
NAPSA .... National Association of Pretrial Service Agencies (AD)
NAPSA .... National Association of Public Service Advertisers [*British*] (DBA)
NAPSA .... National Association of Pupil Services Administrators (EA)
NAPSAA .... National Association of Public School Adult Administrators [*Later, NAPSAE*]
NAPSAC .... International Association of Parents and Professionals for Safe Alternatives in Childbirth [*Association retains acronym of its former name*] (EA)
NAPSAC .... National Association for the Protection from Sexual Abuse of Adults and Children with Learning Disabilities (BUAC)
NAPSAC .... Naval Atomic Planning, Support, and Capabilities Report (NG)
NAPSAE .... National Association for Public School Adult Educators [*Later, NAPCAE*] (EA)
NAPSAP .... Naval Airship Program for Sizing and Performance (MCD)
Nap's bones ... Napier's Bones [*First slide rule*] (AD)
NAPSEC .... National Association of Private Schools for Exceptional Children (EA)
NAPSEO .... National Association of Public Sector Equal Opportunity Officers
NAPSG .... National Association of Principals of Schools for Girls (EA)
NAPSIC .... North American Power Systems Interconnection Committee [*US and Canada*] [*Electric power*]
NAPSIS .... Navy Air Pollution Source Information System
NAPSLO .... National Association of Professional Surplus Lines Offices (EA)
NAPSOE .... National Association of Public Service Organization Executives (EA)
NAPSS .... National Association of Professional Secretarial Services [*Later, PASS*] (EA)
NAPSS .... Numerical Analysis Problem Solving System
NAPSV .... National Association of Private Security Vaults (EA)
Napt .... Napton's Reports [*4 Missouri*] [*A publication*] (DLA)
NAPT .... National Association for Poetry Therapy (EA)
NAPT .... National Association for Proton Therapy (NTPA)
NAPT .... National Association for Pupil Transportation (EA)
NAPT .... National Association for the Prevention of Tuberculosis [*British*] (DI)
NAPT .... National Association of Percussion Teachers (BUAC)
NAPT .... National Association of Physical Therapists (EA)
NAPT .... Naval Air Primary Training
NAPT .... Nordic Association of Plumbers and Tinsmiths (EAIO)
NAPTC .... Naval Air Primary Training Command
NAPTC .... Naval Air Propulsion Test Center [*Later, NAPC*]
NAPTCA .... National Alliance for the Prevention and Treatment of Child Abuse (EA)
NAPTC-AED ... Naval Air Propulsion Test Center - Aeronautical Engine Department
NAPTC-ATD ... Naval Air Propulsion Test Center - Aeronautical Turbine Department
NAPTCC .... National Association of Psychiatric Treatment Centers for Children (EA)
NAPTC-OP ... Naval Air Propulsion Test Center - Operations and Plant Engineering Department
NAPTC-PE ... Naval Air Propulsion Test Center - Propulsion Technology and Project EngineeringDepartment
NAPTCRO ... Naval Air Primary Training Command Regional Office
NAPTDC .... National Association of Professional Truck Driving Champions (EA)
NAPTE .... National Association of Part-Time and Temporary Employees
NaPTEC .... National Primary Teacher Education Conference (AIE)
NAPTIC .... National Air Pollution Technical Information Center [*of National Air Pollution Control Administration*] [*Also, APTIC*] (DIT)
Napton .... Napton's Reports [*4 Missouri*] [*A publication*] (DLA)
NAPTR .... National Association of Property Tax Representatives [*Defunct*] (EA)
NAPTS .... National Association of Public Television Stations [*Later, APB*] (EA)
NAPTW .... National Association of Pet Trade Wholesalers (BUAC)
NAPU .... National Association of Professional Upholsterers [*Defunct*] (EA)
NAPU .... Nuclear Auxiliary Power Unit
NAPUBFAC ... Naval Air Publication Facility (MCD)
NAPUS .... National Association of Postmasters of the United States (EA)
NAPUS .... Nuclear Auxiliary Power Unit System
NAPV .... National Association of Prison Visitors [*British*] (BI)
NAPVD .... National Association for the Prevention of Venereal Disease (AD)
NAPVI .... National Association for Parents of the Visually Impaired (EA)
NAPVO .... National Association of Passenger Vessel Owners (EA)
NAPW .... National Association of Personnel Workers (EA)
NAPWA .... National Association of People with AIDS (EA)
NAPWDA .... North American Police Work Dog Association (EA)
NAPWPT .... National Association of Professional Word Processing Technicians [*Philadelphia, PA*] (EA)
NAQ .... Narssarssuaq [*Denmark*] [*Geomagnetic observatory code*]
NAQAP .... National Association of Quality Assurance Professionals (EA)
NAQDC .... National Air Quality Data Center [*Australia*]
NAQF .... North Atlantic Quality Figure
NAQI .... National Air Quality Index (AD)
NAQMC .... North African Quartermaster Section [*World War II*]
NAQP .... National Association of Quick Printers (EA)

NAQUADAT...	National Water Quality Data Bank [*Environment Canada*] [*Information service or system*] (IID)
NAR	Air Continental, Inc. [*ICAO designator*] (FAAC)
NAR	Nagase Analbuminemia Rat
NAR	Nara [*Japan*] [*Seismograph station code, US Geological Survey*] (SEIS)
NAR	Narcotic (ROG)
NAR	Nare [*Colombia*] [*Airport symbol*] (OAG)
Nar	Narragansett (AD)
NAR	Narration [*Films, television, etc.*]
NAR	Narrow (AAG)
NAR	Narrow (AD)
nar	Nasal Airway Resistance [*Medicine*]
NAR	National Archives and Records Service, Washington, DC [*OCLC symbol*] (OCLC)
NAR	National Asbestos Registry [*Environmental Protection Agency*] (GFGA)
NAR	National Association for the Retarded (DMAA)
NAR	National Association of Realtors (EA)
NAR	National Association of Rocketry (EA)
NAR	Naval Air Reserve
NAR	Naval Auxiliary Reserve
NAR	Naval Research and Development
NAR	Navy Ammunition Reclassification
NAR	Nelson Aldrich Rockefeller (AD)
NAR	Neo Aristero Revma [*Greece*] [*Political party*] (ECED)
NAR	Net Advertising Revenue [*Television*] [*British*]
NAR	Net Assimilation Rate [*Botany*]
nar	Net Assimilation Rate (AD)
NAR	No Action [*or Answer*] Required (NVT)
nar	No Apparent Rate (AD)
NAR	Noise-Adding Radiometer
NAR	Nordic Association for Rehabilitation [*Denmark*] (EAIO)
NAR	Nordiska Akademiker Radet [*Nordic Academic Council - NAC*] [*Defunct*] (EA)
NAR	North American Review [*A publication*] (BRI)
NAR	North American Rockwell Corp. [*Later, Rockwell International Corp.*] (MCD)
NAR	North American Route [*Aviation*]
NAR	North American Royalties (AD)
NAR	North Australia Railway
NAR	Northern Alberta Railways Co. [*AAR code*]
NAR	Nose Alone Reference [*Aviation*] (MCD)
NAR	Not According to Routine
NAR	Notice of Ammunition Reclassification [*Navy*] (NG)
NAR	Nuclear Acoustic Resonance
NAR	Nuclear Androgen Receptor [*Endocrinology*]
NAR	Nuclear Assessment Routine (MCD)
NAR	Nuclei Armati Rivoluzionari [*Armed Revolutionary Nuclei*] [*Italian*] (PD)
NAR	Nucleic Acids Research [*A publication*]
NAR	Numerical Analysis Research (MCD)
NARA	Narcotics Addict Rehabilitation Act [*1966*]
NARA	National Air Resources Act (GFGA)
NARA	National Alliance for Rural Action (EA)
NARA	National Aquatic Resources Agency [*Sri Lanka*] [*Marine science*] (OSRA)
NARA	National Archives and Records Administration [*Independent government agency*] [*Formerly, NARS*]
NARA	National Association for the Rescue of Animals [*British*] (DI)
NARA	National Association of Recovered Alcoholics [*Defunct*] (EA)
NARA	National Association of Rehabilitation Agencies (EA)
NARA	National Association of Republican Attorneys (EA)
NARA	National Association of Review Appraisers (EA)
NARA	Naval Aircraft Restorers Association (EA)
NARA	Nippon Australian Relations Agreement (AD)
NARA	North American Radio Archives (EA)
NARA	North American Radon Association [*Defunct*] (EA)
NARA	North American Regional Alliance of IATA [*International Amateur Theatre Association*] (EA)
NARA	North American Rhea Association (NTPA)
NARA	Northern Auto Racing Association [*Sanctioning organization*]
NARAA	National Association of Recruitment Advertising Agencies [*Defunct*] (EA)
NARACC	National Association for Research and Action in Community Care [*British*] (DI)
NARACS	National Radio Communications System [*FAA*] (TAG)
NARAD	Naval Air Research and Development (MUGU)
NARAD	Navy Research and Development (AD)
NARADCOM	Natick Research and Development Command [*Army*]
NARAG	National Association of Ratepayers' Action Groups [*British*] (DI)
NARAL	National Abortion Rights Action League (EA)
NARAL	National Association for the Repeal of Abortion Laws
NARAL	Net Advertising Revenue after Levy [*Television*] [*British*]
NARAL PAC	National Abortion and Reproductive Rights Action League-Political Action Committee
NARAMU	National Association of Review Appraisers and Mortgage Underwriters (NTPA)
NARANEXOS	Name, Rate, Service Number, and Expiration of Obligated Service [*Navy*]
NARANO	Name, Rate, and Service Number [*Navy*]
NARAS	National Academy of Recording Arts and Sciences (EA)
NARASO	Nevada Association Race and Sports Book Operators (EA)
NARASPO	Navy Regional Airspace Officer (MUGU)
NARAT	NATO Request for Air Transport Support [*Military*]
NARATE	Navy Automatic RADAR Test Equipment (KSC)
NARATE	Northrop Automatic RADAR Test System (SAA)
NARAVA	National Archives and Records Administration Volunteer Association (EA)
NARB	Narcotic Addict Rehabilitation Branch [*National Institute of Mental Health*]
NARB	National Advertising Review Board [*New York, NY*] (EA)
NARB	National Assembly of Religious Brothers (EA)
NARB	National Assocation of Radio Broadcasters (NTCM)
NARB	National Association for Regional Ballet [*Later, RDA*]
NARB	National Association of Referees in Bankruptcy [*Later, National Conference of Bankruptcy Judges*] (EA)
NARB	National Association of Retired Bankers [*Later, RBA*] (EA)
NARB	Navy Art Review Board (DNAB)
NARB	Nonazeotropic Refrigerant Blend
NARBA	North American Regional Broadcasting Agreement [*To minimize interference between AM stations*]
NARBC	National Angora Rabbit Breeders Club (EA)
NARBL	Net Advertising Revenue before Levy [*Television*] [*British*]
NARBW	National Association of Railway Business Women (EA)
narc	Narcotic (AD)
NARC	Narcotics [*FBI standardized term*]
narc	Narcotics Agent (AD)
NARC	Narcotism [*Chemical dependency*] (DAVI)
NARC	National Agricultural Research Center
NARC	National Amateur Retriever Club (EA)
NARC	National Archives and Records Service (AD)
NARC	National Army Revolutionary Committee [*or Council*] [*Laos*]
NARC	National Association for Retarded Children (AEBS)
NARC	National Association for Retarded Citizens [*Later, ARC*] (EA)
NARC	National Association of Regional Councils (EA)
NARC	National Association of Retired Catholics (AD)
NARC	Naval Air Research Center (DNAB)
NARC	Naval Air Reserve Center (DNAB)
NARC	Naval Alcohol Rehabilitation Center (DNAB)
NARC	Nonautomatic Relay Center (AABC)
NARC	North American Riders Club (EA)
NARC	North American Rockwell Corp. [*Later, Rockwell International Corp.*] (MCD)
NARC	Northern Automobile Racing Club [*Sanctioning organization*]
NARC	Nuclear Age Resource Center (EA)
NARC	Nucleus Arcuatus (DMAA)
NARCA	National Antidrug Reorganization and Coordination Act
NARCA	National Association of Retail Collection Attorneys (NTPA)
NARCE	National Association of Retired Civil Employees [*Later, NARFE*] (EA)
NARCF	National Association of Residential Care Facilities (NTPA)
NARCF	National Association of Retail Clothiers and Furnishers [*Later, MRA*] (EA)
NARCINT	Narcotics Intelligence [*Military*] (ADDR)
NARCL	Nuclear Accident Response Capability Listing (MCD)
narco	Narcolepsy [*Neurology*] (DAVI)
narco	Narcotic (AD)
NARCO	Narcotics Commission [*United Nations*] (AD)
narco	Narcotics Hospital (DAVI)
narco	Narcotics Officer (AD)
narco	Narcotics Treatment Center (DAVI)
NARCO	National Aeronautical Corp. (MCD)
narcocard	Narcotic-Addict Registration Card (AD)
narcodollars	Narcotic Traffic Dollars (AD)
NARCOG	Narcotics Coordination Group [*CIA*]
NARCOM	Narration, Commentary [*Motion pictures*]
NARCOM	North Atlantic Relay Communication Satellite
Narconon	Narcotics Anonymous [*An association*] (AD)
Nar Conv	Nares' Penal Convictions [*1815*] [*A publication*] (DLA)
NAR CORP	North American Rockwell Corp. [*Later, Rockwell International Corp.*]
narcos	Narcotics (AD)
narcos	Narcotics Police Officers (AD)
narcot	Narcotic (AD)
narcotest	Narcotics Test (AD)
Narcotics L Bull	Narcotics Law Bulletin [*A publication*] (DLA)
narco-traf	Narcotics Traffick (AD)
narcs	Narcotics (AD)
narcs	Narcotics Agents (AD)
narcs	Narcotics Hospital (AD)
narcs	Narcotics Officers (AD)
narcs	Narcotics Treatment Centers (AD)
NARCU	National Association of Railroad and Utility Commissioners (NTCM)
NARCUP	National Association for Retired Credit Union People (AD)
NArd	Ardsley Public Library, Ardsley, NY [*Library symbol Library of Congress*] (LCLS)
NARD	National Association of Regimental Drummers (AD)
NARD	National Association of Retail Druggists (EA)
NARD	National Association of Rudimental Drummers [*Defunct*]
NARD	Navy Alcohol Rehabilitation Drydock (DNAB)
nard	Spikenard (AD)
NARDA	National Appliance and Radio TV Dealers Association (IAA)
NARDA	National Association of Retail Dealers of America (EA)
NARDA	Naval Air Research and Development Activities (SAA)
NARDAC	Navy Regional Data Automation Center
NARDACWASHDC	Navy Regional Data Automation Center, Washington, DC (DNAB)
NArdCG	CIBA-GEIGY Corp., Corporate Library, Ardsley, NY [*Library symbol*] [*Library of Congress*] (LCLS)
NARDELOG	Navy Rapid Delivery Logistics (AFIT)
NARDET	Naval Air Reserve Detachment (DNAB)

NARDIC....... Navy Research and Development Information Center
NARDIS....... Navy Automated Research and Development Information System [*Later, NAVWUIS*]
Nar Div........ Narodni Divadlo [*National Theater*] [*Czechoslavakia*] (AD)
NARDIV....... Naval Air Reserve Divisions
NARDIV(FA)... Naval Air Reserve Division (Fleet Air) (DNAB)
NARDV....... National Association Rainbow Division Veterans (EA)
NARE......... National Association for Remedial Education [*British*]
NARE......... North Atlantic Regional Experiment [*Ozone measurement*]
NAREA....... National Association of Real Estate Appraisers (EA)
Na_{reab}......... Sodium Reabsorption Rate [*Biochemistry*] (DAVI)
NAREB........ National Association of Real Estate Boards [*Later, National Association of Realtors*] (EA)
NAREB........ National Association of Real Estate Brokers
NAREBB...... National Association of Real Estate Buyer Brokers (EA)
NAREC........ National Association of Real Estate Companies (EA)
NAREC........ Naval Research Electronic Computer
narec .... Naval Research Electronic Computer (AD)
NAREE........ National Association of Real Estate Editors (EA)
NaREIA....... National Real Estate Investors Association (NTPA)
NAREIF........ National Association of Real Estate Investment Funds [*Later, NAREIT*] (EA)
NAREIM....... National Association of Real Estate Investment Managers (NTPA)
NAREIT........ National Association of Real Estate Investment Trusts (EA)
NARELLO...... National Association of Real Estate License Law Officials (EA)
NAREMCO..... National Records Management Council (EA)
NAREP........ National Association of Real Estate Professionals (NTPA)
NARESU...... Naval Air Reserve Unit (DNAB)
NARETPA..... National Agricultural Research, Extension, and Teaching Policy Act of 1977
NARETU....... Naval Air Reserve Electronics Training Unit (DNAB)
NARF .... American Rehabilitation Association [*Formerly, National Association of Rehabilitation Facilities*] (EA)
NARF .... National Association of Rehabilitation Facilities (EA)
NARF .... National Association of Retail Furnishers (AD)
NARF .... Native American Rights Fund (EA)
NARF .... Natural Axial Resonant Frequency (PDAA)
narf........... Natural Axial-Resonant Frequency (AD)
NARF .... Naval Aerospace Research Facility
NARF .... Naval Air Reserve Force
NARF .... Naval Air Rework Facility
NARF .... Navy Arctic Research Facility
NARF .... Nuclear Aerospace Research Facility (IEEE)
NARF .... Nuclear Aircraft Research Facility (AD)
NARFE........ National Association of Retired Federal Employees (EA)
NARFFO...... Naval Air Rework Facility Field Office (DNAB)
NARFS........ Naval Air Reserve Force Squadron (DNAB)
NARGA........ National Association of Retail Grocers of Australia (AD)
NARGOM...... North American Research Group on Management (PDAA)
NARGUS ...... National Association of Retail Grocers of the United States [*Later, NGA*] (EA)
NARHA........ North American Riding for the Handicapped Association (EA)
NARHC........ National Association of River and Harbor Contractors [*Later, NADC*] (EA)
NARHS........ National Auto Racing Historical Society (EA)
NARI .... National Agriculture Research Institute (WDAA)
NARI .... National AIDS Research Institute [*India*]
NARI .... National Alliance for Reduction of Imprisonment [*Defunct*] (EA)
NARI .... National Association of Recycling Industries [*Later, ISRI*] (EA)
NARI .... National Association of Rehabilitation Instructors (EA)
NARI .... National Association of Residents and Interns (EA)
NARI .... National Association of the Remodeling Industry (EA)
NARI .... National Atmospheric Research Institute (AD)
NARI .... Native American Research Institute (EA)
NARI .... Nuclear Aerospace Research Institute [*Air Force*]
NARIC........ National Academic Recognition Information Centre (AIE)
NARIC........ National Rehabilitation Information Center (EA)
NARICM....... National Association of Retail Ice Cream Manufacturers [*Later, NICYRA*] (EA)
Nar Inv .... Narcotics Investigation (AD)
NARISCO...... North American Rockwell Information Systems Co.
NARIST....... Naristillae [*Nasal Drops*] [*Pharmacy*]
narist.......... Naristillae [*Nasal Drops*] [*Latin*] (AD)
NARK......... Nikolai Andreyvich Rimsky-Korsakov
Narkomvneshtorg... Narodny Komissariat Vneshney Torgovli [*People's Commissariate of Foreign Trade*] [*Russian*] (AD)
NARKOMVNUDEL... Narodnyi Komissariat Vnutrennikh Del [*People's Commissariat of Internal Affairs (1917-1946)*] [*Also known as NKVD Soviet secret police organization*]
NARL .... National Aero Research Laboratory [*Canada*] (PDAA)
NARL .... Naval Arctic Research Laboratory
NARL .... No Adverse Response Level [*Medicine*] (HCT)
NARM .... National Association of Recording Merchandisers (EA)
NARM .... National Association of Relay Manufacturers (EA)
NARM .... National Association of Restaurant Managers [*Scottsdale, AZ*] (EA)
NARM .... National Association of Retail Merchants (EA)
NARM .... Naturally Occurring or Accelerator-Produced Radioactive Material
NARM .... Naval Resource Model (MCD)
N-arm .... Nuclear Armament (AD)
NARMC....... National Association of Regional Media Centers (EA)
NARMC....... National Association of Resident Management Corporations (NTPA)
NARMC....... Naval Aerospace and Regional Medical Center [*Bureau of Medicine*]
NARMCO...... National Research and Manufacturing Co. (AD)
N-armed ...... Nuclear-Armed (AD)
NARMFD...... National Association of Retail Meat and Food Dealers

NARMH........ National Association for Rural Mental Health (EA)
NARMIC....... National Action/Research on the Military Industrial Complex (EA)
NArmN....... North Castle Library, Armonk, NY [*Library symbol Library of Congress*] (LCLS)
NARMP....... National Antibacterial Residue Minimization Program [*Australia*]
NARMPU...... Naval Air Reserve Mobile Photographic Unit (DNAB)
NARMU...... Naval Air Reserve Maintenance Units
NARN......... National Association of Registered Nurses (EA)
NARND....... National Association of Radio News Directors (IAA)
NARO........ National Agricultural Research Organization [*Netherlands*] (ECON)
NARO........ National Association of Reimbursement Officers [*Washington, DC*] (EA)
NARO......... National Association of Royalty Owners (EA)
NARO.......... North American Regional Office (AD)
NAROCTESTSTA... Naval Air Rocket Test Station
NARP........ National Administrative Rehabilitation Programme [*United Nations program*]
NARP........ National Association for Registered Plans (EA)
NARP........ National Association of Railroad Passengers (EA)
NARP........ National Association of Reunion Managers (NTPA)
NARP........ Neurogenic Muscle Weakness, Ataxia, and Retinitis Pigmentosa [*Medicine*]
NARP........ New Australian Republican Party [*Political party*]
NARP........ Nonaqueous Reversed Phase [*Chromatography*]
NARP........ Nuclear Weapons Accident Report Procedures (AD)
NARPA....... National Air Rifle and Pistol Association [*British*]
NARPA....... National Association for Rights Protection and Advocacy (EA)
NARPD....... National Association for the Relief of Paget's Disease [*British*]
NARPM....... National Association of Residential Property Managers (NTPA)
NARPO....... National Association of Retired Police Officers [*British*] (DBA)
NARPPS....... National Association of Rehabilitation Professionals in the Private Sector (EA)
NARPTR....... National Association of Railroad Property Tax Representatives (NTPA)
NARPV....... National Association for Remotely Piloted Vehicles (MCD)
NARR........ Narrator [*or Narration*]
NARRD .... National Association of Record Retailer Dealers [*Defunct*] (EA)
Nar Rep Bul... Narodna Republika Bulgaria [*Bulgarian People's Republic*] [*Political party*] (AD)
Narr Mod ..... Narrationes Modernae [*Style's English King's Bench Reports*] [*1646-55*] [*A publication*] (DLA)
NARRP....... National Association of Recreation Resource Planners (NTPA)
NARRS....... National Association of Radio Reading Services (EA)
NARS......... Narrative Accomplishment Reporting System [*Department of Agriculture*] [*Information service or system*] (IID)
NARS......... National Acupuncture Research Society (EA)
NARS......... National Agricultural Research Systems (ECON)
NARS......... National Annual Report Service [*NYSE*]
NARS......... National Archives and Records Service [*of GSA*] [*Washington, DC Later, NARA*]
NARS......... National Association of Radiation Survivors (EA)
NARS......... National Association of Radiator Specialists [*British*] (DBA)
NARS......... National Association of Radiotelephone Systems [*Later, Telocator Network of America*] (EA)
NARS......... National Association of Rail Shippers (EA)
NARS......... National Association of Refunders and Shoppers [*Defunct*] (EA)
NARS......... National Association of Rehabilitation Secretaries (EA)
NARS......... Naval Air Rescue Service (MUGU)
NARS......... New Atlantean Research Society [*Defunct*] (EA)
NARS......... Nonaffiliated Reserve Section
NARS......... Northampton Activity Rating Scale [*Psychology*]
NARS......... North Atlantic Radio System
NARSA....... National Automotive Radiator Service Association (EA)
NARS-A1..... National Archive and Record Service-Automation 1 (NITA)
NARSAB...... National Association of Rail Shippers Advisory Boards (EA)
NARSAD...... National Alliance for Research on Schizophrenia and the Depressions (EA)
NARSC....... National Association of Reinforcing Steel Contractors (EA)
NARSIS....... National Association for Road Safety Instruction in Schools (AD)
NARSLL....... National Association to Reform State Liquor Laws [*Later, National Association to Reform State Drinking Ages*] [*Defunct*] (EA)
NARST....... National Association for Research in Science Teaching (EA)
NARSTC....... Naval Air Rescue Training Command
NARSUP ...... Navy Acquisition Regulations Supplement
NARSVA....... National Archives and Record Service Volunteer Association [*Later, NARAVA*] (EA)
NARSVPD .... National Association of Retired Senior Volunteer Program Directors (EA)
NART .... National Association for Remedial Teaching (AEBS)
NART .... National Association of Recreation Therapists [*Later, NTRS*] (EA)
NART .... New Adult Reading Test
NART .... North American Racing Team [*Auto racing*]
NARTA........ North American Restaurant and Tavern Alliance (EA)
NARTB........ National Association of Radio and Television Broadcasters [*Later, NAB*]
NARTC........ National Association of Railroad Trial Counsel (EA)
NARTC........ Naval Air Research Training Command
NARTC........ Naval Air Rocket Test Center (MUGU)
NARTC........ North America Regional Test Center (NATG)
NARTCE....... National Association for Released Time Christian Education (EA)
NARTE........ National Association of Radio and Telecommunications Engineers (EA)
NARTEL .... North Atlantic Radio Telephone Committee
NARTH........ National Association of Research and Therapy of Homosexuality (EA)

NARTM	National Association of Rope and Twine Merchants (AD)
NARTRANS...	North American Rockwell Training and Services [*Obsolete*]
NARTS	National Association of Radio Telephone Systems [*Later, Telocator Network of America*] (IAA)
NARTS	National Association of Reporter Training Schools [*Defunct*] (EA)
NARTS	National Association of Resale and Thrift Shops (EA)
NARTS	Naval Aeronautics Test Station
NARTS	Naval Air Rocket Test Station
NARTU	Naval Air Reserve Training Unit
NARU	Natural Rate of Unemployment [*Economics*]
NARU	Naval Air Reserve Unit (NVT)
NARU	North Australian Research Unit (AD)
NARUC	National Association of Regulatory Utility Commissioners (EA)
NARUCE	National Association of Regulatory Utility Commission Engineers (IAA)
NARUS	Navy Aircraft Resources Utilization Study
NARVRE	National Association of Retired and Veteran Railroad Employees (EA)
NARW	National Assembly of Religious Women (EA)
NARW	National Association of Refrigerated Warehouses [*Later, IARW*] (EA)
NARWA	Nordic Agricultural Research Workers Association (EA)
NARWACL...	North American Regional World Anti-Communist League (AD)
NAS	N-Acetylserotonin [*Biochemistry*]
NAS	Narcotics Affairs Section [*Foreign service*]
NAS	Narrow-Angle Sensor
NAS	Nasal
nas.............	Nasal (AD)
NAS	Nasangga [*Fiji*] [*Seismograph station code, US Geological Survey*] (SEIS)
NAS	Nassau [*Bahamas*] [*Airport symbol*] (OAG)
NAS	National Academy of Sciences [*Washington, DC*]
NAS	National Academy of Songwriters (EA)
NAS	National Academy of Sports (EA)
NAS	National Adoption Society (WDAA)
NAS	National Advanced Systems (HGAA)
NAS	National Advocates Society (EA)
NAS	National Aerospace Standards (MCD)
NAS	National Aerospace Standards Industrial Association (AAGC)
NAS	National Agricultural Society (NADA)
NAS	National Aircraft Standards
NAS	National Airspace System [*NASA*]
NAS	National Alliance for Salvation [*Sudan*] [*Political party*] (MENA)
NAS	National Aquarium Society (EA)
NAS	National Aquatic School [*Red Cross*]
NAS	National Association of Sanitarians [*Later, NEHA*] (EA)
NAS	National Association of Scholars (EA)
NAS	National Association of Schoolmasters [*British*]
NAS	National Association of Shopfitters [*British*] (BI)
NAS	National Association of Shopkeepers [*British*] (DBA)
NAS	National Association of Specialized Carriers, Marietta GA [*STAC*]
NAS	National Association of Stevedores (EA)
NAS	National Association of Supervisors [*Later, Federal Managers Association*] (EA)
NAS	National Astrological Society [*Defunct*] (EA)
NAS	National Audubon Society (EA)
NAS	National Autistic Society [*British*]
NAS	National Aviation System [*FAA*]
NAS	National Avionics Society (EA)
NAS	National Seastar [*Vancouver Stock Exchange symbol*]
NAS	Native American Studies (AD)
NAS	Naval Air Service
NAS	Naval Air Station
NAS	Naval Air Systems Command, Washington, DC [*OCLC symbol*] (OCLC)
NAS	Naval Audit Service (DOMA)
NAS	Navigation Avoidance System (KSC)
NAS	Navy Advisory Section [*Vietnam*] (VNW)
NAS	Neonatal Abstinence Syndrome (DAVI)
NAS	Neonatal Airleak Syndrome [*Medicine*] (DMAA)
NAS	NetWare Access Server [*Computer science*]
NAS	Network Access Switch [*Telecommunications*] (MCD)
NAS	Network Application Support [*Computer science*] (BTTJ)
NAS	Network-Attached Storage [*Computer science*]
NAS	Neuroallergic Syndrome [*Medicine*] (DMAA)
NAS	New Attack Submarine [*Navy*] (MUSM)
NAS	Newsreel Access Systems, Inc. [*Also, an information service or system*] (IID)
NAS	No Added Salt [*Medicine*]
n-a-s............	No Added Salt (AD)
NAS	Nocturnal Adoration Society (EA)
NAS	Noise Abatement Society [*British*]
NAS	Non-Assessable Stock [*Investment term*] (MHDW)
NAS	Nonavailability Statement [*Military*]
NAS	Non-Indigenous Aquatic Species [*Marine science*] (OSRA)
NAS	Nonlinear Antenna System
NAS	NORAD Alert System (MCD)
NAS	Nord Amerikanischer Sangerbund (EA)
NAS	Normalized Alignment Score
NAS	North American Shale [*Geology*]
NAS	North American Supply [*World War II*]
NAS	Northeast Aviation Services Ltd. [*British ICAO designator*] (FAAC)
NAS	Nozzle Actuating System [*Aerospace*] (MCD)
NAS	Numerical Aerodynamic Simulation [*NASA supercomputer system*]
NAS	Numerical Analysis Subroutines [*Computer science*] (BUR)
NAS	Numerical and Atmospheric Sciences Network [*NASA*]
NAS	Nursery Association Secretaries [*Later, Nursery Association Executives*] (EA)
NAS	Nursing Auxiliary Service [*British*]
NASA	National Acoustical Suppliers Association [*Defunct*] (EA)
NASA	National Advertising Sales Association (EA)
NASA	National Aeronautics and Space Act of 1958
NASA	National Aeronautics and Space Administration [*Washington, DC*]
NASA	National Aerospace Services Association [*Defunct*] (MCD)
NASA	National Appliance Service Association (EA)
NASA	National Association of School Affiliates (EA)
NASA	National Association of Schools of Art (EA)
NASA	National Association of Securities Administrators
NASA	National Association of Shippers' Agents [*Washington, DC*] (EA)
NASA	National Association of State Archeologists (EA)
NASA	National Association of Synagogue Administrators (EA)
NASA	National Automobile Salesmen's Association
NASA	Naval Aircraft Safety Activity (SAA)
NASA	Newspaper Advertising Sales Association (EA)
NASA	North American Sailing Association (AD)
NASA	North American Saxophone Alliance (AD)
NASA	North American Securities Administrators Association [*Also, NASAA*] (EA)
NASA	North American Shippers Association (EA)
NASA	North American Singers Association (EA)
NASA	North American Swiss Alliance (EA)
NASA	North Atlantic Seafood Association [*Defunct*] (EA)
NASA	North Atlantic Shippers Association (DS)
NASAA	National Aeronautics and Space Administration Act (AD)
NASAA	National Assembly of State Arts Agencies (EA)
NASAA	National Association of State Approval Agencies (EA)
NASAA	National Association of Student Activity Advisers (EA)
NASAA	North American Securities Administrators Association [*Topeka, KS*] (EA)
NASA-AEC ...	National Aeronautics and Space Administration and Atomic Energy Commission (SAA)
NASAB	National Association of Shippers Advisory Boards (EA)
NASABCA	National Aeronautics and Space Administration Board of Contract Appeals
NASA-CF Florida...	National Aeronautics and Space Administration - Cocoa Beach, Florida (AD)
NASA-CO	National Aeronautics and Space Administration - Cleveland, Ohio (AD)
NASACRE.....	National Association for Standing Advisory Councils for Religious Education (AIE)
NASACT	National Association of State Auditors, Comptrollers, and Treasurers (EA)
NASACU........	National Association of State Approved Colleges and Universities (EA)
NASAD	National Association of Schools of Art and Design (EA)
NASAD	National Association of Sport Aircraft Designers (EA)
NASADAD ...	National Association of State Alcohol and Drug Abuse Directors (EA)
NASAE	National Association of Supervisors of Agricultural Education (EA)
NASA-EC California...	National Aeronautics and Space Administration - Edwards, California (AD)
NASAEN.......	National Association for State-Enrolled Assistant Nurses (AD)
NASAERC....	NASA Electronic Research Center (IAA)
NASAF	Northwest African Strategic Air Force [*British military*] (DMA)
NASA FAR Supp...	National Aeronautics and Space Administration FAR Supplement [*A publication*] (AAGC)
NASAGA	North American Simulation and Gaming Association (EA)
NASA-GM Maryland...	National Aeronautics and Space Administration - Greenbelt, Maryland (AD)
NASA-HA Alabama...	National Aeronautics and Space Administration - Huntsville, Alabama (AD)
NASAHOE	National Association of Supervisors and Administrators of Health Occupations Education (EA)
NASA-HT......	National Aeronautics and Space Administration - Houston, Texas (AD)
NASAKOM....	Nasional, Agama, Kommunist [*Indonesian President Sukarno's policy of unity among National, Religious, and Communist forces*]
Nasakom	Nationalist-Communist (AD)
NASA-KSC ...	National Aeronautics and Space Administration - Kennedy Space Center
NASAL	National Association of Single Adult Leaders (EA)
NASAL	Network of Single Adult Leaders (EA)
NASA LST Telescope...	National Aeronautics and Space Administration Large Space Telescope (AD)
NASA-LV Virginia...	National Aeronautics and Space Administration - Langley Field, Virginia (AD)
NASA-MC California...	National Aeronautics and Space Administration - Moffett Field, California (AD)
NASAMECU..	Natura Sanat, Medicus Curat [*Nature Heals, the Doctor Cures*] [*Title of collected talks by Dr. Georg Groddeck, published in 1913*]
NASA-MSC...	National Aeronautics and Space Administration - Manned Spacecraft Center
NAS & FCA...	National Automatic Sprinkler and Fire Control Association (AD)
NASANX.......	Naval Air Station Annex (DNAB)
NASAO........	National Association of State Aviation Officials (EA)
NASAOCARE...	National Association of State Aviation Officials Center for Aviation Research and Education (EA)
NASAP........	National Association of Student Affairs Professionals (NTPA)
NASAP........	Navy Alcohol Safety Action Program (DNAB)
NASAP........	Network Analysis for Systems Applications Program [*Computer program*] [*NASA*]

NASAP.........	Nonproliferation Alternative Systems Assessment Program [*Nuclear energy*] (NRCH)
NASAP.........	North American Society of Adlerian Psychology (EA)
NASAP.........	Nuclear Alternative System Assessment Program
NASAPOFF...	Navy Alcohol Safety Action Program Office (DNAB)
NASAPR.......	National Aeronautics and Space Administration Procurement Regulations
NASAPRD	National Aeronautics and Space Administration Procurement Regulations Directive
NASAR.........	National Association for Search and Rescue (EA)
NASA/RECON...	National Aeronautics and Space Administration Remote Console
NASARR.......	North American Search and Range RADAR [*Military*]
NASA-SC California...	National Aeronautics and Space Administration - Santa Monica, California (AD)
NASASP.......	National Association State Agencies for Surplus Property (EA)
NASASPS....	National Association of State Administrators and Supervisors of Private Schools (EA)
NASA-STAR...	NASA Scientific and Technical Reports (NITA)
NASA/STIF...	National Aeronautics and Space Administration/Scientific and Technical Information Facility
NASATE.......	National Association of Substance Abuse Trainers and Educators (EA)
NASA-TR......	NASA Tank Reactor
NASB..........	Nancy Ann Story Book [*Doll collecting*]
NASB..........	National Association of School Boards (OICC)
NASB..........	National Association of Spanish Broadcasters (EA)
NASB..........	National Association of State Boards of Accountancy (AAGC)
NASB..........	Navigational Aid Support Base
NASB..........	New American Standard Bible [*A publication*] (BJA)
NASB..........	North American Savings Bank FSB [*NASDAQ symbol*] (SAG)
NASB..........	North Amer Svgs Bk [*NASDAQ symbol*] (TTSB)
NASBA.........	National Association of State Boards of Accountancy [*New York, NY*] (EA)
NASBA.........	National Automobile Safety Belt Association [*British*]
NASBA.........	Nucleic Acid Sequence-Based Amplification [*Biochemistry*]
NASBCO.......	National Association of School Bus Contract Operators [*Later, NSTA*] (EA)
NASBE.........	National Association of State Boards of Education (EA)
NASBE.........	National Association of Supervisors of Business Education [*Fort Lauderdale, FL*] (EA)
NASBERM....	Naval Air Station, Bermuda
NASBIC.......	National Association of Small Business Investment Companies [*Washington, DC*] (EA)
NASBITE......	National Association of Small Business International Trade Educators (NTPA)
NASBLA.......	National Association of State Boating Law Administrators (EA)
NASBO........	National Association of State Budget Officers (EA)
NASBO........	North African Shipping Board [*World War II*]
NASBOE.......	National Association of Supervisors of Business and Office Education [*Later, NASBE*]
NASBOSA	National Academy of Sciences Board on Ocean Science Affairs (PDAA)
NASBP........	National Association of Surety Bond Producers [*Bethesda, MD*] (EA)
NASBS........	North American Skull Base Society (EA)
NASC..........	National Aeronautics and Space Council [*Terminated, 1973*]
NASC..........	National Aircraft Standards Committee
NASC..........	National Alliance for Safer Cities (EA)
NASC..........	National Alliance of Senior Citizens (EA)
NASC..........	National Aloe Science Council [*Later, IASC*] (EA)
NASC..........	National Amalgamated Society of Coopers [*A union*] [*British*]
NASC..........	National Aquatic Sports Camps (EA)
NASC..........	National Association of Scaffolding Contractors [*British*] (DBA)
NASC..........	National Association of School Counselors [*Defunct*] (EA)
NASC..........	National Association of Service Contractors [*Defunct*] (EA)
NASC..........	National Association of Solar Contractors (EA)
NASC..........	National Association of Specialized Carriers [*Defunct*] (EA)
NASC..........	National Association of Student Councils (EA)
NASC..........	National Athletic Steering Committee (EA)
NASC..........	NATO Supply Center
NASC..........	Naval Aircraft Standards Committee (AFIT)
NASC..........	Naval Air Systems Command
NASC..........	Navy Aviation Safety Center (MUGU)
NASC..........	North American Shale Composite [*Geology*]
NASC..........	North American Sporting Clays [*An association*]
NASC..........	North American Sports Camps
NASC..........	North America Supply Council
NASC..........	North Atlantic Salmon Convention [*Marine science*] (OSRA)
NASC..........	Northwest Association of Schools and Colleges (EA)
NASCA........	National Association for Corporate Speaker Activities [*Reston, VA*] (WDMC)
NASCA........	National Association of State Cable Agencies (EA)
NASCA........	National Association of State Conservation Agencies [*Washington, DC*]
NASCA........	North American Swing Club Association (EA)
NASCAP.......	NASA Charging Analyzer Program (MCD)
NASCAR.......	National Association for Stock Car Advancement and Research (AD)
NASCAR.......	National Association for Stock Car Auto Racing (EA)
NASCAR.......	National Association of Sports Car Racing (AD)
NASCAS.......	National Academy of Sciences Committee on Atmospheric Science
NASCAT.......	National Association of Securities and Commercial Law Attorneys (EA)
NASCC........	National Association of Service and Conservation Corps (EA)
NASCCD.......	National Association of State Catholic Conference Directors (EA)
NASCCEN.....	Naval Air Systems Command Representative, Central
NAS-CD........	National Academy of Sciences - Chemistry Division
NASCD........	National Association for Sickle Cell Disease (EA)
NASCD........	National Association of Soil Conservation Districts [*Later, National Association of Conservation Districts*]
NASCDC......	National Association for Sick Child Daycare Centers (PAZ)
NASCDD	National Association of State Civil Defense Directors [*Later, NEMA*] (EA)
NASCH........	National Association of Swimming Clubs for the Handicapped [*British*] (DBA)
NASCIS.......	National Acute Spinal Cord Injury Study
NASCL	North American Student Cooperative League
NASCLANT...	Naval Air Systems Command Representative, Atlantic
NASCMVE....	National Academy of Sciences Committee on Motor Vehicle Emissions (PDAA)
NASCO........	National Academy of Sciences Committee on Oceanography
NASCO........	National Association of Security Companies (NTPA)
NASCO........	National Association of Smaller Communities (EA)
NASCO........	National Association of State Charity Officials (EA)
NASCO........	National Automotive Service Co. (AD)
NASCO........	National Scientific Committee on Oceanography [*Marine science*] (MSC)
NASCO........	North American Students of Cooperation (EA)
NASCO........	North Atlantic Salmon Conservation Organization [*Edinburgh, Scotland*] (EAIO)
NASCOE......	National Association of ASCS [*Agricultural Stabilization and Conservation Service*] County Office Employees (EA)
Nascom	NASA Communications
NASCOM......	NASA Communications Network
NASCOM......	NASA Worldwide Communications Network (MCD)
NASCOM......	National Aeronautics and Space Administration Tracking Network (AD)
NASCOM......	National Airspace Communications System
NASCOM......	Naval Air Systems Command (MCD)
NASCom......	Naval Air Systems Command (AD)
NASCOMIS...	Naval Air Station/Command Management Information System (MCD)
NASCOP......	NASA Communications Operating Procedures (MCD)
NAS/COW	National Academy of Sciences/Committee on Water [*Marine science*] (MSC)
NASCP........	National Association of Sports for Cerebral Palsy [*Later, USCPAA*] (EA)
NASCP........	North American Society for Corporate Planning [*Later, PF*] (EA)
NASCPA......	North American Study Center for Polish Affairs (EA)
NASCPAC....	Naval Air Systems Command Representative, Pacific
NASCPD......	National Association of Senior Companion Project Directors (EA)
NASCPNCLA...	Naval Air Systems Command Representative, Naval Air Training Command, Pensacola [*Florida*]
NASCRIST....	Naval Air Station Corpus Christi
NASCRL......	Naval Air Systems Command Representative, Atlantic
NASCRP......	Naval Air Systems Command Representative-Pacific (MCD)
NASCS........	National Association of Shoe Chain Stores [*Later, FDRA*] (EA)
NASCSP......	National Association for State Community Service Programs (EA)
NASCUMC....	National Association of Schools and Colleges of the United Methodist Church (EA)
NASCUS......	National Association of State Credit Union Supervisors (EA)
NASD	National Amalgamated Stevedores and Dockers (AD)
NASD	National Association for Staff Development [*British*] (DET)
NASD	National Association of Schools of Dance (EA)
NASD	National Association of Schools of Design [*Later, NASA*]
NASD	National Association of Securities Dealers [*Washington, DC*] (EA)
NASD	National Association of Selective Distributors [*Defunct*] (EA)
NASD	National Association of Service Dealers (EA)
NASD	Naval Air [*or Aviation*] Supply Depot
NASD	Naval Aviation Supply Depot (AD)
NASD	Nippon Advanced Ship Design (AD)
NASDA........	National Association of Sign and Display Advertisers [*Defunct*]
NASDA........	National Association of State Departments of Agriculture (EA)
NASDA........	National Association of State Development Agencies (EA)
NASDA........	National Space Development Agency [*Japan*]
NASDA........	North American South Devon Association (EA)
NASDAC......	National Aviation Safety Data Analysis Center [*FAA*] (TAG)
NASDAD	National Association of Seventh-Day Adventist Dentists (EA)
NASDAGS ...	National Association of State Directors of Administration and General Service (EA)
NASDAPC	National Association of State Drug Abuse Program Coordinators [*Later, NASADAD*] (EA)
NASDAQ	National Association of Securities Dealers Automated Quotations [*Over-the-counter stock quotations*] [*Bunker Ramo Corp. Trumbell, CT*] [*Information service or system*]
Nasdaq	National Association of Securities Dealers Automated Quotations [*The full name is the Nasdaq Stock Market*] [*Washington, DC*] (WDMC)
NASDAQS ...	National Association of Security Dealers Automated Quotation System (AD)
NASDCD	National Association of State Directors of Child Development
NASDDDS	National Association of State Directors of Developmental Disability Services (NTPA)
NASDDP	National Association of State Directors for Disaster Preparedness [*Later, NEMA*] (EA)
NASDI.........	National Association of Selective Distributors (EA)
NASDIEGO ...	Naval Air Station San Diego
NASDIM.......	National Association of Securities Dealers and Investment Managers [*Securities and Investment Board*] [*British*]
NASDLET.....	National Association of State Directors of Law Enforcement Training
NASDM.......	National Association of Special Delivery Messengers [*Later, APWU*] [*AFL-CIO*] (EA)
NASDME......	National Association of State Directors of Migrant Education (EA)

NASDS......... National Amalgamated Stevedores' and Dockers' Society [*A union*] [*British*]

NASDS......... National Association of Scuba Diving Schools [*Later, CA*] [*Commercial firm*] (EA)

NASDS......... Naval Aviation Supply Distribution System (AFIT)

NASDS......... North American Sheep Dog Society (EA)

NASDSE....... National Association of State Directors of Special Education [*Database producer*]

NASDSSE..... National Association of State Directors and Supervisors of Secondary Education [*Later, NASSDSE*] (EA)

NASDT......... Naval Aviators' Speech Discrimination Test

NASDT......... North American Society for Dialysis and Transplantation (EA)

NASDTEC.... National Association of State Directors of Teacher Education and Certification (EA)

NASDU........ National Amalgamated Stevedores and Dockers Union [*British*] (BI)

NASDVA...... National Association of State Directors of Veterans Affairs (EA)

NASDVE....... National Association of State Directors of Vocational Education (EA)

NASDVTEC.. National Association of State Directors of Vocational-Technical Education (NTPA)

NASE.......... National Academy of School Executives [*of American Association of School Administrators*]

NASE.......... National Academy of Stationary Engineers [*British*] (DAS)

NASE.......... National Association for the Self-Employed [*Fort Worth, TX*] (EA)

NASE.......... National Association for the Study of Epilepsy (DAVI)

NASE.......... National Association of Stationary Engineers (AD)

NASE.......... National Association of Steel Exporters [*Defunct*] (EA)

nase........... Neutral Atom Space Engine (AD)

NASE.......... Nonacoustic Submarine Effects (NVT)

NASEA........ National Association of Student Employment Administrators (EA)

NASEA........ Native American Science Education Association [*Defunct*] (EA)

NASEAB...... Naval Air Systems Effectiveness Advisory Board

NASEAN...... National Association for State Enrolled Assistant Nurses

NASECODE.. Numerical Analysis of Semiconductor Devices and Integrated Circuits [*Computer science*]

NASEDIO..... National Association of State Education Department Information Officers (EA)

NASEES....... National Association for Soviet and East European Studies [*British*]

NASEM........ National Association of Satellite Equipment Manufacturers [*Defunct*] (EA)

NASEMP...... National Association of State Educational Media Professionals (EA)

NASEMSD... National Association of State EMS Directors (EA)

NASEN........ National Association for Special Educational Needs (AIE)

NASEN........ National Association of State Enrolled Nurses [*British*] (BI)

NASEO........ National Association of State Energy Officials (NTPA)

NASEPA....... National Association of State Environmental Programs Agencies [*Marine science*] (MSC)

NAS/ESB...... National Academy of Sciences/Environmental Studies Board [*Marine science*] (MSC)

NASF.......... National Aboriginal Sports Foundation (AD)

NASF.......... National American Studies Faculty [*Defunct*] (EA)

NASF.......... National Arts Stabilization Fund [*Defunct*] (EA)

NASF.......... National Association of State Foresters (EA)

NASF.......... Native American Scholarship Fund [*An association*] (EA)

NASF.......... NIC [*Naval Intelligence Center*] Analyst Support Facility

NASF.......... North American Soccer Foundation [*Defunct*] (EA)

NASF.......... Numerical Aerodynamic Simulation Facility

NASFA........ National Association of State Facilities Administrators (EA)

NASFAA...... National Association of Student Financial Aid Administrators (EA)

NASFCA...... National Automatic Sprinkler and Fire Control Association (EA)

NASFCB...... National Association of Specialty Food and Confection Brokers (EA)

NASFM....... National Association of State Fire Marshals (NTPA)

NASFM....... National Association of Store Fixture Manufacturers (EA)

NASFO........ National Asset Seizure and Forfeiture Office (AD)

NASFT........ National Association for the Specialty Food Trade (EA)

NASFW....... National Association of Solid Fuel Wholesalers [*British*] (DBA)

NASG.......... National Alliance for Spiritual Growth (EA)

NASGA........ North American Strawberry Growers Association (EA)

NAS-GB....... Noise Abatement Society of Great Britain (AD)

NASGC....... National Association of Small Government Contractors (EA)

NAS/GRB..... National Academy of Sciences/Geophysical Research Board [*Marine science*] (MSC)

NASGS........ North African Secretary General Staff [*World War II*]

NASGTMO... Naval Air Station Guantanamo

NASGW....... National Association of Sporting Goods Wholesalers (EA)

NASH.......... Nahariya to Ashkelon [*Proposed name for possible "super-city" formed by the urban sprawl between these two*] [*Israel*]

Nash........... Nashville [*Tennessee*] (AD)

NASH.......... National Association of Safety at Home [*British*] (DBA)

NASH.......... National Association of Specimen Hunters (AD)

NASHA........ National Association for Speech and Hearing Action (EA)

NASHA........ North American Survival and Homesteading Association (AD)

NASHAC...... National Association for Safety and Health in the Arts and Crafts (EA)

NASHAW..... National Association for Statewide Health and Welfare (EA)

NASHC....... National All States Hobby Club [*Defunct*] (EA)

NashCtr....... Nashville Country Club [*Associated Press*] (SAG)

NashF......... Nash Finch Co. [*Associated Press*] (SAG)

NASHOC..... North American Student Humanist Organizing Committee [*Defunct*] (EA)

Nash Pl....... Nash's Ohio Pleading and Practice [*A publication*] (DLA)

NASHRD...... National Association of State Human Resource Directors (EA)

Nashua....... Nashua Corp. [*Associated Press*] (SAG)

NASI.......... National Alssociation of Systems Integrators (CDE)

NASI.......... NetWare Asynchronous Services Interface [*Computer science*] (PCM)

NASI.......... Nigerian Army School of Infantry

NASI.......... Novell Asynchronous Services Interface

NASIB......... Naval Air Station, Imperial Beach (DNAB)

NASIC......... Northeast Academic Science Information Center

NASID......... National Association of the Sixth Infantry Division (EA)

NASIG........ North African Signal Section [*World War II*]

NASIG........ North American Serials Group (EA)

NASILP....... National Association of Self-Instructional Language Programs (EA)

NASIMD...... National Association of the Sixth Infantry/Motorized Division [*Later, NASID*] (EA)

Nas Inst...... Nasmith's Institutes of English Private Law [*1873*] [*A publication*] (DLA)

Nas Inst Priv... Nasmith's Institutes of English Private Law [*1873*] [*A publication*] (DLA)

Nas Inst Pub... Nasmith's Institutes of English Public Law [*1873*] [*A publication*] (DLA)

NASIP......... National Aviation Safety Inspection Program [*RSPA*] (TAG)

NASIR......... Nuclear Amplification by Stimulated Isomer Radiation (SAA)

NASIRC....... NASA Automated Systems Incident Response Capability

NASIRE....... National Association of State Information Resource Executives (AAGC)

NASIS......... NASA Aerospace Safety Information System

NASIS......... National Association for State Information Systems (EA)

NASIS......... NATO Subject Indicator System (NATG)

NASISS....... National Association of Sailing Instructors and Sailing Schools (EA)

NASJA........ North American Ski Journalists Association (EA)

NASJAX...... Naval Air Station Jacksonville

NASJE........ National Association of State Judicial Educators

NASL.......... Nasal (DAVI)

NASL.......... National Association of State Lotteries (EA)

NASL.......... Naval Applied Science Laboratory

NASL.......... North American Soccer League [*Defunct*] (EA)

NASLAKE.... Naval Air Station Lakehurst

NASLAT...... National Association of Securities and Commercial Law Attorneys (NTPA)

NASLI......... National Association for Senior Living Industries (EA)

NASLPA...... North American Soccer League Players Association [*Defunct*] (EA)

NASLR........ National Association of State Land Reclamationists (EA)

NASLS........ National Association of Small Loan Supervisors (EA)

NASM......... National Air and Space [*Warfare*] Model [*Air Force*]

NASM......... National Air and Space Museum [*Smithsonian Institution*] [*Formerly, NAM*]

NASM......... National Association for School Magazines [*British*] (BI)

NASM......... National Association of Sandwich Manufacturers [*Defunct*] (EA)

NASM......... National Association of Schools of Music (EA)

NASM......... National Association of Service Managers (EA)

NASM......... National Association of Service Merchandising (EA)

NASM......... National Association of State Militia (EA)

NASM......... National Association of Surrogate Mothers (EA)

NASM......... Naval Aviation School of Medicine

NASMA....... Parti Nasionalis Malaysia [*Political party*] (FEA)

NASMAC..... Naval Air Software Management Advisory Committee (MCD)

NASMAP..... NAS Management Automation Program [*FAA*] (TAG)

NASMAR..... National Association of Sack Merchants and Reclaimers [*British*] (BI)

NASMBCM... National Association of Sanitary Milk Bottle Closure Manufacturers [*Defunct*] (EA)

NASMD....... National Association of Medicaid Directors (EA)

NASMD....... National Association of School Music Dealers (EA)

NASMD....... National Association of Sewing Machine Dealers [*Defunct*] (EA)

NASMD....... National Association of Sewing Machine Distributors [*Defunct*] (EA)

NASMD....... National Association of Sheet Music Dealers [*Later, NAMM*] (EA)

NASMD....... Northamerican Association of Sheet Metal Distributors [*Later, division of NHAW*] (EA)

NASMHPD... National Association of State Mental Health Program Directors (EA)

NASMI........ National Association of Secondary Material Industries [*Later, NARI*] (EA)

NAS(MISC)... North American Supply Committee, Miscellaneous [*World War II*]

NASML........ National Air and Space Museum Library [*Smithsonian Institute*] (AD)

NASMO....... National Association of School Meals Organisers [*British*] (DBA)

NASMO....... NATO Starfighter Management Office

NASMP....... National Association of Sales and Marketing Professionals [*Defunct*] (EA)

NASMV....... National Association on Standard Medical Vocabulary (EA)

NASN......... National Air Sampling Network [*Public Health Service*]

NASN......... National Air Surveillance Network [*Environmental Protection Agency*]

NASN......... National Association of School Nurses (EA)

NAS/NAE..... National Academy of Sciences/National Academy of Engineering [*Marine science*] (MSC)

NAS/NAE-SECAN... NAS/NAE [*National Academy of Sciences/National Academy of Engineering*] Science and Engineering Committee Advisory to NOAA [*National Oceanic and Atmospheric Administration*] [*Defunct*] (USDC)

NAS/NAE-SECAN... National Academy of Sciences/National Academy of Sciences Engineering Science and Engineering Committee Advisory to NOAA[*National Oceanic and Atmospheric Administration*] [*Marine science*] (OSRA)

NASNI........ Naval Air Station North Island

NAS-NRC..... National Academy of Sciences - National Research Council (EA)

NASNSA...... National Association of Special Needs State Administrators (EA)

NASO.......... Natchez & Southern Railway Co. [*AAR code Terminated*]

NASO.......... National Adult School Organisation [*British*]

NASO.......... National Association of Sports Officials (EA)

NASO.......... National Astrological Society [*Defunct*] (EA)

NASO.......... National Astronomical Space Observatory

NASO.......... Naval Aviation Supply Office

NASO	Nonacoustic Sensor Operator [*Military*] (CAAL)
NAS/OAB	National Academy of Sciences/Ocean Affairs Board [*Marine science*] (MSC)
NASOC	North American Singer Owners Club (EA)
NASOH	North American Society for Oceanic History (EA)
NASOPT	Network Analysis System with Optimization Facility [*NASA*] (IAA)
NA So Rhod	Southern Rhodesia Native Appeal Court Reports [*A publication*] (DLA)
NASORLO	National Association of State Outdoor Recreation Liaison Officers (EA)
NAS/OSB	National Academy of Sciences/Ocean Sciences Board [*Marine science*] (MSC)
NASP	National Achievement Scholarship Program [*National Merit Scholarship Corp.*] (AEBS)
NASP	National Aerospace Plane (AAGC)
NASP	National Aerospace Plane Program [*NASA, DoD*]
NASP	National Airport System Plans [*Department of Transportation*]
NASP	National Airspace System Plan [*FAA*] (TAG)
NASP	National Alternative Schools Program
NASP	National Association for the Southern Poor (EA)
NASP	National Association of School Psychologists (EA)
NASP	National Association of Schools and Publishers (EA)
NASP	National Association of Securities Professionals (EA)
NASP	National Association of Single Persons (EA)
NASP	National Atmospheric Sciences Program
NASP	National Aviation System Plan [*A publication*]
NASP	Naval Air Survivability Program (MCD)
NASP	Navy Advanced SATCOM [*Satellite Communications*] Program (ANA)
NASP	Negro, Anglo-Saxon Protestant
NASPA	National Association for Public Accountants (HGAA)
NASPA	National Association of Student Personnel Administrators (EA)
NASPA	National Society of Public Accountants (MCD)
NaSPA	National Systems Programmers Association (EA)
NASPA	North American Soccer Players Association [*Later, NASLPA*] (EA)
NASPAA	National Association of Schools of Public Affairs and Administration (EA)
NASPAC	National Airspace System Performance Analysis Capability [*FAA*] (TAG)
NASPALS	Nas Precision Approach and Landing System [*FAA*] (TAG)
Nas Par	Nasionale Party [*National Party*] [*Political party*] (AD)
NASPD	National Association of Plumbing Specialty Distributors (NTPA)
NASPD	National Association of State Park Directors (EA)
NASPD	National Association of Steel Pipe Distributors (EA)
NASPE	National Association for Sport and Physical Education (EA)
NASPE	National Association of State Personnel Executives (EA)
NASPE	North American Society of Pacing and Electrophysiology (EA)
NASPENSA	Naval Air Station Pensacola
Nas Pers	Nasionale Pers [*National Press*] [*South Africa*] (AD)
NASPG	North American Society for Pediatric Gastroenterology [*Later, NASPGN*] (EA)
NASPGN	North American Society for Pediatric Gastroenterology and Nutrition (EA)
NASPHV	National Association of State Public Health Veterinarians (EA)
NASPL	North American Association of State and Provincial Lotteries (NTPA)
NASPM	National Association of Seed Potato Merchants [*British*] (BI)
NASPM	National Association of Slipper and Playshoe Manufacturers (EA)
NASPO	National Airspace System Program Office [*FAA*] (MCD)
NASPO	National Alliance of Statewide Preservation Organizations (EA)
NASPO	National Association of State Purchasing Officials (EA)
NASPO	NATO Starfighter Production Organization
NASPPR	National Association of Service Providers in Private Rehabilitation (NTPA)
NASPR	NASA Procurement Regulation (KSC)
NASPRFMR	National Association of Superintendents of Public Residential Facilities for theMentally Retarded
NASPSM	National Association of Shirt, Pajama, and Sportswear Manufacturers [*Later, AAMA*]
NASPSPA	North American Society for the Psychology of Sport and Physical Activity (EA)
Na-Spt	Sodium Spot [*Urine Test*] [*Biochemistry*] (DAVI)
NASQAN	National Stream Quality Accounting Network [*Department of the Interior*]
NASQUON	Naval Air Station Quonset Point
NASR	National Annual Symposium on Reliability [*IEEE*] (MCD)
NASR	National Association of Sitter Registries [*Defunct*] (EA)
NASR	National Association of Solvent Recyclers (EA)
NASR	National Association of Swine Records (EA)
NASRA	National Association of State Retirement Administrators (EA)
NASRC	National Association of State Racing Commissioners [*Later, ARCI*] (EA)
NASRC	North American Salmon Research Center [*Later, Atlantic Salmon Research Institute*] [*Canada Research center*] (RCD)
NASRC	North Atlantic Salmon Research Center [*Marine science*] (MSC)
NASRN	National Association of State Radio Networks (EA)
NASRO	National Association of Shooting Range Owners (EA)
NASRP	National Association of Special and Reserve Police [*Defunct*]
NASRP	National Association of State Recreation Planners (EA)
NASRPM	National Association of State River Program Managers (EA)
NASRR	North American Search and Range RADAR [*Military*]
NASRS	Not Available Status Report System [*DoD*]
NASRU	Naval Air Systems Command Reserve Unit (MCD)
NASRWCBL	National Amalgamated Society of Railway Wagon and Carriage Builders and Lifters [*A union*] [*British*]
NASS	Narrow Angle Sun Sensor (SAA)
NASS	Nassau (ROG)
Nass	Nassau, Bahamas (AD)
NASS	National Accident Sampling System [*National Highway Traffic Safety Admini stration*] [*Washington, DC*]
NASS	National Agricultural Statistics Service [*Department of Agriculture*] [*Information service or system*] (IID)
NASS	National Aids Support System [*Military*] (SAA)
NASS	National Alliance for Safe Schools (EA)
NASS	National Alliance of Supermarket Shoppers (EA)
NASS	National Ankylosing Spondylitis Society [*British*] (DBA)
NASS	National Association for Small Schools [*British*] (DI)
NASS	National Association of Saw Shops (EA)
NASS	National Association of School Superintendents (AD)
NASS	National Association of Secretarial Services [*St. Petersburg, FL*] (EA)
NASS	National Association of Secretaries of State (EA)
NASS	National Association of Specialized Schools [*Defunct*] (EA)
NASS	National Association of Steel Stockholders (MHDB)
NASS	National Association of Suggestion Systems (EA)
NASS	National Association of Summer Sessions [*Later, NAASS*]
NASS	Naval Air Signal School
NASS	Naval Armaments Stores System (PDAA)
NASS	Navigation Satellite System (PDAA)
NASS	Navy Advent Ship Station (SAA)
NASS	Network Access Switching Subsystem [*Telecommunications*] (MCD)
NASS	North African Special Service Section [*World War II*]
NASS	North American Shagya-Arabian Society (EA)
NASS	North American Spine Society (EA)
NASS	North American Super Sports [*Defunct*] (EA)
NAS(S)	North American Supply Committee, Scientific Subcommittee [*World War II*]
NASSA	National Aerospace Services Association [*Defunct*] (EA)
NASSA	National Art School Students' Association [*Australia*]
NASSAM	National Association for the Self-Supporting Active Ministry (EA)
NASS & LS	National Association of State Savings and Loan Supervisors [*Later, ACSSS*] (EA)
NASSB	National Association of Supervisors of State Banks [*Later, CSBS*] (EA)
NASSC	National Alliance on Shaping Safer Cities [*Later, NASC*] (EA)
NASSCO	National Association of Sewer Service Companies (EA)
NASSCO	National Steel & Shipbuilding Co.
NASSCOM	National Association of Software and Service Companies
NASSD	National Association of School Security Directors (EA)
NASSD	National Association of Sign Supply Distributors (NTPA)
NASSD	North American Society of Scaffold Professionals (NTPA)
NASSDC	National Social Science Documentation Centre [*Information service or system*] (IID)
NASSDE	National Association of State Supervisors of Distributive Education (EA)
NASSDOC	National Social Science Documentation Centre [*Information service or system*] (IID)
NASSDSE	National Association of State Supervisors and Directors of Secondary Education (EA)
NAS/SEC	National Academy of Sciences' Site Evaluation Committee
NASSH	North American Society for Sport History (EA)
NASSHE	National Association of State Supervisors of Home Economics [*Later, NASSVHE*]
NASSL	National Association of Spanish Speaking Librarians (EA)
NASSLEO	National Association of School Safety and Law Enforcement Officers (NTPA)
NASSM	National Association of Scissors and Shears Manufacturers (EA)
NASSM	National Association of State Supervisors of Music (EA)
NASSM	North American Society for Sport Management (EA)
NASSO	National Association of Socialist Students' Organizations [*Political party*] (AD)
NASSP	National Association of Secondary School Principals (EA)
NASSP	North American Society for Social Philosophy (EA)
NASSP-B	National Association of Secondary School Principals. Bulletin [*A publication*] (BRI)
NASSPE	National Alliance of Spanish-Speaking People for Equality (EA)
NASSR	Nahichevan Autonomous Soviet Socialist Republic (AD)
NASSS	National Association of Support for Small Schools [*British*] (DBA)
NASSS	North American Society for the Sociology of Sport (EA)
NASSSA	National Association of State Social Security Administrators [*Later, NCSSSA*] (EA)
NASSTA	National Association of Secretaries of State Teachers Associations [*Later, NCSEA*] (EA)
NASSTIE	National Association of State Supervisors of Trade and Industrial Education (EA)
NASSTRAC	National Small Shipments Traffic Conference [*Acronym now used as official name of association*] (EA)
NASSTRAC	National Small Shipments Traffic Council
NASSVHE	National Association of State Supervisors of Vocational Home Economics (EA)
NAST	National Association of Schools of Theatre (EA)
NAST	National Association of State Treasurers (EA)
NAST	Navigation/Attack Systems Trainer (PDAA)
NAST	Navy Advent Ship Terminal (SAA)
NAST	Nuclear Accident Support Team [*Canada*]
NASTA	National Association of State Text Book Administrators (EA)
NASTAD	National Alliance of State and Territorial AIDS [*Acquired Immune-Deficiency Syndrome*] Directors (EA)
NASTAD	Naval Acoustic Sensor Training Aids Department (DNAB)
NASTAR	National Standard Race [*Skiing*]
NASTAT	North American Society of Teachers of the Alexander Technique (EA)

NASTBD....... National Association of State Text Book Directors [*Later, NASTA*] (EA)
Nastc .... Nastech Pharmaceutical Co., Inc. [*Associated Press*] (SAG)
NASTC .... Naval Air Station Twin Cities (DNAB)
NASTD .... National Association of State and Territorial Apprenticeship Directors [*Bureau of Apprenticeship and Training*] [*Department of Labor*]
NASTD .... National Association of State Telecommunications Directors (EA)
Nastech .... Nastech Pharmaceutical Co., Inc. [*Associated Press*] (SAG)
NASTEMP ..... National Association of State Educational Media Professionals (EA)
NASTI .... Naval Air Station, Terminal Island (AD)
NASTI .... Next Assembly Support Table Index [*Aerospace*] (MCD)
NASTL .... National Anti-Steel-Trap League (EA)
NASTOCK..... North American Stock Market [*I. P. Sharp Associates*] [*Canada Information service or system*]
NASTPHV..... National Association of State and Territorial Public Health Veterinarians [*Later, NASPHV*] (EA)
NASTRAN .... NASA Structural Analysis [*Computer program*]
NAS/TRB...... National Academy of Sciences/Transportation Board [*Marine science*] (MSC)
NASTS .... National Association for Science, Technology, and Society (EA)
NASTT .... North American Society for Trenchless Technology (EA)
NASTX .... Phoenix Equity Opportunities Cl.A [*Mutual fund ticker symbol*] (SG)
NASU .... National Adult School Union [*British*] (DAS)
NASU .... National Association of State Universities [*Later, NASULGC*]
NASU .... National Association of System 3 Users (IAA)
NASU .... Navy Air Support Unit
NASU .... Navy Underwater Sound Laboratory (MUGU)
NASU .... North American Singers Union (EA)
NASUA .... National Association of State Units on Aging (EA)
NASUCA....... National Association of State Utility Consumer Advocates (EA)
NASULGC ... National Association of State Universities and Land-Grant Colleges (EA)
NASUP......... National Association on Service to Unmarried Parents (EA)
NAS-UWT .... National Association of Schoolmasters - Union of Women Teachers [*British*]
NASV .... International Academy of Sports Vision [*Formerly, National Academy of Sports Vision*] (EAIO)
NASV .... National Academy of Sports Vision (EA)
NASVG........ Nordic Association for Study and Vocational Guidance [*See also NRSY*] (EAIO)
NASVH........ National Association of State Veterans Homes (EA)
NASVO .... National Association of State Vocal Organizations (EA)
NASW .... National Association of Science Writers (EA)
NASW .... National Association of Social Workers (EA)
NASW .... National Association of Social Workers National Committee on Lesbian and Gay Issues (EA)
NASW .... North American Slope Water [*Oceanography*] (MSC)
NASWA .... North American Shortwave Association (EA)
NASWF .... Naval Air Special Weapons Facility
NASWHP..... National Association of Sheltered Workshops and Homebound Programs [*Later, NARF*] (EA)
NASWM .... National Association of Scottish Woollen Manufacturers [*British*] (BI)
NASWS........ National Aeronautics and Space Administration White Sands [*Proving ground*]
NASWSO..... National Association of Soft Water Service Operators [*Later, WQA*]
NAT............. Information Content Natural Unit [*Information theory*]
NAT............. N-Acetyltransferase [*An enzyme*]
NAT............. N-Acetyltryptophan [*Biochemistry*]
NAT............. NASA Apollo Trajectory (KSC)
NAT............. NASA STI [*Scientific and Technical Information*] Facility, BWI Airport, MD [*Baltimore-Washington International*] [*OCLC symbol*] (OCLC)
NAT............. Natal [*Brazil*] [*Airport symbol*] (OAG)
NAT............. Natal [*Neonatology*] (DAVI)
Nat............. Natalia (AD)
Nat............. Natalie (AD)
Nat............. Natasha (AD)
Nat............. Nathalie (AD)
Nat............. Nathan (AD)
Nat............. Nathaniel (AD)
nat............. Nation (AD)
Nat............. Nation [*A publication*] (BRI)
NAT............. Nation
Nat............. National (AD)
nat............. National (AD)
NAT............. National
NAT............. National Academy of Teaching (EA)
NAT............. National Agency for Tourism
NAT............. National Air Transport (SAA)
NAT............. National Arbitration Tribunal [*British*]
NAT............. National Association of Toolmakers [*A union*] [*British*]
NAT............. National Drug Co. [*Research code symbol*]
NAT............. Nationalist (WDAA)
Nat............. Nationalist (ODBW)
NAT............. Nationality (AAG)
Nat............. National Party [*Australia Political party*]
NAT............. National Transport, Inc.
NAT............. Native (AAG)
nat............. Native (AD)
NAT............. Nativity [*Church calendars*] (ROG)
NAT............. Natrolite [*A zeolite*]
NAT............. Natural (AAG)
nat............. Natural (AD)
Nat............. Natural (ODBW)
nat............. Naturalist (AD)
nat............. Naturalization (AD)

Nat............. Naturalized [*Botany*]
NAT............. Natural Unit (IAA)
Nat............. Nature [*or Naturalist*]
nat............. Nature (AD)
NAT............. Naturist (WDAA)
NAT............. Natus [*Birth*] [*Latin*]
nat............. Natuurkunde [*Natural Science*] [*Dutch*] (AD)
NAT............. Naval Air Technical Services Facility (MUGU)
NAT............. Naval Air Terminal
NAT............. Naval Air Training
NAT............. Naval Anthropomorphic Teleoperater (DNAB)
NAT............. Navigational Aids Technician (DNAB)
NAT............. Nearly Airborne Truck (PDAA)
NAT............. Network Address Translation [*Computer science*]
NAT............. Network Analysis Team
NAT............. Network Analysis Technique (IAA)
NAT............. New Age Thinking
NAT............. New Attainment Target (AIE)
NAT............. Nitric Acid Trihydrate [*Inorganic chemistry*]
NAT............. Nitrosoanatabine [*Also, NAtB*] [*Organic chemistry*]
NAT............. No Action Taken
NAT............. Non-Verbal Ability Tests [*Intelligence test*]
NAT............. Nordic American Tanker Shipping Ltd. [*AMEX symbol*] (SAG)
NAT............. Normal Allowed Time (IEEE)
nat............. Normal Allowed Time (AD)
NAT............. North African Theater [*World War II*]
NAT............. North Atlantic Air, Inc. [*ICAO designator*] (FAAC)
NAT............. North Atlantic Region [*USTTA*] (TAG)
NAT............. North Atlantic Regional Area [*Aviation*]
NAT............. North Atlantic Treaty
NAT............. Not Attending Training
NATA .... N-Acetyl-Tryptophan-Amide [*Organic chemistry*]
NATA .... N-Acetyltyramine [*Biochemistry*]
NATA .... Narcotic Addict Treatment Act of 1974
NATA .... National Airfreight Trucking Alliance (EA)
NATA .... National Air Transportation Association (EA)
NATA .... National Association of Tax Accountants [*Defunct*] (EA)
NATA .... National Association of Tax Administrators (EA)
NATA .... National Association of Teachers' Agencies (EA)
NATA .... National Association of Teachers of Agriculture [*Australia*]
NATA .... National Association of Temple Administrators (EA)
NATA .... National Association of Testing Authorities (IAA)
NATA .... National Association of Transportation Advertising [*Later, Transit Advertising Association*]
NATA .... National Athletic Trainers Association (EA)
NATA .... National Automated Transportation Association (AD)
NATA .... National Automobile Transporters Association [*Detroit, MI*] (EA)
NATA .... National Automotive Trade Association
NATA .... National Aviation Trades Association
NATA .... North American Tasar Association (EA)
NATA .... North American Telecommunications Association (EA)
NATA .... North American Telephone Association (EA)
NATA .... North American Trakehner Association (EA)
NATA .... North American Travel Association [*Defunct*] (EA)
NATA .... North Atlantic Treaty Alliance
Nat Absten... National Abstentionalist (AD)
NATAD........ National Association of Textile and Apparel Distributors [*Defunct*] (EA)
NATAF........ Northwest African Tactical Air Force [*World War II*]
Natal LJ....... Natal Law Journal [*South Africa*] [*A publication*] (DLA)
Natal LM .... Natal Law Magazine [*South Africa*] [*A publication*] (DLA)
Natal LQ...... Natal Law Quarterly [*South Africa*] [*A publication*] (DLA)
Natal LR...... Natal Law Reports [*South Africa*] [*A publication*] (DLA)
NatAlt .... Natural Alternatives International [*Associated Press*] (SAG)
NA T & N.... Selected Decisions of the Native Appeal Court, Transvaal and Natal [*A publication*] (DLA)
NATAPROBU... National Association of Professional Bureaucrats [*Later, INATAPROBU*]
Nat Arc .... National Archives (AD)
NATARI........ National Association of Traffic Accident Reconstructionists and Investigators (EA)
NATAS .... National Academy of Television Arts and Sciences (EA)
NATAS .... National Appropriate Technology Assistance Service [*Butte, MT*] [*Department of Energy*] (GRD)
NATAS .... North American Thermal Analysis Society (EA)
Nat Assn ..... National Association (AD)
natat .... Natation (AD)
NATaT......... National Association of Towns and Townships (EA)
NatAutoC .... National Auto Credit, Inc. Holding [*Associated Press*] (SAG)
NATAW .... National Association of Textile and Apparel Wholesalers [*Later, NATAD*] (EA)
NATB .... National Automobile Theft Bureau (EA)
NATB .... Naval Air Training Base
NATB .... Naval Training Bulletin
NAtB .... Nitrosoanatabine [*Organic chemistry*]
NATB .... Nonreading Aptitude Test Battery [*US Employment Service*] [*Department of Labor*]
Nat Bank Reg... National Bankruptcy Register Reports [*United States*] [*A publication*] (DLA)
Nat Bankr Law... National Bankruptcy Law [*A publication*] (DLA)
Nat Bankr N & R... National Bankruptcy News and Reports [*A publication*] (DLA)
Nat Bankr R... National Bankruptcy Register [*United States*] [*A publication*] (DLA)
Nat Bankr Reg... National Bankruptcy Register [*United States*] [*A publication*] (DLA)

Nat Bankr Rep...   National Bankruptcy Register Reports [United States]
                   [A publication] (DLA)
Nat Bar J.....   National Bar Journal [A publication] (DLA)
NATBASES...   Naval Air Training Bases
Nat BC.......   National Bank Cases [United States] [A publication] (DLA)
NatBev.........   National Beverage Corp. [Associated Press] (SAG)
NATBF.........   Northwest African Tactical Bomber Force [World War II]
Nat BJ.........   National Bar Journal [A publication] (DLA)
Nat BR.........   National Bankruptcy Register [United States] [A publication] (DLA)
Nat Brev.....   Fitzherbert's Natura Brevium [A publication] (DLA)
NAT BUR ECON RES...   National Bureau of Economic Research (WDAA)
Nat Bur Econ Res...   National Bureau of Economic Research (AD)
Nat Bur Stand Circ...   National Bureau of Standards Circular [A publication] (AD)
NAtC ....   Columbia-Greene Community College, Athens, NY [Library symbol
                   Library of Congress] (LCLS)
NATC ....   National Air Taxi Conference (SAA)
NATC ....   National Air Traffic Controllers (AD)
NATC ....   National Air Transportation Conferences [Later, NATA]
NATC ....   National Alcohol Tax Coalition (EA)
NATC ....   National Association of Taurine Clubs
NATC ....   National Association of Tax Consultants (EA)
NATC ....   National Association of Telemarketing Consultants [Defunct] (EA)
NATC ....   Naval Air Test Center
NATC ....   National Air Training Center
NATC ....   Naval Air Training Command (CAAL)
NATC ....   Nordic Amateur Theatre Council (EAIO)
NATC ....   Nordic Automobile Technical Committee [Defunct Denmark] (EAIO)
NATC ....   North Atlantic Training Council (NATG)
NATC ....   Northwest African Training Command [World War II]
NATC ....   Noval Air Test Center (IAA)
NATCA ....   National Air Traffic Controllers Association (EA)
NATCA ....   National Association of Trial Court Administrators (EA)
NATCA ....   North American Trap Collector Association (EA)
NATCC ....   Northwest African Troop Carrier Command [World War II]
NATCD ....   National Association of Tobacco & Confectionery Distributors (AC)
NATCEM ....   National Cemetery
NATCENTATHLIT...   National Centre for Athletic Literature (NITA)
NATCG ....   National Association of Training Corps for Girls [British] (BI)
Natch ....   Natchez (AD)
natch ....   Naturally (AD)
NATCO ....   National Association of Transit Consumer Organizations (EA)
NATCO ....   National Automatic Tool Co.
NATCO ....   National Coordinator [Marine science] (MSC)
NATCO ....   National Tank Co. (AD)
NATCO ....   Navy Air Traffic Coordinating Officer
NATCO ....   North American Transplant Coordinators Organization (EA)
NATCO ....   Northern Advanced Technologies Corp. [Research center] (RCD)
NATCO ....   Nuclear Auditing and Testing Co.
natcol ....   Natural Color (AD)
NATCOL ....   Natural Food Colours Association [Basel, Switzerland] (EAIO)
natcom ....   National Communications (AD)
NATCOM ......   National Communications Symposium [IEEE]
NATCOM ......   National Conference on Communications (MCD)
NATCOM ......   NATO Communication (NATG)
Nat Con ......   Nature Conservancy (BARN)
NatConv ....   National Convenience Stores [Associated Press] (SAG)
NATCS ....   National Air Traffic Control Service (IEEE)
NATCS ....   National Air Traffic Control System (NATG)
Nat D ....   De Natura Deorum [of Cicero] [Classical studies] (OCD)
NATD ....   National Association of Teachers of Dancing [British] (DBA)
NATD ....   National Association of Telecommunications Dealers (EA)
NATD ....   National Association of Test Directors (EA)
NATD ....   National Association of Tobacco Distributors (EA)
NATD ....   National Association of Tool Dealers [British] (BI)
NATD ....   National Diagnostics, Inc. [NASDAQ symbol] (SAG)
NATD ....   Natl Diagnostics [NASDAQ symbol] (TTSB)
NATDEC ....   Naval Air Training Division Engineering Command (DNAB)
NATDEFSM...   National Defense Service Medal [Military decoration]
Nat Dem .....   National Democrats [Political party] (AD)
NatDiag ....   National Diagnostics, Inc. [Associated Press] (SAG)
NATDP.........   National Agricultural Text-Digitizing Project [National Agricultural
                   Library]
NATDS ....   National Association of Truck Driving Schools (EA)
NATDS ....   Naval Air Tactical Data System (MCD)
NATDS ....   Navy Automated Transportation Data System (DNAB)
NATDW ....   National Diagnostics Wrrt [NASDAQ symbol] (TTSB)
NATE..........   National Association for Teachers of Electronics [Defunct] (EA)
NATE..........   National Association for the Teaching of English (AD)
NATE..........   National Association of Teachers of English
NATE..........   National Association of Temple Educators (EA)
NATE..........   Native American Teacher Education (AD)
NATE..........   Neutral Atmosphere Temperature Experiment
NATEBE........   National Association of Teacher Educators for Business Education
                   [DeKalb, IL] (EA)
NATEBOE.....   National Association of Teacher Educators for Business and Office
                   Education [Later, NATEBE] (EA)
NATEC ....   Naval Air Technical Evaluation Center (IAA)
NATEC ....   Naval Air Training and Experimental Command
NATECHTRA...   Naval Air Technical Training (DNAB)
NATECHTRACEN...   Naval Air Technical Training Center
NATECHTRAU...   Naval Air Technical Training Unit
NATECOM ....   Naval Airship Training and Experimentation Command
NatEdu ....   National Education Corp. [Associated Press] (SAG)
NATEF ....   National Automotive Technicians Education Foundation (EA)

NATEFACS ...   National Association of Teacher Educators for Family and Consumer
                   Sciences (NTPA)
NATEL.........   Nortronics Automatic Test Equipment Language [Computer science]
NATELCA .....   National Association for Teaching English and other Community
                   Languages to Adults [Formerly, NATELSA] (AIE)
NatEng........   National Energy Group [Associated Press] (SAG)
NATES ....   National Analysis of Trends in Emergency Systems [Canada] (MSC)
NATESA ....   National Alliance of Television and Electronics Services
                   Associations (IAA)
NATESA ....   National Association of Television and Electronic Servicers of
                   America [N ESSDA] [Absorbed by] (EA)
NATESLA .....   National Association for Teaching English as a Secondary Language
                   to Adults [British] (DI)
NATESTCEN...   Naval Air Test Center
NATEVHE .....   National Association of Teacher Educators for Vocational Home
                   Economics (EA)
NATEX ....   National Stock Exchange [Dissolved, 1975]
NATF.........   National Automobile Theft Bureau
NATF.........   Naval Air Test Facility
NATF.........   Navy Advanced Tactical Fighter (MCD)
NATF.........   New Arrivals Task Force (MCD)
NATFACS .....   National Association of Teachers of Family and Consumer
                   Sciences (NTPA)
NATFB ....   National Archives Trust Fund Board
NATFC ....   North American Toyah Fan Club (EA)
Nat Fed.......   National Federation (AD)
NatFGs.........   National Fuel Gas Co. [Associated Press] (SAG)
NATFHE ....   National Association of Teachers in Further and Higher Education
                   [British]
Nat For ....   National Forum [A publication] (BRI)
NATFREQU....   Natural Frequency (IAA)
NATF-SI ......   Naval Air Test Facility - Ship Installations
NATG ....   National Association of Training Groups [British] (DBA)
NATGA ....   National Amateur Tobacco Growers' Association [British] (BI)
NAT GAL......   National Gallery [London] (WDAA)
Nat Gal ......   National Gallery (AD)
NatGam ......   National Gaming Corp. [Associated Press] (SAG)
Nat Geog Mag...   National Geographic Magazine [A publication] (AD)
NatGolf ....   National Golf Properties [Associated Press] (SAG)
NatGsO ....   National Gas & Oil Co. [Associated Press] (SAG)
NATH ....   Nathan's Famous [NASDAQ symbol] (TTSB)
NATH ....   Nathan's Famous, Inc. [NASDAQ symbol] (NQ)
Nathan........   Nathan's Common Law of South Africa [A publication] (DLA)
Nathans ....   Nathan's Famous, Inc. [Associated Press] (SAG)
Nath B ....   Nathaniel Bowditch (AD)
NATHE ....   National Associations of Teachers of Home Economics [British]
NATHHAN ...   National Challenged Homeschoolers Associated Network (PAZ)
nat hist......   Natural History (AD)
Nathl..........   Nathaniel (AD)
NatHlth ....   Natural Health Trends Corp. [Associated Press] (SAG)
NatHme ....   National Home Centers [Commercial firm Associated Press] (SAG)
NatHP ....   Nationwide Health Properties, Inc. [Associated Press] (SAG)
NATI...........   National Instrument Corp. [NASDAQ symbol] (SAG)
NATIBO ....   North American Technology and Industrial Base Organization
NATICH.......   National Air Toxics Information Clearinghouse [Environmental
                   Protection Agency] (GFGA)
NATIDC.......   Netherlands-Australia Trade and Industrial Development Council
                   (AD)
NATIE.........   National Association for Trade and Industrial Education (EA)
NATII ....   National Association of Trade and Industrial Instructors (EA)
NATINADS...   NATO Integrated Air Defense System (NATG)
Nat Inc Tax Mag...   National Income Tax Magazine [A publication] (DLA)
NatInst.........   National Instrument Corp. [Associated Press] (SAG)
nation ....   Nationality (AD)
National ADDA...   National Attention-Deficit Disorder Association (EA)
National PTA...   National Congress of Parents and Teachers (PAZ)
NATIP.........   Navy Technical Information Program
NATIS ....   National Information Systems [Later, GIP] [UNESCO]
NATIS ....   Naval Air Training Information System
NATIS ....   North Atlantic Treaty Information Service (NATG)
NATIV ....   Nativity
Nativ...........   Nativity (AD)
NATIV ....   North American Test Instrument Vehicle [Air Force test rocket]
NATIVE ....   North American Test Instrument Vehicle [Air force test rocket] (IAA)
Nat J Leg Ed...   National Journal of Legal Education [A publication] (DLA)
NATK ....   North American Technologies Corp. [NASDAQ symbol] (SAG)
NATK ....   North Amer Technologies Group [NASDAQ symbol] (TTSB)
NATKE ....   National Association of Theatrical and Kine Employees (AD)
NATKE ....   National Association of Theatrical and Kinema Employees [British]
                   (DI)
NATL...........   NAI Technologies [NASDAQ symbol] (SAG)
NATL...........   National (AAG)
natl ....   National (AD)
Natl............   National (AL)
NATL...........   National Agricultural Transportation League [Defunct] (EA)
NATI...........   Natl Instruments [NASDAQ symbol] (TTSB)
NATL...........   Naval Aeronautical Turbine Laboratory
N Atl ....   North Atlantic (AD)
N Atlantic Reg Bus L Rev...   North Atlantic Regional Business Law Review
                   [A publication] (DLA)
NATLAS ....   National Testing Laboratory Accreditation Scheme [Military British]
Nat Law Guild Q...   National Lawyers Guild Quarterly [A publication] (DLA)
NatlBev.......   National Beverage Corp. [Associated Press] (SAG)
NatlCity.......   National City Corp. [Associated Press] (SAG)
Natl Civ Rev...   National Civic Review [A publication] (ILCA)

N Atl Cur	North Atlantic Current (AD)
Nat L Guild Q...	National Lawyers Guild Quarterly [*A publication*] (DLA)
Nat Lib	National Liberal (AD)
NatLib..........	National Liberal Party [*Australia Political party*]
Nat Lib	National Library of Canada (AD)
NATLIBCAN...	National Library of Canada (AD)
NATLIBNZ	National Library of New Zealand (AD)
Nat'l Income Tax Mag...	National Income Tax Magazine [*A publication*] (DLA)
Nat LJ	Natal Law Journal [*South Africa*] [*A publication*] (DLA)
Nat'l Legal Mag...	National Legal Magazine [*A publication*] (DLA)
Nat LM	Natal Law Magazine [*South Africa*] [*A publication*] (DLA)
Natlm...........	Naturalism (VRA)
Nat Louis U...	National-Louis University (GAGS)
Nat'l Pub Empl Rep...	National Public Employment Reporter [*A publication*] (DLA)
Nat LQ	Natal Law Quarterly [*South Africa*] [*A publication*] (DLA)
Nat LR	Natal Law Reports [*South Africa*] [*A publication*] (ILCA)
Nat L Rec	National Law Record [*A publication*] (DLA)
NatlReg	National Registry [*Associated Press*] (SAG)
Nat L Rep ...	National Law Reporter [*A publication*] (DLA)
Natl Rep Sys...	National Reporter System (DLA)
Nat L Rev ...	National Law Review [*A publication*] (DLA)
NatlRV	National R.V. Holdings, Inc. [*Associated Press*] (SAG)
Nat'l School L Rptr...	National School Law Reporter [*A publication*] (DLA)
NATLSEMICON...	National Semiconductor Corp. (IAA)
NatlStl	National Steel Corp. [*Associated Press*] (SAG)
NATM	National Association of Trailer Manufacturers (NTPA)
NATM	New Austrian Tunnel Method [*Civil engineering*]
NATMA	National Award and Trophy Manufacturers Association (EA)
NATMAC	National Air Traffic Management Advisory Committee [*British*]
NATMAP	National Mapping (AD)
NATMATMUS...	National Automotive and Truck Model and Toy Museum of the United States
NATMC	National Advanced Technology Management Conference
NatMFS........	National Medical Financial Services Corp. [*Associated Press*] (SAG)
NATMH	National Association of Teachers of the Mentally Handicapped [*British*]
NatMicr........	Natural Microsystems Corp. [*Associated Press*] (SAG)
NATMILCOMSYS...	National Military Command System
NAT MON	National Monument (WDAA)
Nat Mon	National Monument (AD)
NATMSACT...	Naval Air Training Support Facility (AAGC)
Nat Mus	Natal Museum (AD)
NATMUS......	National Automobile and Truck Museum of the United States
NATMUS......	National Automotive and Truck Museum of United States (EA)
Nat Mus	National Museum (AD)
NATN	National Association of Theatre Nurses [*British*] (BI)
NATN	National Association of Traveling Nurses
NATNAV	North Atlantic Navigation
NATNAVDENCEN...	National Naval Dental Center (DNAB)
NATNAVMEDCEN...	National Naval Medical Center [*Bethesda, MD*]
NATNAVRESMASTCONRADSTA...	National Naval Reserve Master Control Radio Station (DNAB)
Natn Bank Mon Sum...	National Bank. Monthly Summary [*A publication*]
Natn Bank Mon Sum Aust Cond...	National Bank of Australasia. Monthly Summary of Australian Conditions [*A publication*]
Natnet..........	National Network [*Telecommunications British*]
Natn Farmer...	National Farmer [*A publication*]
NatnGv03.....	Nations Government Income Term 2003 [*Associated Press*] (SAG)
NatnGv04.....	Nations Government Income Term 2004 [*Associated Press*] (SAG)
Natn Hosp ..	National Hospital [*A publication*]
Natn Parks J...	National Parks Journal [*A publication*]
Natn Rehab Digest...	National Rehabilitation Digest [*A publication*]
NatnsBal......	Nations Balanced Target Maturity Fund [*Associated Press*] (SAG)
NatnsBk.......	NationsBank Corp. [*Associated Press*] (SAG)
Natn Times Mag...	National Times Magazine [*A publication*]
NATO	Narrow-Angle Target of Opportunity [*Photography*] [*NASA*]
NATO	National Association of Taxicab Owners [*Later, ITA*] (EA)
NATO	National Association of Telephone Operators [*A union*] [*British*]
NATO	National Association of Theatre Owners (EA)
NATO	National Association of Trailer Owners (EA)
NATO	National Association of Travel Organizations [*Later, TIA*] (EA)
NATO	No Action, Talk Only (DICI)
NATO	North African Theater of Operations [*World War II*]
NATO	North American Treat Organization [*AIA*] (TAG)
NATO	North Atlantic Treaty Organization [*Facetious translation: "No Action, Talk Only"*] [*Brussels, Belgium*]
NATOA.........	National Association of Telecommunications Officers and Advisors (EA)
NATO AEW...	North Atlantic Treaty Organization Airborne Early Warning Program
NATO-AGARD...	North Atlantic Treaty Organization - Advisory Group for Aeronautical Research and Development
Nat Obs	National Observer [*A publication*] (AD)
NATODC.......	North Atlantic Treaty Organization Defense College (DNAB)
NATODEFCOL...	North Atlantic Treaty Organization Defense College (DNAB)
NATOELLA ...	North Atlantic Treaty Organization - European Long Lines Agency
NatOilwll	National Oilwell, Inc. [*Associated Press*] (SAG)
NAT-OJT	National On-the-Job Training Program [*Department of Labor*]
NATO-LRSS...	North Atlantic Treaty Organization - Long-Range Scientific Studies
NATO MC	North Atlantic Treaty Organization Military Committee
NATOMILOCGRP...	North Atlantic Treaty Organization - Military Oceanography Group (NATG)
NATOPS.......	Naval Air Training and Operating Procedures Standardization (MCD)
Nat Ord........	Natural Order [*Botany*] (BARN)
NATO-RDPP...	North Atlantic Treaty Organization - Multilateral Research and Development Production Program

NATOSAT.....	North Atlantic Treaty Organization Satellite
NATO-SC......	North Atlantic Treaty Organization - Science Committee
NATOUSA......	North African Theater of Operations, United States Army [*World War II*]
NATP	National Association of Tax Practitioners (EA)
NATP	Natl Power plc [*LO, exchange symbol*] (TTSB)
NATPA	North America Taiwanese Professors' Association (EA)
NAT PAC......	National PAC [*Political Action Committee*] (EA)
NATPE	National Association of Television Program Executives (NTCM)
NATPE	NATPE [*National Association of Television Program Executives*] International (EA)
Nat Peop	Native Peoples [*A publication*] (BRI)
nat phil.......	Natural Philosophy (AD)
Nat Phil	Natural Philosophy (BARN)
Nat Pk	National Park (BARN)
NATPN........	North African Transportation Section [*World War II*]
NatProc.......	National Processing, Inc. [*Associated Press*] (SAG)
NatProp.......	National Propane Partners LP [*Associated Press*] (SAG)
NATPS	National Association of Trade Protection Societies [*British*] (DBA)
NATR	Natchez Trace Parkway [*National Park Service designation*]
NATR	National Association of Tenants and Residents [*British*] (BI)
NATR	National Association of Toy Retailers [*British*] (BI)
NATR	National Representative [*Red Cross*]
Nat R	National Review [*A publication*] (BRI)
natr............	Natrium [*Sodium*] [*Latin*] (AD)
NATR	Natrium [*Sodium*] [*Pharmacy*]
NATR	Natural Resources
NATR	Nature's Sunshine Prod [*NASDAQ symbol*] (TTSB)
NATR	Nature's Sunshine Products, Inc. [*NASDAQ symbol*] (NQ)
NATR	No Additional Traffic Reported [*Aviation*]
NATR	Nordischer Amator Theater Rat [*Nordic Amateur Theatre Council - NATC*] (EAIO)
NATRA	National Association of Television and Radio Announcers (NTCM)
NATRA	National Association of Television and Radio Artists [*Inactive*]
NATRA	Naval Air Training Command (AFIT)
NATRACOM...	Naval Air Training Command (DNAB)
NATRADIVENGCOM...	Naval Air Training Division Engineering Command (DNAB)
NATRAP.......	Narrow-Band Transmission of RADAR Pictures (MCD)
NATRC........	North American Trail Ride Conference (EA)
NatRe	National Re Corp. [*Associated Press*] (SAG)
NatRecd......	National Record Mart, Inc. [*Associated Press*] (SAG)
Nat Reg	National Register, Edited by Mead [*1816*] [*A publication*] (DLA)
Nat Rept Syst...	National Reporter System (DLA)
NATRFD.......	National Association of Television-Radio Farm Directors [*Later, NAFB*] (EA)
NATRI	National Association of Treasurers of Religious Institutes (EA)
NATRI	Navy Training Requirements Information
NATRIP........	National Association of Tax Reducing Income Plans (NTPA)
NatrlHlth......	Natural Health Trends Corp. [*Associated Press*] (SAG)
NATRON	National Cash Register Electronic Data Processing System (MCD)
NAT-RPG......	North Atlantic Treaty Regional Planning Group (NATG)
NatrSun	Natures Sunshine Products [*Associated Press*] (SAG)
NATS	National Activity to Test Software
NATS	National Air Toxics Strategy [*Environmental Protection Agency*] (GFGA)
NATS	National Air Traffic Services [*British*]
NATS	National Association of Teachers of Singing (EA)
NATS	National Association of Temporary Services [*Alexandria, VA*] (EA)
NATS	National Association of Textile Supervisors (EA)
Nats	Nationalists (AD)
NATS	National Secs [*NASDAQ symbol*] (TTSB)
NATS	National Securities Corp. [*NASDAQ symbol*] (NQ)
Nats	Natsionalnyii [*National*] [*Russian*] (AD)
NATS	Naval Air Test Station (AD)
NATS	Naval Air Transport Service
NATS	Needlework and Accessories Trade Show (ITD)
NATS	Negative Authorization Terminal System [*Computer science*] (MHDB)
NATS	New Aircraft Tool System [*Army*]
NATS	Noise Abatement Test System (FAAC)
NATS	Nordisk Avisteknisk Samarbetsnamnd [*Nordic Joint Technical Press Board*] [*Sweden*] (EAIO)
NATS	North American Truffling Society (EA)
NATSA	National Associated Truck Stops and Associates (EA)
NATSAA	NATO Air Traffic Service Advisory Agency (NATG)
NATSC	National Association of Training School Chaplains (EA)
NATSC	National Association of Trap and Skeet Clubs (EA)
NAT SC	Natural Sciences (WDAA)
NAT SC D ...	Doctor of Natural Science (WDAA)
Nat ScD	Doctor of Natural Science (AD)
Nat Sci Fdn...	National Science Foundation (AD)
NATSECM.....	National Security Medal
Nat Sec Soc...	National Secular Society (AD)
Nat Semi	National Semiconductor Corp.
NATSEMI	National Semiconductor Inc. (AD)
NATSF	Naval Air Technical Services Facility (MCD)
NATSFERRY...	Naval Air Transport Service, Ferry Command [*World War II*]
NATSFQADIVLANT...	Naval Air Technical Services Facility, Quality Assurance Division, Atlantic (DNAB)
NATSFQADIVPAC...	Naval Air Technical Services Facility, Quality Assurance Division, Pacific (DNAB)
NATSIEP	National Aboriginal and Torres Strait Islander Education Policy [*Australia*]
NATSJA........	National Association of Training School and Juvenile Agencies [*Later, NAJCA*] (EA)
NATSLANT...	Naval Air Transport Service, Atlantic Wing [*World War II*]

NATSO.........	National Association of Truck Stop Operators (EA)
NATSOPA....	National Society of Operative Printers and Assistants [*British*]
NAT sound...	Natural Sound [*Broadcasting*] (WDMC)
NATSPAC.....	Naval Air Transport Service, Pacific Wing [*World War II*]
NATSPG.......	North Atlantic Systems Planning Group [*Military*] (WDAA)
NATSRA.......	North American Thermal Soil Recycling Association (NTPA)
NATSS........	National Association of Temporary and Staffing Services (NTPA)
NAT-STD......	NATO STANAG International Standards
NATSU........	Naval Air Technical Services Unit (NVT)
NATSU........	Nominated Air Traffic Service Unit (DA)
Nat Sup.......	National Superannuation (AD)
NatSurg.......	National Surgery Centers, Inc. [*Associated Press*] (SAG)
NATSYN.......	Natural and Synthetic [*Type of long-wearing rubber, which is actually wholly synthetic*]
NATT...........	National Association of Teachers of Travellers [*British*] (DBA)
NATT...........	National Association of Towns and Township Officials (EA)
NATT...........	Naval Air Technical Training
N ATT	Naval Attache (WDAA)
N Att	Naval Attache (AD)
NAtt	Stevens Memorial Library, Attica, NY [*Library symbol Library of Congress*] (LCLS)
NATTA	Network of Alternative Technology and Technology Assessment (EAIO)
NATTA	North American Trackless Trolley Association (EA)
N-attack.......	Nuclear Attack (AD)
Nat Tax Mag...	National Tax Magazine [*A publication*] (DLA)
NATTC	National Tank Truck Carriers (AD)
NATTC	Naval Air Technical Training Center
NATTCDET ..	Naval Air Technical Training Center Detachment (DNAB)
NATTCL.......	Naval Air Technical Training Center, Lakehurst (DNAB)
NATTFU	National Transsexual-Transvestite Feminization Union (EA)
NATTKE.......	National Association of Theatrical, Television, and Kine Employees [*A union*] [*British*] (DCTA)
NATTS	National Association of Trade and Technical Schools (EA)
NATTS	Naval Air Turbine Test Station
NATTS	North American Transvestite/Transsexual Society [*Defunct*] (EA)
NATTS-ATL..	Naval Air Turbine Test Station - Aeronautical Turbine Laboratory
NATTU	Naval Air Technical Training Unit
Nat U	Nations Unies [*United Nations*] [*French*] (AD)
NATU	Naval Aircraft Torpedo Unit
Nat UL Rev...	National University. Law Review [*1921-31*] [*A publication*] (DLA)
Nat Uni	National University (AD)
natur	Naturalist (AD)
NATUR........	Naturalist (WDAA)
NATURBTESTSTA...	Naval Air Turbine Test Station
Nature Struct Biol...	Nature Structural Biology (MEC)
NaturlAlt......	Natural Alternatives International [*Associated Press*] (SAG)
NATUS........	Naturalized United States Citizen
NATUSA.......	North African Theater of Operations (AD)
NATUSA.......	North African Theater, United States Army [*World War II*]
NATVA	National All Terrain Vehicle Association (EA)
NATVAS	National Academy of Television Arts and Sciences (EA)
NatVisn	National Vision Associates [*Associated Press*] (SAG)
NATW	National Association of Texaco Wholesalers (EA)
NATW	National Association of Town Watch (EA)
NATW	Natural Wonders [*NASDAQ symbol*] (TTSB)
NATW	Natural Wonders, Inc. [*NASDAQ symbol*] (SAG)
NATWA	National Auto and Truck Wreckers Association [*Later, ADRA*] (EA)
NATwA	North American Tiddlywinks Association (EA)
NATWARCOL...	National War College [*Later, UND*] [*DoD*] (DNAB)
NATWC	National War College [*Later, UND*] [*DoD*]
NatWest......	National Westminster [*Bank*]
NATWF	North American Tug of War Federation (EA)
NATWJ........	National Alliance of Third World Journalists (EA)
NatWndr	Natural Wonders, Inc. [*Associated Press*] (SAG)
NATWP	Naval Air Transport Wing, Pacific
NAT WS	Nordic Amer Tanker Ship Wrrt [*AMEX symbol*] (TTSB)
naty	Naturally (AD)
NaTY...........	Sodium Hydrogen Phosphate-Tryptone-Yeast Extract [*Growth medium*] [*Microbiology*]
Natzd	Naturalized [*Biology*] (BARN)
NAU	Confederation Nordique des Cadres, Techniciens, et Autres Responsables [*Nordic Confederation of Supervisors, Technicians, and Other Managers*] (EAIO)
NAU	Nalcus Resources [*Vancouver Stock Exchange symbol*]
NAU	Napuka [*Marquesas Islands*] [*Airport symbol*] (OAG)
NAU	Narcotics Assistance Unit [*Department of State*]
Nau..............	Nauruan (AD)
Nau.............	Nauru Island (AD)
nau	Nautica [*Nautical*] [*Spanish*] (AD)
NAU	Naval Administrative Unit
NAU	Network Access Unit [*Telecommunications*]
NAU	Network Addressable Unit (NITA)
NAU	Network Address [*or Addressable*] Unit [*Computer science*] (BUR)
NAU	Network Administration Utilities [*Honeywell*] (NITA)
NAU	Noise Augmentation Unit [*Military*] (CAAL)
NAU	Nordic Confederation of Supervisors, Technicians, and Other Managers [*Formerly, Nordic Union of Foremen*] (EA)
NAU	North Arizona University (AD)
NAu.............	Seymour Library, Auburn, NY [*Library symbol Library of Congress*] (LCLS)
NAUA..........	National Aircraft Underwriters' Association (AD)
NAUA..........	National Automobile Underwriters Association [*Later, ISO*] (EA)
NAUB..........	National Association of Urban Bankers (EA)

NAuC	Cayuga County Community College, Auburn, NY [*Library symbol Library of Congress*] (LCLS)
NAUE	New and Unused Equipment (MCD)
NAUF	Name and Address Update File [*IRS*]
NAUFMA......	National Association of Urban Flood Management Agencies [*Later, NAFSWMA*] (EA)
NAUFOF.......	North American UFO Federation [*Defunct*] (EA)
NAUFRED	National Association of Used Fitness and Rehabilitation Equipment Dealers (NTPA)
NAUFWP.....	National Association of University Fisheries and Wildlife Programs (NTPA)
NAUG..........	National AppleWorks Users Group (EA)
nauga	Naugahide (AD)
NAUHF........	Northern Area Ultrahigh Frequency Radio System [*Green Pine*] (MCD)
NAuHi	Cayuga County Historical Society, Auburn, NY [*Library symbol Library of Congress*] (LCLS)
NAUI	National Association of Underwater Instructors (EA)
NAUL	Netherland-America University League [*Defunct*] (EA)
NAULAS......	North American Union Life Assurance Society [*Chicago, IL*] (EA)
NAUM	National Association of Uniform Manufacturers [*Later, NAUMD*] (EA)
NAUMD........	National Association of Uniform Manufacturers and Distributors (EA)
NAuMH	Auburn Memorial Hospital, Learning Resources Center, Auburn, NY [*Library symbol Library of Congress*] (LCLS)
NAUN	Nearest Active Upstream Neighbor [*Computer science*]
NAU-OLC	North American Union of Sisters of Our Lady of Charity (TOCD)
NAUP	National Association of Unemployed Persons [*Defunct*] (EA)
NAUPA	National Amalgamated Union of Shop Assistants [*A union*] [*British*]
NAUPA	National Association of Unclaimed Property Administrators (EA)
NAURI.........	Nonaccelerating-Unemployment Rate of Inflation [*Economics*]
NAurW	Wells College, Aurora, NY [*Library symbol Library of Congress*] (LCLS)
NAUS	National Aerospace Utilization System (NOAA)
NAUS	National Association for Uniformed Services (EA)
NAuS	Seward House, Auburn, NY [*Library symbol Library of Congress*] (LCLS)
NAUSAWC ...	National Amalgamated Union of Shop Assistants, Warehousemen, and Clerks [*A union*] [*British*]
NAUS/SMW...	National Association for Uniformed Services and Society of Military Widows (NTPA)
NAuT..........	Auburn Theological Seminary, Auburn, NY [*Library symbol Library of Congress Obsolete*] (LCLS)
NAUT	Nautica Enterprises [*NASDAQ symbol*] (TTSB)
NAUT	Nautica Enterprises, Inc. [*NASDAQ symbol*] (SAG)
NAUT	Nautical (AAG)
naut	Nautical (AD)
NAUTIC.......	Naval Autonomous Intelligent Console (PDAA)
Nautica.......	Nautica Enterprises, Inc. [*Associated Press*] (SAG)
NAUTIS-F....	Naval Autonomous Information System-Frigate (DOMA)
NAUTO........	Nautophone
NAUTS........	Nautical Miles (ROG)
NAUTT	National Association of Unions in the Textile Trade [*British*] (DCTA)
NAUW..........	National Association of University Women (EA)
NAUWS........	Naval Advanced Undersea Weapons School
n aux b.......	New Auxiliary Boiler (AD)
NAV	Narrows [*Virginia*] [*Seismograph station code, US Geological Survey*] (SEIS)
NAV	National American Veterans
NAV	National Association of Videographers [*Defunct*] (EA)
NAV	Natividade [*Brazil*] [*Airport symbol*] (AD)
Nav	Navaho (AD)
nav.............	Navajo [*MARC language code Library of Congress*] (LCCP)
NAV	Naval (MSA)
Nav.............	Naval (AD)
nav.............	Naval (AD)
NAV	Naval Artillery Volunteers [*British*] (ROG)
Nav.............	Navarra (AD)
Nav.............	Navarre (AD)
Nav.............	Navassa Island (AD)
NAV	Nav Flight Planning [*Czech Republic*] [*FAA designator*] (FAAC)
nav.............	Navigable (AD)
NAV	Navigate (AAG)
nav.............	Navigation (AD)
NAV	Navigation (GAVI)
NAV	Navigator (DSUE)
Nav.............	Navistar International Corp. [*Associated Press*] (SAG)
NAV	Navistar International Corp. [*NYSE symbol*] (SPSG)
NAV	Navistar Intl [*NYSE symbol*] (TTSB)
NAV	Navy (AAG)
NAV	Net Annual Value [*Business term*] (ADA)
NAV	Net Asset Value
NAV	Next Generation Advanced Vehicle [*Nippon Steel Corp.*]
NAV	Nonalcoholic Volunteers
NAV	North American Ventures, Inc. [*Vancouver Stock Exchange symbol*]
NAV	Visual Navigation (MCD)
NAVA	National Association for Variable Annuities
NAVA	National Association for Veterinary Acupuncture (EA)
NAVA	National Association of Veterinary Assistants [*Defunct*] (EA)
NAVA	National Audio-Visual Association [*Later, ICIA*] (EA)
NAVA	Navajo National Monument
NAVA	Net Asset Value (AD)
NAVA	North American Vexillological Association (EA)
NAVABSCOLLU...	Navy Absentee Collection Unit (DNAB)
NAVAC........	National Audiovisual Aids Centre [*British*]
NAVACAD	Naval Academy

NA Vacc....... North American Vaccine, Inc. [*Associated Press*] (SAG)
NAVACCTGFINCEN... Navy Accounting and Finance Center (DNAB)
NAVACD....... Naval Academy (DNAB)
navaco......... Navigation Action Cutout (AD)
NAVACO....... Navigation Action Cutout Switchboard
NAVACT....... All Navy Activities [*A dispatch to all activities in an area*]
NAVACTDET... Naval Activities Detachment (DNAB)
NAVAD......... Naval Administrator At [*Place*]
NAVADCOM... Naval Administrative Command
NAVADGP..... Naval Advisory Group
NAVADGRU... Naval Advisory Group (CINC)
NAVADGRU... Navy Administrative Group
NAV-ADMIN... Navigation-Administration [*Inquiry program*] (AFIT)
NAVADMINCOM... Naval Administrative Command (DNAB)
NAVADMINO... Navy Administrative Office [*or Officer*]
NAVADMINU... Naval Administration Unit (MUGU)
NAVADMINUANX... Naval Administrative Unit Annex (DNAB)
NAVADS....... Navy Automated Transport Documentation System (DNAB)
NAVADUNIT... Naval Administrative Unit
NAVADUNSEAWPNSCOL... Naval Advanced Undersea Weapons School (DNAB)
NAVADVUSEAWPNSCOL... Naval Advanced Undersea Weapons School (MUGU)
NAVAE....... National Association for Vietnamese American Education (EA)
NAVAER....... Navy Aeronautics
NAVAERAUDOFC... Navy Area Audit Office [*London*] (DNAB)
NAVAEROMEDCEN... Naval Aeronautical Medical Center
NAVAERORECOV... Naval Aerospace Recovery Facility
NAVAERORECOVF... Naval Aerospace Recovery Facility (AD)
NAVAERORECOVFAC... Naval Aerospace Recovery Facility
NAVAEROSPMEDINST... Naval Aerospace Medical Institute
NAVAEROSPMEDRSCHINST... Naval Aerospace Medical Research Institute (DNAB)
NAVAERO(SP)OMEDRSCHLAB... Naval Aerospace Medical Research Laboratory (DNAB)
NAVAERO(SP)RECFAC... Naval Aerospace Recovery Facility (DNAB)
NAVAERO(SP)REGMEDCEN... Naval Aerospace Medical Center (DNAB)
NAVAGLOBE... Long-Distance Navigation System, Global [*Air Force*]
NAVAID....... Navigation Aid
NAVAID....... Navigational Aid (DNAB)
NAVAIDE...... Naval Aide
NAVAIDSUPPUNIT... Navigational Aids Support Unit (DNAB)
NAVAIR....... Naval Air Systems Command
NAVAIR....... Naval Air Systems Command Headquarters (USDC)
NAVAIRANDACT... Naval Air Research and Development Activities (MUGU)
NAVAIRDEVCEN... Naval Air Development Center [*Also, NADC, NADEVCEN*] (MUGU)
NAVAIRDEVU... Naval Air Development Unit (MUGU)
NAVAIRECONTECHSUPCEN... Naval Air Reconnaissance Technical Support Center
NAVAIRENGCEN... Naval Air Engineering Center [*Closed*]
NAVAIRENGCENFO... Naval Air Engineering Center Field Office (DNAB)
NAVAIRENGLAB... Naval Air Engineering Laboratory (DNAB)
NAVAIRENGRCEN... Naval Air Engineering Center [*Closed*]
NAVAIRENGRFAC... Naval Air Engineering Facility (MUGU)
NAVAIRESCEN... Naval Air Reserve Center (DNAB)
NAVAIRESFORRON... Naval Air Reserve Force Squadron (DNAB)
NAVAIRESMOPIXU... Naval Air Reserve Mobile Photographic Unit (DNAB)
NAVAIRESU... Naval Air Reserve Unit (DNAB)
NAVAIREWORKF... Naval Air Rework Facility
NAVAIREWORKFAC... Naval Air Rework Facility
NAVAIRFAC... Naval Air Facility
NAVAIRINST... Naval Air Systems Command Instruction
NavAirInstr... Naval Air Command Instruction (AAGC)
NAVAIRINTO... Naval Air Intelligence Office (MUGU)
NAVAIRLANT... Naval Air Force, Atlantic Fleet
NAVAIRLOGOFF... Naval Air Logistics Office (DNAB)
NAVAIRLOGTASKFORREP... Naval Air Logistics Task Force Representative (DNAB)
NAVAIRMAINTRAGRU... Naval Air Maintenance Training Group (DNAB)
NAVAIRMATCEN... Naval Air Material Center [*Also, NAMATCEN, NAMC*] (MUGU)
NAVAIRMINDEFDEVU... Naval Air Mine Defense Development Unit (MUGU)
NAVAIRNEWS... Naval Aviation News [*A publication*] (DNAB)
NAVAIRPAC... Naval Air Force, Pacific Fleet
NAVAIRPROPCEN... Naval Air Propulsion Center (GRD)
NAVAIRPROPTESTCEN... Naval Air Propeller Test Center
NAVAIRRES... Naval Air Reserve
NAVAIRREWORKF... Naval Air Rework Facility (AD)
NAVAIRSTA... Naval Air Station (DNAB)
NAVAIRSUPPU... Naval Air Support Unit
NAVAIRSYSCO... Naval Air Systems Command (MCD)
NAVAIR SYSCOM... Naval Air System Command (DOMA)
NAVAIRSYSCOM... Naval Air Systems Command
NAVAIRSYSCOMFLEREADREP... Naval Air Systems Command Fleet Readiness Representative (DNAB)
NAVAIRSYSCOMFLESUPREPCEN... Naval Air Systems Command Fleet Supply Representative Center (DNAB)
NAVAIRSYSCOMHQ... Naval Air Systems Command Headquarters
NAVAIRSYSCOMMETSYSDIV... Naval Air Systems Command, Meteorological Systems Division (DNAB)
NAVAIRSYSCOMREP... Naval Air Systems Command Representative
NAVAIRSYSCOMREPAC... Naval Air Systems Command Representative, Pacific
NAVAIRSYSCOMREPCENT... Naval Air Systems Command Representative, Central
NAVAIRSYSCOMREPLANT... Naval Air Systems Command Representative, Atlantic
NAVAIRSYSCOMREP PNCLA... Naval Air Systems Command Representative, Naval Air Training Command, Pensacola [*Florida*]
NAVAIRSYSCOMTARANDSYSDIV... Naval Air Systems Command Target and Range Systems Command (DNAB)
NAVAIRTECHREP... Naval Air Systems Command Technical Representative (DNAB)
NAVAIRTECHSERVFAC... Naval Air Technical Services Facility (MUGU)

NAVAIRTERM... Naval Air Terminal (DNAB)
NAVAIRTESTCEN... Naval Air Test Center (MUGU)
NAVAIRTESTCENT... Naval Air Test Center (GRD)
NAVAIRTESTFAC... Naval Air Test Facility (MUGU)
NAVAIRTESTFACSHIPINSTAL... Naval Air Test Facility - Ship Installations (DNAB)
NAVAIRTORPU... Naval Aircraft Torpedo Unit (MUGU)
NAVAIRTRACEN... Naval Air Training Center
NAVAIRTU ... Naval Air Training Unit (MUGU)
NAVAIRTURBTESTSTA... Naval Air Turbine Test Station (MUGU)
NAVAL .... National Audio Visual Aids Library (AIE)
Naval E........ Naval Engineer (PGP)
NAVALOT..... Allotment Division [*Navy*]
NAVALREHCEN... Naval Alcohol Rehabilitation Center (DNAB)
NAVALREHDRYDOCK... Navy Alcohol Rehabilitation Drydock (DNAB)
NAVALT....... Navy Alterations
NAVAMDEP... Naval Ammunition Depot [*Charleston, SC*]
NAVAMPROENGCEN... Naval Ammunition Production Engineering Center (DNAB)
NAVANTRA... Naval Air Advanced Training Center
NAVANTRACOM... Naval Air Advanced Training Command
NAVAP........ National Association of VA [*Veterans Administration*] Physicians (EA)
NAVAPD....... National Association of VA [*Veterans' Administration*] Physicians and Dentists (NTPA)
NAVAPI........ North American Voltage and Phase Indicator (IEEE)
NAVAPSCIENCLAB... Naval Applied Science Laboratory (DNAB)
NAVAR........ Navigation Air RADAR (IAA)
NAVAR........ Navigation and Ranging (IAA)
NAVAR......... Navigation RADAR
NAVARA....... Navy Appellate Review Activity
Nav Arch..... Naval Architect [*Academic degree*]
NAVAREAAUDSVC... Naval Area Audit Service
NAVARHO..... Navigation and Radio Homing [*Aviation*]
NAVARMDEP... Naval Armament Depot
Navarre........ Navarre Corp. [*Associated Press*] (SAG)
NAVASCOPE... Navigation Airborne RADAR Scope [*Air Force*]
NAVASCREEN... Navigation RADAR Screen [*Air Force*]
NAVASTROGRU... Navy Astronautics Group (MUGU)
NAVASTROGRUHQTRINJFAC... Navy Astronautics Group Headquarters, Tracking and Injection Facility (DNAB)
NAVASTROGRUP... Navy Astronautics Group (SAA)
NAVASWDATACEN... Navy Antisubmarine Warfare Data Center
NAVASWDATCEN... Navy Antisubmarine Warfare Data Center (DNAB)
NAVATAC..... Navy Antiterrorism Analysis Center (COE)
NAVATR....... Naval Air Systems [*Command Headquarters*] [*Marine science*] (OSRA)
NAVAUD ..... Navy Auditor
NAVAUDO.... Navy Audit Office (DNAB)
NAVAUDSVC... Director, Naval Audit Service
NAVAUDSVCAP... Naval Audit Service, Capital Area (DNAB)
NAVAUDSVCHQ... Naval Audit Service Headquarters (DNAB)
NAVAUDSVCNE... Naval Audit Service, Northeast Area (DNAB)
NAVAUDSVCSE... Naval Audit Service, Southeast Area (DNAB)
NAVAUDSVCWEST... Naval Audit Service, Western Area (DNAB)
NavAus .... Navigation in Australian Waters (AD)
NAVAUTH .... Naval Authority
NAVAUTODINSCEN... Navy Automatic Digital Network Switching Center (DNAB)
NAVAVCEN... Naval Audio-Visual Center (DNAB)
NAVAVENGSERVU... Naval Aviation Engineering Services Unit [*Philadelphia, PA*] (DNAB)
NAVAVENGSERVUDET... Naval Aviation Engineering Service Unit Detachment (DNAB)
NAVAVIONICFAC... Naval Avionics Facility [*Later, NAC*] (MUGU)
NAVAVIONICSCEN... Naval Avionics Center (DNAB)
NAVAVMEDCEN... Naval Aviation Medical Center (DNAB)
NAVAVMUSEUM... Naval Aviation Museum [*Pensacola, FL*] (DNAB)
NAVAVNENGRSERVU... Naval Aviation Engineering Service Unit [*Philadelphia, PA*] (DNAB)
NAVAVNLOGCEN... Naval Aviation Logistics Center (NVT)
NAVAVNLOGCENDET... Naval Aviation Logistics Center Detachment (DNAB)
NAVAVNLOGCENFSO... Naval Aviation Logistics Center Field Service Office (DNAB)
NAVAVNLOGCENMETALABOPS... Naval Aviation Logistics Center Meteorology Calibration Laboratory Operations (DNAB)
NAVAVNMEDCEN... Naval Aviation Medical Center (DNAB)
NAVAVNSAFECEN... Naval Aviation Safety Center
NAVAVNSCOLCOM... Naval Aviation School Command
NAVAVNWEPSFAC... Naval Aviation Weapons Facilities
NAVAVNWPNSFAC... Naval Aviation Weapons Facilities (DNAB)
NAVAVNWPNSFACDET... Naval Aviation Weapons Facility Detachment (DNAB)
NAVB .... National Association of Volunteer Bureaus [*British*] (EAIO)
NAVBALTAP... Allied Naval Forces, Baltic Approaches [*NATO*] (NATG)
NAVBALTAP... Naval Forces Baltic Approaches [*NATO*] (AD)
NAVBASE..... Naval Base
NAVBASELANT... Naval Bases Atlantic
NAVBASEPAC... Naval Bases Pacific
NAVBCHGRU... Naval Beach Group (DNAB)
NAVBCHPHIBREFTRAGRU... Navy Beach Amphibious Refresher Training Group (DNAB)
NAVBCSTSVCDET... Navy Broadcasting Service Detachment (DNAB)
NAVBCSTSVCDETTASA... Navy Broadcasting Service Detachment Television Audio Support Activity (DNAB)
NAVBCSTSVCWASHDC... Navy Broadcasting Service, Washington, DC (DNAB)
NAVBE......... National Association for Vocational Business Education (AEBS)
NAVBEACHGRU... Naval Beach Group (CINC)
NAVBIODYNLAB... Naval Biodynamics Laboratory (DNAB)
NAVBIOLAB... Naval Biological Laboratory (MUGU)
NAVBIOSCILAB... Naval Biosciences Research Laboratory (DNAB)

NAVBIT........ Naval Basic Instrument Trainer (PDAA)
navbm........ Naval Ballistic Missile (AD)
NAVBM........ Navy Ballistic Missile
NAVBMC...... Navy Ballistic Missile Committee
NAVBOILAB... Navy Boiler Laboratory
nav brz........ Naval Bronze (AD)
Nav Bs......... Naval Base (AD)
NAVC .... Naval Aviation Cadet
NAVC .... North American Voyageur Council (EA)
NAVCAD....... Naval Aviation Cadet
NavCad....... Naval Cadet (AD)
NAVCALAB... Navy Calibration Laboratory (DNAB)
NAVCALABANX... Navy Calibration Laboratory Annex (DNAB)
NAVCALABMSG... Navy Calibration Laboratory Meteorology Support Group (DNAB)
NAVCALABOPS... Navy Calibration Laboratory Operations (DNAB)
NAVCALS.... Naval Communication Area Local Station (NVT)
NAVCAMS.... Naval Communication Area Master Station (NVT)
NAVCAMSEASTPAC... Naval Communication Area Master Station, Eastern Pacific (DNAB)
NAVCAMSLANT... Naval Communication Area Master Station, Atlantic (DNAB)
NAVCAMSMED... Naval Communication Area Master Station, Mediterranean (DNAB)
NAVCAMSOAM... Naval Communication Area Master Station, South America (DNAB)
NAVCAMSSPECCOMDIVLANT... Naval Communication Area Master Station, Special Communications Division, Atlantic (DNAB)
NAVCARGOHANBN... Naval Cargo Handling Battalion
NAVCAT........ Naval Career Appraisal Team (MUGU)
NAVCAT........ Naval Construction Action Team [*Vietnam*] (VNW)
NAVCBCEN... Naval Construction Battalion Center
NAVCC......... Naval Communications Center (MCD)
NAVCENFRACO... Navy Central Freight Control Office
NAVCENT..... Allied Naval Forces, Central Europe [*NATO*]
NAVCENT..... Naval Forces [*US*] Central [*Command*] (DOMA)
NAVCG......... Coast Guard Publication [*Formerly, NCG*]
NAVCHAPGRU... Navy Cargo Handling and Port Group (NVT)
NAVCHAPGRUDET... Navy Cargo Handling and Port Group Detachment (DNAB)
NAVCINSUPPACT... Navy Counterintelligence Support Activity (DNAB)
NAVCINTSUPPCEN... Navy Counterintelligence Support Center (DNAB)
NAVCINTSUPPGRU... Navy Counterintelligence Support Unit (DNAB)
NAVCIVENGLAB... Navy Civil Engineering Laboratory (DNAB)
NAVCIVENGRLAB... Naval Civil Engineering Laboratory
NAVCJ .... National Association on Volunteers in Criminal Justice [*Later, IAJV*] (EA)
NAVCLODEP... Naval Clothing Depot
NAVCLOTEXTOFC... Navy Clothing and Textile Office (DNAB)
NAVCLOTEXTRSCHFAC... Navy Clothing and Textile Research Facility [*Natick, MA*] (DNAB)
NAVCLOTEXTRSCHU... Navy Clothing and Textile Research Unit
NAVCLOTHTEXOFC... Navy Clothing and Textile Office (DNAB)
NAVCM......... Navigation Countermeasure (IAA)
NAVCM......... Navigation Countermeasures and Deception
NavCm......... Navigation Countermeasures and Deception (AD)
NAVCMD...... Navigation Command
NAVCOASTSYSCEN... Naval Coastal Systems Center [*Panama City, FL*] (DNAB)
NAVCOM...... Naval Communications [*System*]
navcom........ Navigation Communication (AD)
NAVCOMCOM... Naval Communications Command
NAVCOMM..... Naval Communications [*System*]
NAVCOMMAREA... Naval Communications Area (NVT)
NAVCOMMCOM... Naval Communications Command
NAVCOMMDET... Naval Communication Station Detachment (DNAB)
NAVCOMMDETSPECCOMMDIV... Naval Communication Station Detachment, Special Communications Division (DNAB)
NAVCOMMFAC... Naval Communications Facility (NVT)
NAVCOMMHQ... Naval Communications Headquarters (DNAB)
NAVCOMMIS... Naval Communications Command Management Information System (MCD)
NAVCOMMOPNET... Naval Communications Operation Network (DNAB)
NAVCOMMSTA... Naval Communication Station
NAVCOMMSTASPECCOMMDIV... Naval Communication Station, Special Communications Division (DNAB)
NAVCOMMSYS... Naval Communication System (MUGU)
NAVCOMMSYSSUPPACT... Naval Communications System Support Activity (DNAB)
NAVCOMMTRACEN... Naval Communications Training Center (MUGU)
NAVCOMMU... Naval Communication Unit
NAVCOMMUNR... Naval Communications Unit, Naval Reserve (IAA)
NAVCOMPARS... Naval Communications Processing and Routing System (MCD)
NAVCOMPT... Office of the Comptroller of the Navy
NAVCOMPTINST... Office of the Comptroller of the Navy Instruction
NAVCOMPTMAN... Naval Comptroller Manual
NAVCOMSYSSUPPACT... Naval Command Systems Support Activity (DNAB)
NAVCOMSYSSUPPCEN... Naval Command Systems Support Center (DNAB)
NAVCOMSYSTO... Navy Commissary Store (DNAB)
NAVCOMSYSTORE... Navy Commissary Store
NAVCOMU ... Naval Communications Unit
NAVCON ...... Naval Countermeasures (CINC)
NAVCON ...... Navigation Control Systems (RDA)
Nav Const.... Naval Constructor [*Academic degree*]
NAVCONSTRACEN... Naval Construction Training Center (DNAB)
NAVCONSTRAU... Naval Construction Training Unit (DNAB)
NAVCONSTREGT... Naval Construction Regiment (DNAB)
NAVCONTDEP... Navy Contracting Department (DNAB)
NAVCONTRACEN... Naval Construction Training Center
NAVCONVHOSP... Naval Convalescent Hospital

NAVCORCOURSECEN... Naval Correspondence Course Center (DNAB)
NAVCORRCUSUNIT... Navy Correctional Custody Unit (DNAB)
NAVCOSSACT... Naval Command Systems Support Activity
NAVCOSSCEN... Naval Command Systems Support Center (DNAB)
NAVCRUITAREA... Navy Recruiting Area
NAVCRUITBRSTA... Navy Recruiting Branch Station (DNAB)
NAVCRUITCOM... Navy Recruiting Command (DNAB)
NAVCRUITCOMORIENTUNIT... Navy Recruiting Command Orientation Unit (DNAB)
NAVCRUITCOMSAT... Navy Recruiting Command Standardization and Audit Team (DNAB)
NAVCRUITCOMYPFLDREP... Navy Recruiting Command Youth Programs Field Representative (DNAB)
NAVCRUITDIST... Navy Recruiting District (DNAB)
NAVCRUITEXHIBCEN... Navy Recruiting Exhibit Center (DNAB)
NAVCRUITEXHIBCENCAT... Navy Recruiting Exhibit Center Catalog (DNAB)
NAVCRUITRACOM... Navy Recruit Training Command (DNAB)
NAVCRUITSTA... Navy Recruiting Station
NAVCSG....... National Archives Volunteers Constitution Study Group [*Defunct*] (EA)
NAVCURRSUPPGRULANTFLT... Naval Current Support Group, Atlantic Fleet (DNAB)
NAVCURRSUPPGRUNAVEUR... Naval Current Support Group, Naval Forces, Europe (DNAB)
NAVCURRSUPPGRUPACFLT... Naval Current Support Group, Pacific Fleet (DNAB)
NAVCURSERV... Naval Courier Service
NAVCURSERVDET... Naval Courier Service Detachment (DNAB)
NAVCURSERVHQ... Naval Courier Service Headquarters
NAVD .... National Association of Video Distributors (EA)
NAVD .... North American Vertical Datum [*National Oceanic and Atmospheric Administration*]
NAVD88...... North American Vertical Datum of 1988 (USDC)
NAVDAB...... Navy Ocean Experimental Acoustic Data Bank (MSC)
NAVDAC...... Naval Data Automation Command (MCD)
NAVDAC...... Navigation Data Assimilation Center (AD)
navdac........ Navigation Data Assimilation Computer (AD)
NAVDAC...... Navigation Data Assimilation Computer
NAVDAD...... Navigationally-Derived Air Data (MCD)
NAVDAF ...... Navy Data Automation Center (DNAB)
NAVDAMCONTRACEN... Navy Damage Control Training Center
NAVDAR...... Naval Defense Acquisition Regulations (MCD)
NAVDATACEN... Naval Data Center (DNAB)
NAVDEFEASTPAC... Naval Defense Forces, Eastern Pacific (DNAB)
NAVDEGSTA... Navy Degaussing Station (DNAB)
NAVDEGSTALANT/PAC... Naval Degaussing Station, Atlantic/Pacific
NAVDENCEN... Naval Dental Center
NAVDENCLINIC... Naval Dental Clinic
NAVDENSCOL... Naval Dental School
NAVDENTECHSCOL... Naval Dental Technicians School
NAVDEP...... Naval Deputy [*NATO*] (NATG)
Nav Dep...... Naval Deputy [*NATO*] (AD)
NAVDEPCENT... Naval Deputy to Commander-in-Chief, Allied Forces, Central Europe [*NATO*] (NATG)
NAVDEPNOAA... Naval Deputy National Oceanic and Atmospheric Administration (DNAB)
NAVDEPT...... Navy Department
NAVDES...... Navy Design Selection List
NAVDESCOL... Naval Destroyer School (NVT)
NAVDESSCOL... Naval Destroyer School
NAVDET...... Naval Detachment
NAVDEVTRACEN... Navy Development Training Center
NAVDI......... National Association for Ventilator Dependent Individuals (EA)
NAVDIS...... Naval District
NAVDISBAR... Navy Disciplinary Barracks (DNAB)
NAVDISCBAR... Naval Disciplinary Barracks
NAVDISCOM... Navy Disciplinary Command
NAVDISEAVECTORCONCEN... Navy Disease Vector Control Center
NAVDISP...... Naval Dispensary
NAVDIST...... Naval District
NAVDISVECTTECOLCONCEN... Navy Disease Vector Ecology and Control Center (DNAB)
NAVDIVSALVTRACEN... Naval Diving and Salvage Training Center (DNAB)
NAVDOC...... Navy Department Orientation Course (NG)
NAVDOCKS... Bureau of Yards and Docks Publications [*Obsolete Navy*]
NAVDOCSP... Bureau of Yards and Docks Publications [*Obsolete Navy*]
NAVDRUGREHCEN... Naval Drug Rehabilitation Center (DNAB)
NAVE .... National Assessment of Vocational Education [*Department of Education*] (GFGA)
Nav E.......... Naval Engineer [*Academic degree*]
NAVEA...... National Adult Vocational Education Association (EA)
NAVEAMS...... Navigational Warning East Atlantic and Mediterranean [*Navy*] (PDAA)
NavEams..... Navigation in the Eastern Atlantic and the Mediterranean (AD)
NAVEARB..... Navy Employee Appeals Review Board (DNAB)
NavEast...... Navigation along the East Coast of Asia (AD)
NAVEASTOCEANCEN... Naval Eastern Oceanography Center (DNAB)
NAVED....... National Association of Visual Education Dealers [*Later, National Audio-Visual Association*] (AEBS)
NAVEDTRA... Naval Education and Training Command (MCD)
NAVEDTRA... Naval Education and Training Program Development Center [*Pensacola, FL*]
NAVEDTRACOM... Naval Education and Training Center [*or Command*] (DNAB)
NAVEDTRAPRODEVCEN... Naval Education and Training Program Development Center [*Pensacola, FL*] (DNAB)
NAVEDTRAPRODEVCENCODIV... Naval Education and Training Program Development Center Coordination Division (DNAB)

NAVEDTRAPRODEVCENDET... Naval Education and Training Program Development Center Detachment (DNAB)
NAVEDTRASUPPCEN... Naval Education and Training Support Center (DNAB)
NAVEDTRASUPPCENLANT... Naval Education and Training Support Center, Atlantic (DNAB)
NAVEDTRASUPPCENPAC... Naval Education and Training Support Center, Pacific (DNAB)
NAVEDTRASUPPCENPACNCFA... Naval Education and Training Support Center, Pacific, Navy Campus for Achievement (DNAB)
NAVEL .... Naloxone, Atropine, Valium, Epinephrine, Lidocaine [*Medicine*] (DMAA)
NAVELEC ..... Naval Electronics System Command (IAA)
NAVELECS ... Naval Electronic Systems Command (SAA)
NAVELECSYSCOM... Naval Electronics Systems Command
NAVELECSYSCOMCENLANTDIV... Naval Electronics Systems Command, Central Atlantic Division
NAVELECSYSCOMHQ... Naval Electronics Systems Command Headquarters
NAVELECSYSCOMNEDIV... Naval Electronics Systems Command, Northeast Division
NAVELECSYSCOMSEDIV... Naval Electronics Systems Command, Southeast Division
NAVELECSYSCOMWESTDIV... Naval Electronics Systems Command, Western Division
NAVELEM .... Navy Element (DNAB)
NAVELEX ..... Naval Electronics Systems Command
NAVELEX ..... Naval Electronic Systems Command Headquarters (USDC)
NAVELEXACTS... Naval Electronic Systems Command Activities (DNAB)
NAVELEXDET... Naval Electronic Systems Command Detachment (DNAB)
NAVELEXENGOFF... Naval Electronics Engineering Office (DNAB)
NAVELEXINST... Naval Electronics Systems Command Instruction
NAVELEXSITEREP... Naval Electronic Systems Command, Site Representative (DNAB)
NAVELEXSYSCOMCENDET... Naval Electronic Systems Command Center Detachment (DNAB)
NAVELEXSYSCOMDIV... Naval Electronic Systems Command Division (DNAB)
NAVELEXSYSCOMMIDWESTDIV... Naval Electronic Systems Command, Midwest Division (DNAB)
NAVELEXSYSCOMSEDIV... Naval Electronic Systems Command, Southeast Division (DNAB)
NAVELEXSYSTRAPUBMO... Naval Electronic Systems Command Training and Publications Management Office (DNAB)
NAVELEXTECHREP... Naval Electronic Systems Command Technical Representative (DNAB)
NAVELXSYSCOMTECHLREP... Naval Electronic Systems Command Technician Liaison Representative (DNAB)
NAVEMSCEN... Navy Electromagnetic Spectrum Center (DNAB)
NAVENENVSA... Navy Energy and Environmental Support Activity (DNAB)
NAVENGRXSTA... Naval Engineering Experiment Station
NAVENPVNTMEDU... Navy Environmental and Preventive Medicine Unit (DNAB)
NAVENVPREDRSCHFAC... Naval Environmental Prediction Research Facility (MCD)
NAVENVRHLTHCEN... Navy Environmental Health Center (DNAB)
NAVENVSUPPCEN... Navy Environmental Support Center (DNAB)
NAVENVSUPPO... Navy Environmental Support Office [*Obsolete*] (DNAB)
NAVEODFAC... Naval Explosive Ordnance Disposal Facility
NAVEODTECHCE... Naval Explosive Ordnance Disposal Technology Center [*Indian Head, MD*]
NAVEODTECHCEN... Naval Explosive Ordnance Disposal Technology Center [*Indian Head, MD*] (DNAB)
NAVESNP..... National Association of Vocational Education Special Needs Personnel (EA)
NAVETC .... Navy Educational Tape Catalog (DNAB)
NAVEURWWMCCS DP... Naval Forces, Europe, Worldwide Military Command Control System, Data Processing (DNAB)
NAVEURWWMCCS EMSKD... Naval Forces, Europe, Worldwide Military Command Control System, Employment Schedule (DNAB)
NAVEURWWMCCS MOVREP... Naval Forces, Europe, Worldwide Military Command Control System, Movement Reports (DNAB)
NAVEURWWMCCS NAVFORSTA... Naval Forces, Europe, Worldwide Military Command Control System, Naval Forces Status (DNAB)
NAVEX .... Navigation Exercise [*Navy*] (NVT)
navex .... Navigation Exercise (AD)
NAVEX .... Norton AntiVirus Extension
NAVEXAM .... Naval Examining Board
NAVEXAMBD... Naval Examining Board (DNAB)
NAVEXAMCEN... Navy Examination Center
NAVEXAMCENADVAUTHLIST... Naval Examining Center Advancement Authorization List (DNAB)
NAVEXENGLANDCOM... Navy Exchange, England Complex (DNAB)
NAVEXHIBCEN... Naval Exhibit Center
NAVEXOS..... Executive Office of the Secretary [*Navy*]
NAVF .... Naval Avionics Facility [*Later, NAC*] (AFIT)
NAVF .... Norges Allmennvitenskapelige Forskningsrad [*Norwegian Research Council for Science and the Humanities*] [*Information service or system*] (IID)
NAVFAC .... Naval Facilities Engineering Command [*Formerly, Bureau of Yards and Docks*]
NAVFAC .... Naval Facilities Engineering Command Headquarters (USDC)
NAVFAC .... Naval Facility
NAVFAC .... Navy Faces (NITA)
NAVFACCHESDIV... Naval Facilities Engineering Command, Chesapeake Division (DNAB)
NAVFACDM... Naval Facilities Engineering Command Design Manuals
NAVFACENG... Naval Facilities Engineering Command (CAAL)
NAVFACENGCOM... Naval Facilities Engineering Command [*Formerly, Bureau of Yards and Docks*]

NAVFACENGCOMCHESDIV... Naval Facilities Engineering Command, Chesapeake Division (DNAB)
NAVFACENGCOMCONTR... Naval Facilities Engineering Command Contractor (DNAB)
NAVFACENGCOMHQ... Naval Facilities Engineering Command Headquarters (DNAB)
NAVFACENGCOMLANTDIV... Naval Facilities Engineering Command, Atlantic Division (DNAB)
NAVFACENGCOMNORDIV... Naval Facilities Engineering Command, Northern Division (DNAB)
NAVFACENGCOMPACDIV... Naval Facilities Engineering Command, Pacific Division (DNAB)
NAVFACENGCOMSODIV... Naval Facilities Engineering Command, Southern Division (DNAB)
NAVFACENGCOMWESDIV... Naval Facilities Engineering Command, Western Division (DNAB)
NAVFACENSYSCOM... Naval Facilities Engineering Systems Command
NAVFACINST... Naval Facilities Engineering Command Instructions
NAVFACLANTDIV... Naval Facilities Engineering Command, Atlantic Division (DNAB)
NAVFACLANT/PAC... Naval Facilities Atlantic/Pacific
NAVFACNORDIV... Naval Facilities Engineering Command, Northern Division (DNAB)
NAVFACOC... Naval Facility Operational Center (DNAB)
NAVFACP..... Naval Facilities Engineering Command Publications
NAVFAC P-68... Naval Facilities Engineering Command Contracting Manual [*A publication*] (AAGC)
NAVFACSODIV... Naval Facilities Engineering Comamnd, Southern Division (DNAB)
NAVFAC-TP-AD... Naval Facilities Engineering Command Technical Publications - Administration
NAVFAC-TP-MO... Naval Facilities Engineering Command Technical Publications - Maintenance Operation
NAVFAC-TP-PL... Naval Facilities Engineering Command Technical Publications - Planning
NAVFAC-TP-PU... Naval Facilities Engineering Command Technical Publications - Public Utilities
NAVFACWESDIV... Naval Facilities Engineering Command, Western Division (DNAB)
NAVFAMALWACT... Navy Family Allowance Activity
NAVFE .... Naval Forces Far East (AD)
NAVFEC .... Naval Facilites (AD)
NAVFEC .... Naval Facilities Engineering Command [*Formerly, Bureau of Yards and Docks*]
NAVFECENGCOM... Naval Facilities Engineering Command (AD)
NAVFECO..... Naval Facilities Engineering Command (PDAA)
NAVFINCEN... Navy Finance Center
NAVFINCEN-CLEVE... Navy Finance Center - Cleveland [*Ohio*] (DNAB)
NAVFINCEN-WASH... Navy Finance Center - Washington, DC (DNAB)
NAVFINOFF... Navy Finance Office
NAVFITWEPSCOL... Navy Fighter Weapons School (DNAB)
NAVFLDINTO... Navy Field Intelligence Office (DNAB)
NAVFLDOPINTO... Naval Field Operational Intelligence Office
NAVFLDOPSUPPGRU... Naval Field Operations Support Group
NAVFLIGHTPREPSCOL... Naval Flight Preparatory School
NAVFLITHTDEMORON... Navy Flight Demonstration Squadron (DNAB)
NAVFOODMGTM... Navy Food Management Team (DNAB)
NAVFOR....... Naval Forces (AD)
NAVFORJAP... Naval Air Forces, Japan (AD)
NAVFORKOR... Naval Air Forces, Korea (AD)
NAVFORSTAT... Naval Force Status Report (NVT)
NAVFRCOORD... Navy Frequency Coordinator (DNAB)
NAVFROF... Navy Freight Office
NAVFSSO..... Navy Food Services Office (DNAB)
NAVFSSO..... Navy Food Service Systems Office
NAVFUELDEP... Naval Fuel Depot
NAVFUELSUPO... Naval Fuel Supply Office
NAVFW .... Norton AntiVirus for Firewalls [*Symantec*] [*Computer science*]
NAVG .... Navigators Group [*NASDAQ symbol*] (TTSB)
NAVG .... [*The*] Navigators Group, Inc. [*NASDAQ symbol*] (NQ)
NAVGDENSCOL... Naval Graduate Dental School (DNAB)
NAVGEN ...... Navy General Publications
NavgGp... [*The*] Navigators Group, Inc. [*Associated Press*] (SAG)
NAVGMSCHOL... Navy Guided Missile School
NAVGMU...... Navy Guided Missile Unit
NAVGP......... Naval Advisory Group
NAVGRU...... Naval Group
NAVGSUP .... Navigational Guidance Support (NVT)
NAVGUN ...... Naval Gun Factory [*Later, NWF*]
NAVH .... National Aid to Visually Handicapped (AD)
NAVH .... National Association for Visually Handicapped (EA)
NAVH .... National Association of Voluntary Hostels [*British*] (DBA)
NAVHARS .... Navigation Heading and Altitude Reference System [*Aviation*] (PDAA)
NAVHET...... National Association of Vocational Home Economics Teachers (EA)
NAVHISTCEN... Naval History Center (DNAB)
NAVHISTDISPLAYCEN... Navy Historical Display Center
NAVHLTHRSCHC... Naval Health Research Center
NAVHLTHRSCHCEN... Naval Health Research Center (DNAB)
NAVHO......... National Association of Voluntary Help Organisers [*British*] (DBA)
NAVHOME... Naval Home [*Philadelphia, PA*]
NAVHOMERESINFOSYS... Naval Home Resident Information System (DNAB)
NAVHOSINGACT... Naval Housing Activity (DNAB)
NAVHOSP .... Naval Hospital
NAVHOSPCORPSCOL... Naval Hospital Corps School
NAVHOUSINGACT... Naval Housing Activity

NAVHT .... National Association of Vocational Homemakers Teachers [*Later, National Association of Vocational Home Economics Teachers*] (EA)

Nav I .... Navassa Island (AD)

NAVI .... Norton AntiVirus

NAVIC .... Navy Information Center (MCD)

navicert .... Naval Inspection Certificate (AD)

NAVICERT .... Navigation Certificate [*Paper issued by British government to merchant vessel, certifying that cargo was non-contraband, that is, not consigned to Germany*] [*World War II*]

NAVID .... Navigation Aid (NASA)

NAVIG .... Navigation

NAVIGA .... Welt Organisation fur Schiffsmodellbau und Schiffsmodellsport [*World Organization for Modelship Building and Modelship Sport*] [*Austria*] (EAIO)

NAVILCO ...... Navy International Logistics Control Office (MCD)

NAVIMAC ..... Naval Immediate Area Coordinator (DNAB)

NavInd .... Navigation in the Indian Ocean (AD)

NAVINFO ...... Navy Information Office (DNAB)

NAVINRELACT ... Navy Internal Relations Activity (DNAB)

NAVINSGEN ... Naval Inspector General

NAVINTCOM ... Naval Intelligence Command

NAVINTCOMINST ... Naval Intelligence Command Instructions

NAVINTCOMM ... Naval Intelligence Command

NAVINTEL ..... Naval Intelligence

NAVINTSUPPCEN ... Naval Intelligence Support Center (DNAB)

NAVINVSERV ... Naval Investigative Service (DNAB)

NAVINVSERVHQ ... Naval Investigative Service Headquarters (NVT)

NAVINVSERVO ... Naval Investigative Service Office

NAVINVSERVOREP ... Naval Investigative Service Office Representative (DNAB)

NAVINVSERVRA ... Naval Investigative Service Resident Agent (DNAB)

NAVION .... North American Aviation, Inc. [*Later, Rockwell International Corp.*] [*Acronym also used to refer to light aircraft of World War II*]

NAVISLO ...... Naval Interservice Liaison Office (DNAB)

Navistar .... Navistar International Corp. [*Associated Press*] (SAG)

NAVJAC .... North American Vane Jump Angle Computer

NAVJAG .... Judge Advocate General's Office Publications [*Navy*]

NAVJIT .... Naval Jet Instrument Trainer

NAVJNTSERVACT ... Naval Joint Services Activity (DNAB)

NAVJUSTSCOL ... Naval Justice School

NAVL .... National Anti-Vaccination League [*British*] (BI)

NAVL .... Navigation Light (IAA)

NAVLEGSERVOFF ... Naval Legal Service Office (DNAB)

NAVLEGSERVOFFDET ... Naval Legal Service Office Detachment (DNAB)

NAVLIAGRU ... Naval Liaison Group (DNAB)

NAVLINKSTA ... Naval Link Station (DNAB)

NAVLIS .... Navy Logistics Information System

NAVLO .... Naval Liaison Officer

NAVLOGENGRU ... Naval Logistics Engineering Group (DNAB)

NAVLOGSIP ... Navy Logistic Support Improvement Plan (NG)

NAVLOS .... Navy Liaison Officer for Scouting (DNAB)

NAVMAA ...... Naval Mutual Aid Association (DNAB)

NAVMAC ...... Navy Manpower and Material Analysis Center (DNAB)

NAVMACPAC ... Navy Manpower and Material Analysis Center, Pacific (DNAB)

NAVMACS ..... Naval Modular Automated Communications System (NVT)

NAVMAIRCOMCON ... Naval and Maritime Air Communications-Electronics Conference [*NATO*]

NAVMAP ...... Navy Missile Analysis Program (MCD)

NAVMAR ...... Naval Forces, Marianas (AD)

NAVMARCORESTRACEN ... Navy and Marine Corps Reserve Training Center

NAVMAREXHIBCEN ... Navy-Marine Corps Exhibit Center (DNAB)

NAVMARJUDACT ... Navy-Marine Corps Judiciary Activity

NAVMARTRIJUDCIR ... Navy-Marine Corps Trial Judiciary Court (DNAB)

NAVMARTRIJUDCIRBROFF ... Navy-Marine Corps Trial Judiciary Court Branch Office (DNAB)

NAVMARTRIJUDIC ... Navy-Marine Corps Trial Judiciary (DNAB)

NAVMASSO ... Navy Maintenance and Supply Systems Office (DNAB)

NAVMASSO ... Navy Management Systems Support Office (AAGC)

NAVMASSODET ... Navy Maintenance and Supply Systems Office Detachment (DNAB)

NAVMASSODETPAC ... Navy Maintenance and Supply Systems Office Detachment, Pacific (DNAB)

NAVMAT ...... Naval Material Command [*Formerly, NMSE*] (MCD)

NAVMATCOM ... Naval Material Command [*Formerly, NMSE*]

NAVMATCOMSUPPACT ... Naval Material Command Support Activity

NAVMAT COOPLAN ... Naval Material Command Contingency/Emergency Planning (DNAB)

NAVMATDATASYSGRU ... Naval Material Data Systems Group (DNAB)

NAVMATDET ... Naval Material Command Detachment (DNAB)

NAVMATEVALU ... Naval Material Evaluation Unit (DNAB)

NAVMATINST ... Naval Material Command Instruction

NAVMATMOCON ... Navy Material Movement Control Plan

NAVMATRANSOFC ... Naval Material Transportation Office (DNAB)

NAVMC .... Navy-Marine Corps

NAVMEC .... Naval Manpower Engineering Center (MCD)

NAVMED ...... Naval Aerospace Medical Institute (MCD)

NAVMED ...... Naval Medicine

NAVMEDADMINU ... Navy Medical Administrative Unit (DNAB)

NAVMEDATASERVCEN ... Naval Medical Data Service Center

NAVMEDCEN ... Navy Medical Center (DNAB)

NAVMEDCOM ... Naval Medical Command (ANA)

NAVMEDFLDRSCHLAB ... Navy Medical Field Research Laboratory (DNAB)

NAVMEDIS ..... Navy Medical Information System

NAVMEDLAB ... Naval Medical Laboratory (DNAB)

NAVMEDLABDET ... Naval Medical Laboratory Detachment (DNAB)

NAVMEDMATSUPPCOM ... Naval Medical Materiel Support Command (DNAB)

NAVMEDNPRSCHU ... Navy Medical Neuropsychiatric Research Unit (DNAB)

NAVMEDRSCHDEVCOM ... Naval Medical Research and Development Command (DNAB)

NAVMEDRSCHINST ... Naval Medical Research Institute

NAVMEDRSCHINSTDET ... Navy Medical Research Institute Detachment (DNAB)

NAVMEDRSCHU ... Naval Medical Research Unit

NAVMEDRSCHUDET ... Naval Medical Research Unit Detachment (DNAB)

NAVMEDRSHCHLAB ... Navy Medical Research Laboratory (DNAB)

NAVMEDSCOL ... Naval Medical School

NAVMEDSUPPU ... Navy Medical Support Unit (DNAB)

NAVMGTSYSCEN ... Naval Management Systems Center (MCD)

NAVMIC .... Naval Maritime Intelligence Center [*Formerly, NISC and then NTIC*] (DOMA)

NAVMILPERSCOM ... Naval Military Personnel Command (MCD)

NAVMINCOMEASTA ... Navy Mine Countermeasures Station

NAVMINDEFLAB ... Navy Mine Defense Laboratory [*Later, NCSC*]

NAVMINDEP ... Naval Mine Depot

NAVMINENGRFAC ... Naval Mine Engineering Facility

NAVMINWARTRACEN ... Naval Mine Warfare Training Center

NAVMIRO .... Naval Material Industrial Resources Office

NAVMIS .... Naval Mission

NAVMIS .... Navy Management Information System (MCD)

NAVMISCEN ... Naval Missile Center [*Point Mugu, CA*] (MCD)

NavMisCen ... Naval Missile Center (AD)

NAVMISFAC ... Naval Missile Facility [*Also, NMF*] (MUGU)

NAVMMAC ... Navy Manpower and Material Analysis Center (NVT)

NAVMMACLANT ... Navy Manpower and Material Analysis Center, Atlantic

NAVMMACPAC ... Navy Manpower and Material Analysis Center, Pacific

NAVMOBCONSTBN ... Navy Mobile Construction Battalion

NAVMORTOFF ... Navy Mortuary Office (DNAB)

NAVMTO ...... Navy Material Transportation Office

NAVMTO ...... Navy Movement and Transportation Office

NAVMTONORVA ... Naval Military Transportation Office, Norfolk, Virginia (DNAB)

NAVMTOREP ... Naval Military Transportation Office Representative (DNAB)

NAVMUTAID ... Navy Mutual Aid

NAVN .... Naval Aviation News

NAVNET .... Navigation Network (NVT)

NAVNET .... Navy Network (DOMA)

NAVNETDEP ... Naval Net Depot

NAVNON ...... Allied Naval Forces, North Norway [*NATO*] (NATG)

NAVNON ...... Naval Forces, Northern Norway [*NATO*] (AD)

NavNoPac .... Navigation in the North Pacific (AD)

NavNorlant ... Navigation in the North Atlantic (AD)

NAVNORTH ... Allied Naval Forces, Northern Europe [*NATO*]

NAVNUPWRSCOL ... Navy Nuclear Power School (DNAB)

NAVNUPWRTRAU ... Naval Nuclear Power Training Unit (MCD)

NAVNUPWRU ... Naval Nuclear Power Unit

NAVO .... National Association of Volvo Owners [*Defunct*] (EA)

NAVO .... Naval Oceanographic Office (USDC)

NAVOBS ...... Naval Observatory (MUGU)

NAVOBSY ..... Naval Observatory [*Navy*]

NAVOBSYFLAGSTAFFSTA ... Naval Observatory Flagstaff [*Arizona*] Station

NAVOBSYSTA ... Naval Observatory Station (DNAB)

NAVOCEANCOM ... Naval Oceanography Command Support System (GFGA)

NAVOCEANCOMCEN ... Naval Oceanography Command Center (DNAB)

NAVOCEANCOMDET ... Naval Oceanography Command Detachment (MCD)

NAVOCEANCOMFAC ... Naval Oceanography Command Facility (DNAB)

NAVOCEANCOMMDET ... Naval Oceanography Communications Detachment (DNAB)

NAVOCEANDISTO ... Naval Oceanographic District Office

NAVOCEANO ... Naval Oceanographic Office [*Also known as NOO; formerly, HO, NHO, USNHO*] [*Bay St. Louis, MS*]

NavOceanO ... Naval Oceanographic Officer (AD)

NAVOCEANOAIRSUPPGRU ... Naval Oceanographic Office Aircraft Support Squadron (DNAB)

NAVOCEANODET ... Naval Oceanographic Office Detachment (DNAB)

NAVOCEANOFC ... Naval Oceanographic Office (DNAB)

NAVOCEANPROFAC ... Naval Ocean Processing Facility (DNAB)

NAVOCEANSURVINFOCEN ... Naval Ocean Surveillance Information Center (DNAB)

NAVOCEANSYSCEN ... Naval Ocean Systems Center [*Formerly, NELC*] (DNAB)

NAVOCEANSYSCENLAB ... Naval Ocean Systems Center Laboratory (DNAB)

NAVOCEANSYSCENLABDET ... Naval Ocean Systems Center Laboratory Detachment (DNAB)

NAVOCFORMED ... Naval On-Call Force, Mediterranean [*NATO*] (NATG)

NAVOCS .... Naval Officer Candidate School

NAVOLF .... Navy Outlying Landing Field (DNAB)

NAVOPFAC ... Naval Operating Facility

NAVOPHTHALSUPPTRACT ... Naval Ophthalmic Support and Training Activity (DNAB)

NAVOPNET ... Naval Operations Network (CINC)

NAVOPSUPPGRU ... Naval Operations Support Group (DNAB)

NAVOPSUPPGRULANT ... Naval Operations Support Group, Atlantic

NAVOPSUPPGRUPAC ... Naval Operations Support Group, Pacific

NAVORD ...... Naval Ordnance (MUGU)

NAVORD ...... Naval Ordnance Systems Command [*Later, Naval Sea Systems Command*]

NAVORD ...... Naval Ordnance Systems Command Headquarters (USDC)

NAVORDCH ... Naval Ordnance Chart (MCD)

NAVORDENGFAC ... Naval Ordnance Engineering Facility (DNAB)

NAVORDFAC ... Naval Ordnance Facility

NAVORD ILS/MIS ... Naval Ordnance Systems Command, Integrated Logistics Support / Management Information System (DNAB)

NAVORDINST ... Naval Ordnance Systems Command Instruction

NAVORDLABFIELDIV ... Naval Ordnance Laboratory Field Division (DNAB)

NAVORDLIST... Navy Ordnance List (DNAB)
NAVORDMISTESTFAC... Naval Ordnance Missile Test Facility
NAVORDSTA... Naval Ordnance Station
NAVORDSTADET... Naval Ordnance Station Detachment (DNAB)
NAVORD-SWOP... Naval Ordnance Systems Command, Special Weapons Ordnance Publication
NAVORDSYSCO... Naval Ordnance Systems Command [*Later, Naval Sea Systems Command*] (MCD)
NAVORDSYSCOM... Naval Ordnance Systems Command [*Later, Naval Sea Systems Command*]
NAVORDSYSCOMHQ... Naval Ordnance Systems Command Headquarters
NAVORDSYSSUPPO... Naval Ordnance Systems Support Office
NAVORDSYSSUPPO... Naval Ordnance Systems Support Office (DNAB)
NAVORDSYSSUPPOLANT... Naval Ordnance Systems Support Office, Atlantic (DNAB)
NAVORDSYSSUPPOPAC... Naval Ordnance Systems Support Office, Pacific (DNAB)
NAVORDTECHREP... Naval Ordnance Technical Representative (MCD)
NAVORDTESTU... Naval Ordnance Test Unit
NAVORDU.... Naval Ordnance Unit
NAVORECSUPPACT... Naval Officer Record Support Activity (DNAB)
NAVOROUS... Naval Order of the United States [*Later, NOUS*] [*An association*] (EA)
NAVOSH ...... Navy Occupational Safety and Health (MCD)
NAVOSH DAP/MIS... Navy Occupational Safety and Deficiency Abatement/ Management Information System
NAVOSTAT... Navigation by Visual Observation of Satellites (DNAB)
NAVP .... National Association of Vision Professionals (EA)
NAVPA .... National Association of Veterans Program Administrators (EA)
NAVPAC....... Navigation Package (DNAB)
NAVPACEN... Navy Public Affairs Center (DNAB)
NAVPAOEASCO... Naval Public Affairs Office, East Coast
NAVPAOMWEST... Naval Public Affairs Office, Midwest
NAVPAOWESCO... Naval Public Affairs Office, West Coast
NAVPBRO... Naval Plant Branch Representative Officer (DNAB)
NAVPC .... National Association of Vision Program Consultants [*Later, NAVP*] (EA)
NAVPECO..... Naval Production Equipment Control Office
NAVPECOS... Navy Pentagon Computer Services Division (DNAB)
NAVPEP ..... Navy Program Evaluation Procedures
NAVPERS..... Bureau of Naval Personnel [*Also, BNP, BUPERS*]
NAVPERS..... Naval Personnel (AD)
NAVPERSCEN... Naval Personnel Center
NAVPERSINST... Bureau of Naval Personnel Instruction
NAVPERS-PRD... Bureau of Naval Personnel - Personnel Research Division
NAVPERSPROGSUPPACT... Naval Personnel Program Support Activity
NAVPERSRANDCEN... Naval Personnel Research and Development Center
NAVPERSRANDCENWB... Naval Personnel Research and Development Center, Washington [*DC*] Branch (DNAB)
NAVPERSRANDLAB... Navy Personnel Research and Development Laboratory
NAVPERSREACT... Naval Personnel Research Activity
NAVPERSRSCHACT... Naval Personnel Research Activity
NAVPETOFF... Navy Petroleum Office
NAVPETRAU... Naval Petroleum Training Unit (DNAB)
NAVPETRES... Naval Petroleum Reserves
NAVPETRESO... Naval Petroleum Reserves Office
NAVPGCOL... Navy Postgraduate College
NAVPGSCOL... Naval Postgraduate School
NAVPHIBASE... Naval Amphibious Base (MUGU)
NAVPHIBASELANT... Naval Amphibious Base Atlantic
NAVPHIBSCOL... Naval Amphibious School (NVT)
NAVPHIL... Naval Forces - Philippines (AD)
NAVPHOTOCEN... Naval Photographic Center
NAVPLANTDEVU... Naval Plant Development Unit (DNAB)
NAVPLANTREP... Naval Plant Representative Office [*or Officer*] (MCD)
NAVPLANTREPO... Naval Plant Representative Office [*or Officer*]
NAVPLANTTECHREP... Naval Plant Technical Representative (DNAB)
NAVPO .... National Association of Van Pool Operators [*Later, Association of Commuter Transportation*] (EA)
NAVPOLAROCEANCEN... Naval Polar Oceanography Center (DNAB)
NAVPOOL .... Navigation Parameter Common Pool (NASA)
NAVPOOL .... Navigation [*Parameter Common*] Pool
NAVPORCO... Naval Port Control Office [*or Officer*]
NAVPORCOF... Naval Port Control Office [*or Officer*]
NAVPORTCO... Naval Port Control Office [*Or Officer*] (DNAB)
NAVPOSTGRADSCOL... Naval Postgraduate School
NAVPOWFAC... Naval Powder Factory
NAVPrD........ Navistar Intl Cv Jr D Pref [*NYSE symbol*] (TTSB)
NAVPREFLIGHTSCOL... Naval Preflight School
NAVPrG........ Navistar Intl $6 cm Cv Pfd [*NYSE symbol*] (TTSB)
NAVPRIMSTDEPT... Navy Primary Standards Department (DNAB)
NAVPRIS...... Naval Prison
NAVPRO...... Naval Plant Representative Office [*or Officer*]
NAVPROPLT... Naval Propellant Plant (DNAB)
NAVPROV .... Naval Proving Ground [*Dahlgren, VA*]
NAVPTO...... Navy Passenger Transportation Office (DNAB)
NAVPUB....... Naval Publications (AD)
NAVPUB....... Navy Publications and Printing Service
NAVPUBFORMCEN... Naval Publications and Forms Center (MCD)
NAVPUBINST... Navy Publications and Printing Service Instruction
NAVPUBPRINTO... Navy Publications and Printing Office
NAVPUBPRINTSERV... Naval Publications and Printing Service (DNAB)
NAVPUBPRINTSERVO... Navy Publications and Printing Service Office
NAVPUBSCONBD... Navy Department Publications Control Board
NAVPUBWKSCEN... Navy Public Works Center
NAVPUBWKSDEPT... Navy Public Works Department (DNAB)

NAVPUR ...... Navy Purchasing Office
NAVPURDEP... Navy Purchasing Department (DNAB)
NAVPURO.... Navy Purchasing Office
NAVPVNTMEDU... Navy Preventive Medicine Unit
NAVR .... Navarre Corp. [*NASDAQ symbol*] (SAG)
NAVR .... Navigator (WGA)
NAVRA......... National Association of Volunteer Referral Agencies [*Australia*]
NAVRADCO... Naval Regional Active Duty Cryptologic Officer (DNAB)
NAVRADCON... Naval Radiological Control
NAVRADLDEFLAB... Navy Radiological Defense Laboratory
NAVRADRECFAC... Naval Radio Receiving Facility (DNAB)
NAVRADSTA... Naval Radio Station
NAVRADTRANSFAC... Naval Radio Transmitting Facility (DNAB)
NAVRDSATCOMMGRU... Naval Research and Development Satellite Communications Group (MUGU)
NAVRECCEN... Naval Recreation Center (DNAB)
NAVRECONTACSUPPCENLANT... Naval Reconnaissance and Tactical Support Center, Atlantic (DNAB)
NAVRECONTECHSUPPCEN... Naval Reconnaissance and Technical Support Center
NAVRECONTECHSUPPCENLANT... Naval Reconnaissance and Technical Support Center, Atlantic (DNAB)
NAVRECONTECHSUPPCENPAC... Naval Reconnaissance and Technical Support Center, Pacific (DNAB)
NAVRECSTA... Naval Receiving Station (NVT)
NAVREF .... National Association of Veterans' Research and Education Foundations (NTPA)
NAVREGAIRCARCONO... Navy Regional Air Cargo Central [*or Control*] Office (DNAB)
NAVREGCONTO... Navy Regional Contracting Office (DNAB)
NAVREGCONTODET... Navy Regional Contracting Office Detachment (DNAB)
NAVREGDENCEN... Navy Regional Dental Center (DNAB)
NAVREGDENCENBRFAC... Navy Regional Dental Center Branch Facility (DNAB)
NAVREGDENCLIN... Navy Regional Dental Clinic (DNAB)
NAVREGFINCEN... Navy Regional Finance Center
NAVREGFINCENBRKLN... Navy Regional Finance Center, Brooklyn [*New York*] (DNAB)
NAVREGFINCENGLAKES... Navy Regional Finance Center, Great Lakes (DNAB)
NAVREGFINCENNORVA... Navy Regional Finance Center, Norfolk, Virginia (DNAB)
NAVREGFINCENPEARL... Navy Regional Finance Center, Pearl Harbor [*Hawaii*] (DNAB)
NAVREGFINCENSDIEGO... Navy Regional Finance Center, San Diego [*California*] (DNAB)
NAVREGFINCENSFRAN... Navy Regional Finance Center, San Francisco [*California*] (DNAB)
NAVREGFINOFC... Navy Regional Finance Office (DNAB)
NAVREGMEDCEN... Naval Regional Medical Center (DNAB)
NAVREGMEDCENBRCLINIC... Naval Regional Medical Center Branch Clinic (DNAB)
NAVREGMEDCENBRHOSP... Naval Regional Medical Center Branch Hospital (DNAB)
NAVREGMEDCENCLINIC... Naval Regional Medical Center Clinic (DNAB)
NAVREGMEDCENDET... Naval Regional Medical Center Detachment (DNAB)
NAVREGPEO... Naval Regional Plant Equipment Office [*or Officer*] (DNAB)
NAVREGPROCO... Navy Regional Procurement Office (DNAB)
NAVREGS .... Navy Regulations
NAVREL .... Navy Relief Society
NAVREPFAC... Naval Repair Facility (MCD)
NAVRES .... Naval Reserve
NAVRESCEN... Naval Research Center (DNAB)
NAVRESCEN... Naval Reserve Center (DNAB)
NAVRESCOMICEDEFOR... Naval Reserve Commander, Iceland Defense Force (DNAB)
NAVRESFOR... Naval Reserve Force (DNAB)
NAVRESLAB... Naval Research Laboratory [*ONR*]
NAVRESMANPOWERCEN... Naval Reserve Manpower Center
NAVRESMANPWRCEN... Naval Reserve Manpower Center (DNAB)
NAVRESMIDSCOL... Naval Reserve Midshipmen's School
NAVRESO .... Navy Resale System Office (PDAA)
NAVRESO .... Navy Resale Systems Office (DNAB)
NAVRESOFSO... Navy Resale Systems Field Support Office (DNAB)
NAVRESOREACT... Naval Reserve Officer Recording Activity (DNAB)
NAVRESOREP... Navy Resale Systems Office Representative (DNAB)
NAVRESREDCOM... Naval Reserve Readiness Command (DNAB)
NAVRESREDCOMREG... Naval Reserve Readiness Command Region (DNAB)
NAVRESSECGRP... Naval Reserve Security Group (DNAB)
NAVRESSO... Navy Resale and Services Support Office
NAVRESSOFO... Navy Resale and Services Support Office, Field Office (DNAB)
NAVRESTRA... Naval Reserve Training (DNAB)
NAVRESTRACEN... Naval Reserve Training Center
NAVRESTRACOM... Naval Reserve Training Command
NAVRESTRAFAC... Naval Reserve Training Facility (DNAB)
NAVRESUBDET... Naval Reserve Submarine Detachment (DNAB)
NAVRESUPPOFC... Naval Reserve Support Office (DNAB)
NAVRESUPPOFCDET... Naval Reserve Support Office Detachment (DNAB)
NAVRETRAINCOM... Naval Retraining Command
NAVROM... Romanian Merchant Marine (AD)
NAVROUTE... Navy Routing Office
NAVRSCHLAB... Naval Research Laboratory [*ONR*]
NAVS .... National Anti-Vivisection Society (EA)
NAVS .... National Association of Variety Stores [*Defunct*] (EA)
NAVS .... Navigation System
NAVS .... North American Vegetarian Society (EA)
NAVSAFECEN... Naval Safety Center
NAVSANDA... Bureau of Supplies and Accounts [*Later, NSUPSC*] [*Navy*]
NAVSAT .... Navigational Satellite [*NASA*]
navsat.......... Navigational Satellite (AD)

NavSat......... Navigation in the South Atlantic (AD)
NAVSATCOMMDET... Navy Satellite Communications Detachment (DNAB)
NAVSATCOMMFAC... Navy Satellite Communications Facility (DNAB)
NAVSATCOMMNET... Navy Satellite Communications Network (DNAB)
NAVSCAP..... Allied Naval Forces, Scandinavian Approaches [NATO] (NATG)
NAVSCAP..... Naval Forces, Scandinavian Approaches [NATO] (AD)
NAVSCIADV... Naval Science Advisor (DNAB)
NAVSCIENTECHINTCEN... Naval Scientific and Technical Intelligence Center
NAVSCITECHGRUFE... Naval Scientific and Technical Group, Far East (DNAB)
NAVSCOLCEOFF... Naval Civil Engineer Corps Officers School (DNAB)
NAVSCOLCOM... Naval Schools Command
NAVSCOLCOM NORVA... Naval Schools Command, Norfolk, Virginia
NAVSCOLCONST... Naval Schools Construction
NAVSCOLCRYPTOREP... Naval School of Cryptographic Repair (DNAB)
NAVSCOLCYROGENICS... Naval School of Cryogenics (DNAB)
NAVSCOLDEEPSEADIVER... Navy School for Deep Sea Divers (DNAB)
NAVSCOLEOD... Naval School of Explosive Ordnance Disposal (DNAB)
NAVSCOLHOSPADMIN... Naval School of Hospital Administration (DNAB)
NAVSCOLMINWAR... Naval School of Mine War (DNAB)
NAVSCOLMINWARFARE... Naval Mine Warfare School
NAVSCOLPHYDISTMGT... Naval School of Physical Distribution Management
　　(DNAB)
NAVSCOLTRANSMGT... Naval School of Transportation Management (DNAB)
NAVSCSCOL... Naval Supply Corps School
NAVSCSCOLDET... Naval Supply Corps School Detachment (DNAB)
NAVSEA....... Naval Avionics Support Equipment Appraisal (NG)
NAVSEA....... Naval Sea [formerly, Ship] Systems Command (MCD)
NAVSEAADSO... Naval Sea Systems Command Automated Data Systems Office
　　(DNAB)
NAVSEAADSODET... Naval Sea Systems Command Automated Data Systems
　　Office Detachment (DNAB)
NAVSEACARCOORD... Naval Sea Cargo Coordinator (DNAB)
NAVSEACARCOR... Navy Sea Cargo Coordinator (NVT)
NAVSEACEN... Naval Sea Support Center (DNAB)
NAVSEACENFSO... Naval Sea Support Center, Fleet Support Office (DNAB)
NAVSEACENHAWLAB... Naval Sea Support Center, Hawaii Laboratory (DNAB)
NAVSEACENLANT... Naval Sea Support Center, Atlantic (MCD)
NAVSEACENLANTDET... Naval Sea Support Center, Atlantic Detachment (DNAB)
NAVSEACENPACDET... Naval Sea Support Center, Pacific Detachment (DNAB)
NAVSEACENREP... Naval Sea Support Center Representative (DNAB)
NAVSEACENTLANT... Naval Sea Support Center - Atlantic (AD)
NAVSEACENTPAC... Naval Sea Support Center - Pacific (AD)
NAVSEACOHREP... Naval Sea Systems Command Complex Overhaul
　　Representative (DNAB)
NAVSEADET... Naval Sea Systems Command Detachment (DNAB)
NAVSEAMATREP... Naval Sea Systems Command Material Representative (DNAB)
NAVSEAMQAO... Naval Sea Systems Command Material Quality Assessment
　　Office (DNAB)
NAVSEASYSCOM... Naval Sea [Formerly, Ship] Systems Command (DNAB)
NAVSEASYSCOMGTOWESTPAC... Naval Sea Systems Command Management
　　Office, Western Pacific (DNAB)
NAVSEASYSCOMHQ... Naval Sea Systems Command Headquarters (DNAB)
NAVSEATECHREP... Naval Sea Systems Command Technical Representative
　　(DNAB)
NAVSEC....... Naval Ship Engineering Center
NAVSECENGRFAC... Naval Security Engineering Facility
NAVSECGRU... Naval Security Group
NAVSECGRUACT... Navy Security Group Activity
NAVSECGRUACTFO... Naval Security Group Activity Field Office (DNAB)
NAVSECGRUACTSPECOMMDIV... Naval Security Group Activity, Special
　　Communications Division (DNAB)
NAVSECGRUCOM... Naval Security Group Command (MCD)
NAVSECGRUDET... Naval Security Group Detachment
NAVSECGRUHQ... Navy Security Group Headquarters
NAVSECGRUMGDAT... Naval Security Group Command Management Data (DNAB)
NAVSECGRU MIS... Naval Security Group Management Information System
　　(DNAB)
NAVSECINST... Naval Ship Engineering Center Instruction
NAVSECMECHSDIV... Naval Ship Engineering Center, Mechanicsburg
　　[Pennsylvania] Division (DNAB)
NAVSECNORDIV... Naval Ship Engineering Center, Norfolk Division
NAVSECPHILA... Naval Ship Engineering Center, Philadelphia Division
NAVSECPHILAD... Naval Ship Engineering Center Philadelphia Division
NAVSECPHILADIV... Naval Ship Engineering Center, Philadelphia Division
NAVSECSDIEGODIV... Naval Ship Engineering Center, San Diego [California]
　　Division (DNAB)
NAVSECSTA... Naval Security Station
NAVSEEACT... Naval Shore Electronics Engineering Activity
NAVSEEC..... Naval Electronics Systems Command Headquarters
NAVSEG....... Navigation Satellite Executive Steering Group
NAVSERVSCOLCOM... Naval Service School Command
NAVSEX... Naval Standing Exercises (NATG)
NAVSHIP...... Naval Ship Systems Command [Later, NAVSEA, NSSC]
NAVSHIPCOM... Naval Ship Systems Command (AD)
NAVSHIPENGCEN... Naval Ship Engineering Center
NAVSHIPENGSUPPACT... Naval Ship Engineering Support Activity
NAVSHIPLO... Navy Shipbuilding Office
NAVSHIPMISENGSYS... Naval Ships Missile Systems Engineering System (DNAB)
NAVSHIPMISYSENGSTA... Naval Ship Missile System Engineering Station
NAVSHIPREPFAC... Naval Ship Repair Facility
NAVSHIPREPO... Naval Ship Repair Officer (DNAB)
NAVSHIPRSCHDEVCEN... Naval Ship Research and Development Center [Also,
　　DTNSRDC] (DNAB)
NAVSHIPRSCHDEVCENANNA... Naval Ship Research and Development Center,
　　Annapolis [Maryland] Division (DNAB)

NAVSHIPS ... Naval Ship Systems Command [Later, NAVSEA, NSSC]
NAVSHIPS ... Naval Ship Systems Command Headquarters [Formerly, BuShips]
　　(USDC)
NAVSHIPSA... Navy Shipbuilding Scheduling Activity
NAVSHIPSINST... Naval Ship Systems Command Instruction
NAVSHIPSO... Navy Shipbuilding Scheduling Office
NAVSHIPSTO... Navy Ships' Store Office (DNAB)
NAVSHIPSYSCOM... Naval Ship Systems Command [Later, NAVSEA, NSSC]
NAVSHIPSYSCOMHQ... Naval Ship Systems Command Headquarters
NAVSHIPTECHSMAN... Navy Ship Technical Manual (DNAB)
NAVSHIPWPNSYSENGSTA... Naval Ship Weapon Systems Engineering Station
　　[Port Hueneme, CA] (DNAB)
NAVSHIPWPNSYSENGSTADET... Naval Ship Weapon Systems Engineering Station
　　Detachment (DNAB)
NAVSHIPWPNSYSENGSTAREP... Naval Ship Weapon Sytems Engineering Station
　　Representative (DNAB)
NAVSHIPY ... Naval Shipyard (SAA)
NAVSHIPYD... Naval Shipyard
NavShipyd... Naval Shipyard (AD)
NAVSIT .... Navy Scholarship Information Team (DNAB)
NAVSMO...... Navigation Satellite Management Office
NAVSO......... Naval Supply Office
NAVSO......... Navy, Secretary's Office
NAVSO......... Navy Staff Offices
NavSoPac ... Navigation of the South Pacific (AD)
NAVSOUTH... Allied Naval Forces, Southern Europe [NATO] (NATG)
NAVSOUTH... Naval Forces, Southern Europe (AD)
NAVSPACCOM... Naval Space Command (DOMA)
NAVSPASUR... Naval Space Surveillance [Center or System]
NAVSPASYSAC... Naval Space Systems Activity (DNAB)
NAVSPEC... Navy Specification (AAGC)
NAVSPECWAR... Naval Special Warfare (MUSM)
NAVSPECWARGP... Naval Special Warfare Group (AABC)
NAVSPECWARGRAUDET... Naval Special Warfare Group Detachment (DNAB)
NAVSPECWARGRU... Naval Special Warfare Group (NVT)
NAVSPECWARU... Naval Special Warfare Unit (DNAB)
NAVSPECWARUDET... Naval Special Warfare Unit Detachment (DNAB)
NAVSSES... Naval Ship Systems Engineering Station
NAVSSESDET... Naval Ship Systems Engineering Station Detachment (DNAB)
NAVSTA....... Naval Station
NAVSTAG...... Naval Standardization Agreement [NATO]
NAVSTALANT... Naval Stations Atlantic
NAVSTAPAC... Naval Stations Pacific
NAVSTAR..... Navigation Satellite Tracking and Ranging [Later, GPS] [Air Force]
NAVSTAR..... Navigation System Using Time and Ranging (AD)
NAVSTAR..... Navy Study of Transport Aircraft Requirements
NAVSTAR-GPS... Navigation Satellite Tracking and Ranging Global Positioning
　　System [Air Force] (MCD)
NAVSTD...... Navy Standard (AAGC)
NAVSTIC...... Naval Scientific and Technical Intelligence Center
NAVSTKWARCEN... Naval Strike Warfare Center (DOMA)
NAVSTRIP... Navy Standard Requisitioning and Issuing Procedure
NAVSUBBASE... Naval Submarine Base
NAVSUBINSURV... Naval Sub-Board of Inspection and Survey (DNAB)
NAVSUBMEDCEN... Naval Submarine Medical Center
NAVSUBMEDRSCHLAB... Naval Submarine Medical Research Laboratory (DNAB)
NAVSUBSCOL... Naval Submarine School
NAVSUBSUPPBASE... Naval Submarine Support Base (DNAB)
NAVSUBSUPPBASEDET... Naval Submarine Support Base Detachment (DNAB)
NAVSUBSUPPFAC... Navy Submarine Support Facility (DNAB)
NAVSUBTRACENPAC... Naval Submarine Training Center, Pacific (DNAB)
NAVSUP....... Naval Supplies
NAVSUP....... Naval Supply Systems Command [Formerly, Bureau of Supplies and
　　Accounts] (MCD)
NAVSUPACT... Naval Support Activity (NVT)
NAVSUPCEN... Naval Supply Center
NAVSUPDEP... Naval Supply Depot (DNAB)
NAVSUPDEPT... Naval Supply Department (DNAB)
NAVSUPFORANT... Naval Support Forces, Antarctica
NAVSUPGRU... Naval Support Group (NVT)
NAVSUPINST... Naval Supply Systems Command Instruction
NAVSUPMIS... Navy Supply Management Information System
NAVSUPO .... Navy Supply Office (DNAB)
NAVSUPOANX... Navy Supply Office Annex (DNAB)
NAVSUPORANT... Naval Support Forces, Antarctica (AD)
NAVSUPPACT... Naval Supply [or Support] Activity
NAVSUPPACTDET... Naval Support Activity Detachment (DNAB)
NAVSUPPFOR... Naval Support Force
NAVSUPPFORANTARCTIC... Naval Support Forces, Antarctic
NAVSUPRANDDFAC... Navy Supply Research and Development Facility (DNAB)
NAVSUPRANDFA... Naval Supply Research and Development Facility
NAVSUPSYSCOM... Naval Supply Systems Command [Formerly, Bureau of
　　Supplies and Accounts]
NAVSUPSYSCOMHQ... Naval Supply System Command Headquarters
NAVSURFAC... Naval Surface Force, Pacific
NAVSURFLANT... Naval Surface Force, Atlantic (DNAB)
NAVSURFLANTREADSUPPGRU... Naval Surface Force, Atlantic Readiness Support
　　Group (DNAB)
NAVSURFPACDAT... Naval Surface Force, Pacific Dependents' Assistance Team
　　(DNAB)
NAVSURFWPNCEN... Naval Surface Weapons Center (PDAA)
NAVSURMISYS... Naval Surface Missile Systems (MCD)
NAVSWC...... Naval Surface Warfare Center [Silver Spring, MD]
NAVSWC...... Naval Surface Weapons Center [Later, NSWC] (CAAL)
NAVSWCFAC... Naval Surface Weapons Center Facility (DNAB)

NAVSWCREP... Naval Surface Weapons Center Representative (DNAB)
NAVSWOP ... Naval Special Weapons Ordnance Publication
NAVSYD....... Naval Shipyard
NAVTA .... National Automatic Vendors' Trade Association (EA)
navtac........... Navigation Tactical (AD)
NAVTAC .... Navigation Tactical (AD)
NAVTAC .... Tactical Navigation System
NAVTACDATASYSDEVSITE... Naval Tactical Data Systems Development and Evaluation Site (DNAB)
NAVTACDOCACT... Navy Tactical Doctrine Activity
NAVTACDOCDEVPRODACT... Navy Tactical Doctrine Development and Production Activity (DNAB)
NAVTACINTEROPSUPPACT... Navy Tactical Interoperability Support Activity (DNAB)
NAVTACINTEROPSUPPACTDET... Navy Tactical Interoperability Support Activity Detachment (DNAB)
NAVTACSAT... Naval Tactical Satellite (DNAB)
NAVTACSTANS... Naval Tactical Standards (MCD)
NAVTACSUPPACT... Navy Tactical Support Activity (NVT)
NAVTAG .... Naval Tactical Game
NAVTAG .... Navy Tactical Action Game
NAVTASC...... Naval Telecommunications Automation Support Center (DNAB)
NAVTASCDETLANT... Naval Telecommunications Automation Support Center, Atlantic (DNAB)
NAVTASCDETPAC... Naval Telecommunications Automation Support Center, Pacific (DNAB)
NAVTEC .... National Association of Vocational-Technical Education Communicators (EA)
NAVTECHJAP... Naval Technical Mission to Japan
NAVTECHMISJAP... Naval Technical Mission to Japan (DNAB)
NAVTECHREP... Naval Technical Representative
NAVTECHTRACEN... Naval Air Technical Training Center
NAVTECHTRACENDET... Naval Technical Training Center Detachment (DNAB)
NAVTECMISEU... Naval Technical Mission in Europe
NAVTELCOM... Naval Telecommunications Command
NAVTELSYSIC... Naval Telcommunications System Integration Center (DNAB)
NAVTIS .... National Vessel Traffic Information System (AD)
NAVTIS .... Naval Training Information System (MCD)
NAVTIS ADS... Naval Training Information System with Automated Data Systems (DNAB)
NAVTNG....... Navigator Training [Air Force]
NAVTNGSq... Navigator Training Squadron [Air Force]
NAVTORPSTA... Naval Torpedo Station
NAVTP .... National Association of Vertical Transportation Professionals
NAVTRA .... Naval Training Command
NAVTRACEN... Naval Training Center (DNAB)
NAVTRACOM... Naval Training Command
NAVTRADEV... Naval Training Device Center
NAVTRADEVCEN... Naval Training Device Center
NAVTRADEVSUPCEN... Naval Training Devices Supply Center (DNAB)
NAVTRADISTCEN... Naval Training and Distribution Center
NAVTRAEQUIPC... Naval Training Equipment Center
NAVTRAEQUIPCEN... Naval Training Equipment Center
NAVTRAEQUIPCENFEO... Naval Training Equipment Center Field Office (DNAB)
NAVTRAEQUIPCENREPCEN... Naval Training Equipment Center, Representative for the Center (DNAB)
NAVTRAEQUIPCENREPLANT... Naval Training Equipment Center Representative, Atlantic (DNAB)
NAVTRAEQUIPCENREPPAC... Naval Training Equipment Center Representative, Pacific (DNAB)
NAVTRAFSAT... Navigational/Traffic-Control Satellite (MCD)
NAVTRAIDSCEN... Naval Training Aids Center
NAVTRAINST... Naval Training Support Command Instruction (MCD)
NAVTRANSCO... Naval Transportation Coordinating Office
NAVTRAPUBCEN... Naval Training Publications Center (MCD)
NAVTRASAT... Navigation/Traffic Control Satellite (MCD)
NAVTRASCOL... Naval Training School
NAVTRASTA... Naval Training Station
NAVTRASYSCEN... Naval Training Systems Center [Orlando, FL]
NAVUSEARANDCEN... Naval Undersea Research and Development Center (MCD)
NAVUSEARESDEVCEN... Naval Undersea Research and Development Center
NAVUSEAWARCEN... Naval Undersea Warfare Center
NAVUWSEC... Naval Underwater Weapons Systems Engineering Center (AD)
NAVUWSES... Naval Underwater Systems Engineering Center
NAVUWSOUNDLAB... Naval Underwater Sound Laboratory [Later, NUSC]
NAVVF .... National Association of the Van Valkenburg Family (EA)
NAVWAG...... Naval Warfare Analysis Group
NAVWARCOL... Naval War College
Nav War C Rev... Naval War College. Review [A publication] (DLA)
NAVWASS... Navigation and Weapon-Aiming Subsystem (MCD)
NAVWEARSCHFA... Navy Weather Research Facility
NAVWEASERV... Naval Weather Service Command
NAVWEPEVALFAC... Naval Weapons Evaluation Facility [Kirtland Air Force Base, NM] (DNAB)
NAVWEPS.... Bureau of Naval Weapons [Obsolete]
NAVWESA.... Naval Weapons Engineering Support Activity
NAVWESS.... National Aviation Weather System Study (NOAA)
NAVWESTOCEANCEN... Naval Western Oceanographic Center (DNAB)
NAVWPNCEN... Naval Weapons Center (MCD)
NAVWPNENGSUPPACT... Naval Weapons Engineering Support Activity (DNAB)
NAVWPNEVALFAC... Naval Weapons Evaluation Facility [Kirtland Air Force Base, NM]
NAVWPNLAB... Naval Weapons Laboratory [Later, NSWC]
NAVWPNQAO... Naval Weapons Quality Assurance Office [Washington, DC]
NAVWPNQUALASSURO... Naval Weapons Quality Assurance Office [Washington, DC]

NAVWPNSCEN... Naval Weapons Center
NAVWPNSERVO... Naval Weapons Services Office [Also, NWSO, WEPSO]
NAVWPNSTA... Naval Weapons Station (MCD)
NAVWPNSTRACEN... Naval Weapons Training Center (DNAB)
NAVWPNSUPPACT... Naval Weapons Support Activity (DNAB)
NAVWPNSUPPCEN... Naval Weapons Support Center (DNAB)
NAVWPNSYSANALO... Naval Weapons Systems Analysis Office
NAVWUIS ..... Navy Work Unit Information Service (IID)
NAVXDIVINGU... Navy Experimental Diving Unit
NAVYCAB..... Navy Contract Adjustment Board (AAGC)
NAVYEO....... Navigator's Yeoman [British military] (DMA)
NAW .... Narathiwat [Thailand] [Airport symbol] (OAG)
NAW .... National Agricultural Workers Union
NAW .... National Association for Women (NADA)
NAW .... National Association of Wholesaler-Distributors [Washington, DC] (EA)
NAW .... National Association of Wholesalers (NADA)
NAW .... National Association of Widows [British] (DI)
NAW .... Negative Afterwave [Microelectrode recording]
NAW .... Newair [Denmark ICAO designator] (FAAC)
N/AW .... Night/Adverse Weather Evaluator (IEEE)
NAW .... Non-All-Weather (CINC)
NAW .... North African Waters
NAW .... Northwest African Waters
NAWA .... National Academy of Western Art (EA)
NAWA .... National Apple Week Association [Later, NAM] (EA)
NAWA .... National Association of Women Artists (EA)
NAWA .... North American Warmblood Association (EA)
NAWAC ..... National Aviation Weather Advisory Committee [Marine science] (OSRA)
NAWAC ..... National Weather Analysis Center [Air Force, Navy]
NAWAF ..... Navy with Air Force
NAWAPA ..... North American Water and Power Alliance
NAWAR....... Navy with Army
NAWARCOL... Naval War College (MUGU)
NAWAS .... National Attack Warning System [Military] (IAA)
NAWAS .... National Warning System [Civil Defense]
NAWatch..... North American Watch Corp. [Associated Press] (SAG)
NAWAU........ National Aviation Weather Advisory Unit [Federal Aviation Administration] (USDC)
NAWB....... National Association of Wine and Beer Makers [British] (DBA)
NAWB....... National Association of Wine Bottlers [Later, NWA] (EA)
NAWBM....... National Association of Window Blind Manufacturers [British] (BI)
NAWBO....... National Association of Women Business Owners [Chicago, IL] (EA)
NAWC .... National Art Workers Community [Later, FCA] (EA)
NAWC .... National Association for Women in Careers [Later, NAFWIC] (EA)
NAWC .... National Association of Water Companies (EA)
NAWC .... National Association of Waterproofing Contractors (NTPA)
NAWC .... National Association of Women's Centers [Defunct] (EA)
NAWC .... National Association of Women's Clubs [British] (DBA)
NAWC .... Naval Air Warfare Center (DOMA)
NAWC .... Naval War College
NAWC .... North American Watch Corp. [NASDAQ symbol] (SAG)
NAWC .... North Atlantic Women's Conference (PSS)
NAWCAS...... National Association of Women's and Children's Apparel Salesmen [Later, Bureau of Wholesale Sales Representatives] (EA)
NAWCC .... National Association of Watch and Clock Collectors (EA)
NAWCC .... National Association of Women in Chambers of Commerce (EA)
NAWCC .... North American Wetlands Conservation Council (COE)
NAWCH .... National Association for the Welfare of Children in Hospital [British]
NAWCJ .... National Association of Women in Criminal Justice (EA)
NAWCM ...... National Association of Wiping Cloth Manufacturers [Later, IAWCM] (EA)
NAWCWD .... Naval Air Warfare Center Weapons Divison
NAWCWPNS... Naval Air Warfare Center Weapons Division
NAWD .... Notice of Award
NAWDA........ North American Working Dog Association (EA)
NAWDAC...... National Association for Women Deans, Administrators, and Counselors (EA)
NAWDC .... National Association of Waste Disposal Contractors [British] (DCTA)
NAWDC .... National Association of Women Deans and Counselors [Later, NAWDAC] (EA)
NAWDEX...... National Water Data Exchange [United States Geological Survey] [Reston, VA] [Information service or system]
NAWDP........ National Association of Workforce Development Professionals (NTPA)
NAWE .... National Association for Women in Education (NTPA)
NAWE .... National Association of Waterfront Employers (NTPA)
NAWESA ..... Naval Weapons Engineering Support Activity (PDAA)
NAWF .... National Aborigine Welfare Fund [Australia] (NADA)
NAWF .... Nodes Above White Flower [Botany]
NAWF .... North American Waterfowl Federation
NAWF .... North American Wildlife Foundation (EA)
NAWF .... North American Wolf Society (EA)
NAWFA .... North Atlantic Westbound Freight Association (DS)
NAWFC .... National Association of Wholesale Fur Cleaners
NAWFC .... National Association of Women Federal Contractors [Later, NAWGC] (EA)
NAWFMP...... North American Waterfowl Management Plan of 1986 (COE)
NAWG .... National Association of Wheat Growers (EA)
NAWGA .... National-American Wholesale Grocers' Association
NAWGC .... National Association of Women Government Contractors [Defunct] (EA)
NAWGF .... National Association of Wheat Growers Foundation (EA)
NAWGP......., National Agenda for Women's Grants Program [Australia]

NAWH..........	National Association of Women in Horticulture [*Defunct*] (EA)
NAWH..........	Norwegian-American Historical Museum (AD)
NAWHP........	National Association of Women's Health Professionals (NTPA)
NAWHSL......	National Association of Women Highway Safety Leaders (EA)
NAWiC........	National Association for Women in Careers [*Later, NAFWIC*] (EA)
NAWIC........	National Association of Women in Construction (EA)
NAWID........	National Association of Water Institute Directors (EA)
NAWID........	National Association of Writing Instrument Distributors (EA)
NAWJ..........	National Association of Women Judges (EA)
NAWK..........	National Association of Warehouse Keepers [*British*] (DBA)
NAWL..........	National Association of Women Lawyers (EA)
NAWL..........	North American Iterative Weighted Least Squares (SAA)
NAWLA........	North American Wholesale Lumber Association (EA)
NAWM........	National Association of Wool Manufacturers [*Later, American Textile Manufacturers Institute*] (EA)
NAWM........	Naval Air Weapons Meet (MUGU)
NAWMD........	National Association of Waste Material Dealers [*Later, NARI*]
NAWME.......	National Average Weekly Male Earning
NAWMP........	National Association of Waste Material Producers [*Defunct*] (EA)
NAWMP........	Naval Aviation Weapons Maintenance Program (MCD)
NAWND.......	National Association of Wholesale Newspaper Distributors (DGA)
NAWP..........	National Anti-Waste Programme [*British*] (DCTA)
NAWP..........	National Association for Widowed People [*Later, IAWP*] (EA)
NAWP..........	National Association of Women Pharmacists [*British*] (DBA)
NAWPA........	North American Water and Power Alliance
NAWPB........	National Association of Wholesale Pie Bakers (EA)
NAWPB........	National Association of Wine Producers and Bottlers [*Later, NWA*] (EA)
NAWPC........	National Aircraft War Production Council [*World War II*]
NAWPF........	National Aviation Weather Processing Facility [*FAA*] (TAG)
NAWPF........	North American Wildlife Park Foundation (EA)
NAWPM........	National Association of Wholesale Paint Merchants [*British*] (BI)
NAWPS........	National Association of Word Processing Specialists [*Later, WPS*] (EA)
NAWPU........	National Association of Water Power Users [*British*] (DBA)
NAWQC........	National Ambient Water Quality Criteria (WPI)
NAWR..........	National Assembly of Women Religious
NAWRSRF ...	New Age World Religious and Scientific Research Foundation (EA)
NAWS..........	National Agricultural Workers Survey
NAWS..........	National Aviation Weather System
NAWS..........	Naval Air Weapons Station
NAWS..........	NORAD Attack Warning System (MCD)
NAWS..........	North African War Shipping [*World War II*]
NAWS..........	North American Wolf Society (EA)
NAWSS........	North American Wilderness Survival School
NAWT..........	National Animal Welfare Trust (WDAA)
NAWT..........	National Association of Waste Transporters (NTPA)
NAWTPD......	Naval All Weather Testing Program Detachment
NAWTS........	National Association of World Trade Secretaries [*Later, AWTCE*] (EA)
NAWU..........	National Agricultural Workers Union (EA)
NAWU..........	National Asphalt Workers' Union [*A union*] [*British*]
NAWW..........	National Association of Wheat Weavers (EA)
NAWWO.......	National Association of Woolen and Worsted Overseers [*Later, NATS*] (EA)
NAX	Ewa, HI [*Location identifier FAA*] (FAAL)
NAX	New Arcadia Explorations [*Vancouver Stock Exchange symbol*]
NAX	Norwegian Air Shuttle, AS [*FAA designator*] (FAAC)
NAXSTA	Naval Air Experimental Station
NAY	Navegacion y Servicios Aereos Canarios SA [*Spain ICAO designator*] (FAAC)
NAY	New Alster Energy [*Vancouver Stock Exchange symbol*]
NAYA	North American Yngling Association . (EA)
NAYC	National Association of Youth Clubs [*British*] (DI)
NAYCEO	National Association of Youth and Community Education Officers [*British*] (DI)
NAYGTA......	North American Youth Glider Training Association
NAYO	National Association of Youth Orchestras (EAIO)
NAYPCAS.....	National Association of Young People's Counselling and Advisory Services [*British*] (DI)
NAYPIC........	National Association of Young People in Care [*British*]
NAYRE	National Association for Year-Round Education (EA)
NAYRU........	North American Yacht Racing Union (EA)
NAYSI	North American Youth Sport Institute (EA)
NAYT	National Association of Youth Theatres [*British*] (DBA)
NAYTA	National Association of Youth Training Agencies (AIE)
NAYW	National Association for Young Writers [*Defunct*] (EA)
NAZ.............	Nazarene
Naz	Nazir (BJA)
NAZ.............	Normal Analytical Zone [*Chemistry*]
NAZ.............	Nuveen Arizona Premium Income [*NYSE symbol*] (SAG)
NAZ.............	Nuveen AZ Prem Inc. Muni Fd [*NYSE symbol*] (TTSB)
NAZ.............	Servicios Aereos del Nazas SA de CV [*Mexico ICAO designator*] (FAAC)
NAZI.............	Nationalsozialistische Deutsche Arbeiterpartei [*National Socialist German Workers' Party, 1919-45*] [*Political party*]
NB..............	Brooklyn Public Library, Brooklyn, NY [*Library symbol Library of Congress*] (LCLS)
NB..............	Nabonidus and Belshazzar (BJA)
NB..............	Nail Bed (DMAA)
NB..............	Nanobarn [*Unit of Measure*]
NB..............	Narrowband
nb	Narrowband (IDOE)
NB..............	Narrow Beam (NATG)
NB..............	National Battlefield (BARN)

NB..............	National Board
NB..............	NationsBank Corp. [*NYSE symbol*] (SPSG)
NB..............	Naval Base
NB..............	Navigation Base (NASA)
NB..............	Navy Band
NB..............	Neath and Brecon Railway [*Wales*]
NB..............	Nebraska (IAA)
Nb..............	Nebraska State Library, Lincoln, NE [*Library symbol Library of Congress*] (LCLS)
NB..............	Needle Biopsy [*Surgical procedure*] (DAVI)
NB..............	Negative Binomial Distribution [*Statistics*]
NB..............	Negri Body (AAMN)
NB..............	Nemzeti Bank [*National Bank*] [*Hungarian*]
NB..............	Neo-Babylonian [*or New Babylonian*] (BJA)
NB..............	Network Booter [*Computer science*] (BYTE)
NB..............	Neuro-Behccet [*Syndrome*] [*Medicine*] (DMAA)
NB..............	Neuroblast [*Cytology*]
NB..............	Neuroblastoma [*Medicine*] (DMAA)
NB..............	Neurometric Battery (DMAA)
NB..............	Neurometric Test Battery [*Neurometrics*]
NB..............	Neutral Buoyancy [*Navy*] (SSD)
NB..............	New Benloe's Reports, English King's Bench [*1531-1628*] [*A publication*] (DLA)
NB..............	New Boiler
NB..............	Newborn
NB..............	New Bottom [*On ships*]
NB..............	New Brunswick [*Canadian province*] [*Postal code*]
NB..............	New Brunswick Reports [*A publication*] (DLA)
NB..............	New Business
NB..............	New Haven Airways [*ICAO designator*] (AD)
NB..............	Next Brochure
NB..............	Nimbus [*Cloud*] [*Meteorology*]
Nb..............	Niobium [*See Cb*] [*Chemical element*]
NB..............	Nitrobenzene [*Organic chemistry*]
NB..............	Nitrogen Base (NASA)
NB..............	Nitrous Oxide-Barbiturate [*Organic chemistry*] (MAE)
NB..............	No Ball [*Cricket*]
NB..............	No Bias [*Relay*] [*Electronics*]
NB..............	No Bid [*or Bidders*]
NB..............	No Bowel Movement [*Gastroenterology*] (DAVI)
NB..............	Noise Blanker
N/B..............	Noise Power/Bandwidth
NB..............	Nomenclature Board [*Tasmania, Australia*]
NB..............	Nominal Bore [*Tubing*]
NB..............	Nonbattle [*Army*] (AABC)
NB..............	Nonbusiness [*IRS*]
NB..............	Nordiska Batradet [*Nordic Boat Council*] [*Sweden*] (EAIO)
NB..............	Nordlands Bank [*Norway*]
NB..............	Normal Bowel Movement [*Gastroenterology*] (DAVI)
NB..............	Normoblast [*Hematology*] (AAMN)
NB..............	Northampton & Bath Railroad Co. [*AAR code*]
NB..............	Northbound
NB..............	North Britain [*i.e., Scotland*]
NB..............	Not a Bean [*Penniless*] [*Facetious translation of NB, Nota Bene (Note Well)*] (DSUE)
NB..............	Nota Bene [*Note Well*] [*Latin*]
nb	Nota Bene [*Note Well*] [*Latin*] (WDMC)
NB..............	Not Bent [*Freight*]
NB..............	Not Blind [*Experimental conditions*]
NB..............	Notch-Bend (PDAA)
NB..............	Nuclear Blank (NRCH)
NB..............	Nuclear Boiler (NRCH)
NB..............	Nucleus Basalis [*Brain anatomy*]
NB..............	Nulla Bona [*No Goods*] [*Latin Legal term*] (DLA)
Nb..............	Numbers [*Old Testament book*] (BJA)
NB2	Norsar Array Site 02B00 [*Norway*] [*Seismograph station code, US Geological Survey*] (SEIS)
NB 2d	New Brunswick Reports, Second Series [*A publication*] (DLA)
NB3	Norsar Array Site 03B00 [*Norway*] [*Seismograph station code, US Geological Survey*] (SEIS)
NB4	Norsar Array Site 04B00 [*Norway*] [*Seismograph station code, US Geological Survey*] (SEIS)
NB5	Norsar Array Site 05B00 [*Norway*] [*Seismograph station code, US Geological Survey*] (SEIS)
NBA	Amateur Astronomers Association, Brooklyn, NY [*Library symbol Library of Congress*] (LCLS)
NBa	Davenport Library, Bath, NY [*Library symbol Library of Congress*] (LCLS)
NBA	Narrowband Allocation
NBA	Narrowband Analyzer
NBA	Narrow-Beam Adapter
NBA	National Ballet of America
NBA	National Band Association (EA)
NBA	National Bank Act of 1863
NBA	National Bankers Association [*Washington, DC*] (EA)
NBA	National Bankruptcy Act [*1898*]
NBA	National Bar Association (EA)
NBA	National Basketball Association (EA)
NBA	National Beefmaster Association (EA)
NBA	National Benevolent Association of the Christian Church [*Disciples of Christ*] (EA)
NBA	National Benzole and Allied Products Association [*British*] (BI)
NBA	National Biographical Association (EA)
NBA	National Bison Association (NTPA)
NBA	National Boat Association (EA)

NBA	National Book Awards [*Discontinued*]
NBA	National Bowling Association (EA)
NBA	National Boxing Association (NADA)
NBA	National Boxing Association of America [*Later, WBA*]
NBA	National Braille Association (EA)
NBA	National Brassfoundry Association [*British*] (BI)
NBA	National Broadcasting Authority [*Bangladesh*] (EY)
NBA	National Broiler Association [*Later, NBC*]
NBA	National Buffalo Association (EA)
NBA	National Building Agency [*British*]
NBA	National Business Association (EA)
NBA	National Butterfly Association (EA)
NBA	National Button Association
NBA	N-Bromoacetamide [*Organic chemistry*]
NBA	N-Butylamine [*Organic chemistry*]
NBA	Net Book Agreement [*British*]
NBA	Net Building Area (ADA)
NBA	New Brunswick Area (SAA)
NBA	Nickel-Base Alloy
NBA	Non-Weight-Bearing Ambulation [*Orthopedics*] (DAVI)
NBA	North British Academy
NBA	North East Bolivian Airways [*ICAO designator*] (FAAC)
NBAA	Amateur Astronomers Association, Brooklyn, NY [*Library symbol*] [*Library of Congress*] (LCLS)
NBAA	National Business Aircraft Association (EA)
NBab	Babylon Public Library, Babylon, NY [*Library symbol Library of Congress*] (LCLS)
NBAB	Biological Station, Fisheries and Oceans Canada [*Station de Biologie, Peches et Oceans Canada*] St. Andrews, New Brunswick [*Library symbol National Library of Canada*] (NLC)
NBab	Neo-Babylonian [*or New Babylonian*] (BJA)
NBAC	National Bioethics Advisory Commission
NBAC	National Biotechnology Advisory Committee [*Canada*]
NBAC	National Black Alcoholism Council (EA)
NBACA	National Broadcast Association for Community Affairs (NTPA)
NBACCH	Charlotte County Historical Society, Inc., St. Andrews, New Brunswick [*Library symbol National Library of Canada*] (NLC)
NBAD	National Bank of Abu Dhabi
NBAD	Naval Bases Air Defense
NBAD	N-beta-Alanyldopamine [*Biochemistry*]
NBADA	National Barrel and Drum Association [*Later, NABADA - The Association of Container Reconditioners*] (EA)
NBAF	National Blonde d'Aquitaine Foundation (EA)
NBAGLE	National Black Alliance for Graduate Level Education [*Defunct*] (EA)
NBAJ	National Buffalo Association Juniors [*Defunct*] (EA)
NBAK	National Bancorp of Alaska, Inc. [*NASDAQ symbol*] (NQ)
NBAK	Natl Bancorp(AK) [*NASDAQ symbol*] (TTSB)
N balance	Nitrogen Balance [*Medicine*] (WDAA)
NBald	Baldwin Public Library, Baldwin, NY [*Library symbol Library of Congress*] (LCLS)
NBaldBE	Brookside Elementary School, Baldwin, NY [*Library symbol Library of Congress*] (LCLS)
NBaldCE	Collidge Elementary School, Baldwin, NY [*Library symbol Library of Congress*] (LCLS)
NBaldGE	Grand Avenue Elementary School, Baldwin, NY [*Library symbol*] [*Library of Congress*] (LCLS)
NBaldHE	Harbor Elementary School, Baldwin, NY [*Library symbol Library of Congress*] (LCLS)
NBaldHJ	Harbor Junior High School, Baldwin, NY [*Library symbol Library of Congress*] (LCLS)
NBaldLE	Lenox Elementary School, Baldwin, NY [*Library symbol Library of Congress*] (LCLS)
NBaldME	Meadow Elementary School, Baldwin, NY [*Library symbol Library of Congress*] (LCLS)
NBaldMiE	Milburn Elementary School, Baldwin, NY [*Library symbol Library of Congress*] (LCLS)
NbaldPE	Plaza Elementary School, Baldwin, NY [*Library symbol Library of Congress*] (LCLS)
NBaldPrE	Prospect Elementary School, Baldwin, NY [*Library symbol Library of Congress*] (LCLS)
NBaldSE	Shubert Elementary School, Baldwin, NY [*Library symbol Library of Congress*] (LCLS)
NBaldSH	Baldwin Senior High School, Baldwin, NY [*Library symbol Library of Congress*] (LCLS)
NBaldStE	Steele Elementary School, Baldwin, NY [*Library symbol Library of Congress*] (LCLS)
NB Alsk	National Bancorp of Alaska, Inc. [*Associated Press*] (SAG)
NB & BA	National Bed-and-Breakfast Association (EA)
NB & C	Norfolk, Baltimore & Carolina Line [*Steamship*] (MHDB)
NBAO	New Brunswick Area Office [*Later, NBL*] [*AEC*]
NBAPA	National Black American Paralegal Association (NTPA)
NBar	Barker Free Library, Barker, NY [*Library symbol Library of Congress*] (LCLS)
nbar	Nanobar [*One billionth of a bar*]
NBAR	Non-Binding Allocation of Responsibility (COE)
NBAR	Nonbinding Preliminary Allocation of Responsibility [*Environmental Protection Agency*] (FFDE)
NBaryU	Unified Theological Seminary, Barrytown, NY [*Library symbol*] [*Library of Congress*] (LCLS)
NBAS	Neonatal Behavioural Assessment Scale [*Developed by Brazelton*]
NBAS-K	Neonatal Behavioral Assessment Scale-Kansas Revision (EDAC)
NBASLH	National Black Association for Speech, Language and Hearing (EA)
NBat	Richmond Memorial Library, Batavia, NY [*Library symbol Library of Congress*] (LCLS)
NBatC	Genesee Community College, Batavia, NY [*Library symbol Library of Congress*] (LCLS)
NBatGB	Genesse-Wyoming Board of Cooperative Education Services, Batavia, NY [*Library symbol*] [*Library of Congress*] (LCLS)
NBatGH	Genesee Memorial Hospital, Batavia, NY [*Library symbol Library of Congress*] (LCLS)
NBatHHi	Holland Purchase Historical Society, Batavia, NY [*Library symbol Library of Congress*] (LCLS)
NBatStJ	Saint Jerome Hospital, Medical Library, Batavia, NY [*Library symbol Library of Congress*] (LCLS)
NBatV	United States Veterans Administration Hospital, Library Service, Batavia, NY [*Library symbol Library of Congress*] (LCLS)
NBAU	No Business as Usual (EA)
NBaVA	United States Veterans Administration Hospital, Bath, NY [*Library symbol Library of Congress*] (LCLS)
NBAW	Notable Black American Women [*A publication*]
NBAWADU	National Black Anti-War Anti-Draft Union (EA)
NBayv	Bayville Free Library, Bayville, NY [*Library symbol Library of Congress*] (LCLS)
NBayvE	Bayville Elementary School, Bayville, NY [*Library symbol*] [*Library of Congress*] (LCLS)
NBayvI	Bayville Intermediate School, Bayville, NY [*Library symbol*] [*Library of Congress*] (LCLS)
NBayvP	Bayville Primary School, Bayville, NY [*Library symbol*] [*Library of Congress*] (LCLS)
NbB	Beatrice Public Library, Beatrice, NE [*Library symbol Library of Congress*] (LCLS)
NBB	Brooklyn Museum, Brooklyn, NY [*Library symbol Library of Congress*] (LCLS)
NBB	Narrowband Beam [*Physics*]
NBB	National Bank of Bahrain (EY)
NBB	National Bank of Brunei
NBBA	National Bed and Breakfast Association (NTPA)
NBBA	National Beep Baseball Association (EA)
NBBA	National Black Business Alliance
NBB & L	National Bath, Bed, and Linen Show (ITD)
NBBB	National Better Business Bureau (NADA)
NBBC	Bibliotheque Medicale, Hopital Regional Chaleur [*Medical Library, Chaleur Regional Hospital*] Bathurst, New Brunswick [*Library symbol National Library of Canada*] (NLC)
NBBC	National Black Business Council
NBBCC	College Communautaire du New Brunswick, Bathurst, New Brunswick [*Library symbol National Library of Canada*] (NLC)
NBBDA	National Burlap Bag Dealers Association [*Later, Textile Bag and Packaging Association*] (EA)
NbBe	Bellevue Public Library, Bellevue, NE [*Library symbol Library of Congress*] (LCLS)
NBB-E	Brooklyn Museum, Wilbour Library of Egyptology, Brooklyn, NY [*Library symbol Library of Congress*] (LCLS)
NBBE	National Board for Bakery Education [*British*] (BI)
NbBea	Beatrice Public Library, Beatrice, NE [*Library symbol*] [*Library of Congress*] (LCLS)
NbBeL	Bellevue Public Library, Bellevue, NE [*Library symbol*] [*Library of Congress*] (LCLS)
NBBI	National Blue Books, Inc. [*Canoga Park, CA*] [*Publisher*]
NBBI	National Board of Boiler and Pressure Vessel Inspectors (NTPA)
NBBI	Nederlands Bureau voor Bibliotheekwezen en Informatieverzorging [*Netherlands Organization for Libraries and Information Services*] [*Information service or system*] (IID)
NBBL	National Bath, Bed, and Linen Association (EA)
NbBla	Blair Public Library, Blair, NE [*Library symbol Library of Congress*] (LCLS)
NBBLA	National Bath, Bed, and Linen Association [*Later, NBBL*] (EA)
NbBlaD	Dana College, Blair, NE [*Library symbol Library of Congress*] (LCLS)
NBBLC	National Black on Black Love Campaign (EA)
NBBMA	National Beauty and Barber Manufacturers Association [*Later, ABA*] (EA)
NBBMK	Mussee de Kent, Bouctouche, New Brunswick [*Library symbol National Library of Canada*] (NLC)
NBBN	Nepisiguit Centennial Public Library, Bathurst, New Brunswick [*Library symbol National Library of Canada*] (NLC)
Nb-BPH	Nebraska Library Commission, Library for Blind and Physically Handicapped, Lincoln, NE [*Library symbol Library of Congress*] (LCLS)
NBBPVI	National Board of Boiler and Pressure Vessel Inspectors (EA)
NBBQA	National Barbecue Association
NbBro	Broken Bow Carnegie Library, Broken Bow, NE [*Library symbol Library of Congress*] (LCLS)
NBBS	New British Broadcasting Station (NADA)
NBBWM	Central New Brunswick Woodmen's Museum, Boiestown, New Brunswick [*Library symbol National Library of Canada*] (NLC)
NBC	Beaufort, SC [*Location identifier FAA*] (FAAL)
NBC	Brooklyn College, Brooklyn, NY [*Library symbol Library of Congress*] (LCLS)
NBC	Concordia College, Seward, NE [*OCLC symbol*] (OCLC)
NBC	Cook [*N. B.*] Corp. Ltd. [*Toronto Stock Exchange symbol Vancouver Stock Exchange symbol*]
NBC	Narrowband Conducted (IEEE)
NBC	National Baseball Congress (EA)
NBC	National Basketball Congress (NADA)
NBC	National Battlefields Commission [*See also CCBN*]
NBC	National Beagle Club (EA)
NBC	National Beef Congress
NBC	National Bibliographic Control
NBC	National Biscuit Co. (EFIS)

NBC .... National Board for Certification in Dental Laboratory Technology (EA)
NBC .... National Book Committee [Defunct]
NBC .... National Book Council [Later, NBL] [United Kingdom]
NBC .... National Bowling Council (EA)
NBC .... National Boxing Council [British]
NBC .... National Boys' Club (WDAA)
NBC .... National Braille Club [Later, NBA] (EA)
NBC .... National Broadcasters' Club (NTCM)
NBC .... National Broadcasting Co., Inc. [New York, NY]
NBC .... National Broadcasting Commission (NADA)
NBC .... National Broiler Council (EA)
NBC .... National Broom Council [Later, NBMC] (EA)
NBC .... National Building Code
NBC .... National Building Code of Canada (HGAA)
NBC .... National Bus Co. [British]
NBC .... Natural Background Clutter
NBC .... Natural Birth Control
NBC .... Navy Beach Commando
NBC .... Neumann Boundary Conditions
NBC .... Newfoundland Base Command [Army World War II]
NBC .... Nies Babylonian Collection [Yale University] (BJA)
NBC .... Nigerian Broadcasting Corp.
NBC .... Noise Balancing Circuit (DEN)
NBC .... Noise Balancing Control (IAA)
NBC .... Nonbattle Casualty (NVT)
NBC .... Nordic Boat Council (EA)
NBC .... Nostalgia Book Club
NBC .... Nuclear, Biological, and Chemical [Warfare]
NBC .... Number Base Conversion
NBCA .... Campbellton Centennial Public Library, New Brunswick [Library symbol National Library of Canada] (NLC)
NBCA .... National Band Council of Australia
NBCA .... National Bareboat Charter Association (NTPA)
NBCA .... National Baseball Congress of America (NADA)
NBCA .... National Beagle Club of America (EA)
NBCA .... National Bituminous Concrete Association [Later, NAPA] (EA)
NBCA .... National Business Circulation Association (EA)
NBCA .... Navy Department Board of Contract Appeals [1944-50] (AAGC)
NBCAA .... National Bible College Athletic Association (PSS)
NBCAC .... Chaleur Library Region, Campbellton, New Brunswick [Library symbol National Library of Canada] (NLC)
NBCAM .... Campobello Public Library, New Brunswick [Library symbol National Library of Canada] (BIB)
NBCAP .... National Becaon Code Allocation Plan (FAAC)
NBCBP .... Bibliotheque Publique Mgr. Paquet, Caraquet, New Brunswick [Library symbol National Library of Canada] (NLC)
NBCC .... National Baby Care Council [Defunct] (EA)
NBCC .... National Beauty Career Center (EA)
NBCC .... National Bidders Control Center
NBCC .... National Bituminous Coal Commission [Functions transferred to Department of the Interior, 1939]
NBCC .... National Black Chamber of Commerce (EA)
NBCC .... National Board for Certified Counselors (EA)
NBCC .... National Book Critics Circle (EA)
NBCC .... National Breast Cancer Coalition
NBCC .... National Budget and Consultation Committee [Defunct] (EA)
NBCC .... National Building Code of Canada
NBCC .... National Bureau for Co-Operation in Child Care [British]
NBCC .... National Business Career Center (EA)
NBCC .... Netherlands British Chamber of Commerce (DS)
NBCC .... Nevoid Basal-Cell Carcinoma [Oncology]
NBCC .... Nigerian British Chamber of Commerce [London] (DCTA)
NBCC .... Nuclear, Biological, and Chemical Contamination (DOMA)
NBCC .... Nuclear, Biological, Chemical, Conventional [Warfare]
NBCCA .... National Business Council for Consumer Affairs [Terminated, 1974] [Department of Commerce] (EGAO)
NBCCC .... Miramichi Campus, New Brunswick Community College [Campus Miramichi, College Communautaire du Nouveau-Brunswick], Chatham, New Brunswick [Library symbol National Library of Canada] (NLC)
NBCCC .... National Black Catholic Clergy Caucus (EA)
NBCCC .... National Bureau for Co-Operation in Child Care [British] (BI)
NBC-CDTP ... National Board for Certification - Certified Dental Technician Program (EA)
NBCCH .... National Board for Certified Clinical Hypnotherapists (NTPA)
NBCCS .... Nevoid Basal Cell Carcinoma Syndrome [Oncology] (DMAA)
NBCD .... Natural Binary-Coded Decimal
NBCD .... Negate BCD [Binary-Coded Decimal] Number [Computer science]
NBCD .... Nuclear, Biological, and Chemical Defense (NATG)
NBCDCE .... Nuclear, Biological, and Chemical Defense Control Element [Military]
NBCDI .... National Black Child Development Institute (EA)
NBCDL .... National Board for Certification of Dental Laboratories [Later, CDL] (EA)
NBCDX .... Nuclear, Biological, and Chemical Defense Exercise [NATO] (NATG)
NBCE .... Nuclear, Biological, and Chemical Element
NbCen.......... Hards Memorial Library, Central City, NE [Library symbol Library of Congress] (LCLS)
NbCenC........ Nebraska Central College, Central City, NE [Library symbol Library of Congress Obsolete] (LCLS)
NBCFAE .... National Black Coalition of Federal Aviation Employees (EA)
NBCFD .... Naval Base Consolidated Fire Department (DNAB)
NBCG........... National Bulk Commodities Group [Australia]
NBCGT......... National Business Consortium for the Gifted and Talented [Defunct] (EA)

NbCh........... Chadron Public Library, Chadron, NE [Library symbol Library of Congress] (LCLS)
NBCH .... Historical Society Nicolas Denys, Societe Historique Nicolas Denys, Caraquet, New Brunswick [Library symbol National Library of Canada] (NLC)
NBCHD........ Health Sciences Library, Hotel-Dieu Hospital, Chatham, New Brunswick [Library symbol National Library of Canada] (BIB)
NBCHR........ Bibliotheque de la Sante, Centre Hospitalier Restigouche, Campbellton, New Brunswick [Library symbol National Library of Canada] (BIB)
NbChS .... Chadron State College, Chadron, NE [Library symbol Library of Congress] (LCLS)
NBCI .... NBC Internet
NBCI .... Nigerian Bank for Commerce and Industry
NBCIA .... National Blue Crab Industry Association (EA)
NBCL .... National Beauty Culturists' League (EA)
NBCL .... National Birth Control League
NBCLEO .... National Black Caucus of Local Elected Officials (NTPA)
NBCM .... Miramichi Natural History Society, Chatham, New Brunswick [Library symbol National Library of Canada] (NLC)
NBCMA .... Mussee Acadien, Caraquet, New Brunswick [Library symbol National Library of Canada] (NLC)
NBCMu .... Brooklyn Children's Museum, Brooklyn, NY [Library symbol Library of Congress] (LCLS)
NbCo........... Columbus Public Library, Columbus, NE [Library symbol Library of Congress] (LCLS)
NbCoC .... Platte Technical Community College, Columbus, NE [Library symbol Library of Congress] (LCLS)
NBCOT .... National Board for Certification of Orthopaedic Technologists (EA)
NBCP .... Brooklyn College of Pharmacy, Brooklyn, NY [Library symbol Library of Congress] (LCLS)
NBCP .... National Bladder Cancer Project [National Cancer Institute]
NBCPC .... National Board for Cardiovascular and Pulmonary Credentialing [Later, Cardiovascular Credentialing International - CCI] (EA)
NbCr........... Crete Public Library, Crete, NE [Library symbol Library of Congress] (LCLS)
NbCrD......... Doane College, Crete, NE [Library symbol Library of Congress] (LCLS)
NBCRS .... Nuclear-Biological-Chemical Reconnaissance System [Military]
NBCS .... National Black Communicators Society (EA)
NBCS .... St. Thomas University, Fredericton, New Brunswick [Library symbol National Library of Canada] (NLC)
NBCSA .... National Black Catholic Seminarians Association (EA)
NBCSDA....... National Broom Corn and Supply Dealers Association (EA)
NBCSH .... La Societe Historique de Clair, Inc., New Brunswick [Library symbol National Library of Canada] (NLC)
NBCSI .... National Board of the Coat and Suit Industry [Defunct] (EA)
NBCSL .... National Black Caucus of State Legislators (EA)
NBcs TX....... National Bancshares Corp. of Texas [Associated Press] (SAG)
NBCU .... National Bureau of Casualty Underwriters [Later, ISO] (EA)
NBC USA .... National Baptist Convention, USA (EA)
NBCV .... Narrowband Coherent Video (IEEE)
NBCVHA....... Le Village Historique Acadien, Caraquet, New Brunswick [Library symbol National Library of Canada] (NLC)
NBCW .... National Bird Cage Week
NBCW .... National Board of Catholic Women [British]
NBCWRS...... Nuclear, Biological, and Chemical Warning and Reporting System
NBD .... Doane College, Crete, NE [OCLC symbol] (OCLC)
NBD .... Narrowband Detector
NBD .... National Bank of Dubai
NBD .... National Detroit Corp. (EFIS)
NBD .... NBD Bancorp, Inc. [NYSE symbol] (SPSG)
NBD .... Negative Binomial Distribution [Statistics]
NBD .... Neurogenic Bladder Dysfunction [Medicine]
NBD .... Neurologic Bladder Dysfunction [Medicine] (DB)
NBD .... Neutral Beam Divider
NBD .... Nitrobenzoxadiazole [Organic chemistry]
nbd .... No Big Deal [Internet language] [Computer science]
NBD .... Nondirectional Beacon
NBD .... Norbornadiene [Organic chemistry]
NBD .... Nucleotide Binding Domain [Biochemistry]
NBDA .... National Barrel and Drum Association
NBDA .... National Bicycle Dealers Association (EA)
NBDA .... National Black Deaf Advocates (EA)
NBDC .... National Blood Data Center [American Blood Commission] [Information service or system] (IID)
NBDC .... National Bomb Data Center
NBDCA .... National Baptist Deacons Convention of America (EA)
NBDE .... National Bureau of Document Examiners (EA)
NBDEA .... National Beverage Dispensing Equipment Association (EA)
NBDF .... Narrow Band Device - Fix
NBDF .... Narrowband Dicke-Fix [Electronics] (CET)
NBDFB .... Nitrobenzenediazonium Tetrafluoroborate [Organic chemistry]
NBDFX........ Narrowband Dicke-Fix [Electronics] (MSA)
NBDKH........ Keillor House Museum, Dorchester, New Brunswick [Library symbol National Library of Canada] (NLC)
NBDL .... Narrowband Data Line
NBDL .... Narrowband Data Link (IAA)
NBDL .... Naval Biodynamics Laboratory (GRD)
NBDM .... Miramichi Salmon Museum, Inc., Doaktown, New Brunswick [Library symbol National Library of Canada] (NLC)
NBDMO........ N-Bromo(dimethyl)oxazolidinone [Organic chemistry]
NB-DNJ....... N-Butyldeoxynojirimycin [Biochemistry]
NBDP.......... Narrow-Band Direct Printing (OTD)
NBD-PS........ Nitrobenzoxadiazole Phosphatidylserine [Biochemistry]

NBDRRM ..... Restigouche Regional Museum, Dalhousie, New Brunswick [*Library symbol National Library of Canada*] (NLC)
NBDS .... Nuclear Burst Detection Systems (MCD)
NBDVS .... Narrow Band Digital Voice System [*Telecommunications*] (LAIN)
NBE .... Dallas, TX [*Location identifier FAA*] (FAAL)
NbE .... Exeter Public Library, Exeter, NE [*Library symbol Library of Congress*] (LCLS)
NBE .... Near Band Edge (AAEL)
NBE .... Neutron Binding Energy
NBE .... Newburyport Birders' Exchange (EA)
NBE .... Nominal Band Edge
NBE .... Normal Binocular Experience [*Ophthalmology*]
NbE .... North by East
NBE .... Nova Beaucage Mines Ltd. [*Toronto Stock Exchange symbol*]
NBE .... Nuclear Binding Energy
NBEA .... National Ballroom and Entertainment Association (EA)
NBEA .... National Black Evangelical Association (EA)
NBEA .... National Broadcast Editorial Association (EA)
NBEA .... National Business Education Association [*Reston, VA*] (EA)
NBEBR .... Bibliotheque Regionale du Haut Saint-Jean, Edmundston, New Brunswick [*Library symbol National Library of Canada*] (NLC)
NBEC .... National Business and Education Council (OICC)
NBECC .... New Brunswick Community College, Edmundston, New Brunswick [*Library symbol National Library of Canada*] (NLC)
NBECS .... Nonresidential Building Energy Comsumption Survey [*Department of Energy*] (GFGA)
NBed .... Bedford Free Library, Bedford, NY [*Library symbol Library of Congress*] (LCLS)
NBEDC .... National Black Economic Development Conference
NBedh .... Bedford Hills Free Library, Bedford Hills, NY [*Library symbol Library of Congress*] (LCLS)
NBEF .... National Bowhunter Education Foundation (EA)
NBel .... Bellport Memorial Library, Bellport, NY [*Library symbol Library of Congress*] (LCLS)
NBelf .... Belfast Public Library, Belfast, NY [*Library symbol Library of Congress*] (LCLS)
NBelL .... Long Island Library Resources Council, Inc., Bellport, NY [*Library symbol Library of Congress*] (LCLS)
NBellm .... Bellmore Memorial Library, Bellmore, NY [*Library symbol Library of Congress*] (LCLS)
NBellmCM ... Wellington C. Mepham High School, Bellmore, NY [*Library symbol*] [*Library of Congress*] (LCLS)
NBellmGJ .... Grand Avenue Junior High School, Bellmore, NY [*Library symbol*] [*Library of Congress*] (LCLS)
NBellmKH ... John F. Kennedy High School, Bellmore, NY [*Library symbol*] [*Library of Congress*] (LCLS)
NBellmR ...... C.H. Reinhard School, Bellmore, NY [*Library symbol*] [*Library of Congress*] (LCLS)
NBellmSE ... Shore Road Elementary School, Bellmore, NY [*Library symbol*] [*Library of Congress*] (LCLS)
NBellmWE ... Winthrop Avenue Elementary School, Bellmore, NY [*Library symbol*] [*Library of Congress*] (LCLS)
NBelS .... Suffolk Cooperative Library System, Bellport, NY [*Library symbol Library of Congress*] (LCLS)
NBEMM .... Musee de Madawaska, Edmundston, New Brunswick [*Library symbol National Library of Canada*] (NLC)
N Ben .... New Benloe's Reports, English King's Bench [*1531-1628*] [*A publication*] (DLA)
N Benl .... New Benloe's Reports, English King's Bench [*1531-1628*] [*A publication*] (DLA)
NBEO .... National Board of Examiners in Optometry (EA)
NBEOPS .... National Board of Examiners for Osteopathic Physicians and Surgeons [*Later, NBOME*] (EA)
NB Eq .... New Brunswick Equity Reports [*A publication*] (DLA)
NB Eq Ca .... New Brunswick Equity Cases [*A publication*] (DLA)
NB Eq R ...... New Brunswick Equity Reports [*A publication*] (DLA)
NB Eq Rep... New Brunswick Equity Reports [*A publication*] (DLA)
NBER .... National Bureau of Economic Research (EA)
NBER .... National Bureau of Engineering Registration
NBERA .... National Bicentennial Ethnic-Racial Alliance
NBerG .... Gillam-Grant Community Center Library, Bergen, NY [*Library symbol Library of Congress*] (LCLS)
NBernN .... Bernardsville News, Bernardsville, NJ [*Library symbol Library of Congress*] (LCLS)
NBerR .... Bergen Reading Center, Bergen, NY [*Library symbol Library of Congress*] (LCLS)
NBES .... National Business Equipment Survey [*British*]
NBESLM ...... Centre Universitaire Saint-Louis Maillet, Edmundston, New Brunswick [*Library symbol National Library of Canada*] (NLC)
NBet .... Bethpage Public Library, Bethpage, NY [*Library symbol Library of Congress*] (LCLS)
NBET .... National Business Entrance Test [*Education*] (AEBS)
NBetCaE ...... Campagne Elementary School, Bethpage, NY [*Library symbol Library of Congress*] (LCLS)
NBetCE .... Central Elementary School, Bethpage, NY [*Library symbol Library of Congress*] (LCLS)
NBETF .... Neutral-Beam Engineering Test Facility [*Lawrence Berkeley Laboratory*] [*Terminated Department of Energy*] (GRD)
NBetG .... Grumman Aerospace Corp., Bethpage, NY [*Library symbol Library of Congress*] (LCLS)
NBetH .... Mid-Island Hospital, Bethpage, NY [*Library symbol Library of Congress*] (LCLS)
NBethKJ....... John F. Kennedy Junior High School, Bethpage, NY [*Library symbol Library of Congress*] (LCLS)

NBethSH ...... Bethpage Senior High School, Bethpage, NY [*Library symbol Library of Congress*] (LCLS)
NBetKE .... Kramer Elementary School, Bethpage, NY [*Library symbol Library of Congress*] (LCLS)
NBetKJ........ John F. Kennedy Junior High School, Bethpage, NY [*Library symbol*] [*Library of Congress*] (LCLS)
NBetSH .... Bethpage Senior High School, Bethpage, NY [*Library symbol*] [*Library of Congress*] (LCLS)
NBetWE .... John H. West Elementary School, Bethpage, NY [*Library symbol*] [*Library of Congress*] (LCLS)
NBF .... Brooklyn Friends School, New York, NY [*Library symbol Library of Congress*] (LCLS)
NBF .... Narrowband Filter
NBF .... National Bed Federation [*British*] (DBA)
NBF .... National Birman Fanciers (EA)
NBF .... National Boating Federation (EA)
NBF .... National Burn Federation (EA)
NBF .... Neutral Buoyancy Facility [*Navy*] (MCD)
NBF .... New Biotechnology Firm
NBF .... New Business Funds (MCD)
NBF .... Nordisk Barnkirurgisk Forening [*Scandinavian Association of Paediatric Surgeons - SAPS*] [*Denmark*] (EAIO)
NBF .... Northbay Financial Corp. [*AMEX symbol*] (SPSG)
NBF .... North Bergen Federation of Public Libraries [*Library network*]
NBF .... Northwest AHEC [*Area Health Education Center*] - Bowman Gray School of Medicine, Taylorsville, NC [*OCLC symbol*] (OCLC)
NBF .... Nucleotide Binding Fold [*Genetics*]
NBFA .... National Baseball Fan Association (EA)
NBFA .... National Business Forms Association [*Alexandria, VA*] (EA)
NBFA .... New Business Fund Authorization (MCD)
NBFA .... Provincial Archives of New-Brunswick [*Archives Provinciales du Nouveau-Brunswick*] Fredericton, New Brunswick [*Library symbol National Library of Canada*] (NLC)
NBFAA .... National Burglar and Fire Alarm Association (EA)
NBFAFA .... Archives, Diocese of Fredericton, Anglican Church of Canada, New Brunswick [*Library symbol National Library of Canada*] (NLC)
NBFAG .... Research Station, Agriculture Canada [*Station de Recherches, Agriculture Canada*] Fredericton, New Brunswick [*Library symbol National Library of Canada*] (NLC)
NBFB .... Beaverbrook Collection, New Brunswick Archives, Fredericton, New Brunswick [*Library symbol National Library of Canada*] (NLC)
NbFb .... Fairbury Public Library, Fairbury, NE [*Library symbol Library of Congress*] (LCLS)
NbFbC.......... Southeast Community College, Fairbury, NE [*Library symbol Library of Congress*] (LCLS)
NBFBS .... New Brunswick Barristers Society, Fredericton, New Brunswick [*Library symbol National Library of Canada*] (NLC)
NbFC.......... Central Lutheran Theological Seminary, Fremont, NE [*Library symbol Library of Congress*] (LCLS)
NBFC.......... New Brunswick Library Service, Fredericton, New Brunswick [*Library symbol National Library of Canada*] (NLC)
NbFc .... Woods Memorial Library, Falls City, NE [*Library symbol Library of Congress*] (LCLS)
NbFcP.......... Woods Memorial Library, Falls City, NE [*Library symbol*] [*Library of Congress*] (LCLS)
NBFDEC .... Dr. Everett Chalmers Hospital, Fredericton, New Brunswick [*Library symbol National Library of Canada*] (NLC)
NBFE.......... Maritimes Forest Research Centre, Environment Canada [*Centre de Recherches Forestieres des Maritimes, Environnement Canada*] Fredericton, New Brunswick [*Library symbol National Library of Canada*] (NLC)
NBFED .... New Brunswick Department of Education, Fredericton, New Brunswick [*Library symbol National Library of Canada*] (NLC)
NBFFO .... National Board of Fur Farm Organizations (EA)
NBFHR........ New Brunswick Department of Historical Resources, Fredericton, New Brunswick [*Library symbol National Library of Canada*] (NLC)
NBFI.......... Non-Bank Financial Institutions [*Ghana*]
NBFI.......... Non-Bank Financial Intermediary (ADA)
NBFJS........ Sunbury West Historical Society, Fredericton Junction, New Brunswick [*Library symbol National Library of Canada*] (NLC)
NBFJWO ...... National Bureau of Federated Jewish Women's Organizations (EA)
NBFKL .... Kings Landing Historical Settlement, Fredericton, New Brunswick [*Library symbol National Library of Canada*] (NLC)
NBFL.......... Legislative Library [*Bibliotheque Legislative*] Fredericton, New Brunswick [*Library symbol National Library of Canada*] (NLC)
NBFLM........ Photogrammetry Branch, New Brunswick Department of Lands and Mines, Fredericton, New Brunswick [*Library symbol National Library of Canada*] (NLC)
NBFM.......... Narrowband Frequency Modulation [*Radio*]
NBFMM........ Medley Memorial Library, Christ Church Cathedral, Fredericton, New Brunswick [*Library symbol National Library of Canada*] (NLC)
NBFNR........ New Brunswick Department of Natural Resources and Energy, Fredericton, New Brunswick [*Library symbol National Library of Canada*] (NLC)
NBFO.......... National Black Feminist Organization
NBFP.......... New Brunswick Power, Fredericton, New Brunswick [*Library symbol National Library of Canada*] (NLC)
NBFPO.......... Premier's Office, Province of New Brunswick, Fredericton, New Brunswick [*Library symbol National Library of Canada*] (NLC)
NbFr.......... Fremont Public Library, Fremont, NE [*Library symbol Library of Congress*] (LCLS)
NBFR .... Not Before [*ICAO designator*] (FAAC)
NbFrM.......... Midland Lutheran College, Fremont, NE [*Library symbol Library of Congress*] (LCLS)

NBFRP .... New Brunswick Research and Productivity Council, Fredericton, New Brunswick [*Library symbol National Library of Canada*] (NLC)
NBFS .... National Bird-Feeding Society (EA)
NBFS .... New Balanced File Organization Scheme (MHDB)
NBFS .... Societe d'Histoire de la Riviere Saint Jean, Fredericton, New Brunswick [*Library symbol National Library of Canada*] (BIB)
NBFSS .... New Brunswick Department of Social Services, Fredericton, New Brunswick [*Library symbol National Library of Canada*] (NLC)
NBFT .... Bureau de Traduction, Gouvernement du Nouveau-Brunswick [*Translation Bureau, Governement of New Brunswick*] Fredericton, New Brunswick [*Library symbol National Library of Canada*] (NLC)
NBFTR .... New Brunswick Department of Transportation, Fredericton, New Brunswick [*Library symbol National Library of Canada*] (NLC)
NBFU .... National Board of Fire Underwriters [*Later, AIA*] (EA)
NBFU .... University of New Brunswick, Fredericton, New Brunswick [*Library symbol National Library of Canada*] (NLC)
NBFUA .... Archives and Special Collections Department, University of New Brunswick, Fredericton, New Brunswick [*Library symbol National Library of Canada*] (NLC)
NBFUE .... Engineering Library, University of New Brunswick, Fredericton [*Library symbol National Library of Canada*] (BIB)
NBFUL .... Law Library, University of New Brunswick, Fredericton, New Brunswick [*Library symbol National Library of Canada*] (NLC)
NBFUM .... Map Room, Government Documents Department, University of New Brunswick, Fredericton, New Brunswick [*Library symbol National Library of Canada*] (NLC)
NBFY .... York-Sunbury Historical Society, Fredericton, New Brunswick [*Library symbol National Library of Canada*] (NLC)
NBFYR .... York Regional Library, Fredericton, New Brunswick [*Library symbol National Library of Canada*] (NLC)
NBFYRC .... New Brunswick Department of Youth, Recreation and Cultural Resources, Fredericton, New Brunswick [*Library symbol National Library of Canada*] (NLC)
NBG .... Bowman Gray School of Medicine, Winston-Salem, NC [*OCLC symbol*] (OCLC)
NBG .... Brooklyn Botanic Garden, Brooklyn, NY [*Library symbol Library of Congress*] (LCLS)
NbG .... Grand Island Public Library, Grand Island, NE [*Library symbol Library of Congress*] (LCLS)
NBG .... National Bank of Greece
NBG .... Naval Beach Group (NVT)
NBG .... New Orleans, LA [*Location identifier FAA*] (FAAL)
NBG .... Nieuwe Vertaling Nederlands Bijbelgenootschap [*A publication*] (BJA)
NBG .... No Blasted Good [*Slang*]
NBG .... No Bloody Good [*British slang*]
NBG .... Nuclear Beta Gauge
NBGA .... National Bingo Game Association [*British*] (DBA)
NBGACF .... Canadian Forces Base, Gagetown, New Brunswick [*Library symbol National Library of Canada*] (NLC)
NBGFCC .... New Brunswick Community College, Grand Falls, New Brunswick [*Library symbol National Library of Canada*] (NLC)
NBGFH .... Grand Falls Historical Society, New Brunswick [*Library symbol National Library of Canada*] (NLC)
NBGG .... Grand Manan Historical Society, Grand Harbour, Grand Manan Island, New Brunswick [*Library symbol National Library of Canada*] (NLC)
NbGi .... Grand Island Public Library, Grand Island, NE [*Library symbol*] [*Library of Congress*] (LCLS)
NBGMM .... Grand Manan Museum, Grand Harbour, Grand Manan Island, New Brunswick, [*Library symbol National Library of Canada*] (NLC)
NBGQA .... National Building Granite Quarries Association (EA)
NBGRN .... Narrow Band Gaussian Random Noise (PDAA)
NBGS .... New Bedford Glass Society [*Defunct*] (EA)
NBH .... Hastings College, Hastings, NE [*OCLC symbol*] (OCLC)
NbH .... Hastings Public Library, Hastings, NE [*Library symbol Library of Congress*] (LCLS)
NBH .... National Bank of Hungary
NBH .... National Bellas Hess [*Inc.*] [*Commercial firm*]
NBH .... Network Busy Hour [*Telecommunications*] (TEL)
NBH .... North Bay [*Hawaii*] [*Seismograph station code, US Geological Survey Closed*] (SEIS)
NBHA .... National Bicentennial Hospitality Alliance [*American Revolution Bicentennial Administration*]
NBHA .... National Builders' Hardware Association [*Later, DHI*] (EA)
NbHC .... Hastings College, Hastings, NE [*Library symbol Library of Congress*] (LCLS)
NBHCA .... Albert County Historical Society, Inc., Hopewell Cape, New Brunswick [*Library symbol National Library of Canada*] (NLC)
NBHCA .... National Belgian Hare Club of America [*Defunct*] (EA)
NbHCC .... Central Technical Community College, Hastings, NE [*Library symbol Library of Congress*] (LCLS)
NbHCro .... Crosier Fathers' Library, Hastings, NE [*Library symbol Library of Congress*] (LCLS)
NbHi .... Nebraska State Historical Society, Lincoln, NE [*Library symbol Library of Congress*] (LCLS)
NbHo .... Holdrege-Phelps County Library, Holdrege, NE [*Library symbol Library of Congress*] (LCLS)
NBHPA .... National Black Health Planners Association (EA)
NBHS .... National Bureau for Handicapped Students [*British*] (CB)
NBi .... Binghamton Public Library, Binghamton, NY [*Library symbol Library of Congress*] (LCLS)
NBI .... Nabisco Brands, Inc. [*Toronto Stock Exchange symbol*]
NBI .... Nathaniel Branden Institute
NBI .... National BankAmericard, Inc. [*Later, Visa USA, Inc.*]

NBI .... National Bridge Inventory [*FHWA*] (TAG)
NBI .... Neutral Beam Injection (MCD)
NBI .... Nielsen Broadcast Index [*A. C. Nielsen Co.*] (NTCM)
NBI .... No Bone Injury [*Medicine*]
NBI .... Nonbattle Injuries
NBI .... Northern Business Information, Inc. [*New York, NY*] [*Information service or system*] (TSSD)
NBI .... Nothing but Initials [*Initialism is name of commercial word processor firm*]
NBI .... Nuclear Burst Indicator (NATG)
NBIA .... National Business Incubation Association
NBIAP .... National Biological Impact Assessment Program [*Computer science*] (IID)
NBiBT .... Broome Technical Community College, Binghamton, NY [*Library symbol Library of Congress*] (LCLS)
NBIC .... National Business Information Center [*Dun & Bradstreet*]
NBIE .... National Burn Information Exchange [*Information service or system*] (CRD)
NBiF .... Four County Library System, Binghamton, NY [*Library symbol Library of Congress*] (LCLS)
NBiL .... Our Lady of Lourdes Hospital, Binghamton, NY [*Library symbol Library of Congress*] (LCLS)
NBIO .... North American Biologicals, Inc. [*NASDAQ symbol*] (NQ)
NBIP .... National Biomonitoring Inventory Program [*Department of Energy*] (MSC)
NBIRF .... National Brain Injury Research Foundation (EA)
NBiRM .... Roberson Museum and Science Center, Binghamton, NY [*Library symbol*] [*Library of Congress*] (LCLS)
NBIS .... National Bridge Inspection Standards [*FHWA*] (TAG)
NBiSC .... New York State Supreme Court Law Library, Binghamton, NY [*Library symbol Library of Congress*] (LCLS)
NBiSEG .... New York State Electric & Gas Corp., Binghamton, NY [*Library symbol Library of Congress*] (LCLS)
NBiSL .... Singer Co., Link Division, Binghamton, NY [*Library symbol Library of Congress*] (LCLS)
NBiSU .... State University of New York at Binghamton, Binghamton, NY [*Library symbol Library of Congress*] (LCLS)
NBIT .... New Bedford Institute of Technology [*Massachusetts*]
NBIX .... Neurocrine Biosciences [*NASDAQ symbol*] (TTSB)
NBIX .... Neurocrine Biosciences, Inc. [*NASDAQ symbol*] (SAG)
NBJ .... Kingsbrook Jewish Medical Center, Brooklyn, NY [*Library symbol Library of Congress*] (LCLS)
NBJ .... National Bar Journal [*A publication*] (DLA)
NbK .... Kearney Public Library, Kearney, NE [*Library symbol Library of Congress*] (LCLS)
NBK .... Kingsborough Community College of the City University of New York, Brooklyn, NY [*Library symbol Library of Congress*] (LCLS)
NBK .... Nabu Network Corp. [*Toronto Stock Exchange symbol*]
NBK .... National Bank of Kuwait
NBK .... Natural Born Killers [*Movie title*]
NBK .... Nebelkerze [*Smoke-Candle*] [*German military - World War II*]
NBK .... Nordisk Bilteknisk Kommitte [*Nordic Automobile Technical Committee - NATC*] [*Defunct Denmark*] (EAIO)
NBKC .... Kingsborough Community College of the City University of New York, Brooklyn, NY [*Library symbol*] [*Library of Congress*] (LCLS)
NBkCmce ..... Northern Bank of Commerce [*Associated Press*] (SAG)
NBkCmce ..... Northwest Bank of Commerce [*Oregon*] [*Associated Press*] (SAG)
NbKi .... Kimball Public Library, Kimball, NE [*Library symbol Library of Congress*] (LCLS)
N Bkpt R ..... National Bankruptcy Register Reports [*United States*] [*A publication*] (DLA)
N Bkpt Reg... National Bankruptcy Register Reports [*United States*] [*A publication*] (DLA)
N Bk R .... National Bankruptcy Register Reports [*United States*] [*A publication*] (DLA)
NbKS .... Kearney State College, Kearney, NE [*Library symbol Library of Congress*] (LCLS)
NBL .... Brooklyn Law School, Brooklyn, NY [*Library symbol Library of Congress*] (LCLS)
NbL .... Lincoln City Libraries, Lincoln, NE [*Library symbol Library of Congress*] (LCLS)
NBL .... National Basketball League (NADA)
NBL .... National Bicycle League (EA)
NBL .... National Book League [*Formerly, NBC*]
NBL .... National Business League [*Washington, DC*] (EA)
NBL .... Naval Biosciences Laboratory [*Research center*]
NBL .... Navy Basic Logistic [*Plan*]
NBL .... Nebraska Library Commission, Lincoln, NE [*OCLC symbol*] (OCLC)
NBL .... New Brunswick Laboratory [*Formerly, NBAO*] [*Argonne, IL*] [*Department of Energy*]
NBL .... Night Bombardment - Long Distance [*Air Force*]
NBL .... No Berth List [*Shipping*] (DS)
NBL .... Noble Affiliates [*NYSE symbol*] (TTSB)
NBL .... Noble Affiliates, Inc. [*NYSE symbol*] (SPSG)
NBL .... Norbaska Mines Ltd. [*Toronto Stock Exchange symbol*]
nbl .... Normoblast [*Hematology*]
NBL .... Not Bloody Likely [*British slang*]
NBL .... Nuclear Bomb Line (CINC)
NBIa .... Blauvelt Free Library, Blauvelt, NY [*Library symbol Library of Congress*] (LCLS)
NBLA .... National Businesswomen's Leadership Association [*Defunct*] (EA)
NBIaD .... Dominican College, Blauvelt, NY [*Library symbol Library of Congress*] (LCLS)
NBLB .... Nebraska Law Bulletin [*A publication*] (DLA)
NBLC .... National Business Law Council [*Formerly, NABLT*] (EA)

Nb-LC .... Nebraska Public Library Commission, Lincoln, NE [*Library symbol Library of Congress*] (LCLS)
NBLCC .... National Black Lay Catholic Caucus (EA)
NBLD .... Narrowband Linear Detector (MCD)
NbID .... Noble Drilling Corp. [*Associated Press*] (SAG)
NBLE .... Nearly Best Linear Estimator [*Statistics*]
NbleDr .... Noble Drilling Corp. [*Associated Press*] (SAG)
NBLiCH .... Long Island College Hospital, Brooklyn, NY [*Library symbol Library of Congress*] (LCLS)
NBLiHi .... Long Island Historical Society, Brooklyn, NY [*Library symbol Library of Congress*] (LCLS)
NBLiU .... Long Island University, Brooklyn, NY [*Library symbol Library of Congress*] (LCLS)
NbLL .... Lincoln City Libraries, Lincoln, NE [*Library symbol*] [*Library of Congress*] (LCLS)
NbLNP .... United States Department of the Interior, National Park Service, Midwest Archaeological Center, Lincoln, NE [*Library symbol Library of Congress*] (LCLS)
NbLo .... Loup City Township Library, Loup City, NE [*Library symbol Library of Congress*] (LCLS)
NBLP .... National Bureau for Lathing and Plastering [*Later, International Institute for Lath and Plaster*] (EA)
NBLR .... National Black Leadership Roundtable (EA)
Nb-LR .... Nebraska Legislative Council, Reference Library, Lincoln, NE [*Library symbol Library of Congress*] (LCLS)
NBLR .... North Borneo Law Reports [*A publication*] (DLA)
NBLSA .... National/Black Law Student Association (EA)
NbLSc .... Southeast Community College, Lincoln, NE [*Library symbol Library of Congress*] (LCLS)
NbLU .... Union College, Lincoln, NE [*Library symbol Library of Congress*] (LCLS)
NbLVA .... United States Veterans Administration Hospital, Lincoln, NE [*Library symbol Library of Congress*] (LCLS)
NbLW .... Nebraska Wesleyan University, Lincoln, NE [*Library symbol Library of Congress*] (LCLS)
NBm .... Briarcliff Manor Public Library, Briarcliff Manor, NY [*Library symbol Library of Congress*] (LCLS)
NbM .... McCook Public Library, McCook, NE [*Library symbol Library of Congress*] (LCLS)
NBM .... Medical Research Library of Brooklyn, Brooklyn, NY [*Library symbol Library of Congress*] (LCLS)
NBM .... National Building Museum (EA)
NBM .... National Bureau of Metrology
NBM .... Nation's Balanced Target Maturity Fund [*NYSE symbol*] (SAG)
NBM .... Nations Bal Target Mat Fd [*NYSE symbol*] (TTSB)
NBM .... Navy Basic Modernization [*Plan*]
NBM .... Nitro-Form Bind Medium [*Analytical biochemistry*]
NBM .... No Bowel Movement [*Medicine*] (DMAA)
NBM .... Nonbook Materials (ADA)
NBM .... Normal Bone Marrow [*Medicine*] (DMAA)
NBM .... Normal Bowel Movement [*Medicine*] (DMAA)
NBM .... Nothing by Mouth
NBM .... Nuclear Ballistic Missile
NBM .... Nucleus Basalis Magnocellularis [*Cytology*]
nbM .... Nucleus Basalis of Meynert [*Brain anatomy*]
NBMAIA .... National Broom Manufacturers and Allied Industries Association [*Later, NBMC*] (EA)
NBmB .... Briarcliff College, Briarcliff Manor, NY [*Library symbol Library of Congress*] (LCLS)
NBMB .... National Bus Military Bureau (EA)
NBMB .... N Binary Digits-M Binary Digits (NITA)
NBMBAA .... National Black MBA [*Master of Business Administration*] Association [*Chicago, IL*] (EA)
NbMC .... McCook Community College, McCook, NE [*Library symbol Library of Congress*] (LCLS)
NBMC .... National Bar Mitzvah Club [*Later, AZYF*] (EA)
NBMC .... National Black Media Coalition (EA)
NBMC .... National Black Music Caucus - of the Music Educators National Conference (EA)
NBMC .... National Broom and Mop Council [*Defunct*]
NBMC .... National Businessmen's Council [*Defunct*] (EA)
NBMCM .... Minto Coal Museum, New Brunswick [*Library symbol National Library of Canada*] (NLC)
NBMCR .... Non-Book Materials Cataloguing Rules (NITA)
NBMDA .... National Building Material Distributors Association (EA)
NBMDR .... National Bone Marrow Donor Registry (EA)
NBME .... Medgar Evers College of the City University of New York, Brooklyn, NY [*Library symbol Library of Congress*] (LCLS)
NBME .... National Board of Medical Examiners (EA)
NBMG .... Navigational Bombing and Missile Guidance (MCD)
NBMGS .... Navigational Bombing and Missile Guidance System (AAG)
NBMHD .... Hopital Docteur Georges - L. Dumont [*Docteur Georges - L. Dumont Hospital*]Moncton, New Brunswick [*Library symbol National Library of Canada*] (NLC)
NbMi .... Milford Public Library, Milford, NE [*Library symbol Library of Congress*] (LCLS)
NbMiS .... Southeast Community College, Milford, NE [*Library symbol Library of Congress*] (LCLS)
NBmK .... King's College, Briarcliff Manor, NY [*Library symbol Library of Congress*] (LCLS)
NbML .... McCook Public Library, McCook, NE [*Library symbol*] [*Library of Congress*] (LCLS)
NBmlA .... Adirondack Historical Association Museum Library, Blue Mountain Lake, NY [*Library symbol Library of Congress*] (LCLS)

NBMMH .... Health Sciences Library, The Moncton Hospital, New Brunswick [*Library symbol National Library of Canada*] (NLC)
NBMO .... Nonbonding Molecular Orbital [*Physical chemistry*]
NBMOA .... National Black McDonald's Operators Association (EA)
NBMOAL .... Atlantic Lottery Corp. [*Societe des Loteries de l'Atlantique*], Moncton, New Brunswick [*Library symbol National Library of Canada*] (NLC)
NBMOCC .... New Brunswick Community College, Moncton, New Brunswick [*Library symbol National Library of Canada*] (NLC)
NBMOF .... Fisheries and Oceans Canada [*Peches et Oceans Canada*] Moncton, New Brunswick [*Library symbol National Library of Canada*] (NLC)
NBMOLM .... Lutz Mountain Heritage Foundation, Inc., Moncton, New Brunswick [*Library symbol National Library of Canada*] (NLC)
NBMOM .... Moncton Museum, New Brunswick [*Library symbol National Library of Canada*] (NLC)
NBMORE .... Canada Department of Regional Industrial Expansion [*Ministere de l'Expansion Industrielle Regionale*] Moncton, New Brunswick [*Library symbol National Library of Canada*] (NLC)
NBMOTA .... Airworthiness Library, Atlantic Region, Transport Canada [*Bibliotheque de la Navigabilite Aerienne, Region de l'Atlantique, Transports Canada*], Moncton, New Brunswick [*Library symbol National Library of Canada*] (NLC)
NBMOTAR .... Atlantic Regional Library, Transport Canada [*Bibliotheque Regionale de l'Atlantique, Transports Canada*], Moncton, New Brunswick [*Library symbol National Library of Canada*] (NLC)
NBMOU .... Universite de Moncton, New Brunswick [*Library symbol National Library of Canada*] (NLC)
NBMOUA .... Archives Acadiennes, Universite de Moncton, New Brunswick [*Library symbol National Library of Canada*] (NLC)
NBMOUD .... Bibliotheque de Droit, Universite de Moncton, New Brunswick [*Library symbol National Library of Canada*] (NLC)
NBMOW .... Albert-Westmorland-Kent Regional Library, Moncton, New Brunswick [*Library symbol National Library of Canada*] (NLC)
NBMR .... NATO Basic Military Requirements (AABC)
NBMR .... Northern Bengal Mounted Rifles [*British military*] (DMA)
NBMS .... National Bulk Mail System [*Postal Service*]
NBMT .... NATO Basic Military Techniques (NATG)
NBmtT .... Bear Mountain Trailside Museum, Bear Mountain, NY [*Library symbol*] [*Library of Congress*] (LCLS)
NBMUX .... Neub. & Berman Munic. Secs. Trust [*Mutual fund ticker symbol*] (SG)
Nbn .... Nabonidus (BJA)
NBN .... Narrow Band Nerve [*Neurology*] (DAVI)
NBN .... Narrowband Network
NBN .... Narrowband Noise
NBN .... National Bank of Nigeria Ltd.
NBN .... National Bibliography Number
NBN .... National Black Network [*A radio network*]
NBN .... National Book Number [*British*]
NBN .... Nationality Broadcasting Network [*Cable-television system*]
NBN .... Network for Better Nutrition (EA)
NBN .... Neubabylonisches Namenbuch zu den Geschaeftsurkunden [*A publication*] (BJA)
NBN .... Newborn Nursery [*Medicine*]
NBN .... Newcastle Broadcasting Network [*Australian company broadcasting in Papua New Guinea*] (FEA)
NBN .... Nixdorf Broadband Network [*Communications*] [*British*]
NBN .... North British Airlines Ltd. [*ICAO designator*] (FAAC)
NBN .... Old Manse Library, Newcastle, New Brunswick [*Library symbol National Library of Canada*] (NLC)
NBNA .... National Bank of North America [*New York*]
NBNA .... National Black Nurses Association (EA)
NBNAM .... Archives of the Miramichi Historical Society, Newcastle, New Brunswick [*Library symbol National Library of Canada*] (NLC)
NbNb .... Neubabylonisches Namenbuch zu den Geschaeftsurkunden [*A publication*] (BJA)
NbNc .... Nebraska City Public Library, Nebraska City, NE [*Library symbol Library of Congress*] (LCLS)
NBNC .... New York City Community College of the City University of New York, Brooklyn, NY [*Library symbol Library of Congress*] (LCLS)
NBNC .... Noted but Not Corrected (MCD)
NbNcM .... Morton-James Public Library, Nebraska City, NE [*Library symbol*] [*Library of Congress*] (LCLS)
NBNDH .... New Denmark Historical Museum, New Brunswick [*Library symbol National Library of Canada*] (NLC)
NbNf .... Norfolk Public Library, Norfolk, NE [*Library symbol Library of Congress*] (LCLS)
NbNfN .... Northeast Technical Community College, Norfork, NE [*Library symbol Library of Congress*] (LCLS)
NBNM .... Health Sciences Library, Miramichi Hospital, Newcastle, New Brunswick [*Library symbol National Library of Canada*] (NLC)
NbNp .... North Platte Public Library, North Platte, NE [*Library symbol Library of Congress*] (LCLS)
NbNpM .... Mid-Plains Community College, North Platte, NE [*Library symbol Library of Congress*] (LCLS)
NBNR .... National Bankruptcy News and Reports [*A publication*] (DLA)
NBN Rep .... National Bankruptcy News and Reports [*A publication*] (DLA)
NBo .... Bolivar Free Library, Bolivar, NY [*Library symbol Library of Congress*] (LCLS)
NBO .... Nairobi [*Kenya*] [*Airport symbol*] (OAG)
NBO .... National Bank of Oman Ltd. SAO (EY)
NBO .... Navy Bureau of Ordnance [*Obsolete*]
NBO .... Nebo Air Co. Ltd. [*Former USSR*] [*FAA designator*] (FAAC)
NBO .... Network Buildout (IEEE)
NBO .... Nonbed Occupancy (AAMN)

NBO	Nonbridging Oxygen [*Materials science*]
NBO	Nordiska Kooperativa och Allmannyttiga Bostadsforetags Organisation [*Organization of Cooperative and Non-Profit Making Housing Enterprises in the Nordic Countries*] (EAIO)
NBO	Normal-Branch Oscillation [*Astronomy*]
NBO	Norsar Array Site 01B00 [*Norway*] [*Seismograph station code, US Geological Survey*] (SEIS)
NBO	Omaha Public Library, Omaha, NE [*OCLC symbol*] (OCLC)
NbO	Omaha Public Library, Omaha, NE [*Library symbol Library of Congress*] (LCLS)
NBO	Oromocto Public Library, New Brunswick [*Library symbol National Library of Canada*] (NLC)
NBOA	National Ballroom Operators Association [*Later, National Ballroom and Entertainment Association*]
NBOA	National Business Owners Association (EA)
NbOB	Boys Town Center for the Study of Youth Development, Omaha, NE [*Library symbol Library of Congress*] (LCLS)
NbOC	Creighton University, Omaha, NE [*Library symbol Library of Congress*] (LCLS)
NBOC	Network Building Out Capacitor [*Telecommunications*] (TEL)
NBOC	Northern Bank of Commerce [*NASDAQ symbol*] (SAG)
NBOC	Northern Bk Comm Ore [*NASDAQ symbol*] (TTSB)
NBOC	Northwest Bank of Commerce [*Oregon*] [*NASDAQ symbol*] (SAG)
NbOC-A	Creighton University, Alumni Library, Omaha, NE [*Library symbol Library of Congress*] (LCLS)
NbOC-D	Creighton University, School of Dentistry, Omaha, NE [*Library symbol Library of Congress*] (LCLS)
NbOC-H	Creighton University, Health Sciences Library, Omaha, NE [*Library symbol Library of Congress*] (LCLS)
NbOC-L	Creighton University, School of Law, Omaha, NE [*Library symbol Library of Congress*] (LCLS)
NbOC-M	Creighton University, School of Medicine and School of Pharmacy, Omaha, NE [*Library symbol Library of Congress*] (LCLS)
NbOD	Duchesne College, Omaha, NE [*Library symbol Library of Congress*] (LCLS)
NbOg	Goodall City Library, Ogallala, NE [*Library symbol Library of Congress*] (LCLS)
NbOGS	Church of Jesus Christ of Latter-Day Saints, Genealogical Society Library, OmahaBranch, Omaha, NE [*Library symbol Library of Congress*] (LCLS)
NBoh	Connetquot Public Library, Bohemia, NY [*Library symbol Library of Congress*] (LCLS)
NBohCH	Connetquot High School, Bohemia, NY [*Library symbol Library of Congress*] (LCLS)
NbOJ	Joslyn Art Museum, Omaha, NE [*Library symbol Library of Congress*] (LCLS)
NBoL	Bolivar Free Library, Bolivar, NY [*Library symbol*] [*Library of Congress*] (LCLS)
NBoIS	Marcella Sembrich Memorial Studio, Bolton Landing, NY [*Library symbol*] [*Library of Congress*] (LCLS)
N (Bomb)	Neutron Bomb
NbOMC	Metropolitan Technical Community College, Omaha, NE [*Library symbol Library of Congress*] (LCLS)
NBOME	National Board of Osteopathic Medical Examiners (EA)
NbONPS	United States National Park Service, Midwest Regional Office, Omaha, NE [*Library symbol Library of Congress*] (LCLS)
NbOP	Presbyterian Theological Seminary, Omaha, NE [*Library symbol Library of Congress*] (LCLS)
NBOR	Network Building Out Resistor [*Telecommunications*] (TEL)
NBOR	Nucleus of Basal Optic Root [*Neuroanatomy*]
NbOsc	Osceola Public Library, Osceola, NE [*Library symbol Library of Congress*] (LCLS)
NBOT	National Board of Orthopaedic Technologists [*British*] (DAVI)
NbOU	University of Nebraska at Omaha, Omaha, NE [*Library symbol Library of Congress*] (LCLS)
NbOV	United States Veterans Administration Hospital, Omaha, NE [*Library symbol Library of Congress*] (LCLS)
NbOW	Westside Community Schools, Omaha, NE [*Library symbol*] [*Library of Congress*] (LCLS)
NBp	Bayport-Blue Point Public Library, Blue Point, NY [*Library symbol Library of Congress*] (LCLS)
NBP	Name Binding Protocol [*Computer science*]
NBP	National Battlefield Park (BARN)
NBP	National Booster Program (AAG)
NBP	National Braille Press (EA)
NBP	National Business Publications [*Later, ABP*] (EA)
NBP	Needs-Based Payment [*Job Training and Partnership Act*] (OICC)
NBP	Neutral Bitter Principle [*Pharmacy*]
NBP	New Birth Party [*Cyprus*] [*Political party*]
NBP	(Nitrobenzyl)pyridine [*Organic chemistry*]
NBP	NonBacterial Prostatis [*Medicine*]
NBP	Normal Boiling Point
NBP	Northern Border Partners Ltd. [*NYSE symbol*] (SPSG)
NBP	Northern Border Ptnrs L.P. [*NYSE symbol*] (TTSB)
NBP	Nucleic Acid Binding Protein [*Biochemistry*]
NBP	Peru State College Library, Peru, NE [*OCLC symbol*] (OCLC)
NBP	Pratt Institute, Brooklyn, NY [*Library symbol Library of Congress*] (LCLS)
NBPA	National Back Pain Association (EAIO)
NBPA	National Bark Producers Association (EA)
NBPA	National Basketball Players Association (EA)
NBPA	National Beverage Packaging Association (EA)
NBPA	National Black People's Assembly (EA)
NBPA	National Black Police Association (EA)
NBPA	National Building Products Association [*Defunct*] (EA)

NBPA	Navy Board for Production Awards
NBPASV	Southern Victoria Historical Society, Perth-Andover, New Brunswick [*Library symbol National Library of Canada*] (NLC)
NBPB	National Biotechnology Policy Board
NBPC	National Black Political Convention [*1972*]
NBPC	National Black Programming Consortium (EA)
NBPC	National Border Patrol Council (EA)
NBPDW	National Brotherhood of Packinghouse and Dairy Workers [*Formerly, NBPW*] (EA)
NBPE	National Board of Podiatry Examiners
NBPE	National Board of Polygraph Examiners [*Later, APA*] (EA)
NbPerS	Peru State College, Peru, NE [*Library symbol Library of Congress*] (LCLS)
NBPHA	N-Benzoyl(phenyl)hydroxylamine [*Organic chemistry*]
NBPI	National Board for Prices and Incomes [*British*]
NBPI	Newspaper Benevolent and Provident Institution [*British*] (DGA)
NBPIW	National Brotherhood of Packinghouse and Industrial Workers (EA)
NbPI	Plattsmouth Public Library, Plattsmouth, NE [*Library symbol Library of Congress*] (LCLS)
NBPM	Narrowband Phase Modulation (MCD)
NBPM	Network-Based Project Management (PDAA)
NBPMC	National Bureau of Professional Management Consultants (NTPA)
NBPME	National Board of Podiatric Medical Examiners (EA)
NBPNPA	National Board of Pediatric Nurse Practitioners and Associates [*Later, NCBPNP/N*] (EA)
NBPO	NATO Bullpup Production Organization [*Missiles*] (NATG)
NBPol	Polytechnic Institute of New York, Brooklyn, NY [*Library symbol Library of Congress*] (LCLS)
NBPol-G	Polytechnic Institute of New York, Long Island Graduate Center, Farmingdale, NY [*Library symbol Library of Congress*] (LCLS)
NBpP	Bayport-Blue Point Public Library, Blue Point, NY [*Library symbol*] [*Library of Congress*] (LCLS)
NBPP	National Black Political Party
NBPRP	National Board for the Promotion of Rifle Practice (EA)
NBPRS	National Black Public Relations Society (NTPA)
NBPS	National Backgammon Players Society [*British*] (DBA)
NBPTE	National Board of Physical Therapy Examiners (EA)
NBPTS	National Board for Professional Teaching Standards (EA)
NBPu	Brooklyn Public Library, Brooklyn, NY [*Library symbol*] [*Library of Congress*] (LCLS)
NBPW	National Brotherhood of Packinghouse Workers [*Later, NBPDW*]
NBQ	Nitro(benzothiazolo)quinolinium Perchlorate [*Antineoplastic drug*]
NBR	Nabors Industries [*AMEX symbol*] (TTSB)
NBR	Nabors Industries, Inc. [*AMEX symbol*] (SPSG)
NBR	Narrowband Radiated (IEEE)
NBR	National Bankruptcy Register Reports [*United States*] [*A publication*] (DLA)
NBR	National Board of Review of Motion Pictures
NBR	National Buildings Record [*British*]
NBR	Neighborhood Business Revitalization [*Program*]
NBR	Net Borrowing Requirement [*Banking*] (MHDW)
NBR	New Beginnings Resources [*Vancouver Stock Exchange symbol*]
NBR	New Brunswick Reports [*Maritime Law Book Co. Ltd.*] [*Canada Information service or system A publication*] (CRD)
NBR	[*The*] Nightly Business Reports [*Television program*]
NBR	Nitrile Butadiene-Acrylonitrile Rubber (AAEL)
NBR	Nitrile-Butadiene Rubber
NBR	Nonborrowed Reserve [*Banking*]
NBR	Nonbreathing
NBR	North British Railway
NBR	Nuclear Boiler Rated (NRCH)
NBR	Null Balance Recorder
NBR	Number (KSC)
NBR	Number of Bids Received [*DoD*]
NBR	Nursing Boards Review [*Course*] [*American Journal of Nursing*]
NBR 2d	New Brunswick Reports, Second Series [*A publication*] (DLA)
NBRA	National Barrel Racing Association
NBRA	National Basketball Referees Association (NTPA)
NBRA	National Brain Research Association (EA)
NbRal	Ralston Public Library, Ralston, NE [*Library symbol Library of Congress*] (LCLS)
NBR All	Allen's New Brunswick Reports [*Canada A publication*] (DLA)
NBR Ber	Berton's New Brunswick Reports [*A publication*] (DLA)
NBRC	National Black Republican Council (EA)
NBRC	National Board for Respiratory Care (EA)
NBRCA	Atlantic Institution, Correctional Service Canada [*Etablissement Atlantique, Service Correctionnel Canada*], Renous, New Brunswick [*Library symbol National Library of Canada*] (BIB)
NBR Carl	Carleton's New Brunswick Reports [*A publication*] (DLA)
NBR Chip	Chipman's New Brunswick Reports [*1825-35*] [*A publication*] (DLA)
NbRcW	Willa Cather Pioneer Memorial, Red Cloud, NE [*Library symbol Library of Congress*] (LCLS)
NBre	Brewster Public Library, Brewster, NY [*Library symbol Library of Congress*] (LCLS)
NBREH	L'Eglise Historique St-Henri-De-Barachois, Robichaud, New Brunswick [*Library symbol National Library of Canada*] (NLC)
NBren	Brentwood Public Library, Brentwood, NY [*Library symbol Library of Congress*] (LCLS)
NBrenEJ	East Junior High School, Brentwood, NY [*Library symbol*] [*Library of Congress*] (LCLS)
NBrenIMC	District Instructional Media Center, Brentwood, NY [*Library symbol Library of Congress*] (LCLS)
NBrenSJ	Saint Joseph's College, Brentwood, NY [*Library symbol Library of Congress*] (LCLS)
NB Rep	New Brunswick Reports [*A publication*] (DLA)

NB Rev Stat... New Brunswick Revised Statutes [*Canada*] [*A publication*] (DLA)
NBRF .... National Biomedical Research Foundation [*Georgetown University*] [*Research center*]
NBRG........... National Basic Reference Graphic (MCD)
NBR Han...... Hannay's New Brunswick Reports [*12, 13 New Brunswick*] [*A publication*] (DLA)
NBri .... Bay Shore-Brightwaters Public Library, Brightwaters, NY [*Library symbol Library of Congress*] (LCLS)
NBrih .... Hampton Library, Bridgehampton, NY [*Library symbol Library of Congress*] (LCLS)
NBR Kerr .... Kerr's New Brunswick Reports [*A publication*] (DLA)
NBRL .... Naval Biomedical Research Laboratory
NBRL .... Naval Blood Research Laboratory [*Bureau of Medicine*]
NBRMP........ National Board of Review of Motion Pictures (EA)
NBRN .... Nestart Library, Richibucto, New Brunswick [*Library symbol National Library of Canada*] (NLC)
NBrockU ..... State University of New York, College at Brockport, Brockport, NY [*Library symbol Library of Congress*] (LCLS)
NBron .... Bronxville Public Library, Bronxville, NY [*Library symbol Library of Congress*] (LCLS)
NBronC .... Concordia College, Bronxville, NY [*Library symbol Library of Congress*] (LCLS)
NBronSL ...... Sarah Lawrence College, Bronxville, NY [*Library symbol Library of Congress*] (LCLS)
NBroo .... Brookhaven Free Library, Brookhaven, NY [*Library symbol Library of Congress*] (LCLS)
NBrooHS...... Bellport Senior High School, Brookhaven, NY [*Library symbol Library of Congress*] (LCLS)
NBRP & B.... Pugsley and Burbridge's New Brunswick Reports [*A publication*] (DLA)
NBRP & T.... Pugsley and Trueman's New Brunswick Reports [*A publication*] (DLA)
NBRPC........ New Brunswick Research and Productivity Council
NBR Pug...... Pugsley's New Brunswick Reports [*A publication*] (DLA)
NBR Pugs.... Pugsley's New Brunswick Reports [*1876-93*] [*Canada*] [*A publication*] (DLA)
NBRSA........ National Bench Rest Shooters Association (EA)
NBRT .... National Board for Respiratory Therapy [*Formerly, ARIT*] [*Later, NBRC*] (EA)
NBR Tru...... Trueman's New Brunswick Reports [*A publication*] (DLA)
N Bruns ...... New Brunswick Reports [*A publication*] (DLA)
NBrunS........ New Brunswick Scientific Co., Inc. [*Associated Press*] (SAG)
NbRVt.......... Neubabylonische Rechts- und Verwaltungstexte [*A publication*] (BJA)
NbRVu .... Neubabylonische Rechts- und Verwaltungsurkunden Uebersetzt und Erlaeutert [*A publication*] (BJA)
NBS .... Bureau of Ships Publications [*Obsolete Navy*]
NBS .... Kekaha, Kauai, HI [*Location identifier FAA*] (FAAL)
NBS .... Narrowband Search (MCD)
NBS .... National Australia Bank. Monthly Summary [*A publication*] (ADA)
NBS .... National Bakery School [*British*] (BI)
NBS .... National Battlefield Site (BARN)
NBS .... National Biological Survey [*Department of the Interior*]
NBS .... National Blood Service (WDAA)
NBS .... National Bookkeepers' Society (EA)
NBS .... National Book Sale [*British*]
NBS .... National Bridal Service (EA)
NBS .... National Broadcasting Service [*Trinidad and Tobago*] (EY)
NBS .... National Broadcasting Service [*New Zealand*]
NBS .... National Broadcasting System
NBS .... National Brotherhood of Skiers (EA)
NBS .... National Bureau of Standards [*Department of Commerce*] [*Later, NIST*]
NBS .... National Bureau of Standards, Gaithersburg, MD [*OCLC symbol*] (OCLC)
NBS .... National Business Systems, Inc. [*Toronto Stock Exchange symbol*]
NBS .... National Button Society (EA)
NBS .... Natural Black Slate (MSA)
NBS .... Navigational Bombing System [*British military*] (DMA)
NBS .... N-Bromosuccinimide [*Organic chemistry*]
NBS .... Needs-Based Staffing (ADA)
NBS .... Neighborhood Bible Studies (EA)
NBS .... Netherland Benevolent Society of New York [*Later, Netherlands-America CommunityAssociation*] (EA)
NBS .... Neurobehavioral Scale
NBS .... Neutral Buoyancy Simulator [*Navy*] (MCD)
NBS .... Nevoid Basal Cell Carcinoma Syndrome [*Oncology*] (DMAA)
NBS .... New British Standard [*Imperial wire gauge*]
NBS .... New Brunswick Scientific Co., Inc.
NBS .... Newcastle Business School [*British*] (ODBW)
NBS .... Night Bombardment - Short Distance [*Air Force*]
NBS .... Nijmegen Breakage Syndrome [*Medicine*] (DMAA)
NBS .... Nimbus Aviation [*British ICAO designator*] (FAAC)
NBS .... No Bacteria Seen [*Clinical microbiology*]
NBS .... Nonbaseline Software Library (MCD)
NBS .... Nordiska Byggforskningsorgans Samarbetsgrupp [*Nordic Building Research Cooperation Group*] [*Iceland*] (EAIO)
NBS .... Normal Blood Serum (MAE)
NBS .... Normal Bowel Sounds [*Gastroenterology*] (DAVI)
NBS .... Normal Burro Serum [*Biochemistry*] (DAVI)
NBS .... Normandy Base Section [*World War II*]
NBS .... Nothing Before Something [*Library cataloguing*] (DGA)
NBS .... Nuclear Backscattering Spectroscopy (EDCT)
NBS .... Nucleotide Binding Site [*Genetics*]
NBS .... Numeric Backspace Character [*Computer science*]
NBS .... Numismatic Bibliomania Society (EA)

NBS .... Saint John Regional Library, New Brunswick [*Library symbol National Library of Canada*] (NLC)
NbS............. Scottsbluff Public Library, Scottsbluff, NE [*Library symbol Library of Congress*] (LCLS)
NBSA .... National Bakery Suppliers Association (EA)
NBS-A .... National Bureau of Standards - Atomic (SAA)
NBSA .... Nurses' Board of South Australia
NBSAB .... Fort Beausejour Museum, Sackville, New Brunswick [*Library symbol National Library of Canada*] (NLC)
NBSAC .... National Boating Safety Advisory Council [*Department of Transportation*] [*Washington, DC*] (EGAO)
NBSACW...... Canadian Wildlife Service, Environment Canada [*Service Canadien de la Faune, Environnement Canada*] Sackville, New Brunswick [*Library symbol National Library of Canada*] (NLC)
NBSAE .... Norwegian-British-Swedish Antarctic Expedition [*1949-52*]
NBSAM .... Mount Allison University, Sackville, New Brunswick [*Library symbol National Library of Canada*] (NLC)
NBSARM...... Ross Memorial Library, St. Andrews, New Brunswick [*Library symbol National Library of Canada*] (BIB)
NBSBL .... National Bureau of Standards Boulder Laboratories
NBSC .... Health Sciences Library, Centracare Saint John, Inc., New Brunswick [*Library symbol National Library of Canada*] (NLC)
NBSC .... National Bank of South Carolina (EFIS)
NBSC .... National Black Sisters' Conference (EA)
NBSC .... New Brunswick Scient [*NASDAQ symbol*] (TTSB)
NBSC .... New Brunswick Scientific Co., Inc. [*NASDAQ symbol*] (NQ)
NBSC .... Nitrobenzenesulfenyl Chloride [*Organic chemistry*]
NBSCA........ National Beauty Salon Chain Association [*Later, ICSA*] (EA)
NBSCCST.... National Bureau of Standards Center for Computer Sciences and Technology (DIT)
NBSCM .... Centre Marin, Shippagan, New Brunswick [*Library symbol National Library of Canada*] (NLC)
NBSCU .... Centre Universitaire de Shippagan, New Brunswick [*Library symbol National Library of Canada*] (NLC)
NBSD .... Night Bombardment - Short Distance [*Air Force*] (IEEE)
NBSDI .... National Brands Soft Drinks Institute (EA)
NBsdQ .... Queensborough Community College of the City University of New York, Bayside, NY [*Library symbol Library of Congress*] (LCLS)
NbSe .... Seward Public Library, Seward, NE [*Library symbol Library of Congress*] (LCLS)
NbSeT......... Concordia Teachers College, Seward, NE [*Library symbol Library of Congress*] (LCLS)
NBSF .... Nitrobenzenesulfonyl Fluoride [*Organic chemistry*]
NBSFS .... National Bureau of Standards Frequency Standard (IEEE)
NBSG .... National Biotherapy Study Group (EA)
NbSHS .... Hiram Scott College, Scottsbluff, NE [*Library symbol Library of Congress Obsolete*] (LCLS)
NBSI .... North Bancshares [*NASDAQ symbol*] (TTSB)
NBSI .... North Bancshares, Inc. [*NASDAQ symbol*] (SAG)
NbSi........... Sidney Public Library, Sidney, NE [*Library symbol Library of Congress*] (LCLS)
NBSIR .... National Bureau of Standards Interagency Reports
NBSL .... New York City School Library System, Brooklyn, NY [*Library symbol Library of Congress*] (LCLS)
NBSLD .... National Bureau of Standards Load Determination [*Computer program*]
NBSM .... New Brunswick Museum, Saint John, New Brunswick [*Library symbol National Library of Canada*] (NLC)
NBSMA .... National Boot and Shoe Manufacturers' Association [*Later, FIA*]
NbSN .... Nebraska Western College, Scottsbluff, NE [*Library symbol Library of Congress*] (LCLS)
NBSPA .... National Bark and Soil Producers Association (NTPA)
NBSQH .... Quaco Historical and Library Society, St. Martins, New Brunswick [*Library symbol National Library of Canada*] (NLC)
NBSR .... National Bureau of Standards Reactor
NBSRH........ Health Sciences Library, Saint John Regional Hospital [*Bibliotheque des Sciences de la Sante, Hopital Regional de Saint-Jean*], New Brunswick [*Library symbol National Library of Canada*] (NLC)
NBSS .... National Bank Surveillance System
NBSS .... National British Softbill Society (BI)
NBSS .... Naval Beach Signal Section
NBsSH .... Southside Hospital, Bay Shore, NY [*Library symbol Library of Congress*] (LCLS)
NBS-SIS....... NBS-Standard Information Services (NITA)
NBSSSC....... St. Croix Public Library, St. Stephen, New Brunswick [*Library symbol National Library of Canada*] (NLC)
NBSSX .... Neub. & Berman Focus Fund [*Mutual fund ticker symbol*] (SG)
NBST .... Narrowband Subscriber Terminal (CET)
NBST .... National Board for Science and Technology [*Ireland*] (PDAA)
NBST .... [*The*] New Braunfels & Servtex Railroad, Inc. [*AAR code*]
NbSt............ Nimbostratus [*Cloud*] [*Meteorology*] (AIA)
NBSTAC....... St. Andrews Campus, New Brunswick Community College [*Library symbol National Library of Canada*] (BIB)
NBS/TAD...... National Bureau of Standards/Technical Analysis Division (NOAA)
NB Stat .... New Brunswick Statutes [*Canada*] [*A publication*] (DLA)
NBStF......... Saint Francis College, Brooklyn, NY [*Library symbol Library of Congress*] (LCLS)
NBSTIM .... Le Musee St-Isidore, Inc., New Brunswick [*Library symbol National Library of Canada*] (NLC)
NBStJC........ Saint Joseph's College, Brooklyn, NY [*Library symbol Library of Congress*] (LCLS)
NbSu........... Superior Carnegie Library, Superior, NE [*Library symbol Library of Congress*] (LCLS)
NBSU........... University of New Brunswick, Saint John, New Brunswick [*Library symbol National Library of Canada*] (NLC)

NBSUH......... Kings County Historical Society, Sussex, New Brunswick [*Library symbol National Library of Canada*] (NLC)

NBSU-M....... State University of New York at Brooklyn, Medical Research Library, Brooklyn, NY [*Library symbol*] [*Library of Congress*] (LCLS)

NBSUS......... Sussex Public Library, New Brunswick [*Library symbol National Library of Canada*] (NLC)

NBSV .... Narrowband Secure Voice System [*Army*] (CAAL)

NBSVS......... Narrowband Secure Voice System [*Army*] (MCD)

NBSVS......... Saint John Vocational School, New Brunswick [*Library symbol National Library of Canada*] (NLC)

NBT............. Brunswick, ME [*Location identifier FAA*] (FAAL)

NBT............. Nagoya Bumpy Torus [*Military*]

NBT............. Narrow-Beam Transducer [*National Ocean Survey*]

NBT............. National Bancshares Corp. of Texas [*AMEX symbol*] (SAG)

NBT............. Natl Bacshares Texas [*AMEX symbol*] (TTSB)

NBT............. Navigator Bombardier Training [*Air Force*] (AFM)

NBT............. Negative Balance Test (IAA)

NBT............. Netherlands Board of Tourism (EA)

NBT............. Networks for Biotechnology

NBT............. Neurobiotin [*Biochemical labelling compound*]

NBT............. Neutral Buoyancy Trainer [*Navy*] (MCD)

NBT............. New Brunswick Telephone Co. Ltd. [*Toronto Stock Exchange symbol*]

NBT............. Nimbus Beacon Transmitter

NBT............. Nitroblue Tetrazolium [*A stain*] [*Hematology*]

NBT............. Normal Breast Tissue [*Medicine*] (DB)

NBT............. Northern Ballet Theatre [*England*]

NBT............. Null-Balance Transmissometer (IEEE)

NBTA .... National Basketball Trainers Association (EA)

NBTA .... National Baton Twirling Association (EA)

NBTA .... National Board of Trial Advocacy (EA)

NBTA .... National Business Teachers Association (NADA)

NBTA .... National Business Travel Association (EA)

NBTA .... National Bus Traffic Association (EA)

NBTB .... NBT Bancorp. [*NASDAQ symbol*] (SAG)

NBT Bcp ...... NBT Bancorp [*Associated Press*] (SAG)

NBTC .... New Brands and Their Companies [*Formerly, NTN*] [*A publication*]

NBTC .... New Brunswick Teachers College

NBT-DF........ Nitroblue Tetrazolium Diformazan [*A stain*] [*Hematology*]

NBTDR......... Narrowband Time Domain Reflectometry (MCD)

NBTE........... Nonbacterial Thrombotic Endocarditis [*Cardiology*]

NbTe .... Tekamah Carnegie Public Library, Tekamah, NE [*Library symbol Library of Congress*] (LCLS)

NBTF........... National Brain Tumor Foundation (EA)

NBTF........... National Building Trades Federation [*A union*] [*British*]

NBTH .... Bibliotheque Medicale, Hotel-Dieu Saint-Joseph-De-Tracadie, New Brunswick [*Library symbol National Library of Canada*] (BIB)

NBTI............ Nitrobenzylthioinosine [*Organic chemistry*]

NBTL........... National Battery Test Laboratory [*Department of Energy*]

NBTL........... Naval Boiler and Turbine Laboratory

NBTM.......... Le Musee Historique de Tracadie, New Brunswick [*Library symbol National Library of Canada*] (NLC)

NBTNF......... Newborn, Term, Normal, Female [*Obstetrics*]

NBTNM......... Newborn, Term, Normal, Male [*Obstetrics*]

NBTPI.......... National Book Trade Provident Institution [*British*] (DGA)

NBTPS .... National Book Trade Provident Society [*British*] (DI)

NBTR .... Narrowband Tape Recorder

NBTS .... National Blood Transfusion Service

NBTS .... New Boston Tracking Station (SAA)

NBTS .... New Brunswick Theological Seminary [*New Jersey*]

NBTS .... Northern Baptist Theological Seminary [*Lombard, IL*]

NBTT .... Net Barter Terms of Trade

NBTY .... NBTY, Inc. [*NASDAQ symbol*] (SAG)

NBu............. Buffalo and Erie County Public Library, Buffalo, NY [*Library symbol Library of Congress*] (LCLS)

NBU .... Glenview, IL [*Location identifier FAA*] (FAAL)

NBU .... NBU Mines Ltd. [*Toronto Stock Exchange symbol*]

nbu .... Nebraska [*MARC country of publication code Library of Congress*] (LCCP)

NBU .... New Better than Used [*Statistics*]

NBU .... Nordiska Bankmannaunionen [*Confederation of Nordic Bank Employees' Unions*] (EA)

NBU .... University of Nebraska at Omaha, Omaha, NE [*OCLC symbol*] (OCLC)

NbU .... University of Nebraska, Lincoln, NE [*Library symbol Library of Congress*] (LCLS)

NBuA .... Allied Corp., Specialty Chemicals Division, Buffalo, NY [*Library symbol Library of Congress*] (LCLS)

NbU-A.......... University of Nebraska, Agriculture Library, Lincoln, NE [*Library symbol Library of Congress*] (LCLS)

NBuAA .... Acres American, Inc., Buffalo, NY [*Library symbol Library of Congress*] (LCLS)

NBuACE ...... United States Army, Corps of Engineers, Buffalo, NY [*Library symbol*] [*Library of Congress*] (LCLS)

NBuAK .... Albright-Knox Art Gallery, Buffalo Fine Arts Academy, Buffalo, NY [*Library symbol Library of Congress*] (LCLS)

NBuAn .... Andco, Inc., Buffalo, NY [*Library symbol Library of Congress*] (LCLS)

NBuB .... Buffalo Society of Natural Sciences, Buffalo Museum of Science, Buffalo, NY [*Library symbol Library of Congress*] (LCLS)

NBuBA .... Bell Aerosystems Co., Buffalo, NY [*Library symbol Library of Congress*] (LCLS)

NBuBE .... Buffalo and Erie County Public Library, Buffalo, NY [*Library symbol*] [*Library of Congress*] (LCLS)

NBuBLH ...... Bry-Lin Hospital, Buffalo, NY [*Library symbol Library of Congress*] (LCLS)

NBuBM .... Brystol-Myers Pharmaceuticals R & D, Buffalo, NY [*Library symbol*] [*Library of Congress*] (LCLS)

NBuBO .... Buffalo Organization for Social and Technological Innovation, Inc. (BOSTI), Buffalo, NY [*Library symbol Library of Congress*] (LCLS)

NBuBR .... Biblial Research Institute, Inc., Buffalo, NY [*Library symbol*] [*Library of Congress*] (LCLS)

NBuC .... State University of New York, College at Buffalo, Buffalo, NY [*Library symbol Library of Congress*] (LCLS)

NBuCA .... Cornell Aeronautical Laboratory, Buffalo, NY [*Library symbol Library of Congress*] (LCLS)

NBuCBL ...... Christel, Bean & Linihan, Buffalo, NY [*Library symbol*] [*Library of Congress*] (LCLS)

NBuCC .... Canisius College, Buffalo, NY [*Library symbol Library of Congress*] (LCLS)

NBuCEC ...... CECOS International, Buffalo, NY [*Library symbol Library of Congress*] (LCLS)

NBuCH .... Children's Hospital, Buffalo, NY [*Library symbol Library of Congress*] (LCLS)

NBuCo .... Buffalo Color Corp., Buffalo, NY [*Library symbol Library of Congress*] (LCLS)

NBuCoH ...... Buffalo Columbus Hospital, Buffalo, NY [*Library symbol*] [*Library of Congress*] (LCLS)

NBuD .... D'Youville College, Buffalo, NY [*Library symbol Library of Congress*] (LCLS)

NBuDa .... Daemen College, Buffalo, NY [*Library symbol Library of Congress*] (LCLS)

NBuDD .... DeLancey Divinity School, Buffalo, NY [*Library symbol Library of Congress Obsolete*] (LCLS)

NBuDY .... E. I. Du Pont de Nemours & Co., Yerkes Research Laboratory, Buffalo, NY [*Library symbol Library of Congress*] (LCLS)

NBUE .... New Better than Used in Expectation [*Statistics*]

NBuEC .... Erie Community College-North, Buffalo, NY [*Library symbol Library of Congress*] (LCLS)

NBuEC-C ..... Erie Community College-North, City Campus, Buffalo, NY [*Library symbol Library of Congress*] (LCLS)

NBuEC-U ..... Erie Community College-North, Urban Center, Buffalo, NY [*Library symbol Library of Congress*] (LCLS)

NBuEE .... Ecology and Environment, Inc., Buffalo, NY [*Library symbol Library of Congress*] (LCLS)

NBuEMH ...... Edward J. Meyer Memorial Hospital Medical Library, Buffalo, NY [*Library symbol Library of Congress*] (LCLS)

NBuF .... Falcon Research & Development, Inc., Buffalo, NY [*Library symbol Library of Congress*] (LCLS)

NBUF .... National Black United Front (EA)

NBUF .... National Black United Fund (EA)

NBuG .... Grosvenor Reference Division, Buffalo and Erie County Public Library, Buffalo, NY [*Library symbol Library of Congress*] (LCLS)

NBuGC .... Graphic Controls Corp., Buffalo, NY [*Library symbol Library of Congress*] (LCLS)

NBuGD .... Goldome FSB, Bufflo, NY [*Library symbol*] [*Library of Congress*] (LCLS)

NBuGH .... Buffalo General Hospital, Buffalo, NY [*Library symbol Library of Congress*] (LCLS)

NBuGH-N ..... Buffalo General Hospital, School of Nursing, Buffalo, NY [*Library symbol Library of Congress*] (LCLS)

NBuHi .... Buffalo and Erie County Historical Society, Buffalo, NY [*Library symbol Library of Congress*] (LCLS)

NBuHSA....... Health Systems Agency of Western New York, Inc., Buffalo, NY [*Library symbol Library of Congress*] (LCLS)

NBuKMH ..... Kenmore Mercy Hospital, Medical Library, Buffalo, NY [*Library symbol*] [*Library of Congress*] (LCLS)

NbU-L .... University of Nebraska, College of Law, Lincoln, NE [*Library symbol Library of Congress*] (LCLS)

NBuLH .... Lafayette General Hospital, Buffalo, NY [*Library symbol Library of Congress*] (LCLS)

NBuLTV........ LTV Aerospace & Defense Co., Buffalo, NY [*Library symbol*] [*Library of Congress*] (LCLS)

NBuM .... Medaille College, Buffalo, NY [*Library symbol Library of Congress*] (LCLS)

NbU-M .... University of Nebraska, College of Medicine, Omaha, NE [*Library symbol Library of Congress*] (LCLS)

NBuMM........ Marine Midland Services Corp., Technical Information Center, Buffalo, NY [*Library symbol Library of Congress*] (LCLS)

NBuNCE....... National Center for Earthquake Engineering, Research Information Services, State, Buffalo, NY [*Library symbol*] [*Library of Congress*] (LCLS)

NBuPC .... Buffalo Psychiatric Center, Buffalo, NY [*Library symbol Library of Congress*] (LCLS)

NBuPL .... Pennwalt Corp., Lucidol Division, Buffalo, NY [*Library symbol Library of Congress*] (LCLS)

NBuRH........ Rosary Hill College, Buffalo, NY [*Library symbol Library of Congress Obsolete*] (LCLS)

NBuRSI........ Reichert Scientific Instruments, Buffalo, NY [*Library symbol*] [*Library of Congress*] (LCLS)

NBUSA........ United States Army, Fort Hamilton Post Library, Fort Hamilton, Brooklyn, NY [*Library symbol Library of Congress*] (LCLS)

NBuSCA ...... SCA Chemical Services, Inc., Buffalo, NY [*Library symbol Library of Congress*] (LCLS)

NBuSCH ...... Sisters of Charity Hospital, Buffalo, NY [*Library symbol Library of Congress*] (LCLS)

NBuSD .... Buffalo City School District, Buffalo, NY [*Library symbol*] [*Library of Congress*] (LCLS)

NBuSFH....... St. Francis Hospital of Buffalo, Buffalo, NY [*Library symbol*] [*Library of Congress*] (LCLS)

NBuSK	Spencer Kellogg Division, Textron, Inc., Buffalo, NY [*Library symbol Library of Congress*] (LCLS)
NBuSMH	Sheehan Memorial Emergency Hospital, Buffalo, NY [*Library symbol Library of Congress*] (LCLS)
NBuSR	Sierra Research Corp., Buffalo, NY [*Library symbol Library of Congress*] (LCLS)
NBuStM	Saint Mary's School for the Deaf, Buffalo, NY [*Library symbol Library of Congress*] (LCLS)
NBuTC	Trocaire College, Buffalo, NY [*Library symbol Library of Congress*] (LCLS)
NBuU	State University of New York at Buffalo, Buffalo, NY [*Library symbol Library of Congress*] (LCLS)
NBuU-A	State University of New York at Buffalo, Art Library, Buffalo, NY [*Library symbol Library of Congress*] (LCLS)
NBuU-AR	State University of New York at Buffalo, Archives, Buffalo, NY [*Library symbol Library of Congress*] (LCLS)
NBuU-BA	State University of New York at Buffalo, Bell Annex, Buffalo, NY [*Library symbol Library of Congress*] (LCLS)
NBuU-BS	State University of New York at Buffalo, Bell Science Library, Buffalo, NY [*Library symbol Library of Congress*] (LCLS)
NBuU-C	State University of New York at Buffalo, Chemistry Library, Buffalo, NY [*Library symbol Library of Congress*] (LCLS)
NBuU-CT	University of Buffalo Foundation, Inc., Center for Tomorrow, State University of New York at Buffalo, Amherst, NY [*Library symbol*] [*Library of Congress*] (LCLS)
NBuU-D	State University of New York at Buffalo, Documents Library, Buffalo, NY [*Library symbol Library of Congress*] (LCLS)
NBuU-E	State University of New York at Buffalo, Educational Opportunity Center, Buffalo, NY [*Library symbol Library of Congress*] (LCLS)
NBuU-H	State University of New York at Buffalo, Health Sciences Library, Buffalo, NY [*Library symbol Library of Congress*] (LCLS)
NBuU-HA	State University of New York at Buffalo, Harriman Library, Buffalo, NY [*Library symbol Library of Congress*] (LCLS)
NBuU-L	State University of New York at Buffalo, Law Library, Buffalo, NY [*Library symbol Library of Congress*] (LCLS)
NBuU-LL	State University of New York at Buffalo, Library Literature Library, Buffalo, NY [*Library symbol Library of Congress*] (LCLS)
NBuU-LS	State University of New York at Buffalo, Library Science Library, Buffalo, NY [*Library symbol Library of Congress*] (LCLS)
NBuU-Mu	State University of New York at Buffalo, Music Library, Buffalo, NY [*Library symbol Library of Congress*] (LCLS)
NBuU-P	State University of New York at Buffalo, Physics Library, Buffalo, NY [*Library symbol Library of Congress*] (LCLS)
NBuU-PO	State University of New York at Buffalo, Poetry Library, Buffalo, NY [*Library symbol Library of Congress*] (LCLS)
NBuU-R	State University of New York at Buffalo, Reference, Buffalo, NY [*Library symbol Library of Congress*] (LCLS)
NBuU-RL	State University of New York at Buffalo, Ridge Lea, Buffalo, NY [*Library symbol Library of Congress*] (LCLS)
NBuU-RP	State University of New York at Buffalo, Roswell Park Memorial Institute, Buffalo, NY [*Library symbol Library of Congress*] (LCLS)
NBuU-SE	State University of New York at Buffalo, Science and Engineering Library, Buffalo, NY [*Library symbol Library of Congress*] (LCLS)
NBuVA	United States Veterans Administration Hospital, Buffalo, NY [*Library symbol Library of Congress*] (LCLS)
NBuVM	Villa Maria College of Buffalo, Buffalo, NY [*Library symbol Library of Congress*] (LCLS)
NBuVNA	Visiting Nursing Association of Buffalo, Buffalo, NY [*Library symbol Library of Congress*] (LCLS)
NBuW	Worthington Compressor & Engine International, Buffalo, NY [*Library symbol Library of Congress*] (LCLS)
NBuWeP	Westwood Pharmaceuticals, Inc., Buffalo, NY [*Library symbol Library of Congress*] (LCLS)
NBUWH	Carleton County Historical Society, Upper Woodstock, New Brunswick [*Library symbol National Library of Canada*] (NLC)
NBuWNED	WNED-TV, Buffalo, NY [*Library symbol Library of Congress*] (LCLS)
NBuX	XACO, Inc., Buffalo, NY [*Library symbol*] [*Library of Congress*] (LCLS)
NBV	Net Book Value (TEL)
NbV	Valentine Public Library, Valentine, NE [*Library symbol Library of Congress*] (LCLS)
NBVA	National Bulk Vendors Association (EA)
NBVA	United States Veterans Administration Hospital, Brooklyn, NY [*Library symbol Library of Congress*] (LCLS)
NBV Ad	New Brunswick Vice Admiralty Reports [*A publication*] (DLA)
NBVA-O	United States Veterans Administration Hospital, Outpatient Clinic, Brooklyn, NY [*Library symbol Library of Congress*] (LCLS)
NBVCXO	Narrowband Voltage-Controlled Crystal Oscillator
NBVF	National Burn Victim Foundation (EA)
NBVM	Narrow-Band Voice Modulation (PDAA)
NBVO	National Black Veterans Organization [*Defunct*] (EA)
NBW	L. P. Fisher Public Library, Woodstock, New Brunswick [*Library symbol National Library of Canada*] (NLC)
NBW	National Barristers' Wives [*Later, NABBS*] (EA)
NBW	National Book Week (NTCM)
NBW	Natural Bandwidths [*Spectroscopy*]
NBW	Nebraska Wesleyan University, Lincoln, NE [*OCLC symbol*] (OCLC)
NBW	Noise Bandwidth
nbw	Noise Bandwidth (IDOE)
NBW	Normal Birth Weight
NbW	North by West
NBWA	National Beer Wholesalers' Association (EA)
NBWA	National Blacksmiths and Welders Association (EA)
NBWA	National Buddhist Women's Associations (EA)
NbWayS	Wayne State College, Wayne, NE [*Library symbol Library of Congress*] (LCLS)
NBWH	Carleton Memorial Hospital, Woodstock, New Brunswick [*Library symbol National Library of Canada*] (BIB)
NBWHP	National Black Women's Health Project (EA)
NbWi	Dvoracek Memorial Library, Wilber, NE [*Library symbol Library of Congress*] (LCLS)
NBWPLC	National Black Women's Political Leadership Caucus (EA)
NBWROP	Naval Bureau of Weapons Reserve Ordnance Plant
NBWTAU	National British Women's Total Abstinence Union (EAIO)
NBWV	Victoria-Carleton Courthouse, Woodstock, New Brunswick [*Library symbol National Library of Canada*] (NLC)
NBWY	York Regional Library, Headquarters No. 2, Woodstock, New Brunswick [*Library symbol National Library of Canada*] (NLC)
NBX	Jeffersn-Pilot 7.25% `ACES' [*NYSE symbol*] (TTSB)
NBX	Jefferson Pilot [*NYSE symbol*] (SAG)
NBX	Nabire [*Indonesia*] [*Airport symbol*] (OAG)
NBY	Nearest Besselian Year
NBY	Nutrient Broth Yeast [*Microbiology*]
NbY	York Public Library, York, NE [*Library symbol Library of Congress*] (LCLS)
NbYC	York College, York, NE [*Library symbol Library of Congress*] (LCLS)
NBYLC	National Black Youth Leadership Council (EA)
NBysSH	Bay Shore Senior High School, Bay Shore, NY [*Library symbol Library of Congress*] (LCLS)
nc----	Central America [*MARC geographic area code Library of Congress*] (LCCP)
NC	Chloropicrin Stannic Chloride [*Inorganic chemistry*]
NC	La Nouvelle Clio [*Brussels*] [*A publication*] (BJA)
NC	NACCO Indus Inc. Cl'A' [*NYSE symbol*] (TTSB)
NC	Name Control [*IRS*]
NC	Nano Crystal (AAEL)
nc	Nanocurie [*Pne billionth of a curie*]
NC	Narrowband Communicative Services [*Telecommunications*]
NC	Narrow Coverage
NC	Nasal Cannula [*Medicine*] (MEDA)
NC	Nashville, Chattanooga & St. Louis [*Louisville & Nashville Railroad Co.*] [*AAR code*]
NC	Natal Carabiniers [*British military*] (DMA)
NC	National Catholic News Service
NC	National Cemetery (IIA)
NC	National Center (IAA)
NC	National Certificate (WDAA)
NC	National Churches [*A publication*]
NC	National Coarse [*Thread*]
NC	National Colonialist Party [*Australia Political party*]
NC	National Cooperatives [*Later, UNICO*] [*An association*]
NC	National Curriculum [*Education*] (AIE)
NC	Native Cavalry [*British military*] (DMA)
NC	NATO Center (NATG)
NC	NATO Confidential (NATG)
NC	Natural Cytotoxic [*Cells*] [*Immunochemistry*]
NC	Nature Conservancy [*NERC*] [*British*]
NC	Naval Cadet [*British*] (ROG)
NC	Naval Correspondence
NC	Navigation Computer
NC	Navigation Console
NC	Navy Component
NC	Navy Cross
NC	Neanderthal Conservative [*Slang*]
NC	Nearly Commensurate Model [*Physics*]
NC	Necrosis
Nc	Negative Wave in Children [*Neurophysiology*]
NC	Neighborhood Coalition (EA)
NC	Nerve Center [*An association*] (EA)
NC	Nerve Conduction
NC	Net Capital [*Business term*]
NC	Net Charter [*Business term*] (DS)
NC	Net Control (MCD)
NC	Net Cost
NC	Netilmicin-Clindamycin [*Antibiotic combination*]
NC	Network Card [*British Rail*]
NC	Network Channel [*Broadcasting*] (NTCM)
NC	Network Computer (PCM)
NC	Network Computing
NC	Network Congestion [*Telecommunications*] (TEL)
NC	Network Connect
NC	Network Control (IAA)
NC	Network Controller
NC	Network Countdown
NC	Neural Crest [*Anatomy*]
NC	Neurocirculatory [*Medicine*] (DAVI)
NC	Neurologic Check [*Medicine*]
NC	Neutral Current [*Physics*]
NC	Neutralization Capacitor (IAA)
NC	Neutralizing Capacitance [*or Coil*] (DEN)
NC	Neutron Controller [*Nuclear energy*] (NRCH)
N/C	New Account (ROG)
NC	Newair [*ICAO designator*] (AD)
NC	New Caledonia [*ANSI two-letter standard code*] (CNC)
NC	New Canada Press
NC	New Cases (Bingham's New Cases) in Common Pleas [*1834-40*] [*A publication*] (DLA)
NC	New Cavendish Books [*Publisher*] [*British*]
N/C	New Charter [*Navigation*]

NC	New Church (ROG)
NC	New Construction [Navy]
NC	New Consultants [A publication]
NC	New Crop
NC	Neylan Conference (EA)
NC	Nickel Cadmium (IAA)
NC	Nickel Clad
NC	Night Coach [Airline designation]
N-C	Nightingale-Conant [Audio publisher]
NC	Nippon Club (EA)
NC	Nitrocellulose [Organic chemistry]
NC	Nixdorf Computer (IAA)
NC	NOAA [National Oceanic and Atmospheric Administration] Corps (USDC)
NC	No Casualty (MAE)
NC	No Change
NC	No Charge
NC	No Circuits
NC	No Coil (MSA)
NC	No Collaterals [Medicine]
NC	No Comment (NASA)
N/C	No Complaints [Medicine]
NC	No Connection [Valve pins] [Radio] [Technical drawings]
nc	No Connection (IDOE)
NC	No Contact
NC	No Contest [Sports]
NC	No Cost (AAG)
NC	No Credit (WGA)
NC	Noise Correlation (MSA)
NC	Noise Criteria (NAKS)
NC	Noise Criterion
NC	Noiseless Camera (NTCM)
NC	Nominal Correction
NC	Nominating Committee [American Occupational Therapy Association]
NC	Noncallable (EBF)
NC	Noncallable Bond [Investment term]
NC	Noncoin (IAA)
NC	Noncollectable
NC	Non-Color Sensitized Emulsion [Also called color-blind emulsion] (WDMC)
NC	Noncommercial [Rate] [Value of the English pound]
NC	Noncommissioned
NC	Noncomplex (MCD)
NC	Noncompliance [Noncompliant] (DAVI)
NC	Nonconforming
NC	Nonconformist [Indicating religious preference] [Military British]
NC	Non-Continuous Liner [Shipping] (DS)
NC	Noncontributory (DAVI)
NC	Nonconversational (IAA)
NC	Non-Crystalline (OA)
NC	Non-Curling [Photographic film] (ROG)
NC	Nonlinear Capacitance
NC	Nonrecurring Costs (AAGC)
NC	Nordic Council
NC	NORDLEK Council (EAIO)
NC	Normal Children
NC	Normal Control
NC	Normal Copy [Oncology]
NC	Normally Closed [Switch]
NC	Norman Conquest [of England, 1066]
NC	Normocephalic [On physical examination] [Medicine] (DAVI)
NC	North Carolina [Postal code]
NC	North Carolina Railroad
NC	North Carolina Reports [A publication] (DLA)
Nc	North Carolina State Library, Raleigh, NC [Library symbol Library of Congress] (LCLS)
NC	North Carolina Supreme Court Reports [A publication] (DLA)
NC	North Central Airlines, Inc. [ICAO designator] (OAG)
NC	North Coast (ADA)
NC	Northcor Resources Ltd. [Vancouver Stock Exchange symbol]
NC	North Country (ROG)
NC	Northern Command
NC	Northern Consolidated Airlines, Inc.
NC	Northrop Corp. (KSC)
NC	Norwegian Club (EA)
NC	Nose Cone [Aviation] (AFM)
N/C	Nose Cone [Aerospace] (NAKS)
NC	Not Carried
NC	Not Coded (MCD)
NC	Not Competitive [Rejected research proposals] [National Institutes of Health]
NC	Not Completed [Medicine] (DMAA)
NC	Not Connected [Electronics] (DEN)
NC	Not Controlled [Experimental conditions]
N/C	Not Critical (NASA)
NC	Not Cultured (MAE)
NC	Notes of Cases at Madras (Strange) [A publication] (DLA)
NC	Notes of Cases, English Ecclesiastical and Maritime Courts [1841-50] [A publication] (DLA)
NC	Novo Cruzado [Brazilian currency]
NC	Nuclear Capability
NC	Nuclear Congress
NC	Nuclear-Cytoplasmic [Ratio] [Cytology] (MAE)
NC	Nucleocapsid (DB)
NC	Nucleus of Ciliated Cell
NC	Nuestra Cuenta [Our Account] [Business term Spanish]
NC	™Nuff Ced∫ [Enough Said] [Slang]
NC	Numbering Counter [Computer science] (OA)
NC	Numerical Control [Computer science]
NC	Nurse Corps [Military]
NC	Sagrada Biblia [1944] [Eloino Nacar Fuster and Alberto Colunga] (BJA)
NC	Sandoz Pharmaceuticals [Research code symbol]
nc	Sodium Carbonate [CIPW classification] [Geology]
NC	Warner-Lambert Pharmaceutical Co. [Research code symbol]
NC1	Navy Counselor First Class (DNAB)
NC1	Nominal Correction 1 [Phasing Maneuver] [NASA] (NAKS)
NC3	Norsar Array Site 03C00 [Norway] [Seismograph station code, US Geological Survey] (SEIS)
NC³A	Nuclear Command, Control, and Communications Assessment (COE)
NC³D	National Coordinating Center for Curriculum Development
NC5	Norsar Array Site 05C00 [Norway] [Seismograph station code, US Geological Survey] (SEIS)
NC-17	No Children under 17 Admitted [Movie rating]
NCa	Canton Free Library, Canton, NY [Library symbol Library of Congress] (LCLS)
NCA	College of New Caledonia Library [UTLAS symbol]
NCA	Jacksonville, NC [Location identifier FAA] (FAAL)
NCA	National Campaign for the Arts [British] (DBA)
NCA	National Camping Association (EA)
NCA	National Candle Association (EA)
NCA	National Canners Association [Later, NFPA] (EA)
NCA	National Capital Award
NCA	National Carousel Association (EA)
NCA	National Cashmere Association [Defunct] (EA)
NCA	National Caterers Association [Later, ICA] (EA)
NCA	National Cathedral Association (EA)
NCA	National Cattlemens Association (EA)
NCA	National Caves Association (EA)
NCA	National Caving Association [British] (DBA)
NCA	National Ceramic Association [Later, ICA] (EA)
NCA	National Certificate of Agriculture [British]
NCA	National Certification Agency (DMAA)
NCA	National Certification Agency for Medical Laboratory Personnel (EA)
NCA	National Chaplain's Association (EA)
NCA	National Charcoal Association
NCA	National Chastity Association (EA)
NCA	National Cheerleaders Association (EA)
NCA	National Childminding Association [British] (EAIO)
NCA	National Chiropractic Association [Universal Chiropractic Association and American Chiropratic Association] [Later, American Chiropractic Association] [Formed by a merger of]
NCA	National Christian Association (EA)
NCA	National Civic Association
NCA	National Club Association (EA)
NCA	National Coal Association (EA)
NCA	National Coal Authority [Australia]
NCA	National Coffee Association of the United States of America (EA)
NCA	National Color-Bred Association (EA)
NCA	National Command Authorities
NCA	National Commission on Accrediting [Later, COPA] (EA)
NCA	National Communication Agencies (NATG)
NCA	National Communications Association (EA)
NCA	National Composition Association [Later, NCPA] (EA)
NCA	National Computer Association (EA)
NCA	National Concilio of America (EA)
NCA	National Confectioners Association of the United States (EA)
NCA	National Conference of Artists (EA)
NCA	National Congressional Analysis Corp. (IID)
NCA	National Constables Association (EA)
NCA	National Constructors Association (EA)
NCA	National Contesters Association (EA)
NCA	National Contingency Account (OICC)
NCA	National Cosmetology Association (EA)
NCA	National Costumers Association (EA)
NCA	National Council for Aviculture [British] (DBA)
NCA	National Council on Alcoholism [Later, NCADD] (EA)
NCA	National Council on the Aging [Washington, DC]
NCA	National Council on the Arts [of NFAH]
NCA	National Coursing Association [Later, NGA] (EA)
NCA	National Cranberry Association
NCA	National Creameries Association [Later, NMPF] (EA)
NCA	National Credit Association (NADA)
NCA	National Cricket Association [British]
NCA	National Crop Acreage Program [Department of Agriculture]
NCA	Naval Center for Cost Analysis
NCA	Naval Command Assistant
NCA	Naval Communications Annex
NCA	Navy Contract Administrator
NCA	NCA Minerals [Vancouver Stock Exchange symbol]
NCA	N-Carboxy Anhydride [Organic chemistry]
NCA	N-Chloroacetamide [Organic chemistry]
NCA	N-Chloroethylnorapomorphine [Organic chemistry, biochemistry]
NCA	Network Career Advancement Institute [Telecommunications service] (TSSD)
NCA	Network Computing Architecture [Computer science] (TNIG)
NCA	Network for Community Activities
NCA	Neurocirculatory Asthenia [Medicine]
NCA	Neutrophil Chemotactic Activity [Clinical chemistry]
NCA	New Communities Administration [HUD]

NCA .... Newfoundland Club of America (EA)
NCA .... News & Current Affairs (WDAA)
NCA .... Nickel-Copper Alloy (MSA)
NCA .... Nippon Cargo Airlines [*Japan*]
NCA .... Nippon Cargo Airlines Co. Ltd. [*Japan ICAO designator*] (FAAC)
NCA .... No Copies Available (ADA)
NCA .... No Coupons Attached (DLA)
NCA .... Nodulocystic Acne [*Medicine*] (DMAA)
NCA .... Noise Control Act (EG)
NCA .... Noise Control Association (EA)
NCA .... Noncombat Aircraft [*Military*] (MCD)
NCA .... Noncontractile Area (DB)
NCA .... Noncontractual Authorization
NCA .... Nonorganic Ceramic Adhesive
NCA .... Nonspecific Cross-Reacting Antigen [*Immunology*]
NCA .... Normal Coordinate Analysis
NCA .... North Caicos [*British West Indies*] [*Airport symbol*] (OAG)
NCA .... North Carolina Court of Appeals Reports [*A publication*] (DLA)
NCA .... North Central Association of Colleges and Secondary Schools [*Later, NCACS*]
NCA .... North Central Bible College, Minneapolis, MN [*OCLC symbol*] (OCLC)
NCA .... North Coast Airlines [*Australia*]
NCA .... Northern Communications Area [*Military*]
NCA .... Northern Consolidated Airlines, Inc.
NCA .... Northwest Computing Association
NCA .... Nuclear and Chemical Agency [*Army*]
NCA .... Nuclear Cerebral Angiogram [*Medicine*] (DMAA)
NCA .... Nurse Consultants Association (EA)
NCA .... Nuveen California Municipal Fund [*NYSE symbol*] (SPSG)
NCA .... Nuveen CA Muni Val Fd [*NYSE symbol*] (TTSB)
NcA............ Pack Memorial Public Library, Asheville, NC [*Library symbol Library of Congress*] (LCLS)
NCAA .... National Center for Audio Tapes Archive (EA)
NCAA .... National Center on Arts and the Aging (EA)
NCAA .... National Change of Address Association [*Commercial firm New York, NY*] (EA)
NCAA .... National Collegiate Athletic Association (EA)
NCAA .... National Command Authority Aircraft-747 [*MTMC*] (TAG)
NCAA .... National Credit Adjustment Association [*New York, NY*] (EA)
NCAA .... NATO Civil Air Augmentation (DOMA)
NCAA .... Naval Civilian Administrators Association [*Later, NCMA*] (EA)
NCAA .... Nonnuclear Consumable Annual Analysis (MCD)
NCAAA......... National Center of Afro-American Artists
NCAAA......... National Council of Affiliated Advertising Agencies [*Later, First Network of Affiliated Advertising Agencies*] (EA)
NcAAB .... Asheville-Buncombe Technical Institute, Asheville, NC [*Library symbol Library of Congress*] (LCLS)
NCAAC......... Northern California Athletic Conference (PSS)
NCAADA....... National Community Action Agency Directors Association [*Formerly, NCAAEDA*] [*Later, NACAA*] (EA)
NCAADACCB... National Commission on Accreditation of Alcoholism and Drug Abuse Counselor Credentialing Bodies (EA)
NCAAE......... National Council of Administrators of Adult Education (EA)
NCAAEDA..... National Community Action Agency Executive Directors Association (EA)
NcAAH .... Appalachian Hall Medical Library, Asheville, NC [*Library symbol*] [*Library of Congress*] (LCLS)
NCAAL .... National Conference of African American Librarians
NcAAP .... Amcel Propulsion Co., Asheville, NC [*Library symbol Library of Congress*] (LCLS)
NCAAP......... National Coalition for Adequate Alcoholism Programs [*Defunct*] (EA)
NCAB .... National Association of Citizen Advice Bureaux [*British*]
NCAB .... National Cancer Advisory Board
NCAB .... National Collegiate Athletic Bureau [*Later, NCSS*] (EA)
NCAB .... National Committee for Amateur Baseball [*Later, USBF*]
NCAB .... Navy Contract Adjustment Board
NCABC......... National Catholic Association for Broadcasters/Communicators (EA)
NCABC......... National Citizens' Advice Bureaux Committee [*British*] (BI)
NcAbd.......... Page Memorial Library, Aberdeen, NC [*Library symbol*] [*Library of Congress*] (LCLS)
NCABHP....... National Center for the Advancement of Blacks in the Health Professions (EA)
NcAbMR ...... North Carolina Marine Resources Center, Bogue Banks Library, Atlantic Beach, NC [*Library symbol Library of Congress*] (LCLS)
NcAC........... Cecils Junior College, Asheville, NC [*Library symbol*] [*Library of Congress*] (LCLS)
NCAC .... National Cancer Advisory Committee [*Australia*]
NCAC .... National Catholic Action Coalition [*Defunct*] (EA)
NCAC .... National Christian Action Coalition [*Defunct*] (EA)
NCAC .... National Civil Aviation Council [*British*] (BI)
NCAC .... National Clean Air Coalition [*Defunct*] (EA)
NCAC .... National Coalition Against Censorship (EA)
NCAC .... National Consumer Advisory Council
NCAC .... National Copyright Advisory Committee (NADA)
NCAC .... National Council Against Conscription [*World War I*] [*British*]
NCAC .... National Council of Acoustical Consultants (EA)
NCAC .... Navy Combat Art Collection (DNAB)
NCAC .... Nordic Customs Administrative Council (EA)
NCAC .... North Carolina Administrative Code [*A publication*] (AAGC)
NCAC .... North Coast Athletic Conference (PSS)
NCAC .... Northern Combat Area Command [*Myanmar*]
NCACC......... National Collection of Animal Cell Cultures (DB)
NCACC......... National Conference of Appellate Court Clerks (EA)
NCACE......... National Capital Association for Cooperative Education (MCD)
NCACME...... National Center for Adult, Continuing, and Manpower Education [*Office of Education*]
NCACP......... National Campaign for the Abolition of Capital Punishment [*Founded in 1955*] [*British*]
NCACPS....... National Coalition to Abolish Corporal Punishment in Schools (EA)
NCACS......... National Coalition of Alternative Community Schools (EA)
NCACS......... North Central Association of Colleges and Schools (EA)
NCAD .... New Cumberland Army Depot [*Pennsylvania*] (AABC)
NCAD .... Notice of Cancellation at Anniversary Date [*Insurance*] (DCTA)
NCADD......... National Commission Against Drunk Driving (EA)
NCADD......... National Council on Alcoholism and Drug Dependence (EA)
NCADH......... National Committee Against Discrimination in Housing [*Defunct*] (EA)
NCADI.......... National Clearinghouse for Alcohol and Drug Abuse Information (PAZ)
NCADI .... National Clearinghouse for Alcohol and Drug Information [*US Public Health Service*] [*Information service or system*] (IID)
NC Admin Code... North Carolina Administrative Code [*A publication*] (DLA)
NCADP......... National Coalition Against the Death Penalty (EA)
NCADP......... National Coalition to Abolish the Death Penalty (EA)
NCADV......... National Coalition Against Domestic Violence (EA)
NC Adv Legis Serv... North Carolina Advance Legislative Service (Michie) [*A publication*] (DLA)
NCAE .... National Center for Alcohol Education [*National Institutes of Health*]
NCAE .... National Center for Audio Experimentation [*Defunct*] (EA)
NCAE .... National College of Agricultural Engineering [*British*] (ARC)
NCAE .... National Conference on Airborne Electronics (MCD)
NCAE .... National Council for Alcohol Education (DMAA)
NCAE .... National Council of Agricultural Employers (EA)
NCAEE .... National Committee on Art Education for the Elderly [*Defunct*] (EA)
NCAEF .... National Ceramic Association Educational Foundation (EA)
NCAEG......... National Confederation of American Ethnic Groups (EA)
NCAEI .... National Conference on the Application of Electrical Insulation
NCAES .... National Center for Analysis of Energy Systems (HGAA)
NCAF .... National Clean Air Fund (GFGA)
NCAF .... National Committee Against Fluoridation [*National Health Federation - NHF*] [*Absorbed by*] (EA)
NCAF .... National Community Action Foundation (EA)
NCAFB......... Normal Crop Acreage Farm Base
NCAFP......... National Committee on American Foreign Policy (EA)
NCAG .... National Council on the Arts and Government (EA)
NcAh........... Ahoskie Public Library, Ahoskie, NC [*Library symbol Library of Congress*] (LCLS)
NCAH .... National Committee, Arts for the Handicapped [*Later, VSA*] (EA)
NCAHCP....... National Council on Alternative Health Care Policy (EA)
NcAHE .... Mountain Area Health Education Center, Health Sciences Library, Asheville, NC [*Library symbol Library of Congress*] (LCLS)
NCAHE......... National Commission on Allied Health Education [*American Occupational Therapy Association*]
NCAHF .... National Council Against Health Fraud (EA)
NcAHH......... Highland Hospital, Medical Library, Asheville, NC [*Library symbol Library of Congress*] (LCLS)
NcAhRC .... Roanoke-Chowan Technical Institute, Ahoskie, NC [*Library symbol Library of Congress*] (LCLS)
NCAHRN ...... National Central American Health Rights Network (EA)
NCAHUAC .... National Committee to Abolish the House Un-American Activities Committee [*Later, NCARL*] (EA)
NCAI .... Aitutaki [*Cook Islands*] [*ICAO location identifier*] (ICLI)
NCAI .... National Clearinghouse for Alcohol Information [*Rockville, MD*] [*National Institutes of Health*]
NCAI .... National Coalition for Adult Immunization
NCAI .... National Congress of American Indians (EA)
NCAI .... National Council of American Importers [*Later, AAEI*] (EA)
NCAI .... National Council on Alcoholism, Inc. (NADA)
NCA-I.......... Neighborhood Cleaners Association-International (NTPA)
NCAIAE .... National Center for American Indian Alternative Education (EA)
NCAIANMHR... National Center for American Indian and Alaska Native Mental Health Research (EA)
NCAIC .... Nuclear Chemical Accident Incident Control (MCD)
NCAIE .... National Center for American Indian Education [*Later, NCAIAE*] (EA)
NCAIE .... National Council of the Arts in Education [*Later, ACAE*] (EA)
NCAIED........ National Center for American Indian Enterprise Development (EA)
NCAIL .... National Council Against Illegal Liquor [*Defunct*] (EA)
NCAIP .... National Consumer Affairs Internship Program [*Defunct*] (EA)
NCAIR.......... National Center for Automated Information Retrieval (IID)
NCAIR.......... North Carolina Association for Institutional Research (EDAC)
NCAJ .... National Center for Administrative Justice [*Formerly, CAJ*] (EA)
NCA/JCS ...... National Command Authorities and Joint Chiefs of Staff
NCAJL.......... National Council on Art in Jewish Life (EA)
NCaL........... Canton Free Library, Canton, NY [*Library symbol*] [*Library of Congress*] (LCLS)
NCAL .... National Centre for Athletics Literature (AIE)
NCAL .... National Committee for Adult Literacy [*British*] (DI)
N Cal .... New Caledonia
NcAlb.......... Albemarle-Stanly County Public Library, Albemarle, NC [*Library symbol Library of Congress*] (LCLS)
NcAlbS......... Stanly Technical Institute, Albemarle, NC [*Library symbol Library of Congress*] (LCLS)
NCALHBCU... National Consortium of Arts and Letters for Historically Black Colleges and Universities (EA)
NCALI .... National Clearinghouse for Alcohol Information [*National Institutes of Health*] (IID)
NCALL .... National Council on Agricultural Life and Labor Research Fund (EA)
NcAlP.......... Pamlico Technical Institute, Alliance, NC [*Library symbol Library of Congress*] (LCLS)

NCalv .... Baiting Hollow Free Library, Calverton, NY [*Library symbol Library of Congress*] (LCLS)
NCAM .... National Center for Advanced Materials [*Later, Berkeley Center for Advanced Materials*]
NCAM .... Network Communication Access Method
N-CAM .... Neural Cell Adhesion Molecule [*Biochemistry*]
NCAMI .... National Committee Against Mental Illness [*Defunct*] (EA)
NCAMLP ...... National Certification Agency for Medical Laboratory Personnel (MAE)
NCAMP .... National Coalition Against the Misuses of Pesticides (EA)
NCAMR .... Nordic Council for Arctic Medical Research (EA)
NCAN .... Incan Superior Ltd. [*AAR code*]
NCAN .... National Catholic AIDS Network (EA)
NCAN .... National Citizens Action Network (EA)
NCAN .... National Coalition of American Nuns (EA)
NCAN .... National Committee for Amnesty Now (EA)
NCaN .... North Country Reference and Research Resources Council, Canton, NY [*Library symbol Library of Congress*] (LCLS)
NCAnA .... Anson Technical Institute, Ansonville, NC [*Library symbol Library of Congress*] (LCLS)
NCanC .... Community College of the Finger Lakes, Canandaigua, NY [*Library symbol Library of Congress*] (LCLS)
NcANCC .... United States National Oceanic and Atmospheric Administration, National ClimaticCenter, Ashville, NC [*Library symbol Library of Congress*] (LCLS)
NcAnd .... Andrews Carnegie Library, Andrews, NC [*Library symbol Library of Congress*] (LCLS)
NC & B .... Naval Courts and Boards
NC & CS ...... Navigation Command and Control System
NC & SL ...... Nashville, Chattanooga & St. Louis Railway (IIA)
NC & ST L .... Nashville, Chattanooga & St. Louis Railway
NCANH........ National Council for the Accreditation of Nursing Homes (NADA)
NCanHi .... Ontario County Historical Society, Canandaigua, NY [*Library symbol Library of Congress*] (LCLS)
NCaNNH ...... Northern New York Health Information Cooperative, Canton, NY [*Library symbol Library of Congress*] (LCLS)
NCanV .... United States Veterans Administration Hospital, Canandaigua, NY [*Library symbol Library of Congress*] (LCLS)
NCAO .... National Commission on Air Quality [*Environmental Protection Agency*] (ERG)
NCAO .... Naval Civil Affairs Officer [*World War II*]
N-CAP .... National Coalition Against Pornography (EA)
NCAP .... National Coalition of Abortion Providers (NTPA)
NCAP .... Naval Combat Air Patrol (DNAB)
NCAP .... Neighborhood Community Action Program
NCAP .... Nematic Curvilinear Aligned Phase [*Emulsion film used in windows*] [*Taliq Corp.*]
NCAP .... New Car Assessment Program [*Automobile testing*]
NCAP .... Night Combat Air Patrol [*Military*]
NCAP .... Nonlinear Circuit Analysis Program (MCD)
NCAP .... Nordic Council for Animal Protection (EA)
NCAP .... Northwest Coalition for Alternatives to Pesticides (GNE)
NCAP .... Nucleotide Column Affinity for Purification [*Biochemical analysis*]
N-CAP .... Nurses Coalition for Action in Politics
NCAPC .... National Center for Air Pollution Control [*Public Health Service*] [*Obsolete*]
NCAPI .... Nuveen California Premium Income Municipal Fund [*Associated Press*] (SAG)
NCAPO .... National Council of Adoptive Parents Organizations [*NACAC*] [*Absorbed by*]
NC App .... North Carolina Appellate Reports [*A publication*] (AAGC)
NC App .... North Carolina Court of Appeals Reports [*A publication*] (DLA)
NCAPS .... Naval Control and Protection of Shipping (NVT)
NCapV .... United States Veterans Administration Hospital, Medical Library, Castle Point, NY [*Library symbol*] [*Library of Congress*] (LCLS)
NCAQ .... National Commission on Air Quality (GNE)
NCAR .... National Center for Association Resources (EA)
NCAR .... National Center for Atmospheric Research [*Boulder, CO*] [*National Science Foundation*] (GRD)
NCAR .... National Conference on the Advancement of Research (EA)
NCAR .... Navy Center for Acquisition Research [*Monterey, CA*]
NCAR .... Nonconformance and Corrective Action Reporting System [*NASA*] (KSC)
N Car .... North Carolina (DLA)
N Car .... North Carolina Reports [*A publication*] (DLA)
Nc-Ar .... North Carolina State Department of Archives and History, Raleigh, NC [*Library symbol Library of Congress*] (LCLS)
NcAr............. Sallie H. Jenkins Memorial Public Library, Aulander, NC [*Library symbol*] [*Library of Congress*] (LCLS)
NCARAI .... Navy Center for Applied Research in Artificial Intelligence [*Washington, DC*] (GRD)
NCARB .... National Council of Architectural Registration Boards (EA)
NCaRC .... North Country Reference and Research Resources Council, Canton, NY [*Library symbol Library of Congress Obsolete*] (LCLS)
NCARF .... National Committee for Amish Religious Freedom (EA)
NCARL .... National Committee Against Repressive Legislation (EA)
N Car Law Rep... Carolina Law Repository (Reprint) [*North Carolina*] [*A publication*] (DLA)
NCARMD...... National Commission on Arthritis and Related Musculoskeletal Disease
NCarNG........ North Carolina Natural Gas Corp. [*Associated Press*] (SAG)
N Carolina Cases... North Carolina Cases [*A publication*] (DLA)
NCARP .... Collegiate Association for Research of Principle (EA)
N Car Rep ... North Carolina Reports [*A publication*] (DLA)
NCAS .... National Coalition Against Surrogacy (EA)

NCAS .... National Coalition of Advocates for Students (EA)
NCAS .... National Collegiate Association for Secretaries [*Defunct*] (EA)
NCAS .... Neocarzinostatin [*Zinostatin*] [*Antineoplastic drug*]
NcA-S .... Pack Memorial Public Library, Sondley Reference Library, Asheville, NC [*Library symbol Library of Congress*] (LCLS)
NCaS .... Saint Lawrence University, Canton, NY [*Library symbol Library of Congress*] (LCLS)
NCASA .... National Campaign Against Solvent Abuse [*British*] (DBA)
NCASA .... National Coalition Against Sexual Assault (EA)
NCASA .... Naval Civil Affairs Staging Area
NCASAA....... National Court Appointed Special Advocates Association (EA)
NcAsbC........ Randolph Public Library, Asheboro, NC [*Library symbol Library of Congress*] (LCLS)
NcAsbH........ Randolph Hospital, Inc., Asheboro, NC [*Library symbol*] [*Library of Congress*] (LCLS)
NcAsbR........ Randolph Technical Institute, Asheboro, NC [*Library symbol Library of Congress*] (LCLS)
NCASC .... National Capital Administrative Support Center [*Marine science*] (OSRA)
NCASC .... National Council of Acupuncture Schools and Colleges (EA)
NCASC .... Nordic Council for Adult Studies in Church [*See also NKS*] (EAIO)
NCASEPS .... North Central Alaskan Seasonal Earned Premium Scale [*Aviation*] (AIA)
NCASF .... National Council of American-Soviet Friendship (EA)
NCASI .... National Council of the Paper Industry for Air and Stream Improvement (EA)
NCAT .... Atiu [*Cook Islands*] [*ICAO location identifier*] (ICLI)
NCAT .... National Catalog (AEPA)
NCAT .... National Center for Advanced Technology [*Vienna, VA*]
NCAT .... National Center for Appropriate Technology (EA)
NCAT .... National Center for Audiotape [*Later, NCATA*] (EA)
NCAT .... National Centre for Alternative Technology [*British*]
NCAT .... National Council of Athletic Training (NTPA)
NCAT .... National Program for Clear Air Turbulence [*Air Force*]
NCAT .... Naval College Aptitude Test (NVT)
NC/AT .... Normal Cephalic Atraumatic [*Medicine*] (DMAA)
NCATA .... National Cable Antenna Television Association of Canada (NTCM)
NCATA .... National Center for Audiotape Archive [*Defunct*] (EA)
NCATA .... National Coalition of Arts Therapy Associations (EA)
NCATB .... National Congress of Animal Trainers and Breeders (EA)
NCATE .... National Council for Accreditation of Teacher Education (EA)
NCATH .... National Campaign Against Toxic Hazards (EA)
NcATH .... Thoms Rehabilitation Hospital, Medical Library, Asheville, NC [*Library symbol*] [*Library of Congress*] (LCLS)
NcAu .... Sallie H. Jenkins Memorial Public Library, Aulander, NC [*Library symbol Library of Congress*] (LCLS)
NcAU .... University of North Carolina at Asheville, Asheville, NC [*Library symbol Library of Congress*] (LCLS)
NCaUA .... State University of New York, Agricultural and Technical College, Canton, NY [*Library symbol Library of Congress*] (LCLS)
NCAV .... National Coursing Association of Victoria [*Australia*]
NcAV .... United States Veterans Administration, Hospital Library Service, Asheville, NC [*Library symbol Library of Congress*] (LCLS)
NCAVAE .... National Committee for Audio-Visual Aids in Education [*British*]
NCAVC .... National Center for the Analysis of Violent Crime [*Quantico, VA*] [*Department of Justice*] (GRD)
NCAW .... National Council for Animal Welfare (NADA)
NCAWA .... National Coinamatic Auto Wash Association [*Later, ICA/NCC*]
NCAWE .... National Council of Administrative Women in Education (EA)
NCAWP .... National Council for Alternative Work Patterns (EA)
NCAWRR ..... National Committee Against War, Racism, and Repression
NCAYR .... National Chaplains Association for Youth Rehabilitation [*Defunct*]
NCazC.......... Cazenovia College, Cazenovia, NY [*Library symbol Library of Congress*] (LCLS)
NCB .... Barber-Scotia College, Concord, NC [*OCLC symbol*] (OCLC)
NCB .... Nanyang Commercial Bank [*China*]
NCB .... National Cargo Bureau (EA)
NCB .... National Central Bureau [*INTERPOL term*]
NCB .... National Children's Bureau [*British*]
NCB .... National Classification Board [*American Trucking Association*]
NCB .... National Coal Board [*British*]
NCB .... National Codification Bureau [*NATO*] (NATG)
NCB .... National Collection of Industrial Bacteria [*British*]
NCB .... National College of Business (IAA)
NCB .... National Commercial Bank [*Saudi Arabia*]
NCB .... National Commercial Bank [*Jamaica*]
NCB .... National Compliance Board [*New Deal*]
NCB .... National Conservation Bureau [*Defunct*]
NCB .... National Cooperative Bank (USGC)
NCB .... Naval Communications Board
NCB .... Naval Construction Battalion
NCB .... Navy Comptroller Budget (NG)
NCB .... Nederlandse Credietbank NV [*Financial institution*] [*Netherlands*] (EY)
NCB .... NetBIOS [*Network Basic Input/Output System*] Control Block [*Computer science*]
NCB .... Net Clearing Balance [*Finance*]
NCB .... Netherlands Convention Bureau (EA)
NCB .... Network Connect Block [*Computer science*] (CIST)
NCB .... Network Control Block
NCB .... New Century Bible [*A publication*] (BJA)
NCB .... New Crime Buffer
NCB .... Nickel-Cadmium Battery
NCB .... Nippon Credit Bank [*Japan*]
NCB .... No Claim Bonus [*Insurance*] (ADA)

NCB .... No Code Blue [*For terminal cases*] [*Medicine*] (DAVI)
NCB .... Noncallable Bond [*Investment term*]
NCB .... North Caribou Flying Service Ltd. [*Canada ICAO designator*] (FAAC)
NCB .... Northwest Cherry Briners Association (EA)
NcBa .... Mitchell County Library, Bakersville, NC [*Library symbol Library of Congress*] (LCLS)
NCBA .... National Candy Brokers Association (EA)
NCBA .... National Catholic Band Association (NTPA)
NCBA .... National Catholic Bandmasters' Association (EA)
NCBA .... National Cattle Breeders Association [*British*] (DBA)
NCBA .... National Caucus and Center on Black Aged (EA)
NCBA .... National Chinchilla Breeders of America [*Later, ECBC*] (EA)
NCBA .... National Color-Bred Association (EA)
NCBA .... National Commodity and Barter Association (EA)
NCBA .... National Cooperative Business Association (EA)
NCBA .... National Council on Black Aging (EA)
NCBAE .... No-Claim Bonus as Earned [*Insurance*] (ODBW)
NcBaneL ..... Lees-McRae College, Banner Elk, NC [*Library symbol Library of Congress*] (LCLS)
NCBBC .... National Council of Bible Believing Churches [*Later, CBBC*] (EA)
NcBc .... Marianna Black Library, Bryson City, NC [*Library symbol Library of Congress*] (LCLS)
NCBC .... National Commerce Bancorp [*NASDAQ symbol*] (NQ)
NCBC .... National Committee for the Berne Convention [*Defunct*] (EA)
NCBC .... Natl Commerce Bancorp [*NASDAQ symbol*] (TTSB)
NCBC .... Naval Construction Battalion Center
NCBC .... New Century Bible Commentary [*A publication*]
NCBC .... North Carolina Biotechnology Center [*Research center*] (RCD)
NcBcF .... Fontana Regional Library, Bryson City, NC [*Library symbol Library of Congress*] (LCLS)
NCBCS .... National Conference of States on Building Codes and Standards (OICC)
NcBe .... Belmont Abbey College, Belmont, NC [*Library symbol Library of Congress*] (LCLS)
NCBE .... National City Bancshares [*NASDAQ symbol*] (SAG)
NCBE .... National Clearinghouse for Bilingual Education [*Wheaton, MD*]
NCBE .... National Conference of Bar Examiners (EA)
NCBE .... National Conference of Bar Executives [*Later, NABE*] (EA)
NCBE .... National Council for Better Education (EA)
NCBE .... Natl City Bancshares [*NASDAQ symbol*] (TTSB)
NCBE .... North County Business Exchange
NcBea .... Cateret County Public Library, Beaufort, NC [*Library symbol Library of Congress*] (LCLS)
NCBEA .... National Catholic Business Education Association [*Emporia, KS*] (EA)
NCBEA .... North Central Business Education Association (AEBS)
NcBeaAE ...... United States Marine Fisheries Service, Southeast Fisheries Center, Beaufort Laboratory, Beaufort, NC [*Library symbol Library of Congress*] (LCLS)
NCBEC .... National Center for Business and Economic Communication [*American University*] [*Research center*] (RCD)
NCBEE .... National Council of State Boards of Engineering Examiners [*Later, NCEE*] (IAA)
NCBEL .... [*The*] New Cambridge Bibliography of English Literature [*A publication*]
NCBES .... National Council of Black Engineers and Scientists (NTPA)
NcBeSH .... Sacred Heart College, McCarthy Library, Belmont, NC [*Library symbol Library of Congress*] (LCLS)
NcBesL .... Lithium Corp. of America, Ellestad Research Library, Bessemer City, NC [*Library symbol Library of Congress*] (LCLS)
NCBF .... National Conference of Bar Foundations (EA)
NCBF .... Non-Conventional Brake Fluid [*Automotive engineering*]
NCBFAA ...... National Customs Brokers and Forwarders Association of America [*New York, NY*]
NCBFE .... National Center for a Barrier Free Environment (EA)
NCBG .... National Coalition of Black Gays (EA)
ncbh-- .... British Honduras [*MARC geographic area code Library of Congress*] (LCCP)
NCBH .... National Coalition to Ban Handguns [*Later, CSGV*] (EA)
NCBHC .... National Committee on Black and Hispanic Concerns (EA)
NCBI .... National Center for Biotechnology Information (IID)
NCBI .... National Cotton Batting Institute (EA)
NCBIAE .... National Council of BIA [*Bureau of Indian Affairs*] Educators (EA)
NCBJ .... National Conference of Bankruptcy Judges (EA)
NCBJS .... National Council of Beth Jacob Schools [*Later, FCBJS*] (EA)
NcBl .... Bridger Memorial Public Library, Bladenboro, NC [*Library symbol Library of Congress*] (LCLS)
NCBL .... National Conference of Black Lawyers (EA)
NCBL .... Natural Convection Boiling Loops
NCBLG .... National Coalition of Black Lesbians and Gays (EA)
NcBlm .... Black Mountain Public Library, Black Mountain, NC [*Library symbol Library of Congress*] (LCLS)
NCBLRDC ... National Coalition of Black Lung and Respiratory Disease Clinics (EA)
NcBlv .... Phillip Leff Memorial Library, Beulaville, NC [*Library symbol Library of Congress*] (LCLS)
NCBM .... National City Bancorp [*NASDAQ symbol*] (NQ)
NCBM .... National Conference of Black Mayors (EA)
NCBM .... National Council on Business Mail (EA)
NCBM .... Natl City Bancorp'n [*NASDAQ symbol*] (TTSB)
NCBMP .... National Coalition of Black Meeting Planners (EA)
NCBMP .... National Council of Building Material Producers [*A union*] [*British*]
NcBo .... Watauga County Library, Boone, NC [*Library symbol Library of Congress*] (LCLS)

NcBoA .... Appalachian State University, Boone, NC [*Library symbol Library of Congress*] (LCLS)
NcBoHE .... Northwest Area Health Education Center, Boone, NC [*Library symbol*] [*Library of Congress*] (LCLS)
NcBoNM ...... New River Area Mental Health, Boone, NC [*Library symbol*] [*Library of Congress*] (LCLS)
NCBOR .... No Claim Bonus on Renewal [*Insurance*] (AIA)
NCBP .... National Conference of Bar Presidents (EA)
NCBPD .... National Consortium for Black Professional Development (EA)
Nc-BPH .... North Carolina Library for the Blind and Physically Handicapped, Raleigh, NC [*Library symbol Library of Congress*] (LCLS)
NCBPNP/N .. National Certification Board of Pediatric Nurse Practitioners and Nurses (EA)
NCBR .... National Center for Bilingual Research [*National Institute of Education*] [*Research center*] (RCD)
NCBR .... Near Commercial Breeder Reactor [*Also, PLBR*]
NcBre .... Transylvania County Library, Brevard, NC [*Library symbol Library of Congress*] (LCLS)
NcBreC .... Brevard College, Brevard, NC [*Library symbol Library of Congress*] (LCLS)
NCBS .... National Cage Bird Show (EA)
NCBS .... National Consumer Board for Stuttering (EA)
NCBS .... National Council for Black Studies (EA)
NCBSA .... National Candy Brokers and Salesmen's Association [*Later, NCBA*] (EA)
NcBsG .... Gardner-Webb College, Boiling Springs, NC [*Library symbol Library of Congress*] (LCLS)
NcBuC .... Campbell College, Buies Creek, NC [*Library symbol Library of Congress*] (LCLS)
NcBuC-L ...... Campbell University, Law Library, Buies Creek, NC [*Library symbol*] [*Library of Congress*] (LCLS)
NcBur .... Central North Carolina Regional Library, Burlington, NC [*Library symbol Library of Congress*] (LCLS)
NcBurAT ..... AT&T Technologies Inc., Technical Library, Burlington, NC [*Library symbol*] [*Library of Congress*] (LCLS)
NcBurgP ...... Pender County Library, Burgaw, NC [*Library symbol Library of Congress*] (LCLS)
NcBurgP-H .. Pender County Library, Hampstead Branch Library, Hampstead, NC [*Library symbol*] [*Library of Congress*] (LCLS)
NcBurT .... Technical Institute of Alamance, Burlington, NC [*Library symbol Library of Congress*] (LCLS)
NcBurWE ..... Western Electric Co., Technical Library, Burlington, NC [*Library symbol Library of Congress*] (LCLS)
NcButM .... Murdoch Center, School Library, Butner, NC [*Library symbol Library of Congress*] (LCLS)
NcBv .... Yancey County Public Library, Burnsville, NC [*Library symbol Library of Congress*] (LCLS)
NCBVA .... National Concrete Burial Vault Association (EA)
NCBVP .... National Coalition on Black Voter Participation (EA)
NCBW .... National Cage Bird Week Association [*Defunct*] (EA)
NCBW .... National Coalition of 100 Black Women (EA)
NCBWA .... National Collegiate Baseball Writers Association (EA)
NcBy .... Palmico County Library, Bayboro, NC [*Library symbol Library of Congress*] (LCLS)
NCC .... Chadron State College, Chadron, NE [*OCLC symbol*] (OCLC)
NCC .... NAACOG [*Nurses Association of the American College of Obstetricians and Gynecologists*] Certification Corp. (EA)
NCC .... NASA Class Code (NASA)
NCC .... National Cadet Corps (NADA)
NCC .... National Cambridge Collectors (EA)
NCC .... National Cancer Center (EA)
NCC .... National Can Corp. (EFIS)
NCC .... National Capital Commission [*Canada*]
NCC .... National Capon Council [*Defunct*] (EA)
NCC .... National Caravan Council Ltd. [*British*] (BI)
NCC .... National Carbon Co. (MCD)
NCC .... National Career Center (EA)
NCC .... National Carwash Council [*Later, ICA*] (EA)
NCC .... National Castings Council [*Defunct*] (EA)
NCC .... National Certification Commission (NTPA)
NCC .... National Certification Corporation for the Obstetric, Gynecologic and Neonatal Nursing Specialties (EA)
NCC .... National Certified Counselor (DHP)
NCC .... National Chile Center [*Formerly, NCCSC*] (EA)
NCC .... National Citizens Coalition [*Canada*]
NCC .... National Citizens Committee. Bulletin [*A publication*]
NCC .... National City Corp. [*NYSE symbol*] (CTT)
NCC .... National Clearing Corp. [*National Association of Securities Dealers*]
NCC .... National Clients Council (EA)
NCC .... National Climatic Center [*National Oceanic and Atmospheric Administration*]
NCC .... National Coaches Council [*Later, ANCC*] (EA)
NCC .... National Coal Council [*Department of Energy*] [*Arlington, VA*] (EGAO)
NCC .... National Communications Club (EA)
NCC .... National Communications Command [*Army*] (RDA)
NCC .... National Communications Commission [*Uganda*] (ECON)
NCC .... National Company of Crossbowmen [*Defunct*] (EA)
NCC .... National Computer Center [*IRS*]
NCC .... National Computer Conference
NCC .... National Computer Council (NADA)
NCC .... National Computing Centre [*Manchester, England*]
NCC .... National Conference on Citizenship (EA)
NCC .... National Congressional Club (EA)
NCC .... National Consumer Council [*British*] (ILCA)

NCC .... National Consumers Congress [*Later, NCL*]
NCC .... National Container Committee [*Later, Uniform Classification Committee*] (EA)
NCC .... National Coordinating Committee (USGC)
NCC .... National Coordinating Committee for the Promotion of History (EA)
NCC .... National Coordinating Committee to End the War [*Organization formed in 1965*] (VNW)
NCC .... National Coordinating Council on Drug Abuse Education and Information [*Later, NCCDE*] (EA)
NCC .... National Coordination Committee [*Responsible for administering the Work Incentive Program*]
NCC .... National Cotton Council of America (EA)
NCC .... National Council Against Conscription [*World War I*] [*British*]
NCC .... National Council of Churches of Christ in the USA (EA)
NCC .... National Counselor Certification [*Psychology*]
NCC .... National Crime Commission
NCC .... National Cryptologic Command [*National Security Agency*]
NCC .... National Cultural Center [*Later, John F. Kennedy Center for the Performing Art s*]
NCC .... National Curriculum Council [*British*] (ECON)
NCC .... Native Council of Canada
NCC .... Natl City Corp. [*NYSE symbol*] (TTSB)
NCC .... Natural Circulation Cooldown [*Nuclear energy*] (NUCP)
NCC .... Naturally Commutated Cycloconverter [*Electronics*] (EECA)
NCC .... Nature Conservancy Council [*British*]
NCC .... Navajo Community College [*Chinle, AZ*]
NCC .... Naval Command College (DOMA)
NCC .... Naval Component Command (CINC)
NCC .... Navigation Computer Control
NCC .... Navigation Control Console
NCC .... Navy Command Center (MCD)
NCC .... Navy Cost Center
NCC .... NetWare Console Commander [*Frye Computer Systems*] [*Telecommunications*] (PCM)
NCC .... NetWare Control Center [*Novell, Inc.*] [*Computer science*] (PCM)
NCC .... Network Communications Corp.
NCC .... Network Computer Center (OA)
NCC .... Network Control Center [*Telecommunications*]
NCC .... Network Control Computer (HGAA)
NCC .... Network Coordination Center [*NASA*]
NCC .... Network of Concerned Correspondents (EA)
NCC .... Neural Crest Cell [*Cytology*]
NCC .... Neuronal Correlate of Consciousness
NCC .... New Chancery Cases (Younge and Collyer) [*1841-43*] [*England*] [*A publication*] (DLA)
NCC .... New Chemical Compound [*Food science*]
NCC .... New Common Carriers
NCC .... New Computer Center [*Social Security Administration*]
NCC .... New Construction and Conversion [*Navy*] (AFIT)
NCC .... New Consultants and Consulting Organizations Directory [*A publication*]
NCC .... Newfoundland Capital Corp. Ltd. [*Toronto Stock Exchange symbol*]
NCC .... Newspaper Comics Council [*Later, NFC*] (EA)
NCC .... Niagara County Community College [*UTLAS symbol*]
NCC .... Nitrogen Charging Console
NCC .... Noise Control Committee
NCC .... Nominal Corrective Combination (MCD)
NCC .... Noncancelable Commitment (SDI)
NCC .... Noncarbohydrate Craver [*Nutrition*]
NCC .... Noncombatant Corps [*British*]
NCC .... NORAD Control Center [*Military*]
NCC .... Nordic Choral Committee (EAIO)
NCC .... Normal-Control Children [*Psychology*]
NCC .... Normally Closed Contact [*Switch*] (IAA)
NCC .... North Calotte Committee [*See also NKK*] [*Nordic Council of Ministers*] [*Finland*] (EAIO)
NCC .... North Central College [*Naperville, IL*]
NCC .... North Central Conference (PSS)
NCC .... North Coast Air Services Ltd. [*Canada ICAO designator*] (FAAC)
NCC .... Northwest Christian College [*Oregon*]
NCC .... Notre Cause Commune [*Benin*] [*Political party*] (EY)
NCC .... Numerical Control Code
NCC .... Nursing Clerical Coordinator
NcC .... Public Library of Charlotte and Mecklenburg County, Charlotte, NC [*Library symbol Library of Congress*] (LCLS)
NcCA .... Arthur Andersen & Co., Carolinas Central Library, Charlotte, NC [*Library symbol*] [*Library of Congress*] (LCLS)
NCCA .... Nash Car Club of America (EA)
NCCA .... National Carpet Cleaners Association [*British*] (EAIO)
NCCA .... National Catholic Camping Association [*Defunct*] (EA)
NCCA .... National Catholic Council on Alcoholism and Related Drug Problems (EA)
NCCA .... National Cedar Chest Association [*Defunct*] (EA)
NCCA .... National Center for Child Advocacy
NCCA .... National Center for Community Action (EA)
NCCA .... National Chemical Credit Association (EA)
NCCA .... National Child Care Association (NTPA)
NCCA .... National Clergy Council on Alcoholism and Related Drug Problems (EA)
NCCA .... National Club Cricket Association [*British*] (BI)
NCCA .... National Coil Coaters Association (EA)
NCCA .... National Collegiate Conference Association (EA)
NCCA .... National Columbia Challenger Association (EA)
NCCA .... National Commission for the Certification of Acupuncture (EA)
NCCA .... National Commission for the Certification of Acupuncturists (EA)

NCCA .... National Committee on Central America (EA)
NCCA .... National Concrete Contractors Association [*Later, ASCC*] (EA)
NCCA .... National Cotton Council of America [*Memphis, TN*]
NCCA .... National Council for Critical Analysis [*Defunct*] (EA)
NCCA .... National Council for Culture and Art (EA)
NCCA .... National Court Clubs Association [*Later, IRSA*] (EA)
NCCA .... Naval Center for Cost Analysis
NCCA .... Negligence and Compensation Cases, Annotated [*A publication*] (DLA)
NCCA .... Nordic Committee for Central Africa [*Defunct*] (EA)
NCCA 3d ...... Negligence and Compensation Cases, Annotated, Third Series [*A publication*] (DLA)
NCCAA .... National Christian College Athletic Association (EA)
NCCAC .... National Catholic Conference of Airport Chaplains (EA)
NCCACS .... National Council of Columbia Associations in Civil Service (EA)
NCCAE .... National Conference of Catholic Art Educators (AEBS)
NCCAE .... National Council of County Association Executives (EA)
NCCAFV .... National Council on Child Abuse and Family Violence (EA)
NcCaLM .... United States Naval Medical Field Research Laboratory, Camp Lejeune, NC [*Library symbol Library of Congress*] (LCLS)
NcCaLMC .... United States Marine Corps, Marine Corps Base General Library, Camp Lejeune, NC [*Library symbol Library of Congress*] (LCLS)
NcCaLNM ... United States Navy, Naval Regional Medical Center, Library, Camp Lejeune, NC [*Library symbol Library of Congress*] (LCLS)
NCCAN .... National Center on Child Abuse and Neglect [*Department of Health and Human Services*] [*Washington, DC*]
NCCAN .... National Clearinghouse on Child Abuse and Neglect Information (PAZ)
NCCA NS .... Negligence and Compensation Cases, Annotated, New Series [*A publication*] (DLA)
NCCAP .... National Certification Council for Activity Professionals (NTPA)
NcCar .... Moore County Library, Carthage, NC [*Library symbol Library of Congress*] (LCLS)
NCCAS .... National Center of Communication Arts and Sciences (EA)
NCCAS .... National Council for Clean Air and Streams
NCCAT .... National Committee for Clear Air Turbulence (KSC)
NCCB .... National Carpenters Craft Board [*Defunct*] (EA)
NCCB .... National Citizens Committee for Broadcasting (EA)
NCCB .... National Conference of Catholic Bishops (EA)
NCCB .... National Consumer Cooperative Bank
NCCB .... National Council to Combat Blindness [*Also known as Fight for Sight - FS*] (EA)
NCCBA .... National Caucus and Center on Black Aged (EA)
NCCBI .... National Coordinating Committee of the Beverage Industry
NCCBMI ...... National Consortium for Computer Based Music Instruction [*University of Delaware*] [*Research clearinghouse*] (EA)
NCCBN .... National Council of Churches Broadcasting Network (NTCM)
NCCC .... National Cambodia Crisis Committee [*Defunct*] (EA)
NCCC .... National Cancer Cytology Center [*Later, NCC*] (EA)
NCCC .... National Catholic Cemetery Conference (EA)
NCCC .... National Certified Career Counselor (DHP)
NCCC .... National Civilian Community Corps
NCCC .... National Conference of Catholic Charities (EA)
NCCC .... National Conservative Congressional Committee (EA)
NCCC .... National Consumer Credit Consultants (EA)
NCCC .... National Council of Churches of Christ in the USA [*Later, NCC*] (EA)
NCCC .... National Council of Community Churches [*Later, ICCC*] (EA)
NCCC .... National Council of Corvette Clubs (EA)
NCCC .... Norris Cotton Cancer Center [*Dartmouth-Hitchcock Medical Center*] [*Research center*] (RCD)
NCCCC .... National Coalition for Campus Child Care (EA)
NCCCC .... National Council for Credentialing Career Counselors (DHP)
NCCCC .... Naval Command, Control Communications Center (IAA)
NCCCC .... North Central Community College Conference (PSS)
NCCCCA ...... National Collegiate Cross Country Coaches Association [*Later, USCCCA*] (EA)
NCCCD .... National Center Confraternity of Christian Doctrine (EA)
NCCCD .... National Center for Computer Crime Data (EA)
NcCCed .... Cedalion Systems, Inc., Information Resources, Charlotte, NC [*Library symbol*] [*Library of Congress*] (LCLS)
NcCCel .... Celanese Fibers Co., Technical Information Center, Charlotte, NC [*Library symbol Library of Congress*] (LCLS)
NCCCHE ...... National Certification Commission in Chemistry and Chemical Engineering (IAA)
NCCCLC ...... Naval Command Control Communications Laboratory Center
NcCCP .... Central Piedmont Community College, Charlotte, NC [*Library symbol Library of Congress*] (LCLS)
NCCCP .... National Center for Community Crime Prevention (EA)
NCCCR .... National Citizens Committee for Community Relations [*Defunct*]
NCCCWA ...... National Cotton Compress and Cotton Warehouse Association [*Later, CWAA*] (EA)
NcCD .... Duke Power Co., Information Systems Library, Charlotte, NC [*Library symbol*] [*Library of Congress*] (LCLS)
NCCD .... National Center for Chronic Disease Control [*Public Health Service*]
NCCD .... National College for Criminal Defense (EA)
NCCD .... National Council for Community Development (EA)
NCCD .... National Council for Criminal Defense (EA)
NCCD .... National Council on Crime and Delinquency (EA)
NCCDC .... National Center for Chronic Disease Control (DAVI)
NcCDD .... Duke Power Co., David Nabow Library, Charlotte, NC [*Library symbol*] [*Library of Congress*] (LCLS)
NCCDE .... National Coordinating Council on Drug Education [*Formerly, NCC*]
NCCDL .... National College of Criminal Defense Lawyers and Public Defenders (DLA)
NCCDN .... National Consortium of Chemical Dependency Nurses (EA)

NCCDPC....... NATO Command, Control, and Information Systems and Automatic Data Processing Committee (NATG)

NCCD-R & I... National Council on Crime and Delinquency, Research and Information Division [*Research center*] (RCD)

NCCDS......... National Cooperative Crohn's Disease Study

NCCDS......... Network Control Center Data System (SSD)

NCCE .... National Center for Community Education (EA)

NCCE .... National Coalition for Consumer Education (EA)

NCCE .... National Commission for Cooperative Education (EA)

NCCE .... National Committee for Citizens in Education (EA)

NCCE .... Nordic Committee for Commercial Education [*See also NKH*] [*Odense, Denmark*] (EAIO)

NCCEA .... Neurosensory Center Comprehensive Examination for Aphasia (DAVI)

NCCED .... National Congress for Community Economic Development (EA)

NCCEM .... National Coordinating Council on Emergency Management (EA)

NCCEM .... National Council of Catholic Employers and Managers (EA)

NCCEWV ..... National Coordinating Committee to End the War in Vietnam [*Defunct*]

NCCF .... National Cancer Care Foundation (EA)

NCCF .... National Commission on Consumer Finance [*Terminated*]

NCCF .... National Council on Community Foundations [*Later, CF*] (EA)

NCCF .... Network Communications Control Facility [*IBM program product*]

NCCFL .... National Catholic Conference on Family Life (EA)

NCCG .... National Council on Compulsive Gambling [*Later, NAPG*] (EA)

NCCG .... Navy Central Clearance Group (DNAB)

NCCGDP ...... National Council of Chairmen of Graduate Departments of Psychology

NcCGS .... Church of Jesus Christ of Latter-Day Saints, Genealogical Society Library, Charlotte North Carolina Branch, Charlotte, NC [*Library symbol Library of Congress*] (LCLS)

NcCh .... Chapel Hill Public Library, Chapel Hill, NC [*Library symbol Library of Congress*] (LCLS)

NCCH .... National Council of Community Hospitals (EA)

NCCH .... National Council to Control Handguns [*Later, HCI*] (EA)

NCCH .... Nurses' Central Clearing House (AIE)

NCCHB......... National Committee on Concerns of Hispanics and Blacks [*Defunct*] (EA)

NCCHC .... National Commission on Correctional Health Care (EA)

NCCHE .... National Chicano Council for Higher Education [*Defunct*] (EA)

NCCHI .... National Cap and Cloth Hat Institute (EA)

NcCHM .... Helms, Mullis & Johnston Law Library, Charlotte, NC [*Library symbol*] [*Library of Congress*] (LCLS)

NCCHR......... National Commission on Confidentiality of Health Records [*Defunct*] (EA)

NCCHS .... National Commission on Community Public Health Services

NcCI .... IBM Corp., Library/15C, Charlotte, NC [*Library symbol Library of Congress*] (LCLS)

NCCI .... Nashville Country Club [*NASDAQ symbol*] (SAG)

NCCI .... National Commission on Coping with Interdependence (EA)

NCCI .... National Council on Compensation Insurance [*New York, NY*] (EA)

NCCI .... North Central Computer Institute [*Research center*] (RCD)

NCC/IBL .... Nederlandse Centrale Catalogus/Interbibliothecair Leenverkeer System [*Netherlands Central Catalogue/Interlibrary Loan System*] [*Consortium of the Royal Library and University Libraries*] [*Information service or system*] (IID)

NCCIJ.......... National Catholic Conference for Interracial Justice (EA)

NCCIP .... National Center for Clinical Infant Programs (EA)

NCCIP .... Nordic Cooperation Committee for International Politics, Including Conflict and Peace Research (EA)

NCCIR .... National Catholic Commission for Industrial Relations [*Australia*]

NCCIS .... NATO Command, Control, and Information System (NATG)

NCCIW .... Nashville Country Club Wrrt [*NASDAQ symbol*] (TTSB)

NcCJ .... Johnson C. Smith University, Charlotte, NC [*Library symbol Library of Congress*] (LCLS)

NCCJ........... National Conference of Christians and Jews (EA)

NCCJP & A... National Clearinghouse for Criminal Justice Planning and Architecture [*Defunct*] (EA)

NCCK .... Noncoherent Carrier Keying (IAA)

NCCL .... National Citizen Communication Lobby (EA)

NCCL .... National Conference of Catechetical Leadership (NTPA)

NCCL .... National Council for Civil Liberties [*British*]

NCCL .... National Council of Canadian Labour

NCCL .... National Council of Catholic Laity [*Defunct*] (EA)

NCCL .... National Council of Coal Lessors

NcCla .... Hocutt-Ellington Memorial Library, Clayton, NC [*Library symbol Library of Congress*] (LCLS)

NCC-LAW..... North Carolina Center for Laws Affecting Women, Inc. [*Research center*] (RCD)

NcCIH .... Haywood Technical Institute, Clyde, NC [*Library symbol Library of Congress*] (LCLS)

NcCli........... Sampson-Clinton Public Library, Clinton, NC [*Library symbol Library of Congress*] (LCLS)

NcCliS .... Sampson Technical Institute, Clinton, NC [*Library symbol Library of Congress*] (LCLS)

NCCLS .... National Committee for Clinical Laboratory Science

NCCLS .... National Committee for Clinical Laboratory Standards (EA)

NCCLS .... National Consumer Center for Legal Services [*Later, NRCCLS*] (EA)

NCCLVP ...... National Coordinating Committee on Large Volume Parenterals (BABM)

NCCM .... Master Chief Navy Counselor [*Navy rating*] (DNAB)

NcCM.......... Mecklenburg County Medical Society, Charlotte, NC [*Library symbol Library of Congress*] (LCLS)

NCCM .... National Council of Catholic Men (EA)

NCCMA .... National Corporate Cash Management Association (EA)

NCCMCU...... National Committee to Commemorate the Millenium of Christianity in the Ukraine (EA)

NCCMGI ...... National Clearinghouse for Corporate Matching Gift Information (EA)

NCCMHC...... National Council of Community Mental Health Centers (EA)

NCCMHS...... National Consortium for Child Mental Health Services (EA)

NCCMIRS..... Navy Civilian Career Management Inventory and Referral System (DNAB)

NcCML........ Medical Library of Mecklenburg County, Inc., Charlotte, NC [*Library symbol Library of Congress*] (LCLS)

NCCML .... National Committee for Careers in the Medical Laboratory [*Defunct*] (EA)

NCCMP .... National Coordinating Committee for Multiemployer Plans (EA)

NCCMP .... Navy Civilian Career Management Program (DNAB)

NCCMT .... National Committee for Careers in Medical Technology [*Later, NCCML*] (EA)

NCCN .... National Comprehensive Cancer Network [*Medical*]

NCCN .... National Council of Catholic Nurses [*Defunct*] (EA)

NCCN .... New Century Cyclopedia of Names [*A publication*]

NCCNA .... National Clearinghouse on Child Neglect and Abuse [*HEW*]

NCCNHR....... National Citizens Coalition for Nursing Home Reform (EA)

NcCo........... Concord Public Library, Concord, NC [*Library symbol Library of Congress*] (LCLS)

NCCO .... Neodymium, Cerium, Copper, Oxide [*Inorganic chemistry*]

NcCoB......... Barber-Scotia College, Concord, NC [*Library symbol Library of Congress*] (LCLS)

NcCoC......... Cabarrus County Library, Concord, NC [*Library symbol*] [*Library of Congress*] (LCLS)

NcCoCH....... Cabarrus County Health Department, Concord, NC [*Library symbol Library of Congress*] (LCLS)

NcCoi......... Currituck County Public Library, Coinjock, NC [*Library symbol Library of Congress*] (LCLS)

NcCol.......... Polk County Public Library, Columbus, NC [*Library symbol Library of Congress*] (LCLS)

NcCola........ Tyrrell County Public Library, Columbia, NC [*Library symbol Library of Congress*] (LCLS)

NcConC........ Concordia College, Conover, NC [*Library symbol Library of Congress Obsolete*] (LCLS)

NC Conf ...... North Carolina Conference Reports [*A publication*] (DLA)

NC Conf Rep... North Carolina Conference Reports [*A publication*] (DLA)

NCCOP......... National Corporation for the Care of Old People [*British*] (BI)

NcCorD........ Duke Power Co., Information Resource Center, Cornelius, NC [*Library symbol Library of Congress*] (LCLS)

NCCOS........ National Committee for Certificates in Office Studies [*British*]

NCCOSC....... Naval Command, Control, and Ocean Surveillance Center [*Formerly, NOSC and other activities*] (DOMA)

NCCP .... National Center for Children in Poverty (EA)

NCCP .... National Chinese Curriculum Project [*Australia*]

NCCP .... National Clearinghouse for Commuter Programs (EA)

NCCP .... National Coordinated Cataloging Program [*Library science*]

NCCP .... National Council on City Planning

NCCP .... NATO Commanders Communications Publication (NATG)

NCCP .... Navigation Control Console Panel

NCCP .... Northern California Cancer Program [*Research center*] (RCD)

NCCPA .... National Cinder Concrete Products Association (EA)

NCCPA .... National Commission on Certification of Physician's Assistants (EA)

NCCPA .... National Council of College Publications Advisers (EA)

NCCPAP....... National Conference of CPA [*Certified Public Accountant*] Practitioners [*New York, NY*] (EA)

NCCPB .... National Council of Commercial Plant Breeders (EA)

NCCPC........ NATO Civil Communications Planning Committee (NATG)

NCCPG........ National Council for the Conservation of Plants and Gardens (PDAA)

NCCPL .... National Community Crime Prevention League (EA)

NcCpM........ United States Marine Corps, Air Station, Cherry Point, NC [*Library symbol Library of Congress*] (LCLS)

NCCPS .... National Citizens Commission for the Public Schools (AEBS)

NCCPT .... National Congress of Colored Parents and Teachers (AEBS)

NCCPV .... National Commission on the Causes and Prevention of Violence (EA)

NcCQ .... Queens College, Charlotte, NC [*Library symbol Library of Congress*] (LCLS)

nccr--.......... Costa Rica [*MARC geographic area code Library of Congress*] (LCCP)

NCCR.......... National Coalition for Cancer Research (EA)

NCCR.......... National Committee for Cultural Resources (EA)

NCCR.......... National Council for Children's Rights (EA)

NCCR.......... National Council for Community Relations [*Later, NCMPR*] (EA)

NCCR.......... National Council of Chain Restaurants (NTPA)

NCCR.......... Network Control Center Representative (SSD)

NCCR.......... New Construction/Conversion Requirements System [*Navy*]

NCCRE......... National Consumers Committee for Research and Education [*Later, NCL*] (EA)

NCCRI......... National Catholic Coalition for Responsible Investment (EA)

NcCS........... Charlotte-Mecklenburg Schools, Staff Development Center, Charlotte, NC [*Library symbol Library of Congress*] (LCLS)

NCCS .... National Carriers Contract Services [*National Freight Consortium*] [*British*]

NCCS .... National Catholic Committee on Scouting (EA)

NCCS .... National Catholic Community Service [*Defunct*] (EA)

NCCS .... National Catholic Conference for Seafarers (EA)

NCCS .... National Center for Charitable Statistics (EA)

NCCS .... National Center for Constitutional Studies (EA)

NCCS .... National Christ Child Society (EA)

NCCS .... National Climbing Classification System

NCCS .... National Coalition for Cancer Survivorship (EA)

NCCS .... National Command and Control System

NCCS .... National Council for Community Services to International Visitors [*Later, NCIV*]
NCCS .... Navy Camera Control System
NCCS .... Navy Command and Control System (NVT)
NCCS .... Nordic Church Council for Seamen [*Denmark*] (EAIO)
NCCS .... Nordic Council for Church Studies (EA)
NCCSA .... National Council for the Church and Social Action (EA)
NCCSA .... Nature Conservation Council of South Australia
NCCSC .... National Coordinating Center in Solidarity with Chile [*Later, NCC*] (EA)
NCCSC .... Northern California Collegiate Ski Conference (PSS)
NcCSC .... Sandoz Chemical, Charlotte, NC [*Library symbol*] [*Library of Congress*] (LCLS)
NCCSCE .... National Council on Community Services and Continuing Education (EA)
NcCSH .... Sun-Health, Inc., Charlotte, NC [*Library symbol*] [*Library of Congress*] (LCLS)
NcCSI........... SIM International Resource Center, Charlotte, NC [*Library symbol*] [*Library of Congress*] (LCLS)
NCCSL .... National Center for Cross-Cultural Studies in Law [*Monash University*] [*Australia*]
NCCSS .... North Central Conference on Summer Schools (EA)
NCCT .... National Council for Civic Theatres Ltd. [*British*] (BI)
NCCTA .... National Council of Chemical Technician Affiliates
NCCTS .... National Catholic Conference for Total Stewardship (EA)
NCCU .... National Conference of Canadian Universities
NCCU .... Newborn Convalescent Care Unit [*Medicine*]
NCCU .... North Carolina Central University [*Durham*]
NcCU .... University of North Carolina at Charlotte, Charlotte, NC [*Library symbol Library of Congress*] (LCLS)
NCC/USA...... National Council of Churches of Christ in the USA (NTCM)
NCCUSL........ National Commission for Creation of Uniform State Laws
NCCUSL .... National Conference of Commissioners on Uniform State Laws (EA)
NcCuW......... Western Carolina University, Cullowhee, NC [*Library symbol Library of Congress*] (LCLS)
NCCV .... National Center for Church Vocations [*Later, NCVC*] (EA)
NCCV .... New Construction and Conversion [*Navy*]
NCCVL .... Northern California Collegiate Volleyball League (PSS)
NCCW .... National Chamber of Commerce for Women [*New York, NY*] (EA)
NCCW .... National Council of Career Women
NCCW .... National Council of Catholic Women (EA)
NCCWAO...... National Council of Community World Affairs Organizations (EA)
NCCWHO ..... National Citizens Committee for the World Health Organization [*Later, AAWH*] (EA)
NCCY .... National Committee for Children and Youth [*Later, NCOCY*] (EA)
NCCY .... National Council of Catholic Youth [*Defunct*] (EA)
NcCyL .... Lord Corp. Research and Development Library, Cary, NC [*Library symbol*] [*Library of Congress*] (LCLS)
NcCyS .... SAS Institute, Inc., Cary, NC [*Library symbol*] [*Library of Congress*] (LCLS)
NCCYSA .... National Conference of Catholics in Youth Serving Agencies [*Defunct*] (EA)
nccz--.......... Canal Zone [*MARC geographic area code Library of Congress*] (LCCP)
NcD.............. Duke University, Durham, NC [*Library symbol Library of Congress*] (LCLS)
NCD .... National Center for the Diaconate [*Later, NAAND*] (EA)
NCD .... National Commission for Democracy [*Ghana*] [*Political party*]
NCD .... National Commission on Diabetes
NCD .... National Compliance Database [*Environmental Protection Agency*] (AEPA)
NCD .... National Control Data
NCD .... National Council on Drugs [*Defunct*] (EA)
NCD .... Natural Circular Dichroism [*Optics*]
NCD .... Navy Cargo Document (DNAB)
NCD .... Navy Contracting Directives (MCD)
NCD .... Negotiable Certificate of Deposit (ADA)
NCD .... Negotiated Critical Dates [*Telecommunications*] (TEL)
NCD .... Nemine Contradicente [*No One Contradicting*] [*Latin Legal term*] (DLA)
NCD .... Network Cryptographic Device
NCD .... Neurocirculatory Dystonia [*Medicine*] (DMAA)
NCD .... New Component Design (IAA)
NCD .... Nicotinamide Cytosine Dinucleotide [*Biochemistry*]
NCD .... Nitrogen Clearance Delay (DMAA)
NCD .... No Can Do [*From pidgin English*]
NCD .... No Claim Discount [*Insurance*] (AIA)
NCD .... Noncallable Deposit [*Investment term*]
NCD .... Non-Communicable Disease
NCD .... Non-Cumulative Dividend [*Business term*] (MHDW)
NCD .... Nonlinear Control Design [*Computer science*]
NCD .... Nordic Committee on Disability (EAIO)
NCD .... Nordic Council for the Deaf [*See also DNR*] (EAIO)
NCD .... Normal Childhood Diseases (DAVI)
NCD .... Normal Childhood Disorders [*Medicine*]
NCD .... Normalized Cumulative Deviation
NCD .... North Central Dairy Forwarders Tariff Bureau, Minneapolis MN [*STAC*]
NCD .... North Central Division [*Army Engineers*]
NCD .... Norton Change Directory [*Computer science*]
NCD .... Not Considered Disabling [*Medicine*] (MAE)
NCD .... Not Considered Disqualifying
NCD .... Notice of Credit Due
NCD .... Nova Scotia College of Art and Design Library [*UTLAS symbol*]
NCD .... Nuclear Commission Date (DNAB)

NCD .... Numerically Controlled Drafting (MCD)
NCDA.......... National Career Development Association (EA)
NCDA.......... National Center for Drug Analysis [*St. Louis*] [*FDA*]
NCDA.......... National Ceramic Dealers Association (EA)
NCDA.......... National College of District Attorneys
NCDA.......... National Community Development Association (EA)
NCDA.......... National Council on Drug Abuse [*Defunct*] (EA)
NCDAC........ National Civil Defense Advisory Council (EA)
NcDaD .... Davidson College, Davidson, NC [*Library symbol Library of Congress*] (LCLS)
NCDAD........ National Council for Diplomats in Art and Design [*British*] (BI)
NCDAI........ National Clearinghouse for Drug Abuse Information [*Public Health Service*] [*Rockville, MD*]
NcDaIG .... Gaston College, Dallas, NC [*Library symbol Library of Congress*] (LCLS)
NcDan......... Stokes County Public Library, Danbury, NC [*Library symbol Library of Congress*] (LCLS)
NCDAPA....... National Curtain, Drapery, and Allied Products Association [*Later, HFPA*]
NcD-B .... Duke University, Fuqua School of Business, Durham, NC [*Library symbol Library of Congress*] (LCLS)
NCDB.......... National Center for Drugs and Biologics [*FDA*]
NCDB.......... National Commercial and Development Bank [*Dominica*]
NCDB.......... National Compliance Database [*Environmental Protection Agency*] (AEPA)
NCDBC........ National Center for the Development of Bilingual Curriculum (EA)
NCDC.......... National Catholic Development Conference (EA)
NCDC.......... National Center for Disease Control [*Public Health Service*]
NCDC.......... National Centers for Disease Control (NADA)
NCDC.......... National Climatic Data Center [*National Oceanic and Atmospheric Administration Information service or system*] (IID)
NCDC.......... National Coalition for a Democratic Constitution [*Political group*] [*South Korea*]
NCDC.......... National Committee for the Day Care of Children [*Later, DCCA*]
NCDC.......... National Communicable Disease Center (MCD)
NCDC.......... National Criminal Defense College (EA)
NCDC.......... Naval Contract Distribution Center
NCDC.......... New Community Development Corp. [*HUD*]
NCDC.......... Nitro(carboxyphenyl)diphenylcarbamate [*Biochemistry*]
NCDC.......... Norchenodeoxycholic Acid [*Biochemistry*]
NCDCA........ National Child Day Care Association (EA)
NCDCF........ National Civil Defense Computer Facility
NCDCR........ North Carolina Department of Cultural Resources
NCDCV........ Neonatal Calf Diarrhea Coronavirus
NcD-D .... Duke University, Divinity School, Durham, NC [*Library symbol Library of Congress*] (LCLS)
NCDD.......... No Change in the Due Date (AFM)
NCDD-CCD... National Conference of Diocesan Directors of Religious Education (EA)
NCDDRE-CCD... National Conference of Diocesan Directors of Religious Education - CCD [*Continuing Christian Development*] (EA)
NcDe........... Denton Public Library, Denton, NC [*Library symbol Library of Congress*] (LCLS)
NCDE .... National Coalition for Democracy in Education [*Defunct*] (EA)
NCDF .... National Computer Dealer Forum (EA)
NCDH .... National Committee Against Discrimination in Housing (EA)
NCDHM........ National Children's Dental Health Month [*American Dental Association*]
NCDI .... Network Computing Devices, Inc. [*NASDAQ symbol*] (SAG)
NCDIE .... Network Computing Devices [*NASDAQ symbol*] (TTSB)
NcD-L .... Duke University, School of Law, Durham, NC [*Library symbol Library of Congress*] (LCLS)
NCDL .... National Canine Defence League [*British*] (DI)
NCDM .... Numerically Controlled Drafting Machine (MCD)
NcD-MC .... Duke University, Medical Center, Durham, NC [*Library symbol Library of Congress*] (LCLS)
NCDO.......... Navy Central Disbursing Office
NcDo........... Surry County-Dobson Library, Dobson, NC [*Library symbol Library of Congress*] (LCLS)
NcDoS .... Surry Community College, Dobson, NC [*Library symbol Library of Congress*] (LCLS)
NCDP .... Namibie Christelike Demokratiese Party [*Namibian Christian Democratic Party*] [*Political party*] (PPW)
NCDP .... Navigation Control/Display Panel (MCD)
NCDPEH....... National Coalition for Disease Prevention and Environmental Health
NCDRC........ National Catholic Disaster Relief Committee (EA)
NCDRE........ National Conference of Directors of Religious Education (NTPA)
NCDS .... National Center for Disability Services (EA)
NCDS .... National Center for Dispute Settlement [*American Arbitration Association*] [*Later, CDS*]
NCDS .... National Child Development Study [*British*]
NCDS .... National Council for the Divorced and Separated [*British*] (DBA)
NCDS .... Naval Combat Data System
NCDS .... Navy Combat Direction System (MCD)
NCDS .... Numerical Control Distribution System [*Computer science*] (MHDI)
NCDT .... National Council for Drama Training [*British*]
NCDT .... Noble-Collip Drum Trauma [*Physiology*]
NCDT .... Non-Chargeable Downtime
NCDT .... North Carolina Dance Theater
NCDT & E .... Naval Combat Demolition Training and Experimental Base [*Maui, HI*] (KSC)
NCDT & EBASE... Naval Combat Demolition Training and Experimental Base [*Maui, HI*]
NCDTO........ National Council of Dance Teacher Organizations [*Later, NDCA*] (EA)

NcDu............ Dunn Public Library, Dunn, NC [*Library symbol Library of Congress*] (LCLS)
NCDU.......... Naval Combat Demolition Unit
NCDU.......... Navigation Control and Display Unit
NcDubB........ Bladen Technical College, Dublin, NC [*Library symbol Library of Congress*] (LCLS)
NcDur.......... Durham City-County Public Library, Durham, NC [*Library symbol Library of Congress*] (LCLS)
NcDurBC...... Blue Cross & Blue Shield of North Carolina, Durham, NC [*Library symbol Library of Congress*] (LCLS)
NcDurBD..... Becton, Dickinson & Co., Research Center Library, Research Triangle Park, Durham, NC [*Library symbol Library of Congress*] (LCLS)
NcDurC........ North Carolina Central University, Durham, NC [*Library symbol Library of Congress*] (LCLS)
NcDurCG...... Ciba-Geigy Corp., Biotechnology Library, Durham, NC [*Library symbol*] [*Library of Congress*] (LCLS)
NcDurCL...... North Carolina Central University, School of Library Science, Durham, NC [*Library symbol Library of Congress*] (LCLS)
NcDurCR...... Chemstrand Research Center, Inc., Durham, NC [*Library symbol Library of Congress*] (LCLS)
NcDurEP...... United States Environmental Protection Agency, Office of Administration, LibraryServices Branch, Park, Durham, NC [*Library symbol Library of Congress*] (LCLS)
NcDurF........ Forest History Society, Inc., Durham, NC [*Library symbol*] [*Library of Congress*] (LCLS)
NcDurG........ Glaxo, Inc., Durham, NC [*Library symbol*] [*Library of Congress*] (LCLS)
NcDurGH...... Durham County General Hospital, Medical Library, Durham, NC [*Library symbol Library of Congress*] (LCLS)
NcDurHS...... United States National Environmental Health Sciences Center, Durham, NC [*Library symbol Library of Congress*] (LCLS)
NcDurIBM...... International Business Machines Corp., IBM CPD Library, Durham, NC [*Library symbol Library of Congress*] (LCLS)
NcDurIF....... International Fertility Research Program, Durham, NC [*Library symbol Library of Congress*] (LCLS)
NcDurIT....... Chemical Industry institute of Toxicology, Durham, NC [*Library symbol*] [*Library of Congress*] (LCLS)
NcDurL........ Liggett & Myers, Inc. [*Later, Liggett Group, Inc.*], Durham, NC [*Library symbol Library of Congress*] (LCLS)
NcDurM....... Monsanto Triangle Park Development Center, Durham, NC [*Library symbol Library of Congress*] (LCLS)
NcDurMi...... Microelectronics Center Library, Durham, NC [*Library symbol*] [*Library of Congress*] (LCLS)
NcDurNH...... National Humanities Center, Durham, NC [*Library symbol Library of Congress*] (LCLS)
NcDurRa...... Radian Corp. Library, Durham, NC [*Library symbol*] [*Library of Congress*] (LCLS)
NcDurRT...... Research Triangle Institute, Technical Library, Durham, NC [*Library symbol Library of Congress*] (LCLS)
NcDurSci..... North Carolina School of Science and Mathematics, Durham, NC [*Library symbol Library of Congress*] (LCLS)
NcDurST...... North Carolina Science and Technology Research Center, Durham, NC [*Library symbol Library of Congress*] (LCLS)
NcDurT........ Durham Technical Institute, Durham, NC [*Library symbol Library of Congress*] (LCLS)
NcDurUC...... Union Carbide Agricultural Products Co., Inc., Research Triangle Park, Durham, NC [*Library symbol Library of Congress*] (LCLS)
NcDurV........ United States Veterans Administration Hospital, Durham, NC [*Library symbol Library of Congress*] (LCLS)
NcDurW....... Wellcome Research Laboratories, Durham, NC [*Library symbol Library of Congress*] (LCLS)
NcDurW-Gv... Burroughs Wellcome & Co., Greenville, NC [*Library symbol Library of Congress*] (LCLS)
NCDV.......... Nebraska Calf Diarrhea Virus
NCDVD........ National Conference of Diocesan Vocation Directors (EA)
NcD-W......... Duke University, Woman's College, Durham, NC [*Library symbol Library of Congress*] (LCLS)
NcE............. Bladen County Public Library, Elizabethtown, NC [*Library symbol Library of Congress*] (LCLS)
NCe............. Middle Country Public Library, Centereach, NY [*Library symbol Library of Congress*] (LCLS)
NCE............. Nasa Cotopaxi [*Ecuador*] [*Seismograph station code, US Geological Survey*] (SEIS)
NCE............. National College of Education [*Illinois*]
NCE............. National Commission for Education (AIE)
NCE............. National Committee on the Emeriti (EA)
NCE............. National Council of Exchangors (EA)
NCE............. Navy Calibration Equipment List
NCE............. Navy Civil Engineer [*A publication*]
NCE............. Negative Contrast Echocardiography [*Medicine*] (DB)
NCE............. Network Connection Element
NCE............. Network Control Elements (MCD)
NCE............. Network Control Engine [*Synoptics Communications, Inc.*]
NCE............. Neuritis of the Cauda Equina [*Medicine*]
NCE............. Newark College of Engineering [*New Jersey*]
NCE............. New Catholic Edition [*Bible*]
NCE............. New Catholic Encyclopedia [*A publication*]
NCE............. New Chemical Entity
NCE............. Nice [*France*] [*Airport symbol*] (OAG)
NCE............. No Change in Estimates
NCE............. Nomadic Computing Environment
NCE............. Noncommercial Education [*FCC*] (NTCM)
NCE............. Nonconvulsive Epilepsy [*Medicine*]
NCE............. Normal Calomel Electrode [*Electrochemistry*]

NCE............. Normal Chick Embryo
NCE............. Normal Curve Equivalent [*Testing*] (EDAC)
NCE............. Northcoast Executive Airlines [*ICAO designator*] (FAAC)
NCE............. NTID [*National Technical Institute for the Deaf*] Center on Employment (PAZ)
NCE............. Nuclear Capability Evaluation
NCE............. Nuclear Capability Exercise [*Army*] (AABC)
NCE............. Nuclear/Chemical Environment [*Battlefield condition*] (RDA)
NCEA.......... National Catholic Educational Association (EA)
NCEA.......... National Center for Economic Alternatives (EA)
NCEA.......... National Center for Environmental Assessment (AEPA)
NCEA.......... National Christian Education Association (EA)
NCEA.......... National College Education and Admissions Foundation (EA)
NCEA.......... National Community Education Association (EA)
NCEA.......... National Consortium for Education Access (EA)
NCEA.......... National Council for Educational Awards [*Ireland*]
NCEA.......... N-(Carboxyethyl)alanine [*Biochemistry*]
NCEarc........ National Conference of Executives of the Arc (NTPA)
NCEAS........ National Center for Ecological Analysis and Synthesis
NcEB........... Bladen Technical Institute, Elizabethtown, NC [*Library symbol Library of Congress*] (LCLS)
NcEb........... East Bend Public Library, East Bend, NC [*Library symbol*] [*Library of Congress*] (LCLS)
NCEB.......... National Center for Educational Brokering [*Defunct*] (EA)
NCEB.......... National Council for Environmental Balance (EA)
NCEB.......... NATO Communications Electronics Board
NCEB.......... North Coast Energy [*NASDAQ symbol*] (TTSB)
NCEBP........ North Coast Energy Cv'B'Pfd [*NASDAQ symbol*] (TTSB)
NCEBVS...... National Chronic Epstein-Barr Virus Syndrome Association (EA)
NCEBW....... North Coast Energy Wrrt [*NASDAQ symbol*] (TTSB)
NCEC.......... National Center for Educational Communication [*Office of Education*]
NCEC.......... National Chemical Emergency Centre [*Atomic Energy Authority*] [*Didcot, Oxon., England*]
NCEC.......... National Christian Education Council [*Church of England*]
NCEC.......... National Commission for Electrologist Certification (EA)
NCEC.......... National Committee for an Effective Congress (EA)
NCEC.......... National Construction Employers Council [*Defunct*] (EA)
NCEC.......... North Coast Export Co. [*An association Defunct*] (EA)
NCECA........ National Council on Education for the Ceramic Arts (EA)
NC Ecc........ Notes of Cases, English Ecclesiastical and Maritime Courts [*1841-50*] [*A publication*] (DLA)
NCECD........ National Commission for Economic Conversion and Disarmament (EA)
NCECE........ National Council of Elected County Executives (EA)
NCECF........ National Children's Eye Care Foundation (EA)
NCECG........ National Coalition to Expand Charitable Giving [*Defunct*] (EA)
NCECS........ North Carolina Educational Computing Services (NITA)
NCECW....... National Center for the Early Childhood Work Force (EA)
NcEd........... Eden Public Library, Eden, NC [*Library symbol*] [*Library of Congress*] (LCLS)
NCED.......... National Center on Employment of the Deaf (EA)
NCEDC........ Northern California Earthquake Data Center
NCedHS....... Lawrence High School, Cedarhurst, NY [*Library symbol*] [*Library of Congress*] (LCLS)
NCEDL........ National Committee for Effective Design Legislation (EA)
NcEdR......... Rockingham County Public Library, Eden, NC [*Library symbol*] [*Library of Congress*] (LCLS)
NcEdR-M...... Mayodan Public Library, Mayodan, NC [*Library symbol*] [*Library of Congress*] (LCLS)
NcEdR-R...... Rockingham County Public Library, Reidsville Branch Library, Reidsville, NC [*Library symbol Library of Congress*] (LCLS)
NcEdR-S...... Stoneville Public Library, Stoneville, NC [*Library symbol*] [*Library of Congress*] (LCLS)
NcEdt.......... Shepard-Pruden Memorial Library, Edenton, NC [*Library symbol Library of Congress*] (LCLS)
NCEE.......... National Catholic Educational Exhibitors (EA)
NCEE.......... National Center on Education and Employment [*New York, NY Department of Education*] (GRD)
NCEE.......... National Congress for Educational Excellence (EA)
NCEE.......... National Council of Engineering Examiners (EA)
NCEEC........ Nested Cone Extendable Exit Cone (MCD)
NCEEF........ National Committee for Electrical Engineering Films
NCEER........ National Center for Earthquake Engineering Research [*Buffalo, NY*] (GRD)
NCEES........ National Council of Examiners for Engineering and Surveying (NTPA)
NCEF.......... National Calling and Emergency Frequencies (CET)
NCEF.......... National Commission on Electronic Funds Transfers (MHDW)
NCEF.......... Nomads' Charitable and Educational Foundation [*Australia*]
NCEF.......... Non-Circumcision Educational Foundation (EA)
NCEFF........ National Committee for Education in Family Finance (EA)
NCE-FM...... Noncommercial Educational FM [*Frequency Modulation*] [*Telecommunications*] (OTD)
NCEFR........ National Council of Erectors, Fabricators, and Riggers (EA)
NCEFT........ National Commission on Electronic Fund Transfers
NCEHAI....... National Committee on Ethics of the Hearing Aid Industry [*Defunct*] (EA)
NCEHELP.... National Conference of Executives of Higher Education Loan Plans [*Later, NCHELP*] (EA)
NCEHP........ National Center for the Exploration of Human Potential (EA)
NCEHPHP.... National Council on the Education of Health Professionals in Health Promotion (DAVI)
NCEHS........ National Center for Environmental Health Strategies (EA)
NcEl........... Kemp Memorial Library, Ellerbe, NC [*Library symbol Library of Congress*] (LCLS)
NCEL.......... Naval Civil Engineering Laboratory

NCEL............ Navy Contractor Experience List
NCEL............ Nuclear Certified Equipment List (DNAB)
NcElc .... East Albemarle Regional Library, Elizabeth City, NC [*Library symbol Library of Congress*] (LCLS)
NcElcA .... College of the Albemarle, Elizabeth City, NC [*Library symbol Library of Congress*] (LCLS)
NcElcE .... Elizabeth City State University, Elizabeth City, NC [*Library symbol Library of Congress*] (LCLS)
NcElcP .... Pasquotank-Camden Library, Elizabeth City, NC [*Library symbol Library of Congress*] (LCLS)
NcElcR .... Roanoke Bible College, Mary E. Griffith Memorial Library, Elizabeth City, NC [*Library symbol Library of Congress*] (LCLS)
NcElk .... Elkin Public Library, Elkin, NC [*Library symbol Library of Congress*] (LCLS)
NcElon .... Elon College, Elon College, NC [*Library symbol Library of Congress*] (LCLS)
NcElonCH .... Historical Society of the Southern Convention, Congregation of Christian Churches, Elon College, NC [*Library symbol Library of Congress*] (LCLS)
NcElonP .... Primitive Baptist Library, Elon College, NC [*Library symbol Library of Congress*] (LCLS)
NCEM.......... National Center for Electron Microscopy [*Berkeley, CA*] [*Lawrence Berkeley Laboratory*] [*Department of Energy*]
NCEMC .... National Committee on the Education of Migrant Children [*of the National Child Labor Committee*] (EA)
NCEMCH ...... National Center for Education in Maternal and Child Health (EA)
NCEMMH ...... National Center, Educational Media and Materials for the Handicapped [*Defunct*] (EA)
NCEMP .... National Center for Energy Management and Power
NCEMT........ National Center for Excellence in Metalworking Technology [*Navy*]
NcEn............ Lilly Pike Sullivan Municipal Library, Enfield, NC [*Library symbol Library of Congress*] (LCLS)
NCEN .... National Commission on Egg Nutrition
NCEN .... North Central
NcEnk .... American Enka Corp., Enka, NC [*Library symbol Library of Congress*] (LCLS)
NCentBsh..... North Central Bancshares, Inc. [*Associated Press*] (SAG)
N Cent School L Rev... North Central School Law Review [*A publication*] (DLA)
NCEO .... National Center for Employee Ownership (EA)
NCEO .... National Center for Exploitation of the Oceans
NCEOA .... National Council of Educational Opportunity Associations (EA)
NCEP .... National Center for Education in Politics [*Defunct*] (EA)
NCEP .... National Centers for Environmental Prediction [*Marine science*] (OSRA)
NCEP .... National Cholesterol Education Program Coordinating Committee [*National Institutes of Health*] (EGAO)
NCEP .... National Council for the Encouragement of Patriotism (EA)
NCEP .... National Council on Employment Policy (EA)
NCEPI .... National Center for Environmental Publications and Information (AEPA)
NcEr............ Erwin Public Library, Erwin, NC [*Library symbol Library of Congress*] (LCLS)
NCER .... National Center for Earthquake Research [*US Geological Survey*]
NCER .... National Conference on Electromagnetic Relays
NCER .... National Council on Educational Research [*Later, NCERI*] [*Department of Education Washington, DC*]
NCERACCS... National Coalition to End Racism in America's Child Care System (EA)
NCERD .... National Center for Educational Research and Development [*HEW*]
NCERT .... National Council for Educational Research and Training (WDAA)
nces-- .... El Salvador [*MARC geographic area code Library of Congress*] (LCCP)
NCES .... National Center for Education Statistics [*Office of Education*] [*Later, CES*]
NCES .... National Council for Educational Standards (AIE)
NCES .... New Careers in Employment Security (OICC)
NCES .... Normal Curve Equivalent Scores [*Testing*] (EDAC)
NCES .... North Central Experiment Station [*University of Minnesota*] [*Research center*] (RCD)
NCES .... North Country Educational Services [*Library network*]
NCESA .... National Class E Scow Association (EA)
NCESGR....... National Committee for Employer Support of the Guard and Reserve (EA)
NCET............ National Center for Educational Technology [*Office of Education*]
NCET............ National Coastal Ecosystems Team [*Office of Biological Services, United States Fish and Wildlife Service*] (MSC)
NCET............ National Conference of English Teachers (BARN)
NCET............ National Council for Educational Technology [*British*]
NCETA .... National Center for Education and Training in Addictions [*Australia*]
NCEUS .... National Commission on Employment and Unemployment Statistics [*Bureau of Labor Statistics*] (GFGA)
NCEW .... National Conference of Editorial Writers (EA)
NCEY .... National Committee on Employment of Youth [*National Child Labor Committee*] (EA)
NCEZ........... National Coalition for Enterprise Zones [*San Diego, CA*] (EA)
NCF............. Narramore Christian Foundation (EA)
NCF............. National Cancer Foundation
NCF............. National Chamber Foundation (EA)
NCF............. National Civics Federation
NCF............. National Clayware Federation [*British*] (DBA)
NCF............. National Commission on a Free and Responsible Media (EA)
NCF............. National Communications Forum [*National Engineering Consortium, Inc.*] [*Chicago, IL*] [*Telecommunications*] (TSSD)
NCF............. National Conservative Foundation (EA)
NCF............. National Consumer Federation (NADA)

NCF............. National Control Facility [*FAA*] (TAG)
NCF............. National Craniofacial Foundation [*Later, ICF*] (EA)
NCF............. National Cristina Foundation (EA)
NCF............. NATO Composite Force
NCF............. Naval Communications Facility (MUGU)
NCF............. Naval Construction Force (NVT)
NCF............. Nerve Cell Food
NCF............. Net Cash Flow
NCF............. NetWare Configuration File [*Computer science*]
NCF............. Network Control Facility (COE)
NCF............. Neutrophil Chemotactic Factor [*Hematology*]
NCF............. Neutrophil Cytosol Factor [*Cytology*]
NCF............. Newton-Cotes Formula [*Mathematics*]
NCF............. No Clean Flux Process [*Computer manufacturing*] (PCM)
NCF............. No Conscription Fellowship [*England, World War I*]
NCF............. No Containment Failure [*Environmental science*] (COE)
NCF............. Nominal Characteristics File (IEEE)
NCF............. Noncold Front [*Meteorology*]
NCF............. Nonflammable Cellulosic Foam
NCF............. Nuclear Capable Forces (MCD)
NCF............. Nucleonics Calibration Facility (RDA)
NCF............. Nugget Coombs Foundation for Indigenous Studies [*Australia*]
NCF............. Nurses Christian Fellowship (EA)
NCFA .... Narcolepsy and Cataplexy Foundation of America (EA)
NCFA .... National Cat Fanciers' Association [*Defunct*] (EA)
NCFA .... National Collection of Fine Arts [*Later, National Mus eum of American Art*]
NCFA .... National Collegiate Football Association (EA)
NCFA .... National Commercial Finance Association (EA)
NCFA .... National Commission of Fine Arts (NADA)
NCFA .... National Committee for Adoption (EA)
NCFA .... National Consumer Finance Association (EA)
NCFA .... National Council for Adoption [*Formerly National Committee for Adoption*] (PAZ)
NCFA .... Naval Campus for Achievement (NVT)
NCFA .... North Carolina Forestry Association (WPI)
NCFA .... North Central Field Area
NCFA .... Nurses' Christian Fellowship of Australia
NCFAE .... National Council of Forestry Association Executives (EA)
NCFAP .... Naval Campus for Achievement Program (MCD)
NcFayC .... Cumberland County Public Library, Fayetteville, NC [*Library symbol Library of Congress*] (LCLS)
NcFayC-F..... Cumberland County Public Library, North Carolina Foreign Language Center, Fayetteville, NC [*Library symbol Library of Congress*] (LCLS)
NcFayCFH.... Cape Fear Valley Hospital, Medical Library, Fayetteville, NC [*Library symbol Library of Congress*] (LCLS)
NcFayH........ Fayetteville Area Health Education Foundation, Inc., Fayetteville, NC [*Library symbol Library of Congress*] (LCLS)
NcFayM .... Methodist College, Fayetteville, NC [*Library symbol Library of Congress*] (LCLS)
NcFayR .... Rutledge College, Fayetteville, NC [*Library symbol Library of Congress*] (LCLS)
NcFayS .... Fayetteville State University, Fayetteville, NC [*Library symbol Library of Congress*] (LCLS)
NcFayT .... Fayetteville Technical Institute, Fayetteville, NC [*Library symbol Library of Congress*] (LCLS)
NcFayV .... United States Veterans Administration Medical Center, Fayetteville, NC [*Library symbol Library of Congress*] (LCLS)
NcFb .... United States Army, Special Services Library System, Fort Bragg, NC [*Library symbol Library of Congress*] (LCLS)
NcFbH.......... United States Army, Womack Army Hospital, Fort Bragg, NC [*Library symbol Library of Congress*] (LCLS)
NcFbIM........ United States Army, Institute for Military Assistance, Marquat Memorial Library, Fort Bragg, NC [*Library symbol Library of Congress*] (LCLS)
NcFc .... Mooneyham Public Library, Forest City, NC [*Library symbol Library of Congress*] (LCLS)
NCFC .... National Coalition for a Free Cuba (EA)
NCFC .... National Commercial Finance Conference [*Later, NCFA*] (EA)
NCFC .... National Congress for Men and Children [*An association*] (PAZ)
NCFC .... National Council of Farmer Cooperatives (EA)
NCFCA .... National Congress of Floor Covering Associations [*Defunct*] (EA)
NCFD .... National Corporate Fund for Dance (EA)
NCFD .... New Computer Family D (SAA)
NCFDA .... National Council on Federal Disaster Assistance
NCFDAL .... National Committee for Fair Divorce and Alimony Laws (EA)
NCFDITFS ... National Committee for the Full Development of Instructional Television Fixed Services [*ITFS regulation*] (NTCM)
NCFE........... National Campaign for Freedom of Expression
NCFE........... National Center for Financial Education (EA)
NCFE........... National Committee for Full Employment [*Defunct*] (EA)
NCFE........... National Commodity Futures Examination
NCFEAD ...... National Council for Foundation Education in Art and Design (AIE)
NCFEPS .... National Commission for Full Employment Policy Studies (OICC)
NCFES .... North Central Forest Experiment Station [*St. Paul, MN*] [*Department of Agriculture*] (GRD)
NCFFR .... National Commission on Fraudulent Financial Reporting [*Defunct*] (EA)
NCFI............ National Cold Fusion Institute [*Closed June 30, 1991*]
NCFI............ North Carolina Alliance of Community (TBD)
NCFIS .... National Center for Freedom of Information Studies (EA)
NCFJE .... National Committee for the Furtherance of Jewish Education (EA)
NCFL........... National Catholic Forensic League (EA)
NCFL........... National Center for Family Literacy (PAZ)

NCFLIS .... National Council on Foreign Language and International Studies (EA)
NCFM........... National Coalition of Free Men (EA)
NCFM........... National Commission on Food Marketing
NCFMF........ National Committee for Fluid Mechanics Films
NCFMS .... Naval Comptroller Financial Management Service
NCFNP .... National Committee for a Freedom Now Party [Defunct] (EA)
NCFO .... National Conference of Firemen and Oilers (NTPA)
NCFP .... National Conference on Fluid Power (EA)
NCFPC .... National Center for Fish Protein Concentrate [Fish and Wildlife Service]
NCFPC .... National Commission on Fire Prevention and Control
NCFPI .... National Clearinghouse for Family Planning Information [Database]
NCFPS .... National Center for Family Planning Services [Health Services and Mental Health Administration, HEW]
NcFr............ Macon County Public Library, Franklin, NC [Library symbol Library of Congress] (LCLS)
NCFR .... National Campaign for Firework Reform [British] (DBA)
NCFR .... National Council for Family Reconciliation (EA)
NCFR .... National Council on Family Relations (EA)
NCFRF .... National Cystic Fibrosis Research Foundation [Later, Cystic Fibrosis Foundation] (EA)
NcFrt........... Franklinton Public Library, Franklinton, NC [Library symbol Library of Congress] (LCLS)
NCFS .... National College of Foot Surgeons (EA)
NCFS .... National Committee on Films for Safety [Defunct] (EA)
NCFS .... National Conference of Friendly Societies [British] (DBA)
NCFS .... Near Constant Force Suspension
NCFS .... Noncontingent Footshock
NCFSA .... National Chronic Fatigue Syndrome Association (EA)
NCFSD .... NORAD Cost Factors and System Data [Military] (MCD)
NCFSFA .... National Chronic Fatigue Syndrome and Fibromyalgia Association [Formerly, National Chronic Fatigue Syndrome Association] (EA)
NCFSK .... Noncoherent Frequency Shift Keying
NCFSU .... Naval Construction Force Support Unit (NVT)
NCFT........... National Council for Families and Television (EA)
NCFTF .... National Consumer Fraud Task Force (EA)
NCFTJ......... National Conference on Federal Trial Judges (EA)
NcFv .... Farmville Public Library, Farmville, NC [Library symbol Library of Congress] (LCLS)
NCFVP .... National Center for Film and Video Preservation (EA)
NCFVSI .... National Council for Fishing Vessel Safety and Insurance (EA)
NCG .... Coast Guard Publication [Later, NAVCG]
NcG............. Greensboro Public Library, Greensboro, NC [Library symbol Library of Congress] (LCLS)
NCG .... Nanochannel Glass
NCG .... National Contractors Group [British] (DBA)
NCG .... National Council for the Gifted (EA)
NCG .... Network Control Group [Manned Space Flight Network]
NCG .... New College Graduate (BARN)
NCG .... Nickel-Coated Graphite [Materials technology]
NCG .... Nicotine Chewing Gum (PDAA)
NCG .... Noncondensible Gases
NCG .... North Carolina Nat Gas [NYSE symbol] (TTSB)
NCG .... Nova-Cogesco Resources, Inc. [Toronto Stock Exchange symbol]
NCG .... Nuclear Cratering Group [Later, EERA] [Army]
NCG .... Nueva Casas Grandes [Mexico] [Airport symbol] (AD)
NCG .... Null Command Generator
NCG .... Numerical Control Graphics (MCD)
NcGa........... Gaston-Lincoln Regional Library, Gastonia, NC [Library symbol Library of Congress] (LCLS)
NCGA .... National Church Goods Association (EA)
NCGA .... National Collegiate Gymnastics Association (PSS)
NCGA .... National Computer Graphics Association (EA)
NCGA .... National Corn Growers Association (EA)
NCGA .... National Cotton Ginners' Association (EA)
NCGA .... National Council on Governmental Accounting (EA)
NcGA .... North Carolina Agricultural and Technical State University, Greensboro, NC [Library symbol Library of Congress] (LCLS)
NcGaH .... Gaston Memorial Hospital, Inc., Medical Library, Gastonia, NC [Library symbol Library of Congress] (LCLS)
NcGaL.......... Gaston-Lincoln Regional Library, Gastonia, NC [Library symbol] [Library of Congress] (LCLS)
NcGAT .... AT&T Technologies Inc., Legal Library, Greensboro, NC [Library symbol] [Library of Congress] (LCLS)
NcGav .... Gates County Library, Gatesville, NC [Library symbol Library of Congress] (LCLS)
NcGB .... Bennett College, Greensboro, NC [Library symbol Library of Congress] (LCLS)
NcGBI .... Burlington Industries, Inc., Information Services Library, Greensboro, NC [Library symbol Library of Congress] (LCLS)
NcGBur .... Burlington Industries, Inc., Information Services Library, Greensboro, NC [Library symbol Library of Congress] (LCLS)
NcGC .... Greensboro College, Greensboro, NC [Library symbol Library of Congress] (LCLS)
NCGC .... National Catholic Guidance Conference [Later, ARVIC] (EA)
NCGCC........ National Convention of Gospel Choirs and Choruses (EA)
NcGCG .... Ciba-Geigy Corp., Technical Information Service, Greensboro, NC [Library symbol Library of Congress] (LCLS)
NcGCH .... Wesley Long Community Hospital, Inc., Greensboro, NC [Library symbol Library of Congress] (LCLS)
NcGCL .... Center for Creative Leadership, Greensboro, NC [Library symbol Library of Congress] (LCLS)
NcGCM .... Cone Mills Corp., Greensboro, NC [Library symbol Library of Congress] (LCLS)
NCGE .... National Council for Geographic Education (EA)

NC Gen Stat... General Statutes of North Carolina [A publication] (DLA)
NCGEP .... National Council on Graduate Education in Psychology
NcGf............ Granite Falls Public Library, Granite Falls, NC [Library symbol Library of Congress] (LCLS)
NcGG .... Guilford College, Greensboro, NC [Library symbol Library of Congress] (LCLS)
NCGG......... National Committee for Geodesy and Geophysics (MCD)
NcGGil .... Gilbarco Corp. Library, Greensboro, NC [Library symbol Library of Congress] (LCLS)
NcGGT .... Guilford Technical Community College, Learning Resource Center, Greensboro, NC [Library symbol Library of Congress] (LCLS)
NcGH .... Moses H. Cone Memorial Hospital, Medical Library, Greensboro, NC [Library symbol Library of Congress] (LCLS)
NCGIC .... National Cartographic and Geographic Information Center [Geological Survey] [Reston, VA Database]
NCGIF .... National Cherry Growers and Industries Foundation (EA)
NCGIS .... National Council of Guilds for Infant Survival (EA)
NcGL........... Lorillard Research Center, Greensboro, NC [Library symbol Library of Congress] (LCLS)
NCGLC .... National Caucus of Gay and Lesbian Counselors (EA)
NCGMCTC.... National Chevy/GMC Truckin' Club [Defunct] (EA)
NcGo........... Wayne County Public Library, Goldsboro, NC [Library symbol Library of Congress] (LCLS)
NcGoCH .... Cherry Hospital, Learning Resource Center, Goldsboro, NC [Library symbol Library of Congress] (LCLS)
NcGoO .... O'Berry Center, Professional Library, Goldsboro, NC [Library symbol Library of Congress] (LCLS)
NcGoW .... Wayne Community College, Goldsboro, NC [Library symbol Library of Congress] (LCLS)
NcGPS .... Greensboro Public Schools, Greensboro, NC [Library symbol Library of Congress] (LCLS)
NCGR .... National Center for Genome Resources
NCGR .... National Clonal Germplasm Repository [Corvallis, OR] [Agricultural Research Service] [Department of Agriculture] (GRD)
NCGR .... National Council for GeoCosmic Research (EA)
NCGR .... National Council on Gene Resources (EA)
NcGrE .... East Carolina University, Greenville, NC [Library symbol Library of Congress] (LCLS)
NcGrE-H...... East Carolina University, Health Sciences Library, Greenville, NC [Library symbol Library of Congress] (LCLS)
NcGrP .... Pitt Technical Institute, Greenville, NC [Library symbol Library of Congress] (LCLS)
NcGrS .... Sheppard Memorial Library, Greenville, NC [Library symbol Library of Congress] (LCLS)
NCGS .... National Coalition of Girls Schools (NTPA)
NCGS .... National Cooperative Gallstone Study
NCGS .... New Century Gilders Society [A union] [British]
NCGS .... Nuclear Criteria Group Secretariat [Air Force Weapons Laboratory] [Kirtland Air Force Base, NM]
NCGS .... Nuclear Criteria Group Secretary (NAKS)
NCGSTDS .... National Coalition of Gay Sexually Transmitted Disease Services [Defunct] (EA)
ncgt--.......... Guatemala [MARC geographic area code Library of Congress] (LCCP)
NcGU .... University of North Carolina at Greensboro, Greensboro, NC [Library symbol Library of Congress] (LCLS)
NcGWE .... Western Electric Co., Legal Library, Greensboro, NC [Library symbol Library of Congress] (LCLS)
NCGWR....... National Center for Ground Water Research [Stillwater, OK] [Environmental Protection Agency] (GRD)
NCH .... Hamilton & Kirkland Colleges, Clinton, NY [Library symbol Library of Congress] (LCLS)
NCH .... Nachingwea [Tanzania] [Airport symbol] (OAG)
NCH .... National Center for Homeopathy (EA)
NCH .... National Center on Educational Media and Materials for the Handicapped, Columbus, OH [Inactive] [OCLC symbol] (OCLC)
NCH .... National Children's Home [British]
NCH .... National Clearinghouse [Public Health Service]
NCH .... National Coalition for the Homeless (EA)
NCH .... National Cocaine Hotline
NCH .... National Committee on Housing
NCH .... National Council on the Humanities [Washington, DC]
NCH .... NCH Corp. [Formerly, National Chemsearch Corp.] [NYSE symbol] (SPSG)
NCH .... Negative Channel [Computer science] (IAA)
NCH .... Network Connection Handler
NCH .... Nielson Clearing House [A.C. Nielson Co.] (DOAD)
NCH .... Notched
NCH .... Number [or Name] Changed [Telephone Listing] (BARN)
NCha........... Chatham Public Library, Chatham, NY [Library symbol Library of Congress] (LCLS)
NcHa........... Hamlet Public Library, Hamlet, NC [Library symbol Library of Congress] (LCLS)
NCHA.......... National Campers and Hikers Association (EA)
NCHA.......... National Capital Housing Authority
NCHA.......... National Crossbow Hunters Association (EA)
NCHA.......... National Cutting Horse Association (EA)
NCHA.......... Northern Collegiate Hockey Association (PSS)
NCHAA .... National Cutting Horse Association of Australia
NChaL......... Chatham Public Library, Chatman, NY [Library symbol] [Library of Congress] (LCLS)
NcHal.......... Halifax County Library, Halifax, NC [Library symbol Library of Congress] (LCLS)
NChap.......... Chappaqua Library, Chappaqua, NY [Library symbol Library of Congress] (LCLS)

NcHaR .... Richmond Technical Institute, Hamlet, NC [*Library symbol Library of Congress*] (LCLS)

NcHav.......... Havelock-Craven County Public Library, Havelock, NC [*Library symbol Library of Congress*] (LCLS)

NcHavCr ...... Craven Community College, Havelock Learning Center, Havelock, NC [*Library symbol*] [*Library of Congress*] (LCLS)

NcHay.......... Moss Memorial Library, Hayesville, NC [*Library symbol Library of Congress*] (LCLS)

NCHC .... National Clogging and Hoedown Council (EA)

NCHC .... National Collegiate Honors Council (EA)

NCHC .... National Council of Health Centers [*Formerly, NCHCS*] [*Later, AHCA*] (EA)

NCHCA .... National Commission for Health Certifying Agencies (EA)

NCHCS .... National Council of Health Care Services (EA)

NCHCT .... National Center for Health Care Technology [*US Congress agency*]

NCHDI .... National Center for Hearing Dog Information [*Later, HDRC*] (EA)

NcHe.......... H. Leslie Perry Memorial Library, Henderson, NC [*Library symbol Library of Congress*] (LCLS)

NCHE .... National Center for Health Education (EA)

NCHE .... National Committee on Household Employment

NCHE .... National Council for History Education (EA)

NCheH .... Saint Joseph Intercommunity Hospital, Cheektowaga, NY [*Library symbol Library of Congress*] (LCLS)

NCHELP .... National Council of Higher Education Loan Programs (EA)

NCHEML ...... National Chemical Laboratory (MCD)

NCHEMS ...... National Center for Higher Education Management Systems (EA)

NCHER .... National Center for Homecare Education and Research [*Defunct*] (EA)

NCHES .... National Child Health and Education Study [*University of Bristol*] [*British*]

NcHeV .... Vance County Technical Institute, Henderson, NC [*Library symbol Library of Congress*] (LCLS)

NCHF .... Navy Cargo Handling Force (COE)

NcHf............ Perquimans County Library, Hertford, NC [*Library symbol Library of Congress*] (LCLS)

NCHFCI .... National Committee to Honor the Fourteenth Centennial of Islam (EA)

NCHFFA .... National Council of Health Facilities Finance Authorities (NTPA)

N CHG .... Normal Charge (MHDB)

NCHGD .... National Clearinghouse for Human Genetic Diseases [*Later, NCEMCH*] [*Public Health Service*] [*Information service or system*] (IID)

NCHGR .... National Center for Human Genome Research

NCHHA .... National Council of Homemakers and Home Health Aides

NCHHHSO.... National Coalition of Hispanic Health and Human Services Organizations (EA)

NCHI .... National Council of the Housing Industry (EA)

NcHil .... Confederate Memorial Library, Hillsboro, NC [*Library symbol Library of Congress*] (LCLS)

NCHLA .... National Committee for a Human Life Amendment (EA)

NCHLRR ...... National Commission on Human Life, Reproduction, and Rhythm (EA)

NCHLS .... National Council on Health Laboratory Services (EA)

NCHM .... National Center for Housing Management (EA)

NCHMHHSO... National Coalition of Hispanic Mental Health and Human Services Organizations [*Later, NCHHHSO*]

NCHMI .... National Centers for Health and Medical Information, Inc. [*Research center*] (RCD)

NCHMOS...... Negative Channel Metal-Oxide Semiconductor (IAA)

NCHMT .... National Capital Historical Museum of Transportation (EA)

ncho--.......... Honduras [*MARC geographic area code Library of Congress*] (LCCP)

NCHO .... National Chicano Health Organization (EA)

NcHp.......... High Point Public Library, High Point, NC [*Library symbol Library of Congress*] (LCLS)

NCHP .... National Corp. for Housing Partnerships

NCHP .... Nickel-Chromium Honeycomb Panel

NCHPA .... National Center for Health Promotion and Aging (EA)

NcHpC .... High Point College, High Point, NC [*Library symbol Library of Congress*] (LCLS)

NCHPC .... National Consortium for High Performance Computing (DDC)

NCHPD .... National Council on Health Planning and Development

NcHpH .... High Point Regional Hospital Medical Library, High Point, NC [*Library symbol*] [*Library of Congress*] (LCLS)

NCHR.......... National Coalition for Haitian Refugees (EA)

NCHR.......... National Coalition for Human Rights (EA)

N Ch R......... Nelson's English Chancery Reports [*A publication*] (DLA)

NCHRP .... National Cooperative Highway Research Program

NCHRTM...... National Clearing House of Rehabilitation Training Materials [*Oklahoma State University*] [*Information service or system*] (IID)

NcHs.......... Hudson Library, Highlands, NC [*Library symbol Library of Congress*] (LCLS)

NCHS .... National Center for Health Statistics [*Public Health Service*] [*Hyattsville, MD Originator and database*]

NCHS .... National Committee on Homemaker Service [*Superseded by NHC*] (EA)

NCHSR .... National Center for Health Services Research

NCHSR .... National Center for Health Services Research and Health Care Technology Assessment [*Rockville, MD*] [*Public Health Service*] (GRD)

NCHSR & D... National Center for Health Services Research and Development [*Later, NCHSR*] [*HEW*]

NCHSRD ...... National Center for Health Services Research and Development [*Later, NCHSR*] [*HEW*]

NcHu.......... Hudson Public Library, Hudson, NC [*Library symbol Library of Congress*] (LCLS)

NcHv.......... Henderson County Public Library, Hendersonville, NC [*Library symbol Library of Congress*] (LCLS)

NcHvH .... Blue Ridge Technical Institute, Hendersonville, NC [*Library symbol Library of Congress*] (LCLS)

NcHvME ...... Mother Earth News, Hendersonville, NC [*Library symbol Library of Congress*] (LCLS)

NCHVR........ National Center for HIV [*Human Immunodeficiency Virus*] Virology Research [*Australia*]

NCHVRFE..... National College for Heating, Ventilating, Refrigeration, and Fan Engineering (MCD)

NCHW .... National Council of Hispanic Women (EA)

NCHWPPTA... National Conference of Health, Welfare, and Pension Plans, Trustees and Administrators [*Later, International Foundation of Employee Benefit Plans*] (EA)

NcHy.......... Elbert Ivey Memorial Library, Hickory, NC [*Library symbol Library of Congress*] (LCLS)

NcHyC .... Catawba Valley Technical Institute, Hickory, NC [*Library symbol Library of Congress*] (LCLS)

NcHyCH ...... Catawba Memorial Hospital, Northwest AHEC Library at Hickory, Hickory, NC [*Library symbol*] [*Library of Congress*] (LCLS)

NcHyCM ...... Catawba Area Mental Health Center, Hickory, NC [*Library symbol*] [*Library of Congress*] (LCLS)

NcHyFH........ Glenn R. Frye Memorial Hospital, Hickory, NC [*Library symbol*] [*Library of Congress*] (LCLS)

NcHyL.......... Lenoir Rhyne College, Hickory, NC [*Library symbol Library of Congress*] (LCLS)

NcHyMH ...... Hickory Memorial Hospital Library, Hickory, NC [*Library symbol*] [*Library of Congress*] (LCLS)

NcHyS.......... Siecor Corp., Technical Information Center, Hickory, NC [*Library symbol Library of Congress*] (LCLS)

NCi.......... Central Islip Public Library, Central Islip, NY [*Library symbol Library of Congress*] (LCLS)

nCi.......... Nanocurie [*One billionth of a curie*]

NCI.......... Naphthalene Creosote, Iodoform [*Powder for lice*]

NCI.......... National Cancer Institute [*Database producer*] [*Bethesda, MD*] [*National Institutes of Health*] [*Department of Health and Human Services*]

NCI.......... National Captioning Institute (EA)

NCI.......... National Cheese Institute (EA)

NCI.......... National Components, Inc. (EFIS)

NCI.......... National Computer Index [*National Computing Centre Ltd.*] [*British Information service or system*] (CRD)

NCI.......... National Computer Institute (MCD)

NCI.......... National Computing Industries (NITA)

NCI.......... National Council for Inordinacy (EA)

NCI.......... National Critics Institute (EA)

NCI.......... Natural Casing Institute [*Later, International Natural Sausage Casing Institute*] (EA)

NCI.......... Naval Cost Inspector

NCI.......... Navigation Control Indicator (MCD)

NCI.......... Necocli [*Colombia*] [*Airport symbol*] (OAG)

NCI.......... Negative Chemical Ionization [*Spectrometry*]

NCI.......... Network Communications International [*Telecommunications service*] (TSSD)

NCI.......... Network Computer, Inc. (IGQR)

NCI.......... Neutral Countries Intelligence [*of Ministry of Economic Warfare*] [*British World War II*]

NCI.......... New Community Instrument [*European Community*] (MHDB)

NCI.......... New Creation Institute (EA)

NCI.......... No Common Interest

NCI.......... No-Cost Item (AAG)

NCI.......... Nomenclature Control Index (MCD)

NCI.......... Nominal Correction I [*Phasing maneuver*] (MCD)

NCI.......... Noncoded Information [*Computer science*] (IBMDP)

NCI.......... Noncoherent Integration

NCI.......... Noncriterion Ischemic (DMAA)

NCI.......... North Conway Institute (EA)

NCI.......... Northeast Computer Institute (HGAA)

NCI.......... Notice of Change Inception (MCD)

NCI.......... Notice of Change Incorporation (MCD)

NCI.......... Nuclear Capability Inspection (CINC)

NCI.......... Nuclear Contour Index [*Cytology*]

NCI.......... Nuclear Control Institute (EA)

NCI.......... Nurse Competency Inventory

NCI.......... Nursing Care Integration [*Medicine*] (DMAA)

NCI.......... Nursing Citation Index

NCI.......... Office of New Concepts and Initiatives [*Air Force*] (TEL)

NCI.......... Southwest New Jersey Consortium for Health Information Service, Voorhees, NJ [*OCLC symbol*] (OCLC)

NCIA .... National Cavity Installation Association [*British*]

NCIA .... National Center on Institutions and Alternatives (EA)

NCIA .... National Crop Insurance Association [*Shawnee Mission, KS*] (EA)

NCIAC .... National Construction Industry Arbitration Committee (EA)

NCIAC .... North Central Intercollegiate Athletic Conference (PSS)

NCIAED .... National Center for Information and Advice on Educational Disadvantage

NCIB .... National Charities Information Bureau (EA)

NCIB .... National Collection of Industrial Bacteria [*British*]

NCI Bldg ...... NCI Building Systems [*Associated Press*] (SAG)

NCIBRD........ National Center for Integrated Bioremediation Research & Development [*Initiated in Michigan with government funding, 1994*]

NCIC .... National Cancer Institute of Canada

NCIC .... National Career Information Center [*Defunct*] (EA)

NCIC .... National Cartographic Information Center [*United States Geological Survey*] [*Reston, VA*]
NCIC .... National Commission on the Indian Canadian
NCIC .... National Congress of Italian Canadians
NCIC .... National Construction Industry Council (EA)
NCIC .... National Crime Information Center [*FBI*] [*Washington, DC*]
NCIC .... National Crop Insurance Council [*Inactive*] (EA)
NCIC .... Network Communications Interface, Common (MCD)
NCIC .... Non-Circumcision Information Center (EA)
NCIC .... Nonconfidential Information Center (AEPA)
NCIC .... Northwest Coastal Information Center [*Marine science*] (MSC)
NCIC .... Northwest Conference of Independent Colleges (PSS)
NCICA .... National Counter Intelligence Corps Association (EA)
NCIC Ops ..... North Carolina Industrial Commission Advance Sheets [*A publication*] (DLA)
NCICU .... National Council of Independent Colleges and Universities [*Later, NAICU*]
NCID .... National Council for Industrial Defense (EA)
NCIDQ .... National Council for Interior Design Qualification (EA)
NCIE .... National Coalition for Indian Education (EA)
NCIES .... National Center for the Improvement of Educational Systems [*Office of Education*]
NCIES .... National Committee for International Education through Satellites (EA)
NCIESD .... National Conference on International Economic and Social Development [*Later, IDC*]
NCIH .... National Conference on Industrial Hydraulics
NCIH .... National Council for International Health (EA)
NCIHC .... National Council for Interior Horticultural Certification (EA)
NCII .... National Council for Industrial Innovation (EA)
NCII .... National Council of Individual Investors
NCIJC .... National Council of Independent Junior Colleges [*Defunct*]
NCIL .... National Council on Independent Living (EA)
NCILT .... National Centre for Industrial Language Training [*British*] (DI)
NCIMA .... National Cellulose Insulation Manufacturers Association
NCIMC .... National Council of Industrial Management Clubs [*Later, IMC*] (EA)
NCIMS .... National Conference on Interstate Milk Shipments
NCIMS .... Negative Chemical Ionization Mass Spectra
NCIMS .... Numerical Control Information Management System (MCD)
NCIN .... National Credit Information Network
NCIN .... North Carolina Information Network [*Library network*]
NCINAS .... National Council of Industrial Naval Air Stations (EA)
NCINASEO ... National Council of Industrial Naval Air Stations Employee Organizations [*Formerly, NCNASEO*] (EA)
NCIO .... National Congress of Inventors Organizations (EA)
NCIO .... National Council on Indian Opportunity (EA)
NCIP .... National Council for Industrial Peace [*Defunct*] (EA)
NCIP .... No Change in Price (MCD)
NCIP .... Non-Contributory Invalid Pension [*British*] (DI)
NCIP .... North American Collections Inventory Project [*Established 1982*] [*Library science*]
NCIPA .... National Committee for Independent Political Action (EA)
NCIPLA .... National Council of Intellectual Property Law Associations (EA)
NCIR .... National Center for Immigrants' Rights [*Later, NILC*] (EA)
NCIR .... National Center for Initiative Review (EA)
NCIR .... National Conference on Industrial Research
NCIRF .... National Center for Initiative Review Foundation [*Defunct*] (EA)
NCIRLS .... North Central Regional Library System [*Library network*]
NCIS .... Nadir Climate Interferometer Spectrometer (MCD)
NCIS .... National Chemical Information System (DIT)
NCIS .... National Coalition of Independent Scholars
NCIS .... National Council of Independent Schools [*Later, National Association of Independent Schools*] (AEBS)
NCIS .... National Credit Information Service [*TRW, Inc.*] [*Long Beach, CA Credit-information databank*]
NCIS .... National Criminal Intelligence Service (WA)
NCIS .... National Criminal Investigation Service (WDAA)
NCIS .... National Crop Insurance Services (EA)
NCIS .... Navy Cost Information System
NCIS .... Nuclear Criticality Information System [*Lawrence Livermore National Laboratory*] [*Information service or system*] (IID)
NCISC .... Naval Counterintelligence Support Center
NCISD .... National Coalition on Immune System Disorders (EA)
NCISE .... National Center for Improving Science Education (EA)
NCiSH .... Central Islip State Hospital, Central Islip, NY [*Library symbol Library of Congress*] (LCLS)
NCISS .... National Council of Investigation and Security Services (EA)
NCIT .... National Committee for Insurance Taxation (EA)
NCIT .... National Council of Independent Truckers [*Defunct*] (EA)
NCIT .... National Council of Inland Transport [*British*] (DBA)
NCIT .... Numerical Control Inspection Tape (MCD)
NCITC .... National Clothing Industry Training Committee [*Australia*]
NCITD .... National Committee on International Trade Documentation [*MARAD*] (TAG)
NCITD .... National Council on International Trade Documentation [*In association name: NCITD - The International Trade Facilitation Council*] (EA)
NCITR .... National Center for Intermedia Transport Research [*Los Angeles, CA*] (GRD)
NCITS .... National Committee for Information Technology Standards [*Washington, DC*] (DDC)
NCITT .... National Committee for the In-Service Training of Teachers [*Scotland*] (AIE)
NCIU .... Network Common Interface Unit
NCIU .... Network Common Interference Unit (MCD)
NCIU .... Network Communications Interface, Unique
NCIV .... National Council for International Visitors (EA)
NcJ .... Jamestown Public Library, Jamestown, NC [*Library symbol*] [*Library of Congress*] (LCLS)
NCJ .... Johnson C. Smith University, James B. Duke Memorial Library, Charlotte, NC [*OCLC symbol*] (OCLC)
NCJ .... Needle Catheter Jejunostomy [*Medicine*] (DMAA)
NCJA .... National Criminal Justice Association (EA)
NcJa .... Onslow County Public Library, Jacksonville, NC [*Library symbol Library of Congress*] (LCLS)
NcJaC .... Coastal Carolina Community College, Jacksonville, NC [*Library symbol Library of Congress*] (LCLS)
NcJac .... Northampton County Memorial Library, Jackson, NC [*Library symbol Library of Congress*] (LCLS)
NcJacL .... Northampton County Memorial Library, Jackson, NC [*Library symbol*] [*Library of Congress*] (LCLS)
NcJaMC .... United States Marine Corps, Marine Corps Air Station, Special Services for Station Library, New River Base, Jacksonville, NC [*Library symbol Library of Congress*] (LCLS)
NCJAR .... National Council for Japanese American Redress [*Defunct*] (EA)
NCJAVM .... National Council on Jewish Audio-Visual Materials (EA)
NCJC .... National Conference of Judicial Councils [*Defunct*] (EA)
NCJCC .... National Council of Jewish Correctional Chaplains [*Later, AJCCA*] (EA)
NCJCJ .... National Council of Juvenile Court Judges [*Later, NCJFCJ*] (EA)
NCJCS .... National Conference of Jewish Communal Service [*Later, CJCS*] (EA)
NCJD .... National Coalition for a Just Draft (EA)
NCJD .... National Congress of Jewish Deaf (EA)
NCJE .... National Council for Jewish Education [*Later, CJE*] (EA)
NCJF .... National Center for Jewish Film (EA)
NCJFCJ .... National Council of Juvenile and Family Court Judges (EA)
NcJG .... Guilford Technical Institute, Jamestown, NC [*Library symbol Library of Congress*] (LCLS)
NCJISN .... National Council of Jewish Invalids Survivors of Nazism [*Later, CHSD*] (EA)
NCJISS .... National Criminal Justice Information and Statistics Service
NCJJ .... National Center for Jobs and Justice (EA)
NCJJ .... National Center for Juvenile Justice (EA)
NCJMS .... National Center for Job Market Studies [*Commercial firm Washington, DC*] (EA)
NcJo .... Jonesville-Arlington Public Library, Jonesville, NC [*Library symbol Library of Congress*] (LCLS)
NCJO .... National Council of Junior Outdoorsmen (EA)
NCJ of L ...... North Carolina Journal of Law [*A publication*] (DLA)
NCJPS .... National Center for Jewish Policy Studies
NCJR .... National Coalition for Jail Reform [*Defunct*] (EA)
NCJRS .... National Criminal Justice Reference Service [*Department of Justice*] [*Information service or system*]
NcJRS .... Ragsdale Senior High School, Jamestown, NC [*Library symbol*] [*Library of Congress*] (LCLS)
NCJSB .... National Commission on Jobs and Small Business [*Defunct*] (EA)
NCJSC .... National Criminal Justice Statistics Center
NCJT .... Nordic Committee of Journalism Teachers (EA)
NCJW .... National Council of Jewish Women (EA)
NCJWA .... National Council of Jewish Women of Australia
NCK .... Camden County College, Voorhees, NJ [*OCLC symbol*] (OCLC)
NcK .... Kinston-Lenoir County Public Library, Kinston, NC [*Library symbol Library of Congress*] (LCLS)
NCK .... Nagycenk [*Hungary*] [*Geomagnetic observatory code*]
NCK .... Neck
NCK .... Nickelodeon Industries Corp. [*Vancouver Stock Exchange symbol*]
NCK .... Norman, Craig & Kummel [*Advertising agency*]
NcKa .... Cannon Memorial YMCA Public Library, Kannapolis, NC [*Library symbol Library of Congress*] (LCLS)
NCKA .... National Catholic Kindergarten Association (AEBS)
NcKbMR .... North Carolina Marine Resources Center, Fort Fisher, Kure Beach, NC [*Library symbol Library of Congress*] (LCLS)
NcKC .... Kinston-Lenoir County Public Library, Caswell Center Library, Kinston, NC [*Library symbol Library of Congress*] (LCLS)
NcKeD .... Duplin County, Dorothy Wightman Library, Kenansville, NC [*Library symbol Library of Congress*] (LCLS)
NcKeS .... James Sprunt Technical Institute, Kenansville, NC [*Library symbol Library of Congress*] (LCLS)
NcKg .... King Public Library, King, NC [*Library symbol Library of Congress*] (LCLS)
NcKiK .... Kittrell College, Kittrell, NC [*Library symbol Library of Congress*] (LCLS)
NcKL .... Lenoir Community College, Kinston, NC [*Library symbol Library of Congress*] (LCLS)
NCKL .... North Central Kansas Libraries System [*Library network*]
NcKm .... Jacob S. Mauney Memorial Library, Kings Mountain, NC [*Library symbol Library of Congress*] (LCLS)
NcKn .... Kenly Public Library, Kenly, NC [*Library symbol*] [*Library of Congress*] (LCLS)
NCKWM .... National Committee for the Korean War Memorial [*Later, KWVM*] (EA)
NCL .... Camden County Library, Voorhees, NJ [*OCLC symbol*] (OCLC)
NCL .... Financial
NCL .... National Carriers Ltd. [*British*] (DCTA)
NCL .... National Center for the Laity (EA)
NCL .... National Central Library [*United Kingdom*]
NCL .... National Character Laboratory (EA)
NCL .... National Chemical Laboratory
NCL .... National Civic League (EA)

NCL............. National Coalition for Literacy (EA)
NCL............. National Commuter Airways [*British ICAO designator*] (FAAC)
NCL............. National Consumers League (EA)
NCL............. National Council of Labour [*British*] (DCTA)
NCL............. National Cycle League (EA)
NCL............. Navy Calibration Laboratory
NCL............. Navy Code Logistic [*Plan*]
NCL............. Network Control Language
NCL............. Neuronal Ceroid Lipofuscinosis [*Medicine*]
NCL............. New Caledonia [*ANSI three-letter standard code*] (CNC)
NCL............. Newcastle [*England*] [*Airport symbol*] (OAG)
NCL............. Node Compatibility List [*Telecommunications*] (TEL)
NCL............. Noise Control Laboratory [*Pennsylvania State University*] [*Research center*] (RCD)
NCL............. Norfolk, VA [*Location identifier FAA*] (FAAL)
NCL............. Norwegian Caribbean Lines
NCL............. Nucleolin (DMAA)
NCL............. Numerically Controlled Lathe
NCL............. NuVeen Ins CA Prem Inc Muni 2 [*NYSE symbol*] (TTSB)
NCL............. Nuveen Insured California Premium Income Municipal II [*NYSE symbol*] (SPSG)
NcL............. Scotland County Memorial Library, Laurinburg, NC [*Library symbol Library of Congress*] (LCLS)
NCLA......... National C-Lark Association (EA)
NCLA......... National Council of Local Administrators of Vocational Education and Practical Arts (EA)
NCLAN........ National Crop Loss Assessment Network
NCL & SW... National Conference of Lawyers and Social Workers
NC Law Repos... North Carolina Law Repository [*A publication*] (DLA)
NC Law Repository... North Carolina Law Repository (Reprint) [*A publication*] (DLA)
NCLC......... National Catholic Liturgical Conference (EA)
NCLC......... National Caucus of Labor Committees
NCLC......... National Chamber Litigation Center (EA)
NCLC......... National Child Labor Committee (EA)
NCLC......... National Christian Life Community of the United States of America (EA)
NCLC......... National Consumer Law Center (EA)
NCLC......... National Council of Labour Colleges
NCLC......... National Council on Legal Clinics [*Later, CLEPR*]
NCLC......... Nineteenth Century Literary Criticism [*A publication*]
NCLC......... Noncombatant Labour Corps [*British*]
NCLCH........ National Civil Liberties Clearing House [*Defunct*] (EA)
NCLCI........ National Christian Leadership Conference for Israel (EA)
NCLD......... National Center for Law and Deafness [*Formerly, National Center for Law and the Deaf*] (EA)
NCLD......... National Center for Law and the Deaf (EA)
NCLD......... National Center for Learning Disabilities (EA)
NCLD......... Williamsport District Library Center [*Library network*]
NCLE......... National Contact Lens Examiners (EA)
NcLeC......... Caldwell County Public Library, Lenoir, NC [*Library symbol Library of Congress*] (LCLS)
NcLeCT...... Caldwell Community College and Technical Institute, Lenoir, NC [*Library symbol Library of Congress*] (LCLS)
NCLEHA...... National Conference of Local Environmental Health Administrators (EA)
NCLER........ National Clearinghouse on Licensure, Enforcement, and Regulation (EA)
NCLEX........ National Council Licensure Examination
NCLEX-RN ... National Council Licensure Examination for Registered Nurses
NCLF........... National Coalition to Legalize Freedom (EA)
NCLG......... National Committee for Latin and Greek (EA)
NCLG......... National Conference of Lieutenant Governors (EA)
NCLH......... National Center for Law and the Handicapped [*Defunct*] (EA)
NCLHA....... National Conference of Law Historians of America (EA)
NCLI........... National Committee for Labor Israel [*Later, NCLIIHC*] (EA)
NCLIIHC...... National Committee for Labor Israel-Israel Histadrut Campaign (EA)
NcLil........... Harnett County Public Library, Lillington, NC [*Library symbol Library of Congress*] (LCLS)
NcLiL.......... Lincoln County Memorial Library, Lincolnton, NC [*Library symbol Library of Congress*] (LCLS)
NClinc.......... Clinton Corners Reading Center, Clinton Corners, NY [*Library symbol Library of Congress*] (LCLS)
NCLIP .... North Coast Life Ins Cv'A'Pfd [*NASDAQ symbol*] (TTSB)
NCLIP .... North Coast Life Insurance Co. [*NASDAQ symbol*] (SAG)
NCLIS .... National Commission on Libraries and Information Science [*Washington, DC*]
NCLIS .... National Council for Languages and International Studies (EA)
NcLit........... Littleton Public Library, Littleton, NC [*Library symbol Library of Congress*] (LCLS)
NCLJ........... North Carolina Law Journal [*A publication*] (DLA)
NcLjUM....... United Methodist Church, Commission on Archives and History, Lake Junaluska, NC [*Library symbol Library of Congress*] (LCLS)
NcLk .... Rockingham County Library, Leaksville, NC [*Library symbol Library of Congress*] (LCLS)
NCLLF........ National Civil Liberties Legal Foundation [*Inactive*] (EA)
NcLo........... Franklin County Library, Louisburg, NC [*Library symbol Library of Congress*] (LCLS)
NCLO......... Naval Communication Liaison Officer (IAA)
NcLo-B........ Franklin County Library, Bunn Branch Library, Bunn, NC [*Library symbol*] [*Library of Congress*] (LCLS)
NcLoC......... Louisburg College, Louisburg, NC [*Library symbol Library of Congress*] (LCLS)
NCLP .... National Conference on Law and Poverty
NCLP .... National Contract Laboratory Program (COE)

NCLP .... Numerically Controlled Line Plotter
NCLPWA...... National Council of Local Public Welfare Administrators (EA)
NCLR .... National Center for Legislative Research [*Defunct*] (EA)
NCLR .... National Center for Lesbian Rights (EA)
NCLR .... National Coalition for Land Reform (EA)
NCLR .... National Council for Labor Reform (EA)
NCLR .... National Council of La Raza (EA)
NCL Rep...... North Carolina Law Repository [*A publication*] (DLA)
NCL Reps..... North Carolina Law Repository (Reprint) [*A publication*] (DLA)
NCLS .... National Clearinghouse for Legal Services [*Legal Services Corp.*] [*Information service or system*] (IID)
NCLS .... National Committee for Liberation of Slovakia (EA)
NCLS .... National Conference of Lawyers and Scientists [*Joint project of the American Association for the Advancement of Science and the American Bar Association*]
NCLS .... National Conference of State Legislatures [*Australia*]
NCLS .... North Country Library System [*Library network*]
NcLS .... Saint Andrews Presbyterian College, Laurinburg, NC [*Library symbol Library of Congress*] (LCLS)
NCLT .... Night Carrier Landing Trainer [*Navy*]
NCLTA........ National Cigar Leaf Tobacco Association [*Defunct*] (EA)
NcLu .... Robeson County Public Library, Lumberton, NC [*Library symbol Library of Congress*] (LCLS)
NcLuH........ Southeastern General Hospital, Medical Library, Lumberton, NC [*Library symbol Library of Congress*] (LCLS)
NcLuR........ Robeson Technical Institute, Lumbarton, NC [*Library symbol Library of Congress*] (LCLS)
NcLxD .... Davidson County Public Library, Lexington, NC [*Library symbol Library of Congress*] (LCLS)
NcLxDC...... Davidson County Community College, Lexington, NC [*Library symbol Library of Congress*] (LCLS)
NCm............ Center Moriches Free Public Library, Center Moriches, NY [*Library symbol Library of Congress*] (LCLS)
NCM........... Court Martial Reports, Navy Cases [*A publication*] (DLA)
NCM........... Mars Hill College, Mars Hill, NC [*OCLC symbol*] (OCLC)
NCM........... Nailfold Capillary Microscope (DAVI)
NCM........... National Center for Men (EA)
NCM........... National Coal Model [*Department of Energy*] (GFGA)
NCM........... National Coastal Monitoring (USDC)
NCM........... National College of Music [*British*] (DI)
NCM........... National Congress for Men (EA)
NCM........... National Corvette Museum
NCM........... National Cursillo Movement (EA)
NCM........... Natural Clay Mosaic (DICI)
NCM........... Navy Commendation Medal
NCM........... Navy Correspondence Manual
NCM........... Net Control Master (MCD)
NCM........... Network Control Module
NCM........... Newcastle Conservatorium of Music [*Australia*]
NCM........... New Moon [*Queensland*] [*Airport symbol*] (AD)
NCM........... Nicaraguan Campaign Medal
NCM........... Nippon Calculating Machine Co. [*Japan*] (PDAA)
NCM........... Nitrocellulose Membrane
NCM........... No Compromise Majority [*An association*] (EA)
NCM........... Noise Canceling Microphone
NCM........... Non Compos Mentis [*Not of Sound Mind*] [*Latin*] (LWAP)
NCM........... Noncorrosive Metal
NCM........... Noncrew Member
NCM........... Nordic Council of Ministers (EAIO)
NCM........... Nordic Council on Medicines [*See also NLN*] (EAIO)
NCM........... Normal Human Colon Mucosal [*Cells*]
NCM........... North Carolina Motor Carriers Association [*STAC*]
NCM........... Northern Conservatory of Music [*Maine*]
NCM........... Northern Cruise Master (SAA)
NCM........... Notice of Commencement of Manufacture [*Toxic Substances Control Act*] [*Environmental Protection Agency*] (EPA)
NCM........... Numerical Controlled Machine
NCM........... Nurse Case Manager (DMAA)
NCM........... Nuveen California Municipal Income [*NYSE symbol*] (SPSG)
NCMA .... National Campus Ministry Association (EA)
NCMA .... National Catalog Managers Association (EA)
NCMA .... National Ceramic Manufacturers Association
NCMA .... National Childminding Association [*British*] (DBA)
NCMA .... National Concrete Masonry Association (EA)
NCMA .... National Contract Management Association (EA)
NCMA .... National Corporate Medical Associates [*An association*]
NCMA .... National Council of Millinery Associations (EA)
NCMA .... National Council of Moving Associations (EA)
NCMA .... Naval Civilian Manager's Association (EA)
NCMA .... Newspaper Credit Managers' Association (EA)
NcMad........ Madison Public Library, Madison, NC [*Library symbol Library of Congress*] (LCLS)
NCMAF ...... National Conference on Ministry to the Armed Forces (EA)
NCMAG...... National Computer Center Management Advisory Group (COE)
NcMaM...... McDowell Technical Institute, Marion, NC [*Library symbol Library of Congress*] (LCLS)
NcMaMC..... McDowell County Public Library, Marion, NC [*Library symbol Library of Congress*] (LCLS)
NcMan........ Dare County Library, Manteo, NC [*Library symbol Library of Congress*] (LCLS)
NcManA...... College of the Albemarle, Dare County Center Library, Manteo, NC [*Library symbol*] [*Library of Congress*] (LCLS)
NcManMR.... North Carolina Marine Resources Center, Roanoke Island Resource Library, Manteo, NC [*Library symbol Library of Congress*] (LCLS)

NcMarM.......	Madison County Public Library, Marshall, NC [*Library symbol Library of Congress*] (LCLS)
NcMauDC	North Carolina Department of Corrections, Eastern Correctional Center Library, Maury, NC [*Library symbol*] [*Library of Congress*] (LCLS)
NcMax	Gilbert Patterson Memorial Public Library, Maxton, NC [*Library symbol Library of Congress*] (LCLS)
NCMC	National Capital Management Corp. [*NASDAQ symbol*] (NQ)
NCMC	National Center on Missing Children (NADA)
NCMC	National Coalition for Marine Conservation (EA)
NCMC	National Conference of Metropolitan Courts
NCMC	Natl Capital Mgmt [*NASDAQ symbol*] (TTSB)
NCMC	Natural Cell-Mediated Cytotoxicity [*Immunochemistry*]
NCMC	N-Carboxymethylchitosan [*Biochemistry*]
NCMC	NORAD Cheyenne Mountain Complex [*Military*] (AABC)
NCMC	Nordic Council for Music Conservatories (EA)
NCMC	Numerically-Controlled Machine Center (IAA)
NcMccC........	Carteret Technical Institute, Morehead City, NC [*Library symbol Library of Congress*] (LCLS)
NcMccH	McCain Hospital, Medical Library, McCain, NC [*Library symbol Library of Congress*] (LCLS)
NcMccS	Sandhills Youth Center, McCain, NC [*Library symbol Library of Congress*] (LCLS)
NCMCE	National Council of Minority Consulting Engineers (IAA)
NCMCG........	National Construction Machinery Credit Group [*Park Ridge, IL*] (EA)
NCMD	National Center for Municipal Development (EA)
NCMDA	National Coin Machine Distributors Association (EA)
NCMDA	National Commission on Marijuana and Drug Abuse [*Presidential advisory committee, terminated 1973*]
NCMDLRJO...	National Council of Marriage and Divorce Law Reform and Justice Organizations (EA)
NCME..........	National Center for Mediation Education (EA)
NCME..........	National Council on Measurement in Education (EA)
NCME..........	Network for Continuing Medical Education (EA)
NCME..........	Northern Counties Motor & Engineering Co. Ltd. [*British*] (DCTA)
NCME..........	Numerically Controlled Machine Equipment
NCMEA	National Catholic Music Educators Association [*Later, NPM*] (EA)
NCMEC	National Center for Missing and Exploited Children (EA)
NCMES	Numerically-Controlled Measuring and Evaluating System (IAA)
NCMESD	National Coalition for More Effective School Discipline (EA)
NCMET........	Nonclosed Shell Many Electron Theory [*Physics*]
NcMf...........	Murfreesboro Public Library, Murfreesboro, NC [*Library symbol Library of Congress*] (LCLS)
NCMF..........	National Carvers Museum Foundation [*Defunct*] (EA)
NCMF..........	National Church Music Fellowship [*Defunct*]
NcMfC.........	Chowan College, Murfreesboro, NC [*Library symbol Library of Congress*] (LCLS)
NCMFST	National Committee for Motor Fleet Supervisor Training (EA)
NcMG..........	Graham Evangelistic Association, Montreat, NC [*Library symbol Library of Congress*] (LCLS)
NCMG..........	Mangaia [*Cook Islands*] [*ICAO location identifier*] (ICLI)
NCMH	National Clearinghouse for Mental Health Information (NITA)
NCMH	National Committee for Mental Health (DAVI)
NCMH	National Committee for Mental Hygiene (DAVI)
NCMH	National Committee on Maternal Health (EA)
NCMH	National Council for Monday Holidays
NcMhC.........	Mars Hill College, Mars Hill, NC [*Library symbol Library of Congress*] (LCLS)
NCMHC.......	National Community Mental Healthcare Council (NTPA)
NCMHC.......	National Community Mental Heathcare Council (EA)
NcMHi.........	Historical Foundation of the Presbyterian and Reformed Churches, Montreat, NC [*Library symbol Library of Congress*] (LCLS)
NCMHI	National Clearinghouse for Mental Health Information [*Public Health Service*] [*Rockville, MD Database*] [*HEW*]
NCMHS.......	National Conference on Mental Health Statistics [*Department of Health and Human Services*] (GFGA)
NCMI	National Coin Machine Institute (EA)
NCMI	National Committee Against Mental Illness (EA)
NCMI	National Council of Music Importers [*Later, NCMIE*]
NCMI	National Country Maintenance Index (IAA)
NCMIE	National Council of Music Importers and Exporters (EA)
NcMiP.........	Pfeiffer College, Misenheimer, NC [*Library symbol Library of Congress*] (LCLS)
NCMJ..........	National Contract Management Journal [*A publication*] (AAGC)
NCMK	Mauke [*Cook Islands*] [*ICAO location identifier*] (ICLI)
NCMLB	National Council of Mailing List Brokers [*Later, MLBPA*] (EA)
NcMM..........	Montreat-Anderson College, Montreat, NC [*Library symbol Library of Congress*] (LCLS)
NCmM	Museum Manor of Saint George, Center Moriches, NY [*Library symbol Library of Congress*] (LCLS)
NCMM	Nuveen California Municipal Market Opportunity Fund [*Associated Press*] (SAG)
NCmMM	Museum Manor of Saint George, Center Moriches, NY [*Library symbol*] [*Library of Congress*] (LCLS)
NCMN	Manuae [*Cook Islands*] [*ICAO location identifier*] (ICLI)
NCMO	Navigational Aids/Communications Management Office [*Air Force*] (CET)
NcMoBH	Broughton Hospital, Staff Library, Morganton, NC [*Library symbol Library of Congress*] (LCLS)
NcMoc	Davie County Public Library, Mocksville, NC [*Library symbol Library of Congress*] (LCLS)
NcMoFM......	Foothills Area Mental Health, North Carolina School for the Deaf, Morganton, NC [*Library symbol*] [*Library of Congress*] (LCLS)
NcMoGH	Grace Hospital, Medical Library, Morganton, NC [*Library symbol*] [*Library of Congress*] (LCLS)
NcMoM........	Morganton-Burke Library, Inc., Morganton, NC [*Library symbol Library of Congress*] (LCLS)
NcMon	Union County Public Library, Monroe, NC [*Library symbol Library of Congress*] (LCLS)
NcMorB.......	Bell Northern Research, Inc., Learning Resources Center, Morrisville, NC [*Library symbol*] [*Library of Congress*] (LCLS)
NcMoW........	Western Piedmont Community College, Morganton, NC [*Library symbol Library of Congress*] (LCLS)
NcMoWC......	Western Carolina Center, Staff Library, Morganton, NC [*Library symbol Library of Congress*] (LCLS)
NcMoWCC.....	Western Correctional Center, Morganton, NC [*Library symbol*] [*Library of Congress*] (LCLS)
NCMP	National Commission for Manpower Policy [*Department of Labor*]
NCMP	National Commission on Materials Policy
NCMP	Navy Capabilities and Mobilization Plan (DOMA)
NCMPA	National Corrugated Metal Pipe Association [*Later, NCSPA*] (EA)
NCMPR	National Council for Marketing and Public Relations (EA)
NCMR	Matiaro [*Cook Islands*] [*ICAO location identifier*] (ICLI)
NCMR	National Committee for Monetary Reform (EA)
NCMR	Nonconforming Material Report
NCMR	North Canterbury Mounted Rifles [*British military*] (DMA)
NCMRED......	National Council on Marine Resources and Engineering Development [*Later, ICMSE*]
NCMS	National Center for Manufacturing Sciences [*Research center*]
NCMS	National Classification Management Society (EA)
NCMS	National Council of Marine Sciences
NCMS	Numerically-Controlled Machine System (IAA)
NCMS	Numerically-Controlled Manufacture System (IAA)
NCMT.........	Numerically Controlled Machine Tool
NcMta	Mount Airy Public Library, Mount Airy, NC [*Library symbol Library of Congress*] (LCLS)
NCMTA	National Council of Marine Trade Associations
NcMtaC.......	Crossroads Center, Mount Airy, NC [*Library symbol*] [*Library of Congress*] (LCLS)
NcMtC........	Mount Olive College, Mount Olive, NC [*Library symbol Library of Congress*] (LCLS)
NCMTE	National Council on Medical Technology Education [*Defunct*]
NCMTI	Noncoherent Moving Target Indicator (MCD)
NCMTT........	National Council for Mother Tongue Teaching (AIE)
NcMu	Murphy Public Library, Murphy, NC [*Library symbol Library of Congress*] (LCLS)
NCMUE	National Council on Measurements Used in Education [*Later, National Council on Measurement in Education*] (AEBS)
NcMuN........	Nantahala Regional Library, Murphy, NC [*Library symbol Library of Congress*] (LCLS)
NcMuT	Tri-County Technical Institute, Murphy, NC [*Library symbol Library of Congress*] (LCLS)
NcMv	Mooresville Public Library, Mooresville, NC [*Library symbol Library of Congress*] (LCLS)
NCMV	Northern Cereal Mosaic Virus [*Plant pathology*]
n-cn--.........	Canada [*MARC geographic area code Library of Congress*] (LCCP)
NCN	National Airlines (Chile), SA [*FAA designator*] (FAAC)
NCN	National Cardiovascular Network
NCN	National Christian Network [*Cable-television system*]
NCN	National Computer Network Corp. [*Information service or system*] (IID)
NCN	National Council of Nurses [*British*] (DI)
NCN	Navy Control Number (MCD)
NCN	Network Control Node
NCN	Nixdorf Communications Network [*Nixdorf*] [*Germany*]
NCN	Non-Casein Nitrogen (OA)
NCNA..........	National Council of Nonprofit Associations
NCNA..........	National Council on Noise Abatement (EA)
NCNA..........	New China News Agency
n-cn-ab.......	Alberta [*MARC geographic area code Library of Congress*] (LCCP)
NCNASEO	National Council of Naval Air Stations Employee Organizations [*Later, NCINASEO*] (EA)
NCNB..........	National Center for Nonprofit Boards (EA)
NCNB..........	North Carolina National Bank (EFIS)
n-cn-bc.......	British Columbia [*MARC geographic area code Library of Congress*] (LCCP)
NcNbC........	Craven Technical Institute, New Bern, NC [*Library symbol Library of Congress*] (LCLS)
NcNbCP	Craven-Pamlico-Carteret Regional Library, New Bern, NC [*Library symbol Library of Congress*] (LCLS)
NCNC	National Captive Nations Committee (EA)
NCNC	National Council of Nigeria and the Cameroons [*Political party*]
NCNC	Normochromic Normocytic [*Medicine*] (MEDA)
NCNC	Normochromic, Normocytic Anemia [*Hematology*] (DAVI)
NCNCA........	Normochromic, Normocytic Anemia [*Hematology*] (DAVI)
NCND	Neither Confirm nor Deny
NCNE	National Campaign for Nursery Education [*British*]
NCNE	National Center for Neighborhood Enterprise (EA)
NcNep.........	Newport Public Library, Newport, NC [*Library symbol*] [*Library of Congress*] (LCLS)
NCNEVAW....	National Communications Network for the Elimination of Violence Against Women [*NCADV*] [*Absorbed by*] (EA)
NcNew	Avery-Morrison Public Library, Newland, NC [*Library symbol Library of Congress*] (LCLS)
NCNGD	Not Crushed or Not Ground
n-cnh-.........	Hudson Bay [*MARC geographic area code Library of Congress*] (LCCP)
n-cnm-........	Maritime Provinces [*MARC geographic area code Library of Congress*] (LCCP)
n-cn-mb.......	Manitoba [*MARC geographic area code Library of Congress*] (LCCP)

n-cn-nf.......... Newfoundland [*MARC geographic area code Library of Congress*] (LCCP)

n-cn-nk........ New Brunswick [*MARC geographic area code Library of Congress*] (LCCP)

n-cn-ns........ Nova Scotia [*MARC geographic area code Library of Congress*] (LCCP)

n-cn-nt........ Northwest Territories [*MARC geographic area code Library of Congress*] (LCCP)

N/CNO........... Navy/Chief of Naval Operations (AAG)

n-cn-on........ Ontario [*MARC geographic area code Library of Congress*] (LCCP)

NCNP........... National Child Nutrition Project (EA)

NCNP........... National Conference for New Politics [*Organization formed in 1966 to support peace candidates*] (VNW)

n-cnp-........... Prairie Provinces [*MARC geographic area code Library of Congress*] (LCCP)

n-cn-pi......... Prince Edward Island [*Canada*] [*MARC geographic area code Library of Congress*] (LCCP)

NCNPSA...... National Conference of Non-Profit Shipping Associations (EA)

ncnq--........... Nicaragua [*MARC geographic area code Library of Congress*] (LCCP)

n-cn-qu........ Quebec [*MARC geographic area code Library of Congress*] (LCCP)

NCNR........... National Center for Nursing Research [*Bethesda, MD*] [*Department of Health and Human Services*] (GRD)

NCNS........... Nassau [*Cook Islands*] [*ICAO location identifier*] (ICLI)

NCNS........... National Catholic News Service (EA)

NCNS........... North Central Name Society (EA)

n-cn-sn........ Saskatchewan [*MARC geographic area code Library of Congress*] (LCCP)

NcNt............ Catawba County Library, Newton, NC [*Library symbol Library of Congress*] (LCLS)

NCNTUCW ... National Commission on New Technological Uses of Copyrighted Works [*Terminated, 1978*] [*Library of Congress*]

NcNv............ Harold D. Cooley Library, Nashville, NC [*Library symbol*] [*Library of Congress*] (LCLS)

NCNW........... National Congress of Neighborhood Women (EA)

NCNW........... National Council of Negro Women (EA)

NCNW........... Nearly Certain New Work (MCD)

NcNw............ Wilkes County Public Library, North Wilkesboro, NC [*Library symbol Library of Congress*] (LCLS)

NcNwA......... Appalachian Regional Library, North Wilkesboro, NC [*Library symbol Library of Congress*] (LCLS)

NCNY.......... Netherland Club of New York (EA)

NCNY.......... Newswomen's Club of New York (EA)

n-cn-yk .... Yukon Territory [*MARC geographic area code Library of Congress*] (LCCP)

NCo............ Commack Public Library, Commack, NY [*Library symbol Library of Congress*] (LCLS)

NCO .... National Commission for Information and Conscientization on Development Cooperation [*Netherlands*]

NCO .... National Council of Obesity (EA)

NCO .... Nationalist Chams Organization (EA)

NCO .... Negotiated Consent Order [*Environmental Protection Agency*] (ERG)

NCO .... Net Control (CAAL)

NCO .... Net Control Outstation [*Military*] (DOMA)

NCO .... Network Control Office [*Telecommunications*] (TEL)

NCO .... New Consultants [*A publication*]

NCO .... Noncombatant Evacuation Order [*Navy*] (CINC)

NCO .... Noncombat Operations [*Military*] (CAAL)

NCO .... Noncommissioned Officer [*Military*]

NCO .... Non Compliance Order [*Environmental Protection Agency*]

NCO .... Norsar Array Site 01C00 [*Norway*] [*Seismograph station code, US Geological Survey*] (SEIS)

NCO .... North Canadian Oils Ltd. [*Toronto Stock Exchange symbol*]

NCO .... North Carolina Department of Transportation, Raleigh, NC [*OCLC symbol*] (OCLC)

NCO .... Nuclear Control Order [*Military*] (MUSM)

NCO .... Number-Controlled Oscillator

NCO .... Nuveen California Municipal Market Opportunities [*NYSE symbol*] (SPSG)

NCO .... Nuveen CA Muni Mkt Oppt [*NYSE symbol*] (TTSB)

NCOA......... National Campground Owners Association (EA)

NCOA......... National Change of Address Service [*US Postal Service*]

NCOA......... National Chevelle Owners Association (EA)

NCOA......... National Condominium Owners Association [*Defunct*]

NCOA......... National Corvette Owners' Association (EA)

NCOA......... National Council on the Aging (EA)

NCOA......... Noncommissioned Officer Academy [*Military*] (AABC)

NCOA......... Non-Commissioned Officers Association of the United States of America (EA)

NCoBJ.......... Burr Junior High School, Commack, NY [*Library symbol*] [*Library of Congress*] (LCLS)

NCOBPS...... National Conference of Black Political Scientists (EA)

NCOBQ........ Noncommissioned Officer Bachelor Quarters [*Military*] (AFM)

N'COBRA ..... National Coalition of Blacks for Reparations in America (ECON)

NCobUA....... State University of New York, Agricultural and Technical College at Cobleskill, Cobleskill, NY [*Library symbol Library of Congress*] (LCLS)

NCOC........... National Commission on Organized Crime (NADA)

NCOC........... National Council on Organized Crime (EA)

NCOC........... Noncommissioned Officer Course (VNW)

NCoCE........ Cedar Road Elementary School, Commack, NY [*Library symbol*] [*Library of Congress*] (LCLS)

NCOCY........ National Council of Organizations for Children and Youth (EA)

NCOD........... National Catholic Office for the Deaf (EA)

NCOD........... National Coming Out Day [*An association*] (EA)

NCOD........... National Coming Out Day Campaign (EA)

NCOD........... National Commission on Orphan Diseases [*Department of Health and Human Services*] (GFGA)

NCODE .... National Clearinghouse on Development Education [*Information service or system*] (IID)

NCODP......... Noncommissioned Officer Development Program [*Army*] (INF)

NCO-ER........ Noncommissioned Officer Evaluation Reporting [*Army*] (INF)

NCOES........ Noncommissioned Officer Education System [*Military*] (AABC)

NC of A........ Newfoundland Club of America (EA)

NCOG........... NCO Group, Inc. [*NASDAQ symbol*] (SAG)

NcOG........... Richard H. Thornton Memorial Library, Oxford, NC [*Library symbol Library of Congress*] (LCLS)

NCOGD........ National Council for the Observance of Grandparent's Day (EA)

NCO Grp ..... NCO Group, Inc. [*Associated Press*] (SAG)

NCOHC........ Northern California Occupational Health Center [*University of California*] [*Research center*] (RCD)

NCO/HPCC ... National Coordination Office for High Performance Computing and Communications

NCoHS-N ..... North High School, Commack, NY [*Library symbol*] [*Library of Congress*] (LCLS)

NCoHS-S...... South High School, Commack, NY [*Library symbol*] [*Library of Congress*] (LCLS)

NCOI........... National Council for the Omnibus Industry [*British*]

NCOIC........ Noncommissioned Officer-in-Charge [*Military*]

NCoIE........ Indian Hollow Elementary School, Commack, NY [*Library symbol*] [*Library of Congress*] (LCLS)

NCOIL........ National Conference of Insurance Legislators (EA)

NCOL........... National Council on Occupational Licensing [*Formerly, COL*] [*Defunct*] (EA)

NCOLANT..... Net Control Officer, Atlantic [*Navy*] (DNAB)

NCOLG......... National Coordinating Office for Latin and Greek [*Later, NCLG*] (EA)

NCoInA .... Albany Area Board of Cooperative Education Services, Colonie, NY [*Library symbol*] [*Library of Congress*] (LCLS)

NCOLP......... Noncommissioned Officer Logistics Program [*Army*] (AABC)

NCOLS......... Noncommissioned Officers' Leadership School [*Air Force*] (AFM)

NCOLUG ...... North Carolina Online User Group (NITA)

NCOM........... NEC Computerised Operation and Maintenance System (NITA)

NCOM........... News Communications [*NASDAQ symbol*] (TTSB)

NCOM........... News Communications, Inc. [*NASDAQ symbol*] (SAG)

NCOMBL...... Noncombustible (MSA)

NCOMD........ National Committee on the Observance of Mothers' Day [*Later, MDC*] (EA)

NCOMDR ..... National Clearinghouse on Marital and Date Rape (EA)

NCOMED...... Net Control Officer, Mediterranean [*Navy*] (DNAB)

NCOMM........ Naval Communications Command

NCOMP......... National Catholic Office for Motion Pictures [*Later, Office for Film and Broadcasting*]

NCOMR........ National Clearinghouse on Marital Rape [*Later, NCOMDR*] (EA)

NCON........... Encon Systems [*NASDAQ symbol*] (SAG)

NCoNE........ North Ridge Elementary School, Commack, NY [*Library symbol*] [*Library of Congress*] (LCLS)

NCoOE........ Old Farms Elementary School, Commack, NY [*Library symbol*] [*Library of Congress*] (LCLS)

NCooHi .... New York State Historical Association, Cooperstown, NY [*Library symbol Library of Congress*] (LCLS)

NCOOM........ Noncommissioned Officers' Open Mess [*Military*] (AFM)

NCop........... Copiague Memorial Public Library, Copiague, NY [*Library symbol Library of Congress*] (LCLS)

NCOP........... National Council on Philanthropy [*Later, IS*] (EA)

NCOP........... New Choreographers On Point

NCOPA......... National Conference of Police Associations (EA)

NCOPAC....... Net Control Officer, Pacific [*Navy*] (DNAB)

NCOPD......... National Catholic Office for Persons with Disabilities (EA)

NCOPDP ...... Noncommissioned Officer Professional Development Program [*Army*] (INF)

NCOPDR ...... NCO [*Noncommissioned Officer*] Professional Development Ribbon [*Military decoration*] (GFGA)

NCOPE......... National Council of Preservation Executives (EA)

NCOPF......... National Council for One Parent Families [*British*]

NCopH......... Lakeside Hospital, Copiague, NY [*Library symbol Library of Congress*] (LCLS)

NCopHS .... Copiague High School, Copiague, NY [*Library symbol*] [*Library of Congress*] (LCLS)

NCoRE .... Rolling Hills Elementary School, Commack, NY [*Library symbol*] [*Library of Congress*] (LCLS)

NCorf........... Corfu Free Library, Corfu, NY [*Library symbol Library of Congress*] (LCLS)

NCorn.......... Cornwall Public Library, Cornwall, NY [*Library symbol Library of Congress*] (LCLS)

NCornB......... Harvard Black Rock Forest, Cornwall, NY [*Library symbol Library of Congress*] (LCLS)

NCorni.......... Corning Public Library, Corning, NY [*Library symbol Library of Congress*] (LCLS)

NCorniC........ Corning Glass Works, Corning, NY [*Library symbol Library of Congress*] (LCLS)

NCorniCC..... Corning Community College, Corning, NY [*Library symbol Library of Congress*] (LCLS)

NCorniFL...... College Center of the Finger Lakes, Corning, NY [*Library symbol Library of Congress*] (LCLS)

NCorniM........ Corning Museum of Glass, Corning, NY [*Library symbol Library of Congress*] (LCLS)

NCorniS .... Southern Tier Library System, Corning, NY [*Library symbol Library of Congress*] (LCLS)

NCort........... Cortland Free Library, Cortland, NY [*Library symbol Library of Congress*] (LCLS)

NCORT .... National Catholic Office for Radio and Television [*Later, Office for Film and Broadcasting*]
NCortHi .... Cortland County Historical Society, Cortland, NY [*Library symbol Library of Congress*] (LCLS)
NCortSC .... Smith-Corona Laboratory, Cortland, NY [*Library symbol Library of Congress*] (LCLS)
NCortU .... State University of New York, College at Cortland, Cortland, NY [*Library symbol Library of Congress*] (LCLS)
NCOS .... Comite de Liaison des Organisations Non-Gouvernmentales de Developpement aupres des Communautes Europeennes [*Liaison Committee of Development Non-Governmental Organizations to the European Communities*] (EAIO)
NCOS .... National Centre for Orchestral Studies [*Goldsmiths' College*] [*British*] (CB)
NCOS .... National Commission on Space [*Terminated, 1986*] (EGAO)
NCOS .... National Commission on Superconductivity [*Presidential advisory commission*] (EGAO)
NCOS .... National Council on Stuttering (EA)
NCOS .... Non-Concurrent Operating System [*Sperry UNIVAC*]
NCOSCC .... National Central Office for the Suppression of Counterfeit Currency [*British*]
NCoSJ .... Saw Mill Junior High School, Commack, NY [*Library symbol*] [*Library of Congress*] (LCLS)
NCOSTA .... National Council of Officers of State Teachers Associations (EA)
NcOtV .... United States Veterans Administration Hospital, Oteen, NC [*Library symbol Library of Congress*] (LCLS)
NCoWE .... Wood Park Elementary School, Commack, NY [*Library symbol*] [*Library of Congress*] (LCLS)
NCOWFL .... National Center on Women and Family Law (EA)
NCoxHi .... Greene County Historical Society, Inc., Coxsakie, NY [*Library symbol Library of Congress*] (LCLS)
NcP .... Given Memorial Library, Pinehurst, NC [*Library symbol Library of Congress*] (LCLS)
NCP .... National Cancer Program [*National Institutes of Health*]
NCP .... National Caries Program [*Public Health Service*] (GRD)
NCP .... National Car Parks [*British*]
NCP .... National Choreography Project
NCP .... National Circus Project (EA)
NCP .... National Climate Program [*Rockville, MD*] [*National Oceanic and Atmospheric Administration*]
NCP .... National Collegiate Players (EA)
NCP .... National Commission on Productivity [*Later, National Productivity Council*]
NCP .... National Commodity-Processing Program [*Department of Agriculture*] (GFGA)
NCP .... National Contingency Plan [*Hazardous wastes*] [*Environmental Protection Agency*]
NCP .... National Convention Party [*Gambia*] [*Political party*] (PPW)
NCP .... National Council of Psychotherapists and Hypnotherapy Register [*British*] (DBA)
NCP .... National Council on Philanthropy [*Later, IS*]
NCP .... National Curriculum Project
NCP .... National Cycling Proficiency (BARN)
NCP .... National Inventory Control Point [*Military*]
NCP .... National Oil and Hazardous Substances Contingency Plan
NCP .... Natural Clay Pavers (DICI)
NCP .... Naval Capabilities Plan
NCP .... N-Chlorothiophosphoramide [*Organic chemistry*]
NCP .... N-Cholorpiperidine [*Organic chemistry*]
NCP .... Nepali Congress Party [*Political party*] (EY)
NCP .... Net Combat Power
NCP .... Net Community Productivity (FFDE)
NCP .... Net Control Procedure
NCP .... Netherlands and Colonial Philately
NCP .... NetWare Core Protocol [*Computer science*]
NCP .... Network Control Point [*Telecommunications*]
NCP .... Network Control Processor [*Telecommunications*] (TSSD)
NCP .... Network Control Program [*IBM Corp.*] [*Telecommunications*] (BUR)
NCP .... Network Control Protocol [*Telecommunications*]
NCP .... New Call to Peacemaking (EA)
NCP .... New Communities Program [*Defunct*] (EA)
NCP .... New Community Projects [*A publication*]
NCP .... Nickel-Chromium Panel
NCP .... Nitrogen Charge Panel [*Later, MRAC*] (AAG)
NCP .... No Caffeine [*or*] Pepper (DAVI)
NCP .... No-Copy Paper
NCP .... Noctilucent Cloud Particles
NCP .... Noncarbon Paper (IAA)
NCP .... Noncollagen Protein
NCP .... Noncompliance Penalty [*Environmental Protection Agency*] (EPA)
NCP .... Non-Conformance Penalties [*Automotive emissions standards*]
NCP .... Non-Custodial Parent
NCP .... Non-United States Coalition Partner (DOMA)
NCP .... Normal Circular Pitch (MSA)
NCP .... North Celestial Pole [*Astronomy*]
NCP .... Not Copy Protected [*Computer science*] (IGQR)
NCP .... Nuclear Contingency Plan (MCD)
NCP .... Numerically-Controlled Peripheral (IAA)
NCP .... Nursing Care Plan
NCP .... Nuveen California Performance Plus Municipal [*NYSE symbol*] (SPSG)
NCP .... Nuveen CA Perf Plus Muni [*NYSE symbol*] (TTSB)
NCPA .... National Center for Policy Alternatives [*Later, CPA*] (EA)
NCPA .... National Coalition of Patriotic Americans (EA)
NCPA .... National Committee for the Prevention of Alcoholism and Drug Dependency [*Later,NCPADD*] (EA)
NCPA .... National Composition and Prepress Association (EA)
NCPA .... National Conservation Policy Act [*1979*]
NCPA .... National Cottonseed Products Association (EA)
NCPA .... National Crime Prevention Association [*Defunct*] (EA)
NCPAC .... National Conservative Political Action Committee (EA)
NCPAD .... National Council on Psychological Aspects of Disability (EA)
NCPADD .... National Committee for the Prevention of Alcoholism and Drug Dependency (EA)
NCPAG .... National CPA [*Certified Public Accountant*] Group [*Later, BKR International*] (EA)
NCPAMA .... Noise Control Product and Materials Association [*Later, NCA*] (IAA)
NCPAMT .... National Coalition of Psychiatrists Against Motorcoach Therapy (EA)
N-CPAP .... Nasal Continuous Positive Airway Pressure [*Medicine*] (DMAA)
NCPAS .... National Computer Program Abstract Service, Inc. (IID)
NC/PAT .... National Council for the Public Assessment of Technology [*Defunct*]
NCPB .... National Cancer Policy Board
NcPb .... Pinebluff Public Library, Pinebluff, NC [*Library symbol Library of Congress*] (LCLS)
NCPC .... National Cancer Pain Coalition
NCPC .... National Capital Planning Commission [*Formerly, NCPPC*]
NCPC .... National Chrysler Products Club (EA)
NCPC .... National Citizens Participation Council (EA)
NCPC .... National Coal Policy Conference [*Defunct*] (EA)
NCPC .... National Collegiate Poultry Club
NCPC .... National Crime Prevention Council (EA)
NCPC .... Nose Cone Protective Covering [*Aviation*]
NCPCA .... National Center for the Prosecution of Child Abuse (EA)
NCPCA .... National Committee for Peace in Central America [*Defunct*] (EA)
NCPCA .... National Committee for Prevention of Child Abuse (EA)
NCPCA .... National Committee to Prevent Child Abuse (EA)
NCPCC .... National Clearinghouse for Poison Control Centers (EA)
NCpCE .... Cherry Lane Elementary School, Carle Place, NY [*Library symbol*] [*Library of Congress*] (LCLS)
NCPCF .... National Coalition for the Protection of Children and Families (EA)
NCPCINST .... Naval Civilian Personnel Command Instructions (MCD)
NCPCO .... National Climate Program Coordinating Office
NCPCR .... National Center for Prevention and Control of Rape [*National Institutes of Health*]
NCPCU .... National Council of Postal Credit Unions (NTPA)
NCPD .... National Catholic Office for Persons with Disabilities (EA)
NCPD .... Navy Current Procurement Directive
NCPDM .... National Council of Physical Distribution Management
NCPDP .... National Council for Prescription Drug Programs (EA)
NCPDS .... Navy Civilian Personnel Data System
NCPE .... National Committee on Pay Equity (EA)
NCPE .... National Council for Preservation Education
NCPE .... Noncardiac Pulmonary Edema [*Medicine*]
NCPEA .... National College Physical Education Association [*Later, NCPEAM*] (EA)
NCPEA .... National Conference of Professors of Educational Administration [*Later, NAPEHE*] (EA)
NCPEAM .... National College Physical Education Association for Men [*Later, NAPEHE*]
NCPEARL .... National Coalition for Public Education and Religious Liberty (EA)
NCPEG .... Navy Contractor Performance Evaluation Group
NCPEP .... New Century Policies Educational Programs (EA)
NCPERL .... National Coalition for Public Education and Religious Liberty (EA)
NCPERS .... National Conference on Public Employee Retirement Systems (EA)
NcPeS .... Pembroke State University, Pembroke, NC [*Library symbol Library of Congress*] (LCLS)
NCPF .... National Council on Private Forests (EA)
NcPfO .... Olin Corp., Ecusta-Film Technical Library, Pisgah Forest, NC [*Library symbol Library of Congress*] (LCLS)
NCPG .... National Catholic Pharmacists Guild of the United States (EA)
NCPG .... National Committee on Planned Giving (NFD)
NCPG .... National Council on Problem Gambling (EA)
NCPG .... Nozzleless Center-Perforated Grain (MCD)
NCPGG .... National Center for Petroleum Geology and Geophysics [*Australia*]
NCPH .... National Council on Public History [*Database producer*] (EA)
NCpHS .... Carle Place High School, Carle Place, NY [*Library symbol*] [*Library of Congress*] (LCLS)
NCPI .... National Clay Pipe Institute (EA)
NCPI .... National Committee on Property Insurance [*Boston, MA*] (EA)
NCPI .... National Computer Program Index (IAA)
NCPI .... National Conference on Parent Involvement (EA)
NCPI .... National Crime Prevention Institute (EA)
NCPI .... Navy Civilian Personnel Instructions
NCPIE .... National Coalition for Parent Involvement in Education
NCPIE .... National Conference on Prescription Medicine Information and Education
NCPIE .... National Council of Patient Information and Education (EA)
NCPIM .... National Commission to Prevent Infant Mortality
NCPL .... Kirkland Town Library, Clinton, NY [*Library symbol*] [*Library of Congress*] (LCLS)
NCPL .... National Center for Preservation Law (EA)
NCPL .... National Collegiate Parachuting League (EA)
NCPLA .... National Council of Patent Law Associations [*Later, NCIPLA*] (EA)
NCPLD .... Noncoupled
NcPly .... Washington County Library, Plymouth, NC [*Library symbol Library of Congress*] (LCLS)
NcPlyP .... Pettigrew Regional Library, Plymouth, NC [*Library symbol Library of Congress*] (LCLS)

NcPm .... Charles H. Stone Memorial Library, Pilot Mountain, NC [*Library symbol Library of Congress*] (LCLS)
NCPM .... National Centre for Popular Music [*England*] (WDAA)
NCPM .... National Clay Pot Manufacturers (EA)
NCPM .... National Conference of Personal Managers (EA)
NCPM .... Noncritical Phase Matching (IAA)
NCPMA .... National Clay Pot Manufacturers Association (NTPA)
NCPMA .... Noise Control Products and Materials Association [*Later, NCA*] (EA)
ncpn-- .... Panama [*MARC geographic area code Library of Congress*] (LCCP)
NCPNFUNW... National Coalition for a Policy of No-First-Use of Nuclear Weapons (EA)
NCPO .... National Chronic Pain Outreach Association (EA)
NCPO .... National Climate Program Office [*National Oceanic and Atmospheric Administration*]
NCPO .... Nordic Council for Physical Oceanography (EA)
NcPo .... United States Air Force, Pope Air Force Base, Base Library, Pope AFB, NC [*Library symbol Library of Congress*] (LCLS)
NCPOA .... National Chief Petty Officers' Association (EA)
NCPOA .... National Chronic Pain Outreach Association, Inc. (PAZ)
NcPolA .... Anson Technical College, Learning Resources Center, Polk Campus, Polkton, NC [*Library symbol Library of Congress*] (LCLS)
NCPP .... National Coal Policy Project
NCPP .... National Council on Public Policy (EA)
NCPP .... National Council on Public Polls (EA)
NCPPB .... National Collection of Plant Pathogenic Bacteria (DMAA)
NCPPC .... National Capital Park and Planning Commission [*Later, NCPC*]
NCPPP .... National Council for Public-Private Partnerships (EA)
NCPPR .... National Center for Public Policy Research (EA)
NCPQWL ...... National Center for Productivity and Quality of Working Life [*Later, National Productivity Council*]
NCPR .... National Championship Poker Run [*American Motorcyclists Association*]
NCPR .... National Congress of Petroleum Retailers [*Later, SSDA*] (EA)
NCPR .... No Cardiopulmonary Resuscitation [*For terminal patients*] (DAVI)
NCpRE .... Rushmore Elementary School, Carle Place, NY [*Library symbol*] [*Library of Congress*] (LCLS)
NCPRP .... National Coastal Pollution Research Program [*Environmental Protection Agency*] (MSC)
NCPRR .... National Congress for Puerto Rican Rights (EA)
NCPRV .... National Congress of Puerto Rican Veterans (EA)
NCPRV .... National Council of Puerto Rican Volunteers [*Defunct*] (EA)
NCPS .... National Cat Protection Society (EA)
NCPS .... National Circus Preservation Society (EA)
NCPS .... National Coalition to Prevent Shoplifting (EA)
NCPS .... National Commission on Product Safety
NCPS .... National Commission on the Public Service [*Defunct*] (EA)
NCPS .... Nigerian College of Petroleum Studies [*Kaduna, Northern Nigeria*]
NCPS .... Non-Contributory Pension Scheme (DLA)
NCPS .... Nuclear Contingency Planning System (MCD)
NCPSA .... National Child Passenger Safety Association [*Later, NPSA*] (EA)
NCPSC .... National Committee on Paper Stock Conservation
NCPSF .... National Council of Professional Services Firms [*Later, PSC*] (EA)
NCPSIDS ...... National Center for the Prevention of Sudden Infant Death Syndrome (EA)
NCPSSM ...... National Committee to Preserve Social Security and Medicare (EA)
NCPT .... National Conference on Power Transmission (EA)
NCPT .... National Congress of Parents and Teachers [*Later, National PTA*] (EA)
NCPT .... Nationally-Certified Psychiatric Technician
NCPT .... Navy Central Planning Team [*NATO*] (NATG)
NCPTA .... National Confederation of Parent Teacher Associations [*British*]
NCPTCAN ..... National Center for the Prevention and Treatment of Child Abuse and Neglect (EA)
NCPTF .... National Campaign for a Peace Tax Fund (EA)
NCPTO .... National China Painting Teachers Organization [*Later, IPAT*] (EA)
NCPTWA ...... National Clearinghouse for Periodical Title Word Abbreviations [*ANSI*]
NCPUA .... National Committee on Pesticide Use in Agriculture [*Canada*]
NCP/VS .... NCP Virtual Storage (NITA)
NCPVS .... Network Control Program Virtual Storage [*Telecommunications*] (IAA)
NCPW .... National Country Party of Western Australia [*Political party*]
NCPWB .... National Certified Pipe Welding Bureau (EA)
NCPWSF ...... National Congenital Port Wine Stain Foundation (EA)
NCPY .... Penrhyn [*Cook Islands*] [*ICAO location identifier*] (ICLI)
NCPYA .... National Conference of Public Youth Agencies [*Defunct*] (EA)
NCQ .... Marietta, GA [*Location identifier FAA*] (FAAL)
NCQA .... National Committee for Quality Assurance (EA)
NCQHC .... National Committee for Quality Health Care (EA)
NCQIE .... National Coalition for Quality Integrated Education (EA)
NCQR .... National Council for Quality and Reliabiltiy [*British*] (BI)
NCR .... Air Sur [*Spain ICAO designator*] (FAAC)
NCR .... National Capital Region
NCR .... National Cash Register [*Computer science*] (NADA)
NCR .... National Cash Register Co. [*Later, NCR Corp.*] [*Computer manufacturer*]
NCR .... National Civic Review [*A publication*] (BRI)
NCR .... National Coalition for Research in Neurological and Communicative Disorders (EA)
NCR .... National Coalition for Research in Neurological Disorders (EA)
NCR .... National Council of Resistance for Liberty and Independence [*Iran*] (PD)
NCR .... Naval Construction Regiment (NVT)
NCR .... Navy Code Room
NCR .... Network Change Request [*NASA*] (KSC)
NCR .... Network Control Room [*Television*]
NCR .... Neutrophil Complement Rosettes [*Hematology*]
NCR .... New Cinema Review [*A publication*]
N Cr .... New York Criminal Reports [*A publication*] (DLA)
NCR .... Nickerson, C. R., San Francisco CA [*STAC*]
NCR .... Nicorandil [*Biochemistry*]
NCR .... Nitrile-Chloroprene Rubber
NCR .... No Calibration Required (MCD)
NCR .... No Canadian Rights
NCR .... No Carbon Required (NG)
NCR .... Noncoding Region [*Genetics*]
NCR .... Non-Combat Ready [*Military*] (SAA)
NCR .... Noncompliance Report [*Environmental Protection Agency*] (EPA)
NCR .... Nonconformance Record [*NASA*] (KSC)
NCR .... Nonconformance Report [*Nuclear energy*] (NRCH)
NCR .... Nonconserved Region [*Genetics*]
NCR .... Non-Selective Catalyst Reduction [*Diesel engine emissions*]
NCR .... Normotensive Control (DB)
NCR .... North Carolina Register [*A publication*] (AAGC)
NCR .... Northern Central Railway [*British*] (ROG)
NCR .... Notification of Change Report (NRCH)
NCR .... Nucal Resources Ltd. [*Vancouver Stock Exchange symbol*]
NCR .... Nuclear (AAG)
NCR .... Nuclear Cytoplasmic Ratio [*Cytology*]
NCR .... Ontario Library Service - Voyageur [*UTLAS symbol*]
NcR .... Wake County Public Libraries, Raleigh, NC [*Library symbol Library of Congress*] (LCLS)
NcRa .... Hoke County Public Library, Raeford, NC [*Library symbol Library of Congress*] (LCLS)
NCRA .... National Cancer Registrar's Association (NTPA)
NCRA .... National Cellular Resellers' Association (EA)
NCRA .... National Center on Rural Aging (EA)
NCRA .... National Championship Racing Association [*Auto racing*]
NCRA .... National Coalition of Redevelopment Agencies (EA)
NCRA .... National Cooperative Refinery Association [*Commercial firm*] (EA)
NCRA .... National Cooperative Research Act [*1984*]
NCRA .... National Correctional Recreational Association (EA)
NCRA .... National Council of Research Administrators
NCRA .... National Court Reporters Association
NCRA .... National Crew and Rowing Association (PSS)
NCRAC .... National Community Relations Advisory Council [*Later, NJCRAC*] (EA)
NCRC .... National Catholic Resettlement Council (EA)
NCRC .... National Cave Rescue Commission
NCRC .... National Committee for a Representative Congress (EA)
NCRC .... National Community Reinvestment Coalition
NCRC .... Nickel-Cadmium Rechargeable Cell
NcR-C .... Wake County Public Libraries, Cameron Village Regional Library, Raleigh, NC [*Library symbol*] [*Library of Congress*] (LCLS)
NCRC/AODA... National Certification Reciprocity Consortium/Alcoholism and Other Drug Abuse (EA)
NCRCH .... Nordic Committee of the Research Councils for the Humanities (EA)
NcRCPL .... Carolina Power & Light Co., Technical Library, Raleigh, NC [*Library symbol Library of Congress*] (LCLS)
NCRCRD ...... North Central Regional Center for Rural Development [*Iowa State University*] [*Research center*] (RCD)
NCRD .... National Council on Resource Development (EA)
NCRD .... National Council to Repeal the Draft [*Defunct*] (EA)
NCRDA .... National Center for Research into Drug Abuse [*Australia*]
NCRDC .... National Capital Region, District of Columbia (MCD)
NcRDC .... North Carolina Department of Corrections, Central Prison School, Raleigh, NC [*Library symbol Library of Congress*] (LCLS)
NCRDC .... Northern Colorado Research-Demonstration Center [*Colorado State University*] [*Research center*] (RCD)
NcRDD .... North Carolina Department of Human Resources, Dorothea Dix Hospital, F. T. Fuller Staff Library, Raleigh, NC [*Library symbol Library of Congress*] (LCLS)
NCRDL .... Nautical Charting Research and Development Laboratory [*National Oceanic and Atmospheric Administration*]
NCRDS .... National Coal Resources Data System [*Geological Survey*] [*Databank*] [*Information service or system*] (IID)
NCRDTA ...... National Council of Refuse Disposal Trade Associations
NCRE .... National Conference on Research in English (EA)
NCRE .... National Council on Rehabilitation Education (EA)
NCRE .... Naval Construction Research Establishment [*British*] (AAG)
NC Reg .... North Carolina Register [*A publication*] (AAGC)
NcReH .... Annie Penn Hospital, Medical Library, Reidsville, NC [*Library symbol Library of Congress*] (LCLS)
NCREIF .... National Council of Real Estate Investment Fiduciaries (EA)
NCREL .... North Central Regional Educational Laboratory [*Elmhurst, IL*] [*Department of Education*] (GRD)
NC Rep .... North Carolina Reports [*A publication*] (DLA)
NC Rep Appendix... North Carolina Reports, Appendix [*A publication*] (DLA)
NC Reports... North Carolina Reports [*A publication*] (DLA)
NcRf .... Eden Public Library, Eden, NC [*Library symbol Library of Congress*] (LCLS)
NCRF .... National Court Reporters Foundation
NcR-F .... Wake County Public Libraries, Fuquay-Varina Public Library, Fuquay-Varina, NC [*Library symbol*] [*Library of Congress*] (LCLS)
NCRFCL .... National Commission on Reform of Federal Criminal Laws
NCRFP .... National Council for a Responsible Firearms Policy [*Defunct*] (EA)
NCRFRA ...... National Committee to Repeal the Federal Reserve Act (EA)
NCRFSCU .... National Commission on the Role and Future of State Colleges and Universities [*Defunct*] (EA)
NCRG .... Avarua/Rarotonga International [*Cook Islands*] [*ICAO location identifier*] (ICLI)

NcRGM .... North Carolina Department of Human Resources, The Governor Morehead School, Raleigh, NC [*Library symbol Library of Congress*] (LCLS)

NcRGP .... State of North Carolina, Governor's Press Office State Capital Building, Raleigh, NC [*Library symbol*] [*Library of Congress*] (LCLS)

NcRGS .... Church of Jesus Christ of Latter-Day Saints, Genealogical Society Library, Raleigh Branch, Raleigh, NC [*Library symbol Library of Congress*] (LCLS)

NCRH .... National Center for Radiological Health [*Public Health Service*]

NCRH .... North Coast Railroad Historical Society (EA)

NcRH .... W. W. Holding Technical Institute, Raleigh, NC [*Library symbol Library of Congress*] (LCLS)

NcRHR .... North Carolina Department of Human Resources, Public Health Library, Raleigh, NC [*Library symbol Library of Congress*] (LCLS)

NCRI .... National Center for Resource Innovations

NCRI .... National Coastal Resources Research and Development Institute [*Newport, OR*] [*Department of Commerce*] (GRD)

NCRI .... National Consumer Research Institute (EA)

NCRIB .... Naval Communications Improvement Review Board (DNAB)

NCRIC .... National Chemical Response and Information Center [*Established by the Chemical Manufacturers Association to provide information and advice during emergencies*]

NCRIPTAL .... National Center for Research to Improve Postsecondary Teaching and Learning [*Ann Arbor, MI*] [*Department of Education*] (GRD)

NCRIS .... National Committee to Restore Internal Security (EA)

NcRJP .... Jaakko Poyry, Inc., Raleigh, NC [*Library symbol*] [*Library of Congress*] (LCLS)

NCRK .... Rakahanga [*Cook Islands*] [*ICAO location identifier*] (ICLI)

NCRL .... National Canners Association Research Laboratory

NCRL .... National Citizens Radio League (IAA)

NCRLC .... National Catholic Rural Life Conference (EA)

NCRLC .... National Committee on Regional Library Cooperation

NCRLL .... National Conference on Research in Language and Literacy (NTPA)

NCRLS .... National Committee for Russian Language Study [*American Association for the Advancement of Slavic Studies*] (EDAC)

NCRLS .... National Committee of Religious Leaders of Safety (EA)

NcRM .... Meredith College, Raleigh, NC [*Library symbol Library of Congress*] (LCLS)

NCRM .... National Conference on Radiation Measurements

NCRM .... Nordic Council for Railway Music (EA)

NcRm .... Thomas Hackney Braswell Memorial Library, Rocky Mount, NC [*Library symbol Library of Congress*] (LCLS)

NcRMA .... North Carolina Museum of Art in Raleigh, Raleigh, NC [*Library symbol Library of Congress*] (LCLS)

NcRMC .... Meredith College, Raleigh, NC [*Library symbol*] [*Library of Congress*] (LCLS)

NCRMD .... National Capital Region, Maryland (MCD)

NcRmE .... Edgecombe Technical College, Learning Resources Center, Rocky Mount, NC [*Library symbol Library of Congress*] (LCLS)

NcRMG .... Measurements Group, Inc., Raleigh, NC [*Library symbol Library of Congress*] (LCLS)

NcRmHE ...... Area L AHEC Library, Rocky Mount, NC [*Library symbol*] [*Library of Congress*] (LCLS)

NcRmN .... Nash Technical Institute, Rocky Mount, NC [*Library symbol Library of Congress*] (LCLS)

NcRMNH ...... North Carolina State Museum of Natural History, Raleigh, NC [*Library symbol Library of Congress*] (LCLS)

NcRMNH-B ... North Carolina State Museum of Natural History, H. H. Brimley Memorial Library, Raleigh, NC [*Library symbol Library of Congress*] (LCLS)

NcRmW .... North Carolina Wesleyan College, Rocky Mount, NC [*Library symbol*] [*Library of Congress*] (LCLS)

NCRND .... National Committee for Research in Neurological Disorders [*Later, NCR*] (EA)

NcRNO .... News and Observer Publishing Co., Raleigh, NC [*Library symbol*] [*Library of Congress*] (LCLS)

NcRNR .... North Carolina Department of Natural Resources and Community Development, Raleigh, NC [*Library symbol*] [*Library of Congress*] (LCLS)

NCRNT .... National Committee for Rescue from NAZI Terror [*British*]

NcRo .... Rockingham-Richmond County Library, Rockingham, NC [*Library symbol Library of Congress*] (LCLS)

NcRob .... Bemis Memorial Library, Robbinsville, NC [*Library symbol Library of Congress*] (LCLS)

NcRobS .... Snowbird Community Library, Robbinsville, NC [*Library symbol Library of Congress*] (LCLS)

NCroh .... Croton Free Library, Croton-On-Hudson, NY [*Library symbol Library of Congress*] (LCLS)

NCrohH .... Hudson Institute, Croton-On-Hudson, NY [*Library symbol Library of Congress*] (LCLS)

NcRop .... Roper Community Library and Resource Center, Inc., Roper, NC [*Library symbol*] [*Library of Congress*] (LCLS)

NCROPA ...... National Campaign for the Reform of the Obscene Publications Acts [*British*] (DBA)

NcRoS .... Sandhills Regional Library, Rockingham, NC [*Library symbol Library of Congress*] (LCLS)

NcRov .... Robersonville Public Library, Robersonville, NC [*Library symbol Library of Congress*] (LCLS)

NcRox .... Person County Public Library, Roxboro, NC [*Library symbol Library of Congress*] (LCLS)

NcRoxP .... Person Technical Institute, Roxboro, NC [*Library symbol Library of Congress*] (LCLS)

NCRP .... National Climatic Research Program

NCRP .... National Commission on Radiological Protection

NCRP .... National Committee for Responsible Patriotism (EA)

NCRP .... National Committee for Responsive Philanthropy (EA)

NCRP .... National Council for Research and Planning (EA)

NCRP .... National Council on Radiation Protection and Measurements [*Later, NCRPM*]

NcRP .... Peace College, Raleigh, NC [*Library symbol Library of Congress*] (LCLS)

NCR paper ... No Carbon Required Paper

NCRPC .... National Capital Regional Planning Council [*Terminated, 1966*]

NCRPCV ...... National Council of Returned Peace Corps Volunteers (EA)

NCRPE .... National Council on Religion and Public Education (EA)

NcRPI .... North Carolina Department of Public Instruction, Education Information Services, Raleigh, NC [*Library symbol*] [*Library of Congress*] (LCLS)

NCRPM .... National Council on Radiation Protection and Measurements (EA)

NcRPS .... Pointer & Spruill Library, Raleigh, NC [*Library symbol*] [*Library of Congress*] (LCLS)

NCRR .... National Center for Research Resources [*National Institutes of Health*]

NCRR .... National Center for Resource Recovery [*Defunct*]

NCRR .... National Credit Union Administration Rules and Regulations

NCRR .... Nordic Council of Reindeer Research (EAIO)

NcRr .... Roanoke Rapids Public Library, Roanoke Rapids, NC [*Library symbol Library of Congress*] (LCLS)

NCRRC .... National Committee to Reopen the Rosenberg Case (EA)

NCRRF .... Norris Communications Corp. [*NASDAQ symbol*] (SAG)

NcRRH .... Rex Hospital Library, Raleigh, NC [*Library symbol*] [*Library of Congress*] (LCLS)

NCRRHA ...... National Confederation of Registered Rest Home Associations [*British*] (DBA)

NCRRRC ...... North Country Reference and Research Resources Council [*Information service or system*] (IID)

NCRS .... National Clearinghouse on Revenue Sharing [*Defunct*]

NCRS .... National Committee for Rural Schools [*Defunct*] (EA)

NCRS .... National Corvette Restorers Society (EA)

NcRS .... North Carolina State University at Raleigh, Raleigh, NC [*Library symbol Library of Congress*] (LCLS)

NCRSA .... National Commercial Refrigeration Sales Association (EA)

NcRSA .... Saint Augustine's College, Raleigh, NC [*Library symbol Library of Congress*] (LCLS)

NcRSh .... Shaw University, Raleigh, NC [*Library symbol Library of Congress*] (LCLS)

NcRSM .... Saint Mary's Junior College, Raleigh, NC [*Library symbol Library of Congress*] (LCLS)

NcRS-P .... North Carolina State University at Raleigh, Photocopy Services, Raleigh, NC [*Library symbol*] [*Library of Congress*] (LCLS)

NCRSR .... National Congenital Rubella Syndrome Registry [*Centers for Disease Control*]

NcRS-V .... North Carolina State University, School of Veterinary Medicine, Raleigh, NC [*Library symbol Library of Congress*] (LCLS)

NCRT .... National College of Rubber Technology (PDAA)

NCRTE .... National Center for Research on Teacher Education [*East Lansing, MI*] [*Department of Education*] (GRD)

NCR/TSI .... NCR Telecommunication Services, Inc. (TSSD)

NcRu .... Norris Public Library, Rutherfordton, NC [*Library symbol Library of Congress*] (LCLS)

NCRUCE ...... National Conference of Regulatory Utility Commission Engineers (EA)

NcRuR .... Rutherford County Library, Inc., Rutherfordton, NC [*Library symbol Library of Congress*] (LCLS)

NCRV .... National Committee for Radiation Victims (EA)

NCRVA .... National Capital Region, Virginia (MCD)

NCRVD .... National Conference of Religious Vocation Directors [*Later, NRVC*] (EA)

NCRVDM ...... National Conference of Religious Vocation Directors of Men [*Later, NCRVD*] (EA)

NCRVE .... National Center for Research in Vocational Education (EA)

NCRW .... National Council for Research on Women (EA)

NcRWCM ..... Wake County Hospital System, Wake County Medical Center, Raleigh, NC [*Library symbol Library of Congress*] (LCLS)

NcRWHD ...... Wake County Health Department, Raleigh, NC [*Library symbol*] [*Library of Congress*] (LCLS)

NCRWS .... National Campaign for Radioactive Waste Safety (EA)

NCRY .... National Commission on Resources for Youth

NCS .... National Cartoonists Society (EA)

NCS .... National Cemetery System

NCS .... National Center for Stuttering (EA)

NCS .... National Chrysanthemum Society (EA)

NCS .... National Commemorative Society [*Defunct*]

NCS .... National Committee on Safety

NCS .... National Communications System [*DoD*]

NCS .... National Compliance Strategy (GNE)

NCS .... National Computer Systems, Inc.

NCS .... National Conference on Solicitations (EA)

NCS .... National Consensus Standards (MCD)

NCS .... National Conservation Strategy (GNE)

NCS .... National Convenience Stores, Inc. [*NYSE symbol*] (SPSG)

NCS .... National Corrosion Service [*British*] (IRUK)

NCS .... National Council of Stutterers [*Later, NCOS*] (EA)

NCS .... National Crime Squad (WDAA)

NCS .... National Crime Stoppers [*Later, ACF*] (EA)

NCS .... National Crime Survey [*University of Michigan*] [*Database*]

NCS .... National Cryptologic School [*National Security Agency*]

NCS .... Nationwide Cellular Service, Inc. (EFIS)

NCS .... Naval Canteen Service [*British military*] (DMA)

NCS .... Naval Communications Station [*or System*]
NCS .... Naval Compass Stabilizer (PDAA)
NCS .... Naval Control of Shipping [*NATO*] (NATG)
NCS .... Navigational Computer Set (MCD)
NCS .... Navigation Control Simulator
NCS .... N-Chlorosuccinimide [*Organic chemistry*]
NCS .... NCR [*NCR Corp.*] Century Software
NCS .... Nearest Cross Street (ADA)
NCS .... Needlework and Craft Showcase (ITD)
NCS .... Neocarzinostatin [*Zinostatin*] [*Antineoplastic drug*]
NCS .... Nerve Conduction Studies [*Neurology*] (DAVI)
NCS .... Net Control Station [*Communications*] [*Amateur radio*]
NCS .... Network Communications Server [*J & L Information Systems*]
NCS .... Network Communication Standard (AAEL)
NCS .... Network Communication System (IAA)
NCS .... Network Control Station (IAA)
NCS .... Network Control System
NCS .... Network Coordination Station
NCS .... Network Co-ordination System (NITA)
NCS .... Newborn Calf Serum [*Immunology*]
NCS .... Newcastle [*South Africa*] [*Airport symbol*] (OAG)
NCS .... Nielsen Coverage Service [*A.C. Nielson Co.*] (DOAD)
NCS .... Nineteenth Century Series [*A publication*]
NCS .... NMIC [*National Military Intelligence Center*] Control Subsystem
NCS .... No Checking Signal [*Telecommunications*] (TEL)
NCS .... No Concentrated Sweets [*Medicine*] (DMAA)
NCS .... Noncallable Security [*Investment term*]
NCS .... Noncircumferential Stenosis [*Medicine*] (DMAA)
NCS .... Non-Collimated Source (PDAA)
NCS .... Non-Conventional System [*Post coordinate indexing*] (NITA)
NCS .... Noncoronary Sinus [*Cardiology*] (AAMN)
NCS .... Noncritical Sensitive [*DoD*]
NCS .... Noncrystalline Solid [*Physics*]
NCS .... Noncrystallographic Symmetry [*Chemistry*]
NCS .... Nonwater Cooling System
NCS .... North Carolina State Library, Raleigh, NC [*OCLC symbol*] (OCLC)
NCS .... Northern Cross Society (EA)
NCS .... Nuclear-Chicago Solubilizer
NCS .... Nuclear Components Spare (IAA)
NCS .... Nuclear Criticality Safety (NRCH)
NCS .... Nuclear-Powered Container Ship (PDAA)
NCS .... Nucleolar Channel System
NCS .... Nucleus Support Crew [*Navy*] (DNAB)
NCS .... Nueva Concepcion [*El Salvador*] [*Seismograph station code, US Geological Survey Closed*] (SEIS)
NCS .... Numerical Category Scaling
NCS .... Numerical Control Society [*Later, NCS/AIMTECH*] (EA)
NCS .... Numerical Control System (IAA)
NCS .... Nutation Control System (MCD)
NCS .... Simpson Air Ltd. [*Canada ICAO designator*] (FAAC)
NCSA .... National Capital Speakers Association (EA)
NCSA .... National Carl Schurz Association [*Defunct*] (EA)
NCSA .... National Center for Statistics and Analysis [*National Highway Traffic Safety Administration*] [*Washington, DC*] (GRD)
NCSA .... National Center for Supercomputer Applications (NITA)
NCSA .... National Center for Supercomputing Applications [*University of Illinois*] [*National Science Foundation*] [*Research center*] (RCD)
NCSA .... National Church Secretaries Association [*Defunct*] (EA)
NCSA .... National Club Sports Association (EA)
NCSA .... National Coffee Service Association [*Vienna, VA*] (EA)
NCSA .... National Collegiate Ski Association (EA)
NCSA .... National Committee for Senior Americans (EA)
NCSA .... National Committee of State Associations
NCSA .... National Computational Science Alliance [*Supercomputing center*]
NCSA .... National Computer Security Association [*Computer science*] (PCM)
NCSA .... National Confectionery Salesmen's Association of America (EA)
NCSA .... National Construction Software Association (EA)
NCSA .... National Contract Sweepers Association [*Later, NCSI*] (EA)
NCSA .... National Council of Seamen's Agencies [*Later, ICOSA*] (EA)
NCSA .... National Crushed Stone Association [*Later, NSA*] (EA)
NCSA .... National Cued Speech Association (EA)
NCSA .... National Customs Service Association [*Later, NTEU*] (EA)
NCSA .... Newsagency Council of South Australia
NCSA .... Newspaper Collectors Society of America (EA)
NCSA .... No Charge Storage Agreement (AAGC)
NCSA .... Non-Chemical Shift Anisotropy [*Physical chemistry*]
NCSA .... Noncommercial Spot Announcement [*Public service announcement*] (NTCM)
NCSAB .... National Council of State Agencies for the Blind (EA)
NCSABMT... National Campaign to Save the ABM [*Antiballistic missile*] Treaty [*Defunct*] (EA)
NcSaC.......... Central Carolina Technical Institute, Sanford, NC [*Library symbol Library of Congress*] (LCLS)
NCSAC .... National Catholic Social Action Conference [*Defunct*] (EA)
NCSAC .... National Child Support Advocacy Coalition (EA)
NCSAC .... Nuclear Cross Sections Advisory Committee
NcSaCi......... Cilco, Sanford, NC [*Library symbol*] [*Library of Congress*] (LCLS)
NCSAG........ Nuclear Cross Section Advisory Group (NRCH)
NCS/AIMTECH... Numerical Control Society/AIMTECH [*Association for Integrated Manufacturing Technology*] (EA)
NcSaL.......... Lee County Library, Sanford, NC [*Library symbol Library of Congress*] (LCLS)
NcSal........... Rowan Public Library, Salisbury, NC [*Library symbol Library of Congress*] (LCLS)

NcSalC........ Catawba College, Salisbury, NC [*Library symbol Library of Congress*] (LCLS)
NcSaLCL..... Lee County Library, Sanford, NC [*Library symbol*] [*Library of Congress*] (LCLS)
NcSaI-E....... Rowan Public Library East Branch, Rockwell, NC [*Library symbol*] [*Library of Congress*] (LCLS)
NcSaIL........ Livingstone College, Salisbury, NC [*Library symbol Library of Congress*] (LCLS)
NcSaIR........ Rowan Technical Institute, Salisbury, NC [*Library symbol Library of Congress*] (LCLS)
NcSaIRH..... Rowan Memorial Hospital Area, Health Education Center, Salisbury, NC [*Library symbol Library of Congress*] (LCLS)
NcSaI-S....... Rowan Public Library, South Rowan Branch, Landis, NC [*Library symbol Library of Congress*] (LCLS)
NcSaITM..... Tri-County Mental Health Center, Salisbury, NC [*Library symbol*] [*Library of Congress*] (LCLS)
NcSaIVA..... United States Veterans Administration Center, Medical Library, Salisbury, NC [*Library symbol Library of Congress*] (LCLS)
NCSAnet..... [*The*] National Center for Supercomputing Applications Network [*Computer science*] (TNIG)
NCSAP........ National Council for Single Adoptive Parents (EA)
NCSASR...... National Center for Small-Angle Scattering Research [*Oak Ridge, TN*] [*Department of Energy*] (GRD)
NCSAW....... National Catholic Society for Animal Welfare [*Later, ISAR*] (EA)
NCSB .... National Centre for School Biotechnology (AIE)
NCSBCS...... National Conference of States on Building Codes and Standards (EA)
NCSBEE ...... National Council of State Boards of Engineering Examiners [*Later, NCEE*] (EA)
NCSBI .... National Council for Small Business Innovation
NcSbJ .... North Carolina Justice Academy, Salemburg, NC [*Library symbol Library of Congress*] (LCLS)
NCSBMD..... National Council for Small Business Management Development [*Later, ICSB*] (EA)
NCSBN .... National Council of State Boards of Nursing (EA)
NcSbP......... Southwood College, Salemburg, NC [*Library symbol Library of Congress*] (LCLS)
NCSC .... National Catholic Stewardship Council (EA)
NCSC .... National Center for State Courts (EA)
NCSC .... National Child Safety Council (EA)
NCSC .... National Communication System Circulars
NCSC .... National Computer Security Center (IGQR)
NCSC .... National Computer Security Council
NCSC .... National Council of Senior Citizens (EA)
NCSC .... National Council on Schoolhouse Construction [*Later, CEFP*] (EA)
NCSC .... Naval Coastal Systems Center [*Panama City, FL*]
NCSC .... Navy Command Support Center (MCD)
NCSC .... North Carolina State College
Nc-SC .... North Carolina State Supreme Court, Raleigh, NC [*Library symbol Library of Congress*] (LCLS)
NCSCBHEP... National Center for the Study of Collective Bargaining in Higher Education and the Professions (EA)
NCSCC .... National Championship Stock Car Racing [*Later, NASCAR*]
NCSCCY ..... National Council of State Committees for Children and Youth (EA)
NCSCEE ...... National Council of State Consultants in Elementary Education [*Defunct*] (EA)
NCSCI .... National Center for Standards and Certification Information [*Gaithersburg, MD*] [*Database*] [*National Institute of Standards and Technology*]
NCSCJ .... National Conference of Special Court Judges (EA)
NCSCJPA ..... National Conference of State Criminal Justice Planning Administrators [*Later, NCJA*] (EA)
NCSCL .... National Committee for Sexual Civil Liberties (EA)
NcScn .... Scotland Neck Memorial Library, Scotland Neck, NC [*Library symbol Library of Congress*] (LCLS)
NCSCPAS.... National Center for the Study of Corporal Punishment and Alternatives in the Schools (EA)
NCSCR .... North Carolina State College Reactor
NCSCT .... National Center for School and College Television
NCSD .... National Child Safety Development [*British*]
NCSD .... National Council on Student Development (EA)
NCSDCJC..... National Council of State Directors of Community Junior Colleges (NTPA)
NCSDR........ National Commission on Sleep Disorders Research
NCSE .... National Center for Science Education (EA)
NCSE .... National Commission on Safety Education [*Defunct*] (EA)
NCSE .... National Committee on Secondary Education [*of NASSP*]
NCSE .... National Council for Special Education [*British*]
NcSe........... Selma Public Library, Selma, NC [*Library symbol*] [*Library of Congress*] (LCLS)
NCSEA .... National Child Support Enforcement Association (EA)
NCSEA .... National Community School Education Association [*Later, NCEA*] (EA)
NCSEA .... National Council of State Education Associations (EA)
NCSEE .... National Coalition for Sex Equity in Education (EA)
NCSEER ..... National Council for Soviet and East European Research (EA)
NCSEES ..... Nordic Committee for Soviet and East European Studies (EA)
NCSEMSTC... National Council of State Emergency Medical Services Training Coordinators (EA)
NC Sess Laws... Session Laws of North Carolina [*A publication*] (DLA)
NCSEX .... Naval Control of Shipping Exercises
NCSF .... National Catholic Society of Foresters (EA)
NCSF .... National Cold Storage Federation [*British*] (DBA)
NCSF .... National College Student Foundation [*Defunct*] (EA)
NCSFA........ National Conference of State Fleet Administrators (EA)

NCSFI .... National Coalition to Stop Food Irradiation (EA)
NCSFP .... National Council on Synthetic Fuels Production [*Later, CSF*] (EA)
NCSFWI .... National Coalition to Stop Food and Water Irradiation (EA)
NCSG .... National Chimney Sweep Guild (EA)
NCSGC......... National Council of State Garden Clubs (EA)
NCSGSO ...... National Conference of State General Service Officers [*Later, NASDAGS*] (EA)
NcSh .... Cleveland County Memorial Library, Shelby, NC [*Library symbol Library of Congress*] (LCLS)
NCsh .... Cold Spring Harbor Public Library, Cold Spring Harbor, NY [*Library symbol Library of Congress*] (LCLS)
NCSH .... National Clearinghouse for Smoking and Health [*Public Health Service*]
NCSH .... Newton College of the Sacred Heart [*Later, Newton College*] [*Massachusetts*]
NCSHA .... National Council of State Housing Agencies (NTPA)
NCSHA .... Naval Communications System Headquarters Activity (SAA)
NCshB .... Cold Spring Harbor Biological Laboratory, Cold Spring Harbor, NY [*Library symbol Library of Congress*] (LCLS)
NcShC .... Cleveland County Technical Institute, Shelby, NC [*Library symbol Library of Congress*] (LCLS)
NCshL .... Cold Spring Harbor Public Library, Cold Spring Harbor, NY [*Library symbol*] [*Library of Congress*] (LCLS)
NCS Hlt........ NCS Healthcare, Inc. [*Associated Press*] (SAG)
NCSHPO ...... National Conference of State Historic Preservation Officers (EA)
NCSHSA ...... National Council of State Human Service Administrators (EA)
NCshWM..... Whaling Museum Society, Inc., Cold Spring Harbor, NY [*Library symbol Library of Congress*] (LCLS)
NCSI .... National Communication System Instructions
NCSI .... National Contract Sweepers Institute (EA)
NCSI .... National Convenience Stores, Inc. [*NASDAQ symbol*] (SAG)
NCSI .... National Council for Stream Improvement (EA)
NCSI .... National Council of Savings Institutions (EMRF)
NCSI .... National Council of Self-Insurers [*Chicago, IL*] (EA)
NCSI .... National Curriculum Study Institute [*Associaton for Supervision and Curriculum Development*] (EDAC)
NCSI .... Network Communications Services Interface [*Computer science*] (PCM)
NCSIT .... National Coalition to Support Indian Treaties (EA)
NCSITSG...... National Community Services Industry Training Steering Group [*Australia*]
NCSJ........... National College of the State Judiciary (DLA)
NCSJ........... National Conference on Soviet Jewry (EA)
NCSJ........... Naval Communication Station, Japan
NcSj............ United States Air Force, Seymour Johnson Air Force Base, Base Library, Seymour Johnson AFB, NC [*Library symbol Library of Congress*] (LCLS)
NCSL .... National Center for Service-Learning [*Defunct*] (EA)
NCSL .... National Civil Service League [*Defunct*] (EA)
NCSL .... National Conference of Standards Laboratories (EA)
NCSL .... National Conference of State Legislatures (EA)
NCSL .... National Council of State Legislatures (WPI)
NCSL .... Naval Coastal Systems Laboratory [*Later, NCSC*]
NCSL .... Naval Code and Signal Laboratory
NCSL .... Near-Coincident Site Lattice [*Crystallography*]
NCSLA .... National Conference of State Liquor Administrators (EA)
NCSLL .... National Conference of State Legislative Leaders [*Later, NCSL*] (EA)
NCSLO .... Naval Control of Shipping Liaison Officer
NCSM .... National Communication System Memoranda
NCSM .... National Council of Supervisors of Mathematics (EA)
NCSMHC ..... National Council for the Single Mother and Her Child [*Australia*]
NcSmJ......... Johnston County Technical Institute, Smithfield, NC [*Library symbol Library of Congress*] (LCLS)
NCSMX .... National Campaign to Stop the MX [*Defunct*] (EA)
NcSn........... Greene County Public Library, Snow Hill, NC [*Library symbol Library of Congress*] (LCLS)
NCSN .... National Computer Service Network (EA)
NCSN .... National Council for School Nurses [*of AAHPER*]
NCSNE......... Naval Control of Shipping in Northern European Command Area [*NATO*] (NATG)
NCSO .... National Council of Salesmen's Organizations [*New York, NY*] (EA)
NCSO .... Naval Control of Shipping Officer
NCSO .... Naval Control of Shipping Operations
NCSO .... Naval Control Service Office [*World War II British Routing Service*]
NCSOICC..... North Carolina State Occupational Information Coordinating Committee (EDAC)
NcSopS-L .... Southport-Brunswick County Library, Leland Branch Library, Leland, NC [*Library symbol Library of Congress*] (LCLS)
NcSopS-W ... Southport-Brunswick County Library, West Brunswick Branch Library, Shallotte, NC [*Library symbol Library of Congress*] (LCLS)
NCSORG ..... Naval Control of Shipping Organization
NCSP .... National Center for Surrogate Parenting [*Later, IAI*] [*Commercial firm*] (EA)
NCSP .... National Conference on State Parks [*Later, NRPA*] (EA)
NCSP .... National Crime Stop Program (EA)
NCSP .... Naval Communication Station, Philippines (DNAB)
NCSP .... Nordic Committee on Salaries and Personnel [*Nordic Council of Ministers*] [*Copenhagen, Denmark*] (EAIO)
NcSp .... Southern Pines Public Library, Southern Pines, NC [*Library symbol Library of Congress*] (LCLS)
NcSpa .... Alleghany County Public Library, Sparta, NC [*Library symbol Library of Congress*] (LCLS)
NCSPA .... National Corrugated Steel Pipe Association (EA)
NCSPA .... North Carolina State Ports Authority
NCSPAA....... National Council of School Press and Advisers Association

NCSPAE....... National Council of State Pharmaceutical Association Executives (EA)
NCSPAE....... National Council of State Pharmacy Association Executives (NTPA)
NCSPAS....... National Conference of State Pharmaceutical Association Secretaries [*Later, NCSPAE*]
NcSph.......... Spring Hope Public Library, Spring Hope, NC [*Library symbol Library of Congress*] (LCLS)
NcSpi........... Spindale Public Library, Spindale, NC [*Library symbol Library of Congress*] (LCLS)
NcSpiI.......... Isothermal Community College, Spindale, NC [*Library symbol Library of Congress*] (LCLS)
NcSpiR......... Rutherford County Library, Inc., Spindale, NC [*Library symbol*] [*Library of Congress*] (LCLS)
NCSPP .... National Center for Social Policy and Practice (EA)
NcSppA........ Avery-Mitchell-Yancey Regional Library, Spruce Pine, NC [*Library symbol Library of Congress*] (LCLS)
NcSppM....... Mayland Technical Institute, Spruce Pine, NC [*Library symbol Library of Congress*] (LCLS)
NcSpr.......... Spray Public Library, Spray, NC [*Library symbol*] [*Library of Congress*] (LCLS)
NCSPS .... National Committee for Support of the Public Schools [*Later, NCCE*] (EA)
NcSpS.......... Sandhills Community College, Southern Pines, NC [*Library symbol Library of Congress*] (LCLS)
NCSPWA..... National Council of State Public Welfare Administrators [*Later, NCSHSA*] (EA)
NCSR.......... National Centre for Systems Reliability [*Research center British*] (CB)
NCSRA........ National Conference of State Retail Associations (EA)
NCSS .... National Cactus and Succulent Society [*British*] (BI)
NCSS .... National Center for Social Statistics [*HEW*]
NCSS .... National Collegiate Sports Services (EA)
NCSS .... National Commission on Supplies and Shortages [*Terminated, 1977*]
NCSS .... National Conference of Shomrim Societies (EA)
NCSS .... National Conference of State Societies (EA)
NCSS .... National Conference on Student Services (EA)
NCSS .... National Conversational Software Systems, Inc.
NCSS .... National Cooperative Soil Survey
NCSS .... National Council for the Social Studies (EA)
NCSS .... National Council of Social Service [*British*]
NCSS .... National Crash Severity Study [*National Highway Traffic Safety Administration*]
NCSS .... Navy Command Support System (MCD)
NCSS .... NCS HealthCare `A' [*NASDAQ symbol*] (TTSB)
NCSS .... NCS Healthcare, Inc. [*NASDAQ symbol*] (SAG)
NCSS .... Nordic Council of Ski Schools (EAIO)
NCSS .... Number Cruncher Statistical System [*Computer software*] (PCM)
NCSSA........ Naval Command Systems Support Activity
NCSSAD...... National Council of Secondary School Athletic Directors (EA)
NCSSB .... National Coalition for Seat Belts on School Buses (EA)
NCSSC........ Naval Command Systems Support Center
NCSSE .... National Coalition to Support Sexuality Education [*Fact sheet published by the Sexuality Information and Education Coalition of the United States (SIECUS)*] (PAZ)
NCSSFL .... National Council of State Supervisors of Foreign Languages (EA)
NCSSIA........ National Council of State Self-Insurers Associations [*Later, NCSI*] (EA)
NCSSM .... National Council of State Supervisors of Music (EA)
NCSSM .... North Carolina School of Science and Mathematics [*Free, residential public high school for gifted students*]
NCSSMA...... National Council of Social Security Management Associations (EA)
NCSSSA...... National Conference of State Social Security Administrators (EA)
NCSSW .... Nordic Committee of Schools of Social Work (EAIO)
NcSt........... Iredell Public Library, Statesville, NC [*Library symbol Library of Congress*] (LCLS)
NCST .... National Center for Software Technology [*India*] (DDC)
NCST .... National Certification Skills Test [*Psychiatry*]
NCST .... National Coalition for Science and Technology [*Defunct*] (EA)
NCSTAR....... National Committee of Shatnez Testers and Researchers (EA)
NCSTAS .... National Council of Scientific and Technical Art Societies [*Later, IG*] (EA)
NCSTD .... National Council of State Travel Directors (EA)
NcStH.......... Iredell Memorial Hospital, Statesville, NC [*Library symbol*] [*Library of Congress*] (LCLS)
NCstLf......... North Coast Life Insurance Co. [*Associated Press*] (SAG)
NcStMC....... Mitchell College, Statesville, NC [*Library symbol Library of Congress*] (LCLS)
NcStpR........ Robeson Technical Institute, St. Pauls, NC [*Library symbol Library of Congress Obsolete*] (LCLS)
NCSTR......... NATO Communication System Technical Recommendation (NATG)
NC Str......... Strange's Notes of Cases, Madras [*1798-1816*] [*A publication*] (DLA)
NC/STRC...... North Carolina Science and Technology Research Center [*North Carolina Department of Commerce*] [*Research center*] (RCD)
NCSTS .... National Conference of State Transportation Specialists (EA)
NCSTSR....... National Conference of Superintendents of Training Schools and Reformatories [*Later, International Conference of Administrators Residential Centers for Youth -ICA*] (EA)
NCSU .... Network Channel Service Unit [*Computer science*] (TNIG)
NCSU .... North Carolina State University [*Raleigh*]
NcSupB........ Brunswick Technical College, Supply, NC [*Library symbol Library of Congress*] (LCLS)
NCSW .... National Conference of Social Workers
NCSW .... National Conference on Social Welfare [*Defunct*] (EA)
NCSW .... National Council for the Single Woman and Her Dependants Ltd. [*British*] (BI)

NcSw .... Swannanoa Public Library, Swannanoa, NC [*Library symbol Library of Congress*] (LCLS)

NcSwC .... Chemtronics, Inc., Swannanoa, NC [*Library symbol*] [*Library of Congress*] (LCLS)

NCSWCL ...... National [*Presidential*] Commission on State Workmen's Compensation Laws

NCSWD .... National Center for Solid Waste Disposal [*Later, National Center for Resource Recovery*] (EA)

NCSWD .... National Center for the Study of Wilson's Disease (EA)

NCSWD .... National Council for the Single Woman and Her Dependants (EA)

NCSWDI .... National Combination Storm Window and Door Institute [*Defunct*] (EA)

NcSwW .... Warren Wilson College, Swannanoa, NC [*Library symbol Library of Congress*] (LCLS)

NCSX .... Shipping Control Exercise [*NATO exercises*] (NATG)

NcSy .... Jackson County Public Library, Sylva, NC [*Library symbol Library of Congress*] (LCLS)

NCSY .... National Conference of Synagogue Youth (EA)

NcSyS .... Southwestern Technical Institute, Sylva, NC [*Library symbol Library of Congress*] (LCLS)

NCT .... Name Changed To

NCT .... National Centre of Tribology [*Risley Nuclear Laboratories*] [*British*] (CB)

NCT .... National Chamber of Trade [*British*] (BI)

NCT .... National Childbirth Trust [*British*]

NCt .... National College Television [*Cable-television system*] (WDMC)

N Ct .... Native Court [*Ghana*] [*A publication*] (DLA)

NCT .... NATO Comparative Testing (RDA)

NCT .... Neoclassical Radiation Theory

NCT .... Nerve Conduction Tests [*Neurology*] (DAVI)

NCT .... Nerve Conduction Time [*neurology*] (DAVI)

NCT .... Net Cost of Transport

NCT .... Network Control Terminal (MCD)

NCT .... Neural Crest Tumor [*Oncology*]

NCT .... Neutral Contour Technology [*Automotive engineering*]

NCT .... New Curing Technology

NCT .... Nicoya [*Costa Rica*] [*Airport symbol*] (AD)

NCT .... Night Closing Trunks [*Telecommunications*] (TEL)

NCT .... Noise Cancellation Technology (PS)

NCT .... Non-Chargeable Time (DGA)

NCT .... Non-Competitive Tenders [*Business term*] (MHDW)

NCT .... Non-Contact Time (AIE)

NCT .... Nordic Cooperation on Telecommunications (EAIO)

NCT .... North Coast Industries Ltd. [*Vancouver Stock Exchange symbol*]

NCT .... Northern Cultural Trust [*South Australia*]

NCT .... Number Connection Test

NcTA .... Edgecombe County Memorial Library, Tarboro, NC [*Library symbol Library of Congress*] (LCLS)

NCTA .... National Cable Television Association (EA)

NCTA .... National Capital Transportation Agency [*Functions transferred to Washington Metropolitan Area Transit Authority*]

NCTA .... National Cattle Theft Act

NCTA .... National Ceramic Teachers Association (EA)

NCTA .... National Child Transport Association (NTPA)

NCTA .... National Christmas Tree Association (EA)

NCTA .... National Council for Technological Awards [*British*]

NCTA .... National Council for the Traditional Arts (EA)

NCTA .... Navajo Code Talkers Association (EA)

NCTA .... North Country Trail Association (EA)

NcTaE .... Edgecombe County Technical Institute, Tarboro, NC [*Library symbol Library of Congress*] (LCLS)

NcTaH .... Edgecomb General Hospital Library, Tarboro, NC [*Library symbol*] [*Library of Congress*] (LCLS)

NCTAM .... National Committee for Theoretical and Applied Mechanics [*British*]

NCTAMS ...... Naval Computer and Telecommunications Area Master Station (DOMA)

NcTa-P .... Edgecombe County Memorial Library, Pinetops Branch, Pinetops, NC [*Library symbol Library of Congress*] (LCLS)

NcTayA .... Alexander County Public Library, Taylorsville, NC [*Library symbol Library of Congress*] (LCLS)

NCTC .... National Cancer Institute Tissue Culture [*Medium*]

NCTC .... National Catholic Theatre Conference (EA)

NCTC .... National Collection of Type Cultures [*British*]

NCTC .... Naval Communications Training Center

NCTC .... Naval Computer and Telecommunications Command (DOMA)

NCTC .... Naval Construction Training Center

NCTCA .... National Collegiate Track Coaches Association (EA)

NCTCA .... National Council of Teachers for Critical Analysis (AEBS)

NCTCP .... National Coalition of Title I/Chapter I Parents (EA)

NCTD .... National College of Teachers of the Deaf [*British*]

NCTE .... National Council for Textile Education (EA)

NCTE .... National Council for Torah Education (EA)

NCTE .... National Council of Teachers of English

NCTE .... Network Channel Terminating Equipment [*Telecommunications*]

NCTE .... No-Cost Time Extension (MCD)

NCTE .... North Central Turfgrass Exposition [*Illinois Turfgrass Foundation*] (TSPED)

NCTEPS ...... National Commission on Teacher Education and Professional Standards [*Defunct*] (EA)

NC Term R... North Carolina Term Reports [*A publication*] (DLA)

NC Term Rep... North Carolina Term Reports [*A publication*] (DLA)

NCTET .... National Coalition for Technology Education and Training

NCTF .... National Check Traders Federation [*British*] (BI)

NCTF .... National Corporate Theatre Fund (EA)

NCTFC .... North Central Texas Film Cooperative [*Library network*]

NCTGA .... National Christmas Tree Growers Association [*Later, National Christmas Tree Association*] (EA)

NcTh .... Thomasville Public Library, Thomasville, NC [*Library symbol Library of Congress*] (LCLS)

NcThCH .... Community General Hospital Library, Thomasville, NC [*Library symbol*] [*Library of Congress*] (LCLS)

NcThDM .... Davidson Area Mental Health Center, Thomasville, NC [*Library symbol*] [*Library of Congress*] (LCLS)

NCTI .... National Cable Television Institute (EA)

NCTI .... National Consumer Testing Institute (BARN)

NCTI .... Noise Cancellation Tech [*NASDAQ symbol*] (TTSB)

NCTI .... Noise Cancellation Technologies, Inc. [*NASDAQ symbol*] (SAG)

NCTIP .... National Coalition of ESEA [*Elementary and Secondary Education Act*] Title I Parents (EA)

NCTIP .... National Committee on the Treatment of Intractable Pain (EA)

NCTJ .... National Council for the Training of Journalists [*British*]

NCTL .... National Commercial Temperance League [*British*] (BI)

NCTM .... National Council of Teachers of Mathematics (EA)

NCTO .... Naval Central Torpedo Office

NCTO .... Navy Clothing and Textile Supply Office

NCTP .... National Cryptologic Training Plan (MCD)

NCTPD .... National Council for Teacher-Centred Professional Development [*British*] (DBA)

NCTPI .... Nuveen Connecticut Premium Income Municipal Fund [*Associated Press*] (SAG)

NcTr .... Montgomery County Public Library, Troy, NC [*Library symbol Library of Congress*] (LCLS)

NCTR .... National Center for Telephone Research [*Louis Harris and Associates*] [*Commercial firm*] (EA)

NCTR .... National Center for Therapeutic Riding (EA)

NCTR .... National Center for Toxicological Research [*Department of Health and Human Services*] [*Jefferson, AR*]

NCTR .... National Council on Teacher Retirement (EA)

NCTR .... Naval Commercial Traffic Regulations

NCTR .... Noncooperative Target Recognition (MCD)

NCTR .... Nordic Council for Tax Research (EA)

NCTR .... Taylor's North Carolina Term Reports [*A publication*] (DLA)

NCTRC .... National Council for Therapeutic Recreation Certification (EA)

NcTrDC .... North Carolina Department of Corrections, Troy, NC [*Library symbol*] [*Library of Congress*] (LCLS)

NCT Rep ...... North Carolina Term Reports [*A publication*] (DLA)

NCTRF .... Navy Clothing and Textile Research Facility [*Natick, MA*]

NCTRH .... National Council for Therapy and Rehabilitation through Horticulture (EA)

NcTrM .... Montgomery Technical Institute, Troy, NC [*Library symbol Library of Congress*] (LCLS)

NCTRP .... National Cooperative Transit Research and Development Program [*TRB*] (TAG)

NCTRU .... Navy Clothing and Textile Research Unit (MCD)

NCTS .... National Center for Tourism Studies [*Australia*]

NCTS .... National Council of Technical Schools (EA)

NCTS .... Navy Civilian Technical Specialist (MCD)

NCTS .... Northeast Corridor Transportation System [*Boston to Washington high-speed transportation*]

NCTSI .... National Council of Technical Service Industries [*Later, Contract Services Association of America - CSA*]

NCTT .... National Committee on Tunneling Technology

NCTT .... Nuclear Certification Test Team (MCD)

NCTTA .... National Competitiveness Technology Transfer Act [*1989*] [*Department of Energy*]

NCTTF .... Northern Counties Textile Trades' Federation [*British*] (DCTA)

NCTU .... Northern Carpet Trades Union [*British*] (DCTA)

NCTV .... National Coalition on Television Violence (EA)

NCTV .... National College Television [*Cable-television system*]

NCTW .... National Conference of Tuberculosis Workers [*Later, CLAS*] (EA)

NCTWU .... National Cigar and Tobacco Workers' Union [*British*]

NCTWX .... Nicholas II Fund [*Mutual fund ticker symbol*] (SG)

NcTy .... Lanier Library Association, Inc., Tryon, NC [*Library symbol Library of Congress*] (LCLS)

NCtyB .... National City Bancorp [*Associated Press*] (SAG)

NCtyBn .... National City Bancshares [*Associated Press*] (SAG)

NcTyI .... Isothermal Community College, Polk Campus, Tryon, NC [*Library symbol Library of Congress*] (LCLS)

NCTYL .... National College for the Training of Youth Leaders [*British*] (BI)

NCu .... Cuba Library, Cuba, NY [*Library symbol Library of Congress*] (LCLS)

NCU .... National Communications Union [*British*]

NCU .... National Conference for Unification [*South Korea Political party*] (PPW)

NCU .... National Cutlery Union [*British*]

NCU .... National Cyclists' Union [*British*]

NCU .... Naval Communications Unit (IAA)

NCU .... Navigation Computer Unit

NCU .... Navigation Control and Display Unit (MCD)

NCU .... Network Configuration Utility [*Telecommunications*]

NCU .... Network Control Unit [*Computer science*]

NCU .... New Cinch Uranium [*Vancouver Stock Exchange symbol*]

NCU .... Nitrogen Control Unit (AAG)

NCU .... Nonconforming Use (ADA)

ncu .... North Carolina [*MARC country of publication code Library of Congress*] (LCCP)

NCU .... Nozzle Control Unit [*NASA*]

NCU .... Number Crunching Unit (MHDB)

NCU .... Nuveen California Premium Income Municipal (SPSG)

NCU .... Nuveen California Premium Income Municipal Fund [*AMEX symbol*] (SAG)

NCU .... Nuveen CA Prem Inc. Muni [*AMEX symbol*] (TTSB)
NCU .... Union College, Lincoln, NE [*OCLC symbol*] (OCLC)
NcU .... University of North Carolina, Chapel Hill, NC [*Library symbol Library of Congress*] (LCLS)
NCUA .... National Credit Union Administration
NCUA .... National Credit Union Association (NADA)
NCUAAE ..... National Council of Urban Administrators of Adult Education (OICC)
NcU-BPR ...... University of North Carolina, Bureau of Public Records, Collection and Research,Chapel Hill, NC [*Library symbol Library of Congress*] (LCLS)
NCUC .... National Commission on Unemployment Compensation (NADA)
NCUC .... North Carolina Utilities Commission Reports [*A publication*] (DLA)
NCUC .... Nuclear Chemistry Users Committee
NCUCIF ...... National Credit Union Share Insurance Fund (EBF)
NCU(E) .... National Communications Union, Engineering Group [*British*]
NCUEA .... National Center for Urban Ethnic Affairs (EA)
NCUEA .... National Council of Urban Education Associations (EA)
NCUES .... National Center for Urban Environmental Studies [*Defunct*] (EA)
NCUF .... National Computer Users Forum [*National Computing Center*] (PDAA)
NCUG .... National Centrex Users Group (CIST)
NCUG .... Nevada COBOL [*Common Business-Oriented Language*] Users Group [*Defunct*] (EA)
NCUGAE ...... National Computer User Group in Agricultural Education (NITA)
NcU-H .... University of North Carolina, Division of Health Affairs, Chapel Hill, NC [*Library symbol Library of Congress*] (LCLS)
NCUI .... National Center for Urban and Industrial Health [*Public Health Service*]
NcU-IG .... University of North Carolina, Institute of Government Library, Chapel Hill, NC [*Library symbol Library of Congress*] (LCLS)
NCuL .... Cuba Library, Cuba, NY [*Library symbol*] [*Library of Congress*] (LCLS)
NcU-L .... University of North Carolina, Law Library, Chapel Hill, NC [*Library symbol Library of Congress*] (LCLS)
NcU-LS .... University of North Carolina at Chapel Hill, Library School, Chapel Hill, NC [*Library symbol Library of Congress*] (LCLS)
NCUMA .... National Credit Union Management Association (EA)
NCUMC .... National Council for the Unmarried Mother and Her Child [*British*] (ILCA)
NcU-MS .... University of North Carolina, Institute of Marine Sciences, Morehead City, NC [*Library symbol Library of Congress*] (LCLS)
NCUP .... National Conference of University Professors (AIE)
NCUP .... No Commission until Paid
NCUPI .... National Coalition for Universities in the Public Interest [*Defunct*] (EA)
NCUPM .... National Council of United Presbyterian Men (EA)
NcU-Pop ...... University of North Carolina, Carolina Population Center, Technical Information Service, Chapel Hill, NC [*Library symbol Library of Congress*] (LCLS)
NCUPRSE .... National Consortium of Universities Preparing Rural Special Educators [*Defunct*] (EA)
NCUR .... National Committee for Utilities Radio (MCD)
NCUR .... National Conferences on Undergraduate Research [*An association*]
NCURA .... National Council of University Research Administrators (EA)
NCUSA .... Navy Club of the United States of America (EA)
NCUSAA ...... Navy Club of the United States of America Auxiliary (EA)
NCUSAR ...... National Council on US-Arab Relations (EA)
NCUSCR ...... National Committee on United States-China Relations (EA)
NCUSCT .... National Council for US-China Trade [*Later, USCBC*] (EA)
NCUSIF .... National Credit Union Share Insurance Fund
NCUSIOGT ... National Council of the United States, International Organization of Good Templars (EA)
NCUTLO .... National Committee on Uniform Traffic Laws and Ordinances (EA)
NCUUA .... National Council for Universal and Unconditional Amnesty [*For Vietnam-War resisters*] [*Defunct*] (EA)
NCV .... Navigation Computer Unit
NCV .... Nerve Conduction Velocity [*Electrophysiology*]
NCV .... Net Calorific Value (PDAA)
NCV .... No Commercial Value [*Business term*]
NCV .... No Core Value [*Business term*]
NCV .... No Customs Value (DS)
NCV .... Non-Cholera Vibrios [*Microbiology*]
NCV .... Normalized Critical View
NCVA .... National Center for Voluntary Action [*Later, NVC*]
NcVal .... Valdese Public Library, Valdese, NC [*Library symbol Library of Congress*] (LCLS)
NcValH .... Valdese General Hospital, Valdese, NC [*Library symbol*] [*Library of Congress*] (LCLS)
NCVC .... National Catholic Vocation Council [*Defunct*] (EA)
NCVC .... National Congress on Volunteerism and Citizenship [*Bicentennial event, 1976*]
NCVE .... National Council on Vocational Education [*Department of Education Washington, DC*] (EGAO)
NCVECS .... National Center for Vehicle Emissions Control and Safety [*Colorado State University*]
NCVHS .... National Committee on Vital and Health Statistics [*Department of Health and Human Services*] (GFGA)
NCVL .... Northeast College Volleyball League (PSS)
NCVO .... National Council for Voluntary Organisations [*British*] (ILCA)
NCVOTE .... National Center for Vocational, Occupational, and Technical Education [*Office of Education*]
NCVP .... Natural Circulation Verification Program [*Nuclear energy*] (NRCH)
NCVP .... Noncapsid Viral Protein [*Biochemistry*]
NCVQ .... National Council for Vocational Qualifications [*British*]
NCVR .... National Conference of Vicars for Religious (EA)

NCVS .... National Credential Verification Service (MCD)
NCVS .... National Crime Victimization Survey [*Department of Justice*] (ECON)
NCVS .... Nerve Conduction Velocity Studies [*Medicine*] (MEDA)
NCW .... National Council of Women of Great Britain (BI)
NCW .... National Council of Women of the United States (EA)
NCW .... Newberry College, Newberry, SC [*OCLC symbol*] (OCLC)
NCW .... Nose Cone Warhead [*Aviation*] (NATG)
NCW .... Not Complied With [*Military*]
NcW .... Wilmington Public Library, Wilmington, NC [*Library symbol Library of Congress*] (LCLS)
NcWa .... George H. and Laura E. Brown Library, Washington, NC [*Library symbol Library of Congress*] (LCLS)
NCWA .... National Candy Wholesalers Association (EA)
NCWA .... National Children's Wear Association [*British*] (EAIO)
NCWA .... NATO Civil Wartime Agency (NATG)
NCWA .... Newsagency Council of Western Australia
NCWA .... Northeast College Wrestling Association (PSS)
NcWaB .... Beaufort County Technical Institute, Washington, NC [*Library symbol Library of Congress*] (LCLS)
NcWaBHM ... Beaufort, Hyde, Martin Regional Library, Washington, NC [*Library symbol Library of Congress*] (LCLS)
NcWad .... Anson County Library, Wadesboro, NC [*Library symbol Library of Congress*] (LCLS)
NcWadAS .... Anson County Senior High School, Medial Center, Wadesboro, NC [*Library symbol*] [*Library of Congress*] (LCLS)
NcWal .... Thelma Dingus Bryant Library, Wallace, NC [*Library symbol Library of Congress*] (LCLS)
NCWAO .... National Council of World Affairs Organizations (EA)
NcWarW ...... Warren County Memorial Library, Warrenton, NC [*Library symbol Library of Congress*] (LCLS)
NCWAS .... National Coal Workers Autopsy Study
NcWaw .... Warsaw Public Library, Warsaw, NC [*Library symbol Library of Congress*] (LCLS)
NcWayH ...... Haywood County Public Library, Waynesville, NC [*Library symbol Library of Congress*] (LCLS)
NcWayH-C ... Haywood County Public Library, Canton Branch, Canton, NC [*Library symbol Library of Congress*] (LCLS)
NCWBA .... National Conference of Women's Bar Associations (EA)
NCWC .... National Carwash Council
NCWC .... National Catholic Welfare Conference [*Later, USCC*] (EA)
NCWC .... National Catholic Welfare Conference News Service (NTCM)
NCWC .... National Council of Women Chiropractors (EA)
NCWC .... National Council of Women of Canada
NcWc .... Walnut Cove Public Library, Walnut Cove, NC [*Library symbol Library of Congress*] (LCLS)
NcWC .... Wilmington Public Library, College Square Branch, Wilmington, NC [*Library symbol*] [*Library of Congress*] (LCLS)
NcWCF .... Cape Fear Technical Institute, Wilmington, NC [*Library symbol Library of Congress*] (LCLS)
NcWcL .... Walnut Cove Public Library, Walnut Cove, NC [*Library symbol*] [*Library of Congress*] (LCLS)
NCWD .... National Coalition for Women in Defense (EA)
NcWea .... Bess Tilson Sprinkle Memorial Library, Weaverville, NC [*Library symbol Library of Congress*] (LCLS)
NcWel .... Weldon Memorial Library, Weldon, NC [*Library symbol Library of Congress*] (LCLS)
NcWelc .... North Davidson Public Library, Welcome, NC [*Library symbol Library of Congress*] (LCLS)
NcWelH .... Halifax County Technical Institute, Weldon, NC [*Library symbol Library of Congress*] (LCLS)
NcWeR .... Rockingham Community College, Wentworth, NC [*Library symbol Library of Congress*] (LCLS)
NCWFC .... National Council of Women of Free Czechoslovakia (EA)
NCWFD .... National Committee for World Food Day [*Later, USNCWFD*] (EA)
NcWfSB .... Southeastern Baptist Theological Seminary, Wake Forest, NC [*Library symbol Library of Congress*] (LCLS)
NCWGA .... Natural Colored Wool Growers Association (EA)
NCWGB .... National Council of Women of Great Britain (DI)
NcWGE .... General Electric Co., WMD Technical Library, Wilmington, NC [*Library symbol Library of Congress*] (LCLS)
NCWGE .... National Coalition for Women and Girls in Education (EA)
NcWhC .... Columbus County Public Library, Whiteville, NC [*Library symbol Library of Congress*] (LCLS)
NcWHE .... Wilmington Area Health Education Center Medical Library, Wilmington, NC [*Library symbol*] [*Library of Congress*] (LCLS)
NcWhS .... Southeastern Community College, Whiteville, NC [*Library symbol Library of Congress*] (LCLS)
NcWil .... Wilson County Public Library, Wilson, NC [*Library symbol Library of Congress*] (LCLS)
NcWilA .... Atlantic Christian College, Wilson, NC [*Library symbol Library of Congress*] (LCLS)
NcWilB .... Beddingfield High School Library, Wilson, NC [*Library symbol*] [*Library of Congress*] (LCLS)
NcWilC .... Carolina Discipliana Library, Wilson, NC [*Library symbol Library of Congress*] (LCLS)
NcWilE .... North Carolina Department of Human Resources, Eastern North Carolina School for the Deaf, Wilson, NC [*Library symbol Library of Congress*] (LCLS)
NcWilF .... Fike High School Library, Wilson, NC [*Library symbol*] [*Library of Congress*] (LCLS)
NcWilH .... Wilson Memorial Hospital, Wilson, NC [*Library symbol*] [*Library of Congress*] (LCLS)
NcWilHS ...... Hunt High School Library, Wilson, NC [*Library symbol*] [*Library of Congress*] (LCLS)

NcWill .... Martin Memorial Library, Williamston, NC [*Library symbol Library of Congress*] (LCLS)
NcWilIM ...... Martin Technical Institute, Williamston, NC [*Library symbol Library of Congress*] (LCLS)
NcWilW .... Wilson County Technical Institute, Wilson, NC [*Library symbol Library of Congress*] (LCLS)
NcWin .... Wingate College, Wingate, NC [*Library symbol Library of Congress*] (LCLS)
NcWind .... Lawrence Memorial Library, Windsor, NC [*Library symbol Library of Congress*] (LCLS)
NcWintA ...... Albermarle Regional Library, Winton, NC [*Library symbol Library of Congress*] (LCLS)
NCWIS .... New Computerized World Information Service [*Information service or system*] (IID)
NcWiW .... Wilkes Community College, Wilkesboro, NC [*Library symbol Library of Congress*] (LCLS)
NcWj .... Ashe County Public Library, West Jefferson, NC [*Library symbol Library of Congress*] (LCLS)
NCWM .... National Conference on Weights and Measures (EA)
NCWM .... National Congress of Women in Music (EA)
NcWMM ...... Miller-Motte Business College, Wilmington, NC [*Library symbol*] [*Library of Congress*] (LCLS)
NcWN .... New Hanover County Public Library, Wilmington, NC [*Library symbol Library of Congress*] (LCLS)
NcWNC .... New Hanover County Public Library, Carolina Beach Branch Library, Carolina Beach, NC [*Library symbol*] [*Library of Congress*] (LCLS)
NCWNSW .... National Council of Women of New South Wales [*Australia*]
NCWP .... National Communications Working Party [*Australia Political party*]
NCWP .... Near Coastal Waters Program (WPI)
NCWPA .... National Committee for Women in Public Administration (EA)
NCWPA .... National Council for the Welfare of Prisoners Abroad [*British*] (DI)
NCWPTF ...... National Council for a World Peace Tax Fund (EA)
NCWQ .... National Commission on Water Quality [*National Academy of Sciences*]
NCWQ .... National Council of Women of Queensland [*Australia*]
NCWR .... Nordic Council for Wildlife Research (EAIO)
NCWRU .... North Central Watershed Research Unit [*Department of Agriculture*] (GRD)
NcWs .... Forsyth County Public Library System, Winston-Salem, NC [*Library symbol Library of Congress*] (LCLS)
NCWS .... Non-Community Water System [*Environmental Protection Agency*]
NCWSA .... National Collegiate Water Ski Association (EA)
NcWsA .... North-West AHEC Library at Winston-Salem, Bowman-Gray School of Medicine, Winston-Salem, NC [*Library symbol*] [*Library of Congress*] (LCLS)
NcWsAT .... AT & Technologies, Inc., Winston-Salem, NC [*Library symbol*] [*Library of Congress*] (LCLS)
NcWsAT-R ... AT & T Technologies, Inc., Winston-Salem, NC [*Library symbol*] [*Library of Congress*] (LCLS)
NCWSBA ...... National Council of Wool Selling Brokers of Australia
NcWs-C .... Forsyth County Public Library, Clemmons Branch Library, Clemmons, NC [*Library symbol Library of Congress*] (LCLS)
NcWs-E .... Forsyth County Public Library, East Winston Branch, Winston-Salem, NC [*Library symbol Library of Congress*] (LCLS)
NcWsF .... Forsyth Technical Institute, Winston-Salem, NC [*Library symbol Library of Congress*] (LCLS)
NcWsFM ..... Forsyth-Stokes Area Mental Health Center, Winston-Salem, NC [*Library symbol*] [*Library of Congress*] (LCLS)
NcWs-K .... Forsyth County Public Library, Kernersville Branch Library, Kernersville, NC [*Library symbol Library of Congress*] (LCLS)
NcWsM .... Moravian Archives, Winston-Salem, NC [*Library symbol Library of Congress*] (LCLS)
NcWsMES ... Museum of Early Southern Decorative Arts, MESDA Library, Winston-Salem, NC [*Library symbol Library of Congress*] (LCLS)
NcWsMM ..... Moravian Music Foundation, Winston-Salem, NC [*Library symbol Library of Congress*] (LCLS)
NcWsN .... North Carolina School of the Arts, Winston-Salem, NC [*Library symbol Library of Congress*] (LCLS)
NcWs-R .... Forsyth County Public Library, Reynolda Manor Branch, Winston-Salem, NC [*Library symbol Library of Congress*] (LCLS)
NcWsR .... Reynolds Tobacco Co., Winston-Salem, NC [*Library symbol*] [*Library of Congress*] (LCLS)
NcWsRI .... Reynolds Industries, Corporate Library, Winston-Salem, NC [*Library symbol Library of Congress*] (LCLS)
NcWsR-M .... Reynolds Tobacco Co., Marketing Development Intelligence Center, Winston-Salem, NC [*Library symbol Library of Congress*] (LCLS)
NcWsR-R .... Reynolds Tobacco Co., Research and Development Technical Information Services, Winston-Salem, NC [*Library symbol Library of Congress*] (LCLS)
NcWs-RS ..... Forsyth County Public Library, Rural Hall/Stanleyville Branch Library, Rural Hall, NC [*Library symbol Library of Congress*] (LCLS)
NcWs-S .... Forsyth County Public Library, Southside Branch, Winston-Salem, NC [*Library symbol Library of Congress*] (LCLS)
NcWsS .... Salem College, Winston-Salem, NC [*Library symbol Library of Congress*] (LCLS)
NcWs-T .... Forsyth County Public Library, Thruway Branch, Winston-Salem, NC [*Library symbol*] [*Library of Congress*] (LCLS)
NcWsU .... Winston-Salem State University, Winston-Salem, NC [*Library symbol Library of Congress*] (LCLS)
NcWsW .... Wake Forest University, Winston-Salem, NC [*Library symbol Library of Congress*] (LCLS)
NcWsW-B .... Wake Forest University, Babcock Graduate School of Management, Winston-Salem, NC [*Library symbol Library of Congress*] (LCLS)

NcWsWE ...... Western Electric Co., Lexington Road Technical Library, Winston-Salem, NC [*Library symbol Library of Congress*] (LCLS)
NcWsWE-R ... Western Electric Co., Reynolda Road Technical Library, Winston-Salem, NC [*Library symbol Library of Congress*] (LCLS)
NcWsW-L ..... Wake Forest University, Law Library, Winston-Salem, NC [*Library symbol Library of Congress*] (LCLS)
NcWsW-M ... Wake Forest University, Bowman Gray School of Medicine, Wake Forest, NC [*Library symbol Library of Congress*] (LCLS)
NCWT .... National Council of Women of Tasmania [*Australia*]
NCWTF .... Naval Commander Western Task Force
NCWTM ...... National Council on Wholistic Therapeutics and Medicine [*Defunct*] (EA)
NCWU .... National Catholic Women's Union (EA)
NcWU .... University of North Carolina at Wilmington, Wilmington, NC [*Library symbol Library of Congress*] (LCLS)
NCWUS .... National Council of Women of the United States (WDAA)
NCWUSA ..... National Council of Women of the United States of America (DI)
NCWV .... National Council of Women of Victoria [*Australia*]
NCWW .... National Commission on Working Women (EA)
NCWWA ...... National Council of Women of Western Australia
NCX .... Corpus Christi, TX [*Location identifier FAA*] (FAAL)
NCX .... NCN Exploration & Development [*Vancouver Stock Exchange symbol*]
NCX .... North Carolina Central University, Durham, NC [*OCLC symbol*] (OCLC)
NCY .... Annecy [*France*] [*Airport symbol*] (OAG)
NcY .... Hyconeechee Regional Library, Yanceyville, NC [*Library symbol Library of Congress*] (LCLS)
NCY .... Nancy Aviation [*France ICAO designator*] (FAAC)
NCY .... National Collaboration for Youth (EA)
N-CY .... Natural-Colored Yellow [*Diamonds*]
NCY .... New Century Resources [*Vancouver Stock Exchange symbol*]
NCY .... North Central Yiddish (BJA)
NCY .... Yorktown, VA [*Location identifier FAA*] (FAAL)
NCYA .... National Catholic Youth Association [*British*] (BI)
NcYad .... Yadkin County Public Library, Yadkinville, NC [*Library symbol Library of Congress*] (LCLS)
NCYC .... National Catholic Youth Council
NCYC .... National Collection of Yeast Cultures [*AFRC Institute of Food Research*] [*British Information service or system*] (IID)
NCYC .... National Council of Yacht Clubs (EA)
N CYC BN ... Northern Cyclist Battalion [*British military*] (DMA)
NCYC CAT .... National Collection of Yeast Cultures Catalogue [*Norwich Laboratory*] [*Norfolk, England*] [*Information service or system*] [*A publication*] (IID)
NCYD .... National Center for Youth with Disabilities (EA)
NCYF .... National Crusaders Youth Federation (EA)
NCYFS .... National Children and Youth Fitness Study [*HHS*]
NcYG .... Gunn Memorial Public Library, Yanceyville, NC [*Library symbol Library of Congress*] (LCLS)
NCYI .... National Council of Young Israel (EA)
NCYL .... National Center for Youth Law (EA)
NcYo .... Youngsville Public Library, Youngsville, NC [*Library symbol Library of Congress*] (LCLS)
NCYOF .... National CYO [*Catholic Youth Organizations*] Federation (EA)
NCYP .... National Conference of Yeshiva Principals (EA)
NCYRE .... National Council for Year-Round Education [*Later, NAYRE*] (EA)
NCYSI .... National Clearinghouse for Youth Sports Information [*Operated by the National Alliance for Youth Sports*] (PAZ)
NCYSP .... National Committee on Youth Suicide Prevention (EA)
NCYWA ...... Nordic Child and Youth Welfare Alliance (EA)
NCz .... New Cruzado [*Monetary unit*] [*Brazil*] (BARN)
NcZG .... Glaxo, Inc., Zebulon, NC [*Library symbol*] [*Library of Congress*] (LCLS)
ND .... Aerospatiale [*Societe Nationale Industrielle Aerospatiale*] [*France ICAO aircraft manufacturer identifier*] (ICAO)
ND .... Diploma in Naturopathy [*British*]
ND .... Doctor of Naturopathic Medicine (PGP)
ND .... Doctor of Naturopathy
ND .... Doctor of Nursing (PGP)
ND .... Named (ROG)
ND .... Narrowband Distributive Services [*Telecommunications*]
ND .... NASA [*National Aeronautics and Space Administration*] Document
ND .... Nasal Deformity (DAVI)
ND .... National Debt
ND .... National Diploma [*Academic degree*] (AIE)
ND .... Native Defect (AAEL)
ND .... Natural Death [*Medicine*]
ND .... Natural Draught
ND .... Naval Dispensary
ND .... Naval Distillate Fuel (NVT)
ND .... Naval District
ND .... Naval Draftsman (ROG)
ND .... Navigation Display (MCD)
ND .... Navy Department
N-D .... N-Dimensional (MCD)
ND .... Nea Demokratia [*New Democracy*] [*Greece*] [*Political party*] (PPE)
N/D .... Need Date (MCD)
ND .... Negative Declaration (NRCH)
ND .... Negatives and Deposition (DGA)
Nd .... Neodymium [*Chemical element*]
ND .... Neonatal Death [*Medicine*] (MAE)
ND .... Neoplastic Disease [*Medicine*]
ND .... Nervous Debility [*Medicine*]
ND .... Net Debt

ND	Network Directorate (SSD)
ND	Neurologic Deficit [Medicine]
ND	Neuropathic Doctor (BARN)
ND	Neurotic Depression [Psychiatry]
ND	Neutral Density [Photography]
ND	Neutral Density Filter (WDMC)
ND	Neutral-Drive [Automotive engineering]
ND	Neutron Diffraction (MCD)
ND	Newcastle Disease [Virus] [Also, NDV]
ND	New Dawn [An association] (EA)
ND	New Deal (DAS)
ND	New Deck [On ships]
ND	New Democracy [European political movement] (ECON)
ND	New Developments Research Branch [Bureau of Naval Personnel] [Washington, DC]
ND	New Directions [Later, Democratic Alternatives - DA] (EA)
ND	New Donor (AAEL)
ND	New Dramatists (EA)
ND	New Drug
ND	New Drugs [A publication]
Nd................	Newfoundland Reports [A publication] (DLA)
ND	News Director (NTCM)
ND	Newsletters Directory [Later, NIP] [A publication]
ND	Next Day [Stock exchange term] (SPSG)
ND	Next Day's Delivery
ND	Nickajack Dam [TVA]
ND	Nippondenso Co. [Toyota Motor Corp.]
ND	No Data
ND	No Date [of publication]
nd	No Date (VRA)
ND	No Decision [Sports]
ND	Node Dissection [Medicine]
N/D	No Defects
ND	No Detect
ND	No Discount [Business term] (DS)
ND	No Disease [Medicine]
ND	No Drawing [Engineering]
ND	Nondelay [Military]
ND	Nondelivery [Shipping]
ND	Non-Denominational
ND	Non-Descript (WDMC)
N/D	Nondestructive
ND	Nondetectable [Medicine] (DB)
ND	Nondeterministic (IAA)
ND	Nondiabetic [Medicine]
ND	Nondirectional (IAA)
ND	Nondirectional Antenna
ND	Nondirectional Microphone (WDMC)
ND	Nondirector (IAA)
ND	Nondisabling [Medicine]
ND	Non Disponible [Not Available] [French]
N/D	Non-Drinker [Medicine]
ND	Nonduty [Military]
ND	Nordair [ICAO designator] (AD)
ND	Nordair Ltd. [Canada ICAO designator] (OAG)
ND	Normal Delivery [Obstetrics]
ND	Normal Development [Pediatrics] (DAVI)
ND	North Dakota [Postal code]
Nd................	North Dakota State Library, Bismarck, ND [Library symbol Library of Congress] (LCLS)
ND	North Dakota Supreme Court Reports [1890-1953] [A publication] (DLA)
ND	Northern District (DLA)
ND	Nose Down [Aviation]
ND	Nose Drops [Pharmacy] (DAVI)
ND	Nostra Domina [Our Lady] [Latin]
ND	Not Dated [Banking, bibliography]
nd	Not Dated (EBF)
ND	Not Detected [or Detectable] [Medicine]
ND	Not Determined [Medicine]
ND	Not Diagnosed [Medicine]
ND	Not Directly (DGA)
ND	Not Done
ND	Nothing Doing [Amateur radio slang]
ND	Notre Dame Sisters (TOCD)
ND	Nouvelle Droite [New Right] [France] [Political party] (WDAA)
ND	Nuclear Device (AAG)
Nd................	Number of Dissimilar Matches
ND	Number of Document [Online database field identifier]
ND	Nursing Doctorate
ND	Ny Demokrati [New Democracy] [Sweden Political party] (EY)
ND	Romania [License plate code assigned to foreign diplomats in the US]
ND	University of Notre Dame [Indiana]
nd	Updated (VRA)
Nd2..............	Nord-Aviation 262 [Airplane code]
NDA	Bandanaira [Indonesia] [Airport symbol] (OAG)
NDA	Naphthalenedicarboxaldehyde [Organic chemistry]
NDA	National Dairy Association (NADA)
NDA	National Dairymen's Association, Inc. [British] (BI)
NDA	National Dance Association (EA)
NDA	National Defense Act
NDA	National Defense Area (AABC)
NDA	National Democratic Alliance [Sierra Leone] [Political party] (EY)
NDA	National Democratic Alliance [Sudan] [Political party]

NDA	National Dental Association (EA)
NDA	National Denturist Association (EA)
NDA	National Diploma in Agriculture [British]
NDA	National Dome Association [Later, NDC] (EA)
NDA	National Door Association [Defunct]
NDA	National Drilling Association (NTPA)
NDA	NAUI [National Association of Underwater Instructors] Diving Association (EA)
NDA	Naval Discipline Act [British military] (DMA)
NDA	Neutral Detector Assembly
NDA	Nevada (ROG)
NDA	New Desk Accessories [Utility program] [Apple Computers, Inc.] [Computer science]
NDA	New Drug Application [FDA]
NDA	Newspaper Design Award (DGA)
NDA	Ninos de las Americas [Children of the Americas] (EAIO)
NDA	No Data Available [Computer science]
NDA	No Demonstrable Antibody [Medicine] (MAE)
NDA	No Detectable Activity
NDA	No Diagnosis of Anything
NDA	Nonadecanoic Acid [Organic chemistry]
NDA	Nondestructive Assay
NDA	Nondimensional Analysis
NDA	Non-Disclosure Agreement (WDMC)
NDA	Nonresonant Deflection Amplifier
NDA	Nordair Ltd. [Toronto Stock Exchange symbol]
NDA	Northern Airways, Inc. [ICAO designator] (FAAC)
NDA	Nuclear Device Association (AAG)
NDA	[The] Nuzi Dialect of Akkadian [A publication] (BJA)
NDAA	National Dental Assistants Association (EA)
NDAA	National District Attorneys Association (EA)
NDAAC	Navy Drug and Alcohol Advisory Council (DNAB)
NDA & LB	Naval District Affairs and Logistics Branch
NDAB	Numerical Data Advisory Board [National Academy of Sciences] [Information service or system] (IID)
NDAC	National Defense Advisory Commission [World War II]
NDAC	National Defense Advisory Committee (NADA)
NDAC	NATO Data-Buoy System [National Oceanic and Atmospheric Administration]
NDAC	No Data Accepted [Computer science] (IAA)
NDAC	North Dakota Administrative Code [A publication] (AAGC)
NDAC	North Dakota Agricultural College
NDAC	Nuclear Defense Affairs Committee [NATO]
NDACP	Navy Drug Abuse Control Program (DNAB)
NDACS	Navy Drug Abuse Counselor School (DNAB)
NDACS	Network Diagnostic and Control Systems (ADA)
NDACSS	Navy Department Advisory Committee on Structural Steel
ND Admin Code...	North Dakota Administrative Code [A publication] (DLA)
NDAFA	National Directory of Accounting Firms and Accountants [A publication]
ND Agr E	National Diploma in Agricultural Engineering [British]
N DAK	North Dakota (AAG)
N Dak	North Dakota Reports [A publication] (DLA)
ND Ala	United States District Court for the Northern District of Alabama (DLA)
NDAM	New Disk Access Method [Computer science] (MHDI)
NDANG	North Dakota Air National Guard (MUSM)
NDAP	Nationalsozialistische Deutsche Arbeiterpartei [National Socialist German Workers' Party, 1919-45] [Political party] (PPW)
NDAPTA	National Drivers Association for the Prevention of Traffic Accidents [Defunct] (EA)
NDARC	National Drug and Alcohol Research Center [University of New South Wales] [Australia]
NDAT	Nondestructible Aiming Target
NDAT	Non-Destructive Assay Technique [Military] (PDAA)
NData	National Data Corp. [Associated Press] (SAG)
NDATUS	National Drug and Alcohol Treatment Utilization Survey [Department of Health and Human Services] (GFGA)
NDB	National Discount Brokers Group [NYSE symbol] [Formerly, Sherwood Group] (SG)
NDB	Nautical Directional Beacon (IAA)
NDB	Naval Disciplinary Barracks
NDB	Navy Department Bulletin [A publication]
NDB	Net Debit Balance
NDB	Net Decision Benefit (NUCP)
NDB	Nondirectional Beacon (AFM)
NDB	Nouadhibou [Mauritania] [Airport symbol] (OAG)
NDB	Nuclear Depth Bomb (NVT)
NDB	Numeric Data Base [INPADOC] [Computer science]
NDBA	National Data Base on Aging (EDAC)
NDBA	National Deaf Bowling Association (EA)
NDBA	New Directions in Biblical Archaeology [A publication] (BJA)
NDBA	Nitrosodibutylamine [Organic chemistry]
NDBB	North Dakota Bar Brief [A publication] (DLA)
NdBC	Bismarck Junior College, Bismarck, ND [Library symbol Library of Congress] (LCLS)
NDBC	National Data Buoy Center [National Oceanic and Atmospheric Administration Also, an information service or system] (IID)
NDBC	National Day of Bread Committee [Defunct] (EA)
NDBC	National Dry Bean Council (EA)
NDBC	National Duckpin Bowling Congress (EA)
NDBCA	Navy Department Board of Contract Appeals
NDBDM	Navy Department Board of Decorations and Medals (DNAB)
NDBDP	National Data Buoy Development Project [Later, NDBO] [Coast Guard] (MSC)

NdBH .... Bismarck Hospital, School of Nursing Library, Bismarck, ND [*Library symbol Library of Congress*] (LCLS)

NdBHD .... North Dakota State Health Department, Bismarck, ND [*Library symbol Library of Congress*] (LCLS)

NdBHwy ...... North Dakota State Highway Department, Bismarck, ND [*Library symbol Library of Congress*] (LCLS)

NDBI .... National Dairymen's Benevolent Institution, Inc. [*British*] (BI)

NDBL .... National Deaf-Blind League [*British*] (EAIO)

NDBLO .... Not to Descend Below [*Aviation*] (FAAC)

NdBM .... Mary College, Bismarck, ND [*Library symbol Library of Congress*] (LCLS)

NDBMS .... Network Database Management System

NDBO .... National Data Buoy Office [*Marine science*] (OSRA)

NDBO .... NOAA [*National Oceanic and Atmospheric Administration*] Data Buoy Office [*or Operation*] (IID)

NdBoU .... North Dakota State University, Bottineau Branch, Bottineau, ND [*Library symbol Library of Congress*] (LCLS)

NDBP .... National Data Buoy Program [*National Oceanic and Atmospheric Administration*] (GFGA)

NdBPI .... North Dakota State Department of Public Instruction, Bismarck, ND [*Library symbol Library of Congress*] (LCLS)

NDBPSA ...... Non-Denominational Bible Prophecy Study Association (EA)

NdBPW .... North Dakota State Public Welfare Board, Bismarck, ND [*Library symbol Library of Congress*] (LCLS)

NdBQ .... Quain and Ramstad Clinic, Bismarck, ND [*Library symbol Library of Congress*] (LCLS)

NDBS .... National Data Buoy System

NDBS .... Naval Despatch Boat Service

NDBULCUMED... Navy Department Bulletins, Cumulative Editions [*A publication*]

NdBV .... Bismarck [*Veterans Memorial*] Public Library, Bismarck, ND [*Library symbol Library of Congress*] (LCLS)

NDC .... Air Nordic SWE Aviation, AB [*Sweden*] [*FAA designator*] (FAAC)

NDC .... Naphthalene Dicarboxylate [*Organic chemistry*]

NDC .... Natick Development Center [*Massachusetts*] [*Army*]

NDC .... National Dairy Council (EA)

NDC .... National Data Communication

NDC .... National Data Corp. [*NYSE symbol*] (SPSG)

NDC .... National Debt Commission [*Australia*]

NDC .... National Defence College [*British*]

NDC .... National Defence Committee [*Ghana*] [*Political party*] (PPW)

NDC .... National Defence Company [*British military*] (DMA)

NDC .... National Defence Contribution [*British*]

NDC .... National Defence Corps [*British*]

NDC .... National Defence College [*Australia*]

NDC .... National Defense Corps (NADA)

NDC .... National Defense Council (KSC)

NDC .... National Democratic Club (EA)

NDC .... National Democratic Congress [*Ghana*] [*Political party*] (ECON)

NDC .... National Democratic Congress [*Grenada*] [*Political party*] (EY)

NDC .... National Design Council [*Canada*]

NDC .... National DeSoto Club (EA)

NDC .... National Development Corp. [*Dominica*] (EY)

NDC .... National Development Council (EA)

NDC .... National Directory of Churches, Synagogues, and Other Houses of Worship [*A publication*]

NDC .... National Disaster Coalition

NDC .... National Distributing Co., Inc. (EFIS)

NDC .... National Diving Council

NDC .... National Dome Council (EA)

NDC .... National Drug Code [*FDA*]

NDC .... National Duckling Council [*Defunct*] (EA)

NDC .... Natl Data [*NYSE symbol*] (TTSB)

NDC .... NATO Defense College [*Also, NADC, NADEFCOL*] (NATG)

NDC .... Natural Distribution Certificate (WDAA)

NDC .... Naval Data Center

NDC .... Naval Dental Clinic

NDC .... Naval Doctrine Command (COE)

NDC .... Navigation Display and Computer (MCD)

NDC .... Negative Differential Conductivity (OA)

NDC .... Network Data Control (MCD)

NDC .... Network Diagnostic Control

NDC .... Neurologic Disease Control

NDC .... New Democratic Coalition

NDC .... New Die Cast [*Honda Motor Co. Ltd.*]

NDC .... New Directions in Creativity Program (EDAC)

NDC .... New Dramatists Committee [*Later, ND*] (EA)

NDC .... Nippon Decimal Classification [*Library science*]

NDC .... No Date Club [*Brooklyn girls - no dates for the duration*] [*World War II*]

NDC .... No Direct Charge

NDC .... Noise Dose Count (IAA)

NDC .... Nondifferentiated Cell [*Medicine*] (DMAA)

NDC .... Non-Double-Couple [*Seismology*]

NDC .... NORAD Direction Center [*Military*]

NDC .... Normalized Device Coordinates [*Computer science*]

NDC .... Northern Development Co. [*British*] (ECON)

NDC .... Northwest Drama Conference (EA)

NDC .... Notice of Drawing Change [*Navy*] (DNAB)

NDC .... Notre Dame College [*Missouri, New Hampshire, Ohio*]

NDC .... Notre Dame College, Manchester, NH [*Inactive*] [*OCLC symbol*] (OCLC)

NDC .... Noyes Data Corp.

NDC .... Nuclear Data Committee (NRCH)

NDC .... Nuclear Design and Construction [*British*]

NDC .... Nuclear Design Calculations [*Program*]

NDCA .... Naphthalenedicarboxylic Acid [*Organic chemistry*]

NDCA .... National Dance Council of America (EA)

NDCA .... National Deaf Children's Association [*British*]

NDCA .... National Drilling Contractors Association (EA)

NDCA .... Nuclear Development Corp. of America

NDCAC .... North Dakota College Athletic Conference (PSS)

ND Cal .... United States District Court for the Northern District of California (DLA)

NdCan .... Cando Public Library, Cando, ND [*Library symbol Library of Congress*] (LCLS)

NDCC .... National Defense Cadet Corps

NDCC .... Navy Department Corrosion Committee

NDCC .... Nondirectional Cross-Country (MCD)

NDCC .... North Dakota Century Code [*A publication*]

NDCCC .... National Defense Communications Control Center (MCD)

NDCD .... National Drug Code Directory [*FDA*] [*A publication*]

NDCDAR .... National Defense Committee of the Daughters of the American Revolution (EA)

NDCEE .... National Defense Center for Environmental Excellence [*DoD*] (RDA)

ND Cent Code... North Dakota Century Code [*A publication*] (DLA)

NDCF .... National Defense Council Foundation (EA)

NDCG .... Nursing Development Conference Group (DMAA)

NdCo .... Cooperstown Public Library, Cooperstown, ND [*Library symbol Library of Congress*] (LCLS)

NDColl .... National Defence College [*British*]

NDCP .... Navy Decision Coordinating Paper

NDCP .... Navy Development Concept Paper (CAAL)

NDC-PS .... No Drawing Change Project Slip

NdCr .... Divide County Library, Crosby, ND [*Library symbol Library of Congress*] (LCLS)

NDCS .... National Deaf Children's Society [*British*] (BI)

NDCT .... Natural Draft Cooling Tower [*Nuclear energy*] (NRCH)

NDCT .... Non-Secure Data Communication Terminal (DWSG)

NDD .... Duke University Library, Durham, NC [*OCLC symbol*] (OCLC)

NDd .... Dundee Library, Dundee, NY [*Library symbol Library of Congress*] (LCLS)

NDD .... National Diploma in Dairying [*British*]

NDD .... National Diploma in Design [*British*]

NDD .... Navigation and Direction Division [*British military*] (DMA)

NDD .... Negotiation Decision Document [*Environmental Protection Agency*] (EPA)

NDD .... Net Defence Department [*Navy British*]

NDD .... New Democratic Dimensions (EA)

NDD .... Nitro(dimethyl)dihydrobenzofuran [*Organic chemistry*]

NDD .... No Dialysis Days [*Nephrology*] (DAVI)

NDD .... Nondeferred Development (MCD)

NDD .... Norton Disk Doctor [*Computer science*]

NDD .... Novo Redondo [*Angola*] [*Airport symbol*] (AD)

NDD .... Nuclear Detection Device (MCD)

NDD .... Sumbe [*Angola*] [*Airport symbol*] (OAG)

NDd .... Woman's Study Club & Library, Dundee, NY [*Library symbol*] [*Library of Congress*] (LCLS)

NDD & RF ..... Naval Dry Dock and Repair Facility

NDDC .... National Defeat Dukakis Campaign (EA)

NDDC .... Navy Department Duty Chaplain (DNAB)

NDDC .... NORAD Division Direction Center [*Military*] (AABC)

NdDe .... Devils Lake Carnegie Library, Devils Lake, ND [*Library symbol Library of Congress*] (LCLS)

NdDeH .... Mercy Hospital, Devils Lake, ND [*Library symbol Library of Congress*] (LCLS)

NDDEIC .... National Digestive Diseases Education and Information Clearinghouse [*Public Health Service*] [*Later, NDDIC*] (IID)

NdDeL .... Lake Region Junior College, Devils Lake, ND [*Library symbol Library of Congress*] (LCLS)

NDDG .... National Diabetes Data Group [*British*]

NdDi .... Dickinson Public Library, Dickinson, ND [*Library symbol Library of Congress*] (LCLS)

NDDIC .... National Digestive Diseases Information Clearinghouse (EA)

NdDiS .... Dickinson State College, Dickinson, ND [*Library symbol Library of Congress*] (LCLS)

NdDiStJ .... Saint Joseph Hospital, Dickinson, ND [*Library symbol Library of Congress*] (LCLS)

NDDN .... National Dry Deposition Network (GNE)

NDDO .... Neglect of Diatomic Differential Overlap [*Quantum mechanics*]

NDDP .... NATO Defense Data Program (AABC)

NDDS .... National Disability Data System [*Social Security Administration*] (GFGA)

NDDS .... Nuclear Detonation Detection System (DOMA)

NDE .... IndyMac Mortgage Holdings [*NYSE symbol*] [*Formerly, INMC Mortgage Holdings*]

NDE .... Mandera [*Kenya*] [*Airport symbol*] (OAG)

NDE .... National Defense Education

NDE .... National Defense Emergency [*Headquarters*] (MCD)

NDE .... National Dinghy Exhibition [*British*]

NDE .... Navy Department Establishments [*British*]

NDE .... N-Demethylencainide [*Organic chemistry*]

NDE .... Near-Death Experience

NDE .... Nevada Desert Experience (EA)

NDE .... No Date Established

NDE .... No Delay Expected

NDE .... Nondestructive Evaluation

NDE .... Nondestructive Examination [*Nuclear energy*] (NRCH)

NDE .... Nondiabetic Extremity [*Medicine*] (DMAA)

NDE .... Nonlinear Differential Equations

NDE .... Notodden [*Norway*] [*Airport symbol*] (AD)

NDEA	National Defense Education Act [1958]
NDEA	National Defense Emergency Authorization
NDEA	National Display Equipment Association [British] (BI)
NDEA	Nitrosodiethylamine [Organic chemistry]
nDEA	No Deviation of Electrical Axis [On electrocardiogram] [Cardiology] (DAVI)
N de Aqi	Nicholas de Aquila [Flourished, 1197-1217] [Authority cited in pre-1607 legal work] (DSA)
NDEC	NDE Environmental Corp. [NASDAQ symbol] (NQ)
NDEI	National Defense Education Institute
NDEITA	National Dance-Exercise Instructor's Training Association (EA)
NDEL	Non-Destructive Evaluation Laboratory [NASA]
NDELA	Nitrosodiethanolamine [Also, NDEOL] [Organic chemistry]
NdEIN	State Normal and Industrial School, Ellendale, ND [Library symbol Library of Congress Obsolete] (LCLS)
NdEIT	Trinity Bible Institute, Ellendale, ND [Library symbol Library of Congress] (LCLS)
NDemP	National Democratic Party [British]
NDEOL	Nitrosodiethanolamine [Also, NDELA] [Organic chemistry]
NDEP	Nevada Division of Environmental Protection
NDER	National Defense Executive Reserve
NDERR	National Defense Executive Reserve Roster [of the CSC]
NDERWF	Navy Department Employees Recreation and Welfare Fund (MCD)
NDES	Normal Digital Echo Suppressor [Telecommunications] (TEL)
NDETP	National Drug Education Training Program [HEW]
NDeUA	State University of New York, Agricultural and Technical College at Delhi, Delhi, NY [Library symbol Library of Congress] (LCLS)
NDEW	Nuclear Directed-Energy Weapon
NDEW	Nuclear-Driven Directed-Energy Weapon
NDex	Dexter Free Library, Dexter, NY [Library symbol Library of Congress] (LCLS)
NDEX	Newspaper Index [Bell & Howell Co.] [Database]
NDf	Dobbs Ferry Public Library, Dobbs Ferry, NY [Library symbol Library of Congress] (LCLS)
NdF	Fargo Public Library, Fargo, ND [Library symbol Library of Congress] (LCLS)
NDF	Nacelle Drag Efficiency [Factor] [Aerospace]
NDF	Nandi [Fiji] [Seismograph station code, US Geological Survey] (SEIS)
NDF	National Democratic Front [Pakistan] [Political party] (FEA)
NDF	National Democratic Front [Philippines] [Political party] (FEA)
NDF	National Democratic Front [Myanmar] [Political party] (FEA)
NDF	National Democratic Front [Iran] [Political party] (PD)
NDF	National Democratic Front [Guyana] [Political party] (EY)
NDF	National Democratic Front [Yemen] [Political party] (PD)
NDF	National Diploma in Forestry [British]
NDF	National Dividend Foundation (EA)
NDF	National Drilling Federation [Later, IDF] (EA)
NDF	Naval Dairy Farm
NDF	Naval Defence Force [British military] (DMA)
NDF	Navy Distillate Fuel (DNAB)
NDF	Neutral Density Filter
NDF	Neutral Detergent Fiber [Food analysis]
NDF	New Democratic Forum (EA)
NDF	New Dimensions Foundation (EA)
NDF	New Dosage Form [Medicine] (MAE)
NDF	Nicolas-Durand-Favre [Disease] [Medicine] (DB)
NDF	Night Defense Fire (DNAB)
NDF	No Defect Found
NDF	No Diagnostic Findings [Medicine] (DMAA)
NDF	No Disease Found (DAVI)
NDF	Nondipole Field [Electromagnetism]
NDF	Nonlinear Distortion Factor [Telecommunications] (OA)
NDF	Nonrecursive Digital Filter [Navy] (IAA)
NDFA	National Dietary Foods Association [Later, NNFA] (EA)
NDFA	National Drama Festivals Association [British] (BI)
NdFA	North Dakota State University, Fargo, ND [Library symbol Library of Congress] (LCLS)
NdFC	Cass County Court House, Fargo, ND [Library symbol Library of Congress] (LCLS)
NDFC	National Days Fan Club (EA)
NdFD	Dakota Clinic, Fargo, ND [Library symbol Library of Congress] (LCLS)
NDFEA	Northwest Dried Fruit Export Association [Defunct] (EA)
nd filter	Neutral-Density Filter [Photography] (WDMC)
NDfL	Dobbs Ferry Public Library, Dobbs Ferry, NY [Library symbol] [Library of Congress] (LCLS)
NDFL	National Defense Foreign Language [Fellowship]
ND Fla	United States District Court for the Northern District of Florida (DLA)
NdFM	Masonic Grand Lodge Library, Fargo, ND [Library symbol Library of Congress] (LCLS)
NDfM	Mercy College, Dobbs Ferry, NY [Library symbol Library of Congress] (LCLS)
NdFMG	Masonic Grand Lodge, Fargo, ND [Library symbol] [Library of Congress] (LCLS)
NdFN	Neuropsychiatric Hospital, Fargo, ND [Library symbol Library of Congress] (LCLS)
NDFS	Non-Dwelling Floor Space (SAA)
NDfS	Stauffer Chemical Co., Eastern Research Center, Dobbs Ferry, NY [Library symbol Library of Congress] (LCLS)
NdFStJ	Saint John's Hospital, Fargo, ND [Library symbol Library of Congress] (LCLS)
NdFStL	Saint Luke's Hospital, Fargo, ND [Library symbol Library of Congress] (LCLS)
NdFStLN	Saint Luke's School of Nursing, Fargo, ND [Library symbol Library of Congress] (LCLS)
NDFTA	National Dried Fruit Trade Association [British] (DBA)
NdFVA	United States Veterans Administration Hospital, Fargo, ND [Library symbol Library of Congress] (LCLS)
NDFYP	Navy Department Five Year Plan
NdG	Grand Forks Public Library, Grand Forks, ND [Library symbol Library of Congress] (LCLS)
NDG	National Dance Guild [Later, ADG]
NDG	National Distribution Guide [Mailing technique]
NDG	No Date Given (AFM)
NDGA	National Depression Glass Association (EA)
NDGA	National Dog Groomers Association (EA)
NDGA	Nordihydroguaiaretic Acid [Antioxidant, food additive]
ND GA	United States District Court for the Northern District of Georgia (DLA)
NDGAA	National Dog Groomers Association of America (EA)
NDGE	NATO Air Defense Ground Environment
NdGIT	United States Air Force Institute of Technology, Grand Forks AFB, ND [Library symbol Library of Congress] (LCLS)
NDGL	Neodymium-Doped Glass LASER
NDGO	Navy Department General Order
NdGrC	Carnegie Bookmobile Library, Grafton, ND [Library symbol Library of Congress] (LCLS)
NDGS	National Defense General Staff (NATG)
NDGS	National Duncan Glass Society (EA)
NdGUH	Grand Forks United Hospital, Grand Forks, ND [Library symbol Library of Congress] (LCLS)
NDGW	Native Daughters of the Golden West (EA)
NDH	Delhi [India] [Airport symbol] (AD)
NDH	National Defense Headquarters [Canada]
NDH	National Diploma in Horticulture [British]
NDH	Natural Disaster Hospitals [Public Health Service]
NDH	New Departure Hyatt Division [General Motors Corp.]
NDH	Royal North Devonshire Yeomanry Hussars [British military] (DMA)
NdHa	Harvey Public Library, Harvey, ND [Library symbol Library of Congress] (LCLS)
NDHA	National Dental Hygienists' Association (EA)
NDHA	National District Heating Association [Later, IDHCA] (EA)
NDHFP	New Developments Human Factors Program [Navy]
NdHi	State Historical Society of North Dakota, Bismarck, ND [Library symbol Library of Congress] (LCLS)
NDHQ	National Defence Headquarters [Canada]
NDHS	Nimbus Data Handling System
NDHX	Natural Draft Heat Exchanger [Nuclear energy] (NRCH)
NDI	Dickinson State College, Dickinson, ND [OCLC symbol] (OCLC)
NDI	KS Nordic Air, Denmark [ICAO designator] (FAAC)
NDI	Namudi [Papua New Guinea] [Airport symbol] (OAG)
NDI	National Dance Institute (EA)
NDI	National Death Index [Department of Health and Human Services] (GFGA)
NDI	National Democratic Institute for International Affairs
NDI	National Design, Inc. (PCM)
NDI	Nephrogenic Diabetes Insipidus [Endocrinology]
NDI	Network Development and Implementation Group [National Research Council of Canada]
NDI	New Delhi [India] [Seismograph station code, US Geological Survey] (SEIS)
NDI	Nielsen Drug Index [Marketing] (DOAD)
NDI	Nissan Design International
NDI	No-Dig International [A publication]
NDI	Noise Depreciation Index
NDI	Non-Combat Development Item
NDI	Nondestructive Inspection (AFM)
NDI	Non-Developmental Item [Military] (INF)
NDI	Non-Development [or Developmental] Issue [or Item]
NDI	Nondevelopment Item (MCD)
NDI	Numerical Designation Index (IEEE)
NDIA	National Defense Industrial Association
NDIA	New Denver International Airport (COE)
NDiag	National Diagnostics, Inc. [Associated Press] (SAG)
NDIC	National Diabetes Information Clearinghouse [Public Health Service] (IID)
NDIC	NATO Defense Information Complex (NATG)
NDIC	Nuclear Data Information Center [ORNL]
NDIC	Nuclear Desalination Information Center
NDICE	Non-Developmental Items Candidate Evaluation
NDIIA	National Democratic Institute for International Affairs (EA)
ND Ill	United States District Court for the Northern District of Illinois (DLA)
NDIMC	NATO Defense Information Management Committee (NATG)
ND Ind	United States District Court for the Northern District of Indiana (DLA)
ND Iowa	United States District Court for the Northern District of Iowa (DLA)
NDIR	Nondispersive Infrared [Analyzer]
NDIR	Non-Dispersive Infrared Spectroscopy (AAEL)
NDIRA	Nondispersive Infrared Analysis (COE)
NDIS	National Document and Information Service [Australia]
NDIS	Network Driver Interface Specification [Computer science] (PCM)
NDIS	Nissan Direct Ignition System [Automotive engineering]
NDIS	North Dakota State Industrial School
NDIU	National Drugs Intelligence Unit [Metropolitan Police] [British]
NDIY	North Devon Imperial Yeomanry [British military] (DMA)
NdJ	Alfred Dickey Free Library, Jamestown, ND [Library symbol Library of Congress] (LCLS)
NDJ	Jamestown College, Jamestown, ND [OCLC symbol] (OCLC)
NDJ	N'Djamena [Chad] [Airport symbol] (OAG)

NdJC .... Jamestown College, Jamestown, ND [*Library symbol Library of Congress*] (LCLS)
NDJCC .... North Dakota Junior College Conference (PSS)
NdJF .... North Dakota Farmers Union Resource Library, Jamestown, ND [*Library symbol Library of Congress*] (LCLS)
NdJN .... Northern Prairie Wildlife Research Center, Jamestown, ND [*Library symbol Library of Congress*] (LCLS)
NdJSH .... State Hospital, Jamestown, ND [*Library symbol Library of Congress*] (LCLS)
NDK .... Namorik [*Marshall Islands*] [*Airport symbol*] (OAG)
NDK .... Nucleoside Diphosphate Kinase [*An enzyme*]
NDK .... South Weymouth, MA [*Location identifier FAA*] (FAAL)
NDL .... Duke University, Law Library, Durham, NC [*OCLC symbol*] (OCLC)
NDL .... National Defence Headquarters Library [*UTLAS symbol*]
NDL .... National Democratic League [*Early British political party*]
NDL .... National Demographics & Lifestyles, Inc.
NDL .... National Diet Library [*Japan*]
NDL .... National Digital Library (TELE)
NDL .... Natural Daylight
NDL .... Needle (MSA)
NDL .... Neon Discharge Lighting [*Automotive lighting*]
NDL .... Network Database Language [*Telecommunications*] (OSI)
NDL .... Network Definition Language [*Burroughs Corp.*]
NDL .... Ni-Cal Developments Ltd. [*Vancouver Stock Exchange symbol*]
NDL .... No Decompression Limit
NDL .... Norddeutscher Lloyd [*German steamship company*]
Nd-L .... North Dakota State Law Library, Bismarck, ND [*Library symbol Library of Congress*] (LCLS)
NDL .... Nuclear Data Link System [*Nuclear Regulatory Commission*]
NDL .... Nuclear Defense Laboratory [*Army*]
NDL .... Nuclear Diagnostic Laboratories, Inc. (EFIS)
NDL .... Numerical Drawing List
NDLB .... National Dock Labour Board [*British*]
NDLC .... Network Data Link Control
NdLibC .... North Dakota State Library Commission, Bismarck, ND [*Library symbol Library of Congress*] (LCLS)
NDLOA .... National Disabled Law Officers Association (EA)
NDLT .... N-Channel Depletion-Load Triode Inverter
ndlwk .... Needlework (VRA)
NDM .... Ferrocarriles Nacionales de Mexico [*AAR code*]
NDM .... Mary College, Library, Bismarck, ND [*OCLC symbol*] (OCLC)
NDM .... Nadym Airlines [*Russian Federation*] [*ICAO designator*] (FAAC)
NDM .... National Dried (Milk) [*Brand name for the British government's dried milk for babies - manufacturer undisclosed*]
NDM .... N-Desmethyl-Methsuximide [*Biochemistry*] (AAMN)
NDM .... Negative Differential Mobility (IEEE)
NDM .... Neutron Dose Monitor
NDM .... New Democratic Movement (EA)
NDM .... New Dimensions in Medicine
NDM .... Newspaper Designated Market (WDMC)
NDM .... NOAA [*National Oceanic and Atmospheric Administration*] Directives Manual (NOAA)
NDM .... Nomad Energy & Resources [*Vancouver Stock Exchange symbol*]
NDM .... North Durham Militia [*British military*] (DMA)
NDMA .... National Dimension Manufacturers Association (EA)
NDMA .... National Door Manufacturers Association [*Later, NWWDA*]
NDMA .... National Dress Manufacturers Association [*Later, AMA*] (EA)
NDMA .... Nitrosodimethylaniline [*Chemistry*] (DAVI)
NDMA .... N-Nitrosodimethylamine [*Also, DMN, DMNA*] [*Organic chemistry*]
NDMA .... Nonprescription Drug Manufacturers Association (EA)
NdMan .... Mandan Public Library, Mandan, ND [*Library symbol Library of Congress*] (LCLS)
NdManMH .... North Dakota Memorial Mental Health and Retardation Center, Mandan, ND [*Library symbol Library of Congress*] (LCLS)
NdManN .... North Dakota Industrial School, Mandan, ND [*Library symbol Library of Congress*] (LCLS)
NdManNG .... United States Northern Great Plains Research Center, Mandan, ND [*Library symbol Library of Congress*] (LCLS)
NdMayS .... Mayville State College, Mayville, ND [*Library symbol Library of Congress*] (LCLS)
NDMB .... National Defense Mediation Board [*World War II*]
NDMC .... NATO Defense Manpower Committee (NATG)
NDMC .... N-Desmethylclobazam [*Biochemistry*]
NDMDA .... National Depressive and Manic Depressive Association (EA)
NdMin .... Minot Public Library, Minot, ND [*Library symbol Library of Congress*] (LCLS)
NdMinAF .... United States Air Force, Base Library, Minot AFB, ND [*Library symbol Library of Congress*] (LCLS)
NdMinIT .... United States Air Force Institute of Technology, Minot AFB, ND [*Library symbol Library of Congress*] (LCLS)
NdMinN .... Northwest Bible College, Minot, ND [*Library symbol Library of Congress*] (LCLS)
NdMinS .... Minot State College, Minot, ND [*Library symbol Library of Congress*] (LCLS)
NdMinT-M .... Trinity Medical Center, August Cameron Medical Library, Minot, ND [*Library symbol Library of Congress*] (LCLS)
NdMinT-N .... Trinity Medical Center, School of Nursing, Minot, ND [*Library symbol Library of Congress*] (LCLS)
ND Miss .... United States District Court for the Northern District of Mississippi (DLA)
NDML .... Neutral Data Manipulation Language [*Computer science*]
NdMo .... Mott Public Library, Mott, ND [*Library symbol Library of Congress*] (LCLS)
NDMPI .... Nitrosodimethylpiperazinium Iodide [*Organic chemistry*]
NDMS .... National Debt Management System [*Social Security Administration*] (GFGA)
NDMS .... National Disaster Medical System
NDMS .... Netware Distributed Management Services [*Novell, Inc.*] (PCM)
NDMS .... Network Design and Management System
NDMS .... Noise Deficiency Management System
NDMS .... Non-Directional Mud-and-Snow (PDAA)
NDMSP .... Navy Department Mobilization Security Plan (NG)
NDMTB .... Nondeployment Mobilization Troop Basis (AABC)
NDMTP .... National Defense Manufacturing Technology Plan
NDMWC .... National Domestic Meatworks Wholesalers Council [*Australia*]
NDN .... National Diffusion Network [*Department of Education*] [*Information service or system*] (IID)
NDN .... National Directory of Newsletters and Reporting Services [*A publication*]
NDN .... New Data Network (IAA)
NDN .... Ninety-Nine Cent Only Stores [*NYSE symbol*] (SAG)
NDN .... Nonsynaptic Diffusion Neurotransmission [*Neurology*]
NDN .... Nu-Dawn Resources, Inc. [*Vancouver Stock Exchange symbol*]
nDNA .... Deoxyribonucleic Acid, Nuclear [*Biochemistry, genetics*]
NDNHI .... North Dakota Natural Heritage Inventory [*North Dakota State Department of Natural Resources*] [*Bismarck*] [*Information service or system*] (IID)
NDNO .... National Directory of Nonprofit Organizations [*A publication*]
NDNT .... Not Dressed nor Tanned
NDNY .... United States District Court for the Northern District of New York (DLA)
NDO .... National Debt Office [*British*]
NDO .... Navy Disbursing Office
NDO .... Negotiate Downward Only (MCD)
NDO .... Network Development Office [*Library of Congress*]
NDOA .... National Dog Owners' Association [*British*] (BI)
NDOC .... Neurological Dysfunctions of Children [*Test*]
ND Ohio .... United States District Court for the Northern District of Ohio (DLA)
ND Okla .... United States District Court for the Northern District of Oklahoma (DLA)
NDOP .... Navy Designated Overhaul Point (CAAL)
NDOS .... National Defense Operations Section [*FCC*]
NDOS .... New Disc Operating System (NITA)
NDp .... Deer Park Public Library, Deer Park, NY [*Library symbol Library of Congress*] (LCLS)
NDP .... National Democracy Party [*Thailand*] [*Political party*] (PPW)
NDP .... National Democratic Party [*Rhodesia and Nyasaland*] [*Political party*]
NDP .... National Democratic Party [*Sierra Leone*] [*Political party*] (EY)
NDP .... National Democratic Party [*Morocco*] [*Political party*] (PPW)
NDP .... National Democratic Party [*Grenada*] [*Political party*] (PPW)
NDP .... National Democratic Party [*India*] [*Political party*] (PPW)
NDP .... National Democratic Party [*Egypt*] [*Political party*] (PPW)
NDP .... National Democratic Party [*Iraq*] [*Political party*] (BJA)
NDP .... National Democratic Party [*Namibia*] [*Political party*] (PPW)
NDP .... National Democratic Party [*Solomon Islands*] [*Political party*] (PPW)
NDP .... National Democratic Party [*Pakistan*] [*Political party*] (PD)
NDP .... Nationaldemokratische Partei [*National Democratic Party*] [*Austria Political party*] (PPW)
NDP .... National Determination Party (EA)
NDP .... National Development Party [*Montserrat*] [*Political party*] (EY)
NDP .... National Diocesan Press [*Later, Episcopal Communicators*] (EA)
NDP .... National Diploma in Poultry Husbandry [*British*]
NDP .... National Disclosure Policy [*Military*] (MCD)
NDP .... Nationalist Democracy Party [*Turkey Political party*] (PPW)
NDP .... Nationwide Demonstration Program
NDP .... Naval Doctrine Publication (DOMA)
NDP .... Navy Department Personnel
NDP .... Neighborhood Development Program [*Urban renewal*]
NDP .... Net Dietary Protein (MAE)
NDP .... Net Domestic Product [*Business term*] (PDAA)
NDP .... Neurological Disorders Program [*National Institute of Neurological and Communicative Disorders and Stroke*]
NDP .... Neutron Depth Profiling [*Analytical chemistry*]
NDP .... New Democratic Party [*Facetious translations: "Never Dies Politically," "No Dreams of Prosperity"*] [*Canada Political party*] (PPW)
NDP .... New Democratic Party [*South Korea Political party*] (PPW)
NDP .... New Democratic Party [*St. Vincent*] [*Political party*] (PPW)
NDP .... New Democratic Party [*Seychelles*] [*Political party*] (EY)
NDP .... Night Defensive Position [*Military*]
NDP .... Normal Diametral Pitch (MSA)
NDP .... Nuclear Desalination Plant
NDP .... Nuclear Disarmament Party [*Australia Political party*]
NDP .... Nucleoside Diphosphate [*Biochemistry*]
NDP .... Numeric Data Processor
NDP .... Pensacola, FL [*Location identifier FAA*] (FAAL)
NDPA .... National Decorated Packaging Association
NDPA .... National Decorating Products Association (EA)
NDPA .... National Directory Publishing Association (NTPA)
NDPA .... Nitrosodipropylamine [*Also, DPN, DPNA*] [*Organic chemistry*]
NDPB .... National Drug Policy Board [*Department of Justice*] (GFGA)
NDPB .... Non-Departmental Public Body [*British*]
NDPBC .... National Duck Pin Bowling Congress [*Later, NDBC*] (EA)
NDPC .... National Democratic Policy Committee (EA)
NDPC .... National [*Military Information*] Disclosure Policy Committee
NDPC .... National Dropout Prevention Center (EA)
NDPC .... National Drowning Prevention Coalition (EA)
NDpCal .... Net Dietary Protein Energy Ratio (WDAA)

NDPD.......... National Data Processing Division [*Environmental Protection Agency*] (GFGA)

NDPD.......... Nationaldemokratische Partei Deutschlands [*German National Democratic Party*] [*Political party*]

NDPF.......... NASA Data Processing Facility (MCD)

NDPhA........ N-Nitrosodiphenylamine [*Organic chemistry*]

NDpHS........ Deer Park High School, Deer Park, NY [*Library symbol*] [*Library of Congress*] (LCLS)

NDPIC........ Navy Department Program Information Center

NDPK.......... Nucleoside Diphosphokinase [*An enzyme*]

NDPK.......... Nucleotide Diphosphate Kinase [*An enzyme*]

NDPL.......... National Democratic Party of Liberia [*Political party*] (EY)

NDPN.......... National Dropout Prevention Network (EA)

NDPP.......... (Nitrobenzyl)(Diethylaminophenylazo)-pyridinium Bromide [*Reagent*]

NDPR.......... NATO Defense Planning Review (NATG)

NDPR.......... Nuclear Duty Position Roster (MCD)

NDPRP........ National Defense Project Rating Plan

NDPS.......... National Data Processing Service [*British*] (DCTA)

NDPS.......... Novell Distributed Print Services [*Computer science*]

NDQ............ NASA Delta Quotation (MCD)

ND(Q).......... Nominal Defendant (Queensland) [*Australia*]

NDR............ Andrea Airlines SA [*Peru*] [*ICAO designator*] (FAAC)

NDR............ Nador [*Morocco*] [*Airport symbol*] (AD)

NDR............ National Derby Rallies (EA)

NDR............ National Dog Registry (EA)

NDR............ National Driver Register

NDR............ National Drug Co. [*Research code symbol*]

NDR............ Negative Differential Resistance [*Electronics*]

NDR............ Neonatal Death Rate [*Medicine*] (DMAA)

NDR............ Net Difference Report (IAA)

NDR............ Network Data Reduction

NDR............ Network Data Representation [*Computer science*]

NDR............ Neutral Detergent Residue [*Food analysis*]

NDR............ New Dimensions Radio (EA)

NDR............ Nondestructive Read [*Computer science*]

NDR............ Norddeutscher Rundfunk [*Radio network*] [*Germany*]

NDR............ Normal Daily Requirement [*Military*]

NDR............ Normal Detrusor Reflex (DMAA)

NDR............ Normotensive Donor Rat

NDR............ Nuclear Double Resonance [*Analytical chemistry*]

NDRA.......... National Deafblind & Rubella Association (WDAA)

NDRA.......... Nostalgia Drag Race Association (EA)

NDRB.......... New Developments Research Branch [*Navy*] (MCD)

NDRC.......... National Defense Research Committee [*of Office of Scientific Research and Development*] [*World War II*]

NDRE.......... Norwegian Defense Research Establishment

ND Res Found Bull... North Dakota Research Foundation Bulletin [*A publication*]

NDRF.......... National Debt Repayment Foundation (EA)

NDRF.......... National Defense Reserve Fleet [*Maritime Administration, Department of Commerce*]

NDRG.......... NATO Defense Research Group (NATG)

NDRI.......... National Diabetes Research Interchange [*Research center*] (RCD)

NDRI.......... Naval Dental Research Institute

NDRL.......... Notre Dame Radiation Laboratory [*University of Notre Dame*] [*Research center*] (RCD)

NDRM......... Neesby Delayed Release Mechanism [*Medicine*]

NDRO.......... Nondestructive Read Only [*Computer science*] (IAA)

NDRO.......... Nondestructive Readout [*Computer science*]

NDRP.......... New Democratic Republican Party [*South Korea Political party*] (EY)

NDRS.......... National Driver Register Service [*Department of Transportation*]

NDRS.......... Nuclear Definition and Reporting System (AAG)

NDRSWG..... NATO Data Requirements and Standards Working Group (NATG)

NDRT.......... Nelson-Denny Reading Test (EDAC)

NDRW......... Nondestructive Read/Write [*Computer science*]

NDryT......... Tompkins-Cortland Community College, Division of Instructional and Learning Resources, Dryden, NY [*Library symbol Library of Congress*] (LCLS)

NDS............ Congregation of Notre Dame de Sion [*Roman Catholic women's religious order*]

NDS............ National Dahlia Society [*British*] (DBA)

NDS............ National Decision Systems [*Information service or system*] (IID)

NDS............ National Defense Stockpile [*Collection of materials essential to the defense industry*]

NDS............ National Design Specification [*For wood construction*] (WPI)

NDS............ National Dioxin Study [*Environmental Protection Agency*] (GFGA)

NDS............ National Disposal Site [*Environmental Protection Agency*] (GFGA)

NDS............ Naval Dental School

NDS............ Navigation Development Satellite (MCD)

NDS............ Navigation Display System

NDS............ Navy Data System

NDS............ Navy Directive System (NVT)

NDS............ Navy Display System

NDS............ Needs [*Automotive advertising*]

NDS............ NetWare Directory Services [*Novell, Inc.*] [*Computer science*] (PCM)

NDS............ Network Data Series (MHDI)

NDS............ Network Development System (IAA)

NDS............ Neurologic Disability Score

NDS............ Neutral-Drive Switch [*Automotive engineering*]

NDS............ Neutron Doped Silicon (IAA)

NDS............ New Drug Submission [*Medicine*] (DB)

NDS............ Nicholas Data [*Vancouver Stock Exchange symbol*]

NDS............ Nominal Detectable Signal (IAA)

NDS............ Noncommunications Detection System (MCD)

NDS............ Non-Developmental Software

NDS............ Nonparametric Detection Scheme [*Communication signal*]

NDS............ Nordic Demographic Society (EA)

NDS............ Nordstress (Australia) Pt Ltd. [*FAA designator*] (FAAC)

NDS............ Normal Dog Serum [*Medicine*] (DMAA)

NDS............ North Dakota State Library Commission, Bismarck, ND [*OCLC symbol*] (OCLC)

NDS............ Novell Directory Service [*Computer Networking*] (PCM)

NDS............ NPIC [*National Photographic Interpretation Center*] Data System (MCD)

NDS............ Nuclear Data Sheets [*National Academy of Sciences*]

NDS............ Nuclear Detection Satellite

NDS............ Nuclear Detection System (MCD)

NDS............ Nuclear Detonation Detection System

NDSA.......... National Disposal Services Association (EA)

NDSB.......... Narcotic Drugs Supervisory Body [*UN*]

NDSB.......... Navy Dependents School Branch

ND/SB.......... Nuclear Depth/Strike Bomb (DOMA)

NDSC.......... National Down Syndrome Congress (EA)

NDSC.......... Network for the Detection of Stratospheric Change [*New Zealand*] (USDC)

NDSE.......... Nondeliverable Support Equipment

NDSEG........ National Defense Science and Engineering

NDSEG........ National Defense Science and Engineering Graduate

ND Sess Laws... Laws of North Dakota [*A publication*] (DLA)

NDSF.......... National Defense Sealift Fund (DOMA)

NDSF.......... North Dakota School of Forestry

NDSL.......... National Direct [*formerly, Defense*] Student Loan [*later, Perkins Loan*] [*Department of Education*]

NDSL.......... Non Domestic Substances List [*Canada*]

NDSM......... National Defense Service Medal [*Military decoration*]

NDSN.......... National Drug Strategy Network (EA)

NDSN.......... Nobody Don't Say Nothing

NDSN.......... Nordson Corp. [*NASDAQ symbol*] (NQ)

NDSOS........ Navy Deep Sea Oceanographic System

NDSS.......... National Down Syndrome Society (EA)

NDSS.......... National DS Society

NDSTC......... Naval Diving and Salvage Training Center (DNAB)

NDSU.......... North Dakota State University

NDT............ Ferrocarril Nacional de Tehuantepec [*AAR code*]

NDT............ National Diploma in the Science and Practice of Turfculture and Sports Ground Management [*British*]

NDT............ Net Data Throughout

NDT............ Network Description Table (MHDI)

NDT............ Neuro-Developmental Treatment [*Physical therapy*]

NDT............ Nevada Dance Theatre

NDT............ New Dictionary of Thoughts [*A publication*]

NDT............ New Dimensions [*Vancouver Stock Exchange symbol*]

NDT............ Nil-Ductility Temperature [*Metallurgy*]

NDT............ Nil-Ductility Transition [*Metallurgy*] (IEEE)

NDT............ No Dial Tone [*Of a telephone*] (WDMC)

NDT............ Noise Detection Threshold (DMAA)

NDT............ Nondestructive Test (DMAA)

NDT............ Nondestructive Testing

NDT............ Non-Lethal Disabling Technology

NDT............ Nuclear Detection Test (IAA)

NDTA.......... National Defense Transportation Association (EA)

NDTA.......... National Dental Technicians Association [*Defunct*] (EA)

NDTA.......... Neurodevelopmental Treatment Association (EA)

NDTA.......... Non-Destructive Testing Association of Australia

NDT & E...... Nondestructive Testing and Evaluation Programs [*Pennsylvania State University*] [*Research center*] (RCD)

NDTC.......... National Drug Trade Conference (EA)

NDTC.......... Naval Device Training Center

NDTC.......... Nondestructive Testing Center (IEEE)

NDTE.......... North Dakota Tracer Experiment (USDC)

ND Tex......... United States District Court for the Northern District of Texas (DLA)

NDTF.......... Nondestructive Test Facility (MCD)

Ndthl.......... Neanderthal (VRA)

NDTI.......... Nondestructive Testing and Inspection

NDTIAC....... Non-Destructive Testing Information Center [*Army Materials and Mechanics Research Center*] (PDAA)

NDTIB.......... Nondestructive Testing and Inspection Building

NDTL.......... Nondestructive Test Laboratory (MCD)

NDTMA........ National Drain Tile Manufacturers Association [*Defunct*] (EA)

NDTMA........ Non Destructive Testing Management Association (NTPA)

NDTP.......... Nuclear Data Tape Program

NDTRAN...... Notre Dame Translator [*Programming language*] [*1977*] [*Computer science*] (CSR)

NDTT.......... Nil-Ductility Transition Temperature [*Metallurgy*]

NDU............ National Defense University [*DoD*]

NDU............ National Defense University, Washington, DC [*OCLC symbol*] (OCLC)

NDU............ National Democratic Union [*Zimbabwe*] [*Political party*] (PPW)

NDU............ Navigation Display Unit [*Military*]

NDU............ NDU Resources [*Vancouver Stock Exchange symbol*]

NDU............ Nederlandse Dagbladunie

N/D/U.......... None Done Up [*Bookselling*]

ndu............ North Dakota [*MARC country of publication code Library of Congress*] (LCCP)

NDU............ Nuclear Data Unit [*International Atomic Energy Agency*] (DIT)

NDU............ Rundu [*Namibia*] [*Airport symbol*] (OAG)

NdU............ University of North Dakota, Grand Forks, ND [*Library symbol Library of Congress*] (LCLS)

NDUC.......... Nimbus Data Utilization Center

NdU-El........ University of North Dakota, Ellendale Branch, Ellendale, ND [*Library symbol Library of Congress Obsolete*] (LCLS)

NDUF .... National Democratic United Front [*Later, FNDF*] [*Myanmar*] [*Political party*]　(PD)

NdU-L .... University of North Dakota, Law Library, Grand Forks, ND [*Library symbol Library of Congress*]　(LCLS)

NdU-M .... University of North Dakota, Medical Library, Grand Forks, ND [*Library symbol Library of Congress*]　(LCLS)

NDunBH .... Brooks Memorial Hospital Medical Center, Dunkirk, NY [*Library symbol Library of Congress*]　(LCLS)

NDUP .... Nonduplicate

NDUSTA .... New Duty Station [*Navy*]

NDUUV .... Nondispersive Ultraviolet

NDUV .... Non-Dispersive Ultraviolet Spectroscopy　(AAEL)

NDV .... Newcastle Disease Virus [*Also, ND*]

NDV .... Not to Delay Delivery

NDV .... Not to Delay Vessel

NDV .... Nuclear Delivery Vehicle

NDV .... Valley City State College, Valley City, ND [*OCLC symbol*]　(OCLC)

NDV .... Washington, DC [*Location identifier FAA*]　(FAAL)

NdVc .... Valley City Public Library, Valley City, ND [*Library symbol Library of Congress*]　(LCLS)

NdVcT .... Valley City State College, Valley City, ND [*Library symbol Library of Congress*]　(LCLS)

NDVI .... Normalized Difference Vegetation Index [*Plant biota*]

NDW .... Naval District Washington

NDW .... North Dakota State School of Science, Mildred Johnson Library, Wahpeton, ND [*OCLC symbol*]　(OCLC)

NDW .... Norton Desktop for Windows [*Symantec Corp.*] [*Computer science*]　(PCM)

NDWAC .... National Drinking Water Advisory Council [*Environmental Protection Agency*]

NdWah .... Leach Public Library, Wahpeton, ND [*Library symbol Library of Congress*]　(LCLS)

NdWahS ..... North Dakota State School of Science, Wahpeton, ND [*Library symbol Library of Congress*]　(LCLS)

NDWBA .... National Deaf Women's Bowling Association　(EA)

NdWi .... James Memorial Library, Williston, ND [*Library symbol Library of Congress*]　(LCLS)

NdWiU .... University of North Dakota, Williston Branch, Williston, ND [*Library symbol Library of Congress*]　(LCLS)

NdWiW .... West Plains Rural Library, Williston, ND [*Library symbol Library of Congress*]　(LCLS)

NDWP .... National Demonstration Water Project　(EA)

NDWRRI ...... North Dakota Water Resources Research Institute [*Fargo, ND*] [*Department of the Interior*]　(GRD)

NDWU .... National Domestic Workers Union　(EA)

NDX .... Northern Dynasty Explorations Ltd. [*Toronto Stock Exchange symbol Vancouver Stock Exchange symbol*]

NDxhBJ .... Burr's Lane Junior High School, Dix Hills, NY [*Library symbol Library of Congress*]　(LCLS)

NDxhFE .... Forest Park Elementary School, Dix Hills, NY [*Library symbol*] [*Library of Congress*]　(LCLS)

NDxhH .... Half Hollow Hills Community Public Library, Dix Hills, NY [*Library symbol*] [*Library of Congress*]　(LCLS)

NDxhHH-E .... Half Hollow Hills High School East, Dix Hills, NY [*Library symbol Library of Congress*]　(LCLS)

NDxhHH-W ... Half Hollow Hills High School West, Dix Hills, NY [*Library symbol Library of Congress*]　(LCLS)

NDxhHT .... Half Hollow Hills District Teacher's Center, Dix Hills, NY [*Library symbol Library of Congress*]　(LCLS)

NDY .... Dahlgren, VA [*Location identifier FAA*]　(FAAL)

NDY .... Neodymium-Doped Yttralox [*Ceramic*]

NDY .... Nonresonant Deflection Yoke

NDY .... Sanday [*Scotland*] [*Airport symbol*]　(OAG)

Nd:YAG .... Neodymium-Doped: Yttrium Aluminum Garnet [*LASER technology*]

NDYL .... Neodymium-Doped YAG [*Yttrium Aluminum Garnet*] LASER

NDZ .... Milton, FL [*Location identifier FAA*]　(FAAL)

NE .... Air New England [*ICAO designator*]　(AD)

Ne .... Algemeen Rijksarchief te s'Gravenhage (Central State Archives), The Hague, Netherlands [*Library symbol Library of Congress*]　(LCLS)

NE .... Left Nationalists [*Spain Political party*]　(PPW)

NE .... Narcotics Education [*An association*]　(EA)

NE .... National Emergency

NE .... National Estate

NE .... National Exchequer [*British*]

NE .... National Executive　(ADA)

NE .... National Exhibition [*British*]

NE .... Naval Engineer [*Academic degree*]

NE .... Navy Evaluation

NE .... Near East　(BJA)

NE .... Nebraska [*Postal code*]

NE .... Negative Expectancy [*Psychometrics*]

NE .... Negatives and Etching　(DGA)

NE .... Negotiated Exit [*Telecommunications*]　(OSI)

Ne .... Nehemiah [*Old Testament book*]　(BJA)

NE .... Neiva [*Sociedade Construtora Aeronautica Neiva Ltda.*] [*Brazil ICAO aircraft manufacturer identifier*]　(ICAO)

NE .... Neomycin [*Antibacterial compound*]

NE .... Neon [*Chemical element*]

ne .... Neon　(VRA)

Ne .... Neon [*Chemical element*]　(ODBW)

ne .... Nephelite [*CIPW classification*] [*Geology*]

NE .... Nephropathia Epidemica [*Medicine*]

NE .... Nerve Ending　(MAE)

NE .... Nerve Excitability [*Test*]

NE .... Net Earnings

ne .... Netherlands [*MARC country of publication code Library of Congress*]　(LCCP)

NE .... Netherlands

NE .... Neumann-Electroporation [*Gene technology*]

NE .... Neural Excitation [*neurology*]　(DAVI)

NE .... Neurologic Examination [*Medicine*]

NE .... Neutral Endopeptidase [*An enzyme*]

NE .... Neutral Excitation

NE .... New Edition

NE .... New Editions [*Record label*]

NE .... New Engine [*On ships*]

NE .... New England

NE .... [*The*] New English Bible [*1961*] [*A publication*]　(BJA)

NE .... New Executable [*Computer science*]　(PCM)

NE .... News Editor　(ADA)

NE .... Niacin Equivalent

NE .... Nickel Equivalent [*Coinage*]

NE .... Niger [*ANSI two-letter standard code*]　(CNC)

NE .... Night Experimental [*British military*]　(DMA)

NE .... Nodal Exchange　(MCD)

NE .... No Earthly Chance　(DSUE)

NE .... No Ectopy [*Medicine*]　(MEDA)

NE .... No Effects

NE .... Noise-Equivalent　(IAA)

NE .... Nonelastic [*Medicine*]　(MAE)

NE .... Non-English Speaker [*Airline notation*]

NE .... Nonessential

NE .... Norepinephrine [*Also known as NA: Noradrenaline*] [*Biochemistry*]

NE .... Normal Excitability [*Medicine*]

NE .... Normally Energized　(NRCH)

NE .... Northeast

NE .... Northeast Airlines, Inc. [*Obsolete*]

NE .... North Eastern Reporter [*A publication*]　(DLA)

NE .... Not Elevated [*Laboratory science*]　(DAVI)

NE .... Not Employed

NE .... Not Engaged

NE .... Not Enlarged [*Medicine*]

NE .... Not Entitled [*British military*]　(DMA)

NE .... Not Equal [*Relational operator*]

NE .... Not Equal To　(NITA)

NE .... Not Evaluated　(INF)

NE .... Not Examined [*Medicine*]

NE .... Not Exceeding

N/E .... Not Explosive

NE .... Notice of Exception　(MCD)

NE .... Nuclear Electric　(WDAA)

NE .... Nuclear Energy　(COE)

NE .... Nuclear Engineer

NE .... Nuclear Envelope [*Cytology*]

NE .... Nuclear Explosive

NE .... Nuclear Extract [*Cytology*]

NE .... Nursing Educator　(AAMN)

NE 2d .... North Eastern Reporter, Second Series [*West*] [*A publication*]　(AAGC)

NE-10 .... Northeast-10 Conference　(PSS)

NEa .... Eastchester Public Library, Eastchester, NY [*Library symbol Library of Congress*]　(LCLS)

NEA .... Nashville Entertainment Association　(EA)

NEA .... National Economic Association　(EA)

NEA .... National Editorial Association [*Later, NNA*]　(EA)

NEA .... National Education Association　(EA)

NEA .... National Electronic Associations [*Later, NESSDA*]

NEA .... National Employment Association [*Later, NAPC*]　(EA)

NEA .... National Endowment for the Arts

NEA .... National Energy Accounts [*Department of Commerce*] [*Information service or system*]　(IID)

NEA .... National Energy Act　(GFGA)

NEA .... National Erectors Association　(EA)

NEA .... Natural Energy Association [*British*]

NEA .... Nearctic Resources, Inc. [*Toronto Stock Exchange symbol*]

NEA .... Near-Earth Asteroid [*Astronomy*]

NEA .... Near Eastern Affairs [*Department of State*]

NEA .... Neath [*Welsh depot code*]

NEA .... Negative Electron Affinity [*Photocathode*]

NEA .... Nelson & Albemarle Railway [*AAR code*]

NEA .... Nenana [*Alaska*] [*Seismograph station code, US Geological Survey*]　(SEIS)

NEA .... Neoplasm Embryonic Antigen　(DB)

NEA .... Network Equivalent Analysis

NEA .... New England Airlines, Inc. [*ICAO designator*]　(FAAC)

NEA .... New Entitlement Authority

NEA .... Newsletter Editors' Association [*Australia*]

NEA .... Newspaper Enterprise Association [*A syndicate*]

NEA .... No Evidence of Abnormality [*Medicine*]　(DMAA)

NEA .... Noise-Equivalent Angle　(MCD)

NEA .... Northeast Airlines, Inc. [*Obsolete*]

NEA .... Northeast Asia　(CINC)

NEA .... Northern Examining Association [*British*]

NEA .... Nuclear Energy Agency [*See also AEN*] [*Organization for Economic Cooperation and Development*]　(EAIO)

NEA .... Null Error Amplifier

NEA .... Nutrition Education Association　(EA)

NeAA .... Gemeente Archief van Amsterdam, Amsterdam, Netherlands [*Library symbol Library of Congress*]　(LCLS)

NEAA .... National Employment Assistance Act　(OICC)

NEAA	Norwegian Elkhound Association of America (EA)
NEAAN	Non-Essential Amino Acid N [*Biochemistry*] (PDAA)
NEAATS	Northeast Asia Association of Theological Schools
NEAB	Northern Examinations and Assessment Board (AIE)
NEABFGP	New England Advisory Board for Fish and Game Problems [*Defunct*] (EA)
NEabG	Genesee County Landmark Society, East Bethany, NY [*Library symbol Library of Congress*] (LCLS)
NEAC	New English Art Club [*British*]
NEAC	Nippon Electric Automatic Computer (IEEE)
NEAC	Northeast Air Command
NEACDS	Naval Emergency Air Cargo Delivery System (CAAL)
NEACH	New England Automated Clearing House Association
NEACP	National Emergency Airborne Command Post [*Pronounced "kneecap"*] [*Modified Boeing 747 jet to be used as a military control center by the President or Vice President during a nuclear war or other crisis*]
NEACRP	Nuclear Energy Agency Committee on Reactor Physics [*OECD*] (EY)
NEACSS	New England Association of Colleges and Secondary Schools [*Later, NEASC*] (EA)
NEA-DB	NEA [*Nuclear Energy Agency*] Data Bank [*OECD*] [*Information service or system*] (IID)
NEADS	National Education for Assistance Dog Services [*Formerly, New England Assistance Dog Service*] (PAZ)
NEADS	Near East and African Development Service
NEADS	Network Engineering Administrative Data System [*AT & T*]
NEADS	Northeast Atlantic Dynamics Studies [*Marine science*] (MSC)
NEADW	Northeast Atlantic Deep Water [*Oceanography*]
NEAF	Near East Air Force [*British*]
NEAFC	North-East Atlantic Fisheries Commission [*British*] (EAIO)
NEAFCS	National Extension Association of Family & Consumer Sciences (NTPA)
NEAGC	National Early American Glass Club (EA)
NEAHI	Near East Animal Health Institute
NEAM	Nonvolatile Electrically Alterable Memory
NEAN	National Execution Alert Network (EA)
NEANDC	Nuclear Energy Agency Nuclear Data Committee [*OECD*] (EY)
NEANMCC	Navy Element Alternate National Military Command Center (MCD)
NEanpHE	Harley Avenue Elementary School, East Northport, NY [*Library symbol Library of Congress*] (LCLS)
NeAO	Rijksinstituut voor Orlogsdocumentatie, Amsterdam, Netherlands [*Library symbol Library of Congress*] (LCLS)
NEAP	National Energy Audit Program [*Canada*]
NEAPD	Northeastern Air Procurement District
NEAQ	Northern Electricity Authority of Queensland [*Australia*]
NEAR	National Emergency Alarm Repeater [*Civil defense warning system for homes*]
NEAR	Nationwide/Worldwide Emergency Ambulance Return
NEAR	Near-Earth Asteroid Rendezvous (MCD)
NEAR	New England Action Research Project
NEAR	Nielsen Engineering & Research, Inc.
NEARA	New England Antiquities Research Association (EA)
NEARELF	Near East Land Forces [*British military*] (DMA)
NEARNAVDIST	Nearest Naval District
NEARnet	[*The*] New England Academic and Research Network [*Computer science*] (TNIG)
NEARO	New England Albanian Relief Organization
NEARP	New England Appalachian Research Project [*University of Maine at Orono*] [*Research center*] (RCD)
NEARS	Navy Evaluation of Advanced Reconnaissance Systems
NEARS	Near Earth Asteroid Returned Samples [*NASA, proposed*]
NEARTIP	Near-Term Improvement Program [*For torpedos*] (MCD)
NEARYP	National Employers Association of Rayon Yarn Producers [*British*] (BI)
NEAS	National Engineering Aptitude Search
NEAS	National European American Society (EA)
NEAS	Near East Archaeological Society (EA)
NEAS	Newsletter of Engineering Analysis Software [*A publication*] (MCD)
NEASA	Near Eastern, African, and South Asian Affairs [*Department of State*]
NEASC	New England Association of Schools and Colleges (EA)
NEASCUS	New England Association of School, College, and University Staffing
NEASIM	Network Analytical Simulator (PDAA)
NEASP	Navy Enlisted Advanced School Program
NEaspHS	Eastport High School, Eastport, NY [*Library symbol Library of Congress*] (LCLS)
NeAT	Koninklijk Instituut voor de Tropen, Amsterdam, Netherlands [*Library symbol Library of Congress*] (LCLS)
NEAT	National Cash Register Electronic Autocoding Technique [*Computer science*] (IAA)
NEAT	National Electronic Autocoding Technique (MHDB)
NEAT	Navy Electronics Application Trainer
NEAT	Navy Embarked Advisory Team
NEAT	NCR [*NCR Corp.*] Electronic Autocoding Technique [*Computer science*]
NEAT	Near-Earth Asteroid Tracking
NEAT	New Enhanced Advanced Technology (CIST)
NEAT	New Enhanced Technology
NEATE	New England Association of Teachers of English (AEBS)
NEATICC	Northeast Asia Tactical Information Communications Center (DNAB)
NEATO	North East Asian Treaty Organization (NATG)
NeAU	University of Amsterdam, Amsterdam, Netherlands [*Library symbol Library of Congress*] (LCLS)
NEAuC	Christ the King Seminary, East Aurora, NY [*Library symbol Library of Congress*] (LCLS)
NEAuF	Fisher-Price Toys, East Aurora, NY [*Library symbol Library of Congress*] (LCLS)
NEAuH	Elbert Hubbard Library Museum, East Aurora, NY [*Library symbol Library of Congress*] (LCLS)
NEAuS	Saint John Vianney Seminary, East Aurora, NY [*Library symbol Library of Congress*] (LCLS)
NEawNE	North Side Elementary School, East Williston, NY [*Library symbol Library of Congress*] (LCLS)
NEB	Department of Aeronautics State of Nebraska [*FAA designator*] (FAAC)
NEB	National Energy Board [*Canada*]
NEB	National Enterprise Board [*Later, BTG*] [*British*]
NEB	Nebelwerfer [*German six-barrelled mortar*] (DSUE)
NEB	Nebraska
Neb	Nebraska (ODBW)
Neb	Nebraska Supreme Court Reports [*A publication*] (DLA)
NEB	Nebula [*Spray*] [*Pharmacy*]
NEB	Neuroepithelial Bodies [*Anatomy*]
NEB	New England Business Services [*NYSE symbol*] (SAG)
NEB	New England Bus Svc [*NYSE symbol*] (TTSB)
NEB	New England Motor Rate Bureau Inc., Burlington MA [*STAC*]
NEB	[*The*] New English Bible [*1961*] [*A publication*]
NEB	Nissim Ezra Benjamin [*Shanghai*] (BJA)
NEB	Noise-Equivalent Bandwidth
NEB	Nonenzymatic Maillard Browning [*Food technology*]
NEB	North-Eastbound [*Aviation*] (FAAC)
NEB	North Equatorial Belt [*Planet Jupiter*]
NEB	Nuclear Energy Board [*Republic of Ireland*] (NUCP)
NEB	Nuclear Envelope Breakdown [*Also, NEBD*] [*Cytology*]
Neb	United States District Court for the District of Nebraska (DLA)
NEBA	North East Bolivian Airways [*ICAO designator*] (FAAC)
Neb Admin R	Nebraska Administrative Rules and Regulations [*A publication*] (DLA)
NEBB	National Environmental Balancing Bureau (EA)
NEBBA	Northeastern Bird-Banding Association [*Later, AFO*] (EA)
NEBBS	Naval Environmental Bulletin Board System
Nebby	Negative-Equity Baby Boomer [*Lifestyle classification*]
NEBD	Nuclear Envelope Breakdown [*Also, NEB*] [*Cytology*]
NEbE	Northeast by East
NEBHE	New England Board of Higher Education [*Information service or system*]
NEBI	National Employee Benefits Institute [*Washington, DC*] (EA)
NEBIC	New England Bibliographic Instruction Collection
NEBIS	North of England Biotechnology Information Service [*University of Newcastle-Upon-Tyne Medical School*] [*England*] [*Information service or system*] (IID)
NEBIT	New and Expanding Business and Industry Training (OICC)
NEBK	National Enterprise Bank [*Washington, DC*] (NQ)
Neb LB	Nebraska Law Bulletin [*A publication*] (DLA)
Neb Leg N	Nebraska Legal News [*A publication*] (DLA)
NEBM	No Eating between Meals
NEBMA	Neben-Munitionsanstalt [*Branch ammunition depot*] [*German military - World War II*]
NEbN	Northeast by North
NEBOSH	National Examination Board in Occupational Safety and Health (PDAA)
NEBR	Nebraska (AAG)
Nebr	Nebraska (ODBW)
Nebr	Nebraska Reports [*A publication*] (DLA)
Neb RC	Nebraska Railway Commission Reports [*A publication*] (DLA)
Neb Rev Stat	Revised Statutes of Nebraska [*A publication*] (DLA)
Nebr LB	Nebraska Law Bulletin [*A publication*] (DLA)
NEBS	New England Business Service, Inc. [*NASDAQ symbol*] (NQ)
NEBSS	National Examinations Board in Supervisory Studies [*British*]
Neb Sup Ct J	Nebraska Supreme Court Journal [*A publication*] (DLA)
NEBUL	Nebula [*Spray*] [*Pharmacy*]
NEBULA	Natural Electronic Business User's Language [*International Computers Ltd.*]
Neb (Unof)	Nebraska Unofficial Reports [*A publication*] (DLA)
Neb Unoff	Nebraska Unofficial Reports [*A publication*] (DLA)
NE Bus	New England Business Services [*Associated Press*] (SAG)
NEBW	Nonvacuum Electron Beam Welding
Neb WCC	Nebraska Workmen's Compensation Court. Bulletin [*A publication*] (DLA)
NEC	National Economic Council [*Defunct*] (EA)
NEC	National Economists Club (EA)
NEC	National Ecumenical Coalition (EA)
NEC	National Education Center for Paraprofessionals in Mental Health (EA)
NEC	National Education Corp. [*NYSE symbol*] (SPSG)
NEC	National Egg Council [*Later, PEIA*] (EA)
NEC	National Electoral Commission [*Nigeria*] (ECON)
NEC	National Electrical Code
NEC	National Electronics Conference (AEBS)
NEC	National Electronics Council (NITA)
NEC	National Emblem Club (EA)
NEC	National Emergency Council [*Abolished, 1939*]
NEC	National Employers' Committee
NEC	National Empowerment Consortium [*Investment group*] [*South Africa*]
NEC	National Engineering Consortium (EA)
NEC	National Entertainment Conference [*Later, NECAA*] (EA)
NEC	National Exchange Club (EA)
NEC	National Executive Committee [*British*] (DCTA)
NEC	National Executive Council (WDAA)
NEC	National Exhibition Centre [*British*]

NEC	National Extension College [*England*]
NEC	Natl Education [*NYSE symbol*] (TTSB)
NEC	Naval Examining Center
NEC	Naval Exercise Coordinator (CINC)
NEC	Naval Exhibit Center
NEC	Navy Enlisted Classification (NG)
NEC	Navy Enlisted Code
NEC	Nebraska State Railway Commission [*STAC*]
NEC	NEC Corp. [*Associated Press*] (SAG)
NEC	Necessary (AABC)
NEC	Necessity
NEC	Necochea [*Argentina*] [*Airport symbol*] (OAG)
NEC	Necrotizing Enterocolitis [*Medicine*]
NEC	Negro Ensemble Company [*A theatre group*]
NEC	Netherlands Electrotechnical Committee
NEC	Neuroendocrine Cell [*Cytology*]
NEC	Neuroendocrine Convertase (DMAA)
NEC	New England College, Henniker, NH [*OCLC symbol*] (OCLC)
NEC	New England Conservatory of Music (BARN)
NEC	New England Council (EA)
NEC	Newspaper Editor's Course [*Defense Information School*] (DNAB)
NEC	Nippon Electric Co. [*Japan*]
NEC	No-Error Check (IAA)
NEC	No Essential Changes (DMAA)
NEC	No Eye Contact [*Psychology*]
NEC	Noise-Equivalent Charge (PDAA)
NEC	Nonengineering Change (DNAB)
NEC	Nonesterified Cholesterol (DMAA)
NEC	Northeast Conference (PSS)
NEC	Northeast Conference on the Teaching of Foreign Languages (EA)
NEC	North East Corner [*Freemasonry*]
NEC	Northeast Corridor [*Railroad line*] (EGAO)
NEC	North Equatorial Current [*Oceanography*] (MSC)
NEC	Northern European Command [*NATO*] (NATG)
NEC	Northern European Countries
NEC	Northern Europe Committee [*NATO*] (NATG)
NEC	Not Else Classified (DMAA)
nec	Not Elsewhere Classified (ODBW)
NEC	Not Elsewhere Classified
NEC	Notes of English Ecclesiastical Cases [*A publication*] (DLA)
NEC	Nuclear Energy Center (NRCH)
NEC	Nuclear Energy Commission (USDC)
NEC	Nucleus of Epidermal Cell
NEC	Nursing Ethics Committee (DMAA)
NECA	National Electrical Contractors Association (EA)
NECA	National Employment Counseling Association (EA)
NECA	National Employment Counselors Association (EA)
NECA	National Episcopal Coalition on Alcohol [*Later, NECAD*] (EA)
NECA	National Exchange Carrier Association (EA)
NECA	National Explorers and Collectors Association (EA)
NECA	Near East College Association (EA)
NECA	N-Ethylcarboxamide Adenosine [*Biochemistry*]
NECA	Numismatic Error Collectors of America (EA)
NECAA	National Entertainment and Campus Activities Association [*Formerly, NEC*] (EA)
NECAC	New England College Athletic Conference (PSS)
NECAD	National Episcopal Coalition on Alcohol and Drugs (EA)
NECAF	National Electromagnetic Compatibility Analysis Facility [*Department of Commerce*] (PDAA)
NECAP	NASA Energy-Cost Analysis Program
NECAP	Navigation Equipment Capability Analysis (KSC)
NECAP	Nutmeg Electric Companies Atomic Project
NECAR	National Engineers Commission on Air Resources (PDAA)
NECAR	New Electric Car [*Daimler-Benz AG*] (PS)
NECB	New England Comm Bancorp'A' [*NASDAQ symbol*] (TTSB)
NECB	New England Community Bancorp, Inc. [*NASDAQ symbol*] (SAG)
NE CBcp	New England Community Bancorp, Inc. [*Associated Press*] (SAG)
NECC	National Education Computer Center
NECC	National Emergency Coordination Center (BARN)
NECC	New England Collegiate Conference
NECC	New England Congressional Caucus [*Defunct*] (EA)
NECC	Northeast Computer Center [*Military*] (AABC)
NECC	North Equatorial Countercurrent [*Oceanography*]
NECC	Northern Essex Community College [*Haverhill, MA*]
NECCAC	Northeast Community College Athletic Conference (PSS)
NECCB	National Education Council of the Christian Brothers [*Later, RECCB*] (EA)
NECCO	New England Confectionery Co.
NECCO	Northern Essex Community College [*Haverhill, MA*]
NECCTA	National Educational Closed-Circuit Television Association [*British*]
NECCWA	New England College Conference Wrestling Associaton (PSS)
NECDC	New England Consumer Development Council
NECEA	National Engineering Construction Employers Association [*British*] (DBA)
NECEC	New England Catholic Education Center (AEBS)
NECF	National Exchange Club Foundation for the Prevention of Child Abuse (EA)
NECG	National Engineering Council for Guidance (EA)
NECH	National Employment Clearing House [*American Chemical Society*]
NECH	National Event Clearinghouse Database [*National Event Clearinghouse, Inc.*] [*Information service or system*] (CRD)
NECHE	Northeastern Colorado Hail Experiment
NECHI	Northeastern Consortium for Health Information [*Library network*]
NECI	Noise Exposure Computer Integrator (PDAA)
NECIES	North East Coast Institution of Engineers and Shipbuilders (EAIO)
NECIP	Northeast Corridor Improvement Project [*Department of Transportation*]
NECIS	Naval Environmental Compliance Information System
NECIS	NEC Information Systems, Inc. [*Boxborough, MA*]
NECK	Neck [*Commonly used*] (OPSA)
NECLC	National Emergency Civil Liberties Committee (EA)
NECM	New England Conference Management [*Australia*]
NECM	New England Conservatory of Music [*Boston, MA*]
NECMA	New England County Metropolitan Areas
NECMD	Newark Contract Management District (SAA)
NECNVA	New England Committee for Nonviolent Action [*Later, CNVA*] (EA)
NECO	Nippon Electric Co. (IAA)
NECO	Nuclear Engineering Co., Inc.
NECOE	New England Center for Organizational Effectiveness (EA)
NECOP	Nutrient-Enhanced Coastal Ocean Productivity [*Marine science*] (OSRA)
NECOS	Communication Net Control Station [*Navy*] (NVT)
NECOS	Northern European Chiefs of Staff [*NATO*] (NATG)
NECP	National Eye Care Project [*Foundation of the American Academy of Ophthalmology*] (EA)
NECP	New England College of Pharmacy
NECP	Nonengineering Change Proposal
NECPA	National Emergency Command Post Afloat
NECPA	National Energy Conservation Policy Act [*1978*]
NECPL	NATO Exploratory Conference on Production Logistics (NATG)
NECPR	New External Cardiopulmonary Resuscitation
NECPWA	Northeast Club for Pre-War Austins [*British*] (EAIO)
NECQ	National Electronics Component Qualification System (AAEL)
NECRMP	Northeast Corridor Regional Modeling Project [*Environmental Protection Agency*] (GFGA)
Necro	Necrofile [*A publication*]
NECROL	Necrology (WDAA)
necrp	Necropolis (VRA)
NECS	National Electrical Code Standards
NECS	National Elephant Collectors Society (EA)
NECS	Nationwide Educational Computer Service (IEEE)
NECSS	Nuclear Energy Center Site Survey (NRCH)
NECTA	National Electric Comfort Trade Association [*Defunct*] (EA)
NECTAR	Network of European CNS [*Central Nervous System*] Transplantation and Restoration
NECTEC	National Electronics and Computer Technology Center [*Thailand*] (DDC)
NECTP	Northeast Corridor Transportation Project
NECWA	New England College Wrestling Association (PSS)
NECY	Necessary
NECY	Necessity (WDAA)
NED	Naphthylethylenediamine Dihydrochloride [*Organic chemistry*]
NED	National Endowment for Democracy (EA)
NED	Naval Equipment Department [*British military*] (DMA)
NED	Navigation Error Data (MUGU)
Ned	Nedarim (BJA)
NED	NeverEnding Disk [*Computer software*] [*Sytron Corp.*] (PCM)
NED	Newark [*Delaware*] [*Seismograph station code, US Geological Survey*] (SEIS)
NED	New Editor [*Computer program*] [*Air Force*] (MCD)
NED	New England Division [*Army Engineers*]
NED	New English Dictionary [*i.e., the Oxford English Dictionary*]
NED	No-Effect Dose [*Medicine*] (LDT)
NED	No Evidence of Disease
NED	No Expiration Date
NED	Nonenzymatic Glycosylation [*Biochemistry*] (DAVI)
NED	Normal Equivalent Deviation
NED	North, East, and Down
NED	Northeastern University, Boston, MA [*OCLC symbol*] (OCLC)
NED	Nuclear Energy Division [*General Electric Co.*]
NED	Nuclear Engineering Directorate [*Army*]
NEDA	National Economic Development Association
NEDA	National Electronic Distributors Association (EA)
NEDA	National Emergency Defense Airlift
NEDA	National Environmental Development Association (EA)
NEDA	National Equipment Distributors Association [*Defunct*] (EA)
NEDA	National Exhaust Distributors Association [*Later, NEDA/USA*] (EA)
Neda	Nedarim (BJA)
NEDA/CAAP	National Environmental Development Association/Clean Air Act Project [*Defunct*] (EA)
NEDA/GRND	National Environmental Development Association/Ground Water Project (EA)
NEDA/USA	National Exhaust Distributors Association/Undercar Specialists Association [*Defunct*] (EA)
NEDC	National Economic Development Council [*Nickname: Neddie*] [*British*]
NeDC	New England Document Conservation Center, Andover, MA [*Library symbol Library of Congress*] (LCLS)
NEDCC	New England Document Conservation Center [*Information service or system*] (IID)
NEDCC	Northeast Document Conservation Center
NEDCO	Non-Electronic Part Data Collection (PDAA)
NEDCO	Northeast Dairy Cooperative Federation [*Defunct*] (EA)
NEDECO	Netherlands Engineering Consultants
NEDED	Naval Explosive Development Engineering Department (DNAB)
NEDEL	No Epidemiologically Detectable Exposure Level [*Medicine*] (HCT)
NEDELA	Network Definition Language [*Computer science*] (PDAA)
NEDEP	Navy Enlisted Dietetic Education Program
NEDEPA	Nea Demokratiki Parataxi [*Cyprus*] [*Political party*] (PPE)
NeDF	New England Data Film, Inc., Milford, CT [*Library symbol Library of Congress*] (LCLS)

NEDI .... Nobel Education Dynamics, Inc. [*NASDAQ symbol*] (SAG)
NEDIPA .... Nea Demokratiki Parataxi [*Cyprus*] [*Political party*] (PPW)
NEDIPS .... NEC Dataflow Image Processing System (NITA)
NEDIS .... National Environmental Data and Information Service [*Marine science*] (MSC)
NEDL .... New England Deposit Library
NEDI .... Nobel Ed Dynamics [*NASDAQ symbol*] (TTSB)
NEDLC .... National Economic Development and Law Center [*Berkeley, CA*] [*Research center*] (EA)
NEDLIB .... Networked European Deposit Library (TELE)
NEDN .... Naval Environmental Data Network
NEDN .... Naval Worldwide Environmental Data Network (MCD)
NEDO .... National Eating Disorders Organization
NEDO .... National Economic Development Office [*British*]
NEDRES .... National Environmental Data Referral Service [*Online database*] [*National Oceanic and Atmospheric Administration Washington, DC*]
NEDS .... National Emissions Data System [*Environmental Protection Agency Information service or system*]
NEDS .... Naval Environmental Data System (CAAL)
NEDS .... Naval Environmental Display Station (CAAL)
NEDS .... New Enlisted Distribution System (NVT)
NEDS .... Nonviolent Explosive Destructive System (MCD)
NEDSA .... Nonerasing Deterministic Stack Automation [*Computer science*] (IAA)
NEDT .... National Educational Development Test
NEDT .... Noise-Equivalent Differential Temperature
NeDTH .... Technische Hogeschool Delft, Delft, Netherlands [*Library symbol Library of Congress*] (LCLS)
NEDTRA .... Naval Education and Training Command (MCD)
NEDU .... Navy Experimental Diving Unit [*Panama City, FL*]
NEE .... National Electrical Effect
NEE .... National Electrology Educators (EA)
NEE .... Needle Electrode Examination [*Medicine*] (DMAA)
NEE .... Net Ecosystem Exchange [*Biology*]
NEE .... New England Express [*Steamship*] (MHDW)
NEE .... Noise-Equivalent Energy (MCD)
NEE .... Noise Equivalent Exposure [*Photonics*]
NEE .... Norethindrone/Ethinyl Estradiol [*Oral contraceptive*]
NEE .... Northeast Airlines [*FAA designator*] (FAAC)
NEE .... Northeast Express Regional Airlines, Inc. [*ICAO designator*] (FAAC)
NEEB .... North Eastern Electricity Board [*British*]
NEEC .... National Environmental Enforcement Council [*National Association of Attorneys General*] (EPA)
NEEC .... National Export Expansion Council [*Terminated, 1973*] [*Department of Commerce*]
NEEC .... Not Entailing Excessive Cost [*Environmental technology*]
NEEC .... Nuclear Explosion Effects Center
NEED .... National Energy Education Development Project (EA)
NEED .... National Environmental Education Development [*Program of National Park Service*] [*Defunct*]
NEED .... Native Employment and Educational Development [*Canada*]
NEED .... Near East Emergency Donations
Need .... Needham's Annual Summary of Tax Cases [*England*] [*A publication*] (DLA)
NEED .... Need, Inc. [*An association*] (EA)
NEED .... Negro Education Emergency Drive
NEED .... New Employment Expansion and Development [*Canada*]
NEEDHA .... National Electrical Engineering Department Heads Association (EA)
NEEDIS .... National Enterprise Education Development and Information Service (AIE)
NEEDS .... NASA End-to-End Data Systems
NEEDS .... National Emergency Employment Data System (NITA)
NEEDS .... Navy Education and Employment Development System (MCD)
NEEDS .... Neighborhood Environmental Evaluation and Decision System [*Health Services and Mental Health Administration*]
NEEDS .... New England Educational Data Systems
NEEDS-IR ..... NIKKEI Economic Electronic Databank Service - Information Retrieval [*Information service or system Japan*] (IID)
NEEDS-TS .... NIKKEI Economic Electronic Databank Service - Time Sharing [*Information service or system Japan*] (IID)
NEEE .... Near East Equine Encephalomyelitis [*Medicine*] (DMAA)
NeEinP .... Philips Research Laboratories, Eindhoven, Netherlands [*Library symbol Library of Congress*] (LCLS)
NeEinT .... Technische Hogeschool te Eindhoven, Eindhoven, Netherlands, [*Library symbol Library of Congress*] (LCLS)
NEEITC .... National Electrical and Electronic Industry Training Committee [*Australia*]
NEEJ .... National Environmental Enforcement Journal [*National Association of Attorneys General*] [*A publication*] (EPA)
NEEL .... National Environmental Education Landmarks [*Department of the Interior*]
NEELS .... National Emergency Equipment Locator System [*Environment Canada*] [*Information service or system*] (CRD)
NEEMIS .... New England Energy Management Information System
NEEP .... Negative End Expiratory Pressure [*Medicine*]
NEEP .... New England Economic Project (NITA)
NEEP .... Nuclear Electronics Effects Program
NE'ER .... Never (ROG)
NEERI .... National Environmental Engineering Research Institute
NEERS .... National Earthquake Early Reporting System (NOAA)
NEES .... Naval Engineering Experiment Station
NEES .... New England Electric System
NEESA .... Naval Energy and Environmental Support Activity
NEESAB .... National Energy Extension Service Advisory Board [*Department of Energy Washington, DC*] (EGAO)

NEET .... Navy Extended Electrode Technique (PDAA)
NEETF .... National Environmental Education and Training Foundation [*An association*] (PS)
NEETS .... Naval Electronics Environmental Training System (MCD)
NEETU .... National Engineering and Electrical Trade Union [*Republic of Ireland*] (BI)
NEEWSSOP... NATO Europe Early Warning System Standard Operating Procedures (NATG)
NEF .... National Educators Fellowship [*Later, CEAI*]
NEF .... National Energy Foundation (EA)
NEF .... National Extra Fine [*Thread*]
NEF .... Naval Emergency Fund [*A budget category*]
NEF .... Near East Foundation (EA)
NEF .... Negative-Regulatory Factor [*Genetics*]
NeF .... Nephritic Factor [*Clinical medicine*]
NEF .... New Education Fellowship [*Later, WEF*]
NEF .... No Further Clearance Required [*Aviation*] (FAAC)
NEF .... Noise-Equivalent Flux
NEF .... Noise Exposure Forecast [*Aircraft*]
NEF .... Nordiska.Ekonomiska Forskningsradet [*Nordic Economic Research Council - NERC*] (EAIO)
NEF .... Nurses Educational Funds (EA)
NEF .... Scudder New Europe Fund [*NYSE symbol*] (SPSG)
NEFA .... Narcotic Educational Foundation of America (EA)
NEFA .... New European Fighter Aircraft (PS)
NEFA .... Nonesterified Fatty Acid [*Biochemistry*]
NEFARS .... Nuclear Effects from Analysis of Residual Signatures
NEFBRACS... Nearfield Bearing and Range Accuracy Calibration System (PDAA)
NEFC .... Near East Forestry Commission
NEFC .... New England Football Conference (PSS)
NEFC .... Northeast Fisheries Center [*Department of Commerce*] [*Woods Hole, MA*]
NEFCO .... New England Fish Co.
NEFD .... Noise-Equivalent Flux Density
NEFDA .... New England Fisheries Development Association (EA)
NEFDF .... New England Fisheries Development Foundation [*Later, NEFDA*] (EA)
NEFE .... New England Fish Exchange (EA)
NEFEC .... Northeast Fisheries Center [*National Marine Fisheries Service*] (USDC)
NEFES .... Northeastern Forest Experiment Station [*Department of Agriculture*] [*Broomall, PA*] (GRD)
NEFGX .... New England Growth [*Mutual fund ticker symbol*] (SG)
NEFI .... New England Fuel Institute
NEFMC .... New England Fisheries Management Council
NEFMO .... NATO European Fighter Management Organization (MCD)
NEFO .... National Electronics Facilities Organization
NEFOS .... New Emerging Forces
NEFP .... New England Free Press [*Publisher*]
NEFPS .... National Enginemen and Firemen's Protection Society [*A union*] [*British*]
NEFSA .... National Education Field Service Association [*Defunct*] (EA)
NEG .... Energy East [*NYSE symbol*] [*Formerly, New York State E&G*]
NEG .... National Environmental Group (EFIS)
Neg. .... Nega'im (BJA)
NEG .... Negate a Binary Number [*Computer science*]
NEG .... Negation (WDAA)
NEG .... Negative (AAG)
neg .... Negative (VRA)
NEG .... Neglect [*FBI standardized term*]
NEG .... Negligible (AAG)
NEG .... Negotiable (ADA)
NEG .... Negril [*Jamaica*] [*Airport symbol*] (OAG)
NEG .... Negro
NEG .... Numerical Experimentation Group [*Marine science*] (OSRA)
NEGA .... National Ex-Offender Grant Alliance [*Defunct*] (EA)
NEGA .... New England Gerontological Association (EA)
Negb .... Negotiable
Neg C .... Negligence Cases [*Commerce Clearing House*] [*A publication*] (DLA)
Neg Cas ...... Bloomfield's Manumission (or Negro) Cases [*New Jersey*] [*A publication*] (DLA)
NEGD .... Negotiated (ROG)
NEGDEF .... Navy Enlisted Ground Defense Emergency Force
NEGF .... Neurite Growth-Promoting Factor (DMAA)
NEGI .... National Federation of Engineering and General Ironfounders [*British*] (BI)
Neg Inst....... Negotiable Instrument [*Legal term*] (DLA)
NEGISTOR ... Negative Resistor (PDAA)
NEGIT .... Negative Impedance Transistor [*Electronics*] (IAA)
Negl .... Negligence
Negl & Comp Cas Ann... Negligence and Compensation Cases, Annotated [*A publication*] (DLA)
Negl & Comp Cas Ann 3d... Negligence and Compensation Cases, Annotated, Third Series [*A publication*] (DLA)
Negl & Comp Cas Ann (NS)... Negligence and Compensation Cases, Annotated, New Series [*A publication*] (DLA)
Negl Cas..... Negligence Cases [*Commerce Clearing House*] [*A publication*] (DLA)
Negl Cas 2d... Negligence Cases, Second Series [*Commerce Clearing House*] [*A publication*] (DLA)
NEGN .... Negotiation (ROG)
NEGOA........ Northeast Gulf of Alaska [*Marine science*] (MSC)
NEGOT .... Negotiable [*Legal shorthand*] (LWAP)
NEGPED .... Negotiator's Planned Execution Date (MCD)
NEGPR .... Negative Print
NEGPT .... Negative Print (VRA)

NEGRO......... National Economic Growth and Reconstruction Organization [*Black entrepreneurial organization*]
NEGRO........ New England Grass Roots Organization
Negro Cas ... Bloomfield's Manumission (or Negro) Cases [*New Jersey*] [*A publication*] (DLA)
NEGRS......... Negative Report Submitted [*Army*] (AABC)
NEGRSBM.... Negative Report Submitted [*Army*] (AABC)
negs............ Negatives [*Film*] (WDMC)
NEGTAX....... Negative Tax (MHDW)
NEGX.......... National Energy Group [*NASDAQ symbol*] (SAG)
NEGX.......... Natl Energy Group`A' [*NASDAQ symbol*] (TTSB)
NEGX.......... Negate a Binary Number with Extend [*Computer science*]
NEGY.......... Neutral-Equivalent Gasoline Yield [*Petroleum chemistry*]
NEH .... East Carolina University, Health Sciences Library, Greenville, NC [*OCLC symbol*] (OCLC)
NEh .... East Hampton Free Library, East Hampton, NY [*Library symbol Library of Congress*] (LCLS)
NEH .... National Endowment for the Humanities
Neh .... Nehemiah [*Old Testament book*]
NEH .... Nuclear Effects Handbook
NEHA .... National Environmental Health Association (EA)
NEHA .... National Executive Housekeepers Association (EA)
NeHB .... Bureau voor de Industriele Eigendom, Bibliotheek Octrooiraad, The Hague, Netherlands [*Library symbol Library of Congress*] (LCLS)
NEHC .... National Extension Homemakers Council (EA)
NEHE .... Nurses for Environmental Health Education (DAVI)
NEHEP .... National Eye Health Education Program [*Information service or system*] (IID)
NEHF .... National Eye and Health Foundation (EA)
NEHGS......... New England Historic Genealogical Society (EA)
NEHI .... Northwest Educators of the Hearing Impaired (EDAC)
NeHKB .... Koninklijke Bibliotheek [*Royal Library*], The Hague, Netherlands [*Library symbol Library of Congress*] (LCLS)
NEHRC......... New England History Resources Center [*University of New England*] [*Australia*]
NEHRP......... National Earthquake Hazards Reduction Program [*Federal Emergency Management Agency*] [*Washington, DC*] (EGAO)
NeHSU......... Staatsuitgeverij Christoffel Plantijnstaat (State Printing Office), The Hague, Netherlands [*Library symbol Library of Congress*] (LCLS)
NEi.............. East Islip Public Library, East Islip, NY [*Library symbol Library of Congress*] (LCLS)
NEI.............. Narcotics Education, Inc. (EA)
NEI.............. National Elevator Industry (NTPA)
NEI.............. National Enterprises (EFIS)
NEI.............. National Estuarine Inventory
NEI.............. National Eye Institute [*Formerly, NINDB*] [*Department of Health and Human Services Bethesda, MD*] [*National Institutes of Health*]
NEI.............. Nature Expeditions International (GNE)
NEI.............. Neipperg [*Federal Republic of Germany*] [*Seismograph station code, US Geological Survey*] (SEIS)
NEI.............. Netherlands East Indies
NEI.............. New Enterprise Institute [*University of Southern Maine*] [*Research center*] (RCD)
NEI.............. New Equipment Introduction [*Army*] (AABC)
NEI.............. Noise-Equivalent Input
NEI.............. Noise-Equivalent Intensity
NEI.............. Noise Equivalent Irradiance (CIST)
NEI.............. Non Est Inventus [*It Has Not Been Found or Discovered*] [*Latin*]
NEI.............. Nordic Energy Index [*Database*] [*Nordic Atomic Libraries Joint Secretariat*] [*Denmark*] [*Information service or system*] (IID)
NEI.............. Northern Electric Industries [*British*]
NEI.............. Northern Engineering Industries [*Commercial firm British*]
nei .... Not Elsewhere Included or Indicated (EBF)
NEI.............. Not Elsewhere Indicated
NEI.............. Nouvelles Equipes Internationales [*Later, European Christian Democratic Union*]
NEI.............. Nuclear Energy Institute (NTPA)
NEIAL.......... North East Iowa Academic Libraries [*Library network*]
NEIB............ Northeast Indiana Banc [*NASDAQ symbol*] (TTSB)
NEIB............ Northeast Indiana Bancorp, Inc. [*NASDAQ symbol*] (SAG)
NEIC............ National Earthquake Information Center [*US Geological Survey*]
NEIC............ National Electronic Information Corp. [*Information service or system*] (IID)
NEIC............ National Energy Information Center [*Department of Energy*] [*Washington, DC*]
NEIC............ National Enforcement Investigations Center [*Environmental Protection Agency*] (EG)
NEIC............ National Equivalence Information Centre (AIE)
NEIC............ NATO Equipment Interpretation Course (MCD)
NEIC............ New England Information Center [*Information service or system*]
NEIC............ Northeast Independent Conference (PSS)
NEIC............ North East Insurance [*NASDAQ symbol*] (TTSB)
NEIC............ North East Insurance Co. [*NASDAQ symbol*] (NQ)
NEICA .... National Energy Information Center Affiliate [*University of New Mexico*] (IID)
NEICE.......... North of England Institute for Christian Education
NEIDA.......... Network of Educational Innovation for Development in Africa (EAIO)
NEIDS.......... North East Interim Data System (WDAA)
NEIED.......... National Educational Institute for Economic Development (EA)
NEIETC........ New England Interstate Environmental Training Center
NEIF............ Near-Earth Instrumentation Facility [*NASA*] (KSC)
NEII............. National Elevator Industry, Inc. (EA)
NEIL............ Neon Indicating Light
NEIL............ Nordic Energy Index, Literature [*Database*] [*Nordic Atomic Libraries Joint Secretariat*] [*Information service or system*] (CRD)

NeimM......... Neiman-Marcus Group [*Associated Press*] (SAG)
NeINBc........ Northeast Indiana Bancorp, Inc. [*Associated Press*] (SAG)
NE Ins .... North East Insurance Co. [*Associated Press*] (SAG)
NEIPG .... National Electronic Industries Procurement Group
NEIR .... Narrative End Item Report [*NASA*] (KSC)
NEIR .... Neither (ROG)
NEIRLS .... Northeast Regional Library System [*Library network*]
NEIS .... National Earthquake Information Service [*United States Geological Survey*] (IID)
NEIS .... National Emissions Inventory System [*Database*] [*Environment Canada*] [*Information service or system*] (CRD)
NEIS .... National Engineering Information System (BUR)
NEIS .... National Environmental Information Symposium
NEIS .... Nuclear Energy Information Service [*An association*] (EA)
NEISA .... New England Intercollegiate Sailing Association
NEISS .... National Electronic Injury Surveillance System [*Consumer Product Safety Commission*] [*Washington, DC Databank*]
NEIT............ New Equipment Introductory Team [*Army*] (AABC)
NEITA.......... National Excellence in Teaching Award [*Australia*]
NEIULS .... Northeast Iowa Union List of Serials
NEIWPCC..... New England Interstate Water Pollution Control Commission
NEIX .... Nordic Energy Index [*Database*] [*Nordic Atomic Libraries Joint Secretariat*] [*Information service or system*] (CRD)
NEJ .... Seattle, WA [*Location identifier FAA*] (FAAL)
NEJA .... National Entertainment Journalists Association [*Defunct*] (EA)
NEJS .... Near Eastern and Judaistic Studies (BJA)
NEK .... Naval Equerry to the King
NEKASA ...... New England Knitwear and Sportswear Association (EA)
NEKDA .... New England Kiln Drying Association (EA)
NEKL .... Northeast Kansas Library System [*Library network*]
NEKOA .... New England Knitted Outerwear Association [*Later, NEKASA*] (EA)
NEL .... East Carolina University, Department of Library Science, Greenville, NC [*OCLC symbol*] (OCLC)
NEl .... Greenburgh Public Library, Elmsford, NY [*Library symbol Library of Congress*] (LCLS)
NEL .... Lakehurst, NJ [*Location identifier FAA*] (FAAL)
NEL .... National Electronics Laboratory (IDOE)
NEL .... National Emancipation League [*Nigeria*]
NEL .... National Engineering Laboratory [*Superseded IAT*] [*Gaithersburg, MD*] [*National Institute of Standards and Technology*]
NEL .... National Engineering Laboratory [*Scotland*]
NEL .... National Epilepsy League [*Later, EFA*] (EA)
NEL .... Naval Command Control Communications Laboratory Center
NEL .... Naval Electronics Laboratory
NEL .... Naval Explosive Laboratory
NEL .... Navy Electronics Laboratory [*San Diego, CA*]
NEL .... Nelson [*Nevada*] [*Seismograph station code, US Geological Survey*] (SEIS)
Nel .... Nelson's English Chancery Reports [*A publication*] (DLA)
NEL .... Neon Light (IAA)
NEL .... New England Mutual Life Insurance Co. (EFIS)
NEL .... New English Library [*Publishers*] [*British*]
NEL .... NewTel Enterprises Ltd. [*Toronto Stock Exchange symbol*]
NEL .... No Effect Level (ADA)
NEL .... Non-English Language
NEL .... Nonspecific Excitability Level [*Animal behavior*]
NEL .... Northern Extratropical Land [*Geography*]
NEL .... Nuclear Energy Laboratory [*Research center*] (RCD)
NEL .... Nuclear Engineering Laboratory [*University of Utah*] [*Research center*] (RCD)
NELA........... National Electric Light Association
NELA........... National Employment Lawyers Association (EA)
NELA........... New England Library Association
NELA........... Northeastern Loggers Association (EA)
NELAC......... National Environment Laboratory Accreditation Conference [*Environmental Protection Agency*]
NELAT......... Navy Electronics Laboratory Assembly Tester
NELATS........ Naval Electronics Laboratory Automatic Tester System (DNAB)
NELB........... New England Library Board [*Library network*]
NELC........... Naval Electronics Laboratory Center [*Later, NOSC*]
NELCON NZ... National Electronics Conference, New Zealand [*IEEE*]
Nel CR .... Nelson's English Chancery Reports [*A publication*] (DLA)
NEld............ Sunshine Hall Free Library, Eldred, NY [*Library symbol Library of Congress*] (LCLS)
NELEC......... Nonelectric
NELEX........ Naval Electronics Systems Command Headquarters
NELIA......... Nuclear Energy Liability Insurance Association [*Later, ANI*] (EA)
NELIAC........ Naval Electronics Laboratory International ALGOL Compilers
NELINET...... New England Library Information Network
NELIS.......... Noncommunications Emitter Location and Identification System (MCD)
NELIS-A .... Noncommunications Emitter Location and Identification System - Airborne
NELL........... Nellcor, Inc. [*NASDAQ symbol*] (NQ)
NELL........... Nellcor Puritan Bennett [*NASDAQ symbol*] (TTSB)
Nell............. Nell's Reports [*1845-55*] [*Ceylon*] [*A publication*] (DLA)
NELLCO .... New England Law Library Consortium, Inc. [*Harvard Law School*] [*Information service or system*] (IID)
Nellcor........ Nellcor, Inc. [*Associated Press*] (SAG)
NElle........... Ellenville Public Library, Ellenville, NY [*Library symbol Library of Congress*] (LCLS)
NElm........... Steele Memorial Library of Elmira and Chemung County, Elmira, NY [*Library symbol Library of Congress*] (LCLS)
NELMA........ Northeastern Lumber Manufacturers Association (EA)

NEImC .... Elmira College, Elmira, NY [*Library symbol Library of Congress*] (LCLS)

NEImhC .... City Hospital at Elmhurst, Elmhurst, NY [*Library symbol Library of Congress*] (LCLS)

NEImHi .... Chemung County Historical Society, Elmira, NY [*Library symbol Library of Congress*] (LCLS)

NEImM .... Mount Saviour Monastery, Elmira, NY [*Library symbol Library of Congress*] (LCLS)

NEImo .... Elmont Public Library, Elmont, NY [*Library symbol Library of Congress*] (LCLS)

NEImoAE ...... Alden Terrace Elementary School, Elmont, NY [*Library symbol*] [*Library of Congress*] (LCLS)

NEImoCCE ... Clara H. Carlson Elementary School, Elmont, NY [*Library symbol*] [*Library of Congress*] (LCLS)

NEImoCE ...... Covert Elementary School, Elmont, NY [*Library symbol Library of Congress*] (LCLS)

NEImoDE ...... Dutch Broadway Elementary School, Elmont, NY [*Library symbol*] [*Library of Congress*] (LCLS)

NEImoGE ..... Gotham Avenue Elementary School, Elmont, NY [*Library symbol*] [*Library of Congress*] (LCLS)

NEImoMH ...... Elmont Memerial High School, Elmont, NY [*Library symbol*] [*Library of Congress*] (LCLS)

NEImoSE ...... Stewart Elementary School, Elmont, NY [*Library symbol Library of Congress*] (LCLS)

NEImP .... Elmira Psychiatric Center, Elmira, NY [*Library symbol Library of Congress*] (LCLS)

NEImsAr ..... Weschester County Archives, Elmsford, NY [*Library symbol*] [*Library of Congress*] (LCLS)

NEImSC .... Supreme Court Law Library-Elmira, Elmira, NY [*Library symbol*] [*Library of Congress*] (LCLS)

NEImsSW ...... Southern Westchester BOCES School, Elmsford, NY [*Library symbol*] [*Library of Congress*] (LCLS)

NELOS .... Navy Electronics Laboratory Operating System

NELP .... National Employment Law Project [*New York, NY*] (EA)

NELP .... Navy Environmental Leadership Program

NELP .... North East London Polytechnic [*School*] [*England*]

NELPAC .... National Engineering Laboratory's Thermophysical Properties Package [*British Information service or system*] (IID)

NELPIA .... Nuclear Energy Liability Property Insurance Association [*Later, ANI*]

NeLR .... Rijksuniversiteit Leiden, Leiden, Netherlands [*Library symbol Library of Congress*] (LCLS)

NELRC .... National Epilepsy Library and Resource Center [*Epilepsy Foundation of America*] [*Information service or system*] (IID)

NELS .... National Educational Longitudinal Survey

NELS .... National Environmental Laboratories [*Proposed*]

Nels .... Nelson's English Chancery Reports [*A publication*] (DLA)

Nels 8vo ...... Nelson's English Chancery Reports [*A publication*] (DLA)

NELS:88 .... National Education Longitudinal Study of 1988 [*Department of Education*] (GFGA)

NELSA .... Northeast Library Service Area [*Library network*]

Nels Abr ...... Nelson's Abridgment of the Common Law [*A publication*] (DLA)

Nels Cler ..... Nelson's Rights of the Clergy [*A publication*] (DLA)

Nels F .... Finch's English Chancery Reports, by Nelson [*1673-81*] [*A publication*] (DLA)

Nels Fol ...... Finch's English Chancery Reports, by Nelson [*1673-81*] [*A publication*] (DLA)

Nels Lex Man ... Nelson's Lex Maneriorum [*A publication*] (DLA)

NelsnB .... Nelson [*Thomas*], Inc. [*Associated Press*] (SAG)

NelsnT .... Nelson [*Thomas*], Inc. [*Associated Press*] (SAG)

NELSON .... News Editing and Layout System of Newspapers (DGA)

Nelson (Eng) ... Nelson's English Chancery Reports [*A publication*] (DLA)

Nelson's Rep. ... Nelson Tempore Finch [*1673-81*] [*A publication*] (DLA)

NELTS .... Number of Elements Loaded [*Army*]

NeLV .... Koninklijk Instituut voor Taal-, Land-, en Volkenkunde, Leiden, Netherlands [*Library symbol Library of Congress*] (LCLS)

NELV .... Nerine Latent Virus [*Plant pathology*]

NELWA .... New England Lumber Women's Association [*Defunct*] (EA)

NEm .... East Meadow Public Library, East Meadow, NY [*Library symbol Library of Congress*] (LCLS)

NEM .... Metropolitan Technical Community College, Omaha, NE [*OCLC symbol*] (OCLC)

nem .... Nahrungs Einheit Milch [*Nahrungsteinheit Milch*] [*Nutritional milk unit*] [*Dietetics*] (DAVI)

Nem .... Nemean [*of Pindar*] [*Classical studies*] (OCD)

NEM .... Nemuro [*Japan*] [*Seismograph station code, US Geological Survey*] (SEIS)

NEM .... N-Ethylmaleimide [*Also, NEMI*] [*Organic chemistry*]

NEM .... N-Ethylmorpholine [*Organic chemistry*]

nEM .... NetworkMCI Enterprise Management

NEM .... New Electronic Media (NTCM)

NeM .... New England Micrographics, Inc., Waltham, MA [*Library symbol Library of Congress*] (LCLS)

NEM .... Newmont Mining [*NYSE symbol*] (TTSB)

NEM .... Newmont Mining Corp. [*NYSE symbol*] (SPSG)

NEM .... Nickel Electroformed Mold

NEM .... Nonelectronic Maintenance

NEM .... Noram Environment [*Vancouver Stock Exchange symbol*]

NEM .... Not Elsewhere Mentioned

nem .... Not Elsewhere Mentioned (EBF)

NEMA .... National Early Music Association [*British*] (DBA)

NEMA .... National Eclectic Medical Association [*Defunct*] (EA)

NEMA .... National Educational Management Association (EA)

NEMA .... National Electrical Manufacturers Association (EA)

NEMA .... National Electricity Manufacturers' Association (NITA)

NEMA .... National Emergency Management Association (EA)

NEMA .... National Emergency Medicine Association (EA)

NEMA .... Nematode [*Threadworm*]

NEMA .... Nematron Corp. [*NASDAQ symbol*] (SAG)

NEMAC .... National Energy Management Advisory Committee [*British*]

NEMAC .... Normal Error Model Analysis Chart

NEMAG .... Negative Effective Mass Amplifiers and Generators

NEMAS .... New England Marine Advisory Service

NEMAS .... Nursing Education Module Authoring System

NEMATOL .... Nematology

NEmBGE .... Bowling Green Elementary School, East Meadow, NY [*Library symbol Library of Congress*] (LCLS)

NEmBWE ..... Barnum Woods Elementary School, East Meadow, NY [*Library symbol Library of Congress*] (LCLS)

NEMC .... National Export Meatworks Council [*Australia*]

NEMC .... New England Medical Center [*Boston, MA*]

NEMCA .... NATO Electromagnetic Compatibility Agency (NATG)

NEMCA .... Non-Faradaic Electrochemical Modification of Catalytic Activity [*Chemistry*]

NEMCC .... Nonessential Motor Control Center (AAG)

NEMCH .... New England Medical Center Hospitals

NEmCJS .... W. T. Clarke Junior-Senior High School, East Meadow, NY [*Library symbol Library of Congress*] (LCLS)

NEM CON ..... Nemine Contradicente [*No One Contradicting*] [*Latin Legal term*]

nem con .... Nemine Contradicente [*No One Contradicting*] [*Latin*] (WA)

NEMD .... Nonequilibrium Molecular Dynamics [*Chemical property simulation technique*]

NEMD .... Nonspecific Esophageal Motility Disorder [*Gastroenterology*] (DAVI)

NEMD .... Nonspecific Esophageal Motor Dysfunction [*Medicine*]

NEMDA .... Northeastern Minnesota Development Association

NEM DISS .... Nemine Dissentiente [*No One Dissenting*] [*Latin*]

NEMEA .... New England Media Evaluators Association

NEMEDRI ..... North European and Mediterranean Routing Information [*Naval Oceanographic Office*]

NEMEX .... National Energy Management Exhibition and Conference (ITD)

NEMG T RL .. New England MG ™T∫Register Ltd. (EA)

NEmH .... Meadowbrook Hospital, East Meadow, NY [*Library symbol Library of Congress*] (LCLS)

NEMI .... National Elevator Manufacturing Industry [*Later, NEII*] (EA)

NEMI .... N-Ethylmaleimide [*Also, NEM*] [*Organic chemistry*]

NEMIC .... New England Materials-Instruction Center

NEMISYS .... New Mexico Information System [*Library network*]

NEmL .... East Meadow Public Library, East Meadow, NY [*Library symbol*] [*Library of Congress*] (LCLS)

NEMLA .... New England Modern Language Association (AEBS)

NEmMC .... Nassau County Medical Center, East Meadow, NY [*Library symbol Library of Congress*] (LCLS)

NEmMcE ...... McVey Elementary School, East Meadow, NY [*Library symbol Library of Congress*] (LCLS)

NEMMCO ...... National Electricity Market Management Company, Ltd. [*Australia*] [*Commercial firm*]

NEmME .... Meadowbrook Elementary School, East Meadow, NY [*Library symbol Library of Congress*] (LCLS)

NEmMH .... East Meadow High School, East Meadow, NY [*Library symbol*] [*Library of Congress*] (LCLS)

NEmNHi ...... Nassau County Historical Museum, East Meadow, NY [*Library symbol Library of Congress*] (LCLS)

NEMO .... Naval Experimental Manned Observatory

NEMO .... Never Ever Mention Outside [*Secret computer toy project of Axlon, Inc.*]

NeMO .... New Millennium Observatory

NEMO .... Nonempirical Molecular Orbitals [*Atomic physics*]

NEMO .... Not Emanating Main Office [*Remote broadcast*] (NTCM)

NEMO .... Nuclear Exchange Model

NEMP .... Nuclear Electromagnetic Propagation

NEMP .... Nuclear Electromagnetic Pulse (AABC)

NEmPE .... Parkway Elementary School, East Meadow, NY [*Library symbol Library of Congress*] (LCLS)

NEMPS .... National Environmental Monitoring and Prediction System (MCD)

NEMQO .... Non Est Mortale Quod Opto [*It Is No Mortal Thing I Desire*] [*Motto of Friedrich III, Duke of Schleswig-Holstein-Gottorp (1597-1659)*] [*Latin*]

NEMR .... National E [*Electronic*]-Mail Registry [*Information service or system*] (TSSD)

NEMRA .... National Electrical Manufacturers Representatives Association (EA)

NEMRB .... New England Motor Rate Bureau

NEMRIP .... New England Marine Resources Information Program [*University of Rhode Island*] [*Later, NEMAS*]

NEMS .... National Aeronautics and Space Administration [*NASA*] Equipment Management System (AAGC)

NEMS .... National Exchange Market System

NEMS .... Near-Earth Magnetospheric Satellite

NEMS .... Nimbus E Microwave Spectrometer [*Meteorology*]

NEMSPA ...... National EMS [*Emergency Medical Service*] Pilots Association (EA)

NEMT .... Naval Emergency Monitoring Teams (PDAA)

NEMTA .... New England Men's Track Association (PSS)

NEMVAC ...... Noncombatant Emergency and Evacuation Plan (NVT)

NE-MWCC .... Northeast-Midwest Congressional Coalition (EA)

NEmWJ .... Woodland Junior High School, East Meadow, NY [*Library symbol*] [*Library of Congress*] (LCLS)

NEN .... New Eyes for the Needy (EA)

NEN .... North-East Airlines Ltd. [*Nigeria*] [*FAA designator*] (FAAC)

NEN .... Northstar Energy Corp. [*Toronto Stock Exchange symbol*]

NEN .... Whitehouse, FL [*Location identifier FAA*] (FAAL)

NENCL .... Nonenclosure

NE/ND .... New Edition / No Date [*of Publication*] (DGA)

NENEP	Navy Enlisted Nursing Education Program
NENG	New England
NEngEl	New England Electric System [*Associated Press*] (SAG)
NEngInv	New England Investment Companies Ltd. [*Associated Press*] (SAG)
N Eng J Med	New England Journal of Medicine (MEC)
N Eng J Prison L	New England Journal on Prison Law [*A publication*] (DLA)
N Eng Rep	New England Reporter [*A publication*] (DLA)
NEnI	International Business Machines Corp., Systems Development Library, Endicott, NY [*Library symbol Library of Congress*] (LCLS)
N ENMLD	Not Enameled [*Freight*]
NEnoVM	James Vernon Middle School, East Norwich, NY [*Library symbol*] [*Library of Congress*] (LCLS)
NEO	National Electrolysis Organization [*Later, SCME*] (EA)
NEO	National Energy Office [*Executive Office of the President*]
NEO	Near-Earth Object [*Astronomy*]
NEO	Near-Earth Orbit
NEO	Neoarsphenamine [*or Neosalvarsan*] [*Medicine*]
NEO	Neocomian [*Paleontology*]
NEO	Neomycin [*Antibiotic compound*]
NEO	Neonatal [*Medicine*]
NEO	Neopharm, Inc. [*AMEX symbol*] (SAG)
NEO	Noncombatant Evacuation Operation [*Army*] (INF)
NEO	Noncombatant Evacuation Order [*Army*] (AABC)
NEO	Northeastern Operations Office [*NASA*]
NEO	Northeast Oklahoma R. R. [*AAR code*]
NEO	Pensacola, FL [*Location identifier FAA*] (FAAL)
NEOB	New Executive Office Building [*Washington, DC*]
NEOC	National Earth Observations Center [*National Oceanic and Atmospheric Administration*]
NEOCOMP	New Computational Formulas
NEOCON	National Exposition of Contract Interior Furnishings
NEOCON	Neoconservative
NEOCON	Neomycin, Colistin, Nystatin [*Antineoplastic drug regimen*]
NEOCS	Navy Enlisted Occupational Classification System (NVT)
NEODA	National Edible Oil Distributors Association [*British*] (DBA)
NEODA	Naval Explosive Ordnance Disposal Association
NEODF	Naval Explosive Ordnance Disposal Facility
NEO-DHC	Neohesperidin Dihydrochalcone [*Also, NHDC*] [*Sweetening agent*]
NEODTC	Naval Explosive Ordnance Disposal Technology Center [*Indian Head, MD*] (DNAB)
NEOF	No Evidence of Failure (MCD)
NEOF	Nordic Engineer Officers' Federation (EA)
NEOG	Neogen Corp. [*NASDAQ symbol*] (NQ)
Neogen	Neogen Corp. [*Associated Press*] (SAG)
NEOL	Neolens, Inc. [*NASDAQ symbol*] (NQ)
Neol	Neolithic (VRA)
NEOL	Neologism
NEOM	NeoMedia Technologies, Inc. [*NASDAQ symbol*] (SAG)
NEOMAL	Northeastern Ohio Major Academic Libraries [*The College of Wooster*] [*Wooster, OH Later, NEOMARL*] [*Library network*]
NEOMARL	Northeast Ohio Major Academic and Research Libraries [*Library network Information service or system*] (IID)
NeoMd	NeoMedia Technologies, Inc. [*Associated Press*] (SAG)
NeoMdia	NeoMedia Technologies, Inc. [*Associated Press*] (SAG)
NEOME	New Electroactive Organic Materials for Electronics [*Esprit*]
NEOP	Neoprobe Corp. [*NASDAQ symbol*]
NEOP	New England Order of Protection [*Later, Woodmen of the World Life Insurance Society*] (EA)
NeoPath	NeoPath, Inc. [*Associated Press*] (SAG)
Neophrm	Neopharm, Inc. [*Associated Press*] (SAG)
NEO-PI	NEO [*Neuroticism, Extraversion, Openness to Experience*] Personality Inven tory [*Personality development test*] [*Psychology*]
Neopr	Neoprobe Corp. [*Associated Press*] (SAG)
Neoprobe	Neoprobe Corp. [*Associated Press*] (SAG)
NEOPW	Neoprobe Corp. Wrrt'E' [*NASDAQ symbol*] (TTSB)
NeoRx	NeoRx Corp. [*Associated Press*] (SAG)
NEOS	NeoStar Retail Group [*NASDAQ symbol*] (SAG)
NeoStar	NeoStar Retail Group [*Associated Press*] (SAG)
NEOT	NeoTherapeutics, Inc. [*NASDAQ symbol*] (SAG)
NeoTher	NeoTherapeutics, Inc. [*Associated Press*] (SAG)
NeoThr	NeoTherapeutics, Inc. [*Associated Press*] (SAG)
NEOU	Navigators' and Engineering Officers' Union [*British*]
Neoz	Neozyme Corp. [*Associated Press*] (SAG)
N/EP	Name on End-Paper [*Antiquarian book trade*]
NEP	National Education Program
NEP	National Emphasis Program [*Occupational Safety and Health Administration*]
NEP	National Energy Plan (COE)
NEP	National Energy Program [*or Plan*] [*Canada*]
NEP	National Estuary Program [*Federal government*]
NEP	Natural Effects Processor
NEP	Near-Earth Phase [*NASA*]
NEP	Nearest Equivalent Product
NEP	Needle Exchange Program
NEP	Negative Equally Probable
NEP	Negative Expiratory Pressure [*Medicine*]
NEP	Nemzeti Egyseg Partja [*Party of National Unity*] [*Hungary Political party*] (PPE)
Nep	Nepal (VRA)
nep	Nepali [*MARC language code Library of Congress*] (LCCP)
NEP	NEPC Airlines [*India*] [*FAA designator*] (FAAC)
NEP	Nepean Public Library [*UTLAS symbol*]
NEP	Nephrology [*Medical specialty*] (DHSM)
Nep	Nepos [*First century BC*] [*Classical studies*] (OCD)
NEP	Neptune (ROG)
NEP	Nerve-Ending Particle (OA)
NEP	Net Ecosystem Production [*Biology*]
NEP	N-Ethylpyrrolidinone [*Organic chemistry*]
NEP	Network Entry Point (AAGC)
NEP	Neutral Endopeptidase [*An enzyme*]
N-Ep	Neutralizing Epitope [*Immunogenetics*]
NEP	Neverending Program (IAA)
NEP	New Economic Policy [*Program of former USSR, 1921-28; also US wage/price freeze and controls of Nixon Administration, 1971*]
NEP	New Edition Pending [*Publishing*]
NEP	New England Plant (NRCH)
NEP	New Equipment Practice
NEP	Newton Extrapolation Ploynominal (IAA)
NEP	No Evidence of Pathology [*Medicine*] (DMAA)
NEP	Noise-Equivalent Power
NEP	Nominal Entry Point [*Aerospace*] (NAKS)
NEP	Nonelectronic Part
NEP	Nonelutable Polar Compounds [*Analytical chemistry*]
NEP	Non-English-Proficient
NEP	Normal Entry Point (MCD)
NEP	Nuclear Electric Propulsion [*System*]
NEP	Nu Pacific Resources Ltd. [*Vancouver Stock Exchange symbol*]
NEPA	National Enginemen's Protection Association [*A union*] [*British*]
NEPA	National Environmental Policy Act (EG)
NEPA	National Environmental Policy Act of 1969
NEPA	National Environmental Protection Agency [*China*]
NEPA	National Euchre Players Association (EA)
NEPA	Northeast Pacific Area
NEPA	Nuclear Energy for Propulsion of Aircraft
NEPAL	National Egg Packers' Association Ltd. [*British*] (BI)
NEP & P	New England Printer and Publisher [*A publication*] (DGA)
NEPB	National Energy Protection Board
NEPBC	Northeastern Pennsylvania Bibliographic Center [*King's College*] [*Wilkes-Barre, PA*] [*Library network*]
NEPC	New England Power Co.
NEPCC	North East Pacific Culture Collection [*of marine organisms*] [*University of British Columbia*]
NEPCO	New England Provision Co.
NEPCON	National Electronic Packaging and Production Conference
NEPD	No Evidence of Pulmonary Disease (DAVI)
NEPD	Noise-Equivalent Power Density
NEPDB	Navy Environmental Protection Data Base [*Obsolete*]
NEPE	National Emergency Planning Establishment [*Canada*]
NEPE	Nez Perce National Historical Park
NEPE	Nitrate Ester Plasticized Polyethylene (PDAA)
NEPEA	New England Project on Education of the Aging [*Defunct*] (EA)
NEPEC	National Earthquake Prediction Evaluation Council [*US Geological Survey*]
NEPEX	New England Power Exchange
neph	Nephrite (VRA)
NEPH	Nephrology
NEPHAT	Northeastern Pacific Hurricane Analog Tracker
NEPHGE	Nonequilibrium pH Gradient Gel Electrophoresis
NEPHIS	Nested Phrase Indexing System [*Automated indexing system*] [*University of Western Ontario*]
NEPI	National Environmental Policy Institute [*Washington, D.C.*]
NEPIA	Nuclear Energy Property Insurance Association [*Later, ANI*] (EA)
NEPIS	N-Ethyl(phenylisoxazolium)sulfonate [*Organic chemistry*]
NEPL	National Endowment for the Preservation of Liberty [*Foundation created by Carl Channell to collect funds for Nicaraguan CONTRAs*]
NEPMA	National Engine Parts Manufacturers Association (EA)
NEPMU	Navy Environmental and Preventive Medicine Unit (NVT)
NEPN	Near-Earth Phase Network [*NASA*] (KSC)
NEPO	NATO Equipment Policy Objective (NATG)
NEPO	New Entrant Prison Officer (WDAA)
NEPOOL	New England Power Pool
NEPP	National Energy Policy Plan
NEPPCO	Northeastern Poultry Producers Council [*Later, PEIA*] (EA)
NEPR	NATO Electronic Parts Recommendations (AABC)
NEPr	Noble Drilling $1.50 Cv Pfd [*NYSE symbol*] (TTSB)
NEPR	Nuclear Explosion Pulse Reaction (AAG)
NEPRA	National Electric Power Regulatory Authority [*Pakistan*]
NEPRAC	National Electron Probe Resource for Analysis of Cells [*Harvard University*] [*Research center*] (RCD)
NEPRF	Naval Environmental Prediction Research Facility
NEPRS	New Equipment Personnel Requirements Summary [*Army*]
NEPS	National Economic Projections Series [*NPA Data Services, Inc.*] [*Information service or system*] (CRD)
NEPS	National Estuarine Pollution Study [*Federal Water Quality Administration*] (MSC)
NEPSS	Navy Environmental Protection Support Service
NEPSWL	New England Plant, Soil, and Water Laboratory [*Department of Agriculture*] [*Research center*] (RCD)
NEPT	Neptune (WDAA)
NEPT	No Evidence of Pulmonary Tuberculosis [*Medicine*]
NEPTUNE	North-Eastern Electronic Peak Tracing Unit and Numerical Evaluator (IEEE)
NEPU	Northern Elements Progression Union [*Nigeria*] [*Political party*]
NEQ	New England Quarterly [*A publication*] (BRI)
NEQ	Not Equal (EECA)
NER	Air Newark, Inc. [*ICAO designator*] (FAAC)
NEr	East Rockaway Public Library, East Rockaway, NY [*Library symbol Library of Congress*] (LCLS)

NER	National Educational Radio
NER	National Emissions Report [*Environmental Protection Agency*] (GFGA)
NER	National Engineers Register (IAA)
NER	Near East Report [*A publication*] (BJA)
Ner.	Neriglissar (BJA)
Ner.	Nero [*of Suetonius*] [*Classical studies*] (OCD)
NER	Nervine [*Medicine*] (ROG)
NER	Network for Economic Rights [*Defunct*] (EA)
NER	Neutral External Rotation [*Sports medicine*]
NER	Never-Exceed Redline [*Aerospace*] (AAG)
NER	New England Reporter [*A publication*] (DLA)
NER	Niger [*ANSI three-letter standard code*] (CNC)
NER	No Evidence of Recurrence [*Medicine*] (MAE)
NER	Noise-Equivalent Radiance
NER	Nonconformance Event Record [*NASA*] (KSC)
NER	Nonionizing Electromagnetic Radiation
NER	North Eastern Railway [*British*]
NER	Northeastern Regional Library, Cimarron, NM [*OCLC symbol*] (OCLC)
NER	North Eastern Reporter [*Commonly cited NE*] [*A publication*] (DLA)
NER	Not Economically Repairable
NER	Nuclear Electric Resonance (PDAA)
NER	Nucleotide-Excision Repair
NERA	National Economic Research Associates
NERA	National Emergency Relief Administration
NERA	Naval Enlisted Reserve Association (EA)
Nera	Nera & Musica [*Record label*] [*Norway*]
NERA	New England Reading Association (AEBS)
NeraAS	Nera AS [*Associated Press*] (SAG)
NERAC	New England Research Application Center [*University of Connecticut*]
NERAIC	North European Region Air Information Center (NATG)
NERAM	Network Reliability Assessment Model (PDAA)
NERAy	Nera-AS [*NASDAQ symbol*] (SAG)
NERAY	Nera AS ADS [*NASDAQ symbol*] (TTSB)
NERBC	New England River Basin Commission
NERBS	National Electric Rate Book by States [*A publication*]
NERC	National Electronic Reliability Council (NTCM)
NERC	National Electronics Research Council
NERC	National English Rabbit Club [*British*] (BI)
NERC	National Environmental Research Center [*Later, CERL*] [*Environmental Protection Agency*]
NERC	National Environmental Research Council (NITA)
NERC	National Environment Resource Council [*British*] (NRCH)
NERC	National Equal Rights Council (EA)
NERC	Natural Environment Research Council [*Research center British*] (IRC)
NERC	New England Regional Commission [*Terminated, 1981*] [*Department of Commerce*]
NERC	Newton-Evans Research Co., Inc. [*Ellicott City, MD*] [*Information service or system*] (TSSD)
NERC	Nordic Economic Research Council (EA)
NERC	North American Electric Reliability Council (EA)
NERC	Nuclear Energy Research Center [*Also, CEEN, SCK*] [*Belgium*]
NERC	Regional Conference for the Near East [*UN Food and Agriculture Organization*]
NErCE	Centre Elementary School, East Rockaway, NY [*Library symbol Library of Congress*] (LCLS)
NERCIC	Northeast Regional Coastal Information Center [*Marine science*] (MSC)
NERCOE	New England Resource Center for Occupational Education
NERCOM	New England Regional Commission [*Department of Commerce*] [*Terminated, 1981*] (EGAO)
NERCOMM	New England Regional Commission [*Terminated, 1981*] [*Department of Commerce*] (NOAA)
NERComP	New England Regional Computing Program, Inc. [*Boston, MA*]
NERCP	Naval European Research Contract Program (NG)
NERD	Newman's Electronic Rhyming Dictionary [*Computer software*] (PCM)
NERD	No Evidence of Recurrent Disease [*Medicine*] (MAE)
NERDA	New England Rural Development Association
NERDAS	NASA Earth Resources Data Annotation System (MCD)
NERDC	Northeast Regional Data Center [*University of Florida*] [*Research center*] (RCD)
NEREM	Northeast Electronics Research and Engineering Meeting
NE Rep	New England Reporter [*A publication*] (DLA)
NE Rep	North Eastern Reporter [*Commonly cited NE*] [*A publication*] (DLA)
NEREP	Nuclear Execution and Reporting Plan (COE)
NE Reporter	North Eastern Reporter [*Commonly cited NE*] [*A publication*] (DLA)
NE Repr	North Eastern Reporter [*Commonly cited NE*] [*A publication*] (DLA)
NERF	National Eye Research Foundation [*Later, NEHF*] (EA)
NERHL	Northeastern Radiological Health Laboratory [*Massachusetts*]
NErHS	East Rockaway High School, East Rockaway, NY [*Library symbol*] [*Library of Congress*] (LCLS)
NERI	National Electronics Research Initiative [*British*]
NERIS	National Educational Resources Information Service [*British*]
NERIS	National Energy Referal Information System (NITA)
NERIT	Northeast Regional Implementation Team [*Army Corps of Engineers*]
NERL	National Ecological Research Laboratory [*Environmental Protection Agency*]
NE Rlty	New England Realty Associates Ltd. [*Associated Press*] (SAG)
NERMLS	New England Regional Medical Library Service (EA)
NERN	National Educational Radio Network [*Defunct*] (NTCM)
NERO	National Energy Resources Organization (EA)
NERO	Near-Earth Rescue and Operations [*NASA*]

NERO	Noninvasive Evaluation of Radiation Output [*Medicine*] (DMAA)
NERO	Nuclear Effects Rocket Operations
NERO	Sodium [*Na*] Experimental Reactor of Zero Power [*British*] (DEN)
NEROC	Northeast Radio Observatory Corp.
NEROS	Northeast Regional Oxidant Study [*Environmental Protection Agency*] (GFGA)
NERP	National Environmental Research Park [*Marine science*] (MSC)
NERP	Nicaraguan Exile Relocation Program [*CIA*]
NERPG	Northern European Regional Planning Group [*NATO*] (NATG)
NERPRC	New England Regional Primate Research Center [*Harvard University*] [*Research center*] (RCD)
NERRA	New Equipment Resources Requirements Analysis [*Army*] (AABC)
NErRE	Rhame Elementary School, East Rockaway, NY [*Library symbol Library of Congress*] (LCLS)
NERRS	National Estuarine Research Reserve System (USDC)
NERS	Neurotic/Endogenous Rating Scale (DB)
NERSA	Centrale Nucleaire Europeenne a Neutrons Rapides SA [*France*] (PDAA)
NERSA	Northeast Rail Service Act [*1981*] [*Also, NRSA*]
NERSE	Nutrition, Exercise, Relaxation, Sleep, and Enjoyment
NERSICA	National Established Repair, Service, and Improvement Contractors Association [*Later, National Remodelers Association*]
NERSP	Navy Environmental Remote Sensing Program
NERU	Nursing Education Research Unit
NERV	Nervous [*Medicine*]
NERV	Nuclear Emergency Recovery Vehicle (NUCP)
NERV	Nuclear Emulsion Recovery Vehicle (MUGU)
NERV	Nuclear Energy Research Vehicle
NERVA	Nuclear Engine for Rocket Vehicle Application [*NASA*]
NErWE	Waverly Park Elementary School, East Rockaway, NY [*Library symbol*] [*Library of Congress*] (LCLS)
NERX	NeoRx Corp. [*NASDAQ symbol*] (NQ)
NERXP	NeoRx $2.4375 Cv Exch Pfd [*NASDAQ symbol*] (TTSB)
NERXW	Neorx Corp. Wrrt [*NASDAQ symbol*] (TTSB)
NES	National Eczema Society [*British*]
NES	National Election Studies [*Conducts national surveys of the American electorate*]
NES	National Energy Software [*Department of Energy Information service or system*] (CRD)
NES	National Energy Strategy [*Department of Energy*] (ECON)
NES	National Enuresis Society (EA)
NES	National Estimating Society [*Later, SCEA*] (EA)
NES	National European American Society
NES	National Eutrophication Survey [*Environmental Protection Agency*]
NES	Naval Examination Service [*British military*] (DMA)
NES	Naval Experimenting Station
NES	Near Eastern Society (EA)
NES	Near Eastern Studies [*A publication*] (BJA)
NES	Near-End Suppressor (IAA)
NES	Nesmont Industry [*Vancouver Stock Exchange symbol*]
NES	Netherlands' Ecological Society [*Multinational association*] (EAIO)
NES	N-Ethylsuccinimide [*Organic chemistry*]
NES	Network Environmental Systems, Inc. (EFIS)
NES	Neurobehavioral Evaluation System
NES	New Earnings Survey [*British*]
NES	New England Electric System [*NYSE symbol*] (SPSG)
NES	New England El Sys [*NYSE symbol*] (TTSB)
NES	New Enlisted System [*Navy*] (DNAB)
NES	News Election Service [*Vote-counting consortium of the major TV networks and two wire services*]
NES	Nintendo Entertainment System [*Video game*]
NES	Noise-Equivalent Signal (IEEE)
NES	Non-English-Speaking (ADA)
NES	Nonerasable Storage [*Computer science*]
NES	Nordeste, Linhas Aereas Regionais SA [*Brazil*] [*ICAO designator*] (FAAC)
NES	Nordic Ergonomic Society (EAIO)
NES	Nordiska Ergonomisallskapet [*Nordic Ergonomic Society*] (EAIO)
NES	Northeast Environmental Services, Inc. (EFIS)
NES	Not Elsewhere Specified
NES	Nuclear Export Signal [*Biochemistry*]
NES	Numerical Engineering Society [*British*] (DBA)
NESA	John H. Nelson Environmental Study Area [*University of Kansas*] [*Research center*] (RCD)
NESA	National Eagle Scout Association (EA)
NESA	National Electric Sign Association (EA)
NESA	National Emission Standards Act [*1967*]
NESA	National Employment Service Act [*1933*]
NESA	National Energy Services Association (NTPA)
NESA	National Energy Specialist Association (EA)
NESA	National Environmental Specialist Association (EA)
NESA	National Environmental Study Areas Program [*National Park Service*] [*Defunct*]
NESA	Near East and South Asia [*Department of State*]
NE/SA	Near East/South Asia Council of Overseas Schools (EA)
NESA	New England School of Art
NESAC	National Environmental Services Administration Committee [*Marine science*] (MSC)
NESB	National Environmental Specimen Bank [*Energy Research and Development Administration*]
NESB	Non-English-Speaking Background (ADA)
NESB1	Number of Equally Strong Beams [*Military*] (CAAL)
NESB1	First Generation Non-English-Speaking Background
NESB2	Second Generation Non-English-Speaking Background
NESBA	National Earth Shelter Builders Association [*Defunct*] (EA)

NESBA	National Executive of Small Business Agencies [*Australia*]
NESC	National Electrical Safety Code [*Also, NEC*] (NTCM)
NESC	National Electric Safety Code (SAA)
NESC	National Energy Software Center [*Department of Energy*] [*Information service or system*] (IID)
NESC	National Enquiry into Scholarly Communication
NESC	National Environmental Satellite Center [*Formerly, National Weather Satellite Center*] [*Later, National Environmental Satellite Service*]
NESC	National Environmental Supercomputing Center (AEPA)
NESC	National Environmental Svc. [*NASDAQ symbol*] (TTSB)
NESC	National Executive Service Corps [*New York, NY*] (EA)
NESC	Naval Electronics Systems Command
NESC	Navy Electromagnetic Spectrum Center (DNAB)
NESC	Neuroepithelial Stem Cells [*Medicine*]
NESC	Non-English-Speaking Country
NESC	Nuclear Engineering and Scientific Congress (MCD)
NESCA	National Environmental Systems Contractors Association [*Later, ACCA*] (EA)
NESCAC	New England Small College Athletic Conference
NESCAUM	North East States for Coordinated Air Use Management
NESCNSC	Net Evaluation Subcommittee, National Security Council (AABC)
NESCO	National Energy Supply Corp. [*Proposed*]
NESCO	National Engineering Science Co.
NESCO	Naval Environmental Support Office [*Marine science*] (MSC)
NESCO	Nigerian Electricity Supply Corp. African Workers' Union
NESCTM	National Environmental Satellite Center Technical Memoranda (NOAA)
NESCWS	Nonessential Services Chilled Water System [*Nuclear energy*] (NRCH)
NESDA	National Electronic Service Dealers Association [*Later, NESSDA*] (EA)
NESDA	National Equipment Servicing Dealers Association (EA)
NESDEC	New England School Development Council (EA)
NESDIS	National Environmental Satellite, Data, and Information Service [*Washington, DC National Oceanic and Atmospheric Administration*] (GRD)
NESDRES	National Environmental Data Referral Service [*Marine science*] (OSRA)
NESE	Neue Ephemeris fuer Semitische Epigraphik [*Wiesbaden*] [*A publication*] (BJA)
NESEA	Naval Electronic Systems Engineering Activity
NESEC	Naval Electronics Systems Engineering Center (MCD)
NESEP	Navy Enlisted Scientific Education Program
NESF	Normal Engineered Safety Features [*Nuclear energy*] (NRCH)
NESHAP	National Emission Standards for Hazardous Air Pollutants [*Environmental Protection Agency*]
NESHAPS	National Emission Standard for Hazard Air Pollutants [*Environmental science*] (COE)
NESHAPS	National Emission Standards for Hazardous Air Pollutants (WPI)
NESIP	Naval Explosive Safety Improvement Program
NESIP/POA & M...	Naval Explosive Safety Improvement Program / Plan of Action and Milestones (DNAB)
NESL	Northeast Shipbuilders Ltd. [*Commercial firm British*]
NESLA	New England Shoe and Leather Association (EA)
NEsM	Mount Saint Alphonsus Seminary, Esopus, NY [*Library symbol Library of Congress*] (LCLS)
NESMRA	New England Super-Modified Racing Association
NESN	NATO English-Speaking Nations
NESN	New England Sports Network [*Cable-television system*]
NESO	Naval Air Engineering Support Office [*Norfolk, VA*]
NESO	Naval Electronic Sensor Operator [*Canadian Navy*]
NESO	Naval Engineering Service Office (MCD)
NESO	Navy Environmental Support Office [*Obsolete*]
NESO	Northeastern Society of Orthodontists (DMAA)
NESOSC	New England Society of Open Salts Collectors (EA)
NESP	National Environmental Studies Project [*Defunct*] (EA)
NESP	Navy EHF [*Extremely High Frequency*] Satellite Program (DOMA)
NESP	Nurse Education Support Program
NESR	Natural Environment Support Room (MCD)
NESR	Noise-Equivalent Spectral Radiance [*Physics*]
NESRA	National Employee Services and Recreation Association (EA)
NESS	NASA Expert Simulation System (NITA)
NESS	National Easter Seal Society (EA)
NESS	National Emergency Steel Specification [*World War II*]
NESS	National Environmental Satellite Service [*National Oceanic and Atmospheric Administration Telecommunications*] (TEL)
NESS	Network and Evaluation Simulation System (NITA)
NESS	Northeast Satellite Systems [*Avoca, PA*] [*Telecommunications*] (TSSD)
NESS	Nuclear Effects Simulation Study
NESSDA	National Electronic Sales and Service Dealers Association (EA)
NEssDS	Dunlap Society, Essex, NY [*Library symbol Library of Congress*] (LCLS)
NESSEC	Naval Electronics Systems Security Engineering Center (MCD)
NEST	National Emergency Survivable Troop System (AABC)
NEST	Naval Experimental Satellite Terminal (IEEE)
NEST	New and Emerging Sciences and Technologies
NEST	New El Salvador Today (EA)
NEST	New Expanding Shelter Technology [*Residential construction*]
NEST	Nonelectric Stimulus Transfer
NEST	Novell Embedded Systems Technology [*Novell, Inc.*] [*Computer science*]
NEST	Nuclear Effects Support Team
NEST	Nuclear Emergency Search Team [*Department of Energy*]
NEST	Nuclear Explosive Simulation Technique

NESTA	National Earth Science Teachers Association (EA)
NESTED	Naval Electronic Systems Test and Evaluation Detachment
NESTEF	Naval Electronic Systems Test and Evaluation Facility
NESTEV.......	Naval Electronics Systems Test and Evaluation (IAA)
NESTOR.......	Netherlands Educational and Scientific Titles for Online Retrieval (TELE)
NESTOR.......	Neutron Source Thermal Reactor [*British*] (DEN)
NESTS	Nonelectric Stimulus Transfer System
NestU..........	Northeast Utilities [*Associated Press*] (SAG)
NESW	Nonessential Service Water Relay Pump [*Nuclear energy*] (IAA)
NET	Centre for Agricultural Publications and Documents, Wageningen, Netherlands [*OCLC symbol*] (OCLC)
NET	Nasoendotracheal Tube [*Medicine*]
NET	National Educational Television [*Later, EBC*]
NET	National Empowerment Television
NET	National Environmental Testing, Inc. (EFIS)
NET	National Estate Tasmania [*Australia*]
NET	National Evangelization Teams (EA)
NET	Negative Entropy Trap
NET	Nerve Excitability Test [*Medicine*] (DMAA)
NET	Net Energy Thrust
NET	Net Equivalent Temperature
NET	Net Explosive Weight (MSA)
NET	NETI Technologies, Inc. [*Vancouver Stock Exchange symbol*]
NET	Netto [*Lowest*]
NET	Network [*Telecommunications*] (AAG)
net	Network (WDMC)
NET	Network Aviation Services (NIG) Ltd. [*FAA designator*] (FAAC)
NET	Neuroectodermal Tumor [*Medicine*] (DMAA)
NET	Neuroelectric Therapy [*Substance detoxification*]
NET	Neuroendocrine Tumor [*Medicine*] (DMAA)
NET	New Equipment Training [*Army*] (AABC)
NET	New Era Technologies, Inc. [*Washington, DC*] [*Telecommunications*] (TSSD)
NET	Newton Emission Theory [*Physics*]
NET	Next European Torus [*Formerly, Joint European Torus (JET)*]
NET	Nimbus Experiment Team [*NASA*]
NET	Nitrigin Eireann Teoranta [*Nationalized industry*] [*Ireland*] (EY)
NET	No Electronic Theft [*Act*]
NET	No Evidence of Tumor [*Medicine*]
NET	Noise-Equivalent Temperature
NET	Noise Evaluation Test (IAA)
NET	Nonlethal Entanglement Technology
NET	Nonradiative Energy Transfer [*Physics*]
NET	Norepinephrine Transporter [*Medicine*] (DMAA)
NET	Norethisterone [*Oral contraceptive ingredient*]
NET	Norme Europeene de Telecommunications [*Telecommunications*] (OSI)
NET	North European Oil Royalty Trust [*NYSE symbol*] (SPSG)
NET	North Europn Oil Rty Tr [*NYSE symbol*] (TTSB)
NET	Not Earlier Than
NET	Nuclear Effects Test
NET	Nuclear Emergency Teams [*DASA*]
NET	Nuclear Energy Team
NET	Nuclear Engineer Trainee
NET	Number of Element Types
NETA	International Electrical Testing Association (EA)
NETA	National Employment and Training Association [*Upland, CA*] (EA)
NETA	National Environmental Training Association (EA)
NETA	Network Associates [*NASDAQ symbol*] [*Formerly, McAfee Associates*] (SG)
NETA	New England Telecommunications Association (CIST)
NETA	Northeast Test Area [*Military*] (MCD)
NETAC	Nuclear Energy Trade Associations' Conference
NETANAL	Network Analysis (PDAA)
NETAPPS	Net Ad-Produced Purchases [*Advertising*]
NetBEUI	NetBIOS [*Network Basic Input/Output System*] Extended User Interface [*Microsoft Corp.*] (PCM)
NETBIOS	Network Basic Input/Output System [*Computer software*]
NetBIOS	Network Basic Input/Output System [*Computer science*] (DOM)
NETC	National Emergency Training Center
NETC	National Emergency Transportation Center
NETC	Naval Education and Training Center [*or Command*] (NVT)
NETC	NETCM On-Line Comm Svcs [*NASDAQ symbol*] (TTSB)
NETC	Netcom On-Line Communications Services, Inc. [*NASDAQ symbol*] (SAG)
NETC	New England Theatre Conference (EA)
NETC	New England Trail Conference (EA)
NETC	No Explosion of the Total Contents [*Business term*] (DCTA)
NETC	Northeast Transportation Coalition
NET CDF	Network Common Data Format [*Computer science*]
NETCHE	Nebraska Educational Television Council for Higher Education, Inc. [*Library network*]
NETCO	North Western Employes Transportation Corp. [*Successor to Chicago & North Western Railway*]
Netcom	Netcom On-Line Communictions Services, Inc. [*Associated Press*] (SAG)
NETCOM	Network Communications
NETCOM	Network Control Communications [*Deep Space Instrumentation Facility, NASA*]
NETCON	Network Control [*Computer science*] (MHDB)
NETD	Noise-Equivalent Temperature Difference [*Thermography*]
NETDC	New England Trophoblastic Disease Center
NETDP	National Environmental Technology Demonstration Program (BCP)
NETDS	Near-Earth Tracking and Data System

NETE............ Naval Engineering Test Establishment [*Canadian Armed Forces*] (PDAA)
NETE............ Network of European Teacher Education (AIE)
NETF............ Netframe Systems [*NASDAQ symbol*] (SAG)
NETF... Nuclear Energy Test Facility (AFM)
NETF............ Nuclear Engineering Test Facility (AAG)
NETFIPCBR... Naval Education and Training Financial Information Processing Branch (DNAB)
NETFMS........ Naval Education and Training Financial Management System (DNAB)
Netframe....... Netframe Systems [*Associated Press*] (SAG)
NETFS......... National Educational Television/Film Service (WGA)
NETG.......... National Education Training Group (EFIS)
NETG.......... Network General [*NASDAQ symbol*] (TTSB)
NETG.......... Network General Corp. [*NASDAQ symbol*] (CTT)
NetGALA...... Network of Gay and Lesbian Alumni Associations (EA)
NETGEN....... Network Generation [*Computer science*] (MHDB)
NETH.......... National Employ the Handicapped Week
NETH.......... Netherlands
Neth........... Netherlands (ODBW)
Neth Ant..... Netherlands Antilles
Netherl Intl L Rev... Netherlands Yearbook of International Law [*The Hague, Netherlands*] [*A publication*] (DLA)
Neth Int'l L Rev... Netherlands International Law Review [*A publication*] (DLA)
Nethl.......... Netherlands (VRA)
Neth P........ Netherlands Pharmacopoeia [*A publication*]
NETHW........ National Employ the Handicapped Week (OICC)
Neth YB Int'l Law... Netherlands Yearbook of International Law [*A publication*] (DLA)
NETI........... Network Technologies International, Inc. [*Ann Arbor, MI*] [*Telecommunications*] (TSSD)
Netiquette.... Internet Etiquette [*Computer science*]
NETISA........ Naval Education and Training Information Systems Activity (DNAB)
NETK........... Network Express [*NASDAQ symbol*] (TTSB)
NETK........... Network Express, Inc. [*NASDAQ symbol*] (SAG)
NETL........... National Export Traffic League [*New York, NY*] (EA)
NETL........... NetLive Communications, Inc. [*NASDAQ symbol*] (SAG)
NETL........... Nuclear Engineering Teaching Laboratory [*University of Texas at Austin*] [*Research center*] (RCD)
NetLive...... NetLive Communications, Inc. [*Associated Press*] (SAG)
NETLS........ Northeast Texas Library System [*Library network*]
NETLS/DPL... Northeast Texas Library System/Dallas Public Library Film Service [*Library network*]
NET Ltd....... Nigerian External Telecommunications Ltd. [*Lagos*]
NETM.......... NetManage, Inc. [*NASDAQ symbol*] (SAG)
N et M........ Nocte et Mane [*Night and Morning*] [*Pharmacy*]
n et m........ Nocte et Mane [*Latin*] [*Night and Morning*] [*Pharmacy*] (DAVI)
NETMA........ Nobody Ever Tells Me Anything [*Executive complaint*]
Netmed....... Netmed, Inc. [*Associated Press*] (SAG)
NETMIS....... Naval Education and Training Management Information System (MCD)
Netmng........ NetManage, Inc. [*Associated Press*] (SAG)
NETMUX...... Network Multiplexer (NITA)
NET/NLT..... No Earlier Than/No Later Than (MCD)
NETOP........ Network Operator Process [*Computer science*] (MHDB)
NETOPS....... Nuclear Emergency Team Operations (AFM)
NETP.......... New Equipment Training Program [*Army*] (AABC)
NetPC......... Network Personal Computer (IGOR)
NETPDC....... Naval Education and Training Program Development Center [*Pensacola, FL*] (DNAB)
NETR .... NATO Electronic Technical Recommendation (PDAA)
NETR .... No Essential Traffic Reported [*Aviation*]
NETR .... Nuclear Engineering Test Reactor [*Air Force*]
NETRA......... New England Trail Rider Association (EA)
NETRB......... New England Territory Railroad Bureau
NETRC........ National Educational Television and Radio Center [*Later, EBC*] (EA)
NETREM...... Net Requirementes Estimation Model (PDAA)
NETR-FTC... New England Territory Railroads Freight Traffic Committee
Netrix.......... Netrix Corp. [*Associated Press*] (SAG)
NETRJE........ Network Remote Job Entry [*Telecommunications*] (OSI)
NE TR S NUM... Ne Tradas sine Nummo [*Cash on Delivery*] [*Latin*]
NETS.......... National Electronics Teachers' Service [*Defunct*]
NETS.......... Nationwide Emergency Telecommunications System [*DoD*]
NETS.......... Navy Engineering Technical Services (NG)
NETS.......... Nebraska Electronic Transfer System
NETS.......... Network Electrical Technique System (IAA)
NETS.......... Network Event Theater [*NASDAQ symbol*] (TTSB)
NETS.......... Network Event Theatre, Inc. [*NASDAQ symbol*] (SAG)
NETS.......... Network for Electronic Transfers System
NETS.......... Network of Employees for Traffic Safety [*NHTSA*] (TAG)
NETS.......... Network Techniques
NETS.......... Network Testing Section [*Social Security Administration*]
NETS.......... Neurodysfunction Eye Test System [*Medical*]
NETS.......... New Examiner Training School [*Federal Home Loan Bank Board*]
NETSC........ Naval Education and Training Support Center (DNAB)
NETSCL....... Naval Education and Training Support Center, Atlantic (DNAB)
NETSCP...... Naval Education and Training Support Center, Pacific (DNAB)
Netscpe...... Netscape Communications Corp. [*Associated Press*] (SAG)
NETSET....... Network Synthesis and Evaluation Technique [*Computer science*]
NETSET....... Network Systems and Evaluation Technique (NITA)
NETSIM....... [*Traffic*] Network Simulation [*TXDOT*] (TAG)
NETSL........ New England Technical Services Librarians
Netsmrt....... Netsmart Technologies, Inc. [*Associated Press*] (SAG)
NETSO........ Northern European Transhipment Organization [*NATO*] (NATG)
NETSP........ New Equipment Training Support Package
NetSrce........ NetSource Communications, Inc. [*Associated Press*] (SAG)

NETSS .... National Electronic Telecommunications System for Surveillance [*Center for Disease Control*]
NetStar .... NetStar, Inc. [*Associated Press*] (SAG)
NETSW....... Network Event Theater Wrrt [*NASDAQ symbol*] (TTSB)
NETT.......... Netter Digital Entertainment [*NASDAQ symbol*] (TTSB)
NETT.......... Netter Digital Entertainment, Inc. [*NASDAQ symbol*] (SAG)
NETT.......... Net Tons [*Shipping*]
NETT.......... Network Environmental Technology Transfer [*Europe*] [*An association*]
NETT.......... New Employment, Transition, and Training [*Department of Labor*] (OICC)
NETT.......... New Equipment Training Team [*Army*]
NETTEL...... Network Telecommunications, Inc. [*Denver, CO*] [*Telecommunications*] (TSSD)
Netter .... Netter Digital Entertainment, Inc. [*Associated Press*] (SAG)
NetterD........ Netter Digital Entertainment, Inc. [*Associated Press*] (SAG)
NETTSP........ New Equipment Training Test Support Package (MCD)
NETTW........ Netter Digital Entm't Wrrt [*NASDAQ symbol*] (TTSB)
NETV.......... Nebraska ETV [*Educational Television*] Network [*Lincoln, NE*] [*Telecommunications*] (TSSD)
NetV.......... NetVantage, Inc. [*Associated Press*] (SAG)
NETVA........ NetVantage, Inc. [*NASDAQ symbol*] (SAG)
NETVA........ NetVantage Inc.'A' [*NASDAQ symbol*] (TTSB)
NetVant........ NetVantage, Inc. [*Associated Press*] (SAG)
NETVU........ NetVantage Inc. Unit [*NASDAQ symbol*] (TTSB)
NETVW....... NetVantage Inc. Wrrt'A' [*NASDAQ symbol*] (TTSB)
NETVZ........ NetVantage Inc. Wrrt'B' [*NASDAQ symbol*] (TTSB)
NetwkAp ..... Network Appliance Corp. [*Associated Press*] (SAG)
NetwkE .... Network Event Theatre, Inc. [*Associated Press*] (SAG)
Networth...., Networth, Inc. [*Associated Press*] (SAG)
netwrkg....... Networking (BARN)
NETX.......... Network Equipment Technologies, Inc. (MHDW)
NEU .... (Naphthyl)ethyl Urea [*Organic chemistry*]
NEU .... Neuchatel [*Switzerland*] [*Seismograph station code, US Geological Survey Closed*] (SEIS)
Neu............. Neuraminic Acid [*Biochemistry*]
neu............. Neurilemma [*Neurology*] (DAVI)
NEU .... Transportes Aereos Neuquinos Sociedad de Estado [*Argentina ICAO designator*] (FAAC)
NEUC.......... National Engine Use Council [*Defunct*] (EA)
NEUCC........ Northern European Universities Computer Centre [*Denmark*] (PDAA)
Neucrine...... Neurocrine Biosciences, Inc. [*Associated Press*] (SAG)
NEUDATA..... Neutron Data Under Direct Access (NITA)
NEUFCH....... Neufchatel [*Imprint*] (ROG)
NEUG.......... National Epson Users Group (EA)
NEUM .... Non-European Unity Movement [*South Africa*] (PD)
Neumed....... Neuromedical Systems, Inc. [*Associated Press*] (SAG)
neur........... Neurology [*Medicine*] (MAE)
NeUR.......... Rijksuniversiteit te Utrecht, Utrecht, Netherlands [*Library symbol Library of Congress*] (LCLS)
NEUR-A....... Neurogenic Battery Acute (DAVI)
Neurex........ Neurex Corp. [*Associated Press*] (SAG)
Neurgn........ Neurogen Corp. [*Associated Press*] (SAG)
NEURO......... Neurology [*or Neurological*]
NEurO.......... North European Oil Royalty Trust [*Associated Press*] (SAG)
NEUROBIOL... Neurobiology
NEUROL....... Neurology
NEUROLGST... Neurobiologist
Neuropath.... Neuropathology [*or Neuropathologist*] (DAVI)
Neuro-Surg... Neurosurgeon (BABM)
Neuro-Surg... Neurosurgery [*or Neurosurgeon*] (DAVI)
NeuroTc...... Neurobiological Technologies, Inc. [*Associated Press*] (SAG)
NEURS........ Navy Energy Usage Reporting System (DNAB)
NEUS.......... New Extensions for Utilizing Scientists, Inc.
NEUS.......... Northeastern United States
NEUS.......... Nuclear-Electric Unmanned Spacecraft
NEUSSN....... Northeastern United States Seismic Network (NRCH)
NEUT.......... Neuter
NEUT.......... Neutral (AAG)
neut............ Neutrophil [*Hematology*]
neut equiv... Neutralization Equivalent [*Chemistry*]
NEUTN........ Neutralization [*Electronics*] (ECII)
NEV........... Nederlandse Ecologen Vereniging [*Netherlands Ecological Society*] [*Multinational association*] (EAIO)
NEV........... Negative Expected Value
NEV........... Neighborhood Electric Vehicle
NEV........... Net Economic Value
NEV........... Neutral-to-Earth Voltage [*Electrical power transmission*]
NEV........... Nevada (AAG)
Nev........... Nevada (ODBW)
Nev........... Nevada Supreme Court Reports [*A publication*] (DLA)
NEV........... Nevis [*Leeward Islands*] [*Airport symbol*] (OAG)
NEV........... Nieghborhood Electric Vehicle
NEV........... Nuevo Energy [*NYSE symbol*] (TTSB)
NEV........... Nuevo Energy Co. [*NYSE symbol*] (SPSG)
NEV........... Nuevo Financing I [*NYSE symbol*] (SAG)
NEVA .... North Eastern Vecturists Association
Nevada Rep... Nevada Reports [*A publication*] (DLA)
Nevada Repts... Nevada Reports [*A publication*] (DLA)
Nev Admin Code... Nevada Administrative Code [*A publication*] (DLA)
Nev & M... Nevile and Manning's English King's Bench Reports [*A publication*] (ILCA)
Nev & Mac... Neville and Macnamara's Railway Cases [*1855-1950*] [*A publication*] (DLA)

Nev & MacN... Neville and Macnamara's Railway and Canal Cases [1855-1950] [A publication] (DLA)

Nev & Man... Nevile and Manning's English King's Bench Reports [A publication] (DLA)

Nev & Man Mag Cas... Nevile and Manning's English Magistrates' Cases [A publication] (DLA)

Nev & Mcn... Neville and Macnamara's Railway Cases [England] [A publication] (DLA)

Nev & M (Eng)... Nevile and Manning's English King's Bench Reports [A publication] (DLA)

Nev & MKB... Nevile and Manning's English King's Bench Reports [A publication] (DLA)

Nev & MMC... Nevile and Manning's English Magistrates' Cases [A publication] (DLA)

Nev & P....... Nevile and Perry's English King's Bench Reports [1836-38] [A publication] (DLA)

Nev & P....... Nevile and Perry's English Magistrates' Cases [1836-37] [A publication] (DLA)

Nev & PKB... Nevile and Perry's English King's Bench Reports [1836-38] [A publication] (DLA)

Nev & P Mag Cas... Nevile and Perry's English Magistrates' Cases [1836-37] [A publication] (DLA)

Nev & PMC... Nevile and Perry's English Magistrates' Cases [1836-37] [A publication] (DLA)

NEVATV .... Nebraska VA Television Network [Telecommunications service] (TSSD)

NEVE............ Nonempirical Valence-Electron [Physics]

NevEngy ...... Nevada Energy Co., Inc. [Associated Press] (SAG)

NEVLESS ..... Nevertheless (ROG)

NEVOT .... Network Voice Terminal [Telecommunications]

Nev PSC Op... Nevada Public Service Commission Opinions [A publication] (DLA)

NevPw .... Nevada Power Co. [Associated Press] (SAG)

Nev Rev Stat... Nevada Revised Statutes [A publication] (DLA)

Nev SBJ .... Nevada State Bar Journal [A publication] (DLA)

Nev Stats..... Statutes of Nevada [A publication] (DLA)

Nev St Bar J... Nevada State Bar Journal [A publication] (DLA)

NEVX .... Nerine Virus X [Plant pathology]

NEW............ Hawarden BAE [British ICAO designator] (FAAC)

NEW............ National Electronics Week

NEW............ National Energy Watch [Edison Electric Institute]

NEW............ Native Egg White

NEW............ Navy Early Warning

NEW............ Net Economic Welfare [Economic indicator]

NEW............ Net Explosive Weight (AFM)

new............ Newari [MARC language code Library of Congress] (LCCP)

NEW............ Newark [Diocesan abbreviation] [New Jersey] (TOCD)

NEW............ New College of California, San Francisco, CA [OCLC symbol] (OCLC)

New............ Newell's Illinois Appeal Reports [A publication] (DLA)

NEW............ New England Air Express, Inc. [ICAO designator] (FAAC)

NEW............ New England Inv Cos. L.P. [NYSE symbol] (TTSB)

NEW............ New England Investment Companies [Formerly, Reich & Tang Ltd.] [NYSE symbol] (SPSG)

NEW............ New Orleans, LA [Location identifier FAA] (FAAL)

NEW............ Newport [Quebec] [Geomagnetic observatory code]

NEW............ Newport [Washington] [Seismograph station code, US Geological Survey] (SEIS)

NEW............ Newtec Industries Ltd. [Vancouver Stock Exchange symbol]

NEW............ Newton

NEW............ Non-Traditional Employment for Women

NEW............ Nuclear Energy Women [Defunct] (EA)

NEW............ Nursery Education Week (AEBS)

NEW............ Nvest L.P. [NYSE symbol] [Formerly, New England Investment Companies]

NEw .... Thomas E. Ryan Public Library, East Williston, NY [Library symbol Library of Congress] (LCLS)

NEW8C .... New England Women's 8 Conference (PSS)

NEWA .... National Electrical Wholesalers Association

NEWA .... Nuclear Energy Writers Association [Defunct]

NEWAC .... NATO Electronic Warfare Advisory Committee (NATG)

NEWAC .... New England Women's Athletic Conference (PSS)

New Ad....... New Advocate [A publication] (BRI)

NewAD......... Newspaper Archive Developments Ltd., New Haven, CT [Library symbol Library of Congress] (LCLS)

New Age...... New Age Journal [A publication] (BRI)

NewAge .... New Age Media Fund [Associated Press] (SAG)

NEW AM ..... Berlin, VT [AM radio station call letters] (BROA)

NEW AM ..... Madisonville, TX [AM radio station call letters] (BROA)

NewAm......... New America High Income Fund [Associated Press] (SAG)

New Am Cyc... New American Cyclopaedia [A publication] (ROG)

New Ann Reg... New Annual Register [London] [A publication] (DLA)

Newark L Rev... University of Newark. Law Review [A publication] (DLA)

NEWB .... Newberry Bancorp [NASDAQ symbol] (TTSB)

NEWB .... Newberry Bancorp, Inc. [NASDAQ symbol] (SAG)

Newb .... Newberry's United States District Court, Admiralty Reports [A publication] (DLA)

NEWB .... Newbury [Municipal borough in England]

Newb Adm ... Newberry's United States District Court, Admiralty Reports [A publication] (DLA)

New Benl.... New Benloe's Reports, English King's Bench [1531-1628] [A publication] (DLA)

New B Eq Ca ... New Brunswick Equity Cases [A publication] (DLA)

New B Eq Rep... New Brunswick Equity Reports [A initialism] (DLA)

Newberry..... Newberry's United States District Court, Admiralty Reports [A publication] (DLA)

Newberry Adm (F)... Newberry's United States District Court, Admiralty Reports [A publication] (DLA)

Newberry's Ad Rep... Newberry's United States District Court, Admiralty Reports [A publication] (DLA)

NewbNk....... Newbridge Networks, Inc. [Associated Press] (SAG)

Newbon .... Newbon's Private Bills Reports [1895-99] [England] [A publication] (DLA)

New Br .... New Brunswick Reports [A publication] (DLA)

New Br Eq (Can)... New Brunswick Equity Reports [Canada] [A publication] (DLA)

New Br Eq Cas (Can)... New Brunswick Equity Cases [Canada] [A publication] (DLA)

New Br R..... New Brunswick Reports [A publication] (DLA)

Newbyth ...... Newbyth's Manuscript Decisions, Scotch Session Cases [A publication] (DLA)

NEWC .... Newcastle [Name of two cities in England]

NEWC .... Newcor, Inc. [NASDAQ symbol] (SAG)

NewCare..... New Care Health Corp. [Associated Press] (SAG)

New Cas ..... New Cases (Bingham's New Cases) [A publication] (DLA)

New Cas Eq... New Cases in Equity [8, 9 Modern Reports] [1721-55] [A publication] (DLA)

NEWCC .... Northeastern Weed Control Conference [Later, NEWSS] (EA)

NEWC L ...... Newcastle-Under-Lyme [City in England] (ROG)

NEWCN ...... New Construction [Navy]

Newcor .... Newcor, Inc. [Associated Press] (SAG)

NewDay ..... New Day Beverage, Inc. [Associated Press] (SAG)

Newell........ Newell Co. [Associated Press] (SAG)

Newell........ Newell's Appeals Reports [48-90 Illinois] [A publication] (DLA)

Newell Defam... Newell on Defamation, Slander, and Libel [A publication] (DLA)

Newell Eject... Newell's Treatise on the Action of Ejectment [A publication] (DLA)

Newell Mal Pros... Newell's Treatise on Malicious Prosecution [A publication] (DLA)

Newell Sland & L... Newell on Slander and Libel [A publication] (DLA)

New Eng...... New England Reporter [A publication] (DLA)

New Eng Cons Music... New England Conservatory of Music (GAGS)

NEWENGGRU... New England Group (DNAB)

New Engl Univ Bull... New England University. Bulletin [A publication]

New Eng R.... New England Reporter [A publication] (DLA)

New Eng Rep... New England Reporter [A publication] (DLA)

New Eng Sch Law... New England School of Law (GAGS)

New ER....... New England Review [A publication] (BRI)

NEWF......... Newfoundland [with Labrador, a Canadian province]

NewfEx .... Newfield Exploration [Associated Press] (SAG)

NEWFLD ...... Newfoundland [with Labrador, a Canadian province]

Newfld LR ... Newfoundland Law Reports [A publication] (DLA)

Newf LR ...... Newfoundland Law Reports [A publication] (DLA)

NEW FM ..... Alberta, VA [FM radio station call letters] (BROA)

NEW FM ..... Pukatawagan, Manitoba [FM radio station call letters] (BROA)

NEWFO .... Newfoundland [with Labrador, a Canadian province]

Newfoundl LR... Newfoundland Law Reports [A publication] (DLA)

Newfoundl R... Newfoundland Reports [A publication] (DLA)

Newfoundl Sel Cas... Newfoundland Select Cases [A publication] (DLA)

NEWFS .... New England Wild Flower Society (EA)

Newf S Ct ... Newfoundland Supreme Court Decisions [A publication] (DLA)

Newf Sel Cas... Newfoundland Select Cases [A publication] (DLA)

NEWH .... New Horizons Worldwide, Inc. [NASDAQ symbol] (SAG)

Newhal .... Newhall Land & Farming Co. [Associated Press] (SAG)

New Hamp... New Hampshire Reports [A publication] (DLA)

New Hamp R... New Hampshire Reports [A publication] (DLA)

New Hamp Rep... New Hampshire Reports [A publication] (DLA)

New Hampshire Rep... New Hampshire Reports [A publication] (DLA)

NewHrz....... New Horizons Savings & Loan Association [Associated Press] (SAG)

NEWI .... New West Eyeworks [NASDAQ symbol] (TTSB)

NEWI .... New West Eyeworks, Inc. [NASDAQ symbol] (SAG)

NEWIL .... Northeast Wisconsin Intertype Libraries [Library network]

New Ir Jur ... New Irish Jurist and Local Government Review [1900-05] [A publication] (DLA)

NEWISA....... New England Women's Intercollegiate Sailing Association

New J Chem... New Journal of Chemistry (MEC)

New Jersey... New Jersey Law Reports [A publication] (DLA)

New Jersey Eq... New Jersey Equity Reports [A publication] (DLA)

New Jersey Equity... New Jersey Equity Reports [A publication] (DLA)

New Jersey Leg Rec... New Jersey Legal Record [A publication] (DLA)

New Jersey L Rev... New Jersey Law Review [A publication] (DLA)

New Jersey SBA Qu... New Jersey State Bar Association. Quarterly [A publication] (DLA)

New Journ ... New Journalist [A publication]

NEWLC .... NATO Electronic Warfare Liaison Committee

Newl Ch PR... Newland's Chancery Practice [A publication] (DLA)

Newl Ch Prac... Newland's Chancery Practice [A publication] (DLA)

Newl Cont... Newland on Contracts [1806] [A publication] (DLA)

NEWLON...... New London, Connecticut [Navy]

NEWM .... New England and World Missions (EA)

NEW M .... New Mexico (ROG)

New Mag Cas... New Magistrates' Cases (Bittleston, Wise, and Parnell) [1844-51] [A publication] (DLA)

Newm Conv... Newman on Conveyancing [A publication] (DLA)

New Mex BA... New Mexico State Bar Association, Minutes [A publication] (DLA)

New Mex SBA... New Mexico State Bar Association, Report of Proceedings [A publication] (DLA)

NEWMOA..... Northeast Waste Management Officials Association

NEW MOONS... NASA Evaluation with Models of Optimized Nuclear Spacecraft

NewmtM....... Newmont Mining [Associated Press] (SAG)

New Nat Brev... New Natura Brevium [A publication] (DLA)

New NB .... New Natura Brevium [A publication] (DSA)

NEwNE........	North Side Elementary School, East Williston, NY [*Library symbol*] [*Library of Congress*] (LCLS)
NEWOT........	Naval Electronic Warfare Operator Trainer (MCD)
NewOv........	Newscorp Overseas Ltd. [*Associated Press*] (SAG)
NEWP.........	Newport [*England*]
NEWP.........	Newport Corp. [*NASDAQ symbol*] (NQ)
NEWPEX......	Northeast Wood Products Expo [*In company name, NEWPEX, Inc.*] (TSPED)
NEWPIL.......	NADGE [*NATO Air Defense Ground Environment*] Early Warning Program Information Leaflet (NATG)
NEWPIN.......	New Parent-Infant Network (AIE)
NEWPOSITREP...	New [*Corrected*] Position Report (NVT)
New Pract Case...	New Practice Cases [*1844-48*] [*A publication*] (DLA)
New Pr Cases..	New Practice Cases [*1844-48*] [*A publication*] (DLA)
Newpt.........	Newport Corp. [*Associated Press*] (SAG)
NEWQ.........	Newquay [*Urban district in England*]
NEWR.........	New England Realty Associates Ltd. [*NASDAQ symbol*] (NQ)
New R	New Republic [*A publication*] (BRI)
NEWRADS ..	Nuclear Explosion Warning and Radiological Data System
New Rep......	Bosanquet and Puller's New Reports, English Common Pleas [*1804-07*] [*A publication*] (DLA)
New Rep......	New Reports [*1862-65*] [*England*] [*A publication*] (DLA)
NEWRIT.......	Northeast Water Resources Information Terminal (IID)
NEWRZ.......	New Englad Rlty Assoc L.P. [*NASDAQ symbol*] (TTSB)
NEWS	Naval Electronic Warfare Simulator
NEWS	Neighborhood Environmental Workshops (EA)
NEWS	NetWare Early-Warning System [*Frye Computer Systems, Inc.*] [*Computer science*] (PCM)
NEWS	Network Extensible Window System [*Computer science*]
NEWS	New England Wild Flower Society (EA)
NEWS	New European Wide Warranty System [*General Motors Corp.*]
NEWS	New Product Early Warning System
NewSAfr.......	New South Africa Fund [*Associated Press*] (SAG)
NEWSAR......	Nuclear Energy Waste Space Transportation and Removal (GFGA)
New Sci.......	New Scientist [*A publication*] (BRI)
NewsCm......	News Communications, Inc. [*Associated Press*] (SAG)
NEWSCOMP...	Newspaper Composition (PDAA)
NewsCorp	News Corp Ltd. [*Associated Press*] (SAG)
NewsCp	[*The*] News Corp. Ltd. [*Associated Press*] (SAG)
New Series...	Martin's Louisiana Reports, New Series [*A publication*] (DLA)
New Sess Cas...	New Session Cases (Carrow, Hamerton, and Allen) [*1844-51*] [*A publication*] (DLA)
NEWSL	Newsletter
Newsl Aust Coll Ed Qd...	Australian College of Education. Queensland Chapter. Newsletter [*A publication*]
Newsl Aust Natn Ass Ment Hlth...	Australian National Association for Mental Health. Newsletter [*A publication*]
Newsl Leg Act...	Newsletter on Legislative Activities [*Council of Europe*] [*A publication*] (DLA)
Newsl Statist Soc Aust...	Statistical Society of Australia. Newsletter [*A publication*]
NEWSLTR	Newsletter
NEWSS	Northeastern Weed Science Society [*Formerly, NEWCC*] (EA)
NewSvg	Newnan Savings Bank [*Associated Press*] (SAG)
NEW T	Newcastle-Upon-Tyne [*City in England*] (ROG)
NEWT.........	Newton [*England*]
NEWT.........	Not Environmentally Worse Than (WDAA)
New TB.......	New Technical Books [*A publication*] (BRI)
New Term Rep...	Dowling and Ryland's English King's Bench Reports [*A publication*] (DLA)
New Term Rep...	New Term Reports [*A publication*] (DLA)
NEWTS	Naval Electronic Warfare Training System
NewWrld......	New World Communictions Corp. [*Associated Press*] (SAG)
New York......	New York Magazine [*A publication*] (BRI)
New York Att'y Gen Annual Rep...	New York Attorney General Reports [*A publication*] (DLA)
New York City BA Bul...	Bulletin. Association of the Bar of the City of New York [*A publication*] (DLA)
New York R...	New York Court of Appeals Reports [*A publication*] (DLA)
New York Rep...	New York Court of Appeals Reports [*A publication*] (DLA)
New York Supp...	New York Supplement [*A publication*] (DLA)
New Yugo L...	New Yugoslav Law [*A publication*] (DLA)
NEWZAD	New Zealand Army Detachment (CINC)
New Zeal Jur R...	New Zealand Jurist Reports [*A publication*] (DLA)
New Zeal L...	New Zealand Law Reports [*A publication*] (DLA)
New Zeal LR...	New Zealand Law Reports [*A publication*] (DLA)
NEX.............	National Exchange, Inc. [*McLean, VA*] [*Telecommunications*] (TSSD)
NEX.............	Nonepoxide Xanthophyll [*Organic chemistry*]
NEX.............	Northern Executive Aviation Ltd. [*British ICAO designator*] (FAAC)
NEX.............	Nose to Ear to Xiphoid [*Medicine*]
N EX	Not Exceeding [*Freight*]
NEXAFS	Near-Edge X-Ray Absorption Fine Structure [*For study of surfaces*]
NEXAIR.......	Next Generation Upper Air System [*National Weather Service*]
NEXCO........	National Association of Export Companies [*New York, NY*] (EA)
NEXCOM......	Navy Exchange Service Command
NexGen........	NexGen, Inc. [*Associated Press*] (SAG)
NEXRAD.......	Next Generation Weather RADAR [*National Weather Service*]
Nexstar........	NeXstar Pharmaceuticals [*Associated Press*] (SAG)
NEXT..........	Nationwide Evaluation of X-Ray Trends
NEXT..........	NATO Experimental Tactics (NATG)
NEXT..........	Near-End Crosstalk [*Bell System*]
NExt...........	New Experiences in Teaching [*Mathematics*]
NEXT..........	New/Experimental Techniques (MCD)
NEXT..........	NextHealth, Inc. [*NASDAQ symbol*] (SAG)
NexT	Nexus Telecommunication Systems Ltd. [*Associated Press*] (SAG)
NextelCm.....	Nextel Communications [*Commercial firm Associated Press*] (SAG)

NextHlth	NextHealth, Inc. [*Associated Press*] (SAG)
NEXUS	Nature and Earth United with Science [*Brand of hair products*]
NEXUS	Nucleus Expert User System (NITA)
NEXUS	Numerical Examination of Urban Smog (IAA)
NexusTel	Nexus Telecommunication Systems Ltd. [*Associated Press*] (SAG)
NEY...........	Neomycin Egg Yolk [*Agar*] [*Microbiology*]
NEY...........	Neyland [*British depot code*]
NEY...........	Northeastern Yiddish [*Language, etc.*] (BJA)
NEYO	New York City National Park Service Group
NEZP	Net Euphotic Zone Production [*Oceanography*]
NEZP	Nezperce Railroad Co. [*AAR code*]
NF..............	Air Vanuatu [*Airline code*] [*Australia*]
NF..............	Eaton Laboratories, Inc. [*Research code symbol*]
NF..............	EJA/Newport [*ICAO designator*] (AD)
NF..............	Fujisawa Pharmaceutical Co. [*Japan*] [*Research code symbol*]
NF..............	Nafcillin [*An antibiotic*]
nF..............	Nanofarad [*One billionth of a farad*]
NF..............	Nanofiltration
NF..............	Narodni Fronta [*National Front*] [*Former Czechoslovakia*] [*Political party*] (PPE)
NF..............	National Federation of Nonpublic School State Accrediting Associations (NTPA)
NF..............	National Fine [*Thread*]
NF..............	National Forest (IIA)
NF..............	National Formulary [*A publication listing standard drugs*]
NF..............	National Foundation
NF..............	National Front [*British Political party*] (CDAI)
NF..............	Natural Flat
NF..............	Natural Flood (MCD)
NF..............	Natural Food (MCD)
NF..............	Near Face [*Technical drawings*]
NF..............	Nebramycin Factor [*An antibacterial compound*]
NF..............	Necrotising Fasciitis [*Medicine*] (WDAA)
NF..............	Negro Female
NF..............	Neighborhood Final Fade
NF..............	Nephritic Factor [*Clinical medicine*]
NF..............	Nested or Flat [*Freight*]
NF..............	Neue Folge [*New Series*] [*Bibliography*] [*German*]
NF..............	Neurofibromatosis [*Medicine*]
NF..............	Neurofibromatosis, Inc. [*An association*] (EA)
NF..............	Neurofilament [*Neurophysiology*]
NF..............	Neutral Fraction
NF..............	Neutron Flux [*Nuclear energy*] (NRCH)
N/F.............	Neutrons per Fission
NF..............	Newfoundland [*with Labrador, a Canadian province*] [*Postal code*]
NF..............	Newfoundland Reports [*A publication*] (DLA)
NF..............	New French [*Language, etc.*] (ROG)
NF..............	Newspaper Fund (EA)
NF..............	Nichibei Fujinkai [*An association*] (EA)
NF..............	Nickel Faced (DGA)
NF..............	Niederfrequenz [*Audio Frequency*] [*German military - World War II*]
NF..............	Nieman Foundation (EA)
NF..............	Nieuw Front [*New Front*] [*Suriname*] [*Political party*] (EY)
NF..............	Night Fighter Aircraft
NF..............	Night Frequency [*Aviation*] (IAA)
NF..............	Nitrofluoranthene [*Organic chemistry*]
NF..............	Nobel Foundation (EA)
NF..............	No Flash [*Phototypesetting*] (DGA)
NF..............	No Fly [*Shrewd tradesman*] [*Slang British*] (DSUE)
NF..............	No Fool
NF..............	No Form (AAG)
NF..............	No Funds [*Banking*]
n/f.............	No Funds (WDMC)
NF..............	Noise Factor
NF..............	Noise Figure
NF..............	Noise Frequency (MSA)
NF..............	Noise Fuse (MCD)
NF..............	None Found [*Medicine*]
NF..............	Nonferrous
NF..............	Nonfiction (NTCM)
NF..............	Nonfiler [*IRS*]
NF..............	Nonfiltered
NF..............	Non-Fragments (NITA)
NF..............	Nonfunction (AAMN)
NF..............	Nonfundable
NF..............	Nonne-Froin [*Syndrome*] [*Medicine*] (DB)
NF..............	Nonwhite Female
NF..............	Noranda Forest, Inc. [*Toronto Stock Exchange symbol Vancouver Stock Exchange symbol*]
NF..............	Nordiska Fabriksarbetarefederationen [*Nordic Federation of Factory Workers Unions - NFFWU*] (EAIO)
NF..............	Nordmanns-Forbunder [*Norsemen's Federation*] (EA)
NF..............	Norfolk [*Virginia*] [*Navy Yard*]
NF..............	Norfolk Island [*ANSI two-letter standard code*] (CNC)
NF..............	Normal Flow [*Medicine*]
NF..............	Normal Form [*Database design rule*] [*Computer science*] (PCM)
NF..............	Normal Formula
NF..............	Normal Frequency [*Telecommunications*] (NTCM)
NF..............	Norman French [*Language, etc.*]
NF..............	Norsk Front [*Norwegian Front*] (PD)
NF..............	Northern Foundation [*Canada*] (EAIO)
NF..............	Northern French [*Language, etc.*] (ROG)
NF..............	North Following [*Astronomy*]
NF..............	Northumberland Fusiliers [*British military*] (DMA)
NF..............	Nose Fairing [*Missiles*]

NF	Nose Fuse [*Aviation*]
NF	Not Fertilized
NF	Not Fordable [*Maps and charts*]
NF	Not Found [*Telephone listing*] [*Telecommunications*] (TEL)
NF	Nouveau Franc [*New Franc*] [*Monetary unit Introduced in 1960*] [*France*]
NF	Nuclear Factor [*Cytology*]
NF	Nuclear Red Fast [*A dye*]
NF	Nutrition Foundation [*Later, ILSI-NF*]
NF	Royal Northumberland Fusiliers [*Military unit*] [*British*]
NF1	Neurofibromatosis Type 1 [*Medicine*]
NFA	Cast Metals Association (EA)
NFA	Naga Federal Army [*India*]
NFA	Natal Field Artillery [*British military*] (DMA)
NFA	National Faculty Association (NADA)
NFA	National Faculty Association of Community and Junior Colleges [*Later, NEA Higher Education Council*]
NFA	National Families in Action (EA)
NFA	National Farmers' Association [*Republic of Ireland*] (BI)
NFA	National Federation of Anglers [*British*] (BI)
NFA	National Film Archive [*British Film Institute*]
NFA	National Film, Television, and Sound Archives [*Ottawa*] [*UTLAS symbol*]
NFA	National Finance Adjusters (NTPA)
NFA	National Fire Academy (COE)
NFA	National Firearms Act
NFA	National Firearms Association [*Canada*]
NFA	National Fishermen's Association [*Australia*]
NFA	National Fitness Association [*Later, NHCA*] (EA)
NFA	National Florist Association (EA)
NFA	National Flute Association (EA)
NFA	National Food Administration
NFA	National Foremen's Association [*A union*] [*British*]
NFA	National Forensic Association (EA)
NFA	National Foundation for Asthma (EA)
NFA	National Foundry Association (EA)
NFA	National Franchisee Association (EA)
NFA	National Freedom Academy (EA)
NFA	National Front of Ahvaz [*Iran*]
NFA	National Frumps of America (EA)
NFA	National Futures Association (EA)
NFA	Natural Food Associates (EA)
NFA	Naval Fuel Annex
NFA	Net Financial Assets (BARN)
NFA	New Farmers of America [*Later, FFA*] (EA)
NFA	New Fighter Aircraft (MCD)
NFA	News and Feature Assistant (WDMC)
nfa	News and Feature Assistant [*An employee of a TV network*] (WDMC)
NFA	Night Fighter Association
NFA	Nitrogen Filling Assembly
NFA	Nixon Family Association (EA)
NFA	No Fire Area [*Military*] (INF)
NFA	No Fixed Abode
NFA	No Flow Assemblies (COE)
NFA	No Further Action
NFA	Nondeterministic Finite Automaton
NFA	Non-Financial Agreement (OICC)
NFA	Non-Food Agricultural [*Commodity Price Index*] (ECON)
NFA	Nonhydroxylated Fatty Acid [*Organic chemistry*]
NFA	North Flying AS [*Denmark ICAO designator*] (FAAC)
NFA	Northwest Festivals Association (EA)
NFA	Northwest Fisheries Association (EA)
NFA	Northwest Forestry Association (EA)
NFA	Not for Attribution [*Military*]
NFA	Not Forgotten Association [*British*] (DBA)
NFA	Nuclear Free America (EA)
NFA	Nutritional Foods Association [*Australia*]
NFAA	National Fashion Accessories Association (NTPA)
NFAA	National Federation of Advertising Agencies [*Later, IFAA*] (EA)
NFAA	National Field Archery Association (EA)
NFAA	National Forum for the Advancement of Aquatics (EA)
NFAA	National Foundation for Advancement in the Arts (EA)
NFAA	Neuro-Fibromatosis Association of Australia
NFAA	Nordic Forwarding Agents Association [*Defunct*] (EA)
NFAA	Northern Federation of Advertisers Associations [*Stockholm, Sweden*] (EAIO)
NFAA	Nuclear Fuel Assurance Act
NFAAUM	National Federation of Asian American United Methodists (EA)
NFAC	Arnolds Cove Public Library, Newfoundland [*Library symbol National Library of Canada*] (NLC)
NFAC	National Food and Agricultural Council (NADA)
NFAC	National Foreign Assessment Center [*CIA*]
NFAC	National Foundation for Asthmatic Children at Tucson [*Later, NFA*] (EA)
NFAC	National Franchise Association Coalition (EA)
NFAC	National Full-Scale Aerodynamics Complex [*Ames Research Center, CA*] [*NASA*]
NFAC	Naval Facilities Engineering Command Headquarters
NFACJC	National Faculty Association of Community and Junior Colleges [*Later, NEA Higher Education Council*]
NFADB	National Family Association for Deaf-Blind [*Sponsored by the Helen Keller National Center for Deaf-Blind Youths and Adults (HKNC)*] (PAZ)
NFAF	Naval Fleet Auxiliary Force
NFAH	National Federation of American Hungarians (EA)
NFAH	National Federation of Hungarian-Americans
NFAH	National Foundation on the Arts and Humanities
NFAHA	National Foundation on the Arts and Humanities Act [*1965*]
NFAHS	National Foundation for Affordable Housing Solutions (EA)
NFaiB	Board of Cooperative Educational Services - Monroe I, Fairport, NY [*Library symbol Library of Congress*] (LCLS)
NFAIO	National Federation of Asian Indian Organizations in America [*Later, NFIAA*] (EA)
NFAIS	National Federation of Abstracting and Indexing Services (NITA)
NFAIS	National Federation of Abstracting and Information Services (EA)
NFAIS	National Federation of American Information Services [*International Council of Scientific Unions*]
NFAL	National Foundation of Arts and Letters (WDAA)
NFAM	National Foundation for the Australian Musical
NFAM	Network File Access Method
NFAN	National Filter Analysis Network [*Environmental Protection Agency*] (GFGA)
NFANA	Norwegian Fjord Association of North America (EA)
NF & F	Natural Food and Farming [*A publication*]
NFAP	Nerve Fiber Action Potentials [*Neurophysiology*]
NFAP	Network File Access Protocol
NFAP	Nuclear Free Australia Party [*Political party*]
NFAPC	National Fisheries Adjustment Program Committee [*Australia*]
NFar	Farmingdale Public Library, Farmingdale, NY [*Library symbol Library of Congress*] (LCLS)
NFAR	No Further Action Required (DAVI)
NFarB	BioResearch, Inc., Farmingdale, NY [*Library symbol Library of Congress*] (LCLS)
NFarEE	East Memorial Elementary School, Farmingdale, NY [*Library symbol Library of Congress*] (LCLS)
NFarF	Fairchild-Hiller Corp. [*Later, Fairchild Industries, Inc.*], Republic Aviation Division, Farmingdale, NY [*Library symbol Library of Congress*] (LCLS)
NFarHS	Howitt School, Farmingdale, NY [*Library symbol*] [*Library of Congress*] (LCLS)
NFarNE	Northside Elementary School, Farmingdale, NY [*Library symbol*] [*Library of Congress*] (LCLS)
NFARS	NORAD Forward Automated Reporting System (MCD)
NFarSH	Farmingdale Senior High School, Farmingdale, NY [*Library symbol*] [*Library of Congress*] (LCLS)
NFarUA	State University of New York, Agricultural and Technical College at Farmingdale, Farmingdale, NY [*Library symbol Library of Congress*] (LCLS)
NFarWP	Woodward Parkway School, Farmingdale, NY [*Library symbol*] [*Library of Congress*] (LCLS)
NFAS	National Field Archery Society [*British*] (DBA)
NFASG	National Fashion Accessories Salesmen's Guild (EA)
NFAT	Nuclear Factor for Activated T-Cells [*Genetics*]
NFAWSR	North Fork American Wild and Scenic River (COE)
NFay	Fayetteville Free Library, Fayetteville, NY [*Library symbol Library of Congress*] (LCLS)
NFB	Booth Memorial Hospital, Flushing, NY [*Library symbol Library of Congress*] (LCLS)
NFB	Mount Clemens, MI [*Location identifier FAA*] (FAAL)
NFB	National Federation of the Blind (EA)
NFB	National Film Board [*Canada*] (WDMC)
NFB	National Film Board of Canada [*UTLAS symbol*]
NFB	National Foundation for the Blind (DMAA)
NFB	Naval Frontier Base
NFB	Negative Feedback (DEN)
NFB	New Fibers International [*Vancouver Stock Exchange symbol*]
NFB	Niagara Frontier Tariff Bureau, Inc., Buffalo NY [*STAC*]
NFB	Node of First-Fruiting Branch [*Botany*] (OA)
NFB	No Feed Back (AEBS)
NFB	Nonfermenting Bacteria
NFB	North Fork Bancorp [*NYSE symbol*] (SPSG)
NFBA	National Family Business Association [*Tarzana, CA*] (EA)
NFBA	National Farm Borrowers Association (EA)
NFBA	National Food Brokers Association (EA)
NFBA	National Frame Builders Association (EA)
NFBC	National Family Business Council [*Northbrook, IL*] (EA)
NFBC	National Film Board of Canada
NFBC	Newfoundland Base Command [*Army World War II*]
NFBC	North Fork Bancorp (MHDW)
NFBCA	National Federation of Blind Citizens of Australia
NFBF	Bishops Falls Public Library, Newfoundland [*Library symbol National Library of Canada*] (NLC)
NFBF	National Farm Bureau Federation
NFBG	National Federation of Badger Groups [*British*] (DBA)
NFBI	Bell Island Public Library, Newfoundland [*Library symbol National Library of Canada*] (NLC)
NFBI	Netherlands Flower-Bulb Institute [*Defunct*] (EA)
NFBI	Nonresidential Fixed Business Investment (MCD)
NFBN	National Food Bank Network (EA)
NFBO	Bonavista Public Library, Newfoundland [*Library symbol National Library of Canada*] (NLC)
NFBOT	Botwood Public Library, Newfoundland [*Library symbol National Library of Canada*] (NLC)
NFBPA	National Forum for Black Public Administrators (EA)
NFBPM	National Federation of Builders' and Plumbers' Merchants [*British*] (BI)
NFBPT	National Federation for Biblio/Poetry Therapy (EA)
NFBPW	National Federation of Business and Professional Women's Clubs (WGA)

NFBPWC	National Federation of Business and Professional Women's Clubs (EA)
NFBQ	Rural District Memorial Library, Badgers Quay, Newfoundland [*Library symbol National Library of Canada*] (NLC)
NFBR	Bay Roberts Public Library, Newfoundland [*Library symbol National Library of Canada*] (NLC)
NFBR	National Foundation for Biomedical Research [*An association*]
NFBR	National Foundation for Brain Research (EA)
NFBRI	Brigus Public Library, Newfoundland [*Library symbol National Library of Canada*] (NLC)
NFBS	National Freehold Building Society [*British*]
NFBSS	National Federation of Bakery Students' Societies [*British*] (BI)
NFBTE	National Federation of Building Trades Employers [*British*] (DCTA)
NFBTO	National Federation of Building Trades Operatives [*British*]
NFBU	Buchans Public Library, Newfoundland [*Library symbol National Library of Canada*] (NLC)
NFBU	National Federation of Bus Users [*British*]
NFBU	National Fire Brigades Union (ROG)
NFBUK	National Federation for the Blind [*British*] (DBA)
NFBUR	Burgeo Public Library, Newfoundland [*Library symbol National Library of Canada*] (NLC)
NFBURI	Burin Public Library, Newfoundland [*Library symbol National Library of Canada*] (NLC)
NFBV	Baie Verte Public Library, Newfoundland [*Library symbol National Library of Canada*] (NLC)
NFBWA	National Federation of Buddhist Women's Associations [*Later, BCAFBWA*]
NFBWW	Nordic Federation of Building and Wood Workers (EA)
NFC	Carbonear Public Library, Newfoundland [*Library symbol National Library of Canada*] (NLC)
NFC	Name Formula Card
NFC	National Farm Coalition [*Defunct*] (EA)
NFC	National Federated Craft (EA)
NFC	National Fenestration Council [*Later, PGMC*] (EA)
NFC	National Fertility Center (DAVI)
NFC	National Film Carriers (EA)
NFC	National Finance Center (USDC)
NFC	National Firebird Club (EA)
NFC	National Fire Code
NFC	National Food Conference Association (EA)
NFC	National Football Conference [*of NFL*]
NFC	National Forensic Center (EA)
NFC	National Fraternal Congress [*Later, NFCA*]
NFC	National Freight Consortium (WDAA)
NFC	National Freight Corp. [*British*]
NFC	National Fructose Center (EA)
NFC	National Fund Chairman [*or Co-chairman*] [*Red Cross*]
NFC	Native Forest Council (EA)
NFC	Navy Federal Credit Union
NFC	Navy Finance Center
NFC	Near-Frictionless Carbon
NFC	Negative Factor Counting
NFC	Negative Feedback Circuit
nfc	Newfoundland [*MARC country of publication code Library of Congress*] (LCCP)
NFC	News for Farmer Cooperatives [*A publication*]
NFC	Newsline Fan Club (EA)
NFC	Newspaper Features Council (EA)
NFC	NFC Ltd. [*Associated Press*] (SAG)
NFC	NFC PLC [*AMEX symbol*] (SPSG)
NFC	NFC plc ADS [*AMEX symbol*] (TTSB)
NFC	Nighttime Fatal Crash
NFC	No Further Clearance Required (KSC)
NFC	No Further Consequences (NRCH)
NFC	Nonfavorably Considered (DAVI)
NFC	Nordisk Forening for Cellforskning [*Nordic Society for Cell Biology - NSCB*] (EAIO)
NFC	Nose Fairing Container [*Missiles*]
NFC	Not Favorably Considered
NFC	Nuclear Fuel Cycle (NUCP)
NFC	Numbered Fleet Commander (DOMA)
NFCA	Carmanville Public Library, Newfoundland [*Library symbol National Library of Canada*] (NLC)
NFCA	National Family Caregivers Association (NTPA)
NFCA	National Federation of Community Associations [*British*] (DI)
NFCA	National Floor Covering Association [*Canada*] (EAIO)
NFCA	National Foster Care Association [*British*] (EAIO)
NFCA	National Fraternal Congress of America [*Naperville, IL*] (EA)
NFCA	National Fuel Credit Association [*Defunct*]
NFCA	Near-Field Calibration Array (PDAA)
NFCA	Nonfuel Core Array [*Nuclear energy*] (NRCH)
NFCAA	National Fencing Coaches Association of America (EA)
NFCADA	National Family Council Against Drug Abuse [*Formerly, NFCDA*] (EA)
NFC(ALLOT)	Navy Finance Center (Allotments Division) (DNAB)
NFCARW	National Federation of Cuban-American Republican Women (EA)
NFCAT	Joseph E. Clouter Memorial Library, Catalina, Newfoundland [*Library symbol National Library of Canada*] (NLC)
NFCB	Corner Brook City Public Library, Newfoundland [*Library symbol National Library of Canada*] (NLC)
NFCB	National Federation of Community Broadcasters (EA)
NFCBF	Newfoundland Department of Forest Resources and Lands, Corner Brook, New Foundland [*Library symbol National Library of Canada*] (NLC)
NFCBFT	Fisher Institute of Applied Arts and Technology, Corner Brook, Newfoundland [*Library symbol National Library of Canada*] (NLC)
NFCBM	Sir Wilfred Grenfell College, Memorial University, Corner Brook, Newfoundland [*Library symbol National Library of Canada*] (NLC)
NFCBR	Regional Library, Corner Brook, Newfoundland [*Library symbol National Library of Canada*] (NLC)
NFCBRO	National Federation of Citizen Band Radio Operators (EA)
NFCBW	Western Memorial Hospital, Corner Brook, Newfoundland [*Library symbol National Library of Canada*] (NLC)
NFCC	National Family Conciliation Council [*British*] (DI)
NFCC	National Farm-City Council (EA)
NFCC	National Foundation for Consumer Credit [*Silver Spring, MD*] (EA)
NFCC	National Free Clinic Council [*Superseded by NCAHCP*]
NFCC	Neighborhood Family-Care Center (MEDA)
NFC(CAD)	Navy Finance Center (Central Accounts Division) (DNAB)
NFCCE	National Fellowship of Child Care Executives (EA)
NFC-CLEVE	Navy Finance Center - Cleveland [*Ohio*] (DNAB)
NFCCS	National Federation of Catholic College Students [*Defunct*] (EA)
NFCDA	National Family Council on Drug Addiction [*Later, NFCADA*] (EA)
NFCDCU	National Federation of Community Development Credit Unions [*New York, NY*] (EA)
NFCDS	National Federation of Clubs for Divorced and Separated [*British*] (BI)
NFCE	Centreville Public Library, Newfoundland [*Library symbol National Library of Canada*] (NLC)
NFCEO	National Foundation for Conservation and Environmental Officers [*Defunct*] (EA)
NFCF	Churchill Falls Public Library, Newfoundland [*Library symbol National Library of Canada*] (NLC)
NFCF	National Federation of City Farms [*British*] (EAIO)
NFCG	National Federation of Consumer Groups [*British*] (ILCA)
NFCGA	National Federation of Constructional Glass Associations [*British*] (BI)
NFCGC	National Federation of Coffee Growers of Colombia [*See also FNCC*] (EA)
NFCGH	Carbonear General Hospital, Newfoundland [*Library symbol National Library of Canada*] (NLC)
NFCH	Cow Head Public Library, Newfoundland [*Library symbol National Library of Canada*] (NLC)
NFCH	National Foundation for the Chemically Hypersensitive (EA)
NFCI	Change Islands Public Library, Newfoundland [*Library symbol National Library of Canada*] (NLC)
NFCI	National Federation of Clay Industries [*British*] (BI)
NFCIS	Nuclear Fuel Cycle Information System [*Database*] [*International Atomic Energy Agency*] [*United Nations*] (DUND)
NFCJ	National Forum on Criminal Justice [*Formerly, NICD*] [*Inactive*] (EA)
NFCL	Clarenville Public Library, Newfoundland [*Library symbol National Library of Canada*] (NLC)
NFC-L	National Fisheries Center - Leetown [*Department of the Interior*] (GRD)
NFCM	National Front Constitutional Movement [*British*]
NFCO	Cormack Public Library, Newfoundland [*Library symbol National Library of Canada*] (NLC)
NFCO	National Federation of Community Organizations [*British*] (EAIO)
NFCP	Channel/Port Aux Basques Public Library, Newfoundland [*Library symbol National Library of Canada*] (NLC)
NFCPG	National Federation of Catholic Physicians' Guilds (EA)
NFCPO	National Forum of Catholic Parent Organizations [*Defunct*] (EA)
NFCR	National Foundation for Cancer Research (EA)
NFCRC	National Fisheries Contaminant Research Center (EA)
NFCS	National Federation of Catholic Seminarians [*Defunct*] (EA)
NFCS	National Federation of Construction Supervisors [*British*] (BI)
NFCS	Naval Field Contracting System (AAGC)
NFCS	Night-Fire [*Rifle*] Control Sight [*Army*]
NFCS	Nuclear Forces Communications Satellite
NFCSG	Cape St. George Public Library, Newfoundland [*Library symbol National Library of Canada*] (NLC)
NFCSIT	National Federation of Cold Storage and Ice Trades [*British*] (BI)
NFCT	National Federation of Class Teachers (AIE)
NFCT	Nonfederal Control Tower [*For chart use only*]
NFCTA	National Federation of Continuative Teachers' Associations [*British*]
NFCTA	National Federation of Corn Trade Associations [*British*] (BI)
NFCTA	National Fibre Can and Tube Association [*Later, CCTI*] (EA)
NFCU	Navy Federal Credit Union
NFCUS	National Federation of Canadian University Students
NFCW	Cartwright Public Library, Newfoundland [*Library symbol National Library of Canada*] (BIB)
NFC-WASH	Navy Finance Center - Washington, DC (DNAB)
NFCYM	National Federation for Catholic Youth Ministry (EA)
NFD	Dover Public Library, Newfoundland [*Library symbol National Library of Canada*] (BIB)
NFD	Eurowings (NFD & RFG Luftverhehrs AG) [*Germany ICAO designator*] (FAAC)
NFD	National Faculty Directory [*A publication*]
NFD	National Fax Directory [*A publication*]
NFD	National Federation for Decency (EA)
NFD	National Federation of Drapers and Allied Traders Ltd. [*Republic of Ireland*] (BI)
NFD	Naval Fuel Depot
NFD	Neurofibrillary Degeneration [*Medicine*]
NFD	Neutron Flux Density [*Nuclear energy*]
NFD	Newfoundland [*with Labrador, a Canadian province*]
NFD	Newfoundland Tracking Station
NFD	No Fixed Date
NFD	No Foreign Dissemination [*Intelligence classification*] (MCD)

NFD .... Norfolk, Franklin & Danville Railway Co. [*AAR code*]
NFD .... Northern Frontier District [*Kenya*]
NFD .... Nueva Fuerza Democratica [*New Democratic Force*] [*Colorado Political party*] (EY)
NFDA .... National Fastener Distributors Association (EA)
NFDA .... National Food Distributors Association (EA)
NFDA .... National Funeral Directors Association (EA)
NFDC .... Dark Cove Public Library, Newfoundland [*Library symbol National Library of Canada*] (NLC)
NFDC .... National Father's Day Committee (EA)
NFDC .... National Federation of Demolition Contractors [*British*] (EAIO)
NFDC .... National Fertilizer Development Center [*Tennessee Valley Authority*] [*Muscle Shoals, AL*]
NFDC .... National Flight Data Center [*FAA*]
NFDCAMD... National Food, Drug, and Cosmetic Association of Manufacturers and Distributors [*Defunct*] (EA)
NFDD .... National Flight Data Digest [*FAA*] (TAG)
NFDF .... National Flag Day Foundation (EA)
NFDH .... Daniels Harbour Public Library, Newfoundland [*Library symbol National Library of Canada*] (NLC)
NFDH .... National Foundation of Dentistry for the Handicapped (EA)
NFDL .... Deer Lake Public Library, Newfoundland [*Library symbol National Library of Canada*] (NLC)
NFDM .... Nonfat Dry Milk
NFDMA .... National Funeral Directors and Morticians Association (EA)
NFDPM .... National Federation of Data Processing Manufacturing (NITA)
NFDPS .... National Flight Data Processing System [*ICAO*] (DA)
NFDR .... Neurofacial-Digitorenal Syndrome [*Medicine*] (DMAA)
NFDRS .... National Fire Danger Rating System [*US Forest Service*]
NFDW .... National Federation of Democratic Women (EA)
NFE .... Fentress, VA [*Location identifier FAA*] (FAAL)
NFE .... National Faculty Exchange (EA)
NFE .... Naval Facilities Engineering Command, Alexandria, VA [*OCLC symbol*] (OCLC)
NFE .... Near Free Electron (AAEL)
NFE .... Nearly Free Electron [*Physics*] (OA)
NFE .... Network Front End
NFE .... News from Ethiopia [*A publication*]
NFE .... Nitride Forming Element [*Metal treating*]
NFE .... Nitrogen-Free Extract [*Analytical chemistry*]
NFE .... Nonferrous Extract (DMAA)
NFE .... Nonformal Education
NFE .... Northwest Fruit Exporters (NTPA)
NFE .... Nose Fairing Exit [*Missiles*]
NFE .... Not Fully Equipped [*of aircraft*] [*Air Force*]
NFEA .... National Federated Electrical Association (MHDB)
NFEA .... National Federation of Export Associations [*New York, NY*] (EA)
NFEA .... Newspaper Farm Editors of America (EA)
NFEA .... Non-Fleet Experienced Aviator (NVT)
NFEAC .... National Foundation for Education in American Citizenship (EA)
NFEC .... National Food and Energy Council (EA)
NFEC .... National Foundation for Environmental Control (EA)
NFEC .... Naval Facilities Engineering Command [*Formerly, Bureau of Yards and Docks*] (IEEE)
NFEC .... Newspaper Food Editors Conference (EA)
NFECC .... National Fusion Energy Computer Center [*Lawrence Livermore National Laboratory*] (MCD)
NFED .... National Foundation for Ectodermal Dysplasias (EA)
NFEF .... National Free Enterprise Foundation [*Australia*]
NFER .... National Foundation for Educational Research [*British*] (DET)
NFER .... National Foundation for Educational Research in England and Wales (IID)
NFER .... National Foundation for Eye Research (EA)
NFER .... Nonferrous
NFERF .... National Fisheries Education and Research Foundation (EA)
NFESC .... Naval Facilities Engineering Service Center (BCP)
NFET .... N-Channel Junction Field-Effect Transistor (IDOE)
NFETA .... National Foundry and Engineering Training Association [*British*]
NFETM .... National Federation of Engineers' Tools Manufacturers (MHDB)
NFEW .... National Forum for Executive Women [*Washington, DC*] (EA)
NFEWA .... Newspaper Food Editors and Writers Association (EA)
NFF .... Fogo Public Library, Newfoundland [*Library symbol National Library of Canada*] (NLC)
NFF .... Jacksonville, FL [*Location identifier FAA*] (FAAL)
NFF .... Natal Field Force [*British military*] (DMA)
NFF .... National Fatherland Front [*Afghanistan*] [*Political party*] (FEA)
NFF .... National Federation of Fishermen [*Inactive*] (EA)
NFF .... National Federation of Fishmongers [*British*] (DBA)
NFF .... National Fitness Foundation (EA)
NFF .... National Flag Foundation (EA)
NFF .... National Flood Frequency Program [*Computer science*]
NFF .... National Football Foundation and Hall of Fame (EA)
NFF .... National Forum Foundation (EA)
NFF .... National Froebel Foundation [*British*] (BI)
NFF .... Naval Fuel Facility
NFF .... Nemzeti Fueggetlensegi Front [*National Independence Front*] [*Hungary Political party*] (PPE)
NFF .... New Forests Fund (EA)
NFF .... No Fault Found (MCD)
NFF .... No Frills Fund
Nff .... Nordisk Forening for Folkendansforskning [*Nordic Association for Folk Dance Research*] [*Sweden*] (EAIO)
NFF .... Nuclear Freeze Foundation [*Defunct*] (EA)
NFF .... Numbered Fleet Flagship [*Navy*]
NFFA .... Ba [*Fiji*] [*ICAO location identifier*] (ICLI)

NFFA .... National Flying Farmers Association [*Later, International Flying Farmers*]
NFFA .... National Folk Festival Association [*Later, National Council for the TraditionalArts*]
NFFA .... National Frozen Food Association (EA)
NFFAO .... National FFA [*Future Farmers of America*] Organization (EA)
NFFC .... Nancy Fisher Fan Club (EA)
NFFC .... National Family Farm Coalition (EA)
NFFC .... National Fantasy Fan Club for Disneyana Enthusiasts
NFFC .... National Film Finance Corp. [*British*] (BI)
NFFDA .... National Frozen Food Distributors Association [*Later, NFFA*]
NFFDF .... National Fraternal Flag Day Foundation [*Defunct*] (EA)
NFFE .... National Federation of Federal Employees (EA)
NFFF .... Nandi [*Fiji*] [*ICAO location identifier*] (ICLI)
NFFF .... National Fantasy Fan Federation
NFFF .... National Federation of Fish Friers [*British*] (BI)
NFFGB .... National Federation of Flemish Giant Breeders [*Later, NFFGRB*]
NFFGRB ...... National Federation of Flemish Giant Rabbit Breeders (EA)
NFFH .... Fox Harbour Public Library, Newfoundland [*Library symbol National Library of Canada*] (NLC)
NFFI .... Not Fit for Issue [*Navy*]
NFFL .... Northern Forest Fire Laboratory [*Later, Intermountain Fire Sciences Laboratory*] [*Research center*] (RCD)
NFFN .... Nandi/International [*Fiji*] [*ICAO location identifier*] (ICLI)
NFFO .... Fortune Public Library, Newfoundland [*Library symbol National Library of Canada*] (NLC)
NFFO .... Malolo Lailai [*Fiji*] [*ICAO location identifier*] (ICLI)
NFFO .... National Federation of Fishermen's Organisations (EAIO)
NFFO .... Non-Fossil Fuel Obligation [*Pronounced "Noffo"*] [*Nuclear power*]
NFFPT .... National Federation of Fruit and Potato Trades [*British*] (BI)
NFFQO .... National Federation of Freestone Quarry Owners [*British*] (BI)
NFFR .... Freshwater Public Library, Newfoundland [*Library symbol National Library of Canada*] (NLC)
NFFR .... National Foundation for Facial Reconstruction (EA)
NFFR .... Rabi [*Fiji*] [*ICAO location identifier*] (ICLI)
NFFS .... National Foundation of Funeral Service (EA)
NFFS .... Non-Ferrous Founders Society (EA)
NFFTU .... National Federation of Furniture Trade Unions [*British*] (BI)
NFFWU .... Nordic Federation of Factory Workers Unions (EA)
NFG .... Gander Public Library, Newfoundland [*Library symbol National Library of Canada*] (NLC)
NFG .... Nagaland Federal Government [*India*]
NFG .... National Freight Group
NFG .... National Fuel Gas Co. [*NYSE symbol*] (SPSG)
NFG .... Natl Fuel Gas [*NYSE symbol*] (TTSB)
NFG .... Northwest Fruit Growers (EA)
NFG .... Oceanside, CA [*Location identifier FAA*] (FAAL)
NFGA .... Garnish Public Library, Newfoundland [*Library symbol National Library of Canada*] (NLC)
NFGAU .... Gaultois Public Library, Newfoundland [*Library symbol National Library of Canada*] (BIB)
NFGB .... Grand Bank Public Library, Newfoundland [*Library symbol National Library of Canada*] (NLC)
NFGBM .... Medical Library, Melville Hospital, Goose-Bay, Newfoundland [*Library symbol National Library of Canada*] (BIB)
NFGBM .... National Fellowship of Grace Brethren Ministers (EA)
NFGC .... National Federation of Grain Cooperatives [*Later, NCFC*] (EA)
NFGCA .... National Federation of Grandmother Clubs of America (EA)
NFGF .... Regional Library, Grand Falls, Newfoundland [*Library symbol National Library of Canada*] (NLC)
NFGFC .... Central Region Libraries, Grand Falls, Newfoundland [*Library symbol National Library of Canada*] (NLC)
NFGFH .... Central Newfoundland Hospital, Grand Falls, Newfoundland [*Library symbol National Library of Canada*] (NLC)
NFGFHA ...... Harmsworth Public Library, Grand Falls, Newfoundland [*Library symbol National Library of Canada*] (NLC)
NFGJPH .... James Paton Memorial Hospital, Gander, Newfoundland [*Library symbol National Library of Canada*] (NLC)
NFGL .... Glenwood Public Library, Newfoundland [*Library symbol National Library of Canada*] (NLC)
NFGLO .... Glovertown Public Library, Newfoundland [*Library symbol National Library of Canada*] (NLC)
NFGMIC ...... National Federation of Grange Mutual Insurance Companies [*Glastonbury, CT*] (EA)
NFGND .... National Foundation for Genetics and Neuromuscular Disease [*Later, NGF*]
NFGNE .... National Fund for Graduate Nursing Education [*Defunct*]
NFGO .... Goulds Public Library, Newfoundland [*Library symbol National Library of Canada*] (BIB)
NFGOCM ..... National Forum of Greek Orthodox Church Musicians (EA)
NFGOPC ...... National Federation of the Grand Order of Pachyderm Clubs (EA)
NFGR .... Greenspond Public Library, Newfoundland [*Library symbol National Library of Canada*] (NLC)
NFGS .... National Federation of Gramophone Societies (EAIO)
NFGS .... National Fenton Glass Society (EA)
NFH .... Holyrood Public Library, Newfoundland [*Library symbol National Library of Canada*] (BIB)
NFH .... National Federation of Hairdressers (WDAA)
NFH .... National Fish Hatchery
NFH .... Native Field Hospital [*British military*] (DMA)
NFH .... Nonfamilial Hematuria [*Medicine*] (DMAA)
NFHA .... National Federation of Housing Associations [*British*] (DBA)
NFHA .... National Fox Hunters Association (EA)
NFHANA ...... Norwegian Fjord Horse Association of North America [*Later, NFANA*] (EA)

NFHAS .... National Faculty of Humanities, Arts, and Sciences (EA)

NFHB .... Harbour Breton Public Library, Newfoundland [*Library symbol National Library of Canada*] (NLC)

NFHBA .... Hare Bay Public Library, Newfoundland [*Library symbol National Library of Canada*] (NLC)

NFHC .... National Federation of Hispanics in Communication (EA)

NFHC .... National Federation of Housing Coops [*British*] (DBA)

NFHC .... National Federation of Housing Counselors (EA)

NFHC .... National Foot Health Council [*Defunct*] (EA)

NFHC .... National Foundation for History of Chemistry (EA)

NFHCF .... National Flotation Health Care Foundation (EA)

NFHD .... National Foundation for the Handicapped and Disabled [*Defunct*] (EA)

NFHE .... Hermitage Public Library, Newfoundland [*Library symbol National Library of Canada*] (NLC)

NFHE .... Non-Irradiated Fuel Handling Equipment [*Nuclear energy*] (NRCH)

NFHEA .... National Farm Home Editors Association [*Defunct*] (EA)

NFHG .... Harbour Grace Public Library, Newfoundland [*Library symbol National Library of Canada*] (NLC)

NFHH .... Harrys Harbour Public Library, Newfoundland [*Library symbol National Library of Canada*] (NLC)

NFhM .... Medical Society of the County of Queens, Forest Hills, NY [*Library symbol Library of Congress*] (LCLS)

NFHO .... Caaf Ho Nandi [*Fiji*] [*ICAO location identifier*] (ICLI)

NFHO .... National Federation of Housestaff Organizations (EA)

NFHON .... National Federation of Hispanic Owned Newspapers (NTPA)

NFHPER ...... National Foundation for Health, Physical Education, and Recreation [*Defunct*]

NFHRL .... National Fish Health Research Laboratory [*Department of the Interior*] [*Kearneysville, WV*] (GRD)

NFHTP .... National Federation of Hebrew Teachers and Principals [*Defunct*] (EA)

NFHV .... Happy Valley Public Library, Newfoundland [*Library symbol National Library of Canada*] (NLC)

NFI .... Narrow Fabrics Institute (EA)

NFI .... National Fisheries Center [*Marine science*] (OSRA)

NFI .... National Fisheries Institute (EA)

NFI .... Natural Food Institute [*Defunct*] (EA)

NFI .... Naturfreunde-Internationale [*International Friends of Nature - IFN*] (EAIO)

NFI .... Net Fundable Issues (DNAB)

NFI .... News Features of India [*Press agency*]

NFI .... New Signet Resources [*Vancouver Stock Exchange symbol*]

NFI .... Nielsen Food Index [*Marketing*] (DOAD)

NFI .... No Further Service (Inspections)

NFI .... Noise Figure Indicator

NFI .... Not Further Identified (MCD)

NFIA .... National Families in Action [*An association*] (EA)

NFIA .... National Feed Ingredients Association (EA)

NFIA .... National Flood Insurance Act of 1968 (COE)

NFIA .... National Flood Insurers Association [*Defunct*] (EA)

NFIA .... National Forest Industries Association [*Australia*]

NFIA .... Nonappropriated Fund Instrumentalities Act

NFIAA .... National Federation of Indian American Associations (EA)

NFIB .... National Federation of Independent Business [*San Mateo, CA*] (EA)

NFIB .... National Foreign Intelligence Board [*Formerly, USIB*] [*Military*]

NFIC .... National Foundation for Ileitis and Colitis (EA)

NFIC .... National Fraud Information Center

NFICA .... National Federation Interscholastic Coaches Association (EA)

NFICA .... National Forest Industries Campaign Association [*Australia*]

NFICSC .... National Foundation for Ileitis and Colitis Sports Council (EA)

NFID .... National Foundation for Infectious Diseases (EA)

NFIE .... National Foundation for the Improvement of Education (EA)

NFIL .... Nuclear Factor Interleukin [*Genetics*]

NFIMA .... National Federation Interscholastic Music Association (EA)

NFIOA .... National Federation Interscholastic Officials Association (EA)

NFIP .... National Flood Insurance Program [*Federal Emergency Management Agency*]

NFIP .... National Foreign Intelligence Program [*DoD*]

NFIP .... National Foundation for Infantile Paralysis [*Later, MDBDF*]

NFIPA .... National Fire Protection Association (WPI)

NFIPS .... National Flood Insurance Program System [*Federal Emergency Management Agency*] (GFGA)

NFIR .... National Federation of Indian Railwaymen

NFIRF .... Nature Farming International Research Foundation (EAIO)

NFIRS .... National Fire Incident Reporting System [*Federal Emergency Management Agency*] (GFGA)

NFIS .... Naval Fighting Instruction School

NFISDA .... National Federation Interscholastic Speech and Debate Association (EA)

NFisi .... Fishers Island Library Association, Fishers Island, NY [*Library symbol Library of Congress*] (LCLS)

NFisk .... Blodgett Memorial Library, Fishkill, NY [*Library symbol Library of Congress*] (LCLS)

NFISM .... National Federation of Iron and Steel Merchants [*British*] (BI)

NFISYD .... National Federation of Independent Scrap Yard Dealers (EA)

NFITC .... National Forest Industries Training Council [*Australia*]

NFIU .... National Federation of Independent Unions

NFJ .... Milton, FL [*Location identifier FAA*] (FAAL)

NFJC .... National Foundation for Jewish Culture (EA)

NFJGD .... National Foundation for Jewish Genetic Diseases (EA)

NFJM .... National Foundation for Junior Museums [*Later, NSYF*]

NFJMC .... National Federation of Jewish Men's Clubs (EA)

NFK .... Norfolk Island [*ANSI three-letter standard code*] (CNC)

NFK .... Nuclear Factor Kappa (DMAA)

NFKK .... Nordisk Forening for Klinisk Kemi [*Scandinavian Society for Clinical Chemistry - SSCC*] [*Finland*] (EAIO)

NFKP .... Kings Point Public Library, Newfoundland [*Library symbol National Library of Canada*] (NLC)

NFKPA .... National Federation of Kidney Patients Association [*British*] (DI)

NFL .... Fallon, NV [*Location identifier FAA*] (FAAL)

NFL .... Labrador City Public Library, Newfoundland [*Library symbol National Library of Canada*] (NLC)

NFL .... National Federation of Laymen (EA)

NFL .... National Film Library (NADA)

NFL .... National Football League (EA)

NFL .... National Forensic League (EA)

NFL .... National Foresters League (NADA)

NFL .... National Fund Leadership [*Group*] [*Red Cross*]

NFL .... Naval Standard Flange (MSA)

NFL .... Nerve Fiber Layer [*Neurology*] (DAVI)

NFL .... Neurofilament Protein, Light Polypeptide (DMAA)

NFL .... Newfoundland and Prince Edward Island Reports [*Maritime Law Book Co. Ltd.*] [*Canada Information service or system*] (CRD)

NFL .... Newfoundland Light & Power Co. Ltd. [*Toronto Stock Exchange symbol*]

NFL .... Newlands Field Laboratory [*University of Nevada - Reno*] [*Research center*] (RCD)

NFL .... No Field Lubrication (PDAA)

NFL .... No Fire Line [*Military*]

NFL .... No Phone Listed [*Cablegram marking*] [*British*]

NFL .... Normal Female Liver [*Hepatology*]

NFL .... Northaire Freight Lines Ltd. [*ICAO designator*] (FAAC)

NFL .... Nurses for Laughter

NFL .... Nuveen Ins FL Prem Inc. Muni [*NYSE symbol*] (TTSB)

NFL .... Nuveen Insured Florida Premium Income Municipal [*NYSE symbol*] (SPSG)

NFLA .... L'Anse Au Loup Public Library, Newfoundland [*Library symbol National Library of Canada*] (NLC)

NFLA .... National Football League Alumni (EA)

NFLA .... National Front for the Liberation of Angola (EA)

NFLA .... Nuclear-Free Local Authorities (WDAA)

NFLC .... National Federation of Land Councils [*Australia*]

NFLC .... Northern Forest Lands Council (WPI)

NFLCC .... National Fishing Lure Collectors Club (EA)

NFLCP .... National Federation of Local Cable Programmers (EA)

NFLD .... Nerve Fiber Layer Defect [*Medicine*] (DMAA)

NFLD .... Newfoundland [*with Labrador, a Canadian province*]

Nfld .... Newfoundland [*Canada*] (DD)

Nfld .... Newfoundland Supreme Court Decisions [*Canada*] [*A publication*] (DLA)

NFLD .... Northfield Laboratories [*NASDAQ symbol*] (TTSB)

NFLD .... Northfield Laboratories, Inc. [*NASDAQ symbol*] (SAG)

Nfld LR .... Newfoundland Law Reports [*A publication*] (DLA)

Nfld R .... Newfoundland Reports [*A publication*] (DLA)

Nfld Rev Stat... Newfoundland Revised Statutes [*Canada*] [*A publication*] (DLA)

NFLDS .... National Fire Loss Data System [*Military*] (PDAA)

Nfld Sel Cas... Newfoundland Select Cases [*A publication*] (DLA)

Nfld Stat ..... Newfoundland Statutes [*Canada*] [*A publication*] (DLA)

NFLE .... Lewisporte Public Library, Newfoundland [*Library symbol National Library of Canada*] (NLC)

NFLF .... National Family Life Foundation (EA)

NFLF .... Nylon Full-Line Filter

NFLHB .... Blow Me Down School/Public Library, Lark Harbour, Newfoundland [*Library symbol National Library of Canada*] (NLC)

NFLI .... Northern Fraternal Life Insurance (EA)

NFLI .... Nutrition For Life International, Inc. [*NASDAQ symbol*] (SAG)

NFLI .... Nutrition For Life Intl. [*NASDAQ symbol*] (TTSB)

NFLIO .... Training Department, Iron Ore Co. of Canada, Labrador City, Newfoundland [*Library symbol National Library of Canada*] (NLC)

NFLIW .... Nutrition For Life Intl. Wrrt [*NASDAQ symbol*] (TTSB)

NflkSo .... Norfolk Southern Corp. [*Associated Press*] (SAG)

NFLO .... Lourdes Public Library, Newfoundland [*Library symbol National Library of Canada*] (NLC)

NFlp .... Floral Park Public Library, Floral Park, NY [*Library symbol Library of Congress*] (LCLS)

NFLPA .... National Football League Players Association (EA)

NFLPA .... National Free Lance Photographers Association (EA)

NFlpBE .... Floral Park-Bellerose Elementary School, Floral Park, NY [*Library symbol*] [*Library of Congress*] (LCLS)

NFlpCE .... John Lewis Childs Elementary School, Floral Park, NY [*Library symbol*] [*Library of Congress*] (LCLS)

NFlpMH .... Floral Park Memeorial High School, Floral Park, NY [*Library symbol*] [*Library of Congress*] (LCLS)

NFLPN .... National Federation of Licensed Practical Nurses (EA)

NFlpSH .... Sewanhaka High School, Floral Park, NY [*Library symbol*] [*Library of Congress*] (LCLS)

NFLQI .... Nuveen Florida Quality Income Municipal Fund [*Associated Press*] (SAG)

NFLS .... La Scie Public Library, Newfoundland [*Library symbol National Library of Canada*] (NLC)

NFLS .... Nicolet Federated Library System [*Library network*]

NFLSV .... National Front for the Liberation of South Vietnam

NFLTHC ...... National Foundation for Long Term Health Care [*Defunct*] (EA)

NFLU .... Lumsden Public Library, Newfoundland [*Library symbol National Library of Canada*] (NLC)

NFM .... Conception Bay South Public Library, Manuels, Newfoundland [*Library symbol National Library of Canada*] (NLC)

NFM .... Midland Lutheran College, Fremont, NE [*OCLC symbol*] (OCLC)

NFM .... Narrowband Frequency Modulation [*Radio*]

NFM............ Neurofilament Protein, Medium Polypeptide (DMAA)
NFM............ New Frontiers of Medicine [*An association*] (EA)
NFM............ Next Full Moon [*Freemasonry*] (ROG)
NFM............ Noise Figure Meter
NFM............ Nonfat Milk (OA)
NFM............ Nonferrous Metal
NFM............ Northern Fowl Mite [*Immunology*]
NFM............ North-Finding Module (RDA)
NFMA........... Marystown Public Library, Newfoundland [*Library symbol National Library of Canada*] (NLC)
NFMA........... National Federation of Municipal Analysts (NTPA)
NFMA........... National Fireplace Makers Association [*British*] (BI)
NFMA........... National Footwear Manufacturers Association [*Later, FIA*]
NFMA........... National Forest Management Act (GFGA)
NFMA........... Needleroom Felt Manufacturers Association [*British*] (DBA)
NFMA........... Northwest Farm Managers Association (EA)
NFMA........... November, February, May, and August [*Denotes quarterly payments of interest or dividends in these months*] [*Business term*]
NFMAA......... National Federation Music Adjudicator Association (EA)
NFMC........... National Federation of Music Clubs (EA)
NFMC........... National Film Music Council [*Defunct*]
NFMD........... National Foundation for Muscular Dystrophy
NFMD........... National Foundation for the March of Dimes (NADA)
NFME........... National Fund for Medical Education (EA)
NFME........... Nordic Federation for Medical Education [*Denmark*] (EAIO)
NFMHA......... National Federation of Milk Hauler Associations (EA)
NFMHJ......... John B. Wheeler Memorial Library, Musgrave Harbour, Newfoundland [*Library symbol National Library of Canada*] (NLC)
NFMHO......... National Foundation Manufactured Home Owners (EA)
NFMLTA....... National Federation of Modern Language Teachers Associations (EA)
NFMM.......... National Fellowship of Methodist Musicians (EA)
NFMN.......... National Fallout Monitoring Network
NFMOA......... National Fish Meal and Oil Association (EA)
NFMP.......... Mount Pearl Public Library, Newfoundland [*Library symbol National Library of Canada*] (NLC)
NFMP.......... National Federation of Master Painters and Decorators of England and Wales (BI)
NFMP.......... Nonferrous Metal Powder
NFMPC........ Non-Ferrous Metals Producers Committee (EA)
NFMR.......... National Foundation for Metabolic Research [*Defunct*] (EA)
NFMR.......... Non-Linear Ferromagnetic Resonance (PDAA)
NFMR.......... Nordisk Forening for Medisinsk Radiologi [*Scandinavian Radiological Society - SRS*] (EAIO)
NFMRAD...... Null Filter Mobile RADAR (PDAA)
NFMS.......... National Federation of Music Societies [*British*]
NFMS.......... National Fetal Mortality Survey [*Department of Health and Human Services*] (GFGA)
NFMS.......... Navy Fleet Material Support (MCD)
NFMS.......... Nitrogen Flow Measuring System
NFMS.......... Noise Figure Meter System
NFMS.......... Nonfat Milk Solids (OA)
NFMSAEG.... Naval Fleet Missile System Analysis and Evaluation Group
NFMSAEGA.. Naval Fleet Missile System Analysis and Evaluation Group Annex (MCD)
NFMSO........ Navy Fleet Material Support Office (DNAB)
NFMT.......... National Federation of Meat Traders [*British*] (BI)
NFMT.......... Navy Food Management Team (DNAB)
NFMWC....... National Federation of Master Window Cleaners [*British*] (DBA)
NFMY.......... National Festival of Music for Youth (AIE)
NFN .... National Fathers' Network [*An association*] (PAZ)
NFN .... National Federation of Non-Profits (NTPA)
NFN .... Newly Founded Nest [*Ornithology*]
NFN .... No Form Necessary
NFN .... No Further Need (MUGU)
NFn .... Not for Resuscitation [*Medicine*] (WDAA)
NFN .... Nouvelle Front NAZI [*New NAZI Front*] [*French*] (PD)
NFNA .... National Flight Nurses Association (EA)
NFNA .... Nausori/International [*Fiji*] [*ICAO location identifier*] (ICLI)
NFNA .... Norris Arm Public Library, Newfoundland [*Library symbol National Library of Canada*] (NLC)
NFNB .... Bureta [*Fiji*] [*ICAO location identifier*] (ICLI)
NFND .... Deumba [*Fiji*] [*ICAO location identifier*] (ICLI)
NFND .... National Foundation for Neuromuscular Diseases [*Later, NGF*] (EA)
NFNG .... Ngau [*Fiji*] [*ICAO location identifier*] (ICLI)
NFNH .... Lauthala Islands [*Fiji*] [*ICAO location identifier*] (ICLI)
NFNID .... National Foundation for Non-Invasive Diagnostics (EA)
NFNK .... Lakemba [*Fiji*] [*ICAO location identifier*] (ICLI)
NFNL .... Lambasa [*Fiji*] [*ICAO location identifier*] (ICLI)
NFNLI .... Labrador Inuit Association, Nain, Newfoundland [*Library symbol National Library of Canada*] (NLC)
NFNLI .... Labrador Unit Association, Nain, Newfoundland [*Library symbol National Library of Canada*] (NLC)
NFNM .... Matei [*Fiji*] [*ICAO location identifier*] (ICLI)
NFNN .... Vanuabalavu [*Fiji*] [*ICAO location identifier*] (ICLI)
NFNO .... Koro [*Fiji*] [*ICAO location identifier*] (ICLI)
NFNP .... National Food and Nutrition Policy [*Australia*]
NFNP .... Norris Point Public Library, Newfoundland [*Library symbol National Library of Canada*] (NLC)
NFNR .... Rotuma [*Fiji*] [*ICAO location identifier*] (ICLI)
NFNS .... Neurofibromatosis-Noonan Syndrome [*Medicine*] (DMAA)
NFNS .... Savusavu [*Fiji*] [*ICAO location identifier*] (ICLI)
N FNSHD .... Not Finished [*Freight*]
NFNTU .... National Federation of Furniture Trade Union [*British*]
NFNU .... Bua [*Fiji*] [*ICAO location identifier*] (ICLI)

NFNU .... National Federation of Nurses' Unions [*See also FNSII*]
NFNV .... Vatukoula [*Fiji*] [*ICAO location identifier*] (ICLI)
NFNW .... Wakaya [*Fiji*] [*ICAO location identifier*] (ICLI)
NFNWF .... Navy Fleet Numerical Weather Facility [*Marine science*] (MSC)
NFO .... National Family Opinion
NFO .... National Farmers Organization (EA)
NFO .... Naval Flight Officer
NFO .... Navy Finance Office
NFO .... News from the Ukraine [*A publication*]
NFO .... Normal Fuel Oil (DNAB)
NFO .... Norvell Family Organization (EA)
NFO .... Not Fully Open (MCD)
NFOAPA...... National Federation of Old Age Pensioners' Associations [*British*] (BI)
NFO(B)........ Naval Flight Officer (Bombardier) (DNAB)
NFOBA........ National Fats and Oils Brokers Association [*Defunct*] (EA)
NFOC .... Naval Facility Operational Center (DNAB)
NFOC .... Naval Flight Officer Candidate (DNAB)
NFO(C)........ Naval Flight Officer (Controller) (DNAB)
NFOF .... Fiji [*Fiji*] [*ICAO location identifier*] (ICLI)
NFOFL .... National Federation of Officers for Life (EA)
NFOHA........ National Federation of Off-Licence Holders Associations of England and Wales (BI)
NFO(I)......... Naval Flight Officer (RADAR Intercept) (DNAB)
NFOIO .... Naval Field Operational Intelligence Office (NVT)
NFOIODET... Naval Field Operational Intelligence Office Detachment (DNAB)
NFOM .... Near Field Optical Microscopy (AAEL)
NFO(N) .... Naval Flight Officer (Navigator) (DNAB)
NFOO .... Naval Forward Observing Officer [*British military*] (DMA)
NFOP .... National Fraternal Order of Police (NTPA)
NFOP .... Old Perlican Public Library, Newfoundland [*Library symbol National Library of Canada*] (NLC)
NFoPA .... National Forest Products Association [*Washington, DC*]
NFOR .... NFO Research [*NASDAQ symbol*] (TTSB)
NFOR .... NFO Research, Inc. [*NASDAQ symbol*] (SAG)
NFO Rs....... NFO Research, Inc. [*Associated Press*] (SAG)
NFOSG .... Naval Field Operations Support Group
NFOV .... Narrow Field of View
NFP .... Marietta, GA [*Location identifier FAA*] (FAAL)
NFP .... Nandrolone Furylpropionate [*Pharmacology*]
NFP .... National Family Partnership [*An association*] (EA)
NFP .... National Federation of Parents for Drug-Free Youth (EA)
NFP .... National Federation Party [*Fiji*] [*Political party*] (PPW)
NFP .... National Fire Academy Library, Emmitsburg, MD [*OCLC symbol*] (OCLC)
NFP .... National Focal Points (DCTA)
NFP .... Nationalist Front for Progress [*Solomon Islands*] [*Political party*] (FEA)
NFP .... Natural Family Planning
NFP .... Neighborhood Facilities Program (OICC)
NFP .... Network for Fitness Professionals [*Australia*]
NFP .... Neurofilament Protein [*Neurophysiology*]
NFP .... New Federalist Party (EA)
NFP .... New Forests Project (EA)
NFP .... New Frontier Party [*Japan*] [*Political party*]
NFP .... N-Formylmethionylphenylalanine [*Biochemistry*]
NFP .... Nonflare Proton
NFP .... Norfolk Petroleum Ltd. [*Vancouver Stock Exchange symbol*]
NFP .... Normal Failure Period
NFP .... Northern Frontier Province [*Kenya*]
NFP .... Not for Profit (ADA)
NFP .... Not for Publication (ADA)
NFP .... Placentia Public Library, Newfoundland [*Library symbol National Library of Canada*] (NLC)
NFPA .... National Federation of Paralegal Associations (EA)
NFPA .... National Fire Protection Association (EA)
NFPA .... National Flaxseed Processors Association (EA)
NFPA .... National Flexible Packaging Association [*Later, FPA*] (EA)
NFPA .... National Flight Paramedics Association (EA)
NFPA .... National Fluid Power Association (EA)
NFPA .... National Food Processors Association (EA)
NFPA .... National Forest Products Association (EA)
NFPA .... National Foster Parent Association (EA)
NFPA .... Natural Family Planning Association of Connecticut (EA)
NFPA .... Pasadena Public Library, Newfoundland [*Library symbol National Library of Canada*] (NLC)
NFPB .... National Friends of Public Broadcasting
NFPC .... National Federation of Plastering Contractors [*British*] (BI)
NFPC .... National Federation of Priests' Councils (EA)
NFPC .... National Forest Planning Committee (WPI)
NFPC .... Pouch Cove Public Library, Newfoundland [*Library symbol National Library of Canada*] (NLC)
NFPCA .... National Fire Prevention and Control Administration [*Later, United States Fire Administration*] [*Department of Commerce*]
NFPDC .... National Federation of Painting and Decorating Contractors [*British*] (DBA)
NFPDHE....... National Federation of Plumbers and Domestic Heating Engineers [*British*] (BI)
NFPE........... NATO Force Planning Exercise (NATG)
NFPE........... Non-Financial Public Enterprise [*British*]
NFPEC .... Curran Memorial Library, Port Au Port East, Newfoundland [*Library symbol National Library of Canada*] (NLC)
NFPEDA....... National Farm and Power Equipment Dealers Association [*Later, NAEDA*] (EA)
NF/PFOG...... National Federation of Parents and Friends of Gays (EA)

NFPHC .... National Federation of Permanent Holiday Camps Ltd. [*British*] (BI)
NFPI .... National Frozen Pizza Institute (EA)
NFPL .... Point Leamington Public Library, Newfoundland [*Library symbol National Library of Canada*] (NLC)
NFPLA .... National Foundation for Professional Legal Assistants (EA)
NFPM .... Nuclear Flight Propulsion Module (KSC)
NFPMA .... National Feeder Pig Marketing Association (EA)
NFPMA .... National Foundation for Peroneal Muscular Atrophy (EA)
NFPMC .... National Farm Products Marketing Council [*Canada*]
NFPNS .... Natural Family Planning National Secretariat [*Australia*]
NFPO .... National Federation of Professional Organizations (EA)
NFPO .... National Federation of Property Owners [*British*] (BI)
NFPOC .... National Federation of Post Office Clerks [*Later, APWU*]
NFPOD .... National Foundation for the Prevention of Oral Disease [*Defunct*] (EA)
NFPR .... National Fund for Research into Poliomyelitis and Other Crippling Diseases [*British*] (BI)
NFPRHA ...... National Family Planning and Reproductive Health Association (EA)
NFPS .... Naval Flight Preparatory School
NFPS .... Naval Future Policy Staff [*British*]
NFPS .... Navy Field Purchase Systems (NG)
NFPS .... Nuclear Flight Propulsion System (AAG)
NFPS .... Port Saunders Public Library, Newfoundland [*Library symbol National Library of Canada*] (NLC)
NFPTC .... National Federation of Postal and Telegraph Clerks [*A union*] [*British*]
NFPW .... National Federation of Press Women (EA)
NFPW .... National Federation of Professional Workers [*British*] (DI)
NFPW .... Port Au Port West School/Public Library, Newfoundland [*Library symbol National Library of Canada*] (NLC)
NFQ .... Night Frequency (FAAC)
NFQC .... Queens College, Flushing, NY [*Library symbol Library of Congress*] (LCLS)
NFR .... National Field Research [*British*]
NFR .... National Film Board Reference Library [*UTLAS symbol*]
NFR .... Naturvetenskapliga forskingsradet [*Swedish Natural Science Research Council*]
NFR .... Near-Field Recording [*Computer science*] (PCM)
NFR .... Negative Flux Rate (IEEE)
NFR .... Nephron Filtration Rate [*Physiology*]
NFR .... Net Financing Requirement
NFR .... Net Flux Radiometer [*Instrumentation*]
NFR .... New Frontier Petroleum Corp. [*Vancouver Stock Exchange symbol*]
NFR .... No Further Requirement
NFR .... Nordisk Forening for Rehabilitering [*Nordic Association for Rehabilitation*] (EAIO)
N FR .... Northern French [*Language, etc.*] (ROG)
NFR .... Not for Resuscitation [*Hospital patient classification*]
NFR .... Nuclear Fission Reactor
NFR .... Nursing Field Representative [*Red Cross*]
NFR-90 .... NATO Frigate for the 1990s
NFRA .... National Forest Recreation Association (EA)
NFRA .... Robert's Arm Public Library, Newfoundland [*Library symbol National Library of Canada*] (BIB)
NFRAP .... No Further Response Action Planned (BCP)
NFRC .... National Federation of Roofing Contractors [*British*] (EAIO)
NFRC .... National Fenestration Rating Council (EA)
NFRC .... National Finals Rodeo Committee (EA)
NFRC .... National Forest Research Council (WPI)
NFRC .... National Forest Reservation Commission [*Terminated, 1976; functions transferred to Department of Agriculture*]
NFRCD .... National Fund for Research into Crippling Diseases [*British*] (DI)
NFred .... Darwin R. Barker Library Association, Fredonia, NY [*Library symbol Library of Congress*] (LCLS)
NFredCB ..... Chautauqua County Board of Cooperative Educational Services, Fredonia, NY [*Library symbol*] [*Library of Congress*] (LCLS)
NFredU .... State University of New York, College at Fredonia, Fredonia, NY [*Library symbol Library of Congress*] (LCLS)
NFree .... Freeport Memorial Library, Freeport, NY [*Library symbol Library of Congress*] (LCLS)
NFreeAE ..... Archer Elementary School, Freeport, NY [*Library symbol Library of Congress*] (LCLS)
NFreeAtE ..... Caroline G. Atkinson Elementary School, Freeport, NY [*Library symbol*] [*Library of Congress*] (LCLS)
NFreeBE ...... Bayview Avenue Elementary School, Freeport, NY [*Library symbol*] [*Library of Congress*] (LCLS)
NFreeCE ..... Columbus Elementary School, Freeport, NY [*Library symbol Library of Congress*] (LCLS)
NFreeDH ...... Doctors Hospital, Freeport, NY [*Library symbol Library of Congress*] (LCLS)
NFreeDJ ..... Dodd Junior High School, Freeport, NY [*Library symbol Library of Congress*] (LCLS)
NFreeEC ...... Early Childhood Center, Freeport, NY [*Library symbol*] [*Library of Congress*] (LCLS)
NFreeGE ...... Leo F. Giblyn Elementary School, Freeport, NY [*Library symbol*] [*Library of Congress*] (LCLS)
NFreeH .... Freeport Hospital, Freeport, NY [*Library symbol Library of Congress*] (LCLS)
NFreeHS ..... Freeport High School, Freeport, NY [*Library symbol Library of Congress*] (LCLS)
NFRH .... Rocky Harbour Public School, Newfoundland [*Library symbol National Library of Canada*] (NLC)
NFRM .... National Foundation for Research in Medicine (EA)
NFRMC .... National Foundation for Rural Medical Care [*Defunct*] (EA)
NFRN .... National Federation of Retail Newsagents [*British*]

NFRP .... Marie S. Penney Memorial Library, Ramea, Newfoundland [*Library symbol National Library of Canada*] (NLC)
NFRRC .... Nuclear Fuel Recovery and Receiving Center (NRCH)
NFRS .... National Fancy Rat Society [*British*] (DBA)
NFRW .... National Federation of Republican Women (EA)
NFS .... Fayetteville State University, Fayetteville, NC [*OCLC symbol*] (OCLC)
NFs .... Franklin Square Public Library, Franklin Square, NY [*Library symbol Library of Congress*] (LCLS)
NFS .... National Aeronautics and Space Administration FAR Supplement [*A publication*] (AAGC)
NFS .... National Federation of Settlements [*Later, UNCA*]
NFS .... National Fertility Study
NFS .... National Field Service Corp. [*Suffern, NY*] [*Telecommunications*] (TSSD)
NFS .... National Film Society [*Defunct*] (EA)
NFS .... National Fire Service [*British*]
NFS .... National Flying Service [*British*]
NFS .... National Food Situation [*Series*] [*A publication*]
NFS .... National Food Survey [*British*]
NFS .... National Forest Service (COE)
NFS .... National Forest System (GNE)
NFS .... National Fuchsia Society (EA)
NFS .... Naval Flying Station [*British*]
NFS .... Navy Facilities System
NFS .... Navy Field Service
NFS .... Network File System
NFS .... Neutron Flux Spectra [*Nuclear energy*]
NFS .... Nitrofuraldehyde Semicarbazone [*Germicide*]
NFS .... Nitrogen Flow System
NFS .... No Fracture Seen [*Medicine*] (DMAA)
NFS .... Noise Frequency Spectrum
NFS .... Nonfriendly Submarines (MCD)
NFS .... Nordiska Forbundet for Statskunskap [*Nordic Political Science Association - NPSA*] [*Norway*] (EAIO)
NFS .... Not for Sale
NFS .... Not on Flying Status
NFS .... Nozzle Flow Sensor (MCD)
NFS .... Nuclear Fuel Services Fuel Fabrication Plant
NFS .... Nuclear Fuel Services Plant (NRCH)
NFS .... NWFS Capital Financing Trust [*NYSE symbol*] (SAG)
NFSA .... National Federation of Sea Anglers [*British*]
NFSA .... National Fertilizer Solutions Association (EA)
NFSA .... National Field Selling Association (NTPA)
NFSA .... National Fire Sprinkler Association (EA)
NFSA .... National Food Service Association (EA)
NFSA .... National Food Standards Agreement [*Australia*]
NFSA .... Navy Field Safety Association (EA)
NFSA .... New Fuel Storage Area (NRCH)
NFSA .... News from Saudi Arabia [*A publication*] (BJA)
NFSA .... Provincial Archives of Newfoundland and Labrador, St. John's, Newfoundland [*Library symbol National Library of Canada*] (NLC)
NFSAG .... Research Station, Agriculture Canada [*Station de Recherches, Agriculture Canada*] St. John's, Newfoundland [*Library symbol National Library of Canada*] (NLC)
NFSAIC .... Charles Curtis Memorial Hospital, International Grenfell Association, St. Anthony, Newfoundland [*Library symbol National Library of Canada*] (NLC)
NFSAIS .... National Federation of Science Abstracting and Indexing Services [*Later, NFAIS*] (EA)
NFSAL .... St. Alban's Public Library, Newfoundland [*Library symbol National Library of Canada*] (NLC)
NFSAN .... St. Anthony Public Library, Newfoundland [*Library symbol National Library of Canada*] (NLC)
NFS & NC .... National Federation of Settlements and Neighborhood Centers [*Later, UNCA*] (EA)
NFSANS ...... Naskapi School/Public Library, Sops Arm, Newfoundland [*Library symbol National Library of Canada*] (NLC)
NFSB .... Spaniards Bay Public Library, Newfoundland [*Library symbol National Library of Canada*] (NLC)
NFSBC .... Boys' Club, St. John's, Newfoundland [*Library symbol National Library of Canada*] (NLC)
NFSBCS .... Cape Shore Public Library, St. Brides, Newfoundland [*Library symbol National Library of Canada*] (NLC)
NFSBS .... Bay St. George Community College, Stephenville, Newfoundland [*Library symbol National Library of Canada*] (NLC)
NFSC .... National Federation of Stamp Clubs (EA)
NFSC .... Seal Cove Public Library, Newfoundland [*Library symbol National Library of Canada*] (NLC)
NFSCA .... Children's and Adults' Library, St. John's, Newfoundland [*Library symbol National Library of Canada*] (NLC)
NFSCAEE ..... Environment Division, Newfoundland Department of Consumer Affairs and Environment, St. John's, Newfoundland [*Library symbol National Library of Canada*] (NLC)
NFSCCU .... National Federation of Savings and Cooperative Credit Unions [*British*] (DBA)
NFSCF .... Newfoundland and Labrador Institute of Fisheries and Marine Technology (Marine Institute), St. John's, New Foundland [*Library symbol National Library of Canada*] (NLC)
NFsCH .... H. Frank Carey High School, Franklin Square, NY [*Library symbol*] [*Library of Congress*] (LCLS)
NFSCJ .... Dr. Charles A. Janeway Child Health Centre, St. John's, Newfoundland [*Library symbol National Library of Canada*] (NLC)
NFSCR .... Children's Rehabilitation Centre, St. John's, Newfoundland [*Library symbol National Library of Canada*] (NLC)
NFSCSW ...... National Federation of Societies for Clinical Social Work (EA)

NFSCT .... Cabot Institute of Applied Arts and Technology, St. John's, Newfoundland [*Library symbol National Library of Canada*] (NLC)

NFSCTM ...... Topsail Campus Resource Centre, Cabot Institute of Applied Arts and Technology, St. John's, Newfoundland [*Library symbol National Library of Canada*] (NLC)

NFSD .... National Aeronautics and Space Administration FAR Supplement Directive (AAGC)

NFSD .... National Federation of Spiritual Directors (EA)

NFSD .... National Fraternal Society of the Deaf [*Mount Prospect, IL*] (EA)

NFSD .... Nonfused (MSA)

NFSE .... National Federation for the Self-Employed and Small Businesses [*British*] (DBA)

NFSE .... National Federation of Sales Executives [*Later, Sales and Marketing Executives International*]

NFSE .... National Federation of Self Employed [*British*]

NFSEC .... Newfoundland Forest Research Centre, Environment Canada [*Centre de RecherchesForestieres de Terre-Neuve, Environnement Canada*] St. John's, Newfoundland [*Library symbol National Library of Canada*] (NLC)

NFSEEP .... National Foundation for the Study of Equal Employment [*Washington, DC*] (EA)

NFSF .... National Freedom Shrine Foundation (EA)

NFSF .... NFS Financial Corp. [*NASDAQ symbol*] (NQ)

NFSF .... North-West Atlantic Fisheries Centre, Fisheries and Oceans Canada [*Centre de Pecheries de l'Atlantique du Nord-Ouest, Peches et Oceans Canada*] St. John's, Newfoundland [*Library symbol National Library of Canada*] (NLC)

NFSFJG .... St. Judes Central High School Public Library/Bay St. George South Public LibraryLibrary, St. Fintans, Newfoundland [*Library symbol National Library of Canada*] (NLC)

NFSFS .... Newfoundland Forest Service, St. John's, Newfoundland [*Library symbol National Library of Canada*] (NLC)

NFSG .... National Federation of Students of German (EA)

NFSG .... Newfoundland Public Library Services, St. John's, Newfoundland [*Library symbol National Library of Canada*] (NLC)

NFSG .... Provinical Reference and Resource Library, Newfoundland Public Library Services, St. John's, New Foundland [*Library symbol National Library of Canada*] (NLC)

NFSGE .... St. Georges Public Library, Newfoundland [*Library symbol National Library of Canada*] (NLC)

NFSGGH ...... C. A Pippy Jr. Medical Library, Grace General Hospital, St. John's, Newfoundland [*Library symbol National Library of Canada*] (NLC)

NFSGGHN .... School of Nursing, Grace General Hospital, St. John's, Newfoundland [*Library symbol National Library of Canada*] (NLC)

NFSGH .... General Hospital Corp., St. John's, Newfoundland [*Library symbol National Library of Canada*] (NLC)

NFSGHN ...... Nursing Education, General Hospital Corp., St. John's, Newfoundland [*Library symbol National Library of Canada*] (NLC)

NFSGO .... Gosling Library, St. John's, Newfoundland [*Library symbol National Library of Canada*] (NLC)

NFSH .... National Federation of Spiritual Healers (EA)

NFSH .... Southern Harbour Public Library, Newfoundland [*Library symbol National Library of Canada*] (NLC)

NFSHC .... National Federation of State Humanities Councils (EA)

NFSHE .... Health Education Division, Newfoundland Department of Health, St. John's, Newfoundland [*Library symbol National Library of Canada*] (NLC)

NFSHPH .... Public Health Nursing Division, Newfoundland Department of Health, St. John's, Newfoundland [*Library symbol National Library of Canada*] (NLC)

NFSHSA .... National Federation of State High School Associations (EA)

NFSHSAA ..... National Federation of State High School Athletic Associations [*Later, NFSHSA*] (EA)

NFSICA .... Institute of Chartered Accountants of Newfoundland, St. John's, Newfoundland [*Library symbol National Library of Canada*] (NLC)

NFsJE .... John Street Elementary School, Franklin Square, NY [*Library symbol Library of Congress*] (LCLS)

NFSJL .... Law Library, Newfoundland Department of Justice, St. John's, Newfoundland [*Library symbol National Library of Canada*] (NLC)

NFSK .... Kindale Public Library, Stephenville, Newfoundland [*Library symbol National Library of Canada*] (NLC)

NFSK .... Narrowband Frequency Shift Keying (MCD)

NFSL .... Legislative Library, St. John's, Newfoundland [*Library symbol National Library of Canada*] (NLC)

NFSL .... Newnan Savings Bank [*NASDAQ symbol*] (NQ)

NFSL .... Newnan Svgs Bank FSB [*NASDAQ symbol*] (TTSB)

NFSL .... No Fighter Suitably Located (SAA)

NFSL .... Nucleus Fleet Sealift

NFSLA .... St. Lawrence Public Library, Newfoundland [*Library symbol National Library of Canada*] (NLC)

NFSLG .... St. Lunaire-Griquet Public Library, St. Lunaire, Newfoundland [*Library symbol National Library of Canada*] (NLC)

NFSLP .... Central Records Library, Newfoundland Light and Power Co. Ltd., St. John's, Newfoundland [*Library symbol National Library of Canada*] (NLC)

NFSLS .... Law Society of Newfoundland, St. John's, Newfoundland [*Library symbol National Library of Canada*] (NLC)

NFSM .... Memorial University, St. John's, Newfoundland [*Library symbol National Library of Canada*] (NLC)

NFSM .... National Fraternity of Student Musicians (EA)

NFSM .... Queen Elizabeth II Library, Memorial University of Newfoundland, St. John's, Newfoundland [*Library symbol National Library of Canada*] (NLC)

NFSMA .... National Fruit and Syrup Manufacturers Association (EA)

NFSMA .... Provincial Planning Office, Newfoundland Department of Municipal Affairs, St. John's, Newfoundland [*Library symbol National Library of Canada*] (NLC)

NFSME .... Newfoundland Department of Mines and Energy, St. John's, Newfoundland [*Library symbol National Library of Canada*] (NLC)

NFSMEC ...... Curriculum Materials Centre, Education Library, Memorial University, St. John's,Newfoundland [*Library symbol National Library of Canada*] (NLC)

NFSMED ...... Education Library, Memorial University, St. John's, Newfoundland [*Library symbol National Library of Canada*] (NLC)

NFSMEM ...... Publications and Information Section, Mineral Development Division Library, Newfoundland Department of Mines and Energy, St. John's, Newfoundland [*Library symbol National Library of Canada*] (NLC)

NFSMG .... Department of Geography, Memorial University, St. John's, Newfoundland [*Library symbol National Library of Canada*] (NLC)

NFSMLS ...... Library Studies Program, Memorial University of Newfoundland, St. John's, Newfoundland [*Library symbol National Library of Canada*] (BIB)

NFSMM .... Health Sciences Library, Memorial University, St. John's, Newfoundland [*Library symbol National Library of Canada*] (NLC)

NFSMMH ...... Maritime History Archive, Memorial University, St. John's, Newfoundland [*Library symbol National Library of Canada*] (BIB)

NFSMO .... Ocean Engineering Centre, Memorial University, St. John's, Newfoundland [*Library symbol National Library of Canada*] (NLC)

NFSN .... NATO French-Speaking Nations

NFsNH .... North Junior-Senior High School, Franklin Square, NY [*Library symbol*] [*Library of Congress*] (LCLS)

NFSNI .... National Research Council IRAP [*Industrial Research Assistance Program*], St. John's, Newfoundland [*Library symbol National Library of Canada*] (NLC)

NFSNL .... Newfoundland and Labrador Hydro, St. John's, Newfoundland [*Library symbol National Library of Canada*] (NLC)

NFSNLD .... Newfoundland and Labrador Development Corp., St. John's, Newfoundland [*Library symbol National Library of Canada*] (NLC)

NFSNM .... Marine Dynamics Branch, Canada Institute for Scientific and Technical Information, National Research Council [*Direction de la Dynamique Marine Institut Canadien de l'Information Scientifique et Technique, Conseil National de Recherches*], St. John's, Newfoundland [*Library symbol National Library of Canada*] (NLC)

NFSNO .... National Federation for Specialty Nursing Organizations (EA)

NFSO .... Navy Fuel Supply Office

NFSP .... National Federation of Sub-Postmasters [*British*] (DBA)

NFSP .... Non-Flight Switch Panel

NFSP .... Springdale Public Library, Newfoundland [*Library symbol National Library of Canada*] (NLC)

NFsPE .... Polk Street Elementary School, Franklin Square, NY [*Library symbol*] [*Library of Congress*] (LCLS)

NFSPR .... Provincial Reference Library, St. John's, Newfoundland [*Library symbol National Library of Canada*] (NLC)

NFSPS .... National Federation of State Poetry Societies (EA)

NFSQ .... Queen's College, St. John's, Newfoundland [*Library symbol National Library of Canada*] (NLC)

NFSRA .... National Fitness Southern Recreation Association [*Australia*]

NFSRD .... Newfoundland Department of Rural Development, St. John's, Newfoundland [*Library symbol National Library of Canada*] (NLC)

NFSREX .... Canada Department of Regional Industrial Expansion [*Ministere de l'Expansion Industrielle Regionale*] St. John's, Newfoundland [*Library symbol National Library of Canada*] (NLC)

NFSS .... National Fallout Shelter Survey [*Civil Defense*]

NFSS .... National Federation of Sailing Schools [*British*]

NFSS .... National Finch and Softbill Society (EA)

NFSS .... Nucleus Fleet Scientific Support

NFSSC .... St. Clare's Mercy Hospital, St. John's, Newfoundland [*Library symbol National Library of Canada*] (NLC)

NFSSCN ...... School of Nursing, St. Clare's Mercy Hospital, St. John's, Newfoundland [*Library symbol National Library of Canada*] (NLC)

NFSSW .... Newfoundland Status of Women Council, St. John's, Newfoundland [*Library symbol National Library of Canada*] (NLC)

NFST .... Newfoundland Department of Tourism, St. John's, Newfoundland [*Library symbol National Library of Canada*] (NLC)

NFSTA .... Newfoundland Teachers' Association, St. John's, Newfoundland [*Library symbol National Library of Canada*] (NLC)

NFSTC .... Stephenville Crossing Public Library, Newfoundland [*Library symbol National Library of Canada*] (NLC)

NFSTCG ...... Canadian Coast Guard [*Garde Cotiere Canadienne*] St. John's, Newfoundland [*Library symbol Obsolete National Library of Canada*] (NLC)

NFSTPG .... National Foundation for the Study and Treatment of Pathological Gambling [*Defunct*] (EA)

NFSTR .... Medical Library, Sir Thomas Roddick Hospital, Stephenville, Newfoundland [*Library symbol National Library of Canada*] (NLC)

NFSU .... Nonflying Support Unit

NFSU .... Summerford Public Library, Newfoundland [*Library symbol National Library of Canada*] (NLC)

NFSU .... Suva/Nausori [*Fiji*] [*ICAO location identifier*] (ICLI)

NFSVP .... National Forest Service Volunteers Program (EA)

NFsWE .... Washington Street Elementary School, Franklin Square, NY [*Library symbol*] [*Library of Congress*] (LCLS)

NFSWH .... Health Services, Waterford Hospital, St. John's, Newfoundland [*Library symbol National Library of Canada*] (NLC)

NFSWMM .... National Federation of Scale and Weighing Machine Manufacturers [*British*] (DBA)

NFsWS .... Willow Road School, Franklin Square, NY [*Library symbol*] [*Library of Congress*] (LCLS)

NFT............	National Film and Television Sound Archives [*National Film Board of Canada*] [*UTLAS symbol*]
NFT.............	National Film Theatre [*British*]
NFT.............	Navigation Flight Test [*Aviation*] (DA)
NFT.............	Navy Flight Test (MCD)
NFT.............	Nefteyugansk Aviation Division [*Russian Federation*] [*ICAO designator*] (FAAC)
NFT	Networks File Transfer
NFT.............	Neurofibrillary Tangle [*Brain anatomy*]
NFT.............	Newfoundland Telephone Co. Ltd. [*Toronto Stock Exchange symbol*]
NFT.............	New Frontiers in Theology [*A publication*] (BJA)
NFT.............	N-Formimidoylthienamycin [*Biochemistry*]
NFT.............	No Filing Time [*Aviation*]
NFT.............	Non-Firing Test [*Military*]
NFT.............	Non-Functional Test (SAA)
NFT.............	Normal Fuel-Oil Tank (MSA)
NFT.............	Nutrient Film Technique
NFTA............	National Federation of Taxicab Associations [*British*] (DBA)
NFTA............	National Feminist Therapist Association (EA)
NFTA............	National Fillings Trades Association [*British*] (DBA)
NFTA............	National Freight Transportation Association [*Rocky River, OH*] (EA)
NFTA............	New Feminist Talent Associates (EA)
NFTA............	Night-Fire [*Rifle*] Training Aid [*Army*] (INF)
NFTA............	Nitrogen Fixing Tree Association [*University of Hawaii*] [*Research center*] (RCD)
NFTB............	National Federation of Temple Brotherhoods (EA)
NFTB............	Naval Fleet Training Base
NFTB............	Niagara Frontier Tariff Bureau
NFTB............	Nuclear Flight Test Base
NFTC............	National Foreign Trade Council [*New York, NY*] (EA)
NFTC............	National Furniture Traffic Conference (EA)
NFTD............	Normal, Full Term Delivery [*Obstetrics*]
NFTE............	Eua [*Tonga*] [*ICAO location identifier*] (ICLI)
NFTF............	Night Fighting Training Facility [*Army*] (PPW)
NFTF............	Tongatapu/Fua'Amotu International [*Tonga*] [*ICAO location identifier*] (ICLI)
NFTL............	Ha'Apai Lifuka [*Tonga*] [*ICAO location identifier*] (ICLI)
NFTMS.........	National Federation of Terrazzo-Mosaic Specialists [*British*] (BI)
NFTN	Nuku'Alofa [*Tonga*] [*ICAO location identifier*] (ICLI)
NFTO	Niuafo'Ou [*Tonga*] [*ICAO location identifier*] (ICLI)
NFTO	Torbay Public Library, Newfoundland [*Library symbol National Library of Canada*] (NLC)
NFTP............	Niuatoputapu [*Tonga*] [*ICAO location identifier*] (ICLI)
NFTR	Trepassey Public Library, Newfoundland [*Library symbol National Library of Canada*] (NLC)
NFTS............	National Federation of Temple Sisterhoods (EA)
NFTS............	National Film and Television School [*British*]
NFTS............	Naval Flight Training School
NFTS............	Women of Reform Judaism, the Federation of Temple Sisterhoods (EA)
NFTSA	National Film, Television, and Sound Archives [*Canada*]
NFTSD	Normal Full-Term Spontaneous Delivery [*Obstetrics*] (DAVI)
NFtT.............	Fort Ticonderoga Association Museum and Library, Fort Ticonderoga, NY [*Library symbol Library of Congress*] (LCLS)
NFtT.............	Nonorganic Failure to Thrive [*Neonatology*] [*Pediatrics*] (DAVI)
NFTV............	Vava'u [*Tonga*] [*ICAO location identifier*] (ICLI)
NFTW..........	National Federation of Telephone Workers [*Later, CWA*]
NFTW..........	National Federation of Tobacco Workers [*A union*] [*British*]
NFTW..........	Twillingate Public Library, Newfoundland [*Library symbol National Library of Canada*] (NLC)
NFTY...........	North American Federation of Temple Youth (EA)
NFTZ...........	Non Free Trade Zone (DS)
NFU	National Farmers' Union [*British*]
NFU	National Film Unit (BARN)
NFU	Niho Fukushi University [*UTLAS symbol*]
NFU	Not for Us [*Communications*]
NFUCWC......	National Foundation for Unemployment Compensation and Workers Compensation (EA)
NFUF	Codroy Valley Public Library, Upper Ferry, Newfoundland [*Library symbol National Library of Canada*] (NLC)
NFUI	Upper Island Cove Public Library, Newfoundland [*Library symbol National Library of Canada*] (NLC)
NFV.............	National Field Volunteer [*Red Cross*]
NFV.............	Naval Forces Vietnam (VNW)
NFV.............	No Further Visits [*Medicine*]
NFV.............	Nordischer Friseurverband [*Nordic Association of Hairdressers*] [*Sweden*] (EAIO)
NFV.............	Point Barrow, AK [*Location identifier FAA*] (FAAL)
NFV.............	Victoria Public Library, Newfoundland [*Library symbol National Library of Canada*] (NLC)
NFVA	Net Free Vent Area [*Roofing*]
NFVC	National Frozen Vegetable Council [*Later, FVC*] (EA)
NFVLS	National Federation of Voluntary Literacy Schemes [*British*]
NFVOA	Northern Fishing Vessel Owners Association [*Defunct*] (EA)
NFVP	National Film and Video Productions [*Australia*]
NFVT	National Federation of Vehicle Trades [*British*] (BI)
NFW............	Lakehurst, NJ [*Location identifier FAA*] (FAAL)
NFW............	Non-Fuel-Wasting (MCD)
NFW............	Nursed Fairly Well [*Medicine*] (DMAA)
NFWA	National Farm Workers of America
NFWA	National Furniture Warehousemen's Association [*Later, NMSA*] (EA)
NFWA	Neuromuscular Foundation of Western Australia
NFWA	Wabush Public Library, Newfoundland [*Library symbol National Library of Canada*] (NLC)
NFWBO.........	National Foundation for Women Business Owners
NFWC	National Fire Waste Council
NFWD	New Field Wildcat Drilling [*Petroleum technology*]
NFWE..........	Edgar L. M. Roberts Memorial Library, Woodypoint, Newfoundland [*Library symbol National Library of Canada*] (NLC)
NFWE..........	National Federation of Woman's Exchanges (EA)
NFWF	National Fish and Wildlife Foundation (EPA)
NFWG	National Federation of Wholesale Grocers and Provision Merchants [*British*] (BI)
NFWH	National Foundation for Wholistic Medicine [*Defunct*] (EA)
NFWH	Whitbourne Public Library, Newfoundland [*Library symbol National Library of Canada*] (NLC)
NFWHF	National Fresh Water Fishing Hall of Fame
NFWI	National Federation of Women's Institutes [*British*]
NFWI	Windsor Memorial Public Library, Newfoundland [*Library symbol National Library of Canada*] (NLC)
NFWIN	Winterton Public Library, Newfoundland [*Library symbol National Library of Canada*] (NLC)
NFWM	National Farm Worker Ministry (EA)
NFWPM	National Federation of Wholesalers and Poultry Merchants [*British*] (DBA)
NFWS	Navy Fighter Weapons School (DNAB)
NFWT	National Foundation of Wheelchair Tennis (EA)
NFWV	Wesleyville Public Library, Newfoundland [*Library symbol National Library of Canada*] (NLC)
NFWW	National Federation of Women Workers [*British*]
NFX.............	Newfield Exploration [*NYSE symbol*] (TTSB)
NFX.............	Newfield Exploration Co. [*NYSE symbol*] (SPSG)
NFX.............	Nuclear Factor X (DMAA)
NFXD	National Fax Directory [*A publication*]
NFXF	National Fragile X Foundation (EA)
NFY.............	Notify [*Telecommunications*] (TEL)
NFYD	Notified [*Telecommunications*] (TEL)
NFYFC	National Federation of Young Farmers' Clubs (EAIO)
NFZ.............	National Front of Zimbabwe (PPW)
NFZ.............	(Nitro)furfuralsemicarbazone [*Organic chemistry*]
NFZ.............	No Fire Zone [*Military*]
NFZ.............	Nuclear Free Zone (AFM)
NFZR	Nuclear Free Zone Registry [*Defunct*] (EA)
NG	Green Hills Aviation [*ICAO designator*] (AD)
ng	Nanogram [*One billionth of a gram*]
NG	Narrow Gage (NAKS)
NG	Narrow Gauge
NG	Nasogastric [*Medicine*]
NG	National Gallery [*London*]
NG	National Gathering [*Jordan*] [*A publication*] (BJA)
NG	National Grange (EA)
NG	National Grid [*British Ordnance Survey maps*]
NG	National Guard [*or Guardsman*]
NG	Natural Gas
NG	Natural Gas Shutoff [*NFPA pre-fire planning symbol*] (NFPA)
NG	Natural, Grazed [*Agriculture*]
NG	Naval Gunfire (SAA)
NG	Navy General [*MCD files*]
NG	NAZI Government (BJA)
NG	Negative Glow (IDOE)
NG	Neopentyl Glycol [*Organic chemistry*]
NG	Nephridial Gland
NG	New Genus
NG	New Gnostics Special Interest Group (EA)
NG	New Granada
NG	New Group
NG	New Growth [*Medicine*]
NG	New Guinea
NG	Newly Generated
ng	Niger [*MARC country of publication code Library of Congress*] (LCCP)
NG	Nigeria [*ANSI two-letter standard code*] (CNC)
NG	Nitrogen Gauge (MCD)
NG	Nitroglycerin [*Also, GTN, NTG*] [*Explosive, vasodilator*]
NG	Nitroguanidine [*Organic chemistry*]
NG	Noble Gases [*Nuclear energy*] (NRCH)
NG	Noble Grand
NG	Noble Guard [*Freemasonry*] (ROG)
NG	Nodose Ganglion [*Medicine*] (DB)
NG	No Go [*i.e., an unacceptable arrangement*]
NG	No Good [*Similar to IC - Inspected and Condemned*]
NG	No Gum [*Philately*]
NG	Non-Government (OTD)
NG	Nongraduate
NG	Normal Graduate
NG	Normotensive Group [*Cardiology*]
NG	Norwegian
NG	Norwegium [*Chemistry*] (ROG)
NG	Nose Gear [*Aviation*] (MCD)
NG	Not Given (ADA)
NG	Not Good
NG	Not Guilty
NG	Nottingham [*Postcode*] (ODBW)
NG	Nuclear Galaxy (BARN)
NG	Royal North Gloucestershire Militia [*British military*] (DMA)
NGA	National Gallery of Art [*Washington, DC*]
NGA	National Gallery of Art, Washington, DC [*OCLC symbol*] (OCLC)
NGA	National Gallery of Australia
NGA	National Gallery of Canada Library [*UTLAS symbol*]
NGA	National Gardening Association (EA)

NGA	National Glass Association (EA)
NGA	National Gliding Association [*Later, SSA*]
NGA	National Governors' Association (EA)
NGA	National Grant Agency
NGA	National Graphical Association [*British printers' union*]
NGA	National Greyhound Association (EA)
NGA	National Grocers Association (EA)
NGA	National Guardianship Association (NTPA)
NGA	NATO Guidelines Area (NATG)
NGA	Natural Gas Association (EPA)
NGA	Naval Gunfire Assistant
NGA	Needlework Guild of America [*Later, NGAI*] (EA)
NGA	Nigeria [*ANSI three-letter standard code*] (CNC)
NGA	Nutrient Gelatin Agar [*Microbiology*]
NGA	WAAC (Nigeria) Ltd. Nigeria Airways [*ICAO designator*] (FAAC)
NGA	Young [*Australia Airport symbol*] (OAG)
NGAA	National Girls Athletic Association [*Defunct*]
NGAA	Natural Gasoline Association of America [*Later, GPA*]
NGAB	Abaiang [*Kiribati*] [*ICAO location identifier*] (ICLI)
NGaC	Capuchin Theological Seminary, Garrison, NY [*Library symbol Library of Congress*] (LCLS)
NGAC	National Greenhouse Advisory Committee [*Australia*]
NGAC	National Guard Air Corps (WDAA)
NGAD	Nobody Gives a Damn
NGADA	National Graphic Arts Dealers Association (EA)
NGAI	NGA [*Needlework Guild of America*], Inc. (EA)
NGAL	Chestatee Regional Library [*Library network*]
NGAM	Noble Gas Activity Monitor (IEEE)
NG & A	National Gift and Art Association (EA)
NGAO	New Governmental Advisory Organizations [*A publication*]
NGAPI	Nuveen Georgia Premium Income Municipal Fund [*Associated Press*] (SAG)
NGARP	National Guard and Army Reserve Policy
NGAS	Naval Gunfire Air Spotting
NGAS	Needs-Based Goal Attainment Scale (EDAC)
NGATM	New Generation Air Traffic Manager (GAVI)
NGAUS	National Guard Association of the United States (EA)
NGAYA	National Gay Alliance for Young Adults (EA)
NGAZ	NATO Gazetteer (MCD)
NGB	Army National Guard Bureau (BCP)
NGB	National Garden Bureau (EA)
NGB	National Governing Body [*United States Olympic Committee*]
NGB	National Guard Base
NGB	National Guard Bureau [*Army*]
ngb	Natural Gum Blend [*Philately*]
NGB	Neues Goettinger Bibelwerk [*A publication*] (BJA)
NGBR	Beru [*Kiribati*] [*ICAO location identifier*] (ICLI)
NGBRI	Not Guilty by Reason of Insanity
NGc	Garden City Public Library, Garden City, NY [*Library symbol Library of Congress*] (LCLS)
NGC	Gloucester County College, Voorhees, NJ [*OCLC symbol*] (OCLC)
NGC	National Gallery of Canada
NGC	National Gambling Commission (NADA)
NGC	National Gasohol Commission [*Defunct*] (EA)
NGC	National General Corp. (EFIS)
NGC	National Giro Centre [*British*] (DCTA)
NGC	National Glass Clubs (EA)
NGC	National Gloster Club (EA)
NGC	National Goose Council (NTPA)
NGC	National Governors Conference [*Later, NGA*] (EA)
NGC	National Guild of Churchmen (EA)
NGC	National Guinea Club
NGC	National Gypsy Council [*British*] (DBA)
NGC	Natural Gas Clearinghouse
ngc	Natural Gum Crease [*Philately*]
NGC	Near Galactic Catalog
NGC	New General Catalogue [*Astronomy*]
NGC	Newmont Gold [*NYSE symbol*] (TTSB)
NGC	Newmont Gold Co. [*NYSE symbol*] (SPSG)
NGC	Noise Generator Card
NGC	Nordic Geodetic Commission (EA)
NGC	North Georgia College [*Dahlonaga*]
NGC	Nozzle Gap Control [*Aerospace*] (AAG)
NGC	Nucleus Reticularis Gigantocellularis [*Brain anatomy*]
NGcA	Adelphi University, Garden City, NY [*Library symbol Library of Congress*] (LCLS)
NGCAA	National Golf Clubs Advisory Association [*British*] (DBA)
Ng-CAM	Neuralglial Cell Adhesion Model [*Biochemistry*]
NGCC	National Guard Computer Center
NGCC	North German Coal Control [*Post-World War II*]
NGcCC	Nassau Community College, Garden City, NY [*Library symbol Library of Congress*] (LCLS)
NGC Cp	NGC Corp. [*Associated Press*] (SAG)
NGCDO	North German Coal Distribution Organization [*Post-World War II*]
NGcE	Endo Laboratories, Inc., Garden City, NY [*Library symbol Library of Congress*] (LCLS)
NGcG	George Mercer, Jr., School of Theology, Garden City, NY [*Library symbol Library of Congress*] (LCLS)
NGcHE	Homestead Elementary School, Garden City, NY [*Library symbol*] [*Library of Congress*] (LCLS)
NGCIC	Natural Gas Consumers Information Center (EA)
NGcJ	Garden City Junior High School, Garden City, NY [*Library symbol*] [*Library of Congress*] (LCLS)
NGcLE	Locust Elementary School, Garden City, NY [*Library symbol*] [*Library of Congress*] (LCLS)

NGCM	Navy Good Conduct Medal
NGCMA	National Golf Car Manufacturers Association (NTPA)
NGcMH	Mineola High School, Garden City Park, NY [*Library symbol Library of Congress*] (LCLS)
NGCMS	National Guild of Community Music Schools [*Later, NGCSA*] (EA)
NGcN	Nassau Academy of Medicine, Garden City, NY [*Library symbol Library of Congress*] (LCLS)
NGcNe	Newsday, Garden City, NY [*Library symbol Library of Congress*] (LCLS)
NGcNLS	Nassau Library System, Garden City, NY [*Library symbol Library of Congress*] (LCLS)
NGCOW	National Gypsum Wrrt [*NASDAQ symbol*] (TTSB)
NGCP	National Guild of Catholic Psychiatrists (EA)
NGcpMH	Mineola High School, Garden City Park, NY [*Library symbol*] [*Library of Congress*] (LCLS)
NGcR	Nassau County Research Library, Garden City, NY [*Library symbol Library of Congress*] (LCLS)
NGCR	Next Generation Computer Resources (DWSG)
NGCSA	National Guild of Community Schools of the Arts (EA)
NGcSAE	Stratford Avenue Elementary School, Garden City, NY [*Library symbol*] [*Library of Congress*] (LCLS)
NGcSE	Stewart Avenue Elementary School, Garden City, NY [*Library symbol*] [*Library of Congress*] (LCLS)
NGcSH	Garden City Senior High School, Garden City, NY [*Library symbol*] [*Library of Congress*] (LCLS)
NGcSS	Scully, Scott, Murphy, and Presser, Garden City, NY [*Library symbol Library of Congress*] (LCLS)
NGcStP	Saint Paul's School, Garden City, NY [*Library symbol*] [*Library of Congress*] (LCLS)
NGCT	Navy General Classification Test (DNAB)
NGD	National Grassland Demonstration [*British*]
NGD	National Guild of Decoupeurs (EA)
NGD	New Golden Sceptre Minerals Ltd. [*Toronto Stock Exchange symbol Vancouver Stock Exchange symbol*]
Ngd	Nitrosoguanidine [*Biochemistry*]
NGDA	National Glass Dealers Association [*Later, NGA*] (EA)
NGDB	National Geochemical Data Bank [*Natural Environment Research Council*] [*Information service or system*] (IID)
NGDBFC	Nitty Gritty Dirt Band Fan Club (EA)
NGDC	National Geophysical Data Center [*Later, NGSDC*] [*Boulder, CO*] [*National Oceanic and Atmospheric Administration*] (MCD)
NGDF	National Grave's Disease Foundation
NGDS	Naval Graduate Dental School
NGE	National Grain Exchange [*Australia*]
NGE	Navigation Guidance Equipment (MCD)
NGE	New York State E&G [*NYSE symbol*] (TTSB)
NGE	New York State Electric & Gas Corp. [*NYSE symbol*] (SPSG)
NGE	N'Gaoundere [*Cameroon*] [*Airport symbol*] (OAG)
NGEC	National Gypsy Education Council [*British*]
NGEDA	National Guard Executive Directors Association (NTPA)
n gen	New Genus [*Biology*] (BARN)
NGEN	Noise Generator (MSA)
NGeno	Wadsworth Library, Geneseo, NY [*Library symbol*] [*Library of Congress*] (LCLS)
NGenoA	Livingston County Archives, Geneseo, NY [*Library symbol Library of Congress*] (LCLS)
NGenoLS	Livingston-Steuben-Wyoming Educational Communication Center (BOCES), Geneseo, NY [*Library symbol Library of Congress*] (LCLS)
NGenoU	State University of New York, College at Geneseo, Geneseo, NY [*Library symbol Library of Congress*] (LCLS)
NGEPr	N.Y. State E&G, 3.75% Pfd [*NYSE symbol*] (TTSB)
NGEPrD	N.Y. State E&G Adj Rt B Pfd [*NYSE symbol*] (TTSB)
NGEPrE	N.Y. State E&G 7.40% Pfd [*NYSE symbol*] (TTSB)
NGEPSSC	Navy Graduate Education Program Select Study Committee [*Terminated, 1975*] (EGAO)
NGF	Kaneohe, HI [*Location identifier FAA*] (FAAL)
NGF	National Gaucher Foundation (EA)
NGF	National Genetics Foundation [*Defunct*] (EA)
NGF	National Golf Foundation (EA)
NGF	Nations Government Income Term Trust 2004 [*NYSE symbol*] (SAG)
NGF	Nations Gvt Inc. Term Tr 2004 [*NYSE symbol*] (TTSB)
NGF	Natural Guard Fund [*Defunct*] (EA)
NGF	Naval Gun Factory [*Later, NWF*]
NGF	Naval Gunfire
NGF	Nerve Growth Factor [*A protein*] [*Biochemistry*]
NGF	Nevada Goldfields Corp. [*Toronto Stock Exchange symbol*]
NGF	New Games Foundation [*Defunct*] (EA)
NGF	New Guinea Force [*Army World War II*]
NGF	Northern Group of Forces [*Commonwealth of Independent States*] (NATG)
NGFA	National Grain and Feed Association (EA)
NGFCF	Nevada Goldfields Corp. (MHDW)
NGFEX	Naval Gunfire Exercise (NVT)
NGFF	Funafuti [*Tuvalu*] [*ICAO location identifier*] (ICLI)
NGFLO	Naval Gunfire Liaison Officer
NGFLT	Naval Gunfire Liaison Team
NGFO	Nanumea [*Tuvalu*] [*ICAO location identifier*] (ICLI)
NGFO	Naval Gunfire Officer
NGFP	National Graduate Fellowship Program [*Department of Education*] (GFGA)
NGFR	Nerve Growth Factor Receptor [*Neurobiology*]
NGFS	National Grigsby Family Society (EA)
NGFS	Naval Gunfire Support (NVT)
NGFT	National Guard on Field Training Exercises

NGFT .... Naval Gunfire Liaison Team (MUGU)
NGFU .... Funafuti/International [*Tuvalu*] [*ICAO location identifier*] (ICLI)
NGG .... Air Trans NG Group Moldova [*FAA designator*] (FAAC)
NGG .... Negative Grid Generator
NGGA .... National Greentown Glass Association (EA)
NGGC .... National Grape Growers Cooperative (NTPA)
NGGR .... Nonglucogenic/Glucogenic Ratio (DB)
NGH .... Hobart and William Smith Colleges, Geneva, NY [*Library symbol Library of Congress*] (LCLS)
NGH .... NASA Grant Handbook
NGH .... National Guard [*Hawaii*] [*Seismograph station code, US Geological Survey*] (SEIS)
NGH .... National Guild of Hypnotists (EA)
NGHA .... 91st General Hospital Association (EA)
NGHBRHD.... Neighborhood
NGHEF .... National Gay Health Education Foundation (EA)
NGI .... National Garden Institute
NGI .... Nations Government Income Term Trust [*NYSE symbol*] (SPSG)
NGI .... Nations Gvt Inc. Term Tr 2003 [*NYSE symbol*] (TTSB)
NGI .... Natural Gas Industry [*Australia*]
NGI .... Next Generation Internet [*Computer science*]
NGI .... Ngau [*Fiji*] [*Airport symbol*] (OAG)
NGI .... Not Guilty by Reason of Insanity
NGI .... Nuclear Globulin Inclusions (DMAA)
NGI .... Nurses' Global Impressions (DB)
NGI .... N-W Group, Inc. [*Toronto Stock Exchange symbol*]
NGIB .... National Geodetic Information Branch [*National Oceanic and Atmospheric Administration*]
NGIC .... National Geodetic Information Center [*National Oceanic and Atmospheric Administration*] (IID)
NGIC .... National Guard Intelligence Center [*USA*]
NGiG .... Gibco/Invenex, Grand Island, NY [*Library symbol Library of Congress*] (LCLS)
NGiHC .... Hooker Chemicals & Plastics Corp., Corporate Technical and Services Center Research Library, Grand Island, NY [*Library symbol Library of Congress*] (LCLS)
NGIPSCA...... National GI Pipe Smokers Club of America (EA)
NGISC .... National Gambling Impact Study Commission
NgIU .... University of Ibadan, Ibadan, Nigeria [*Library symbol Library of Congress*] (LCLS)
n giv .... Not Given (DAVI)
NGJ .... Beaufort, SC [*Location identifier FAA*] (FAAL)
NGJ .... Nigerian Geographical Journal [*A publication*]
NGJA .... National Gymnastics Judges Association (EA)
NGJC .... North Greenville Junior College [*South Carolina*]
NGK .... New Greek [*Language, etc.*]
NGK .... Niemegk [*German Democratic Republic*] [*Geomagnetic observatory code*]
n-gl-- .... Greenland [*MARC geographic area code Library of Congress*] (LCCP)
NGl .... Harborfields Public Library, Greenlawn, NY [*Library symbol*] [*Library of Congress*] (LCLS)
NGL .... Natural Gas Liquids
NGL .... Natural Ground Level
NGL .... Neodymium Glass LASER
NGL .... Neon Glow Lamp
NGL .... NGC Corp. [*NYSE symbol*] (TTSB)
NGL .... No Gimbal Lock
NGL .... No Greater Love (EA)
NGL .... Normalair-Garrett Ltd. [*British*] (IRUK)
NGL .... North Gasline [*Alaska*] [*Seismograph station code, US Geological Survey*] (SEIS)
NGL .... Nose Gear Launch (MCD)
NGL .... Trident NGL Holdings, Inc. [*NYSE symbol*] (SPSG)
NGlc .... Glen Cove Public Library, Glen Cove, NY [*Library symbol Library of Congress*] (LCLS)
NGlcC .... Community Hospital at Glen Cove, Glen Cove, NY [*Library symbol Library of Congress*] (LCLS)
NGlcCE .... Coles Elementary School, Glen Cove, NY [*Library symbol*] [*Library of Congress*] (LCLS)
NGlcCoE ...... Connolly Elementary School, Glen Cove, NY [*Library symbol*] [*Library of Congress*] (LCLS)
NGlcDE .... Deasy Elementary School, Glen Cove, NY [*Library symbol*] [*Library of Congress*] (LCLS)
NGlcF-L .... Friends Academy, Lower School, Glen Cove, NY [*Library symbol*] [*Library of Congress*] (LCLS)
NGlcF-U ...... Friends Academy, Upper School, Glen Cove, NY [*Library symbol*] [*Library of Congress*] (LCLS)
NGlcGE .... Gribbin Elementary School, Glen Cove, NY [*Library symbol*] [*Library of Congress*] (LCLS)
NGlcHS........ Glen Cove High School, Glen Cove, NY [*Library symbol*] [*Library of Congress*] (LCLS)
NGlcLE .... Landing Elementary School, Glen Cove, NY [*Library symbol*] [*Library of Congress*] (LCLS)
NGlcM .... Garvie's Point Museum, Glen Cove, NY [*Library symbol Library of Congress*] (LCLS)
NGlcMS .... Glen Cove Middle School, Glen Cove, NY [*Library symbol Library of Congress*] (LCLS)
NGlcP .... Pall Corp., Glen Cove, NY [*Library symbol Library of Congress*] (LCLS)
NGlcW .... Webb Institute of Naval Architecture, Glen Cove, NY [*Library symbol Library of Congress*] (LCLS)
NGlf .... Crandall Library, Glens Falls, NY [*Library symbol Library of Congress*] (LCLS)

NGlfAC......... Adirondack Community College, Glens Falls, NY [*Library symbol Library of Congress*] (LCLS)
NGlH .... Hazeltine Corp., Greenlawn, NY [*Library symbol*] [*Library of Congress*] (LCLS)
NGlhC .... New York Chiropractic College, Glen Head, NY [*Library symbol Library of Congress*] (LCLS)
NGlhES .... Glen Head Elementary School, Glen Head, NY [*Library symbol Library of Congress*] (LCLS)
NGlhGE .... Glenwood Landing Elementary School, Glen Head, NY [*Library symbol*] [*Library of Congress*] (LCLS)
NGlhNH....... North Shore High School, Glen Head, NY [*Library symbol*] [*Library of Congress*] (LCLS)
NGlhNJ .... North Shore Junior High School, Glen Head, NY [*Library symbol Library of Congress*] (LCLS)
NGlHS .... Harborfields High School, Greenlawn, NY [*Library symbol*] [*Library of Congress*] (LCLS)
NGLIOGT..... National Grand Lodge, International Order of Good Templars [*Later, NCUSIOGT*] (EA)
NGlo .... Gloversville Free Library, Gloversville, NY [*Library symbol*] [*Library of Congress*] (LCLS)
NGLO .... Naval Gunfire Liaison Officer
NGLR .... Neodymium Glass LASER Rod
NGLS .... Non-Governmental Liaison Service [*World Resources Institute*]
NGLTF .... National Gay and Lesbian Task Force (EA)
NGlwES .... Glenwood Landing Elementary School, Glenwood Landing, NY [*Library symbol Library of Congress*] (LCLS)
N GLZD ...... Not Glazed [*Freight*]
NGM .... Agana Naval Air Station [*FAA*] (TAG)
ngm .... Nanogram [*Measurement*] (DAVI)
NGM .... Nested Grid Model [*Marine science*] (OSRA)
NGM .... NetWare Global Messaging [*Computer science*] (CDE)
NGM .... Neutron-Gamma Monte Carlo [*Computer science*]
NGM .... New Ridge Resources [*Vancouver Stock Exchange symbol*]
NGM .... Nitrogen Generation Module [*NASA*]
NGM .... Noise Generation Mechanism
NGMA .... Maiana [*Kiribati*] [*ICAO location identifier*] (ICLI)
NGMA .... National Gadget Manufacturers Association
NGMA .... National Gas Measurement Association (EA)
NGMA .... National Geoscience Mapping Accord [*Australia*]
NGMA .... National Gospel Music Association (EA)
NGMA .... National Grants Management Association (AAGC)
NGMA .... National Greenhouse Manufacturers Association (EA)
NGMK .... Marakei [*Kiribati*] [*ICAO location identifier*] (ICLI)
ng/ml .... Nanograms [*One billionth of a gram*] per Milliliter
NGMN .... Makin [*Kiribati*] [*ICAO location identifier*] (ICLI)
NGN .... Nagano [*Japan*] [*Seismograph station code, US Geological Survey*] (SEIS)
NGN .... Nargana [*Panama*] [*Airport symbol*] (OAG)
NGN .... National Geographic Names Data Base [*Geological Survey*] [*Database*]
NGN .... News Group Newspapers [*British*]
NGN .... NRG Resources Ltd. [*Vancouver Stock Exchange symbol*]
NGNA .... National Gerontological Nursing Association (NTPA)
NGNC .... Non-Government Non-Catholic [*School*]
NGNF .... National Guard Not in Federal Service
NG/NS .... Next Generation/Notional System [*Army*]
NGNU .... Nikunau [*Kiribati*] [*ICAO location identifier*] (ICLI)
NGO .... Nago [*Ryukyu Islands*] [*Seismograph station code, US Geological Survey*] (SEIS)
NGO .... Nagoya [*Japan*] [*Airport symbol*] (OAG)
NGO .... National Gas Outlet [*Thread*]
NGO .... Naval Gunfire Officer
NGO .... Navy Guidance Official [*British*]
NGO .... Neuro-Genetic Optimizer (PCM)
NGO .... Nitroglycerin Ointment [*Pharmacy*] (CPH)
NGO .... Non-Gazetted Officer [*India*] (WDAA)
NGO .... Nongovernmental Observer
NGO .... Nongovernmental Organization [*Generic term*]
NGOC .... Naval Gunfire Operations Center
NGOC .... North German Oil Control [*Post-World War II*]
NGOCD .... Non-Governmental Organization Committee on Disarmament (EA)
NGO Committee... Non-Governmental Organizations Committee on UNICEF (EA)
NGOCS........ National Guard Officer Candidate School
NGoH .... Hillside Hospital, Glen Oaks, NY [*Library symbol Library of Congress*] (LCLS)
NGON.......... Onotoa [*Kiribati*] [*ICAO location identifier*] (ICLI)
NGos........... Goshen Library and Historical Society, Goshen, NY [*Library symbol Library of Congress*] (LCLS)
NGosA .... Arden Hill Hospital Medical Library, Goshen, NY [*Library symbol Library of Congress*] (LCLS)
NGou .... Reading Room Association Library, Gouveneur, NY [*Library symbol Library of Congress*] (LCLS)
NGowH .... Tri-County Memorial Hospital, Gowanda, NY [*Library symbol Library of Congress*] (LCLS)
NGP .... Corpus Christi, TX [*Location identifier FAA*] (FAAL)
NGP .... Greensboro Public Library, Greensboro, NC [*OCLC symbol*] (OCLC)
NGP .... Nano Glass Pellet
NGP .... Natural Gas Pressure
NGP .... Nearest Grid Point (PDAA)
NGP .... Network Graphics Protocol
NGP .... Neue Grosse Partei [*New Great Party*] [*Germany Political party*] (PPW)
NGP .... New Gatineau Pulp [*Pulp and paper technology*]
NGP .... N-Glycidylpyrrolidone [*Organic chemistry*]
Ngp............. Nominal Group [*Linguistics*]

NGP	Northern Galactic Pole
NGP	North Galactic Pole
NGPA	National Gas Policy Act (GFGA)
NGPA	National Guard Personnel, Army
NGPA	Natural Gas Policy Act [1978]
NGPA	Natural Gas Processors Association [Later, GPA] (EA)
NGPEC	National Guard Professional Education Center [North Little Rock, AR]
NGPL	Natural Gas Plant Liquids [DOE] (TAG)
NGPP	National Guild of Professional Paperhangers (EA)
NGPRP	Northern Great Plains Resource Program [Dept. of the Interior, Dept. of Agriculture and Environmental Protection Agency] (PDAA)
NGPRS	Northern Great Plains Research Center [Department of Agriculture] [Research center] (RCD)
NGPSA	Natural Gas Pipeline Safety Act [1968]
NGPSA	Natural Gas Processors Suppliers Association [Later, GPSA] (EA)
NGPT	National Guild of Piano Teachers (EA)
NGQ	Nongovernment Quarters (AFM)
NGR	Narrow Gauge Railways Ltd. [Wales]
NGR	Narrow Gauze Roll [Medicine]
NGR	Nasogastric Replacement [Medicine] (DMAA)
NGR	National Guard Register
NGR	National Guard Regulations
N GR	New Greek [Language, etc.] (ROG)
N-GR	New York State Library, General Reference Library, Albany, NY [Library symbol Library of Congress] (LCLS)
NGR	Nigerum [Papua New Guinea] [Airport symbol] (OAG)
NGR	Non-Grain-Raising [Coating technology]
NGR	Norgold Resources [Vancouver Stock Exchange symbol]
NGR	Nuclear Gamma Ray Spectroscopy (EDCT)
NGRA	National Gay Rights Advocates [Defunct] (EA)
NGRC	National Government of the Republic of China
NGRC	National Greyhound Racing Club [British] (DI)
NGRE	Negative Glucocorticoid Response Element [Biochemistry]
NGRF	National Ghost Ranch Foundation (EA)
NGRI	Not Guilty by Reason of Insanity
NGrl	Greenwood Lake Public Library, Greenwood, NY [Library symbol Library of Congress] (LCLS)
NGrlHS	Harborfields High School, Greenlawn, NY [Library symbol Library of Congress] (LCLS)
NGrn	Great Neck Library, Great Neck, NY [Library symbol Library of Congress] (LCLS)
NGrnBE	Baker Elementary School, Great Neck, NY [Library symbol Library of Congress] (LCLS)
NGrnKE	Kennedy Elementary School, Great Neck, NY [Library symbol Library of Congress] (LCLS)
NGrnKJE	Kensington-Johnson Elementary School, Great Neck, NY [Library symbol Library of Congress] (LCLS)
NGrnLE	Lakeville Elementary School, Great Neck, NY [Library symbol Library of Congress] (LCLS)
NGrnMiS	John L. Miller-Great Neck North High School, Great Neck, NY [Library symbol] [Library of Congress] (LCLS)
NGrnMS	Great Neck South Middle School, Great Neck, NY [Library symbol Library of Congress] (LCLS)
NGrnNA	Network Analysis Corp., Great Neck, NY [Library symbol Library of Congress] (LCLS)
NGrnNM	Great Neck North Middle School, Great Neck, NY [Library symbol] [Library of Congress] (LCLS)
NGrnPE	Parkville Elementary School, Great Neck, NY [Library symbol Library of Congress] (LCLS)
NGrnS	Sperry Rand Corp., Sperry Gyroscope Division, Great Neck, NY [Library symbol Library of Congress] (LCLS)
NGrnSH	Great Neck South Senior High School, Great Neck, NY [Library symbol Library of Congress] (LCLS)
NGrnSRE	Saddle Rock Elementary School, Great Neck, NY [Library symbol Library of Congress] (LCLS)
NGroT	Tompkins-Cortland Community College, Groton, NY [Library symbol Library of Congress Obsolete] (LCLS)
NGrpAg	United States Department of Agriculture, Plum Island Animal Disease Laboratory Library, Greenport, NY [Library symbol·Library of Congress] (LCLS)
NGrpEH	Eastern Long Island Hospital, Greenport, NY [Library symbol Library of Congress] (LCLS)
NGRS	Narrow Gauge Railway Society [British]
NGRS	National Geodetic Reference System [National Oceanic and Atmospheric Administration]
NGRS	National Goals Research Staff
NGS	General Air Services Ltd. [Nigeria] [ICAO designator] (FAAC)
NGS	Nagasaki [Japan] [Airport symbol] (OAG)
NGS	National Gardens Scheme Charitable Trust (EAIO)
NGS	National Gas Straight [Thread]
NGS	National Genealogical Society (EA)
NGS	National Geodetic Survey [National Oceanic and Atmospheric Administration]
NGS	National Geodetic System (OTD)
NGS	National Geographic Service
NGS	National Geographic Society (EA)
NGS	National Geriatrics Society (EA)
NGS	National Gladiolus Society (EA)
NGS	National Goldfish Society
NGS	National Graniteware Society (EA)
NGS	Natural Ground Surface
NGS	Naval Gunfire Support
NGS	Neutral Gear Switch [Automotive engineering]
NGS	Neutral Grain Spirits
NGS	No Gallstones [Medicine]
NGS	Nominal Guidance Scheme (OA)
NGS	Non-Immune [or Normal] Goat Serum
NGS	Normal Goat Serum (DMAA)
NGS	Nuclear Generating Station (BARN)
NGS	Nucleonic Gauging System
NGSA	National Golf Salesmen Association [Defunct] (EA)
NGSA	Natural Gas Supply Association (EA)
NGSA	Nerve Growth Stimulating Activity [Biochemistry]
NGSC	National Gay Student Center [Defunct] (EA)
NGSC	National Gender Selection Center (EA)
NGSCO	National Geodetic Survey Operations Center [National Oceanic and Atmospheric Administration]
NGSDC	National Geophysical and Solar-Terrestrial Data Center [National Oceanic and Atmospheric Administration] (IID)
NGSEF	National Geographic Society Education Foundation (EA)
NGSF	Noble Gas Storage Facility (NRCH)
NGSFO	Naval Gunfire Support Forward Observer [British]
NGSIC	National Geodetic Survey Information Center [National Oceanic and Atmospheric Administration] (IID)
NGSLO	Naval Gunfire Support Liaison Officer
NGSM	National Gold Star Mothers [Defunct] (EA)
NGSMA	Natural Gasoline Supply Men's Association [Later, GPSA]
NGSNY	National Guard State of New York (HGAA)
NGSP	National Geodetic Satellite Program [NASA]
NGSP	National Grain Sorghum Producers (NTPA)
NGSP	National Guilds of St. Paul (EA)
NGSP	Nonglycosylated Serum Protein
NGSQ	National Genealogical Society Quarterly [A publication] (BRI)
NGSS	Non-Government Schools' Secretariat [South Australia]
NGSSO	Naval Gunfire Support Staff Officer
NGST	Next Generation Space Telescope [NASA]
NGSTDC	National Geophysical and Solar-Terrestrial Data Center [National Oceanic and Atmospheric Administration]
NGT	Berclair, TX [Location identifier FAA] (FAAL)
NGT	Eastern American Natural Gas Trust [NYSE symbol] (SAG)
NGT	Eastern AmerNatlGasTr`SPERs' [NYSE symbol] (TTSB)
NGT	Nagatsuro [Irozaki] [Japan] [Seismograph station code, US Geological Survey] (SEIS)
NGT	NASA Ground Terminal (MCD)
NGT	Nasogastric Tube [Medicine] (CPH)
NGT	National Gas Taper [Thread]
NGT	National Guard Technician (MCD)
NGT	National Guild of Telephonists [British] (BI)
NGT	Natural Gas Temperature
NGT	Neon Globe Tube
NGT	New Generation Truck [Concept vehicle]
NGT	Next Generation Trainer [Air Force]
NGT	Night
NGT	Noise Generator Tube
NGT	Nominal Grouping Technique
NGT	Nonsymmetric Gravitational Theory
NGT	Northern General Transport Co. [British] (DCTA)
NGT	Not Greater Than
NGTA	National Gas Transportation Association (NTPA)
NGTA	Next Generation Trainer Aircraft (MCD)
NGTA	Nonguaranteed Trade Arrears (IMH)
NGTA	Tarawa/Bonriki International [Kiribati] [ICAO location identifier] (ICLI)
NGTB	Abemama [Kiribati] [ICAO location identifier] (ICLI)
NGTC	National Grain Trade Council (EA)
NGTE	National Gas Turbine Establishment [British]
NGTE	Tabiteuea (North) [Kiribati] [ICAO location identifier] (ICLI)
NGTF	National Gay Task Force [Later, NGLTF] (EA)
NGTG	NCAR [National Center for Atmospheric Research] GARP Task Group [Global Atmospheric Research Program]
NGTM	Tamana [Kiribati] [ICAO location identifier] (ICLI)
NGTO	Nonouti [Kiribati] [ICAO location identifier] (ICLI)
NGTP	Natural Gas Tank Pressure
NGTR	Arorae [Kiribati] [ICAO location identifier] (ICLI)
NGTS	Tabiteuea (South) [Kiribati] [ICAO location identifier] (ICLI)
NGTT	Natural Gas Tank Temperature
NGTT	Tarawa/Betio [Kiribati] [ICAO location identifier] (ICLI)
NGTU	Butaritari [Kiribati] [ICAO location identifier] (ICLI)
NGU	Nachalnik Glavnoyo Upravlenia [Chief of Main Directorate] [Soviet military rank]
nGU	Nano-Goldblatt Units [Clinical chemistry]
NGU	Nongonococcal Urethritis [Medicine]
NGU	Norfolk, VA [Location identifier FAA] (FAAL)
NGU	University of North Carolina, Greensboro, Greensboro, NC [OCLC symbol] (OCLC)
NGUAX	Neub. & Berman Guardian Fund [Mutual fund ticker symbol] (SG)
N GUI	New Guinea Territory (WDAA)
N Guin	New Guinea
NGUK	Aranuka [Kiribati] [ICAO location identifier] (ICLI)
NGuNA	New York State Nurses Association, Guilderland, NY [Library symbol Library of Congress] (LCLS)
NGUS	National Guard of the United States
NGUT	National Group of Unit Trusts [British] (DI)
NGV	Angoavia Angola [FAA designator] (FAAC)
NGV	Natural Gas for Vehicles
NGV	Natural Gas Vehicle
NGV	New Goldcore Ventures [Vancouver Stock Exchange symbol]
NGV	Nozzle Guide Vanes [Aviation] (AIA)
NGVC	National Guard Volunteer Corps [British military] (DMA)
NGVC	Natural Gas Vehicle Coalition (NTPA)

NGVD.......... National Geodetic Vertical Datum [*National Oceanic and Atmospheric Administration*]
NGvHI......... Harbor Hill Intermediate School, Greenvale, NY [*Library symbol*] [*Library of Congress*] (LCLS)
NGvP.......... Long Island University, C. W. Post Center, Greenvale, NY [*Library symbol Library of Congress*] (LCLS)
NGVP.......... Natural Gas Vehicle Partnership
NGVR.......... New Guinea Volunteer Reserve
NGW.......... Corpus Christi, TX [*Location identifier FAA*] (FAAL)
NGW.......... Gardner-Webb College, Boiling Springs, NC [*OCLC symbol*] (OCLC)
NGW.......... National Gallery of Art, Washington, DC
NGW.......... No Gift Wrap [*Mail-order catalogs*]
NGWA.......... National Ground Water Association (NTPA)
NGWIC......... National Ground Water Information Center [*National Water Well Association*] [*Information service or system*] (IID)
NGX.......... Northgate Explor [*NYSE symbol*] (TTSB)
NGX.......... Northgate Exploration Ltd. [*NYSE symbol Toronto Stock Exchange symbol*] (SPSG)
NGYN.......... National Gay Youth Network (EA)
NGZ.......... Alameda, CA [*Location identifier FAA*] (FAAL)
NH .... All Nippon [*ICAO designator*] (AD)
NH .... Editions Nouveaux Horizons [*US government imprint*]
NH .... Hamilton Public Library, Hamilton, NY [*Library symbol Library of Congress*] (LCLS)
NH .... Nahum [*Bible*]
nH .... Nanohenry [*One billionth of a henry*] (IEEE)
NH .... Nash-Healey [*Model of automobile, now out of production*]
NH .... National Heritage [*British*] [*An association*] (DBA)
NH .... National Highway
NH .... National Hunt [*British*]
NH .... NATO Helicopter [*NH-90*] (DOMA)
NH .... Natriuretic Hormone (DB)
NH .... Natural History [*A publication*] (BRI)
NH .... Naval Home [*Philadelphia, PA*]
NH .... Naval Hospital
NH .... Neo-Hebrew (BJA)
NH .... Neonatal Hepatitis [*Medicine*] (DB)
NH .... Neonatal Hypothyroidism [*Cretinism*] [*Medicine*]
NH .... Never Hinged [*Philately*]
NH .... New Hampshire [*Postal code*]
Nh .... New Hampshire State Library, Concord, NH [*Library symbol Library of Congress*] (LCLS)
NH .... New Hampshire Supreme Court Reports [*A publication*] (DLA)
NH .... New Haven [*Connecticut*]
NH .... New Head [*Also, NL*] [*News stories*] (NTCM)
NH .... New High [*Investment term*]
NH .... New York, New Haven & Hartford R. R. [*AAR code*]
N/H .... Next Higher Assembly [*Engineering*]
NH .... Nike Hercules [*Surface-to-air missile system*] (MCD)
NH .... Nodal-His [*Medicine*] (MEDA)
NH .... Nodular Histiocytic [*Lymphoma*] [*Oncology*] (DAVI)
NH .... Nominal Height (MCD)
NH .... Nonhandicapped
NH .... Nonhuman (MAE)
NH .... Nonhygroscopic
NH .... Norfolk Howard [*Refers to a bed-bug*] [*Slang*] (DSUE)
NH .... Northern Canada Mines Ltd. [*Toronto Stock Exchange symbol*]
NH .... Northern Hemisphere
Nh .... Northern Hogsucker [*Ichthyology*]
NH .... Northumberland Hussars [*British military*] (DMA)
NH .... Not Held
NH .... Novikoff Hepatoma [*Medicine*] (DB)
NH .... Nursing Home
NH₃ .... Ammonia (GNE)
NHA .... American Foundation for Management Research, Hamilton, NY [*Library symbol Library of Congress*] (LCLS)
NHA .... Nahanni Mines Ltd. [*Toronto Stock Exchange symbol*]
NHA .... National Fashion Accessories Association (EA)
NHA .... National Hairdressers' Association [*British*] (BI)
NHA .... National Handbag Association (EA)
NHA .... National Hay Association (EA)
NHA .... National Health Agencies (EA)
NHA .... National Health Association
NHA .... National Hearing Association (EA)
NHA .... National Hemophilia Association (DAVI)
NHA .... National Heritage Act [*Protects national treasures from sale out of the country*] [*British*]
NHA .... National Hide Association [*Later, USHSLA*] (EA)
NHA .... National Hobo Association (EA)
NHA .... National Hockey Association [*to 1917*]
NHA .... National Holiness Association [*Later, CHA*] (EA)
NHA .... National Homeowners Association (EA)
NHA .... National Homeschool Association (EA)
NHA .... National Housewives Association [*British*] (DBA)
NHA .... National Housing Act [*1934, 1954*]
NHA .... National Housing Administration
NHA .... National Housing Agency [*Superseded by HHFA, 1947; then by HUD, 1965*]
NHA .... National Humanities Alliance (EA)
NHA .... National Hunters Association (EA)
NHA .... National Hydrogen Association (NTPA)
NHA .... National Hydropower Association (EA)
NHA .... National Hypertension Association (EA)
NHA .... National Hypoglycemia Association (EA)
NHA .... Nationwide Hotel Association

NHA .... New Homemakers of America [*Later, FHA*] (EA)
NHA .... New Humanity Alliance (EA)
NHA .... Next Higher Assembly [*Engineering*]
NHA .... Next Higher Authority (MUGU)
NHA .... Nhatrang [*Vietnam*] [*Seismograph station code, US Geological Survey Closed*] (SEIS)
NHA .... Nitrohippuric Acid [*Organic chemistry*]
NHA .... Nonhydrogen Atom [*Chemistry*]
NHA .... Nonspecific Hepatocellular Abnormality [*Medicine*] (MAE)
NHA .... Northwest Hardwood Association [*Later, WHA*] (EA)
NHA .... Nutritional Health Alliance
NHAAP.......... National Heart Attack Alert Program
NHAC .... National Health Awareness Center [*Later, NHSAC*] (EA)
NHACE .... National Hispanic Association of Construction Enterprises (EA)
NHACES .... New Hampshire Association for Computer Education Statewide (EDAC)
NHACFC.......... National Health Agencies for the Combined Federal Campaign [*Formerly, FSCNHA*] [*Later, NVHA*] (EA)
NH Act.......... National Housing Act [*1934, 1954*] (DLA)
NH Admin Code... New Hampshire Code of Administrative Rules [*A publication*] (DLA)
NH Admin Rules Ann... New Hampshire Code of Administrative Rules Annotated [*A publication*] (AAGC)
NHAES .... New Hampshire Agricultural Experiment Station [*University of New Hampshire*] [*Research center*] (RCD)
NHaHS .... Harborfields High School, Harborfields, NY [*Library symbol*] [*Library of Congress*] (LCLS)
NHAIAC.......... National Highway Accident and Injury Analysis Center
NHAM .... National Hose Assemblies Manufacturers Association [*Defunct*]
NHamB .... Hampton Bays Public Library, Hampton Bays, NY [*Library symbol Library of Congress Obsolete*] (LCLS)
NHamH.......... Hilbert College, Hamburg, NY [*Library symbol Library of Congress*] (LCLS)
N Hamp .... New Hampshire Reports [*A publication*] (DLA)
NHampB .... Hampton Bays Public Library, Hampton Bays, NY [*Library symbol Library of Congress*] (LCLS)
N Hamp Rep... New Hampshire Reports [*A publication*] (DLA)
N Hampshire Rep... New Hampshire Reports [*A publication*] (DLA)
NH & C .... Railway and Canal Cases [*1835-55*] [*England*] [*A publication*] (DLA)
NH&RA .... National Housing & Rehabilitation Association (NTPA)
NH & S.......... Needham, Harper & Steers [*Advertising agency*]
NH & S .... Nuclear Hardening and Survivability
NHANES.......... National Health and Nutritional Examination Survey
NHANG .... New Hampshire Air National Guard (MUSM)
NHaOM.......... Oldfield Middle School, Harborfield, NY [*Library symbol*] [*Library of Congress*] (LCLS)
NHapS .... Suffolk County Department of Health Service, Hauppauge, NY [*Library symbol*] [*Library of Congress*] (LCLS)
NHapSA .... Suffolk Academy of Medicine, Hauppauge, NY [*Library symbol Library of Congress*] (LCLS)
Nh-Ar .... New Hampshire Department of Administration and Control, Division of Archives and Records Management, Concord, NH [*Library symbol Library of Congress*] (LCLS)
NHAR.......... Next Higher Assembly Removal Frequency [*Engineering*] (MCD)
NHarC .... Harriman College, Harriman, NY [*Library symbol Library of Congress*] (LCLS)
NHARC.......... Nursing Home Advisory and Research Council (EA)
NHarn .... Harrison Public Library, Harrison, NY [*Library symbol Library of Congress*] (LCLS)
NHarnC .... Westchester County Courthouse, Harrison, NY [*Library symbol*] [*Library of Congress*] (LCLS)
NHas.......... Hastings-On-Hudson Public Library, Hastings-On-Hudson, NY [*Library symbol Library of Congress*] (LCLS)
NHAS .... National Healthcare Antifraud Association [*Address unknown*] (EA)
NHAS .... National Hearing Aid Society (EA)
NHASA .... National Handbag and Accessories Salesmen's Association (EA)
NHasI.......... Institute of Society, Ethics, and Life Sciences, The Hastings Center, Hastings- On-Hudson, NY [*Library symbol Library of Congress*] (LCLS)
NHAT .... Neutron Hardness Assurance Test
NHauS .... Suffolk County Department of Health Service, Hauppauge, NY [*Library symbol Library of Congress*] (LCLS)
NHAW.......... Northamerican Heating and Airconditioning Wholesalers Association (EA)
NHAW.......... Notable Hispanic American Women [*A publication*]
NHB .... Kodiak [*Alaska*] [*Airport symbol*] (AD)
NHB .... NASA Handbook (KSC)
NHB .... National Harbours Board [*Canada*]
NHB .... National Health Board
NHB .... National Naval Medical Center [*Maryland*] [*Seismograph station code, US Geological Survey Closed*] (SEIS)
NHB .... New Hibernian [*Vancouver Stock Exchange symbol*]
NHB .... Nitro(hydroxy)benzoic Acid [*Organic chemistry*]
NHBC .... National House Building Council [*British*]
NHBE .... Normal Human Bronchial Epithelial [*Cells*]
NHBPCC.......... National High Blood Pressure Coordinating Committee
NHBPEP.......... National High Blood Pressure Education Program
NHBPM.......... National Housebuilders' and Plumbers' Merchants [*British*] (DI)
NHBRA.......... National Housebuilders' Registration Association [*British*] (DI)
NHBRC.......... National House-Builders Registration Council [*British*] (ILCA)
NHBS .... Navy Headquarters Budgeting System (GFGA)
NHBS/NHPS... Navy Headquarters Budgeting System/Navy Headquarters Programming System (GFGA)
NHBW .... National Hook-Up of Black Women (EA)

NHC .... Colgate University, Hamilton, NY [*Library symbol Library of Congress*] (LCLS)
NHC .... National Havurah Committee (EA)
NHC .... National Healthcare Ltd. [*AMEX symbol*] (SPSG)
NHC .... National Health Council (EA)
NHC .... National Heart Council (EA)
NHC .... National Homecaring Council [*Later, FHH*] (EA)
NHC .... National Horse Carriers Association, Inc., Frankfort KY [*STAC*]
NHC .... National Housing Center (EA)
NHC .... National Housing Conference (EA)
NHC .... National Housing Council [*of the HHFA*] [*Abolished, 1965*]
NHC .... National Humanities Center (EA)
NHC .... National Hunt Committee [*British*] (DI)
NHC .... National Hunt Cup [*British*] (ROG)
NHC .... National Hurricane Center [*National Weather Service*]
NHC .... Native High Court Reports [*South Africa*] [*A publication*] (DLA)
NHC .... Natl Healthcare L.P. [*AMEX symbol*] (TTSB)
NHC .... Natural Hydrocarbon [*Organic chemistry*]
NHC .... Navy Department Library, Naval Historical Center, Washington, DC [*OCLC symbol*] (OCLC)
NHC .... Neighborhood Health Center [*Generic term*] (DHSM)
NHC .... Neohemocyte [*An artificial red blood cell*]
NHC .... Neonatal Hypocalcemia [*Medicine*] (DB)
NHC .... New Haven [*Connecticut*] [*Seismograph station code, US Geological Survey Closed*] (SEIS)
NHC .... N-Hexylcarborane [*Rocket fuel*] (RDA)
NHC .... Nicaraguan Humanitarian Coalition (EA)
NHC .... Nonhistone Chromosomal Protein [*Genetics*] (MAE)
NHC .... Normal-Hexylcarbane (MCD)
NHC .... Northwest Horticultural Council (EA)
NHCA .... National Hairdressers and Cosmetologists Association (EA)
NHCA .... National Health Club Association (EA)
NHCA .... National Hearing Conservation Association (EA)
NHCA .... National Hispanic Congress on Alcoholism [*Defunct*] (EA)
NHCA .... National Hispanic Council on Aging (EA)
NHCAA .... National Health Care Anti-Fraud Association (EA)
NHCAP .... Native Hawaiian Culture and Arts Program [*An association*] (EA)
NHCC .... NASA Headquarters Computer Center
N-HCC .... Nash-Healey Car Club (EA)
NHCC .... National Havurah Coordinating Committee (EA)
NHCC .... National Health Care Campaign [*Defunct*] (EA)
NHCC .... National Hebrew Culture Council (EA)
NHCC .... National Hispanic Corporate Council (EA)
NHCE .... Non-Highly Compensated Employee
NHCES .... National Health Care Expenditures Study (DHSM)
NHCFD .... National Health Care Foundation for the Deaf [*Later, Deaf-REACH*] (EA)
NHCI .... National Home Centers [*NASDAQ symbol*] (SAG)
NhCla .... Fiske Free Library, Claremont, NH [*Library symbol Library of Congress*] (LCLS)
NHCoA .... National Hispanic Council on Aging (EA)
NHCP .... National HUMINT Collection Plan (MCD)
NHCP .... Nonhistone Chromosomal Protein [*Genetics*]
NHCS .... National Health Care Survey [*Department of Health and Human Services*] (GFGA)
NHCS .... National Home Center Show (ITD)
NHCSA .... National Historic Communal Societies Association [*Later, CSA*] (EA)
NhCSp .... Saint Paul's School, Concord, NH [*Library symbol Library of Congress*] (LCLS)
NhCT .... New Hampshire Technical Institute, Concord, NH [*Library symbol Library of Congress*] (LCLS)
NHCU .... Nursing Home Care Unit [*Veterans Administration*]
NHCUC .... New Hampshire College and University Council, Library Policy Committee [*Library network*]
NhD .... Dartmouth College, Hanover, NH [*Library symbol Library of Congress*] (LCLS)
NHD .... Doctor of Natural History (WDAA)
NHD .... National History Day (EA)
NHD .... New Harding Group, Inc. [*Toronto Stock Exchange symbol*]
NHD .... Normal Hair Distribution [*Medicine*] (DAVI)
NHD .... Not Heard [*Communications*]
NHDA .... National Huntington's Disease Association [*Later, HDSA*] (EA)
NHDAA .... National Home Demonstration Agents' Association [*Later, NAEHE*] (EA)
NhD-BE .... Dartmouth College, Business Administration and Engineering Library, Hanover, NH [*Library symbol Library of Congress*] (LCLS)
NHDC .... National Hansen's Disease Center (DMAA)
NHDC .... National Home Demonstration Council [*Later, NEHC*] (EA)
NHDC .... NATO HAWK Documentation Center [*Missiles*] (NATG)
NHDC .... Naval Historical Display Center
NHDC .... Neohesperidin Dihydrochalcone [*Also, NEO-DHC*] [*Sweetening agent*]
NhD-D .... Dartmouth College, Dana Biomedical Library, Hanover, NH [*Library symbol Library of Congress*] (LCLS)
NHDF .... Normal Human Diploid Fibroblast [*Medicine*] (DMAA)
NhD-H .... Dartmouth College, Hood Museum, Hanover, NH [*Library symbol*] [*Library of Congress*] (LCLS)
NHDI .... Notch Die [*Tool*] (AAG)
NhD-K .... Dartmouth College, Kresge Physical Sciences Library, Hanover, NH [*Library symbol Library of Congress*] (LCLS)
NHDL .... Nonhigh Density Lipoprotein [*Medicine*] (DMAA)
NHDNA .... Nucleohistone Deoxyribonucleic Acid
NhDo .... Dover Public Library, Dover, NH [*Library symbol Library of Congress*] (LCLS)

NhD-P .... Dartmouth College, Paddock Music Library, Hanover, NH [*Library symbol*] [*Library of Congress*] (LCLS)
NHDS .... National Health Data System (DMAA)
NHDS .... National Hospital Discharge Survey
NHDS .... Nonhazardous Dry Solid [*Shipping classification*]
NHDSC .... National Hot Dog and Sausage Council (EA)
NHE .... National Housing Endowment (EA)
NHE .... Nitrogen Heat Exchange
NHE .... Normal Hydrogen Electrode
NHE .... North Hennepin Community College Library, Brooklyn Park, MN [*OCLC symbol*] (OCLC)
NHE .... Nuclease-Hypersensitive Element [*Biochemistry*]
NHEA .... National Higher Education Association (EA)
NHEB .... National Home Enlargement Bureau [*British*] (DI)
N HEB .... New Hebrew [*Language, etc.*] (ROG)
N HEB .... New Hebrides (ROG)
NHEDLP ...... National Housing and Economic Development Law Project
NHEF .... National Health Education Foundation
NHEFS .... NHANES [*National Health and Nutritional Examination Survey*] Epidemiologic Follow-Up Study [*Department of Health and Human Services*] (GFGA)
NHEK .... Normal Human Epidermal Keratinocyte
NHeLP .... National Health Law Program (EA)
NHELP .... New Hitachi Effective Library for Programming (NITA)
NHem .... Hempstead Public Library, Hempstead, NY [*Library symbol Library of Congress*] (LCLS)
NHEM .... Normal Human Epidermal Melanocyte [*Cytology*]
NHemB .... Burns & Roe, Inc., Branch Library, Hempstead, NY [*Library symbol Library of Congress*] (LCLS)
NHemCE ..... William S. Covert School, Hempstead, NY [*Library symbol*] [*Library of Congress*] (LCLS)
NHemFE ..... Franklin School, Hempstead, NY [*Library symbol*] [*Library of Congress*] (LCLS)
NHemFuE .... Fulton School, Hempstead, NY [*Library symbol*] [*Library of Congress*] (LCLS)
NHemGH ..... Hempstead General Hospital, Medical Center, Hempstead, NY [*Library symbol Library of Congress*] (LCLS)
NHemH .... Hofstra University, Hempstead, NY [*Library symbol Library of Congress*] (LCLS)
NHemJE ...... Jackson Elementary School, Hempstead, NY [*Library symbol*] [*Library of Congress*] (LCLS)
NHEML .... National Hurricane and Experimental Meteorology Laboratory [*Marine science*] (MSC)
NHemLE ...... Ludlum School, Hempstead, NY [*Library symbol*] [*Library of Congress*] (LCLS)
NHemLJ ...... Lawrence Road Junior High School, Hempstead, NY [*Library symbol*] [*Library of Congress*] (LCLS)
NHemME ..... Marshall School, Hempstead, NY [*Library symbol*] [*Library of Congress*] (LCLS)
NHemMS ..... Hempstead Middle School, Hempstead, NY [*Library symbol*] [*Library of Congress*] (LCLS)
NHemNH ..... Nassau County Department of Health, Hempstead, NY [*Library symbol Library of Congress*] (LCLS)
NHemNHR ... Nassau County Department of Health, Division of Laboratories and Research, Hempstead, NY [*Library symbol Library of Congress*] (LCLS)
NHemPE ...... Prospect School, Hempstead, NY [*Library symbol*] [*Library of Congress*] (LCLS)
NHemSH ..... Hempstead Senior High School, Hempstead, NY [*Library symbol*] [*Library of Congress*] (LCLS)
NHemWE .... Washington School, Hempstead, NY [*Library symbol*] [*Library of Congress*] (LCLS)
NHen .... Henderson Free Library, Henderson, NY [*Library symbol Library of Congress*] (LCLS)
NHEN .... National Holistic Education Network (EA)
NHENMA ..... National Hand Embroidery and Novelty Manufacturers Association [*Defunct*] (EA)
NHEP .... Nicaragua-Honduras Education Project (EA)
NHERI .... National Home Education Research Institute (EA)
NHerkCHi .... Herkimer County Historical Society, Herkimer, NY [*Library symbol Library of Congress*] (LCLS)
NHerrSH ..... Herricks Senior High School, Herricks, NY [*Library symbol*] [*Library of Congress*] (LCLS)
NHES .... National Health Enhancement Systems, Inc. [*NASDAQ symbol*] (NQ)
NHES .... National Health Examination Survey [*Department of Health and Human Services*] (GFGA)
NHES .... National Humane Education Society (EA)
NHES .... Natl Health Enhacement Sys [*NASDAQ symbol*] (TTSB)
NHESA .... National Higher Education Staff Association [*Defunct*] (EA)
NHESP .... Natural Heritage and Endangered Species Program [*Massachusetts State Division of Fisheries and Wildlife*] [*Also, an information service or system*] (IID)
NHew .... Hewlett-Woodmere Public Library, Hewlett, NY [*Library symbol Library of Congress*] (LCLS)
NHewE .... Hewlett Elementary School, Hewlett, NY [*Library symbol Library of Congress*] (LCLS)
NHewFC ...... Franlin Early Childhood Center, Hewlett, NY [*Library symbol*] [*Library of Congress*] (LCLS)
NHewFE ...... Franklin Elementary School, Hewlett, NY [*Library symbol Library of Congress*] (LCLS)
NHewLD ...... Lawrence Country Day School, Hewlett, NY [*Library symbol*] [*Library of Congress*] (LCLS)
NHewOE ...... Ogden Elementary School, Hewlett, NY [*Library symbol Library of Congress*] (LCLS)

NHewSH	G. W. Hewlett Senior High School, Hewlett, NY [*Library symbol*] [*Library of Congress*] (LCLS)
NHewWM	Woodmere Middle School, Hewlett, NY [*Library symbol*] [*Library of Congress*] (LCLS)
NhExP	Phillips Exeter Academy, Exeter, NH [*Library symbol Library of Congress*] (LCLS)
NHF	National Hairdressers' Federation [*British*] (BI)
NHF	National Handicapped Foundation (EA)
NHF	National Headache Foundation (EA)
NHF	National Health Federation (EA)
NHF	National Health Foundation (NADA)
NHF	National Heart Foundation (NADA)
NHF	National Hemophilia Foundation (EA)
NHF	National Humanities Faculty [*Later, NFHAS*] (EA)
NHF	National Hunting and Fishing [*In "NHF" Day*] [*National Rifle Association*]
NHF	National Hydrocephalus Foundation (EA)
NHF	Nausori Highlands [*Fiji*] [*Seismograph station code, US Geological Survey*] (SEIS)
NHF	Naval Historical Foundation (EA)
NHF	New Halfa [*Sudan*] [*Airport symbol*] (OAG)
NHF	Nonimmune Hydrops Fetalis [*Medicine*] (DMAA)
NHF	Nordiska Handikappforbundet [*Nordic Association for the Handicapped - NAH*] (EAIO)
NHF	Nordisk Herpetologisk Forening [*Scandinavian Herpetological Society - SHS*] (EAIO)
NHF	Nordisk Hydrologisk Forening [*Nordic Association for Hydrology - NAH*] [*Denmark*] (EAIO)
NHFA	National Home Furnishings Association (EA)
NHFF	National Historical Fire Foundation (EA)
NHFL	National Home Fashions League (EA)
NHFP	New Hebrides Federal Party [*Political party*] (PPW)
NhFr	Franklin Public Library, Franklin, NH [*Library symbol Library of Congress*] (LCLS)
NHFRA	National Hay Fever Relief Association [*Defunct*] (EA)
NHG	Newhawk Gold Mines Ltd. [*Toronto Stock Exchange symbol Vancouver Stock Exchange symbol*]
NHG	New High German [*Language, etc.*]
NHG	Normal Human Globulin [*or anticancer substance derived from NHG*] [*Biochemistry*]
NHG	Northern Hemisphere Glaciation
NHGJ	Normal Human Gastric Juice [*Medicine*] (DMAA)
NHGRI	National Human Genome Research Institute (HGEN)
NHH	Neither Help nor Hinder
NHH	Neurohypophyseal Hormone (DB)
NhHaCR	United States Army, Cold Regions Research and Engineering Laboratory, Hanover, NH [*Library symbol Library of Congress*] (LCLS)
NHHC	National Home Health Care Corp. [*NASDAQ symbol*] (SPSG)
NHHC	Natl Home Health Care [*NASDAQ symbol*] (TTSB)
NhHen	Tucker Free Library, Henniker, NH [*Library symbol Library of Congress*] (LCLS)
NhHenN	New England College, Henniker, NH [*Library symbol Library of Congress*] (LCLS)
NhHi	New Hampshire Historical Society, Concord, NH [*Library symbol Library of Congress*] (LCLS)
NhHopA	New Hampshire Antiquarian Society, Hopkinton, NH [*Library symbol Library of Congress*] (LCLS)
NHHRA	National Hereford Hog Record Association (EA)
NH-HY	Harvard University, Harvard-Yenching Institute [*Chinese-Japanese Library*],Cambridge, MA [*Library symbol Library of Congress*] (LCLS)
NHI	Jacksonville, FL [*Location identifier FAA*] (FAAL)
NHI	Naphtali Herz Imber (BJA)
NHI	Nathan Hale Institute (EA)
NHI	National Health Insurance [*British*]
NHI	National Health Investors [*NYSE symbol*] (SPSG)
NHI	National Heart Institute [*Later, NHLI, NHLBI*] [*National Institutes of Health*]
NHI	National Highway Institute
NHI	National Hobby Institute [*Defunct*]
NHI	National Housing Institute (EA)
NHI	National Humanities Institute (EA)
NHI	Nelson Holdings International Ltd. [*Toronto Stock Exchange symbol Vancouver Stock Exchange symbol*]
NHi	New York Historical Society, New York, NY [*Library symbol Library of Congress*] (LCLS)
NHI	Nielsen Home Video Index [*A. C. Nielsen Co.*] (NTCM)
NHIA	National Holography and Imaging Association (EA)
NHIC	NASA Hazards Identification Committee (KSC)
NHIC	National Health Information Clearinghouse [*Public Health Service*] [*Later, ODPHP Health Information Center*] (IID)
NHIC	National Heritage Insurance Co.
NHIC	National Home Improvement Council [*Later, NARI*] (EA)
NHick	Hicksville Free Public Library, Hicksville, NY [*Library symbol Library of Congress*] (LCLS)
NHickAd	Hicksville Administration, Hicksville, NY [*Library symbol Library of Congress*] (LCLS)
NHickBE	Burns Elementary School, Hicksville, NY [*Library symbol Library of Congress*] (LCLS)
NHickCE	Old Country Elementary School, Hicksville, NY [*Library symbol Library of Congress*] (LCLS)
NHickDLE	Dutch Lane Elementary School, Hicksville, NY [*Library symbol Library of Congress*] (LCLS)
NHickEE	East Elementary School, Hicksville, NY [*Library symbol Library of Congress*] (LCLS)
NHickFE	Fork Elementary School, Hicksville, NY [*Library symbol Library of Congress*] (LCLS)
NHickHT	Holy Trinity Diocesan High School, Hicksville, NY [*Library symbol*] [*Library of Congress*] (LCLS)
NHickL	Long Island Lighting Co., Hicksville, NY [*Library symbol*] [*Library of Congress*] (LCLS)
NHickLE	Lee Elementary School, Hicksville, NY [*Library symbol Library of Congress*] (LCLS)
NHickOL	Our Lady of Mercy School, Hicksville, NY [*Library symbol*] [*Library of Congress*] (LCLS)
NHickSH	Hicksville Senior High School, Hicksville, NY [*Library symbol Library of Congress*] (LCLS)
NHickWE	Willet Elementary School, Hicksville, NY [*Library symbol Library of Congress*] (LCLS)
NHickWoE	Woodland Avenue Elementary School, Hicksville, NY [*Library symbol*] [*Library of Congress*] (LCLS)
NHIF	Brain Injury Association [*Formerly, National Head Injury Foundation*] (EA)
NHIF	National Head Injury Foundation (EA)
NHig	Highland Free Library, Highland, NY [*Library symbol Library of Congress*] (LCLS)
NHigfL	Ladycliff College, Highland Falls, NY [*Library symbol Library of Congress*] (LCLS)
NHigm	Rushmore Memorial Library, Highland Mills, NY [*Library symbol Library of Congress*] (LCLS)
NHIP	Natl Hlth Inv 8.50%Cv Pfd [*NYSE symbol*] (TTSB)
NHIP	Nursing Home Improvement Program [*National Institute of Mental Health*]
NHIR	Natural History Information Retrieval System [*Smithsonian Institution*]
NHIR	New Hope & Ivyland Railroad Co. [*AAR code*]
NHIS	National Health Interview Survey [*Department of Health and Human Services*] (GFGA)
NHIS	Navy Hazardous Materials Information System (DNAB)
NHIS	New Hampshire International Speedway [*Loudon*]
NHIS	Nuclear Hardening Interceptor Structure
NHIS	Nursing Home Information Service (EA)
NHISCH	National Health Interview Survey of Child Health [*Department of Health and Human Services*]
NHIY	Northumberland Hussars Imperial Yeomanry [*British military*] (DMA)
NHJA	National Hunter and Jumper Association (EA)
NHjI	International Business Machines Corp., Components Division Library, Hopewell Junction, NY [*Library symbol Library of Congress*] (LCLS)
NHK	Nippon Hoso Kyokai [*Japanese national broadcasting system*] (NTCM)
NHK	Normal Human Kidney [*Medicine*] (DMAA)
NHK	Patuxent River, MD [*Location identifier FAA*] (FAAL)
NhKe	Keene Public Library, Keene, NH [*Library symbol Library of Congress*] (LCLS)
NhKeHi	Historical Society of Cheshire County, Keene, NH [*Library symbol Library of Congress*] (LCLS)
NhKeK	Keene State College, Keene, NH [*Library symbol Library of Congress*] (LCLS)
NHKidQ	New Horizon Kids Quest, Inc. [*Associated Press*] (SAG)
NHKYA	National Hand Knitting Yarn Association [*Later, NHKYC*] (EA)
NHKYC	National Hand Knitting Yarn Committee [*Defunct*] (EA)
NHL	Hamilton Public Library, Hamilton, NY [*Library symbol*] [*Library of Congress*] (LCLS)
NHL	National Historic Landmark
NHL	National Hockey League (EA)
NHL	Negro Heritage Library
NHL	Newhall Land & Farming Co. [*NYSE symbol*] (SPSG)
NHL	Newhall Land/Farming [*NYSE symbol*] (TTSB)
NHL	Nodular Histiocytic Lymphoma [*Oncology*]
NHL	Non-Hodgkin's Lymphoma [*Oncology*]
NHL	Nordic Federation of Heart and Lung Associations (EA)
NHL	Normal Human Lymphocyte
NHL	Northcal Resources [*Vancouver Stock Exchange symbol*]
NHL	Notes from Hume's Lectures [*A publication*] (DLA)
NHLA	National Hardwood Lumber Association (EA)
NHLA	National Health Lawyers Association (EA)
NHLA	National Hispanic Leadership Agenda (EA)
NHLA	National Housewives' League of America (EA)
NHLA	National Housewives League of America for Economic Security (EA)
NHLBAC	National Heart, Lung, and Blood Advisory Council [*National Institutes of Health*]
NHLBCA	National Hockey League Booster Clubs Association (EA)
NHLBI	National Heart, Lung, and Blood Institute [*Bethesda, MD*] [*National Institutes of Health*]
NHLBIC	National Heart, Lung, and Blood Information Center (PAZ)
NHLC	National Hispanic Leadership Conference (EA)
NHLC	National Home Loans Corp. [*British*]
NhLe	Lebanon Public Library, Lebanon, NH [*Library symbol Library of Congress*] (LCLS)
NhLeHi	Lebanon Historical Society, Lebanon, NH [*Library symbol Library of Congress*] (LCLS)
NHLF	National Heritage Lottery Fund [*British*] (WDAA)
NHLI	National Heart and Lung Institute [*Later, NHLBI*] [*National Institutes of Health*]
NHLP	National Housing Law Project (EA)
NHLPA	National Hockey League Player's Association (EA)
NHL Rep	New Hampshire Law Reporter [*A publication*] (DLA)
NHltCre	National Healthcare Ltd. [*Associated Press*] (SAG)

NhM............ Manchester City Library, Manchester, NH [*Library symbol Library of Congress*] (LCLS)
NHM .... Natural History Museum [*British*]
NHM .... Niihama [*Japan*] [*Seismograph station code, US Geological Survey Closed*] (SEIS)
NHM .... Nitrosohexamethyleneimine [*Organic chemistry*]
NHM .... No Hot Metal [*Photocomposition*]
NHM .... Nonhostile Missing [*Military*] (CINC)
NHM .... Normal Human Milk
NHM .... Nozzle Hinge Moment
NHM .... Nuclear Hyperfine Magnetic [*Rare-earth alloy*]
NHM .... University of New Hampshire, Durham, NH [*OCLC symbol*] (OCLC)
NHMA .... National Handle Manufacturers Association [*Defunct*] (EA)
NHMA .... National Housewares Manufacturers Association (EA)
NHMC .... National Hispanic Media Coalition (EA)
NHMC .... National Hispanic Media Conference (EA)
NHMC .... Normal Human Mammary Cell
NHMEL .... National High Magnetic Field Laboratory
NHMF .... National Heritage Memoiral Fund (WDAA)
NHMF .... National Heritage Memorial Fund (AIE)
NHMFL .... National High Magnetic Field Laboratory [*Florida State University*]
NHMILCOM... NATO HAWK Military Committee [*Missiles*] (AABC)
NHML .... Non-Hodgkin's Malignant Lymphoma [*Oncology*] (DMAA)
NhMND .... Notre Dame College, Manchester, NH [*Library symbol Library of Congress*] (LCLS)
NHMO .... NATO HAWK Management Office [*Missiles*] (NATG)
NHmpTh ...... New Hampshire Thrift Bancshares, Inc. [*Associated Press*] (SAG)
NHMRC....... National Health and Medical Research Council (DAVI)
NHMRC .... National Hotel & Motel Reservations Corp.
NhMSA .... Saint Anselm's College, Manchester, NH [*Library symbol Library of Congress*] (LCLS)
NhMV.......... United States Veterans Administration Hospital, Manchester, NH [*Library symbol Library of Congress*] (LCLS)
NHN .... National Homes Network [*British*] (DI)
NHN .... Nebraska HealthNetwork [*Information service or system*] (IID)
NHN .... Northern Horizon [*Vancouver Stock Exchange symbol*]
NhNa .... Nashua Public Library, Nashua, NH [*Library symbol Library of Congress*] (LCLS)
NhNaR .... Rivier College, Nashua, NH [*Library symbol Library of Congress*] (LCLS)
NhNaS .... Sanders Associates, Inc., Technical Library, Nashua, NH [*Library symbol Library of Congress*] (LCLS)
NhNelC .... Colby Junior College for Women [*Later, CSC*], New London, NH [*Library symbol Library of Congress*] (LCLS)
NHNP .... New Hebrides National Party [*Political party*] (FEA)
NHNR.......... National Highway Needs Report [*Department of Transportation*]
NHO .... M/I Schottenstein Homes [*NYSE symbol*] (TTSB)
NHO .... National Hospice Organization (EA)
NHO .... Navy Hydrographic Office [*Later, NOO*]
NHO .... Northern Hemisphere Observatory [*Canary Islands*] (PDAA)
NHOA .... National Hemi Owners Association (EA)
NHolb .... Sachem Public Library, Holbrook, NY [*Library symbol Library of Congress*] (LCLS)
NHolbHS...... Sachem High School North, Holbrook, NY [*Library symbol Library of Congress*] (LCLS)
NHolbSJ ...... Seneca Junior High School, Holbrook, NY [*Library symbol Library of Congress*] (LCLS)
NHoll .... Community Free Library, Holley, NY [*Library symbol Library of Congress*] (LCLS)
NHOP.......... National Hurricane Operations Plan (DNAB)
NHorizn........ New Horizon Kids Quest, Inc. [*Associated Press*] (SAG)
NHorW........ Westinghouse Electric Corp., Engineering Library, Horseheads, NY [*Library symbol Library of Congress*] (LCLS)
NHOS........... Naval Hospital
NHP .... National Hamiltonian Party (EA)
NHP .... National Historic Park (BARN)
NHP .... National Housing Partnership [*HUD*]
NHP .... National Humanitarian Party [*Political party Australia*]
NHP .... Nationwide Health Prop [*NYSE symbol*] (TTSB)
NHP .... Nationwide Health Properties, Inc. [*NYSE symbol*] (SPSG)
NHP .... Natural History Press (DGA)
NHP .... Neighborhood Health Program [*Generic term*]
NHP .... Net Horsepower [*Engineering*]
NHP .... Network Host Protocol
NHP .... New Haven Free Public Library, New Haven, CT [*OCLC symbol*] (OCLC)
NHP .... New Health Practitioners [*Nurse practitioners and physician assistants*]
NHP .... NHP, Inc. [*Associated Press*] (SAG)
NHP .... Nitrogen High Pressure
NHP .... Nominal Horsepower
NHP .... Nonhistone Protein (DB)
NHP .... Nonhuman Primate
NHP .... Noninverted Hand Position [*Neuropsychology*]
NHP .... Normal Hearing Peer [*of the hearing-impaired*]
NHP .... Normal Human-Pooled Plasma
NHP .... Nuclear Heart Pacer
NHP .... Nursing Home Placement (DAVI)
NHPA .... National Hispanic Psychological Association [*Defunct*] (EA)
NHPA .... National Historic Preservation Act (GNE)
NHPA .... National Historic Preservation Act of 1966
NHPA .... National Horseshoe Pitchers Association of America (EA)
NH-PA......... Nurse Healers - Professional Associates (NTPA)
NHPA .... Nurse Healers - Professional Associates (EA)
NHPAA........ National Historic Preservation Act Amendments of 1980 (COE)

NHPAA........ National Horseshoe Pitchers Association of America (EA)
NHPC .... National Health Planning Council (DMAA)
NHPC .... National Historical Publications Commission [*Later, NHPRC*]
NHPDA .... National Honey Packers and Dealers Association (EA)
NHPDPA ...... National Health Promotion and Disease Prevention Act of 1976 (COE)
NHPF .... National Health Policy Forum (EA)
NhPHi .... Peterborough Historical Society, Peterborough, NH [*Library symbol Library of Congress*] (LCLS)
NHPI .... NHP, Inc. [*NASDAQ symbol*] (SAG)
NHPIC .... National Health Planning Information Center [*Public Health Service*] [*Database*] (IID)
NHpJR .... James Roosevelt Library, Hyde Park, NY [*Library symbol Library of Congress Obsolete*] (LCLS)
NHPLO .... NATO HAWK Production and Logistics Organization [*France*] (NATG)
NhPIS .... Plymouth State College of the University of New Hampshire, Plymouth, NH [*Library symbol Library of Congress*] (LCLS)
NHPMA .... Northern Hardwood and Pine Manufacturers Association [*Defunct*] (EA)
NHPN .... National Highway Planning Network [*FHWA*] (TAG)
NHPO .... NATO HAWK Production Organization [*Missiles*]
NhPoA .... Portsmouth Athenaeum, Portsmouth, NH [*Library symbol Library of Congress*] (LCLS)
NhPoS .... Strawbery Banke, Portsmouth, NH [*Library symbol Library of Congress*] (LCLS)
NHPP .... National Health Professions Placement Network
NHPP .... National Hormone and Pituitary Program (EA)
NHpR .... Franklin D. Roosevelt Library, Hyde Park, NY [*Library symbol Library of Congress Obsolete*] (LCLS)
NHPRC........ National Historical Publications and Records Commission [*Formerly, NHPC*] [*Washington, DC*]
NHPRO .... National Historical Publications and Records Commission
NHPRO .... Nitrosohydroxyproline [*Organic chemistry*]
NHPSCR ...... New Hampshire Public Service Commission Reports [*A publication*] (DLA)
NHPYR .... Nitrosohydroxypyrrolidine [*Organic chemistry*]
NHQ .... NASA Headquarters
NHQ .... National Headquarters
NHQ .... Nuclear Hyperfine Quadrupolar [*Rare-earth alloy*]
NHQC .... National Hispanic Quincentennial Commission (EA)
NHQRA .... Nursing Home Quality Reform Act
NHR .... National Heritage (EFIS)
NHR .... National Housewives Register [*British*]
NHR .... National Hunt Rules [*British*]
NHR .... Net Histocompatibility Ratio
NHR .... New Hampshire Reports [*A publication*] (DLA)
NHR .... North Hart Resources [*Vancouver Stock Exchange symbol*]
NHR .... Nova/Husky Research Corp. Ltd. [*UTLAS symbol*]
NHRA .... National Hot Rod Association (EA)
NHRA .... National Housing and Rehabilitation Association (EA)
NHRA .... National Human Resources Association (NTPA)
NHRA .... Next Higher Repairable Assembly (MCD)
NHRAC........ National Health Resources Advisory Committee [*Terminated, 1978*] [*General Services Administration*] (EGAO)
NHRAIC....... Natural Hazards Research and Applications Information Center [*University of Colorado - Boulder*] [*Research center*] (RCD)
NHRAW....... Northamerican Heating, Refrigeration, and Airconditioning Wholesalers Association (NTPA)
NHRB.......... National Health Review Board [*Proposed medical-care price regulator*] (ECON)
NHRC .... National Health Research Center (DAVI)
NHRC .... National Human Rights Committee (EA)
NHRC .... National Human Rights Congress [*Australia*]
NHRC .... Naval Health Research Center (GRD)
NHRCPPUS... National Human Rights Campaign for Political Prisoners in the US (EA)
NHRD.......... National Health Planning and Resource Development Act [*1974*] (DHSM)
NHRDP .... National Health Research and Development Program [*Canada*]
NHRE .... National Hail Research Experiment
NH Rep ...... New Hampshire Reports [*A publication*] (DLA)
NH Rev Stat... New Hampshire Revised Statutes [*A publication*] (AAGC)
NH Rev Stat Ann... New Hampshire Revised Statutes, Annotated [*A publication*] (DLA)
NHRI .... National Health Research Institutes [*Taiwan*]
NHRI .... National Hydrology Research Institute [*Canada*]
NHRL .... National Hurricane Research Laboratory [*Later, AOML*]
NHRL .... Northern Hemisphere Reference Line [*Geology*]
NHRP .... National Heart Research Project (EA)
NHRP .... National Hurricane Research Project
NHRP .... Next Hop Resolution Protocol [*Computer science*]
NHRR.......... New Haven Railroad
NHRRC........ National Hybrid Rice Research Center [*China*]
NHRS .... New Hampshire Revised Statutes [*A publication*] (DLA)
NHrzWrld...... New Horizons Worldwide, Inc. [*Associated Press*] (SAG)
NHS .... Das Nordhebraeische Sagenbuch [*A publication*] (BJA)
NhS .... Kelley Memorial Library, Salem, NH [*Library symbol Library of Congress*] (LCLS)
NHS .... Nag Hammadi Studies [*A publication*] (BJA)
NHS .... Nathaniel Hawthorne Society (EA)
NHS .... National Handcraft Society [*Commercial firm*] (EA)
NHS .... National Handicapped Sports (EA)
NHS .... National Health Service [*British*]
NHS .... National Health Survey
NHS .... National Highway System

NHS .... National Historical Society [*Commercial firm*] (EA)
NHS .... National Historic Site (BARN)
NHS .... National Honor Society (EA)
NHS .... National Huguenot Society (EA)
NHS .... Native Human Serum Pooled [*Hematology*] (DAVI)
NHS .... Natural Human Serum
NHS .... Naval Honor Schools (AFIT)
NHS .... Neighborhood Housing Services [*Generic term*]
NHS .... New Hampshire State Library, Concord, NH [*OCLC symbol*] (OCLC)
NHS .... New Hampshire Tracking Station
NHS .... N-Hydroxysuccinimide [*Organic chemistry*]
NHS .... Nikon Historical Society (EA)
NHS .... Normal Horse Serum
NHS .... Normal Human Serum
NHS .... North Hampton [*South Carolina*] [*Seismograph station code, US Geological Survey Closed*] (SEIS)
NHSA .... National Handicapped Skiers Association [*British*] (DBA)
NHSA .... National Head Start Association (EA)
NHSA .... National Heart Savers Association (EA)
NHSA .... National Highway Safety Administration [*Formerly, NHSB; later, NHTSA*] [*Department of Transportation*]
NHSA .... National Home Service Association [*Defunct*] (EA)
NHSA .... National Horse Show Association of America (EA)
NHSA .... Natural Health Society of Australia
NHSA .... Naval Historical Society of Australia
NHSA .... Negro Historical Society of America
NHSA .... Neighborhood Housing Services of America (EA)
NHSAA .... National Horse Show Association of America (EA)
NHSAC .... National Health and Safety Awareness Center [*Defunct*] (EA)
NHSAC .... National Highway Safety Advisory Committee
NHSACA ...... National High School Athletic Coaches Association (EA)
NHSAS .... National Health Service Audit Staff [*Department of Health and Social Security*] [*British*]
NHSB .... National High School Band Institute (EA)
NHSB .... National Highway Safety Bureau [*Later, NHSA, NHTSA*] [*Department of Transportation*]
NHsBE .... Birchwood Elementary School, Huntington Station, NY [*Library symbol*] [*Library of Congress*] (LCLS)
NHSBVA ...... National High School Boys Volleyball Association (EA)
NHSC .... National Health Service Corps [*Department of Health and Human Services*]
NHSC .... National Highway Safety Council (NADA)
NHSC .... National Home Study Council (EA)
NHSC .... National Horse Show Commission (EA)
NHsCE .... Countrywood Elementary School, Huntington Station, NY [*Library symbol*] [*Library of Congress*] (LCLS)
NHSCP .... National Household Survey Capability Program [*United Nations*]
NHSCVO ...... National Health Screening Council for Volunteer Organizations (EA)
NHSD .... National Health Survey Division [*of OSG*]
NHSD .... NATO HAWK Support Department [*Missiles*] (NATG)
NHSF .... National Hispanic Scholarship Fund (EA)
NHSF .... National Horse Show Foundation (EA)
NHsH .... Half Hollow Hills Community Public Library, Huntington Station, NY [*Library symbol Library of Congress*] (LCLS)
NHsK .... KLD Associates, Inc., Huntington Station, NY [*Library symbol*] [*Library of Congress*] (LCLS)
NHSL .... New Horizons Savings & Loan Association [*NASDAQ symbol*] (SPSG)
NHSL .... NHS Financial [*NASDAQ symbol*] (TTSB)
NHSM .... No Hepatosplenomegaly [*On physical examination*] [*Gastroenterology*] (DAVI)
NHsME .... Maplewood Elementary School, Huntington Station, NY [*Library symbol*] [*Library of Congress*] (LCLS)
NHsMJ .... Memorial Junior High School, Huntington Station, NY [*Library symbol*] [*Library of Congress*] (LCLS)
NHsOE .... Oakwood Elementary School, Huntington Station, NY [*Library symbol*] [*Library of Congress*] (LCLS)
NHSP .... N-Hydroxysuccinimidyl Palmitate [*Organic chemistry*]
NHSR .... National Hospital Service Reserve [*British*]
NHSRA .... National Handicapped Sports and Recreation Association [*Later, NHS*] (EA)
NHSRA .... National High School Rodeo Association (EA)
NHSS .... National Herb Study Society (EA)
NHsS .... South Huntington Public Library, Huntington Station, NY [*Library symbol Library of Congress*] (LCLS)
NHsSAHS .... Saint Anthony's High School, Huntington Station, NY [*Library symbol*] [*Library of Congress*] (LCLS)
NHsSE .... Silaswood Elementary School, Huntington Station, NY [*Library symbol*] [*Library of Congress*] (LCLS)
NHsSJH .... Henry L. Stinson Junior High School, Huntington Station, NY [*Library symbol*] [*Library of Congress*] (LCLS)
NHSV .... Normal Hourly Space Velocity [*Emission control*]
NHsW .... Walt Whitman Birthplace Association, Huntington Station, NY [*Library symbol Library of Congress*] (LCLS)
NHsWH .... Walt Whitman High School, Huntington Station, NY [*Library symbol*] [*Library of Congress*] (LCLS)
NHT .... Corpus Christi, TX [*Location identifier FAA*] (FAAL)
NHT .... Nationwide Housing Trust [*British*]
NHT .... Nernst Heat Theorem [*Physics*]
NHT .... Nonpenetrating Head Trauma [*Medicine*] (DMAA)
NHT .... Now Hear This (EFIS)
NHT .... Nursing Home Type (ADA)
NHTB .... New Hampshire Thrift [*NASDAQ symbol*] (TTSB)
NHTB .... New Hampshire Thrift Bancshares, Inc. [*NASDAQ symbol*] (NQ)
NHTC .... Natural Health Trends Corp. [*NASDAQ symbol*] (SAG)

NHTCW .... Natural Health Trends Wrrt'A' [*NASDAQ symbol*] (TTSB)
NHTCZ .... Natural Health Trends Wrrt'B' [*NASDAQ symbol*] (TTSB)
NHTD .... NASA Headquarters Telephone Directory
NHTP .... Nursing Home-Type Patient
NHTPC .... National Housing and Town Planning Council [*British*]
NHTS .... New Hampshire Tracking Station (SAA)
NHTSA .... National Highway Traffic Safety Administration [*Formerly, NHSB, NHSA*] [*Department of Transportation*]
NHTSA .... National Highway Transportation Safety Administration (EBF)
NHTU .... Naval Hovercraft Trials Unit
NHu .... Huntington Public Library, Huntington, NY [*Library symbol Library of Congress*] (LCLS)
nhu .... New Hampshire [*MARC country of publication code Library of Congress*] (LCCP)
NhU .... University of New Hampshire, Durham, NH [*Library symbol Library of Congress*] (LCLS)
NHUBW .... National Hook-Up of Black Women (EA)
NHUC .... National Highway Users Conference [*Later, HUF*]
NHuCE .... Cuba Hill Elementary School, Huntington, NY [*Library symbol Library of Congress*] (LCLS)
NHudC .... Columbia-Greene Community College, Hudson, NY [*Library symbol Library of Congress*] (LCLS)
NHudDAR .... Daughters of the American Revolution, Hendrick Hudson Chapter, Hudson, NY [*Library symbol Library of Congress*] (LCLS)
NHudHi .... Columbia County, New York Official Historian, Hudson, NY [*Library symbol Library of Congress*] (LCLS)
NhudO .... Olana State Historic Site, Hudson, NY [*Library symbol*] [*Library of Congress*] (LCLS)
NHuEJ .... Elwood Junior High School, Huntington, NY [*Library symbol Library of Congress*] (LCLS)
NHuFE .... Flower Hill Elementary School, Huntington, NY [*Library symbol*] [*Library of Congress*] (LCLS)
NHuFJ .... Finley Junior High School, Huntington, NY [*Library symbol Library of Congress*] (LCLS)
NHuGH .... John H. Glenn High School, Huntington, NY [*Library symbol*] [*Library of Congress*] (LCLS)
NHuH .... Huntington Hospital, Huntington, NY [*Library symbol Library of Congress*] (LCLS)
NHuHAE ...... Harley Avenue Elementary School, Huntington, NY [*Library symbol*] [*Library of Congress*] (LCLS)
NHuHE .... Huntington Elementary School, Huntington, NY [*Library symbol*] [*Library of Congress*] (LCLS)
NHuHi .... Huntington Historical Society, Huntington, NY [*Library symbol Library of Congress*] (LCLS)
NHuHS .... Huntington High School, Huntington, NY [*Library symbol Library of Congress*] (LCLS)
NHuI .... Immaculate Conception Seminary, Huntington, NY [*Library symbol Library of Congress*] (LCLS)
NHuJE .... Jefferson Elementary School, Huntington, NY [*Library symbol*] [*Library of Congress*] (LCLS)
NHuL .... Huntington Public Library, Huntington, NY [*Library symbol*] [*Library of Congress*] (LCLS)
NHuMHS ...... Madonna Heights High School, Huntington, NY [*Library symbol*] [*Library of Congress*] (LCLS)
NhuSE .... Southdown Elementary School, Huntington, NY [*Library symbol*] [*Library of Congress*] (LCLS)
NHusk .... KLD Associates, Inc., Huntington Station, NY [*Library symbol Library of Congress*] (LCLS)
NHusMJ .... Memorial Junior High School, Huntington Station, NY [*Library symbol Library of Congress*] (LCLS)
NHusWH ...... Walt Whitman High School, Huntington Station, NY [*Library symbol Library of Congress*] (LCLS)
NHuTJ .... R. K. Toaz Junior High School, Huntington, NY [*Library symbol Library of Congress*] (LCLS)
NHV .... Nuku Hiva [*French Polynesia*] [*Airport symbol*] (OAG)
NHvL .... Long Island Lighting Co., Hicksville, NY [*Library symbol Library of Congress*] (LCLS)
NHW .... National Health and Welfare Mutual Life Insurance Association [*Formerly, NHWRA*] (EA)
NHW .... Neuhebraeisches Woerterbuch [*A publication*] (BJA)
NHW .... New Hospital for Women [*1904*] [*British*] (ROG)
NHW .... Night Hawk Resources Ltd. [*Vancouver Stock Exchange symbol*]
NhWalHi ...... Walpole Historical Society, Walpole, NH [*Library symbol Library of Congress*] (LCLS)
NHWK .... Harris Computer Systems [*NASDAQ symbol*] (TTSB)
NHWK .... Harris Computer Systems Corp. [*NASDAQ symbol*] (SAG)
NHWM .... Normal Human White Matter (DB)
NHWP .... Northeast Hazardous Waste Project [*Environmental Protection Agency*] (GFGA)
NHWRA .... National Health and Welfare Retirement Association [*Later, NHW*] (EA)
NHWS .... National Hurricane Warning Service [*National Weather Service*]
NHWU .... Non-Heatset Web Unit (EA)
NHWZSP ..... National Highway Work Zone Safety Program
NHX .... Albany, GA [*Location identifier FAA*] (FAAL)
nhx .... Narthex (VRA)
NHY .... NIPSCO Industries [*NYSE symbol*] (TTSB)
NHY .... Norsk Hydro AS [*NYSE symbol*] (SPSG)
NHY .... Northumberland Hussars Yeomanry [*British military*] (DMA)
NHyF .... General Services Administration, National Archives and Record Service, Franklin D. Roosevelt Library, Hyde Park, NY [*Library symbol Library of Congress*] (LCLS)
NHZ .... Brunswick, ME [*Location identifier FAA*] (FAAL)
NHZ .... Nominal Hazard Zone [*Environmental science*] (COE)

NI............... [*First*] Cranial Nerve [*Second cranial nerve is NII, etc., through NVIII*] [*Medicine*] (DAVI)
NI............... Das Neue Israel [*A publication*] (BJA)
NI............... NAMBA [*North American Model Boating Association*] International (EA)
NI............... National Income
NI............... National Insurance [*British*]
NI............... National Interest
NI............... National Intervenors [*Defunct*] (EA)
NI............... Nation Institute (EA)
NI............... Nation of Ishmael [*An association*] (EA)
NI............... Native Infantry [*Indian Armed Forces regiment*]
NI............... Nautical Institute [*British*] (EAIO)
NI............... Naval Instructor [*British*]
NI............... Naval Intelligence
NI............... Need International [*An association*] (EA)
NI............... Negotiable Instrument
NI............... Netherlands Indies [*Later, Republic of Indonesia*]
NI............... Net Income
NI............... Net Interest
NI............... Network Identification [*Broadcasting*] (NTCM)
NI............... Network International (EA)
NI............... Neuraminidase Inhibition [*Medicine*] (DMAA)
NI............... Neurointermediate Lobe [*Of the pituitary*]
NI............... Neurological Impairment
NI............... Neurological Institute
NI............... Neurologically Intact [*Medicine*]
NI............... Neutralization Index [*Medicine*] (DMAA)
NI............... Neutraminidase Inhibition (PDAA)
NI............... New Impression [*Publishing*]
NI............... New Internationalist [*Australia A publication*]
NI............... New Ireland
NI............... New Issue [*Publishing*]
NI............... News International [*An association*] (EA)
NI............... Niagara Institute (EA)
NI............... Nicaragua [*ANSI two-letter standard code*] (CNC)
Ni............... Nickel [*Chemical element*]
ni............... Nickel (VRA)
Ni............... Nicolaus de Tudeschis [*Deceased, 1445*] [*Authority cited in pre-1607 legal work*] (DSA)
Ni............... Nicolaus Furiosus [*Flourished, 12th century*] [*Authority cited in pre-1607 legal work*] (DSA)
NI............... Night (AABC)
NI............... NIPSCO Industries [*NYSE symbol*] (SPSG)
NI............... Nitrogen [*Chemical element*]
NI............... No Imprint (ADA)
NI............... No Information
NI............... No Interaction [*Medicine*]
NI............... Noise Index
N/I............... Noise to Interference Ratio [*Telecommunications*] (TEL)
NI............... No Issue
NI............... Non-Aligned [*Political group*] [*EC*] (ECED)
NI............... Noninductive (DEN)
NI............... Non-Inhibitable Interrupt (MHDB)
NI............... Non-Interlaced (CDE)
NI............... Nonintervention
NI............... Noninvasive Index [*Medicine*]
NI............... Nonviolence International (EA)
NI............... Normal Impurity [*Metals*]
NI............... Normal Inferior
NI............... Northern Indiana Public Service Co. [*NYSE symbol*] (SAG)
NI............... Northern Indiana Railway
NI............... Northern Ireland
NI............... Northern Ireland Law Reports [*A publication*] (DLA)
NI............... North Indiana Public Service Co. [*AMEX symbol*] (SAG)
NI............... North Island [*New Zealand*] (BARN)
NI............... Notice of Information [*Computer science*]
NI............... Not Identified
NI............... Not Illustrated [*Publishing*]
NI............... Not In
NI............... Not Indicated [*Laboratory science*] (DAVI)
NI............... Not Informed
NI............... Not Inoculated
NI............... Not Interested
NI............... Not Isolated
NI............... Not Issued (AAG)
NI............... Nuclear Instrumentation (NRCH)
NI............... Nuclear Island (NRCH)
NI............... Numerical Index (BUR)
NI............... Numismatics International (EA)
NI............... Tompkins County Public Library, Ithaca, NY [*Library symbol Library of Congress*] (LCLS)
NIA............... National Ice Association [*Later, PIA*] (EA)
NIA............... National Iceboat Authority
NIA............... National Impala Association (EA)
NIA............... National Income Accounts
NIA............... National Inholders Association [*Database producer*] (EA)
NIA............... National Institute on Aging [*Bethesda, MD*] [*National Institutes of Health*]
NIA............... National Insulation Association (NTPA)
NIA............... National Insulator Association (EA)
NIA............... National Insurance Association [*Chicago, IL*] (EA)
NIA............... National Intelligence Authority [*1946-1947*]
NIA............... National International Academy
NIA............... National Involvement Association (EA)

NIA............... National Irrigation Administration (NADA)
NIA............... Naval Intelligence Activity (DOMA)
NIA............... Navy Industrial Association [*Later, NSIA*]
NIA............... Neighborhood Improvement Association (BARN)
NIA............... Neighborhoods-in-Action [*An association*] (EA)
NIA............... Nephelometric Immunoassay [*Analytical chemistry*]
NIA............... Nephelometric Inhibition Assay [*Analytical chemistry*] (MAE)
NIA............... Net Internal Area
NIA............... Neuromuscular Integrative Action
NIA............... Newspaper Institute of America (EA)
NIA............... Nickel-Iron Alloy
NIA............... Nitroisatoic Anhydride [*Organic chemistry*]
NIA............... No Information Available
NIA............... No Input Acknowledge [*Computer science*]
NIA............... Norfolk Island [*Australia Seismograph station code, US Geological Survey Closed*] (SEIS)
NIA............... Norfolk Island Airlines [*Australia ICAO designator*] (FAAC)
NIA............... Nutrition Institute of America [*Inactive*] (EA)
NIAA............... National Independent Agents' Association [*Australia*]
NIAA............... National Indian Athletic Association (EA)
NIAA............... National Industrial Advertisers Association [*Later, B/PAA*]
NIAA............... National Institute of Animal Agriculture [*Defunct*] (EA)
NIAA............... Northern Iowa Athletic Association (PSS)
NIAAA............... National Institute on Alcohol Abuse and Alcoholism [*Rockville, MD*] [*Public Health Service*] [*Department of Health and Human Services*]
NIAAA............... National Interscholastic Athletic Administrators Association (EA)
NIAA-DTF............... National Industry Associations Anti-Dumping Task Force [*Australia*]
NIAB............... National Institute of Agricultural Botany (WDAA)
NIAB............... Naval Intelligence Advisory Board (DNAB)
NIABS............... National Institute for Applied Behavioral Science
NIABY............... Not in Anyone's Back Yard (PA)
NIAC............... NASA Industrial Application Center [*University of Southern California*] [*Los Angeles*] [*Information service or system*] (IID)
NIAC............... NASA Industrial Applications Center [*University of Pittsburgh*] [*Pittsburgh, PA*]
NIAC............... National Industry Advisory Committee [*Terminated, 1986*] [*FCC*]
NIAC............... National Information and Analysis Center
NIAC............... National Insulation and Abatement Contractors Association (EA)
NIAC............... National Insurance Advisory Committee [*British*] (DCTA)
NIAC............... Nebraska-Iowa Athletic Conference (PSS)
NIAC............... Northern Ireland Automation Centre [*Queen's University of Belfast*] (CB)
NIAC............... Nuclear Insurance Association of Canada
NIAC............... Nutritional Information and Analysis Center [*Illinois Institute of Technology and Institute of Food Technologists*] (IID)
NIACA............... National Indirect Air Carrier Association [*Defunct*] (EA)
NIACE............... National Institute for the Advancement of Career Education [*Defunct*] (EA)
NIACE............... National Institute of Adult Continuing Education [*British*]
NIACRO............... Northern Ireland Association for the Care and Resettlement of Offenders (DI)
NIACT............... Night Action [*American diplomat's jargon*]
NIAD............... National Institute on Adult Daycare (EA)
NIADA............... National Independent Automobile Dealers Association (EA)
NIADA............... National Institute of American Doll Artists (EA)
NIADDK............... National Institute of Arthritis, Diabetes, and Digestive and Kidney Diseases [*National Institutes of Health*] (EA)
NIAE............... National Institute for Architectural Education (EA)
NIAE............... National Institute of Agricultural Engineering [*Research center British*] (IRC)
NIAF............... National Italian American Foundation (EA)
NIAG............... NATO Industrial Advisory Group (MCD)
NIAG............... Niagara (ROG)
Niag............... Niagara Corp. [*Associated Press*] (SAG)
NIAG............... Niagara Corp. [*NASDAQ symbol*] (SAG)
Niagara U............... Niagara University (GAGS)
NiagCp............... Niagara Corp. [*Associated Press*] (SAG)
NIAGW............... Niagar Corp. Wrrt [*NASDAQ symbol*] (TTSB)
NIAH............... National Indian AIDS Hotline (EA)
NIAID............... National Institute of Allergy and Infectious Diseases [*of National Institutes of Health*] [*Department of Health and Human Services Bethesda, MD*]
NIAJ............... Niagara Junction Railway Co. [*Absorbed into Consolidated Rail Corp.*] [*AAR code*]
NIAL............... National Institute of Arts and Letters [*Later, AAIAL*] (EA)
NIAL............... Network for Informal Adult Learning (AIE)
NIAL............... Not In Active Labor [*Obstetrics*] (DAVI)
NIALSA............... Northwest Indiana Area Library Services Authority [*Library network*]
NIAM............... National Institute of Advertising Management
NiaM............... Niagara Mohawk Power Corp. [*Associated Press*] (SAG)
NIAMDD............... National Institute of Arthritis, Metabolism, and Digestive Diseases [*Formerly, NIAMD*] [*Later, NIADDK*] [*National Institutes of Health*]
NiaMP............... Niagara Mohawk Power Corp. [*Associated Press*] (SAG)
NIAMS............... National Institute of Arthritis and Musculoskeletal and Skin Diseases [*Bethesda, MD*] [*Department of Health and Human Services*] (GRD)
NIAMSD............... National Institute of Arthritis and Musculoskeletal and Skin Diseases [*Department of Health and Human Services*] (GFGA)
NIAMSK............... National Institute of Arthritis and Musculoskeletal and Skin Diseases
NI & C............... Nippon Information and Communication [*Joint venture of IBM Corp. Japan and Nippon Telegraph and Telephone*]
NI & RT............... Numerical Index and Requirement Table (MCD)
NIANSW............... Nursery Industry Association of New South Wales [*Australia*]
NIAP............... National Income and Products [*Economics*]

NIAP	Noninverting Amplifier Pair
NIAR	National Institute of Agrobiological Resources [*Japan*]
NIAR	National Institute of Atmospheric Research
NIAR	Neutron-Induced Autoradiography
NIAS	National Institute for Advanced Studies (EA)
NIAS	National Institute of Aeronautical Sciences
NIAS	National Institute of Airworthiness Surveyors [*Australia*]
NIASA	National Insurance Actuarial and Statistical Association [*Later, ISO*]
NIASE	National Institute for Automotive Service Excellence
NIAT	Non-Indexable Address Tag (SAA)
NIAT	Nursery Industry Association of Tasmania [*Australia*]
NIAWA	Nursery Industry Association of Western Australia [*Australia*]
NIAWR	National Institute on Aging, Work, and Retirement [*Washington, DC*] (EA)
NIB	National Identification Bureau [*British*]
NIB	National Industries for the Blind (EA)
NIB	National Information Bureau [*Information service or system*] (EA)
NIB	National Institute for the Blind (EA)
NIB	National Investment Bank [*Ghana*] (EY)
NIB	Navigation Information Bulletin
NIB	Negative Impedance Booster [*Electronics*]
NIB	Negative Ion Beam
NIB	Negative Ion Blemish
NIB	Network Interface Board
NIB	New Iberia Bancorp [*AMEX symbol*] (TTSB)
NIB	New Iberia Bancorp, Inc. [*AMEX symbol*] (SAG)
NIB	Nigeria International Bank Ltd.
NIB	Node Initialization Block [*Computer science*] (IBMDP)
NIB	Noninterference Basis
NIB	Nordic Investment Bank (GNE)
NIB	Not to Interface Base
NIBA	National Industrial Belting Association (EA)
NIBA	National Insurance Buyers Association
NIBA	Nebraska Independent Bankers Association (TBD)
NIBAA	National Insurance Brokers' Association of Australia
NIBC	Northern Ireland Base Command [*World War II*]
NIBCA	National Intercollegiate Boxing Coaches Association (EA)
NIberia	New Iberia Bancorp, Inc. [*Associated Press*] (SAG)
NIberiaB	New Iberia Bancorp [*Associated Press*] (SAG)
NIBESA	National Independent Bank Equipment and Systems Association [*Park Ridge, IL*] (EA)
NIBGE	National Institute of Biotechnology and Genetic Engineering [*Pakistan*]
NIBID	National Investment Bank for Industrial Development [*Greece*]
NIBJL	National Information Bureau for Jewish Life (EA)
NIBL	National Industrial Basic Language (MHDB)
NIBL	National Industrial Basketball League (EA)
NIBM	National Institute for Burn Medicine (EA)
NIBMAR	No Independence before Majority African Rule [*British policy in regard to Rhodesia*]
NIBOR	New York Interbank Official Rate
NIBP	Noninvasive Blood Pressure [*Medicine*] (DMAA)
NIBRA	National Independent Bicycle Rep Association [*Defunct*] (EA)
NIBS	National Institute of Building Sciences (EA)
NIBS	National Interim Bankruptcy System (AAGC)
NIBS	Neural, Informational, and Behavioral Science
NIBS	Neutral Industry Booking System (AAGC)
NIBS	Nippon Institute of Biological Sciences (DAVI)
NIBS	Nuffield Interactive Book System [*British*] (TELE)
NIBSC	National Institute for Biological Standards and Control [*British*]
NIBTN	Nitroisobutametriol Trinitrate [*An explosive*]
NIC	Cornell University, Ithaca, NY [*Library symbol Library of Congress*] (LCLS)
NIC	Naphthylisocyanate [*Organic chemistry*]
NIC	National Impeachment Coalition [*Defunct*] (EA)
NIC	National Incomes Commission [*Nickname: Nicky*] [*British*]
NIC	National Indications Center [*Disbanded*] [*DoD*]
NIC	National Industrial Council (EA)
NIC	National Informatics Center [*India*] [*Information service or system*]
NIC	National Information Clearinghouse [*for Infants with Disabilities and Life-Threatening Conditions*] (PAZ)
NIC	National Information Clearinghouse for Infants with Disabilities and Life-Threatening Conditions
NIC	National Institute of Corrections [*Department of Justice*]
NIC	National Institute of Creativity [*Defunct*] (EA)
NIC	National Institute of Credit [*New York, NY*] (EA)
NIC	National Insurance Certificate [*British*]
NIC	National Insurance Contribution [*British*] (ECON)
NIC	National Insurance Contributions [*British*]
NIC	National Integrated Services Digital Network Council
NIC	National Intelligence Committee
NIC	National Interagency Council on Smoking and Health [*New York, NY*]
NIC	National Interfraternity Conference (EA)
NIC	National Interrogation Center [*Military*]
NIC	National Interstate Council of State Boards of Cosmetology (EA)
NIC	National Inventors Council [*Terminated, 1974*] [*National Institute of Standards and Technology*]
NIC	Natural Image Computer (PDAA)
NIC	Nauru Island Council [*Australia*]
NIC	Naval Intelligence Code [*World War II British*]
NIC	Naval Intelligence Command
NIC	Navigation Information Center
NIC	Navy Information Center
NIC	Nearly Instantaneous Compounding (MCD)
NIC	Neck Injury Criteria [*Automotive safety testing*]
NIC	Negative Immittance Converter [*Electronics*]
NIC	Negative Impedance Converter [*Electronics*]
NIC	Negative Ion Chamber
NIC	Neighborhood Info Centers Project (EA)
NIC	Neonatal Intensive Care
NIC	Netherlands Information Combine [*Delft*] [*Information service or system*] (IID)
NIC	Net Interest Cost [*Investment term*]
NIC	Network Information Center [*Advanced Research Projects Agency*] [*DoD*]
NIC	Network Interface Card [*Computer science*]
NIC	Network Interface Control
NIC	Neurogenic Intermittent Claudication [*Medicine*] (DMAA)
NIC	New Community Instrument for Borrowing & Lending (WDAA)
NIC	New Initial Commissions [*Business term*]
NIC	New International Commentary on the New Testament [*A publication*] (BJA)
NIC	Newly Industrializing Country (ECON)
NIC	Newspaper Indexing Center [*Flint, MI*]
NIC	Newsprint Information Committee [*Defunct*] (EA)
Nic	Nicander [*Second century BC*] [*Classical studies*] (OCD)
NIC	Nicaragua [*ANSI three-letter standard code*] (CNC)
Nic	Nicaragua (VRA)
NIC	Nicaraguan Information Center (EA)
NIC	Nickling Resources, Inc. [*Vancouver Stock Exchange symbol*]
Nic	Nicolaus de Tudeschis [*Deceased, 1445*] [*Authority cited in pre-1607 legal work*] (DSA)
NIC	Nicosia [*Cyprus*] [*Airport symbol*] (AD)
Nic	Nicotinyl Alcohol [*Biochemistry*] (MAE)
nic	Niger-Congo [*MARC language code Library of Congress*] (LCCP)
NIC	Nineteen-Hundred Indexing and Cataloging (DIT)
NIC	NIPSCO Capital Markets [*NYSE symbol*] (SAG)
NIC	NIPSCO Cap Mkt 7.75% Debt Sec [*NYSE symbol*] (TTSB)
NIC	Noise Isolation Class (PDAA)
NIC	Nominal Index Card (WDAA)
NIC	Non-Intel [*Corp.*]-Compatible Chips [*Computer science*]
NICA	Non-Intervention in Chile [*An association*] (EA)
NIC	Noninvasive Carotid [*Study*] [*Cardiology*] (DAVI)
NIC	Northern Illinois Commuter [*ICAO designator*] (FAAC)
NIC	Northern Intercollegiate Conference (PSS)
NIC	Not in Contact [*Electronics*] (DEN)
NIC	Not in Contract [*Technical drawings*]
NIC	Nudist Information Center [*Defunct*] (EA)
NICA	National Ice Carving Association (EA)
NICA	National Indian Counselors Association (EA)
NICA	National Institute of Conveyancing Agents [*British*] (DBA)
NICA	National Insulation Contractors Association [*Later, NIAC*] (EA)
NICA	National Interfaith Coalition on Aging (EA)
NICA	Netherlands Indies Civil Affairs Organization [*World War II*]
NICA	Nicaragua Interfaith Committee for Action (EA)
NICA	Nicaraguense de Aviacion SA [*Nicaragua*] [*ICAO designator*] (FAAC)
NICAC	Nebraska Intercollegiate Athletic Conference (PSS)
NiCad	Nickel-Cadmium
NICAD	Nickel Cadmium (NG)
Nic Adult Bast	Nicolas' Adulterine Bastardy [*1836*] [*A publication*] (DLA)
NICAM	Near-Instantaneous Companded Audio Multiplex (WDAA)
NICAM	Near-Instantaneous Companding Audio Multiplex (WDAA)
NICAM	Near Instantaneously Companded Audio Multiplex
Nic & Fl Reg	Nicoll and Flaxman on Registration [*A publication*] (DLA)
NICAP	National Investigations Committee on Aerial Phenomena
NICAP	Nuveen Insured California Premium Income Municipal [*Associated Press*] (SAG)
NICAP2	Nuveen Insured California Premium Income Municipal Fund 2 [*Associated Press*] (SAG)
NICAR	Nicaragua
NICARD	Navy/Industry Cooperative Research and Development Program (MCD)
NICAS	Nuveen Insured California Select Tax Free [*Associated Press*] (SAG)
NICATELSAT	Nicaraguan Telecommunication by Satellite [*Commercial firm*]
NICB	National Industrial Conference Board [*Later, TCB*] (EA)
NICB	National Insurance Crime Bureau (NTPA)
Nic Bel	Nicolaus Bellonus [*Flourished, 1542-47*] [*Authority cited in pre-1607 legal work*] (DSA)
Nic Boe	Nicolaus Boerius [*Authority cited in pre-1607 legal work*] (DSA)
NICC	National Industrial Conservation Conference
NICC	National Inventory Control Center (MCD)
NICC	Nationalized Industries Computer Committee (NITA)
NICC	Neonatal Intensive Care Center (DAVI)
NICC	Nevis Island Cultural Center of the US (EA)
NICCYH	National Information Center for Children and Youth with Handicaps (EA)
NICD	National Information Center on Deafness (EA)
NICD	National Institute on Crime and Delinquency [*Later, NFCJ*] (EA)
NICD	Nickel Cadmium (MCD)
Ni-Cd	Nickel-Cadmium
NICDA	National Imported Car Dealers Association (EA)
NICE	National Information Conference and Exposition [*Associated Information Managers*]
NICE	National Institute for Computers in Engineering [*Defunct*] (EA)
NICE	National Institute for Consumer Education
NICE	National Institute of Ceramic Engineers (EA)
NICE	Nationally-Integrated Caring Employees [*Union*] [*British*] (DI)
NICE	National Society of Fund Raisers Institute of Continuing Education [*Former name of the National Society of Fund Raising Executives Foundation*] (NFD)

NICE............. Network Information and Control Exchange [*Computer science*] (CIST)
NICE............. Noninvasive Carotid Examination [*Cardiology*] (DAVI)
NICE............. Noninvasive Cerebrovascular Examination [*Cardiology*] (DAVI)
NICE............. Nonlinear, Iterative Constrained Estimator (MCD)
NICE............. Nonprofit International Consortium for Eiffel (EA)
NICE............. Normal Input-Output Control Executive [*Computer science*]
NICE............. Northern Indiana Consortium for Education [*Library network*]
NICE³ .... National Industrial Competitiveness through Efficiency: Energy, Environment, andEconomics [*Environmental Protection Agency*]
NICEC .... National Institute for Careers Education and Counselling [*Research center British*] (IRC)
NICEDD........ National Institute for Continuing Education in Developmental Disabilities (EA)
NICEIC .... National Inspection Council for Electrical Installation Contracting [*British*]
NICEL........... National Institute for Citizen Education in the Law (EA)
Nic Elec....... Nicolson's Elections in Scotland [*A publication*] (DLA)
NICEM .... National Information Center for Educational Materials (NITA)
NICEM .... National Information Center for Educational Media [*Later, AV Online*] (EA)
NICER.......... Northern Ireland Council for Educational Research (AIE)
NICET.......... National Institute for Certification in Engineering Technologies (EA)
NICEY......... NICE-Systems ADR [*NASDAQ symbol*] (TTSB)
NICF........... National Institute of Carpet Fitters [*British*] (DBA)
NICG .... National Interagency Coordination Group [*National Atmospheric Electricity Hazards Program*] (MCD)
NICH .... National Information Center for the Handicapped (EA)
NICH .... Nitches, Inc. [*NASDAQ symbol*] (SAG)
NICH .... Non-Intervention in Chile [*An association*] (EA)
Nic Ha C...... Nicholl, Hare, and Carrow's Railway and Canal Cases [*1835-55*] [*A publication*] (DLA)
Nich Adult Bast... Nicholas on Adulterine Bastardy [*A publication*] (DLA)
Nic H & C..... Nicholl, Hare, and Carrow's Railway and Canal Cases [*1835-55*] [*A publication*] (ILCA)
NICHCY........ National Information Center for Children and Youth with Disabilities (PAZ)
NICHD.......... National Institute of Child Health and Human Development [*Bethesda, MD*] [*National Institutes of Health*] (GRD)
Nich H & C... Nicholl, Hare, and Carrow's Railway and Canal Cases [*1835-55*] [*A publication*] (DLA)
NICHHD .... National Institute of Child Health and Human Development [*National Institutes of Health*]
Nicholl H & C... Nicholl, Hare, and Carrow [*1835-55*] [*A publication*] (DLA)
Nichols-Cahill... Nichols-Cahill's Annotated New York Civil Practice Acts [*A publication*] (DLA)
Nicholson .... Nicholson's Manuscript Decisions, Scotch Session Cases [*A publication*] (DLA)
NICHROME... Nickel Chromium [*Alloy*] [*Trade name*]
NichRs......... Nichols Research Corp. [*Associated Press*] (SAG)
NICI .... National Insulation Certification Institute (EA)
NICI .... National Interagency Counterdrug Institute [*Camp San Luis Obispo, CA*] (DOMA)
NICI .... Negative Ion Chemical Ionization [*Spectrometry*]
NICIMS......... Negative Ion Chemical Ionization Mass Spectroscopy
NICIS .... Nikon Intracellular Calcium Ion System
NICJ........... National Institute for Consumer Justice
NICK .... Name Information Correlation Key
NICK .... Nature's Initial Cosmic Kickstart
NICK .... Nickelodeon [*Cable television channel*]
nick........... Nickname
NICLC .... National Institute on Community-Based Long-Term Care (EA)
NICLF......... Ni-Cal Developments Ltd. (MHDW)
NICLOG....... National Information Center for Local Government Records [*Canada*]
NICM .... National Institute for Campus Ministries (EA)
NICM .... National Institute of Comparative Medicine (DAVI)
NICMA .... National Ice Cream Mix Association (EA)
NICMA .... National Industrial Cafeteria Managers Association [*Later, SFM*] (EA)
NICMC .... National Institute of Certified Moving Consultants (NTPA)
NICMOS...... Near-Infrared Camera and Multiobject Spectrograph [*Astronomy*]
NICN .... Navy Item Control Number (MCD)
NICNT .... New International Commentary on the New Testament [*A publication*] (BJA)
NICO .... National Insurance Consumer Organization (EA)
NICO .... Navy Indochina Clearing Office (DNAB)
NICO .... Navy Inventory Control Office
Nico............ Nicolaus de Tudeschis [*Deceased, 1445*] [*Authority cited in pre-1607 legal work*] (DSA)
NICOA......... National Independent Coal Operators Association [*Defunct*] (EA)
NICOA......... National Indian Council on Aging (EA)
Nico Alex..... Nicolaus de Alexandria [*Authority cited in pre-1607 legal work*] (DSA)
NICOL......... National Insurance Corp. of Liberia (EY)
NICOL......... New Integrated Computer Language
NICOL......... Nineteen-Hundred Commercial Language
Nicolas .... Proceedings and Ordinances of the Privy Council, Edited by Sir Harry Nicolas [*A publication*] (DLA)
Nicollet........ Nicollet Process Engineering, Inc. [*Associated Press*] (SAG)
NICOP......... Navy Industry Cooperation Plan
NICOP......... Nickel Copper
NICOR......... NICOR, Inc. [*Formerly, Northern Illinois Gas Co.*] [*Associated Press*] (SAG)
NICORD ...... Navy/Industry Cooperative Research and Development Program
NICOS........ Newfoundland Institute for Cold Ocean Science [*Memorial University of Newfoundland*] [*Canada Research center*] (RCD)
NICOV.......... National Information Center on Volunteerism [*Later, NVC*] (EA)

NICP .... National Inventory Control Point [*Military*]
NICP .... NOAA [*National Oceanic and Atmospheric Administration*] Interoceanic Canal Project (NOAA)
NICP .... Nuclear Incident Control Plan
Nic R .... Nicolaus Rufulus [*Flourished, 13th century*] [*Authority cited in pre-1607 legal work*] (DSA)
NICRA........ National Ice Cream Retailers Association [*Later, NICYRA*] (EA)
NICRA........ Northern Ireland Civil Rights Association
NICRAD....... Navy/Industry Cooperative Research and Development
NICRISP....... Navy Integrated Comprehensible Repairable Item Scheduling Program
NICRO .... National Institute for Crime Prevention and Rehabilitation of Offenders
NICS .... NAS Interfacility Communications System [*FAA*] (TAG)
NICS .... National Airspace System Interfacility Communications System (FAAC)
NICS .... National Instant Check System
NICS .... National Institute for Chemical Studies (EA)
NICS .... National Insurance Contributions System [*Department of Health and Social Security*] [*British*]
NICS .... NATO Integrated Communications System (NATG)
NICS .... Network Integrity Control System
NICS .... Newly Industrialized Countries (DFIT)
NICS .... Nissan's Induction Control System [*Automotive engineering*]
NICSA .... National Investment Company Service Association (NTPA)
NICSBC ...... National Interstate Council of State Boards of Cosmetology (NTPA)
NICSE .... National Institute for Child Support Enforcement [*Commercial firm*] (EA)
NICSEM ...... National Information Center for Special Education Materials [*University of Southern California*] [*Los Angeles, CA*]
NICSEM/NIMIS... National Information Center for Special Education Material/ National Instructional Material Information System (EDAC)
NICSH........ National Interagency Council on Smoking and Health [*Defunct*] (EA)
Nic Sic Do ... Nicolaus (Siculus Doctor) de Tudeschis [*Deceased, 1445*] [*Authority cited in pre-1607 legal work*] (DSA)
NICSMA ...... NATO Integrated Communications System Management Agency (NATG)
NICSO .... NATO Integrated Communications System Organization [*Brussels, Belgium*] (NATG)
NICSX .... Nicholas Fund [*Mutual fund ticker symbol*] (SG)
NIC-TRANS... Naval Intelligence Command - Translation Division
NICU .... Neonatal [*or Newborn*] Intensive Care Unit
NICU .... Neurological Intensive Care Unit [*Medicine*]
NICU .... Neurosurgical Intensive Care Unit [*Medicine*] (DMAA)
NICU .... Newborn Intensive Care Unit [*Medicine*] (DB)
NICU .... Nonimmunologic Contact Urticaria [*Medicine*] (DMAA)
NICUFO .... National Investigations Committee on Unidentified Flying Objects (EA)
NICWM .... National Information Center on Women and the Military [*Later, WMP*] (EA)
NICYRA........ National Ice Cream and Yogurt Retailers Association (EA)
NID .... Inyokern, CA [*Location identifier FAA*] (FAAL)
NID .... National Institute for the Deaf (WDAA)
NID .... National Institute of Drycleaning [*Later, IFI*] (EA)
NID .... National Institute of Dyslexia [*Defunct*] (EA)
NID .... National Intelligence Daily [*CIA*] [*A publication*] (MUSM)
NID .... Naval Intelligence Database (DOMA)
NID .... Naval Intelligence Division [*British*]
NID .... Negligible Individual Dose [*Environmental Protection Agency*]
NID .... Network In-Dial [*Automatic Voice Network*] (CET)
NID .... Network Interface Device [*Telecommunications*]
NID .... New Interactive Display [*NEC*] [*Computer science*] (PCM)
NID .... New International Dictionary [*Webster's*] [*A publication*]
Nid .... Niddah (BJA)
NID .... Nonequilibrium Ionospheric Disturbance [*Geophysics*]
NID .... Nonillusion Direction [*Ophthalmology*]
NID .... Noninsulin-Dependent [*Diabetes*] [*Endocrinology*] (DAVI)
NID .... Non-Internal Development [*DoD*]
NID .... Northern Ireland District
NID .... Nuclear Instruments and Detectors [*IEEE*] (MCD)
NIDA .... 99th Infantry Division Association (EA)
NIDA .... National Independent Dairy-Food Association (EA)
NIDA .... National Industrial Distributors Association [*Philadelphia, PA*] (EA)
NIDA .... National Institute on Drug Abuse [*Department of Health and Human Services*] [*Rockville, MD*]
NIDA .... National Insurance Development Act of 1975
NIDA .... Northeastern Industrial Developers Association
NIDA .... Numerically Integrated Differential Analyzer [*Computer science*]
NIDA Res Mono... National Institute on Drug Abuse Research Monographs (MEC)
NIDC .... National Insurance Development Corp. [*Government-sponsored organization*]
NIDC .... Newly Industrialized Developing Country
NIDCC.......... National Internal Defense Coordination Center [*Army*] (AABC)
NIDCD.......... National Institute on Deafness and Other Communication Disorders [*National Institutes of Health*] (EGAO)
NIDD .... Non-Insulin-Dependent Diabetes [*Medicine*]
NIDDK........ National Institute of Diabetes and Digestive and Kidney Diseases [*Public Health Service*] [*Also, an information service or system*] (IID)
NIDDKD ...... National Institute of Diabetes and Digestive and Kidney Diseases [*Department of Health and Human Services*] (GFGA)
NIDDM........ Non-Insulin-Dependent Diabetes Mellitus [*Medicine*]
NIDDY......... Non-Insulin-Dependent Diabetes in the Young [*Medicine*] (DMAA)
NiDI .... Nickel Development Institute (EAIO)
NIDL .... Network Interface Definition Language [*Computer science*]

NIDLR:........ Office of the Director of Law Reform, Northern Ireland (DLA)
NIDM .... National Institute for Disaster Mobilization (EA)
NIDM .... Noninsulin-Dependent Diabetes Mellitus [*Endocrinology*] (DAVI)
NIDN .... Navy Intelligence Data Network (MCD)
NIDOC......... National Information and Documentation Center
NIDOCD .... National Institute on Deafness and Other Communication Disorders [*NIH*]
NIDR .... National Institute for Dispute Resolution (EA)
NIDR .... National Institute of Dental Research [*Public Health Service*] [*Bethesda, MD*]
NIDR .... Networked Information Discovery and Retrieval (TELE)
NIDRR .... National Institute on Disability and Rehabilitation Research [*Washington, DC Department of Education*] (GRD)
NIDS .... National Institute of Diaper Services [*Defunct*]
NIDS .... National Inventory of Documentary Sources [*British*]
NIDS .... National Investor Data Service (EA)
NIDS .... Navigation Instrument Development Unit
NIDS .... Network Interface Data System [*NASA*]
NIDS .... Nonionic Detergent Soluble (DMAA)
NIDS .... Nuclear Integrated Data System
NIE............. NASA Interface Equipment (MCD)
NIE............. National Index of Ecosystems [*Australia*]
NIE............. National Institute for the Environment [*Proposed government agency*]
NIE............. National Institute of Education [*Department of Education*] [*Washington, DC*]
NIE............. National Institute of Education, Washington, DC [*OCLC symbol*] (OCLC)
NIE............. National Intelligence Estimate
NIE............. Negative Ion Erosion
NIE............. Netherlands Institute of Ecology
NIE............. Neutron Ionization Effect
NIE............. Newly-Industrialized Economy
NIE............. Newspaper in Education Program
NIE............. Niedzica [*Poland*] [*Seismograph station code, US Geological Survey*] (SEIS)
NIE............. Not Included Elsewhere
NIEA.......... National Indian Education Association (EA)
NIEAC .... National Indian Education Advisory Committee [*Terminated, 1974*] [*Department of the Interior*] (EGAO)
NIECC .... National Industrial Energy Conservation Council (MCD)
NIEF........... National Ironfounding Employers Association [*British*] (BI)
NIEHS .... National Institute of Environmental Health Sciences [*Research Triangle Pa rk, NC*] [*National Institutes of Health*]
NIEHS .... National Institute of Environmental Health Service [*Marine science*] (OSRA)
NIEI........... National Indoor Environmental Institute (EPA)
NIEI........... National Institute of Electromedical Information (EA)
niel........... Niello (VRA)
NIEM.......... National Industrial Engineering Mission (AABC)
Nient Cul ..... Nient Culpable [*Not Guilty*] [*Latin Legal term*] (DLA)
NIEO.......... New International Economic Order
NIEP.......... National Independent Energy Producers (NTPA)
NIER.......... National Industrial Equipment Reserve [*of DMS*]
NIER.......... National Institute for Educational Research (NITA)
NIERC .... Northern Ireland Economic Research Centre
NIES........... National Intelligence Estimates [*Summaries of foreign policy information and advice prepared for the president*] [*Known informally as "knees"*]
NIESR .... National Institute of Economic and Social Research [*British*]
NIETB......... National Imagery Exploitation Target Base (MCD)
NIETS......... National Imagery Exploitation Tasking Study
NIETU .... National Independent Enginemen's Trade Union [*British*]
NIEU .... Negro Industrial and Economic Union
NIF............ National Ichthyosis Foundation (EA)
NIF............ National Ignition Facility [*Lawrence Livermore National Laboratory*] [*Department of Energy*] (PS)
NIF............ National Income Forecasting (ADA)
NIF............ National Innovation Fund [*South Africa*]
NIF............ National Institute for the Family (EA)
NIF............ National Interfraternity Foundation (EA)
NIF............ National Inventors Foundation (EA)
NIF............ National Investment Fund [*Poland*] [*Finance*]
NIF............ National Iranian Front [*Political party*]
NIF............ National Islamic Front [*Sudan*] [*Political party*]
NIF............ National Issues Forums (EA)
NIF............ Navy Industrial Fund
NIF............ Negative Inspiratory Force [*Medicine*]
NIF............ Network Information Files [*Burroughs Corp.*]
NIF............ Neutrophil Immobilizing Factor (DMAA)
NIF............ Neutrophil Migration Inhibition Factor
NIF............ New Israel Fund (EA)
NIF............ Nickel-Iron Film
NIF............ Nifedipine [*Pharmacology*]
nif............ Nitrogen-Fixing [*Biology*] (BARN)
NIF............ Noise Improvement Factor (IEEE)
NIF............ Nonintestinal Fibroblast [*Medicine*] (DMAA)
NIF............ Note-Issuance Facility [*Banking*]
NIF............ Not Industrially Funded [*Military*]
NIF............ Not in File
NIF............ Nuclear Information File (AFM)
NIF............ Nuveen Prem Insured Muni Inc. [*NYSE symbol*] (TTSB)
NIFA.......... Nuveen Premium Insured Municipal Income [*NYSE symbol*] (SPSG)
NIFA.......... National Intercollegiate Flying Association (EA)
NIFAC........ Night Forward Air Controller [*Aircraft*]
NIFADCS...... National Institute of Furnace and Air Duct Cleaning Specialists (EA)

NIFAST .... National Industrial Fire and Safety Centre (ACII)
NIFB........... National Institute of Farm Brokers [*Later, NIFLB*] (EA)
NIFC........... National Interagency Firefighting Center
NIFDA......... National Independent Flag Dealers Association (NTPA)
NIFDA......... National Institutional Food Distributor Associates (EA)
NIFE........... Nomenclature-in-Federal Employment
NIFEGS .... Northern Ireland Further Education Guidance Service (AIE)
NIFER .... National Institute for Full Employment Research [*Department of Labor*] (OICC)
NIFES......... National Industrial Fuel Efficiency Service [*British*]
NIFF........... Nordiska Ickekommersielles Fonogramproducenters Forening [*Nordic Association of Non-Commercial Phonogram Producers - NANPP*] (EAIO)
NIFFTE........ Noncooperative Identification Friend or Foe Technology Evaluation (RDA)
NIFI........... National Institute for the Foodservice Industry (EA)
NIFL........... Finger Lakes Library System, Ithaca, NY [*Library symbol Library of Congress*] (LCLS)
NIFLB......... National Institute of Farm and Land Brokers [*Later, FLI*] (EA)
NIFLP......... Nuveen Insured Florida Premium Income Municipal Fund [*Associated Press*] (SAG)
NIFM.......... Northwest Independent Forest Manufacturers (WPI)
NIFMS .... NAVAIR [*Naval Air Systems Command*] Industrial Finance Management System (MCD)
NIFO .... Next In, First Out [*Queuing technique*]
NIFOB .... Non-Injurious Free-on-Board
NIFP........... National Institute for Federal Procurement (AAGC)
NIFP........... National Institute of Fresh Produce [*British*] (DBA)
NIFRS......... Navy Industrial Fund-Reporting System (MCD)
NIFS........... National Institute for Farm Safety (EA)
NIFS........... NT [*New Technology*] File System [*Microsoft Corp.*]
NIFTE......... Neon Indicator Functional Test Equipment
NIFTI.......... Near-Isotropic Flux Turbulence Instrument [*Oceanography*]
NIFTP......... Network Independent File Transfer Program (HGAA)
NIFTP......... Network Independent File Transfer Protocol (PDAA)
NIFTS......... Naval Integrated Flight Training System (MCD)
NI/FWM....... New, Incorporated/Fourth World Movement (EA)
NIG........... Aero Contractors Company of Nigeria Ltd. [*ICAO designator*] (FAAC)
NIG........... National Institute of Genetics [*Japan*]
NIG........... Nationwide Investigations Group [*British*]
NIG........... Naval Inspector General
NIG........... Negative Ion Generator (ADA)
NIG........... Niger [*Black*] [*Pharmacy*]
NIG........... Nigeria
NIG........... Nikunau [*Kiribati*] [*Airport symbol*] (OAG)
NIG........... Nonimmunoglobulin [*Medicine*] (DB)
NIG........... Nude Ionization Gauge
NIGA.......... National Indian Gaming Association (NTPA)
NIGA.......... Neutron-Induced Gamma Activity (AABC)
NIGA.......... Nuclear-Induced Ground Radioactivity (NATG)
NIG&P .... Nanjing Institute of Geology and Paleontology [*China*]
Nig Ann Int'l L... Nigerian Annual of International Law [*A publication*] (DLA)
Nig Bar J..... Nigerian Bar Journal [*A publication*] (DLA)
Nig BJ .... Nigerian Bar Journal [*A publication*] (DLA)
NIGCS........ National Imperial Glass Collectors Society (EA)
NIGDA........ National Industrial Glove Distributors Association (EA)
NIGEC .... National Institute for Global Environmental Change [*University of Southern California and Department of Energy*]
Nigeria Bar J... Nigerian Bar Journal. Annual Journal of the Nigeria Bar Association [*Lagos, Nigeria*] [*A publication*] (DLA)
Nigeria LR... Nigeria Law Reports [*A publication*] (DLA)
Nigerian Ann Int'l L... Nigerian Annual of International Law [*A publication*] (DLA)
Nigerian LJ... Nigerian Law Journal [*A publication*] (DLA)
NIGHTCAP ... Night Combat Air Patrol [*Military*] (NVT)
Nig Lawy Q.. Nigeria Lawyer's Quarterly [*A publication*] (DLA)
Nig LJ........ Nigerian Law Journal [*A publication*] (DLA)
Nig LQ .... Nigeria Lawyer's Quarterly [*A publication*] (ILCA)
Nig LQR...... Nigerian Law Quarterly Review [*A publication*] (DLA)
Nig LR .... Nigeria Law Reports [*A publication*] (DLA)
NIGMS........ National Institute of General Medical Sciences [*National Institutes of Health*] [*Bethesda, MD*]
NIGP .... Nanjing Institute of Geology and Paleontology [*China*]
NIGP .... National Institute of Governmental Purchasing (EA)
Nigr .... Nigeria (VRA)
Nigr .... Nigrinus [*of Lucian*] [*Classical studies*] (OCD)
NIGS.......... Non-Inertial Guidance Set (SAA)
NIH............ Hoffmann-La Roche, Inc. [*Research code symbol*]
NIH............ National Institute for the Humanities [*Yale University*] [*National Endowment for the Humanities*]
NIH............ National Institute of Hardware [*British*] (BI)
NIH............ National Institute of Housecraft [*British*] (BI)
NIH............ National Institute on the Holocaust [*Later, AFIP*] (EA)
NIH............ National Institutes of Health [*Public Health Service*] [*Bethesda, MD*]
NIH............ New Inn Hall [*British*] (ROG)
NIH............ Nonimmune Hydrops [*Medicine*]
NIH............ North Irish Horse [*Military unit*] [*British*]
NIH............ Not Invented Here (NITA)
NIH............ Not Invented Here Syndrome [*Business Management*]
NIHB.......... National Indian Health Board (EA)
NIHC.......... Northern Ireland House of Commons
NIHCA........ Northern Ireland Hotels and Caterers Association (ODBW)
NIHD.......... Noise-Induced Hearing Damage [*Medicine*] (MEDA)
NIHE.......... National Institute for Higher Education [*Defunct*] (ACII)
NIHERST...... National Institute of Higher Education (Research, Science, and Technology) [*Spain*]

NIHF .... Nonimmune Hydrops Fetalis [*Medicine*]
NIHGR .... National Institute for Human Genome Research [*National Institutes of Health*] (BARN)
NIHHD .... National Institute of Health and Human Development
NIHi .... DeWitt Historical Society of Tompkins County, Ithaca, NY [*Library symbol Library of Congress*] (LCLS)
NIHL .... Noise-Induced Hearing Loss
NIHOE .... Nitrogen, Helium, and Oxygen Experiment (DNAB)
NIHR .... National Institute of Handicapped Research [*Department of Health and Human Services*] [*Later, NIDRR*] [*Washington, DC*]
NIHS .... National Institute of Hypertension Studies - Institute of Hypertension School ofResearch (EA)
NIHS .... NAVEUR Intelligence Highlights Summary (MCD)
NIHTA .... Northern Ireland Head Teachers' Association
NIHYSOB ..... Now I Have You, Son of a Bitch [*Term coined by Kenneth Blanchard, author of "The One-Minute Manager"*]
NII .... National Industries, Inc. (EFIS)
NII .... National Information Infrastructure [*Proposed 1992*] [*Telecommunications*]
NII .... National Intergroup (EFIS)
NII .... NATO Item Identification (NATG)
NII .... Negative Immittance Inverter (PDAA)
NII .... Neruonal Intranuclear Inclusion [*Neurophysiology*]
NII .... Net Interest Income (TDOB)
NII .... Niigata [*Japan*] [*Seismograph station code, US Geological Survey*] (SEIS)
NII .... Nuclear Installations Inspectorate [*British*]
NIIA .... Nonisotropic Immunoassay
NIIC .... Ithaca College, Ithaca, NY [*Library symbol Library of Congress*] (LCLS)
NIIC .... National Injury Information Clearinghouse [*Consumer Product Safety Commission*]
NIIC .... NORAD Intelligence Indications Center (MCD)
NIIC .... Northern Illinois Intercollegiate Conference (PSS)
NIICP .... No Increase in Contract Price
NIICU .... National Institute of Independent Colleges and Universities (EA)
NIIG .... NATO Item Identification Guide (NATG)
NIIN .... National Item Identification Number (MCD)
NII Nor........ NII Norsat International, Inc. [*Associated Press*] (SAG)
NIIO .... New International Information Order (NITA)
NIIP .... National Institute of Industrial Psychology (PDAA)
NIIP .... Net International Investment Position
NIIRS .... National Imagery Interpretation Rating Scale (MCD)
NIIS .... National Institute of Infant Services [*Later, NADS*]
NIIS .... New Image Industries [*NASDAQ symbol*] (TTSB)
NIIS .... New Image Industries, Inc. [*NASDAQ symbol*] (NQ)
NIIS .... New Item Introductory Schedule (AAGC)
NIIS .... Niagara Institute for International Studies [*Canada*]
NIIS .... Nuclear Issues Information Service (IID)
NIIT .... National Information Infrastructure Testbed [*Telecommunications*] (PCM)
NIIU .... Neozyme Corp. [*NASDAQ symbol*] (SAG)
NIJ .... National Institute of Justice (USGC)
NIJ .... New Irish Jurist [*A publication*] (DLA)
NIJD .... National Institute of Judicial Dynamics [*Defunct*] (EA)
NIJH .... National Institute for Jewish Hospice (EA)
NIJJDP .... National Institute for Juvenile Justice and Delinquency Prevention
NIJR .... New Irish Jurist [*A publication*] (DLA)
NIK .... Boston, MA [*Location identifier FAA*] (FAAL)
NIK .... Nickel [*Watchmaking*] (ROG)
NIK .... Nickel Rim Mines Ltd. [*Toronto Stock Exchange symbol*]
NIK .... Nikolski [*Alaska*] [*Seismograph station code, US Geological Survey Closed*] (SEIS)
nik .... Northern Ireland [*MARC country of publication code Library of Congress*] (LCCP)
NIK .... Novye Inostrannyye Knigi [*New Foreign Books*] [*A publication*]
NIKA .... Northern Ireland Korfball Association (EAIO)
NikeB .... Nike, Inc. [*Associated Press*] (SAG)
NIKKEI .... Nihon Keizai Shimbun, Inc. [*Tokyo, Japan*] (IID)
NIKOS .... New Internet Knowledge Systems [*Computer science*] (DDC)
NIL .... Negotiable Instruments Law (DLA)
NIL .... Neurointermediate Lobe [*Neuroanatomy*]
NIL .... Nilore [*Pakistan*] [*Seismograph station code, US Geological Survey*] (SEIS)
NIL .... Nitrogen Inerting Line (IEEE)
NIL .... No Limit (NASA)
NIL .... Nothing in Light Disease [*Nephrotic Syndrome*] (DAVI)
NIL .... Nothing to Send [*Amateur radio shorthand*] (WDAA)
NIL .... Not in Labor [*Medicine*]
NIL .... Nuclear-Induced Lightning
NILA .... National Industrial Leather Association [*Later, NIBA*] (EA)
NILab .... Northern Ireland Labour Party [*Political party Defunct*]
NILB .... National Indian Lutheran Board (EA)
NILC .... National Immigration Law Center (EA)
NILE .... National Institute of Labor Education [*Defunct*] (EA)
NILE .... Naval Inflatable Life-Saving Equipment [*British military*] (DMA)
NILE .... Number of Inverters Along Any Loop is Even (MHDI)
NILE & CJ.... National Institute of Law Enforcement and Criminal Justice [*Law Enforcement Assistance Administration*]
NILECJ......... National Institute of Law Enforcement and Criminal Justice [*Law Enforcement Assistance Administration*]
Niles Reg .... Niles' Weekly Register [*A publication*] (DLA)
NILF .... Not in Labor Force (GFGA)
NILFP .... National Institute of Locker and Freezer Provisioners [*Later, AAMP*] (EA)

NILGOSC...... Northern Ireland Local Government Officers Superannuation Committee
NIIH .... Herkimer County Community College, Ilion, NY [*Library symbol Library of Congress*] (LCLS)
NILI............. Netsah Israel Lo Yeshakker (BJA)
NILI............. Newark Island Layered Intrusion [*Geology*] [*Canada*]
NILIC .... Northern Illinois Iowa Conference (PSS)
NILKY .... No Income, Lots of Kids [*Lifestyle classification*]
NILN .... Nylon Insert Lock Nut
NILO .... Naval Intelligence Liaison Officer (NVT)
NILP............ Northern Ireland Labour Party [*Political party Defunct*] (PPW)
NILPT .... National Institute for Low Power Television [*Defunct*] (EA)
NILR .... Northern Ireland Law Reports [*A publication*] (DLA)
NILRC .... Northern Illinois Learning Resources Cooperative [*Library network*]
Nil Reg .... Niles' Weekly Register [*A publication*] (DLA)
NILS .... Naval Intelligence Locating Summary (MCD)
NILS .... Newsletter of International Labour Studies [*Netherlands*]
NILS .... Northern Illinois Library System [*Library network*]
NILS .... Nuclear Instrument Landing System
NILT .... National Institute for Lay Training [*Defunct*] (EA)
NILTC .... National Industrial Language Training Centre (AIE)
NILUG .... National Independent Lynx User Group (NITA)
NIM .... National Impact Model [*Environmental Protection Agency*] (ERG)
NIM .... Naval Inspector of Machinery
NIM .... Net Interest Margin [*Banking*]
NIM .... Networked Interactive Multimedia
NIM .... Network Injection Molding
NIM .... Network Interface Machine [*Datapac*]
NIM .... Network Interface Module [*Telecommunications*] (TSSD)
NIM .... Network Interface Monitor
NIM .... Neurological Impress Method (EDAC)
NIM .... Newspapers in Microform (NITA)
NIM .... Niamey [*Niger*] [*Airport symbol*] (OAG)
NIM .... Night Intruder Mission [*Air Force*]
NIM .... No Immediate Miracles [*Acronym and facetious translation derived from turning President Gerald Ford's anti-inflation WIN buttons upside down*] [*See WIN entry*]
NIM .... Noninterrupt Mode
NIM .... NORAD Intelligence Memorandum (MCD)
NIM .... Normal Integration Mode
NIM .... North Irish Militia [*Military unit*] [*British*]
NIM .... Nothing in Mind [*Acronym and facetious translation derived from turning President Gerald Ford's anti-inflation WIN buttons upside down*] [*See WIN entry*]
NIM .... Nuclear Instrumentation Module
NIM .... Nuveen Select Maturities Muni [*NYSE symbol*] (TTSB)
NIM .... Nuveen Select Maturities Municipal [*NYSE symbol*] (SPSG)
NIM .... Nylon Insulation Material
NIM .... University of North Carolina at Asheville, Asheville, NC [*OCLC symbol*] (OCLC)
NIMA .... National Imagery and Mapping Agency [*Military*]
NIMA .... National Institute on Mental Health
NIMA .... National Insulation Manufacturers Association [*Later, Thermal Insulation Manufacturers Association*] (EA)
NIMA .... Noninherited Maternal Antigen [*Genetics*] [*Immunology*]
NIMAB .... National Indian Manpower Advisory Board
NIMAC .... National Interscholastic Music Activities Commission [*Defunct*] (EA)
NIMBAS ...... The Netherlands Insitute for MBA Studies
NIMBIN .... Nuclear Instrumentation Modular Bin
NIMBUS ...... Network Information Management Client-Based User Service [*Marine science*] (OSRA)
Nimbus........ Nimbus CD International, Inc. [*Associated Press*] (SAG)
NIMBUS-7.... NOAA [*National Oceanic and Atmospheric Administration*] Satellite (USDC)
NIMBY .... Not in My Back Yard [*i.e., garbage incinerators, prisons, roads, etc.*]
NIMC .... National Institute of Management Counsellors (EA)
NIMC .... National Institute of Municipal Clerks [*Later, IIMC*]
NIMC .... Nodding Image Motion Compensation [*Instrumentation*]
NIMCGA....... Northern Indiana Muck Crop Growers Association [*Defunct*] (EA)
NIMCP .... NATO Information Management Control Point (NATG)
NIME .... National Institute for Multicultural Education [*Defunct*] (EA)
NIMEX .... Nomenclature for Imports and Exports [*European Community*] (PDAA)
NIMEY .... Not in My Election Year [*Slang*]
NIMFR .... National Institutes of Marriage and Family Relations (EA)
NIMFY .... Not in My Front Yard [*i.e., Garbage incinerators, landfills, etc.*]
NIMH .... National Institute of Medical Herbalists [*British*]
NIMH .... National Institute of Mental Health [*Rockville, MD*] [*Department of Health and Human Services*]
NiMH .... Nickel-Metal Hydride [*Organic chemistry*] (PS)
NIMIC .... NATO [*North Atlantic Treaty Organization*] Insensitive Munitions Information Center
NIMIC .... Not in My Insurance Company [*Insurance slang*]
NIMIS .... National Instructional Materials Information System
NIMIT .... Nimbus Integration and Test [*NASA*] (KSC)
NIMJ........... Near Infrared Miniaturized Jammer
NIML .... National Independence Movement of Latvia [*Political party*]
NIMLO .... National Institute of Municipal Law Officers (EA)
NIMLO Mun L Rev... National Institute of Municipal Law Officers. Municipal Law Review [*A publication*] (DLA)
NIMMA .... Northern Ireland Mixed Marriage Association
NIMMP .... National Institute of Marine Medicine and Pharmacology [*Proposed*] [*National Institutes of Health*]
NIMMS .... Nineteen-Hundred Integrated Modular Management System
NIMP .... National Intern Matching Program [*Later, NRMP*] (EA)

NIMP	New and Improved Materials and Processes (PDAA)
N IMP	New Impression [*Publishing*] (DGA)
NIMPA	National Independent Meat Packers Association [*Later, NMA*] (EA)
NIMPH	Network Interface Message Processing Host [*NERComP*]
NIMPHE	Nuclear Isotope Monopropellant Hydrazine Engine
NIMQ	Not in My Queue (WDAA)
NIMR	National Institute for Medical Research [*British*]
NIMR	Navy Industrial Management Reviews (NG)
NIMROD	National Institute for Medical Research Online Database (PDAA)
NIMROD	Nineteen-Hundred [*Computer*] Management and Recovery of Documentation (PDAA)
NIMROD	Northern Illinois Meteorological Research on Downbursts [*National Center for Atmospheric Research*]
NIMRS	Navy Integrated Message Reporting System (MCD)
NIMS	National Infant Mortality Survey [*Department of Health and Human Services*] (GFGA)
NIMS	National Information Management System
NIMS	National Ingredient Marketing Specialists (EA)
NIMS	Nationwide Improved Mail Service [*Postal Service*]
NIMS	Near Infrared Mapping Spectrometer [*Instrument on Galileo spacecraft*] [*NASA*]
NIMS	North American Ingredient Marketing Specialists (NTPA)
NIMSC	Nuclear Instrumentation Modular System (MCD)
NIMSC	Nonconsumable Item Materiel Support Code [*Military*] (AFIT)
NIMSCO	NODC [*National Oceanographic Data Center*] Index to Instrument Measures Subsurface Current Observations [*Marine science*] (MSC)
NIMSDP	Non-Innovator Multiple Source Drug Product
NIMSR	Nonconsumable Item Materiel Support Request [*Military*] (AFIT)
NIMT	National Institute for Music Theater [*Defunct*] (EA)
NIMTECH	New and Improved Technology [*British*]
NIMTOF	Not in My Term of Office [*Government slang*]
NIMTOO	Not in My Term of Office (PA)
NIN	National Information Network [*ASTIA*]
NIN	National Inservice Network
NIN	Neighbors in Need [*An association*]
NIN	Nine Inch Nails [*Rock music group*]
NIN	Nine West Group [*NYSE symbol*] (TTSB)
NIN	Nine West Group, Inc. [*NYSE symbol*] (SPSG)
NIN	Ninhydrine [*Chemical agent used in espionage*]
NIN	Ninilchik [*Alaska*] [*Seismograph station code, US Geological Survey Closed*] (SEIS)
NIN	Ninilchik, AK [*Location identifier FAA*] (FAAL)
NIN	Norsat International, Inc. [*Vancouver Stock Exchange symbol*]
NINA	National Institute Northern Accelerator (PDAA)
NINA	Neutron Instruments for Nuclear Analysis (PDAA)
NINA	No Irish Need Apply [*Classified advertising*]
NINB	National Institute of Neurology and Blindness (WDAA)
NINCDS	National Institute of Neurological and Communicative Disorders and Stroke [*Formerly, NINDS*] [*Public Health Service Bethesda, MD*]
NINDB	National Institute of Neurological Diseases and Blindness [*Later, NEI, NINDS*] [*National Institutes of Health*]
NINDC	Northern Independence Conference (PSS)
NInDE	Elementary School No. 2, Inwood, NY [*Library symbol*] [*Library of Congress*] (LCLS)
NINDS	National Institute of Neurological Diseases and Stroke [*Formerly, NINDB*] [*Later, NINCDS*] [*National Institutes of Health*]
NINDS	National Institute of Neurological Disorders and Stroke
NIndTP	National Independent Teenage Party [*British*]
NINE	National Infertility Network Exchange [*An association*] (EA)
NINE	Ninth-Plate (VRA)
NINE	Number Nine Visual Tech [*NASDAQ symbol*] (TTSB)
NINE	Number Nine Visual Technology, Inc. [*NASDAQ symbol*] (SAG)
Nine-C Lit	Nineteenth-Century Literature [*A publication*] (BRI)
NINES	Norfolk Information Exchange Scheme (NITA)
NineWest	Nine West Group, Inc. [*Associated Press*] (SAG)
NINFRA	National Independent Nursery Furniture Retailers Association (EA)
NINIA	Nephelometric Inhibition Immunoassay [*Analytical chemistry*]
Nink	No Income, No Kids [*Lifestyle classification*]
NINO	No Inspector, No Operator (ODBW)
NINOW	Non-Interest-Bearing Negotiable Order of Withdrawal [*Banking*]
NINR	National Institute for Nursing Research
NINS	Northern Ireland News Service [*Information service or system*] (IID)
NINST	Non-Instrument Runway [*Aviation*] (DA)
NINST	Nose Instantaneous [*Aerospace*]
NINVS	Noninvasive Neurovascular Study [*Medicine*] (DAVI)
NInWE	Elementary School No. 4, Inwood, NY [*Library symbol*] [*Library of Congress*] (LCLS)
NINYP	Nuveen Insured New York Premium Income Municipal [*Associated Press*] (SAG)
NINYS	Nuveen Insured New York Select Tax Free Income [*Associated Press*] (SAG)
NIO	National Institute of Oceanography [*British*] (IID)
NIO	National Intelligence Officer (MCD)
NIO	Naval Inspector of Ordnance
NIO	Navigational Information Office
NIO	Navy Institute of Oceanography
NIO	Nieuwe Internationale Orde [*Netherlands*]
NIO	Niobium [*See Cb*] [*Chemical element*] (ROG)
NIO	Nioki [*Zaire*] [*Airport symbol*] (OAG)
NIO	Northern Ireland Office
NIO	Nuveen Ins Muni Oppt Fd [*NYSE symbol*] (TTSB)
NIO	Nuveen Insured Municipal Opportunity Fund [*NYSE symbol*] (SPSG)
NIOBE	Numerical Integration of the Boltzmann Transport Equation
NIOD	Network In-Out Dial [*Automatic Voice Network*] (CET)
NIOF	National Institute of Oceanography and Fisheries [*Egypt*] [*Marine science*] (OSRA)
NIOG	Nationalized Industries Overseas Group [*British*] (DCTA)
NIOK	National Institute for Overseas Koreans (EA)
NIOK	Nederlands Instituut voor Onderzoek in de Katalyse [*Netherlands Institute for Catalysis Research*]
NIOP	National Institute of Oilseed Products (EA)
NIOPSWL	New Input/Output Program Status Word Location [*Computer science*] (MHDI)
NIOS	Nixdorf Integrated Office System (HGAA)
NIOS	Northern Ireland Orchid Society (EAIO)
NIOSH	National Institute for Occupational Safety and Health [*Public Health Service*] [*Cincinnati, OH Database producer*]
NIOSHTIC	National Institute for Occupational Safety and Health Technical Information Center [*Database*] [*NIOSH*] [*Information service or system*] (CRD)
NIOSHTIC	NIOSH Technical Information Center (NITA)
NIOTC	Naval Inshore Operations Training Center (NVT)
NIOZ	Netherlands Institute for Sea Research [*Marine science*] (OSRA)
NIp	Island Park Public Library, Island Park, NY [*Library symbol Library of Congress*] (LCLS)
NIP	Jacksonville, FL [*Location identifier FAA*] (FAAL)
NIP	Mononitroiodophenyl [*Organic chemistry*] (DAVI)
NIP	NADGE [*NATO Air Defense Ground Environment*] Improvement Plan (NATG)
NIP	Namibia Independence Party [*Political party*] (PPW)
NIP	National Identification Program for the Advancement of Women in Higher EducationAdministration (EA)
NIP	National Impatient Profile (MEDA)
NIP	National Independence Party [*Namibia*] [*Political party*] (PPW)
NIP	National Industrial Partner
NIP	National Inspection Plan [*RSPA*] (TAG)
NIP	National Institute of Polarology [*Research center British*] (IRUK)
NIP	National Integration Party [*Liberia*] [*Political party*] (EY)
NIP	National Intelligence Priorities (MCD)
NIP	National Inventory Programme [*National Museums of Canada*] [*Later, CHIN*]
NIP	Naval Institute Press [*Publisher*]
NIP	Naval Intelligence Professionals (EA)
NIP	Navy Interceptor Program
NIP	Negative Inspiratory Pressure [*Medicine*] (DAVI)
NIP	Neighbourhood Improvement Program [*Canada*]
NIP	Network Input Processor [*Computer science*] (MCD)
NIP	Network Interface Processor (MCD)
NIP	New Impact Resources, Inc. [*Vancouver Stock Exchange symbol*]
NIP	New Incentive Package (ADA)
NIP	Newsletters in Print [*Formerly, ND*] [*A publication*]
NIP	Nipple (AAG)
NIP	Nipponese
NIP	No Infection Present [*Medicine*] (DMAA)
NIP	Nonimpact Printer
NIP	Normal Impact Point
NIP	Normal Incidence Pyrheliometer (PDAA)
NIP	Normal Investment Practice
NIP	Notice of Intelligence Potential [*Military*] (AFM)
NIP	Notice of Intent to Purchase [*DoD*]
NIP	Not in Practice (CMD)
NIP	Nucleus Initialization Program [*Computer science*]
NIP	Numeric Indicator Performance
NIP	Numero d'Identification Personnel [*Personal Identification Number - PIN*]
NIPA	National Income and Product Accounts [*The WEFA Group*] [*Information service*] [*Information service or system*] (CRD)
NIPA	National Institute of Pension Administrators [*Santa Ana, CA*] (EA)
NIPA	National Institute of Public Affairs
NIPA	N-Isopropylacrylamide [*Organic chemistry*]
NIPA	Noninherited Paternal Antigen [*Genetics*] [*Immunology*]
NIPA	Noninterference Performance Assessment
NIPA	Nordens Institut pa Aland [*Nordic Institute in Aland - NIA*] [*Finland*] (EAIO)
NIPA	Northern Ireland Ploughing Association (EAIO)
NIPA	Northern Ireland Police Authority
NIPA	Notice of Initiation of Procurement Action (NRCH)
NIPAGRAM	National Income and Product Account Data by Mailgram [*NTIS*]
NIPALS	Noniterative Partial Least Squares [*Algorithm*]
NIP & TB	Northern Ireland Postal and Telecommunications Board
NIPC	N-Isopropylcarbazole [*Organic chemistry*]
NIPCC	National Industrial Pollution Control Council [*Terminated, 1973*] [*Department of Commerce*]
NIPD	Not in the Public Domain
NIPDE	National Initiative for Product Data Exchange
NIPDWR	National Interim Primary Drinking Water Regulations [*Environmental Protection Agency*]
NIPDWS	National Interim Primary Drinking Water Standards [*Environmental Protection Agency*]
NIPE	Noninvasive Peripheral Vascular Examination [*or Evaluation*] (DAVI)
NIPER	National Institute for Petroleum and Energy Research [*Formerly, BETC*] [*Department of Energy Bartlesville, OK*]
NIPERA	Nickel Producers Environmental Research Association
NIPF	Nonindustrial Private Forest Owners (WPI)
NIPF	Northern Ireland Peace Forum
NIPFDA	National Independent Poultry and Food Distributors Association (EA)
NIPGM	National Institute on Park and Grounds Management (EA)
NIPH	National Institute of Poultry Husbandry [*British*] (BI)
NIPH	National Institute of Public Health

NIpHE	Francis X. Hegarty Elementary School, Island Park, NY [*Library symbol*] [*Library of Congress*] (LCLS)
NIPHL	Noise-Induced Permanent Hearing Loss (PDAA)
NIPHLE	National Institute of Packaging, Handling, and Logistic Engineers (EA)
NIPILS	New Irish Professionals in London [*Lifestyle classification*]
NIPIM2	Nuveen Insured Premium Income Municipal Fund 2 [*Associated Press*] (SAG)
NIPIMn	Nuveen Insured Premium Income Municipal Fund [*Associated Press*] (SAG)
NIPIMS	NAVMAT Instructional Procurement Inventory Monitoring System (MCD)
NIPIR	Nuclear Immediate Photo Interpretation Report (MCD)
NIpL	Lincoln Orens School, Island Park, NY [*Library symbol*] [*Library of Congress*] (LCLS)
NIPM	National Institute of Public Management (EA)
NIPN	NEC Corp. [*NASDAQ symbol*] (SAG)
NIP/NLG	National Immigration Project of the National Lawyers Guild (EA)
NIPNY	NEC Corp. ADR [*NASDAQ symbol*] (TTSB)
NIPO	Negative Input, Positive Output
NIPOLOS	Nonimpact Off-Line Operating System [*Computer science*]
NIPP	National Institute for Public Policy (EA)
NIPP	National Intelligence Projection for Planning (AFM)
NIPP	Net Income per Partner [*Business term*]
NIPP	Nonimpact Printing Process (MCD)
NIPPE	National Income per Person Employed
NIPPING	Nonimpact Printing (DGA)
NippnTT	Nippon Telegraph & Telephone Co. [*Associated Press*] (SAG)
NIPR	National Industrial Plant Reserve
NIPR	Naval Intelligence Publication Register (NVT)
ni pr.	Nisi Prius [*Unless Before*] [*Legal term Latin*] (WGA)
NIPr	North'n Ind Pub Sv.4 1/4%cmPfd [*AMEX symbol*] (TTSB)
NIPrA	North'n Ind Pub Sv Adj RtA Pfd [*NYSE symbol*] (TTSB)
NI PRI	Nisi Prius [*Unless Before*] [*Legal term Latin*]
NIPS	National Information Processing System [*Military*]
NIPS	National Institute for Public Services
NIPS	National Inventory of Pollution Sources [*Database*] [*Environment Canada*] [*Information service or system*] (CRD)
NIPS	Nationwide Integrated Postal Service [*Postal Service*]
NIPS	Naval Intelligence Processing System
NIPS	Navy Information Policy Summaries (NG)
NIPS	New Inventory Pricing Systems (MCD)
NIPS	Nippon Information Processing System [*Nippon Shuppan Hanbai, Inc.*] [*Database*]
NIPS	NIPSCO Capital Markets [*Associated Press*] (SAG)
NIPS	NMCS Information Processing System (NITA)
NIPS	Northern Indiana Public Service Co. [*Associated Press*] (SAG)
NIPSA	Northern Ireland Public Service Alliance (EAIO)
NIPSCO	NIPSCO Industries [*Associated Press*] (SAG)
NIPSSA	Naval Intelligence Processing System Support Activity
NIPT	New Information Processing Technology Project [*Japan*] (ECON)
NIPTS	Noise-Induced Permanent Threshold Shift [*Hearing*]
NIR	Beeville, TX [*Location identifier FAA*] (FAAL)
NIr	Irvington Public Library, Irvington, NY [*Library symbol Library of Congress*] (LCLS)
NIR	National Inventory Record [*DoD*]
NIR	Near Infrared (ECII)
NIR	Near-Infrared Reflectance (DB)
NIR	Near Infrared Region
NIR	Nerve Impulse Recorder
NIR	Networked Information Resource (TELE)
NIR	Network Information Retrieval
NIR	New Ireland Review [*A publication*] (ROG)
NIR	Next Inferior Rank
NIR	Next Instruction Register (NITA)
NIR	Nitrite Reductase [*An enzyme*]
NIR	No Individual Requirement (MSA)
NIR	Noninductive Resistor
NIR	Non-Insulin-Requiring [*Medicine*]
NIR	Norskair [*Norway ICAO designator*] (FAAC)
N Ir	Northern Ireland Law Reports [*A publication*] (DLA)
NIR	Northern Ireland Railways Co. Ltd.
NIRL	Nose Impact Rocket (NATG)
NIRA	National Industrial Recovery Act [*1933*]
NIRA	National Industrial Recovery Administration (WDAA)
NIRA	National Industrial Recreation Association [*Later, NESRA*] (EA)
NIRA	National Industrial Reserve Act of 1948
NIRA	National Intercollegiate Rodeo Association (EA)
NIRA	National Iridology Research Association (NTPA)
NIRA	Navy Industrial Relations Activity (DNAB)
NIRA	Navy Internal Relations Activity (DNAB)
NIRA	Near Infrared Reflectance Analysis
NIRA	Nitrite Reductase (DB)
NIRAP	Naval Industrial Reserve Aircraft Plant (MUGU)
NIRAS	National Institute of Research and Advanced Studies [*Proposed*]
NIRB	National Industrial Recovery Board [*Terminated, 1935*]
NIRB	Nuclear Insurance Rating Bureau
NIRC	National Industrial Relations Court [*British*]
NIRC	National Information Retrieval Colloquium [*Later, Benjamin Franklin Colloquium on Information Science*]
NIRC	National Institute of Rug Cleaning [*Superseded by AIDS International*] (EA)
NIRC	Negative Ion Recombination Chamber
NIRCF	National Immigration, Refugee and Citizenship Forum (EA)
NIRD	National Institute for Research in Dairying [*British*]
NIRD	Nonimmune Renal Disease [*Medicine*] (DMAA)
NIRDR	Nonintegrated RADAR (MCD)
NIRE	National Institute for Rehabilitation Engineering (EA)
N IRE	Northern Ireland
NIREB	National Institute of Real Estate Brokers [*Later, Realtors National Marketing Institute*] (EA)
NIREX	Nuclear Industry Radioactive Waste Executive [*British*] (ECON)
NIRI	National Information Research Institute
NIRI	National Investor Relations Institute [*Washington, DC*] (EA)
NIRL	Negligible Individual Risk Level (GNE)
N Ir LR	Northern Ireland Law Reports [*A publication*] (DLA)
NIRM	Network for Information Retrieval in Mammology
NIRMA	Nuclear Information and Records Management Association (EA)
NIRMP	National Intern and Resident Matching Program (DAVI)
NIRNS	National Institute for Research in Nuclear Science [*British*]
NIRO	Nike-Iroquois [*Rockets*]
NIROC	National Institute of Red Orange Canaries and All Other Cage Birds (EA)
NIROP	Naval Industrial Reserve Ordnance Plant (MCD)
NIROS	Near Infrared Oxygen Sufficiency Scope [*Monitors oxygen delivery to brain during surgery*] (DAVI)
NIROS	Nixdorf Real-Time Operating System (NITA)
NIRPL	Navy Industrial Readiness Planning List (NG)
N Ir Pub Gen Acts	Northern Ireland Public General Acts [*A publication*] (DLA)
NIRS	National Inorganic and Radionuclides Survey [*Environmental Protection Agency*]
NIRS	National Institute for Radiological Science [*Japan*]
NIRS	Near Infrared Reflectance Spectroscopy [*Britton Chance*]
NIRS	Nuclear Information and Resource Service
NIRSA	National Intramural-Recreational Sports Association (EA)
N Ir Stat	Northern Ireland Statutes [*A publication*] (DLA)
NIRTS	National Income Realty Trust [*NASDAQ symbol*] (NQ)
NIRTS	Natl Inc. Rlty Tr SBI [*NASDAQ symbol*] (TTSB)
NIRTS	New Integrated Range Timing System
NIrvH	Lake Shore Hospital, Irving, NY [*Library symbol Library of Congress*] (LCLS)
NIs	Islip Public Library, Islip, NY [*Library symbol Library of Congress*] (LCLS)
NIS	NASA Interface System (MCD)
NIS	National Income Statistics [*British*]
NIS	National Information Systems [*Later, GIP*] [*UNESCO*] (BUR)
NIS	National Information Systems, Inc. [*Information service or system*] (IID)
NIS	National Institute of Science (EA)
NIS	National Insurance Surcharge [*A separately accounted tax on employment*] [*British*]
NIS	National Intelligence Service (NADA)
NIS	National Intelligence Summary (MCD)
NIS	National Intelligence Survey
NIS	National Interdepartmental Seminar [*Military*]
NIS	National Inventory System [*Department of Agriculture*] (GFGA)
NIS	NATO Identification System
NIS	Naval Intelligence School
NIS	Naval Investigative Service
NIS	Navy Inspection Service
NIS	Negative Ion Source
NIS	Negotiation Information System
NIS	Neighborhood Information Service
NIS	Network Information Service
NIS	Network Information Services (NITA)
NIS	Network Information System [*AT & T*]
NIS	Network Interface System
NIS	Neutron Inelastic Scattering
NIS	Neutron Instrumentation System (IEEE)
NIS	Newly-Independent States [*Of former Soviet Union*]
NIS	News and Information Service [*National Broadcasting Co.*]
NIS	Nicaraguense de Aviacion SA [*Nicaragua*] [*ICAO designator*] (FAAC)
NIS	Nickel-Iron System
NIS	Night Illumination System
NIS	N-Iodosuccinimide [*Organic chemistry*]
NIS	No Intermediate Storage [*Industrial engineering*]
NIS	Noise Information System [*Environmental Protection Agency*] (IID)
NIS	Nonconsumable Item Subgroup [*Military*] (AFIT)
NIS	Nonimmune Sheep Serum (DB)
NIS	Normal Incidence Spectrometer (PDAA)
NIS	Not in Stock
NIS	NOVA Corp. [*NYSE symbol*] (TTSB)
NIS	Nova Corp. (Georgia) [*NYSE symbol*] (SAG)
NIS	Nuclear Instrumentation System (NRCH)
NIS	Shekel (ODBW)
NISA	National Inconvenienced Sportsmen's Association [*Later, NHSRA*] (EA)
NISA	National Industrial Sand Association (EA)
NISA	National Industrial Service Association [*Later, EASA*]
NISA	National Industrial Stores Association (EA)
NISA	National Institute of Supply Associations
NISA	Northeast Intercollegiate Sailing Association (PSS)
NISA	Numerically Integrated Elements for System Analysis (MCD)
NISARC	National Information Storage and Retrieval Center
NISBCO	National Interreligious Service Board for Conscientious Objectors (EA)
Nisbet	Nisbet of Dirleton's Scotch Session Cases [*1665-77*] [*A publication*] (DLA)
NISBS	National Institute of Social and Behavioral Science (EA)
NISC	National Independent Study Center [*Civil Service Commission*]

NISC	National Industrial Space Committee
NISC	National Industry Safety Committee (NADA)
NISC	National Information Services Corp. (IID)
NISC	National Institute of Senior Centers (EA)
NISC	National Intelligence Study Center (EA)
NISC	National Inter Seminary Council
NISC	National Intramural Sports Council
NISC	Naval Intelligence Support Center
NISCA	National Interscholastic Swimming Coaches Association of America (EA)
NISCO	Nuclear Installation Services Co. (NRCH)
NISCON	National Industrial Safety Conference (PDAA)
NISCR	South Central Research Library Council, Ithaca, NY [Library symbol Library of Congress] (LCLS)
NISC-TRANS	Naval Intelligence Support Center Translation Division
NISCUE	National Institute for State Credit Union Examination [McLean, VA] (EA)
NISD	National Institute of Steel Detailing (EA)
NISDA	Northeast Intercollegiate Swimming and Diving Association (PSS)
N-ISDN	National ISDN [Integrated Services Digital Network] [Telecommunications]
NISE	Neighborhood Information Sharing Exchange [Defunct] (EA)
NISE	Normalized Integral Squared Error
NISEC	National Institute for the Study of Educational Change
NISEC	Northern Ireland Schools Examination Council (AIE)
NISEE	National Information Service for Earthquake Engineering (EA)
NISG	National Institute of Student Governments [Defunct] (EA)
NISG	Navy Installation Survey Group
NISGAZ	National Intelligence Survey Gazetteer
NISGUA	Network in Solidarity with the People of Guatemala (EA)
NISH	National Industries for the Severely Handicapped (EA)
NISH	National Information Sources on the Handicapped [Clearinghouse on the Handicapped] [Database]
NISH	National Institute of Senior Housing (EA)
NISH	Nonisotopic In Situ Hybridization [Analytical biochemistry]
NISHQ	Naval Investigative Service Headquarters
NI-SIL	Nickel-Silver
Nisi Prius & Gen T Rep	Nisi Prius and General Term Reports [Ohio] [A publication] (DLA)
Nisi Prius Rep	Ohio Nisi Prius Reports [A publication] (DLA)
NISL	National Indoor Soccer League [Australia]
NISL	National Intercollegiate Swimming League (PSS)
NISLAPP	National Institute for Science, Law, and Public Policy (EA)
NISM	Non-Deterministic Incomplete Sequential Machine (PDAA)
NISMART	National Incidence Studies of Missing, Abducted, Runaway, and Thrownaway Children
NISMF	Naval Inactive Ship Maintenance Facility
NISMO	Nissan Motorsports
NISO	National Information Standards Organization - Z39 (EA)
NISO	Naval Investigative Service Office (NVT)
NISOA	National Intercollegiate Soccer Officials Association (EA)
NISOD	National Institute for Staff and Organizational Development (OICC)
NISOR	Naval Investigative Service Office Representative (DNAB)
NISP	National Industrial Security Program [A publication] (AAGC)
NISP	National Information System for Psychology
NISP	Navy Integrated Space Program (NG)
NISP	Nuclear Weapons Intelligence Support Plan (COE)
NISP	NUWEP [Nuclear Weapon] Intelligence Support Plan [Military]
NISPA	National Information System for Physics and Astronomy (NITA)
NISPOM	National Industrial Security Program Manual [A publication] (AAGC)
NISR	National Intelligence Situation Report (MCD)
NISR	Navy Initial Support Requirement (AFIT)
NISRA	National Industrial Salvage and Recovery Association [British] (BI)
NISRA	National Intercollegiate Squash Racquets Association (EA)
NISRA	Naval Investigative Service Resident Agent (NVT)
NISREGFORENSICLAB	Naval Investigative Service Regional Forensic Laboratory (DNAB)
NISS	National Information of Software and Services (AIE)
NISS	National Institute of Social Sciences (EA)
NISS	New Information Systems and Services [A publication]
Nissan	Nissan Motor Co. Ltd. [Associated Press] (SAG)
NISSM	Navy Interim Surface Ship Model (CAAL)
NISSOL	NAVAIR [Naval Air Systems Command] Initial Supply Support Outfitting List (MCD)
NISSPO	NATO Identification System Special Project Office
NISSU	Naval Investigative Service Satellite Unit (DNAB)
NIST	National Information System for Science and Technology (NITA)
NIST	National Institute for Standards and Technology
NIST	National Institute of Science and Technology (NADA)
NIST	National Institute of Standards and Technology [Formerly, NBS] [Gaithersburg, MD] [Department of Commerce]
NIST	National Intelligence Support Team (COE)
NIST-7	National Institute of Standards and Technology, Seventh Generation (MED)
N/ISTA	National/International Safe Transit Association (NTPA)
NISTA	Northern Independent Steel Training Association (AIE)
NISTARS	Naval Integrated Storage Tracking and Retrieval System
NIST-EEEL	National Institute of Standards & Technology - Electronics and EE Lab
NISTF	National Information Systems Task Force [Society of American Archivists] [Information service or system] (IID)
NISU	National Injury Surveillance Unit [Australia]
NISUS	Neutron Intermediate Standard Uranium Source (PDAA)
NISW	National Institute of Social Work [British]
NISW	Naval In-Shore Warfare (PDAA)
NISWA	National Indian Social Workers Association (EA)
NIT	Midwest Aviation Corp. [ICAO designator] (FAAC)
NIT	National Institute of Technology
NIT	National Instructional Television [Superseded by AIT] (EA)
NIT	National Intelligence Test [Psychology]
NIT	National Intelligence Topic (MCD)
NIT	National Invitation Tournament [Basketball]
NIT	Negative Income Tax
NIT	Network Information Technology
NIT	Network Interface Task [Computer science] (CIST)
NIT	New Information Technology
NIT	Nitrum [Chemistry] (ROG)
NIT	None in Town [Bookselling]
NIT	Non-Intelligent Terminal (NITA)
NIT	Nonlinear Inertialess Three-Pole [Telecommunications] (OA)
NIT	Norfolk International Terminal
NIT	Normal Incidence Technique [Structural testing]
NIT	Nuclear Irradiation Test
NIT	Nurses in Transition (EA)
NITA	National Indoor Tennis Association [Formerly, ITA] [Later, NTA] (EA)
NITA	National Industrial Television Association [Later, ITVA] (EA)
NITA	National Institute for Trial Advocacy (EA)
NITA	National Instructional Television Association (NTCM)
NITA	National Intravenous Therapy Association [Later, INS] (EA)
NITB	Northern Ireland Tourist Board
NITB	Tompkins-Seneca-Tioga Board of Cooperative Educational Services, Ithaca, NY [Library symbol] [Library of Congress] (LCLS)
NITC	National Information Technology Committee [Thailand] (DDC)
NITC	National Information Transfer Centre (NITA)
NITC	National Instructional Television Center (NTCM)
NITC	National Intelligence Tasking Center [CIA]
NITCCU	Northern Information Technology Centre Consultancy Unit (NITA)
Nitches	Nitches, Inc. [Associated Press] (SAG)
NITE	Navy Integrated Terminal Evaluation
NITE	Night Imaging Thermal Equipment [Army] (INF)
NITEC	National Information Technology in Education Centre (ACII)
NITEDEVRON	Night Development Squadron
NITEOP	Night Imaging Through Electro-Optic Package [Military British]
NITEP	National Incinerator Testing and Evaluation Program [Environmental Protection Agency] (GFGA)
NITEWOG	Naval Integrated Test and Evaluation Working Group (MCD)
NITF	National Imagery Transmission Format (DOMA)
NITF	National Interreligious Task Force (EA)
NITFSJ	National Interreligious Task Force on Soviet Jewry (EA)
NITINOL	Nickel Titanium Naval Ordnance Laboratory [An alloy named by William Buehler of the NOL] (KSC)
Nitinol	Nitinol Medical Technologies, Inc. [Associated Press] (SAG)
NITL	National Industrial Traffic League (EA)
NITL	National Industrial Transportation League (EA)
NITM	National Income Tax Magazine [A publication] (DLA)
NITMDA	National Indoor Track Meet Directors Association (EA)
NIT OX	Nitrous Oxide [Laughing gas] (AAMN)
NITP	National Industrial Training Program [Canada]
NITP	National Institutional Training Program [Canada]
NITP	Nibbling Template
NITPA	National Institutional Teacher Placement Association [Later, ASCUS]
NITPICKERS	National Institute of Technical Processors, Information Consultants, Keyword Experts, and Retrieval Specialists [Fictitious organization]
NITRAS	Navy Integrated Training Resources and Administration System (NVT)
NITRC	National Indian Training and Research Center (EA)
NITRO	National Independent Textiles Retailers Organizations (NTPA)
NITRO	Nitrocellulose (WDAA)
NITRO	Nitrogen [Chemical element]
nitro	Nitroglycerin [Pharmacy]
NITRO	Sodium Nitroprusside [Pharmacology] (DAVI)
NITROS	Nitrostarch (AAG)
NITSTL	Nitride Steel
NITU	Notice of Interim Trail Use [Interstate Commerce Commission]
NITUC	National Independent Truckers Unity Council [Defunct] (EA)
NITV	National Iranian Television (NADA)
NIU	NATO Interface Unit (MCD)
NIU	Naval Intelligence Unit
NIU	Navigation Interface Unit [Navy] (CAAL)
NIU	Network Interface Unit [Computer science]
NIU	Niue [ANSI three-letter standard code] (CNC)
NIU	Niumate [Tonga] [Seismograph station code, US Geological Survey Closed] (SEIS)
NIU	Northern Illinois University [Dekalb, IL]
NIU	University of Northern Iowa, Cedar Falls, IA [OCLC symbol] (OCLC)
NIUC	National Independent Union Council [Later, NFIU]
NIUE	Alofi/Niue International [Niue Island] [ICAO location identifier] (ICLI)
NIUF	National Inshore Union of Fishermen [British]
NIULPE	National Institute for Uniform Licensing of Power Engineers'
NIUW	National Institute for Urban Wildlife (EA)
NIV	National Institute of Victimology (EA)
NIV	Negative Ion Vacancy
NIV	Neutron-Induced Voltage (NUCP)
NIV	Newbury International Ventures, Inc. [Vancouver Stock Exchange symbol]
NIV	New International Version [of the Bible] [A publication]
NIV	Nivalenol [A mycotoxin]
NIV	Nodule-Inducing Virus
NIVA	National Independent Vendors Association [Defunct] (EA)

NIVC .... National Interactive Video Centre [*British*]

NIVEA .... Night Vision Equipment for Armor

NIVR .... Netherlands Agency for Aerospace Programs

NIW .... National Industrial Workers Union

NIW .... Naval Inshore Warfare Project

NIW .... Nonlethal Incapacitating Weapon

NIWC .... National Institute for Women of Color   (EA)

NIWC .... Naval Inshore Warfare Command   (NVT)

NIWFA .... National Intercollegiate Women's Fencing Association   (EA)

NIWG .... National Institute for the Word of God   (EA)

NIWKC .... National Institute of Wood Kitchen Cabinets [*Later, KCMA*]

NIWL .... National Institute for Work and Learning   (EA)

NIWR .... National Institutes for Water Resources   (NTPA)

NIWS .... National Institute on Workshop Standards [*Defunct*]   (EA)

NIWS .... National Integrated Wage Structure   (ADA)

NIWS .... News Information Weekly Service

NIWTU .... Naval Inshore Warfare Task Unit   (MCD)

NIWU .... National Industrial Workers Union   (EA)

NIX............. Nioro [*Mali*] [*Airport symbol*]   (OAG)

Nix............. Nixa [*Record label*] [*Great Britain, etc.; including Vanguard label re-issues*]

NIX............. Nix-O-Tine Pharmaceuticals Ltd. [*Vancouver Stock Exchange symbol*]

NIX............. Pacific Beach, WA [*Location identifier FAA*]   (FAAL)

Nix Dig ...... Nixon's Digest of Laws [*New Jersey*] [*A publication*]   (DLA)

Nix F.......... Nixon's Forms [*A publication*]   (DLA)

NIXT........... Normal Incidence X-Ray Telescope

NIY............. Norfolk, VA [*Location identifier FAA*]   (FAAL)

NIY............. Northamptonshire Imperial Yeomanry [*British military*]   (DMA)

NIY............. Northumberland Imperial Yeomanry [*British military*]   (DMA)

NIYC .... National Indian Youth Council   (EA)

NIZ............. Nizhne-Angarsk [*Former USSR Seismograph station code, US Geological Survey*]   (SEIS)

NIZC .... National Industrial Zoning Committee   (EA)

NJ .... Namakwaland Lugdiens [*ICAO designator*]   (AD)

NJ .... Namakwaland Lugdiens Bpk [*South Africa*] [*ICAO designator*]   (ICDA)

nJ .... Nanojoule [*One billionth of a joule*]

NJ .... Napierville Junction Railway Co. [*AAR code*]

NJ .... Nasojejunal [*Medicine*]

NJ .... Network Junction [*Telecommunications*]   (OA)

NJ .... Neue Justiz. Zeitschrift fuer Recht und Rechtswissenschaft [*Berlin, German Democratic Republic*] [*A publication*]   (DLA)

NJ .... New Jaguar [*Jaguar PLC*]

NJ .... New Japan Aircraft Maintenance Co. Ltd. [*Japan ICAO aircraft manufacturer identifier*]   (ICAO)

NJ .... New Jason [*Charter-party clause*] [*Business term*]   (DS)

NJ .... New Jersey [*Postal code*]

Nj .... New Jersey State Library, Trenton, NJ [*Library symbol Library of Congress*]   (LCLS)

NJ .... New Jersey Supreme Court Reports [*A publication*]   (DLA)

NJ .... New Journalism [*Refers to specific style, as that of writer Tom Wolfe*]

NJ .... Non Justifying [*Typography*]   (DGA)

NJ .... Notice of Judgment (Official) [*Legal term*]   (DLA)

NJ .... Nylon Jacket

NJA .... National Jail Association [*Later, AJA*]   (EA)

NJA .... National Jewellers' Association [*British*]   (BI)

NJA .... National Jogging Association [*Later, ARFA*]   (EA)

NJA .... National Jousting Association   (EA)

NJA .... National Judges Association   (EA)

NJA .... New Jewish Agenda   (EA)

NJA .... Nozzle Jetevator Assembly

NJA .... Sky Air Cargo Services (UK) Ltd. [*British ICAO designator*]   (FAAC)

NJAA .... National Junior Angus Association   (EA)

NjAc .... Atlantic City Free Public Library, Atlantic City, NJ [*Library symbol Library of Congress*]   (LCLS)

NJAC .... National Joint Advisory Council [*on labor-management relations*] [*British*]

NJAC .... New Jersey Administrative Code [*A publication*]

NJAC .... New Jersey Athletic Conference   (PSS)

NjAcCoC ..... Atlantic County Clerk, Atlantic City, NJ [*Library symbol Library of Congress*]   (LCLS)

NjAcFA........ United States Federal Aviation Administration, National Aviation Facilities Experimental Center, Atlantic City, NJ [*Library symbol Library of Congress*]   (LCLS)

NjAcJ .... Jewish Record, Atlantic City, NJ [*Library symbol Library of Congress*]   (LCLS)

NjAcP.......... Press Publishing Co., Atlantic City, NJ [*Library symbol Library of Congress*]   (LCLS)

NjAcPI .... Popolo Italiano, Atlantic City, NJ [*Library symbol Library of Congress*]   (LCLS)

NjAcR .... Atlantic City Reporter, Atlantic City, NJ [*Library symbol Library of Congress*]   (LCLS)

NJ Admin Code... New Jersey Administrative Code [*A publication*]   (DLA)

NJAG .... National Jewish Artisans Guild [*Defunct*]   (EA)

NJAIC.......... New Jersey Asparagus Industry Council   (EA)

NjAl .... Allentown Public Library, Allentown, NJ [*Library symbol Library of Congress*]   (LCLS)

NjAlA .... Allentown Printing Service, Allentown, NJ [*Library symbol Library of Congress*]   (LCLS)

NjAlB .... Allentown Borough Hall, Allentown, NJ [*Library symbol Library of Congress*]   (LCLS)

NjAlHi......... Allentown Historical Society, Allentown, NJ [*Library symbol Library of Congress*]   (LCLS)

NJam .... James Prendergast Free Library, Jamestown, NY [*Library symbol Library of Congress*]   (LCLS)

NJamC......... Chautauqua-Cattaraugus Library System, Jamestown, NY [*Library symbol Library of Congress*]   (LCLS)

NJamCC...... Jamestown Community College, Jamestown, NY [*Library symbol Library of Congress*]   (LCLS)

NJamH........ Jamestown General Hospital, Jamestown, NY [*Library symbol Library of Congress*]   (LCLS)

NJamW........ Woman's Christian Association Hospital, Jamestown, NY [*Library symbol Library of Congress*]   (LCLS)

NJANG .... New Jersey Air National Guard   (MUSM)

NJAR .... New Jersey Administrative Reports [*A publication*]

NjAs............ Asbury Park Free Public Library, Asbury Park, NJ [*Library symbol Library of Congress*]   (LCLS)

NjAsP.......... Asbury Park Press, Asbury Park, NJ [*Library symbol Library of Congress*]   (LCLS)

NjAsS.......... Spotlight Magazine, Asbury Park, NJ [*Library symbol Library of Congress*]   (LCLS)

NjAt .... Atlantic Highlands Public Library Association, Atlantic Highlands, NJ [*Library symbol Library of Congress*]   (LCLS)

NjAuV......... Weekly Visitor, Audubon, NJ [*Library symbol Library of Congress*]   (LCLS)

NjAveT........ Tabloid Lithographers, Inc., Avenel, NJ [*Library symbol Library of Congress*]   (LCLS)

NjAvH .... Herald, Avalon, NJ [*Library symbol Library of Congress*]   (LCLS)

NJB............. Appalachian State University, Boone, NC [*OCLC symbol*]   (OCLC)

NjB............. Bridgeton Free Public Library, Bridgeton, NJ [*Library symbol Library of Congress*]   (LCLS)

NJB............. New Jerusalem Bible [*1985*] [*A publication*]   (ODCC)

NjBa........... Bayonne Free Public Library, Bayonne, NJ [*Library symbol Library of Congress*]   (LCLS)

NjBaF.......... Facts of Bayonne Publishing Co., Bayonne, NJ [*Library symbol Library of Congress*]   (LCLS)

NjBaFAR ..... Federal Archives and Records Center, General Services Administration, Bayonne, NJ [*Library symbol Library of Congress*]   (LCLS)

NjBaNSRF.... United States Naval Supply Research and Development Facility, Bayonne, NJ [*Library symbol Library of Congress*]   (LCLS)

NjBAP......... Cumberland County Advertiser-Press, Inc., Bridgeton, NJ [*Library symbol Library of Congress*]   (LCLS)

NjBarHi....... Barrington Historical Society, Barrington, NJ [*Library symbol Library of Congress*]   (LCLS)

NjBas.......... Bernards Township Library, Inc., Basking Ridge, NJ [*Library symbol Library of Congress*]   (LCLS)

NjBb........... Bound Brook Memorial Library, Bound Brook, NJ [*Library symbol Library of Congress*]   (LCLS)

NjBbA......... American Cyanamid Co., Organic Chemicals Division, Bound Brook, NJ [*Library symbol Library of Congress*]   (LCLS)

NjBbC .... Bound Brook Chronicle, Bound Brook, NJ [*Library symbol Library of Congress*]   (LCLS)

NJBBF .... National Judo Black Belt Federation of the USA   (EA)

NjBbU .... Union Carbide Plastics Co., Bound Brook, NJ [*Library symbol Library of Congress*]   (LCLS)

NjBCoC .... Cumberland County Clerk, Bridgeton, NJ [*Library symbol Library of Congress*]   (LCLS)

NjBe........... Belleville Free Public Library, Belleville, NJ [*Library symbol Library of Congress*]   (LCLS)

NjBeA......... Ad-Print, Belleville, NJ [*Library symbol Library of Congress*]   (LCLS)

NjBeacO ...... Daily Observer, Beachwood, NJ [*Library symbol Library of Congress*]   (LCLS)

NjBel.......... Belmar Public Library, Belmar, NJ [*Library symbol Library of Congress*]   (LCLS)

NjBelvCoC ... Warren County Clerk, Belvidere, NJ [*Library symbol Library of Congress*]   (LCLS)

NjBelvW ...... Warren County Library, Belvidere, NJ [*Library symbol Library of Congress*]   (LCLS)

NjBer.......... Bergenfield Free Public Library, Bergenfield, NJ [*Library symbol Library of Congress*]   (LCLS)

NjBerl .... Marie Fleche Memorial Library, Berlin, NJ [*Library symbol Library of Congress*]   (LCLS)

NjBern........ Bernardsville Library Association, Bernardsville, NJ [*Library symbol Library of Congress*]   (LCLS)

NjBernN...... Bernardsville News, Bernardsville, NJ [*Library symbol Library of Congress*]   (LCLS)

NjBeT......... Belleville Telegram, Belleville, NJ [*Library symbol Library of Congress*]   (LCLS)

NjBh........... Berkley Heights Public Library, Berkley Heights, NJ [*Library symbol Library of Congress*]   (LCLS)

NjBl .... Bloomfield Public Library, Bloomfield, NJ [*Library symbol Library of Congress*]   (LCLS)

NjBla .... Gloucester Township [*Blackwood*] Library, Blackwood, NJ [*Library symbol Library of Congress*]   (LCLS)

NjBlaC .... Camden County College, Blackwood, NJ [*Library symbol Library of Congress*]   (LCLS)

NjBlaCG...... Camden-Gloucester Newspapers, Blackwood, NJ [*Library symbol Library of Congress*]   (LCLS)

NjBlaiP .... Blairstown Press, Blairstown, NJ [*Library symbol Library of Congress*]   (LCLS)

NjBlC .... Bloomfield College, Bloomfield, NJ [*Library symbol Library of Congress*]   (LCLS)

NjBlHi......... Historical Society of Bloomfield, Bloomfield, NJ [*Library symbol Library of Congress*]   (LCLS)

NjBlI .... Independent Press, Bloomfield, NJ [*Library symbol Library of Congress*]   (LCLS)

NjBIM .... Academy of Medicine of New Jersey, Bloomfield, NJ [*Library symbol Library of Congress*]   (LCLS)

NjBIS .... Shering Corp., Bloomfield, NJ [*Library symbol Library of Congress*] (LCLS)

NjBIW .... Westinghouse Electric Corp., Lamp Division, Bloomfield, NJ [*Library symbol Library of Congress*] (LCLS)

NjBN .... Bridgeton Evening News, Bridgeton, NJ [*Library symbol Library of Congress*] (LCLS)

NjBo .... Bogota Public Library, Bogota, NJ [*Library symbol Library of Congress*] (LCLS)

NjBoo .... Holmes Library, Boonton, NJ [*Library symbol Library of Congress*] (LCLS)

NjBooT .... Times-Bulletin, Boonton, NJ [*Library symbol Library of Congress*] (LCLS)

NjBorHi .... Bordentown Historical Society, Bordentown, NJ [*Library symbol Library of Congress*] (LCLS)

NjBorL .... Lorraine Publishing, Inc., Bordentown, NJ [*Library symbol Library of Congress*] (LCLS)

NjBriCN .... Plainfield Courier-News, Bridgewater, NJ [*Library symbol Library of Congress*] (LCLS)

NjBrigT .... Brigantine Times, Brigantine, NJ [*Library symbol Library of Congress*] (LCLS)

NjBro .... Mendham Township Library, Brookside, NJ [*Library symbol Library of Congress*] (LCLS)

NjBrS .... Seacoast Newspapers, Brick Town, NJ [*Library symbol Library of Congress*] (LCLS)

NjBu .... Library Co. of Burlington, Burlington, NJ [*Library symbol Library of Congress*] (LCLS)

NjBuHi .... Burlington County Historical Society, Burlington, NJ [*Library symbol Library of Congress*] (LCLS)

NjButA .... Argus Printing & Publishing Co., Butler, NJ [*Library symbol Library of Congress*] (LCLS)

NjC .... Chatham Public Library, Chatham, NJ [*Library symbol Library of Congress*] (LCLS)

NJC .... Natchez Junior College [*Mississippi*]

NJC .... National Jewish Center [*Australia*]

NJC .... National Jewish Coalition (EA)

NJC .... National Joint Council (AIE)

NJC .... National Judicial College (EA)

NJC .... National Security Caucus Institute (EA)

NJC .... Navarro Junior College [*Texas*]

NJC .... Navy Job Classification Manual

NJC .... New Jersey Central Railroad

NJC .... Newton Junior College [*Massachusetts*]

NJC .... Norfolk Junior College [*Nebraska*]

NjCa .... Camden Free Public Library, Camden, NJ [*Library symbol Library of Congress*] (LCLS)

NJCAA .... National Job Corps Alumni Association [*Washington, DC*] (EA)

NJCAA .... National Junior College Athletic Association (EA)

NjCaC .... Cooper Medical Center, Camden, NJ [*Library symbol Library of Congress*] (LCLS)

NjCaHi .... Camden County Historical Society, Camden, NJ [*Library symbol Library of Congress*] (LCLS)

NjCal .... Caldwell Free Public Library, Caldwell, NJ [*Library symbol Library of Congress*] (LCLS)

NjCalC .... Caldwell College, Caldwell, NJ [*Library symbol Library of Congress*] (LCLS)

NjCalP .... Caldwell Progress, Caldwell, NJ [*Library symbol Library of Congress*] (LCLS)

NjCaN .... Camden News, Camden, NJ [*Library symbol Library of Congress*] (LCLS)

NjCapS .... Star and Wave, Cape May, NJ [*Library symbol Library of Congress*] (LCLS)

NJCAPT & C... National Joint Council for Administrative, Professional, Technical, and ClericalStaff [*British*]

NjCaRD .... Radio Corp. of America, Communications Systems Division, Camden, NJ [*Library symbol Library of Congress*] (LCLS)

NjCarpD .... E. I. Du Pont de Nemours & Co., Carney's Point Development Laboratory, Carney's Point, NJ [*Library symbol Library of Congress*] (LCLS)

NjCaSH .... Catholic Star Herald, Camden, NJ [*Library symbol Library of Congress*] (LCLS)

NjCaUR .... Union Reporter, Camden, NJ [*Library symbol Library of Congress*] (LCLS)

NJCBI .... National Joint Council for the Building Industry [*British*] (DCTA)

NJCBSPT ..... New Jersey College Basic Skills Placement Test (EDAC)

NjCC .... Chatham Courier, Chatham, NJ [*Library symbol Library of Congress*] (LCLS)

NJCC .... National Joint Computer Committee [*of ACM, AIEE, IRE*] [*Superseded by AFIPS*]

NJCC .... Northeastern Junior College of Colorado [*Sterling*]

NJCCA .... National Japanese Canadian Citizens' Association

NJCCOE ...... Nordic Joint Committee of Commercial and Office Executives (EA)

NJCDE .... Nordic Joint Committee for Domestic Education (EA)

NjCE .... Chatham Township Echoes, Chatham, NJ [*Library symbol Library of Congress*] (LCLS)

NJCEC .... NATO Joint Communications-Electronics Committee (NATG)

NJCF .... National Juvenile Court Foundation (EA)

NjCg .... Cedar Grove Public Library, Cedar Grove, NJ [*Library symbol Library of Congress*] (LCLS)

NjCh .... Cherry Hill Free Public Library, Cherry Hill, NJ [*Library symbol Library of Congress*] (LCLS)

NJ Ch .... New Jersey Equity Reports [*A publication*] (DLA)

NJCHC .... National Joint Council for Handicapped Children [*British*]

NjChCP .... Courier Post, Cherry Hill, NJ [*Library symbol Library of Congress*] (LCLS)

NjChe .... Chester Free Public Library, Chester, NJ [*Library symbol Library of Congress*] (LCLS)

NjChJ .... Jewish Federation of Camden County, Cherry Hill, NJ [*Library symbol Library of Congress*] (LCLS)

NjChM .... Cherry Hill Medical Center, Cherry Hill, NJ [*Library symbol Library of Congress*] (LCLS)

NjChSG .... Shoppers Guide, Cherry Hill, NJ [*Library symbol Library of Congress*] (LCLS)

NjChSN .... Suburban Newspaper Group, Cherry Hill, NJ [*Library symbol Library of Congress*] (LCLS)

NjCiL .... Cinnaminson Little Paper, Cinnaminson, NJ [*Library symbol Library of Congress*] (LCLS)

NjCl .... Clark Free Public Library, Clark, NJ [*Library symbol Library of Congress*] (LCLS)

NJCL .... Network Job Control Language [*Computer science*]

NJCLAFB...... National Joint Council for Local Authority Fire Brigades [*British*]

NJCLD .... National Joint Committee for Learning Disabilities

NJCLE .... Institute for Continuing Legal Education, New Jersey (DLA)

NjClif .... Clifton Public Library, Clifton, NJ [*Library symbol Library of Congress*] (LCLS)

NjClifB .... New Jersey Business Review, Clifton, NJ [*Library symbol Library of Congress*] (LCLS)

NjClifI .... Clifton Independent Prospector, Clifton, NJ [*Library symbol Library of Congress*] (LCLS)

NjClifL .... Clifton Leader, Clifton, NJ [*Library symbol Library of Congress*] (LCLS)

NjClifP .... Clifton Publishing Co., Clifton, NJ [*Library symbol Library of Congress*] (LCLS)

NjClifPE .... Post Eagle Publishing Co., Clifton, NJ [*Library symbol Library of Congress*] (LCLS)

NjClifW .... Woodward-Clyde Consultants, Clifton, NJ [*Library symbol Library of Congress*] (LCLS)

NjClinH .... Hunterdon Review, Clinton, NJ [*Library symbol Library of Congress*] (LCLS)

NjClp .... Cliffside Park Public Library, Cliffside Park, NJ [*Library symbol Library of Congress*] (LCLS)

NjClpP .... Palisades Printing Corp., Cliffside Park, NJ [*Library symbol Library of Congress*] (LCLS)

NjCmCo .... Cape May County Library, Cape May Court House, NJ [*Library symbol Library of Congress*] (LCLS)

NjCmCoC ..... Cape May County Clerk, Cape May Court House, NJ [*Library symbol Library of Congress*] (LCLS)

NjCmG .... Cape May County Gazette, Cape May Court House, NJ [*Library symbol Library of Congress*] (LCLS)

NjCo .... Collingswood Free Public Library, Collingswood, NJ [*Library symbol Library of Congress*] (LCLS)

NjCoB .... Christian Beacon, Collingswood, NJ [*Library symbol Library of Congress*] (LCLS)

NjCoC .... Collingswood Publishing Co., Collingswood, NJ [*Library symbol Library of Congress*] (LCLS)

NjColS .... South Jersey Ad-Visor, Cologne, NJ [*Library symbol Library of Congress*] (LCLS)

NjConC .... College of Saint Elizabeth, Convent Station, NJ [*Library symbol Library of Congress*] (LCLS)

NJCOS .... National Jewish Committee on Scouting (EA)

NjCoT .... Camden County Times, Collingswood, NJ [*Library symbol Library of Congress*] (LCLS)

NjCr .... Cranford Public Library, Cranford, NJ [*Library symbol Library of Congress*] (LCLS)

NJCRAC .... National Jewish Community Relations Advisory Council (EA)

NjCrbP .... Cranbury Press, Cranbury, NJ [*Library symbol Library of Congress*] (LCLS)

NjCrC .... Cranford Citizen & Chronicle, Cranford, NJ [*Library symbol Library of Congress*] (LCLS)

NjCrHi .... Cranford Historical Society, Cranford, NJ [*Library symbol Library of Congress*] (LCLS)

NjCrU .... Union College, Cranford, NJ [*Library symbol Library of Congress*] (LCLS)

NJCS .... National Jewish Committee on Scouting (EA)

NJCSA .... National Juvenile Court Services Association (EA)

NJCSE .... National Jewish Civil Service Employees (EA)

NjD .... Dover Public Library, Dover, NJ [*Library symbol Library of Congress*] (LCLS)

NjDA .... Daily Advance, Dover, NJ [*Library symbol Library of Congress*] (LCLS)

NJDA .... National Juvenile Detention Association (EA)

NjDC .... County College of Morris, Dover, NJ [*Library symbol*] [*Library of Congress*] (LCLS)

NJDDC .... New Jersey Development Disabilities Council (EDAC)

NjDe .... Denville Free Public Library, Denville, NJ [*Library symbol Library of Congress*] (LCLS)

NjDeC .... Citizen of Morris County, Denville, NJ [*Library symbol Library of Congress*] (LCLS)

NJDEP .... New Jersey Department of Environmental Protection

NJDFC .... New Jersey Devils Fan Club (EA)

NjDPA .... United States Army, Armament Research and Development Command, Science and Technical Library, Dover Site, Dover, NJ [*Library symbol Library of Congress*] (LCLS)

NJE .... Network Job Entry

NJE .... New Jersey Equity Reports [*A publication*] (DLA)

Nj-E .... New Jersey State Library, Department of Education, Trenton, NJ [*Library symbol Library of Congress*] (LCLS)

NJE .... Office of Cancer and Toxic Substances Research, Trenton, NJ [*OCLC symbol*] (OCLC)

NjEa............. Eatontown Public Library, Eatontown, NJ [*Library symbol Library of Congress*] (LCLS)

NjEb............. East Brunswick Public Library, East Brunswick, NJ [*Library symbol Library of Congress*] (LCLS)

NjEbGS .... Church of Jesus Christ of Latter-Day Saints, Genealogical Society Library, East Brunswick Stake Branch, East Brunswick, NJ [*Library symbol Library of Congress*] (LCLS)

NjEbS.......... Sentinel Publishing Co., East Brunswick, NJ [*Library symbol Library of Congress*] (LCLS)

NjEdE.......... Engelhard Minerals & Chemicals Corp. [*Later, Engelhard Corp.*], Research Library, Edison, NJ [*Library symbol Library of Congress*] (LCLS)

NjEdM.......... Middlesex County College, Edison, NJ [*Library symbol Library of Congress*] (LCLS)

NjEgN .... Egg Harbor News, Egg Harbor City, NJ [*Library symbol Library of Congress*] (LCLS)

NjEh............. East Hanover Public Library, East Hanover, NJ [*Library symbol Library of Congress*] (LCLS)

NjEli............. Elizabeth Free Public Library, Elizabeth, NJ [*Library symbol Library of Congress*] (LCLS)

NjEliCoC ...... Union County Clerk, Elizabeth, NJ [*Library symbol Library of Congress*] (LCLS)

NjEliJ.......... Daily Journal, Elizabeth, NJ [*Library symbol Library of Congress*] (LCLS)

NjEIT........... Elmer Times, Elmer, NJ [*Library symbol Library of Congress*] (LCLS)

NjEn............. Englewood Library, Englewood, NJ [*Library symbol Library of Congress*] (LCLS)

NjEncL......... Thomas J. Lipton, Inc., Englewood Cliffs, NJ [*Library symbol Library of Congress*] (LCLS)

NjEncStP...... Saint Peter's College, Englewood Cliffs, NJ [*Library symbol Library of Congress*] (LCLS)

NJE/NJI........ Network Job Entry, Including Network Job Interface

NjEnP.......... Englewood Press, Englewood, NJ [*Library symbol Library of Congress*] (LCLS)

NjEnPa......... Palisades Newspapers, Englewood, NJ [*Library symbol Library of Congress*] (LCLS)

NjEnS.......... North Jersey Suburbanite, Englewood, NJ [*Library symbol Library of Congress*] (LCLS)

NjEo............. East Orange Free Public Library, East Orange, NJ [*Library symbol Library of Congress*] (LCLS)

NjEoA.......... Advocate, East Orange, NJ [*Library symbol Library of Congress*] (LCLS)

NjEoS.......... Sokol USA, East Orange, NJ [*Library symbol Library of Congress*] (LCLS)

NjEoU .... Upsala College, East Orange, NJ [*Library symbol Library of Congress*] (LCLS)

NjEoV.......... United States Veterans Administration Hospital, East Orange, NJ [*Library symbol Library of Congress*] (LCLS)

NJ Eq.......... New Jersey Equity Reports [*A publication*] (DLA)

NJ Eq R........ New Jersey Equity Reports [*A publication*] (DLA)

NJ Equity...... New Jersey Equity Reports [*A publication*] (DLA)

NJer............. Jericho Public Library, Jericho, NY [*Library symbol Library of Congress*] (LCLS)

NJerC.......... Long Island Association of Commerce and Industry, Jericho, NY [*Library symbol Library of Congress*] (LCLS)

NJerCE........ Cantiague Elementary School, Jericho, NY [*Library symbol*] [*Library of Congress*] (LCLS)

NJerHS .... Jericho Senior High School, Jericho, NY [*Library symbol Library of Congress*] (LCLS)

NJerJE........ George Jackson Elementary School, Jericho, NY [*Library symbol Library of Congress*] (LCLS)

NJerS.......... Staff Supermarket Associates, Inc., Jericho, NY [*Library symbol Library of Congress*] (LCLS)

N Jersey R.... New Jersey Law Reports [*A publication*] (DLA)

NJESS.......... Nigerian Journal of Economic and Social Studies [*A publication*]

NjEwB.......... Bergen Citizen, Edgewater, NJ [*Library symbol Library of Congress*] (LCLS)

NjEwJJ......... Johnson & Johnson Dental Product Co., East Windsor, NJ [*Library symbol Library of Congress*] (LCLS)

NJF............. Cherry Point, NC [*Location identifier FAA*] (FAAL)

NjF............. Fair Lawn Free Public Library, Fair Lawn, NJ [*Library symbol Library of Congress*] (LCLS)

NJF............. Nordiska Journalistforbundet [*Nordic Association of Journalists Unions - NAJU*] (EAIO)

NJF............. Nordiske Jordbrugsforskeres Forening [*Nordic Agricultural Research Workers Association - NARWA*] (EAIO)

NJF............. Scandinavian Agricultural Research Workers' Association

NJFA........... National Justice Foundation of America (EA)

NJFAA......... Federal Aviation Administration, Eastern Region Library, Jamaica, NY [*Library symbol Library of Congress*] (LCLS)

NJFC........... Norma Jean Fan Club (EA)

NJFD........... Notices of Judgment, United States Food and Drug Administration [*A publication*] (DLA)

NjFdA.......... United States Army, Special Services Post Library, Fort Dix, NJ [*Library symbol Library of Congress*] (LCLS)

NjFf............. Fairfield Free Public Library, Fairfield, NJ [*Library symbol Library of Congress*] (LCLS)

NjFhUGA...... United States Golf Association, Far Hills, NJ [*Library symbol Library of Congress*] (LCLS)

NjFlCoC ...... Hunterdon County Clerk, Flemington, NJ [*Library symbol Library of Congress*] (LCLS)

NjFID .... Hunterdon County Democrat, Flemington, NJ [*Library symbol Library of Congress*] (LCLS)

NjFlH .... Hunterdon County Library, Flemington, NJ [*Library symbol Library of Congress*] (LCLS)

NjFlHi .... Hunterdon County Historical Society, Flemington, NJ [*Library symbol Library of Congress*] (LCLS)

NjFlM........... Hunterdon Medical Center, Flemington, NJ [*Library symbol Library of Congress*] (LCLS)

NjFmE-TD .... United States Army, Electronics Command, Technical Documents Branch, Fort Monmouth, NJ [*Library symbol Library of Congress*] (LCLS)

NjFmS.......... United States Army, Signal School, Fort Monmouth, NJ [*Library symbol Library of Congress*] (LCLS)

NjFNB.......... Shopper-News Beacon, Fair Lawn, NJ [*Library symbol Library of Congress*] (LCLS)

NjFp............. Florham Park Public Library, Florham Park, NJ [*Library symbol Library of Congress*] (LCLS)

NjFpEx......... Exxon Research & Engineering Co., Engineering Information Center, Florham Park, NJ [*Library symbol Library of Congress*] (LCLS)

NjFpN.......... Florham Park Community News, Florham Park, NJ [*Library symbol Library of Congress*] (LCLS)

NjFr............. Freehold Public Library, Freehold, NJ [*Library symbol Library of Congress*] (LCLS)

NJFR........... National Joint Fiction Reserve

NjFraS.......... Suburban News, Franklin Lakes, NJ [*Library symbol Library of Congress*] (LCLS)

NjFrCoC .... Clerk of Monmouth County, Freehold, NJ [*Library symbol Library of Congress*] (LCLS)

NjFrHi.......... Monmouth County Historical Association, Freehold, NJ [*Library symbol Library of Congress*] (LCLS)

NjFrM.......... Monmouth County Library, Freehold, NJ [*Library symbol Library of Congress*] (LCLS)

NjFrS.......... Schreiber Publishing Co., Freehold, NJ [*Library symbol Library of Congress*] (LCLS)

NjFrtD.......... Delaware Valley News, Frenchtown, NJ [*Library symbol Library of Congress*] (LCLS)

NjFrvA .... Advertiser, Franklinville, NJ [*Library symbol Library of Congress*] (LCLS)

NjFvW.......... West New Yorker, Inc., Fairview, NJ [*Library symbol Library of Congress*] (LCLS)

NJG............. Glassboro State College, Glassboro, NJ [*OCLC symbol*] (OCLC)

NJG............. Nachtjagugeschwader [*Night Fighter*] [*German*]

NJG............. Nice Jewish Girl [*Slang*]

NjGaB.......... Bergen Gazette, Inc., Garfield, NJ [*Library symbol Library of Congress*] (LCLS)

NjGaG.......... Garfield Guardian, Garfield, NJ [*Library symbol Library of Congress*] (LCLS)

NjGb .... Glassboro Public Library, Glassboro, NJ [*Library symbol Library of Congress*] (LCLS)

NjGbS.......... Glassboro State College, Glassboro, NJ [*Library symbol Library of Congress*] (LCLS)

NJGFE......... Nordic Joint Group for Forest Entomology (EA)

NjGiD.......... E. I. Du Pont de Nemours & Co., Eastern Laboratory Library, Gibbstown, NJ [*Library symbol Library of Congress*] (LCLS)

NjGl............. Gloucester City Library, Gloucester City, NJ [*Library symbol Library of Congress*] (LCLS)

NjGIN.......... Gloucester City News, Gloucester City, NJ [*Library symbol Library of Congress*] (LCLS)

NjGlri.......... Glen Ridge Free Public Library, Glen Ridge, NJ [*Library symbol Library of Congress*] (LCLS)

NjGlriA......... Associated Technical Services, Inc., Glen Ridge, NJ [*Library symbol Library of Congress*] (LCLS)

NjGrbR......... Raritan Valley Hospital, Greenbrook, NJ [*Library symbol Library of Congress*] (LCLS)

NjGrHi.......... Cumberland County Historical Society, Greenwich, NJ [*Library symbol Library of Congress*] (LCLS)

NJGSC .... National Jewish Girl Scout Committee (EA)

NjH............. Haddonfield Public Library, Haddonfield, NJ [*Library symbol Library of Congress*] (LCLS)

NJHA .... National Junior Horticultural Association (EA)

NjHaC.......... Centenary College for Women, Hackettstown, NJ [*Library symbol Library of Congress*] (LCLS)

NjHack......... Johnson Free Public Library, Hackensack, NJ [*Library symbol Library of Congress*] (LCLS)

NjHackR....... Bergen Record, Hackensack, NJ [*Library symbol Library of Congress*] (LCLS)

NjHam......... Hammonton Public Library, Hammonton, NJ [*Library symbol Library of Congress*] (LCLS)

NjHamN........ News Publishing Co., Hammonton, NJ [*Library symbol Library of Congress*] (LCLS)

NjHanS........ Sandoz, Inc., Hanover, NJ [*Library symbol Library of Congress*] (LCLS)

NjHarN......... Diamond Shamrock Corp., Harrison, NJ [*Library symbol Library of Congress*] (LCLS)

NjHarR......... Radio Corp. of America, Electronics Division, Harrison, NJ [*Library symbol Library of Congress*] (LCLS)

NjHas........... Hasbrouck Heights Free Public Library, Hasbrouck Heights, NJ [*Library symbol Library of Congress*] (LCLS)

NjHaS .... Star Gazette, Hackettstown, NJ [*Library symbol Library of Congress*] (LCLS)

NjHaSG........ Star Gazette, Hackettstown, NJ [*Library symbol*] [*Library of Congress*] (LCLS)

NjHasO........ Observer, Hasbrouck Heights, NJ [*Library symbol Library of Congress*] (LCLS)

NjHawD........ Dodds Publishing Co., Hawthorne, NJ [*Library symbol Library of Congress*] (LCLS)

NjHawP........ Hawthorne Press, Inc., Hawthorne, NJ [*Library symbol Library of Congress*] (LCLS)

NjHb .... Hillsborough Public Library, Hillsborough, NJ [*Library symbol Library of Congress*] (LCLS)

NJHC .... National Jewish Hospitality Committee (EA)

NjHh .... Haddon Heights Public Library, Haddon Heights, NJ [*Library symbol Library of Congress*] (LCLS)

NJHHCC ...... National Joint Heavy and Highway Construction Committee (EA)

NjHHi .... Historical Society of Haddonfield, Haddonfield, NJ [*Library symbol Library of Congress*] (LCLS)

NjHi .... New Jersey Historical Society, Newark, NJ [*Library symbol Library of Congress*] (LCLS)

NjHibP .... High Bridge Painting Co., High Bridge, NJ [*Library symbol Library of Congress*] (LCLS)

NjHig .... Hightstown Memorial Library, Hightstown, NJ [*Library symbol Library of Congress*] (LCLS)

NjHigG .... Hightstown Gazette, Hightstown, NJ [*Library symbol Library of Congress*] (LCLS)

NjHigN .... NL Industries, Inc., Hightstown, NJ [*Library symbol Library of Congress*] (LCLS)

NjHigP .... Peddie School, Hightstown, NJ [*Library symbol Library of Congress*] (LCLS)

NjHil .... Hillside Free Public Library, Hillside, NJ [*Library symbol Library of Congress*] (LCLS)

NjHilT .... Hillside Times, Hillside, NJ [*Library symbol Library of Congress*] (LCLS)

NJH/NAC ...... National Jewish Hospital/National Asthma Center [*Later, National Jewish Center for Immunology and Respiratory Medicine*] (EA)

NjHo .... Hoboken Free Public Library, Hoboken, NJ [*Library symbol Library of Congress*] (LCLS)

NjHoGF .... General Foods Corp., Hoboken, NJ [*Library symbol Library of Congress*] (LCLS)

NjHolB .... Bell Telephone Laboratories, Inc., Technical Information Library, Holmdel, NJ [*Library symbol Library of Congress*] (LCLS)

NjHop .... Hopewell Public Library, Hopewell, NJ [*Library symbol Library of Congress*] (LCLS)

NjHopM .... Hopewell Museum, Hopewell, NJ [*Library symbol Library of Congress*] (LCLS)

NjHopN .... Hopewell Valley News, Hopewell, NJ [*Library symbol Library of Congress*] (LCLS)

NjHoS .... Stevens Institute of Technology, Hoboken, NJ [*Library symbol Library of Congress*] (LCLS)

NjHowB .... Booster Press, Howell, NJ [*Library symbol Library of Congress*] (LCLS)

NJHS .... National Junior Honor Society (EA)

NjI .... Free Public Library of Irvington, Irvington, NJ [*Library symbol Library of Congress*] (LCLS)

NJI .... Network Job Interface

NJI .... New Jersey Institute of Technology, Newark, NJ [*OCLC symbol*] (OCLC)

NJIC .... National Joint Industrial Council [*Pharmacology British*]

NJIFR .... Notices of Judgment, Federal Insecticide, Fungicide, and Rodenticide Act [*A publication*] (DLA)

NJII .... New Jersey, Indiana & Illinois Railroad Co. [*AAR code*]

NJIS .... National Jewish Information Service (for the Propagation of Judaism) [*Defunct*] (EA)

NJIT .... New Jersey Institute of Technology (GAGS)

NjJ .... Jersey City Free Public Library, Jersey City, NJ [*Library symbol Library of Congress*] (LCLS)

NJJ .... Jersey City State College, Jersey City, NJ [*OCLC symbol*] (OCLC)

NJJ .... Niijima [*Japan*] [*Seismograph station code, US Geological Survey Closed*] (SEIS)

NjJa .... Library at Jamesburg, Jamesburg, NJ [*Library symbol Library of Congress*] (LCLS)

NjJacN .... Jackson News, Jackson, NJ [*Library symbol Library of Congress*] (LCLS)

NjJacP .... Jackson Township Publishing Co., Jackson, NJ [*Library symbol Library of Congress*] (LCLS)

NjJJ .... Jewish Standard, Jersey City, NJ [*Library symbol Library of Congress*] (LCLS)

NjJJJ .... Jersey Journal, Jersey City, NJ [*Library symbol Library of Congress*] (LCLS)

NjJS .... Jersey City State College, Jersey City, NJ [*Library symbol Library of Congress*] (LCLS)

NjJStP .... Saint Peter's College, Jersey City, NJ [*Library symbol Library of Congress*] (LCLS)

NjJUB .... Urner-Barry Publications, Jersey City, NJ [*Library symbol Library of Congress*] (LCLS)

NJK .... El Centro, CA [*Location identifier FAA*] (FAAL)

NJK .... Kean College of New Jersey, Union, NJ [*OCLC symbol*] (OCLC)

NjK .... Kearny Public Library, Kearny, NJ [*Library symbol Library of Congress*] (LCLS)

NjKeHS .... Keansburg High School, Keansburg, NJ [*Library symbol*] [*Library of Congress*] (LCLS)

NjKey .... Keyport Free Public Library, Keyport, NJ [*Library symbol Library of Congress*] (LCLS)

NjKO .... Kearny Observer, Kearny, NJ [*Library symbol Library of Congress*] (LCLS)

NjKWT .... Western Electric Co., Kearny, NJ [*Library symbol Library of Congress*] (LCLS)

NjL .... Lodi Memorial Library, Lodi, NJ [*Library symbol Library of Congress*] (LCLS)

NJL .... New Jersey Law Reports [*A publication*] (DLA)

NJL .... New Jersey State Library, Trenton, NJ [*OCLC symbol*] (OCLC)

NJLA .... New Jersey Library Association

NjLaHi .... Lake Hopatcong Historical Society, Lake Hopatcong, NJ [*Library symbol Library of Congress*] (LCLS)

NjLak .... Lakewood Public Library, Lakewood, NJ [*Library symbol Library of Congress*] (LCLS)

NjLakC .... Ocean County Citizen, Lakewood, NJ [*Library symbol Library of Congress*] (LCLS)

NjLakG .... Georgian Court College, Lakewood, NJ [*Library symbol Library of Congress*] (LCLS)

NjLakhM ...... Manchester Publishing Co., Lakehurst, NJ [*Library symbol Library of Congress*] (LCLS)

NjLakT .... Ocean County Daily Times, Lakewood, NJ [*Library symbol Library of Congress*] (LCLS)

NjLamB .... Lambertville Beacon, Lambertville, NJ [*Library symbol Library of Congress*] (LCLS)

NJ Law .... New Jersey Law Reports [*A publication*] (DLA)

NJ Law N .... New Jersey Law News [*A publication*] (DLA)

NjLawR .... Rider College, Lawrenceville, NJ [*Library symbol Library of Congress*] (LCLS)

NJ Law Rep... New Jersey Law Reports [*A publication*] (DLA)

NJLC .... National Juvenile Law Center [*Later, NCYL*] (EA)

NjLe .... Leonia Public Library, Leonia, NJ [*Library symbol Library of Congress*] (LCLS)

NjLedW .... West Morris Star Journal, Ledgewood, NJ [*Library symbol Library of Congress*] (LCLS)

NJ Leg Rec... New Jersey Legal Record [*A publication*] (DLA)

NjLF .... Felician College, Lodi, NJ [*Library symbol Library of Congress*] (LCLS)

NjLf .... Little Falls Free Public Library, Little Falls, NJ [*Library symbol Library of Congress*] (LCLS)

NJLFC .... New Jersey Film Circuit [*Library network*]

NjLh .... Lake Hiawatha Public Library, Lake Hiawatha, NJ [*Library symbol Library of Congress*] (LCLS)

NjLhP .... Pennysaver Publishing Co., Lake Hiawatha, NJ [*Library symbol Library of Congress*] (LCLS)

NjLi .... Free Public Library of Livingston, Livingston, NJ [*Library symbol Library of Congress*] (LCLS)

NjLin .... Linden Free Public Library, Linden, NJ [*Library symbol Library of Congress*] (LCLS)

NjLincB .... Brookdale Community College, Lincroft, NJ [*Library symbol Library of Congress*] (LCLS)

NjLinEx .... Exxon Research & Engineering Co., Company and Literature Information Center Library, Linden, NJ [*Library symbol Library of Congress*] (LCLS)

NjLinEx-M ..... Exxon Research & Engineering Co., Medical Research Library, Linden, NJ [*Library symbol Library of Congress*] (LCLS)

NjLivStB ...... Saint Barnabas Medical Center, Staff Library, Livingston, NJ [*Library symbol Library of Congress*] (LCLS)

NjLiW .... West Essex Tribune, Livingston, NJ [*Library symbol Library of Congress*] (LCLS)

NjLob .... Long Branch Public Library, Long Branch, NJ [*Library symbol Library of Congress*] (LCLS)

NjLp .... Lincoln Park Public Library, Lincoln Park, NJ [*Library symbol Library of Congress*] (LCLS)

NjLP .... Paci Press, Lodi, NJ [*Library symbol Library of Congress*] (LCLS)

NjLpBHi .... Beavertown Historical Society, Lincoln Park, NJ [*Library symbol Library of Congress*] (LCLS)

NjLpH .... Lincoln Herald, Lincoln Park, NJ [*Library symbol Library of Congress*] (LCLS)

NjLPP .... Paci Press, Lodi, NJ [*Library symbol*] [*Library of Congress*] (LCLS)

NJL Rep ...... New Jersey Law Reports [*A publication*] (DLA)

NJL Rev ...... New Jersey Law Review [*A publication*] (DLA)

NjLwR .... Record Breeze, Lindenwold, NJ [*Library symbol Library of Congress*] (LCLS)

NjLy .... Lyndhurst Public Library, Lyndhurst, NJ [*Library symbol Library of Congress*] (LCLS)

NjLyL .... Leader Publications, Lyndhurst, NJ [*Library symbol Library of Congress*] (LCLS)

NjLyoV .... United States Veterans Administration Hospital, Lyons, NJ [*Library symbol Library of Congress*] (LCLS)

NjM .... Free Public Library of the Borough of Madison, Madison, NJ [*Library symbol Library of Congress*] (LCLS)

NJM .... Montclair State College, Upper Montclair, NJ [*OCLC symbol*] (OCLC)

NJM .... New Jersey Miscellaneous Reports [*A publication*] (DLA)

NJM .... Swansboro, NC [*Location identifier FAA*] (FAAL)

NJMA .... National Jail Managers Association [*Later, AJA*] (EA)

NjMah .... Free Public Library of the Township of Mahwah, Mahwah, NJ [*Library symbol Library of Congress*] (LCLS)

NjMahR .... Ramapo College of New Jersey, Mahwah, NJ [*Library symbol Library of Congress*] (LCLS)

NjMal .... Franklin Township Public Library, Malaga, NJ [*Library symbol Library of Congress*] (LCLS)

NjMan .... Manasquan Public Library, Manasquan, NJ [*Library symbol Library of Congress*] (LCLS)

NjManhT ...... Times Beacon Co., Manahawkin, NJ [*Library symbol Library of Congress*] (LCLS)

NjManS .... Coast Star, Manasquan, NJ [*Library symbol Library of Congress*] (LCLS)

NjMap .... Maplewood Memorial Library, Maplewood, NJ [*Library symbol Library of Congress*] (LCLS)

NjMapW ...... Worrall Publishing Co., Maplewood, NJ [*Library symbol Library of Congress*] (LCLS)

NjMat .... Matawan Joint Free Public Library, Matawan, NJ [*Library symbol Library of Congress*] (LCLS)

NjMatB .... Bayshore Independent, Matawan, NJ [*Library symbol Library of Congress*] (LCLS)

NjMatHi .... Madison Township Historical Society, Matawan, NJ [*Library symbol Library of Congress*] (LCLS)

NjMayO........ Our Town, Maywood, NJ [*Library symbol Library of Congress*] (LCLS)

NJMC............ National Jewish Music Council [*Later, Jewish Welfare Board Jewish Music Council*] (EA)

NjMcUSAF ... United States Air Force, Base Library, McGuire Air Force Base, NJ [*Library symbol Library of Congress*] (LCLS)

NjMD .... Drew University, Madison, NJ [*Library symbol Library of Congress*] (LCLS)

NJMDC .... NORAD Joint Manual Direction Center [*Military*]

NjMD-T .... Drew University, Theological School, Madison, NJ [*Library symbol Library of Congress*] (LCLS)

NjMe............ Free Public Library, Metuchen, NJ [*Library symbol Library of Congress*] (LCLS)

NjME............ Madison Eagle, Madison, NJ [*Library symbol Library of Congress*] (LCLS)

NjMedR .... Central Record, Medford, NJ [*Library symbol Library of Congress*] (LCLS)

NjMen.......... Mendham Public Library, Mendham, NJ [*Library symbol Library of Congress*] (LCLS)

NjMenO .... Observer-Tribune, Mendham, NJ [*Library symbol Library of Congress*] (LCLS)

NjMF............ Fairleigh Dickinson University, Madison, NJ [*Library symbol Library of Congress*] (LCLS)

NjMhB .... Burlington County Area Reference Library, Mount Holly, NJ [*Library symbol Library of Congress*] (LCLS)

NjMhCoC ..... Burlington County Clerk, Mount Holly, NJ [*Library symbol Library of Congress*] (LCLS)

NjMhH .... Burlington County Herald, Mount Holly, NJ [*Library symbol Library of Congress*] (LCLS)

NjMHi .... Madison Historical Society, Madison, NJ [*Library symbol Library of Congress*] (LCLS)

NjMhL .... Burlington County Lyceum [*Mount Holly Public Library*], Mount Holly, NJ [*Library symbol Library of Congress*] (LCLS)

NjMhPM ...... Burlington County Prison Museum, Mount Holly, NJ [*Library symbol Library of Congress*] (LCLS)

NJMI .... Catholic Medical Center of Brooklyn & Queens, Inc., Jamaica, NY [*Library symbol*] [*Library of Congress*] (LCLS)

NJMI............ Mary Immaculate Hospital, School of Nursing, Jamaica, NY [*Library symbol Library of Congress*] (LCLS)

NjMi............ Middletown Township Free Public Library, Middletown, NJ [*Library symbol Library of Congress*] (LCLS)

NJMI............ New Junior Maudsley Inventory [*Psychology*]

NjMiA .... Advisor, Middletown, NJ [*Library symbol Library of Congress*] (LCLS)

NjMiC .... Courier, Middletown, NJ [*Library symbol Library of Congress*] (LCLS)

NjMid........... Middlesex Public Library, Middlesex, NJ [*Library symbol Library of Congress*] (LCLS)

NjMil .... Millburn Free Public Library, Millburn, NJ [*Library symbol Library of Congress*] (LCLS)

NjMilt .... Milltown Public Library, Milltown, NJ [*Library symbol Library of Congress*] (LCLS)

NjMilv .... Millville Public Library, Millville, NJ [*Library symbol Library of Congress*] (LCLS)

NjMilvHi ...... Wheaton Historical Association, Millville, NJ [*Library symbol Library of Congress*] (LCLS)

NjMilvM....... Millville Daily, Millville, NJ [*Library symbol Library of Congress*] (LCLS)

NjMiP .... Middletown Township Public Library, Middletown, NJ [*Library symbol*] [*Library of Congress*] (LCLS)

NJ Mis........ New Jersey Miscellaneous Reports [*A publication*] (DLA)

NJ Misc....... New Jersey Miscellaneous Reports [*A publication*] (DLA)

NJ Mis R .... New Jersey Miscellaneous Reports [*A publication*] (DLA)

NjMj............ South Brunswick Free Public Library, Monmouth Junction, NJ [*Library symbol Library of Congress*] (LCLS)

NjMIA .... Atlantic County Library, Mays Landing, NJ [*Library symbol Library of Congress*] (LCLS)

NjMIAC .... Atlantic Community College, Mays Landing, NJ [*Library symbol Library of Congress*] (LCLS)

NjMICoC ...... Atlantic County Clerk, Mays Landing, NJ [*Library symbol Library of Congress*] (LCLS)

NjMIR .... Atlantic County Record, Mays Landing, NJ [*Library symbol Library of Congress*] (LCLS)

NjMo............ Joint Free Public Library of Morristown and Morris Township, Morristown, NJ [*Library symbol Library of Congress*] (LCLS)

NjMoAT........ American Telephone & Telegraph Co., Morristown Corporate Marketing Library, Morristown, NJ [*Library symbol Library of Congress*] (LCLS)

NjMoCoC ..... Morris County Clerk, Morristown, NJ [*Library symbol Library of Congress*] (LCLS)

NjMoH .... Morristown Memorial Hospital, Morristown, NJ [*Library symbol Library of Congress*] (LCLS)

NjMoHP .... Morristown National Historical Park, Morristown, NJ [*Library symbol Library of Congress*] (LCLS)

NjMon.......... Montclair Free Public Library, Montclair, NJ [*Library symbol Library of Congress*] (LCLS)

NjMonM....... Montclair Times, Montclair, NJ [*Library symbol Library of Congress*] (LCLS)

NjMor .... Moorestown Free Library, Moorestown, NJ [*Library symbol Library of Congress*] (LCLS)

NjMorR .... Radio Corp. of America, Missile and Surface Radar Division, Moorestown, NJ [*Library symbol Library of Congress*] (LCLS)

NjMou.......... Mountain Lakes Public Library, Mountain Lakes, NJ [*Library symbol Library of Congress*] (LCLS)

NjMouHi ...... Mountain Lakes Historical Society, Mountain Lakes, NJ [*Library symbol Library of Congress*] (LCLS)

NjMov .... Montvale Free Public Library, Montvale, NJ [*Library symbol Library of Congress*] (LCLS)

NjMovL .... Lehn & Fink Products Co., Montvale, NJ [*Library symbol Library of Congress*] (LCLS)

NjMp .... Morris Plains Public Library, Morris Plains, NJ [*Library symbol Library of Congress*] (LCLS)

NJMP .... New Jewish Media Project [*JMS*] [*Absorbed by*] (EA)

NjMpN .... Morris News-Bee, Morris Plains, NJ [*Library symbol Library of Congress*] (LCLS)

NjMpW .... Warner-Lambert Research Institute, Morris Plains, NJ [*Library symbol Library of Congress*] (LCLS)

NJMR .... Nordisk Verbane Musik Rad [*Nordic Council for Railway Music - NCRM*] (EAIO)

NjMs............ Maple Shade Public Library, Maple Shade, NJ [*Library symbol Library of Congress*] (LCLS)

NJMS............ New Jersey Medical School [*Newark*]

NjMsP........... Maple Shade Progress Press, Maple Shade, NJ [*Library symbol Library of Congress*] (LCLS)

NjMuA .... Air Reduction Co., Inc., Central Research Department Library, Murray Hill, NJ [*Library symbol Library of Congress*] (LCLS)

NjMuB .... Bell Telephone Laboratories, Inc., Murray Hill, NJ [*Library symbol Library of Congress*] (LCLS)

NjMuhHi ...... Harrison Township Historical Society, Mullica Hill, NJ [*Library symbol Library of Congress*] (LCLS)

NJN............. College of Medicine and Dentistry of New Jersey, Newark, NJ [*OCLC symbol*] (OCLC)

NjN............. Newark Public Library, Newark, NJ [*Library symbol Library of Congress*] (LCLS)

NJN............. New Jersey Network [*Trenton*] [*Telecommunications service*] (TSSD)

NjNA .... United States Attorney's Office, Law Library, Newark, NJ [*Library symbol Library of Congress*] (LCLS)

NjNAA.......... New Jersey Afro-American, Newark, NJ [*Library symbol Library of Congress*] (LCLS)

NjNb .... New Brunswick Free Public Library, New Brunswick, NJ [*Library symbol Library of Congress*] (LCLS)

NjNbH .... Home News, New Brunswick, NJ [*Library symbol Library of Congress*] (LCLS)

NjNbJJ .... Johnson & Johnson, Research Center, New Brunswick, NJ [*Library symbol Library of Congress*] (LCLS)

NjNbM .... Middlesex General Hospital, New Brunswick, NJ [*Library symbol Library of Congress*] (LCLS)

NjNbS .... New Brunswick Theological Seminary, New Brunswick, NJ [*Library symbol Library of Congress*] (LCLS)

NjNbSI .... Squibb-Beechnut, Inc., New Brunswick, NJ [*Library symbol Library of Congress*] (LCLS)

NjNbSp .... New Brunswick Spokesman, New Brunswick, NJ [*Library symbol Library of Congress*] (LCLS)

NjNbStP .... Saint Peter's Medical Center, New Brunswick, NJ [*Library symbol Library of Congress*] (LCLS)

NjNC .... New Jersey Institute of Technology, Newark, NJ [*Library symbol Library of Congress*] (LCLS)

NjNCM .... New Jersey College of Medicine and Dentistry, Newark, NJ [*Library symbol Library of Congress*] (LCLS)

NjNE .... Essex County College, Newark, NJ [*Library symbol Library of Congress*] (LCLS)

NjNeP .... New Egypt Press, New Egypt, NJ [*Library symbol Library of Congress*] (LCLS)

NjNet .... Dennis Memorial Library, Newton, NJ [*Library symbol Library of Congress*] (LCLS)

NjNetcN....... News Leader, Netcong, NJ [*Library symbol Library of Congress*] (LCLS)

NjNetCoC ..... Sussex County Clerk, Newton, NJ [*Library symbol Library of Congress*] (LCLS)

NjNetDB .... Don Bosco College, Newton, NJ [*Library symbol Library of Congress*] (LCLS)

NjNetH .... New Jersey Herald, Newton, NJ [*Library symbol Library of Congress*] (LCLS)

NjNetS .... Sussex County Library, Newton, NJ [*Library symbol Library of Congress*] (LCLS)

NjNetSHi...... Sussex County Historical Society, Newton, NJ [*Library symbol Library of Congress*] (LCLS)

NjNhBHi...... Bergen County Historical Society, North Hackensack, NJ [*Library symbol Library of Congress*] (LCLS)

NjNI .... Ironbound Crier, Newark, NJ [*Library symbol Library of Congress*] (LCLS)

NjNIJS .... Institute of Jazz Studies, Rutgers, the State University, Newark, NJ [*Library symbol*] [*Library of Congress*] (LCLS)

NjNIM .... International Musician, Newark, NJ [*Library symbol Library of Congress*] (LCLS)

NjNIT .... Italian Tribune, Newark, NJ [*Library symbol Library of Congress*] (LCLS)

NjNJL........... Jewish Ledger, Newark, NJ [*Library symbol Library of Congress*] (LCLS)

NjNJN .... Jewish News, Newark, NJ [*Library symbol Library of Congress*] (LCLS)

NjNL .... Luso-Americano, Newark, NJ [*Library symbol Library of Congress*] (LCLS)

NjNLH.......... New Jersey Labor Herald, Newark, NJ [*Library symbol Library of Congress*] (LCLS)

NjNN .... Nite-Lite, Newark, NJ [*Library symbol Library of Congress*] (LCLS)

NjNoA .... Atlantic County Advertiser, Northfield, NJ [*Library symbol Library of Congress*] (LCLS)

NjNoa .... North Arlington Free Public Library, North Arlington, NJ [*Library symbol Library of Congress*] (LCLS)

NjNoaP .... North Arlington Free Public Library, North Arlington, NJ [*Library symbol*] [*Library of Congress*] (LCLS)

NjNor .... Norwood Public Library, Norwood, NJ [*Library symbol Library of Congress*] (LCLS)

NjNp .... New Providence Memorial Library, New Providence, NJ [*Library symbol Library of Congress*] (LCLS)

NjNpD .... Dispatch, New Providence, NJ [*Library symbol Library of Congress*] (LCLS)

NjNpHi .... New Providence Historical Society, New Providence, NJ [*Library symbol Library of Congress*] (LCLS)

NjNpI .... Independent Press, New Providence, NJ [*Library symbol Library of Congress*] (LCLS)

NjNPSE .... Public Service Electric & Gas Co., Newark, NJ [*Library symbol*] [*Library of Congress*] (LCLS)

NjNT .... Tribuna di North Jersey, Newark, NJ [*Library symbol Library of Congress*] (LCLS)

NjNu .... Nutley Free Public Library, Nutley, NJ [*Library symbol Library of Congress*] (LCLS)

NjNuH .... Hoffmann-La Roche, Inc., Scientific Library, Nutley, NJ [*Library symbol Library of Congress*] (LCLS)

NjNuHi .... Nutley Historical Society, Nutley, NJ [*Library symbol Library of Congress*] (LCLS)

NjNuS .... Sun-Bank Newspapers, Nutley, NJ [*Library symbol Library of Congress*] (LCLS)

NJNY .... New Jersey & New York R. R. [*AAR code*]

NjO .... Free Public Library of the City of Orange, Orange, NJ [*Library symbol Library of Congress*] (LCLS)

NjOak .... Oakland Public Library, Oakland, NJ [*Library symbol Library of Congress*] (LCLS)

NjOaS .... Shore Publishers, Inc., Oakhurst, NJ [*Library symbol Library of Congress*] (LCLS)

NjOcM .... Ocean City Historical Museum, Ocean City, NJ [*Library symbol Library of Congress*] (LCLS)

NjOcS .... Sentinel Ledger, Ocean City, NJ [*Library symbol Library of Congress*] (LCLS)

NjOgT .... Ocean Grove Times, Ocean Grove, NJ [*Library symbol Library of Congress*] (LCLS)

NjOrd .... Oradell Public Library, Oradell, NJ [*Library symbol Library of Congress*] (LCLS)

NjOrdB .... Burns & Roe, Inc., Oradell, NJ [*Library symbol Library of Congress*] (LCLS)

NJosnU .... United Health Services, Wilson Hospital, Johnson City, NY [*Library symbol Library of Congress*] (LCLS)

NJostF .... Fulton-Montgomery Community College, Johnstown, NY [*Library symbol Library of Congress*] (LCLS)

NjOtR .... Fleming H. Revell Co., Old Tappan, NJ [*Library symbol Library of Congress*] (LCLS)

NjOW .... Worrall Publications, Inc., Orange, NJ [*Library symbol Library of Congress*] (LCLS)

NJP .... National Jury Project (EA)

NJP .... Network Job Processing

NJP .... Nonjudicial Punishment [*Military*]

NjP .... Princeton University, Princeton, NJ [*Library symbol Library of Congress*] (LCLS)

NJP .... Warminster, PA [*Location identifier FAA*] (FAAL)

NJP .... William Patterson College of New Jersey, Wayne, NJ [*OCLC symbol*] (OCLC)

NjPA .... American Cyanamid Co., Agricultural Division, Princeton, NJ [*Library symbol Library of Congress*] (LCLS)

NjP-A .... Art Museum of Princeton University, Princeton, NJ [*Library symbol*] [*Library of Congress*] (LCLS)

NJPA .... National Juice Products Association (EA)

NjPalN .... Bergen News, Palisades Park, NJ [*Library symbol Library of Congress*] (LCLS)

NjPar .... Paramus Public Library, Paramus, NJ [*Library symbol Library of Congress*] (LCLS)

NjParB .... Bergen Community College, Paramus, NJ [*Library symbol Library of Congress*] (LCLS)

NjParkHi ...... Pascack Historical Society and Museum, Park Ridge, NJ [*Library symbol Library of Congress*] (LCLS)

NjParkP .... Pascack Publications Corp., Park Ridge, NJ [*Library symbol Library of Congress*] (LCLS)

NjParR .... Ridgewood Newspapers, Paramus, NJ [*Library symbol Library of Congress*] (LCLS)

NjParT .... Town News, Paramus, NJ [*Library symbol Library of Congress*] (LCLS)

NjPas .... Passaic Public Library, Passaic, NJ [*Library symbol Library of Congress*] (LCLS)

NjPasC .... Passaic Citizen, Passaic, NJ [*Library symbol Library of Congress*] (LCLS)

NjPasCS ...... Catholic Sokol Printing Co., Passaic, NJ [*Library symbol Library of Congress*] (LCLS)

NjPasE .... Eastern Catholic Life, Passaic, NJ [*Library symbol Library of Congress*] (LCLS)

NjPasH .... Herald News, Passaic, NJ [*Library symbol Library of Congress*] (LCLS)

NjPat .... Paterson Free Public Library, Paterson, NJ [*Library symbol Library of Congress*] (LCLS)

NjPatCoC ..... Passaic County Clerk, Paterson, NJ [*Library symbol Library of Congress*] (LCLS)

NjPatNe .... News, Paterson, NJ [*Library symbol Library of Congress*] (LCLS)

NjPatPHi ...... Passaic County Historical Society, Paterson, NJ [*Library symbol Library of Congress*] (LCLS)

NjPatSA .... Saint Anthony's Guild, Franciscan Monastery, Paterson, NJ [*Library symbol Library of Congress*] (LCLS)

NjPatV .... Voce Italiana, Paterson, NJ [*Library symbol Library of Congress*] (LCLS)

NjPauR .... Record, Paulsboro, NJ [*Library symbol Library of Congress*] (LCLS)

NjPauS .... Mobil Research & Development Corp., Paulsboro, NJ [*Library symbol Library of Congress*] (LCLS)

NJPC .... National Joint Practice Commission (DMAA)

NjPD .... Daily Princetonian, Princeton, NJ [*Library symbol Library of Congress*] (LCLS)

NJPDDATC... National Joint Painting, Decorating, and Drywall Apprenticeship and Training Committee (EA)

NjPE .... Educational Testing Service, Princeton, NJ [*Library symbol Library of Congress*] (LCLS)

NjPeB .... Burlington County College, Pemberton, NJ [*Library symbol Library of Congress*] (LCLS)

NjPegR .... Penns Grove Record, Penns Grove, NJ [*Library symbol Library of Congress*] (LCLS)

NjPenP .... Pennsauken Resume, Pennsauken, NJ [*Library symbol Library of Congress*] (LCLS)

NjPeqB .... Beacon, Pequannock, NJ [*Library symbol Library of Congress*] (LCLS)

NjPera .... Perth Amboy Free Public Library, Perth Amboy, NJ [*Library symbol Library of Congress*] (LCLS)

NjPeraSo ..... Universum Sokol Publishers, Perth Amboy, NJ [*Library symbol Library of Congress*] (LCLS)

NjPeraSt ...... Saint John's Church, Perth Amboy, NJ [*Library symbol Library of Congress*] (LCLS)

NjPERS .... E. R. Squibb & Sons, Princeton, NJ [*Library symbol Library of Congress*] (LCLS)

NjPeT .... Times Advertising Printing Co., Pemberton, NJ [*Library symbol Library of Congress*] (LCLS)

NjPF .... FMC Corp., Princeton, NJ [*Library symbol Library of Congress*] (LCLS)

NjP-G .... Princeton University, Gest Library, Princeton, NJ [*Library symbol Library of Congress*] (LCLS)

NjPh .... Phillipsburg Free Public Library, Phillipsburg, NJ [*Library symbol Library of Congress*] (LCLS)

NJPHA .... National Junior Polled Hereford Association (EA)

NJPHC .... National Junior Polled Hereford Council [*Later, NJPHA*] (EA)

NjPHi .... Historical Society of Princeton, Princeton, NJ [*Library symbol Library of Congress*] (LCLS)

NjPhP .... Free Press, Phillipsburg, NJ [*Library symbol Library of Congress*] (LCLS)

NjPI .... Institute for Advanced Study, Princeton, NJ [*Library symbol Library of Congress*] (LCLS)

NjPi .... McCowan Memorial Library, Pitman, NJ [*Library symbol Library of Congress*] (LCLS)

NjPiM .... McCowan Memorial Library, Pitman, NJ [*Library symbol*] [*Library of Congress*] (LCLS)

NjPJ .... Robert Wood Johnson Foundation Library, Princeton, NJ [*Library symbol Library of Congress*] (LCLS)

NjPl .... Emanuel Einstein Free Public Library, Pompton Lakes, NJ [*Library symbol Library of Congress*] (LCLS)

NjPla .... Plainfield Public Library, Plainfield, NJ [*Library symbol Library of Congress*] (LCLS)

NjPlaM .... Muhlenberg Hospital, Plainfield, NJ [*Library symbol Library of Congress*] (LCLS)

NjPlaSDB.... Seventh Day Baptist Historical Society, Plainfield, NJ [*Library symbol Library of Congress*] (LCLS)

NjPlaT .... Plainfield Times, Plainfield, NJ [*Library symbol Library of Congress*] (LCLS)

NjPlaV .... Voice, Plainfield, NJ [*Library symbol Library of Congress*] (LCLS)

NjPleM .... Mainland Journal, Pleasantville, NJ [*Library symbol Library of Congress*] (LCLS)

NjPM .... Mobil Research & Development Corp., Central Research Division Library, Princeton, NJ [*Library symbol Library of Congress*] (LCLS)

NJPMB .... Navy Jet-Propelled-Missile Board

NjPMC .... Medical Center at Princeton, Princeton, NJ [*Library symbol Library of Congress*] (LCLS)

NjPoiO .... Ocean County Leader, Point Pleasant Beach, NJ [*Library symbol Library of Congress*] (LCLS)

NjPoR .... Richard Stockton State College, Pomona, NJ [*Library symbol Library of Congress*] (LCLS)

NjPP .... Princeton Packet, Inc., Princeton, NJ [*Library symbol Library of Congress*] (LCLS)

NjPpE .... Eastern Historical Commission, Prospect Park, NJ [*Library symbol Library of Congress*] (LCLS)

NjP-Pop .... Princeton University, Office of Population Research, Princeton, NJ [*Library symbol Library of Congress*] (LCLS)

NjPPP .... Princeton Public Library, Princeton, NJ [*Library symbol Library of Congress*] (LCLS)

NjPRCA .... Radio Corp. of America, Laboratories Division, Princeton, NJ [*Library symbol Library of Congress*] (LCLS)

NjPS .... Princeton Shopping News, Princeton, NJ [*Library symbol Library of Congress*] (LCLS)

NjP-SC .... Princeton University, Princeton Special Collection, Princeton, NJ [*Library symbol*] [*Library of Congress*] (LCLS)

NjPStJ .... Saint Joseph's College, Princeton, NJ [*Library symbol Library of Congress*] (LCLS)

NjPT .... Princeton Theological Seminary, Princeton, NJ [*Library symbol Library of Congress*] (LCLS)

NjPTe .... Textile Research Institute, Princeton, NJ [*Library symbol Library of Congress*] (LCLS)

NjPTT .... Town Topics, Inc., Princeton, NJ [*Library symbol Library of Congress*] (LCLS)

NjPW .... Western Electric Co., Inc., Engineering Research Center, Princeton, NJ [*Library symbol Library of Congress*] (LCLS)

NjPwAT .... American Telephone & Telegraph Co. Resource Center, Piscataway, NJ [*Library symbol Library of Congress*] (LCLS)

NjPwC .... Colgate-Palmolive Co., Technical Information Center, Piscataway, NJ [*Library symbol Library of Congress*] (LCLS)

NjPwIE .... Institute of Electrical and Electronics Engineers, Piscataway, NJ [*Library symbol Library of Congress*] (LCLS)

NJQ .... Queens Borough Public Library, Jamaica, NY [*Library symbol Library of Congress*] (LCLS)

NJQH .... Queens Hospital Center, Jamaica, NY [*Library symbol Library of Congress*] (LCLS)

NJR .... New Jersey Register [*A publication*] (DLA)

NJR .... New Jersey Resources [*NYSE symbol*] (TTSB)

NJR .... New Jersey Resources Corp. [*NYSE symbol*] (SPSG)

NJR .... New JEWEL Regime [*Grenada*]

NJR .... Nonjob Routed [*Military*] (AFIT)

NjR .... Rutgers-[*The*] State University, New Brunswick, NJ [*Library symbol Library of Congress*] (LCLS)

NJRA .... National Juvenile Restitution Association [*Later, ARA*] (EA)

NjRah .... Rahway Public Library, Rahway, NJ [*Library symbol Library of Congress*] (LCLS)

NjRahB .... Bauer Publishing & Printing Ltd., Rahway, NJ [*Library symbol Library of Congress*] (LCLS)

NjRahM ...... Merck, Sharp & Dohme [*Later, Merck & Co., Inc.*] Research Laboratory, Research Library, Rahway, NJ [*Library symbol Library of Congress*] (LCLS)

NjRam .... Ramsey Free Public Library, Ramsey, NJ [*Library symbol Library of Congress*] (LCLS)

NjRamH ...... Home and Store News, Ramsey, NJ [*Library symbol Library of Congress*] (LCLS)

NjRamI .... Immaculate Conception Theological Seminary, Ramsey, NJ [*Library symbol Library of Congress*] (LCLS)

NjRarO .... Ortho Pharmaceutical Corp., Raritan, NJ [*Library symbol Library of Congress*] (LCLS)

NjRarOD ...... Ortho Diagnostics, Raritan, NJ [*Library symbol Library of Congress*] (LCLS)

NjRb .... Red Bank Public Library, Red Bank, NJ [*Library symbol Library of Congress*] (LCLS)

NjRbR .... Daily Register, Red Bank, NJ [*Library symbol Library of Congress*] (LCLS)

NJRC .... National Jewish Resource Center (EA)

NJRC .... New Jersey Board of Railroad Commissioners Annual Reports [*A publication*] (DLA)

NjRdR .... Riverdale Publishing Co., Riverdale, NJ [*Library symbol Library of Congress*] (LCLS)

NJ Rep .... New Jersey Law Reports [*A publication*] (DLA)

NJ Re Tit N... New Jersey Realty Title News [*A publication*] (DLA)

NJ Rev Stat... New Jersey Revised Statutes [*A publication*] (DLA)

NjRf .... Ridgefield Public Library, Ridgefield, NJ [*Library symbol Library of Congress*] (LCLS)

NjRh .... Rocky Hill Public Library, Rocky Hill, NJ [*Library symbol Library of Congress*] (LCLS)

NjRiv .... Riverside Public Library, Riverside, NJ [*Library symbol Library of Congress*] (LCLS)

NjRive .... River Edge Free Public Library, River Edge, NJ [*Library symbol Library of Congress*] (LCLS)

NjR-L .... Rutgers-[*The*] State University, Rutgers-Camden School of Law, Camden, NJ [*Library symbol Library of Congress*] (LCLS)

NjR-NL .... Rutgers, The State University, Law School Library-Newark, Newark, NJ [*Library symbol*] [*Library of Congress*] (LCLS)

NjRo .... Roseland Public Library, Roseland, NJ [*Library symbol Library of Congress*] (LCLS)

NjRocM .... Morris County News, Rockaway, NJ [*Library symbol Library of Congress*] (LCLS)

NjRos .... Roselle Free Public Library, Roselle, NJ [*Library symbol Library of Congress*] (LCLS)

NJROTC ...... Naval Junior Reserve Officer Training Corps

NjRp .... Ridgefield Park Free Public Library, Ridgefield Park, NJ [*Library symbol Library of Congress*] (LCLS)

NjRpS .... Sun Bulletin, Ridgefield Park, NJ [*Library symbol Library of Congress*] (LCLS)

NjR-S .... Rutgers-[*The*] State University, College of South Jersey, Camden, NJ [*Library symbol Library of Congress*] (LCLS)

NJRsc .... New Jersey Resources [*Associated Press*] (SAG)

NjRu .... Rutherford Free Public Library, Rutherford, NJ [*Library symbol Library of Congress*] (LCLS)

NjRuB .... Becton, Dickinson & Co., Rutherford, NJ [*Library symbol Library of Congress*] (LCLS)

NjRuF .... Fairleigh Dickinson University, Rutherford, NJ [*Library symbol Library of Congress*] (LCLS)

NjRw .... Ridgewood Library, Ridgewood, NJ [*Library symbol Library of Congress*] (LCLS)

NjRwN .... Ridgewood News, Ridgewood, NJ [*Library symbol Library of Congress*] (LCLS)

NjRwPHi ..... Paramus Historical and Preservation Society, Ridgewood, NJ [*Library symbol Library of Congress*] (LCLS)

NJS .... New Jersey Superior Court Reports [*A publication*] (DLA)

NJS .... Noise Jammer Simulator [*Telecommunications*] (TEL)

NJS .... Stockton State College, Pomona, NJ [*OCLC symbol*] (OCLC)

NjS .... Summit Free Public Library, Summit, NJ [*Library symbol Library of Congress*] (LCLS)

NJSA .... New Jersey Statutes, Annotated [*A publication*]

NjSabN .... News Dispatch, Saddle Brook, NJ [*Library symbol Library of Congress*] (LCLS)

NjSalCoC ..... Salem County Clerk, Salem, NJ [*Library symbol Library of Congress*] (LCLS)

NjSalHi .... Salem County Historical Society, Salem, NJ [*Library symbol Library of Congress*] (LCLS)

NjSalS .... Sunbeam Publishing Co., Salem, NJ [*Library symbol Library of Congress*] (LCLS)

NJSBAQ ...... New Jersey State Bar Association. Quarterly [*A publication*] (DLA)

NjSbB .... Beachcomber, Ship Bottom, NJ [*Library symbol Library of Congress*] (LCLS)

NjSbbU .... Saint Sophia Ukrainian Orthodox Seminary, South Bound Brook, NJ [*Library symbol Library of Congress*] (LCLS)

NJSBJ .... New Jersey State Bar Journal [*A publication*] (DLA)

NJSBTA Ops... New Jersey State Board of Tax Appeals, Opinions [*A publication*] (DLA)

NjSC .... Ciba Pharmaceutical Co., Research Library, Summit, NJ [*Library symbol Library of Congress*] (LCLS)

NjSCC .... Summit City Clerk, Summit, NJ [*Library symbol Library of Congress*] (LCLS)

NjScp .... Scotch Plains Public Library, Scotch Plains, NJ [*Library symbol Library of Congress*] (LCLS)

NjScpT .... Times, Scotch Plains, NJ [*Library symbol Library of Congress*] (LCLS)

NJSD .... National Joint Service Delegations (NATG)

NJSDC .... New Jersey State Data Center [*New Jersey State Department of Labor*] [*Trenton*] [*Information service or system*] (IID)

NjSe .... Secaucus Free Public Library, Secaucus, NJ [*Library symbol Library of Congress*] (LCLS)

NjSeH .... Secaucus Home News, Secaucus, NJ [*Library symbol Library of Congress*] (LCLS)

NJ Sess Law Serv... New Jersey Session Law Service [*A publication*] (DLA)

NjSewG .... Gloucester County College, Sewell, NJ [*Library symbol Library of Congress*] (LCLS)

NjSewHi ...... Washington Township Historical Society, Sewell, NJ [*Library symbol Library of Congress*] (LCLS)

NJSGA .... National Junior Santa Gertrudis Association (EA)

NjSGS .... Church of Jesus Christ of Latter-Day Saints, Genealogical Society Library, Caldwell Branch, Summit, NJ [*Library symbol Library of Congress*] (LCLS)

NjSH .... Summit Herald, Summit, NJ [*Library symbol Library of Congress*] (LCLS)

NjShO .... Ocean County Review, Seaside Heights, NJ [*Library symbol Library of Congress*] (LCLS)

NJSHS .... National Junior Science and Humanities Symposium

NjSicTR .... Cape May County Times and Seven Mile Beach Reporter, Sea Isle City, NJ [*Library symbol Library of Congress*] (LCLS)

NJSN .... National Job Sharing Network (EA)

NJSO .... National Jazz Service Organization (EA)

NjSo .... Somerville Free Public Library, Somerville, NJ [*Library symbol Library of Congress*] (LCLS)

NjSoa .... South Amboy Public Library, South Amboy, NJ [*Library symbol Library of Congress*] (LCLS)

NjSoaP .... South Amboy Publishing Co., South Amboy, NJ [*Library symbol Library of Congress*] (LCLS)

NjSobC .... Central Post, South Brunswick, NJ [*Library symbol Library of Congress*] (LCLS)

NjSoCo .... Somerset County Library, Somerville, NJ [*Library symbol Library of Congress*] (LCLS)

NjSoCoC ...... Somerset County Clerk, Somerville, NJ [*Library symbol Library of Congress*] (LCLS)

NjSoE .... Ethicon, Inc., Somerville, NJ [*Library symbol Library of Congress*] (LCLS)

NjSoH .... Somerset Hospital, Somerville, NJ [*Library symbol Library of Congress*] (LCLS)

NjSoHR .... Hoechst-Roussel Pharmaceuticals, Inc., Somerville, NJ [*Library symbol Library of Congress*] (LCLS)

NjSoM .... Somerset Messenger-Gazette, Somerville, NJ [*Library symbol Library of Congress*] (LCLS)

NjSomHi ...... Atlantic County Historical Society, Somers Point, NJ [*Library symbol Library of Congress*] (LCLS)

NjSoo .... South Orange Public Library, South Orange, NJ [*Library symbol Library of Congress*] (LCLS)

NjSooS .... Seton Hall University, South Orange, NJ [*Library symbol Library of Congress*] (LCLS)

NjSooS-L ..... Seton Hall University, Law Library, Newark, NJ [*Library symbol Library of Congress*] (LCLS)

NjSop .... South Plainfield Free Public Library, South Plainfield, NJ [*Library symbol Library of Congress*] (LCLS)

NjSopA .... American Smelting & Refining Co., Research Department Library, South Plainfield,NJ [*Library symbol Library of Congress*] (LCLS)

NjSopP .... PAMCAM, Inc., South Plainfield, NJ [*Library symbol Library of Congress*] (LCLS)

NjSoS .... Somerset County College, Somerville, NJ [*Library symbol Library of Congress*] (LCLS)

NjSosS .... Somerset Spectator, Somerset, NJ [*Library symbol Library of Congress*] (LCLS)

NjSoVA .... United States Veterans Administration Supply Depot, Somerville, NJ [*Library symbol Library of Congress*] (LCLS)

NjSp .... Springfield Free Public Library, Springfield, NJ [*Library symbol Library of Congress*] (LCLS)

NjSpl .... Spring Lake Public Library, Spring Lake, NJ [*Library symbol Library of Congress*] (LCLS)

NjSpW .... Western Electric Co., Springfield, NJ [*Library symbol Library of Congress*] (LCLS)

NJST .... New Jersey Steel [*NASDAQ symbol*] (TTSB)

NJST .... New Jersey Steel Corp. [*NASDAQ symbol*] (NQ)

NjSt .... Passaic Township Public Library, Stirling, NJ [*Library symbol Library of Congress*] (LCLS)

NJ Stat Ann (West)... New Jersey Statutes, Annotated (West) [*A publication*] (DLA)

NJ St BJ ...... New Jersey State Bar Journal [*A publication*] (DLA)

NJ Stl .... New Jersey Steel Corp. [*Associated Press*] (SAG)

NjStR .... Recorder Publishing Co., Stirling, NJ [*Library symbol Library of Congress*] (LCLS)

NjStrK .... John F. Kennedy Memorial Hospital, Stratford, NJ [*Library symbol Library of Congress*] (LCLS)

NjSu .... Roxbury Public Library, Succasunna, NJ [*Library symbol Library of Congress*] (LCLS)

NJ Sup .... New Jersey Superior Court Reports [*A publication*] (DLA)

NJ Super .... New Jersey Superior Court Reports [*A publication*] (DLA)

NjSw .... Swedesboro Free Public Library, Swedesboro, NJ [*Library symbol Library of Congress*] (LCLS)

NjSwN .... Swedesboro News, Swedesboro, NJ [*Library symbol Library of Congress*] (LCLS)

NJT .... National Jewish Television [*Cable-television system*]

NJT .... Societe Novajet [*France ICAO designator*] (FAAC)

NjT............... Trenton Free Public Library, Trenton, NJ [*Library symbol Library of Congress*] (LCLS)

NJT .... Trenton State College, Trenton, NJ [*OCLC symbol*] (OCLC)

NjTCP .... Commercial Printing Co., Trenton, NJ [*Library symbol Library of Congress*] (LCLS)

NjTea........... Teaneck Public Library, Teaneck, NJ [*Library symbol Library of Congress*] (LCLS)

NjTeaF........ Fairleigh Dickinson University, Teaneck, NJ [*Library symbol Library of Congress*] (LCLS)

NjTeaL......... Luther College, Teaneck, NJ [*Library symbol Library of Congress*] (LCLS)

NjTen........... Tenafly Public Library, Tenafly, NJ [*Library symbol Library of Congress*] (LCLS)

NJTL .... National Junior Tennis League (EA)

NjTM........... Monitor, Trenton, NJ [*Library symbol Library of Congress*] (LCLS)

NjTMC .... Mercer County Community College, Trenton, NJ [*Library symbol Library of Congress*] (LCLS)

NjTPP .... Planned Parenthood of Mercer Area, Trenton, NJ [*Library symbol Library of Congress*] (LCLS)

NjTR .... Rider College, Trenton, NJ [*Library symbol Library of Congress*] (LCLS)

NjTrCo .... Ocean County Public Library, Toms River, NJ [*Library symbol Library of Congress*] (LCLS)

NjTrCoC...... Ocean County Clerk, Toms River, NJ [*Library symbol Library of Congress*] (LCLS)

NjTrO .... Ocean County College, Toms River, NJ [*Library symbol Library of Congress*] (LCLS)

NjTrR .... Reporter, Toms River, NJ [*Library symbol Library of Congress*] (LCLS)

NjTS............. Trenton State College, Trenton, NJ [*Library symbol Library of Congress*] (LCLS)

NjTSch......... Schweats, Inc., Trenton, NJ [*Library symbol Library of Congress*] (LCLS)

NjTStF .... Saint Francis Medical Center, Health Science Library, Trenton, NJ [*Library symbol Library of Congress*] (LCLS)

NjTTr .... Trentonian, Trenton, NJ [*Library symbol Library of Congress*] (LCLS)

NjTTT.......... Trenton Times Newspapers, Trenton, NJ [*Library symbol Library of Congress*] (LCLS)

nju .... New Jersey [*MARC country of publication code Library of Congress*] (LCCP)

NJU............. Nordic Judo Union (EAIO)

NJU............. Northern Jiaotong Univeristy [*China*]

NjU .... Union Township Public Library, Union, NJ [*Library symbol Library of Congress*] (LCLS)

NjUbI .... International Flavors & Fragrances, Inc., Union Beach, NJ [*Library symbol Library of Congress*] (LCLS)

NjUc............ Union City Free Public Library, Union City, NJ [*Library symbol Library of Congress*] (LCLS)

NjUcD .... Dispatch, Union City, NJ [*Library symbol Library of Congress*] (LCLS)

NjUcS .... Shield, Union City, NJ [*Library symbol Library of Congress*] (LCLS)

NjUcSM .... Saint Michael's Passionist Monastery, Union City, NJ [*Library symbol Library of Congress*] (LCLS)

NjUJ............. Jewish Community News, Union, NJ [*Library symbol Library of Congress*] (LCLS)

NjUN .... Kean College of New Jersey, Union, NJ [*Library symbol Library of Congress*] (LCLS)

NjUpM .... Montclair State College, Upper Montclair, NJ [*Library symbol Library of Congress*] (LCLS)

NjUpM-C...... China Institute of New Jersey, Montclair State College, Upper Montclair, NJ [*Library symbol Library of Congress*] (LCLS)

NJUS .... Netherlands Jurisprudence (NITA)

NjUS .... Suburban Publishing Co., Union, NJ [*Library symbol Library of Congress*] (LCLS)

NjUsrHi........ Upper Saddle River Historical Committee, Upper Saddle River, NJ [*Library symbol Library of Congress*] (LCLS)

NJV............. Nederlandse Juristenvereniging [*Netherlands Lawyers Association*] (ILCA)

NjV.............. Vineland Free Public Library, Vineland, NJ [*Library symbol Library of Congress*] (LCLS)

NjVC .... Cumberland County College, Vineland, NJ [*Library symbol Library of Congress*] (LCLS)

NjVcP........... Ventnor City Public Library, Ventnor City, NJ [*Library symbol*] [*Library of Congress*] (LCLS)

NJVGA .... National Junior Vegetable Growers Association [*Later, NJHA*] (EA)

NjVHi .... Vineland Historical and Antiquarian Society, Vineland, NJ [*Library symbol Library of Congress*] (LCLS)

NjVT............. Times Journal, Vineland, NJ [*Library symbol Library of Congress*] (LCLS)

NJW............. Norris Junction [*Wyoming*] [*Seismograph station code, US Geological Survey*] (SEIS)

NjW .... Wayne Public Library, Wayne, NJ [*Library symbol Library of Congress*] (LCLS)

NjWa .... Warren Township Public Library, Warren, NJ [*Library symbol Library of Congress*] (LCLS)

NjWas.......... Washington Free Public Library, Washington, NJ [*Library symbol Library of Congress*] (LCLS)

NjWasW ...... Washington Star, Washington, NJ [*Library symbol Library of Congress*] (LCLS)

NJWB.......... National Jewish Welfare Board [*Later, JWB*]

NjWdHi .... Gloucester County Historical Society, Woodbury, NJ [*Library symbol Library of Congress*] (LCLS)

NjWdT .... Woodbury Daily Times, Woodbury, NJ [*Library symbol Library of Congress*] (LCLS)

NjWef .... Westfield Memorial Library, Westfield, NJ [*Library symbol Library of Congress*] (LCLS)

NjWefW ...... Wyckoff Printing Co., Westfield, NJ [*Library symbol Library of Congress*] (LCLS)

NjWem .... Haddon Township Free Library, Westmont, NJ [*Library symbol Library of Congress*] (LCLS)

NjWemT ...... Camden County Times, Westmont, NJ [*Library symbol Library of Congress*] (LCLS)

NjWesny...... West New York Public Library, West New York, NJ [*Library symbol Library of Congress*] (LCLS)

NjWew........ Westwood Free Public Library, Westwood, NJ [*Library symbol Library of Congress*] (LCLS)

NjWewP....... Pascack Valley Community Life, Westwood, NJ [*Library symbol Library of Congress*] (LCLS)

NjWewW...... Westwood Publications, Westwood, NJ [*Library symbol Library of Congress*] (LCLS)

NjWF .... Fairleigh Dickinson University, Wayne, NJ [*Library symbol Library of Congress*] (LCLS)

NjWhi .... Whippanong Public Library, Whippany, NJ [*Library symbol Library of Congress*] (LCLS)

NjWhiB .... Bell Telephone Laboratories, Inc., Technical Information Library, Whippany, NJ [*Library symbol Library of Congress*] (LCLS)

NjWhiM .... Morris County Free Library, Whippany, NJ [*Library symbol Library of Congress*] (LCLS)

NjWhiR........ Regional Weekly News, Whippany, NJ [*Library symbol Library of Congress*] (LCLS)

NjWhsH .... Hunterdon Review, Whitehouse Station, NJ [*Library symbol Library of Congress*] (LCLS)

NjWi .... Willingboro Public Library, Willingboro, NJ [*Library symbol Library of Congress*] (LCLS)

NjWilH......... Williamstown High School, Williamstown, NJ [*Library symbol Library of Congress*] (LCLS)

NjWiT .... Burlington County Times, Willingboro, NJ [*Library symbol Library of Congress*] (LCLS)

NjWlM .... Monmouth College, West Long Beach, NJ [*Library symbol Library of Congress*] (LCLS)

NjWMN .... Matzner Suburban Newspapers, Wayne, NJ [*Library symbol Library of Congress*] (LCLS)

NjWo .... West Orange Free Public Library, West Orange, NJ [*Library symbol Library of Congress*] (LCLS)

NjWoE .... Edison National Historic Site, West Orange, NJ [*Library symbol Library of Congress*] (LCLS)

NjWolA........ Alphonsus College, Woodcliff Lake, NJ [*Library symbol Library of Congress*] (LCLS)

NjWoo .... Free Public Library of Woodbridge, Woodbridge, NJ [*Library symbol Library of Congress*] (LCLS)

NjWooN....... News-Tribune, Woodbridge, NJ [*Library symbol Library of Congress*] (LCLS)

NjWor.......... Wood Ridge Memorial Library, Wood Ridge, NJ [*Library symbol Library of Congress*] (LCLS)

NjWP .... William Paterson College of New Jersey, Wayne, NJ [*Library symbol Library of Congress*] (LCLS)

NJWPC .... National Jobs with Peace Campaign (EA)

NjWw .... Wildwood Crest Public Library, Wildwood, NJ [*Library symbol*] [*Library of Congress*] (LCLS)

NjWwHi .... Wildwood Historical Commission, Wildwood, NJ [*Library symbol Library of Congress*] (LCLS)

NjWwL......... Wildwood Leader, Wildwood, NJ [*Library symbol Library of Congress*] (LCLS)

NjWwP......... National Association of Precancel Collectors, Wildwood, NJ [*Library symbol Library of Congress*] (LCLS)

NjWy........... Wyckoff Free Public Library, Wyckoff, NJ [*Library symbol Library of Congress*] (LCLS)

NjWyN .... Wyckoff News, Wyckoff, NJ [*Library symbol Library of Congress*] (LCLS)

NJY............. Newjay Resources Ltd. [*Vancouver Stock Exchange symbol*]

NJY............. York College of the City University of New York, Jamaica, NY [*Library symbol Library of Congress*] (LCLS)

NjZaA.......... Alma White College, Zarephath, NJ [*Library symbol Library of Congress*] (LCLS)

Nk .... Naik [*British military*] (DMA)

NK.............. Natural Killer [*Cell*] [*Immunochemistry*]

NK.............. Neck (AAG)

NK.............. Neon Komma [*New Party*] [*Greek Political party*] (PPE)

NK.............. Neurokinin [*Biochemistry*]

NK.............. New Kingdom [*Egyptology*] (ROG)

NK.............. Next of Kin

NK.............. Nielsen-Kellerman

NK	Nippon Kaiji Kyokai [*Japanese ship classification society*] (DS)
NK	No Ketones [*Organic chemistry*] (DAVI)
NK	No Kidding [*An association Canada*] (EAIO)
NK	Nomemklatur Kommission [*Commission on Nomenclature*] [*Germany*] (DAVI)
NK	Nordiska Kemistradet [*Chemical Societies of the Nordic Countries*] (EAIO)
NK	Normal Keratinocyte (DB)
NK	North Korean
NK	Not Known
n/k	Not Known (DMAA)
NK	Nuclear Kill
NKa	Katonah Village Library, Katonah, NY [*Library symbol Library of Congress*] (LCLS)
NKA	National Kindergarten Association [*Defunct*] (EA)
NKA	Neurokinin A [*Biochemistry*]
NKA	Nikiskha [*Alaska*] [*Seismograph station code, US Geological Survey*] (SEIS)
NKA	No Known Allergies [*Medicine*]
NKA	Norcanair [*Canada ICAO designator*] (FAAC)
NKA	Nordisk Kontaktorgan for Atomenergisporgsmal [*Nordic Liaison Committee for Atomic Energy*] (EAIO)
NKA	North Korean Army
NKA	Now Known As (DLA)
NKABEA	National Korean American Bilingual Educators Association [*Defunct*] (EA)
NKAF	Natural Killer-Cell Activating Factor [*Immunology*]
NKAF	North Korean Air Force
NKAO	Nagorno-Karabakh Autonomous Oblast
NKB	Bear Stearns Companies, Inc. [*AMEX symbol*] (SAG)
NKB	Neurokinin B [*Biochemistry*]
NKB	Nordiska Kommitten for Byggbestammelser [*Nordic Committee on Building Regulations - NCBR*] [*Finland*] (EAIO)
NKB	Norges Kommunalbank [*Bank*] [*Norway*]
NKBA	National Kitchen and Bath Association (EA)
NKC	Merrill Lynch & Co. [*AMEX symbol*] (SAG)
NKC	National Kidney Centre [*British*] (CB)
NKC	Natural Killer Cells [*Microbiology*] (DAVI)
nkc	New Brunswick [*MARC country of publication code Library of Congress*] (LCCP)
NKC	Nonketotic Coma [*Medicine*] (DMAA)
NKC	Nouakchott [*Mauritania*] [*Airport symbol*] (OAG)
NKCA	National Kitchen Cabinet Association [*Later, KCMA*] (EA)
NKCA	National Knife Collectors Association (EA)
NKCA	Natural Killer Cell Activity [*Medicine*] (DMAA)
NKCF	Natural Killer (Cell) Cytotoxic Factor [*Immunochemistry*]
NKCP	North Kalimantan Communist Party [*Malaysia*] [*Political party*] (PD)
NKDA	No Known Drug Allergies [*Medicine*]
NKDC	Nonketotic Diabetic Coma [*Medicine*] (CPH)
NKDF	National Kidney Disease Foundation [*Later, NKF*] (EA)
NKDS	Navy Key Distribution System (CAAL)
NKE	Nake [*Ryukyu Islands*] [*Seismograph station code, US Geological Survey Closed*] (SEIS)
NKE	Nike, Inc. Class B [*NYSE symbol*] (SPSG)
NKE	NIKE, Inc. Cl'B' [*NYSE symbol*] (TTSB)
NKE	Nortek Capital Corp. [*Formerly, Nortek Energy Corp.*] [*Vancouver Stock Exchange symbol*]
NKendOHi	Orleans County Historical Society, Kendall, NY [*Library symbol Library of Congress*] (LCLS)
NKEWA	New Kuban Education and Welfare Association (EA)
NKF	National Kidney Foundation (EA)
NKF	Nordiske Kvinners Fredsnettverk [*Nordic Women's Peace Network*] [*Denmark, Finland, Norway, and Sweden*] (EAIO)
NKF	Nordisk Konstforbund [*Nordic Art Association*] [*Norway*] (EAIO)
NKFA	No Known Food Allergies [*Medicine*] (DMAA)
NKFO	Nordisk Kollegium for Fysisk Oceanografi [*Nordic Council for Physical Oceanography - NCPO*] (EAIO)
NKFTA	National Kosher Food Trade Association [*Defunct*] (EA)
NKG	Nanjing [*China*] [*Airport symbol*] (OAG)
NkG	Newton K. Gregg, Novato, CA [*Library symbol Library of Congress*] (LCLS)
NKGB-NKVD	Narodnyi Komissariat Gosudarstvennoe Bezopasnosti-Narodnyi Komissariat Vnutrennikh Del [*Later, KGB*]
NKH	Kaneohe Bay, HI [*Location identifier FAA*] (FAAL)
NKH	Nonketotic Hyperglycemia [*Endocrinology*] (DAVI)
NKH	Nonketotic Hyperosmotic [*Medicine*] (MAE)
NKH	Nordisk Komite for Handelsundervisning [*Nordic Committee for Commercial Education - NCCE*] [*Odense, Denmark*] (EAIO)
NKHA	National Kerosene Heater Association (EA)
NKHA	Nonketotic Hyperosmolar Acidosis [*Medicine*]
NKHHC	Nonketotic Hyperosmolar Hyperglycemis Coma [*Also, HHNK*] [*Medicine*]
NKHS	Nonketotic Hyperosmolar Syndrome [*Biochemistry*] (DAVI)
NKHS	Normal Krebs-Henseleit Solution (DB)
NKI	Nash-Kelvinator International [*Automobile manufacturer, now out of production*]
NKI	Nikolski [*Alaska*] [*Seismograph station code, US Geological Survey*] (SEIS)
NKiB	Benedictine Hospital, Medical Library, Kingston, NY [*Library symbol Library of Congress*] (LCLS)
NKiC	Children's Home of Kingston, Kingston, NY [*Library symbol Library of Congress*] (LCLS)
NKID	Narodnyi Komissariat Inostrannykh Del [*People's Commissariat of Foreign Affairs*] [*Former USSR*] (LAIN)
NKID	Noodle Kidoodle [*NASDAQ symbol*] (TTSB)
NKID	Noodle Kidoodle, Inc. [*NASDAQ symbol*] (SAG)
NKiHL	Kingston Hospital Libraries, Kingston, NY [*Library symbol Library of Congress*] (LCLS)
NKiI	International Business Machines Corp., Kingston, NY [*Library symbol Library of Congress*] (LCLS)
NKipM	United States Merchant Marine Academy, Kings Point, NY [*Library symbol Library of Congress*] (LCLS)
NKJV	New King James Version of the Bible [*A publication*]
NKK	Nordkalottkommitten [*North Calotte Committee - NCC*] [*Finland*] (EAIO)
NKK	Novo-Kazalinsk [*Former USSR Geomagnetic observatory code*]
NKL	Nemeth-Kellner Leukemia
NKL	New Keel [*On ships*]
NKL	New Kelore Mines Ltd. [*Toronto Stock Exchange symbol*]
NKL	Nickel
NKL C	Nkolo [*Zaire*] [*Airport symbol*] (AD)
NKL C	Nickel Copper [*Freight*]
NKL FCD	Nickel Faced (DGA)
NKM	Nakhla [*Morocco*] [*Seismograph station code, US Geological Survey*] (SEIS)
NKM	University of North Carolina at Charlotte, Charlotte, NC [*OCLC symbol*] (OCLC)
NKMA	National Knitwear Manufacturers Association (EA)
NKMA	No Known Medication Allergies (DAVI)
NKMB	Nordisk Kollegium for Marinbiologi [*Nordic Council for Marine Biology - NCMB*] (EAIO)
NKMU	National Kangaroo Monitoring Unit [*Australia*]
NKN	Neurokinin (DMAA)
NKN	North Korean Navy
NKO	Narodnyi Komissariat Oborony [*People's Commissariat of Defense*] [*Existed until 1946*] [*Former USSR*]
NKO	Need to Know Only [*Espionage*]
NKOA	National Knitted Outerwear Association [*Later, NKSA*] (EA)
NKOT	Nu-kote Holding'A' [*NASDAQ symbol*] (TTSB)
NKOT	Nu-Kote Holding, Inc. [*NASDAQ symbol*] (SAG)
NKOTB	New Kids on the Block [*Music group*]
NKP	Nakorn Phanom [*Air base northeast of Bangkok*]
NKP	Nasionale Konserwatiewe Party [*National Conservative Party*] [*South Africa*] [*Political party*] (PPW)
NKP	New Kensington [*Pennsylvania*] [*Seismograph station code, US Geological Survey Closed*] (SEIS)
NKP	New Korea Party [*South Korea*]
NKP	Norges Kommunistiske Parti [*Norwegian Communist Party*] [*Political party*] (PPE)
NKPA	National Kraut Packers Association (EA)
NKPA	North Korean People's Army
NKpaH	Kings Park State Hospital, Kings Park, NY [*Library symbol Library of Congress*] (LCLS)
NKpK	Keuka College, Keuka Park, NY [*Library symbol Library of Congress*] (LCLS)
NKPR	Innkeepers USA Trust [*NASDAQ symbol*] (SAG)
NKP RTAB	Nakhon Phanom Royal Thai Air Base [*Leased by USAF during the Vietnam War*] (VNW)
NKR	Nakanohara [*Japan*] [*Seismograph station code, US Geological Survey*] (SEIS)
NKR	New Kenrell Resources [*Vancouver Stock Exchange symbol*]
NKR	Nordisk Konservatorierad [*Nordic Council for Music Conservatories - NCMC*] (EAIO)
NKR	Normal Rat Kidney (DB)
N KR	Norwegian Krone [*Monetary unit*]
NKRC	No Known Relatives or Concerned
NKS	Network of Kindred Spirits (EA)
NKS	Nordisk Kirkelig Studierad [*Nordic Council for Adult Studies in Chruch - NCASC*] (EAIO)
NKSA	National Knitwear and Sportswear Association (EA)
NKSC	National Korean Studies Center [*Australia*]
NKSF	Natural Killer-Cell Stimulatory Factor [*Immunology*]
NKT	Cherry Point, NC [*Location identifier FAA*] (FAAL)
NKT	Nankipoo [*Tennessee*] [*Seismograph station code, US Geological Survey*] (SEIS)
NKT	None Kept in Town
NKU	Nakusp Resources Ltd. [*Vancouver Stock Exchange symbol*]
NKU	Nkaus [*Lesotho*] [*Airport symbol*] (OAG)
NKUDIC	National Kidney and Urologic Diseases Information Clearinghouse (EA)
NKUSA	Neturei Karta of USA (EA)
NKVD	Narodnyi Kommissariat Vnutrennikh Del [*People's Commissariat for Internal Affairs*] [*Former USSR*] (NADA)
NKVMF	Narodnyy Komissariat Voyenno-Morskogo Flota [*People's Commissariat of the Navy*] [*Former USSR*] (LAIN)
NKX	San Diego, CA [*Location identifier FAA*] (FAAL)
N Ky St LF	Northern Kentucky State Law Forum [*A publication*] (DLA)
NKYu	Narodnyy Komissariat Yustitsii [*People's Commissariat of Justice*] [*Former USSR*] (LAIN)
NKz	Kwanza (ODBW)
NKZ	Nuclear Killing Zone [*Military British*]
NL	Air Liberia [*ICAO designator*] (AD)
nl----	Great Lakes [*MARC geographic area code Library of Congress*] (LCCP)
NL	Lima Public Library, Lima, NY [*Library symbol Library of Congress*] (LCLS)
NL	Nailable [*Technical drawings*]
nl	Nanoliter [*One billionth of a liter*] (MAE)
NL	Nasolacrimal [*Medicine*] (DAVI)
NL	Natick Laboratories [*Army*] (MCD)

NL............	National Lakeshore (BARN)
NL............	National Lead (EFIS)
NL............	National League of Professional Baseball Clubs (EA)
NL............	National Liberal [British politics]
NL............	National Library [Canada]
NL............	Native Language (BARN)
NL............	Naturalist's Library [A publication]
NL............	Natural Language [Computer software]
NL............	Natural Log [or Logarithm] (WDAA)
NL............	Naval Lighter
NL............	Navigating Lieutenant [Navy British] (ROG)
N/L...........	Navigation/Localizer (IEEE)
NL............	Navy League of the United States
NL............	Navy Library (WDAA)
NL............	Navy List [British military] (DMA)
NL............	Nebenlager [Branch Camp] [German military - World War II]
NL............	Nelson's Lutwyche, English Common Pleas Reports [A publication] (DLA)
NL............	Neon Lamp (KSC)
NL............	Netherlands [ANSI two-letter standard code] (CNC)
NL............	Net Loss
NL............	Neurilemmona [Oncology]
NL............	Neutral Lipid (DB)
nl.............	New Caledonia [MARC country of publication code Library of Congress] (LCCP)
NL............	New Latin [Language, etc.]
NL............	New Lead [Also, NH] [News stories] (NTCM)
NL............	New Leader [A publication] (BRI)
nl.............	New Line (WDMC)
NL............	New Line [Computer science]
NL............	New London, Connecticut [Navy]
NL............	Newsletter (WDMC)
N-L...........	New York State Library, Law Library, Albany, NY [Library symbol Library of Congress] (LCLS)
NL............	Night Letter
NL............	NL Industries, Inc. [Formerly, National Lead Co.] [NYSE symbol] (SPSG)
NL............	Nodular Lymphoma [Oncology] (DAVI)
N/L...........	No Ledger (SAA)
NL............	No Liability (ADA)
NL............	No License [Traffic offense charge]
NL............	No Limit (NASA)
NL............	No Liner (DS)
NL............	No Load
NL............	Non-Labeled [Tape] [Computer science]
NL............	Non Licet [It Is Not Permitted] [Latin]
NL............	Nonlinear
NL............	Non Liquet [It Is Not Clear] [Latin]
NL............	Non-Loaded (NITA)
NL............	Nonlocking
NL............	Non Longe [Not Far] [Latin]
NL............	Nonprogrammer Language [Computer science] (PDAA)
NL............	Normal (DAVI)
n/l............	Normal Limits
NL............	Normal Lungs
NL............	North Latitude
NL............	Nose Left [Aviation] (MCD)
NL............	Not Listed (AFM)
NL............	Not Located
NL............	Nulead [Journalism] [Slang] (WDMC)
NL............	Nurses for Laughter [Defunct] (EA)
NL............	Nyhan-Lesch [Syndrome] [Medicine] (DB)
NLA...........	Children's Leukemia Research Association [Formerly, National Leukemia Association] (EA)
NLA...........	National Landscape Association (EA)
NLA...........	National Leather Association (EA)
NLA...........	National Leukemia Association (EA)
NLA...........	National Liberation Army [Bolivia]
NLA...........	National Librarians Association (EA)
NLA...........	National Libraries Authority
NLA...........	National Library Act
NLA...........	National Library of Australia (NITA)
NLA...........	National Library of Canada, Cataloguing Branch [UTLAS symbol]
NLA...........	National Lime Association (EA)
NLA...........	National Limousine Association (EA)
NLA...........	National Locksmiths Association (EA)
NLA...........	NATO Lot Acceptance (MCD)
NLA...........	Navy League of Australia
NLA...........	Ndola [Zambia] [Airport symbol] (OAG)
NLA...........	Neiltown Air Ltd. [Canada ICAO designator] (FAAC)
NLA...........	Net Lettable Area
NLA...........	Neuroleptanalgesia [Altered state of awareness] [Medicine] (AAMN)
NLA...........	Neuroleptic Anesthesia
NLA...........	Neuroleptoanesthesia [Medicine] (DMAA)
NLA...........	New Large Airplane
NLA...........	New Libertarian Alliance (EA)
NLA...........	Next Lower Assembly (MCD)
NLA...........	Nine Lives Associates (EA)
NLA...........	Nonlinear Amplifier
NLA...........	Nonuniform Linear Array
NLA...........	Normalized Load Access (NITA)
NLA...........	Normalized Local Address [Computer science] (CIST)
NLA...........	Normal Lactase Activity [Medicine] (DMAA)
NLA...........	Norris-LaGuardia Act (MHDB)
NLA...........	Northwestern Lumbermen's Association (EA)

NLAA	National Legal Aid Association
NLAAM	N-Desmethyl-levo-alpha-Acetylmethadol [Opiate]
NLABS	Natick Laboratories [Army] (AABC)
NLAC	National Listen America Club (EA)
NLacOH	Our Lady of Victory Hospital, Lackawanna, NY [Library symbol Library of Congress] (LCLS)
NLADA........	National Legal Aid and Defender Association (EA)
NLADA Brief...	National Legal Aid and Defender Association Briefcase [A publication] (DLA)
NLakrHS	Sachem High School South, Lake Ronkonkoma, NY [Library symbol Library of Congress] (LCLS)
NLAL..........	Nodule-Like Alveolar Lesion [Medicine] (DB)
NLanEB	Erie No. 1 Board of Coopertive Educational Services, Lancaster, NY [Library symbol] [Library of Congress] (LCLS)
NLANR	National Laboratory for Applied Network Research (DDC)
NLanS........	Scott Aviation, Lancaster, NY [Library symbol] [Library of Congress] (LCLS)
NLAP	National Lab Audit Program (COE)
NLAPW	National League of American Pen Women (EA)
NLar..........	Larchmont Public Library, Larchmont, NY [Library symbol Library of Congress] (LCLS)
NLAS	National Lum and Abner Society (EA)
NLaw	Peninsula Public Library, Lawrence, NY [Library symbol Library of Congress] (LCLS)
NLawBS.......	Brandeis School, Lawrence, NY [Library symbol] [Library of Congress] (LCLS)
NLawCE	Central Elementary School, Lawrence, NY [Library symbol Library of Congress] (LCLS)
NLawChE.....	Cedarhurst Elementary School, Lawrence, NY [Library symbol Library of Congress] (LCLS)
NLawDE.......	Donahue Elementary School, Lawrence, NY [Library symbol Library of Congress] (LCLS)
NLawJH	Lawrence Junior High School, Lawrence, NY [Library symbol Library of Congress] (LCLS)
NLawPE	Peninsula Elementary School, Lawrence, NY [Library symbol Library of Congress] (LCLS)
NLawSH.......	Lawrence Senior High School, Lawrence, NY [Library symbol] [Library of Congress] (LCLS)
NLawWE......	Wansee Elementary School, Lawrence, NY [Library symbol Library of Congress] (LCLS)
NLB...........	National Labor Board (WDAA)
NLB...........	National Library for the Blind
NLB...........	National Library of Canada, Locations Division [UTLAS symbol]
NLB...........	National Lighting Bureau (EA)
NLB...........	Needle Liver Biopsy [Medicine] (DMAA)
NLB...........	No Lunch Break
NLB...........	Nuclear Light Bulb
NLBA.........	National Lead Burning Association (EA)
NLBA.........	National Licensed Beverage Association (EA)
NLB & D	National League for the Blind and Disabled [British] (DBA)
NLBC	National Livestock Brand Conference [Later, International Livestock Brand Conference]
NLBD.........	National League of the Blind and Disabled [A union] [British] (DCTA)
NLBI..........	National League of the Blind of Ireland (EAIO)
NLBMDA.....	National Lumber and Building Material Dealers Association (EA)
NLBRA.......	National Little Britches Rodeo Association (EA)
NLC...........	Lemoore, CA [Location identifier FAA] (FAAL)
NLC...........	NADGE [NATO Air Defense Ground Environment] Logistics Committee (NATG)
NLC...........	Nalco Chemical [NYSE symbol] (TTSB)
NLC...........	Nalco Chemical Co. [NYSE symbol] (SPSG)
NLC...........	National Laboratory Center [Bureau of Alcohol, Tobacco, and Firearms] [Rockville, MD] (GRD)
NLC...........	National Labour Congress [Nigeria] (ECON)
NLC...........	National Lawyers Club (EA)
NLC...........	National Leadership Committee [Military]
NLC...........	National Leadership Council [Defunct] (EA)
NLC...........	National League of Cities (EA)
NLC...........	National Legislative Conference [Later, NCSL] (EA)
NLC...........	National Legislative Council [Later, NCSL]
NLC...........	National Liberal Club [British]
NLC...........	National Liberation Committee [South Africa]
NLC...........	National Liberty Committee (EA)
NLC...........	National Library of Canada
NLC...........	National Library of Canada, Ottawa, ON, Canada [OCLC symbol] (OCLC)
NLC...........	National Library of China
NLC...........	National Lifeguard Championships (EA)
NLC...........	National Liturgical Commission [Catholic Church] [Australia]
NLC...........	National Location Code [Civil Defense]
NLC...........	National Logistical Command (MCD)
NLC...........	National Lutheran Council [Later, LC/USA] (EA)
NLC...........	Navy Law Center (DNAB)
NLC...........	Negro Labor Committee [Defunct] (EA)
NLC...........	Nematic Liquid Crystal [Physical chemistry]
NLC...........	Network Language Center (MHDB)
NLC...........	New Liberal Club [Shin Jiyu Club] [Japan] (PPW)
NLC...........	New Line Character [Keyboard] [Computer science] (MDG)
NLC...........	New Location Code [Military]
NLC...........	New Orleans & Lower Coast Railroad Co. [AAR code]
NLC...........	News and Letters Committee (EA)
NLC...........	Next Linear Collider [Proposed]
NLC...........	Noctilucent Clouds
NLC...........	Node Location Code (PDAA)
NLC...........	Noise-Level Cable

NLC.............	Nordic Literature Committee [*Copenhagen, Denmark*] (EAIO)
NLC.............	Northern Libraries Colloquy (EA)
NLC.............	Northland Library System [*Library network*]
NLCA	Norlaudanosolinecarboxylic Acid [*Biochemistry*]
NLCA	Norlithocholic Acid [*Biochemistry*]
NLCA	Norwegian Lutheran Church of America (IIA)
NLCAA	National Little College Athletic Association [*Later, NSCAA*] (EA)
NLCAB	National Library of Canada Advisory Board
NLCACBC.....	National League of Cuban American Community-Based Centers (EA)
NLCC	Navy League Cadet Corps (EA)
NLCD	National Liberation Council Decree [*1966-69*] [*Ghana*] [*A publication*] (DLA)
NLCEA	Naval Laboratory Centers' Employee Association (DNAB)
NLCH	National Legislative Council for the Handicapped (EA)
NLCIF.........	National Light Castings Ironfounders' Federation [*British*] (BI)
NLCM..........	National Lutheran Campus Ministry (EA)
NLCMDD......	National Legal Center for the Medically Dependent and Disabled (EA)
NLCOA	National Leadership Coalition on AIDS [*Acquired Immune Deficiency Syndrome*] (EA)
NLCP	Navy Logistics Capabilities Plan
NLCP-FY	Navy Logistics Capabilities Plan - Fiscal Year (DNAB)
NLCPI	National Legal Center for the Public Interest (EA)
NLCS	National Computer Systems, Inc. [*NASDAQ symbol*] (NQ)
NLCS	National League Championship Series [*Baseball*]
NLCS	National Lutheran Commission on Scouting [*Defunct*] (EA)
NLCS	Natl Computer Sys [*NASDAQ symbol*] (TTSB)
NLCS	Nordic Leather Chemists Society [*Formerly, IVLIC Scandinavian Section*] (EA)
NLCSDHRES...	National Labor Committee in Support of Democracy and Human Rights in El Salvador (EA)
NLCSE	Non-Linear Charge Storage Element (PDAA)
NLCSJ.........	National Lawyers Committee for Soviet Jewry (EA)
NLCWC	National Lincoln-Civil War Council (EA)
NLD	Namakwaland Lugdiens (EDMS) BPK [*South Africa ICAO designator*] (FAAC)
NLD	NASA Launch Director
NLD	Nasolacrimal Duct [*Medicine*] (DAVI)
NLD	National League for Democracy [*Myanmar*] [*Political party*] (EY)
NLD	National Legal Databases (IID)
NLD	National Legion of Decency [*Later, National Catholic Office for Motion Pictures*] (EA)
NLD	Naval Electrical Department [*British military*] (DMA)
NLD	Naval Lighter [*Pontoon*] Dock
NLD	Necrobiosis Lipoidica Diabeticorum [*Medicine*]
NLD	Netherlands [*ANSI three-letter standard code*] (CNC)
NLD	No Load (MSA)
NLD	Northland Bank [*Toronto Stock Exchange symbol Vancouver Stock Exchange symbol*]
NLD	Not in Line of Duty [*as of an injury*] [*Military*]
NLD	Nuevo Laredo [*Mexico*] [*Airport symbol*] (OAG)
NLDA	National Livestock Dealers Association [*Later, Livestock Marketing Association*] (EA)
NLDA	National Luggage Dealers Association (EA)
NLDB	Natural Language Data Base
NLDC	National Legal Data Center [*Defunct*] (EA)
NLDF	National Leigh's Disease Foundation (EA)
NLDF	Naval Local Defense Forces
NLDM	Network Logical Data Manager (NITA)
NLDN	National Lightning Detection Network
NLDV	National League of Disabled Voters (EA)
NLE	National Livestock Exchange [*Defunct*] (EA)
NLE	Nonlinear Element
Nle	Norleucine [*A nonessential amino acid*] [*Biochemistry*]
NLE	Northern Commuter Airlines [*New Zealand*] [*ICAO designator*] (FAAC)
NLEA	National Lumber Exporters Association [*Later, AHEC*] (EA)
NLEA	Nutrition Labeling and Education Act [*1990*] [*Food and Drug Administration*]
NLEACH	Northleach [*England*]
NLEC..........	National Law Enforcement Council (EA)
NLEC..........	National Lutheran Educational Conference [*Later, LECNA*] (EA)
NLEEF	National Law Enforcement Emergency Frequency (LAIN)
NLEF	National Legislative Education Foundation (EA)
NLEF	National Lupus Erythematosus Foundation [*Defunct*] (EA)
NLEMA........	National Lutheran Editors and Managers Association [*Defunct*] (EA)
NLEOMF	National Law Enforcement Officers Memorial Fund (EA)
NLer...........	Woodward Memorial Library, LeRoy, NY [*Library symbol Library of Congress*] (LCLS)
NLerHi........	LeRoy Historical Society, LeRoy, NY [*Library symbol Library of Congress*] (LCLS)
NLETS........	National Law Enforcement Telecommunications System
NLETS........	National Law Enforcement Teletype System (COE)
Nleu..........	Norleucine (DB)
NLev	Levittown Public Library, Levittown, NY [*Library symbol Library of Congress*] (LCLS)
NLEV..........	National Low-Emission Vehicles
NLevAE........	Abbey Lane Elementary School, Levittown, NY [*Library symbol*] [*Library of Congress*] (LCLS)
NLevDH........	Division Avenue High School, Levittown, NY [*Library symbol*] [*Library of Congress*] (LCLS)
NLevEC........	Levittown Memorial Education Center, Levittown, NY [*Library symbol*] [*Library of Congress*] (LCLS)
NLevGE........	Gardiners Avenue Elementary School, Levittown, NY [*Library symbol*] [*Library of Congress*] (LCLS)

NLevGGE	Geneva N. Gallow Elementary School, Levittown, NY [*Library symbol*] [*Library of Congress*] (LCLS)
NLevI	Island Trees Public Library, Levittown, NY [*Library symbol Library of Congress*] (LCLS)
NLevIH	Island Trees High School, Levittown, NY [*Library symbol Library of Congress*] (LCLS)
NLevIJ	Island Trees Memorial Junior High School, Levittown, NY [*Library symbol Library of Congress*] (LCLS)
NLevJSE	J. Fred Sparke Elementary School, Levittown, NY [*Library symbol*] [*Library of Congress*] (LCLS)
NLevLE	Lee Road Elementary School, Levittown, NY [*Library symbol*] [*Library of Congress*] (LCLS)
NLevMH	General Douglas McArthur High School, Levittown, NY [*Library symbol*] [*Library of Congress*] (LCLS)
NLevMSE	Michael F. Stokes Elementary School, Levittown, NY [*Library symbol*] [*Library of Congress*] (LCLS)
NLevNE........	Northside Elementary School, Levittown, NY [*Library symbol*] [*Library of Congress*] (LCLS)
NLevSJ	Jonas E. Salk Junior High School, Levittown, NY [*Library symbol*] [*Library of Congress*] (LCLS)
NLevSLE	Summit Lane Elementary School, Levittown, NY [*Library symbol*] [*Library of Congress*] (LCLS)
NLevSNE	Seaman Neck Elementary School, Levittown, NY [*Library symbol*] [*Library of Congress*] (LCLS)
NLevWM	Wisdom Middle School, Levittown, NY [*Library symbol*] [*Library of Congress*] (LCLS)
NLew	Lewiston Public Library, Lewiston, NY [*Library symbol Library of Congress*] (LCLS)
NLewStM	Mount Saint Mary's Hospital, Lewiston, NY [*Library symbol Library of Congress*] (LCLS)
NLf.............	Little Falls Public Library, Little Falls, NY [*Library symbol Library of Congress*] (LCLS)
NLF.............	Nasolabial Fold [*Medicine*] (DAVI)
NLF.............	National Fuelcorp Ltd. [*Vancouver Stock Exchange symbol*]
NLF.............	National League of Families of Prisoners and Missing in Southeast Asia
NLF.............	National Legal Foundation (EA)
NLF.............	National Liberal Federation [*British*]
NLF.............	National Liberation Front [*Vietnam*] [*Political party*]
NLF.............	National Liberation Front [*Aden*] [*Political party*]
NLF.............	National Liberation Front [*South Africa*] [*Political party*] (PD)
NLF.............	National Liberation Front [*Myanmar*] [*Political party*] (PD)
NLF.............	Navigation Light Flasher
NLF.............	Nearest Landing Field
NLF.............	Neonatal Lung Fibroblast [*Medicine*] (DMAA)
NLF.............	Neutral Lipid Fraction [*Biochemistry*]
NLF.............	New Leadership Fund (EA)
NLF.............	No-Load Funds
NLF.............	Nonlactose Fermenting [*Organism*] [*Medicine*] (DB)
NLF.............	North Luzon Force [*Army World War II*]
NLF.............	Westair Aviation, Inc. [*Canada ICAO designator*] (FAAC)
NLFA..........	National Lamb Feeders Association (EA)
NLFA..........	National Livestock Feeders Association [*Later, NCA*] (EA)
NLFED	Naval Landing Force Equipment Depot
NLFM..........	Noise-Level Frequency Monitor
NLFMA........	National Law Firm Marketing Association (EA)
NLFPA	National Liberation Front Party Apparatus [*Algeria*]
NLFS..........	Nucleus Landing Force Staff (DNAB)
NLFSV	National Liberation Front of South Vietnam [*Political party*]
NLFT..........	No-Load Frame Time
NLG	National Gas & Oil Corp. [*AMEX symbol*] (SPSG)
NLG	National Lawyers Guild (EA)
NLG	Natl Gas & Oil [*AMEX symbol*] (TTSB)
NLG	Nelson Lagoon [*Alaska*] [*Airport symbol*] (OAG)
NLG	North Louisiana & Gulf Railroad Co. [*AAR code*]
NLG	Nose Landing Gear [*Aviation*]
NLG	Null Line Gap
NLG	Numismatic Literary Guild (EA)
NLGA..........	National Lumber Grading Agency [*Canada*]
NLGAWVA.....	National Legion of Greek-American War Veterans in America (EA)
NLGC	Nauru Local Government Council [*Australia*]
NLGC	Noise-Level Gain Control (MCD)
NLGDA........	National Lawn and Garden Distributors Association (EA)
NLGHA........	National Lesbian and Gay Health Association (EA)
NLGHF	National Lesbian and Gay Health Foundation (EA)
NLGI	National Lubricating Grease Institute (EA)
NLGLA........	National Lesbian and Gay Lawyers Association (NTPA)
NLGLP	National Laboratory Gene Library Project (HGEN)
NLGPDC.......	National Lawyer's Guild Peace and Disarmament Committee [*Later, NLGPDS*] (EA)
NLGPDS......	National Lawyer's Guild Peace and Disarmament Society (EA)
NLGPDS......	National Lawyer's Guild Peace and Disarmament Subcommittee (EA)
NLGQ	National Lawyers Guild Quarterly [*A publication*] (DLA)
NLH	New Lao Hak [*Lao Patriotic Front*] [*Vietnam*] [*Political party*]
NLH	New Life Hamlet [*See also NLHS, NLHZ*] [*Vietnam*] [*Military*]
NLH	Non-Locating Head [*Engineering*] (OA)
NLHA..........	National Leased Housing Association [*Washington, DC*] (EA)
NLHO..........	National Latina Health Organization (EAIO)
NLHRSA.......	National Left-Handers Racquet Sports Association (EA)
NLHS	New Lao Hak Sat [*New Life Hamlet*] [*See also NLH Vietnam*] [*Military*]
NLHZ	New Lao Hak Zat [*New Life Hamlet*] [*See also NLH, NLHS Vietnam*] [*Military*]
NLI.............	National Landscape Institute
NLI.............	National Language Interface (NITA)

NLI..............	National Leadership Institute [*Defunct*] (EA)
NLI..............	National Library of Ireland (AIE)
NLI..............	National Limestone Institute [*Later, NSA*] (EA)
NLI..............	Neodymium LASER Illuminator
NLI..............	New Learning Initiative (AIE)
NLI..............	Noise Limit Indicator
NLI..............	Nonlinear Interpolating (IEEE)
NLI..............	Northern Lights College Library [*UTLAS symbol*]
NLI..............	NovaNET Learning
NLIA..........	National Languages Institute of Australia
NLib............	Liberty Public Library, Liberty, NY [*Library symbol Library of Congress*] (LCLS)
NLIC...........	National Landslide Information Center [*US Geological Survey*]
NLIC...........	National Lead Information Center (AEPA)
NLicL..........	LaGuardia Community College of the City University of New York, Long Island Cit y, NY [*Library symbol Library of Congress*] (LCLS)
NLicP..........	PepsiCo, Inc., Research Library, Long Island, NY [*Library symbol Library of Congress*] (LCLS)
NLIF...........	Nonlinear Interference Filter [*Electronics*]
NLIHC........	National Low Income Housing Coalition (EA)
NLin...........	Lindenhurst Memorial Library, Lindenhurst, NY [*Library symbol Library of Congress*] (LCLS)
NLIN..........	NOAA [*National Oceanic and Atmospheric Administration*] Library and Information Network [*Marine science*] (OSRA)
NLin...........	Nonlinear
NL Ind	NL Industries, Inc. [*Formerly, National Lead Co.*] [*Associated Press*] (SAG)
NLinHS	Lindenhurst High School, Lindenhurst, NY [*Library symbol*] [*Library of Congress*] (LCLS)
NLinJS........	Lindenhurst Junior High School, Lindenhurst, NY [*Library symbol*] [*Library of Congress*] (LCLS)
NLIS..........	National Lesbian Information Service
NLIS..........	Navy Logistics Information System
NLISA........	National League of Insured Savings Associations [*Later, NSLL*] (EA)
NLJ...........	Nagpur Law Journal [*India*] [*A publication*] (DLA)
NLJ...........	New Law Journal [*A publication*] (ILCA)
NLK...........	Neuroleukin [*Biochemistry*]
NLK...........	Norfolk Island [*Airport symbol*] (OAG)
NLK...........	Norlink Air Ltd. [*British ICAO designator*] (FAAC)
NLKF.........	Nonlinear Kalman Filter
NLL...........	National Aeronautical Research Institute [*Netherlands*] (SAA)
NLL...........	National Lacrosse League [*Disbanded*]
NLL...........	National Lending Library for Science and Technology [*Later, BLLD*] [*British Library*]
NLL...........	National Liberal League [*Later, NLSCS*] (EA)
NLL...........	Negative Logic Level
NLL...........	New England School of Law Library, Boston, MA [*OCLC symbol*] (OCLC)
NLL...........	New Library of Law [*Harrisburg, PA*] [*A publication*] (DLA)
NLL...........	New Library of Law and Equity [*England*] [*A publication*] (DLA)
NLL...........	New Life League (EA)
NLL...........	New London [*Connecticut*] Laboratory [*Navy*] (DNAB)
NLL...........	Normal Liquid Level [*Engineering*]
NLL...........	Northern Limit Line [*Korea*]
NLL...........	Nullagine [*Australia Airport symbol*] (OAG)
NLLC..........	National Labor Law Center (EA)
NLLC..........	National Languages and Literacy Council [*Australia*]
NLLS..........	Nonlinear Least Square [*Mathematics*]
NLLSQ........	Nonlinear Least Squares [*Computer program*]
NLLST........	National Lending Library for Science and Technology [*Later, BLL*] [*British*]
NL LT.........	Net Laying Light (SAA)
NLM..........	National Language Mediator
NLM..........	National Library of Medicine [*Public Health Service*] [*Bethesda, MD Database producer*]
NLM..........	National Library of Medicine, Bethesda, MD [*OCLC symbol*] (OCLC)
NLM..........	Natural Language Mode [*Computer science*]
NLM..........	Naval Ordnance Lab [*Maryland*] [*Seismograph station code, US Geological Survey Closed*] (SEIS)
NLM..........	Nederlands Luchtvaart Maatschappij [*Airline*] [*Netherlands*]
NLM..........	NetWare Loadable Module [*Computer science*] (DDC)
NLM..........	Network Loadable Module (GAVI)
NLM..........	New Library of Music [*A publication*]
NLM..........	Noise Level Monitor (DMAA)
NLM..........	Nonlinear Mapping (MCD)
NLM..........	Nuclear Level Mixing [*Physics*]
NLMA.........	National Lumber Manufacturers Association [*Later, NFPA*] (EA)
NLMA.........	Northeastern Lumber Manufacturers Association
NLMBX	Neub. & Berman Ltd. Maturity Bond Fund [*Mutual fund ticker symbol*] (SG)
NLMC..........	National Latino Media Coalition [*Citizen's group*] (NTCM)
NLMC..........	National League of Masonic Clubs (EA)
NLMC..........	Nordic Labour Market Committee (EAIO)
NLMC..........	North Lilly Mining Co. [*NASDAQ symbol*] (NQ)
NLMC..........	North Lily Mining [*NASDAQ symbol*] (TTSB)
NLME..........	Non-Linear Material Effect (PDAA)
NLMF.........	National Labor-Management Foundation (EA)
NLMF.........	Nucleus of Longitudinal Muscle Fiber
NLMFA........	No-Load Mutual Fund Association (EA)
NLMS..........	Navigational Lane Marking System [*Navy*] (DOMA)
NLMS..........	Navy Logistics Management School
NLMS..........	Numerical Largeness of More Significant [*Statistics*]
NLMWT........	National Liberation Movement of Western Togoland
NLN	National League for Nursing (EA)

NLN	National Library Network
NLN	New Line Cinema (EFIS)
NLN	New Lintex Minerals [*Vancouver Stock Exchange symbol*]
NLN	No Longer Needed (AABC)
NLN	Nordiska Lakemedelsnamnden [*Nordic Council on Medicines - NCM*] (EAIO)
NLN	Northwest Missouri Library Network [*Library network*]
NLNA	National Landscape Nurserymen's Association [*Later, NLA*] (EA)
NLNE	National League for Nursing Education (DAVI)
NLnet..........	[*The*] Newfoundland and Labrador Network [*Canada*] [*Computer science*] (TNIG)
NLNGNE	National League of Nursing Graduate Nursing Examination (GAGS)
NLNP	National Library Network Program (AEPA)
NLNR	Nonlinear (MSA)
NLNS	New Lightweight Night Sight (INF)
NLO	Nasolacrimal Occlusion [*Medicine*]
NLO	Naval Liaison Officer
NLO	No-Limit Order
NLO	Nonlinear Optics (IEEE)
NLob..........	Long Beach Public Library, Long Beach, NY [*Library symbol Library of Congress*] (LCLS)
NLobBK.......	Blackhealth Kindergarten School, Long Beach, NY [*Library symbol*] [*Library of Congress*] (LCLS)
NLobES.......	East School, Long Beach, NY [*Library symbol Library of Congress*] (LCLS)
NLobH	Long Beach Memorial Hospital, Long Beach, NY [*Library symbol Library of Congress*] (LCLS)
NLobJH.......	Long Beach Junior High School, Long Beach, NY [*Library symbol Library of Congress*] (LCLS)
NLobLE.......	Lido Elementary School, Long Beach, NY [*Library symbol Library of Congress*] (LCLS)
NLobLS.......	Lindell Boulevard School, Long Beach, NY [*Library symbol Library of Congress*] (LCLS)
NLobM.......	Long Beach Middle School, Long Beach, NY [*Library symbol*] [*Library of Congress*] (LCLS)
NLobMS.......	Magnolia School, Long Beach, NY [*Library symbol Library of Congress*] (LCLS)
NLobSH.......	Long Beach Senior High School, Long Beach, NY [*Library symbol Library of Congress*] (LCLS)
NLobWE.......	West Elementary School, Long Beach, NY [*Library symbol Library of Congress*] (LCLS)
NLock	Lockport Public Library, Lockport, NY [*Library symbol Library of Congress*] (LCLS)
NLockH........	Lockport Memorial Hospital, Doctor's Library, Lockport, NY [*Library symbol Library of Congress*] (LCLS)
NLockMt......	Mount View Health Facility, Lockport, NY [*Library symbol Library of Congress*] (LCLS)
NLockNHi....	Niagara County Historical Society, Lockport, NY [*Library symbol Library of Congress*] (LCLS)
NLOGM.......	Navy Liaison Office for Guided Missiles (MCD)
NLOMA	National Lutheran Outdoors Ministry Association (EA)
NLONTEVDET...	New London Test and Evaluation Detachment [*Navy*]
NLOP	Nonlinear Optical Polymer
NLOrLanyard...	Netherlands Orange Lanyard [*Military decoration*]
NLOS	Natural Language Operating System
NLOS	Nonline of Sight
NLOS-AT/AD..	Nonline-of-Sight Antitank/Air Defense Vehicle [*Army*]
NLOS-CA.....	Non-Line-of-Sight-Combined Arms System (INF)
NLOS/IOE....	Nonline-of-Sight / Internal Operator Equipment (DWSG)
NLOS-R.......	Non-Line-of-Sight-Rear [*Army*] (DOMA)
NLouvGS......	Church of Jesus Christ of Latter-Day Saints, Genealogical Society Library, Albany New York Stake Branch, Loudonville, NY [*Library symbol Library of Congress*] (LCLS)
NLouvS........	Siena College, Loudonville, NY [*Library symbol Library of Congress*] (LCLS)
NLowLH......	Lewis County General Hospital, Medical Library, Lowville, NY [*Library symbol Library of Congress*] (LCLS)
NLp..........	Lake Placid Public Library, Lake Placid, NY [*Library symbol Library of Congress*] (LCLS)
NLP..........	Narodnoliberalna Partiia [*National Liberal Party*] [*Bulgaria*] [*Political party*] (PPE)
NLP..........	National Labour Party [*Sierra Leone*] [*Political party*] (EY)
NLP..........	National Land for People [*An association*] (EA)
NLP..........	National League of Postmasters of the United States
NLP..........	National Liberal Party [*Bermuda*] [*Political party*] (EY)
NLP..........	National Liberation Party [*Gambia*] [*Political party*] (PPW)
NLP..........	National Realty Ltd. [*AMEX symbol*] (SPSG)
NLP..........	Natl Realty L.P. [*AMEX symbol*] (TTSB)
NLP..........	Natural Language Processing [*Computer science*]
NLP..........	Natural Law Party [*Australia Political party*]
NLP..........	Neglected Language Program
NLP..........	Neighborhood Loan Program
NLP..........	Nelspruit [*South Africa*] [*Airport symbol*] (OAG)
NLP..........	Net Level Premium [*Insurance*]
NLP..........	Neurolinguistic Programming
NLP..........	New Left Party [*Political party Australia*]
NLP..........	Nodular Liquifying Panniculitis [*Dermatology*] (DAVI)
NLP..........	No Light Perception [*Ophthalmology*]
NLP..........	Nonlinear Programming [*Algorithm*]
NLP..........	Normal Light Perception [*Physiology*] (MAH)
NLPC	n-Laurylpyridinium Chloride [*Detergent*]
NLPGA........	National LP-Gas Association (EA)
NLPM..........	National League of Postmasters of the United States (EA)
NLPM..........	Newspaper Lines per Minute (DGA)

NLPNEF .... National Licensed Practical Nurses Educational Foundation [*Defunct*] (EA)
NLPQ .... Natural Language Processing System for Queuing Problems [*Computer science*] (PDAA)
NLPR .... National Laboratory of Psychical Research [*British*]
NLPS .... Natural Language Processing Segment [*Computer science*]
NLpSA .... Lake Placid School of Art, Fine Arts Library, Lake Placid, NY [*Library symbol Library of Congress*] (LCLS)
NLpT .... Tissue Culture Association, Lake Placid, NY [*Library symbol Library of Congress*] (LCLS)
NLPTL .... National Lutheran Parent-Teacher League (EA)
NLQ .... Natural Language Query [*Software*] [*Battelle Software Products Center*]
NLQ .... Near Letter Quality [*Computer printer*]
NLQ .... Nigeria Lawyer's Quarterly [*A publication*] (DLA)
NLQ .... Nonlinear Quantization [*Telecommunications*] (NTCM)
NLQ .... Not Letter Quality (NITA)
NLQR .... Nigeria Law Quarterly Review [*A publication*] (DLA)
NLR .... Nagpur Law Reports [*India*] [*A publication*] (DLA)
NLR .... Natal Law Reports [*India*] [*A publication*] (DLA)
NLR .... National Liquid Reserves Money Market Fund
NLR .... National Research Laboratory [*Netherlands*] (GAVI)
NLR .... NATO Liaison Representative (MCD)
NLR .... Neodymium LASER Range-Finder
NLR .... Net Liquidity Ratio (PDAA)
NLR .... Newfoundland Law Reports [*A publication*] (DLA)
NLR .... New Law Reports [*Ceylon*] [*A publication*] (DLA)
N-LR .... New York State Library, Legislative Reference Library, Albany, NY [*Library symbol Library of Congress*] (LCLS)
NLR .... Nigeria Law Reports [*A publication*] (DLA)
NLR .... Noise Load Ratio
NLR .... Nolan Resources Ltd. [*Vancouver Stock Exchange symbol*]
NLR .... Nonlinear Regression [*Mathematics*]
NLR .... Nonlinear Resistance (IDOE)
NLR .... Nonlinear Resistive
NLR .... Nonlinear Resistor [*Electronics*] (ECII)
NLR .... North London Railway [*British*]
NLR .... Nyasaland Law Reports [*A publication*] (DLA)
NLR .... South African Law Reports, Natal Province Division [*1910-46*] [*A publication*] (DLA)
NLRA .... National Labor Relations Act [*1935*]
NLRA .... National Lakes and Rivers Association [*Defunct*] (EA)
NLRB .... National Labor Relations Board [*Department of Labor*] [*Washington, DC*]
NLRB .... National Labor Relations Board Decisions and Orders [*A publication*] (DLA)
NLRB Ann Rep... National Labor Relations Board Annual Report [*A publication*] (DLA)
NLRB Dec... National Labor Relations Board Decisions [*A publication*] (DLA)
NLRBP .... National Labor Relations Board Professional Association
NLRBPA ...... National Labor Relations Board Professional Association (EA)
NLRBU .... National Labor Relations Board Union (EA)
NLRCA .... National Lilac Rabbit Club of America (EA)
NLRCCAP..... National Legal Resource Center for Child Advocacy and Protection [*Later, ABACCL*] (EA)
NL Rev .... Northeastern Law Review [*A publication*] (DLA)
NLRG .... Narrow-Line Radio Galaxy
NLRG .... Navy Long-Range Guidance
NLROG........ Navy Long-Range Objectives Group (DNAB)
NLR (OS).... Natal Law Reports, Old Series [*1867-72*] [*South Africa*] [*A publication*] (DLA)
NLRSS .... Navy Long-Range Strategic Study
NLRU .... Nordens Liberale og Radikale Ungdom [*Nordic Liberal and Radical Youth*] (EAIO)
NLS............. Nassau Library System [*Library network*]
NLS............. National Language Support [*Computer science*] (PCM)
NLS............. National Launch System (ECON)
NLS............. National Library of Scotland (NITA)
NLS............. National Library Service for the Blind and Physically Handicapped [*Also, NLS /BPH*] [*Library of Congress*]
NLS............. National Longitudinal Survey [*Statistics*]
NLS............. National Longitudinal Surveys of Labor Market Experience [*Ohio State University*] [*Columbus*] [*Information service or system*] (IID)
NLS............. Natural Law Society (EA)
NLS............. Navigating Light System
NLS............. Negative Lens Systems
NLS............. Neodymium LASER System
NLS............. Network Library System
NLS............. Network License System [*Computer science*] (CIST)
NLS............. New Least Square (PDAA)
NLS............. No-Load Speed
NLS............. No-Load Start
NLS............. Non-Linear Least Squares [*Statistics*]
NLS............. Nonlinear Smoothing
NLS............. Nonlinear Systems
NLS............. Nordic Language Secretariat [*See also SLN*] [*Norway*] (EAIO)
NLS............. Nordiske Laererorganisationers Samrad [*Council of Nordic Teachers' Association*] [*Sweden*] (EAIO)
NLS............. Normal Lymphocyte Supernatant (DB)
NLS............. North Carolina Central University, School of Library Science, Durham, NC [*OCLC symbol*] (OCLC)
NLS............. Nuclear Localization Signal [*Biochemistry*]
NLS............. Nuclear Location Sequence [*Cytology*]
NLS............. On-Line System [*Stanford Research Institute*] [*Computer science*]

NLSA .... National Liquor Stores Association (EA)
NLSA .... National Lithuanian Society of America (EA)
NLSA .... National Locksmith Suppliers Association (EA)
NLSBA .... National Lincoln Sheep Breeders' Association (EA)
NLS/BPH..... National Library Service for the Blind and Physically Handicapped [*Also, NLS*] [*Library of Congress Computer science*] (IID)
NLSC .... National Logistics Supply Center [*Marine science*] (OSRA)
NLSC .... Navy Lockheed Service Center
NLSC .... Northeastern Louisiana State College
NLSCS .... National League for Separation of Church and State (EA)
NLSF .... National Life Share Foundation (EA)
NLSF .... Navy Logistics Support Force (DOMA)
NLsH .... Frederic R. Harris, Inc., Lake Success, NY [*Library symbol Library of Congress*] (LCLS)
NLSI........... National Library of Science and Invention [*British*] (DIT)
NLSLS .... National Library of Scotland Lending Services (NITA)
NLsM .... Medical Society of the State of New York, Lake Success, NY [*Library symbol Library of Congress*] (LCLS)
NLSMA .... National Lamp and Shade Manufacturers' Association (IAA)
NLSMA .... National Longitudinal Study of Mathematical Abilities
NLSMB .... National Live Stock and Meat Board (EA)
NLSP .... Neighborhood Legal Services Program
NLSP .... NetWare Link Services Protocol [*Novell, Inc.*] (PCM)
NLSPA .... National Live Stock Producers Association (EA)
NLSPN .... National List of Scientific Plant Names [*Department of Agriculture*] (IID)
NLSS .... Navy Logistics Systems School
NLSS .... New London Submarine School [*Navy*] (MCD)
NLSSA .... National Litigation Support Services Association (NTPA)
NLSST .... Nonlinear Sea Surface Temperature (USDC)
NLST........... Nonlisted Name [*Telecommunications*] (TEL)
NLSU .... National League for Social Understanding (EA)
NLSY .... National Longitudinal Study of Youth
NLT .... Negative Line Transmission [*Noise limiter*] (IAA)
NLT .... Net Long Ton
NLT .... Newfoundland Labrador Air Transport Ltd. [*Canada ICAO designator*] (FAAC)
NLT .... New London Training Unit [*Navy*]
NLT .... Night Letter [*Telegraphic communications*]
NLT .... Noise Limiter (IAA)
NLT .... Normal Lube-Oil Tank (MSA)
NLT .... Normal Lymphocyte Transfer [*Immunochemistry*]
NLT .... Not Later Than
NLT .... Not Less Than
NLT .... Nucleus Lateralis Tuberis (DMAA)
NLTA .... National Lawn Tennis Association (WDAA)
NLTA .... National League of Teachers' Associations [*Defunct*] (EA)
NLTC .... National Livestock Tax Committee [*Later, NCA*] (EA)
NLTCDP ...... National Long-Term Care Channeling Demonstration Program [*Department of Health and Human Services*] (GFGA)
NLTE .... Nonlocal Thermodynamic Equilibrium
NLTF........... National Leather Trades Federation [*A union*] [*British*]
NLTNIF .... National Low-Temperature Neutron Irradiation Facility [*Oak Ridge, TN*] [*Department of Energy*] (GRD)
NLTRA .... National Land Title Reclamation Association (EA)
NLTS .... Near Launch Tracking System
NLU .... Naval Field Liaison Unit (DNAB)
NLU .... Normal Latch Up (COE)
NLUC .... National Land Use Classification (PDAA)
NLUF .... National LASER Users Facility [*Rochester, NY*] [*Department of Energy*] (GRD)
NLUS .... Navy League of the United States (EA)
NLUTS .... National Labourers' Union Trade Society [*British*]
NLv .... Locust Valley Public Library, Locust Valley, NY [*Library symbol Library of Congress*] (LCLS)
NLV .... Narcissus Latent Virus
NLVA .... National Licensed Victuallers Association [*British*] (DBA)
NLvBI.......... Bayville Intermediate School, Locust Valley, NY [*Library symbol Library of Congress*] (LCLS)
NLvHS .... Locust Valley High School, Locust Valley, NY [*Library symbol Library of Congress*] (LCLS)
NLvI............ Locust Valley Intermediate School, Locust Valley, NY [*Library symbol Library of Congress*] (LCLS)
NLvMP........ A.M. MacArthur Primary School, Locust Valley, NY [*Library symbol*] [*Library of Congress*] (LCLS)
NLVP .... NASA Launch Vehicle Planning Project (MCD)
NLVR .... Nonlinear Vacuum Regulator Valve [*Automotive engineering*]
NLW .... National Lawyers Wives (EA)
NLW .... National Library of Wales (WDAA)
NLW .... National Library Week
NLW .... Nominal Line Width
NLWF.......... Futuna/Pointe Vele [*Wallis and Futuna Islands*] [*ICAO location identifier*] (ICLI)
NLWW .... Wallis/Hififo [*Wallis and Futuna Islands*] [*ICAO location identifier*] (ICLI)
NLX............. NLX Resources, Inc. [*Toronto Stock Exchange symbol*]
NLY............. Northerly
NLynAE........ Atlantic Avenue School, Lynbrook, NY [*Library symbol*] [*Library of Congress*] (LCLS)
NLynd .... Yates Community Library, Lyndonville, NY [*Library symbol Library of Congress*] (LCLS)
NLynDE .... Davidson Avenue Elementary School, Lynbrook, NY [*Library symbol*] [*Library of Congress*] (LCLS)
NLyndHi...... Lyndonville Historical Society, Lyndonville, NY [*Library symbol Library of Congress*] (LCLS)

NLynHS........	Lynbrook High School, Lynbrook NY [*Library symbol*] [*Library of Congress*] (LCLS)
NLynME.......	Marion Street Elementary School, Lynbrook, NY [*Library symbol*] [*Library of Congress*] (LCLS)
NLynNM.......	North Middle School, Lynbrook, NY [*Library symbol*] [*Library of Congress*] (LCLS)
NLynSM.......	Lynbrook South Middle School, Lynbrook, NY [*Library symbol*] [*Library of Congress*] (LCLS)
NLynWPE.....	Waverly Park Elementary School, Lynbrook, NY [*Library symbol Library of Congress*] (LCLS)
nm----..........	Gulf of Mexico [*MARC geographic area code Library of Congress*] (LCCP)
NM...............	Mt. Cook Airlines [*ICAO designator*] (AD)
NM...............	Nachmittag [*Afternoon*] [*German*]
NM...............	Nanomemory (IAA)
nm............	Nanometer [*One billionth of a meter*]
nM............	Nanomole [*One billionth of a mole*]
NM............	Narrow Market [*Investment term*]
NM...............	Nationalist Movement (EA)
NM...............	National Magazine Co. Ltd. [*Publisher*] [*British*]
NM...............	National Match
NM...............	National Media Corp. [*NYSE symbol*] (SPSG)
NM...............	National Monument (GNE)
NM...............	National Motor Volunteers [*British military*] (DMA)
NM...............	Nations Ministries (EA)
NM...............	Natl Media Corp. [*NYSE symbol*] (TTSB)
NM...............	Natriuretic Material [*Physiology*]
NM...............	Naturally Occurring Mutants
NM...............	Nautical Mile [*6,080 feet*]
NM...............	Naval Mission (AFIT)
NM...............	Navigation Multiplexer [*Navy*] (CAAL)
NM...............	Navy Mines (MCD)
NM...............	Near Match (MCD)
nm...............	Near-Metacentric [*Botany*]
NM...............	Near Mint [*Condition*] [*Numismatics, deltiology, etc.*]
NM...............	Negro Male
NM...............	Neiman-Marcus
NM...............	Netherlands Museum [*Later, HHT*] (EA)
NM...............	Net Imports [*Economics*]
NM...............	Network Manager (MCD)
NM...............	Neuromotor [*Neurology*] (DAVI)
NM...............	Neuromuscular
NM...............	Newly Molded
NM...............	New Material [*FAR clauses*] (AAGC)
NM...............	New Measurement
NM...............	New Mexico [*Postal code*]
Nm...............	New Mexico State Library, Santa Fe, NM [*Library symbol Library of Congress*] (LCLS)
NM...............	New Mexico Supreme Court Reports [*A publication*] (DLA)
NM...............	New Mexico Territorial Court (DLA)
NM...............	New Moon [*Moon phase*]
N/m...............	Newton per Meter
N-M...............	New York State Library, Medical Library, Albany, NY [*Library symbol Library of Congress*] (LCLS)
Nm...............	Nicotiana mesophilia [*Tobacco*]
NM...............	Nictitating Membrane [*Animal anatomy*]
NM...............	Night and morning (DAVI)
NM...............	Night Message
NM...............	Nitrogen Mustard [*Also, HN, M, MBA*] [*Antineoplastic drug, war-gas base*]
NM...............	Nitromethane [*Organic chemistry*]
NM...............	Nocte et Mane [*Night and Morning*] [*Pharmacy*]
NM...............	Nodular Melanoma [*Oncology*]
NM...............	Nodular Mixed Lymphoma [*Onocology*] (DAVI)
NM...............	Noise Meter (MSA)
NM...............	No Mark
N/m...............	No Mark (EBF)
NM...............	Nomen Masculinam [*Masculine Name*] [*Latin*] (ROG)
NM...............	No Message
NM...............	Nonmagnetic (IAA)
NM...............	Nonmetallic
NM...............	Nonmotile [*Microbiology*]
NM...............	Nonwhite Male
NM...............	Nordiska Metallarbetaresekretariatet [*Nordic Metalworkers Secretariat - NMS*] (EAIO)
NM...............	Normetadrenaline [*Biochemistry*] (DAVI)
NM...............	Notice to Mariner
N/M...............	Not Marked [*Business term*]
NM...............	Not Married
NM...............	Not Meaningful
NM...............	Not Measurable [*or Measured*]
n/m...............	Not Mentioned [*Medicine*]
NM...............	Noun Modifier [*Linguistics*]
NM...............	Nuclear Magnetic
NM...............	Nuclear Magnetron (MSA)
NM...............	Nuclear Measurement (IAA)
NM...............	Nuclear Medicine
NM...............	Nuclear Membrane (DB)
Nm...............	Numbers [*Old Testament book*]
NM...............	Nutmeg (ADA)
NM...............	Nux Moschata [*Nutmeg*] [*Pharmacology*] (ROG)
N/m^2............	Newtons per Square Meter [*Pascals*] (IDOE)
NmA...............	Albuquerque Public Library, Albuquerque, NM [*Library symbol Library of Congress*] (LCLS)
NMA...............	Miami, FL [*Location identifier FAA*] (FAAL)

NMA............	Minute Men of America (NADA)
NMA............	Naphthalenemethylamine [*Reagent*] [*Organic chemistry*]
NMA............	Nashville Music Association [*Later, NEA*] (EA)
NMA............	National Malaria Association (DAVI)
NMA............	National Management Association [*Dayton, OH*] (EA)
NMA............	National Management Award [*GAMC*]
NMA............	National Marina Association [*Defunct*] (EA)
NMA............	National Maritime Alliance (NTPA)
NMA............	National Maritime Authority [*Australia*]
NMA............	National Meat Association [*Formerly, NIMPA*] (EA)
NMA............	National Medical Association (EA)
NMA............	National Microfilm Association [*Later, National Micrographics Association, now AIIM*] [*Trade association*]
NMA............	National Microform Association (NITA)
NMA............	National Micrographics Association [*Later, AIIM*] [*Trade association*] (EA)
NMA............	National Midwives Association (EA)
NMA............	National Military Authority (NATG)
NMA............	National Mime Association [*Later, NMTA*] (EA)
NMA............	National Mining Association (NTPA)
NMA............	National Motorists Association (EA)
NMA............	National Museum of Antiquities in Scotland
NMA............	National Music Academy [*Australia*]
NMA............	National Mustang Association (EA)
NMA............	NATO Military Authorities (NATG)
NMA............	Natural Marketing Association [*Woodland Hills, CA*] (EA)
NMA............	Navy Mutual Aid Association (EA)
NMA............	Needle Makers Association [*British*] (BI)
NMA............	Negligee Manufacturers Association [*Later, IAMA*]
NMA............	Netherlands Military Administration [*World War II*]
NMA............	Neue Mozart-Ausgabe [*A publication*]
NMA............	Neurogenic Muscular Atrophy [*Medicine*]
NMA............	New Music Articles [*A publication*]
NMA............	Nicaragua Medical Aid (EA)
NMA............	N-Methylaspartate [*Organic chemistry*]
NMA............	N-Methylaspartic Acid [*An amino acid*]
NMA............	N-Methylolacrylamide [*Organic chemistry*]
NMA............	Noma Industries Ltd. [*Toronto Stock Exchange symbol*]
NMA............	Non-Marine Association [*Lloyd's Underwriters*] (AIA)
NMA............	Nonmass Analyzed [*Photovoltaic energy systems*]
NMA............	Nonmedical Attendant (AABC)
NMA............	Nonprofit Management Association (EA)
NMA............	Nonresonant Magnetic Amplifier
NMA............	Normal Method of Acquisition (MCD)
NMA............	Northwest Mining Association (EA)
NMA............	Nuveen Muni Advantage Fd [*NYSE symbol*] (TTSB)
NMA............	Nuveen Municipal Advantage Fund [*NYSE symbol*] (SPSG)
NMA............	University of Albuquerque, Albuquerque, NM [*OCLC symbol*] (OCLC)
NMa............	Wead Library, Malone, NY [*Library symbol Library of Congress*] (LCLS)
NMAA	National Machine Accountants Association [*Later, DPMA*]
NMAA	National Metal Awning Association [*Defunct*] (EA)
NMAA	National Mobilization Against AIDS [*Acquired Immune Deficiency Syndrome*] (EA)
NMAA	National Multimedia Association of America (DDC)
NMAA	National Museum of African Art [*Smithsonian Institution*]
NMAA	Navy Mutual Aid Association
NMAA	Nursing Mothers' Association of Australia
NmAAc.........	Albuquerque Academy, Albuquerque, NM [*Library symbol*] [*Library of Congress*] (LCLS)
NmAACF......	ACF Industries, Inc., Albuquerque, NM [*Library symbol Library of Congress*] (LCLS)
NmAAF	United States Air Force, Weapons Laboratory, Kirtland Air Force Base, Albuquerque, NM [*Library symbol Library of Congress*] (LCLS)
NmAAM	United States Army, Medical Library, Sandia Base, Albuquerque, NM [*Library symbol Library of Congress*] (LCLS)
NMAB	National Market Advisory Board [*SEC*]
NMAB	National Materials Advisory Board (EA)
N-MAb	Neutralizing Monoclonal Antibody [*Immunology*]
NMAB	N-Monochloro(amino)butyric Acid [*Organic chemistry*]
NmABD........	BDM Corp., Albuquerque, NM [*Library symbol*] [*Library of Congress*] (LCLS)
NMAC	National Medical Audiovisual Center [*of the National Library of Medicine*] [*LHNCBC*] [*Absorbed by*] (EA)
NMAC	National Minority AIDS [*Acquired Immune Deficiency Syndrome*] Council (EA)
NMAC	Naval Missile and Astronautics Center
NMAC	Near Midair Collision
NMAC	Nissan Motor Acceptance Corp.
NMAC	Nuclear Materials Accounting and Control
NMACT	Nuclear Materials Accounting Control Team [*British*] (NUCP)
NmADAS......	United States Defense Atomic Support Agency, Sandia Base, Albuquerque, NM [*Library symbol Library of Congress*] (LCLS)
NmA-EP	Albuquerque Public Library, Ernie Pyle Memorial Branch, Albuquerque, NM [*Library symbol Library of Congress*] (LCLS)
NMAF	National Medical Association Foundation [*Defunct*] (EA)
NMAFA	National Museum of African Art [*Smithsonian Institution*] (GFGA)
NMAG	Nonmagnetic (MSA)
N Mag Ca ...	New Magistrates' Cases [*England*] [*A publication*] (DLA)
NmAGen.......	New Mexico Genealogical Society, Inc., Albuquerque, NM [*Library symbol Library of Congress*] (LCLS)
NmAGS........	Church of Jesus Christ of Latter-Day Saints, Genealogical Society Library, Albuquerque Branch, Albuquerque, NM [*Library symbol Library of Congress*] (LCLS)

NMah............ Mahopac Library Association, Mahopac, NY [*Library symbol Library of Congress*] (LCLS)

NmAHS........ Honeywell Sperry Inc., Defense System Division, Albuquerque, NM [*Library symbol*] [*Library of Congress*] (LCLS)

NMAHSTC.... National Museum of American History, Science, Technology, and Culture [*Smithsonian Institution*]

NmAI........... Alamogordo Public Library, Alamogordo, NM [*Library symbol Library of Congress*] (LCLS)

NmAL........... Lovelace Foundation for Medical Education and Research, Albuquerque, NM [*Library symbol Library of Congress*] (LCLS)

NMAL........... Northeast Marine Animal Lifeline

NmA-LG....... Albuquerque Public Library, Los Griegos Branch, Albuquerque, NM [*Library symbol Library of Congress*] (LCLS)

NMalv.......... Malverne Public Library, Malverne, NY [*Library symbol Library of Congress*] (LCLS)

NMalvDE...... Davison Elementary School, Malverne, NY [*Library symbol Library of Congress*] (LCLS)

NMalvHM...... Howard T. Herber Middle School, Malverne, NY [*Library symbol*] [*Library of Congress*] (LCLS)

NMalvLE...... Lindner Elementary School, Malverne, NY [*Library symbol Library of Congress*] (LCLS)

NMalvSH...... Malverne Senior High School, Malverne, NY [*Library symbol*] [*Library of Congress*] (LCLS)

NMam.......... Mamaroneck Free Library, Mamaroneck, NY [*Library symbol Library of Congress*] (LCLS)

NmAM.......... Montessori School, Albuquerque, NM [*Library symbol Library of Congress*] (LCLS)

NMamL........ Mamaroneck Free Library, Mamaroneck, NY [*Library symbol*] [*Library of Congress*] (LCLS)

NM & S....... Bureau of Medicine and Surgery Publications [*Navy*]

NM&SA........ National Moving & Storage Association [*MTMC*] (TAG)

NManh......... Manhasset Public Library, Manhasset, NY [*Library symbol Library of Congress*] (LCLS)

NManhH...... North Shore Hospital, Manhasset, NY [*Library symbol Library of Congress*] (LCLS)

NManhJH.... Manhasset Junior High School, Manhasset, NY [*Library symbol*] [*Library of Congress*] (LCLS)

NManhJSH... Manhasset Junior-Senior High School, Manhasset, NY [*Library symbol Library of Congress*] (LCLS)

NManhM...... Manhasset Medical Center Hospital, Manhasset, NY [*Library symbol Library of Congress*] (LCLS)

NManhME.... Munsey Park Elementary School, Manhasset, NY [*Library symbol*] [*Library of Congress*] (LCLS)

NManhSE.... Shelter Rock Elementary School, Manhasset, NY [*Library symbol*] [*Library of Congress*] (LCLS)

NManhSH... Manhasset Senior High School, Manhasset, NY [*Library symbol*] [*Library of Congress*] (LCLS)

NManhSM.... Saint Mary's Boys High School, Manhasset, NY [*Library symbol*] [*Library of Congress*] (LCLS)

NMANX........ Neub. & Berman Manhattan Fund [*Mutual fund ticker symbol*] (SG)

NMAP.......... Navy Military Assistance Programs

NmA-PP....... Albuquerque Public Library, Prospect Park Branch, Albuquerque, NM [*Library symbol Library of Congress*] (LCLS)

NM App....... New Mexico Court of Appeals (DLA)

NmAr........... Artesia Public Library, Artesia, NM [*Library symbol Library of Congress*] (LCLS)

NMar........... Marcellus Free Library, Marcellus, NY [*Library symbol Library of Congress*] (LCLS)

Nm-Ar.......... New Mexico State Records Center and Archives, Santa Fe, NM [*Library symbol Library of Congress*] (LCLS)

NMARC........ Navy and Marine Corps Acquisition Review Committee [*Terminated, 1975*] (MCD)

NMarcP........ Marcy Psychiatric Center, Marcy, NY [*Library symbol Library of Congress*] (LCLS)

NmArP......... Artesia Public Library, Artesia, NM [*Library symbol*] [*Library of Congress*] (LCLS)

NMas........... Henry H. Warren Memorial Library, Massena, NY [*Library symbol Library of Congress*] (LCLS)

NMAS.......... National Map Accuracy Standards (PDAA)

NMAS.......... National Marine Advisory Service [*National Oceanic and Atmospheric Administration*] (MSC)

NmAS.......... Sandia Corp., Albuquerque, NM [*Library symbol Library of Congress*] (LCLS)

NMasL......... Massena Public Library, Massena, NY [*Library symbol*] [*Library of Congress*] (LCLS)

NMasMH..... Massena Memorial Hospital, Massena, NY [*Library symbol*] [*Library of Congress*] (LCLS)

NMass......... Massapequa Public Library, Massapequa, NY [*Library symbol Library of Congress*] (LCLS)

NMassAJ..... J. Lewis Ames Junior High School, Massapequa, NY [*Library symbol*] [*Library of Congress*] (LCLS)

NMassBE..... Birch Elementary School, Massapequa, NY [*Library symbol Library of Congress*] (LCLS)

NMassBH..... Berner High School, Massapequa, NY [*Library symbol Library of Congress*] (LCLS)

NMassELE... East Lake Elementary School, Massapequa, NY [*Library symbol Library of Congress*] (LCLS)

NMassFE..... Fairfield Elementary School, Massapequa, NY [*Library symbol Library of Congress*] (LCLS)

NMassHE..... Hawthorn Elementary School, Massapequa, NY [*Library symbol Library of Congress*] (LCLS)

NMassHS..... Masspequa High School, Massapequa, NY [*Library symbol*] [*Library of Congress*] (LCLS)

NMassLE..... Lockhart Elementary School, Massapequa, NY [*Library symbol Library of Congress*] (LCLS)

NMassMJ.... J.P. McKenna Junior High School, Massapequa, NY [*Library symbol*] [*Library of Congress*] (LCLS)

NMassSE.... Charles E. Schwarting Elementary School, Massapequa, NY [*Library symbol*] [*Library of Congress*] (LCLS)

NMassUE.... Unqua Elementary School, Massapequa, NY [*Library symbol Library of Congress*] (LCLS)

NMat............ Mattituck Free Library, Mattituck, NY [*Library symbol Library of Congress*] (LCLS)

NMAT........... Night-Time Marine Air Temperature

NMATP......... Navy Military Assistance Training Program (NG)

Nmatrn......... Nematron Corp. [*Associated Press*] (SAG)

NMAU.......... Naval Medical Administration Unit (DNAB)

NmAU.......... University of Albuquerque, Albuquerque, NM [*Library symbol Library of Congress*] (LCLS)

NmAVA........ United States Veterans Administration Hospital, Albuquerque, NM [*Library symbol Library of Congress*] (LCLS)

NMAX.......... Nonwireline Multiple-Access Communications Exchange System (PDAA)

NMb............. Mastics-Moriches-Shirley Community Library, Mastic Beach, NY [*Library symbol Library of Congress*] (LCLS)

NMB............. Namib Air (Pty) Ltd. [*Namibia*] [*ICAO designator*] (FAAC)

NMB............. National Marine Board [*British World War II*]

NMB............. National Maritime Board

NMB............. National Meat Brokers [*Australia*]

NMB............. National Mediation Board [*Department of Labor*]

NMB............. National Metric Board

NMB............. National Motel Brokers (EA)

NMB............. National Mutual Benefit [*Madison, WI*] (EA)

NMB............. Naval Meteorological Branch [*British*]

NMB............. Naval Minecraft Base

NMB............. Naval Model Basin

NMB............. Neuromuscular Blockade [*Medicine*]

NMB............. New Methylene Blue [*Organic chemistry*]

NMB............. Nippon Miniature Bearing Corp. (EFIS)

NMB............. Noise, Measurement Buoy

NMB............. No Military Branch

NMB............. Not Member of a Branch

NMBA.......... National Marine Bankers Association [*Chicago, IL*] (EA)

NMBA.......... Neuromuscular Blocking Agent

NMBA.......... (Nitrosomethylamino) Butyric Acid [*Organic chemistry*]

NMBC.......... National Minority Business Campaign [*Later, NMBD*] (EA)

NMBC.......... National Minority Business Council [*New York, NY*] (EA)

NMbCH........ Bayview Community Hospital, Mastic Beach, NY [*Library symbol Library of Congress*] (LCLS)

NMBD.......... National Minority Business Directories [*Minneapolis, MN*] (EA)

NmBeN........ Northwestern Regional Library, Belen, NM [*Library symbol Library of Congress*] (LCLS)

NMBF.......... National Manufacturers of Beverage Flavors [*Defunct*] (EA)

NMBHF........ Naismith Memorial Basketball Hall of Fame (EA)

NMBMMR..... New Mexico Bureau of Mines and Mineral Resources [*New Mexico Institute of Mining and Technology*] [*Research center*] (RCD)

NMbr........... Millbrook Library, Millbrook, NY [*Library symbol*] [*Library of Congress*] (LCLS)

NMBR.......... NATO Military Basic Requirement (MCD)

NMbrB......... Bennett College, Millbrook, NY [*Library symbol Library of Congress*] (LCLS)

NMBS.......... Nationale Maatschappij der Belgische Spoorwegen [*Railway*] [*Belgium*] (EY)

NMBS.......... Nimbus CD International, Inc. [*NASDAQ symbol*] (SAG)

NMBS.......... Nimbus CD Intl. [*NASDAQ symbol*] (TTSB)

NMBT.......... New Main Battle Tank [*Military*] (RDA)

NMBT.......... New Milford Bank & Trust Co. [*NASDAQ symbol*] (CTT)

NMBT.......... New Milford BK & Tr Conn [*NASDAQ symbol*] (TTSB)

NmC............ Carlsbad Public Library, Carlsbad, NM [*Library symbol Library of Congress*] (LCLS)

NMC............ Marine Corps Publications [*Later, NAVMC*]

NMC............ Meredith College, Raleigh, NC [*OCLC symbol*] (OCLC)

NMC............ Nail Manufacturers Council (EA)

NMC............ Natal Medical Corps [*British military*] (DMA)

NMC............ National Magazine Co.

NMC............ National Mail Centers, Inc. [*Telecommunications service*] (TSSD)

NMC............ National Manpower Council

NMC............ National Marine Center (USDC)

NMC............ National Maritime Council [*Defunct*] (EA)

NMC............ National Mastitis Council (EA)

NMC............ National Medical Care

NMC............ National Memorials Committee [*Australia*]

NMC............ National Message Center [*Overland Park, KS*] (TSSD)

NMC............ National Meteorological Center [*National Oceanic and Atmospheric Administration Information service or system*] (IID)

NMC............ National Migrant Clearinghouse (OICC)

NMC............ National Military Council [*Surinam*] (PD)

NMC............ National Missionary Council [*Australia*]

NMC............ National Motorsports Committee (EA)

NMC............ National Mouse Club [*British*] (BI)

NMC............ National Museum of Canada

NMC............ National Music Camp [*Interlochen, MI*]

NMC............ National Music Council (EA)

NMC............ NATO Manual on Codification (NATG)

NMC............ Naval Material Command [*Formerly, NMSE*]

NMC............ Naval Medical Center [*Bethesda, MD*]

NMC............ Naval Memorandum Correction (NVT)

NMC............ Naval Missile Center [*Point Mugu, CA*]

NMC............ Naval Mission Center (KSC)

NMC............ NAVA [*National Audio-Visual Association*] Materials Council (EA)

NMC............	Navigation Map Computer
NMC............	Navy Mail Clerk
NMC............	Navy Memorandum Correction
NMC............	Nebraska Motor Carriers Association, Petroleum Carriers' Conference, Inc., OmahaNE [*STAC*]
NMC............	Net Matchable Cost
NMC............	Network Management Center [*Computer science*]
NMC............	Network Management Console [*Industrial Networking, Inc.*]
NMC............	Network Measurement Center
NMC............	Neuromuscular Control [*Medicine*] (DMAA)
NMC............	Nine Mile Canyon [*California*] [*Seismograph station code, US Geological Survey*] (SEIS)
NMC............	Noble Metal Catalyst [*Automotive engineering*]
NMC............	No More Credit [*Business term*] (ADA)
NMC............	Non-Metropolitan Counties [*British*]
NMC............	Non-Mission Capable [*Military*] (INF)
NMC............	Nonmotor Condition [*Medicine*] (DMAA)
NMC............	Northern Montana College [*Havre*]
NMC............	Northwestern Michigan College [*Traverse City*]
NMC............	Not Mission Capable (MCD)
NMC............	Nuclear Metal Conference
NMC............	Nucleus Reticularis Magnocellularis [*Medicine*] (DMAA)
NMC............	Numac Energy [*AMEX symbol*] (SPSG)
NMC............	Nurse Managed Center (MEDA)
NMC............	Nursery Marketing Council (EA)
NMC............	Nursing Mothers Counsel [*An association*] (EA)
NMC............	Public Archives of Canada, National Map Collection [*UTLAS symbol*]
NMC............	San Francisco, CA [*Location identifier FAA*] (FAAL)
NMCA	National Marble Club of America (EA)
NMCA	National Meat Canners Association (EA)
NMCA	National Military Command Authority (NVT)
NMCA	National Mossberg Collectors Association (EA)
NMCA	National Motorcycle Commuter Association [*Defunct*] (EA)
NMCA	National Musclecar Association (EA)
NMCA	Navy Mothers' Clubs of America (EA)
N-McAb	Neutralizing Monoclonal Antibody [*Immunology*]
NMCAC	National Motor Carrier Advisory Committee [*MTMC*] (TAG)
NMCB	National Metric Conversion Board (NADA)
NMCB	National Munitions Control Board [*World War II*]
NMCB	National Museum of Canada Bulletin [*A publication*]
NMCB	Navy Mobile Construction Battalion (CINC)
NMCC	National Management Career Curriculum [*Office of Personnel Management*] (GFGA)
NMCC	National Manpower Coordinating Committee [*Department of Labor*]
NMCC	National Military Command Center [*DoD*]
NMCC	Navy-Marine Corps Council [*Defunct*] (EA)
NMCC	Network Management Control Center [*Telecommunications*]
NMCC	Nonmyeloid Cell Content (DB)
NMCC	Northeast-Midwest Congressional Coalition (EA)
NMCCDDA ...	National Model Cities Community Development Directors Association [*Later, NCDA*] (EA)
NMCCIS	NATO Military Command and Control and Information System (NATG)
NMCDA	National Model Cities Directors Association [*Later, NCDA*] (EA)
NMCEC	Navy-Marine Corps Exhibit Center
NMCES	National Medical Care Expenditures Survey [*Department of Health and Human Services*] (GFGA)
NMCGB	National Music Council of Great Britain (EAIO)
NMCGRF	Navy-Marine Corps-Coast Guard Residence Foundation
NMCHC	National Maternal and Child Health Clearinghouse (EA)
NMCI	National Multicultural Institute (EA)
NmCiN	Northeastern Regional Library, Cimarron, NM [*Library symbol*] [*Library of Congress*] (LCLS)
NMCIRD	Naval Material Command Industrial Resources Detachment (DNAB)
NMCJS	Naval Member, Canadian Joint Staff
NmCl	Clovis-Carver Public Library, Clovis, NM [*Library symbol Library of Congress*] (LCLS)
NMCL	Navy Missile Center Laboratory (KSC)
NmCla	Albert W. Thompson Memorial Library, Clayton, NM [*Library symbol Library of Congress*] (LCLS)
NMCLA	Bethesda Military Librarians Group [*Library network*]
NmCIA	United States Air Force, Cannon Air Force Base, Clovis, NM [*Library symbol Library of Congress*] (LCLS)
NmClaP	Albert W. Thompson Memorial Library, Clayton, NM [*Library symbol*] [*Library of Congress*] (LCLS)
NMCLK	Navy Mail Clerk
NMCM	Navy and Marine Corps Medal [*Military decoration*]
NMCM	Not Mission Capable, Maintenance (NVT)
NMCO	Navy Material Cataloging Office
NMCOM	Naval Material Command [*Formerly, NMSE*] (MCD)
NmCP	United States Potash Co., Carlsbad, NM [*Library symbol Library of Congress*] (LCLS)
NMCRB	Navy Military Construction Review Board
NMCRC	Navy-Marine Corps Reserve Center (NVT)
NMCRS	Navy-Marine Corps Relief Society
NMCRTC	Navy and Marine Corps Reserve Training Center
NMCS	National Medic-Card [*Commercial firm*] (EA)
NMCS	National Medicinal Chemistry Symposium
NMCS	National Military Command System
NMCS	Navy Mine Countermeasures Station (MUGU)
NMCS	Not Mission Capable, Supply (MCD)
NMCS	Nuclear Materials Control System (IEEE)
NMCSA	Navy Material Command Support Activity
NMCSHA	National Morgan Cutting and Stock Horse Association (EA)
NMCSS	National Military Command System Standards (AFM)

NMCSSC	National Military Command System Support Center (AABC)
NMCUES	National Medical Care Utilization and Expenditure Survey [*Department of Health and Human Services A publication*] (DHSM)
NmD	Deming Public Library, Deming, NM [*Library symbol Library of Congress*] (LCLS)
NMD	NASA Management Delegations (MCD)
NMD	National Missile Defense [*DoD*]
NMD	Naval Mine Depot
NMD	Navy Marine Diesel Fuel
NMD	Netmed, Inc. [*AMEX symbol*] (SAG)
NMD	Nonmonetary Determination [*Unemployment insurance*] (OICC)
NMD	Normal Muscle Development (DAVI)
NMD	Nu-Media Industry International [*Vancouver Stock Exchange symbol*]
NMD	Nutrition Monitoring Division [*Department of Agriculture*] (GFGA)
NMDA	National Marine Distributors Association (EA)
NMDA	National Medical and Dental Association (EA)
NMDA	National Metal Decorators Association (EA)
NMDA	National Midas Dealers Association (EA)
NMDA	National Motorcycle Dealers Association [*Later, NMRA*] (EA)
NMDA	National Motorcycle Dismantelers Association (EA)
NMDA	National Motor Drivers' Association [*A union*] [*British*]
NMDA	N-Methyl-D-Aspartic Acid [*An amino acid*]
NMDA	Nonresonant Magnetic Deflection Amplifier
NMDAR	N-Methyl-D-Aspartic Acid Receptor [*Neurochemistry*]
nMDC	Native Macrophage-Derived Chemokine [*Immunology*]
NMDC	Nonmagnetic Drill Collar [*Well drilling technology*]
NMDCEF	National Medico-Dental Conference for the Evaluation of Fluoridation [*Later, Medical-Dental Committee on Evaluation of Fluoridation*] (EA)
NMDF	Navy Management Data File (DNAB)
NMDG	N-Methyl-D-Glucamine [*Biochemistry*]
NMD/GBR	National Missile Defense-Ground Based RADAR [*Army*] (RDA)
NMDIS	National Marine Data and Information Service [*China*] [*Marine science*] (OSRA)
NMDIS	National Music and Disability Information Service [*British*]
NMDL	Naval Mine Defense Laboratory [*Naval Facilities Engineering Command*] [*Panama City, FL*]
NMDL	Navy Management Data List (NG)
NMDL	Navy Material Data List
NMDP	National Marrow Donor Program [*Department of Health and Human Services*]
NMDP	Neomenthyldiphenylphosphine [*Organic chemistry*]
NMDPI	Nuveen Maryland Premium Income Municipal Fund [*Associated Press*] (SAG)
NMDR	Nuclear Magnetic Double Resonance
NMDRP	National Military Discharge Review Project (EA)
NMDS	Naval Mine Disposal School
NMDS	Network Management Directory Services (NITA)
NMDS	New Music Distribution Service (EA)
NMDS	Nonmetric Multidimensional Scaling [*Statistics*]
NMDSC	Naval Medical Data Service Center (DNAB)
NMDSG	Naval Material Data Systems Group (DNAB)
NMDU	Newspaper and Mail Deliverers Union of New York and Vicinity (EA)
NMDY	Nonresonant Magnetic Deflection Yoke
NMDZ	NATO Maritime Defense Zone (NATG)
NmE	Espanola Public Library, Espanola, NM [*Library symbol Library of Congress*] (LCLS)
NME	National Marriage Encounter (EA)
NME	National Military Establishment [*Designated Department of Defense, 1949*]
NME	Naval Material Establishment (DOMA)
NME	Necrolytic Migratory Erythema [*Dermatology*]
NME	Newly Maturing Economy [*Business term*]
NME	New Molecular Entity [*Chemistry*]
NME	New Musical Express [*A publication*] (WDAA)
NME	Nightmute [*Alaska*] [*Airport symbol*] (OAG)
NME	Nissan Motorsports Europe
NME	Noise-Measuring Equipment
NME	Nonsupervisory Manufacturing Engineer
NME	Norton Mobile Essentials [*Symantec*]
NMEA	National Marine Educators Association (EA)
NMEA	National Marine Electronics Association (EA)
NMEBA	National Marine Engineers' Beneficial Association (EA)
NMEC	National Metric Education Center [*Western Michigan University*]
NMEC	Nuclear Material Control Center (NUCP)
NMed	Lee-Whedon Memorial Library, Medina, NY [*Library symbol Library of Congress*] (LCLS)
NMED	New Mexico Environmental Department
NMEDA	National Mobility Equipment Dealers Association (NTPA)
NMedH	Medina Memorial Hospital, Medina, NY [*Library symbol Library of Congress*] (LCLS)
NMedia	National Media Corp. [*Associated Press*] (SAG)
NMEF	Naval Mine Engineering Facility
NMEFC	National Marine Environmental Forecasting Center [*China*] [*Marine science*] (OSRA)
NMEG	Nisei Mass Evacuation Group
NMEIA	National Machine Embellishment Instructors and Artists (NTPA)
NMEIA	National Machine Embroidery Instructors Association (EA)
NMEIAA	National Machine Embroidery Instructors Association of America (EA)
NMEL	Navy Marine Engineering Laboratory [*Later, David W. Taylor Naval Ship Research and Development Center*] (KSC)
NMelA	Airborne Institute Laboratories, Melville, NY [*Library symbol Library of Congress*] (LCLS)

NMeIH .... Holzmacher, McLendon & Murrell, Inc., Melville, NY [*Library symbol Library of Congress*] (LCLS)

NMeIL .... Litcom Library, Melville, NY [*Library symbol Library of Congress*] (LCLS)

NMeIS .... Suffolk State School, Melville, NY [*Library symbol Library of Congress*] (LCLS)

NMeISC .... Sagamore Children's Center, Melville, NY [*Library symbol Library of Congress*] (LCLS)

NmEN .... Northern Regional Library, Espanola, NM [*Library symbol Library of Congress*] (LCLS)

NMERI .... New Mexico Engineering Research Institute [*University of New Mexico*] [*Research center*] (RCD)

NMerk .... Merrick Public Library, Merrick, NY [*Library symbol Library of Congress*] (LCLS)

NMerkBE ..... Birch Elementary School, Merrick, NY [*Library symbol*] [*Library of Congress*] (LCLS)

NMerk CE .... Chatterton Elementary School, Merrick, NY [*Library symbol*] [*Library of Congress*] (LCLS)

NMerkCH ..... Sanford H. Calhoun High School, Merrick, NY [*Library symbol*] [*Library of Congress*] (LCLS)

NMerkF .... Five Towns College, Merrick, NY [*Library symbol Library of Congress*] (LCLS)

NMerkLE ..... Lakeside Elementary School, Merrick, NY [*Library symbol*] [*Library of Congress*] (LCLS)

NMerkMJ ..... Merrick Avenue Junior High School, Merrick, NY [*Library symbol*] [*Library of Congress*] (LCLS)

NMES .... National Medical Expenditure Survey [*Department of Health and Human Services*] (GFGA)

NMES .... Naval Marine Engineering Station

NMET .... Naval Mobile Environmental Team (COE)

NMEU .... Naval Material Evaluation Unit (DNAB)

NMEX .... New Mexico

N Mex Highlands U ... New Mexico Highlands University (GAGS)

N Mex Inst M&T ... New Mexico Institute of Mining and Technology (GAGS)

N Mex St U ... New Mexico State University (GAGS)

NMF .... Boston, MA [*Location identifier FAA*] (FAAL)

NmF .... Farmington Public Library, Farmington, NM [*Library symbol Library of Congress*] (LCLS)

NMF .... National Marfan Foundation (EA)

NMF .... National Medical Fellowships (EA)

NMF .... National Migraine Foundation [*Later, National Headache Foundation - NHF*] (EA)

NMF .... National Motor Freight Traffic Association Inc., Agent, Washington DC [*STAC*]

NMF .... National Myoclonus Foundation [*Defunct*] (EA)

NMF .... Naval Missile Facility [*Also, NAVMISFAC*]

NMF .... Navy Management Fund

NMF .... New Master File

NMF .... N-Methylformamide [*Antineoplastic compound*]

NMF .... N-Methyl Fucosamine [*Organic chemistry*]

NMF .... Nonmaster File [*Computer science*]

NMF .... Nonmember Firm [*of NYSE*]

NMF .... Nonmigrating Fraction [*of spermatozoa*] [*Medicine*]

NMF .... Nonprofit Mailers Federation (EA)

NMF .... Nonuniform Magnetic Field

NMF .... Nordiska Maskinbefalsfederationen [*Nordic Engineer Officers' Federation - NEOF*] (EAIO)

NMFA .... National Military Family Association (EA)

NMFC .... National Magazine and Film Carriers (NTPA)

NMFC .... National Magazine, Book, and Film Carriers Conference (NTPA)

NMFC .... National Motor Freight Classification

NMFCR .... National Motor Freight Classification Rules

NMFEC .... National Medical Foundation for Eye Care [*Later, AAO*] (EA)

NMFECC ..... National Magnetic Fusion Energy Computer Center [*Department of Energy*] (MCD)

NmFGS .... Church of Jesus Christ of Latter-Day Saints, Genealogical Society Library, Farmington Branch, Farmington, NM [*Library symbol Library of Congress*] (LCLS)

NMFHAWAREA ... Naval Missile Facility, Hawaiian Area (MUGU)

NMFHG .... National Master Farm Homemakers Guild (EA)

NMFI .... National Master Facility Inventory [*Department of Health and Human Services*] (GFGA)

NmfL .... National Microfilms Ltd., Dublin, Ireland [*Library symbol*] [*Library of Congress*] (LCLS)

NMFMA .... National Mutual Fund Managers Association [*Defunct*] (EA)

NMFPA .... Naval Missile Facility, Point Arguello

NMFPM .... Naval Missile Facility, Point Mugu [*California*] (SAA)

NMFR .... NAPALM [*National ADP Program for AMC Logistics Management*] Master File Record

NMFRL .... Naval Medical Field Research Laboratory [*Camp Lejeune, NC*]

NmFs .... Fort Sumner Public Library, Fort Sumner, NM [*Library symbol Library of Congress*] (LCLS)

NMFS .... National Marine Fisheries Service [*Formerly, Bureau of Commercial Fisheries*] [*National Oceanic and Atmospheric Administration Washington, DC*]

NMFS .... National Medical Financial Services Corp. [*NASDAQ symbol*] (SAG)

NMFS .... National Mortality Followback Survey [*National Center for Health Statistics*]

NMFS .... Natl Medical Finl Svcs [*NASDAQ symbol*] (TTSB)

NMFS .... Night Missile Flash Simulator (MCD)

NMFT .... New Material Flight Tests

NMFTA .... National Motor Freight Traffic Association [*Alexandria, VA*] (EA)

NMFWA .... National Military Fish and Wildlife Association (EA)

NMFWA .... Neuromuscular Foundation of Western Australia

NmG .... Gallup Public Library, Gallup, NM [*Library symbol Library of Congress*] (LCLS)

NMG .... Navy Metrication Group (DNAB)

NMG .... Navy Military Government

NMG .... Neiman-Marcus Group [*NYSE symbol*] (SPSG)

NM (G) .... New Mexico Reports (Gildersleeve) [*1852-89*] [*A publication*] (DLA)

NMG .... New Orleans, LA [*Location identifier FAA*] (FAAL)

NMG .... Numerical Master Geometry [*System*]

NMG .... San Miguel [*Panama*] [*Airport symbol*] (OAG)

NMGA .... National Military Guidance Association (EA)

NMGC .... National Marriage Guidance Council [*British*] (ILCA)

NMGCS .... National Milk Glass Collectors Society

NmGr .... Mother Whiteside Memorial Library, Grants, NM [*Library symbol Library of Congress*] (LCLS)

NMGRA .... National Museum and Gallery Registration Association (EA)

NMh .... Library of Poultney Bigelow, Malden-On-Hudson, NY [*Library symbol*] [*Library of Congress*] (LCLS)

NMH .... Nautical Miles per Hour

NMH .... New Mexico Highlands [*New Mexico*] [*Seismograph station code, US Geological Survey*] (SEIS)

NMH .... New Mexico Highlands University, Las Vegas, NM [*OCLC symbol*] (OCLC)

NMH .... N-Methylhydroxylamine [*Organic chemistry*]

NmHa .... Hatch Public Library, Hatch, NM [*Library symbol Library of Congress*] (LCLS)

NMHA .... National Mental Health Association (EA)

NMHA .... National Minority Health Association (EA)

NMHA .... National Mobile Home Association (EA)

NmHARL ...... Aeromedical Library, 6571st Aeromedical Research Laboratory, Holloman AFB, NM [*Library symbol Library of Congress*] (LCLS)

NMHC .... National Materials Handling Centre [*Cranfield Institute of Technology*] [*British*] (CB)

NMHC .... National Multi Housing Council (EA)

NMHC .... Nonmethane Hydrocarbons [*Organic chemistry*]

NMHCA .... National Mental Health Consumers' Association (EA)

NMHCC .... National Managed Health Care Congress (HGEN)

NMHCSHC ... National Mental Health Consumer Self-Help Clearinghouse (EA)

NMHF .... National Manufactured Housing Federation (EA)

NMHFA .... National Manufactured Housing Finance Association [*Defunct*] (EA)

NmHi .... Historical Society of New Mexico, Santa Fe, NM [*Library symbol Library of Congress*] (LCLS)

NmHo .... Hobbs Public Library, Hobbs, NM [*Library symbol Library of Congress*] (LCLS)

NmHoC .... New Mexico Junior College, Hobbs, NM [*Library symbol Library of Congress*] (LCLS)

NmHORA ...... United States Air Force, Office of Research Analyses, Technical Library, Holloman AFB, Albuquerque, NM [*Library symbol Library of Congress*] (LCLS)

NmHoSW ..... College of the Southwest, Hobbs, NM [*Library symbol Library of Congress*] (LCLS)

NM/HR .... Nautical Mile/Hour (MCD)

NMHS .... National Maritime Historical Society (EA)

NMHSPE ...... New Mexico High School Proficiency Examination (EDAC)

NMHT .... National Museum of History and Technology [*Later, National Museum of American History*] (GRD)

NMHU .... New Mexico Highlands University [*Las Vegas, NM*]

NMI .... Minot State College, Minot, ND [*OCLC symbol*] (OCLC)

NMI .... NASA Management Instruction (KSC)

NMI .... NASA Management Issuance (MCD)

NMI .... National Macaroni Institute (EA)

NMI .... National Maglev Initiative [*Department of Transportation*]

NMI .... National Maintenance Index (IAA)

NMI .... National Manpower Institute [*Later, NIWL*] (EA)

NMI .... National Maritime Institute [*British*]

NMI .... Nautical Mile

nmi .... Nautical Mile (NAKS)

NMI .... New Material Introductory [*Team*] [*Military*]

NMI .... Nissan Motorsports International [*Automotive competition*]

NMI .... No Middle Initial

NMI .... Nonmajor Item (MCD)

NMI .... Nonmasking [*or Nonmaskable*] Interrupt

NMI .... Northeast-Midwest Institute (EA)

NMI .... Northwest Microfilm, Inc. [*Information service or system*] (IID)

NMI .... Nuclear Magnetic Imaging

NMI .... Nuclear Metals, Inc.

NMI .... Nuveen Municipal Income Fund [*NYSE symbol*] (SPSG)

NMi .... Thrall Library, Middletown, NY [*Library symbol Library of Congress*] (LCLS)

NMIA .... National Military Intelligence Association (EA)

NMIAPO .... New Montreal International Airport Project [*Canada*]

NMIB .... New Material Introductory Briefing [*Military*] (MCD)

NMIBT .... New Material Introductory Briefing Team [*Military*] (MCD)

NMIC .... National Maritime Intelligence Center [*Created in 1992 from intelligence activities in the Washington, D.C., area*] [*Navy*] (DOMA)

NMIC .... National Meat Industry Council (EA)

NMIC .... National Military Information Center

NMIC .... National Missile Industry Conference (AAG)

NMIC .... Not Made in Canada [*Business term*]

NMICSS .... NMIC [*National Military Information Center*] Support System (MCD)

NMIDA .... N-Methyliminodiacetic Acid [*Organic chemistry*]

NMidp .... Middleport Free Library, Middleport, NY [*Library symbol Library of Congress*] (LCLS)

NMidpF .... FMC Corp., Niagara Chemical Division, R and D Library, Middleport, NY [*Library symbol Library of Congress*] (LCLS)

NMIHS .... National Maternal and Infant Health Survey [*Department of Health and Human Services*] (GFGA)

NMil .... Millerton Free Library, Millerton, NY [*Library symbol Library of Congress*] (LCLS)

NMIL .... New Materiel Introductory Letter [*Army*] (AABC)

NMILA .... NASA Merritt Island Launch Area (SAA)

NMilBc .... New Milford Savings Bank [*Associated Press*] (SAG)

NMilt .... Sarah Hull Hallock Free Library, Milton, NY [*Library symbol Library of Congress*] (LCLS)

NMIMT .... New Mexico Institute of Mining and Technology [*Socorro*]

NMin .... Mineola Memorial Library, Mineola, NY [*Library symbol Library of Congress*] (LCLS)

NMinH .... Nassau Hospital, Mineola, NY [*Library symbol Library of Congress*] (LCLS)

NMinHe .... Hampton Elementary School, Mineola, NY [*Library symbol Library of Congress*] (LCLS)

NMinJE .... Jackson Avenue Elementary School, Mineola, NY [*Library symbol Library of Congress*] (LCLS)

NMinME ...... Meadow Elementary School, Mineola, NY [*Library symbol Library of Congress*] (LCLS)

NMinMJ .... Mineola Junior High School, Mineola, NY [*Library symbol Library of Congress*] (LCLS)

NMinMS ...... Mineola Middle School, Mineola, NY [*Library symbol*] [*Library of Congress*] (LCLS)

NMinNCL ..... Nassau County Law Library, Mineola, NY [*Library symbol Library of Congress*] (LCLS)

NMiOC .... Orange County Community College, Middletown, NY [*Library symbol Library of Congress*] (LCLS)

NMIP .... New Major Investment Program [*Australia*]

NMIQI .... Nuveen Michigan Quality Income Municipal Fund [*Associated Press*] (SAG)

NMiR .... Ramapo Catskill Library System, Middletown, NY [*Library symbol Library of Congress*] (LCLS)

NMIRO .... Naval Material Industrial Resources Office

NMIS .... National Military Indications System (MCD)

NMIS .... Naval Manpower Information System

NMIS .... Newspapers Mutual Insurance Society Ltd. [*British*] (BI)

NMIS .... Nuclear Materials Information System

NMIS .... Nuclear Materials Inventory System (NRCH)

NMIS .... Nursing Management Information System (DMAA)

NMISMAN ..... Navy Manpower Information System Manual (DNAB)

NMIST .... National Military Intelligence Support Team [*Defense Intelligence Agency*] (DOMA)

NMIT .... New Materiel Introductory Team [*Army*] (AABC)

NMITC .... Navy and Marine Corps Intelligence Training Center (DOMA)

NMIU .... Nordic Meat Industry Union (EA)

NMIW .... Northwest Marine Iron Works (AAGC)

NmJ .... Jal Public Library, Jal, NM [*Library symbol Library of Congress*] (LCLS)

NMJ .... Neuromuscular Junction [*Anatomy*]

NM (J) .... New Mexico Reports (Johnson) [*A publication*] (DLA)

NMJC .... National Men's Judo Championships [*British*]

NMJC .... Northeastern Mississippi Junior College [*Senatobia*]

NMJC .... Northwest Mississippi Junior College

NMJL .... National Mah Jongg League (EA)

NMK .... Cape May, NJ [*Location identifier FAA*] (FAAL)

NMK .... Niagara Mohawk Power Corp. [*NYSE symbol*] (SPSG)

NMK .... Niagara Mohawk Pwr [*NYSE symbol*] (TTSB)

NMKL .... Nordisk Metodikkommitte for Livsmedel [*Nordic Committee on Food Analysis*] (EAIO)

NMKPr .... Niagara Moh Pwr Adj Rt A Pfd [*NYSE symbol*] (TTSB)

NMKPrA .... Niag Moh Pwr 3.40% Pfd [*NYSE symbol*] (TTSB)

NMKPrB .... Niag Moh Pwr 3.60% Pfd [*NYSE symbol*] (TTSB)

NMKPrC .... Niag Moh Pwr 3.90% Pfd [*NYSE symbol*] (TTSB)

NMKPrD .... Niag Moh Pwr 4.10% Pfd [*NYSE symbol*] (TTSB)

NMKPrE .... Niag Moh Pwr 4.85% Pfd [*NYSE symbol*] (TTSB)

NMKPrG .... Niag Moh Pwr 5.25% Pfd [*NYSE symbol*] (TTSB)

NMKPrI .... Niag Moh Pwr 7.72% Pfd [*NYSE symbol*] (TTSB)

NMKPrK .... Niagara Mohawk Pwr Adj C Pfd [*NYSE symbol*] (TTSB)

NMKPrM .... Niagara Moh Pwr 9.50% Pfd [*NYSE symbol*] (TTSB)

NML .... Narragansett Marine Laboratory [*University of Rhode Island*]

NML .... National Magnet Laboratory

NML .... National Measurement Laboratory [*Gaithersburg, MD*] [*National Institute of Standards and Technology*] (GRD)

NML .... National Medical Library (DAVI)

NML .... National Metrology Laboratory (ACII)

NML .... National Municipal League (EA)

NML .... National Music League (EA)

NML .... Native Machine Language [*Computer science*]

NML .... Nautical Mile

NML .... Naval Materials Management (SAA)

NML .... Navy Management List (AFIT)

NML .... New Mathematical Library [*School Mathematics Study Group*]

Nm-L .... New Mexico Supreme Court Law Library, Santa Fe, NM [*Library symbol Library of Congress*] (LCLS)

NML .... Nodular Mixed Lymphoma [*Oncology*] (DAVI)

NML .... No Man's Land [*Medical slang, cardiology*]

NML .... Normal

NML .... Nuclear Magnetic Logging (IAA)

NML .... Nuclear Magnetism Log (PDAA)

NML .... University of New Mexico, School of Law, Albuquerque, NM [*OCLC symbol*] (OCLC)

NmLa .... Mesa Public Library, Los Alamos, NM [*Library symbol Library of Congress*] (LCLS)

NmLaS .... Los Alamos Scientific Laboratory, Los Alamos, NM [*Library symbol Library of Congress*] (LCLS)

NmLaS-M .... Los Alamos Scientific Laboratory, Medical Library, Los Alamos, NM [*Library symbol Library of Congress*] (LCLS)

NmLaU .... University of New Mexico, Los Alamos, NM [*Library symbol Library of Congress*] (LCLS)

NMLC .... Normalized Mass Loss Coefficient [*Nuclear energy*] (NUCP)

NmLc .... Thomas Branigan Memorial Library, Las Cruces, NM [*Library symbol Library of Congress*] (LCLS)

NmLcU .... New Mexico State University, Las Cruces, NM [*Library symbol Library of Congress*] (LCLS)

NMLO .... National Media Liaison Officer

NmLor .... Lordsburg-Hidalgo Public Library, Lordsburg, NM [*Library symbol Library of Congress*] (LCLS)

NmLov .... Lovington Public Library, Lovington, NM [*Library symbol Library of Congress*] (LCLS)

NmLovS ...... Southeastern Regional Library Center, Lovington, NM [*Library symbol Library of Congress*] (LCLS)

NMLR .... Nigerian Monthly Law Reports [*1964-65*] [*A publication*] (DLA)

NMLRA .... National Muzzle Loading Rifle Association (EA)

NMLS .... National Microwave Landing System (MCD)

NMLT .... New Material Laboratory Tests

NmLv .... Las Vegas Carnegie Library, Las Vegas, NM [*Library symbol Library of Congress*] (LCLS)

NmLvH .... New Mexico Highlands University, Las Vegas, NM [*Library symbol Library of Congress*] (LCLS)

NmLvSH ...... New Mexico State Hospital, Las Vegas, NM [*Library symbol Library of Congress*] (LCLS)

NMM .... Meridian, MS [*Location identifier FAA*] (FAAL)

NMM .... NASA Management Manual

NMM .... National Maritime Museum [*British*]

NMM .... Network Measurement Machine [*Computer Network*] (IAA)

NMM .... Neutron Magnetic Moment

NMM .... New Madrid [*Missouri*] [*Seismograph station code, US Geological Survey Closed*] (SEIS)

NMM .... New Mexico Military Institute, Roswell, NM [*OCLC symbol*] (OCLC)

NMM .... N-Methylmorpholine [*Organic chemistry*]

NMM .... Nodular Malignant Melanoma [*Medicine*] (DB)

NMM .... Nonne-Milroy-Meige [*Syndrome*] [*Medicine*] (DB)

NMM .... Norsemont Mining [*Vancouver Stock Exchange symbol*]

NMM .... Nuclear Materials Management

NMMA .... National Macaroni Manufacturers Association [*Later, NPA*] (EA)

NMMA .... National Maintenance Management Association [*Defunct*] (EA)

NMMA .... National Marine Manufacturers Association (EA)

NMMC .... National Adult Education Clearinghouse (NAEC)/National Multimedia Center for Adult Education [*Information service or system Defunct*] (IID)

NMMC .... National Marina Manufacturers Consortium [*Defunct*] (EA)

NmMeB .... Bent-Mescalero School Library, Mescalero, NM [*Library symbol Library of Congress*] (LCLS)

NMMFO .... Navy Maintenance Management Field Office

NMMFO(W) ... Navy Maintenance Management Field Office (West) (DNAB)

NMMHMO ..... Network and Mixed Model Health Maintenance Organization [*Insurance*] (WYGK)

NMMHOF ..... National Mobile/Manufactured Home Owners Foundation [*Later, NFMHO*] (EA)

NMMI .... New Mexico Military Institute [*Roswell*] (MCD)

NMML .... National Marine Mammal Laboratory [*National Marine Fisheries Service*]

NMMLC .... New Moon Matchbox and Label Club (EA)

NMMM .... Navy Maintenance and Material Management System [*Also known as MMM, NMMMS, 3M*]

NMMMS .... Navy Maintenance and Material Management System [*Also known as MMM, NMMM, 3M*]

NmMS .... Montezuma Seminary, Montezuma, NM [*Library symbol Library of Congress*] (LCLS)

NMMSB .... Non-Nuclear Munitions Safety Board

NMMSN .... National Marine Mammal Stranding Network (EA)

NMMSS .... Nuclear Materials Management and Safeguards System (NRCH)

NMMW .... Near Millimeter Wave System [*Telecommunications*] (TEL)

NMN .... Nicotinamide-Mononucleotide [*Biochemistry*]

NMN .... No Middle Name

NMN .... Normetanephrine [*Also, Methylnorepinephrine*] [*Biochemistry*]

NMN .... NRD Mining Ltd. [*Vancouver Stock Exchange symbol*]

NMNA .... National Male Nurse Association [*Later, AAMN*] (EA)

NMNase .... Nicotinamidenucleotide Phosphoribohydrolase [*An enzyme*]

NMND .... Naval Magazine and Net Depot

NMNFO .... Navy Maintenance Field Office (NVT)

NMNH .... National Museum of National History

NMNH .... National Museum of Natural History [*Smithsonian Institution*]

NMNRU .... National Medical Neuropsychiatric Research Unit (DMAA)

NMNRU .... Naval Medical Neuropsychiatric Research Unit

NMNS .... National Museum of Natural Sciences [*National Museums of Canada*] [*Research center*] (RCD)

NMO .... Long Beach, CA [*Location identifier FAA*] (FAAL)

NMO .... National Medical Organisation (ACII)

NMO .... National Mobility Office [*British*]

NMO .... Navy Management Office

NMO .... N-Methylmorpholine N-Oxide [*Organic chemistry*]

NMO .... Noble Mines & Oils Ltd. [*Toronto Stock Exchange symbol*]

NMO .... Normal Manual Operation (KSC)

NMO .... Normal Mode Operation

NMO .... Norman [*Oklahoma*] [*Seismograph station code, US Geological Survey Closed*] (SEIS)

NMO .... Number of Critical Micro-Operations [*Computer science*] (MHDI)

NMO	Nuveen Municipal Market Opportunities [*NYSE symbol*] (SPSG)
NMO	Nuveen Muni Mkt Oppt [*NYSE symbol*] (TTSB)
NMOA	National Mail Order Association [*Los Angeles, CA*] (EA)
NMOC	Non-Methane Organic Compound [*Environmental chemistry*]
NMOCOD	[*The*] Nonmateriel Objectives Coordinating Document [*Army*] (RDA)
NMOG	Non-Methane Organic Gas [*Organic chemistry*]
nmol	Nanomole [*One billionth of a mole*] (MAE)
NMoN	New York Ocean Science Laboratory, Montauk, NY [*Library symbol Library of Congress*] (LCLS)
NMONA	National Mail Order Nurserymen's Association [*Later, MAN*] (EA)
NMontr	Hendrick Hudson Free Library, Montrose, NY [*Library symbol Library of Congress*] (LCLS)
NMontrVA	United States Veterans Administration Hospital, Montrose, NY [*Library symbol Library of Congress*] (LCLS)
NMOP	National Mission Operating Procedures (AAG)
NMOPI	Nuveen Missouri Premium Income Municipal Fund [*Associated Press*] (SAG)
NMOR	Nitrosomorpholine [*Also, NNM*] [*Organic chemistry*]
NMOS	Negative Channel Metal-Oxide Semiconductor
NMOS	Network Mission and Operations Support
NMOS	Nonvolatile Metal-Oxide Semiconductor (MCD)
NMOSAW	Naval and Military Order of the Spanish-American War (EA)
NMP	National Maintenance Point [*Military*] (AABC)
NMP	National Meter Programming (NRCH)
NMP	National Municipal Policy [*Environmental Protection Agency*] (EPA)
NMP	Naval Management Program
NMP	Naval Medical Publication
NMP	Naval Message Processing (MCD)
NMP	Navigational Microfilm Projector
NMP	Navy Manning Plan (NVT)
NMP	Nederlands Middenstands Partij [*Netherlands Middle Class Party*] [*Political party*] (PPE)
NMP	Net Material Product [*Economics*]
NMP	Network Management Protocol [*Computer science*] (TNIG)
NM/P	New Material/Process (MCD)
NMP	N-Methylphenazium [*Organic chemistry*]
NMP	N-Methylphthalimide [*Organic chemistry*]
NMP	N-Methylpyrrolidone [*Organic chemistry*]
NMP	Normal Menstrual Period [*Gynecology*] (MAE)
NMP	Not Machine Pressed
NMP	Nucleoside Monophosphate [*Biochemistry*]
NMP	Nuveen Michigan Premium Income Municipal [*NYSE symbol*] (SPSG)
NMP	Nuveen MI Prem Inc. Muni [*NYSE symbol*] (TTSB)
NmP	Portales Public Library, Portales, NM [*Library symbol Library of Congress*] (LCLS)
NMPA	National Motorsports Press Association (EA)
NMPA	National Music Publishers' Association (EA)
NMPA	NATO Maritime Patrol Aircraft (NATG)
NMPA	New Mexico Philatelic Association (EA)
NMPA	(Nitrosomethylamino) Propionic Acid [*Organic chemistry*]
NMPA	Nitrosomethylpropylamine [*Organic chemistry*]
NMPASC	NATO Maritime Patrol Aircraft Steering Committee (NATG)
NMPATA	National Music Printers and Allied Trades Association (EA)
NMPB	National Millinery Planning Board [*Defunct*] (EA)
NMPC	National Maintenance Publications Center [*Army*] (AABC)
NMPC	National Milk Publicity Council [*British*] (BI)
NMPC	National Minority Purchasing Council [*Later, NMSDC*] (EA)
NMPC	National Moratorium on Prison Construction [*Defunct*] (EA)
NMPC	Naval Military Personnel Command (ANA)
NMPC	NutraMax Products, Inc. [*NASDAQ symbol*] (SAG)
NMPCRECSREDIVREGOFF	Naval Military Personnel Command, Recreational Services Division, Regional Office (DNAB)
NMPD	Nitromethylpropanediol [*Organic chemistry*]
NMPDN	National Materials Property Data Network (EA)
NmPE	Eastern New Mexico University, Portales, NM [*Library symbol Library of Congress*] (LCLS)
NMPF	National Milk Producers Federation (EA)
NMPF	Normal Magnitude Probability Function
NMPFT	National Museum of Photography, Film & Television (WDAA)
NMPG	New Mexico Proving Ground [*Army*]
NMPIS	National Marine Pollution Information System [*Marine science*] (OSRA)
NMPIS	National Marine Pollution Information Systems (USDC)
NMPL	New Material Planning Letter (MCD)
NMPNC	Naval Medical Program for Nuclear Casualties
NMPNS	Nine Mile Point Nuclear Station (NRCH)
NMPO	Navy Motion Picture Office
NMPO	Nordic Master Painters' Organization (EA)
NMPP	Nautical Miles per Pound (MCD)
NMPP	Nouvelles Messageries de la Presse Parisienne [*Paris press distribution agency*]
NMPPO	National Marine Pollution Program Office [*Marine science*] (OSRA)
NMPS	Matritech, Inc. [*NASDAQ symbol*] (SAG)
NMPS	Nautical Miles per Second
NMPS	Navy Motion Picture Service
NMPSMOPIXDISTOFF	Navy Motion Picture Service, Motion Picture Distribution Office (DNAB)
NMPTP	N-Methyl(phenyl)tetrahydropyridine [*Biochemistry*]
NMPX	Navy Motion Picture Exchange
NMQAAC	National Mammography Quality Assurance Advisory Committee [*U.S. Food and Drug Administration*]
NMQR	New Music Quarterly Review [*Record label*]
NMQUE	Nocte Maneque [*Night and Morning*] [*Pharmacy*]
NMR	Centre for Nuclear Magnetic Resonance [*University of Warwick*] [*British*] (CB)

NMR	Nappamerrie [*Queensland*] [*Airport symbol*] (AD)
NMR	Natal Mounted Rifles [*British military*] (DMA)
NMR	National Military Representatives with SHAPE [*NATO*]
NMR	National Milk Record [*British*] (BI)
NMR	National Missile Range (KSC)
NMR	National Museum of Racing (EA)
NMR	Natural Magnetic Remanence [*Geophysics*]
NMR	Naval Medical Research Institute, Washington, DC [*OCLC symbol*] (OCLC)
NMR	Naval Missile Range
NMR	Navy Management Review [*A publication*]
NMR	Neomar Resources Ltd. [*Toronto Stock Exchange symbol*]
NMR	Neonatal Mortality Rate [*Medicine*] (DMAA)
NMR	Neonatal Mortality Risk [*Medicine*]
NMR	New Material Release (MCD)
NMR	News Media Representative (COE)
NMR	Nictitating Membrane Response [*Neurophysiology*]
NMR	Nielsen Media Research [*NYSE symbol*] [*Formerly, Cognizant Corp.*]
NMR	N. M. De Rothschild & Co. [*Merchant bank*] [*British*]
NMR	NMR of America, Inc. [*Associated Press*] (SAG)
NMR	No Maintenance Requirement (NVT)
NMR	No Master Record [*Military*] (AFIT)
NMR	Nonconforming Material Report (MCD)
NMR	Normal Mode Rejection
NMR	Nuclear Magnetic Relaxation
NMR	Nuclear Magnetic Resonance [*Also, NUMAR*] [*Atomic physics*]
nmr	Nuclear Magnetic Resonance (HGEN)
NmR	Roswell Carnegie Library, Roswell, NM [*Library symbol Library of Congress*] (LCLS)
NMR	San Juan, PR [*Location identifier FAA*] (FAAL)
NmRa	Arthur Johnson Memorial Library, Raton, NM [*Library symbol Library of Congress*] (LCLS)
NMRA	National Marine Representatives Association (EA)
NMRA	National Mine Rescue Association
NMRA	National Mobile Radio Association [*Defunct*] (EA)
NMRA	National Model Railroad Association (EA)
NMRA	National Motorcycle Racing Association (EA)
NMRA	National Motorcycle Retailers Association [*Defunct*] (EA)
NMRA	National Mud Racing Association
NMR & DA	Navy Material Redistribution and Disposition Administration
NMR & DO	Navy Material Redistribution and Disposal Office [*or Officer*]
NMRAS	Nuclear Material Report and Analysis System [*Energy Research and Development Administration*]
NMRB	National Mutual Royal Bank [*Australia*] (ADA)
NMRC	National Maritime Research Center [*Maritime Administration*] [*Also, an information service or system*] (IID)
NMRC	National Meat Retail Council [*Australia*]
NMRC	National Men's Resource Center (EA)
NMRC	National Microelectronics Research Centre (NITA)
NMRC	Navy Material Redistribution Center
NMRC	Neuromuscular Research Center [*Boston University*]
NMRD	Nuclear Magnetic Relaxation Dispension [*Physics*]
NMRDC	Naval Medical Research and Development Command (MCD)
NmRE	Eastern New Mexico University, Roswell Campus, Roswell, NM [*Library symbol Library of Congress*] (LCLS)
NMREC	National Maritime Resource Center [*MARAD*] (TAG)
NM Reg	New Mexico Register [*A publication*] (AAGC)
NMRF	Navy-Marine Corps Residence Foundation (DNAB)
NMRG	Navy Mid-Range Guidance
NMRI	National Mass Retailing Institute [*New York, NY*] (EA)
NMRI	National Medical Research Institute (MAE)
NMRI	Naval Medical Research Institute
NMRI	Nuclear Magnetic Resonance Imaging
NMRL	Naval Medical Research Laboratory
NMRLIT	Nuclear Magnetic Resonance Literature System [*Chemical Information Systems, Inc.*] [*Information service or system*]
NmRM	New Mexico Military Institute, Roswell, NM [*Library symbol Library of Congress*] (LCLS)
NMRN	National Meteorological Rocket Network
NMRO	Navy Mid-Range Objectives
NMRP	National Migrant Resource Program (EA)
NMRP	Nuclear Magnetic Resonance Program
NMRR	NMR of America [*NASDAQ symbol*] (TTSB)
NMRR	NMR of America, Inc. [*NASDAQ symbol*] (NQ)
NMRR	Normal-Mode Rejection Ratio [*Electronics*] (BARN)
NMRS	National Mobile Radio System [*Later, Telocator Network of America*] (EA)
NMRS	Navy Manpower Requirements System (NVT)
NMRS	Nuclear Magnetic Resonance Spectroscopy (DMAA)
NMRS	Numerous (FAAC)
NMRT	New Members Round Table [*American Library Association*]
NMRT	Nimbus Meteorological Radiation Tape [*NASA*]
NMRTC	Navy and Marine Corps Reserve Training Center
NMRU	Naval Medical Research Unit
NmRu	Ruidoso Public Library, Ruidoso, NM [*Library symbol Library of Congress*] (LCLS)
NMRX	Numerex Corp. [*NASDAQ symbol*] (SAG)
NMS	Ancient Egyptian Arabic Order Nobles of the Mystic Shrine (EA)
NMS	Namsang [*Myanmar*] [*Airport symbol*] (OAG)
NMS	National Management Systems [*Information service or system*] (IID)
NMS	National Marine Service, Inc. (EFIS)
NMS	National Maritime System [*MARAD*] (TAG)
NMS	National Market System
NMS	National Master Specification [*Construction Specifications Canada*] [*Information service or system*] (IID)

NMS............	National Measurement System [*National Institute of Standards and Technology*]
NMS............	National Medicine Society [*British*]
NMS............	National Military Strategy (DOMA)
NMS............	National Mobility Scheme [*British*]
NMS............	Natural Mortality Schedule [*Biology*]
NMS............	Naval Medical School (MCD)
NMS............	Naval Meteorological Service
NMS............	Navigation Management System (PDAA)
NMS............	Navy Mid-Range Study
NMS............	NetWare Management System [*Novell, Inc.*] (PCM)
NMS............	Network Management Services [*Ohio Bell Communications, Inc.*] [*Cleveland, OH*] [*Telecommunications*] (TSSD)
NMS............	Network Management Signal [*Telecommunications*] (TEL)
NMS............	Network Management System (DA)
NMS............	Network Measurement System [*Computer network*]
NMS............	Neuroleptic Malignant Syndrome
NMS............	Neuromuscular Stimulator [*Neurology*] (DAVI)
NMS............	Neuro-Musculo-Skeletal [*Medicine*]
NMS............	Neutral Mass Spectrometer [*Instrumentation*]
NMS............	Neutron Monitoring System [*Nuclear energy*] (NRCH)
NMS............	New Manning System [*Army*] (MCD)
NMS............	New Mexico State Library, Santa Fe, NM [*OCLC symbol*] (OCLC)
NMS............	New Mexico Statutes [*A publication*] (DLA)
NMS............	New Music Seminar
NMS............	New Music Society [*Australia*]
NMS............	Nitrogen Measuring System
NMS............	Noise Measuring Set [*Telecommunications*] (TEL)
NMS............	Nonmajor System (MCD)
NMS............	Nonmedical Science Category (DAVI)
NMS............	Non-Metric Multidimensional Scaling (PDAA)
NMS............	Nonprofit Management Strategies [*A publication*]
NMS............	Nordic Metalworkers Secretariat (EA)
NMS............	Normal Market Size Transaction
NMS............	Normal Mouse Serum
NMS............	Nuclear Materials Safeguards
NMS............	Nuclear-Powered Merchant Ship (PDAA)
NmS............	Santa Fe City and County Public Library, Santa Fe, NM [*Library symbol Library of Congress*] (LCLS)
NMSA.........	National Metal Spinners Association (EA)
NMSA.........	National Middle School Association (EA)
NMSA.........	National Moving and Storage Association (EA)
NMSA.........	New Mexico Statutes Annotated [*A publication*] (AAGC)
NMSA.........	Nonnuclear Munitions Storage Area [*Air Force*] (DOMA)
NMSA.........	Nonstandard Metropolitan Statistical Area
NMSA.........	North Atlantic Treaty Organization [*NATO*] Mutual Support Act (AAGC)
NMSB.........	Navy Manpower Survey Board
NMSB.........	NewMil Bancorp [*NASDAQ symbol*] (TTSB)
NMSB.........	New Milford Savings Bank [*NASDAQ symbol*] (NQ)
NmSC.........	College of Santa Fe, Santa Fe, NM [*Library symbol Library of Congress*] (LCLS)
NMSC.........	National Main Street Center (EA)
NMSC.........	National Maple Syrup Council [*Later, NAMSC*]
NMSC.........	National Merit Scholarship Corp. (EA)
NMSC.........	Naval Medical Supply Unit (DNAB)
NMSC.........	Navy Management Systems Center (PDAA)
NMSC.........	Nerve and Muscle Stimulating Current
NMSC.........	Nonmelanoma Skin Cancer [*Medicine*]
NMSC.........	Non-Military Supplies Committee [*Combined Production and Resources Board*] [*British World War II*]
NMSC.........	Northeast-Midwest Senate Coalition (EA)
NMSC.........	Northwest Missouri State College [*Later, Northwest Missouri State University*]
NMSC.........	Nutrition Management [*NASDAQ symbol*] (SAG)
NmSc.........	Silver City Public Library, Silver City, NM [*Library symbol Library of Congress*] (LCLS)
NMSCA.......	Navy Material Command Support Activity (PDAA)
NMSCA.......	Nutrition Mgmt Svcs'A' [*NASDAQ symbol*] (TTSB)
NmSCS.......	College of Santa Fe, Santa Fe, NM [*Library symbol*] [*Library of Congress*] (LCLS)
NmScSW.....	Southwestern Regional Library, Silver City, NM [*Library symbol Library of Congress*] (LCLS)
NMSCW......	Nutrition Mgmt Svcs Wrrt [*NASDAQ symbol*] (TTSB)
NmScW.......	Western New Mexico University, Silver City, NM [*Library symbol Library of Congress*] (LCLS)
NMSD.........	National Match Support Detachment [*Ammunition supplier*]
NMSD.........	National Military Strategy Document (DOMA)
NMSD.........	Naval Medical Supply Depot
NMSD.........	Next Most Significant Digit [*Computer science*]
NMSDC.......	National Minority Supplier Development Council (EA)
NMSE.........	Naval Material Support Establishment [*After 1966, NAVMAT, NMCOM, NMC*]
NMSF.........	Normalized Mean Square Error (DMAA)
NMSHC.......	Bureau of Medicine and Surgery Hospital Corps Publication [*Later, NAVMED*] [*Navy*]
NMSI.........	National Mini-Storage Institute [*Defunct*] (EA)
NMSI.........	National Museum of Science & Industry (WDAA)
NMSIDS.......	Near-Miss Sudden Infant Death Syndrome [*Medicine*] (DMAA)
NMSK.........	Namesake (ABBR)
NMSL.........	National Maximum Speed Limit [*NHTSA*] (TAG)
NmSM.........	Museum of New Mexico, Santa Fe, NM [*Library symbol Library of Congress*] (LCLS)
NMSM.........	New Mexico School of Mines (AAG)

NmSM-A......	Museum of New Mexico, Laboratory of Anthropology, Santa Fe, NM [*Library symbol Library of Congress*] (LCLS)
NMSMK......	Numismatic (ABBR)
NMSMTST ...	Numismaticist (ABBR)
NMSO.........	NATO Maintenance and Support Operation (AFM)
NMSO.........	Naval Manpower Survey Office (NVT)
NMSO.........	N-Methylnitroanisole [*Organic chemistry*]
NMSO.........	Nuclear Missile Safety Office [*or Officer*] (AFM)
NmSo.........	Socorro Public Library, Socorro, NM [*Library symbol Library of Congress*] (LCLS)
NmSoI........	New Mexico Institute of Mining and Technology, Socorro, NM [*Library symbol Library of Congress*] (LCLS)
NmSP.........	New Mexico State Penitentiary Library, Santa Fe, NM [*Library symbol Library of Congress*] (LCLS)
NMSP.........	New Mon State Party [*Myanmar*] [*Political party*]
NMSP.........	N-Methylspiperone [*Biochemistry*]
NmSp.........	Springer Public Library, Springer, NM [*Library symbol Library of Congress*] (LCLS)
NmSpP.......	Springer Public Library, Springer, NM [*Library symbol*] [*Library of Congress*] (LCLS)
NMSQT......	National Merit Scholarship Qualifying Test
NmSr.........	Moise Memorial Library, Santa Rosa, NM [*Library symbol Library of Congress*] (LCLS)
NMSRA......	National Master Shoe Rebuilders Association (EA)
NMSRC......	National Middle School Resource Center (EA)
NMSS.........	NASCOM [*Naval Air Systems Command*] Manual Scheduling System
NMSS.........	National Meteorological Satellite System (IAA)
NMSS.........	National Multiple Sclerosis Society (EA)
NMSS.........	National Multipurpose Space Station
NMSS.........	Natural Microsystems [*NASDAQ symbol*] (TTSB)
NMSS.........	Natural Microsystems Corp. [*NASDAQ symbol*] (SAG)
NMSS.........	Nemesis (ABBR)
NMSS.........	Office of Nuclear Materials Safety and Safeguards [*Nuclear Regulatory Commission*]
NMSSA......	National Multiple Sclerosis Society of Australia
NMSSA......	NATO Maintenance Supply Service Agency [*Later, NAMSO*]
NMSSO......	Navy Maintenance and Supply Systems Office (DNAB)
NMSSS......	NATO Maintenance Supply Service System
NMSST......	Naval Manpower Shore Survey Team (NVT)
NmSStJ.......	Saint John's College in Santa Fe, Santa Fe, NM [*Library symbol Library of Congress*] (LCLS)
NMST.........	New Materials System Test [*Obsolete Nuclear energy*]
NM Stat Ann...	New Mexico Statutes, Annotated [*A publication*] (DLA)
NMSU.........	Naval Motion Study Unit [*British*]
NMSU.........	New Mexico State University
NmSuAF......	United States Air Force, Sacramento Peak Observatory, Sunspot, NM [*Library symbol Library of Congress*] (LCLS)
NMSVA......	Navy Mail Service Veterans Association (EA)
NMSZ.........	New Madrid Seismic Zone [*Geology*]
NMT............	Barrow, AK [*Location identifier FAA*] (FAAL)
NMT............	National Museum of Transport [*Later, TMA*] (EA)
NMT............	Neuromuscular Tension [*Medicine*]
NMT............	Neuromuscular Transmission [*Physiology*]
NMT............	New Mexico Institute of Mining and Technology, Socorro, NM [*OCLC symbol*] (OCLC)
NMT............	N-Methyltransferase (DB)
NMT............	N-Monomethyltryptamine [*Organic chemistry*]
NMT............	N-Myristoyl Acyltransferase [*An enzyme*]
NMT............	Noble-Metal-Coated Titanium [*Anode*]
NMT............	No More Than [*Pharmacy*] (DAVI)
NMT............	No More Trouble [*Coates' brand of cotton thread*] (ROG)
NMT............	Nonmetalic [*Technical drawings*]
NMT............	Nordic Mobile Telephone [*Radio-telephone system for car users*] [*Denmark, Finland, Norway, Sweden*]
NMT............	Nordic Mobile Telephone Network (NITA)
NMT............	Northwest Marine Trade Association (EA)
NMT............	Norwegian Method of Tunnelling [*Civil engineering*]
NMT............	Notification of Master Tool (NASA)
NMT............	Not More Than
NMT............	Nuclear Medicine Technology
NMT............	Number of Module Types
NMT............	Nuveen MA Prem Inc. Muni Fd [*NYSE symbol*] (TTSB)
NMT............	Nuveen Massachusetts Premium Income Municipal Fund [*NYSE symbol*] (SPSG)
NMTA.........	National Manpower Training Association [*Later, NETA*] (EA)
NMTA.........	National Metal Trades Association [*Later, AAIM*] (EA)
NMTA.........	National Movement Theatre Association (EA)
NMTBA.......	National Machine Tool Builders' Association [*Later, AMT*] (EA)
NMTBD.......	No More to Be Done [*Medicine*]
NMTC.........	Naval Mine Testing Center (MCD)
NMTC.........	Naval Missile Testing Center
NMTC.........	North Metropolitan Tramways Co. [*British*] (ROG)
NMTC.........	Nucleon-Meson Transport Code
NMTCB.......	Nuclear Medicine Technology Certification Board (EA)
NMTD.........	Nonmetastatic Trophoblastic Disease [*Medicine*] (DMAA)
NMTD.........	Nuclear Materials Transfer Document
NMTF.........	National Market Traders Federation [*British*] (DBA)
NMTF.........	National Metal Trades Federation [*British*] (DBA)
NMTF.........	Naval Mine Test Facility
NMTFA.......	National Master Tile Fixers Association [*British*] (DBA)
NMTHC.......	Nonmethane Total Hydrocarbons [*Organic chemistry*]
NmTHF.......	Harwood Foundation, Taos, NM [*Library symbol Library of Congress*] (LCLS)
NMTI..........	Nitinol Medical Technologies, Inc. [*NASDAQ symbol*] (SAG)

NMtK .... Mount Kisco Public Library, Mount Kisco, NY [*Library symbol Library of Congress*] (LCLS)

NmTKC .... Kit Carson Memorial Foundation, Inc., Taos, NM [*Library symbol Library of Congress*] (LCLS)

NMTLK........ Nonmetallic (ABBR)

NMTN .... National Music Theater Network (EA)

NMTO .... Navy Material Transportation Office

NMTP .... National Means Test Proposal

NMTR .... Nuclear Materials Transfer Report

NmTr .... Truth Or Consequences Public Library, Truth Or Consequences, NM [*Library symbol Library of Congress*] (LCLS)

NMTS.......... National Milk Testing Service

NMTS.......... Navy Military Technical Specialist (MCD)

NMTS.......... Neuromuscular Tension State [*Medicine*] (DMAA)

NMTS.......... Noise Measurement Test Set

NmTu .... Tucumcari Public Library, Tucumcari, NM [*Library symbol Library of Congress*] (LCLS)

NmTuE........ Eastern Plains Regional Library, Tucumcari, NM [*Library symbol Library of Congress*] (LCLS)

NMtv .... Mount Vernon Public Library, Mount Vernon, NY [*Library symbol Library of Congress*] (LCLS)

NMTX.......... Novametrics Medical Systems [*NASDAQ symbol*] (SAG)

NMTX.......... Novametrix Medical Systems, Inc. [*NASDAQ symbol*] (NQ)

NMTX.......... Novametrix Med Sys [*NASDAQ symbol*] (TTSB)

NMTXW .... Novametrix Med Sys Wrt'A' [*NASDAQ symbol*] (TTSB)

NMTXZ .... Novametrix Med Sys Wrrt'B' [*NASDAQ symbol*] (TTSB)

NMU .... Brunswick, ME [*Location identifier FAA*] (FAAL)

NMU .... National Maritime Union (USDC)

NMU .... National Maritime Union of America (EA)

NMU .... National Museums of Canada Library [*UTLAS symbol*]

NMU .... Network Monitor Unit [*Telecommunications*] (TSSD)

NMU .... Neuromuscular Unit [*Medicine*]

nmu .... New Mexico [*MARC country of publication code Library of Congress*] (LCCP)

NMU .... Nitrosomethylurea [*Also, MNU*] [*Organic chemistry*]

NMU .... Nordic Musicians' Union (EA)

NMU .... Northern Michigan University [*Marquette*]

NmU .... University of New Mexico, Albuquerque, NM [*Library symbol Library of Congress*] (LCLS)

NMUC .... National Medical Utilization Committee [*HEW*]

NmU-L .... University of New Mexico, Law Library, Albuquerque, NM [*Library symbol Library of Congress*] (LCLS)

NmU-M .... University of New Mexico, Library of the Medical Sciences, School of Medicine and Bernalillo County Medical Society, Albuquerque, NM [*Library symbol Library of Congress*] (LCLS)

NMuP.......... Muttontown Preserve, Muttontown, NY [*Library symbol Library of Congress*] (LCLS)

NMV........... Nitrogen Manual Valve (MCD)

NMVCA .... National Military Vehicle Collectors Association [*Defunct*]

NMVO .... Navy Manpower Validation Office (DNAB)

NMVOC ...... Nonmethane Volatile Organic Carbon [*Environmental chemistry*]

NMVOLANT... Navy Manpower Validation Office, Atlantic (DNAB)

NMVOPAC... Navy Manpower Validation Office, Pacific (DNAB)

NMVP .... Navy Manpower Validation Program (NG)

NMVSA .... Navy Manpower Validation Support Activity

NMVSAC...... National Motor Vehicle Safety Advisory Council (EA)

NMVTA .... National Motor Vehicle Theft Act

NMvUA .... State University of New York, Agricultural and Technical College at Morrisville,Morrisville, NY [*Library symbol Library of Congress*] (LCLS)

NMW .... Astoria, OR [*Location identifier FAA*] (FAAL)

NMW .... Naval Mine Warfare (DOMA)

NMW .... Normal Molecular Weight

NMW .... Western Carolina University, Cullowhee, NC [*OCLC symbol*] (OCLC)

NMWA .... National Military Wives Association [*Later, NMFA*] (EA)

NMWA .... National Mineral Wool Association [*Later, MIMA*]

NMWC .... National Migrant Workers Council [*Farmington Hills, MI*] (EA)

NMWC .... Nelson, Marlborough, and West Coast Regiment [*British military*] (DMA)

NMWC .... New Mexico Western College

NMWIA .... National Mineral Wool Insulation Association [*Formerly, NMWA*] [*Later, MIMA*] (EA)

NMWL .... Normal Molecular Weight, Low in Extractables

NmWM .... White Sands Missile Range Library, White Sands Missile Range, NM [*Library symbol Library of Congress*] (LCLS)

NMWP .... National Migrant Worker Program [*Department of Labor*]

NMWQL ...... National Marine Water Quality Laboratory [*Environmental Protection Agency*] (MSC)

NMWS .... Naval Mine Warfare School

NMWTC ...... Naval Mine Warfare Training Center

NMWTS ...... Naval Mine Warfare Test Station

NMWTS ...... Naval Mine Warfare Training School

n-mx-- .... Mexico [*MARC geographic area code Library of Congress*] (LCCP)

NMxAr .... New Mexico & Arizona Land Co. [*Associated Press*] (SAG)

NMxB.......... Board of Cooperative Educational Services, Regional Resource Center, Mexico, NY [*Library symbol Library of Congress*] (LCLS)

NMY........... Mayville State College, Mayville, ND [*OCLC symbol*] (OCLC)

NMY........... Nonresonant Magnetic Yoke

NMY........... Nuveen Maryland Premium Income Municipal Fund [*NYSE symbol*] (SPSG)

NMY........... Nuveen MD Prem Inc. Muni Fd [*NYSE symbol*] (TTSB)

NMyM.......... Maryknoll Fathers Seminary, Maryknoll, NY [*Library symbol Library of Congress*] (LCLS)

NMZ........... Norman Resources Ltd. [*Vancouver Stock Exchange symbol*]

NMZ........... Willow Grove, PA [*Location identifier FAA*] (FAAL)

NN .... Air Trails [*ICAO designator*] (AD)

N:N .... Azo Group [*Chemical group with two nitrogen atoms*] (MEDA)

nn .... Footnotes (DLA)

NN .... Names (ABBR)

NN .... NASA Notice

NN .... National Neighbors (EA)

NN .... National Networker [*An association*] (EA)

NN .... Natural, Nongrazed [*Agriculture*]

NN .... Nearest Neighbor [*Mathematics*] [*Computer search term*]

NN .... Necessary Nuisance [*i.e., a husband*] [*Slang*]

NN .... Neonatal (DAVI)

NN .... Nerves

nn .... Nervi Nerves [*Neurology*] [*Latin*] (DAVI)

NN .... Neural Network (AAEL)

NN .... Neurotics Nomine [*British*]

NN .... Neutral and Nonaligned [*Nations*]

NN .... Nevada Northern Railway Co. [*AAR code*]

NN .... Newbridge Networks [*NYSE symbol*] (TTSB)

NN .... Newbridge Networks, Inc. [*NYSE symbol*] (SAG)

nn .... New Hebrides [*MARC country of publication code Library of Congress*] (LCCP)

NN .... New Nationals [*Political party Australia*]

NN .... Newspaper News [*A publication*]

NN .... New York Public Library, New York, NY [*Library symbol Library of Congress*] (LCLS)

NN .... Nicaragua Network (EA)

NN .... Nicaragua Network Education Fund (EA)

NN .... Nigerian Navy

NN .... Noise Network (WDAA)

nn .... Nomen Nescio [*Unknown*] [*Latin*] (GPO)

nn .... Nomen Novum [*New Name*] [*Latin*] (DAVI)

NN .... Nomina [*Names*] [*Latin*]

NN .... No Name

NN .... Non-Nuclear Lance (MCD)

NN .... Non-Participating National (OTD)

NN .... Noon

NN .... Normalnull [*Mean Sea Level*] [*German*]

N/N .... Normocytic/Normochromic Anemia (DAVI)

NN .... Northampton [*Postcode*] (ODBW)

NN .... Northwestern National (EFIS)

NN .... Notes [*Finance*]

NN .... Not Nested [*Freight*]

NN .... Not Normal

N/N .... Not North Of

N/N .... Not to Be Noted [*Business term*]

NN .... Nouns

NN .... Nuclear Network (EA)

NN .... Nucleon-Nucleon

N/N .... Nurses' Notes (MAE)

NN .... Nurturing Network [*An association*] (EA)

NNA .... American Geographical Society, New York, NY [*Library symbol Library of Congress*] (LCLS)

NNA .... Nana [*Peru*] [*Seismograph station code, US Geological Survey*] (SEIS)

NNA .... National Neckwear Association (EA)

NNA .... National Needlework Association (EA)

NNA .... National Newman Apostolate

NNA .... National News Agency [*Lebanon*]

NNA .... National Newspaper Association (EA)

NNA .... National Notary Association (EA)

NNA .... National Notion Association [*Later, AHSA*] (EA)

NNA .... National Numismatic Association (EA)

NNA .... Neutral/Nonaligned [*Countries*]

NNA .... New Nadina Explorations [*Vancouver Stock Exchange symbol*]

NNA .... New Network Architecture

NNA .... N-Nitrosamine [*Organic chemistry*]

NNA .... Nonhistone Nucleoprotein Antibodies [*Immunochemistry*]

NNA .... Normochromic, Normocytic Anemia (DAVI)

NNAA .... Augusta Warshaw Advertising Library, New York, NY [*Library symbol Library of Congress*] (LCLS)

NNAA .... National Newman Alumni Association [*Defunct*] (EA)

NNAA .... Native North American Almanac [*A publication*]

NNAAI........ American Alpine Club, New York, NY [*Library symbol Library of Congress*] (LCLS)

NNAAr......... American Arbitration Association, New York, NY [*Library symbol Library of Congress*] (LCLS)

NNAB......... American Bible Society, New York, NY [*Library symbol Library of Congress*] (LCLS)

NNABA........ American Bankers Association, New York, NY [*Library symbol Library of Congress*] (LCLS)

NNAC .... National Native American Cooperative (EA)

NNAC .... National Noise Abatement Council [*Defunct*]

NNACC........ National Native American Chamber of Commerce [*Defunct*] (EA)

NNACS........ American Cancer Society, New York, NY [*Library symbol Library of Congress*] (LCLS)

NNAD .... Anti-Defamation League of B'nai B'rith, New York, NY [*Library symbol Library of Congress*] (LCLS)

NNADAP ..... National Native Alcohol and Drug Abuse Program [*Canada*]

NNAdv .... American Association of Advertising Agencies, New York, NY [*Library symbol Library of Congress*] (LCLS)

NNAF .... American Foundation for the Blind, New York, NY [*Library symbol Library of Congress*] (LCLS)

NNAFS........ National Newman Association of Faculty and Staff [*Defunct*] (EA)

NNAG.......... American Gas Association, New York, NY [*Library symbol Library of Congress*] (LCLS)

NNAG........... NATO Naval Advisory Group (NATG)
NNAG........... NATO Naval Armaments Group (NATG)
NNAI .... American Irish Historical Society, New York, NY [*Library symbol Library of Congress*] (LCLS)
NNAIA.......... American Institute of Certified Public Accountants, New York, NY [*Library symbol Library of Congress*] (LCLS)
NNAIAA........ American Institute of Aeronautics and Astronautics, Technical Information Service, New York, NY [*Library symbol*] [*Library of Congress*] (LCLS)
NNAIL .... Austrain Institute Library, New York, NY [*Library symbol*] [*Library of Congress*] (LCLS)
NNAIP .... American Institute of Physics, New York, NY [*Library symbol Library of Congress*] (LCLS)
NNAJ .... American Jewish Committee, New York, NY [*Library symbol Library of Congress*] (LCLS)
NNAJN .... American Journal of Nursing Co., New York, NY [*Library symbol Library of Congress*] (LCLS)
NNAKC......... American Kennel Club, New York, NY [*Library symbol Library of Congress*] (LCLS)
NNAL .... American Academy of Arts and Letters, New York, NY [*Library symbol Library of Congress*] (LCLS)
NNAMA........ American Management Associations, New York, NY [*Library symbol Library of Congress*] (LCLS)
NNAMM .... American Merchant Marine Library Association, New York, NY [*Library symbol Library of Congress*] (LCLS)
NNAN.......... American Numismatic Society, New York, NY [*Library symbol Library of Congress*] (LCLS)
NNAn .... Anthology Film Archives, New York, NY [*Library symbol Library of Congress*] (LCLS)
NNan .... Nanuet Public Library, Nanuet, NY [*Library symbol Library of Congress*] (LCLS)
NNAnF .... Anthology Film Archives, New York, NY [*Library symbol*] [*Library of Congress*] (LCLS)
NNanL .... Nanuet Public Library, Nanuet, NY [*Library symbol*] [*Library of Congress*] (LCLS)
NNAP .... NAVAIR [*Naval Air Systems Command*] Naval Aviation Plan (MCD)
NNAPS......... Night Navigation and Pilotage System
NNAPW........ National Network of Asian and Pacific Women (EA)
NNAS.......... Neonatal Narcotic Abstinence Syndrome [*Medicine*] (DMAA)
NNASA........ American National Standards Institute, New York, NY [*Library symbol Library of Congress*] (LCLS)
NNASF .... American-Scandinavian Foundation, New York, NY [*Library symbol Library of Congress*] (LCLS)
NNASovM ..... American-Soviet Medical Society, New York, NY [*Library symbol Library of Congress Obsolete*] (LCLS)
NNASP .... American Society for Psychical Research, New York, NY [*Library symbol Library of Congress*] (LCLS)
NNAT .... American Telephone & Telegraph Co., Corporate Research Library, New York, NY [*Library symbol Library of Congress*] (LCLS)
NNAUR .... Australian Consulate-General, Australian Reference Library, New York, NY [*Library symbol*] [*Library of Congress*] (LCLS)
NNAuS .... National Audubon Society, New York, NY [*Library symbol Library of Congress*] (LCLS)
N/NAVEXOS... Navy/Executive Offices (AAG)
NNAVS......... Association for Voluntary Sterilization, Inc., International Project, New York, NY [*Library symbol Library of Congress*] (LCLS)
NNAW .... Native North American Writers [*A publication*]
NNAy .... American Home Products Corp., Ayerst Medical Library, New York, NY [*Library symbol Library of Congress*] (LCLS)
NNB .... Association of the Bar of the City of New York, New York, NY [*Library symbol Library of Congress*] (LCLS)
NNB .... National Needlecraft Bureau (EA)
NNB .... National News Bureau [*Commercial firm*] (EA)
NNB .... New Natura Brevium [*A publication*] (DSA)
NN-B .... New York Public Library, Albert A. and Henry W. Berg Collection, New York, NY [*Library symbol Library of Congress*] (LCLS)
NNb .... North Babylon Public Library, North Babylon, NY [*Library symbol Library of Congress*] (LCLS)
NNB .... Northumberland and Newcastle Board of Education [*UTLAS symbol*]
NNBa .... Barnard College, Columbia University, New York, NY [*Library symbol Library of Congress*] (LCLS)
NNBA.......... National Nurses in Business Association (EA)
NN Ball........ NN Ball & Roller, Inc. [*Associated Press*] (SAG)
NNBBC......... Bernard M. Baruch College of the City University of New York, New York, NY [*Library symbol Library of Congress*] (LCLS)
NNbBE .... Belmont Elementary School, North Babylon, NY [*Library symbol*] [*Library of Congress*] (LCLS)
NNBC.......... Bronx Community College, New York, NY [*Library symbol Library of Congress*] (LCLS)
NNBC.......... National Network of Bilingual Centers (EA)
NNBCLA....... Negative Negabinary Carry-Look-Ahead Adder [*Computer science*] (MHDI)
NNbe .... North Bellmore Public Library, North Bellmore, NY [*Library symbol Library of Congress*] (LCLS)
NNbeDE .... Dinkelmeyer Elementary School, North Bellmore, NY [*Library symbol Library of Congress*] (LCLS)
NNbeGE .... Gunther Elementary School, North Bellmore, NY [*Library symbol Library of Congress*] (LCLS)
NNbeJJ........ Jerusalem Avenue Junior High School, North Bellmore, NY [*Library symbol*] [*Library of Congress*] (LCLS)
NNbeNE .... Newbridge Road Elementary School, North Bellmore, NY [*Library symbol*] [*Library of Congress*] (LCLS)
NNbePE .... Park Elementary School, North Bellmore, NY [*Library symbol Library of Congress*] (LCLS)

NNBeS .... Bentley School, New York, NY [*Library symbol Library of Congress*] (LCLS)
NNbeSME .... Saw Mill Elementary School, North Bellmore, NY [*Library symbol Library of Congress*] (LCLS)
NNBG.......... New York Botanical Garden, Bronx, NY [*Library symbol Library of Congress*] (LCLS)
NNbHS .... North Babylon High School, North Babylon, NY [*Library symbol*] [*Library of Congress*] (LCLS)
NNBI .... Beth Israel Medical Center, New York, NY [*Library symbol Library of Congress*] (LCLS)
NNBIS .... National Narcotics Border Interdiction System
NNBL .... National Negro Business League [*Later, National Business League*]
NNbL .... North Babylon Public Library, North Babylon, NY [*Library symbol*] [*Library of Congress*] (LCLS)
NNbLE .... William E. De Luca Jr. Elementary School, North Babylon, NY [*Library symbol*] [*Library of Congress*] (LCLS)
NNBLI .... British Information Services, New York, NY [*Library symbol Library of Congress*] (LCLS)
NNBMC........ Borough of Manhattan Community College, New York, NY [*Library symbol Library of Congress*] (LCLS)
NNbMJ........ Robert Moses Junior High School, North Babylon, NY [*Library symbol*] [*Library of Congress*] (LCLS)
NNbPE .... Parliment Place Elementary School, North Babylon, NY [*Library symbol*] [*Library of Congress*] (LCLS)
NN-Br.......... New York Public Library, Branch Library System, New York, NY [*Library symbol Library of Congress*] (LCLS)
NNBR.......... NN Ball & Roller [*NASDAQ symbol*] (TTSB)
NNBR.......... NN Ball & Roller, Inc. [*NASDAQ symbol*] (SAG)
NNBS .... Biblical Seminary in New York, New York, NY [*Library symbol Library of Congress*] (LCLS)
NNBSC......... Bank Street College of Education, New York, NY [*Library symbol Library of Congress*] (LCLS)
NNbWE .... Woods Road Elementary School, North Babylon, NY [*Library symbol*] [*Library of Congress*] (LCLS)
NNC .... Columbia University, New York, NY [*Library symbol Library of Congress*] (LCLS)
NNC .... Naga National Council [*India*] (PD)
NNC .... Natal Native Contingent [*British military*] (DMA)
NNC .... National Namibia Concerns (EA)
NNC .... National Neighborhood Coalition (EA)
NNC .... National Network Congestion Signal (NITA)
NNC .... National News Council (EA)
NNC .... National Nomad Club [*Defunct*] (EA)
NNC .... National Nuclear Corp. [*British*]
NNC .... National Nudist Council [*Defunct*] (EA)
NNC .... National Nutrition Consortium [*Defunct*] (EA)
NNC .... Navy Nurse Corps
NNC .... Neutral Nations Committee [*CINCPAC*] (CINC)
NN/C .... Night Noise Group C [*Aircraft*]
NNC .... Nolan, Norton & Co., Inc., Lexington, MA [*OCLC symbol*] (OCLC)
NNC .... Non-Noise Certificated Aircraft (DA)
NNC .... Northern Navigation Co. Ltd. [*AAR code*]
NNC .... Northwest Nazarene College [*Nampa, ID*]
NNC .... Notice of Noncompliance (EPA)
NNC .... Nuance (ABBR)
NNC .... Nudist National Committee (EA)
NNC .... Nuveen NC Prem Inc. Muni [*NYSE symbol*] (TTSB)
NNC .... Nuveen North Carolina Premium Income Municipal Fund [*NYSE symbol*] (SPSG)
NNC-A......... Columbia University, Avery Library of Architecture, New York, NY [*Library symbol Library of Congress*] (LCLS)
NNCA.......... National Newman Chaplains Association [*Later, CCMA*] (EA)
NNCAA........ National Negro County Agents Association (EA)
NNCAM........ Cravath, Swaine & Moore, New York, NY [*Library symbol*] [*Library of Congress*] (LCLS)
NNCar......... Carnegie Corp. of New York, New York, NY [*Library symbol Library of Congress*] (LCLS)
NNCB.......... [*The*] College Board, New York, NY [*Library symbol*] [*Library of Congress*] (LCLS)
NNC-B......... Columbia University, Biological Sciences Library, New York, NY [*Library symbol Library of Congress*] (LCLS)
NNC-BE....... Columbia University, Business-Economic Library, New York, NY [*Library symbol*] [*Library of Congress*] (LCLS)
NNCBN........ City Bank, North America, New York, NY [*Library symbol*] [*Library of Congress*] (LCLS)
NNCBS........ Columbia Broadcasting System, Inc., New York, NY [*Library symbol Library of Congress*] (LCLS)
NNCC.......... Chemists' Club, New York, NY [*Library symbol Library of Congress*] (LCLS)
NNCC.......... National Network Control Centre [*Communications*] [*British*]
NNCC.......... National Nursing Consultative Committee [*Australia*]
NNCC.......... Navy Nurse Corps Candidate (DNAB)
NNCCA........ Canadian Centre for Architecture, New York, NY [*Library symbol*] [*Library of Congress*] (LCLS)
NNCCG........ Canadian Consulate General Library, New York, NY [*Library symbol*] [*Library of Congress*] (LCLS)
NNCCVTE..... National Network for Curriculum Coordination in Vocational and Technical Education (OICC)
NNCE .... Carnegie Endowment for International Peace, New York, NY [*Library symbol Library of Congress*] (LCLS)
NNC-EA....... Columbia University, East Asiatic Library, New York, NY [*Library symbol Library of Congress*] (LCLS)
NNCEF .... Child Education Foundation, New York, NY [*Library symbol Library of Congress Obsolete*] (LCLS)

NNCenC .... Century Association, New York, NY [*Library symbol Library of Congress*] (LCLS)

NNCEP .... Centro de Estudios Puertorriquenos, New York, NY [*Library symbol Library of Congress*] (LCLS)

NNCF .... Commonwealth Fund, New York, NY [*Library symbol Library of Congress*] (LCLS)

NNCF .... National Newman Club Federation [*Defunct*] (EA)

NNCFo .... Council on Foundations, New York, NY [*Library symbol Library of Congress*] (LCLS)

NNCFR .... Council on Foreign Relations, New York, NY [*Library symbol Library of Congress*] (LCLS)

NNC-G .... Columbia University, Lamont-Doherty Geological Observatory, Palisades, NY [*Library symbol Library of Congress*] (LCLS)

NNCG .... Norwegian Consulate General, New York, NY [*Library symbol*] [*Library of Congress*] (LCLS)

NNCh .... Chadbourne & Parke, New York, NY [*Library symbol*] [*Library of Congress*] (LCLS)

NNCI .... College of Insurance, New York, NY [*Library symbol Library of Congress*] (LCLS)

NNCit .... Cities Service Co., Corporate Library, New York, NY [*Library symbol Library of Congress*] (LCLS)

NNC-L .... Columbia University, Law Library, New York, NY [*Library symbol Library of Congress*] (LCLS)

NNC-M .... Columbia University, Medical Library, New York, NY [*Library symbol Library of Congress*] (LCLS)

NNCN .... Northern Nigeria Case Notes [*A publication*] (DLA)

NNCo .... Collectors Club, New York, NY [*Library symbol Library of Congress*] (LCLS)

NNcoM .... Moore-Cottrell Subscription Agencies, Inc., North Cohocton, NY [*Library symbol Library of Congress*] (LCLS)

NNConE .... Consolidated Edison Co., Inc., New York, NY [*Library symbol Library of Congress*] (LCLS)

NNCoo .... Cooper Union for the Advancement of Science and Art, New York, NY [*Library symbol Library of Congress*] (LCLS)

NNCorI .... Cornell University, New York State School of Industrial and Labor Relations, Sanford V. Lenz Library, New York, NY [*Library symbol*] [*Library of Congress*] (LCLS)

NNCorM .... Cornell University, Medical College, New York, NY [*Library symbol Library of Congress*] (LCLS)

NNCorM-A ... New York Hospital-Cornell Medical Center Archives, New York, NY [*Library symbol*] [*Library of Congress*] (LCLS)

NNCorM-D ... Cornell University, Medical College, Oskar Diethelm Historical Library, New York, NY [*Library symbol*] [*Library of Congress*] (LCLS)

NNC-P .... Columbia University, College of Pharmacy, New York, NY [*Library symbol Library of Congress*] (LCLS)

NNCP .... Pfizer, Inc., New York, NY [*Library symbol Library of Congress*] (LCLS)

NNCPI .... Nuveen North Carolina Premium Income Municipal Fund [*Associated Press*] (SAG)

NNCPL .... College of Police Science, New York, NY [*Library symbol Library of Congress*] (LCLS)

NNCPM .... New York College of Podiatric Medicine, New York, NY [*Library symbol Library of Congress*] (LCLS)

NNC-Pop ..... Columbia University, International Institute for the Study of Human Reproduction, Center for Population and Family Health, New York, NY [*Library symbol Library of Congress*] (LCLS)

NNC-Ps .... Columbia University, Psychology Library, New York, NY [*Library symbol Library of Congress*] (LCLS)

NNcR .... Roberts Wesleyan College, North Chili, NY [*Library symbol Library of Congress*] (LCLS)

NNCre .... Creedmore Psychiatric Center, Queens Village, New York, NY [*Library symbol Library of Congress*] (LCLS)

NNCREW ..... National Network of Commercial Real Estate Women (NTPA)

NNCS .... Child Study Association of America, New York, NY [*Library symbol Library of Congress*] (LCLS)

NNCSC .... National Neutron Cross Section Center [*AEC*] (MCD)

NNC-T .... Columbia University, Teachers College, New York, NY [*Library symbol Library of Congress*] (LCLS)

NNC-Typ ..... Columbia University, American Typefounders' Library, New York, NY [*Library symbol Library of Congress*] (LCLS)

NNCU-C .... City University of New York, Central Office, New York, NY [*Library symbol*] [*Library of Congress*] (LCLS)

NNCU-G .... City University of New York, Graduate Center, New York, NY [*Library symbol Library of Congress*] (LCLS)

NNCU-L .... City University of New York, Law School, Flushing, NY [*Library symbol Library of Congress*] (LCLS)

NNCU-T .... City University of New York, Division of Teacher Education, New York, NY [*Library symbol Library of Congress*] (LCLS)

NND .... Dover Publications, New York, NY [*Library symbol Library of Congress*] (LCLS)

NND .... National Network Dialing [*Telecommunications*] (TEL)

NND .... National Number Dialing [*Telecommunications*] (DCTA)

NND .... Naval Net Depot

NND .... Neo-Natal Death [*Medicine*]

NND .... New and Nonofficial Drugs [*AMA*]

NND .... Nonspecific Nonerosive Duodenitis [*Medicine*] (DMAA)

NNDC .... National Naval Dental Center

NNDC .... National New Democratic Coalition (EA)

NNDC .... National Nuclear Data Center [*Department of Energy*] [*Database producer*] (IID)

NNDCG .... Danish Consulate General, Reference Library, New York, NY [*Library symbol*] [*Library of Congress*] (LCLS)

NNDE .... Nearest-Neighbor Distance Error [*Algorithm*]

NNDP .... Debevoise & Plimpton, New York, NY [*Library symbol*] [*Library of Congress*] (LCLS)

NNDP .... Naga National Democratic Party [*India*] [*Political party*] (PPW)

NNDPA .... N-Nitrosodiphenylamine [*Organic chemistry*]

NNDPW .... Davis, Polk & Wardwell, Law Library, New York, NY [*Library symbol Library of Congress*] (LCLS)

NNDR .... National Non-Domestic Rate [*British*]

NNDSS .... National Notification Disease Surveillance System [*Centers for Disease Control*]

NNDTC .... National Nondestructive Testing Centre [*Atomic Energy Authority*] [*Information service or system*] (IID)

NNE .... Engineering Societies Library, New York, NY [*Library symbol Library of Congress*] (LCLS)

NNE .... Neonatal Necrotizing Enterocolitis [*Medicine*] (AAMN)

NNE .... Noise and Number Exposure (PDAA)

NNE .... Nonneuronal Enolase [*Medicine*] (DMAA)

NNE .... Nonneuron-Specific Enolase [*An enzyme*]

NNE .... Nonstandard Negro English

NNE .... North-Northeast

NNEA .... National Negro Evangelical Association [*Later, NBEA*]

NNEB .... National Nursery Examination Board

NNebg .... Newburgh Free Library, Newburgh, NY [*Library symbol Library of Congress*] (LCLS)

NNebgE .... Epiphany Apostolic College, Newburgh, NY [*Library symbol Library of Congress*] (LCLS)

NNebgL .... Ninth Judicial District Law Library, Newburgh, NY [*Library symbol Library of Congress*] (LCLS)

NNebgM .... Mount Saint Mary College, Newburgh, NY [*Library symbol*] [*Library of Congress*] (LCLS)

NNebgWM ... Washington's Headquarters Museum, Newburgh, NY [*Library symbol*] [*Library of Congress*] (LCLS)

NNEC .... Explorers Club, New York, NY [*Library symbol Library of Congress*] (LCLS)

NNec .... New City Free Library, New City, NY [*Library symbol Library of Congress*] (LCLS)

NNECA .... National Network of Episcopal Clergy Associations (EA)

NNECH .... National Nutrition Education Clearing House [*Society for Nutrition Education*] (IID)

NNecL .... New City Free Library, New City, NY [*Library symbol*] [*Library of Congress*] (LCLS)

NNEF .... Educational Film Library Association, New York, NY [*Library symbol Library of Congress*] (LCLS)

NNef .... Newfane Public Library, Newfane, NY [*Library symbol Library of Congress*] (LCLS)

NNefH .... Inter-Community Memorial Hospital, Newfane, NY [*Library symbol Library of Congress*] (LCLS)

NNefL .... Newfane Free Library, Newfane, NY [*Library symbol*] [*Library of Congress*] (LCLS)

NNegbM ...... Mount St. Mary College, Newburgh, NY [*Library symbol Library of Congress*] (LCLS)

NNegbWM ... Washington's Headquarters Museum, Newburgh, NY [*Library symbol Library of Congress*] (LCLS)

NNehpHH ..... Herricks High School, New Hyde Park, NY [*Library symbol Library of Congress*] (LCLS)

NNEL .... Equitable Life Assurance Society of the United States, Medical Library, New York, NY [*Library symbol Library of Congress*] (LCLS)

NNEL-M ...... Equitable Life Assurance Society of the United States, Medical Library, New York, NY [*Library symbol Library of Congress*] (LCLS)

NNepa .... Elting Memorial Library, New Paltz, NY [*Library symbol Library of Congress*] (LCLS)

NNepaSU ..... State University of New York, College at New Paltz, New Paltz, NY [*Library symbol Library of Congress*] (LCLS)

NNer .... New Rochelle Public Library, New Rochelle, NY [*Library symbol Library of Congress*] (LCLS)

NNerAIS ...... United States Army, Information School, Fort Slocum, New Rochelle, NY [*Library symbol Library of Congress*] (LCLS)

NNerC .... College of New Rochelle, New Rochelle, NY [*Library symbol Library of Congress*] (LCLS)

NNerI .... Iona College, New Rochelle, NY [*Library symbol Library of Congress*] (LCLS)

NNES .... National Nuclear Energy Series [*of AEC-sponsored books*]

NNESCC ...... Northern New England Small College Conference (PSS)

NNEU .... Naval Nuclear Evaluation Unit

NNEW .... Ernst & Whinney, Audit Management Services, New York, NY [*Library symbol Library of Congress*] (LCLS)

NNEWD .... North-Northeastward (FAAC)

NNEXF .... Newscope Resources Ltd. [*NASDAQ symbol*] (SAG)

NNF .... Fordham University, New York, NY [*Library symbol Library of Congress*] (LCLS)

NNF .... Namibia National Front [*Political party*] (PPW)

NNF .... National Nephrosis Foundation [*Later, NKF*]

NNF .... National Neurofibromatosis Foundation (PAZ)

NNF .... National Newman Foundation [*Defunct*] (EA)

NNF .... National Newspaper Foundation (EA)

NNF .... National Nothing Foundation [*Defunct*] (EA)

NNF .... Nordisk Neurokirurgisk Forening [*Scandinavian Neurosurgical Society - SNS*] (EAIO)

NNF .... Nordisk Neurologisk Forening [*Scandinavian Neurological Association - SNA*] (EAIO)

NNF .... Northern Nurses Federation [*Norway*]

NNF .... Nuveen Ins. NY Prem Inc. Muni [*NYSE symbol*] (TTSB)

NNF .... Nuveen Insured New York Premium Income Municipal [*NYSE symbol*] (SPSG)

NNFA	National Nutritional Foods Association (EA)
NNFB	Ford, Bacon & Davis, Inc., New York, NY [*Library symbol Library of Congress*] (LCLS)
NNFBC	First Boston Corporation, New York, NY [*Library symbol Library of Congress*] (LCLS)
NNFC	Finch College, New York, NY [*Library symbol Library of Congress*] (LCLS)
NNFE	Free Europe Committee, New York, NY [*Library symbol Library of Congress*] (LCLS)
NNFF	Ford Foundation, New York, NY [*Library symbol Library of Congress*] (LCLS)
NNFF	National Neurofibromatosis Foundation (EA)
NNFF	Not Nested or Folded Flat [*Freight*]
NNFF-FL	Ford Foundation, Ford Foundation Library, New York, NY [*Library symbol Library of Congress*] (LCLS)
NNFFu	Franklin Furnance Archives, New York, NY [*Library symbol*] [*Library of Congress*] (LCLS)
NNFI	French Institute/Alliance Francaise, New York, NY [*Library symbol Library of Congress*] (LCLS)
NNFIT	Fashion Institute of Technology, New York, NY [*Library symbol Library of Congress*] (LCLS)
NNF-L	Fordham University, Law Library, New York, NY [*Library symbol Library of Congress*] (LCLS)
NNFL	Religious Society of Friends [*Quakers*], New York, NY [*Library symbol Library of Congress*] (LCLS)
NNF-LC	Fordham University, Library at Lincoln Center, New York, NY [*Library symbol Library of Congress*] (LCLS)
NNFM	Grand Lodge of New York, F & AM Library and Museum, New York, NY [*Library symbol Library of Congress*] (LCLS)
NNFoC	Foundation Center Library, New York, NY [*Library symbol Library of Congress*] (LCLS)
NNFoM	Forbes Magazine, Inc., New York, NY [*Library symbol Library of Congress*] (LCLS)
NNFP	Nuclear Nitrogen Fixation Plant
NNFr	Frick Art Reference Library, New York, NY [*Library symbol Library of Congress*] (LCLS)
NNF-RS	Fordham University, Institute of Contemporary Russian Studies, New York, NY [*Library symbol Library of Congress*] (LCLS)
NNFS	Nordic Narrow/16mm Film Society (EA)
NNFT	National Federation of Textiles, New York, NY [*Library symbol Library of Congress*] (LCLS)
NNFU	Nuclear Nonfirst Use
NNG	General Theological Seminary of the Protestant Episcopal Church, New York, NY [*Library symbol Library of Congress*] (LCLS)
NNG	Nanning [*China*] [*Airport symbol*] (OAG)
NNG	National Network of Grantmakers
NNG	National Number Group (NITA)
NNG	Nonspecific Nonerosive Gastritis [*Medicine*] (DMAA)
NNGA	Northern Nut Growers Association (EA)
NNGBSW	National Network of Graduate Business School Women [*Knoxville, TN*] (EA)
NNGI	National Aeronautics and Space Administration, Goddard Institute for Space Studies, New York, NY [*Library symbol*] [*Library of Congress*] (LCLS)
NNGoe	Goethe House, German Cultural Institute, New York, NY [*Library symbol Library of Congress*] (LCLS)
NNGr	Grolier Club, New York, NY [*Library symbol Library of Congress*] (LCLS)
NNGS	Church of Jesus Christ of Latter-Day Saints, Genealogical Society Library, New York Branch, New York, NY [*Library symbol Library of Congress*] (LCLS)
NNGu	Solomon R. Guggenheim Museum, New York, NY [*Library symbol Library of Congress*] (LCLS)
NNH	Hispanic Society of America, New York, NY [*Library symbol Library of Congress*] (LCLS)
NNH	Natal Native Horse [*British military*] (DMA)
NNH	National Humanities Center, Research Triangle Park, NC [*OCLC symbol*] (OCLC)
NNH	Nordiska Namnden for Handikappfragor [*Nordic Committee on Disability - NCD*] [*Sweden*] (EAIO)
NNHA	National Novice Hockey Association [*Later, HNA*] (EA)
NNHC	Hostos Community College, New York, NY [*Library symbol Library of Congress*] (LCLS)
NNHC	Natal Native High Court Reports [*1899-1915*] [*South Africa*] [*A publication*] (DLA)
NNHCF-C	Holy Cross Friary, Juniper Carol Library, New York, NY [*Library symbol Library of Congress*] (LCLS)
NNHE	New York City Board of Higher Education, New York, NY [*Library symbol Library of Congress*] (LCLS)
NNHeb	Hebrew Union College - Jewish Institute of Religion, New York, NY [*Library symbol Library of Congress*] (LCLS)
NNHH	Harlem Hospital Center, Medical Library, New York, NY [*Library symbol Library of Congress*] (LCLS)
NNHHR	Hughes, Hubbard & Reed, New York, NY [*Library symbol*] [*Library of Congress*] (LCLS)
NNHL	National Novice Hockey League [*Later, NNHA*] (EA)
NNHol	Holland Society of New York, New York, NY [*Library symbol Library of Congress*] (LCLS)
NNHor	Horticultural Society of New York, Inc., New York, NY [*Library symbol Library of Congress*] (LCLS)
NNhp	New Hyde Park Public Library, New Hyde Park, NY [*Library symbol Library of Congress*] (LCLS)
NNhpDE	Denton Avenue Elementary School, New Hyde Park, NY [*Library symbol*] [*Library of Congress*] (LCLS)
NNhpGE	Garden City Park School, New Hyde Park, NY [*Library symbol*] [*Library of Congress*] (LCLS)
NNhpH	Hillside Public Library, New Hyde Park, NY [*Library symbol Library of Congress*] (LCLS)
NNhpHE	Hillside Grade School, New Hyde Park, NY [*Library symbol*] [*Library of Congress*] (LCLS)
NNhpHH	Herricks High School, New Hyde Park, NY [*Library symbol*] [*Library of Congress*] (LCLS)
NNhpJ	Long Island Jewish Hospital, New Hyde Park, NY [*Library symbol Library of Congress*] (LCLS)
NNhpME	Manor-Oaks-William R. Bowie School, New Hyde Park, NY [*Library symbol*] [*Library of Congress*] (LCLS)
NNhpMH	New Hyde Park Memorial High School, New Hyde Park, NY [*Library symbol*] [*Library of Congress*] (LCLS)
NNhpNE	New Hyde Park Road School, New Hyde Park, NY [*Library symbol*] [*Library of Congress*] (LCLS)
NNHR	New York City Human Resources Administration, New York, NY [*Library symbol Library of Congress*] (LCLS)
NNHS	Hospital for Special Surgery, New York, NY [*Library symbol Library of Congress*] (LCLS)
NNHS	National Nursing Home Survey [*Department of Health and Human Services*] (GFGA)
NNhS	Special Metals Corp., New Hartford, NY [*Library symbol Library of Congress*] (LCLS)
NNHuC	Hunter College of the City University of New York, New York, NY [*Library symbol Library of Congress*] (LCLS)
NNHWW	H.W. Wilson Co., Bronx, NY [*Library symbol*] [*Library of Congress*] (LCLS)
NNI	National Newspaper Index [*Information Access Co.*] [*Bibliographic database*] [*Information service or system*] (IID)
NNI	Net National Income [*Economics*]
NNI	Net-Net Income [*Business term*]
NNI	Network Node Interface [*Computer science*]
NNI	New Nickerie [*Surinam*] [*Airport symbol*] (AD)
NNI	Noise and Number Index
NNI	Noise Nuisance Index (PDAA)
NNI	Nonnuclear Instrumentation (NRCH)
NNI	Nucleon-Nucleon Interaction
NNI	Office of Naval Intelligence Publications
NNIA	American Institute of Aeronautics and Astronautics, New York, NY [*Library symbol Library of Congress*] (LCLS)
NNia	Niagara Falls Public Library, Niagara Falls, NY [*Library symbol Library of Congress*] (LCLS)
NNiaA	Airco Speer Research & Development Laboratories, Niagara Falls, NY [*Library symbol Library of Congress*] (LCLS)
NNiaB	Bell Aerospace Textron, Technical Library, Niagara Falls, NY [*Library symbol Library of Congress*] (LCLS)
NNiaC	Niagara County Community College, Niagara Falls, NY [*Library symbol Library of Congress*] (LCLS)
NNiaCa	Carborundum Co., Niagara Falls, NY [*Library symbol Library of Congress*] (LCLS)
NNiaD	E. I. Du Pont de Nemours & Co., Electrochemical Department, Niagara Falls, NY [*Library symbol Library of Congress*] (LCLS)
NNiaEM	Elkem Metals Co., Niagara Falls, NY [*Library symbol Library of Congress*] (LCLS)
NNiaH	Hooker Chemical Corp. [*Later, Hooker Chemicals & Plastics Corp.*], Niagara Falls, NY [*Library symbol Library of Congress*] (LCLS)
NNiaHC	Hooker Chemicals & Plastics Corp., Business Library, Niagara Falls, NY [*Library symbol Library of Congress*] (LCLS)
NNiaM	Moore Business Forms, Niagara Falls, NY [*Library symbol Library of Congress*] (LCLS)
NNiaMed	Niagara Falls Memorial Medical Center, Medical Library, Niagara Falls, NY [*Library symbol Library of Congress*] (LCLS)
NNiaN	National Lead Co., Research Library, Niagara Falls, NY [*Library symbol Library of Congress*] (LCLS)
NNiaNC	NIACET Corporation, Niagara Falls, NY [*Library symbol Library of Congress*] (LCLS)
NNiaNL	Nioga Library System, Niagara Falls, NY [*Library symbol Library of Congress*] (LCLS)
NNiaO	Occidental Chemical Corp., Technical Information Center, Niagra Falls, NY [*Library symbol*] [*Library of Congress*] (LCLS)
NNiaSE	Sohio Engineered Materials Co., Research and Development Library, Niagara Falls, NY [*Library symbol*] [*Library of Congress*] (LCLS)
NNiaTC	TAM Ceramics, Inc., Niagara Falls, NY [*Library symbol Library of Congress*] (LCLS)
NNiaTV	Trott Vocational High School, Niagara Falls, NY [*Library symbol Library of Congress*] (LCLS)
NNiaU	Niagara University, Niagara University, NY [*Library symbol Library of Congress*] (LCLS)
NNiaUC	Union Carbide Corp., Niagara Falls, NY [*Library symbol Library of Congress*] (LCLS)
NNICC	National Narcotics Intelligence Consumers Committee [*Drug Enforcement Administration*] [*Washington, DC*] (EGAO)
NNIIC	Istituto Italiano Di Cultura Biblioteca, New York, NY [*Library symbol*] [*Library of Congress*] (LCLS)
NNIIE	Institute of International Education, New York, NY [*Library symbol Library of Congress*] (LCLS)
NNIMD	Institute for Muscle Disease, New York, NY [*Library symbol Library of Congress Obsolete*] (LCLS)
NNIND	International Nickel Co., Technical Library, New York, NY [*Library symbol Library of Congress*] (LCLS)
NNInS	Insurance Society of New York, New York, NY [*Library symbol Library of Congress*] (LCLS)
NNIP	Institute of Public Administration, New York, NY [*Library symbol Library of Congress*] (LCLS)

NNIPF .... International Planned Parenthood Federation, Documentation and Publications Center, New York, NY [*Library symbol Library of Congress*] (LCLS)

NNIR .... Industrial Relations Counselors, New York, NY [*Library symbol Library of Congress*] (LCLS)

NNIRR .... National Network for Immigrant and Refugee Rights (EA)

NNIS .... Library for Intercultural Studies, Inc., New York, NY [*Library symbol Library of Congress*] (LCLS)

NNIS .... National Nosocomial Infections Study [*Medicine*] (DMAA)

NNIS .... National Nosocomial Infections Surveillance [*Medicine*]

NNIS .... Nonnuclear Instrumentation System (NRCH)

NNISS .... Nosocomial Infections Surveillance System [*Center for Disease Control*]

NNJ .... Jewish Theological Seminary of America, New York, NY [*Library symbol Library of Congress*] (LCLS)

NNJ .... Nakano [*Japan*] [*Seismograph station code, US Geological Survey*] (SEIS)

NNJ .... Nuveen New Jersey Premium Income Municipal [*NYSE symbol*] (SPSG)

NNJ .... Nuveen NJ Prem Inc. Muni [*NYSE symbol*] (TTSB)

NNJef .... Jefferson School of Social Science, New York, NY [*Library symbol Library of Congress Obsolete*] (LCLS)

NNJH .... Joint Health Library, New York, NY [*Library symbol Library of Congress Obsolete*] (LCLS)

NNJHK .... Jenny Hunter's Kindergarten and Primary Training School, New York, NY [*Library symbol Library of Congress Obsolete*] (LCLS)

NNJJ .... John Jay College of Criminal Justice, New York, NY [*Library symbol Library of Congress*] (LCLS)

NNJS .... Japan Society Library, New York, NY [*Library symbol*] [*Library of Congress*] (LCLS)

NNJu .... Juilliard School of Music, New York, NY [*Library symbol Library of Congress*] (LCLS)

NNK .... Naknek [*Alaska*] [*Airport symbol*] (OAG)

NNK .... Nic-Nik Resources [*Vancouver Stock Exchange symbol*]

NNK .... Nicotine-Derived Nitrosaminoketone

NNK .... Nonnuclear Kill

NNKRAS .... Non-Nuclear Kill Requirements and Applications Study [*Military*]

NNL .... Beeville, TX [*Location identifier FAA*] (FAAL)

NNL .... Herbert H. Lehman College of the City University of New York, New York, NY [*Library symbol Library of Congress*] (LCLS)

NN-L .... New York Public Library, Research Library for the Performing Arts at Lincoln Center, New York, NY [*Library symbol Library of Congress*] (LCLS)

NNL .... Ninilchik [*Alaska*] [*Seismograph station code, US Geological Survey*] (SEIS)

NNL .... Nondalton [*Alaska*] [*Airport symbol*] (OAG)

NNL .... No Net Loss

NNL .... Non-Nuclear Lance Missile (PDAA)

NNLBI .... Leo Baeck Institute, New York, NY [*Library symbol Library of Congress*] (LCLS)

NNLC .... Lutheran Council in the USA, New York, NY [*Library symbol Library of Congress*] (LCLS)

NNLC .... Ngwane National Liberatory Congress [*Swaziland*]

NNLDA .... National Network of Learning Disabled Adults (EA)

NNLehman.... Lehman Corp., New York, NY [*Library symbol Library of Congress*] (LCLS)

NNLH .... Lenox Hill Hospital, Medical Library, New York, NY [*Library symbol Library of Congress*] (LCLS)

NNLI .... New York Law Institute, New York, NY [*Library symbol Library of Congress*] (LCLS)

NNLM .... National Network of Libraries of Medicine

NNLN .... Northern Nigeria Legal Notes [*A publication*] (DLA)

NNLP .... National Natural Landmarks Program (WPI)

NNLR .... Law Reprints, New York, NY [*Library symbol*] [*Library of Congress*] (LCLS)

NNLR .... Northern Nigeria Law Reports [*A publication*] (DLA)

NNLS .... New York Law School Library, New York, NY [*Library symbol Library of Congress*] (LCLS)

NNM .... American Museum of Natural History, New York, NY [*Library symbol Library of Congress*] (LCLS)

NNM .... Davidson College, Davidson, NC [*OCLC symbol*] (OCLC)

NNM .... Neonatal Mortality [*Medicine*] (DMAA)

NN-M .... New York Public Library, Municipal Reference Library, New York, NY [*Library symbol Library of Congress*] (LCLS)

NNM .... Next (or Nearest) New Moon [*Freemasonry*] (ROG)

NNM .... Nicolle-Novy-MacNeal [*Medium*] [*Microbiology*] (DAVI)

NNM .... N-Nitrosomorpholine [*Also, NMOR*] [*Organic chemistry*]

NNM .... No Neutral Mode

NNm .... North Merrick Public Library, North Merrick, NY [*Library symbol Library of Congress*] (LCLS)

NNM .... Nuveen New York Municipal Income [*AMEX symbol*] (SPSG)

NNMa .... Marymount Manhattan College, New York, NY [*Library symbol Library of Congress*] (LCLS)

NNMAI .... Museum of the American Indian, New York, NY [*Library symbol Library of Congress*] (LCLS)

NNMan .... Manhattan College, New York, NY [*Library symbol Library of Congress*] (LCLS)

NNMB .... Methodist Board of Missions, New York, NY [*Library symbol Library of Congress*] (LCLS)

NNmBJ .... Brookside Junior High School, North Merrick, NY [*Library symbol Library of Congress*] (LCLS)

NNMC .... Mannes College of Music, New York, NY [*Library symbol Library of Congress*] (LCLS)

NNMC .... National Naval Medical Center [*Bethesda, MD*]

NNmCE .... Camp Avenue Elementary School, North Merrick, NY [*Library symbol*] [*Library of Congress*] (LCLS)

NNMcGraw... McGraw-Hill, Inc., New York, NY [*Library symbol Library of Congress*] (LCLS)

NNME .... Mid-European Studies Center, New York, NY [*Library symbol Library of Congress*] (LCLS)

NNMec......... General Society of Mechanics and Tradesmen, New York, NY [*Library symbol Library of Congress*] (LCLS)

NNMel .... Andrew W. Mellon Foundation, New York, NY [*Library symbol Library of Congress*] (LCLS)

NN-Mel .... New York Public Library, Mellon Microfilm Collection, New York, NY [*Library symbol Library of Congress*] (LCLS)

NNMer .... Mercantile Library Association, New York, NY [*Library symbol Library of Congress*] (LCLS)

NNMF .... Markle Foundation, New York, NY [*Library symbol Library of Congress*] (LCLS)

NNmFE .... Harold D. Fayette Elementary School, North Merrick, NY [*Library symbol*] [*Library of Congress*] (LCLS)

NNMH .... Montefiore Hospital, New York, NY [*Library symbol Library of Congress*] (LCLS)

NNMi .... Millenium Film Workshop, New York, NY [*Library symbol Library of Congress*] (LCLS)

NNML .... Metropolitan Life Insurance Co., New York, NY [*Library symbol Library of Congress*] (LCLS)

NNMLC .... Medical Library Center of New York, New York, NY [*Library symbol Library of Congress*] (LCLS)

NNMM .... Metropolitan Museum of Art, New York, NY [*Library symbol Library of Congress*] (LCLS)

NNMMA........ Museum of Modern Art, New York, NY [*Library symbol Library of Congress*] (LCLS)

NNMMA-F.... Museum of Modern Art, Film Study Center, New York, NY [*Library symbol Library of Congress*] (LCLS)

NNMMA-U ... Metropolitian Museum of Art, Uris Library and Resources Center, New York, NY [*Library symbol*] [*Library of Congress*] (LCLS)

NNMM-C...... Metropolitan Museum of Art, The Cloisters Library, New York, NY [*Library symbol*] [*Library of Congress*] (LCLS)

NNMM-CI..... Metropolitan Museum of Art, Costume Institute, New York, NY [*Library symbol Library of Congress*] (LCLS)

NNmN .... North Merrick Public Library, North Merrick, NY [*Library symbol*] [*Library of Congress*] (LCLS)

NNMO .... Mobil Oil Corp., Secretariat Library, New York, NY [*Library symbol*] [*Library of Congress*] (LCLS)

NnmOE .... Old Mill Road Elementary School, North Merrick, NY [*Library symbol*] [*Library of Congress*] (LCLS)

NNMoMA ..... Museum of Modern Art, New York, NY [*Library symbol Library of Congress*] (LCLS)

NNMP .... Motion Picture Association of America, Inc., Research Department Library, New York, NY [*Library symbol Library of Congress*] (LCLS)

NNMPA........ Museum of Primitive Art, New York, NY [*Library symbol Library of Congress*] (LCLS)

NNmPE .... Park Avenue Elementary School, North Merrick, NY [*Library symbol*] [*Library of Congress*] (LCLS)

NN-MPH ...... New York Public Library, Public Health Division, New York, NY [*Library symbol Library of Congress*] (LCLS)

NNMR .... Missionary Research Library, New York, NY [*Library symbol Library of Congress*] (LCLS)

NNMRR........ New York Metropolitan Reference and Research Library Agency, Inc., New York, NY [*Library symbol Library of Congress*] (LCLS)

NNMS .... Manhattan State Hospital, New York, NY [*Library symbol Library of Congress*] (LCLS)

NNMS .... National Nutrition-Monitoring System [*Department of Agriculture*] (GFGA)

NNMS .... Nazareth National Motor Speedway [*Pennsylvania*]

NNMSB......... Nonnuclear Munitions Safety Board [*Military*]

NNMSCP....... Nonnuclear Munitions Safety Control Program [*Military*]

NNMSE .... Network Node Manager Special Edition

NNMSG........ Nonnuclear Munitions Safety Group [*Air Force*] (AFM)

NNMSGP....... Nonnuclear Munitions Safety Group [*Air Force*]

NNMSK........ Memorial Sloan-Kettering Cancer Center, New York, NY [*Library symbol Library of Congress*] (LCLS)

NNMSM .... Manhattan School of Music, New York, NY [*Library symbol Library of Congress*] (LCLS)

NNMT .... Newport News Marine Terminal

NNMtS .... Mount Sinai Hospital, New York, NY [*Library symbol Library of Congress*] (LCLS)

NNMtSM ...... Mount Sinai School of Medicine of the City University of New York, New York, NY [*Library symbol Library of Congress*] (LCLS)

NNMtSV .... College of Mount Saint Vincent, New York, NY [*Library symbol Library of Congress*] (LCLS)

NNMus......... Museum of the City of New York, New York, NY [*Library symbol Library of Congress*] (LCLS)

NNN .... Commercial Net Lease Realty, Inc. [*NYSE symbol*] (SAG)

NNN .... Commercial Net Lease Rlty [*NYSE symbol*] (TTSB)

NNN .... Nannies Need Nannies Association [*British*] (DBA)

NNN .... National Navy Notice

NNN .... National Nostalgic Nova (EA)

NNN .... Next Nearest Neighbor [*Chemical physics*]

NNN .... Nicolle-Novy-MacNeal [*Medium*] [*Medicine*] (MEDA)

NNN .... Nitrosonornicotine [*Organic chemistry*]

NNN .... N-Nitrosonornicotine [*Organic chemistry*]

NNN .... No National Name

NNN .... No No Nanette [*Broadway musical*]

NNN .... Noramco Mining Corp. [*Toronto Stock Exchange symbol Vancouver Stock Exchange symbol*]

NNN .... Novy, MacNeal, and Nicolle's Medium [*Medicine*] (MAE)

NNNA .... No Name, No Address

NNNAM .... New York Academy of Medicine, New York, NY [*Library symbol Library of Congress*] (LCLS)

NNNASA ...... National Aeronautical and Space Administration, Institute for Space Studies, NewYork, NY [*Library symbol Library of Congress*] (LCLS)

NNNBC .... National Broadcasting Co., Inc., General Library, New York, NY [*Library symbol Library of Congress*] (LCLS)

NNNBC-I ..... National Broadcasting Co., Inc., Information Unit, Research Department, New York, NY [*Library symbol Library of Congress*] (LCLS)

NNNC .... New York Chamber of Commerce, New York, NY [*Library symbol Library of Congress*] (LCLS)

NNNCC-Ar .... New York County Clerk Archives, Division of Old Records, New York, NY [*Library symbol*] [*Library of Congress*] (LCLS)

NNNCL .... New York County Lawyers Association, New York, NY [*Library symbol Library of Congress*] (LCLS)

NNNCR .... National Council for Resources on Women, New York, NY [*Library symbol*] [*Library of Congress*] (LCLS)

NNNDO .... Neglect of Non-Neighbor Differential Overlap [*Physics*]

NNNDR .... Narcotic and Drug Research, Inc., New York, NY [*Library symbol*] [*Library of Congress*] (LCLS)

NNNeI .... Netherlands Information Service, New York, NY [*Library symbol Library of Congress*] (LCLS)

NNNGB .... New York Genealogical and Biographical Society, New York, NY [*Library symbol Library of Congress*] (LCLS)

NNNH .... National Health Agencies Library, New York, NY [*Library symbol Library of Congress Obsolete*] (LCLS)

NNNHi .... Naval History Society, New York, NY [*Library symbol Library of Congress Obsolete*] (LCLS)

NNNM .... New York Medical College, Flower and Fifth Avenue Hospitals, New York, NY [*Library symbol Library of Congress*] (LCLS)

NNNMCA ..... New Museum of Contemporary Art, New York, NY [*Library symbol*] [*Library of Congress*] (LCLS)

NNNPsan ..... New York Psychoanalytic Institute, New York, NY [*Library symbol Library of Congress*] (LCLS)

NNNPSC ..... National No-Nukes Prison Support Collective (EA)

NNNPsI .... New York State Department of Mental Hygiene, Psychiatric Institute, New York, NY [*Library symbol Library of Congress*] (LCLS)

NNNS .... New School for Social Research, New York, NY [*Library symbol Library of Congress*] (LCLS)

NNNSB .... National Society for the Prevention of Blindness, New York, NY [*Library symbol Library of Congress*] (LCLS)

NNNT .... New York Theological Seminary, New York, NY [*Library symbol Library of Congress*] (LCLS)

NNNTSH ...... Naukove Tovarystvo Imeni Shevchenka (Shevchenko Scientific Society, Inc.), New York, NY [*Library symbol Library of Congress*] (LCLS)

NNNWA .... N. W. Ayer & Son, New York, NY [*Library symbol Library of Congress*] (LCLS)

NNO .... Naga Nationalist Organization [*India*]

NNO .... No New Orders [*Medical Records*] (DAVI)

NNO .... Nord-Nord-Ouest [*North-Northwest*] [*French*]

NNO .... Northern Orion Explorations [*Vancouver Stock Exchange symbol*]

NNO .... Nuveen N.Y. Muni Market Opportunity (EFIS)

NNOA .... National Naval Officers Association (EA)

NNOC .... National Network Operations Center [*Ottawa, ON*] [*Telecommunications*] (TSSD)

NNomAE ...... Albany Avenue Elementary School, North Massapequa, NY [*Library symbol*] [*Library of Congress*] (LCLS)

NNomEE ...... Eastplain Elementary School, North Massapequa, NY [*Library symbol*] [*Library of Congress*] (LCLS)

NNomPH ...... Plainedge High School, North Massapequa, NY [*Library symbol*] [*Library of Congress*] (LCLS)

NNomPJ ...... Sylvia Packard Junior High School, North Massapequa, NY [*Library symbol*] [*Library of Congress*] (LCLS)

NNOPE .... Naturists and Nudists Opposing Pornographic Exploitation (EA)

NNopo .... Northport Public Library, Northport, NY [*Library symbol Library of Congress*] (LCLS)

NNopo-E ...... Northport Public Library, East Northport Branch, East Northport, NY [*Library symbol Library of Congress*] (LCLS)

NNopoHS ..... Northport High School, Northport, NY [*Library symbol*] [*Library of Congress*] (LCLS)

NNopoJH .... Northport Junior High School, Northport, NY [*Library symbol*] [*Library of Congress*] (LCLS)

NNopoVA ..... United States Veterans Administration Hospital, Northport, NY [*Library symbol Library of Congress*] (LCLS)

NNOR .... Nonnuclear Ordnance Requirement (MCD)

NNorP .... Norwich Pharmacal Co., Norwich, NY [*Library symbol Library of Congress*] (LCLS)

nNOS .... Neuronal Nitric Oxide Synthase [*An enzyme*]

NNosCE .... Sea Cliff Elementary School, North Shore, NY [*Library symbol*] [*Library of Congress*] (LCLS)

NnosJH .... North Shore Junior High School, North Shore, NY [*Library symbol*] [*Library of Congress*] (LCLS)

NNosSH ...... North Shore Senior High School, North Shore, NY [*Library symbol*] [*Library of Congress*] (LCLS)

NNOt .... New York Orthopaedic Hospital, New York, NY [*Library symbol Library of Congress*] (LCLS)

NNot .... North Tonawanda Public Library, North Tonawanda, NY [*Library symbol Library of Congress*] (LCLS)

NNotD .... DeGraff Memorial Hospital, North Tonawanda, NY [*Library symbol Library of Congress*] (LCLS)

NNotHC .... Hooker Chemicals & Plastics Corp., Durez Division Library, North Tonawanda, NY [*Library symbol Library of Congress*] (LCLS)

NNotL .... Lawless Container Corp., North Tonawanda, NY [*Library symbol Library of Congress*] (LCLS)

NNotP .... North Tonawanda Public Library, North Tonawanda, NY [*Library symbol*] [*Library of Congress*] (LCLS)

n nov .... Nomen Novum [*New Name*] [*Latin*] [*Pharmacy*] (DAVI)

N NOV .... Nomen Novum [*New Name*] [*Latin*] (BABM)

NNP .... Needle-Nosed Probe

NNP .... Negative Node Point

NNP .... Neonatal Nurse Practitioner (DAVI)

NNP .... Nerve Net Pulse [*Neurobiology*]

NNP .... Net National Product [*Economics*]

NNP .... Nuveen New York Performance Plus Municipal [*NYSE symbol*] (SPSG)

NNP .... Nuveen NY Perform Plus Muni [*NYSE symbol*] (TTSB)

NNPA .... National Negro Press Association [*Defunct*] (EA)

NNPA .... National Newspaper Promotion Association [*Later, INPA*] (EA)

NNPA .... National Newspaper Publishers Association (EA)

NNPA .... Nuclear Nonproliferation Act [*1975*]

NNPA .... Port Authority of New York and New Jersey, New York, NY [*Library symbol Library of Congress*] (LCLS)

NNParS .... Parsons School of Design, New York, NY [*Library symbol Library of Congress*] (LCLS)

NNPaul .... Paul, Weiss, Rifkind, Wharton & Garrison, Law Library, New York, NY [*Library symbol Library of Congress*] (LCLS)

NNPaW .... Payne Whitney Clinic, New York, NY [*Library symbol Library of Congress*] (LCLS)

NNPC .... Nigerian National Petroleum Corp. (ECON)

NNPC .... Pace College, New York, NY [*Library symbol Library of Congress*] (LCLS)

NNPC-L .... Pace University, Law Library, White Plains, NY [*Library symbol Library of Congress*] (LCLS)

NNPE-NC .... National Council of the Protestant Episcopal Church, New York, NY [*Library symbol Library of Congress*] (LCLS)

NNPennie .... Pennie, Edmonds, Morton, Taylor & Adams, New York, NY [*Library symbol Library of Congress*] (LCLS)

NNPf .... Carl H. Pforzheimer Library, New York, NY [*Library symbol Library of Congress*] (LCLS)

NNPH-O .... Institute of Ophthalmology, Presbyterian Hospital, New York, NY [*Library symbol Library of Congress*] (LCLS)

NNPHR .... New York City Public Health Research Laboratory, New York, NY [*Library symbol Library of Congress*] (LCLS)

NNPHW .... National New Professional Health Workers [*Later, NPSAPHA*] (EA)

NNPI .... Naval Nuclear Propulsion Information (MCD)

NNPIA .... Polish Institute of Art and Sciences in America, Inc., Research Library, New York, NY [*Library symbol*] [*Library of Congress*] (LCLS)

NNPlan .... Planning Assistance, Inc., New York, NY [*Library symbol Library of Congress*] (LCLS)

NNPM .... Pierpont Morgan Library, New York, NY [*Library symbol Library of Congress*] (LCLS)

NNPopC .... Population Council, New York, NY [*Library symbol Library of Congress*] (LCLS)

NNPPFA .... Planned Parenthood Federation of America, Inc., Katharine Dexter McCormick Library, New York, NY [*Library symbol Library of Congress*] (LCLS)

NNPPNYC .... Planned Parenthood of New York City, Inc., Abraham Stone Memorial Library, Margaret Sanger Center, New York, NY [*Library symbol Library of Congress*] (LCLS)

NNPRM .... United Presbyterian Mission Library of the United Presbyterian Church in the USA, New York, NY [*Library symbol Library of Congress*] (LCLS)

NNPS .... Navy Nuclear Power School (DNAB)

NNPS .... Norco Nuclear Power Station (NRCH)

NNPSPP .... National Non-Point Source Pollution Program (GNE)

NNPTU .... Naval Nuclear Power Training Unit (DNAB)

NNPU .... Naval Nuclear Power Unit [*Obsolete*]

NNR .... City College of City University of New York, New York, NY [*Library symbol Library of Congress*] (LCLS)

NNR .... National Nature Reserve [*British*]

NNR .... National Number Routed [*Telecommunications*] (TEL)

NNR .... Nearest-Neighbor Rule [*Mathematics*]

NNR .... Nevada North Resources [*Vancouver Stock Exchange symbol*]

NNR .... New and Nonofficial Remedies [*A publication*]

NNR .... Nordiska Nykterhetsradet [*Nordic Temperance Council - NTC*] (EAIO)

NNR .... Northern NORAD [*North American Air Defense*] Region (SAA)

NNRA .... National Negro Republican Assembly [*Defunct*]

NNRB .... National Neurological Research Bank [*Veterans Administration Medical Center*] [*Research center*] (RCD)

NNRB .... Recording for the Blind, Inc., New York, NY [*Library symbol Library of Congress*] (LCLS)

NNRDC .... National Nuclear Rocket Development Center [*Also known as NRDS*]

NNRDF .... National Nuclear Rocket Development Facility (AAG)

NNRecA .... National Recreation Association [*Later, NRPA*], New York, NY [*Library symbol Library of Congress*] (LCLS)

NNreP .... Regional Plan Association, Inc., Library, New York, NY [*Library symbol Library of Congress*] (LCLS)

NNRF .... National Neurological Research Foundation (EA)

NNRG .... Nevada Energy Co., Inc. [*NASDAQ symbol*] (SAG)

NNRGA .... Nevada Energy [*NASDAQ symbol*] (TTSB)

NNRH .... Roosevelt Hospital, Medical Library, New York, NY [*Library symbol Library of Congress*] (LCLS)

NNRIS.......... Nebraska Natural Resources Information System [*Nebraska State Natural Resources Commission*] [*Lincoln*] [*Information service or system*] (IID)

NNRo........... Theodore Roosevelt Association, New York, NY [*Library symbol Library of Congress*] (LCLS)

NNRocF....... Rockefeller Foundation, New York, NY [*Library symbol Library of Congress*] (LCLS)

NNRocFA..... Rockefeller Family & Associates, Inc., Office Library, New York, NY [*Library symbol Library of Congress*] (LCLS)

NNRoI......... Rochdale Institute, New York, NY [*Library symbol Library of Congress*] (LCLS)

NNRom........ Romanian Library, New York, NY [*Library symbol Library of Congress*] (LCLS)

NNRRB........ R. R. Bowker Co., New York, NY [*Library symbol Library of Congress*] (LCLS)

NNRT.......... Non-Nucleoside Reverse Transcriptase [*Biochemistry*]

NNRT.......... Racquet and Tennis Club, New York, NY [*Library symbol Library of Congress*] (LCLS)

NNRTI......... Non-Nucleoside Reverse Transcriptase Inhibitor [*Biochemistry*]

NNRTI......... Nonnucleoside Reverse Transcriptase Inhibitor [*Medicine*] (TAD)

NNRU.......... Rockefeller University, New York, NY [*Library symbol Library of Congress*] (LCLS)

NNRU-P....... Rockefeller University, Population Council, Bio-Medical Library, New York, NY [*Library symbol Library of Congress*] (LCLS)

NNRY.......... Nunnery (ABBR)

NNRYS........ National Network of Runaway and Youth Services (EA)

NNS .... National Narrowcast Service [*Public Broadcasting Service*] [*Arlington, VA*] [*Telecommunications service*] (TSSD)

NNS .... National Natality Survey

NNS .... National Network Services (NITA)

NNS .... National Newspaper Syndicate

NNS .... Navy Navigation Satellite

NNS .... Navy News Service (DOMA)

NNS .... Neonatal Society [*British*] (DBA)

NNS .... Neural Network Simulator

NNS .... Newhouse News Service (WDMC)

NNS .... Newport News Shipbuilding (DOMA)

NNS .... New York Society Library, New York, NY [*Library symbol Library of Congress*] (LCLS)

NNS .... Non-Native Speakers (EDAC)

NNS .... Nonnuclear Safety (NRCH)

NNS .... Nonnutritive Sweetener

NNS .... Norfolk Naval Shipyard [*Portsmouth, VA*] (MCD)

NNs............. North Salem Free Library, North Salem, NY [*Library symbol Library of Congress*] (LCLS)

NNS .... Nucleon-Nucleon Scattering

NNSA.......... National Nurses Society on Addictions (EA)

NNSaB........ Salomon Brothers, New York, NY [*Library symbol Library of Congress*] (LCLS)

NNSAE........ Society of Automotive Engineers, New York, NY [*Library symbol Library of Congress*] (LCLS)

NNSAR........ Sons of the American Revolution, Empire State Society Library, New York, NY [*Library symbol Library of Congress*] (LCLS)

NNSAS........ Skadden, Arps, Slate, Meagher & Flom, New York, NY [*Library symbol Library of Congress*] (LCLS)

NNSB .... Simmons-Boardman Publishing Corp., New York, NY [*Library symbol Library of Congress Obsolete*] (LCLS)

NNSB & DDCO... Newport News Shipbuilding & Dry Dock Co. (DNAB)

NNSC.......... Neutral Nations Supervisory Commission

NN-Sc .... New York Public Library, Schomburg Collection, New York, NY [*Library symbol Library of Congress*] (LCLS)

NNSC.......... NSF [*National Science*] Network Service Center [*Internet*] (TNIG)

NNSC.......... Smithsonian Institution, Cooper-Hewitt Museum of Decorative Arts and Design, New York, NY [*Library symbol*] [*Library of Congress*] (LCLS)

NNSDO .... National Nursing Staff Development Organization (NTPA)

NNSeag .... Joseph E. Seagram & Sons, Inc., New York, NY [*Library symbol Library of Congress*] (LCLS)

NNSG.......... NASCOM [*NASA Communications Network*] Network Scheduling Group

NNShA........ Shubert Archive, New York, NY [*Library symbol*] [*Library of Congress*] (LCLS)

NNSIHi........ Staten Island Historical Society, New York, NY [*Library symbol Library of Congress*] (LCLS)

NNSII .... Staten Island Institute of Arts and Sciences, New York, NY [*Library symbol Library of Congress*] (LCLS)

NNSIS......... Swedish Information Service, New York, NY [*Library symbol*] [*Library of Congress*] (LCLS)

NNSJD .... Cathedral of Saint John the Divine, New York, NY [*Library symbol Library of Congress*] (LCLS)

NNSN.......... No National Stock Number (AABC)

NNSNP........ National Network in Solidarity with the Nicaraguan People (EA)

NNSPG........ National Network in Solidarity with the People of Guatemala (EA)

NNSPo........ Standard & Poor's Corp., New York, NY [*Library symbol Library of Congress*] (LCLS)

NNSR.......... Sons of the Revolution in the State of New York, New York, NY [*Library symbol Library of Congress*] (LCLS)

NNSS.......... Navy Navigational Satellite System

NNSS.......... Shearman & Sterling Library, New York, NY [*Library symbol*] [*Library of Congress*] (LCLS)

NNSSS........ South Street Seaport Museum, New York, NY [*Library symbol*] [*Library of Congress*] (LCLS)

NNSTB .... Simpson, Thacher & Bartlett, Law Library, New York, NY [*Library symbol*] [*Library of Congress*] (LCLS)

NNStJ .... St. John's University, Jamaica, NY [*Library symbol Library of Congress*] (LCLS)

NNStL......... Saint Luke's Hospital, Richard Walker Bolling Memorial Medical Library, New York, NY [*Library symbol Library of Congress*] (LCLS)

NNStOD...... Standard Oil Co. (New Jersey), New York, NY [*Library symbol Library of Congress*] (LCLS)

NNSTWG..... Nonnuclear Survivability Technology Working Group (AFIT)

NNSU-MC .... State University of New York, Maritime College, Fort Schuyler, Bronx, NY [*Library symbol Library of Congress*] (LCLS)

NNSU-Op .... State University of New York, College of Optometry, New York, NY [*Library symbol Library of Congress*] (LCLS)

NNSW......... Nonnuclear Strategic Warfare

NNSWM....... National Network for Social Work Managers (EA)

NNSY.......... Norfolk Naval Shipyard [*Portsmouth, VA*]

NNT .... Nan [*Thailand*] [*Airport symbol*] (OAG)

NNT .... Nanotec Canada, Inc. [*Vancouver Stock Exchange symbol*]

NNT .... Nearest Neighbor Tool [*Mathematical technique*] (USDC)

NNT .... New York Times, New York, NY [*Library symbol Library of Congress*] (LCLS)

NNT .... Notice Number Tracking (MCD)

NNT .... Number Needed to Treat

NNTAICH...... Technical Assistance Information Clearing House, New York, NY [*Library symbol Library of Congress*] (LCLS)

NNTax......... Tax Foundation, Inc., New York, NY [*Library symbol Library of Congress*] (LCLS)

NNTC .... National Nondestructive Testing Centre [*Atomic Energy Authority*] [*Information service or system*] (IID)

NNTC .... Norwich and Norfolk Terrier Club (EA)

NNTC .... Teachers College, New York, NY [*Library symbol Library of Congress*] (LCLS)

NNTEP........ Northern Nigeria Teacher Education Project [*University of Wisconsin*] (AEBS)

NNTF.......... Traphagen School of Fashion, New York, NY [*Library symbol Library of Congress*] (LCLS)

NNTIA......... Teachers Insurance and Annuity Association of America, New York, NY [*Library symbol*] [*Library of Congress*] (LCLS)

NNTM......... Tobacco Merchants Association of the United States, New York, NY [*Library symbol Library of Congress*] (LCLS)

NNTN......... Not Necessarily the News [*Cable television comedy program*]

NNTP .... National Nuclear Test Plan [*Later, NNTRP*]

NNTP .... Network News Transfer Protocol (TELE)

NNTP .... Network News Transport Protocol [*Telecommunications*]

NNTRP........ National Nuclear Test Readiness Program [*Formerly, NNTP*]

NNTT .... National New Technology Telescope [*Proposed*] [*National Science Foundation*]

NNttR......... Rockefeller Archive Center, Rockefeller University, North Tarrytown, NY [*Library symbol*] [*Library of Congress*] (LCLS)

NNU .... Nanuque [*Brazil*] [*Airport symbol*] (AD)

NNU .... Neonatal Unit [*Medicine*] (DMAA)

NNU .... Net Nitrogen Utilization [*Medicine*] (DAVI)

NNU .... New York University, New York, NY [*Library symbol Library of Congress*] (LCLS)

NNU .... Nordic Numismatic Union (EAIO)

NNU-B .... New York University, Graduate School of Business Administration, New York, NY [*Library symbol Library of Congress*] (LCLS)

NNU-C .... New York University, School of Commerce, New York, NY [*Library symbol Library of Congress*] (LCLS)

NNU-D .... New York University, College of Dentistry, New York, NY [*Library symbol Library of Congress*] (LCLS)

NNU-ES....... New York University, Engineering and Science Library, New York, NY [*Library symbol Library of Congress*] (LCLS)

NNU-F......... New York University, Fales Collection, New York, NY [*Library symbol Library of Congress*] (LCLS)

NNU-FA....... New York University, Institute of Fine Arts, New York, NY [*Library symbol Library of Congress*] (LCLS)

NNU-G .... New York University, Wall Street Library, New York, NY [*Library symbol Library of Congress*] (LCLS)

NNU-H .... New York University, University Heights Library, Bronn, NY [*Library symbol Library of Congress*] (LCLS)

NNUH......... United Hospital Fund of New York, New York, NY [*Library symbol Library of Congress*] (LCLS)

NNU-IEM..... New York University, Institute of Environmental Medicine, Tuxedo Park, NY [*Library symbol Library of Congress*] (LCLS)

NNU-L......... New York University, School of Law, New York, NY [*Library symbol Library of Congress*] (LCLS)

NNU-LA....... New York University, Fobert F. Wagner Labor Archives, New York Labor Records Survey, New York, NY [*Library symbol*] [*Library of Congress*] (LCLS)

NNU-M........ New York University, Medical Center, New York, NY [*Library symbol Library of Congress*] (LCLS)

NNUN......... United Nations Library, New York, NY [*Library symbol Library of Congress*] (LCLS)

NNUnC........ University Club, New York, NY [*Library symbol Library of Congress*] (LCLS)

NNUN-CF .... United Nations Childrens Fund, New York, NY [*Library symbol Library of Congress*] (LCLS)

NNUni......... Unipub, Inc., New York, NY [*Library symbol Library of Congress*] (LCLS)

NNUnionC.... Union Club, New York, NY [*Library symbol Library of Congress*] (LCLS)

NNUnionL.... Union League Club, New York, NY [*Library symbol Library of Congress*] (LCLS)

NNUN-PA.... United Nations Fund for Population Activities, New York, NY [*Library symbol Library of Congress*] (LCLS)

NNUN-W ...... United Nations, Woodrow Wilson Memorial Library, New York, NY [*Library symbol Library of Congress*] (LCLS)

NNU-T .... New York University, Tamiment Library, New York, NY [*Library symbol Library of Congress*] (LCLS)

NNUT .... Union Theological Seminary, New York, NY [*Library symbol Library of Congress*] (LCLS)

NNUT-Mc ..... Union Theological Seminary, McAlpin Collection, New York, NY [*Library symbol Library of Congress*] (LCLS)

NNUVAN ...... Ukrainian Academy of Arts and Sciences in the United States, New York, NY [*Library symbol Library of Congress*] (LCLS)

NNUVE .... Nonnegative Unbiased Variance Estimator [*Statistics*]

NNU-W .... New York University, Washington Square Library, New York, NY [*Library symbol Library of Congress*] (LCLS)

NNU-We .... New York University, Joe Weinstein Residence Halls Library, New York, NY [*Library symbol Library of Congress*] (LCLS)

NNV .... National Naval Volunteers

NNVAB .... United States Veterans Administration Hospital, Bronx, NY [*Library symbol Library of Congress*] (LCLS)

NNVAM .... United States Veterans Administration Hospital (Manhattan), New York, NY [*Library symbol Library of Congress*] (LCLS)

NNW .... North-Northwest

NNWB .... Navy Nuclear Weapons Bulletin [*A publication*]

NNWB .... Net National Well Being

NNWC .... Nonnuclear Weapons Country

NNWF .... National Network of Women's Funds (EA)

NNWFG .... Wilkie, Farr & Gallagher, New York, NY [*Library symbol Library of Congress*] (LCLS)

NNWG .... Wenner-Gren Foundation for Anthropological Research, New York, NY [*Library symbol Library of Congress*] (LCLS)

NNWH .... Nonnormal Working Hours

NNWH .... Walter Hampden Memorial Library, New York, NY [*Library symbol Library of Congress*] (LCLS)

NNWhit .... Whitney Museum of American Art, New York, NY [*Library symbol Library of Congress*] (LCLS)

NNWI .... Neonatal Narcotic Withdrawal Index [*Medicine*] (DMAA)

NNWM .... William Douglas McAdams, Inc., Medical Library, New York, NY [*Library symbol Library of Congress*] (LCLS)

NNWML .... Wagner College, Staten Island, NY [*Library symbol Library of Congress*] (LCLS)

NNWO .... Navy Nuclear Weapons Officer (DNAB)

NNWP .... National Network of Women Philanthropists (NFD)

NNWRN .... North-Norwestern (FAAC)

NNWS .... National Network of Women in Sales [*Defunct*] (EA)

NNWS .... Nonnuclear Weapons State

NNWSI .... Nevada Nuclear Waste Storage Investigations

NNWWD ...... North-Westward (FAAC)

NNY .... Nanyang [*China*] [*Airport symbol*] (OAG)

NNY .... Nuveen New York Municipal Fund [*NYSE symbol*] (SPSG)

NNY .... Nuveen NY Muni Val Fd [*NYSE symbol*] (TTSB)

NNy .... Nyack Library, Nyack, NY [*Library symbol Library of Congress*] (LCLS)

NNYAB .... National Network of Youth Advisory Boards (EA)

NNYC .... Yale Club, New York, NY [*Library symbol Library of Congress*] (LCLS)

NNYD .... Norfolk Navy Yard [*Virginia*] [*Later, Norfolk Naval Shipyard*]

NNYI .... YIVO Institute for Jewish Research, New York, NY [*Library symbol Library of Congress*] (LCLS)

NNYIQ .... Nuveen New York Investment Quality Municipal Fund [*Associated Press*] (SAG)

NNyM .... Nyack Missionary College, Nyack, NY [*Library symbol Library of Congress*] (LCLS)

NNYMCA ...... Young Men's Christian Association, National Council Historical Library, New York, NY [*Library symbol*] [*Library of Congress*] (LCLS)

NNYMCA-GC... Young Men's Christian Association, Grand Central Branch Library, New York, NY [*Library symbol Library of Congress*] (LCLS)

NNYMCA-NC... Young Men's Christian Association, National Council Historical Library, New York, NY [*Library symbol Library of Congress*] (LCLS)

NNYMI .... Nuveen New York Municipal Income Fund [*Associated Press*] (SAG)

NNYMV .... Nuveen New York Municipal Value Fund [*Associated Press*] (SAG)

NNYSQ .... Nuveen New York Select Quality Municipal Fund [*Associated Press*] (SAG)

NNYU .... Yeshiva University, New York, NY [*Library symbol Library of Congress*] (LCLS)

NNYU-HJ ...... Yeshiva University, Mendel Gottesman Library of Hebraica Judaica, New York, NY [*Library symbol Library of Congress*] (LCLS)

NNYU-M ...... Yeshiva University, Albert Einstein College of Medicine, Bronx, NY [*Library symbol Library of Congress*] (LCLS)

NNYU-S .... Yeshiva University, Stern College, New York, NY [*Library symbol Library of Congress*] (LCLS)

NNZ .... New York Zoological Society, New York, NY [*Library symbol Library of Congress*] (LCLS)

NNZ .... Point Sur, CA [*Location identifier FAA*] (FAAL)

NNZCG .... New Zealand Consulate General, Library, New York, NY [*Library symbol*] [*Library of Congress*] (LCLS)

NNZi .... Zionist Archives and Library, New York, NY [*Library symbol Library of Congress*] (LCLS)

NO .... Air North [*ICAO designator*] (AD)

NO .... Lifts Not Operating [*Skiing*]

NO .... Nachalnik Otdelenia [*Chief of Department*] [*Soviet military rank*]

NO .... Narcotics Officer

NO .... National Office

NO .... National Office, Office of Federal Contract Compliance Programs (AAGC)

NO .... National Outlook: an Australian Christian Monthly [*A publication*] (APTA)

NO .... Native Officer [*British military*] (DMA)

NO .... Natural Orbital [*Physical chemistry*]

NO .... Natural Order [*Botany*]

NO .... Naval Observatory [*Navy*]

NO .... Naval Officer

NO .... Navigation Officer

NO .... Negative [*British naval signaling*]

NO .... New Options (EA)

NO .... New Order [*Defunct*] (EA)

NO .... New Orleans [*Louisiana*]

NO .... Nitric Oxide

NO .... Nitrogen Monoxide

NO .... Nitrogen Oxide [*Emission control*] [*Automotive engineering*]

NO .... Noah (ABBR)

No .... Nobelium [*Chemical element*]

NO .... Nocturia [*Urology*] (DAVI)

n/o .... None Obtained [*Medicine*]

NO .... Nonobese [*Medicine*] (DMAA)

NO .... Nonofficial

NO .... Nonoriginal

N/O .... No Orders [*Business term*]

NO .... No Palpable Nodes [*Oncology*]

NO .... Nord-Ouest [*Northwest*] [*French*]

NO .... Normally Open [*Switch*]

NO .... North

NO .... North Central Airlines, Inc.

NO .... Northern (ABBR)

N/O .... North Of [*In outdoor advertising*] (WDMC)

NO .... Norway [*ANSI two-letter standard code*] (CNC)

no .... Norway [*MARC country of publication code Library of Congress*] (LCCP)

NO .... Nose [*Horse racing*]

NO .... Notes [*Online database field identifier*]

NO .... Not for Off [*Kennedy Space Center Distribution*] (NAKS)

NO .... Not Or [*Logical operator*] [*Computer science*]

N/O .... Not Otherwise

NO .... Not Our Publication

N/O .... Not Out [*Bookselling*]

NO .... November (ADA)

NO .... Nuestra Orden [*Our Order*] [*Spanish Business term*]

NO .... Number (EY)

No .... Number (EBF)

no .... Number (WDMC)

NO .... Numero [*In Number*] [*Pharmacy*] (ROG)

NO .... Nurse's Office (DMAA)

NO .... Nursing Officer [*British*]

NO .... Oneida Library, Oneida, NY [*Library symbol Library of Congress*] (LCLS)

NO2 .... Nitrogen Dioxide

NO3 .... Nitrate (GNE)

No9Vis .... Number Nine Visual Technology, Inc. [*Associated Press*] (SAG)

NOA .... National Oceanographic Association

NOA .... National Officers Association (EA)

NOA .... National Onion Association (EA)

NOA .... National Opera Association (EA)

NOA .... National Optical Association [*Later, NAOO*]

NOA .... National Optometric Association (EA)

NOA .... National Orchestral Association (EA)

NOA .... National Outboard Association [*Defunct*] (EA)

NOA .... National Outdoorsmen's Association [*Defunct*] (EA)

NOA .... NATO Oil Authority (NATG)

NOA .... Natural Optical Activity

NOA .... Natural Orange Aroma

NOA .... Nature of Action [*Military*] (AFM)

NOA .... Network-Oriented Analysis and Transformation Unit [*Computer science*] (MHDB)

NOA .... New London, CT [*Location identifier FAA*] (FAAL)

NOA .... New Obligational Authority

NOA .... Norontair [*Canada ICAO designator*] (FAAC)

NOA .... Northwest Orient Airlines, Inc.

NOA .... Notice of Availability (MCD)

NOA .... Not Operationally Assigned

N-O-A .... Not-Or-And [*Computer science*]

NOA .... Not Otherwise Authorized

NOA .... Nueva Organizacion Antiterrorista [*New Anti-Terrorist Organization*] [*Guatemala*] (PD)

NOA .... University of North Carolina, Chapel Hill Library School, Chapel Hill, NC [*OCLC symbol*] (OCLC)

NOAA .... National Oceanic and Atmospheric Administration [*Rockville, MD*] [*Pronounced "Noah"*]

NOAA .... Nonoperating Aircraft Authorization

NOAADN ...... National Organization for Advancement of Associate Degree Nursing (EA)

NOAA-FSL.... NOAA [*National Oceanic and Atmospheric Administration*]-Forecast Systems Lab

NOAA-JTRE... National Oceanic and Atmospheric Administration Joint Tsunami Research Effort

NOAA-NOS... National Oceanic and Atmospheric Administration - National Ocean Service (DNAB)

NOAA-NWS... National Oceanic and Atmospheric Administration - National Weather Service (DNAB)

NOAA-PMEL... National Oceanic and Atmospheric Administration Pacific Marine Environmental Laboratory

NOAA-TR-NMFS-Circ... National Oceanic and Atmospheric Administration Technical Report-National MarineFisheries Service-Circular [*A publication*] (PDAA)

NOAA-TR-NMFS-SSRF... National Oceanic and Atmospheric Administration-Technical Report-National MarineFisheries Service-Special Scientific Report Fisheries (PDAA)

NOAB.......... National Outdoor Advertising Bureau [*Defunct*] (EA)
NOAC.......... National Operations and Automation Conference (HGAA)
No a/c.......... No Account (EBF)
NOAC.......... Nuclear Operations Analysis Center [*Department of Energy*] [*Information service or system*] (IID)
NOACT.......... Naval Overseas Air Cargo Terminal
NOACT.......... No Action (MUGU)
NOACTLANT... Naval Ordnance Activities, Atlantic
NOACTPAC... Naval Ordnance Activities, Pacific
NOaD.......... Dowling College, Oakdale, NY [*Library symbol Library of Congress*] (LCLS)
NOAD.......... National Organization for Apraxia and Dyspraxia (EA)
No Adams St C... North Adams State College (GAGS)
NOADN........ National Oceanic and Atmospheric Data Network
NOADN........ National Organization for Associate Degree Nursing (EA)
NOADN........ National Organization for Associate Degree Nursing (NTPA)
No Adv........ No Advice (EBF)
NOAEL.......... No Observed Adverse Effect Level [*Toxicology*] (EG)
NOaf.......... Oakfield Public Library (Haxton Memorial), Oakfield, NY [*Library symbol Library of Congress*] (LCLS)
NOAFIRM..... Affirmative Replies Neither Required nor Desired (MUGU)
NOAG.......... Naval Objectives Analysis Group
NOAH.......... Narrow-Band Optimization of the Alignment of Highways (PDAA)
NOAH.......... National Ocean Agency Headquarters
NOAH.......... National Organization for Albinism and Hypopigmentation (EA)
NOAH.......... New York Online Access to Health Home Page [*Database*]
NOAH.......... Norwegian Adapted HAWK [*Hughes Aircraft Co.*]
NOAHS.......... New Opportunities in Animal Health Sciences
NOaJH.......... Oakdale-Bohemia Junior High School, Oakdale, NY [*Library symbol Library of Congress*] (LCLS)
NOALA........ Noise-Operated Automatic Level Adjustment
NOAM.......... Noan Mizrachi [*American Zionist organization*]
NOAM.......... Nuclear Ordnance Air Force Materiel [*Military*] (AFIT)
NOAMTRAC... North America Trail Complex (EA)
NO & LC..... New Orleans & Lower Coast Railroad Co. (IIA)
NOAO.......... National Optical Astronomy Observatories [*Tucson, AZ*] [*National Science Foundation*]
NOAO.......... Navy Officers, Accounts Office (MUGU)
NOAP.......... National Ocean Access Project (EA)
NOAP.......... Naval Overseas Air Cargo Terminal, Pearl (MUGU)
NOAP.......... Navy Oil Analysis Program (NG)
NOAPP.......... National Organization of Adolescent Pregnancy and Parenting (EA)
NOAPP.......... National Organization on Adolescent Pregnancy, Parenting, and Prevention (PAZ)
NOAPS.......... National Oil and Acrylic Painters Society
NOAR.......... National Organization for an American Revolution (EA)
NOARB........ New Orleans Army Base (SAA)
No Ariz U..... Northern Arizona University (GAGS)
NOARL.......... National Oceanographic and Atmospheric Research Laboratory (USDC)
NOARL.......... Naval Ocean and Atmosphere Research Laboratory [*USA*] [*Marine science*] (OSRA)
NOART........ New Orleans Army Terminal
NOB.......... National Oil Board (NATG)
NOB.......... Naval Operating Base
NOB.......... Naval Order of Battle
NOB.......... Naval Ordnance Bulletin [*A publication*]
NOB.......... Nobeoka [*Japan*] [*Seismograph station code, US Geological Survey*] (SEIS)
NOB.......... Nobile [*Nobly*] [*Music*] (ROG)
NOB.......... Nobility (ABBR)
NOB.......... Nobis [*With Us*] [*Latin*] (ROG)
NOB.......... Noble (ABBR)
NOB.......... Non-Biased Optical Bistable [*Device*] (AAEL)
NOB.......... Nonobese [*A diabetic mouse strain*]
NOB.......... North Bay Cooperative Library System, Santa Rosa, CA [*OCLC symbol*] (OCLC)
NOB.......... Norwest Corp. [*NYSE symbol*] (SPSG)
NOB.......... Notes over Bonds [*Finance*] (NUMA)
NOB.......... Not on Bonus
NOB.......... Nuclear Order of Battle (AFM)
NOB.......... Number of Bursts
NOB.......... San Francisco, CA [*Location identifier FAA*] (FAAL)
NOBA.......... Nitrosobenzamide [*Organic chemistry*]
NOBAR........ National Organization for Birthfathers and Adoption Reform (EA)
NOBC.......... National Office for Black Catholics (EA)
NOBC.......... National Order of Battlefield Commissions (EA)
NOBC.......... National Organization of Bar Counsel (EA)
NOBC.......... Naval Officer Billet Classifications [*or Code*]
NOBCA........ National Organization of Black College Alumni (EA)
NOBCCE....... National Organization of Black Chemists and Chemical Engineers [*Later, NOPABCCE*] (EA)
NOBCChE..... National Organization for Professional Advancement of Black Chemists and Chemical Engineers
NOBCO........ National Organization of Black County Officials (EA)
NOBDUCHAR... Naval Operating Base, Dutch Harbor, Aleutians
NOBE.......... Nordstrom, Inc. [*NASDAQ symbol*] (NQ)
NoBeFi........ Fiskeridirektoratet [*Directorate of Fisheries*], Bergen-Nordens, Norway [*Library symbol Library of Congress*] (LCLS)

Nobel.......... Nobel Insurance Ltd. [*Associated Press*] (SAG)
NobelEd....... Nobel Education Dynamics, Inc. [*Associated Press*] (SAG)
NOBELS........ New Office and Business Education Learning System
NoBeU.......... Universitetet i Bergen [*University of Bergen*], Bergen, Norway [*Library symbol Library of Congress*] (LCLS)
NOBFRAN.... Naval Operating Base, San Francisco, California
NOBH.......... Nobility Homes [*NASDAQ symbol*] (TTSB)
NOBH.......... Nobility Homes, Inc. [*NASDAQ symbol*] (NQ)
NobiltyH....... Nobility Homes, Inc. [*Associated Press*] (SAG)
NOBIN.......... Stichting Nederlands Orgaan voor de Bevordering van de Informatieverzorging [*Netherlands Organization for Information Policy*] [*Information service or system Defunct*] (IID)
NOBL.......... Nobel Insurance Ltd. [*NASDAQ symbol*] (NQ)
NoblAf........ Noble Affiliates, Inc. [*Associated Press*] (SAG)
NOBLE........ National Organization of Black Law Enforcement Executives (EA)
Noble.......... Noble's Current Court Decisions [*New York*] [*A publication*] (DLA)
NobleR........ Noble Roman's, Inc. [*Associated Press*] (SAG)
NOBLF........ Nobel Insurance [*NASDAQ symbol*] (TTSB)
NobltyH....... Nobility Homes [*Associated Press*] (SAG)
NOBMN....... Nobleman (ABBR)
NoBncshs.... North Bancshares, Inc. [*Associated Press*] (SAG)
NOBNEWT.... Naval Operating Base, Newport, Rhode Island
NoBordr....... Northern Border Partners Ltd. [*Associated Press*] (SAG)
NOBP.......... Nitrosobenzopyrone [*Organic chemistry*]
NOBR.......... Nobler (ABBR)
NOBS.......... Naval Observatory [*Navy*]
NOBS.......... Naval Operating Base Supplies (DNAB)
N Obs.......... Nihil Obstat [*Official Approval*] [*Latin*]
NOBS.......... Nonanoyloxybenzene (EDCT)
NOBS.......... Nonanoyloxybenzene Sulfonate [*Laundry bleach activator*]
NOBS.......... Nursing Observation of Behaviour Syndromes (DB)
NOBSOLO.... Naval Operating Base, Coco Solo, Canal Zone
NOBST........ Noblest (ABBR)
NOBSY........ Naval Observatory [*Navy*]
NOBT.......... New Orleans Board of Trade (EA)
NOBT.......... Nobility (ABBR)
NOBTRIN .... Naval Operating Base, Trinidad
NOBTS.......... Naval Order of Battle Textual Summary (MCD)
NOBWN....... Noblewomen (ABBR)
NOBY.......... Nobly (ABBR)
NOC.......... Ascor Flyservice AS [*Norway ICAO designator*] (FAAC)
NOC.......... National Oceanographic Center [*Marine science*] (MSC)
NOC.......... National Oceanographic Council (NADA)
NOC.......... National Offshore Council (EA)
NOC.......... National Olympic Committee (NADA)
NOC.......... National Olympic Committees
NOC.......... National Online Circuit [*Defunct*] (EA)
NOC.......... National Opportunity Camps for the Pre-Teen Child (EA)
NOC.......... Natural Organic Carbon
NOC.......... Naval Operations Center (NVT)
NOC.......... Navy Officer's Classification
NOC.......... Network Operation Center [*Bell System*]
NOC.......... Network Operations Control [*NASA*] (KSC)
NOC.......... New Orleans Consortium [*Library network*]
noc.......... Noctis [*Night*] [*Medicine*]
NOC.......... Nominal Operating Cell [*Photovoltaic energy systems*]
NOC.......... Nonionic Organic Compound [*Organic chemistry*]
NOC.......... Non-Ionic Organic Contaminant [*Environmental chemistry*]
NOC.......... Normally Open Contact [*Switch*] (IAA)
NOC.......... Norris Communications Corp. [*Vancouver Stock Exchange symbol*]
NOC.......... Northrop Corp. [*NYSE symbol*] (SPSG)
NOC.......... Northrop Grumman [*NYSE symbol*] (TTSB)
NOC.......... Northrop Grumman Corp. [*NYSE symbol*] (SAG)
NOC.......... Northwest Ohio Consortium [*Library network*]
NOC.......... Norwegian Government Office of Culture [*Record label*]
NOC.......... Notation of Content [*Aerospace*]
NOC.......... Notice of Cancellation (AAGC)
NOC.......... Notice of Change (MCD)
NOC.......... Notice of Commencement (EPA)
NOC.......... Notice of Contents [*Indexing*]
NOC.......... Not Otherwise Classified
NOC.......... Not Otherwise Coded (GFGA)
NOC.......... Nuclear Operations Center (MCD)
NOC.......... Nuclear Ordnance Commission [*Military*] (AFIT)
NOC.......... Numerical Optimisation Centre [*British*]
NOC.......... Nuttall Ornithological Club (EA)
NOc.......... Oceanside Free Library, Oceanside, NY [*Library symbol Library of Congress*] (LCLS)
NOC.......... University of North Carolina, Chapel Hill, Chapel Hill, NC [*OCLC symbol*] (OCLC)
NOCA.......... National Organization for Competency Assurance (EA)
NOCA.......... National Organization for Competency Assurance (NTPA)
NOCA.......... Nitrosooxazolidinecarboxylic Acid [*Organic chemistry*]
NOCA.......... North Cascades National Park
No Ca Ecc & Mar... Notes of Cases, English Ecclesiastical and Maritime Courts [*1841-50*] [*A publication*] (DLA)
No Car Ag & Tech... North Carolina Agricultural & Technical State University (GAGS)
No Car Cent U... North Carolina Central University (GAGS)
No Car St U (Raleigh)... North Carolina State University (Raleigh) (GAGS)
NOcaS .... Shaker Museum Foundation, Inc., Old Catham, NY [*Library symbol Library of Congress*] (LCLS)
No Cas LJ.... Notes of Cases, Law Journal [*A publication*] (DLA)
NOCB.......... New Orleans City Ballet

NocBE........... Walter S. Boardman Elementary School, Oceanside, NY [*Library symbol*] [*Library of Congress*] (LCLS)
NOCC........... NATO Oil Crisis Contingent (NATG)
NOCC........... Navigation Operational Checkout Computer
NOCC........... Navigation Operator's Control Console
NOCC........... Network Operations Control Center [*Manned Space Flight Network, NASA*]
NOCCC........ No Control Circuit Contacts (MSA)
NOCC/JTWC... Naval Oceanography Command Center/Joint Typhoon Warning Center
NOCD........... Not Our Class, Dear [*Slang*]
NOCE........... New Orleans Commodity Exchange (EA)
NOCEM........ National Organization for Civic Education & Election Monitoring [*Lira, Uganda*]
NOCERCC.... National Organization for Continuing Education of Roman Catholic Clergy (EA)
NOCF........... National Office Computer Facility [*IRS*]
NOCF........... Naval Oceanography Command Facility (DNAB)
NocFE........... Elementary School #3, Oceanside, NY [*Library symbol*] [*Library of Congress*] (LCLS)
NOcH........... South Nassau Communities Hospital, Oceanside, NY [*Library symbol Library of Congress*] (LCLS)
NOCHA........ National Off-Campus Housing Association [*Defunct*] (EA)
NOCI........... Nederlandse Organisatie voor Chemische Informatie (NITA)
NOCI........... Non Orthogonal Configuration Interaction (AAEL)
NOCIG........ Night Only Calligraphic Image Generator
NOC II.......... Nuclear Operations Concept II [*Military*]
NO-CIRC ..... National Organization of Circumcision Information Resource Centers (EA)
NOCIRC........ National Organization of Circumcision Information Resource Centers (PAZ)
NOCM........... National Organization for Changing Men (EA)
NOCM........... Nuclear Ordnance Commodity Manager (AFM)
NocME........... Elementary School #8, Oceanside, NY [*Library symbol*] [*Library of Congress*] (LCLS)
NocMS........... Oceanside Middle School, Oceanside, NY [*Library symbol*] [*Library of Congress*] (LCLS)
NOCN........... National Ocean Communications Network (USDC)
NOCN........... National Open College Network (AIE)
NocNE........... Elementary School #5, Oceanside, NY [*Library symbol*] [*Library of Congress*] (LCLS)
NOCO........... Noise Correlation
NOCO........... Nuclear Ordnance Cataloging Officer [*Military*]
NOCO........... Nuclear Ordnance Catalog Office [*DoD*]
NOCONIT..... No Continuing Interest (NG)
NOCONTRACT... Not Releasable to Contractors (MCD)
NOCOPS ...... NORAD Combat Operations System (MCD)
NOCOR .... Neglect of Core Orbitals [*Physical chemistry*]
NOCP........... Network Operator Control Program
NOCSA........ National Olympic Committee of South Africa (ECON)
NOCSAE....... National Operating Committee on Standards for Athletic Equipment (EA)
NOcSE .... Florence A. Smith School, Oceanside, NY [*Library symbol*] [*Library of Congress*] (LCLS)
NocSH .... Oceanside Senior High School, Oceanside, NY [*Library symbol*] [*Library of Congress*] (LCLS)
NOCT .... Navy Overseas Cargo Terminals
NOCT .... Nocte [*At Night*] [*Pharmacy*] (ROG)
noct .... Nocturnal (CPH)
NOCT .... Nominal [*or Normal*] Operating Cell Temperature [*Photovoltaic energy systems*]
NOCT MANEQ... Nocte Maneque [*Night and Morning*] [*Pharmacy*]
NOD............. National Organization on Disability (EA)
NOD............. Naval Ordnance Department [*British*]
NOD............. Naval Ordnance Depot
NOD............. Navy Operational Deception (MCD)
NOD............. Network Operations Directive [*NASA*] (KSC)
NOD............. Network Out-Dial [*Automatic Voice Network*] (CET)
NOD............. New Offshore Dischargement (NATG)
NOD............. Night Observation Device
NOD............. Noise Output Device
NOD............. Nondefinitive Pattern [*Laboratory science*] (DAVI)
NOD............. Nonobese Diabetic [*Mouse strain*]
NOD............. Norris Dam [*TVA*]
NOD............. Notice of Decision (COE)
NOD............. Notice of Deficiency (EPA)
NOD............. Notify of Death (DAVI)
NODA........... National Operatic and Dramatic Association (EAIO)
NODA........... National Orientation Directors Association (EA)
NODA........... National Outdoor Drama Association [*Defunct*] (EA)
NODA........... Normal-Octyl & -Deyl Adipate [*Organic chemistry*]
NODAC........ Naval Ordnance Data Automation Center
NODAC........ Navy Occupational Development and Analysis Center (DNAB)
No Dak St U... North Dakota State University (GAGS)
NODAL........ Network-Oriented Data Acquisition Language
NODAN .... Noise-operated Device for Antinoise [*Telecommunications*] (TEL)
NODAP........ Nonlinear Distortion Analysis Program [*Bell System*]
NODAS........ Network-Oriented Data Acquisition System (MHDI)
NODC........... National Oceanographic Data Center [*Databank originator*] [*Washington, DC*] [*National Oceanic and Atmospheric Administration*]
NODC........... Naval Oceanographic Distribution Center
NODC........... Naval Operating Development Center
NODC........... Non-OPEC Developing Country (NUCP)

NODCAB ...... National Oceanographic Data Center Advisory Board [*National Oceanic and Atmospheric Administration*] (NOAA)
NODCC........ Noble Order, Descendants of the Conqueror and His Companions (EA)
NODDS......... Naval Oceanographic Data Distribution System
NODE........... National Organization of Downsized Employees
NODE........... Noise Diode [*Electronics*] (IAA)
NODEL......... Not to Delay
NODESTA.... Will Not Depart This Station [*Army*] (AABC)
NODEX........ New Offshore Dischargement Exercise (NATG)
NODI........... Notice of Delayed [*or Delinquent*] Item
NODIS.......... No Distribution [*Military security classification*] (AFM)
NODIS.......... Northern Ohio Data and Information Service [*Cleveland State University*] [*Information service or system*] (IID)
NODL.......... National Office for Decent Literature [*Defunct*]
NODL.......... Not on Drawing List (MCD)
NODLR........ Night Observation Device, Long-Range [*Army*] (RDA)
NODM.......... Ferrocarril Nor-Oeste de Mexico [*Mexico North Western Railroad*] [*AAR code*]
NODM.......... National Organization of Dance and Mime [*British*] (DBA)
NODMR......... Night Observation Device, Medium-Range [*Army*]
NODRA......... National One Design Racing Association (EA)
NODS.......... National Oversight Database (AEPA)
NODS.......... Navy Overseas Dependents School
NODS.......... Near-Object Detection Sensor [*Automotive electronics*]
NODS.......... Near Obstacle Detection System [*General Motors-Delco Co.*]
NOE........... Nap of the Earth [*Night helicopter flight*] [*Army*]
NOE........... No Ophthalmologic Examination [*Medicine*]
NOE........... No Other Entry (ADA)
NOE........... NORAD Operational Evaluation (MCD)
NOE........... Norden-Norddeich [*Germany*] [*Airport symbol*]
NOE........... Notice of Exception
NOE........... Notice of Execution
NOE........... Not Otherwise Enumerated
NOE........... Nuclear Overhauser Effect
NOE........... Nuclear Overhauser Enhancement (DB)
NOEA.......... National Outdoor Events Association [*British*] (DBA)
No East Rep... Northeastern Reporter [*Commonly cited NE*] [*A publication*] (DLA)
NOEB.......... NATO Oil Executive Board (NATG)
NOEB-E........ NATO Oil Executive Board - East
NOEB-W...... NATO Oil Executive Board - West
NOEC.......... No Effects Concentration [*British environmental standard*]
NOEC .... No Observed Effect Concentration [*Toxicology*]
NOECC........ Northeast College Conference (PSS)
NOECOMM... Nap-of-the-Earth Communications [*Night helicopter flight*]
NOED .... New Oxford English Dictionary [*Proposed*]
NOEDS......... Nuclear Overhauser Enhancement Difference Spectrometry
NOEF.......... Naval Ordnance Engineering Facility (DNAB)
NOEHI......... No One Else Has It [*Lexicography*]
No E III U..... Northeastern Illinois University (GAGS)
NOEL .... National Organization of Episcopalians for Life (EA)
NOEL .... National Ornament and Electric Lights Christmas Association (EA)
NOEL .... Naval Ordnance Electronics Laboratory
NOEL .... Noel Group [*NASDAQ symbol*] (TTSB)
NOEL .... Noel Group, Inc. [*NASDAQ symbol*] (SAG)
NOEL .... No Observed Effect Level [*Toxicology*]
No E La U..... Northeast Louisiana University (GAGS)
NoelGp .... Noel Group, Inc. [*Associated Press*] (SAG)
NOELS .... New Office Education Learning System
No E Mo St U... Northeast Missouri State University (GAGS)
No E Ohio U... Northeastern Ohio University (GAGS)
NOEP.......... Neue Oekonomische Politik [*New Economic Policy*] [*Germany*]
NOES.......... National Operational Environmental Satellite Service (MCD)
NOESS......... National Operational Environmental Satellite System
No E St U ..... Northeastern State University (GAGS)
NoestUt........ Northeast Utilities [*Associated Press*] (SAG)
NOESY......... Nuclear Overhauser Effect Spectroscopy
No et Vet Test... Novi et Veteris Testamenti (DSA)
NOEU.......... Naval Ordnance Experimental Unit
No E U.......... Northeastern University (GAGS)
NOEV .... NORAD Operational Evaluation (IAA)
NOF........... Fonnafly AS [*Norway ICAO designator*] (FAAC)
NOF........... National Oceanographic Facility [*Marine science*] (OSRA)
NOF........... National Optical Font [*Typography*]
NOF........... National Osteopathic Foundation (EA)
NOF........... National Osteoporosis Foundation (EA)
NOF........... Naval Operating Facility
NOF........... Naval Ordnance Facility
NOF........... NCR [*NCR Corp.*] Optical Font (MCD)
NOF........... Network Operations and Facilities
NOF........... Network Operations Forum [*Exchange Carriers Standards Association*] [*Telecommunications*]
NOF........... Neurite Outgrowth Factor [*Biochemistry*]
NOF........... Nickel Offsets Ltd. [*Toronto Stock Exchange symbol*]
NOF........... Nitrosyl Fluoride (SAA)
NOF........... NOTAM Office
NOF .... St. Petersburg, FL [*Location identifier FAA*] (FAAL)
NOFA.......... National Office Furniture Association [*Later, NOPA*] (EA)
NOFA.......... Natural Organic Farmers Association (EA)
NOFA.......... Notice of Funding Availability [*Department of Housing and Urban Development*] (GFGA)
NOFAD........ Naval Ocean Floor Analysis Division (DNAB)
N of Cas ..... Notes of Cases at Madras (Strange) [*A publication*] (DLA)
N of Cas ...... Notes of Cases, English Ecclesiastical and Maritime Courts [*1841-50*] [*A publication*] (DLA)

NOFI .... National Oil Fuel Institute [*Later, NOJC*] (EA)
NOFIN .... No Further Information
NoFkBc .... North Fork Bancorp [*Associated Press*] (SAG)
NOFMA .... National Oak Flooring Manufacturers Association (EA)
NOFOA .... Naval Office for Occupied Areas [*World War II*]
NOFODIS ..... No Foreign Dissemination [*Intelligence classification*]
NOFORN ...... Not Releasable to Foreign Nationals [*Military security classification*]
NOFRC .... Northern Forest Research Centre [*Canadian Forestry Service of Agriculture Canada*] [*Research center*] (RCD)
NOFS .... National Option and Futures Society [*Defunct*] (EA)
NOFT .... Naval Overseas Freight Terminal
NOFT .... Nonorganic Failure-to-Thrive [*Medicine*] (DMAA)
NOFT .... Notification of Foreign Travel (AFM)
NOFTT .... Nonorganic Failure-to-Thrive [*Medicine*] (MEDA)
NOG .... Arizona-Nogales [*Mexico*] [*Airport symbol*] (AD)
NOG .... North Carolina Natural Gas [*NYSE symbol*] (SAG)
NOG .... NSAPAC Operations Group
NOG .... Nuclear Ordnance Group [*Air Force*] (MCD)
NOG .... Numbering
NOg .... Ogdensburg Public Library, Ogdensburg, NY [*Library symbol Library of Congress*] (LCLS)
NOGA .... National Osteopathic Guild Association (EA)
NOGAD .... Noise-Operated Gain-Adjusting Device
NOGAPS ...... Navy Operational Global Atmospheric Prediction System
NOGGA .... National Ornamental Goldfish Growers Association (EA)
NOgH .... A. Barton Hepburn Hospital, Ogdensburg, NY [*Library symbol Library of Congress*] (LCLS)
NOGL .... Naval Ordnance Gauge Laboratory
NOGL .... Nizam's Own Golgonda Lancers [*British military*] (DMA)
NOGLSTP..... National Organization of Gay and Lesbian Scientists and Technical Professionals (EA)
NOgM .... Mater Dei College, Ogdensburg, NY [*Library symbol Library of Congress*] (LCLS)
NOGM .... No Gammopathy Detected [*Biochemistry*] (DAVI)
NOgRM .... Remington Art Memorial Museum, Ogdensburg, NY [*Library symbol*] [*Library of Congress*] (LCLS)
NOGS .... Night Observation Gunship (MCD)
NOgSH .... Saint Lawrence State Hospital, Ogdensburg, NY [*Library symbol Library of Congress*] (LCLS)
NOgW .... Wadhams Hall Seminary College, Ogdensburg, NY [*Library symbol Library of Congress*] (LCLS)
NOH .... Chicago, IL [*Location identifier FAA*] (FAAL)
NOH .... Night Observation Helicopter (MCD)
NOH .... University of North Carolina, Health Science Library, Chapel Hill, NC [*OCLC symbol*] (OCLC)
NOHA .... Nutrition for Optimal Health Association (EA)
NOHARMM... National Organization to Halt the Abuse and Routine Mutilation of Males (EA)
NOHIC .... National Oral Health Information Clearinghouse (PAZ)
NOHIMS...... Navy Occupational Health Information Management System
NoHo .... North of Houston Street [*Artists' colony in New York City*] [*See also SoHo, SoSo, TriBeCa*]
NOHOL........ Not Holding [*a given course or altitude*] [*Aviation*]
NOHP .... Not Otherwise Herein Provided
NOHQI .... Nuveen Ohio Quality Income Municipal Fund [*Associated Press*] (SAG)
NOHS .... National Oceanographic Hazard Survey (NITA)
NOHS .... National Organization of Human Services [*Defunct*] (EA)
NOHSCP ..... National Oil and Hazardous Substances Contingency Plan [*Environmental Protection Agency*] (ERG)
NOHSE........ National Organization of Human Service Education (EA)
NOHSM....... National Occupational Health Survey of Mining [*Department of Health and Human Services*] (GFGA)
NOHSN .... National Organization of Hospital Schools of Nursing [*Defunct*] (EA)
NOI .... Detroit, MI [*Location identifier FAA*] (FAAL)
NOI .... National Oilwell, Inc. [*NYSE symbol*] (SAG)
NOI .... National Opera Institute (EA)
NOI .... Nation of Islam [*Religion*]
NOI .... NAVWEPS ORDALT Instruction (MCD)
NOI .... Netherlands Offset Industry
NOI .... Net Operating Income
NOI .... Node Operator Interface (NITA)
NOI .... Noise Com, Inc. (SPSG)
NOI .... Nonoperational Intelligence
NOI .... Notice of Inquiry (IEEE)
NOI .... Notice of Intent (MCD)
NOI .... Notice of Intention
NOI .... Not Otherwise Identified (NG)
NOI .... Not Otherwise Indexed
NOIA .... National Ocean Industries Association (EA)
NOIAW .... National Organization of Italian-American Women (EA)
NOIBN......... Not Otherwise Identified [*or Indicated*] by Name [*Military*] (AABC)
NOIBN......... Not Otherwise Indexed by Name [*Tariffs*]
NOIC .... National Oceanographic Instrumentation Center [*National Oceanic and Atmospheric Administration*]
NOIC .... National Osteopathic Interfraternity Council (EA)
NOIC .... Naval Ocean Intelligence Center (DOMA)
NOIC .... Naval Officer-in-Charge
NOIC .... Navy Operational Intelligence Center [*Now Naval Maritime Intelligence Center (NAVMIC)*] (DOMA)
NOICC .... National Occupational Information Coordinating Committee [*Washington, DC*]
NOIE .... Naval Ordnance Inspection Establishment [*Ministry of Defence*] [*British*] (PDAA)
NOII .... Non-Occlusive Intestinal Ischemia [*Medicine*] (DMAA)

No III U......... Northern Illinois University (GAGS)
NOIO .... Naval Ordnance Inspecting Officer
NOIS .... National Occupational Information Service
NOISE .... National Organisation of Initiatives for Social Education [*British*] (DBA)
NOISE .... National Organization for Improving School Environments [*Defunct*] (EA)
NOISE .... National Organization to Insure a Sound-Controlled Environment (EA)
NOISE .... National Organization to Insure Survival Economics (EA)
NOISE .... Noise Information Service
NoiseCT....... Noise Cancellation Technologies, Inc. [*Associated Press*] (SAG)
Noise Reg Rep... Noise Regulation Reporter [*Bureau of National Affairs*] [*A publication*] (DLA)
NOITU .... National Organization of Industrial Trade Unions (EA)
NOIWON ...... National Operations and Intelligence Watch Officers Network (MCD)
NOIZ .... Micronetics, Inc. [*NASDAQ symbol*] (NQ)
NOIZ .... Micronetics Wireless [*NASDAQ symbol*] (TTSB)
NOJ .... Kodiak, AK [*Location identifier FAA*] (FAAL)
NOJ .... New Orleans Jassband (WDAA)
NOJC .... National Oil Jobbers Council [*Later, PMAA*] (EA)
NOJC .... New Orleans Jazz Club (EA)
NOJC .... Northern Oklahoma Junior College
NOJSM .... National Office of Jesuit Social Ministries (EA)
NOK .... Next of Kin
NOK .... Nokia Corp. [*NYSE symbol*] (SAG)
NOK .... Noril'sk [*Former USSR Geomagnetic observatory code*]
NOKD .... Not Our Kind, Dear [*Slang*]
No Kent U..... Northern Kentucky University (GAGS)
Nokia .... Nokia Corp. [*Associated Press*] (SAG)
NOKL .... Northwestern Oklahoma Railroad Co. [*AAR code*]
Nok Mort ..... Nokes' Mortgages and Receiverships [*3rd ed.*] [*1951*] [*A publication*] (DLA)
NOKW .... NAZI Oberkommando der Wehrmacht [*NAZI Armed Forces High Command*] [*World War II German*] (BJA)
NOL .... National Old Lacers [*Later, IOL*] (EA)
NOL .... National Ordnance Laboratory
NOL .... National Overseas Airline Co. [*Egypt*] [*ICAO designator*] (FAAC)
NOL .... Naval Ordnance Laboratory [*Later, NSWC*]
NOL .... Net Operating Loss
NOL .... New Orleans - Loyola [*Louisiana*] [*Seismograph station code, US Geological Survey*] (SEIS)
Nol............ Nolan's English Magistrates' Cases [*A publication*] (DLA)
Nol............ Nolan's English Settlement Cases [*A publication*] (DLA)
NOL .... Normal Operational Loss [*Nuclear energy*]
NOL .... Normal Overload
NOL .... Norse Oriental Lines (MHDW)
NOL .... Northland Oils Ltd. [*Toronto Stock Exchange symbol*]
NOl .... Olean Public Library, Olean, NY [*Library symbol Library of Congress*] (LCLS)
NOLA .... National Association for Outlaw and Lawman History (EA)
NOLA .... Northeastern Ohio Library Association [*Library network*]
NOLAC........ National Organization of Liaison for Allocation of Circuit (NATG)
Nolan......... Nolan on the Poor Laws [*A publication*] (DLA)
Nolan......... Nolan's English Magistrates' Cases [*A publication*] (DLA)
Noland........ Noland Co. [*Associated Press*] (SAG)
NOLAP........ Non-Linear Analysis Program (PDAA)
NOLC .... National Obscenity Law Center (IID)
NOLC .... National One-Liners Club (EA)
NOLC .... Naval Ordnance Laboratory Corona
nol con .... Nolo Contendere [*I Do Not Wish to Contend*] [*Legal term*] [*Latin*] (BARN)
NOID .... Dresser Industries, Inc., Dresser Clark Division, Olean, NY [*Library symbol Library of Congress*] (LCLS)
NOLD .... Noland Co. [*NASDAQ symbol*] (NQ)
NOLDAR ...... Noludar [*A hypnotic*] [*Roche laboratories*] (DAVI)
NOLDC........ Non-Oil Less-Developed Country
NOLEO .... Notice to Law Enforcement Officials
NOIH .... Olean General Hospital, Olean, NY [*Library symbol Library of Congress*] (LCLS)
NOLHGA ...... National Organization of Life and Health Guaranty Associations [*An association*]
NOLM .... Nonlinear Optical Loop Mirror [*Optical computing*]
Nol Mag ...... Nolan's English Magistrates' Cases [*A publication*] (DLA)
NOL-MDI..... Naval Ordnance Laboratory Miss Distance Indicator
NOLO .... No Live Operator (NG)
NOLOC........ No Location (AABC)
NOLPE .... National Organization on Legal Problems of Education (EA)
NOLPE Sch LJ... NOLPE [*National Organization on Legal Problems of Education*] School Law Journal [*A publication*] (DLA)
NOLPE School LJ... NOLPE [*National Organization on Legal Problems of Education*] School Law Journal [*A publication*] (DLA)
NOLPE School L Rep... NOLPE [*National Organization on Legal Problems of Education*] School Law Reporter [*A publication*] (DLA)
Nol PL .... Nolan on the Poor Laws [*A publication*] (DLA)
NOL PROS... Nolle Prosequi [*Unwilling to Prosecute*] [*Legal term Latin*]
NOLS .... National Oceanographic Laboratory System
NOLS .... National Organization for Legal Services (EA)
NOLS .... National Outdoor Leadership School
NOISFH........ Saint Francis Hospital, Olean, NY [*Library symbol Library of Congress*] (LCLS)
NolSL.......... Cattaraugus-Allegany School Library System, Olean, NY [*Library symbol*] [*Library of Congress*] (LCLS)
NOLSW........ National Organization Legal Services Workers (NTPA)
NOLTESTFAC... Naval Ordnance Laboratory Test Facility (SAA)

NOLTF	Naval Ordnance Laboratory Test Facility
NOL/WO	Naval Ordnance Laboratory, White Oak [*Maryland*]
NOM	National Online Meeting [*Conference*] (IT)
NOM	National Organization for Men (EA)
NOM	National Organization for Men Legal Defense and Education Fund
NOM	Natural Organic Matter
NOM	Network Operations Manager [*Manned Space Flight Network, NASA*]
NOM	Network Output Multiplexer [*Telecommunications*] (MCD)
NOM	Newspapers on Microfilm
NOM	Nomad River [*Papua New Guinea*] [*Airport symbol*] (OAG)
NOM	Noman [*Italy*] [*FAA designator*] (FAAC)
NOM	Nome [*Alaska*] [*Seismograph station code, US Geological Survey Closed*] (SEIS)
NOM	Nomenclature (AAG)
NOM	Nominal (AAG)
NOM	Nominate (AFM)
Nom.	Nominating (AL)
NOM	Nominative
NOM	Norbeau Mines, Inc. [*Toronto Stock Exchange symbol*]
NOM	Normal Extraocular Movements [*Ophthalmology*] (DAVI)
NOM	Number of Open Microphones
NOM	Nuveen Missouri Premium Income Municipal Fund [*AMEX symbol*] (SPSG)
NOM	Nuveen MO Prem, Inc. Muni [*AMEX symbol*] (TTSB)
NOM	Opa Locka, FL [*Location identifier FAA*] (FAAL)
NOMA	National Office Management Association [*Later, AMS*]
NOMA	National Oil Marketers Association [*Defunct*] (EA)
NOMA	National Organization of Minority Architects (EA)
NOMAD	National Organisational Management Database
NOMAD	National Organization of Miniaturists and Dollers (EA)
NOMAD	Navy Oceanographic Meteorological Association (USDC)
NOMAD	Navy Oceanographic Meteorological Automatic Device
NOMAD	Navy Operation and Maintenance Aviation Deck (MCD)
NOMAD	Nozzle Materials Application and Design (MCD)
NOMAG	Nonmagnetic (IAA)
NOMb	Nitric Oxide Myoglobin [*Food technology*]
NOMBOS	Nonmine Bottom Objects [*Navy*] (NVT)
NOMC	National Organization for Migrant Children [*Later, NCEMC*] (EA)
nom cons	Nomen Conservandum [*Retained Name*] [*Latin*]
NOMD	Nominated (ABBR)
NOMDA	National Office Machine Dealers Association (EA)
nom dub	Nomen Dubium [*Doubtful Name*] [*Latin*]
NOME	National Origin Minority Education [*New Hampshire Department of Education*] (EDAC)
NOMEE	Nominee [*Legal shorthand*] (LWAP)
NOMEN	Nomenclature (AFM)
NOMES	New England Offshore Mining Experiment Study (NOAA)
NOMG	Nominating (ABBR)
NOMI	Nonocclusive Mesenteric Infarction [*Medicine*] (AAMN)
NOMI	Nonocclusive Mesenteric Ischemia [*Medicine*]
No Mich U	Northern Michigan University (GAGS)
nom illeg	Nomen Illegitimum [*Illegitimate Name*] [*Latin*]
NOMIN	Nominative (WDAA)
nom inval	Nomen Invalidum [*Name Not Valid*] [*Latin*]
NOMIS	National Online Manpower Information System [*Manpower Services Commission*] [*Information service or system*] (IID)
NOMIS	Naval Ordnance Management Information System
NOMIS	Nuclear Operations and Maintenance Information Service (IID)
NOML	Nominal (ROG)
NOMLM	Nominalism (ABBR)
NOMLT	Nominalist (ABBR)
NOMLY	Nominally (ABBR)
NOMMA	National Ornamental and Miscellaneous Metals Association (EA)
NOM MUD ...	Nomen Nudum [*A Name without Designation*] [*Latin*] (BABM)
NOMN	Nomination
nom nov	Nomen Novum [*New Name*] [*Latin*]
nom nud	Nomen Nudum [*Invalid Name*] [*Biology, taxonomy*] [*Latin*]
NOMOP	No Record of Mustering-Out Payment (DNAB)
NOMOTC	National Organization of Mothers of Twins Clubs (EA)
nom prov	Nomen Provisiorum [*Provisional Name*] [*Latin*]
NOMR	Nominator (ABBR)
nom rej	Nomen Rejiciendum [*Rejected Name*] [*Latin*]
NOMRP	Normal Return Point (MCD)
NOMS	Network Operations Management System [*Computer science*]
NOMS	Nuclear Operations Monitoring System (MCD)
NOMSA	National Office Machine Service Association [*Paramount, CA*] (EA)
NOMSS	National Operational Meteorological Satellite System
NOMSS	Navy Oceanographic and Meteorological Support System (MCD)
nom superfl...	Nomen Superfluum [*Superfluous Name*] [*Latin*]
NOMTF	Naval Ordnance Missile Test Facility
NOMTS	Naval Ordnanace Missile Test Station [*White Sands Missile Range, NM*] (GRD)
NOMUS	Nordisk Musikkomite [*Nordic Music Committee*] (EAIO)
NOMV	Nominative (ABBR)
NOMW	National Organizational of Mall Walkers
NOMW	National Organization of Mall Walkers (EA)
NON	National Organization for Non-Parents [*Later, NAOP*]
NON	Nonouti [*Kiribati*] [*Airport symbol*] (OAG)
NON	Normine Resources Ltd. [*Vancouver Stock Exchange symbol*]
NON	North Norway (NATG)
NON	Notice of Noncompliance (EPA)
No N	Novae Narrationes [*New Counts*] [*1516*] [*A publication*] (DLA)
NONA	Notice of Nonavailability
Nonacq	Nonacquiescence by Commissioner in a Tax Court or Board of Tax Appeals Decision [*United States*] [*Legal term*] (DLA)

NONADD	Nonadditivity [*Statistics*]
NON AL OCC...	Non Alibi Occurrit [*It Occurs in No Other Place*] [*Latin*] (ROG)
NON-BUS	Nonbusiness [*IRS*]
NONCAN	Noncancellable [*Insurance*]
NONCIT	Noncitizen (AABC)
NON-CM	Noncumulative (ABBR)
NONCNST	Nonconsent
NONCOHO ...	Noncoherent Oscillator (MCD)
noncoll	Noncollinear (MHDI)
NONCOM	Noncommissioned Officer [*Military*]
NON COM ...	Non Compos Mentis [*Not in Sound Mind*] [*Latin*] (ROG)
NONCOMECM...	Noncommunications Electronics Countermeasures [*Military*] (AABC)
NONCOMJAM...	Noncommunications Jamming [*Military*] (AABC)
NONCON	Nonconformist
NON CUL	Non Culpabilis [*Not Guilty*] [*Latin*] (ROG)
NON-CUM	Non-Cumulative [*Business term*]
Non-cum	Noncumulative (EBF)
NOND	Non Detected [*Laboratory science*] (DAVI)
NONE	National Organization for Non-Enumeration (EA)
NONE	New Orleans & Northeastern R. R. [*AAR code*]
NONEG	Negative Replies Neither Required nor Desired
NOneoC	Hartwick College, Oneonta, NY [*Library symbol Library of Congress*] (LCLS)
NOneoU	State University of New York, College at Oneonta, Oneonta, NY [*Library symbol Library of Congress*] (LCLS)
NONF	Nonfasting [*Laboratory science*] (DAVI)
NONFLMB	Nonflammable
NON-FRAG ...	Non-Fragmentation [*Bomb*]
NONGAP	Nonlinear Grain Analysis Program (MCD)
N/ONI	Navy/Office of Naval Intelligence (AAG)
NONLIN	Nonlinear (IAA)
NONMAGCI...	Nonmagnetic Cast Iron (IAA)
NON-MSA	Non-Standard Metropolitan Statistical Area (OICC)
NON/NOV	Notices of Noncompliance/Notices of Violation [*Navy*]
NON-NSN	Not Assigned a National Stock Number
NON OBS	Non Obstante [*Notwithstanding*] [*Latin*]
NON OBST ..	Non Obstante [*Notwithstanding*] [*Latin*] (ROG)
NONP	Nonpackaged
NONP	Nonpareil (ADA)
NONP	Non-Precision Approach Runway [*Aviation*] (DA)
NONPAR	Nonparticipating [*Insurance*]
Non-Par	Non-Participating Provider
NONPAYT	Nonpayment (ROG)
NONPERF	Nonperforated (ABBR)
NONPF	National Organization of Nurse Practitioner Faculties (NTPA)
nonpoly	Nonpolychrome (VRA)
NONPROF	Nonprofessional
NON PROS ..	Non Prosequitur [*Does Not Prosecute*] [*Latin*]
N/ONR	Navy/Office of Naval Research (AAG)
Non-REM	Nonrapid Eye Movement [*Type of sleep*] (MAE)
NON REP	Non Repetatur [*Do Not Repeat*] [*Pharmacy*]
Non Repetat...	Non Repetatur [*Do Not Repeat*] [*Pharmacy*]
NON RES	Nonresident (WDAA)
NONRSNT ...	Nonresonant (IAA)
NONS	Nonspecific [*Laboratory science*] (DAVI)
NONSAP	Nonlinear Structural Analysis Program [*Computer science*]
non segs	Nonsegmented Neutrophils [*Medicine*] (CPH)
NON SEQ	Non Sequitur [*It Does Not Follow*] [*Latin*]
NONSKED	Nonscheduled (ABBR)
NON-SLIP	Non-Speech Language Initiation Program
NONSTAND...	Nonstandard (WDAA)
NONSTD	Nonstandard
NONStY	Non-Standard Yiddish (BJA)
NONSUB	Nonsubmarine [*Navy*] (NVT)
NONSYN	Nonsynchronous
NONTSDSL...	Not Included in Technical Service Demand Stockage Lists [*Army*] (AABC)
NONTT	Nonentity (ABBR)
NONUM	Notional Number (NVT)
non-vis	Nonvisualization (DAVI)
NON-VON	Non-Von Neumann [*Experimental computer, not based on the principles of Von Neumann computer design, under construction at Columbia University*]
NON-VTG	Non-Voting [*Business term*]
Non-vtg	Nonvoting (EBF)
NOO	Naoro [*Papua New Guinea*] [*Airport symbol*] (OAG)
NOO	National Organization Order (USDC)
NOO	Naval Oceanographic Office [*Also known as NAVOCEANO; formerly, HO, NHO, USNHO*]
NOO	Naval Oceanographic Office, Washington, DC [*Inactive*] [*OCLC symbol*] (OCLC)
NOO	Nevada Operations Office [*Department of Energy*]
NOO	Notice of Obligation [*Military*] (AFM)
NOOB	Not Out of Bed [*Medicine*] (DAVI)
NOOD	National Offshore One-Design [*Boating regatta*]
NOOD	Nitric Oxide Optical Detector
NoodKid	Noodle Kidoodle, Inc. [*Associated Press*] (SAG)
No of Cas Madras...	Notes of Cases at Madras (Strange) [*A publication*] (DLA)
NOOIAC	National Offshore Operations Industry Advisory Committee [*Coast Guard*]
Nooney	Nooney Realty Trust, Inc. [*Associated Press*] (SAG)
NOOOA	NORAD Office of Operational Analysis (IAA)
NO-OP	Flight Not Operating [*Travel industry*]
NOOP	No Operation [*Computer science*]

no-op	No Operator [Telemarketing] (WDMC)
NOOS	Nuclear Orbit-to-Orbit Shuttle [NASA]
NOO-SP	Naval Oceanographic Office Special Publication
NoOU	Not One of Us [Slang]
NoOU	Universitetet i Oslo [University of Oslo], Oslo, Norway [Library symbol Library of Congress] (LCLS)
NoOU-M	Universitetet i Oslo, Matematisk-Naturvitenskapelige Fakultet [University of Oslo, Department of Mathematics and Natural Sciences], Oslo, Norway [Library symbol Library of Congress] (LCLS)
NOP	Brooklyn, NY [Location identifier FAA] (FAAL)
NOP	National Onderzoek Persmedia [Database] [Stichting Nationaal Onderzoek Persmedia] [Netherlands] [Information service or system] (CRD)
NOP	National Opinion Poll
NOP	National Oracy Project (AIE)
NOP	National Outpatient Profile [Medicine] (MEDA)
NOP	Naval Oceanographic Publication
NOP	Naval Officer Procurement
NOP	Naval Ordnance Plant
NOP	Navigation Operating Procedure
NOP	Navy Objectives Plan
NOP	Near Object Probe (SAA)
NOP	Net Orders Processed [Business term] (DOAD)
NOP	Network Operations Procedure [Manned Space Flight Network, NASA]
NOP	Newscorp Overseas Ltd. [NYSE symbol] (SPSG)
NOP	Noncoherent Optical Processor
NOP	Nonoperating (KSC)
NOP	No Operation [Computer science]
NOP	Normal Operating Procedure (NRCH)
NOP	North Oscura Peak [White Sands Missile Range] [Army]
NOP	Notice of Procurement [Navy] (NG)
NOP	Not Otherwise Provided
nop	Not Otherwise Provided (EBF)
NOP	Not Our Publication
NOP	Novair-Aviacao Geral SA [Portugal ICAO designator] (FAAC)
NOP	Nuclear Operations (COE)
NOP	Nuclear Operations Plan (MCD)
NOP	Nuclear Ordnance Platoon [Marine Corps] (NVT)
NOP	Null Operation [Computer science]
NOP	Number of Openings [Technical drawings]
NOP	Number of Passes (MSA)
NOP	Numerical Oceanographic Prediction (PDAA)
NOPA	National Office Products Association (EA)
NOPA	National Oilseed Processors Association (EA)
NOPA	Network Operations Performance Analysis [Manned Space Flight Network, NASA]
NOPAA	National Office Products Association of Australia
NOPABCCE	National Organization for Professional Advancement of Black Chemists and Chemical Engineers (EA)
NOPAC	North Pacific [Aviation] (FAAC)
NOPAR	Do Not Pass to Air Defense RADAR [Air Traffic Control] (FAAC)
NOPAT	Net Operating Profit after Tax
NOPB	New Orleans Public Belt Railroad [AAR code]
NOPC	Naval Oceanographic Processing Center (DOMA)
NOPCL	Naval Officer Personnel Circular Letter
NOPCO	National Oil Products Co. [Later, NOPCO Chemical Co.]
NOPD	New Orleans Police Department [Initialism also used as title of TV series]
NOPE	National Organization of Poll-Ettes (EA)
NOPE	Naturists and Nudists Opposing Pornographic Exploitation (EA)
NOPE	New Orleans Port of Embarkation
NOPE	No Promotion [Refers to lack of publicity in the record business]
NOPE	Not on Planet Earth [Waste management slang]
NOPEC	Non-OPEC [Oil producing countries which are not members of OPEC]
NOPEOL	National Organization to Promote English as the Official Language (EA)
NOPES	Non-Occupational Pesticide Exposure Study [Environmental Protection Agency] (GFGA)
NOPF	National Oceanographic Processing Facility (DOMA)
NOPF	Naval Oceanographic Processing Facility (ANA)
NOPF	Naval Ordnance Plant, Forest Park [Illinois]
nopf	Not Otherwise Provided For (EBF)
NOPHN	National Organization for Public Health Nursing (HGAA)
NOPHYSRET	Not Required to Take New Physical Provided No Material Change since Recent Retirement Physical [Military]
NOPI	Naval Ordnance Plant Institute (MCD)
NOPL	Naval Ordnance Plant, Louisville [Kentucky]
NOPMS	Network-Oriented Project Management System (PDAA)
NOP-N	Nordiska Publiceringsnamnden for Naturvetenskap [Nordic Publishing Board in Science] (EAIO)
NOPN	Normally Open [Switch]
NOPO	Nuclear Operations Planning Office (COE)
NOPOL	No Pollution
NOPPA	National Ocean Pollution Planning Act of 1978
NOPPA	Nitroso(oxopropyl)propylamine [Organic chemistry]
NOPPO	National Ocean Pollution Program Office (GNE)
NOPPrA	Newscp Pverseas Ltd Pref [NYSE symbol] (TTSB)
NOPPrB	Newscp Overseas Ltd Adj Pref [NYSE symbol] (TTSB)
NOPR	Notice of Proposed Rule Making [Federal agencies]
NOPRI	National Orthotic and Prosthetic Research Institute (EA)
NOPROCAN	If Not Already Processed, Orders Cancelled [Military]
NOPS	National Ocean Policy Study [US Senate]
NOPS	Nike Operator Proficiency Scale [Army]
NOPS	Noncoherent Optical Processing System
NOPT	No Procedure Turn Required [Aviation]
NOPUS	National Occupant Protection Use Survey [NHTSA] (TAG)
NoPVDM	N'Oubliez Pas Vos Decorations Maconniques [Do Not Forget Your Masonic Regalia] [Freemasonry] [French]
NOPWC	National Old People's Welfare Council (NADA)
NO-PYR	N-Nitrosopyrrolidine [Also, NYPR] [Biochemistry, organic chemistry]
NOQUIS	Nucleonic Oil Quantity Indication System [Air Force]
NOR	AS Norving [Norway ICAO designator] (FAAC)
NOR	National Organization for Rehabilitation [British]
nor	Nitrogen ohne Radikal [Chemical prefix]
NOR	Nitrogen Oxide Reduction [Research in automotive air pollution]
NOR	Nonoperational Ready (NVT)
NOR	Non-Ordinary Resident [British]
NOR	Noradrenaline [or Norepinephrine] [Endocrinology] (DAVI)
NOR	Noranda, Inc. [Toronto Stock Exchange symbol Vancouver Stock Exchange symbol]
NOR	Norbornadiene [Also, NBD] [Organic chemistry]
NOR	Nord [Greenland] [Seismograph station code, US Geological Survey Closed] (SEIS)
NOR	Nordfjordur [Iceland] [Airport symbol] (OAG)
NOR	Nordisk Organ for Reinforskning [Nordic Council of Reindeer Research] [Norway] (EAIO)
NOR	Norhtwestern Corp. [NYSE symbol] [Formerly, Northwestern Pub. Svc.]
Nor	Norma [Constellation]
NOR	Normal (KSC)
NOR	Norman
NOR	Normandale Community College, Bloomington, MN [OCLC symbol] (OCLC)
NOR	North
NOR	North Central Airlines, Inc.
NOR	Norway [ANSI three-letter standard code] (CNC)
Nor	Norway (VRA)
nor	Norwegian [MARC language code Library of Congress] (LCCP)
NOR	Norwich [City in England] (ROG)
NOR	Norwich [Diocesan abbreviation] [Connecticut] (TOCD)
NOR	Notice of Readiness [Shipping]
NOR	Notice of Revision
NOR	Not Operationally Ready [Military] (AFM)
NOR	Not Or [Logical operator] [Computer science]
NOR	Nucleolar Organizer Region [in chromosomes]
NOR	Nucleolus Organizer Region [Genetics] (DOG)
NOR	Number of Rounds [Military] (CINC)
NOR	San Diego, CA [Location identifier FAA] (FAAL)
NORA	National Oil Recyclers Association (GNE)
NORA	National Online Regulatory Access [Data Development, Inc.] [Information service or system] (CRD)
NORA	Norwegian Zero Power Reactor Assembly
NORAC	No Radio Contact [Aviation]
NORAD	North American Aerospace Defense Command [FAA] (TAG)
NORAD	North American Air Defense [Integrated United States-Canada command]
NORAD	North American Air Defense Command (AAGC)
NORAD	Norwegian Agency for International Development
NORADCOC	North American Air Defense Combat Operations Center [Military] (AFM)
NORAD CPX	North American Air Defense Command Post Exercise (SAA)
NORADCRU	North American Air Defense Orientation Cruise (NVT)
NORADEX	North American Air Defense Exercise (NVT)
Noradr	Noradrenaline [Norepinephrine] [Endocrinology] (DAVI)
NorAE	Norwegian Antarctic Expedition [1956-]
NORAID	Irish Northern Aid Committee (EA)
NORAID	Norwegian Agency for International Development
NORAIL	Northrop Overhead Rail Assembly and Installation Line (SAA)
NORAIM	Not Operationally Ready, Aircraft Intermediate Maintenance [Military] (DNAB)
Noram	Noram Energy Corp. [Associated Press] (SAG)
Noram	Noram Financing I [Associated Press] (SAG)
NoramE	Noram Energy Corp. [Formerly, Arkla, Inc.] [Associated Press] (SAG)
Norand	Norand Corp. [Associated Press] (SAG)
NORAP	Northwestern Alumni Players
NORAPS	Navy Operational Regional Atmospheric Prediction System (MCD)
NORASDEFLANT	North American Antisubmarine Defense Force, Atlantic (NATG)
NORATS	Navy Operational Radio and Telephone Switchboard (NVT)
NOrb	Orangeburg Public Library, Orangeburg, NY [Library symbol Library of Congress] (LCLS)
NORBA	National Off-Road Bicycle Association [Later, USCF] (EA)
NOrbR	Rockland State Hospital, Medical Library, Orangeburg, NY [Library symbol Library of Congress] (LCLS)
NORBS	Northern Base Section [Corsica]
NORC	National Oceanographic Records Center
NORC	National Opinion Research Center [University of Chicago]
NORC	Naturally Occurring Retirement Community
NORC	Naval Ordnance Research Calculator [or Computer] [Naval Ordnance Proving Ground]
Norc	Norcross' Reports [23-24 Nevada] [A publication] (DLA)
NORC	Normal Curve [Laboratory science] (DAVI)
Norc	Normally Occurring Retirement Community
NORC	Nuclear Ordnance Record Card (NVT)
NOrc	Orchard Park Public Library, Orchard Park, NY [Library symbol Library of Congress] (LCLS)
NorCACHA	North Carolina Automated Clearing House Association (TBD)
NORCALSEC	Northern California Section, Western Sea Frontier

NORCANUKUS... Norway, Canada, United Kingdom, United States (DOMA)
NORCAP ...... National Organisation of Counselling Adoptees and Their Parents [British] (DBA)
NOrcE .... Erie Community College-South, Orchard Park, NY [Library symbol Library of Congress] (LCLS)
NorcEB........ Erie-Cattaraugus Board of Cooperative Educational Services, Orchard Park, NY [Library symbol] [Library of Congress] (LCLS)
NORCO .... National Oil Recovery Corp.
NorCran ...... Northland Cranberries [Associated Press] (SAG)
NORCUS ...... Northwest College and University Association for Science [Richland, WA] [Department of Energy]
NORD......... Bureau of Ordnance Publication [Later, NAVORD] [Navy]
NORD......... National Organization for Rare Disorders (EA)
NORD......... Naval Ordnance
NORD......... Norsk Data (NITA)
NORD......... Not Ordered, This Part of Package (DAVI)
NORDA .... Naval Oceanographic Research and Development Administration [USA] [Marine science] (OSRA)
NORDA .... Naval Ocean Research and Development Activity [Bay St. Louis, MS]
NORDEK ...... Nordic Customs Union (EBF)
NORDEK ...... Norway, Denmark, Finland, Sweden [Nordic Economic Community] [Trade bloc]
NORDEL ...... Organization for Nordic Electrical Cooperation (EA)
NORDIATRANS... Association for Nordic Transplant and Dialysis Personnel (EAIO)
Nordic........ Nordic American Tanker Shipping Ltd. [Associated Press] (SAG)
NORDICOM... Nordic Documentation Center for Mass Communication Research [Database ori ginator] [Finland Information service or system] (IID)
NORDINFO... Nordiska Samarbetsorganet for Vetenskaplig Information [Nordic Council for Scientific Information and Research Libraries] [Finland] (EAIO)
NORDITA ..... Nordic Institute for Theoretic Atomic Physics [Later, NIIP] (EY)
NORDO .... No Radio
Nord P .... Nordic Pharmacopoeia [A publication]
NordPac...... Nord Pacific Ltd. [Associated Press] (SAG)
NordPc........ Nord Pacific Ltd. [Associated Press] (SAG)
NordRs........ Nord Resources Corp. [Associated Press] (SAG)
NORDSAT ..... Scandinavian Countries Broadcast Satellite (MCD)
Nordser........ Nordisk Samkatalog foer Seriella Medicinska Publikationer [Karolinska Institutets Bibliotek och Informationscentral] [Sweden Information service or system] (CRD)
Nordsn......... Nordson Corp. [Associated Press] (SAG)
Nordst......... Nordstrom, Inc. [Associated Press] (SAG)
NORDTEL..... Nordiskt Samarbete Inom Telekommunikation [Nordic Cooperation on Telecommunications] [Finland] (EAIO)
NORDUnet ... [The] Nordic University Network (TNIG)
NORE......... Northeast
NOREASTNAVFACENGCOM... Northeast Division Naval Facilities Engineering Command
NOREC......... No Record
NOREC......... Northern Environmental Council [Defunct] (EA)
NORECHAN... Northeast Subarea Channel (NATG)
NOREF........ No Reference
NOREP........ No Reply Received
NOREP........ Not Reportable
NORESS....... Norwegian Regional Seismic Array
Norex......... Norex America, Inc. [Associated Press] (SAG)
NOREX........ Nuclear Operational Readiness Exercise (NVT)
NORF......... Norfolk [County in England]
Norf........... Norfolk [County in England] (ODBW)
NORFISH ..... North Pacific Fisheries Project (NOAA)
NORFLK....... Norfolk [County in England]
NORFORM .... Not Releasable to Foreign Nationals
Nor Fr........ Norman French [Language, etc.] (DLA)
NORGD .... National Organization for the Rights of Guide Dogs (EA)
NORGLAC ... Northern Great Lakes Area Council
NORGRAPH... Northeast Graphics Conference and Printing Show [Printing Industry Association of Connecticut and Western Massachusetts] (TSPED)
NORI.......... National Office for the Rights of the Indigent [Later, LDF]
NORIANE ..... Normes et Reglements Informations Automatisees en Ligne [Automated Standards and Regulations Information Online] [Database French Association for Standardization] [Information service or system] (IID)
NORIF........ Natural Oocyte Retrieval Intravaginal Fertilization [Alternative to traditional in-vitro fertilization (IVF)] (PAZ)
NORIMB....... Norimberge [Nuremberg] [Imprint] (ROG)
NORIP......... NORAD Intelligence Plan [Military] (AABC)
NORIS......... North Island (MUGU)
NORIV......... No Arrival Report [Aviation] (FAAC)
NORK........ [The] New Orleans Rhythm Kings [Jazz band]
NORKZ........ Norsk-Data AS (MHDW)
Norland........ Norland Medical Systems, Inc. [Associated Press] (SAG)
NORLANT ..... North Atlantic Area (MUGU)
NORLANTAACS... North Atlantic Airways and Air Communications Service (SAA)
NORLANTEX... North Atlantic - Training Exercise (MCD)
NorldCr........ Northland Cranberries, Inc. [Associated Press] (SAG)
NORLEU....... Norleucine [A nonessential amino acid] [Biochemistry]
norleu........ Norleucine [Biochemistry] (DAVI)
NORM......... National Office Resources Management [IRS]
NORM......... National Organization for Raw Materials (EA)
NORM......... Naturally Occurring Radioactive Material (FFDE)
Norm .... Norma [Constellation]
NORM......... Normal [or Normalize] (AAG)
NORM......... Norman [or Normandy]

NORM......... Normative Operating Reporting Method
NORM......... Normetal [AAR code]
NORM......... Not Operationally Ready Maintenance [Military] (NG)
NORM......... Not Operational Ready Materiel [Military] (AFIT)
NORM......... Nuclear Operational Readiness Maneuver (NVT)
NORM......... Nuclear Ordnance Readiness Manpower
NORMARC ... Norwegian MARC (NITA)
NORMATERM... Normalisation, Automatisation de la Terminologie [Standardization and Automation of Terminology] [Databank] [France] [Information service or system] (IID)
NORMCLSD... Normally Closed [Switch] [Electronics] (IAA)
NORMET...... Normetanephrine [Also, Methylnorepinephrine] [Biochemistry] (AAMN)
NORM(F)..... Not Operationally Ready Maintenance - Flyable [Military] (MCD)
NORM(G).... Not Operationally Ready Maintenance - Grounded [Military] (MCD)
NORML....... National Organization for the Reform of Marijuana Laws (EA)
NORML....... National Organization for the Reinforcement of Marijuana Laws (NADA)
NORML....... National Organization for the Repeal of Marijuana Laws (NADA)
NORML....... Normal (DAVI)
NORMOPN... Normally Open [Switch] [Electronics] (IAA)
NORMSHOR... Normal Tour of Shore Duty
NORO......... Not Operationally Ready Other [Military] (AFM)
NOROEC ...... NORAD Operational Employment Concept [Military] (AABC)
NORP......... New Oil Reference Price
NORP......... Nord Pacific Ltd. [NASDAQ symbol] (SAG)
NORPAC ...... Naval Overhaul and Repair Pacific (MUGU)
NORPAC ...... Northern Pacific Railway Co.
NORPAC ...... North Pacific [Military]
Nor Pat....... Norman. Letters Patent [1853] [A publication] (DLA)
NORPAX ...... North Pacific Experiment [National Science Foundation]
NORPI......... No Pilot Balloon Observation Will Be Filed Next Collection Unless Weather Changes Siginificantly [NWS] (FAAC)
NOrpOHi ...... Oyster Pond Historical Society, Orient Point, NY [Library symbol Library of Congress] (LCLS)
Nor Pro Pr ... North's Probate Practice [Illinois] [A publication] (DLA)
NORPY....... Nord Pacific Ltd ADR [NASDAQ symbol] (TTSB)
NORQR .... NORAD Qualitative Requirement [Military] (AABC)
NORR......... No Reply Received (FAAC)
Norr........... Norris' Reports [82-96 Pennsylvania] [A publication] (DLA)
NORRA .... National Off-Road Racing Association
NORRD .... No Reply Received (NOAA)
Norrell........ Norrell Corp. [Associated Press] (SAG)
NORRF........ Norris Communications [NASDAQ symbol] (TTSB)
Norris .... Norris' Reports [82-96 Pennsylvania] [A publication] (DLA)
Norris & L Perpetuities... Norris and Leach on Rule Against Perpetuities [A publication] (DLA)
NorrisC........ Norris Communications Corp. [Associated Press] (SAG)
Norris Seamen... Norris' Law of Seamen [A publication] (DLA)
Norr Peake... Norris' Edition of Peake's Law of Evidence [A publication] (DLA)
NORRS .... Naval Operational Readiness Reporting Systems
NORS......... National Organization for River Sports (EA)
NORS......... New Old Replacement Stock [Automotive parts]
NORS......... Not Operationally Ready for Service [Military] (VNW)
NORS......... Not Operationally Ready Supply [Military]
NORS......... Not Operationally Ready System [Military]
NORSAIR .... Not Operationally Ready Supply Aviation Items Report [Military]
NORSAR ...... Norwegian Seismic Array [Royal Norwegian Council for Scientific and Industrial Research]
NORSAT....... Norwegian Satellite System
NORSEACENT... North Sea Subarea (NATG)
NORSEC....... Northern Security Exhibition [British] (ITD)
NORSEX....... Norwegian Remote Sensing Experiment [in marginal ice zone]
NORSF........ Not Operationally Ready Supply Flyable [Military] (MCD)
NORS-G .... Not Operationally Ready for Service - Grounded (VNW)
NORSG .... Not Operationally Ready Supply Grounded [Military] (NG)
NORSIB....... NORAD Space Intelligence Bulletin [DoD]
Norsk........ Norsk Hydro [Associated Press] (SAG)
NORSN .... Not Operationally Ready Supply Nongrounded [Military] (NG)
NORSNET .... National Oceanographic Reference Station Network (NOAA)
NORSOLS .... Northern Solomons Area
NORST....... No Restrictions (FAAC)
Norstan...... Norstan, Inc. [Associated Press] (SAG)
NORSTAR .... Norden Search Terrain Avoidance RADAR (SAA)
NorSys....... Nortech Systems, Inc. [Associated Press] (SAG)
NORT......... Nuclear Ordnance Readiness Test (NVT)
NORTAM..... Northrop Terminal Attrition Model (SAA)
NORTEB...... Norwegian Telecommunications Users Group
Nortek........ Nortek, Inc. [Associated Press] (SAG)
Nortel .... Northern Telecom [Canada]
NorTel........ Northern Telecom Ltd. [Associated Press] (SAG)
Nortel100 ... Nortel Inversora SA [Associated Press] (SAG)
North .... Northampton County Reporter [Pennsylvania] [A publication] (DLA)
NORTH....... Northerly (ABBR)
NORTH....... Northern (ABBR)
NORTH....... Northern Operations of Rail Transportation and Highways [Alaska]
North .... Reports Tempore Northington [Eden. English Chancery Reports] [1757-67] [A publication] (DLA)
NORTHAG .... North [European] Army Group [NATO]
Northam ...... Northampton Law Reporter [Pennsylvania] [A publication] (DLA)
Northam Law Rep... Northampton County Law Reporter [Pennsylvania] [A publication] (DLA)
Northam L Rep... Northampton Law Reporter [Pennsylvania] [A publication] (DLA)
Northamp Co Repr... Northampton County Reporter [Pennsylvania] [A publication] (DLA)

Northampton Co Rep... Northampton County Reporter [*Pennsylvania*] [*A publication*] (DLA)
North & G.... North and Guthrie's Appeals Reports [*68-80 Missouri*] [*A publication*] (DLA)
NORTHANTS... Northamptonshire [*County in England*]
Northbay...... Northbay Financial Corp. [*Associated Press*] (SAG)
North Car J Int'l L & Comm... North Carolina Journal of International Law and Commercial Regulation [*A publication*] (DLA)
North Carolina College LJ... North Carolina College Law Journal [*A publication*] (DLA)
North Co ...... Northampton County Reporter [*Pennsylvania*] [*A publication*] (DLA)
North Co Rep... Northampton County Reporter [*Pennsylvania*] [*A publication*] (DLA)
North Co R (PA)... Northampton County Reporter [*Pennsylvania*] [*A publication*] (DLA)
NORTHD ...... Northumberland [*County in England*] (ROG)
North Ken'y SL Rev... Northern Kentucky State Law Review [*A publication*] (DLA)
NORTHM...... Northumberland (ABBR)
NORTH'N .... Northampton [*City in England*] (ROG)
Northop U.... Northop University (GAGS)
North Pr....... North's Probate Practice [*Illinois*] [*A publication*] (DLA)
Northrim...... Northrim Bank [*Associated Press*] (SAG)
Northrop ULJ... Northrop University. Law Journal of Aerospace, Energy, and the Environment [*A publication*] (DLA)
North St L... North. Study of the Laws [*1824*] [*A publication*] (DLA)
NORTHUM ... Northumberland [*County in England*]
Northum ...... Northumberland County Legal News [*Pennsylvania*] [*A publication*] (DLA)
NORTHUMB... Northumberland [*County in England*] (ROG)
Northumb .... Northumberland [*County in England*] (ODBW)
Northumb Co... Northumberland County Legal News [*Pennsylvania*] [*A publication*] (DLA)
Northumberland Co Leg Jour... Northumberland Legal Journal [*Pennsylvania*] [*A publication*] (DLA)
Northumberland LJ... Northumberland Legal Journal [*Pennsylvania*] [*A publication*] (DLA)
Northumb Legal J... Northumberland Legal Journal [*Pennsylvania*] [*A publication*] (DLA)
Northumb LJ... Northumberland Legal Journal News [*Pennsylvania*] [*A publication*] (DLA)
Northumb LN... Northumberland Legal Journal [*Pennsylvania*] [*A publication*] (DLA)
Northum Co Leg N... Northumberland County Legal News [*Pennsylvania*] [*A publication*] (ILCA)
Northum Leg J... Northumberland Legal Journal [*Pennsylvania*] [*A publication*] (DLA)
Northum Leg J (PA)... Northumberland Legal Journal [*Pennsylvania*] [*A publication*] (DLA)
Northum Leg N (PA)... Northumberland County Legal News [*Pennsylvania*] [*A publication*] (DLA)
Northwestern U... Northwestern University (GAGS)
North WLJ ... Northwestern Law Journal [*A publication*] (DLA)
Northw Rep... Northwestern Reporter [*Commonly cited NW*] [*A publication*] (DLA)
NORTIC........ NORAD [*North American Aerospace Defense Command*] Technical Intelligence Center (DOMA)
NORTLANT... North Atlantic
Nort LC........ Norton's Leading Cases on Inheritance [*India*] [*A publication*] (DLA)
NortMc........ Norton McNaughton, Inc. [*Associated Press*] (SAG)
Norton .... Norton's Cases on Hindu Law of Inheritance [*1870-71*] [*India*] [*A publication*] (DLA)
NORTR........ Nortronics Corp.
NortrpG........ Northrop Grumman Corp. [*Formerly, Northrup Corp.*] [*Associated Press*] (SAG)
NorTrst .... Northern Trust Corp. [*Associated Press*] (SAG)
NorTst........ Northern Trust Corp. [*Associated Press*] (SAG)
NORVA........ Norfolk, Virginia [*Navy*]
NORVAGRP... Norfolk, Virginia Group [*Navy*]
NORVAL....... Norvaline [*Biochemistry*]
NORVIC....... Norvicensis [*Norwich*] [*Imprint*] (ROG)
NORVIPS ..... Northrup Voice Interruption Priority System (MUGU)
NORW......... Norway [*or Norwegian*]
NORW......... Norwich [*City in England*] (ROG)
NORWEB...... Northwestern Electricity Board (NADA)
Norweb .... NORWEB PLC [*Associated Press*] (SAG)
NORWELD ... Northwest Library District [*Library network*]
NORWESSEAFRON... Northwestern Sea Frontier
NORWESSEC... Northwestern Sector, Western Sea Frontier
Norwest........ Norwest Corp. [*Associated Press*] (SAG)
NORWESTLANT... Northwest Atlantic [*Military*]
NORWESTNAVFACENGCOM... Northwest Division Naval Facilities Engineering Command
NorwFn........ Norwich Financial Corp. [*Associated Press*] (SAG)
NORWICH.... Knickers Off Ready When I Come Home [*Correspondence*] (DSUE)
NorwlkSv ..... Norwalk Savings Society [*Associated Press*] (SAG)
Norwood ...... Norwood Promotional Products [*Associated Press*] (SAG)
Norwt........ Norwest Corp. [*Associated Press*] (SAG)
NORWY........ NORWEB PLC [*NASDAQ symbol*] (SAG)
NOS .... National Ocean Service [*Formerly, Coast and Geodetic Survey*] [*Washington, DC National Oceanic and Atmospheric Administration*]
NOS .... National Ocean Survey. (NOAA)
NOS .... National Office Staff [*American Occupational Therapy Association*]
NOS .... National Operational Satellite
NOS .... National Oratorio Society [*Defunct*] (EA)
NOS .... National Osteoporosis Society [*British*]
NOS .... NATO Office of Security (NATG)

NOS .... Naval Ordnance Station
NOS .... Nederlandse Omroep Stichting [*Radio and television network*] [*Netherlands*]
NOS .... Network Operating System
NOS .... Network Queueing System [*Computer science*] (CIST)
NOS .... New Old Stock [*Automotive parts*]
NOS .... Night Observation Sight [*Air Force*]
NOS .... Night Observation System [*Navy*] (CAAL)
NOS .... Night Operation System [*Aviation*]
NOS .... Nimbus Operational System
NOS .... Nine O'Clock Service (WDAA)
NOS .... Nitric Oxide Synthase [*An enzyme*]
NOS .... Non-Ocular Source [*Physiology*]
NOS .... Nonoriented Satellite
NOS .... Nopaline Synthase [*An enzyme*]
NOS .... Northern State College Library, Aberdeen, SD [*OCLC symbol*] (OCLC)
NOS .... Northstar Resources Ltd. [*Toronto Stock Exchange symbol*]
NOS .... Norway Airlines [*ICAO designator*] (FAAC)
NOS .... Nosing (ABBR)
NOS .... Nossi-Be [*Madagascar*] [*Airport symbol*] (OAG)
NOS .... Nostalgia [*A radio station format*] (WDMC)
NOS .... Not Off Sanctions (WDAA)
NOS .... Not on Shelf (ADA)
NOS .... Not Otherwise Specified (AFM)
NOS .... Not Otherwise Stated
nos.............. Not Otherwise Stated (EBF)
NOS .... Nouvel Ordre Social [*New Social Order*] [*Switzerland*] (PD)
NOS .... Number of Stops (IAA)
NOS .... Numbers (AAG)
nos.............. Numbers (WDMC)
NOs.............. Oswego City Library, Oswego, NY [*Library symbol Library of Congress*] (LCLS)
NOSA............ National Occupational Safety Association (NADA)
NOSA............ National Outerwear and Sportswear Association (EA)
NOSAC............ National Offshore Safety Advisory Committee [*Coast Guard*]
NOSAD........ National Organization for Seasonal Affective Disorder (EA)
NOSALF .... Nordiska Samfundet for Latinamerika Forskning [*Nordic Association for Research on Latin America*] [*Sweden*] (EAIO)
NOSAP........ National Ocean Survey Analytical Plotter [*NOAA*] (PDAA)
NOSB............ National Organic Standards Board
NOSBE........ Network Operating System/Batch Environment
NOSC............ Naval Ocean Systems Center [*Formerly, NELC*]
NOSC............ Naval Ordnance Systems Command [*Later, Naval Sea Systems Command*]
NOSC............ Nonoscillating
NOsC .... Oswego County Library System, Oswego, NY [*Library symbol*] [*Library of Congress*] (LCLS)
NOSCL........ Naval Ocean Systems Center Laboratory (DNAB)
NOSCP........ National Ocean Sediment Coring Program (NOAA)
NOSD............ Nosed (ABBR)
NoSdeSv..... North Side Savings Bank [*Associated Press*] (SAG)
NOSE .... National Odd Shoe Exchange (EA)
NOSE .... Neighbors Opposing Smelly Emissions [*Student legal action organization*]
NOSE .... Neotronics Olfactory Sensing Equipment [*Neotronics Scientific*] (PS)
NOSG............ Nosing (ABBR)
NOSGLANT... Naval Operations Support Group, Atlantic
NOSGPAC...... Naval Operations Support Group, Pacific
NOSH............ Hain Food Group [*NASDAQ symbol*] (TTSB)
NOSH............ Hain Food Group, Inc. [*NASDAQ symbol*] (SAG)
NOS-H .... Nordiska Samarbetsnamnden for Humanistisk Forskning [*Nordic Committee of the Research Councils for the Humanities - NCRCH*] (EA)
NOsH .... Oswego Hospital, Oswego, NY [*Library symbol*] [*Library of Congress*] (LCLS)
NOsHi .... Oswego County Historical Society, Oswego, NY [*Library symbol Library of Congress*] (LCLS)
NOsI............. International Business Machines Corp., Oswego, NY [*Library symbol Library of Congress*] (LCLS)
NOSIC.......... Naval Ocean Surveillance Information Center
NOSIC.......... Naval Operations Support Information Center [*Navy*]
NOSIC.......... Neurologic Outcome Scale for Infants and Children [*Medicine*] (DMAA)
NOSIE .... Nurses Observation Scale for Inpatient Evaluation [*Psychiatry*]
NOSIG.......... No Significant Change [*Used to qualify weather phenomena*]
NOSIH.......... Naval Ordnance Station, Indian Head (MCD)
NOSINS........ Nosiness (ABBR)
NOSL .... Naval Ordnance Station, Louisville [*Kentucky*]
NOSL .... Night-Day Optical Survey of Lightning [*NASA*]
NOSL .... Night/Day Optical Survey of Thunderstorm Lightning (NAKS)
NOSLA.......... National Oil Scouts and Landmen's Association [*Later, IOSA*]
NOSL-QA ..... Naval Ordnance Station, Louisville Quality Assurance Department [*Kentucky*]
NOS-LSCR ... National Ocean Survey Lake Survey Center [*National Oceanic and Atmospheric Administration*]
NOSM .... Navy Occupation Service Medal
NOSM .... Noise Diotic, Signal Monaural (PDAA)
NOSMO........ Norden Optics Setting, Mechanized Operation [*Air Force bombsight*]
NOS-N .... Samarbetsnamnden for de Nordiska Naturvetenskapliga Forskningraden [*Joint Committee of the Nordic Natural Science Research Councils - JCNNSRC*] (EA)
NOSO.......... Naval Ordnance Supply Office (MUGU)
NOSP .... National Ophthalmic Speakers Programme [*Canada*]
NOSP .... Naval Ordnance Special Projects

NOSP	Network Operations Support Plan [*NASA*] (KSC)
NOSP	Network Operation Support Program [*Computer science*]
NOSPL	No Special Observation Taken [*NWS*] (FAAC)
NOSR	National Office for Social Responsibility (EA)
NOSS	National Oceanic Satellite System (MCD)
NOSS	National Oceanic Survey Satellite (NAKS)
NOSS	National Ocean Survey System [*Cooperative program of governmental agencies*]
NOSS	National Office Support System (NITA)
NOSS	National Orbiting Space Station
NOSS	Navy Ocean Surveillance System
NOSS	Nimbus Operational Satellite System [*GSFC/USWB*]
NOss	Ossining Public Library, Ossining, NY [*Library symbol Library of Congress*] (LCLS)
NOSSA	New Orleans Steamship Association (EA)
NOSSCR	National Organization of Social Security Claimants' Representatives (EA)
NOSSO	Naval Ordnance Systems Support Office (MCD)
NOSSOLANT	Naval Ordnance Systems Support Office, Atlantic
NOSSOPAC	Naval Ordnance Systems Support Office, Pacific
NOSSOREP	Naval Ordnance Systems Support Office Representative (DNAB)
NOST	Knights of the Square Table (EA)
NOST	Nuclear Operational Systems Test
NOSTA	National Ocean Science and Technology Agency
NOSTA	Naval Ophthalmic Support and Training Activity
No St C	Northern State College (South Dakota) (GAGS)
NoStPw	Northern States Power Co. [*Associated Press*] (SAG)
NOSTS	National Ocean Survey Tide Station [*Marine science*] (MSC)
NOsU	State University of New York, College at Oswego, Oswego, NY [*Library symbol Library of Congress*] (LCLS)
NOS/VE	Network Operating System / Virtual Environment (HGAA)
NOT	New Organization Training
NOT	New Orleans Terminal [*AAR code*]
NOT	Nocturnal Oxygen Therapy [*Medicine*] (DMAA)
NOT	Nordic Optical Telescope
NOT	Noront Resources Ltd. [*Vancouver Stock Exchange symbol*]
NOT	Notary (WDAA)
NOT	Notation (ROG)
NOT	Noted
NOT	Notice (ROG)
NOT	Notion
NOT	Not Our Title [*Publishing*] (WDMC)
NOT	Nucleus of the Optic Tract [*Eye anatomy*]
NOT	Number of Turns (IAA)
NOTA	National Organ Transplant Act [*1984*]
NOTA	None of the Above [*Politics*]
NOTACGENSEA	Nontactical Generator, Southeast Asia
NOTACK	No Attack Area [*Military*] (NVT)
NOTAD	Notice to Airmen Address
NOTAEI	National Old Timers' Association of the Energy Industry (EA)
NOTAL	Not at All
NOTAL	Not to, nor Needed by, All
NOTAM	Notice to Airmen
NOTAM	Notice to Mariners (DOMA)
NOTAP	Navy Occupational Task Analysis Program (NVT)
NOTAR	No-Tail Rotor [*Helicopters*]
NOTARC	National Old Timers Auto Racing Club (EA)
NOTAS	Notice to Airmen Summary
NOTB	National Ophthalmic Treatment Board [*British*]
NOTBA	National Ophthalmic Treatment Board Association [*British*]
NOTC	Naval Ordnance Test Center (KSC)
NOTC	NOAA [*National Oceanic and Atmospheric Administration*] Operational Telecommunications Coordinator (NOAA)
Not Cas	Notes of Cases at Madras (Strange) [*A publication*] (DLA)
Not Cas	Notes of Cases, English Ecclesiastical and Maritime Courts [*1841-50*] [*A publication*] (DLA)
Not Cas Ecc & M	Notes of Cases, English Ecclesiastical and Maritime Courts [*1841-50*] [*A publication*] (DLA)
Not Cas Madras	Notes of Cases at Madras (Strange) [*A publication*] (DLA)
NOTCOMM	Not Commissioned [*Military*]
Notc on Fac	Notcutt on Factories and Workshops [*2nd ed.*] [*1879*] [*A publication*] (DLA)
Not Dec	Notes of Decisions [*Martin's North Carolina Reports*] [*A publication*] (DLA)
Not Dig	Boddam and Greenwood's Notanda Digest [*A publication*] (DLA)
Not Dign	Notitia Dignitatum [*Classical studies*] (OCD)
note	Footnote in Cross-Reference [*Publishing*]
NOTEF	National Organ Transplant Education Foundation (EA)
NOTEMPS	Nontemporary Storage System (MCD)
NOTES	National Organization of Telecommunications Engineers and Scientists [*Washington, DC Telecommunications*] (TSSD)
Notes	Notes (Music Library Association) [*A publication*] (BRI)
Notes Higher Ed	Notes on Higher Education [*A publication*]
Notes of Ca	Notes of Cases [*England*] [*A publication*] (DLA)
Notes of Cas	Notes of Cases, English Ecclesiastical and Maritime Courts [*1841-50*] [*A publication*] (DLA)
Notes of Cases	Notes of Cases, English Ecclesiastical and Maritime Courts [*1841-50*] [*A publication*] (DLA)
Notes on US	Notes on United States Reports [*A publication*] (DLA)
No Test	Novum Testamentum (DSA)
NO-TFA	National Old-Time Fiddlers' Association (EA)
NOTIF	Notification
NOTIN	Notification (ROG)
NOTIP	Night Observation Television in a Pod
NOTIP	Northern-Tier Integration Project [*Military*] (DNAB)
NOTIS	Network Operations Trouble Information System [*Telecommunications*] (TEL)
NOTIS	Northwestern Online Total Integrated System [*Northwestern University Library*] [*Library automation project*] [*Information service or system*] (IID)
Not J	Notaries Journal [*A publication*] (DLA)
N-O-T-L	Niagara-On-The-Lake [*Ontario*]
NOTL	Notarial (ROG)
NOTM	National Organization of Tutoring and Mentoring Centers (EA)
NOTM	New Orleans, Texas & Mexico [*AAR code*]
NOTMAR	Notice to Mariner (NVT)
NoTN	Norges Tekniske Vitenskapsakademi [*Norwegian Academy for Technical Sciences*], Trondheim, Norway [*Library symbol Library of Congress*] (LCLS)
NOTN	Notion (ABBR)
NoTNG	Norges Geologiske Undersoeklse Biblioteket [*Geological Survey of Norway*], Trondheim, Norway [*Library symbol*] [*Library of Congress*] (LCLS)
NOTNO	Notional Number (NVT)
NOTO	Non-Official Trade Organisation [*British*]
NOTO	Numbering Tool (AAG)
NOTOF	Notice to Airmen Office
Not Op	Wilmot's Notes of Opinions and Judgments [*A publication*] (DLA)
NOTOX	No Toxic Incinerator Group [*Political party*]
NOTOX	Not to Exceed (NOAA)
Not Pub	Notary Public (EBF)
NOTR	National Order of Trench Rats (EA)
Notrad	No Traditions [*Internet*]
Notre Dame Est Plan Inst	Notre Dame Estate Planning Institute. Proceedings [*A publication*] (DLA)
Notre Dame J Leg	Notre Dame Journal of Legislation [*A publication*] (DLA)
NOTRTR	National Organization of Test, Research, and Training Reactors [*Later, TRTR*] (EA)
NOTS	Naval Ocean Transport Service [*Changed to MSTS in 1949 now MSC*] (DOMA)
NOTS	Naval Ordnance Test Station
NOTS	Naval Overseas Transport Service
NOTS	NOAA [*National Oceanic and Atmospheric Administration*] Operational Telecommunications System (NOAA)
NOTS	Nuclear Orbit Transfer Stage (PDAA)
NOT SAFE	National Organization Taunting Safety and Fairness Everywhere (EA)
Nott & Hop	Nott and Hopkins' Reports [*United States Court of Claims*] [*A publication*] (DLA)
Nott & Hunt	Nott and Huntington's Reports [*1-7 United States Court of Claims*] [*A publication*] (DLA)
Nott & McC	Nott and McCord's South Carolina Reports [*A publication*] (DLA)
Nott & M'C (SC)	Nott and M'Cord's South Carolina Reports [*A publication*] (DLA)
NOTTM	Nottingham [*County in England*]
Nott Mech L	Nott on the Mechanics' Lien Law [*A publication*] (DLA)
NOTTS	Nottinghamshire [*County in England*]
Notts	Nottinghamshire [*County in England*] (ODBW)
NOTU	Naval Operational Training Unit
NOTU	Naval Ordnance Test Unit
NoTU	Universitetet i Trondheim [*University of Trondheim*], Trondheim, Norway [*Library symbol Library of Congress*] (LCLS)
NOTUN	Notice of Unreliability
NoTU-T	Universitetet i Trondheim, Norges Tekniske Hogskole [*University of Trondheim, Norwegian Institute of Technology*], Trondheim-NTH, Norway [*Library symbol Library of Congress*] (LCLS)
NoTU-V	Universitetet i Trondheim, Kongelige Norske Videnskabers Selskabs [*University of Trondheim, Royal Norwegian Society of Sciences and Letters*], Trondheim, N orway [*Library symbol Library of Congress*] (LCLS)
NOTWG	Notwithstanding
NOTWSTG	Notwithstanding
NOTWT	Do Not Transmit by Radio (NATG)
NOTY	Notary (ROG)
NOU	Naval Ordnance Unit
NOU	Noumea [*New Caledonia*] [*Airport symbol*] (OAG)
NOU	Nouvelles (NITA)
NOU	Sitka, AK [*Location identifier FAA*] (FAAL)
NOUR	Nourish (ABBR)
NOURD	Nourished (ABBR)
NOURG	Nourishing (ABBR)
NOURT	Nourishment (ABBR)
NOUS	Naval Order of the United States (EA)
Nouv Rev	Nouvelle Revue de Droit Francais [*Paris*] [*A publication*] (DLA)
NOV	Avianova SpA [*Italy ICAO designator*] (FAAC)
NOV	Huambo [*Angola*] [*Airport symbol*] (OAG)
NOV	Nodamura Virus
NOV	Non Obstante Veredicto [*Judgment Notwithstanding*] [*Latin Legal term*] (DLA)
NOV	Nonoccluded Virus
NOV	Notice of Violation [*Nuclear energy*] (NRCH)
NOV	NovaCare [*NYSE symbol*] (SPSG)
NOV	Nova Lisboa [*Angola*] [*Airport symbol*] (AD)
NOV	Novamin, Inc. [*Toronto Stock Exchange symbol*]
NOV	Novara [*Sicily*] [*Seismograph station code, US Geological Survey*] (SEIS)
NOV	Novation [*Legal term*] (DLA)
NOV	Novel (ROG)
NOV	Novelist (ABBR)
Nov	Novellae [*Classical studies*] (OCD)
NOV	November (AAG)
Nov	November (ODBW)

nov............. Novembre [*November*] [*French*] (ASC)
NOV .... Novitiate (ROG)
nov............. Novum [*New*] [*Latin*] (MAE)
NOVA.......... National Organization for Victim Assistance (EA)
NOVA.......... National Outdoor Volleyball Association [*Defunct*] (EA)
NOVA.......... National Overhead Evaluation Assessment [*Term for the restructuring process begun at E. F. Hutton after the October 1987 stock market collapse*]
NOVA.......... Network Organization via Advanced Architecture [*Marubeni Corp.*]
NOVA.......... Northern Valley Private Industry Council [*Sunnyvale, CA*] (ECON)
Nova............ Nova Corp. [*Associated Press*] (SAG)
NOVA.......... Nova Omega Ventura Apollo [*General Motors automobiles*]
NOVA.......... Nurses Organization of Veterans Affairs (EA)
NOVA.......... Nutritional Oncology Vascular Access
NovaCre....... NovaCare [*Associated Press*] (SAG)
Novadig....... Novadigm, Inc. [*Associated Press*] (SAG)
Novatk........ Novatek International, Inc. [*Associated Press*] (SAG)
NOVATOR .... Novye Torit [*Newly Flattened*] [*KGB term for newly recruited agent abroad*]
Nova U .... Nova University (GAGS)
Novavx........ Novavax, Inc. [*Associated Press*] (SAG)
NOVC.......... Novice (ABBR)
NOVCAM...... Nonvolatile Charge-Addressed Memory [*Computer science*] (PDAA)
NOV/CD....... Notice of Violation / Compliance Demand (EPA)
Nov Com Fragm... Novae Comoediae Fragmenta in Papyris Reperta Exceptis Menandreis [*A publication*] (OCD)
NOVE .... NOMOS Verlagskatalog [*NOMOS Datapool*] [*Information service or system*] (IID)
NOVEL .... Narrative Output Vocabulary Editing Language [*Psychiatric test*]
Novell......... Novell, Inc. [*Associated Press*] (SAG)
Noven.......... Noven Pharmaceuticals, Inc. [*Associated Press*] (SAG)
NOVI .... Novitron International, Inc. [*NASDAQ symbol*] (SAG)
NOVICE........ Night Operational Vision and the Individual Combat Engineer (MCD)
Novitrn........ Novitron International, Inc. [*Associated Press*] (SAG)
NOVL.......... Novell, Inc. [*NASDAQ symbol*] (NQ)
NOVLT........ Novelty
Novlus......... Novellus Systems, Inc. [*Associated Press*] (SAG)
NOVM......... No Obvious Value Mail [*Postal service*]
Novmtx .... Novametrics Medical Systems [*Associated Press*] (SAG)
Novmtx .... Novametrix Medical Systems, Inc. [*Associated Press*] (SAG)
NOVN.......... Noven Pharmaceuticals [*NASDAQ symbol*] (TTSB)
NOVN.......... Noven Pharmaceuticals, Inc. [*NASDAQ symbol*] (NQ)
NOV N .... Novum Nomen [*New Name*] [*Latin*] (BABM)
nov n .... Novum Nomen [*New Name*] [*Latin*] (DAVI)
NovoNdk...... Novo Nordisk AS [*Associated Press*] (SAG)
Novoste .... Novoste Corp. [*Associated Press*] (SAG)
NOVP.......... Novantrone, Oncovin, Vinblastine, Prednisone [*Antineoplastic drug*] (CDI)
NOVRAM...... Non-Volatile Random Access Memory [*Computer science*]
NOVRAM...... Nonvolotile Static RAM (NITA)
NOVS.......... National Office of Vital Statistics [*Public Health Service*] [*Obsolete*]
Nov Sc Dec... Nova Scotia Decisions [*A publication*] (DLA)
Nov Sc LR ... Nova Scotia Law Reports [*A publication*] (DLA)
NOV SP........ Novum Species [*New Species*] [*Latin*] (BABM)
nov sp .... Novum Species [*New species*] [*Latin*] (DAVI)
NOVST........ Novelist (ABBR)
NOVT .... Novelty (ABBR)
NOVT .... Novoste Corp [*NASDAQ symbol*] (TTSB)
NOW............ MAI Systems [*AMEX symbol*] (TTSB)
NOW............ MAI Systems Corp. [*AMEX symbol*] (SAG)
NOW............ National Organization for Women (EA)
NOW............ National Organizations of the World [*A publication*]
NOW............ National Overhaul Warranty [*Automotive engineering*]
NOW............ Negotiable Order of Withdrawal [*Banking*]
NOW............ Neighbors of Woodcraft [*Portland, OR*] (EA)
NOW............ Network Order Wire [*Military*] (CAAL)
NOW............ News of the World [*A publication*] (DGA)
NOW............ Nonhazardous Oil Field Waste [*Environmental Protection Agency*] (FFDE)
NOW............ Northway Explorations Ltd. [*Toronto Stock Exchange symbol*]
NOW............ Nurture-Outreach-Witness [*Religion*]
NOW............ Nutrition on the Web [*Internet site for teens*]
NOW............ Port Angeles, WA [*Location identifier FAA*] (FAAL)
NOW............ Royal Norwegian Air Force [*ICAO designator*] (FAAC)
NOW account... Negotiable Order of Withdrawal Account (EBF)
NOWAI........ Neshei Ubenos Agudath Israel [*Antwerp*] (BJA)
NOWAPA...... North American Water and Power Alliance (NADA)
NOWD......... Northward (ABBR)
No West Rep... Northwestern Reporter [*Commonly cited NW*] [*A publication*] (DLA)
NOweWJ...... Wheatley Junior-Senior High School, Old Westbury, NY [*Library symbol Library of Congress*] (LCLS)
NOwHC-U .... Old Westbury School of the Holy Child, Upper School, Old Westbury, NY [*Library symbol*] [*Library of Congress*] (LCLS)
NOWIS........ National Older Workers Information System [*American Association of Retired Persons*] [*Information service or system Defunct*] (IID)
NOWL .... National Order of Women Legislators (EA)
NOW LDEF... NOW [*National Organization for Women*] Legal Defense and Education Fund (EA)
NOWL/NFWL... National Order of Women Legislators/National Foundation for Women Legislators (NTPA)
NOWME .... National Organisation for Women's Management Education [*British*] (DI)
No W Mo St U... Nortwest Missouri State University (GAGS)
NOwNC .... New York College of Osteopathic Medicine, Old Westbury, NY [*Library symbol Library of Congress*] (LCLS)

NOwNI .... New York Institute of Technology, Old Westbury, NY [*Library symbol Library of Congress*] (LCLS)
NOwNI-C...... New York Institute of Technology, Commack Center Library, Commack, NY [*Library symbol Library of Congress*] (LCLS)
NOwNI-CI.... New York Institute of Technical, Central Islip, NY [*Library symbol*] [*Library of Congress*] (LCLS)
NOwNI-N...... New York Institute of Technology, New York, NY [*Library symbol Library of Congress*] (LCLS)
No W Okla St U... Northwestern Oklahoma State University (GAGS)
NOWPA....... National Osteopathic Women Physician's Association (EA)
NOWP-OM.... National Older Workers Programs - Operation Mainstream [*Department of Labor*]
NOWR......... Nuclear Ordnance War Reserve [*Military*] (AFIT)
NOWRA........ National Onsite Waste Water Recycling Association (AEPA)
NOWSA....... National One-Write Systems Association (EA)
Nowsc......... Nowsco Well Services Ltd. [*Associated Press*] (SAG)
No W St U La... Northwestern State University of Louisiana (GAGS)
NOwU .... State University of New York, College at Old Westbury, Oyster Bay, NY [*Library symbol Library of Congress*] (LCLS)
NOWUS........ Normal Operation with Unscram [*Nuclear energy*] (NRCH)
NOwWJ........ Wheatley Junior-Senior High School, Old Westbury, NY [*Library symbol*] [*Library of Congress*] (LCLS)
NOWWN ...... National Organization of World War Nurses (EA)
NOX .... Air Nordic in Vasteras AB [*Sweden ICAO designator*] (FAAC)
NOx............. Nitrogen Oxide (COE)
NOX .... Nitrous Oxide [*Laughing gas*]
NOX .... Novavax, Inc. [*AMEX symbol*] (SAG)
NOX .... Noxious (ABBR)
NOx............. Oxford Memorial Library, Oxford, NY [*Library symbol Library of Congress*] (LCLS)
NOXA .... Naphth-2yl-Oxyacetic Acid (LDT)
NOXA .... Naphthoxyacetic Acid [*Organic chemistry*]
NOXO .... Noxso Corp. [*NASDAQ symbol*] (NQ)
Noxso.......... Noxso Corp. [*Associated Press*] (SAG)
NOXY .... Noxiously (ABBR)
NOXZEMA.... Knocks Eczema [*Acronym, brand name for skin cream, said to be taken from this phrase*]
NOY .... Not Out Yet
Noy .... Noy's English King's Bench Reports [*1559-1649*] [*A publication*] (DLA)
NOy............. Oyster Bay-East Norwich Public Library, Oyster Bay, NY [*Library symbol Library of Congress*] (LCLS)
Noy Ch U ..... Noyes on Charitable Uses [*A publication*] (DLA)
Noye .... Grounds and Maxims of English Law, by William Noye [*A publication*] (DLA)
Noy (Eng) .... Noy's English King's Bench Reports [*1559-1649*] [*A publication*] (DLA)
Noye's Max... Maxims of the Laws of England, by William Noye [*A publication*] (DLA)
NOyHS .... Oyster Bay High School, Oyster Bay, NY [*Library symbol Library of Congress*] (LCLS)
Noy Max..... Noy's Maxims [*A publication*] (DLA)
NOyRE .... Theodore Roosevelt Elementary School, Oyster Bay, NY [*Library symbol*] [*Library of Congress*] (LCLS)
NOYS........... National Organization for Youth Safety [*NHTSA*] (TAG)
NOyStD........ Saint Dominic High School, Oyster Bay, NY [*Library symbol*] [*Library of Congress*] (LCLS)
NOZ .... Elizabeth City, NC [*Location identifier FAA*] (FAAL)
NOZ .... No Operating Zone (DA)
NOZ .... Nozzle (AAG)
NOZE .... US National Ozone Expedition [*1986*] [*McMurdo Station, Antarctica*]
NP................ Adriance Memorial Library, Poughkeepsie, NY [*Library symbol Library of Congress*] (LCLS)
NP................ Desert Pacific [*ICAO designator*] (AD)
np---- .... Great Plains [*MARC geographic area code Library of Congress*] (LCCP)
NP................ Nacionalista Party [*Philippines*]
NP................ Name of Publisher (NITA)
NP................ Nameplate
NP................ NAPALM [*Naphthenic and Palmitic Acids*] (NATG)
NP................ [*The*] Narragansett Pier Railroad Co. Inc. (IIA)
NP................ Nasal Prongs [*For administration of oxygen*] (DAVI)
NP................ Nasionale Party van Suid-Afrika [*National Party of South Africa*] [*Political party*] (PPW)
NP................ Nasionale Party van Suidwesafrika [*National Party of South West Africa*] [*Namibia*] [*Political party*] (PPW)
NP................ Nasopharyngeal [*or Nasopharynx*] [*Medicine*]
NP................ Nationalist Parnellite [*British*] (ROG)
NP................ Nationalist Party [*Philippines*] [*Political party*] (PPW)
NP................ Nationalist Party [*Malta*] [*Political party*] (PPE)
NP................ National Parks [*A publication*] (BRI)
NP................ National Party [*Papua New Guinea*] [*Political party*] (PPW)
NP................ National Pipe [*Thread*]
NP................ National Police (CINC)
NP................ National Porkettes (EA)
NP................ National Power PLC [*NYSE symbol*] (SAG)
NP................ National Primary (OTD)
NP................ National Publishing Co. [*Philadelphia*]
NP................ Nation Party [*Turkey*] [*Political party*] (PPW)
NP................ Natural Passivation [*Metallurgy*]
NP................ Naval Party [*British military*] (DMA)
NP................ Naval Patrol [*British military*] (DMA)
NP................ Naval Pattern [*British military*] (DMA)
NP................ Naval Pension [*British*] (ROG)
NP................ Naval Police [*British*] (ROG)

NP	Naval Prison
NP	Naval Publication (IEEE)
NP	Neap Tide
NP	Near Point
NP	Needle Position [*on dial*]
NP	Negative Prescreening [*Marketing*]
NP	Negative Pressure (NRCH)
NP	Neo-Punic (BJA)
NP	Nepal [*ANSI two-letter standard code*] (CNC)
np	Nepal [*MARC country of publication code Library of Congress*] (LCCP)
Np	Neper [*A unit on a natural logarithmic scale*]
Np	Neptunium [*Chemical element*]
NP	Neptunium (NAKS)
NP	Net Position [*Business term*]
NP	Net Price [*Business term*] (MHDW)
NP	Net Proceeds
NP	Net Profit
NP	Network Planning [*Computer science*]
NP	Network Program (NASA)
NP	Network Project [*An association*] (EA)
NP	Neuritic Plaque [*Pathology*]
NP	Neuropathology [*Medicine*]
NP	Neurophysin [*Biochemistry*]
NP	Neurophysiological
NP	Neuropsychiatric
N/P	Neuro-Psychiatry [*Medical Officer designation*] [*British*]
NP	Newly Presented (DMAA)
NP	New Paragraph
np	New Paragraph (WDMC)
NP	New Party (EA)
NP	New Patient
NP	New Pattern [*British military*] (DMA)
np	New Pence [*Monetary unit in Great Britain since 1971*]
NP	New Permutations
NP	New Point [*Used in correcting manuscripts, etc.*]
NP	Newport [*Rhode Island*]
NP	New Position
NP	New Providence
N/P	Newspaper
NP	Nickel Plated [*Guns*]
NP	Niemann-Pick [*Disease*] [*Medicine*] (DB)
NP	Nippon Investment Corp. [*Vancouver Stock Exchange symbol*]
NP	Nisi Prius [*Unless Before*] [*Legal term Latin*]
NP	Nitrogen-Phosphorus [*Chemistry*] (MAE)
NP	Nitrophenide [*Pharmacology*]
NP	Nitrophenoacetylamino Caproate
NP	Nitropropane [*Organic chemistry*]
NP	Nitro Proved [*Rifle mark*] (DICI)
NP	Nitroprusside [*A vasodilator*]
NP	Nitropyrene [*Organic chemistry*]
NP	Nitrosopiperidine [*Organic chemistry*]
NP	Nobel Prize
NP	Nomen Proprium [*Proper Name*] [*Latin*]
NP	Nominal Horsepower (IAA)
NP	Nondeterministic Polynomial [*Mathematics*]
NP	Nonpapillate [*Type of seed*] [*Botany*]
NP	Nonparticipating [*Insurance or finance*]
NP	Non-Patents (NITA)
N/P	Nonpayment (ROG)
NP	Nonperson
NP	Nonpolarized [*Computer science*]
NP	Nonpolice (BARN)
NP	Nonpractising Member [*Chiropody*] [*British*]
NP	Nonprint [*Computer science*] (IAA)
NP	Nonprocurable
NP	Nonprofit (BARN)
NP	Nonpropelled (AAG)
NP	Nonylphenol [*Organic chemistry*]
NP	No Paging
NP	No Parity
NP	No Party with the Name of the Recipient of the Message [*International telex abbreviation*] (WDMC)
NP	No Pin [*Electronics*] (OA)
NP	No Place [*of publication*] [*Bibliography*]
np	No Place (WDMC)
np	No Place of Publication (WDAA)
NP	No Predators [*Ecology*]
NP	No Print [*Telecommunications*] (TEL)
NP	No Printer Listed (NTCM)
NP	No Prospect [*In sports*]
NP	No Protest [*Banking*]
NP	No Publisher Listed (NTCM)
NP	Normal Phase [*Chromatography*]
NP	Normal Pitch (ADA)
NP	Normal Plasma [*Medicine*] (MAE)
NP	Normal Pregnancy [*Medicine*]
NP	Normal Pressure
NP	Normal Profit [*Business term*] (MHDW)
NP	Northern Pacific Railway Co. (MHDW)
NP	Northern Pine [*Utility pole*] [*Telecommunications*] (TEL)
NP	North Pole [*Also, PN*]
NP	Notary Public
Np	Notary Public (WDAA)
np	Notary Public (WDAA)

N/P	Notes Payable [*Finance*] (DFIT)
NP	Not Perceptible [*Medicine*]
NP	Not Performed
NP	Not Planned
NP	Not Practiced [*Medicine*]
NP	Not Preferred
NP	Not Present (DAVI)
NP	Not Pressed or Glazed [*Paper*] (DGA)
NP	Not Printed (ILCA)
N/P	Not Provided (KSC)
NP	Noun Phrase [*Linguistics*]
NP	Nucleoplasmic [*Index*] [*Cytology*]
NP	Nucleoprotein [*Biochemistry*]
NP	Nucleoside Phosphorylase [*An enzyme*]
np	Nucleotide Pair [*Genetics*] (DOG)
np	Nucleotide Phosphorylase (DB)
NP	Nucleus Pulposus [*Medicine*] (DAVI)
N_p	Number of Primary Turns (IDOE)
NP	Number of Primary Turns (IAA)
NP	Number of Steps, Polynomial Time [*Mathematics*]
NP	Nursed Poorly [*Medicine*] (DMAA)
NP	Nurse Practitioner
NP	Nursing Procedure
NP	Nurturing Parent [*Psychology*] (DHP)
NP	Ohio Nisi Prius Reports [*A publication*] (DLA)
NP0	Negative-Positive-Zero
NPA	Committee for a National Peace Academy [*Later, N-PAC*] (EA)
NPA	Napan [*West Irian, Indonesia*] [*Airport symbol*] (AD)
NPA	Naphthylphthalamic Acid [*Organic chemistry*]
NPA	Naptalam (EDCT)
NPA	National Paddleball Association (EA)
NPA	National Panel of Arbitrators
NPA	National Paperboard Association [*Later, API*]
NPA	National Paralegal Association (EA)
NPA	National Parenthood Association (NADA)
NPA	National Parents Association
NPA	National Parking Association (EA)
NPA	National Parks and Access to the Countryside Act [*Town planning*] [*British*]
NPA	National Parks Association [*Later, NPCA*] (EA)
NPA	National Particleboard Association (EA)
NPA	National Pasta Association (EA)
NPA	National Patrolmen's Association
NPA	National Pawnbrokers Association (EA)
NPA	National Payphone Association (EA)
NPA	National Peace Academy
NPA	National Pediculosis Association (EA)
NPA	National People's Action (EA)
NPA	National Perinatal Association (EA)
NPA	National Peripheral Association (EA)
NPA	National Personnel Associates
NPA	National Pet Association [*Defunct*] (EA)
NPA	National Petroleum Association [*Later, NPRA*]
NPA	National Pharmaceutical Alliance (NTPA)
NPA	National Pharmaceutical Association [*Washington, DC*]
NPA	National Phlebotomy Association (EA)
NPA	National Pigeon Association [*Defunct*] (EA)
NPA	National Pilots Association [*Defunct*] (EA)
N/P	National Pistol Association [*British*] (DI)
NPA	National Pituitary Agency [*Later, NHPP*]
NPA	National Planning Association (EA)
NPA	National Plastercraft Association (EA)
NPA	National Playbus Association [*British*] (DBA)
NPA	National Podiatry Association [*Later, NPMA*] (EA)
NPA	National Poker Association (EA)
NPA	National Portage Association [*British*] (DBA)
NPA	National Ports Authority [*British*]
NPA	National Postmasters Auxiliary (EA)
NPA	National Poultry Association [*Australia*]
NPA	National Prescription Audit
NPA	National Preservers Association [*Later, International Jelly and Preserve Association*] (EA)
NPA	National Priority Area [*Military*]
NPA	National Proctologic Association (EA)
NPA	National Production Authority [*Functions merged into BDSA, 1953*]
NPA	National Productivity Authority (MHDB)
NPA	National Prohibition Act
NPA	National Psychological Association [*Defunct*] (EA)
NPA	Naval Procurement Account
NPA	Navy Postal Affairs Section Publication
NPA	Navy Purchasing Activity (AFIT)
NPA	Near Point Accommodation [*Ophthalmology*]
NPA	Neighborhood Publication Area Report [*Bureau of the Census*] (GFGA)
NPA	Network Program Analysis by ADI [*Area of Dominant Influence*] [*Arbitron Ratings Co.*] [*Information service or system*] (CRD)
NPA	Neutrons per Absorption (DEN)
NPA	New People's Army [*Philippines*] (PD)
NPA	New Populist Action [*Defunct*] (EA)
NPA	New Product Announcements [*Predicasts, Inc.*] [*Cleveland, OH*] [*Information service or system*] (IID)
NPA	Newsletter Publishers Association (NTPA)
NPA	Newspaper Publishers' Association [*British*] (DCTA)
NPA	Nine Pin Association [*Schauenburg, Federal Republic of Germany*] (EAIO)

NPA	Nonbuffered Pyrophosphatase Activity
NPA	Non-Par Approved
NPA	Non-Principal Axis
NPA	No Previous Admission [*Medicine*] (MEDA)
NPA	No Price Available [*Business term*] (ADA)
NPA	Normal Pressure Angle
NPA	Northern Pipeline Agency [*Ottawa, ON*]
NPA	Notice of Proposed Amendment (DA)
NPA	Novel Plasminogen Activator [*Anticlotting agent*]
NPA	N-Propylamine [*Organic chemistry*]
NPA	Nuclear Plant Analyzer (NRCH)
NPA	Numbering Plan Area [*Bell System*] [*Telecommunications*]
NPA	Numerical Production Analysis (IEEE)
NPA	Pensacola, FL [*Location identifier FAA*] (FAAL)
NPA	PTS [*Predicasts, Inc.*] New Product Announcements/Plus [*Information service or system*] (IID)
NPAA	National Park Academy of the Arts (EA)
NPAA	National Photographic Art Archive [*Victoria and Albert Museum*] [*British*]
NPAA	National Postal Arts Association (EA)
NPAA	Noise Pollution and Abatement Act (GFGA)
NPAACT	National Parks Association of the Australian Capital Territory
NPAB	Navy Price Adjustment Board
NPAB	Nuclear Power Advisory Board (PDAA)
NPABC	National Public Affairs Center for Television (NADA)
NPAC	National Parks Advisory Council [*Australia*]
N-PAC	National Peace Academy Campaign [*Formerly, NPA*] (EA)
NPAC	National Peace Action Coalition
NPAC	National Plantation Advisory Committee
NPAC	National Political Action Committee (EA)
NPAC	National Program for Acquisitions and Cataloging [*Library of Congress*]
NPAC	National Project in Agricutural Communication (PDAA)
NPAC	Navy Procurement Assignment Committee
NPAC	Northeast Parallel Architectures Center [*Syracuse University*] [*Research center*] (RCD)
NPAC	Northern Pipeline Agency Canada [*See also APNC*]
NPACI	National Partnership for Advanced Computational Infrastructure [*Supercomputing Center*]
NPACI	National Production Advisory Council on Industry [*British*]
NPACOE	National Panhellenic Association of Central Office Executives (EA)
NPACSE	National Political Action Committee for Scientists and Engineers
NPACT	National Public Affairs Center for Television [*Defunct*]
NPAED	National Progress Association for Economic Development (EA)
NPAF	National Peace Academy Foundation (EA)
NPAF	National Picture & Frame Co. [*NASDAQ symbol*] (SAG)
NPAF	National Pledge of Allegiance Foundation (EA)
NPA(G)R	National Parks and Access to the Countryside (Grants) Regulations [*Town planning*] [*British*]
NPAH	Nitrated Polycyclic Aromatic Hydrocarbons [*Automotive emissions*] [*Organic chemistry*]
NPAI	Network Protocol Addressing Information [*Telecommunications*] (OSI)
NPAI	Nevada Public Affairs Institute [*University of Nevada - Reno*] [*Research center*] (RCD)
NPals	Palisades Free Library, Palisades, NY [*Library symbol Library of Congress*] (LCLS)
NPAM	Navy Priorities and Allocations Manual (DNAB)
NPAM	Nonpermanent Active Militia
NPAN	National Plan for Australian Newspapers
NP & GT Rep...	Nisi Prius and General Term Reports [*Ohio*] [*A publication*] (DLA)
NP & OSR ...	Naval Petroleum and Oil Shale Reserve
NP & PA ...	National Paperbox and Packaging Association (EA)
NPANX	Naval Potomac Annex
NPAP	National Psychological Association for Psychoanalysis (EA)
NPAP	Navy Public Affairs Plan (DNAB)
NPAP	Niue People's Action Party [*Political party*] (EY)
NPAR	Negative-Positive Acknowledgment and Retransmission [*Telecommunications*] (IAA)
NPAR	Nonstandard Part Approval Request (MCD)
NPAR	Nuclear Plant Aging Research Program (COE)
NP/ARCA	National Pacific/Asian Resource Center on Aging (EA)
NPAS	National Policy Assistance Standards (AAGC)
NPAS	Normalized Photoacoustic Signal [*Instrumentation*]
NPASO	National Postsecondary Agriculture Student Organization (EA)
NPAT	National Political Awareness Test [*Sent to all candidates in presidential, congressional, gubernatorial, and most state legislative races*]
NPat............	Patchogue Library, Patchogue, NY [*Library symbol Library of Congress*] (LCLS)
NPatB	Brookhaven Town Hall, Historical Collection, Patchogue, NY [*Library symbol Library of Congress*] (LCLS)
NPatBH	Brookhaven Memorial Hospital, Patchogue, NY [*Library symbol Library of Congress*] (LCLS)
NPatSJ.........	Saint Joseph's College, Patchogue, NY [*Library symbol Library of Congress*] (LCLS)
NPAV	National Parks Association of Victoria [*Australia*]
NPAWT	National Plan of Action for Women in TAFE [*Technical and Further Education*] [*Australia*]
NPB	NADGE [*NATO Air Defense Ground Environment*] Policy Board (NATG)
NPB	National Park Board (NADA)
NPB	National Parole Board [*Canada*]
NPB	National Planning Board [*Terminated, 1944; superseded by National Resources Board*]
NPB	National Plant Board (EA)

NPB	National Plumbing Bureau (NTPA)
NPB	National Prayer Breakfast (EA)
NPB	National Productivity Board (NADA)
NPB	Neutral Particle Beam (MCD)
NPB	Newspaper Bag (ROG)
NPB	Nodal Premature Beat [*Cardiology*]
NPB	Nonplasminogen Binding [*Hematology*]
NPB	Nonprimate Biosatellite
NPB	Non-Protein Bound [*Medicine*] (DMAA)
NPB	Norfolk & Portsmouth Belt Line Railroad Co. [*AAR code*]
NPBA	National Palomino Breeders Association [*Inactive*]
NPBA	National Paper Box Association [*Formerly, NPBMA; later NP & PA*] (EA)
NPBA	National Perinatal Bereavement Association [*Defunct*] (EA)
NPBA	National Pig Breeders' Association [*British*] (BI)
NPBA	National Pocket Billiards Association (EA)
NPBA	National Police Bloodhound Association (EA)
NPBA	National Poro Beautician Association [*Defunct*] (EA)
NPBA	Natural Product Broker Association [*St. Augustine, FL*] (EA)
NPBC	National Penn Bancshares, Inc. [*NASDAQ symbol*] (NQ)
NPBC	National Progressive Broadcast Coalition [*Defunct*] (EA)
NPBC	Natl Penn Bancshares [*NASDAQ symbol*] (TTSB)
NPBE	National Political Button Exchange [*An association Defunct*] (EA)
NPBE	Nitrophenyl Butyl Ether [*Organic chemistry*]
NPBE	Nonlinear Poisson-Boltzmann Equation [*Physical chemistry*]
NPBEA	National Poultry, Butter, and Egg Association [*Defunct*] (EA)
NPBI	National Pretzel Bakers Institute [*Defunct*] (EA)
NPBMA	National Paper Box Manufacturers Association (EA)
NPBOA	National Party Boat Owners Alliance (EA)
NPBRO	Naval Plant Branch Representative Office
NPBS	Navy Personnel Billeting System (DNAB)
NPBSA	National Paper Box Supplies Association [*Defunct*] (EA)
NPBW	Neutral Particle Beam Weapon [*Military*] (MUSM)
NPC	NASA Procurement Circular
NPC	NASA Publication Control (KSC)
NPC	Nasopharyngeal Carcinoma [*Medicine*]
NPC	National Packaging Confederation [*British*] (DBA)
NPC	National Panhellenic Conference (EA)
NPC	National Patent Council (EA)
NPC	National Peace Council [*British*]
NPC	National Peach Council (EA)
NPC	National Peanut Council (EA)
NPC	National People's Congress [*Nigeria*] [*Political party*]
NPC	National People's Congress [*China*] [*Political party*] (PPW)
NPC	National Periodicals Center
NPC	National Personnel Consultants [*Later, NAPC*] [*Defunct*] (EA)
NPC	National Petroleum Council [*Department of Energy*] (EA)
NPC	National Pharmaceutical Council (EA)
NPC	National Philatelic Center [*Australia*]
NPC	National Philatelic Collections [*Smithsonian Institution*]
NPC	National Pizza Co. (EFIS)
NPC	National Playwrights Conference (EA)
NPC	National Plumbing Code
NPC	National Poetry Circle [*Cambridge*] [*British*]
NPC	National Ports Council [*British*]
NPC	National Potato Council (EA)
NPC	National Press Club (EA)
NPC	National Prime Contractor (NATG)
NPC	National Processing Centre [*Marine science*] (MSC)
NPC	National Productivity Council [*Inactive*]
NPC	National Publicity Council for Health and Welfare Services [*Later, NPRC*]
NPC	Native Preacher Co. [*An association*] (EA)
NPC	NATO Parliamentarians' Conference
NPC	NATO Pipeline Committee
NPC	NATO Programming Center (NATG)
NPC	Nauru Phosphate Commission [*Australia*]
NPC	Naval Personnel Committee [*British military*] (DMA)
NPC	Naval Photographic Center
NPC	Navy Policy Council
NPC	Navy Procurement Circular
NPC	Near Point of Convergence [*Ophthalmology*]
NPC	Needle Punch Card
NPC	Neplanocin A [*Biochemistry*]
NPC	Neuropsychiatry Clerical Procedure [*Navy*]
NPC	Neuropsychiatry Clerical Technician [*Navy*]
NPC	New Practice Cases [*Legal*] [*British*]
NPC	New Practice Cases. Bail Court [*1844-48*] [*A publication*] (DLA)
NP-C	Niemann-Pick Type C [*Disease*] [*Medicine*]
NPC	Ninety Pound Charge
NPC	Nisi Prius Cases [*England*] [*A publication*] (DLA)
NPC	Nitrogen Purge Control
NPC	Nodal Premature Contraction [*Cardiology*] (MAE)
NPC	Nominal Protection Coefficient [*Business term*]
NPC	Nonparenchymal Cell (DB)
NPC	Nonphased Color [*Television signals*] (NTCM)
NPC	Nonplayer Characters [*Computer science*]
NPC	Nonprinting Character [*Computer science*]
NPC	Nonproductive Cough [*Medicine*] (DAVI)
NPC	No Previous Carrier [*Insurance*]
NPC	No Previous Complaint [*Medicine*] (DAVI)
NPC	Normal Phase Chromatography
NPC	Northern Pacific Conference (PSS)
NPC	North Pacific Coast Freight Bureau, Seattle WA [*STAC*]
NPC	North Pacific Industry [*Vancouver Stock Exchange symbol*]

NPC	North Polar Cap [*A filamentary mark on Mars*]
NPC	NPC International, Inc. [*Associated Press*] (SAG)
NPC	Nuclear Pore Complex [*Protein*]
NPC	Nuclear Power Co. (NRCH)
NPC	Nursing and Personal Care
NPC	Nuveen Ins CA Prem Inc. Muni [*NYSE symbol*] (TTSB)
NPC	Nuveen Insured California Premium Income Municipal [*NYSE symbol*] (SPSG)
NPC	Public Library of Charlotte and Mecklenburg County, Charlotte, NC [*OCLC symbol*] (OCLC)
NPCa	Nasopharyngeal Carcinoma [*Medicine*] (MAE)
NPCA	National Paint and Coatings Association (EA)
NPCA	National Parks and Conservation Association (EA)
NPCA	National Peace Corps Association (EA)
NPCA	National Peer Counseling Association (DHP)
NPCA	National Pest Control Association (EA)
NPCA	National Pig Carvers Association (EA)
NPCA	National Plastercraft Association (EA)
NPCA	National Precast Concrete Association (EA)
NPCA	National Progressive Consumers Alliance (EA)
NPCBW	National Political Congress of Black Women (EA)
NPCC	National Poison Control Center (DAVI)
NPCC	National Pop Can Collectors (EA)
NPCC	Northeast Power Coordinating Council [*Regional power council*]
NPCC	North Peralta Community College [*California*]
NPCCI	Notification Procedures for Confidential Commercial Information (COE)
NPC/COES	National Panhellenic Conference of Central Office Executives (EA)
NPCD	National Association of Parish Coordinators/Directors of Religious Education (EA)
NPCDN........	National Private Circuit Digital Network (PDAA)
NPCF	National Pollution Control Foundation
NPCFB	North Pacific Coast Freight Bureau
NPCI	National Potato Chip Institute [*Later, SFA*]
NPCI	NPC International, Inc. [*NASDAQ symbol*] (SAG)
NPCI	NPC Intl. [*NASDAQ symbol*] (TTSB)
NPCIL	Nuclear Power Corp. of India Ltd.
NPC Intl	NPC International, Inc. [*Associated Press*] (SAG)
NPCL	North Pacific Coast Line (MHDB)
N-PCL	Not-for-Profit Corp. Law [*New York, NY A publication*]
NP-CLT	Neuropsychiatry Clerical Procedure Technician [*Navy*]
NPCMW	North Pacific Central Mode Water [*Marine science*] (OSRA)
NPCN	National Poison Center Network (EA)
NPCNU........	Neopentyl(chloroethyl)nitrosourea [*Biochemistry*]
NPCO	Negative Patient-Care Outcome [*Medicine*] (WDAA)
N-P, Complete...	Nondeterministic Polynomial Complete Problem [*Mathematics*]
NPCP	Nairobi Peoples' Convention Party
NPCP	National Prostatic Cancer Project
NPCR	No Periodic Calibration Required (MCD)
NPCR	No Programmed Calibration Required (MCD)
NPCS	National Population Control Secretariat [*Australia*]
NP-CT	Naval Personnel Conversion Tables
NP Cult	Nasopharyngeal Culture [*Bacteriology*] (CPH)
NPCW	National Pork Council Women (EA)
NPD	Napped (ABBR)
NPD	Narcissistic Personality Disorder [*Medicine*] (DMAA)
NPD	NASA Policy Directive
NPD	NASA Program Director (SSD)
NPD	Nationaldemokratische Partei Deutschlands [*National Democratic Party of Germany*] [*Germany Political party*] (PPE)
NPD	National Niemann Pick Disease Foundation (EA)
NPD	National Paint Distributors (EA)
NPD	National Party for Democracy [*Zambia*] [*Political party*] (EY)
NPD	National Patent Development Corp. [*AMEX symbol*] (SPSG)
NPD	National Philanthropy Day (NFD)
NPD	National Policy Debate [*Nuclear energy*] (NRCH)
NPD	National Power Demonstration (IEEE)
NPD	National Program Director
NPD	National Program for Dermatology
NPD	Natl Patent Devel [*AMEX symbol*] (TTSB)
NPD	Natriuretic Plasma Dialysate [*Medicine*] (MAE)
NPD	Navy Procurement Directives
NPD	Nees Politikes Dynameis [*New Political Forces*] [*Greek Political party*] (PPE)
NPD	Negative Pressure Device [*Medicine*] (DMAA)
NPD	Neimann-Pick Disease (CPH)
NPD	Network Protection Device [*Telecommunications*] (TEL)
NPD	Network Protective Device (NITA)
NPD	New Product Development [*Business term*]
NPD	New Providence Development Co. Ltd. [*Toronto Stock Exchange symbol*]
NPD	Newspaper Press Directory [*A publication*] (DGA)
NPD	Niemann-Pick Disease [*Medicine*]
NPD	Night Perimeter Defense
NPD	Nitrogen-Phosphorus Detector [*Analytical instrumentation*]
NPD	Nitrogen, Phosphorus Gas Chromatographic Detector [*Spectroscopy*]
NPD	Nominal Percent Defective
NPD	Nonparental Ditype [*Genetics*]
NPD‘	No Pathologic Diagnosis [*Medicine*] (BARN)
NPD	No Pay Due [*Military*] (ADDR)
NPD	No Payroll Division
NPD	North Pacific Division [*Army World War II*]
NPD	North Pacific Drift [*Oceanography*]
NPD	North Polar Distance

NPD	Nouveau Parti Democratique [*New Democratic Party*] [*Canada Political party*] (EAIO)
NPD	N-Player Prisoneris Dilemma
NPD	Nuclear Power Demonstration [*of a reactor*]
NPD	Nuclear Power Division (SAA)
NPD	South African Law Reports, Natal Province Division [*A publication*] (DLA)
NPDA	National Pharmaceutical Distributors' Association [*Australia*]
NPDA	National Plywood Distributors Association (EA)
NPDA	National Privy Diggers Association (EA)
NPDA	National Pyrotechnic Distributors Association [*APA*] [*Absorbed by*] (EA)
NPDA	Network Problem Determination Aid (NITA)
NPDA	Network Problem Determination Application [*Computer science*]
NPDAA	National Pharmaceutical Direct Advertising Association [*Defunct*] (EA)
NPDB	National Practitioner Data Bank [*Information service or system*] (IID)
NPDB	Nuclear Plant Databank (NRCH)
NPDBA	National Pet Dealers and Breeders Association [*Defunct*] (EA)
NPDC	Dutchess Community College, Poughkeepsie, NY [*Library symbol Library of Congress*] (LCLS)
NPDC	National Patent Development Corp.
NPDC	National Peace Day Celebration (EA)
NPDC	National Planning Data Corp. [*Information service or system*] (IID)
NPDC	National Poetry Day Committee (EA)
NPDC	Neurofibromatosis-Pheochromocytoma-Duodenal Carcinoid [*Syndrome*] [*Medicine*] (DMAA)
NPDCM........	Dutchess County Mental Health Center, Poughkeepsie, NY [*Library symbol Library of Congress*] (LCLS)
NPDDE........	Nitrophenyl Dodecyl Ether [*Organic chemistry*]
NPDE	Nonlinear Partial Differential Equation
NPDEA	National Professional Driver Education Association (AEBS)
NPDES	National Pollutant Discharge Elimination System [*Environmental Protection Agency*]
NPDF	Normal Probability Distribution Function
NPDI	Nonperformance of Duty because Imprisoned [*Navy*]
NPDL	Nodular Poorly Differentiated Lymphocyte
NPDM	Navy Program Decision Meeting (DOMA)
NPDN..........	Nordic Public Data Network [*Denmark, Finland, Iceland, Norway and Sweden*] (PDAA)
NPDNA	Nucleoprotamine Deoxyribonucleic Acid
NPDO..........	Nacelle Product Development Organization (MCD)
NPDO..........	Non-Profit Distributing Organization (PDAA)
NPDR..........	NCO Professional Development Ribbon [*Military decoration*]
NPDR..........	Nonproliferative Diabetic Retinopathy [*Medicine*] (MAE)
NPDS	National Pollutant Discharge Elimination System [*Environmental Protection Agency*] (ERG)
NPDS	Nuclear Particle Detection System (KSC)
NPDSA........	National Public Domain Software Archive (AIE)
NPDU	Naval Plant Development Unit (DNAB)
NPDU	Network Protocol Data Unit [*Telecommunications*] (OSI)
NPDW.........	North Pacific Deep Water [*Oceanography*]
NPDWG	Networking Project for Disabled Women and Girls (EA)
NPDWR.......	National Primary Drinking Water Regulations [*Environmental Protection Agency*]
NPE	Elizabeth City State University, Elizabeth City, NC [*OCLC symbol*] (OCLC)
NPE	Napier [*New Zealand*] [*Airport symbol*] (OAG)
NPE	Nasal Physical Examination
NPE	National Plastic Exposition
NPE	National Population Enquiry
NPE	Natural Parity Exchange [*Physics*] (OA)
NPE	Naval Pilot Evaluation (MUGU)
NPE	Navy Preliminary Evaluation
NPE	Network Processing Element (NITA)
NPE	New Preliminary Evaluation (MCD)
NPE	Nonpolluting Engine [*Rocketdyne/Commonwealth Edison Co.*]
NPE	Nonpotential Energy [*of molecules*]
NPE	Nonylphenol Ethoxylate [*Organic chemistry*]
NPE	Nuclear Photographic Emulsion
NPE	Nuclear Planning and Execution System (MCD)
NPE	Nuclear Power Engineering (IAA)
NPE	Nuveen Ins Prem Inc. Muni [*NYSE symbol*] (TTSB)
NPE	Nuveen Insured Premium Income Municipal [*NYSE symbol*] (SPSG)
NPEA	National Patio Enclosure Association (EA)
NPEA	National Printing Equipment Association [*Later, NPES*] (EA)
NPEB	Nonparametric Empirical Bayes [*Statistics*]
NPEC	National Panhellenic Editors Conference (EA)
NPEC	Native Plants Extracts Cooperative [*Australia*]
NPEC	Nuclear Power Engineering Committee [*Nuclear Regulatory Commission*] (NRCH)
NPECCD.......	National Public Education Campaign on Clinical Depression
NPED	Nuclear-Powered Energy Depot
NPee...........	Field Library, Inc., Peekskill, NY [*Library symbol Library of Congress*] (LCLS)
NPEF..........	New Product Evaluation Form
NPel...........	Pelham Public Library, Pelham, NY [*Library symbol Library of Congress*] (LCLS)
NPELRA	National Public Employer Labor Relations Association (EA)
NPEO	Nonylphenol Polyethoxylate [*Organic chemistry*]
NPER	National Public Employment Reporter Database [*Information service or system*] (IID)
NPerbA	J. N. Adam Developmental Center, Perrysburg, NY [*Library symbol Library of Congress*] (LCLS)
NPES	National Printing Equipment and Supply Association (EA)

NPES .... National Printing Equipment Show
NPE(S) .... Nuclear Planning and Execution (Service) (DOMA)
NPES .... Nuclear Planning and Execution System (COE)
NPESO .... NAVSHIPS [*Naval Ship Systems Command*] Plant Equipment Support Office
NPET .... Nicollet Process Engineering, Inc. [*NASDAQ symbol*] (SAG)
NPET .... Nicollet Process Engr [*NASDAQ symbol*] (TTSB)
NPET .... Nonpetroleum
NPEV .... Nonpolio Enterovirus [*Infectious Diseases*] (DAVI)
NPEX .... Normal Priority Exit (IAA)
NPF .... Names Project Foundation (EA)
NPF .... National Paraplegia Foundation (EA)
NPF .... National Park Foundation (EA)
NPF .... National Parkinson Foundation (EA)
NPF .... National Pharmaceutical Foundation (EA)
NPF .... National Piano Foundation (EA)
NPF .... National Pig Fair [*British*] (ITD)
NPF .... National Poetry Foundation (EA)
NPF .... National Police Force [*South Vietnam*] (VNW)
NPF .... National Policy Forum
NPF .... National Press Foundation (EA)
NPF .... National Progressive Front [*Iraq*] [*Political party*] (PPW)
NPF .... National Psoriasis Foundation (EA)
NPF .... Naval Parachute Facility (MCD)
NPF .... Naval Powder Factory
NPF .... Naval Procurement Fund [*Budget appropriation title*]
NPF .... NAVSTAR [*Navigation Satellite Tracking and Ranging*] Processing Facility (MCD)
NPF .... Net Propulsion Force (MCD)
NPF .... Network Pulse Forming
NPF .... Neutrons per Fission (DEN)
NPF .... Newspaper Press Fund (DGA)
NPF .... Newtonian Potential Function [*Mathematics*]
NPF .... Nicaragua Peace Fleet [*Defunct*] (EA)
NPF .... Nonpublic Funds [*Canadian Forces*]
NPF .... Nordisk Plastikkirurgisk Forening [*Scandinavian Association of Plastic Surgeons - SAPS*] (EAIO)
NPF .... North Pyrenean Fault [*Geology*]
NPF .... Not Provided For
npf .... Not Provided For (ODBW)
NPF .... Nuclear Power Facility (NRCH)
NPF .... Nuveen Premium Municipal Income [*NYSE symbol*] (SPSG)
NPF .... Nuveen Prem Muni Income [*NYSE symbol*] (TTSB)
NPFA .... National Peanut Festival Association (EA)
NPFA .... National Playing Fields Association [*British*]
NPFA .... National Prepared Food Association (NTPA)
NPF & PP .... Naval Prison Farms and Prison Personnel [*Budget appropriation title*]
NPFC .... National Pro-Family Coalition (EA)
NPFC .... Naval Publications and Forms Center
NPFC .... North Pacific Fisheries Commission (NOAA)
NPFC .... North Pacific Fur Seal Commission [*Defunct*]
NPFDA .... National Poultry and Food Distributors Association (NTPA)
NPFF .... National Police Field Force [*Military*]
NPFF .... Normal Probability Frequency Function
NPFFA .... National Prepared Frozen Food Association (EA)
NPFFG .... National Plant, Flower, and Fruit Guild (EA)
NPFFPA .... National Prepared Frozen Food Processors Association [*Later, NPFFA*] (EA)
NPFI .... National Plant Food Institute [*Later, TFI*] (EA)
NPFID .... Nitrogen-Phosphorus-Flame Ionization Detector [*Instrumentation*]
NPFL .... National Patriotic Front of Liberia [*Political party*] (EY)
NPFM .... Neural Pulse Frequency Modulation (PDAA)
NPFMC .... Northern Prawn Fishery Management Committee [*Australia*]
NPFMC .... North Pacific Fishery Management Council [*National Oceanic and Atmospheric Administration*] (GFGA)
NPFO .... Nuclear Power Field Office (IEEE)
NPFR .... Normalized Peak Filling Rate [*Cardiology*]
NPFRC .... North Pacific Fisheries Research Center [*National Oceanic and Atmospheric Administration*]
NPFS .... Naval Preflight School
NPFS .... No Prior or Current Federal Service (AABC)
NPFSC .... North Pacific Fur Seal Commission [*Defunct*]
NPFT .... Neurotic Personality Factor Test [*Psychology*]
NPFTA .... National Personal Fitness Trainers Association (EA)
NPFZ .... North Pyrenean Fault Zone [*Geology*]
NPG .... Napping (ABBR)
NPG .... National Peace Garden (EA)
NPG .... National Portrait Gallery [*Smithsonian Institution*]
NPG .... NATO Planning Group (NATG)
NPG .... Naval Proving Ground [*Dahlgren, VA*]
NPG .... Negative Population Growth (EA)
NPG .... Neopentylglycol [*Organic chemistry*]
NPG .... Nevada Proving Ground (BARN)
NPG .... New Performance Gallery [*San Francisco*]
NPG .... Nonprocessor Grant (IAA)
NPG .... Nonunit Personnel Generator (DOMA)
NPG .... Normalized Electron-Peak to Gamma-Peak [*Electronics*] (OA)
NPG .... Normalized Programming Generator (IAA)
NPG .... Not Paged [*Publishing*]
NPG .... N-Phenylglycine [*Organic chemistry*]
NPG .... Nuclear Planning Group [*NATO*]
NPG .... Nuclear Power Group [*British Defunct*] (NUCP)
NPG .... Nuveen GA Prem Inc Muni [*AMEX symbol*] (TTSB)
NPG .... Nuveen Georgia Premium Income Municipal Fund [*AMEX symbol*] (SPSG)

NPG .... Ontario Library Service Nipigon/Thunder Bay Public Library [*UTLAS symbol*]
NPGA .... National Propane Gas Association (NTPA)
NPGA .... National Pygmy Goat Association (EA)
NPGB .... (Nitrophenyl)guanidinobenzoate [*Organic chemistry*]
NPGC .... National Pell Grant Coalition (EA)
NPG-GMA .... N-Phenylglycine Glycidyl Methacrylate [*Organic chemistry*]
NPGLINAC .. Naval Postgraduate School Linear Accelerator
NPGPA .... Non-Powder Gun Products Association (EA)
NPGS .... National Plant Germplasm System [*Department of Agriculture*]
NPGS .... Naval Postgraduate School
NPGS .... Nuclear Power Generating Station (NRCH)
NPGTC .... National Prairie Grouse Technical Council (EA)
NPH .... Association of Nordic Paper Historians [*See also FNPH*] [*Sweden*] (EAIO)
NPH .... Nalcap Holdings, Inc. [*Vancouver Stock Exchange symbol*]
NPH .... Natural Period in Heave
NPH .... Natural Protamine Hagadorn [*Insulin*]
NPH .... Natural Protein Hagedorn (DB)
NPH .... Nephi [*Utah*] [*Airport symbol*] (OAG)
NPH .... Neurophysin [*Biochemistry*]
NPH .... Neutral Protamine Hagedorn [*Insulin suspension*]
NPH .... No Previous History [*Medicine*] (DAVI)
NPH .... No Profit Here [*Business term*]
NPH .... Normal Paraffin Hydrocarbon
NPH .... Normal Pressure Hydrocephalus [*Medicine*]
NPh. .... Northern Phoenician (BJA)
NPH .... North Pit [*Hawaii*] [*Seismograph station code, US Geological Survey*] (SEIS)
NPHA .... Nanga Parbat/Haramosh Axis [*Himalayan geology*]
NPHA .... National Park Hospitality Association (NTPA)
NPHA .... National Peer Helpers Association (EA)
NPhA .... National Pharmaceutical Association (EA)
NPHA .... National Plott Hound Association (EA)
NPHA .... National Prison Hospice Association (NTPA)
NPHB .... Nonphotochemical Hole Burning [*Spectrometry*]
NPhD .... Doctor of Natural Philosophy
NPHE .... Nitrophenyl Hexyl Ether [*Organic chemistry*]
NPHOE .... Nitrophenyl Hydroxyoctyl Ether [*Organic chemistry*]
NPHPRS ...... National Public Health Program Reporting System [*Department of Health and Human Services*]
NPHR .... National Foreign Intelligence Plan for Human Resources (MCD)
NPhR .... Neue Philologische Rundschau [*A publication*] (BJA)
NPHRC .... National Pediatric HIV Resource Center (PAZ)
NPHS .... Northwick Park Heart Study (DAVI)
NPHWA .... National Presbyterian Health and Welfare Association [*Later, PHEWA*]
NPhx .... Nasopharynx [*Anatomy*] (DAVI)
NPI .... International Business Machines Corp., Systems Development Division, Poughkeepsie, NY [*Library symbol Library of Congress*] (LCLS)
NPI .... Narcissistic Personality Inventory [*Psychology*] (EDAC)
NPI .... National Paralegal Institute (EA)
NPI .... National Parkinson Institute
NPI .... National Pollutant Inventory
NPI .... National Presto Industries, Inc. (EFIS)
NPI .... National Provident Institution [*Wales*]
NPI .... National Purchasing Institute (EA)
NPI .... Net Premium Income [*Insurance*] (AIA)
NPI .... NeuroPsychiatric Institute [*UCLA*]
NPI .... NEXRAD [*Next Generation Weather Radar*] Product Interface [*Marine science*] (OSRA)
NPI .... Nonprocedural Interface [*Computer science*]
NPI .... No Present Illness
NPI .... No Previous Information [*to tip off a US Customs Service seizure*]
NPI .... Normick Perron, Inc. [*Toronto Stock Exchange symbol*]
NPI .... North Pocatello Valley [*Idaho*] [*Seismograph station code, US Geological Survey*] (SEIS)
NPI .... Nucleoplasmic Index [*Medicine*] (DMAA)
NPI .... Numbering Plan Indicator [*Computer science*] (TNIG)
NPI .... Nuveen Prem Income Muni [*NYSE symbol*] (TTSB)
NPI .... Nuveen Premium Income Municipal Fund, Inc. [*NYSE symbol*] (SPSG)
NPIA .... Nanny Pop-Ins Association [*Defunct*] (EA)
NPIA .... National Photography Instructors Association (EA)
NPIAS .... National Plan of Integrated Airport Systems [*BTS*] [*FAA*] (TAG)
NPIC .... National Pesticide Information Clearinghouse [*Later, NPTN*] (EA)
NPIC .... National Pharmacy Insurance Council [*Defunct*] (EA)
NPIC .... National Photographic Intelligence Center (MUSM)
NPIC .... National Photographic Interpretation Center [*CIA*]
NPIC .... Naval Photographic Interpretation Center
NPIC .... Neurogenic Peripheral Intermittent Claudication [*Medicine*] (DMAA)
NPIC .... Nitrosopipecolic Acid [*Organic chemistry*]
NPie .... Piermont Public Library, Piermont, NY [*Library symbol Library of Congress*] (LCLS)
NPIF .... National Peace Institute Foundation (EA)
NPIG .... Nuclear Power Information Group [*British*] (NUCP)
NPIN .... National Parent Information Network
NPIN .... Negative-Positive-Intrinsic-Negative [*Electron device*] (MSA)
NPIP .... National Poultry Improvement Plan (EA)
NPIP .... Nitrosopiperidine [*Also, NP*] [*Organic chemistry*]
NPIPF .... Newspaper and Printing Industries Pension Fund [*British*] (BI)
NPiPNA .... N-Paraffins, iso-Paraffins, Naphthenes and Aromatics [*Gasoline analysis*]
NPIR .... No Periodic Inspection Required [*Military*] (AFIT)

NPIRG.........	National Public Interest Research Group (EA)
NPIRI..........	National Printing Ink Research Institute (EA)
NPIRS..........	National Pesticide Information Retrieval System [*Purdue University*] [*West Lafayette, IN Database*]
NPIS	National Physics Information System [*American Institute of Physics*] [*New York, NY*] (DIT)
NP/IS	National Premium Incentive Show (ITD)
NPIS	New Product Information Service [*Department of Commerce*]
NPIS	Nuclear Plant Island Structure (NRCH)
NPITI	National Project for the Improvement of Televised Instruction [*National Association of Educational Broadcasters*]
NPIU	Network Processing and Interface Unit (NITA)
NPIU	Numerical Processing and Interface Unit [*Computer science*] (MHDB)
NPIW	North Pacific Intermediate Water [*Marine science*] (OSRA)
NPIX	Network Peripherals [*NASDAQ symbol*] (TTSB)
NPIX	Network Peripherals, Inc. [*NASDAQ symbol*] (SAG)
NPJ.............	Corpus Christi, TX [*Location identifier FAA*] (FAAL)
NPj.............	Port Jefferson Free Library, Port Jefferson, NY [*Library symbol Library of Congress*] (LCLS)
NPjES	Port Jefferson Elementary School, Port Jefferson, NY [*Library symbol Library of Congress*] (LCLS)
NPjMH........	John T. Mather Memorial Hospital, Port Jefferson, NY [*Library symbol Library of Congress*] (LCLS)
NPJPA	National Prune Juice Packers Association (EA)
NPjs............	Port Jefferson Station-Terryville Public Library, Port Jefferson Station, NY [*Library symbol Library of Congress*] (LCLS)
NPjSCH.......	Saint Charles Hospital, Port Jefferson, NY [*Library symbol Library of Congress*] (LCLS)
NPJT	Nonparoxysmal Atrioventricular Junction Tachycardia [*Cardiology*]
NPjVH.........	Earl L. Vandermeulen High School, Port Jefferson, NY [*Library symbol Library of Congress*] (LCLS)
NPK	Nationale Partij Kombinatie [*National Party Alliance*] [*Surinam*] [*Political party*] (PPW)
NPK	National Presto Industries, Inc. [*NYSE symbol*] (SPSG)
NPK	Natl Presto Indus [*NYSE symbol*] (TTSB)
NPK	Nitrogen, Phosphorus, Potassium [*Fertilizer components*]
NPK	Noble Peak Resources Ltd. [*Vancouver Stock Exchange symbol*]
NPK	Nodal Point Keying
NPKA	National Paving and Kerb Association [*British*] (DBA)
NPL.............	Free Public Library of Newark, Newark, NJ [*OCLC symbol*] (OCLC)
NPL.............	Nameplate (MSA)
NPL.............	Naples [*Italy*] [*Seismograph station code, US Geological Survey Closed*] (SEIS)
NPL.............	National Physical Laboratory [*Research center British*] (IRC)
NPL.............	National Physics Laboratory (KSC)
NPL.............	National Priorities List [*Hazardous wastes*] [*Environmental Protection Agency*]
NPL.............	National Propane Partners LP [*NYSE symbol*] (SAG)
NPL.............	National Puzzlers' League (EA)
NPL.............	Natural Processing Language [*Computer science*] (HGAA)
NPL.............	Neon Pilot Light
NPL.............	Neoproteolipid [*Hematology*]
NPL.............	Nepal [*ANSI three-letter standard code*] (CNC)
NPL.............	Nepheline Resources Ltd. [*Vancouver Stock Exchange symbol*]
NPL.............	Newfoundland Public Library Services [*UTLAS symbol*]
NPL.............	New Plymouth [*New Zealand*] [*Airport symbol*] (OAG)
NPL.............	New Process Line (IAA)
NPL.............	New Product Line
NPL.............	New Programming Language [*1974*] [*Later, PL/1*] [*Computer science*]
NPL.............	Nodular Poorly Differentiated Lymphoma [*Oncology*] (DAVI)
NPL.............	Noise Pollution Level
NPL.............	Nonparametric Multipoint Linkage [*Mathematics*]
NPL.............	Nonpartisan League [*Political party in North Dakota opposed by the IVA*]
NPL.............	Nonpersonal Liability
NPL.............	Nonprogramming Language (IAA)
NPL.............	Nonstandard Parts List (MCD)
NPL.............	No Perception of Light [*Ophthalmology*] (CPH)
NPL.............	Normal Power Level (KSC)
npl	Noun, Plural [*Grammar*] (CDAI)
NPL.............	Numerical Parts List
NPL.............	Numerical Preference List [*Military*] (AFIT)
NPl.............	Plainview-Old Bethpage Public Library, Plainview, NY [*Library symbol Library of Congress*] (LCLS)
NPLA	National Perishable Logistics Association (NTPA)
NPla...........	Plattsburgh Public Library, Plattsburgh, NY [*Library symbol Library of Congress*] (LCLS)
NPlaB	Bellarmine College, Plattsburgh, NY [*Library symbol Library of Congress*] (LCLS)
NPlaC	Champlain College, Plattsburgh, NY [*Library symbol Library of Congress Obsolete*] (LCLS)
NPLAC	National People Living with AIDS [*Acquired Immune Deficiency Syndrome*] Coalition [*Australia*]
NPlaCC	Clinton Community College, Plattsburgh, NY [*Library symbol Library of Congress*] (LCLS)
NPlaCEF	Clinton-Essex-Franklin Library System, Plattsburgh, NY [*Library symbol Library of Congress*] (LCLS)
NPlaCN	Champlain Valley School of Nursing, Plattsburgh, NY [*Library symbol Library of Congress*] (LCLS)
NPL-AERO ...	National Physical Laboratory, Aerodynamics Division [*British*]
NPLAN	National Plan for Australian Newspapers
NPlaP	Champlain Valley Physicians Hospital, Plattsburgh, NY [*Library symbol Library of Congress*] (LCLS)
NPlaU	State University of New York, College at Plattsburgh, Plattsburgh, NY [*Library symbol Library of Congress*] (LCLS)
NPIBE	Old Bethpage Elementary School, Plainview, NY [*Library symbol Library of Congress*] (LCLS)
NPIBM	Plainview-Old Bethpage Middle School, Plainview, NY [*Library symbol*] [*Library of Congress*] (LCLS)
NPLC	National Pedigree Livestock Council (EA)
NPLC	National Product Liability Council (EA)
NPLC	Normal Phase Liquid Chromatography
NPICH	Central General Hospital, Plainview, NY [*Library symbol Library of Congress*] (LCLS)
NPLD	National Pro-Life Democrats (EA)
NPIe...........	Mount Pleasant Public Library, Pleasantville, NY [*Library symbol Library of Congress*] (LCLS)
NPLEI.........	National Police Law Enforcement Institute (EA)
NPIeP	Pace University Westchester, Pleasantville, NY [*Library symbol Library of Congress*] (LCLS)
NPLF..........	National Preservation Loan Fund [*National Trust for Historic Preservation*]
NPLG	Navy Program Language Group
NPLG	Night Plane Guard Station (NVT)
NPLG	Night Plane Landing Guard (NVT)
NPIGS........	Church of Jesus Christ of Latter-Day Saints, Genealogical Society Library, Plainview Branch, Plainview, NY [*Library symbol Library of Congress*] (LCLS)
NPIJE	Jamaica Elementary School, Plainview, NY [*Library symbol Library of Congress*] (LCLS)
NPIKH	John F. Kennedy High School, Plainview, NY [*Library symbol Library of Congress*] (LCLS)
NPIMC	Nassau County Medical Center, Plainview Division, Plainview, NY [*Library symbol Library of Congress*] (LCLS)
NPIMM	H.B. Mattlin Middle School, Plainview, NY [*Library symbol*] [*Library of Congress*] (LCLS)
NPInRI........	New Plan Realty Trust [*Associated Press*] (SAG)
NPLO	NATO Production and Logistics Organization (NATG)
NP-L PAC....	National Pro-Life Political Action Committee [*Defunct*] (EA)
NPIPE	Pasadena Elementary School, Plainview, NY [*Library symbol Library of Congress*] (LCLS)
NPIPwE.......	Parkway Elementary School, Plainview, NY [*Library symbol Library of Congress*] (LCLS)
NPLR	Nyasaland Protectorate Law Reports [*A publication*] (ILCA)
NPLS	Nonplus (ABBR)
NPLSD........	Nonplused (ABBR)
NPISH........	Plainview-Old Bethpage Senior High School, Plainview, NY [*Library symbol Library of Congress*] (LCLS)
N/PLT.........	Name Plate [*Automotive engineering*]
NPLTC	National Public Law Training Center (EA)
N PLUR.......	Neuter Plural [*Grammar*] (OCD)
NPM	Counts per Minute (IDOE)
NPM	Marist College, Poughkeepsie, NY [*Library symbol Library of Congress*] (LCLS)
NPM	Narrowband Phase Modulation (DEN)
NPM	National Association of Pastoral Musicians (EA)
NPM	National Program Manager [*Environmental Protection Agency*] (GFGA)
NPM	Natural Particulate Matter [*Oceanography*]
NPM	Naval Provost Martial [*British*]
NPM	Navy Programming Manual
NPM	Neonatal-Perinatal Medicine [*Medical specialty*] (DHSM)
Np/m..........	Neper per Meter
NPM	Network Performance Monitor (NITA)
NPM	New Privateer Mines [*Vancouver Stock Exchange symbol*]
NPM	Non-Print Media [*Advertising*]
NPM	North Pahute Mesa [*Nevada*] [*Seismograph station code, US Geological Survey*] (SEIS)
NPM	Nothing per Mouth [*Medicine*] (DMAA)
NPM	Nuveen Prem Income Muni 2 [*NYSE symbol*] (TTSB)
NPM	Nuveen Premium Income Municipal 2 [*NYSE symbol*] (SPSG)
NPMA	National Piano Manufacturers Association of America [*Later, PMAI*] (EA)
NPMA	National Podiatric Medical Association (EA)
NPMA	National Property Management Association (EA)
NPMA	Navy Personnel Management Academy (DNAB)
NPMA	Newspaper Purchasing Management Association (EA)
NPMC	National Pecan Marketing Council (EA)
NPMCA	National Paper Marketing Council of Australia
NPMG	NATO Patriot Management Group (MCD)
NPMH	Mid-Hudson Libraries, Poughkeepsie, NY [*Library symbol Library of Congress*] (LCLS)
NPMHU	National Postal Mail Handlers Union (EA)
NPMI	Nordic Pool for Marine Insurance [*Helsinki, Finland*] (EA)
NPMP	National Pesticide Monitoring Program [*Later, National Contaminant Biomonitoring Program*] [*US Fish and Wildlife Service*]
NPMR	National Premium Manufacturers Representatives [*Later, IMRA*] (EA)
NPMTC	Navy Pacific Missile Test Center (MCD)
NPMTT........	Nuclear Propulsion Mobile Training Team [*Military*] (CAAL)
NPN	NASA Part Number (MCD)
NPN	National Particulate Network [*Environmental Protection Agency*] (GFGA)
NPN	National Party of Nigeria [*Political party*] (PPW)
NPN	National Performance Network (EA)
NPN	National Prevention Network (EA)
NPN	National Prices Network
N-P-N	Negative-Positive-Negative [*Transistor*] (CET)
NPN	New Product Network [*Television*]

NPN	New Pseudonyms and Nicknames [*A publication*]
NPN	Non-Par Not Approved
NPN	Nonprotein Nitrogen [*Analytical chemistry*]
NPN	Normal Propyl Nitrate (MCD)
NPNA	No Protest Nonacceptance [*Banking*]
NPNCA	National Parks and Nature Conservation Authority [*Australia*]
NPNCF	Nicene and Post-Nicene Christian Fathers [*A publication*] (ODCC)
NPNP	Negative-Positive-Negative-Positive [*Transistor*]
NP NS	Ohio Nisi Prius Reports, New Series [*A publication*] (DLA)
NPO	Naphthylphenyloxazole [*Biochemical analysis*]
NPO	NASA Pasadena Office (MCD)
NPO	National [*or New*] Post Office Building
NPO	National Project Office
NPO	Naval Port Officer
NPO	Navy Post Office
NPO	Navy Program Objectives (NG)
NPO	Navy Purchasing Office
NPO	Negative Positive Zero (IAA)
NPO	Neighborhood Patrol Office [*or Officer*]
NPO	New Personnel Orientation (MCD)
NPO	New Philharmonic Orchestra [*British*]
NPO	Nil per Os [*Nothing by Mouth*] [*Medicine*]
NPO	Non Per Os [*Nothing by Mouth*] [*Latin*] (BABM)
NPO	No Part on Order (MCD)
NPO	Norpet Resources Ltd. [*Toronto Stock Exchange symbol*]
NPO	Not Pickled Ordinary [*Metal industry*]
NPO	Nuclear Plant Operator (NRCH)
NPO	Nuclear Propulsion Office
NPO	Nucleus Preopticus (DMAA)
NPO	Preoptic Nucleus (DB)
NPO	Strategic Systems Project Office, Washington, DC [*OCLC symbol*] (OCLC)
NPOAA	National Police Officers Association of America (EA)
NPOC	National Point of Contact (PDAA)
NPOC	Navy Polar Oceanographic Center (DNAB)
NPOC	Nonpurgeable Organic Carbon
NPODS	Navy Publishing on Demand System (AAGC)
NPOE	Nitrophenyl Octyl Ether [*Organic chemistry*]
NPOEV	Nuclear-Powered Ocean Engineering Vehicle [*Minisub*]
NP Ohio	Ohio Nisi Prius Reports [*A publication*] (DLA)
NPO/HS	Nulla per Os Hora Somni [*Nothing by Mouth at Bedtime*] [*Latin Pharmacy*] (MAH)
NPOI	Navy Prototype Optical Interferometer
NPOL	Nuclear Pollution [*Environmental science*] (COE)
NPOLA	Navy Purchasing Office, Los Angeles
NPOMHWMGL...	National Post Office Mail Handlers, Watchmen, Messengers, and Group Leaders [*Later, NPMHU*] (EA)
NPOPR	Not Paid on Prior Rolls
NPoq	Beekman Community Library Reading Center, Poughquag, NY [*Library symbol Library of Congress*] (LCLS)
NP or D	No Place or Date
NPOS	Nitrite Positive [*Organic chemistry*] (DAVI)
NPOS	Nurses Professional Orientation Scale (DMAA)
NPOST	Nonperturbative Open-Shell Theory [*Physics*]
NPot	Potsdam Public Library, Potsdam, NY [*Library symbol Library of Congress*] (LCLS)
NPotC	Clarkson College of Technology, Potsdam, NY [*Library symbol Library of Congress*] (LCLS)
NPotU	State University of New York, College at Potsdam, Potsdam, NY [*Library symbol Library of Congress*] (LCLS)
NPour	Hiram Halley Memorial Library, Pound Ridge, NY [*Library symbol*] [*Library of Congress*] (LCLS)
NPP	National Patriotic Party [*Liberia*] [*Political party*] (EY)
NPP	National Peach Partners [*Defunct*] (EA)
NPP	National People's Party [*Pakistan*] [*Political party*] (FEA)
NPP	National Periodicals Publications, Inc.
NPP	National Policy Paper [*Army*] (AABC)
NPP	National Pretreatment Program [*Metal finishing technology*]
NPP	National Priority Program [*NHTSA*] (TAG)
NPP	National Prison Project (EA)
NPP	National Procurement Point [*Military*] (RDA)
NPP	National Progressive Party [*Iraq*] [*Political party*] (BJA)
NPP	National Prohibition Party (EA)
NPP	Naval Propellant Plant
NPP	Navy Propellant Plant (DNAB)
NPP	Negative Picture Phase
NPP	Nemzeti Paraszt Part [*National Peasant Party*] [*Hungary Political party*] (PPE)
NPP	Neodymium Pentaphosphate [*Inorganic chemistry*]
NPP	Net Primary Productivity
NPP	Network Power Processor [*Acme Electric Corp.*] [*Computer science*] (PCM)
NPP	Network Protocol Processor
NPP	New Patriotic Party [*Ghana*] [*Political party*] (ECON)
NPP	New People's Party [*North Korea Political party*] (FEA)
NPP	New Physics Project (AIE)
NPP	New Product Planning (IAA)
NPP	New Progressive Party [*Puerto Rico*] [*Political party*]
NPP	Nigerian People's Party [*Political party*] (PPW)
NPP	Nitrophenyl Phosphate [*Biochemical analysis*]
NPP	Nitrophenylprolinol [*Organic chemistry*]
NPP	Nitropropenyl Pivalate [*Organic chemistry*]
NPP	Non-Penetrating Periscope [*DARPA*]
NPP	No Passed Proof
NPP	Normal Pool Plasma [*Clinical chemistry*]
NPP	North American Power [*Vancouver Stock Exchange symbol*]
NPP	Nozzleless Performance Program Module (MCD)
NPP	N-Pentylpalmitamide [*Organic chemistry*]
NPP	Nuclear Power Plant (IEEE)
NPP	Nurse Practitioner Project
NPP	Nuveen Performance Plus Municipal [*NYSE symbol*] (SPSG)
NPP	Nuveen Perform Plus Muni [*NYSE symbol*] (TTSB)
NPPA	National Parks and Primitive Areas
NPPA	National Pickle Packers Association [*Later, PPI*]
NPPA	National Pizza and Pasta Association (EA)
NPPA	National Press Photographers Association (EA)
NPPA	National Probation and Parole Association [*Later, NCCD*]
NPPAC	National and Provincial Parks Association of Canada
NPPAG	National Program Production and Aquisition Grant [*Corporation for Public Broadcasting*] [*Radio*] (NTCM)
NPPase	Nitrophenylphosphatase (DB)
NPPB	National Poisons and Pesticides Board [*Sweden*]
NPPB	National Potato Promotion Board (EA)
NPPB	Nitro(Phenylpropylamino) Benzoate [*Organic chemistry*]
NPPC	National Pork Producers Council (EA)
NPPC	National Power Policy Committee [*World War II*]
NPPC	Navy Programming Planning Council
NPPC	Nuclear Power Plant Co. Ltd.
NPPC	Numeric Parts Preference Code [*Military*] (AFIT)
NPPC	Nursing Professional Practice Council (DMAA)
NPPD	(Nitrophenyl)pentadienal [*Tracer chemical*] [*Organic chemistry*]
NPPE	Negative Pressure Pulmonary Edema [*Medicine*] (DMAA)
NPPE	Nitrophenyl Pentyl Ether [*Organic chemistry*]
NPPE	Nuclear Power Propulsion Evaluation (NG)
NPPF	National Poultry Producers Federation [*Defunct*] (EA)
NPPI	Navy Program Progress Item (CAAL)
NPPI	Negative Pressure Patient Isolator [*Medicine*] (WDAA)
NPPI	Norwood Promotional Prd [*NASDAQ symbol*] (TTSB)
NPPI	Norwood Promotional Products [*NASDAQ symbol*] (SAG)
NPPL	National Parks and Public Lands [*Victoria, Australia*]
NPPL	Neuropsychopharmacology Laboratory [*Wayne State University*] [*Research center*]
NPPN	Nitroxyperoxypropyl Nitrate [*Environmental chemistry*]
NPPN	NUDO [*Namibia United Democratic Organization*] Progressive Party of Namibia [*Political party*] (PPW)
NPPO	Navy Program Planning Office
NPPO	Navy Publications and Printing Office
NP.PP	Natl Power PLC Interim ADS [*NYSE symbol*] (TTSB)
NPP/QAS	Naval Propellant Plant Quality Assurance Department [*Indian Head, MD*]
NPPR	Nationalist Party of Puerto Rico (NADA)
NPPR	Navy Program Progress Report
NPPR	Nonproductive Procurement Directive
NPPRE	Nitrophenyl Propyl Ether [*Organic chemistry*]
NPPS	Navy Planning and Programming System
NPPS	Navy Publications and Printing Service
NPPSBO	Navy Publications and Printing Service Branch Office
NPPSIS	National Parent to Parent Support & Information Systems, Inc.
NPPSMO	Navy Publications and Printing Service Management Office
NPPSO	Navy Publications and Printing Service Office
NPPSSOEASTDIV...	Navy Publications and Printing Service, Southeastern Division (DNAB)
NPPSWESTDIV...	Navy Publications and Printing Service, Western Division (DNAB)
NPPTA	National Public Parks Tennis Association (EA)
NPPTS	Nuclear Power Plant Training Simulator (PDAA)
NPPW	National Poison Prevention Week
NPQAA	Natural Products Quality Assurance Alliance
NPR	Napier [*New Zealand*] [*Seismograph station code, US Geological Survey Closed*] (SEIS)
NPR	Napper (ABBR)
NPR	Narodowa Partia Robotnicza [*National Workers Party*] [*Poland Political party*] (PPE)
NPR	National Aeronautics and Space Administration Procurement Regulation [*A publication*] (AAGC)
NPR	National Parks and Access to the Countryside Regulations [*Town planning*] [*British*]
NPR	National Performance Review [*A publication*]
NPR	National Public Radio [*Washington, DC Telecommunications*] (TSSD)
NPR	Naval Petroleum Reserves
NPR	Naval Plant Representative
NPR	Navy Payroll (DNAB)
NPR	Navy Preliminary Revision (DNAB)
NPR	Navy Procurement Regulation
NPR	Negro Puerto Rican
NPR	Neoricans in Puerto Rico (EA)
NPR	Neptune Resources Corp. [*Toronto Stock Exchange symbol*]
NPR	Net Pool Return
NPR	Net Protein Ratio [*Nutrition*]
NPR	New Plan Realty Trust SBI [*NYSE symbol*] (SPSG)
NPR	New Plan Rlty Tr SBI [*NYSE symbol*] (TTSB)
NPR	New Production Reactor [*Department of Energy*]
NPR	Night Press Rate [*of newspapers*]
NPR	Nisi Prius Reports [*A publication*] (DLA)
NPR	Noise Power Ratio
NPR	Noise Prediction and Reduction
NPR	Noise Preferential Route [*Aviation*] (DA)
NPR	Nonprocessor Request (IAA)
NPR	Nonproduction Release (MCD)
NPR	Normal Pulse Rate [*Medicine*] (DMAA)
NPR	North Polar Region

NPR	Notice of Program Reimbursement (MEDA)
NPR	Notice of Proposed Rule Making [*Federal agencies*] (GFGA)
NPR	Nozzle Pressure Ratio [*Aviation*]
NPR	Nuclear Paramagnetic Resonance (MCD)
NPR	Nuclear Posture Review [*DoD*]
NPR	Nuclear Power Reactor
NPR	Nuclear Pulse Rocket [*NASA*]
NPR	Nucleoside Phosphoribosyl (DMAA)
NPR	Numerical Position Readout (IAA)
NPr	Pearl River Public Library, Pearl River, NY [*Library symbol Library of Congress*] (LCLS)
NPrA	American Cyanamid Co., Lederle Laboratories, Pearl River, NY [*Library symbol Library of Congress*] (LCLS)
NPRA	National Parks and Recreation Act of 1978 (COE)
NPRA	National Parks and Recreation Association (NADA)
NPRA	National Personal Robot Association [*Later, NSRA*] (EA)
NPRA	National Petroleum Refiners Association (EA)
NPRA	Naval Personnel Research Activity
NPRA	Newspaper Personnel Relations Association (EA)
NPR&D	Navy Property Redistribution and Disposal (AAGC)
NPRC	National Personnel Records Center [*National Archives and Records Service*]
NPRC	National Polystyrene Recycling Co.
NPRC	National Project on Resource Coordination for Justice Statistics and Information [*Canada*]
NPRC	National Public Relations Council of Health and Welfare Services [*Formerly, NPC*]
NPRC	National Puerto Rican Coalition (EA)
NPRC	Newspaper Production and Research Center
NPRC	Nonproliferation Program Review Committee [*US, multiagency*]
NPRC	Nuclear Power Range Channel (IEEE)
NPRC (CPR)	National Personnel Records Center (Civilian Personnel Records) [*National Archives and Records Service*] (AFM)
NPRCG	Nuclear Public Relations Contact Group
NPRC (MPR)	National Personnel Records Center (Military Personnel Records) [*National Archives and Records Service*] (AFM)
NPRD	NASA Procurement Regulation Directive
NPRD	Nonelectronic Parts Reliability Data (MCD)
NPRD	Nuclear Plant Reliability Data
NPRDA	National Precure Retread Dealers Association [*Defunct*] (EA)
NPRDC	National Public Resources Defense Council (NUCP)
NPRDC	Navy Personnel Research and Development Center (GRD)
NPRDL	Naval Personnel Research and Development Laboratory
NPRDS	Nuclear Plant Reliability Data System (NRCH)
NPRF	National Priority Reserve Fund [*Australia*]
NPRF	National Puerto Rican Forum (EA)
NPRF	Northrop Pulse Radiation Facility
NPRFT	Nonprofit (ABBR)
NPRI	National Psychiatric Reform Institute
NPRL	Navy Prosthetics Research Laboratory
NPRL	Nonprocedural Referencing Language
NPRM	Neopharm Inc. [*NASDAQ symbol*] (TTSB)
NPRM	Notice of Proposed Rule Making [*Federal agencies*]
NPRMW	Neopharm Inc. Wrrt [*NASDAQ symbol*] (TTSB)
NPRN	Neoprene [*Synthetic rubber*]
NPRN	North American Public Relations Network (NTPA)
NPRO	NaPro Bio Therapeutics [*NASDAQ symbol*] (TTSB)
NPRO	NaPro BioTherapeutics, Inc. [*NASDAQ symbol*] (SAG)
NPRO	Naval Petroleum Reserves Office
NPRO	Navy Plant Representative Office
NPRO	N-Nitrosoproline [*Organic chemistry*]
NPROA	Nitrosoprolylalanine [*Organic chemistry*]
NPROG	Nitrosoprolylglycine [*Organic chemistry*]
NPROW	Napro Biotheraputics Wrrts [*NASDAQ symbol*] (TTSB)
NPRPA	Naval Petroleum Reserves Production Act (AAGC)
NPRR	National Public Relations Roundtable [*Defunct*]
NPRR	Net Pool Return Rule
NPRS	NASA Procurement Regulation Supplement
NPRS	Negative Poll Response State (IAA)
NPRS	Newpark Resources, Inc. [*NASDAQ symbol*] (SAG)
NPRS	Nonpersistent (FAAC)
NPRTSN	Nonpartisan (ABBR)
NPRTSNSP	Nonpartisanship (ABBR)
NPRTX	Neub. & Berman Partners Fund [*Mutual fund ticker symbol*] (SG)
NPRV	Nitrogen Pressure Relief Valve (MCD)
NPRWC	National Puerto Rican Women's Caucus [*Defunct*] (EA)
NPS	Counts per Second (IDOE)
NPS	Honolulu, HI [*Location identifier FAA*] (FAAL)
NPS	Narcotics Prevention Service (NADA)
NPS	NASA Planning Studies (KSC)
NPS	Nationale Partij Suriname [*Surinam National Party*] [*Political party*] (PPW)
NPS	National Park Service [*Department of the Interior*]
NPS	National Parole Service [*Canada*]
NPS	National Periodicals System
NPS	National Permit Strategy [*Environmental Protection Agency*] (GFGA)
NPS	National Pesticide Survey [*Environmental Protection Agency*] (GFGA)
NPS	National Philatelic Society [*Defunct*] (EA)
NPS	National Phone Services, Inc.
NPS	National Poetry Secretariat [*British*] [*An association*] (DBA)
NPS	National Poetry Series
NPS	National Pony Society [*British*] (DI)
NPS	National Prisoner Statistics [*An association*]
NPS	Naval Postgraduate School
NPS	Navy Personnel Survey

NPS	Navy Primary Standards (MSA)
NPS	Neapolis [*Greece*] [*Seismograph station code, US Geological Survey*] (SEIS)
NPS	Negative Potential Shifts [*Neurophysiology*]
NPS	Network Processing Supervisor [*Honeywell, Inc.*]
NPS	Network Processor System (NITA)
NPS	Neutral Pressure Switch
NPS	Newspaper Pagination System [*Typography*] (DGA)
NPS	Night Photographic System
NPS	Nitrophenyl Sulfenyl [*Organic chemistry*]
Nps	Nitrophenylthio(nitrophenylsulfonyl) [*Biochemistry*]
NPS	Noise Power Spectra [*Spectrometry*]
NPS	Nominal Pipe Size (SAA)
NPS	Noncumulative Preferred Stock [*Investment term*] (MHDW)
NPS	Nonperishable Subsistence
NPS	Non-Pneumatic Spare [*Automotive engineering*]
NPS	Nonpoint Source [*Environmental Protection Agency*] (AEPA)
NPS	Nonpoint Source Pollution [*Agricultural engineering*]
NPS	Non-Prior Service (MCD)
NPS	No-Par Stock [*Investment term*] (MHDW)
NPS	No Prior Service [*Military*]
NPS	Normalized Plateau Slope
NPS	Normal Pipe Size
NPS	North Polar Sequence
NPS	Northwestern Public Service Co. [*NYSE symbol*] (SPSG)
NPS	Northwestern Pub Svc [*NYSE symbol*] (TTSB)
NPS	Nuclear and Plasma Sciences (MCD)
NPS	Nuclear Planning System (COE)
NPS	Nuclear-Powered Ship (NVT)
NPS	Nuclear Power Source
NPS	Nuclear Power System
NPS	Numerical Plotting System (NRCH)
NPS	NWPS Capital Financing Tr PERCS [*NYSE symbol*] (SAG)
NPSA	National Passenger Safety Association [*Defunct*] (EA)
NPSA	National Pecan Shellers Association (EA)
NPSA	National Pegboard Systems Association (EA)
NPSA	National Psychic Science Association (EA)
NPSA	New Program Status Area (IEEE)
NPSA	Novitiate of Saint Andrew-On-Hudson, Poughkeepsie, NY [*Library symbol Library of Congress*] (LCLS)
NPSAPHA	New Professionals Section of the American Public Health Association (EA)
NPSAS	National Postsecondary Student Aid Study [*Department of Education*] (GFGA)
NPSB	National Prisoner Statistics Bulletin [*Department of Justice*]
NPSB	News Print Service Bureau
NPS BBS	Nonpoint Source Electronic Bulletin Board System [*Environmental Protection Agency*] (AEPA)
NPSC	Naval Personnel Separation Center
NPSC	New Paradigm Sftwr [*NASDAQ symbol*] (TTSB)
NPSC	New Paradigm Software [*NASDAQ symbol*] (SAG)
NPSC-CL	Nursing Policy Studies Centre [*University of Warwick*] [*British*] (CB)
NPS-CL	Nitrophenyl Sulfenyl Chloride
NPS/CPSU/UW	National Park Service Cooperative Park Studies Unit, University of Washington [*Research center*] (RCD)
NPSCW	New Paradigm Software Wrrt [*NASDAQ symbol*] (TTSB)
NPSD	Naval Photographic Services Depot
NPSD	Neutron Power Spectral Density (OA)
NPSD	Noise Power Spectre Density
NPSDN	Nordic Packet Switched Data Network (NITA)
NPSE	National Premium Sales Executives (EA)
NPSE	Navy Peridontal Screening Examination (DNAB)
NPSF	National Pipe Straight Fine [*Mechanical engineering*]
NPSF	National Straight Pipe Threads for Dry Seal Pressure Tight Joints
NPSFR	Net Public Sector Financing Requirement [*Business term*]
NPSH	National Straight Pipe Threads for Hose Couplings and Nipples
NPSH	Net Positive Suction Head [*Pumps*]
NPSH	Nonprotein Sulfhydryl [*Biochemistry*]
NPSH	Not Positive Suction Head (COE)
NPSHA	Net Positive Suction Head Available [*Pumps*] (PDAA)
NPSHR	Net Positive Suction Head Required [*Chemical or food processing*]
NPSI	National Pipe Straight Intermediate [*Mechanical engineering*]
NPSI	Network Control Program Packet Switching Interface [*Computer science*] (HGAA)
NPSI	Nursing Performance Simulation Instrument
NPSL	National Professional Soccer League [*Later, NASL*]
NPSL	National Straight Pipe Threads for Locknuts and Locknut Pipe Threads
NPSM	Non-Productive Standard Minute (PDAA)
NPSMS	Nonpoint Source Management System (WPI)
NPSNL	South Eastern New York Library Resources Council, Poughkeepsie, NY [*Library symbol*] [*Library of Congress*] (LCLS)
NPSO	Nonpaired Spatial Orbitals [*Atomic physics*]
NPSP	National People's Salvation Party [*Zambia*] [*Political party*] (EY)
NPSP	Net Positive Static Pressure (NASA)
NPSP	Net Positive Suction Pressure [*Cryogenics*]
NPSP	N-Phenylselenenylphthalimide [*Organic chemistry*]
NPSP	NPS Pharmaceutical, Inc. [*NASDAQ symbol*] (SAG)
NPSP	NPS Pharmaceuticals [*NASDAQ symbol*] (TTSB)
NPsP	Paul Smiths College, Paul Smiths, NY [*Library symbol Library of Congress*] (LCLS)
NPSPA	National Pecan Shellers and Processors Association (EA)
NPS Phm	NPS Pharmaceutical, Inc. [*Associated Press*] (SAG)
NPSPrA	NWPS Cap Fin 8.125% Tr Sec 1 [*NYSE symbol*] (TTSB)
NPSR	No Primary Staff Responsibility [*Army*] (AABC)

NPSRA......... National Professional Squash Racquets Association (EA)
NPSRC......... National Professional Standards Review Council [*Terminated, 1982*] [*HEW*] (EGAO)
NPSRI.......... National Public Services Research Institute
NPSS .... IEEE Nuclear and Plasma Sciences Society (EA)
NPSS .... National Police and Security Service [*Republic of Vietnam*]
NPSS .... National Proficiency Survey Series [*Scannell*] (TES)
NPSS .... Noms Propres Sud-Semitiques [*A publication*] (BJA)
NPSS .... Non-Public School Section [*American Association of School Librarians*]
NPSS .... Nordic Post Security Service
NPSS .... Nuclear and Plasma Science Symposium (MCD)
NPST .... Native Pituitary-Derived Somatotropin [*Endocrinology*]
NPST .... Native Porcine Somatotropin [*Endocrinology*]
NPSTN .... National Public Switched Telecommunications Network (MHDI)
NPSWL........ New Program Status Word Location
NPT .... Nasal Provocation Test [*Immunology*]
NPT .... National Periodic Test [*Telecommunications*] (OTD)
NPT .... National Petroleum Corp. Ltd. [*Toronto Stock Exchange symbol*]
NPT .... National Pipe Taper [*Mechanical engineering*]
NPT .... National Taper Pipe [*Thread*]
NPT .... Navy Pointer Tracker (MCD)
NPT .... Neomycin Phosphotransferase [*An enzyme*]
NPT .... Neoprecipitin Test [*Oncology*]
NPT .... Neopyrithiamine Hydrochloride [*Chemistry*] (DAVI)
NPT .... Network Planning Technique [*Computer science*] (IEEE)
NPT .... Neuropsychiatry
NPT .... Neuropsychiatry Technician [*Navy*]
NPT .... New Periodical Titles [*of British Union Catalogue of Periodicals*]
NPT .... Newport [*Rhode Island*] [*Airport symbol*] (OAG)
NPT .... Newport Ebbw Junction [*British depot code*]
NPT .... New Product Tiers [*Telecommunications*] (OTD)
NPT .... Nocturnal Penile Tumescence [*Psychiatry*]
NPT .... Non-Packet Mode Terminal (MHDB)
NPT .... Non-Proliferation Treaty (MUSM)
NPT .... Non-Punch Through (AAEL)
NPT .... Nonpyramidal Tract
NPT .... Normal Pressure and Temperature
NPT .... Nuclear Non-Proliferation Treaty [*United Nations*] (ECON)
NPT .... Nucleoside Phosphotransferase (DB)
NPT .... Nuveen Prem Income Muni 4 [*NYSE symbol*] (TTSB)
NPT .... Nuveen Premium Income Municipal Fund IV [*NYSE symbol*] (SPSG)
NPT .... Portland Terminal R. R. Co. [*Formerly, Northern Pacific Terminal R. R.*] [*AAR code*]
NPTA .... National Paper Trade Association (EA)
NPTA .... National Passenger Traffic Association [*Later, NBTA*] (EA)
NPTA .... National Perishable Transportation Association (EA)
NPTA .... National Piano Travelers Association (EA)
NPTA .... National Postal Transport Association [*Later, APWU*]
NPTA .... New Periodical Title Abbreviations [*A publication*]
NPTA .... Nordstrom Personal Touch America [*E-mail shopping service*]
NPTC .... National Postal and Travelers Censorship [*Army*] (AABC)
NPTC .... National Private Truck Council (NTPA)
NPTC .... National Proficiency Test Council (AIE)
NPtc .... Port Chester Public Library, Port Chester, NY [*Library symbol Library of Congress*] (LCLS)
NPTCO .... National Postal and Travelers Censorship Organization [*Army*] (AABC)
NPtcU .... United Hospital, Port Chester, NY [*Library symbol Library of Congress*] (LCLS)
NPTD .... Nitrogen Phosphorus Thermionic Detector [*Instrumentation*]
NPT/E.......... Navy Parachute Team / East Coast (DNAB)
NPte............ Port Ewen Free Library, Port Ewen, NY [*Library symbol Library of Congress*] (LCLS)
NPTF........... National Taper Pipe Threads for Dry Seal Pressure Tight Joints
NPTF........... Nuclear Power Task Force
NPTF........... Nuclear Proof Test Facility [*Proposed, but never built*] (NRCH)
NPTFB .... National Park Trust Fund Board [*Later, NPF*]
NPTG .... Nuclear Power Task Group [*Navy*] (MCD)
NPTH .... NeoPath, Inc. [*NASDAQ symbol*] (SAG)
NPTI........... Nissan Performance Technology, Inc.
NPtjer .... Port Jervis Free Public Library, Port Jervis, NY [*Library symbol Library of Congress*] (LCLS)
NPTL........... National Police Testing Laboratories (EA)
NPTL........... Nuptial (ABBR)
NPTN .... National Pesticide Telecommunication Network (EA)
NPTN .... National Public Telecomputing Network (TNIG)
NPTR .... National Parachute Test Range (MCD)
NPTR .... National Taper Pipe Threads for Railing Fixtures
NPTRL .... Naval Personnel and Training Research Laboratory [*Formerly, Personnel Research Activity*]
NPTS .... Nationwide Personal Transportation Study [*Department of Transportation*] (GFGA)
NPTS .... Nationwide Personal Transportation Survey [*BTS*] [*FHWA*] (TAG)
NPTSM .... Nepotism (ABBR)
NPTST .... Nepotist (ABBR)
NPTU .... Naval Petroleum Training Unit (DNAB)
NPT/W......... Navy Parachute Team / West Coast (DNAB)
NPtw........... Port Washington Public Library, Port Washington, NY [*Library symbol Library of Congress*] (LCLS)
NptwDE........ Daly Elementary School, Port Washington, NY [*Library symbol Library of Congress*] (LCLS)
NPtwGE....... Guggenheim Elementary School, Port Washington, NY [*Library symbol Library of Congress*] (LCLS)

NPtwJSE.:.... John Philip Sousa Elementary School, Port Washington, NY [*Library symbol*] [*Library of Congress*] (LCLS)
NptwME .... Manorhaven Elementary School, Port Washington, NY [*Library symbol Library of Congress*] (LCLS)
NPtwMSE..... Main Street Elementary School, Port Washington, NY [*Library symbol Library of Congress*] (LCLS)
NPtwSH....... Paul D. Schreiber High School, Port Washington, NY [*Library symbol*] [*Library of Congress*] (LCLS)
NPtwSSE...... South Salem Elementary School, Port Washington, NY [*Library symbol Library of Congress*] (LCLS)
NPtwWJ....... Carrie Palmer Weber Junior High School, Port Washington, NY [*Library symbol*] [*Library of Congress*] (LCLS)
NPTWZI .... North Pacific Trade Winds Zone Investigation (NOAA)
NPTZ........... North Pacific Transition Zone [*Marine science*] (OSRA)
NPU .... National Pharmaceutical Union (PDAA)
NPU .... National Postal Union [*Later, APWU*]
NPU .... Naval Parachute Unit
NPU .... Navigation Processor Unit (MCD)
NPU .... Ne Plus Ultra [*No Further; i.e., the pinnacle of attainment*] [*French*]
NPU .... Net Protein Utilization [*Nutrition*]
NPU .... Network Processing Unit
NPU .... Newspaper Press Union (DGA)
NPU .... Nitrogen Pressure Unit (MCD)
NPU .... Nitrogen Purge Unit (MCD)
NPU .... Nordic Postal Union (EA)
NPU .... Not Passed Urine [*Medicine*]
NPUD .... National Party for Unity and Democracy [*Mauritania*] [*Political party*] (EY)
NPUG.......... National Prime User Group (GNE)
NPUI .... Nursing Process Utilization Inventory (DMAA)
NPUP .... National Progressive Unionist Party [*Egypt*] [*Political party*] (PPW)
NPur .... Purchase Free Library, Purchase, NY [*Library symbol Library of Congress*] (LCLS)
NPurMC .... Manhattanville College, Purchase, NY [*Library symbol Library of Congress*] (LCLS)
NPurU .... State University of New York, College at Purchase, Purchase, NY [*Library symbol Library of Congress*] (LCLS)
NPurW .... Westchester Academy of Medicine, Purchase, NY [*Library symbol Library of Congress*] (LCLS)
NPV .... National Present Volume Method [*Management*]
NPV .... Naturpolitische Volkspartei [*People's Party for Nature Policy*] [*Germany Political party*] (PPW)
NPV .... Negative Predictive Value [*Experimentation*]
NPV .... Net Present Value [*Accounting*]
NPV .... New Plymouth Ventures, Inc. [*Vancouver Stock Exchange symbol*]
NPV .... Nitrogen Pressure Valve (KSC)
NPV .... Nonpropulsive Vent (KSC)
NPV .... No Par Value [*Stock exchange term*]
NPV .... Nuclear Polyhedrosis Virus
NPV .... Nuveen VA Prem Inc. Muni Fd [*NYSE symbol*] (TTSB)
NPV .... Nuveen Virginia Premium Income Municipal Fund [*NYSE symbol*] (SPSG)
NPV .... Vassar College, Poughkeepsie, NY [*Library symbol Library of Congress*] (LCLS)
NPVCE .... Net Present Value for Current Expendable Launch Vehicles [*NASA*] (KSC)
NPVH .... Net Present Value at the Horizon (PDAA)
NPVLA .... National Paint, Varnish, and Lacquer Association [*Later, NPCA*] (EA)
NPV-Mu .... Vassar College, George Sherman Dickerson Music Library, Poughkeepsie, NY [*Library symbol*] [*Library of Congress*] (LCLS)
NPVNE .... Net Present Value for New Expendable Launch Vehicles [*NASA*] (KSC)
NPVS .... No-Par-Value Stock [*Stock exchange term*]
NPVSH .... Net Present Value for Space Shuttle [*NASA*] (KSC)
NPW .... International Union of Allied Novelty and Production Workers
NPW .... National Party of Western Australia [*Political party*]
NPW .... Network for Professional Women [*Hartford, CT*] (EA)
NPW .... Nuveen WA Prem Inc. Muni Fd [*AMEX symbol*] (TTSB)
NPW .... Nuveen Washington Premium Income Municipal Fund [*AMEX symbol*] (SPSG)
NPWA .... National Pure Water Association [*British*]
NPWAC .... National Parks and Wildlife Advisory Council [*Tasmania, Australia*]
NPwADS .... National Power PLC [*Associated Press*] (SAG)
NPWC .... National Press Women's Club (NTCM)
NPWC .... Navy Public Works Center
NPWD .... Navy Public Works Department
NPWFNSW.... National Parks and Wildlife Foundation of New South Wales [*Australia*]
NPWIC .... National Prisoner of War Information Center (DOMA)
NPWOA .... National Piggly Wiggly Operators Association (SAG)
NPWRC .... Northern Prairie Wildlife Research Center [*Jamestown, ND*] [*Department of the Interior*] (GRD)
NPWS .... NATO Planning Workshop (NATG)
NPX .... New Pioneer Exploration [*Vancouver Stock Exchange symbol*]
NPX .... Norpropoxyphene (DB)
NPX .... Nuveen Ins Prem Inc. Muni 2 [*NYSE symbol*] (TTSB)
NPX .... Nuveen Insured Premium Income Municipal Fund [*NYSE symbol*] (SPSG)
NPY .... Neuropeptide Y [*Biochemistry*]
NPY .... Nuveen PA Prem Inc. Muni 2 [*NYSE symbol*] (TTSB)
NPY .... Nuveen Pennsylvania Premium Income Municipal [*NYSE symbol*] (SPSG)
NPy .... Penn Yan Public Library, Penn Yan, NY [*Library symbol Library of Congress*] (LCLS)
NPYLI .... Neuropeptide Y-Like Immunoreactivity [*Medicine*] (DB)

NPYR	Nitrosopyrrolidine [*Also, NYPYR*] [*Organic chemistry*]
NPYRR	N-Nitrosopyrrolidine [*Organic chemistry*]
NPZ	New Plymouth [*New Zealand*] [*Seismograph station code, US Geological Survey Closed*] (SEIS)
NPZ	North Pyrenean Zone [*Geology*]
NQ	Cumberland Airlines [*ICAO designator*] (AD)
NQ	Net Quick Assets
NQ	Neural Quantum [*Theory*] [*Sensory discrimination*]
nq	Nicaragua [*MARC country of publication code Library of Congress*] (LCCP)
NQ	Quoque Library, Quoque, NY [*Library symbol Library of Congress*] (LCLS)
NQA	Memphis, TN [*Location identifier FAA*] (FAAL)
NQA	National Quality Award [*LIMRA, NALU*]
NQA	National Quilting Association (EA)
NQA	Net Quick Assets
NQA	North Carolina Agricultural and Technical State University, Greensboro, NC [*OCLC symbol*] (OCLC)
NQA	Nursing Quality Assurance (DMAA)
NQAA	Nuclear Quality Assurance Agency
NQB	National Quotation Bureau [*Stock market*]
NQB	No Qualified Bidders [*Investment term*] (DFIT)
NQC	NASA Quality Control (KSC)
NQC	National Quotations Committee [*of the National Association of Securities Dealers*]
NQC	Nuclear Quality Control (DNAB)
NQC	Nuveen CA Inv Qual Muni [*NYSE symbol*] (TTSB)
NQC	Nuveen California Investment Quality Municipal Fund [*NYSE symbol*] (SPSG)
NQCC	Nuclear Quadrupole Coupling Constant [*Physics*]
NQD	Nonquaded [*Telecommunications*] (TEL)
NQD	Notice of Quality Discrepancy
NQE	Nuclear Quality Engineering (DNAB)
NQF	Nuveen FL Inv Qua Muni [*NYSE symbol*] (TTSB)
NQF	Nuveen Florida Investment Quality Municipal [*NYSE symbol*] (SPSG)
NQHR	National Quarter Horse Registry (EA)
NQI	Kingsville, TX [*Location identifier FAA*] (FAAL)
NQI	Nuveen Ins Qual Muni [*NYSE symbol*] (TTSB)
NQI	Nuveen Insured Quality Municipal [*NYSE symbol*] (SPSG)
NQIC	National Quality Information Centre [*Institute of Quality Assurance*] [*Information service or system*] (IID)
NQJ	Nuveen New Jersey Investment Quality Municipal [*NYSE symbol*] (SPSG)
NQJ	Nuveen NJ Inv Qua Muni [*NYSE symbol*] (TTSB)
NQKA	Northwest Quoin Key Association [*Defunct*] (EA)
NQL	National Quick Lube Ltd. [*Vancouver Stock Exchange symbol*]
NQL	North Queensland Libraries: A Directory [*Australia A publication*]
NQL	Nouveau Quartier Latin [*Paris bookstore*]
NQL	Nuclear Quadrupole Interaction [*Physics*]
NQLA	North Queensland Logging Association [*Australia*]
NQM	Midway/Henderson Naval Station, HI [*Location identifier FAA*] (FAAL)
NQM	Navy Quality Management
NQM	Nuveen Investment Quality Municipal [*NYSE symbol*] (SPSG)
NQM	Nuveen Inv Quality Muni [*NYSE symbol*] (TTSB)
NQMFP	North Queensland Multifunction Polis [*Australia*]
NQN	Neuquen [*Argentina*] [*Airport symbol*] (OAG)
NQN	Nuveen New York Investment Quality Municipal Fund [*NYSE symbol*] (SPSG)
NQN	Nuveen NY Inv Qual Muni [*NYSE symbol*] (TTSB)
NQN	Transportes Aereos Neuquen [*Argentina ICAO designator*] (FAAC)
NQO	Nitroquinoline Oxide [*Organic chemistry*]
NQOS	Not Quite Our Sort (IIA)
NQP	Nuveen PA Inv Qua Muni [*NYSE symbol*] (TTSB)
NQP	Nuveen Pennsylvania Investment Quality Municipal [*NYSE symbol*] (SPSG)
NQPA	National Quarter Pony Association (EA)
NQPC	National Quartz Producers Council (EA)
NQPP	National Quarantine Publicity Program [*Australia*]
NQR	New Quebec Raglan Mines Ltd. [*Toronto Stock Exchange symbol*]
NQR	Non-Quadratic Residues (MHDB)
NQR	Nuclear Quadrupole Resonance [*Frequencies*]
NQRC	National Quadraphonic Radio Committee
NQRR	Nuclear Quadrupole Resonance Response
NQS	Nuveen Select Quality Municipal [*NYSE symbol*] (SPSG)
NQS	Nuveen Select Qual Muni [*NYSE symbol*] (TTSB)
NQSO	Nonqualified Stock Options (WYGK)
NQT	Network Quality Tester (NITA)
NQT	Newly Qualified to Teach (GFGA)
NQT	Nonlanguage Qualification Test
NQT	Nor-Quest Resources Ltd. [*Vancouver Stock Exchange symbol*]
NQTGCA	North Queensland Tobacco Growers Cooperative Association [*Australia*]
NQTV	North Queensland Television [*Australia*]
NQU	Not Quite Us [*Lower in social status*] [*Slang British*]
NQU	Nuqui [*Colombia*] [*Airport symbol*] (OAG)
NQU	Nuveen Qual Income Muni Fd [*NYSE symbol*] (TTSB)
NQU	Nuveen Quality Income Municipal Fund [*NYSE symbol*] (SPSG)
NQWMI	Non-Q-Wave Myocardial Infarction [*Cardiology*] (CPH)
NQX	Key West, FL [*Location identifier FAA*] (FAAL)
NQY	Newquay [*England*] [*Airport symbol*] (OAG)
NR	Bosanquet and Puller's New Reports, English Common Pleas [*1804-07*] [*A publication*] (DLA)
NR	Nachrichtenregiment [*Signal Regiment*] [*German military - World War II*]
NR	Narrow Resonance [*Nuclear energy*] (NRCH)
NR	Natal Reports [*South Africa*] [*A publication*] (DLA)
NR	National Range
NR	National Recovery Act
NR	National Recovery Administration [*Voided by Supreme Court, 1935*]
NR	National Register (COE)
NR	National Report (OICC)
NR	National Reporter [*Maritime Law Book Co. Ltd.*] [*Canada Information service or system*] (CRD)
NR	National Reserve [*British military*] (DMA)
NR	NATO Restricted (NATG)
NR	Natural Resources
NR	Natural Rubber
NR	Nauru [*ANSI two-letter standard code*] (CNC)
NR	Naval Rating
NR	Naval Reactors (GAAI)
NR	Naval Reserve
NR	Navigational RADAR
NR	Navy Regulations
NR	Near (EY)
nr	Near (VRA)
NR	Negative Resistance [*Electronics*]
NR	Net Register [*Shipping*]
NR	Neural Retina [*Ophthalmology*]
NR	Neutral Red [*An indicator*]
NR	Neutral-Reverse [*Automotive engineering*]
NR	Newpark Resources [*NYSE symbol*] (TTSB)
NR	New Range (IAA)
NR	New Reports [*1862-65*] [*England*] [*A publication*] (DLA)
NR	Next Renewal
NR	Next to Reading Matter [*Also, NRM*] [*Advertising*] (NTCM)
NR	Nicaraguan Resistance [*An association*] (EA)
NR	Nicolaus Rufulus [*Flourished, 13th century*] [*Authority cited in pre-1607 legal work*] (DSA)
nr	Nigeria [*MARC country of publication code Library of Congress*] (LCCP)
NR	Nigeria Regiment [*British military*] (DMA)
NR	Nitrate Reductase [*An enzyme*]
NR	Nitrile Rubber [*Organic chemistry*]
NR	Nodal Rhythm [*Cardiology*] (DAVI)
NR	Noise Rating (NASA)
NR	Noise Ratio
NR	Noise Ration
NR	Noise Reduction (IAA)
NR	Nonconformance Report [*Nuclear energy*] (NRCH)
NR	Nonlinear Resistance (IAA)
NR	Nonrated
NR	Nonreactive [*Relay*]
NR	Nonrebreathing [*Medicine*] (AAMN)
NR	Nonrecoverable (IEEE)
NR	Nonrefundable [*Airline fare code*]
NR	Nonregistered (AABC)
NR	Non Repetatur [*Do Not Repeat*] [*Pharmacy*]
NR	Nonresident [*British*]
NR	Nonresponder [*Strain of mice*]
NR	Non-Response (WDMC)
NR	Nonreturnable [*Beverage bottles*]
NR	Nonreversing (IAA)
NR	Nonspecific Gene Resistance [*Genetics*]
NR	No Radiation (MAE)
NR	NORAD Region (IAA)
N/R	No Record (AAG)
NR	No Refill [*Pharmacy*]
NR	No Release (AAG)
NR	No Remittance
NR	No Report [*Medicine*]
NR	No Requirement
NR	No Residency Requirement [*Voter registration*]
NR	No Response [*Medicine*]
NR	Norfolk Rangers [*British military*] (DMA)
NR	Norgold Russet Potato
NR	No Risk [*Business term*]
NR	Normal (MAE)
NR	Normal Range
NR	Normal Record [*Medicine*] (DAVI)
NR	Normal Responder
NR	Normotensive Rat [*Medicine*] (DMAA)
NR	Northern Range [*Navigation*]
NR	Northern Rhodesia [*Later, Zambia*]
NR	North Riding [*England*] (ROG)
NR	North River [*New York, New Jersey*]
NR	Northward Aviation Ltd. (MHDW)
NR	Nose Right [*Aviation*] (MCD)
N/R	Notes Receivable
NR	Notice of Rating Required [*Civil Service*]
N/R	Notice of Readiness [*Shipping*]
NR	Not Rated
NR	Not Readable
NR	Not Recorded
N/R	Not Remarkable [*Medicine*]
NR	Not Reported
NR	Not Required
NR	Not Resolved (MAE)
N/R	Not Responsible For
NR	Nuchal Rigidity [*Medicine*]
NR	Nuclear Radiation

NR	Nuclear Radiology [*Medical specialty*] (DHSM)
NR	Nuclear Reactor
NR	Nuclear Research Submarine (MCD)
NR	Nuestra Remesa [*Our Remittance*] [*Spanish Business term*]
NR	Nufort Resources, Inc. [*Toronto Stock Exchange symbol*]
NR	Number (AAG)
NR	Number of Runs
NR	Nurse
NR	Nursing Representative [*Red Cross*]
NR	Nursing Services (HCT)
NR	Nutritive Ratio
NR	Nystagmus Recorder
NR	Reynold's Number [*Viscosity*] (MAE)
NR	Rochester Public Library, Rochester, NY [*Library symbol Library of Congress*] (LCLS)
nr----	Rocky Mountain Region [*MARC geographic area code Library of Congress*] (LCCP)
NR	Submersible Research Vehicle (Nuclear Propulsion) [*Navy ship symbol*]
NRA	Coupeville, WA [*Location identifier FAA*] (FAAL)
NRA	Narrandera [*Australia Airport symbol*] (OAG)
NRA	NASA Research Announcement
NRA	National Racing Authority (NADA)
NRA	National Reclamation Association [*Later, National Water Resources Association*] (EA)
NRA	National Record of Achievement [*British*] (DET)
NRA	National Recovery Act
NRA	National Recovery Administration [*Voided by Supreme Court, 1935*]
NRA	National Recreation Area [*National Park Service*] (GFGA)
NRA	National Recreation Association [*Later, NRPA*] (EA)
NRA	National Reform Association (EA)
NRA	National Register of Archives [*Historical Manuscripts Commission*] [*British*]
NRA	National Rehabilitation Association (EA)
NRA	National Remodelers Association [*Later, NARI*]
NRA	National Renderers Association (EA)
NRA	National Republican Alliance [*Australia*]
NRA	National Resistance Army [*Uganda*] (PD)
NRA	National Restaurant Association (EA)
NRA	National Retirement Association [*Australia*]
NRA	National Rifle Association (NADA)
NRA	National Rifle Association of America (EA)
NRA	National Rivers Authority [*British*]
NRA	National Roads Authority [*1997*] [*Malawi*]
NRA	National Roommate Association [*Later, ASRS*] (EA)
NRA	National Rounders Association [*British*] (BI)
NRA	NATO Refugees Agency (NATG)
NRA	Naval Radio Activity
NRA	Naval Reserve Association (EA)
NRA	Navy Recruiting Area (DNAB)
NRA	Negative Resistance Amplifier (PDAA)
NRA	Net Rentable Area (ADA)
NRA	Network Resolution Area
NRA	New Era Development Ltd. [*Vancouver Stock Exchange symbol*]
NRA	New Regional Airliner
NRA	Nitra Air [*Slovakia*] [*FAA designator*] (FAAC)
NRA	Nitrate Reductase (DB)
NRA	Non-Recurrrence Action (SAA)
NRA	Nonredundant Array
NRA	Nonregistered Accountable [*Military*]
NRA	Nonresident Alien
NRA	No Repair Action [*Military*]
NRA	Normal Retirement Age
NRA	North River [*Alaska*] [*Seismograph station code, US Geological Survey*] (SEIS)
NRA	Nothing Recorded Against [*Security investigation result*] [*British*]
NRA	Nuclear Radiation Absorber
NRA	Nuclear Reaction Analysis
NRA	Nuclear Regulatory Agency
NRA	Nucleus Raphe Alatus [*Neurology*]
NRA	Nucleus Retroambigualis [*Neurology*] (DAVI)
NRA	St. Augustine's College, Raleigh, NC [*OCLC symbol*] (OCLC)
NRAA	National Railway Appliances Association [*Later, REMSA*] (EA)
NRAA	National Rehabilitation Administration Association (NTPA)
NRAA	National Renal Administrators Association (EA)
NRAA	National Rifle Association of America
NRAB	American Baptist Historical Society, Rochester, NY [*Library symbol Library of Congress*] (LCLS)
NRAB	National Railroad Adjustment Board
NRAB	National Railroad Adjustment Board Awards [*A publication*] (DLA)
NRAB	Naval Reserve Aviation Base
NRAB (1st D)	United States National Railroad Adjustment Board Awards, First Division [*A publication*] (DLA)
NRAB (2d D)	United States National Railroad Adjustment Board Awards, Second Division [*A publication*] (DLA)
NRAB (3d D)	United States National Railroad Adjustment Board Awards, Third Division [*A publication*] (DLA)
NRAB (4th D)	United States National Railroad Adjustment Board Awards, Fourth Division [*A publication*] (DLA)
NRAC	National Resources Analysis Center
NRAC	National Rural Advisory Council (NADA)
NRAC	Natural Resources Audit Council
NRAC	Naval Research Advisory Committee
NRACCO	Navy Regional Air Cargo Central [*or Control*] Office
NRAD	National Racquetball Association of the Deaf (EA)

NRAD	No Risk After Discharge [*Shipping*]
NRADUSA	National Racquetball Association of the Deaf of the USA [*Later, NRAD*] (EA)
NRAF	Naval Reserve Auxiliary Field
NRAF	Navy Recruiting Aids Facility (DNAB)
NRAF	Not Running at Finish [*Automobile racing*]
NRAG	Naval Research Advisory Group (KSC)
NRAI	National Residential Appraisers Institute (EA)
NRAL	New York State Appellate Division, Law Library, Rochester, NY [*Library symbol Library of Congress*] (LCLS)
NRAM	Non-Volatile Random Access Memory [*Computer science*]
NRAMEG	National Restaurant Association Marketing Executives Group [*Defunct*] (EA)
NRAMRG	National Restaurant Association Market Research Group [*Defunct*] (EA)
NR & HC	National Rivers and Harbors Congress [*Later, WRC*]
NRans	Ransomville Free Library, Ransomville, NY [*Library symbol Library of Congress*] (LCLS)
NRAO	National Radio Astronomy Observatory [*Charlottesville, VA*] [*National Science Foundation*] (GRD)
NRAO	Navy Regional Accounts Office
NRAP	Naturally Radioactive Product (NRCH)
NRAS	National Radio Astronomy Observatory [*Charlottesville, VA*] [*National Science Foundation*] (GRD)
NRAS	Navy Readiness Analysis System
NRAS	Nuclear Release Authentication System [*Seventh Army*] (AABC)
NRASF	National Registry of Ambulatory Surgical Facilities (EA)
NRAT	Nonrationed (AABC)
NRB	Mayport, FL [*Location identifier FAA*] (FAAL)
NRB	National Religious Broadcasters (EA)
NRB	National Research Bureau [*Commercial firm*] (EA)
NRB	National Resources Board [*Terminated, 1935; functions transferred to National Resources Committee*]
NRB	National Roads Board (NADA)
NRB	Natural Rubber Bureau [*Later, MRB*] (EA)
NRB	Naval Reactor Branch (MUGU)
NRB	Naval Repair Base
NRB	Navy Recruiting Bureau
NRB	Navy Reservation Bureau
NRB	New Redundancy Benefit [*To reduce unemployment*] [*British*]
NRB	Nonconformance Review Board [*Nuclear Regulatory Commission*] (NRCH)
NRB	Nonrejoining Break [*Medicine*] (DMAA)
NRB	Non-Reportable Birth [*Medicine*] (MEDA)
NRB	Nuclear Reactors Branch [*AEC*]
NRB1CL	Nuclear Reactor Operator, First-Class Badge [*Military decoration*] (GFGA)
NRB2CL	Nuclear Reactor Operator, Second-Class Badge [*Military decoration*] (GFGA)
NRBA	National Radio Broadcasters Association [*NAB*] [*Absorbed by*] (EA)
NRBA	National Registered Builders Association [*British*] (DBA)
NRBBAS	Nuclear Reactor Operator, Basic Badge [*Military decoration*] (GFGA)
NRBC	National Rare Blood Club [*Later, NRBC/NYBC*] (EA)
NRBC	Normal Red Blood Cell [*Medicine*] (DMAA)
NRBC	Nucleated Red Blood Cell
NRBC/NYBC	National Rare Blood Club/New York Blood Center (EA)
NRBE	Native Races of the British Empire [*A publication*]
NRBF	Number of Rounds between Failures [*Quality control*] (MCD)
NRBL	Bausch & Lomb, Inc., Rochester, NY [*Library symbol Library of Congress*] (LCLS)
NRBL-S	Bausch & Lomb, Inc., SOFLENS Division, Technical Information Center, Rochester, NY [*Library symbol Library of Congress*] (LCLS)
NRBP	Natural Resource-Based Product
NRBP	New Reports of Bosanquet and Puller [*A publication*] (DLA)
NRBQ	New Rhythm and Blues Quartet [*Rock music group*]
NRBQ	Nurses' Registration Board of Queensland [*Australia*]
NRBS	Navy Recruiting Branch Station (DNAB)
NRBS	Nonrebreathing System [*Medicine*] (DAVI)
NRBSUPV	Nuclear Reactor Operator, Shift Supervisor Badge [*Military decoration*] (GFGA)
NRC	Crows Landing, CA [*Location identifier FAA*] (FAAL)
NRC	NAC RE Corp. [*NYSE symbol*] (SAG)
NRC	National Racquetball Club (EA)
NRC	National Radio Club [*Defunct*] (EA)
NRC	National Radio Conference [*Broadcast regulations*] (NTCM)
NRC	National Railroad Construction and Maintenance Association, Inc. (EA)
NRC	National Ramah Commission (EA)
NRC	National Reading Conference (EA)
NRC	National Realty Club [*New York, NY*] (EA)
NRC	National Realty Committee [*Washington, DC*] (EA)
NRC	National Reconditioning Order [*National Weather Service*] (USDC)
NRC	National Records Center
NRC	National Recycling Coalition (EA)
NRC	National Recycling Corp. (EFIS)
NRC	National Redemption Council [*Ghana*]
NRC	National Referral Center [*Defunct*] (EA)
NRC	National Register Criteria (COE)
NRC	National Remodelers Council [*Later, NAHB/RC*] (EA)
NRC	National Reprographic Centre for Documentation [*British*]
NRC	National Republican Club
NRC	National Republican Convention [*Nigeria*] [*Political party*]
NRC	National Research Center (NATG)
NRC	National Research Corp.

NRC	National Research Council [*National Academy of Sciences*] [*Washington, DC*]
NRC	National Research Council, Canada [*Research center*] (IRC)
NRC	National Resistance Committee (EA)
NRC	National Resource Center for Paraprofessionals in Special Education and Related Human Services (EA)
NRC	National Resources Committee [*Functions transferred to National Resources Planning Board*]
NRC	National Response Center [*Environmental Protection Agency*]
NRC	National Retreat Centre [*British*] (CB)
NRC	National Riding Committee [*Later, ANRC*] (EA)
NRC	National Rocket Club [*Later, NSC*]
NRC	National Rural Center (EA)
NRC	Natural Resources Center [*University of Alabama*] [*Research center*] (RCD)
NRC	Natural Resources Council of America (EA)
NRC	Natural Rights Center (EA)
NRC	Naval Radio Compass (IAA)
NRC	Naval Radiological Control (DNAB)
NRC	Naval Records Club [*Later, INRO*]
NRC	Naval Recreation Center (DNAB)
NRC	Naval Research Co. - Reserves
NRC	Naval Retraining Command
NRC	Navy Reconnaissance Center (MCD)
NRC	Navy Recruiting Command (DNAB)
NRC	Navy Reserve Centers (NVT)
NRC	Negative Resistance Characteristic [*Electrophysiology*]
NRC	Netherlands Red Cross
NRC	Net Replacement Cost [*Accounting*]
NRC	Networking Routing Center (MHDB)
NRC	Network Reliability Coordinator
NRC	Neutron Radiation Capture
NRC	New Research Centers [*A publication*]
NRC	New Right Coalition (EA)
NRC	Newspaper Research Council (EA)
NRC	Nitrogen Consumption Rate (DB)
NRC	Noise-Rating Curve (OA)
NRC	Noise Reduction Coefficient [*of insulation*]
NRC	Nonrecurring Costs [*Accounting*] (KSC)
NRC	Non-Reusable Containers (GNE)
NRC	Non-unit-Related Cargo (DOMA)
NRC	Norco Resources [*Vancouver Stock Exchange symbol*]
NRC	Normal Retinal Correspondence
NRC	North Carolina State University, Raleigh, NC [*OCLC symbol*] (OCLC)
NRC	Norwegian Refugee Council
NRC	Notch Root Contraction (OA)
NRC	Not Recommended for Children (ADA)
NRC	Not Routine Care [*Medicine*]
NRC	Nuclear Radiation Center [*Washington State University*] [*Research center*] (RCD)
NRC	Nuclear Recycling Consultants (EA)
NRC	Nuclear Regulatory Commission [*Washington, DC*]
NRC	Nuclear Research Council
NRC	Nutrition-Related Complications [*Medicine*]
NRCA	National Reamer Collectors Association (EA)
NRCA	National Rebel Class Association (EA)
NRCA	National Recovery and Collection Association (EA)
NRCA	National Redbone Coonhound Association (EA)
NRCA	National Refrigeration Contractors Association (NTPA)
NRCA	National Rehabilitation Counseling Association (EA)
NRCA	National Resources Council of America
NRCA	National Retail Credit Association [*Later, ICA*]
NRCA	National Roofing Contractors Association (EA)
NRC-ACAC	National Research Council Army Countermine Advisory Committee
NRCAR	Nuclear Regulatory Commission Acquisition Regulation (AAGC)
NRCC	National Registry in Clinical Chemistry (EA)
NRCC	National Republican Coalition for Choice (EA)
NRCC	National Republican Congressional Committee (EA)
NRCC	National Research Council of Canada
NRCC	National Resource for Computation in Chemistry [*Lawrence Berkeley Laboratory*] [*Terminated, 1981*]
NRCC	Naval Regional Contracting Center (AAGC)
NRCC	NORAD Region Combat Center [*Military*]
NRCCL	Norwegian Research Centre for Computers and Law (NITA)
NRCCLS	National Resource Center for Consumers of Legal Services (EA)
NRCCS	National Research Council Committee on Salmonella (EA)
NRCD	National Redemption Council Decree [*Ghana*] [*A publication*] (DLA)
NRCd	National Reprographic Centre for Documentation [*Hatfield Polytechnic Institute*] [*Hertfordshire, England Evaluation and information group*] [*Information service or system*]
NRCd	National Reprographic Centre for Documentation Study (NITA)
NRCDA	North Region Cooperative Development Agency [*British*]
NRCDES	National Research Council Division of Earth Sciences [*Marine science*] (OSRA)
NRC/DME	National Research Council of Canada, Division of Mechanical Engineering [*Research center*] (RCD)
NRCHB	Naval Reserve Cargo-Handling Battalion
NRCHMI	National Resource Center on Homelessness and Mental Illness (EA)
NRCHTB	Naval Reserve Cargo-Handling Training Battalion
NRCI	National Radio Co., Inc. (IAA)
NRCI	National Rainbow Coalition, Inc. (EA)
NRCI	National Red Cherry Institute (EA)
NRCI	Nuclear Regulatory Commission Issuances [*A publication*] (DLA)
NRCL	National Research Council Library (DIT)
NRCL	Nonrenal Clearance [*Medicine*] (DMAA)

NRCLS	National Resource Center for Consumers of Legal Services (DLA)
NRC-MAC	National Research Council - Mine Advisory Committee
NRC/MAI	National Railroad Construction and Maintenance Association, Inc. (EA)
NRCMC	National Resource Center for Minority Contractors (EA)
NRCMCA	National Radiator Core Manufacturing Credit Association [*Later, NRMCA*] (EA)
NRCMF	NRC Master File (NITA)
NRC-NAS	National Research Council - National Academy of Sciences (AAG)
NRCP	Nonreinforced Concrete Pipe [*Technical drawings*]
NRCPR	Nuclear Regulatory Commission Procurement Regulation (AAGC)
NRCPS	National Research Council on Peace Strategy (EA)
NRCR	Colgate-Rochester Divinity School, Rochester, NY [*Library symbol Library of Congress*] (LCLS)
NRCS	National Resources Conservation Service (PA)
NRCS	National Roller Canary Society [*British*] (BI)
NRCS	Normalized RADAR Cross Section
NRCS	United States Natural Resources Conservation Service
NRCSA	National Registration Center for Study Abroad (EA)
NRCSA	Neurological Resources Center of South Australia
NRCSL	National Research Center on Student Learning [*University of Pittsburgh*] [*Research center*] (RCD)
NRCSM	Narcissism (ABBR)
NRCST	Narcissist (ABBR)
NRCST	National Referral Center for Science and Technology (MCD)
NRCTK	Narcotic (ABBR)
NRC-TOX	National Research Council - Committee on Toxicology
NRCV	Consolidated Vacuum Corp., Rochester, NY [*Library symbol Library of Congress*] (LCLS)
NRCWA	National Resource Center on Women and AIDS [*Acquired Immune Deficiency Syndrome*] (EA)
NRCX	Nuclear Regulary Commission (EBF)
NRCYS	National Resource Center for Youth Services (EA)
NRD	Aeronardi SpA [*Italy ICAO designator*] (FAAC)
NRD	National Range Division [*Air Force*]
NRD	National Range Documentation (MUGU)
NRD	National Registered Designer [*British*]
NRD	Natural Resource Damage [*Environmental science*]
NRD	Natural Resources Division [*An association*] (EAIO)
NRD	Naval Radio Direction Finder (IAA)
NRD	Naval Recruiting Department [*British military*] (DMA)
NRD	Naval Research and Development (KSC)
NRD	Navy Recruiting District (DNAB)
NRD	Negative Resistance Diode
NRD	Nominal Rim Diameter [*Automotive engineering*]
NRD	Nonrenal Death (MAE)
NRD	Nonreplenishable Demand
NRD	Norderney [*Germany Airport symbol*] (OAG)
NRD	Nordlingen [*Federal Republic of Germany*] [*Seismograph station code, US Geological Survey Closed*] (SEIS)
NRD	Nord Resources [*NYSE symbol*] (TTSB)
NRD	Nord Resources Corp. [*NYSE symbol*] (SPSG)
NRD	No Record of Destination [*Aviation*]
NRD	Normal Retirement Date
NR/D	Not Required, but Desired
NRD	Nuclear Radiation Detector
NRD	Nucleus Raphe Dorsalis [*Neuroanatomy*]
NRD	Office of Naval Research and Development
NRDB	National Residue Database
NRDB	Nonreversing, Dynamic Braking (IAA)
NRDC	N-Arginine Dibasic Convertase [*An enzyme*]
NRDC	Natick Research and Development Center [*Army*] (INF)
NRDC	National Research & Development Corp. [*Later, BTG*] [*British*]
NRDC	National Resources Defence Council (ECON)
NRDC	National Respiratory Disease Conference (DAVI)
NRDC	National Retail Distribution Certificate [*British*]
NRDC	National Running Data Center, Inc. [*Defunct*] (EA)
NRDC	Natural Resources Defense Council
NRDC	Navy Relief Society, Washington, DC, Auxiliary
NRDC	Navy Research and Development Committee
NRDCA	National Roof Deck Contractors Association (EA)
NRDEC	Natick Research Development and Engineering Center [*Army*] (INF)
NRDF	Non-Recursive Digital File (NITA)
NRDF	Nonrecursive Digital Filter [*Navy*]
NRDFS	Naval Radio Direction Finder Service
NRDI	National Rural Development Institute (EA)
NRDL	Naval Radiological Defense Laboratory
NRDL	Navy Radiological Defense Laboratory (DNAB)
NRDLS	National Rural Development Leaders School (OICC)
NRDM	Nuclear Weapons Reconnaissance Data Manual (COE)
NRDO	National Research and Development Organization (WDAA)
NRDO	Navy Radio (NOAA)
NRDR	Non-Resetting Data Reconstruction (PDAA)
NRDR-CF	Non-Resetting Data Reconstruction with Continuous Feedback (PDAA)
NRDR-DF	Non-Resetting Data Reconstruction with Discrete Feedback (PDAA)
NRDS	Nuclear Rocket Detection System [*NASA*]
NRDS	Nuclear Rocket Development Station
NRDSCG	Naval Research and Development Satellite Communications Group (SAA)
NRDU-V	Navy Research and Development Unit - Vietnam (MCD)
NRE	Aviones Are, SA de CV [*Mexico*] [*FAA designator*] (FAAC)
NRE	Eastman Kodak Co., Rochester, NY [*Library symbol Library of Congress*] (LCLS)
NRE	National Real Estate Corp. [*NYSE symbol*] (SPSG)

NRE	National Resource Explorations Ltd. [*Toronto Stock Exchange symbol Vancouver Stock Exchange symbol*]
NRE	Natl Re Corp. [*NYSE symbol*] (TTSB)
NRE	Naval Research Establishment
NRE	Negative Regulatory Element [*Genetics*]
NRE	Negative Resistance Effect
NRE	Negative Resistance Element [*Electronics*] (IAA)
NRE	New and Renewable Energy (PDAA)
NRE	New York Revised Laws [*A publication*] (DLA)
NRE	Nonrecurring Engineering (AAEL)
NRE	Nonrecurring Engineering Expense
NRE	Nonrotating Earth (NATG)
NRE	Not Receiving Additional Irrigation [*Agriculture*]
NRE	Nuclear Radiation Effect
NRE	Nuclear Receptor Element [*Biochemistry*]
NRE	Nuclear Rocket Engine (AAG)
NRe	[*Reynolds*] Number [*Aerodynamics*] (BARN)
NRE	Point Mugu, CA [*Location identifier FAA*] (FAAL)
NRE-A	Eastman Kodak Co., Apparatus Division, Rochester, NY [*Library symbol Library of Congress*] (LCLS)
NREA	National Rural Education Association (EA)
NREAN	Northern Rivers Energy Action Network [*Australia*]
NRE-B	Kodak (Near East) Ltd., Beirut, Lebanon [*Library symbol Library of Congress*] (LCLS)
NREB	Naval Reserve Evaluation Board (DNAB)
NREBX	Mgn. Stanley D. Witter Natural Resources Cl.B [*Mutual fund ticker symbol*] (SG)
NREC	National Reconnaissance Executive Committee (LAIN)
NREC	National Resources Evaluation Center [*of OEP*] [*Nuclear effects*]
NREC	Natural Resources and Environment Committee [*Victoria, Australia*]
NRECA	National Rural Electric Cooperative Association (EA)
NREd	Eastman Dental Center, Basil G. Bibby Library, Rochester, NY [*Library symbol Library of Congress*] (LCLS)
NRed	Red Hook Public Library, Red Hook, NY [*Library symbol Library of Congress*] (LCLS)
NRedL	Red Hook Public Library, Red Hook, NY [*Library symbol*] [*Library of Congress*] (LCLS)
NRE-E	Eastman Kodak Co., Engineering Division, Rochester, NY [*Library symbol Library of Congress*] (LCLS)
NREEC	Natural Resources and Environmental Education Center [*Oklahoma State University*] [*Research center*] (RCD)
NREF	North Russia Expeditionary Force [*World War I*] [*Canada*]
NREFA	National Real Estate Fliers Association [*Later, Real Estate Aviation Chapter*] (EA)
NREH	Normal Renin Essential Hypertension [*Medicine*] (DMAA)
NREH	Nuclear Radiation Effects Handbook (SAA)
NRE-L	Kodak Ltd., Recordak Division, London, United Kingdom [*Library symbol Library of Congress*] (LCLS)
NREL	National Renewable Energy Laboratory [*Department of Energy*]
NRE-M	Eastman Kodak Co., Health and Safety Laboratory, Rochester, NY [*Library symbol Library of Congress*] (LCLS)
NREM	Nonrapid Eye Movement [*Type of sleep*]
NREMS	Nonrapid Eye Movement Sleep [*Neurology*] (DAVI)
NREMT	National Registry of Emergency Medical Technicians (EA)
NREMT-P	National Registry of Emergency Medical Technicians - Paramedics (DAVI)
NREN	National Research and Education Network [*Federal government*]
NRenSA	Saint Anthony-On-Hudson Theological Seminary, Rensselaer, NY [*Library symbol Library of Congress*] (LCLS)
NRenSW	Sterling-Winthrop Research Institute, Rensselaer, NY [*Library symbol Library of Congress*] (LCLS)
NRE-P	Eastman Kodak Co., Photographic Technology Library, Rochester, NY [*Library symbol Library of Congress*] (LCLS)
NREP	Name Removed from End-Paper [*Antiquarian book trade*]
NREP	National Registry of Environmental Professionals (EA)
NREP	National Reliability Evaluation Program [*Nuclear Regulatory Commission*]
NREP	Neutron Resonance Escape Probability [*Nuclear energy*] (NRCH)
NRE-R	Eastman Kodak Co., Research Laboratories, Rochester, NY [*Library symbol Library of Congress*] (LCLS)
NRERC	National Rural Education Research Consortium [*Defunct*] (EA)
NRES	Natural Resources, Energy, and Environment [*Office of Management and Budget*]
NRES	Naval Receiving Station
NRES	Nichols Research [*NASDAQ symbol*] (TTSB)
NRES	Nichols Research Corp. [*NASDAQ symbol*] (NQ)
NRETN	Nonreturn
NREVSS	National Respiratory and Enteric Virus Surveillance System
NRF	National Republican Foundation (EA)
NRF	National Research Foundation [*Research center*] (RCD)
NRF	National Research Foundation [*South Africa*]
NRF	National Retail Federation (EA)
NRF	National Roofing Foundation (EA)
NRF	National Rowing Foundation (EA)
NRF	National Rural Fellows (EA)
NRF	Naval Reactor Facility
NRF	Naval Repair Facility
NRF	Naval Reserve Fleet [*or Force*]
NRF	Neurite Retraction Factor [*Biochemistry*]
NRF	Neurosciences Research Foundation (DAVI)
NRF	Newport Restoration Foundation (EA)
NRF	Nitrogen Rejection Facility [*Process engineering*]
NRF	No Redeeming Features
NRF	No Reflight
NRF	No Reinforcement [*Psychology*]

NRF	Normal Renal Function [*Medicine*] (DMAA)
NRF	Not Running at the Finish [*Automobile racing term*]
NRF	Nuclear Resonance Fluorescence (IAA)
NRF	Nutrition Research Foundation [*Australia*]
NRF	R. T. French Co., Rochester, NY [*Library symbol Library of Congress*] (LCLS)
NRFA	National Retail Florists Association [*Defunct*]
NRFA	National Retail Furniture Association [*Later, NHFA*] (EA)
NRFB	Never Removed from Box [*Doll collecting*]
NRFBS	National Research Foundation for Business Statistics (EA)
NRFC	National Railroad Freight Committee (EA)
NRFC	Navy Regional Finance Center
NRFC-B	Navy Regional Finance Center, Brooklyn [*New York*] (DNAB)
NRFC-GL	Navy Regional Finance Center, Great Lakes (DNAB)
NRFC-N	Navy Regional Finance Center, Norfolk [*Virginia*] (DNAB)
NRFC-PH	Navy Regional Finance Center, Pearl Harbor [*Hawaii*] (DNAB)
NRFC-SD	Navy Regional Finance Center, San Diego [*California*] (DNAB)
NRFC-SF	Navy Regional Finance Center, San Francisco [*California*] (DNAB)
NRFD	Not Ready for Data
NRFEA	National Retail Farm Equipment Association [*Later, NFPEDA*]
NRFF	National Research Foundation for Fertility [*Inactive*] (EA)
NRFI	National Rail Freight Initiative [*Australia*]
NRFI	Nonrecurring Finished Intelligence (MCD)
NRFI	Not Ready for Issue
NRFL	National Rugby Football League (NADA)
NRFMAU	Naval Reserve Fleet Management Assistance Unit (DNAB)
NRFO	Navy Regional Finance Office
NRFS	Naval Reserve Force Study Group (DNAB)
NRFSA	Navy Radio Frequency Spectrum Activity
NRFSEA	National Reciprocal and Family Support Enforcement Association [*Later, NCSEA*] (EA)
NRFU	Nonresponse Follow-Up [*Bureau of the Census*] (GFGA)
NRG	Energy (ABBR)
NRG	Nautical Research Guild (EA)
NRG	Naval Research Group
NRG	Northern Rhodesia Gazette [*A publication*] (DLA)
NRG	Ross Aviation, Inc. [*ICAO designator*] (FAAC)
NRG	Tri-Lite, Inc. [*AMEX symbol*] (SPSG)
NRGA	National Rice Growers Association [*Defunct*] (EA)
NRGas	Rochester Gas & Electric Corp., Technical Information Center, Rochester, NY [*Library symbol Library of Congress*] (LCLS)
NRGC	Nucleus Reticularis Gigantocellularis [*Neuroanatomy*]
NRGD-SC	Stromberg-Carlson Corp., Rochester, NY [*Library symbol Library of Congress*] (LCLS)
NRGE	George Eastman House, Rochester, NY [*Library symbol Library of Congress*] (LCLS)
NRGI	National Energy Group [*NASDAQ symbol*] (SAG)
NRGN	Neurogen Corp. [*NASDAQ symbol*] (NQ)
NRGR	General Railway Signal Co., Rochester, NY [*Library symbol Library of Congress*] (LCLS)
NRGS	Church of Jesus Christ of Latter-Day Saints, Genealogical Society Library, Rochester Branch, Rochester, NY [*Library symbol Library of Congress*] (LCLS)
NRH	Natural Rate Hypothesis [*Economics*]
NRH	Nodular Regenerative Hyperplasia [*of liver*] [*Medicine*]
NRH	Nonready Hours
NRH	No Reply Heard [*ICAO designator*] (FAAC)
NRHA	National Radio Heritage Association (EA)
NRHA	National Reining Horse Association (EA)
NRHA	National Retail Hardware Association (EA)
NRHA	National Roller Hockey Association of Great Britain (BI)
NRHA	National Rural Health Association (EA)
NRHA	Northern Rivers Hydrophonic Association [*Australia*]
NRhbA	Astor Home for Children, Rhinebeck, NY [*Library symbol Library of Congress*] (LCLS)
NRHC	National Rental Housing Council [*Later, NMHC*] (EA)
NRHC	National Rivers and Harbors Congress [*Later, WRC*]
NRHC	National Rural Housing Coalition (EA)
NRHCA	National Rural Health Care Association [*Formerly, NRPCA*] (EA)
NRhDH	Long Island Doctors' Hospital, Roslyn Heights, NY [*Library symbol Library of Congress*] (LCLS)
NRHE	Nonregenerative Heat Exchanger [*Nuclear energy*] (NRCH)
NRHGC	National Republican Heritage Groups (Nationalities) Council (EA)
NRHi	Rochester Historical Society, Rochester, NY [*Library symbol Library of Congress*] (LCLS)
NRHP	National Register of Historic Places [*A publication*]
NRHP	National Register of Hypnotherapists and Psychotherapists [*British*] (DBA)
NRHS	National Railway Historical Society (EA)
NRHS	New Royal Horticultural Society [*British*]
NRHSA	National Retail Hobby Store Association (NTPA)
NRHU	National Rural Health Unit [*Australia*]
NRHX	Nonregenerative Heat Exchanger [*Nuclear energy*] (NRCH)
NRI	National Radio Institute
NRI	National Research Institute [*Audience research organization*] (NTCM)
NRI	National Resource Inventory [*US database on erosion*]
NRI	National Rivers Inventory (GNE)
NRI	Natural Resources Institute [*University of Greenwich*] [*British*]
NRI	Natural Resources International
NRI	Net Radio Interface [*Telecommunications*] (TEL)
NRI	Neurological and Related Intervention [*Medicine*]
NRI	Neutral Regular Insulin
NRI	New Records, Inc. [*Record label*]
NRI	New Ring Index [*of chemical compounds*] [*A publication*]
NRI	Nomura Research Institute (NITA)

NRI	Nonrecurring Installation Charge [*Telecommunications*] (TEL)
NRI	Nonrecurring Investment (NASA)
NRI	Nonrepairable Item (MCD)
NRI	Nonresident Instruction (MCD)
NRI	Non-Respiratory Infection [*Medicine*] (DMAA)
NRI	Noril'sk [*Former USSR Seismograph station code, US Geological Survey*] (SEIS)
NRI	Novagold Resources, Inc. [*Toronto Stock Exchange symbol*]
NRI	Number of Records Ignored (SAA)
NRIA	Narrow Resonance Infinite Absorber (PDAA)
NRIA	National Railroad Intermodal Association [*Defunct*] (EA)
NRIAD	National Register of Industrial Art Designers [*British*] (DAS)
NRIC	National Rehabilitation Information Center [*Catholic University of America*] [*Bibliographic Database*] [*Washington, DC*]
NRIC	Negative Return in Cartridge [*Advanced photo system*]
NRIC	Non-Reciprocal Impedance Converter (PDAA)
NRIC	Nuclear Research Information Center [*American Nuclear Center*] [*Information service or system*] (IID)
NRICH	National Resource Institute on Children and Youth with Handicaps [*Defunct*] (EA)
NRID	National Registry [*NASDAQ symbol*] (SAG)
NRIIA	National Republican Institute for International Affairs (EA)
NRIM	Narrow Resonance Infinite Mass [*Nuclear energy*] (NRCH)
NRIM	Northrim Bank [*NASDAQ symbol*] (SAG)
NRIMS	National Research Institute for Mathematical Sciences [*South Africa*]
NRIP	Navy Reserve Intelligence Program (MCD)
NRIP	Number of Rejected Initial Pickups
NRIPMVLIC	Nonresident Interprovince Motor Vehicle Liability Insurance Card [*For travel in Canada*]
NRIS	Natural Resource Information System [*Department of the Interior*]
NRIS	New Mexico Natural Resources Information System [*New Mexico State Department of Natural Resources*] [*Santa Fe*] (IID)
NRIUW	Naval Reserve Inshore Undersea Warfare (DNAB)
NRJ	Natural Resources Journal [*A publication*] (BRI)
NRJ	Non-Reciprocal Junction (PDAA)
NRK	Newark (ABBR)
NRK	Normal Rat Kidney
NRK	Normotensive Rat Kidney
NRK	Norrkoping [*Sweden*] [*Airport symbol*] (OAG)
NRK	Norsk Rikskringkasting [*Norwegian Broadcasting Corporation*]
NRK	Nurek [*Former USSR Seismograph station code, US Geological Survey Closed*] (SEIS)
NRKF	Normal Rat Kidney Fibroblast [*Cytology*]
NRkpJH	Rocky Point Junior-Senior High School, Rocky Point, NY [*Library symbol Library of Congress*] (LCLS)
NRL	Naneco Resources Ltd. [*Vancouver Stock Exchange symbol*]
NRL	National Reference Library [*British*] (NUCP)
NRL	National Registry for Librarians (EA)
NRL	National Research Laboratory
NRL	National Research Library [*Canada*] (DIT)
NRL	National Resources Library
NRL	Naval Research Laboratory [*Washington, DC Seismograph station code, US Geological Survey Closed*] (SEIS)
NRL	Naval Research Laboratory, Washington, DC [*OCLC symbol*] (OCLC)
NRL	Network Restructuring Language
NRL	New York Revised Laws [*A publication*] (DLA)
NRL	Night Ration Locker (MSA)
NRL	Normal Rated Load
NRL	Normal Response Level
NRL	Norrell Corp. [*NYSE symbol*] (SAG)
NRL	Norske Reindriftsamers Lansforbund [*Norway*]
NRL	North Ronaldsay [*Scotland*] [*Airport symbol*] (OAG)
NRL	Nuclear Reactor Laboratory [*Massachusetts Institute of Technology*] [*Research center*] (RCD)
NRL	Nuclear Weapons Reconnaissance List (COE)
NRL	Nucleus Reticularis Lateralis (DB)
NRLA	Network Repair Level Analysis
NRLA	Northeastern Retail Lumbermen's Association (EA)
NRLC	National Railway Labor Conference (EA)
NRLC	National Right to Life Committee (EA)
NRLCA	National Rural Letter Carriers' Association (EA)
NRLCHESBAYDET	Naval Research Laboratory, Chesapeake Bay Detachment (DNAB)
NRLD	Norland Medical Systems [*NASDAQ symbol*] (TTSB)
NRLD	Norland Medical Systems, Inc. [*NASDAQ symbol*] (SAG)
NRLDA	National Retail Lumber Dealers Association [*Later, NLBMDA*]
NRL/EOTPO	Naval Research Laboratory Electro-Optical Technology Program Office [*Washington, DC*]
NRLETF	National Right to Life Educational Trust Fund (EA)
NRLF	Lincoln First Bank of Rochester, Rochester, NY [*Library symbol Library of Congress*] (LCLS)
NRLFLTSUPPDET	Naval Research Laboratory, Flight Support Detachment (DNAB)
NRLGY	Neurology
NRLM	National Research Lab of Metrology [*Japan*]
NRLN	Northern Regional Legal Notice [*1954-61*] [*Nigeria*] [*A publication*] (DLA)
NRLP	National Railway Labor Panel [*World War II*]
NRLR	Northern Rhodesia Law Reports [*A publication*] (DLA)
NRLREP	Naval Research Laboratory Representative (DNAB)
NRLSI	National Reference Library of Science and Invention [*of the British Museum*]
NRLSITEDET	Naval Research Laboratory, Field Site Detachment (DNAB)
NRLSPECPROJDET	Naval Research Laboratory, Special Projects Detachment (DNAB)

NRL/SVIC	Naval Research Laboratory Shock and Vibration Information Center [*ONR*]
NRLUWSREFDET	Naval Research Laboratory, Underwater Sound Reference Detachment (DNAB)
NRM	Nara [*Mali*] [*Airport symbol*] (OAG)
NRM	National Railway Museum (WDAA)
NRM	National Registry of Microbiologists (DAVI)
NRM	National Resistance Movement [*Uganda*] (PD)
NRM	National Revolutionary Movement [*France*]
NRM	Natural Remanent Magnetism [*or Magnetization*]
NRM	Natural Resource Management
NRM	Naval Reserve Medal
NRM	Next to Reading Matter [*Advertising*] (WDMC)
NRM	Nonrecurring Maintenance [*NASA*] (KSC)
NRM	Normalize (DEN)
NRM	Normal Response Mode
NRM	Norm-Referenced Measurement [*Education*]
NRM	Northair Mines Ltd. [*Toronto Stock Exchange symbol Vancouver Stock Exchange symbol*]
NRM	Northern Rocky Mountains
NRM	North Rainier Mesa [*Nevada*] [*Seismograph station code, US Geological Survey*] (SEIS)
NRM	Nucleus Reticularis Magnocellularis (DB)
NRM	Rochester Museum and Science Center, Rochester, NY [*Library symbol Library of Congress*] (LCLS)
NRMA	National Reloading Manufacturers Association (EA)
NRMA	National Retail Merchants Association [*New York, NY*] (EA)
NRMA	Nuclear Records Management Association (EA)
NRMADI	Non Recedet Malum a Domo Ingrati [*Evil Shall Not Depart from the House of theUngrateful*] [*(After Prov., XVII. 13) Motto of Julius, Duke of Braunschweig-Wolfenbuttel (1529-89)*] [*Latin*]
NRMC	Monroe Community College, Rochester, NY [*Library symbol Library of Congress*] (LCLS)
NRMC	National Records Management Council (EA)
NRMC	National Resources Management Corp.
NRMC	Naval Records Management Center
NRMC	Naval Regional Medical Center (NVT)
NRMC	Naval Reserve Manpower Center
NRMC	Northeast Rat and Mouse Club (EA)
NRMCA	National Radiator Manufacturing Credit Association (EA)
NRMCA	National Ready Mixed Concrete Association (EA)
NRMCEN	Naval Records Management Center
NRME	Notched, Returned, and Mitred Ends [*Construction*]
NRMEC	North American Rockwell Microelectronics Co. [*Obsolete*]
NRMF	New Road Map Foundation (EA)
NRMI	National Record Mart, Inc. [*NASDAQ symbol*] (SAG)
NRMI	National Registry of Myocardial Infarction
NRMI	Natl Record Mart [*NASDAQ symbol*] (TTSB)
NRMIUW	Naval Reserve Mobile Inshore Undersea Warfare (DNAB)
NRML	Monroe County Library System, Rochester, NY [*Library symbol Library of Congress*] (LCLS)
NRML	Normal (WGA)
NRMLC	Normalcy (ABBR)
NRMLT	Normality (ABBR)
NRMLY	Normally (ABBR)
NRMLZ	Normalize (ABBR)
NRMLZD	Normalized (ABBR)
NRMLZG	Normalizing (ABBR)
NRMLZN	Normalization (ABBR)
NRMLZR	Normalizer (ABBR)
NRMM	National Register of Microform Masters [*Library of Congress*]
NRMM	NATO Reference Mobility Model
NRMOMAGU	Naval Reserve Mobile Mine Assembly Group (DNAB)
NRMP	National Records Management Program (AEPA)
NRMP	National Resident Matching Program (EA)
NRMRL	National Risk Management Research Laboratory [*Environmental Protection Agency*] (AEPA)
NRMS	National Registry of Medical Secretaries (EA)
NRMS	Natural Resource Management System [*Army Corps of Engineers*] [*Database*]
NRMS	Naval Reserve Midshipmen's School
NRMS	Neutralization-Reionization Mass Spectrometry
NRMS	Nominal Root Mean Square (IAA)
NRMS	Norman Rockwell Memorial Society (EA)
NRMT	Northern Rocky Mountain Trench [*Geology*]
NRMTC	Nordoff-Robbins Music Therapy Centre Ltd. [*British*] (CB)
NRMU	Natural Resources Management [*Organization of Eastern Caribbean States*]
NRMU	Northern Rhodesia European Mineworkers' Union
NRMV	Normative (ABBR)
NRMVY	Normatively (ABBR)
NRMW	Margaret Woodbury Strong Museum, Rochester, NY [*Library symbol Library of Congress*] (LCLS)
NRN	Naryn [*Former USSR Seismograph station code, US Geological Survey*] (SEIS)
NRN	National Resource Network [*Commercial firm*] (EA)
NRN	Natural Radioactive Nuclides
NRN	Negative Run Number [*Computer science*] (OA)
NRN	Northern
NRN	Royal Netherlands Navy [*ICAO designator*] (FAAC)
nRNA	Ribonucleic Acid, Nuclear [*Biochemistry, genetics*]
NRNC	Nazareth College of Rochester, Rochester, NY [*Library symbol Library of Congress*] (LCLS)
NRND	Norand Corp. [*NASDAQ symbol*] (SAG)
NRNFC	National Rick Nelson Fan Club (EA)

NRNHD .... Nixon, Hargrave, Devans & Doyle, Rochester, NY [*Library symbol*] [*Library of Congress*] (LCLS)
NRNLR .... Northern Region of Nigeria Law Reports [*A publication*] (DLA)
NRNP .... Nuclear Ribonucleoprotein [*Medicine*] (DMAA)
NRNR .... National Rotorcraft Noise Reduction [*Program to reduce noise of helicopters*]
NRNS .... Nearness (ABBR)
NRO .... National Range Operations (RDA)
NRO .... National Reconnaissance Office [*Air Force/CIA*]
NRO .... National Reconnaissance Organization [*CIA*]
NRO .... Naval Research Objectives
NRO .... Navy Retail Office (AFIT)
NRO .... Negative Resistance Oscillator [*Electronics*]
NRO .... Nobeyama Radio Observatory
NRO .... Nonresident-Owned Funds [*Investment term*]
NRO .... Not RAM [*Reliability, Availability, and Maintainability*] Oriented
NRock .... Rockville Centre Public Library, Rockville Centre, NY [*Library symbol Library of Congress*] (LCLS)
NRockH .... Mercy Hospital, Rockville Centre, NY [*Library symbol Library of Congress*] (LCLS)
NRockHE ..... Hewett Elementary School, Rockville Centre, NY [*Library symbol Library of Congress*] (LCLS)
NRockL .... Lakeview Public Library, Rockville Centre, NY [*Library symbol Library of Congress*] (LCLS)
NRockM .... Molloy College, Rockville Centre, NY [*Library symbol Library of Congress*] (LCLS)
NRockRE ..... Riverside School, Rockville Centre, NY [*Library symbol*] [*Library of Congress*] (LCLS)
NRockSMS ... South Side Middle School, Rockville Centre, NY [*Library symbol*] [*Library of Congress*] (LCLS)
NRockSSH ... South Side Senior High School, Rockville Centre, NY [*Library symbol*] [*Library of Congress*] (LCLS)
NRockWE ..... Wilson Elementary School, Rockville Centre, NY [*Library symbol Library of Congress*] (LCLS)
NRockWR .... Woodfield Road School, Rockville Centre, NY [*Library symbol*] [*Library of Congress*] (LCLS)
NRockWS ..... Floyd B. Watson School, Rockville Centre, NY [*Library symbol*] [*Library of Congress*] (LCLS)
NROE .... Naval Reactor Organic Experiment
nroff .... Nontypesetting Runoff [*Computer science*] (CDE)
NRom .... Jervis Library Association, Rome, NY [*Library symbol Library of Congress*] (LCLS)
NROM .... Noble Roman's, Inc. [*NASDAQ symbol*] (NQ)
NROM .... Noble Romns [*NASDAQ symbol*] (TTSB)
NRomA .... Rome Air Development Center, Rome, NY [*Library symbol Library of Congress*] (LCLS)
NRomAF ...... United States Air Force, Base Library, Griffiss Air Force Base, Rome, NY [*Library symbol Library of Congress*] (LCLS)
NRomAF-R ... United States Air Force, Rome Air Development Center, Griffiss, NY [*Library symbol Library of Congress*] (LCLS)
NROMM .... Netherlands Register of Microform Masters (TELE)
NROO .... Naval Reactors Operations Office
NRoos .... Roosevelt Community Library, Roosevelt, NY [*Library symbol Library of Congress*] (LCLS)
NRoosCE ..... Centennial Elementary School, Roosevelt, NY [*Library symbol*] [*Library of Congress*] (LCLS)
NRoosDP ..... Daniels Primary Center, Roosevelt, NY [*Library symbol*] [*Library of Congress*] (LCLS)
NRoosJH ..... Roosevelt Junior-Senior High School, Roosevelt, NY [*Library symbol*] [*Library of Congress*] (LCLS)
NRoosPK .... Prekindergarten School, Roosevelt, NY [*Library symbol*] [*Library of Congress*] (LCLS)
NRoosRE ..... Theadore Roosevelt Elementary School, Roosevelt, NY [*Library symbol*] [*Library of Congress*] (LCLS)
NRoosWE .... Washington-Rose Elementary School, Roosevelt, NY [*Library symbol*] [*Library of Congress*] (LCLS)
NROPS .... New Riders of the Purple Sage [*Rock music group*]
NROS .... Naval Reserve Officer School
NRosl .... Bryant Library, Roslyn, NY [*Library symbol Library of Congress*] (LCLS)
NRoslH .... Saint Francis Hospital, Roslyn, NY [*Library symbol Library of Congress*] (LCLS)
NRoslhEI ..... East Hills Intermediate School, Roslyn Heights, NY [*Library symbol*] [*Library of Congress*] (LCLS)
NRoslhHP .... Heights Primary School, Roslyn Heights, NY [*Library symbol*] [*Library of Congress*] (LCLS)
NRoslhHS ... Roslyn High School, Roslyn Heights, NY [*Library symbol*] [*Library of Congress*] (LCLS)
NRoslhJH .... Roslyn Junior High School, Roslyn Heights, NY [*Library symbol*] [*Library of Congress*] (LCLS)
NRoslHS ...... Roslyn High School, Roslyn, NY [*Library symbol Library of Congress*] (LCLS)
NRoslhWI .... Willets Road Intermediate School, Roslyn Heights, NY [*Library symbol Library of Congress*] (LCLS)
NRoslJH ...... Roslyn Junior High School, Roslyn, NY [*Library symbol Library of Congress*] (LCLS)
NROSS .... Navy Remote Ocean Sensing System [*Proposed*]
NROTC .... Naval Reserve Officers' Training Corps
NROTCBA .... National Reserve Officers' Training Corps Band Association (AEBS)
NROTCU ...... Naval Reserve Officers' Training Corps Unit (DNAB)
NROTCUNAVADMINU ... Naval Reserve Officers' Training Corps Unit and Administrative Unit (DNAB)
NROVA .... National Record of Vocational Achievement (AIE)
NRP .... National Religious Party [*Hamiflaga Hadatit Leumit*] [*Israel*] [*Political party*] (PPW)

NRP .... National Reporting Program [*National Institute of Mental Health*] [*Department of Health and Human Services*] (GFGA)
NRP .... National Republican Party [*Guyana*] [*Political party*] (EY)
NRP .... National Resistance Party [*Political party*] (BJA)
NRP .... National Review Panel [*Work Incentive Program*] [*Department of Labor*]
NRP .... National Route Program (GAVI)
N/RP .... Neoclassical/Rational Planning
NRP .... Net Rating Point [*Advertising*] (DOAD)
NRP .... Net Rating Points [*Media ratings*] (NTCM)
NRP .... Network Resource Planning [*Computer science*] (CIST)
NRP .... Neurosciences Research Program [*Massachusetts Institute of Technology*]
NRP .... Nevis Reformation Party [*Political party*]
NRP .... New Republic Party [*South Africa*] [*Political party*] (PPW)
NRP .... New Rhodesia Party [*Political party*]
NRP .... Noise Review Program [*Navy*] (DNAB)
NRP .... Nonregistered Publication
NRP .... Nonreportable Property [*Military*]
NRP .... Nonstationary Random Process
NRP .... Non-unit Related Personnel [*Military*] (DOMA)
NRP .... Normal Rated Power
NRP .... Notice of Research Project
NRP .... NRP, Inc. [*Associated Press*] (SAG)
NRP .... Nuclear Reform Project (EA)
NRP .... Nucleus Reticularis Parvocellularis (DB)
NRP .... Nuwe Republiekparty [*New Republic Party*] [*Political party Afrikaans*]
NRP .... People's Republican Party [*Turkey Political party*]
NRP .... Pfaudler Technical Library, Rochester, NY [*Library symbol Library of Congress*] (LCLS)
NRpA .... Ayerst Science Laboratory, Rouses Point, NY [*Library symbol Library of Congress*] (LCLS)
NRPA .... National Recreation and Park Association (EA)
NRPA .... Non-Redundant Pinhole Array (PDAA)
NRPAC .... Naval Reserve Public Affairs Co.
NRPAI .... National Rifle and Pistol Association of Ireland (EAIO)
NRPAIN .... National Register of Prominent Americans and International Notables (EA)
NRPB .... National Radiological Protection Board [*British*]
NRPB .... National Research Planning Board
NRPB .... National Resources Planning Board [*Abolished, 1943*]
NRPB .... Naval Research Planning Board (DNAB)
NRPB .... Naval Reserve Policy Board (DNAB)
NRPB .... Nickerson RPB Ltd. [*British*] (IRUK)
NRPC .... National Railroad Passenger Corp. [*Government rail transportation*]
NRPC .... National Register Publishing Co. [*Information service or system*] (IID)
NRPC .... Naval Reserve Personnel Center (DNAB)
NRPC .... Nucleus Reticularis Pontis Caudalis (DB)
NRPCA .... National Rural Primary Care Association [*Later, NRHCA*] (EA)
NRPD .... National Radiological Protection Board [*British*]
NRPEO .... Naval Regional Plant Equipment Office [*or Officer*] (DNAB)
NRPF .... National Railroad Pension Forum [*Defunct*] (EA)
NRPF .... National Retinitis Pigmentosa Foundation [*Later, RPFFB*] (EA)
NRPG .... National Retinoblastoma Parents Group (EA)
NRPG .... Nucleus Reticularis Paragigantocellularis (DB)
NRPH .... Park Ridge Hospital, Medical Library, Rochester, NY [*Library symbol Library of Congress*] (LCLS)
NRPIO .... Naval Registered Publications Issuing Office
NRPJ .... Nezavisna Radnicka Partija Jugoslavije [*Independent Labor Party of Yugoslavia*] [*Political party*]
NRPlanP ...... Planned Parenthood of Rochester and Monroe County, Rochester, NY [*Library symbol Library of Congress*] (LCLS)
NRPM .... Nonregistered Publications Memoranda
NRPM .... Nuclear Weapons Reconnaissance Planning Manual (COE)
NRPO .... Naval Regional Procurement Office
NRPP .... Pennwalt Corp., Pharmaceutical Division Research Library, Rochester, NY [*Library symbol Library of Congress*] (LCLS)
NRPRA .... Natural Rubber Producers' Research Association [*British*] (BI)
NRPS .... Naval Radiological Protection Service (PDAA)
NRPS .... New Riders of the Purple Sage [*Rock music group*]
NRPS .... Non-Ribosomal Peptide Synthetase [*An enzyme*]
NRPSA .... National Retail Pet Supply Association [*Defunct*] (EA)
NRPSGA ...... National Retail Pet Store and Groomers Association (EA)
NRPTC .... National Register of Potentially Toxic Chemicals (GNE)
NRR .... Naval Research Reactor
NRR .... Naval Research Requirement
NRR .... Naval Reserve Requirement (MCD)
NRR .... Negative Radial Rake (IAA)
NRR .... Negative Resistance Repeater [*Electronics*] (IAA)
NRR .... Net Reproduction Rate [*Medicine*] (DMAA)
NRR .... Net Reproductive Rate
NRR .... Net Retail Requirements
NRR .... Noise Reduction Rating [*Audio technology*] (EG)
NRR .... No Response Required
NRR .... No Resume Required
NRR .... Northern Rhodesia Regiment
NRR .... North Reno [*Nevada*] [*Seismograph station code, US Geological Survey*] (SEIS)
NRR .... Note, Record, Report [*Medical records and nursing*] (DAVI)
NRR .... Nuclear Rocket Reactor
NRR .... Office of Nuclear Reactor Regulation [*Nuclear Regulatory Commission*]
NRR .... Roosevelt Roads, PR [*Location identifier FAA*] (FAAL)
NRRA .... National Rail Regulatory Authority [*Australia*]
NRRA .... National Resource Recovery Association (EA)

NRRA..........	National Risk Retention Association (EA)
NRRA..........	National Romany Rights Association (WDAA)
NRRAD	Narrated (ABBR)
NRRAG	Narrating (ABBR)
NRRAN	Narration (ABBR)
NRR & C	Russell and Chesley's Nova Scotia Reports [*A publication*] (DLA)
NRRAR	Narrator (ABBR)
NRRAS........	Navy Readiness Reporting and Analysis System (MCD)
NRRAV........	Narrative (ABBR)
NRRB..........	National Recovery Review Board [*Terminated, 1934*]
NRRC..........	National Rex Rabbit Club (EA)
NRRC..........	Naval Research Reserve Co.
NRRC..........	Northern Regional Research Center [*Formerly, NRRL*] [*Peoria, IL*] [*Department of Agriculture*]
NRRC..........	Nuclear Risk Reduction Center (DOMA)
NRRD..........	Norstan, Inc. [*NASDAQ symbol*] (NQ)
NRRF..........	Naval Radio Receiving Facility (DNAB)
NRRF..........	Naval Reserve Readiness Facility (DNAB)
NRRFSS......	National Research and Resource Facility for Submicron Structures [*Cornell University*] [*Research center*] (RCD)
NRRI..........	National Regulatory Research Institute [*Ohio State University*] [*Research center*] (RCD)
NRRI..........	Natural Resources Research Institute [*Research center*] (RCD)
NRRI..........	Rochester Institute of Technology, Rochester, NY [*Library symbol Library of Congress*] (LCLS)
NRRI-C	Rochester Institute of Technology, Melbert B. Cary, Jr. Graphic Arts Collection,Rochester, NY [*Library symbol Library of Congress*] (LCLS)
NRRL..........	Northern Regional Research Laboratory [*Later, NRRC*] [*Department of Agriculture*]
NRRO..........	Naval Radio Research Observatory (IAA)
NRRO..........	Nuclear Radiation-Resistant Oils (NRCH)
NRRP..........	National Reservoir Research Program [*Department of the Interior*] (GRD)
NRRP..........	Sybron Corp., Rochester, NY [*Library symbol Library of Congress*] (LCLS)
NRRPC.........	National Rural and Resources Press Club [*Australia*]
NRRR..........	Rochester Reference Research and Resources Council, Rochester, NY [*Library symbol Library of Congress*] (LCLS)
NRRS..........	Naval Radio Research Station
NRRS..........	Nebraska Reading Retrieval System (EDAC)
NRRS..........	No Remaining Radiation Service [*Unit*] [*Military*]
NRS...........	Atlantic Richfield Co. [*ICAO designator*] (FAAC)
NRS...........	Imperial Beach, CA [*Location identifier FAA*] (FAAL)
NRS...........	Name Registration Scheme [*Telecommunications*] (OSI)
NRS...........	National Radio Station (IAA)
NRS	National Readership Survey [*British*]
NRS	National Real Estate Service [*Canada*]
NRS	National Reemployment Service
NRS	National Referral System [*British*] (DCTA)
NRS	National Reporter System [*Database*] [*Maritime Law Book Co. Ltd.*] [*Information service or system*] (CRD)
NRS	National Runaway Switchboard (EA)
NRS	Nationwide Refrigeration Supplies [*British*]
NRS	Naval Radio Station
NRS	Naval Receiving Station
NRS	Naval Recruiting Service [*British military*] (DMA)
NRS	Naval Recruiting Station
NRS	Naval Research Section [*Library of Congress*] (MCD)
NRS	Naval Rocket Society (IAA)
NRS	Navy Records Society [*British*] (DBA)
NRS	Navy Relief Society (EA)
NRS	Network Resource Server [*J & L Information Systems*]
NRS	Neurobehavioral Rating Scale [*Medicine*] (DMAA)
NRS	Nevada Revised Statutes [*A publication*]
NRS	Newborn Rights Society (EA)
NRS	New Rural Society [*HUD project*]
NRS	Night Reconnaissance System
NRS	Nitrogen Recharge Station
NRS	Nonconformance Reporting System (NASA)
NRS	Nonconforming Reporting System
NRS	Non-Rising Stem [*Valve*] (DICI)
NRS	Normal Rabbit Serum [*Culture medium*]
NRS	Normal Rat Serum [*Hematology*]
NRS	Normal Reference Serum (MAE)
NRS	Nuclear Radiation Shield
NRS	Nuclear Reaction Spectrometry (BARN)
NRS	Nuclear Rocket Shuttle (KSC)
NRS	Numerical Rating Scale (DMAA)
NRS	Numerical Rating System [*Insurance*]
NRS	Nurse (ABBR)
NRSA..........	National Remote Sensing Agency [*India*]
NRSA..........	National Rental Service Association (EA)
NRSA..........	National Research Service Awards [*Department of Health and Human Services*]
NRSA..........	National Rose Society of Australia
NRSA..........	Natural Rubber Shippers Association (EA)
NRSA..........	Northeast Rail Service Act [*1981*] [*Also, NERSA*]
NRSB..........	Saint Bernard's Seminary and College, Rochester, NY [*Library symbol Library of Congress*] (LCLS)
NRSC..........	National Radio Systems Committee
NRSC..........	National Remote Sensing Centre [*Royal Aircraft Establishment Space Department*] [*British*] (CB)
NRSC..........	National Republican Senatorial Committee (EA)
NRSC..........	Naval Reserve Supply Company (DNAB)
NRSC..........	Nordic Road Safety Council [*See also NTR*] [*Helsinki, Finland*] (EAIO)
NRSCC.......	National Reference System in Clinical Chemistry (DAVI)
NRSCC.......	National Registry System for Chemical Compounds (DIT)
NRSCO.......	Navy Recruiting Station Commanding Officer
NRSD..........	Nursed (ABBR)
NRSDNC......	Nonresidence (ABBR)
NRSDNT......	Nonresident (ABBR)
NRSE..........	Neuron-Restrictive Silencer Element [*Neurogenesis*]
NRSE..........	Nurse (ABBR)
NRSe..........	Sear-Brown Associates, PC, Rochester, NY [*Library symbol Library of Congress*] (LCLS)
NRSED.......	Nursed (ABBR)
NRSEG.......	Nursing (ABBR)
NRSEMD.....	Nursemaid (ABBR)
NRSEP.......	National Roster of Scientific and Engineering Personnel (IAA)
NRSF........	National Rehabilitation and Service Foundation (EA)
NRSF........	National Reye's Syndrome Foundation (EA)
NRSF........	Neuron-Restrictive Silencer Factor [*Neurogenesis*]
NRSFPS......	National Reporting System for Family Planning Services [*National Institutes of Health*]
NRSG..........	Naval Reserve Security Group (DNAB)
NRSG..........	Nursing
NRSH........	Nourish (ABBR)
NRSHD.......	Nourished (ABBR)
NRSHG	Nourishing (ABBR)
NRSHNT	Nourishment (ABBR)
NRSI..........	National Reading Styles Institute
NRSITD.......	Near-Sighted (ABBR)
NRSITNS.....	Near-Sightedness (ABBR)
NRSJ	Saint John Fisher College, Rochester, NY [*Library symbol Library of Congress*] (LCLS)
NRSL..........	Navy Radio and Sound Laboratory (IAA)
NRSO..........	Navy Resale Systems Office
NRSP..........	National Remote Sensing Program [*Marine science*] (OSRA)
NRSP..........	National Remote Sensing Programme (USDC)
NRS(R)........	Naval Radio Station (Receiving) (DNAB)
nrsry..........	Nursery
NRS(S)........	Naval Radio Station (Sending) (DNAB)
NRSSC.......	National Rural and Small Schools Consortium (EA)
NRSSG.......	Nuclear Reactor Systems Safety Group [*Air Force*]
NRSSGP	Nuclear Reactor Systems Safety Group [*Air Force*]
NRSSO.......	Navy Resale and Services Support Office (DNAB)
NRSTCTV	Nonrestrictive (ABBR)
NRSTK	Narcisistic (ABBR)
NRSTP	National Register of Scientific and Technical Personnel (IAA)
NRSV........	Necrotic Ringspot Virus [*of prunes*]
NRSV........	New Revised Standard Version [*1989*] [*A publication*] (ODCC)
NRSW........	Nuclear River Service Water (IEEE)
NRSY........	Nordiska Forbundet for Studie- och Yrkesvagledning [*Nordic Association for Study and Vocational Guidance - NASVG*] (EAIO)
NRSY	Nursery
NRT...........	Burroughs Wellcome & Co., Research Triangle Park, NC [*OCLC symbol*] (OCLC)
nrt...............	Narrator [*MARC relator code*] [*Library of Congress*] (LCCP)
NRT	National Rally Terminology [*Automotive competition*]
NRT	National Recreation Trail (COE)
NRT	National Repertory Theatre Foundation [*Defunct*] (EA)
NRT	National Resource Trustee (BCP)
NRT	National Response Team [*RSPA*] (TAG)
NRT	National Response Team for Oil and Hazardous Materials Spills [*Environmental Protection Agency Washington, DC*] (EGAO)
NRT	Navy Reserve Training
NRT	Near-Real Time
NRT	Neighbours of the Roundtable (EA)
NRT	Net Registered Tonnage
NRT	Net Register Tons [*Shipping*]
NRT	Network Readiness Test (KSC)
NRT	Neuromuscular Re-Education Techniques (DAVI)
NRT	Nicotine-Replacement Therapy [*Medicine*]
NRT	Nonradiating Target
NRT	Nonreal Time
NRT	Nonrequestor Terminal (IAA)
NRT	Normal Rated Thrust (AAG)
NRT	Norm-Referenced Testing [*Education*]
NRT	Nortel Inversora 10%'MEDS' [*NYSE symbol*] (TTSB)
NRT	Nortel Inversora SA [*NYSE symbol*] (SAG)
NRT	Northfield [*Vermont*] [*Seismograph station code, US Geological Survey Closed*] (SEIS)
NRT	Notion Round Table (EA)
NRT	Nucleus Reticularis Thalami [*Neuroanatomy*]
NRT	Taylor Instrument Cos., Rochester, NY [*Library symbol Library of Congress*] (LCLS)
NRT	Tokyo-Narita [*Japan*] [*Airport symbol*] (OAG)
NRTA	National Retired Teachers Association, Division of AARP (EA)
NRTAC........	National Recreation Trails Advisory Committee (COE)
NRTAC........	National Road Trauma Advisory Council [*Australia*]
NRT & CMA...	National Retail Tea and Coffee Merchants Association
NRTB	Naval Reserve Training Branch
NRTC	National Retail Trade Centre (EAIO)
NRTC	Naval Reserve Training Center
NRTC	Nonreal-Time Conversion Subsystem [*Space Flight Operations Facility, NASA*]
NRTCOMD ...	Naval Reserve Training Command
NRTDAS.......	Nonreal-Time Data Automation System [*NASA*] (IAA)

NRTEC	National Rural Teacher Education Consortium [*National Rural Development Institute*] [*Later, NRSSC*] (EA)
NRTF	National Recreation Trails Fund (COE)
NRTF	Naval Radio Transmitting Facility (DNAB)
NRTH	North (ABBR)
NrthFce	North Face, Inc. (The) [*Associated Press*] (SAG)
NRTHSD	Northside
NRTHUM	Northumberland [*County in England*] (ROG)
NRTI	National Rehabilitation Training Institute [*Defunct*] (EA)
NRTI	Nooney Realty Trust [*NASDAQ symbol*] (TTSB)
NRTI	Nooney Realty Trust, Inc. [*NASDAQ symbol*] (NQ)
NRTI	Nucleoside Revenue Transcript Inhibitor [*Biochemistry*]
NRTIPT	Naval Reserve Training in Port (NVT)
NRTK	Nonreceptor Tyrosine Kinase [*An enzyme*]
NRTL	Nationally Recognized Testing Laboratory (COE)
NRTL	Non-Random Two-Liquid [*Equation of state*]
NRTO	National Remotivation Therapy Organization (EA)
NRTOI	National Range Technical Operating Instructions [*NASA*] (KSC)
NRTP	Nucleus Reticularis Tegmenti Pontis [*Neuroanatomy*]
NRTR	Near-Real-Time Reconnaissance (MCD)
NRTR	Nurture (ABBR)
NRTRD	Nurtured (ABBR)
NRTRG	Nurturing (ABBR)
NRTS	National Reactor Test Station [*INEL*] (NRCH)
NRTS	Not Repairable This Ship [*Navy*] (AFIT)
NRTS	Not Reparable This Station
NRTSC	Naval Reconnaissance and Technical Support Center
NRTSCPAC ...	Naval Reconnaissance and Technical Support Center, Pacific (DNAB)
NRTWC	National Right to Work Committee (EA)
NRTWLDEF ...	National Right to Work Legal Defense and Education Foundation [*Also, NRWLDF*] (EA)
NRTY	Norton McNaughton [*NASDAQ symbol*] (TTSB)
NRTY	Norton McNaughton, Inc. [*NASDAQ symbol*] (SAG)
NRU	National Reactor Universal
NRU	National Research Universal [*Nuclear reactor*] [*Canada*]
NRU	National Rural Utilities Cooperative Finance Corp. [*NYSE symbol*] (SAG)
NRU	Natural Resource Unit [*Environmental unit*]
NRU ....../......	Nauru [*ANSI three-letter standard code*] (CNC)
NRU	Network Resource Unit (MHDB)
NRU	Neuropsychiatric Research Unit [*Navy*]
NRU	Neutral Red Uptake (DMAA)
N Ru	Nicolaus Rufulus [*Flourished, 13th century*] [*Authority cited in pre-1607 legal work*] (DSA)
NRU	Nitrogen Rejection Unit [*Process engineering*]
NRU	Nonreplaceable Unit (IAA)
NRU	Not Recently Used [*Replacement algorithm*] [*Computer science*] (BYTE)
NRU	University of Rochester, Rochester, NY [*Library symbol Library of Congress*] (LCLS)
NRU-A	University of Rochester, Memorial Art Gallery, Rochester, NY [*Library symbol Library of Congress*] (LCLS)
NRUCFC	National Rural Utilities Cooperative Finance Corp. (EA)
NRU-M	University of Rochester, School of Medicine and Dentistry, Rochester, NY [*Library symbol Library of Congress*] (LCLS)
NRU-Mus	University of Rochester, Eastman School of Music; Rochester, NY [*Library symbol Library of Congress*] (LCLS)
NRurU45	National Rural Utilities Cooperative Finance Corp. [*Associated Press*] (SAG)
NRUS	Neighbors Are Us (PA)
NRU-W	University of Rochester, Women's College, Rochester, NY [*Library symbol Library of Congress*] (LCLS)
NRV	Navarre Resources [*Vancouver Stock Exchange symbol*]
NRV	Nerve (ABBR)
NRV	Net Realizable Value
NRV	Neubabylonische Rechts- und Verwaltungsurkunden [*A publication*] (BJA)
NRV	Nonrevenue [*Passengers or cargo*] [*Transportation*]
NRV	Northamptonshire Rifle Volunteer Corps [*British military*] (DMA)
NRV	North Carolina State University, School of Veterinary Medicine, Raleigh, NC [*OCLC symbol*] (OCLC)
NRV	North Vancouver Airlines Ltd. [*Canada*] [*FAA designator*] (FAAC)
NRV	Nucleus Reticularis Ventralis (DB)
NRVA	Net Realizable Value Accounting (ADA)
NRVC	National Religious Vocation Conference (EA)
NRvCH	Central Suffolk Hospital, Riverhead, NY [*Library symbol Library of Congress*] (LCLS)
NRVD	Nerved (ABBR)
NRVG	Nerving (ABBR)
NRVH	National RV Holdings, Inc. [*NASDAQ symbol*] (SAG)
NRVH	Natl R.V.Holding [*NASDAQ symbol*] (TTSB)
NRVI	Nervy (ABBR)
NRVLS	Nerveless (ABBR)
NRVMA	National Roadside Vegetation Management Association (EA)
NRVOC	National RV [*Recreational Vehicle*] Owners Club (EA)
NRvS	Suffolk County Historical Society, Riverhead, NY [*Library symbol Library of Congress*] (LCLS)
NRVSBL	Nonreversible
NRvSL	Supreme Court Law Library, Tenth Judicial District, Riverhead, NY [*Library symbol Library of Congress*] (LCLS)
NRVU	Nervous (ABBR)
NRVUNS	Nervousness (ABBR)
NRVUS	Nervous (ABBR)
NRVUSNS	Nervousness (ABBR)

NRVUSY	Nervously (ABBR)
NRVUY	Nervously (ABBR)
NRVWRKG ..	Nerve-Wracking (ABBR)
NRW	New Right Watch [*An association*] (EA)
NRW	Nonradioactive Waste [*Nuclear energy*] (NRCH)
NRW	Norwegian (ABBR)
NRW	Nuclear RADWASTE (IEEE)
NRW	Number of Remaining Words
NR/WA	National Rep/Wholesaler Association (EA)
NRWA	National Rural Water Association (EA)
NRWC	National Right to Work Committee (EA)
NRWD	Narrowed (ABBR)
NRWG	Narrowing (ABBR)
NRWG	Neutron Radiography Working Group [*EURATOM*]
NRW-KA	National Registry of Willys-Knight Automobiles [*Later, W-O-KR*]
NRWLDEF ...	National Right to Work Legal Defense and Education Foundation [*Later, NRWLDF*] (EA)
NRWLDF	National Right to Work Legal Defense Foundation (EA)
NRWMDD	Narrow-Minded (ABBR)
NRWMDDNS ..	Narrow-Mindedness (ABBR)
NRWO	Nuclear RADWASTE [*Radioactive Waste*] Operator (IAA)
NRWV	Nonradioactive Waste Vent [*Nuclear energy*] (NRCH)
NRX	National Research Experiment [*Canadian reactor*]
NRX	NERVA [*Nuclear Engine for Rocket Vehicle Application*] Reactor Experiment
NRX	Nuclear Engine Reactor Experiment (NRCH)
NRX	Nuclear Reactor, Experimental
NRX	Xerox Corp., Rochester, NY [*Library symbol Library of Congress*] (LCLS)
NRX(C)	Nonreturn-to-Zero (Change) Recording
NRX-CX	Nuclear Engine Reactor Critical Assembly (SAA)
NRX-EST	NERVA [*Nuclear Engine for Rocket Vehicle Applications*] Reactor Experiment-EngineSystem Test (SAA)
NRY	Nearly (ABBR)
NRy	Rye Free Reading Room, Rye, NY [*Library symbol Library of Congress*] (LCLS)
NRyHi	Rye Historical Society, Rye, NY [*Library symbol Library of Congress*] (LCLS)
NRyS	Sloan-Kettering Institute for Cancer Research, Rye, NY [*Library symbol Library of Congress*] (LCLS)
NRZ	Nonreturn to Zero [*Data transmission*]
NRZ	Null Reception Zone
NRZ1	Nonreturn to Zero Change on One (BUR)
NRZC	Nonreturn to Zero Change
NRZI	Nonreturn to Zero Inverted [*Recording method*]
NRZI	NRZ Indicator (NITA)
NRZL	Nonreturn to Zero Level
NRZL	Nonreturn to Zero Logic (MCD)
NRZM	Nonreturn to Zero Mark
NRZ-S	Non-Return to Zero-Space (MCD)
NS	Graduate of the Royal Naval Staff College, Greenwich [*British*]
NS	Nachalnik Sektora [*Chief of Sector*] [*Soviet military rank*]
ns	Nanosecond [*One billionth of a second*] [*Also, nsec*]
NS	Naram-Sin (BJA)
NS	Narodna Stranka [*People's Party*] [*Montenegro*] [*Political party*] (EY)
NS	Narodnye Sotsialisty [*Popular Socialists*] [*Former USSR Political party*] (PPE)
N-S	Nassi-Schneiderman [*Computer science*]
NS	National Savings [*British*]
NS	National Scientific [*Vancouver Stock Exchange symbol*]
NS	National Seashore (BARN)
NS	National Service [*in the armed forces*] [*British*]
NS	National Society
NS	National Sojourners (EA)
NS	National Special [*Thread*]
NS	National Standard (IEEE)
NS	National Steel [*NYSE symbol*] (SPSG)
NS	National Strategy
NS	National Samling [*National Union*] [*Norway*] (PD)
NS	Natl Steel 'B' [*NYSE symbol*] (TTSB)
NS	NATO Secret (NATG)
NS	NATO Surveillance (NATG)
NS	Natural Sciences
NS	[*The*] Naturist Society (EA)
NS	Naval School (MCD)
NS	Naval Shipyard
NS	Naval Station
NS	Naval Stores [*British*]
NS	Navigation Subsystem (OA)
NS	NAVSHIPS [*Naval Ship Systems Command*] Publication
NS	Near Side [*Technical drawings*]
NS	Near Space
NS	Nederlandse Spoorwegen [*Netherlands Railways*]
NS	Neo Sumerian (BJA)
NS	Nephrosclerosis [*Medicine*]
NS	Nephrotic Syndrome [*Medicine*] (DAVI)
NS	Nerine Society [*Defunct*] (EA)
NS	Nervous System
NS	Net Sales (MHDW)
NS	Net Surplus
NS	Network Service [*Computer science*] (TNIG)
NS	Neue Sachlichkeit [*New Objectivity*] [*Pre-World War II group of German artists*]
NS	Neuroelectric Society [*Defunct*] (EA)
NS	Neurologic Signs [*Medicine*] (CPH)

NS..............	Neurologic Survey [*Medicine*] (MAE)
NS................	Neurosecretory
NS................	Neurosurgery [*Medicine*]
NS................	Neuro-Syphilis [*Medicine*]
NS................	Neurotic Score [*Psychology*]
N/S..............	Neutrons per Second
NS................	Newport Steel Corp. (EFIS)
NS................	News [*A radio station format*] (WDMC)
NS................	New School
NS................	New Series [*Bibliography*]
NS................	New Side
NS................	Newspaper Society [*British*]
n/s...............	Newsstand [*Also N/S*] (WDMC)
NS................	New Statesman [*A publication*] (BRI)
NS................	New Style
NS................	New System [*Computer science*]
NS................	Next System [*Computer science*]
NS................	Nickel Silver [*Used in minting coins*]
NS................	Nickel Steel
Ns...............	Nielsbohrium [*Proposed name and symbol for recently-discovered element*]
NS................	Nietzsche Society (EA)
NS................	Nimbostratus [*Cloud*] [*Meteorology*]
NS................	Nitrogen Supply
NS................	Nitrogen System
NS................	Nobelstiftelsen [*Nobel Foundation - NF*] (EAIO)
NS................	Nockian Society (EA)
NS................	Nodular Sclerosis [*Medicine*] (AAMN)
NS................	Noise Sensitivity (IAA)
NS................	Noise Supressor [*Radio*] (NTCM)
NS................	Nonscheduled
NS................	Nonschizophrenic [*Psychology*]
NS................	Nonsequenced (IAA)
NS................	Nonserviceable (MSA)
NS................	Nonshorting (IAA)
NS................	Nonskew (IAA)
NS................	Nonslip (ABBR)
NS................	Nonsmutted [*Plant pathology*]
NS................	Nonspecified
NS................	Nonstandard (AABC)
NS................	Nonstatus Candidates May Apply [*Civil Service*]
NS................	Nonstimulation
NS................	Nonstop [*Aviation*]
NS................	Nonstructural [*Protein*] (DB)
NS................	Nonsymptomatic [*Medicine*] (MAE)
NS................	Nordisk Speditorforbund [*Nordic Forwarding Agents Association - NFAA*] [*Defunct*] (EAIO)
NS................	Nordisk Svommeforbund [*Nordic Swimming Federations Association - NSFA*] (EAIO)
NS................	Norfolk Southern Railway Co. [*AAR code*]
NS................	Normally Shut (NRCH)
NS................	Normal Saline
NS................	Normal Segment
NS................	Normal Serum
NS................	Normal Sodium (DB)
N/S..............	North Sea - Nonrigid Airship [*Royal Naval Air Service*] [*British*]
N/S..............	North Side [*In outdoor advertising*] (WDMC)
NS................	North Somerset Imperial Yeomanry [*British military*] (DMA)
NS................	North-South
NS................	No Sample (MAE)
NS................	No Scramble (IAA)
NS................	Nose [*Horse racing*]
ns	No Sequelae [*Aftereffects*] [*Medicine*] (MAE)
NS................	No Sound [*Script notation*] (NTCM)
NS................	No Sparring (DS)
NS................	No Specimen [*Medicine*]
N/S..............	No Stamp [*Deltiology*]
NS................	No Stimulation [*Neurophysiology*]
NS................	Nostro Signore [*Our Lord*]
NS................	No Surgery Performed
NS................	Notre Seigneur [*Our Lord*] [*French*]
NS................	Not Seen
NS................	Not Significant
NS................	Not Specified
ns	Not Specified (EBF)
NS................	Not Sprinklered [*Insurance*]
NS................	Not Stated
NS................	Not Stocked
NS................	Not Stung
NS................	Not Sufficient
n/s...............	Not Sufficient (WDMC)
NS................	Not Suitable
NS................	Not Suppressed
NS................	Not Switchable (MCD)
NS................	Noun Substantive [*Grammar*] (ROG)
NS................	Nourishing Stout [*Brewing*] (ROG)
NS................	Nova Scotia [*Canadian province*] [*Postal code*]
NS................	Noxious Stimuli
NS................	Noxious Substances (COE)
NS................	Nuclear Safety (COE)
NS................	Nuclear Science
NS................	Nuclear Sclerosis [*Ophthalmology*]
NS................	Nuclear Ship
NS................	Nuclear Shuttle (NASA)
NS................	Nuclear Submarine
NS................	Nuclear Systems
NS................	Nuernberger [*ICAO designator*] (AD)
N_s	Number of Secondary Turns (IDOE)
NS................	Number of Secondary Turns (IAA)
NS................	Numismatic Society
NS................	Nursing Services
NS................	Nursing Sister [*Navy British*]
NS................	Nutrition Society [*British*] (EAIO)
NS................	Nylon Suture [*Medicine*]
NS................	Nzingha Society (EA)
ns................	Sodium Metasilicate [*CIPW classification*] [*Geology*]
Ns................	Surface Refractivity (CET)
NSa	Bancroft Public Library, Salem, NY [*Library symbol Library of Congress*] (LCLS)
NSA	Naphthalene Sulfonic Acid [*Organic chemistry*]
NSA	Napoleonic Society of America (EA)
NSA	National Safety Association (NADA)
NSA	National Sawmilling Association [*British*] (BI)
NSA	National Scrabble Association (EA)
NSA	National Secretaries Association (International) [*Later, PSI*] (EA)
NSA	National Security Act (AAG)
NSA	National Security Agency [*Acronym is facetiously translated as No Such Agency or Never Say Anything because of staffers' reluctance to give interviews*] [*DoD*]
NSA	National Security Agency, Fort George G. Meade, MD [*OCLC symbol*] (OCLC)
NSA	National Security Archive
NSA	National Security Area (COE)
NSA	National Seniors' Association [*Australia*]
NSA	National Service Acts [*British*]
NSA	National Sheep Association [*British*] (DBA)
NSA	National Shellfisheries Association (EA)
NSA	National Sheriffs' Association (EA)
NSA	National Shipping Authority [*Department of Commerce*]
NSA	National Showmen's Association (EA)
NSA	National Shuffleboard Association (EA)
NSA	National Silo Association [*Later, ISA*] (EA)
NSA	National Skating Association of Great Britain
NSA	National Ski Association of America [*Later, United States Ski Association*]
NSA	National Slag Association (EA)
NSA	National Slate Association (EA)
NSA	National Smokers Alliance
NSA	National Snurfing Association (EA)
NSA	National Society of Accountants (NTPA)
NSA	National Society of Andersonville (EA)
NSA	National Society of Artists (EA)
NSA	National Society of Auctioneers [*Later, National Auctioneers Association*]
NSA	National Softball Association (EA)
NSA	National Sound Archive [*British Library*]
NSA	National Speakers Association (EA)
NSA	National Spiritual Alliance of the USA (EA)
NSA	National Sports Association (EA)
NSA	National Sprint Association [*British*] (DBA)
NSA	National Sprouting Association (EA)
NSA	National Standards Association (NADA)
NSA	National Standards Association, Inc. [*Bethesda, MD*]
NSA	National Stereoscopic Association (EA)
NSA	National Stone Association (EA)
NSA	National Stroke Association (EA)
NSA	National Student Association [*Later, USSA*]
NSA	National Students Association (NADA)
NSA	National Sunflower Association (EA)
NSA	National System Architecture
NSA	Nausea (KSC)
NSA	Naval Stock Account
NSA	Naval Supply Account
NSA	Naval Support Activity [*Vietnam*]
NSA	Navy Supply Annex (AFIT)
NSA	Neighborhood Strategy Area [*Program*] [*HUD*]
NSA	Nepal Studies Association (EA)
NSA	Network Software Associates, Inc.
NSA	Neurological Society of America (DAVI)
NSA	Neurological Society of Australasia
NSA	Neurosurgical Society of America (EA)
NSA	New Sabina Resources Ltd. [*Vancouver Stock Exchange symbol*]
NSA	New Shipborne Aircraft [*Canada*]
NSA	New South Africa Fund [*NYSE symbol*] (SAG)
NSA	Nichiren Shoshu Soka Gakkai of America [*Buddhist organization*] (EA)
NSA	Nile Safaris Aviation [*Sudan*] [*ICAO designator*] (FAAC)
NSA	Nitrosylsulfuric Acid [*Inorganic chemistry*]
NSA	Node Switching Assembly (SSD)
NSA	Noise Suppressor Assembly
NSA	Nominal Stress Approach (PDAA)
NSA	Nonsequenced Acknowledgment (IAA)
NSA	Non-Sterling Area (PDAA)
NSA	Nonylsuccinic Acid [*Organic chemistry*]
NSA	Noosa [*Australia Airport symbol*] (OAG)
NSA	Normal Serum Albumin [*Clinical chemistry*]
NSA	Northeastern Saengerbund of America (EA)
NSA	North Sea Assets [*Investment firm*] [*British*]
NSA	North-South Acceleration
NSA	Norwegian Seamen's Association (EA)

NSA .... No Salt Added
nsa .... No Salt Added (DMAA)
NSA .... No Serious Abnormality (DAVI)
NSA .... No Significant Abnormalities [*Medicine*]
NSA .... No Significant Anomaly [*Medicine*] (DMAA)
NSA .... Not Seasonally Adjusted [*US Census terminology*]
NSA .... Nuclear Science Association (NADA)
NSA .... Nuclear Stock Association [*British*] (DBA)
NSA .... Nuclear Suppliers Association (EA)
NSA .... Nuclear Systems Analysis
NSA .... Number of Signals Averaged (DMAA)
NSA .... Nursery School Association [*British*] (BARN)
NSAA .... National Sales Achievement Award [*NALU*]
NSAA .... National Ski Areas Association (EA)
NSAA .... National Space and Aeronautics Agency (MCD)
NSAA .... National Sulphuric Acid Association [*British*] (DBA)
NSAA .... National Supply Association of America [*Later, NSDA*] (EA)
NSAA .... National Surgical Assistant Association (NTPA)
NSAA .... Norwegian Singers Association of America (EA)
NSAAB .... National Security Agency Advisory Board [*Fort George G. Meade, MD*] (EGAO)
NSAAC .... Atlantic Co-Operator, Antigonish, Nova Scotia [*Library symbol National Library of Canada*] (NLC)
NSABA .... National Spiritual Assembly of Baha'is of Australia
NSABP .... National Surgical Adjuvant Breast and Bowel Project (DAVI)
NSABP .... National Surgical Adjuvant Breast Project
NSAC .... National Society for Autistic Children [*British*]
NSAC .... National Society of Accountants for Cooperatives (EA)
NSAC .... National Spiritualist Association of Churches (EA)
NSAC .... National Sport Aviation Council [*Defunct*] (EA)
NSAC .... National Student Action Center (EA)
NSAC .... National Student Aid Coalition [*Defunct*] (EA)
NSAC .... Nova Scotia Agricultural College
NSAC .... NSAC, the National Society for Children and Adults with Autism (EA)
NSAC .... Nuclear Safety Advisory Committee (NUCP)
NSAC .... Nuclear Safety Analysis Center [*Electric Power Research Institute*] (NRCH)
NSACG .... Nuclear Strike Alternate Control Group (NATG)
NSACS .... National Society for the Abolition of Cruel Sports [*British*] (BI)
NSACS .... Naval Ships Advanced Communications System (SAA)
NSACSS .... National Security Agency/Central Security Service (AABC)
NSAD .... National Society of Art Directors (EA)
NSAD .... Naval Support Activity, Da Nang [*Vietnam*] (VNW)
NSAD .... Naval Support Activity Detachment (DNAB)
NSAD .... Nuclear Safety Analysis Document (KSC)
NSADN .... Daily News, Amherst, Nova Scotia [*Library symbol National Library of Canada*] (NLC)
NSAE .... National Society for Art Education [*British*]
NSAE .... National Society of Architectural Engineers (EA)
NSAF .... National Sanitation Foundation (IAA)
NSAF .... Naval Supply Account Fund
NSAFC .... National Service Armed Forces Act [*British*]
NSAFF .... National Society Against Factory Farming [*British*] (DBA)
NSAG .... Negative Channel Self-Aligned Gate (IAA)
NSAGT .... New South African Group Test [*Intelligence test*]
NSAH .... Heritage Association of Antigonish, Nova Scotia [*Library symbol National Library of Canada*] (NLC)
NSAI .... Nashville Songwriters Association, International (EA)
NSAI .... National Standards Authority of Ireland [*Irish Science and Technology Agency*] (IRC)
NSAI .... Need Satisfaction of Activity Interview
NSAI .... Nonsteroidal Anti-Inflammatory [*Pharmacochemistry*]
NSAI .... NSA International [*NASDAQ symbol*] (TTSB)
NSAI .... NSA International, Inc. [*NASDAQ symbol*] (SAG)
NSAIA .... Nonsteroidal Anti-Inflammatory Agent
NSAID .... Nonsteroidal Anti-Inflammatory Drug
NSAIN .... Indian and Northern Affairs Canada [*Affaires Indiennes et du Nord Canada*],Amherst, Nova Scotia [*Library symbol National Library of Canada*] (BIB)
NSA Int .... NSA International, Inc. [*Associated Press*] (SAG)
NSAJ .... National Secretariat Australia Jaycees
NSAL .... National Society of Arts and Letters (EA)
NSALC .... Nonsmoking Attributable Lung Cancer
NSalDH .... Salamanca District Hospital, Salamanca, NY [*Library symbol Library of Congress*] (LCLS)
NSALO .... National Security Agency Liaison Officer
NSAM .... National Security Agency Memorandum
NSAM .... Naval School of Aviation Medicine
NSAM .... Norwegian Advanced Surface to Air Missile System
NSAMC .... Cumberland Regional Library, Amherst, Nova Scotia [*Library symbol National Library of Canada*] (NLC)
NS Am Law Register ... American Law Register (Reprint) [*Ohio*] [*A publication*] (DLA)
NSAMRMS ... Maritime Resource Management Service [*Service d'Amenagement des Ressources des Maritimes*] Amherst, Nova Scotia [*Library symbol National Library of Canada*] (NLC)
NSAN .... Nissan Motor Co. Ltd. [*NASDAQ symbol*] (NQ)
NSan .... Sanborn-Pekin Free Library, Sanborn, NY [*Library symbol Library of Congress*] (LCLS)
NS & E .... New Systems and Enhancements (MCD)
NS & L .... NS & L Bancorp, Inc. [*Associated Press*] (SAG)
NS & S .... New Statesman & Society [*A publication*] (BRI)
NS & SO .... Nervous System and Sense Organs
NS & T .... National Status and Trends (GNE)
NS & T .... Naval Science and Tactics
NSanF .... National Sanitation Foundation
NSANL .... Non-Sectarian Anti-NAZI League (EA)
NSanO .... Orleans-Niagara Board of Cooperative Educational Services, Associates Special Educational Instruction Materials Center, Sanborn, NY [*Library symbol Library of Congress*] (LCLS)
NSanO-C .... Orleans-Niagara Board of Cooperative Educational Services, Educational Communications Center, Sanborn, NY [*Library symbol Library of Congress*] (LCLS)
NSanO-S .... Orleans-Niagara Board of Cooperative Educational Services, Sanborn, NY [*Library symbol*] [*Library of Congress*] (LCLS)
NSANY .... Nissan Motor Co. ADR [*NASDAQ symbol*] (TTSB)
NSAP .... Apia [*Western Samoa*] [*ICAO location identifier*] (ICLI)
NSAP .... National Socialist Action Party [*British*]
NSAP .... National Society for Animal Protection (EA)
NSAP .... Navy Science Assistance Program (CAAL)
NSAP .... Network Service Access Point [*Telecommunications*] (OSI)
NSAPAC .... National Security Agency Pacific (CINC)
NSAPEA .... Nordic Society Against Painful Experiments on Animals (EA)
NSAPI .... Netscape Server [*Computer science*] (PCM)
NSAPI .... Netscape Server API [*All-Purpose Interface*] [*Computer science*]
NSAR .... Annapolis Valley Regional Library, Annapolis Royal, NS [*Library symbol National Library of Canada*] (NLC)
NSAR .... Nitrososarcosine [*Organic chemistry*]
NSARC .... Navy Systems Acquisition Review Council
NSARF .... Fort Anne Museum, Annapolis Royal, Nova Scotia [*Library symbol National Library of Canada*] (NLC)
NSAS .... National Society of Appraiser Specialists (NTPA)
NSAS .... Naval Support Activity, Saigon [*Vietnam*] (VNW)
NSAS .... Near Infrared Spectral Analysis Software
NSAS .... Nonscheduled Air Services (AAG)
NSAS .... Nuclear Sealed Authentication System (AABC)
NSAS .... St. Francis Xavier University, Antigonish, Nova Scotia [*Library symbol National Library of Canada*] (NLC)
NSASAB .... National Security Agency Scientific Advisory Board [*Ft. George G. Meade, MD*] (EGAO)
NSASC .... Chemistry Department, St. Francis Xavier University, Antigonish, Nova Scotia [*Library symbol National Library of Canada*] (NLC)
NSAT .... NATO Small Arms Test (MCD)
NSAT .... NAVMAT [*Navy Material Command*] Special Assistance Team (DNAB)
NSAT .... NII Norsat International, Inc. [*NASDAQ symbol*] (SAG)
NSATE .... NII Norsat Intl. [*NASDAQ symbol*] (TTSB)
NSATS .... NAVMAT [*Navy Material Command*] Selected Acquisitions Tracking System (DNAB)
NSAU .... Asau [*Western Samoa*] [*ICAO location identifier*] (ICLI)
NSau .... Saugerties Public Library, Saugerties, NY [*Library symbol Library of Congress*] (LCLS)
NSauF .... Ferroxcube Corp., Suagerties, NY [*Library symbol Library of Congress*] (LCLS)
NSA-US .... National Spiritual Assembly of the Baha'is of the US (EA)
NSAW .... National Society of Asphalt Workers [*A union*] [*British*]
NSay .... Sayville Library, Sayville, NY [*Library symbol Library of Congress*] (LCLS)
NSB .... Bimini-North [*Bahamas*] [*Airport symbol*] (OAG)
NSB .... Nationaal-Socialistische Beweging [*National Socialist Movement*] [*Netherlands Political party*] (PPE)
NSB .... National Savings Bank [*British*]
NSB .... National Science Board [*National Science Foundation*]
NSB .... National Small Business Association [*Later, NSBU*]
NSB .... National Socialist Board [*Dutch National Socialist Party of 1931; later, Dutch NAZI Party*] [*Political party*]
NSB .... NATO Security Board (NATG)
NSB .... Naval Standardization Board
NSB .... Naval Studies Board [*National Academy of Sciences*] (DOMA)
NSB .... Naval Submarine Base
NSB .... Near Surface Burst (MCD)
NSB .... Network of Small Businesses [*Lyndhurst, OH*] (EA)
NSB .... Newsprint Service Bureau [*Later, API*] (EA)
NSB .... Nonspecific Binder
NSB .... Non-Statutory Body
NSB .... Nonsustained Breakdown (IAA)
NSB .... Nordisk Sammanslutning for Barnavard [*Nordic Child and Youth Welfare Alliance - NCYWA*] (EA)
NSB .... Nord-Sud [*Benin*] [*ICAO designator*] (FAAC)
NSB .... Norges Statsbaner [*Norwegian State Railways*]
NSB .... Northern Soviet Boundary
NSB .... Not Separately Billed
NSBA .... National Saanen Breeders Association (EA)
NSBA .... National Safe Boating Association (EA)
NSBA .... National School Band Association [*British*] (DBA)
NSBA .... National School Boards Association (EA)
NSBA .... National Semi-Professional Baseball Association (EA)
NSBA .... National Sheep Breeders' Association [*British*] (BI)
NSBA .... National Shrimp Breeders Association (EA)
NSBA .... National Small Business Association [*Later, NSBU*]
NSBA .... National Snaffle Bit Association (EA)
NSBA .... National Sugar Brokers Association (EA)
NSBB .... National Society for Business Budgeting [*Later, PEI*]
NSBBA .... National Small Business Benefits Association (EA)
NSBC .... National Safe Boating Council (EA)
NSBC .... National Safety Belt Coalition [*NHTSA*] (TAG)
NSBC .... National Shoeboard Conference (EA)
NSBC .... National Student Book Club
NSBC .... Natural Science Book Club
NS Bcp .... NS Bancorp, Inc. [*Associated Press*] (SAG)

NSBCSH.......	Cape Sable Historical Society, Barrington, Nova Scotia [*Library symbol National Library of Canada*] (NLC)
NSBD	Narrow Spectral Band Detection
NSBD	National Society of Bank Directors [*Formerly, NABD*] [*Later, ASBD*] (EA)
NSBDM.......	DesBrisay Museum and National Exhibit Centre, Bridgewater, Nova Scotia [*Library symbol National Library of Canada*] (NLC)
NSBE	National Society of Black Engineers (EA)
NSBEO	National Sonic Boom Evaluation Office [*Air Force*] (MCD)
NSBET	National Society of Biomedical Equipment Technicians (EA)
NSBF	National Scientific Balloon Facility [*Palestine, TX*] [*NASA*]
NSBGCA.......	National Small Business Government Contractors Association [*Defunct*] (EA)
NSBGW.......	National Society of Brushmakers and General Workers [*A union*] [*British*] (DCTA)
NSBI	NS Bancorp, Inc. [*NASDAQ symbol*] (SAG)
NSbIA	Institute of Advanced Studies of World Religions, Stony Brook, NY [*Library symbol Library of Congress*] (LCLS)
NSBISS.......	NATO Security Bureau Industrial Security Section (NATG)
NSBJH	James House, Bridgetown, Nova Scotia [*Library symbol National Library of Canada*] (NLC)
NSBK	North Side Savings Bank [*NASDAQ symbol*] (NQ)
NSBL	Lighthouse Publishing Ltd., Bridgewater, Nova Scotia [*Library symbol National Library of Canada*] (NLC)
NSBLE	Leader, Berwick, Nova Scotia [*Library symbol National Library of Canada*] (NLC)
NSBM	Monitor, Bridgetown, Nova Scotia [*Library symbol National Library of Canada*] (NLC)
NSBMA	National Small Business Men's Association [*Later, NSBU*]
NSBNL........	Naval Submarine Base - New London (MCD)
NSBP	National Society of Black Physicists (EA)
NSBPA	National Shrimp Breaders and Processors Association (EA)
NSBPH........	National Library Service for the Blind and Physically Handicapped [*Library of Congress Washington, DC Library network*]
NSBR	Register, Berwick, Nova Scotia [*Library symbol National Library of Canada*] (NLC)
NSBRH........	Bear River Historical Society, Nova Scotia [*Library symbol National Library of Canada*] (NLC)
NSBRO........	National Service Board for Religious Objectors [*Later, NISBCO*] (EA)
NSBS	South Shore Regional Library, Bridgewater, Nova Scotia [*Library symbol National Library of Canada*] (NLC)
NSbSM	Suffolk Museum at Stony Brook, Stony Brook, NY [*Library symbol Library of Congress*] (LCLS)
NSBSSA.......	National Strict Baptist Sunday School Association [*British*]
NSBSSN.......	South Shore News, Bridgewater, Nova Scotia [*Library symbol National Library of Canada*] (NLC)
NSbSU	State University of New York at Stony Brook, Stony Brook, NY [*Library symbol Library of Congress*] (LCLS)
NSbSU-H	State University of New York at Stony Brook, Health Sciences Library, Stony Brook, NY [*Library symbol Library of Congress*] (LCLS)
NSBT	National Swiss Battle Tank (MCD)
NSBT	Not Series by Title (MCD)
NSBU	National Small Business United [*Washington, DC*] (EA)
NSBVCA.......	Victoria County Archives and Museum, Baddeck, Nova Scotia [*Library symbol National Library of Canada*] (NLC)
NSBWC.......	National Safe Boating Week Committee [*Later, NSBC*]
NSBWK.......	Western King's Memorial Hospital, Berwick, Nova Scotia [*Library symbol National Library of Canada*] (NLC)
NSC	Arthur D. Little, Inc. [*Research code symbol*]
NSC	Bristol-Myers Co. [*Research code symbol*]
NSC	Hoffmann-La Roche, Inc. [*Research code symbol*]
NSC	NASCAR [*National Association for Stock Car Auto Racing*] Street Classics [*Later, WW*] (EA)
NSC	National Cancer Institute [*Research code symbol*]
NSC	National Safety Corp.
NSC	National Safety Council (NADA)
NSC	National Safflower Council [*Defunct*] (EA)
NSC	National Savings Certificates [*British*] (DAS)
NSC	National Savings Committee [*British*]
NSC	National Science Council [*Irish*] (MSC)
NSC	National Security Council
NSC	National Semiconductor Corp.
NSC	National Service Center
NSC	National Shrimp Congress (EA)
NSC	National Simulation Council (SAA)
NSC	National Slavic Convention (EA)
NSC	National Smallgoods Council [*Australia*]
NSC	National Snorkellers Club [*British*] (DBA)
NSC	National Society of Chauffeurs [*A union*] [*British*]
NSC	National Society of Computer/Genealogists [*Defunct*] (EA)
NSC	National Society of Cwens (EA)
NSC	National Space Club (EA)
NSC	National Space Council
NSC	National Spiritualist Church [*British*]
NSC	National Staff Committee [*Nurses and midwives*] [*British*]
NSC	National Standards Commission (NADA)
NSC	National Stinson Club (EA)
NSC	National Supercomputer Center (CIST)
NSC	National Supply Class [*Military*] (AFIT)
NSC	National Surface Cleaning, Inc. (EFIS)
NSC	National Survey of Children
NSC	National Synthetics Collection [*Smithsonian Institution*]
NSC	NATO [*North Atlantic Treaty Organization*] Science Committee (EAIO)
NSC	NATO Steering Committee (NATG)
NSC	NATO Supply Center (NATG)
NSC	NATO Supply Classification
NSC	Naval Coastal Systems Center [*Florida*]
NSC	Naval Safety Center (MCD)
NSC	Naval School Command
NSC	Naval Sea Cadets
NSC	Naval Space Command (MCD)
NSC	Naval Staff College (DOMA)
NSC	Naval Supply Center
NSC	Navigation and Sensor Computer
NSC	Navigation Star Catalogue
NSC	Navy Service Center
NSC	Net Sale Certificate (DGA)
NSC	Network Service Center [*Telecommunications*]
NSC	Network Switching Center [*Telecommunications*] (TEL)
NSC	Network Systems Corp. [*Brooklyn Park, MN*] [*Telecommunications*] (TSSD)
NSC	Neurosecretory Cells
NSC	Newscope Resources Ltd. [*Toronto Stock Exchange symbol*]
NSC	New Session Cases [*Scotland*] [*A publication*] (DLA)
NSC	Newtex SS [*Steamship company*] [*AAR code*]
NSC	Nicaragua Solidarity Campaign (EAIO)
NSC	Nippon Steel Corp. [*Japan*]
NSC	Nodal Switching Center
NSC	Noise Suppression Circuit (DEN)
NSC	Nomenclature Sequence Code [*Navy*] (AFIT)
NSC	Nominal Single Dose [*Pharmacology*] (DAVI)
NSC	Non-Service-Connected
NSC	Norfolk Southern [*NYSE symbol*] (TTSB)
NSC	Norfolk Southern Railway [*NYSE symbol*] (SPSG)
NSC	Northeastern State College [*Oklahoma*]
NSC	North Star Conference (PSS)
NSC	North Stonington [*Connecticut*] [*Seismograph station code, US Geological Survey*] (SEIS)
NSC	No Significant Change [*Medicine*]
NSC	No Significant Cloud [*Meteorology*] (FAAC)
NSC	Nothing So Called [*Bookselling*]
NSC	Not Service-Connected [*Medicine*] (MEDA)
nsc.............	Nova Scotia [*MARC country of publication code Library of Congress*] (LCCP)
NSC	NSC Corp. [*Associated Press*] (SAG)
NSC	Nuclear Science Center [*Louisiana State University*] [*Research center*] (RCD)
NSC	Numerical Sequence Code
NSC	Nursing Sentence Completions [*Nursing school test*]
NSC	Salem College, Winston-Salem, NC [*OCLC symbol*] (OCLC)
NSCA.........	NASCOM [*NASA Communications Network*] Assembly
NSCA.........	National Satellite Cable Association [*Defunct*] (EA)
NSCA.........	National Scrip Collectors Association (EA)
NSCA.........	National Senior Citizens Association [*Commercial firm*] (EA)
NSCA.........	National Shrimp Canners Association
NSCA.........	National Ski Credit Association (EA)
NSCA.........	National Soccer Coaches Association of America (EA)
NSCA.........	National Society for Clean Air [*British*] (DCTA)
NSCA.........	National Society of Commercial Agents [*Australia*]
NSCA.........	National Sound and Communications Association (EA)
NSCA.........	National Spinal Cord Association (DHP)
NSCA.........	National Sporting Clays Association
NSCA.........	National Strength and Conditioning Association (EA)
NSCA.........	National Subacute Care Association (EA)
NSCA.........	National Systems Contractors Association (NTPA)
NSCA.........	Natural Sausage Casings Association [*British*] (DBA)
NSCA.........	Northwest Salmon Canners Association (EA)
NSCA.........	Nova Scotia College of Art
NSCA.........	Nutrient Starch Cycloheximide Agar [*Microbiology*]
NSca..........	Scarsdale Public Library, Scarsdale, NY [*Library symbol Library of Congress*] (LCLS)
NSCAA........	National Small College Athletic Association (EA)
NSCAA........	National Soccer Coaches Association of America (NTPA)
NSCAA........	[*The*] National Society for Children and Adults with Autism 2 [*Formerly, NSAC*]
NSCAA........	Nutrient Starch Cycloheximide Antibiotic Agar [*Microbiology*]
NSCAE........	National Standards Council of American Embroiderers [*Later, CAE*] (EA)
NSCAEU.......	National Service Conference of the American Ethical Union (EA)
NSCAH........	National Student Campaign Against Hunger [*Later, NSCAHH*] (EA)
NSCAHH.......	National Student Campaign Against Hunger and Homelessness (EA)
NSCAMP.....	National Stock Control and Maintenance Point [*Army*] (AFIT)
NSC & MP...	National Stock Control and Maintenance Point [*Army*] (AABC)
NSCAR........	National Society of the Children of the American Revolution (EA)
NSCAS........	Archelaus Smith Museum, Centreville (Shelburne Co.), Nova Scotia [*Library symbol National Library of Canada*] (NLC)
NSCAT........	NASA [*or NROSS*] Scatterometer [*Instrumentation*]
N-SCATT......	Navy Scatterometer (MCD)
NSCAV........	National Safety Council of Australia, Victoria Division
NSCB	NBSC Corp. [*NASDAQ symbol*] (NQ)
NSCB	Nordic Society for Cell Biology (EA)
NSCC	National Securities Clearing Corp.
NSCC	National Service Coordinating Committee [*Ministry of Labour and National Service*] [*British World War II*]
NSCC	National Siamese Cat Club (EA)
NSCC	National Social Conditioning Camps [*Later, NOC*] (EA)
NSCC	National Society for Crippled Children (DAVI)
NSCC	Naval Sea Cadet Corps (NVT)

NSCC	Navy Sea Cargo Coordinator (DNAB)
NSCC	New Sudan Council of Churches
NSCC	North Shore Community College [Beverly, MA]
NSCC	NSC Corp. [NASDAQ symbol] (SAG)
NSCC	Nuclear Services Closed Cooling (IEEE)
NSCCA	National Society for Crippled Children and Adults [Later, NESS] (EA)
NSCCA	National Sports Car Club of America
NSCCA	Nuclear Safety Cross-Check Analysis (DOMA)
NSCCF	Canadian Forces Base, Cornwallis, Nova Scotia [Library symbol National Library of Canada] (NLC)
NSCCFE	Ensign, Canadian Forces Base, Cornwallis, Nova Scotia [Library symbol National Library of Canada] (NLC)
NSCCLO	Naval Sea Cadet Corps Liaison Officer (DNAB)
NSCCM	Cumberland County Museum, Amherst, Nova Scotia [Library symbol National Library of Canada] (NLC)
NSCD	National School Development Council (AEE)
NSCD	Nonservice-Connected Disability (MAE)
NSCD	Nuclear Service Control Date (DNAB)
NSCDA	National Society of Colonial Dames of America (EA)
N Sc Dec	Nova Scotia Decisions [A publication] (DLA)
NSCDET	Naval Supply Center Detachment (DNAB)
NSCDP	Non-Sexist Child Development Project (EA)
NSCDRF	National Sickle Cell Disease Research Foundation [Defunct] (EA)
NSCE	NetSource Communications, Inc. [NASDAQ symbol] (SAG)
NSCEC	National School Curriculum Center for Educational Computing [Defunct] (EA)
NSCEE	National Schools Committee for Economic Education (EA)
NSCEO	National Society of Chief Executive Officers [Defunct] (EA)
NSCF	National Skin Cancer Foundation [Later, SCF] (EA)
NSCF	National Student Christian Federation [Later, UCM] (EA)
NSCF	Naval Small Craft Facilities
NSCF	Northstar Computer Forms [NASDAQ symbol] (TTSB)
NSCF	Northstar Computer Forms, Inc. [NASDAQ symbol] (SAG)
NSCFA	National Support Center for Families of the Aging [Defunct] (EA)
NSCG	Northeastern Spoon Collectors Guild (EA)
NSCH	Canso Historical Society, Nova Scotia [Library symbol National Library of Canada] (NLC)
NSch	Schenectady County Public Library, Schenectady, NY [Library symbol Library of Congress] (LCLS)
NSchC	Schenectady County Community College, Schenectady, NY [Library symbol Library of Congress] (LCLS)
NSchE	Ellis Hospital, Schenectady, NY [Library symbol Library of Congress] (LCLS)
NSCHF	National Sprint Car Hall of Fame [Iowa]
NSchGEKA	General Electric Co., Knolls Atomic Laboratory, Technical Library, Schenectady, NY [Library symbol Library of Congress] (LCLS)
NSchGEM	General Electric Co., Main Library, Schenectady, NY [Library symbol Library of Congress] (LCLS)
NSchGER	General Electric Co., Research Laboratory, Schenectady, NY [Library symbol Library of Congress] (LCLS)
NSchGERB	General Electric Co., R and D Center, Branch Library, Schenectady, NY [Library symbol Library of Congress] (LCLS)
NSchHLC	Capital District Library Council, Schenectady, NY [Library symbol Library of Congress] (LCLS)
NSchM	Mohawk Valley Library Association, Schenectady, NY [Library symbol Library of Congress] (LCLS)
NSchoCHi	Schoharie County Historical Society, Schoharie, NY [Library symbol Library of Congress] (LCLS)
NSchSC	Schenectady Chemicals, Inc., Schenectady, NY [Library symbol Library of Congress] (LCLS)
N Sch Social Research	[The] New School for Social Research (GAGS)
NSchStC	Saint Clare's Hospital, Physicians' Library, Schenectady, NY [Library symbol Library of Congress] (LCLS)
NSchU	Union College, Schenectady, NY [Library symbol Library of Congress] (LCLS)
NSCI	NASCOM System Control Interface [NASA] (MCD)
NSCI	National Surgery Centers, Inc. [NASDAQ symbol] (SAG)
NSCI	Natl Surgery Centers [NASDAQ symbol] (TTSB)
NSCIA	National Spinal Cord Injury Association (EA)
NSCIA	National Supervisory Council for Intruder Alarms [British] (DBA)
NSCIC	National Security Council Intelligence Committee [Inactive]
NSCIC	National Soybean Crop Improvement Council
NSCID	National Security Council Intelligence Directive [Pronounced "nee-sid"] (AFM)
NSCIF	National Spinal Cord Injury Foundation [Formerly, NPF] [Later, NSCIA] (EA)
NSCIG	National Security Council Interdepartmental Group (MCD)
NSCISC	National Spinal Cord Injury Statistical Center Database [University of Alabama in Birmingham] [Information service or system] (CRD)
NSCL	National Superconducting Cyclotron Laboratory [Michigan State University] [National Science Foundation] [Research center] (RCD)
NSCLC	National Senior Citizens Law Center (EA)
NSCLC	Non-Small-Cell Lung Cancer [Oncology]
NSCLS	North State Cooperative Library System [Library network]
NSCM	National Society of Cycle Makers [A union] [British]
NSCM	NATO Supply Code for Manufacturing (MCD)
NSCM	Non-Stockpile Chemical Materiel [Military] (RDA)
NSCN	National Socialist Council of Nagaland [India] (PD)
NSCNC	Nascence (ABBR)
NSCNQH	North Queens Heritage Society, Caledonia, Nova Scotia [Library symbol National Library of Canada] (NLC)
NSCNT	Nascent (ABBR)
NSCO	National Scientific Committee on Oceanography
NSCO	Naval Sea Cargo Coordinator (DNAB)

NSCORT	NASA Specialized Center for Research and Training
NSCP	National Society of Compliance Professionals (EA)
NSCP	Naval Stores Conservation Program
NSCP	Navy Staffing Criteria Program
NSCP	Netscape Communications [NASDAQ symbol] (TTSB)
NSCP	Netscape Communications Corp. [NASDAQ symbol] (SAG)
NSCPA	National Society of Certified Public Accountants (EA)
NSCPC	National Student Consumer Protection Council (EA)
NSCPS	Naval Supply Center, Puget Sound [Bremerton, WA] (DNAB)
NSCPT	National Society for Cardiovascular and Pulmonary Technology (EA)
NSCR	National Society for Cancer Relief [British]
NSCR	National Sport Custom Registry (EA)
NSCR	Non-Selective Catalytic Reduction [Chemistry]
NSCR	Nuclear Science Center Reactor
NSCRC	National Stock Car Racing Commission
NSCRDFO	National Study Commission on Records and Documents of Federal Officials
NSCS	National Scouting Collectors Society (EA)
NSCS	National Security Council System (COE)
NSCS	National Sisters Communications Service [Later, CCM] (EA)
NSCS	National Small Craft School [Red Cross]
NSCS	Naval Strategic Communications Simulator (MCD)
NSCS	Navy Supply Corps School
NSCS	Night Shift Call System (DMAA)
NSCS	North Star Computer Society (EA)
NSCS	Universite Sainte-Anne, Church Point, Nova Scotia [Library symbol National Library of Canada] (NLC)
NSCSA	Centre Acadien, Universite Sainte-Anne, Church Point, Nova Scotia [Library symbol National Library of Canada] (BIB)
NSCSC	National School Calendar Study Committee
NSCSCC	National Standard for Common System Component Characteristics (MCD)
NSCSL	National Center for Service Learning (EBF)
NSCSWD	No Small Craft or Storm Warnings are Being Displayed [Weather]
NSCT	National Students Center for Thailand
NSCT	Niagara, St. Catharines & Toronto [AAR code]
NSCTE	National Society of College Teachers of Education [Later, SPE] (EA)
NSCTI	National Society for Cardiopulmonary Technology, Inc. (DAVI)
NSCTRN	Nonsectarian (ABBR)
NSCVPT	National Society for Cardiovascular and Pulmonary Technology (EA)
NSCVR	National Student Campaign for Voter Registration (EA)
NSCW	National Society of Cycle Workers [A union] [British]
NSD	Dartmouth Regional Library, Dartmouth, Nova Scotia [Library symbol National Library of Canada] (NLC)
NSD	Ferrosan [Denmark] [Research code symbol]
NSD	Geldert and Oxley's Nova Scotia Decisions [7-9 Nova Scotia Reports] [1866-75] [Canada] [A publication] (DLA)
NSD	Nairobi Sheep Disease [Medicine] (DMAA)
NSD	National Aeronautics and Space Administration Standard Detonator (NAKS)
NSD	National Silage Demonstration [British]
NSD	National Smooth Dancers (DICI)
NSD	National Standard Co. [NYSE symbol] (SAG)
NSD	Naval Stores Department [British military] (DMA)
NSD	Naval Supply Depot
NSD	Navy Support Date (NG)
NSD	Neonatal Staphylococcal Disease [Medicine] (DB)
NSD	Network Status Display
NSD	New Spirit Research [Vancouver Stock Exchange symbol]
NSD	Next Most Significant Digit [Computer science]
NSD	Night Sleep Deprivation [Medicine] (DMAA)
NSD	Noise Suppression Device
NSD	Nominal Single Dose [Medicine] (DB)
NSD	Nominal Standard Dose [Medicine]
NSD	Non-Self-Destroying
NSD	Nonsequential Disk [Computer science] (IAA)
NSD	Normal, Spontaneous Delivery [Obstetrics]
NSD	Normal Standard Dose [Oncology radiation]
NSD	Norsk Samfunnsvitenskapelig Datatjeneste [Norwegian Social Science Data Services] [Information service or system] (IID)
NSD	Northside Aviation Ltd. [British ICAO designator] (FAAC)
NSD	No Significant Defects [or Deficiency] [Medicine]
NSD	No Significant Deviation [Medicine]
NSD	No Significant Difference [Medicine]
NSD	No Significant Disease [Medicine]
NSD	United States Library of Congress, Washington, DC [OCLC symbol] (OCLC)
NSDA	National Soft Drink Association (EA)
NSDA	National Spasmodic Dysphonia Association (EA)
NSDA	National Sprayer and Duster Association (EA)
NSDA	National Supply Distributors Association [Dayton, OH] (EA)
NSDA	National Surplus Dealers Association (EA)
NSDA	Naval Supply Depot Annex
NSDA	Nissan Safety Device Advisor [Driver information system]
NSDA	Non-Self Destruct Alternative [Army]
NSDA	Nonsteroid Dependent Asthmatic [Medicine] (DAVI)
NSDAB	Non-Self-Deployable Aircraft and Boats (MCD)
NSDAP	Nationalsozialistische Deutsche Arbeiterpartei [National Socialist German Workers' Party, 1919-45] [Political party]
NSDAP-AO	NSDAP Auslands- und Aufbauorganisation (EA)
NSDAR	National Society, Daughters of the American Revolution (EA)
NSDAT	Naval School of Dental Assisting and Technology (DNAB)
NSDAVNDEPT	Naval Supply Depot Aviation Department (DNAB)

NSDB	Bedford Institute of Oceanography [*Institut Oceanographique de Bedford*] Dartmouth, Nova Scotia [*Library symbol National Library of Canada*] (NLC)
NSDB	National Science Development Board
NSDB	NSD Bancorp [*NASDAQ symbol*] (SAG)
NSD Bc	NSD Bancorp [*Associated Press*] (SAG)
NSDBE	National Society, Daughters of the British Empire (EA)
NSDBR	National Society, Daughters of the Barons of Runnemede (EA)
NSDC	Courier, Digby, Nova Scotia [*Library symbol National Library of Canada*] (NLC)
NSDC	National School Development Council (EA)
NSDC	National Serials Data Centre [*British Library*] (PDAA)
NSDC	National Square Dance Convention (EA)
NSDC	National Staff Development Committee [*Australia*]
NSDC	National Staff Development Council (EA)
NSDC	Naval Special Devices Center (SAA)
NSDC	Nonsuppurative Destructive Cholangitis [*Medicine*]
NSDC	NORAD Sector Direction Center [*Military*]
NSDC	Northern Shipowners' Defence Club [*See also NORDISK*] (EAIO)
NSDCM	NORAD Sector Direction Center Manual [*Military*]
NSDD	National Security Decision Directive
NSDDET	Naval Supply Depot Detachment (DNAB)
NSDDS	Dartmouth District School Board, Nova Scotia [*Library symbol National Library of Canada*] (NLC)
NSDE	Environment Canada [*Environnement Canada*] Dartmouth, Nova Scotia [*Library symbol National Library of Canada*] (NLC)
NSDEA	National Soda Dispensing Equipment Association (EA)
NS Dec	Nova Scotia Decisions [*A publication*] (DLA)
NSDEQ	National Society, Descendants of Early Quakers (EA)
NSDF	National Student Drama Festival [*British*]
NSDF	Navy Standard Distillate Fuel (NVT)
NSDG	Digby General Hospital, Nova Scotia [*Library symbol National Library of Canada*] (NLC)
NSDGH	Dartmouth General Hospital, Nova Scotia [*Library symbol National Library of Canada*] (NLC)
NSDH	Hermes Electronics Ltd., Dartmouth, Novia Scotia [*Library symbol National Library of Canada*] (NLC)
NSDI	National Sales Development Institute
NSDI	National Spatial Data Infrastructure [*BTS*] (TAG)
NSDJA	National Sash and Door Jobbers Association (EA)
NSDL	National Soil Dynamics Laboratory [*Auburn, AL*] [*Department of Agriculture*] (GRD)
NSDL	Navy Standard Distribution List (MCD)
NSDLANT/PAC	Naval Supply Depots, Atlantic/Pacific
NSDLMM	National Society of Descendants of Lords of the Maryland Manors (EA)
NSDM	Mirror, Digby, Nova Scotia [*Library symbol National Library of Canada*] (NLC)
NSDM	National Security Decision Memorandum [*Air Force*]
NSDM	New School for Democratic Management [*Inactive*] (EA)
NSDM	Nuclear Sediment Density Meter (PDAA)
NSDMM	MacLaren Plansearch Ltd., Dartmouth, Nova Scotia [*Library symbol National Library of Canada*] (NLC)
NSDNHM	North Highlands Museum, Dingwall, Nova Scotia [*Library symbol National Library of Canada*] (NLC)
NSDNSH	Nova Scotia Hospital, Dartmouth, Nova Scotia [*Library symbol National Library of Canada*] (NLC)
NSDO	National Seed and Development Organisation [*British*]
NSDP	NASCOM System Development Plan
NSDP	National Serials Data Program [*Library of Congress*] (EA)
NSDP	National Society of Denture Prosthetists [*Later, ADP*]
NSDP	Norfolk Sample Drug Program
NSDR	National Ships Destination Room (NATG)
NSDR	National Silver Dollar Roundtable (EA)
NSDR	No-son Dependency Ratio [*Demographics*]
NSDRV	Dartmouth Regional Vocational School, Dartmouth, Nova Scotia [*Library symbol National Library of Canada*] (NLC)
NSDS	Navy School, Diving and Salvage (NVT)
NSDS	Neutron Spectrometer Digital System
NSDSA	Naval Sea Data Support Activity (NVT)
NSDTA	National Staff Development and Training Association (EA)
NSDU	Network Service Data Unit [*Telecommunications*] (OSI)
NSDUP	National Society, Daughters of Utah Pioneers (EA)
NSDV	Netted Secure Digital Voice (MCD)
NSDWR	National Secondary Drinking Water Regualtions (GNE)
NSE	Milton, FL [*Location identifier FAA*] (FAAL)
NSE	Nagoya Stock Exchange [*Japan*] (NUMA)
NSE	National Sales Executives
NSE	National Seafood Educators (EA)
NSE	National Society for Epilepsy [*British*]
NSE	National Stock Exchange [*Dissolved, 1975*]
NSE	National Student Exchange (EA)
NSE	National Support Elements [*British military*] (DMA)
NSE	Natural Space Environment
NSE	Naval Shore Establishment
NSE	Naval Support Element (DOMA)
NSE	Navier-Stokes Equation
NSE	Navigation Support Equipment
NSE	Network Service Element [*Telecommunications*] (OSI)
NSE	Network SouthEast [*British Rail*] (ECON)
NSE	Network Systems Engineer (SSD)
NSE	Neuron-Specific Enolase [*Formerly, NSP*] [*An enzyme*]
NSE	Neuropsychological Status Examination [*Psychology*]
NSE	Neutral Stream Etch (AAEL)
NSE	New York Stock Exchange (EBF)
NSE	Nitroguanidine Support Element (MCD)
NSE	Noise (ABBR)
NSE	Nonsecurity Exemption [*Military*]
NSE	Nonspecific Esterase [*An enzyme*]
NSE	North Steaming Error (SAA)
NSE	Northwest Sports Enterprises Ltd. [*Vancouver Stock Exchange symbol*]
NSE	Nuclear Science and Engineering [*A publication*]
NSE	Nuclear Statistical Equilibrium [*Physics*]
NSE	Nuclear Support Equipment
NSE	Nuclear Systems Engineering
NSE	Number of Simultaneous Engagements [*Military*]
NSE	Satena Servicios de Aeronavegacion A Territorios Nac [*Colombia*] [*ICAO designator*] (FAAC)
NSEA	National Standards Educators Association (EA)
NSea	Seaford Public Library, Seaford, NY [*Library symbol Library of Congress*] (LCLS)
NSeacES	Sea Cliff Elementary School, Sea Cliff, NY [*Library symbol*] [*Library of Congress*] (LCLS)
NSEAD	National Society for Education in Art and Design (EAIO)
NSeaHE	Seaford Harbor Elementary School, Seaford, NY [*Library symbol*] [*Library of Congress*] (LCLS)
NSeaME	Seaford Manor Elementary School, Seaford, NY [*Library symbol*] [*Library of Congress*] (LCLS)
NSeaMH	Massapequa General Hospital, Seaford, NY [*Library symbol Library of Congress*] (LCLS)
NSeaMS	Seaford Middle School, Seaford, NY [*Library symbol*] [*Library of Congress*] (LCLS)
NSeaP	Plainedge Public Library, Seaford, NY [*Library symbol Library of Congress*] (LCLS)
NSeaSH	Seaford Senior High School, Seaford, NY [*Library symbol*] [*Library of Congress*] (LCLS)
NSeaTM	Tackapausha Museum, Seaford, NY [*Library symbol Library of Congress*] (LCLS)
nsec	Nanosecond [*One billionth of a second*] [*Also, ns*]
NSEC	National Security Group, Inc. [*NASDAQ symbol*] (SAG)
NSEC	National Service Entertainments Council [*British*]
NSEC	National Society of Environmental Consultants (EA)
NSEC	Natl Security Group [*NASDAQ symbol*] (TTSB)
NSEC	Naval Ship Engineering Center (MCD)
NSecln	National Security Group, Inc. [*Associated Press*] (SAG)
NSECINST	Naval Ship Engineering Center Instruction
NSEDP	National Sex Equity Demonstration Project (EDAC)
NSEE	National Society for Experiential Education (NTPA)
NSEEC	Naval Shore Electronics Engineering Center [*Terminated, 1966*] (MCD)
NSEF	National SANE Education Fund (EA)
NSEF	National Student Educational Fund (EA)
NSEF	Navy Security Engineering Facility
NSEF	New Society Educational Foundation (EA)
NSel	Middle Country Public Library, Selden Branch, Selden, NY [*Library symbol Library of Congress*] (LCLS)
NSELA	National Science Education Leadership Association (NTPA)
NSelC	Suffolk County Community College, Selden, NY [*Library symbol Library of Congress*] (LCLS)
NSelC-E	Suffolk County Community College, Eastern Campus, Riverhead, NY [*Library symbol Library of Congress*] (LCLS)
NSelC-W	Suffolk County Community College, Western Campus, Brentwood, NY [*Library symbol Library of Congress*] (LCLS)
NSELH	East Lake Ainslie Historical Society, Nova Scotia [*Library symbol National Library of Canada*] (BIB)
NSELS	Noiseless (ABBR)
NSem	National Semiconductor Corp. [*Associated Press*] (SAG)
NSEM	Nederlandsche Standard Electric Maatschappij (NITA)
NSEMA	National Spray Equipment Manufacturers Association (EA)
NSEN	Network Simulations Engineer (SSD)
NSENS	Noisiness (ABBR)
NSEP	National Security and Emergency Preparedness
NSEP	National Security Education Program [*The Academy for Educational Development*]
NS/EQ	New Source and Environmental Questionnaire [*Environmental Protection Agency*] (EG)
NSERC	Natural Sciences and Engineering Research Council of Canada [*Research center*] (IRC)
NSERI	National Solar Energy Research Institute [*Energy Research and Development Administration*]
NSES	National Security Electronic Surveillance
NSES	National Society of Electrotypers and Stereotypers [*British*] (BI)
NSetSP	Society for the Preservation of Long Island Antiquities, Setauket, NY [*Library symbol Library of Congress*] (LCLS)
NSewCH	H.F. Carey High School, Sewanhaka, NY [*Library symbol*] [*Library of Congress*] (LCLS)
NSewEH	Elmont Memorial High School, Sewanhaka, NY [*Library symbol Library of Congress*] (LCLS)
NSewNH	New Hyde Park Memorial High School, Sewanhaka, NY [*Library symbol*] [*Library of Congress*] (LCLS)
NSewSJ	Stanforth Junior High School, Sewanhaka, NY [*Library symbol Library of Congress*] (LCLS)
NSF	Camp Springs, MD [*Location identifier FAA*] (FAAL)
NSF	National Salvation Front [*Romania*] [*Political party*]
NSF	National Sanitation Foundation (EA)
NSF	National Schizophrenia Fellowship [*British*]
NSF	National Science Foundation (EA)
NSF	National Science Foundation, Washington, DC [*OCLC symbol*] (OCLC)

NSF............ National Scoliosis Foundation (EA)
NSF............ National Sex Forum [*Later, ET*] (EA)
NSF............ National Sharecroppers Fund (EA)
NSF............ National Ski Federation (BARN)
NSF............ National Soaring Foundation (EA)
NSF............ National Squash Federation [*British*] (DBA)
NSF............ National Stockbrokers Forum [*Later, CFC*] (EA)
NSF............ National Strike Force [*Marine science*] (MSC)
NSF............ Naval Stock Fund
NSF............ Naval Supersonic Facility
NSF............ Naval Supply Force
NSF............ Naval Support Force (MCD)
NSF............ Navy Security Force
NSF............ Navy Special Fuel
NSF............ Navy Stock Fund (DOMA)
NSF............ Negotiated Search Facility [*Information retrieval*]
NSF............ NEM [*N-Ethylmaleimide*]-Sensitive Fusion [*Biochemistry*]
NSF............ N-ethylinaleimide Sensitive Fusion
NSF............ N-Ethylmaleimide-Sensitive Fusion (protein) [*Organic chemistry*]
NSF............ Net Square Feet (MCD)
NSF............ Neutron Scattering Facility [*Oak Ridge, TN*] [*Oak Ridge National Laboratory*] [*Department of Energy*] (GRD)
NSF............ Nitrogen Supply Flask
NSF............ Nodular Subepidermal Fibrosis [*Dermatology*] (DAVI)
NSF............ Noncancerous Skin Fibroblast [*Medicine*]
NSF............ Non-Spin-Flip [*Solid state physics*]
NSF............ Nonsterile Field Soil [*Agronomy*]
NSF............ Nonstock Fund
NSF............ Nordiska Skattevetenskapliga Forskningradet [*Nordic Council for Tax Research - NCTR*] (EAIO)
NSF............ Not Sufficient Funds [*Banking*]
nsf............ Not Sufficient Funds [*Banking*] (ODBW)
NSF............ Nuclear Safety Facility
NSF............ Nuclear Science Foundation (IAA)
NSF............ Nuclear Structure Facility [*British*]
NSFA .... Faleolo/International [*Western Samoa*] [*ICAO location identifier*] (ICLI)
NSFA .... National Science Foundation Act [*1950*]
NSFA .... Naval Support Force, Antarctica (DNAB)
NSFA .... Nordic Swimming Federations Association (EA)
NSFAC .... National Student Financial Aid Council [*Later, NASFAA*] (EA)
NSFAR .... National Science Foundation Acquisition Regulation [*A publication*] (AAGC)
NSFB .... New School of Family Birthing (EA)
NSFC .... Nancy Sinatra Fan Club (EA)
NSFC .... National Small Flows Clearinghouse [*Environmental Protection Agency*] (AEPA)
NSFC .... National Society of Film Critics
NSFC .... Nat Stuckey Fan Club [*Defunct*] (EA)
NSFC .... Natural Science Foudation of China
NSFC .... Natural Science Foundation of China
NSFC .... Northern States Financial Corp. [*NASDAQ symbol*] (SAG)
NSFC .... Northern States Finl [*NASDAQ symbol*] (TTSB)
NSFCCDLR... National Society of Fathers for Child Custody and Divorce Law Reform [*Later, FER*] (EA)
NSFD .... Notice of Structural or Functional Deficiency
NSFFC .... National Save the Family Farm Coalition (EA)
NSFG .... National Survey of Family Growth
NSFH .... North-South Fine, Hundreds
NSFI........... Fagali'I [*Western Samoa*] [*ICAO location identifier*] (ICLI)
NSF-I .... National Science Fair - International
NSF/IDOE.... National Science Foundation Office for the International Decade of Ocean Exploration
NSfK .... Nordiska Samarbetsradet for Kriminologi [*Scandinavian Research Council for Criminology - SRCC*] [*Finland*] (EAIO)
NSFL.......... National Sanitation Foundation Laboratory
NSFNET ...... National Science Foundation Network
NSFO .... Navy Special [*or Standard*] Fuel Oil
NSFORT....... Non-Standard FORTRAN [*Computer science*] (PDAA)
NSFP .... Natural Suppressor Factor Protein (DB)
NSFP .... Non-Sodium Fire Protection [*Nuclear energy*] (NRCH)
NSFPA .... National Suppliers to Food Processors Association (EA)
NSFPR .... National Science Foundation Procurement Regulation [*A publication*] (AAGC)
NSFR .... National Society of Fund Raisers [*Later, NSFRE*] (EA)
NSFR .... Nitroxide Stable Free Radical [*For tissue NMR*]
NSFRC .... National Silver Fox Rabbit Club (EA)
NSFRE .... National Society of Fund Raising Executives (EA)
NSFRE Foundation... National Society of Fund Raising Executives Foundation [*Formerly the National Society of Fund Raisers Institute of Continuing Education and the National Society of Fund Raising Executives*] (NFD)
NSFRE Institute... Former name of the National Society of Fund Rainsing Executives Foundation (NFD)
NSFS .... National Society for Shut-Ins (EA)
NSFS .... Net Section Fracture Strength (PDAA)
NSfSC .... Sullivan County Community College, South Fallsburg, NY [*Library symbol Library of Congress*] (LCLS)
NSF/STAH.... National Science Foundation Program for Science and Technology Aid to the Handicapped
NSFT .... North-South Fine, Tens
NSFTD .... Normal, Spontaneous, Full Term Delivery [*Obstetrics*]
NSFTL......... National Sanitation Foundation Testing Laboratory, Inc. (MSA)
NSFU .... Needle Stampers' and Filers' Union [*British*]
NSFU .... North-South Fine, Units

NSG .... Aircompany Liana JSA [*Ukraine*] [*FAA designator*] (FAAC)
NSG .... National Society for Graphology (EA)
NSG .... National Steering Group (AIE)
NSG .... National Supply Group [*Military*] (AFIT)
NSG .... Naval Security Group
NSG .... Network Support Group (NITA)
NSG .... Neurosecretory Granules
NSG .... Newspaper Systems Group (EA)
NSG .... Non-Statutory Guidance [*British*] (DET)
NSG .... Non-Statutory Guidelines (WDAA)
NSG .... North Seeking Gyro
NSG .... Not So Good
NSG .... Nuclear Suppliers' Group [*Australia*] (ECON)
NSG .... Nursing
NSGA .... National Sand and Gravel Association [*Later, NAA*] (EA)
NSGA .... National Sporting Goods Association (EA)
NSGA .... Naval Security Group Activity
NSGC .... National Self Government Committee (EA)
NSGC .... National Society of Genetic Counselors (EA)
NSGC .... National Swine Growers Council [*Later, NPPC*] (EA)
NSGC .... Naval Security Group Command (DNAB)
NSGCC .... Coastal Courier, Glace Bay, Nova Scotia [*Library symbol National Library of Canada*] (NLC)
NSGCFA....... Aurora, Canadian Forces Base, Greenwood, Nova Scotia [*Library symbol National Library of Canada*] (NLC)
NSGCH .... Naval Security Group Command Headquarters
NSGCT .... Nonsiminomatous Germ Cell Turmors [*Medicine*] (MEDA)
NSGCTT .... Nonseminomatous Germ Cell Tumors of the Testes
NSGD .... National Sea Grant Depository [*National Oceanic and Atmospheric Administration Information service or system*] (IID)
NSGD .... National Support Group for Dermatomyositis (EA)
NSGD .... National Support Group for PM/DM [*Formerly, National Support Group for Dermatomyositis*] (EA)
NS-GFW...... Noise Substest of the Goldman-Fristoe-Woodcock Auditory Skills Test Battery (EDAC)
NSGIB .... NAVSHIPS [*Naval Ship Systems Command*] General Information Book
NSGLS .... Nordisk Sekretariat for Gartneri- Land-, og Skovarbejderforbund [*Nordic Secretariat for Agricultural and Horticultural Workers - NSAHW*] [*Denmark Defunct*] (EAIO)
NSGN .... Noise Generator (CET)
NSGOC........ Naval Security Group Orientation Course (DNAB)
NSGOC........ Old Court House Museum, Guysborough, Nova Scotia [*Library symbol National Library of Canada*] (NLC)
NS Grp .... NS Group, Inc. [*Associated Press*] (SAG)
Nsg Sta ...... Nursing Station (DAVI)
NSGT .... National Aeronautics and Space Administration Ground Terminal (NAKS)
NSGT .... Non-Self-Governing Territories [*United Nations*]
NSGTMEM ... National Society of General Tool Makers, Engineers, and Machinists [*A union*] [*British*]
NSGTP .... Naval Security Group Training Publication (DNAB)
NSGW .... National Society of Glass Workers [*A union*] [*British*]
NSGW .... Native Sons of the Golden West (EA)
NSH .... Halifax City Regional Library, Nova Scotia [*Library symbol National Library of Canada*] (NLC)
NSh .... John Jermain Memorial Public Library, Sag Harbor, NY [*Library symbol Library of Congress*] (LCLS)
NSH .... Nashua Corp. [*NYSE symbol*] (SPSG)
NSH .... Nashville [*Diocesan abbreviation*] [*Tennessee*] (TOCD)
NSH .... National Society for Histotechnology (EA)
NSH .... National Society of Hypnotherapists (EA)
NSH .... Naval School of Health Sciences, Bethesda, MD [*OCLC symbol*] (OCLC)
NSH .... Nordisk Samarbeidskomite for Husstellundervisning [*Nordic Joint Committee for Domestic Education - NJCDE*] (EAIO)
NSH .... Northern-Southern Hybrid [*Hemoglobin phenotype of Rana pipiens*]
NSH .... Not So Hot [*Slang*]
NSHA .... National Steeplechase and Hunt Association (EA)
NSHA .... National Stock Horse Association (EA)
NSHAC-FP ... National Self-Help Action Center - Food Program (EA)
NSHAG........ Art Gallery of Nova Scotia, Halifax, Nova Scotia [*Library symbol National Library of Canada*] (NLC)
NSHANSS .... Synod Office, Diocese of Nova Scotia, Anglican Church of Canada, Halifax, Nova Scotia [*Library symbol National Library of Canada*] (NLC)
NSHAR......... Algas Resources Ltd., Halifax, Nova Scotia [*Library symbol National Library of Canada*] (NLC)
NSHAVI....... [*The*] Atlantic Provinces Resource Centre for the Visually-Impaired, Halifax, Nova Scotia [*Library symbol National Library of Canada*] (NLC)
NSHBS......... Nova Scotia Barristers Society, Halifax, Nova Scotia [*Library symbol National Library of Canada*] (NLC)
NSHC .... Cambridge Military Library, Halifax, Nova Scotia [*Library symbol National Library of Canada*] (NLC)
NSHC.......... National Self-Help Clearinghouse (EA)
NSHC.......... National Silver-Haired Congress (EA)
NSHC.......... National Syrian Hamster Council [*British*] (DBA)
NSHC.......... North Sea Hydrographic Commission [*of the International Hydrographic Organization*] [*Belgium*]
NSHCA........ Nova Scotia College of Art and Design, Halifax, Nova Scotia [*Library symbol National Library of Canada*] (NLC)
NSHCB........ Music and Record Library, Canadian Broadcasting Corp. [*Musicotheque et Discotheque, Societe Radio-Canada*] Halifax, Nova Scotia [*Library symbol National Library of Canada*] (NLC)

NSHCBC....... Canadian British Consultants Ltd., Halifax, Nova Scotia [*Library symbol National Library of Canada*] (NLC)

NSHCBF....... Film Library, CBHT-TV, Halifax, Nova Scotia [*Library symbol National Library of Canada*] (NLC)

NSHCD.......... Law Library, Cox, Downie & Co., Halifax, Nova Scotia [*Library symbol National Library of Canada*] (NLC)

NSHCDD...... Nova Scotia Commission on Drug Dependency, Halifax, Nova Scotia [*Library symbol National Library of Canada*] (NLC)

NSHCFM...... Maritime Command Museum, Canadian Forces Base, Halifax, Nova Scotia [*Library symbol National Library of Canada*] (BIB)

NSHCH.......... Camp Hill Hospital, Halifax, Nova Scotia [*Library symbol National Library of Canada*] (NLC)

NSHCIC........ National Solar Heating and Cooling Information Center [*Later, CAREIRS*]

NSHCIC........ Nova Scotia Communications and Information Centre, Halifax, Nova Scotia [*Library symbol National Library of Canada*] (NLC)

NSHD.......... Dalhousie University, Halifax, Nova Scotia [*Library symbol National Library of Canada*] (NLC)

NSHD.......... Nodular Sclerosing Hodgkin's Disease [*Medicine*] (DMAA)

NSHDA......... Archives, Dalhousie University, Halifax, Nova Scotia [*Library symbol National Library of Canada*] (BIB)

NSHDAG...... Nova Scotia Department of the Attorney-General, Halifax, Nova Scotia [*Library symbol National Library of Canada*] (NLC)

NSHDCA...... Nova Scotia Department of Consumer Affairs, Halifax, Nova Scotia [*Library symbol National Library of Canada*] (NLC)

NSHDD........ Nova Scotia Department of Industry, Trade, and Technology, Halifax, Nova Scotia [*Library symbol National Library of Canada*] (NLC)

NSHDE......... Nova Scotia Department of the Environment, Halifax, Nova Scotia [*Library symbol National Library of Canada*] (NLC)

NSHDEA....... Resource Centre, Ecology Action Centre, Dalhousie University, Halifax, Nova Scotia [*Library symbol National Library of Canada*] (NLC)

NSHDF......... Nova Scotia Department of Fisheries, Halifax, Nova Scotia [*Library symbol National Library of Canada*] (NLC)

NSHDH........ Nova Scotia Department of Transportation, Halifax, Nova Scotia [*Library symbol National Library of Canada*] (NLC)

NSHDIP........ Institute of Public Affairs, Dalhousie University, Halifax, Nova Scotia, [*Library symbol National Library of Canada*] (NLC)

NSHDIR........ School of Resources and Environmental Studies, Dalhousie University, Halifax, Nova Scotia [*Library symbol National Library of Canada*] (NLC)

NSHDL.......... Law School, Dalhousie University, Halifax, Nova Scotia [*Library symbol National Library of Canada*] (NLC)

NSHDLS....... School of Library Service, Dalhousie University, Halifax, Nova Scotia [*Library symbol National Library of Canada*] (NLC)

NSHDM........ W. K. Kellogg Health Sciences Library, Dalhousie University, Halifax, Nova Scotia [*Library symbol National Library of Canada*] (NLC)

NSHDMA...... Map Library, Dalhousie University, Halifax, Nova Scotia [*Library symbol National Library of Canada*] (NLC)

NSHDOL...... Nova Scotia Department of Labour and Manpower, Halifax, Nova Scotia [*Library symbol National Library of Canada*] (NLC)

NSHDOM..... Nova Scotia Department of Mines, Halifax, Nova Scotia [*Library symbol National Library of Canada*] (NLC)

NSHDOS...... Dalhousie Ocean Studies Programme, Dalhousie University, Halifax, Nova Scotia [*Library symbol National Library of Canada*] (NLC)

NSHDR........ Cultural Affairs Library, Nova Scotia Department of Tourism and Culture, Halifax, Nova Scotia [*Library symbol National Library of Canada*] (NLC)

NSHDS......... MacDonald Science Library, Dalhousie University, Halifax, Nova Scotia [*Library symbol National Library of Canada*] (NLC)

NSHDS......... National Society for Hebrew Day Schools (NTPA)

NSHE........... [*The*] New Schaff-Herzog Encyclopaedia of Religious Knowledge [*A publication*] (BJA)

NSHEB......... North of Scotland Hydro-Electric Board (ECON)

NShei.......... Shelter Island Public Library Society, Shelter Island, NY [*Library symbol Library of Congress*] (LCLS)

NSherb........ Sherburne Public Library, Sherburne, NY [*Library symbol Library of Congress*] (LCLS)

NSHF........... Fisheries and Oceans Canada [*Peches et Oceans Canada*] Halifax, Nova Scotia [*Library symbol National Library of Canada*] (NLC)

NSHF........... Scotia-Fundy Regional Library, Fisheries and Oceans Canada [*Bibliotheque de la Region Scotia-Fundy, Peches et Oceans Canada*], Halifax, Nova Scotia [*Library symbol National Library of Canada*] (NLC)

NSHFIF........ Federal-Provincial Taxation and Fiscal Relations Library, Nova Scotia Departmentof Finance, Halifax, Nova Scotia [*Library symbol National Library of Canada*] (NLC)

NSHH.......... Nova Scotia Department of Health, Halifax, Nova Scotia [*Library symbol National Library of Canada*] (NLC)

NSHHC........ Halifax County Regional Library, Lower Sackville, Nova Scotia [*Library symbol National Library of Canada*] (NLC)

NSHHE........ Halifax Herald Ltd., Nova Scotia [*Library symbol National Library of Canada*] (NLC)

NSHHI.......... Health Services Library, Halifax Infirmary, Nova Scotia [*Library symbol National Library of Canada*] (NLC)

NSHHR........ Nova Scotia Human Rights Commission, Halifax, Nova Scotia [*Library symbol National Library of Canada*] (NLC)

NSHHS......... Hantsport and Area Historical Society, Nova Scotia [*Library symbol National Library of Canada*] (NLC)

NSHIAP........ Atlantic Regional Library, Parks Canada [*Bibliotheque Regionale de l'Atlantique, Parcs Canada*] Halifax, Nova Scotia [*Library symbol National Library of Canada*] (NLC)

NSHIC.......... International Centre for Ocean Development, Halifax, Nova Scotia [*Library symbol National Library of Canada*] (BIB)

NSHJ .... Canada Department of Justice [*Ministere de la Justice*] Halifax, Nova Scotia [*Library symbol National Library of Canada*] (NLC)

NSHK........... University of King's College, Halifax, Nova Scotia [*Library symbol National Library of Canada*] (NLC)

NSHKH......... Izaak Walton Killam Hospital for Children, Halifax, Nova Scotia [*Library symbol National Library of Canada*] (NLC)

NSHKJ......... School of Journalism, University of King's College, Halifax, Nova Scotia [*Library symbol National Library of Canada*] (NLC)

NSHKMGM... Kitz, Matheson, Green & MacIsaac Law Firm, Halifax, Nova Scotia [*Library symbol National Library of Canada*] (NLC)

NSHL........... Legislative Library, Halifax, Nova Scotia [*Library symbol National Library of Canada*] (NLC)

NSHLA......... Nova Scotia Legal Aid, Halifax, Nova Scotia [*Library symbol National Library of Canada*] (NLC)

NSHLP......... Liberal Party of Nova Scotia, Halifax [*Library symbol National Library of Canada*] (BIB)

NSHM.......... Atlantic Regional Laboratory, National Research Council [*Laboratoire Regionalde l'Atlantique, Conseil National de Recherches du Canada*] Halifax, Nova Scotia [*Library symbol National Library of Canada*] (NLC)

NSHMA......... Nova Scotia Department of Municipal Affairs, Halifax, Nova Scotia [*Library symbol National Library of Canada*] (NLC)

NSHMBA....... National Society of Hispanic MBAs (EA)

NSHMC......... Maritime Conservatory of Music, Halifax, Nova Scotia [*Library symbol National Library of Canada*] (NLC)

NSHMCA....... Archives, Maritime Conference, United Church of Canada Halifax, Nova Scotia [*Library symbol National Conference of Commissioners on Uniform State Laws*] (BIB)

NSHMCR...... Law Library, McInnes, Cooper & Robertson, Halifax, Nova Scotia [*Library symbol National Library of Canada*] (NLC)

NSHML........ Martec Ltd., Halifax, Nova Scotia [*Library symbol National Library of Canada*] (NLC)

NSHMM...... Maritime Museum of the Atlantic, Halifax, Nova Scotia [*Library symbol National Library of Canada*] (NLC)

NSHMO....... Mobil Oil Canada Ltd., Halifax, Nova Scotia [*Library symbol National Library of Canada*] (NLC)

NSHMS........ Nova Scotia Museum, Halifax, Nova Scotia [*Library symbol National Library of Canada*] (NLC)

NSHMT......... Regional Library, Canadian Coast Guard [*Bibliotheque Regionale, Garde CotiereCanadienne*] Dartmouth, Nova Scotia [*Library symbol National Library of Canada*] (NLC)

NSHMTT..... Information Resource Centre, Maritime Tel & Tel, Halifax, Nova Scotia [*Library symbol National Library of Canada*] (NLC)

NSHN.......... Defence Research Establishment Atlantic, Canada Department of National Defence [*Centre de Recherches pour la Defense Atlantique, Ministere de la Defense Nationale*] Dartmouth, Nova Scotia [*Library symbol National Library of Canada*] (NLC)

NSHND........ Reference and Recreational Library (Stadacona), Canada Department of National Defence [*Bibliotheque de Consultation et de Lecture (Stadacona), Ministere de la Defense Nationale*] Halifax, Nova Scotia [*Library symbol National Library of Canada*] (NLC)

NSHNF........ National Film Board [*Office National du Film*], Halifax, Nova Scotia [*Library symbol National Library of Canada*] (NLC)

NSHNI.......... Nova Scotia Nautical Institute, Halifax, Nova Scotia [*Library symbol National Library of Canada*] (NLC)

NSHNP......... Nova Scotia Newspaper Project, Halifax [*Library symbol National Library of Canada*] (BIB)

NSHNS......... Ships Recreational Library, Canadian Forces Base Halifax [*Bibliotheque Recreative, Base des Forces Canadiennes Halifax*], Nova Scotia [*Library symbol National Library of Canada*] (BIB)

NSHO........... Naval Service Headquarters, Ottawa (DNAB)

NShor.......... Shoreham-Wading River Public Library, Shoreham, NY [*Library symbol Library of Congress*] (LCLS)

NShorHS...... Shoreham-Wading River High School, Shoreham, NY [*Library symbol Library of Congress*] (LCLS)

NSHP........... Nova Scotia Public Archives, Halifax, Nova Scotia [*Library symbol National Library of Canada*] (NLC)

NSHPC......... Corporate Research and Information Centre, Nova Scotia Power Corp., Halifax, Nova Scotia [*Library symbol National Library of Canada*] (NLC)

NSHPH......... Atlantic School of Theology, Halifax, Nova Scotia [*Library symbol National Library of Canada*] (NLC)

NSHPI.......... Planning Information Office, City of Halifax, Nova Scotia [*Library symbol National Library of Canada*] (NLC)

NSHPL......... Nova Scotia Union Catalogue, Nova Scotia Provincial Library, Halifax, Nova Scotia [*Library symbol National Library of Canada*] (NLC)

NSHPLX....... Reference Services, Nova Scotia Provinical Library, Halifax, Nova Scotia [*Library symbol National Library of Canada*] (NLC)

NSHPT......... Neonatal Severe Hyperparathyroidism [*Medicine*] (DMAA)

NSHPW........ Atlantic Regional Library, Public Works Canada [*Bibliotheque Regionale de l'Atlantique, Travaux Publics Canada*] Halifax, Nova Scotia [*Library symbol National Library of Canada*] (NLC)

NSHQ........... Naval Service Headquarters [*Canada*]

NSHQ........... Naval Staff Headquarters [*British military*] (DMA)

NShr............ John C. Hart Memorial Library, Shrub Oak, NY [*Library symbol Library of Congress*] (LCLS)

NSHR........... National Show Horse Registry (EA)

NSHR........... Nova Scotia Research Foundation, Dartmouth, Nova Scotia [*Library symbol National Library of Canada*] (NLC)

NSHRC........ National Self-Help Resource Center [*Defunct*] (EA)

NSHRC........ National Shared Housing Resource Center (EA)

NSHRC........ Nova Scotia Rehabilitation Centre, Halifax, Nova Scotia [*Library symbol National Library of Canada*] (NLC)

NSHRCA ...... Roman Catholic Archdiocesan Archives, Halifax, Nova Scotia [*Library symbol National Library of Canada*] (BIB)

NSHRL .... Nova Scotia Regional Libraries, Halifax, Nova Scotia [*Library symbol National Library of Canada*] (NLC)

NSHRP .... Photogrammetry Division, Nova Scotia Research Foundation, Halifax, Nova Scotia [*Library symbol Obsolete National Library of Canada*] (NLC)

NSHS .... National Slavic Honor Society (EA)

NSHS .... Naval School of Health Sciences [*Bethesda, MD*]

NSHS .... St. Mary's University, Halifax, Nova Scotia [*Library symbol National Library of Canada*] (NLC)

NSHSDET .... Naval School of Health Sciences Detachment (DNAB)

NSHSG .... Sable Gas Systems Ltd., Halifax, Nova Scotia [*Library symbol National Library of Canada*] (NLC)

NSHSMC ...... Stewart, MacKeen & Covert Law Firm, Halifax, Nova Scotia [*Library symbol National Library of Canada*] (NLC)

NSHSP .... Social Development Division Library, Social Planning Department, City of Halifax, Nova Scotia [*Library symbol National Library of Canada*] (NLC)

NSHSPT ...... Ferguson Library for Print Handicapped Students, Patrick Power Library, St. Mary's University, Halifax, Nova Scotia [*Library symbol National Library of Canada*] (NLC)

NSHSS .... Nova Scotia Department of Community Services, Halifax, Nova Scotia [*Library symbol National Library of Canada*] (NLC)

NSHSW .... Maritime School of Social Work, Halifax, Nova Scotia [*Library symbol National Library of Canada*] (NLC)

NSHT .... Technical University of Nova Scotia, Halifax, Nova Scotia [*Library symbol National Library of Canada*] (NLC)

NSHTI .... Nova Scotia Institute of Technology, Halifax, Nova Scotia [*Library symbol National Library of Canada*] (NLC)

NSHTU .... Nova Scotia Teachers Union, Halifax, Nova Scotia [*Library symbol National Library of Canada*] (NLC)

NSHV .... Mount Saint Vincent University, Halifax, Nova Scotia [*Library symbol National Library of Canada*] (NLC)

NSHVA .... Art Gallery, Mount Saint Vincent University, Halifax, Nova Scotia [*Library symbol National Library of Canada*] (NLC)

NSHVGH ..... Health Sciences Library, Victoria General Hospital, Halifax, Nova Scotia [*Library symbol National Library of Canada*] (NLC)

NSHVH .... Halifax Regional Vocational School, Nova Scotia [*Library symbol National Library of Canada*] (NLC)

NSHVTT .... Nova Scotia Department of Advanced Education and Job Training, Halifax, Nova S cotia [*Library symbol National Library of Canada*] (NLC)

NSHW .... Atlantic Region, Atmospheric Environment Service, Environment Canada [*Bureau Regional de l'Atlantique, Service de l'Environnement Atmospherique, Environnement Canada*] Halifax, Nova Scotia [*Library symbol National Library of Canada*] (NLC)

NShW .... Sag Harbor Whaling and Historical Museum, Sag Harbor, NY [*Library symbol*] [*Library of Congress*] (LCLS)

NSI .... Handbook of North-Semitic Inscriptions [*A publication*] (BJA)

NSI .... NASA Science Internet

NSI .... NASA [*National Aeronautical and Space Administration*] Standard Indicator

NSI .... NASA Standard Initiator (NASA)

NSI .... National Security Index of the American Security Council [*A publication*] (DLA)

NSI .... National Security Information (NRCH)

NSI .... National Service Industries, Inc. [*NYSE symbol*] (SPSG)

NSI .... National Service [*Life*] Insurance

NSI .... National Shipbuilding Initiative [*MARAD*] (TAG)

NSI .... National Shoe Institute (EA)

NSI .... National Space Institute [*Later, NSS*] (EA)

NSI .... National Supervisory Inspectorate [*British*] (EECA)

NSI .... Natl Service Indus [*NYSE symbol*] (TTSB)

NSI .... Naval Science Instructor (DNAB)

NSI .... Negative Self-Image [*Psychology*]

NSI .... Network Solutions, Inc.

NSI .... Network Strategies, Inc. [*Fairfax, VA*] [*Telecommunications*] (TSSD)

NSI .... Network Support, Inc.

NSI .... Neurosciences Institute (DAVI)

NSI .... Next Sequential Instruction

NSI .... Nielsen Station Index [*Nielsen Media Research*] [*Information service or system*]

NSI .... Nitrogen Solubility Index [*Analytical chemistry*]

NSI .... Noise Source Instrumentation

NSI .... Nonsatellite Identification

NSI .... Nonsequenced Information (IAA)

NSI .... Non-Specific Illness (WDAA)

NSI .... Nonspecific Sexually Transmitted Infection [*Medicine*]

NSI .... Nonstandard Item

NSI .... Nonstocked Item

NSI .... Non-Syncytium-Inducing [*Cytology*]

NSI .... Norsk Senter for Informatikk [*Norwegian Center for Informatics*] [*Information service or system*] (IID)

NSI .... North-South Institute [*Canada*] (EAIO)

NSI .... Norton Simon, Inc. (EFIS)

NSI .... No Signs of Infection [*Medicine*] (DMAA)

NSI .... Not Seriously Injured [*Environmental science*] (COE)

NSI .... Nuclear Safety Inspection (NVT)

NSI .... Nuclear Safety Institute

NSI .... Nuclear Services International

NSI .... Nuclear Status Indicator (DNAB)

NSI .... Nuclear Surety Inspection

NSI .... San Nicolas Island, CA [*Location identifier FAA*] (FAAL)

NSI-1 .... NASA [*National Aeronautics and Space Administration*] Standard Initiator -Type 1 [*Formerly, SMSI*] (NASA)

NSIA .... National Security and International Affairs [*Office of Management and Budget*]

NSIA .... National Security Industrial Association (EA)

NSIAC .... National Student Involvement Assistance Center [*Boston University*] [*Defunct*]

NSIAC .... Northern Sun Intercollegiate Athletic Conference (PSS)

NSIAD .... National Security and International Affairs Division (AAGC)

NSIC .... National Spinal Injuries Centre [*Stoke Mandeville Hospital*] [*British*] (CB)

NSIC .... National Storage Industry Consortium

NSIC .... National Strategy Information Center (EA)

NSIC .... Naval Security and Investigative Command

NSIC .... Next Senior in Command [*Navy*]

NSIC .... Northern Sun Intercollegiate Conference (PSS)

NSIC .... Noster Salvator Iesus Christus [*Our Savior, Jesus Christ*] [*Latin*]

NSIC .... Nuclear Safety Information Center

NSIC .... Nuclear Strike Information Center

NSiC .... Staten Island Community College, Staten Island, NY [*Library symbol Library of Congress Obsolete*] (LCLS)

NSiCS .... College of Staten Island, St. George Campus, Staten Island, NY [*Library symbol Library of Congress*] (LCLS)

NSICU .... Neurosurgical Intensive Care Unit [*Medicine*] (DMAA)

NSID .... National Society of Interior Designers [*Later, ASID*]

NSIDC .... National Snow and Ice Data Center [*National Oceanic and Atmospheric Administration*] (GFGA)

NSIDH .... National System of Interstate and Defense Highways (AFIT)

NSidHi .... Sidney New York Historical Society, Sidney, NY [*Library symbol*] [*Library of Congress*] (LCLS)

NSidS .... Bendix Corp., Electrical Components Division, Engineering Library, Sidney, NY [*Library symbol Library of Congress*] (LCLS)

NSIDS .... National Shut-In Day Society (EA)

NSIDSC .... National Sudden Infant Death Syndrome Clearinghouse (EA)

NSIDSF .... National Sudden Infant Death Syndrome Foundation (EA)

NSIDSF .... SIDS Alliance (EA)

NSIEE .... National Society for Internships and Experiential Education (EA)

NSIF .... National Swine Improvement Federation (EA)

NSIF .... Near Space Instrumentation Facility [*NASA*] (KSC)

NSiIR .... New York State Department of Mental Hygiene, Institute for Basic Research in Mental Retardation, Staten Island, NY [*Library symbol Library of Congress*] (LCLS)

NSIL .... National Seafood Inspection Laboratory [*Pascagoula, MS*] [*Department of Commerce*] (GRD)

NSIL .... Nonsaturating Inverter Logic (IAA)

NSILA .... Nonsuppressible Insulin-Like Activity [*Cytochemistry*]

NSiIStC .... Saint Columban's Seminary, Silver Creek, NY [*Library symbol Library of Congress Obsolete*] (LCLS)

NSiND .... Notre Dame College of Staten Island, Staten Island, NY [*Library symbol Library of Congress*] (LCLS)

NSIPA .... National Society of Insurance Premium Auditors (EA)

NSIPS .... NRL [*Naval Research Laboratory*] Satellite Image Processing System [*Marine science*] (OSRA)

NSIR .... Nosier (ABBR)

NSiRC .... Richmond College, Staten Island, NY [*Library symbol Library of Congress Obsolete*] (LCLS)

NSIS .... NASA Software Information System (SSD)

NSIS .... National Shut-In Society (EA)

NSIS .... National Survey of Instructional Staff [*Department of Education*] (GFGA)

NSISL .... New South Intercollegiate Swimming League (PSS)

NSiSV .... Saint Vincent's Medical Center of Richmond, Staten Island, NY [*Library symbol Library of Congress*] (LCLS)

NSIT .... Insight Enterprises, Inc. [*NASDAQ symbol*] (SAG)

NSIT .... Insiht Enterprises [*NASDAQ symbol*] (TTSB)

NSIT .... Not Safe in Taxis

NSITF .... National Ship Installations Test Facility

NSIX .... Neuromedical Systems [*NASDAQ symbol*] (TTSB)

NSIX .... Neuromedical Systems, Inc. [*NASDAQ symbol*] (SAG)

NSIY .... North Somerset Imperial Yeomanry [*British military*] (DMA)

NSJ .... Nuestro Senor Jesucristo [*Our Lord, Jesus Christ*] [*Spanish*]

NSJC .... National Society of Journeymen Curriers [*A union*] [*British*]

NSJC .... Noster Salvator Jesus Christus [*Our Savior, Jesus Christ*] [*Latin*]

NSJC .... Notre Seigneur Jesus Christ [*Our Lord, Jesus Christ*] [*French*]

NSK .... Nippon Seiko Kabushiki Kaisha [*Japan*]

NSK .... Not Specified by Kind (MHDI)

NSKC .... National Safe Kids Campaign (EA)

NSKER .... Efamol Research Institute, Kentville, Nova Scotia [*Library symbol National Library of Canada*] (NLC)

NSKIP .... Nordiska Samarbetskommitten for Internationell Politik [*Nordic Cooperation Committee for International Politics, Including Conflict and Peace Research*] (EAIO)

NSKKR .... Kings Regional Vocational School, Kentville, Nova Scotia [*Library symbol National Library of Canada*] (NLC)

NSKL .... Wildlife Division, Nova Scotia Department of Lands and Forests, Kentville, Nova Scotia [*Library symbol National Library of Canada*] (NLC)

NSKOK .... Old Kings Courthouse Heritage Museum, Kentville, Nova Scotia [*Library symbol National Library of Canada*] (NLC)

NSKR .... Research Station, Agriculture Canada [*Station de Recherches, Agriculture Canada*] Kentville, Nova Scotia [*Library symbol National Library of Canada*] (NLC)

NSKVH .... Valley Health Services Association, Kentville, Nova Scotia [*Library symbol National Library of Canada*] (NLC)

NSL .... Nasal (ABBR)

NSL............	Nasion-Sella Line [*Brain anatomy*]
NSL............	National Science Laboratories (KSC)
NSL............	National Science Library [*Later, Canada Institute for Scientific and Technical Information*] (DIT)
NSL............	National Service League [*British military*] (DMA)
NSL............	National Soccer League (EA)
NSL............	National Standards Laboratory [*Formerly, IBS, IMR*] [*National Institute of Standards and Technology*]
NSL............	National Story League (EA)
NSL............	Naval Submarine League (EA)
NSL............	Naval Supersonic Laboratory
NSL............	Navigating Sub-Lieutenant [*Navy British*] (ROG)
NSL............	Navy Standards Laboratory
NSL............	Navy Stock List
NSL............	Net Switching Loss [*Telecommunications*] (TEL)
NSL............	New Special Libraries [*A publication*]
NSL............	Nonstandard Label [*Computer science*]
NSL............	Nonstockage List
NSL............	Northrup Space Laboratories (KSC)
NSL............	Norwood & St. Lawrence Railroad Co. [*AAR code*]
NSL............	Not Stock Listed
NSL............	Nuclear Safety Line
NSI............	Saranac Lake Free Library, Saranac Lake, NY [*Library symbol Library of Congress*] (LCLS)
NSLA	Louisbourg Archives, Nova Scotia [*Library symbol National Library of Canada*] (NLC)
NSLA	National Society of Literature and the Arts (EA)
NSLA	National Staff Leasing Association (EA)
NSLAL	Nova Scotia Land Survey Institute, Lawrencetown, Nova Scotia [*Library symbol National Library of Canada*] (NLC)
NSLB	NS&L Bancorp [*NASDAQ symbol*] (TTSB)
NSLB	NS & L Bancorp, Inc. [*NASDAQ symbol*] (SAG)
NSLC	Naval Sea Logistics Center
NSLC	Nuclear Safety and Licensing Commission
NSLF...........	Fortress of Louisbourg, Canada National Historic Park [*Forteresse de Louisbourg, Parc Historique National*] Nova Scotia [*Library symbol National Library of Canada*] (NLC)
NSLF...........	National Socialist Liberation Front (NADA)
NSLF...........	Nonself
NSLFM........	Fisheries Museum of the Atlantic, Lunenburg, Nova Scotia [*Library symbol National Library of Canada*] (NLC)
NSLFP	Fort Point Museum, La Have, Nova Scotia [*Library symbol National Library of Canada*] (NLC)
NSIH	General Hospital of Saranac Lake, Saranac Lake, NY [*Library symbol Library of Congress*] (LCLS)
NSLHS	Lunenburg Heritage Society, Nova Scotia [*Library symbol National Library of Canada*] (NLC)
NSLI...........	National Service Life Insurance
NSLI...........	National Street Law Institute (EA)
NSLIN	Nonstandard Line Item Number [*Army*] (AABC)
NSLL...........	National Save-a-Life League [*Defunct*] (EA)
NSLL...........	National Savings and Loan League [*Formerly, NLISA*] (EA)
NSLLS	Lockeport Little School Museum, Nova Scotia [*Library symbol National Library of Canada*] (NLC)
NSINC.........	North Country Community College, Saranac Lake, NY [*Library symbol Library of Congress*] (LCLS)
NSLP	National School Lunch Program [*Department of Agriculture*]
NSLPE	Progress-Enterprise, Lunenburg, Nova Scotia [*Library symbol National Library of Canada*] (NLC)
NSLQCM	Queens County Museum, Liverpool, Nova Scotia [*Library symbol National Library of Canada*] (NLC)
NSLR	Nova Scotia Law Reports [*A publication*] (DLA)
NSLRB	National Steel Labor Relations Board [*New Deal*]
NSLRS	National School Labor Relations Service [*Later, LMRS*] (EA)
NSLS	National Synchrotron Light Source [*Brookhaven National Laboratory*]
NSLS	North Suburban Library System, Wheeling, IL [*Library network*]
NSLSA	National Surf Life Saving Association of America [*Later, USLA*] (EA)
NSLSRA	National Society of Live Stock Record Associations (EA)
NSIT...........	Trudeau Institute, Saranac Lake, NY [*Library symbol Library of Congress*] (LCLS)
N/S-LTI-G/T...	National/State Leadership Training Institute on Gifted and Talented (EA)
NSIW	Will Rogers Memorial Fund, Saranac Lake, NY [*Library symbol Library of Congress*] (LCLS)
NSLY	Nasally (ABBR)
NSLY	Noisily (ABBR)
NSM............	National Search and Rescue Manual (COE)
NSM............	National Security Management [*Military*]
NSM............	National Security Medal [*Military decoration*]
NSM............	National Selected Morticians (EA)
NSM............	National Semiconductor Corp. [*NYSE symbol*] (SPSG)
NSM............	National Serviceman [*British military*] (DMA)
NSM............	National Soaring Museum (DICI)
NSM............	National Socialist Movement (EA)
NSM............	Natl Semiconductor [*NYSE symbol*] (TTSB)
NSM............	Naval School of Music
NSM............	Network Security Module
NSM............	Network Space Monitor (SAA)
NSM............	Network Status Monitor [*NASA*] (KSC)
NSM............	Neurosecretory Material (MAE)
NSM............	Neurosecretory Motoneurons
NSM............	New Schools Movement [*Defunct*] (EA)
NSM............	New Smoking Material [*A wood cellulose-based tobacco substitute*]
NSM............	Nice Safe Man [*Slang*]
NSM............	Nitsanim [*Israel*] [*Later, AMT*] [*Geomagnetic observatory code*]
NSM............	Noise Source Meter
NSM............	Nonantigenic Specific Mediator (DB)
NSM............	Nondeterministic Sequential Machine (IAA)
NSM............	Norseman [*Australia Airport symbol*] (OAG)
NSM............	Northern Student Movement [*Defunct*] (EA)
NSM............	North-South Map [*Via orbiter*]
NSM............	Nutrient Sporulation Medium [*Medicine*] (DMAA)
NSm............	Smithtown Public Library, Smithtown, NY [*Library symbol Library of Congress*] (LCLS)
N-S/M²	Newton Second per Square Meter (WDAA)
NSMA	Maota [*Western Samoa*] [*ICAO location identifier*] (ICLI)
NSMA	National Scale Men's Association (EA)
NSMA	National Seasoning Manufacturers Association (EA)
NSMA	National Second Mortgage Association [*Center Square, PA*] (EA)
NSMA	National Shoe Manufacturers Association [*Later, FIA*] (EA)
NSMA	National Soup Mix Association [*Defunct*] (EA)
NSMAPMAWOL...	Not So Much a Programme, More a Way of Life [*British television program*]
NSMATCC	NATO Small Arms Test Control Commission (MCD)
NSMC	National Security Management Course [*National Defense University*] (GFGA)
NSMC	National Student Marketing Corp.
NSMC	Naval Submarine Medical Center
NSMCA	National Spirit, Metropolitan Club of America (EA)
NSMCM	Naval Supplement, Manual for Courts-Martial [*United States*] [*A publication*] (DLA)
NSME..........	Eastern Counties Regional Library, Mulgrave, Nova Scotia [*Library symbol National Library of Canada*] (NLC)
NSMEX	Examiner, Middleton, Nova Scotia [*Library symbol National Library of Canada*] (NLC)
NSMFA	North Sea Mine Force Association (EA)
NSMG	Naval School of Military Government
NSMG & A....	Naval School of Military Government and Administration
NSmGH	Smithtown General Hospital, Smithtown, NY [*Library symbol Library of Congress*] (LCLS)
NSMH	Nuclear Systems Material Handbook (NRCH)
NSMHC	National Society for Mentally Handicapped Children [*British*] (BI)
NSmHSE	Smithtown High School East. Smithtown, NY [*Library symbol*] [*Library of Congress*] (LCLS)
NSmHSW.....	Smithtown High School West, Smithtown, NY [*Library symbol*] [*Library of Congress*] (LCLS)
NSML..........	Low-Sodium Meal [*Airline notation*] (ADA)
NSMM	Macdonald Museum, Middleton, Nova Scotia [*Library symbol National Library of Canada*] (NLC)
NSMM	National Society of Metal Mechanics [*A union*] [*British*] (DCTA)
NSMM	National Sustainment Maintenance Management [*Army*]
NSMO	NASTRAN [*NASA Structural Analysis*] Systems Management Office
NSMP	National Society of Master Patternmakers [*British*] (BI)
NSMP	National Society of Mural Painters (EA)
NSMP	Navy Support and Mobilization Plan (NVT)
NSMPA	National Screw Machine Products Association (EA)
NSMR	National Society for Medical Research (EA)
NSMR	Non-Store Marketing Report [*A publication*]
NSMRL	Naval Submarine Medical Research Laboratory
NSMRSE	National Study of Mathematics Requirements for Scientists and Engineers
NSMRTS	Nuclear Submarine Maneuvering Room Training Simulator (PDAA)
NSMS	National Safety Management Society (EA)
NSMS	National Sheet Music Society (EA)
NSMS	Network Server Management System [*Tylink Corp.*]
NSMS	Soldiers Memorial Hospital, Middleton, Nova Scotia [*Library symbol National Library of Canada*] (NLC)
NSMSES	Naval Ship Missile System Engineering Station
NSMSESDETLANT...	Naval Ship Missile System Engineering Station Detachment, Atlantic (MUGU)
NSmSJH	Saint John's Smithtown Hospital, Smithtown, NY [*Library symbol Library of Congress*] (LCLS)
NSMT..........	National Society of Master Thatchers [*British*] (DBA)
NSMT..........	National Society of Medical Technologists
NSMV	Valley Mirror, Middleton, Nova Scotia [*Library symbol National Library of Canada*] (NLC)
NSMW	Naval Schools Mine Warfare
NSN	Military Sealift Command, Washington, DC [*OCLC symbol*] (OCLC)
NSN	National Stock Number (MCD)
NSN	NATO Stock Number (NATG)
NSN	Nelson [*New Zealand*] [*Airport symbol*] (OAG)
NSN	Nephrotoxic Serum Nephritis [*Medicine*] (DMAA)
NSN	Nicotine-Stimulated Neurophysin [*Biochemistry*]
NSN	North Star Network [*Defunct*] (EA)
NSN	No Stock Number
Nsn	Number of Similar Negative Matches
NSN	Nurses Support Network [*Later, NIT*] (EA)
NSNA	National Socialist Nederlandse Arbeiders Partij [*Netherlands group favoring integration of the Netherlands into the German reich*] [*World War II*]
NSNA	National Student Nurses' Association (EA)
NSNA	Newcomen Society in North America (EA)
NSNC	National Society of Newspaper Columnists (NTPA)
NSNC	Nova Scotia Normal College
NSNCE	Nuisance (ABBR)
NSNCL	Nonsensical (ABBR)
NSND	Nonsymptomatic, Nondisabling (MAE)
NSND	Normal Saline Nose Drops [*Pharmacology*] (DAVI)
NSNE	Nappan Experimental Farm, Nova Scotia [*Library symbol National Library of Canada*] (NLC)

NSNEW	National Society of New England Women (EA)
NSNF	Nonstrategic Nuclear Forces (MCD)
NSnfG	GTE Sylvania, Inc., Electronic Components Group, Seneca Falls, NY [*Library symbol Library of Congress*] (LCLS)
NSNGA	Aberdeen Hospital, New Glasgow, Nova Scotia [*Library symbol National Library of Canada*] (NLC)
NSNGE	Evening News, New Glasgow, Nova Scotia [*Library symbol National Library of Canada*] (NLC)
NSNGH	New Glasgow Senior High School, Nova Scotia [*Library symbol National Library of Canada*] (BIB)
NSNGP	Pictou-Antigonish Regional Library, New Glasgow, Nova Scotia [*Library symbol National Library of Canada*] (NLC)
NSNHC	Cabot Archives, Neil's Harbour, Nova Scotia [*Library symbol National Library of Canada*] (NLC)
NSNMDR	National Stock Number Master Data Records (MCD)
NSNMK	Kentville Publishing, New Minas, Nova Scotia [*Library symbol National Library of Canada*] (NLC)
NSNP	No Space, No Print [*Computer science*] (MHDI)
NSNRP	Nonstock Numbered Repair Parts
NSNS	Nonsense (ABBR)
NSNSCLY	Nonsensically (ABBR)
NSO	NASA Support Operation (KSC)
NSO	National Security Office [*or Officer*] (GFGA)
NSO	National Service Officer [*Ministry of Labour and National Service*] [*British World War II*]
NSO	National Solar Observatory [*Tucson, AZ*] [*National Science Foundation*] (GRD)
NSO	National Standardization Office [*US Army Materiel Command*]
NSO	National Symphony Orchestra
NSO	Naval Staff Officer
NSO	Naval Store Officer [*British*]
NSO	Navy Subsistence Office (DNAB)
NSO	Neighborhood Service Organization
NSO	Neosporin Ointment [*Medicine*] (CPH)
NSO	Network Support Office [*NASA*]
NSO	Next Standing Order
NSO	Nitrogen, Sulfur, and Oxygen [*In chemical compounds*]
NSO	Noise Suppression Oscillator (MCD)
NSO	Nonferrous Smelter Order [*Environmental Protection Agency*]
nso	Northern Sotho [*MARC language code Library of Congress*] (LCCP)
NSO	North State Cooperative Library System, Willows, CA [*OCLC symbol*] (OCLC)
NSO	No Spares Ordered (AAG)
NSO	Nuclear Safety Office [*or Officer*] [*Air Force*] (AFM)
NSO	Nucleus Supraopticus (DMAA)
NSO	Numeric Stockage Objective [*Items*] [*DoD*]
NSO	Scone [*Australia Airport symbol*] (OAG)
NSo	Somers Library, Somers, NY [*Library symbol Library of Congress*] (LCLS)
NSOA	National School Orchestra Association (EA)
NSOA	National Symphony Orchestra Association (EA)
NSOA	Nuclear Safety Operational Analysis (NRCH)
NSoa	Rogers Memorial Library, Southampton, NY [*Library symbol Library of Congress*] (LCLS)
NSoaH	Southampton Hospital, Southampton, NY [*Library symbol Library of Congress*] (LCLS)
NSoaS	Long Island University, Southampton College, Southampton, NY [*Library symbol Library of Congress*] (LCLS)
NSOB	New Senate Office Building
NSOC	National SIGINT [*Signal Intelligence*] Operations Center (MCD)
NSOC	Navy Satellite Operations Center (NVT)
NSOC	New South Conference (PSS)
NSOC	Norbornene Spiroorthocarbonate [*Organic chemistry*]
NSOD	Naval School of Ordnance Disposal
NSOEA	National Stationery and Office Equipment Association [*Later, NOPA*] (EA)
NSOF	Naval Status of Forces (MCD)
NSOF	Navy Special Operations Force (AABC)
NSOG	Navy Special Operations Group [*SEALS that operated in Vietnam*] (VNW)
NSOGA	National Seniors' Open Golf Association (EA)
NSoHi	Somers Historical Society, Somers, NY [*Library symbol Library of Congress*] (LCLS)
NSOHSC	National Survey of Oral Health in School Children [*Department of Health and Human Services*] (GFGA)
NSOJ	Journal, Oxford, Nova Scotia [*Library symbol National Library of Canada*] (NLC)
NSOM	Near Field Scanning Optical Microscopy
NSoo	Southold Free Library, Southold, NY [*Library symbol Library of Congress*] (LCLS)
NSOP	National Second Opinion Program (EA)
NSOPCD	National Society of Old Plymouth Colony Descendants (EA)
NSOPF	National Survey of Postsecondary Faculty [*Department of Education*] (GFGA)
NSOR	No Shop Order Required
NSos	South Salem Library, South Salem, NY [*Library symbol Library of Congress*] (LCLS)
NSOSG	North Sea Oceanographical Study Group [*British*]
NSP	NASA Support Plan (KSC)
NSP	National Salvation Party [*Milli Selamet Partisi*] [*Turkey Political party*] (PPW)
NSP	National Sea Products Ltd. [*Toronto Stock Exchange symbol*]
NSP	National Search and Rescue Plan (COE)
NSP	National Seopsengwe Party [*Bophuthatswana*] [*Political party*] (PPW)

NSP	National Ski Patrol System (EA)
NSP	National Socialist Party [*New Zealand*] [*Political party*] (PD)
NSP	National Society of Painters [*A union*] [*British*]
NSP	National Society of Professors [*Later, NEA Higher Education Council*] (EA)
NSP	National Space Program (AAG)
NSP	National Stolen Property
NSP	National Stuttering Project (EA)
NSP	Native Signal Processing [*Computer science*] (PCM)
NSP	Navigational Satellite Program [*NASA*] (IAA)
NSP	Navy Safety Program (DNAB)
NSP	Navy Space Project
NSP	Navy Standard Part
NSP	Navy Support Plan
NSP	Neighborhood Statistics Program [*Bureau of the Census*] (GFGA)
NSP	Net Social Profitability
NSP	Network Service Provider [*Telecommunications*]
NSP	Network Services Protocol [*Digital Equipment Corp.*] [*Telecommunications*] (TEL)
NSP	Network Signal Processor (NASA)
NSP	Network Support Plan [*NASA*] (KSC)
NSP	Network Support Processor (NITA)
NSP	Neurological Shellfish Poisoning (USDC)
NSP	Neuron-Specific Protein [*Later, NSE*] [*Biochemistry*]
NSP	Neurotoxic Shellfish Poisoning [*Medicine*]
NSP	New Species
NSP	Nominal Stagnation Point
NSP	Non-Self-Propelled
NSP	Nonseries Parallel (IAA)
NSP	Nonspecific Prostatitis [*Medicine*] (ADA)
NSP	Nonstandard Part
NSP	Nonstorage Protein [*Food technology*]
NSP	Nonstructural Protein (DMAA)
NSP	Nordiska Sjoforsakringspoolen [*Nordic Pool for Marine Insurance - NPMI*] (EA)
NSP	Normal Serum Pool
NSP	Normal Superphosphate [*Fertilizer*]
NSP	Northern States Power Co. [*NYSE symbol*] (SPSG)
NSP	Northern States Pwr [*NYSE symbol*] (TTSB)
NSP	No Separate Billing Price (MCD)
NSP	Nose Shipping Plug
NSP	Not Separately Priced (NG)
NSP	N-Succinylperimycin (DB)
NSP	Nuclear Strike Plan [*Army*] (AABC)
Nsp	Number of Similar Positive Matches
NSP	Numeric Space Character [*Computer science*]
NSP	Numeric Subroutine Package [*Computer science*] (CIST)
NSP	Nutritional Support Panel [*Dietetics*] (DAVI)
nsp	Species Nova [*New Species*] [*Latin*] (EES)
NSP	St. Andrews Presbyterian College, Laurinburg, NC [*OCLC symbol*] (OCLC)
NSPA	Advocate, Pictou, Nova Scotia [*Library symbol National Library of Canada*] (NLC)
NSPA	National Scholastic Press Association (EA)
NSPA	National Shrimp Processors Association (EA)
NSPA	National Socialist Party of America (EA)
NSPA	National Society of Public Accountants [*Alexandria, VA*] (EA)
NSPA	National Soybean Processors Association [*Later, NOPA*] (EA)
NSPA	National Split Pea Association [*Defunct*]
NSPA	National Standard Parts Association [*Later, ASIA*]
NSPA	National State Printing Association (EA)
NSPA	Navy Shore Patrol Administration (WDAA)
NSPA	Pictou Advocate, Nova Scotia [*Library symbol National Library of Canada*] (NLC)
NSPAC	National Security Political Action Committee [*Defunct*] (EA)
NSPAR	Nonstandard Part Approval Request
NSpaT	Saint Thomas Aquinas College, Sparkill, NY [*Library symbol Library of Congress*] (LCLS)
NSPB	National Society to Prevent Blindness (EA)
NSPB	Prevent Blindness America [*Formerly, National Society to Prevent Blindness*] (EA)
NSPBB	Burning Bush Museum, Pictou, Nova Scotia [*Library symbol National Library of Canada*] (BIB)
NSPB/PBA	National Society to Prevent Blindness/Prevent Blindness America (NTPA)
NSPC	National Security Planning Commission
NSPC	National Society of Painters in Casein (EA)
NSPC	National Sound-Program Center [*Telecommunications*] (TEL)
NSPC	National Standard Plumbing Code Committee (EA)
NSPC	National Straight Pipe Threads in Pipe Couplings
NSPCA	National Society for the Prevention of Cruelty to Animals
NSPCA	National Society of Painters in Casein and Acrylic (EA)
NSPCB	National Society for the Preservation of Covered Bridges (EA)
NSPCC	National Society for the Prevention of Cruelty to Children
NSPCC	Naval Ships Parts Control Center (MCD)
NSPCM	National Society for Prevention of Cruelty to Mushrooms (EA)
NSPD	Naval Shore Patrol Detachment
NSPE	National Society of Professional Engineers (EA)
NSPE	Navy Senior Procurement Executive (AAGC)
NSPE	Specimen Unobtainable [*Laboratory science*] (DAVI)
NSpeB	Board of Cooperative Educational Services (BOCES), Spencerport, NY [*Library symbol Library of Congress*] (LCLS)
N-SPECS	Navy Specifications (AAGC)
NSPF	National Swimming Pool Foundation (EA)
nspf	Not Specially Provided For (EBF)

NSPF	Not Specifically Provided For
NSPFEA	National Spray Painting and Finishing Equipment Association [*Later, NSEMA*] (EA)
NSPG	National Security Planning Group
NSPH	Neonatal Severe Hyperparathyroidism [*Medicine*] (DMAA)
NSPHM	Port Hastings Museum and Archives, Nova Scotia [*Library symbol National Library of Canada*] (NLC)
NSPI	National Society for Performance and Instruction (EA)
NSPI	National Society for Programmed Instruction (IAA)
NSPI	National Spa and Pool Institute (EA)
NSPI	National Spatial Data Infrastructure [*BTS*] (TAG)
NSPI	Nonstorage Protein Isolate [*Food technology*]
NSPIAE	National Society of Professional Insurance Agency Executives (NTPA)
NSPIE	National Society for the Promotion of Industrial Education [*Later, AVA*]
NSPKU	National Society for Phenylketonuria and Allied Disorders [*British*] (DBA)
NSPLO	NATO Sidewinder Production and Logistics Organization [*Missiles*] (NATG)
NSPMH	McCulloch House, Pictou, Nova Scotia [*Library symbol National Library of Canada*] (NLC)
NSPNC	North Cumberland Historical Society, Pugwash, Nova Scotia [*Library symbol National Library of Canada*] (NLC)
NSPO	NATO Sea Sparrow Project Office (MCD)
NSPO	NATO Sidewinder Production Organization [*Missiles*] (NATG)
NSPO	NATO Sidewinder Program Office [*Missiles*] (NATG)
NSPO	Naval Ship Production Overseer [*British*]
NSPO	Naval Space Projects Office
NSPO	Navy Special Projects Office
NSPO	Nuclear Systems Project Office [*Air Research and Development Command*] [*Air Force*] (AAG)
NS-POG	NAVSHIPS [*Naval Ship Systems Command*] Propulsion Operating Guides
NSPP	National Serials Pilot Project
NSPP	Nuclear Safety Pilot Plant [*ORNL*]
NSPPrA	Non'n St Pwr Minn,$3.60 Pfd [*NYSE symbol*] (TTSB)
NSPPrB	No'n St Pwr Minn,$4.08 Pfd [*NYSE symbol*] (TTSB)
NSPPrC	No'n Pwr Minn,$4.10 Pfd [*NYSE symbol*] (TTSB)
NSPPrE	No's St Pwr Minn.$4.16 Pfd [*NYSE symbol*] (TTSB)
NSPPrG	No'n St Pwr Minn,$4.56 Pfd [*NYSE symbol*] (TTSB)
NSPPrH	No'n St Pwr Minn,$6.80 Pfd [*NYSE symbol*] (TTSB)
NSPPrI	No'n St Pwr Minn,$7.00 Pfd [*NYSE symbol*] (TTSB)
NSPR	National Society for Park Resources (EA)
NSPR	National Society of Patient Representatives of the American Hospital Association (EA)
NSPR	National Society of Pershing Rifles (EA)
NSPR	Nonstandard Part Approval Request
NSPR	Record, Parrsboro, Nova Scotia [*Library symbol National Library of Canada*] (NLC)
NSPRA	National School Public Relations Association (EA)
NSPRCA	National Society for Patient Representation and Consumer Affairs (NTPA)
NSPRCA	National Society of Patient Representation and Consumer Affairs of the American Hospital Association (EA)
NSPrD	No'n St Pwr Minn,$4.11 Pfd [*NYSE symbol*] (TTSB)
NSPRDS	New Systems Personnel Requirements Data System [*Navy*]
NSPRM	National Society of Professional Resident Managers (EA)
NSPRT	Nonsupport (ABBR)
NSPRV	Pictou Regional Vocational School, Nova Scotia [*Library symbol National Library of Canada*] (NLC)
NSprvCH	Bertrand Chaffee Hospital, Springville, NY [*Library symbol Library of Congress*] (LCLS)
NSPS	National Ski Patrol System (EA)
NSPS	National Society of Professional Sanitarians (EA)
NSPS	National Society of Professional Surveyors (EA)
NSPS	National Standards of Performance for Stationary Sources (ACII)
NSPS	National Stockpile Purchase Specification [*for metals*]
NSPS	National Sweet Pea Society [*British*] (BI)
NSPS	New Source Performance Standards [*Environmental Protection Agency*] (AEPA)
NSPS	Nonsynchronous Pulse Suppression (MCD)
NSPS	Nuclear Safety Protection System (NRCH)
NSPS	Nuclear Strike Planning System (MCD)
NSPSE	National Society of Painters, Sculptors, and Engravers [*British*] (DI)
NSPSH	Parrsboro Shore Historical Society, Parrsboro, Nova Scotia [*Library symbol National Library of Canada*] (BIB)
NSPSS	Scotia Sun, Port Hawkesbury, Nova Scotia [*Library symbol National Library of Canada*] (NLC)
NSPST	National Society of Pharmaceutical Sales Trainers (EA)
NSPV	Nandina Stem-Pitting Virus [*Plant pathology*]
NSPV	Number of Scans per Vehicle (OA)
NSPVT	Nonsustained Polymorphic Ventricular Tachycardia [*Cardiology*] (DAVI)
NSPw	Northern States Power Co. [*Associated Press*] (SAG)
NSPWA	National Society Patriotic Women of America
NSQ	Neuroticism Scale Questionnaire [*Psychology*]
NSQ	Not Sufficient Quantity [*Clinical chemistry*]
NSQ	Nurse Satisfaction Questionnaire
NSQC	National Society of Quality Circles [*British*] (DBA)
NSR	Mount Vernon, WA [*Location identifier FAA*] (FAAL)
NSR	Nasoseptal Reconstruction [*Otorhinolaryngology*] (DAVI)
NSR	Natinal Securities & Research Corp. (EFIS)
NSR	National Air Charter PT [*Indonesia*] [*ICAO designator*] (FAAC)
NSR	National Scientific Register

NSR	National Security Review (AAGC)
NSR	National Shipping Report [*NATO*]
NSR	National Shipping Representative (NATG)
NSR	National Shorthand Reporter [*A publication*]
NSR	National Singles Registry (EA)
NSR	National Slow Rate (NASA)
NSR	National Swine Registry (NTPA)
NSR	NATO Staff Requirements (MCD)
NSR	Naval Supply Requirement (DNAB)
NSR	Net Survival Rate
NSR	Neutron Source Reactor
NSR	New Source Review [*A publication*] (EPA)
NSR	Night Sky Radiation
NSR	Nitrile Silicone Rubber [*Organic chemistry*]
NSR	Noise-to-Signal Ratio (IAA)
NSR	Nominal Slow Rate [*NASA*] (KSC)
NSR	Nonspecific Reaction [*Medicine*] (DMAA)
NSR	Norair Science Report (SAA)
NSR	Nordic Shooting Region (EAIO)
NSR	Nordiska Skidskolans Rad [*Nordic Council of Ski Schools - NCSS*] [*Finland*] (EAIO)
NSR	Nordiska Skogsarbetsstudiernas Rad [*Nordic Research Council on Forest Operations*] [*Sweden*] (EAIO)
NSR	Nordisk Skuespillerrad [*Nordic Actors' Council - NAC*] [*Sweden*] (EAIO)
NSR	Norfolk Southern Railway Co. [*NYSE symbol*] (SAG)
NSR	Normal Sinus Rhythm [*Medicine*] (DMAA)
NSR	Normal Slow Rate Maneuver (NASA)
NSR	Norske Samers Riksforbund [*Norway*]
NSR	Northern Sea Route (NATG)
NSR	North Staffordshire Railway [*British*] (ROG)
NSR	No Sign of Recurrence [*Medicine*] (DMAA)
NSR	No Staff Responsibility [*Army*] (AABC)
NSR	Not Seen Regularly [*Medicine*] (DAVI)
NSR	Nova Scotia Provincial Library [*UTLAS symbol*]
NSR	Nova Scotia Regiment [*Canada*] (DMA)
NSR	NSR Resources, Inc. [*Toronto Stock Exchange symbol*]
NSR	Nuclear Spin Relaxation [*Physics*]
NSR	Nuclear Structure References [*Brookhaven National Laboratory*] [*Information service or system*]
NSR	Nutrient Supply Rate [*Oceanography*]
NSRA	National Scooter Riders Association [*British*] (DBA)
NSRA	National Service Robot Association (EA)
NSRA	National Shoe Retailers Association (EA)
NSRA	National Shorthand Reporters Association (EA)
NSRA	National Ski Retailers Association (EA)
NSRA	National Smallbore Rifle Association [*British*]
NSRA	National Society for Research into Allergy [*British*]
NSRA	National Street Rod Association (EA)
NSRA	National Swim and Recreation Association (EA)
NSRA	Nuclear Safety Research Association [*See also GAKK*] [*Japan*] (NRCH)
NSRB	National Security Resources Board [*Functions transferred to ODM, 1953*]
NSRB	Nuclear Safety Review Board (NRCH)
NSRBD	National Security Resources Board [*Functions transferred to ODM, 1953*] (GFGA)
NSRC	National SIDS Resource Center (EA)
NSRC	National Silver Rabbit Club (EA)
NSRC	National Stereophonic Radio Committee
NSRC	NeoSynthesis Research Centre [*Sri Lanka*] (EAIO)
NSRC	North Stratford Railroad Corp. [*AAR code*]
NSR Coch ...	Cochran's Nova Scotia Reports [*1859*] [*A publication*] (DLA)
NSR Coh	Cohen's Nova Scotia Reports [*A publication*] (DLA)
NSRD	National Security Resources Development
NSRDB	National SIGINT [*Signal Intelligence*] Requirements Database (MCD)
NSRDC	National Standards Reference Data Center
NSRDC	[*David W. Taylor*] Naval Ship Research and Development Center (AAGC)
NSRDC/A	Naval Ship Research and Development Center, Annapolis [*Maryland*] Division (DNAB)
NSRDC(AD)...	Naval Ship Research and Development Center (Annapolis Division)
NSRDCANNADIV...	Naval Ship Research and Development Center, Annapolis [*Maryland*] Division (DNAB)
NSRDF	Naval Supply Research and Development Facility
NSRDL	Naval Ship Research and Development Laboratory (MCD)
NSRDL/A	Naval Ship Research and Development Laboratory, Annapolis [*Maryland*]
NSRDL/PC ...	Naval Ship Research and Development Laboratory, Panama City [*Florida*] [*Later, NCSC*]
NSRDS	National Standard Reference Data System [*Gaithersburg, MD*] [*National Institute of Standards and Technology*]
NSREA	National Society of Real Estate Appraisers (NTPA)
NSREC	National Society's Religious Education Centre (AIE)
NSREF	National Society for Real Estate Finance [*Washington, DC*] (EA)
NS Rev Stat...	Nova Scotia Revised Statutes [*Canada*] [*A publication*] (DLA)
NSRF	National Stroke Recovery Foundation (EA)
NSRF	Naval Ship Repair Facility (MCD)
NSRF	Naval Strategic Reserve Fleet
NSRFC	Nova Scotia Research Foundation Corp. [*Crown Corp.*] [*Canada*] (IRC)
NSRG & O ...	Nova Scotia Reports, by Geldert and Oxley [*A publication*] (DLA)
NSRG & R ...	Nova Scotia Reports, by Geldert and Russell [*A publication*] (DLA)
NSRJ	Nova Scotia Reports (James) [*A publication*] (DLA)
NSR (James)...	Nova Scotia Reports (James) [*Canada*] [*A publication*] (DLA)

NSRL	National SIGINT [*Signal Intelligence*] Requirements List (MCD)
NSRL	Nuclear Structure Research Laboratory (NRCH)
NSRM	National Strategy for Rangeland Management [*Australia*]
NSRMCA.....	National Star Route Mail Contractors Association (EA)
NSRMP	Net Survival Rate for Monocyclic Process
NSRN..........	National School Resource Network [*Defunct*] (EA)
NSRO..........	Navy Resale System Office (PDAA)
NSR Old	Oldright's Nova Scotia Reports [*A publication*] (DLA)
NSRP..........	National Search and Rescue Plan
NSRP	National States Rights Party (EA)
NSRP..........	Neutral Seat Reference Point (MCD)
NSRP	Nonstandard Part Request
NSRP..........	Nontechnical Support Real Property
NSRP..........	Nordic Society for Radiation Protection [*See also NSFS*] [*Helsinki, Finland*] (EAIO)
NSRPr..........	NorfolkSo'nRy$2.60cmPfd [*NYSE symbol*] (TTSB)
NSR PSU	Non Self-Representing Primary Sampling Unit [*Bureau of the Census*] (GFGA)
NSRQCE......	National Symposium on Reliability and Quality Control in Electronics (MCD)
NSRR..........	Normal Sinus Rate and Rhythm [*Cardiology*] (DAVI)
NSRR..........	Nuclear Safety Research Reactors (NRCH)
NSRR & C ...	Russell and Chesley's Nova Scotia Reports [*10-12 Nova Scotia Reports*] [*1875-79*] [*A publication*] (DLA)
NSRR & G ...	Russell and Geldert's Nova Scotia Reports [*A publication*] (DLA)
NSRS	National Scholarship Research Service [*Information service or system*] (IID)
NSRS	National Shoreline Refuse Survey [*British*]
NSRS	National Spatial Reference System [*Marine science*] (OSRA)
NSRS	National Supply Radio Station (MCD)
NSRS	Naval Supply Radio Station
NSRT	Near-Surface Radiation Thermometer
NSRT	Near Surface Reference Temperature [*Oceanography*]
NSRT	North South Roundtable (EAIO)
NSR Thom ...	Thomson's Nova Scotia Reports [*A publication*] (DLA)
NSRU..........	North Star Universal [*NASDAQ symbol*] (TTSB)
NSRU..........	North Star Universal, Inc. [*NASDAQ symbol*] (NQ)
NSrU	Ulster County Community College, Stone Ridge, NY [*Library symbol Library of Congress*] (LCLS)
NSRW..........	Nuclear Service Raw Water (IEEE)
NSR Wall....	Wallace's Nova Scotia Reports [*6 Nova Scotia Reports*] [*1884-1907*] [*A publication*] (DLA)
NSRWP.......	Nuclear Service Raw Water Pump [*Electronics*] (IAA)
NSRy	Norfolk Southern Railway Co. [*Associated Press*] (SAG)
NSS	National Sample Survey (PDAA)
NSS	National Sculpture Society (EA)
NSS	National Search and Rescue Secretariat [*Canada*] (DA)
NSS	National Secular Society [*British*] (DBA)
NSS	National Seismic Stations
NSS	National Serigraph Society [*Defunct*]
NSS	National Service Secretariat (EA)
NSS	National Slovak Society of the USA
NSS	National Snapdragon Society (EA)
NSS	National Space Society (EA)
NSS	National Space Station [*NASA*] (IAA)
NSS	National Speleological Society (EA)
NSS	National Staff Side [*British*]
NSS	National Stockpile Site
NSS	National Study Service [*Defunct*] (EA)
NSS	National Supply System (MCD)
NSS	National Surveillance Scheme (WDAA)
NS/S	Native Seeds/SEARCH [*Southwestern Endangered Arid-Land Resource Clearing House*] (EA)
NSS	Naval Sea Systems Command, Washington, DC [*OCLC symbol*] (OCLC)
NSS	Naval Security Station (NVT)
NSS	Naval Simulation System [*DoD*]
NSS	Naval Strategic Study
NSS	Navigation Subsystem Switchboard
NSS	Navy Secondary Standards (MSA)
NSS	Navy Shore Station (IAA)
NSS	Navy Standard Score (DNAB)
NSS	Navy Strategic Study
NSS	Navy Supply System
NSS	Network Supervisor System
NSS	Network Support System [*Computer science*]
NSS	Network Synchronization Subsystem [*Telecommunications*] (TEL)
NSS	Neurological Soft Signs [*Occupational therapy*]
NSS	Neuropathy Symptom Score
NSS	Neutral Safety Switch [*Automotive engineering*]
NSS	Neutral Speed Stability (PDAA)
NSS	Neutron Scattering Society
NSS	Neutron Spectrometer System
NSS	[*The*] Newburgh & South Shore Railway Co. [*AAR code*]
NSS	New Statesman and Society [*A publication*]
NSS	Nitrogen Supply Subsystem
NSS	Nitrogen Supply System [*or Subsystem*] (AAG)
NSS	NMIC [*National Military Information Center*] Support System (MCD)
NSS	Nodding Subdish System
NSS	Noise Suppressor System (MCD)
NSS	Non-Salt Sensitive
NSS	Non-Sea Salt
NSS	Non-Self-Sustaining [*Container ship*] (MCD)
NSS	Nonstandard Facilities Setup [*Computer science*]
NSS	Nordiska Kommitten for Samordning av Elektriska Sakerhetsfragor [*Nordic Committee for Coordination of Electrical Safety Matters*] (EAIO)
NSS	Nordiska Statistiska Sekretariatet [*Nordic Statistical Secretariat*] (EAIO)
NSS	Normal Saline Solution
NSS	Northstar Aviation, Inc. [*ICAO designator*] (FAAC)
NSS	Northwest Steam Society (EA)
NSS	Nortronics System Support
NSS	Not Statistically Significant (MAE)
NSS	NS Group [*NYSE symbol*] (SPSG)
NSS	Nuclear Science Symposium (PDAA)
NSS	Nuclear Steam System (NRCH)
NSSA	National Sanitary Supply Association [*Later, ISSA*] (EA)
NSSA	National Scholastic Surfing Association (EA)
NSSA	National Science Supervisors Association (EA)
NSSA	National Senior Sports Association (EA)
NSSA	National Sjogren's Syndrome Association (EA)
NSSA	National Skeet Shooting Association (EA)
NSSA	National Sportscasters and Sportswriters Association (EA)
NSSA	National Suffolk Sheep Association (EA)
NSSA	National Sunday School Association [*Defunct*] (EA)
NSSA	National Swim School Association (EA)
NSSA	Navy Space Systems Activity [*Los Angeles, CA*] (MCD)
NSSA	Nematological Society of Southern Africa (EAIO)
NSSA	New York Skirt and Sportswear Association (EA)
N-SSA	North-South Skirmish Association (EA)
NSSA	Nova Scotia Society of Artists [*1922-72*] [*Canada*] (NGC)
NSSAB	National Selective Service Appeal Board [*of SSS*] [*Inactive since 1975*]
NSSAC	National Society, Sons of the American Colonists [*Defunct*] (EA)
NSS&FFA.....	National Soft Serve and Fast Food Association (NTPA)
NSSAR	National Society, Sons of the American Revolution (EA)
NSSB	National Society of Scabbard and Blade (EA)
NSSB	Norwich Financial [*NASDAQ symbol*] (TTSB)
NSSB	Norwich Financial Corp. [*NASDAQ symbol*] (NQ)
NSSC	Cape Breton Regional Library, Sydney, Nova Scotia [*Library symbol National Library of Canada*] (NLC)
NSSC	Napco Security Sys [*NASDAQ symbol*] (TTSB)
NSSC	Napco Security Systems, Inc. [*NASDAQ symbol*] (NQ)
NSSC	NASA Safety Standards Committee
NSSC	National School Safety Center
NSSC	National Society for the Study of Communication [*Later, ICA*] (EA)
NSSC	National Soil Survey Committee [*Canada*]
NSSC	National Space Science Center [*British*]
NSSC	Naval Sea [*formerly, Ship*] Systems Command
NSSC	Neutral Sulfite Semichemical [*Pulp*]
NSSC	Neutral Sulfite Semimechanical Process (EDCT)
NSSCB	Cape Breton Post, Sydney, Nova Scotia [*Library symbol National Library of Canada*] (NLC)
NSSCBD......	Cape Breton Development Corp., Sydney, Nova Scotia [*Library symbol National Library of Canada*] (NLC)
NSSCBH......	Cape Breton Hospital, Sydney, Nova Scotia [*Library symbol National Library of Canada*] (NLC)
NSSCC	National Space Surveillance Control Center
NSSCDS	Naval Small Ship Combat Data System (SAA)
NSSCG........	Canadian Coast Guard College [*College de la Garde Cotiere Canadienne*] Sydney, Nova Scotia [*Library symbol National Library of Canada*] (NLC)
NSSCM	Shelburne County Museum, Nova Scotia [*Library symbol National Library of Canada*] (NLC)
NSSCO........	Coast Guard, Shelburne, Nova Scotia [*Library symbol National Library of Canada*] (NLC)
NSSCS	Non-Self-Sustaining Containership [*Environmental science*] (COE)
NSSD	National Strategy for Sustainable Development [*Australia*]
NSSDC	National Space Science Data Center [*Greenbelt, MD*] [*NASA*] (MCD)
NSSDP	National Society of Sons and Daughters of the Pilgrims (EA)
NSsE..........	Empire State College, Saratoga Springs, NY [*Library symbol Library of Congress*] (LCLS)
NSSE	National Society for the Study of Education (EA)
NSSE	National Study of School Evaluation (EA)
NSSEA	National School Supply and Equipment Association (EA)
NSSEB	Non-Social Security Equivalent Benefit
NSSET	National Symposium on Space Electronics and Telemetry [*IEEE*] (MCD)
NSSF	National Shooting Sports Foundation (EA)
NSSF	National Social Science Foundation [*Proposed in 1966*]
N/SSF	Novice, Society of St. Francis
NSSFA	National Single Service Food Association (EA)
NSSFC	National Severe Storms Forecast Center [*National Oceanic and Atmospheric Administration*]
NSSFC	National Society of Student Film Critics [*Defunct*] (EA)
NSSFFA	National Soft Serve and Fast Food Association (EA)
NSSFNS......	National Scholarship Service and Fund for Negro Students (EA)
NSSG	National Ski Study Group [*Defunct*]
NSSHA	National Spotted Saddle Horse Association (EA)
NSSHA	National Student Speech and Hearing Association [*Later, NSSLHA*] (EA)
NSSHCF	Canadian Forces Base Barrington, Stone Horse, Nova Scotia [*Library symbol National Library of Canada*] (NLC)
NSSHDC	National Spanish Speaking Housing Development Corp.
NSSHET	Newcomen Society for the Study of the History of Engineering and Technology [*British*] (EAIO)
NSSI	Nuclear Support Services, Inc. [*NASDAQ symbol*] (NQ)

NS-SIB......... NAVSHIPS [*Naval Ship Systems Command*] Ship Information Booklets
NSSIC.......... National Student Strike Information Center [*Brandeis University*]
NSSJD......... Community of the Nursing Sisters of St. John the Divine [*Anglican religious community*]
NSSK........... National Society of Student Keyboardists (EA)
NSSK........... North-South Station-Keeping (PDAA)
NSSL........... National Seed Storage Laboratory [*Department of Agriculture*] [*Fort Collins, CO*] (GRD)
NSSL........... National Service Star Legion (EA)
NSSL........... National Severe Storms Laboratory [*National Oceanic and Atmospheric Administration*] [*Research center*]
NSSL........... National Society of State Legislators [*Later, NCSL*]
NSSL........... National Survey of State Laws [*A publication*]
NSSLC......... National Social Science and Law Center (EA)
NSSLHA....... National Student Speech Language Hearing Association (EA)
NSSLP......... National Social Science and Law Project (EA)
NSSM.......... National Security Study Memorandum [*Obsolete*]
NSSM.......... Navy Spread Spectrum MODEM (MCD)
NSSMM........ Memorial High School, Sydney Mines, Nova Scotia [*Library symbol National Library of Canada*] (NLC)
NSSMS........ NATO Sea Sparrow Missile System
NSSN.......... National Speed Sport News [*A publication*]
NSSN.......... National Standard Shipping Note (DS)
NSSN.......... National Standards Systems Network
NSSNF........ Naval Strategic Systems Navigation Facility
NSSO.......... National Society of Student Organists [*Later, NSSK*] (EA)
NSSO.......... National Solar Space Observatory [*NASA*]
NSSO.......... Navy Ships' Store Office [*PX*]
NSSP.......... National Severe Storms Project [*National Oceanic and Atmospheric Administration*]
NSSP.......... National Shellfish Sanitation Program [*Food and Drug Administration*] (GFGA)
NSSP.......... National Syrian Socialist Party [*Lebanon*] [*Political party*]
NSSP.......... Nava Sama Samaja Party [*New Equal Society Party*] [*Sri Lanka*] [*Political party*] (PPW)
NSSP.......... Neutralization Self-Solidification Process (PDAA)
NSSP.......... Nonreporting Secondary Stock Point (AFIT)
NSSP.......... Normal Size, Shape, and Position [*On examination*] [*Anatomy*] (DAVI)
NSSPAVAF... Normal Size, Shape, and Position Anteverted, and Anteflexed [*Uterus*] [*On examination*] [*Gynecology*] (DAVI)
NSSR.......... National Spotted Swine Record (EA)
NSSR.......... New School for Social Research [*New York, NY*]
NSSR.......... Nordic Society of Space Research
NSSR.......... Record, Springhill, Nova Scotia [*Library symbol National Library of Canada*] (NLC)
NSSRA........ National Ski & Snowboard Retailers Association (NTPA)
NSSRI......... Nervous System Sports-Related Injury [*Medicine*]
NSSRM........ Soluth Rawdon Museum, Nova Scotia [*Library symbol National Library of Canada*] (NLC)
NSSS.......... National Sewage Sludge Survey [*Environmental Protection Agency*]
NSSS.......... National Space Surveillance System
NSSS.......... Nuclear Steam Supply System [*Vendor*] (NRCH)
NSsS.......... Skidmore College, Saratoga Springs, NY [*Library symbol Library of Congress*] (LCLS)
NSsSA........ Southern Adirondack Library System, Saratoga Springs, NY [*Library symbol Library of Congress*] (LCLS)
NSsSC........ Supreme Court Library at Saratoga Springs, Saratoga Springs, NY [*Library symbol*] [*Library of Congress*] (LCLS)
NSSSE........ National Study of Secondary School Evaluation [*Later, NSSE*] (EA)
NSSSRH...... St. Rita's Hospital, Sydney, Nova Scotia [*Library symbol National Library of Canada*] (NLC)
NSSSS........ Nuclear Steam Supply Shutoff System (NRCH)
NSST.......... Nonspecific ST Segment Changes [*On electroencephalogram*] [*Cardiology*] (DAVI)
NSST.......... Northwestern Syntax Screening Test [*Education*]
NSSTA........ National Structured Settlements Trade Association (EA)
NS Stat....... Nova Scotia Statutes [*Canada*] [*A publication*] (DLA)
NSSTC........ National Small Shipments Traffic Conference (EA)
NSSTE........ National Society of Sales Training Executives [*Orlando, FL*] (EA)
NSSTT........ Nonspecific ST and T [*Wave on electrocardiogram*] [*Cardiology*] (DAVI)
NSSU.......... National Steam Service Union [*British*]
NSSU.......... National Sunday School Union [*British*]
NSSUP........ National Society of the Sons of Utah Pioneers (EA)
NSSX.......... National Sanitary Supply Co. [*NASDAQ symbol*] (NQ)
NSSX.......... Natl Sanitary Supply [*NASDAQ symbol*] (TTSB)
NSSX.......... University College of Cape Breton, Sydney, Nova Scotia [*Library symbol National Library of Canada*] (NLC)
NSSXA........ Archives and General Library, College of Cape Breton, Sydney, Nova Scotia [*Library symbol National Library of Canada*] (NLC)
NSSY.......... Norwalk Savings Society [*NASDAQ symbol*] (SAG)
NSSYA........ National Small Sailing Yacht Association (EA)
NST............ Aviacion Ejecutiva del Noroeste SA de CV [*Mexico ICAO designator*] (FAAC)
NST............ Nasty (ABBR)
NST............ National Skills Training
NST............ National Standard Taper (IAA)
NST............ National Symposium on Telemetering (MCD)
NST............ Navy Shipboard Terminal
NST............ Navy Standard Teleprinter (DOMA)
NST............ Nest (ABBR)
NST............ Nesting Module (MCD)
NST............ Network Support Team [*NASA*] (KSC)
NST............ Newfoundland Standard Time [*Aviation*] (AIA)
NST............ New Serial Titles [*A publication of Library of Congress*]
NST............ New Serial Titles, Library of Congress, Washington, DC [*OCLC symbol*] (OCLC)
NST............ Noise Source Tube
NST............ Noise, Spikes, and Transients (PDAA)
NST............ Nonshivering Thermogenesis [*Physiology*]
NST............ Nonslip Tread [*Technical drawings*]
NST............ Nonstress Test [*Gynecology*]
NST............ Normal Sphincter Tone [*Gastroenterology*] (DAVI)
NST............ North Solomon Trench [*Geoscience*]
NST............ Not Sooner Than
NST............ Nuclear and Space Talks (DOMA)
NST............ Nuclear Spin Tomography (DB)
NST............ Numerical Surveying Technique (PDAA)
NST............ Nutritional Support Team [*Dietetics*] (DAVI)
NSTA.......... Anesta Corp. [*NASDAQ symbol*] (SAG)
NSTA.......... National Safe Transit Association (EA)
NSTA.......... National School Transportation Association (EA)
NSTA.......... National Science Teachers Association (EA)
NSTA.......... National Security Traders Association [*Later, STA*] (EA)
NSTA.......... National Shoe Traveler's Association (EA)
NSTA.......... National Spasmodic Torticollis Association (EA)
NSTA.......... National Squash Tennis Association (EA)
NSTA.......... Nova Scotia Agricultural College, Truro, Nova Scotia [*Library symbol National Library of Canada*] (NLC)
NS-TAB....... NAVSHIPS [*Naval Ship Systems Command*] Training Aid Bulletins
NSTAC........ National Security Telecommunications Advisory Committee (NITA)
NSTAF........ National Solar Technical Audience File [*Solar Energy Research Institute*] [*Database*]
NSTAG........ National Science and Technology Advisory Group [*Australia*]
NStand....... National Standard Co. [*Associated Press*] (SAG)
NSTAP........ National Strategic Targeting and Attack Policy (CINC)
NSTARS...... Navy Standard Tracking and Retrieval System (MCD)
NStarU........ North Star Universal, Inc. [*Associated Press*] (SAG)
NSTB.......... Biblio-Tech Ltd., Three Fathom Harbor, Nova Scotia [*Library symbol National Library of Canada*] (NLC)
NSTB.......... National Science and Technology Board [*Singapore*]
NStBU......... St. Bonaventure University, St. Bonaventure, NY [*Library symbol Library of Congress*] (LCLS)
NSTC.......... Colchester - East Hants Regional Library, Truro, Nova Scotia [*Library symbol National Library of Canada*] (NLC)
NSTC.......... National Science and Technology Council [*Formerly, FCCSET*]
NSTC.......... National Security Training Commission [*Expired, 1957*]
NSTC.......... National Shade Tree Conference [*Later, ISA*]
NSTC.......... National Spiritualist Teachers Club (EA)
NSTC.......... Nineteenth Century Short Title Catalogue [*Avero Publications Ltd.*] [*Information service or system British*] (CRD)
NSTC.......... Nonsmokers' Travel Club [*Defunct*] (EA)
NSTC.......... Not Subject to Call (MHDB)
NSTC.......... Nova Scotia Teachers College [*Canada*]
NSTC.......... Nova Scotia Technical College
NSTCH........ Colchester Historical Society, Truro, Nova Scotia [*Library symbol National Library of Canada*] (BIB)
NST-D......... Navy Standard Transmission [*Dension hydraulics*] (CAAL)
NSTD.......... Nested [*Packaging*]
NSTD.......... Non-System Training Devices [*USA*]
NSTDB........ National Strategic Target Data Base (CINC)
NSTDH........ National STD [*Sexually Transmitted Disease*] Hotline (EA)
NSTDN........ Daily News, Truro, Nova Scotia [*Library symbol National Library of Canada*] (NLC)
NSTDP........ National Society of Tole and Decorative Painters (EA)
N-STDS....... Navy Standards (AAGC)
NSTE.......... National Society of Telephone Employees [*A union*] [*British*]
NSTEP........ National Spit Tobacco Education Program [*An initiative of Oral Health America*]
NSTEP........ Naval Scientist Training and Exchange Program (DNAB)
NSTF.......... Fraser Culture Centre, Tatamagouche, Nova Scotia [*Library symbol National Library of Canada*] (NLC)
NSTF.......... National Scholarship Trust Fund [*An affiliate of the Graphic Arts Technical Foundation*]
NSTF.......... Near Surface Test Facility [*Nuclear energy*] (NUCP)
NSTF.......... Neutron Sensor Testing Facility (IAA)
NSTF.......... Nuclear Science and Technology Facility [*State University of New York at Buffalo*] [*Research center*] (RCD)
NSTFI......... Nuveen Select Tax Free Income Portfolio [*Associated Press*] (SAG)
NSTFI2....... Nuveen Select Tax Free Income Portfolio 2 [*Associated Press*] (SAG)
NSTFI3....... Nuveen Select Tax Free Income Portfolio 3 [*Associated Press*] (SAG)
NSTG.......... Nesting (ABBR)
NSTG.......... Nuclear Strike Target Graphic (MCD)
NSTI........... NASCOM [*NASA Communications Network*] Simulation Traffic Interface (SSD)
NSTIC......... Naval Science and Technology Information Centre (NITA)
NSTIC......... Naval Scientific and Technical Information Centre [*Later, DRIC*] [*British*] (MCD)
NSTIC......... Navy Scientific and Technical Intelligence Center (IEEE)
NSTICLANT... Naval Scientific and Technical Intelligence Center, Atlantic (DNAB)
NSTICPAC.... Naval Scientific and Technical Intelligence Center, Pacific (DNAB)
NSTIM......... Islands Museum and Tourist Bureau, Tiverton, Nova Scotia [*Library symbol National Library of Canada*] (NLC)
NStj............ Margaret Reaney Memorial Library, St. Johnsville, NY [*Library symbol*] [*Library of Congress*] (LCLS)
NSTK.......... Nastech Pharmaceutical [*NASDAQ symbol*] (TTSB)

NSTK	Nastech Pharmaceuticals [*NASDAQ symbol*] (SAG)
NSTKW	Nastech Pharmaceutical Wrrt [*NASDAQ symbol*] (TTSB)
NSTL	National Software-Testing Laboratories [*Computer science*]
NSTL	National Space Technology Laboratories [*Formerly, MTF*] [*Mississippi*] [*NASA*]
NSTL	National Strategic Target Line [*or List*] (AFM)
NSTL	Nestled (ABBR)
NSTL	Nuclear Services and Training Laboratory [*Ohio State University*] [*Research center*] (RCD)
NSTLG	Nestling (ABBR)
NSTLG	Nostalgia (ABBR)
NSTLGC	Nostalgic (ABBR)
NSTM	Naval School Transportation Management
NSTM	Navy Ship Technical Manual (CAAL)
NSTM	Navy Standard Test Model (CAAL)
NSTM	Nordiska Skeppstekniska Mote [*Joint Committee of Nordic Marine Technology - JCNMT*] (EAIO)
NS-TMI	NAVSHIPS [*Naval Ship Systems Command*] Technical Manual Index
NSTN	Nonstandard Telephone Number [*Telecommunications*] (TEL)
NSTN	[*The*] Nova Scotia Technology Network [*Canada*] [*Computer science*] (TNIG)
NSTNS	Nastiness (ABBR)
NSTO	New System Training Office [*Army*]
NSTO	Non Statutory Training Organisation [*British*]
NSTOA	National Ski Touring Operators' Association (EA)
NSTP	National Society of TV Producers (NTCM)
NSTP	Nuffield Service Teaching Project
NSTPS	Law Library, Patterson, Smith, Mathews & Grant, Truro, Nova Scotia [*Library symbol National Library of Canada*] (NLC)
NSTR	Naval Sea Systems Command Technical Representative
NSTR	Northstar Health Services, Inc. [*NASDAQ symbol*] (SAG)
NSTR	Record, Truro, Nova Scotia [*Library symbol National Library of Canada*] (NLC)
NSTRE	Northstar Health Svcs [*NASDAQ symbol*] (TTSB)
NSTS	National Sea Training Schools [*British*]
NSTS	National Securities Trading System
NSTS	National Space Transportation System
NSTS	National Student Traffic Safety Program [*National Commission on Safety Education*] [*Washington, DC*] (AEBS)
NST-S	National Support Team-Sarajevo [*Military*]
NSTS	Navy Stockpile to Target Sequence
NSTS	NCC [*Navy Command Center*] Security Test System
NSTSPO	National Space Transportation System Program Office (SSD)
NSTT	National Sea Training Trusts [*British*] (DS)
NSTT	Naval Strategy Think Tank (DOMA)
NSTT	Nonseminomatous Testicular Tumor [*Medicine*] (DMAA)
NSTT	Nova Scotia Teachers' College, Truro, Nova Scotia [*Library symbol National Library of Canada*] (NLC)
NSTTF	National Solar Thermal Test Facility [*Sandia National Laboratories*]
NSTU	Pago Pago/International, Tutuila Island [*American Samoa*] [*ICAO location identifier*] (ICLI)
NST-V	Navy Standard Transmission [*Vickers hydraulics*] (CAAL)
NSTW	National Science and Technology Week [*An annual outreach program begun in 1985 by the National Science Foundation*]
NSTX	National Spherical Torus Experiment [*Plasma physics*]
NSTY	Nastily (ABBR)
NSU	Naval Scout Unit
NSU	Neckarsulm [*Location in Wuerttemberg, Germany, of NSU Werke, automobile manufacturer; initialism used as name of its cars*]
NSU	Neighborhood Stabilization Unit (LAIN)
NSU	Network Service Unit (NITA)
NSU	Neurosurgical Unit [*Medicine*] (DMAA)
NSU	Nitrogen Supply Unit (AAG)
NSU	Nonspecific Urethritis [*Medicine*]
NSU	North Stansbury [*Utah*] [*Seismograph station code, US Geological Survey*] (SEIS)
NSU	Nuova Sinistra Unita [*New United Left*] [*Italy Political party*] (PPE)
NSUA	Nigerian Students Union in the Americas (EA)
NSuf	Suffern Free Library, Suffern, NY [*Library symbol Library of Congress*] (LCLS)
NSufA	Avon Products, Inc., Suffern, NY [*Library symbol Library of Congress*] (LCLS)
NSufR	Rockland Community College, Suffern, NY [*Library symbol Library of Congress*] (LCLS)
NSUK	Nichiren Shoshu of the UK [*Buddhist organization*] (DI)
NSUP	Naval Supply Systems Command Headquarters
NSUPSC	Naval Supply Systems Command [*Formerly, Bureau of Supplies and Accounts*] (MCD)
NSURG	Neurosurgery [*Medicine*]
NSUS	Newcomen Society of the United States (EA)
NSv	Finkelstein Memorial Library, Spring Valley, NY [*Library symbol Library of Congress*] (LCLS)
NSV	National Socialist Vanguard (EA)
NSV	Negative Supply Voltage
NSV	Net Sales Value (BUR)
NSV	Netted Secure Voice [*Military*] (CAAL)
NSV	Neurosecretory Vesicle [*Neuroanatomy*]
NSV	Noise, Shock, and Vibration (PDAA)
NSV	Nonautomatic Self-Verification [*Computer science*] (MDG)
NSV	Nonspecific Vaginitis [*Medicine*]
NSV	Nonspinning Vehicle
NSV	Nova Scotia Savings & Loans Co. [*Toronto Stock Exchange symbol*]
NSV	Nuclear Service Vessel
NSVA	Navy Seabee Veterans of America (EA)
NSVA	New South Wales Vigoro Association [*Australia*]

NSVC	National Sisters Vocation Conference [*Later, NRVC*] (EA)
NSVD	Normal Spontaneous Vaginal Delivery [*Obstetrics*] (DMAA)
NSVEA	Natural-Source Vitamin E Association (EA)
NSVP	National School Volunteer Program (EA)
NSVP	National Student Volunteer Program [*Later, NCSL*] (EA)
N/SVQ	National/Scottish Vocational Qualification (WDAA)
NSVRA	National Stenomask Verbatim Reporters Association (NTPA)
NSVT	Nonsustained Ventricular Tachycardia [*Medicine*] (CPH)
NSW	Ansett Airlines of New South Wales [*Australia ICAO designator*] (FAAC)
NSW	National Software Works
NSW	Naval Special Warfare (NVT)
NSW	New South Wales (WA)
NSW	NSP [*National Aeronautical and Space Administration Support Plan*] Status Word
NSWA	Acadia University, Wolfville, Nova Scotia [*Library symbol National Library of Canada*] (NLC)
NSWA	National Social Welfare Assembly [*Later, National Assembly of National Voluntary Health and Social Welfare Organizations*] (EA)
NSWA	National Soft Wheat Association [*Later, MNF*] (EA)
NSWA	National Stripper Well Association (EA)
NSWA	North Shore Writers Alliance (EA)
NSW Adm	New South Wales Reports, Admiralty [*A publication*] (DLA)
NSWAEM	New South Wales Assemblies' Evangelic Mission [*Australia*]
NSWAG	Department of Geography, Acadia University, Wolfville, Nova Scotia [*Library symbol Obsolete National Library of Canada*] (NLC)
NSWAGTC	New South Wales Association of Gifted and Talented Children [*Australia*]
NSWAHP	New South Wales Association of Health Professions [*Australia*]
NSWALC	New South Wales Adult Literacy Council [*Australia*]
NS Wales L	New South Wales Law [*A publication*] (DLA)
NS Wales LR Eq	New South Wales Law Reports, Equity [*A publication*] (DLA)
NSWAP	National Socialist White American Party [*Political party*]
NSWAPA	New South Wales Amateur Pistol Association [*Australia*]
NSWAR	New South Wales Arbitration Reports [*A publication*] (DLA)
NSWAS	New South Wales Association of Sephardim [*Australia*]
NSWAWL	New South Wales Animal Welfare League [*Australia*]
NSWAWPA	New South Wales Amateur Water Polo Association [*Australia*]
NSWB	New South Wales Bushmen [*British military*] (DMA)
NSWBA	New South Wales Bar Association [*Australia*]
NSWBA	New South Wales Basketball Association [*Australia*]
NSWBA	New South Wales Bridge Association [*Australia*]
NSWBAC	New South Wales Buying Advisory Center [*Australia*]
NSWBACE	New South Wales Board of Adult and Community Education [*Australia*]
NSWBBA	New South Wales Bloodhorse Breeders' Association [*Australia*]
NSWBC	Black Cultural Centre for Nova Scotia, Westphal [*Library symbol National Library of Canada*] (BIB)
NSWBCS	New South Wales Bookmakers' Cooperative Society [*Australia*]
NSWBGA	New South Wales Bowling Greenkeepers' Association [*Australia*]
NSWBIC	New South Wales Banana Industry Committee [*Australia*]
NSWBJE	New South Wales Board of Jewish Education [*Australia*]
NSW Bktcy Cas	New South Wales Reports, Bankruptcy Cases [*A publication*] (DLA)
NSWBL	New South Wales Basketball League [*Australia*]
NSWBS	New South Wales Board of Surveyors [*Australia*]
NSWBSA	New South Wales Board Sailing Association [*Australia*]
NSWC	Naval Surface Warfare [*or Weapons*] Center [*Dahlgren, VA*]
NSWCA	New South Wales Canoe Association [*Australia*]
NSWCA	New South Wales Coal Association [*Australia*]
NSWCA	New South Wales Council on the Aging [*Australia*]
NSW CAC Report	New South Wales Corporate Affairs Commission. Report [*Australia A publication*]
NSWCAF	Naval Surface Weapons Center Acoustic Facility (GRD)
NSWCC	New South Wales Canine Council [*Australia*]
NSWCC	New South Wales Council of Churches [*Australia*]
NSWCCFT	New South Wales Council for Children's Films and Television [*Australia*]
NSWCCU	New South Wales Churches Cricket Union [*Australia*]
NSWC/DL	Naval Surface Weapons Center, Dahlgren Laboratory
NSWC Eq	New South Wales Law Reports, Equity [*A publication*] (DLA)
NSWCF	New South Wales Cycling Federation [*Australia*]
NSWCFA	New South Wales Canning Fruitgrowers' Association [*Australia*]
NSWCFVI	New South Wales Chamber of Fruit and Vegetable Industries [*Australia*]
NSWCGA	New South Wales Cane Growers' Association [*Australia*]
NSWCGA	New South Wales Cherry Growers' Association [*Australia*]
NSWCGA	New South Wales Chicken Growers' Association [*Australia*]
NSWCGC	New South Wales Citrus Growers' Council [*Australia*]
NSWCHS	New South Wales Cooperative Housing Society [*Australia*]
NSWCMACA	New South Wales Chinese Martial Arts and Cultural Association [*Australia*]
NSWCMC	New South Wales Chicken Meat Council [*Australia*]
NSWCMOA	New South Wales Coal Mine Owners' Association [*Australia*]
NSWCOA	New South Wales Colliery Officials' Association [*Australia*]
NSWCOHO	New South Wales Council of Heritage Organizations [*Australia*]
NSWCOTA	New South Wales Council on the Aging [*Australia*]
NSWCPA	New South Wales Coal Proprietors' Association [*Australia*]
NSWCPC	New South Wales Child Protection Council [*Australia*]
NSWCRL	New South Wales Law Reports, Supreme Court [*A publication*] (DLA)
NSWCSA	New South Wales Churches Soccer Association [*Australia*]
NSWCSA	New South Wales Cold Storage Association [*Australia*]
NSWCTA	New South Wales Council of Tourist Associations [*Australia*]
NSWCUA	New South Wales Credit Unit Association [*Australia*]

NSWCUA...... New South Wales Cricket Umpires' Association [*Australia*]
NSWCUEA... New South Wales Credit Union Employers' Association [*Australia*]
NSWC/WOL... Naval Surface Weapons Center, White Oak Laboratory
NSWCYMCA... New South Wales Council of the Young Men's Christian
   Associations [*Australia*]
NSWDAA...... New South Wales Domestic Abattoirs Association [*Australia*]
NSWDAA...... New South Wales Drug and Alcohol Authority [*Australia*]
NSWDAHAC... National Society Women Descendants of the Ancient and Honorable
   Artillery Company (EA)
NSWDBA...... New South Wales Deer Breeders' Association [*Australia*]
NSW Dept Forestry Bull... New South Wales. Department of Forestry. Bulletin
   [*Australia A publication*]
NSWDFA...... New South Wales Dairy Farmers' Association [*Australia*]
NSWDFA...... New South Wales Deer Farmers' Association [*Australia*]
NSWDFB...... New South Wales Dried Fruits Board [*Australia*]
NSWDIC...... New South Wales Dairy Industry Conference [*Australia*]
NSWDPA...... New South Wales Dairy Products Association [*Australia*]
NSWDSC...... New South Wales Dam Safety Committee [*Australia*]
NSWDU...... New South Wales Debating Union [*Australia*]
NSWEEU...... New South Wales Education Exports Unit [*Australia*]
NSWEK .... Eastern King's Memorial Hospital, Wolfville, Nova Scotia [*Library
   symbol National Library of Canada*] (NLC)
NSWEPC...... New South Wales Egg Producers' Cooperative [*Australia*]
NSWEPOWA... New South Wales Ex-Prisoners of War Association [*Australia*]
NSW Eq Rep... New South Wales Law Reports, Equity [*A publication*] (DLA)
NSWETF ...... New South Wales Education and Training Foundation [*Australia*]
NSWFA .... New South Wales Farmers' Association [*Australia*]
NSWFB .... New South Wales Fire Brigades [*Australia*]
NSWFBEU ... New South Wales Fire Brigade Employee's Union [*Australia*]
NSWFC .... New South Wales Fitness Council [*Australia*]
NSWFCHA... New South Wales Farm and Country Holiday Association [*Australia*]
NSWFF .... New South Wales Folk Federation [*Australia*]
NSWFG .... New South Wales Furniture Guild [*Australia*]
NSWFGA...... New South Wales Flower Growers' Association [*Australia*]
NSWFGHC .. New South Wales Free Growers' Horticultural Council [*Australia*]
NSWFHU...... New South Wales Friends of the Hebrew University [*Australia*]
NSWFIA...... New South Wales Farmers' Industrial Association [*Australia*]
NSWFIC ...... New South Wales Fishing Industry Council [*Australia*]
NSWFITC..... New South Wales Food Industry Training Council [*Australia*]
NSWFITC..... New South Wales Furniture Industry Training Council [*Australia*]
NSWFMC...... New South Wales Flour Millers' Council [*Australia*]
NSWFPA...... New South Wales Forest Products Association [*Australia*]
NSWFPCA.... New South Wales Federation of Parents and Citizens' Associations
   [*Australia*]
NSWFS .... New South Wales Fabian Society [*Australia*]
NSWFTO...... New South Wales Film and Television Office [*Australia*]
NSWG......... Naval Special Warfare Group (NVT)
NSWG.......... North Sea Working Group [*Advisory Committee on Pollution of the
   Sea*]
NSWG......... Nuclear Safety Working Group (CINC)
NSWGA...... New South Wales Golf Association [*Australia*]
NSWGB........ New South Wales Grains Board [*Australia*]
NSWGBOTA... New South Wales Greyhound Breeders, Owners and Trainers
   Association [*Australia*]
NSWGC........ New South Wales Gun Club [*Australia*]
NSWGCB...... New South Wales Guild of Craft Bookbinders [*Australia*]
NSWGCHS... New South Wales Group of Cooperative Housing Societies
   [*Australia*]
NSWGCSUA... New South Wales Glass and Ceramic Silica Users' Association
   [*Australia*]
NSW Geol Survey Mineral Resour... New South Wales. Geological Survey. Mineral
   Resources [*Australia A publication*]
NSWGFL...... New South Wales Gridiron Football League [*Australia*]
NSWGFM...... New South Wales Guild of Furniture Manufacturers [*Australia*]
NSWGIS ...... New South Wales Government Information Service [*Australia*]
NSWGMA...... New South Wales Girls' Marching Association [*Australia*]
NSWGMA...... New South Wales Glass Merchants' Association [*Australia*]
NSWGTC ...... New South Wales Government Travel Center [*Australia*]
NSWH.......... Wolfville Historical Museum, Nova Scotia [*Library symbol National
   Library of Canada*] (NLC)
NSWHA........ New South Wales Hockey Association [*Australia*]
NSWHCA...... New South Wales Homeless Children's Association [*Australia*]
NSWHEA...... New South Wales Horticultural Exporters' Association [*Australia*]
NSWHGA ...... New South Wales Hospital Group Apprentices Scheme [*Australia*]
NSWHJ......... Hants Journal, Windsor, Nova Scotia [*Library symbol National Library
   of Canada*] (NLC)
NSWHPAC ... New South Wales Hospitals Planning Advisory Center [*Australia*]
NSWHRA ...... New South Wales Hot Rod Association [*Australia*]
NSWHS........ New South Wales Humanist Society [*Australia*]
NSWHTA...... New South Wales Hardcourt Tennis Association [*Australia*]
NSWI .... National Safe Workplace Institute (EA)
NSWICCA ..... New South Wales Indo-China Chinese Association
NSWID......... New South Wales Institute of Dieticians [*Australia*]
NSWIG......... New South Wales Industrial Gazette [*Australia A publication*]
NSW Inc Acts... New South Wales Incorporated Acts [*A publication*] (DLA)
NSW Ind Arbtn... New South Wales Industrial Arbitration Cases [*A publication*]
   (DLA)
NSW Ind Arbtn Cas... New South Wales Industrial Arbitration Cases
   [*A publication*] (DLA)
NSW Indus Arb R... New South Wales Industrial Arbitration Reports
   [*A publication*] (DLA)
NSWIP........ New South Wales Institute of Physiotherapy [*Australia*]
NSWIP........ New South Wales Institute of Psychotherapy [*Australia*]
NSWJB .... New South Wales Judgements Bulletin [*Australia A publication*]
NSWJBD ...... New South Wales Jewish Board of Deputies [*Australia*]

NSWJCU...... New South Wales Junior Cricket Union [*Australia*]
NSWJHS ...... New South Wales Jersey Herd Society [*Australia*]
NSWJT......... Materials Laboratory Library, Nova Scotia Department of
   Transportation, Windsor Junction, Nova Scotia [*Library symbol
   National Library of Canada*] (NLC)
NSWJWM ... New South Wales Jewish War Memorial [*Australia*]
NSWKE...... King's-Edgehill School, Windsor, Nova Scotia [*Library symbol
   National Library of Canada*] (NLC)
NSWL .... Naval Surface Warfare Laboratory
NSWL .... New South Wales Lotteries [*Australia*]
NSW Land App... New South Wales Land Appeal Court Cases [*A publication*]
   (DLA)
NSW Land App Cts... New South Wales Land Appeal Courts (DLA)
NSW Law Repts... New South Wales Law Reports [*A publication*]
NSWLC .... New South Wales Leagues Club [*Australia*]
NSWLHPB.... New South Wales Ladies Highland Pipe Band [*Australia*]
NSW Local Gov't R... New South Wales Local Government Reports
   [*A publication*] (DLA)
NSWLRC...... New South Wales Law Reform Commission [*Australia*] (ILCA)
NSWLSEA ... New South Wales Live Stock Exporters' Association [*Australia*]
NSWMA...... National Soft Wheat Millers Association [*Later, MNF*] (EA)
NSWMA...... National Solid Wastes Management Association (EA)
NSWMA...... New South Wales Marching Association [*Australia*]
NSWMA...... New South Wales Midwives' Association [*Australia*]
NSWMB ...... New South Wales Medical Board [*Australia*]
NSWMEA ..... New South Wales Meat Exporters' Association [*Australia*]
NSWMEQB.... New South Wales Migrant Employment and Qualifications Board
   [*Australia*]
NSWMH....... New South Wales Masonic Hospital [*Australia*]
NSWMIA...... New South Wales Meat Industry Authority [*Australia*]
NSWNA....... New South Wales Netball Association [*Australia*]
NSWNCA...... New South Wales National Coursing Association [*Australia*]
NSWNGA .... New South Wales Nut Growers' Association [*Australia*]
NSWNPWS.... New South Wales National Parks and Wildlife Service [*Australia*]
NSWNRB ..... New South Wales Nurses' Registration Board [*Australia*]
NSWO......... Nuclear Surface Warfare Officer [*Navy*] (DOMA)
NSWODA ..... New South Wales Oyster Distributors' Association [*Australia*]
NSWOTA...... New South Wales Occupational Therapy Association [*Australia*]
NSWOTA...... New South Wales Operating Theatre Association [*Australia*]
NSWOTA...... New South Wales Organic Traders' Association [*Australia*]
NSWP......... Non-Soviet Warsaw Pact (NATG)
NSWPA....... New South Wales Poker Association [*Australia*]
NSWPA........ New South Wales Polo Association [*Australia*]
NSWPACC.... New South Wales Police Aero Club Company [*Australia*]
NSWPBA...... New South Wales Pipe Band Association [*Australia*]
NSWPC........ New South Wales Parachute Council [*Australia*]
NSWPC........ New South Wales Parents' Council [*Australia*]
NSWPC........ New South Wales Prices Commission [*Australia*]
NSWPEA...... New South Wales Physical Education Association [*Australia*]
NSWPGA...... New South Wales Professional Golfers' Association [*Australia*]
NSWPL........ New South Wales Police Legacy [*Australia*]
NSWPMOA.... New South Wales Public Medical Officers' Association [*Australia*]
NSWPOA..... New South Wales Property Owners' Association [*Australia*]
NSWPP........ National Socialist White People's Party [*Formerly, American NAZI
   Party*] (EA)
NSWPP .... New South Wales Parliamentary Papers [*A publication*]
NSWPR....... Newspaper
NSW Priv Com Papers... New South Wales Privacy Committee. Papers [*Australia
   A publication*]
NSWPSPOA... New South Wales Public Service Professional Officers' Association
   [*Australia*]
NSW Pub Acts... New South Wales Public Acts [*A publication*] (DLA)
NSW Pub Stat... New South Wales Public Statutes [*A publication*] (DLA)
NSWRA........ New South Wales Rifle Association [*Australia*]
NSWRA........ New South Wales Rowing Association [*Australia*]
NSWRAA...... New South Wales Rural Assistance Authority [*Australia*]
NSW Railway & Tramway Mag... New South Wales Railway and Tramway
   Magazine [*Australia A publication*]
NSWRCSA ... New South Wales Registered Cereal Seedgrowers' Association
   [*Australia*]
NSWRFAC.... New South Wales Recreational Fishing Advisory Council [*Australia*]
NSWRFL...... New South Wales Rugby Football League [*Australia*]
NSWRFS..... New South Wales Rod Fishers' Society [*Australia*]
NSWRITC.... New South Wales Rural Industry Training Committee [*Australia*]
NSWRLIFA... New South Wales Rugby League Insurance Finance Agency
   [*Australia*]
NSWRTA...... New South Wales Road Transport Association [*Australia*]
NSWRTEHF... New South Wales Railway and Transport Employees' Hospital Fund
   [*Australia*]
NSWRTLA.... New South Wales Right to Life Association [*Australia*]
NSWRTM..... New South Wales Rail Transport Museum [*Australia*]
NSWRTTC.... New South Wales Road Transport Training Council [*Australia*]
NSWS .... National Surface Water Survey (GNE)
NSWS .... Nuclear Service Water System (NRCH)
NSWSA........ New South Wales Ski Association [*Australia*]
NSWSA........ New South Wales Softball Association [*Australia*]
NSWSA........ New South Wales Swimming Association [*Australia*]
NSWSACW... New South Wales Standing Advisory Committee on Wheat [*Australia*]
NSWSBA...... New South Wales Sheepbreeders' Association [*Australia*]
NSWSCC...... New South Wales Society for Crippled Children [*Australia*]
NSWSCC ..... New South Wales State Cancer Committee [*Australia*]
NSWSCR...... New South Wales Supreme Court Reports [*A publication*] (DLA)
NSW S Ct Cas... New South Wales Supreme Court Cases [*A publication*] (DLA)
NSW S Ct R... New South Wales Supreme Court Reports [*A publication*] (DLA)
NSWSDA...... New South Wales Soft Drink Association [*Australia*]

NSWSES :..... Naval Ship Weapon Systems Engineering Station [*Port Hueneme, CA*]
NSWSF .... New South Wales Soccer Federation [*Australia*]
NSWSGA...... New South Wales Seed Growers' Association [*Australia*]
NSWSHS...... New South Wales School of Hypnotic Sciences [*Australia*]
NSWSJC ...... New South Wales Show Jumping Council [*Australia*]
NSWSK .... New South Wales Shorinjiryu Karate-do Association [*Australia*]
NSWSMBA.... New South Wales Stud Merino Breeders' Association [*Australia*]
NSWSO .... New South Wales Superannuation Office [*Australia*]
NSWSRCTG... New South Wales Sales Representatives and Commercial Travellers' Guild [*Australia*]
NSWSS .... New South Wales Supply Service [*Australia*]
NSWSTC ...... New South Wales Science and Technology Council [*Australia*]
NSWSTM ..... New South Wales School of Therapeutic Massage [*Australia*]
NSWTA .... National Senior Women's Tennis Association (EA)
NSWTAFEC... New South Wales Technical and Further Education Commission [*Australia*]
NSWTC .... New South Wales Taxi Council [*Australia*]
NSWTC .... New South Wales Tourism Commission [*Australia*]
NSWTC .... New South Wales Travel Center [*Australia*]
NSWTEU ..... New South Wales Theatrical Employees' Union [*Australia*]
NSWTG .... Naval Special Warfare Task Group (CAAL)
NSWTITC ..... New South Wales Timber Industry Training Council [*Australia*]
NSWTLMB ... New South Wales Tobacco Leaf Marketing Board [*Australia*]
NSWU .... Naval Special Warfare Unit (DOMA)
NSWVRA...... New South Wales Video Retailers' Association [*Australia*]
NSWWA .... New South Wales Wrestling Association [*Australia*]
NSWWA .... North Shore Women Writers Alliance [*Later, NSWA*] (EA)
NSWWAC.... New South Wales Women's Advisory Council [*Australia*]
NSWWH....... West Hants Historical Society Museum, Windsor, Nova Scotia [*Library symbol National Library of Canada*] (NLC)
NSWWJA ..... New South Wales Women Justices' Association [*Australia*]
NSW Worker's Comp R... New South Wales Worker's Compensation Reports [*A publication*] (DLA)
NSWWP .... New South Wales Water Polo [*Australia An association*]
NSWWSA..... New South Wales Water Ski Association [*Australia*]
NSWWSBA.... New South Wales Wool Selling Brokers' Association [*Australia*]
NSXB .... Neutron Star X-Ray Binary [*Astrophysics*]
NSY .... Naval Shipyard
NSY .... New Scotland Yard
NSY .... Noisy (ABBR)
NSY .... North Salopian Yeomanry [*British military*] (DMA)
NSY .... North Somerset Yeomanry [*British military*] (DMA)
NSY .... Nursery (DAVI)
NSy .... Onondaga County Public Library, Syracuse, NY [*Library symbol Library of Congress*] (LCLS)
NSY .... Western Counties Regional Library, Yarmouth, Nova Scotia [*Library symbol National Library of Canada*] (NLC)
NSyA........... Allied Corp., Solvay Process Division, Syracuse, NY [*Library symbol Library of Congress*] (LCLS)
NSYA .... National School Yearbook Association [*Later, NSY/NA*]
NSyAF......... United States Air Force, Hancock Air Base Library, Syracuse, NY [*Library symbol Library of Congress*] (LCLS)
NSyAg......... Agway, Inc., Syracuse, NY [*Library symbol Library of Congress*] (LCLS)
NSyBL......... Bristol Laboratories, Syracuse, NY [*Library symbol Library of Congress*] (LCLS)
NSyC........... Carrier Corp., Syracuse, NY [*Library symbol Library of Congress*] (LCLS)
NSYC .... Courrier de la Nouvelle-Ecosse, Yarmouth, Nova Scotia [*Library symbol National Library of Canada*] (NLC)
NSyCA .... United States Court of Appeals, Syracuse, NY [*Library symbol Library of Congress*] (LCLS)
NSYCDA...... Archives, Diocese of Yarmouth, Catholic Church, Nova Scotia [*Library symbol National Library of Canada*] (NLC)
NSyCH .... Crouse-Irving Hospital, Syracuse, NY [*Library symbol Library of Congress*] (LCLS)
NSYD .... Naval Shipyard
NSYDCN ..... Diocese of Central New York, Syracuse, NY [*Library symbol Library of Congress*] (LCLS)
NSyEd......... Educational Opportunity Center, Syracuse, NY [*Library symbol Library of Congress*] (LCLS)
NSYF .... Natural Science for Youth Foundation (EA)
NSYFG .... Fundy Group Publications, Yarmouth, Nova Scotia [*Library symbol National Library of Canada*] (NLC)
NSyGE .... General Electric Co., Syracuse, NY [*Library symbol Library of Congress*] (LCLS)
NSyGH .... Community-General Hospital, Syracuse, NY [*Library symbol Library of Congress*] (LCLS)
NSYHM....... Research Library, Yarmouth County Historical Society, Yarmouth, Nova Scotia [*Library symbol National Library of Canada*] (NLC)
NSyL .... LeMoyne College, Syracuse, NY [*Library symbol Library of Congress*] (LCLS)
NSyLG .... Loretto Geriatric Center, Educational Resource Center, Syracuse, NY [*Library symbol Library of Congress*] (LCLS)
NSyMR .... Maria Regina College, Syracuse, NY [*Library symbol Library of Congress*] (LCLS)
NSyN .... City Normal School, Syracuse, NY [*Library symbol Library of Congress Obsolete*] (LCLS)
NSY/NA....... National School Yearbook/Newspaper Association [*Defunct*] (EA)
NSyo........... Syosset Public Library, Syosset, NY [*Library symbol Library of Congress*] (LCLS)
NSyOB .... Onondaga-Courtland-Madison Board of Cooperative Education Service, Syracuse, NY [*Library symbol*] [*Library of Congress*] (LCLS)

NSyoBaE..... Baylis Elementary School, Syosset, NY [*Library symbol Library of Congress*] (LCLS)
NSyoBE....... Berry Hill Elementary School, Syosset, NY [*Library symbol Library of Congress*] (LCLS)
NSyOC .... Onondaga Community College, Syracuse, NY [*Library symbol Library of Congress*] (LCLS)
NSyoF .... Fairchild Space and Defense System, Syosset, NY [*Library symbol Library of Congress*] (LCLS)
NSyoG .... United States Geological Survey, Water Resources Division, Syosset, NY [*Library symbol Library of Congress*] (LCLS)
NSyoH .... Syosset Hospital, Syosset, NY [*Library symbol Library of Congress*] (LCLS)
NSyOHi....... Onondaga Historical Association, Syracuse, NY [*Library symbol Library of Congress*] (LCLS)
NSyoOL .... Onondaga Library System, Syracuse, NY [*Library symbol Library of Congress*] (LCLS)
NSyoOL....... Our Lady of Mercy Academy, Syosset, NY [*Library symbol*] [*Library of Congress*] (LCLS)
NSyoP......... PRD Electronics, Inc., Information Center Library, Syosset, NY [*Library symbol Library of Congress*] (LCLS)
NSyoRE....... Robbins Elementary School, Syosset, NY [*Library symbol Library of Congress*] (LCLS)
NSyoSGE..... South Grove Elementary School, Syosset, NY [*Library symbol Library of Congress*] (LCLS)
NSyoSH ...... Syosset Senior High School, Syosset, NY [*Library symbol*] [*Library of Congress*] (LCLS)
NSyoSRE..... Split Rock Elementary School, Syosset, NY [*Library symbol Library of Congress*] (LCLS)
NSyoSwJ ..... South Woods Junior High School, Syosset, NY [*Library symbol*] [*Library of Congress*] (LCLS)
NSyoTJ .... Harry B. Thompson Junior High School, Syosset, NY [*Library symbol*] [*Library of Congress*] (LCLS)
NSyoVE....... Village Elementary School, Syosset, NY [*Library symbol Library of Congress*] (LCLS)
NSyoWE...... Willits Elementary School, Syosset, NY [*Library symbol Library of Congress*] (LCLS)
NSyoWhE.... Whitman Elementary School, Syosset, NY [*Library symbol Library of Congress*] (LCLS)
NSYR .... Medical Library, Yarmouth Regional Hospital, Nova Scotia [*Library symbol National Library of Canada*] (BIB)
NSyR .... Syracuse Research Corp., Syracuse, NY [*Library symbol*] [*Library of Congress*] (LCLS)
NSYS .... Nortech Systems [*NASDAQ symbol*] (TTSB)
NSYS .... Nortech Systems, Inc. [*NASDAQ symbol*] (SAG)
NSySC .... New York State Supreme Court Law Library, Syracuse, NY [*Library symbol*] [*Library of Congress*] (LCLS)
NSySJ .... Saint Joseph's Hospital, School of Nursing and Medical Library, Syracuse, NY [*Library symbol*] [*Library of Congress*] (LCLS)
NSYSP .... National Summer Youth Sports Program
NSySU-F...... State University of New York, College of Environmental Sciences and Forestry at Syracuse University, Syracuse, NY [*Library symbol Library of Congress*] (LCLS)
NSySU-M.... State University of New York, Upstate Medical Center, Syracuse, NY [*Library symbol Library of Congress*] (LCLS)
NSyT........... Technology Club of Syracuse, Syracuse, NY [*Library symbol Library of Congress*] (LCLS)
NSyU .... Syracuse University, Syracuse, NY [*Library symbol Library of Congress*] (LCLS)
NSyU-CE...... Syracuse University, Library of Continuing Education at Syracuse, Syracuse, NY [*Library symbol Library of Congress*] (LCLS)
NSyU-G........ Syracuse University, Educational Resources Center of the All-University Gerontology Center, Syracuse, NY [*Library symbol Library of Congress*] (LCLS)
NSyVA .... United States Veterans Administration Hospital, Syracuse, NY [*Library symbol Library of Congress*] (LCLS)
NSZP .... Nemzeti Szabadelvu Part [*National Liberal Party*] [*Hungary Political party*] (PPE)
NT.............. Iraq-Saudi Arabia Neutral Zone [*ANSI two-letter standard code*] (CNC)
NT.............. Lake State Airways [*ICAO designator*] (AD)
N-T............. Nal-Tel [*Race of maize*]
nT................ Nanotesla
NT................ Narrower Term [*Indexing*]
NT................ Naso-Tracheal [*Medicine*]
NT................ National Taranesc [*National Peasant Party*] [*Romania*] [*Political party*] (PPE)
NT................ National Team
NT................ National Theatre [*Great Britain*]
NT................ National Trust (WDAA)
NT................ National Trust for Historic Preservation
NT................ Natty (ABBR)
NT................ Naturalization Test
NT................ Naval Training
NT................ Navy Type (MSA)
NT................ Neap Tide
NT................ Near Term
NT................ Neat [*Plain*] [*Bookbinding*] (ROG)
NT.'............. Neonatal Tetanus
NT................ Neotetrazolium
NT................ Nephrostomy Tube [*Nephrology*] (DAVI)
NT................ Nested-Task [*Computer science*] (BYTE)
NT................ Net (WDAA)
NT................ Netilmicin-Ticarcillin [*Antibiotic combination*]
NT................ Nett [*Net*] [*British*] (ROG)
NT................ Net Tax [*IRS*]

N/t	Net Terms [*Business term*] (DS)	NTA	National Translator Association (EA)
NT	Net Tons [*Shipping*]	NTA	National Trappers Association (EA)
NT	Network Terminal (MCD)	NTA	National Triton Association (EA)
NT	Network Termination [*Telecommunications*]	NTA	National Trolleybus Association [*British*]
NT	Neural Tube [*Anatomy*]	NTA	National Troubleshooting Association (NTPA)
NT	Neurologically Typical [*Psychology*]	NTA	National Tuberculosis Association [*Later, American Lung Association*] (EA)
NT	Neurotensin [*Biochemistry*]		
NT	Neurotoxin [*Biochemistry*]	NTA	National Tutoring Association (NTPA)
NT	Neurotrophin [*Neurobiology*]	NTA	National Type Approval (PDAA)
NT	Neuter (WGA)	NTA	Natural Thymocytotoxic Autoantibody (DB)
NT	Neutralization Test [*Chemistry*]	NTA	Naval Technical Assistants
NT	Neutralizing (MAE)	NTA	Navy Technical Assessment (MCD)
NT	Neutral Zone [*Internet country code*]	NTA	Navy Technician Authorization (NG)
NT	Neutron Transmitter [*Nuclear energy*] (NRCH)	NTA	Near-Terminal Area [*Airports*]
NT	Nevada Territory [*Prior to statehood*]	NTA	Neher Tetrode Amplifier
NT	News/Talk [*Radio programming format*] (WDMC)	NTA	Net Tangible Assets [*Business term*] (ADA)
NT	New Taiwan	NTA	Net Technical Assessment (MCD)
NT	New Technology [*Microsoft operating system*] [*Computer science*] (PCM)	NTA	Nevada Test Site Array [*Nevada*] [*Seismograph station code, US Geological Survey*] (SEIS)
N/T	New Terms [*Business term*]	NTA	New Towns Act [*Town planning*] [*British*]
NT	New Territories [*Hong Kong*]	NTA	Nielsen Television Area (WDAA)
NT	New Testament (WDAA)	NTA	Nitrilotriacetic Acid [*Organic chemistry*]
NT	New Thailand Dollar [*Monetary unit*]	NTA	Northern Textile Association (EA)
nt	Newton (NASA)	NTA	Northern Thunderbird Air Ltd. [*Canada ICAO designator*] (FAAC)
NT	Newton	NTA	Northwest Territory Alliance (EA)
NT	New Towns [*British*]	NTA	Norwegian Telecommunications Administration [*or Agency*] [*Oslo*]
NT	New Translation	NTA	Nuclear Test Aircraft
Nt	Nicotiana tabacum [*Tobacco*]	NTA	Nurse Training Act
NT	Night (ROG)	NTa	Warner Library, Tarrytown, NY [*Library symbol Library of Congress*] (LCLS)
NT	Night Telegram		
NT	Night Trunk [*Business term*] (DCTA)	NTAA	National Travelers Aid Association (EA)
nt	Nit [*Unit of luminance*]	NTAA	Tahiti/FAAA [*French Polynesia*] [*ICAO location identifier*] (ICLI)
NT	Niton (ABBR)	NTAB	Nephrotoxic Antibody [*Medicine*] (MAE)
NT	Node Tracker [*Frye Computer Systems*] [*Telecommunications*] (PCM)	NTAB	Northern Territory Architects' Board [*Australia*]
N/T	None in Town [*Bookselling*]	NTAB	Notable (ABBR)
N/T	Nonmeasured Time	NTAB	Nuclear Technical Advisory Board [*American National Standards Institute*]
NT	Non-T Cell [*Cytology*]		
NT	Nontender (DAVI)	NTABY	Notably (ABBR)
NT	Nontight (AAG)	NTAC	National Technical Assistance Center on Family Violence [*Defunct*] (EA)
NT	Nontryptophan [*Protein-bound fluorescence*]		
NT	Nontumorous [*Medicine*] (DB)	NTAC	Naval Training Aids Center (DNAB)
NT	Nontypeable (MAE)	NTAC	New Technology Access Centre (AIE)
NT	Nordiska Transportarbetarefederationen [*Nordic Transportworkers' Federation - NTF*] (EAIO)	NTACF	Northern Territory Anti-Cancer Foundation
		NTACS	Nationwide Truck Activity Survey [*BTS*] [*FHWA*] (TAG)
NT	Nordisk Traebeskyttelsesrad [*Nordic Wood Preservation Council - NWPC*] (EAIO)	NTAF	Naval Training Aids Facility (DNAB)
		NTAG	Network Technical Architecture Group [*Library of Congress*]
NT	Normalized and Tempered (MCD)	NTaGF	General Foods Technical Center Library, Tarrytown, NY [*Library symbol Library of Congress*] (LCLS)
NT	Normal Temperature (ADA)		
NT	Normal Tour	NTaHi	Historical Society of the Tarrytowns, Tarrytown, NY [*Library symbol Library of Congress*] (LCLS)
NT	Northern Telecom Ltd. [*NYSE symbol*] (SPSG)		
NT	Northwest Territories [*Postal code*] [*Canada*]	NTAI	Nam Tai Electronics, Inc. [*NASDAQ symbol*] (NQ)
NT	Nortriptyline [*Antidepressant drug*]	NTaI	Washington Irving Home, Sleepy Hollow Restorations, Tarrytown, NY [*Library symbol Library of Congress*] (LCLS)
NT	Note [*Online database field identifier*]		
N/T	No Terms [*Shipping*]	NTAIDSC	Northern Territory AIDS [*Acquired Immune Deficiency Syndrome*] Council [*Australia*]
NT	No Test		
NT	No Tillage [*Agriculture*]	NTAIF	Nam Tai Electronics [*NASDAQ symbol*] (TTSB)
NT	No Tool (SAA)	NTaM	Marymount College, Tarrytown, NY [*Library symbol Library of Congress*] (LCLS)
NT	No Trace [*Counterintelligence*]		
NT	No Transmission [*Telecommunications*]	NTAM	New Testament Archaeology Monographs [*A publication*] (BJA)
NT	No Trump [*in game of bridge*]	NTAN	Nitrilotriacetonitrile [*Organic chemistry*]
NT	Not Tender (DAVI)	NT & SA	National Trust & Savings Association (MHDB)
NT	Not Tested	NTAP	National Targeting and Attack Policy (CINC)
NT	Not Titled [*Accounting*]	NTAP	National Track Analysis Program [*Aviation*] (FAAC)
NT	Not Typical	NTAP	Network Appliance [*NASDAQ symbol*] (TTSB)
NT	Novum Testamentum [*New Testament*] [*of the Bible*]	NTAP	Network Appliance Corp. [*NASDAQ symbol*] (SAG)
NT	Nuclear Transfer	NTAP	Notices to Airmen Publication [*A publication*] (FAAC)
NT	Nucleotidase [*An enzyme*] (DAVI)	NTap	Tappan Free Library, Tappan, NY [*Library symbol Library of Congress*] (LCLS)
nt	Nucleotide [*Genetics*] (DOG)		
NT	Nuisance Tax (MHDW)	NTA Proceedings	National Tax Association. Proceedings [*A publication*] (DLA)
NT	Numbering Transmitter	NTAR	Nonviolent Techniques Against Rape [*An association*] (EA)
NT	Nurse Technician	NTAR	Rurutu [*French Polynesia*] [*ICAO location identifier*] (ICLI)
NT	Thermal Necrosis [*Roentgenology*]	NTARH	National Teen Age Republican Headquarters (EA)
NT	Troy Public Library, Troy, NY [*Library symbol Library of Congress*] (LCLS)	NTARS	National Transportation Analysis Regions [*FHWA*] (TAG)
		NTARY	Notary (ABBR)
NT-1	Network Terminator Type 1 (PCM)	NTAS	Northern Territory Archives Service [*Australia*]
NTA	Fujisawa Pharmaceutical Co. [*Japan*] [*Research code symbol*]	NTaS	Sleepy Hollow Restorations, Tarrytown, NY [*Library symbol Library of Congress*] (LCLS)
NTA	Naphthoyltrifluoroacetone [*Organic chemistry*]		
NTA	Narcotics Treatment Administration [*Washington, DC*]	NTAT	Tubuai/Mataura [*French Polynesia*] [*ICAO location identifier*] (ICLI)
NTA	National Tabletop Association (EA)	NTATC	National Transportation Apprenticeship and Training Conference [*Bureau of Apprenticeship and Training*] [*Department of Labor*]
NTA	National Tattoo Association (EA)		
NTA	National Tax Association [*Later, NTA-TIA*] (EA)	NTA-TIA	National Tax Association - Tax Institute of America (EA)
NTA	National Tax Association-Tax Institute of America (NTPA)	NTATN	Notation (ABBR)
NTA	National Taxidermists Association [*Defunct*] (EA)	NTATNL	Notational (ABBR)
NTA	National Taxpayers Alliance (EA)	NTaUC	Union Carbide Corp., Tarrytown Technical Center, Tarrytown, NY [*Library symbol Library of Congress*] (LCLS)
NTA	National Teachers Association (AEE)		
NTA	National Technical Association (EA)	NtAust	National Australia Bank [*Associated Press*] (SAG)
NTA	National Telecommunications Agency	NTAVL	Not Available (NOAA)
NTA	National Telefilm Associates, Inc. (NTCM)	NTB	National Target Base (MCD)
NTA	National Tennis Academy [*Commercial firm*] (EA)	NTB	National Test Bed [*Military*] (SDI)
NTA	National Tennis Association [*Later, IRJA*] (EA)	NTB	Nontariff Barrier [*Kennedy Round*]
NTA	National Threshers Association (EA)	NTB	Nontumor-Bearing
NTA	National Tour Association (EA)	NTB	Norsk Telegrambyra [*Norwegian News Agency*]
NTA	National Tourism Administration [*China*] (EY)	NTB	Northumbria Tourist Board [*British*] (DCTA)
NTA	National Tourist Association (NADA)	NTB	Notable (ABBR)
		NTB	No Talent Bum [*Slang*]

NTB............ Nuclear Test Ban
NTBA .... National Tour Brokers Association (EA)
NTBA .... Northern Territory Bowls Association [*Australia*]
NTBB .... National Temporal Bone Banks Program of the DRF [*Deafness Research Foundation*] (EA)
N/TBC .... Nontuberculous [*Medicine*] (DAVI)
NTBIC .... Northern Territory Buffalo Industry Council [*Australia*]
NTBK .... Notebook (ABBR)
NTBM.......... NU-Tech Bio-Med [*NASDAQ symbol*] (TTSB)
NTBM.......... Nu-Tech Bio Med, Inc. [*NASDAQ symbol*] (SAG)
NTBPSC....... Nepal, Tibet, and Bhutan Philatelic Study Circle (EA)
NTBR .... National Temporal Bone Registry
NTBR .... Not to Be Resuscitated
NTBRB .... Northern Territory Building Referees' Board [*Australia*]
NTBS .... Northern Territory Board of Studies [*Australia*]
NT BUR STNDS... National Bureau of Standards [*Department of Commerce*] (WDAA)
NTBY .... Notably (ABBR)
NTC............ Gibson Aviation [*ICAO designator*] (FAAC)
NTC............ National Tasking Center (MCD)
NTC............ National Teachers Corps
NTC............ National Team Championship [*Swimming*] [*British*] (ROG)
NTC............ National Teen Challenge (EA)
NTC............ National Telecommunications Conference [*IEEE*]
NTC............ National Telemedia Council (EA)
NTC............ National Television Center [*Telecommunications*] (TEL)
NTC............ National Territorial Command (MCD)
NTC............ National Test Center (NATG)
NTC............ National Thanksgiving Commission (EA)
NTC............ National Theatre Conference (EA)
NTC............ National Thrift Committee [*Defunct*] (EA)
NTC............ National Timesharing Council (EA)
NTC............ National Traditionalist Caucus (EA)
NTC............ National Trails Council (EA)
NTC............ National Training Center [*Red Cross*] [*Charlottesville, VA*]
NTC............ National Training Center [*Military*] (INF)
NTC............ National Translations Center [*John Crerar Library*] [*Information service or system*]
NTC............ National Transportation Center [*Large city situated at a key junction of rail, air, and highway transportation*] [*Postal Service*]
NTC............ National Travel Club [*Commercial firm*] (EA)
NTC............ National Treatment Consortium for Alcohol and Other Drugs (EA)
NTC............ National Troopers Coalition (EA)
NTC............ Naturally Occurring Top Component [*Virology*]
NTC............ Nautical Training Corps [*British military*] (DMA)
NTC............ Naval Training Center
NTC............ Naval Training Command
NTC............ Navy Test Controller (DNAB)
NTC............ Negative Temperature Coefficient
NTC............ Negative Thermal Coefficient (IAA)
NTC............ Neotetrazolium Chloride [*A dye*]
NTC............ Network Transmission Committee [*Video Transmission Engineering Committee*] (NTCM)
NTC............ Nissan Technical Center [*Automobile manufacturing*]
NTC............ Nordic Temperance Council (EA)
NTC............ Nordic Theater Committee [*Later, NTDC*] (EAIO)
NTC............ Normal Tour of Duty Completed
ntc .... Northwest Territories [*MARC country of publication code Library of Congress*] (LCCP)
NTC............ Norwich Terrier Club [*Later, NNTC*] (EA)
NTC............ Notice
NTC............ No Traffic Reported [*Air Traffic Control*] (FAAC)
NTC............ Nucleon Transport Code
NTC............ Nu-Trans Cooperative (EA)
NTC............ Nuveen Connecticut Premium Income Municipal Fund [*NYSE symbol*] (SPSG)
NTC............ Nuveen CT Prem Inc. Muni [*NYSE symbol*] (TTSB)
NTCA .... National Telephone Cooperative Association (EA)
NTCA .... National Tile Contractors Association (EA)
NTCA .... National Town Class Association (EA)
NTCA .... National Tribal Chairman's Association [*Defunct*] (EA)
NTCA .... N-Nitrosothioazolidine Carboxylic Acid [*Organic chemistry*]
NTCA .... Northern Territory Cricket Association [*Australia*]
NtCapit .... National Capital Management Corp. [*Associated Press*] (SAG)
NTCAVAL ..... Notice of Availability
NTC/AW ...... National Training Center / Air Warrior System (DWSG)
NTCB .... (Nitro)thiocyanatobenzoic Acid [*Organic chemistry*]
NTCB .... Northern Territory Convention Bureau [*Australia*]
NTCB .... Noticeable (ABBR)
NTCBY .... Noticeably (ABBR)
NTCC .... Naval Tactical Communications Center (MCD)
NTCC .... Naval Telecommunications Center (DOMA)
NTCC .... Neutron Transport Computer Code
NTCC .... Nimbus Technical Control Center
NTCC .... Northern Territory Conservation Commission [*Australia*]
NTCCDET .... Naval Telecommunications Center Detachment (DNAB)
NTCCS .... Naval Tactical Command and Control System (PDAA)
NTCD .... Nitro(thiocyano)benzoic Acid [*Organic chemistry*]
NTCD .... Noticed (ABBR)
NTCDC .... Northern Territory Counter Disaster Council [*Australia*]
NTCF .... National Telemarketing Fulfillment Center
NTCF.......... National Toxic Campaign Fund [*An association*]
NTCFA .... Northern Territory Commercial Fishermen's Association [*Australia*]
NTCFA .... Northern Territory Crab Fishermen's Association [*Australia*]
NTCG .... Noticing (ABBR)

NTCGA........ Northern Territory Community Government Association [*Australia*]
NTCHA........ National Taxi and Car Hire Association [*British*] (BI)
NTCHBA....... National Trust Closely Held Business Association (EA)
NTCI........... National Training Center - Phase I (MCD)
NTCKR........ Nutcracker (ABBR)
NTCL........... Nautical
NTCLP........ Northern Territory Country Liberal Party [*Australia Political party*]
NTCMA........ National Traditional Country Music Association [*Later, NTMA*] (EA)
NtCmcBc...... National Commerce Bancorp [*Associated Press*] (SAG)
NTCMP........ Northern Territory Chamber of Mines and Petroleum [*Australia*]
NtCnv.......... National Convenience Stores, Inc. [*Associated Press*] (SAG)
NTCOSS....... Northern Territory Council of Social Service [*Australia*]
NTCOTA....... Northern Territory Council on the Aging [*Australia*]
NTCP........... Near-Term Construction Permit [*Nuclear energy*] (NRCH)
NTCP........... Nightcap (ABBR)
NTCP........... Non-Traditional Casting Project (EA)
NtCptr......... National Computer Systems, Inc. [*Associated Press*] (SAG)
NTCS........... Nonverbal Test of Cognitive Skills [*Intelligence test*]
NTCS-A........ Navy Tactical Command System Afloat (DOMA)
NTCSD........ Naval Training Center, San Diego
NTCSOC....... Naval Telecommunications Command Satellite Operations Center (MCD)
NTCT........... National Tennis Center Trust [*Australia*]
NTCTA .... Northern Territory Clay Target Association [*Australia*]
NTD .... Das Neue Testament Deutsch. Neues Goettinger Bibelwerk [*A publication*] (BJA)
NTD .... NASA Test Director (MCD)
NTD .... National Tap Dance Co. of Canada
NTD .... National Technology Databank [*Singapore*] (DDC)
NTD .... National Theatre of the Deaf (EA)
NTD .... National Transit Database [*FTA*] (TAG)
NTD .... Naval Training Department [*British military*] (DMA)
NTD .... Neural Tube (Closure) Defect [*Medicine*]
NTD .... Neutron Transmutation Doped [*Silicon for semiconductor use*]
NTD .... Neutron Transmutation Doping (AAEL)
NTD .... New Tyee Resources [*Vancouver Stock Exchange symbol*]
NTD .... Nitroblue Tetrazolium Dye [*Test*] [*Laboratory science*] (DAVI)
NTD .... Noise Tone Difference (DMAA)
NTD .... Nontight Door
NTD .... N-Tone International Ltd. [*Vancouver Stock Exchange symbol*]
NTD .... Nuclear Test Directorate [*Air Force*]
NTD .... Port Hueneme, CA [*Location identifier FAA*] (FAAL)
NTDA .... National Trade Development Association (WDAA)
NTDA .... National Trailer Dealers Association (EA)
NTDA .... National Tyre Distributors Association [*British*] (DBA)
NTDA .... Navy Tactical Doctrine Activity (NVT)
NTDAAM....... National Trust for the Development of African American Men (EA)
NTDAB .... Northern Territory Drug and Alcohol Board [*Australia*]
NTDB .... National Trade Data Bank (EGAO)
NTDB .... National Trade Database (ACII)
NTDC .... NanoTechnology Development Corp.
NTDC .... Naval Training Devices Center [*Port Washington, LI*]
NTDC .... Nordic Theatre and Dance Committee (EAIO)
NTDDPA....... Navy Tactical Doctrine Development and Production Activity
NTDE .... North Dakota Tracer Experiment [*Marine science*] (OSRA)
NtDentex...... National Dentex Corp. [*Associated Press*] (SAG)
NTDG .... National Teaching Development Grant [*Australia*]
NTDI .... NATO Target Data Inventory (MCD)
NTDO .... Navy Technical Data Office [*of the Office of Naval Material*]
NTDPMA....... National Tool, Die, and Precision Machining Association [*Later, NTMA*] (EA)
NTDRA........ National Tire Dealers and Retreaders Association (EA)
NTDS .... Naval Technical Data System (IAA)
NTDS .... Navy Tactical Data System
NTDS .... Northern Telecom Data Systems (NITA)
NTDSC........ Nondestructive Testing Data Support Center [*DoD*] (MCD)
NTDS/LBTS... Naval Tactical Data System / Land-Based Test Site (DNAB)
NTE .... Nantes [*France*] [*Airport symbol*] (OAG)
NTE .... National Teacher Examination
NTE .... National Transportation Exchange
NTE .... National Treasury Employees Union
NTE .... Navy Technical Evaluation (NG)
NTE .... Navy Teletypewriter Exchange [*Later, NTX*]
NTE .... Negative Thermal Expansion [*Physics*]
NTE .... Network Terminating Equipment [*Telecommunications*] (IAA)
NTE .... Neuropathy Target Esterase [*Medicine*] (DMAA)
NTE .... Neurotoxic Esterase [*Medicine*] (DMAA)
NTE .... Neutron Transient Effect
NTE .... Nontactical Equipment
NTE .... Northern Eagle Mines [*Vancouver Stock Exchange symbol*]
NTE .... Not to Exceed [*Aviation*]
NTE .... Nursing the Environment
NTEA .... National Tax Equality Association (EA)
NTEA .... National Telecommunications Electronics Administration
NTEA .... National Time Equipment Association (EA)
NTEA .... National Truck Equipment Association (EA)
NTeam........ National TechTeam, Inc. [*Associated Press*] (SAG)
NTEC .... National Telecommunications Education Committee [*North American Telecommunications Association*] [*Washington, DC Telecommunications service*] (TSSD)
NTEC .... National Traction Engine Club [*British*] (DBA)
NTEC .... Naval Training Equipment Center
NTEC .... Neose Technologies [*NASDAQ symbol*] (TTSB)
NTech......... National Technical Systems, Inc. [*Associated Press*] (SAG)
NTECPE....... Naval Training Equipment Center, Project Engineer

NTEF............	National Tennis Educational Foundation [*Later, NTFHF*] (EA)
NTEG	Integ Inc. [*NASDAQ symbol*] (SAG)
NTEI.............	New Technical Education Initiative (AIE)
NTE/IOTE	Navy Technical Evaluation/Initial Operational Test and Evaluation (MCD)
NTEL............	No-Toxic-Effect Level [*Toxicology*] (LDT)
NTelpd..........	Northwest Teleproductions, Inc. [*Associated Press*] (SAG)
NTEO	Northern Territory Electoral Office [*Australia*]
NTEP............	National Type Evaluation Program [*Environmental Protection Agency*]
NTER	Normalized Transmission Energy Requirement
N Terr..........	Northern Territory
N Terr Austl Ord...	Northern Territorial Ordinances [*Australia A publication*] (DLA)
NTES............	Northern Territory Emergency Service [*Australia*]
N-TEST	Nuclear Testing (WDAA)
NTET............	National Traction Engine Trust [*British*] (DBA)
NTEU	National Treasury Employees Union (EA)
NTeZ............	North Temperate Zone [*Planet Jupiter*]
NTF.............	National Tactical Force (NATG)
NTF.............	National Tennis Foundation [*Formerly, NTEF*] [*Later, NTFHF*] (EA)
NTF.............	National Test Facility [*Military*] (SDI)
NTF.............	National Theater File [*Theater Sources, Inc.*] [*Information service or system Defunct*] (IID)
NTF.............	National Tidal Facility [*Flinders University*] [*Australia*]
NTF.............	National Trainers Federation [*British*] (DBA)
NTF.............	National Transonic Facility [*NASA*]
NTF.............	National Transport Federation [*Australia*]
NTF.............	National Turkey Federation (EA)
NTF.............	Naval Task Force
NTF.............	Navy Technological Forecast
NTF.............	Neurotrophic Factor [*Medicine*] (DMAA)
NTF.............	Nigerian Trust Fund [*African Development Bank*]
NTF.............	Nordic Transportworkers' Federation [*See also NT*] (EAIO)
NTF.............	Nordisk Thoraxkirurgisk Forening [*Scandinavian Association for Thoracic and Cardiovascular Surgery - SATCS*] (EAIO)
NTF.............	Normal Throat Flora [*Medicine*] (DMAA)
NTF.............	No Trouble Found
NTF.............	Nuclear Test Facility
NTFA...........	National Teaching-Family Association (EA)
NTFA...........	National Track and Field Association [*Superseded by ANG*] (EA)
NTFAO.........	National Task Force on Autocratic Options (EA)
NTFC...........	National Telemarketing Fulfillment Center
NTFC...........	National Television Film Council (EA)
NTFC...........	NATO Tactical Fighter Center
NTFC...........	Nonlinear Transient Fuel Film Compsensation [*Automotive fuel system*]
NTFDC.........	Non Theatrical Film Distributors Council (EA)
NTFEEG........	National Task Force on Education for Economic Growth (EA)
NTFHF	National Tennis Foundation and Hall of Fame [*Later, ITHOF*] (EA)
NTFIC..........	Northern Territory Fishing Industry Council [*Australia*]
NTFITC.........	Northern Territory Fishing Industry Training Committee [*Australia*]
NTFL...........	National Touch Football Leagues (EA)
NTFNC	Northern Territory Field Naturalists' Club [*Australia*]
NTFND.........	No Trouble Found [*Aviation*] (FAAC)
NTFP...........	National Task Force on Prostitution (EA)
NTFS...........	Network of Tropical Fisheries Scientists [*Marine science*] (OSRA)
NTFS...........	Northern Territory Fire Service [*Australia*]
NTFS...........	NT File System [*Computer science*]
NTFTA.........	National Toy Fox Terrier Association (EA)
NTFWTC	NATO Tactical Fighter Weapons Training Center
NTFY...........	Notify (AFM)
NTG............	Nitroglycerin [*Also, GTN, NG*] [*Explosive, vasodilator*]
NTG............	Nitrosoguanidine [*Organic chemistry*]
NTG............	Nontactical Generator (RDA)
NTG............	Non-Technical Generator [*Army*]
NTG............	Nontoxic Goiter [*Medicine*]
NTG............	Nontreatment Group [*Medical research*] (DAVI)
NTG............	Normal Triglyceridemic (DB)
NTG............	N-Tolylglycine [*Organic chemistry*]
NTG............	Nuclear Test Gage [*Environmental science*] (COE)
NTGA..........	Anaa [*French Polynesia*] [*ICAO location identifier*] (ICLI)
NTGA..........	National Tabletop and Giftware Association (NTPA)
NTGA..........	National Traveler's Gasoline Advisory (DICI)
NTGB..........	Fangatau [*French Polynesia*] [*ICAO location identifier*] (ICLI)
NTGC..........	Tikehau [*French Polynesia*] [*ICAO location identifier*] (ICLI)
NTGD..........	Apataki [*French Polynesia*] [*ICAO location identifier*] (ICLI)
NTGE...........	Reao [*French Polynesia*] [*ICAO location identifier*] (ICLI)
NTGF...........	Fakarava [*French Polynesia*] [*ICAO location identifier*] (ICLI)
NTGH..........	Hikueru [*French Polynesia*] [*ICAO location identifier*] (ICLI)
NTGI...........	Manihi [*French Polynesia*] [*ICAO location identifier*] (ICLI)
NTGIS	National Transit Geographic Information System [*FTA*] (TAG)
NTGJ...........	Totegegie [*French Polynesia*] [*ICAO location identifier*] (ICLI)
NTGK..........	Kaukura [*French Polynesia*] [*ICAO location identifier*] (ICLI)
NTGK..........	New Testament Greek (BARN)
NTGL..........	Fakahina [*French Polynesia*] [*ICAO location identifier*] (ICLI)
NTGM	Makemo [*French Polynesia*] [*ICAO location identifier*] (ICLI)
NTGMA........	Northern Territory Girls' Marching Association [*Australia*]
NTGMB........	Northern Territory Grain Marketing Board [*Australia*]
NTGN..........	Napuka [*French Polynesia*] [*ICAO location identifier*] (ICLI)
NTGO..........	Nitroglycerine Ointment [*Pharmacy*]
NTGO..........	Tatakoto [*French Polynesia*] [*ICAO location identifier*] (ICLI)
NTGP..........	Northern Territory Government Publications [*Australia*]
NTGP..........	Puka Puka [*French Polynesia*] [*ICAO location identifier*] (ICLI)
NTGPE.........	Northern Territory Government Pipeline Executive [*Australia*]
NTGPO........	Northern Territory Government Printing Office [*Australia*]
NTGQ..........	Pukarua [*French Polynesia*] [*ICAO location identifier*] (ICLI)

NTGR	Aratica [*French Polynesia*] [*ICAO location identifier*] (ICLI)
NTGR	New Testament Greek (BJA)
NTGS	Northwest Territory Genealogical Society (EA)
NTG SL	Nitroglycerin Sublingual [*Pharmacology*] (DAVI)
NtGsO	National Gas & Oil Corp. [*Associated Press*] (SAG)
NTGT	Takapoto [*French Polynesia*] [*ICAO location identifier*] (ICLI)
NTGU	Arutua [*French Polynesia*] [*ICAO location identifier*] (ICLI)
NTGV	Mataiva [*French Polynesia*] [*ICAO location identifier*] (ICLI)
NTGW	Nukutavake [*French Polynesia*] [*ICAO location identifier*] (ICLI)
NTGY	Tureia [*French Polynesia*] [*ICAO location identifier*] (ICLI)
NTH	Hudson Valley Community College, Troy, NY [*Library symbol Library of Congress*] (LCLS)
NtH	Natural Health Trends Corp. [*Associated Press*] (SAG)
NTH	New Testament Handbooks [*A publication*]
NTH	Northern Platinum [*Vancouver Stock Exchange symbol*]
NTHA	National Temple Hill Association (EA)
NTHA	Northern Territory Hockey Association [*Australia*]
NTHC	Northern Territory Housing Commission [*Australia*]
NTHCS	National Toothpick Holder Collector's Society (EA)
NthCsE	North Coast Energy [*Associated Press*] (SAG)
NthCst	North Coast Energy, Inc. [*Associated Press*] (SAG)
NthCstE	North Coast Energy [*Associated Press*] (SAG)
NTHEST	Northeast
NTHESTN	Northeastern
NTHEX	Northeast Investors Tr. [*Mutual fund ticker symbol*] (SG)
NthfldLb	Northfield Laboratories, Inc. [*Associated Press*] (SAG)
Nthgat	Northgate Exploration Ltd. [*Associated Press*] (SAG)
NtHHlt	National Home Health Care Corp. [*Associated Press*] (SAG)
NTHL	National Treasure Hunters League [*Defunct*] (EA)
NthLily	North Lilly Mining Co. [*Associated Press*] (SAG)
NtHlt	National Health Investors [*Associated Press*] (SAG)
NtHlthE	National Health Enhancement Systems, Inc. [*Associated Press*] (SAG)
NtHltl	National Health Investors [*Associated Press*] (SAG)
Nthmb	Northumberland [*County in England*] (WGA)
NTHN	Northern
Nthn	Northern (TBD)
NthnTch	Northern Technologies International [*Associated Press*] (SAG)
NTHP	National Trust for Historic Preservation (EA)
NTHRN	Northern
NthStat	Northern States Financial Corp. [*Associated Press*] (SAG)
NthstCF	Northstar Computer Forms, Inc. [*Associated Press*] (SAG)
NthstrHl	Northstar Health Services, Inc. [*Associated Press*] (SAG)
NTHV	Near-Term Hybrid Vehicle (PDAA)
NTHWST	Northwest
NTHWSTN	Northwestern
NTHZ	N-Nitrosothiazolidine [*Organic chemistry*]
NTI	Bintuni [*Indonesia*] [*Airport symbol*] (OAG)
NTI	Nadic-Terminated Imide [*Polymer technology*]
NTI	National Tactical Interface (MCD)
NTI	National Technology Initiative [*Program introduced by President Bush in February 1992*]
NTI	National Theatre Institute (EA)
NTI	National Trade Index
NTI	Naval Travel Instructions
NTI	Nesbitt Thomson, Inc. [*Toronto Stock Exchange symbol Vancouver Stock Exchange symbol*]
NTI	NeuROM Technology, Inc.
NTI	Neuropsychiatric Interest Checklist
NTI	Nielsen Television Index [*Nielsen Media Research*] [*Information service or system*]
NTI	Noise Transmission Impairment [*Telecommunications*]
NTI	Nonthyroidal Illness [*Medicine*]
NTI	Nordman [*Idaho*] [*Seismograph station code, US Geological Survey Closed*] (SEIS)
NTI	Northern Technology International [*AMEX symbol*] (SPSG)
NTI	No Travel Involved [*Military*]
NTIA	National Telecommunications and Information Administration [*Department of Commerce*] [*Washington, DC*]
NTIAC	Nondestructive Testing Information Analysis Center [*Army Materials and Mechanics Research Center*] [*Watertown, MA*]
NTIB	National Technology and Industrial Base (AAGC)
NTIC	Immaculate Conception Seminary, College of Philosophy, Troy, NY [*Library symbol Library of Congress*] (LCLS)
NTIC	National Training and Information Center (EA)
NTIC	Naval Technical Intelligence Center [*Pronounced N-tech; Formerly, NISC, now NAVMIC*] (DOMA)
NTIC	Nondestructive Testing Information Center [*Battelle Memorial Institute*] [*Databank*] [*Information service or system*] (IID)
NTICED	National Training Institute for Community Economic Development (EA)
NTICL	National Technical Information Centre and Library (NITA)
NTID	National Technical Institute for the Deaf [*Rochester Institute of Technology*] [*Research center*]
NTIES	National Treatment Improvement Evaluation Study [*Department of Health and Human Services*]
NTIF	National Taxpayers' Investigative Fund (EA)
NTIG	Nontreated Immunoglobulin [*Medicine*] (DMAA)
NTIH	Normal Terminate Interrupt Handler (MCD)
NTII	Neurobiological Technologies, Inc. [*NASDAQ symbol*] (SAG)
NTIK	Nontactical Instrumentation Kit [*Military*] (DWSG)
NTIMS	Negative-Ion Thermal Ionization Mass Spectrometry
NTIOC	No Travel Involved for Officer Concerned [*Military*]
N-TIP	National Technology Investment Programme [*Canada*]
NTIP...........	National Turkey Improvement Plan

NTIPP .... Navy Technical Information Presentation Program (MCD)
NTIPS .... Navy Technical Information Presentation System (MCD)
NTIR .... Nederlands Tijdschrift voor Internationaal Recht [*Netherlands A publication*] (ILCA)
NTIR .... Nontechnical Intelligence Report
NTIRA .... National Trucking Industrial Relations Association (EA)
NTIS .... National Technical Information Service [*Department of Commerce*] [*Springfield, VA Database producer and database*]
NTIS .... NEC [*Nippon Electric Company*]-Toshiba Information Systems, Inc. [*Japan*]
NTIS .... Nondestructive Testing Information System (SAA)
NTISSC .... National Telecommunications and Information System Security Committee (NITA)
NTITC .... National Tourism Industry Training Council [*Australia*]
NTITS .... Northern Territory Interpreter and Translator Service [*Australia*]
NTJ .... Nigeria Trade Journal [*A publication*]
NTJCAC .... Northern Texas Junior College Athletic Conference (PSS)
NTK .... Need to Know (MCD)
NTK .... Newton Tool Kit [*Computer science*]
NTK .... Nontactical Kit [*Military*] (DWSG)
NTK .... Nordisk Teaterkomite [*Nordic Theater Committee - NTC*] (EAIO)
NTK .... Nortek, Inc. [*NYSE symbol*] (SPSG)
NTK .... Nunatak [*Alaska*] [*Seismograph station code, US Geological Survey*] (SEIS)
NTK .... Tustin, CA [*Location identifier FAA*] (FAAL)
NTKR .... Takaroa [*French Polynesia*] [*ICAO location identifier*] (ICLI)
NTL .... Jacksonville, NC [*Location identifier FAA*] (FAAL)
NTL .... National
ntL .... National (DD)
NTL .... National Technology Ltd. (NITA)
NTL .... National Temperance League [*Later, ACAP*] (EA)
NTL .... National Tennis League
NTL .... National Testing Laboratories [*Australia*]
NTL .... National Training Laboratories [*Later, NTLI*] (EA)
NTL .... Natural Thermo Luminescence (IAA)
NTL .... Neon Test Light
NTL .... Newcastle [*Australia Airport symbol*] (OAG)
NTL .... Night Telegraph Letter
NTL .... Nonthreshold Logic (IAA)
NTL .... Nonuniform Transmission Line [*Computer science*] (IAA)
NTL .... Northair Aviation Ltd. [*British ICAO designator*] (FAAC)
NTL .... Northern Technol Intl. [*AMEX symbol*] (TTSB)
NTL .... Northern Telecom Ltd. [*Toronto Stock Exchange symbol Vancouver Stock Exchange symbol*]
NTL .... Northern Territory Library [*Australia*]
NTL .... No Time Lost [*Military*]
NTL .... NovAtel Communications Ltd. [*UTLAS symbol*]
NTL .... Novosti Tehnikskoi Literatury (NITA)
NTL .... Nuclear Technology Laboratory [*Stanford University*] (MCD)
NTL .... Nuclear Thermionics Laboratory
NTL .... Nuclear Transport Ltd. [*British*] (IRUK)
NTLA .... National Toy Libraries Association [*British*] (EAIO)
NTLA .... Nebraska Test of Learning Aptitude [*Education*]
NTLAT .... Northern Territory Land Acquisition Tribunal [*Australia*]
NTLB .... Northern Territory Land Board [*Australia*]
NTLC .... National Tax-Limitation Committee (EA)
NTLC .... National Trades and Labour Congress [*Canada*]
NTLC .... National Traffic Law Center [*MHTSA*] (TAG)
NtlCity .... National City Corp. [*Associated Press*] (SAG)
NTLDO .... Navy Terminal Leave Disbursing Office
NTLEN .... Nutlet Length [*Botany*]
NTLF .... National Taxpayers Legal Fund (EA)
NTLF .... Northern Troops and Landing Force
NTLGA .... Northern Territory Local Government Association [*Australia*]
NTLGGC .... Northern Territory Local Government Grants Commission [*Australia*]
NTLI .... Neurotensin-Like Immunoreactivity
NTLI .... NTL Institute (EA)
NtlInco .... National Income Realty Trust [*Associated Press*] (SAG)
NtlIns .... National Insurance Group [*Associated Press*] (SAG)
NtlPict .... National Picture & Frame Co. [*Associated Press*] (SAG)
NtlRlty .... National Realty Ltd. [*Associated Press*] (SAG)
NTLS .... National Truck Leasing System (EA)
NTLS .... Non-Transposed Loop Sensor (PDAA)
NTLSEA .... Northern Territory Live Stock Exporters' Association [*Australia*]
NtlSecs .... National Securities Corp. [*Associated Press*] (SAG)
NtlWire .... National Wireless Holdings, Inc. [*Associated Press*] (SAG)
NtlWstA .... National Westminster Bank Ltd. [*Associated Press*] (SAG)
NTM .... Narrowband Trunk Module [*Telecommunications*]
NTM .... National Technical Means [*For monitoring compliance with the provisions of an agreement*]
NTM .... NAVAIR Test Manual (MCD)
NTM .... Nazarene Theological Seminary, Kansas City, MO [*OCLC symbol*] (OCLC)
NTM .... Net Ton Mile [*Shipping*]
NTM .... New Tribes Mission (EA)
NTM .... Night Message (MSA)
NTM .... Nontariff Measures
NTM .... Non-Transition Metal (MCD)
NTM .... Nontuberculous Mycobacteria [*Medicine*] (DMAA)
NTM .... Non-Tuberculous Mycobacteria [*Microbiology*]
NTM .... Normal Transmitting Male [*Genetics*]
NTM .... North American Airlines, Inc. [*Canada ICAO designator*] (FAAC)
NtM .... Norton Micro Images, Inc., Trenton, NJ [*Library symbol Library of Congress*] (LCLS)
NTM .... Notice to Mariners
NTM .... Not to My Knowledge
NTMA .... National Tank Manufacturers Association [*Defunct*] (EA)
NTMA .... National Terrazzo and Mosaic Association (EA)
NTMA .... National Tooling and Machining Association (EA)
NTMA .... National Traditional Music Association (EA)
NTMB .... Nontuberculous Mycobacterium [*A bacterium*] (DAVI)
NTMD .... Nuku Hiva [*French Polynesia*] [*ICAO location identifier*] (ICLI)
NTME .... Naval Technical Mission in Europe
NtMerc .... National Mercantile Bancorp [*Associated Press*] (SAG)
NTMG .... Nutmeg Federal Savings & Loan Association [*NASDAQ symbol*] (SAG)
NTMG .... Nutmeg Fedl Svgs & Loan [*NASDAQ symbol*] (TTSB)
NTMI .... Net Ton of Molten Iron
NTMI .... Nontransmural Myocardial Infarction [*Cardiology*] (CPH)
NTMICP .... National Topographic Map Inventory Control Point
NTMJ .... Naval Technical Mission to Japan
NTML .... National Tillage Machinery Laboratory [*Department of Agriculture*] [*Research center*] (GRD)
NTMN .... Hiva-Oa/Atuana [*French Polynesia*] [*ICAO location identifier*] (ICLI)
NTMN .... National Thrift and Mortgage News [*A publication*]
NTMNG .... Nontoxic, Multinodular Goiter [*Medicine*] (DAVI)
NTMP .... Nike Target Measurements Program
NTMP .... Nitrate Motion Picture (VRA)
NTMP .... Ua Pou [*French Polynesia*] [*ICAO location identifier*] (ICLI)
NTMPA .... Northern Territory Marine and Ports Authority [*Australia*]
NTMT .... Navigation Tender Maintenance Training (DNAB)
NTMU .... Ua Huka [*French Polynesia*] [*ICAO location identifier*] (ICLI)
NTMVSA .... National Traffic and Motor Vehicle Safety Act
NTMWG .... Nuclear Test Monitoring Working Group [*Military*]
NTN .... National Airways Corp. (Pty) Ltd. [*South Africa ICAO designator*] (FAAC)
NTN .... National TeleAccess Network [*Database of physician opportunities*]
NTN .... National Telecommunications Network [*Rockville, MD*] (TSSD)
NTN .... National Towing News [*A publication*] (EAAP)
NTN .... National Trends Network (EPA)
NTN .... Nephrotoxic Nephritis [*Medicine*]
NTN .... Network Terminal Number [*Telecommunications*]
NTN .... Network Termination Number [*Computer science*] (TNIG)
NTN .... Neutral Twisted Nematic [*Computer science*] (PCM)
NTN .... Neutron [*A nuclear particle*] (MSA)
NTN .... Newton [*Diocesan abbreviation*] [*Melkite United States*] (TOCD)
NTN .... Newton College, Newton, MA [*Inactive*] [*OCLC symbol*] (OCLC)
NTN .... New Trade Names [*Later, NBTC*] [*A publication*]
NTN .... Normanton [*Australia Airport symbol*] (OAG)
NTN .... Northern Territory News [*A publication*]
NTN .... Norton Co., Coated Abrasive Division, R and D Department, Troy, NY [*Library symbol Library of Congress*] (LCLS)
NTN .... NTN Canada, Inc. [*Associated Press*] (SAG)
NTN .... NTN Communications [*AMEX symbol*] (TTSB)
NTN .... NTN Communications, Inc. [*AMEX symbol*] (SPSG)
NTNA .... Northern Territory Nurserymen's Association [*Australia*]
NTNC .... NTN Canada, Inc. [*NASDAQ symbol*] (SAG)
NTNC .... NTN Cda [*NASDAQ symbol*] (TTSB)
NTN Cda .... NTN Canada, Inc. [*Associated Press*] (SAG)
NTNCom .... NTN Communications, Inc. [*Associated Press*] (SAG)
NTNCWS .... Non-Transient Non-Community Water System [*Environmental Protection Agency*]
NTNF .... Norges Teknisk-Naturvitenskapelige Forskningsraad [*Online database*]
NTNG .... Nitrate Negative (VRA)
NTNV .... Narcissus Tip Necrosis Virus [*Plant pathology*]
NTNYT .... Not the New York Times [*A publication*]
NTO .... Name To (AAG)
NTO .... National Tenants Organization [*Defunct*] (EA)
NTO .... National Turnover [*Economics*]
NTO .... Natural Transition Orbitals [*Atomic physics*]
NTO .... Naval Technology Office [*Arlington, VA*] (GRD)
NTO .... Naval Transport Officer
NTO .... Network Terminal Operator
NTO .... Network Terminal Option [*Computer science*]
NTO .... New Technology Opportunities [*Program*] [*US government*]
NTO .... Nitrogen Tetroxide [*Inorganic chemistry*]
NTO .... Nonorthogonal Timing Error (IAA)
NTO .... Non-Target Organism (EES)
NTO .... Nontraditional Occupations
NTO .... No Try On [*Purchaser did not have a fitting*] [*Merchandising slang*]
NTO .... Not Taken Out [*Insurance*]
NTO .... Santo Antao [*Cape Verde Islands*] [*Airport symbol*] (OAG)
NTOC .... Naval Telecommunications Operations Center (DNAB)
NTOCDET .... Naval Telecommunications Operations Center Detachment (DNAB)
NTOF .... National Traumatic Occupational Fatalities [*Surveillance system run by National Institute for Occupational Safety and Health*]
NTOFMS .... Neutral Time-of-Flight Mass Spectroscopy [*Aviation*]
NTOL .... Near-Term Operating License [*Nuclear energy*] (NRCH)
NTOL .... Normal Takeoff and Landing [*Aviation*] (MCD)
NTOMC .... National Tung Oil Marketing Cooperative [*Defunct*] (EA)
NTonHi .... Historical Society of the Tonawandas, Tonawanda, NY [*Library symbol Library of Congress*] (LCLS)
NTonL .... Union Carbide Corp., Linde Division, Tonawanda, NY [*Library symbol Library of Congress*] (LCLS)
NTonS .... Sheridan Park Hospital, Inc., Tonawanda, NY [*Library symbol Library of Congress*] (LCLS)
NTOP .... New Technology Opportunities Program [*US government*]
NTORS .... Naval Torpedo Station

NTOS .... Natural Therapeutic and Osteopathic Society and Register [British] (DBA)
NTOTC .... National Training and Operational Technology Center [Environmental Protection Agency] (IID)
NTP .... Nathian [Pakistan] [Seismograph station code, US Geological Survey] (SEIS)
NTP .... National Tasking Plan [Military]
NTP .... National Toxicology Program [Department of Health and Human Services] [Research Triangle Park, NC]
NTP .... National Transportation Policy
NTP .... Naval Tactical Publication (NVT)
NTP .... Naval Telecommunications Procedures (NVT)
NTP .... Naval Telecommunications Publication (NVT)
NTP .... Navy Technological Projections
NTP .... Navy Training Plan (NVT)
NTP .... Near Time Processing (IAA)
NTP .... Network Terminal Protocol
NTP .... Network Terminating Point [Telecommunications] (TEL)
NTP .... Network Termination Processor
NTP .... Network Test Panel [NASA] (KSC)
NTP .... Network Time Protocol
NTP .... Neuronal Thread Protein [Biology]
NTP .... Nistransair [Republic of Moldova] [FAA designator] (FAAC)
NTP .... Nitrol Paste [Pharmacology] (DAVI)
NTP .... Nitroprusside [A vasodilator]
NTP .... Nonzero Temperature Plasma
NTP .... Normal Temperature and Pressure [Medicine]
NTP .... Notice to Proceed (KSC)
NTP .... No Title Page [Bibliography]
NTP .... Nuclear Test Plant
NTP .... Nuclear Thermal Propulsion (COE)
NTP .... Nuclear Transportation Project (EA)
NTP .... Nucleoside Triphosphate [Biochemistry]
NTP .... Number of Theoretical Plates
NTP .... Numerical Tape Punch
NTP .... Sodium Nitroprusside [An antihypertensive and reagent] [Pharmacology] (DAVI)
NTPA .... National Tractor Pullers Association (EA)
NTPA .... National Trotting Pony Association [Later, ITPA]
NTPA .... Naval Technical Proficiency Assist (NVT)
NTPA .... Northern Territory Planning Authority [Australia]
NTPA .... Northern Territory Police Association [Australia]
NTPAC .... Northern Territory Planning Appeals Committee [Australia]
NtPatnt .... National Patent Development Corp. [Associated Press] (SAG)
NTPAW .... National Transportation Public Affairs Workshop
NTPC .... National Technical Processing Center
NTPC .... National Temperance and Prohibition Council (EA)
NTPC .... Naval Training Publications Center
NTPC .... Navy Training Plan Conference
NTPD .... Normal Temperature, Pressure Differential (MCD)
NTPDLB .... Northern Territory Plumbers and Drainers Licensing Board [Australia]
NTPE .... Non-Tactical Peripheral Equipment [Military]
NtPenn .... National Penn Bancshares, Inc. [Associated Press] (SAG)
NTPF .... National Tile Promotion Federation [Defunct] (EA)
NTPF .... Near-Term Prepositioning Forces [Navy]
NTPF .... Number of Terminals per Failure [Computer science]
NTPG .... National Textile Processors Guild [Defunct] (EA)
NTPH .... Nucleosidetriphosphate Pyrophosphatase [An enzyme]
NTPHINB ...... National Trust for Places of Historic Interest or Natural Beauty [British] (EAIO)
NTPI .... Navy Technical Proficiency Inspection (NG)
NTPI .... Nuclear Training Proficiency Inspection [Navy] (DOMA)
NTP/IDCSP ... Navy Test Plan for Initial Defense Communications Satellite Program (DNAB)
NTPL .... Navy Technical Proficiency List
NTPL .... Nut Plate (AAG)
NTPNC .... Northern Territory Place Names Committee [Australia]
NTPO .... National Transuranic Waste Program Office [Department of Energy] (GAAI)
NTPO .... Nitrilotrimethylenephosphonic Acid [Organic chemistry]
NTPOC .... Navy Technical Point of Contact (DOMA)
NTPP .... Normal through Patch Panel (MCD)
NTPR .... Nuclear Targeting Policy Review (MCD)
NtPrest .... National Presto Industries, Inc. [Associated Press] (SAG)
NTPS .... Naval Test Pilot School
NTPS .... Near-Term Prepositioned Ships
NTPWA .... Northern Territory Power and Water Authority [Australia]
NtPwADS ..... National Power PLC [Associated Press] (SAG)
NtPwIntr ...... National Power PLC [Associated Press] (SAG)
NTQ .... National Trust of Queensland [Australia]
NTQ .... Nebennieren, Thymus, Quotient [Test] [Medicine]
NTR .... National Tape Repository (EA)
NTR .... National Transcontinental Railway [Canada]
NTR .... Navigational Time Reference (AAG)
NTR .... Navy Technical Representative (MCD)
NTR .... Negative True Rake (IAA)
NTR .... Nernst-Thomson Rule [Physics]
NTR .... Net-of-Tax Rate (ECON)
NTR .... Neutron Test Reactors (KSC)
NTR .... New Technology Report
NTR .... Next Task Register
NTR .... Noise Temperature Ratio (AAG)
NTR .... Nontranslated Region [Genetics]
NTR .... Nordiska Trafiksakerhetsradet [Nordic Road Safety Council - NRSC] [Finland] (EAIO)

NTR .... Nordisk Tolladministrativt Rad [Nordic Customs Administrative Council - NCAC] (EAIO)
NTR .... No Texts Required [Education]
NTR .... Nothing to Report
NTR .... No Traffic Reported [Aviation]
NTR .... No Treatment Required [Medicine] (WDAA)
NTR .... Nuclear Test Reactor [Also known as GETR]
NTR .... Nutrition
NTR .... Rensselaer Polytechnic Institute, Troy, NY [Library symbol Library of Congress] (LCLS)
NTRA .... National Television Rental Association [British]
NTRA .... National Trailer Rental Association (EA)
NTRA .... National Tumor Registrars Association (EA)
NTRA .... National Tyre Recycling Association [British] (DBA)
NTRA .... Northern Territory Rifle Association [Australia]
N Trans S Dec... National Transportation Safety Board Decisions [A publication] (DLA)
NTRC .... National Tourism Review Commission
NTRC .... National Toxins Research Center (DMAA)
NTRC .... Natural Toxins Research Center [Public Health Service] (GRD)
NTRC .... Northern Territory Rural College [Australia]
NTRDA .... National Tuberculosis and Respiratory Diseases Association [Later, American Lung Association]
NT Rep .... New Term Reports, English Queen's Bench [A publication] (DLA)
NT Repts ..... New Term Reports, English Queen's Bench [A publication] (DLA)
NTRG .... New Testament Reading Guide [Collegeville, MN] [A publication] (BJA)
NTRGLB .... Northern Territory Racing, Gaming and Liquor Board [Australia]
NTRL .... NASA Technology Readiness Level (SSD)
NTRL .... Natural
NTRL .... Naval Training Research Laboratory (WDAA)
NtrlH .... Natural Health Trends Corp. [Associated Press] (SAG)
NTRLLy .... Naturally
NTRM .... Nitrogen-Tillage-Residue Management (GNE)
NTRMA .... National Tile Roofing Manufacturing Association (EA)
NTRP .... No Traffic Reported [Aviation] (FAAC)
NTRS .... National Therapeutic Recreation Society (EA)
NTRS .... Nationwide Trailer Rental System
NTRS .... Northern Trust [NASDAQ symbol] (TTSB)
NTRS .... Northern Trust Corp. [NASDAQ symbol] (NQ)
NTRS .... Russell Sage College, Troy, NY [Library symbol Library of Congress] (LCLS)
NTRU .... Northern Territory Rugby Union [Australia]
NTRX .... Netrix Corp. [NASDAQ symbol] (SAG)
NTrZ .... North Tropical Zone [Planet Jupiter]
NTS .... Cirrus Air, Inc. [ICAO designator] (FAAC)
NTS .... Namens Trau- und Sterberegister der Judenschaft [A publication] (BJA)
NTS .... Narodno Trudovoi Soyuz [People's Labor Union] [Frankfurt, Federal Republic of Germany] (PD)
NTS .... NASA Test Support
NTS .... Nasotracheal Suction [Medical procedure] (DAVI)
NTS .... National Technical Systems
NTS .... National Technical Systems Inc. [Commercial firm]
NTS .... National Thespian Society [Later, ITS] (EA)
NTS .... National Traffic System [Amateur radio]
NTS .... National Transportation Statistics [or Survey] [Department of Transportation]
NTS .... National Transportation System [BTS] (TAG)
NTS .... National Travel Survey [Census Bureau]
NTS .... National Trust for Scotland (DI)
NTS .... National Tulip Society [Defunct] (EA)
NTS .... Naval Target Subdivision [G-2, SHAEF]
NTS .... Naval Telecommunications System (NVT)
NTS .... Naval Torpedo Station
NTS .... Naval Training School
NTS .... Naval Training Station
NTS .... Naval Transportation Service [Later, MSC]
NTS .... Navigational Technology Satellite (MCD)
NTS .... Navigation Technology Satellite (PDAA)
NTS .... Navigation Technology System (IAA)
NTS .... Navigator Training Squadron [Air Force]
NTS .... Navy Technology Satellite
NTS .... Near Term Schedule (MCD)
NTS .... Negative Torque Signal (MSA)
NTS .... Network/TDRSS [Tracking and Data Relay Satellite System] [NASA] (MCD)
NTS .... Nevada Test Site [Department of Energy]
NTS .... New Tube Shelter [British]
NTS .... Nitroglycerin Transdermal System [Pharmacy]
NTS .... Nontariff Size
NTS .... Nontemporary Storage [Personal property]
NTS .... Non-Traffic Sensitive [Costs] [Telecommunications]
NTS .... Nontranscribed Spacer [Genetics]
NTS .... Nordiske Teleansattes Samarbeidsorgan [Nordic Telecommunications Association] (EAIO)
NTS .... Notch Tensile Strength (OA)
NTS .... Notes [Finance]
Nts .... Notes (EBF)
NTS .... Not to Scale [Drafting]
NTS .... Nuclear Test Site (MCD)
NTS .... Nuclear Test Stage (AAG)
NTS .... Nucleus Tractus Solitarii [Brain anatomy]
NTS .... Number of Theoretical Stages [Chemical engineering]
NTS .... Nutrition Today Society [Defunct] (EA)

NTS............. Samaritan Hospital, Troy, NY [Library symbol Library of Congress] (LCLS)
NTSA .... National Tay-Sachs Association [Later, NTSAD] (EA)
NTSA .... National Technical Services Association (EA)
NTSA .... National Traffic Safety Agency [Federal Highway Administration]
NTSA .... National Trails System Act (COE)
NTSA .... National Training Systems Association (EA)
NTSA .... National Truck and Trailer Tank Institute [Later, Tank Conference of the Truck Trailer Manufacturers Association]
NTSA .... National Transportation Safety Association [Defunct] (EA)
NTSA .... National T-Shirt Association (EA)
NTSA .... National Tuberous Sclerosis Association (EA)
NTSA .... Naval Telecommunications System Architect (MCD)
NTSA .... Navy Tactical Support Activity (DNAB)
NTSA .... Northern Territory Softball Association [Australia]
NTSA .... Norway Technical Science Academy
NTSAD .... National Tay-Sachs and Allied Diseases Association (EA)
NtSanit .... National Sanitary Supply Co. [Associated Press] (SAG)
NTSB .... National Threat Safety Bureau
NTSB .... National Transportation Safety Board [Independent government agency] [Washington, DC]
NTSB .... Northern Territory Surveyor Board [Australia]
NTSC .... National Science and Technology Council (DDC)
NTSC .... National Tax Strike Coalition (EA)
NTSC .... National Technical Systems, Inc. [NASDAQ symbol] (NQ)
NTSC .... National Television Standard Code [Video equipment] (RDA)
NTSC .... National Television Standards Committee
NTSC .... National Television System Committee [Formed in 1936]
NTSC .... Natl Technical Sys [NQS] (TTSB)
NTSC .... Naval Training Systems Center [Orlando, FL]
NTSC .... Nonextrusion Texturized Soy Concentrate
NTSC .... North Texas State College [Later, North Texas State University]
NTSCH .... Naval Training School
NTSDS .... Near-Term Swimmer Defense System
NTSE .... Naval Telecommunications System Engineer (MCD)
NTSE .... Nontactical Support Equipment (MCD)
NTSEA .... National Trade Show Exhibitors Association [Later, IEA] (EA)
NTS EIS ...... Nevada Test Site Environmental Impact Statement
NtSemi .... National Semiconductor Corp. [Associated Press] (SAG)
NTSF .... National Technical Scholarship Foundation (AEBS)
NTSF .... Nonextrusion Texturized Soy Flour
NTSH .... Near-Term Scout Helicopter [Army]
NTSI .... National Tire Svcs [NASDAQ symbol] (TTSB)
NTSI .... National Tribunal of Second Instance [Catholic Church] [Australia]
NTSI .... Nonextrusion Texturized Soy Isolate
NTSK .... Nordiska Tele-Satelit Kommitton [Norway]
NTSM.......... Saint Mary's Hospital, Troy, NY [Library symbol Library of Congress] (LCLS)
Ntsmrt .... Netsmart Technologies, Inc. [Associated Press] (SAG)
NTSO .... NASA Test Support Office (KSC)
NTSR .... National Tunis Sheep Registry (EA)
NTSR .... NetStar, Inc. [NASDAQ symbol] (SAG)
NTSRI .... National Tunis Sheep Registry (NTPA)
NTSRP .... Nontechnical Services Real Property
NTSRVA ...... Nevada Test Site Radiation Victim Association (EA)
NTSSC .... Northern Territory School Sports Council [Australia]
NTST .... Netsmart Technologies, Inc. [NASDAQ symbol] (SAG)
NTSTN .... Naval Telecommunications System Test Node (CAAL)
NtSvIn .... National Service Industries, Inc. [Associated Press] (SAG)
NTT............. Nasotracheal Tube [Medicine] (DAVI)
NTT............. National Training Team [Operated by the Helen Keller National Center for Deaf-Blind Youths and Adults (HKNC)] (PAZ)
NTT............. National Tree Trust (WPI)
NTT............. Nearly Total Thyroidectomy [Medicine] (DMAA)
NTT............. New Technology Telescopes [Under development]
NTT............. Nippon Tel & Tel ADS [NYSE symbol] (TTSB)
NTT............. Nippon Telegraph & Telephone Co. [NYSE symbol] (SAG)
NTT............. Nippon Telegraph & Telephone Corp. [Telecommunications and videotex company] [Japan]
NTT............. Non-Tactical Tape [Military]
NTT............. Nuiatoputapu [Tonga] [Airport symbol] (OAG)
NTT............. Number Theoretic Transform (MHDI)
NTTA .... National Tobacco Tax Association (EA)
NTTAB .... Northern Territory Totalizator Agency Board [Australia]
NTTB .... Bora Bora/Motu-Mute [French Polynesia] [ICAO location identifier] (ICLI)
NTTBR .... Nineteen Thirty-Two Buick Registry (EA)
NTTC .... National Tank Truck Carriers [Alexandria, VA] (EA)
NTTC .... National Technology Transfer Center [NASA]
NTTC .... Naval Technical Training Center
NTTC.......... NAVFAC [Naval Facilities Engineering Command] Technical Training Center
NTTCIW ...... National Technical Task Committee on Industrial Wastes
NTTE .... Non-Tactical Training Equipment [Military]
NTTE .... Tetiaroa [French Polynesia] [ICAO location identifier] (ICLI)
NTTF .... Networking and Telecommunications Task Force [Computer science] (TNIG)
NTTF.......... Network Test and Training Facility [Goddard Space Flight Center]
NTTFX........ Hancock(J) Global Technology [Mutual fund ticker symbol] (SG)
NTTG .... Rangiroa [French Polynesia] [ICAO location identifier] (ICLI)
NTTH .... Huahine/Fare [French Polynesia] [ICAO location identifier] (ICLI)
NTTLC........ Northern Territory Trades and Labor Council [Australia]
NTTM......... Moorea/Temae [French Polynesia] [ICAO location identifier] (ICLI)
NTTO .... Hao [French Polynesia] [ICAO location identifier] (ICLI)
NTTP .... Maupiti [French Polynesia] [ICAO location identifier] (ICLI)
NTTPC........ Nippon Telegraph & Telephone Public Corp. [Telecommunications] (IAA)

NTTR .... Naval Torpedo Testing Range
NTTR .... Nontactical Telecommunications Requirement [Army] (AABC)
NTTR .... Raiatea/Uturoa [French Polynesia] [ICAO location identifier] (ICLI)
NTTRL .... National Tissue Typing Reference Laboratory (PDAA)
NTTS .... National Technology Transfer Center
NTTT .... Tahiti [French Polynesia] [ICAO location identifier] (ICLI)
NTTTTI .... National Truck Tank and Trailer Tank Institute [Later, Tank Conference of the Truck Trailer Manufacturers Association]
NTTX.......... Mururoa [French Polynesia] [ICAO location identifier] (ICLI)
NTU .... National Taxpayers Union (EA)
NTU .... National Technological University [Fort Collins, CO]
NTU .... National Tenants Union [Defunct] (EA)
NTU .... Naval Training Unit
NTU .... Navy Toxicology Unit
NTU .... Nephelometric Turbidity Unit [Analytical chemistry]
NTU .... Network Terminating [or Termination] Unit
NTU .... New Threat Upgrade [Military] (CAAL)
NTU .... Nonimmune Transfer Utensil [i.e., spoon] [Slang]
NTU .... Nordisk Trafikskoleunion [Nordic Union of Motor Schools Associations - NUMSA] [Finland] (EAIO)
NTU .... Normal Trading Unit
NTU .... Not Taken Up
NTU .... Nuclear Training Unit (MCD)
NTU .... Number of Transfer Units
NTU .... Oceana, VA [Location identifier FAA] (FAAL)
NTUC .... National Trades Union Congress (NADA)
NTUC .... National Trade Union Congress [Singapore]
NTUC .... National Trade Union Council [Hungary]
NTUC .... National Trade Union Council for Human Rights (EA)
NTUC .... Nigerian Trade Union Congress
NTUC .... Nyasaland Trade Union Congress
NTuc .... Tuckahoe Public Library, Tuckahoe, NY [Library symbol Library of Congress] (LCLS)
NTucW........ Westchester County Historical Society, Tuckahoe, NY [Library symbol Library of Congress] (LCLS)
NTULC .... Negro Trade Union Leadership Council
NTuPSC ...... Sunmount Development Center, Staff Library, Tupper Lake, NY [Library symbol Library of Congress] (LCLS)
NTUV .... Vahitahi [French Polynesia] [ICAO location identifier] (ICLI)
NTuxp .... Tuxedo Park Library, Tuxedo Park, NY [Library symbol Library of Congress] (LCLS)
NTuxpl .... International Paper Co., Corporate Research and Development Division, Technical Information Center, Tuxedo Park, NY [Library symbol Library of Congress] (LCLS)
NTV .... Nerve Tissue Vaccine [Medicine] (DMAA)
NTV .... Nervous Tissue Vaccine (AAMN)
NTV .... Nippon Television Network Corp. [Japan]
NTV .... Nontactical Vehicle [Army]
NTV .... NTV Oil Services Industries, Inc. [Vancouver Stock Exchange symbol]
NTVA .... Nondeterministic Time Variant Automation [Mathematics] (IAA)
NTVEI......... New Technical and Vocational Education Initiative (AIE)
NTVLRO...... National Television Licensing and Records Office [British]
NTVS .... Navy Television System
NTVT .... Non-Toxic Vinyl Tubing
NTVU .... National Trust Volunteer Unit [British] (EAIO)
NTW........... Navigator Training Wing [Military]
NTW........... Non-Pressure Thermit Welding (PDAA)
NTW........... Nose, Tail, Waist [Aviation]
NTWA .... National Trust of Western Australia
NTWA .... National Turf Writers Association (EA)
NtwExp .... Network Express, Inc. [Associated Press] (SAG)
NTWH .... National Theatre Workshop of the Handicapped (EA)
NTWK .... Network (MSA)
NTWK .... Network Long Distance [NASDAQ symbol] (TTSB)
NTWK .... Network Long Distance, Inc. [NASDAQ symbol] (SAG)
NtwkC .... Network Connection, Inc. [Associated Press] (SAG)
NtwkCn .... Network Connection, Inc. [Associated Press] (SAG)
NtwkEq .... Network Equipment Technologies, Inc. [Associated Press] (SAG)
NtwkG .... Network General Corp. [Associated Press] (SAG)
NtwkLng ...... Network Long Distance, Inc. [Associated Press] (SAG)
NtwkPeri...... Network Periphrals, Inc. [Associated Press] (SAG)
NtwkSix ...... Network Six, Inc. [Associated Press] (SAG)
NtWnLf .... National Western Life Insurance Co. [Associated Press] (SAG)
NTWRK ...... Network
NTWRKNG .. Networking
NTWS .... New Threat Warning System [Military]
NTWS .... Nontrack while Scan
NtWst.......... National Westminster Bank Ltd. [Associated Press] (SAG)
NtWstmin ..... National Westminster Bank Ltd. [Associated Press] (SAG)
NT WT .... Net Weight
nt wt .... Net Weight (WDAA)
NTX........... National Teletypewriter Exchange (IAA)
NTX........... Naval Teletypewriter Exchange [Formerly, NTE]
NTX........... Neonatal Thymectomy [Medicine]
NTX........... Networking and Expansion [Computer science] (PCM)
NTX........... Northern Air Service, Inc. [ICAO designator] (FAAC)
NTX........... Nuveen Texas Quality Income [NYSE symbol] (SPSG)
NTX........... Nuveen TX Qual Income Muni [NYSE symbol] (TTSB)
NTXQI .... Nuveen Texas Quality Income [Associated Press] (SAG)
NTY........... Sun City [South Africa] [Airport symbol] (OAG)
NTZ........... Indstrie Natuzzi ADS [NYSE symbol] (TTSB)
NTZ........... Industrie Natuzzi [NYSE symbol] (SPSG)
NTZ........... Iraq-Saudi Arabia Neutral Zone [ANSI three-letter standard code] (CNC)

NTZ	Nitazoxanide [*Medicine*] (TAD)
NTZ	Normal Transformation Zone (DMAA)
NTZ	Northern Transgressive Zone [*Geology*]
NTZ	North Temperate Zone [*Planet Jupiter*]
NU	Lipnur [*Indonesia*] [*ICAO aircraft manufacturer identifier*] (ICAO)
NU	Nachalnik Uprovlenja [*Chief of Directorate*] [*Soviet military rank*]
NU	Name Unknown
nU	Nanounit [*One billionth of a standard unit*]
NU	National Union (EA)
NU	National Unity Party [*British Political party*]
NU	NATO Unclassified (NATG)
nu	Nauru [*MARC country of publication code Library of Congress*] (LCCP)
NU	Nebraska University (MCD)
NU	Nebraska Unofficial Reports [*A publication*] (DLA)
NU	Neurology (DAVI)
NU	New Ulm [*Diocesan abbreviation*] [*Minnesota*] (TOCD)
NU	New Uses [*Research test*] [*Psychology*]
Nu	Ngultrum [*Monetary unit*] [*Bhutan*] (BARN)
NU	Niue [*ANSI two-letter standard code*] (CNC)
NU	Northeast Utilities [*NYSE symbol*] (SPSG)
NU	Northern Union [*Rugby*] [*British*] (DAS)
NU	Northrop Unit [*Of hydrolytic enzyme activity*]
NU	North Up [*Automotive engineering*]
NU	Norwich Union (WDAA)
NU	Nose Up [*Aviation*]
NU	Nothing Unsatisfactory (MHDB)
NU	Not Used
Nu	Nucleolus [*Cytology*]
nu	Nude [*Mouse*] [*Medicine*] (DMAA)
NU	Nu-Gro Corp. [*Toronto Stock Exchange symbol*]
NU	Nullified Unpostable [*Computer science*]
Nu	Numbers [*Old Testament book*] (BJA)
NU	Number Unobtainable [*Telecommunications*]
Nu	Nusselt Number [*IUPAC*]
NU	Southwest Airlines [*ICAO designator*] (AD)
NUA	Nations Unies des Animaux [*United Animal Nations - UAN*] (EA)
NUA	Net Unrealized Appreciation Tax
NUA	Network User Address
NUA	Network Users Association [*Defunct*] (EA)
NUA	Not Under the Act
NUA	Nuclear Agency [*Army*]
NUA	Nuna Air AS [*Denmark ICAO designator*] (FAAC)
NUAAW	National Union of Agricultural and Allied Workers [*British*]
NUABA	National United Affiliated Beverage Association (EA)
NUAC	National Urban Affairs Council (EA)
NUAD	Nucleus Average Optical Density [*Microscopy*]
NUADC	National Underwater Accident Data Center
NUAT	Nordisk Union for Alkoholfri Trafikk [*Scandinavian Union for Non-Alcoholic Traffic - SUNAT*] (EA)
NUATFAC	Nordiska Unionen for Arbetsledare, Tekniska Funktionarer och andra Chefer [*Nordic Confederation of Supervisors, Technicians and Other Managers*] (EAIO)
NUB	National Union of Busmen [*British*]
NUB	Navy Uniform Board (DNAB)
NUB	Northumberland Mines Ltd. [*Toronto Stock Exchange symbol*]
Nub	Nubes [*Clouds*] [*of Aristophanes*] [*Classical studies*] (OCD)
nub	Nubian [*MARC language code Library of Congress*] (LCCP)
NUBA	National UHF [*Ultrahigh Frequency*] Broadcasters Association (EA)
NUBC	National Uniform-Billing Committee [*Insurance*] (DAVI)
NUBE	National Union of Bank Employees [*Later, Banking, Insurance, and Finance Union*] (DCTA)
NUBF	National Union of British Fishermen
NUBIC	Nuclear Bunkered Instrumentation Center (MCD)
NUBICWOPS	Nuclear, Biological, and Chemical Warfare Operations [*Military*]
NUBLU	New Basic Logic Unit [*Computer science*] (MHDI)
NUBOMCWKT	National Union of Blastfurnacemen, Ore Miners, Coke Workers, and Kindred Trades [*British*] (DCTA)
NUBS	National Unemployment Benefit System [*Department of Health and Social Security*] [*British*]
NUBSO	National Union of Boot and Shoe Operatives [*British*]
NUBTC	National Union of Boot Top Cutters [*British*]
NUC	National Unification Council [*Philippines*] [*Political party*] (FEA)
NUC	National Union of Carriers [*British*]
NUC	National University Consortium for Telecommunications in Teaching (EA)
NUC	National Urban Coalition (EA)
NUC	Naval Undersea Center [*Later, NOSC*] (MCD)
NUC	Naval Undersea Research and Development Center [*Marine science*] (OSRA)
NUC	Navy Unit Commendation [*Military decoration*]
NUC	New University Conference
NUC	Non-Uniformity Correction
NUC	Nuclear
NUC	Nucleated
Nuc	[*A*] Nucleoside [*Also, N*]
NUC	Nucleus (WDAA)
NUC	Nucorr Petroleums Ltd. [*Toronto Stock Exchange symbol*]
NUC	Nuveen California Quality Income Municipal [*NYSE symbol*] (SPSG)
NUC	Nuveen CA Qual Income Muni [*NYSE symbol*] (TTSB)
NUC	San Clemente Island, CA [*Location identifier FAA*] (FAAL)
NUCA	National Utility Contractors' Association (EA)
NUCAA	National United Church Association of America (EA)
NUCAL	National Union Catalog Author List
NUCAP	Nuclear Cannon Projectile [*Army*]
NUCAP	Nuclear Capability [*Military*]
NUCAP	Nuclear Capability Report (CINC)
Nucaps	National Union of Civil and Public Servants [*British*] (DBA)
NUCAS	Nuclear Authentication System
NUCAW	National Union of Clerks and Administrative Workers [*British*]
NUCBO	National Uniform Certification of Building Operators (EA)
NUCC	North Up Cursor Centered [*Automotive engineering*]
NUCDEF	Nuclear Defense (AABC)
NUCDETS	Nuclear Detonation Detection and Reporting System (AABC)
Nuc E	Nuclear Engineer
NUCEA	National University Continuing Education Association (EA)
NUCEX	Nuclear Exercise [*Also, NUKEX*] (NVT)
NUCFO	Nuclear Force Posture
NUCH	Nucha [*Nape of the Neck*] [*Latin*] (ROG)
NUCIA	National Union of Cooperative Insurance Agents [*British*]
NUCINT	Nuclear Intelligence (MCD)
NUCISE	National Union of Cooperative Insurance Society Employees [*British*]
NUCL	Nuclear
NUCL	Nucleus
Nuc L Bull	Nuclear Law Bulletin [*A publication*] (ILCA)
NUCLE	Nuclear
Nuclear Reg Rep (CCH)	Nuclear Regulation Reports (Commerce Clearing House) [*A publication*] (DLA)
NUCLENOR	Controles Nucleares del Norte, SA [*Spain*]
NUCLEX	Nuclear Industries Exhibition
NUCLEX	Nuclear Loadout Exercise [*Military*] (NVT)
Nucl Phys	Nuclear Physics (MEC)
NUCM	North Up Cursor Moving [*Automotive engineering*]
NUCM	Nuclear Metals [*NASDAQ symbol*] (TTSB)
NUCM	Nuclear Metals, Inc. [*NASDAQ symbol*] (NQ)
NUCMC	National Union Catalog of Manuscript Collections [*Library of Congress*]
NucMet	Nuclear Metals, Inc. [*Associated Press*] (SAG)
NUCMUN	Nuclear Munitions (RDA)
NUCO	National Union of Certified Officers [*British*]
NUCO	NuCo2 Inc. [*NASDAQ symbol*] (TTSB)
NUCO	Numerical Code (NATG)
NuCo2	NuCo2, Inc. [*Associated Press*] (SAG)
NUCOL	Numerical Control Language [*Computer science*] (PDAA)
NUCOM	Nuclear Effects on Joint Force Communications (MCD)
NUCOM	Numerical Contouring Mechanism
Nucor	Nucor Corp. [*Associated Press*] (SAG)
NUCP	National Union of Czechoslovak Protestants in America and Canada [*Defunct*] (EA)
NUC PHY	Nuclear Physics (WDAA)
NUCPS	National Union of Civil and Public Servants [*British*]
NUCPWR	Nuclear Powered (NVT)
NucReaOpBasBad	Nuclear Reactor Operator, Basic Badge [*Military decoration*] (AABC)
NucReaOpFCBad	Nuclear Reactor Operator, First-Class Badge [*Military decoration*] (AABC)
NucReaOpSCBad	Nuclear Reactor Operator, Second-Class Badge [*Military decoration*] (AABC)
NucReaOpSftSupvBad	Nuclear Reactor Operator, Shift Supervisor Badge [*Military decoration*] (AABC)
NUCREP	Nuclear Damage Report (AABC)
NUCS	National Union of Christian Schools [*Later, CSI*] (EA)
NUCS	National Union of Club Stewards [*British*] (DBA)
NUCSAM	Nuclear Surface-to-Air Missile (NVT)
NUCSE	National Union of Czechoslovak Students in Exile (EA)
NUCSEQ	Nucleotide Sequencing Search System [*NIH/EPA Chemical Information System*] [*Database*]
NUCSTAT	Nuclear Operational Status Report (NATG)
NUCUAA	National United Church Ushers Association of America (EA)
NUCURES	Northeastern University Center for Urban and Regional Economic Studies [*Research center*] (RCD)
NUCWA	Nuclear Weapons Accounting (MCD)
NUCWAR	Nuclear War
NUCWARN	Nuclear Warning Message [*Military*] (ADDR)
NUCWPN	Nuclear Weapon (AABC)
NUCWPNSTRACEN	Nuclear Weapons Training Center
NUD	Adak, AK [*Location identifier FAA*] (FAAL)
NUD	En Nahud [*Sudan*] [*Airport symbol*] (AD)
NUD	National Union of the Deaf [*British*]
NUD	Naval Unit Disseminator (RDA)
NUD	Nebraska University Disease or N. Underdahl Disease [*A disease of swine named both for the place where it was originally identified and for the person who isolated the causative agent*]
NUD	Nonulcer Dyspepsia [*Gastroenterology*] (DAVI)
NUDA & GO	National Union of Domestic Appliances and General Operatives [*British*] (DBA)
NUDAC	Nuclear Data Center (IAA)
NUDAGMW	National Union of Domestic Appliance and General Metal-Workers [*British*] (DCTA)
NUDAGO	National Union of Domestic Appliances & General Operatives (WDAA)
NUDAP	Nuclear Detonating Data Points (MCD)
NUDAW	National Union of Shop Distributive and Allied Workers [*British*]
NUDBTW	National Union of Dyers, Bleachers, and Textile Workers [*British*] (DCTA)
NUDET	Nuclear Detection (MCD)
NUDET	Nuclear Detonation (COE)
NUDET	Nuclear Detonation Evaluation Technique (MCD)
NUDETS	Nuclear Detection and Reporting System
NUDETS	Nuclear Detonation Detection and Reporting System

NUDO........... National United Democratic Organization [*Namibia*] [*Political party*] (PPW)
NUDORE...... Nuclear Doctrine Organization and Equipment (MCD)
NUDWSS .... National Union of Docks, Wharves, and Shipping Staffs [*British*]
NUE .... Nitrogen Utilization Efficiency [*Ecology*]
NUE .... Niue [*Niue Island*] [*Seismograph station code, US Geological Survey*] (SEIS)
NUE .... Nucor Corp. [*NYSE symbol*] (SPSG)
NUE .... Nuremberg [*Germany Airport symbol*] (OAG)
NUEA .... National University Extension Association [*Later, NUCEA*] (EA)
NUERA .... Nuclear Extended Range Aircraft [*Proposed*] [*Air Force*]
NUESNA...... National Union of Eritrean Students - North America (EA)
NUET .... National Union of Elementary Teachers [*British*]
NuevEn .... Nuevo Energy Co. [*Associated Press*] (SAG)
NUEW .... National Union of Eritrean Women - North America (EA)
NUF .... National Ulcer Foundation (EA)
NUF .... National Unifying Force [*Zimbabwe*] [*Political party*] (PPW)
NUF .... National Union of Firemen [*British*] (DAS)
NUF .... National Unity Front [*Poland Political party*] (PPW)
NUF .... National Urban Fellows (EA)
NUF .... Natural Uranium Fuel
NUF .... Nordisk Urologisk Forening [*Scandinavian Association of Urology - SAU*] (EAIO)
NUF .... Nuveen Florida Quality Income Municipal [*NYSE symbol*] (SPSG)
NUF .... Nuveen FL Qual Income Muni [*NYSE symbol*] (TTSB)
NUFAM........ Nuclear Fire Planning and Assessment Model (MCD)
NUFCW....... National Union of Funeral and Cemetery Workers [*British*] (BI)
NUFD.......... Naval Unit, Fort Detrick [*Maryland*]
NUFDC........ Northgate Universal Floppy Drive Controller [*Computer science*]
NUFGW....... National Union of Flint Glassworkers [*British*] (DBA)
NUFI .... National Unfinished Furniture Institute [*Defunct*] (EA)
NUFLAT ...... National Union of Footwear, Leather, and Allied Trades [*British*] (DCTA)
NUFLV .... National United Front for the Liberation of Vietnam (EA)
NUFON........ Northern UFO Network [*British*]
NUFP .... Not Used for Production (AAG)
NUFP .... Number of Uncorrected Flight Plans (SAA)
NUFRONLIV... National United Front for the Liberation of Vietnam (EA)
NUFS .... National United Front of Somalia [*Political party*] (EY)
NUFS .... National Utility Financial Statement Model [*Department of Energy*] (GFGA)
NUFSO......... National Union of Funeral Service Operatives [*British*] (DI)
NUFTIC .... Nuclear Fuels Technology Information Center (DIT)
NUFTO......... National Union of Furniture Trade Operatives [*British*]
NUFUCO ...... Nuclear Fuel Cost (PDAA)
NUG............ Federation of NCR [*NCR Corp.*] User Groups (EA)
NUG............ National Union of Glovers [*British*] (SAG)
NUG............ Necrotizing Ulcerative Gingivitis [*Dentistry*]
NUG............ Nonutility Generator
NUGMW........ National Union of General and Municipal Workers [*British*]
NUGS.......... Nonutility Generating Source
NUGSAT....... National Union of Gold, Silver, and Allied Trades [*British*] (DCTA)
NUH............ National Union for the Homeless (EA)
NUHADI .... Nuclear Helicopter Air Density Indicating [*System*] [*Army*]
NUHC.......... Nu Horizons Electronics [*NASDAQ symbol*] (TTSB)
NUHC.......... Nu-Horizons Electronics Corp. [*NASDAQ symbol*] (SAG)
NUHELI........ Nuclear Helicopter Lift Indicator [*KSC*]
NUHKW........ National Union of Hosiery and Knitwear Workers [*British*] (DCTA)
NuHoriz........ Nu-Horizons Electronics Corp. [*Associated Press*] (SAG)
NUI .... National University of Ireland
NUI .... NetWare Users International
NUI .... Networks Unlimited, Inc. [*Defunct*] (EA)
NUI .... Network User Identifier [*or Identification*] [*Password*]
NUI .... Notebook User Interface [*Penpoint*] [*Computer science*]
NUI .... NUI Corp. [*NYSE symbol*] (SPSG)
NUI .... Nuiqsut [*Alaska*] [*Airport symbol*] (OAG)
NUI .... Number User Identification (DMAA)
NUI .... Patuxent River, MD [*Location identifier FAA*] (FAAL)
NUIA .... National United Italian Associations (EA)
NUIC .... National Urban Indian Council (EA)
NUIR .... National Union for Independence and Revolution [*Chad*] [*Political party*]
NUIS .... National Union of Iraqi Students [*British*] (DI)
NUIS .... Navy Unit Identification System (NVT)
NUIU .... New University Industrial Unit [*New University of Ulster*] [*Research center British*]
NUIW .... National Union of Insurance Workers [*British*] (DCTA)
NUJ............. National Union of Journalists [*British*]
NUJMB .... Northern Universities Joint Matriculation Board (AIE)
NUK .... Nukutavake [*French Polynesia*] [*Airport symbol*] (OAG)
NUKE .... Nuclear
NUKEX......... Nuclear Exercise [*Also, NUCEX*] (NVT)
NUKFAT ...... National Union of Knitwear, Footwear & Apparel Trades (WDAA)
NUKO.......... Nuko Information Sys [*NASDAQ symbol*] (TTSB)
NUKO.......... Nuko Information Systems, Inc. [*NASDAQ symbol*] (SAG)
NukoInfo....... Nuko Information Systems Inc. [*Associated Press*] (SAG)
NuKote......... Nu-Kote Holding, Inc. [*Associated Press*] (SAG)
NUL .... National and University Library [*Israel*] (BJA)
NUL .... National Union for Liberation [*Philippines*] [*Political party*] (PPW)
NUL .... National Urban League (EA)
NUL .... New Universal Library [*A publication*]
NUL .... New Upper Lateral [*Botany*]
NUL .... Nihon University [*UTLAS symbol*]
NUL .... Non-GSE [*Ground Support Equipment*] Utilization List [*NASA*] (NASA)

NUL .... No Upper Limit (MHDW)
NUL .... Nu-Lady Gold Mines [*Vancouver Stock Exchange symbol*]
NUL .... Nulato [*Alaska*] [*Airport symbol*] (OAG)
NUL .... Nulato, AK [*Location identifier FAA*] (FAAL)
NUL .... Null (OSI)
NUL .... Null Character [*Keyboard*] [*Computer science*]
NULAC .... Nuclear Liquid Air Cycle Engine
NULACE ...... Nuclear Liquid Air Cycle Engine
NULBA .... National United Licensees Beverage Association [*Later, NUABA*] (EA)
NULC .... National Union of Liberal Clubs [*British*] (DBA)
NULCAIS ..... Northwestern University Library Computer-Assisted Information Service (OLDSS)
NULCW........ National Union of Lift and Crane Workers [*British*]
NULEOA ...... National United Law Enforcement Officers Association (EA)
NULF .... National United Liberation Front [*Myanmar*] [*Political party*] (FEA)
nullip .... Nullipara [*obstetrics*] (DAVI)
NULMW........ National Union of Lock and Metal Workers [*British*] (DCTA)
NULO .... NASA Unmanned Launch Operations (MCD)
NULO .... National Union of Labour Organisers [*British*] (DBA)
NULOR......... Neuron Location and Ranging
NULS .... National Underwater Laboratory System [*Marine science*] (MSC)
NULS .... Net Unit-Load Size (MHDB)
NULU .... New Library Utility
NUM............ Error in Use of Numbers [*Used in correcting manuscripts, etc.*]
NUM............ National Union of Mineworkers [*South Africa*]
NUM............ National Unity Movement [*Sierra Leone*] [*Political party*] (EY)
Num............ Numa [*of Plutarch*] [*Classical studies*] (OCD)
NUM............ Numadu [*Japan*] [*Seismograph station code, US Geological Survey Closed*] (SEIS)
NUM............ Number [*or Numerator, or Numeric*]
Num............ Numbers [*Old Testament book*]
NUM............ Numeral [*or Numerical*]
NUM............ Nurse Unit Manager
NUM............ Nuveen Michigan Quality Income Municipal [*NYSE symbol*] (SPSG)
NUM............ Nuveen MI Qual Income Muni [*NYSE symbol*] (TTSB)
NUMA.......... National Underwater and Marine Agency (MCD)
NUMA.......... Nonuniform - Memory - Access [*Computer science*]
NUMA.......... Nuclear Mitotic Apparatus [*Medicine*] (DMAA)
NUMAC........ Northumbrian Universities Multiple Access Computer (NITA)
Numac......... Numac Energy [*Associated Press*] (SAG)
NUMAR........ Nuclear Magnetic Resonance [*Also, NMR*]
Numar .... Numar Corp. [*Associated Press*] (SAG)
NUMARC...... Nuclear Management and Resources Council (EA)
NUMARCOM... Nuclear Power for Marine Purposes Committee (MCD)
NUMAS........ Numerical Multifactor Assessment System (ADA)
NUMAST...... National Union of Marine Aviation and Shipping Transport [*British*]
NUMB.......... Numbered
Numb.......... Numbers [*Old Testament book*]
NUMBR........ Number (DAVI)
NUMC.......... Newcastle University Mountaineering Club [*Australia*]
NUMD.......... Numed Home Health Care, Inc. [*NASDAQ symbol*] (SAG)
Numd.......... Numed Home Health Care, Inc. [*Associated Press*] (SAG)
NUMD.......... NuMED Home Hlth Care [*NASDAQ symbol*] (TTSB)
NUMDW........ NuMED Home Health Care Wrrt [*NASDAQ symbol*] (TTSB)
NUMEC........ Nuclear Materials & Equipment Corp.
NUMEC........ Nuclear Uranium Materials and Equipment Corp. (GAAI)
Numed......... Numed Home Health Care, Inc. [*Associated Press*] (SAG)
NumedH ...... Numed Home Health Care, Inc. [*Associated Press*] (SAG)
NUMEPS...... Numeric Meta Language Processing System (PDAA)
NUMERALS... Numerical Analysis System (BUR)
Numerex....... Numerex Corp. [*Associated Press*] (SAG)
Numid.......... Numidian
NUMIS......... Navy Uniform Management Information System
NUMIS......... Numismatics
NUMISM....... Numismatics
Num Lock .... Numeric Lock [*Computer science*]
NUMM.......... National Union of Masters and Mates [*British*]
NUMMI........ New United Motor Manufacturing, Inc. [*Joint venture of Toyota Motor Corp . and General Motors Corp.*]
NUMR.......... Numar Corp. [*NASDAQ symbol*] (SAG)
NumR .... Numbers Rabbah
NUMS.......... Nuclear Materials Security (NRCH)
NUMS.......... Nu-Med, Inc. (EFIS)
NUMS.......... Numerous (ROG)
NUMSA........ National Union of Metalworkers of South Africa
NUMW.......... National Unemployed Workers' Movement [*British*]
NUN............ Network User Name [*Telecommunications*] (OSI)
NUN............ Nunasi-Central Airlines Ltd. [*Canada ICAO designator*] (FAAC)
NUN............ Nuveen New York Quality Income Municipal [*NYSE symbol*] (SPSG)
NUN............ Nuveen NY Qual Income Muni [*NYSE symbol*] (TTSB)
NUN............ Pensacola, FL [*Location identifier FAA*] (FAAL)
NUn............ Uniondale Public Library, Uniondale, NY [*Library symbol Library of Congress*] (LCLS)
NUNA........... Not Used on Next Assembly (AAG)
NUnCCE....... Cornelius Court Elementary School, Uniondale, NY [*Library symbol*] [*Library of Congress*] (LCLS)
NUnCE .... California Elementary School, Uniondale, NY [*Library symbol Library of Congress*] (LCLS)
NUnH.......... Uniondale High School, Uniondale, NY [*Library symbol Library of Congress*] (LCLS)
NUnLJ......... Lawrence Junior High School, Uniondale, NY [*Library symbol Library of Congress*] (LCLS)
NUnNE........ Northern Parkway Elementary School, Uniondale, NY [*Library symbol*] [*Library of Congress*] (LCLS)

NUnSE	Smith Elementary School, Uniondale, NY [*Library symbol Library of Congress*] (LCLS)
NUnStA	Saint Agnes Cathedral High School, Uniondale, NY [*Library symbol*] [*Library of Congress*]
NUnTHJ	Turtle Hook Junior High School, Uniondale, NY [*Library symbol Library of Congress*] (LCLS)
NUnWE	Walnut Elementary School, Uniondale, NY [*Library symbol Library of Congress*] (LCLS)
NUO	Nugold Enterprises Corp. [*Vancouver Stock Exchange symbol*]
NUO	Nuveen Ohio Quality Income Municipal [*NYSE symbol*] (SPSG)
NUO	Nuveen OH Qual Incme Muni [*NYSE symbol*] (TTSB)
NUOL	Naval Underwater Ordnance Laboratory (NOAA)
NUOM	Northern Union of Operative Masons [*British*]
NUOS	Naval Underwater Ordnance Station
NUP	Nationalist Unionist Party [*Sudan*]
NUP	National Umma Party [*Sudan*] [*Political party*]
NUP	National Union of Protestants
NUP	National United Party [*Vanuatu*] [*Political party*] (EY)
NUP	National Unity Party [*British Political party*] (EA)
NUP	Negro Universities Press (AEBS)
NUP	New Union Party [*Later, IUP*] (EA)
NUP	Nunapitchuk [*Alaska*] [*Airport symbol*] (OAG)
NUPAD	Nuclear-Powered Active Detection System
NUpB	United States Brookhaven National Laboratory, Upton, NY [*Library symbol Library of Congress*] (LCLS)
NUpB & PW	National Union of Printing, Bookbinding, and Paperworkers [*British*] (DGA)
NUpB-MH	United States Brookhaven National Laboratory, Medical Research Center Hospital, Upton, NY [*Library symbol Library of Congress*] (LCLS)
NUPBP	National Union of Printing, Bookbinding, and Paperworkers [*British*]
NUPDTU	National Union of Painters and Decorators Trade Union [*British*]
NUPE	National Union of Public Employees [*British*]
NUPEC	Nuclear Power Engineering Test Center (NRCH)
NUPGE	National Union of Provincial Government Employees [*Canada*]
NUPLEX	Nuclear Complex
NUPOC	Nuclear Propulsion Officer Candidate [*Navy*]
NUPOC-S	Nuclear Propulsion Officer Candidate - Submarine (DNAB)
NUPPS	Nonuniform Progressive Phase Shift (IAA)
NUPS	Nordic Union of Private Schools (EA)
NUPT	National Union of Press Telegraphists [*British*] (DGA)
NUPWR	Nuclear Power [*or Powered*] (DNAB)
NUPWRU	Nuclear Power Unit (DNAB)
NUQ	Mountain View, CA [*Location identifier FAA*] (FAAL)
NUR	Natchez, Urania & Ruston Railway Co. [*AAR code*]
NUR	National Union of Railwaymen [*British*]
NUR	Net Unduplicated Research
Nur	Nitrosourea [*Biochemistry*]
NUR	Nonuniformity Ratio
NUR	Nurmijarvi [*Finland*] [*Seismograph station code, US Geological Survey*] (SEIS)
NUR	Nurse (AABC)
NUR	Nuspar Resources [*Vancouver Stock Exchange symbol*]
NURA	National Union of Rate-Payers' Associations [*British*] (BI)
NuraTL	Nur Advanced Technologies Ltd. [*Associated Press*] (SAG)
NURB	National Uniform Business Rate [*British*]
NURB	Neville Upper Reservoir Buffer [*Medicine*] (DMAA)
NURBS	Nonuniform Rational B-Spline [*A type of spline*] [*Computer science*]
NURBS	Nonuniform Relational B-Spline [*Micro Cadam 3-D*] [*Computer science*]
NURC	National Undersea Research Center [*Virgin Islands*]
NURC	National Union of Railway Clerks [*British*]
NURC	National Union of Retail Confectioners [*British*] (BI)
NURDC	Naval Undersea Research and Development Center
NURE	National Uranium Resource Evaluation [*Program*] [*Energy Research and Development Administration*]
NURED	Nuclear Requirements Determination [*Military*]
NUREG	Nuclear Regulatory Commission
NUREM	Nuclear Requirements Methodology [*Military*]
NUREP	New York University Resonance Escape Probability [*Code*] [*Nuclear energy*] (NRCH)
NUREQ	Nuclear Requirements [*Military*]
NUREX	Nuclear Requirements Extrapolation [*Model*] (MCD)
NU/RF	National Urban/Rural Fellows (EA)
NURF	National Utility Reference File [*Department of Energy*]
NURF	Nucleosome Remodeling Factor [*Analytical biochemistry*]
NURIG	Navy Utility Regulatory Intervention Group (DNAB)
NUROC	Nuclear Rocket Project (SAA)
NURP	National Undersea Research Program [*Department of Commerce*] (GRD)
NURP	Nationwide Urban Runoff Program [*Water pollution*]
NURP	NOAA [*National Oceanic and Atmospheric Administration*] Undersea Research Program [*Marine science*] (OSRA)
NURS	International Nursing Services, Inc. [*NASDAQ symbol*] (SAG)
NURS	International Nursing Svcs [*NASDAQ symbol*] (TTSB)
NURS	Nursery
Nurs	Nurses (AL)
Nurs	Nursing (AL)
NURS	Nursing
NURsc	New Jersey Resources [*Associated Press*] (SAG)
NURSE	Nurses Underrepresented in Social Equality (BABM)
NURSE	Nursing
NURSEDETS	Nurse Detachments [*Army*]
NURSW	International Nursing Wrrt [*NASDAQ symbol*] (TTSB)
NURSW	Nursing System-Wide

NURT	National Union of Retail Tobacconists [*British*] (BI)
NURTE	Nur Advanced Technologies Ltd. [*NASDAQ symbol*] (SAG)
NUS	National Union of Scalemakers [*British*] (DCTA)
NUS	National Union of Seamen [*British*]
NUS	National Union of Students [*British*]
NUS	National University of Singapore
NUS	National Utility Services [*British*]
NUS	New Upper Stage [*NASA*] (KSC)
NUS	Nominal Ultimate Strength (IAA)
NUS	Nonuniformly Spaced (IAA)
NUS	Norsup [*Vanuatu*] [*Airport symbol*] (OAG)
NUS	Nuclear Utility Services
NUS	NUS Corp. (GAAI)
NUS	Nu Skin Enterprises [*NYSE symbol*] [*Formerly, Nu Skin Asia Pacific*]
NUS	Nu-Start Resource Corp. [*Vancouver Stock Exchange symbol*]
n-us--	United States [*MARC geographic area code Library of Congress*] (LCCP)
n-usa-	Appalachian Area [*MARC geographic area code Library of Congress*] (LCCP)
NUSA	National Union of Shop Assistants [*British*] (DAS)
N/USA	National/United Service Agencies
NUSA	Neighborhoods USA (EA)
NUSA	Ninth United States Army
NUSAC	Nuclear Sciences Advisory Committee [*Department of Energy/ National Science Foundation*]
NUSACC	National United States-Arab Chamber of Commerce (EA)
n-us-ak	Alaska [*MARC geographic area code Library of Congress*] (LCCP)
n-us-al	Alabama [*MARC geographic area code Library of Congress*] (LCCP)
n-us-ar	Arkansas [*MARC geographic area code Library of Congress*] (LCCP)
NUSAR	Nuclear Sweep and RADAR (IAA)
NUSAS	National Union of South African Students
NUSAS	Navy Underwater Swimmer Assault System (SAA)
NUSAT	Northern Utah Satellite
n-us-az	Arizona [*MARC geographic area code Library of Congress*] (LCCP)
NUSC	Naval Underwater Systems Center
NUSC	Naval Underwater Systems Center/Command (USDC)
n-usc-	North Central States [*MARC geographic area code Library of Congress*] (LCCP)
n-us-ca	California [*MARC geographic area code Library of Congress*] (LCCP)
NUSCAT	New Airborne Scatterometer (MCD)
NUSCDET	Naval Underwater Systems Center Detachment (DNAB)
NUSC/NL	Naval Underwater Systems Center, New London [*Connecticut*]
NUSC/NPT	Naval Underwater Systems Center, Newport [*Rhode Island*]
n-us-co	Colorado [*MARC geographic area code Library of Congress*] (LCCP)
NUSCOT	Nuclear Submarine Control Trainer (PDAA)
n-us-ct	Connecticut [*MARC geographic area code Library of Congress*] (LCCP)
NUSD	Nucleus Sum Optical Density [*Microscopy*]
n-us-dc	District of Columbia [*MARC geographic area code Library of Congress*] (LCCP)
n-us-de	Delaware [*MARC geographic area code Library of Congress*] (LCCP)
n-use-	Northeast (United States) [*MARC geographic area code Library of Congress*] (LCCP)
NUSEC	Naval Underwater Systems Engineering Center (MUGU)
NUSFDB	NUS [*National University of Singapore*] Financial Database [*Information service or system*] (IID)
n-us-fl	Florida [*MARC geographic area code Library of Congress*] (LCCP)
n-us-ga	Georgia [*MARC geographic area code Library of Congress*] (LCCP)
NUSGGMW	National Union of Stove Grate and General Metal Workers [*British*]
NUSGW	National Union of Stove and Grate Workers [*British*]
NUSH	Nucleus Shape [*Microscopy*]
n-us-hi	Hawaii [*MARC geographic area code Library of Congress*] (LCCP)
n-us-ia	Iowa [*MARC geographic area code Library of Congress*] (LCCP)
n-us-id	Idaho [*MARC geographic area code Library of Congress*] (LCCP)
n-us-il	Illinois [*MARC geographic area code Library of Congress*] (LCCP)
n-us-in	Indiana [*MARC geographic area code Library of Congress*] (LCCP)
n-us-ks	Kansas [*MARC geographic area code Library of Congress*] (LCCP)
n-us-ky	Kentucky [*MARC geographic area code Library of Congress*] (LCCP)
n-usl-	Middle Atlantic States [*MARC geographic area code Library of Congress*] (LCCP)
NUSL	Naval Underwater Sound Laboratory [*Later, NUSC*]
n-us-la	Louisiana [*MARC geographic area code Library of Congress*] (LCCP)
n-usm-	Mississippi River and Basin [*MARC geographic area code Library of Congress*] (LCCP)
n-us-ma	Massachusetts [*MARC geographic area code Library of Congress*] (LCCP)
n-us-md	Maryland [*MARC geographic area code Library of Congress*] (LCCP)
n-us-me	Maine [*MARC geographic area code Library of Congress*] (LCCP)
n-us-mi	Michigan [*MARC geographic area code Library of Congress*] (LCCP)
n-us-mn	Minnesota [*MARC geographic area code Library of Congress*] (LCCP)
n-us-mo	Missouri [*MARC geographic area code Library of Congress*] (LCCP)
n-us-ms	Mississippi [*MARC geographic area code Library of Congress*] (LCCP)
n-us-mt	Montana [*MARC geographic area code Library of Congress*] (LCCP)
NUSMWCHDE	National Union of Sheet Metal Workers, Coppersmiths, Heating and Domestic Engineers [*British*] (DCTA)
n-usn-	New England [*MARC geographic area code Library of Congress*] (LCCP)
n-us-nb	Nebraska [*MARC geographic area code Library of Congress*] (LCCP)
n-us-nc	North Carolina [*MARC geographic area code Library of Congress*] (LCCP)
n-us-nd	North Dakota [*MARC geographic area code Library of Congress*] (LCCP)

n-us-nh........ New Hampshire [*MARC geographic area code Library of Congress*] (LCCP)

n-us-nj......... New Jersey [*MARC geographic area code Library of Congress*] (LCCP)

n-us-nm...... New Mexico [*MARC geographic area code Library of Congress*] (LCCP)

n-us-nv....... Nevada [*MARC geographic area code Library of Congress*] (LCCP)

n-us-ny....... New York [*MARC geographic area code Library of Congress*] (LCCP)

n-uso-........ Ohio River and Basin [*MARC geographic area code Library of Congress*] (LCCP)

n-us-oh....... Ohio [*MARC geographic area code Library of Congress*] (LCCP)

n-us-ok....... Oklahoma [*MARC geographic area code Library of Congress*] (LCCP)

n-us-or....... Oregon [*MARC geographic area code Library of Congress*] (LCCP)

NUSOS....... Nuclear Underwater Sound Source (NG)

n-usp-........ Pacific and Mountain States [*MARC geographic area code Library of Congress*] (LCCP)

n-us-pa....... Pennsylvania [*MARC geographic area code Library of Congress*] (LCCP)

NUSPRAW ... National Union of Storeworkers, Packers, Rubber and Allied Workers [*Australia*]

n-us-ri........ Rhode Island [*MARC geographic area code Library of Congress*] (LCCP)

NUSRL....... Navy Underwater Sound Reference Laboratory

n-uss-........ Missouri River and Basin [*MARC geographic area code Library of Congress*] (LCCP)

NUSS.......... National Union of School Students [*British*] (DI)

NUSS.......... Nuclear Safety Standard (PDAA)

n-us-sc....... South Carolina [*MARC geographic area code Library of Congress*] (LCCP)

n-us-sd....... South Dakota [*MARC geographic area code Library of Congress*] (LCCP)

NUSSE....... Nonuniform Simple Surface Evaporated Model (MCD)

n-ust-........ Southwest (United States) [*MARC geographic area code Library of Congress*] (LCCP)

n-us-tn....... Tennessee [*MARC geographic area code Library of Congress*] (LCCP)

n-us-tx....... Texas [*MARC geographic area code Library of Congress*] (LCCP)

NUSU.......... Nuclear Superheating (SAA)

n-usu-........ Southern States [*MARC geographic area code Library of Congress*] (LCCP)

NUSU-CX .... Nuclear Superheat Critical Experiment (SAA)

NUSUM....... Nuclear Detonation Summary (NVT)

NUSUM....... Numerical Summary Report [*Military*] (AFM)

n-us-ut....... Utah [*MARC geographic area code Library of Congress*] (LCCP)

n-us-va....... Virginia [*MARC geographic area code Library of Congress*] (LCCP)

n-us-vt....... Vermont [*MARC geographic area code Library of Congress*] (LCCP)

n-usw-........ Northwest (United States) [*MARC geographic area code Library of Congress*] (LCCP)

n-us-wa...... Washington [*MARC geographic area code Library of Congress*] (LCCP)

n-us-wi....... Wisconsin [*MARC geographic area code Library of Congress*] (LCCP)

n-us-wv...... West Virginia [*MARC geographic area code Library of Congress*] (LCCP)

n-us-wy...... Wyoming [*MARC geographic area code Library of Congress*] (LCCP)

NUSZ.......... Nucleus Size [*Microscopy*]

NUT .... Mauna Loa Macadamia 'A' [*NYSE symbol*] (TTSB)

NUT .... Mauna Loa Macadamia Partners LP [*NYSE symbol*] (SPSG)

NUT .... National Union of Teachers [*British*]

NUT .... Nautilus Resources Ltd. [*Vancouver Stock Exchange symbol*]

N-U-T.......... Newcastle-Upon-Tyne [*City in England*]

NUT .... Number Unobtainable Tone [*Telecommunications*] (TEL)

NUt .... Utica Public Library, Utica, NY [*Library symbol Library of Congress*] (LCLS)

NUTA.......... National Used Truck Association

NUtC........... Utica College of Syracuse University, Utica, NY [*Library symbol Library of Congress*] (LCLS)

NU-TEC....... Nuclear Detection [*Radiation monitoring device*] (WDAA)

Nu-Tech...... Nu-Tech Bio Med, Inc. [*Associated Press*] (SAG)

NUTEX....... Nuclear Tactical Exercise

NUTG.......... National Union of Townswomen's Guilds [*British*]

NUtGE........ General Electric Co., Utica, NY [*Library symbol Library of Congress*] (LCLS)

NUTGW....... National Union of Tailors and Garments Workers [*British*]

NUtHi......... Oneida Historical Society, Utica, NY [*Library symbol Library of Congress*] (LCLS)

NUTI .... NASCOM User Traffic Interface [*NASA*] (MCD)

NUTIS .... Numerical and Textile Information System (PDAA)

NUTL .... Nonuniform Transmission Line (IAA)

NUtM .... Munson-Williams-Proctor Institute, Utica, NY [*Library symbol Library of Congress*] (LCLS)

NUTM .... Nutmeg Industries, Inc. (MHDW)

NutmgFd...... Nutmeg Federal Savings & Loan Association [*Associated Press*] (SAG)

NUtMI........ Utica Mutual Insurance Co., Utica, NY [*Library symbol Library of Congress*] (LCLS)

NUtMM ...... Masonic Medical Research Laboratory, Utica, NY [*Library symbol Library of Congress*] (LCLS)

NUtMV .... Mohawk Valley Community College, Utica, NY [*Library symbol Library of Congress*] (LCLS)

NUtMVL...... Mohawk Valley Learning Resource Center, Utica Psychiatric Center, Utica, NY [*Library symbol Library of Congress*] (LCLS)

NUtMY....... Mid-York Library System, Utica, NY [*Library symbol Library of Congress*] (LCLS)

NUTN .... National Union of Trained Nurses [*British*] (DI)

NUTN .... National University Teleconference Network [*Stillwater, OK*] [*Telecommunications*] (TSSD)

NUTP .... National Uranium Tailings Program [*Canada*]

NUtP .... Utica Psychiatric Center, Utica, NY [*Library symbol Library of Congress*] (LCLS)

NUTPW....... National Union of Tin Plate Workers [*British*]

NUTR .... Nutrition (AABC)

NUTRAT...... Nuclear Uses Technology Reaction Analysis Team

NUTRI......... Nutrition

NUTRL........ Nutritional

NutrLf .... Nutrition For Life International, Inc. [*Associated Press*] (SAG)

NutrLfe ...... Nutrition for Life International, Inc. [*Associated Press*] (SAG)

Nutrmax..... NutraMax Products, Inc. [*Associated Press*] (SAG)

NutrMg....... Nutrition Management [*Associated Press*] (SAG)

NutrMgt...... Nutrition Management [*Associated Press*] (SAG)

NUTS .... New Universal Terminology Subjects

NUtSC......... New York State Supreme Court Law Library, Utica, NY [*Library symbol Library of Congress*] (LCLS)

NUtSU........ State University of New York, College at Utica-Rome, Utica, NY [*Library symbol Library of Congress*] (LCLS)

NUTT .... National Union of Tobacco Trades [*British*]

NUTTAB...... Nutrient Data Table

NUTX .... Nucleus Texture [*Microscopy*]

NUU .... New Universal Union (EA)

NUU .... New University of Ulster [*Ireland*] (DI)

NUUSFE...... National Union of United States Forces Employees [*South Korea*]

NUUT .... National Union of Uncertified Teachers [*British*]

NUV .... Near Ultraviolet

NUV .... Norges Unge Venstre [*Norway*]

NUV .... Nuveen Municipal Value Fund, Inc. [*NYSE symbol*] (SPSG)

NUV .... Nuveen Muni Value Fd [*NYSE symbol*] (TTSB)

NuvAZ........ Nuveen Arizona Premium Income [*Associated Press*] (SAG)

NUVB .... National Union of Vehicle Builders [*British*]

NuvCal....... Nuveen California Municipal Value Fund [*Associated Press*] (SAG)

NuvMu....... Nuveen Municipal Value Fund, Inc. [*Associated Press*] (SAG)

NuvPI........ Nuveen Premium Income Municipal Fund, Inc. [*Associated Press*] (SAG)

NuvPI2....... Nuveen Premium Income Municipal Fund 2 [*Associated Press*] (SAG)

NuvPI4....... Nuveen Premium Income Municipal Fund 4 [*Associated Press*] (SAG)

NuvPP........ Nuveen Performance Plus Municipal Fund [*Associated Press*] (SAG)

NuvQInc..... Nuveen Quality Income Municipal Fund [*Associated Press*] (SAG)

NuvSel....... Nuveen Select Quality [*Associated Press*] (SAG)

NUVW........ National Union of Vehicular Workers [*British*]

NuvWA....... Nuveen Washington Premium Income Municipal Fund [*Associated Press*] (SAG)

NUW .... National Universities Week [*Canada*]

NUW .... Nu-West Group Ltd. [*Toronto Stock Exchange symbol*]

NUW .... Whidbey Island, WA [*Location identifier FAA*] (FAAL)

NUWA........ National Unemployed Workers Association (NADA)

NUWATI...... Nuclear Work Authorization Technical Instruction (DNAB)

NUWAX....... Nuclear Weapons Accident Exercises

NUWC........ Naval Undersea Warfare Center [*Later, NURDC*]

NUWDAT...... National Union of Wallcoverings, Decorative and Allied Trades [*British*] (DGA)

NUWEDS...... Nuclear Weapons Emergency Destruct System [*Navy*] (ANA)

NUWEP........ Nuclear Weapon Employment Policy (MCD)

NUWEP........ Nuclear Weapons Effect Planning

NUWES .... Naval Undersea Warfare Engineering Station (MCD)

NUWES .... Naval Underwater Weapons Evaluation Station

NUWMF....... Naval Undersea Warfare Museum Foundation (PDAA)

NUWPNSTRACEN... Nuclear Weapons Training Center (MCD)

NUWPNSUPANX... Nuclear Weapons Supply Annex

NUWPNTRACEN... Nuclear Weapons Training Center

NUWPNTRACENLANT... Nuclear Weapons Training Center, Atlantic

NUWPNTRACENPAC... Nuclear Weapons Training Center, Pacific

NUWRES...... Naval Underwater Weapons Research and Engineering Station

NUWS .... Naval Underwater Weapons Station (MCD)

NUWSAMBS... National United Women's Societies of the Adoration of the Most Blessed Sacrament (EA)

NUWSEC...... Naval Underwater Weapons Systems Engineering Center

NUWT .... National Union of Women Teachers [*British*] (DAS)

NUWT .... Northeast Utilities [*NASDAQ symbol*] (SAG)

NuWt .... Nu-West Industries, Inc. [*Associated Press*] (SAG)

NUWTW....... Northeast Utils Wrrt [*NASDAQ symbol*] (TTSB)

NUWW........ National Union of Women Workers (MHDB)

NUYC.......... Nordic Union of Young Conservatives (EA)

NV............... Naamloze Vennootschap [*Limited Company, Corporation*] [*Netherlands*] (GPO)

NV............... Naked Vision

nV............... Nanovolt [*One billionth of a volt*] (IEEE)

NV.....,........ Near Vertical [*Aerospace*]

NV............... Needle Valve

NV............... Negative Variation [*Medicine*] (MAE)

NV............... Nerve and Vein [*Medicine*] (DAVI)

NV............... Net Value

NV............... Neurovascular [*Anatomy*]

NV............... Neutralization Value (IAA)

NV............... Nevada [*Postal code*]

Nv............... Nevada State Library, Carson City, NV [*Library symbol Library of Congress*] (LCLS)

NV............... New Version [*of the Bible*]

NV............... Next Visit [*Medicine*]

NV..............	Night Vision Device [*Optics*]
NV..............	Nonvaccinated
NV..............	Nonvenereal [*Medicine*]
NV..............	Nonveteran
nv	Non Vidi [*Not Seen*] [*Latin*]
NV..............	Nonvintage [*Wine*]
nv	Nonvirulent [*Pathology*]
nv	Non Visus [*Not Seen*] [*Latin*] (EES)
NV..............	Nonvolatile
NV..............	Nonvoting [*Investment term*]
NV..............	Nord-Viscount Corp.
NV..............	Normal Value [*Clinical chemistry*]
NV..............	Norske Veritas [*Norwegian ship classification society*] (DS)
NV..............	North Anna [*Virginia*] [*Seismograph station code, US Geological Survey Closed*]
N-V	Northrop-Ventura (SAA)
NV..............	Northwest Territorial Airways [*ICAO designator*] (AD)
NV..............	Not Vaccinated [*Medicine*]
N/V.............	No Value [*Legal term*] (DLA)
NV..............	Nozzle Vanes (AAG)
NV..............	Nuisance Value (MHDB)
N/V.............	Number of Engine Revolutions per Minute per Vehicle Miles per Hour [*Automotive engineering*]
NVA.............	Nationale Volksarmee [*National Peoples' Army*] [*Germany*]
NVA.............	National Variety Artists [*Defunct*] (EA)
NVA.............	National Velthrow Association (EA)
NVA.............	National Veterans Association (EA)
NVA.............	National Viatical Association (ECON)
NVA.............	National Villa Association [*British*] (BI)
NVA.............	National Vista Alliance (EA)
NVA.............	National Vulvodynia Association [*Disseminate information about vulvar pain and establish support networks across the country*] [*Medicine*]
NVA.............	Native Vegetation Authority [*South Australia*]
NVA.............	Near Visual Acuity [*Medicine*]
NVA.............	Negative Vorticity Advection [*NWS*] (FAAC)
NVA.............	Neiva [*Colombia*] [*Airport symbol*] (OAG)
NVA.............	Nile Valley Aviation Co. [*Egypt*] [*ICAO designator*] (FAAC)
NVA.............	Non-Violent Alternatives [*An association*] (EA)
NvA.............	Normalized Volt-Ampere
NVA.............	North Vietnamese Army
Nva.............	Norvaline [*Biochemistry*]
NVA.............	NOVA Corp.(Cda) [*NYSE symbol*] (TTSB)
NVA.............	Nova Corp. of Alberta [*Later, Nova Corp.*] [*NYSE symbol Toronto Stock Exchange symbol*] (SPSG)
NVA.............	No Voltage Amplification [*Electronics*] (IAA)
NVA.............	N-Vinylacetamide [*Organic chemistry*]
NVAC...........	Natal Voluntary Ambulance Corps [*British military*] (DMA)
NVAC...........	National Vaccine Advisory Committee [*Reports to Congress, Health and Human Services*]
NVAC...........	North Vietnamese Army Captured
NVAC...........	Sunny Von Bulow National Victim Advocacy Center [*Later, NVC*] (EA)
NVACP.........	Neighborhoods, Voluntary Associations and Consumer Protection [*Environmental Protection Agency*] (ERG)
NVAF	North Vietnamese Air Force
NVAFB	North Vandenberg Air Force Base (NASA)
NVAL	National Vision Associates [*NASDAQ symbol*] (SAG)
NVAL	Natl Vision Associates [*NASDAQ symbol*] (TTSB)
Nval	Norvaline (DB)
NVAL	Not Available
NValHi.........	Columbia County Historical Library, Valatie, NY [*Library symbol Library of Congress*] (LCLS)
NValhM........	Westchester Medical Center, Valhalla, NY [*Library symbol Library of Congress*] (LCLS)
NValhW	Westchester Community College, Valhalla, NY [*Library symbol Library of Congress*] (LCLS)
NVAN..........	Non-Violent Anarchist Network (EA)
NV & EOL....	Night Vision and Electro-Optics Laboratory [*Army*] (RDA)
NV & H........	Nuclear Survivability and Hardening
NVAPI.........	Nuveen Virginia Premium Income Municipal Fund [*Associated Press*] (SAG)
Nv-Ar	Nevada State Library, Division of State Archives, Carson City, NV [*Library symbol Library of Congress*] (LCLS)
NVAR..........	Normalized Variance (PDAA)
NVAS	Night Vision Attack System
NVAS	North Vietnamese Army Suspect
NVASD........	Night Vision Aerial Surveillance Device
NVASS........	Night Vision Airborne Surveillance System
NVATA........	National Vocational Agricultural Teachers' Association (EA)
NVB	Inco Ltd. [*NYSE symbol*] (SAG)
NVB	Napa Valley Bancorp (EFIS)
NVB	National Volunteer Brigade [*South African equivalent of the British Home Guard*]
NVB	Navigational Base (KSC)
NVB	Nederlandse Volksbeweging [*Dutch People's Movement*] [*Political party*] (PPE)
NVB	Neurovascular Bundle [*Medicine*] (DB)
NVB	Night Vision Binocular
Nvb	November (CDAI)
NVBA	National Veteran Boxers Association (EA)
NvBc	Boulder City Library, Boulder City, NV [*Library symbol Library of Congress*] (LCLS)
NvBcBM......	United States Bureau of Mines, Boulder City Metallurgy Research Laboratories, Boulder City, NV [*Library symbol Library of Congress*] (LCLS)
NvBcER.......	United States Energy Research and Development Administration, Boulder City Metallurgy Research Laboratories, Boulder City, NV [*Library symbol Library of Congress*] (LCLS)
NVBF	Nordisk Vetenskapliga Bibliotekarie-Forbundet [*Scandinavian Federation of Research Librarians*]
NvBL	Lehman Caves National Monument, Baker, NV [*Library symbol Library of Congress*] (LCLS)
NVC	National Victim Center (EA)
NVC	National Victims of Crime (EA)
NVC	National Video Clearinghouse [*Defunct*] (EA)
NVC	National Video Corp.
NVC	National Volunteer Center (EA)
NVC	Nonverbal Communication (ADA)
NVC	Noverco, Inc. [*Toronto Stock Exchange symbol*]
NVC	Nuriootpa Viticulture Center [*Australia*]
NVC	Nuveen California Select Quality Municipal [*NYSE symbol*] (SPSG)
NVC	Nuveen CA Select Qual Muni [*NYSE symbol*] (TTSB)
NvC	Ormsby Public Library, Carson City, NV [*Library symbol Library of Congress*] (LCLS)
NVCA	National Valentine Collectors' Association (EA)
NVCA	National Van Conversion Association (EA)
NVCA	National Vehicle Conversion Association
NVCA	National Venture Capital Association [*Arlington, VA*] (EA)
NvCAQI	Nuveen California Quality Income Municipal [*Associated Press*] (SAG)
NVCC	Northern Virginia Community College
NVCF	National Victims of Crime Foundation (EA)
NVCH	National Volunteer Clearinghouse for the Homeless [*Defunct*] (EA)
NvCIQ	Nuveen California Investment Quality Municipal Fund [*Associated Press*] (SAG)
NV-CJD.......	New Variant Creutzfeldt-Jakob Disease [*Medicine*]
NvCMI........	Nuveen California Municipal Income Fund [*Associated Press*] (SAG)
NVCPP.......	Nuveen California Performance Plus Municipal Fund [*Associated Press*] (SAG)
NVCS	Nissan Valve Control System [*Automotive engineering*]
NvCSQ	Nuveen California Select Quality Municipal Fund [*Associated Press*] (SAG)
NVCT	Nonverbal Classification Test
NVCZ	N-Vinylcarbazole [*Organic chemistry*]
NVD	Nausea, Vomiting, Diarrhea [*Medicine*]
NVD	Neck Vein Distention [*Medicine*]
NVD	Neovascularization of the Disc [*Ophthalmology*] (DAVI)
NVD	Neurovesicle Dysfunction [*Medicine*] (DMAA)
NVD	Nevada, MO [*Location identifier FAA*] (FAAL)
NVD	Newcastle Virus Disease [*Veterinary medicine*] (MAE)
NVD	Night Vision Device [*Optics*]
NVD	Nonvalvular Disease [*Medicine*] (DMAA)
NVD	Nonvalvular Heart Disease (MAE)
NVD	Normal Vaginal Delivery [*Medicine*] (DMAA)
NVD	North Vancouver District Public Library [*UTLAS symbol*]
NVD	No Value Declared [*Business term*] (DCTA)
NVD	No Venous Distention [*Medicine*] (MEDA)
NVD	Number of Vessels Diseased [*Medicine*] (DB)
NVDA	National Vitamin Distributors Association (EA)
NVDM	Network Virtual Data Manager [*Computer science*] (IAA)
NVDM	Novadigm, Inc. [*NASDAQ symbol*] (SAG)
NVDML.......	Network Virtual Data Management Language [*Telecommunications*] (OSI)
NVE...........	Colvin Aviation, Inc. [*ICAO designator*] (FAAC)
NvE............	Elko County Library, Elko, NV [*Library symbol Library of Congress*] (LCLS)
NVE...........	Native Valve Endocarditis [*Medicine*]
NVE...........	Neovascular Edema [*Ophthalmology*] (DAVI)
NVE...........	Neovascularization Elsewhere [*Cardiology*] (DAVI)
NVE...........	Night Vision Equipment (MCD)
NVE...........	Nonvisual Eyepiece
NVe...........	Vestal Public Library, Vestal, NY [*Library symbol Library of Congress*] (LCLS)
NVEBW	Non-Vacuum Electron Beam Welding (PDAA)
NVEF..........	National Vocational Educational Foundation (EA)
NVeGS........	Church of Jesus Christ of Latter-Day Saints, Genealogical Society Library, Ithaca Branch, Vestal, NY [*Library symbol Library of Congress*] (LCLS)
NvEHi.........	Northeastern Nevada Historical Society, Elko, NV [*Library symbol Library of Congress*] (LCLS)
NVEL..........	Navel
NVeL..........	Vestal Public Library, Vestal, NY [*Library symbol*] [*Library of Congress*] (LCLS)
NvEIGS	Church of Jesus Christ of Latter-Day Saints, Genealogical Society Library, Ely Branch, Ely, NV [*Library symbol Library of Congress*] (LCLS)
NVEOC........	Night Vision and Electro-Optics Center [*Fort Belvoir, VA*] [*US Army Communications-Electronics Command*] (RDA)
NVEOD........	Night Vision and Electro Optics Directorate [*Army*] (RDA)
NVEOL........	Night Vision and Electro-Optics Laboratory [*Army*] (GRD)
NVEPDC......	National Vocational Educational Professional Development Consortium [*Later, NVEPDF*] (EA)
NVEPDF......	National Vocational Educational Professional Development Foundation [*Later, NVEF*] (EA)
NVESD........	Night Vision and Electronic Sensors Directorate [*Army*] (RDA)
NVETS	National Vocational Education and Training System [*Australia*]
NVF...........	Nasal Visual Field (DB)

NVF............ National Vitamin Foundation (EA)
NVF............ National Vitiligo Foundation (EA)
NVF............ National Volunteer Force (WDAA)
NVF............ Nordisk Vejteknisk Forbund [*Nordic Association of Road and Traffic Engineering*] (EAIO)
NVFC .... National Volunteer Fire Council (EA)
NVFEL......... National Vehicle and Fuel Emissions Laboratory
NVFET......... Non-Volatile Field-Effect-Transistor [*Electronics*]
NvFGS .... Church of Jesus Christ of Latter-Day Saints, Genealogical Society Library, Fallon Branch, Fallon, NV [*Library symbol Library of Congress*] (LCLS)
NVFI........... National Vitiligo Foundation (PAZ)
NvFL........... Nuveen Florida Investment Quality Municipal Fund [*Associated Press*] (SAG)
NVFR .... Night Visual Flight Rating
NVG .... National Trust Co. [*Toronto Stock Exchange symbol*]
NVG .... Neovascular Glaucoma (DAVI)
NVG .... Neoviridogrisein [*Antibacterial*]
NVG .... Night Vision Goggles
NVG .... Night Vision Group
NVGA .... National Vocational Guidance Association (EA)
NVGGA .... Napa Valley Grape Growers Association (EA)
NVGI .... National Voluntary Groups Institute (EA)
NvGM......... Mormon Station State Park, Genoa, NV [*Library symbol Library of Congress*] (LCLS)
NVGS.......... Night Vision Goggle Sensor (DWSG)
NVGTN........ Navigation
NvH............ Henderson District Public Library, Henderson, NV [*Library symbol Library of Congress*] (LCLS)
NVH .... National R.V. Holdings [*NYSE symbol*]
NVH .... Nitrogen Vent Header [*Nuclear energy*] (NRCH)
NVH .... Noise, Vibration, Harshness [*Automotive technology*]
NVHA .... National Voluntary Health Agencies (EA)
NvHi........... Nevada State Historical Society, Reno, NV [*Library symbol Library of Congress*] (LCLS)
NvHV-A........ United States Veterans Administration Hospital, Ambulatory Care Service, Henderson, NV [*Library symbol Library of Congress*] (LCLS)
NVI .... Night Vision Imaging (DWSG)
NVI............. Non-Value Indicator [*Type of postage stamp*] (ODBW)
NVI............. Normalized Vegetation Index [*Meteorology*]
NVIC .... National Vaccine Information Center
NVIC .... Navigational and Vessel Inspection Circular [*Coast Guard*] (GFGA)
NVIC .... N-Viro International [*NASDAQ symbol*] (TTSB)
NVIC .... N-Viro International Corp. [*NASDAQ symbol*] (SAG)
NVICP......... National Vaccine Injury Compensation Program (PAZ)
NVIEW........ NVIEW Corp. [*Associated Press*] (SAG)
NVII .... Navy Vocational Interest Inventory (NVT)
NvIMO........ Nuveen Insurance Municipal Opportunity Fund [*Associated Press*] (SAG)
NvInQI........ Nuveen Insured Quality Fund [*Associated Press*] (SAG)
NvIQI.......... Nuveen Investment Quality Municipal Fund [*Associated Press*] (SAG)
N-ViroInt...... N-Viro International Corp. [*Associated Press*] (SAG)
NVIS .... Nearly Vertical Incident Skywave [*Propagation model*] (MCD)
nVision .... N-Vision, Inc. [*Associated Press*] (SAG)
NVK .... Milton, FL [*Location identifier FAA*] (FAAL)
NVK .... Narvik [*Norway*] [*Airport symbol*] (OAG)
NVL .... Hunting Aviation Services Ltd. [*British ICAO designator*] (FAAC)
NvL............ Las Vegas Public Library, Las Vegas, NV [*Library symbol Library of Congress*] (LCLS)
NVL............ Night Vision Laboratory [*Army*]
NVL............ Novolazarevskaya [*Antarctica*] [*Seismograph station code, US Geological Survey*] (SEIS)
NVLA .... National Vehicle Leasing Association (EA)
NVLA .... National Viewers' and Listeners' Association [*British*]
NVLAP .... National Association of Voluntary laboratory Accreditation Practices
NVLAP .... National Voluntary Laboratory Accreditation Program [*Gaithersburg, MD*] [*National Institute of Standards and Technology*]
NvLBM........ Basic Magnesium, Inc., Las Vegas, NV [*Library symbol Library of Congress Obsolete*] (LCLS)
NvLC........... Clark County Library, Las Vegas, NV [*Library symbol Library of Congress*] (LCLS)
NVLC .... National Veterans Law Center [*Defunct*] (EA)
NvLGS .... Church of Jesus Christ of Latter-Day Saints, Genealogical Society Library, Las Vegas Branch, Las Vegas, NV [*Library symbol Library of Congress*] (LCLS)
NvLN........... University of Nevada, Las Vegas, NV [*Library symbol Library of Congress*] (LCLS)
NVLS .... Novellus Systems [*NASDAQ symbol*] (TTSB)
NVLS .... Novellus Systems, Inc. [*NASDAQ symbol*] (CTT)
NVM............ National Voter Mobilization [*Defunct*] (EA)
NVM............ Nativity of the Virgin Mary
NVM............ Nonvolatile Matter
NVM............ Nonvolatile Memory [*Computer science*] (HGAA)
NVM............ Non-Volatile Random Access Memory [*Computer science*]
NVM............ Nova Marketing Ltd. [*Vancouver Stock Exchange symbol*]
NVMA .... National Veterinary Medical Association (WDAA)
NVMA .... Noise and Vibration Monitor Analyzer [*Military*] (CAAL)
NvMAd .... Nuveen Municipal Advantage Fund [*Associated Press*] (SAG)
NvMAP........ Nuveen Massachusetts Premium Income Municipal Fund [*Associated Press*] (SAG)
NvMcK........ Kinnear Public Library, McGill, NV [*Library symbol Library of Congress*] (LCLS)
NvMiD .... Douglas County Library, Minden, NV [*Library symbol Library of Congress*] (LCLS)

NvMIPI........ Nuveen Michigan Premium Income Municipal [*Associated Press*] (SAG)
NvMO.......... Nuveen Municipal Opportunity Fund [*Associated Press*] (SAG)
NVMS .... Night Visibility Measuring Set
Nvmt........... Novametrics Medical Systems [*Associated Press*] (SAG)
Nvmt........... Novametrix Medical Systems, Inc. [*Associated Press*] (SAG)
NvMul......... Nuveen Municipal Income Fund [*Associated Press*] (SAG)
NvMus........ Nevada State Museum, Capital Complex, Carson City, NV [*Library symbol Library of Congress*] (LCLS)
NVMV .... Nicotiana Velutina Mosaic Virus [*Plant pathology*]
NVN .... Nirvana Industries Ltd. [*Vancouver Stock Exchange symbol*]
NVN .... Non-Von Neumann
NVN .... North Vietnam (VNW)
NVN .... Noun-Verb-Noun [*Education of the hearing-impaired*]
NVN .... Nuveen New York Select Quality Municipal [*NYSE symbol*] (SPSG)
NVN .... Nuveen NY Selct Qual Muni [*NYSE symbol*] (TTSB)
NVNA .... Non-Volatile Nitrosamine [*Organic chemistry*]
NVNAF .... North Vietnamese Air Force
NvNJ .... Nuveen New Jersey Investment Quality Municipal Fund [*Associated Press*] (SAG)
NvNJPI........ Nuveen New Jersey Premium Income Municipal [*Associated Press*] (SAG)
NVNN.......... North Vietnamese Navy
NvNoIC .... Clark County Community College, North Las Vegas, NV [*Library symbol Library of Congress*] (LCLS)
NVNTA .... Night Vision Net Technical Assessment (MCD)
NvNYP .... Nuveen New York Performance Plus Municipal Fund [*Associated Press*] (SAG)
NvNYQI .... Nuveen New York Quality Income Municipal [*Associated Press*] (SAG)
NVO .... Coalition of National Voluntary Organizations [*Also, National Voluntary Organizations*] (AC)
NVO .... Nevada Operations Office [*Department of Energy*] (MCD)
NVO .... New Vehicle Order
NVO .... Nonverbal Operation
NVO .... Nonvessel Operator [*Shipping*]
NVO .... Nonvolatile Organic [*Residue of thermal processing*]
NVO .... Novo Nordisk A/S ADR [*NYSE symbol*] (SPSG)
NVOAD .... National Voluntary Organizations Active in Disaster (EA)
NVOC .... Nitroveratryloxycarbonyl [*Organic radical*]
NVOC .... Nonvessel-Owning Carrier [*Shipping*] (DS)
NVOCC .... Nonvessel Operating Common Carrier [*Shipping*]
NVOCC .... Non-Vessel Operating Container Carrier
NVOCC .... Nonvessel-Owning Common Carrier [*Shipping*] (DS)
NVOD .... Near Video on Demand (WDAA)
NvoFn .... Nuevo Financing I [*Associated Press*] (SAG)
NVOI .... National Voice of Iran [*Clandestine, Soviet-backed radio station*]
NVOILA .... National Voluntary Organizations for Independent Living for the Aging (EA)
NVOO.......... Nevada Operations Office [*Department of Energy*]
NVOP .... National Veteran's Outreach Program (EA)
NVORDCH ... Naval Ordnance Chart
NVP .... National Vaccine Program [*National Institutes of Health*]
NVP .... Nausea and Vomiting in Pregnancy
NVP .... Nevada Power Co. [*NYSE symbol*] (SPSG)
NVP .... Nevirpine [*Organic chemistry*]
NVP .... Nominal Velocity of Propagation [*Electronics*] (PCM)
NVP .... N-Vinylpyrrolidone [*Organic chemistry*]
NVPA .... National Visual Presentation Association (EA)
NvPA.......... Nuveen Pennsylvania Investment Quality Municipal Fund [*Associated Press*] (SAG)
NvPAP2........ Nuveen Pennsylvania Premium Income Municipal Fund [*Associated Press*] (SAG)
NvPIM......... Nuveen Premier Insured Municipal Income Fund [*Associated Press*] (SAG)
NvPMI......... Nuveen Premium Municipal Income Fund [*Associated Press*] (SAG)
NVPO .... Nuclear Vehicle Projects Office [*NASA*]
NVPOWG ..... NASA/VAFB [*National Aeronautical and Space Administration/ Vandenburg Air Force Base*] Payload Operations Working Group
NVPP .... National Vehicle Population Poll (COE)
NVPP .... National Vehicle Population Profile
NVPS .... Night Vision Pilotage System [*Military*]
NVP-U......... Nationale Volkspartij - Unie [*National United People's Party*] [*Netherlands Antilles*] [*Political party*] (PPW)
NVQ .... National Vocational Qualification (WDAA)
NVQ .... National Vocation Qualification [*British*]
NVR .... National Video Resources
NVR .... Naval Vessel Register (MCD)
NVR .... Nonvolatile Residue (NAKS)
NVR .... Norfolk Volunteer Regiment [*British military*] (DMA)
NVR .... No Verification Required (NASA)
NVR .... No Voltage Release [*Electronics*]
NVR .... NVA [*North Vietnam Army*] Regulars (VNW)
NVR .... NVR, Inc. [*AMEX symbol*] (SPSG)
NVRAM .... Nonvolatile Random-Access Memory [*Computer science*]
NVRC .... National Retirees Volunteer Coalition [*An association*]
NvREr .... United States Energy Research Development Administration, Reno, NV [*Library symbol Library of Congress*] (LCLS)
NvRFM........ Grand Lodge of the Free and Accepted Masons of the State of Nevada, Reno, NV [*Library symbol Library of Congress*] (LCLS)
NvRGS .... Church of Jesus Christ of Latter-Day Saints, Genealogical Society Library, Reno Branch, Reno, NV [*Library symbol Library of Congress*] (LCLS)
NvRH .... Harrah's Automobile Collection and Pony Express Museum, Reno, NV [*Library symbol Library of Congress*] (LCLS)

NVRIA.......... National Vision Research Institute of Australia
NvRNC......... National College of the State Judiciary, Law Library, Reno, NV [*Library symbol Library of Congress*] (LCLS)
NVRS.......... National Vegetable Research Station [*Research center British*] (IRC)
NVRS.......... Night Vision Reconnaissance System
NVRS.......... Numerical Value Rating System [*Navy*]
NvRW.......... Washoe County Library, Reno, NV [*Library symbol Library of Congress*] (LCLS)
NvRWL....... Washoe County Law Library, Reno, NV [*Library symbol Library of Congress*] (LCLS)
NVR.WS...... NVR Inc. Wrrt [*AMEX symbol*] (TTSB)
NVs.............. Henry Waldinger Memorial Library, Valley Stream, NY [*Library symbol Library of Congress*] (LCLS)
NVS .... Narrowband Voice Security
NVS .... National Vegetable Society [*British*] (DBA)
NVS .... Neurological Vital Signs [*Medicine*]
NVS .... Neutron Velocity Selector
NVS .... Night Vision Safety [*Automotive rear-view mirrors*]
NVS .... Night Vision System
NVS .... Nonvoting Stock [*Investment term*]
NVS .... Novosibirsk [*Former USSR Seismograph station code, US Geological Survey*] (SEIS)
NVS .... Number of Video Samples
NVS .... Southeastern Baptist Theological Seminary, Wake Forest, NC [*OCLC symbol*] (OCLC)
NVSA .... Ablow [*Vanuatu*] [*ICAO location identifier*] (ICLI)
NVSA .... Natuurbestuurvereniging van Suidelike Afrika [*Southern African Wildlife Management Association - SAWMA*] [*Pretoria, South Africa*] (EAIO)
NVSA .... Nematologiese Vereniging van Suidelike Afrika [*Nematological Society of Southern Africa*] (EAIO)
NVsAE......... Alden Terrace Elementary School, Valley Stream, NY [*Library symbol*] [*Library of Congress*] (LCLS)
NVsBAE....... Brooklyn Avenue School, Valley Stream, NY [*Library symbol*] [*Library of Congress*] (LCLS)
NVsBE......... William L. Buck School, Valley Stream, NY [*Library symbol*] [*Library of Congress*] (LCLS)
NVSC .... Sola [*Vanuatu*] [*ICAO location identifier*] (ICLI)
NVsCE......... Robert W. Carbonaro School, Valley Stream, NY [*Library symbol*] [*Library of Congress*] (LCLS)
NVsCSE....... Clear Stream Avenue Elementary School, Valley Stream, NY [*Library symbol*] [*Library of Congress*] (LCLS)
NVsCSH....... Central Senior High School, Valley Stream, NY [*Library symbol Library of Congress*] (LCLS)
NVSD .... Lo-Linua [*Vanuatu*] [*ICAO location identifier*] (ICLI)
NVSD .... National Vital Statistics Division [*National Center for Health Statistics*] [*Obsolete*]
NVSD .... Night Vision System Development [*Military*]
NVsDE .... Devet Elementary School, Valley Stream, NY [*Library symbol Library of Congress*] (LCLS)
NVSDS......... New Vehicle Satisfaction with Dealer Service [*Quality research*]
NVSE .... Emae [*Vanuatu*] [*ICAO location identifier*] (ICLI)
NVSF .... Graig Cove [*Vanuatu*] [*ICAO location identifier*] (ICLI)
NVsFE......... Forest Elementary School, Valley Stream, NY [*Library symbol Library of Congress*] (LCLS)
NVsFH .... Franklin General Hospital, Valley Stream, NY [*Library symbol Library of Congress*] (LCLS)
NVSG .... Longana [*Vanuatu*] [*ICAO location identifier*] (ICLI)
NVSH.......... Nonvocal Severely Handicapped
NVSH.......... Sara [*Vanuatu*] [*ICAO location identifier*] (ICLI)
NVsHE .... Howell Road School, Valley Stream, NY [*Library symbol*] [*Library of Congress*] (LCLS)
NVSL .... Lamap [*Vanuatu*] [*ICAO location identifier*] (ICLI)
NVSL .... National Veterinary Services Laboratory [*Ames, IA*] [*Department of Agriculture*] (GRD)
NVSM .... Lamen-Bay [*Vanuatu*] [*ICAO location identifier*] (ICLI)
NVSM .... Nonvolatile Semiconductor Memory (MCD)
NVSMD......... Nonvolatile Semiconductor Memory Device (PDAA)
NVsMJH....... Memorial Junior High School, Valley Stream, NY [*Library symbol Library of Congress*] (LCLS)
NvSMM........ Nuveen Select Maturities Municipal Fund [*Associated Press*] (SAG)
NVSN.......... Maewo-Naone [*Vanuatu*] [*ICAO location identifier*] (ICLI)
NVSN.......... N-Vision, Inc. [*NASDAQ symbol*] (SAG)
NVsNSH....... Valley Stream North High School, Valley Stream, NY [*Library symbol*] [*Library of Congress*] (LCLS)
NVSNW........ n-Vision Inc. Wrrt [*NASDAQ symbol*] (TTSB)
NVSO .... Lonorore [*Vanuatu*] [*ICAO location identifier*] (ICLI)
NVsOE .... Ogden Elementary School, Valley Stream, NY [*Library symbol*] [*Library of Congress*] (LCLS)
N-VSOS........ Non-Verbal Scale of Suffering [*Personality development test*] [*Psychology*]
NVSP .... Norsup [*Vanuatu*] [*ICAO location identifier*] (ICLI)
NVSR .... Redcliff [*Vanuatu*] [*ICAO location identifier*] (ICLI)
NVSS .... National Vital Statistics System [*Department of Health and Human Services*] (GFGA)
NVSS .... Nonvolatile Suspended Solids [*Environmental chemistry*]
NVSS .... Normal-Variant Short Stature [*Medicine*]
NVSS .... Santo/Pekoa [*Vanuatu*] [*ICAO location identifier*] (ICLI)
NVsSAE........ Shaw Avenue Elementary School, Valley Stream, NY [*Library symbol*] [*Library of Congress*] (LCLS)
NVsSSH....... South Senior High School, Valley Stream, NY [*Library symbol Library of Congress*] (LCLS)
NVST .... Tongoa [*Vanuatu*] [*ICAO location identifier*] (ICLI)
NVSU .... Ulei [*Vanuatu*] [*ICAO location identifier*] (ICLI)
NVSV .... Valesdir [*Vanuatu*] [*ICAO location identifier*] (ICLI)

NVSW.......... Walaha [*Vanuatu*] [*ICAO location identifier*] (ICLI)
NVsWE........ Willow Elementary School, Valley Stream, NY [*Library symbol Library of Congress*] (LCLS)
NVsWhE....... Wheeler Elementary School, Valley Stream, NY [*Library symbol Library of Congress*] (LCLS)
NVSX .... South West Bay [*Vanuatu*] [*ICAO location identifier*] (ICLI)
NVSZ .... North West Santo [*Vanuatu*] [*ICAO location identifier*] (ICLI)
NVT.............. Navegantes [*Brazil*] [*Airport symbol*] (OAG)
NVT.............. Nelson Vending Technology Ltd. [*Toronto Stock Exchange symbol*]
NVT.............. Nerve, Vein, and Tendon (DAVI)
NVT.............. Network Validation Testing [*Telecommunications*] (CIST)
NVT.............. Network Virtual Terminal
NVT.............. Neuton Velocity Time (IAA)
NVT.............. Norton Villiers Triumph [*Automobile manufacturer*] [*British*]
NVT.............. Novell Virtual Terminal [*Novell, Inc.*] [*Computer science*] (PCM)
NVT.............. Nuisance Valve Tactics
NVTA .... National Visiting Teachers Association (EA)
NVTCS......... Nissan Valve Timing Control System
NVTG .... Norton Villiers Triumph Group [*Automobile manufacturer*] [*British*]
NVTHLSS..... Nevertheless (ROG)
NV-THS....... National Vocational-Technical Honor Society (EA)
NVTK .... Novatek International, Inc. [*NASDAQ symbol*] (SAG)
NVTOC......... Nonvolatile Total Organic Carbon [*Environmental chemistry*]
NVTS .... National Vocational Training Service
NVTS .... Null Voltage Test Set (MCD)
NVTWUGBI... National Vehicular Traffic Workers' Union of Great Britain and Ireland
nvu.............. Nevada [*MARC country of publication code Library of Congress*] (LCCP)
NvU.............. University of Nevada, Reno, NV [*Library symbol Library of Congress*] (LCLS)
NVUE .... NVIEW Corp. [*NASDAQ symbol*] (SAG)
NVVA .... Anatom [*Vanuatu*] [*ICAO location identifier*] (ICLI)
NVVA .... Napa Valley Vintners Association (EA)
NVVB .... Aniwa [*Vanuatu*] [*ICAO location identifier*] (ICLI)
NVVC .... National Vietnam Veterans Coalition (EA)
NVVCCG...... North Vietnamese and Viet Cong Collecting Group [*Defunct*] (EA)
NVVD .... Dillon's Bay [*Vanuatu*] [*ICAO location identifier*] (ICLI)
NVVF .... Futuna [*Vanuatu*] [*ICAO location identifier*] (ICLI)
NVVI .... Ipota [*Vanuatu*] [*ICAO location identifier*] (ICLI)
NVVJ.......... Forari [*Vanuatu*] [*ICAO location identifier*] (ICLI)
NVVK .... Lenakel [*Vanuatu*] [*ICAO location identifier*] (ICLI)
NVVQ .... Quoin Hill [*Vanuatu*] [*ICAO location identifier*] (ICLI)
NVVRS......... National Vietnam Veterans Readjustment Study [*Veterans Administration*]
NVVV .... Port-Vila/Bauerfield [*Vanuatu*] [*ICAO location identifier*] (ICLI)
NVWA .... National Volkswagen Association (EA)
NVWLA .... Napa Valley Wine Library Association (EA)
NVWSC........ Nonvolatile Whole Smoke Condensate [*Environmental chemistry*] (AAMN)
NVX .... North American Vaccine [*AMEX symbol*] (TTSB)
NVX .... North American Vaccine, Inc. [*AMEX symbol*] (SAG)
NVY .... Royal Navy [*British ICAO designator*] (FAAC)
NW.............. Naked Weight
NW.............. Naked Wire (IAA)
nW.............. Nanowatt [*One billionth of a watt*]
NW.............. Narrow Widths [*Construction*]
NW.............. Nasal Wash [*Medicine*] (DMAA)
NW.............. NASA Waiver (KSC)
NW.............. National Westminster Bancorp, Inc. [*NYSE symbol*] (SPSG)
NW.............. National Women's Conference Committee [*Formerly, CCNWC*] (EA)
NW.............. Natl Westminster ADS [*NYSE symbol*] (TTSB)
NW.............. Nat-War Alliance [*Defunct*] (EA)
NW.............. Naval Air Systems Command
NW.............. Net Weight
NW.............. Network (NASA)
NW.............. Network Cells [*Botany*]
NW.............. Net Worth
NW.............. Neville and Winther's Acid
NW.............. New
NW.............. Newsweek [*A publication*] (BRI)
NW.............. New Wave [*Style of music*]
NW.............. New World [*Translation of the Holy Scriptures*] [*A publication*] (BJA)
NW.............. Nominal Width (NATG)
NW.............. Norfolk & Western Railway Co. [*AAR code*]
NW.............. Normal Waste [*Nuclear energy*] (NRCH)
NW.............. Norman-Wood Disease [*Medicine*] (DB)
NW.............. North Wales
NW.............. Northwest
NW.............. North-Western Provinces, High Court Reports [*India*] [*A publication*] (DLA)
NW.............. North Western Reporter [*National Reporter System*] [*A publication*] (DLA)
NW.............. Northwest Orient Airlines, Inc. [*ICAO designator*]
NW.............. Nor-Weberine [*Biochemistry*]
NW.............. Nose Wheel [*Aviation*] (MCD)
NW.............. Not Waiverable (COE)
NW.............. Now
NW.............. No Wait [*Industrial engineering*]
NW.............. No Wind [*Air*] Position [*Navigation*]
NW.............. Nuclear Warfare
NW.............. Nuclear Weapon (NG)
nw----.......... West Indies [*MARC geographic area code Library of Congress*] (LCCP)
NW2............ New River [*California*] [*Seismograph station code, US Geological Survey*] (SEIS)

NW 2d	North Western Reporter, Second Series [*West*] [*A publication*] (AAGC)
NWA	Moheli [*Comoro Islands*] [*Airport symbol*] (OAG)
NWA	Narrogin [*Australia Seismograph station code, US Geological Survey*] (SEIS)
NWA	National Water Alliance (EA)
NWA	National Waterfowl Alliance, Waterfowl USA [*Later, WUSA*] (EA)
NWA	National Watermelon Association (NTPA)
NWA	National Water Well Association, Worthington, OH [*OCLC symbol*] (OCLC)
NWA	National Weather Association (EA)
NWA	National Welders Association [*A union*] [*British*]
NWA	National Wellness Association (EA)
NWA	National Wine Association [*Defunct*] (EA)
NWA	National Wrestling Alliance (DAVI)
NWA	National Writers Association (NTPA)
NWA	Naval Warfare Analysis (MCD)
NWA	Naval Weapons Annex
NWA	Navy Wifeline Association (EA)
NWA	New Work Authorized (MCD)
NWA	New World Alliance [*Defunct*] (EA)
NWA	Niggers with Attitude [*Rap recording group*]
NWA	Northumbrian Water Authority [*British*] (DCTA)
NWA	Northwest Airlines (MHDB)
NWA	Northwest Airlines, Inc. [*ICAO designator*] (FAAC)
NWA	Northwest Orient Airlines, Inc. (MCD)
NWA	Nothin' Worth Askin' [*Rap recording group*]
NWAA	National Wheelchair Athletic Association (EA)
NWAA	National Women's Automotive Association [*Defunct*] (EA)
NWAACC	Northwest Athletic Association of Community Colleges (PSS)
NWAAF	Northwest African Air Forces [*World War II*]
NWAB	Necks with Any Boy [*Slang*]
NWAC	National Weather Analysis Center [*Air Force, Navy*]
NWAC	National Wheelchair Athletic Committee
NWAC	National Women's Advisory Council (NADA)
NWAC	Native Women's Association of Canada
NWAC	Northeast Women's Athletic Conference (PSS)
NWAC	Northwest Airlines'A' [*NASDAQ symbol*] (TTSB)
NWAC	Northwest Airlines Corp. [*NASDAQ symbol*] (SAG)
NWadd	Hepburn Library, Waddington, NY [*Library symbol Library of Congress*] (LCLS)
NWAFC	Northwest and Alaska Fisheries Center [*National Marine Fisheries Service*] [*Department of Commerce*] [*Research center*] (RCD)
NWAG	Naval Warfare Analysis Group
NWAHACA ...	National Warm Air Heating and Air Conditioning Association [*Later, ACCA*] (EA)
NWAI	Nuclear Weapons Acceptance Inspection (NG)
NWAIB	Nuclear Weapon Accident Investigation Board (AABC)
NWald	Josephine-Louise Public Library, Walden, NY [*Library symbol Library of Congress*] (LCLS)
NWall	Wallkill Public Library, Wallkill, NY [*Library symbol Library of Congress*] (LCLS)
NWan	Wantagh Public Library, Wantagh, NY [*Library symbol Library of Congress*] (LCLS)
NWanE	Wantagh Elementary School, Wantagh, NY [*Library symbol Library of Congress*] (LCLS)
NWanFLE	Forest Lake Elementary School, Wantagh, NY [*Library symbol Library of Congress*] (LCLS)
NWanJH	Wantagh Junior High School, Wantagh, NY [*Library symbol*] [*Library of Congress*] (LCLS)
NWanJS	Wantagh Junior-Senior High, Wantagh, NY [*Library symbol Library of Congress*] (LCLS)
NWanME	Mandalay Elementary School, Wantagh, NY [*Library symbol Library of Congress*] (LCLS)
NWanSH	Wantagh Senior High School, Wantagh, NY [*Library symbol*] [*Library of Congress*] (LCLS)
NWanSPE	Sunrise Park Elementary School, Wantagh, NY [*Library symbol Library of Congress*] (LCLS)
NWAO	Narrogin [*Australia Seismograph station code, US Geological Survey*] (SEIS)
NWAP	National White American Party (BJA)
NWapA	Mount Alvernia Seminary, Wappingers Falls, NY [*Library symbol*] [*Library of Congress*] (LCLS)
NWAPP	National Woman Abuse Prevention Project (EA)
nwaq--	Antigua [*MARC geographic area code Library of Congress*] (LCCP)
NWas	Moffat Library Association, Washingtonville, NY [*Library symbol Library of Congress*] (LCLS)
NWASC	Northwest Association of Schools and Colleges (DHP)
NWatfG	General Electric Co., Silicone Products Department, Waterford, NY [*Library symbol Library of Congress*] (LCLS)
NWatt	Roswell P. Flower Memorial Public Library, Watertown, NY [*Library symbol Library of Congress*] (LCLS)
NWattJ	Jefferson Community College, Watertown, NY [*Library symbol Library of Congress*] (LCLS)
NWattJHi	Jefferson County Historical Society, Watertown, NY [*Library symbol Library of Congress*] (LCLS)
NWattKH	Samaritan Keep Nursing Home, Medical Library, Watertown, NY [*Library symbol Library of Congress*] (LCLS)
NWattMH	Mercy Hospital of Watertown, Watertown, NY [*Library symbol Library of Congress*] (LCLS)
NWattN	North Country Library System, Watertown, NY [*Library symbol Library of Congress*] (LCLS)
NWatvlA	Watervliet Arsenal Library, Watervliet, NY [*Library symbol Library of Congress*] (LCLS)
NWAVL	Now Available (NOAA)

NWB	National Wiring Bureau [*Defunct*] (EA)
NWB	Naval Weapons Bulletin
NWB	Nederlandse Waterschapsbank NV [*Waterschaps Bank of the Netherlands*]
NWB	New War Department Building [*Obsolete*]
NWB	Non-Weight-Bearing [*Orthopedics and physical therapy*] (DAVI)
NWB	Northwestbound [*ICAO designator*] (FAAC)
NWB	North Western Bell (HGAA)
NWB	Northwest Towboat Tariff Bureau, Inc., Seattle WA [*STAC*]
NWB	No Weight-Bearing [*orthopedics*] (DAVI)
NWBA	National Wheelchair Basketball Association (EA)
nwbb--	Barbados [*MARC geographic area code Library of Congress*] (LCCP)
NWBB	Noumea [*New Caledonia*] [*ICAO location identifier*] (ICLI)
NwbBc	Newberry Bancorp, Inc. [*Associated Press*] (SAG)
nwbc--	Barbuda [*MARC geographic area code Library of Congress*] (LCCP)
NWbC	Cardion Electronics, Woodbury, NY [*Library symbol Library of Congress*] (LCLS)
NWBC	National Women's Business Council
NWBC	National Wooden Box Council [*Later, NWPCA*] (EA)
nwbf--	Bahamas [*MARC geographic area code Library of Congress*] (LCCP)
NWBHI	Nuclear Weapon Burst Height Indicator
NWbN	Northwest by North
NWBW	National Women Bowling Writers Association (EA)
NWbW	Northwest by West
NWbW	Waldemar Medical Research Foundation, Woodbury, NY [*Library symbol Library of Congress*] (LCLS)
NWC	National Waco Club (EA)
NWC	National War College [*Later, UND*] [*DoD*]
NWC	National Warning Center [*Civil Defense*]
NWC	National Water Center (EA)
NWC	National Water Commission [*Terminated, 1973*]
NWC	National Water Council [*British*] (DCTA)
NWC	National Waterfowl Council (EA)
NWC	National Watershed Congress (EA)
NWC	National Waterways Conference (EA)
NWC	National Wiretap Commission [*Department of Justice*]
NWC	National Women's Coalition [*Defunct*] (EA)
NWC	National Woodie Club (EA)
NWC	National Writers Club (EA)
NWC	Nationwide Cellular Service, Inc. (EFIS)
NWC	Naval War College
NWC	Naval Weapons Center
NWC	Net Working Capital
NWC	Net Worth Certificate (EBF)
NWC	New ACS Ltd. [*United Republic of Tanzania*] [*FAA designator*] (FAAC)
NWC	New World Club (EA)
NWC	New World Coalition (EA)
NWC	Northwest Cape
NWC	Northwest College [*Washington*]
NWC	North West Community College Library [*UTLAS symbol*]
NWC	Nuclear War Capability (AAG)
NWC	Nuclear Weapons Complex (COE)
NWC	Nuclear Weapons Control
NWC	Wingate College, Wingate, NC [*OCLC symbol*] (OCLC)
NWCA	National Water Carriers Association
NWCA	National Woodcarvers Association (EA)
NWCA	National Wrestling Coaches Association (EA)
NWCA	National Writing Centers Association (NTPA)
NWCA	Navy Wives Clubs of America (EA)
NWCA	NewCare Health [*NASDAQ symbol*] (TTSB)
NWCA	New Care Health Corp. [*NASDAQ symbol*] (SAG)
NWCA	Northwest Cherry Briners Association
NWCAA	National War College Alumni Association
NWCAEU	National Women's Conference of the American Ethical Union (EA)
NWC/ARP	Naval War College Advanced Research Program [*Newport, RI*]
NWCC	National Water Co. Conference [*Later, NAWC*]
NWCC	National Women's Conference Committee (EA)
NWCC	Neutron Well Coincidence Counter [*Nuclear energy*] (NRCH)
NWCC	Northwest Christian College [*Oregon*]
NWCC	Noumea/La Tontouta [*New Caledonia*] [*ICAO location identifier*] (ICLI)
NWCCA	Naval Weapons Center, Corona Annex [*California*]
NWC/CAR	Naval War College Center for Advanced Research [*Newport, RI*]
NWCCL	Naval Weapons Center, Corona Laboratories [*California*]
NWCCS	Naval Worldwide Command and Control System (MCD)
NWCDC	North West Cooperative Development Council [*British*]
NWCF	New Waste Calcining Facility [*Nuclear energy*] (NUCP)
NWCG	New World Communic Grp'A' [*NASDAQ symbol*] (TTSB)
NWCG	New World Communictions Corp. [*NASDAQ symbol*] (SAG)
NWCG	Nuclear Weapons Coordinating Group
NWCHA	Northwest Clearing House Association (TBD)
NWCI	New World Coffee [*NASDAQ symbol*] (TTSB)
NWCI	New World Coffee, Inc. [*NASDAQ symbol*] (SAG)
NWCIEP	Nation-Wide Committee on Import-Export Policy [*Defunct*] (EA)
nwcj--	Cayman Islands [*MARC geographic area code Library of Congress*] (LCCP)
NwCm	News Communications, Inc. [*Associated Press*] (SAG)
NWCME	National Winter Convention on Military Electronics [*IEEE*] (MCD)
NWC/NW	Naval War College / Naval Warfare Course (DNAB)
nwco--	Curacao Group [*MARC geographic area code Library of Congress*] (LCCP)
NWCP	National Wetlands Conservation Project [*Defunct*] (EA)
NWCP	Navy Weight-Control Program (DNAB)
NWCR	Naval War College Review [*A publication*]

NWCR.......... Nuclear Weapons Correction Report [*Army*] (AABC)
NWCRB........ Navy War Contracts Relief Board
NWCS.......... NATO-Wide Communications System (NATG)
NWCS.......... Nuclear Weapons Control System
NWCTU........ National Woman's Christian Temperance Union (WDAA)
nwcu.......... Cuba [*MARC geographic area code Library of Congress*] (LCCP)
NWD........... Naval Weapons Directory
NWD........... Network Wide Directory
NWD........... New World Dictionary [*A publication*]
NWD........... Northwest Air Services Ltd. [*Nigeria*] [*ICAO designator*] (FAAC)
NWD........... Northwest Drug Co. Ltd. [*Toronto Stock Exchange symbol*]
NWD........... Number of Words (MSA)
NWDA.......... National Wholesale Druggists' Association (EA)
NWDA.......... National Wine Distributors' Association (EA)
NwDay......... New Day Beverage, Inc. [*Associated Press*] (SAG)
NWDC.......... National Wildlife Defence Council (USDC)
NWDC.......... National Wildlife Defense Council [*Marine science*] (OSRA)
NWDC.......... Navigation/Weapon Delivery Computer (PDAA)
NWDC.......... Northwest Drama Conference (EA)
NWDC/S....... Navigation/Weapons Delivery Computer/System
NWDEN........ Number of Words per Entry (MSA)
NWDGA........ National Wholesale Dry Goods Association [*Later, NATAD*]
NWdmA........ Woodmere Academy, Woodmere, NY [*Library symbol*] [*Library of Congress*] (LCLS)
NWdmE........ No. 6 Elementary School, Woodmere, NY [*Library symbol*] [*Library of Congress*] (LCLS)
NWDO.......... National Workforce Development Office (COE)
nwdq--........ Dominica [*MARC geographic area code Library of Congress*] (LCCP)
nwdr--......... Dominican Republic [*MARC geographic area code Library of Congress*] (LCCP)
NWDS.......... National Water Data System [*US Geological Survey*] [*Reston, VA*]
NWDS.......... Navigation/Weapons Delivery System
NWDS.......... Network Wide Directory System (MHDI)
NWDS.......... Noah Worcester Dermatological Society (EA)
NWDS.......... Number of Words
NWDSEN...... Number of Words per Entry
NWE........... Narrow Width Effect (IAA)
NWE........... Newline Resources Ltd. [*Vancouver Stock Exchange symbol*]
NWE........... Northwest Aero Associates, Inc. [*FAA designator*] (FAAC)
NWE........... Nuclear Weapons Effects
NWe........... Westbury Memorial Public Library, Westbury, NY [*Library symbol Library of Congress*] (LCLS)
NWEA.......... National Women's Economic Alliance [*Washington, DC*] (EA)
NWEA.......... National Wood Energy Association (EA)
NWEAF........ National Women's Economic Alliance Foundation (NTPA)
NWEB.......... Northwestern Electricity Board [*British*]
NWeBE........ Board of Cooperative Educational Services, Nassau Education Resource Center, Westbury, NY [*Library symbol Library of Congress*] (LCLS)
NWeBGE...... Bowling Green Elementary School, Westbury, NY [*Library symbol*] [*Library of Congress*] (LCLS)
NWebPH...... Pilgrim Hospital, West Brentwood, NY [*Library symbol Library of Congress*] (LCLS)
NWEC.......... Nuclear Weapons Effects Course (MCD)
NWeCJS...... W. Tresper Clarke Junior-Senior High School, Westbury, NY [*Library symbol*] [*Library of Congress*] (LCLS)
NWED.......... Nuclear Weapon Effects Development
NWeDE........ Drexel Elementary School, Westbury, NY [*Library symbol*] [*Library of Congress*] (LCLS)
NWEE.......... National Women's Employment and Education [*Defunct*] (EA)
NWEF.......... National Women's Education Fund (EA)
NWEF.......... Naval Weapons Evaluation Facility [*Kirtland Air Force Base, NM*]
NWEF.......... New World Education Fund (EA)
NWEF.......... North Western Expeditionary Force [*Norway*] [*World War II*]
NWEF.......... Nuclear Weapons Education Fund (EA)
NWef.......... Patterson Library, Westfield, NY [*Library symbol*] [*Library of Congress*] (LCLS)
NWefHi........ Chautauqua County Historical Society, Westfield, NY [*Library symbol Library of Congress*] (LCLS)
NWefMH...... Westfield Memorial Hospital, Inc., Westfield, NY [*Library symbol Library of Congress*] (LCLS)
NWehb......... Westhampton Free Library, Westhampton Beach, NY [*Library symbol Library of Congress*] (LCLS)
NWehbJH..... Westhampton Beach Junior High School, Westhampton Beach, NY [*Library symbol Library of Congress*] (LCLS)
NWeJH........ Westbury Junior High School, Westbury, NY [*Library symbol*] [*Library of Congress*] (LCLS)
NWel.......... David A. Howe Public Library, Wellsville, NY [*Library symbol Library of Congress*] (LCLS)
NWEL.......... Nuclear Weapons Effects Laboratory
NWelH........ Jones Memorial Hospital, Wellsville, NY [*Library symbol Library of Congress*] (LCLS)
NWeM......... Metco, Inc., Westbury, NY [*Library symbol Library of Congress*] (LCLS)
NWEO......... Nuclear Weapon Effects Office [*DoD*] (RDA)
NWEO......... Nuclear Weapon Employment Officer (AABC)
NWEP......... Nuclear Weapons Effects Panel
NWePLE...... Powell's Lane Elementary School, Westbury, NY [*Library symbol*] [*Library of Congress*] (LCLS)
NWePSE...... Park School Early Childhood Center, Westbury, NY [*Library symbol*] [*Library of Congress*] (LCLS)
NWEQ........ Northwest Equity Corp. [*NASDAQ symbol*] (TTSB)
NWER......... Nuclear Weapons Effects Research [*Army*]
NWER/T...... Nuclear Weapons Effects Research and Testing [*Army*] (RDA)
NWES......... Nuclear Weapons Electronic Specialist (AABC)

NWes.......... Olive Free Library Association, West Shokan, NY [*Library symbol Library of Congress*] (LCLS)
NWESA....... Naval Weapons Engineering Support Activity (MCD)
NWesbHS..... West Bablyon High School, West Babylon, NY [*Library symbol*] [*Library of Congress*] (LCLS)
NWesbJH..... West Babylon Junior High School, West Babylon, NY [*Library symbol*] [*Library of Congress*] (LCLS)
NWeSH....... Westbury Senior High School, Westbury, NY [*Library symbol*] [*Library of Congress*] (LCLS)
NWesyM...... Suffolk Marine Museum, West Sayville, NY [*Library symbol Library of Congress*] (LCLS)
NWET......... Nuclear Weapon Effects Test
nweu--........ Sint Eustatius [*MARC geographic area code Library of Congress*] (LCCP)
NWevNS...... West Valley Nuclear Services Co., West Valley, NY [*Library symbol Library of Congress*] (LCLS)
NWF........... International Women's Forum [*National Women's Forum*] [*Acronym is based on former name,*] (EA)
NWF........... National War Formulary
NWF........... National War Fund
NWF........... National Welfare Fund (WDAA)
NWF........... National Wildlife Federation (EA)
NWF........... Naval Weapons Factory [*Formerly, NGF*]
NWF........... Naval Working Fund [*Navy, Coast Guard*]
NWF........... New Wilderness Foundation (EA)
NWF........... New World Foundation (EA)
NWF........... Nuclear Waste Fund (NUCP)
NWF........... Numerical Weather Facility
NWFA......... National Wholesale Furniture Association (EA)
NWFA......... National Wood Flooring Association (EA)
NWFA......... Northwest Farm Managers Association (EA)
NWFA......... Northwest Fisheries Association (EA)
NWFAL....... Nation-Wide Fallout (SAA)
NWFC......... Nuclear Weapons Freeze Campaign (EA)
NWFF......... North West Frontier Fellowship (EA)
NWFI......... Non-Woven Fabrics Institute [*Defunct*] (EA)
NWFMA...... Northwest Farm Managers Association
NWFP........ North-West Frontier Province [*Pakistan*] (PD)
NWFP........ Nuclear Weapons Fire Planning (MCD)
NWFP........ Rocky Flats/Nuclear Weapons Facilities Project [*Organization with goal of nuclear disarmament*] [*Defunct*] (EA)
NWF Pak ... North West Frontier, Pakistan (ILCA)
NWFS........ NetWare File System [*Computer science*]
NWFS........ NWS Capital Financing Trust [*Associated Press*] (SAG)
NWFSPCN... Nahanni National Park, Parks Canada [*Parc National Nahanni, Parcs Canada*] Fort Simpson, Northwest Territories [*Library symbol National Library of Canada*] (NLC)
NWFSPCW... Wood Buffalo National Park, Parks Canada [*Parc National Wood Buffalo, Parcs Canada*] Fort Smith, Northwest Territories [*Library symbol National Library of Canada*] (NLC)
NWFST .... Thebacha College Library, Fort Smith, Northwest Territories [*Library symbol National Library of Canada*] (NLC)
NWFWA...... Northwest Forest Workers Association [*Defunct*] (EA)
NWFZ......... Nuclear Weapons-Free Zone
NWG......... National Wire Gauge
NWG........... New Goliath Minerals Ltd. [*Toronto Stock Exchange symbol Vancouver Stock Exchange symbol*]
nwga--......... Greater Antilles [*MARC geographic area code Library of Congress*] (LCCP)
NWGA......... National Wool Growers Association [*Later, ASIA*] (EA)
NWGA......... Northwest Guides Association [*Defunct*]
nwgd.......... Grenada [*MARC geographic area code Library of Congress*] (LCCP)
NWGDE....... Nordic Working Group on Development Education [*Nordic Council of Ministers*] [*Denmark*] (EAIO)
nwgp--......... Guadeloupe [*MARC geographic area code Library of Congress*] (LCCP)
NWGP......... Nuclear War Graphics Project [*Defunct*] (EA)
nwgs-- .... Grenadines [*MARC geographic area code Library of Congress*] (LCCP)
NWGS......... Naval Warfare Gaming System
NWGSFW.... National Working Group on Screw Fly Worm [*Australia*]
NWGWU .... National Warehouse and General Workers' Union [*British*]
NWH........... Nawa Air Transport [*Hungary ICAO designator*] (FAAC)
NWH........... New Hombre Resources [*Vancouver Stock Exchange symbol*]
NWH........... Normal Working Hours
NWh........... West Hempstead Public Library, West Hempstead, NY [*Library symbol Library of Congress*] (LCLS)
NWHA......... National Wholesale Hardware Association (EA)
NWHC......... National Women's Health Coalition [*Later, IWHC*]
NWHC......... Naval Weapons Handling Center
NWhCE....... Cornwell Avenue School, West Hempstead, NY [*Library symbol*] [*Library of Congress*] (LCLS)
NWHF......... National Wildlife Health Foundation (EA)
NWHF......... National Women's Hall of Fame (EA)
NWhh.......... Whitehall Free Library, Whitehall, NY [*Library symbol*] [*Library of Congress*] (LCLS)
NWhHS....... West Hempstead High School, West Hempstead, NY [*Library symbol*] [*Library of Congress*] (LCLS)
nwhi--......... Hispaniola [*MARC geographic area code Library of Congress*] (LCCP)
NWHI......... Northwestern Hawaiian Islands
NWHL........ National Wildlife Health Laboratory [*Department of the Interior*] (GRD)
NWHL........ Naval Weapons Handling Laboratory

NWhMS	West Hempstead Middle School, West Hempstead, NY [*Library symbol*] [*Library of Congress*] (LCLS)
NWHN	National Women's Health Network (EA)
NWHP	National Women's History Project (EA)
NWhp	White Plains Public Library, White Plains, NY [*Library symbol Library of Congress*] (LCLS)
NWhpG	College of White Plains, White Plains, NY [*Library symbol Library of Congress*] (LCLS)
NWhpI	IBM Library Processing Center, White Plains, NY [*Library symbol Library of Congress*] (LCLS)
NWhpNC	Nynex Corp., White Plains, NY [*Library symbol*] [*Library of Congress*] (LCLS)
NWhpNH	New York Hospital, Westchester Division, White Plains, NY [*Library symbol Library of Congress*] (LCLS)
NWhpSC	New York State Supreme Court Law Library, White Plains, NY [*Library symbol Library of Congress*] (LCLS)
NWhpT	Texaco Inc., Corp. Library, White Plains, NY [*Library symbol*] [*Library of Congress*] (LCLS)
NWhpTI	Temple Israel Library, White Plains, NY [*Library symbol Library of Congress*] (LCLS)
NWhpW	Westchester Library System, White Plains, NY [*Library symbol Library of Congress*] (LCLS)
NWHRC	National Women's Health Resource Center (EA)
NWHRN	Northwest Territories Public Library Services, Hay River, Northwest Territories [*Library symbol National Library of Canada*] (NLC)
NWHSLC	Northern Wisconsin Health Science Library Cooperative [*Library network*]
nwht--	Haiti [*MARC geographic area code Library of Congress*] (LCCP)
NWhWE	George Washington School, West Hempstead, NY [*Library symbol*] [*Library of Congress*] (LCLS)
NWI	National Wetlands Inventory
NWI	Netherlands West Indies
NWI	Networking and World Information [*Electronic information and communications exchange service*]
NWI	Norwich [*England*] [*Airport symbol*] (OAG)
NWI	Nuclear Weapons Inventory (SSD)
NWI	Nuinsco Resources Ltd. [*Toronto Stock Exchange symbol*]
NWi	West Islip Public Library, West Islip, NY [*Library symbol Library of Congress*] (LCLS)
NWIAC	Arctic College, Iqualuit, Northwest Territories [*Library symbol National Library of Canada*] (BIB)
NWIB	National Westminster Investment Bank [*British*]
NWIC	National Water Information Clearinghouse [*Proposed*] [*US Geological Survey*]
NWIC	National Women's Insurance Center (EA)
NWIC	Northeast Women's Intercollegiate Association (PSS)
NWICO	New World Information and Communications Order [*UNESCO*]
NWiH	Good Samaritan Hospital, West Islip, NY [*Library symbol Library of Congress*] (LCLS)
NWII	Inuvik Scientific Resource Centre, Indian and Northern Affairs Canada [*CentreScientifique de Ressources d'Inuvik, Affaires Indiennes et du Nord Canada*], Northwest Territories [*Library symbol National Library of Canada*] (NLC)
NWIIE	Eastern Arctic Research Laboratory, Indian and Northern Affairs Canada [*Laboratoire de Recherches Arctique de l'Est, Affaires Indiennes et du Nord Canada*], Igloolik, Northwest Territories [*Library symbol National Library of Canada*] (BIB)
NWiIP	Willard Psychiatric Center, Willard, NY [*Library symbol Library of Congress*] (LCLS)
NWiIs	Wilson Free Library, Wilson, NY [*Library symbol Library of Congress*] (LCLS)
NWiIsHi	Wilson Historical Society, Wilson, NY [*Library symbol Library of Congress*] (LCLS)
NwImag	New Image Industries, Inc. [*Associated Press*] (SAG)
NWin	Windham Public Library, Windham, NY [*Library symbol Library of Congress*] (LCLS)
NWIO	New World Information Order [*Term coined by the Nonaligned Countries at their Fifth Summit Meeting in 1976*]
NWIP	Naval Warfare Information Publication
NWIP	Naval Warfare Intercept Procedures (MCD)
NWIP	North Wales Independent Press
NWIR	National Wireless Holdings, Inc. [*NASDAQ symbol*] (SAG)
NWIR	Natl Wireless Hldgs [*NASDAQ symbol*] (TTSB)
NWIRP	Naval Weapons Industrial Reserve Plant (AFM)
NWIS	National Water Information System [*Department of the Interior*] (GFGA)
NWIS	Naval Weaponeering Information Sheet (MCD)
NWISO	Naval Weapons Industrial Support Office (DNAB)
NWIT	Nuclear Waste Isolation Technology (NUCP)
NWIYRA	North West Intercollegiate Yacht Racing Association
NWJA	National Wholesale Jewelers Association [*Later, AJDA*] (EA)
nwjm	Jamaica [*MARC geographic area code Library of Congress*] (LCCP)
NWK	Network Equipment Technologies, Inc. [*NYSE symbol*] (SPSG)
NWK	Network Equip Tech [*NYSE symbol*] (TTSB)
NWK	Norwalk Public Library, Norwalk, CT [*Inactive*] [*OCLC symbol*] (OCLC)
NwkCmp	Network Computing Devices, Inc. [*Associated Press*] (SAG)
NwkIm	Network Imaging Corp. [*Associated Press*] (SAG)
NwkImg	Network Imaging Corp. [*Associated Press*] (SAG)
NWKLS	Northwest Kansas Library System [*Library network*]
NWL	National Water Lift Co. (MCD)
NWL	National Women's League of the United Synagogue of America [*Later, AWL*] (EA)
NWL	Natural Wavelength
NWL	Naval Weapons Laboratory [*Later, NSWC*]
NWL	Newell Co. [*NYSE symbol*] (SPSG)
NWL	Newline Development [*Vancouver Stock Exchange symbol*]
NWL	Normal Water Leg [*Nuclear energy*] (NRCH)
NWL	Normal Water Level (IAA)
NWL	North Wright Air, Ltd. [*Canada*] [*FAA designator*] (FAAC)
nwla--	Lesser Antilles [*MARC geographic area code Library of Congress*] (LCCP)
NWLA	National Women and the Law Association (EA)
NWLA	Northern Woods Logging Association (EA)
NW Law Rev...	Northwestern Law Review [*A publication*] (DLA)
NWLB	National War Labor Board [*World War II*]
NWLC	National Women's Law Center (EA)
NWL/D	Naval Weapons Laboratory / Dahlgren [*Virginia*] (DNAB)
NWldP	New World Power Corp. (The) [*Associated Press*] (SAG)
NWldPwr	[*The*] New World Power Corp. [*Associated Press*] (SAG)
NWLDYA	National Wholesale Lumber Distributing Yard Association (EA)
NWLF	National Watermen and Lightermen's Federation [*A union*] [*British*]
NWLF	New World Liberation Front
nwli--	Leeward Islands [*MARC geographic area code Library of Congress*] (LCCP)
NWLI	National Western Life Insurance Co. [*NASDAQ symbol*] (NQ)
NWLIA	Natl Western Life Ins'A' [*NASDAQ symbol*] (TTSB)
NWL Rev	North Western Law Review [*Chicago*] [*A publication*] (DLA)
NWLS	Northwest Wisconsin Library System [*Library network*]
NWM	Morris County Free Library, Whippany, NJ [*OCLC symbol*] (OCLC)
NWM	Newfields Minerals Ltd. [*Toronto Stock Exchange symbol*]
NWM	New Ways Ministry (EA)
NWM	New World Monkey
NWM	Northwest Monsoon
NWM	United States Military Academy, West Point, NY [*Library symbol Library of Congress*] (LCLS)
NWMA	National Woodwork Manufacturers Association [*Formerly, NDMA*] [*Later, NWWDA*] (EA)
NWMA	Northwest Mining Association (EA)
NWMAF	National Women's Martial Arts Federation (EA)
NWMC	National Wool Marketing Corp. (EA)
NWMC	Northwest Michigan College
NWMF	National Women's Music Festival (EA)
NWMF	Nuclear Weapons Maintenance Foreman (AABC)
NwMilfd	New Milford Bank & Trust Co. [*Associated Press*] (SAG)
nwmj--	Montserrat [*MARC geographic area code Library of Congress*] (LCCP)
NWMKT	Newmarket [*Urban district in England*]
NWML	National Women's Mailing List (EA)
NWMP	North-West Mounted Police [*Later, RCMP*] [*Canada*]
nwmq--	Martinique [*MARC geographic area code Library of Congress*] (LCCP)
NWMRS	National Waste Minimization and Recycling Strategy [*Australia*]
NWMS	Nazarene World Mission Society (EA)
NWMS	Nuclear Weapons Maintenance Specialist (AABC)
NwmtG	Newmont Gold Co. [*Associated Press*] (SAG)
NWMTI	Northwest Medical Team International
NWN	National Workers Network [*Defunct*] (EA)
NWN	Newcan Minerals [*Vancouver Stock Exchange symbol*]
NWN	New Warrior Network [*An association*] (EA)
NWN	Nonwhite Noise
NWN	Northwestern
NWN	Northwinds Northern Ltd. [*Canada ICAO designator*] (FAAC)
NWN	Nuclear Waste News [*Business Publishers, Inc.*] [*No longer available online*] [*Information service or system*] (CRD)
nwna--	Netherlands Antilles [*MARC geographic area code Library of Congress*] (LCCP)
NWNet	Northwestern States Network [*Computer science*] (TNIG)
NWNG	Northwest Natural Gas [*NASDAQ symbol*] (TTSB)
NWNG	Northwest Natural Gas Co. [*NASDAQ symbol*] (NQ)
NWNSA	National Women's Neckwear and Scarf Association (EA)
NW-NW	No Work - No Woo [*Slogan adopted by women war workers in Albina shipyards in Portland, Oregon, who agreed not to date men who were absent from work*] [*World War II*]
NWO	Directory of National Women's Organizations [*A publication*]
NWO	NASA Washington Office (KSC)
NWO	Netherlands Organization for Scientific Research
NWO	New Work Opportunities [*A publication*]
NWO	New World Order [*Bush administration*]
NWO	Nonwoven Oriented
NWO	Nuclear Weapons Officer
NWOA	National Woodland Owners Association (EA)
NWOBHM ...	New Wave of British Heavy Metal [*Rock music type, 1979-81*]
NWOC	Naval Weather and Oceanographic Center (DOMA)
NWOFC	Numerical Weather and Oceanographic Forecasting Center [*Marine science*] (MSC)
NWOO	NATO Wartime Oil Organization (NATG)
NWOR	Neworld Bancorp, Inc. [*NASDAQ symbol*] (NQ)
NWP	National Water Project [*Later, RCAP*] (EA)
NWP	National Woman's Party (EA)
NWP	National Writing Project (EA)
NWP	Nationwide Outdoor Recreation Plan [*Bureau of Outdoor Recreation*]
NWP	NATO and Warsaw Pact [*Projects*] (NATG)
NWP	Naval Warfare Procedures (MCD)
NWP	Naval Warfare Publications
NWP	Naval Weapons Plant (AAG)
NWP	Naval Weapons Publications
NWP	Northwestern Pacific Railroad Co. [*AAR code*]
NWP	North-Western Provinces, High Court Reports [*India*] [*A publication*] (DLA)

NWP	Northwest Passage (ROG)
NWP	Northwest Plastics, Inc. (EFIS)
NWP	Northwest Provinces
NWP	Nuclear Waste Project [*Defunct*] (EA)
NWP	Numerical Weather Prediction
NWP	NWP Resources [*Vancouver Stock Exchange symbol*]
NWp...........	Williston Park Public Library, Williston Park, NY [*Library symbol Library of Congress*] (LCLS)
NWPA.........	Nuclear Waste Policy Act (NRCH)
NWPA.........	Nuclear Waste Policy Act of 1982 (GAAI)
NWPAG.......	NATO Wartime Preliminary Analysis Group (NATG)
NwPar.........	New Paradigm Software [*Associated Press*] (SAG)
NWPB.........	National Watermelon Promotion Board
NWPC.........	National Women's Political Caucus (EA)
NWPC.........	[*The*] New World Power Corp. [*NASDAQ symbol*] (SAG)
NWPC.........	Northwest Provinces Code [*India*] [*A publication*] (DLA)
NWPCA.......	National Wooden Pallet and Container Association (EA)
NWPCB.......	Naval Warfare Planning Chart Bases (MCD)
NWPCE.......	New World Power [*NASDAQ symbol*] (TTSB)
NWPCP.......	National Wetlands Priority Conservation Plan (COE)
NWpCsE.....	Center Street Elementary School, Williston Park, NY [*Library symbol*] [*Library of Congress*] (LCLS)
NWPF.........	National Water Purification Foundation
NWPF.........	Nonwoven Polyester Fabric
NWPHC.......	Northwest Provinces, High Court Reports [*India*] [*A publication*] (DLA)
NwpkRs	Newpark Resources, Inc. [*Associated Press*] (SAG)
NWPL	Naval Warfare Publications Library (NVT)
NWPMA......	National Wooden Pallet Manufacturers Association [*Later, NWPCA*] (EA)
NWPO.........	Northwest Pacific Oceanographers [*An association*] (NOAA)
NWPOG.......	Numerical Weather Prediction Operational Grid (SAA)
NWPP	Nationwide Permit Program [*Army Corps of Engineers*] (GFGA)
NWPPCA......	Auyuittuq National Park, Parks Canada [*Parc National Auyuittuq, Parcs Canada*] Pangnirtung, Northwest Territories [*Library symbol National Library of Canada*] (NLC)
nwpr--........	Puerto Rico [*MARC geographic area code Library of Congress*] (LCCP)
NWPrA........	Natl Westminster Pref'A'ADS [*NYSE symbol*] (TTSB)
NWPrB........	Natl Westminster Pref'B'ADS [*NYSE symbol*] (TTSB)
NWPS	National Wilderness Preservation System
NWPS	Northwestern Public Service Co. [*Associated Press*] (SAG)
NWPS	NWPS Capital Financing Tr PERCS [*Associated Press*] (SAG)
NWPSC.......	Nationwide Postal-Strike Contingency Plan (DNAB)
NWPU.........	Numerical Weather Prediction Unit (DNAB)
NWPW........	Naval Weapons Plant, Washington, DC
NWPX.........	Northwest Pipe [*NASDAQ symbol*] (TTSB)
NWPYVO......	National Working Party of Youth Volunteer Organisers (AIE)
NWQ	Northwest Digital Ltd. [*Toronto Stock Exchange symbol*]
NWQI.........	National Water Quality Inventory [*Environmental Protection Agency*]
NWQL.........	National Water Quality Laboratory
NWQSS........	National Water Quality Surveillance System [*Dicontinued, 1981*] [*Environmental Protection Agency*]
NWR	National Welfare Rights (WDAA)
NWR	National Wildlife Refuge (WDAA)
NWR	National Women's Register [*British*] (DBA)
NWR	Navy Weapons Requirement
NWR	Next Word Request
NWR	NOAA [*National Oceanic and Atmospheric Administration*] Weather Radio (NOAA)
NWR	Normotensive Wistar Rat (DB)
NWR	North Western Railway [*India*]
NWR	Northwestern Reporter [*Commonly cited NW*] [*A publication*] (DLA)
NWR	North Western Reporter [*Legal*]
NWR	Nuclear Weapons Report [*Army*] (AABC)
NWRA.........	National Waterbed Retailers Association (EA)
NWRA.........	National Water Resources Association (EA)
NWRA.........	National Wheel and Rim Association (EA)
NWRA.........	National Wildlife Refuge Association (EA)
NWRA.........	National Wildlife Rehabilitators Association (EA)
NWRA.........	National Women's Rowing Association [*Later, USRA*] (EA)
NWRC.........	National Weather Records Center [*Later, National Climatic Center*] [*National Oceanic and Atmospheric Administration*]
NWRC.........	National Wildflower Research Center (EA)
NWRC.........	Naval Warfare Research Center (MCD)
NWRC.........	Nebraska Water Resources Center [*University of Nebraska - Lincoln*] [*Research center*] (RCD)
NWRC.........	Northeast Watershed Research Center [*University Park, PA*] [*Department of Agriculture*] (GRD)
NWREL	Northwest Regional Educational Laboratory [*Portland, OR*] [*Research center*]
NW Rep	Northwestern Reporter [*Commonly cited NW*] [*A publication*] (DLA)
NWREP.......	Nuclear Weapons Report (COE)
NW Repr.....	North Western Reporter [*A publication*] (DLA)
NW Rev Ord...	Northwest Territories Revised Ordinances [*Canada*] [*A publication*] (DLA)
NWRF	Naval Weather Research Facility
NWRHB.......	North West Regional Health Board [*Tasmania, Australia*]
NWRI	National Water Research Institute [*Environment Canada*] [*Research center*] (RCD)
NwrldCf........	New World Coffee, Inc. [*Associated Press*] (SAG)
NWRLF	New World Radical Liberation Front (NADA)
NWRN.........	Northwestern (FAAC)
NWRO.........	National Welfare Rights Organization [*Defunct*]
NWRS	National Wildlife Refuge System (WDAA)

NWRS.........	North-West Recording Society [*Record label*]
NWRS.........	Nuclear Weapons Requirements Study (CINC)
NwRSA	Northwest Region Spinners Association (EA)
NWRT	National Wildlife Rescue Team (EA)
NWRWA......	North West Regional Water Authority [*Tasmania, Australia*]
NWS	National Watercolor Society (EA)
NWS	National Waterways Study [*Marine science*] (MSC)
NWS	National Weather Service [*Formerly, US Weather Bureau*] [*Silver Spring, MD*] [*National Oceanic and Atmospheric Administration*]
NWS	National Winter Sports [*Association*] [*Defunct*] (EA)
NWS	Naval Weapons Station
NWS	Navy Weather Service
NWS	[*The*] News Corp. Ltd. [*NYSE symbol*] (SPSG)
NWS	News Corp. Ltd ADS [*NYSE symbol*] (TTSB)
NWS	New Workers Scheme (AIE)
NWS	New World Society
NWS	Nimbus Weather Satellite
NWS	Non-Heatset Web Section (NTPA)
NWS	Normal Water Surface (ADA)
NWS	North Warning System (MCD)
NWS	North-West Semitic (BJA)
NWS	Northwest States (ROG)
NWS	Norway Station [*South Africa*] [*Later, SNA*] [*Geomagnetic observatory code*]
NWS	Nose Wheel Steering [*Aviation*]
NWS	Nowsco Well Service Ltd. [*Toronto Stock Exchange symbol*]
NWS	Nuclear Weapons State
NWS	Nuclear Weapon State
NWSA	National Water Slide Association (EA)
NWSA	National Welding Supply Association (EA)
NWSA	National Wheelchair Softball Association (EA)
NWSA	National Winter Sports Association
NWSA	National Women's Studies Association (EA)
NWSA	National Women's Suffrage Association (WDAA)
NWSA	Naval Weapons Support Activity
NWSA	Naval Weather Service Association (EA)
NWSA	Nose Wheel Steering Amplifier [*Aviation*] (MCD)
NWSA	Nuclear Weapons Supply Annex
NWSA Jnl ...	NWSA Journal [*A publication*] (BRI)
NWSAP.......	Naval Weapons Station Acceptance Program (MCD)
NWSB	National Wage Stabilization Board [*Superseded NWLB, 1945; terminated, 1947*]
NWSB	Northwest Savings Bank [*NASDAQ symbol*] (SAG)
NWSB	Nuclear Warfare Status Branch (CINC)
nwsb--........	Saint-Barthelemy [*MARC geographic area code Library of Congress*] (LCCP)
NWSC.........	National Water Safety Congress (EA)
NWSC.........	National Weather Satellite Center [*Later, National Environmental Satellite Service*]
NWSC.........	National Weather Service Center (MCD)
NWSC.........	National Women's Student Coalition (EA)
NWSC.........	Naval Weapons Support Center (MCD)
NWSC.........	Naval Weather Service Command
NWSCA.......	National Water and Soil Conservation Agency (BARN)
NWSCC.......	Nuclear Weapons System Control Console (MCD)
NWSC/CR....	Naval Weapons Support Center, Crane [*Indiana*]
Nwscop.......	Newscope Resources Ltd. [*Associated Press*] (SAG)
NWS-CR......	National Weather Service-Central Region (PDAA)
NWSD.........	Naval Weather Service Detachment [*or Division*]
nwsd--........	Saba [*MARC geographic area code Library of Congress*] (LCCP)
NWSED.......	Naval Weather Service Environmental Detachment [*Navy*]
NWSEO.......	National Weather Service Employees Organization (EA)
NWS-ER......	National Weather Service-Eastern Region (PDAA)
NWSF	Northwest Sea Frontier
NWSF	Nuclear Weapons Storage Facility [*Army*] (AABC)
NWSFO.......	NWS [*National Weather Service*] Forecast Office [*Marine science*] (OSRA)
NWSG.........	Nuclear War Study Group (EA)
NWSG.........	Nuclear Weapon Systems Surety Group [*Army*]
NWsH.........	Houghton College, Buffalo Campus, West Seneca, NY [*Library symbol Library of Congress*] (LCLS)
NWSH.........	National Weather Service Headquarters
NWsHeaC ...	Health Care Plan Medical Center, West Seneca, NY [*Library symbol Library of Congress*] (LCLS)
NWSI	New World Services, Inc.
NWSIA........	National Water Supply Improvement Association [*Later, IDA*] (EA)
NWSLF	Nowsco WellService [*NASDAQ symbol*] (TTSB)
NWSLF	Nowsco Well Services [*NASDAQ symbol*] (SAG)
NWSM........	Nuclear Weapons Stockpile Memorandum
NWSO.........	Naval Weapons Services Office [*Also known as NAVWPNSERVO, WEPSO*]
NWSO.........	Naval Weather Service Office
nwspa.........	Newspaper (VRA)
NWSPr........	News Corp. Ltd Pfd ADS [*NYSE symbol*] (TTSB)
NWSRFS......	National Weather Service River Forecast System (NOAA)
NWSRS........	National Wild and Scenic Rivers System
NWSS	National Weather Satellite System (KSC)
NWSS	National Wool Sorters' Society [*A union*] [*British*] (DCTA)
NWSS	Navy WWMCCS [*World-Wide Military Command and Control System*] Standardization Software
NWSS	Network Six, Inc. [*NASDAQ symbol*] (SAG)
NWSS	Nuclear Weapons Support Section [*Army*] (AABC)
NWsS.........	West Seneca State School, West Seneca, NY [*Library symbol Library of Congress*] (LCLS)
NWSSG.......	Nuclear Weapons System Safety Group

NWSSG........ Nuclear Weapons System Satellite Group [*Military*] (IAA)
NWSSGP....... Nuclear Weapons System Safety Group
NWS-SR ..... National Weather Service-Southern Region (PDAA)
NWST .... NewStar Media [*NASDAQ symbol*] [*Formerly, Dove Entertainment*]
nwst-- .... St. Martin (Sint Maarten) [*MARC geographic area code Library of Congress*] (LCCP)
NwstAirl....... Northwest Airlines Corp. [*Associated Press*] (SAG)
NwstEqty...... Northwest Equity Corp. [*Associated Press*] (SAG)
NWSTG .... National Weather Service Telecommunications Gateway
NWSTG .... NWS [*National Weather Service*] Telecommunications Gateway [*Marine science*] (OSRA)
NwStlWr...... Northwestern Steel & Wire Co. [*Associated Press*] (SAG)
NwstSBk ..... Northwest Savings Bank [*Associated Press*] (SAG)
NWSTTC ..... National Weather Service Technical Training Center
nwsv-- .... Swan Islands [*MARC geographic area code Library of Congress*] (LCCP)
NWSW .... Northwestern Steel & Wire Co. [*NASDAQ symbol*] (SAG)
NWSW .... Nothwestern Steel & Wire [*NASDAQ symbol*] (TTSB)
NWS-WR ..... National Weather Service-Western Region (PDAA)
NWSY .... Naval Weapons Station, Yorktown [*Virginia*]
N WT .... Net Weight
NWT............. New World Translation (of the Holy Scriptures) [*A publication*] (BJA)
NWT............. Nonwatertight [*Packaging*] (AAG)
NWT............. Northwestern Terminal R. R. [*AAR code*]
NWT............. Northwestern Utilities Ltd. [*Toronto Stock Exchange symbol*]
NWT............. Northwest Territorial Airways [*Canada ICAO designator*] (FAAC)
NWT............. Northwest Territories [*Canada*]
NWT............. Nowata [*Papua New Guinea*] [*Airport symbol*] (OAG)
NWT............. Nylon Wire Tie
NWTA .... National Waterways Transport Association [*British*]
NWTA .... National Woman's Trucking Association [*Defunct*] (EA)
NWTA .... National Wool Trade Association [*Defunct*] (EA)
NWTA .... North West Territory Alliance (EA)
NWTB .... Northwestern Tariff Bureau
NWTB .... North West Tourist Board [*British*] (DCTA)
NWTC .... National Wetlands Technical Council (EA)
NWTC .... Naval Weapon Test Center [*China Lake, California*] [*Navy*]
NWTC .... Northern Warfare Training Center [*Army*] (MCD)
NWTC .... Nuclear Weapons Training Center
nwtc-- .... Turks and Caicos Islands [*MARC geographic area code Library of Congress*] (LCCP)
NWTCL .... Nuclear Weapons Training Center, Atlantic (DNAB)
NWTCP .... Nuclear Weapons Training Center, Pacific (DNAB)
NWTD .... Nonwatertight Door (ADA)
NWTDB .... Naval Warfare Tactical Data Base (DOMA)
NWTEC .... National Wool Textile Export Corp. [*British*] (BI)
NW Terr...... Northwest Territories, Supreme Court Reports [*A publication*] (DLA)
NWTF........... National Wild Turkey Federation (EA)
NWTG .... Nuclear Weapons Training Group (DNAB)
NWTGL .... Nuclear Weapons Training Group, Atlantic (DNAB)
NWTGP .... Nuclear Weapons Training Group, Pacific (DNAB)
NWTH .... Networth, Inc. [*NASDAQ symbol*] (SAG)
NWTI .... National Wood Tank Institute (EA)
NWTI .... Nuclear Weapons Technical Inspections
NWTK .... North West Token Kai [*An association*] (EA)
NWTL .... Northwest Teleprod'ns [*NASDAQ symbol*] (TTSB)
NWTL .... Northwest Teleproductions, Inc. [*NASDAQ symbol*] (NQ)
NWTLR .... North West Territories Law Reports [*A publication*] (DLA)
NWTO .... Network for Work Time Options [*San Francisco, CA*] (EA)
NWT Ord...... Northwest Territories Ordinances [*Canada*] [*A publication*] (DLA)
NWTP .... Naval Warfare Tactical Publication (DNAB)
NWTR .... North West Territories Reports [*1885-1907*] [*Canada*] [*A publication*] (DLA)
nwtr--.......... Trinidad and Tobago [*MARC geographic area code Library of Congress*] (LCCP)
NWTRB .... Nuclear Waste Technical Review Board [*Nuclear energy*] (EGAO)
NWTRCC..... National War Tax Resistance Coordinating Committee (EA)
NWT Rev Ord... Northwest Territories Revised Ordinances [*Canada A publication*] (DLA)
NWTS .... National Waste Terminal Storage [*For radioactive wastes*]
NWTS .... National Wilms' Tumor Study [*Oncology*]
NWTS .... Naval Weapons Test Station
NWT/S .... Nuclear Weapons Technician/Specialist (AAG)
NWTSG .... National Wilms' Tumor Study Group [*Oncology*]
NWU .... National Workers Union (NADA)
NWU .... National Writers Union (EA)
NWU .... Nebraska Wesleyan University
NWU .... Northwestern University School of Law (DLA)
NWU .... Nose Wheel Up [*Aviation*]
nwuc-- .... United States Miscellaneous Caribbean Islands [*MARC geographic area code Library of Congress*] (LCCP)
NWUIS .... Navy Work Unit Information System (DNAB)
NWUS .... Northwestern United States
NWV .... Newcoast Silver Mines [*Vancouver Stock Exchange symbol*]
NWV .... Norfolk, VA [*Location identifier FAA*] (FAAL)
nwvb-- .... Virgin Islands, British [*MARC geographic area code Library of Congress*] (LCCP)
NWvH .... Millard Fillmore Suburban Hospital, Williamsville, NY [*Library symbol*] [*Library of Congress*] (LCLS)
nwvi-- .... Virgin Islands of the US [*MARC geographic area code Library of Congress*] (LCCP)
nwvr............. Virgin Islands [*MARC geographic area code Library of Congress*] (LCCP)
NWvS........... Sanders Associates, Inc., Williamsville, NY [*Library symbol Library of Congress*] (LCLS)

NWW .... Newgate Resources [*Vancouver Stock Exchange symbol*]
NWW .... New Ways to Work (EA)
NWW .... North West Airline [*Australia ICAO designator*] (FAAC)
NWW .... Nose Wheel Well [*Aviation*] (MCD)
NWWA .... National Water Well Association [*Database producer*] (EA)
NWWA .... North-West Water Authority [*British*] (DCTA)
NWWA .... Tiga, Iles Loyaute [*New Caledonia*] [*ICAO location identifier*] (ICLI)
NWWC .... Ile Art/Wala, Iles Belep [*New Caledonia*] [*ICAO location identifier*] (ICLI)
NWWC .... National White Wyandotte Club [*Defunct*] (EA)
NwWCof...... New World Coffee, Inc. [*Associated Press*] (SAG)
NWWCSS..... Naval Worldwide Command Support System (MCD)
NWWD .... Kone [*New Caledonia*] [*ICAO location identifier*] (ICLI)
NWWDA ...... National Wood Window and Door Association (EA)
NWWE .... Ile Des Pins/Moue [*New Caledonia*] [*ICAO location identifier*] (ICLI)
NwWEye ...... New West Eyeworks, Inc. [*Associated Press*] (SAG)
NWWF .... Voh [*New Caledonia*] [*ICAO location identifier*] (ICLI)
NWWH .... Houailou/Nesson [*New Caledonia*] [*ICAO location identifier*] (ICLI)
NWWI .... Hienghene/Henri Martinet [*New Caledonia*] [*ICAO location identifier*] (ICLI)
nwwi-- .... Windward Islands [*MARC geographic area code Library of Congress*] (LCCP)
NWWJ .... Poum [*New Caledonia*] [*ICAO location identifier*] (ICLI)
NWWK .... Koumac [*New Caledonia*] [*ICAO location identifier*] (ICLI)
NWWL .... Lifou/Ouanaham, Iles Loyaute [*New Caledonia*] [*ICAO location identifier*] (ICLI)
NWWM .... Noumea/Magenta [*New Caledonia*] [*ICAO location identifier*] (ICLI)
NWWN .... Noumea [*New Caledonia*] [*ICAO location identifier*] (ICLI)
NWWO .... Ile Ouen/Edmond-Cane [*New Caledonia*] [*ICAO location identifier*] (ICLI)
NWWOX .... Phoenix Aberdeen Worldwide Opportunities [*Mutual fund ticker symbol*] (SG)
NWWQ .... Mueo/Nickel [*New Caledonia*] [*ICAO location identifier*] (ICLI)
NWWR .... Mare/La Roche, Iles Loyaute [*New Caledonia*] [*ICAO location identifier*] (ICLI)
NWWS .... NOAA [*National Oceanic and Atmospheric Administration*] Weather Wire Service (NOAA)
NWWS .... Plaine Des Lacs [*New Caledonia*] [*ICAO location identifier*] (ICLI)
NWWU .... Touho [*New Caledonia*] [*ICAO location identifier*] (ICLI)
NWWV .... Ouvea/Ouloup, Iles Loyaute [*New Caledonia*] [*ICAO location identifier*] (ICLI)
NWWW .... Noumea/La Tontouta [*New Caledonia*] [*ICAO location identifier*] (ICLI)
NWWY .... Ouaco/Paquiepe [*New Caledonia*] [*ICAO location identifier*] (ICLI)
NWX .... National Westminster Bank PLC [*NYSE symbol*] (SAG)
NWX .... New Minex Resources Ltd. [*Vancouver Stock Exchange symbol*]
nwxi-- .... St. Christopher-Nevis-Anguilla [*MARC geographic area code Library of Congress*] (LCCP)
nwxk-- .... St. Lucia [*MARC geographic area code Library of Congress*] (LCCP)
nwxm-- .... St. Vincent [*MARC geographic area code Library of Congress*] (LCCP)
NWXPrA...... Natl Westminster Bk Ex Cap Sec [*NYSE symbol*] (TTSB)
NWY .... New Penn Energy [*Vancouver Stock Exchange symbol*]
NWy............. Wyoming Free Public Library, Wyoming, NY [*Library symbol Library of Congress*] (LCLS)
NWY .... Yellowknife Public Library, Northwest Territories [*Library symbol National Library of Canada*] (NLC)
NWya........... Wyandanch Public Library, Wyandanch, NY [*Library symbol Library of Congress*] (LCLS)
NWyaHEC .... LaFrancis Hardiman Early Childhood Center, Wyandanch, NY [*Library symbol*] [*Library of Congress*] (LCLS)
NWyaHS ...... Wyandanch Memorial High School, Wyandanch, NY [*Library symbol*] [*Library of Congress*] (LCLS)
NWyaKE...... Martin Luther King Elementary School, Wyandanch, NY [*Library symbol*] [*Library of Congress*] (LCLS)
NWyaOMS ... Milton Olive Middle School, Wyandanch, NY [*Library symbol*] [*Library of Congress*] (LCLS)
NWyaSE....... Straightpath Elementary School, Wyandanch, NY [*Library symbol*] [*Library of Congress*] (LCLS)
NWYC .... Court Library, Department of Justice, Yellowknife, Northwest Territories [*Library symbol National Library of Canada*] (BIB)
NWYC .... National Write Your Congressman [*An association*] (EA)
NWYCC....... National Write Your Congressman [*Also known as National Write Your Congressman Club*] (EA)
NWYCJ .... Cooper-Johnson, Yellowknife, Northwest Territories [*Library symbol National Library of Canada*] (BIB)
NWYD.......... Dene Nation, Yellowknife, Northwest Territories [*Library symbol National Library of Canada*] (BIB)
NWYECW..... Canadian Wildlife Service, Environment Canada [*Service Canadien de la Faune, Environnement Canada*] Yellowknife, Northwest Territories [*Library symbol National Library of Canada*] (NLC)
NWYEEP ...... Assessment and Coordination Branch, Environmental Protection Service, Environment Canada [*Direction de l'Evaluation et de la Coordination, Service de la Protection de l'Environnement, Environnement Canada*] Yellowknife, Northwest Territories [*Library symbol National Library of Canada*] (NLC)
NWYGI......... Government Library, Government of the Northwest Territories, Yellowkn ife, Northwest Territories [*Library symbol National Library of Canada*] (NLC)
NWYIN........ Indian and Northern Affairs Canada [*Affaires Indiennes et du Nord Canada*] Yellowknife, Northwest Territories [*Library symbol National Library of Canada*] (NLC)

NWYND....... Northern Region Information System (NORIS), Canada Department of National Defence [*Reseau d'Information de la Region du Nord (NORIS), Ministere de la DefenseNationale*] Yellowknife, Northwest Territories [*Library symbol National Library of Canada*] (NLC)

NWYOS....... Dr. Otto Schaefer Health Resource Centre, Yellowknife, Northwest Territories [*Library symbol National Library of Canada*] (NLC)

NWYPC....... Parks Canada [*Parcs Canada*] Yellowknife, Northwest Territories [*Library symbol National Library of Canada*] (NLC)

NWYPW....... Technical Resource Centre, Department of Public Works and Highways, Government of the Northwest Territories, Yellowknife, Northwest Territories [*Library symbol National Library of Canada*] (BIB)

NWYRR....... Renewable Resources Library, Government of the Northwest Territories, Yellowknife, Northwest Territories [*Library symbol National Library of Canada*] (NLC)

NWYWNH .... Prince of Wales Northern Heritage Centre, Government of the Northwest Territories, Yellowknife, Northwest Territories [*Library symbol National Library of Canada*] (NLC)

NX.............. Net Exports
NX.............. New Zealand Air Charter [*ICAO designator*] (AD)
nx .... Norfolk Island [*MARC country of publication code Library of Congress*] (LCCP)
NX.............. Normal to X-Axis (MCD)
NX.............. Nose to X-Axis (MCD)
NX.............. Not Exceeding
NX.............. Not Expendable (MUGU)
nx .... Nourishment [*Dietetics*] (DAVI)
NX.............. Quanex Corp. [*NYSE symbol*] (SPSG)
NXA .... Nodal Exchange Area (MHDB)
NXA .... Nolisair International, Inc. [*Canada ICAO designator*] (FAAC)
NXA .... Norex America [*AMEX symbol*] (TTSB)
NXA .... Norex America, Inc. [*AMEX symbol*] (SPSG)
NXA .... Norex Industries [*AMEX symbol*] [*Formerly, Norex America*] (SG)
NXA .... Siem Industries [*AMEX symbol*] [*Formerly, Norex Industries*]
NXA .... Wake County Public Library, Raleigh, NC [*OCLC symbol*] (OCLC)
NXB .... Neurotoxin B
NXC .... Nuveen Ins CA Sel Tax-Free Inc. [*NYSE symbol*] (TTSB)
NXC .... Nuveen Insured California Select Tax-Free Income [*NYSE symbol*] (SPSG)
NXCI .... National Xeriscape Council, Inc. [*An association*] (EA)
NXCO .... Neurex Corp. [*NASDAQ symbol*] (SAG)
NXDO .... Nike-X Development Office [*Army*] (AABC)
NXGN .... NexGen, Inc. [*NASDAQ symbol*] (SAG)
NXI.............. Oak Harbor, WA [*Location identifier FAA*] (FAAL)
NXL.............. Napoleon Exploration [*Vancouver Stock Exchange symbol*]
NXL.............. New Plan Excel Realty Trust [*Formerly, New Plan Excel Realty*] [*NYSE symbol*]
n-xl-- .... St. Pierre and Miquelon [*MARC geographic area code Library of Congress*] (LCCP)
NXM............ Non-Existent Memory (MHDB)
NXM............ Noramex Minerals [*Vancouver Stock Exchange symbol*]
NXMIS .... Nike-X Management Information System [*Army*]
NXN .... Milton, FL [*Location identifier FAA*] (FAAL)
NXN .... No Christian Name
NXN .... Nuveen Ins NY Sel Tax-Free Inc. [*NYSE symbol*] (TTSB)
NXN .... Nuveen Insured New York Select Tax-Free Income [*NYSE symbol*] (SPSG)
NXP .... Noxe Resources Corp. [*Vancouver Stock Exchange symbol*]
NXP .... Nuveen Select Tax-Free Inc. [*NYSE symbol*] (TTSB)
NXP .... Nuveen Select Tax-Free Income [*NYSE symbol*] (SPSG)
NXP .... Twentynine Palms, CA [*Location identifier FAA*] (FAAL)
NXPM .... Nike-X Project Manager [*Army*] (AABC)
NXPO .... Nike-X Program [*or Project*] Office [*Army*]
NXPRG......... Nike-X Program Review Group [*Army*] (AABC)
NXQ .... Nuveen Selct Tax-Free Inc. 2 [*NYSE symbol*] (TTSB)
NXQ .... Nuveen Select Tax-Free Income 2 [*NYSE symbol*] (SPSG)
NXR .... Noncrossing Rule
NXR .... Nuveen Selct Tax-Free Inc. 3 [*NYSE symbol*] (TTSB)
NXR .... Nuveen Select Tax-Free Income 3 [*NYSE symbol*] (SPSG)
NXS .... Nexus Resources Corp. [*Vancouver Stock Exchange symbol Toronto Stock Exchange symbol*]
NXSM .... Nike-X System Manager [*Army*] (AABC)
NXSMO .... Nike-X System Manager's Office [*Army*]
NXSO .... Nike-X Support Office [*Army*]
NXSPC......... Nexus Telecommunication Systems Ltd. [*NASDAQ symbol*] (SAG)
NXSR .... Non-Extraction Steam Rate (PDAA)
NXT............. Next
NXTR .... NeXstar Pharmaceutical [*NASDAQ symbol*] (SAG)
NXTR .... NeXstar Pharmaceuticals [*NASDAQ symbol*] (TTSB)
NXUL .... Nexus Telecommunication Systems Ltd. [*NASDAQ symbol*] (SAG)
NXULF .... Nexus Telecomm Sys Wrrt [*NASDAQ symbol*] (TTSB)
NXUS .... Nexus Telecommunication Systems Ltd. [*NASDAQ symbol*] (SAG)
NXUSF .... Nexus Telecommns Sys Ltd [*NASDAQ symbol*] (TTSB)
NXUW .... Nexus Telecommunication Systems Ltd. [*NASDAQ symbol*] (SAG)
NXUWF........ Nexus Telecommuns Sys Wrrt'A' [*NASDAQ symbol*] (TTSB)
NXUZ .... Nexus Telecommunication Systems Ltd. [*NASDAQ symbol*] (SAG)
NXUZF .... Nexus Telecommuns Sys Wrrt'B' [*NASDAQ symbol*] (TTSB)
NXW .... University of North Carolina, Wilmington, Wilmington, NC [*OCLC symbol*] (OCLC)
NXWPC........ Nexus Telecommunication Systems Ltd. [*NASDAQ symbol*] (SAG)
NXX .... Willow Grove, PA [*Location identifier FAA*] (FAAL)
NXZPC .... Nexus Telecommunication Systems Ltd. [*NASDAQ symbol*] (SAG)
NY............... John Dewey [*Final letters of his first and last name used as a pseudonym*] [*American author, 1859-1952*]

NY.............. Navy Yard
NY.............. Nelen Yubu [*A publication*] (APTA)
NY.............. Net Yield
NY.............. New Year
NY.............. New York [*Naval Shipyard*]
NY.............. New York [*City or state*] [*Postal code*]
NY.............. New York Airways, Inc. [*ICAO designator*]
NY.............. New York Court of Appeals Reports [*A publication*] (DLA)
NY.............. New Yorker [*A publication*] (BRI)
NY.............. Noorduyn Aviation Ltd. [*Canada ICAO aircraft manufacturer identifier*] (ICAO)
NY.............. Normal to Y-Axis (MCD)
NY.............. Northamptonshire Yeomanry [*British military*] (DMA)
NY.............. Northumberland Yeomanry [*British military*] (DMA)
NY.............. Nose to Y-Axis (NASA)
NY.............. No Year [*of publication*] [*Bibliography*]
NY.............. Nuclear Yellow [*A fluorescent dye*]
NY.............. Nuclear Yield
NY.............. Nyasaland (ROG)
NY.............. Yonkers Public Library, Yonkers, NY [*Library symbol Library of Congress*] (LCLS)
NY 2d .... New York Court of Appeals Reports, Second Series [*A publication*] (DLA)
NYA .... National Yogurt Association (EA)
NYA .... National Youth Administration [*Terminated, 1943*]
NYA .... National Youth Alliance (EA)
NYA .... Neighborhood Youth Administration (OICC)
NYA .... New York Airways, Inc. [*Air carrier designation symbol*]
NYA .... Not Yet Answered
nya............ Nyanja [*MARC language code Library of Congress*] (LCCP)
NYAB .... National Youth Advisory Board [*Environmental Protection Agency*]
NYAB .... New York Air Brake Co.
NYABIC........ New York Association for Brain Injured Children
NYACH........ New York Automated Clearing House (TBD)
NY Admin Code... Official Compilation of Codes, Rules, and Regulations of the State of New York [*A publication*] (DLA)
NYADS........ New York Air Defense Sector (SAA)
NYAES-C...... New York Agricultural Experiment Station (Cornell University) [*Research center*] (RCD)
NYAIC .... New York Association of Industrial Communicators [*Later, NY/IABC*] (EA)
NYAL .... National Yugoslav Army of Liberation [*World War II*]
NYALR .... New Yorkers for Abortion Law Repeal (EA)
NYAM .... New York Academy of Medicine
NYAM .... New York Academy of Music
NYAMP .... New York Advertising Media Planners [*Defunct*] (EA)
NYANA .... New York Association for New Americans (EA)
NY & E .... New York & Erie Railroad
NY & NE...... New York & New England Railroad [*Nickname: Now You Are Nearing Eternity*]
NY & NH...... New York & New Haven Railroad
NYANG........ New York Air National Guard (MUSM)
NY Ann Ca... New York Annotated Cases [*A publication*] (DLA)
NY Ann Cas... New York Annotated Cases [*A publication*] (DLA)
NY Anno Cas... New York Annotated Cases [*A publication*] (DLA)
NY Anno Dig... New York Annotated Digest [*A publication*] (ILCA)
NY Annot Dig... New York Annotated Digest [*A publication*] (DLA)
NYap........... Middle Island Central Public Library, Yaphank, NY [*Library symbol Library of Congress*] (LCLS)
NYAP .... New York Assembly Program [*Computer science*]
NYAP .... New York Average Price per Share [*Stock market*]
NY App Dec... New York Court of Appeals Decisions [*A publication*] (DLA)
NY App Div... New York Supreme Court, Appellate Division Reports [*A publication*] (DLA)
NYAS .... New York Academy of Sciences (EA)
NYB .... National Youth Bureau [*British*]
NYB .... New York Bancorp [*NYSE symbol*] (SAG)
NYB .... New York Bancorp Inc. [*AMEX symbol*] (SPSG)
NYB .... New York Bight [*Oceanography*] (MSC)
NYBA .... North York Board of Education [*UTLAS symbol*]
NYBA .... National Young Buddhist Association [*Defunct*] (EA)
NYBagel ...... New York Bagel Enterprises, Inc. [*Associated Press*] (SAG)
NYB & M ..... New York, Boston & Montreal Railroad
NY Bank Law... New York Banking Law [*A publication*] (DLA)
NYBC .... National Yiddish Book Center (EA)
NYBC .... New York Business Communicators [*Later, NY/IABC*] (EA)
NY Bcp .... New York Bancorp [*Associated Press*] (SAG)
NY Bcp .... New York Bancorp, Inc. [*Associated Press*] (SAG)
NYBE .... National Yiddish Book Exchange (EA)
NYBFU......... New York Board of Fire Underwriters (BARN)
NYBG .... New York Botanical Garden
NYBOS........ Navy Yard, Boston, Massachusetts [*Obsolete*]
NYBPE .... New York Business Press Editors [*New York, NY*] (EA)
NYBS .... New York Bagel Enterprises, Inc. [*NASDAQ symbol*] (SAG)
NYBS .... New York Browning Society (EA)
NYBSBC...... New York Bureau of State Building Codes (BARN)
NYBT .... Boyce Thompson Institute for Plant Research, Yonkers, NY [*Library symbol Library of Congress*] (LCLS)
NYBT .... New York Board of Trade [*New York, NY*] (EA)
NYC .... Charley [*Nevada*] [*Seismograph station code, US Geological Survey Closed*] (SEIS)
NYC .... Neighborhood Youth Corps [*Department of Labor*] [*Terminated*]
NYC .... New York Central R. R. [*Later, Penn Central*] [*AAR code*]
NYC .... New York Circus (EA)
NYC .... New York City

NYC	New York, Motor Carrier Conference [*STAC*]
NYC	New York [*New York*]/Newark [*New Jersey*] [*Airport symbol*] (OAG)
NYC	New York, NY [*Location identifier FAA*] (FAAL)
NYCA	New York Court of Appeals Reports [*A publication*] (DLA)
NYCAC	New York Collegiate Athletic Conference (PSS)
NYC & HR	New York Central & Hudson River Railroad
NYC & HRR	New York Central & Hudson River Railroad (ROG)
NYC & SL	New York, Chicago and St. Louis Railroad Co. (IIA)
NYC & STL	New York, Chicago & St. Louis Railroad Co.
NY Cas Err	Caines' New York Cases in Error [*A publication*] (DLA)
NY Cas in Error	Caines' New York Cases in Error [*A publication*] (DLA)
NYCATC	New York City Athletic Conference (PSS)
NYCB	New York City Ballet
NYCBA	New York City Bar Association. Bulletin [*A publication*] (DLA)
NYCBA Bull	Bulletin. Association of the Bar of the City of New York [*A publication*] (DLA)
NYCBAN	New York Center Beacon Alphanumerics [*FAA*]
NYCC	New York Candy Club (EA)
NYCC	New York City Commission for the United Nations, Consular Corps, and International Business (EA)
NYCCA	New York Cocoa Clearing Association (EA)
NYCCC	New York City Community College
NYCCD	New York Current Court Decisions [*A publication*] (DLA)
NYCCH	New York Advance Digest Service (Commerce Clearing House), Cited by Year [*A publication*] (DLA)
NYCCI	New York Corset Club (EA)
NYCDC	New York Curtain and Drapery Club (EA)
NYCE	New York Cash Exchange [*Automated teller machine network*]
NYCE	New York Cocoa Exchange [*Later, CSCE*]
NYCE	New York, Commodities Exchange
NYCE	New York Cotton Exchange (EA)
NYCE	New York Curb Exchange [*Later, AMEX*]
NYCER	New York Conference on Electronic Reliability (MCD)
NYCFMA	New York Credit and Financial Management Association [*New York, NY*] (EA)
NY Ch	Chancery Sentinel [*New York*] [*A publication*] (DLA)
NYCH	National Youth Coalition on Housing [*Australia*]
NYCHA	New York Clearing House Association [*New York, NY*] (EA)
NYCHARL	Navy Yard, Charleston, South Carolina
NY Ch Sent	New York Chancery Sentinel [*A publication*] (DLA)
NYCI	New York City's First [*First beluga whale born at the New York Aquarium, 1981*] [*Pronounced "Nicky"*]
NY City Ct	New York City Court [*A publication*] (DLA)
NY City Ct Rep	New York City Court Reports [*A publication*] (DLA)
NY City Ct Supp	New York City Court Reports, Supplement [*A publication*] (DLA)
NY City Hall Rec	New York City Hall Recorder [*A publication*] (ILCA)
NY City H Rec	New York City Hall Recorder [*A publication*] (DLA)
NY Civ Prac Law & R	New York Civil Practice Law and Rules [*A publication*] (DLA)
NY Civ Pro	New York Civil Procedure [*A publication*] (DLA)
NY Civ Proc	New York Civil Procedure [*A publication*] (ILCA)
NY Civ Proc (NS)	New York Civil Procedure, New Series [*A publication*] (DLA)
NY Civ Proc R	New York Civil Procedure Reports [*A publication*] (DLA)
NY Civ Proc Rep	Civil Procedure Reports [*New York*] [*A publication*] (DLA)
NY Civ Proc R NS	New York Civil Procedure Reports, New Series [*A publication*] (DLA)
NY Civ Pro R	New York Civil Procedure Reports [*A publication*] (ILCA)
NY Civ Pro R NS	New York Civil Procedure Reports, New Series [*A publication*] (ILCA)
NY Civ Pr Rep	New York Civil Procedure Reports [*A publication*] (ILCA)
NYCMA	New York Clothing Manufacturers Association (EA)
NYCMD	New York Contract Management District (SAA)
NYCME	New York Clothing Manufacturers Exchange [*Later, NYCMA*] (EA)
NYCN	New York Connecting Railroad [*AAR code*]
NYCO	New York City Opera
NYCO	NYCOR, Inc. [*NASDAQ symbol*] (NQ)
NYCOA	NYCOR Inc.'A' [*NASDAQ symbol*] (TTSB)
NY Code R	New York Code Reporter [*A publication*] (DLA)
NY Code Rep	New York Code Reporter [*A publication*] (DLA)
NY Code Rep NS	New York Code Reports, New Series [*A publication*] (DLA)
NY Code Report	New York Code Reporter [*A publication*] (DLA)
NY Code Report NS	New York Code Reporter, New Series [*A publication*] (DLA)
NY Code Reports NS	New York Code Reports, New Series [*A publication*] (DLA)
NY Code Reptr	New York Code Reporter [*A publication*] (DLA)
NY Code Reptr NS	New York Code Reporter, New Series [*A publication*] (DLA)
NY Code R NS	New York Code Reports, New Series [*A publication*] (DLA)
NY Cond	New York Condensed Reports [*1881-82*] [*A publication*] (DLA)
Nycor	NYCOR, Inc. [*Associated Press*] (SAG)
NY Co Rem	New York Code of Remedial Justice [*A publication*] (DLA)
NYCP	Civil Procedure Reports [*New York*] [*A publication*] (DLA)
NY Cr	New York Criminal Reports [*A publication*] (DLA)
NY Crim	New York Criminal Reports [*A publication*] (DLA)
NY Crim R	New York Criminal Reports [*A publication*] (DLA)
NY Crim Rep	New York Criminal Reports [*A publication*] (DLA)
NYCRR	New York Codes, Rules, and Regulations [*A publication*] (DLA)
NY Cr R	New York Criminal Reports [*A publication*] (DLA)
NY Cr Rep	New York Criminal Reports [*A publication*] (DLA)
NYCS	New York Cipher Society (EA)
NYCSA	New York Coat and Suit Association (EA)
NYCSA	New York College Stores Association
NYCSCE	New York Coffee, Sugar, and Cocoa Exchange
NYCSE	New York Coffee and Sugar Exchange [*Later, CSCE*] (EA)
NYCSG	New York Constitution Study Group (EA)
NYCSLS	New York C. S. Lewis Society (EA)
NYCSMA	National Young Christian Students' Movement of Australia
NY Ct App	New York Court of Appeals (DLA)
NYCTC	New York City Technical College
NYCTCG	New York Cold Type Composition Group [*Later, TANY*] (EA)
NYCTN	New York Cotton Exchange (EBF)
NYCTNCA	New York Cotton Exchange, Citrus Associates
NYCUC	New York City Urban Corps (EA)
NYD	Navy Yard
NYD	New York Datum (NRCH)
NYD	New York Dock Railway [*AAR code*]
NYD	Not Yet Diagnosed [*Facetious translation: "Not Yet Dead"*] [*Medicine*]
NYD	Not Yet Discovered (DMAA)
NYD	Nycomed ASA ADS [*NYSE symbol*] (TTSB)
NY Daily L Gaz	New York Daily Law Gazette [*A publication*] (DLA)
NY Daily L Reg	New York Daily Law Register [*A publication*] (DLA)
NY Daily Reg	New York Daily Register [*A publication*] (DLA)
NY Daily Tr	New York Daily Transcript, Old and New Series [*A publication*] (DLA)
NYDCC	New York Drama Critics Circle (EA)
NY Dep't R	New York Department Records [*A publication*] (DLA)
NYDF	National Youth Development Foundation [*Defunct*] (EA)
NYDISS	New York Disposal Surveillance System [*U.S. Army Corps of Engineers*]
NYDLWC Dec	New York State Department of Labor. Court Decisions of Workmen's Compensation [*A publication*] (DLA)
NYDO	National Youth Development Officer (AIE)
NYDP	Neighborhood Youth Development Program
NYDR	New York Department Reports [*A publication*] (DLA)
Nye	Nye's Reports [*18-21 Utah*] [*A publication*] (DLA)
NYEC	National Youth Employment Coalition (EA)
NYEG	New York State Electric & Gas Corp. [*Associated Press*] (SAG)
NY El Cas	New York Election Cases [*A publication*] (DLA)
NY Elec Cas	New York Election Cases [*A publication*] (DLA)
NY Elect Cas	New York Election Cases [*A publication*] (DLA)
NYER	Nyer Med Group [*NASDAQ symbol*] (TTSB)
NYER	Nyer Medical Group [*NASDAQ symbol*] (SAG)
NyerMd	Nyer Medical Group [*Associated Press*] (SAG)
NYES	Elizabeth Seton College, Yonkers, NY [*Library symbol Library of Congress*] (LCLS)
NYET LC	Not Yet in Library of Congress [*Suggested name for the Library of Congress computer system*]
NYETR	New York Estate Tax Reports [*Prentice-Hall, Inc.*] [*A publication*] (DLA)
NYEWW	New York Exchange for Woman's Work [*New York, NY*] (EA)
NYF	National Yeomen F [*Defunct*] (EA)
NYF	National Youth Foundation [*Australia*]
NYF	New York Foundation
NYF	New York Futures Exchange
NYFBT	New York Film Board of Trade [*Defunct*] (EA)
NYFBX	Mgn. Stanley D. Witter N.Y. Tax Free Cl.B [*Mutual fund ticker symbol*] (SG)
NYFC	New York Film Critics (EA)
NYFCC	New York Futures Clearing Corp. [*New York Futures Exchange*]
NYFD	New York Fashion Designers [*Later, NYFDF*] (EA)
NYFDF	New York Fashion Designers and Foundation [*Defunct*] (EA)
NYFE	New York Futures Exchange [*Pronounced "knife"*]
NYFEA	National Young Farmer Educational Association (EA)
NYFFFBA	New York Foreign Freight Forwarders and Brokers Association [*New York, NY*] (EA)
NYFRF	New York Fertility Research Foundation [*Later, FRF*] (EA)
NYFUO	New York Federation of Urban Organizations
NYFWA	New York Financial Writers' Association (EA)
NYG	Geigy Pharmaceuticals, Yonkers, NY [*Library symbol Library of Congress*] (LCLS)
NYG	New York State Library, Albany, NY [*OCLC symbol*] (OCLC)
NYG	Nyge Aero AB [*Sweden ICAO designator*] (FAAC)
NYG	Quantico, VA [*Location identifier FAA*] (FAAL)
NYGBS	New York Genealogical and Biographical Society (EA)
NYGC	New York Governor's Conference
NYGJB	New York Guild for Jewish Blind [*Later, JGB*]
NYH	New York Helicopter Corp. [*ICAO designator*] (FAAC)
NYHA	National Yacht Harbour Association [*British*] (BI)
NYHA	New York Heart Association [*Classifications I, II, III, and IV*] [*Cardiology*] (DAVI)
NYHA	New York Heart Associaton (MEDA)
NYHC	New York Health Care, Inc. [*NASDAQ symbol*] (SAG)
NYhI	International Business Machines Corp., Thomas J. Watson Research Center, Yorktown Heights, NY [*Library symbol Library of Congress*] (LCLS)
NYHIthC	New York Health Care, Inc. [*Associated Press*] (SAG)
NYhP	Putnam North Westchester S.L.S., Yorktown Heights, NY [*Library symbol*] [*Library of Congress*] (LCLS)
NYHSL	New York Health and Safety Laboratory [*Energy Research and Development Administration*]
NYHT	New York Herald Tribune [*Defunct newspaper*]
NYI	Sunyani [*Ghana*] [*Airport symbol*] (OAG)
NY/IABC	New York/International Association of Business Communicators [*New York, NY*] (EA)
NYIBC	New York International Ballet Competition
NYIBC	New York Islanders Booster Club (EA)
NYIBS	New York International Bible Society (EA)
NYIC	New York Iroquois Conference (EA)
NYICD	New York Institute for Child Development (EA)
NYIDA	New York Importers and Distillers Association (EA)
NYIE	New York Insurance Exchange
NYIF	New York Index - Finance [*Stock market*]

NYIF............	New York Institute of Finance (ECON)
NYII.............	New York Index - Industrials [Stock market]
NYIL............	Netherlands Yearbook of International Law [A publication] (DLA)
NYIT............	New York Index - Transportation [Stock market]
NYIT............	New York Institute of Technology
NYIU............	New York Index - Utilities [Stock market]
NYJ.............	Joshua Tree [Nevada] [Seismograph station code, US Geological Survey Closed] (SEIS)
NYJ.............	National Young Judaea (EA)
NYJO	National Youth Jazz Orchestra [British]
NY Jud Rep...	New York Judicial Repository [A publication] (DLA)
NY Jud Repos...	New York Judicial Repository [A publication] (DLA)
NY Jur	New York Jurisprudence [A publication] (DLA)
NY Jur	New York Jurist [A publication] (DLA)
NYK	New York [City]
NYK	North York Public Library [UTLAS symbol]
NYKGRP	New York Group [Navy]
NYL............	Neodymium YAG [Yttrium Aluminum Garnet] LASER
NYL............	Nylon (MSA)
NYL............	Yuma, AZ [Location identifier FAA] (FAAL)
NY Law Bul...	New York Monthly Law Bulletin [A publication] (DLA)
NY Law Gaz ...	New York Law Gazette [A publication] (DLA)
NY Law (McKinney)...	McKinney's Consolidated Laws of New York [A publication] (DLA)
NY Law Sch...	New York Law School (GAGS)
NYLB	[The] New York & Long Branch Railroad Co. [Absorbed into Consolidated Rail Corp.] [AAR code]
NYLC	National Young Life Campaign [British]
NYLC	National Youth Leadership Council (EA)
NYLC Ann	New York Leading Cases, Annotated [A publication] (DLA)
NYL Cas	New York Leading Cases [A publication] (DLA)
NYLE & W.....	New York, Lake Erie & Western Railroad [Later, EL] [Nickname: Now You Lay Easy and Wait]
NY Leg N.....	New York Legal News [1880-82] [A publication] (DLA)
NY Leg Obs...	New York Legal Observer (Owen) [A publication] (DLA)
NY Leg Reg...	New York Legal Register [A publication] (DLA)
NYLEX USA...	New York Leather Exposition [American European Trade and Exhibition Center]
NYLG	New York Law Group [Later, BAHRGNY] (EA)
NYL Gaz	New York Law Gazette [A publication] (DLA)
NY LIFE	New York Life (EFIS)
NYLO	New York Legal Observer [A publication] (DLA)
NYLR	Neodymium YAG [Yttrium Aluminum Garnet] LASER Range-Finder
Ny LR	Nyasaland Law Reports [South Africa] [A publication] (DLA)
NYLRB	New York State Labor Relations Board Decisions [A publication] (DLA)
NYLRB Dec...	New York State Labor Relations Board Decisions and Orders [A publication] (DLA)
NYL Rec	New York Law Record [A publication] (DLA)
NYLS	New York Law School
NYLS	New York State Longitudinal Study (EDAC)
NYLSMA	New York Lamp and Shade Manufacturers Association (EA)
NYLS Stud L Rev...	New York Law School. Student Law Review [A publication] (DLA)
NYLTI..........	National Youth Leadership Training Institute
NYM............	Climax Mine [Nevada] [Seismograph station code, US Geological Survey Closed] (SEIS)
NYM............	New York Mercantile Exchange
NYM............	New York Movers Tariff Bureau, Inc., New York NY [STAC]
nym	Nyamwezi [MARC language code Library of Congress] (LCCP)
NYM............	NYMAGIC, Inc. [Formerly, New York Marine & General Insurance Co.] [NYSE symbol] (SPSG)
NYMA	New York City Metropolitan Area
NYMA	New York Mounters Association [New York, NY] (EA)
NYMAGC.......	NYMAGIC, Inc. [Formerly, New York Marine & General Insurance Co.] [Associated Press] (SAG)
NYMC	New York Medical College [Valhalla, NY]
NYME..........	New York Mercantile Exchange (EA)
NY Med C....	New York Medicine College (GAGS)
NYMEX	New York Mercantile Exchange (EA)
NYMI	Navy Yard, Mare Island, California
NY Misc.......	New York Miscellaneous Reports [A publication] (DLA)
NY Misc 2d...	New York Miscellaneous Reports. Second Series [A publication] (DLA)
NYMM	New York Merchandise Mart
NYMNEX	New York Mercantile Exchange
NYMO	National Youth Ministry Organization (EA)
NY Mo Law Bul...	New York Monthly Law Bulletin [A publication] (DLA)
NY Mo L Bul...	New York Monthly Law Bulletin [A publication] (DLA)
NY Mo LR....	New York Monthly Law Reports [A publication] (DLA)
NY Mo L Rec...	New York Monthly Law Record [A publication] (DLA)
NY Month L Bul...	New York Monthly Law Bulletin [A publication] (DLA)
NY Month LR...	New York Monthly Law Reports [A publication] (DLA)
NY Month L Rep...	New York Monthly Law Reports [A publication] (DLA)
NY Monthly Law Bul...	New York Monthly Law Bulletin [A publication] (DLA)
NYMPH	Nymphomaniac (DSUE)
nymphm	Nymphaeum (VRA)
NYMPHO.......	Nymphomaniac (DSUE)
NYMS	New York Microscopical Society (EA)
NY Mun Gaz...	New York Municipal Gazette [A publication] (DLA)
NYN	NYNEX Corp. [NYSE symbol] (SPSG)
NYN	Nyngan [Australia Airport symbol] (OAG)
NYNCY........	NYNEX CableCommsGrpADS Unit [NASDAQ symbol] (TTSB)
NYNCY........	Nynex Cable Communications Group PLC [NASDAQ symbol] (SAG)
NYNEX	New York New England Exchange [Telecommunications]
Nynex	NYNEX Corp. [Associated Press] (SAG)
NYNH & H ...	New York, New Haven & Hartford R. R.
NYNJDDA	New York and New Jersey Dry Dock Association [Defunct] (EA)
NYNMA	New York New Media Association (IGQR)
NYNOR	Navy Yard, Norfolk, Virginia
NYNS	New York Naval Shipyards [Obsolete]
NYNS-ML	New York Naval Shipyard, Material Laboratory (MCD)
NynxCbl.......	Nynex Cable Communications Group PLC [Associated Press] (SAG)
NYNYD........	New York Navy Yard (DNAB)
NYNYK	Navy Yard, New York, New York
NYO	National Youth Orchestra [British] (DI)
NYO	New York Oils Ltd. [Toronto Stock Exchange symbol]
NYO	New York Operations [AEC] (MCD)
NYO	Not Yet Operating (DA)
nyo.............	Nyoro [MARC language code Library of Congress] (LCCP)
NYo.............	Youngstown Free Library, Youngstown, NY [Library symbol Library of Congress] (LCLS)
NYO & W.....	New York, Ontario & Western Railway Co.
NYOD..........	New York Ordnance District [Military] (MUGU)
NY Off Dept R...	New York Official Department Reports [A publication] (DLA)
NYOL	New York On-Line [Information service or system] (IID)
NYoOF	Old Fort Niagara Association, Youngstown, NY [Library symbol Library of Congress] (LCLS)
NY Op Att Gen...	Opinions of the Attorneys-General of New York [A publication] (DLA)
NY Ops Atty Gen...	Opinions of the Attorney General of New York [A publication] (DLA)
NYOSL........	New York Ocean Science Laboratory
NYP	New York-Pennsylvania League [Baseball]
NYP	New York Press (WDMC)
NYP	New York Public Library, Serials, New York, NY [OCLC symbol] (OCLC)
NYP	Not Yet Published
NYPA	New York Port Authority
NYPAA	National Yellow Pages Agency Association [Tucson, AZ] (EA)
NYP & B	New York, Providence & Boston Railroad
NYPC	New York Pigment Club (EA)
NYPD	New York Police Department [Initialism also used as title of TV series]
NYPE	New York Port of Embarkation [Military]
NYPE	New York Produce Exchange [Defunct] (EA)
NYPF	National Young Professionals Forum (EA)
NYPFO........	New York Air Force Procurement Field Office
NYPH	Navy Yard, Pearl Harbor, Hawaii
NYPHIL........	Navy Yard, Philadelphia, Pennsylvania
NYPIRG.......	New York Public Interest Research Group
NYPL	New York Public Library [New York, NY]
NYPLC	National Youth Pro-Life Coalition (EA)
NYPLR	New York Prime Loan Rate [Finance] (DS)
NYPM	National Yellow Pages Monitor (EFIS)
NYPM	National Yokefellow Prison Ministry [Later, YPM] (EA)
NYPM	Navy Youth Program Manager (MCD)
NYPMA	New York Paper Merchants Association (EA)
NYPO	New York Publicity Outlet [A publication] (WDMC)
NYPOE	New York Port of Embarkation [Military]
NYPORT.......	Navy Yard, Portsmouth, New Hampshire
NYPR	New York Practice Reports [A publication] (DLA)
NYPR	N-Nitrosopyrrolidine [Also, NO-PYR] [Biochemistry, organic chemistry]
NYPRPG	New York Publishers Rights and Permissions Group (EA)
NY Pr Rep ...	New York Practice Reports [A publication] (DLA)
NYPS	National Yellow Pages Service
NYPS	Navy Yard, Puget Sound [Bremerton], Washington
NYP-SA.......	National Yellow Pages Service Association (WDMC)
NYPSO	New York Philharmonic Symphony Orchestra
NYPYR........	Nitrosopyrrolidine [Also, NPYR] [Organic chemistry]
NYR	National Young Republicans (NADA)
NYR	Neodymium YAG [Yttrium Aluminum Garnet] Range-Finder
NYR	New York Court of Appeals Reports [A publication] (DLA)
NYR	Not Yet Reported [Air Force]
NYR	Not Yet Required (MUGU)
NYR	Not Yet Returned [Military]
NYR	Nuclear Yield Requirement (NATG)
NYR	Receiver Site [Nevada] [Seismograph station code, US Geological Survey Closed] (SEIS)
NYRA	New York Racing Authority [Cable-television system]
NYRAPG	New York Rights and Permissions Group (EA)
NYRB	New York Review of Books [A publication] (BRI)
NYRC	New York Railroad Commission Reports [A publication] (DLA)
NY Rec	New York Record [A publication] (DLA)
NY Reg	New York Daily Register [A publication] (DLA)
NY Rep	New York Court of Appeals Reports [A publication] (DLA)
NY Reps	New York Court of Appeals Reports [A publication] (DLA)
NY Reptr.....	New York Reporter [A publication] (ILCA)
NYRFC........	New York Rangers Fan Club (EA)
NYRL	New York Revised Laws [A publication] (DLA)
NYRMA	New York Raincoat Manufacturers Association (EA)
NYRRC........	New York Road Runners Club (EA)
NYRS	New York Revised Statutes [A publication] (DLA)
NYRS	New Youth Research Survey [Religious education test]
NYS	New York Shavians (EA)
NYS	New York State
NYS	New York State Electric & Gas Corp. [Associated Press] (SAG)
NYS	New York State Reporter [A publication] (DLA)
NYS	New York State Union List, Albany, NY [OCLC symbol] (OCLC)

NYS .... New York Supplement [A publication] (DLA)
NYS .... Not Yet Specified
NYS .... Syncline Ridge [Nevada] [Seismograph station code, US Geological Survey Closed] (SEIS)
NYS .... Yonkers School System, Yonkers, NY [Library symbol Library of Congress] (LCLS)
NYS 2d .... New York Supplement, Second Series [A publication] (DLA)
NYSA .... New York Shipping Association (EA)
NYSAC .... New York State Athletic Commission (BARN)
NYSASS .... New York State Association of Service Stations [Later, NYSASSRS] (EA)
NYSASSRS... New York State Association of Service Stations and Repair Shops (EA)
NYSBA Bull... New York State Bar Association. Bulletin [A publication] (DLA)
NY S B BULL... New York State Bar Bulletin [A publication] (LWAP)
NYSC .... New York Shipbuilding Corp.
NYSC .... Thompson and Cook's New York Supreme Court Reports [A publication] (DLA)
NYSCA .... National Youth Sports Coaches Association (EA)
NYSCAT .... New York State Union Catalog of Film and Video [Mid-Hudson Library System] [Information service or system] (IID)
NYSCS .... New York State Colonization Society [Defunct] (EA)
NYS Ct .... New York Superior Court Reports [A publication] (DLA)
NYSD .... New York Society for the Deaf [Formerly, JSD] (EA)
NYSDA .... New York State Security Dealers Association (EA)
NYSDEC .... New York State Department of Environmental Conservation
NYS DEC...... New York State Department of Environmental Conservation (BCP)
NYSDR .... New York State Department Reports [A publication] (DLA)
NYSE .... New York Stock Exchange [New York, NY] (EA)
NYSE .... New York Stock Exchange Guide [Commerce Clearing House] [A publication] (DLA)
NYSEG .... New York State Electric & Gas Corp. [Associated Press] (SAG)
NY Sen J ..... New York Senate Journal [A publication] (DLA)
NYSERDA .... New York State Energy Research and Development Authority
NYSERNET.. New York State Educational and Research Network
NYSERNet.... New York State Education and Research Network, Inc. [Telecommunications service] (TSSD)
NYSF .... National Youth Science Foundation
NYSFTCA ..... New York State Fruit Testing Cooperative Association (EA)
NYSGI .... New York Sea Grant Institute [Albany, NY] [Department of Commerce] (GRD)
NYSIIS .... New York State Identification and Intelligence System
NYSILL .... New York State Interlibrary Loan [Network]
NYSILL .... New York State Inter-Library Loans System (NITA)
NYSNY .... New York Naval Shipyard (New York)
NYSP .... New York School of Printing (DGA)
NYSPCC....... New York Society for the Prevention of Cruelty to Children
NY Spec Term R... Howard's New York Practice Reports [A publication] (DLA)
NY Spec Term Rep... Howard's New York Practice Reports [A publication] (DLA)
NYSPI .... New York State Psychiatric Institute [New York State Office of Mental Hygiene] [Research center] (RCD)
NYSR .... New York State Reporter [A publication] (DLA)
NYSSA .... New York Society of Security Analysts [New York, NY] (EA)
NYSSDA....... New York State Safe Deposit Association [New York, NY] (EA)
NYSSF .... National Youth Sports Safety Foundation (EA)
NYSSTF .... New York State Science and Technology Foundation (RDA)
NY St .... New York State Reporter [A publication] (DLA)
NYST .... Nystagmus [Medicine]
NY State R... New York State Reporter [A publication] (DLA)
NY State Rep... New York State Reporter [A publication] (DLA)
NY St Ba A... New York State Bar Association. Bulletin [A publication] (DLA)
NY St Bull ... New York State Bulletin (AAGC)
NY St Dept Rep... New York State Department Reports [A publication] (DLA)
NYStJ.......... Saint Joseph's Seminary, Dunwoodie, Yonkers, NY [Library symbol Library of Congress] (LCLS)
NY St R .... New York State Reporter [A publication] (DLA)
NY St Rep ... New York State Reporter [A publication] (DLA)
NY St Repr... New York State Reporter [A publication] (DLA)
NY Sup Ct.... New York Supreme Court Reports [A publication] (DLA)
NY Sup Ct Rep... Thompson and Cook's New York Supreme Court Reports [A publication] (DLA)
NY Sup Ct (T & C)... Thompson and Cook's New York Supreme Court Reports [A publication] (DLA)
NY Super..... New York Superior Court Reports [A publication] (DLA)
NY Super Ct... New York Superior Court Reports [Various reporters] [A publication] (DLA)
NY Super Ct R... New York Superior Court Reports [A publication] (DLA)
NY Super Ct Rep... New York Superior Court Reports [A publication] (DLA)
NY Supl ...... New York Supplement [A publication] (DLA)
NY Supp ...... New York Supplement [A publication] (DLA)
NY Supp 2d... New York Supplement, Second Series [A publication] (DLA)
NY Suppl ..... New York Supplement [A publication] (DLA)
NY Supr...... New York Superior Court Reports [A publication] (DLA)
NY Supr Ct... New York Superior Court Reports [A publication] (DLA)
NY Supr Ct R... New York Superior Court Reports [A publication] (DLA)
NY Supr Ct Rep... New York Superior Court Reports [A publication] (DLA)
NY Supr Ct Repts (T & C)... New York Supreme Court Reports, by Thompson and Cook [A publication] (DLA)
NY Suprm Ct... New York Supreme Court Reports [A publication] (DLA)
NYSV .... Narcissus Yellow Stripe Virus [Plant pathology]
NYSW .... New York, Susquehanna & Western Railroad Co. [AAR code]
NYSWAC ...... New York State Women's Collegiate Athletic Conference (PSS)
NYSWGGI .... New York State Wine Grape Growers, Inc. (EA)
NYT............. National Youth Theatre [British]
NYT............. New Yiddish Theater (BJA)

NYT............. New York Testing Laboratories, Inc.
NYT............. [The] New York Times Co. [AMEX symbol] (SPSG)
NYTA .... New York Theatre Annual [A publication]
NYTA .... New York Times CI'A' [AMEX symbol] (TTSB)
NY Tax Cas... New York Tax Cases [Commerce Clearing House] [A publication] (DLA)
NYTB .... New York Theatre Ballet
NYTBIO .... [The] New York Times Biographical File [The New York Times Co.] [Information service or system] (CRD)
NYTBR .... New York Times Book Review [A publication] (BRI)
NYTCL .... New York Temperance Civic League [Later, AYE] (EA)
NYTEI .... New York Tax Exempt Income Fund [Associated Press] (SAG)
Nytest .... NYTEST Environmental, Inc. [Associated Press] (SAG)
NY Them ..... New York Themis [New York City] [A publication] (DLA)
NYT/IB .... New York Times Information Bank
NY Tim .... [The] New York Times Co. [Associated Press] (SAG)
NYTIS .... New York Times Information Service, Inc. [Mead Data Central] [Database originator and host] (IID)
NYTLa .... New York Times (Late Edition) [A publication] (BRI)
NYTLC .... New York Taxi & Limousine Commission (WDAA)
NYTNS .... New York Times News Service
NYTR .... New York Term Reports (Caines' Reports) [A publication] (DLA)
NY Trans ..... New York Transcript [Numbers 1-11] [1861 New York City] [A publication] (DLA)
NY Trans App... New York Transcript Appeals Reports [A publication] (DLA)
NY Trans NS... New York Transcript, New Series [New York City] [A publication] (DLA)
NY Trans Rep... New York Transcript Reports [A publication] (DLA)
NYT Rep ...... Caines' Term Reports [New York] [A publication] (DLA)
NYTS .... New York Theological Seminary
NYTS .... Nytest Environmental [NASDAQ symbol] (TTSB)
NYTS .... NYTEST Environmental, Inc. [NASDAQ symbol] (NQ)
NYTTS .... New York Turtle and Tortoise Society (EA)
nyu............. New York [MARC country of publication code Library of Congress] (LCCP)
NYU .... New York University
NYU .... Nyaung-U [Myanmar] [Airport symbol] (OAG)
NYU Conf Charitable... New York University. Conference on Charitable Foundations. Proceedings [A publication] (DLA)
NYU Conf Charitable Fdn... New York University. Conference on Charitable Foundations. Proceedings [A publication] (DLA)
NYU Conf on Char Found Proc... Conference on Charitable Foundations. Proceedings. New York University [A publication] (DLA)
NYUL Center Bull... New York University. Law Center. Bulletin [A publication] (DLA)
NYULT .... New York University School of Continuing Education, Continuing Education in Law and Taxation [A publication] (DLA)
NY Unconsol Laws... New York Unconsolidated Laws (McKinney) [A publication] (DLA)
NYUP .... New York University Press (DGA)
NYU Rev Law & Soc... New York University. Review of Law and Social Change [A publication] (DLA)
NYUTI .... New York University Tax Institute (DLA)
NYV .... Vern [Nevada] [Seismograph station code, US Geological Survey Closed] (SEIS)
NYVTX .... Davis New York Venture CI.A [Mutual fund ticker symbol] (SG)
NYWA .... National Youth Work Alliance (EA)
NYWASH...... Navy Yard, Washington, DC [Obsolete]
NYWC .... New York Wine Council (EA)
NYWCC........ New York Water Color Club [1890-1941] (NGC)
NY Week Dig... New York Weekly Digest [A publication] (DLA)
NY Weekly Dig... New York Weekly Digest [A publication] (DLA)
NYWF .... New York World's Fair
NYWGF........ New York Wine/Grape Foundation (EA)
NY Wkly Dig... New York Weekly Digest [A publication] (DLA)
NYYP .... New York Yellow Pages, Inc.
NYZP .... New York Zoological Park
NYZS .... New York Zoological Society
NZ .... Air New Zealand Ltd. (Domestic Division) [ICAO designator] (ICDA)
Nz .... National Library of New Zealand, Wellington, New Zealand [Library symbol] [Library of Congress] (LCLS)
NZ.............. Neutrality Zone
NZ.............. New Mexico & Arizona Land Co. [AMEX symbol] (SPSG)
NZ.............. New Mexico/Ariz Land [AMEX symbol] (TTSB)
nz.............. New Zealand [MARC country of publication code Library of Congress] (LCCP)
NZ.............. New Zealand [ANSI two-letter standard code] (CNC)
NZ.............. New Zealand National Airways Corp. [ICAO designator]
NZ.............. New Zealand Reports [A publication] (DLA)
N-Z............. Nike-Zeus [Missiles] (AAG)
NZ.............. Normal Acceleration
NZ.............. Normal to Z-Axis (MCD)
NZ.............. Nose to Z-Axis (MCD)
NZ.............. Nuclear Zone
NZA............ Niobium Zinc Alloy
NZAA.......... Auckland/International [New Zealand] [ICAO location identifier] (ICLI)
NZAF.......... New Zealand Air Force (DAS)
NzAGS .... Church of Jesus Christ of Latter-Day Saints, Genealogical Society Library, Auckland Branch, Auckland, New Zealand [Library symbol Library of Congress] (LCLS)
NZAK.......... Auckland [New Zealand] [ICAO location identifier] (ICLI)
NZAP.......... New Zealand Associated Press (BARN)
NZAP.......... Taupo [New Zealand] [ICAO location identifier] (ICLI)
NZ App Rep... New Zealand Appeal Reports [A publication] (DLA)
NZAPS .... Nike-Zeus Automatic Programming System [Missiles]

NZAQ	Auckland [*New Zealand*] [*ICAO location identifier*] (ICLI)
NZAR	Ardmore [*New Zealand*] [*ICAO location identifier*] (ICLI)
NzAU	Auckland University, Auckland, New Zealand [*Library symbol Library of Congress*] (LCLS)
NZ Awards...	New Zealand Awards, Recommendations, Agreements, Etc. [*A publication*] (DLA)
NZB..............	New Zealand Black [*Mice hybrids*]
NZB..............	Nonzero Binary (NASA)
NZB..............	Royal New Zealand Ballet
NZBC	New Zealand Broadcasting Commission (WDAA)
NZBC	New Zealand Broadcasting Corp.
NZBS	New Zealand Broadcasting Service
NZC.............	Jacksonville, FL [*Location identifier FAA*] (FAAL)
NZC.............	New Zealand Chocolate [*Mouse*] (DMAA)
NZC.............	New Zealand Cross (DAS)
NZCA	Campbell Island [*New Zealand*] [*ICAO location identifier*] (ICLI)
NZCER	New Zealand Council for Educational Research (WDAA)
NzCGS	Church of Jesus Christ of Latter-Day Saints, Genealogical Society Library, Canterbury Branch, Christchurch, New Zealand [*Library symbol Library of Congress*] (LCLS)
NZCH	Christchurch/International [*New Zealand*] [*ICAO location identifier*] (ICLI)
NZCI............	Chatham Island/Tuuta [*New Zealand*] [*ICAO location identifier*] (ICLI)
NZCM	McMurdo Sound, Antarctica [*New Zealand*] [*ICAO location identifier*] (ICLI)
NZCO	Christchurch [*New Zealand*] [*ICAO location identifier*] (ICLI)
NZ Col LJ	New Zealand Colonial Law Journal [*A publication*] (DLA)
NzCSI-A	New Zealand Department of Scientific and Industrial Research, Antarctic Division, Christchurch, New Zealand [*Library symbol Library of Congress*] (LCLS)
NZ Ct App ...	New Zealand Court of Appeals (DLA)
NZ Ct Arb.....	New Zealand Court of Arbitration (DLA)
NZD	Nonzero Digit (ECII)
NZDF	Christchurch/International [*New Zealand*] [*ICAO location identifier*] (ICLI)
NZDN	Dunedin [*New Zealand*] [*ICAO location identifier*] (ICLI)
NZE.............	Glenview, IL [*Location identifier FAA*] (FAAL)
NZE.............	North Zenith East
NZE.............	Nzerekore [*Guinea*] [*Airport symbol*] (AD)
N Zea..........	New Zealand (VRA)
NZEF	New Zealand Employers' Federation (ODBW)
NZEF	New Zealand Expeditionary Force (WDAA)
NZEFIP........	New Zealand Expeditionary Force in the Pacific (WDAA)
NZEI	New Zealand Educational Institute (WDAA)
NZF.............	Near Zero Field
NZFL	New Zealand Federation of Labor (ODBW)
NZFOE	New Zealand Futures and Options Exchange (NUMA)
NZG	Near Zero Gravity
NZG	North Carolina School of the Arts, Winston-Salem, NC [*OCLC symbol*] (OCLC)
NZ Gaz LR ...	New Zealand Gazette Law Reports [*A publication*] (DLA)
NZGLR	New Zealand Gazette Law Reports [*A publication*] (DLA)
NZGS	Gisborne [*New Zealand*] [*ICAO location identifier*] (ICLI)
NZHK	Hokitika [*New Zealand*] [*ICAO location identifier*] (ICLI)
NZHN	Hamilton [*New Zealand*] [*ICAO location identifier*] (ICLI)
NZHO	Wellington [*New Zealand*] [*ICAO location identifier*] (ICLI)
NZIC...........	New Zealand Institute of Chemistry
NZIER	New Zealand Institute of Economic Research
NZ Ind Arb...	New Zealand Industrial Arbitration Awards [*A publication*] (DLA)
NZJ	Naze [*Ryukyu Islands*] [*Seismograph station code, US Geological Survey*] (SEIS)
NZJ	Santa Ana, CA [*Location identifier FAA*] (FAAL)
NZJP...........	New Zealand Justice of the Peace [*1876-77*] [*A publication*] (DLA)
NZ Jur	New Zealand Jurist [*1873-78*] [*A publication*] (DLA)
NZ Jur Mining Law...	Jurist Reports, New Series, Cases in Mining Law [*New Zealand*] [*A publication*] (DLA)
NZ Jur NS....	New Zealand Jurist, New Series [*A publication*] (DLA)
NZKB	Wellington/Kilbirnie [*New Zealand*] [*ICAO location identifier*] (ICLI)
NZKI	Kaikoura [*New Zealand*] [*ICAO location identifier*] (ICLI)
NZKL..........	Wellington/Kelburn [*New Zealand*] [*ICAO location identifier*] (ICLI)
NZKMB	New Zealand Kiwifruit Marketing Board
NZKT	Kaitaia [*New Zealand*] [*ICAO location identifier*] (ICLI)
NZKX	Kaitaia [*New Zealand*] [*ICAO location identifier*] (ICLI)
NZL.............	New Zealand [*ANSI three-letter standard code*] (CNC)
NZ Law Soc N...	New Zealand Law Society. Newsletter [*A publication*] (DLA)
NZLGR	Local Government Reports [*New Zealand*] [*A publication*] (DLA)
NZLJMC.......	New Zealand Law Journal, Magistrates' Court Decisions [*A publication*] (DLA)
NZLO	New Zealand Liaison Officer
NZLP	New Zealand Labour Party [*Political party*] (PPW)
NZLR	New Zealand Law Reports [*A publication*] (DLA)
NZLRCA	New Zealand Law Reports, Court of Appeal [*A publication*] (DLA)
NZM............	Mount Cook Airlines [*New Zealand*] [*ICAO designator*] (FAAC)
NZMF..........	Milford Sound [*New Zealand*] [*ICAO location identifier*] (ICLI)
NZMN	New Zealand Merchant Navy (DAS)
NZMS...........	New Zealand Meteorological Service [*Marine science*] (OSRA)
NZN	Niedersachsischer Zeitschriftennachweis [*Deutsches Bibliotheksinstitut*] [*Germany Information service or system*] (CRD)
NZNB	New Zealand Naval Board [*Wellington*]
NZNFC	Norma Zimmer National Fan Club (EA)
NZNP	New Plymouth [*New Zealand*] [*ICAO location identifier*] (ICLI)
NZNR	Napier [*New Zealand*] [*ICAO location identifier*] (ICLI)
NZNS	Nelson [*New Zealand*] [*ICAO location identifier*] (ICLI)
NZNV	Invercargill [*New Zealand*] [*ICAO location identifier*] (ICLI)
NZO	New Zealand Obese [*Mouse*] [*Medicine*] (DMAA)
NZOH	Ohakea [*New Zealand*] [*ICAO location identifier*] (ICLI)
NZOI	New Zealand Oceanographic Institute
NZ Ords.......	Ordinances of the Legislative Council of New Zealand [*A publication*] (DLA)
NZOU..........	Oamaru [*New Zealand*] [*ICAO location identifier*] (ICLI)
NZP.............	National Zoological Park [*Smithsonian Institution*]
NZPA	New Zealand Press Association
NZPCC	New Zealand Privy Council Cases [*A publication*] (DLA)
NZPC Cas	New Zealand Privy Council Cases [*A publication*] (DLA)
NZPM	Palmerston North [*New Zealand*] [*ICAO location identifier*] (ICLI)
NZPO	New Zealand Post Office [*Telecommunications*]
NZPP	Paraparaumu [*New Zealand*] [*ICAO location identifier*] (ICLI)
NZQN	Queenstown [*New Zealand*] [*ICAO location identifier*] (ICLI)
NZR	New Zealand Red [*Rabbit*] [*Medicine*] (DMAA)
NZ Rep	New Zealand Reports, Court of Appeals [*A publication*] (DLA)
NZ Repr Stat...	Reprint of the Statutes of New Zealand [*A publication*] (DLA)
NZRFU	New Zealand Rugby Football Union
NZRN	Raoul Island [*New Zealand*] [*ICAO location identifier*] (ICLI)
NZRO	Rotorua [*New Zealand*] [*ICAO location identifier*] (ICLI)
NZRR	New Zealand Rough Riders [*Military*] (ROG)
NZR Regs & B...	Rules, Regulations, and By-Laws under New Zealand Statutes [*A publication*] (DLA)
NZS.............	Nonzero Sum [*Genetics*]
NZSC	New Zealand Supreme Court [*A publication*] (DLA)
NZSEAFRON...	New Zealand Sea Frontier
NZSG	Non-Zero-Sum Game (MHDW)
NZ Stat	Statutes of New Zealand [*A publication*] (DLA)
NZ Stat Regs...	New Zealand Statutory Regulations [*A publication*] (DLA)
NZT.............	Nonzero Test (IAA)
NZT.............	Nonzero Transfer
NZT.............	Telecom Corp. New Zealand [*NYSE symbol*] (SPSG)
NZT.............	Telecom Corp. New Zealand ADS [*NYSE symbol*] (TTSB)
NZTBR	New Zealand Taxation Board of Review Decisions [*A publication*] (DLA)
NZTG	Tauranga [*New Zealand*] [*ICAO location identifier*] (ICLI)
NZTJWG	Nike-Zeus Target Joint Working Group [*Missiles*] (MUGU)
NZTO	New Zealand Tourism Office (EA)
NZTP..........	New Zealand Tourist and Publicity Office [*Later, NZTO*] (EA)
NZTS	New Zealand Treaty Series [*A publication*] (DLA)
NZTU	Timaru [*New Zealand*] [*ICAO location identifier*] (ICLI)
NZTV..........	Nike-Zeus Target Vehicle [*Missiles*] (IAA)
NzTvGS........	Church of Jesus Christ of Latter-Day Saints, Genealogical Society Library, Temple View Branch, Temple View, New Zealand [*Library symbol Library of Congress*] (LCLS)
NZW............	New Zealand White [*Mice hybrids*]
NZW............	South Weymouth, MA [*Location identifier FAA*] (FAAL)
NZWA	Chatham Island/Waitangi [*New Zealand*] [*ICAO location identifier*] (ICLI)
NZWB	Woodbourne [*New Zealand*] [*ICAO location identifier*] (ICLI)
NZWG	Wigram [*New Zealand*] [*ICAO location identifier*] (ICLI)
NzWGAL	General Assembly Library, Wellington, New Zealand, [*Library symbol Library of Congress*] (LCLS)
NzWGS	Church of Jesus Christ of Latter-Day Saints, Genealogical Society Library, Wellington Stake Branch, Wellington, New Zealand [*Library symbol Library of Congress*] (LCLS)
NZWK	Whakatane [*New Zealand*] [*ICAO location identifier*] (ICLI)
NzWMW.......	New Zealand Ministry of Works and Development, Head Office Library, Wellington, New Zealand [*Library symbol Library of Congress*] (LCLS)
NZWN	Wellington/International [*New Zealand*] [*ICAO location identifier*] (ICLI)
NzWNA	National Archives, Wellington, New Zealand [*Library symbol Library of Congress*] (LCLS)
NZWP	Whenuapai [*New Zealand*] [*ICAO location identifier*] (ICLI)
NZWQ	Wellington [*New Zealand*] [*ICAO location identifier*] (ICLI)
NZWR	Whangarei [*New Zealand*] [*ICAO location identifier*] (ICLI)
NZWS	Westport [*New Zealand*] [*ICAO location identifier*] (ICLI)
NZWU	Wanganui [*New Zealand*] [*ICAO location identifier*] (ICLI)
NZY	San Diego, CA [*Location identifier FAA*] (FAAL)
NZYM	Synthetech, Inc. [*NASDAQ symbol*] (NQ)
NZZA	Auckland [*New Zealand*] [*ICAO location identifier*] (ICLI)
NZZC...........	Christchurch [*New Zealand*] [*ICAO location identifier*] (ICLI)
NZZO	Auckland [*New Zealand*] [*ICAO location identifier*] (ICLI)
NZZW..........	Wellington [*New Zealand*] [*ICAO location identifier*] (ICLI)

O
By Acronym

O	Absence of Sex Chromosome (DAVI)
O	An Oige [*The Irish Youth Hostels Association*] [*Founded in 1931*]
o	Deamino [*As substituent on nucleoside*] [*Biochemistry*]
O	Horizontal Opposed [*Aircraft engine*]
O	Law Opinions [*A publication*] (DLA)
O	New Orleans [*Louisiana*] [*Mint mark, when appearing on US coins*] [*Obsolete*]
O	None (DAVI)
O	Nonmotile [*Laboratory science*] (DAVI)
O	Oasis
O	Oath
O	Oberst [*Colonel*] [*German military - World War II*]
O	Obiit [*He, or She, Died*] [*Latin*]
O	Object
O	Objective
O	Oblast [*Governmental subdivision in USSR corresponding to a province or state*]
O	Oboe [*Phonetic alphabet*] [*World War II*] (DSUE)
O	Observation Aircraft [*Designation for all US military aircraft*]
O	Observer
O	Obsolescent (AFIT)
O	Obstetrics [*Medicine*] (MAE)
O	Obvious (STED)
O	Occasional [*Concerning occurrence of species*]
O	Occidental
O	Occipital (STED)
O	Occiput [*Medicine*]
O	Occlusal [*Dentistry*]
O	Occupation (ADA)
O	Occurrence
O	Ocean [*Maps and charts*]
O	Octal [*Number system with a base of eight*] [*Computer science*] (BUR)
O	Octarius [*Pint*] [*Pharmacy*]
O	Octavo [*Book from 20 to 25 centimeters in height*] [*Bibliography*]
O	October
O	Octupole [*Physics*] (OA)
O	Oculus [*Eye*] [*Latin*]
O	Odericus [*Flourished, 1166-1200*] [*Authority cited in pre-1607 legal work*] (DSA)
O	Off
O	Offered [*Stock exchange term*] (SPSG)
O	Office [*or Officer*]
O	Office of Operations [*Coast Guard*]
O	Official [*Rate*] [*Value of the English pound*]
O	Often (STED)
O	Ohio
O	Ohio Reports [*A publication*] (DLA)
O	Ohio State Library, Columbus, OH [*Library symbol Library of Congress*] (LCLS)
O	Ohm [*Electricity*]
O	Ohne [*Antigen*] [*Immunology*]
O	Oil
o	Oil (VRA)
O	Oklahoma (DLA)
O	Old
O	Olivine Subgroup [*Fayalite, forsterite*] [*CIPW classification Geology*]
O	Omicron [*Fifteenth letter of the Greek alphabet*] (NASA)
O	Omnipol Foreign Trade Corp. [*Former Czechoslovakia*] [*ICAO aircraft manufacturer identifier*] (ICAO)
O	Omnivore
O	Oncovin [*Leurocristine, Vincristine*] [*Also, LCR, V, VC, VCR*] [*Antineoplastic drug*]
O	Ongoing
O	Only
O	Ontario (DLA)
O	Ontario Reports [*A publication*] (DLA)
O	Ontario Securities Commission [*Canada*]
O	Opacity (MCD)
O	Open [*Dancing position*]
O	Open-Air Places [*Parks, pools, etc.*] [*Public-performance tariff class*] [*British*]
O	Open Circuit
O	Opening
O	Operand [*Computer science*]
O	Operating Room Attendant [*Ranking title*] [*British Royal Navy*]
O	Operation
O	Operator
O	[*Telephone*] Operator (WDMC)
O	Operon [*Genetics*]
O	Ophthalmology [*Medical Officer designation*] [*British*]
O	Opium [*Slang*]
O	Optimus [*Best*] [*Latin*]
O	Optional Dishes [*School meals*] [*British*]
O	Options [*Computer science*] [*Telecommunications*]
O	Oral [*Medicine*]
O	Orange [*Color*] [*Medicine*] (DMAA)
O	Orange [*Phonetic alphabet*] [*Royal Navy World War I Pre-World War II*] (DSUE)
O	Orange [*Maps and charts*]
O	Orbit [*Medicine*] (DAVI)
O	Orchid Flowering [*Horticulture*]
O	Ordained
O	Order
O	Orderly [*Medicine*] (DAVI)
O	Orders Group [*British military*] (DMA)
O	Ordinance
O	Ordinary
O	Ordinary Level [*School graduating grade*] [*British*]
O	Ordinary Ray [*Direction of*]
O	Ordinate [*Mathematics*] (MSA)
O	Ordinis [*By the Order Of*] [*Latin*]
O	Ordnance
O	Ordonnanzoffizier [*Special-Missions Staff Officer*] [*German military - World War II*]
O	Oregon (ROG)
O	Oregon Reports [*A publication*] (DLA)
O	Organ
O	Organic [*Soil*]
O	Organism [*Psychology*]
O	Organization
O	Organized Naval Reserve
O	Orient [*Freemasonry*]
O	Oriental
O	Origin
o	Origin (IDOE)
O	Original
O	Orotidine [*One-letter symbol; see Ord*]
o	Ortho [*Chemistry*]
O	Orthodox [*Judaism*]
O	Orthopedic (STED)
O	Os [*Bone*] [*Latin*]
O	Oscar [*Phonetic alphabet*] [*International*] (DSUE)
O	Oscillation or Fluctuation in Behavior [*Psychology*]
O	Oscillators [*JETDS nomenclature*] [*Military*] (CET)
O	Osphradium [*An organ in mollusks*]
O	Osten [*East*] [*German*]
O	Ostiole [*Biology*]
O	Other
O	Other Program (NTCM)
O	Otto's United States Supreme Court Reports [*91-107 United States*] [*A publication*] (DLA)
O	Ouest [*West*] [*French*]
O	Out
O	Outboard (DS)
O	Outfield [*Baseball*]
O	Outlay (GFGA)
O	Outlet
O	Output (BUR)
o	Output (IDOE)
O	Outside Cylinders [*Trains*] [*British*]
O	Outside Edge [*Skating*]
O	Ovary
O	Ovation (WGA)
O	Oven
O	Over
O	Overall (IAA)
O	Overall Rating [*Broadcasting*]
O	Overcast
o	Overruled [*Ruling in cited case expressly overruled*] [*Used in Shepard's Citations*] [*Legal term*] (DLA)
O	Overseer

O	Ovule [*Botany*]
O	Owner
O	Oxford [*County borough in England*]
O	Oxidative (STED)
O	Oxygen [*Chemical element*]
O	Realty Income [*NYSE symbol*] (TTSB)
O	Realty Income Corp. [*NYSE symbol*] (SAG)
O	Respirations [*on anesthesia chart*] (DAVI)
O	Shoulder Season [*Airline fare code*]
O	Solicitor's Opinion [*A publication*] (DLA)
O	South African Law Reports, Orange Free State Provincial Division [*1910-46*] [*A publication*] (DLA)
O	Without Film [*Bacteriology*] (DAVI)
O1	Ensign [*Navy*]
O1	Organized Naval Reserve Seagoing
O1	Second Lieutenant [*Air Force, Army, Marine Corps*]
O2	Both Eyes [*Pharmacy*]
O2	First Lieutenant [*Air Force, Army, Marine Corps*]
O2	Lieutenant Junior Grade [*Navy*]
O2	Organized Naval Reserve Aviation
O$_2$	Oxygen (IDOE)
O-2A	Oligodendrocytes and Type 2 Astrocytes [*Neurology*]
O$_2$ Cap	Oxygen Capacity (MAE)
O$_2$sat	Oxygen Saturation (MAE)
O$_2$V	Oxygen Ventilation Equivalent [*Laboratory science*] (DAVI)
O3	Captain [*Air Force, Army, Marine Corps*]
O3	Lieutenant [*Navy*]
O$_3$	Ozone (PS)
O4	Lieutenant Commander [*Navy*]
O4	Major [*Air Force, Army, Marine Corps*]
O40	October 4th Organization (EA)
O5	Commander [*Navy*]
O5	Lieutenant Colonel [*Air Force, Army, Marine Corps*]
O6	Captain [*Navy*]
O6	Colonel [*Air Force, Army, Marine Corps*]
O7	Brigadier General [*Air Force, Army, Marine Corps*]
O7	Commodore [*Navy*]
O8	Major General [*Air Force, Army, Marine Corps*]
O8	Rear Admiral [*Navy*]
O9	Lieutenant General [*Air Force, Army, Marine Corps*]
O9	Vice Admiral [*Navy*]
O10	Admiral [*Navy*]
O10	General [*Air Force, Army, Marine Corps*]
OA	Almonte Public Library, Ontario [*Library symbol National Library of Canada*] (NLC)
O-A	Objective Analytic Batteries [*Personality development test*] [*Psychology*]
OA	Objective Aperture [*Microscopy*]
OA	Objective Area [*Military*]
OA	Oblate Sisters of the Assumption [*Roman Catholic religious order*]
OA	Obligation Authority [*Army*]
OA	Obstacle Avoidance (MCD)
OA	Occipital Artery [*Anatomy*]
OA	Occiput Anterior [*Medicine*]
OA	Ocean Acre [*Marine science*] (MSC)
O/A	Offer Accepted (ADA)
OA	Office Address (WDAA)
OA	Office Audit [*IRS*]
OA	Office Automation
OA	Office for Accreditation [*American Library Association*]
OA	Office of Administration [*NASA*]
OA	Office of Applications [*NASA*]
OA	Office of Audits (COE)
OA	Office of Operations Analysis [*Arms Control and Disarmament Agency*] (GRD)
OA	Office of the Administrator
OA	Officers Association [*British military*] (DMA)
OA	Official Assignee (ROG)
OA	Ohio Appellate Reports [*A publication*] (DLA)
OA	Oil-Immersed Self-Cooled [*Transformer*] (IEEE)
OA	Old Account [*Banking*]
OA	Old Age
OA	Old Assyrian (BJA)
OA	Oleic Acid [*Medicine*] (DMAA)
OA	Olymbiaki Aeroporia [*Olympic Airlines*]
OA	Olympic Airways [*Greece*] [*ICAO designator*] (OAG)
OA	Omniantenna
OA	Omnirange Antenna (IAA)
OA	On Acceptance [*Business term*]
oa	On Acceptance (EBF)
OA	On Account [*Business and trade*]
OA	On Account Of
O/A	On Application (NITA)
OA	On Arrival (ADA)
O/A	On or About (WDAA)
o/a	On or About (WDMC)
O/A	Open Access [*Library shelves*] (DGA)
OA	Open Account
OA	Open Agility
OA	Open Annealed [*Metal industry*]
OA	Open Architecture [*Telecommunications*] (IAA)
OA	Opera America [*An association*] (EA)
OA	Operand Address (NITA)
OA	Operand Address Register [*Computer science*]
OA	Operating Agency

OA	Operating Aircraft
OA	Operating Assemblies [*JETDS nomenclature*] [*Military*] (CET)
OA	Operating Authorization
OA	Operational Advice
OA	Operational Aft (MCD)
OA	Operational Amplifier [*Telecommunications*] (TEL)
OA	Operational [*or operations*] Analysis
OA	Operationally Available (NATG)
OA	Operation Analysis [*or Analyst*] (WDAA)
OA	Operation Appreciation (EA)
O/A	Operations/Administration (SSD)
OA	Operations Advisor [*NASA*]
OA	Operations Area
OA	Operator Access (IAA)
OA	Opiate Analgesia
OA	Optical Adjunct
OA	Optic Atrophy (CPH)
OA	Optoacoustic [*Cell*]
OA	Oral Alimentation [*Gastroenterology*] (DAVI)
OA	Oral Apparatus [*Zoology*]
OA	Orbital Assembly (MCD)
OA	Orbit Analysis
OA	Orbit Analyst (MCD)
OA	Orbiter Access Arm [*NASA*]
O/A	Order Authority (MCD)
OA	Order of AHEPA [*Also known as American Hellenic Educational Progressive Association*] (EA)
OA	Order of Alhambra
OA	Order of Australia (WDAA)
OA	Order of the Alhambra (EA)
OA	Order of the Arrow (EA)
O/A	Ordnance Alteration (MCD)
OA	Ordnance Artificer [*Obsolete Navy British*]
OA	Organic Acid (AAEL)
OA	Organizational Analysis
OA	Organizational Assessment
O/A	Original-Abfuellung [*On estate-bottled German wine labels*]
OA	Originating Agency (SAA)
OA	Orlando Aerospace [*Martin Marietta*] (RDA)
OA	Oro Americano [*American Gold*] [*Spanish Business term*]
OA	Osborne Association (EA)
OA	Osteoarthritis [*Medicine*]
OA	Osteogenesis Imperfecta [*Brittle bone disease*]
OA	Other Appointments
OA	Other Articles
OA	Oudh Appeals [*India*] [*A publication*] (DLA)
O/A	Our Account [*Business term*]
O/A	Outer Anchorage [*Navigation*]
OA	Output Amplitude
OA	Output Axis
OA	Ovalbumin [*Also, OV, OVA, OVAL*] [*Biochemistry*]
OA	Overachievers Anonymous (EA)
OA	Overall [*Technical drawings*]
OA	Overeaters Anonymous (EA)
OA	Overfire Airport [*Combustion technology*]
OA	Overtime Authorization (AAG)
OA	Oxalic Acid [*Organic chemistry*] (AAMN)
OA	Services to the Aged under the Older Americans Act [*Public human service program*] (PHSD)
OA 2d	Ohio Appellate Reports, Second Series [*A publication*] (DLA)
OAA	Hereditary Order of Armigerous Augustans (EA)
OAA	Nora, AK [*Location identifier FAA*] (FAAL)
OAA	o-Aminoacetanilide [*Organic chemistry*]
OAA	Obstetric Anaesthetists Association [*British*] (DBA)
OAA	Office of Administrative Appeals [*U.S. Department of Labor*] (BARN)
OAA	Office of Aviation Affairs [*Army*]
OAA	Old-Age Assistance [*Superseded by SSI*] [*HEW*]
OAA	Older Americans Act [*1965*]
OAA	Older Americans Almanac [*A publication*]
OAA	Ontario Association of Architects [*1890*] [*Canada*] (NGC)
OAA	Optical Acquisition Aid [*Deep Space Instrumentation Facility, NASA*]
OAA	Opticians Association of America (EA)
OAA	Orbiter Access Arm [*NASA*] (NASA)
OAA	Orbiter Alternate Airfield [*NASA*] (MCD)
OAA	Order of Australia Association
OAA	Organic Acidemia Association (EA)
OAA	Organisation des Nations Unies pour l'Alimentation et l'Agriculture [*Food and Agriculture Organization of the United Nations*]
OAA	Organization of Athletic Administrators [*Defunct*] (EA)
OAA	Orient Airlines Association (EA)
OAA	Other Acronymic Agencies
OAA	Outdoor Advertising Association (BARN)
OAA	Outdoor Advertising Association of Great Britain (BUAC)
OAA	Oxaloacetic [*or Oxalacetic*] Acid [*Organic chemistry*]
OAA	Oxley Aviation [*Australia ICAO designator*] (FAAC)
OAAA	Oceania Amateur Athletic Association (EAIO)
OAAA	Order of Americans of Armorial Ancestry (EA)
OAAA	Outdoor Advertising Association of America [*Washington, DC*] (EA)
OAAA	Outdoor Advertising Association of Australia, Inc. (BUAC)
OAAB	Objective-Analytic Anxiety Battery [*Psychology*]
OAAC	Ocean Affairs Advisory Committee [*Department of State*] (MSC)
OAAC	Older Americans Advocacy Commission [*HEW*]
OAAC	Outdoor Advertising Association of Canada (BUAC)
OAAD	Amdar [*Afghanistan*] [*ICAO location identifier*] (ICLI)
OAAD	Ovarian Ascorbic Acid Depletion [*Test*]

OAADM	Ovarian Ascorbic Acid Depletion Material
OAAIS	Office of Administrative Analysis, Information, and Statistics [*Red Cross*]
OAAK	Andkhoi [*Afghanistan*] [*ICAO location identifier*] (ICLI)
OA & C	Ohio Circuit Court Decisions [*A publication*] (DLA)
OA & M	Operations, Administration, and Maintenance [*Telecommunications*]
OA & MS	Office of Administration and Management Services [*Employment and Training Administration*] [*Department of Labor*]
OA & S	Other Arms and Services [*Military*]
OAAPS	Organization for Afro-Asian Peoples Solidarity
OAARD	Office of the Assistant Administrator for Research and Development [*HEW*]
OAAS	Asmar [*Afghanistan*] [*ICAO location identifier*] (ICLI)
OAA/S	Observer's Assessment of Alertness / Sedation Scale [*Medicine*]
OAAS	Ontario Association of Agricultural Societies [*Canada*] (BUAC)
OAASA	Office of the Administrative Assistant to the Secretary of the Army
OAASN	Office of the Administrative Assistant to the Secretary of the Navy
OAAT	Ortho-Aminoazotoluene [*A dye*] [*Organic chemistry*]
OAAU	Organization of Afro-American Unity
OAAU	Orthogonal Array Arithmetic Unit [*Computer science*]
OAAV	Organization of African-American Veterans (EA)
OAB	Attawapiskat Band Library, Ontario [*Library symbol National Library of Canada*] (BIB)
OAB	Moab, UT [*Location identifier FAA*] (FAAL)
OAB	Oakland [*California*] Army Base (VNW)
OAB	Ocean Affairs Board [*National Academy of Sciences*] (MSC)
OAB	Old-Age Benefits
OAB	Olive Advisory Board [*Defunct*] (EA)
OAB	Ordnance Assembly Building (MUGU)
OAB	Organisation Africaine du Bois [*African Timber Organization*] (EAIO)
OAB	Outer Air Battle [*Navy*] (ANA)
OAB	Overseas Affairs Branch [*Army*]
OAB	Overseas Appointments Bureau [*Christian Education Movement*] [*British*] (AEBS)
OAB	Owners Abroad Aviation Ltd. [*British ICAO designator*] (FAAC)
OAB	Oxford Annotated Bible [*New York*] [*A publication*] (BJA)
OABA	Burleigh-Anstruther and Chandos Union Public Library, Apsley, Ontario [*Library symbol National Library of Canada*] (BIB)
OABA	Outdoor Amusement Business Association (EA)
OABD	Behsood [*Afghanistan*] [*ICAO location identifier*] (ICLI)
OABETA	Office Appliance and Business Equipment Trades Association (HGAA)
OABG	Baghlan [*Afghanistan*] [*ICAO location identifier*] (ICLI)
OABK	Bandkamalkhan [*Afghanistan*] [*ICAO location identifier*] (ICLI)
OABN	Bamyan [*Afghanistan*] [*ICAO location identifier*] (ICLI)
OABP	Organic Anion Binding Protein [*Biochemistry*]
OABR	Bamar [*Afghanistan*] [*ICAO location identifier*] (ICLI)
OABS	Sarday [*Afghanistan*] [*ICAO location identifier*] (ICLI)
OABT	Bost [*Afghanistan*] [*ICAO location identifier*] (ICLI)
OABT	Ortho-Aminobenzenethiol [*Organic chemistry*]
OAC	Acton Public Library, Ontario [*Library symbol National Library of Canada*] (NLC)
OAC	Cleveland Institute of Art, Cleveland, OH [*OCLC symbol*] (OCLC)
OAC	Oceanic Affairs Committee (BUAC)
OAC	Oceanic Area Control [*Aviation*] (FAAC)
OAC	Oceanographic Advisory Committee [*Navy Oceanographer*] (USDC)
OAC	Office of Academic Computing [*Research center*] (RCD)
OAC	Officer Advanced Course [*Army*] (INF)
OAC	Ohio Administrative Code [*A publication*] (AAGC)
OAC	Ohio Athletic Conference (PSS)
OAC	On Approved Credit
OAC	Ontario Agricultural College [*Canada*]
OAC	Ontario Appeal Cases [*Database*] [*Maritime Law Book Co. Ltd.*] [*Information service or system*] (CRD)
OAC	Ontario Arts Council
OAC	Open Air Campaigners, US (EA)
OAC	Operating Agency Code (AFM)
OAC	Operation Anti-Christ (EA)
OAC	Operation of Aircraft Costs (DNAB)
OAC	Operations Analysis Center
OAC	Operations Analysis Chief [*Air Force*]
OAC	Optical Absorption Coefficient (AAEL)
OAC	Optical Acceleration Cancellation [*Vision*]
OAC	Optical Area Correlator
OAC	Optimal Automatic Control
OAC	Optimized Aftercooled [*Truck engineering*]
OAC	Optimum Approach Course [*Navy*] (NVT)
OAC	Ordnance Ammunition Command [*Merged with Munitions Command*] [*Army*]
OAC	Ordo ab Chao [*Order Out of Chaos*] [*Freemasonry*] [*Latin*]
OAC	Oregon Administrative Code [*A publication*] (AAGC)
OAC	Oriental Airlines Ltd. [*Nigeria*] [*ICAO designator*] (FAAC)
OAC	Original Acquisition Cost (AAGC)
OAC	Original Air Conditioning (IIA)
OAC	Outdoor Advertising Council (BUAC)
OAC	Outer Approach Channel
OAC	Overseas Automotive Club (EA)
OACB	Charburjak [*Afghanistan*] [*ICAO location identifier*] (ICLI)
OACC	Chakhcharan [*Afghanistan*] [*ICAO location identifier*] (ICLI)
OACC	Oceanic Area Control Centre
OACC	Older Americans Consumer Cooperative [*Washington, DC*] (EA)
OACD	Office of Agricultural and Chemical Development [*of TVA*]
OACDT	Outback Areas Community Developmnent Trust [*Australia*]
OACES	Ocean-Atmosphere Carbon Exchange Study [*Marine science*] (OSRA)
OACG	Office of the Assistant Comptroller General (AAGC)
OACH	Acton High School, Ontario [*Library symbol National Library of Canada*] (NLC)
OACI	Optical Automatic Car Identification
OACI	Organisation de l'Aviation Civile Internationale [*International Civil Aviation Organization*] [*French United Nations*]
OACI	Organizacion de Aviacion Civil Internacional [*International Civil Aviation Organization*] [*Spanish United Nations*] (DUND)
OACII	Operational Approved Configuration Identification Index (SAA)
OACIS	Ocean-Atmospheric Climatic Interaction Studies
OACIS	Oregon Advanced Computing Institute [*Research center*] (RCD)
OACO	Operation and Checkout [*NASA*] (IAA)
OAC of S	Office of the Assistant Chief of Staff [*Military*]
OACP	Canada Publishing Corp., Agincourt, Ontario [*Library symbol National Library of Canada*] (BIB)
OACP	Operational Analysis Code Package (PDAA)
OACR	Office of the Admiral Commanding Reserves [*Navy British*]
OACS	Office of the Assistant Chief of Staff [*Military*] (AAG)
OACSA	Office of the Assistant Chief of Staff for Automation and Communications [*Military*] (MCD)
OACSAC	Office of the Assistant Chief of Staff for Automation and Communications [*Military*]
OACSC-E	Office of the Assistant Chief of Staff for Communications-Electronics (AABC)
OACSEA	Older American Community Service Employment Act [*1975*]
OACSFOR	Office of the Assistant Chief of Staff for Force Development [*Army*]
OACSI	Office of the Assistant Chief of Staff for Intelligence [*Army*]
OACSIM	Office of the Assistant Chief of Staff for Information Management [*Military*]
OACT	Office of the Actuary [*Department of Health and Human Services*] (GFGA)
OACT	Officer, Airman, Civilian, and Total (MCD)
OACT	Organisation Africaine de Cartographie et de Teledetection [*Algeria*] (EAIO)
OACT	Ormone Adrenocorticotropina [*Italian Medicine*]
OAD	Adria Laboratories, Inc., Columbus, OH [*OCLC symbol*] (OCLC)
OAD	Obstructive Airway Disease [*Medicine*]
OAD	Office of Administration
OAD	Officers' Accounts Division [*Navy*]
OAD	Officers' Assignment Division, The Adjutant General's Office [*Army*]
OAD	Opening of Anterior Digestive [*Gland*]
OAD	Operational Active Data [*Navy*]
OAD	Operational Analysis Division [*Air Force*]
OAD	Operational Availability Data [*Military*]
OAD	Operational Availability Date [*Nuclear Regulatory Commission*] (GFGA)
OAD	Optical Activity Detection
OAD	Orbiter Atmospheric Drag [*NASA*]
OAD	Ordered, Adjudged, and Decreed (WDAA)
OAD	Ordered to Active Duty (AABC)
OAD	Ordering and Distributing (IAA)
OAD	Organic Anionic Dye [*Medicine*] (DMAA)
OAD	Organizations and Agencies Directories Series [*A publication*]
OAD	Original Air Date [*of program's first telecast*]
OAD	Overall Absolute Deviation [*Mathematics*]
OAD	Overall Depth (WDAA)
OAD	Overall Dimensions (IAA)
OAD	Oxford American Dictionary [*A publication*]
OAD	Special Audit Division (AAGC)
OADAB	Office of the Assistant Director of the Army Budget
OADAP	Office of Alcoholism and Drug Abuse Prevention [*Department of Health and Human Services*]
OADC	Oleate-Albumin-Dextrose-Catalase [*Medium*] (DMAA)
OADC	Oleic Acid, Albumin, Dextrose, Catalase
OADD	Dawlatabad [*Afghanistan*] [*ICAO location identifier*] (ICLI)
OA/DDP	Office Automation / Distributed Data Processing (MHDI)
OADEMQA	Office of Acid Deposition, Environmental Monitoring, and Quality Assurance [*Environmental Protection Agency*] (GFGA)
OADF	Darra-I-Soof [*Afghanistan*] [*ICAO location identifier*] (ICLI)
OA-DG	Occupational Area Defense Grouping (DNAB)
OADG	Open Architecture Development Group [*IBM Corp.*] (CDE)
OADH	One-Arm Dove Hunt Association (EA)
OADH	Organization of Advanced Disabled Hobbyists (EA)
OADMS	Office of Automated Data Management Services [*General Services Administration*]
OADMT	Oliphant Auditory Discrimination Memory Test [*Medicine*] (STED)
OAdN	Ohio Northern University, Ada, OH [*Library symbol Library of Congress*] (LCLS)
OADPS	Office of Automatic Data Processing Services (AAGC)
OADR	Office of Agricultural Defense Relations [*New Deal*]
OADR	Originating Agency Determination Required (MCD)
OADS	Omnidirectional Air Data System
OADV	Devar [*Afghanistan*] [*ICAO location identifier*] (ICLI)
OADW	Wazakhwa [*Afghanistan*] [*ICAO location identifier*] (ICLI)
OADZ	Darwaz [*Afghanistan*] [*ICAO location identifier*] (ICLI)
OAE	NOAA [*National Oceanic and Atmospheric Administration*]-LISD Seattle Center, Seattle, WA [*OCLC symbol*] (OCLC)
OAE	Occupational and Adult Education [*Office of Education*] (OICC)
OAE	Oceanic Anoxic Event
OAE	Office of Analysis and Evaluation [*Environmental Protection Agency*] (EPA)
OAE	Officer of Arms Extraordinary [*College of Arms/Heralds' College*] [*British*]
OAE	Old Antarctic Explorer
OAE	Operational Area Evaluation [*Environmental science*] (COE)

OAE............	Optical Alignment Equipment
OAE............	Optima Energy Corp. [*Vancouver Stock Exchange symbol*]
OAE............	Orbiting Astronomical Explorer [*NASA*] (IIA)
OAE............	Orchestra of the Age of Enlightenment [*British*]
OAE............	Organization of Architectural Employees
OAE............	Orzeck Aphasia Evaluation [*Psychology*]
OAE............	Oscillating-Analyzer Ellipsometer (PDAA)
OAE............	Otoacoustic Emission [*Audiology*]
OAE............	Otoacoustic Emission [*Medicine*] (STED)
OAEC	Essa Centennial Library, Angus, Ontario [*Library symbol National Library of Canada*] (BIB)
OAEFT.........	Astorville Branch, East Ferris Township Public Library, Ontario [*Library symbol National Library of Canada*] (NLC)
OAEK	Keshm [*Afghanistan*] [*ICAO location identifier*] (ICLI)
OAEM	Eshkashem [*Afghanistan*] [*ICAO location identifier*] (ICLI)
OAEQ	Islam Qala [*Afghanistan*] [*ICAO location identifier*] (ICLI)
OAET	Elma Township Public Library, Atwood, Ontario [*Library symbol National Library of Canada*] (NLC)
OAF.............	Austrian Air Ambulance [*ICAO designator*] (FAAC)
OAF.............	Occidentale Afrique Francaise [*French West Africa*]
OAF.............	Office of Alcohol Fuels [*Department of Energy*]
OAF.............	Officer Assignment Folder [*Military*] (AFM)
OAF.............	Ontario Ministry of Agriculture and Food [*UTLAS symbol*]
OAF.............	Open Air Factor
OAF.............	Options for Animals Foundation (EA)
OAF.............	Orbital Antenna Farm (PDAA)
OAF.............	Origin Address Field [*Computer science*] (IBMDP)
OAF.............	Orthodox and Anglican Fellowship (EA)
OAF.............	Osteoclast Activating Factor [*Endocrinology*]
OAF.............	Oxygen Alternate Fill
OAFB	Offutt Air Force Base [*Nebraska*] (AAG)
OAFC	Arden Branch, Frontenac County Library, Ontario [*Library symbol National Library of Canada*] (BIB)
OAFC	Occupational Analysis Field Center
OAFC	Office of Air Force Chaplains
OAFC	Official Aerrage Fan Club [*Defunct*] (EA)
OAFD	Orbiter Air Flight Deck [*NASA*] (MCD)
OAFG	Khost-O-Fering [*Afghanistan*] [*ICAO location identifier*] (ICLI)
OA/FI	Operational Assurance/Fault Isolation (MCD)
OAFIE	Office of Armed Forces Information and Education
OAFM..........	On or After Full Moon [*Freemasonry*] (ROG)
OAFR	Farah [*Afghanistan*] [*ICAO location identifier*] (ICLI)
OAFT	Official Air Freight Tariffs
OAFTO	Orbiter Atmospheric Flight Test Office [*NASA*] (NASA)
OAFZ	Faizabad [*Afghanistan*] [*ICAO location identifier*] (ICLI)
OAG	Oblique Anterior Gauche [*Left Anterior Oblique Position*] [*Medicine*]
OAG	Office of the Adjutant General [*Military*] (MCD)
OAG	Office of the Attorney-General
OAG	Official Airline Guide, Inc. [*ICAO designator*] (FAAC)
OAG	Official Airline Guides, Inc. [*Information service or system*] (IID)
OAG	Oleoyl(acetyl)glycerol [*Organic chemistry*]
OAG	Online Airlines Guide [*A publication*]
OAG	Open Angle Glaucoma [*Ophthalmology*]
OAG	Open Applications Group [*An association*] (NTPA)
OAG	Opinions of the Attorney General
OAG	Optical Alignment Group
OAG	Orange [*Australia Airport symbol*] (OAG)
OAGA	Ghaziabad [*Afghanistan*] [*ICAO location identifier*] (ICLI)
OAGB	Osteopathic Association of Great Britain
OAGCM	Ocean-Atmosphere General Circulation Model [*Oceanography*]
OAGD	Gader [*Afghanistan*] [*ICAO location identifier*] (ICLI)
OAG-EE	Official Airline Guide-Electronic Edition [*Official Airline Guides, Inc.*] [*Database*]
OAGG	Gage Educational Publishing Ltd., Agincourt, Ontario [*Library symbol National Library of Canada*] (NLC)
OAGL	Gulistan [*Afghanistan*] [*ICAO location identifier*] (ICLI)
OAGM	Ghelmeen [*Afghanistan*] [*ICAO location identifier*] (ICLI)
OAG Massachusetts...	Massachusetts Attorney General Reports [*A publication*] (DLA)
OAGN	Ghazni [*Afghanistan*] [*ICAO location identifier*] (ICLI)
OAGS	Gasar [*Afghanistan*] [*ICAO location identifier*] (ICLI)
OAG West Virginia...	West Virginia Attorney General Reports [*A publication*] (DLA)
OAGZ	Gardez [*Afghanistan*] [*ICAO location identifier*] (ICLI)
OAH	Ancaster High and Vocational School, Ontario [*Library symbol National Library of Canada*] (NLC)
OAH	Office of Aboriginal Health [*Australia*]
OAH	Organization of American Historians (EA)
OAH	Ovarian Androgenic Hyperfunction [*Medicine*] (DMAA)
OAH	Overall Height [*Automotive specifications*]
OAH	Overhead Air Hoist
OAHE	Hazrat Eman [*Afghanistan*] [*ICAO location identifier*] (ICLI)
OAHJ	Hajigak [*Afghanistan*] [*ICAO location identifier*] (ICLI)
OAHN	Khwahan [*Afghanistan*] [*ICAO location identifier*] (ICLI)
OAHR	Herat [*Afghanistan*] [*ICAO location identifier*] (ICLI)
OAHS	O-Acetylhomoserine (thiol)-lyase [*An enzyme*]
OAI.............	Office of Analysis and Inspections [*Department of Health and Human Services*] (GFGA)
OAI.............	Office of Audit and Inspection [*Energy Research and Development Administration*]
OAI.............	Office of Audit and Investigation [*United States Geological Survey*]
OAI.............	Ohio Aerospace Institute
OAI.............	Open Application Interface
OAI.............	Optical Associates Inc. (NITA)
OAI.............	Outside Air Intake (NRCH)
OAIAC	Operational Area Industry Advisory Committee [*Civil Defense*]
OAIB	Old-Age Insurance Benefit (MHDB)
OAID	Older Americans Information Directory [*A publication*]
OAIDE	Operational Assistance and Instructive Data Equipment
OAIM	Office of Aviation Information Management [*Department of Transportation*] [*Information service or system*] (IID)
OAINN.........	Ohio Aerospace Institute Neural Networks (HGEN)
OAIP	Ontario Assessment Instrument Pool [*Educational test*] [*Canada*]
OAIP	Organic Ablative Insulative Plastic
OAIS	Opinion, Attitude, and Interest Survey [*Psychology*]
OAIW	International Waxes Ltd., Agincourt, Ontario [*Library symbol National Library of Canada*] (NLC)
OAJ	Ajax Public Library, Ontario [*Library symbol National Library of Canada*] (NLC)
OAJ	Jacksonville [*North Carolina*] [*Airport symbol*] (OAG)
OAJ	Jacksonville, NC [*Location identifier FAA*] (FAAL)
OAJ	Open Apophyseal Joint (DB)
OAJ	Opening Altitude Judgement [*Parachuting*] (DICI)
OAJL	Jalalabad [*Afghanistan*] [*ICAO location identifier*] (ICLI)
OAJS	Jabul Saraj [*Afghanistan*] [*ICAO location identifier*] (ICLI)
OAJW	Jawand [*Afghanistan*] [*ICAO location identifier*] (ICLI)
OAk	Akron Public Library, Akron, OH [*Library symbol Library of Congress*] (LCLS)
OAK	Oakfield [*New York*] [*Seismograph station code, US Geological Survey Closed*] (SEIS)
OAK	Oak Indus [*NYSE symbol*] (TTSB)
OAK	Oak Industries, Inc. [*NYSE symbol*] (SPSG)
OAK	Oakland [*California*] [*Airport symbol*]
OAK	Oakland Operations Office (DOGT)
OAK	Oakwood College, Huntsville, AL [*OCLC symbol*] (OCLC)
OAK	Oakwood Petroleums Ltd. [*Toronto Stock Exchange symbol*]
OAK	Oklahoma-Arkansas-Kansas League [*Old baseball league*]
OAK	Older Americans Corps [*Proposed*]
OAK	Optical Alignment Kit (MCD)
OAK	Organization for the Advancement of Knowledge (EA)
OAK	Overhaul Alignment Kit (MCD)
OAK	San Francisco [*California*] Oakland [*Airport symbol*] (OAG)
OAKA	Koban [*Afghanistan*] [*ICAO location identifier*] (ICLI)
OAKB	Kabul Ad [*Afghanistan*] [*ICAO location identifier*] (ICLI)
OAKC	Oakhurst Capital, Inc. [*NASDAQ symbol*] (SAG)
OAKC	Oakhurst Co. [*NASDAQ symbol*] (TTSB)
OAKC	Oakhurst Co., Inc. [*NASDAQ symbol*] (SAG)
OAkCh	Akron Child Guidance Center, Akron, OH [*Library symbol Library of Congress*] (LCLS)
OAKD	Kamdesh [*Afghanistan*] [*ICAO location identifier*] (ICLI)
OAKE	Organization of American Kodaly Educators (EA)
OAkF	Firestone Tire & Rubber Co., Akron, OH [*Library symbol Library of Congress*] (LCLS)
OAKF	Oak Hill Financial [*NASDAQ symbol*] (TTSB)
OAKF	Oak Hill Financial, Inc. [*NASDAQ symbol*] (SAG)
OAKG	Khojaghar [*Afghanistan*] [*ICAO location identifier*] (ICLI)
OAkGr	B. F. Goodrich Co., Akron, OH [*Library symbol Library of Congress*] (LCLS)
OAkGy	Goodyear Tire & Rubber Co., Akron, OH [*Library symbol Library of Congress*] (LCLS)
OakHill	Oak Hill Financial, Inc. [*Associated Press*] (SAG)
OakHill	Oak Hill Sportswear Corp. [*Associated Press*] (SAG)
OakHillF	Oak Hill Financial, Inc. [*Associated Press*] (SAG)
Oakhurst	Oakhurst Capital, Inc. [*Associated Press*] (SAG)
Oakhurst	Oakhurst Co., Inc. [*Associated Press*] (SAG)
OakInds	Oak Industries, Inc. [*Associated Press*] (SAG)
OAKIX	Oakmark International Fund [*Mutual fund ticker symbol*] (SG)
OAKJ	Kajaki [*Afghanistan*] [*ICAO location identifier*] (ICLI)
OAkk	Old Akkadian (BJA)
OAKL	Konjak-I-Logar [*Afghanistan*] [*ICAO location identifier*] (ICLI)
Oakland U ...	Oakland University (GAGS)
Oakly	Oakly, Inc. [*Associated Press*] (SAG)
OAKM	Kamar [*Afghanistan*] [*ICAO location identifier*] (ICLI)
OAKMX	Oakmark Fund [*Mutual fund ticker symbol*] (SG)
OAKN	Kandahar [*Afghanistan*] [*ICAO location identifier*] (ICLI)
OAKR	Kaldar [*Afghanistan*] [*ICAO location identifier*] (ICLI)
OAKS	Khost [*Afghanistan*] [*ICAO location identifier*] (ICLI)
OAKS	River Oaks Furniture [*NASDAQ symbol*] (TTSB)
OAKS	River Oaks Furniture, Inc. [*NASDAQ symbol*] (SAG)
OAKT	Kalat [*Afghanistan*] [*ICAO location identifier*] (ICLI)
OAKT	Oak Technology [*NASDAQ symbol*] (TTSB)
OAKT	Oak Technology, Inc. [*NASDAQ symbol*] (SAG)
OakTch	Oak Technology, Inc. [*Associated Press*] (SAG)
OAkU	University of Akron, Akron, OH [*Library symbol Library of Congress*] (LCLS)
OAkU-L	University of Akron, School of Law, Akron, Ohio [*Library symbol Library of Congress*] (LCLS)
Oakwood......	Oakwood Homes Corp. [*Associated Press*] (SAG)
OAKX	Kabul [*Afghanistan*] [*ICAO location identifier*] (ICLI)
OAKZ	Karez-I-Mir [*Afghanistan*] [*ICAO location identifier*] (ICLI)
OAL	Alliston Memorial Public Library, Ontario [*Library symbol National Library of Canada*] (BIB)
OAL	Audit Liaison Division (AAGC)
OAL	Coaldale, NV [*Location identifier FAA*] (FAAL)
OAL	National Oceanic and Atmospheric Administration, Miami Branch, Miami, FL [*OCLC symbol*] (OCLC)
OAL	Office of Arts and Libraries [*British*]
OAL	Olympic Airways SA [*Greece*] [*ICAO designator*] (FAAC)
OAL	Operational Applications Laboratory [*Air Force*]
OAL	Operations and Logistics (IAA)
OAL	Order Action List [*Military*] (DNAB)

OAL.............	Order of Ancient Lights
OAL.............	Ordnance Aerophysics Laboratory
OAL.............	Overall Length [Automotive specifications]
OAL.............	Overall Level (NASA)
OALAC	Amherstview Branch, Lennox and Addington County Public Library, Ontario [Library symbol National Library of Canada] (NLC)
OALAC	Older Americans' Legal Action Center (DICI)
OAIB	Babcock & Wilcox Co., Alliance, OH [Library symbol Library of Congress] (LCLS)
OALC	Ogden Air Logistics Center (MCD)
OALDCE	Oxford Advanced Learner's Dictionary of Current English
OALF............	Organic Acid Labile Fluoride [Chemistry] (AAMN)
OALF............	Oromo Abo Liberation Front [Ethiopia] [Political party] (EY)
OALG	Logar [Afghanistan] [ICAO location identifier] (ICLI)
OALJ	Office of Administrative Law Judges [Department of Agriculture] (GFGA)
OALL............	Allenford Branch, Bruce County Public Library, Ontario [Library symbol National Library of Canada] (NLC)
OALL............	Lal [Afghanistan] [ICAO location identifier] (ICLI)
OALL............	Ossification of Anterior Longitudinal Ligament [Medicine] (STED)
OAIM	Mount Union College, Alliance, OH [Library symbol Library of Congress] (LCLS)
OALM..........	Of a Like Mind [An association] (EA)
OALM..........	Optical Address Light Modulator [Instrumentation]
OALMA	Orthopedic Appliance and Limb Manufacturers Association [Later, AOPA]
OALN	Laghman [Afghanistan] [ICAO location identifier] (ICLI)
OALOS	Office for Ocean Affairs and the Law of the Sea [United Nations] (GNE)
OALS	Observer Air Lock System (OA)
OALS	Office of Arid Lands Studies [University of Arizona] [Research center] (RCD)
OALS	Orbiter Automatic Landing System (MCD)
OALT............	Operational Acceptable Level of Traffic [FAA] (TAG)
O ALT HOR...	Omnibus Alternis Horis [Every Other Hour] [Pharmacy] (ROG)
OAM.............	Oamaru [New Zealand] [Airport symbol] (OAG)
OAM.............	Office of Administration and Management [Employment and Training Administration] [Department of Labor]
OAM.............	Office of Aerospace Medicine [NASA] (MCD)
OAM.............	Office of Alternative Medicine [National Institutes of Health]
OAM.............	Office of Automation and Manpower [Department of Labor] [See also OMAT]
OAM.............	Office of Aviation Medicine [FAA]
OAM.............	One Australian Movement [Political party]
OAM.............	Onze Alma Mater (BJA)
OAM.............	Open-Air Mission
OAM.............	Operations, Administration, and Maintenance (CIST)
OAM.............	Operations and Management (MCD)
OAM.............	Optimum Artillery Mix (SAA)
OAM.............	Orbital Assembly Module (MCD)
OAM.............	Order of Ancient Maccabees (BJA)
OAM.............	Organization and Methods [Military] (AFIT)
OAM.............	Orthopedic Appliance Mechanic [Navy]
OAM.............	Oscillator Activity Monitor [Telecommunications] (TEL)
OAM.............	Outer Acrosomal Membrane [Medicine] (DMAA)
OAMA	Office Automation Management Association (EA)
OAMA	Ogden Air Material Area [AFLC]
OAMA	Oil Appliance Manufacturers' Association [British] (BI)
OAMAC	Oceanic and Atmospheric Management Advisory Committee [National Oceanic and Atmospheric Administration] (EGAO)
OAMCE	Optical Alignment, Monitoring, and Calibration Equipment
OAMDG........	Omnia ad Majorem Dei Gloriam [All to the Greater Glory of God] [Latin]
OAME	Orbital Attitude and Maneuvering Electronics
OAMEX	Ocean-Atmosphere Exchange Processes [Marine science] (MSC)
OAMF...........	Fort Malden National Historic Park, Amherstburg, Ontario [Library symbol National Library of Canada] (NLC)
OAMHS........	Ameliasburgh Historical Society, Ontario [Library symbol National Library of Canada] (BIB)
OAMK	Mukur [Afghanistan] [ICAO location identifier] (ICLI)
OAMN	Maimama [Afghanistan] [ICAO location identifier] (ICLI)
OAMN	Operations and Maintenance, Navy (AFIT)
OAMP	Optical Analog Matrix Processing
OAMS	Mazar-I-Sharif [Afghanistan] [ICAO location identifier] (ICLI)
OAMS	Office of Administrative and Management Systems [Social Security Administration]
OAMS	Optical Angular Motion Sensor
OAMS	Orbital Altitude and Maneuvering System (IAA)
OAMS	Orbital Attitude and Maneuvering System [NASA]
OAMS	Organic and Atmospheric Mass Spectrometer (KSC)
OAMT...........	Munta [Afghanistan] [ICAO location identifier] (ICLI)
OAN	Curriculum Resources Centre, Niagara South Board of Education, Allanburg, Ontario [Library symbol National Library of Canada] (BIB)
OAN	NMFS [National Marine Fisheries Service] Southeast Fisheries Center, Beaufort Laboratory, Beaufort, NC [OCLC symbol] (OCLC)
OAN	Ocean Aids to Navigation [Coast Guard]
OAN	Omega Arts Network (EA)
OANA	Organisation of Asian News Agencies (BUAC)
OANA	Organization of Asia-Pacific News Agencies [Malaysia] (EY)
OAND	Origin and Destination (NITA)
O & A	Observation and Assessment [Medicine]
O & A	October and April [Denotes semiannual payments of interest or dividends in these months] [Business term]

O & A (Date)...	Oath and Acceptance Date [Date from which a military officer's commissioned service runs]
O & B	Opium and Belladonna [Pharmacy] (MAE)
O & C	Onset and Course [of a disease] [Medicine]
o & c	Onset and Course [Medicine] (AD)
O & C	Operation and Checkout [NASA]
O&C.............	Operations and Control (NAKS)
O & C	Oxford and Cambridge Schools Examination Board [British] (DCTA)
O & CC	Order and Change Control (AAG)
o & cc	Order and Change Control (AD)
O & CM	Organist and Choir Master (ROG)
O & C/O........	Operation and Checkout [O & C is preferred] [NASA] (KSC)
O & D	Origin and Destination [Aviation]
o & d	Origin and Destination (AD)
O & E	Observation and Evaluation [Medicine] (DAVI)
O & E	Observation and Examination [Medicine]
O & E	Operations and Engineering
o & e	Operations and Engineering (AD)
O & F	Organizations and Functions (MCD)
O & FN	Ordnance and Facilities - Navy
O & FS	Operations and Flight Support [NASA] (NASA)
O&G.............	Obstetrics and Gynecology (DMAA)
O & G/PF	Oil and Gas/Pipeline Facilities
O & I	Operations and Intelligence [Section] [Army] (INF)
o & i	Organizational and Intermediate (AD)
O & I	Outline and Installation (MCD)
O & IR	Operation and Inspection Record (KSC)
O & K	Orenstein & Koppel (AD)
O & LS	Ocean and Lake Surveys [Budget appropriation title] [Navy]
O & M	Ogilvy & Mather [Advertising agency]
O & M	Ohio & Morenci Railroad (IIA)
O&M.............	Operating and Maintenance [USCG] (TAG)
O & M	Operation and Maintenance (DOMA)
O&M.............	Operations and Maintenance (CIST)
O & M	Operations and Management
O & M	Organization and Management
O & M	Organization and Methods (AABC)
O & M	Orientation and Mobility [for the blind]
O & MA	Operation and Maintenance Activities (AAG)
O&MA...........	Operation and Maintenance, Army (AAGC)
O & M-DA.....	Operation and Maintenance, Defense Agencies [DoD]
O & MF........	Operation and Maintenance Facilities (MUGU)
O & MFH......	Operation and Maintenance, Family Housing [Army] (AABC)
O & MMC	Operations and Maintenance, Marine Corps
O & MN	Operation and Maintenance, Navy
O & MN	Overhaul and Maintenance, Navy (MCD)
O & MNR	Operation and Maintenance, Naval Reserve (NVT)
O & N	Oregon & Northwestern Railroad Co. (IIA)
O&O.............	On and Off (DMAA)
O & O	One and Only (IIA)
O & O	Operational and Organizational (RDA)
O & O	Organization and Operation
O & O	Owned and Operated
O & OP	Organizational and Operational Plan [Army]
O & OS	Ordnance and Ordnance Stores [Navy]
OANDOS	Ordnance and Ordnance Stores [Coast Guard]
O & P	Operations and Procedures (KSC)
O & P	Ova and Parasites [Medicine]
O & PC	Owl and the Pussy Cat [Poem by Edward Lear, 1871]
O & R	Ocean and Rail [Shipping]
o&r	Ocean and Rail (EBF)
OANDR	Operation and Regulation
O & R	Overhaul and Repair
O & S	Operation and Support Funds [DoD] (RDA)
O & S	Operations and Support (MCD)
O & S	Optics and Sensors Program
O & S	Over and Short Account [Business term]
O & SCMIS ...	Operating and Support Costs Management Information System
O & S HA	Operating and Support Hazard Analysis
O & ST	Order and Shipping Time [Military] (MCD)
O & T	Operations and Training [Military]
O & T	Organization and Training [Military]
OANDT........	Organization and Training Division [Supreme Headquarters Allied Powers Europe] (NATG)
O & T	Oyer and Terminer [Hear and Determine] [Legal term] (DLA)
O & W	Oldest and Wisest [Nickname for President Ronald Reagan]
O & W	Oneida & Western Railroad (IIA)
O & W	Ontario & Western Railroad [Nickname: Old and Weary]
O & W Dig...	Oldham and White's Digest of Laws [Texas] [A publication] (DLA)
O & Y	Olympia & York [Commercial firm Canada] (ECON)
OANFE	Operational Aircraft Not Fully Equipped (NG)
OANI	Office of the Administrator of Norfolk Island [Australia]
OANM	On or After New Moon [Freemasonry] (ROG)
OANR	Nawor [Afghanistan] [ICAO location identifier] (ICLI)
OANR	Office of Air, Noise, and Radiation [Environmental Protection Agency] (ERG)
OANS	Occupied Area News Service [Military] (IAA)
OANS	Salang-I-Shamali [Afghanistan] [ICAO location identifier] (ICLI)
OANT	Normanby Township Community and School Library, Ayton, Ontario [Library symbol National Library of Canada] (NLC)
OA/NWOB	Open Allotments/Navy-Wide Operating Budgets (MCD)
OAO	Arkhangelsk 2 Aviation Division [Former USSR] [FAA designator] (FAAC)
OAO	National Oceanic and Atmospheric Administration, Miami, Miami, FL [OCLC symbol] (OCLC)

OAO	Office of Aircraft Operations [*Miami, FL*] [*National Oceanic and Atmospheric Administration*] (GRD)
OAO	One and Only [*A favorite girl or boy friend*]
OAO	Operational and Organizational (MCD)
OAO	Orbited Assembly Operation
OAO	Orbiting Astronomical Observatory [*NASA*]
OAO	Orthogonalized Atomic Orbital (OA)
OAO	Outdoor Adventure Online [*America Online*]
OAOAF	Operations Analysis Office, Air Force (MCD)
OAOAFLC	Operations Analysis Office, Air Force Logistics Command (MCD)
OAOB	Obeh [*Afghanistan*] [*ICAO location identifier*] (ICLI)
OAOG	Urgoon [*Afghanistan*] [*ICAO location identifier*] (ICLI)
OAOI	On and Off Instruments [*Aviation*]
OAOO	Deshoo [*Afghanistan*] [*ICAO location identifier*] (ICLI)
OAOP	Older Adult Offender Project [*of the Alston Wilkes Society*] (EA)
OAOR	Oxygen Adsorption, Out-gassing, and Chemical Reduction (PDAA)
OAP	NMFS [*National Marine Fisheries Service*] Northeast Fisheries Center, WoodsHole, MA [*OCLC symbol*] (OCLC)
OAP	Observation Amphibian Plane [*Coast Guard*]
OAP	Occupational Ability Patterns [*Psychologic test*] (STED)
OAP	Occupational Aptitude Pattern [*US Employment Service*] [*Department of Labor*]
OAP	Oceanic Automation Program [*FAA*] (TAG)
OAP	Office of Adolescent Pregnancy [*Medicine*] (BABM)
OAP	Office of Aerial Phenomena [*Air Force*]
OAP	Office of Aircraft Production [*World War II*]
OAP	Office of Air Programs [*Obsolete Environmental Protection Agency*]
OAP	Office of Alien Property [*World War II*] (DLA)
OAP	Office of Antarctic Programs [*National Science Foundation*] [*Later, Division of Polar Programs*]
OAP	Office of Atomic Programs [*DoD*]
OAP	Office of the Director of Aerospace Programs [*Air Force*]
OAP	Offset Aiming Point (AFM)
OAP	Oil Analysis Program [*Military*] (AFIT)
OAP	Old-Age Pension [*or Pensioner*]
OAP	On-Axis Pointing (PDAA)
OAP	Oncovin [*Vincristine*], Ara-C, Prednisone [*Antineoplastic drug regimen*]
OAP	Operation Angel Plane (EA)
OAP	Operations and Procedures (IAA)
OAP	Ophthalmic Arterial Pressure [*Medicine*]
OAP	Ophthalmic Artery Pressure [*Medicine*] (STED)
OAP	Optical Augmentation Project
OAP	Optically Active Polymer
OAP	Ordinary Alterations Plan [*Navy*] (OAG)
OAP	Organic Ablative Plastic
OAP	Ortho-Aminoacetophenone [*Organic chemistry*]
OAP	Orthogonal Array Processor [*Computer*]
OAP	Osteoarthropathy [*Medicine*] (MAE)
OAP	Outlet Absolute Pressure
OAP	Outline Acquisition Plan [*Army*]
OAP	Overall Average Percentage (DNAB)
OAP	Over Fire Air Port
OAP	Oxygen at Atmospheric Pressure
OAPBC	Office for Advancement of Public Black Colleges [*of the National Association of State Universities and Land Grant Colleges*] (EA)
OAP-BLEO	Oncovin [*Vincristine*] ARA-C [*Cytarabine or cytosine arabinoside*] Prednisone, Bleomycin [*Antineoplastic drug regimen*] (DAVI)
OAPC	Office of Alien Property Custodian [*World War II*]
OAPCA	Organotin Antifouling Paint Control Act of 1988
OAPCB	Old-Age-Pensioner CBer [*Experienced citizens band radio operator*]
OAPEC	Organization of Arab Petroleum Exporting Countries [*See also OPAEP*] [*OPEC Kuwait*] [*Absorbed by*]
OAPEP	Organisation Arabe des Pays Exportateurs de Petrole [*Organization of Arab Petroleum Exporting Countries*]
OAPG	Paghman [*Afghanistan*] [*ICAO location identifier*] (ICLI)
OAPJ	Pan Jao [*Afghanistan*] [*ICAO location identifier*] (ICLI)
OAPM	Optimal Amplitude and Phase Modulation
OAPNA	Organization of Asian-Pacific News Agencies (BUAC)
OAPO	Eastern Pacific Tuna Fishing Organization [*Marine science*] (OSRA)
OAPP	Office of Adolescent Pregnancy Programs [*HEW*]
O App	Ohio Appellate Reports [*A publication*] (DLA)
O App 2d	Ohio Appellate Reports, Second Series [*A publication*] (DLA)
OAPS	Orbit Adjust Propulsion Subsystem [*NASA*]
OAPU	Overseas Air Preparation Unit [*British military*] (DMA)
OAPWL	Overall Power Watt Level (PDAA)
OAQ	National Climatic Center, Ashville, NC [*OCLC symbol*] (OCLC)
OAQ	Observatorio Astronomico de Quito [*Ecuador*] [*Seismograph station code, US Geological Survey*] (SEIS)
OAQ	Order of Architects of Quebec [*1974, founded 1890 as PQAA*] [*Canada*] (NGC)
OAQD	Qades [*Afghanistan*] [*ICAO location identifier*] (ICLI)
OAQK	Qala-I-Nyazkhan [*Afghanistan*] [*ICAO location identifier*] (ICLI)
OAQM	Kron Monjan [*Afghanistan*] [*ICAO location identifier*] (ICLI)
OAQN	Qala-I-Naw [*Afghanistan*] [*ICAO location identifier*] (ICLI)
OAQPS	Office of Air Quality Planning and Standards [*Environmental Protection Agency*]
OAQPSTTN	Office of Air Quality Planning and Standards Technology Transfer Network [*Environmental Protection Agency*] (AEPA)
OAQQ	Qarqin [*Afghanistan*] [*ICAO location identifier*] (ICLI)
OAQR	Qaisar [*Afghanistan*] [*ICAO location identifier*] (ICLI)
OAQS	Online Associative Query System (NITA)
OAR	Arnprior Public Library, Ontario [*Library symbol National Library of Canada*] (NLC)
OAR	Augustinian Recollect Sisters (TOCD)
OAR	Monterey/Fort Ord, CA [*Location identifier FAA*] (FAAL)
OAR	Offender Aid and Restoration (EA)
OAR	Office of Aerospace Research [*Air Force*]
OAR	Office of AIDS Research [*National Institute of Health*]
OAR	Office of Air and Radiation [*Environmental Protection Agency*] (GFGA)
OAR	Office of Analysis and Review [*Army, Navy*]
OAR	Office of Oceanic and Atmospheric Research [*National Oceanic and Atmospheric Administration*]
OAR	Ohio Appellate Reports [*A publication*] (DLA)
OAR	Ohio Art [*AMEX symbol*] (TTSB)
OAR	[*The*] Ohio Art Co. [*AMEX symbol*] (SPSG)
O-Ar	Ohio State Archives, Columbus, OH [*Library symbol Library of Congress*] (LCLS)
OAR	Ontario Appeal Reports [*A publication*] (DLA)
OAR	Open Architecture Receiver [*Telecommunications*]
OAR	Operand Address Register [*Computer science*] (IAA)
OAR	Operational Address Register [*Computer science*] (IAA)
OAR	Operational Availability and Reliability [*Military*]
OAR	Operation Assessment and Readiness [*Environmental science*] (COE)
OAR	Operations Analysis Report
OAR	Operations and Regulations (IAA)
OAR	Operator Authorization Record [*Computer science*] (IBMDP)
OAR	Optical Angle Readout
OAR	Optical Automatic Ranging
OAR	ORDALT [*Ordnance Alterations*] Accomplishment Requirement (NG)
OAR	Ordering as Required (MHDB)
OAR	Order of the Augustinian Recollects [*Roman Catholic men's religious order*]
OAR	Ordnance Allowance Report [*Navy*]
OAR	Ordnance Alteration Reporting
OAR	Ordnance Alteration Requirement (NG)
OAR	Organized Air Reserve
OAR	Orientation/Alertness Remediation (STED)
OAR	Original Action Record
OAR	Other Administrative Reasons [*Medicine*] (MAE)
OAR	Over All Rate [*Real estate*] (DICI)
OAR	Overhaul and Repair
OAR	Overtime Authorization Request (MCD)
OAR	Oxford Applied Research [*Software manufacturer*] [*British*]
OARAC	Office of Air Research Automatic Computer
OARB	Azilda Branch, Rayside-Balfour Public Library, Ontario [*Library symbol National Library of Canada*] (NLC)
OARB	Oakland Army Base [*California*] (AABC)
OARBC	Boeing of Canada Ltd., Arnprior, Ontario [*Library symbol National Library of Canada*] (BIB)
OARC	Ordinary Administrative Radio Conference
OARD	Arthur District High School, Arthur, Ontario [*Library symbol National Library of Canada*] (NLC)
OARDC	Ohio Agricultural Research and Development Center [*Ohio State University*] [*Research center*] (RCD)
OARG	Uruzgan [*Afghanistan*] [*ICAO location identifier*] (ICLI)
OARM	Dilaram [*Afghanistan*] [*ICAO location identifier*] (ICLI)
OARM	Middlesex County Public Library, Arva, Ontario [*Library symbol National Library of Canada*] (NLC)
OARM	Office of Administration and Resources Management [*Environmental Protection Agency*] (GFGA)
OARMS	Armstrong Community Library, Ontario [*Library symbol National Library of Canada*] (NLC)
OAR-N	Office of Analysis and Review, Navy (MUGU)
OARnet	[*The*] Ohio Academic Resources Network [*Computer science*] (TNIG)
OARP	Office of Advanced Research Programs [*Later, OART*] [*NASA*]
OARP	Operator Accelerated Retraining Program [*Nuclear energy*] (NRCH)
OARP	Rimpa [*Afghanistan*] [*ICAO location identifier*] (ICLI)
OARS	Ocean Area Reconnaissance Satellite [*Antisubmarine warfare*]
OARS	Ocean Atmosphere Response Studies [*Marine science*] (MSC)
OARS	Ocean Reconnaissance Submarine [*NATO*] (LAIN)
OARS	Office Automation Reporting Service (NITA)
OARS	On-Line Automated Reference Service [*Library science*]
OARS	Opening Automated Report Service [*NYSE*]
OART	Oakland Army Terminal [*California*]
OART	Office of Advanced Research and Technology [*Later, OAST*] [*NASA*]
OAR/USA	Offender Aid and Restoration USA [*An association*] (EA)
OAS	O-Acetylserine (thiol)-lyase [*An enzyme*]
OAS	Oasis [*Board on Geographic Names*]
OAS	Oasis Residential [*NYSE symbol*] (SPSG)
OAS	Obstacle Assessment Surface [*Aviation*] (DA)
OAS	Occupational Aspiration Scale [*Education*]
OAS	Occupied Areas Section [*Military government*]
OAS	Offensive Air Support (MCD)
OAS	Offensive Attack System (DOMA)
OAS	Offensive Avionics System
OAS	Office Automation System (NASA)
OAS	Office for Advanced Studies (AAG)
OAS	Office of Administrative Systems [*Department of Agriculture*] (GFGA)
OAS	Office of Airline Statistics [*U.S. Department of Transportation*] (BARN)
OAS	Office of Oceanic and Atmospheric Services [*National Oceanic and Atmospheric Administration*] (MSC)
OAS	Office of the Assistant for Study Support [*Air Force*]
OAS	Office of the Assistant Secretary [*Defense*] [*Navy*]
OAS	Ohio Academy of Science (PDAA)
OAS	Oklahoma Academy of Science (BUAC)
OAS	Old Age and Survivors' Insurance (IAA)

OAS	Old-Age Security
OAS	Olley Air Service Ltd.
OAS	Oman Aviation Services Co. [*ICAO designator*] (FAAC)
OAS	On Active Service
OAS	Open-Hearth Acid Steel
OAS	Operational Announcing System (IAA)
OAS	Optical Alignment Sights [*NASA*]
OAS	Optical Array Spectrometer
OAS	Optical Augmentation System
OAS	Optics and Sensors [*Program*] (MCD)
OAS	Optoacoustic Spectrometry [*Also, PAS*]
OAS	Oral Allergy Syndrome [*Medicine*] (DMAA)
OAS	Orbiter Aeroflight Simulator [*NASA*] (NASA)
OAS	Orbiter Atmospheric Simulator [*NASA*] (MCD)
OAS	Orbiter Avionics System [*NASA*] (NASA)
OAS	Orbitor Avionics Simulator [*NASA*]
OAS	Organisation de l'Armee Secrete [*Secret Army Organization*] [*France*] (PD)
OAS	Organizational Accounting Structure (IAA)
OAS	Organization of American States (EA)
OAS	Organization of Arab Students in the USA and Canada (EA)
OAS	Oriental and African Studies
OAS	Origin-of-Assembly Sequence [*Genetics*]
OAS	Orthopedic Appliance Service
OAS	Osmotically Active Substance [*Medicine*] (DMAA)
OAS	Other Active Military Service (DNAB)
OAS	Other Approved Studies (ADA)
OAS	Output Amplitude Stability
OAS	Oxygen Activated Sludge (DICI)
OAS²	Secret Army Organisation [*Algeria*] (BUAC)
OAS²	Officer Accession/Separation System (MCD)
OASAF	Office of Assistant Secretary of Air Force
OASAF	Optical Active Surface Approach Fuze
OASA (FM)	Office of the Assistant Secretary of the Army (Financial Management) (MUGU)
OASA (I & L)	Office of the Assistant Secretary of the Army (Installations and Logistics) (MUGU)
OASAM	Office of the Assistant Secretary for Administration and Management [*Department of Labor*]
OASA(M & RA)	Office of the Assistant Secretary of the Army (Manpower and Reserve Affairs)
OASA (R & D)	Office of the Assistant Secretary of the Army (Research and Development) (MUGU)
OASARDA	Office of the Assistant Secretary of the Army (Research, Development and Aquisition) (RDA)
OASAS	Office of Alcoholism and Substance Abuse Services [*U.S. Department of Health and Human Services*] (BARN)
OASB	Sarobi [*Afghanistan*] [*ICAO location identifier*] (ICLI)
OASBO	Office of Asbestos and Small Business Ombudsman [*Environmental Protection Agency*]
OAsC	Ashland College, Ashland, OH [*Library symbol Library of Congress*] (LCLS)
OASC	Office of Advanced Scientific Computing [*National Science Foundation*]
OASCB	Orbiter Avionics Software Control Board [*NASA*] (NASA)
OASCMIS	Operating and Support Costs Management Information System (MCD)
OASD	Office of the Assistant Secretary of Defense
OASD	Shindand [*Afghanistan*] [*ICAO location identifier*] (ICLI)
OASD(AE)	Office of the Assistant Secretary of Defense (Applications Engineer) (MCD)
OASD-C	Office of the Assistant Secretary of Defense - Comptroller
OASDG	Alexandria Branch, Stormount, Dundas, and Glengarry County Public Library, Ontario [*Library symbol National Library of Canada*] (NLC)
OASD(HA)	Office of the Assisant Secretary of Defense (Health Affairs) (DNAB)
OASDHI	Old-Age, Survivors, Disability, and Health Insurance [*Program*] [*Social Security Administration*]
OASDI	Old-Age, Survivors, and Disability Insurance [*Program*] [*Social Security Administration*]
OASD/IL	Office of the Assistant Secretary of Defense/Installations and Logistics (MCD)
OASD/ISA	Office of the Assistant Secretary of Defense/International Security Affairs (CINC)
OASD/ISP	Office of the Assistant Secretary of Defense for International Security Policy (SDI)
OASD(MRA)	Office of the Assistant Secretary of Defense (Manpower and Reserve Affairs)
OASD (MRA & L)	Office of Assistant Secretary of Defense (Manpower-Reserve Affairs and Logistics) (MCD)
OASD(PA)	Office of the Assistant Secretary of Defense (Public Affairs) (NTCM)
OASD(R & D)	Office of the Assistant Secretary of Defense (Research and Development) (MCD)
OASD(SA)	Office of the Assistant Secretary of Defense (Systems Analysis) (CINC)
OASD(S & L)	Office of the Assistant Secretary of Defense (Supply and Logistics) [*Obsolete*] (MCD)
OASD(T)	Office of the Assistant Secretary of Defense (Telecommunications)
OAS/EOM	Organization of American States Electoral Observation Mission
OASES	Open Access Satellite Education Services (EDAC)
OASES	Organization for American-Soviet Exchanges (EA)
OASET	Office of the Assistant Secretary for Employment and Training [*Department of Labor*]
OASF	Orbiting Astronomical Support Facility (MCD)
OASFP	Old Alliance Society of French Polishers [*A union*] [*British*]
OASG	Office Automation Specialist Group (NITA)
OASG	Sheberghan [*Afghanistan*] [*ICAO location identifier*] (ICLI)
OASH	Obstructive Asymmetrical Septal Hypertrophy [*Medicine*] (CPH)
OASH	Office of the Assistant Secretary for Health [*Department of Health and Human Services*]
OASHA	Operating and Support Hazard Analysis (MCD)
OASHDI	Old Age Survivors Health and Disability Program [*Health insurance*] (GHCT)
OAsht	Ashtabula County District Library, Ashtabula, OH [*Library symbol Library of Congress*] (LCLS)
OAshtK	Kent State University, Ashtabula Regional Campus, Ashtabula, OH [*Library symbol Library of Congress*] (LCLS)
OASI	Office Automation Society International (EA)
OASI	Old-Age and Survivors Insurance [*Program*] [*Social Security Administration*]
OASI	Old America Stores [*NASDAQ symbol*] (TTSB)
OASI	Old Americia Stores, Inc. [*NASDAQ symbol*] (SAG)
OASIA	Office of the Assistant Secretary for International Affairs [*Department of the Treasury*]
OASIS	Occupational Aptitude Survey and Interest Schedule
OASIS	Ocean All-Source Information System
OASIS	Oceanic and Atmospheric Scientific Information System [*National Oceanic and Atmospheric Administration*] (MCD)
OASIS	Office Administration Simulation Study
OASIS	Onboard at Site Invoicing System [*IBM Computer Program*]
OASIS	Online Administrative Information System [*Computer science*] (IAA)
OASIS	Online Automotive Service Information System [*Ford Motor Co.*]
OASIS	Open Access Same-Time Information Service [*Joint venture from IBM and TradeWave Corp.*]
OASIS	Operational Analysis and System Interface System
OASIS	Operational and Supportability Implementation System [*FAA*] (TAG)
OASIS	Operational Applications of Special Intelligence System (MCD)
OASIS	Operational Automatic Scheduling Information System (MUGU)
OASIS	Operation Analysis Strategic Interaction Simulator [*Nuclear war games*]
OASIS	Optimized Air-to-Surface Infrared Seeker
OASIS	Order, Accounting, Stock, Invoicing and Statistics (MHDB)
OASIS	Order and Schedules Input System (MCD)
OASIS	Organization for Applied Science in Society
OASIS	Organized Adoption Search Information Services (EA)
OASIS	Outlook and Situation Information System [*Department of Agriculture*] [*Defunct*] (IID)
OASIS	Outpatient Appointment Scheduling and Information System
OASIS	Over-the-Horizon Airborne Sensor Information System [*Navy*] (DOMA)
OASIS	Ownership Accountability of Selected Secondary Items Stocked
OASIS-AS	Occupational Aptitude Survey and Interest Schedule - Aptitude Survey [*Vocational guidance test*]
OASIS-IS	Occupational Aptitude Survey and Interest Schedule - Interest Schedule [*Vocational guidance test*]
OasisR	Oasis Residential, Inc. [*Associated Press*] (SAG)
OasisRsd	Oasis Residential, Inc. [*Associated Press*] (SAG)
OASK	Serka [*Afghanistan*] [*ICAO location identifier*] (ICLI)
OASL	Salam [*Afghanistan*] [*ICAO location identifier*] (ICLI)
OASM	Office of Aerospace Medicine [*NASA*] (KSC)
OASM	Ohm-Ampere-Second Meter [*System of units*]
OASM	Samangan [*Afghanistan*] [*ICAO location identifier*] (ICLI)
OASMA	Offensive Air Support Mission Analysis (MCD)
OASMS	Ordnance Ammunition Surveillance and Maintenance School [*Army*]
OASN	Office of the Assistant Secretary of the Navy
OASN	Sheghnan [*Afghanistan*] [*ICAO location identifier*] (ICLI)
OASN(FM)	Office of the Assistant Secretary of the Navy for Financial Management
OASN(I & L)	Office of the Assistant Secretary of the Navy for Installations and Logistics
OASN(M/RA)	Office of the Assistant Secretary of the Navy (Manpower and Reserve Affairs)
OASN(M/RA/L)	Office of the Assistant Secretary of the Navy (Manpower, Reserve Affairs, and Logistics)
OASN(P & RF)	Office of the Assistant Secretary of the Navy for Personnel and Reserve Force
OASN(R & D)	Office of the Assistant Secretary of the Navy for Research and Development
OAS-OGN	Organization of American States-Observer Group in Nicaragua
OASP	Organic Acid Soluble Phosphorus
OASP	Over-All Sound Pressure (PDAA)
OASP	Sare Pul [*Afghanistan*] [*ICAO location identifier*] (ICLI)
OASPL	Overall Sound Pressure Level
OASPrA	Oasis Residential $2.25'A' Pfd [*NYSE symbol*] (TTSB)
OASR	Office of Aeronautical and Space Research [*Later, OART*] [*NASA*]
OASR	Sabar [*Afghanistan*] [*ICAO location identifier*] (ICLI)
OAss	Old Assyrian (BJA)
OASS	Salang-I-Junubi [*Afghanistan*] [*ICAO location identifier*] (ICLI)
OASSO	Operational Applications of Satellite Snowcover Observations [*NASA*]
OAsT	Ashland Theological Seminary, Ashland, OH [*Library symbol Library of Congress*] (LCLS)
OAST	Office of Aeronautical and Space Technology [*Formerly, OART*] [*NASA*]
OAST	Order and Shipping Time [*Military*] (AFIT)
OAST	Overland Air Superiority Training [*Navy*] (DOMA)
OAST	Shur Tepa [*Afghanistan*] [*ICAO location identifier*] (ICLI)
OASTP	Office of the Assistant Secretary for Technology Policy [*U.S. Department of Commerce*] (BARN)
OASU	Oceanographic Air Survey Unit
OASV	Orbital Assembly Support Vehicle

OASW	Office of the Assistant Secretary of War [*World War II*]
OASYS	Obstacle Avoidance System [*Army*] (RDA)
OASYS	Office Automation System
OASYS	Order Allocation System
OAT	Atikokan Public Library, Ontario [*Library symbol National Library of Canada*] (NLC)
OAT	Ocean Acoustic Tomography
OAT	Office for Advanced Technology [*Air Force*]
OAT	On-Air Test [*Telecommunications*] (DOAD)
OAT	One at a Time
OAT	Open-Air Theater
OAT	Operating Ambient Temperature
OAT	Operational Acceptance Test
OAT	Operational Air Traffic (NATG)
OAT	Optical Adaptive Technique
OAT	Optometry Admissions Test (GAGS)
OAT	Ornithineaminotransferase [*An enzyme*]
OAT	Outer Atmospheric Temperature (IAA)
OAT	Outside Air Temperature [*Aviation*]
OAT	Overall Test
OAT	Oxide-Aligned Transistor [*Electronics*] (PDAA)
OAT	Oxoacid Aminotransferase Inhibition (DB)
OAT	Quaker Oats [*NYSE symbol*] (TTSB)
OAT	Quaker Oats Co. [*NYSE symbol Toronto Stock Exchange symbol*] (SPSG)
OAT	Sogervair/Transoceanic Aviation [*France ICAO designator*] (FAAC)
OATA	Optical Acquisition and Tracking Aid Assembly
OATC	Oceanic Air Traffic Center
OATC	Overseas Air Traffic Control
OATD	Toorghondi [*Afghanistan*] [*ICAO location identifier*] (ICLI)
OATG	Tashkurghan [*Afghanistan*] [*ICAO location identifier*] (ICLI)
OATH	Atikokan High School, Ontario [*Library symbol National Library of Canada*] (NLC)
OATHS	One-in-a-Thousand Society (EA)
OATK	Kotal [*Afghanistan*] [*ICAO location identifier*] (ICLI)
OATM	Atikokan Centennial Museum, Ontario [*Library symbol National Library of Canada*] (BIB)
OATM	Orbiter Antenna Test Model [*NASA*]
OATMEAL	Optimum Allocation of Test and Equipment Manpower Against Logistics
OATN	Tereen [*Afghanistan*] [*ICAO location identifier*] (ICLI)
OATP	On-Aircraft Test Procedure (MCD)
OATP	Operational Acceptance Test Procedure (NRCH)
OATQ	Taluqan [*Afghanistan*] [*ICAO location identifier*] (ICLI)
OATS	Office Automation Technology Services [*AT&T*] (CIST)
OATS	Office of Air Transportation Security [*FAA*]
OATS	On-Board Acoustic Tracking System [*Navy*] (CAAL)
OATS	Open Architecture Test System (MCD)
OATS	Optical Attitude Transfer System (SSD)
OATS	Optimum Aerial Target Sensor
OATS	Orbit and Attitude Tracking (GAVI)
OATS	Original Article Tear Sheets
OATS	Original Article Tearsheet Service (NITA)
OATS	Original Article Text Service
OATS	Outdoor Advertising Total System (PDAA)
OATS	Overall Test Set
OATS	Over Armor Technology Synthesis (RDA)
OATS	Wild Oats Markets, Inc. [*NASDAQ symbol*] (SAG)
OATUU	Organisation of African Trade Union Unity [*Formerly, AATUF, ATUC*] [*See also OUSA Accra, Ghana*] (EAIO)
OATW	Tewara [*Afghanistan*] [*ICAO location identifier*] (ICLI)
OATZ	Tesak [*Afghanistan*] [*ICAO location identifier*] (ICLI)
OAU	Aurora Public Library, Ontario [*Library symbol National Library of Canada*] (NLC)
OAU	Ohio University, Athens, OH [*Library symbol Library of Congress*] (LCLS)
OAU	Operator Assistance Unit (NITA)
OAU	Optical Alignment Unit
OAU	Organization for African Unity (NADA)
OAU	Organization of African Unity
OAU	Original Sixteen To One Mine [*PC, exchange symbol*] (TTSB)
OAU	Oriol Avia [*Russian Federation*] [*ICAO designator*] (FAAC)
OAUH	Aurora Historical Society, Ontario [*Library symbol National Library of Canada*] (NLC)
OAUHS	PRECIS Project, Aurora High School, Ontario [*Library symbol National Library of Canada*] (NLC)
OAULC	OAU [*Organization of African Unity*] Liberation Committee [*Addis Ababa, Ethiopia*] (EAIO)
OAUM	Aurora Museum, Ontario [*Library symbol National Library of Canada*] (BIB)
OAUS	Sterling Drug Ltd., Aurora, Ontario [*Library symbol National Library of Canada*] (BIB)
OAU/STRC	Organization of African Unity Scientific and Technical Research Commission [*Marine science*] (MSC)
OAUYCE	York County Board of Education, Aurora, Ontario [*Library symbol National Library of Canada*] (NLC)
OAUZ	Kunduz [*Afghanistan*] [*ICAO location identifier*] (ICLI)
O-A-V	Object-Attribute-Value
OAV	Oculoauriculovertebral Dysplasia [*Medicine*] (MAE)
OAV	Omni-Aviacao e Tecnologia Lda. [*Portugal ICAO designator*] (FAAC)
OAV	Operational Aerospace Vehicle
OAVC of SA	Office of the Assistant Vice Chief of Staff, Army [*Later, OAVCSA*] (AABC)
OAVCSA	Office of the Assistant Vice Chief of Staff, Army [*Formerly, OAVC of SA*] (AABC)

OAVD	Oculoauriculovertebral Dysplasia [*Medicine*] (MEDA)
OAVE	Occupational, Adult, and Vocational Education (OICC)
OAvG	B. F. Goodrich Chemical Co. [*of B. F. Goodrich Co.*], Development Center Library, Avon Lake, OH [*Library symbol Library of Congress*] (LCLS)
OAVP	Older Americans Volunteer Program [*ACTION*]
OAVSDG	Avonmore Branch, Stormont, Dundas, and Glengarry County Public Library, Ontario [*Library symbol National Library of Canada*] (BIB)
OAVTME	Office of Adult, Vocational, Technical, and Manpower Education [*Office of Education*]
OAW	Old Abandoned Well (WDAA)
OAW	Optically Assisted Winchester [*Computer science*]
OAW	Overall Width
OAW	Oxyacetylene Welding
OAWCS	Overseas Air Weapons Control System
OAWM	Office of Air and Water Measurement [*National Institute of Standards and Technology*]
OAWOP	Ontario Police College, Aylmer West, Ontario [*Library symbol National Library of Canada*] (NLC)
OAWP	Office of Air and Water Programs (OICC)
OAWP	Operations Analysis Working Paper [*NASA*] (KSC)
OAWR	Office of Agricultural War Relations [*World War II*]
OAWR	Office of Atmospheric Water Resources [*Bureau of Reclamation*]
OAWRMR	Other Acquisition War Reserve Material Requirements (MCD)
OAWU	Wurtach [*Afghanistan*] [*ICAO location identifier*] (ICLI)
OAWZ	Wazirabad [*Afghanistan*] [*ICAO location identifier*] (ICLI)
OAX	Oaxaca [*Mexico*] [*Airport symbol*] (OAG)
OAX	Oaxaca [*Mexico*] [*Seismograph station code, US Geological Survey*] (SEIS)
OAX	Operational Aviation Services - Australia [*ICAO designator*] (FAAC)
OAY	Moses Point, AK [*Location identifier FAA*] (FAAL)
OAY	NOAA [*National Oceanic and Atmospheric Administration*] Geophysical Fluid Dynamics Laboratory, Princeton, NJ [*OCLC symbol*] (OCLC)
OAYM	Aylmer District Museum, Ontario [*Library symbol National Library of Canada*] (BIB)
OAYQ	Yangi Qala [*Afghanistan*] [*ICAO location identifier*] (ICLI)
OAYR	Outstanding Airman of the Year Ribbon [*Military decoration*] (AFM)
OAZB	Zebak [*Afghanistan*] [*ICAO location identifier*] (ICLI)
OAZG	Zaranj [*Afghanistan*] [*ICAO location identifier*] (ICLI)
OB	Brockville Public Library, Ontario [*Library symbol National Library of Canada*] (NLC)
OB	Brought Over (ROG)
Ob	Obadiah [*Old Testament book*]
OB	Oberlerchner [*Joseph Oberlerchner Holzindustrie*] [*Austria ICAO aircraft manufacturer identifier*] (ICAO)
ob	Obese
OB	Obeum [*Nickname for toilets at Cambridge University*] [*Slang British*] (DSUE)
OB	Obidiah [*Old Testament*]
OB	Obiit [*He, or She, Died*] [*Latin*]
ob	Obiter [*Incidentally*] [*Latin*] (GPO)
OB	Obituary Notice (DSUE)
OB	Objection (ROG)
OB	Objective [*Microscopy*]
OB	Objective Benefit (MAE)
OB	Obligation (ROG)
OB	Obligation Bond
OB.	Obliteration
OB	Oblong
ob	Oblong [*Bookbinding*] (WDMC)
OB	Oboe
ob	Oboe (WDAA)
OB	Obolus [*Coin*] [*Latin*] (ADA)
OB	O'Brien Energy & Resources Ltd. [*Toronto Stock Exchange symbol*]
OB	Obscure (KSC)
OB	Observation (WGA)
OB	Observed Bearing [*Navigation*]
OB	Obsolete (AABC)
OB	Obstetrician
OB	Obstetrics [*Medicine*]
OB	Obtuse Bisectrix [*Crystallography*]
OB +	Occult Blood Positive [*Medicine*] (DAVI)
OB	Occult Bleeding [*Medicine*]
OB	Occupational Behavior
OB	Ocean Bottom
OB	Octal-to-Binary [*Computer science*] (BUR)
OB	Octave Band
O-B	Oerlikon-Buehrle [*Switzerland*]
OB	Off-Broadway (WGA)
OB	Offensive Back [*Football*]
OB	Official Board of Ballroom Dancing [*British*] (BI)
OB	Official Bulletin. International Commission for Air Navigation [*A publication*] (DLA)
OB	Oil Bearing (DCTA)
OB	Oil Bomb
OB	Old Babylonian (BJA)
OB	[*The*] Old Bailey [*London court*]
OB	Old Bonded [*Whiskey*] (ROG)
OB	Old Boy [*Communications operators' colloquialism*]
OB	Old Buildings [*British Admiralty*]
OB	Oligoclonal Band [*Analytical biochemistry*]
OB	Ombudsman for Business [*Department of Commerce*]
OB	On Being: the Servant's Servant [*A publication*] (APTA)

OB	On Board
O/B	Onboard (NAKS)
OB	Opal Air [ICAO designator] (AD)
OB	Opening of Books
OB	Operating Base [Navy]
OB	Operating Budget (AFM)
OB	Operational Base [Navy]
OB	Operation Brotherhood
OB	Optometrists' Board [Australian Capital Territory]
OB	Or Better [Business term]
OB	Ordered Back
OB	Order of Battle [Military]
OB	Order of Burma [British military] (DMA)
OB	Order of the Bath
OB	Ordnance Battalion [Navy]
OB	Ordnance Board [Navy]
OB	Oregon Ballet
OB	Orgelbuechlein [Little Organ Book] [Bach Music]
OB	Orientalische Bibliographie [A publication] (BJA)
OB	Ortsbatterie [Local Battery] [German military - World War II]
OB	Outboard
OB	Outbound (WDAA)
OB	Out-of-Business (OICC)
OB	Output Buffer [Computer science]
OB	Output Bus [Computer science]
OB	Outside Broadcast (EY)
OB	Outside Bugs [Nonresident staff at a school] [British] (DSUE)
OB	Outward Bound (EA)
OB	Over Bath [Classified advertising] (ADA)
OB	Overboard (AAG)
OB	Overseas Brats [Commercial firm] (EA)
OB	Overseas Broadcast [or Broadcasting] (IAA)
OB	Owena Bank [Nigeria]
OB	Own Brand (MHDB)
OB	Oxford Biographies [A publication]
OB	Peru [International civil aircraft marking] (ODBW)
OBA	Barrie Public Library, Ontario [Library symbol National Library of Canada] (NLC)
OBA	Oasis Bungera [Antarctica] [Seismograph station code, US Geological Survey Closed] (SEIS)
OBA	Oberhasli Breeders of America (EA)
OBA	Object Behavior Analysis [Computer science]
OBA	Octave Band Analyzer
OBA	Off Boresight Angle (MCD)
OBA	Office of Business Administration [Later, Office of Administration] [NASA]
OBA	Office of Business Affairs [Northern Territory, Australia]
OBA	Office of Business Analysis [Information service or system] (IID)
OBA	Open Broadcasting Authority [Noncommercial TV channel] [British]
OBA	Operating Basis Accident [Environmental science] (COE)
OBA	Operating Budget Authority (MCD)
OBA	Optical Base Assembly (KSC)
OBA	Optical Brightening Agents
OBA	Ornithyl-Beta-Alanine [Biochemistry]
OBA	Outward Bound Australia
OBA	Over Burner Air
OBA	Oxygen Breathing Apparatus
OBAA	Oil Burning Apparatus Association (BUAC)
OBAALA	Organisation for Black Arts Advancement and Learning Activities [British]
Obad	Obadiah [Old Testament book]
OBAD	Object Average Optical Density [Microscopy]
OBAD	Operating Budget Authority Document [Military] (AFIT)
OBADRS	Octave Band Automatic Data Reduction System
OBAG	Georgian Bay Regional Library, Barrie, Ontario [Library symbol National Library of Canada] (NLC)
OBAGC	Georgian College of Applied Arts and Technology, Barrie, Ontario [Library symbol National Library of Canada] (NLC)
OBAL	Balmertown Public Library, Ontario [Library symbol National Library of Canada] (NLC)
OBAN	Bancroft Public Library, Ontario [Library symbol National Library of Canada] (NLC)
OBAN	Operating Budget Account Number [Air Force]
OB & F	Ollivier, Bell, and Fitzgerald's Court of Appeal Reports [1878-80] [New Zealand] [A publication] (DLA)
OB & F (CA)	Ollivier, Bell, and Fitzgerald's Court of Appeal Reports [1878-80] [New Zealand] [A publication] (DLA)
OB & FNZ	Ollivier, Bell, and Fitzgerald's New Zealand Reports [A publication] (DLA)
OB & F (SC)	Ollivier, Bell, and Fitzgerald's Supreme Court Reports [New Zealand] [A publication] (DLA)
OB & PA	Office of Budget and Program Analysis [Department of Agriculture] (GFGA)
OBANU	United Public Library, Carlow, Dungannon, and Mayo Townships, Bancroft, Ontario [Library symbol National Library of Canada] (BIB)
OBAP	Organization of Black Airline Pilots (EA)
OBAR	Ohio Bar (NITA)
OBarb	Barberton Public Library, Barberton, OH [Library symbol Library of Congress] (LCLS)
OBarn	Barnesville Public Library, Barnesville, OH [Library symbol Library of Congress] (LCLS)
OBAS	Organ Builders' Amalgamated Society [A union] [British]
OBAS	Simcoe County Co-Op, Barrie, Ontario [Library symbol National Library of Canada] (NLC)

OBAT	Augusta Township Public Library, Brockville, Ontario [Library symbol National Library of Canada] (NLC)
OBat	Clermont County Public Library, Batavia, OH [Library symbol Library of Congress] (LCLS)
OBatC	Clermont General and Technical College, Batavia, OH [Library symbol Library of Congress] (LCLS)
OBatH	Clermont Mercy Hospital, Batavia, OH [Library symbol Library of Congress] (LCLS)
OBAWS	On-Board Aircraft Weighing System (MCD)
OBB	Barry's Bay Public Library, Ontario [Library symbol National Library of Canada] (NLC)
OBB	Obbligato [Essential] [Music]
OBB	Obsidian Butte [California] [Seismograph station code, US Geological Survey] (SEIS)
OBB	Oesterreichische Bundesbahnen [Austrian Federal Railways]
OBB	Old Battleship [Navy]
OBB	On-Board Buffer (CIST)
OBB	Operation Better Block
OBB	Own Bed Bath [Medicine] (DMAA)
OBB	Oxybisbenzene [Organic chemistry]
OBBB	Bahrain [Bahrain] [ICAO location identifier] (ICLI)
OBBD	Official Board of Ballroom Dancing [British]
OBBFC	Official Betty Boop Fan Club (EA)
OBBI	Bahrain/International [Bahrain] [ICAO location identifier] (ICLI)
Obbl	Obbligato [Essential] [Music]
OBBM	Brant County Historical Museum, Brantford, Ontario [Library symbol National Library of Canada] (NLC)
Obbmo	Obbligatissimo [Your Obedient Servant] [Italian]
OBBMV	Madawaska Valley District High School, Barry's Bay, Ontario [Library symbol National Library of Canada] (NLC)
OBBO	Observation Balloon
OBC	Barwick Community Library, Ontario [Library symbol National Library of Canada] (BIB)
OBC	Obock [Djibouti] [Airport symbol] (OAG)
OBC	Oceania Basketball Confederation [Australia] (EA)
OBC	Off Boresight Correction [Military] (CAAL)
OBC	Officer Basic Course [Military]
OBC	Ohio Bell Communications, Inc. [Cleveland] [Telecommunications] (TSSD)
OBC	Old Bottle Club of Great Britain (BUAC)
OBC	Old Boys' Corps [Military British]
OBC	On-Board Checkout [Aircraft]
OBC	On-Board Computer (MCD)
OBC	On-Board Controller [Telecommunications]
OBC	One Big Computer [Proposed model for automation of the New York and American stock exchanges]
OBC	Optical Bar Camera [NASA] (LAIN)
OBC	Order of British Columbia [Canada] (DD)
OBC	Ouachita Baptist College [Arkadelphia, AR] [Later, OBU]
OBC	Outboard Boating Club of America [Defunct] (EA)
OBC	Outside Back Cover [Publishing] (WDMC)
OBC	Overseas Bankers' Club [British]
OBC	Overseas Book Centre
OBC	Oxide-Coated Brush Cathode
OBCA	Office of Bank Customer Affairs [FDIC]
OBCAB	Albion-Bolton Branch, Town of Caledon Public Libraries, Bolton, Ontario [Library symbol National Library of Canada] (NLC)
OBCCL	Canada Cement Lafarge Ltd., Belleville, Ontario [Library symbol National Library of Canada] (NLC)
OBCE	On-Board Checkout Equipment (MCD)
OBCE	Operational Baseline Cost Estimate [Army]
OBCGEH	Housewares and Home Entertainment Department, Canada General Electric Co. Ltd., Barrie, Ontario [Library symbol National Library of Canada] (NLC)
OBCH	Overseas Booksellers' Clearing House (DGA)
OBCI	Ocean Bio-Chem [NASDAQ symbol] (TTSB)
OBCI	Ocean Bio-Chem, Inc. [NASDAQ symbol] (NQ)
OBCI	On-Board Controller Interface [Telecommunications]
OBCO	On-Board Checkout [NASA] (KSC)
OB/CP	Observation/Command Post (DNAB)
OBCP	Ortho-Benzyl-para-chlorophenol [Disinfectant]
OBCR	Optical Bar Code Reader (NITA)
OBCS	Chromatographic Specialties Ltd., Brockville, Ontario [Library symbol National Library of Canada] (NLC)
OBCS	On-Board Checkout Subsystem [NASA] (NASA)
OBCS	On-Board Checkout [Instrumentation] System
Obd	Obadiah [Old Testament book] (BJA)
OBD	Odorant-Binding Protein (DB)
OBD	Office of Business Development [Economic Development Administration]
o/bd	Oil on Board (VRA)
OBD	Omnibearing Distance
OBD	On-Board Diagnostics [Chrysler Corp.'s computer system]
OBD	Open Blade Damper (OA)
OBD	Operational Base Development (AAG)
OBD	Operation Buckle Down [NHTSA] (TAG)
OBD	Optical Beam Deflection
OBD	Organic Brain Disease
OBD	Organization for Black Designers
OBDB	On-Board Data Bank (DNAB)
OBDC	Open Database Connectivity [Computer science]
OBDD	Ordered Bicontinuous Double Diamond [Phase structure]
OBDE	Dollman Electronics Canada Ltd., Brampton, Ontario [Library symbol National Library of Canada] (NLC)
OBDII	On-oard Diagnostics-Second Generation

OB DK	Observation Deck (WDAA)
OBDO	Oceanographic, Boarding, and Diving Officer [*Navy British*]
OBDT	Obedient
OBDV	Oat Blue Dwarf Virus [*Plant pathology*]
OBE	Belleville Public Library, Ontario [*Library symbol National Library of Canada*] (NLC)
OBE	Oberlin College, Oberlin, OH [*OCLC symbol*] (OCLC)
OBE	Office of Biological Education (DAVI)
OBE	Office of Business Economics [*Later, Office of Economic Analysis*] [*Department of Commerce*]
OBE	Officer of the Most Excellent Order of the British Empire (WDAA)
OBE	Officer of the Order of the British Empire (NGC)
OBE	Okeechobee, FL [*Location identifier FAA*] (FAAL)
OBE	On-Board Equipment
OBE	One-Boson Exchange [*Physics*] (OA)
OBE	Operating Basis Earthquake [*Nuclear reactor*] (NRCH)
OBE	Operating Basis Event (IEEE)
OBE	Order of the British Empire [*Facetious translations: Old Boiled Egg, Other Buggers' Efforts*]
OBE	Ottawa Board of Education, Library Services Centre [*UTLAS symbol*]
OBE	Outcome-Based Education [*School reform*]
OBE	Outerback End
OBE	Out-of-Body Experience [*Parapsychology*]
OBE	Overcome [*or Overtaken*] by Events
OBEA	Oregon Business Education Association (EDAC)
OBEAB	Beaverton Branch, Brock Township Public Library, Ontario [*Library symbol National Library of Canada*] (BIB)
OBEAR	Beardmore Public Library, Ontario [*Library symbol National Library of Canada*] (NLC)
OBEATE	Beaverton-Thorah Eldon Historical Society, Inc., Ontario [*Library symbol National Library of Canada*] (NLC)
OBEC	Organization for Economic Cooperation and Development (EBF)
OBECO	Outboard Engine Cutoff [*NASA*] (KSC)
OBED	Beamsville District Secondary School, Ontario [*Library symbol National Library of Canada*] (NLC)
OBed	Bedford Public Library, Bedford, OH [*Library symbol Library of Congress*] (LCLS)
OBedF	Ferro Corp., Chemical Library, Bedford, OH [*Library symbol Library of Congress*] (LCLS)
OBEDS	Deloro Stellite Co., Belleville, Ontario [*Library symbol National Library of Canada*] (BIB)
OBEE	Beeton Public Library, Ontario [*Library symbol National Library of Canada*] (BIB)
OBEGOSC	Organizational Effectiveness General Officer Steering Committee (MCD)
OBEH	Hastings County Historical Society, Belleville, Ontario [*Library symbol National Library of Canada*] (BIB)
OBEHP	Hastings and Prince Edward County Health Unit, Belleville, Ontario [*Library symbol National Library of Canada*] (BIB)
OBEL	Loyalist College of Applied Arts and Technology, Belleville, Ontario [*Library symbol National Library of Canada*] (NLC)
OBELF	Fleming Branch, Lincoln Public Library, Beamsville, Ontario [*Library symbol National Library of Canada*] (BIB)
OBEM	Beachville Ye Olde Museum, Ontario [*Library symbol National Library of Canada*] (BIB)
OBEM	Object-Based Equipment Model (AAEL)
OBEM	One-Boson Exchange Model
OBEM	Operational Battery Effectiveness Model (MCD)
OBEMLA	Office of Bilingual Education and Minority Language Affairs [*Department of Education*] (GFGA)
O Ben	Old Benloe's Reports, English Common Pleas [*1486-1580*] [*A publication*] (DLA)
O Benl	Old Benloe's Reports, English Common Pleas [*1486-1580*] [*A publication*] (DLA)
OBEP	One-Boson Exchange Potential
OBEr	OB [*Out-of-the-Body*] Experient [*Parapsychology*]
OBER	Office of Biological and Environmental Research (HGEN)
OBerB	Baldwin-Wallace College, Berea, OH [*Library symbol Library of Congress*] (LCLS)
OBERS	Office of Business Economics Research Service (NRCH)
OBERST	Oberstimme [*Upper Part*] [*Music*]
OBERW	Oberwerk [*Upper Work*] [*Music*]
OBES	Office of Basic Energy Sciences (COE)
OBES	Office of Basic Energy Services [*Department of Energy*]
OBES	Orthonormal Basis of an Error Space [*Statistics*]
OBESA	Stephens-Adamson, Belleville, Ontario [*Library symbol National Library of Canada*] (NLC)
OBESG	Office of Basic Energy Science/Geosciences [*Department of Energy*]
OBESSU	Organising Bureau of European School Student Unions (EAIO)
OBEWS	On-Board Electronic Warfare Simulation [*Air Force*]
OBEX	Object Exchange [*Computer science*] (PCM)
OBF	Octave Band Filter
OBF	One-Bar Function (OA)
OBF	Operational Base Facility
OBF	Organ Blood Flow [*Physiology*]
OBF	Ottawa Board of Education, Library Services Centre (Films) [*UTLAS symbol*]
OBF	Output Buffer Full [*Computer science*] (IAA)
OBFAR	Burks Falls, Armour, and Ryerson Union Library, Burks Falls, Ontario [*Library symbol National Library of Canada*] (NLC)
OBFC	Barriefield Branch, Frontenac County Library, Ontario [*Library symbol National Library of Canada*] (BIB)
OBFC	O'Leary Brothers Fan Club (EA)
OBFM	On or Before Full Moon [*Freemasonry*] (ROG)
OBFNO	Northern Ontario Public School Principals' Association, Burks Falls, Ontario [*Library symbol National Library of Canada*] (NLC)
OBFS	Octave Band Filter Set
OBFS	Offshore Bulk Fuel System
OBFS	Organization of Biological Field Stations (EA)
OBFS	Overseas Base Facilities Summary [*Navy*]
Ob G	Obergericht [*Court of Appeal*] [*German*] (DLA)
OBG	Oberg Industries Ltd. [*Vancouver Stock Exchange symbol*]
OBG	Obigarm [*Former USSR Seismograph station code, US Geological Survey Closed*]
OBG	Obstetrics-Gynecology [*Medicine*]
OBG	Oldie but Goodie [*Music*]
OBgCE	Conneaut Elementary School, Bowling Green, OH [*Library symbol*] [*Library of Congress*] (LCLS)
OBgCrE	Crim Elementary School, Bowling Green, OH [*Library symbol*] [*Library of Congress*] (LCLS)
OBgJH	Bowling Green Junior High School, Bowling Green, OH [*Library symbol*] [*Library of Congress*] (LCLS)
OBgKE	Kenwood Elementary School, Bowling Green, OH [*Library symbol*] [*Library of Congress*] (LCLS)
OBgRE	Ridge Elementary School, Bowling Green, OH [*Library symbol*] [*Library of Congress*] (LCLS)
OBGS	On-Board Gunnery Simulator (PDAA)
OBGS	Orbital Bombardment Guidance System
OBgSH	Bowling Green Senior High School, Bowling Green, OH [*Library symbol*] [*Library of Congress*] (LCLS)
OBgSME	South Main Elementary School, Bowling Green, OH [*Library symbol*] [*Library of Congress*] (LCLS)
OBGT	Old Babylonian Grammatical Texts [*A publication*] (BJA)
OBgU	Bowling Green State University, Bowling Green, OH [*Library symbol Library of Congress*] (LCLS)
OBgU-C	Bowling Green State University, Center for Archival Collections, Bowling Green, OH [*Library symbol Library of Congress*] (LCLS)
OB-GYN	Obstetrician-Gynecologist (PAZ)
OB-GYN	Obstetrics-Gynecology [*Medicine*]
OBH	Office Busy Hour [*Telecommunications*] (TEL)
OBH	Oil Bath Heater
OBH	Old Berkeley Hunt [*British*]
OBH	Old Berkshire Hounds [*British*]
OBH	Old Highland Blend [*Whisky*] (ROG)
OBH	Operational Biomedical Harness
OBH	Wolbach, NE [*Location identifier FAA*] (FAAL)
OBHFC	Official Bobby Hart Fan Club (EA)
OBHT	Tecumseh Township Public Library, Bond Head, Ontario [*Library symbol National Library of Canada*] (BIB)
OBI	Obidos [*Brazil*] [*Airport symbol*] (AD)
OBI	Obihiro [*Japan*] [*Seismograph station code, US Geological Survey*] (SEIS)
OBI	Obligated Involuntary Officer [*Military*]
OBI	Office du Baccalaureat International [*International Baccalaureate Office - IBO*] (EAIO)
OBI	Office of Basic Instrumentation [*National Bureau of Standards*]
OBI	Old Babylonian Inscriptions [*A publication*] (BJA)
OBI	Omnibearing Indicator [*Radio*]
OBI	Online Book Initiative [*Trademark name*] [*Internet*]
OBI	Open-Back Inclinable
OBI	Open-Back Inclinable Press [*Manufacturing term*]
OBI	Open Buying on the Internet [*Computer science*]
OBI	Operation Blessing International [*An association*]
OBI	Order of British India
OBI	Organisation du Baccalaureat International [*International Baccalaureate Organisation - IBO*] (EAIO)
OBI	Osaka Bioscience Institute [*Japan*]
OBIC	Optical Beam Induced Current [*Electronics*] (AAEL)
O BID	Omni Bidus [*Every Two Days*] [*Pharmacy*] (ROG)
OBIE	Obie Media Corp. [*NASDAQ symbol*] (SAG)
ObieMed	Obie Media Corp. [*Associated Press*] (SAG)
OBIFC	Osmond Boys International Fan Club (EA)
OBIFCO	On-Board In-Flight Checkout (MCD)
OBIG	Oesterreichisches Bundesinstitut fuer Gesundheitswesen [*Austrian National Institute for Public Health*] [*Information service or system*] (IID)
OBIGGS	On-Board Inert Gas Generator System [*Aviation*] (MCD)
O BIH	Omni Bihora [*Every Two Hours*] [*Pharmacy*] (ROG)
OBINXTO	Obit in Christo [*Died in Christ*] [*Latin*]
OBIPS	Optical Band Imager and Photometer System [*Aerospace*]
OBIS	Optimum Burn-In Screening
OBIS	Outdoor Biology Instructional Strategies [*National Science Foundation project*]
OBIT	Obiit [*He, or She, Died*] [*Latin*]
Obit	Obiter [*A publication*]
obit	Obituary [*Journalism*] [*Also, ob*] (WDMC)
OBIT	Obituary Notice (DSUE)
OBIU	On-Board Interface Unit (DWSG)
OBIWR	Whitefish River Band Public Library, Birch Island, Ontario [*Library symbol National Library of Canada*] (NLC)
OBJ	Intermediate Object Code File [*Computer science*]
OBJ	Object (AAG)
obj	Object (VRA)
obj	Objection (WDAA)
OBJ	Objection (WDAA)
OBJ	Objective
OBJ	Oklahoma Bar Association. Journal [*A publication*] (DLA)
OBJ	Operation Buster-Jangle [*Atomic weapons testing*]
OBJ	Orthodox Black Jews (BJA)

ObjDes.........	Object Design, Inc. [*Associated Press*] (SAG)
OBJN	Objection
ObjSoft	ObjectSoft Corp. [*Associated Press*] (SAG)
ObjSys........	Objective Systems Integrators, Inc. [*Associated Press*] (SAG)
OBJV...........	Objective (MSA)
OBK	Northbrook, IL [*Location identifier FAA*] (FAAL)
OBK	Organisation pour l'Amenagement et le Developpement du Bassin de la Riviere Kagera [*Organization for the Management and Development of the Kagera River Basin - KBO*] (EAIO)
OBL.............	League of Off-Broadway Theatres and Producers (EA)
OBL.............	Object-Based Language (AAEL)
OBL.............	Oblast [*Governmental subdivision in USSR corresponding to a province or state*]
OBL.............	Obligation (ADA)
OBL.............	Obligato [*Obbligato*] [*Music*] (ROG)
OBL.............	Oblique (AABC)
obl...............	Oblique (STED)
OBL.............	Oblong
obl...............	Oblong [*Bookbinding*] (WDMC)
OBL.............	Oceanic Boundary Layer
OBL.............	Office of Business Loans [*Economic Development Administration*]
OBL.............	One Block Look-Ahead [*Computer science*]
OBL.............	Operational Base Launch [*Air Force*]
OBL.............	Order Bill of Lading [*Shipping*]
OBL.............	Outside of the Battery Limits [*Engineering economics*]
OBL.............	Outstanding Balance List [*IRS*]
OBla...........	Blanchester Public Library, Blanchester, OH [*Library symbol Library of Congress*] (LCLS)
OBLAC	Bath Branch, Lennox and Addington County Public Library, Ontario [*Library symbol National Library of Canada*] (NLC)
OBLACS	Sandburst Branch, Lennox and Addington County Public Library, Bath, Ontario [*Library symbol National Library of Canada*] (BIB)
OBLAT	Oblatum [*Cachet*] [*Pharmacy*]
OBLAUTH.....	Obligation Authority [*Army*] (AABC)
OBIC	Bluffton College, Bluffton, OH [*Library symbol Library of Congress*] (LCLS)
OBIC-M........	Bluffton College, Mennonite Historical Library, Bluffton, OH [*Library symbol Library of Congress*] (LCLS)
OBLG	Obligate (AABC)
OBLH	Bloomfield-Hallowell Union Library, Bloomfield, Ontario [*Library symbol National Library of Canada*] (BIB)
OBLI...........	Oxford and Bucks Light Infantry [*Military unit*] [*British*]
Oblig...........	Obligation (TBD)
OBLIGN........	Obligation (ROG)
OBLISERV.....	Obligated Services of [*numbers of months indicated*] Required [*Navy*]
OBLISERVNATRA...	Obligated to Serve Three and One-Half Years Following Date of Completion of Training within the Naval Air Training Command
OBLISERVONEASIX...	Obligated to Serve on Active Duty One Year for Each Six Months Schooling or Fraction Thereof [*Navy*]
OBLISERVTHREETIME...	Obligated to Serve on Active Duty a Period Three Times the Length of Period of Education [*Navy*]
OBLISERVTWOYR...	Obligated to Serve on Active Duty a Period of Two Years [*Navy*]
OBLN	Obligation (AFM)
OBLR	Blind River Public Library, Ontario [*Library symbol National Library of Canada*] (NLC)
OBLu..........	Old Babylonian Version of Lu [*A publication*] (BJA)
OBlv...........	Bliss Memorial Public Library, Bloomville, OH [*Library symbol Library of Congress*] (LCLS)
OBM...........	Aviaobshemash [*Former USSR*] [*FAA designator*] (FAAC)
OBM...........	Morobe [*Papua New Guinea*] [*Airport symbol*] (OAG)
OBM...........	Oberlin College, Conservatory of Music, Library, Oberlin, OH [*OCLC symbol*] (OCLC)
OBM...........	Ocean Biogeochemical Model
OBM...........	Ogilvy Benson & Mather Ltd. (EFIS)
OBM...........	Optimal Body Mass [*Ecology*]
OBM...........	Ordnance Bench Mark (IAA)
OBM...........	Oriental Boat Mission [*Later, International Missions*] (EA)
OBM...........	Ulan Bator [*Mongolia*] [*Seismograph station code, US Geological Survey Closed*] (SEIS)
OBMA	Outboard Boat Manufacturers Association [*Later, NMMA*] (EA)
OBMC	Officers' Basic Military Corps [*Air Force*]
OBMC	Outbound Midcourse Correction [*NASA*] (KSC)
OBMP	Bruce Mines and Plummer Additional Union Public Library, Bruce Mines, Ontario [*Library symbol National Library of Canada*] (NLC)
OBMS	Objectives-Based Management System (ADA)
OBN	Oban [*Scotland*] [*Airport symbol*] (OAG)
OBN	Obninsk [*Former USSR Seismograph station code, US Geological Survey*] (SEIS)
OBN	Occult Blood Negative [*Medicine*] (DAVI)
OBN	Office Balancing Network [*Telecommunications*] (TEL)
OBN	Office of Biochemical Nomenclature [*NAS-NRC*]
OBN	On-Board Navigation
OBN	Out-of-Band Noise
OBNA	Only But Not All (NITA)
OBNE	Department 9911, Northern Telecom Ltd., Belleville, Ontario [*Library symbol National Library of Canada Obsolete*] (NLC)
OBNM	On or Before New Moon [*Freemasonry*] (ROG)
OBNTC	Old Boys Network Turtle Club (EA)
OBO	Obihiro [*Japan*] [*Airport symbol*] (OAG)
OBO	Obock [*Djibouti*] [*Seismograph station code, US Geological Survey*] (SEIS)
OBO	Official Business Only (AFM)

OBO	Oil/Bulk/Ore Carrier [*Multipurpose bulk carrier*] (DS)
OBO	Or Best Offer [*Classified advertising*]
OBO	Orbital Bomber (IAA)
OBO	Order Book Official [*Investment term*]
OBO	Order by Order
O/B/O	Ore/Bulk/Oil [*Bulk carrier vessel*]
OBO	Organization of Bricklin Owners (EA)
OBOA	Ontario Building Officials Association [*Canada*] (AAGC)
OB/OD	Open Burning/Open Detonation [*Military*]
OBOE	Observed Bombing of Enemy
OBOE	Offensive Burst Operating Environment
OBOE	Offshore Buoy-Observing Equipment (PDAA)
OBOF	Old Buffer over Forty [*Elderly recruits*] [*World War I*] [*British*]
OBOG	On-Board Oxygen-Generation [*For military aviation*]
OBOGS	On-Board Oxygen Generating System [*Navy*] (CAAL)
OBOLC	Caledon Public Libraries, Bolton, Ontario [*Library symbol National Library of Canada*] (NLC)
OBOM	Bowmanville Museum, Ontario [*Library symbol National Library of Canada*] (BIB)
OBON...........	Newcastle Public Library Board, Bowmanville, Ontario [*Library symbol National Library of Canada*] (NLC)
OBONF.........	Bonfield Public Library, Ontario [*Library symbol National Library of Canada*] (NLC)
OBOS	Our Bodies Ourselves [*A publication*]
OBP	Occult Blood Positive [*Medicine*] (DAVI)
OBP	Occupational Back Pain
OBP	Octyl Benzyl Phthalate (EDCT)
OBP	Odorant-Binding Protein [*Biochemistry*]
OBP	Oil Breather Pressure
OBP	On-Base Percentage [*Baseball*]
OBP	On-Board Processor
OBP	On-Line Benefits Processing
OBP	Open Break Position [*Dancing*]
OBP	Outer (Edge of) Basal Piece
OBP	Ova, Blood, and Parasites [*Medicine*] (MAE)
obp	Oxygen at High Pressure (AD)
OBPA	Outer Banks Protection Act (AAGC)
OBPA	Oxybisphenoxarsine [*Organic chemistry*]
OB PH	Oblique Photography (WDAA)
OBPH	People Helping People, Inc., Brantford, Ontario [*Library symbol National Library of Canada*] (NLC)
OBQ	Optometrists' Board of Queensland
OBR	Bradford Public Library, Ontario [*Library symbol National Library of Canada*] (NLC)
OBR	Office of Budget and Reports
OBR	One-Button-Recording [*Video technology*]
OBR	Optical Bar Code
OBR	Optical Bar Code Reader (MHDB)
OBR	Optical Bar Recognition [*Commonly known as a bar code*] (WDMC)
OBR	Origin of Bidirectional Replication [*Genetics*]
OBR	Outboard Recorder [*Computer science*] (BUR)
OBR	Owens, B. R., Montebello CA [*STAC*]
OBRA	Brampton Public Library, Ontario [*Library symbol National Library of Canada*] (NLC)
OBRA	Office of Business Research and Analysis [*Department of Commerce*]
OBRA	Omnibus Budget Reconciliation Act [*1987*]
OBRA	Omnibus Budget Reconciliation Act of 1990 (COE)
OBRA	Overseas Broadcasting Representatives Association (IAA)
OBRAC	Bracebridge Public Library, Ontario [*Library symbol National Library of Canada*] (NLC)
OBRAD........	Oblate Radial (PDAA)
OBRAM........	Chinguacousy Township Public Library, Bramalea, Ontario [*Library symbol National Library of Canada*] (NLC)
OBRAMB.......	Bell Northern Research, Bramalea, Ontario [*Library symbol National Library of Canada*] (NLC)
OBRANT.......	Northern Telecom, Brampton, Ontario [*Library symbol National Library of Canada*] (NLC)
OBRAPA......	Archives, Region of Peel, Brampton, Ontario [*Library symbol National Library of Canada*] (BIB)
OBRASC......	Brampton Campus, Sheridan College, Brampton, Ontario [*Library symbol National Library of Canada*] (BIB)
OBRC	Operating Budget Review Committee [*Military*]
OBRER........	Blind River Refinery, Eldorado Resources Ltd., Ontario [*Library symbol National Library of Canada*] (NLC)
OBRET	Old Breton [*Language, etc.*]
OBrG	B. F. Goodrich Co., Technical Library, Brecksville, OH [*Library symbol Library of Congress*] (LCLS)
OBRH	Home Care Program, Brockville, Ontario [*Library symbol National Library of Canada*] (BIB)
OBRI	Belle River Public Library, Ontario [*Library symbol National Library of Canada*] (NLC)
O Bridg........	Orlando Bridgman's English Common Pleas Reports [*A publication*] (DLA)
O Bridg (Eng)...	Orlando Bridgman's English Common Pleas Reports [*A publication*] (DLA)
O Bridgm.....	Orlando Bridgman's English Common Pleas Reports [*A publication*] (DLA)
O'Brien	O'Brien's Upper Canada Reports [*A publication*] (DLA)
OBRIG	Brighton Public Library, Ontario [*Library symbol National Library of Canada*] (BIB)
O'Bri Lawy...	O'Brien's Lawyer's Rule of Holy Life [*A publication*] (DLA)
O'Bri ML.......	O'Brien's Military Law [*A publication*] (DLA)
OBRIS.........	Smith Township Public Library, Bridgenorth, Ontario [*Library symbol National Library of Canada*] (BIB)

OBRIT..........	Britt Area Community Library, Britt, Ontario [*Library symbol National Library of Canada*] (NLC)
OBRIT..........	Old British [*Language, etc.*]
OBRM..........	W. Ross MacDonald School, Brantford, Ontario [*Library symbol National Library of Canada*] (NLC)
OBRMR.........	Mississauga Reserve Library, Blind River, Ontario [*Library symbol National Library of Canada*] (NLC)
OBRNR........	Oil Burner
OBRO..........	Oxford-On-Rideau Township Public Library, Burritt's Rapids, Ontario [*Library symbol National Library of Canada*] (BIB)
OBROW.......	Ochotnicza Brygada Robotnicza Obrony Warszawy [*A publication*] (BJA)
OBRP..........	On-Board Repair Parts [*Navy*]
OBRP..........	Pauline Johnson College, Brantford, Ontario [*Library symbol National Library of Canada*] (NLC)
OBRPH.........	Library Resources & Information Centre, Brockville Psychiatric Hospital, Ontario [*Library symbol National Library of Canada*] (NLC)
OBRR..........	Obstetric Recovery Room (STED)
OBRT..........	Brantford Public Library, Ontario [*Library symbol National Library of Canada*] (NLC)
OBrV..........	United States Veterans Administration Hospital, Brecksville, OH [*Library symbol Library of Congress*] (LCLS)
OBRWI........	[*The*] Woodland Indian Cultural Educational Centre, Brantford, Ontario [*Library symbol National Library of Canada*] (NLC)
OBS	Aubenas [*France*] [*Airport symbol*] (OAG)
OBS	Obesity [*Medicine*] (DMAA)
OBS	Obligations (ROG)
Obs	Obscene [*Legal term*]
obs...........	Obscura (VRA)
OBS	Obscurant
OBS	Obscure (ADA)
OBS	Observation (ROG)
OBS	Observatory
OBS	Observe
Obs	Observer (London) [*A publication*] (BRI)
OBS	Obsolete (AAG)
obs...........	Obsolete (STED)
OBS	Obstacle (AABC)
Obs	Obstacle Light [*Aviation*] (DA)
OBS	Obstetrical Service [*Medicine*] (MAE)
OBS	Obstetrics [*Medicine*]
OBS	Obstruction (WGA)
OBS	Ocean Bottom Seismometer [*California*] [*Seismograph station code, US Geological Survey Closed*] (SEIS)
OBS	Ocean Bottom Station
OBS	Office of Biological Service [*Marine science*] (MSC)
OBS	Office of Boating Safety [*Coast Guard*]
OBS	Official Bulletin Station [*Amateur radio*]
OBS	Old Babylonian Sumerian (BJA)
OBS	Old Bailey's Sessions Papers [*A publication*] (DLA)
OBS	Omnibearing Selector [*Radio*]
OBS	On-Board Spares [*Army*]
OBS	On-Board System [*Navy*] (CAAL)
OBS	Online BookStore [*Commercial firm*]
OBS	On-Line Business Systems, Inc. [*Information service or system*] (IID)
OBS	Open-Back Stationary Press [*Manufacturing term*]
OBS	Open-Hearth Basic Steel
OBS	Opera Ballet School (DICI)
OBS	Operand Buffering System [*Computer science*] (IAA)
OBS	Operational Bioinstrumentation System [*NASA*]
OBS	Operational Biomedical Sensors (NASA)
OBS	Operational Biomedical Systems (KSC)
OBS	Optical Beam Scanner
OBS	Optical Beam Steering
OBS	Orange Badge Scheme [*Disabled parking permit*] [*British*]
OBS	Orbital Bombardment System
OBS	Organic Brain Syndrome [*Psychiatry*]
OBS	Organization Breakdown Structure [*Computer science*] (PCM)
OBS	Organized Behavioral System (WDMC)
OBS	Oriental and Biblical Studies [*A publication*] (BJA)
OBS	OSIS [*Ocean Surveillance Information System*] Baseline System [*Navy*]
OBS	Ottawa Board of Education, Library Services Centre (Software) [*UTLAS symbol*]
OBS	Oxford Bibliographical Society (DGA)
OBS	Sidney Township Public Library, Batawa, Ontario [*Library symbol National Library of Canada*] (BIB)
OBSC..........	Obscure
OBSC..........	Obscured Light [*Navigation signal*]
OBSCIS........	Offender Based State Corrections Information System (OICC)
OBSD..........	Object Sum Optical Density [*Microscopy*]
OBSD..........	Observed
obsd..........	Observed (STED)
OBSD..........	Optical Beam Steering Device
OBSERV.......	Observatory
OBSH..........	Object Shape [*Microscopy*]
OBSH..........	Oxybis(benzenesulfonylhydrazine) [*Organic chemistry*]
OBSHT........	Obstacle Height
OBSL..........	St. Lawrence College [*College Saint-Laurent*], Brockville, Ontario [*Library symbol National Library of Canada*] (NLC)
Obs Lt.........	Observer Lieutenant [*British military*] (DMA)
OBSN..........	Observation (AAG)
OBSNFL.......	Observation Flight (IAA)
OBSOL.........	Obsolescent

Obsoles	Obsolescent
OBSP	Obiit sine Prole [*Died without Issue*] [*Latin*]
OBSP	Old Bailey's Sessions Papers [*Legal term British*]
OBSPL	Octave Band Sound Pressure Level
OBSPM	Obiit sine Prole Masculus [*He, or She, Died without Male Issue*] [*Latin*]
OBSR	Observation
OBSRON	Observation Squadron
OBSRVTRY...	Observatory
OBSS	Ocean Bottom Scanning SONAR
Obs Spot......	Observation Spot [*Control point*] [*Nautical charts*]
OBST	Obstacle (AFM)
OBST	Obstetric
Obst	Obstetrician (STED)
OBST	Obstetrics [*Medicine*]
obst	Obstipation (STED)
OBST	Obstruction (AFM)
obstet	Obstetric (STED)
OBSTET.......	Obstetrics [*Medicine*]
obstl	Obstruction Light (AD)
OBSTN	Obstruction (MSA)
Obstr	Obstruction
obstr	Obstruction (AD)
OBSTRN.......	Obstetrician [*Medicine*]
OBSUED.......	Oberbefehlshaber Suedost [*Headquarters, Commander-in-Chief, South*] [*Southern Germany and several army groups on the Eastern Front*] [*German military - World War II*]
OBSUM........	Order of Battle Summary [*Military*] (MCD)
OBSV	Observation (IAA)
obsv	Observation (AD)
obsv	Observatory (AD)
OBSV	Observatory (IAA)
OBSV	Observer
obsv	Observer (AD)
OBSVE	Observe (ROG)
OBSY	Observatory (AABC)
ob syn	Organic Brain Syndrome [*Medicine*] (AD)
OBSZ	Object Size [*Microscopy*]
OBT	Obedient
obt	Obedient (AD)
obt	Obiit [*He Died*] [*Latin*] (AD)
OBT	Obiit [*He, or She, Died*] [*Latin*]
OBT	Observer Training [*Army*]
obt	Obtained (STED)
OBT	On-Board Trainer [*Navy*] (CAAL)
OBT	Oriental Bank & Trust [*NYSE symbol*] (TTSB)
OBT	Overseas Branch Transfer (AD)
OBT	Sisters Oblates to the Blessed Trinity (TOCD)
OBTA	Oak Bark Tanners' Association (AD)
OBTAINDORSETRANS...	Obtain Endorsement to Transport (DNAB)
OBTD	Obtained
obtd	Obtained (AD)
OBTEX	Offboard Targeting Experiments (GAVI)
OBTG	Obtaining (ROG)
OBTN	Obtain (ROG)
obts	Offender-Based Transaction Statistics (AD)
OBTS	Offender Base Transaction Statistical System [*Department of Justice*] [*Database*] [*Information service or system*] (IID)
OBTS	Organizational Behavior Teaching Society (EA)
OBTVR........	Office for Battlefield Technical Vulnerability Reduction [*Army*] (RDA)
OBTW	Oh, By the Way [*Computer hacker terminology*] (NHD)
OBTX	Object Texture [*Microscopy*]
OBU	Burlington Public Library, Ontario [*Library symbol National Library of Canada*] (NLC)
OBU	Kobuk [*Alaska*] [*Airport symbol*] (OAG)
OBU	Kobuk, AK [*Location identifier FAA*] (FAAL)
OBU	Offshore Banking Unit
OBU	Oklahoma Baptist University
OBU	One Big Union [*A reference to Canada*]
OBU	Operational Base Unit [*British military*] (DMA)
OBU	Operative Bootmakers Union (AD)
OBU	Operative Builders' Union [*British*]
OBU	OSIS [*Ocean Surveillance Information System*] Baseline Upgrade [*Navy*]
OBU	Ouachita Baptist University [*Arkadelphia, AR*] [*Formerly, OBC*]
OBUC..........	Canada Centre for Inland Waters [*Centre Canadien des Eaux Interieures*], Burlington, Ontario [*Library symbol National Library of Canada*] (NLC)
OBUCC........	Canadian Canners Ltd., Burlington, Ontario [*Library symbol National Library of Canada*] (NLC)
OBUFBL.......	Bayfield Laboratory, Ocean Science and Surveys, Fisheries and Oceans Canada [*Laboratoire Bayfield, Science et Leves Oceaniques, Peches et Oceans Canada*] Burlington, Ontario [*Library symbol National Library of Canada*] (NLC)
OBUJB	Joseph Brant Memorial Hospital, Burlington, Ontario [*Library symbol National Library of Canada*] (BIB)
OBUL	Lord Elgin High School, Burlington, Ontario [*Library symbol National Library of Canada*] (NLC)
O Bul	Old Bulgarian (AD)
OBulg.........	Old Bulgarian [*Language*] (BARN)
OBUR.........	Burford Public Library, Ontario [*Library symbol National Library of Canada*] (BIB)
OBur..........	Burton Public Library, Burton, OH [*Library symbol Library of Congress*] (LCLS)
o/bur..........	Oil on Burlap (VRA)

OB-US.........	Obstetrical Ultrasound (STED)
OBUS.........	Obstetric Ultrasound [*Microcomputer system dealing with results of obstetric ultrasound examinations*]
OBUTS........	Organ Builders' United Trade Society [*A union*] [*British*]
OBUV.........	Operative Bakers' Union of Victoria [*Australia*]
OBv..............	Bellevue Public Library, Bellevue, OH [*Library symbol Library of Congress*] (LCLS)
OBV.............	Bobcaygeon Branch, Victoria County Public Library, Ontario [*Library symbol National Library of Canada*] (BIB)
OBV	Obligated Volunteer Officer [*Military*]
OBV	Obstacle Breaching Vehicle [*Military*]
OBV	Obverse
obv..............	Obverse (AD)
obv..............	Obvious (AD)
obv..............	Ocean Boarding Vessel (AD)
OBV	Ocean Boarding Vessel
OBV	Octane Blending Value (PDAA)
obv..............	Octane Blending Value (AD)
OBV	On-Balance Volume [*Measurement devised by stock market technician Joseph Granville*]
OBV	Operation Big Vote (EA)
OBV	Oxidizer Bleed Valve (NASA)
OBVP	Obiit Vita Patris [*He, or She, Died in the Lifetime of His, or Her, Father*] [*Latin*]
obvy............	Obviously (AD)
Obw.............	Oberwerk [*Highest Organ Bank*] [*German*] (AD)
OBW	Oberwerk [*Upper Work*] [*Music*]
OBW	Observation Window
obw.............	Observation Window (AD)
OBW	Oxford Bible Warehouse [*British*] (ROG)
OBWC	Westinghouse Canada, Inc., Burlington, Ontario [*Library symbol National Library of Canada*] (NLC)
OBWO	O-Type Backward-Wave Oscillator (IDOE)
OBX.............	Oslo Stock Exchange [*Norway*] (NUMA)
OBy.............	Old Byblian (BJA)
OBZ.............	Outer Border Zone [*Geology*]
OC...............	Air California [*Air carrier designation symbol*] (AD)
OC...............	Cornwall Public Library, Ontario [*Library symbol National Library of Canada*] (NLC)
OC...............	Degrees Celsius
OC...............	Jersey. Ordres du Conseil [*A publication*] (DLA)
OC...............	Oberlin College (AD)
OC...............	Object Class [*Military*]
O/C..............	Object Classification (NG)
OC...............	Objective Capability
OC...............	Oblate College (AD)
OC...............	Observation Car [*British*]
OC...............	Observer-Controller [*Army*] (INF)
OC...............	Observer Corps [*Became ROC, 1941*] [*British*]
OC...............	Obsessive Compulsive (PAZ)
OC...............	Obstacle Clearance (PDAA)
oc...............	Obstetrical Conjugate [*Medicine*] (AD)
OC...............	Obstetric Conjugate [*Pelvic measurement*] [*Gynecology*]
OC...............	Obstruction Chart
OC...............	Occidental
OC...............	Occidental College (AD)
OC...............	Occipital Cortex [*Brain anatomy*]
OC...............	Occlusocervical [*Dentistry*]
OC...............	Occulentum [*Medicine*] (CPH)
Oc...............	Occulting Light [*Navigation signal*]
OC...............	Occupied [*International telex abbreviation*] (WDMC)
OC...............	Occurs (MDG)
OC...............	Ocean
Oc...............	Ocean (AD)
oc...............	Ocean (AD)
OC...............	Oceanographic Devices [*JETDS nomenclature*] [*Military*] (CET)
O/C..............	O'Clock (ROG)
Oc...............	Octahedral [*Molecular geometry*]
OC...............	October (ADA)
Oc...............	Octyl [*Biochemistry*]
OC...............	Ocular [*Microscopy*]
OC...............	Oculentum [*Eye Ointment*] [*Pharmacy*]
OC...............	Odessa College (AD)
oc...............	Odor Control (AD)
OC...............	Odor Control
OC...............	Oedipus Coloneus [*of Sophocles*] [*Classical studies*] (OCD)
OC...............	Of Course
OC...............	Off-Camera [*Film*] (WDMC)
OC...............	Off Center (WGA)
OC...............	Offensive Center [*Football*]
OC...............	Office Call [*Medicine*]
OC...............	Office Consultation (AD)
OC...............	Office Copy
OC...............	Office of Censorship [*Terminated, 1945*] [*Military*]
OC...............	Office of Compliance [*U.S. Food and Drug Administration*]
OC...............	Office of the Commissioner [*Office of Education*]
OC...............	Office of the Comptroller
O/C..............	Officer Cadet [*British military*] (DMA)
OC...............	Officer Candidate [*Military*]
OC...............	Officer Commanding [*Military*]
OC...............	Officer in Charge (AD)
OC...............	Officer of the Order of Canada
OC...............	Officer, Order of Canada [*Decoration*] (CMD)
OC...............	Officers' Cook
OC...............	Official Circular [*Poor Law Board, etc.*] [*A publication*] (DLA)
OC...............	Official Classification
OC...............	Off-Machine Coated [*Paper*] (DGA)
OC...............	Ohio College (AD)
OC...............	Oil Cooler
o/c..............	Oil on Canvas (VRA)
OC...............	Okolona College (AD)
OC...............	Old Carthusian
OC...............	Old Category Code (NITA)
OC...............	Old Catholic
OC...............	Old Chap [*Amateur radio shorthand*] (WDAA)
O/C..............	Old Charter [*Business and trade*]
OC...............	Old Cheltonian [*British*] (ROG)
OC...............	Old Code [*Louisiana Code of 1808*] [*A publication*] (DLA)
OC...............	Old Crop
OC...............	Oleoresin Capsicum (BARN)
OC...............	Olivet College (AD)
OC...............	Olympic College (AD)
OC...............	On Call (BUR)
oc...............	On Camera (AD)
OC...............	On Camera (WDMC)
OC...............	On Cards
OC...............	On Center [*Technical drawings*]
oc...............	On Center (AD)
OC...............	On-Condition (NASA)
oc...............	On-Condition (NAKS)
OC...............	On Consignment (MHDB)
OC...............	On Course [*Navigation*]
OC...............	Online Chronicle (NITA)
OC...............	Only Child
OC...............	Ope Consilio [*By Aid and Counsel*] [*Latin Legal term*] (DLA)
OC...............	Open Charter [*Business term*]
oc...............	Open Charter
OC...............	Open Chock [*Shipfitting*]
OC...............	Open Circuit
oc...............	Open Circuit (NAKS)
OC...............	Open Circular [*Configuration of DNA*] [*Microbiology*]
O/C..............	Open/Closed [*Mouth*] [*Doll collecting*]
OC...............	Open Collector (IAA)
OC...............	Open College (AIE)
OC...............	Open Contract
O/C..............	Open Cover [*Shipping*]
o/c..............	Open Cover (AD)
oc...............	Open Cup (AD)
OC...............	Open Cup [*Electronics*]
OC...............	Opera-Comique [*Comic Opera*] [*French*] (AD)
OC...............	Opera Company (AD)
OC...............	Operating Characteristic
OC...............	Operating Coil (IAA)
OC...............	Operating Company
OC...............	Operating Curve (NRCH)
OC...............	Operational Capability (AAG)
OC...............	Operational Check (MCD)
OC...............	Operational Computer (IEEE)
OC...............	Operation Code (IAA)
OC...............	Operation CORK [*Joan B. Kroc Foundation*] [*CORK is derived from the foundation name*] [*Defunct*] (EA)
OC...............	Operation Crossroads [*Atomic weapons testing*]
OC...............	Operations Center [*Military*]
OC...............	Operations Chief [*Deep Space Network, NASA*]
OC...............	Operations Conductor (MUGU)
OC...............	Operations Control
O/C..............	Operations Critical (MCD)
OC...............	Operator Circuit [*Telecommunications*] (IAA)
OC...............	Operator Command (NITA)
OC...............	Opere Citato [*In the Work Cited*] [*Latin*] (WDAA)
OC...............	Opportunity Cost (MHDB)
OC...............	Optical Cavity [*LASER technology*] (EECA)
OC...............	Optic Chiasm [*Anatomy*]
OC...............	Optometric Corp. (AD)
OC...............	Oral Care [*Denistry*] (DAVI)
oc...............	Oral Contraceptive [*Medicine*] (AD)
OC...............	Oral Contraceptive [*Endocrinology*]
OC...............	Orbital Check (MCD)
oc...............	Orbital Check [*NASA*] (NAKS)
OC...............	Order Canceled
OC...............	Order Card
OC...............	Order in Council [*A publication*] (DLA)
OC...............	Orderly Corporal [*British*]
OC...............	Order of Cistercians [*Roman Catholic religious order*]
OC...............	Ordinary Capital Account [*Inter-American Development Bank*]
OC...............	Ordinary Chondrite [*A type of meteorite*]
OC...............	Ordnance Chart (MCD)
OC...............	Ordnance College [*Military British*] (ROG)
OC...............	Ordo Charitatis [*Fathers of the Order of Charity*] [*Roman Catholic religious order*]
OC...............	Organic Carbon
OC...............	Organizational Chart
o/c..............	Organized Crime (AD)
OC...............	Organochlorine [*Also, OCL*] [*Organic chemistry*]
OC...............	Organo Corale [*Choir Organ*] [*Latin*] (AD)
OC...............	Organ of Consultation
OC...............	Oriel College (AD)
OC...............	Oriens Christianus [*A publication*] (ODCC)
OC...............	Original Claim (MAE)
OC...............	Original Cosmopolitans [*Defunct*] (EA)

OC .... Original Cover
OC .... Orion Capital [*NYSE symbol*] (TTSB)
OC .... Orion Capital Corp. [*NYSE symbol*] (SPSG)
OC .... Orlando College (AD)
OC .... Orphans' Court (DLA)
OC .... Osteocalcin [*Biochemistry*]
OC .... Osteochondritis (DB)
OC .... Otero College (AD)
OC .... Oudh Cases [*India*] [*A publication*] (DLA)
OC .... Out Cold [*Slang*]
OC .... Outer Canthus (DB)
OC .... Outflow Channels [*A filamentary mark on Mars*]
OC .... Outing Club
OC .... Outlet Contact
O/C .... Out of Charge [*Customs*]
OC .... Output Computer
OC .... Outside Circumference (MSA)
OC .... Outsiders Club (EAIO)
O/C .... Overcharge
o/c .... Overcharge (AD)
OC .... Overcurrent
oc .... Overcurrent (NAKS)
oc .... Overdraft Charge [*Banking*] (AD)
OC .... Overseas Chinese (AD)
OC .... Overseas Commands [*Air Force*]
OC .... Overseas Country (ODBW)
O/C .... Over-the-Counter [*Also, OTC*] [*Stock exchange term*]
OC .... Over-the-Horizon Compressed (MCD)
OC .... Oxidation Catalyst [*Automotive engineering*]
OC .... Oxygen Consumed
OC .... Oxygen Cutting [*Welding*]
OC .... Public Library of Cincinnati and Hamilton County, Cincinnati, OH [*Library symbol Library of Congress*] (LCLS)
OC-5 .... Organizing Committee for a Fifth Estate (AD)
OCA .... Aeroservicios Carabobo CA (ASERCA) [*Venzuela*] [*ICAO designator*] (FAAC)
OCA .... Campbellford Branch, Northumberland County Public Library, Ontario [*Library symbol National Library of Canada*] (NLC)
OCA .... Carmelite Vietnamese of Our Lady of Mt. Carmel (TOCD)
OCA .... Cincinnati Art Museum, Cincinnati, OH [*Library symbol Library of Congress*] (LCLS)
OCA .... Creighton University, Alumni Library, Omaha, NE [*OCLC symbol*] (OCLC)
OCA .... Observatoire de la Cote d'Azur [*France*]
OCA .... Obsessive-Compulsive Anonymous (EA)
OCA .... Obstacle Clearance Altitude [*Aviation*] (DA)
oca .... Ocarina (AD)
OCA .... Ocean Control Authority
OCA .... Oceanic Control Area [*ICAO*]
OCA .... Ocean Reef Club [*Florida*] [*Airport symbol*] (OAG)
OCA .... Oceans and Coastal Areas
OCA .... Oculocutaneous Albinism [*Medicine*] (DAVI)
OCA .... Offensive Counterair [*Army*] (ADDR)
OCA .... Office, Comptroller of the Army
OCA .... Office of Competitive Assessment [*Department of Commerce*]
OCA .... Office of Computing Activities [*Later, DCR*] [*National Science Foundation*]
OCA .... Office of Congressional Affairs [*Energy Research and Development Administration*]
OCA .... Office of Consumer Advisor [*USDA*]
OCA .... Office of Consumer Affairs [*US Postal Service ombudsman*]
OCA .... Office of the City Attorney (AD)
OCA .... Office of the Community Advocate [*Australian Capital Territory*]
OCA .... Officers' Caterer [*Navy British*]
OCA .... Ohio College Association (AD)
OCA .... Ohio Courts of Appeals Reports [*A publication*] (DLA)
OCA .... Oil Company of Australia (AD)
OCA .... Old Comrades Association [*British military*] (DMA)
OCA .... Oldsmobile Club of America (EA)
OCA .... Olivopontocerebellar Atrophy [*Medicine*] (DMAA)
OCA .... Olympic Council of Asia [*Hawaii, Kuwait*] (EAIO)
OCA .... Oncovin [*Vincristine*] Cyclophosphamide, Adriamycin [*Doxorubicin*] [*Antineoplastic drug regimen*] (DAVI)
OCA .... Ontario College of Agriculture
OCA .... Ontario College of Art
OCA .... Opencast Coal Act [*Town planning*] [*British*]
OCA .... Open College of Arts [*British*]
OCA .... Open Communication Architecture (CIST)
OCA .... Open Communications Architecture (AD)
OCA .... Operational Control Authority [*NATO*]
OCA .... Operation Crossroads Africa (EA)
OCA .... Oral Contraceptive Agent [*Endocrinology*]
OCA .... Order of the Crown in America [*Later, TOCA*] (EA)
OCA .... Oregon Corrections Association (AD)
OCA .... Organisation Combat Anarchiste [*Anarchist Combat Organization*] [*France Political party*] (PPW)
OCA .... Organizacion de las Cooperativas de America [*Organization of the Cooperatives of America - OCA*] (EAIO)
OCA .... Organization of Chinese Americans (EA)
OCA .... [*The*] Orthodox Church of America
OCA .... Osteopathic Cranial Association [*Later, CA*]
OCA .... Otterhound Club of America (EA)
OCA .... Outstanding Claims Advance [*Insurance*] (AIA)
OCA .... Oxychloride Cement Association [*Defunct*]
OCAA .... Oklahoma City-Ada-Atoka Railway Co. [*AAR code*]

OCAA .... Organization of Central American Armies (AD)
OCAAF .... Order of the Chief of the Army Air Forces
OCAAR .... Occupational Accidents Analysis and Reporting
OCAB .... Cannington Branch, Brock Township Public Library, Ontario [*Library symbol National Library of Canada*] (BIB)
OCAB .... Overseas Correspondents Association Bangladesh (BUAC)
OCAC .... Ocean Acre Project [*Marine science*] (MSC)
OCAC .... Office of the Chief of Air Corps [*World War II*]
OCAC .... Officer Commanding Administrative Centre [*World War I*] [*British*]
OCAC .... Operations, Control, and Analysis Center (DOMA)
OCad .... Cadiz Public Library, Cadiz, OH [*Library symbol Library of Congress*] (LCLS)
OCAD .... Occlusive Cartoid Artery Disease [*Medicine*] (DMAA)
OCAD .... Orcad, Inc. [*NASDAQ symbol*] (SAG)
OCADA .... Office of the Chief, Air Defense Artillery
OCADS .... Oklahoma City Air Defense Sector (SAA)
OCAE .... United States Army Engineer Division, Ohio River, Technical Library, Cincinnati,OH [*Library symbol Library of Congress*] (LCLS)
OCAF .... Office, Chief of Aerospace (SAA)
OCAF .... Oklahomans for Children and Families
OCAFF .... Office, Chief of Army Field Forces
OCAI .... Orthodontic Centers of Amer [*NASDAQ symbol*] (TTSB)
OCAI .... Orthodontic Centers of America, Inc. [*NASDAQ symbol*] (SAG)
OCAJ .... American Jewish Periodical Center, Cincinnati, OH [*Library symbol Library of Congress*] (LCLS)
OCAJA .... American Jewish Archives, Cincinnati, OH [*Library symbol Library of Congress*] (LCLS)
OCal .... Caldwell Public Library, Caldwell, OH [*Library symbol Library of Congress*] (LCLS)
OCAL .... Ocal, Inc. [*NASDAQ symbol*] (SAG)
Ocal .... Ocal, Inc. [*Associated Press*] (SAG)
Ocal .... Octo Archives, Inc., Laurel, MD [*Library symbol*] [*Library of Congress*] (LCLS)
ocal .... On-Line Cryptanalytic Aid Language [*Computer science*] (AD)
OCAL .... Online Cryptanalytic Aid Language [*Computer science*]
OCAL .... Organization of Communist Action in Lebanon (PD)
OCAL .... Overseas Containers of Australia, Ltd. (AD)
OCAL .... [*The*] Oxford Companion to American Literature [*A publication*]
OCALC .... Oklahoma City Air Logistic Center [*Formerly, OCAMA*] (MCD)
O'Callaghan New Neth... O'Callaghan's History of New Netherland [*A publication*] (DLA)
OCAM .... Common Organization of African, Malagasy, and Mauritian States (EBF)
OCAM .... Office, Computing, and Accounting Machinery
OCAM .... Organisation Commune Africaine et Mauricienne [*African and Mauritian Common Organization*] [*Formerly, Organisation Commune Africaine et Malgache*]
OCAMA .... Oklahoma City Air Materiel Area [*Later, OCALC*]
OCAMA-SED... Oklahoma City Air Materiel Area [*later, OCALC*] Service Engineering Division
OCamd .... Preble County District Library, Camden Branch, Camden, OH [*Library symbol Library of Congress*] (LCLS)
OCAMM .... Organisation Commune Africaine, Malgache, et Mauricienne [*African, Malagasy, and Mauritian Common Organization*] [*Formerly, Organisation Commune Africaine et Malgache Later, OCAM*]
OCan .... Canton Public Library Association, Canton, OH [*Library symbol Library of Congress*] (LCLS)
OCAN .... Officer Candidate Airman
OC & E .... Oregon, California, and Eastern Railroad (AD)
OC & R .... Operations, Commitments, and Requirements [*Military*]
OC & S .... Ordnance Center and School [*Army*] (RDA)
OCanK .... Kent State University, Stark County Regional Campus, Canton, OH [*Library symbol Library of Congress*] (LCLS)
OCanM .... Malone College, Canton, OH [*Library symbol Library of Congress*] (LCLS)
OCanS .... Stark County District Library, Canton, OH [*Library symbol Library of Congress*] (LCLS)
OCanW .... Walsh College, Canton, OH [*Library symbol Library of Congress*] (LCLS)
OCAO .... Athenaeum of Ohio, Eugene H. Maly Library, Cincinnati, OH [*Library symbol*] [*Library of Congress*] (LCLS)
OCAP .... Capreol Public Library, Ontario [*Library symbol National Library of Canada*] (NLC)
OCAP .... Open Channel Air Preheater [*Heat exchanger*]
OCAPO .... Office of Compliance Analysis and Program Operations [*Environmental Protection Agency*] (GFGA)
OCAQ .... Ordre de Comptables Agrees du Quebec [*Canada*] (DD)
OCAR .... Cargill Branch, Bruce County Public Library, Ontario [*Library symbol National Library of Canada*] (NLC)
OCAR .... Office of the Chief, Army Reserve (AABC)
OCARD .... Cardinal Public Library, Ontario [*Library symbol National Library of Canada*] (BIB)
OCareyS ...... Our Lady of Carey Seminary, Carey, OH [*Library symbol Library of Congress*] (LCLS)
OCarm .... Calced Carmelites (TOCD)
OCarm .... Carmelite Fathers and Brothers (TOCD)
ocarm .... Carmelite Fathers and Brothers (TOCD)
OCarm .... Carmelite Nuns of the Ancient Observance (TOCD)
OCarm .... Carmelite Sisters (Corpus Christi) (TOCD)
OCarm .... Carmelite Sisters for Aged and Infirm (TOCD)
OCarm .... Congregation of Our Lady of Mount Carmel (TOCD)
OCarm .... Institute of the Sisters of Our Lady of Mt. Carmel (TOCD)
OCARM .... Order of Brothers of the Blessed Virgin Mary of Mount Carmel [*Rome, Italy*] (EAIO)

OCART .... Cartier Public Library, Ontario [*Library symbol National Library of Canada*] (NLC)
OCart .... Order of Carthusians [*Roman Catholic religious order*]
ocart .... Order of Carthusians (TOCD)
OCartSC ...... Saint Charles Seminary, Carthagena, OH [*Library symbol Library of Congress*] (LCLS)
OCAS .... Office, Coordinator of Army Studies (AABC)
OCAS .... Office of Carrier Accounts and Statistics [*of CAB*]
OCAS .... Office of Civil Aviation Security (AD)
OCAS .... Office of the Chief of Air Service [*World War II*]
OCAS .... Officer-in-Charge of Armament Supply
OCAS .... Ohio Casualty [*NASDAQ symbol*] (TTSB)
OCAS .... Ohio Casualty Corp. [*NASDAQ symbol*] (NQ)
OCAS .... Ohio College of Applied Science
OCAS .... Online Cryptanalytic Aid System [*Computer science*] (IEEE)
OCAS .... Ordnance Configuration Accounting System [*Navy*]
OCAS .... Organization of Central American States [*See also ODECA*] [*San Salvador, El Salvador*] (EAIO)
OCAS .... Out of Controlled Airspace [*Aviation*] (FAAC)
OCASA .... Overseas Chinese Association of South Australia
O Cat .... Old Catalan (AD)
OCAT .... Optometric College Aptitude Test (WDAA)
OCAT .... Optometry College Admissions Test (WDAA)
OCATOUR ... Office National Centrafricain du Tourisme (EY)
OCAU .... Observation, Classification, and Allocation Unit (WDAA)
OCAW .... Oil, Chemical, and Atomic Workers (AD)
OCAW .... Oil, Chemical, and Atomic Workers International Union (EA)
OCAW .... Organization of Chinese American Women (EA)
OCB .... Cache Bay Public Library, Ontario [*Library symbol National Library of Canada*] (NLC)
OCB .... Cincinnati Bible Seminary, Cincinnati, OH [*Library symbol Library of Congress*] (LCLS)
OCB .... Officer Career Brief [*Resume*] [*Military*]
OCB .... Officers' Cadet Battalion [*British*]
OCB .... Off-Machine Coated Board [*Paper*] (DGA)
OCB .... Offshore Certification Bureau [*British*] (CB)
OCB .... Oil [*Operated*] Circuit Breaker
ocb .... Oil Circuit Breaker (AD)
OCB .... Oil Collection Basin (NRCH)
OCB .... Oil Control Board [*British*]
OCB .... Operations Coordinating Board [*Terminated, 1961*] [*National Security Council*]
OCB .... Outgoing Calls Barred [*Telecommunications*] (TEL)
OCB .... Output Current Booster
OCB .... Override Control BITS [*Binary Digits*] [*Computer science*]
OCB .... Over-the-Counter Batch [*Stock exchange term*] (MHDW)
OCBA .... Ortho-Chlorobenzoic Acid [*Organic chemistry*]
OCBC .... Ortho-Chlorobenzyl Chloride [*Organic chemistry*]
OCBC .... Overseas Chinese Banking Corp. (AD)
OCBF .... Outer Cortical Blood-Flow [*Medicine*] (DB)
OCBH .... Bethesda Base Hospital, Information Resource Center, Cincinnati, OH [*Library symbol Library of Congress*] (LCLS)
OC/B/L .... Ocean Bill of Lading [*Shipping*]
oc b/l .... Ocean Bill of Lading (AD)
OCBN .... Ortho-Chlorobenzonitrile [*Organic chemistry*]
OCBOA .... Other Comprehensive Bases of Accounting (ADA)
OCBR .... Other than Cost Base Review [*DoD*]
OCBR .... Output Channel Buffer Register [*Computer science*] (IAA)
OCB(S) .... Oil Control Board, Supply [*British*]
OCC .... CARSTAB Corp., Research Library, Cincinnati, OH [*Library symbol Library of Congress*] (LCLS)
OCC .... Coca [*Ecuador*] [*Airport symbol*] (OAG)
OCC .... Object-Centered Coordinate (DMAA)
OCC .... Object Class Code [*Military*] (AFM)
OCC .... Occasionally
occ .... Occasionally (AD)
occ .... Occipital [*or Occiput*] [*Anatomy*] (MAE)
OCC .... Occluded Corrosion Cell (PDAA)
OCC .... Occlusion
OCC .... Occultation [*Astronomy*]
Occ .... Occulting (AD)
OCC .... Occulting Light [*Navigation signal*]
OCC .... Occupation (AFM)
occ .... Occupation (AD)
OCC .... Occupied (IAA)
OCC .... Occupied Command Center [*Military*]
OCC .... Occurrence
Occ .... Occurs (ILCA)
OCC .... Ocean City College [*Maryland*]
OCC .... Ocean Coordinating Committee [*IEEE*] (MSC)
OCC .... Ocean Cruising Club [*British*] (DI)
OCC .... Oceanic Control Center (OA)
OCC .... OCLC [*Online Computer Library Center*] Library, Columbus, OH [*OCLC symbol*] (OCLC)
OCC .... Octagon Car Club [*Later, MOCC*] (EAIO)
OCC .... Octal Correction Cards [*Computer science*]
OCC .... Ocutech Canada [*Vancouver Stock Exchange symbol*]
OCC .... Office of Cancer Communications [*Department of Health and Human Services*] (GFGA)
OCC .... Office of Chemical Control (COE)
occ .... Office of Contract Compliance (NAKS)
OCC .... Office of Contract Compliance [*NASA*] (NASA)
OCC .... Office of the Chief Counsel [*U.S. Food and Drug Administration*]
OCC .... Office of the Comptroller of the Currency [*Department of the Treasury*]

OCC .... Office of the Director of Command, Control, and Communications [*Air Force*]
OCC .... Officers' Chief Cook
OCC .... Official Custodian of Charities [*British*]
OCC .... Offshore Construction Council (BUAC)
OCC .... Offshore Craft Conference (BUAC)
OCC .... Offsite Coordination Center [*Environmental science*] (COE)
OCC .... Ohio Circuit Reports [*or Decisions*] [*A publication*] (DLA)
OCC .... Ohio College of Chiropody
OCC .... Ohio Conservation Consortium [*Library network*]
OCC .... Oklahoma Crime Commission (AD)
OCC .... Old Corrugated Container [*Paper recycling*]
OCC .... Olney Communication College (AD)
OCC .... Olympic Committee Congress
OCC .... Omnibus Crime Control and Safe Streets Act [*1968*]
OCC .... Onondaga Community College (AD)
OCC .... Open Channel Cooperative
OCC .... Open Circuit Characteristic (IAA)
OCC .... Operating Characteristics Curve
OCC .... Operational Computer Complex (KSC)
OCC .... Operations Control Center [*or Console*] (AFM)
occ .... Operations Control Center (NAKS)
OCC .... Operator Control Command (BUR)
OCC .... Operator Control Console [*Canadian Navy*]
OCC .... Operator's Computer Console
OCC .... Oppenheimer Capital Ltd. [*NYSE symbol*] (SPSG)
OCC .... Oppenheimer Cap L.P. [*NYSE symbol*] (TTSB)
OCC .... Optical Circuit and Component (NITA)
OCC .... Option Clearing Corp.
OCC .... Oral Cholecystography [*Medicine*] (DMAA)
OCC .... Oral Contraceptive Council [*Defunct*] (EA)
OCC .... Orange Carpet Crowd [*An association*]
OCC .... Orange Coast College [*Formerly, OCJC*] [*Costa Mesa, CA*]
OCC .... Order of Calced Carmelites [*Roman Catholic religious order*] (DICI)
OCC .... Ordnance Command Converter [*Military*] (IAA)
OCC .... Ordo Carmelitarum Calceatorum [*Carmelites*] [*Roman Catholic religious order*]
OCC .... Organic Carbon Cycle
OCC .... Organic Consultative Committee [*Victoria, Australia*]
OCC .... Organisation Combat Communiste [*Communist Combat Organization*] [*France Political party*] (PPW)
OCC .... Osborne Computer Corporation (NITA)
OCC .... Other Common Carrier [*Telecommunications*]
OCC .... Other Communications Company
OCC .... Outer Critics Circle (EA)
OCC .... Output Circuit Check [*Electronics*]
OCCA .... Ocean Cargo Clearance Authority (DOMA)
OCCA .... Office, Chief of Civil Affairs
OCCA .... Officer-in-Charge of Civilian Affairs [*in newly occupied countries*] [*Army World War II*]
OCCA .... Oil and Colour Chemists' Association
OCCA .... Omnibus Crime Control Act of 1970 (OICC)
OCCA .... Organized Crime Control Act of 1970
OCCAC .... Ohio Community College Athletic Conference (PSS)
OCCAS .... Occasional
occas .... Occasional (AD)
Occas .... Occasional Light [*Navigation signal*]
OCCASL ...... Occasional
OCCB .... Operational Configuration Control Board (AFM)
OCCB .... Organized Crime Control Bureau (LAIN)
OCC-BL .... Occult Blood [*Medicine*] (DAVI)
OCCBP .... Organization for Collectors of Covered Bridge Postcards (EA)
OCCC .... Oil Control Coordination Committee (AD)
OCCC .... Oocyte-Corona-Cumulus Complex
OCCC .... Open Chest Cardiac Compression [*Cardiology*] (DAVI)
OCCC .... Orange County Community College (AD)
OCCC .... Organized Crime-Control Commission [*California*] (AD)
OCCCA .... Office of Congressional, Community, and Consumer Affairs
OCCCE .... Organization for Coordination and Cooperation in the Control of Major Endemic Diseases
Oc C Cm O... Office of the Chief Chemical Officer (AD)
OCCD .... Com Dev Ltd., Cambridge, Ontario [*Library symbol National Library of Canada*] (NLC)
occd .... Occupied (AD)
OCCDC .... Oregon Coastal Conservation and Development Commission (AD)
OCC-E .... Office of the Chief of Communications-Electronics [*Army*] (AABC)
OCCE .... Oklahoma Citizen's Commission on Education (EDAC)
OCCEDCA .... Organization for Co-Ordination in Control of Endemic Diseases in Central Africa (EA)
OCCF .... Oklahoma City Community Foundation (AD)
OCCF .... Operator Communication and Control Facility [*IBM Corp.*]
OCCF .... Optical Cable [*NASDAQ symbol*] (TTSB)
OCCF .... Optical Cable Corp. [*NASDAQ symbol*] (SAG)
OCCGE .... Organisation de Coordination et de Cooperation pour la Lutte Contre les Grandes Endemies [*Organization for Co-Ordination and Co-Operation in the Control of Major Endemic Diseases*] (EAIO)
OCCGERMDL... Army of Occupation of Germany Medal [*Military decoration*]
OCCH .... Children's Hospital Research Foundation, Research Library, Cincinnati, OH [*Library symbol Library of Congress*] (LCLS)
OCCH .... Office, Chief of Chaplains [*Formerly, OC of Ch*] [*Army*] (AABC)
Occ Heal ANZ.. Occupational Health Australia and New Zealand [*A publication*]
OCCI .... Optical Coincidence Coordinate Indexing (PDAA)
Occidental C... Occidental College (GAGS)
OCCIM .... Christ Hospital Institute of Medical Research, Research Library, Cincinnati, OH [*Library symbol Library of Congress*] (LCLS)

OCCIN.......... Process Technology Department, Inco Ltd., Copper Cliff, Ontario [*Library symbol National Library of Canada*] (BIB)
occip.......... Occipital (AD)
OCCIP.......... Occiput [*Anatomy*] (WDAA)
OcciPet.......... Occidental Petroleum Corp. [*Associated Press*] (SAG)
OcciPt.......... Occidental Petroleum Corp. [*Associated Press*] (SAG)
OCCIS.......... Operational Command and Control Intelligence System [*Army*] (AABC)
OCCIS.......... Operations Command and Control Information System [*Military*]
occl.......... Occlude (AD)
OCCL.......... Ontario Community College Librarians [*Canada*] (AD)
OCCM.......... Office of Commercial Communications Management (AFM)
OCCM.......... Open Chest Cardiac Massage [*Cardiology*] (DAVI)
OCCM.......... Optical Counter-Countermeasures
OCCMDL.......... Army of Occupation Medal [*Military decoration*]
OCCMED.......... Occupational Medicine (AABC)
OCCMH.......... Cambridge Memorial Hospital, Ontario [*Library symbol National Library of Canada*] (BIB)
OCCMLC.......... Office, Chief, Chemical Corps [*Army*]
OCCMLO.......... Office of the Chief Chemical Officer [*Military*]
OCCMS.......... Occupational Measurement Squadron [*Air Force*]
OCCN.......... Occasion
Occ N.......... Occasional Notes, Canada Law Times [*A publication*] (DLA)
Occ Newsl .. Occasional Newsletter [*American Bar Association, Committee on Environmental Law*] [*A publication*] (ILCA)
OCC NS.......... Ohio Circuit Court Reports, New Series [*A publication*] (DLA)
OCCO.......... Office Canadien de Commercialisation des Oeufs
OCCO.......... Office of the Chief Chemical Officer [*Military*] (AAG)
OCCP.......... Octachlorocyclopentene [*Organic chemistry*]
OCCP.......... Outside Communications Cable Plant (CET)
Occ Pap Univ NSW... University of New South Wales. Occasional Papers [*A publication*]
OCCPR.......... Open-Chest Cardiopulmonary Resuscitation
OCCR.......... Cramahe Township Public Library, Castleton, Ontario [*Library symbol National Library of Canada*] (BIB)
OCCR.......... Overseas Custody (Child Removal)
OCCS.......... Oce Copy Control System (NITA)
OCCS.......... Office of Combined Chiefs of Staff [*World War II*]
OCCS.......... Office of Computer and Communication Systems (NITA)
OCCS.......... Officer Career Counseling System [*Army*] (RDA)
OCCS.......... Operational Command and Control System [*Army*] (AABC)
OCCS.......... Optical Contrast Contour Seeker
OCCSA.......... Ordnance and Chemical Center and School [*Army*] (MCD)
OCCSA.......... Ohio Correctional and Court Services Association (AD)
OCCSPEC.......... Occupational Specialities [*A publication*] (DNAB)
OCCT.......... Collingwood Township Public Library, Clarksburg, Ontario [*Library symbol National Library of Canada*] (NLC)
occ th.......... Occupational Therapy (AD)
OccTh.......... Occupational Therapy [*or Therapist*] (DAVI)
OccuHlt.......... Occupational Health & Rehabilitation, Inc. [*Associated Press*] (SAG)
OCCULT.......... Optical Covert Communications Using LASER Transceivers (MCD)
OCCULT.......... Ordered Computer Collation of Unprepared Literary Texts
occup.......... Occupation (AD)
OCCUP.......... Occupational
OCCUPON.......... Occupation (ROG)
OCCUPTN.......... Occupation
OCCUPTNL... Occupational
OccuSys.......... OccuSystems, Inc. [*Associated Press*] (SAG)
OCCWC.......... Office of Chief of Counsel, War Crimes [*Allied German Occupation Forces*]
OCD.......... Carmelitas del Sagrado Corazon (TOCD)
OCD.......... Carmelite Sisters of the Most Sacred Heart of Los Angeles (TOCD)
OCD.......... Discalced Carmelite Fathers (TOCD)
ocd.......... Discalced Carmelite Friars (TOCD)
OCD.......... Discalced Carmelite Nuns (TOCD)
OCD.......... Obsessive-Compulsive Disorder [*Psychology*]
ocd.......... Obsessive Compulsive Disorder [*Medicine*] (AD)
OCD.......... Occupation Centres for Defectives [*British*]
OCD.......... Ocean Chemistry Division [*Atlantic Oceanographic and Meteorological Laboratory*] (USDC)
OCD.......... Office of Child Development [*HEW*]
OCD.......... Office of Civil Defense
OCD.......... Office of Civilian Defense [*Within Office of Emergency Management*] [*World War II*]
OCD.......... Office of Community Development [*HUD*]
OCD.......... Office of the Center Director [*U.S. Food and Drug Admistration*]
OCD.......... Offshore and Coastal Dispersion (GNE)
OCD.......... Ohio Circuit Court Decisions [*A publication*] (DLA)
OCD.......... Online Communications Drive [*or Driver*] [*Computer science*] (WDAA)
ocd.......... On-Line Communications Driver [*Computer science*] (AD)
ocd.......... Operational Capability Date (AD)
OCD.......... Operational Capability Date (AAG)
OCD.......... Operational Capability Demonstration (AAGC)
OCD.......... Operational Capability Development
OCD.......... Operational Concept Document
OCD.......... Operations Concept Document
ocd.......... Optical Character Definition [*Computer science*] (AD)
OCD.......... Ordnance Classification of Defects [*Navy*]
OCD.......... Ordo Carmelitarum Discalceatorum [*Order of Discalced, or Barefoot, Carmelites*] [*Roman Catholic religious order*]
OCD.......... Osteochondritis Dissecans [*Medicine*]
OCD.......... Other Checkable Deposits [*Federal Reserve system*] (GFGA)
O/C/D.......... Out of Collector's District [*Bookselling*] (ROG)
OCD.......... Ovarian Cholesterol Depletion [*Test*]
ocd.......... Ovarian Cholesterol Depletion [*Medicine*] (AD)

OCD.......... Overhaul Consumption Data
OCD.......... [*The*] Oxford Classical Dictionary [*A publication*] (ODCC)
OCD.......... Oxygen Cost Diagram (DMAA)
o/cdbd.......... Oil on Cardboard (VRA)
OCDD.......... Octachlorodibenzodioxin [*Organic chemistry*]
OCDD.......... On-Line Call Detail Delivery [*AT&T*] (CIST)
OCDE.......... Organisation de Cooperation et de Developpement Economiques [*Organization for Economic Cooperation and Development - OECD*] [*France*] (EAIO)
OCDE.......... Organizacion de Cooperacion y Desarrollo Economicos [*Organization for Economic Cooperation and Development - OECD*] [*Spain*] (MSC)
OCDETF.......... Organized Crime Drug Enforcement Task Force
OCDF.......... Operations Control and Display Facility [*Military*] (RDA)
OCDM.......... Office of Civil and Defense Mobilization [*Merged with Office of Emergency Planning*]
OCDM.......... Offshore and Coastal Dispersion Model [*Environmental science*] (COE)
OCDMS.......... On-Board Checkout and Data Management System (MCD)
OCDN.......... Order for Correction of Defect of Nonconformance
OCDQ.......... Organizational Climate Description Questionnaire
OCDr.......... Drackett Co., Research and Development Library, Cincinnati, OH [*Library symbol Library of Congress*] (LCLS)
OCDR.......... Office of Collateral Development Responsibility (AFM)
OCDR.......... Officer Control Distribution Report
OCDR.......... Orbiter Critical Design Review [*NASA*] (NASA)
OCDRE.......... Organic-Cooled Deuterium Reactor Experiment [*Nuclear energy*]
OCDS.......... Overseas College of Defence Studies [*British*]
OCDS.......... Secular Order of Discalced Carmelites [*Rome, Italy*] (EAIO)
O/CDT.......... Officer Cadet [*Military*] (WDAA)
O/Cdt.......... Officer-Cadet (AD)
OCDU.......... Optics Coupling Data [*or Display*] Unit [*Guidance and navigation*] (KSC)
OCE.......... Edgecliff College, Cincinnati, OH [*Library symbol Library of Congress*] (LCLS)
OCE.......... Helicocean [*France ICAO designator*] (FAAC)
OCE.......... Ocean City [*Maryland*] [*Airport symbol*] (OAG)
OCE.......... Ocean Color Experiment [*NASA*]
OCE.......... Ocean Covered Earth (OA)
Oce.......... Oceanic [*Record label*]
OCE.......... Odessa Commodity Exchange [*Ukraine*] (EY)
OCE.......... Office, Chief of Engineers [*Army*]
OCE.......... Office of Career Education [*Office of Education*]
OCE.......... Office of Coastal Environment [*National Oceanic and Atmospheric Administration*]
OCE.......... Office of Criminal Enforcement [*Environmental Protection Agency*] (EPA)
OCE.......... Office of Cultural Exchange [*Department of State*]
OCE.......... Office of the Chief Economist (AAGC)
OCE.......... Office of the Director of Civil Engineering [*Air Force*]
OCE.......... Officer Commanding Exercises [*Military*]
OCE.......... Officer Conducting the Exercise [*Navy, Coast Guard*] [*Military*]
OCE.......... Officer Corps Engineers
OCE.......... Omega Chi Epsilon [*Honor society*] (EA)
OCE.......... OMGUS [*Office of Military Government, United States*] Civilian Employees Association [*Post-World War II, Germany*]
OCE.......... Ontario College of Education
OCE.......... Open Collaborative Environment [*Apple Computer, Inc.*]
oce.......... Operational Control Equipment (AD)
OCE.......... Oregon, California & Eastern Railway Co. [*AAR code*]
OCE.......... Oregon College of Education
OCE.......... Organizational Climate Exercise II [*Test*] (TMMY)
OCE.......... Oscillating Current Element
OCE.......... Other Controllable Expenses (MEDA)
OCEA.......... Outstanding Civil Engineering Achievement [*Award*] [*American Society of Civil Engineers*]
OCEAC.......... Organisation de Coordination pour la Lutte Contre les Endemies en Afrique Centrale [*Organization for Co-Ordination in Control of Endemic Diseases in Central Africa - OCCEDCA*] (EAIO)
OCEAN.......... Oceanographic Coordination, Evaluation, and Analysis Network
OCEAN.......... Organisation de la Communaute Europeenne des Avitailleurs des Navires [*Ship Suppliers' Organization of the European Community - SSOEC*] [*Hague, Netherlands*] (EAIO)
OCEANAV.......... Naval Oceanography Command [*Marine science*] (MSC)
OCEANAV.......... Oceanographer of the Navy
OCEANAVINST... Naval Oceanographic Office Instruction
OceanB.......... Ocean Bio-Chem, Inc. [*Associated Press*] (SAG)
OCEANDEVRON... Oceanographic Development Squadron [*Navy*] (DNAB)
Ocean E.......... Ocean Engineer (PGP)
Oceaner.......... Oceaneering International, Inc. [*Associated Press*] (SAG)
OceanF.......... Ocean Financial Corp. [*Associated Press*] (SAG)
OCEANIC.......... Ocean Network Information Center [*Information service or system*] (IID)
Ocean Inst ... Oceanografiska Institute [*Oceanographic Institute*] [*Goeteborg, Sweden*] (AD)
OCEANLANT... Ocean Subarea (Atlantic) [*NATO*] (NATG)
Ocean Man... Ocean Management [*A publication*] (ILCA)
oceano.......... Oceanologist (AD)
oceanog.......... Oceanography (AD)
OCEANOG.......... Oceanography
OceanOpt.......... Ocean Optique Distributors, Inc. [*Associated Press*] (SAG)
OCEANS.......... Omnibus Conference on Experimental Aspects of NMR [*Nuclear Magnetic Resonance*] Spectroscopy (MUGU)
OCEANSYSLANT... Ocean Systems, Atlantic
OCEANSYSPAC... Ocean Systems, Pacific

OCED .... Office of Comprehensive Employment Development [*Department of Labor*]

OCED .... Organization for Economic Co-Operation and Development (WPI)

OCedC .... Cedarville College, Cedarville, OH [*Library symbol Library of Congress*] (LCLS)

OCEFT .... Corbeil Branch, East Ferris Township Public Library, Ontario [*Library symbol National Library of Canada*] (NLC)

OCEI .... Ocean Construction Equipment Inventory (DNAB)

OCel .... Dwyer-Mercer County District Library, Celina, OH [*Library symbol Library of Congress*] (LCLS)

OCEL .... Optical Coating Evaluation Laboratory (AD)

OCEL .... Oxford Companion to English Literature [*A publication*] (AD)

OCELAC .... Camden East Branch, Lennox and Addington County Library, Ontario [*Library symbol National Library of Canada*] (NLC)

OCEleC .... Cincinnati Electronics Corporation, Cincinnati, OH [*Library symbol Library of Congress*] (LCLS)

O Celt .... Old Celtic (AD)

OCEml .... Emery Industries, Inc., Research Library, Cincinnati, OH [*Library symbol Library of Congress*] (LCLS)

OCEN .... Oce-Van der Grinten NV [*Netherlands NASDAQ symbol*]

OCENY .... Oce-van der Grinten ADR [*NASDAQ symbol*] (TTSB)

Oce-NY .... Oce-Van der Grinten NV [*Associated Press*] (SAG)

OCEO .... Office of the Commissioner for Equal Opportunity [*Australia*]

OCEP .... Office of Community Employment Programs [*Department of Labor*]

OCEPA .... United States Environmental Protection Agency, Cincinnati, OH [*Library symbol Library of Congress*] (LCLS)

OCESL .... Office of Criminal Enforcement and Special Litigation (COE)

OCf .... Chagrin Falls Public Library, Chagrin Falls, OH [*Library symbol Library of Congress*] (LCLS)

OCF .... Obsessive Compulsive Foundation (EA)

OCF .... Ocala [*Florida*] [*Airport symbol*] (OAG)

OCF .... Ocala, FL [*Location identifier FAA*] (FAAL)

OCF .... Office of the Chief of Finance [*Military*]

OCF .... Officers' Christian Fellowship of the USA (EA)

OCF .... Officiating Chaplain to the Forces [*Military British*]

OCF .... On-Board Computational Facility [*NASA*] (NASA)

OCF .... Open Channel Flow

OCF .... Open Computing Facility

OCF .... Operational Control Facility (SAA)

OCF .... Operator Console Facility [*Computer science*] (IBMDP)

OCF .... Orbiter Computational Facility [*NASA*] (NASA)

ocf .... Originally Cultured Formulation (AD)

OCF .... Ossining Correctional Facility [*Sing Sing*] (AD)

OCF .... Owens-Corning [*NYSE symbol*] (TTSB)

OCF .... Owens-Corning Fiberglas Corp. [*NYSE symbol*] (SPSG)

OCF .... Ozenji Critical Facility [*Nuclear reactor*] [*Japan*]

OCFA .... Overseas Christian Fellowship Australia

OCF & A ...... Office, Chief of Finance and Accounting [*Army*] (AABC)

OCFC .... Cloyne Branch, Frontenac County Library, Ontario [*Library symbol National Library of Canada*] (BIB)

OCFC .... Ocean Financial Corp. [*NASDAQ symbol*] (SAG)

OCFC .... Overseas Combined Federal Campaign [*Red Cross*]

OCFDA .... United States Food and Drug Administration, Cincinnati, OH [*Library symbol Library of Congress*] (LCLS)

OCFMFP ...... Ontario Centre for Farm Machinery and Food Processing Technology, Chatham, Ontario [*Library symbol National Library of Canada*] (NLC)

OCF-ML .... Organisation Communiste de France - Marxiste-Leniniste [*Communist Organization of France - Marxist-Leninist*] (PPW)

OCFNT .... Occuluded Front [*NWS*] (FAAC)

OCFP .... Office of Commercial and Financial Policy [*Department of Commerce*]

OCFP .... Operator Command Function Processor [*Computer science*] (MHDI)

OCFR .... Oxford Committee for Family Relief [*British*] (AD)

OCFR .... Oxford Committee for Famine Relief [*British*] (DI)

OCFT .... Office of Curriculum Frameworks and Textbooks (AD)

OCG .... Cincinnati General Hospital, Medical Library, Cincinnati, OH [*Library symbol Library of Congress*] (LCLS)

OCG .... Occupational Changes in a Generation [*Socioeconomics*]

OCG .... OCG Technology, Inc. [*Associated Press*] (SAG)

OCG .... Oesterreichische Computer Gesellscahft [*Austrian Computer Society*] [*German*] (AD)

OCG .... Office of Challenge Grants [*National Endowment for the Humanities*] (BARN)

OCG .... Office of the Commanding General [*Army*]

OCG .... Office of the Comptroller General (AAGC)

ocg .... Omnicardiogram [*Medicine*] (AD)

OCG .... Omnicardiogram [*Medicine*] (DMAA)

OCG .... Optimal Code Generation

OCG .... Oral Cholecystography [*or Cholecystogram*] [*Radiology*]

OCG .... Orbital Curve of Growth [*Mathematics*]

OCG .... Osborne & Chappel Goldfields US [*Toronto Stock Exchange symbol*]

OCGA .... Oxygen Consumption Gauge

OCGA .... Official Code of Georgia, Annotated [*A publication*] (DLA)

OCGH .... Cornwall General Hospital, Ontario [*Library symbol National Library of Canada*] (NLC)

OCGI .... Omni Capital Group (EFIS)

OCGM .... Office of Cabinet and Government Management [*Australia*]

OCGS .... Church of Jesus Christ of Latter-Day Saints, Genealogical Society Library, Cincinnati Branch, Cincinnati, OH [*Library symbol Library of Congress*] (LCLS)

OCGSH .... Good Samaritan Hospital, Medical Library, Cincinnati, OH [*Library symbol Library of Congress*] (LCLS)

OCGT .... OCG Technology [*NASDAQ symbol*] (TTSB)

OCGT .... OCG Technology, Inc. [*NASDAQ symbol*] (NQ)

OCGT .... Open-Cycle Gas Turbine (PDAA)

OCH .... Chesley Branch, Bruce County Public Library, Ontario [*Library symbol National Library of Canada*] (NLC)

OCh .... Chillicothe and Ross County Public Library, Chillicothe, OH [*Library symbol Library of Congress*] (LCLS)

OCH .... Hebrew Union College - Jewish Institute of Religion, Cincinnati, OH [*Library symbol Library of Congress*] (LCLS)

OCH .... Nacogdoches, TX [*Location identifier FAA*] (FAAL)

OCH .... Obedience Champion [*Dog show term*]

OCH .... Obstacle Clearance Height [*Aviation*] (FAAC)

OCH .... Ochre [*Philately*] (ROG)

och. .... Ochre (AD)

OCH .... Office for Communication in the Humanities (NITA)

OCH .... Oral Contraceptive Hormone (DB)

OCH .... Orbiter Common Hardware [*NASA*] (NASA)

OCH .... Order of the Compassionate Heart (EA)

OCH .... Organ Clearing House (EA)

OCH .... Outpatient Clinic (Hospital) [*Veterans Administration*]

OCHA .... Chatham Public Library, Ontario [*Library symbol National Library of Canada*] (NLC)

OCHA .... Oregon Clearing House Association (TBD)

OChaG .... Geauga County Public Library, Chardon, OH [*Library symbol Library of Congress*] (LCLS)

OCHAH .... Chatham Public General Hospital, Ontario [*Library symbol National Library of Canada*] (NLC)

OCHAK .... Chatham-Kent Museum, Chatham, Ontario [*Library symbol National Library of Canada*] (NLC)

OCHAKC ...... Kent County Public Library, Chatham, Ontario [*Library symbol National Library of Canada*] (NLC)

OCHAMPUS... Office for the Civilian Health and Medical Program of the Uniformed Services (AABC)

OCHAMPUS... Office of Civilian Health and Medical Program of the Uniformed Services (USGC)

OCHAMPUSEUR... Office of the Civilian Health and Medical Program of the Uniformed Services in Europe (DNAB)

OCHAP .... Chapleau Public Library, Ontario [*Library symbol National Library of Canada*] (NLC)

OCharlys ..... OCharleys, Inc. [*Associated Press*] (SAG)

OCHAT .... Thames Arts Centre, Chatham, Ontario [*Library symbol National Library of Canada*] (NLC)

OCHC .... Operator Call Handling Center [*Telecommunications*] (TEL)

OCHCB .... Huron County Board of Education, Clinton, Ontario [*Library symbol National Library of Canada*] (NLC)

OCHDC .... Hilton Davis Chemical Co., Cincinnati, OH [*Library symbol Library of Congress*] (LCLS)

OCHERB .... Chelmsford Branch, Rayside-Balfour Public Library, Chelmsford, Ontario [*Library symbol National Library of Canada*] (NLC)

OCHIN .... Norton Co. Electric, Chippewa, Ontario [*Library symbol National Library of Canada*] (NLC)

OC-HLTHLB.. Occupational Health Labels [*Army*]

OCHM .... Haldimand County Museum Board, Cayuga, Ontario [*Library symbol National Library of Canada*] (NLC)

OCHP .... Cincinnati Historical Society, Cincinnati, OH [*Library symbol Library of Congress*] (LCLS)

OCHR .... Oil Catcher

OCHRE .... Optical Character Recognition Engine (PDAA)

OCHS .... Old Colony Historical Society (AD)

OCHSDG ...... Chesterville Branch, Stormont, Dundas, and Glengarry County Public Library, Ontario [*Library symbol National Library of Canada*] (BIB)

OChU .... Ohio University, Chillicothe Branch Campus, Chillicothe, OH [*Library symbol Library of Congress*] (LCLS)

OCHWL........ Wollaston and Limerick Public Library, Coe Hill, Ontario [*Library symbol National Library of Canada*] (BIB)

OCI .... Integrated Revolutionary Organizations [*Cuba*] (PPW)

OCI .... Occlude (DA)

OCI .... Ocean Color Imager [*Meteorology*] [*NASA*]

OCI. .... O.C. International [*Formerly, Orient Crusades Gospel Outreach*] (EA)

OCI .... Office of Community Investment [*Federal Home Loan Bank Board*]

OCI .... Office of Computer Information [*Department of Commerce*] [*Originator and database*]

OCI .... Office of Corollary Interest [*DoD*]

OCI .... Office of Criminal Investigation [*Environmental Protection Agency*] (EPA)

OCI .... Office of Current Intelligence (MCD)

OCI .... Office of the Coordinator of Information (AD)

OCI .... Old Canada Investment Corp. Ltd. [*Toronto Stock Exchange symbol*]

OCI .... Olympic Council of Ireland (EAIO)

OCI .... Ontario Cancer Institute [*UTLAS symbol*]

OCI .... Open Circuit Inductance (IAA)

OCI .... Operational Checkout Instruction (AD)

OCI .... Operation Child Identification [*Defunct*] (EA)

OCI .... Operator Control Interface (OA)

OCI .... Optically-Coupled Insulator (IAA)

OCI .... Optically Coupled Isolator

OCI .... Organisation Communiste Internationaliste [*Internationalist Communist Organization*] [*France Political party*] (PPW)

OCI .... Organisation de la Conference Islamique [*Organization of the Islamic Conference - OIC*] [*Jeddah, Saudi Arabia*] (EAIO)

OCI .... Organizational Climate Index [*Test*]

OCI .... Organizational Conflict of Interest (AAGC)

oci .... Organization Conflict of Interest (AD)

OCI .... Organized Crime Intelligence Unit [*Law Enforcement Assistance Administration*]

OCI .... Oryzacystatins I [*Biochemistry*]

OCI............ Outpatient Clinic (Independent) [*Veterans Administration*]

OCI............ Oxide Control and Indication (NRCH)

OCIA........... Organic Crop Improvement Association (EA)

OCIAA........ Office of Coordinator of Inter-American Affairs [*World War II*]

OCIB........... Beausoleil Indian Band Library, Christian Island, Ontario [*Library symbol National Library of Canada*] (BIB)

OCIB........... Organized Crime Intelligence Bureau (AD)

OCIC........... Officer Commanding in Charge [*Facetious acronym*] [*Army British*] (DSUE)

OCIC........... Organisation Catholique Internationale du Cinema et de l'Audiovisuel [*International Catholic Organization for Cinema and Audiovisual*] (EAIO)

OCIE............ Organizational Clothing and Individual Equipment [*Military*]

OCIEP......... Office of the Commissioners of Inquiry for Environment and Planning [*Australia*]

OCIF............ Out Card in File

OCII............ Oryzacystatins II [*Biochemistry*]

OCIL............ Office of Community and Intergovernmental Liaison [*Environmental Protection Agency*] (GFGA)

OCIMF......... Oil Companies International Marine Forum [*British*] (EAIO)

OCINFO....... Office of the Chief of Information [*Military*]

OCIR........... Office of Community and Intergovernmental Relations (COE)

OCIR........... Operational Capability Inprovement Request Out of Commission, In Reserve [*Vesselstatus*] (DNAB)

OCirP.......... Pickaway County District Public Library, Circleville, OH [*Library symbol Library of Congress*] (LCLS)

OCIS........... Oacis Healthcare Holdings Corp. [*NASDAQ symbol*] (SAG)

OCIS........... Oacis Heathcare Hldgs [*NASDAQ symbol*] (TTSB)

OCIS........... Office for Church in Society (EA)

OCIS........... Office of Computing and Information Services [*University of Georgia*] [*Research center*] (RCD)

OCIS........... Organized Crime Information System [*Federal Bureau of Investigation*] [*Information service or system*] (IID)

OCIS........... OSHA [*Occupational Safety and Health Administration*] Computerized Information System [*Environmental science*]

OCIS........... Oxford Centre for Islamic Studies [*British*]

OcisHlth...... Oacis Healthcare Holdings Corp. [*Associated Press*] (SAG)

OCist........... Cistercian Fathers (TOCD)

ocist............ Cistercian Fathers (TOCD)

OCist........... Cisterdan Nuns (TOCD)

O CIST......... Ordinis Cisterciensis [*Cistercian Order*] (ROG)

OCITA.......... Office of the Chemical Industry Trade Advisor

OCIU........... Optical Cable Interface Unit (MCD)

OCJ............. Ocho Rios [*Jamaica*] [*Airport symbol*] (OAG)

OCJ............. Optional Construction Joint

OCJA........... Oklahoma Criminal Justice Association (AD)

OCJC........... Orange Coast Junior College [*California*] [*Later, OCC*]

OCJCS......... Office of the Chairman, Joint Chiefs of Staff (MCD)

OCJH.......... Jewish Hospital, Medical Library, Cincinnati, OH [*Library symbol Library of Congress*] (LCLS)

OCJH-N....... Jewish Hospital, School of Nursing, Cincinnati, OH [*Library symbol Library of Congress*] (LCLS)

OCJP........... Office of Criminal Justice Planning (AD)

OCJP........... Office of Criminal Justice Program (OICC)

OCK............ Chalk River Public Library, Ontario [*Library symbol National Library of Canada*] (BIB)

OCK............ Kent State University, Stark County Regional Campus, Canton, OH [*OCLC symbol*] (OCLC)

OCK............ Operation Control Key [*Computer science*] (IAA)

OCKA.......... Atomic Energy of Canada [*L'Energie Atomique du Canada*] Chalk River, Ontario [*Library symbol National Library of Canada*] (NLC)

OCKE.......... Petawawa National Forestry Institute, Canadian Forestry Service, Environment Canada [*Institut Forestier National Petawawa, Service Canadien des Forets, Environnement Canada*] Chalk River, Ontario [*Library symbol National Library of Canada*] (NLC)

OCl............. Cleveland Public Library, Cleveland, OH [*Library symbol Library of Congress*] (LCLS)

OCL............. Ocean Cargo Line (AD)

OCL............. Ocellus

OCL............. Office of Congressional Liaison [*Environmental Protection Agency*] (GFGA)

OCL............. Offshore Commercial Loan

OCL............. Oil City Lubricants Ltd. [*Vancouver Stock Exchange symbol*]

OCL............. Old Light Cruiser [*Navy symbol*]

OCL............. Operational Check List (MUGU)

OCL............. Operational Control Level

OCL............. Operation Control Language [*Computer programming*]

ocl............. Operator Control Language (AD)

OCL............. Operators Control Language [*Computer science*] (BUR)

ocl............. Optical Communications Linkage (AD)

OCL............. Ordnance Circular Letter

OCL............. Organochlorine [*Also, OC*] [*Organic chemistry*]

OCL............. Orthopedic Casting Laboratory (DAVI)

OCL............. Outgoing Correspondence Log (AAG)

OCL............. Overall Connection Loss [*Telecommunications*] (TEL)

OCL............. Overhaul Cycle Limit

OCL............. Over-Night Cargo Ltd. [*Nigeria*] [*ICAO designator*] (FAAC)

OCL............. Overseas Container Line (AD)

OCL............. Overseas Containers Ltd. (AD)

OCL............. Overseas Currency Loan

OCIA.......... Alcan Aluminum Co., Cleveland, OH [*Library symbol Library of Congress*] (LCLS)

OCLA.......... Office of Congressional and Legislative Affairs [*U.S. Department of Interior*] (BARN)

OCLA........... Oregon Compiled Laws Annotated [*A publication*]

OCL/ACT...... Overseas Container Lines and Associated Container Transport (AD)

OCLAE......... Organizacion Continental Latinoamericana de Estudiantes [*Latin American Continental Students' Organization*] (EAIO)

OCIAM......... Arthur G. McKee & Co., Cleveland, OH [*Library symbol Library of Congress*]

OCLaw......... Cincinnati Law Library Association, Cincinnati, OH [*Library symbol Library of Congress*] (LCLS)

OCIBE......... Board of Education, Cleveland, OH [*Library symbol Library of Congress*] (LCLS)

OCIBHS....... Benedictine High School, Cleveland, OH [*Library symbol Library of Congress*] (LCLS)

OCI-BPH...... Ohio Regional Library, Braille and Talking Books Division, Cleveland Public Library, Cleveland, OH [*Library symbol Library of Congress*] (LCLS)

OCIBS......... Blessed Sacrament Seminary, Cleveland, OH [*Library symbol Library of Congress*] (LCLS)

OCIC........... Cleveland Clinic Educational Foundation, Cleveland, OH [*Library symbol Library of Congress*] (LCLS)

OCLC.......... Ohio College Library Center (BARN)

OCLC.......... Online Computer Library Center [*Formerly, Ohio College Library Center. Initialism used in reference to cataloging system it developed*] [*Information service or system*]

OCICC......... Cuyahoga Community College, Cleveland, OH [*Library symbol Library of Congress*] (LCLS)

OCICh......... Christian Science Reading Room, Cleveland, OH [*Library symbol Library of Congress*] (LCLS)

OCICIM........ Cleveland Institute of Music, Cleveland, OH [*Library symbol Library of Congress*] (LCLS)

OCICo.......... Cuyahoga County Public Library, Cleveland, OH [*Library symbol Library of Congress*] (LCLS)

OCID........... Dyke College, Cleveland, OH [*Library symbol Library of Congress*] (LCLS)

OCLD.......... Oil-Cooled

OCIDe.......... Deaconess Hospital, Medical Library, Cleveland, OH [*Library symbol Library of Congress*] (LCLS)

OCLDP-K..... Open Court Language Development Program: Kindergarten (EDAC)

OCLE........... Continuing Legal Education, University of Oklahoma Law Center (DLA)

OCIFRB....... Federal Reserve Bank of Cleveland, Cleveland, OH [*Library symbol Library of Congress*] (LCLS)

OCIG........... Glidden Co. Research Library, Cleveland, OH [*Library symbol Library of Congress*] (LCLS)

OCIGC......... Garden Center of Greater Cleveland, Cleveland, OH [*Library symbol Library of Congress*] (LCLS)

OCIGI.......... Gould, Incorporated, Gould Information Center, Cleveland, OH [*Library symbol Library of Congress*] (LCLS)

OCIh........... Cleveland Heights-University Heights Public Library, Cleveland Heights, OH [*Library symbol Library of Congress*] (LCLS)

OCLI............ Curve Lake Indian Band Library, Ontario [*Library symbol National Library of Canada*] (BIB)

OCLI............ Optical Coating Lab [*NASDAQ symbol*] (TTSB)

OCLI............ Optical Coating Laboratories, Inc. (PCM)

OCLI............ Optical Coating Laboratory, Inc. [*NASDAQ symbol*] (NQ)

OCLIPS....... Operational Climate Prediction and Services [*Marine science*] (OSRA)

OCIJC.......... John Carroll University, Cleveland, OH [*Library symbol Library of Congress*] (LCLS)

OCIL............ General Electric Co., Light Research Laboratory, Cleveland, OH [*Library symbol Library of Congress*] (LCLS)

OCLL........... Office, Chief of Legislative Liaison [*Military*]

OCILH......... Lakeside Hospital, Cleveland, OH [*Library symbol Library of Congress*] (LCLS)

OCLloyd....... Lloyd Library and Museum, Cincinnati, OH [*Library symbol Library of Congress*] (LCLS)

OCIMA........ Cleveland Museum of Art, Cleveland, OH [*Library symbol Library of Congress*] (LCLS)

OCIMGH....... Cleveland Metropolitan General Hospital, Cleveland, OH [*Library symbol Library of Congress*] (LCLS)

OCIMN........ Cleveland Museum of Natural History, Cleveland, OH [*Library symbol Library of Congress*] (LCLS)

OCIMt......... Mount Sinai Hospital, Cleveland, OH [*Library symbol Library of Congress*] (LCLS)

OCINASA...... National Aeronautics and Space Administration, Lewis Research Center, Cleveland, OH [*Library symbol Library of Congress*] (LCLS)

OCIND......... Notre Dame College, Cleveland, OH [*Library symbol Library of Congress*] (LCLS)

OCLNR........ Oil Cleaner

OCIP........... Park Synagogue, Cleveland, OH [*Library symbol Library of Congress*] (LCLS)

OCLR.......... Oil Cooler

OCIRC.......... Rowfant Club, Cleveland, OH [*Library symbol Library of Congress*] (LCLS)

OCISA.......... Cleveland Institute of Art, Cleveland, OH [*Library symbol Library of Congress*] (LCLS)

OCISS......... Saint Stanislaus Seminary, Cleveland, OH [*Library symbol Library of Congress*] (LCLS)

OCIStJ........ Saint John College of Cleveland, Cleveland, OH [*Library symbol Library of Congress*] (LCLS)

OCIStM........ Saint Mary's Seminary, Cleveland, OH [*Library symbol Library of Congress*] (LCLS)

OCITem........ Temple Library, Tiffereth Israel Congregation, Cleveland, OH [*Library symbol Library of Congress*] (LCLS)

OCIU........... Cleveland State University, Cleveland, OH [*Library symbol Library of Congress*] (LCLS)

OCLU .... Overseas Container Line Unit (AD)

OCIU-L......... Cleveland-Marshall College of Law, Cleveland State University, Cleveland, OH [*Library symbol Library of Congress*] (LCLS)

OCIUr........... Ursuline College, Pepper Pike, OH [*Library symbol Library of Congress*] (LCLS)

OCLUS......... Outside Continental Limits of United States [*Military*]

OCIV .... United States Veterans Administration Hospital, Cleveland, OH [*Library symbol Library of Congress*] (LCLS)

OCIW .... Case Western Reserve University, Cleveland, OH [*Library symbol Library of Congress*] (LCLS)

OCIW-H........ Case Western Reserve University, Cleveland Health Sciences Library, Cleveland, OH [*Library symbol Library of Congress*] (LCLS)

OCIWHi......... Western Reserve Historical Society, Cleveland, OH [*Library symbol Library of Congress*] (LCLS)

OCIWHi-AM... Western Reserve Historical Society, Frederick C. Crawford Auto-Aviation Museum, Cleveland, OH [*Library symbol Library of Congress*] (LCLS)

OCIW-L........ Case Western Reserve University, Law Library, Cleveland, OH [*Library symbol*] [*Library of Congress*] (LCLS)

OCIW-LS...... Case Western Reserve University, School of Library Science, Cleveland, OH [*Library symbol Library of Congress*] (LCLS)

OCIW-S........ Case Western Reserve University, Sears Library, Cleveland, OH [*Library symbol Library of Congress*] (LCLS)

OCIW-SS...... Case Western Reserve University, School of Applied Social Science, Cleveland, OH [*Library symbol Library of Congress*] (LCLS)

OCM........... Cincinnati Masonic Temple, Cincinnati, OH [*Library symbol Library of Congress*] (LCLS)

OCM........... Creighton University, Health Sciences Library, Omaha, NE [*OCLC symbol*] (OCLC)

OCM........... Matchedash Public Library, Coldwater, Ontario [*Library symbol National Library of Canada*] (BIB)

OCM........... Office of Compliance Monitoring [*Environmental Protection Agency*] (GFGA)

OCM........... Office of Country Marketing [*Department of Commerce*] (IMH)

OCM........... Office of the Commission [*Nuclear energy*] (NRCH)

OCM........... Ohm Centimeter (IAA)

OCM........... Oil Content Monitor [*Navy*] (CAAL)

ocm .... Oil Content Monitor (AD)

OCM........... On-Camera Meteorologist

OCM........... On-Condition Maintenance (AABC)

OCM........... One-Channel Map [*Computer science NASA*]

OCM........... Optical Contour Maximization [*Chemistry*]

OCM........... Optical Countermeasures

OCM........... Ordnance Committee Meeting (AAG)

OCM........... Ordnance Committee Minutes [*Military*]

OCM........... Ordo Constantini Magni [*International Constantinian Order*] (EA)

OCM........... Organic Content Monitor (NASA)

ocm .... Organic Content Monitor (NAKS)

OCM........... Origin of Columellar Muscle

OCM........... Oscillator and Clock Module

OCM........... Outline of Cultural Materials [*Human Relations Area Files*] [*Information retrieval*]

OCM........... Oxford Companion to Music [*A publication*] (AD)

OCMA......... Oxidative Coupling of Methane [*Chemistry*]

OCMA......... Oil Companies' Materials Association [*British*] (BI)

OCMCEN...... Occupational Measurement Center [*Air Force*]

OCMH......... Madonna House Library, Combermere, Ontario [*Library symbol National Library of Canada*] (NLC)

OCMH......... Office of the Chief of Military History [*Army*]

OCMI.......... Officer-in-Charge, Marine Inspection Office [*Coast Guard*]

OCMiI......... Cincinnati Milacron, Inc., Research Library, Cincinnati, OH [*Library symbol Library of Congress*] (LCLS)

OCMiIC........ Cincinnati Milacron, Inc., Corporate Information Center, Cincinnati, OH [*Library symbol*] [*Library of Congress*] (LCLS)

OCMiI-T....... Cincinnati Milacron, Inc., Technical Information Center, Cincinnati, OH [*Library symbol Library of Congress*] (LCLS)

OCM-LP....... Organizacao Comunista Marxista-Leninista Portuguesa [*Portuguese Communist Organization, Marxist-Leninist*] [*Political party*] (PPE)

OCMLR .... Organisation Communiste Marxiste-Leniniste de la Reunion [*Reunionese Communist Organization, Marxist-Leninist*] [*Political party*] (PPW)

OCMM .... Office of Civilian Manpower Management [*Later, Office of Civilian Personnel*] [*Navy*]

OCMMINST... Office of Civilian Manpower Management Instruction [*Navy*]

OCMM-N...... Office of Civilian Manpower Management - Navy

OCMN .... Merrell-National Laboratories, Cincinnati, OH [*Library symbol Library of Congress*] (LCLS)

OCMODL...... Operating Cost Model

OCMR .... On-Condition Maintenance Rate (MCD)

OCMR .... Ontario Centre for Materials Research [*Canada Research center*] (RCD)

OCMS .... On-Board Checkout and Monitoring System [*NASA*] (KSC)

OCMS .... Operative Crate Makers' Society [*A union*] [*British*]

OCMS .... Optional Calling Measured Service [*Telecommunications*] (TEL)

OCMS .... Ordnance Command Management System

OCMS .... Ordnance Committee Meeting Standards (AAG)

OCMSq .... Occupational Measurement Squadron [*Air Force*]

OCMU .... Ocmulgee National Monument

OCN .... Canadian Park Service, Environment Canada [*Service Canadien des Parcs, Environnement Canada*], Cornwall, Ontario [*Library symbol National Library of Canada*] (NLC)

OCN .... Ocean

OCN .... Oceanair-Transportes Aereos Regional SA [*Portugal ICAO designator*] (FAAC)

OCN .... Oceanside, CA [*Location identifier FAA*] (FAAL)

OCN .... Oculomotor Nucleus [*Eye anatomy*]

OCN .... Office of the Commissioner of Namibia (BUAC)

OC-N .... Office of the Comptroller of the Navy

OCN .... Open College Network (AIE)

OCN .... Operation Completion Notice (AAG)

OCN .... Optimal Channel Network [*Physics*]

OCN .... Optimal Climate Normals [*Climatology*]

OCN .... Orcana Resources Ltd. [*Vancouver Stock Exchange symbol*]

OCN .... Order Control Number (NASA)

OCN .... Organization Change Notice

OCN .... Organized Crime Narcotics Program [*Department of Justice*]

OCN .... Over Castle Rock [*New York*] [*Seismograph station code, US Geological Survey*] (SEIS)

OCNAUD ..... Oficina del Coordinador de las Naciones Unidas para la Ayuda en los Desastres [*Office of the Coordinator of the United Nations for Help in Disasters*] [*Spanish*] (AD)

OCNAV....... Office of the Oceanographer of the Navy

Ocn Bch ..... Ocean Beach (AD)

OCNC......... Coniston Branch, Nickel Centre Public Library, Ontario [*Library symbol National Library of Canada*] (NLC)

OCNew....... New Church Library, Cincinnati, OH [*Library symbol Library of Congress Obsolete*] (LCLS)

OCnf......... Canal Fulton Public Library, Canal Fulton, OH [*Library symbol Library of Congress*] (LCLS)

OCNGA....... Officer-in-Charge of National Guard Affairs

OCNGH ...... Garden Hill Branch, Northumberland County Public Library, Campbellcroft, Ontario [*Library symbol National Library of Canada*] (BIB)

OCNGS....... Oyster Creek Nuclear Generating Station (NRCH)

OCNHT....... North Himsworth Township Public Library, Callander, Ontario [*Library symbol National Library of Canada*] (NLC)

OCNIOS...... National Institute for Occupational Safety and Health, Cincinnati, OH [*Library symbol Library of Congress*] (LCLS)

OCNL .... Occasional

ocnl .... Occasional (AD)

OCNLY .... Occasionally

OCNM .... Oregon Caves National Monument (AD)

OCNM .... Organization of the Crimean Tatar National Movement (BUAC)

OCNMAP .... Ocean Map [*Marine science*] (OSRA)

OCNO .... Office of the Chief of Naval Operations

OCNPP ...... Oyster Creek Nuclear Power Plant (NRCH)

OCNPR....... Operation and Conservation of Naval Petroleum Reserves [*Budget appropriation title*]

OCNS .... Oklahoma City NORAD [*North American Air Defense*] Sector (SAA)

OCNSW ...... Outdoor Club of New South Wales [*Australia*]

OCNWU...... Organizing Committee for a National Writers Union (EA)

OCO .... Cobourg Public Library, Ontario [*Library symbol National Library of Canada*] (NLC)

OCo........... Columbus Public Library, Columbus, OH [*Library symbol Library of Congress*] (LCLS)

OCO .... Object Code Only (HGAA)

OCO .... Office, Chief of Ordnance [*Army*]

OCO .... Office of Central Operations [*Bureau of Health Insurance*]

OCO .... Office of Civil Operations [*Coordinated US civilian pacification efforts in Vietnam*] (VNW)

OCO .... Off-Load Control Officer [*Navy*] (ANA)

OCO .... Old Cornish [*Language, etc.*]

OCO .... OMS [*Orbital Maneuvering Subsystem*] Cutoff [*NASA*] (NASA)

OCO .... One-Cancels-the-Other Order [*Business term*]

OCO .... Ontario College of Ophthalmology [*Canada*] (AD)

oco........... Open-Close-Open (AD)

OCO .... Open-Close-Open [*Technical drawings*]

OCO .... Operating Capital Outlay (WPI)

OCO .... Operational Capability Objective [*Army*]

OCO .... Operational Checkout (AAG)

OCO .... Operations Console Operator (MUGU)

OCO .... Optically-Coupled Oscillator [*Instrumentation*]

OCO .... Ordnance Corps Order (AAG)

OCO .... Public Library of Columbus and Franklin County, Columbus, OH [*OCLC symbol*] (OCLC)

OCOA.......... Art Gallery of Cobourg, Ontario [*Library symbol National Library of Canada*] (NLC)

OCoa.......... Columbiana Public Library, Columbiana, OH [*Library symbol Library of Congress*] (LCLS)

OCOA.......... Organismo Coordinador de Operaciones Antisubversivas [*Coordinating Organism of Antisubversive Operations*] [*Uruguay*] (AD)

OCoAC........ American Ceramic Society, Columbus, OH [*Library symbol Library of Congress*] (LCLS)

OCOAP........ Oscillating-Compensator Oscillating-Analyzer Polarimeter (PDAA)

OCoB .... Battelle-Columbus Laboratories, Columbus, OH [*Library symbol Library of Congress*] (LCLS)

OCOB .... Cobalt Public Library, Ontario [*Library symbol National Library of Canada*] (BIB)

OCOBD....... Cobden Public Library, Ontario [*Library symbol National Library of Canada*] (BIB)

OCoBex....... Bexley Public Library, Columbus, OH [*Library symbol Library of Congress*] (LCLS)

OCoC......... Capital University, Columbus, OH [*Library symbol Library of Congress*] (LCLS)

OCOC .... Cochrane Public Library, Ontario [*Library symbol National Library of Canada*] (NLC)

OCOCC........ Ontario CAD/CAM Centre, Cambridge, Ontario [*Library symbol National Library of Canada*] (NLC)

OCoC-L	Capital University, School of Law, Columbus, OH [Library symbol Library of Congress] (LCLS)
OCoCT	Columbus Technical Institute, Columbus, OH [Library symbol Library of Congress] (LCLS)
OCoCU	Capital University, Columbus, OH [Library symbol] [Library of Congress] (LCLS)
OCoD	Ohio Dominican College, Columbus, OH [Library symbol Library of Congress] (LCLS)
OCOD	Organization for Cooperation in Overseas Development [Canada] (EAIO)
OCoE	Evangelical Lutheran Theological Seminary, Columbus, OH [Library symbol Library of Congress] (LCLS)
OCOE	Office of the Chief of Engineers [Army] (RDA)
OCoF	Franklin University, Columbus, OH [Library symbol Library of Congress] (LCLS)
OC of AC	Office of the Chief of Air Corps [World War II]
OC of AS	Office of the Chief of Air Staff [World War II]
OC of Ch	Office, Chief of Chaplains [Later, OCCH] [Army] (AABC)
OC of F	Office of the Chief of Finance [Military]
OC of ORD	Office, Chief of Ordnance [Army]
OC of SA	Office, Chief of Staff, Army (AABC)
OC of SptS	Office of the Chief of Support Services [Army] (AABC)
OC of T	Office, Chief of Transportation [Army]
OCoG	Grandview Heights Library, Columbus, OH [Library symbol Library of Congress] (LCLS)
OCOGF	General Foods Ltd., Cobourg, Ontario [Library symbol National Library of Canada] (NLC)
OCoGS	Church of Jesus Christ of Latter-Day Saints, Genealogical Society Library, Columbus Branch, Columbus, OH [Library symbol Library of Congress] (LCLS)
OCOKA	Observation and Fields of Fire, Cover and Concealment, Obstacles, Key Terrain, Avenues of Approach (MCD)
OCOL	Collingwood Public Library, Ontario [Library symbol National Library of Canada] (NLC)
OCOLB	Colborne Public Library, Ontario [Library symbol National Library of Canada] (BIB)
OCoLC	OCLC Online Computer Library Center, Dublin, OH [Library symbol] [Library of Congress] (LCLS)
OCoLC	Ohio College Library Center, Columbus, OH [Library symbol Library of Congress] (LCLS)
OCOLD	Coldwater Memorial Public Library, Ontario [Library symbol National Library of Canada] (BIB)
OCOM	Oficina Central de Organizacion y Metodos [Central Office of Organization and Methods] [Spain] (AD)
OCOM	Outlet Communications, Inc. [NASDAQ symbol] (NQ)
OCOMS	Office of Community Services [Military]
OComS	Office of Community Services (AD)
OCON	Northumberland and Newcastle Board of Education, Cobourg, Ontario [Library symbol National Library of Canada] (NLC)
OCON	Orders for Correction of Nonconformance [Navy] (NG)
OCoNC	National Center on Educational Media and Materials for the Handicapped, Columbus, OH [Library symbol Library of Congress] (LCLS)
OConCL	Carnegie Public Library, Conneaut, OH [Library symbol] [Library of Congress] (LCLS)
OCONT	Oil Control
OConUS	Outside Continental Limits of the United States (AD)
OCONUS	Outside Continental United States [Military]
OCOO	Cookstown Public Library, Ontario [Library symbol National Library of Canada] (BIB)
OCoO	Ohioana Library, Columbus, OH [Library symbol Library of Congress] (LCLS)
OCOO	Osteopathic College of Ophthalmology and Otorhinolaryngology (EA)
OCOO	Osteopathic Colleges of Ophthalmology and Otolaryngology-Head and Neck Surgery (EA)
OCOP	Outline Contingency Operation Plan (COE)
OCoR	Riverside Methodist Hospital, Columbus, OH [Library symbol Library of Congress] (LCLS)
OCORD	Office, Chief of Ordnance [Army]
O Corn	Old Cornish (AD)
OCoSH	Columbus State Hospital, Columbus, OH [Library symbol Library of Congress] (LCLS)
OCOT	Office, Chief of Transportation [Army]
OCoV	Center for Vocational and Technical Education, Ohio State University, Columbus, OH [Library symbol Library of Congress] (LCLS)
OCoY	Young Men's Christian Association, Columbus, OH [Library symbol Library of Congress] (LCLS)
OCP	Carleton Place Public Library, Ontario [Library symbol National Library of Canada] (NLC)
OCP	Obstacle [or Obstruction] Clearance Panel [Aviation] (OA)
OCP	Occupational Cluster Program (OICC)
OCP	Ocean Culture Product
OCP	Octacalcium Phosphate [Inorganic chemistry]
OCP	Ocular Cicatricial Pemphigoid [Ophthalmology]
OCP	Office of Civilian Personnel [Military]
OCP	Office of Commercial Programs [NASA]
OCP	Office of Consumer Protection (AD)
OCP	Office of Cultural Presentations (AD)
OCP	Office of the Chief of Protocol [US Department of State] (AD)
OCP	Officer Candidate Programme [British military] (DMA)
OCP	Official Crude Prices [Petroleum Intelligence Weekly] [Information service or system] (CRD)
OCP	Oficina Central de Personal [Central Personnel Office] [Spain] (AD)
OCP	Onchocerciasis Chemotherapy Project [WHO]
OCP	Onchocerciasis Control Program [World Health Organization] (BUAC)
OCP	One-Component Plasma
OCP	Ontario College of Pharmacy
OCP	Open Circuit Potential (PDAA)
OCP	Operating [or Operational] Control Procedure (MSA)
OCP	Operational Capability Plan [Army]
OCP	Operational Checkout Procedure [NASA] (KSC)
OCP	Operational Communications Plan (MCD)
OCP	Operational Configuration Processing (COE)
OCP	Operational Control Panel
OCP	Operations Control Plan (AAG)
OCP	Optical Character Printing
OCP	Oral Contraceptive Pill [Gynecology] [Pharmacology] (DAVI)
OCP	Orbital Combustion Process (PDAA)
OCP	Orbital Control Program (SAA)
OCP	Orbital Correction Program [NASA] (KSC)
OCP	Order Code Processor [International Computers Ltd.]
OCP	Organizational Competitiveness Program [Motivational program]
OCP	Orientalia Christiana Periodica [A publication] (ODCC)
OCP	Ortho-Chlorophenol [Organic chemistry]
OCP	Ostacalcium Phosphate [A fertilizer]
OCP	Out of Commission for Parts (AFM)
OCP	Output Control Program
OCP	Output Control Pulse (NASA)
ocp	Output Control Pulses (AD)
OCP	Ova, Cysts, Parasites [Gastroenterology] (DAVI)
OCP	Overland Common Point [Imported item] [Business term]
ocp	Overland Common Points (AD)
OCP	Overload Control Process [Telecommunications] (TEL)
OCP	Overseas Common Point [Exported item] [Business term]
OCP	Owners and Contractors Protective [Insurance]
OCP	Oxford Concordance Project (NITA)
OCP	Public Library of Cincinnati and Hamilton County, Cincinnati, OH [OCLC symbol] (OCLC)
OCPA	Office, Chief of Public Affairs [Army]
OCPA	Office of Congressional and Public Affairs [FCC] (TSSD)
OCPA	Ortho-Chlorophenoxyacetic Acid [Organic chemistry]
OCPA	Ortho-Chlorophenylacetic Acid [Organic chemistry]
OCPCA	Oil and Chemical Plant Constructors' Association [British]
OCPCJR	Office of Crime Prevention and Criminal Justice Research (AD)
OCPD	Occult Constrictive Pericardial Disease [Cardiology] (CPH)
OCPD	Officer-in-Charge Police District (AD)
OCPDB	Organic Chemical Producers Data Base (NITA)
OCPED	Office de Commercialisation du Poisson d'Eau Douce [Freshwater Fish Marketing Corp. - FFMC]
OCPG	Goodwood Data Systems Ltd., Carleton Place, Ontario [Library symbol National Library of Canada] (NLC)
OCPG	Procter & Gamble Co., Cincinnati, OH [Library symbol Library of Congress] (LCLS)
OCPG-H	Procter and Gamble Co., Health and Beauty Library, Cincinnati, OH [Library symbol] [Library of Congress] (LCLS)
OCPG-I	Procter & Gamble Co., Ivorydale Technical Center, Cincinnati, OH [Library symbol Library of Congress] (LCLS)
OCPG-Mv	Procter & Gamble Co., Miami Valley Laboratories, Cincinnati, OH [Library symbol Library of Congress] (LCLS)
OCPG-Sw	Procter & Gamble Co., Sharon Woods Technical Center, Technical Library, Cincinnati, OH [Library symbol Library of Congress] (LCLS)
OCPG-Wh	Procter & Gamble Co., Winton Hill Technical Center, Cincinnati, OH [Library symbol Library of Congress] (LCLS)
OCPH	Providence Hospital, Medical Library, Cincinnati, OH [Library symbol Library of Congress] (LCLS)
OCPINST	Office of Civilian Personnel Instruction [Navy] (MCD)
OCPL	Leigh Instruments Ltd., Carleton Place, Ontario [Library symbol National Library of Canada] (NLC)
OCPL	Oklahoma City Public Library (AD)
OCPL	Onondaga Library System [Library network]
OCPL	Orange County Public Library [Florida]
OCPLACS	Ontario Cooperative Program in Latin American and Caribbean Studies [Research center] (RCD)
OCPM	Optically Connected Parallel Machines [Computer science]
OCPNA	Ortho-Chloro-para-nitroaniline [Organic chemistry]
OCPO	Office of Civilian Personnel Operations [Air Force]
OCPO	Office of Computer Processing Operations [Social Security Administration]
OCPO	Operations Cargo Passenger Office (DNAB)
OCPP	Orbiter Cloud Photopolarimeter [NASA]
OCPP	(Ortho-Chlorophenoxy)propionic Acid [Organic chemistry]
OCPR	Office of Claims and Payments Requirements [Social Security Administration]
OCPR	Office of Collateral Policy Responsibility (AFM)
OCPR	Operation and Conversion of Naval Petroleum Reserves (DNAB)
OCPS	I. P. Sharp Associates Ltd., Carleton Place, Ontario [Library symbol National Library of Canada] (NLC)
OCPS	Office Canadien du Poisson Sale [Canadian Saltfish Corporation]
OCPS	Office of Census and Population Studies [British]
OCPS	Officer Candidate Preparatory School (DNAB)
OCPS	Oxygen Cabin Pressurization Section [NASA] (KSC)
OCPSF	Organic Chemical, Plastic, and Synthetic Fiber
OCPW	Office of Chief of Psychological Warfare (LAIN)
OCQ	Membre de l'Ordre des Chimistes du Quebec [Canada] (DD)
OCQ	Oconto, WI [Location identifier FAA] (FAAL)
OCQ	Oneida Ltd. [NYSE symbol] (SPSG)
OCQM	Office of Chief Quartermaster [Military]
OCR	Creemore Public Library, Ontario [Library symbol National Library of Canada] (BIB)

OCR	Norcross, GA [*Location identifier FAA*] (FAAL)
OCR	Occupational Safety and Health Control Report [*Navy*]
OCR	O'Connell Ranch [*California*] [*Seismograph station code, US Geological Survey*] (SEIS)
OCR	Oculocardiac Reflex [*Physiology*]
OCR	Office for Civil Rights [*Department of Education*]
OCR	Office of Civilian Requirements [*Division of War Production Board*] [*World War II*]
OCR	Office of Civil Rights [*Environmental Protection Agency*] (GFGA)
OCR	Office of Coal Research [*Energy Research and Development Administration*]
OCR	Office of Collateral Responsibility (AFM)
OCR	Office of Community Relations (COE)
OCR	Office of Coordinating Responsibility [*Air Force*]
OCR	Office of the County Recorder (AD)
OCR	Oil Circuit Recloser
O Cr	Oklahoma Criminal Reports [*A publication*] (DLA)
OCR	Omnicare, Inc. [*NYSE symbol*] (SPSG)
OCR	Operational Capability Release
OCR	Operational Change Report [*Military*] (NVT)
OCR	Operational Control Record [*Nuclear energy*] (NRCH)
OCR	Operations Capability Reference (SSD)
OCR	Operations Control Room [*Military*] (CAAL)
OCR	Optical Character Reader [*Computer science*]
ocr	Optical Character Reader [*Computer science*] (AD)
OCR	Optical Character Recognition [*Computer science*]
OCR.	Optical Character Resolution [*Ligature Co.*] (PCM)
OCR	Optimum Charge Regulator
OCR	Optional Character Reader [*Computer science*] (DA)
OCR	Oracle Resources [*Vancouver Stock Exchange symbol*]
OCR	Order Control Record (SAA)
OCR	Order of Corporate Reunion [*British*]
OCR	Order of the Crown of Rumania
OCR	Ordo Reformatorum Cisterciensium [*Cistercians, Trappists*] [*Roman Catholic men's religious order*]
OCR	Organic-Cooled Reactor [*Nuclear energy*] (OA)
OCR	Organisation for the Collaboration of Railways [*See also OSShD*] [*Warsaw, Poland*] (EAIO)
OCR	Organization Change Request
OCR	Organized Crime and Racketeering Section [*Department of Justice*] (DLA)
OCR	Output Control Register
OCR	Over Consolidated Ratio [*Nuclear energy*] (NUCP)
OCR	Overcurrent Relay (MSA)
OCR	Overhaul Component Requirement [*NASA*] (KSC)
OCR	Overhead Component Requirement (IAA)
OCR	Oxidizable Carbon Ratio
OCRA	Optical Character Recognition - ANSI Standard (Font A) [*Computer science*]
OCRA	Organisation Clandestine de la Revolution Algerienne [*Secret Organization of the Algerian Revolution*] [*France*] (AD)
OCRA	Overseas Company Registration Agents Ltd. (ECON)
OCRB	Optical Character Recognition - ANSI Standard (Font B) [*Computer science*]
OCRB	Optical Character Recognition Bar [*Computer science*] (IAA)
OCRBI	Organization for Cooperation in the Roller Bearings Industry [*Warsaw, Poland*] (EAIO)
O Cr C	Oudh Criminal Cases [*India*] [*A publication*] (DLA)
OCRCWA	Outcare Civil Rehabilitation Council of Western Australia
OCRD	Ocean Climate Research Division [*Pacific Marine Environmental Laboratory*] (USDC)
OCRD	Office, Chief of Research and Development [*Army*]
OCRE	Office of Conservation and Renewable Energy (COE)
OCRE	Optical Character Recognition Equipment [*Computer science*] (AABC)
ocre	Optical Character Recognition Equipment [*Computer science*] (AD)
OCRE	Organizations Concerned about Rural Education (AD)
oCRF	Ovine Corticotrophin Releasing Factor [*Endocrinology*]
OCRHA	Overseas Command Records Holding Area [*Army*]
OCRI	Office Canadien pour un Renouveau Industriel [*Canadian Office for Industrial Revival*]
OCRIT	Office of Combat Indentification Technology [*Army*]
OCRIT	Optical Character Recognizing Intelligent Terminal [*Computer science*] (IAA)
ocrit	Optical Character-Recognizing Intelligent Terminal [*Computer science*] (AD)
OCRM	Ocean and Coastal Resource Management (GNE)
OCRM	Office of Coastal Resource Management (USDC)
OCRM	Officer Commanding Royal Marines [*British military*] (DMA)
OCRM	Orbiter Crash and Rescue Manuals [*NASA*]
OCRR	Office of the Coordinator, Regulatory Reform [*Canada*]
OCRS	Oculocerebrorenal Syndrome [*Medicine*] (DMAA)
OCRS	Ontario Centre for Remote Sensing [*Canada*]
OCRS	Optical Character Recognition System (NITA)
OCRS	Organisation Commune des Regions Sahariennes [*Common Organization of the Saharan Regions*]
OCRS	Organized Crime and Racketeering Section [*Department of Justice*]
OCRSDG	Crysler Branch, Stormont, Dundas, and Glengarry County Library, Ontario [*Library symbol National Library of Canada*] (BIB)
OCRSF	Organized Crime and Racketeering Strike Force (AD)
OcrstLb	Ocurest Laboratories, Inc. [*Associated Press*] (SAG)
OCRU	Office of Communication and Research Utilization (AD)
OCRUA	Optical Character Recognition Users Association [*Later, RTUA*] (EA)
OCRW	Raymond Walters General and Technical College, Cincinnati, OH [*Library symbol Library of Congress*] (LCLS)

OCRWM	Office of Civilian Radioactive Waste Management [*Oak Ridge National Laboratory*]
OCRX	OncoRx, Inc. [*NASDAQ symbol*] (SAG)
OCS	Cities Service Co., Technical Center - Energy Resources Group, Research Library, Tulsa, OK [*OCLC symbol*] (OCLC)
OCS	Obsessive Compulsive Scale [*Psychology*] (EDAC)
OCS	Obstacle Clearance Surface (AD)
OCS	Ocean Color Scanner (PDAA)
OCS	Ocean Culture System
OCS	Octachlorostyrene [*Organic chemistry*]
OCS	Octopine Synthase [*An enzyme*]
OCS	Office, Chief of Staff [*Army*]
OCS	Office Cleaning Service [*Commercial firm British*]
OCS	Office Computer System (IAA)
OCS	Office for Consumer Services [*HEW*]
OCS	Office of Civilian Supply [*Division of War Production Board*]
OCS	Office of Commercial Services [*Department of Commerce*]
OCS	Office of Communication Systems [*Air Force*]
OCS	Office of Community Services [*Family Support Administration*] [*Department of Health and Human Services*] (GFGA)
OCS	Office of Community Services [*Bureau of Indian Affairs*]
OCS	Office of Computing Services [*Georgia Institute of Technology*] [*Research center*] (RCD)
OCS	Office of Contract Settlement [*Functions transferred to GSA, 1949; now obsolete*]
OCS	Office of the Chief Scientist
OCS	Office of the Chief Surgeon [*Military*]
OCS	Officer Candidate School [*Military*]
OCS	Officers' Chief Steward [*Navy*]
OCS	Old Church Slavonic [*Language, etc.*]
OCS	On-Board Checkout System [*NASA*]
ocs	Onboard Checkout System [*NASA*] (NAKS)
ocs	On Company Service (AD)
OCS	Open Canalicular System [*Hematology*]
OCS	Open-Circuit-Stable
OCS	Operational Call Sign (IAA)
OCS	Operational Characteristics (NATG)
OCS	Operational Control Segment (SSD)
OCS	Operations Control System
OCS	Operator's Connection Set (IAA)
OCS	Optical Character Scanner [*Computer science*]
OCS	Optical Communicator System (MCD)
OCS	Optical Computer System (IAA)
OCS	Optical Contact Sensor
OCS	Optical Contrasting Seeker (MCD)
OCS	Optimum Coordinated Shipboard [*or Shorebased*] Allowance List (DNAB)
OCS	Orbit Computation System (MCD)
OCS	Orbit Correction Subsystem (NOAA)
OCS	Order of the Cross Society (EA)
OCS	Organe de Controle des Stupefiants [*Narcotic Drug Control Organization*] [*France*] (AD)
OCS	Oriel Computer Services Ltd. (NITA)
OCS	Oriental Ceramic Society (EA)
OCS	Oriental Chair of Solomon [*Freemasonry*]
OCS	Oriented Cellular Structure
OCS	Ornithodoros Coriaceus Spirochete [*Entomology*]
OCS	Outer Continental Shelf
ocs	Outler Continental Shelf (AD)
OCS	Outpatient Clinci Substation [*Medicine*] (DAVI)
OCS	Outpatient Clinic Substation [*Veterans Administration*]
OCS	Output Control Subsystem
OCS	Overload Control Subsystem [*Telecommunications*] (TEL)
OCS	Overseas Civil Servants (AD)
OCS	Overseas Communication Service [*India*] (BUAC)
OCS	Overseas Courier Service (AD)
OCS	Overspeed Control System (AAG)
OCS	Saint Thomas Institute, Cincinnati, OH [*Library symbol Library of Congress*] (LCLS)
OCSA	Office, Chief of Staff, Army
OCSA	Ohio Collegiate Soccer Association (PSS)
OCSA	Orchid Society of South Australia
OCSA	Outstanding Civilian Service Award
OCSAA	Official Committee on Service Attaches and Advisers [*British*]
OCSAB	Office of Contract Settlement Appeal Board [*Abolished, 1952*]
OCSAB	Outer Continental Shelf Advisory Board [*Marine science*] (MSC)
OCSAN	Organisation pour la Conservation du Saumon de l'Atlantique Nord [*North Atlantic Salmon Conservation Organization*] [*Scotland*] (EAIO)
OCSC	Outer Continental Shelf Committee [*Congressional committee*] (MSC)
OCSD	Obsessive Compulsive Spectrum Disorder [*Psychology*]
OCSD	Oculocraniosomatic Disease [*Medicine*] (DMAA)
OCSDG	Stormont, Dundas, and Glengarry County Public Library, Cornwall, Ontario [*Library symbol National Library of Canada*] (NLC)
OCSDGL	Stormont, Dundas, and Glengarry Law Association, Cornwall, Ontario [*Library symbol National Library of Canada*] (BIB)
OCSE	Office of Child Support Enforcement [*Department of Health and Human Services*]
OCSEA	Outer Continental Shelf Environmental Assessment [*Marine science*] (MSC)
OCSEAC	Outer Continental Shelf Environmental Studies Advisory Commission [*Department of the Interior*] (MSC)
OCSEAP	Outer Continental Shelf Environmental Assessment Program [*Department of Commerce, Department of the Interior*]

OCSEF .... Outer Continental Shelf Events File [*Department of the Interior*] (MSC)
OCSEP .... Outer Continental Shelf Energy Program [*Marine science*] (MSC)
OCSF .... Office Contents Special Form [*Insurance*]
ocsf............. Office Contents Special Form [*Inventor*] (AD)
OCSIGO....... Office of the Chief Signal Officer
OCSL .... Oriel Computer Services Limited (NITA)
OCSL .... St. Lawrence College [*College Saint-Laurent*], Cornwall, Ontario [*Library symbol National Library of Canada*] (NLC)
OCSLA .... Outer Continental Shelf Lands Act
OCSLAA ...... Outer Continental Shelf Lands Act Amendments of 1978 (COE)
OCSM .... Organization of Canadian Symphony Musicians [*See also OMOSC*]
OCSM .... Outer Continental Shelf Oil and Gas Supply Model [*Department of Energy*] (GFGA)
ocsn............. Occasion (AD)
ocsnl............ Occasional (AD)
ocsnly.......... Occasionally (AD)
ocso............. [*The*] Cistercians Order of the Strict Observance, Trappists (TOCD)
OCSO .... Office of the Chief Signal Officer
OCSO .... Order of Cistercian Nuns of the Strict Observance [*Roman Catholic religious order*]
OCSO .... Order of Cistercians of the Strict Observance [*Trappists*] [*Roman Catholic men's religious order*]
OCSOT .... Overall Combat Systems Operability Test (NVT)
OCSP .... Office of Cued Speech Programs [*Gallaudet College*] [*Research center*] (RCD)
OCSP .... Out of Commission, Special [*Vessel status*] (DNAB)
OCSPC .... Outer Continental Shelf Policy Committee [*California*] (AD)
OCSPWAR ... Office of the Chief of Special Warfare [*Army*]
OCSR .... Optical Cable Signal Repeater (MCD)
OCSR .... Serpent River Band Public Library, Cutler, Ontario [*Library symbol National Library of Canada*] (NLC)
OCSS .... Office of the Chief of Support Services [*Army*]
OCST .... Office of Cable Signal Theft [*National Cable Television Association*] (NTCM)
OCST .... Office of Commercial Space Transportation [*NASA*]
OCST .... Overcast (AABC)
ocst.............. Overcast (AD)
OCStFH .... Saint Francis/Saint George Hospital, Cincinnati, OH [*Library symbol Library of Congress*] (LCLS)
OCStG .... Saint Gregory Seminary, Cincinnati, OH [*Library symbol Library of Congress*] (LCLS)
OCSTL .... On-Board Checkout System Test Language [*NASA*] (KSC)
OCSW .... Objective Crew-Served Weapon
OCT............. Cincinnati Technical College, Cincinnati, OH [*Library symbol Library of Congress OCLC symbol*] (LCLS)
OCT............. Object Classification Test (DMAA)
OCT............. Octagon (AAG)
oct .... Octagon (AD)
OCT............. Octahedral [*Molecular geometry*] (IAA)
OCT............. Octal [*Number system with a base of eight*] [*Computer science*] (CET)
oct .... Octal (AD)
oct .... Octane (AD)
OCT............. Octane (AAG)
OCT............. Octanol [*Organic chemistry*]
Oct.............. Octans [*Constellation*] (WDAA)
Oct.............. Octanus [*Constellation*]
OCT............. Octarius [*Pint*] [*Pharmacy*]
OCT............. Octave (ADA)
oct .... Octave (AD)
Oct.............. Octavius (AD)
oct .... Octavo (AD)
OCT............. Octavo [*Book from 20 to 25 centimeters in height*] [*Bibliography*]
oct .... Octet (AD)
Oct.............. October (AD)
OCT............. October (EY)
oct .... Octobre [*October*] [*French*] (ASC)
OCT............. Octuple (MSA)
OCT............. Office, Chief of Transportation [*Army*]
OCT............. Office of Critical Tables [*NAS-NRC*]
OCT............. Officer Candidate Test [*Army*]
OCT............. Officer Classification Test
OCT............. Operational Climatic Testing (MCD)
OCT............. Operational Cycle Time
OCT............. Operations Control Team [*Deep Space Network, NASA*]
OCT............. Optical Coherence Tomography [*Medicine*]
OCT............. Optical Contract Seeker (MCD)
OCT............. Optimal Control Theory
OCT............. Optimal Cutting Temperature [*Material for tissue fixation*]
OCT............. Oral Contraceptive Therapy [*Endocrinology*] (AAMN)
OCT............. Orbital Circularization Technique
OCT............. Organisation Communiste des Travailleurs [*Communist Organization of Workers*] [*France Political party*] (PPW)
OCT............. Ornithine Carbamoyltransferase [*Also, OTC*] [*An enzyme*]
OCT............. Ortho-Chlorotoluene [*Organic chemistry*]
OCT............. Orthotopic Cardiac Transplantation [*Medicine*] (DMAA)
OCT............. Output Clock Trigger (IAA)
OCT............. Overseas Countries and Territories [*Common Market*]
OCT............. Oxford Classical Texts [*A publication*] (OCD)
OCT............. Oxytocin Challenge Test [*Medicine*]
OCTA .... Oceanic Control Area [*Aviation*] (DA)
OCTA .... Octanucleotide [*Biochemistry*]
OCTA .... Octapentadiene [*Toxic chemical*]
OCTA .... On-Line Corporation Tax Assessment [*British*]

OCTA .... Oregon-California Trails Association (EA)
OCTA .... Ortho-Cyclohexanediaminetetraacetic Acid [*Also, DCTA*] [*Organic chemistry*]
OCTA .... Outsized Cargo Tanker Aircraft
OCTAHDR .... Octahedral
OCTANE....... Operations Control Technique for Actuals Number Extraction (MCD)
OCTAP .... Of Concern to Air Passengers [*Group affiliated with PATCO*] (EA)
OCTB .... Oxford Church Textbooks [*A publication*]
OCTC .... Operator's Control Transfer Channel [*Electronics*] (ECII)
OCTD .... Ornithine Carbamoyltransferase Deficiency [*Medicine*]
OCTD .... Other Connective Tissue Diseases [*Medicine*]
OCTD .... Overlap Connective Tissue Disease [*Medicine*] (DMAA)
octe .... Optical Component Testing and Evaluation (AD)
Octel .... Octel Communications [*Associated Press*] (SAG)
OCTG .... Oil Country Tubular Goods [*Metal industry*]
OCTH .... Town of Haldimand Public Libraries, Caledonia, Ontario [*Library symbol National Library of Canada*] (NLC)
OCTHB .... Office, Chief of Transportation, Historical Branch [*Army*]
OCTI............ Office Central des Transports Internationaux par Chemins de Fer [*Central Office for International Railway Transport*] (EAIO)
OCTI............ Ordnance Corps Technical Instruction
OCTL .... Octel Communications [*NASDAQ symbol*] (TTSB)
OCTL .... Octel Communications Corp. [*NASDAQ symbol*] (NQ)
OCTL .... Open-Circuited Terminating Line (IAA)
OCTL .... Open-Circuited Transmission Line
Octn .... Octanus [*Constellation*]
oct pars .... Octava Pars [*Eighth Part*] [*Latin*] (AD)
OCTR .... Octoraro Railway, Inc. [*AAR code*]
O/CTR .... Over Center [*Automotive engineering*]
OCTRF .... Ontario Cancer Treatment and Research Foundation [*Canada*] (BUAC)
octr prot .... Octrooi Protectie [*Patent Protected*] [*Dutch*] (AD)
OCT/RR........ Off Course Target/Remote Reference Display (NG)
OCTS .... Open Cooperative Test System [*Trademark of NCR Corp.*]
OCTS .... Optical Cable Transmission System (MCD)
Oct Str .... Octavo Strange [*Strange's Select Cases on Evidence*] [*A publication*] (DLA)
OCTU .... Officer Cadet Training Unit [*Military British*]
octup .... Octuplus [*Eightfold*] [*Latin*] (MAE)
octupl .... Octuplicate (AD)
octv............. Open-Circuit Television (AD)
OCTV .... Open-Circuit Television
OCU .... Observation Care Unit [*Medicine*] (DAVI)
OCU .... Oceanroutes, Inc., Palo Alto, CA [*OCLC symbol*] (OCLC)
OCU .... Office Channel Unit (IAA)
OCU .... Oklahoma City University
OCU .... Operational Control Unit
OCU .... Operational Conversion Unit (NATG)
ocu.............. Operational Conversion Unit (AD)
OCU .... Order of Christian Unity [*British*]
OCU .... Orderwire Operator Control Unit (MCD)
OCU .... Over-the-Counter Control Unit [*Stock exchange term*] (MHDW)
OCU .... University of Cincinnati, Cincinnati, OH [*Library symbol Library of Congress*] (LCLS)
OCUA.......... Ontario Council on University Affairs [*Canada*] (AD)
OCU-B......... University of Cincinnati, Biology Library, Cincinnati, OH [*Library symbol Library of Congress*] (LCLS)
OCUC .... Oxford and Cambridge Universities Club [*British*] (DAS)
OCU-DA .... University of Cincinnati, Design, Architecture, and Art Library, Cincinnati, OH [*Library symbol Library of Congress*] (LCLS)
OCU-E .... University of Cincinnati, Engineering Library, Cincinnati, OH [*Library symbol Library of Congress*] (LCLS)
OCUFA .... Ontario Confederation of University Facility Associations [*Canada*] (AD)
OCUG.......... Union Gas Ltd., Chatham, Ontario [*Library symbol National Library of Canada*] (NLC)
OCUG.......... Union Graduate School, Cincinnati, OH [*Library symbol Library of Congress*] (LCLS)
OCU-Geo...... University of Cincinnati, Geology-Geography Library, Cincinnati, OH [*Library symbol Library of Congress*] (LCLS)
ocul............. Oculis [*To the Eyes*] [*Latin*] (AD)
OCUL .... Oculo [*To the Eye*] [*Pharmacy*]
OCUL .... Ocurest Laboratories, Inc. [*NASDAQ symbol*] (SAG)
OCU-L.......... University of Cincinnati, Law Library, Cincinnati, OH [*Library symbol Library of Congress*] (LCLS)
OCULENT ..... Oculentum [*Eye Ointment*] [*Pharmacy*]
oculent .... Oculentum [*Eye Ointment*] [*Latin*] (AD)
OCU-M......... University of Cincinnati, School of Medicine, Cincinnati, OH [*Library symbol Library of Congress*] (LCLS)
OCU-Math .... University of Cincinnati, Mathematics Library, Cincinnati, OH [*Library symbol Library of Congress*] (LCLS)
OCuME......... Milton Elementary School, Custar, OH [*Library symbol*] [*Library of Congress*] (LCLS)
OCU-Mu....... University of Cincinnati, College Conservatory of Music, Cincinnati, OH [*Library symbol Library of Congress*] (LCLS)
OCU-N .... University of Cincinnati, College of Nursing, Cincinnati, OH [*Library symbol Library of Congress*] (LCLS)
OCU-Ph........ University of Cincinnati, Physics Library, Cincinnati, OH [*Library symbol Library of Congress*] (LCLS)
OCUS .... Oblate Conference of the United States (EA)
OCUSI.......... United States Industrial Chemicals Co., Research Center Library, Cincinnati, OH [*Library symbol Library of Congress*] (LCLS)
OCV .... Bering Sea, AK [*Location identifier FAA*] (FAAL)
OCV .... Ocana [*Colombia*] [*Airport symbol*] (OAG)
OCV .... Oil Check Valve

OCV	Old Aircraft Carrier [*Navy symbol*]
OCV	Open-Circuit Voltage
ocv	Open-Circuit Voltage (AD)
OCV	Opimian California Vineyards Corp. [*Toronto Stock Exchange symbol*]
OCV	Ordinary Conversational Voice [*Medicine*]
OCV	Ordre des Chevaliers du Verseau [*Knights of Aquarius Order*] (EAIO)
OCV	Overriding Cam Valve
OCV	United States Veterans Administration Hospital, Cincinnati, OH [*Library symbol Library of Congress*] (LCLS)
OCVD	Open-Circuit Voltage Decay [*In silicon devices*]
OCV-L	Oil Control Valve - Low-Speed
OCVRA	Overseas Citizens Voting Rights Act
oc vu	Ocean View (AD)
OCW	Oklahoma College for Women
OCW	Old Cars Weekly [*A publication*]
OCW	Orange Cyan Wideband (IAA)
OCW	Washington, NC [*Location identifier FAA*] (FAAL)
OCW	Waterloo Regional Library, Waterloo, Ontario [*Library symbol National Library of Canada*] (NLC)
OCWCIB	Organizing Committee of the World Congress on Implantology and Bio-Materials [*See also COCMIB*] [*Rouen, France*] (EAIO)
OCWCT	West Carleton Township Public Library, Carp, Ontario [*Library symbol National Library of Canada*] (BIB)
OCWFLU	Operative Coachmakers' and Wheelwrights' Federal Labour Union [*British*]
OCWN	Ocwen Financial Corp. [*NASDAQ symbol*] (SAG)
OcwnFin	Ocwen Financial Corp. [*Associated Press*] (SAG)
OCX	Object Linking and Embedding Control Extension [*Computer science*] (IGQR)
OCX	Onex Corp. [*Toronto Stock Exchange symbol*]
OCX	Xavier University, Cincinnati, OH [*Library symbol Library of Congress*] (LCLS)
OCXO	Oven-Controlled Crystal Oscillator
OCY	Young Men's Mercantile Library Association, Cincinnati, OH [*Library symbol Library of Congress*] (LCLS)
OCZ	Lincoln, NE [*Location identifier FAA*] (FAAL)
OCZ	Ocean Container Zebrugge (AD)
OCZ	Operational Control Zone (MCD)
OCZM	Office of Coastal Zone Management [*National Oceanic and Atmospheric Administration*]
OD	Aerovias Condor de Colombia Ltda. (AEROCONDOR) [*Colombia ICAO designator*] (ICDA)
OD	Delaware County District Library, Delaware, OH [*Library symbol Library of Congress*] (LCLS)
OD	Doctor of Ophthalmology (WDAA)
OD	Doctor of Optometry
OD	Doctor of Osteopathy (WDAA)
OD	Drug Overdose [*Emergency Medicine*] (DAVI)
OD	Dundas Public Library, Ontario [*Library symbol National Library of Canada*] (NLC)
OD	Emerald Airlines [*ICAO designator*] (AD)
OD	Obiter Dicta [*Legal term Latin*] (DLA)
OD	Observable Difference
OD	Observed Drift
O-D	Obstacle-Dominance [*Medicine*] (DMAA)
OD	Occupational Disease
OD	Oceanographic Datastation [*Telecommunications*] (TEL)
od	Och Dylika [*And the Like*] [*Swedish*] (AD)
OD	Octal-to-Decimal [*Computer science*] (BUR)
OD	Ocular Density [*Ophthalmology*]
OD	Ocular Dominance [*Opthalmology*]
OD	Oculus Dexter [*Right Eye*] [*Ophthalmology*]
od	Oculus Dexter [*Right Eye*] [*Latin*] (AD)
Od	Odeon [*Record label*] [*Europe, etc.*]
Od	Odericus [*Flourished, 1166-1200*] [*Authority cited in pre-1607 legal work*] (DSA)
Od	Odofredus [*Deceased, 1265*] [*Authority cited in pre-1607 legal work*] (DSA)
od	Odur [*or*] [*German*] (AD)
Od	Odyssey [*of Homer*] [*Classical studies*] (OCD)
OD	Office Decision [*United States Internal Revenue Bureau*] [*A publication*] (DLA)
OD	Office of Disability [*Department of Health and Human Services*] (GFGA)
OD	Office of the Director
OD	Officer of the Day [*or Deck*] [*Also, OOD*] [*Navy*]
OD	Ohio Decisions [*A publication*] (DLA)
OD	Oil Desurger
OD	Oil Distribution (DNAB)
OD	Oil Drainage
OD	Old Dutch [*Language, etc.*]
OD	Olive Drab [*Color often used for military clothing and equipment*]
od	Olive Drab (WDAA)
OD	Omnes Dies [*Every Day*] [*Pharmacy*]
OD	Once a Day [*or Daily*] (DAVI)
O/D	On Deck (KSC)
OD	On Demand [*Business term*]
od	On Demand (AD)
O/D	On Dock (MCD)
OD	On Duty
OD	One Day (SAA)
od	Only Daughter (WDAA)
OD	Onrechtmatige Daad [*Tort or Tortious Act*] [*Netherlands*] (ILCA)
OD	Open Drain (IAA)
OD	Open Drop
OD	Operational Downlink/Downlist (NASA)
OD	Operational DownList
OD	Operation Description
OD	Operations Directive [*or Director*]
OD	Operations Division
OD	Optical Density
od	Optical Density (AD)
OD	Optical Disk [*Computer science*] (TELE)
OD	Opus Dei (EA)
OD	Orbit Determination
OD	Orbiter (Operational) Downlink [*NASA*]
OD	Order Dienst [*Netherlands first organized resistance group, 1940*] [*World War II*]
OD	Order of Daedalians (EA)
OD	Order of DeMolay (EA)
O/D	Order of Deportation
OD	Ordinary Seaman [*British*] (DMA)
OD	Ordnance Corps [*Army*] (GFGA)
OD	Ordnance Data [*Inspection and test data*]
OD	Ordnance Department [*or Division*]
OD	Ordnance Document [*Navy*]
OD	Ordnance Drawing
OD	Ordnungsdienst [*Military Police Service*] [*German military - World War II*]
od	Organizational Development (AD)
OD	Organization Development [*Human resources*] (WYGK)
od	Original Design (AD)
OD	Original Design
OD	Original Dirac [*Vacuum model*] [*Physics*]
OD	Originally Derived
OD	Origin and Destination [*Aviation*] (AFM)
O/D	Origin and Destination [*OST*] (TAG)
OD	Osseous Defect [*Medicine*]
OD	Other Denomination [*British military*] (DMA)
OD	Outer Diameter [*Mechanical engineering*]
OD	Out-of-Date
OD	Output Data (IEEE)
OD	Output Disable
OD	Output Display [*Computer science*] (IAA)
OD	Outside Diameter
od	Outside Diameter (AD)
OD	Outside Dimension
OD	Outstanding Debt [*Finance*] (MHDB)
od	Oven Dried (AD)
OD	Oven Dry
OD	Overall Depth [*Typography*] (DGA)
OD	Overburden Drill (PDAA)
OD	Overdose [*of narcotics*]
od	Overdose (AD)
OD	Overdraft [*or Overdrawn*] [*Banking*]
OD	Overdrawn [*Banking*] (WDAA)
OD	Overdrive (AAG)
od	Overdrive (AD)
Od	Overdue
OD	Overload Detection [*Telecommunications*] (TEL)
OD	Overtly Diabetic [*Medicine*]
OD	Oxygen Drain (MCD)
O-D	Zero Dimensional (AAEL)
OD3	Optical Digital Data Disk
ODA	Civic Democratic Alliance [*Czech Republic*] [*Political party*] (BUAC)
ODa	Dayton and Montgomery County Public Library, Dayton, OH [*Library symbol Library of Congress*] (LCLS)
ODA	Occipitodextra Anterior [*A fetal position*] [*Medicine*] (AAMN)
oda	Occipito-Dextra Anterior (AD)
ODA	Octal Debugging Aid [*Computer science*]
Oda	Odessa (AD)
ODa	Offa's Dyke Association [*British*] (DBA)
ODA	Office Document Architecture [*Telecommunications*] (TSSD)
ODA	Office of Debt [*or Depreciation*] Analysis [*Department of the Treasury*]
ODA	Office of Drug Abuse (AD)
ODA	Office of the Defense Attache [*Foreign Service*]
ODA	Office of the Deputy Administrator (COE)
ODA	Office of the District Administrator (AD)
ODA	Office of the District Attorney (AD)
ODA	Official Development Aid [*or Assistance*]
ODa	Old Danish (AD)
ODA	Omnidirectional Antenna
ODA	Ontario Dental Association [*Canada*] (BUAC)
ODA	Operational Data Analysis
ODA	Operational Design and Analysis (IEEE)
ODA	Optical Diffraction Analysis [*Microscopy*]
ODA	Orphan Drug Ace [*1983*] (BARN)
ODA	Oscillating Doublet Antenna
ODA	Oscillator/Doubler/Amplifier
ODA	Other Design Activity (MSA)
ODA	Ouadda [*Central African Republic*] [*Airport symbol*] (AD)
ODA	Overseas Development Administration [*British*] (EAIO)
ODA	Overseas Development Agency [*British*]
ODA	Overseas Development Aid
ODA	Overseas Development Assistance (AD)
ODA	Overseas Doctors Association in the United Kingdom [*British*]
ODA	Oxydianiline [*Organic chemistry*]

ODAA — Aden/International [*People's Democratic Republic of Yemen*] [*ICAO location identifier*] (ICLI)
ODaA — Dayton Art Institute, Dayton, OH [*Library symbol Library of Congress*] (LCLS)
ODAA — Office of Dependent Area Affairs [*Department of State*]
ODAB — Beihan [*People's Democratic Republic of Yemen*] [*ICAO location identifier*] (ICLI)
ODAC — Old Dominion Athletic Conference (PSS)
ODAC — On Demand Analyzer Computer
ODACA — Original Doll Artists Council of America (EA)
ODaCox — Cox Coronary Heart Institute, Dayton, OH [*Library symbol Library of Congress*] (LCLS)
ODADAS — Ohio Department of Alcohol and Drug Addiction Services
ODADC — Omnidirectional Air Data Computer (MCD)
ODaE — Engineers' Club of Dayton, Dayton, OH [*Library symbol Library of Congress*] (LCLS)
ODAF — Aden [*People's Democratic Republic of Yemen*] [*ICAO location identifier*] (ICLI)
ODAG — Al-Gheida [*People's Democratic Republic of Yemen*] [*ICAO location identifier*] (ICLI)
ODaGH — Grandview Hospital, Dayton, OH [*Library symbol Library of Congress*] (LCLS)
ODaGL — Church of Jesus Christ of Latter-Day Saints, Genealogical Society Library, Dayton Ohio Branch, Dayton, OH [*Library symbol Library of Congress*] (LCLS)
ODaGMI — General Motors Corp., Inland Manufacturing Division, Engineering Library, Dayton, OH [*Library symbol Library of Congress*] (LCLS)
ODaGS — Good Samaritan Hospital, Dayton, OH [*Library symbol Library of Congress*] (LCLS)
ODALC — Ogden Air Logistics Center (MCD)
ODALE — Office of Drug Abuse Law Enforcement [*Later, Drug Enforcement Administration*] [*Department of Justice*]
ODALS — Omnidirectional Approach Lighting System [*Aviation*] (FAAC)
ODAM — Mukeiras [*People's Democratic Republic of Yemen*] [*ICAO location identifier*] (ICLI)
ODaMC — Barney Children's Medical Center, Dayton, OH [*Library symbol Library of Congress*] (LCLS)
ODaMCo — Mead Corp., Dayton, OH [*Library symbol Library of Congress*] (LCLS)
ODaMNH — Dayton Museum of Natural History, Dayton, OH [*Library symbol Library of Congress*] (LCLS)
ODaMR — Monsanto Research Corp., Dayton Laboratory, Dayton, OH [*Library symbol Library of Congress*] (LCLS)
ODAMS — Open Water Disposal Area Management Simulation [*US Army Corps of Engineers*]
ODaMVH — Miami Valley Hospital, Dayton, OH [*Library symbol Library of Congress*] (LCLS)
ODAN — Kamaran [*People's Democratic Republic of Yemen*] [*ICAO location identifier*] (ICLI)
ODaN — National Cash Register Co., NCR Library, Dayton, OH [*Library symbol Library of Congress*] (LCLS)
ODAN — Old Danish [*Language, etc.*]
O'D & Br Eq Dig — O'Donnell and Brady's Irish Equity Digest [*A publication*] (DLA)
OD and MC — Operational Direction and Management Control (NATG)
OD & RD — Overseas Discharge and Replacement Depot
ODaNR — North Research Stillwater Pioneers, Dayton, OH [*Library symbol Library of Congress*] (LCLS)
ODaNT — National Cash Register Co., Technical Library, Dayton, OH [*Library symbol Library of Congress*] (LCLS)
ODA/ODIF — Office Document Architecture/Office Document Interchange Format (DOMA)
O-DAP — Oncovin [*Vincristine*], Dianhydrogalactitol, Adriamycin, Platinol [*Cisplatin*] [*Antineoplastic drug regimen*]
ODAP — Operation Data Analysis Program (IAA)
ODAP — Perim [*People's Democratic Republic of Yemen*] [*ICAO location identifier*] (ICLI)
ODAPI — Open Database Applications Program Interface [*Microsoft Corp.*]
ODAPS — Oceanic Display and Planning System [*Air traffic control*]
ODAPS — Operational OGE [*Operational Ground Equipment*] Data Acquisition and Patch Subsystem (GAVI)
ODAQ — Qishn [*People's Democratic Republic of Yemen*] [*ICAO location identifier*] (ICLI)
ODAR — Optical Detection and Ranging (DNAB)
ODAR — Riyan [*People's Democratic Republic of Yemen*] [*ICAO location identifier*] (ICLI)
ODAS — Ocean Data Acquisition Systems
ODAS — Ocean Data Acquisition Systems, Aids and Devices [*Marine science*] (OSRA)
ODAS — Ocean Dynamics Advisory Subcommittee [*NASA*] (MSC)
ODAS — Oral Deaf Adults Section [*Later, OHIS*] (EA)
ODAS — Socotra [*People's Democratic Republic of Yemen*] [*ICAO location identifier*] (ICLI)
ODaSC — Sinclair Community College, Dayton, OH [*Library symbol Library of Congress*] (LCLS)
ODASD — Office of the Deputy Assistant Secretary of Defense
ODaSR — Standard Register Co., Engineering and Research Library, Dayton, OH [*Library symbol Library of Congress*] (LCLS)
ODaStE — Saint Elizabeth Hospital, Dayton, OH [*Library symbol Library of Congress*] (LCLS)
ODaStL — Saint Leonard College, Dayton, OH [*Library symbol Library of Congress*] (LCLS)
ODAT — Ataq [*People's Democratic Republic of Yemen*] [*ICAO location identifier*] (ICLI)
odat — One Day at a Time (AD)

ODaTS — United Theological Seminary, Dayton, OH [*Library symbol Library of Congress*] (LCLS)
ODaU — University of Dayton, Dayton, OH [*Library symbol Library of Congress*] (LCLS)
ODaU-L — University of Dayton, Law Library, Dayton, OH [*Library symbol Library of Congress*] (LCLS)
ODaUM — United Methodist Church, Commission on Archives and History, Dayton, OH [*Library symbol Library of Congress*] (LCLS)
ODaU-M — University of Dayton, Marian Library, Dayton, OH [*Library symbol Library of Congress*] (LCLS)
ODaV — United States Veterans Administration Center, Library Services, Dayton, OH [*Library symbol Library of Congress*] (LCLS)
ODaWU — Wright State University, Dayton, OH [*Library symbol Library of Congress*] (LCLS)
ODaWU-H — Wright State University, School of Medicine, Fordham Library, Dayton, OH [*Library symbol Library of Congress*] (LCLS)
ODaWU-W — Wright State University, Western Ohio Branch Campus, Celina, OH [*Library symbol Library of Congress*] (LCLS)
ODB — Air Service [*Mali*] [*ICAO designator*] (FAAC)
ODB — Cordoba [*Spain*] [*Airport symbol*] (OAG)
ODB — Ocean Data Buoy [*Marine science*] (MSC)
ODB — Odontoblast
ODB — Office of Dependency Benefits
ODB — Oil-Degrading Bacteria
ODB — Operational Database (SSD)
ODB — Operational Data Book [*NASA*] (NAKS)
ODB — Opiate-Directed Behavior
odb — Opiate-Directed Behavior (AD)
ODB — Output Data Buffer
ODB — Output Display Branch [*Computer science*] (IAA)
ODB — Output to Display Buffer [*Computer science*]
odb — Output to Display Buffer [*Computer science*] (AD)
ODB — Oven Dry Basis
ODB — Overseas Development Bank [*Investors' Overseas Services*]
ODB — Oxydibenzil [*Organic chemistry*]
ODBA — Ocean Dumping Ban Act [*1988*]
ODBA — Oregon Dairy Breeders Association (BUAC)
ODBC — Official Doctor of Broken Computers
ODBC — Open Database Connectivity [*Computer science*]
ODBMS — On-Board Database Management System (SSD)
ODC — Oceanographic Data Center (MCD)
ODC — Odometer Data Computer [*Developed by Mileage Validator, Inc.*]
ODC — Office of Defense Cooperation (DOMA)
ODC — Office of Deputy Chief of Staff Programs and Resources [*Air Force*]
ODC — Officer Data Card
ODC — Ohio Dominican College, Columbus, OH [*OCLC symbol*] (OCLC)
ODC — Oil-Dri Corp. of America [*NYSE symbol*] (SPSG)
ODC — Oligodendrocyte [*Also, OLG*] [*Cytology*]
ODC — One-Directional Control [*Engineering*]
ODC — Online Data Capture
ODC — Operational Data Center [*Deep Space Network, NASA*]
ODC — Operational Document Control
ODC — Operation Desert Capture [*DoD*]
ODC — Operation Design Criteria (MCD)
ODC — Optical Disc Controller (NITA)
ODC — Orbital Data Collector
ODC — Order of Discalced Carmelites [*Roman Catholic religious order*]
ODC — Ordinary Decent Criminal [*British prison slang for other than a political prisoner*]
ODC — Organization Development Council [*Defunct*] (EA)
ODC — Original Design Cutoff (AAG)
ODC — Oritidine Decarboxylase (DMAA)
ODC — Ornithine Decarboxylase [*An enzyme*]
ODC — Oscilloscope Digital Control
ODC — Other Direct Costs [*Accounting*]
odc — Other Direct Costs (AD)
odc — Outer Dead Center (AD)
ODC — Outer Dead Center (DNAB)
ODC — Outpatient Diagnostic Center (STED)
ODC — Output Data Control
ODC — Overseas Development Corp. (AD)
ODC — Overseas Development Corporation (NADA)
ODC — Overseas Development Council (EA)
ODC — Overseas Diplomacy Coordinator (DNAB)
ODC — Oxford Decimal Classification
ODC — Oxygen Dissociation Curve [*Medicine*] (DMAA)
ODC — Oxyhaemoglobin Dissociation Curve (PDAA)
ODC — Ozone-Depleting Compound [*Environmental chemistry*]
ODCA — Ocean Dumping Control Act [*Canada*] (MSC)
ODCA — Organizacion Democrata Cristiana de America [*Christian Democratic Organization of America - CDOA*] [*Caracas, Venezuela*]
ODCC — Ohio Decisions, Circuit Court [*Properly cited Ohio Circuit Decisions*] [*A publication*] (DLA)
ODCC — On-Board Digital Computer Control
ODCC — One-Design Class Council (EA)
ODCC — Oxford Dictionary of the Christian Church
ODCC — United States One-Design Class Council (EA)
ODCDR — Orbiter Delta CDR [*NASA*] (GFGA)
ODCH — Ordinary Disease of Childhood (STED)
ODCM — Office of Defense and Civilian Mobilization [*See also OCDM*] (MUGU)
ODCM — Off-Site Dose Calculation Manual [*Nuclear energy*] (NRCH)
ODC of S — Office of the Deputy Chief of Staff [*World War II*]
ODCP — One-Digit Code Point [*Telecommunications*] (TEL)
ODCPC — Order of Descendants of Colonial Physicians and Chirurgiens [*Defunct*] (EA)

ODCR	Officer Distribution Control Report [*Navy*] (NG)
ODCS	Office of the Deputy Chief of Staff [*World War II*]
ODCS	Online Data Compression System (PDAA)
ODCSCD	Office of the Deputy Chief of Staff, Combat Developments [*Army*]
ODCSI	Office of the Deputy Chief of Staff for Intelligence
ODCSLOG	Office of the Deputy Chief of Staff for Logistics [*Army*] (AABC)
ODCSO	Office of Data Collection and Survey Operations [*Bureau of Labor Statistics*]
ODCSOPS	Office of the Deputy Chief of Staff for Operations and Plans [*Army*]
ODCSPER	Office of the Deputy Chief of Staff for Personnel [*Army*]
ODCSRDA	Office of the Deputy Chief of Staff for Research, Development, and Acquisition [*Army*] (AABC)
ODCTI	Old Dominion College Technical Institute (AD)
ODD	Obsessive-Deductive Disorder [*Facetious term for a malady affecting some taxpayers*]
ODD	Obstacle Detection Device
ODD	Ocean Disposal Database [*US Army Corps of Engineers*]
ODD	Oculodentodigital Dysplasia [*Medicine*] (MAE)
ODD	Offboard Deception Device [*Navy*] (CAAL)
ODD	Old Destroyer [*Navy symbol*]
ODD	Oodnadatta [*Australia Airport symbol*] (OAG)
ODD	Operational Detachment Delta [*Antiterrorist unit*] [*Military*] (LAIN)
ODD	Operator Distance Dialing
odd	Operator Distance Dialing (AD)
ODD	Oppositional Defiant Disorder
ODD	Optical Data Digitizer [*Computer science*]
ODD	Optical Data Disc (NITA)
ODD	Optical Digital Data Disk
ODD	Optical Digital Disc (NITA)
ODD	Organizing District Delegate [*British labor*]
ODD	Ouchterlony Double Diffusion Test [*Immunogel assay*]
ODD	Outside Design and Development
ODD	Overseas Deployment Data [*Military*]
ODDA	Office of Deputy Director for Administration [*Marshall Space Flight Center*] (KSC)
ODDD	Optical Digital Data Disk
ODDDR & R	Office of the Deputy Director of Defense Research and Engineering (RDA)
ODDH	On-Board Digital Data Handling
ODDO	Operation Description Distribution Order
ODDP	Office of the Director of Development Planning [*Air Force*] (MCD)
ODDR & E	Office of the Director of Defense Research and Engineering [*Later, Office of the Under Secretary of Defense for Research and Engineering*] [*Army*]
ODDRD	Office of Deputy Director for Research and Development [*Marshall Space Flight Center*] (KSC)
ODDRE	Office of the Director of Defense Research and Engineering [*Later, Office of the Under Secretary of Defense for Research and Engineering*] [*Army*]
ODDS	Oceanographic Digital Data System [*Navy*]
ODDS	Online Data Entry and Display System [*Job Service*] (OICC)
ODDS	Operational Data Delivery Services (MCD)
ODDS	Optical Disk Data System (NITA)
ODDS	Optional Delivery Dispenser System (MCD)
ODE	Delhi Public Library, Ontario [*Library symbol National Library of Canada*] (NLC)
ODE	Odense [*Denmark*] [*Airport symbol*] (OAG)
ODE	O-Desmethylencainide (STED)
ODE	Odessa [*Former USSR Geomagnetic observatory code*]
ODE	Office 97 Developer Edition [*Microsoft*]
ODE	Office of Device Evaluation [*U.S. Food and Drug Administration*]
ODE	Oil Drilling and Exploration (AD)
ODE	Omicron Delta Epsilon [*Fraternity*]
ODE	One Day Event [*Horse-riding*] [*British*] (DI)
ode	One-Day Event (AD)
ODE	One-Dimensional Equilibrium (MCD)
ODE	Online Data Entry (ADA)
ODE	Optical Designation Evaluation (MCD)
ODE	Optimally Designed Experiments
ODE	Orbit Data Editor Assembly [*Space Flight Operations Facility, NASA*]
ODE	Ordinary Differential Equation [*Mathematics*]
ODE	Ortho-Demethylencainide [*Biochemistry*]
ODEAG	Research Station, Agriculture Canada [*Station de Recherches, Agriculture Canada*], Ontario [*Library symbol National Library of Canada*] (NLC)
O'Dea Med Exp	O'Dea's Medical Experts [*A publication*] (DLA)
ODEC	Ocean Design Engineering Corp. (AD)
ODECA	Organizacion de los Estados Centroamericanos [*Organization of Central American States - OCAS*] [*San Salvador, El Salvador*] (EAIO)
ODECO	Ocean Drilling and Exploration Co. (AD)
O Dec Rep	Ohio Decisions Reprint [*A publication*] (DLA)
ODEE	[*The*] Oxford Dictionary of English Etymology [*A publication*]
ODef	Defiance Public Library, Defiance, OH [*Library symbol Library of Congress*] (LCLS)
ODefC	Defiance College, Defiance, OH [*Library symbol Library of Congress*] (LCLS)
ODelp	Delphos Public Library, Delphos, OH [*Library symbol Library of Congress*] (LCLS)
OdeM	Order of Our Lady of Mercy (TOCD)
odem	Order of Our Lady of Mercy (TOCD)
ODENDOR	Optical Detected Electron Nuclear Double Resonance (AAEL)
OD-ENDOR	Optically Detected Electron Nuclear Double Resonance [*Spectroscopy*]
Odeneal	Odeneal's Reports [*9-11 Oregon*] [*A publication*] (DLA)
ODEPA	Organizacion Deportiva Panamericana [*Pan American Sports Organization - PASO*] [*Mexico City, Mexico*] (EAIO)
ODEPA	Oxapentamethylenediethylenephosphoramide [*Pharmacology*]
ODEPLAN	Oficina de Planificacion Nacional [*Office of National Planning*] [*Spain*] (AD)
ODEPR	Optical Detected Electron Paramagnetic Resonance (AAEL)
O Dep Rep	Ohio Department Reports [*A publication*] (DLA)
Oderi	Odericus [*Flourished, 1166-1200*] [*Authority cited in pre-1607 legal work*] (DSA)
ODES	Deseronto Public Library, Ontario [*Library symbol National Library of Canada*] (NLC)
ODES	Ocean Data Evaluation System [*Environmental Protection Agency*] (AEPA)
ODES	Optical Discrimination Evaluation Study [*NASA*] (NASA)
OD-ESR	Optically Detected Electron Spin Resonance [*Spectroscopy*]
ODESSA	Ocean Data Environmental Science Services Acquisition [*Buoy*]
ODESSA	Oceanographic Data for the Environmental Science Services Administration (GFGA)
ODESSA	Organisation der Ehemaligen Schutzstaffel Angehoeriggen [*Organization of Former Members of the Elite Guard*] [*Founded after World War II to smuggle war criminals out of Germany and provide them with false identities*]
ODESUR	Organizacion Deportiva Sudamericana [*An association*] (EAIO)
ODESY	Online Data Entry System [*Burroughs Corp.*]
ODET	Odetics, Inc. [*NASDAQ symbol*] (SAG)
ODETA	Odetics,Inc.'A' [*NASDAQ symbol*] (TTSB)
ODETB	Odetics,Inc.'B' [*NASDAQ symbol*] (TTSB)
Odetics	Odetics, Inc. [*Associated Press*] (SAG)
ODETTE	Organization for Data Exchange through TeleTransmssion in Europe
Odf	Odofredus [*Deceased, 1265*] [*Authority cited in pre-1607 legal work*] (DSA)
ODF	Official Development Finance
ODF	Old Dominion Foundation (AD)
ODF	One-Dimension Flow
ODF	Opacity Distribution Function [*Spectroscopy*]
ODF	Operational Deployment Force (AD)
ODF	Optimal Decision Function
ODF	Orbit Determination Facility (MCD)
ODF	Orientation Distribution Function
ODF	Original Data File (NITA)
ODF	Output Data File
odfc	Outside Diameter of Female Coupling (AD)
ODFFU	Organization for Defense of Four Freedoms for Ukraine (EA)
ODFI	Open Die Forging Institute (EA)
ODFL	Old Dominion Freight Line [*NASDAQ symbol*] (TTSB)
ODFL	Old Dominion Freight Lines, Inc. [*NASDAQ symbol*] (SPSG)
ODFR	Oxygen-Derived Free Radicals [*Biochemistry*]
ODFT	Odd Discrete Fourier Transform (MCD)
ODFW	Oregon Department of Fish and Wildlife Research and Development Section [*Oregon State University*] [*Research center*] (RCD)
ODG	Enid, OK [*Location identifier FAA*] (FAAL)
ODG	Offline Data Generator
ODG	Operational Data Group (MCD)
ODG	Operational Design Group
ODG	Orbit Data Generator [*NASA*]
Odgers	Odgers on Libel and Slander [*A publication*] (DLA)
ODGF	Osteosarcoma-Derived Growth Factor [*Biochemistry*]
Odg Lib	Odgers on Libel and Slander [*A publication*] (DLA)
Odg Pl	Odgers on Principles of Pleading [*20th ed.*] [*1975*] [*A publication*] (DLA)
ODGSE	Operational Development Ground Support Equipment (AAG)
ODGSO	Office of Domestic Gold and Silver Operations [*Department of the Treasury*]
ODH	Highland Secondary School, Dundas, Ontario [*Library symbol National Library of Canada*] (NLC)
ODH	Octanol Dehydrogenase [*An enzyme*]
ODH	Octopine Dehydrogenase [*An enzyme*]
ODH	Ontario Department of Health [*Canada*] (AD)
ODHS	Dundas Historical Society Museum, Ontario [*Library symbol National Library of Canada*] (BIB)
ODHT	Hagerman Township Public Library, Ontario [*Library symbol National Library of Canada*] (NLC)
ODHWS	Office of Defense Health and Welfare Services [*World War II*]
ODI	Nodine, MN [*Location identifier FAA*] (FAAL)
ODI	Odin Industry Ltd. [*Vancouver Stock Exchange symbol*]
ODI	Office Document Index
ODI	Office of Director of Intelligence [*Military*]
ODI	Open Datalink Interface [*Computer science*]
ODI	Open-Door International [*An association*] (AD)
ODI	Open Door International for the Economic Emancipation of the Woman Worker [*Brussels, Belgium*] (EAIO)
ODI	Open Driver Interface [*Computer science*] (CIST)
ODI	Operational Development Inspection (SAA)
ODI	Optical Digital Imagery
ODI	Optonics Devices Incorporated
ODI	Overseas Development Institute (EA)
ODIC	Outside Diameter of Inner Conductor
ODID	Office of the Director of Industrial Demobilization
ODIF	Office Document Interchange Format (HGAA)
ODIFF	Oil Differential
ODIHR	Office for Democratic Institutions & Human Rights [*British*] (WDAA)
ODIL	Overseas Development Institute Ltd. (AD)
ODIN	Online Dakota Information Network [*Information service or system*] (IID)
ODIN	Online Dokumentations und Informationsnetz (NITA)

ODIN .... Online Dokumentations- und Informationsverbund [*Online Documentation and Information Affiliation*]
ODIN .... Operational Display Information Network (MCD)
ODIN .... Optimal [*or Orbital*] Design Integration [*Computer program*]
ODIN .... Orbital Design Integration [*NASA*] (NAKS)
OD Institu .... Organization Development Institute (NTPA)
ODIRP .... Office, Director of Personnel [*Air Force*]
ODIS .... Object Design, Inc. [*NASDAQ symbol*] (SAG)
ODIS .... Ocean Dynamics Information System [*Marine science*] (MSC)
ODIS .... Optical Disk Interface System [*Computer science*]
ODIS .... Orbital Design Integration System
ODIS .... Origin Destination Information System [*US Postal Service*]
ODISC4 .... Office of the Director of Informantion Systems for Command, Control, Communications, and Computers [*Army*]
ODISTA .... Oceanographic Data in Subtrial Areas
ODJ .... Ouanda Djalle [*Central African Republic*] [*Airport symbol*] (AD)
ODJB .... Original Dixieland Jazz Band
ODJS .... Office of the Director, Joint Staff (MCD)
ODK .... Kodiak, AK [*Location identifier FAA*] (FAAL)
ODK .... Omicron Delta Kappa [*Fraternity*]
ODK .... One-Dimensional Kinetics [*Computer program*] (MCD)
ODL .... Cordillo Downs [*South Australia*] [*Airport symbol*] (AD)
ODL .... Object Definition Language [*Computer science*]
ODL .... Oceanic Data Link [*FAA*] (TAG)
ODL .... Office Document Language [*Telecommunications*]
ODL .... Office of Defense Lending [*Department of the Treasury*]
ODL .... Office of the Duchy of Lancaster [*British*]
ODL .... Officer Deficiency Letter [*Navy*] (NVT)
ODL .... Oklahoma Department of Libraries
ODL .... Open and Distance Learning (AIE)
ODL .... Ostwald Dilution Law [*Chemistry*]
ODL .... University of Dayton, Law Library, Dayton, OH [*OCLC symbol*] (OCLC)
ODLAMP ...... One-Dimensional LASER and Mixing Program
ODLB .... Dwight Branch, Lake Of Bays Township Public Library, Ontario [*Library symbol National Library of Canada*] (BIB)
ODLB .... Optical Dispensers' Licensing Board [*New South Wales, Australia*]
ODLI .... Open Data Link Interface [*Computer science*]
ODLRO .... Off-Diagonal Long-Range Order [*Physics*]
odlsq .... Odalisque (VRA)
ODLY .... Orderly (WGA)
ODM .... Methodist Theological School in Ohio, Delaware, OH [*Library symbol Library of Congress*] (LCLS)
ODM .... Odiham FTU [*British ICAO designator*] (FAAC)
ODM .... Office of Defense Mobilization [*Transferred to Office of Defense and Civilian Mobilization, 1958*]
ODM .... Oil Debris Monitor
ODM .... One Day Mission [*NASA*] (KSC)
ODM .... Operational Data Management (KSC)
ODM .... Operational Development Memorandum (AAG)
ODM .... Operations Data Message (MCD)
ODM .... Ophthalmodynamometry [*Ophthalmology*] (MAE)
odm .... Ophthalmodynamometry [*Ophthalmology*] (AD)
ODM .... Optical Diffractogram
ODM .... Optical Disk Memory
ODM .... Optical Display Memory [*Computer science*]
ODM .... Optimized Delivery Model [*Compaq*] [*Computer science*]
ODM .... Optimized Distribution Model [*Compaq Computer Corp.*] [*Computer science*]
ODM .... Orbital Determination Module
ODM .... Order of De Molay (AD)
ODM .... Outboard Data Manager [*Computer science*] (BUR)
ODM .... Overseas Development Ministry [*British*]
ODMA .... Office of the Director of Military Assistance [*Air Force*] (AFM)
ODMA .... Open Document Management API [*Application Programming Interface*] [*Computer science*]
ODMA .... Optical Disc Manufacturing Association (IGQR)
ODMA .... Optical Distributors and Manufacturers Association (AD)
ODMC .... Office for Dependents' Medical Care [*Army*] (AABC)
odmc .... Outside Diameter of Male Coupling (AD)
ODMD .... Delcan, Don Mills, Ontario [*Library symbol National Library of Canada*] (NLC)
ODMF .... Ortho-Demethylfortimicin [*Biochemistry*]
ODMG .... Object Database Management Group [*Computer science*] (CDE)
ODMH .... Ohio Department of Mental Health
ODMIBM ...... IBM Canada Ltd., Don Mills, Ontario [*Library symbol National Library of Canada*] (NLC)
ODMII .... Optical Detected Microwave Induced Impact Ionization (AAEL)
ODMN .... National Research Council, Don Mills, Ontario [*Library symbol National Library of Canada*] (NLC)
ODMO .... Office of Defense Management and Organization [*Military*]
ODMR .... Optically Detected Magnetic Resonance [*Spectroscopy*]
ODMRJ .... Rolf Jensen & Associates Ltd., Don Mills, Ontario [*Library symbol National Library of Canada*] (NLC)
ODMS .... Operational Data Management System [*FAA*] (TAG)
ODMT .... Office of the Director of Military Training
ODMWS .... Wyda Systems Canada, Inc., Don Mills, Ontario [*Library symbol National Library of Canada*] (NLC)
ODN .... Company of Mary [*Roman Catholic women's religious order*]
ODN .... Dalton-Dalton-Newport, Cleveland, OH [*OCLC symbol*] (OCLC)
ODN .... Long Seridan [*Malaysia*] [*Airport symbol*] (OAG)
Odn .... Odense (AD)
Odn .... Odin (AD)
ODN .... Oligodeoxynucleotide [*Biochemistry*]
ODN .... Ophthalmodynamometry [*Ophthalmology*]

ODN .... Organization Development Network (EA)
ODN .... Overseas Development Network (EA)
odn .... Own Doppler Nullifer (AD)
ODN .... Own Doppler Nullifier
ODN .... Oxbridge Directory of Newsletters [*A publication*]
ODNA .... Operational Data and Notices to Airmen [*FAA*]
ODNMR........ Optically-Detected Nuclear Magnetic Resonance [*Spectroscopy*]
ODNP .... Ohio Decisions [*A publication*] (DLA)
ODNR .... Oxford Dictionary of Nursery Rhymes [*A publication*]
ODNRI .... Overseas Development Natural Resources Institute [*British Information service or system*] (IID)
ODNS .... Operations Division of Naval Staff [*British*]
Odo .... Odofredus [*Deceased, 1265*] [*Authority cited in pre-1607 legal work*] (DSA)
ODO .... Odometer [*Automotive engineering*]
ODO .... Office of Disability Operations [*Social Security Administration*] [*Began in 1979*] (OICC)
ODO .... Opeongo High School, Douglas, Ontario [*Library symbol National Library of Canada*] (NLC)
ODO .... Operations Duty Officer (MUGU)
ODO .... Outdoor Officer [*Customs*] [*British*]
ODOB .... Dobie Public Library, Ontario [*Library symbol National Library of Canada*] (BIB)
ODOD.......... Oculodento-Osseous Dysplasia (STED)
ODOE .... Oregon Department of Energy (AD)
OD/OE......... Organizational Development/Organizational Effectiveness (MCD)
ODOF .... Dowling Branch, Onaping Falls Public Library, Ontario [*Library symbol National Library of Canada*] (NLC)
Odof .... Odofredus [*Deceased, 1265*] [*Authority cited in pre-1607 legal work*] (DSA)
Odofr .... Odofredus [*Deceased, 1265*] [*Authority cited in pre-1607 legal work*] (DSA)
Odofre .... Odofredus [*Deceased, 1265*] [*Authority cited in pre-1607 legal work*] (DSA)
ODOM .... Odometer (AAG)
odom .... Odometer (AD)
Odonel Mercandil... Odonellus Mercandilis [*Authority cited in pre-1607 legal work*] (DSA)
odont .... Odontogenic (STED)
Odont.......... Odontology (STED)
ODONT........ Odontology
odont .... Odontology (AD)
OdoorS .... Outdoor Systems, Inc. [*Associated Press*] (SAG)
odop .... Offset Doppler (AD)
ODOP .... Offset Doppler
ODOP.......... Orbital Doppler (IAA)
ODOR.......... Dorion Public Library, Ontario [*Library symbol National Library of Canada*] (NLC)
odoram .... Odoramentum [*Perfume*] [*Latin*] (MAE)
odorat .... Odoratus [*Odorous*] [*Latin*] (MAE)
odorl .... Odorless (AD)
ODOT .... Oregon Department of Transportation
ODOTS .... One-Day One-Trial System (AD)
ODOU .... Douro Public Library, Ontario [*Library symbol National Library of Canada*] (BIB)
ODOW .... Ohio Division of Wildlife
O'Dowd Sh... O'Dowd's Merchant Shipping Act [*A publication*] (DLA)
ODP .... Occipitodextra Posterior [*A fetal position*] [*Medicine*] (AAMN)
odp .... Occipito-Dextra Posterior (AD)
ODP .... Ocean Drilling Program [*Texas A & M University*] [*Research center*] (RCD)
ODP .... Octyl Isodecyl Phthalate [*Organic chemistry*]
ODP .... Oekologisch-Demokratische Partei [*Ecological Democratic Party*] [*Germany Political party*] (PPW)
ODP .... Office Depot [*NYSE symbol*] (TTSB)
ODP .... Office Depot, Inc. [*NYSE symbol*] (SPSG)
ODP .... Office of Defense Planning [*of FRS*]
ODP .... Office of Disability Programs [*Social Security Administration*] (OICC)
ODP .... Office of Disaster Preparedness (AD)
ODP .... Officer Distribution Plan [*Army*]
ODP .... Offshore Drilling Platform
ODP .... Open Data Path (MCD)
ODP .... Open Distributed Processing [*Telecommunications*] (OSI)
ODP .... Open Door Policy
ODP .... Open Dripproof
ODP .... Operational Development Plan [*or Program*]
ODP .... Operational Display Procedure [*NASA*] (NAKS)
ODP .... Optical Data Processing
ODP .... Orbit Determination Program
odp .... Order-Despatched (AD)
ODP .... Orderly Departure Program [*for Vietnamese refugees*] [*United Nations*]
ODP .... Order of the Sons of Divine Providence
ODP .... Organic Development Problem (SAA)
ODP .... Organized Reservists in Drill Pay Status [*Military*]
ODP .... Original Departure Point
ODP .... Original Document Processing
ODP .... Outline Development Plan [*Army*] (AFIT)
ODP .... Output-to-Display Parity Error [*Computer science*] (SAA)
ODP .... Overall Documentation Plan [*NATO*] (NATG)
ODP .... Overlay Demonstration Program [*Military*]
ODP .... Oviposition-Determining Pheromone
ODP .... Ozone-Depleting [*or Depletion*] Potential [*Environmental science*]
ODP .... Ozone Depletion Potential [*Meteorology*]

ODPA............ Organization of Democratic and Popular Action [*Morocco*] [*Political party*] (BUAC)

OD (PA & E)... Office of the Director (Program Analysis and Evaluation) (MCD)

ODPCS.......... Oceanographic Data Processing and Control System (OA)

ODPEX.......... Offshore Drilling and Production Exhibition (PDAA)

ODPHP.......... Office of Disease Prevention and Health Promotion [*US Public Health Service*] [*Information service or system*] (IID)

ODPI............. Office of Director Public Information [*Military*]

ODP/MT........ Organisation pour la Democratie Populaire/Mouvement du Travail [*Burkina Faso*] [*Political party*] (EY)

ODPP........... Office of the Director of Public Prosecutions [*Australia*]

ODPP........... Open Dripproof Protected

ODPR........... Office of the Data Protection Registrar (BUAC)

O'D Pr & Acc.... O'Dedy's Principal and Accessory [*1812*] [*A publication*] (DLA)

ODPS........... Operational Data Processing Squadron

ODPSK.......... Oil Dipstick

ODQ............. On Direct Questioning (DMAA)

ODQ............. Opponens Digiti Quinti [*Muscle*] [*Anatomy*] (DAVI)

ODQ............. [*The*] Oxford Dictionary of Quotations [*A publication*]

ODQM.......... Office of the Division Quartermaster

ODR............. Dryden Public Library, Ontario [*Library symbol National Library of Canada*] (NLC)

ODR............. Oculomotor Delayed Response [*Performance test task*]

ODR............. Office of Defense Representative (COE)

ODR............. Office of Defense Resources [*Civil Defense*]

ODR............. Office of Dissemination and Resources [*HEW*]

ODR............. Official Discount Rate [*Finance*] (ECON)

ODR............. Omnidirectional Range

ODR............. On Display Racks [*Freight*]

ODR............. Operational Design Resolution (SAA)

ODR............. Operator Data Register [*Telecommunications*] (TEL)

ODR............. Optical Data Recognition [*Computer science*]

ODR............. ORDALT [*Ordnance Alterations*] Deficiency Review (MCD)

odr.............. Order (AD)

ODR............. Ordnance Difficulty Report (MCD)

ODR............. Original Data Record

ODR............. Oscillating Disk Rheometer (AAEL)

ODR............. Output Data Redundancy (MCD)

ODR............. Output Definition Register

ODR............. Oxygen Diffusion Rate (OA)

ODR............. Roanoke, VA [*Location identifier FAA*] (FAAL)

ODRAN.......... Operational Drawing Revision Advance Notice (NASA)

ODRC........... Office of Disaster Relief Coordinator [*United Nations*] (WDAA)

ODRC........... Orbiter Data Reduction Center [*NASA*] (MCD)

OD Re.......... Ohio Decisions Reprint [*A publication*] (DLA)

OD Rep........ Ohio Decisions Reprint [*A publication*] (DLA)

ODRI............. Deep River Public Library, Ontario [*Library symbol National Library of Canada*] (NLC)

ODRI............. Office of United States Defense Representative, India [*Army*] (AABC)

ODRL............ Delta Branch, Rideau Lakes Union Library, Ontario [*Library symbol National Library of Canada*] (BIB)

ODRM........... Operations Design Reference Mission (MCD)

ODRN........... Orbiting Data Relay Network

ODRP........... Office of Defense Representative, Pakistan [*Army*]

ODRS........... Orbiting Data Relay System (MCD)

ODRS........... Ore Deposits Research Section [*Pennsylvania State University*] [*Research center*] (RCD)

ODRSS.......... Orbiting Data Relay Satellite System (MCD)

O/DRV.......... Over Drive [*Automotive engineering*]

ODS............. Obstacle Detection System

ODS............. Occupational Demand Schedule (ADA)

ODS............. Ocean Data Station [*Marine science*] (MSC)

ODS............. Octadecylsilane [*Organic chemistry*]

ODS............. Octadeyl(dimethyl)chlorosilane [*Organic chemistry*]

ODS............. Odessa [*Ukraine*] [*Airport symbol*] (OAG)

ODS............. Odessa [*Washington*] [*Seismograph station code, US Geological Survey*] (SEIS)

ODS............. Odessa Explorations Ltd. [*Vancouver Stock Exchange symbol*]

ODS............. Odometer Disclosure Statement

ODS............. Office Dialog System [*Computer science*]

ODS............. Office for Domestic Shipping [*Department of Commerce*]

ODS............. Office of Defender Services (AD)

ODS............. Old Dominion Speedway [*Auto racing*]

ODS............. Open Database Server [*Computer science*]

ODS............. Operating-Differential Subsidy [*Authorized by Merchant Marine Act of 1936*]

ODS............. Operational Data Summary (AAG)

ODS............. Operation Desert Storm [*Military*] (RDA)

ODS............. Operations Directorate Station (SAA)

ODS............. Optical Docking System

ODS............. Optimal Decisions System

ODS............. Orbiter Dynamic Simulator [*NASA*]

ODS............. Ordnance Delivery Schedule [*Navy*] (NG)

ODS............. Orton Dyslexia Society (EA)

ODS............. Osric Dining Society (EA)

ODS............. Output Data Strobe

ODS............. Overall Distance Standard [*for golf balls*] [*Adopted by the United States Golf Association in 1976*]

ODS............. Oxidative-Desulfurization [*Fuel technology*]

ods.............. Oxide Dispersion Strengthened (AD)

ODS............. Oxide Dispersion Strengthened [*Ferrous metallurgy*]

ODS............. Oxygen Depletion Sensor

ODS............. Ozone-Depleting Substance (AAGC)

ODSA........... Oil-Dri Corp. of America (EFIS)

ODSA........... Open Distributed Systems Architecture [*British*]

ODSA........... Operating-Differential Subsidy Agreement [*MARAD*] (TAG)

ODSA........... Overseas Development Service Association (BUAC)

ODSAS.......... Officer Dual Specialty Allocation System

ODSB........... Ocean Data Station Buoy

ODSBA.......... Oxford Down Sheep Breeders Association [*British*] (DBA)

ODSD........... Oversea Duty Selection Date [*Air Force*]

odsd............ Overseas Duty Selection Date (AD)

ODSDG......... Dalkeith Branch, Stormont, Dundas, and Glengarry County Library, Ontario [*Library symbol National Library of Canada*] (BIB)

ODSE........... Open Door Student Exchange (EA)

ODS/FRODS... Observable Differences/Functionally Related Observable Differences (MCD)

ODSI............ Ocean Data Systems, Inc. [*Information service or system*] (IID)

ODSI............ Optical Data Systems [*NASDAQ symbol*] (TTSB)

ODSI............ Optical Data Systems, Inc. [*NASDAQ symbol*] (SAG)

ODSR........... Office of the Director of Scientific Research (AD)

ODSRS.......... Orbiting Deep Space Relay Station (MCD)

ODSS........... Ocean Dumping Surveillance System [*Coast Guard*] (MSC)

ODSS........... Order Delivery Schedule Summary (MCD)

ODSY........... Sayun [*People's Democratic Republic of Yemen*] [*ICAO location identifier*] (ICLI)

ODT............. Occipitodextra Transversa [*A fetal position*] [*Medicine*] (AAMN)

odt.............. Occipito-Dextra Transverse (AD)

ODT............. Ocean Data Transmitter

ODT............. Octal Debugging Technique [*Computer science*] (IEEE)

odt.............. Octal Debugging Technique (AD)

odt.............. Odor Detection Threshold (AD)

ODT............. Odor Detection Threshold (PDAA)

ODT............. Office of Defense Transportation [*Within Office for Emergency Management*] [*World War II*]

ODT............. Oklahoma Department of Transportation

ODT............. Omnidirection Transmission (NVT)

odt.............. One-Day Trials (AD)

odt.............. On-Line Debugging Technique [*Computer science*] (AD)

ODT............. Online Debugging Technique

ODT............. Operational Demand Time [*Military*] (CAAL)

ODT............. Operational Demonstration Test

ODT............. Operational Development Team (IAA)

ODT............. Optical Data Transmission

ODT............. Order-Disorder Transformation

ODT............. Otago Daily Times [*A publication*] (AD)

ODT............. Outside Diameter Tube (MSA)

ODT............. Overseas Deployment Training [*Army*]

ODTAA.......... One Damn Thing After Another [*Title of book by John Masefield*]

ODTACCS..... Office of the Director, Telecommunications, and Command and Control Systems [*DoD*] (PDAA)

ODTC........... Office of Defense Trade Controls (AAGC)

ODTC........... Optic Display Test Chamber

ODTF........... Operational Development Test Facility (AAG)

ODTM........... Orbiter Dynamic Test Model [*NASA*]

ODTS........... Offset Doppler Tracking System (KSC)

ODTS........... Operational Development Test Site (AAG)

ODTS........... Optical Data Transmission System

ODTS........... Optical Discrimination and Tracking System [*Army*]

ODTS........... Organic Dust Toxic Syndrome [*Medicine*]

ODTW.......... Oppositely-Directed Travelling Wave (PDAA)

ODU............. Dunnville Public Library, Ontario [*Library symbol National Library of Canada*] (NLC)

ODU............. Old Dominion University [*Virginia*]

ODU............. Old Dutch [*Language, etc.*]

ODU............. Optical Density Unit

ODU............. Optical Display Unit [*Computer science*] (MCD)

ODU............. Output Display Unit [*Computer science*]

ODUB........... Bibliotheque Publique de Dubreuilville, Ontario [*Library symbol National Library of Canada*] (NLC)

ODUC........... Ohio Data Users Center [*Columbus*] [*Information service or system*] (IID)

ODUM.......... Association of American Youth of Ukrainian Descent (EA)

ODUMP........ Ocean Dumping Permits [*Database*] [*Environment Canada*] [*Information service or system*] (CRD)

ODUN........... Dundalk Public Library, Ontario [*Library symbol National Library of Canada*] (NLC)

od units...... Optical-Density Units (AD)

ODUR........... Durham Public Library, Ontario [*Library symbol National Library of Canada*] (NLC)

ODURF......... Old Dominion University Research Foundation [*Old Dominion University*] [*Research center*] (RCD)

ODUSD(ES)... Office of the Deputy Under Secretary of Defense (Environmental Security) [*DoD*] (RDA)

ODUSD (R & AT)... Office of the Deputy Under Secretary of Defense for Research and Advanced Technology [*DoD*] (RDA)

ODUSM........ Office, Deputy Under Secretary for Manpower [*Navy*]

ODUSN......... Office, Deputy Under Secretary of the Navy

ODV............. Eau-de-Vie [*Taken from the French pronunciation and used to refer to brandy*]

ODVA........... Open DeviceNet Vendors Association (ACII)

ODVAR......... Orbit Determination and Vehicle Attitude Reference

ODVP........... Optimal Digital Voice Processor (MCD)

ODW............. Oak Harbor [*Washington*] [*Airport symbol*] (OAG)

ODW............. Office of Drinking Water [*Environmental Protection Agency*]

ODW............. Ohio Wesleyan University, Delaware, OH [*Library symbol Library of Congress*] (LCLS)

ODW............. Omega Dropwindsonde [*Meteorology*]

ODW............. Oregon Draymen & Warehousemen's Association, Portland OR [*STAC*]

ODW	Organic Dry Weight
ODW	Our Developing World [*An association*] (EA)
ODW	Output Discrete Word (MCD)
ODW	Oven-Dried Weight
ODW	Workers Health and Safety Centre, Don Mills, Ontario [*Library symbol National Library of Canada*] (BIB)
ODWA	Odwalla, Inc. [*NASDAQ symbol*] (SAG)
Odwalla	Odwalla, Inc. [*Associated Press*] (SAG)
ODWC	West Carleton Secondary School, Dunrobin, Ontario [*Library symbol National Library of Canada*] (BIB)
ODWIN	Opening Doors Wider in Nursing [*Project*]
ODWSA	Office of the Directorate of Weapon Systems Analysis [*Army*] (AABC)
O'Dwyer	Jack O'Dwyer's Newsletter [*A publication*] [*New York, NY*] (WDMC)
ODX	Ord, NE [*Location identifier FAA*] (FAAL)
ODY	Odyssey Industries, Inc. [*Toronto Stock Exchange symbol*]
ODY	Odyssey International [*Canada ICAO designator*] (FAAC)
ODZ	Outer Defense Zone
OE	Austria [*International civil aircraft marking*] (ODBW)
OE	Exeter Public Library, Ontario [*Library symbol National Library of Canada*] (NLC)
O/E	Observed versus Expected
OE	OE, Inc. [*Toronto Stock Exchange symbol*]
Oe	Oersted [*Unit of magnetizing intensity*]
oe	Oersted (AD)
OE	Offensive End [*Football*]
OE	Office Equipment
OE	Office of Education [*HEW*]
OE	Office of Energy [*Department of Agriculture*] (GFGA)
OE	Office of Enforcement [*Environmental Protection Agency*] (GFGA)
OE	Oil Emulsion [*Microbiology*]
OE	Oil Equivalent
OE	Old English [*Language, etc.*] [*i.e., before 1150 or 1200*]
OE	Old English [*Typeface*] (WDMC)
OE	Old Etonian [*British*]
OE	Omission Excepted (IAA)
OE	Omissions Excepted
oe	Omissions Excepted (WDAA)
oe	Omissions Expected (AD)
o/e	On Examination (AD)
OE	On Examination [*Medicine*]
OE	Opened Edges [*Publishing*] (DGA)
OE	Open End (MSA)
oe	Open End (AD)
OE	Operating Engineer (NRCH)
OE	Operating Expense
OE	Operational Evaluation [*Army*]
OE	Operation Enterprise [*Hamilton, NY*] (EA)
OE	Operation Enterprise Newsletter [*A publication*]
OE	Operations Engineering (AAG)
OE	Optical/Electrical Conversion [*Telecommunications*]
OE	Optical Emission (MCD)
OE	Orbital Engine ADS [*NYSE symbol*] (SPSG)
OE	Order Entry (DMAA)
O/E	Order/Entry System [*Computer science*] (DHSM)
OE	Ordnance Electrician [*British military*] (DMA)
OE	Ordnance Engineer [*British military*] (DMA)
OE	Oregon Electric Railway Co. [*AAR code*]
OE	Organizational Effectiveness
oe	Organizational Effectiveness (AD)
OE	Organizational Entity
OE	Organizational Error [*Engineering*]
OE	Organo Espressivo [*Swell Organ*] [*Music*]
oe	Organo Espressivo [*Swell Organ*] [*Italian*] (AD)
OE	Orientalium Ecclesiarum [*Decree on the Eastern Catholic Churches*] [*Vatican II document*]
OE	Original Entry [*Computer science*]
OE	Original Equipment [*Automobile industry*]
OE	Original Error [*Navigation*]
OE	Orthoenstatite [*Mineral*]
OE	Other Essays [*Literature*] (ROG)
o/e	Otitis Externa (AD)
OE	Otitis Externa [*Medicine*] (DMAA)
oe	Outdoor Education (AD)
OE	Out Island Airways (OAG)
OE	Outlook Express [*Computer science*] (PCM)
OE	Output Enable [*Semiconductor memory*] (IEEE)
OE	Over-the-Horizon Expanded (MCD)
OE	Own Exchange [*Telecommunications*] (TEL)
OE	Samoan [*ICAO designator*] (AD)
OEA	Archives, City of Etobicoke, Ontario [*Library symbol National Library of Canada*] (BIB)
OEA	Eastern Oklahoma District Library, Muskogee, OK [*OCLC symbol*] (OCLC)
OEA	Oahu Education Association [*Hawaii*] (AD)
OEA	Oblate Education Association [*Defunct*] (EA)
OEA	OEA, Inc. [*NYSE symbol*] (SPSG)
OEA	Office Education Association (EA)
OEA	Office Executives Association (AD)
OEA	Office of Economic Adjustment [*Air Force*] (AFM)
OEA	Office of Economic Analysis [*Formerly, Office of Business Economics*] [*Department of Commerce*]
OEA	Office of Environmental Affairs (AD)
OEA	Office of Environmental Analysis [*Oak Ridge National Laboratory*]
OEA	Office of Ethnic Affairs [*Victoria, Australia*]

OEA	Office of European Associations in Higher Education [*Belgium*] (BUAC)
OEA	Office of Export Administration [*Formerly, OEC*] [*Department of Commerce*]
OEA	Office of External Affairs [*Environmental Protection Agency*] (GFGA)
OEA	Ohio Education Association (AD)
OEA	Operational Effectiveness Analysis (MCD)
OEA	Operator Error Analysis
OEA	Ophthalmic Exhibitors' Association [*British*] (DBA)
OEA	Optometric Editors Association (EA)
OEA	Orchestral Employers' Association [*British*] (BI)
OEA	Ordnance Electrical Artificer [*British military*] (DMA)
OEA	Oregon Education Association (AD)
OEA	Organisation of Europe Aluminium-Smelters (BUAC)
OEA	Organizacion de los Estados Americanos [*Organization of American States - OAS*] [*Spanish*]
OEA	Organizational Expense Accounts [*Army*]
OEA	Outdoor Education Association (EA)
OEA	Overseas Education Association (EA)
OEA	Vincennes, IN [*Location identifier FAA*] (FAAL)
OEAA	Oil Engineering Apprentices Association (AD)
OEAB	Abha [*Saudi Arabia*] [*ICAO location identifier*] (ICLI)
OEac	East Cleveland Public Library, East Cleveland, OH [*Library symbol Library of Congress*] (LCLS)
OEAH	Al-Ahsa [*Saudi Arabia*] [*ICAO location identifier*] (ICLI)
OEal	East Liverpool Carnegie Public Library, East Liverpool, OH [*Library symbol Library of Congress*] (LCLS)
OEALC	Oficina Regional de Educacion para America Latina y el Caribe [*Regional Office for Education in Latin America and the Caribbean-Chile*] (IID)
OEalK	Kent State University, East Liverpool Regional Campus, East Liverpool, OH [*Library symbol Library of Congress*] (LCLS)
OE & TB	Officer Education and Training Branch [*BUPERS*]
OEAP	Operational Error Analysis Program
OEAQ	Outdoor Educators' Association of Queensland [*Australia*]
OEAS	Orbital Emergency Arresting System [*NASA*] (NASA)
OEAS	Organisation Europaischer Aluminium Schmelzhutten [*Organization of European Aluminium Foundries*] (PDAA)
OEAS	Oxygen Enriched Air System (MCD)
OEB	Officers' Organization for Economic Benefits [*Commercial firm*] (EA)
OEB	Oregon Educational Broadcasting (AD)
OEB	Organic Electrolyte Battery
OEBA	El-Baha [*Saudi Arabia*] [*ICAO location identifier*] (ICLI)
OEBA	Office for Economic and Business Affairs [*Department of State*]
OEBH	Bisha [*Saudi Arabia*] [*ICAO location identifier*] (ICLI)
OEBR	Optical Edge Bead Removal (AAEL)
OEBS	Office of Employee Benefits Security [*Department of Labor*]
OEBS	Organic Electrolyte Battery System
OEC	Observed Effect Concentration [*Environmental science*] (ERG)
OEC	Odd-Even Check
Oec	Oeconomica [*of Aristotle*] [*Classical studies*] (OCD)
Oec	Oeconomicus [*of Xenophon*] [*Classical studies*] (OCD)
OEC	Oesterreichischer Aero-Club [*Austrian Aero Club*] [*German*] (AD)
OEC	Office of Emergency Communications [*FCC*] (NTCM)
OEC	Office of Energy Conservation [*Functions transferred to Federal Energy Administration*]
OEC	Office of Export Control [*Later, OEA*] [*World War II*]
OEC	Office on Educational Credit [*Later, OECC*] (EA)
OEC	Ohio Edison [*NYSE symbol*] (TTSB)
OEC	Ohio Edison Co. [*NYSE symbol*] (SPSG)
OEC	Ohio Edison Financing Trust [*NYSE symbol*] (SAG)
OEC	Oil Exporting Countries (AD)
OEC	Ontario Election Decisions [*A publication*] (DLA)
OEC	Open-End Company [*Business term*] (MHDW)
OEC	Open-End Credit [*Business term*] (MHDW)
OEC	Operational Employment Concept [*Army*] (AABC)
OEC	Operational Evaluation Command [*Army*] (DOMA)
OEC	Optical Effect Code
OEC	Optic-Electronic Corp. (RDA)
OEC	Opto-Electronics Center (MCD)
OEC	Orange Empire Conference (PSS)
OEC	Orbital Electron Capture
OEC	Orbiting Experimental Capsule
OEC	Ordnance Equipment Chart
OEC	Organizational Effectiveness Consultants (INF)
OEC	Organizational Entity Code
oec	Organizational Entity Code (AD)
OEC	Overpaid Entry Certificate (DS)
OEC	Overseas Employment Corp. [*Pakistan*] (BUAC)
OEC	Oxygen Equilibrium Curve (DB)
OEC	Oxygen-Evolving Complex [*Photosynthesis*]
OECA	Office of Enforcement and Compliance Assurance [*Environmental Protection Agency*] (AEPA)
OECA	Ontario Educational Communications Authority [*Canada*]
OEC & S	Organizational Effectiveness Center and School [*Army*]
OECC	Office on Educational Credit and Credentials (EA)
OECC	Oregon Educational Computing Consortium (EDAC)
OECCNU	Organizacion para la Educacion la Ciencia, y la Cultura [*Organization for Education, Science, and Culture*] [*United Nations*] (AD)
OECD	Organization for Economic Cooperation and Development [*Formerly, OEEC*]
OECD/ENC	Organization for Economic Cooperation and Development/ Environment Committee [*Marine science*] (MSC)
OECD/MEI	OECD Main Economics Indicators (NITA)
OECD/NIA	OECD National Income Accounts (NITA)

OECE............	Organisation Europeenne de Cooperation Economique [*Organization for European Economic Cooperation - OEEC*] [*Later, OECD See also OCDE France*] (MSC)
OECE............	Organizacion Europea de Cooperacion Economica [*Organization for European Economic Cooperation - OEEC*] [*Later, OECD Spain*]
OECF............	Overseas Economic Cooperation Fund (AD)
OECF............	Overseas Economic Cooperation Fund of Japan (BUAC)
OECIC	Open-End Contract Information Circulars (AAGC)
OECM..........	Office of Enforcement and Compliance Monitoring [*Environmental Protection Agency*] (GFGA)
OEC Md	OEC Medical [*Associated Press*] (SAG)
OECO	Outboard Engine Cutoff [*NASA*]
oeco............	Outboard Engine Cutoff (AD)
OECON........	Offshore Engineering Conference (MCD)
OECON........	Offshore Exploration Conference
OECPrA	Ohio Edison 3.90% Pfd [*NYSE symbol*] (TTSB)
OECPrB	Ohio Edison, 4.40% Pfd [*NYSE symbol*] (TTSB)
OECPrC	Ohio Edison 4.44% Pfd [*NYSE symbol*] (TTSB)
OECPrT	Ohio Edison Fin Tr 9.00% Pfd [*NYSE symbol*] (TTSB)
OECQ	Organisation Europeene pour la Controle de la Qualite GG1European Quality-Control OrganizationGG2 [*France*] (AD)
OECQ	Organisation Europeenne pour la Qualite [*European Organization for Quality -EOQC*] [*Switzerland*]
OECS	Organisation of Eastern Caribbean States (EAIO)
OECS	Organization for the Enforcement of Child Support (EA)
OECS	Organization of East Caribbean States (NADA)
OECSEAS	Organisation of Eastern Caribbean States, Economic Affairs Secretariat [*St. Johns, Antigua*] (EAIO)
OECT............	European Association of the Textile Wholesale Trade [*EC*] (ECED)
OECT............	Oxford Editions of Cuneiform Texts [*A publication*] (BJA)
oecu............	Outboard Engine Cutoff (AD)
OED	Ocean Engineering Division [*Coast Guard*]
OED	Office of Economic Development [*Bureau of Indian Affairs*]
OED	Operational Engineering Detachment (MCD)
OED	Operational Engineering Division [*Central Electricity Generating Board*] [*British*] (IRUK)
OED	Operational Evaluation Demonstration (MCD)
OED	Operation Effectiveness Demonstration (RDA)
OED	Orbiting Energy Depot
OED	Otto Erich Deutsch [*Music cataloger*]
OED	Oxford English Dictionary [*Information service or system A publication*]
OEDA	Office of Energy Data and Analysis [*Functions transferred to Federal Energy Administration*]
OEDC	Office of Engineering Design and Construction [*Tennessee Valley Authority*]
OEDC	Offshore Energy Development Corp. [*NASDAQ symbol*] (SAG)
OEDIPUS	Oxford English Dictionary Inputting, Proofing, and Updating Service
OEDIT	Octal Editor [*Computer science*] (MHDI)
OEDO	Ordnance Engineering Duty Officer
OEDP	Office of Employment Development Programs (AD)
OEDP	Overall Economic Development Program [*Bureau of Indian Affairs*]
OEDR	Dhahran/International [*Saudi Arabia*] [*ICAO location identifier*] (ICLI)
OEDRC........	Optico-Electronic Device for Registering Coincidences (PDAA)
OEDSF	On-Board Experimental Data Support Facility
OEE..............	Ernst & Whinney, Cleveland, OH [*OCLC symbol*] (OCLC)
OEE..............	Essex County Public Library, Essex, Ontario [*Library symbol National Library of Canada*] (NLC)
OEE..............	Office of Educational Exchange [*Department of State*]
OEE..............	Office of the Assistant Secretary for Export Enforcement [*Department of Commerce*] (GFGA)
OEE.............	Ordre de l'Etoile de l'Europe [*Huy, Belgium*] (EAIO)
OEE.............	Outer Enamel Epithelium [*Dentistry*]
oee.............	Outer Enamel Epithelium (AD)
OEE.............	Overall Equipment Effectiveness (AAEL)
OEEC............	Organization for European Economic Cooperation [*Later, OECD*]
OEED	Oxford Encyclopedic English Dictionary [*A publication*]
OEEO	Office of Equal Educational Opportunities [*Office of Education*]
OEEO	Office of Equal Employment Opportunity [*Department of Labor*] (OICC)
OEEPE..........	Organisation Europeenne d'Etudes Photogrammetriques Experimentales [*European Organisation for Experimental Photogrammetric Research*] [*Research Center Netherlands*] (PDAA)
OEER	Oceanographic Equipment Evaluation Range (NOAA)
OEES...........	Interagency Committee on Ocean Exploration and Environmental Services [*Terminated, 1971*] (EGAO)
OEES...........	Organization for Equal Education of the Sexes (EA)
OEET	Office of Environmental Engineering and Technology [*Environmental Protection Agency*] (EPA)
OEETD	Office of Environmental Engineering and Technology Demonstration [*Washington, DC Environmental Protection Agency*] (GRD)
OEF..............	Ear Falls Public Library, Ontario [*Library symbol National Library of Canada*] (NLC)
OEF.............	Oceanic Educational Foundation (EA)
OEF.............	Officeholders Expense Funds [*Slush money*]
OEF.............	Oil Emersion Field [*Biochemistry*] (DAVI)
OEF.............	Open-End Funds [*Investment term*]
OEF.............	Optical Evaluation Facility (RDA)
OEF.............	Osteopathic Educational Foundation (AD)
OEF.............	Overseas Education Fund [*Later, OEFI*] (EA)
OEF.............	Oxford Economic Forecasting (BUAC)
OEF.............	Oxygen Extraction Fraction [*Medicine*] (DMAA)
OEFD	Orbiter Electric Field Detector [*NASA*]
OEFE............	Flos-Elmvale Public Library, Elmvale, Ontario [*Library symbol National Library of Canada*] (BIB)
OEFI............	OEF [*Overseas Educational Fund*] International (EA)
OEG	Eganville Public Library, Ontario [*Library symbol National Library of Canada*] (NLC)
OEG	Occluded Eye Gunsight [*Military*] (INF)
OEG	Operational Exposure Guidance [*Military*] (INF)
OEG	Operations Evaluation Group [*Military*]
OEG	Organization and Equipment Guide [*Army*] (AABC)
OEG	Outdoor Ethics Guild (EA)
OEG	Public Library of Enid and Garfield County, Enid, OK [*OCLC symbol*] (OCLC)
OEGCA........	Old English Game Club of America (EA)
OEGCMJ......	Officer Exercising General Court-Martial Jurisdiction
OEGN	Gizan [*Saudi Arabia*] [*ICAO location identifier*] (ICLI)
OEGS	Gassim [*Saudi Arabia*] [*ICAO location identifier*] (ICLI)
OEGT	Guriat [*Saudi Arabia*] [*ICAO location identifier*] (ICLI)
oegt	Observable Evidence of Good Teaching (AD)
OEGT	Observable Evidences of Good Teaching
OEGT	Office of Education for the Gifted and Talented [*HEW*]
OEH	Baltimore, MD [*Location identifier FAA*] (FAAL)
OEH	Orient Express Hotels (EFIS)
OEHA	Office of Environmental and Health Affairs [*World Bank*] (BUAC)
OEHL	Hail [*Saudi Arabia*] [*ICAO location identifier*] (ICLI)
OEHL	Hoffman-La Roche Ltd., Etobicoke, Ontario [*Library symbol National Library of Canada*] (NLC)
OEHL	Occupational and Environmental Health Laboratory [*Brooks Air Force Base, TX*] [*Air Force*]
OEHMO	Open-Ended Health Maintenance Organization [*Insurance*] (WYGK)
OEI	Ocean Energy [*NYSE symbol*] [*Formerly, Flores & Rucks*] (SG)
OEI	Offshore Ecology Investigation [*Oil study*]
OEI	Oficina de Educacion Iberoamericana [*Ibero-American Bureau of Education - IABE*] [*Madrid, Spain*] (EAIO)
OEI	One Engine Inoperative [*Aviation*]
OEI	Options Exchange Index
OEI	Optoelectronic Isolator
OEI	Organizacion de Estados Iberoamericanos para la Educacion, la Ciencia, y la Cultura [*Organization of Ibero-American States for Education, Science, and Culture*] (EAIO)
OEI	Organizational Entity Identity
oei	Organizational Entity Identity (AD)
OEI	Overall Efficiency Index
OEIAA	Office Equipment Industry Association of Australia
OEIC............	Ocean Engineering Information Centre [*Memorial University of Newfoundland*] [*Information service or system*] (IID)
OEIC............	Open-End Investment Co. [*Investment term*]
OEIC............	Optoelectronic Integrated Circuit [*Computer science*]
OEIC............	Opto-Electronic Integrated Circuits
OEIC............	Overseas Economic Intelligence Committee [*Military*]
OEID	Office of Engineering Infrastructure Development [*Washington, DC National Science Foundation*] (GRD)
OEII............	O'Neill Educational Ideologies Inventory (EDAC)
OEII............	Operation Everest II [*Army*] (RDA)
OEIO	Odds and Ends Input/Output (MCD)
OEIPS	Office of Engineering and Information Processing Standards [*National Bureau of Standards*]
OEIS............	Office of Energy Information Services [*Department of Energy*] (IID)
OEIS............	Orbiter Electrical Interface Simulator [*NASA*]
OEIT............	Open-End Investment Trust [*Investment term*]
OEITFL........	Organisation Europeenne des Industries Transformatrices de Fruits et Legumes [*European Organization of Fruit and Vegetable Processing Industries*] [*Common Market*] [*Belgium*]
OEIU...........	Office Employes International Union [*Later, OPEIU*]
OEJ	Office of Environmental Justice [*Environmental Protection Agency*] (AEPA)
OEJB	Jubail [*Saudi Arabia*] [*ICAO location identifier*] (ICLI)
OEJD...........	Jeddah [*Saudi Arabia*] [*ICAO location identifier*] (ICLI)
OEJH	Office of Environmental Justice Hotline [*Environmental Protection Agency*] (AEPA)
OEJN	Jeddah/King Abdul Aziz International [*Saudi Arabia*] [*ICAO location identifier*] (ICLI)
OEKJ	Al-Kharj [*Saudi Arabia*] [*ICAO location identifier*] (ICLI)
OEKM	Khamis Mushait [*Saudi Arabia*] [*ICAO location identifier*] (ICLI)
OEL.............	Elliot Lake Public Library, Ontario [*Library symbol National Library of Canada*] (NLC)
OEL.............	Eugene Public Library, Eugene, OR [*OCLC symbol*] (OCLC)
OEL.............	Oakley, KS [*Location identifier FAA*] (FAAL)
OEL.............	Occupational Exposure Limit
OEL.............	Ontario Express Ltd. [*Canada ICAO designator*] (FAAC)
OEL.............	Ordnance Engineering Laboratory
OEL.............	Ordnance Equipment List [*Navy*] (NG)
OEL.............	Organizational Equipment List [*Army*]
OELB...........	Oertlicher Landwirtschaftsbetrieb [*Local Agricultural Enterprise*] [*German*]
OELD	Office of the Executive Legal Director [*Nuclear Regulatory Commission*] (GFGA)
OELF	Fort Hope Band Library, Eabamet Lake, Ontario [*Library symbol National Library of Canada*] (BIB)
OELK	Elk Lake Public Library, Ontario [*Library symbol National Library of Canada*] (BIB)
OELM	Elmwood Branch, Bruce County Public Library, Ontario [*Library symbol National Library of Canada*] (NLC)
OELMA	Ohio Educational Library Media Association (EDAC)
OELMN(A)....	Ordnance Electrical Mechanician (Air) [*British military*] (DMA)

OELRR	Office of Economic Liaison and Regulatory Review [*Western Australia*]
OELS	Elliot Lake Secondary School, Ontario [*Library symbol National Library of Canada*] (NLC)
OEly	Elyria Library, Elyria, OH [*Library symbol Library of Congress*] (LCLS)
OElyL	Lorain County Community College, Elyria, OH [*Library symbol Library of Congress*] (LCLS)
OEM	Emo Public Library, Ontario [*Library symbol National Library of Canada*] (NLC)
OEM	Occupational and Environmental Medicine
OEM	Office Equipment Maintenance
OEM	Office for Emergency Management [*World War II*]
OEM	Office of Electronic Machines [*Commercial firm British*]
OEM	Office of Environmental Mediation
OEM	Office of Executive Management
oem	Oil-Emulsion Mud (AD)
OEM	On Equipment Materiel [*Army*] (AABC)
OEM	Open-End Marriage
OEM	Optical Electronic Microscope (WDAA)
OEM	Optical Electron Microscope (PDAA)
oem	Optical Electron Microscope (AD)
OEM	Ordnance Electrical Mechanic [*British military*] (DMA)
OEM	Organizational Element Model
OEM	Original Equipment Manufacturer
oem	Original Equipment Manufacturer (AD)
OEM	Other Equipment Manufacturer (IAA)
OEM	Other Equipment Manufacturers (CMD)
OEM	Own Equipment Material
OEMA	Madinah [*Saudi Arabia*] [*ICAO location identifier*] (ICLI)
OEMA	Office Equipment Manufacturers Association (AD)
OEMA	Office of Educational and Manpower Assistance (OICC)
OEMA	Office of Export Marketing Assistance [*Department of Commerce*]
OEMCP	Optical Effects Module Electronic Controller and Processor [*NASA*]
oemcp	Optical Effects Module Electronic Controller and Processor (AD)
OEMI	Office Equipment Manufacturers Institute [*Later, CBEMA*]
OEMI	Office of Energy, Minerals, and Industry [*Environmental Protection Agency*]
OEMI	Other Equipment Manufacturer's Information (IAA)
OEMN	Ordnance Electrical Mechanician [*British military*] (DMA)
OEMO	One-Electron Molecular Orbital (DB)
OEMP	Office of Environmental Monitoring and Prediction [*Marine science*] (OSRA)
OEMSA	Optical Equipment Manufacturers and Suppliers Association (BUAC)
OEMT	Operational Emergency Management Team [*Environmental science*] (COE)
OEN	Ennismore Township Public Library, Ontario [*Library symbol National Library of Canada*] (BIB)
OEN	Odd-Even Nuclei
oen	Oenanthic (AD)
oen	Oenanthyl (AD)
oen	oenomancy (AD)
oen	oenomel (AD)
oen	oenometer (AD)
oen	oenophilist (AD)
oen	oenophobist (AD)
oen	oenopoetic (AD)
OEN	Ohio Environmental Protection Agency Library, Columbus, OH [*OCLC symbol*] (OCLC)
OEN	Organizational Entity Name
OENCO	Organizational Effectiveness Noncommissioned Officer [*Military*]
OENG	Englehart Public Library, Ontario [*Library symbol National Library of Canada*] (BIB)
OENG	Nejran [*Saudi Arabia*] [*ICAO location identifier*] (ICLI)
OENLA	Enterprise Branch, Lennox and Addington County Library, Ontario [*Library symbol National Library of Canada*] (NLC)
OENR	Oil-Extended Natural Rubber
OENR	Organization for European Nuclear Research
OEO	Office of Economic Opportunity [*Functions transferred to other federal agencies, 1973-75*]
OEO	Office of Equal Opportunity [*NASA*]
OEO	Officers' Eyes Only [*Military*] (NVT)
oeo	Officer's Eyes Only (AD)
OEO	Ordnance Engineer Overseer (AD)
OEO	Ordnance Executive Officer [*Military British*]
OEO	Osceola, WI [*Location identifier FAA*] (FAAL)
OEO	Oversea Employment Office [*Air Force*] (AFM)
OEOA	Office for Emergency Operations in Africa [*United Nations*] (EY)
OEOB	Old Executive Office Building [*Washington, DC*]
OE/OE	Open Entry/Open Exit (OICC)
OEP	Occupational Education Project
OEP	Occupational Exploration Program (OICC)
OEP	Ocean Education Project (EA)
OEP	Odd-Even Predominance [*Organic chemistry*]
OEP	Office of Economic Programs [*of BDSA*]
OEP	Office of Emergency Planning (AD)
OEP	Office of Emergency Preparedness [*formerly, Planning*] [*Terminated, 1973*]
OEP	Office of Energy Planning (COE)
OEP	Office of Energy Programs [*NASA*]
OEP	Office of Environmental Policy [*White House*] [*Marine science*] (OSRA)
OEP	Office of External Programs [*Environmental Protection Agency*] (GFGA)
OEP	Oil-Extended Polymer (IAA)
OEP	Open-Ended Plan [*Human resources*] (WYGK)
OEP	Operand Execution Pipeline [*Computer science*]
OEP	Operational Employment Plan [*Army*]
OEP	Optional Educational Programs (AD)
OEP	Original Element Processor (MHDB)
OEP	Outside Engineering Personnel (MCD)
OEP	Overseas Employment Program [*DoD*]
OEP	Owen Electric Pictures [*Telecommunications service*] (TSSD)
OEP	Preble County District Library, Eaton, OH [*Library symbol Library of Congress*] (LCLS)
OEPA	Hafr Al-Batin Airport [*Saudi Arabia*] [*ICAO location identifier*] (ICLI)
OEPA	Ohio Environmental Protection Agency
OEPAC	Office of the Economic Planning Advisory Council [*Australia*]
OEPER	Office of Environmental Processes and Effects Research [*Environmental Protection Agency Washington, DC*] (GRD)
OEPF	Optometric Extension Program Foundation (EA)
OEPFC	Official Elvis Presley Fan Club (EAIO)
OEPP	Organisation Europeenne et Mediterraneenne pour la Protection des Plantes [*European and Mediterranean Plant Protection Organization - EPPO*] (EAIO)
OEPR	Office of Environmental Project Review [*Department of the Interior*]
OEPR	Office of Extramural Program Review [*Department of Health and Human Services*] (GRD)
OEPS	Office of Educational Programs and Services [*NASA*]
OEPT	Perry Township Public Library Emsdale, Ontario [*Library symbol National Library of Canada*] (NLC)
OEQ	Order of Engineers of Quebec [*Canada*] (PDAA)
OEQ	Organisation Europeenne pour la Qualite [*Switzerland*] (EAIO)
OEQC	Office of Environmental Quality Control (AD)
OER	Odd-Even Rule
OER	Oersted [*Unit of magnetizing intensity*]
OER	Offensive Efficiency Ratio [*Basketball*]
OER	Office of Aerospace Research [*Air Force*] (AD)
OER	Office of Economic Research [*Department of Commerce*]
OER	Office of Energy Research [*Department of Energy Washington, DC*] (GRD)
OER	Office of Energy Research [*University of Illinois*] [*Research center*] (RCD)
OER	Office of Evaluation Research [*University of Illinois at Chicago*] [*Research center*] (RCD)
OER	Office of Exploratory Research [*Environmental Protection Agency Washington, DC*] (GRD)
OER	Officer Effectiveness Report [*Air Force*] (AFM)
OER	Officer Efficiency Report [*Military*]
OER	Officer Engineering Reserve (AD)
OER	Officer Evaluation Report [*Military*] (INF)
OER	Officers' Emergency Reserve [*British*]
OER	Oil Extended Rubber (EDCT)
OER	Operational ELINT Requirements (MCD)
OER	Operational Equipment Requirement (AAG)
OER	Operations Engineering Report (AAG)
OER	Organization for European Research (AD)
oer	Original Equipment Replacement (AD)
OER	Original Equipment Request (AAG)
OER	Ornskoldsvik [*Sweden*] [*Airport symbol*] (OAG)
OER	Osmotic Erythrocyte Resistance
O'ER	Over (ROG)
OER	Overhead Expenditure Request
OER	Oxygen Enhancement Ratio
OER	Oxygen Evolution Reaction (PDAA)
OERA	Omnibus Education Reconciliation Act of 1981
OERAHA	Organisation Europeenne pour des Recherches Astronomiques dans l'Hemisphere Austral [*European Southern Observatory - ESO*] (EAIO)
OERC	Ontario Educational Research Council [*Canada*] (EDAC)
OERC	Optimum Earth Reentry Corridor [*Aerospace*]
oerc	Optimum Earth-Reentry Corridor (AD)
OERCPrD	Ohio Edison 4.56% Pfd [*NYSE symbol*] (TTSB)
OERD	Erin District High School, Erin, Ontario [*Library symbol National Library of Canada*] (NLC)
OERD	Ocean Environment Research Division [*Formerly, MARD, Marine Assessment Research Division and MRRD, Marine Resources Research Division*] [*Marine science*] (OSRA)
OERF	Orthodontic Education and Research Foundation (EA)
OERF	Rafha [*Saudi Arabia*] [*ICAO location identifier*] (ICLI)
OERI	Office of Educational Research and Improvement [*Department of Education Washington, DC*]
OERI	Office of Energy-Related Inventions [*Gaithersburg, MD*] [*National Institute of Standards and Technology*]
OERK	Riyadh/King Khalid International [*Saudi Arabia*] [*ICAO location identifier*] (ICLI)
OERL	Elgin Branch, Rideau Lakes Union Library, Ontario [*Library symbol National Library of Canada*] (NLC)
OERL	Officer Education Research Laboratory [*Air Force*]
OERL	Overall Echo Return Loss
OERP	Overseas Expenditure Reduction Program [*Military*] (AFM)
OERPA	Office of Exploratory Research and Problem Assessment [*National Science Foundation*] (AD)
OERR	Arar [*Saudi Arabia*] [*ICAO location identifier*] (ICLI)
OERR	Office of Emergency and Remedial Response [*Environmental Protection Agency*] (GFGA)
OERS	Officer Evaluation Reporting System [*Army*]
OERS	Organisation Europeenne de Recherches Spatiales
OERT	Succursale d'Embrun, Bibliotheque Publique du Canton de Russell [*Embrun Branch, Russell Township Public Library*] Ontario [*Library symbol National Library of Canada*] (BIB)

OERWM .... Office of Environmental Restoration and Waste Management [*U.S. Department of Energy*] (BARN)

OERY .... Riyadh [*Saudi Arabia*] [*ICAO location identifier*] (ICLI)

OES .... Bureau of Oceans and International Environmental and Scientific Affairs [*Department of State*]

OES .... Espanola Public Library, Ontario [*Library symbol National Library of Canada*] (NLC)

OES .... IEEE Oceanic Engineering Society (EA)

OES .... Occupational Employment Statistics [*Department of Labor*]

OES .... Occupational Exposure Standard [*Environmental chemistry*]

OES .... Office of Economic Stabilization

OES .... Office of Emergency Service [*Federal disaster planning*]

OES .... Office of Employment Security [*Department of Labor*]

OES .... Office of Endangered Species [*Department of the Interior*]

OES .... Office of Examinations and Supervision [*Federal Home Loan Bank Board*]

OES .... Office of Executive Support [*Environmental Protection Agency*] (GFGA)

OES .... Officer Education System [*Army*] (RDA)

OES .... Official Experimental Station [*Amateur radio*]

OES .... Offshore Engineering Society (BUAC)

OES .... Olympus Endoscopy System [*Gastroenterology*] (DAVI)

OES .... Open-Ended Spinning [*Textile industry*]

OES .... Open-Ended System [*Computer science*]

OES .... Operations and Engineering Squadron

OES .... Operations and Equipment Section (SAA)

OES .... Optical Emission Spectroscopy [*Laboratory science*] (DAVI)

OES .... Orbital-Escape System [*NASA*]

OES .... Orbiter Emergency Site [*NASA*] (NASA)

OES .... Order/Entry System [*Computer science*] (OA)

OES .... Order of the Eastern Star [*Freemasonry*] (EA)

OES .... Organisation Europeenne des Scieries [*European Sawmills Organization*] [*EC*] (ECED)

OES .... Organizacion de Estados Americanos [*Organization of American States*] [*Spain*] (AD)

OES .... Organization of European Saw-Mills (BUAC)

OES .... Organization of European States (AD)

OES .... Ostrich Eggshell [*Archeological material*]

OES .... Outgoing Echo Suppressor [*Telecommunications*] (TEL)

OES .... Overseas Educational Service [*Defunct*]

OES .... San Antonio Oeste [*Argentina*] [*Airport symbol*] (OAG)

OESA .... Office of Earth Sciences Applications [*Department of the Interior*] (GRD)

OESA .... Office of Employment Service Administration [*US Employment Service*] [*Department of Labor*]

OESBR .... Oil Extended Styrene Butadiene Rubber (PDAA)

oesbr .... Oil-Extended Styrene-Butadiene Rubber (AD)

OESC .... Open-Ended Systems Corp.

OESCA .... Old English Sheepdog Club of America (EA)

OESCAND .... Old East Scandinavian [*Language, etc.*]

OESD .... Ocean Engineering System Development

OESE .... Office of Elementary and Secondary Education [*Department of Education*]

OES/E .... Office of the Environment (US Department of) State/Environment, Health and Natural Resources (GNE)

OES/EGC ..... Office of the Environment (US Department of) State/Office of Global Change (GNE)

OES/EHC ..... Office of the Environment (US Department of) State/Office of Ecology, Health and Conservation (GNE)

OES/ENP ..... Bureau of Oceans and International Environmental and Scientific Affairs/Environmental and Population Affairs [*Department of State*] (MSC)

OES/ENV ..... Office of the Environment (US Department of) State/Office of Environmental Protection (GNE)

OESH .... Office of Environment, Safety, and Health (COE)

OESH .... Shared Library Services, South Huron Hospital, Exeter, Ontario [*Library symbol National Library of Canada*] (BIB)

OESH .... Sharurah [*Saudi Arabia*] [*ICAO location identifier*] (ICLI)

OESK .... Al-Jouf [*Saudi Arabia*] [*ICAO location identifier*] (ICLI)

OESK .... Osteuropeiska Solidaritetskommitten [*East European Solidarity Committee*] (EAIO)

OESL .... Oceanographic and Environmental Service Laboratory [*Raytheon Co.*]

OESL .... Sulayel [*Saudi Arabia*] [*ICAO location identifier*] (ICLI)

OESLA .... Office of Engineering Standards Liaison and Analysis [*National Bureau of Standards*] (IAA)

OES/N .... Office of the Environment (US Department of) State/Nuclear Energy and Energy Technology Affairs (GNE)

OES/NED ..... Office of the Environment (US Department of) State/Office of Export and Import Control (GNE)

OES/NEP ..... Office of the Environment (US Department of) State/Office of Non-Proliferation and Export Policy (GNE)

OES/NTS ..... Office of the Environment (US Department of) State/Office of Nuclear Technology and Safeguards (GNE)

OES/O .... Office of the Environment (US Department of) State/Oceans and Fisheries Affairs (GNE)

OESO .... Organisation Internationale d'Etudes Statistiques pour les Maladies de l'Oesophage [*International Organization for Statistical Studies on Diseases of the Esophagus*] (EAIO)

OESO .... Organizational Effectiveness Staff Officer [*Military*]

OESOC .... Organizational Effectiveness Staff Officer Course [*Army*]

OES/OFA ..... Bureau of Oceans and International Environmental and Scientific Affairs/Ocean and Fishery Affairs [*Department of State*] (MSC)

OES/OFA ..... Office of the Environment (US Department of) State/Office of Fisheries Affairs (GNE)

OES/OLP ..... Office of the Environment (US Department of) State/Office of Ocean Law and Policy (GNE)

OESOPH ...... Oesophagus

oesoph .... Oesophagus (AD)

OES/OSP ..... Office of the Environment (US Department of) State/Office of Marine Science and Polar Affairs (GNE)

OESP .... O Estado de Sao Paulo [*State of Sao Paulo*] [*Brazil*] [*A publication*] (AD)

OESPCMJ .... Officer Exercising Special Court-Martial Jurisdiction

OESR .... Oil Extended Synthetic Rubber (PDAA)

OESS .... O/ET [*Orbiter/External Tank*] Separation System [*NASA*] (MCD)

OESS .... Office of Engineering Standards Services [*National Bureau of Standards*]

OES/S .... Office of the Environment (US Department of) State/Science and Technology Affairs (GNE)

OESS .... Organizational Effectiveness Survey System [*Army*]

OES/SAT ..... Office of the Environment (US Department of) State/Office of Advanced Technology (GNE)

OES/SCI ..... Bureau of Oceans and International Enviromental and Scientific Affairs/Scientific and Technological Affairs [*Department of State*] (MSC)

OES/SCT ..... Office of Environment (US Department of) State/Office of Cooperative Science and Technology Programs (GNE)

OET .... Objective End Time

OET .... Office of Education and Training (AD)

OET .... Office of Emergency Transportation [*FAA*]

OET .... Office of Engineering and Technology [*Washington, DC FCC*] (GRD)

OET .... Official English Title

OET .... Official Establishments Trust [*Australia*]

OET .... Oldest English Texts

OET .... On Equipment Training (MCD)

O/ET .... Orbiter/External Tank [*NASA*] (NASA)

OET .... Organizacion para Estudios Tropicales [*Organization for Tropical Studies*] (EAIO)

OET .... Overseas Exchange Transactions (AD)

OETA .... Occupied Enemy Territory Administration [*World War II*]

OETA .... Township of Armstrong Public Library [*Bibliotheque Publique Canton Armstrong*], Earlton, Ontario [*Library symbol National Library of Canada*] (BIB)

OET & E ...... Operational Employment Testing and Evaluation (AFM)

OETB .... Ocean Economics and Technology Branch [*United Nations*] (MSC)

OETB .... Offshore Energy Technology Board [*British*]

OETB .... Tabuk [*Saudi Arabia*] [*ICAO location identifier*] (ICLI)

OETC .... Optoelectronics Technology Consortium [*Sponsored by the Department of Defense*]

OETC .... Oregon Educational Technology Consortium

OETC .... Organizational Effectiveness Training Center [*Army*] (MCD)

OETF .... Taif [*Saudi Arabia*] [*ICAO location identifier*] (ICLI)

OETLC .... Office of Economic Trends and Labor Conditions [*Department of Labor*]

OETP .... Operations Experimental Test Plan (IAA)

OETP .... Orbiter Electron Temperature Probe [*NASA*]

OETR .... Turaif [*Saudi Arabia*] [*ICAO location identifier*] (ICLI)

OETT .... Oral Endotracheal Tube [*Medicine*] (STED)

OEu .... Euclid Public Library, Euclid, OH [*Library symbol Library of Congress*] (LCLS)

OEU .... Operation Eyesight Universal [*Canada*] (EAIO)

OEVE .... Office of Earthquakes, Volcanoes, and Engineering [*US Geological Survey*] (AD)

OEW .... Office of Economic Warfare [*World War II*]

OEW .... Open-End Wrench

OEW .... Operational Empty Weight [*Aviation*]

OEW .... Ordinary Electromagnetic Wave

OEW .... Ordnance and Explosive Waste [*Military*]

OEWG .... Open-Ended Working Group (NATG)

OEWG .... Operation, Evaluation Wartime Group (NATG)

OEWJ .... Wejh [*Saudi Arabia*] [*ICAO location identifier*] (ICLI)

OEX .... Office of Educational Exchange [*Department of State*]

OEX .... Oklahoma City, OK [*Location identifier FAA*] (FAAL)

OEX .... Options Exchange [*Finance*]

OEX .... Orbiter Experiments [*NASA*] (MCD)

OEX .... Standard & Poor's 100 Stock Index (DFIT)

OEXP .... Office of Exploration [*NASA*]

OEYN .... Yenbo [*Saudi Arabia*] [*ICAO location identifier*] (ICLI)

OEZ .... Osteuropaeische Zeit [*East European Time*] [*German*] (AD)

OF .... Degrees Fahrenheit

OF .... Fast Airways BV [*Netherlands ICAO designator*] (ICDA)

OF .... Fitted for Oil Fuel [*Ships*]

OF .... Frankford Public Library, Ontario [*Library symbol National Library of Canada*] (BIB)

OF .... Noosa Air [*ICAO designator*] (AD)

OF .... Occipitalfrontal [*Diameter of skull*]

OF .... Occupations Finder [*A publication*] (DHP)

OF .... Oceanographic Facility

OF .... Odd Fellows [*An association*]

Of. .... Official (DAVI)

OF .... Official Files

OF .... Offset Printing Program [*Association of Independent Colleges and Schools specialization code*]

OF .... Offshore Funds [*Investment term*]

OF .... Oil Facility [*International Monetary Fund*]

OF .... Oil-Filled (IAA)

OF .... Oil Fired (ADA)

OF .... Oil Fuel [*British military*] (DMA)

OF .... Old Face [*Typography*]

of .... Old Face (AD)
OF .... Old Field [Botany]
OF .... Old French [Language, etc.]
OF .... One of the Firm [Telecommunications] (TEL)
OF .... Open Forum [An association] (EA)
OF .... Open Full [Container] (DCTA)
OF .... Operating Forces [Navy]
OF .... Operational Fixed
OF .... Operation Friendship (BUAC)
OF .... Operations and Food Analysis
OF .... Operations Following (MCD)
OF .... Ophthalmological Foundation [Later, NSPB]
OF .... Optical Fibre (EECA)
OF .... Optical Frequency
OF .... Optic Fundi (STED)
OF .... Optional Feature (IAA)
OF .... Optional Form
of .... Optional Form (AD)
OF .... Orbital Facility (IAA)
O/F .... Orbital Flight [NASA] (KSC)
OF .... Orbitofrontal
OF .... Order of the Founder [Salvation Army]
OF .... Orphan Foundation [Later, OFA] (EA)
OF .... Orthochromatic Film [Photography] (DGA)
OF .... Oscillator Frequency [Telecommunications] (IAA)
OF .... Osfriends (EA)
OF .... Osmotic Fragility Test
OF .... Osteitis Fibrosa [Medicine] (MAE)
OF .... Osteopathic Foundation [Later, NOF]
OF .... Ostrum-Furst [Syndrome] [Medicine] (STED)
OF .... Other Medical/Surgical Facility (MEDA)
OF .... Outfield [Baseball]
O/F .... Outfit [Doll collecting]
OF .... Output Factor [Computer science] (IEEE)
OF .... Outside Face [Technical drawings]
of .... Outside Face (AD)
Of .... Ovenstone Factor (AD)
OF .... Ovenstone Factor [Medicine] (MAE)
OF .... Overflow
OF .... Overfrequency (MSA)
OF .... Oxbow Falls (AD)
OF .... Oxenstierna Foundation (AD)
Of .... Oxford Foundation (AD)
o/f .... Oxidation/Fermentation (AD)
O-F .... Oxidation-Fermentation [Growth medium]
O/F .... Oxidizer-to-Fuel [Ratio]
o/f .... Oxidizer to Fuel Ratio (AD)
of .... Oxidizing Flame (AD)
OF .... Oxidizing Flame
OF .... Oxydizer-to-Fuel [Ratio]
OF .... Oxygen Fill (NASA)
OFA .... Fairfield County District Library, Lancaster, OH [OCLC symbol] (OCLC)
OFA .... Object Free Area [FAA] (TAG)
OFA .... Office for the Aging (BARN)
OFA .... Office of Family Assistance [Department of Health and Human Services] (GFGA)
OFA .... Office of Federal Activities [Environmental Protection Agency] (GFGA)
OFA .... Office of Financial Analysis [Department of the Treasury]
OFA .... Oficina Alemania [Chile] [Seismograph station code, US Geological Survey] (SEIS)
OFA .... Oil-Immersed Forced-Air-Cooled [Transformer] (IEEE)
OFA .... Oklahoma Forestry Association (WPI)
OFA .... Old Folks Association (AD)
OFA .... Oncofetal Antigen [Immunology]
OFA .... Ontario Film Association [Canada] (BUAC)
OFA .... Optimized Fuel Assembly [Nuclear energy] (NRCH)
OFA .... Order for Assignment [Military] (CAAL)
OFA .... Organic Food Alliance (EA)
OFA .... Organization of Flying Adjusters (NTPA)
OFA .... Organized Flying Adjusters (EA)
OFA .... Orienteering Federation of Australia
OFA .... Oronite Fuel Additive
OFA .... Orphan Foundation of America (EA)
OFA .... Orthopedic Foundation for Animals (EA)
OFA .... Over Fifties Association [Australia]
OFA .... Over Fire Air [Combustion technology]
OFA .... Overseas Family Allowance [British military] (DMA)
OFA .... Owen Family Association (EA)
OFA .... Oxygenated Fuels Association (EA)
OFAA .... Oyster Farmers' Association of Australia
OFAB .... Fort Albany Band Library, Ontario [Library symbol National Library of Canada] (BIB)
OFACS .... Overseas-Foreign Aeronautical Communications Station (MUGU)
OFAD .... Ocean Floor Analysis Division [Later, Sea Floor Division] [NORDA] (EA)
OFAED .... Organization Forecast Authorization Equipment Data [Military] (AFIT)
OFAES .... Oriental Fine Arts Exchange Society [China] (BUAC)
OFAF .... Metallurgical Research Library, Falconbridge Nickel Mines Ltd., Falconbridge, Ontario [Library symbol National Library of Canada] (NLC)
OFAGE .... Orthogonal-Field-Alternation Gel Electrophoresis [Analytical biochemistry]
OFALF .... Omega First Amendment Legal Fund (EA)

OFAM .... Office of Financial and Administrative Management [Department of Labor]
OFANC .... Falconbridge Branch, Nickel Centre Public Library, Ontario [Library symbol National Library of Canada] (NLC)
OFANSW ...... Oyster Farmers' Association of New South Wales [Australia]
OFAR .... Office of Foreign Agricultural Relations [Department of Agriculture]
OFARS .... Overseas-Foreign Aeronautical Receiver Station
OFAS .... Overseas Flight Assistance Service
OFATS .... Overseas-Foreign Aeronautical Transmitter Station
OFavp .... Fairview Park Regional Library, Fairview Park, OH [Library symbol Library of Congress] (LCLS)
OFB .... Oil Forced Blast (IAA)
OFB .... Operational Facilities Branch [NASA] (MCD)
OFB .... Output Feedback (NITA)
OFBM .... Oxidation-Fermentation Basal Medium (STED)
OFC .... Conference on Optical Fiber Communication [Optical Society of America] [Washington, DC] (TSSD)
OFC .... Foleyet Community Library, Ontario [Library symbol National Library of Canada] (NLC)
OFC .... High Court Reports, Orange Free State [A publication] (DLA)
OFC .... Occipitofrontal Circumference [Anatomy]
OFC .... Oceania Football Confederation
OFC .... Oceanography and Fisheries Committee (ASF)
OFC .... Office [or Officer] (AFM)
ofc .... Office (AD)
Ofc .... Office (TBD)
OFC .... Office of Fishery Coordination [World War II]
OFC .... Oil Free Compressor
OFC .... Oldest Finest Canadian [Whiskey] (IIA)
OFC .... Old Fired Copper [Initialism once used as brand name for bourbon]
OFC .... Old French Canadian [Initialism used in Schenley brand of Canadian whisky]
OFC .... One Flow Cascade Cycle (IAA)
OFC .... Open Financial Connectivity [Microsoft Computer Software] [Computer Science]
OFC .... Operational Flight Control [NASA]
OFC .... Opposing Force Component (MCD)
OFC .... Optical Fiber Communication (CIST)
OFC .... Optical File Cabinet [Computer science]
OFC .... Optical Formatter Controller (NITA)
OFC .... Optical Frequency Conversion
OFC .... Orbitofacial Cleft [Medicine] (STED)
OFC .... Oscillation Frequency Control (CIST)
OFC .... Osteitis Fibrosa Cystica [Medicine] (DMAA)
OFC .... Outside Front Cover [Publishing] (NTCM)
OFC .... Overseas Food Corp. (AD)
OFC .... Oxyfuel-Gas Cutting [Welding]
OFCA .... Ontario Federation of Construction Associations [Canada] (AD)
OFCA .... Organisation des Fabricants de Produits Cellulosiques Alimentaires de la CEE [Organization of Manufacturers of Cellulose Products for Foodstuffs in the European Economic Community]
OFC-A .... Oxyfuel-Gas Cutting - Acetylene [Welding]
OFCC .... Office of Federal Contract Compliance [Later, OFCCP] [Department of Labor]
OFCCP .... Office of Federal Contract Compliance Programs [Formerly, OFCC] [Department of Labor]
OFCCP Fed Cont Compl Man... OFCCP Federal Contract Compliance Manual [A publication] (AAGC)
OFCE .... Office [or Officer]
OFCF .... Overseas Farmers Co-Operative Federation Ltd. (BUAC)
OFC-H .... Oxyfuel-Gas Cutting - Hydrogen [Welding]
OFCL .... Official
ofcl .... Official (AD)
Ofcl .... Official (TBD)
Of Cl Pac .... Officium Clerici Pacis [A publication] (DLA)
OFCM .... Office of the Federal Coordinator for Meteorological Services and Research
OFCN .... Organization for Community Networks (IGQR)
OFC-N .... Oxyfuel Cutting - Natural Gas [Welding]
OFCO .... Offensive Counterintelligence Operations (MCD)
OFCOFASSTSECNAV... Office of the Assistant Secretary of the Navy (DNAB)
OFCOFASSTSECNAV(FINMGMT)... Office of the Assistant Secretary of the Navy (Financial Management) (DNAB)
OFCOFASSTSECNAV(INSTALLOG)... Office of the Assistant Secretary of the Navy (Installations and Logistics) (DNAB)
OFCOFASSTSECNAV(PERSRESFOR)... Office of the Assistant Secretary of the Navy (Personnel and Reserve Force) (DNAB)
OFCOFASSTSECNAV(RSCHDEV)... Office of the Assistant Secretary of the Navy (Research and Development) (DNAB)
OFCOFINFO... Office of Information (DNAB)
OFCP .... Ottawa Financial [NASDAQ symbol] (TTSB)
OFCP .... Ottawa Financial Corp. [NASDAQ symbol] (SAG)
OFC-P .... Oxyfuel-Gas Cutting - Propane [Welding]
OFCR .... Officer
OFCS .... Office of Foreign Commercial Services [Abolished 1970, functions transferred to Bureau of International Commerce]
OFCS .... Operational Flight Control System [NASA] (KSC)
OFCSAV ...... Orchardists and Fruit Cool Stores Association of Victoria [Australia]
OFD .... Object Film Distance [Optics]
OFD .... Objective Force Designator (MCD)
OFD .... Occipitofrontal Diameter [of the skull]
OFD .... Ocean Floor Drilling
OFD .... Ocean Freight Differential [MARAD] (TAG)
Ofd .... Offered [Stock exchange term]
OFD .... Ohio Federal Decisions [A publication] (DLA)

OFD	One-Function Diagram
ofd	One-Function Diagram (AD)
OFD	Open-Face Dectector [*Instrumentation*]
ofd	Optical Fire Detector (AD)
OFD	Optical Gun Fire Director [*Military*] (PDAA)
OFD	Oral-Facial-Digital [*Genetics*] (DAVI)
OFD	Oro-Facio-Digital [*Syndrome*] [*Medicine*]
OFD	Oued Fodda [*Algeria*] [*Seismograph station code, US Geological Survey*] (SEIS)
OFDA	Office Furniture Distribution Association (EA)
OFDA	Office of Foreign Disaster Assistance (COE)
OFDA	Office of United States Foreign Disaster Assistance [*Agency for International Development*]
OFDAP	Office of the Field Directorate of Ammunition Plants
OFDC	Official First Day Cover [*Canada Post Corp.*]
OFDC	Ontario Film Development Corp. [*Canada*]
OFDG	Operator Fractionation Decision Guide [*Process control*]
OFDI	Office of Foreign Direct Investments [*Department of Commerce*]
OFDR	Off-Frequency Decoupling Resonance [*Physical chemistry*]
OFDS	Optimal Financial Decision Strategy (MHDI)
OFDS	Orbiter Flight Dynamics Simulator [*NASA*] (NASA)
OFDS	Oxygen Fluid Distribution System [*NASA*] (NASA)
OFE	Odds for Effectiveness [*Navy*]
OFE	Office of Federal Elections [*Later, FEC*]
OFE	Office of Fossil Energy (COE)
OFE	Office of Fuels and Engergy (AD)
OFE	Office of Fusion Energy [*Oak Ridge National Laboratory*]
OFE	Optical Flight Evaluation
OFE	Order for Engagement [*Military*] (CAAL)
OFE	Osteogenic Factor Extract (DB)
OFE	Other Further Education
OFE	Ottawa Fundraising Executives [*Ontario, Canada*]
OFEA	Office of Foreign Economic Administration [*Lend-Lease*] [*World War II*]
OFEA:	Officer Front End Analysis (MCD)
OFEC	Office of Federal Employees Compensation [*Department of Labor*]
OFEC	Office of Foreign Economic Coordination [*World War II*]
OFEC	Wellington County Museum, Fergus, Ontario [*Library symbol National Library of Canada*] (BIB)
OFEHM	Fort Erie Historical Museum, Ontario [*Library symbol National Library of Canada*] (BIB)
OFEMA	Office Francais d'Exportation de Materiel Aeronautique [*French Office for theExportation of Aeronautical Materiel*] (AD)
OFEP	Fort Erie Public Library, Ontario [*Library symbol National Library of Canada*] (NLC)
OFER	Fergus Public Library, Ontario [*Library symbol National Library of Canada*] (NLC)
OFERC	Centre Wellington District High School, Fergus, Ontario [*Library symbol National Library of Canada*] (NLC)
OFERRA	Office of Foreign Economic Relief and Rehabilitation Administration
OFERW	Wellington County Public Library, Fergus, Ontario [*Library symbol National Library of Canada*] (NLC)
OFERWM	Wellington County Museum and Archives, Fergus, Ontario [*Library symbol National Library of Canada*] (BIB)
OFF	Challenge Air Transport, Inc. [*ICAO designator*] (FAAC)
Off	De Officiis [*of Cicero*] [*Classical studies*] (OCD)
OFF	Fort Frances Public Library, Ontario [*Library symbol National Library of Canada*] (NLC)
OFF	Offensive
OFF	Offer
OFF	Offertory
OFF	Office [*or Officer*] (AFM)
off	Office (DD)
OFF	Office for Families (DICI)
OFF	Office of Facts and Figures [*Later, Office of War Information*] [*Military*]
Off	Officer (AD)
OFF	Officers' Family Fund
OFF	Official
Off	Official (STED)
OFF	Offretite [*A zeolite*]
OFF	Omaha, NE [*Location identifier FAA*] (FAAL)
OFF	Organization for Femininity
OFFA	One Fund for All [*An association*] (BUAC)
OFFAR	Office of Fuel and Fuel Additive Registration [*Environmental Protection Agency*]
Off Br	Officina Brevium [*1679*] [*A publication*] (DLA)
Off Brev	Officina Brevium [*1679*] [*A publication*] (DLA)
OFF BUS ONLY...	Official Business Only (DNAB)
OFFC	Office
OffcDpt	Office Depot [*Associated Press*] (SAG)
OFFEE	Offeree [*Legal shorthand*] (LWAP)
OFFEG	Offshore Fossil-Fueled Electric Generators
OFFEN	Offensive [*Ammunition*] (AAG)
offen	Offensive (AD)
OFFENS	Offensive
offeq	Office Equipment (AD)
offer	Offertories (AD)
OFFER	Office of Electricity Regulation [*British*]
Offer	Office of Electricity Regulation [*British*] (WA)
Off Ex	Wentworth's Office of Executors [*A publication*] (DLA)
Off Exec	Wentworth's Office of Executors [*A publication*] (DLA)
offg	Offering (AD)
OFFG	Officiating

Off Gaz Pat Office...	Official Gazette. United States Patent and Trademark Office [*A publication*] (DLA)
OFFI	Official
OFFIC	Official
offic	Official (AD)
OFFIC	Officiate
Office Pubns...	Office Publications (AD)
Officer	Officer's Reports [*1-9 Minnesota*] [*A publication*] (DLA)
Official J Ind Comm Prop...	Official Journal of Industrial and Commercial Property [*Eire*] [*A publication*] (DLA)
Official Rep III Courts Commission...	Official Reports, Illinois Courts Commission [*A publication*] (DLA)
Officmx	Officemax, Inc. [*Associated Press*] (SAG)
OFFINTAC ...	Offshore Installations Technical Advisory Committee (BUAC)
OFFL	Official (AFM)
OFFM	Fort Frances Museum and Cultural Centre, Ontario [*Library symbol National Library of Canada*] (BIB)
OFFMAUTSYS...	Officer Master File Automated System (DNAB)
OFFNAVHIST...	Office of Naval History [*Also, ONH*]
OFFNAVWEASERV...	Office of Naval Weather Service
OFFOR	Offeror [*Legal shorthand*] (LWAP)
OFFP	Fenelon Falls Public Library, Ontario [*Library symbol National Library of Canada*] (BIB)
OFFP	Ovarian Follicular Fluid Peptide [*Endocrinology*]
OFFPROMSYS...	Officer Promotion System (DNAB)
OFFR	Officer
Offr	Officer (AL)
Off Rep	Official Reports of the High Court of the Transvaal [*A publication*] (DLA)
OffshEnr.......	Offshore Energy Development Corp. [*Associated Press*] (SAG)
OFFSHR	Offshore (NVT)
OffsLog	Offshore Logistics, Inc. [*Associated Press*] (SAG)
OFF STA	Officer Status (DNAB)
off-st pkg	Off-Street Parking (AD)
OFFV	Order of First Families of Virginia, 1607-1624/5 (EA)
OFG	Opferfuersorgegesetz (BJA)
OFG	Optical Frequency Generator
OFG	Organic Farmers and Growers Ltd. (BUAC)
OFGAS	Office of Gas Service [*Government body*] [*British*]
Ofgas	Office of Gas Supply [*British*] (WA)
OFGR	Objective Force Gross Requirement [*Army*] (AABC)
OFGSA	Organic Farming and Gardening Society of Australia
OFGST	Organic Farming and Gardening Society of Tasmania [*Australia*]
OFH	Odd Fellows Hall (ROG)
OFH	Oil Field Haulers Association Inc., Austin TX [*STAC*]
OFH	Rutherford B. Hayes Library, Fremont, OH [*Library symbol Library of Congress*] (LCLS)
OFHA	Occipitofrontal Headache [*Medicine*] (DMAA)
OFHA	Oil Field Haulers Association (EA)
OFHC	Oxygen-Free Hard Copper (IAA)
ofhc	Oxygen-Free High-Carbon (AD)
ofhc	Oxygen-Free High Conductivity (AD)
OFHC	Oxygen-Free, High-Conductivity [*Copper*]
OFHC	Oxygen-Free High-Conductivity Copper [*Electronics*] (AAEL)
OFi	Findlay-Hancock County District Public Library, Findlay, OH [*Library symbol Library of Congress*] (LCLS)
OFI	Office of Foreign Investment [*Department of Commerce*]
OFI	Office of the Federal Inspector
OFI	Omni Films International, Inc. (EFIS)
OFI	On-Line Free Form Input [*Computer science*] (MHDI)
OFI	Operational Flight Instrumentation [*NASA*] (NASA)
OFI	Ornamental Fish International (EAIO)
OFI	Oxford Forestry Institute [*University of Oxford*] [*British*] (IRUK)
OFIA	Optical Frame Importers' Association [*British*] (DBA)
OFiC	Findlay College, Findlay, OH [*Library symbol Library of Congress*] (LCLS)
ofic	Oficial [*Official*] [*Spanish*] (AD)
OFIC	Ohio Foundation of Independent Colleges (AD)
OFID	OPEC [*Organization of Petroleum Exporting Countries*] Fund for International Development (EAIO)
O-FID	Oxygen-Flame Ionization Detector
OFIG	Operational Forces Interface Group [*US Army Natick Research, Development, and Engineering Center*] [*Natick, MA*] (RDA)
OFII	Organization for International Investment (NTPA)
OFII	Otto Fuel II [*Military*] (DNAB)
OFINDMAN...	Office of Industrial Management [*Navy*] (DNAB)
OFINTAC	Offshore Installations Technical Advisory Committee [*British Marine science*] (MSC)
OFIR	Oceanic Flight Information Region (IAA)
OFIS	Office Information System (NITA)
OFIS	Operational Flight Information Service [*ICAO*] (DA)
OFIS	U.S. Office Products [*NASDAQ symbol*] (TTSB)
OFIS	US Office Products Co. [*NASDAQ symbol*] (SAG)
OFIX	Office of the Future Information Exchange (NITA)
OFIX	Orthofix International [*NASDAQ symbol*] (SAG)
OFIXF	Orthofix International [*NASDAQ symbol*] (TTSB)
OFJ	Olafsfjordur [*Iceland*] [*Airport symbol*] (OAG)
OFK	Norfolk [*Nebraska*] [*Airport symbol*] (OAG)
OFK	Norfolk, NE [*Location identifier FAA*] (FAAL)
OFK	Oberfeldkommandantur [*Military government area headquarters*] [*German military - World War II*]
OFK	Official Flight Kit [*NASA*] (NASA)
OFK	Optical Flight Kit (NASA)
OFL	Flesherton Public Library, Ontario [*Library symbol National Library of Canada*] (NLC)

OFL............. Official (AABC)
ofl............... Official (AD)
OFL............. Open Fault Locater
OFL............. Optic Fiber Layer
OFL............. Overflow [*Computer science*]
OFL............. Oxidizer Fill Line (AAG)
Oflag........... Offizierlager [*Officer's Prison Camp*] [*German*] (AD)
OFLAG .... Offizierslager [*Permanent Prison Camp for Captured Officers*] [*German military - World War II*]
OFLC........... Office of Foreign Liquidation Commission
OFLD .... Off-Load (NVT)
OFlem......... Old Flemish [*Language, etc.*] (BARN)
OFLIC......... Office of Foreign Liquidation Commission
OFLINPS..... Open Frame Linear Power Supply [*Electronics*] (EECA)
OFLOT .... Office of the National Lottery (BUAC)
OFLT........... Office of Foreign Labor and Trade [*Department of Labor*]
OFLTR .... Oil Filter
OFLUSE ...... For Official Use Only [*Army*]
Ofly............. Offaly (AD)
ofm .... Conventual Franciscans, Friars Minor (TOCD)
OFM............ Franciscan Friars (TOCD)
ofm .... Franciscan Friars, Order of Friars Minor (TOCD)
OFM............ Observation File Maintenance
OFM............ Office of Finance and Management [*Department of Agriculture*] (GFGA)
OFM............ Office of Financial Management [*Bureau of the Budget; later, OMB*]
OFM............ Office of Flight Missions [*NASA*] (MCD)
OFM............ Office of Foreign Missions [*Department of State*]
OFM............ Optofiber Metric Switch
OFM............ Ordnance Field Manual [*Military*]
OFM............ Ordo Fratrum Minorum [*Order of Friars Minor*] [*Observant Franciscans*] [*Roman Catholic religious order*] (EA)
OFM............ Organization Field Maintenance
OFM............ Oriental Fruit Moth [*Entomology*]
OFM............ Orofacial Malformation
OFM............ Our First Men [*Slang*]
OFM............ Out for Maintenance [*Aviation*] (FAAC)
OFM............ Oxygen Fill to Missile (AAG)
OFMC.......... Operational Fixed Microwave Council (IAA)
OFMC.......... Order of Friars Minor Conventual [*Conventuals*] [*Roman Catholic religious order*]
OFMCap....... [*The*] Capuchin Friars (TOCD)
ofmcap........ [*The*] Capuchin Friars, Franciscan Fathers (TOCD)
OFM Cap .... Order of Friars Minor Capuchin [*Capuchins*] [*Roman Catholic religious order*]
OFMConv..... Conventual Franciscans (TOCD)
OFM Conv.... Order of Friars Minor Conventual [*Conventuals*] [*Roman Catholic religious order*]
OFMIS .... Office of Financial and Management Information Systems (OICC)
OFMP.......... Organization of Facility Managers and Planners [*Later, OMERF*] (EA)
OFMS.......... Office of Financial and Management Services [*Department of Labor*]
OFMS.......... Organic-Functionalized Molecular Sieve [*Organic chemistry*]
OFN .... Organization for Flora Neotropica (EA)
OFN .... Ottawa Fundraisers Network [*Ontario, Canada*]
OFN .... Overfull Employment [*Economics*]
OFNCS .... Orange Field Naturalist and Conservation Society [*Australia*]
OFNPS .... Outstate Facility Network Planning System [*Telecommunications*] (TEL)
OFNS .... Observer Foreign News Service (AD)
OFO .... Office of Field Operations [*Employment and Training Administration*] [*Department of Labor*]
OFO .... Office of Flight Operations [*NASA*]
OFO .... Orbiting Frog Otolith [*NASA experimental spacecraft*]
Ofo.............. Orfeo [*Record label*]
OFOBA .... Oils, Fats, and Oilseeds Brokers Association [*Netherlands*] (BUAC)
OFOC .... Old Free Order of Chaldeans [*Freemasonry*] (ROG)
OFOD .... On-Flight Origin and Destination [*International Civil Aviation Organizati on*] [*Information service or system*] (DUND)
OFOFLEGAFFAIRS... Office of Legal Affairs [*Navy*] (DNAB)
OFOM .... Operational Figure of Merit [*Military*] (CAAL)
OFOS .... Opening Filled Other State [*Employment*]
OFP............. Ashland, VA [*Location identifier FAA*] (FAAL)
OFP............. Office of Federal Policy (COE)
OFP............. Oil Filter Pack
OFP............. On-the-Fly Printer
OFP............. Open Fireplace [*Classified advertising*] (ADA)
OFP............. Operating Force Plan
OFP............. Operational Flight Profile [*NASA*] (NASA)
OFP............. Operational Flight Profit
OFP............. Operational Flight Program [*NASA*] (NASA)
OFP............. Operational Format Program [*NASA*] (KSC)
OFP............. Operative Federal Plasterers [*A union*] [*British*]
OFP............. Orbiter Flight Program [*NASA*] (NASA)
OFP............. Order of Friars Preachers [*Dominicans*] (ADA)
OFP............. Ordnance Field Park [*British*]
OFP............. Organizations, Functions, and Programs [*IRS*]
OFP............. Original Flight Plan
OFP............. Oscilloscope Face Plane
OFP............. Ozone Forming Potential [*Exhaust emissions*] [*Automotive engineering*]
OFPA .... Order of the Founders and Patriots of America (EA)
OFPA .... Organic Foods Production Act
OFPANA...... Organic Foods Production Association of North America (EA)

OFPCP .... Organization of Fitness and Personal Care Professionals [*Defunct*] (EA)
OFPF........... Optical Fiber-Pulling Facility (SSD)
OFPM.......... Office of Fiscal Plans and Management [*Bureau of Indian Affairs*]
OFP-MIR...... Ozone-Forming Potential-Maximum Incremental Reactivity [*Exhaust emissions*] [*Automotive engineering*]
OFPP .... Office of Federal Procurement Policy [*Executive Office of the President*] (MCD)
OFPPA .... Office of Federal Procurement Policy Act (COE)
OFPS .... Open Frame Power Supply [*Electronics*] (EECA)
OFPU .... Optical Fiber Production Unit
OFr............. Franklin Public Library, Franklin, OH [*Library symbol Library of Congress*] (LCLS)
OFR............. Ocular Following Reflex [*Ophthalmology*]
OFR............. Off Frequency Rejection [*Radio communications*]
ofr.............. Off Frequency Rejection (AD)
OFR............. Office for Recruitment [*American Library Association*]
OFR............. Office for Research [*American Library Association*]
OfR............. Office for Research (AD)
OFR............. Office of the Federal Register
Ofr.............. Officer (PHSD)
OFR............. Officer Fitness Report [*Navy*] (NVT)
OFR............. Official Failure Rate [*Military*] (AFIT)
OFR............. Oil-Filled Resistor
OFR............. Old French [*Language, etc.*]
O Fr............ Old French (AD)
OFR............. On-Frequency Repeater (IEEE)
OFR............. Open Failure Report [*NASA*] (KSC)
OFR............. Open File Report (MCD)
OFR............. Operational Failure Report (IAA)
OFR............. Operational Fleet Requirements (MCD)
OFR............. Ordering Function Register
OFR............. Over Frequency Relay
OFR............. Overseas Fuel Region (AFIT)
OFR............. Oxidation-Fluorination Ratio (MCD)
OFR............. United Front of Workers (BUAC)
OFRA .... O'Dochartaigh Family Research Association (EA)
OFRAC .... On Farm Research Advisory Committee [*Australia*]
OFR-ALA ..... Office of Recruitment-American Library Association (AD)
OFRF .... Organic Farming Research Foundation
OFRF .... Overland Flow Research Facility [*Army*]
OFRIS .... Old Frisian [*Language, etc.*]
OFris........... Old Frisian (AD)
O Frk .... Old Frankish (AD)
OFRP .... Overseas Family Residence Program [*Military*] (NVT)
OFRR .... Office of Foreign Relief and Rehabilitation [*Obsolete*]
OFRRO .... Office of Foreign Relief and Rehabilitation Operation [*Obsolete*]
OFrS .... Franklin City Schools, Franklin, OH [*Library symbol Library of Congress*] (LCLS)
OFRW .... Oklahoma Federation of Republican Women
OFS............. Fauquier-Strickland Public Library, Fauquier, Ontario [*Library symbol National Library of Canada*] (BIB)
OFS............. Octave Filter Set
OFS............. Office of Field Service [*OSRD*] [*World War II*]
OFS............. Office of Field Services [*Later, Bureau of Domestic Commerce*] [*Department of Commerce*]
OFS............. Office of Oceanographic Facilities and Support [*National Science Foundation*] (USDC)
OFS............. Offset (MSA)
OFS............. Oil from Sludge
OFS............. One-Function Sketch
ofs.............. One-Function Sketch (AD)
OFS............. Ontario Federation of Students [*Canada*] (AD)
OFS............. Operations Fixed Service [*Microwave service*] (NTCM)
OFS............. Optical Fiber Sensor
OFS............. Optical Fuzing System
OFS............. Orange Free State [*South Africa*]
OFS............. Orange Free State Reports, High Court [*1879-83*] [*South Africa*] [*A publication*] (DLA)
OFS............. Orbital [*or Orbiter*] Flight System [*NASA*] (MCD)
OFS............. Orbiter Functional Simulator (NASA)
OFSA .... Ordo Fratrum Sancti Augustini [*Order of St. Augustine - OSA*] [*Rome, Italy*] (EAIO)
OFSB .... Fort Severn Band Library, Ontario [*Library symbol National Library of Canada*] (BIB)
OFSB .... Ordnance Field Service Bulletin [*Military*]
OFSB .... Oriental Federal Savings Bank (EFIS)
OFSC .... Ordnance Field Service Circular [*Military*]
OFSC .... Organization and Finance Subcommittee
OFSCC .... Orbiter Functional Simulator Control Center (MCD)
OFSD .... Operating Flight Strength Diagram
OFSDG........ Finch Branch, Stormont, Dundas, and Glengarry County Public Library, Ontario [*Library symbol National Library of Canada*] (BIB)
OFSE........... Operating Forces Support Equipment (DNAB)
OFSM.......... Operational Flight Safety Monitor (SAA)
OFSMPS ..... Open Frame Switch Mode Power Supply [*Electronics*] (EECA)
OFSO .... Overfill Shutoff Sensor (KSC)
OFSP .... Office of Federal Statistical Policy [*Later, OFSPS*] [*Department of Commerce*]
OFSPS .... Office of Federal Statistical Policy and Standards [*Formerly, OFSP*] [*Department of Commerce*]
OFSSA .... Orange Free State, South Africa (ILCA)
OFST........... Lateral Offset Active Light (GAVI)
OFST.......... Office of the Secretary of the Air Force (AD)

ofst	Offset (VRA)
OFSTED	Office for Standards in Education [*British*] (WDAA)
Ofsted	Office for Standards in Education [*British*] (WA)
OFT	Field Township Public Library, Ontario [*Library symbol National Library of Canada*] (NLC)
OFT	Observed Fire Trainer [*Army*] (RDA)
OFT	Office of Fair Trading [*British*]
OFT	Often
OFT	Ohio Federation of Teachers (AD)
OFT	Operational Feasibility Testing (MCD)
OFT	Operational Flight Trainer
OFT	Optical Fiber Thermometry [*Instrumentation*]
OFT	Optical Fiber Tube
OFT	Optical Fibre Technology
OFT	Optical Fourier Transform
OFT	Optimal Foraging Theory [*Animal behavior*]
OFT	Orbital Flight Test [*NASA*] (NASA)
OFT	Outer Fix Time [*FAA*] (TAG)
OFT	Outfit (MSA)
OFT	Outline Feasibility Test [*Army*]
OFTA	Office for the Aged [*Australia*]
OFTA	Operational Flight Transfer Airframe
OFTB	Offshore Technology Board [*British*]
OFTC	Overseas Finance and Trade Corp. (AD)
OFTD	Oxygen Furnace Tilt Drive
OFTDA	Office of Flight Tracking and Data Acquisition [*NASA*]
OFTDS	Orbital Flight Test Data System [*NASA*] (MCD)
OFTEC	Oil Firing Technical Association for the Petroleum Industry (BUAC)
OFTEL	Office of Telecommunications [*Independent government agency*] [*British*]
Oftel	Office of Telecommunications [*British*] (WDAA)
OFTF	Optical Fibre Transfer Function (EECA)
OFTM	On-Orbit Flight Technique Meeting [*NASA*] (MCD)
OFTMS	Output Format Table Modification Submodule
OFTR	Orbital Flight Test Requirement [*NASA*] (NASA)
OFTS	Office of Technical Services (AD)
OFTS	Office of Transportation Security (AD)
OFTS	Officers Training School (AD)
OFTS	Operational Flight and Tactics Simulator (MCD)
OFTS	Optical Fibre Transmission System (NITA)
OFTS	Overseas Fixed Telecommunications System (AD)
OFTT	Operational Flight and Tactics Trainer (MCD)
OFTT	Organic Failure to Thrive [*Medicine*] (MEDA)
OFU	Floating Units Division [*Coast Guard*]
OFU	Franklin University, Columbus, OH [*OCLC symbol*] (OCLC)
OFU	Ofu Island [*American Samoa*] [*Airport symbol*] (OAG)
OFU	Ofunato [*Japan*] [*Seismograph station code, US Geological Survey*] (SEIS)
OFV	Opposing Forces Vehicle [*Military*]
OFV	Orchid Fleck Virus [*Plant pathology*]
OFW	Objective Family of Weapons
OFW	Off Watch [*Aviation*] (FAAC)
OFW	Operation Fish Watch [*National Oceanic and Atmospheric Administration*] (MSC)
OFW	Opportunities for Women (BUAC)
OFWAT	Oxyfuel-Gas Welding
OFWAT	Office of Water Services [*British*]
Ofwat	Office of Water Services [*British*] (WDAA)
OFWN	Ontario Library Service - Nipigon, Thunder Bay, Ontario [*Library symbol National Library of Canada*] (NLC)
OF/WST	Operational Flight/Weapons System Trainer (NG)
OFX	Open Financial Exchange [*Computer science*]
OFXT	Outer Fix Time [*Aviation*] (FAAC)
OFY	Operation Feed Yourself [*Ghana*] (BUAC)
OFY	Opportunities for Youth [*Canada*] (AD)
OFY	Opportunities for Youth Program [*Canada*]
OFZ	Fort Sill, OK [*Location identifier FAA*] (FAAL)
OFZ	Obstacle Free Zone
OG	Air Guadeloupe [*ICAO designator*] (AD)
OG	Guelph Public Library, Ontario [*Library symbol National Library of Canada*] (NLC)
OG	Obergericht [*Court of Appeal*] [*German*] (DLA)
OG	Oberstes Gericht [*Supreme Court*] [*German*]
OG	Object Glass (MSA)
OG	Obscure Glass
OG	Obstetrics-Gynecology [*Medicine*]
OG	Occlusogingival [*Dentistry*]
OG	Octyl Glucoside [*Organic chemistry*]
OG	Oesterreichische Galerie [*Austrian Gallery*] (AD)
OG	Offensive Guard [*Football*]
OG	Off-Gas [*Nuclear energy*] (NRCH)
OG	Office of Geography [*Functions transferred to Geographic Names Division of Army Topographic Command*] [*Department of the Interior*]
OG	Officer of the Guard [*Army*]
OG	Official Gazette [*PTO*] [*A publication*] (AAGC)
OG	Ogasawara Trench
OG	Ogden Corp. [*NYSE symbol*] (SPSG)
OG	Ogdensburg [*Diocesan abbreviation*] [*New York*] (TOCD)
OG	Ogee [*A molding*] [*Architecture*] (ROG)
OG	Oh, Gee [*Slang*]
og	Oh Gee (AD)
OG	Oil Gauge
og	Oil Gland (AD)
OG	Oil Glands [*In propeller shaft*]

OG	Old Gaelic (AD)
OG	Old German [*Language, etc.*]
OG	Old Girl [*A wife*] [*Slang*]
og	Old Girl (AD)
OG	Old Greasybeard: Tales from the Cumberland Gap [*A publication*]
OG	Oligodendrocyte (DMAA)
OG	Olive Green [*Army*] (ADDR)
OG	Olympic Games
OG	Ongoing (ADA)
OG	On Grade (DAC)
OG	On Ground [*Aviation*]
og	On Ground (AD)
OG	On Guard (AD)
OG	Openly Gay [*An association*] (BUAC)
OG	Operational Group [*World War II*]
OG	Operation Greenhouse [*Atomic weapons testing*]
OG	Optic Ganglion
O/G	Opto/Graphic (AD)
o/g	Opto-Graphic (AD)
o-g	Orange-Green (AD)
OG	Orange Green [*Stain*] [*Medicine*]
OG	Organic Gardening [*A publication*]
OG	Organisation Gestosis [*Basel, Switzerland*] (EAIO)
OG	OR Gate [*Electronics*] (ECII)
OG	Orientation Group [*Air Force*]
OG	Original Gravity (BARN)
OG	Original Gum [*Philately*]
og	Original Gum (AD)
OG	Orogastric [*Feeding*] [*Gastroenterology*] (DAVI)
OG	Outdoor Girl [*Max Factor cosmetic line*]
OG	Outer Gimbal
O/G	Outgoing [*Computer science*]
o/g	Outgoing (AD)
OG	Output Gate [*Computer science*] (IAA)
OG	Outside Guard
OG	Outside Guardian [*Freemasonry*] (ROG)
OG	Oxygen Gage (NAKS)
OG	Oxygen Gauge (NASA)
OG	Zero Gravity
OGA	Obergurgl [*Austria*] [*Seismograph station code, US Geological Survey*] (SEIS)
OGA	Oesterreichische Gesellschaft fur Akupunktur [*Austrian Society of Acupuncture and Auricular Therapy*] (EAIO)
OGA	Ogallala, NE [*Location identifier FAA*] (FAAL)
O/GA	Oil Gauge [*Automotive engineering*]
OGA	Omega Ltd. [*Ukraine*] [*FAA designator*] (FAAC)
OGA	Organic Growers Association [*British*] (DBA)
OGA	Ornamental Growers Association (EA)
OGA	Orogastric Aspirate [*Medicine*] (AAMN)
OGA	Other Government Agencies (COE)
OGA	Outer Gimbal Angle (NASA)
OGA	Outer Gimbal Assembly (NASA)
OGA	Outer Gimbal Axis [*NASA*] (IAA)
OGAC	Galt Collegiate Institute, Cambridge, Ontario [*Library symbol National Library of Canada*] (NLC)
OGAC	Organizational Governance Advisory Committee [*NERComP*]
O Gael	Old Gaelic (AD)
OGAL	Cambridge Public Library, Ontario [*Library symbol National Library of Canada*] (NLC)
OGalG	Gallia County District Library, Gallipolis, OH [*Library symbol Library of Congress*] (LCLS)
OGALL	Cavendish Public Library (G. Galloway), Ontario [*Library symbol National Library of Canada*] (BIB)
OGAMA	Ogden Air Material Area [*AFLC*]
OGAMM	Optical Glass and Macromolecular Materials [*Imaging*]
OGAN	Gananoque Public Library, Ontario [*Library symbol National Library of Canada*] (NLC)
OGANSW	Organic Growers' Association of New South Wales [*Australia*]
OGAR	OGara Co. (The) [*NASDAQ symbol*] (SAG)
OGaraCo	OGara Co. (The) [*Associated Press*] (SAG)
OGAWA	Organic Growers' Association of Western Australia [*Australia*]
OGB	Beriault Branch, Gloucester Public Library, Ontario [*Library symbol National Library of Canada*] (NLC)
OGB	Oesterreichischer Gewerkschaftsbund [*Austrian Trade Union Federation*] [*German*] (AD)
OGB	Orangeburg, SC [*Location identifier FAA*] (FAAL)
OGBD	Orbiter Gamma Burst Detecter [*NASA*]
OGBG	Official Gazette Reports, British Guiana [*A publication*] (DLA)
OGBH	Blackburn Hamlet Branch, Gloucester Public Library, Ontario [*Library symbol National Library of Canada*] (NLC)
OGBKT	Blessed Kateri Tekakwitha School, Gloucester, Ontario [*Library symbol National Library of Canada*] (NLC)
OGBU	Gore Bay Union Public Library, Ontario [*Library symbol National Library of Canada*] (NLC)
OGC	Centennial Collegiate Vocational Institute, Guelph, Ontario [*Library symbol National Library of Canada*] (NLC)
OGc	Grove City Public Library, Grove City, OH [*Library symbol Library of Congress*] (LCLS)
OGC	Oculogyric Crisis [*Medicine*] (DMAA)
OGC	Office of General Counsel
OGC	Order of the Golden Chain (EA)
OGC	Oregon Graduate Center for Study and Research [*Research center*] (RCD)
OGC	Oregon Graduate Centre (BUAC)

OGCF .... Canadian Farm Management Data System, Agriculture Canada [*Systeme Canadien deDonnees sur la Gestion Agricole, Agriculture Canada*] Guelph, Ontario [*Library symbol National Library of Canada*] (NLC)

OGCH .... College Heights Secondary School, Guelph, Ontario [*Library symbol National Library of Canada*] (NLC)

OGCM .... Ocean General Circulation Model [*Atmospheric science*]

OGCMD .... Ogden Contract Management District (SAA)

OGC-N .... Office of General Counsel - NASA

OGCV .... Guelph Collegiate Vocational Institute, Ontario [*Library symbol National Library of Canada*] (NLC)

OGCW .... Cairine Wilson Secondary School, Gloucester, Ontario [*Library symbol National Library of Canada*] (BIB)

OGCWS .... Office of Government Contract Wage Standards (AAGC)

OGD .... Oesophogogastroduodenoscopy [*Medicine*] (WDAA)

OGD .... Ogden [*Utah*] [*Airport symbol*] (AD)

Ogd .... Ogdensburg (AD)

OGD .... Ogdensburg [*New Jersey*] [*Seismograph station code, US Geological Survey*] (SEIS)

Ogd .... Ogden's Reports [*12-15 Louisiana*] [*A publication*] (DLA)

OGD .... Ogden, UT [*Location identifier FAA*] (FAAL)

OGD .... Old Granulomatus Disease (DAVI)

OGD .... Omega Gamma Delta [*Fraternity*] (EA)

OGD .... Open Government Document (PDAA)

OGDA .... Oyster Growers and Dealers Association (EA)

OGDC .... Oil and Gas Development Corp. (AD)

OGDD .... Outgoing/Delay Dial [*Telecommunications*] (TEL)

Ogden .... Ogden Corp. [*Associated Press*] (SAG)

Ogden .... Ogden's Reports [*12-15 Louisiana*] [*A publication*] (DLA)

OGDH .... Oxoglutarate Dehydrogenase [*An enzyme*]

Ogdn .... Ogden Corp. [*Associated Press*] (SAG)

OGDR .... Uniroyal Research Laboratories, Guelph, Ontario [*Library symbol National Library of Canada*] (NLC)

OGE .... Entomological Society of Ontario, Guelph, Ontario [*Library symbol National Library of Canada*] (NLC)

OGE .... Observer Group Egypt [*UN Truce Supervisor Organization*]

OGE .... Office of Government Ethics

OGE .... OGE Energy Corp. [*NYSE symbol*] (SAG)

OGE .... Oklahoma Gas & Elec [*NYSE symbol*] (TTSB)

OGE .... Oklahoma Gas & Electric Co. [*NYSE symbol*] (SPSG)

OGE .... Omaha Grain Exchange [*Defunct*] (EA)

OGE .... Operating [*or Operational*] Ground Equipment

oge .... Operational Ground Equipment (AD)

OGE .... Optional Ground Equipment (AAGC)

OGE .... Optogalvanic Effect (MCD)

OGE .... Oregon Graduate Center, Beaverton, OR [*OCLC symbol*] (OCLC)

OGE .... Osaka Grain Exchange [*Japan*] (NUMA)

OGE .... Out-of-Ground Effect

OGEC .... Organization of Gas Exporting Countries [*Proposed gas cartel*]

OGEDJ .... E. D. Jones Branch, Gloucester Public Library, Ontario [*Library symbol National Library of Canada*] (NLC)

OGE Engy..... OGE Energy Corp. [*Associated Press*] (SAG)

OGEG .... Georgetown District High School, Ontario [*Library symbol National Library of Canada*] (NLC)

OGEH .... Georgetown Branch, Halton Hills Public Libraries, Ontario [*Library symbol National Library of Canada*] (BIB)

OGELR .... Ecole Secondaire Louis-Riel, Gloucester, Ontario [*Library symbol National Library of Canada*] (BIB)

OGELS .... Observer Group in El Salvador

OGEO .... Georgetown Public Library, Ontario [*Library symbol National Library of Canada*] (NLC)

OGeo .... Mary P. Shelton Library, Georgetown, OH [*Library symbol Library of Congress*] (LCLS)

OGEPrA....... Okla Gas & Elec,4% Pfd [*NYSE symbol*] (TTSB)

OGER .... Geraldton Public Library, Ontario [*Library symbol National Library of Canada*] (NLC)

OGer .... Germantown Public Library, Germantown, OH [*Library symbol Library of Congress*] (LCLS)

OGE/RPIE.... Operating Ground Equipment/Real Property Installed Equipment (AFM)

OGES .... Operating Ground Equipment Specification [*Italian*] (AD)

OGEV .... Varian Canada, Inc., Georgetown, Ontario [*Library symbol National Library of Canada*] (NLC)

ogf .... Option Growth Fund (AD)

OGF .... Orogastric Feeding [*Gastroenterology*] (DAVI)

OGF .... Ovarian Growth Factor [*Medicine*]

OGF .... Oxygen Gain Factor [*Medicine*] (DMAA)

OGFC .... Official Gumby Fan Club (EA)

OGFP .... Obtaining Goods by False Pretense

OGFS .... Oil and Gas Field Study [*Department of the Interior*]

OGG .... GasTOPS Ltd., Gloucester, Ontario [*Library symbol National Library of Canada*] (NLC)

OGG .... Kahului [*Hawaii*] [*Airport symbol*] (OAG)

OGG .... Kahului, HI [*Location identifier FAA*] (FAAL)

ogg .... Oggetto [*Object*] [*Italian*] (AD)

OGG .... Organic Geochemistry Group

OGH .... Ovine Growth Hormone (DB)

OGHC .... Hart Chemicals Ltd., Guelph, Ontario [*Library symbol National Library of Canada*] (NLC)

OGHS .... Gloucester High School, Ontario [*Library symbol National Library of Canada*] (BIB)

OGI .... Gould Information Center, Cleveland, OH [*OCLC symbol*] (OCLC)

OGI .... Oceanic Gamefish Investigations [*National Oceanic and Atmospheric Administration*] (MSC)

OGI .... Oculogyral Illusion [*NASA*]

OGI .... Oesterreichische Gesseleschaft fuer Informatik [*Austrian Society for Information Processing*] [*German*] (AD)

OGI .... Off-Gas Isolation [*Nuclear energy*] (NRCH)

OGI .... Ontario Government Information [*Database*] [*Ministry of Culture and Communications*] [*Information service or system*] (CRD)

OGI .... Opera Guilds International (AD)

OGI .... Orientis Graeci Inscriptiones Selectae [*A publication*] (OCD)

OGI .... Outer Grid Injection

OGI .... Oxygen-Glucose Index [*Medicine*] (DMAA)

OGIB .... Occult Gastrointestinal Bleeding [*Medicine*]

OGID .... Outgoing/Immediate Dial [*Telecommunications*] (TEL)

OGIFC .... Original Gilligan's Island Fan Club (EA)

OGIL .... Open General Import Licence [*British*] (DS)

Ogilvie Dict... Ogilvie's Imperial Dictionary of the English Language [*A publication*] (DLA)

OGIP .... Original Gas in Place [*Natural resources*]

OGIS .... Open Geographic Information System

OGJ .... Oil and Gas Journal [*A publication*] (AD)

OGJ .... Outgoing Junction [*Telecommunications*] (TEL)

OGJFR .... John F. Ross Collegiate Vocational Institute, Guelph, Ontario [*Library symbol National Library of Canada*] (NLC)

OGK .... Kenyon College, Gambier, OH [*Library symbol Library of Congress*] (LCLS)

OGL .... Obscure Glass (AAG)

ogl .... Obscure Glass (AD)

OGL .... Open General License [*Import license*] (DS)

OGL .... Oral Glucose Loading [*Endocrinology*]

OGL .... Outgoing Line

OGLA .... Officer Grade Limitations Act of 1954

Oglbay .... Oglebay Norton Co. [*Associated Press*] (SAG)

OGLE .... Oglebay Norton [*NASDAQ symbol*] (TTSB)

OGLE .... Oglebay Norton Co. [*NASDAQ symbol*] (NQ)

OGLE .... Optical Gravitational Lens Experiment [*Astronomy*]

OGLE .... Organization for Getting Legs Exposed [*Group opposing below-the-knee fashions introduced in 1970*]

Oglethorpe U... Oglethorpe University (GAGS)

OGLPFC ...... Official Gary Lewis and the Playboys Fan Club (EA)

OGM .... Office of Grants Management [*Public Health Service*]

OGM .... Office of Guided Missile (IAA)

OGM .... Ontonagon, MI [*Location identifier FAA*] (FAAL)

OGM .... Optimum Gradient Method

OGM .... Ordinary General Meeting

OGM .... Organic Gaseous Mercury [*Environmental chemistry*]

OGM .... Outgoing Message [*Telecommunications*]

OGM .... Outgrowth Medium [*Microbiology*] (DAVI)

OGM .... Outside Gage Marks (SAA)

OGMB .... Mattagami Band Public Library, Gogama, Ontario [*Library symbol National Library of Canada*] (NLC)

OGMC .... Ordnance Guided Missile Center (MCD)

OGMH .... Morrison Hershfield Ltd., Guelph, Ontario [*Library symbol National Library of Canada*] (NLC)

OGMS .... Ordnance Guided Missile School

OGMSD .... Glen Morris Branch, South Dumfries Township Public Library, Ontario [*Library symbol National Library of Canada*] (BIB)

OGMT .... Orbiter Greenwich Mean Time [*NASA*] (MCD)

OGN .... Obstetric, Gynecologic, and Neonatal

OGN .... Yonagunijima [*Japan*] [*Airport symbol*] (OAG)

OGNB .... Orange National Bancorp [*NASDAQ symbol*] (SAG)

OGNB .... Orange Natl Bancorp [*NASDAQ symbol*] (TTSB)

OGNC .... Garson Branch, Nickel Centre Public Library, Ontario [*Library symbol National Library of Canada*] (NLC)

OGNR.......... Oribi Gorge Nature Reserve [*South Africa*] (AD)

OGO .... Abengourou [*Ivory Coast*] [*Airport symbol*] (OAG)

OGO .... City Hall Branch, Gloucester Public Library, Ontario [*Library symbol National Library of Canada*] (NLC)

OGO .... Gould, Inc., Ocean Systems Information Center, Cleveland, OH [*OCLC symbol*] (OCLC)

OGO .... Officer Grade Objectives

OGO .... Oliver Gold Corp. [*Vancouver Stock Exchange symbol*]

OGO .... Orbiting Geophysical Observatory [*NASA*]

OG/OB.......... Office Group/Office Branch [*IRS*]

OGOD .... One Gene One Disorder [*Hypothesis*]

OGOG.......... Gogama Community Library, Ontario [*Library symbol National Library of Canada*] (NLC)

OGOH.......... Huron County Public Library, Goderich, Ontario [*Library symbol National Library of Canada*] (NLC)

OGOHC ...... Huron County Pioneer Museum, Goderich, Ontario [*Library symbol National Library of Canada*] (BIB)

OGOR.......... Goulais River Community Library, Ontario [*Library symbol National Library of Canada*] (NLC)

OGOS.......... Outward Grade of Service (DNAB)

OGP .... Office of Global Programs [*National Oceanic and Atmospheric Administration*] (USDC)

OGP .... Original Gross Premium [*Insurance*] (AIA)

OGP .... Outgoing Message Process [*Telecommunications*] (TEL)

OGPA.......... Office of Governmental and Public Affairs [*Department of Agriculture*] (GFGA)

OGPA.......... Office of the General Purchasing Agent [*Military*]

OGPI .... Optical Glide Path Indicator

OGPr.......... Ogden Corp. $1.875 cm Cv Pfd [*NYSE symbol*] (TTSB)

OGPS.......... Office of Grants and Program Systems [*Department of Agriculture*]

OGPU.......... Obiedinennoye Gosudartsvennoye Politicheskoye Upravlenie [*United State Political Administration*] [*Russian*] (AD)

OGPU	Otdelenie Gosudarstvenni Politcheskoi Upravi [*Special Government Political Administration*] [*Former Soviet secret service organization, also known as GPU Later, KGB*]
OGR	B. F. Goodrich Co., Information Center, Brecksville, OH [*OCLC symbol*] (OCLC)
OGr	Greenville Public Library, Greenville, OH [*Library symbol Library of Congress*] (LCLS)
OGR	Grimsby Public Library and Art Gallery, Ontario [*Library symbol National Library of Canada*] (NLC)
OGR	Office of Government Relations [*Environmental Protection Agency*] (GFGA)
OGR	Office of Government Reports [*New Deal*]
OGR	Official Guide of the Railways [*A publication*] (AD)
OGR	Old Garden Rose [*Pre-1870*] [*Horticulture*]
OGR	Ontario Government Railway [*Canada*] (AD)
OGR	Operation Grass Roots [*Small communities employment service*]
OGR	Order of the Golden Rule (EA)
OGR	Ordnance, Gunnery, and Readiness Division [*Coast Guard*]
OGR	Original Gross Rate [*Insurance*] (AIA)
OGR	ORNL [*Oak Ridge National Laboratory*] Graphite Reactor
OGR	Outgoing Repeater
OGRA	Gravenhurst Public Library, Ontario [*Library symbol National Library of Canada*] (NLC)
OGraD	Denison University, Granville, OH [*Library symbol Library of Congress*] (LCLS)
OGraO	Owens-Corning Fiberglas Corp., Granville, OH [*Library symbol Library of Congress*] (LCLS)
OGRC	Office of Grants and Research Contracts [*NASA*]
OGRE	Greely Public Library, Ontario [*Library symbol National Library of Canada*] (NLC)
OGRE	Optical Grating Reflectance Evaluator (PDAA)
OGRE	Organization of Generally Rotten Enterprises [*Evil organization in television cartoon series "The Drak Pack"*]
OGRL	Outgoing Rural Line [*Telecommunications*] (IAA)
OGRM	Grimsby Museum, Ontario [*Library symbol National Library of Canada*] (BIB)
OGRS	Outgoing Relay Set [*Telecommunications*] (IAA)
OGRS	Outgoing Rural Selector [*Telecommunications*] (IAA)
OGRV	Grand Valley Public Library, Ontario [*Library symbol National Library of Canada*] (NLC)
OGS	Oakland Growth Study [*1932-1964*] [*Sociology*]
OGS	Obsolete General Supplies [*Military*]
OGS	Off-Gas System [*Nuclear energy*] (NRCH)
OGS	Ogdensburg [*New York*] [*Airport symbol*] (OAG)
OGS	Ogdensburg, NY [*Location identifier FAA*] (FAAL)
OGS	Ohio Genealogical Society (EA)
OGS	Ontario Geological Survey [*Ontario Ministry of Northern Development and Mines*] [*Canada*] (IRC)
OGS	Operative Glovers' Society [*A union*] [*British*]
O-GS	Operator-to-General Support [*Maintenance*] (MCD)
OGS	Optical Guidance System
OGS	Oratory of the Good Shepherd [*British*]
OGS	Original Ground Surface
OGS	Outer Glidescope
OGS	Outer Glide Slope [*Aviation*] (NASA)
OGS	Outgoing Secondary Switch (IAA)
OGS	Outgoing Secondary Switches (SAA)
OGS	Overseas Ground Station (MCD)
OGS	Oxogenic Steroid (MAE)
OGS	Oxygen Generation System (NASA)
OGSE	Operational Ground Support Equipment (AAG)
ogse	Operational Ground-Support Equipment (AD)
OGSEL	Operational Ground Support Equipment List (AAG)
OGSESS	Operational Ground Support Equipment Systems Specification (SAA)
OGSGS	Orangeburgh German Swiss Genealogical Society (EA)
OGSI	Ongard Sys [*NASDAQ symbol*] (TTSB)
OGSI	On Gard Systems [*NASDAQ symbol*] (SAG)
OGSM	Office of the General Sales Manager [*Department of Agriculture*]
OGSM	Stone Shop Museum, Grimsby, Ontario [*Library symbol National Library of Canada*] (NLC)
Ogs Med Jur	Ogston's Medical Jurisprudence [*1878*] [*A publication*] (DLA)
OGSO	O-Anon General Service Office [*An association*] (EA)
OGSR	Office of Graduate Studies and Research (AD)
OGST	Overthread Guide Sleeve Tool [*Nuclear energy*] (NRCH)
o-g stain	Orange-Green Stain (AD)
OGSTM	St. Matthew High School, Gloucester, Ontario [*Library symbol National Library of Canada*] (BIB)
OGT	MIS Division, Turnelle Productions Ltd., Gloucester, Ontario [*Library symbol National Library of Canada*] (BIB)
OGT	Office for Gifted and Talented [*Education*]
ogt	On-Going Thing (AD)
OGT	Oppenheimer Multi-Government Trust [*NYSE symbol*] (SPSG)
OGT	Oppenheimer Multi-Gvt Tr [*NYSE symbol*] (TTSB)
OGT	Outgoing Trunk
OGT	Outlet Gas Temperature (MSA)
ogt	Outlet Gas Temperature (AD)
OGTC	Outgoing Toll Center [*Telecommunications*] (IAA)
OGTC	Outgoing Toll Circuit [*Telecommunications*] (IAA)
OGTC	Tudor and Cashel Public Library, Gilmour, Ontario [*Library symbol National Library of Canada*] (BIB)
OGTM	Official Gazette. United States Patent and Trademark Office [*A publication*] (DLA)
OGTT	Oral Glucose Tolerance Test [*Medicine*]
OGU	Occupational Guidance Unit [*Department of Employment*] [*British*]
OGU	Ogden Bay [*Utah*] [*Seismograph station code, US Geological Survey*] (SEIS)
OGU	Orogenital Ulceration [*Medicine*] (DB)
OGU	Outgoing Unit [*Military*]
OGU	Outgoing Unit [*Telecommunications*] (IAA)
OGU	University of Guelph, Ontario [*Library symbol National Library of Canada*] (NLC)
OGV	Outlet Guide Vane
ogv	Outlet Guide Vane (AD)
OGV	Oxygen Gauge Valve (NASA)
OGW	Overhead Ground Wire
OGW	Overload Gross Weight (NG)
OGWE	Education Library, Wellington County Board of Education, Guelph, Ontario [*Library symbol National Library of Canada*] (NLC)
OGWP	Office of Ground Water Protection [*Environmental Protection Agency*] (GFGA)
OGWS	Outgoing/Wink Start [*Telecommunications*] (TEL)
OGX	Ouargla [*Algeria*] [*Airport symbol*] (OAG)
OGY	O'Gyalla [*Later, HRB*] [*Czechoslovakia*] [*Geomagnetic observatory code*]
OGY	OGY Petroleum [*Vancouver Stock Exchange symbol*]
OH	Comair [*ICAO designator*] (AD)
OH	Finland [*International civil aircraft marking*] (ODBW)
OH	Hamilton Public Library, Ontario [*Library symbol National Library of Canada*] (NLC)
oh	Hospitaller Brothers of St. John of God (TOCD)
OH	Hospitaller Brothers of St. John of God (TOCD)
OH	Hospitaller Order of St. John of God [*Roman Catholic men's religious order*]
OH	Hydroxy [*As substituent on nucleoside*] [*Also, HO*] [*Biochemistry*]
OH	Hydroxycorticosteroid [*Endocrinology*] (DAVI)
OH	Hydroxyl Radical (AD)
OH	Oakwood Homes [*NYSE symbol*] (TTSB)
OH	Oakwood Homes Corp. [*NYSE symbol*] (SPSG)
OH	Observation Helicopter
OH	Obstructive Hypopnea (DMAA)
OH	Occipital Horn [*Brain anatomy*]
OH	Occupational Health
OH	Occupational History [*Medicine*]
O-H	Octal-to-Hexadecimal [*Computer science*] (IEEE)
OH	Ocular Herpes [*Medicine*] (AD)
OH	Off Hook [*Computer science*]
OH	Office Hours
oh	Office Hours (AD)
OH	Office of the Handicapped
OH	Official Hostess (BARN)
OH	Ohio [*Postal code*]
Oh	Ohio Courts of Appeals Reports [*A publication*] (DLA)
OH	Ohmic Heating
Oh	Oholoth (BJA)
OH	Old Harrovian (WDAA)
OH	Olduvai Hominid [*Paleoanthropology*]
OH	Oligomer Hybridization (DMAA)
OH	Omega House (AD)
oh	Omni Hora [*Hourly*] [*Latin*] (AD)
OH	Omni Hora [*Every Hour*] [*Pharmacy*]
OH	On Hand
oh	On Hand (AD)
o-H	On-Hudson (AD)
OH	Ontario Hydroelectric [*Canada*]
OH	Open Hearth
oh	Open Hearth (AD)
OH	Open Heart Surgery [*Medicine*]
OH	Opera House (AD)
OH	Operating Hours (MCD)
OH	Operational Handbook [*Marine Corps*] (INF)
OH	Operational Hardware (KSC)
OH	Operator's Handbook
OH	Opposite Hand (OA)
OH	Orah Hayyim Shulhan 'Arukh (BJA)
OH	Oral Hygiene [*Dentistry*] (DAVI)
OH	Originating Hospital [*Aeromedical evacuation*]
OH	Orthostatic Hypotension [*Medicine*]
OH	Osteopathic Hospital (DAVI)
OH	Otago Hussars [*British military*] (DMA)
OH	Outer Housing (COE)
OH	Out Home [*Men's lacrosse position*]
oh	Out Home (AD)
OH	Outlaw HAWK [*Naval Air Development Center*]
OH	Out of Hospital (DMAA)
OH	Outpatient Hospital [*Medicine*]
oh	Oval Head (AD)
OH	Overall Height [*of the Vehicle*] [*TII*] (TAG)
o/h	Overhaul (AD)
OH	Overhaul
OH	Overhead
oh	Overhead (AD)
O/H	Over-the-Horizon Transmission
O/H	Overzuche Handels Maatschappij [*Foreign Trade Company*] [*Dutch*] (ILCA)
OH	Ozar Hatorah (EA)
OH	SFO [*San Francisco and Oakland*] Helicopter Airlines, Inc. [*ICAO designator*] (OAG)
OHA	Chicago, IL [*Location identifier FAA*] (FAAL)

OHA .... Havelock Public Library, Ontario [*Library symbol National Library of Canada*] (BIB)
OHA .... Hydroxyandrostenedione [*Antineoplastic drug*] (CDI)
OHa .... Lane Public Library, Hamilton, OH [*Library symbol Library of Congress*] (LCLS)
OHA .... Occupational Health Administration (AD)
OHA .... Office of Health Affairs [*U.S. Food and Drug Administration*]
OHA .... Office of Hearings and Appeals [*In various federal departments*]
OHA .... Officers' Home Advance (ADA)
OHA .... Off-station Housing Allowance (DOMA)
Oha .... Ohaloth (BJA)
OHA .... OH Aviationa [*France ICAO designator*] (FAAC)
Oh A .... Ohio Appellate Reports [*A publication*] (DLA)
OHA .... Operational Hazard Analysis (NASA)
OHA .... Oral History Association (EA)
OHA .... Oral Hypoglycemic Agent [*Medicine*] (CPH)
OHA .... Oral Hypoglycemic Agents [*Medicine*] (DMAA)
OHA .... Orbital Height Adjustment Maneuver (MCD)
OHA .... Oriental Herb Association (AD)
OHA .... Oscillator Housing Assembly
OHA .... Outside Helix Angle
oha .... Outside Helix Angle (AD)
OHA .... Overseas Housing Allowance
OHA .... Owner Handler Association of America (EA)
OHA .... Oxygen Hemoglobin Affinity (OA)
Oh A 2d ..... Ohio Appellate Reports, Second Series [*A publication*] (DLA)
OHaBHi .... Butler County Historical Society, Hamilton, OH [*Library symbol Library of Congress*] (LCLS)
OHAD .... Dysart Branch, Haliburton County Public Library, Ontario [*Library symbol National Library of Canada*] (BIB)
OHAG .... Art Gallery of Hamilton, Ontario [*Library symbol National Library of Canada*] (NLC)
OHAI .... Haileybury Public Library, Ontario [*Library symbol National Library of Canada*] (NLC)
OHAINC .... Haileybury School of Mines Campus, Northern College of Applied Arts and Technology, Ontario [*Library symbol National Library of Canada*] (BIB)
OHAL .... Haliburton County Public Library, Ontario [*Library symbol National Library of Canada*] (NLC)
OHALM .... Haliburton Highlands Museum, Haliburton, Ontario [*Library symbol National Library of Canada*] (BIB)
OHaMH .... Mercy Hospital, Health Science Library, Hamilton, OH [*Library symbol Library of Congress*] (LCLS)
OHAN .... Hanover Public Library, Ontario [*Library symbol National Library of Canada*] (NLC)
Oh Ap .... Ohio Appellate Reports [*A publication*] (DLA)
OHAPT .... Orleans-Hanna Algebra Prognosis Test (EDAC)
OHARAG ...... Research Station, Agriculture Canada [*Station de Recherches, Agriculture Canada*] Harrow, Ontario [*Library symbol National Library of Canada*] (NLC)
OhArt .... [*The*] Ohio Art Co. [*Associated Press*] (SAG)
OHAS .... Occupational Health and Safety
OHaU .... Miami University, Hamilton Campus, Hamilton, OH [*Library symbol Library of Congress*] (LCLS)
OHB .... L'Equilibre Biologique [*France*] [*Research code symbol*]
OH-B .... Ocean Hill-Brownsville (AD)
OHB .... Orleans Homebuilders [*Montreal Stock Exchange*] [*Formerly, FPA Corp.*]
OHBC .... Oregon Highland Bentgrass Commission (EA)
OHBES .... Schools, Hamilton Board of Education, Ontario [*Library symbol National Library of Canada*] (NLC)
OHBHU .... Hilton Union Public Library, Hilton Beach, Ontario [*Library symbol National Library of Canada*] (NLC)
OHBMS .... On His [*or Her*] Britannic Majesty's Service
OHBP .... Pic Heron Bay Band Public Library, Heron Bay, Ontario [*Library symbol National Library of Canada*] (BIB)
OHC .... Hydroxycholecalciferol [*A form of vitamin D*] (DAVI)
OHC .... Occupational Health Center (KSC)
OHC .... Ocean Heat Convergence
OHC .... Office of Humanities Communication (AD)
OHC .... Office of HUMINT [*Human Intelligence*] Collection [*Military*]
OHC .... O'Higgins [*Antarctica*] [*Seismograph station code, US Geological Survey*] (SEIS)
OHC .... On Board Hard Copier (NASA)
OHC .... Optics Hand Controller (KSC)
OHC .... Order of the Holy Cross [*Episcopalian religious order*]
OHC .... Oriole Homes Corp. [*AMEX symbol*] (SPSG)
OHC .... Ottumwa Heights College [*Iowa*]
OHC .... Outer Hair Cells [*of cochlea*] [*Anatomy*]
ohc .... Outer Hair Cells (AD)
ohc .... Overhead Cam (AD)
OHC .... Over-Head-Cam [*TII*] (TAG)
OHC .... Overhead Camshaft [*Automotive term*]
OHC .... Overhead Cupboards [*Classified advertising*] (ADA)
OHC .... Overseas Hotel Corp. (AD)
OHC.A .... Oriole HomesCv'A' [*AMEX symbol*] (TTSB)
OHCA .... Otter Hound Club of America [*Later, OCA*] (EA)
OHCA .... Out-of-Hospital Cardiac Arrest [*Medicine*] (DMAA)
OHC.B .... Oriole Homes `B' [*AMEX symbol*] (TTSB)
OH-Cbl .... Hydroxycobalamin [*Medicine*] (BABM)
OHCC .... Ordinary High Current Configuration [*Magnetic field*]
Oh Cir Ct .... Ohio Circuit Court Reports [*A publication*] (DLA)
Oh Cir Ct NS.. Ohio Circuit Court Reports, New Series [*A publication*] (DLA)
Oh Cir Dec... Ohio Circuit Decisions [*A publication*] (DLA)
OHCS .... Hydroxycorticosteroid [*Endocrinology*] (AAMN)

OHCS .... Office of Home Care Services (AD)
OHCU .... College Universitaire de Hearst, Ontario [*Library symbol National Library of Canada*] (NLC)
OHD .... Hydroxycholecalciferol (STED)
OHD .... Hydroxyvitamin D (DMAA)
OHD .... Occupational Health Division (COE)
OHD .... Office of Human Development [*Later, OHDS*] [*HEW*]
OHD .... Ohrid [*Former Yugoslavia*] [*Airport symbol*] (OAG)
OHD .... Old Hickory Dam [*TVA*]
OHD .... Ondine-Hirschprung Disease [*Medicine*] (DMAA)
OHD .... One-Hour Duty (IAA)
OHD .... Optical Heterodyne Detection
OHD .... Ordinary Hydrodynamic
ohd .... Organic Hearing Disease [*Medicine*] (AD)
ohd .... Organic Heart Disease [*Medicine*] (AD)
OHD .... Organic Heart Disease [*Medicine*]
OHD .... Overhead Display
OHD .... Overhead Door Corp. (EFIS)
OHD .... Over-the-Horizon Detector [*RADAR*]
OHDA .... Hydroxydopamine [*Also, HDA, HDM*] [*Biochemistry*]
OHD & W ..... Outer Harbor Dock and Wharf (AD)
OHD-B .... Over-the-Horizon Detection RADAR-Backscatter (MCD)
Oh Dec .... Ohio Decisions [*A publication*] (DLA)
Oh Dec Rep.. Ohio Decisions Reprint [*A publication*] (DLA)
OHDET .... Over-the-Horizon Detection [*RADAR*] (SAA)
OHDETS .... Over-the-Horizon Detection System [*RADAR*]
OHDF .... Dofasco, Inc., Hamilton, Ontario [*Library symbol National Library of Canada*] (NLC)
OHDFR .... Research Information Center, DOFASCO, Inc., Hamilton, Ontario [*Library symbol National Library of Canada*] (NLC)
OHDMS .... Operational Hydromet Data Management System (PDAA)
OH-DOC ...... Hydroxydeoxycorticosterone [*Endocrinology*] (DAVI)
OHDS .... Office of Human Development Services [*Formerly, OHD*] [*Department of Health and Human Services*]
OHE .... Hearst Public Library, Ontario [*Library symbol National Library of Canada*] (NLC)
OHE .... Office of Health Economics [*British*]
OHE .... Office of the Housing Expediter [*Terminated, 1951*] (GPO)
OHE .... Oxidizer Heat Exchange (MCD)
OHEA .... Office of Health and Environmental Assessment [*Environmental Protection Agency*] (GFGA)
OHEAT .... Overheat
oheat .... Overheat (AD)
OHEC .... Dr. Harry Paikin Library, Hamilton Board of Education, Ontario [*Library symbol National Library of Canada*] (NLC)
OHEC .... Hamilton Education Centre, Ontario [*Library symbol National Library of Canada*] (NLC)
OhEd .... Ohio Edison Co. [*Associated Press*] (SAG)
OhEd .... Ohio Edison Financing Trust [*Associated Press*] (SAG)
OHEP .... Hepworth Branch, Bruce County Public Library, Ontario [*Library symbol National Library of Canada*] (NLC)
OHER .... Office of Health and Environmental Research [*Department of Energy Washington, DC*]
OHESC .... Ontario Library Service - Escarpment, Hamilton, Ontario [*Library symbol National Library of Canada*] (NLC)
OHET .... Erin Township Public Library, Hillsburgh, Ontario [*Library symbol National Library of Canada*] (NLC)
OHF .... Occupational Health Facility [*NASA*] (KSC)
OHF .... Omsk Hemorrhagic Fever [*Medicine*]
ohf .... Omsk Hemorrhagic Fever (AD)
OHF .... Ordnance Historical Files [*Military*]
ohf .... Overhaul Factor (AD)
OHF .... Overhead Fire (MCD)
OHF .... Overhead Frame (MEDA)
OHF .... Oxalosis and Hyperoxaluria Foundation (EA)
OHFA .... Hydroxy Fatty Acid [*Biochemistry*] (AAMN)
OHFC .... Hartington Branch, Frontenac County Library, Hartington, Ontario [*Library symbol National Library of Canada*] (BIB)
OHFC .... Owen Hart Fan Club (EA)
Oh F Dec ..... Ohio Federal Decisions [*A publication*] (DLA)
OH/FH .... Operating Hour/Flight Hour [*Ratio*]
OHFT .... Overhead Frame Trapeze (STED)
OHG .... Banco OHiggins [*NYSE symbol*] (SAG)
OHG .... Banco O'Higgins ADS [*NYSE symbol*] (TTSB)
OHG .... Offene Handelsgesellschaft [*General Partnership*] [*German*]
OHG .... Old High German [*Language, etc.*]
OHG .... Oral Hypoglycemic [*Endocrinology*] (DAVI)
OHGI .... Over the Hill Gang, International (EA)
OHGS .... Omega Hyperbolic Grid System
OHGVT .... Orbital Horizontal Ground Vibration Test [*NASA*] (NASA)
OHH .... Herrold Hall Learning Resource Center, Zanesville, OH [*OCLC symbol*] (OCLC)
OHH .... Ohio Household Goods Carriers Bureau Inc., Warren OH [*STAC*]
OHH .... Owen Harrison Harding [*of the James W. Ellison novel, "I'm Owen Harrison Harding"*]
OHHA .... Occupational Health Hazard Assessment
OHI .... HUNA International (EA)
OHI .... Occupational Health Institute [*Defunct*] (EA)
OHI .... Ocular Hypertension Indicator
ohi .... Ocular Hypertension Indicator (AD)
OHi .... Ohio Historical Society, Columbus, OH [*Library symbol Library of Congress*] (LCLS)
OHI .... Oil Heat Institute (AD)
OHI .... Oil-Heat Institute of America [*Later, PMAA*]
OHI .... Omega Healthcare Investors [*NYSE symbol*] (SPSG)

OHI	Open Head Injury [*Medicine*] (PAZ)
OHI	Oral Hygiene Index (STED)
OHI	Ordnance Handling Instructions
OHI	Organisation Hydrographique Internationale [*International Hydrographic Organization - IHO*] [*Monte Carlo, Monaco*]
OHI	Other Health Impaired [*Education*]
OHI	State Library of Ohio, Columbus, OH [*OCLC symbol*] (OCLC)
OHIA	Oil-Heat Institute of America [*Later, PMAA*] (KSC)
OHIAA	Hydroxyindolacetic Acid [*Oncology*] (DAVI)
OH-IAA	Hydroxyindoleacetic Acid (STED)
OHIC	ODPHP Health Information Center (EA)
OHiIH	Highland County District Library, Hillsboro, OH [*Library symbol Library of Congress*] (LCLS)
OHiIS	South Hillsboro City Schools, Hillsboro, OH [*Library symbol Library of Congress*] (LCLS)
Ohio	Ohio Supreme Court Reports [*1821-51*] [*A publication*] (DLA)
OHIO	Over the Hill in October [*Used prior to the bombing of Pearl Harbor to typify a recruit's view of US Army life*]
Ohio Abs	Ohio Law Abstract [*A publication*] (DLA)
Ohio Abstract ...	Ohio Law Abstract [*A publication*] (DLA)
Ohio Admin Code ...	Ohio Administrative Code [*Official compilation published by Banks-Baldwin*] [*A publication*] (DLA)
Ohio App	Ohio Appellate Reports [*A publication*] (DLA)
Ohio App 2d ...	Ohio Appellate Reports, Second Series [*A publication*] (DLA)
Ohio Apps ...	Ohio Appellate Reports [*A publication*] (DLA)
Ohio BTA	Ohio Board of Tax Appeals Reports [*A publication*] (DLA)
OhioCa	Ohio Casualty Corp. [*Associated Press*] (SAG)
Ohio CA	Ohio Courts of Appeals Reports [*A publication*] (DLA)
OhioCas	Ohio Casualty Corp. [*Associated Press*] (SAG)
Ohio CC	Ohio Circuit Court Reports [*A publication*] (DLA)
Ohio CC Dec ...	Ohio Circuit Court Decisions [*A publication*] (DLA)
Ohio CC NS ...	Ohio Circuit Court Reports, New Series [*A publication*] (DLA)
Ohio CCR	Ohio Circuit Court Reports [*A publication*] (DLA)
Ohio CCR NS ...	Ohio Circuit Court Reports, New Series [*A publication*] (DLA)
Ohio CD	Ohio Circuit Decisions [*A publication*] (DLA)
Ohio C Dec ...	Ohio Circuit Decisions [*A publication*] (DLA)
Ohio Circ Dec ...	Ohio Circuit Decisions [*A publication*] (DLA)
Ohio Cir Ct	Ohio Circuit Court Decisions [*A publication*] (DLA)
Ohio Cir Ct (NS) ...	Ohio Circuit Court Reports, New Series [*A publication*] (DLA)
Ohio Cir Ct R ...	Ohio Circuit Court Reports [*A publication*] (DLA)
Ohio Cir Ct R NS ...	Ohio Circuit Court Reports, New Series [*A publication*] (DLA)
Ohio Circuits ...	Ohio Circuit Court Decisions [*A publication*] (DLA)
Ohio Cir Dec ...	Ohio Circuit Decisions [*A publication*] (DLA)
Ohio Cond ...	Wilcox's Condensed Ohio Reports [*A publication*] (DLA)
Ohio Cond R ...	Wilcox's Condensed Ohio Reports [*A publication*] (DLA)
Ohio Ct App ...	Ohio Courts of Appeals Reports [*A publication*] (DLA)
Ohio Dec	Ohio Decisions [*A publication*] (DLA)
Ohio Dec NP ...	Ohio Decisions Nisi Prius [*A publication*] (DLA)
Ohio Dec R ...	Ohio Decisions Reprint [*A publication*] (DLA)
Ohio Dec Re ...	Ohio Decisions Reprint [*A publication*] (DLA)
Ohio Dec Rep ...	Ohio Decisions Reprint [*A publication*] (DLA)
Ohio Dec Repr ...	Ohio Decisions Reprint [*A publication*] (DLA)
Ohio Dep't ...	Ohio Department Reports [*A publication*] (DLA)
OhioEd	Ohio Edison Co. [*Associated Press*] (SAG)
Ohio FD	Ohio Federal Decisions [*A publication*] (DLA)
Ohio F Dec ...	Ohio Federal Decisions [*A publication*] (DLA)
Ohio Fed Dec ...	Ohio Federal Decisions [*A publication*] (DLA)
Ohio Gov't ...	Ohio Government Reports [*A publication*] (DLA)
Ohio Jur	Ohio Jurisprudence [*A publication*] (DLA)
Ohio Jur 2d ...	Ohio Jurisprudence, Second Series [*A publication*] (DLA)
Ohio L Abs ...	Ohio Law Abstract [*A publication*] (DLA)
Ohio Law Abs ...	Ohio Law Abstract [*A publication*] (DLA)
Ohio Law Abst ...	Ohio Law Abstract [*A publication*] (DLA)
Ohio Law Bull ...	Weekly Law Bulletin [*Ohio*] [*A publication*] (DLA)
Ohio Law J ...	Ohio Law Journal [*A publication*] (DLA)
Ohio Law R ...	Ohio Law Reporter [*A publication*] (DLA)
Ohio Law Rep ...	Ohio Law Reporter [*A publication*] (DLA)
Ohio Law Repr ...	Ohio Law Reporter [*A publication*] (DLA)
Ohio Laws ...	State of Ohio: Legislative Acts Passed and Joint Resolutions Adopted [*A publication*] (DLA)
Ohio LB	Weekly Law Bulletin [*Ohio*] [*A publication*] (DLA)
Ohio L Bull ...	Ohio Law Bulletin [*A publication*] (DLA)
Ohio Legal N ...	Ohio Legal News [*A publication*] (DLA)
Ohio Legis Bull ...	Ohio Legislative Bulletin (Anderson) [*A publication*] (DLA)
Ohio Legis Serv ...	Ohio Legislative Service [*A publication*] (DLA)
Ohio Leg N ...	Ohio Legal News [*A publication*] (DLA)
Ohio Leg News ...	Ohio Legal News [*A publication*] (DLA)
Ohio LJ	Ohio Law Journal [*A publication*] (DLA)
Ohio Low Dec ...	Ohio Lower Court Decisions [*A publication*] (DLA)
Ohio Lower Dec ...	Ohio Lower Court Decisions [*A publication*] (DLA)
Ohio LR	Ohio Law Reporter [*A publication*] (DLA)
Ohio LR & Wk Bul ...	Ohio Law Reporter and Weekly Bulletin [*A publication*] (DLA)
Ohio L Rep ...	Ohio Law Reporter [*A publication*] (DLA)
OHIO M	Ohio Magazine [*A publication*] (ROG)
Ohio Misc	Ohio Miscellaneous Reports [*A publication*] (DLA)
Ohio Misc 2d ...	Ohio Miscellaneous Reports, Second Series [*A publication*] (DLA)
Ohio Misc 3d ...	Ohio Miscellaneous Reports, Third Series [*A publication*] (DLA)
Ohio Misc Dec ...	Ohio Miscellaneous Decisions [*A publication*] (DLA)
Ohio Monthly Rec ...	Ohio Monthly Record [*A publication*] (DLA)
OHIONET	Ohio Network (NITA)
Ohio (New Series) ...	Ohio State Reports, New Series [*A publication*] (DLA)
Ohio Nisi Prius ...	Ohio Nisi Prius Reports [*A publication*] (DLA)
Ohio Nisi Prius (NS) ...	Ohio Nisi Prius Reports, New Series [*A publication*] (DLA)
Ohio No U ...	Ohio Northern University (GAGS)
Ohio NP	Ohio Nisi Prius Reports [*A publication*] (DLA)
Ohio NP NS ...	Ohio Nisi Prius Reports, New Series [*A publication*] (DLA)
Ohio NS	Ohio State Reports, New Series [*A publication*] (DLA)
Ohio O	Ohio Opinions [*A publication*] (DLA)
Ohio O	Ohio Opinions, Annotated [*A publication*] (DLA)
Ohio O 2d	Ohio Opinions, Second Series [*A publication*] (DLA)
Ohio Op	Ohio Opinions [*A publication*] (DLA)
Ohio Op 2d	Ohio Opinions, Second Series [*A publication*] (DLA)
Ohio Op 3d ...	Ohio Opinions, Third Series [*A publication*] (DLA)
Ohio Ops	Ohio Opinions [*A publication*] (DLA)
Ohio Prob	Ohio Probate Reports, by Goebel [*A publication*] (DLA)
Ohio Prob Ct ...	Goebel's Probate Reports [*Ohio*] [*A publication*] (DLA)
Ohio R	Ohio Report [*A publication*] (DLA)
Ohio R Cond ...	Ohio Reports Condensed [*A publication*] (DLA)
Ohio Rev Code Ann ...	Ohio Revised Code, Annotated [*A publication*] (DLA)
Ohio Rev Code Ann (Anderson) ...	Ohio Revised Code, Annotated (Anderson) [*A publication*] (DLA)
Ohio Rev Code Ann (Baldwin) ...	Ohio Revised Code, Annotated (Baldwin) [*A publication*] (DLA)
Ohio Rev Code Ann (Page) ...	Ohio Revised Code, Annotated (Page) [*A publication*] (DLA)
Ohio S	Ohio State Reports [*A publication*] (DLA)
Ohio S & CP ...	Ohio Superior and Common Pleas Decisions [*A publication*] (DLA)
Ohio S & CP Dec ...	Ohio Superior and Common Pleas Decisions [*A publication*] (DLA)
Ohio SBA Bull ...	Ohio State Bar Association. Bulletin [*A publication*] (DLA)
Ohio SR	Ohio State Reports [*A publication*] (DLA)
Ohio S Rep ...	Ohio State Reports [*A publication*] (DLA)
Ohio St	Ohio State Reports [*A publication*] (DLA)
Ohio St 2d ...	Ohio State Reports, Second Series [*A publication*] (DLA)
Ohio St 3d ...	Ohio State Reports, Third Series [*A publication*] (DLA)
Ohio State ..	Ohio State Reports [*A publication*] (DLA)
Ohio State Rep ...	Ohio State Reports [*A publication*] (DLA)
Ohio State R (NS) ...	Ohio State Reports, New Series [*A publication*] (DLA)
Ohio St R	Ohio State Reports [*A publication*] (DLA)
Ohio St Rep ...	Ohio State Reports [*A publication*] (DLA)
Ohio St Report ...	Ohio State Reports [*A publication*] (DLA)
Ohio St R (NS) ...	Ohio State Reports, New Series [*A publication*] (DLA)
Ohio St U	[*The*] Ohio State University (GAGS)
Ohio SU	Ohio Supreme Court Decisions, Unreported Cases [*A publication*] (DLA)
Ohio Sup & CP Dec ...	Ohio Superior and Common Pleas Decisions [*A publication*] (DLA)
Ohio Supp ...	Ohio Supplement [*A publication*] (DLA)
Ohio Turn ...	Ohio Turnpike (AD)
Ohio U	Ohio University (GAGS)
Ohio Unrep ...	Ohio Supreme Court Decisions, Unreported Cases [*A publication*] (DLA)
Ohio Unrep Jud Dec ...	Pollack's Ohio Unreported Judicial Decisions Prior to 1823 [*A publication*] (DLA)
Ohio Unrept Cas ...	Ohio Supreme Court Decisions, Unreported Cases [*A publication*] (DLA)
Ohio U Pr	Ohio University Press (AD)
OhioVal	Ohio Valley Banc Corp. [*Associated Press*] (SAG)
OHIP	Office of Health and Industry Programs [*U.S. Food and Drug Administration*]
OHIP	Ontario Health Insurance Plan [*Canada*] (CMD)
OHIP	Ontario Hospital Insurance Plan [*Canada*] (AD)
OHIR	Operating House of Ill Repute
OHirC	Hiram College, Hiram, OH [*Library symbol Library of Congress*] (LCLS)
OHirP	Portage County District Library, Hiram, OH [*Library symbol Library of Congress*] (LCLS)
OHIS	Oral Hearing-Impaired Section [*of the Alexander Graham Bell Association for the Deaf*] (EA)
OHI-S	Oral Hygiene Index-Simplified
OHJ	Old-House Journal [*A publication*]
OHJD	John Deere Ltd., Hamilton, Ontario [*Library symbol National Library of Canada*] (NLC)
Oh Jur	Ohio Jurisprudence [*A publication*] (DLA)
OHK	Hawkesbury Public Library, Ontario [*Library symbol National Library of Canada*] (NLC)
OHKAC	Resource Centre, Algonquin College of Applied Arts and Technology [*Centre de Documentation, College Algonquin des Arts Appliques et de la Technologie*], Hawkesbury, Ontario [*Library symbol National Library of Canada*] (BIB)
OHKC	CIP Research Ltd., Hawkesbury, Ontario [*Library symbol National Library of Canada*] (NLC)
OHKGH	Hawkesbury General Hospital, Ontario [*Library symbol National Library of Canada*] (BIB)
OHL	Oberste Herresleitung [*Supreme Headquarters*] [*German*] (AD)
OHL	Ontario Hydro Library [*UTLAS symbol*]
OHL	Oral Hairy Leukoplakia [*Medicine*]
OHL	Overhaul
OHL	Oxford Higher Local Examination [*British*] (ROG)
OHLA	Anthony Pape Memorial Law Library, Hamilton Law Association, Ontario [*Library symbol National Library of Canada*] (BIB)
Oh L Bul	Ohio Law Bulletin [*A publication*] (DLA)
Oh L Ct D	Ohio Lower Court Decisions [*A publication*] (DLA)
OHLEG	East Gwillimbury Public Libraries, Holland Landing, Ontario [*Library symbol National Library of Canada*] (NLC)
Oh Leg N	Ohio Legal News [*A publication*] (DLA)
OHLH	Overhead Heavy Load Handling [*Nuclear energy*] (NRCH)
Ohlinger Fed Practice ...	Ohlinger's Federal Practice [*A publication*] (DLA)
Oh LJ	Ohio Law Journal [*A publication*] (DLA)
Oh L Rep	Ohio Law Reporter [*A publication*] (DLA)

OHM .... McMaster University, Hamilton, Ontario [*Library symbol National Library of Canada*] (NLC)

OHM .... Miami University, Hamilton Campus, Hamilton, OH [*OCLC symbol*] (OCLC)

OHM .... Office of Hazardous Materials [*Department of Transportation*]

OHM .... OHM Corp. [*NYSE symbol*] (SPSG)

OHM .... Ohmmeter [*Engineering*] (AAG)

ohm .... Ohmmeter (AD)

OHM .... Oil and Hazardous Materials Incidence

OHMA .... Archives and Special Collections Division, McMaster University, Hamilton, Ontario [*Library symbol National Library of Canada*] (NLC)

OHMA .... Office of Health and Medical Affairs (GHCT)

OHMAH .... Department of Art and Art History, McMaster University, Hamilton, Ontario [*Library symbol National Library of Canada*] (NLC)

OHMAR .... Oral History in the Mid-Atlantic Region [*An association*]

OHMB .... Health Sciences Library, McMaster University, Hamilton, Ontario [*Library symbol National Library of Canada*] (NLC)

OHMC .... Mohawk College of Applied Arts and Technology, Hamilton, Ontario [*Library symbol National Library of Canada*] (NLC)

OHMcGF ..... Odyssey House McGrath Foundation [*Australia*]

OHMCI .... Office of Her Majesty's Chief Inspector of Schools [*British*] (DET)

OHMCL .... Library Technician Program, Mohawk College of Applied Arts & Technology, Hamilton, Ontario [*Library symbol National Library of Canada*] (NLC)

OHM-CM ..... Ohm-Centimeter (AAG)

ohm-cm ...... Ohm-Centimeter (AD)

OHM Cp ...... OHM Corp. [*Associated Press*] (SAG)

OHMDBA ...... Canadian Baptist Archives, McMaster Divinity College, McMaster University, Hamilton, Ontario [*Library symbol National Library of Canada*] (NLC)

OHMEA .... Office of Hazardous Materials Exemptions and Approvals [*RSPA*] (TAG)

OHMES .... Occupational Health Monitoring and Evaluation System (PDAA)

OHMIS .... Occupational Health Management Information System [*Military*] (GFGA)

Oh Misc ...... Ohio Miscellaneous Reports [*A publication*] (DLA)

OHMM .... Map Library, McMaster University, Hamilton, Ontario [*Library symbol National Library of Canada*] (NLC)

OHMM .... Ohmmeter [*Engineering*]

ohm/m .... Resistence per Meter

OHMO .... Office of Hazardous Materials Operations [*Department of Transportation*] (DLA)

OHMO .... Office of Health Maintenance Organization [*Insurance*] (DHSM)

OHMP .... Oral Health Maintenance Program [*Army*] (AABC)

OHMR .... Office of Hazardous Materials Regulation [*Department of Transportation*] (OICC)

OHMS .... Office of Hazardous Materials Standards [*RSPA*] (TAG)

OHMS .... Onboard Health Monitoring System (AD)

OHMS .... On His [*or Her*] Majesty's Service

OHMS .... Our Helpless Millions Saved [*Title of early film*]

OHMS .... Overhead Machine Screw [*Technical drawings*]

OHMSB .... Oil and Hazardous Materials Spills Branch [*Environmental Protection Agency*] (GRD)

OHMSETT .... Oil and Hazardous Materials Simulated Environmental Test Tank [*Leonardo, NJ*] [*Environmental Protection Agency*]

OHMT .... Office of Hazardous Materials Transportation [*Department of Transportation*] (GFGA)

OHM-TADS... Oil and Hazardous Materials Technical Assistance Data System [*Databank*] [*Environmental Protection Agency*] (IID)

OHMTADS.... Oil and Hazardous Material Technical Assistance Data System [*Environmental Protection Agency*] (AEPA)

OHN .... Hastings Branch, Northumberland County Public Library, Ontario [*Library symbol National Library of Canada*] (BIB)

OHN .... Memphis, TN [*Location identifier FAA*] (FAAL)

OHN .... Occupational Health Nurse [*Government classification*]

OHN .... OHIONET, Columbus, OH [*OCLC symbol*] (OCLC)

OHNC .... Occupational Health Nursing Certificate [*British*]

OHNN .... Otorhinolaryngology and Head/Neck Nurses (EA)

OHNO .... Occupational Health Nursing Officer (AD)

Oh NP .... Ohio Nisi Prius Reports [*A publication*] (DLA)

Oh NP (NS).. Ohio Nisi Prius Reports, New Series [*A publication*] (DLA)

OHNS .... Occupational Health Nursing Sister (AD)

Oh NU Intra LR... Ohio Northern University. Intramural Law Review [*A publication*] (DLA)

OHO .... Ohio Resources Corp. [*Vancouver Stock Exchange symbol*]

Oho .... Oholoth (BJA)

OHO .... Order Holding Office

OHO .... Ordnance Handling Officer [*Navy*] (DOMA)

oho .... Out-of-House Operation (AD)

OHOB .... O'Neill House Office Building [*U.S. House of Representatives*] [*Washington, D.C.*]

OHOHS .... Canadian Centre for Occupational Health and Safety [*Centre Canadien d'Hygieneet de Securite au Travail*] Hamilton, Ontario [*Library symbol National Library of Canada*] (NLC)

Ohol .... Oholoth (BJA)

OHP .... Hydroxypyroline [*Biochemistry*] (AAMN)

OHP .... Oban-Heliport [*Scotland*] [*Airport symbol*] (OAG)

OHP .... Office of Health Physics [*U.S. Food and Drug Administration*]

OHP .... Operational Hydrology Program [*World Meteorological Organization*] (GFGA)

OHP .... Order of the Holy Paraclete [*Anglican religious community*]

OHP .... Outer Helmholtz Plane [*Physics*]

ohp .... Overhead Projection (AD)

OHP .... Overhead Projector (ADA)

OHP .... Oxygen at High Pressure [*Also, HBO, HPO*] (MCD)

OHP .... Oxygen under Hyperbaric Pressure [*For hyperbaric oxygen therapy*] [*Medicine*] (DAVI)

OhP25 .... Ohio Power Co. [*Associated Press*] (SAG)

OH PED ...... Ohne Pedal [*Without Pedal*] [*Music*]

oh Ped .... Ohne Pedale [*Without Pedals*] [*German*] (AD)

OHPO .... Organization Health Program Officer (AFM)

OHPR .... Outstanding Hardware Problem Report (MCD)

Oh Prob ...... Ohio Probate [*A publication*] (DLA)

OHPS .... Oil Hydraulic Power Switch

OHQ .... Overseas Headquarters [*British military*] (DMA)

OHR .... Office of Health Research [*Environmental Protection Agency Washington, DC*] (GRD)

OHR .... Of Human Rights (EA)

OHR .... O'Hara Resources Ltd. [*Vancouver Stock Exchange symbol*]

OHR .... Ohrid [*Yugoslavia*] [*Seismograph station code, US Geological Survey*] (SEIS)

OHR .... Operational Hazard Report [*Air Force*] (AFM)

OHR .... Over-the-Horizon RADAR

OHRB .... Royal Botanical Gardens, Hamilton, Ontario [*Library symbol National Library of Canada*] (NLC)

OHRC .... Redeemer College, Ancaster, Ontario [*Library symbol National Library of Canada*] (NLC)

ohrf .... Overhaul Replacement Factor (AD)

OHRG .... Official Hotel and Resort Guide [*A publication*] (AD)

OHRI .... Occupational Health & Rehabilitation, Inc. [*NASDAQ symbol*] (SAG)

OHRI .... Oral Health Research Institute [*Indiana University*] [*Research center*] (RCD)

OHRI .... Overhaul Recurrent Item (CINC)

OHRI .... Overhaul Removal Interval [*Military*] (AFIT)

OHRI .... Overhaul Removal Item (CINC)

OHRIM .... Office of Human Resource Information Management [*Department of Health and Human Services*] (GFGA)

OHRM .... Office of Human Resources Management [*Environmental Protection Agency*] (GFGA)

OHRR .... Open Heart Recovery Room [*Cardiology*] (DAVI)

OHRS .... Overflow Heat Removal System [*Nuclear energy*] (NRCH)

OHS .... Hamilton Spectator, Ontario [*Library symbol National Library of Canada*] (NLC)

OHS .... Obesity Hypoventilation Syndrome

OHS .... Occupational Health and Safety

OHS .... Occupational Health Services, Inc. [*Secaucus, NJ*] [*Medical databank originator*] [*Information service or system*]

OHS .... Occupational Hearing Service

OHS .... Off-Hook Service [*Telecommunications*] (TEL)

OHS .... Office of Highway Safety [*of BPR*]

OHS .... Ontario Humane Society [*Canada*] (AD)

ohs .... Open-Hearth Steel (AD)

OHS .... Open-Hearth Steel

OHS .... Open Heart Surgery [*Medicine*]

OHS .... Optometric Historical Society (EA)

OHS .... Oral Hygiene Service (AD)

OHS .... Oral Hygiene Society (NADA)

OHS .... Organ Historical Society (EA)

OHS .... Organization Health Survey [*Test*]

OHS .... Organization of Historical Studies (EA)

OHS .... Oval-Headed Screw (DAC)

OHS .... Ovarian Hyperstimulation Syndrome [*Medicine*] (DMAA)

OHS .... Oxford Historical Society [*British*] (ODCC)

OHS .... University of Oregon, Health Sciences Library, Portland, OR [*OCLC symbol*] (OCLC)

OHSA .... Occupational Health and Safety Authority [*Victoria, Australia*]

Oh S & CP... Ohio Superior and Common Pleas Decisions [*A publication*] (DLA)

OHSC .... Oak Hill Sportswear [*NASDAQ symbol*] (TTSB)

OHSC .... Oak Hill Sportswear Corp. [*NASDAQ symbol*] (NQ)

OHSCC .... Steel Company of Canada, Hamilton, Ontario [*Library symbol National Library of Canada*] (NLC)

Oh SCD .... Ohio Supreme Court Decisions, Unreported Cases [*A publication*] (DLA)

OHSCSA ...... Occupational Health and Safety Commission of South Australia

OHSGT .... Office of High-Speed Ground Transportation [*Department of Transportation*]

OHSI .... Omega Health Systems [*NASDAQ symbol*] (TTSB)

OHSI .... Omega Health Systems, Inc. [*NASDAQ symbol*] (SAG)

OHSI .... Oral Health Status Index [*Dentistry*]

OHSIP .... Ontario Health-Services Insurances Plan [*Canada*] (AD)

OHSL .... OHSL Financial Corp. [*NASDAQ symbol*] (SAG)

OHSL Fn ...... OHSL Financial Corp. [*Associated Press*] (SAG)

OHS MSDS... Occupational Health Services Material Safety Data Sheets [*Database*]

OHSPAC ...... Occupational Health-Safety-Programs Accreditation Commission (AD)

OHSRC .... Occupational Health Safety and Rehabilitation Council [*New South Wales, Australia*]

OHSS .... Occupational Health and Safety Staff [*Environmental Protection Agency*] (GFGA)

OHSS .... Ovarian Hyperstimulation Syndrome [*Medicine*] (DMAA)

OHST .... Occupational Health and Safety Technologist

Oh St .... Ohio State Reports [*A publication*] (DLA)

OHST .... Overhead Storage Tank [*Nuclear energy*] (NRCH)

OHSU .... Oregon Health Sciences University (IID)

OHT .... Hornepayne Township Public Library, Ontario [*Library symbol National Library of Canada*] (NLC)

OHT .... Ocean Heat Transport

OHT .... Ocular Hypertensive [*Ophthalmology*]

OHT .... Office of Housing Technology [*National Bureau of Standards*]
OHT .... Ohio Historical Society, Columbus, OH [*OCLC symbol*] (OCLC)
OHT .... Ohio Tank Truck Carriers Bureau, Worthington OH [*STAC*]
OHT .... Overheating Temperature (PDAA)
oht .... Overheating Temperature (AD)
OHT .... Oxygen at High Temperature (OA)
OHTA .... Office of Health Technology Assessment [*HHS*]
OHTA .... Organ Historical Trust of Australia
OHTCS .... Outer Head Temperature Control System [*Nuclear energy*] (NRCH)
OHTE .... Ohmic Heating Toroidal Experiment [*Nuclear fusion device*]
OHTEX .... Ocean Heat Transport Experiment [*Japan*] [*Marine science*] (OSRA)
OHTR .... Theological College of the Canadian Reformed Churches, Hamilton, Ontario [*Library symbol National Library of Canada*] (NLC)
OHTS .... Oil-Hardened Tool Steel
OHu .... Hubbard Public Library, Hubbard, OH [*Library symbol Library of Congress*] (LCLS)
OHU .... Huntsville Public Library, Ontario [*Library symbol National Library of Canada*] (NLC)
ohu .... Ohio [*MARC country of publication code Library of Congress*] (LCCP)
OHU .... Overseas Homeported Units [*Navy*] (NVT)
OHUM .... Muskoka Pioneer Village, Huntsville, Ontario [*Library symbol National Library of Canada*] (BIB)
OHur .... Huron Public Library, Huron, OH [*Library symbol Library of Congress*] (LCLS)
OHV .... Off-Highway Vehicle
OHV .... Overhead Valve
ohv .... Overhead Valve (AD)
OHV .... Overhead Vent (WDAA)
OHVE .... Hanmer Branch, Valley East Public Library [*Succursale Hanmer, Bibliotheque Publique de Valley-East*], Ontario [*Library symbol National Library of Canada*] (NLC)
OHW .... Electronic Systems Library, Westinghouse Canada Ltd., Burlington, Ontario [*Library symbol National Library of Canada*] (NLC)
OHW .... Oak Harbor [*Washington*] [*Seismograph station code, US Geological Survey*] (SEIS)
OHW .... Oxyhydrogen Welding
OHWL .... Wentworth Public Library, Hamilton, Ontario [*Library symbol National Library of Canada*] (NLC)
OHWM .... Open Heart World Mission (EA)
OHWS......... Overhead Wood Screw [*Technical drawings*]
OHY .... Onur Hava Tasimacilik AWMS [*Turkey*] [*ICAO designator*] (FAAC)
OI .... Ingersoll Public Library, Ontario [*Library symbol National Library of Canada*] (NLC)
OI .... Odyssey Institute [*Later, OIC*] (EA)
OI .... Office Instruction (AFM)
OI .... Office of Information (AFM)
OI .... Office of Investigations [*Environmental Protection Agency*] (GFGA)
OI .... Ohashi Institute (EA)
OI .... Oil-Immersed
oi .... Oil-Immersed (AD)
OI .... Oil-Insulated
OI .... Old Icelandic [*Language*] (BARN)
OI .... ONE, Inc. (EA)
OI .... On Instruments [*Aviation*]
OI .... Opener Inhibitor
OI .... Opening of Intestine
OI .... Operating Income [*Accounting*]
OI .... Operating Instructions
OI .... Operational Instrumentation (NASA)
OI .... Operational Intelligence
OI .... Operational Issue [*Military*]
OI .... Operation Identity (EA)
OI .... Operations Interface (MCD)
OI .... Operator Input
OI .... Operator Interface (ACII)
OI .... Opportunistic Infection [*Medicine*]
OI .... Opsonic Index [*Laboratory science*] (DAVI)
OI .... Opsonic Index [*Medicine*]
o/i .... Opsonic Index (AD)
OI .... Optical Isolator [*Nuclear energy*] (NRCH)
OI .... Optimist International (EA)
OI .... Optimum Interpolation [*Marine science*] (OSRA)
OI .... Opto Isolator (AAEL)
OI .... Orbiter Instrumentation [*NASA*] (NASA)
OI .... Orbit [*or Orbital*] Insertion
OI .... Ordinary Interest [*Banking*]
OI .... Organizational/Intermediate (MCD)
OI .... Organization Integration [*Military*]
OI .... Orgasmic Impairment [*Medicine*]
o-i .... Orgasmic Impairment (AD)
OI .... Oriental Institute (AD)
OI .... Orientation Inventory [*Psychology*]
OI .... Orthopedically Impaired
OI .... Osteogenesis Imperfecta [*Medicine*]
OI .... Ote Iwapo [*All That Is Must Be Considered*] [*of OI Committee International, a third-world lobby opposing systematic birth control Swahili*]
OI .... Ours, Inc. (EA)
O-I .... Outer and Inner (DMAA)
OI .... Output Impedance
O/I .... Overseas Investment [*Economics*]
OI .... Owens Illinois [*NYSE symbol*] (SAG)
OI .... Owens-Illinois, Inc. [*NYSE symbol*] (SPSG)
OI .... Oxygen Income [*or Intake*] [*Medicine*]
OI .... Oxygen Index [*Medicine*] (DAVI)

OI .... Oxygen Intact [*Medicine*] (DAVI)
OIA............. Municipal Income Opportunity Trust [*Formerly, Allstate Municipal Income Opportunities Trust*] [*NYSE symbol*] (SPSG)
OIA............. Municipal Income Opp Tr [*NYSE symbol*] (TTSB)
OIA............. Ocean Industries Association (AD)
OIA............. Office of Impact Analysis [*Environmental Protection Agency*] (BARN)
OIA............. Office of Industrial Associates (AD)
OIA............. Office of Inspector and Auditor [*Nuclear Regulatory Commission*] (NRCH)
OIA............. Office of International Activities [*American Chemical Society*]
OIA............. Office of International Administration [*Department of State*]
OIA............. Office of International Affairs [*NASA, HUD*]
OIA............. Oil Import Administration [*Later, Office of Oil and Gas*] [*Department of the Interior*]
OIA............. Oil Insurance Association [*Later, Industrial Risk Insurance*] (EA)
OIA............. Oishiyama A [*Japan*] [*Seismograph station code, US Geological Survey*] (SEIS)
OIA............. Operative Ironmoulders' Association [*A union*] [*British*]
OIA............. Optical Immunoassay [*Clinical chemistry*]
OIA............. Optics Inertial Analyzer (SAA)
OIA............. Orbiter Interface Adapter [*NASA*] (NASA)
OIA............. Organizacion Internacional del Azucar [*International Sugar Organization - ISO*] (EAIO)
OIA............. Outboard Industry Association [*Later, NMMA*] (EA)
OIAA.......... Abadan/International [*Iran*] [*ICAO location identifier*] (ICLI)
OIAA.......... Office of Inter-American Affairs [*Later, BIAA*]
OIAA.......... Office of International Aviation Affairs [*FAA*]
OIA & TU .... Office of Industry Affairs and Technology Utilization [*NASA*]
OIAB.......... Boostan [*Iran*] [*ICAO location identifier*] (ICLI)
OIAB.......... Oil Import Appeals Board (AD)
OIAC.......... Organizacion Internacional de la Aviacion Civil [*International Civil AviationOrganization*] [*Spanish*] (AD)
OIAD .... Dezful [*Iran*] [*ICAO location identifier*] (ICLI)
OIAF........... Office of Information for the Armed Forces (DNAB)
OIAG .... Aghajari [*Iran*] [*ICAO location identifier*] (ICLI)
OIAH .... Gachsaran [*Iran*] [*ICAO location identifier*] (ICLI)
OIAI .... Masjed Soleiman [*Iran*] [*ICAO location identifier*] (ICLI)
OIAJ........... Office for Improvements in the Administration of Justice (AD)
OIAJ........... Omidyeh [*Iran*] [*ICAO location identifier*] (ICLI)
OIAK .... Haft-Gel [*Iran*] [*ICAO location identifier*] (ICLI)
OIAL .... Lali [*Iran*] [*ICAO location identifier*] (ICLI)
OIAM .... Bandar Mahshahr [*Iran*] [*ICAO location identifier*] (ICLI)
OIAN .... Andimeshk [*Iran*] [*ICAO location identifier*] (ICLI)
OI & C .... Office of Investigation and Compliance [*Employment and Training Administration*] [*Department of Labor*]
OI & I .... Office of Invention and Innovation [*Disbanded*] [*National Institute of Standards and Technology*]
OIAS .... Observer Impression Assessment Scale
OIAS .... Occupational Information Access System (WDAA)
OIAT........... Abadan [*Iran*] [*ICAO location identifier*] (ICLI)
OIATU .... Office of Industry Affairs and Technology Utilization [*NASA*]
OIAW .... Ahwaz [*Iran*] [*ICAO location identifier*] (ICLI)
OIB............. Briggs-Lawrence County Public Library, Ironton, OH [*Library symbol Library of Congress*] (LCLS)
OIB............. Iron Bridge Public Library, Ontario [*Library symbol National Library of Canada*] (NLC)
OIB............. Municipal Income Opportunity Trust [*Formerly, Allstate Municipal Income Opportunities Trust*] [*NYSE symbol*] (SPSG)
OIB............. Municipal Income Op Tr II [*NYSE symbol*] (TTSB)
OIB............. Oceanic Island Basalt [*Geology*]
OIB............. Official Information Base
OIB............. Ohio Inspection Bureau (AD)
OIB............. Oishiyama B [*Japan*] [*Seismograph station code, US Geological Survey*] (SEIS)
OIB............. Oklahoma Inspection Bureau (AD)
OIB............. Oligoclonal Immunoglobulin Bands [*Clinical chemistry*]
OIB............. Olympic Installations Board
OIB............. Operating Impedance Bridge (IAA)
OIB............. Operation Instruction Block (NITA)
OIB............. Operations Integration Branch [*NASA*] (KSC)
OIB............. Orbiter Interface Box [*NASA*] (NASA)
OIB............. Ortho-Iodobenzoic (Acid) [*Biochemistry*]
OIBA.......... Abumusa Island [*Iran*] [*ICAO location identifier*] (ICLI)
OIBA.......... Office of Industrial Base Assessment (DOMA)
OIBB.......... Bushehr/Bushehr [*Iran*] [*ICAO location identifier*] (ICLI)
OIBD.......... Bandar Deylam [*Iran*] [*ICAO location identifier*] (ICLI)
OIBF........... Forouz Island [*Iran*] [*ICAO location identifier*] (ICLI)
OIBG.......... Ganaveh [*Iran*] [*ICAO location identifier*] (ICLI)
OIBH.......... Bastak [*Iran*] [*ICAO location identifier*] (ICLI)
OIBI .... Golbandi [*Iran*] [*ICAO location identifier*] (ICLI)
OIBK .... Kish Island [*Iran*] [*ICAO location identifier*] (ICLI)
OIBL .... Bandar Lengeh [*Iran*] [*ICAO location identifier*] (ICLI)
OIBN .... Borazjan [*Iran*] [*ICAO location identifier*] (ICLI)
OIBQ .... Khark Island [*Iran*] [*ICAO location identifier*] (ICLI)
OIBS .... Siri Island [*Iran*] [*ICAO location identifier*] (ICLI)
OIBT........... Bushehr [*Iran*] [*ICAO location identifier*] (ICLI)
OIBV .... Lavan Island [*Iran*] [*ICAO location identifier*] (ICLI)
OIBX .... Tonb Island [*Iran*] [*ICAO location identifier*] (ICLI)
OIC............. Municipal Income Opportunity Trust [*Formerly, Allstate Municipal Income Opportunities Trust*] [*NYSE symbol*] (SPSG)
OIC............. Municipal Income Opp Tr III [*NYSE symbol*] (TTSB)
OIC............. Norwich, NY [*Location identifier FAA*] (FAAL)
OIC............. Objective Individual Combat Weapon
OIC............. Oceanographic Instrumentation Center [*Navy*]
OIC............. Oceans Institute of Canada (IRC)

OIC Octyl Isocyanate [*Organic chemistry*]
OIC Odyssey Institute Corp. (EA)
OIC Offer in Compromise [*IRS*]
OIC Office of Independent Counsel [*U.S. Department of Justice*] (BARN)
OIC Office of Industrial Cooperation [*AEC*]
OIC Office of International Conferences [*Department of State*]
OIC Office of International Cooperation [*in CAA*]
OIC Office of the Insurance Commissioner (AD)
OIC Officer-in-Charge
Oic Officer-in-Charge (WDAA)
OIC Ohio Improved Chesters [*Initialism itself now used as name of breed of swine*]
OIC Oh, I See [*Online dialogue*] (IGQR)
OIC Oil Industry Commission (AD)
OIC Oishiyama C [*Japan*] [*Seismograph station code, US Geological Survey*] (SEIS)
OIC Okinawa Interboard Committee [*Absorbed by Interboard Committee for Christian Work in Japan*] (EA)
OIC Oklahoma Intercollegiate Conference (PSS)
OIC Online Instrument and Control Program [*Computer science*] (NRCH)
OIC Operational Intelligence Centre [*British military*] (DMA)
OIC Operations Instrumentation Coordinator [*NASA*] (KSC)
OIC Operator's Instruction Chart
OIC Opportunities Industrialization Center (OICC)
OIC Optical Integrated Circuit (IEEE)
OIC Optimized Image Compression (PCM)
OIC Orbiter Integrated Checkout [*NASA*] (NASA)
oic Orbiter Integrated Checkout [*NASA*] (NAKS)
O-I-C Order-in-Council [*Canada*]
OIC Order of the Imitation of Christ (TOCD)
oic Order of the Imitation of Christ (TOCD)
O-I-C Organisation Interafricaine du Cafe [*Inter-African Coffee Organization*] [*French*] (AD)
OIC Organisation Internationale Catholique
OIC Organisation Internationale du Commerce [*International Organization for Commerce*] [*France*]
OIC Organization for International Cooperation (EA)
OIC Organization of Islamic Countries
OIC Organization of Islamic Countries [*Intergovernmental group*]
OIC Organization of the Islamic Conference [*See also OCI*] [*Jeddah, Saudi Arabia*] (EAIO)
OIC Overseas Investment Commission (AD)
OICA Azna [*Iran*] [*ICAO location identifier*] (ICLI)
OICA Ontario Institute of Chartered Accountants [*Canada*] (DD)
OIC/A Opportunities Industrialization Centers of America (EA)
OICA Organisation Internationale des Constructeurs d'Automobiles (EAIO)
OICB Baneh [*Iran*] [*ICAO location identifier*] (ICLI)
OICC Bakhtaran [*Iran*] [*ICAO location identifier*] (ICLI)
OICC Officer-in-Charge of Construction [*Navy*]
OICC Operational Intelligence Coordination Center (COE)
OICC Operational Intelligence Crisis Center [*Defense Intelligence Adgency*] (DOMA)
OICC Operations Interface Control Chart (KSC)
OICC Organization of Islamic Capitals and Cities (EA)
OICCFE Officer-in-Charge of Construction, Far East [*Navy*]
OICCSOWESPAC Officer-in-Charge of Construction, South Western Pacific (DNAB)
OICD Abdanan [*Iran*] [*ICAO location identifier*] (ICLI)
OICD Office of International Cooperation and Development [*Department of Agriculture*]
OICD On-Board Information Compression Device [*Aerospace*]
OICE Bijar [*Iran*] [*ICAO location identifier*] (ICLI)
O ICE Old Icelandic [*Language, etc.*] (ROG)
OIcel Old Icelandic [*Language*] (BARN)
OICF Naft-E-Shah [*Iran*] [*ICAO location identifier*] (ICLI)
OICF Oklahoma Independent College Foundation (AD)
OICF Oregon Independent College Foundation (AD)
OICG Ghasre-Shirin [*Iran*] [*ICAO location identifier*] (ICLI)
OICH Islam Abad [*Iran*] [*ICAO location identifier*] (ICLI)
OICI Ilam [*Iran*] [*ICAO location identifier*] (ICLI)
OICI Oficina Internacional Catolica de la Infancia [*International Catholic Child Bureau*]
OICI Organizacion Ibero-Americana de Cooperacion Intermunicipal [*Ibero-American Municipal Organization*] (EAIO)
OICI Organizacion Interamericana de Cooperacion [*Inter-American Cooperation Organ ization*] [*Spanish*] (AD)
OICI Organizacion Interamericana de Cooperacion Intermunicipal [*Interamerican Municipal Organization*]
OICJ Boroujerd [*Iran*] [*ICAO location identifier*] (ICLI)
OICJ Office of International Criminal Justice (AD)
OICK Khorram Abad [*Iran*] [*ICAO location identifier*] (ICLI)
OICL Sare Pole Zahab [*Iran*] [*ICAO location identifier*] (ICLI)
OICM Mehran [*Iran*] [*ICAO location identifier*] (ICLI)
OICM Organisation Internationale pour la Cooperation Medicale [*International Organization for Medical Cooperation*]
OICMA Organisation Internationale Contre le Criquet Migrateur Africain [*International African Migratory Locust Organization*] (EAIO)
OICMATU Officer-in-Charge, Marine Air Traffic Control Unit (DNAB)
OICMILDEPT Officer-in-Charge, Military Department (DNAB)
OICNA Overseas Indian Congress of North America [*Defunct*] (EA)
OICO Office of Integration and Checkout
OICO OI Corp. [*NASDAQ symbol*] (NQ)
OICO Songhor [*Iran*] [*ICAO location identifier*] (ICLI)
OI Corp OI Corp. [*Associated Press*] (SAG)
OICP Office of International Communications Policy (NITA)
OICP Paveh [*Iran*] [*ICAO location identifier*] (ICLI)
OICQ Takab [*Iran*] [*ICAO location identifier*] (ICLI)
OICR Dehloran [*Iran*] [*ICAO location identifier*] (ICLI)
OICR Office of International Commercial Relations [*Department of State*]
OICS Office of Interoceanic Canal Studies [*National Oceanic and Atmospheric Administration*] (NOAA)
OICS Operational Intelligence Collection System
OICS Organe International de Controle des Stupefiants [*International Narcotics Control Board*] (EAIO)
OICS Sanandaj [*Iran*] [*ICAO location identifier*] (ICLI)
OICT Bakhtaran [*Iran*] [*ICAO location identifier*] (ICLI)
OICTP Outline Individual and Collective Training Plan [*Army*]
OICW Objective Individual Combat Weapon [*Army*] (INF)
OICY Malavi [*Iran*] [*ICAO location identifier*] (ICLI)
OICZ Aligoodarz [*Iran*] [*ICAO location identifier*] (ICLI)
OID Object Identification (AAEL)
OID Object Identifier [*Computer science*]
OID Object Interaction Diagram (AAEL)
OID Octal Identifier [*Computer science*] (KSC)
OID Ofensiva de Izquierda Democratica [*Offensive of the Democratic Left*] [*Bolivia*] (PPW)
OID Optoelectronic Imaging Device
OID Order Initiated Distribution
OID Organism Identification Number [*Microbiology*] (DAVI)
OID Original Issue Discount [*Business term*]
oid Original Issue Discount (AD)
OID Original Issue Discount Obligations (TDOB)
OID Outline and Installation Drawing
OIDA Ordnance Industrial Data Agency
OIDC Oil Importing and Developing Country
OIDI Optically Isolated Digital Input
OI DIV Operations/Combat Information Center Division (DNAB)
OIDL Object Interface Definition Language [*Computer science*]
OIDMM Office Internationale de Documentation de Medecine Militaire [*International Office of Documentation on Military Medicine - IODMM*] (EAIO)
OIDO Original Issue Discount Obligations (EBF)
OIDP Oversea Internal Defense Policy [*Army*] (AABC)
OIDPS Oversea Intelligence Data Processing System
OIE Central Library, Albright & Wilson Americas, Islington, Ontario [*Library symbol National Library of Canada*] (NLC)
OIE Office International des Epizooties [*International Office of Epizootics*] [*Research center France*] (IRC)
OIE Office of Indian Education [*Department of Education*] (GFGA)
OIE Office of Inspection and Enforcement [*Nuclear Regulatory Commission*]
OIE Office of International Epizootics (AD)
O/I/E Offsites/Infrastructure/Establishment [*Engineering*]
OIE Operational Independent Evaluator
OIE Optical Incremental Encoder
OIE Optical Infrared Equipment
OIE Organisation Internationale des Employeurs [*International Organization of Employers*]
OIE Overseas Investment Exchange (NUMA)
OIEA Organismo Internacional de Energia Atomica [*International Atomic Energy Agency*] [*Spanish United Nations*] (DUND)
OIEC Office International de l'Enseignement Catholique [*Catholic International Education Office - CIEO*] (EAIO)
OIEO Ocean Instrumentation Engineering Office [*National Oceanic and Atmospheric Administration*] (MSC)
OIER Office of International Economic Research (AD)
OIER Official Intermodal Equipment Register [*Intermodal Publishing Co.*] [*Information service or system*] (IID)
OIES Oxford Institute for Energy Studies [*British*]
OIESA Office of International Economic and Social Affairs [*Department of State*]
OIF American Opportunity Income [*NYSE symbol*] (SPSG)
OIF Amer Opportunity Income [*NYSE symbol*] (TTSB)
OIF Iroquois Falls Public Library, Ontario [*Library symbol National Library of Canada*] (NLC)
OIF Observed Intrinsic Frequency [*Medicine*] (DMAA)
OIF Office for Intellectual Freedom [*American Library Association*]
OIF Office Interconnect Facility [*Computer science*] (BTTJ)
OIF Office of International Finance [*Department of the Treasury*]
OIF Oil Immersion Field (MAE)
OIF Option Institute and Fellowship (EA)
OIF Osteogenesis Imperfecta Foundation (EA)
OIF Osteoinductive Factor [*Biochemistry*]
OIF Other Intelligence File (MCD)
OIFB Boroujen [*Iran*] [*ICAO location identifier*] (ICLI)
OIFC Ghamsar [*Iran*] [*ICAO location identifier*] (ICLI)
OIFC Oil-Insulated, Fan-Cooled
OIFD Ardestan [*Iran*] [*ICAO location identifier*] (ICLI)
OIFF Soffeh [*Iran*] [*ICAO location identifier*] (ICLI)
OIFG Golpaygan [*Iran*] [*ICAO location identifier*] (ICLI)
OIFH Esfahan [*Iran*] [*ICAO location identifier*] (ICLI)
OIFI Semirom [*Iran*] [*ICAO location identifier*] (ICLI)
OIFIG Official Irish FORTH [*Programming language*] Interest Group (EAIO)
OIFJ Najaf Abad [*Iran*] [*ICAO location identifier*] (ICLI)
OIFK Kashan [*Iran*] [*ICAO location identifier*] (ICLI)
OIFL Felavarjan [*Iran*] [*ICAO location identifier*] (ICLI)
OIFM Esfahan [*Iran*] [*ICAO location identifier*] (ICLI)
OIFN Naein [*Iran*] [*ICAO location identifier*] (ICLI)
OIFO Khomeini Shahr [*Iran*] [*ICAO location identifier*] (ICLI)
OIFR Ghomsheh [*Iran*] [*ICAO location identifier*] (ICLI)

OIFS........... Shahrekord [*Iran*] [*ICAO location identifier*] (ICLI)
OIFT........... Esfahan [*Iran*] [*ICAO location identifier*] (ICLI)
OIFU .... Fereidan [*Iran*] [*ICAO location identifier*] (ICLI)
OIFW........... Khomein [*Iran*] [*ICAO location identifier*] (ICLI)
OIFY........... Meymeh [*Iran*] [*ICAO location identifier*] (ICLI)
OIFZ........... Natanz [*Iran*] [*ICAO location identifier*] (ICLI)
OIG .... Ignace Public Library, Ontario [*Library symbol National Library of Canada*] (NLC)
OIG .... Office of the Inspector General [*Army*]
OIG .... Optically Isolated Gate (IEEE)
OIG .... Organisation Intergouvernementale [*Inter-Governmental Organization*] [*French*] (AD)
OIGA........... Astara [*Iran*] [*ICAO location identifier*] (ICLI)
OIGF........... Fouman [*Iran*] [*ICAO location identifier*] (ICLI)
OIGG........... Rasht [*Iran*] [*ICAO location identifier*] (ICLI)
OIGH........... Hashtpar [*Iran*] [*ICAO location identifier*] (ICLI)
OIGIS......... Office of the Inspector-General of Intelligence and Security [*Australia*]
OIGK........... Khailkhal [*Iran*] [*ICAO location identifier*] (ICLI)
OIGL........... Langerood [*Iran*] [*ICAO location identifier*] (ICLI)
OIGM........... Manjil [*Iran*] [*ICAO location identifier*] (ICLI)
OIGN........... Lahijan [*Iran*] [*ICAO location identifier*] (ICLI)
OIGP........... Bandar Anzali [*Iran*] [*ICAO location identifier*] (ICLI)
OIGR........... Office of Industrial Growth and Research [*of BDSA*]
OIGR........... Office of Intergovernmental Relations [*US Congress*] [*Washington, DC*] (GRD)
OIGR........... Roodsar [*Iran*] [*ICAO location identifier*] (ICLI)
OIGT........... Rasht [*Iran*] [*ICAO location identifier*] (ICLI)
OIGU........... Roodbar [*Iran*] [*ICAO location identifier*] (ICLI)
OIH .... Oceanic Institute of Hawaii
OIH .... Office of International Health [*Department of Health and Human Services*]
OIH .... Ortho-Iodohippurate [*Clinical chemistry*] (AAMN)
OIH .... Ovulation-Inducing Hormone [*Endocrinology*]
OIH .... Ovulation-Producing Hormone [*Medicine*] (AD)
OIHA........... Orthoiodohippuric Acid [*Clinical chemistry*] (DAVI)
OIHA........... Takestan [*Iran*] [*ICAO location identifier*] (ICLI)
OIHB........... Asad Abad [*Iran*] [*ICAO location identifier*] (ICLI)
OIHD........... Shahzand [*Iran*] [*ICAO location identifier*] (ICLI)
OIHF........... Tafresh [*Iran*] [*ICAO location identifier*] (ICLI)
OIHG........... Kharaghan [*Iran*] [*ICAO location identifier*] (ICLI)
OIHH........... Hamadan [*Iran*] [*ICAO location identifier*] (ICLI)
OIHJ........... Avaj [*Iran*] [*ICAO location identifier*] (ICLI)
OIHM........... Malayer [*Iran*] [*ICAO location identifier*] (ICLI)
OIHN........... Nahavand [*Iran*] [*ICAO location identifier*] (ICLI)
OIHP........... Office International d'Hygiene Publique [*United Nations*]
OIHQ........... Kangavar [*Iran*] [*ICAO location identifier*] (ICLI)
OIHR........... Arak [*Iran*] [*ICAO location identifier*] (ICLI)
OIHS........... Hamadan [*Iran*] [*ICAO location identifier*] (ICLI)
OIHT........... Hamadan [*Iran*] [*ICAO location identifier*] (ICLI)
OIHU........... Tooyserkan [*Iran*] [*ICAO location identifier*] (ICLI)
OII .... Oceaneering International, Inc. [*NYSE symbol*] (SPSG)
OII .... Oceaneering Intl. [*NYSE symbol*] (TTSB)
OII .... Office of International Investment [*Department of Commerce*]
OII .... Office of Invention and Innovation (AD)
OII .... Oil Investment Institute [*Washington, DC*] (EA)
OII .... Operations Integration Instruction [*NASA*] (NASA)
OII .... Ourobourus Institute (EA)
OIIA........... Abe-Ali [*Iran*] [*ICAO location identifier*] (ICLI)
OIIC........... Kushke Nosrat [*Iran*] [*ICAO location identifier*] (ICLI)
OIIC........... Oil Industry Industrial Committee [*Australia*]
OIID........... Tehran/Doshan Tappeh [*Iran*] [*ICAO location identifier*] (ICLI)
OIIE........... Abyek [*Iran*] [*ICAO location identifier*] (ICLI)
OIIF........... Firouzkouh [*Iran*] [*ICAO location identifier*] (ICLI)
OIIFDRES..... Oficina Internacional de Informacion del Frente Democratico Revolucionario de ElSalvador [*International Information Office of the Democratic Revolutionary Front of El Salvador - IIODRFES*] [*San Jose, Costa Rica*] (EAIO)
OIIG........... Tehran/Ghaleh Morghi [*Iran*] [*ICAO location identifier*] (ICLI)
OIIH........... Mahallat [*Iran*] [*ICAO location identifier*] (ICLI)
OIII........... Tehran/Mehrabad International [*Iran*] [*ICAO location identifier*] (ICLI)
OIIJ........... Karaj [*Iran*] [*ICAO location identifier*] (ICLI)
OIIK........... Ghazvin [*Iran*] [*ICAO location identifier*] (ICLI)
OIIM........... Khoram Dareh [*Iran*] [*ICAO location identifier*] (ICLI)
OIIM........... Overseas Issues Identification Meeting (DNAB)
OIIN........... Delijan [*Iran*] [*ICAO location identifier*] (ICLI)
OIIQ........... Ghom [*Iran*] [*ICAO location identifier*] (ICLI)
OIIR........... Garmsar [*Iran*] [*ICAO location identifier*] (ICLI)
OIIS........... Semnan [*Iran*] [*ICAO location identifier*] (ICLI)
OIIT........... Tehran [*Iran*] [*ICAO location identifier*] (ICLI)
OIIU........... Damghan [*Iran*] [*ICAO location identifier*] (ICLI)
OIIV........... Seveh [*Iran*] [*ICAO location identifier*] (ICLI)
OIIW........... Varamin [*Iran*] [*ICAO location identifier*] (ICLI)
OIIX........... Tehran [*Iran*] [*ICAO location identifier*] (ICLI)
OIJ .... Octarius Duos [*Two Pints*] [*Pharmacy*] (ROG)
OIJ .... Organisation Internationale des Journalistes [*International Organization of Journalists - IOJ*] (EAIO)
OIJSS........... Octarios Duobus cum Semisse [*Two and a Half Pints*] [*Pharmacy*] (ROG)
OIK........... Ocean City, MD [*Location identifier FAA*] (FAAL)
OIKA........... Shahre Babak [*Iran*] [*ICAO location identifier*] (ICLI)
OIKB........... Bandar Abbas [*Iran*] [*ICAO location identifier*] (ICLI)
OIKD........... Darband/Ravar [*Iran*] [*ICAO location identifier*] (ICLI)
OIKE........... Anar [*Iran*] [*ICAO location identifier*] (ICLI)
OIKF........... Baft [*Iran*] [*ICAO location identifier*] (ICLI)
OIKI .... Bandar Khamir [*Iran*] [*ICAO location identifier*] (ICLI)

OIKJ........... Jiroft [*Iran*] [*ICAO location identifier*] (ICLI)
OIKK .... Kerman [*Iran*] [*ICAO location identifier*] (ICLI)
OIKM .... Bam [*Iran*] [*ICAO location identifier*] (ICLI)
OIKN .... Narmashir [*Iran*] [*ICAO location identifier*] (ICLI)
OIKO .... Minab [*Iran*] [*ICAO location identifier*] (ICLI)
OIKQ .... Gheshm Island [*Iran*] [*ICAO location identifier*] (ICLI)
OIKR .... Rafsanjan [*Iran*] [*ICAO location identifier*] (ICLI)
OIKS .... Shahdad [*Iran*] [*ICAO location identifier*] (ICLI)
OIKT .... Kerman [*Iran*] [*ICAO location identifier*] (ICLI)
OIKU .... Hengam Island [*Iran*] [*ICAO location identifier*] (ICLI)
OIKW .... Kahnooj [*Iran*] [*ICAO location identifier*] (ICLI)
OIKX .... Hormoz Island [*Iran*] [*ICAO location identifier*] (ICLI)
OIKY .... Sirjan [*Iran*] [*ICAO location identifier*] (ICLI)
OIKZ .... Zarand [*Iran*] [*ICAO location identifier*] (ICLI)
OIL........... Ocelot Industries Ltd. [*Toronto Stock Exchange symbol*]
OIL........... Office of Intergovernmental Liaison [*Environmental Protection Agency*] (GFGA)
OIL........... Oil City, PA [*Location identifier FAA*] (FAAL)
OIL........... Oklahoma Information Lines [*Oklahoma State Department of Libraries*] [*Oklahoma City*] [*Information service or system*] (IID)
OIL........... Only Input Line (MHDI)
OIL........... Operation Inspection Log (AAG)
OIL........... Orange Indicating Light (MSA)
OIL........... Orbital International Laboratory
OIL........... Ordnance Investigation Laboratory
OIL........... Triton Energy [*NYSE symbol*] (TTSB)
OIL........... Triton Energy Corp. [*NYSE symbol*] (SPSG)
OILA........... Office of International Labor Affairs [*Department of Labor*]
Oil & Gas .... Oil and Gas Reporter [*A publication*] (DLA)
Oil & Gas LR... Oil and Gas Law Review [*A publication*] (DLA)
Oil & Gas Reptr... Oil and Gas Reporter [*A publication*] (DLA)
Oil & Gas Rptr... Oil and Gas Reporter [*A publication*] (DLA)
OILB........... Organisation Internationale de Lutte Biologique Contre les Animaux et les Plantes Nuisibles [*International Organization for Biological Control of Noxious Animals and Plants - IOBC*] (EAIO)
OILD .... Occupationally Induced Lung Disease
OilDri........... Oil-Dri Corp. of America [*Associated Press*] (SAG)
Oilgear .... [*The*] Oilgear Co. [*Associated Press*] (SAG)
oiloff........... Oil Ripoff (AD)
OILSR........... Office of Interstate Land Sales Registration (AD)
OIM........... Office of Industrial Managers [*Navy*]
OIM........... Office of Industrial Mobilization [*of BDSA*]
OIM........... Office of Intergovernmental Management (OICC)
OIM........... Offshore-Installation Manager [*Oil well drilling*]
OIM........... On Its Merits [*British*] (ROG)
OIM........... Orbit Insertion Maneuver
OIM........... Organic Insulating Material
OIM........... Organizational Intermediate Maintenance [*Military*] (AFIT)
OIM........... Oriental Institute Museum [*University of Chicago*] (AD)
OIM........... Orientational Imaging Microscopy (AAEL)
OIM........... Oshima Island [*Japan*] [*Airport symbol*] (OAG)
OIMA........... Torbat-E-Jam [*Iran*] [*ICAO location identifier*] (ICLI)
OIMB........... Birjand [*Iran*] [*ICAO location identifier*] (ICLI)
OIMC........... Office of Information Services (AAGC)
OIMC........... Sarakhs [*Iran*] [*ICAO location identifier*] (ICLI)
OIMD........... Goonabad [*Iran*] [*ICAO location identifier*] (ICLI)
OIME........... Esfarayen [*Iran*] [*ICAO location identifier*] (ICLI)
OIMF........... Ferdous [*Iran*] [*ICAO location identifier*] (ICLI)
OIMG........... Ghaen [*Iran*] [*ICAO location identifier*] (ICLI)
OIMH........... Torbat-E-Heidarieh [*Iran*] [*ICAO location identifier*] (ICLI)
OIMJ........... Emam Shahr [*Iran*] [*ICAO location identifier*] (ICLI)
OIMK........... Nehbandan [*Iran*] [*ICAO location identifier*] (ICLI)
OIML........... Janat Abad [*Iran*] [*ICAO location identifier*] (ICLI)
OIML........... Organisation Internationale de Metrologie Legale [*International Organization of Legal Metrology*] (EAIO)
OIMM........... Mashhad [*Iran*] [*ICAO location identifier*] (ICLI)
OIMN........... Bojnord [*Iran*] [*ICAO location identifier*] (ICLI)
OIMO........... Ghoochan [*Iran*] [*ICAO location identifier*] (ICLI)
OIMP........... Taybad [*Iran*] [*ICAO location identifier*] (ICLI)
OIMQ........... Kashmar [*Iran*] [*ICAO location identifier*] (ICLI)
OIMR........... Fariman [*Iran*] [*ICAO location identifier*] (ICLI)
OIMS........... Orbiter Ion Mass Spectrometer [*NASA*]
OIMS........... Oscillator Instability Measurement System
OIMS........... Sabzevar [*Iran*] [*ICAO location identifier*] (ICLI)
OIMSJ........... Micropower/St. Joseph's High School, Islington, Ontario [*Library symbol National Library of Canada*] (NLC)
OIMT........... Tabas [*Iran*] [*ICAO location identifier*] (ICLI)
OIMV........... Mashhad [*Iran*] [*ICAO location identifier*] (ICLI)
OIMW........... Shirvan [*Iran*] [*ICAO location identifier*] (ICLI)
OIMX........... Shahr Abad [*Iran*] [*ICAO location identifier*] (ICLI)
OIMY........... Neishaboor [*Iran*] [*ICAO location identifier*] (ICLI)
OIMYFC ...... Official International Michael York Fan Club (EA)
OIN........... Oberlin, KS [*Location identifier FAA*] (FAAL)
OI-N .... Office of Information, Navy
OIN........... Organisation Internationale de Normalisation [*International Organization for Standardization*]
OIN........... Organization of International Numismatists
OIN........... Osrodek Informacji Naukowej [*Scientific Information Center*] [*Polish Academy of Sciences Warsaw*] [*Information service or system*] (IID)
OINA........... Amol [*Iran*] [*ICAO location identifier*] (ICLI)
OINA........... Oyster Institute of North America [*Later, SINA*] (EA)
OINB........... Babolsar [*Iran*] [*ICAO location identifier*] (ICLI)
OINC........... Chalous [*Iran*] [*ICAO location identifier*] (ICLI)
OINC........... Officer-in-Charge [*Navy*]

O in C.......... Officer-in-Charge
OINCABCCTC... Officer-in-Charge, Advanced Base Combat Communication Training Center [*Pearl Harbor*] [*Navy*]
OIND.......... Minoo Dasht [*Iran*] [*ICAO location identifier*] (ICLI)
OINE.......... Kalaleh [*Iran*] [*ICAO location identifier*] (ICLI)
OInF.......... Ferro Corp., Independence, OH [*Library symbol Library of Congress*] (LCLS)
OING.......... Gorgan [*Iran*] [*ICAO location identifier*] (ICLI)
OING.......... Organisation Internationale Non-Gouvernementale [*Non-Governmental International Organization*] [*French*] (AD)
OINH.......... Behshahr [*Iran*] [*ICAO location identifier*] (ICLI)
OINI.......... Ghaem Shahr [*Iran*] [*ICAO location identifier*] (ICLI)
OINK.......... Gonbad Ghabous [*Iran*] [*ICAO location identifier*] (ICLI)
Oink.......... One Income, No Kids [*Lifestyle classification*]
OINL.......... Alamdeh [*Iran*] [*ICAO location identifier*] (ICLI)
OINM.......... Mahmood Abad [*Iran*] [*ICAO location identifier*] (ICLI)
OINN.......... Noshahr [*Iran*] [*ICAO location identifier*] (ICLI)
OINO.......... Noor [*Iran*] [*ICAO location identifier*] (ICLI)
OINP.......... Azad Shahr [*Iran*] [*ICAO location identifier*] (ICLI)
OINQ.......... Kelardasht [*Iran*] [*ICAO location identifier*] (ICLI)
OINR.......... Ramsar [*Iran*] [*ICAO location identifier*] (ICLI)
OINS.......... Sari [*Iran*] [*ICAO location identifier*] (ICLI)
OINT.......... Ointment
oint.......... Ointment (AD)
OINV.......... Tonkabon [*Iran*] [*ICAO location identifier*] (ICLI)
OINY.......... Bandar Torkaman [*Iran*] [*ICAO location identifier*] (ICLI)
OINZ.......... Dasht-E-Naz [*Iran*] [*ICAO location identifier*] (ICLI)
OIO.......... Obligated Involuntary Officers [*Used in movie "Spies Like Us"*]
OIO.......... Office of International Operations [*of IRS*]
OIO.......... Oklahomans for Indian Opportunity (AD)
OIO.......... Operations Integration Officer [*NASA*] (MCD)
OIOPSWL.... Old Input/Output Program Status Word Location [*Computer science*] (MHDB)
OIP.......... Eastland, TX [*Location identifier FAA*] (FAAL)
OIP.......... Office of Import Programs [*Functions transferred to Domestic and International Business Administration*] [*Department of Commerce*]
OIP.......... Office of Industrial Programs [*Department of Energy*]
OIP.......... Office of International Programs [*National Science Foundation*]
OIP.......... Oil-in-Place
oip.......... Oil in Place (AD)
OIP.......... Ontario Institute of Painters, Toronto [*1958*] [*Canada*] (NGC)
OIP.......... Operating Internal Pressure [*Nuclear energy*] (NRCH)
OIP.......... Operational Improvement Plan [*or Program*] [*Navy*]
OIP.......... Operational Instruction Pamphlet
OIP.......... Optical Image Processor
OIP.......... Optical Improvement Program [*Army*]
OIP.......... Orbital Improvement Program
OIP.......... Ordnance Installation Plan (MCD)
OIP.......... Organic Insulative Plastic
OIP.......... Organisation Internationale de la Paleobotanique [*International Organization of Paleobotany*]
OIP.......... Organisation Internationale de Psychophysiologie [*International Organization of Psychophysiology - IOP*] (EAIO)
OIP.......... Organisation Internationale pour le Progres [*Austria*] (EAIO)
OIP.......... Organizacion Iberoamericana de Pilotos [*Ibero-American Organization of Pilots - IOP*] [*Mexico City, Mexico*] (EAIO)
OIP.......... Organizing Interstitial Pneumonia [*Medicine*]
oip.......... Oxford India Paper (AD)
OIPA.......... Ortho-Isopropylaniline [*Organic chemistry*]
OIPAAR........ Office of Industrial Personnel Access Authorization Review [*Army*] (AABC)
OIPC.......... Organisation Internationale de Police Criminelle [*International Criminal Police Organization*] [*French*] (AD)
OIPC.......... Organisation Internationale de Protection Civile [*International Civil Defense Organization - ICDO*] (EAIO)
OIPCFC........ Official International Peter Coyote Fan Club (EA)
OIPEEC........ Organisation Internationale pour l'Etude de l'Endurance des Cables [*International Organization for the Study of the Endurance of Wire Ropes - IOSEWR*] (EAIO)
OIPH.......... Office of International Public Health (AD)
Oipi.......... One Income plus Inheritance [*Lifestyle classification*]
OIPMT.......... Optimum Insect Pest Management Trial [*Department of Agriculture*]
OIPO.......... Optimum Installation Position Only (MCD)
OIPR.......... Office of Information, Publications, and Reports [*Department of Labor*]
OIPR.......... Office of Intelligence Policy and Review [*U.S. Department of Justice*] (BARN)
OIPS.......... Optical Image Processing System
OIPT.......... Overarching Integrated Product Team [*Army*]
OIQ.......... Ordre des Ingenieurs du Quebec [*Canada*] (DD)
OIQ.......... Sioux City, IA [*Location identifier FAA*] (FAAL)
OIR.......... Iroquois Public Library, Ontario [*Library symbol National Library of Canada*] (BIB)
OIR.......... Office of Indian Rights [*Department of Justice*]
OIR.......... Office of Industrial Relations [*Superseded, 1966, by Office of Civilian Manpower*] [*Navy*]
OIR.......... Office of Industrial Research [*University of Manitoba*] [*Canada Research center*] (RCD)
OIR.......... Office of Institutional Relations [*Energy Research and Development Administration*]
OIR.......... Office of Inter-American Radio (AD)
OIR.......... Office of International Research [*National Institutes of Health*]
OIR.......... Office of International Resources [*Department of State*]
OIR.......... Okushiri [*Japan*] [*Airport symbol*] (OAG)
OIR.......... Old Irish [*Language, etc.*]
OIr.......... Old Irish (AD)
OIR.......... Online Information Retrieval Ltd. [*Information service or system Defunct*] (IID)
OIR.......... Open Item Review (KSC)
OIR.......... Operations Integration Review (NASA)
OIR.......... Orbiter Infrared Radiometer [*NASA*]
OIR.......... Organisation Internationale de Radiodiffusion [*International Radio Organization*] [*Later, OIRT*]
OIR.......... Other Intelligence Requirements [*Army*] (MCD)
OIR.......... Slov-Air [*Slovakia*] [*ICAO designator*] (FAAC)
OIRA.......... Office of Industrial Resource Administration (AAGC)
OIRA.......... Office of Information and Regulatory Affairs [*Office of Management and Budget*]
OIRA.......... Officials of the Irish Republican Army [*Northern Ireland*]
OIRB.......... Oregon Insurance Rating Bureau (AD)
OIRD.......... Object-to-Image Receptor Distance [*Radiology*] (DAVI)
OIRE.......... Optical Infrared Equipment
OIRM.......... Office and Industrial Records Management (AD)
OIRM.......... Office of Information Resources Management [*General Services Administration*]
OIR-N.......... Office of Industrial Relations, Navy [*Superseded, 1966, by Office of Civilian Manpower*]
OIRS.......... Occupational Interest Rating Scale [*Vocational guidance test*]
OIRS.......... Operation and Inspection Route Sheet (DNAB)
OIRSA.......... Organismo Internacional Regional de Sanidad Agropecuaria [*Regional International Organization of Plant Protection and Animal Health*] [*El Salvador*]
OIRT.......... Organisation Internationale de Radiodiffusion et Television [*International Radio and Television Organization*] [*Formerly, OIR*] (EAIO)
OIS.......... Obstacle Identification Surface [*Aviation*] (DA)
OIS.......... Occupational Information System [*Department of Labor*]
OIS.......... Occupational Interest Survey [*Aptitude test*]
OIS.......... Office of Industrial Security [*DoD*]
OIS.......... Office of Information Services [*Council of State Governments*] [*Lexington, KY*]
OIS.......... Office of Information Systems [*Social and Rehabilitation Service, HEW*]
OIS.......... Office of International Services [*Red Cross*]
OIS.......... Oishiyama [*Japan*] [*Seismograph station code, US Geological Survey*] (SEIS)
OIS.......... OIS Optical Imaging Systems, Inc. [*Associated Press*] (SAG)
OIS.......... Oncology Information Service [*University of Leeds*] [*England*] [*Information service or system*] (IID)
OIS.......... Operating Information System [*Army*]
OIS.......... Operational Insertion System
OIS.......... Operational Instrumentation System
OIS.......... Operational Intercommunication System [*NASA*] (KSC)
ois.......... Operational Intercommunication System (NAKS)
OIS.......... Optical Image Sensor
OIS.......... Optical Imaging Systems (RDA)
OIS.......... Optical Information System [*Computer science*]
ois.......... Orbiter Instrumentation System [*NASA*] (NAKS)
OIS.......... Orbiter Instrumentation Systems [*NASA*] (MCD)
OIS.......... Ounce-Inches per Second (IAA)
OIS.......... Overseas Investors Services (AD)
OISA.......... Abadeh [*Iran*] [*ICAO location identifier*] (ICLI)
OISA.......... Office of International Science Activities [*National Science Foundation*]
OISA.......... Office of International Scientific Affairs (AD)
OIS & T........ Office of Information Systems and Telecommunications [*Veterans Administration*] (TSSD)
OISB.......... Bavanat [*Iran*] [*ICAO location identifier*] (ICLI)
OISC.......... Ardakan-E-Fars [*Iran*] [*ICAO location identifier*] (ICLI)
OISC.......... Oil-Insulated, Self-Cooling
OISCA.......... Organization for Industrial, Spiritual, and Cultural Advancement International [*Tokyo, Japan*] (EAIO)
OISD.......... Darab [*Iran*] [*ICAO location identifier*] (ICLI)
OISDG.......... Ingleside Branch, Stormont, Dundas, and Glengarry County Library, Ontario [*Library symbol National Library of Canada*] (BIB)
OISE.......... Estahbanat [*Iran*] [*ICAO location identifier*] (ICLI)
OISE.......... Office of Industrial Security, Europe [*DoD*]
OISE.......... Ontario Institute for Studies in Education [*University of Toronto*] [*Research center*] (RCD)
OISF.......... Fasa [*Iran*] [*ICAO location identifier*] (ICLI)
OISH.......... Farashband [*Iran*] [*ICAO location identifier*] (ICLI)
OISI.......... Dehbid [*Iran*] [*ICAO location identifier*] (ICLI)
OISI.......... Office of Industrial Security, International [*DoD*] (MCD)
OISI.......... Ophthalmic Imaging Sys [*NASDAQ symbol*] (TTSB)
OISI.......... Ophthalmic Imaging Systems, Inc. [*NASDAQ symbol*] (SAG)
OISJ.......... Jahrom [*Iran*] [*ICAO location identifier*] (ICLI)
OISK.......... Kazeroun [*Iran*] [*ICAO location identifier*] (ICLI)
OISL.......... Lar [*Iran*] [*ICAO location identifier*] (ICLI)
OISLGR........ Office of Industry and State and Local Government Relations [*Energy Research and Development Administration*]
OISM.......... Mamassani [*Iran*] [*ICAO location identifier*] (ICLI)
OISN.......... Neiriz [*Iran*] [*ICAO location identifier*] (ICLI)
OISP.......... Overseas Internal Security Program [*Army*]
OISP.......... Persepolis/Marvdasht [*Iran*] [*ICAO location identifier*] (ICLI)
OISQ.......... Ghir/Karzin [*Iran*] [*ICAO location identifier*] (ICLI)
OISR.......... Lamerd [*Iran*] [*ICAO location identifier*] (ICLI)
OISR.......... Office of Interstate Sales Registration [*HUD*]
OISR.......... Open Item Status Report (NASA)

OISRU..........	Office of Intergovernmental Science and Research Utilization [*National Science Foundation*]
OISS	Office of Information Systems and Services (AAGC)
OISS	Online Information Search Service [*Computer science*] (AD)
OISS	Operational Intelligence Support System (MCD)
OISS	Organizacion Iberoamericana de Seguridad Social [*Ibero-American Social Security Organization*]
OISS	Shiraz/International [*Iran*] [*ICAO location identifier*] (ICLI)
OISSP	Office of Interim Space Station Program [*NASA*]
OIST...........	Operator Integration Shakedown Test
OIST...........	Shiraz [*Iran*] [*ICAO location identifier*] (ICLI)
OISTV	Organisation Internationale pour la Science et la Technique du Vide [*International Organization for Vacuum Science and Technology*] [*French*] (AD)
OISU	Abarghou [*Iran*] [*ICAO location identifier*] (ICLI)
OISW	Kohkiloyeh [*Iran*] [*ICAO location identifier*] (ICLI)
OISX	Khonj [*Iran*] [*ICAO location identifier*] (ICLI)
OISY	Yasouj [*Iran*] [*ICAO location identifier*] (ICLI)
OISZ	Firouzabad [*Iran*] [*ICAO location identifier*] (ICLI)
OIT...........	Object Identification Test
OIT...........	Oblique-Incidence Transmission
OIT...........	Office of International Trade [*Department of Commerce*]
O i T	Officer in Training (AD)
OIT...........	Oil Interceptor Trap
OIT...........	Oita [*Japan*] [*Seismograph station code, US Geological Survey*] (SEIS)
OIT...........	Oita [*Japan*] [*Airport symbol*] (OAG)
O IT	Old Italian [*Language, etc.*] (ROG)
O It	Old Italian (AD)
OIT...........	Ontario Ministry of Industry, Trade, and Technology [*UTLAS symbol*]
OIT...........	Operator Interface Terminal (MCD)
OIT...........	Optimum Insulation Thickness (DICI)
OIT...........	Orbiter Integrated Test [*NASA*] (NASA)
OIT...........	Oregon Institute of Technology, Klamath Falls, OR [*OCLC symbol*] (OCLC)
OIT...........	Organic Integrity Test [*Psychology*]
OIT...........	Organisation Internationale du Travail [*International Labor Organization*] [*French United Nations*] (EAIO)
OIT...........	Organizacion Internacional del Trabajo [*International Labor Organization*] [*Spanish United Nations*] (DUND)
OIT...........	Organization Iberoamericaine de Television (NTCM)
OITA..........	Office of International Tax Affairs [*Department of the Treasury*]
OITA..........	Sarab [*Iran*] [*ICAO location identifier*] (ICLI)
OITAF-NACS...	Organizzazione Internazionale dei Trasporti a Fune [*International Organization for Transportation by Rope*] - North American Continental Section (EA)
OITB..........	Mahabad [*Iran*] [*ICAO location identifier*] (ICLI)
OITC..........	Sardasht [*Iran*] [*ICAO location identifier*] (ICLI)
OITD..........	Marand [*Iran*] [*ICAO location identifier*] (ICLI)
OITDA	Optoelectronic Industry and Technology Development Association [*Japan*]
OITDS	Operations and Intelligence Tactical Data Systems (MCD)
OITF..........	Office of International Trade and Finance [*Department of State*]
OITF..........	Office of International Trade Fairs [*Department of Commerce*]
OITF..........	Organisation Intergouvernementale pour les Transports Internationaux Ferroviaires [*Intergovernmental Organization for International Carriage by Rail*] (EAIO)
OITG..........	Naghadeh [*Iran*] [*ICAO location identifier*] (ICLI)
OITH..........	Khaneh/Piranshahr [*Iran*] [*ICAO location identifier*] (ICLI)
OITI..........	Mianeh [*Iran*] [*ICAO location identifier*] (ICLI)
OITJ..........	Julfa [*Iran*] [*ICAO location identifier*] (ICLI)
OITK..........	Khoy [*Iran*] [*ICAO location identifier*] (ICLI)
OITM..........	Maragheh [*Iran*] [*ICAO location identifier*] (ICLI)
OITN..........	Meshgin Shahr [*Iran*] [*ICAO location identifier*] (ICLI)
OITO..........	Mian Do Ab [*Iran*] [*ICAO location identifier*] (ICLI)
OITP..........	Office for Information Technology Policy [*American Library Association*]
OITP..........	Office of International Trade Promotion [*Department of State*]
OITP..........	Parsabad/Moghan [*Iran*] [*ICAO location identifier*] (ICLI)
OITQ..........	Ahar [*Iran*] [*ICAO location identifier*] (ICLI)
OITR..........	Uromiyeh [*Iran*] [*ICAO location identifier*] (ICLI)
OITS..........	Saghez [*Iran*] [*ICAO location identifier*] (ICLI)
OITT..........	Outpulser, Identifier, Trunk Test
OITT..........	Tabriz [*Iran*] [*ICAO location identifier*] (ICLI)
OITU..........	Makou [*Iran*] [*ICAO location identifier*] (ICLI)
OITV..........	Tabriz [*Iran*] [*ICAO location identifier*] (ICLI)
OITW..........	Azar Shahr [*Iran*] [*ICAO location identifier*] (ICLI)
OITX..........	Sareskand [*Iran*] [*ICAO location identifier*] (ICLI)
OITY..........	Marivan [*Iran*] [*ICAO location identifier*] (ICLI)
OITZ..........	Zanjan [*Iran*] [*ICAO location identifier*] (ICLI)
OIU	Operator Interface Unit [*Computer science*]
OIV	Octarios Quatior [*Four Pints*] [*Pharmacy*] (ROG)
OIV	Office International de la Vigne et du Vin [*International Vine and Wine Office*] (EAIO)
OIV	Overhead Inlet Valve [*Automotive engineering*]
OIV	Oxidizer Isolation Valve (MCD)
oiv	Oxidizer Isolation Valve (NAKS)
OIVA	127th Infantry Veterans Association (EA)
oivs	Orbiter Interface Verification Set [*NASA*] (NAKS)
OIVS	Orbiter Interface Verification Set [*NASA*] (NASA)
OIVV	Office Internationale de la Vigne et du Vin [*International Office of Vines and Wines*] [*French*] (AD)
OIW	Oceanographic Institute of Washington [*Marine science*] (MSC)
OIW	Oceanographic Institute Wellington New Zealand (AD)
OIW	Office of Indigenous Women [*Australia*]
OIW	Oiwake [*Japan*] [*Seismograph station code, US Geological Survey Closed*] (SEIS)
OIW	Order of the Indian Wars (EA)
OIWC	Oil-Insulated, Water-Cooled
OIWP	Oil Industry Working Party (AD)
OIWR	Office of Indian Water Rights [*Bureau of Indian Affairs*]
OIX	Ottawa, IL [*Location identifier FAA*] (FAAL)
OIYA	Ardakan-E-Yazd [*Iran*] [*ICAO location identifier*] (ICLI)
OIYB	Bafgh [*Iran*] [*ICAO location identifier*] (ICLI)
OIYD	Dehshir [*Iran*] [*ICAO location identifier*] (ICLI)
OIYF	Taft [*Iran*] [*ICAO location identifier*] (ICLI)
OIYK	Khor/Jandagh [*Iran*] [*ICAO location identifier*] (ICLI)
OIYM	Mehriz [*Iran*] [*ICAO location identifier*] (ICLI)
OIYN	Khore Beyabanak [*Iran*] [*ICAO location identifier*] (ICLI)
OIYQ	Khezr Abad [*Iran*] [*ICAO location identifier*] (ICLI)
OIYT	Yazd [*Iran*] [*ICAO location identifier*] (ICLI)
OIYY	Yazd [*Iran*] [*ICAO location identifier*] (ICLI)
OIYZ	Ashkezar [*Iran*] [*ICAO location identifier*] (ICLI)
OIZA	Jalagh [*Iran*] [*ICAO location identifier*] (ICLI)
OIZB	Zabol [*Iran*] [*ICAO location identifier*] (ICLI)
OIZC	Chah Bahar/Konarak [*Iran*] [*ICAO location identifier*] (ICLI)
OIZD	Dashtyari [*Iran*] [*ICAO location identifier*] (ICLI)
OIZG	Ghasre Ghand [*Iran*] [*ICAO location identifier*] (ICLI)
OIZH	Zahedan [*Iran*] [*ICAO location identifier*] (ICLI)
OIZI	Iran Shahr [*Iran*] [*ICAO location identifier*] (ICLI)
OIZJ	Jask [*Iran*] [*ICAO location identifier*] (ICLI)
OIZK	Khash [*Iran*] [*ICAO location identifier*] (ICLI)
OIZL	Zabolee [*Iran*] [*ICAO location identifier*] (ICLI)
OIZM	Mirjaveh [*Iran*] [*ICAO location identifier*] (ICLI)
OIZN	Bazman [*Iran*] [*ICAO location identifier*] (ICLI)
OIZO	Sarbaz [*Iran*] [*ICAO location identifier*] (ICLI)
OIZP	Bampoor [*Iran*] [*ICAO location identifier*] (ICLI)
OIZR	Bask [*Iran*] [*ICAO location identifier*] (ICLI)
OIZS	Saravan [*Iran*] [*ICAO location identifier*] (ICLI)
OIZT	Zahedan [*Iran*] [*ICAO location identifier*] (ICLI)
OIZY	Nik-Shahr [*Iran*] [*ICAO location identifier*] (ICLI)
OJ	Air Texana [*ICAO designator*] (AD)
OJ	Jackson Public Library, Jackson, OH [*Library symbol Library of Congress*] (LCLS)
OJ	Ohne Jahr [*Without Date of Publication*] [*Bibliography*] [*German*]
oJ	Ohne Jahr [*Without Year*] [*German*] (AD)
oj	Open-Joint (AD)
OJ	Open-Joisted [*Technical drawings*]
OJ	Open Web Joist [*Technical drawings*]
OJ	Operation Joshua (EA)
OJ	Opium Joint [*Slang*]
OJ	Orange Co. [*NYSE symbol*] (SPSG)
OJ	Orange Juice
oj	Orange Juice (AD)
OJ	Order of Jamaica
OJ	Orenthal James [*Given names of football player O. J. Simpson*]
OJ	Orenthal James Simpson [*Sports personality*] (ECON)
OJ	Originating Junctor [*Telecommunications*] (TEL)
OJ	Orthomode Junction [*Electronics*]
OJ	Orthoplast Jacket [*Orthopedics*] (DAVI)
OJ	Outer Jacket
OJA	Onklos-Jonathan Aramaic (BJA)
OJA	Oriental Pearl Airways Ltd. [*British ICAO designator*] (FAAC)
OJA	Weatherford, OK [*Location identifier FAA*] (FAAL)
OJAC..........	Amman [*Jordan*] [*ICAO location identifier*] (ICLI)
OJ Act..........	Ontario Judicature Act [*A publication*] (DLA)
OJAF..........	Amman [*Jordan*] [*ICAO location identifier*] (ICLI)
OJA-G	Office of the Judge Advocate General [*British*]
OJAI..........	Amman/Queen Alia [*Jordan*] [*ICAO location identifier*] (ICLI)
OJAJ..........	October, January, April, and July [*Denotes quarterly payments of interest or dividends in these months*] [*Business term*]
OJAM..........	Amman/Marka [*Jordan*] [*ICAO location identifier*] (ICLI)
OJapan	Order of Japan (DD)
OJAQ..........	Aqaba [*Jordan*] [*ICAO location identifier*] (ICLI)
OJARS	Office of Justice Assistance, Research, and Statistics [*Department of Justice*]
OJBD	Irbid [*Jordan*] [*ICAO location identifier*] (ICLI)
OJC	North Central Regional Library, Ojibway Cree Project [*UTLAS symbol*]
OJC	Occupied Japan Club (EA)
OJC	Office of Job Corps [*Department of Labor*]
OJC	Olathe, KS [*Location identifier FAA*] (FAAL)
OJC	Order of Jacques-Cartier [*Canada*] (BARN)
OJC	Organisation Juive de Combat [*Jewish Combat Organization*] [*French*] (AD)
OJC	Orlando Junior College [*Florida*]
OJC	Otero Junior College [*La Junta, CO*]
OJC	Overseas Jazz Club (EA)
OJCAC	Ohio Junior College Athletic Conference (PSS)
OJCCT..........	On-Line Journal of Current Clinical Trends (TELE)
OJCE	Orchestre des Jeunes de la Communaute Europeenne [*European Community Youth Orchestra - ECYO*] (EAIO)
OJCN	Jarvis Branch, City of Nanticoke Public Library, Ontario [*Library symbol National Library of Canada*] (BIB)
OJCS	Office of the Joint Chiefs of Staff (AFM)
OJCS..........	Organization of the Joint Chiefs of Staff
OJD..........	Order of Job's Daughters
OJDYD	Office of Juvenile Delinquency and Youth Development [*Later, Youth Development Bureau*] [*HEW*]

OJE .... Okumenischer Jugendrat in Europa [*Ecumenical Youth Council in Europe - EYCE*] (EAIO)
OJE .... On-the-Job Education
OJE .... On-the-Job Evaluation (OICC)
OJE .... On-the-Job Experience
OJE .... Operation Joint Endeavor [*Army*]
OJE .... Orthodox Job Enrichment (PDAA)
OJEC .... Official Journal of the European Communities [*A publication*] (AD)
OJG .... Operation Joint Guard [*Army*]
OJG .... Ordnance Job Guide
OJHF .... Hotel Five [*Jordan*] [*ICAO location identifier*] (ICLI)
OJHR .... Hotel Four [*Jordan*] [*ICAO location identifier*] (ICLI)
oji .... Ojibwa [*MARC language code Library of Congress*] (LCCP)
OJI .... On-the-Job Injuries
oji .... On-the-Job Injuries (AD)
OJJ .... Office of Juvenile Justice (AD)
OJJDP .... Office of Juvenile Justice and Delinquency Prevention [*Department of Justice*] [*Washington, DC*]
OJJO .... Jericho [*Jordan*] [*ICAO location identifier*] (ICLI)
OJJR .... Jerusalem [*Jordan*] [*ICAO location identifier*] (ICLI)
OJL .... Josephine County Library System, Grants Pass, OR [*OCLC symbol*] (OCLC)
OJMF .... Mafraq [*Jordan*] [*ICAO location identifier*] (ICLI)
OJNRF .... O. J. Noer Research Foundation (EA)
OJOP .... Olympic Job Opportunities Program
OJP .... Office of Justice Programs [*Department of Justice*]
OJP .... Ontong Java Plateau [*Geology*]
OJP .... Orlando, FL [*Location identifier FAA*] (FAAL)
OJPR .... Office for Jewish Population Research [*Defunct*] (EA)
OJQ .... Objective Judgment Quotient
OJR .... Old Jamaica Rum (ROG)
oJr .... Old Jamaica Rum (AD)
OJRL .... Optoelectronics Joint Research Laboratory [*Japan*]
OJS .... Las Oblatas de Jesus Sacerdote [*Oblates of Jesus the Priest*] [*Roman Catholic women's religious order*]
OJS .... Optical Jammer Source
OJSA .... Orthomode Junction and Switching Assembly [*Electronics*]
OJT .... On-the-Job Training
ojt .... On-the-Job Training (AD)
OJT .... Over-Water Jet Transport (MCD)
OJTA .... Officer Job/Task Analysis [*Military*]
O Jur .... Ohio Jurisprudence [*A publication*] (DLA)
OJW .... Otjiwarongo [*South-West Africa*] [*Airport symbol*] (AD)
OJY .... Florida Air, Inc. [*ICAO designator*] (FAAC)
OJZ .... White Plains, NY [*Location identifier FAA*] (FAAL)
OJZZ .... Amman [*Jordan*] [*ICAO location identifier*] (ICLI)
OK .... All Right [*From OII Korrect; or from Old Kinderhook, a political club that supported the 1840 presidential campaign of Martin Van Buren*]
OK .... Approved (EBF)
OK .... Correct (EBF)
OK .... Czechoslovak Airlines [*ICAO designator*] (AD)
OK .... Kingston Public Library, Ontario [*Library symbol National Library of Canada*] (NLC)
O-K .... Object-Kowal [*Object in the solar system*]
OK .... Odorless Kerosene
OK .... Ohne Kosten [*Without Cost*] [*German*]
ok .... Ohne Kosten [*Without Cost*] [*German*] (AD)
OK .... Okay [*International telex abbreviation*] (WDMC)
OK .... Okinawa [*Japan*]
OK .... Oklahoma [*Postal code*]
Ok .... Oklahoma Department of Libraries, Oklahoma City, OK [*Library symbol Library of Congress*] (LCLS)
OK .... Okonite (IAA)
OK .... Oktal (IAA)
OK .... Ola Kala [*All Is Well*] [*Greek*]
ok .... Ola Kala [*All is Fine*] [*Greek*] (AD)
OK .... Old Kent Financial [*NYSE symbol*]
OK .... Old Kinderhook (IIA)
OK .... Old Kingdom [*Egyptology*] (ROG)
OK .... Optical Klystron (PDAA)
ok .... Optical Klystron (AD)
OK .... Order of Knights (ADA)
OK .... Oskar Kokoschka [*Austrian painter*] [*1886-1980*]
OK .... Outer Keel
ok .... Outer Keel (AD)
OKA .... Bethany Nazarene College, Bethany, OK [*OCLC symbol*] (OCLC)
OKA .... Kingston Laboratories, Alcan International Ltd., Ontario [*Library symbol National Library of Canada*] (NLC)
OKA .... Okayama [*Japan*] [*Seismograph station code, US Geological Survey*] (SEIS)
OKA .... Okinawa [*Japan*] [*Airport symbol*] (OAG)
OKA .... Otherwise Known As
oka .... Otherwise Known As (AD)
OKA .... Out-of-Kilter Algorithm [*Mathematics*]
OKAA .... Kuwait Directorate General of Civil Aviation [*Kuwait*] [*ICAO location identifier*] (ICLI)
OKAAN .... Optokinetic After-After-Nystagmus [*Ophthalmology*]
OKAB .... Beaverbrook Branch, Kanata Public Library, Ontario [*Library symbol National Library of Canada*] (NLC)
OKAC .... Kuwait [*Kuwait*] [*ICAO location identifier*] (ICLI)
OkAd .... Ada Public Library, Ada, OK [*Library symbol Library of Congress*] (LCLS)
OkAdE .... East Central State College [*Later, East Central Oklahoma State University*], Ada, OK [*Library symbol Library of Congress*] (LCLS)

OKAER .... Radiochemical Co., Atomic Energy of Canada Ltd., [*Societe Radiochimique, L'Energie Atomique du Canada Ltee.*], Kanata, Ontario [*Library symbol National Library of Canada*] (NLC)
OKAF .... Kuwait Air Force [*Kuwait*] [*ICAO location identifier*] (ICLI)
OKAH .... Hazeldean Branch, Kanata Public Library, Ontario [*Library symbol National Library of Canada*] (NLC)
OKAI .... Research & Technology Centre, AMCA International Ltd., Kanata, Ontario [*Library symbol National Library of Canada*] (NLC)
OKAKS .... Synod Office, Diocese of Keewatin, Anglican Church of Canada, Kenora, Ontario [*Library symbol National Library of Canada*] (NLC)
OkAl .... Altus Library, Altus, OK [*Library symbol Library of Congress*] (LCLS)
OKAL .... Aluminum Co. of Canada Ltd., Kingston, Ontario [*Library symbol National Library of Canada*] (NLC)
OkAlS .... Southern Prairie Library System, Altus, OK [*Library symbol Library of Congress*] (LCLS)
OkAlvN .... Northwestern State College, Alva, OK [*Library symbol Library of Congress*] (LCLS)
OKAN .... Kanata Public Library, Ontario [*Library symbol National Library of Canada*] (BIB)
OKAN .... Optokinetic After-Nystagmus [*Ophthalmology*]
OKANA .... Arctec Canada Ltd., Kanata, Ontario [*Library symbol National Library of Canada*] (NLC)
OKAOS .... Synod Office, Diocese of Ontario, Anglican Church of Canada, Kingston, Ontario [*Library symbol National Library of Canada*] (NLC)
OKAP .... Kapuskasing Public Library, Ontario [*Library symbol National Library of Canada*] (NLC)
OkArC .... Chickasaw Library System, Ardmore, OK [*Library symbol Library of Congress*] (LCLS)
OKASG .... St. George's Cathedral, Anglican Church of Canada, Kingston, Ontario [*Library symbol National Library of Canada*] (NLC)
OKAYJ .... A. Y. Jackson High School, Kanata, Ontario [*Library symbol National Library of Canada*] (BIB)
OkB .... Bartlesville Public Library, Bartlesville, OK [*Library symbol Library of Congress*] (LCLS)
OKB .... Kashechewan Band Library, Ontario [*Library symbol National Library of Canada*] (BIB)
OKB .... Oklahoma Baptist University, Shawnee, OK [*OCLC symbol*] (OCLC)
OKB .... Orchid Beach [*Australia Airport symbol*]
OkBERDA ..... United States Energy Research Development Administration, Energy Research Center, Bartlesville, OK [*Library symbol Library of Congress*] (LCLS)
OkBetC .... Bethany Nazarene College, Bethany, OK [*Library symbol Library of Congress*] (LCLS)
OKBK .... Kuwait/International [*Kuwait*] [*ICAO location identifier*] (ICLI)
OkBP .... Phillips Petroleum Co., Research and Development Department, Bartlesville, OK [*Library symbol Library of Congress*] (LCLS)
OkBP-NR ...... Philips Petroleum Co., Exploration and Production Library, Bartlesville, OK [*Library symbol*] [*Library of Congress*] (LCLS)
OkBr .... Bristow Public Library, Bristow, OK [*Library symbol Library of Congress*] (LCLS)
OKBT .... Billings Township Public Library, Kagawong, Ontario [*Library symbol National Library of Canada*] (NLC)
OkBUSM ...... United States Bureau of Mines, Petroleum Research Center, Bartlesville, OK [*Library symbol Library of Congress Obsolete*] (LCLS)
OKC .... Cameron University, Lawton, OK [*OCLC symbol*] (OCLC)
OKC .... Canadian Forces School of Communications and Electronics, Kingston, Ontario [*Library symbol National Library of Canada*] (BIB)
OKC .... Odontogenic Keratocyst [*Medicine*] (DMAA)
OKC .... Okanagan College Learning Resources Centre [*UTLAS symbol*]
OKC .... Oklahoma City [*Oklahoma*] [*Airport symbol*] (OAG)
OKC .... Will Rogers World Airport [*FAA*] (TAG)
OKCAA .... Archives, Archdiocese of Kingston, Catholic Church, Ontario [*Library symbol National Library of Canada*] (NLC)
OkChicW ...... Oklahoma College of Liberal Arts, Chickasha, OK [*Library symbol Library of Congress*] (LCLS)
OKCHN .... Pan-National Congress of the Chechen People [*Russian Federation*]
OKCKT .... King Township Public Library, King City, Ontario [*Library symbol National Library of Canada*] (NLC)
OkCl .... Clinton Public Library, Clinton, OK [*Library symbol Library of Congress*] (LCLS)
OkClaW .... Will Rogers Library, Claremore, OH [*Library symbol Library of Congress*] (LCLS)
OkClW .... Western Plains Library System, Clinton, OK [*Library symbol Library of Congress*] (LCLS)
OKCM .... Canadian Marconi Co., Kanata, Ontario [*Library symbol National Library of Canada*] (NLC)
OKD .... Oklahoma Department of Libraries, Oklahoma City, OK [*OCLC symbol*] (OCLC)
OKD .... Research Centre Library, Du Pont Canada, Inc., Kingston, Ontario [*Library symbol National Library of Canada*] (NLC)
OKD .... Sapporo/Okadama [*Japan*] [*Airport symbol*] (OAG)
OKDBMS ...... Operations Knowledge Data Base Management System [*NASA*]
OKDC .... Du Pont Canada, Inc., Kingston, Ontario [*Library symbol National Library of Canada*] (NLC)
OkDurS .... Southeastern State College, Durant, OK [*Library symbol Library of Congress*] (LCLS)
OKE .... Kenora Public Library, Ontario [*Library symbol National Library of Canada*] (NLC)
OKE .... Metropolitan Library System, Capitol Hill Branch, Oklahoma City, OK [*OCLC symbol*] (OCLC)
OKE .... Okino Erabu [*Japan*] [*Airport symbol*] (OAG)

OKE............ ONEOK, Inc. [*NYSE symbol*] (SPSG)

OKE............ Optical Kerr Effect [*Birefringence induced in an electrical field*]

OkE .... Public Library of Enid and Garfield County, Enid, OK [*Library symbol Library of Congress*] (LCLS)

OKEA .... Kearney and Area Public Library, Kearney, Ontario [*Library symbol National Library of Canada*] (NLC)

OkEdT .... Central State University, Edmond, OK [*Library symbol Library of Congress*] (LCLS)

OKEE........... Keewatin Public Library, Ontario [*Library symbol National Library of Canada*] (NLC)

O'Keefe Ord... O'Keefe's Order in Chancery [*Ireland*] [*A publication*] (DLA)

Oke Fish L... Oke. Fisher Laws [*4th ed.*] [*1924*] [*A publication*] (DLA)

OkEG........... Phillips University, Graduate Seminary, Enid, OK [*Library symbol Library of Congress*] (LCLS)

Oke Game L... Oke. Game Laws [*5th ed.*] [*1912*] [*A publication*] (DLA)

OKEH .... Okehampton [*England*]

OKEM.......... Kemptville Public Library, Ontario [*Library symbol National Library of Canada*] (NLC)

OKEMAF ...... Ontario Ministry of Agriculture and Food, Kemptville, Ontario [*Library symbol National Library of Canada*] (NLC)

Oke Mag Form... Oke. Magisterial Formulist [*19th ed.*] [*1978*] [*A publication*] (DLA)

Oke Mag Syn... Oke. Magisterial Synopsis [*14th ed.*] [*1893*] [*A publication*] (DLA)

OKEMC .... Kemptville College of Agricultural Technology, Ontario [*Library symbol National Library of Canada*] (BIB)

OKEMS .... Earl of March Secondary School, Kanata, Ontario [*Library symbol National Library of Canada*] (NLC)

OKEN .... Old Kent Financial Corp. [*NASDAQ symbol*] (NQ)

OKEN .... Old Kent Finl [*NASDAQ symbol*] (TTSB)

OKentU .... Kent State University, Kent, OH [*Library symbol Library of Congress*] (LCLS)

OkEP........... Phillips University, Enid, OK [*Library symbol Library of Congress*] (LCLS)

OkErC.......... El Reno Junior College Learning Resource Center, El Reno, OK [*Library symbol*] [*Library of Congress*] (LCLS)

OKES .... Georgina Township Public Library, Keswick, Ontario [*Library symbol National Library of Canada*] (NLC)

OKET........... Euphrasia Township Public Library, Kimberley, Ontario [*Library symbol National Library of Canada*] (NLC)

OKetBD........ BDM International, Information Service Center, Kettering, OH [*Library symbol*] [*Library of Congress*] (LCLS)

OKetH .... Kettering Memorial Hospital, Kettering, OH [*Library symbol Library of Congress*] (LCLS)

OKetK .... Charles F. Kettering Foundation, Kettering, OH [*Library symbol Library of Congress*] (LCLS)

Oke Turn...... Oke. Turnpike Laws [*2nd ed.*] [*1861*] [*A publication*] (DLA)

OKF............ Fort Frontenac Library, Canada Department of National Defence [*Bibliotheque Fort Frontenac, Ministere de la Defense Nationale*] Kingston, Ontario [*Library symbol National Library of Canada*] (NLC)

OKFC .... Frontenac County Library, Kingston, Ontario [*Library symbol National Library of Canada*] (NLC)

OKFCSM ...... Frontenac County Schools Museum Association, Kingston, Ontario [*Library symbol National Library of Canada*] (BIB)

OKFI........... Siltronics Ltd., Kanata, Ontario [*Library symbol National Library of Canada*] (NLC)

OkFsAGM..... United States Army, Artillery and Guided Missile School, Fort Sill, OK [*Library symbol Library of Congress*] (LCLS)

OKG .... Oak Grove [*Tennessee*] [*Seismograph station code, US Geological Survey*] (SEIS)

OKG .... Okoyo [*Congo*] [*Airport symbol*] (OAG)

OKG .... Phillips University, Graduate Seminary Library, Enid, OK [*OCLC symbol*] (OCLC)

OKGH.......... Kingston General Hospital, Ontario [*Library symbol National Library of Canada*] (NLC)

OkGoP .... Panhandle State College, Goodwell, OK [*Library symbol Library of Congress*] (LCLS)

OkGuC .... Catholic College of Oklahoma for Women, Guthrie, OK [*Library symbol Library of Congress Obsolete*] (LCLS)

OkGuy......... Guymon City Library, Guymon, OK [*Library symbol Library of Congress*] (LCLS)

OKH .... Oberkommando des Heeres [*Army High Command*] [*German military - World War II*]

OKH .... Okha [*Former USSR Seismograph station code, US Geological Survey*] (SEIS)

OKH .... University of Oklahoma, Health Science Center Library, Oklahoma City, OK [*OCLC symbol*] (OCLC)

OKHD.......... Hotel-Dieu Hospital, Kingston, Ontario [*Library symbol National Library of Canada*] (NLC)

OkHenn........ Hennessey Public Library, Hennessey, OK [*Library symbol Library of Congress*] (LCLS)

OkHi.......... Oklahoma Historical Society, Oklahoma City, OK [*Library symbol Library of Congress*] (LCLS)

OKI............ Choctaw Nation Multi-County Library, McAlester, OK [*OCLC symbol*] (OCLC)

OKI............ Kincardine Branch, Bruce County Public Library, Ontario [*Library symbol National Library of Canada*] (NLC)

OKI............ Ohio-Kentucky-Indiana Regional Planning Authority

OKI............ Oki Island [*Japan*] [*Airport symbol*] (OAG)

OKI............ Okijuku [*Japan*] [*Seismograph station code, US Geological Survey Closed*] (SEIS)

OKIESMO..... Oklahoma Machismo [*Term coined by author Mark Singer*]

OKIL.......... Killaloe Public Library, Ontario [*Library symbol National Library of Canada*] (NLC)

OkIM.......... McUrtain County High Education Program, Idabel, OK [*Library symbol*] [*Library of Congress*] (LCLS)

Okin .... Okinawa (AD)

OKIT........... Kitchener Public Library, Ontario [*Library symbol National Library of Canada*] (NLC)

OKITC .... Learning Resource Centre, Conestoga College of Applied Arts and Technology, Kitchener, Ontario [*Library symbol National Library of Canada*] (NLC)

OKITD .... Doon Pioneer Village, Kitchener, Ontario [*Library symbol National Library of Canada*] (BIB)

OKITM .... Ontario Library Service - Saugeen, Kitchener, Ontario [*Library symbol National Library of Canada*] (NLC)

OKITW......... Kitchener-Waterloo Record, Kitchener, Ontario [*Library symbol National Library of Canada*] (NLC)

OKITWC....... Waterloo County Board of Education, Kitchener, Ontario [*Library symbol National Library of Canada*] (NLC)

OKJ............ Okada Airlines Ltd. [*Nigeria*] [*ICAO designator*] (FAAC)

OKJ............ Okayama [*Japan*] [*Airport symbol*] (OAG)

OKJ............ Oklahoma City Community College, Oklahoma City, OK [*OCLC symbol*] (OCLC)

OKK .... Charles F. Kettering Foundation, Dayton, OH [*OCLC symbol*] (OCLC)

OKK .... Kokomo [*Indiana*] [*Airport symbol*] (OAG)

OKK .... Kokomo, IN [*Location identifier FAA*] (FAAL)

OKKBWP....... One Kind Kiss Before We Part [*Slang*]

OKL............ Lake Ontario Regional Library System, Kingston, Ontario [*Library symbol Obsolete National Library of Canada*] (NLC)

OkL............ Lawton Public Library, Lawton, OK [*Library symbol Library of Congress*] (LCLS)

OKL............ Oberkommando der Luftwaffe [*Air Force High Command*] [*German military - World War II*]

Okl............ Oklahoma (DLA)

OKL............ Oklahoma City [*Diocesan abbreviation*] [*Oklahoma*] (TOCD)

Okl............ Oklahoma Reports [*A publication*] (DLA)

OKL............ University of Oklahoma, Law Library, Norman, OK [*OCLC symbol*] (OCLC)

OKLA .... Oklahoma (AFM)

Okla .... Oklahoma (AD)

Okla .... Oklahoma Criminal Reports [*A publication*] (DLA)

Okla .... Oklahoma Supreme Court Reports [*A publication*] (DLA)

Okla Ap Ct Rep... Oklahoma Appellate Court Reporter [*A publication*] (DLA)

OklaC.......... Oklahoma City (AD)

Okla City U... Oklahoma City University (GAGS)

Okla Cr... Oklahoma Criminal Reports [*A publication*] (DLA)

Okla Crim .... Oklahoma Criminal Reports [*A publication*] (DLA)

Okla CULR... Oklahoma City University. Law Review [*A publication*] (DLA)

OklaG.......... Oklahoma Gas & Electric Co. [*Associated Press*] (SAG)

Okla Gaz........ Oklahoma Gazette [*A publication*] (DLA)

OklaGE........ Oklahoma Gas & Electric Co. [*Associated Press*] (SAG)

Oklahoma ... Oklahoma Reports [*A publication*] (DLA)

Okla ICR ..... Oklahoma Industrial Commission Reports [*A publication*] (DLA)

Okla Lawy ... Oklahoma Lawyer [*A publication*] (DLA)

Okla LJ........ Oklahoma Law Journal [*A publication*] (DLA)

Okl App....... Oklahoma Court of Appeals (DLA)

Okla SBJ...... Oklahoma State Bar Journal [*A publication*] (DLA)

Okla Sess Laws... Oklahoma Session Laws [*A publication*] (DLA)

Okla Sess Law Serv... Oklahoma Session Law Service (West) [*A publication*] (DLA)

Okla Stat ..... Oklahoma Statutes [*A publication*] (DLA)

Okla Stat Ann (West)... Oklahoma Statutes, Annotated (West) [*A publication*] (DLA)

Okla St U..... Oklahoma State University (GAGS)

OkLaU......... Langston University, Langston, OK [*Library symbol Library of Congress*] (LCLS)

OkLC........... Cameron University, Lawton, OK [*Library symbol Library of Congress*] (LCLS)

Okl City UL Rev... Oklahoma City University. Law Review [*A publication*] (DLA)

OkLC-M........ Cameron College, Medical Library Resource Center, Lawton, OK [*Library symbol Library of Congress*] (LCLS)

Okl Cr .... Oklahoma Criminal Reports [*A publication*] (DLA)

Okl Cr R ...... Oklahoma Criminal Reports [*A publication*] (DLA)

OKLEM........ McMichael Canadian Collection, Kleinburg, Ontario [*Library symbol National Library of Canada*] (NLC)

OKLFC......... Official Kate Linder Fan Club (EA)

OKLN .... Northeastern Regional Library, Kirkland Lake, Ontario [*Library symbol National Library of Canada*] (NLC)

OKLN .... Ontario Library Service - James Bay, Kirkland Lake, Ontario [*Library symbol National Library of Canada*] (NLC)

OKLNC........ Kirkland Lake Campus, Northern College, Ontario [*Library symbol National Library of Canada*] (NLC)

Okl St Ann ... Oklahoma Statutes, Annotated [*A publication*] (DLA)

OKLT........... Teck Centennial Public Library, Kirkland Lake, Ontario [*Library symbol National Library of Canada*] (NLC)

OKLU .... Lumonics, Inc., Kanata, Ontario [*Library symbol National Library of Canada*] (NLC)

OKM........... Mitel Corp., Kanata, Ontario [*Library symbol National Library of Canada*] (NLC)

OKM........... Oberkommando der Kriegsmarine [*Navy High Command*] [*German military - World War II*]

OKM........... Oberkommando der Marine [*Naval High Command*] [*Germany*] (AD)

OKM........... Okmulgee, OK [*Location identifier FAA*] (FAAL)

OKM........... Pioneer Multi-County Library, Norman, OK [*OCLC symbol*] (OCLC)

OKMC......... Miller Communications Systems Ltd., Kanata, Ontario [*Library symbol National Library of Canada*] (NLC)

OkMcC .... Choctaw Nation Multi-County Library, McAlester, OK [*Library symbol Library of Congress*] (LCLS)

OkMcO .... Oscar Rose Junior College, Midwest City, OK [*Library symbol Library of Congress*] (LCLS)

OKMD .... Digital Equipment of Canada Ltd., Kanata, Ontario [*Library symbol National Library of Canada*] (NLC)

OKME........... Metro Canada Ltd., Kingston, Ontario [*Library symbol National Library of Canada*] (NLC)

OKMM .... Marine Museum of the Great Lakes at Kingston, Ontario [*Library symbol National Library of Canada*] (NLC)

OkMu .... Muskogee Public Library, Muskogee, OK [*Library symbol Library of Congress*] (LCLS)

OkMuE .... Eastern Oklahoma District Library, Muskogee, OK [*Library symbol Library of Congress*] (LCLS)

OkMuV......... United States Veterans Administration Hospital, Muskogee, OK [*Library symbol Library of Congress*] (LCLS)

OKMV .... Okra Mosaic Virus [*Plant pathology*]

OKN .... Northeastern Oklahoma State University, Tahlequah, OK [*OCLC symbol*] (OCLC)

OKN .... Okmulgee Northern Railway Co. [*AAR code*]

OKN .... Okondja [*Gabon*] [*Airport symbol*] (OAG)

OKN .... Optokinetic Nystagmus [*Ophthalmology*]

OkN .... Pioneer Multi-County Library, Norman, OK [*Library symbol Library of Congress*] (LCLS)

OKNC .... Newbridge Communication Network Corp., Kanata, Ontario [*Library symbol National Library of Canada*] (BIB)

OKNeoAC..... Neo-American Church, the Original Kleptonian [*An association*] (EA)

OkNNS .... National Severe Storms Laboratory, Norman, OK [*Library symbol Library of Congress*] (LCLS)

OKNO........... Kuwait International NOTAM Office [*Kuwait*] [*ICAO location identifier*] (ICLI)

OKO .... Oral Roberts University, Tulsa, OK [*OCLC symbol*] (OCLC)

OKOH........... Penrose Division, Ongwanada Hospital, Kingston, Ontario [*Library symbol National Library of Canada*] (NLC)

OkOk........... Oklahoma County Libraries, Oklahoma City, OK [*Library symbol Library of Congress*] (LCLS)

OkOkB......... Oklahoma Library for the Blind and Physically Handicapped, Oklahoma City, OK [*Library symbol Library of Congress*] (LCLS)

OkOkC.......... Oklahoma Christian College, Oklahoma City, OK [*Library symbol*] [*Library of Congress*] (LCLS)

OkOkCGS .... Oklahoma City Geological Survey, Inc., Oklahoma City, OK [*Library symbol*] [*Library of Congress*] (LCLS)

OkOkD .... Deaconess Hospital, Oklahoma City, OK [*Library symbol Library of Congress*] (LCLS)

OkOke .... Okemah Public Library, Okemah, OK [*Library symbol*] [*Library of Congress*] (LCLS)

OkOkFA....... United States Federal Aviation Administration, Civil Aeromedical Institute, Oklahoma City, OK [*Library symbol Library of Congress*] (LCLS)

OkOkGS ...... Church of Jesus Christ of Latter-Day Saints, Genealogical Society Library, Oklahoma City Branch, Oklahoma City, OK [*Library symbol Library of Congress*] (LCLS)

OkOkK .... Kerr-McGee Corp., Oklahoma City, OK [*Library symbol Library of Congress*] (LCLS)

OkOkM .... Mid-America Bible College, Oklahoma City, OK [*Library symbol*] [*Library of Congress*] (LCLS)

OkOkSO ...... Oklahoma City Community College, Learning Resources Center, Oklahoma City, OK [*Library symbol Library of Congress*] (LCLS)

OkOkU .... Oklahoma City University, Oklahoma City, OK [*Library symbol Library of Congress*] (LCLS)

OkOkU-L ...... Oklahoma City University, Law Library, Oklahoma City, OK [*Library symbol Library of Congress*] (LCLS)

OkOkV......... United States Veterans Administration Hospital, Oklahoma City, OK [*Library symbol Library of Congress*] (LCLS)

OKOT .... Otonabee Township Library, Keen, Ontario [*Library symbol National Library of Canada*] (NLC)

OKP .... Citizens' Parliamentary Club [*Poland*] [*Political party*]

OKP .... Oksapmin [*Papua New Guinea*] [*Airport symbol*] (OAG)

OKP .... O'okiep Copper ADR [*AMEX symbol*] (TTSB)

OKP .... O'Okiep Copper Co. Ltd. [*AMEX symbol*] (SPSG)

OKP .... Optimized Kill Probability

OKP .... Southern Prairie Library System, Altus, OK [*OCLC symbol*] (OCLC)

OkPo........... Ponca City Public Library, Ponca City, OK [*Library symbol Library of Congress*] (LCLS)

OkPoC......... Continental Oil Co., R and D Technical Information Service, Ponca City, OK [*Library symbol Library of Congress*] (LCLS)

OkPot.......... Buckley Public Library, Poteau, OK [*Library symbol Library of Congress*] (LCLS)

OKQ .... Okaba [*Indonesia*] [*Airport symbol*] (OAG)

OKQ .... Queen's University, Kingston, Ontario [*Library symbol National Library of Canada*] (NLC)

OKQA.......... Agnes Etherington Art Centre, Queen's University, Kingston, Ontario [*Library symbol National Library of Canada*] (NLC)

OKQAR........ Archives, Queen's University, Kingston, Ontario [*Library symbol National Library of Canada*] (NLC)

OKQCI.......... Canadian Institute of Guided Ground Transport, Queen's University, Kingston, Ontario [*Library symbol National Library of Canada*] (NLC)

OKQG.......... Department of Geography, Queen's University, Kingston, Ontario [*Library symbol National Library of Canada*] (NLC)

OKQGS........ Department of Geological Sciences, Queen's University, Kingston, Ontario [*Library symbol National Library of Canada*] (NLC)

OKQH.......... Bracken Library, Queen's University, Kingston, Ontario [*Library symbol National Library of Canada*] (NLC)

OKQL .... Law Library, Queen's University, Kingston, Ontario [*Library symbol National Library of Canada*] (NLC)

OKQM .... McArthur College of Education, Queen's University, Kingston, Ontario [*Library symbol National Library of Canada*] (NLC)

OKQMA........ Map Collection, Douglas Library, Queen's University, Kingston, Ontario [*Library symbol National Library of Canada*] (NLC)

OKR .... Optical Key Reader [*Automotive engineering*]

OKR .... Royal Military College of Canada, Kingston, Ontario [*Library symbol National Library of Canada*] (NLC)

OKRC .... Regiopolis - Notre Dame High School, Kingston, Ontario [*Library symbol National Library of Canada*] (NLC)

Ok Reg .... Oklahoma Register [*A publication*] (AAGC)

OKRGI.......... Rutherford and George Island Township Public Library, Killarney, Ontario [*Library symbol National Library of Canada*] (NLC)

OKRS .... Science Engineering Library, Royal Military College of Canada, Kingston, Ontario [*Library symbol National Library of Canada*] (BIB)

OKS .... Ohio Kache Systems Corp.

OKS .... Okanagan Skeena Group Ltd. [*Vancouver Stock Exchange symbol Toronto Stock Exchange symbol*]

OkS .... Oklahoma State University, Stillwater, OK [*Library symbol Library of Congress*] (LCLS)

OKS .... Old King's Scholars Association [*Canterbury, England*]

OKS .... Oshkosh, NE [*Location identifier FAA*] (FAAL)

OKSB .... Southwest Bancorp [*NASDAQ symbol*] (SAG)

OKSBP .... Southwest Bcp 9.2% cm 'A'Pfd [*NASDAQ symbol*] (TTSB)

OkShB.......... Oklahoma Baptist University, Shawnee, OK [*Library symbol Library of Congress*] (LCLS)

OKSL .... St. Lawrence College of Applied Arts and Technology, Kingston, Ontario [*Library symbol National Library of Canada*] (NLC)

OKSMG .... Gibson Medical Library, St. Mary's of the Lake Hospital, Kingston, Ontario [*Library symbol National Library of Canada*] (NLC)

OkS-T........... Oklahoma State University Technical Institute Library, Oklahoma City, OK [*Library symbol Library of Congress*] (LCLS)

OkSt............ Stillwater Public Library, Stillwater, OK [*Library symbol Library of Congress*] (LCLS)

OkS-TBO ...... Oklahoma State University Technical Branch, Okmulgee, OK [*Library symbol*] [*Library of Congress*] (LCLS)

OKT .... [*The*] Oakland Terminal Railway [*Later, OTR*] [*AAR code*]

okt .... Oktober [*October*] [*GRM*] (AD)

okt .... Oktyab [*October*] [*Russian*] (AD)

OKT .... Ollier-Klippel-Trenaunay [*Syndrome*] [*Medicine*] (DB)

OKT .... Oslo Kommune Tunnelbanekontoret [*Oslo Subway System*] (AD)

OkT .... Tulsa City-County Library System, Tulsa, OK [*Library symbol Library of Congress*] (LCLS)

OKT .... University of Tulsa, Tulsa, OK [*OCLC symbol*] (OCLC)

OKT .... Yoakum, TX [*Location identifier FAA*] (FAAL)

OkTA .... American Association of Petroleum Geologists, Energy Resources Library, Tulsa, OK [*Library symbol*] [*Library of Congress*] (LCLS)

OkTahN .... Northeastern State College, Tahlequah, OK [*Library symbol Library of Congress*] (LCLS)

OkTAm .... AMOCO Production Co., Research Center Geology Library, Tulsa, OK [*Library symbol Library of Congress*] (LCLS)

OkTC .... Ceja Corp., Tulsa, OK [*Library symbol Library of Congress*] (LCLS)

OkTCS.......... Cities Service Co., Energy Resources Group, E & P Library, Tulsa, OK [*Library symbol Library of Congress*] (LCLS)

OkTG .... Thomas Gilcrease Institute of American History and Art, Tulsa, OK [*Library symbol Library of Congress*] (LCLS)

OkTGS .... Church of Jesus Christ of Latter-Day Saints, Genealogical Society Library, TulsaBranch, Tulsa, OK [*Library symbol Library of Congress*] (LCLS)

OkTo .... Tonkawa Public Library, Tonkawa, OK [*Library symbol Library of Congress*] (LCLS)

OkTOR .... Oral Roberts University, Learning Resources Center, Tulsa, OK [*Library symbol Library of Congress*] (LCLS)

OkTPA.......... Pan American Oil Corp., Research Library, Tulsa, OK [*Library symbol Library of Congress*] (LCLS)

OkTPh.......... Philbrook Art Center, Tulsa, OK [*Library symbol*] [*Library of Congress*] (LCLS)

Oktronics ..... Oklahoma Electronics (AD)

OkTU........... University of Tulsa, Tulsa, OK [*Library symbol Library of Congress*] (LCLS)

OkTU-L .... University of Tulsa, College of Law, Tulsa, OK [*Library symbol Library of Congress*] (LCLS)

oku.............. Oklahoma [*MARC country of publication code Library of Congress*] (LCCP)

OKU .... Omicron Kappa Upsilon [*Fraternity*]

OkU.............. University of Oklahoma, Norman, OK [*Library symbol Library of Congress*] (LCLS)

OkU-C .... University of Oklahoma, Communication Department, Political Communications Center, Political Commercial Archives, Norman, OK [*Library symbol*] [*Library of Congress*] (LCLS)

OkU-L .... University of Oklahoma, Law School, Norman, OK [*Library symbol Library of Congress*] (LCLS)

OkU-M .... University of Oklahoma, Health Sciences Center, Oklahoma City, OK [*Library symbol Library of Congress*] (LCLS)

OkU-P .... University of Oklahoma, College of Pharmacy, Norman, OK [*Library symbol Library of Congress*] (LCLS)

OKUTD......... Urban Transportation Development Corp., Kingston, Ontario [*Library symbol National Library of Canada*] (NLC)

OkU-TM .... University of Oklahoma, Tulsa Medical College, Tulsa, OK [*Library symbol Library of Congress*] (LCLS)

OkU-W .... University of Oklahoma, Western History Collections, Norman, OK [*Library symbol*] [*Library of Congress*] (LCLS)

OKV .... University of Oklahoma, Library School, Norman, OK [*OCLC symbol*] (OCLC)

OKW .... Brookwood, AL [*Location identifier FAA*] (FAAL)

OKW .... Oberkommando der Wehrmacht [*Armed Forces High Command*] [*German military - World War II*]

OKW	University of Tulsa, College of Law, Tulsa, OK [*OCLC symbol*] (OCLC)
OK W/C	Okay Except for [*with*] the Corrections [*Proofreading*] (WDMC)
OkWeaT	Southwestern State College, Weatherford, OK [*Library symbol Library of Congress*] (LCLS)
OkWo	Woodward Carnegie Library, Woodward, OK [*Library symbol Library of Congress*] (LCLS)
OKX	Central State University, Edmond, OK [*OCLC symbol*] (OCLC)
OKXS	Xenotech Systems, Inc., Kitchener, Ontario [*Library symbol National Library of Canada*] (NLC)
OKY	Oakey [*Queensland*] [*Airport symbol*] (AD)
OKY	Oklahoma City University, Law Library, Oklahoma City, OK [*OCLC symbol*] (OCLC)
OKZ	Phillips University, Zollars Memorial Library, Enid, OK [*OCLC symbol*] (OCLC)
OKZ	Sandersville, GA [*Location identifier FAA*] (FAAL)
OL	London Public Library, Ontario [*Library symbol National Library of Canada*] (NLC)
O/L	Observation/Losing [*Army*] (ADDR)
OL	Occupational Level
OL	Ocean Letter
OL	October League (AD)
ol	Oculus Laevus [*Left Eye*] [*Latin*] (AD)
OL	Oculus Laevus [*Left Eye*] [*Ophthalmology*]
OL	Odd Lot [*Stock exchange term*]
OL	Office Lady [*Japan*] (ECON)
OL	Officer of the Order of Leopold
OL	Official Liquidator [*British*] (ROG)
OL	Ohio Laws [*A publication*] (DLA)
ol	Oil [*Pharmacy*] (CPH)
OL	Oil Level (AAG)
ol	Oil Level (AD)
OL	Oil Lighter [*Shipping*] [*British*]
OL	Oiseau-Lyre [*Record label*] [*France*]
OL	Oldham [*Postcode*] (ODBW)
OL	Old Latin [*Language, etc.*]
OL	Old Leysian (WDAA)
Ol	Oldradus da Ponte de Laude [*Deceased, 1335*] [*Authority cited in pre-1607 legal work*] (DSA)
OL	Oleum [*Oil*] [*Pharmacy*]
ol	Oleum [*Oil*] [*Latin*] (AD)
OL	Oligoblastic Leukemia [*Oncology*]
OL	Olivary [*Neurology*]
ol	Olive [*Philately*]
Ol	Olive [*Political party*] (AD)
ol	Olivine [*CIPW classification*] [*Geology*]
OL	Olsen Line (AD)
Ol	Olympian [*of Pindar*] [*Classical studies*] (OCD)
OL	Olympic
OL	Olympic Lift [*Sports*]
OL	Online
OL	Only Loadable [*Computer science*] (IAA)
OL	Open Learning (AIE)
OL	Open Loop
OL	Operating Level (IEEE)
OL	Operating License
ol	Operating License (AD)
OL	Operating Limit (COE)
OL	Operating Location [*Army*]
OL	Operating Log
OL	Operating Loss
OL	Operational Left [*NASA*] (NAKS)
OL	Operation Liftoff (EA)
O/L	Operations/Logistics
o/l	Operations/Logistics (AD)
OL	Orbital Launch
OL	Order of Lafayette (EA)
OL	Ordinary Leave [*Military*] (AFM)
OL	Ordinary Letter (WDAA)
OL	Ordnance Lieutenant [*Navy British*]
OL	Organization List (MCD)
OL	Original Learning [*Psychometrics*]
OL	Or Less
ol	Or Less (AD)
OL	Oscillating Limiter (IAA)
OL	Ostfriesische Lufttransport GmbH [*Germany ICAO designator*] (ICDA)
OL	Other Line [*Telecommunications*] (TEL)
OL	Outgoing Letter
o/l	Outlook (AD)
OL	Output Latch
OL	Outside Left [*Soccer position*]
OL	Overflow Level
OL	Overhead Line
OL	Overlap
OL	Overlay (NASA)
OL	Overload
OLA	Lakefield Public Library, Ontario [*Library symbol National Library of Canada*] (NLC)
OLA	National Oceanic and Atmospheric Administration, Rockville, MD [*OCLC symbol*] (OCLC)
OLA	Oaklahoma Lumbermen's Association (WPI)
ola	Occipito-Laeva Anterior (AD)
OLA	Occipitolaeva Anterior [*A fetal position*] [*Medicine*] (AAMN)
OLA	Occupiers' Liability Act [*1957*] [*British*] (DCTA)
OLA	Office of Legislative Affairs
OLA	Office of Legislative Analysis [*Environmental Protection Agency*] (GFGA)
OLA/	Official Languages Act [*Canada*]
OLA	Ohio Law Abstract [*A publication*] (DLA)
OLA	Ohio Library Association (AD)
OLA	Oklahoma Library Association (AD)
OLA	Oligonucleotide Ligation Assay [*Analytical biochemistry*]
OLA	Ontario Library Association [*Canada*] (AD)
OLA	Optical Laboratories Association (EA)
OLA	Optical Link in the Atmosphere (PDAA)
OLA	Optimally Localized Averages [*Mathematics*]
OLA	Orbital Lock Assembly
OLA	Orland [*Norway*] [*Airport symbol*] (OAG)
OLA	Osteopathic Libraries Association [*Defunct*] (EA)
OLA	Overview Latin America (EA)
OLAA	Office of Legal Aid Administration
OL Abs	Ohio Law Abstract [*A publication*] (DLA)
OLAC	Offline Adaptive Computer [*Computer science*]
OLAC	Online Audiovisual Catalogers [*An association*] (EA)
OLADE	Organizacion Latin-Americana de Energia [*Latin American Energy Organization*] [*Spanish*] (AD)
OLAFL	Front of Leeds and Lansdowne Public Library, Lansdowne, Ontario [*Library symbol National Library of Canada*] (NLC)
OLAFS	Office of Legal Aid and Family Services
OLAFS	Orbiting and Launch Approach Flight Simulator
OLAG	London Research Center, Agriculture Canada [*Centre de Recherches de London, Agriculture Canada*] London, Ontario [*Library symbol National Library of Canada*] (NLC)
OLAG	Oesterreichische Luftverkehrs Aktiengesellschaft [*Austrian Airlines*]
OLak	Lakewood Public Library, Lakewood, OH [*Library symbol Library of Congress*] (LCLS)
OLakB	Lakewood Board of Education, Lakewood, OH [*Library symbol Library of Congress*] (LCLS)
OLAL	Bibliotheque Publique du Canton d'Alfred [*Alfred Township Public Library*],Lefaivre, Ontario [*Library symbol National Library of Canada*] (BIB)
OLAMINE	Ethanolamine [*Also, EA, Etn*] [*USAN*] [*Organic chemistry*]
OLAN	Landsdowne Public Library, Ontario [*Library symbol National Library of Canada*] (BIB)
OLA-N	Office of Legislative Affairs, Navy (MUGU)
OLAN	On-Board Local Area Network [*Aviation*]
O/LAND	Overland
O/LANDED	Overlanded
OL & T	Owners, Landlords, and Tenants [*Liability insurance*]
ol & t	Owners, Landlords, and Tenants (AD)
OL&T	Owners, Landlords, and Tenants [*Insurance*]
OLanF	Fairfield County District Library, Lancaster, OH [*Library symbol Library of Congress*] (LCLS)
OLanU	Ohio University, Lancaster Branch Campus, Lancaster, OH [*Library symbol Library of Congress*] (LCLS)
OLAP	Online Analytical Processing [*Computer science*] (CDE)
OLAPEC	Organization of Latin American Petroleum Exporting Countries (AD)
OLAR	On-Line Analytical Processing [*Computer science*]
OLAS	Office of Arid Land Studies [*University of Arizona*] (AD)
OLAS	On-Line Acquisitions Systems [*Brodart, Inc.*] [*Book acquisition system*] [*Information service or system*] (IID)
OLAS	Organizacion Latino-Americana de Solidaridad [*Latin American Solidarity Organization*] [*Spanish*] (AD)
OLAS	Organization of Latin American Students (AD)
OLATN	Township of Norfolk Public Library, Langton, Ontario [*Library symbol National Library of Canada*] (NLC)
OLAU	Lanark Union Public Library, Lanark, Ontario [*Library symbol National Library of Canada*] (BIB)
Olav Tryg	Olav Trygvason (AD)
OLB	London Board of Education, Ontario [*Library symbol National Library of Canada*] (NLC)
OLB	Odd-Lot Broker [*Finance*] (MHDW)
OLB	Oertlicher Landwirtschaftsbetrieb [*Local Agricultural Enterprise*] [*German*]
OLB	Official Log Book [*Ship's diary*] (DS)
OLB	Ohio Law Bulletin [*A publication*] (DLA)
OLB	Olbia [*Italy*] [*Airport symbol*] (OAG)
OLB	Omaha, Lincoln & Beatrice Railway Co. [*AAR code*]
OLB	Online Batch (NITA)
OLB	Open Liver Biopsy [*Medicine*] (DMAA)
OLB	Open-Loop Bandwidth [*Also, OLBW*]
OLB	Open Lung Biopsy
OLB	Outer Lead Bond [*Integrated circuit technology*]
OLB	Outside Linebacker [*Football*]
OLBA	Beirut/International [*Lebanon*] [*ICAO location identifier*] (ICLI)
OLBGFC	Official Lane Brody Global Fan Club (EA)
OLBIEN	Olsen's Biomass Energy [*G. V. Olsen Associates*] [*Information service or system*] (CRD)
olbm	Orbital Launched Balistic Missile (AD)
OLBM	Orbital Launched Ballistic Missile [*Military*] (WDAA)
OLBM	Overlay Battle Manager
OLBR	Brescia College, London, Ontario [*Library symbol National Library of Canada*] (NLC)
OlBr	Olive Brown (AD)
OLBR	Operational LASER Beam Recorder
OLBS	OnLine Bookstore
OLBV	Beirut [*Lebanon*] [*ICAO location identifier*] (ICLI)
OLBW	Open-Loop Bandwidth [*Also, OLB*]
olc	Brothers of Our Lady of Providence (TOCD)

OLC.............. Catholic Central High School, London, Ontario [*Library symbol National Library of Canada*] (NLC)
OLC.............. Linfield College, McMinnville, OR [*OCLC symbol*] (OCLC)
OLC.............. Oak Leaf Cluster [*Military decoration*]
OLC.............. Office of Legal Counsel [*Department of Justice*]
Olc............... Olcott's United States District Court Reports, Admiralty [*A publication*] (DLA)
OLC.............. Olema [*California*] [*Seismograph station code, US Geological Survey*] (SEIS)
OLC.............. Oneida, TN [*Location identifier FAA*] (FAAL)
OLC.............. Online Computer [*System*] [*Computer science*]
olc............... On-Line Computer (AD)
OLC.............. Ontario Ladies College
OLC.............. Ontario Library Co-Operative [*UTLAS symbol*]
OLC.............. Open-Loop Control (CIST)
OLC.............. Operation Load Code (MCD)
OLC.............. Operator-Level Chart (AFIT)
OLC.............. Order Location and Control (MCD)
OLC.............. Oubain-Like Compound [*Biochemistry*]
OLC.............. Outgoing Line Circuit
OLC.............. Overseas Liaison Committee [*of the American Council on Education*] [*Later, Division of International Educational Relations of the American Council on Education*] (EA)
OLC.............. Sisters of Our Lady of Charity (TOCD)
OLCA............ Online Circuit Analysis [*System*] [*Computer science*]
Olc Adm....... Olcott's United States District Court Reports, Admiralty [*A publication*] (DLA)
OLCAO......... Orthogonalized Linear Combination of Atomic Orbitals [*Optics*]
OLCC........... Ontario Cancer Clinic, London, Ontario [*Library symbol National Library of Canada*] (NLC)
OLCC........... Optimum Life Cycle Costing (PDAA)
olcc............. Optimum Life-Cycle Costing (AD)
OLCC........... Ordinary Low Current Configuration [*Magnetic field*]
OLCC........... Our Lady of Cincinnati College [*Ohio*]
OLCC........... Overseas Labour Consultative Committee [*British*] (DCTA)
OLCD........... Overseas Liaison and Consultancy Department (NITA)
OLCG........... Clarkson Gordon, London, Ontario [*Library symbol National Library of Canada*] (BIB)
OLCM........... Olicom AS [*NASDAQ symbol*] (SAG)
OLCMF......... Olicom A/S [*NASDAQ symbol*] (TTSB)
Ol Conv........ Oliver's Conveyancing [*A publication*] (DLA)
Olcott.......... Olcott's United States District Court Reports, Admiralty [*A publication*] (DLA)
Olcott Adm (F)... Olcott's United States District Court Reports, Admiralty [*A publication*] (DLA)
Olcott's Adm... Olcott's United States District Court Reports, Admiralty [*A publication*] (DLA)
OLCP........... Online Complex Processing [*Computer science*] (CDE)
OLCPR......... Canadian Peace Research Institute, London, Ontario [*Library symbol National Library of Canada*] (NLC)
OLCR........... Clark Road Secondary School, London, Ontario [*Library symbol National Library of Canada*] (NLC)
O L Cr......... Ordinance Lieutenent-Commander (AD)
OLCR........... Ordnance Lieutenant-Commander [*Navy British*]
OLCR........... Sisters of Our Lady of Charity of Refuge [*Roman Catholic religious order*]
OLCS........... On-Line Computer System (AD)
OLCSSCP..... Children's Psychiatric Research Institute, Ontario Ministry of Community and Social Services, London, Ontario [*Library symbol National Library of Canada*] (NLC)
OLCT.......... Tax Services, Canada Trust Co., London, Ontario [*Library symbol National Library of Canada*] (BIB)
OLCV.......... Century Village, Lang, Ontario [*Library symbol National Library of Canada*] (BIB)
OLD........... Obstructive Lung Disease [*Medicine*] (DMAA)
OLD........... Odd Lot Dealer
OLD........... Office of Legislative Development [*Bureau of Indian Affairs*]
OLD........... Ohio Lower Court Decisions [*A publication*] (DLA)
Old............ Oldradus da Ponte de Laude [*Deceased, 1335*] [*Authority cited in pre-1607 legal work*] (DSA)
Old............ Oldright's Nova Scotia Reports [*A publication*] (DLA)
OLD........... Old Town, ME [*Location identifier FAA*] (FAAL)
OLD........... Online Debug [*Computer science*] (IAA)
OLD........... On-Line Tests and Diagnostics [*Environmental science*] (COE)
OLD........... Open-Loop Damping
OLD........... Operating Level Days
OLD........... Operations and Liquidations Division [*Federal Savings and Loans Insurance Corporation*]
OLD........... Oral Lethal Dose [*Medicine*]
OLD........... Orthochromatic Leukodystrophy [*Medicine*] (DMAA)
OLD........... Our Lady of Deliverance Syriac, Union City [*Diocesan abbreviation*] [*New Jersey*] (TOCD)
OLD........... Oxford Latin Dictionary [*A publication*]
OldAmer...... Old America Stores, Inc. [*Associated Press*] (SAG)
OLDAP........ Online Data Processor (PDAA)
OLDB......... Old National Bancorp [*NASDAQ symbol*] (NQ)
OLDB......... Old Natl Bancorp(Ind) [*NASDAQ symbol*] (TTSB)
OLDB......... On-Line Data Bank [*NASA*] (NAKS)
OLDB......... Online Database [*or Data Bank*]
Old Bailey ... London's Central Criminal Court [*England*] (AD)
Old Bailey Chr... Old Bailey Chronicle [*A publication*] (DLA)
Old Ben...... Benloe in Benloe and Dalison's English Common Pleas Reports [*A publication*] (DLA)
Old Benloe... Benloe in Benloe and Dalison's English Common Pleas Reports [*A publication*] (DLA)

OLDC.......... Online Data Collection [*Computer science*] (MCD)
OLDD.......... Beirut [*Lebanon*] [*ICAO location identifier*] (ICLI)
OldDom...... Old Dominion Freight Lines, Inc. [*Associated Press*] (SAG)
Old Dom U... Old Dominion University (GAGS)
OLD ECC..... Ordinary Linear Differential Equations with Constant Coefficients [*Mathematics*]
Old Ent....... Rastell's Old Entries [*A publication*] (DLA)
OLDERT...... On-Line Executive for Real-Time [*Computer science*] (MHDB)
old-fash...... Old Fashioned (AD)
Oldfos....... Old Established Forces (AD)
OLDFOS...... Old Established Forces [*Military*] (CINC)
OLDHM....... Oldham [*City in England*]
OLDI.......... Online Data Interchange (DA)
OLDIV........ Operations/Lookout and Recognition Division (DNAB)
OldKent...... Old Kent Financial Corp. [*Associated Press*] (SAG)
Old Maid's... Old Maid's Day [*June 4*] (AD)
Old Nat Brev... Old Natura Brevium [*A publication*] (DLA)
OldNB........ Old National Bancorp Industries [*Associated Press*] (SAG)
Oldn Pr....... Oldnall's Sessions Practice [*A publication*] (DLA)
Oldr.......... Oldradus da Ponte de Laude [*Deceased, 1335*] [*Authority cited in pre-1607 legal work*] (DSA)
Oldr.......... Oldright's Nova Scotia Reports [*A publication*] (DLA)
OLDR........ Quick Look Data Reference [*NASA*] (NAKS)
Oldra......... Oldradus da Ponte de Laude [*Deceased, 1335*] [*Authority cited in pre-1607 legal work*] (DSA)
Oldra de Lau... Oldradus da Ponte de Laude [*Deceased, 1335*] [*Authority cited in pre-1607 legal work*] (DSA)
old rep....... Old Repertory (AD)
OldRep....... Old Republic International Corp. [*Associated Press*] (SAG)
Oldr NS...... Oldright's Nova Scotia Reports [*A publication*] (DLA)
OldRp........ Old Republic International Corp. [*Associated Press*] (SAG)
OLDS........ Off-Axis LASER Detection System (MCD)
OLDS........ Offshore Lease Data System [*Department of the Interior*] [*Information service or system*] (IID)
OLDS........ Oldsmobile [*Automotive engineering*]
Olds......... Oldsmobile (AD)
OLDS........ On-Line Detection System [*Nuclear energy*]
OLDS........ Online Display System [*Computer science*]
Old SC...... Old Select Cases [*Oudh, India*] [*A publication*] (DLA)
OldSecBc.... Old Second Bancorp, Inc. [*Associated Press*] (SAG)
OLDSS....... Online Database Search Services Directory [*A publication*]
Old Test...... Old Testament (AD)
OLE.......... Lane Community College, Eugene, OR [*OCLC symbol*] (OCLC)
OLE.......... Leamington Public Library, Ontario [*Library symbol National Library of Canada*] (NLC)
OLe.......... Lebanon Public Library, Lebanon, OH [*Library symbol Library of Congress*] (LCLS)
OLE.......... Object Linking and Embedding [*Windows*] [*Computer science*]
OLE.......... Office for Library Education [*American Library Association*]
OLE.......... Olean [*New York*] [*Airport symbol*] (AD)
OLE.......... Olean, NY [*Location identifier FAA*] (FAAL)
OLE.......... On-Line Encyclopedia [*Hypergraphics Corp.*]
OLE.......... Online Enquiry [*System*]
OLE.......... Ontario Land Economist [*Canada*] (DD)
OLE.......... Oral Language Evaluation [*English and Spanish test*]
OLE.......... Organizational Leadership for Executives [*Military*] (RDA)
OLE.......... Oriole Communication [*Vancouver Stock Exchange symbol*]
OLE.......... Outside Location Engineer (MCD)
OLEA........ Office of Law Enforcement Assistance (AD)
OLeC........ Lebanon Correctional Institution Library, Lebanon, OH [*Library symbol Library of Congress*] (LCLS)
Oleck Corporations... Oleck's Modern Corporation Law [*A publication*] (DLA)
OLED........ Organic Light-Emitting Device [*Photonics*]
OLED........ Organic Light Emitting Diode [*Electronics*]
OLE DB...... OLE Database [*Computer science*]
O Legal News... Ohio Legal News [*A publication*] (DLA)
OLEI......... Point Pelee National Park, Parks Canada [*Parc National de la Pointe-Pelee, Parcs Canada*] Leamington, Ontario [*Library symbol National Library of Canada*] (NLC)
OLELB....... Lyn Branch, Elizabethtown Township Public Library, Ontario [*Library symbol National Library of Canada*] (BIB)
OLEM........ Other Loans Especially Mentioned (EBF)
oleo......... Oleomargarine [*Dietetics*] (DAVI)
oleo......... Oleoresins (AD)
OLEP........ Office of Law Enforcement and Planning (AD)
OLEP........ Office of Law Enforcement Programs [*Federal government*]
OLEP........ Office of Legal Enforcement Policy [*Environmental Protection Agency*] (EPA)
OLEP........ Organization for the Lifelong Establishment of Paternity (EA)
OLER........ Olericulture
olericult..... Olericulture (AD)
OLERT....... Online Executive for Real Time [*Computer science*] (IEEE)
OLES........ Online Editorial System [*Computer science*] (DGA)
OLESS....... Open Learning Electronic Support Services [*Australia*]
O level...... Ordinary Level (ODBW)
O-level...... Ordinary Level Examination [*Education*] (WDAA)
O-levels..... Ordinary Levels [*of educational tests*] (AD)
OLeWHi...... Warren County Historical Society, Lebanon, OH [*Library symbol Library of Congress*] (LCLS)
OLF......... Ohio Library Foundation (AD)
OLF......... Old Low Franconian [*Language, etc.*]
olf......... Olfactory [*Medicine*] (DAVI)
OLF......... Online Filing [*Computer science*] (PDAA)
olf......... On-Line Filing (AD)

OLF.............. Only Living Father [*of Newfoundland's confederation with Canada in 1949*] [*Epithet for Joseph R. Smallwood*]

OLF.............. Open Learning Federation [*British*] (DI)

OLF.............. Orbital Launch Facility

OLF.............. Orbiter Landing Facility [*NASA*] (NASA)

OLF.............. Organ Literature Foundation (EA)

OLF.............. Oromo Liberation Front [*Ethiopia*] [*Political party*] (PD)

OLF.............. Outline Font [*Computer science*] (PCM)

OLF.............. Outlying Field [*Army*]

OLF.............. Wolf Point [*Montana*] [*Airport symbol*] (OAG)

OLF.............. Wolf Point, MT [*Location identifier FAA*] (FAAL)

OLFC............. Fanshawe College of Applied Arts and Technology, London, Ontario [*Library symbol National Library of Canada*] (NLC)

OLFDEMO .... Outline Font Demonstration [*Computer science*]

OLFO............. Open-Loop Feedback Optimal (PDAA)

OLFR .... Olfactory Receptor [*Medicine*] (DMAA)

OLG............. Nordmaling [*Sweden*] [*Airport symbol*] (AD)

OLG............. Oberlandesgericht [*District Court of Appeal*] [*German*] (DLA)

OLG............. Ohio Legislative Service Commission, Columbus, OH [*OCLC symbol*] (OCLC)

OLG............. Old Low German [*Language, etc.*]

OLG............. Oligodendrocyte [*Also, ODC*] [*Cytology*]

OIG.............. Olive Green (AD)

OLG.............. Open-Loop Gain

OLG.............. Sisters of Guadalupe [*Roman Catholic religious order*]

OLG.............. Sisters of Our Lady of the Garden [*Roman Catholic religious order*]

OLGA.......... On-line Guitar Archive [*Internet site*]

OLGC.......... Orthologic Corp. [*NASDAQ symbol*] (SAG)

OLGR.......... [*The*] Oilgear Co. [*NASDAQ symbol*] (NQ)

OLH.............. Huron College, London, Ontario [*Library symbol National Library of Canada*] (NLC)

OLH.............. Old Harbor [*Alaska*] [*Airport symbol*] (OAG)

OLH.............. Old Harbor, AK [*Location identifier FAA*] (FAAL)

OLH.............. Orpen's Light Horse [*British military*] (DMA)

OLH.............. Ovine Lactogenic Hormone [*Endocrinology*] (MAE)

OLH.............. Ovine Luteinizing Hormone [*Endocrinology*]

OLH.............. Oxfordshire Light Horse [*British military*] (DMA)

OLHC........... Old Lyme Holding Corp. [*NASDAQ symbol*] (SAG)

OLHM .... London Historical Museums, Ontario [*Library symbol National Library of Canada*] (BIB)

OLHMIS...... On-Line Hospital Management Information System [*Computer science*]

OI Horse ..... Oliphant's Law of Horses [*6th ed.*] [*1908*] [*A publication*] (DLA)

OLI.............. Lindsay Public Library, Ontario [*Library symbol National Library of Canada*] (NLC)

OLI.............. Ocean Living Institute [*Defunct*] (EA)

OLI.............. Olafsvik [*Iceland*] [*Airport symbol*] (OAG)

OLI.............. Oliktok, AK [*Location identifier FAA*] (FAAL)

OIi.............. Oliver (AD)

OLI.............. Online Information

OLI.............. Open Learning Institute [*UTLAS symbol*]

OLI.............. Open Link Interface (TNIG)

OLI.............. Operation Lifesaver [*An association*] (EA)

OLI.............. Out-of-Line Igniter [*Military*] (CAAL)

OLI.............. Out-of-Line Interrupter (MCD)

OLI.............. Overlay Interceptor

OLI.............. Oxfordshire Light Infantry [*Military unit*] [*British*]

OLiC........... Columbiana County Court House, Lisbon, OH [*Library symbol Library of Congress*] (LCLS)

OLIC........... Online Information Centre (NITA)

OLIC........... On-Line Inspection Centre [*British Gas*] (WDAA)

OL-IC......... Operating Location-Iceland (DNAB)

O-license..... Operator's License (AD)

Olicom........ Olicom AS [*Associated Press*] (SAG)

OLICU........ Little Current Public Library, Ontario [*Library symbol National Library of Canada*] (NLC)

OLICUS........ Sucker Creek Indian Band Public Library, Little Current, Ontario [*Library symbol National Library of Canada*] (NLC)

OLIDS .... Open Loop Insulin Delivery System [*Medicine*] (DMAA)

OLIF............. Orbiter Landing Instrumentation Facilities [*NASA*] (NASA)

OLIFLM....... Online Image Forming Light Modulator

Olig.............. Oligocene (AD)

OLIH .... Lion's Head Branch, Bruce County Public Library, Ontario [*Library symbol National Library of Canada*] (NLC)

OLIM........... Olimpiadas [*Ministerio de Cultura*] [*Spain Information service or system*] (CRD)

OLima........ Lima Public Library, Lima, OH [*Library symbol Library of Congress*] (LCLS)

OLimaAL...... Allen County Law Library, Lima, OH [*Library symbol Library of Congress*] (LCLS)

OLIMCH ...... Open Learning Information and Materials Clearing House [*Australia*]

Olin............. Olin Corp. [*Associated Press*] (SAG)

OLIP........... Online Instrument Package [*Computer science*] (NRCH)

Oliph Hor..... Oliphant's Law of Horses [*6th ed.*] [*1908*] [*A publication*] (DLA)

OLIS............. Listowel Public Library, Ontario [*Library symbol National Library of Canada*] (NLC)

OLIS............. Online Information Services [*Mercer County Community College Library*] (OLDSS)

OLIS............. Oregon Legislative Information System [*Information service or system*]

OLIS............. Oxford Library Information System (TNIG)

OLIS............. Oxford Library Integrated System [*British*] (TELE)

OLIS............. Oxide Layer Isolation Structure

OLISF.......... Frost Campus Library, Sir Sandford Fleming College, Lindsay, Ontario [*Library symbol National Library of Canada*] (NLC)

OLIT........... OPEN LOOK Intrinsic Toolkit

OLitW .... Wagnalls Memorial Library, Lithopolis, OH [*Library symbol Library of Congress*] (LCLS)

OLIV........... Oleum Olivae [*Olive Oil*] [*Pharmacy*] (ROG)

OLIV........... Victoria County Public Library, Lindsay, Ontario [*Library symbol National Library of Canada*] (NLC)

Oliv B & L ... Oliver, Beavan, and Lefroy's English Railway and Canal Cases [*A publication*] (DLA)

Oliv Conv.... Oliver's Conveyancing [*A publication*] (DLA)

Olive.......... Olivera (AD)

OLIVER .... Online Instrumentation via Energetic Radioisotopes [*Computer science*] (PDAA)

OLIVER .... Online Interactive Variable Editing Reporter [*Computer science*] (IAA)

Olivet Naz U... Olivet Nazarene University (GAGS)

Oliv Prec .... Oliver's Precedents [*A publication*] (DLA)

OLIVW .... Walden Public Library, Lively, Ontario [*Library symbol National Library of Canada*] (BIB)

OLJ............. Ohio Law Journal [*A publication*] (DLA)

OLJ............. Order of St. Lazarus of Jerusalem [*British*]

OLJ............. Oudh Law Journal [*India*] [*A publication*] (DLA)

OLJ............. Spokane, WA [*Location identifier FAA*] (FAAL)

OL Jour....... Ohio Law Journal [*A publication*] (DLA)

OL Jour....... Oudh Law Journal [*India*] [*A publication*] (DLA)

OLK............. King's College, London, Ontario [*Library symbol National Library of Canada*] (NLC)

OLK............. Salomon, Inc. [*AMEX symbol*] (SPSG)

OLK............. Salomon Inc, 7.25% ORCL'ELKS' [*AMEX symbol*] (TTSB)

OLK............. Wolf Lake, IN [*Location identifier FAA*] (FAAL)

OLKK .... Tripoli [*Lebanon*] [*ICAO location identifier*] (ICLI)

OLKV .... Tripoli [*Lebanon*] [*ICAO location identifier*] (ICLI)

OLL............. Larder Lake Public Library, Ontario [*Library symbol National Library of Canada*] (BIB)

OLL............. Office of Legislative Liaison (AD)

OLL............. Ollague [*Chile*] [*Seismograph station code, US Geological Survey Closed*] (SEIS)

OLL............. Organic Liquid LASER

OLL............. Our Lady of Lebanon of Los Angeles [*Diocesan abbreviation*] [*California*] (TOCD)

OLL............. Output Logic Level

OLLA........... Office of Lend-Lease Administration [*World War II*]

OLLA........... Oil Lands Leasing Act

OII B & F..... Ollivier, Bell, and Fitzgerald's New Zealand Reports [*A publication*] (DLA)

OLLC........... Office of the Liquor Licensing Commissioner [*South Australia*]

OLLC........... Our Lady of the Lake College [*Texas*]

OLLCR .... Labatt's Central Research Library, London, Ontario [*Library symbol National Library of Canada*] (NLC)

OLLE........... Lake Erie Regional Library System, London, Ontario [*Library symbol National Library of Canada*] (NLC)

OLLE........... Ontario Library Service - Thames, London, Ontario [*Library symbol National Library of Canada*] (NLC)

OLLI........... Online Library Index [*Western Michigan University*]

OLLIE.......... Operation Last Laugh Independence Expenditure [*Political Action Committee opposed to Oliver North's candidacy for United States Senator of Virginia*]

OL LINI SI ... Oleum Lini sine Igne [*Cold-Drawn Linseed Oil*] [*Pharmacy*] (ROG)

Olliv B & F... Ollivier, Bell, and Fitzgerald's New Zealand Reports [*A publication*] (DLA)

OLLL........... Beirut [*Lebanon*] [*ICAO location identifier*] (ICLI)

OLLS........... Online Logical Simulation System [*Computer science*] (KSC)

OLLT........... Office of Libraries and Learning Technologies (NITA)

OLLU .... Our Lady of the Lake University [*Texas*]

OLM........... Lloyd Library and Museum, Cincinnati, OH [*OCLC symbol*] (OCLC)

OLM........... Office for Laboratory Management [*DoD*] (MCD)

OLM........... Olympia [*Washington*] [*Airport symbol*] (AD)

OLM........... Olympia, WA [*Location identifier FAA*] (FAAL)

OLM........... Olympic Financial Ltd [*NYSE symbol*] (TTSB)

OLM........... Online Monitor [*Computer science*]

OLM........... Organic Leach Model [*Landfill technology*]

OLM........... Sisters of Charity of Our Lady of Mercy [*Roman Catholic religious order*]

OLMAT....... Otis Lennon Mental Ability Test (EDAC)

OLMC......... Output Logic Macrocell [*Computer science*]

OLMR......... Office of Labor Management Relations (AD)

OLMR......... Organic Liquid Moderated Reactor

olmr........... Organic Liquid-Moderator Reactor (AD)

Olms........... Decisions of the Judicial Committee of the Privy Council re the British North American Act, 1867, and the Canadian Constitution [*A publication*] (DLA)

OLMS......... Office of Labor-Management Standards [*Department of Labor*]

OLMS......... Osborn Laboratories of Marine Sciences [*New York Zoological Society*] [*Research center*] (RCD)

OLMSA .... Office of Life & Microgravity Sciences & Applications [*NASA*]

Olmsted...... Olmsted's Privy Council Decisions [*1867-1954*] [*A publication*] (DLA)

OLMT......... Organizational Level Maintenance Timer

OLMUG....... Online Librarian's Microcomputer User Group [*Teleconferencing system*]

OLMWPR..... Office of Labor-Management and Welfare-Pension Reports [*Department of Labor*]

OLN........... Colonia Sarmiento [*Argentina*] [*Airport symbol*] (AD)

OLN........... Lane Public Library, Hamilton, OH [*OCLC symbol*] (OCLC)

OLN........... Ohio Legal News [*A publication*] (DLA)

OLN........... Old Man, AK [*Location identifier FAA*] (FAAL)

OLN........... Olin Corp. [*NYSE symbol*] (TTSB)

OLN........... Online News (NITA)

OLO	Longlac Public Library, Ontario [*Library symbol National Library of Canada*] (NLC)
OLO	Olomouc [*Czechoslovakia*] [*Airport symbol*] (AD)
OLO	Olotillo [*Race of maize*]
OLO	Online Operation [*Computer science*]
OLO	Oologah [*Oklahoma*] [*Seismograph station code, US Geological Survey Closed*] (SEIS)
OLO	Operations Launch Order (MUGU)
OLO	Orbital Launch Operation
OLOC	Old Lesbians Organizing for Change [*An association*] (EA)
OLOE	Online Order Entry
OLOF	Levack Branch, Onaping Falls Public Library, Ontario [*Library symbol National Library of Canada*] (NLC)
Olofson	Olofsson Corp. [*Associated Press*] (SAG)
OLOFV	Olofsson Corp. [*NASDAQ symbol*] (SAG)
OLOG	Offshore Logistics [*NASDAQ symbol*] (TTSB)
OLOG	Offshore Logistics, Inc. [*NASDAQ symbol*] (NQ)
OLogC	Logan-Hocking County District Library, Logan, OH [*Library symbol Library of Congress*] (LCLS)
OLOGP	Offshore Logistics, Inc. (MHDW)
OLOGS	Open-Loop Oxygen-Generating System [*Air Force*]
ol ol	Olive Oil (AD)
ol oliv	Oleum Olivae [*Olive Oil*] [*Pharmacy*]
OLOM	Orbiter Lift-Off Mass [*NASA*] (KSC)
OLor	Lorain Public Library, Lorain, OH [*Library symbol Library of Congress*] (LCLS)
OLOS	Oakridge Secondary School, London, Ontario [*Library symbol National Library of Canada*] (NLC)
OLOS	Office for Library Outreach Service [*American Library Association*]
OLOS	Office for Literacy and Outreach Services (AL)
OLOS	Out of Line of Sight (NATG)
olos	Out of Line of Sight (AD)
OLou	Loudonville Public Library, Loudonville, OH [*Library symbol Library of Congress*] (LCLS)
OLOW	Orbiter Lift-Off Weight [*NASA*]
olow	Orbiter Liftoff Weight (AD)
O Lower D ...	Ohio Lower Court Decisions [*A publication*] (DLA)
OLP	Brothers of Our Lady of Providence (TOCD)
OLP	Lewis and Clark College, Portland, OR [*OCLC symbol*] (OCLC)
OLP	Missionaries of the Third Order of St. Francis of Our Lady of the Prairies [*Roman Catholic women's religious order*]
OLP	Observation Landplane [*Coast Guard*]
OLP	Occipitolaeva Posterior [*A fetal position*] [*Medicine*] (AAMN)
olp	Occipito-Laeva Posterior (AD)
OLP	Office of Labor Production [*WPB*] [*World War II*]
OLP	Off-Line Program [*Computer science*]
OLP	Olympic Dam [*Australia Airport symbol*] (OAG)
OLP	One Liberty Properties [*AMEX symbol*] (TTSB)
OLP	One Liberty Properties, Inc. [*AMEX symbol*] (SPSG)
OLP	Online Processor (TEL)
OLP	Online Programming
OLP	Open Learning Programme (AIE)
OLP	Optical Line Pair
OLP	Oral Lichen Plannus [*Medicine*]
OLP	Organizacion para la Liberacion Palestina [*Palestinian Liberation Organization*] [*Spanish*] [*Political party*] (AD)
olp	Original List Price (AD)
OLP	Outside Left Position [*Dancing*]
OLP	Oxygen at Low Pressure (KSC)
OLP	Oxygen Lance Powder (IAA)
OLP	Oxygen Lime Powder [*Steelmaking process*]
OLP	Sisters of Our Lady of Providence [*Roman Catholic religious order*]
olpar	Other Large Phased-Array RADAR (AD)
OLPARS	Online Pattern Analysis and Recognition System [*Computer science*] (MCD)
OL/PBAR	Online Patient Billing and Accounts Receivable System [*Computer science*] (PDAA)
OLPH	London Psychiatric Hospital, Ontario [*Library symbol National Library of Canada*] (NLC)
OLPHS	Parkwood Hospital Services, London, Ontario [*Library symbol National Library of Canada*] (BIB)
OLPP	One Liberty Prop $1.60 Cv Pfd [*AMEX symbol*] (TTSB)
OLPR	Office of Library Personnel Resources [*American Library Association*]
Ol Prec	Oliver's Precedents [*A publication*] (DLA)
OLPS	Online Programming System [*Computer science*]
OLPT	Oxford Library of Practical Theology [*A publication*]
OLPT	Pinchas Troester Library, Congregation B'Nai Israel, London, Ontario [*Library symbol National Library of Canada*] (NLC)
OLQ	Biloxi, MS [*Location identifier FAA*] (FAAL)
OLQ	Officer-Like Qualities [*British military*] (DMA)
olq	Officer-Like Qualities (AD)
OLQ	Olsobip [*Papua New Guinea*] [*Airport symbol*] (OAG)
OLR	Oak-Leaf Roller [*Moth*] [*Entomology*]
OLR	Objective Loudness Rating [*of telephone connections*] (IEEE)
OLR	Office Loop Repeater (MHDB)
OLR	Office of Labor Racketeering [*Department of Labor*]
OLR	Office of Legislative Reference [*Bureau of the Budget; later, OMB*]
OLR	Offline Reader [*Bulletin board*]
OLR	Offline Recovery [*Telecommunications*] (TEL)
OLR	Off Load Route [*Aviation*] (DA)
OLR	Ohio Law Reporter [*A publication*] (DLA)
O-LR	Ohio Legislative Reference Bureau, Columbus, OH [*Library symbol Library of Congress*] (LCLS)
OLR	On-Line Research, Inc. [*Information service or system*] (IID)
OLR	On Location Repair (MCD)
OLR	Ontario Law Reporter [*A publication*] (DLA)
OLR	Ontario Law Reports [*A publication*] (DLA)
OLR	Open-Loop Receiver [*or Response*]
OLR	Open Loop Response (CIST)
OLR	Operator's Local Representative (AIA)
OLR	Organisation pour la Liberation du Rwanda [*Organization for the Liberation of Rwanda*]
OLR	Oudh Law Reports [*India*] [*A publication*] (DLA)
OLR	Outer Lindblad Resonance [*Planetary science*]
OLR	Outgoing Long-Wave Radiation [*Satellite sensed*]
OLR	Overload Relay
olr	Overload Relay (AD)
OLR	Robarts School Library, London, Ontario [*Library symbol National Library of Canada*] (BIB)
OLRAG	London Regional Art Gallery, Ontario [*Library symbol National Library of Canada*] (NLC)
OLRB	Ontario Labor Relations Board [*Canada*] (AD)
OLRB	Ontario Labour Relations Board Monthly Report [*A publication*] (DLA)
O/L-RC	Overload-Reverse Current (NASA)
OL Rep	Ohio Law Reporter [*A publication*] (DLA)
Ol Res	Oleoresin [*Also, OR*] [*Pharmacy*]
ol res	Oleoresin (AD)
OLRI	Office & Factory, Rochevert Industrie, Inc., Lindsay, Ontario [*Library symbol National Library of Canada*] (NLC)
OL RIC	Oleum Ricini [*Castor Oil*] [*Pharmacy*] (ROG)
OLRL	Lyndhurst Branch, Rideau Lakes Union Library, Ontario [*Library symbol National Library of Canada*] (BIB)
OLRM	Medical Library, Ross Memorial Hospital, Lindsay, Ontario [*Library symbol National Library of Canada*] (BIB)
OLRS	Optical LASER Ranging System
OLRT	Online Real Time [*Computer science*]
olrt	On-Line Real Time [*Computer science*] (AD)
OLRV	Olive Latent Ringspot Virus [*Plant pathology*]
OLS	Nogales, AZ [*Location identifier FAA*] (FAAL)
OLS	Office of Legal Services [*of Office of Economic Opportunity*]
OLS	Office of Library Services (AAGC)
OLS	OLS Asia Holdings Ltd. [*Associated Press*] (SAG)
OLS	Olsten Corp. [*NYSE symbol*] (SAG)
OLS	Online Library System (AEPA)
OLS	Online Scan [*Computer science*] (CAAL)
OLS	Online Search (NITA)
OLS	Online System [*Computer science*]
OLS	Ontario Land Surveyor [*Canada*] (ASC)
OLS	Open-Loop System [*Chemical engineering*]
OLS	Operational Launch Station (AAG)
OLS	Operational Linescan System [*Navy*] (ANA)
OLS	Operational Lines of Succession [*Defense readiness*]
OLS	Operation Lifeline Sudan
OLS	Operation...Life Support [*Online lobbying for the television show "My So-Called Life"*]
OLS	Optical Landing System
OLS	Orbiting Lunar Station [*NASA*]
OLS	Ordinary Least Squares [*Statistics*]
OLS	Original Line of Sight
OLS	Overlap Shear
OLS	Sisters of Our Lady of Sorrows [*Roman Catholic religious order*]
OLS	Spartan of Canada Ltd., London, Ontario [*Library symbol National Library of Canada*] (NLC)
OLSA	Off-Line Selectric Analyser [*Computer science*] (IAA)
OLSA	OLS Asia Holdings Ltd. [*NASDAQ symbol*] (SAG)
OLSA	Orbiter Logistics Support Plan [*NASA*]
OLSA	Orbiter/LPS [*Launch Processing System*] Signal Adapter [*NASA*] (NASA)
OLS AH	OLS Asia Holdings Ltd. [*Associated Press*] (SAG)
OL'SAM	Online Database Search Assistance Machine [*Franklin Institute*] [*Information service or system Defunct*] (IID)
OL'SAM	Online Search Assistance Machine (NITA)
OLSASS	Online System Availability and Service Simulation [*Computer science*] (PDAA)
OLSAT	Otis-Lennon School Ability Test [*Education*]
OLSAY	OLS Asia Hlds ADS [*NASDAQ symbol*] (TTSB)
OLSC	Online Scientific Computer [*Computer science*]
olsc	On-Line Scientific Computer (AD)
OLSCA	Orientation Linkage for a Solar Cell Array
OLSCG	Latchford Senior Citizens Group, Ontario [*Library symbol National Library of Canada*] (BIB)
OLSD	Office for Library Service to the Disadvantaged [*American Library Association*]
OLSDG	Lancaster Branch, Stormont, Dundas, and Glengarry County Library, Ontario [*Library symbol National Library of Canada*] (BIB)
OLSE	Ordinary Least-Squares Estimators [*Statistics*]
OLSF	Online Subsystem Facility [*Computer science*] (MCD)
OLSH	Our Lady of the Sacred Heart (ADA)
OLSIDI-F	Oral Language Sentence Imitation Diagnostic Inventory - Format Revised [*Educational test*]
OLSILC	On the Lighter Side, International Lighter Collectors (EA)
OLSIST-F	Oral Language Sentence Imitation Screening Test - Format Revised [*Educational test*]
OLSJ	St. Joseph's Hospital, London, Ontario [*Library symbol National Library of Canada*] (NLC)
OLSOR	Object Location and Small Object Recovery [*Military*] (DNAB)
OLSP	Office of Life Science Programs [*Obsolete NASA*]
OLSP	Operational Logistic Support Plan
OLSP	Orbiter Logistics Support Plan [*NASA*] (NASA)

OLSP	St. Peter's Seminary, London, Ontario [*Library symbol National Library of Canada*] (NLC)
OLSS	Online Software System [*Computer science*] (IEEE)
OLSS	Operational Logistic Support Summary [*Military*] (CAAL)
OLSS	Overseas Limited Storage Site [*Army*]
OLSSDG	Long Sault Branch, Stormont, Dundas, and Glengarry County Public Library, Ontario [*Library symbol National Library of Canada*] (BIB)
Olsten	Olsten Corp. [*Associated Press*] (SAG)
OLSUS	Online System Use Statistics (NITA)
OLSWF	OLS Asia HLDS ADS Wrrt [*NASDAQ symbol*] (TTSB)
OLT	Occipitolaeva Transversa [*A fetal position*] [*Medicine*] (AAMN)
olt	Occipito-Laeva Transverse (AD)
OLT	Oddity-Learning Task [*Psychology*]
OLT	Official Latin Title
Olt	Old Italian (AD)
OLT	Online Test [*Computer science*]
OLT	Orange Light
OLT	Orthotopic Liver Transplantation [*Medicine*]
OLT	Ostfriesische Lufttransport GmbH [*Germany ICAO designator*] (FAAC)
OLT	Oxford Library of Translations [*A publication*]
OLT	United Lodge of Theosophists, London, Ontario [*Library symbol National Library of Canada*] (NLC)
OLTE	Online Test (NITA)
OLTE	Online Test Executive Program [*Computer science*] (PDAA)
OLTE	Organizational Level Test Equipment (MCD)
OLTEP	On-Line Test Executive Program [*IBM Corp.*] [*Computer science*]
OLTL	One Life to Live [*Television program*]
OLTMC	Technical Information Centre, 3M Canada, Inc., London, Ontario [*Library symbol National Library of Canada*] (NLC)
OLTP	On-Line Transaction Processing [*Tandem Computers*]
OLTS	On-Line Mainframe Testing System [*Computer science*] (IAA)
OLTS	Online Test Section (NITA)
OLTS	Online Test System [*Computer science*] (BUR)
OLTS	Online Time Share [*Computer science*]
OLTS	Online Transaction System [*Computer science*] (IAA)
OLTT	Online Teller Terminal
oltt	On-Line Teller Terminal [*Computer science*] (AD)
OLTT	Online Terminal Test [*Computer science*] (IBMDP)
OLU	Columbus [*Nebraska*] [*Airport symbol*] (OAG)
OLU	Outdoing Line Unit (IAA)
OLU	University of Western Ontario, London, Ontario [*Library symbol National Library of Canada*] (NLC)
OLUC	Lucknow Branch, Bruce County Public Library, Ontario [*Library symbol National Library of Canada*] (NLC)
OLUC	Office of Land Use Coordination [*Abolished, 1944*] [*Department of Agriculture*]
OLUC	Online Union Catalog [*Online Computer Library Center, Inc.*] [*Information service or system*] (CRD)
OLuCF	Southern Ohio Correctional Facility, Lucasville, OH [*Library symbol Library of Congress*] (LCLS)
OLUD	Online Update (TEL)
OLUE	Engineering Library, University of Western Ontario, London, Ontario [*Library symbol National Library of Canada*] (BIB)
OLUG	Department of Geography, University of Western Ontario, London, Ontario [*Library symbol National Library of Canada*] (NLC)
OLUG	Office Landscape Users Group [*Later, OPUG*] (EA)
OLUH	University Hospital, London, Ontario [*Library symbol National Library of Canada*] (NLC)
OLUIT	Object Oriented Librarian User Interface Tool (TELE)
OLUL	Law Library, University of Western Ontario, London, Ontario [*Library symbol National Library of Canada*] (NLC)
OLUM	Online Update Control Module (TEL)
OLUM	Sciences Library, Natural Sciences Centre, University of Western Ontario, London, Ontario [*Library symbol National Library of Canada*] (NLC)
OLUMG	MacIntosh Gallery, University of Western Ontario, London, Ontario [*Library symbol National Library of Canada*] (NLC)
OLUNO	Northern Outreach Library Service, University of Western Ontario, London, Ontario [*Library symbol National Library of Canada*] (BIB)
OLURC	London Urban Resource Centre, Ontario [*Library symbol National Library of Canada*] (NLC)
OLUS	Online Update System (RDA)
OLUS	School of Library and Information Science, University of Western Ontario, London, Ontario [*Library symbol National Library of Canada*] (NLC)
OLuS	Scioto Technical College, Lucasville, OH [*Library symbol Library of Congress Obsolete*] (LCLS)
OLUVA	Visual Arts Department, University of Western Ontario, London, Ontario [*Library symbol National Library of Canada*] (NLC)
OLUWP	Office of Land Use and Water Planning [*Abolished, 1976*] [*Department of the Interior*]
olv	Olivaceous (AD)
olv	Olive (AD)
OLV	Olive Branch, MS [*Location identifier FAA*] (FAAL)
OLV	Oliver Resources [*Vancouver Stock Exchange symbol*]
OLV	One-Lung Ventilation [*Medicine*]
olv	On-Line Validation [*Computer science*] (AD)
OLV	Onze Lieve Vrouw [*Our Lady*] [*Dutch*] (AD)
OLV	Open-Frame Low Voltage (IEEE)
OLV	Orbital Launch Vehicle
OLVG	Open-Loop Voltage Gain
OLVH	Medical Library, South Street Campus, Victoria Hospital Corp., London, Ontario [*Library symbol National Library of Canada*] (NLC)
OLVL	Oil Level
O-LVL	Organizational Level (MCD)
OLVM	Our Lady of Victory Missionary Sisters [*Roman Catholic religious order*]
olvn	Olivine [*Philately*]
OLVP	Office of Launch Vehicle Programs [*Obsolete NASA*]
Olwine's LJ (PA)	Olwine's Law Journal [*Pennsylvania*] [*A publication*] (DLA)
OLX	Linn-Benton Community College, Albany, OR [*OCLC symbol*] (OCLC)
OLX	Off-Line Express [*Mustang Software, Inc.*] (PCM)
OLX	On-Line Executive [*Computer science*] (MHDB)
OLY	Olney-Noble, IL [*Location identifier FAA*] (FAAL)
Oly	Olympia (AD)
Oly	Olympic (AD)
OLY	Olympic Aviation SA [*Greece*] [*ICAO designator*] (FAAC)
Olym	Olympia (AD)
OLYM	Olympiad
OLYM	Olympic Financial Ltd. [*NASDAQ symbol*] (NQ)
OLYM	Olympic National Park
OlymF	Olympic Financial Ltd. [*Associated Press*] (SAG)
OlymFn	Olympic Financial Ltd. [*Associated Press*] (SAG)
OLYMP	Olympic Finl Cv Exch Pfd [*NASDAQ symbol*] (TTSB)
Olympic	Olympic National Park, Washington (AD)
OlympStl	Olympic Steel, Inc. [*Associated Press*] (SAG)
OLZ	Oelwein, IA [*Location identifier FAA*] (FAAL)
OM	Air Mongol [*ICAO designator*] (AD)
Om	Book of Omni (AD)
OM	Member of the Order of Merit [*Canada*] (DD)
OM	Minim Fathers (TOCD)
om	Minim Fathers (TOCD)
OM	Mississauga Public Library, Ontario [*Library symbol National Library of Canada*] (NLC)
OM	Obermanual [*Upper Manual*] [*Music*]
OM	Observer's Mate [*British military*] (DMA)
OM	Obtuse Marginal [*Medicine*] (MAE)
OM	Occipitomental [*Diameter of skull*]
OM	Occupational Medal [*as used with special reference to Germany or Japan*] [*Military decoration*]
OM	Occupational Medicine
OM	Oceanography and Meteorology
OM	Ochsner-Mahorner [*Echocardiogram*] (DAVI)
OM	Oculomotor (DB)
OM	Oduma Magazine [*A publication*]
OM	Odyssey of the Mind
OM	Oesterreichische Monatsschrift fuer den Orient (BJA)
OM	Office Manager
OM	Office Messenger [*Military*]
OM	Officine Meccaniche [*Italian auto manufacturer*]
OM	Old Man [*Communications operators' colloquialism*]
om	Old Man (AD)
om	Old Measurement (AD)
OM	Old Measurement
OM	Olympus Mons [*A filamentary mark on Mars*]
OM	Omaha [*Diocesan abbreviation*] [*Nebraska*] (TOCD)
OM	Oman [*IYRU nationality code*] [*ANSI two-letter standard code*] (CNC)
Om	Oman (AD)
om	Omit
OM	Omni Mane [*Every Morning*] [*Pharmacy*]
om	Omni Mane [*Every Morning*] [*Latin*] (AD)
OM	On Margin [*Investment term*]
OM	Opaque Media [*X-ray microscopy*]
OM	Open Market
OM	Open Matching [*Parapsychology*]
OM	Open Mouth [*Doll collecting*]
OM	Opera di Maria [*Work of Mary*] [*An association*] (EAIO)
OM	Opera Mundi [*Book-packaging firm based in Paris*]
OM	Operating Memorandum
OM	Operating Memory (KSC)
OM	Operating Method (COE)
OM	Operational Management [*Computer science*] (IAA)
OM	Operational Mid (NAKS)
OM	Operational Modeling (AAEL)
om	Operational Monitor (AD)
OM	Operational Monitor (IAA)
OM	Operation Mainstream (OICC)
OM	Operation Mobilisation [*Religious movement*] [*British*]
OM	Operation Monkees (EA)
OM	Operations Maintenance
OM	Operations Manager
OM	Operations Manual (NITA)
OM	Operations Memorandum [*Department of Agriculture*] (GFGA)
OM	Operator's Manual
OM	Opticalman [*Navy*] (DAVI)
OM	Optical Master (KSC)
OM	Optical Media [*Computer graphics*]
OM	Optical Microscope (ECII)
OM	Optical Microscopy
OM	Optimus Maximus [*Greatest and Best*] [*Latin*]
OM	Options for Men [*A publication*]
OM	Options Market [*Finance*]
OM	Orbital Maneuvering Engine [*NASA*] (NAKS)
OM	Orbiter Main Engine [*NASA*] (NAKS)
OM	Orbit Modification (IAA)

OM.............	Order of Merit
Om.............	Ordinance Map (AD)
OM.............	Ordnance Mission (AAG)
OM.............	Ordo [*Fratrum*] Minimorum [*Minims of St. Francis of Paul*] [*Roman Catholic men's religious order*]
OM.............	Organic Matter
om.............	Organic Matter (AD)
OM.............	Organizational Maintenance (MCD)
OM.............	Orthogonal Memory (MHDB)
OM.............	Osborne Mendel Rat [*Medicine*] (DMAA)
OM.............	Osmiophilic Layer [*Botany*]
OM.............	Osteomalacia [*Medicine*] (MAE)
OM.............	Osteomyelitis [*Medicine*]
OM.............	Ostmark [*Monetary unit*] [*Germany*]
OM.............	Otitis Media [*Medicine*]
OM.............	Otolitic Membrane [*Otology*]
om.............	Our Memo (AD)
OM.............	Our Message
OM.............	Outboard Marine [*NYSE symbol*] (TTSB)
OM.............	Outer Marker [*Part of an instrument landing system*] [*Aviation*]
om.............	Outer Marker (AD)
OM.............	Outer Membrane [*Biochemistry*]
OM.............	Output Module
OM.............	Outside Manufacturing
O/M...........	Outside of Metal (MSA)
OM.............	Overall Modernity [*Sociological scale*]
OM.............	Overhaul Manual (MCD)
OM.............	Overland Monthly [*A publication*] (ROG)
OM.............	Overseas Mail [*British*]
OM.............	Overseas Minister [*World War I*] [*Canada*]
OM.............	Overt Meditation
OM.............	Overturning Moment
OM.............	Ovulation Method [*Birth control*]
OM.............	Owners Manual
O/M...........	Oxygen-to-Metal [*Ratio*] (NRCH)
OM1............	Opticalman, First Class [*Navy rating*]
OM2............	Opticalman, Second Class [*Navy rating*]
OM3............	Opticalman, Third Class [*Navy rating*]
OMA............	Eppley Airfield [*FAA*] (TAG)
OMA............	Markham Public Library, Ontario [*Library symbol National Library of Canada*] (NLC)
OMA............	Object Management Architecture [*Computer science*] (CDE)
OMA............	Ocean Mining Administration (AD)
OMA............	Oceanography and Marine Assessment [*Marine science*] (OSRA)
OMA............	Office of Management and Administration [*Social Security Administration*] (OICC)
OMA............	Office of Maritime Administration [*Navy*]
OMA............	Office of Maritime Affairs (AD)
OMA............	Office of Military Affairs
OMA............	Office of Military Applications [*Department of Energy*]
OMA............	Office of Military Assistance
OMA............	Office of Minority Affairs [*Department of Agriculture*] (GFGA)
OMA............	Oilskin Manufacturers' Association of Great Britain Ltd. (BI)
OMA............	Oklahoma Military Academy
OMA............	Omaezaki [*Japan*] [*Seismograph station code, US Geological Survey*] (SEIS)
OMA............	Omaha [*Nebraska*] [*Airport symbol*]
Oma............	Omaha, Nebraska (AD)
OMA............	Ontario Medical Association [*Canada*] (AD)
OMA............	Operational Maintenance Activity (NVT)
OMA............	Operation Medicare Alert
OMA............	Operations and Maintenance Appopriation [*Army*]
OMA............	Operations and Maintenance, Army
OMA............	Operations Maintenance Area (NASA)
OMA............	Operations Management Application (SSD)
OMA............	Operations Management Society (NTPA)
OMA............	Operations Monitor Alarm
OMA............	Optical Manufacturers Association (EA)
OMA............	Optical-Mechanical Assembly [*Apollo*] [*NASA*]
OMA............	Optical Multichannel Analyzer [*Spectrometry*]
OMA............	Orbiter Maintenance Area [*NASA*] (MCD)
OMA............	Orderly Marketing Agreement
oma............	Orderly Marketing Arrangement (AD)
OMA............	Organizational Maintenance Activity
OMA............	Oriental Merchants Association [*Defunct*] (EA)
OMA............	Outstanding Merchandising Achievement Award
OMA............	Overall Manufacturers' Association (AD)
OMA............	Overall Manufacturers' Association of Great Britain (BI)
OMAA...........	Abu Dhabi/International [*United Arab Emirates*] [*ICAO location identifier*] (ICLI)
OMAA...........	Occupational Medical Administrators' Association (EA)
OMAA...........	Office of Management Analysis and Audit [*Civil Service Commission*]
OMAAEEC	Organisation Mondiale des Anciens et Anciennes Eleves de l'Enseignement Catholique [*World Organization of Former Pupils of Catholic Schools*] (EAIO)
OMAB..........	Buhasa [*United Arab Emirates*] [*ICAO location identifier*] (ICLI)
OMABP........	Abitibi-Price, Inc., Mississauga, Ontario [*Library symbol National Library of Canada*] (NLC)
OMAC..........	Alkaril Chemicals Ltd., Mississauga, Ontario [*Library symbol National Library of Canada*] (NLC)
OMAC..........	Asab [*United Arab Emirates*] [*ICAO location identifier*] (ICLI)
OMAC..........	Online Manufacturing, Accounting, and Control System
OMAC..........	Online Manufacturing Control (NITA)
OMAC..........	Open Modular Architecture Controller (ACII)
OMAC..........	Operator Measures and Criteria (MCD)
OMACON......	Optimized Magnetohydrodynamic Conversion
OMACS	Online Manufacturing and Control System [*Computer science*] (PDAA)
OMAD	Abu Dhabi/Bateen [*United Arab Emirates*] [*ICAO location identifier*] (ICLI)
OMAD	Madoc Public Library, Ontario [*Library symbol National Library of Canada*] (BIB)
OMAD	Oncovin [*Vincristine*], Methotrexate, Adriamycin, Dactinomycin [*Actinomycin D*] [*Antineoplastic drug regimen*]
OMAD	Optical Mark and Automatic Dialing [*Facsimile transmission*] (DGA)
OMADA	Airway Centre, AES Data Ltd., Mississauga, Ontario [*Library symbol National Library of Canada*] (NLC)
OMAE..........	Emirates Flight Information Region [*United Arab Emirates*] [*ICAO location identifier*] (ICLI)
OMAECL	AECL International, Mississauga, Ontario [*Library symbol National Library of Canada*] (NLC)
OMAF..........	Operations and Maintenance, Air Force
OMAG	Geac Computers International, Markham, Ontario [*Library symbol National Library of Canada*] (NLC)
OMAG	Orbiter Magnetometer [*NASA*]
OMAH	Al Hamra [*United Arab Emirates*] [*ICAO location identifier*] (ICLI)
OMAH	Markham High School, Ontario [*Library symbol National Library of Canada*] (NLC)
OMAHM	Markham District Historical Museum, Ontario [*Library symbol National Library of Canada*] (BIB)
OMAI	Allelix, Inc., Mississauga, Ontario [*Library symbol National Library of Canada*] (NLC)
OMAI	Organisation Mondiale Agudath Israel [*Agudas Israel World Organization - AIWO*] (EAIO)
OMAJ..........	Jebel Dhana [*United Arab Emirates*] [*ICAO location identifier*] (ICLI)
OMAL..........	Al Ain [*United Arab Emirates*] [*ICAO location identifier*] (ICLI)
O'Mal & H ...	O'Malley and Hardcastle's Election Cases [*England*] [*A publication*] (DLA)
OMAM	Abu Dhabi/Al Dhafra [*United Arab Emirates*] [*ICAO location identifier*] (ICLI)
OMAN	Manitouwadge Public Library, Ontario [*Library symbol National Library of Canada*] (NLC)
O-MAN	Overhead Manipulator [*For handling loads in a nuclear environment*]
OMancAH	Alfred Holbrook College, Manchester, OH [*Library symbol Library of Congress Obsolete*] (LCLS)
OMancO.......	Ohio Valley Local District Free Public Library, Manchester, OH [*Library symbol Library of Congress*] (LCLS)
O'M & H	O'Malley and Hardcastle's Election Cases [*England*] [*A publication*] (DLA)
O'M & H El Cas...	O'Malley and Hardcastle's Election Cases [*England*] [*A publication*] (DLA)
OM & MG ...	Organizational Manual and Management Guide
OM & S	Osteopathic Medicine and Surgery
OMANO........	Manotick Public Library, Ontario [*Library symbol National Library of Canada*] (NLC)
OMans	Mansfield Public Library, Mansfield, OH [*Library symbol Library of Congress*] (LCLS)
OMansK	Kingwood Center Library, Mansfield, OH [*Library symbol Library of Congress*] (LCLS)
OMansU	Ohio State University, Mansfield Regional Campus, Mansfield, OH [*Library symbol Library of Congress*] (LCLS)
OMAP	Object Module Assembly Program
OMAP	Operations and Maintenance Application Part [*Telecommunications*]
OMAP	Vaughan Public Library, Maple, Ontario [*Library symbol National Library of Canada*] (NLC)
OMAPC	Astra Pharmaceuticals Canada Ltd., Mississauga, Ontario [*Library symbol National Library of Canada*] (NLC)
OMAPFW	Ontario Ministry of Natural Resources, Maple, Ontario [*Library symbol National Library of Canada*] (NLC)
OMAQ	Quarmain [*United Arab Emirates*] [*ICAO location identifier*] (ICLI)
OMAR	Arzana [*United Arab Emirates*] [*ICAO location identifier*] (ICLI)
omar...........	Congregation of Maronite Monks (TOCD)
OMar	Congregation of Maronite Monks (TOCD)
OMAR	Marathon Public Library, Ontario [*Library symbol National Library of Canada*] (NLC)
OMAR	Office of Medical Applications of Research [*Bethesda, MD*] [*Department of Health and Human Services National Institutes of Health*]
OMAR	Operations and Maintenance, Army Reserve (AABC)
OMAR	Optical Mark Reader [*Computer science*]
omarb.........	Omarbetad [*Revised*] [*Swedish*]
OMarion	Marion Carnegie Public Library, Marion, OH [*Library symbol Library of Congress*] (LCLS)
OMarionU	Ohio State University, Marion Campus, Marion, OH [*Library symbol Library of Congress*] (LCLS)
OMARK	Markdale Public Library, Ontario [*Library symbol National Library of Canada*] (NLC)
OMARNG	Operation and Maintenance, Army National Guard (AABC)
OMARS	Outstanding Media Advertising by Restaurants (AD)
OMAS	Assiginack Public Library, Manitowaning, Ontario [*Library symbol National Library of Canada*] (NLC)
OMAS	Das Island [*United Arab Emirates*] [*ICAO location identifier*] (ICLI)
OMas	Massillon Public Library, Massillon, OH [*Library symbol Library of Congress*] (LCLS)
OMAS	Off-Magic-Angle-Spinning [*Spectroscopy*]
OMAS	One-Man Atmospheric Submersible (PDAA)
OMAS	Operational Miscellaneous Audio Subsystem
OMAST	Massey and Township Public Library, Ontario [*Library symbol Library network*] (NLC)

OMAT............ Matheson Public Library, Ontario [*Library symbol National Library of Canada*] (NLC)

OMAT............ Ocean Measurement and Array Technology [*Navy*] (CAAL)

OMAT............ Office of Manpower, Automation, and Training [*See also OAM*] [*Department of Labor*]

OMATT........... Mattawa Public Library, Ontario [*Library symbol National Library of Canada*] (NLC)

OMAU........... Magnetawan Area Union Public Library, Magnetawan, Ontario [*Library symbol National Library of Canada*] (NLC)

OMAZ........... Zirku [*United Arab Emirates*] [*ICAO location identifier*] (ICLI)

OMB............. Midhurst Branch Library, Ontario [*Library symbol National Library of Canada*] (NLC)

OMB............. Object Management Architecture [*Computer science*]

OMB............. Office of Management and Budget [*Executive Office of the President*] [*Formerly, Bureau of the Budget Washington, DC*]

OMB............. Office of Money and Banking (WPI)

OMB............. Omboue [*Gabon*] [*Airport symbol*] (OAG)

Omb............. Ombudsman (AD)

OMB............. Operational Maintenance Battalion [*Army*] (DOMA)

OMB............. Ordnance Maintenance Bulletin

OMB............. Outboard Motorboat

OMB............. Outer Marker Beacon [*Part of an instrument landing system*] [*Aviation*]

OMB............. Out-of-Home Measurement Bureau [*Later, TABMM*] (EA)

OMBAC........ Old Mission Beach Athletic Club (AD)

OMBC.......... Beak Consultants, Mississauga, Ontario [*Library symbol National Library of Canada*] (NLC)

OMB Circular... Office of Management and Budget Circular (AAGC)

OMBE........... Office of Minority Business Enterprise [*Later, MBDA*] [*Department of Commerce*]

OMBE........... Oxford Mission Brotherhood of the Epiphany [*Anglican religious community*]

OMB/FPPO... Office of Management and Budget/Federal Procurement Policy Office (OICC)

OMBI........... Observation-Measurement-Balancing and Installation [*Production analysis*]

OMBI........... Overcoming Mobility Barriers International (EA)

om bid........ Omnibus Bidendis [*Every Two Days*] [*Latin*] (AD)

OMBR........... Ontario Municipal Board Reports [*A publication*] (DLA)

OMBUU......... Orbiter Midbody Umbilical Unit [*NASA*] (NASA)

OMBVT .... Minesing Branch, Vespra Township Public Library, Ontario [*Library symbol National Library of Canada*] (BIB)

OMBW .... Bangor, Wicklow, McClure, and Monteagle Union Public Library, Maynooth, Ontario [*Library symbol National Library of Canada*] (BIB)

OMBW .... OMB [*Office of Management and Budget*] Watch (EA)

OMC............. Chief Opticalman [*Navy rating*]

OMc............. Herbert Wescoat Memorial Library, McArthur, OH [*Library symbol Library of Congress*] (LCLS)

OMC............. Marietta College, Marietta, OH [*Library symbol Library of Congress*] (LCLS)

OMC............. Mayo Clinic Library, Rochester, MN [*OCLC symbol*] (OCLC)

OMC............. Occupational Medical Center (EFIS)

OMC............. Office of Military Cooperation [*Foreign Service*]

OMC............. Office of Motor Carriers [*FHWA*] [*NHSTA*] [*RSPA*] (TAG)

OMC............. Office of Munitions Control [*Department of State*]

OMC............. Official Mail Center [*Air Force*] (AFM)

OMC............. Off-Machine Coated [*Paper*] (DGA)

OMC............. Omnicom Group [*NYSE symbol*] (TTSB)

OMC............. Omnicom Group, Inc. [*NYSE symbol*] (SPSG)

OMC............. One-Man Control (DNAB)

OMC............. Opel Motorsport Club AG (EA)

OMC............. Open Market Committee [*Also, FOMC*] [*Federal Reserve System*]

OMC............. Operating and Maintenance Costs

OMC............. Operations Monitoring Computer

OMC............. Opticalman, Chief [*Navy rating*] (DNAB)

OMC............. Optical Memory Card [*Computer science*] (CIST)

omc............. Orbiter Maintenance and Checkout [*NASA*] (NAKS)

OMC............. Orbiter Maintenance and Checkout [*NASA*] (NASA)

OMC............. Ordnance Missile Command [*Later, Missile Command*]

OMC............. Ordo Minorum Cappucinorum [*Capuchins*] [*Roman Catholic men's religious order*]

OMC............. Ordo Minorum Conventualium [*Conventual Franciscans*] [*Roman Catholic men's religious order*]

OMC............. Organic Molecular Crystal

OMC............. Orion Molecular Cloud [*Astronomy*]

OMC............. Outboard Marine Corp.

OMC............. Oxford Military College (ROG)

OMC............. Oxford Mission to Calcutta [*British*] (ROG)

OMC............. Oxidized Microcrystalline Waxes (EDCT)

OMC1........... Orion Molecular Cloud 1 [*Astronomy*]

OMCA.......... Ontario Motor Coach Association

OMCA.......... Organic-Moderated Critical Assembly [*Nuclear energy*] (NRCH)

OMCA.......... Otitis Media, Catarrhal, Acute [*Medicine*] (MAE)

OMCB.......... Off-Machine Coated Board [*Paper*] (DGA)

OMCC.......... Open Minded Comics Club [*Defunct*] (EA)

OMCF.......... Operations and Maintenance Control File [*NASA*] (NASA)

OMCF.......... Orbiter Maintenance and Checkout Facility [*NASA*] (NASA)

OMCG.......... Ciba/Geigy Canada Ltd., Mississauga, Ontario [*Library symbol National Library of Canada*] (NLC)

OMCHE .... Organic Material Hydrocarbon Equivalent [*Materials science*]

OMChS .... Otitis Media, Chronic, Suppurating [*Medicine*] (STED)

OMCI........... Organisation Maritime Consultatif Intergouvernementale [*Intergovernmental Maritime Consultative Organization*]

OMCILCR..... Chemical Research Laboratory, CIL, Inc., Mississauga, Ontario [*Library symbol National Library of Canada*] (NLC)

OMcL........... Herbert Wescoat Memorial Library, McArthur, OH [*Library symbol*] [*Library of Congress*] (LCLS)

OMCM .... Master Chief Opticalman [*Navy rating*]

OMCM .... Omnicom Group, Inc. (MHDW)

OMCO .... Official Mail Control Officer (MCD)

OMCR .... Chippewa Resource Centre, Muncey, Ontario [*Library symbol National Library of Canada*] (NLC)

OMCR .... Organic-Moderated Cooled Reactor

OMCR .... Organized Marine Corps Reserve

OMCS .... Office of Motor Carrier Standards [*Federal Highway Administration*]

OMCS .... Senior Chief Opticalman [*Navy rating*]

OMCS .... Sheridan Park Research Community, Cominco Ltd., Mississauga, Ontario [*Library symbol National Library of Canada*] (NLC)

OMCSDG..... Moose Creek Branch, Stormount, Dundas, and Glengarry County Public Library, Ontario [*Library symbol National Library of Canada*] (NLC)

OMCSG .... Canada Systems Group, Mississauga, Ontario [*Library symbol National Library of Canada*] (NLC)

OMCT .... Carnarvon Township Public Library, Mindemoya, Ontario [*Library symbol National Library of Canada*] (NLC)

OMCT .... Office of Motor Carrier Transportation [*Federal Highway Administration*]

OMCT .... Organisation Mondiale Contre la Torture [*World Organization Against Torture*] [*Switzerland*] (EAIO)

OMCTS .... Octamethylcyclotetrasiloxane [*Organic chemistry*]

OMCT/SOST... Organisation Mondiale Contre la Torture/SOS-Torture [*World Organization Against Torture/SOS-Torture*] [*Geneva, Switzerland*] (EAIO)

OM-CVD...... Organometallic Chemical Vapor Deposition [*Also, OM-VPE, MO-CVD, MO-VPE*] [*Semiconductor technology*]

OMCVH........ Credit Valley Hospital, Mississauga, Ontario [*Library symbol National Library of Canada*] (NLC)

OMD .... Doctor of Oriental Medicine

OMD .... Du Pont Canada, Inc., Maitland, Ontario [*Library symbol National Library of Canada*] (NLC)

OMD .... Ocean Margin Drilling [*Program*] [*National Science Foundation*]

OMD .... Ocean Movement Designator

OMD .... Ocular Muscle Dystrophy [*Ophthalmology*] (MAE)

OMD .... Oculoman Dibulodyscephaly (STED)

OMD .... Office of Management Development [*Later, OMPR*] [*NASA*]

omd .... Off-Market Date (AD)

OMD .... Oldsmobile Motor Division [*General Motors Corp.*]

OMD .... O-Methyldopa [*Biochemistry*]

OMD .... Open Macrodefinition

OMD .... Operations and Maintainer Decision

OMD .... Operations and Maintenance Documentation [*NASA*] (NASA)

OMD .... Orbiter Mating Device [*NASA*]

OMD .... Orchestral Manoeuvres in the Dark [*Pop music group*]

OMD .... Ordnance Medical Department [*British military*] (DMA)

OMD .... Organic Mental Disorder [*Neurology*] (CPH)

OMD .... Oriental Medicine Doctor [*Medicine*]

OMDB .... Dubai [*United Arab Emirates*] [*ICAO location identifier*] (ICLI)

OMDB .... Over My Dead Body

OMDC .... Du Pont Canada, Inc., Mississauga, Ontario [*Library symbol National Library of Canada*] (NLC)

OMDCPL ..... Patent & Legal Library, DuPont Canada, Inc., Mississauga, Ontario [*Library symbol National Library of Canada*] (NLC)

OMDEAC..... Dearborn Chemical Co. Ltd., Mississauga, Ontario [*Library symbol National Library of Canada*] (NLC)

OMDG......... Dominion Glass Co. Ltd., Mississauga, Ontario [*Library symbol National Library of Canada*] (NLC)

OMDIR........ Research Library, Duracell, Inc., Mississauga, Ontario [*Library symbol Obsolete National Library of Canada*] (NLC)

OMDL .... Marmora, Deloro, and Lake Union Public Library, Marmora, Ontario [*Library symbol National Library of Canada*] (BIB)

OMDM .... Optomechanical Display Module

OMDO .... Corporate Library, Domglas, Inc., Mississauga, Ontario [*Library symbol National Library of Canada*] (NLC)

OMDP .... Ocean Margin Drilling Program [*National Science Foundation*]

OMDR .... Dunlop Research Centre, Sheridan Park, Mississauga, Ontario [*Library symbol National Library of Canada*] (NLC)

omdr........... Off-Market Date Received (AD)

OMDR .... Operation and Maintainability Data Record

OMDR .... Operations and Maintenance Data Record [*NASA*] (KSC)

OMDR .... Optical Memory Disc Recorder (DOM)

OMDR .... Optic Memory Disk Recorder

OMDS .... Delphax Systems, Mississauga, Ontario [*Library symbol National Library of Canada*] (NLC)

OMDS .... Online Diver Monitoring System

OMDW .... Diversey Wyandotte, Inc., Mississauga, Ontario, [*Library symbol National Library of Canada*] (NLC)

OME .... Erindale College, University of Toronto, Mississauga, Ontario [*Library symbol National Library of Canada*] (NLC)

OME .... Nome [*Alaska*] [*Airport symbol*] (OAG)

OME .... Object Management Extension

OME .... Office of Management Engineer

OME .... Office of Manpower Economics [*Department of Employment*] [*British*]

OME .... Office of Minerals Exploration [*Functions transferred to Geological Survey*] [*Department of the Interior*]

OME .... Office of the Medical Examiner (DAVI)

Ome .... Omega [*Record label*] [*Belgium, etc.*]

OME .... Ometepe [*Nicaragua*] [*Seismograph station code, US Geological Survey*] (SEIS)

OME.............	Open Messaging Environment [*Computer science*] (CDE)
OME.............	Operational Mission Environment (MCD)
OME.............	Orbital [*or Orbiter*] Main Engine [*NASA*] (NASA)
OME.............	Orbital Maneuvering Engine [*NASA*] (KSC)
OME.............	Ordnance Mechanical Engineer [*British military*] (DMA)
OME.............	Organisation Mondiale de l'Emballage [*World Packaging Organization - WPO*] (EAIO)
OME.............	Ormont Explorations Ltd. [*Vancouver Stock Exchange symbol*]
OME.............	Otitis Media with Effusion [*Medicine*]
OMEA..........	Meaford Public Library, Ontario [*Library symbol National Library of Canada*] (NLC)
OMEA..........	Office of Multicultural and Ethnic Affairs [*Australia*]
OMEC..........	Optimized Microminiature Electronic Circuit
OMEC..........	Organization of Mineral Exporting Countries [*Proposed*]
OMED..........	Oxboro Medical International, Inc. [*NASDAQ symbol*] (SAG)
OMED..........	Oxboro Med Intl. [*NASDAQ symbol*] (TTSB)
OMEF..........	Office Machines and Equipment Federation [*British*] (DIT)
OMEF..........	Omega Financial [*NASDAQ symbol*] (TTSB)
OMEF..........	Omega Financial Corp. [*NASDAQ symbol*] (SAG)
OMEG	Omega Environmental [*NASDAQ symbol*] (SPSG)
OMEGA	Off-Road Mobility Evaluation and Generalized Analysis [*Army*]
OMEGA	Operation Model Evaluation Group, Air Force (MCD)
OMEGA	Optimal Missile Engagement Guidance Algorithm (AD)
OmegaEn.....	Omega Environmental, Inc. [*Associated Press*] (SAG)
OmegFn......	Omega Financial Corp. [*Associated Press*] (SAG)
OmegHlt......	Omega Healthcare Investors [*Associated Press*] (SAG)
OMeH	Holden Arboretum, Mento, OH [*Library symbol*] [*Library of Congress*] (LCLS)
OM/EH	Occupational Medicine/Environmental Health Evaluation Center [*Emory University*]
OMEI...........	Office of Minority Economic Impact [*Department of Energy*]
OMEI...........	Other Major End Item [*Military*] (AFIT)
OMEL..........	Orient Mid-East Lines (AD)
OMEN	Ohio Medical Education Network [*Ohio State University*] [*Columbus*] (TSSD)
OMEN	Orthogonal Mini-Embedment (MHDI)
OMEP..........	Office of Marine and Estuarine Protection [*Environmental Protection Agency*] (EPA)
OMEP..........	Organisation Mondiale pour l'Education Prescolaire [*World Organization for Early Childhood Education*] (EAIO)
OMER	Merrickville Public Library, Ontario [*Library symbol National Library of Canada*] (NLC)
OMER	Operations Management Education and Research Foundation (EA)
OMERAD......	Office of Medical Education Research and Development [*Michigan State University*] [*Research center*] (RCD)
OMerc.........	Order of Mercedarians [*Also, MMB*] [*Roman Catholic women's religious order*]
OMERF	Operations Management Education and Research Foundation [*Formerly, OFMP*] (EA)
O-Mess.......	Officer's Mess [*Military*] (AD)
OMET..........	Orbiter Mission Elapsed Time [*NASA*] (MCD)
OMET..........	Ordnance Middle East Tasks [*Military*]
OMET..........	Organization Manning Equipment Table (MCD)
OMETA........	Ordnance Management Engineering Training Agency [*Army*]
OMEW	Office of Missile Electronic Warfare [*Army*] (RDA)
OMEWG	Orbiter Maintenance Engineering Working Group [*NASA*] (NASA)
OMF............	Moose Factory Library, Ontario [*Library symbol National Library of Canada*] (BIB)
OMF............	Object Management Facility [*Computer science*]
OMF............	Object Module File [*Computer science*] (IAA)
OMF............	Object Module Format
OMF............	Office of Management and Finance (AD)
OMF............	Officer Master File [*Army*] (INF)
OMF............	Old Master File
OMF............	Omniflys SA de CV [*Mexico ICAO designator*] (FAAC)
OMF............	Open Media Framework (DOM)
OMF............	Operational Mission Failure (MCD)
OMF............	Operation and Maintenance of Facilities [*Army*]
OMF............	Optical Matched Filter
OMF............	Order Materials For
OMF............	Organizational Master File [*Army*]
OMF............	Oscillatory Magnetic Field
OMF............	Overseas Missionary Fellowship, USA Headquarters (EA)
OMFBAA	Operation and Maintenance of Facilities Budget Activity Account [*Army*] (AABC)
OMFBR	Organic-Moderated Fluidized Bed Reactor
OMFC..........	Overseas Military Forces of Canada [*World War I*]
OMFCA	Operation and Maintenance of Facilities Cost Account [*Army*] (AABC)
OMFCU	Outboard Message Format Conversion Unit (MCD)
OMFD	Mount Forest District High School, Mount Forest, Ontario [*Library symbol National Library of Canada*] (NLC)
OMFE..........	Front of Escott Public Library, Mallorytown, Ontario [*Library symbol National Library of Canada*] (NLC)
OMFJ..........	Fujeirah/International [*United Arab Emirates*] [*ICAO location identifier*] (ICLI)
OMFP..........	Obtaining Money by False Pretense
omfp	Obtaining Money by False Pretenses (AD)
OMFP..........	Ortho-Methylfluorescein Phosphate [*Biochemistry*]
OMFS..........	Office Master Frequency Supply [*Telecommunications*] (TEL)
OMFS..........	Optimum Metric Fastener System
OMFSCA	Operation and Maintenance of Facilities Summary Cost Account [*Army*] (AABC)
OMFT..........	Optical Matched Filter Technique
OMFTS........	Operational Maneuver from the Sea [*Marine Corps*] (DOMA)

OMFUG.......	Other Music for Urban Gormandizers [*Acronym used as subtitle to the New York City nightclub name, CBGB*]
OMFY.......	Front of Yonge Township Public Library, Mallorytown, Ontario [*Library symbol National Library of Canada*] (BIB)
OMG	Aeromega Ltd. [*British ICAO designator*] (FAAC)
OMG	Object Management Group [*Computer science*]
OMG	Office Machines Group [*Business Equipment Manufacturers Association*]
OMG	Office of Marine Geology [*United States Geological Survey*]
OMG	Office of Military Government
OMG	Older Metamorphic Group [*Geology*]
OMG	Oligodendrocyte-Myelin Glycoprotein (DMAA)
OMG	Omega [*Namibia*] [*Airport symbol*] (OAG)
OMG	Omni MultiMedia Group [*AMEX symbol*] (TTSB)
OMG	Omni Multimedia Group, Inc. [*AMEX symbol*] (SAG)
OMG	Operational-Maneuver Group [*Military*]
OMG	Opthalmology Medical Group (AD)
OMG	Osteopathic Medical School Graduate (DMAA)
OMG	Outlaw Motorcycle Gang
OMGA	Golder Associates, Mississauga, Ontario [*Library symbol National Library of Canada*] (NLC)
OMGA	Operations Management Ground Application (SSD)
OmgaHl	Omega Health Systems, Inc. [*Associated Press*] (SAG)
OMGB	Georgian Bay Township Public Library, Mactier, Ontario [*Library symbol National Library of Canada*] (BIB)
OMGB	Office of Military Government for Bavaria [*US Military Government, Germany*]
OMGBS	Office of Military Government for Berlin Sector [*US Military Government, Germany*]
OMGCR........	Research & Development, Gulf Canada Ltd., Mississauga, Ontario [*Library symbol National Library of Canada*] (NLC)
OMGCR........	Technical Library, Petro-Canada Products, Mississauga, Ontario [*Library symbol National Library of Canada*] (NLC)
OMGE	Organisation Mondiale de Gastroenterologie [*World Organization of Gastroenterology - WOG*] [*Edinburgh, Scotland*] (EAIO)
OMGH	Office of Military Government for Hesse [*US Military Government, Germany*]
OMGI	OM Group [*NASDAQ symbol*] (TTSB)
OMGI	OM Group, Inc. [*NASDAQ symbol*] (SAG)
OMGL	Gartner Lee Associates Ltd., Markham, Ontario [*Library symbol National Library of Canada*] (NLC)
OMGR	Omni Insurance Group [*NASDAQ symbol*] (TTSB)
OMGR	Omni Insurance Group, Inc. [*NASDAQ symbol*] (SAG)
OM Grp.......	OM Group, Inc. [*Associated Press*] (SAG)
OMGT..........	Overall Missile Guidance Tests (MCD)
OMGUS........	Office of Military Government, United States
OMGWB.......	Office of Military Government for Wuerttemberg-Baden [*US Military Government, Germany*]
OMH	Health Sciences Library, Mississauga Hospital, Ontario [*Library symbol National Library of Canada*] (BIB)
OMH	Office of Mental Health (DMAA)
OMH	Omega Hydrocarbons Ltd. [*Toronto Stock Exchange symbol*]
OMH	Orumieh [*Iran*] [*Airport symbol Obsolete*] (OAG)
OMHCE........	Organic Material Hydrocarbon Equivalent [*Automotive emissions control*]
OMHL	Occupational Medicine and Hygiene Laboratory [*British*] (IRUK)
OMH-RC	Office of Minority Health Resource Center
OMHT	Hagar Township Public Library, Markstay, Ontario [*Library symbol National Library of Canada*] (NLC)
OMI.............	Middletown Public Library, Middletown, OH [*OCLC symbol*] (OCLC)
OMI.............	Midland Public Library, Ontario [*Library symbol National Library of Canada*] (NLC)
OMI.............	Oblates of Mary Immaculate (TOCD)
omi.............	Oblates of Mary Immaculate (TOCD)
OMI.............	Oblats de Marie Immaculee [*Oblates of Mary Immaculate*] [*Rome, Italy*] (EAIO)
OMI.............	Office of Management Improvement [*Department of Agriculture*]
OMI.............	Office of Management Information [*Military*] (AFIT)
OMI.............	Office of Medical Investigator (DMAA)
OMI.............	Office of Multicultural Interests [*Western Australia*]
OMI.............	Ogilvy & Mather International, Inc. (EFIS)
OMI.............	Ohio Mechanics Institute
OMI.............	Old Myocardial Infarction [*Medicine*]
OMI.............	Olympic Media Information (AD)
OMI.............	OMI Corp. [*Associated Press*] (SAG)
OMI.............	Omnibus Computer Graphics, Inc. [*Toronto Stock Exchange symbol*]
OMI.............	Oocyte Maturation Inhibitor [*Endocrinology*]
OMI.............	Open Market, Inc. (IGQR)
OMI.............	Open Messaging Interface [*Lotus Development Corp.*] (PCM)
OMI.............	Operating Memorandum - Information
OMI.............	Operational Maintenance Instruction (AAG)
OMI.............	Operation Move-In [*New York City*]
omi.............	Operations and Maintenance Instruction (NAKS)
OMI.............	Opinions about Mental Illness [*A questionnaire*]
OMI.............	Optical Measurement Instrument (SAA)
OMI.............	Ordnance Modifications Instructions
OMI.............	Organisation Maritime Internationale [*International Maritime Organization - IMO*] (EAIO)
OMI.............	Organisation Meteorologique Internationale
OMI.............	Organizacion Maritima Internacional [*International Maritime Organization*] [*Spanish United Nations*] (DUND)
OMI.............	Organization for Microinformation
OMI.............	Organizations Master Index [*A publication*]
OMI.............	Other Manufacturing Industries [*Department of Employment*] [*British*]
OMI.............	Our Main Interest (LAIN)

OMI	Owens & Minor [*NYSE symbol*] (TTSB)
OMI	Owens & Minor, Inc. [*NYSE symbol*] (SPSG)
OMIA	Operating, Maintenance, Interest, and Adaptability
OMiabM	Monsanto Research Corp., Mound Laboratory, Miamisburg, OH [*Library symbol Library of Congress*] (LCLS)
OMiabMI	Mead Imaging, Miamisburg, OH [*Library symbol*] [*Library of Congress*] (LCLS)
OMiabMM	Monarch Marking Systems, Pitney Bowes, Chemical Research and Development Library, Miamisburg, OH [*Library symbol Library of Congress*] (LCLS)
OMIBAC	Ordinal Memory Inspecting Binary Automatic Computer (IEEE)
OMIBM	IBM Canada Ltd., Markham, Ontario [*Library symbol National Library of Canada*] (NLC)
OMICA	Organized Migrants in Community Action [*Florida*] [*Defunct*]
OMid	Middletown Public Library, Middletown, OH [*Library symbol Library of Congress*] (LCLS)
OMidAR	Armco, Inc., Research Center, Technical Library, Middletown, OH [*Library symbol Library of Congress*] (LCLS)
OMidH	Middletown Hospital Association, Ada Leonard Memorial Library, Middletown, OH [*Library symbol*] [*Library of Congress*] (LCLS)
OMidU	Miami University, Middletown Campus, Middletown, OH [*Library symbol Library of Congress*] (LCLS)
OMIH	Huronia Historical Park, Midland, Ontario [*Library symbol National Library of Canada*] (NLC)
OMIHM	Halton Region Museum, Milton, Ontario [*Library symbol National Library of Canada*] (BIB)
OMIHS	Institute for Hydrogen Systems, Mississauga, Ontario [*Library symbol National Library of Canada*] (NLC)
OMII	Oxy Metal Industries International (AD)
OMIKK	Orszagos Muszaki Informacios Kozpont es Konyvtar [*National Technical Information Center and Library*] [*Information service or system*] (IID)
OMIL	Milton Public Library, Ontario [*Library symbol National Library of Canada*] (NLC)
OMILD	Mildmay Branch, Bruce County Public Library, Ontario [*Library symbol National Library of Canada*] (NLC)
OMill	Holmes County Public Library, Millersburg, OH [*Library symbol Library of Congress*] (LCLS)
OMILL	Millbrook Public Library, Ontario [*Library symbol National Library of Canada*] (BIB)
OMILV	Milverton Public Library, Ontario [*Library symbol National Library of Canada*] (NLC)
OMiM	Megis Local School District Public Library, Middleport Branch, Middleport, OH [*Library symbol Library of Congress*] (LCLS)
OMIM	Online Mendelian Inheritance in Man [*Genetics*]
OMIM	Outer Mitochondrial Membrane [*Also, OMM*] [*Cytology*]
OMIN	Inco Ltd., Mississauga, Ontario [*Library symbol National Library of Canada*] (NLC)
OMIOM	Original Meaning Is the Only Meaning [*Writing term*]
omiom	Original Meaning is the Only Meaning (AD)
OMIP	Office of Minority Institutions Program [*U.S. Department of the Interior*] (BARN)
OMIS	Office of Management and Information Systems (USGC)
OMIS	Office of Management Information Systems [*Office of Administration and Management*] [*Department of Labor*]
OMIS	Omission (AAG)
OMIS	Operational Management Information System [*Computer science*]
OMIS	Operational Management Information System [*NASA*] (NAKS)
O Misc	Ohio Miscellaneous Reports [*A publication*] (DLA)
OMISS	Operation and Maintenance Instruction Summary Sheet [*NASA*] (NAKS)
OMIT	Mitchell Public Library, Ontario [*Library symbol National Library of Canada*] (NLC)
omit	Orinthine-Decarboxylase, Motility, Indole, Trytophandeaminase (AD)
OMITT	Omittatur [*Let It Be Omitted*] [*Pharmacy*] (ROG)
OMJ	Ohmine [*Japan*] [*Seismograph station code, US Geological Survey*] (SEIS)
OMJ	Orthomode Junction [*Electronics*]
OMJAT	J. A. Turner Professional Library, H. J. A. Brown Education Centre, Mississauga, Ontario [*Library symbol National Library of Canada*] (NLC)
OMK	Omak, WA [*Location identifier FAA*] (FAAL)
OMK	Owl Monkey Kidney [*Cell line*]
omkr	Omdring [*About*] [*Norwegian*] (AD)
OMKR	Outer Marker [*Part of an instrument landing system*] [*Aviation*]
OMKT	Open Market [*NASDAQ symbol*] (TTSB)
OMKT	Open Market, Inc. [*NASDAQ symbol*] (SAG)
OML	One-Man-LAN [*Linked Access Network*] [*PC Interconnect, Inc.*] [*Telecommunications*] (PCM)
OML	Ontario Ministry of Labour Library [*UTLAS symbol*]
OML	Ontario Motor League [*Canada*] (AD)
OML	Operations Manual Letter [*National Weather Service*] (NOAA)
OML	Orbiter Mold Line [*NASA*] (NASA)
OML	Orbiting Military Laboratory (AAG)
OML	Orbitomeatal Line (STED)
OML	Orbitomental Line (DMAA)
OML	Order of Merit List [*Army*] (AABC)
OML	Ordnance Material Letter (SAA)
OML	Ordnance Missile Laboratories (KSC)
OML	Ordnance Muzzle Loading [*British military*] (DMA)
OML	Organic Materials Laboratory [*Watertown, MA*] [*Army*] (GRD)
OML	Organizational Maintenance Level (NVT)
OML	Outer Mold Line (NASA)
OML	Outgoing Matching Loss [*Telecommunications*] (TEL)
OML	Outside Mold Line [*Technical drawings*]
oml	Outside Mold Line (AD)
OML	University of Cincinnati, Marx Law Library, Cincinnati, OH [*OCLC symbol*] (OCLC)
OMLA	Organizational Maintenance Level Activity (MCD)
OMLAC	Oxfordshire Modern Languages Achievement Certificate [*British*] (AIE)
OMLCSA	Old Mine Lamp Collectors Society of America (EA)
OMLE	Organization of Spanish Marxist-Leninists (PD)
OMLIT	One-Man Live Interception Test (SAA)
OMLJ	Officer of Merit, Order of St. Lazarus of Jerusalem (DD)
OMLP	Ohio Midland Light & Power [*AAR code*]
OMLT	[*The*] Learning Tree, Mississauga, Ontario [*Library symbol National Library of Canada*] (NLC)
OMLTA	Ohio Modern Language Teachers Association (EDAC)
OMM	Miami University, Middletown Campus, Middletown, OH [*OCLC symbol*] (OCLC)
OMM	Office of Marine Minerals
OMM	Office of Minerals Mobilization [*Later, OMSF*] [*Department of the Interior*]
OMM	Officer Message Mail [*Military*]
OMM	Officer of the Order of Military Merit [*Canada*] (DD)
OMM	Oil Market Module [*Department of Energy*] (GFGA)
OMM	OMI Corp. [*NYSE symbol*] (TTSB)
OMM	Ommatidium [*Arthropod eye anatomy*]
OMM	Operation and Maintenance Manual
OMM	Ophthalmomandibulomelic [*Dysplasia Syndrome*] [*Medicine*] (STED)
OMM	Orbital Maintenance Mission [*NASA*] (SSD)
OMM	Organisation Meteorologique Mondiale [*World Meteorological Organization - WMO*] (EAIO)
OMM	Organizacion Meteorologica Mundial [*World Meteorological Organization - WMO*] [*Spanish*]
OMM	Organometallic Material
OMM	Outer Mitochondrial Membrane [*Also, OMiM*] [*Cytology*]
OMM	Oxford Medical Manuals [*A publication*]
OMMA	Outboard Motor Manufacturers Association [*Later, MEMA*] (EA)
OMMB	Information Centre, Molson Breweries of Canada Ltd., Mississauga, Ontario [*Library symbol National Library of Canada*] (NLC)
OMMC	Officer Message Mail Center [*Military*]
OMMCS	Ordnance Missile and Munitions Center and School [*Army*]
Om Mer Sh	Omond's Merchant Shipping Acts [*1877*] [*A publication*] (DLA)
OMMH	Orbiter Maintenance Man-Hours [*NASA*] (NASA)
OMMI	Magna International, Inc., Markham, Ontario [*Library symbol National Library of Canada*] (BIB)
OMMI	Oblate Missionaries of Mary Immaculate (TOCD)
OMMIC	Ordnance Maintenance Management Information Center [*Navy*]
OMMLT	Murchison Lyell Township Community Library, Madawaska, Ontario [*Library symbol National Library of Canada*] (NLC)
OMMM	Moore Museum, Mooretown, Ontario [*Library symbol National Library of Canada*] (BIB)
OMMMSA	Oil Mill Machinery Manufacturers and Supply Association (EA)
OMMS	Office of Merchant Marine Safety [*Coast Guard*]
OMMS	Organizational Missile Maintenance Squadron [*Air Force*]
OMM(S)C	Officer Messenger Mail (Sub) Center [*Navy*]
OMMSQA	Office of Modeling, Monitoring Systems, and Quality Assurance [*Environmental Protection Agency*]
OMN	Mansfield-Richland County Public Library, Mansfield, OH [*OCLC symbol*] (OCLC)
OMN	Octamethylnaphthalene [*Organic chemistry*]
OMN	Oculomotor Nerve [*Medicine*] (STED)
OMN	Oman [*ANSI three-letter standard code*] (CNC)
OMN	Omnivorous
OMN	Ormond Beach, FL [*Location identifier FAA*] (FAAL)
OMN	Orthomin
omn 2 hor	Omni Secunda Hora [*Every Two Hours*] [*Latin*] [*Pharmacy*] (DAVI)
OMN BID	Omni Bidus [*Every Two Days*] [*Pharmacy*] (ROG)
OMN BIH	Omni Bihora [*Every Two Hours*] [*Pharmacy*]
omn bih	Omni Bihora [*Every Two Hours*] [*Latin*] (AD)
Omncre	Omnicare, Inc. [*Associated Press*] (SAG)
OMNCS	Office of the Manager National Communications System [*GSA*]
OMNET	Organizational Maintenance New Equipment Training [*Army*] (INF)
OMNG	Operations and Maintenance, National Guard [*Army*]
OMN H	Omni Hora [*Every Hour*] [*Pharmacy*]
OMN HOR	Omni Hora [*Every Hour*] [*Pharmacy*]
OMNI	Omnidirectional
omni	Omnidirectional [*Microphone*] (WDMC)
Omni	Omni Multimedia Group, Inc. [*Associated Press*] (SAG)
omni	Omnirange (AD)
OMNI	Omni-Range (NAKS)
omni	Omnivisual (AD)
omni	Onmidirectional (AD)
OMNI	On-Site Multiple Network Installation [*Thomas & Betts Corp.*]
OMNI	Organizing Medical Networked Information [*British*] (TELE)
Omnicm	Omnicom Group, Inc. [*Associated Press*] (SAG)
OmniIns	Omni Insurance Group, Inc. [*Associated Press*] (SAG)
OmniMult	Omni Multimedia Group, Inc. [*Associated Press*] (SAG)
Omnipt	Omnipoint Corp. [*Associated Press*] (SAG)
OMNIRANGE	Omnidirectional Radio Range (MSA)
OMNITAB	Omnibus Program with Tabular Numerical Functions [*Programming language*] [*1965*] (CSR)
OMNITENNA	Omnirange Antenna
OmniUSA	Omni USA, Inc. [*Associated Press*] (SAG)
OMN MAN	Omni Mane [*Every Morning*] [*Pharmacy*]
omn man	Omni Mane [*Every Morning*] [*Latin*] (AD)
OMNMPS	Operative Machine Needle Makers' Protection Society [*A union*] [*British*]

OMN NOCT...	Omni Nocte [*Every Night*] [*Pharmacy*]
omn noct	Omni Nocte [*Every Night*] [*Latin*] (AD)
omn quad hor...	Omni Quadrante Hora [*Every quarter of An Hour*] [*Latin*] [*Pharmacy*] (DAVI)
OMN QUADR HOR...	Omni Quadrante Horae [*Every Quarter of an Hour*] [*Pharmacy*] (ROG)
OMNT	Northern Telecom, Mississauga, Ontario [*Library symbol National Library of Canada*] (NLC)
OMO	Moonbeam Public Library, Ontario [*Library symbol National Library of Canada*] (BIB)
OMO	Mostar [*Yugoslavia*] [*Airport symbol*] (AD)
OMO	Oblates of the Mother of Orphans (TOCD)
OMO	Office of Marine Operations [*Marine science*] (OSRA)
OMO	Office of the Director of Manpower and Organization [*Air Force*]
OMO	Old Man's Out [*Facetious translation of Omo, a brand of detergent*] [*British*]
OMO	Omoco Holdings [*Vancouver Stock Exchange symbol*]
OMO	One-Man-Operated Bus [*London, England*]
OMO	One Man Operation [*Railroad*] [*British*]
OMO	Open Market Operations [*Economics*]
OMO	Ordinary Money Order
OMO	Singly-Occupied Molecular Orbital [*Physical chemistry*]
OMOAM	Ontario Agricultural Museum, Milton, Ontario [*Library symbol National Library of Canada*] (NLC)
OMOB	Offensive Missile Order of Battle (MCD)
OMODE........	Ordinary Mode (MCD)
OMOL	Oliver Township Public Library, Murillo, Ontario [*Library symbol National Library of Canada*] (BIB)
OMOO	Moosonee Public Library, Ontario [*Library symbol National Library of Canada*] (BIB)
omor	One Man, One Responsibility (AD)
OMorS	Salem Township Public Library, Morrow, OH [*Library symbol Library of Congress*] (LCLS)
OMORSDG ...	Morewood Branch, Stormont, Dundas, and Glengarry County Public Library, Ontario [*Library symbol National Library of Canada*] (BIB)
OMOSC	Organisation des Musiciens d'Orchestres Symphoniques du Canada [*Organization of Canadian Symphony Musicans - OCSM*]
OMOSDG	Morrisburg Branch, Stormont, Dundas, and Glengarry County Public Library, Ontario [*Library symbol National Library of Canada*] (NLC)
OMOT	Metcalfe Branch, Osgoode Township Library, Ontario [*Library symbol National Library of Canada*] (BIB)
OMOTH	Osgoode Township High School Library, Metcalfe, Ontario [*Library symbol National Library of Canada*] (BIB)
OMOV	One Member, One Vote [*System to select parliamentary candidates*] [*British*]
OMP.............	Espe [*Germany*] [*Research code symbol*]
OMP.............	Marion Public Library, Marion, OH [*OCLC symbol*] (OCLC)
OMP.............	Ocean Microwave Package (SSD)
OMP.............	Office of Metric Programs [*Department of Commerce*]
OMP.............	Olfactory Marker Protein [*Biochemistry*]
OMP.............	Oligo-N-methylmorpholinopropylene Oxide [*Pharmacology*]
OMP.............	OM Group, Inc. [*NYSE symbol*] (SAG)
OMP.............	Operating Maintenance Panel (IAA)
OMP.............	Operating Maintenance Procedure (IAA)
OMP.............	Operating Memorandum - Policy
OMP.............	Operations and Maintenance Plan [*NASA*] (NASA)
OMP.............	Optical Mark Printer (NITA)
OMP.............	Organometallic Polymer (CAAL)
omp.............	Organo-Metallic Polymer (AD)
OMP.............	Ormetoprim [*Potentiator for antibacterials*] [*Veterinary medicine*]
OMP.............	Ornithine Monophosphate (DMAA)
OMP.............	Orotidine Monophosphate [*Organic chemistry*]
OMP.............	Outer Membrane Protein [*Biochemistry*]
OMP.............	Output Makeup
OMP.............	Overseas Manpower [*British*]
OMP.............	Oxford Medical Publications [*A publication*]
OMpA...........	American Society for Metals Library, Metals Park, OH [*Library symbol*] [*Library of Congress*] (LCLS)
OMPA	Octamethylpyrophosphoramide [*Insecticide*]
OMPA	Octamethylpyrophosphoramide, Schradan (EDCT)
OMPA	Office of Marine Pollution Assessment [*National Oceanic and Atmospheric Administration*] (ASF)
OMPA	One-Man Pension Arrangement [*Management*]
ompa	One-Man Pension Arrangement (AD)
OMPA	Operating Memorandum - Personnel Assignment
OMPA	Otitis Media, Purulent, Acute [*Medicine*]
OMPA	Outer Membrane Protein A [*Biochemistry*]
OMPC	Office of Municipal Pollution Control [*Environmental Protection Agency*] (GFGA)
OMPC	Overseas Military Personnel Charter (MCD)
OMPD	Office of Mineral Policy Development [*Department of the Interior*]
OMPE.........	Office of Management Planning and Evaluation [*Environmental Protection Agency*] (EPA)
OMPE & R ...	Office of Manpower Policy, Evaluation, and Research [*Department of Labor*]
OMPEC	Offshore Mechanics and Polar Engineering Council
OMPER	Office of Manpower Policy, Evaluation, and Research [*Department of Labor*]
OMPF	Official Military Personnel File [*Army*] (AABC)
ompf	Omphaloskepsis (AD)
OMPI	Ordnance Master Publication Index (MCD)

OMPI	Organisation Mondiale de la Propriete Intellectuelle [*World Intellectual Property Organization - WIPO*] [*Information service or system*] (IID)
OMPI	Organizacion Mundial de la Propiedad Intelectual [*World Intellectual Property Organization*] [*Spanish United Nations*] (DUND)
OMPI	Oxo(mercaptoethyl)(phenyl)imidazolidine [*Biochemistry*]
OMPO	Oahu Metropolitan Planning Organization [*Hawaii*] (AD)
OMPR	Office of Management Planning and Review [*Formerly, OMD*] [*NASA*]
OMPR	Operational Maintainability Problem Reporting (NASA)
OMPR	Optical Mark Page Reader [*Computer science*] (AABC)
ompr	Optical Mark Page Reader (AD)
OMPR	Optical Mark Printer (CIST)
OMPRA	Office of Minerals Policy and Research Analysis (AD)
OMPRA	One-Man Propulsion Research Apparatus [*NASA*]
OMPS	Orbit Maneuvering Propulsion System [*NASA*] (KSC)
OMPSA	Organisation Mondiale pour le Promotion Sociale des Aveugles [*World Council for the Welfare of the Blind - WCWB*] (EAIO)
OMPT	Observed Man [*or Mass*] Point Trajectory [*NASA*] (KSC)
OMPT	Omnipoint Corp. [*NASDAQ symbol*] (TTSB)
OMPU	Oficina Municipale de Planeamiento Urbano [*Municipal Office of Urban Planning*] [*Spain*] (AD)
OMPUS	Official Munitions Production United States
OMPW	Pratt & Whitney Aircraft Ltd., Mississauga, Ontario [*Library symbol National Library of Canada*] (NLC)
OMPX	OCLC Microcomputer Program Exchange (NITA)
OM QUAR HOR...	Omni Quarta Hora [*Every Quarter of An Hour*] [*Latin*] [*Pharmacy*] (DAVI)
OMR	Midland-Ross Corp., Library, Cleveland, OH [*OCLC symbol*] (OCLC)
OMR	Office Methods Research
omr.........	Office Methods Research (AD)
OMR	Office of Marine Resources [*Department of the Interior*] (NOAA)
OMR	Officer Master Record [*Air Force*] (AFM)
OMR	Oligomycin-Resistant (DMAA)
OMR	Online Medical Record (HCT)
OMR	Operational Modification Report (IAA)
OMR	Operation Management Room [*NASA*] (KSC)
OMR	Operations and Maintenance Requirements (NASA)
OMR	Operations Management Room [*NASA*]
OMR	Operations Manager's Report
OMR	Operative Morality Rate [*Statistics*] [*Medicine*] (DAVI)
OMR	Optical Mark Reader [*Computer science*]
omr.........	Optical Mark Reader (AD)
omr.........	Optical Mark Recognition (AD)
OMR	Optical Mark Recognition [*Computer science*] (MCD)
OMR	Optical Meter Relay
OMR	Orad [*Romania*] [*Airport symbol*] (OAG)
OMR	Orbiter Management Review [*NASA*] (NASA)
OMR	Organic Magnetic Resonance
OMR	Organic-Moderated Reactor [*Nuclear energy*]
OMR	Our Material Returned (AAG)
OMR	Overhaul, Maintenance, and Repair (MCD)
OMR	Overhead Materials Requirement [*Manufacturing*]
OMRA	135th Medical Regiment Association (EA)
OMRB	Operating Material Review Board [*NASA*] (NASA)
OMRC	Operational Maintenance Requirements Catalog [*NASA*] (MCD)
OMRC	Optical Mark Reader Card [*Computer science*] (MHDI)
OMRCA	Organic-Moderated Reactor Critical Assembly [*Nuclear energy*]
OMRD	Office of Manpower Research and Development [*National Academy of Sciences*]
OMRD	Overseas Mineral Resource Development (AD)
OMRE	Organic-Moderated Reactor Experiment [*Nuclear energy*]
OMRF	Oklahoma Medical Research Foundation [*University of Oklahoma*] [*Research center*]
OMRF	Orbiter Modification and Refurbishment Facility [*NASA*] (NAKS)
OMRI	Oklahoma Medical Research Institute
OMRI	Open Media Research Institute [*Non-profit news and analysis organization covering Eastern Europe and the former Soviet Union*] (ECON)
OMRK	Ras Al Khaimah/International [*United Arab Emirates*] [*ICAO location identifier*] (ICLI)
OMRM	Manitou Library (Ojibway of Manitou Rapids Indian Band), Manitou Rapids, Ontario [*Library symbol National Library of Canada*] (BIB)
OMRO	Ordnance Materials Research Office [*Later, AMMRC*] [*Army*] (MCD)
OMR/P	Operations and Maintenance Requirements/Plan [*NASA*] (NASA)
OMRR	Ordnance Material Research Reactor [*Nuclear energy*]
OMRS	Operations and Maintenance Requirements Specifications (NASA)
OMRS	Optical Mark Reader Sheet [*Computer science*] (MHDI)
OMRS	Orders and Medals Research Society (EA)
OMRSD	Operational Maintainability Reporting Systems Document [*NASA*] (NASA)
OMRSD.........	Operational Maintenance Requirements and Specifications Document [*NASA*] (NASA)
OMRSD	Operations and Maintenance Requirements and Specification Documentation (NASA)
OMRSD	Operations and Maintenance Requirements and Specifications Documentation
OMRV	Operational Maneuvering Reentry Vehicle (MCD)
OMRW	Optical MASER [*Microwave Amplification by Stimulated Emission of Radiation*] Radiation Weapon (AAG)
OMS.............	Ocean Minesweeper
OMS.............	Octahedral Molecular Sieve [*Inorganic chemistry*]
OMS.............	Office Management System [*Computer science*] (IAA)
OMS.............	Office of Management Services [*Department of Agriculture*]

OMS............	Office of Management Studies (EA)
OMS............	Office of Management Support [*Environmental Protection Agency*] (EPA)
OMS............	Office of Marketing Services [*of BDSA*]
OMS............	Office of Mobile Sources [*Environmental Protection Agency*] (GFGA)
OMS............	Oil Market Simulation Model [*Department of Energy*] (GFGA)
OMS............	Omsk [*Former USSR Airport symbol*] (OAG)
OMS............	On-Board Maintenance System [*Aviation*]
OMS............	One-Minute Superstar [*Actor whose bit part in a television series results in instant stardom*]
OMS............	Opcode MIDI [*Musical Instrument Digital Interface*] System
OMS............	Open Mail System [*Raindrop Software Co.*] (PCM)
OMS............	Open Management System [*Vitalink Communicatons Corp.*]
OMS............	Open Measurement Solution
OMS............	Operational Maintenance System
OMS............	Operational Meteorological Satellite [*NASA*]
OMS............	Operational Mission Summary [*Army*]
OMS............	Operational Mode Summary
OMS............	Operational Monitoring System (MCD)
OMS............	Operations Management System (SSD)
OMS............	Oppenheimer Multi-Sector [*NYSE symbol*] (TTSB)
OMS............	Oppenheimer Multi-Sector Income Trust [*NYSE symbol*] (SPSG)
OMS............	Optical MASER [*Microwave Amplification by Stimulated Emission of Radiation*] System
OMS............	Optical Mass Spectroscopy (AAEL)
OMS............	Optical Modulation System
OMS............	Optimum Mode Selector (CAAL)
OMS............	Oral and Maxillofacial Surgery
oms............	Orbital Maneuvering Subsystem [*NASA*] (NAKS)
oms............	Orbital Maneuvering System [*or Subsystem*] [*NASA*]
OMS............	Orbital Multifunction Satellite
OMS............	Ordnance Machine Shop
OMS............	Organic Mass Spectroscopy
OMS............	Organic Mental Syndrome [*Medicine*] (DMAA)
OMS............	Organisation Mondiale de la Sante [*World Health Organization - WHO*] [*Switzerland*]
OMS............	Organizacion Mundial de la Salud [*World Health Organization*] [*Spanish United Nations*] (DUND)
OMS............	Organizational Maintenance Shop [*Army*]
OMS............	Organizational Maintenance Squadron [*Air Force*] (MCD)
OMS............	Organizational Maintenance Support
OMS............	Oriental Missionary Society [*Later, OMS International*] (EA)
OMS............	Otomandibular Syndrome [*Medicine*] (DMAA)
OMS............	Outdoor Microphone System
OMS............	Output Multiplex Synchronizer
OMS............	Output per Man Shift
oms............	Output per Man Shift (AD)
OMS............	Overnight Message Service [*Diversified Data Processing and Consulting, Inc.*] [*Oak Park, MI*] [*Telecommunications*] (TSSD)
OMS............	Overseas Mission Society [*Defunct*] (EA)
OMS............	Ovonic Memory Switch (PDAA)
OMS............	Spectravac Power Conversion Systems, Inc., Mississauga, Ontario [*Library symbol National Library of Canada*] (NLC)
OMSA	Offshore Marine Service Association [*New Orleans, LA*] (EA)
OMSA	Orders and Medals Society of America (EA)
OMSA	Ordnance Missile Support Agency (SAA)
OMSA	Otitis Media, Suppurative, Acute [*Medicine*]
OMSA	Seaman Apprentice, Opticalman, Striker [*Navy rating*]
OMSA	Simcoe County Archives, Minesing, Ontario [*Library symbol National Library of Canada*] (NLC)
OMSAPC......	Office of Mobile Source Air Pollution Control [*Environmental Protection Agency*]
OMSB	Outcomes Management System Information Board
OMSC	Organisation Mondiale pour la Systemique et la Cybernetique [*World Organization of Systems and Cybernetics*] (EAIO)
OMSC	Otitis Media, Secretory, Chronic [*Medicine*] (DAVI)
OMSC	Otitis Media, Suppurative, Chronic [*Medicine*]
OMSDG........	Maxville Branch, Stormont, Dundas, and Glengarry County Public Library, Ontario [*Library symbol National Library of Canada*] (NLC)
OMSE..........	Office of Management Systems and Evaluation [*Environmental Protection Agency*] (GFGA)
Om Sea	Omond's Law of the Sea [*1916*] [*A publication*] (DLA)
OMSF..........	Office of Manned Space Flight [*NASA*]
OMSF..........	Office of Minerals and Solid Fuels [*Formerly, OMM*] [*Abolished, 1971 Department of the Interior*]
OMSG	Official Mail Study Group [*Defunct*] (EA)
OMSG	Our Message [*Aviation*] (FAAC)
OMSI	Oregon Museum of Science and Industry
OMSIP	Ontario Medical Surgical Insurance Plan [*Canada*] (AD)
OMSITE.......	Oral and Maxillofacial Surgery In-Training Examination
OMSJ..........	Sharjah/International [*United Arab Emirates*] [*ICAO location identifier*] (ICLI)
OMSJB........	St. Jean Bosco Library, Matachewan, Ontario [*Library symbol National Library of Canada*] (BIB)
OMSK	Smith, Kline & French Canada Ltd., Mississauga, Ontario [*Library symbol National Library of Canada*] (NLC)
OMSLMSq ..	Organizational Missile Maintenance Squadron [*Air Force*]
OMSM	Medical Library, Syntex, Inc., Mississauga, Ontario [*Library symbol National Library of Canada*] (NLC)
OMS/MP	Operational Mode Summary/Mission Profiles (MCD)
OMSMT.......	South Marysburgh Township Public Library, Milford, Ontario [*Library symbol National Library of Canada*] (BIB)
OMsn..........	Mason Public Library, Mason, OH [*Library symbol Library of Congress*] (LCLS)
OMSN	Seaman, Opticalman, Striker [*Navy rating*]
OMSP	Operational Maintenance Support Plan [*NASA*] (MCD)
OMSq.........	Organizational Maintenance Squadron [*Air Force*] (AFM)
OMSQA.......	Office of Monitoring Systems and Quality Assurance [*Environmental Protection Agency*] (EPA)
OMSRADS ...	Optimum Mix of Short Range Air Defense Systems
OMST..........	Object Manipulation Speed Test
OMSWG	Operations and Maintenance Security Working Group (SSD)
OMT	McKellar Township Public Library, Ontario [*Library symbol National Library of Canada*] (NLC)
OMT	Metropolitan Toronto Library, Multilanguage Service [*UTLAS symbol*]
OMT	Object Modeling Technique (AAEL)
OMT	Object Modeling Technology [*Ungermann-Bass, Inc.*]
OMT	Ocean Marine Technology [*Vancouver Stock Exchange symbol*]
OMT	Oceanography and Marine Technology [*Defunct*] (USDC)
OMT	Office of Manufacturing Technology [*DARCOM*] [*Army*] (RDA)
OMT	Officiating Minister to the Troops [*British*]
OMT	Ohio Mattress Co. (EFIS)
OMT	Old Merchant Taylors [*School*] [*British*] (ROG)
OMT	Oleoyl Methyl Taurate [*Organic chemistry*]
OMT	O-Methylthreonine [*Biochemistry*]
OMT	O-Methyl Transferase [*An enzyme*]
OMT	Ophthalmic Medical Assistant (DAVI)
OMT	Ophthalmic Medical Technician [*or Technologist*] (HCT)
OMT	Oral Mucosal Transudate [*Clinical chemistry*]
OMT	Ordnance Maintenance Truck [*British*]
OMT	Organizational Maintenance Technician [*Army*] (AABC)
OMT	Organizational Maintenance Trainer (MCD)
OMT	Orthogonal Mode Transducer (IAA)
OMT	Orthomode Transducer [*Electronics*]
omt	Orthomode Transducer (AD)
OMT	Ortho-Mycaminosyltylonolide [*Antibacterial compound*]
OMT	Orthotropic Multicell Tank
OMT	Osteopathic Manipulative Therapy (CPH)
OMT	Other Military Target
OMTA	Office of Management and Technical Assessment [*Environmental Protection Agency*] (GFGA)
OMTA	Ovulation Method Teachers Association (EA)
OMTBP	Octamethyltetrabenzporphyrin [*Organic chemistry*]
OMTC	Ontario Ministry of Transportation and Communications [*Downsview, ON*] [*Telecommunications*] (TSSD)
OMTD	Operator/Maintenance Task Description (DNAB)
OMTN	Other Military Teletypewriter Network (CET)
OMTNS	Over Mountains [*NWS*] (FAAC)
OMTR	Officer Master Tape Record [*Army*] (AABC)
OMTS	Organizational Maintenance Test Station [*Army*]
OMtsjC........	College of Mount St. Joseph-On-The-Ohio, Mount St. Joseph, OH [*Library symbol Library of Congress*] (LCLS)
OMTSS	Ordnance Multiple-Purpose Tactical Satellite System
OMtv	Mount Vernon Public Library, Mount Vernon, OH [*Library symbol Library of Congress*] (LCLS)
OMtvN	Mount Vernon Nazarene College, Mount Vernon, OH [*Library symbol Library of Congress*] (LCLS)
OMU	Operational Mock-Up
OMU	Operative Mechanics' Union [*British*]
OMU	Optical Measuring Unit (KSC)
omu	Optical Measuring Unit (NAKS)
OMUC	Upper Canada Village, Morrisburg, Ontario [*Library symbol National Library of Canada*] (NLC)
OMUP	Organization and Management User Parts [*Telecommunications*] (OSI)
OMV	Oat Mosaic Virus [*Plant pathology*]
OMV	Oblates of the Virgin Mary (TOCD)
omv	Oblates of the Virgin Mary (TOCD)
OMV	Orbital Maneuvering Vehicle [*NASA*]
OMV	Overseas Media Visitor
OMV	Oxygen Manual Valve (NASA)
omv	Oxygen Manual Valve (NAKS)
OMVC	Mattice-Val Cote Public Library, Mattice, Ontario [*Library symbol National Library of Canada*] (BIB)
OMVC	Open Mitral Valve Commissurotomy [*Medicine*]
OMVCC	Orbital Maneuvering Vehicle Control Center [*NASA*] (SSD)
OMVG	Organisation pour la Mise en Valeur du Fleuve Gambie [*Gambia River Basin Organisation*] (EAIO)
OMVI	Operating a Motor Vehicle Intoxicated (MEDA)
OM-VPE	Organometallic Vapor Phase Epitaxy [*Also, OM-CVD, MO-CVD, MO-VPE*] [*Semiconductor technology*]
OMVPE	Organometallic Vapour Phase Epitaxy (AAEL)
OMVTO	Office Motor Vehicle Transportation Officer [*Army*] (AABC)
OMVUIL	Operating Motor Vehicle under the Influence of Liquor [*Traffic offense charge*]
OMVWI	Operating Motor Vehicle while Intoxicated [*Traffic offense charge*]
OMW	Office of the Mining Warden [*Victoria, Australia*]
OMW	Omak [*Washington*] [*Seismograph station code, US Geological Survey*] (SEIS)
OMWG	Object Model Working Group
OMWM	Open Marsh Water Managed [*Ecology*]
OMX	Officemax, Inc. [*NYSE symbol*] (SAG)
OMX	Option Market Index [*Sweden*] (NUMA)
OMX	Xerox Research Centre of Canada, Mississauga, Ontario [*Library symbol National Library of Canada*] (NLC)
OMZ	Oamaru [*New Zealand*] [*Seismograph station code, US Geological Survey*] (SEIS)
OMZ	Oxygen-Minimum Zone [*Oceanography*]
OMZ	Oxymorphonazine [*An analgesic*]

ON .... Air Nauru [ICAO designator] (AD)
ON .... Central Branch, Nepean Public Library, Ontario [Library symbol National Library of Canada] (NLC)
ON .... McKinley Memorial Library, Niles, OH [Library symbol Library of Congress] (LCLS)
ON .... New Order [Revolutionary group] [Italy]
ON .... Octane Number [Fuel terminology]
on .... Octane Number (AD)
ON .... Oculonasal [Anatomy]
ON .... Office Nurse
ON .... Officer's Name (NITA)
ON .... Official Number (DS)
ON .... Off Normal
ON .... Ogden Nash (AD)
ON .... Oil-Immersed Natural-Colled Transformer (IAA)
ON .... Old Norse [Language, etc.]
ON .... Olfactory Nerve [Neuroanatomy]
ON .... Oligonucleotide [Chemistry]
ON .... Omega Navigation (PDAA)
ON .... Omega Neuron [Neuroanatomy]
ON .... Omni Nocte [Every Night] [Pharmacy]
on .... Omni Nocte [Every Night] [Latin] (AD)
ON .... Oncology [Medical specialty] (DHSM)
ON .... Onions (ROG)
on .... Onomastikon [Lexicon] [Greek] (AD)
On .... Onorevole [Honorable] [Italian] (AD)
ON .... Onorevole [Honorable] (EY)
On .... Onsdag [Wednesday] [Danish] (AD)
on .... Onstage [Theater] (WDMC)
ON .... Ontario [Canadian province] [Postal code]
ON .... Ontario Northland Railway [Canada] (AD)
ON .... Opera News [A publication] (BRI)
ON .... Operation Notice (AAG)
ON .... Optic Nerve [Anatomy]
O/N .... Order Notify [Bill of lading] [Shipping]
ON .... Order Number (NITA)
ON .... Ordre Nouveau [New Order] [France] [Political party] (WDAA)
ON .... Oregon [Obsolete] (ROG)
ON .... Original Negative
ON .... Ortho-Novum [A contraceptive] [Ortho Pharmaceutical Corp.] (DAVI)
ON .... Orthopedic Nurse
ON .... Our Neighbours [A publication]
O/N .... Own Name
o/n .... Own Name (AD)
ON .... Oxidation Number (IAA)
ONA .... Nakina Public Library, Ontario [Library symbol National Library of Canada] (BIB)
ONA .... Office of National Assessments [Australia]
ONA .... Onahama [Japan] [Seismograph station code, US Geological Survey] (SEIS)
ONA .... Oneita Industries [NYSE symbol] (SAG)
ONA .... Open Network Architecture [Computer science]
ONA .... Optical Navigation Attachment (WDAA)
ONA .... Orthonitroaniline (DICI)
ONA .... Overseas National Airways [Belgium ICAO designator] (FAAC)
ONA .... Overseas National Airways, Inc.
ONA .... Overseas News Agency
ONA .... Winona [Minnesota] [Airport symbol] (AD)
ONA .... Winona, MN [Location identifier FAA] (FAAL)
ONAC .... Office of Noise Abatement and Control [Environmental Protection Agency]
On a/c .... On Account (EBF)
ONAC .... Operating Network Advisory Committee [NERComP]
ONAIS .... Organization of North American Indian Students [Defunct] (EA)
ONAL .... Off-Net Access Line [Telecommunications] (TEL)
ONAP .... Orbit Navigation Analysis Program
ONAP .... Organisation Nationale d'Anti-Pauvrete [Canada]
ONAS .... Outpatient Nonavailability Statement [DoD]
OnAssign .... On Assignment, Inc. [Associated Press] (SAG)
O-NAV .... On-Board Navigation (MCD)
ONAX .... Overseas National Airways, Inc. [Air carrier designation symbol]
ONB .... Monkey Bay [Malawi] [Airport symbol] (AD)
ONb .... New Breman Public Library, New Breman, OH [Library symbol Library of Congress] (LCLS)
ONB .... North Bay Public Library, Ontario [Library symbol National Library of Canada] (NLC)
ONB .... Octane Number Barrel [Fuel terminology]
ONB .... Old Natura Brevium [A publication] (DLA)
ONB .... Ortho-Nitrobiphenyl [Organic chemistry]
ONBA .... Centre de Ressources, Ecole Secondaire Algonquin, North Bay, Ontario [Library symbol National Library of Canada] (NLC)
ONBCC .... Canadore College, North Bay, Ontario [Library symbol National Library of Canada] (NLC)
Onbcp .... ONBANcorp, Inc. [Associated Press] (SAG)
ONBD .... On Board (NASA)
ONBK .... Onbancorp, Inc. [NASDAQ symbol] (NQ)
ONBKP .... ONBANCorp 6.75% Cv `B' Pfd [NASDAQ symbol] (TTSB)
ONBM .... Belmont and Methuen Township Public Library, Nephton, Ontario [Library symbol National Library of Canada] (BIB)
ONBNU .... Nipissing University College, North Bay, Ontario [Library symbol National Library of Canada] (NLC)
ONBOSUB .... On Board a Submarine [Navy]
ONBOWCOM .... Duty on Board that Vessel when Placed in Commission [Navy]
ONBOWSERV .... Duty on Board that Vessel when Placed in Service [Navy]

ONBP .... Staff Library, North Bay Psychiatric Hospital, Ontario [Library symbol National Library of Canada] (NLC)
ONBT .... Orbiter Neutral Buoyancy Trainer [NASA] (MCD)
ONBT .... Regroupement des Organisations Nationales Benevoles [Also, National Voluntary Organizations] (AC)
ONBWF .... West Ferris Secondary School, North Bay, Ontario [Library symbol National Library of Canada] (NLC)
ONC .... Confederation High School, Nepean, Ontario [Library symbol National Library of Canada] (NLC)
ONC .... Office of Narcotics Coordinator [Later, NARCOG] [CIA]
ONC .... Office of New Careers [HEW]
ONC .... Olivet Nazarene College [Kankakee, IL]
ONC .... Oncology (DAVI)
ONC .... Oncor, Inc. [AMEX symbol] (SAG)
ONC .... On-Site Container (DOMA)
onc .... Ontario [MARC country of publication code Library of Congress] (LCCP)
ONC .... Open Network Computing [Computer science] (PCM)
ONC+ .... Open Network Computing Plus [Computer science] (PCM)
ONC .... Operational Navigation Charts [Air Force]
ONC .... Optimists National Corps [British military] (DMA)
ONC .... Ordinary National Certificate [British]
ONC .... Oregon-Nevada-California [Truck line] (IIA)
ONC .... Organization of Nigerian Citizens
ONC .... Orthopedic Nursing Certificate
ONC .... Overall NATO Command (NATG)
ONCB .... Centennial Branch, Nepean Public Library, Ontario [Library symbol National Library of Canada] (NLC)
ONC/D .... Ordinary National Certificate/Diploma (ACII)
ONCE .... Office of National Cost Estimates [Department of Health and Human Services] (GFGA)
ONCF .... Office National des Chemins de Fer [Moroccan Railways]
ONCFM .... Office National des Chemins de Fer du Maroc [Moroccan Railways] (DCTA)
ONCG-A .... Oncogenic Virus Battery - Acute [Oncology] (DAVI)
ONcM .... Muskingum College, New Concord, OH [Library symbol Library of Congress] (LCLS)
ONCMM .... Cosby, Mason, and Martland Public Library, Noelville, Ontario [Library symbol National Library of Canada] (NLC)
ONCN .... [An] O'Neill Concordance [A publication]
ONCO .... Office of NOAA [National Oceanic and Atmospheric Administration] Corps Operations [Marine science] (OSRA)
OnCo .... On Command Corp. [Associated Press] (SAG)
ONCO .... On Command Corp. [NASDAQ symbol] (SAG)
Onco .... OncoRx, Inc. [Associated Press] (SAG)
Oncogn .... Oncogene Science, Inc. [Associated Press] (SAG)
ONCOL .... Oncologist
OnCom .... On Command Corp. [Associated Press] (SAG)
OnComm .... On Command Corp. [Associated Press] (SAG)
Oncor .... Oncor, Inc. [Associated Press] (SAG)
ONCORE .... On-Command Restartable (MCD)
Oncormd .... OncorMed, Inc. [Associated Press] (SAG)
OncoRx .... OncoRx, Inc. [Associated Press] (SAG)
ONCRC .... Central Resource Centre, Carleton Roman Catholic School Board, Nepean, Ontario [Library symbol National Library of Canada] (NLC)
ONCS .... Oncogene Science [NASDAQ symbol] (TTSB)
ONCS .... Oncogene Science, Inc. [NASDAQ symbol] (NQ)
ONCU .... Cumberland Township Library, Navan, Ontario [Library symbol National Library of Canada] (BIB)
OND .... Office for Network Development [Ottawa, ON] [National Library of Canada Telecommunications service] (TSSD)
OND .... Office of Neighborhood Development (OICC)
OND .... Office of the Nominal Defendant [Australia]
OND .... Ondangua [Namibia] [Airport symbol] (OAG)
OND .... Operator Need Date (NASA)
OND .... Ophthalmic Nursing Diploma
OND .... Ordinary National Diploma [British]
OND .... Orthopaedic Nursing Diploma [British]
OND .... Other Neurological Disorders
OND .... Own Number Dialing [Telecommunications] (OA)
ONDA .... Norwich and District Archives, Norwich, Ontario [Library symbol National Library of Canada] (BIB)
ONDCP .... Office of National Drug Control Policy [Executive Office of the President]
ONDE .... Office of Naval Disability Evaluation (NVT)
ONDI .... Ontrack Data International, Inc. [NASDAQ symbol] (SAG)
ONDS .... Dipix Systems Ltd., Nepean, Ontario [Library symbol National Library of Canada] (NLC)
ONDS .... Optic Nerve Decompression Surgery
ONDS .... Oriental Nocturnal Death Syndrome [Neurology] (DAVI)
ONE .... Banc One Corp. [NYSE symbol] (SPSG)
ONE .... Current Tech [Vancouver Stock Exchange symbol]
ONE .... Current Technology [VS, exchange symbol] (TTSB)
ONe .... Nelsonville Public Library, Nelsonville, OH [Library symbol Library of Congress] (LCLS)
ONE .... Newmarket Public Library, Ontario [Library symbol National Library of Canada] (NLC)
ONE .... Northeastern Ohio University, College of Medicine, Rootstown, OH [OCLC symbol] (OCLC)
ONE .... Office National de l'Energie [National Energy Board - NEB] [Canada]
ONE .... Office Network Exchange [Honeywell, Inc.]
ONE .... Onepusu [Solomon Islands] [Airport symbol Obsolete] (OAG)
ONE .... Onerahi [Whangarei] [New Zealand] [Seismograph station code, US Geological Survey] (SEIS)

ONE	Open Network Environment [*Netscape network*] [*Computer science*]
ONE	Optimum Nutritional Effectiveness [*Brand name of dog food*] [*Ralston Purina Co.*]
O'Neal Neg L	O'Neal's Negro Law of South Carolina [*A publication*] (DLA)
ONEC	OneComm Corp. [*NASDAQ symbol*] (SAG)
OneCm	OneComm Corp. [*Associated Press*] (SAG)
ONEG	O Negative [*Blood type*] [*Hematology and laboratory*] (DAVI)
ONeH	Hocking Technical College, Nelsonville, OH [*Library symbol Library of Congress*] (LCLS)
Oneida	Oneida Ltd. [*Associated Press*] (SAG)
Oneita	Oneita Industries [*Associated Press*] (SAG)
ONELAC	Newburgh Branch, Lennox and Addington County, Ontario [*Library symbol National Library of Canada*] (BIB)
OneLb	One Liberty Properties, Inc. [*Associated Press*] (SAG)
Onelibt	One Liberty Properties, Inc. [*Associated Press*] (SAG)
ONEMRCM	BCC Library, CANMET, Energy, Mines, and Resources Canada [*Bibliotheque du CBC, CANMET, Energie, Mines, et Ressources Canada*], Nepean, Ontario [*Library symbol National Library of Canada*] (NLC)
ONEO	Office of Navajo Economic Opportunity
ONEOK	ONEOK, Inc. [*Associated Press*] (SAG)
ONEP	Office National d'Edition et de Presse [*News agency*] [*Niger*] (EY)
ONEP	Pickering College, Newmarket, Ontario [*Library symbol National Library of Canada*] (NLC)
ONEPI	Office National d'Edition, de Presse, et d'Imprimerie [*Publisher*] [*Benin*] (EY)
OnePrice	One Price Clothing Stores, Inc. [*Associated Press*] (SAG)
ONER	Oceanic Navigational Error Report [*Aviation*] (FAAC)
Onet	Ontario Regional Network [*Canada*] [*Computer science*] (TNIG)
ONEU	Neustadt Village Public Library, Ontario [*Library symbol National Library of Canada*] (NLC)
OneVall	One Valley Bancorp of West Virginia, Inc. [*Associated Press*] (SAG)
ONew	Newark Public Library, Newark, OH [*Library symbol Library of Congress*] (LCLS)
ONewU	Ohio State University, Newark Campus, Newark, OH [*Library symbol Library of Congress*] (LCLS)
OneWve	OneWave, Inc. [*Associated Press*] (SAG)
ONF	Niagara Falls Public Library, Ontario [*Library symbol National Library of Canada*] (NLC)
ONF	Office National du Film du Canada [*National Film Board of Canada - NFB*]
ONF	Old Norman French [*Language, etc.*]
ONF	Old Northern French [*Language, etc.*]
ONF	Optic Nerve Fiber [*Anatomy*]
ONFA	Acres Consulting Services Ltd., Niagara Falls, Ontario [*Library symbol National Library of Canada*] (NLC)
ONFCY	Cyanamid, Niagara Falls, Ontario [*Library symbol National Library of Canada*] (NLC)
ONFJC	John Coutts Library Services Ltd., Niagara Falls, Ontario [*Library symbol National Library of Canada*] (NLC)
ONFLC	Lanmer Consultants Ltd., Niagara Falls, Ontario [*Library symbol National Library of Canada*] (NLC)
ONFM	On or Nearest Full Moon [*Freemasonry*] (ROG)
ONFR	Old Northern French [*Language, etc.*]
ONFWM	Willoughby Historical Museum, Niagara Falls, Ontario [*Library symbol National Library of Canada*] (BIB)
ONFWPL	W. P. London & Associates, Niagara Falls, Ontario [*Library symbol National Library of Canada*] (NLC)
ONG	Donalsonville, GA [*Location identifier FAA*] (FAAL)
ONG	Mornington Island [*Australia Airport symbol*] (OAG)
ONG	Oneok, Inc. (EFIS)
ONG	Ongar [*England*]
ONG	Ongoro [*Peru*] [*Seismograph station code, US Geological Survey Closed*] (SEIS)
ONG	Osteopathic and Naturopathic Guild [*British*] (DBA)
ONGA	Overseas Number Group Analysis [*Telecommunications*] (TEL)
ONGC	Office des Normes Generales du Canada
OnGrd	On Gard Systems [*Associated Press*] (SAG)
OnGrdSy	On Gard Systems [*Associated Press*] (SAG)
ONGRT	North Gower Branch, Rideau Township Library, Ontario [*Library symbol National Library of Canada*] (BIB)
ONGS	Office of National Geodetic Survey [*National Ocean Survey*]
ONH	Office of Naval History [*Also, OFFNAVHIST*]
ONH	Oneonta [*New York*] [*Airport symbol*] (OAG)
ON/H	On the Hatch Cover [*Stowage*] (DNAB)
ONHI	Niagara Historical Society, Niagara-On-The-Lake, Ontario [*Library symbol National Library of Canada*] (NLC)
ONHIC	ODPHP [*Office of Disease Prevention and Health Promotion*] National Health Information Center (IID)
ONI	Moanamani [*Indonesia*] [*Airport symbol*] (OAG)
ONI	Nipigon Public Library, Ontario [*Library symbol National Library of Canada*] (NLC)
ONI	Office of Naval Intelligence
ONI	Oficina Nacional de Informacion [*National Information Office*] [*Press agency Peru*]
ONI	Oni [*Former USSR Seismograph station code, US Geological Survey*] (SEIS)
ONI	Operator Number Identification [*Bell System*]
ONIO	Office of Naval Inspectors of Ordnance
ONIP	Office of National Industry Promotion [*Bureau of Apprenticeship and Training*] [*Department of Labor*]
OnIssues	On the Issues [*A publication*] (BRI)
ONJ	Olivia Newton-John [*Singer*]
ONJSW	J. S. Woodsworth Secondary School, Nepean, Ontario [*Library symbol National Library of Canada*] (NLC)

Onk	Targum Onkelos (BJA)
ONL	New Liskeard Public Library, Ontario [*Library symbol National Library of Canada*] (NLC)
ONL	Office of Naval Liaison [*NASA*] (KSC)
ONL	Ohio Northern University, Law Library, Ada, OH [*OCLC symbol*] (OCLC)
ONL	O'Neill, NE [*Location identifier FAA*] (FAAL)
ONL	Outer Nuclear Layer [*Anatomy*]
ONL	Overnight Loan (ADA)
ONLAC	Lennox and Addington Counties Public Library, Napanee, Ontario [*Library symbol National Library of Canada*] (NLC)
ONLAH	Lennox and Addington Historical Society, Napanee, Ontario [*Library symbol National Library of Canada*] (BIB)
ONLAM	Lennox and Addington Museum, Napanee, Ontario [*Library symbol National Library of Canada*] (NLC)
ONLAS	Optical Night Landing Approach System [*Aviation*] (PDAA)
ONLF	Ogaden National Liberation Front [*Ethiopia*]
ONLICATS	Online Shared Cataloging System [*Computer science*]
ONLP	On-Line Program Development [*Computer science*] (MHDB)
ONIP	Perry County District Library, New Lexington, OH [*Library symbol Library of Congress*] (LCLS)
ONLS	Sunnidale Township Public Library, New Lowell, Ontario [*Library symbol National Library of Canada*] (BIB)
ONLY	Online Yield [*Computer science*]
ONM	Condamine [*Queensland*] [*Airport symbol*] (AD)
ONM	Office of Naval Material [*Later, NMCOM*]
ONM	OncorMed, Inc. [*AMEX symbol*] (SAG)
ONM	Socorro, NM [*Location identifier FAA*] (FAAL)
ONMB	Merivale Road Branch, Nepean Public Library, Ontario [*Library symbol National Library of Canada*] (BIB)
ONMINST	Office of Naval Material Publication Type Instruction
ONMM	On-Board Microwave MODEM [*Telecommunications*] (LAIN)
ONMPC	Office of Naval Material - Permanent Cadre
ONMS	Orbiter Neutral Mass Spectrometer [*NASA*]
ONMSS	Office of Nuclear Materials Safety and Safeguards [*Nuclear Regulatory Commission*]
ONN	Fort Meade, MD [*Location identifier FAA*] (FAAL)
ONN	O'Nyong-Nyong Virus
ONNA	Oh No, Not Again! [*Computer hacker terminology*]
ONNI	Office of National Narcotics Intelligence [*Later, Drug Enforcement Administration*] [*Department of Justice*]
ONNM	On or Nearest New Moon [*Freemasonry*] (ROG)
ONO	Norwood Public Library, Ontario [*Library symbol National Library of Canada*] (BIB)
ONO	Office of Naval Operations
ONO	Ontario [*Oregon*] [*Airport symbol*] (AD)
ONO	Ontario, OR [*Location identifier FAA*] (FAAL)
ONO	Organization of News Ombudsmen (EA)
ONO	Or Nearest [*or Near*] Offer [*Business term*] (ADA)
ONOC	Oceania National Olympic Committee [*Australia*]
ONocHE	Hoover Co., Engineering Division, North Canton, OH [*Library symbol Library of Congress*] (LCLS)
ON-OFF	Oscillatory, Nonoscillatory Flip-Flop [*Computer science*]
ONOL	Niagara-On-The-Lake Public Library, Ontario [*Library symbol National Library of Canada*] (BIB)
Onom	Onomasticon [*of Eusebius*] (BJA)
ONOMAT	Onomatopoeia (ROG)
ONOO	Outline NATO Operational Objective (MCD)
ONOP	Office of Naval Officer Procurement
ONOP	Officer-in-Charge, Branch Office of Naval Officer Procurement (DNAB)
ONowdM	Athenaeum of Ohio, Norwood, OH [*Library symbol Library of Congress*] (LCLS)
ONOZ	Oil Nozzle
ONP	Newport [*Oregon*] [*Airport symbol Obsolete*] (OAG)
ONP	Office of National Programs [*Employment and Training Administration*] [*Department of Labor*]
ONP	Ohio Nisi Prius Reports [*A publication*] (DLA)
ONP	Old Newspaper [*Recycling*]
ONP	Onex Packaging, Inc. [*Toronto Stock Exchange symbol*]
ONP	Open Network Provision
ONP	Operating Nursing Procedure
ONP	Optical Nuclear Polarization (AAEL)
ONP	Original Net Premium [*Insurance*] (AIA)
ONP	Ortho-Nitrophenol [*Organic chemistry*]
ONPA	Office of National Projects Administration [*Department of Labor*]
ONPG	O-Nitrophenyl-beta-D-galactopyranoside [*Test*] [*Microbiology*]
ONPG	O-Nitrophenyl Galactoside (DOG)
ONPG	Operational Nuclear Planning Group [*Military*]
ONP-GAL	Ortho-Nitrophenyl-B-Galactosidase [*Organic chemistry*] (MAE)
ONpK	Kent State University, Tuscarawas County Regional Campus, New Philadelphia, OH [*Library symbol Library of Congress*] (LCLS)
ONPNS	Ohio Nisi Prius Reports, New Series [*1903-13*] [*A publication*] (DLA)
OnPointT	On-Point Technology Systems, Inc. [*Associated Press*] (SAG)
ONPOSR	Office of Naval Petroleum and Oil Shale Reserves
ONPR	Office of New Production Reactors [*U.S. Department of Energy*] (BARN)
ONPR	One Price Clothing Stores, Inc. [*NASDAQ symbol*] (NQ)
ONPR	One Price Clothing Strs [*NASDAQ symbol*] (TTSB)
ONPT	On-Point Technology Systems, Inc. [*NASDAQ symbol*] (SAG)
ONR	Monkira [*Queensland*] [*Airport symbol*] (AD)
ONR	Oboz Narodowo-Radykalny [*Radical Nationalist Camp*] [*Poland Political party*] (PPE)
ONR	Octane Number Requirement [*Automotive engineering*]
ONR	Office of Naval Research [*Arlington, VA*]

ONR	Official Naval Reporter [*British*]
ONR	Ontario Northland Railway
ONR	Operational NonRADAR Directed Flights (NATG)
ONR	Original Net Rate [*Insurance*] (AIA)
ONR	Phillips Petroleum Co., Exploration and Product Library, Bartlesville, OK [*OCLC symbol*] (OCLC)
ONRARO	Office of Naval Research, Area Research Office (DNAB)
ONR BR	Branch Office, Office of Naval Research
ONRBRO	Office of Naval Research Branch Research Office
ONRC	Office of Naval Research, Chicago
ONRDB	Ruth E. Dickinson Branch, Nepean Public Library, Ontario [*Library symbol National Library of Canada*] (BIB)
ONRDET	Office of Naval Research Detachment (DNAB)
ONREAST	Office of Naval Research, East Coast Regional Office (DNAB)
ONRFE	Office of Naval Research, Far East Regional Office (DNAB)
ONRI	Octane Number Requirement Increase [*Automotive engineering*]
ONRL	Office of Naval Research, London
ONRO	ODA Natural Resources Office
ONRRR	Office of Naval Research Resident Representative
ONRS	Oceanic Navigation Research Society (EA)
ONRS	Office of National Range Support (SAA)
ONRT	Office of Naval Research, Tokyo
ONRT	Online Real Time [*Computer science*] (ADA)
ONRWEST	Office of Naval Research, West Coast Regional Office (DNAB)
ONRY	Ogdensburg Bridge & Port Authority [*AAR code*]
ONS	Northwestern School of Law, Lewis and Clark College, Portland, OR [*OCLC symbol*] (OCLC)
ONS	Oconee Nuclear Station (NRCH)
ONS	Office for National Statistics [*British*]
ONS	Office of Nuclear Systems (SAA)
ONS	Off-Normal Switch
ONS	Omega Navigation System
ONS	Oncology Nursing Society (EA)
ONS	Onslow [*Australia Airport symbol Obsolete*] (OAG)
ONS	Open Network Server [*Tylink Corp.*]
ONS	Operational Needs Statement [*Army*]
ONS	Oriental Numismatic Society [*Reading, Berkshire, England*] (EAIO)
ONSDG	Newington Branch, Stormont, Dundas, and Glengarry County Library, Ontario [*Library symbol National Library of Canada*] (BIB)
On Serv	On Service [*A publication*]
ONSHR	On Shore [*NWS*] (FAAC)
ONSI	Orion Network Systems [*NASDAQ symbol*] (TTSB)
ONSI	Orion Network Systems, Inc. [*NASDAQ symbol*] (SAG)
ONSIDIV	On-Sight Surveys Division
OnSiteS	On-Site Sourcing, Inc. [*Associated Press*] (SAG)
Onsl NP	Onslow's Nisi Prius [*A publication*] (DLA)
ONSOD	Omega Navigation System Operations Detail
ONSR	Sir Robert Borden High School, Nepean, Ontario [*Library symbol National Library of Canada*] (BIB)
ONSS	On-Site Sourcing, Inc. [*NASDAQ symbol*] (SAG)
ONST	Outline NATO Staff Target
ONT	Air Ontario Ltd. [*Canada ICAO designator*] (FAAC)
ONT	Office Nationale du Tourisme [*Algeria*] (EY)
ONT	Office of Naval Technology (MCD)
ONT	Ombudsman of the Northern Territory [*Australia*]
ONT	Ontario [*California*] [*Airport symbol*]
ONT	Ontario [*Canadian province*]
Ont	Ontario [*Canada*] (DD)
ONT	Ontario City Library, Ontario, CA [*OCLC symbol*] (OCLC)
ONT	Ontario Northland Railway [*AAR code*]
Ont	Ontario Reports [*A publication*] (DLA)
ONT	Ordinary Neap Tide (WDAA)
ONT	Our New Thread [*Clark thread designation*]
Ont 2d	Ontario Reports, Second Series [*Canada*] [*A publication*] (DLA)
Ont A	Ontario Appeals [*A publication*] (DLA)
ONTAP	Online Training and Practice (NITA)
ONTAP	On-Line Training and Practice File [*Lockheed*] [*Computer science*]
Ont App	Ontario Appeal Reports [*A publication*] (DLA)
Ontario Cons Reg	Ontario Consolidated Regulations [*Canada*] [*A publication*] (DLA)
ONTC	ON Technology [*NASDAQ symbol*] (TTSB)
ONTC	ON Technology Corp. [*NASDAQ symbol*] (SAG)
ON Tch	ON Technology Corp. [*Associated Press*] (SAG)
Ont Dig	Digest of Ontario Case Law [*A publication*] (DLA)
Ont El Cas	Ontario Election Cases [*1884-1900*] [*Canada A publication*] (DLA)
Ont Elec	Ontario Election Cases [*1884-1900*] [*Canada A publication*] (DLA)
Ont Elec C	Ontario Election Cases [*1884-1900*] [*Canada A publication*] (DLA)
Ont Elect	Ontario Election Cases [*1884-1900*] [*Canada A publication*] (DLA)
ONTERIS	Ontario Education Resources Information System [*Ontario Ministry of Education*] [*Toronto*] [*Information service or system*] (IID)
ONTG	Oral Nitroglycerine [*Medicine*]
ONTK	OnTrak Systems [*NASDAQ symbol*] (TTSB)
ONTK	On Trak Systems, Inc. [*NASDAQ symbol*] (SAG)
Ont L	Ontario Law Reports [*A publication*] (DLA)
Ont LJ	Ontario Law Journal [*A publication*] (DLA)
Ont LJ (NS)	Ontario Law Journal, New Series [*A publication*] (DLA)
Ont LR	Ontario Reports [*A publication*] (DLA)
Ont L Rep	Ontario Law Reports [*A publication*] (DLA)
ONTOLT	Onion, Tomato, or Lettuce [*Notation on restaurant checks*]
Ont Pr	Ontario Practice [*A publication*] (DLA)
Ont PR	Ontario Practice Reports [*A publication*] (DLA)
Ont Pr Rep	Ontario Practice Reports [*A publication*] (DLA)
Ont R	Ontario Reports [*A publication*] (DLA)
ONTR	Orders Not to Resuscitate [*Medicine*]
OnTrak	OnTrak Systems, Inc. [*Associated Press*] (SAG)
Ont R & WN	Ontario Reports and Ontario Weekly Notes [*Canada*] [*A publication*] (DLA)
OntrDta	Ontrack Data International, Inc. [*Associated Press*] (SAG)
Ont Reg	Ontario Regulations [*Canada*] [*A publication*] (DLA)
Ont Regs	Ontario Regulations [*Canada A publication*] (DLA)
Ont Rev Regs	Ontario Revised Regulations [*Canada A publication*] (DLA)
Ont Rev Stat	Ontario Revised Statutes [*Canada*] [*A publication*] (DLA)
Ont Rgt	Ontario Regiment [*Canada*] (DMA)
Ont Stat	Ontario Statutes [*Canada*] [*A publication*] (DLA)
Ont Tax Rep (CCH)	Ontario Tax Reporter (Commerce Clearing House) [*A publication*] (DLA)
Ont Week N	Ontario Weekly Notes [*A publication*] (DLA)
Ont Week R	Ontario Weekly Reporter [*A publication*] (DLA)
Ont Wkly N	Ontario Weekly Notes [*A publication*] (DLA)
Ont Wkly Rep	Ontario Weekly Reporter [*A publication*] (DLA)
Ont WN	Ontario Weekly Notes [*A publication*] (DLA)
Ont WR	Ontario Weekly Reporter [*A publication*] (DLA)
Ont WR Op	Ontario Weekly Reporter. Opinions of United States Attorneys General [*A publication*] (DLA)
ONU	Kongoussi [*Upper Volta*] [*Airport symbol*] (AD)
ONU	Ohio Northern University [*Ada, OH*]
ONU	Ohio Northern University, Ada, OH [*OCLC symbol*] (OCLC)
ONU	Ono-I-Lau [*Fiji*] [*Airport symbol Obsolete*] (OAG)
ONU	Optical Network Unit [*Telecommunications*]
ONU	Organisation des Nations Unies [*United Nations French*]
ONU	Organizacion de las Naciones Unidas [*United Nations*] [*Spanish*] (DUND)
ONU	Organizzazione Nazioni Unite [*United Nations*] [*Italian*]
ONUC	Organisation des Nations Unies au Congo [*United Nations Organization in the Congo*]
ONUDI	Organisation des Nations Unies pour le Developpement Industriel [*United Nations Industrial Development Organization*]
ONUDI	Organizacion de las Naciones Unidas para el Desarrollo Industrial [*United Nations Industrial Development Organization*] [*Spanish*] (DUND)
ONU Intra LR	Ohio Northern University. Intramural Law Review [*A publication*] (DLA)
ONULP	Ontario New Universities Library Project
Onuphr De Interp Voc Eccles	Onuphrius. De Interpretatione Vocum Ecclesiae [*A publication*]
ONV	Organisations Nationales Volontaires [*Canada*]
ONVL	Over-the-Nose Vision Line (PDAA)
ONW	Office of Naval Weapons
ONW	On Watch
ONW	Oregon & Northwestern Railroad Co. [*AAR code*]
ONWI	Office of Nuclear Waste Isolation (MCD)
ONWL	Whitefish Lake Band Public Library, Naughton, Ontario [*Library symbol National Library of Canada*] (NLC)
ONWS	Office of Naval Weather Service
ONX	Colon [*Panama*] [*Airport symbol*] (OAG)
ONX	Mount Olive, NC [*Location identifier FAA*] (FAAL)
onx	Onyx (VRA)
ONX	Onyx Petroleum Exploration Co. Ltd. [*Toronto Stock Exchange symbol*]
ONXX	ONYX Pharmaceuticals [*NASDAQ symbol*] (TTSB)
ONXX	Onyx Pharmaceuticals, Inc. [*NASDAQ symbol*] (SAG)
ONY	Olney, TX [*Location identifier FAA*] (FAAL)
ONYX	Onyx Acceptance [*NASDAQ symbol*] (TTSB)
ONYX	Onyx Acceptance Corp. [*NASDAQ symbol*] (SAG)
OnyxAcc	Onyx Acceptance Corp. [*Associated Press*] (SAG)
OnyxPh	Onyx Pharmaceuticals, Inc. [*Associated Press*] (SAG)
OO	Belgium [*International civil aircraft marking*] (ODBW)
OO	Naval Oceanographic Office [*Also known as NOO; formerly, HO, NHO, USNHO*]
OO	Oakly, Inc. [*NYSE symbol*] (SAG)
OO	Oberlin College, Oberlin, OH [*Library symbol Library of Congress*] (LCLS)
OO	Object-Oriented (BYTE)
OO	Observation Officer [*Military*]
OO	Oceanographic Office
OO	Ocean Outlook (EA)
OO	Office of Operations [*Department of Agriculture*] (GFGA)
O/O	Office of Origin (AFM)
OO	Off Ocean (SAA)
OO	Ohio Opinions [*A publication*] (DLA)
OO	Ohne Ort [*Without Place of Publication*] [*Bibliography*] [*German*]
O/O	Oil/Ore [*Ship*] (DS)
OO	Old Orkney [*Whisky*] (ROG)
OO	Once Over [*To examine cursorily*] [*Slang*]
O-o	Once-Over [*Theater*] [*Slang*] (WDMC)
O/O	Only to Order (DGA)
O/O	On Orbit (MCD)
OO	On Order
OO	Oophorectomized [*Gynecology*]
OO	Open Order
OO	Operation Order [*Military*]
OO	Operations Office [*Environmental Protection Agency*] (GFGA)
OO	Operations Officer [*Navy British*]
OO	Orderly Officer [*British*]
O/O	Order Of [*Business term*]
O/o	Order of (EBF)
o/o	Order of (EBF)
OO	Ordnance Office [*or Officer*]
OO	Orthopaedics Overseas (EA)

OO .... Osobyi Otdel [*Counterintelligence surveillance unit in military formation until 1943*] [*Former USSR*]

O/O .... Owner/Operator

O/O .... Owner or Operator (COE)

OO .... Own Occupation [*Banking*]

OO .... Sunaire Lines [*ICAO designator*] (AD)

OO 2d .... Ohio Opinions, Second Series [*A publication*] (DLA)

OOA .... Object of Affections [*Slang*]

OOA .... Object-Oriented Analysis [*Computer science*]

OOA .... Office of Ocean Affairs [*Navy*]

OOA .... Office of the Americas [*An association*] (EA)

OOA .... Olive Oil Association (EA)

OOA .... On or About (WDAA)

OOA .... Open Ocean Area (SAA)

OOA .... Optimum Orbital Altitude (AAG)

OOA .... Oskaloosa, IA [*Location identifier FAA*] (FAAL)

OOA .... Outer Otic Anlage (DMAA)

OOA .... Out of Action (MCD)

OOA .... Out of Area (NVT)

OOA .... Owner Operators of America [*Boston, NY*] (EA)

OOA .... Public Archives [*Archives Publiques*] Ottawa, Ontario [*Library symbol National Library of Canada*]

OOAA .... Olive Oil Association of America [*Later, OOA*] (EA)

OOAC .... Algonquin College of Applied Arts and Technology, Ottawa, Ontario [*Library symbol National Library of Canada*] (NLC)

OOACC .... Colonel By Campus, Algonquin College of Applied Arts and Technology, Ottawa, On tario [*Library symbol National Library of Canada*] (NLC)

OOACF .... Alta Vista Branch, Ontario Cancer Foundation, Ottawa, Ontario [*Library symbol National Library of Canada*] (NLC)

OOACH .... Heron Park Campus, Algonquin College of Applied Arts and Technology, Ottawa, Ontario [*Library symbol National Library of Canada*] (BIB)

OOACL .... Library Technician Program, Algonquin College of Applied Arts & Technology, Ottawa, Ontario [*Library symbol National Library of Canada*] (NLC)

OOACR .... Rideau Campus, Algonquin College of Applied Arts and Technology, Ottawa, On tario, [*Library symbol National Library of Canada*] (NLC)

OOAD .... Object-Oriented Analysis & Design [*Computer science*] (CDE)

OOADE .... Archives Deschatelets (Oblats de Marie-Immaculee), Ottawa, Ontario [*Library symbol National Library of Canada*] (NLC)

OOAEA .... Ethnic Archives of Canada, Public Archives [*Archives Ethniques du Canada, Archives Publiques*] Ottawa, Ontario [*Library symbol National Library of Canada*] (NLC)

OOAECB .... Atomic Energy Control Board [*Commission de Controle de l'Energie Atomique*]Ottawa, Ontario [*Library symbol National Library of Canada*]

OOAER .... Research Co., Atomic Energy of Canada Ltd. [*Societe de Recherches, L'Energie Atomique du Canada Ltee*] Ottawa, Ontario [*Library symbol National Library of Canada*] (NLC)

OOAF .... Bibliotheque de l'Ambassade de France, Ottawa, Ontario [*Library symbol National Library of Canada*] (BIB)

OOAFN .... Assembly of First Nations, Ottawa, Ontario [*Library symbol National Library of Canada*] (NLC)

OOAG .... Libraries Division, Agriculture Canada [*Division des Bibliotheques, Agriculture Canada*] Ottawa, Ontario [*Library symbol National Library of Canada*] (NLC)

OOAGA .... Animal Diseases Research Institute, Agriculture Canada [*Institut de Recherches Veterinaires, Agriculture Canada*] Ottawa, Ontario [*Library symbol National Library of Canada*] (NLC)

OOAGAR ...... Animal Research Institute, Agriculture Canada [*Institut de Recherches Zootechniques, Agriculture Canada*] Ottawa, Ontario [*Library symbol National Library of Canada*] (NLC)

OOAGB .... Plant Research Library, Biosystematics Research Institute, Agriculture Canada [*Bibliotheque de Recherches sur les Vegetaux, Institut de Recherches Biosystematiques, Agriculture Canada*] Ottawa, Ontario [*Library symbol National Library of Canada*] (NLC)

OOAGCH ...... Neatby Library, Agriculture Canada [*Bibliotheque Neatby, Agriculture Canada*] Ottawa, Ontario [*Library symbol National Library of Canada*] (NLC)

OOAGE .... Entomology Research Library, Biosystematics Research Institute, Agriculture Canada [*Bibliotheque de Recherches Entomologiques, Institut de Recherches Biosystematiques, Agriculture Canada*] Ottawa, Ontario [*Library symbol National Library of Canada*] (NLC)

OOAGER ...... Engineering and Statistical Research Centre, Agriculture Canada [*Centre de Recherche Technique et de Statistique, Agriculture Canada*] Ottawa, Ontario [*Library symbol National Library of Canada*] (NLC)

OOAGFP .... Laboratory Services Section, Food Production and Marketing Branch, Agriculture Canada [*Section des Services d'Analyse, Direction de la Production et de la Commercialisation des Aliments, Agriculture Canada*] Ottawa, Ontario [*Library symbol National Library of Canada*] (NLC)

OOAGFR ...... Food Research Centre, Agriculture Canada [*Centre de Recherches sur les Aliments,Agriculture Canada*] Ottawa, Ontario [*Library symbol National Library of Canada*] (BIB)

OOAGO .... Research Station, Agriculture Canada [*Station de Recherches, Agriculture Canada*] Ottawa, Ontario [*Library symbol National Library of Canada*] (NLC)

OOAGSR ...... Soil Research Institute, Agriculture Canada [*Institut de Recherches sur les Sols, Agriculture Canada*] Ottawa, Ontario [*Library symbol National Library of Canada*] (NLC)

OOAI .... AMCA International Ltd., Ottawa, Ontario [*Library symbol National Library of Canada*] (NLC)

OOAK .... Oakville Public Library, Ontario [*Library symbol National Library of Canada*] (NLC)

OOAKA .... Appleby College, Oakville, Ontario [*Library symbol National Library of Canada*] (NLC)

OOAKG .... G. D. Searle Co. of Canada Ltd., Oakville, Ontario [*Library symbol National Library of Canada*] (BIB)

OOAKM .... Oakville Museums, Ontario [*Library symbol National Library of Canada*] (BIB)

OOAKS .... Shell Research Centre, Oakville, Ontario [*Library symbol National Library of Canada*] (NLC)

OOAKSC ...... Sheridan College, Oakville, Ontario [*Library symbol National Library of Canada*] (NLC)

OOAKSCL .... Library Techniques, Sheridan College, Oakville, Ontario [*Library symbol National Library of Canada*] (NLC)

OOAMA .... National Map Collection, Public Archives [*Collection Nationale des Cartes et Plans, Archives Publiques*] Ottawa, Ontario [*Library symbol National Library of Canada*] (NLC)

OOAMA .... Office, Ogden Air Material Area [*AFLC*]

OOAM & S ... On-Orbit Assembly, Maintenance, and Service [*NASA*] (SSD)

OOAMS .... Manuscript Division, Public Archives [*Division des Manuscrits, Archives Publiques*] Ottawa, Ontario [*Library symbol National Library of Canada*] (NLC)

OOANF .... National Film Archives, Public Archives [*Archives Nationales du Film, Archives Publiques*] Ottawa, Ontario [*Library symbol National Library of Canada*] (NLC)

OOAOA .... Archives, Diocese of Ottawa, Anglican Church of Canada, Ontario [*Library symbol National Library of Canada*] (NLC)

OOAR .... Canadian Broadcasting Corp. [*Societe Radio-Canada*] Ottawa, Ontario [*Library symbol National Library of Canada*] (NLC)

OOASH .... Ashbury College, Ottawa, Ontario [*Library symbol National Library of Canada*] (NLC)

OOB .... Bank of Canada [*Banque du Canada*] Ottawa, Ontario [*Library symbol National Library of Canada*] (NLC)

OOB .... Off-Off Broadway [*Theater*]

OOB .... Off Our Backs [*A publication*] (BRI)

OOB .... Opening of Business (MCD)

OOB .... Operations Operating Budget [*Military*] (AFIT)

OOB .... Order of Battle [*Military*] (NVT)

OOB .... Ordnance Office Bulletin [*Military*]

OOB .... Out of Band [*Telecommunications*] (TEL)

OOB .... Out of Bed [*Medicine*]

OOB .... Out of Body [*Parapsychology*]

OOB .... Out of Bounds (IIA)

OOBA .... Brewers Association of Canada, [*Association des Brasseurs du Canada*], Ott awa, Ontario [*Library symbol National Library of Canada*] (NLC)

OOBA .... Off Off Broadway Alliance [*Later, ART/NY*]

OOBBRP .... Out of Bed with Bathroom Privileges [*Medicine*] (DAVI)

OOBC .... Bowmar Canada Ltd., Ottawa, Ontario [*Library symbol National Library of Canada*] (NLC)

OOBE .... Ottawa Board of Education, Ontario [*Library symbol National Library of Canada*] (NLC)

OOBE .... Out-of-Body Experience [*Parapsychology*]

OOBE .... Out-Of-Box Experience [*Computer hacker's terminology*] (PCM)

OOBH .... Information Library, British High Commission, Ottawa, Ontario [*Library symbol National Library of Canada*] (BIB)

OOBLA .... Onset of Blood Lactose Accumulation [*Metabolism*]

OOBM .... Bartonian Metaphysical Society, Ottawa, Ontario [*Library symbol National Library of Canada*] (NLC)

OOBMC .... Bureau of Management Consulting, Department of Supply and Services [*Bureau des Conseillers en Gestion, Ministere des Approvisionnements et Services*] Ottawa, Ontario [*Library symbol National Library of Canada*] (NLC)

OOBMI .... Bell Canada Market Information Centre, Ottawa, Ontario [*Library symbol National Library of Canada*] (NLC)

OOBMM .... Medical Library, Bristol-Myers Pharmaceutical Group, Ottawa, Ontario [*Library symbol National Library of Canada*] (NLC)

OOBR .... Buraimi [*Oman*] [*ICAO location identifier*] (ICLI)

OOC .... Junior Optimist Octagon International [*Formerly, Optimist Octagon Clubs*] (EA)

OOC .... Oberlin College, Conservatory of Music, Oberlin, OH [*Library symbol Library of Congress*] (LCLS)

OOC .... Office of Censorship [*Terminated, 1945*] [*Military*]

OOC .... Office of Corrections [*Victoria, Australia*]

OOC .... Office of Olympic Coordination [*New South Wales, Australia*]

OOC .... Off-On Control

OOC .... Operating Vehicle without Owner's Consent [*Traffic offense charge*]

OOC .... Operational Oceanography Center (USDC)

OOC .... Operation Oceanography Center [*Marine science*] (OSRA)

OOC .... Organized Occupational Curricula

OOC .... Ottawa Public Library [*Bibliotheque Publique d'Ottawa*] Ontario [*Library symbol National Library of Canada*] (NLC)

OOC .... Out of Commission (NVT)

OOC .... Out of Control

OOC .... Over-Ocean Communications

OOC .... Overseas Operating Committee [*World War II*]

OOCAA .... Canadian Astronautics, Ottawa, Ontario [*Library symbol National Library of Canada*] (NLC)

OOCAAS ...... Canadian Automobile Association, Ottawa, Ontario [*Library symbol National Library of Canada*] (BIB)

OOCAB .... Canadian Association of Broadcasters [*Association Canadienne des Radiodiffuseurs*] Ottawa, Ontario [*Library symbol National Library of Canada*] (NLC)

OOCAC.......... Canada Council [*Conseil des Arts du Canada*] Ottawa, Ontario [*Library symbol National Library of Canada*] (NLC)

OOCACR ...... Research and Evaluation Section, Canada Council [*Service de Recherche et d'Evaluation, Conseil des Arts du Canada*], Ottawa, Ontario [*Library symbol National Library of Canada*] (BIB)

OOCACSW ... Documentation Centre, Canadian Advisory Council on the Status of Women [*Centre de Documentation, Conseil Consultatif Canadien de la Situation de la Femme*]Ottawa, Ontario [*Library symbol National Library of Canada*] (NLC)

OOCAM........ Canadian Association of Medical Radiation Technologists, Ottawa, Ontario [*Library symbol National Library of Canada*] (BIB)

OOCANM...... Canadian Museum Association [*Association des Musees Canadiens*], Ottawa, Ontario [*Library symbol National Library of Canada*] (NLC)

OOCAR.......... Canadian Arctic Resources Committee, Ottawa, Ontario [*Library symbol National Library of Canada*] (NLC)

OOCARE...... Care Canada, Ottawa, Ontario [*Library symbol National Library of Canada*] (BIB)

OOCAS.......... Children's Aid Society of Ottawa-Carleton, Ottawa, Ontario [*Library symbol National Library of Canada*] (NLC)

OOCB........... Colonel By Secondary School, Ottawa, Ontario [*Library symbol National Library of Canada*] (NLC)

OOCBC.......... Conference Board of Canada, Ottawa, Ontario [*Library symbol National Library of Canada*] (NLC)

OOCBE.......... Carleton Board of Education, Ottawa, Ontario [*Library symbol National Library of Canada*] (NLC)

OOCBH.......... Human Resources Department, Canadian Broadcasting Corp. [*Departement des Ressources Humaines, Societe Radio-Canada*], Ottawa, Ontario [*Library symbol National Library of Canada*] (BIB)

OOCC........... Carleton University, Ottawa, Ontario [*Library symbol National Library of Canada*] (NLC)

OOCCAH ...... Department of Art History, Carleton University, Ottawa, Ontario [*Library symbol Obsolete National Library of Canada*] (NLC)

OOCCFA...... Canadian Centre for Films on Art [*Centre Canadien du Film sur l'Art*] Ottawa, Ontario [*Library symbol National Library of Canada*] (NLC)

OOCCG......... Geography Department, Carleton University, Ottawa, Ontario [*Library symbol Obsolete National Library of Canada*] (NLC)

OOCCJ.......... Church Council on Justice and Correction [*Conseil des Eglises pour la Justiceet la Criminologie*], Ottawa, Ontario [*Library symbol National Library of Canada*] (BIB)

OOCCL......... County of Carleton Law Library, Ottawa, Ontario [*Library symbol National Library of Canada*] (NLC)

OOCCR.......... Canada Centre for Remote Sensing, Energy, Mines and Resources Canada [*Centre Canadien de Teledetection, Energie, Mines et Ressources Canada*] Ottawa, Ontario [*Library symbol National Library of Canada*] (NLC)

OOCCU.......... Canadian Commission for UNESCO, Ottawa, Ontario [*Library symbol National Library of Canada*] (BIB)

OOCD........... Canadian International Development Agency [*Agence Canadienne de DeveloppementInternational*] Ottawa, Ontario [*Library symbol National Library of Canada*] (NLC)

OOCDA......... Canadian Dental Association, Ottawa, Ontario [*Library symbol National Library of Canada*] (NLC)

OOCDC.......... Computing Devices of Canada, Ottawa, Ontario [*Library symbol National Library of Canada*] (NLC)

OOCDP......... College Dominicain de Philosophie et de Theologie, Ottawa, Ontario [*Library symbol National Library of Canada*] (NLC)

OOCEEC ...... Delegation of the Commission of the European Communities [*Delegation de la C ommission des Communautes Europeennes*], Ottawa, Ontario [*Library symbol National Library of Canada*] (BIB)

OOCES......... Combustion Engineering Superheater Ltd., Ottawa, Ontario [*Library symbol National Library of Canada*] (NLC)

OOCESC....... Centre d'Animation Pedagogique, Conseil des Ecoles Separees Catholiques d'Ottawa, Ontario [*Library symbol National Library of Canada*] (BIB)

OOCF .... Canadian Film Institute [*Institut Canadien du Film*] Ottawa, Ontario [*Library symbol National Library of Canada*] (NLC)

OOCFB......... Canadian Forces Base, Ottawa, Ontario [*Library symbol National Library of Canada*] (BIB)

OOCHA......... Canadian Hospital Association [*Association des Hopitaux du Canada*] Ottawa,Ontario [*Library symbol National Library of Canada*] (NLC)

OOCHAC ...... Catholic Health Association of Canada [*Association Catholique Canadienne de la Sante*], Ottawa, Ontario [*Library symbol National Library of Canada*] (NLC)

OOCHC......... Canadian Horticultural Council [*Conseil Canadien de l'Horticulture*], Ottawa, Ontario [*Library symbol National Library of Canada*] (BIB)

OOCHEO ...... Children's Hospital of Eastern Ontario [*Hopital pour Enfants de l'Est de l'Ontario*] Ottawa, Ontario [*Library symbol National Library of Canada*] (NLC)

OOCHI.......... Chreod International, Ottawa, Ontario [*Library symbol National Library of Canada*] (NLC)

OOCHP......... Common Heritage Programme, Ottawa, Ontario [*Library symbol National Library of Canada*] (BIB)

OOCHR .... Canadian Human Rights Commission [*Commission Canadienne des Droits de la Personne*] Ottawa, Ontario [*Library symbol National Library of Canada*] (NLC)

OOCI............ Department of Consumer and Corporate Affairs [*Ministere de la Consommation etdes Corporations*] Ottawa, Ontario [*Library symbol National Library of Canada*] (NLC)

OOCIC.......... Documentation Centre, Canadian Intergovernmental Conference Secretariat [*Centre de Documentation, Secretariat des Conferences Intergouvernementales Canadiennes*], Ottawa, Ontario [*Library symbol National Library of Canada*] (NLC)

OOCIFE .... Field Exploration Library, Inco Ltd., Copper Cliff, Ontario [*Library symbol National Library of Canada*] (NLC)

OOCIHM....... Canadian Institute for Historical Microreproductions [*Institut Canadien de Microreproductions Historiques*] Ottawa, Ontario [*Library symbol National Library of Canada*] (NLC)

OOCIIPS....... Canadian Institute for International Peace and Security [*Institut Canadien pour la Paix et la Securite Mondiales*] Ottawa, Ontario [*Library symbol National Library of Canada*] (NLC)

OOCIRS........ Canadian Institute for Radiation Safety, Ottawa, Ontario [*Library symbol National Library of Canada*] (NLC)

OOCITT .... Canadian International Trade Tribunal [*Tribunal Canadien du Commerce Exterieur*], Ontario [*Library symbol National Library of Canada*] (BIB)

OOCL .... Capital Library Wholesale, Ottawa, Ontario [*Library symbol National Library of Canada*] (NLC)

OOCLA......... Canadian Library Association, Ottawa, Ontario [*Library symbol National Library of Canada*] (BIB)

OOCLC......... Canadian Labour Congress [*Congres du Travail du Canada*] Ottawa, Ontario [*Library symbol National Library of Canada*] (NLC)

OOCLCG....... Coopers & Lybrand Consulting Group, Ottawa, Ontario [*Library symbol National Library of Canada*] (BIB)

OOCLM .... Canadian Labour Market and Productivity Centre [*Centre Canadien du Marche du Travail et de la Productivite*], Ottawa, Ontario [*Library symbol National Library of Canada*] (NLC)

OOCM .... Canadian Housing Information Centre, Canada Mortgage and Housing Corp. [*Centre Canadien de Documentation sur l'Habitation, Societe Canadienne d'Hypotheques et de Logement*] Ottawa, Ontario [*Library symbol National Library of Canada*] (NLC)

OOCMA........ Canadian Medical Association, Ottawa, Ontario [*Library symbol National Library of Canada*] (NLC)

OOCMC........ Children's Environments Advisory Service, Canada Mortgage and Housing Corp. [*Service Consultatif sur l'Environnement de l'Enfant, Societe Canadienne d'Hypotheques et de Logement*] Ottawa, Ontario [*Library symbol National Library of Canada*] (NLC)

OOCMF .... Office of the Commissioner for Federal Judicial Affairs [*Bureau du Commissaire a la Magistrature Federale*], Ottawa, Ontario [*Library symbol National Library of Canada*] (BIB)

OOCN .... Canadian Nurses' Association [*Association Canadienne des Infirmieres*] Ottawa, Ontario [*Library symbol National Library of Canada*] (NLC)

OOCNET....... Office of Corrections Network

OOCNP......... CNP Resource Centre, Energy, Mines, and Resources Canada [*Centre d'Information EESP, Energie, Mines, et Ressources Canada*] Ottawa, Ontario [*Library symbol National Library of Canada*] (NLC)

OOCO .... Department of Communications [*Ministere des Communications*] Ottawa, Ontario [*Library symbol National Library of Canada*] (NLC)

OOCOAC ...... Consumer's Association of Canada, Ottawa, Ontario [*Library symbol National Library of Canada*] (BIB)

OOCOG .... COGLA [*Canada Oil and Gas Lands Administration*] Ocean Mining Resource Centre , Ottawa, Ontario [*Centre de Ressources sur l'Extraction de Minerais Oceaniques, Administration du Petrole et du Gaz des Terres du Canada*] [*Library symbol National Library of Canada*] (NLC)

OOCOI.......... Cognos, Inc., Ottawa, Ontario [*Library symbol National Library of Canada*] (BIB)

OOCOL......... Commissioner of Official Languages [*Commissaire aux Langues Officielles*] Ottawa, Ontario [*Library symbol National Library of Canada*] (NLC)

OOCOT......... Competition Tribunal [*Tribunal de la Concurrence*], Ottawa, Ontario [*Library symbol National Library of Canada*] (BIB)

OOCOW....... Cowater International, Inc., Ottawa, Ontario [*Library symbol National Library of Canada*] (BIB)

OOCP........... Community Planning Association of Canada [*Association Canadienne d'Urbanisme*] Ottawa, Ontario [*Library symbol National Library of Canada*] (NLC)

OOCPA......... Canadian Payments Association, Ottawa, Ontario [*Library symbol National Library of Canada*] (NLC)

OOCPB......... Planning and Development Library, City of Ottawa, Ontario [*Library symbol National Library of Canada*] (BIB)

OOCPR......... Canadian Public Relations Society [*Societe Canadienne des Relations Publiques*] Ottawa, Ontario [*Library symbol National Library of Canada*] (BIB)

OOCRC......... Canadian Red Cross Society [*Societe Canadienne de la Croix-Rouge*] Ottawa, Ontario [*Library symbol National Library of Canada*] (NLC)

OOCRI.......... Canadian Research Institute for the Avancement of Women [*Institut Canadien deRecherches sur les Femmes*] Ottawa, Ontario [*Library symbol National Library of Canada*] (NLC)

OOCRLF....... Canadian Rights and Liberties Federation, Ottawa, Ontario [*Library symbol National Library of Canada*] (NLC)

OOCRM......... Canadian Royal Mint [*Monnaie Royale Canadienne*] Ottawa, Ontario [*Library symbol National Library of Canada*] (NLC)

OOCS........... Public Service Commission [*Commission de la Fonction Publique*] Ottawa, Ontario [*Library symbol National Library of Canada*] (NLC)

OOCSC......... Canada Safety Council [*Conseil Canadien de la Securite*] Ottawa, Ontario [*Library symbol National Library of Canada*] (NLC)

OOCT .... Canadian Teachers Federation, Ottawa, Ontario [*Library symbol National Library of Canada*] (NLC)

OOCTI .... Canadian Textiles Institute [*Institut Canadien des Textiles*], Ottawa, Ontario [*Library symbol National Library of Canada*] (BIB)

OOCU .... Association of Universities and Colleges of Canada [*Association des Universites et Colleges du Canada*], Ottawa, Ontario [*Library symbol National Library of Canada*] (NLC)

OOCUI .... Canadian Unity Information Office [*Centre d'Information sur l'Unite Canadienne*] Ottawa, Ontario [*Library symbol National Library of Canada*] (NLC)

OOCUS .... CUSO [*Canadian University Service Overseas*], Ottawa, Ontario [*Library symbol National Library of Canada*] (NLC)

OOCVB .... Central Volunteer Bureau of Ottawa-Carleton [*Bureau Central des Benevoles d'Ottawa-Carleton*] Ottawa, Ontario [*Library symbol National Library of Canada*] (BIB)

OOCW .... Canadian Council on Social Development [*Conseil Canadien de Developpement Social*] Ottawa, Ontario [*Library symbol National Library of Canada*] (NLC)

OOCWC .... Canadian Wood Council [*Conseil Canadien du Bois*] Ottawa, Ontario [*Library symbol National Library of Canada*] (NLC)

OOCZ .... Ottawa Citizen, Ontario [*Library symbol National Library of Canada*] (NLC)

OOD .... Object-Oriented Design [*Computer science*]

OOD .... Office of Disability [*Australia*]

OOD .... Office Operations Department

OOD .... Officer of the Day [*or Deck*] [*Also, OD*] [*Navy*]

OOD .... Operations Orientation Director [*NASA*]

OOD .... Orbiter on Dock [*NASA*] (KSC)

OOD .... Woodstown, NJ [*Location identifier FAA*] (FAAL)

OODB .... Dominion Bridge Co. Ltd., Ottawa, Ontario [*Library symbol National Library of Canada*] (NLC)

OODB .... Object-Oriented Database [*Computer science*] (CDE)

OODBMS ...... Object-Oriented Database Management System [*Objectivity, Inc.*] [*Computer science*]

OODBS .... DOBIS (Dortmunder Bibliothekssystem), Ottawa, Ontario [*Library symbol National Library of Canada*] (NLC)

OODCH .... DCH Consultants, Inc., Ottawa, Ontario [*Library symbol National Library of Canada*] (NLC)

OODE .... Office of Overseas Dependent Education [*Military*]

OODEP .... Owner, Officer, Director, or Executive Personnel (MCD)

OODF .... Officer-of-the-Deck (Fleet Task Force Operations) [*Navy*] (DNAB)

OODI .... Officer-of-the-Deck (Independent) [*Navy*] (DNAB)

OODL .... Object-Oriented Dynamic Language [*Computer science*] (PCM)

OODLAC .... Odessa Branch, Lennox and Addington County Library, Ontario [*Library symbol National Library of Canada*] (NLC)

OODLC .... Library Education Services, Data Logic Canada, Ottawa, Ontario [*Library symbol National Library of Canada*] (NLC)

OODM .... Dali Management [*Gestion Dali*], Ottawa, Ontario [*Library symbol National Library of Canada*] (BIB)

OODMR .... DMR Group, Inc., Ottawa, Ontario [*Library symbol National Library of Canada*] (BIB)

OODP .... Department of Supply and Services [*Ministere des Approvisionnements et Services*] Ottawa, Ontario [*Library symbol National Library of Canada*] (NLC)

OODP .... Out-of-Detent Pitch [*Aviation*] (MCD)

OODPS .... Superannuation Division, Compensation Services Branch, Department of Supply and Services [*Division des Pensions de Retraite, Direction des Services de Renumeration, Ministere des Approvisionnements et Services*] Ottawa, Ontario [*Library symbol National Library of Canada*] (NLC)

OODQ .... Oliver Organization Description Questionnaire [*Test*]

OODR .... Out-of-Detent Roll [*Aviation*] (MCD)

OODRC .... Defence Research Establishment Ottawa, Department of National Defence [*Centrede Recherches pour la Defense Ottawa, Ministere de la Defense Nationale*] Ont ario [*Library symbol National Library of Canada*] (NLC)

OODR-MPI .... Optical-Optical Double Resonance Multiphonton Ionization [*Spectrocopy*]

OODSIS .... Directorate of Scientific Information Services, Department of National Defence [*Services d'Information Scientifique, Ministere de la Defense Nationale*] Ottawa, Ontario [*Library symbol National Library of Canada*] (NLC)

OODV .... Orbit-on-Demand Vehicle

OOE .... Department of External Affairs [*Ministere des Affaires Exerieures*] Ottawa,Ontario [*Library symbol National Library of Canada*] (NLC)

OOE .... Office of Employment [*Victoria, Australia*]

OOE .... Office of Energy [*New South Wales, Australia*]

OOE .... Office of Ocean Engineering [*National Oceanic and Atmospheric Administration*] (MSC)

OOE .... Opening of Oesophagus

OOE .... Out-of-Ecliptic Mission [*NASA*] (EGAO)

OOEA .... Embassy of Argentina, Ottawa, Ontario [*Library symbol National Library of Canada*] (BIB)

OOEAB .... Archaeological Research, Environment Canada [*Recherches Archeologiques, Environnement Canada*] Ottawa, Ontario [*Library symbol National Library of Canada*] (NLC)

OOEAPT .... River Road Environmental Technology Centre, Environment Canada [*Centre de Techologie Environnementale de River Road, Environnement Canada*] Ottawa, Ontario [*Library symbol National Library of Canada*] (NLC)

OOEB .... Elisabeth Bruyere Health Center [*Centre de Sante Elisabeth Bruyere*] Ottawa, Ontario [*Library symbol National Library of Canada*] (NLC)

OOEC .... Economic Council of Canada [*Conseil Economique du Canada*] Ottawa, Ontario [*Library symbol National Library of Canada*] (NLC)

OOEC .... Oxford Orthopaedic Engineering Centre [*British*] (IRUK)

OOECS .... ECS [*Energy Conversion Systems*] Power Systems, Inc., Ottawa, Ontario [*Library symbol National Library of Canada*] (NLC)

OOECW .... Canadian Wildlife Service, Environment Canada [*Service Canadien de la Faune, Environnement Canada*] Ottawa, Ontario [*Library symbol National Library of Canada*] (NLC)

OOECWN ...... National Wildlife Research Centre, Canadian Wildlife Service, Environment Canada[*Centre National de Recherche sur la Faune, Service Canadien de la Faune, En vironnement Canada*] Ottawa, Ontario [*Library symbol National Library of Canada*] (NLC)

OOEDC .... Export Development Corp. [*Societe pour l'Expansion des Exportations*] Ottawa, Ontario [*Library symbol National Library of Canada*] (NLC)

OOEE .... Engineering and Economic Research Technologies, Inc., Ottawa, Ontario [*Library symbol National Library of Canada*] (BIB)

OOEIB .... Interpretation Division, Environment Canada - Parks [*Direction de l'Interpretation, Environnement Canada - Parcs*], Ottawa, Ontario [*Library symbol National Library of Canada*] (NLC)

OOEK .... Embassy of Korea, Ottawa, Ontario [*Library symbol National Library of Canada*] (BIB)

OOELB .... Legal Branch, Department of External Affairs [*Direction des Operations Juridiques, Ministere des Affaires Exterieures*] Ottawa, Ontario [*Library symbol National Library of Canada*] (NLC)

OOELC .... Elections Canada, Ottawa, Ontario [*Library symbol National Library of Canada*] (BIB)

OOELS .... Legal Services, Environment Canada [*Services Juridiques, Environnement Canada*] Ottawa, Ontario [*Library symbol National Library of Canada*] (NLC)

OOEMB .... Embassy of Brazil, Ottawa, Ontario [*Library symbol National Library of Canada*] (BIB)

OOEN .... Cameco Research Center, Ottawa, Ontario [*Library symbol National Library of Canada*] (NLC)

OOEO .... Eastern Ontario Regional Library, Ottawa, Ontario [*Library symbol National Library of Canada*] (NLC)

OOEO .... Ontario Library Service - Rideau, Ottawa, Ontario [*Library symbol National Library of Canada*] (NLC)

OOEOB .... Conservation Division, Environment Canada [*Division de la Conservation, Environnement Canada*] Ottawa, Ontario [*Library symbol National Library of Canada*] (NLC)

OOEPC .... Emergency Planning Canada [*Planification d'Urgence Canada*] Ottawa, Ontario [*Library symbol National Library of Canada*] (NLC)

OOEPSE .... Socio-Economic Research Division, Parks Canada Program, Environment Canada [*Division de la Recherche Socio-Economique, Programme Parcs Canada, Environnement Canada*] Ottawa, Ontario [*Library symbol National Library of Canada*] (NLC)

OOESC .... Ecole Secondaire Champlain, Ottawa, Ontario [*Library symbol National Library of Canada*] (NLC)

OOEU .... Euroline, Ottawa, Ontario [*Library symbol National Library of Canada*] (BIB)

OOEY .... Eyretechnics Ltd., Ottawa, Ontario [*Library symbol National Library of Canada*] (NLC)

OOF .... Department of Finance [*Ministere des Finances*] Ottawa, Ontario [*Library symbol National Library of Canada*] (NLC)

OOF .... Offense Only Fighter (MCD)

OOF .... Office of Fisheries [*National Oceanic and Atmospheric Administration*] (GFGA)

OOF .... Office of the Family [*Western Australia*]

OOF .... Office of the Future (IAA)

OOF .... Out of Frame [*Telecommunications*] (ITD)

OOFA .... Documentation Centre, Family Action [*Centre de Documentation, Action Famille*], Ottawa, Ontario [*Library symbol National Library of Canada*] (NLC)

OOFA .... Oblinger/Oplinger Family Association (EA)

O of A .... Order of Amaranth (EA)

OOFC .... Federal Court of Canada [*Cour Federale du Canada*] Ottawa, Ontario [*Library symbol National Library of Canada*] (NLC)

OOFCC .... Farm Credit Corp., Ottawa, Ontario [*Library symbol Obsolete National Library of Canada*] (NLC)

OOFD .... Fahud [*Oman*] [*ICAO location identifier*] (ICLI)

OOFE .... Federal Environmental Assessment Review Office [*Bureau Federal d'Examen des Evaluations Environnementales*], Ottawa, Ontario [*Library symbol National Library of Canada*] (BIB)

OOFF .... Departmental Library, Environment Canada [*Bibliotheque du Ministere, Environnemet Canada*] Ottawa, Ontario [*Library symbol National Library of Canada*] (NLC)

OOFI .... Fisheries and Oceans Canada [*Peches et Oceans Canada*] Ottawa, Ontario [*Library symbol National Library of Canada*] (NLC)

OOFL .... Federal Liberal Agency of Canada, Ottawa, Ontario [*Library symbol National Library of Canada*] (NLC)

OOFM .... Mining Library, Falconbridge Ltd., Onaping, Ontario [*Library symbol National Library of Canada*] (NLC)

OOFP .... Forintek Canada Corp., Ottawa, Ontario [*Library symbol National Library of Canada*] (NLC)

OOFQ .... Firq [*Oman*] [*ICAO location identifier*] (ICLI)

OOFS .... Sport Information Resource Centre [*Centre de Documentation de Reference pour le Sport*] Ottawa, Ontario [*Library symbol National Library of Canada*] (NLC)

OOG .... Geological Survey of Canada [*Commission Geologique du Canada*] Ottawa, Ontario [*Library symbol National Library of Canada*] (NLC)

OOG .... Office of Gambling [*Victoria, Australia*]

OOG .... Office of Oil and Gas [*Functions transferred to Energy Research and Development Administration*] [*Department of the Interior*]

OOG .... Officer of the Guard [*Navy British*]

OOG .... Olive Oil Group [*Later, OOA*] (EA)

OOG .... Oscillating Output Geneva

OOG .... Out of Gauge [*Shipping*] (DCTA)

OOGB .... Ghaba Central [*Oman*] [*ICAO location identifier*] (ICLI)

OOGDC .... Gandalf Data Ltd., Ottawa, Ontario [*Library symbol National Library of Canada*] (NLC)

OOGE .... Canadian Government Expositions Centre, Department of Supply and Services [*Centre des Expositions du Gouvernement Canadien, Ministere des Approvisionnements et Services*] Ottawa, Ontario [*Library symbol National Library of Canada*] (NLC)

OOGG .... Documentation Centre, Goss, Gilroy & Associates, Ottawa, Ontario [*Library symbol National Library of Canada*] (BIB)

OOGGH .... Grace General Hospital, Ottawa, Ontario [*Library symbol National Library of Canada*] (NLC)

OOGH .... Reference Library, Government House [*Salle de Reference, Residence du Gouverneur-General*] Ottawa, Ontario [*Library symbol National Library of Canada*] (NLC)

OOGKS .... Gottlieb Kaylor & Stocks, Ottawa, Ontario [*Library symbol National Library of Canada*] (BIB)

OOGOH .... Gowling & Henderson, Ottawa, Ontario [*Library symbol National Library of Canada*] (NLC)

OOGUI .... Object-Oriented Graphical User Interface [*Computer science*]

OOH .... Heraldry Society of Canada [*Societe Heraldique du Canada*], Ottawa, Ontario [*Library symbol National Library of Canada*] (BIB)

OOH .... Occupational Outlook Handbook [*A publication*] (OICC)

OOH .... Out-of-Hospital (DMAA)

OOHA .... Haima [*Oman*] [*ICAO location identifier*] (ICLI)

OOHC .... Heritage Canada Foundation [*Fondation Canadienne pour la Protection du Patrimoine*] Ottawa, Ontario [*Library symbol National Library of Canada*] (NLC)

OOHG .... Ottawa General Hospital [*Hopital General d'Ottawa*] Ontario [*Library symbol National Library of Canada*] (NLC)

OOHI .... Historical Society of Ottawa Library and the Bytown Historical Museum, Ontario [*Library symbol National Library of Canada*] (NLC)

OOH-OOH ..... On the One Hand, On the Other Hand

OOHUR .... Huronia Regional Centre, Orillia, Ontario [*Library symbol National Library of Canada*] (NLC)

OOI .... Informetrica Ltd., Ottawa, Ontario [*Library symbol National Library of Canada*] (NLC)

OOI .... Memphis, TN [*Location identifier FAA*] (FAAL)

OOI .... Oxygen/Ozone Indicator

OOIA .... Ibra [*Oman*] [*ICAO location identifier*] (ICLI)

OOIB .... Imperial Ballet of Canada, Ottawa, Ontario [*Library symbol National Library of Canada*] (NLC)

OOIC .... Information Centre, Investment Canada [*Centre d'Information, Investissement Canada*] Ottawa, Ontario [*Library symbol National Library of Canada*] (NLC)

OOICC .... Indian Claims Commission [*Commission d'Etude des Revendications des Indiens*] Ottawa, Ontario [*Library symbol National Library of Canada*] (NLC)

OOICCS .... International Council for Canadian Studies [*Conseil International d'Etudes Canadiennes*], Ottawa, Ontario [*Library symbol National Library of Canada*] (BIB)

OOICP .... Phototheque, National Film Board [*Phototheque, Office National du Film*] Ottawa, Ontario [*Library symbol National Library of Canada*] (NLC)

OOID .... International Development Research Centre [*Centre de Recherches pour le Developpement International*] Ottawa, Ontario [*Library symbol National Library of Canada*] (NLC)

OOIDA .... Owner-Operator Independent Drivers Association

OOIHC .... India High Commission, Ottawa, Ontario [*Library symbol National Library of Canada*] (BIB)

OOII .... Ibri [*Oman*] [*ICAO location identifier*] (ICLI)

OOIJC .... International Joint Commission [*Commission Mixte Internationale*], Ottawa, Ontario [*Library symbol National Library of Canada*] (NLC)

OOIN .... Office of the Superintendent of Financial Institutions Canada [*Bureau du Surintendant des Institutions Financieres Canada*] Ottawa, Ontario [*Library symbol National Library of Canada*] (NLC)

OOIP .... Original Oil in Place [*Petroleum*]

OOIPC .... Offices of the Information and Privacy Commissioners of Canada [*Bureaux des Commissaires a l'Information et a la Protection de la Vie Privee du Canada*] Ottawa, Ontario [*Library symbol National Library of Canada*] (NLC)

OOIRB .... Immigration and Refugee Board [*Commission d'Immigration et du Status de Refugie*], Ottawa, Ontario [*Library symbol National Library of Canada*] (BIB)

OOIRP .... Institute for Research on Public Policy [*Institut de Recherches Politiques*], Ottawa, Ontario [*Library symbol National Library of Canada*] (NLC)

OOIRS .... Irving R. Silver Associates Library [*IRSA*], Ottawa, Ontario [*Library symbol National Library of Canada*] (NLC)

OOIT .... Inuit Tapirisat of Canada, Ottawa, Ontario [*Library symbol National Library of Canada*] (NLC)

OOIZ .... Izki [*Oman*] [*ICAO location identifier*] (ICLI)

OOJ .... Department of Justice [*Ministere de la Justice*] Ottawa, Ontario [*Library symbol National Library of Canada*] (NLC)

OOJ .... Obstruction of Justice

OOJN .... Jarf North [*Oman*] [*ICAO location identifier*] (ICLI)

OOK .... On-Off Keying [*Computer science*] (IEEE)

OOK .... Toksook [*Alaska*] [*Airport symbol*] (OAG)

OOKB .... Khasab [*Oman*] [*ICAO location identifier*] (ICLI)

OOkiep .... O'Okiep Copper Co. Ltd. [*Associated Press*] (SAG)

OOL .... Coolangatta [*Queensland*] [*Airport symbol*] (AD)

OOL .... Gold Coast [*Australia Airport symbol*] (OAG)

OOL .... Labour Canada [*Travail Canada*] Ottawa, Ontario [*Library symbol National Library of Canada*] (NLC)

OOL .... Oberlin Public Library, Oberlin, OH [*Library symbol Library of Congress*] (LCLS)

OOL .... Object-Oriented Language [*Computer science*] (BYTE)

OOL .... Office of Oceanography and Limnology [*Smithsonian Institution*] (MCD)

OOL .... Operator-Oriented Language [*Computer science*]

OOL .... Optimized Optical Link

OOL .... Out of Orbit Launch [*NASA*] (LAIN)

OOLAP .... Occupational Safety and Health Branch, Labour Canada [*Direction de la Securite et de l'Hygiene, Travail Canada*] Ottawa, Ontario [*Library symbol National Library of Canada*] (NLC)

OOLC .... Labour College of Canada, Ottawa, Ontario [*Library symbol National Library of Canada*] (NLC)

OOLHMD ...... Optimized Optical Link Helmet-Mounted Display

OOLK .... Lekhwair [*Oman*] [*ICAO location identifier*] (ICLI)

OOLM .... Computing Department, Loeb's MIS, Ottawa, Ontario [*Library symbol National Library of Canada*] (BIB)

OOLML .... Lang, Michener, Lash & Johnston, Ottawa, Ontario [*Library symbol National Library of Canada*] (BIB)

OOLR .... Law Reform Commission [*Commission de Reforme du Droit*] Ottawa, Ontario [*Library symbol National Library of Canada*] (NLC)

OOLR .... Ophthalmology, Otology, Laryngology, Rhinology

OOLR .... Overall Objective Loudness Rating [*of telephone connections*] (IEEE)

OOLRB .... Canada Labour Relations Board [*Conseil Canadien des Relations de Travail*] Ottawa, Ontario [*Library symbol National Library of Canada*] (NLC)

OOLRS .... Research Library, LRS Trimark Ltd., Ottawa, Ontario [*Library symbol National Library of Canada*] (BIB)

OOLUG .... Oklahoma On Line Users Group (NITA)

OOLWB .... Women's Bureau, Labour Canada [*Bureau de la Main-d'Oeuvre Feminine, Travail Canada*] Ottawa, Ontario [*Library symbol National Library of Canada*] (NLC)

OOM .... CANMET [*Canada Centre for Mineral and Energy Technology*] Library, Energy, Mines, and Resources Canada , Ottawa, Ontario [*Bibliotheque CANMET, Energie, Mines, et Ressources Canada*] [*Library symbol National Library of Canada*] (NLC)

OOM .... Cooma [*Australia Airport symbol*] (OAG)

OOM .... Office of Ocean Management [*Marine science*] (MSC)

OOM .... Office of Organization and Management [*NASA*]

OOM .... Officers' Open Mess [*Military*] (AFM)

OOM .... Oomiya [*Japan*] [*Seismograph station code, US Geological Survey Closed*] (SEIS)

OOM .... Open Ocean Mining

OOM .... Open Order Master (MCD)

OOM .... Organized Organic Monolayer [*Organic chemistry*]

OOM .... Original Online Module [*Computer science*] (PDAA)

OOMA .... Masirah [*Oman*] [*ICAO location identifier*] (ICLI)

OOMAD .... Michael A. Dagg Associates [*Michael A. Dagg Associes*], Ottawa, Ontario [*Library symbol National Library of Canada*] (NLC)

OOMFC .... Ompah Branch, Frontenac County Library, Ontario [*Library symbol National Library of Canada*] (BIB)

OOMHC .... Malaysia High Commission, Ottawa, Ontario [*Library symbol National Library of Canada*] (NLC)

OOMHS .... Merivale High School, Ottawa, Ontario [*Library symbol National Library of Canada*] (NLC)

OOMI .... Employment and Immigration Canada [*Emploi et Immigration Canada*] Ottawa, Ontario [*Library symbol National Library of Canada*] (NLC)

OOMIL .... MIL Systems Engineering, Inc., Ottawa, Ontario [*Library symbol National Library of Canada*] (BIB)

OOMJ .... Macera & Jarzyna, Ottawa, Ontario [*Library symbol National Library of Canada*] (BIB)

OOML .... Metropolitan Life Insurance Co., Ottawa, Ontario [*Library symbol National Library of Canada*] (NLC)

OOMM .... Muscat [*Oman*] [*ICAO location identifier*] (ICLI)

OOMM .... Organizational Operations and Maintenance Manual (NASA)

oomm .... Organizational Operations and Maintenance Manual (NAKS)

OOMNA .... National Air Photo Library, Energy, Mines, and Resources Canada [*BibliothequePhotographie Aerienne Nationale, Energie, Mines, et Ressources Canada*], Otta wa, Ontario [*Library symbol National Library of Canada*] (BIB)

OOMO .... Oxford Mills Branch, Oxford-On-Rideau Township Public Library [*Library symbol National Library of Canada*] (BIB)

OOMP .... Physical Metallurgy Division, Energy, Mines and Resources Canada [*Division dela Metallurgie Physique, Energie, Mines et Ressources Canada*] Ottawa, Ontari o [*Library symbol National Library of Canada*] (NLC)

OOMPR .... Microtel Pacific Research Ltd., Ottawa, Ontario [*Library symbol National Library of Canada*] (NLC)

OOMR .... Headquarters Library, Energy, Mines and Resources Canada [*Bibliotheque Centrale, Energie, Mines et Ressources Canada*] Ottawa, Ontario [*Library symbol National Library of Canada*] (NLC)

OOMS .... Muscat/Seeb International [*Oman*] [*ICAO location identifier*] (ICLI)

OOMSD .... Ministry of State for Social Development [*Ministere d'Etat au Developpement Social*] Ottawa, Ontario [*Library symbol National Library of Canada*] (NLC)

OOMSS .... Ministry of State for Science and Technology [*Ministere d'Etat pour les Sciences et la Technologie*], Ottawa, Ontario [*Library symbol National Library of Canada*] (NLC)

OON .... Canada Institute for Scientific and Technical Information, National Research Council (CISTI) [*Institut Canadien de l'Information Scientifique et Technique, Conseil National de Recherches (ICIST)*] Ottawa, Ontario [*Library symbol National Library of Canada*] (NLC)

OON .... Odd-Odd Nuclei

OON .... Officer of the Order of Niger

OONAB .... Administration Building Library, Canada Institute for Scientific and Technical Information [*Bibliotheque de l'Edifice de l'Administration, Institut Canadien de l'Information Scientifique et Technique*] Ottawa, Ontario [*Library symbol National Library of Canada*] (NLC)

OONAM .... Aeronautical and Mechanical Engineering Branch, Canada Institute for Scientific and Technical Information [*Division du Genie Aeronautique et Mecanique, Institut Canadien de l'Information Scientifique et Technique*] Ottawa, Ontario [*Library symbol National Library of Canada*] (NLC)

OONAMC ...... NABU Manufacturing Corp., Ottawa, Ontario [*Library symbol National Library of Canada*] (NLC)

OONBR .... IRC [*Institute for Research in Construction*] Library, National Research Council Canada Ottawa, Ontario [*Bibliotheque IRC (Institut de Recherche en Construction), Conseil National de Recherches Canada*] [*Library symbol National Library of Canada*] (NLC)

OONC .... Chemistry Library, Canada Institute for Scientific and Technical Information [*Division de Chimie, Institut Canadien de l'Information Scientifique et Technique*] Ottawa, Ontario [*Library symbol National Library of Canada*] (NLC)

OONCC .... National Capital Commission [*Commission de la Capitale Nationale*] Ottawa, Ontario [*Library symbol National Library of Canada*] (NLC)

OOND .... Department of National Defence [*Ministere de la Defense Nationale*] Ottawa, Ontario [*Library symbol National Library of Canada*] (NLC)

OONDAT ...... Air Technical Library, Department of National Defence [*Bibliotheque Techniquede l'Aviation, Ministere de la Defense Nationale*] Ottawa, Ontario [*Library symbol National Library of Canada*] (NLC)

OONDC .... Communications and Electronics Engineering Library, Department of National Defence [*Bibliotheque du Genie Electronique et des Communications, Ministere de laDefense National*] Ottawa, Ontario [*Library symbol National Library of Canada*] (NLC)

OONDCP ...... Chief, Construction and Properties, Library, Department of National Defence [*Bibliotheque, Chef - Construction et Immeubles, Ministere de le Defense Nationale*] Ottawa, Ontario [*Library symbol National Library of Canada*] (NLC)

OONDCS ...... Communications Security Establishment, Department of National Defence [*Centrede la Securite des Telecommunications, Ministere de la Defense Nationale*] Ottawa, Ontario [*Library symbol National Library of Canada*] (NLC)

OONDH .... Directorate of History, Department of National Defence [*Bureau du Service Historique, Ministere de la Defense Nationale*] Ottawa, Ontario [*Library symbol National Library of Canada*] (NLC)

OONDIS .... Directorate of Information Services, Department of National Defence [*Servicesd'Information, Ministere de la Defense Nationale*] Ottawa, Ontario [*Library symbol National Library of Canada*] (NLC)

OONDJ .... Judge Advocate General, Department of National Defence [*Jugeavocat General, Ministere de la Defense Nationale*] Ottawa, Ontario [*Library symbol National Library of Canada*] (NLC)

OONDLT .... Land Technical Library, Department of National Defence [*Bibliotheque Technique (Terre), Ministere de la Defense Nationale*] Ottawa, Ontario [*Library symbol National Library of Canada*] (NLC)

OONDM .... National Defence Medical Centre, Department of National Defence [*Centre Medical de la Nationale, Ministere de la Defense Nationale*] Ottawa, Ontario [*Library symbol National Library of Canada*] (NLC)

OONDMC ..... Mapping and Charting Establishment, Department of National Defence [*Service de la Cartographie, Ministere de la Defense Nationale*] Ottawa, Ontario [*Library symbol National Library of Canada*] (NLC)

OONDMT .... Maritime Technical Library, Department of National Defence [*Bibliotheque Technique (Mer), Ministere de la Defense Nationale*] Ottawa, Ontario [*Library symbol National Library of Canada*] (NLC)

OONDORAE... Operational Research and Analysis Establishment, Department of National Defence [*Centre d'Analyse et de Recherche Operationnelle, Ministere de la Defense Nationale*] Ottawa, Ontario [*Library symbol National Library of Canada*] (NLC)

OONDT .... Secretary of State Library at National Defence [*Bibliotheque du Secretariat d'Etat a la Defense Nationale*], Ottawa, Ontario [*Library symbol National Library of Canada*] (NLC)

OONE .... National Energy Board [*Office National de l'Energie*] Ottawa, Ontario [*Library symbol National Library of Canada*] (NLC)

OONFP .... National Farm Products Marketing Council [*Conseil National de Commercialisation des Produits Agricoles*], Ottawa, Ontario [*Library symbol National Library of Canada*] (BIB)

OONG .... National Gallery of Canada [*Galerie Nationale du Canada*] Ottawa, Ontario [*Library symbol National Library of Canada*] (NLC)

OONH .... Department of National Health and Welfare [*Ministere de la Sante Nationale etdu Bien-Etre Social*] Ottawa, Ontario [*Library symbol Obsolete National Library of Canada*] (NLC)

OONHAC .... Federal Centre for AIDS [*Acquired Immune Deficiency Syndrome*], Health Protection Branch, Health and Welfare Canada , Ottawa, Ontario [*Centre Federal du SIDA, Direction Generale de la Protection de la Sante, Sante et Bien-Etre Social Canada*] [*Library symbol National Library of Canada*] (BIB)

OONHBR ...... Banting Research Centre Library, Department of National Health and Welfare [*Bibliotheque du Centre de Recherches Banting, Ministere de la Sante Nationale et du Bien-Etre Social*] Ottawa, Ontario [*Library symbol National Library of Canada*] (NLC)

OONHFV ...... National Clearinghouse on Family Violence, Health and Welfare Canada [*Centre National d'Information sur la Violence dans la Famille, Sante et Bien-Etre Social Canada*], Ottawa, Ontario [*Library symbol National Library of Canada*] (BIB)

OONHH .... Environmental Health Directorate, Health Protection Branch, Department of National Health and Welfare [*Direction de l'Hygiene du Milieu, Direction Generale de la Protection de la Sante, Ministere de la Sante Nationale et du Bien-Etre Social*] Ottawa, Ontario [*Library symbol National Library of Canada*] (NLC)

OONHHP ...... Library Services Division, Health Protection Branch, Health and Welfare Canada [*Service de Bibliotheque, Direction Generale de la Protection de la Sante, Sante et Bien-Etre Social Canada*] Ottawa, Ontario [*Library symbol National Library of Canada*] (NLC)

OONHHS ...... Health Services and Promotion Branch, Department of National Health and Welfare [*Direction Generale des Services et de la Promotion de la Sante, Ministere dela Sante Nationale et du Bien-Etre Social*] Ottawa, Ontario [*Library symbol National Library of Canada*] (NLC)

OONHL .... Laboratory Centre for Disease Control, Health Protection Branch, Department of National Health and Welfare [*Laboratoire de Lutte Contre la Maladie, DirectionGenerale de la Protection de la Sante, Ministere de la Sante Nationale et du Bi en-Etre Social*] Ottawa, Ontario [*Library symbol National Library of Canada*] (NLC)

OONHP .... Vanier Reading Room, Place Vanier, Health Protection Branch, Health and Welfare Canada [*Salle de Lecture de Vanier, Place Vanier, Direction Generale de la Protection de la Sante, Sante et Bien-Etre Social Canada*], Ottawa, Ontario [*Library symbol National Library of Canada*] (NLC)

OONHPP ...... Library Services, Policy, Communications, and Information Branch, Health and Welfare Canada [*Services de Bibliotheque, Direction Generale de la Politique, des Communications, et de l'Information, Sante et Bien-Etre Social Canada*] Ottawa, Ontario [*Library symbol National Library of Canada*] (NLC)

OONIN .... National Institute of Nutrition [*Institut National de la Nutrition*], Ottawa, Ontario [*Library symbol National Library of Canada*] (BIB)

OONL .... National Library of Canada [*Bibliotheque Nationale du Canada*] Ottawa, Ontario [*Library symbol National Library of Canada*] (NLC)

OONLB .... Union Catalogue of Books, National Library of Canada [*Catalogue Collectif desLivres, Bibliotheque Nationale du Canada*] Ottawa, Ontario [*Library symbol National Library of Canada*] (NLC)

OONLC .... Canadiana Acquisitions, National Library of Canada [*Acquisitions pour Canadiana, Bibliotheque Nationale du Canada*] Ottawa, Ontario [*Library symbol National Library of Canada*] (NLC)

OONLD .... Information Technology Services, National Library of Canada [*Services de Technologie de l'Information, Bibliotheque Nationale de Canada*], Ottawa, Ontario [*Library symbol National Library of Canada*] (NLC)

OONLD .... Library Systems Centre, National Library of Canada [*Centre des Systemes de Bibliotheque, Bibliotheque Nationale du Canada*] Ottawa, Ontario [*Library symbol National Library of Canada*] (NLC)

OONLG .... Official Publications, National Library of Canada [*Publications Officielles, Bibliotheque Nationale du Canada*] Ottawa, Ontario [*Library symbol National Library of Canada*] (NLC)

OONLI .... ISDS Canada, National Library of Canada [*ISDS Canada, Bibliotheque Nationale du Canada*], Ottawa, Ontario [*Library symbol National Library of Canada*] (BIB)

OONLMBS.... Multilingual Biblioservice, National Library of Canada [*Biblioservice Multilingue, Bibliotheque Nationale du Canada*] Ottawa, Ontario [*Library symbol National Library of Canada*] (NLC)

OONLN .... Newspaper Division, National Library of Canada [*Division des Journaux Bibliotheque Nationale du Canada*] Ottawa, Ontario [*Library symbol National Library of Canada*] (NLC)

OONLP .... Serials Record, National Library of Canada [*Enregistrement des Publications en Serie, Bibliotheque Nationale du Canada*] Ottawa, Ontario [*Library symbol National Library of Canada*] (NLC)

OONLR .... Retrospective Bibliography, National Library of Canada [*Bibliographie Retrospective, Bibliotheque Nationale du Canada*] Ottawa, Ontario [*Library symbol National Library of Canada*] (NLC)

OONLS .... Union Catalogue of Serials, National Library of Canada [*Catalogue Collectif des Periodiques, Bibliotheque Nationale du Canada*] Ottawa, Ontario [*Library symbol National Library of Canada*] (NLC)

OONM .... National Museums of Canada [*Musees Nationaux du Canada*] Ottawa, Ontario [*Library symbol National Library of Canada*] (NLC)

OONMA .... National Aviation Museum [*Musee National de l'Aviation*], Ottawa, Ontario [*Library symbol National Library of Canada*] (NLC)

OONMC .... Canadian War Museum [*Musee de Guerre du Canada*] Ottawa, Ontario [*Library symbol National Library of Canada*] (NLC)

OONMCC ...... Canadian Conservation Institute, National Museums of Canada [*Institut Canadien de Conservation, Musees Nationaux du Canada*] Ottawa, Ontario [*Library symbol National Library of Canada*] (NLC)

OONMM .... Canadian Museum of Civilization, National Museums of Canada [*Musee Canadien des Civilisations, Musees Nationaux du Canada*] Ottawa, Ontario [*Library symbol National Library of Canada*] (NLC)

OONMNS ..... National Museum of Natural Sciences [*Musee National des Sciences Naturelles*], Ottawa, Ontario [*Library symbol National Library of Canada*] (NLC)

OONMS .... National Museum of Science and Technology [*Musee National des Sciences et de la Technologie*] Ottawa, Ontario [*Library symbol National Library of Canada*] (NLC)

OONORE ...... Bell Northern Research, Ottawa, Ontario [*Library symbol National Library of Canada*] (NLC)

OONP .... Division of Physics, Canada Institute for Scientific and Technical Information [*Division de Physique, Institute Canadien de l'Information Scientifique et Technique*] Ottawa, Ontario [*Library symbol National Library of Canada*] (NLC)

OONR .... Customs and Excise Division, Department of National Revenue [*Division des Douanes et de l'Accise, Ministere du Revenu National*] Ottawa, Ontario [*Library symbol National Library of Canada*] (NLC)

OONR .... Marmul/Nasir [*Oman*] [*ICAO location identifier*] (ICLI)

OONRE .... Electrical Engineering Division, Canada Institute for Scientific and Technical Information [*Division de Genie Electrique, Institut Canadien de l'Information Scientifique et Technique*] Ottawa, Ontario [*Library symbol National Library of Canada*] (NLC)

OONRT .... Taxation Division, Department of National Revenue [*Division de l'Impot, Ministere du Revenu National*] Ottawa, Ontario [*Library symbol National Library of Canada*] (NLC)

OONRTC ...... Centre for Career Development, Revenue Canada - Taxation [*Centre de Developpement Professionnel, Revenu Canada - Impot*] Ottawa, Ontario [*Library symbol National Library of Canada*] (NLC)

OONS .... Sussex Library, Canada Institute for Scientific and Technical Information [*Bibliotheque Sussex, Institut Canadien de l'Information Scientifique et Technique*] Ottawa, Ontario [*Library symbol National Library of Canada*] (NLC)

OONSE .... Natural Sciences and Engineering Research Council of Canada [*Conseil de Recherches en Sciences Naturelles et en Genie du Canada*], Ottawa, Ontario [*Library symbol National Library of Canada*] (NLC)

OONSF .... National Science Film Library [*Cinematheque Nationale Scientifique*] Ottawa, Ontario [*Library symbol National Library of Canada*] (NLC)

OONSI .... North-South Institute [*L'Institut Nord-Sud*], Ottawa, Ontario [*Library symbol National Library of Canada*] (NLC)

OOnt .... Order of Ontario [*Decoration*] [*Canada*] (CMD)

OONU .... Uplands Library, Canada Institute for Scientific and Technical Information [*Bibliotheque d'Uplands, Institut Canadien de l'Information Scientifique et Technique*] Ottawa, Ontario [*Library symbol National Library of Canada*] (NLC)

OONUL .... Union List of Scientific Serials in Canadian Libraries [*Catalogue Collectif des Publications Scientifiques dans les Bibliotheques Canadiennes*] Ottawa, Ontario [*Library symbol National Library of Canada*] (NLC)

OONVRC ...... National Victims Resource Centre [*Centre National de la Documentation sur lesVictimes*] Ottawa, Ontario [*Library symbol National Library of Canada*] (NLC)

OONY .... Opera Orchestra of New York

OONZ .... Nizwa [*Oman*] [*ICAO location identifier*] (ICLI)

OOO .... Earth Physics Branch, Energy, Mines and Resources Canada [*Direction de la Physique du Globe, Energie, Mines et Resources Canada*] Ottawa, Ontario [*Library symbol National Library of Canada*] (NLC)

OOO .... Geophysics Collection, Geological Survey of Canada [*Collection de la Geophysique, Commission Geologique du Canada*], Ottawa, Ontario [*Library symbol National Library of Canada*] (NLC)

OOO .... Grants Pass, OR [*Location identifier FAA*] (FAAL)

OOO .... Office of the Ombudsman

OOO .... Oleum Olivae Optimum [*Best Olive Oil*] [*Pharmacy*] (ROG)

OOO .... Order of Owls (EA)

OOO .... O Sapientia, O Radix, O Adonai [*Three anthems sung in Roman Catholic churches before Christmas*] (ROG)

OOO .... Out of Order [*Telecommunications*] (TEL)

OOOA .... City of Ottawa Archives, Ontario [*Library symbol National Library of Canada*] (NLC)

OOOAG .... Office of the Auditor General [*Bureau du Verificateur General*] Ottawa, Ontario [*Library symbol National Library of Canada*] (NLC)

OOOCF .... Ottawa Clinic, Ontario Cancer Foundation, Ontario [*Library symbol National Library of Canada*] (NLC)

OOOCH .... Ottawa Civic Hospital, Ontario [*Library symbol National Library of Canada*] (NLC)

OOOCM .... Information Services, Ontario Centre for Microelectronics, Nepean, Ontario [*Library symbol National Library of Canada*] (NLC)

OOOF .... Onaping Branch, Onaping Falls Public Library, Ontario [*Library symbol National Library of Canada*] (NLC)

OOOI .... Out-Off-On-In [*Telecommunications*]

OOOL .... Optotek Ltd., Ottawa, Ontario [*Library symbol National Library of Canada*] (NLC)

OOOS .... Object-Oriented Operating System [*Computer science*] (CDE)

OOOTQFUE... Omnipotent Overseer of the Quest for Unsurpassable Excellence [*Rank in the Junior Woodchucks organization mentioned in Donald Duck comic by Carl Barks*]

OOP .... Library of Parliament [*Bibliotheque du Parlement*] Ottawa, Ontario [*Library symbol National Library of Canada*] (NLC)

OOP .... Object-Oriented Programming [*Computer science*]

OOP .... Oceanographic Observations of the Pacific

OOP .... Office of Organization Planning

OOP .... Offline Orthophoto Printer [*Computer science*] (PDAA)

OOP .... Optimum Optical Pump

OOP .... Ounce of Prevention [*A publication*]

OOP .... Out of Pelvis [*Obstetrics*] (DAVI)

OOP .... Out-of-Phase [*Gynecology*]

OOP .... Out of Plane

OOP .... Out of Plant

OOP .... Out of Plaster [*Orthopedics*] (DAVI)

OOP .... Out-of-Pocket [*Costs/expenses*]

OOP .... Out of Pocket Cost

OOP .... Out of Pocket Expense

OOP .... Out of Position (MCD)

OOP .... Out of Print [*Also, OP*] [*Publishing*]

OOP .... Out on Pass (DAVI)

OOPA .... National Arts Centre [*Centre National des Arts*] Ottawa, Ontario [*Library symbol National Library of Canada*] (NLC)

OOPA .... One and Only Parents Association (EA)

OOPAC .... Chaudiere Branch, Departmental Library, Environment Canada [*Succursale Chaudiere, Bibliotheque du Ministere, Environnement Canada*] Ottawa, Ontario [*Library symbol National Library of Canada*] (NLC)

OOPART ...... Out of Place Artifact [*Archeology*]

OOPC .... Management Information Centre, Privy Council Office [*Regie Interne de l'Information, Bureau du Conseil Prive*] Ottawa, Ontario [*Library symbol National Library of Canada*] (NLC)

OOPC .... Office of Operational Planning and Control [*Social Security Administration*]

OOPC .... Owners & Officers of Private Companies [*A publication*]

OOPCF .... Parliamentary Centre for Foreign Affairs and Foreign Trade [*Centre Parlementaire pour les Affaires Etrangeres et le Commerce Exterieur*], Ottawa, Ontario [*Library symbol National Library of Canada*] (NLC)

OOPEC .... Office for Official Publications of the European Communities (ECED)

OOPEC .... Petro-Canada, Ottawa, Ontario [*Library symbol National Library of Canada*] (NLC)

OOPED .... Pylon Electronic Development Co. Ltd., Ottawa, Ontario [*Library symbol National Library of Canada*] (NLC)

OOPF .... Resource Centre, Ottawa Police Force, Ontario [*Library symbol National Library of Canada*] (BIB)

OOPH .... Perley Hospital, Ottawa, Ontario [*Library symbol National Library of Canada*] (NLC)

OOPI .... Petroleum Incentives Program, Energy, Mines and Resources Canada [*Programmes d'Encouragement Petrolier, Energie, Mines et Ressources Canada*] Ottawa, Ontario [*Library symbol National Library of Canada*] (NLC)

OOPIP .... Professional Institute of the Public Service of Canada [*Institut Professionnel de la Fonction Publique du Canada*], Ottawa, Ontario [*Library symbol National Library of Canada*] (BIB)

OOPL .... Object-Oriented Programming Language [*Computer science*] (PCM)

OOPLFC & A... Only Official Peggy Lee Fan Club and Archives (EA)

OOPM .... National Postal Museum [*Musee National des Postes*] Ottawa, Ontario [*Library symbol National Library of Canada*] (NLC)

OOPMF .... Marten Falls Band Library, Ogoki Post, Ontario [*Library symbol National Library of Canada*] (BIB)

OOPMP .... Peat, Marwick & Partners, Ottawa, Ontario [*Library symbol National Library of Canada*] (NLC)

OOPO .... Canada Post [*Postes Canada*] Ottawa, Ontario [*Library symbol National Library of Canada*] (NLC)

OOPOM .... Meriline Branch, Canada Post [*Postes Canada*], Ottawa, Ontario [*Library symbol National Library of Canada*] (BIB)

OOPOR .... Ports Canada, Ottawa, Ontario [*Library symbol National Library of Canada*] (NLC)

OOPS .... Object-Oriented Pieces of Something [*Computer science*]

OOPS .... Object-Oriented Programming (BYTE)

OOPS .... Object-Oriented Programming System (AAEL)

OOPS .... O'Brien's Oil Pollution Service of New Orleans [*Oil spill cleanup service*]

OOPS .... Office for Operations in Political Systems

OOPS .... Off-Line Operating Simulator [*Computer science*]

OOPS .... Online Object Patching System [*Computer science*] (PDAA)

OOPS .... Originals on Permanent Sale

OOPS .... Public Service Staff Relations Board [*Commission des Relations de Travail dans la Fonction Publique*] Ottawa, Ontario [*Library symbol National Library of Canada*] (NLC)

OOPSAC ...... Public Service Alliance of Canada [*Alliance de la Fonction Publique du Canada*] Ottawa, Ontario [*Library symbol National Library of Canada*] (NLC)

OOPSLA .... Object-Oriented Programming Systems, Languages, and Applications [*Computer conference*]

OOPW .... Public Works Canada [*Travaux Publics Canada*] Ottawa, Ontario [*Library symbol National Library of Canada*] (NLC)

OOPWC........ Capital Region Library, Public Works Canada [*Bibliotheque de la Region de la Capitale, Travaux Publics Canada*] Ottawa, Ontario [*Library symbol National Library of Canada*] (NLC)

OOPWR........ Research and Development Laboratories, Public Works Canada [*Laboratoires de Recherche et de Developpement, Travaux Publics Canada*] Ottawa, Ontario [*Library symbol Obsolete National Library of Canada*] (NLC)

OOQ............. Officer of the Quarters

OOQA........... Director-General, Quality Assurance Library, Department of National Defence [*Bibliotheque du Directeur General-Assurance de la Qualite, Ministere de la Defense Nationale*], Ottawa, Ontario [*Library symbol National Library of Canada*] (NLC)

OOQC........... Queensway-Carleton Hospital, Ottawa, Ontario [*Library symbol National Library of Canada*] (NLC)

OOQM.......... Queen Mary Street School, Ottawa, Ontario [*Library symbol National Library of Canada*] (BIB)

OOR............. Mooraberrie [*Queensland*] [*Airport symbol*] (AD)
OOR............. Office for Ordnance Research [*Later, Army Research Office*]
OOR............. Open Ocean Release
OOR............. Operator Override [*Telecommunications*] (TEL)
OOR............. Out of Room (DAVI)
OOR............. Out-of-Roundness [*Manufacturing term*]
OOR............. Oxygen/Ozone Recorder
OOR............. RCMP Headquarters [*Direction Generale de la GRC*] Ottawa, Ontario [*Library symbol National Library of Canada*] (NLC)

OOR............. RCMP [*Royal Canadian Mounted Police*] Law Enforcement Reference Centre , Ottawa, Ontario [*Centre de Documentation Policiere, Gendarmerie Royale du Canada*] [*Library symbol National Library of Canada*] (NLC)

OORA........... Orangeville Public Library, Ontario [*Library symbol National Library of Canada*] (NLC)

OORCS......... Ottawa Roman Catholic Separate School Board, Ontario [*Library symbol National Library of Canada*] (NLC)

OORD........... Indian and Northern Affairs Canada [*Affaires Indiennes et du Nord Canada*] Ottawa, Ontario [*Library symbol National Library of Canada*] (NLC)

OORH........... Riverside Hospital, Ottawa, Ontario [*Library symbol National Library of Canada*] (NLC)

OORI............ Orillia Public Library, Ontario [*Library symbol National Library of Canada*] (NLC)

OORIA.......... J. L. Richard & Associates Ltd., Ottawa, Ontario [*Library symbol National Library of Canada*] (NLC)

OORIGC....... Learning Resources Centre, Georgian College of Applied Arts and Technology, Orillia, Ontario [*Library symbol National Library of Canada*] (NLC)

OORIMT....... Mara Township Public Library, Orillia, Ontario [*Library symbol National Library of Canada*] (BIB)

OORISMH..... OSMH Health Sciences Library, Orillia Soldiers' Memorial Hospital, Ontario [*Library symbol National Library of Canada*] (NLC)

OORM.......... Planning Department Library, Regional Municipality of Ottawa-Carleton, Ottawa, Ontario [*Library symbol National Library of Canada*] (NLC)

OORM.......... Rima [*Oman*] [*ICAO location identifier*] (ICLI)
OORMT........ Transportation-Works Department, Regional Municipality of Ottawa-Carleton, Ottawa, Ontario [*Library symbol National Library of Canada*] (NLC)

OORO........... Royal Ottawa Hospital, Ontario [*Library symbol National Library of Canada*] (NLC)

OORORR..... Royal Ottawa Regional Rehabilitation Centre, Royal Ottawa Hospital, Ontario [*Library symbol National Library of Canada*] (NLC)

OORP........... Rockliffe Park Public Library, Ottawa, Ontario [*Library symbol National Library of Canada*] (BIB)

OORPL......... Communications Research Centre, Department of Communications [*Centre de Recherches sur les Communications, Ministere des Communications*] Ottawa, Ontario [*Library symbol National Library of Canada*] (NLC)

OORQ........... Rostaq [*Oman*] [*ICAO location identifier*] (ICLI)
OORR........... Regional Realty Ltd., Ottawa, Ontario [*Library symbol National Library of Canada*] (BIB)

OOrrW......... Wayne General and Technical College, Orrville, OH [*Library symbol Library of Congress*] (LCLS)

OORS........... RCMP Scientific Information Centre [*Centre d'Information Scientifique de la GRC*] Ottawa, Ontario [*Library symbol National Library of Canada*] (NLC)

OORSFC...... Only Official Rolling Stones Fan Club (EAIO)
OORSS......... CSIS [*Canadian Security Intelligence Service*] Open Information Centre Ontario [*Bibliotheque du SCRS (Service Canadien du Renseignement de Securite), Ottawa*] [*Library symbol National Library of Canada*] (NLC)

OORT........... Canadian Radio-Television and Telecommunications Commission [*Conseil de la Radiodiffusion et des Telecommunications Canadiennes*] Ottawa, Ontario [*Library symbol National Library of Canada*] (NLC)

OORTA......... Roads and Transportation Association of Canada [*Association des Routes et Transports du Canada*] Ottawa, Ontario [*Library symbol National Library of Canada*] (NLC)

OOS............. Occupational Overuse Syndrome
OOS............. Ocean Observing System [*Marine science*] (OSRA)
OOS............. Office of Operations Support [*Law Enforcement Assistance Administration*]
OOS............. On-Orbit Station [*NASA*] (NASA)
OOS............. On-Orbit Station [*NASA*] (NAKS)
OOS............. On-Orbit Support
OOS............. Operational Operating System [*Telecommunications*] (TEL)
OOS............. Orbit-to-Orbit Shuttle [*NASA*]

OOS............. Orbit-to-Orbit Shuttle [*NASA*] (NAKS)
OOS............. Orbit-to-Orbit Stage [*NASA*] (NAKS)
OOS............. Orbit-to-Orbit Stage [*NASA*] (NASA)
OOS............. Out of School (OICC)
OOS............. Out of Sequence (NRCH)
OOS............. Out of Service (NRCH)
OOS............. Out-of-Shot [*Photography*] (ADA)
OOS............. Out of Stock
OOS............. Statistics Canada [*Statistique Canada*] Ottawa Ontario [*Library symbol National Library of Canada*] (NLC)

OOSA........... National Social Services Consultant and Government Relations Officer, Salvation Army Library, Ottawa, Ontario [*Library symbol National Library of Canada*] (BIB)

OOSA........... Salalah [*Oman*] [*ICAO location identifier*] (ICLI)
OOSAR......... Government Relations Office, Spar Aerospace Ltd., Ottawa, Ontario [*Library symbol National Library of Canada*] (BIB)

OOSB........... Smart & Biggar, Ottawa, Ontario [*Library symbol National Library of Canada*] (BIB)

OOSC........... Out-of-Sight Control (MUGU)
OOSC........... Supreme Court of Canada [*Cour Supreme du Canada*] Ottawa, Ontario [*Library symbol National Library of Canada*] (NLC)

OOSCA......... Archives des Soeurs de la Charite d'Ottawa, Ontario [*Library symbol National Library of Canada*] (NLC)

OOSCAC...... Scanada Consultants Ltd., Ottawa, Ontario [*Library symbol National Library of Canada*] (NLC)

OOSCC........ Out-of-Site Control Center (SAA)
OOSCC........ Science Council of Canada [*Conseil des Sciences du Canada*] Ottawa, Ontario [*Library symbol National Library of Canada*] (NLC)

OOSCL......... Census Library, Statistics Canada [*Bibliotheque du Recensement, Statistique Canada*] Ottawa, Ontario [*Library symbol National Library of Canada*] (NLC)

OOSCM........ Census Map Library, Statistics Canada [*Cartotheque du Recensement, Statistique Canada*] Ottawa, Ontario [*Library symbol National Library of Canada*] (NLC)

OOSD........... Object Oriented Structured Design [*Computer science*]
OOSDP........ On-Orbit Station Distribution Panel [*NASA*] (MCD)
OOSG........... Ministry of the Solicitor General [*Ministere du Solliciteur General*] Ottawa, Ontario [*Library symbol National Library of Canada*] (NLC)

OOSGO........ Osgoode Public Library, Ontario [*Library symbol National Library of Canada*] (BIB)

OOSH........... Oshawa Public Library, Ontario [*Library symbol National Library of Canada*] (NLC)

OOSH........... Out of School Hours
OOSH........... Sohar [*Oman*] [*ICAO location identifier*] (ICLI)
OOSHD........ Durham College of Applied Arts and Technology, Oshawa, Ontario [*Library symbol National Library of Canada*] (NLC)

OOSHH........ Education Resource Centre, Oshawa General Hospital, Ontario [*Library symbol National Library of Canada*] (BIB)

OOSHR........ Robert McLaughlin Gallery, Oshawa, Ontario [*Library symbol National Library of Canada*] (NLC)

OOSHT........ Technical Library, Systemhouse Ltd., Ottawa, Ontario [*Library symbol National Library of Canada*] (NLC)

OOSJ........... La Bibliotheque Deschatelets Peres Oblats [*Closed to the public*] Ottawa, Ontario [*Library symbol National Library of Canada*] (NLC)

OOSLM........ Montfort Hospital [*Hopital Montfort*] Ottawa, Ontario [*Library symbol National Library of Canada*] (NLC)

OOSLR........ S. L. Ross Environmental Research, Ottawa, Ontario [*Library symbol National Library of Canada*] (BIB)

OOSM.......... Sahma [*Oman*] [*ICAO location identifier*] (ICLI)
OOSM.......... Surveying and Mapping Library, Cartographic Information and Distribution Centre,Energy, Mines, and Resources Canada [*Bibliotheque des Leves et de Cartograph ies, Centre d'Information et de Distribution Cartographiques, Energie, Mines, et Ressources Canada*] Ottawa, Ontario [*Library symbol National Library of Canada*] (NLC)

OOSMM....... Map Library, Energy, Mines and Resources Canada [*Cartotheque, Energie, Mines et Ressources Canada*] Ottawa, Ontario [*Library symbol National Library of Canada*] (NLC)

OOSN.......... Six Nations Public Library, Ohsweken, Ontario [*Library symbol National Library of Canada*] (BIB)

OOSP........... Patent and Copyright Office, Department of Consumer and Corporate Affairs [*Bureau des Brevets et du Droit d'Auteur, Ministere de la Consommation et des Corporations*] Ottawa, Ontario [*Library symbol National Library of Canada*] (NLC)

OOSPD........ Ocean Observing System Development Panel [*Marine science*] (OSRA)

OOSPX........ St.-Pius X High School, Ottawa, Ontario [*Library symbol National Library of Canada*] (BIB)

OOSQ.......... Saiq [*Oman*] [*ICAO location identifier*] (ICLI)
OOSR........... Sur [*Oman*] [*ICAO location identifier*] (ICLI)
OOSS........... Department of the Secretary of State [*Secretariat d'Etat*] Ottawa, Ontario [*Library symbol National Library of Canada*] (NLC)

OOSS........... Outpatient Ophthalmic Surgery Society (EA)
OOSS........... Overseas Operational Storage Site [*Army*]
OOSSHRC.... Social Sciences and Humanities Research Council of Canada [*Conseil de Recherches en Sciences Humaines du Canada*] Ottawa, Ontario [*Library symbol National Library of Canada*] (NLC)

OOSSTE ...... Terminology and Documentation Branch, Translation Bureau, Department of the Secretary of State [*Direction generale de la Terminologie et de la Documentation,Bureau des Traductions, Secretariat d'Etat*] Ottawa, Ontario [*Library symbol National Library of Canada*] (NLC)

OOSSTE ...... Terminology Library, Information Resource Services Directorate, Secretary of State [*Bibliotheque de la Terminologie, Direction Info-Ressources, Secretariat d'Etat*], Ottawa, Ontario [*Library symbol National Library of Canada*] (NLC)

OOSSTM ...... Multilingual Services Directorate, Translation Bureau, Department of the Secretary of State [*Direction des Services Multilingues, Bureau des Traductions, Secretariat d'Etat*] Ottawa, Ontario [*Library symbol National Library of Canada*] (NLC)

OOSSTR ...... Translation Services Branch, Translation Bureau, Department of the Secretary of State [*Direction Generale des Services de Traduction, Bureau des Traductions,Secretariat d'Etat*] Ottawa, Ontario [*Library symbol National Library of Canada*] (NLC)

OOST .... Standards Council of Canada, Ottawa, Ontario [*Library symbol National Library of Canada*] (BIB)

OOSTI .... Scientific and Technical Information Centre, Laboratory and Scientific Services Division, Revenue Canada Customs and Excise [*Centre d'Information Scientifique et Technique, Division du Laboratoire et des Services Scientifiques, Revenu Canada Douanes et Accise*] Ottawa, Ontario [*Library symbol National Library of Canada*] (NLC)

OOSTM .... Careerware Reference Centre, STM Systems Corp., Ottawa, Ontario [*Library symbol National Library of Canada*] (BIB)

OOSU .... St. Paul University [*Universite St-Paul*] Ottawa, Ontario [*Library symbol National Library of Canada*] (NLC)

OOSUA .... Archives, St. Paul University [*Archives, Universite St-Paul*] Ottawa, Ontario [*Library symbol National Library of Canada*] (NLC)

OOSV .... St. Vincent Hospital [*Hopital St-Vincent*] Ottawa, Ontario [*Library symbol National Library of Canada*] (NLC)

OOSW .... Status of Women Canada [*Condition Feminine Canada*] Ottawa, Ontario [*Library symbol National Library of Canada*] (NLC)

OOSWH .... Soloway, Wright & Houston Law Firm, Ottawa, Ontario [*Library symbol National Library of Canada*] (BIB)

OOT .... Object-Oriented Technology [*Computer science*] (CDE)

OOT .... Oil Out Temperature

OOT .... Onotoa [*Kiribati*] [*Airport symbol*] (OAG)

OOT .... Ootomari [*Former USSR Seismograph station code, US Geological Survey Closed*] (SEIS)

OOT .... Out of Oxygen Tent

OOT .... Out of Tolerance (FAAC)

OOT .... Out-of-Town [*Word processing*]

OOT .... Transport Canada [*Transports Canada*] Ottawa, Ontario [*Library symbol National Library of Canada*] (NLC)

OOTA .... Airworthiness Library, Transport Canada [*Bibliotheque de la Navigabilite Aerienne, Transports Canada*], Ottawa, Ontario [*Library symbol National Library of Canada*] (NLC)

OOTAC .... Airports and Construction Services, Transport Canada [*Service des Aeroports et de la Construction, Transports Canada*] Ottawa, Ontario [*Library symbol National Library of Canada*] (NLC)

OOTAS .... Canadian Aviation Safety Board [*Bureau Canadien de la Securite Aerienne*] Ottawa, Ontario [*Library symbol National Library of Canada*] (NLC)

OOTB .... Tourism Reference and Documentation, Regional Industrial Expansion [*Centre deReference et de Documentation Touristique, Expansion Industrielle Regionale*] , Ottawa, Ontario [*Library symbol National Library of Canada*] (NLC)

OOTC .... Department of Regional Industrial Expansion [*Ministere de l'Expansion Industrielle Regionale*] Ottawa, Ontario [*Library symbol National Library of Canada*] (NLC)

OOTC .... Obligatory On-Topic Comment [*Computer hacker terminology*]

OOTC .... Oceania Olympic Training Center [*Australia*]

OOTC .... Old Old Timers Club (EA)

OOTCI .... Documentation Centre, Communications and Informatics, Transport Canada [*Centre de Documentation, Communications et Informatique, Transports Canada*], Ottawa, Ontario [*Library symbol National Library of Canada*] (BIB)

OOTCO .... Telecommunications Library, Transport Canada [*Bibliotheque de Telecommunications, Transports Canada*], Ottawa, Ontario [*Library symbol National Library of Canada*] (NLC)

OOTCT .... TransCanada Telephone System, Ottawa, Ontario [*Library symbol National Library of Canada*] (NLC)

OOTE .... Out-of-Town Executive

OOTEL .... Telesat Canada, Ottawa, Ontario [*Library symbol National Library of Canada*] (NLC)

OOTFS .... Technical Library AAFBAA, Flight Services Directorate, Transport Canada [*Bibliotheque Technique AAFBAA, Direction Generale du Service des Vols, Transports Canada*], Ottawa, Ontario [*Library symbol National Library of Canada*] (NLC)

OOTH .... Thumrait [*Oman*] [*ICAO location identifier*] (ICLI)

OOTI .... Technical Information Centre, Transport Canada Training Institute [*Centre d'Information Technique, Institut de Formation Transports Canada*], Cornwall, Ontario [*Library symbol National Library of Canada*] (NLC)

OOTIR .... Traffic Injury Research Foundation of Canada [*Fondation de Recherches sur lesBlessures de la Route au Canada*] Ottawa, Ontario [*Library symbol National Library of Canada*] (NLC)

OOTN .... Trade Negotiations Office, External Affairs Canada [*Affaires Exterieures Canada*] Ottawa, Ontario [*Library symbol National Library of Canada*] (NLC)

OOTR .... Tax Court of Canada [*Cour Canadienne de l'Impot*] Ottawa, Ontario [*Library symbol National Library of Canada*] (NLC)

OOTRAT .... Les Traductions Tessier SCC (Division de Multiscript International), Ottawa, Ontario [*Library symbol National Library of Canada*] (BIB)

OOTRS .... Road Safety and Motor Vehicle Regulation Branch, Transport Canada [*Direction de la Securite Routiere et de la Reglementation Automobile, Transports Canada*], Ottawa, Ontario [*Library symbol National Library of Canada*] (NLC)

OOTRT .... Railway Transportation Directorate, Transport Canada [*Direction du Transport Ferroviaire, Transports Canada*] Ottawa, Ontario [*Library symbol National Library of Canada*] (NLC)

OOTSSA .... St. Lawrence Seaway Authority, Transport Canada [*Administration de la Voie Maritime du Saint-Laurent, Transports Canada*] Ottawa, Ontario [*Library symbol National Library of Canada*] (NLC)

OOTT .... National Transportation Agency of Canada [*Office National des Transports du Canada*], Ottawa, Ontario [*Library symbol National Library of Canada*] (NLC)

OOTTD .... Technical Data Resource Centre, Transport Canada [*Centre de la Documentation Technique, Transports Canada*], Ottawa, Ontario [*Library symbol National Library of Canada*] (NLC)

OOTTE .... Telecommunications and Electronics Directorate, Transport Canada [*Direction des Telecommunications et de l'Electronique, Transports Canada*], Ottawa, Ontario [*Library symbol Obsolete National Library of Canada*] (NLC)

OOTW .... Operations Other Than War [*Army*] (INF)

OOU .... Out of Use (IAA)

OOU .... University of Ottawa [*Universite d'Ottawa*] Ontario [*Library symbol National Library of Canada*] (NLC)

OOUA .... Archives, Universite d'Ottawa [*Archives, University of Ottawa*], Ontario [*Library symbol National Library of Canada*] (BIB)

OOUC .... Department of Criminology, University of Ottawa [*Departement de Criminologie,Universite d'Ottawa*] Ontario [*Library symbol National Library of Canada*] (NLC)

OOUD .... Faculty of Civil Law, University of Ottawa [*Faculte de Droit Civil, Universite d'Ottawa*] Ontario [*Library symbol National Library of Canada*] (NLC)

OOUG .... Oregon Online User Group (NITA)

OOUH .... Health Sciences Library, University of Ottawa [*Bibliotheque des Sciences de la Sante, Universite d'Ottawa*] Ontario [*Library symbol National Library of Canada*] (NLC)

OOUI .... Object-Oriented User Interface [*Computer science*]

OOUIC .... Institute of International Cooperation, University of Ottawa [*Institut de Cooperation Internationale, Universite d'Ottawa*] Ontario [*Library symbol National Library of Canada*] (NLC)

OOUM .... Vanier Library, University of Ottawa [*Bibliotheque Vanier, Universite d'Ottawa*] Ontario [*Library symbol National Library of Canada*] (NLC)

OOUMA .... Map Library, University of Ottawa [*Cartotheque, Universite d'Ottawa*] Ontario [*Library symbol National Library of Canada*] (NLC)

OOURC .... Centre de Recherche en Civilisation Canadienne-Francaise, Universite d'Ottawa [*Centre for Research on French Canadian Culture, University of Ottawa*], Ontario [*Library symbol National Library of Canada*] (BIB)

OOUSA .... United States Information Service, Ottawa, Ontario [*Library symbol National Library of Canada*] (NLC)

OOUSC .... Unitarian Service Committee of Canada, Ottawa, Ontario [*Library symbol National Library of Canada*] (BIB)

OOV .... Objects of Verification [*Arms control*] (DOMA)

OOV .... Orbit-to-Orbit Vehicle (MCD)

OOV .... Out of View

OOV .... Out of Vision [*Films, television, etc.*]

OOVIF .... Vanier Institute of the Family [*Institut Vanier de la Famille*] Ottawa, Ontario [*Library symbol National Library of Canada*] (NLC)

OOVV .... Versatile Vickers Systems, Inc., Ottawa, Ontario [*Library symbol National Library of Canada*] (NLC)

OOW .... Officer of the Watch [*Navigation*]

OOW .... Owen Sound Public Library, Ontario [*Library symbol National Library of Canada*] (NLC)

OOWC .... Wordcount, Creative Writing Services, Inc., Ottawa, Ontario [*Library symbol National Library of Canada*] (NLC)

OOWD .... Western Diversification [*Diversification de l'Ouest*], Ottawa, Ontario [*Library symbol National Library of Canada*] (BIB)

OOWGC .... Georgian College Resource Centre, Owen Sound, Ontario [*Library symbol National Library of Canada*] (NLC)

OOWGM .... Health Sciences Library, General & Marine Hospital, Owen Sound, Ontario [*Library symbol National Library of Canada*] (NLC)

OOWGM .... Health Sciences Library, Grey Bruce Regional Health Centre, Owen Sound, Ontario [*Library symbol National Library of Canada*] (NLC)

OOWIC .... West Island College of Ontario, Ottawa [*Library symbol National Library of Canada*] (BIB)

OOWLS .... Sir Wilfrid Laurier High School Library, Carleton Board of Education, Ottawa, Ontario [*Library symbol National Library of Canada*] (BIB)

OOWM .... Owen Sound Museum, County of Grey, Ontario [*Library symbol National Library of Canada*] (BIB)

OOWSRA ..... Omnibus Oregon Wild and Scenic Rivers Act of 1988 (COE)

OOWT .... Tom Thomson Memorial Gallery, Owen Sound, Ontario [*Library symbol National Library of Canada*] (NLC)

OOWU .... Briefing Centre, World University Services of Canada [*Centre de Ressources, Entraide Universitaire Mondiale du Canada*], Ottawa, Ontario [*Library symbol National Library of Canada*] (NLC)

OOX .... XIOS Research Corp., Ottawa, Ontario [*Library symbol National Library of Canada*] (BIB)

OOxM..........	Miami University, Oxford, OH [*Library symbol Library of Congress*] (LCLS)
OOxM-S	Miami University, Scripps Foundation for Research in Population Problems, Oxford, OH [*Library symbol Library of Congress*] (LCLS)
OOYB..........	Yibal [*Oman*] [*ICAO location identifier*] (ICLI)
OOZ	Open Ocean Zone [*Oceanography*]
OOZE	Object-Oriented Z Environment [*Computer science*]
OP...............	Air Panama Internacional [*ICAO designator*] (AD)
Op...............	De Opficio Mundi [*Philo*] (BJA)
OP...............	Dominican Contemplative Nuns (Cloistered) (TOCD)
OP...............	Dominican Contemplative Sisters (TOCD)
OP...............	Dominican Contemplative Sisters (Cloistered) (TOCD)
OP...............	Dominican Rural Missionaries (TOCD)
OP...............	Dominican Sisters (Adrian, MI) (TOCD)
OP...............	Dominican Sisters (Akron, OH) (TOCD)
OP...............	Dominican Sisters (Amityville, NY) (TOCD)
OP...............	Dominican Sisters (Blauvelt, NY) (TOCD)
OP...............	Dominican Sisters (Caldwell, PA) (TOCD)
OP...............	Dominican Sisters (Colombia) (TOCD)
OP...............	Dominican Sisters (Columbus, OH) (TOCD)
OP...............	Dominican Sisters (Ecuador) (TOCD)
OP...............	Dominican Sisters (Edmonds, WA) (TOCD)
OP...............	Dominican Sisters (Fall River, MA) (TOCD)
OP...............	Dominican Sisters (Grand Rapid, MI) (TOCD)
OP...............	Dominican Sisters (Great Bend, KS) (TOCD)
OP...............	Dominican Sisters (Hawthorne, NY) (TOCD)
OP...............	Dominican Sisters (Houston, TX) (TOCD)
OP...............	Dominican Sisters (Justice, IL) (TOCD)
OP...............	Dominican Sisters (Kenosha, WI) (TOCD)
OP...............	Dominican Sisters (Media, PA) (TOCD)
OP...............	Dominican Sisters (Nashville, TN) (TOCD)
OP...............	Dominican Sisters (Newburgh, NY) (TOCD)
OP...............	Dominican Sisters (New Orleans, LA) (TOCD)
OP...............	Dominican Sisters of Carondelet (TOCD)
OP...............	Dominican Sisters of Charity of the Presentation of the Blessed Virgin (TOCD)
OP...............	Dominican Sisters of Mt. Thabor (TOCD)
OP...............	Dominican Sisters of Our Lady of the Most Holy Rosary (TOCD)
OP...............	Dominican Sisters of Our Lady of the Rosary and of Saint Catherine of Siena, Cabra (TOCD)
OP...............	Dominican Sisters of the Roman Congregation (TOCD)
OP...............	Dominican Sisters (Ossining, NY) (TOCD)
OP...............	Dominican Sisters (Oxford, MI) (TOCD)
OP...............	Dominican Sisters (Oxford, South Africa) (TOCD)
OP...............	Dominican Sisters (Racine, WI) (TOCD)
OP...............	Dominican Sisters (San Jose, CA) (TOCD)
OP...............	Dominican Sisters (San Rafael, CA) (TOCD)
OP...............	Dominican Sisters (Sinsinawa, WI) (TOCD)
OP...............	Dominican Sisters (Sparkill, NY) (TOCD)
OP...............	Dominican Sisters (Spokane, WA) (TOCD)
OP...............	Dominican Sisters (Springfield, IL) (TOCD)
OP...............	Dominican Sisters (St. Catherine, KY) (TOCD)
OP...............	Dominican Sisters (Tacoma, WA) (TOCD)
OP...............	Dominican Sisters (Vietnam) (TOCD)
OP...............	Eucharistic Missionaries of St. Dominic (TOCD)
OP...............	Hermanas Dominicanas de la Doctrine Cristiana (TOCD)
OP...............	Marian Society of Dominican Catechists (TOCD)
OP...............	Object Program (IAA)
OP...............	Obligated Position [*Civil Service*]
OP...............	Observation Plane
OP...............	Observation Point [*or Post*]
OP...............	Observation Post [*Military*]
OP...............	Observed Position [*Navigation*]
OP...............	Occasional Paper
OP...............	Occipitoparietal [*Medicine*] (AAMN)
OP...............	Occiput Posterior [*Medicine*]
OP...............	Occupational Psychologist
OP...............	Oceanus Procellarum [*Lunar area*]
OP...............	Octapeptide [*Biochemistry*]
OP...............	Offering Price
OP...............	Office of Personnel [*Department of Agriculture*] (GFGA)
OP...............	Office of Pesticides [*Public Health Service*]
OP...............	Office of Policy [*NASA*]
OP...............	Office of Preparedness (DNAB)
OP...............	Office Pass (AAG)
OP...............	Office Product (IAA)
OP...............	Officer Program [*Military*] (DNAB)
OP...............	Official Publication (ADA)
O/P..............	Off Peak (WDAA)
O-P..............	Off-Price [*A retail outlet selling discounted merchandise*]
o/p	Oil on Panel (VRA)
OP...............	Oil Pressure
OP...............	Oilproof
OP...............	Oil Pump
OP...............	Old Particular [*Marsala*]
OP...............	Old [*Previously seen*] Patient
OP...............	Old Pattern [*British military*] (DMA)
OP...............	Old Persean (WDAA)
OP...............	Old Persian [*Language, etc.*]
OP...............	Old Price [*Riots*] [*Occurred for 67 nights, beginning December 30, 1808, opening night of rebuilt Covent Garden Theatre, London, because of new and higher prices*]
OP...............	Olfactory Peduncle [*Medicine*] (DMAA)
OP...............	Omega Project (EA)
O/P..............	On Proof [*Publishing*] (DGA)
OP...............	Opaque [*Envelopes*]
OP...............	Open [*Stock exchange term*]
OP...............	Opening Pressure [*Medicine*]
OP...............	Opening Price [*Stock exchange term*]
OP...............	Opening Purchase [*Stock exchange term*]
OP...............	Open Policy
OP...............	Open Position [*Dancing*]
op...............	Opera [*Works*] [*Italian*]
OP...............	Opera
Op...............	Opera et Dies [*of Hesiod*] [*Classical studies*] (OCD)
OP...............	Operand [*Computer science*]
op...............	Operate (IDOE)
OP...............	Operate
OP...............	Operating Plan [*Management term*] (MCD)
OP...............	Operating Point (IAA)
OP...............	Operating Policy [*Military*]
OP...............	Operating Procedure [*Management term*] (KSC)
OP...............	Operating Profit [*DoD*]
OP...............	Operation (AFM)
OP...............	Operational (CAAL)
op...............	Operational (IDOE)
OP...............	Operational Priority
OP...............	Operational Procedure (MCD)
OP...............	Operational Project [*Army*] (AABC)
OP...............	Operation Overlord Preparations [*World War II*]
OP...............	Operation Plans
OP...............	Operations (KSC)
OP...............	Operations Order (MCD)
OP...............	Operations Plan (IAA)
OP...............	Operative Procedure
OP...............	Operator [*Computer science*]
op...............	Operator (IDOE)
OP...............	Ophthalmology
OP...............	Opinion (ADA)
O-P..............	Oppenheimer-Phillips [*Process*]
OP...............	Opposed (NVT)
OP...............	Opposite
op...............	Opposite (WDMC)
OP...............	Opposite Prompt [*i.e., the left side*] [*A stage direction*]
OP...............	Optical Probe (AAG)
OP...............	Optical Technician Program [*Association of Independent Colleges and Schools specialization code*]
OP...............	Optime [*Best*] [*Latin*] (ROG)
OP...............	Optional
OP...............	Optional Flag [*Navy British*]
OP...............	Opus [*Work*] [*Latin*]
op...............	Opus (WDMC)
OP...............	Orange Pekoe [*Tea*]
OP...............	Orbital Period (AAG)
OP...............	Orbital Probe [*NASA*]
op...............	Order of Preachers, Dominican Fathers (TOCD)
OP...............	Order of Preachers (Dominicans) (TOCD)
OP...............	Order of Preceptors
OP...............	Order Policy [*Insurance*]
OP...............	Ordinis Praedicatorum [*Of the Order of Preachers, or Dominicans*] [*Latin*]
OP...............	Ordnance Pamphlets
OP...............	Ordnance Personnel
OP...............	Ordnance Publications [*Navy*] (MCD)
OP...............	Ordo Praedicatorum [*Order of Preachers*] [*Dominicans*] [*Roman Catholic religious order*]
OP...............	Organic Phosphates (GNE)
OP...............	Organophoshate (LDT)
OP...............	Organophosphorus [*Organic chemistry*]
OP...............	Orient Press [*Press agency*] [*South Korea*]
OP...............	Original Pack (DB)
OP...............	Original Policy (ADA)
OP...............	Original Premium [*Insurance*]
OP...............	Orthogonal Polynomial (OA)
OP...............	Orthomat Plot (MCD)
OP...............	Osmotic Pressure
OP...............	Osteopoetin [*Biochemistry*]
OP...............	Osteoporosis [*Orthopedics*] (DAVI)
OP...............	Osterogenic Protein
OP...............	Other Papers (ROG)
OP...............	Other People's [*Borrowed money, cigarettes, etc.*] [*Slang*]
OP...............	Other Procurement
OP...............	Other than Psychotic
OP...............	Outer Panel (AAG)
OP...............	Out-of-Press [*Recordings*]
OP...............	Out of Print [*Also, OOP*] [*Publishing*]
op...............	Out of Print [*Publishing*] (WDMC)
OP...............	Outpatient [*Medicine*]
OP...............	Outpost
OP...............	Output (AAG)
o/p	Output
OP...............	Output Primary [*Electronics*]
OP...............	Outside Production
OP...............	Overall Position [*Tertiary entrance*]
OP...............	Over Pressure (AAG)
O/P..............	Overpriced (WDAA)
OP...............	Overprint
op...............	Overprint [*Journalism*] (WDMC)
OP...............	Overproof [*Distilling*]

OP............... Overseas Post (ADA)
OP............... Overtime Pay (MHDB)
OP............... Ovine Prolactin [*Endocrinology*]
O/P............. Ownership Purpose Code [*Army*] (AABC)
OP............... Own Protection (WDAA)
OP............... Oxazolinylphenoxy [*Organic radical*]
OP............... Oxygen Pressure Process [*Ore leach process*]
OP............... Oxygen Purge [*NASA*] (NASA)
OP............... Ozone Protection [*Environmental science*] (COE)
OP............... Paulding County Carnegie Public Library, Paulding, OH [*Library symbol Library of Congress*] (LCLS)
OP............... Perth Public Library, Ontario [*Library symbol National Library of Canada*] (NLC)
OP............... Religious Missionaries of St. Dominic (Spanish Prov.) (TOCD)
OPA............ Kopasker [*Iceland*] [*Airport symbol*] (OAG)
OPa............ Morley Library, Painesville, OH [*Library symbol Library of Congress*] (LCLS)
OPA............ Obscene Publications Act [*British*]
OPA............ Occupational Personality Assessment [*Test*] (TMMY)
OPA............ Office of Petroleum Allocation [*Federal Energy Administration*]
OPA............ Office of Policy Analysis [*Environmental Protection Agency*] (GFGA)
OPA............ Office of Population Affairs [*HEW*]
OPA............ Office of Population Affairs Clearinghouse (EA)
OPA............ Office of Price Administration [*World War II*]
OPA............ Office of Producer Affairs [*Federal Telecommunications Commission*]
OPA............ Office of Program Analysis [*Department of Energy Washington, DC*]
OPA............ Office of Program Appraisal [*Navy*]
OPA............ Office of Public Affairs [*in various government agencies*]
OPA............ Office of the Pardon Attorney [*Department of Justice*]
OPA............ Officer Personnel Act
o/pa........... Oil on Paper (VRA)
OPA............ Oil Pollution Act of 1990 [*MARAD*] (TAG)
OPA............ Onafhankelijke Partij [*Independent Party*] [*Netherlands Political party*] (PPW)
OPA............ Opal Air Pty Ltd. [*Australia*] [*FAA designator*] (FAAC)
OPA............ Opana [*Hawaii*] [*Seismograph station code, US Geological Survey*] (SEIS)
OPA............ Opaque [*Type of ice formation*]
Opa............ Opera of the Month Club [*Record label*]
OPA............ Operations Planning Analysis [*NASA*] (MCD)
OPA............ Operator Priority Access (NITA)
OPA............ O-Phthalaldehyde
OPA............ Optical Parametric Oscillator [*Physics*]
OPA............ Optical Plotting Attachment (WDAA)
OPA............ Optical Publishing Association (EA)
OPA............ Optoelectronic Pulse Amplifier
OPA............ Orbiter Plasma Analyzer [*NASA*]
OPA............ Organophosphorous Acid [*Organic chemistry*]
OPA............ Organ Procurement Agency [*Department of Health and Human Services*] (GFGA)
OPA............ Ortho-Phthaldehyde [*Organic chemistry*]
OPA............ Ortho-Propylaniline
OPA............ Other Procurement, Army (AABC)
OPA............ Output Plate Assembly (MCD)
OPA............ Ovarian Papillary Adenocarcinoma [*Oncology*]
OPA............ Overall Probability of Attack (DNAB)
OPA............ Overhead Precautionary Approach
OPAA.......... Organophosphorous Acid Anhydrase [*An enzyme*]
OPAAW....... Organization of Pan Asian-American Women (EA)
OPAB.......... Abbottabad [*Pakistan*] [*ICAO location identifier*] (ICLI)
OPAC.......... Online Public Access Catalog [*Silicon Valley Information Center - SVIC*] [*San Jose, CA*] [*Information service or system*] (IID)
OPAC.......... Overall Performance Appraisal Certification [*Environmental Protection Agency*] (GFGA)
OPAC.......... Resource Centre, School of Lanark County, Algonquin College of Applied Arts & Technology, Perth, Ontario [*Library symbol National Library of Canada*] (NLC)
OPACK........ Operation Acknowledge [*Computer science*] (MHDI)
OPACS........ Office of Price Administration and Civilian Supply [*Name changed to Office of Price Administration*] [*World War II*]
OPACS........ Order Planning and Control System (MCD)
OPACT........ Organization of Professional Acting Coaches and Teachers (EA)
OPaD.......... Diamond Shamrock Corp., Research Library, Painesville, OH [*Library symbol Library of Congress*] (LCLS)
OPADEC...... Optical Partial Decoy (IAA)
OPADEC...... Optical Particle Decoy
OPADR........ Operand Address [*Computer science*] (IAA)
OPAE.......... Office of Program Analysis and Evaluation [*DoD*]
OPAEP........ Organisation des Pays Arabes Exportateurs de Petrole [*Organization of Arab Petroleum Exporting Countries*] (EAIO)
Op AG......... Opinions of the Attorney General [*A publication*] (DLA)
OPAGREE.... Operational Agreement (DNAB)
OPAGY........ Operating Agency [*Military*]
OPAH.......... Oil Pump Assembly Housing (MCD)
OPAI........... Paisley Branch, Bruce County Public Library, Ontario [*Library symbol National Library of Canada*] (NLC)
OPaL.......... Lake Erie College, Painesville, OH [*Library symbol Library of Congress*] (LCLS)
OPAL.......... Lakehead University, Thunder Bay, Ontario [*Library symbol National Library of Canada*] (NLC)
OPAL.......... Ocean Process Analysis Laboratory [*University of New Hampshire*] [*Research center*] (RCD)
OPAL.......... Older People with Active Lifestyles [*Lifestyle classification*]
OPAL.......... Oncovin [*Vincristine*], Prednisolone, Adriamycin, L-Asparaginase [*Antineoplastic drug regimen*]

OPAL.......... Opal, Inc. [*NASDAQ symbol*] (SAG)
OPAL.......... Operation Alert [*Designed to test ability to recover from an enemy attack*]
OPAL.......... Operational Performance Analysis Language [*Computer science*]
OPAL.......... Operation Plan Analysis Logic [*Search technology*]
OPAL.......... Optical Platform Alignment Linkage
OPAL.......... Orientation Program in American Law [*of AALS*]
OPALE......... Faculty of Education, Lakehead University, Thunder Bay, Ontario [*Library symbol National Library of Canada*] (NLC)
OPALG........ Department of Geography, Lakehead University, Thunder Bay, Ontario [*Library symbol National Library of Canada*] (NLC)
OPALs......... Older People with Active Lifestyles [*Lifestyle classification*]
Opals.......... Older People with an Active Lifestyle [*Lifestyle classification*]
OP AMP...... Operational Amplifier [*Computer science*]
OpAmp........ Operational Amplifier (AAEL)
op amp....... Operational Amplifier (IDOE)
OPANAL...... Operations Analysis [*Navy*] (NG)
OPANAL...... Organismo para la Proscripcion de las Armas Nucleares en la America Latina [*Agency for the Prohibition of Nuclear Weapons in Latin America*] (EAIO)
OP & I........ Office of Patents and Inventions
OP & I........ Office of Publications and Information [*Department of Commerce*]
OP & PB...... Oceanographic Plans and Policy Board (SAA)
OP & R....... Offset Printing and Reprographics [*A publication*] (DGA)
OPAPE........ Organisation Pan-Africaine de la Profession Enseignante [*All Africa Teachers' Organization*] (EAIO)
OPAQ......... Offer Parent-Adolescent Questionnaire [*Personality development test*] [*Psychology*]
OPAQUE...... Optical Atmospheric Quality in Europe (MCD)
OPAR.......... Office of Policy Analysis and Review [*Environmental Protection Agency*] (GFGA)
OPAR.......... Operation Plans Assessment Report [*Environmental science*] (COE)
OPAR.......... Paris Public Library, Ontario [*Library symbol National Library of Canada*] (NLC)
Op Arch...... Opuscula Archaeologica [*A publication*] (OCD)
OPAREA...... Operating Area (CAAL)
op art......... Optical Art (ODBW)
OPAS.......... Occupation Pensions Advisory Service (WDAA)
OPAS.......... Operational Assignment (DA)
OPAS.......... Operational Assistance [*United Nations Development Program*]
OPAS.......... Operational Assistance Scheme [*Of UNDP*] (EBF)
OPAS.......... Operational Public Address System
OPAS.......... Overpass [*Postal Service standard*] (OPSA)
OPASTCO.... Organization for the Protection and Advancement of Small Telephone Companies (EA)
OPat........... Pataskala Public Library, Pataskala, OH [*Library symbol Library of Congress*] (LCLS)
Op Att Gen... Opinions of the Attorneys-General [*United States*] [*A publication*] (DLA)
OPATTI....... Office de Promotion et d'Animation Touristique de Tahiti et ses Iles (EY)
Op Att'y Gen... Opinions of the Attorney General [*A publication*] (DLA)
Op Attys Gen... Opinions of the Attorneys-General [*United States*] [*A publication*] (DLA)
OPB............ Occupational Pensions Board [*British*] (DCTA)
OPB............ Office of the Publication Board [*Department of Commerce*]
OPB............ Open Bay [*Papua New Guinea*] [*Airport symbol*] (OAG)
OPB............ Other People's Butts [*Cigarette butts garnered from ash trays*] [*Slang*]
OPB............ Outpatient Basis [*Medicine*]
OPB............ Oxidizer Preburner (KSC)
OPB............ Pikangikum Band Library, Ontario [*Library symbol National Library of Canada*] (BIB)
OPBAT........ Operation Bahamas, Antilles, and Turks [*Air Force*]
OPBCT........ Providence Bay Branch, Carnarvon Township Public Library, Ontario [*Library symbol National Library of Canada*] (NLC)
OPBDR........ Office of Program and Budget Development and Review [*Bureau of Apprenticeship and Training*] [*Department of Labor*]
OPBE.......... Office of Planning, Budgeting, and Evaluation [*National Institute of Education*]
OPBG.......... Bhagtanwala [*Pakistan*] [*ICAO location identifier*] (ICLI)
OPBL.......... Bela [*Pakistan*] [*ICAO location identifier*] (ICLI)
OPBMA....... Ocean Pearl Button Manufacturers Association [*Defunct*]
OPBN.......... Bannu [*Pakistan*] [*ICAO location identifier*] (ICLI)
OPBOV........ Oxidizer Preburner Oxidizer Valve (NASA)
OPBR.......... Bahawalnagar [*Pakistan*] [*ICAO location identifier*] (ICLI)
OPBU.......... Operating Budget
OPBW.......... Bahawalpur [*Pakistan*] [*ICAO location identifier*] (ICLI)
OPC............ Occult Papillary Carcinoma [*Oncology*]
OPC............ Ocean Policy Committee [*Marine science*] (MSC)
OPC............ Ocean Products Center [*Marine science*] (OSRA)
OPC............ Oculopalatocerebral [*Syndrome*] [*Medicine*] (DMAA)
OPC............ Office de la Protection du Consommateur [*Quebec, PQ*]
OPC............ Office of Policy Coordination (LAIN)
OPC............ Office of Price Control [*World War II*]
OPC............ Office of Primary Concern [*DoD*]
OPC............ Office of Private Cooperation [*Department of State*]
OPC............ Office of Procurement and Contracts [*Department of Housing and Urban Development*] (GFGA)
OPC............ Office of the Protective Commissioner [*Australia*]
OPC............ Ogren, Paul C., South Bend IN [*STAC*]
OPC............ Oil Policy Committee [*Office of Emergency Preparedness*] [*Obsolete*]
OPC............ Oldsmobile Performance Chapter (EA)
OPC............ OLE [*Object Linking and Embedding*] for Process Control (ACII)
OPC............ Oligonucleotide Purification Cartridge [*Chromatography*]

OPC	Olivetti Personal Computers
OPC	One Pound Charge (MCD)
OPC	Online Plotter Controller [California Computer Products, Inc.]
OPC	Open Printed Circuit (IAA)
OPC	Open Promoter Complex [Genetics]
OPC	Operated Preference Controls
OPC	Operation Code
OPC	Operations Code [Army] (IAA)
OPC	Operations Control (IAA)
OPC	Operator Position Controller [Telecommunications]
OPC	Optical Particle Counter (PDAA)
OPC	Optical Phase Conjugator [LASER-aiming device]
OPC	Optical Photoconductor (PCM)
OPC	Optical Photo Coupler
OPC	Optical Proximity Correct (AAEL)
OPC	Optional Calling Plans [Telecommunications] (TEL)
OPC	Orange Pigment Cell
OPC	Ordinary Portland Cement
OPC	Ordnance Procurement Center [Army]
OPC	Organic Photoconductor
OPC	Orion Pictures (EFIS)
OPC	Outer Passenger Cabin
OPC	Outer Proliferative Center [Brain anatomy]
opc	Out of Print and Cancelled [Publishing] (WDMC)
OPC	Out of Print, Canceled [Publishing]
OPC	Outpatient Clinic [Medicine]
OPC	Outpatient Psychiatric Care [Health insurance] (GHCT)
OPC	Overall Performance Category
OPC	Overseas Press Club of America (EA)
OPC	Ownership Purpose and Condition Code [Navy] (DNAB)
OPC	Oxford Pocket Classics [A publication] (ROG)
OPC	Oxypneumocardiogram [Cardiology] (DAVI)
OPC	Perth Courier, Ontario [Library symbol National Library of Canada] (NLC)
OPC	QC Optics [AMEX symbol] (SAG)
OPCA	Occupational Program Consultants Association (EA)
OPCA	Olivopontocerebellar Atrophy [Neurology]
OPCA	Opium Poppy Control Act of 1942
OPCA	Overseas Press Club of America (WDAA)
OP-CAL	Operation California (EA)
Op Cal Att'y Gen	Opinions of the Attorney General of California [A publication] (DLA)
OPCC	Office of Preschool and Child Care [Victoria, Australia]
OPCC	Offutt Air Force Base Processing and Correlation Center (MCD)
OPCC	Optical Product Code Council (EA)
OPCC	Outpatient Psychiatric Care Coverage
Op CCCG	Opinion, Chief Counsel, United States Coast Guard [A publication] (DLA)
OPCE	Operator Control Element [Computer science] (IBMDP)
OPCEN	Operations Center [INTELSAT]
OPCG	Original Print Collectors Group (EA)
OPCGE	Organic/Polymer Crystal Growth Experiment (SSD)
OPCGF	Organic/Polymer Crystal Growth Facility (SSD)
OPCH	Chitral [Pakistan] [ICAO location identifier] (ICLI)
OP CIT	Opere Citato [In the Work Cited] [Latin]
op cit	Opere Citato [In the work cited] [Latin] (WDMC)
OPCIT	Opus Citatum (IAA)
OPCL	Chilas [Pakistan] [ICAO location identifier] (ICLI)
OPCM	Operative Plasterers and Cement Masons International Association of the US and Canada
OPCMIA	Operative Plasterers and Cement Masons International Association of US and Canada (EA)
OPCML	Township of Muskoka Lakes Public Library Board, Port Carling, Ontario [Library symbol National Library of Canada] (BIB)
OPCO	Operating Plan Change Orders [Coast Guard publication]
OPCO	Outside Production Consignment Order
OP-COD	Operating Code [Computer science]
op code	Operation Code (IDOE)
OPCODE	Operations Code [Army] (AABC)
OP-COM	Opera-Comique [Comic Opera] [Music]
OPCOM	Operational Command [Military] (MCD)
OP-COM	Operations-Communications
op-com	Optical Communication (MED)
OPCOMCTR	Operational Command Center [Navy] (NVT)
OPCON	Operational Control [Army] (NVT)
OPCON	Operation Control [Military] (VNW)
OPCON	Operations and Control System (IAA)
OPCON	Operator's Console
OPCON	Optimizing Control [Military]
OPCONCEN	Operational Control Center [Navy]
OPCONCTR	Operational Control Center [Navy] (NVT)
OPCOSAL	Optimum Coordinated Shipboard [or Shorebased] Allowance List
OPCPL	Port Colborne Public Library, Ontario [Library symbol National Library of Canada] (NLC)
OPCR	Chachro [Pakistan] [ICAO location identifier] (ICLI)
OPCR	One-Pass Cold-Rolled [Steel sheets]
OPCS	Office of Population Census and Surveys [British] (ECON)
OPCS	Office of Population Censuses and Surveys [Department of Employment] [British]
OPCS	Operational Planning and Control System [Department of Labor] (OICC)
OPCT	Chirat [Pakistan] [ICAO location identifier] (ICLI)
OPCTR	Operation Counter (IAA)
OPCTR	Operations Center [Military]
OPCV	Office of Planning, Control, and Validation [Social Security Administration]
OPCW	Office of Petroleum Coordination for War [New Deal]
OPCW	Organization for the Prohibition of Chemical Weapons [Proposed, 1992]
OPD	Audit Programs Division (AAGC)
OPD	Delayed Opening
OPD	Observed Position Data
OPD	Obstetric Prediabetic [Medicine] (DMAA)
OPD	Office of Policy Development [Executive Office of the President]
OPD	Office of Program Development [Environmental Protection Agency] (GFGA)
OPD	Officer Personnel Directorate [Army]
OPD	Officer Professional Development [Military] (INF)
OPD	Ohio College of Podiatric Medicine, Cleveland, OH [OCLC symbol] (OCLC)
OPD	One Per Desk (NITA)
OPD	Open Distributed Processing [Computer science] (TELE)
OPD	Opened [Stock exchange term] (SPSG)
OPD	Opening Posterior Digestive [Gland]
OPD	Operand [Computer science]
OPD	Operational Programming Department [Telecommunications] (TEL)
OPD	Operations Division [War Department General Staff] [World War II]
OPD	Operations Planning Division [Manned Spacecraft Center]
OPD	Optical Particle Detector [for evaluating film quality]
OPD	Optical Path Difference (MCD)
OPD	Optical Phase Distortion (PDAA)
OPD	Optical Proximity Detector
OPD	Oral and Pharyngeal Development [Section] [National Institute of Dental Research]
OPD	Orbiting Propellant Depot [NASA]
OPD	Original Pack Dispensing [For drugs] [Packaging]
OPD	Ortho-Phenylenediamine [Organic chemistry]
OPD	'Osef Piskei Din shel ha-Rabanut ha-Rashit le-'Erets Yisrael (BJA)
OPD	Oto-Palato-Digital [Syndrome]
OPD	Outpatient Department [or Dispensary] [Medicine]
OPD	Outpatient Dispensary [Medicine] (DMAA)
OPD	Overall Program Design (OICC)
O/PD	Overpaid (ROG)
OPD	Overseas Policy Defence Committee [British]
OPD	Oxford Paperback Dictionary [A publication]
OPD	Port Dover Centennial Public Library, Ontario [Library symbol National Library of Canada] (NLC)
OPDAC	Optical Data Converter (NOAA)
OPDAG	Original Paper Doll Artists Guild (EA)
OPDAR	Optical Detection and Ranging
OPDARS	Optical Detection and Ranging System (IAA)
OPDATS	Operational Performance Data System
OPDB	Dalbandin [Pakistan] [ICAO location identifier] (ICLI)
OPDC	Overseas Policy Defence Committee [British] (DI)
OPDD	Dadu [Pakistan] [ICAO location identifier] (ICLI)
OPDD	Operational Plan Data Document [Military] (AFM)
O,p-DDD	Ortho, Para-Dichloro-Diphenyldichlorethane [Mitotane] [Antineoplastic drug regimen] (DAVI)
OPDEC	Operational Deception [Navy] (NVT)
OpDent	Operative Dentistry (BABM)
Opdent	Operative Dentistry (DAVI)
OPDET	Operational Detachment (MCD)
OPDEVFOR	Operational Development Forces
OPDG	Dera Ghazi Khan [Pakistan] [ICAO location identifier] (ICLI)
OPDG	Ocular Plethysmodynamography (DB)
OPDI	Dera Ismail Khan [Pakistan] [ICAO location identifier] (ICLI)
OPDI	Operator Please Deliver Immediately
OP DIAP	Open Diapason [Organ stop] [Music]
OPDIF	Operational Planning Identification File [Military]
OPDIN	Ocean Pollution Data and Information Network [Washington, DC Department of Commerce] (GRD)
OPDIN	Ocean Pollution Data Center [Marine science] (OSRA)
OP DIV	Operations/Air Intelligence Photography Division (DNAB)
OPDK	Daharki [Pakistan] [ICAO location identifier] (ICLI)
OPDL	Office of Production and Defense Lending [Department of the Treasury]
OPDO	Oromo People's Democratic Organization [Ethiopia] [Political party] (EY)
OPDOC	Operational Documentation [Military]
OPDP	Officer Professional Development Program [Pronounced "opey-dopey"] [Canadian Navy]
OPDPE	Office of Policy Development Planning and Evaluation [Pronounced "opey dopey"] [NIMH]
OPDR	Office of Primary Development Responsibility (AFM)
OPDS	Office Professional Development System (MCD)
OPDS	Offshore Petroleum Distribution System
OPDU	Operation Protocol Data Unit [Telecommunications] (OSI)
OPDU	Powassan and District Union Public Library, Powassan, Ontario [Library symbol National Library of Canada] (NLC)
OPDUA	Operative Painters amd Decorators' Union of Australia
OPD WDGS	Operations Division, War Department General Staff [World War II]
OPE	Eldorado Nuclear Ltd., Port Hope, Ontario [Library symbol National Library of Canada] (NLC)
OPE	Office of Planning and Evaluation [Office of Personnel Management] (GRD)
OPE	Office of Policy Evaluation [Nuclear energy] (NRCH)
OPE	Office of Postsecondary Education [Department of Education] (GFGA)
OPE	Office of Program Eligibility (AAGC)

OPE.............. Office of Program Evaluation [*Office of Policy, Evaluation, and Research*] [*Department of Labor*]
OPE.............. One-Pion Exchange [*Nuclear energy*]
OPE.............. Open Point Expanding [*Bullet*] (DICI)
OPE.............. Operational Planning Estimate
OPE.............. Operations Project Engineer [*NASA*] (KSC)
OPE.............. Optical Pointing Error
OPE.............. Optical-Probe Experiment [*Giotto probe of Halley's comet*] [*European Space Agency*]
OPE.............. Optimized Processing Element
OPE.............. Orbiting Primate Experiment (MCD)
OPE.............. Oregon, Pacific & Eastern Railway Co. [*AAR code*]
OPE.............. Other Plant Equipment [*DoD*]
OPE.............. Other Project Element (NASA)
OPE.............. Outer Planets Explorer [*NASA*]
OPE.............. Societe 3S Aviation (Aerope) [*France ICAO designator*] (FAAC)
OPE.............. Topeka, KS [*Location identifier FAA*] (FAAL)
OPEAA...... Outdoor Power Equipment Aftermarket Association (EA)
OPEB.......... Bruce County Public Library, Port Elgin, Ontario [*Library symbol National Library of Canada*] (NLC)
OPEC.......... Oil Producers' Economic Cartel (NADA)
OPEC.......... Organization of Petroleum Exporting Countries (NADA)
OPECNA...... OPEC [*Organization of Petroleum Exporting Countries*] News Agency [*See also APOPEC*] [*Vienna, Austria*] (EAIO)
OPECO........ Operations Coordinator [*Marine science*] (MSC)
OP-ED.......... Opposite Editorial Page [*in a newspaper*] [*Usually consists of opinion columns by various guest writers or syndicated columnists*]
op ed.......... Opposite - the Editorial Page [*Newspapers*] (WDMC)
OPED.......... Other Pay Entry Date [*Army*] (AABC)
OPED .... Point Edward Public Library, Ontario [*Library symbol National Library of Canada*] (NLC)
OPEDA........ Organization of Professional Employees of the United States Department of Agriculture (EA)
OPEDA........ Outdoor Power Equipment Distributors Association (EA)
OPEDC........ Overseas Private Enterprise Development Corp. [*Proposed successor to Agency for International Development*]
OPeeO .... Ohio Valley Local District Free Public Library, Peebles Branch, Peebles, OH [*Library symbol Library of Congress*] (LCLS)
OPEF.......... Overall Plume Enhancement Factor [*Space Shuttle*] [*NASA*]
OPEI.......... Office of Public Education and Information [*NASA*]
OPEI.......... Outdoor Power Equipment Institute (EA)
OPEI.......... Outdoor Power Equipment Institute, Inc.
OPEIU........ Office and Professional Employees International Union (EA)
OPEM.......... One-Pion Exchange Model [*Nuclear energy*]
OPEM.......... Pembroke Public Library, Ontario [*Library symbol National Library of Canada*] (NLC)
OPEMA .... Oilfield Production Equipment Manufacturers Association [*Defunct*] (EA)
OPEMAC...... Upper Ottawa Valley Campus Resource Centre, Algonquin College, Pembroke, Ontario [*Library symbol National Library of Canada*] (NLC)
OPEMO........ Ottawa Valley Historical Society, Pembroke, Ontario [*Library symbol National Library of Canada*] (BIB)
OPEN .... Fund for an Open Society (EA)
OPEN .... Oncovin, Prednisone, Etopside, Mitoxantrone [*Antineoplastic drug*] (CDI)
OPEN .... Online Public Education Network
OPEN .... Open Environment [*NASDAQ symbol*] (TTSB)
OPEN .... Open Environment Corp. [*NASDAQ symbol*] (SAG)
OPEN .... Open Protocol Enhanced Network [*Northern Telecom communications network*] [*Canada*]
OPEN .... Open ROUTE Network [*NASDAQ symbol*] [*Formerly, Proteon, Inc.*]
OPEN .... Organisation des Producteurs d'Energie Nucleaire [*Paris, France*] (EAIO)
OPEN .... Origins of Plasma in the Earth's Neighborhood [*Ad Hoc Advisory Committee terminated, 1981*]
OPEN .... Penetanguishene Public Library, Ontario [*Library symbol National Library of Canada*] (BIB)
OPENAH...... Operational Evaluation of Armed Helicopters (MCD)
OPENE .... Ecole Secondaire le Caron, Penetanguishene, Ontario [*Library symbol National Library of Canada*] (BIB)
OPENM .... Mental Health Centre, Penetanguishene, Ontario [*Library symbol National Library of Canada*] (NLC)
OpenMkt..... Open Market, Inc. [*Associated Press*] (SAG)
OpenPln....... Open Plan Systems, Inc. [*Associated Press*] (SAG)
OpenTxt...... Open Text Corp. [*Associated Press*] (SAG)
OpenVis...... OpenVision Technologies, Inc. [*Associated Press*] (SAG)
OPEO.......... Oakland-Pontiac Enthusiast Organization (EA)
OPEO .... Octylphenol Polyethoxylate [*Organic chemistry*]
OPEOS........ Outside Plant Planning, Engineering, and Construction Operations System (MCD)
OPEP .... Orbital-Plane Experiment Package [*NASA*]
OPEPB........ Eastern Pentecostal Bible College, Peterborough, Ontario [*Library symbol National Library of Canada*] (NLC)
OPER .... Office of Policy and Economic Research [*Federal Home Loan Bank Board*] [*Washington, DC*] (GRD)
OPER .... Office of Policy, Evaluation, and Research [*Employment and Training Administration*] [*Department of Labor*]
OPer .... Old Persian [*Language*] (BARN)
OPER .... Operating [*Automotive engineering*]
OPER .... Operation [*or Operational*] (KSC)
Oper............ Operation (TBD)
oper............ Operation (DD)
OPER .... Operator
OPERA........ Operational Analysis (IAA)

OPERA........ Ordnance Pulses Experimental Research Assembly [*Nuclear reactor*]
OPERA........ Out-of-Pile Expulsion and Reentry Apparatus [*Nuclear energy*]
OPERATORS... Optimization Program for Economical Remote Trunk Arrangement and TSPS [*Traffic Service Positions System*] Operator Arrangements [*Telecommunications*] (TEL)
OPERG........ Operating (MDG)
Oper Off..... Operations Officer (TBD)
O-PERS........ Officer Personnel Office (DNAB)
OPers......... Old Persian [*Language*] (BARN)
OPERSCRS... Officer Personnel Course [*Air Force*]
OPersLex.... Old Persian Grammar Texts Lexicon [*A publication*] (BJA)
OPERUN ...... Operation Planning and Execution System for Railway Unified Network (PDAA)
OPES .... Centre de Documentation, Ecole Secondaire de Plantagenet [*Documentation Centre, Plantagenet Secondary School*], Ontario [*Library symbol National Library of Canada*] (BIB)
OPET.......... Organization, Personnel Equipment and Training [*Group*]
OPET.......... Oriented Polyethylene Terephthalate [*Organic chemistry*]
OPET.......... Trent University, Peterborough, Ontario [*Library symbol National Library of Canada*] (NLC)
OPETA .... Trent University Archives, Peterborough, Ontario [*Library symbol National Library of Canada*] (NLC)
OPETAL........ Trent Audio Library Services, Trent University, Peterborough, Ontario [*Library symbol National Library of Canada*] (NLC)
OPETC........ Trent Canal Office, Peterborough, Ontario [*Library symbol National Library of Canada*] (BIB)
OPETCG ...... Canadian General Electric Co. Ltd., Peterborough, Ontario [*Library symbol National Library of Canada*] (NLC)
OPETCM ...... Peterborough Centennial Museum and Archives, Ontario [*Library symbol National Library of Canada*] (BIB)
OPETHS .... Hutchison House Museum, Peterborough Historical Society, Ontario [*Library symbol National Library of Canada*] (BIB)
OPETM........ Map Library, Trent University, Peterborough, Ontario [*Library symbol National Library of Canada*] (NLC)
OPETP .... Peterborough Public Library, Ontario [*Library symbol National Library of Canada*] (NLC)
OPETSF....... Brealy Library, Sir Sandford Fleming College, Peterborough, Ontario [*Library symbol National Library of Canada*] (BIB)
OPETSFD ..... Daniel Library, Sir Sandford Fleming College, Peterborough, Ontario [*Library symbol National Library of Canada*] (BIB)
OPEV .... Petawawa Village and Township Union Public Library, Ontario [*Library symbol National Library of Canada*] (NLC)
OPEVAL .... Operational Evaluation [*Navy*] (NG)
OPEX .... Operational Executive (CIST)
OPEX .... Operational, Executive, and Administrative Personnel Program [*United Nations*]
OPEX .... Operational Extension
OPF.............. Miami, FL [*Location identifier FAA*] (FAAL)
OPF.............. Official Personnel File (MCD)
OPF.............. Official Personnel Folder [*Military*]
OPF.............. One-Piece Folder [*Publishing*] (WDMC)
OPF.............. Open-Pore Foam [*Plastic*]
OPF.............. Operations Flight [*Military*]
OPF.............. Optical Propagation Facility
OPF.............. Orbiter Processing Facility [*NASA*] (NASA)
OPF.............. Overseas Project Fund [*British Overseas Trade Board*] (DS)
OPFA .... Faisalabad [*Pakistan*] [*ICAO location identifier*] (ICLI)
OPFAC........ Operating Facilities [*Coast Guard publication*]
OPFAC........ Operational Facility (RDA)
OPFAD........ Outer-Perimeter Fleet Air Defense
OPFC .... Hinchinbrooke Public Library, Frontenac County Library, Parkham, Ontario [*Library symbol National Library of Canada*] (BIB)
OPFC .... Orbiter Preflight Checklist [*NASA*] (MCD)
OPFCA........ Ornamental Pool and Fountain Constructors Association [*British*] (DBA)
OPFCO........ Operational Program Functional Checkout (MCD)
OPFI.......... Office of Program and Fiscal Integrity (USGC)
OPFM.......... Outlet Plenum Feature Model [*Nuclear energy*] (NRCH)
OPFOR........ Opportunity to Confront the Best Opposing Force [*Army*] (INF)
OPFOR........ Opposing Force [*Military*] (INF)
OPFRC........ Clarendon-Miller Branch, Frontenac County Library, Plevna, Ontario [*Library symbol National Library of Canada*] (NLC)
OPFT.......... Other than Permanent Full-Time (GFGA)
OPFTE........ Other than Permanent Full-Time Equivalent (GFGA)
OPG............ Ocular Pneumoplethysmography (DB)
OPG............ Oculoplethysmograph [*Instrumentation*]
OPG............ Office Of Global Programs [*Marine science*] (OSRA)
OPG............ Office of the Postmaster General [*Obsolete*]
OPG............ Opening
OPG............ Operating
OPG............ Operational Performance Goals
OPG............ Operational Planning Grant (OICC)
OPG............ Operations Planning Group [*Military*]
OPG............ Original Proof Gallon
OPG............ Outside Production Group
OPG............ Overseas Products Group [*Department of Trade*] [*British*]
OPG............ Oxypolygelatin [*Plasma extender*]
Op GA Att'y Gen... Opinions of the Attorney General of Georgia [*A publication*] (DLA)
OPG/CPA...... Oculoplethysmography/Carotid Phonoangiography [*Medicine*] (DAVI)
Op GCT........ Opinion, General Counsel, United States Treasury Department [*A publication*] (DLA)
OPGD.......... Gwadar [*Pakistan*] [*ICAO location identifier*] (ICLI)
OPGE .... OEEC [*Organization for European Economic Cooperation*] Petroleum Industry Emergency Group (NATG)

OP/GSA.........	Office of Preparedness, General Services Administration [*Later, Federal Preparedness Agency*]
OPGSX.........	Oppenheimer Gold & Spl. Minerals [*Mutual fund ticker symbol*] (SG)
OPGT	Gilgit [*Pakistan*] [*ICAO location identifier*] (ICLI)
OPGT	Outer Planets Grand Tour [*NASA*]
OPGUID	Optimum Guidance [*Technique*] (NASA)
OPGW	Optical Groundwire [*Telecommunications*] (TSSD)
OPH	Obliterative Pulmonary Hypertension [*Medicine*]
OPH	Old Parliamentary Hand [*Political*] [*British*]
OPh............	Old Phoenician (BJA)
OPH	Operational Propellant Handling [*NASA*] (AAG)
OPH	Ophicleide [*Musical instrument*]
oph	Ophicleide (WDAA)
Oph	Ophiuchus [*Constellation*]
OPH	Ophthalmodynamometry [*Ophthalmology*]
OPH	Ophthalmolgist
OPH	Ophthalmology [*or Ophthalmoscopy*]
OPH	[*The*] Ophthalmoscope [*London*] [*A publication*] (ROG)
Oph	Ophthalmoscope [*or Ophthalmoscopic*] [*Ophthalmology*] (DAVI)
OPH	Opposite Hand [*Technical drawings*]
OPH	Organophosphorus Hydrolase [*An enzyme*]
OPH	Public Library, Port Hope, Ontario [*Library symbol National Library of Canada*] (NLC)
OPHC	Office of Prepaid Health Care [*Department of Health and Human Services*] (GFGA)
Oph D	Doctor of Ophthalmology
OPHF	Orbital Polarized Hartree-Fock [*Atomic physics*]
Ophi............	Ophiuchus [*Constellation*]
OPHIR.........	Organic Power and Heat Industrial Reactor
Ophn............	Orpheon [*Record label*] [*Poland*]
OPHQ	Karachi [*Pakistan*] [*ICAO location identifier*] (ICLI)
OPHR	Olympic Project for Human Rights
Op Hrs........	Operation Hours (DA)
OPHS	Operational Propellant Handling System [*NASA*] (AAG)
OPHT	Ophthalmic
OPHTH.........	Ophthalmology (AABC)
OPHTHAL....	Ophthalmology
OphtImg......	Ophthalmic Imaging Systems [*Associated Press*] (SAG)
OPHTS	Operational Propellant Handling Test Site [*NASA*] (AAG)
OPHWA.......	Nuclear Products Department, Westinghouse Canada, Inc., Port Hope, Ontario [*Library symbol National Library of Canada*] (NLC)
OPi..............	Flesh Public Library, Piqua, OH [*Library symbol Library of Congress*] (LCLS)
OPI.............	Oculoparalytic Illusion [*Ophthalmology*]
OPI.............	Office of Primary Interest
OPI.............	Office of Programs Integration [*Energy Research and Development Administration*]
OPI.............	Office of Public Information [*NASA*]
OPI.............	Office of Public Information [*UNESCO*]
OPI.............	Off-Site Production Inspection (AAG)
OPI.............	Oil Patch Group, Inc. [*Toronto Stock Exchange symbol*]
OPI.............	Oil Pressure Indicator
OPI.............	Omnibus Personality Inventory [*Psychology*]
OPI.............	One Person's Impact [*An association*] (EA)
OPI.............	Open for Public Inspection [*Patent applications*]
OPI.............	Open Prepress Interface [*Computer science*] (PCM)
OPI.............	Open Protocol Interface [*Telecommunications*]
OPI.............	Optical Publishing, Inc. [*Information service or system*] (IID)
OPI.............	Orbital Position Indicator
OPI.............	Orbiter Payload Interrogator [*NASA*] (MCD)
OPI.............	Ordnance Procedure Instrumentations (AAG)
OPI.............	Ordnance Procurement Instructions [*Army*]
OPI.............	Organophosphate Insecticide
OPI.............	Output Productivity Index
OPI.............	Outside Procurement [*or Purchase*] Inspection (AAG)
OPI.............	Overall Performance Index [*Finance*]
OPI.............	Picton Public Library, Ontario [*Library symbol National Library of Canada*] (NLC)
OPIA	Opto-Precision Instruments Association (NTPA)
OPIAT	Opiates [*Chemical dependency*] [*Pharmacology*] (DAVI)
OPIC	Oficina Permanente Internacional de la Carne [*Permanent International Meat Office*] (EAIO)
OPIC	Overseas Private Investment Corp. [*US International Development Cooperatio n Agency*] [*Washington, DC*]
OPIC	Pickering Public Library, Ontario [*Library symbol National Library of Canada*] (NLC)
OPID	Operational Procedures Interface Document (MCD)
OPIDF	Operational Planning Identification File (MCD)
OPIDN.........	Organophosphate Induced Delayed Neural Toxicity
OPiE...........	Edison State Community College, Piqua, OH [*Library symbol Library of Congress*] (LCLS)
OPIE...........	Ohio Program of Intensive English (EDAC)
OPIET.........	Eco-Tec Ltd., Pickering, Ontario [*Library symbol National Library of Canada*] (NLC)
OPIEW	Older People in Europe Week (WDAA)
OPIG	Picton Gazette, Ontario [*Library symbol National Library of Canada*] (NLC)
OPIL...........	Opalescent Indicating Light
Op III Att'y Gen...	Illinois Attorney General's Opinion [*A publication*] (DLA)
OPIM..........	Order Processing and Inventory Monitoring [*Computer science*]
Opin...........	Opinions of the Attorneys-General [*United States*] [*A publication*] (DLA)
Opinc..........	Options Income (BARN)
OPINE	Operations in a Nuclear Environment [*DoD*]
Opine..........	Option Income [*Business term*]
OPINM.........	North Marysburgh Museum, Picton, Ontario [*Library symbol National Library of Canada*] (BIB)
OpinRsh.......	Opinion Research Corp. [*Associated Press*] (SAG)
OPINT.........	Optical Intelligence
OPINTEL.......	Operational Intelligence
OPIRL.........	Operator Interface Rolling Loop
OPIS	Operational Priority Indicating System (NATG)
OPIS	Orbiter Prime Item Specification [*NASA*] (NASA)
OPIS	Pelee Island Public Library, Ontario [*Library symbol National Library of Canada*] (NLC)
OP(IT).........	Operation Overlord Preparations, Inland Transport [*World War II*]
OPIT	Operator Interface Table (MCD)
OPIT	Oxide-Powder-in-Tube
OPIVITA.......	Outpatient Intravenous Infusion Therapy Association (NTPA)
OPiWU........	Wright State University, Piqua Branch Campus, Piqua, OH [*Library symbol Library of Congress*] (LCLS)
OPJ...........	Ohio Power 8.16% Jr Sub Debs [*NYSE symbol*] (TTSB)
OPJA..........	Jacobabad [*Pakistan*] [*ICAO location identifier*] (ICLI)
Op JAGAF	Opinion, Judge Advocate General, United States Air Force [*A publication*] (DLA)
Op JAGN......	Opinion, Judge Advocate General, United States Navy [*A publication*] (DLA)
OPJC...........	Jacobabad [*Pakistan*] [*ICAO location identifier*] (ICLI)
OPJI...........	Jiwani [*Pakistan*] [*ICAO location identifier*] (ICLI)
Op Judge Adv Gen...	Opinion of the Judge Advocate General (AAGC)
OPK...........	Operative Personenkontrolle [*Operational Person Control*] [*German*]
OPK...........	Optokinetic
OPK...........	Ovulation Predictor Kit
OPKA..........	Cape Monze [*Pakistan*] [*ICAO location identifier*] (ICLI)
Op Kan Att'y Gen...	Opinions of the Attorney General of Kansas [*A publication*] (DLA)
OPKC..........	Karachi/International [*Pakistan*] [*ICAO location identifier*] (ICLI)
OPKD..........	Hyderabad [*Pakistan*] [*ICAO location identifier*] (ICLI)
OPKE..........	Chore [*Pakistan*] [*ICAO location identifier*] (ICLI)
OPKE..........	Knudsen Engineering Ltd., Perth, Ontario [*Library symbol National Library of Canada*] (BIB)
OPKF..........	Gharo [*Pakistan*] [*ICAO location identifier*] (ICLI)
OPKH..........	Khuzdhar [*Pakistan*] [*ICAO location identifier*] (ICLI)
OPKK..........	Karachi/Korangi Creek [*Pakistan*] [*ICAO location identifier*] (ICLI)
OPKL..........	Kalat [*Pakistan*] [*ICAO location identifier*] (ICLI)
OPKN..........	Kharan [*Pakistan*] [*ICAO location identifier*] (ICLI)
OPKO..........	Kohat [*Pakistan*] [*ICAO location identifier*] (ICLI)
OPKR..........	Karachi [*Pakistan*] [*ICAO location identifier*] (ICLI)
OPKT..........	Kohat [*Pakistan*] [*ICAO location identifier*] (ICLI)
Op KY Att'y Gen...	Opinion of Attorney General, State of Kentucky [*A publication*] (DLA)
OPL.............	Air Cote d'Opale [*France ICAO designator*] (FAAC)
OPL.............	Oberlin Public Library, Oberlin, OH [*OCLC symbol*] (OCLC)
OPL.............	Ocean Pressure Laboratory
OPL.............	Office of Presidential Libraries [*National Archives*] (BARN)
OPL.............	Official Publications Library [*The British Library*]
OPL.............	Old Product Line (IAA)
OPL.............	One-Person Library
OPL.............	Opelousas, LA [*Location identifier FAA*] (FAAL)
OPL.............	Open Problem List (NASA)
OPL.............	Operational (AFM)
OPL.............	Operations Plan (KSC)
OPL.............	Optically Pumped LASER (AAEL)
OPL.............	Optical Path Length
OPL.............	Organizer Programming Language [*Computer science*]
OPL.............	Orient-Pacific Line [*Shipping*] (ROG)
OPL.............	Other Party Liability [*Insurance*] (DMAA)
OPL.............	Ottawa Public Library [*UTLAS symbol*]
OPL.............	Outer Plexiform Layer [*Retina*]
OPL.............	Out-of-Phase Loading
OPL.............	Outpost Line
OPL.............	Overpaid Last Account
OPL.............	Ovine Placental Lactogen [*Medicine*] (DMAA)
OPLA	Lahore [*Pakistan*] [*ICAO location identifier*] (ICLI)
Op LA Att'y Gen...	Opinions of the Attorney General of Louisiana [*A publication*] (DLA)
OPLAC.........	Argyle Community Library, Port Loring, Ontario [*Library symbol National Library of Canada*] (NLC)
OPLAN........	Operation Plan [*Army*]
OPLAN SEA...	Operation Plan, Southeast Asia [*Military*]
OPLAW	Operational Law (COE)
OPLC	Organizacion para la Liberacion de Cuba [*Organization for the Liberation of Cuba*] (PD)
OPLC	Overpressure Layer Chromatography
OPLE	Omega Position Location Experiment [*NASA*]
Op Let	Opinion Letter [*A publication*] (DLA)
OPLF..........	Orbiter Processing and Landing Facility [*NASA*] (MCD)
OPLG..........	Oil Plug
OPLH..........	Lahore/Walton [*Pakistan*] [*ICAO location identifier*] (ICLI)
OPLL..........	Loralai [*Pakistan*] [*ICAO location identifier*] (ICLI)
OPLL..........	Ossification of Posterior Longitudinal Ligament [*Orthopedics*] (DAVI)
OPLP..........	Pickle Pat Public Library, Pickle Lake, Ontario [*Library symbol National Library of Canada*] (NLC)
OPLR	Lahore [*Pakistan*] [*ICAO location identifier*] (ICLI)
OPLR	Outpost Line of Resistance
OPLSS	Optimized Portable Life-Support System [*NASA*]
OPM...........	Object Properties Manager
OPM...........	Occult Primary Malignancy [*Oncology*]
OPM...........	Office of Personnel Management [*Supersedes Civil Service Commission*]

OPM............	Office of Planning and Management [*DoD*]
OPM............	Office of Policy and Management [*Environmental Protection Agency*] (GFGA)
OPM............	Office of Procurement and Materiel [*Army*]
OPM............	Office of Production Management [*Superseded by WPB, 1942*]
OPM............	Office of Program Management [*Environmental Protection Agency*] (GFGA)
OPM............	Office of Program Management [*Unemployment Insurance Service*] [*Department of Labor*]
OPM............	Office, Personnel Manager [*Army*] (MUGU)
OPM............	Operating Plane Months [*Navy*] (NG)
OPM............	Operating Procedure for Ministers
OPM............	Operations Message (SSD)
OPM............	Operations per Minute [*Performance measure*]
OPM............	Operator Programming Method [*Computer science*]
OPM............	Ophthalmodynamometry [*Ophthalmology*]
OPM............	Ophthalmoplegic Migraine [*Medicine*] (DB)
OPM............	Optically Projected Map
OPM............	Optical Power Meter
OPM............	Options Pricing Model
OPM............	Ordnance Proof Manual (SAA)
OPM............	Organisasi Papua Merdeka [*Papua Independent Organization*] [*Indonesia*] (PD)
OPM............	Organizacion Politico-Militar [*Politico-Military Organization*] [*Paraguay*] (PD)
OPM............	Oscillating Pressure Method
OPM............	Other People's Money
OPM............	Outer Planet Mission
OPM............	Output per Man (ODBW)
OPM............	Output Position Map [*Computer science*] (OA)
OPM............	Output Processor Module (MCD)
OPM............	Owner President Management Program (DD)
OPM............	Oxford Policy Management [*British*]
OPM............	Perth Museum, Ontario [*Library symbol National Library of Canada*] (NLC)
OPMA	Mangla [*Pakistan*] [*ICAO location identifier*] (ICLI)
OPMA	Office Products Manufacturers Association (EA)
OPMA	Open Pit Mining Association (EA)
OPMA	Ophthalmic Prescription Manufacturers Association [*British*] (DBA)
OPMA	Overseas Press and Media Association [*British*] (EAIO)
OPMAC	Operations for Military Assistance to the Community (PDAA)
OPMACC	Operation Military Aid to the Civil Community [*British military*] (DMA)
OPMARV	Operational Maneuvering Reentry Vehicle (MCD)
OPMC	One Player Median Competitive (PDAA)
OPMCS	Otto Pre-Marital Counseling Schedules [*Psychology*]
OPMD	Officer Personnel Management Directorate [*Military*]
OPME	Office of Personnel Management Evaluation (DNAB)
OPME	Office of Program Management and Evaluation [*Environmental Protection Agency*] (GFGA)
OPMET	Operational Meteorological Information [*ICAO*] (FAAC)
OPMF	Muzaffarabad [*Pakistan*] [*ICAO location identifier*] (ICLI)
OPMG	Office of the Provost Marshal General [*Army*]
OpMG	Oppenheimer Multi-Government Trust [*Associated Press*] (SAG)
OPMH	Occupations for Patients in Mental Hospitals [*British*]
OPMI	Mianwali [*Pakistan*] [*ICAO location identifier*] (ICLI)
OPMI	Open Perfusion Micro-Incubator
OPMI	Operation Microscope [*Surgery*]
Op Minn Att'y Gen...	Opinions of the Attorney General of Minnesota [*A publication*] (DLA)
OPMIS	Optical Propulsion Management Interface System
OPMJ	Moenjodaro [*Pakistan*] [*ICAO location identifier*] (ICLI)
OPMK	Mir Pur Khas [*Pakistan*] [*ICAO location identifier*] (ICLI)
OPMN	Miranshah [*Pakistan*] [*ICAO location identifier*] (ICLI)
OPMN	Port McNicoll Public Library, Ontario [*Library symbol National Library of Canada*] (NLC)
OPMO	Office of Program Management Operations [*Environmental Protection Agency*] (GFGA)
OPMOPLAN...	Operation Missouri Plan [*Program for five-day state funeral planned several years in advance for ex-President Harry Truman*] [*Army*]
OPMPR	Office of Personnel Management Procurement Regulations [*A publication*] (AAGC)
OPMR	Karachi/Masroor [*Pakistan*] [*ICAO location identifier*] (ICLI)
OPMR	Optimal Robotics Corp. [*NASDAQ symbol*] (SAG)
OPMS	Miranshah [*Pakistan*] [*ICAO location identifier*] (ICLI)
OPMS	Office of Physical Measurement Services [*Gaithersburg, MD*] [*National Institute of Standards and Technology*] (GRD)
OPMS	Office of Program Management and Support [*Environmental Protection Agency*] (GFGA)
OPMS	Officer Personnel Management System [*Army*]
OPMS	Outplant Procurement Manufacturing Specification (SAA)
OPMSO	Outside Production Material Sales Order
OPMT..........	Multan [*Pakistan*] [*ICAO location identifier*] (ICLI)
OPMW	Mianwali [*Pakistan*] [*ICAO location identifier*] (ICLI)
OPMX	Optimax Industries, Inc. [*NASDAQ symbol*] (SAG)
OPMX	Otimax Industries [*NASDAQ symbol*] (TTSB)
OPMXZ	Optimax Inds Wrrt'BB' [*NQS*] (TTSB)
OPN	Norwell District Secondary School, Palmerston, Ontario [*Library symbol National Library of Canada*] (NLC)
OPN	Office of the Chief of Naval Operations
OPN	Office Productivity Network [*Computer science*]
OPN	Oil Pan
OPN	Open (AAG)
OPN	Operation
OPN	Opercular Nerve
OPN............	Ophthalmic Nurse (DAVI)
OPN	Opinion (ROG)
OPN	Option (ADA)
OPN	Ora pro Nobis [*Pray for Us*] [*Latin*]
OPN	Osteopontin (DMAA)
OPN	Other Procurement, Navy
OPNAV........	Chief of Naval Operations (AAGC)
OPNAV........	Office of the Chief of Naval Operations
OPNAVCOMMO...	Office of the Chief of Naval Operations, Communications Office (DNAB)
OPNAVINST...	Office of the Chief of Naval Operations Instruction
OPNAVO	Office of the Chief of Naval Operations
OPNAVSUPPACT...	Office of the Chief of Naval Operations, Support Activity (DNAB)
OPNAVSUPPACTDET...	Office of the Chief of Naval Operations, Support Activity Detachment (DNAB)
OPNAVSUPPACT FIG...	Office of the Chief of Naval Operations, Support Activity Flight Information Group (DNAB)
OPNAVSUPPACT TCC...	Office of the Chief of Naval Operations, Support Activity Telecommunications Center (DNAB)
OPNAVSUPPACT WWMCCS DP...	Office of the Chief of Naval Operations, Support Activity, Worldwide Military Command Control System, Data Processing (DNAB)
OPNAVSUPPACT WWMCCS EMPSKED...	Office of the Chief of Naval Operations, Support Activity, Worldwide Military Command Control System, Employment Schedule (DNAB)
OPNAVSUPPACT WWMCCS FORSTAT...	Office of the Chief of Naval Operations, Support Activity, Worldwide Military Command Control System, Force Status (DNAB)
OPNAVSUPPACT WWMCCS MOVREP...	Office of the Chief of Naval Operations, Support Activity, Worldwide Military Command Control System, Movement Reports (DNAB)
OPNAVTCC...	Ofice of the Chief of Naval Operations, Telecommunications Center (DNAB)
OPND..........	Operand (ECII)
Op ND Att'y Gen...	Opinions of the Attorney General of North Dakota [*A publication*] (DLA)
OpnEnv	Open Environment Corp. [*Associated Press*] (SAG)
OPNET	Operator's Training New Equipment Training [*Army*] (INF)
Op Nev Att'y Gen...	Official Opinions of the Attorney General of Nevada [*A publication*] (DLA)
OPNG..........	Opening (AAG)
OPNH..........	Nawabshah [*Pakistan*] [*ICAO location identifier*] (ICLI)
OpnhCa	Oppenheimer Capital Ltd. [*Associated Press*] (SAG)
OPNJC	Ora pro Nobis Jesu Christe [*Pray for Us, Jesus Christ*] [*Motto of Ernst, Duke of Bavaria (1554-1612)*] [*Latin*]
OPNK	Naushki [*Pakistan*] [*ICAO location identifier*] (ICLI)
OPNL	Operational
OPNML	Operations Normal (FAAC)
OPNMR........	Optically Pumped Nuclear Magnetic Resonance [*Physics*]
OPNOTE.......	Operational Note (MCD)
OPNS	Operational Phase [*NASA*] (NAKS)
OPNS	Operations (NASA)
OPNSEVAL & TNGSq...	Operational Evaluation and Training Squadron [*Air Force*]
Op NY Atty Gen...	Opinions of the Attorneys-General of New York [*A publication*] (DLA)
OPo	Megis Local School District Public Library, Pomeroy, OH [*Library symbol Library of Congress*] (LCLS)
OPO	Office of Personnel Operations [*Army*]
OPO	Officer of the Post Office [*British*]
OPO	Oil Pressure Out
OPO	One-Person Operation [*Slang Business term*] (DCTA)
OPO	One Price Only (WDAA)
OPO	Oporto [*Portugal*] [*Airport symbol*] (OAG)
OPO	Optical Parametric Oscillator [*Tunable LASER device*]
OPO	Orbiter Project Office [*NASA*] (MCD)
OPO	Orbiting Planetary Observatory
OPO	Ordnance Personnel Office [*Army*]
OPO	Organ Procurement Organization [*Generic term*] [*Medicine*]
OPO	Organ Procurement Organizations (USGC)
OPO	Other Programmed Operations (IAA)
OPO	Outside Production Order (SAA)
OPO	Outside Purchase Order (SAA)
OPO	Overseas Press Club (NADA)
OPOC	On-Board Pilot-Observer Camera (SAA)
OPOCX	Oppenheimer Discovery [*Mutual fund ticker symbol*] (SG)
OPOEB	Port Elgin Branch, Bruce County Public Library, Ontario [*Library symbol National Library of Canada*] (NLC)
Op Off Legal Counsel...	Opinions of the Office of Legal Counsel [*A publication*] (DLA)
Op Ohio Att'y Gen...	Opinions of the Attorney General of Ohio [*A publication*] (DLA)
OPOK..........	Okara [*Pakistan*] [*ICAO location identifier*] (ICLI)
Op Okla Att'y Gen...	Opinions of the Attorney General of Oklahoma [*A publication*] (DLA)
OPOL	Offshore Pollution Liability Association Ltd. (EA)
OPOL	Optimization-Oriented Language
OPOMP........	Overall Planning and Optimization and Machining Process (MHDI)
OPON..........	Opinion (ROG)
OPOR..........	Ormara [*Pakistan*] [*ICAO location identifier*] (ICLI)
Op Or Att'y Gen...	Opinions of the Attorney General of Oregon [*A publication*] (DLA)
OPORC........	Port Carling Public Library, Ontario [*Library symbol National Library of Canada*] (BIB)
OPORD	Operations Order [*Army*]
OPORPL.......	Oppose Replenishment [*Navy*] (NVT)
OPOS	Optical Property of Orbiting Satellite [*NASA*] (PDAA)

OPOS.......... Outside Production Operation Sheet (MCD)
O-POS......... Oxygen-Dope Polysilicon (PDAA)
OPOSENT..... Oppose Entry [Navy] (NVT)
OPosm......... Portsmouth Public Library, Portsmouth, OH [Library symbol Library of Congress] (LCLS)
OPosmG ...... Goodyear Atomic Corp., Portsmouth, OH [Library symbol Library of Congress] (LCLS)
OPosmS....... Shawnee State College, Portsmouth, OH [Library symbol Library of Congress] (LCLS)
OPosmU ...... Ohio University, Portsmouth Branch Campus, Portsmouth, OH [Library symbol Library of Congress Obsolete] (LCLS)
OPOSORT .... Oppose Sortie [Navy] (NVT)
OPOSS........ Office of Personnel Operations Standards and Systems Office [Army]
OPOSSMS... Options to Purchase or Sell Specific Mortgage-Backed Securities [Merrill Lynch & Co.] [Finance]
OPOSTOR .... Oppose Sortie [Navy] (ANA)
OPOV.......... Oxidizer Preburner Oxidizer Valve (MCD)
OPowS........ Scioto Village High School, Powell, OH [Library symbol Library of Congress] (LCLS)
OPP .... Occiput Posterior Position (DAVI)
OPP .... Octal Print Punch [Computer science]
OPP .... Office of Pesticide Programs [Environmental Protection Agency]
OPP .... Office of Plans and Policy (LAIN)
OPP .... Office of Polar Programs [Later, Division of Polar Programs] [National Science Foundation]
OPP .... Office of Policy and Planning [Office of Policy, Evaluation, and Research] [Department of Labor]
OPP .... Office of Productivity Programs [Office of Personnel Management] (GRD)
OPP .... Office of Program Planning (AAGC)
OPP .... Office of Public Programs [National Archives] (BARN)
OPP .... Office of Public Prosecutions [Northern Territory, Australia]
OPP .... Off-Load Preparation Party [Navy] (ANA)
OPP .... Oncovin [Vincristine], Procarbazine, Prednisone [Antineoplastic drug regimen]
OPP .... Ontario Provincial Police [UTLAS symbol]
OPP .... Open-Pore Polyurethan [Plastic]
OPP .... Operator Preparation Program (IAA)
OPP .... Opponent
OPP .... Opportunity (ADA)
opp .... Opposed (DAVI)
OPP .... Opposed To
OPP .... Opposite (AAG)
opp .... Opposite (WDMC)
OPP .... Oppure [Otherwise] [Music]
OPP .... Organizational Project Plan [Civil Defense]
OPP .... Organization and Personnel Plan [Army]
OPP .... [The] Organization of Plastics Processors
OPP .... Oriented Polypropylene [Plastics technology]
OPP .... Ortho-Phenylphenol [Disinfectant]
OPP .... Other Physical Principles [Defense system]
OPP .... Outer Planet Project
OPP .... Out of Print at Present [Publishing]
opp .... Out of Print at Present [Publishing] (WDMC)
OPP .... Oxidative Pentose Phosphate (PDAA)
OPP .... Oxygen Partial Pressure
OPPA .... Octylphenyl Phosphoric Acid (EDCT)
OPPA .... Octylpyrophosphoric Acid [Organic chemistry]
OPPA .... Office of Publications and Public Affairs [National Endowment for the Humanities] (BARN)
OPPA .... Operation Plan Package Appraisal (AFM)
Op PA Att'y Gen... Opinions of the Attorney General of Pennsylvania [A publication] (DLA)
OPPAR........ Orbiter Project Parts Authorization Request [NASA] (NASA)
OPPAX........ Oppenheimer Global Cl.A [Mutual fund ticker symbol] (SG)
OPPC .... Optima Petroleum Corp. [NASDAQ symbol] (SAG)
OPPC .... Outpatient Professional Psychiatric Clinic [Health insurance] (GHCT)
OPPC .... Parachinar [Pakistan] [ICAO location identifier] (ICLI)
OPPCE........ Opposite Commutator End (IEEE)
OPPCF .... Optima Petroleum [NASDAQ symbol] (TTSB)
OPPD .... Omaha Public Power District
OPPE .... Office of Plans and Program Evaluation (SAA)
OPPE .... Office of Policy, Planning, and Evaluation [Environmental Protection Agency] (GFGA)
OPPE .... Office of Program Planning and Evaluation [National Institutes of Health]
OPPE .... Operational Propulsion Plant Examination [Navy] (NVT)
OPPE .... Operations Planning Project Engineer [Deep Space Instrumentation Facility, NASA]
OPPEX........ Oppenheimer Equity Inc. Cl.A [Mutual fund ticker symbol] (SG)
OPPG .... Oculopneumoplethysmography (DAVI)
OPPG .... Office of Propulsion and Power Generation (SAA)
OPPG .... Panjgur [Pakistan] [ICAO location identifier] (ICLI)
OPP HND ..... Opposite Hand (MSA)
OPPHX........ Oppenheimer High Yield Cl.A [Mutual fund ticker symbol] (SG)
OPPI .... Office of Policy, Planning, and Information [Environmental Protection Agency] (GFGA)
OPPI .... Pasni [Pakistan] [ICAO location identifier] (ICLI)
Opp Int L ..... Oppenheim's International Law [A publication] (DLA)
OPPL .... Orbiter Project Parts List [NASA] (NASA)
OPPLAN ...... Operations Plan (KSC)
OPPM .... Office of Policy and Program Management [Environmental Protection Agency] (GFGA)
OppMS........ Oppenheimer Multi-Sector Income Trust [Associated Press] (SAG)
OPPN .... Pishin [Pakistan] [ICAO location identifier] (ICLI)

OPPOR......... Opportunity (AABC)
OPPORT....... Opportunity (ADA)
OPPOSIT...... Optimization of a Production Process by an Ordered Simulation and Iteration Technique (IEEE)
OPPOSSMS... Options to Purchase or Sell Specified Mortgage-Backed Securities (EBF)
OPPP .... Office of Program Policy and Planning [Social Security Administration] (OICC)
OPPP .... Port Perry High School, Ontario [Library symbol National Library of Canada] (NLC)
OPPR .... Offset Printing Press
OPPR .... Operating Program
OPPS .... Office of Planning and Program Services [Office of Field Operations] [Department of Labor]
OPPS .... Overpressurization Protection Switch (IEEE)
OPPS .... Overpressurization Protection System (IEEE)
OPPS .... Oxygen Partial Pressure Sensor
OPPS .... Peshawar [Pakistan] [ICAO location identifier] (ICLI)
OPPSL .... Office of Private and Public Sector Liaison [Environmental Protection Agency] (GFGA)
OPPSX........ Oppenheimer Growth Cl.A [Mutual fund ticker symbol] (SG)
OPPT .... Office of Pollution Prevention and Toxics [Environmental Protection Agency] (AEPA)
OPPTS .... Office of Prevention, Pesticides, and Toxic Substances [Environmental Protection Agency] (AEPA)
OPPWFA...... Operative Plasteres amd Plaster Workers' Federation of Australia
OPPY .... Opportunity (ROG)
OPQ .... Occupational Personality Questionnaires [Employment test]
OPQ .... Occupying Public Quarters [Military]
OPQS .... Qasim [Pakistan] [ICAO location identifier] (ICLI)
OPQT .... Quetta/Samungli [Pakistan] [ICAO location identifier] (ICLI)
OPR .... Lifts Operating [Skiing]
OPR .... Office of Planning and Research [International Trade Administration] (GRD)
OPR .... Office of Pre-Claims Requirements [Social Security Administration]
OPR .... Office of Primary Responsibility [Air Force]
OPR .... Office of Private Resources [Department of State]
OPR .... Office of Professional Responsibility [Department of Justice]
OPR .... Office of Public Relations [Later, PUBINFO] [Navy]
OPR .... Offsite Procurement Request (IEEE)
OPR .... Old Prussian [Language, etc.]
OPR .... Ontario Practice Reports [A publication] (DLA)
OPR .... Opener (MSA)
OPR .... Open Pool Reactor [Nuclear energy] (NRCH)
OPR .... Operand [Computer science]
OPR .... Operate [or Operator] (AAG)
OPR .... Operational Preference (DA)
OPR .... Operational Project Requirements (AABC)
OPR .... Operations Planning Review (NASA)
OPR .... Operations Procedure (MUGU)
OPR .... Operator
OPR .... OP Resources Ltd. [Vancouver Stock Exchange symbol]
OPR .... Optical Page Reader [Computer science]
OPR .... Optical Pattern Recognition
OPR .... Optimized Palette Reduction [Algorithm] [Computer Presentations, Inc.] (PCM)
OPR .... Optional Parts Request (SAA)
OPR .... Orbit/Payload Recorder [NASA] (MCD)
OPR .... Order Point Recognition (ADA)
OPR .... Outpatient Rate [Medicine] (AFM)
OPR .... Outstanding Performance Rating [Military] (RDA)
OPR .... Overall Pressure Ratio
OPR .... Oxygen Pressure Regulator (MCD)
OPR .... Oxygen Production Rate [Biochemistry]
OPR .... Port Rowan Public Library, Ontario [Library symbol National Library of Canada] (NLC)
OPR .... Santander Overseas Bank [NYSE symbol] (SPSG)
OPRA.......... Observation Post Royal Artillery [British military] (DMA)
OPRA.......... Office Products Reps Association (EA)
OPRA.......... Ohio Penal Racing Association (EA)
OPRA.......... Options Price Reporting Authority [Information service or system] (IID)
OPRAD........ Operations Research and Development Management (PDAA)
OPraem....... Canons Regular of Premontre (TOCD)
opraem....... Canons Regular of Premontre, Premonstratensians, Norbetines (TOCD)
OPraem .... Ordo Canonicorum Regularium Praemonstatenstium [Order of the Canons Regular of Premontre] [Norbertines] [Roman Catholic men's religious order]
OPRAF........ Office of Passenger Rail Franchising [British] (ECON)
OPRD.......... Office of Production Research and Development
OPRD.......... Organic Process Research & Development [A publication]
OPRDY........ Operationally Ready [Army] (AABC)
OPRE .... Prescott Public Library, Ontario [Library symbol National Library of Canada] (NLC)
OPRED........ Operations Reduction [Government term]
OPREDS...... Operational Performance Recording and Evaluation Data System [Military] (CAAL)
OPREG........ Operation Register (IAA)
OPrem .... Ordre de Premontre [Order of the Canons Regular of Premontre] [Rome, Italy] (EAIO)
OPREP........ Operational Reporting [Army]
OPREPS...... Operational Reporting System [Military]
OPREQ........ Operation Request [Computer science] (MHDI)
OPREX........ Operational Exercise [NATO] (NATG)

OPRFLT	Operator Fault (AAG)
oprg	Operating (STED)
OPRG	Oxygenated Fuels Program Reformulated Gasoline
OPRI	Office de la Propriete Industrielle [*Department of Industrial Property*] [*Ministry of Economic Affairs*] (IID)
OPRI	Office de Protection contre les Rayonnements Ionisants [*France*]
OPRIC	Operator in Charge (IAA)
OPRIS	Ohio Project for Research in Information Service (NITA)
OPRK	Opiate Receptor Kappa (DMAA)
OPRK	Rahimyarkhan [*Pakistan*] [*ICAO location identifier*] (ICLI)
OPRL	Ovine Prolactin [*Endocrinology*]
OPRL	Portland Branch, Rideau Lakes Union Library, Ontario [*Library symbol National Library of Canada*] (BIB)
OPRLFT	Operator Fault [*Computer science*] (MHDI)
OPRN	Islamabad/Chaklala [*Pakistan*] [*ICAO location identifier*] (ICLI)
OPRN	Operation
OPRNL	Operational (AAG)
OPRNTL	Operational
OpRobt	Optimal Robotics Corp. [*Associated Press*] (SAG)
OPROM	Optical Programmable Read-Only Memory [*Disk*] (BYTE)
OProv	Old Provencal [*Language*] (BARN)
OPRPrC	Santander Overseas Bk'C'Pfd [*NYSE symbol*] (TTSB)
OPRPrD	Santander Overseas Bk `D'Pfd [*NYSE symbol*] (TTSB)
OPRQ	Shorekote/Rafiqui [*Pakistan*] [*ICAO location identifier*] (ICLI)
OPRR	Office for Protection from Research Risks [*Bethesda, MD*] [*National Institutes of Health*] (GRD)
OPRR	Outside Production Requirement Record (SAA)
OPRRB	Officer Personnel Record Review Board [*Air Force*] (AFM)
OPRRE	Office of Public Roads and Rural Engineering [*Later, Bureau of Public Roads*]
OPRS	Office of Professional Research Services [*American Occupational Therapy Association*]
OPRS	Oil Pressure
OPRS	Operational Planning and Review Systems [*Employment and Training Administration*] [*Department of Labor*]
OPRS	Risalpur [*Pakistan*] [*ICAO location identifier*] (ICLI)
OPRT	Operator Table
OPRT	Orotate Phosphoribosyltransferase (STED)
OPRT	Rawalakot [*Pakistan*] [*ICAO location identifier*] (ICLI)
OPRTNTY	Opportunity
OPRU	Oil Pollution Research Unit [*British*] (ARC)
OPruss	Old Prussian [*Language*] (BARN)
OPRV	Oxygen Pressure Relief Valve (MCD)
OPS	Oblique Photo Sketcher
OPS	Obscene Publications Squad [*British*] (DI)
OPS	Obstacle Planner Software (RDA)
OPS	Occupational Preparation Scheme (AIE)
OPS	Ocean Platform Station [*National Data Buoy Office*] (NOAA)
OPS	Office of Pipeline Safety [*Department of Transportation*]
OPS	Office of Population Surveys [*British*]
OPS	Office of Price Stabilization [*Terminated, 1953*]
OPS	Office of Products Safety [*FDA*]
OPS	Office of Product Standards [*Department of Commerce*] (WDAA)
OPS	Office of Programmatic Systems [*Social Security Administration*]
OPS	Office of Program Services [*US Employment Service*] [*Department of Labor*]
OPS	Office of Public Service [*British*] (WA)
OPS	Office of Publishing Services (AAGC)
OPS	Official Phone Station [*Amateur radio*]
OPS	Official Production System [*Production-system language*]
OPS	Official Public Service Reports [*New York*] [*A publication*] (DLA)
OPS	Off-Premise Station [*Telecommunications*] (TEL)
OPS	Offshore Power Systems (NRCH)
OPS	Oil Pressure Switch
OPS	Oil Production Stock
OPS	Omnidirectional Point Source (PDAA)
OPS	On-Line Process Synthesis [*Computer science*]
OPS	On-Site Inspection Agency [*DoD ICAO designator*] (FAAC)
OPS	Open Pan Sulphitation [*Sugar production*]
OPS	Open Profiling Standard [*Firefly Network*] [*Computer science*]
OPS	Operational Paging System [*NASA*] (KSC)
OPS	Operational Performance Standard [*Aviation*] (DA)
OPS	Operational Power Supply
OPS	Operational Protection System [*Nuclear energy*] (NRCH)
OPS	Operational Sequence [*NASA*] (NAKS)
OPS	Operational Station (SAA)
OPS	Operational Support (MCD)
OPS	Operation and Support (MCD)
OPS	Operations (MCD)
OPS	Operations Division [*NATO*] (NATG)
OPS	Operations per Second (IAA)
OPS	Operations Sequence [*NASA*] (MCD)
OPS	Operations Squadron
OPS	Operations Staff [*Military British*]
OPS	Operator's Subsystem [*Telecommunications*] (TEL)
OPS	Operator System Program [*Manufacturing engineering*] [*Computer science*]
OPS	Ophthalmic Photographers' Society (EA)
Ops	Opinions [*Legal term*] (DLA)
OPS	Opposite Prompters' Side [*i.e., the left side*] [*Stage direction*] (ROG)
OPS	Opposite Surface [*Technical drawings*]
OPS	OPSEC [*Operations Security*] Professional Society (EA)
OPS	Optical Power Spectrum (PDAA)
OPS	Optical Processing System
OPS	Oracle Parallel Server [*Computer science*]
OPS	Orbiter Project Schedules [*NASA*] (NASA)
OPS	Orbiting Primate Spacecraft (MCD)
OPS	Organisation Panamericaine de la Sante [*Pan American Health Organization*] (MSC)
OPS	Oriented Polystyrene [*Plastics technology*]
OPS	Ortho-Phosphoserine [*Biochemistry*]
OPS	Other Personal Services
ops	Out of Print and Searching [*Publishing*] (WDMC)
OPS	Out of Print, Searching [*Publishing*]
OPS	Out of Production Spares (MCD)
OPS	Outpatient Section (DAVI)
OPS	Outpatient Service [*Medicine*]
OPS	Outpatient Supervision [*Medicine*] (DHP)
OPS	Outpatient Surgery [*Health insurance*] (GHCT)
OPS	Outside Production Service (SAA)
OPS	Overhead Positioning System [*AEC*]
OPS	Overpressure [*or Overpressurization*] Protection System [*Nuclear energy*] (NRCH)
OPS	Oxidized Porous Silicon [*Materials science*]
OPS	Oxidizer Particle Size
OPS	Oxygen Purge System [*or Subsystem*] [*NASA*]
OPS	Parry Sound Public Library, Ontario [*Library symbol National Library of Canada*] (NLC)
OPS	Phillips Petroleum Co., Research and Development Department, Bartlesville, OK [*OCLC symbol*] (OCLC)
OpS	Specialist in Optical Science (GAGS)
OPSA	Algonquin Regional Library, Parry Sound, Ontario [*Library symbol Obsolete National Library of Canada*] (NLC)
OPSA	Optimal Pneumatic Systems Analysis (PDAA)
OPSA	Ovarian Papillary Serous Adenocarcinoma [*Medicine*] (DMAA)
Ops AAG POD	United States Post Office Department. Official Opinions of the Solicitor [*A publication*] (DLA)
Ops AG	Opinions of the Attorney General [*A publication*] (DLA)
OPSAM	Optical Storage Access Method [*Computer science*] (PDAA)
OP(S)ARMYJAG	Opinion(s) of the Army Judge Advocate General
OPSAS	Office of Program Support and Advanced Systems (SAA)
OPSATCOM	Optical Satellite Communications (MCD)
Ops Atty Gen	Opinions of the Attorney General [*A publication*] (DLA)
Ops Atty Gen Wisc	Wisconsin Attorney General Reports [*A publication*] (DLA)
OPSB	Orbiter Processing Support Building [*NASA*] (NASA)
OPSB	Sibi [*Pakistan*] [*ICAO location identifier*] (ICLI)
OPSC	Office of Planning Standards and Coordination [*HUD*]
OPSC	Office of the Public Service Commissioner [*Australia*]
OPSC	Optical Security Group [*NASDAQ symbol*] (TTSB)
OPSC	Optical Security Group, Inc. [*NASDAQ symbol*] (SAG)
OPSCAN	Optical Scanning [*Computer science*] (WDAA)
OpScan	Optical Scanning [*Medicine*] (STED)
OPSCOMM	Operations Communications (MCD)
OPSCON	Operations Control [*NASA*] (KSC)
OPSCOP	Operations Control [*Monitor*] Program
OPSCT	Christie Township Public Library, Parry Sound, Ontario [*Library symbol National Library of Canada*] (NLC)
OPSD	Office of Placement Support and Development [*US Employment Service*] [*Department of Labor*]
OPSD	Openside
OPSD	Skardu [*Pakistan*] [*ICAO location identifier*] (ICLI)
OPSDEP	Operations Deputy [*In JCS system*] [*Military*]
OPSE	Optically Pumped Stimulated Emission (AAEL)
OPSEC	Operational Security
OPSEC	Operations per Second (IAA)
OPSEC	Operations Security Program (AAGC)
OPSEC	OPSEC Professionals Society [*Later, OPS*] (EA)
OPSER	Operator Service (CIST)
OPSET	Optimal Set [*of Parameters*] [*Hydrology*]
OPSF	Karachi/Shara-E-Faisal [*Pakistan*] [*ICAO location identifier*] (ICLI)
OP SF	Office of Preparedness, General Services Administration [*later, Federal Preparedness Agency*], Special Facility
OPSF	Orbital Propellant Storage Facility (MCD)
OPSG	Operation Plans Steering Group (DOMA)
OPSHT	Humphrey Township Public Library, Parry Sound, Ontario [*Library symbol National Library of Canada*] (NLC)
OPSI	Optical Sensors [*NASDAQ symbol*] (TTSB)
OPSI	Optical Sensors, Inc. [*NASDAQ symbol*] (SAG)
OPSI	Ordnance Publications for Supply Index [*Military*]
OPSI	Overwhelming Post-Splenectomy Infection [*Medicine*]
OPSIM	Operational Simulator [*Coast Guard*]
OPSIMS	Operational Simulation Subsystem (MCD)
OPSIX	Oppenheimer Strategic Inc. Cl.A [*Mutual fund ticker symbol*] (SG)
Ops JAG	Opinions of the Judge Advocate General, United States Army [*A publication*] (DLA)
OPSK	Sukkur [*Pakistan*] [*ICAO location identifier*] (ICLI)
OPSKS	Optimum Phase Shift Keyed Signals [*Telecommunications*]
OPSM	Office of Public Sector Management [*Australian Capital Territory*]
OPSMB	Organization of Progressive Socialists of the Mediterranean Basin
OPSO	Office of Pipeline Safety Operations [*Department of Transportation*] (DLA)
OPS O	Operations Officer [*Navy*] (DOMA)
Op Sol Dept	Opinions of the Solicitor for the Department of Labor [*United States*] [*A publication*] (DLA)
Op Sol Dept Labor	Opinions of the Solicitor for the Department of Labor Dealing with Workmen's Compensation [*A publication*] (DLA)
Op Solic PO Dep't	Official Opinions of the Solicitor for the Post Office Department • [*A publication*] (DLA)
Op Sol POD	Opinions of the Solicitor for the Post Office Department [*United States*] [*A publication*] (DLA)

OPSP .... Office of Product Standards Policy [*Gaithersburg, MD*] [*Department of Commerce*] (GRD)
OPSP .... Operations Panel [*ICAO*] (DA)
OPSP .... Shekhupura [*Pakistan*] [*ICAO location identifier*] (ICLI)
OPSR .... Office of Pipeline Safety Regulation [*Department of Transportation*] (OICC)
OPSR .... Office of Professional Standards Review [*Medicare and Medicaid*] [*HEW*]
OPSR .... Operations Supervisor [*NASA*] (MCD)
OPSR .... Sargodha [*Pakistan*] [*ICAO location identifier*] (ICLI)
OPSRDY ...... Operations Readiness (MCD)
OPSREP ...... Operations Report [*NATO*] (NATG)
OPSRO .... Office of Professional Standards Review [*Medicare and Medicaid*] Organization [*HEW*]
OPSS .... Orbital Propellant Storage Subsystem (MCD)
OPSS .... Saidu Sharif [*Pakistan*] [*ICAO location identifier*] (ICLI)
OP(ST) .... Operation Overlord Preparations, Service Leave and Travel [*World War II*]
OPST .... Out-of-Pile Systems Test [*Nuclear energy*] (NRCH)
OPSTACOM... Optical Satellite Communications
OPSTAT ...... Operational Status [*Navy*] (NVT)
OPSTATUSREP... Operations Status Report (NATG)
OPST-BQA ... Office of Professional Standards Review-Bureau of Quality Assurance (STED)
OPSTR .... Operating Strength [*Army*] (AABC)
OPSU .... Sui [*Pakistan*] [*ICAO location identifier*] (ICLI)
OPSUB .... Operational SUBPAY (DNAB)
OPSUM .... Operational Summary [*Navy*] (NVT)
OPSUPPFAC... Operational Support Facility (MCD)
OPSW .... Sahiwal [*Pakistan*] [*ICAO location identifier*] (ICLI)
OPSWL .... Old Program Status Word Location
OPS-X .... Operational Teletype Message
OPSYS .... Operating System [*Computer science*]
OPT .... International Finance Corp. [*NYSE symbol*] (SAG)
OPT .... Office of the Public Trustee [*Australian Capital Territory*]
OPT .... Oil Point [*Alaska*] [*Seismograph station code, US Geological Survey*] (SEIS)
OPT .... Oil Pressure Transmitter
OPT .... Operability Testing [*Military*] (CAAL)
OPT .... Operate (WGA)
OPT .... Operational Pressure Transducer (MCD)
OPT .... Operation Prime Time [*Television*]
OPT .... Operations and Telling (SAA)
OPT .... Operations Planning Team [*Air Force*] (DOMA)
OPT .... Opportunities for Professional Transition [*An association*] (EA)
OPT .... Optative [*Grammar*]
OPT .... Optic (IAA)
OPT .... Optical (AAG)
OPT .... Optical Point Transfer
OPT .... Optician
OPT .... Optics
OPT .... Optimization Study [*Nuclear energy*] (NRCH)
OPT .... Optimized Production Technology
OPT .... Optimum (AAG)
OPT .... Optimus [*Best*] [*Latin*]
OPT .... Option [*Shares*]
Opt .... Option (EBF)
OPT .... Option
opt .... Optional (IDOE)
Opt .... Optional (EBF)
OPT .... Optional (AAG)
Opt .... Optometrist (STED)
OPT .... Ortho-Phthaladehyde (DB)
OPT .... Other People's Tobacco [*Slang*]
OPT .... Outpatient [*Medicine*] (AAMN)
OPT .... Outpatient Physical Therapy [*Health insurance*] (GHCT)
OPT .... Outpatient Therapy (DAVI)
OPT .... Outpatient Treatment [*Medicine*]
OPT .... Output Transformer (IAA)
OPT .... Overhead Projection Transparency (MCD)
OPT .... Pakenham Township Public Library, Ontario [*Library symbol National Library of Canada*] (BIB)
OPT .... Payne Theological Seminary, Wilberforce, OH [*OCLC symbol*] (OCLC)
Opta .... Opta Food Ingredients, Inc. [*Associated Press*] (SAG)
OPTA .... Optimal Performance Theoretically Attainable (IEEE)
OPTA .... Organ and Piano Teachers Association [*Defunct*] (EA)
OPTA .... Terbela [*Pakistan*] [*ICAO location identifier*] (ICLI)
OPTACON ... Optical-to-Tactile Converter [*Electronic reader for the blind*]
OPTADS ...... Operations Tactical Data Systems [*Army*] (RDA)
OPTAG .... Optical Aimpoint Guidance System [*Weaponry*]
OPTAG .... Optical Pickoff Two-Axis Gyroscope (SAA)
OPTAN .... Operations Target Analysis [*of strike missions in North Vietnam*]
OPTAR .... Operating Target
OPTAR .... Optical Automatic Ranging
OPTARE ...... Office of Planning, Technical Assistance, Research, and Evaluation [*Washington, DC Department of Commerce*] (GRD)
OPTASK ...... Operational Tasking (DOMA)
OPTAX .... Oppenheimer Municipal Bond Cl.A [*Mutual fund ticker symbol*] (SG)
OPTB .... Operational Program Time Base [*NASA*] (MCD)
OPTC .... Optelecom, Inc. [*NASDAQ symbol*] (NQ)
OptCble ...... Optical Cable Corp. [*Associated Press*] (SAG)
OptclData .... Optical Data Systems [*Associated Press*] (SAG)
OptclDt ...... Optical Data Systems, Inc. [*Associated Press*] (SAG)
Opt Clm ...... Optional Claiming Race (WGA)

OPTCN .... Optician
Opt County Gov't... Optional County Government [*A publication*] (DLA)
Opt D .... Doctor of Optometry
OPT'D .... Optioned [*Automotive advertising*]
OPTE .... Operational Proficiency Training Equipment [*Roland International Corp.*] (MCD)
OPTEC .... Operational Test and Evaluation Command [*Army*] (RDA)
OPTEC .... Optical Properties Technical Evaluation Center
OPTEMPO .... Tempo of Operations (MCD)
Op Tenn Att'y Gen... Opinions of the Attorney General of Tennessee [*A publication*] (DLA)
OPTEV .... Operational Test and Evaluation [*Military*]
OPTEVFOR.... Operational Test and Evaluation Force [*Norfolk, VA*] [*Navy*]
OPTEVFORDET... Operational Test and Evaluation Force Detachment (DNAB)
OptEx .... Optional Exchange [*Dietetics*]
Op Tex Att'y Gen... Opinions of the Attorney General of Texas [*A publication*] (DLA)
OPTH .... Ophthalmic (ROG)
OPTH .... Talhar [*Pakistan*] [*ICAO location identifier*] (ICLI)
OPTI .... Office of Productivity, Technology, and Innovation [*Department of Commerce*]
OPTI .... OPTI, Inc. [*NASDAQ symbol*] (SAG)
OPTIC .... Ophthalmological Products Trade and Industry Conference [*British*] (DBA)
OPTIC .... Optical
OPTIC .... Optical Procedural Task Instruction Compiler
OPTIC .... Oryx Pecos Test Inquiry and Control System (NITA)
Opticam ...... Optics Automation and Management (RDA)
OpticC .... Optical Coating Laboratory, Inc. [*Associated Press*] (SAG)
OPTIM .... Occupational Projections and Training Information for Michigan [*Information service or system*] (IID)
OPTIM .... Order Point Technique for Inventory Management (BUR)
Optima .... Optima Petroleum Corp. [*Associated Press*] (SAG)
OPTIMA ...... Organization for the Phyto-Taxonomic Investigation of the Mediterranean Area [*Berlin, Federal Republic of Germany*] (EAIO)
OptImag ...... Optika Imaging Systems, Inc. [*Associated Press*] (SAG)
Optimax ...... Optimax Industries, Inc. [*Associated Press*] (SAG)
OPTIMUM .... Obtain Increased Productivity through Improved Modernization of Facilities and Updating Maintenance Tools, Equipment, and Methods [*Military*]
OPTIMUS ..... Office of Public Trustee Information Management User System [*Canada*]
OPTINT .... Optical Intelligence (MCD)
OPTIS .... Oxfordshire Project for the Training of Instructors and Supervisors [*British*] (AIE)
OptiSG .... Optical Security Group, Inc. [*Associated Press*] (SAG)
OPTK .... Optika Imaging Systems, Inc. [*NASDAQ symbol*] (SAG)
OPTL .... Optional (MSA)
OPTLC .... Overpressurized Thin-Layer Chromatography
OptIcm .... Optelecom, Inc. [*Associated Press*] (SAG)
OPTM .... Optometry
OPTMTRC .... Optometric
Optmx .... Optimax Industries, Inc. [*Associated Press*] (SAG)
OPTN .... [*The*] National Organ Procurement and Transplantation Network [*Information service or system*] (IID)
OPTN .... Option [*Legal shorthand*] (LWAP)
OPTN .... OPTION CARE [*NASDAQ symbol*] (TTSB)
OPTN .... Option Care, Inc. [*NASDAQ symbol*] (SAG)
OptnCr .... Option Care, Inc. [*Associated Press*] (SAG)
OPTNET ...... Optimum Private Trunk Network Embodying Tandems (PDAA)
OPT-NSC...... Outpatient Treatment/Nonservice-Connected [*Veterans Administration*] (DAVI)
OPTOL .... Optimized Test-Oriented Language [*Computer science*] (PDAA)
OPTOM .... Optometrist
Optom .... Optometry
OPTOMA ...... Ocean Prediction through Observation, Modeling, and Analysis [*Experimental program*]
OPT/OSP ...... Outpatient Physical Therapy/Outpatient Speech Pathology Services [*Department of Health and Human Services*] (GFGA)
OPTQ .... Ocean Optique Distributors, Inc. [*NASDAQ symbol*] (SAG)
OPTQ .... Ocean Optique Dstr [*NASDAQ symbol*] (TTSB)
OPTRA .... Operational Training (DNAB)
OPTRAK...... Optical Tracking and Ranging Kit (PDAA)
OPTRAN...... Operational Transit (GAAI)
OPTRARON... Operational Training Squadron (DNAB)
OPTRX........ Oppenheimer Total Return Cl.A [*Mutual fund ticker symbol*] (SG)
OPTS .... Office of Pesticides and Toxic Substances [*Environmental Protection Agency*]
OPTS .... Office of Program and Technical Services [*Employment and Training Administration*] [*Department of Labor*]
OPTS .... Online Peripheral Test System
OPTS .... Online Program Testing System [*Computer science*] (IAA)
OPTS .... Opta Food Ingredients [*NASDAQ symbol*] (TTSB)
OPTS .... Opta Food Ingredients, Inc. [*NASDAQ symbol*] (SAG)
OPTS .... Organization of Parents through Surrogacy (EA)
OPT-SC .... Outpatient Treatment/Service Connected [*Veterans Administration*] (DAVI)
OptSens ...... Optical Sensors, Inc. [*Associated Press*] (SAG)
OPTT .... Optek Technology [*NASDAQ symbol*] (TTSB)
OPTT .... Taftan [*Pakistan*] [*ICAO location identifier*] (ICLI)
OPTU .... Turbat [*Pakistan*] [*ICAO location identifier*] (ICLI)
OPTU .... Optical Pulse Transmitter Using LASER
OPTV .... Operative
OPTX .... Optex Biomedical [*NASDAQ symbol*] (TTSB)

OPTYP	Opalotype (VRA)
OPTZU	Optical-Pan-Tilt-Zoom Unit (SAA)
OPU	Balimo [Papua New Guinea] [Airport symbol] (OAG)
OPU	Operational Performance Unit (ADA)
OPU	Operations Priority Unit
OPU	Overseas Plexiglas Unit
OPU	Pacific University, Forest Grove, OR [OCLC symbol] (OCLC)
OPU	Unemployed Peoples Union (NADA)
OPUG	Office Planners and Users Group (NTPA)
OPUR	Object Program Utility Routine
OPUS	Octal Program Updating System [Computer science]
OPUS	Offshore Persistent Upwelling Structure
OPUS	Optical Prism Uniformity System
OPUS	Organisation of Professional Users of Statistics
OPUSA	Operation U.S.A. [An association] (EA)
OPUSC	Opuscula [Minor Works] [Latin] (ROG)
OPV	Bedarfsflugunternehmen Dr. L. Polsterer [Austria ICAO designator] (FAAC)
OPV	Offshore Patrol Vessel (DOMA)
OPV	Ohms per Volt
OPV	Optical Path-Length Variation (PDAA)
OPV	Oral Polio Vaccine [Also, Sabin vaccine] (PAZ)
OPV	Oral Poliovirus [Infectious diseases] (DAVI)
OPV	Oral Polio Virus Vaccine
Op VA Att'y Gen	Opinions of the Attorney General and Report to the Governor of Virginia [A publication] (DLA)
OPVN	OpenVision Technologies, Inc. [NASDAQ symbol] (SAG)
OPVN	Open Vision Technology [NASDAQ symbol] (TTSB)
OPW	Objective Personal Weapon
OPW	Oboz Polski Walczacej [A publication] (BJA)
OPW	Office of Public Works (WDAA)
OPW	Opawica Explorations, Inc. [Toronto Stock Exchange symbol]
OPW	Open Pilot Warranty [Insurance] (AIA)
OPW	Operating Weight [Air Force]
OPW	Optical Window
OPW	Opuwa [Namibia] [Airport symbol] (OAG)
OPW	Orthogonalized Plane Wave
OPW	Porter Public Library, Westlake, OH [OCLC symbol] (OCLC)
OPW	Whitney Public Library, Porcupine, Ontario [Library symbol National Library of Canada] (NLC)
OPWA	Office Products Wholesalers Association (NTPA)
Op Wash Att'y Gen	Office of the Attorney General (State of Washington) Opinions [A publication] (DLA)
OPWI	Opiate Withdrawal [Medicine] (DMAA)
Op Wis Att'y Gen	Opinions of the Attorney General of Wisconsin [A publication] (DLA)
OpWldBd	Oppenheimer World Bond Fund [Associated Press] (SAG)
OPWN	Wana [Pakistan] [ICAO location identifier] (ICLI)
OPWS	Orbiter Payload Work Station (MCD)
Op Wyo Att'y Gen	Opinions of the Attorney General of Wyoming [A publication] (DLA)
OPX	Off-Premise Extension [Nuclear energy] (NRCH)
OPX	Orthopyroxene [A silicate mineral]
OPY	Salomon, Inc. [AMEX symbol] (SAG)
OPZ	Opsonized Zymosan [Biochemistry]
OPZB	Zhob [Pakistan] [ICAO location identifier] (ICLI)
OPZONE	Operation Zone (COE)
OQ	Officers' Quarters [Military]
OQ	Oil Quench (IAA)
OQ	Operational Qualification (ACII)
OQ	Optical Quality
OQ	Order Quantity (DNAB)
OQ	Ordre du Quebec [Order of Quebec] [Canada] (DD)
OQ	Royale Airlines [ICAO designator] (AD)
OQA	Operations Quality Assurance [Nuclear energy] (NRCH)
OQA	Optical Quantum Amplifier (PDAA)
OQA	Reidsville, NC [Location identifier FAA] (FAAL)
OQAP	Oil Quality Assessment Program [Society of Automotive Engineers, Inc.]
O-QAR	Optical Quick Access Recorder (GAVI)
OQC	Office of Quality Control [Social and Rehabilitation Service, HEW]
OQC	Operator Quality Control [RADAR]
OQC	Outside Quality Control (KSC)
OQD	Optical Quantum Detector
OQE	Objective Quality Evidence (MCD)
OQG	Optical Quantum Generator
OQI	Oil Quantity Indicator
OQL	Observed Quality Level
OQL	Online Query Language
OQL	Outgoing Quality Level
OQL	Outgoing Quality Limit
OQM	Office of the Quartermaster [Military]
OQMG	Office of the Quartermaster General [Military]
OQP	Optimum Qualification Procedure
O-QPSK	Offset QPSK (NITA)
OQQ	Officer Qualification Questionnaire [Navy] (DOMA)
OQR	Officer's Qualification Record [Army]
OQSMAT	Otis Quick Scoring Mental Abilities Tests [Psychology] (DAVI)
OQT	Officer Qualification Test
OQTD	Operational Qualifications Test Deficiency [Air Force]
OQU	North Kingstown, RI [Location identifier FAA] (FAAL)
OQW	Maquoketa, IA [Location identifier FAA] (FAAL)
OQZ	Union City, TN [Location identifier FAA] (FAAL)
OR	Air Comores [ICAO designator] (AD)
Or	Indian Law Reports, Orissa Series [A publication] (DLA)

OR	Oak Ridge Complex [Department of Energy] [Oak Ridge National Laboratory] (GAAI)
OR	Oak Ridge Operations Office (DOGT)
OR	Objective Reliability (MCD)
OR	Observed Ratio (MCD)
OR	Octane Rating [Automotive engineering]
OR	Octane Requirement [Mechanical engineering]
OR	Odds Ratio [Statistics]
O/R	Office of Record (AFM)
OR	Officer Records [Military] (AFM)
OR	Official Receiver
OR	Official Records
OR	Official Referee
OR	Official Reports, South Africa [A publication] (DLA)
OR	Off-Radial (RDA)
OR	Off-Route [Telecommunications] (OTD)
OR	Oil Rehabilitation Committee [British]
OR	Oil Retention [Enema] [Medicine]
OR	Oil Ring (MSA)
OR	Old Roman (ADA)
OR	Oleoresin [Also, Ol Res] [Pharmacy]
OR	Olfactory Receptor [Biochemistry]
OR	Oligomer Restriction [Genetics]
OR	Omnidirectional Radio Range (MCD)
O/R	On Request
OR	On Return
OR	Ontario Reports [A publication] (DLA)
OR	Open Reduction [Orthopedics] (DAVI)
OR	Open Registry [Flag of convenience] [Shipping] (DS)
OR	Operating Reactor [Nuclear energy] (NRCH)
OR	Operating Resources (AFM)
OR	Operating Room [Medicine]
OR	Operational Equipment Requirement (IAA)
OR	Operationally Ready (MCD)
OR	Operational Readiness [Army]
OR	Operational Reliability [Army] (AABC)
OR	Operational Report (AAG)
OR	Operational Requirement
OR	Operational Research
OR	Operational Right
OR	Operation Reach-Out [Department of Labor]
OR	Operation Record
OR	Operation Rescue (EA)
OR	Operations Request [Military]
OR	Operations Requirements
OR	Operations Research [Computer science]
OR	Operations Review [NASA] (MCD)
OR	Operations Room
OR	Operator (IAA)
OR	Operculum Ridge
OR	Ophthalmic Rete [Bird anatomy]
OR	Opponents' Runs [Baseball]
OR	Optical Reader [Computer science] (BUR)
OR	Optic Radiation (DB)
O+R	Optiram, St. Helier, Jersey, Channel Islands, United Kingdom [Library symbol] [Library of Congress] (LCLS)
OR	Orange
Or	Oratio [A publication] (OCD)
Or	Orationes [of Dio Chrysostomus] [Classical studies] (OCD)
Or	Orationes [of Julian] [Classical studies] (OCD)
OR	Oratorians
OR	Ordered Recorded
OR	Ordering Register (IAA)
OR	Orderly Room
OR	Order of the Road [British] (DBA)
OR	Order Pennant [Navy British]
OR	Order [or Ordering] Register (SAA)
OR	Ordnance Report
OR	Ordnance Requirement
OR	Oregon [Postal code]
Or	Oregon State Library, Salem, OR [Library symbol Library of Congress] (LCLS)
Or	Oregon Supreme Court Reports [A publication] (DLA)
Or	Orestes [of Euripides] [Classical studies] (OCD)
OR	Organized Reserves [Military]
OR	Organ Recovery (EA)
OR	Orient
OR	Oriental (ROG)
OR	Orienting Response [Psychology]
Or	Origen [Deceased circa 254] [Authority cited in pre-1607 legal work] (DSA)
OR	Original (ADA)
O/R	Originator or Recipient [Telecommunications] (OSI)
OR	O-Ring [Automotive engineering]
'Or	'Orlah (BJA)
OR	Orosomucoid [Biochemistry]
or	Orthoclase [CIPW classification] [Geology]
OR	Orthopedic
OR	Orthopedic Research [Medicine]
OR	Oswestry Rangers [British military] (DMA)
OR	Other (ROG)
OR	Other Ranks [Ranks other than officers] [Military]
OR	Outer Roll [Aviation] (MCD)
OR	Out of Range
OR	Output Register (MSA)

OR	Outside Radius [*Technical drawings*]
OR	Outside Right [*Soccer position*]
OR	Overall Report
OR	Overall Resistance (IAA)
OR	Overhaul and Repair
OR	Overload Relay (KSC)
O/R	Overrange [*System or element*] (IEEE)
O/R	Override (KSC)
OR	Over Run (MHDW)
OR	Overseas Replacement [*Military*]
OR	Owasco River [*AAR code*]
OR	Owner's Risk [*Shipping*]
or	Owner's Risk (WDAA)
OR	Own Recognizance [*Legal term*]
O-R	Oxidation-Reduction
OR	Oxygen Enchancement Ratio (IAA)
OR	Oxygen Relief (NASA)
OR	Renfrew Public Library, Ontario [*Library symbol National Library of Canada*] (NLC)
ORA	Montauk Caribbean Airways, Inc. [*ICAO designator*] (FAAC)
ORA	Office of Records Administration [*National Archives*] (BARN)
ORA	Office of Redress Administration [*Department of Justice*]
ORA	Office of Regulatory Affairs [*U.S. Food and Drug Administration*]
ORA	Office of Regulatory Analysis [*Federal Energy Regulatory Commission*]
ORA	Office of Research Administration [*University of Pennsylvania*] [*Research center*] (RCD)
ORA	Office of Research Administration [*North Carolina A & T State University*] [*Research center*] (RCD)
ORA	Office of Research Administration [*St. Louis University*] [*Research center*] (RCD)
ORA	Office of Research Administration [*University of Hawaii*] [*Research center*] (RCD)
ORA	Office of Research Analysis [*Air Force*]
ORA	Office of Rural Affairs [*Victoria, Australia*]
ORA	Oil Refiners Association (NADA)
ORA	Operating Room Attendant [*British military*] (DMA)
ORA	Operational RADAR Directed Flights (NATG)
ORA	Operational Readiness Assessment
ORA	Operation Response Area (MCD)
ORA	Operations Research Analyst [*Army*] (AABC)
ORA	Opportunity Resources for the Arts (EA)
ORA	Optical Reference Axis
ORA	Oran [*Argentina*] [*Airport symbol*] (AD)
ORA	Order for Reinforced Alert (NATG)
Or A	Oregon Court of Appeals Reports [*A publication*] (DLA)
ORA	Organisation de Resistance de l'Armee [*France*]
ORA	Organisation Revolutionnaire Anarchiste [*Revolutionary Anarchist Organization*] [*France Political party*] (PPE)
ORA	Organizacao Revolucionaria Armada [*Terrorist group*] [*Portugal*] (EY)
ORA	Organizational Role Analysis (PDAA)
ORA	Orifice Rod Assembly [*Nuclear energy*] (NRCH)
ORA	Oromo Relief Association [*Ethiopia*]
ORA	Output Reference Axis (IAA)
ORA	Output Register Address
ORA	Ramore Library, Ontario [*Library symbol National Library of Canada*] (BIB)
ORA	Ross Laboratory Library, Columbus, OH [*OCLC symbol*] (OCLC)
ORAAP	Outstanding Reserve Airman Appointment Program
ORAC	Oxygen Radical Absorbance Capacity [*Analytical Chemistry*]
ORACLE	Oak Ridge Automatic Computer and Logical Engine
ORACLE	Observational Research and Classroom Learning Evaluation [*British*] (DET)
ORACLE	Observation Research and Classroom Learning Evaluation (AIE)
ORACLE	On-Line Retrieval and Computational Language for Economists [*Computer science*]
ORACLE	Optical Reception of Announcements by Coded Line Electronics
ORACLE	Optimized Reliability and Component Life Estimate
ORACLE	Optimum Record Automation for Court and Law Enforcement
ORACLE	Optional Reception of Announcements by Coded Line Electronics [*Independent Television "newspaper"*] [*British*] (DI)
ORACLE	Optional Recovery of Announcements by Coded Line Electronics (NITA)
Oracle	Oracle Systems Corp. [*Associated Press*] (SAG)
ORACLE	Ordnance Rapid Area Clearance [*Military*] (CAAL)
ORACLE	Organic Rankine Cycle
ORACLE	Oversight of Resources and Capability for Logistics Effectiveness (PDAA)
ORACT	Operational Readiness and Confidence Test
OrAd	Adams Public Library, Adams, OR [*Library symbol*] [*Library of Congress*] (LCLS)
ORAD	Office of Rural Areas Development [*Later, Rural Community Development Service*] [*Department of Agriculture*]
ORAD	Orbiter RADAR [*NASA*]
Or Admin R ...	Oregon Administrative Rules [*A publication*] (DLA)
Or Admin R Bull...	Oregon Administrative Rules Bulletin [*A publication*] (DLA)
ORADS	Optical Ranging and Detection System
Or Ad Sh	Supreme Court of the State of Oregon Advance Sheets [*A publication*] (DLA)
ORAE	Office de Repartition des Approvisionnements d'Energie [*Canada*]
ORAE	Operational Research and Analysis Establishment (MCD)
OrAg	Agness Community Library, Agness, OR [*Library symbol Library of Congress*] (LCLS)
ORaH	Robinson Memorial Hospital, Ravenna, OH [*Library symbol*] [*Library of Congress*] (LCLS)
OrAh	Washington County Cooperative Library Services, Aloha, OR [*Library symbol*] [*Library of Congress*] (LCLS)
OrAl	Albany Public Library, Albany, OR [*Library symbol Library of Congress*] (LCLS)
ORAL	Oral Access to Library
OrAlBM	United States Bureau of Mines, Education and Training Center, Albany, OR [*Library symbol Library of Congress*] (LCLS)
OrAlC	Linn-Benton Community College, Albany, OR [*Library symbol Library of Congress*] (LCLS)
OrAlH	Albany General Hospital, Albany, OR [*Library symbol Library of Congress*] (LCLS)
Oral Roberts U...	Oral Roberts University (GAGS)
OrAlT	Teledyne-Wah Chang Albany, Albany, OR (LCLS)
OrAm	Amity Public Library, Amity, OR [*Library symbol Library of Congress*] (LCLS)
ORAN	Orange [*Laboratory science*] (DAVI)
ORAN	Orbital Analysis
ORAN	Organisation Regionale Africaine de Normalisation [*African Regional Organization for Standardization - AROS*] (EAIO)
OR&F	Open Reduction and Fixation (DMAA)
OR&F	Operations, Research and Facilities [*Marine science*] (OSRA)
OR & N	Oregon Railroad & Navigation Co.
OR & SP	Office of Research and Sponsored Programs [*Research center*] (RCD)
ORANG	Oregon Air National Guard (MUSM)
Orange	Orange PLC [*Associated Press*] (SAG)
OrangN	Orange National Bancorp [*Associated Press*] (SAG)
OranRk	Orange & Rockland Utilities, Inc. [*Associated Press*] (SAG)
ORANS	Oak Ridge Analytical Systems
Or App	Oregon Reports, Court of Appeal [*A publication*] (DLA)
OrAr	Arlington Public Library, Arlington, OR [*Library symbol Library of Congress*] (LCLS)
Or-Ar	Oregon State Archives, Salem, OR [*Library symbol Library of Congress*] (LCLS)
ORAR	Rainy River Public Library, Ontario [*Library symbol National Library of Canada*] (NLC)
ORAS	Oil Recovery and Separation Technology [*Jastram Werke*]
ORASA	Operational Research and Systems Analysis (PDAA)
OrAshS	Southern Oregon College, Ashland, OR [*Library symbol Library of Congress*] (LCLS)
OrAst	Astor Library, Astoria, OR [*Library symbol Library of Congress*] (LCLS)
OrAstC	Clatsop Community College, Astoria, OR [*Library symbol Library of Congress*] (LCLS)
OrAstM	Columbia River Maritime Museum, Astoria, OR [*Library symbol Library of Congress*] (LCLS)
Orat	Oration [*or Orator or Oratorio*]
Orat	Orator ad M. Brutum [*of Cicero*] [*Classical studies*] (OCD)
ORAT	Oratorical
ORATE	Ordered Random Access Talking Equipment
ORATMS	Off-Route Antitank Mine System (MCD)
ORATS	Operational Readiness Assessment and Training System (MCD)
ORAU	Oak Ridge Associated Universities (EA)
OraVax	OraVax, Inc. [*Associated Press*] (SAG)
ORAW	Oil Remaining after Waterflooding [*Petroleum technology*]
OrB	Beaverton City Library, Beaverton, OR [*Library symbol Library of Congress*] (LCLS)
ORB	Object Request Broker [*Computer science*]
ORB	Oceanic Ridge Basalts
ORB	Oceanographic Research Buoy
ORB	Ocean Research Buoy (IAA)
ORB	Offenders' Review Board [*New South Wales, Australia*]
ORB	Officer Record Brief [*Army*] (AABC)
ORB	Offsets Review Board [*New South Wales, Australia*]
ORB	Omnidirectional Radio Beacon
ORB	Operational Research Branch [*Canada*]
ORB	Operations Record Book [*Air Ministry*] [*British World War II*]
ORB	Optometrists' Registration Board [*Victoria, Australia*]
ORB	Orbe [*Switzerland*] [*Seismograph station code, US Geological Survey Closed*] (SEIS)
Orb	Orbis [*Record label*] [*Germany, etc.*]
ORB	Orbit
ORB	Orbital (KSC)
ORB	Orbital Sciences Corp. [*NYSE symbol*]
ORB	Orbiter [*NASA*] (NASA)
ORB	Orbit Oil & Gas Ltd. [*Toronto Stock Exchange symbol*]
ORB	Order
ORB	Orebro [*Sweden*] [*Airport symbol*] (OAG)
ORB	Organizational Records Branch [*Army*]
ORB	Orr, MN [*Location identifier FAA*] (FAAL)
ORB	Outer Radiation Belt
ORB	Outside Reactor Building [*Nuclear energy*] (NRCH)
Orb	Owners Risk of Breakage (EBF)
ORB	Owner's Risk of Breaking [*Shipping*]
ORB 1-G	Orbiter One-G Trainer [*NASA*] (NASA)
OrBa	Banks Community Library, Banks, OR [*Library symbol Library of Congress*] (LCLS)
ORBA	Erbil [*Iraq*] [*ICAO location identifier*] (ICLI)
ORBACT	Optometrists' Registration Board of the Australian Capital Territory
OrBak	Baker County Public Library, Baker, OR [*Library symbol Library of Congress*] (LCLS)
OrBakSE	Saint Elizabeth Hospital, Baker, OR [*Library symbol Library of Congress*] (LCLS)
OrBan	Bandon Public Library, Bandon, OR [*Library symbol Library of Congress*] (LCLS)

ORBANCO....	Oregon Bank (EFIS)
Or Bar Bull...	Oregon Bar Bulletin [*A publication*] (DLA)
ORBAT........	Order of Battle Report [*Military*] (NATG)
ORBB.........	Sirsenk/Bamarni [*Iraq*] [*ICAO location identifier*] (ICLI)
ORBC.........	Baghdad/Soica Headquarters [*Iraq*] [*ICAO location identifier*] (ICLI)
ORBC.........	Ox Red Blood Cell [*Medicine*] (DMAA)
OrBe..........	Deschutes County Library, Bend, OR [*Library symbol Library of Congress*] (LCLS)
ORBE.........	Open Reciprocating Brayton Engine (PDAA)
OrBeBR......	Bend Research, Inc., Bend, OR [*Library symbol*] [*Library of Congress*] (LCLS)
OrBeC........	Central Oregon Community College, Bend, OR [*Library symbol Library of Congress*] (LCLS)
OrBeCJ	Cascade Junior High School, Bend, OR [*Library symbol*] [*Library of Congress*] (LCLS)
OrBeHS.......	Bend Senior High School, Bend, OR [*Library symbol*] [*Library of Congress*] (LCLS)
OrBeMC......	Saint Charles Medical Center, Medical Library, Bend, OR [*Library symbol Library of Congress*] (LCLS)
OrBeMH......	Mountain View High School, Bend, OR [*Library symbol*] [*Library of Congress*] (LCLS)
OrbEng........	Orbital Engine Corp. Ltd. [*Associated Press*] (SAG)
OrBeOHM.....	Oregon High Desert Museum, Bend, OR [*Library symbol*] [*Library of Congress*] (LCLS)
OrBePJ	Pilot Butte Junior High School, Bend, OR [*Library symbol*] [*Library of Congress*] (LCLS)
OrBFP	Floating Point Systems, Inc., Beaverton, OR [*Library symbol Library of Congress*] (LCLS)
OrBG..........	Oregon Graduate Center, Beaverton, OR [*Library symbol Library of Congress*] (LCLS)
OrBGS........	Church of Jesus Christ of Latter-Day Saints, Genealogical Society Library, Beaverton Branch, Beaverton, OR [*Library symbol Library of Congress*] (LCLS)
ORBI.........	Orbital Sciences Corp. [*NASDAQ symbol*] (SAG)
ORBI.........	Rocky Band No. 1 Indian Band Library, Ontario [*Library symbol National Library of Canada*] (BIB)
ORBIFC.......	Oak Ridge Boys International Fan Club (EA)
ORBIS........	Orbiting Radio Beacon Ionospheric Satellite [*NASA*]
ORBIS........	Ordering and Billing System
ORBIS.........	Oregon Business Information System [*Oregon State Economic Development Department*] [*Information service or system Defunct*] (IID)
ORBIS CAL...	Orbiting Radio Beacon Ionosphere Satellite for Calibration [*NASA*] (PDAA)
ORBIT........	Oak Ridge Binary Internal-Translator
ORBIT........	Objectives-Referenced Bank of Items and Tests (TES)
ORBIT........	Office Research into Buildings and IT (NITA)
ORBIT........	On-Line, Real-Time, Branch Information Transmission [*IBM Corp.*] [*Computer science*]
ORBIT.........	On-Line Reduced Bandwidth Information Transfer [*Computer science*]
ORBIT........	On-Line Retrieval of Bibliographic Text [*Search system*] [*Computer science*]
ORBIT........	ORACLE Binary Internal Translator [*Algebraic programming system*]
ORBIT.........	Orbit, Ballistic Impact, and Trajectory [*Computer*] (MUGU)
Orbit.........	Orbit International Corp. [*Associated Press*] (SAG)
ORBIT........	Order Billing Inventory Technique (PDAA)
ORBK.........	Orbotech Ltd. [*Formerly, Optrotech Ltd.*] [*NASDAQ symbol*] (SPSG)
ORBKF........	Orbotech Ltd Ord [*NASDAQ symbol*] (TTSB)
ORBM.........	Mosul [*Iraq*] [*ICAO location identifier*] (ICLI)
OrBo	Boardman Public Library, Boardman, OR [*Library symbol Library of Congress*] (LCLS)
Orbotch........	Orbotech [*Associated Press*] (SAG)
OrBP..........	Oregon Regional Primate Research Center, Beaverton, OR [*Library symbol Library of Congress*] (LCLS)
Or-BPH	Oregon State Library, Services for the Blind and Physically Handicapped, Salem, OR [*Library symbol Library of Congress*] (LCLS)
ORBR.........	Baghdad/Rasheed [*Iraq*] [*ICAO location identifier*] (ICLI)
OrBroo	Chetco Community Public Library, Brookings, OR [*Library symbol Library of Congress*] (LCLS)
ORBS.........	Baghdad/Saddam International [*Iraq*] [*ICAO location identifier*] (ICLI)
ORBS.........	Off Reservation Boarding School (EDAC)
ORBS.........	Orbital Rendezvous Base System
OrbSci	Orbital Sciences Corp. [*Associated Press*] (SAG)
ORBT.........	Orbit International [*NASDAQ symbol*] (TTSB)
ORBT.........	Orbit International Corp. [*NASDAQ symbol*] (NQ)
OrBT	Tektronix, Inc., Beaverton, OR [*Library symbol Library of Congress*] (LCLS)
OrbtSemi	Orbit Semiconductor Co. [*Associated Press*] (SAG)
Or Bull........	Oregon Bulletin [*A publication*] (AAGC)
ORBV.........	Optometrists' Registration Board of Victoria [*Australia*]
ORBW.........	Baghdad/Muthenna [*Iraq*] [*ICAO location identifier*] (ICLI)
ORBWA.......	Optometrists' Registration Board of Western Australia
ORBZ	Ain Zalah [*Iraq*] [*ICAO location identifier*] (ICLI)
OrC	Corvallis Public Library, Corvallis, OR [*Library symbol Library of Congress*] (LCLS)
ORC	Occupational Research Centre [*Hatfield Polytechnic*] [*British*] (CB)
ORC	Oculo-Reno-Cerebellar [*Syndrome*] [*Medicine*] (DMAA)
ORC	Office of Regional Counsel [*Environmental Protection Agency*] (GFGA)
ORC	Office of Reserve Components [*Army*]
ORC	Office of the Regional Commissioner [*Social Security Administration*] (OICC)
ORC	Officers' Reserve Corps [*Later, Army Reserve*]
ORC	Offshore Racing Council
ORC	Oilseeds Research Council [*Australia*]
ORC	On-Line Reactivity Computer [*Nuclear energy*] (NRCH)
ORC	On-Road Costs [*Motor vehicles*]
orc	Operarios del Reina de Cristo (TOCD)
ORC	Operarios del Reina de Cristo (TOCD)
ORC	Operational Readiness Check
ORC	Operational Reports Control [*Military*] (AFM)
ORC	Operational Requirements Committee [*Ministry of Defence*] [*British*]
ORC	Operations Research Center [*Massachusetts Institute of Technology*] [*Research center*] (KSC)
ORC	Operations Review Committee (COE)
ORC	Opinion Research Center
ORC	Optical Radiation Corp.
ORC	Optical Recording Corp.
ORC	Orange City, IA [*Location identifier FAA*] (FAAL)
ORC	Orange River Colony [*Later, Orange Free State*] [*South Africa*]
ORC	Orbital Research Centrifuge [*NASA*] (KSC)
ORC	Orcadas Del Sur [*Argentina*] [*Geomagnetic observatory code*]
ORC	Orcatech, Inc. [*Toronto Stock Exchange symbol*]
ORC	Orderly Room Corporal [*British*]
ORC	Order of the Red Cross
ORC	Ordnance Rocket Center (KSC)
ORC	Organic Rankine Cycle [*for power generation*] (PDAA)
ORC	Organization Requirements Clerk [*Defense Supply Agency*]
ORC	Organization Resources Counselors (MCD)
ORC	Organized Reserve Corps [*Later, Army Reserve*]
ORC	Origin Recognition Complex [*Genetics*]
ORC	Orthogonal Row Computer
ORC	Outbound RADAR Control
ORC	Overrun Clutch
ORC	Overseas Reconstruction Committee [*British World War II*]
ORC	Overseas Research Center [*Wake Forest University*] [*Research center*] (RCD)
ORC	Owner's Risk of Chafing [*Shipping*]
ORC	Oxidation-Resistant Coating
ORC	Oxidized Regenerated Cellulose [*Hemostatic*] [*Organic chemistry*]
ORC	Ozarks Regional Commission [*Department of Commerce*]
ORC	Reed College, Portland, OR [*OCLC symbol*] (OCLC)
ORC	Reports of the High Court of the Orange River Colony [*South Africa*] [*A publication*] (DLA)
ORCA..........	Ocean Resource Coordination and Assessment [*National Oceanic and Atmospheric Administration*]
ORCA..........	Ocean Resources Conservation Association [*British*]
ORCA..........	Oldtime Radio-Show Collector's Association (EA)
ORCA..........	Online Resource Control Aid [*Computer science*] (HGAA)
ORCA..........	Oregon Caves National Monument
ORCA..........	Organisme Europeen de Recherche sur la Carie [*European Organization for Caries Research*] (EAIO)
ORCA..........	Organized Resistance to Capture in Alaska [*Defunct*] (EA)
Orcad..........	Orcad, Inc. [*Associated Press*] (SAG)
ORCALMIS...	Ordnance Calibration Management Information System [*Navy*] (DNAB)
OrCan	Canby Public Library, Canby, OR [*Library symbol Library of Congress*] (LCLS)
OrCanHS......	Canby Union High School, Canby, OR [*Library symbol Library of Congress*] (LCLS)
ORCATS......	Oldtime Radio Collectors and Traders Society (EA)
OrCb	Coos Bay Public Library, Coos Bay, OR [*Library symbol Library of Congress*] (LCLS)
ORCB..........	Order of Railway Conductors and Brakemen [*Later, United Transportation Union*] (EA)
OrCbS	Southwestern Oregon Community College, Coos Bay, OR [*Library symbol Library of Congress*] (LCLS)
OrCC	Corvallis Clinic, Corvallis, OR [*Library symbol Library of Congress*] (LCLS)
ORCC..........	Ohio Regional Campus Conference (PSS)
ORCC..........	Online Resources Communications Co.
ORCC..........	Outward-Rectifying Chloride Channel [*Biochemistry*]
ORCCA........	Open Road Camper Clubs of America [*Later, ORSAC*] (EA)
ORCEN........	Overseas Records Center [*Military*]
OrCEPA.......	United States Environmental Protection Agency, Corvallis Environmental Research Laboratory, Corvallis, OR [*Library symbol Library of Congress*] (LCLS)
OrCg	W. A. Woodward Memorial Library, Cottage Grove, OR [*Library symbol Library of Congress*] (LCLS)
OrCGS.........	Church of Jesus Christ of Latter-Day Saints, Genealogical Society Library, Corvallis Branch, Corvallis, OR [*Library symbol Library of Congress*] (LCLS)
OrCGSH	Good Samaritan Hospital, Corvallis, OR [*Library symbol Library of Congress*] (LCLS)
ORCH..........	Orchard
orch..........	Orchestra (WDAA)
ORCH..........	Orchestra
ORCHARD....	Orchard [*Commonly used*] (OPSA)
ORCHD	Orchestrated (By) [*Music*]
ORCHIS........	Oak Ridge Computerized Hierarchical Information System [*AEC*] (IID)
ORCHL........	Orchestral [*Music*]
ORCHRD......	Orchard [*Commonly used*] (OPSA)
OrchSHw......	Orchard Supply Hardware Stores Corp. [*Associated Press*] (SAG)
ORCI..........	Opinion Research [*NASDAQ symbol*] (TTSB)
ORCI..........	Opinion Research Crop. [*NASDAQ symbol*] (SAG)
ORCID.........	Optical Readout Cherenkov Imaging Detector [*Computer science*] (PDAA)

OrckitCo........ Orckit Communications Ltd. [*Associated Press*] (SAG)
ORCL .... Oracle Corp. [*NASDAQ symbol*] (TTSB)
ORCL .... Oracle Systems Corp. [*NASDAQ symbol*] (NQ)
OrCIS .... Sunnyside Medical Library, Clackamas, OR [*Library symbol Library of Congress*] (LCLS)
ORCMD........ Orlando Contract Management District (SAA)
OrCMG......... Mid-Valley Genealogical Society, Corvallis, OR [*Library symbol Library of Congress*] (LCLS)
ORCO .... Central Ontario Regional Library, Richmond Hill, Ontario [*Library symbol National Library of Canada*] (NLC)
OrCo .... Coquille Public Library, Coquille, OR [*Library symbol Library of Congress*] (LCLS)
ORCO .... Ontario Library Service - Trent, Richmond Hill, Ontario [*Library symbol National Library of Canada*] (NLC)
OrColHS....... Colton High School, Colton, OR [*Library symbol Library of Congress*] (LCLS)
OrCon .... Condon Public Library, Condon, OR [*Library symbol Library of Congress*] (LCLS)
ORCON .... Observation Report Conversion [*Program*]
ORCON .... Organic Control
ORCON .... Originator Controlled [*Information dissemination*]
ORCON .... Originator-Controlled Information (MCD)
OrCor .... Cornelius Public Library, Cornelius, OR [*Library symbol Library of Congress*] (LCLS)
OrCS .... Oregon State University, Corvallis, OR [*Library symbol Library of Congress*] (LCLS)
ORCS .... Organic Rankine Cycle System [*For power generation*]
ORCS .... Organic Reactions Catalysis Society (EA)
ORCSA......... Orange River Colony, South Africa (ILCA)
OrCS-Ar .... Oregon State University Archives, Corvallis, OR [*Library symbol Library of Congress*] (LCLS)
OrCS-MB...... Oregon State University, Institute of Marine Biology, Coos Bay, OR [*Library symbol Library of Congress*] (LCLS)
OrCS-MSC ... Oregon State University, Hatfield Marine Science Center, Newport, OR [*Library symbol*] [*Library of Congress*] (LCLS)
ORCT .... Orckit Communications Ltd. [*NASDAQ symbol*] (SAG)
OrCuHS........ Culver Senior High School, Culver, OR [*Library symbol*] [*Library of Congress*] (LCLS)
ORCUS......... Operational Research Co., Universal Systems
ORCV .... Outdoor Recreation Center Victoria [*Australia*]
ORCV .... Overriding Cam Valve
ORC youth .... Opinion Research Corporation Youth (NITA)
ORD .... CAP PA Gutierrez [*Hernando R.*] Ordonez [*Mexico ICAO designator*] (FAAC)
ORD .... Chicago [*Illinois*] O'Hare Airport [*Derived from former name: Orchard Field*] [*Airport symbol*]
ORD .... Office for Research and Development [*American Library Association*] (AEBS)
ORD .... Office of Regional Development [*Organization of American States*]
ORD .... Office of Research and Development [*National Oceanic and Atmospheric Administration*] (GFGA)
ORD .... Office of Research and Development [*Washington, DC Environmental Protection Agency*] (GRD)
ORD .... Office of Research Development [*Office of Policy, Evaluation, and Research*] [*Department of Labor*]
ORD .... Office of Rubber Director [*WPB*] [*World War II*]
ORD .... Off-Range Distance (MCD)
ORD .... Ohio River Division [*Army Corps of Engineers*]
ORD .... Once-Run Distillate (PDAA)
ORD .... Operational Readiness Date
ORD .... Operational Readiness Demonstration [*FAA*] (TAG)
ORD .... Operational Ready [*or Readiness*] Data [*NASA*] (GFGA)
ORD .... Operational Requirements Document (COE)
ORD .... Operational Research Division [*Department of National Defence*] [*Canada*]
ORD .... Operations [*or Operational*] Requirement Document
ORD .... Optical Reference Device
ORD .... Optical Rotary Dispersion
ORD .... Orbital Requirements Document
ORD .... Ordained
ORD .... Order
ord .... Order (WDAA)
Ord .... Order (EBF)
ORD .... Orderly
ORD .... Ordinal
ORD .... Ordinance
ORD .... Ordinance (WDAA)
ord .... Ordinary (MSA)
ORD .... Ordinary (MSA)
Ord .... Ordinary (EBF)
ORD .... Ordinary Seaman [*British*]
ORD .... Ordnance (AAG)
ORD .... Ordovician [*Period, era, or system*] [*Geology*]
Ord .... Orotidine [*Also, O*] [*A nucleoside*]
ORD .... Overseas Replacement Depot [*Military*]
ORD .... Owner's Risk of Damage [*Shipping*]
ORDA .... Ober Ramstadt Depot Activity [*Germany*] [*Army*]
ORDA .... Office of Recombinant DNA Activities [*Bethesda, MD*] [*National Institute of Allergy and Infectious Diseases*]
ORDAC......... Overrange Detection and Correction [*Analytical chemistry*]
OrDal .... Dallas Public Library, Dallas, OR [*Library symbol Library of Congress*] (LCLS)
ORDALT....... Ordnance Alterations
Ord Amst .... Ordinance of Amsterdam [*A publication*] (DLA)
Ord Antw ..... Ordinance of Antwerp [*A publication*] (DLA)

ORD BBS .... Office of Research and Development Electronic Bulletin Board System [*Environmental Protection Agency*] (AEPA)
ORD BD ...... Ordnance Board [*Military*] (WDAA)
Ord Bilb....... Ordinance of Bilboa [*A publication*] (DLA)
ORDBN .... Ordnance Battalion
OrdBrd .... Ordnance Board [*British*]
ORDC.......... Orbiter Data Reduction Center [*NASA*]
ORDC.......... Ordnance Corps [*Army*]
ORDC.......... Ordnance Research and Development Center [*Aberdeen Proving Ground, Maryland*] [*Navy*]
ORDCAL....... Ordnance Calibration [*Navy*] (NVT)
ORDCAN ..... Orders Canceled [*Air Force*]
ORDCIT........ Ordnance Department and California Institute of Technology [*Army*] (RDA)
ORDCONCAN... Orders Considered Canceled [*Air Force*]
ORDCONTECH... Ordnance Control Technician (DNAB)
Ord Copen ... Ordinance of Copenhagen [*A publication*] (DLA)
ORDCOR ..... Orders Corrected [*Air Force*]
ORDCORPS... Ordnance Corps [*Army*]
ORDCU .... Occupational Research and Development Coordinating Unit
ORDD.......... Office of Research, Development, and Demonstrations [*Federal Railroad Administration*]
ORDD.......... Ordered (ROG)
ORD DEPT ... Ordnance Department [*Military*] (WDAA)
ORDDIS .... Ordinary Discharge [*Military*]
ORDEAL....... Oak Ridge Data Evaluation and Analysis Language [*Department of Energy*] (PDAA)
ORDEAL....... Orbital Rate Drive Electronics for Apollo and LM [*NASA*]
ORDEAL....... Orbit Rate Display - Earth and Lunar [*NASA*]
ORDENG ..... Ordnance Engineering
ORDER........ On-Line Order Entry System [*Computer science*] (MHDB)
ORDER........ Outstanding Requisitions Defeat Endurance Readiness (DNAB)
ORDET........ Orbit Determination Group
ORDet......... Owner's Risk of Deterioration [*Shipping*]
ORDFAC....... Ordnance Facility
Ord Flor...... Ordinance of Florence [*A publication*] (DLA)
Ord Gen...... Ordinance of Genoa [*A publication*] (DLA)
ORDHAC ..... Ordnance Systems Command Hydroballistics Advisory Committee [*Obsolete Navy*]
Ord Hamb.... Ordinance of Hamburg [*A publication*] (DLA)
ORDINST ..... Ordnance Instruction
ORDIP......... Ordnance Alteration Installation Plan [*Navy*]
ORDIR .... Omnirange Digital RADAR
ORDIS......... Optical Reading Direct Input System (IAA)
ORDIS......... Ordnance Discharge (DNAB)
Ord Konigs... Ordinance of Konigsberg [*A publication*] (DLA)
ORDL.......... Ohio River Division Laboratory [*Army Corps of Engineers*] (KSC)
ORDL-EC..... Ohio River Division Laboratory, Engineer Corps [*Army*] (MCD)
Ord Leg ...... Ordinance of Leghorn [*A publication*] (DLA)
ORDLIS........ Ordnance Logistics Information System [*Navy*]
ORDM .... Ordnance Corps Manual (AAG)
ORDMAINTCO... Ordnance Maintenance Company [*Navy*] (DNAB)
Ord Med Jur... Ordronaux's Medical Jurisprudence [*A publication*] (DLA)
ORDMOD ..... Orders Modified [*Navy*]
ordn .... Ordinance (WDAA)
ORDN.......... Ordnance (KSC)
ORDNA .... Organismes de Radiodiffusion des Pays NonAlignes [*Broadcasting Organizations of Non-Aligned Countries - BONAC*] (EAIO)
ORDNG .... Ordering
ORDNTR ...... Ordinator
ORDO.......... Ordinario [*Ordinarily*] [*Music*] (ROG)
Ordo Nob Urb... Ordo Nobilium Urbium [*of Ausonius*] [*Classical studies*] (OCD)
ORDP.......... Office of Rural Development Policy [*Department of Agriculture*]
ORDP.......... Ordnance Corps Pamphlet [*Army*] (MCD)
ORDPDS...... Offender Rehabilitation Division of the Public Defender Service (EA)
Ord Port...... Ordinance of Portugal [*A publication*] (DLA)
Ord Prus ..... Ordinance of Prussia [*A publication*] (DLA)
ORDR.......... Order
ORDRAT ..... Ordnance Dial Reader and Translator
ORDREV ...... Ordnance Procedures Review [*Military*] (NVT)
Ordr Jud Ins... Ordronaux on Judicial Aspects of Insanity [*A publication*] (DLA)
Ordr Med Jur... Ordronaux's Medical Jurisprudence [*A publication*] (DLA)
Ord Rott...... Ordinance of Rotterdam [*A publication*] (DLA)
ORDRPT ...... Ordnance Report
ORDS.......... Observation Requirements Data Sheet (IAA)
ORDS.......... Office of Research, Demonstrations, and Statistics [*Health Care Financing Administration*]
ORDS.......... Ordinary Shares (WDAA)
ORDSER ..... Ordnance Support Element Review (NVT)
Ord Sgt....... Ordnance Sergeant [*Military*] (DMA)
Ords NZ ...... Ordinances of the Legislative Council of New Zealand [*A publication*] (DLA)
ORDSTA...... Ordnance Station
Ord Swe ..... Ordinance of Sweden [*A publication*] (DLA)
ORDSYSCOM... Ordnance Systems Command [*Formerly, Bureau of Naval Weapons; later, Naval Sea Systems Command*]
ORDT .... Office of Research, Demonstrations, and Training [*Social and Rehabilitation Service, HEW*]
Ord Us .... Ord on Usury [*A publication*] (DLA)
ORDVAC...... Ordnance Variable Automatic Computer
ORDY.......... Ordinary (AABC)
OrE .... Eugene Public Library, Eugene, OR [*Library symbol Library of Congress*] (LCLS)
ORE .... Greendale Aviation Co. [*Nigeria*] [*FAA designator*] (FAAC)
ORE .... Greenfield [*Massachusetts*] [*Airport symbol*] (AD)

ORE .... Obtained Radiation Emittance
ORE .... Occupational Radiation Exposure (NRCH)
ORE .... Oceanographic Research Equipment
ORE .... Office of Regional Economics [Department of Commerce]
ORE .... Office of Research and Evaluation [Bureau of Labor Statistics] (GRD)
ORE .... Officer Responsible for the Exercise [Navy] (NVT)
ORE .... On-Orbit Repair Experiment [NASA] (NASA)
ORE .... On-Orbit Repairs Experiment
ORE .... Operational Readiness [Navy] (NG)
ORE .... Operational Readiness Evaluation [Army]
ORE .... Operational Readiness Exercise [MCD]
ORE .... Optimum Resource Extraction (PDAA)
ORE .... Orange, MA [Location identifier FAA] (FAAL)
ORE .... Oregon (AAG)
Ore .... Oregon (ODBW)
ORE .... Oregon Resources Corp. [Vancouver Stock Exchange symbol]
ORE .... Oregon State University, Corvallis, Corvallis, OR [OCLC symbol] (OCLC)
ORE .... Ornitologia Rondo Esperantlingva [Esperantist Ornithologists' Association] (EAIO)
ORE .... Orthophoto Resolution Enhancer [Army]
ORE .... Output Register Empty (MHDB)
ORE .... Overall Reference Equivalent (NITA)
ORE .... Overhaul, Rebuild, and Exchange (MCD)
ORE .... Overtraining Reversal Effect
OREALC .... Regional Office for Education in Latin America and the Caribbean [UNESCO] [Acronym is based on foreign phrase]
Ore App .... Oregon Court of Appeals Reports [A publication] (DLA)
OrEc .... Echo Public Library, Echo, OR [Library symbol] [Library of Congress] (LCLS)
OREC .... Eramosa Community Library, Rockwood, Ontario [Library symbol National Library of Canada] (NLC)
OREC .... Optimises Rectangles [AERE Harwell] [Software package] (NCC)
OREC .... Oxidation-Resistant Elemental Carbon [Chemistry]
ORECHL .... Centre Hospitalier Le Gardeur, Repentigny, Quebec [Library symbol National Library of Canada] (NLC)
OrECoAr .... Lane County Archives, Eugene, OR [Library symbol Library of Congress] (LCLS)
OrECoL .... Lane County Law Library, Eugene, OR [Library symbol Library of Congress] (LCLS)
ORE/ERO ...... Organisation Regionale de la Federation Internationale Dentaire pour l'Europe [European Regional Organization of the International Dental Federation] (EAIO)
OREF .... Orthopedic Research and Education Foundation [Medicine] (DMAA)
OREG .... Operation Register (IAA)
OREG .... Ordinary Multiple Regression [Statistics]
OREG .... Oregon (AFM)
Oreg .... Oregon (ODBW)
OregMt .... Oregon Metallurgical Corp. [Associated Press] (SAG)
Oregon .... Oregon Reports [A publication] (DLA)
Oreg Rev Stat... Oregon Revised Statutes [A publication] (DLA)
OrEGS .... Church of Jesus Christ of Latter-Day Saints, Genealogical Society Library, Eugene Branch, Eugene, OR [Library symbol Library of Congress] (LCLS)
Oreg SB Bull... Oregon State Bar Bulletin [A publication] (DLA)
Ore Health Sci U... Oregon Health Sciences University (GAGS)
OReilyAu ..... O'Reilly Automotive [Associated Press] (SAG)
OrEL .... Lane Community College, Eugene, OR [Library symbol Library of Congress] (LCLS)
OREL .... Ocean Research and Engineering Laboratory (SAA)
ORELA .... Oak Ridge Electron Linear Accelerator [Oak Ridge, TN] [Department of Energy]
OREM .... Objective Reference Equivalent Measurement (IAA)
OREM .... Office of Research and Evaluation Methods [National Institute of Justice] (GRD)
OREM .... Oregon Metallurgical [NASDAQ symbol] (TTSB)
OREM .... Oregon Metallurgical Corp. [NASDAQ symbol] (NQ)
OREN .... Orthorhombic Enstatite [Geology]
OrENC .... Northwest Christian College, Eugene, OR [Library symbol Library of Congress] (LCLS)
OrEnW .... Wallowa County Library, Enterprise, OR [Library symbol Library of Congress] (LCLS)
OrEnWM ..... Wallowa Memorial Hospital, Burton Carlock Memorial Library, Enterprise, OR [Library symbol Library of Congress] (LCLS)
OREO .... Orbiting Radio Emission Observatory [Satellite]
OREO .... Other Real Estate Owned (EBF)
O Rep .... Ohio Reports [A publication] (DLA)
OrEPM .... Lane County Museum [Formerly, Lane County Pioneer Museum], Eugene, OR [Library symbol Library of Congress] (LCLS)
OREPS .... Operational Research in Electrical Power Systems (PDAA)
ORER .... Official Railway Equipment Register [National Railway Publication Co.] [Information service or system] (IID)
Ore Rev Stat... Oregon Revised Statutes [A publication] (DLA)
ORERP .... Off-Site Radiation Exposure Review Project [Department of Energy]
OrEs .... Estacada Public Library, Estacada, OR [Library symbol Library of Congress] (LCLS)
OrESH .... Sacred Heart General Hospital, Eugene, OR [Library symbol Library of Congress] (LCLS)
OrEsHS .... Estacada High School, Estacada, OR [Library symbol Library of Congress] (LCLS)
Ore St B Bull... Oregon State Bar Bulletin [A publication] (DLA)
OreStl .... Oregon Steel Mills [Associated Press] (SAG)
Ore St U .... Oregon State University (GAGS)
Ore Tax Ct... Oregon Tax Court Reports [A publication] (DLA)

ORETF .... Outdoor Residential Exposure Task Force [A consortium of pesticide manufacturers]
OREX .... Isolyser Co. [NASDAQ symbol] (TTSB)
OREX .... Isolyser Company, Inc. [NASDAQ symbol] (SAG)
ORF .... Norfolk/Virginia Beach [Virginia] [Airport symbol] (OAG)
ORF .... Obesity Research Foundation [British] (DI)
ORF .... Oceanic Research Foundation [Australia]
ORF .... Oesterreichischer Rundfunk [Radio and television network] [Austria]
ORF .... Officers' Recreation Facility
ORF .... Olfactory Research Fund
ORF .... Oman Royal Flight [ICAO designator] (FAAC)
ORF .... Ontario Research Foundation [Canada Research center] (RCD)
ORF .... Open Reading Frame [Genetics]
ORF .... Operational Readiness Float (AABC)
ORF .... Oral Rehydration Fluid
ORF .... Oratorum Romanorum Fragmenta [A publication] (OCD)
Orf .... Orfeo [Record label]
ORF .... Orifice (NASA)
ORF .... Ortho Pharmaceutical Corp. [Research code symbol]
ORF .... Overhaul Replacement Factor (MCD)
ORF .... Owner's Risk of Fire [Shipping]
ORF .... Owner's Risk of Freezing [Shipping]
OrF .... Rogers City Public Library, Forest Grove, OR [Library symbol Library of Congress] (LCLS)
OrFc .... Falls City Public Library, Falls City, OR [Library symbol Library of Congress] (LCLS)
ORFC .... Orifice (AAG)
ORFEUS .... Orbiting Far and Extreme Ultraviolet Spectrometer [Telescope]
OrFFM .... Oregon Masonic Grand Lodge, Forest Grove, OR [Library symbol Library of Congress] (LCLS)
OrFl .... Florence Public Library, Florence, OR [Library symbol Library of Congress] (LCLS)
ORFLS .... Oak Ridge Full Matrix Least Squares
ORFM .... Outlet Region Feature Model [Nuclear energy] (NRCH)
Orf ML .... Orfila's Medecine Legale [A publication] (DLA)
OrFP .... Pacific University, Forest Grove, OR [Library symbol Library of Congress] (LCLS)
OrFS .... Orange Free State (DAS)
ORFS .... Origin Rail Freight [MARAD] (TAG)
ORG .... Glen Robertson Branch, Stormont, Dundas, and Glengarry County Public Library, Ontario [Library symbol National Library of Canada] (BIB)
ORG .... Office of Racing and Gaming [Western Australia]
ORG .... [The] Official Recreation Guide [Applied Information Services, Inc.] [Whitefish, MT] [Information service or system] (IID)
ORG .... Olympics Research Group [University of Calgary] [Canada Research center] (RCD)
ORG .... Operations Research Group
org .... Orange [Philately]
ORG .... Orange [Diocesan abbreviation] [California] (TOCD)
ORG .... Orange, TX [Location identifier FAA] (FAAL)
ORG .... Organ
org .... Organ (WDAA)
ORG .... Organic
ORG .... Organism (ADA)
ORG .... Organization [or Organizational] (AAG)
Org .... Organization (AAGC)
Org .... Organizational (AL)
ORG .... Organogenesis, Inc. [AMEX symbol] (SPSG)
ORG .... Organon [Netherlands] [Research code symbol]
ORG .... Oriental Airlines (Gambia) Ltd. [ICAO designator] (FAAC)
ORG .... Origin (MDG)
Org .... Original (TBD)
ORG .... Original New York Seltzer of Canada Ltd. [Vancouver Stock Exchange symbol]
org .... Originator [MARC relator code] [Library of Congress] (LCCP)
ORG .... Paramaribo [Surinam] Zorg En Hoop Airport [Airport symbol] (OAG)
ORGA .... Organizacion Regional Gallega Autonoma [Regional Galician Autonomy Organization] [Spain Political party] (PPE)
ORGALIME... Organisme de Liaison des Industries Metalliques Europeennes [Liaison Group for the European Engineering Industries] [Brussels, Belgium] (EAIO)
ORGAN .... Organisation Regionale Africaine de Normalisation [African Regional Organization for Standardization - AROS] (EA)
ORGAN .... Organization
Organik........ Organik Technologies, Inc. [Associated Press] (SAG)
organiz........ Organization [or Organizational] (DAVI)
OrGb .... Curry Public Library, Gold Beach, OR [Library symbol Library of Congress] (LCLS)
OrgBehav..... Organizational Behaviour (DD)
ORgC .... Rio Grande College, Rio Grande, OH [Library symbol Library of Congress] (LCLS)
ORGD .... Organized
ORGDP .... Oak Ridge Gaseous Diffusion Plant [Department of Energy]
ORGEL .... Organique et Eau Lourde [Organic liquid and heavy water nuclear reactor]
Org Exp........ Organo Espressivo [Swell Organ] [Music]
OrGH .... Josephine Memorial Hospital, Grants Pass, OR [Library symbol] [Library of Congress] (LCLS)
ORGK........... Organik Technologies [NASDAQ symbol] (TTSB)
ORGK........... Organik Technologies, Inc. [NASDAQ symbol] (SAG)
ORGKL......... Organik Tech Wrrt [NASDAQ symbol] (TTSB)
ORGKW....... Organik Technologies Wrrt'A' [NASDAQ symbol] (TTSB)
ORGKZ......... Organik Technologies Wrrt'B' [NASDAQ symbol] (TTSB)

OrGl .... Gladstone Public Library, Gladstone, OR [*Library symbol Library of Congress*] (LCLS)

ORGL .... Organizational (AFM)

ORGL .... Overall Reading Grade Level (MCD)

OrGIHS .... Gladstone High School, Gladstone, OR [*Library symbol Library of Congress*] (LCLS)

ORGM .... Outdoor Recreation Grants-in-Aid Manual

ORGN .... Organization (AFM)

Orgngn .... Organogenesis, Inc. [*Associated Press*] (SAG)

Orgnik .... Organik Technologies, Inc. [*Associated Press*] (SAG)

ORGNL .... Organizational

ORGO .... Organo [*Organ*] [*Music*] (ROG)

OrGR .... Rogue Community College, Grants Pass, OR [*Library symbol Library of Congress*] (LCLS)

OrGrC .... Mount Hood Community College, Gresham, OR [*Library symbol Library of Congress*] (LCLS)

OrGrGS .... Church of Jesus Christ of Latter-Day Saints, Genealogical Society Library, Gresham Branch, Gresham, OR [*Library symbol Library of Congress*] (LCLS)

ORGSBS ...... Oak Ridge Graduate School of Biomedical Sciences [*Tennessee*]

ORGSC .... Oregon Ryegrass Growers Seed Commission (EA)

ORGT .... Organist

ORGY .... Organization for the Rational Guidance of Youth [*Fictitious organization in film, "The Man from ORGY"*]

ORH .... Occupational Role History [*Psychology*]

ORH .... Office of Rural Health (MEDA)

ORH .... Operational Requirements Handbook

ORH .... Orchard Supply Hardware Strs [*NYSE symbol*] (TTSB)

o-rh .... Orthorhombic [*Crystallography*]

ORH .... Richmond Hill Public Library, Ontario [*Library symbol National Library of Canada*] (NLC)

ORH .... Worcester [*Massachusetts*] [*Airport symbol*] (OAG)

OrHe .... Hermiston Public Library, Hermiston, OR [*Library symbol Library of Congress*] (LCLS)

OrHeGS .... Good Shepherd Hospital, Hermiston, OR [*Library symbol Library of Congress*] (LCLS)

OrHep .... Heppner Public Library, Heppner, OR [*Library symbol Library of Congress*] (LCLS)

OrHepPM ...... Pioneer Memorial Hospital, Heppner, OR [*Library symbol Library of Congress*] (LCLS)

ORHFC .... Official Rocky Horror Fan Club (EA)

OrHi .... Oregon Historical Society, Portland, OR [*Library symbol Library of Congress*] (LCLS)

OrHil .... Hillsboro Public Library, Hillsboro, OR [*Library symbol Library of Congress*] (LCLS)

OrHilHI .... Tuality Health Information Resource Center, Hillsboro, OR [*Library symbol*] [*Library of Congress*] (LCLS)

OrHilT .... Tuality Community Hospital, Hillsboro, OR [*Library symbol Library of Congress*] (LCLS)

OrHilW .... Washington County Law Library, Hillsboro, OR [*Library symbol Library of Congress*] (LCLS)

OrHr .... Hood River County Library, Hood River, OR [*Library symbol Library of Congress*] (LCLS)

OrHx .... Helix Pubic Library, Helix, OR [*Library symbol*] [*Library of Congress*] (LCLS)

Orl .... Independence Public Library, Independence, OR [*Library symbol Library of Congress*] (LCLS)

ORI .... Ocean Research Institute (WDAA)

ORI .... Ocean Resources Institute (COE)

ORI .... Octane Requirement Increase [*Mechanical engineering*]

ORI .... Ocurrence of Reinforcing Information (PDAA)

ORI .... Office of Research and Inventions

ORI .... Office of Research Integrity [*Department of Health and Human Services*]

ORI .... Office of Road Inquiry [*Later, Bureau of Public Roads*]

ORI .... Office Research Institute (NADA)

ORI .... Old Republic International Corp. [*NYSE symbol*] (SPSG)

ORI .... Old Republic Intl. [*NYSE symbol*] (TTSB)

ORI .... Omni Resources, Inc. [*Vancouver Stock Exchange symbol*]

ORI .... Operating and Repair Instruction

ORI .... Operational Readiness Inspection [*Army*]

ORI .... Operational Readiness Instruction [*Military*]

ORI .... Operations Research, Inc. [*Information service or system*]

ORI .... Ophthalmic Research Institute (EA)

ORI .... Oregon Research Institute

ORI .... Orient Air Ltd. [*British ICAO designator*] (FAAC)

ORI .... Orientation Inventory [*Vocational guidance test*]

Ori .... Oriole [*Record label*] [*Great Britain*]

Ori .... Orion [*Constellation*]

ori .... Oriya [*MARC language code Library of Congress*] (LCCP)

ORI .... Outdoor Recreation Institute (EA)

ORI .... Overhaul and Repair Instruction

ORI .... Port Lions [*Alaska*] [*Airport symbol*] (OAG)

ORIA .... Oriental Rug Importers Association of America (EA)

ORIADOC ..... Orientation and Access to Information and Documentation Sources in France [*Commission de Coordination de la Documentation Administrative*] [*Database*]

ORIC .... Oak Ridge Isochronous Cyclotron [*Department of Energy*]

ORIC .... Operational Readiness Inspection Committee [*NASA*]

ORICAT .... Original Cataloguing System (NITA)

ORIDE .... Override (KSC)

ORIE .... Operational Radiation Instrumentation Equipment (SAA)

ORIEN .... Orientation (AABC)

ORIENT .... Orientation

OrientB .... Oriental Bank & Trust [*Associated Press*] (SAG)

ORIF .... Open Reduction with Internal Fixation [*Medicine*]

Orig .... Origen [*Deceased circa 254*] [*Authority cited in pre-1607 legal work*] (DSA)

ORIG .... Origin [*or Original*] (AAG)

orig .... Origin (VRA)

orig .... Original (WDAA)

ORIG .... Originator (MSA)

ORIGAN .... Origanum [*Marjoram*] [*Pharmacology*] (ROG)

ORIG BDS .... Original Boards [*Graphic arts*] (DGA)

ORIGEN2 ...... Oak Ridge Isotope Generation and Depletion Code [*Department of Energy*] (GAAI)

ORIGINATG ... Originating (ROG)

ORIGINS ...... Oklahoma Resources Integrated General Information Network System

ORIGL .... Original (ROG)

ORINS .... Oak Ridge Institute of Nuclear Studies [*Later, ORAU*] (EA)

Orio .... Orion [*Constellation*]

OriolH .... Oriole Homes Corp. [*Associated Press*] (SAG)

ORION .... Online Retrieval of Information over a Network

ORION .... Operational Radio Interferometry Observing Network (MCD)

OrionCap ...... Orion Capital Corp. [*Associated Press*] (SAG)

OrionNS .... Orion Network Systems, Inc. [*Associated Press*] (SAG)

ORIP .... Ripley Branch, Bruce County Public Library, Ontario [*Library symbol National Library of Canada*] (NLC)

ORIPrH .... Old Republic Int 8.75% Pfd'H' [*NYSE symbol*] (TTSB)

Oris .... All India Reporter, Orissa [*A publication*] (DLA)

ORIS .... Office of Regulatory Information Systems [*Energy Regulatory Commission*] (IID)

ORIS .... Officeworker Reader Information Services [*British*]

ORIS .... South Carleton High School, Richmond, Ontario [*Library symbol National Library of Canada*] (NLC)

ORISE .... Oak Ridge Institute for Science and Education [*Oak Ridge Associated Universities*] [*Research center*] (RCD)

Orissa .... All India Reporter, Orissa [*A publication*] (DLA)

ORIT .... Operational Readiness Inspection Team [*Air Force*]

ORIT .... Operational Readiness Inspection Test [*Air Force*]

ORIT .... Organization Regional Interamericana de Trabdjadores [*Inter-American Labor Organization*] [*Spanish*] (BARN)

ORJ .... Corry, PA [*Location identifier FAA*] (FAAL)

ORJ .... Ohio Power Co. [*NYSE symbol*] (SAG)

ORJ .... Oneida Resources, Inc. [*Vancouver Stock Exchange symbol*]

OrJ .... Orange Juice

ORJ .... Orinduik [*Guyana*] [*Airport symbol*] (OAG)

OrJc .... Junction City Public Library, Junction City, OR [*Library symbol Library of Congress*] (LCLS)

OrJe .... Jefferson Public Library, Jefferson, OR [*Library symbol Library of Congress*] (LCLS)

ORJETS .... On-Line Remote Job Entry Terminal System [*Computer science*]

OrJM .... Jacksonville Museum, Jacksonville, OR [*Library symbol Library of Congress*] (LCLS)

OrJvHS .... Jordan Valley High School, Jordan Valley, OR [*Library symbol Library of Congress*] (LCLS)

ORK .... Air Orkney [*British ICAO designator*] (FAAC)

ORK .... Cork [*Ireland*] [*Airport symbol*] (OAG)

OrK .... Klamath County Library, Klamath Falls, OR [*Library symbol Library of Congress*] (LCLS)

ORK .... Orkney [*County in Scotland*] (ROG)

OrKM .... Merle West Medical Center Library, Klamath Falls, OR [*Library symbol*] [*Library of Congress*] (LCLS)

OrKT .... Oregon Technical Institute, Klamath Falls, OR [*Library symbol Library of Congress*] (LCLS)

ORL .... Observed Range Limit

ORL .... Olivetti Research Laboratory Ltd. [*British*] (IRUK)

ORL .... On Air Ltd. [*Canada ICAO designator*] (FAAC)

ORL .... Optimum Repair Level Analysis

ORL .... Orbital Research Laboratory [*NASA*]

ORL .... Ordnance Research Laboratory [*Later, Applied Research Laboratory*] [*Pennsylvania State University*] (MCD)

ORL .... Orion Resources Ltd. [*Vancouver Stock Exchange symbol*]

'Orl .... 'Orlah (BJA)

ORL .... Orlando [*Florida*] [*Airport symbol*] (OAG)

ORL .... Orlando Public Library, Orlando, FL [*OCLC symbol*] (OCLC)

ORL .... Otorhinolaryngology [*Medicine*]

ORL .... Owner's Risk of Leakage [*Shipping*]

ORL .... Red Lake Public Library, Ontario [*Library symbol National Library of Canada*] (NLC)

ORLA .... Optimum Repair Level Analysis [*Air Force*]

ORLA .... Optimum Repair Level Authorization (MCD)

ORLA .... Optimum Report Level Analysis [*Military*]

OrLak .... Lake County Library, Lakeview, OR [*Library symbol*] [*Library of Congress*] (LCLS)

OrLan .... Langlois Public Library, Langlois, OR [*Library symbol Library of Congress*] (LCLS)

Or Laws .... Oregon Laws and Resolutions [*A publication*] (DLA)

Or Laws Adv Sh ... Oregon Laws Advance Sheets [*A publication*] (DLA)

Or Laws Spec Sess ... Oregon Laws and Resolutions [*A publication*] (DLA)

Orl Bridg ...... Orlando Bridgman's English Common Pleas Reports [*A publication*] (DLA)

Orl Bridgman ... Orlando Bridgman's English Common Pleas Reports [*A publication*] (DLA)

Orleans App ... Orleans Court of Appeals [*Louisiana*] (DLA)

Orleans TR ... Orleans Term Reports [*1, 2 Martin*] [*Louisiana*] [*A publication*] (DLA)

OrLeH .... Lebanon Community Hospital, Lebanon, OR [*Library symbol*] [*Library of Congress*] (LCLS)

OrLg............ La Grande Public Library, La Grande, OR [*Library symbol Library of Congress*] (LCLS)

OrLgE.......... Eastern Oregon College, La Grande, OR [*Library symbol Library of Congress*] (LCLS)

OrLgFS .... United States Forest Service, Range and Wildlife Habitat Laboratory, La Grande, OR [*Library symbol Library of Congress*] (LCLS)

OrLgGRH ..... Grande Ronde Hospital, LaGrande, OR [*Library symbol Library of Congress*] (LCLS)

OrLgGS........ Church of Jesus Christ of Latter-Day Saints, Genealogical Society Library, La Grande Branch, La Grande, OR [*Library symbol Library of Congress*] (LCLS)

ORLIS.......... Orts-, Regional-, und Landesplanung Literaturinformationssystem [*Literature Information System for Town and Regional Planning*] [*1974-1978 Database*]

ORLL .... Operational Reports - Lessons Learned [*Army*] (AABC)

OrLo............ Lake Oswego Public Library, Lake Oswego, OR [*Library symbol Library of Congress*] (LCLS)

OrLoHS........ Lake Oswego High School, Lake Oswego, OR [*Library symbol Library of Congress*] (LCLS)

OrLoJS......... Lake Oswego Junior High School, Lake Oswego, OR [*Library symbol Library of Congress*] (LCLS)

OrLoLHS...... Lakeridge High School, Lake Oswego, OR [*Library symbol Library of Congress*] (LCLS)

OrLpHS........ La Pine Senior High School, La Pine, OR [*Library symbol*] [*Library of Congress*] (LCLS)

OrIPID.......... Industrial Design Corp., Portland, OR [*Library symbol*] [*Library of Congress*] (LCLS)

ORLPP........ Office of Research, Legislation, and Program Policies [*Unemployment Insurance Service*] [*Department of Labor*]

ORLS .... Selco Mining Corp., Red Lake, Ontario [*Library symbol National Library of Canada*] (NLC)

Or LSJ .... Oregon Law School Journal [*1902-03*] [*A publication*] (DLA)

ORLSTJ....... St. Joseph Township Public Library, Richards Landing, Ontario [*Library symbol National Library of Canada*] (NLC)

Orl TR......... Orleans Term Reports [*1, 2 Martin*] [*Louisiana*] [*A publication*] (DLA)

ORLY .... O'Reilly Automotive [*NASDAQ symbol*] (SAG)

ORLY .... Overload Relay (IEEE)

ORM .... Northampton [*England*] [*Airport symbol*] (AD)

ORM .... Office of Recycled Materials [*National Bureau of Standards*]

ORM .... Office of Regional Management [*Employment and Training Administration*]

ORM .... Office of Regulated Material [*Environmental Protection Agency*] (GFGA)

ORM .... Off-Road Mobility

ORM .... Off-Route Mine

ORM .... Operators Reference Manual (IAA)

ORM .... Optical Reference Manual

ORM .... Opytnyi Reaktivnyi Motor [*Experimental Reaction Motor*] [*Former USSR*]

orm.............. Ormolu (VRA)

ORM .... Other Regulated Material

ORM .... Overhaul and Repair Manual

ORM .... Overlapping Resolution Mapping [*Computer science*]

ORMA .... Office of Refugee and Migration Affairs [*Department of State*]

OrMaC .... Marylhurst College, Marylhurst, OR [*Library symbol Library of Congress*] (LCLS)

OrMad .... Jefferson County Library, Madras, OR [*Library symbol Library of Congress*] (LCLS)

OrMadHS..... Madras High School, Madras, OR [*Library symbol*] [*Library of Congress*] (LCLS)

OrMadJH ..... Madras Junior High School, Madras, OR [*Library symbol*] [*Library of Congress*] (LCLS)

ORMAK .... Oak Ridge TOKAMAK [*Energy Research and Development Administration*]

ORMAS........ Operational Resource Management Assessment System [*Military*]

OrMc............ McMinnville Public Library, McMinnville, OR [*Library symbol Library of Congress*] (LCLS)

ORMC .... Off-Route [*Smart*] Mine Clearance [*Military*]

OR/MC .... Operational Requirements/Military Characteristics (NG)

OrMcL .... Linfield College, McMinnville, OR [*Library symbol Library of Congress*] (LCLS)

OrMeGS....... Church of Jesus Christ of Latter-Day Saints, Genealogical Society Library, Medford Branch, Medford, OR [*Library symbol Library of Congress*] (LCLS)

OrMeJ.......... Jackson County Library System, Medford, OR [*Library symbol Library of Congress*] (LCLS)

OrMePH....... Providence Hospital, Medford, OR [*Library symbol*] [*Library of Congress*] (LCLS)

OrMeRM ...... Rogue Valley Medical Center, Medford, OR [*Library symbol*] [*Library of Congress*] (LCLS)

OrMf .... Milton-Freewater Public Library, Milton-Freewater, OR [*Library symbol Library of Congress*] (LCLS)

OrMi .... Milwaukie Public Library, Milwaukie, OR [*Library symbol Library of Congress*] (LCLS)

ORMI .... Oak Ridge Military Institute

OrMiCHS...... Clackamas High School, Media Center, Milwaukie, OR [*Library symbol Library of Congress*] (LCLS)

OrMiD .... Dwyer Community Hospital, Medical Library, Milwaukie, OR [*Library symbol Library of Congress*] (LCLS)

OrMiHS........ Milwaukie High School, Milwaukie, OR [*Library symbol Library of Congress*] (LCLS)

OrMiLHS...... La Salle High School, Milwaukie, OR [*Library symbol Library of Congress*] (LCLS)

OrMiPHS...... Rex Putnam High School, Milwaukie, OR [*Library symbol Library of Congress*] (LCLS)

ORMM .... Basrah/Magal [*Iraq*] [*ICAO location identifier*] (ICLI)

ORMOA........ Office for Relations with Military and Occupation Authorities

OrMol .... Molalla Public Library, Molalla, OR [*Library symbol Library of Congress*] (LCLS)

OrMolHS ..... Molalla Senior High School, Molalla, OR [*Library symbol Library of Congress*] (LCLS)

OrMolMS ..... Molalla Mid-High School, Molalla, OR [*Library symbol*] [*Library of Congress*] (LCLS)

OrMon .... Monmouth Library, Monmouth, OR [*Library symbol Library of Congress*] (LCLS)

Ormond........ Ormond's Reports [*19-107 Alabama*] [*A publication*] (DLA)

OrMonO....... Oregon College of Education, Monmouth, OR [*Library symbol Library of Congress*] (LCLS)

ORMONS ..... Operational Readiness Monitoring System (MCD)

OrMonW ...... Western Oregon State College, Monmouth, OR [*Library symbol*] [*Library of Congress*] (LCLS)

OrMp .... Myrtle Point Public Library (Flora M. Laird Library), Myrtle Point, OR [*Library symbol Library of Congress*] (LCLS)

ORMS .... Basrah/Shaibah [*Iraq*] [*ICAO location identifier*] (ICLI)

ORMS .... Operational Readiness Management System

OR/MS .... Operations Research or Management Science

ORMS .... Operative Roller Makers' Society [*A union*] [*British*]

ORMS .... Other Regulated Materials (GNE)

OrMta .... Mount Angel Public Library, Mount Angel, OR [*Library symbol Library of Congress*] (LCLS)

OrMtaC .... Mount Angel College [*Later, Cesar Chavez College*], Mount Angel, OR [*Library symbol Library of Congress*] (LCLS)

ORMU .... Orbital Remote Maneuvering Unit

OrN .... Newberg Library Association, Newberg, OR [*Library symbol Library of Congress*] (LCLS)

ORN .... Oak Ridge National Laboratory, Oak Ridge, TN [*OCLC symbol*] (OCLC)

ORN .... Olfactory Receptor Neuron [*Biochemistry*]

ORN .... Operating Room Nurse [*Medicine*]

ORN .... Oran [*Algeria*] [*Airport symbol*] (OAG)

ORN .... Orange (AAG)

ORN .... Organization of Revolutionaries of the North [*Lebanon*] (PD)

ORN .... Orient Airways [*Pakistan*] [*ICAO designator*] (FAAC)

ORN .... Ornament (MSA)

ORN .... OrNda Healthcorp [*NYSE symbol*] (TTSB)

Orn.............. Ornithine [*Same as DAV*] [*An amino acid*]

ORN .... Ornithine (DB)

ORN .... Ornithology

ORN .... Orthopedic Nurse

ornam.......... Ornament (VRA)

ORNAM........ Ornamental

OrNb .... North Bend Public Library, North Bend, OR [*Library symbol Library of Congress*] (LCLS)

OrNbGS........ Church of Jesus Christ of Latter-Day Saints, Genealogical Society Library, Coos Bay Stake Branch, North Bend, OR [*Library symbol Library of Congress*] (LCLS)

ORND.......... Ornda Healthcorp [*Formerly, Republic Health Corp.*] [*NASDAQ symbol*] (SPSG)

Ornda........... Ornda Healthcorp [*Associated Press*] (SAG)

OrNep .... Newport Public Library, Newport, OR [*Library symbol Library of Congress*] (LCLS)

OrNepH........ Pacific Communities Hospital Library, Newport, OR [*Library symbol*] [*Library of Congress*] (LCLS)

ORNG........... Orange

ORNG........... Orange PLC [*NASDAQ symbol*] (SAG)

OrngCo......... Orange-Co., Inc. [*Associated Press*] (SAG)

OrNGF.......... George Fox College, Newberg, OR [*Library symbol Library of Congress*] (LCLS)

ORNGY .... Orange PLC ADR [*NASDAQ symbol*] (TTSB)

ORNITH........ Ornithology

ORNITHOL ... Ornithology

ORNL .... Oak Ridge National Laboratory [*Oak Ridge, TN*] [*Department of Energy*]

ORNL-PCA ... Oak Ridge National Laboratory Pool Critical Assembly (SAA)

ORNLY-NDP... Oak Ridge National Laboratory Nuclear Data Project [*Database producer*]

ORNMT .... Ornament

ORNTL .... Ornamental

OrNyGS........ Church of Jesus Christ of Latter-Day Saints, Genealogical Society Library, NyssaBranch, Nyssa, OR [*Library symbol Library of Congress*] (LCLS)

OrNyMH....... Malheur Memorial Hospital, J. J. Sarazin Memorial Library, Nyssa, OR [*Library symbol Library of Congress*] (LCLS)

ORO .... Oak Ridge Operations Office (MCD)

ORO .... Office of Regional Operations [*Environmental Protection Agency*] (GFGA)

ORO .... Office of Regional Operations [*Office of Field Operations*] [*Department of Labor*]

ORO .... Official Receiver's Office [*Australia*]

ORO .... Oil Red O [*A stain*]

ORO .... Operations Research Office

ORO .... Orapouche [*An arbovirus*] [*Laboratory science*] (DAVI)

OrO .... Oregon City Public Library, Oregon City, OR [*Library symbol Library of Congress*] (LCLS)

ORO .... Orofino Resources Ltd. [*Toronto Stock Exchange symbol Vancouver Stock Exchange symbol*]

ORO .... Oropa [*Italy*] [*Seismograph station code, US Geological Survey Closed*] (SEIS)

ORO .... Oropouche [*An arbovirus*]

Oro.............. Orotate [*Biochemistry*]

Oro..............	Orotic Acid [*Biochemistry*]
ORO.............	Orthicon Read-Out
ORO.............	Porto Seguro [*Brazil*] [*Airport symbol*] (AD)
ORO.............	Rockland Public Library, Ontario [*Library symbol National Library of Canada*] (NLC)
OrOa............	Oakridge Public Library, Oakridge, OR [*Library symbol Library of Congress*] (LCLS)
OROA...........	Oroamerica, Inc. [*NASDAQ symbol*] (SAG)
Oroamer.......	Oroamerica, Inc. [*Associated Press*] (SAG)
OROAP.........	Organizacion Regional del Oriente para la Administracion Publica [*Eastern Regional Organization for Public Administration*] (EAIO)
OrOC...........	Clackamas County Public Library, Oregon City, OR [*Library symbol Library of Congress*] (LCLS)
OrOCC.........	Clackamas Community College, Oregon City, OR [*Library symbol Library of Congress*] (LCLS)
OROCS.........	Optical Recognition of Chemical Structures Program [*IBM Almaden Research Center*] [*San Jose, CA*]
OrOgCL........	Cooperative Library Network of Clackamas County, Oak Grove, OR [*Library symbol*] [*Library of Congress*] (LCLS)
OrOHS	Oregon City Senior High School, Oregon City, OR [*Library symbol Library of Congress*] (LCLS)
OROM..........	Optical Read-Only Memory [*Computer science*]
OrOn............	Malheur County Library, Ontario, OR [*Library symbol Library of Congress*] (LCLS)
OrOnHR	Holy Rosary Hospital, Weise-Biggs Memorial Medical Library, Ontario, OR [*Library symbol Library of Congress*] (LCLS)
OrOnT	Treasure Valley Community College, Ontario, OR [*Library symbol Library of Congress*] (LCLS)
ORootN........	Northeastern Ohio Universities, College of Medicine, Basic Medical Sciences Library, Rootstown, OH [*Library symbol Library of Congress*] (LCLS)
OROS..........	Optical Read-Only Storage [*Computer science*]
OROS...........	Oral Osmotic [*System for delivering drugs into the bloodstream*] [*Alza Corp. trademark*]
OROS...........	Rosseau Public Library, Ontario [*Library symbol National Library of Canada*] (NLC)
OROSS.........	Operational Readiness-Oriented Supply System [*Army*] (PDAA)
OrOWH	Willamette Falls Community Hospital, Oregon City, OR [*Library symbol Library of Congress*] (LCLS)
OrP	Library Association of Portland [*Public Library for Portland and Multnomah County*], Portland, OR [*Library symbol Library of Congress*] (LCLS)
ORP	Objective Rally [*or Rallying*] Point [*Military*]
ORP	Objective Release Point [*Army*] (INF)
ORP	Occiput Right Posterior Fetal position [*Medicine*] (STED)
ORP	Office of Radiation Programs [*Environmental Protection Agency*]
ORP	Office of Regulatory Programs [*Federal Energy Administration*] [*Obsolete*]
ORP	Officer Requirements Plan (DNAB)
ORP	OFS [*Orbital Flight System*] Retransmission Processor [*NASA*] (GFGA)
ORP	OFS [*Orbiter Functional Simulator*] Retransmission Processor [*NASA*]
ORP	Operational Readiness Panel
ORP	Operational Readiness Platform [*Aviation*] (DA)
ORP	Optical Rotary Power
ORP	Orapa [*Botswana*] [*Airport symbol Obsolete*] (OAG)
ORP	Orbital Rendezvous Procedure (AAG)
ORP	Ordinary, Reasonable, and Prudent [*Legal term*] (BARN)
ORP	Organ Recovery Program (EA)
ORP	Ormara [*Pakistan*] [*Airport symbol*] (AD)
ORP	Outside Right Position [*Dancing*]
ORP	Oxidation-Reduction Potential
ORP	Oxygen-Regulated Protein [*Biochemistry*]
ORP	Phelps Community Library, Redbridge, Ontario [*Library symbol National Library of Canada*] (NLC)
ORPA..........	Orbiter Retarding Potential Analyzer [*NASA*]
ORPA...........	Organizacion Revolucionaria del Pueblo en Armas [*Revolutionary Organization of the People in Arms*] [*Guatemala*] [*Political party*] (PD)
OrP-A...........	Portland City Archives, Portland, OR [*Library symbol Library of Congress*] (LCLS)
OrPAA.........	Arthur Anderson & Co., Portland, OR [*Library symbol Library of Congress*] (LCLS)
OrPAB.........	Academic Book Center, Portland, OR [*Library symbol*] [*Library of Congress*] (LCLS)
OrPB	Bonneville Power Administration, Portland, OR [*Library symbol Library of Congress*] (LCLS)
OrPBC.........	Blue Cross/Blue Shield of Oregon, Portland, OR [*Library symbol*] [*Library of Congress*] (LCLS)
OrPBK.........	Bess Kaiser Foundation Hospital, Medical Library, Portland, OR [*Library symbol Library of Congress*] (LCLS)
OrPC	Cascade College, Portland, OR [*Library symbol Library of Congress*] (LCLS)
ORPC...........	Office of Rail Public Counsel [*Terminated, 1979*] [*Affiliated with Interstate Commerce Commission*]
ORPC...........	Old Radio Program Collectors Club (EA)
OrPCA.........	Roman Catholic Archdiocese of Portland in Oregon, Chancery Office, Portland, OR [*Library symbol Library of Congress*] (LCLS)
OrPCC.........	Concordia College, Portland, OR [*Library symbol Library of Congress*] (LCLS)
OrPCM........	Cedar Mill Community Library, Portland, OR [*Library symbol Library of Congress*] (LCLS)
OrPCNM......	National College of Naturopathic Medicine, Portland, OR [*Library symbol Library of Congress*] (LCLS)
OrPCol	Columbia Christian College, Portland, OR [*Library symbol Library of Congress*] (LCLS)
OrPD	Protestant Episcopal Church, Diocesan Library, Portland, OR [*Library symbol Library of Congress*] (LCLS)
OrPeB	Blue Mountain Community College, Pendleton, OR [*Library symbol Library of Congress*] (LCLS)
OrPeCH.......	Pendleton Community Hospital, Pendleton, OR [*Library symbol Library of Congress*] (LCLS)
OrPEH.........	Emanuel Hospital, Portland, OR [*Library symbol Library of Congress*] (LCLS)
OrPeSA........	Saint Anthony Hospital, Pendleton, OR [*Library symbol Library of Congress*] (LCLS)
OrPeU.........	Umatilla County Library, Pendleton, OR [*Library symbol Library of Congress*] (LCLS)
OrPFW........	United States Fish and Wildlife Service, Portland, OR [*Library symbol Library of Congress*] (LCLS)
OrPGE.........	Portland General Electric Co., Portland, OR [*Library symbol Library of Congress*] (LCLS)
OrPGF.........	Genealogical Forum of Portland, Portland, OR [*Library symbol Library of Congress*] (LCLS)
OrPGH	Good Samaritan Hospital and Medical Center, Portland, OR [*Library symbol Library of Congress*] (LCLS)
OrPGS.........	Church of Jesus Christ of Latter-Day Saints, Genealogical Society Library, Portland Branch, Portland, OR [*Library symbol Library of Congress*] (LCLS)
OrPGSE.......	Church of Jesus Christ of Latter-Day Saints, Genealogical Society Library, Portland East Branch, Portland, OR [*Library symbol Library of Congress*] (LCLS)
ORPH..........	Orphan [*or Orphanage*]
ORPH..........	Orphan Medical, Inc. [*NASDAQ symbol*] (SAG)
ORPH..........	Orphan Med Inc. [*NASDAQ symbol*] (TTSB)
OrphanM......	Orphan Medical, Inc. [*Associated Press*] (SAG)
Orph Frag....	Orphica Fragmenta [*A publication*] (OCD)
ORPHIC.......	Organized Projected Hypotheses for Innovations in Curriculum [*Educational planning*]
OrPHP.........	Holladay Park Hospital, Medical Library, Portland, OR [*Library symbol Library of Congress*] (LCLS)
OrPHS-D	Oregon Health Sciences University, Dental Library, Portland, OR [*Library symbol Library of Congress*] (LCLS)
ORPI...........	Organ Pipe Cactus National Monument
ORPICS.......	Orbital Rendezvous Positioning, Indexing, and Coupling System
OrPK	Bess Kaiser Foundation Hospital, Medical Library, Portland, OR [*Library symbol Library of Congress*] (LCLS)
OrPKF.........	Kaiser Foundation Hospitals, Health Services Research Center, Portland, OR [*Library symbol Library of Congress*] (LCLS)
OrPL	Lewis and Clark College, Portland, OR [*Library symbol Library of Congress*] (LCLS)
ORPL..........	Office de Protection contre les Rayonnements Ionisants [*Office for Protecti on Against Ionizing Radiation*] [*France*]
ORPL..........	Overseas Replacement [*Military*]
OrPL-L.........	Northwestern School of Law, Lewis and Clark College, Portland, OR [*Library symbol Library of Congress*] (LCLS)
ORPM..........	Office of Research Program Management [*Environmental Protection Agency*] (GFGA)
ORPM..........	Orthorhythmic Pacemaker [*Medicine*] (STED)
OrPMB........	Multnomah School of the Bible, Portland, OR [*Library symbol Library of Congress*] (LCLS)
OrPML.........	Multnomah County Law Library, Portland, OR [*Library symbol Library of Congress*] (LCLS)
OrPNA........	Northwest Association of Private Colleges and Universities, Microform Center, Portland, OR [*Library symbol Library of Congress*] (LCLS)
OrPNR	Northwest Regional Educational Laboratory, Information Center Library, Portland,OR [*Library symbol Library of Congress*] (LCLS)
OrPO	Oregonian Publishing Co. Library, Portland, OR [*Library symbol Library of Congress*] (LCLS)
OrPOF.........	Oregon Odd Fellows Grand Lodge, Portland, OR [*Library symbol Library of Congress*] (LCLS)
OrPOj..........	Oregon Daily Journal, Portland, OR [*Library symbol*] [*Library of Congress*] (LCLS)
OrPoL	Hazel M. Lewis Library (Powers Public Library), Powers, OR [*Library symbol*] [*Library of Congress*] (LCLS)
ORPOS........	Office of Regulatory Policy, Oversight, and Supervision [*Federal Home Loan Bank Board*]
OrPP	Port of Portland Library, Portland, OR [*Library symbol Library of Congress*] (LCLS)
OrPPC.........	Portland Community College, Portland, OR [*Library symbol Library of Congress*] (LCLS)
OrPPCP.......	Precision Cast Parts, Portland, OR [*Library symbol*] [*Library of Congress*] (LCLS)
OrPPL.........	Pacific Power & Light Co., Portland, OR [*Library symbol Library of Congress*] (LCLS)
OrPPM........	Providence Medical Center, Portland, OR [*Library symbol Library of Congress*] (LCLS)
OrPPS.........	Portland Public School District, Portland, OR [*Library symbol Library of Congress*] (LCLS)
OrPr...........	Crook County Library, Prineville, OR [*Library symbol Library of Congress*] (LCLS)
OrPR...........	Reed College, Portland, OR [*Library symbol Library of Congress*] (LCLS)
OrPRAM.......	Oregon Royal Arch Masons Grand Chapter Archives, Portland, OR [*Library symbol Library of Congress*] (LCLS)
OrPrC..........	Crook County Library, Prineville, OR [*Library symbol*] [*Library of Congress*] (LCLS)

OrPrH.......... Pioneer Memorial Hospital Library, Prineville, OR [*Library symbol*] [*Library of Congress*] (LCLS)

OrPrK.......... Pilot Rock Public Library, Pilot Rock, OR [*Library symbol*] [*Library of Congress*] (LCLS)

OrPRP.......... Riverside Psychiatric Hospital, Portland, OR [*Library symbol Library of Congress*] (LCLS)

ORPS.......... Occurrence Reporting and Processing System [*Environmental science*] (COE)

ORPS.......... Overseas Return Placement System [*Military*]

OrPS.......... Portland State University, Portland, OR [*Library symbol Library of Congress*] (LCLS)

OrPSMA...... Saint Mary's Academy, Portland, OR [*Library symbol Library of Congress*] (LCLS)

OrPS-MI...... Metropolitan Instructional Support Laboratory, Portland State University, Portland, OR [*Library symbol*] [*Library of Congress*] (LCLS)

OrPStV......... Saint Vincent Hospital and Medical Center, Portland, OR [*Library symbol Library of Congress*] (LCLS)

ORPSU......... Organized Reserve Port Security Unit [*Military*]

OrPT............ Temple Beth Israel, Portland, OR [*Library symbol Library of Congress*] (LCLS)

OrPTC.......... Town Center Library at Tanasbourne, Portland, OR [*Library symbol Library of Congress*] (LCLS)

OrPto........... Port Orford Public Library, Port Orford, OR [*Library symbol Library of Congress*] (LCLS)

OrPU............ University of Portland, Portland, OR [*Library symbol Library of Congress*] (LCLS)

OrPUCA....... United States Court of Appeals, Portland, OR [*Library symbol*] [*Library of Congress*] (LCLS)

Or PUC Ops... Oregon Office of the Public Utilities Commissioner. Opinions and Decisions [*A publication*] (DLA)

OrPUDC....... United States District Court, Central Library, Portland, OR [*Library symbol*] [*Library of Congress*] (LCLS)

OrPV............ United States Veterans Administration Hospital, Portland, OR [*Library symbol Library of Congress*] (LCLS)

OrPW........... Western Evangelical Seminary, Portland, OR [*Library symbol Library of Congress*] (LCLS)

OrPWB......... Western Conservative Baptist Theological Seminary, Portland, OR [*Library symbol Library of Congress*] (LCLS)

OrPWP......... Warner Pacific College, Portland, OR [*Library symbol Library of Congress*] (LCLS)

OrPWS......... Western States Chiropractic College, Portland, OR [*Library symbol Library of Congress*] (LCLS)

OrPWsC....... West Slope Community Library, Portland, OR [*Library symbol Library of Congress*] (LCLS)

ORQ............. Norwalk, CT [*Location identifier FAA*] (FAAL)

ORQ............. Outstanding Performance Rating with Quality Step Increase [*Military*] (DNAB)

ORQMC....... Orderly Room Quartermaster-Corporal [*British military*] (DMA)

ORQMS....... Orderly Room Quartermaster-Sergeant [*British military*] (DMA)

ORR............. Oak Ridge Research Reactor [*ORNL*] (NRCH)

ORR............. Oak Ridge Reservation

ORR............. Office of Ready Reserve [*Army*]

ORR............. Office of Refugee Relief [*Department of Health and Human Services*]

ORR............. Office of Refugee Resettlement (USGC)

ORR............. Office of the Rail Regulator [*British*] (WA)

ORR............. Omnidirectional RADAR Range (IAA)

ORR............. Omnidirectional Radio Range (IAA)

ORR............. Onsager Reciprocal Relations [*Thermodynamics*]

ORR............. Operational Readiness Reporting

ORR............. Operational Readiness Review (NASA)

ORR............. Operational Ready Rate (MCD)

ORR............. Operations Requirements Review (NASA)

ORR............. Optical Ratio Reflector

ORR............. Orbital Rendezvous RADAR (AAG)

ORR............. Orroval Valley, Australia, Tracking Station [*NASA*] (NASA)

ORR............. Orthographic RADAR Restitutor

ORR............. Oudh and Rohilkand Railway Rifles [*British military*] (DMA)

ORR............. Overhaul Replacement Rate

ORR............. Owner's Risk Rates [*Shipping*]

ORR............. Red Rock Public Library, Ontario [*Library symbol National Library of Canada*] (NLC)

ORR............. Rogue Community College Library, Grants Pass, OR [*OCLC symbol*] (OCLC)

ORRA........... Orbit Semiconductor [*NASDAQ symbol*] (SAG)

ORRA........... Oriental Rug Retailers of America (EA)

ORRAS........ Optical Research Radiometrical Analysis System (IEEE)

ORRCAT...... Ridgetown College of Agricultural Technology, Ontario [*Library symbol National Library of Canada*] (NLC)

OrRed.......... Redmond Public Library, Redmond, OR [*Library symbol Library of Congress*] (LCLS)

OrRedDH..... Central Oregon District Hospital, Medical Library, Redmond, OR [*Library symbol Library of Congress*] (LCLS)

OrRedHS...... Redmond Senior High School, Redmond, OR [*Library symbol*] [*Library of Congress*] (LCLS)

OrRedOJ...... Obsidian Junior High School, Redmond, OR [*Library symbol*] [*Library of Congress*] (LCLS)

OrRedTE...... John Tuck Elementary School, Redmond, OR [*Library symbol*] [*Library of Congress*] (LCLS)

Or Rep......... Oregon Reports [*A publication*] (DLA)

Or Rev Stat... Oregon Revised Statutes [*A publication*] (DLA)

ORRMIS....... Oak Ridge Regional Modeling Information System

OrRoD.......... Douglas County Library, Roseburg, OR [*Library symbol Library of Congress*] (LCLS)

OrRoM.......... Douglas County Museum, Roseburg, OR [*Library symbol Library of Congress*] (LCLS)

OrRoMM....... Mercy Medical Center, Roseburg, OR [*Library symbol Library of Congress*] (LCLS)

OrRoU.......... Umpqua Community College, Roseburg, OR [*Library symbol Library of Congress*] (LCLS)

OrRoV.......... United States Veterans Administration Hospital, Roseburg, OR [*Library symbol Library of Congress*] (LCLS)

ORRR........... Oak Ridge Research Reactor [*Department of Energy*] (NRCH)

ORRRC......... Outdoor Recreation Resources Review Commission [*Terminated, 1962*] [*Department of the Interior*]

ORRT............ Operational Readiness and Reliability Test

ORRTA.......... Office of the Registrar of Restrictive Trading Agreements (PDAA)

ORRV............ Off-Road Recreation Vehicle

ORS............. Obligated Reserve Section [*Air Force*] (AFM)

ORS............. Oceanographic Research Ship

ORS............. Octahedral Research Satellite [*NASA*]

ORS............. Office for Research & Statistics [*American Library Association*]

ORS............. Office of Radiation Standards [*AEC*]

ORS............. Office of Regulatory Support [*Environmental Protection Agency*] (GFGA)

ORS............. Office of Rent Stabilization [*Functions transferred to Office of Defense Mobilization, 1953*]

ORS............. Office of Research and Statistics [*Social Security Administration*]

ORS............. Office of Revenue Sharing [*Department of the Treasury*]

ORS............. Official Relay Station [*Amateur radio*]

ORS............. Off-Site Repair and Support (MCD)

ORS............. Oil Recovery System

ORS............. Old Red Sandstone

ORS............. Olfactory Reference Syndrome [*Medicine*] (DMAA)

ORS............. Online Reference Service [*Thunder Bay Public Library*] [*Canada*] (OLDSS)

ORS............. Online Research Systems [*Information service or system*] (IID)

ORS............. On-Line Retrieval System [*Computer science*] (TELE)

ORS............. Operational Reactor Safeguards (DNAB)

ORS............. Operational Research Society [*British*]

ORS............. Operational Research Station [*Air Ministry*] [*British World War II*]

ORS............. Optimal Real Storage (CMD)

ORS............. Oral Electrolyte Solution [*Nutrition*]

ORS............. Oral Rehydration Salts [*or Solution*]

ORS............. Oral Surgeon

ORS............. Orbital Refueling System [*NASA*] (NASA)

ORS............. Orbiter Refueling System [*NASA*]

ORS............. Orbiter Relay Simulator [*NASA*]

ORS............. Orbiting Research Satellite [*NASA*]

ORS............. Orderly Room Sergeant [*British*]

ORS............. Oregon Revised Statutes [*A publication*] (AAGC)

ORS............. Organization Rating Scale

ORS............. Originating Register Sender

ORS............. Orpheus Island [*Australia Airport symbol*]

ORS............. Orsett [*England*]

ORS............. Orsina Resources [*Vancouver Stock Exchange symbol*]

ORS............. Orthopedic Research Society (EA)

ORS............. Orthopedic Surgeon

ORS............. Orthopedic Surgery (STED)

ORS............. Oscillographic Recording System

ORS............. Others

ORS............. Outboard Rotating Shield

ORS............. Outstanding Requisition System (DNAB)

ORS............. Oval Ring Seal

ORS............. Overlay Reproducer System

ORS............. Ownership Reporting System [*Securities and Exchange Commission*] (GFGA)

ORS............. Owner's Risk of Shifting [*Shipping*]

ORS............. Oxfordshire Record Society [*British*] (DBA)

ORS............. Research and Development Library, Shaw Industries, Rexdale, Ontario [*Library symbol National Library of Canada*] (BIB)

ORSA........... Operations Research Society of America (EA)

OR/SA.......... Operations Research/Systems Analysis [*Army*]

ORSA........... Order of Recollects of St. Augustine

ORSA........... Oregon Revised Statutes Annotated [*A publication*]

ORSA........... Osteoclast Resorption Stimulating Activity (DMAA)

OrSa............ Salem Public Library, Salem, OR [*Library symbol Library of Congress*] (LCLS)

OrSaC.......... Chemeketa Community College, Salem, OR [*Library symbol Library of Congress*] (LCLS)

ORSAC......... Oak Ridge Systems Analysis Code

ORSAC......... Open Road ™See America∫ Club [*Defunct*] (EA)

OR/SAEC...... Operations Research/Systems Analysis Executive Course [*Army*]

OrSaGS........ Church of Jesus Christ of Latter-Day Saints, Genealogical Society Library, SalemBranch, Salem, OR [*Library symbol Library of Congress*] (LCLS)

OrSaH.......... Salem Hospital, Salem, OR [*Library symbol Library of Congress*] (LCLS)

OrSaMHi...... Marion County Historical Society, Salem, OR [*Library symbol*] [*Library of Congress*] (LCLS)

OrSan........... Sandy Public Library, Sandy, OR [*Library symbol Library of Congress*] (LCLS)

ORSANCO.... Ohio River Valley Water Sanitation Commission

OrSanHS....... Sandy Union High School, Sandy, OR [*Library symbol Library of Congress*] (LCLS)

ORSAR......... Official Reports, South African Republic [*A publication*] (DLA)

OrSaSH........ Oregon State Hospital, Medical Library, Salem, OR [*Library symbol*] [*Library of Congress*] (LCLS)

OrSaT .... Oregon Department of Transportation, Salem, OR [*Library symbol*] [*Library of Congress*] (LCLS)
OrSaW .... Willamette University, Salem, OR [*Library symbol Library of Congress*] (LCLS)
OrSaWB .... Western Baptist Bible College, Salem, OR [*Library symbol Library of Congress*] (LCLS)
OrSaW-L ...... Willamette University, Law Library, Salem, OR [*Library symbol Library of Congress*] (LCLS)
Or SB Bull ... Oregon State Bar. Bulletin [*A publication*] (ILCA)
ORS(BC) ...... Operational Research Section (Bomber Command) [*British World War II*]
Or-SC .... Oregon Supreme Court, Salem, OR [*Library symbol Library of Congress*] (LCLS)
ORSDI .... Oak Ridge Selective Dissemination of Information [*Department of Energy*] (NASA)
ORSE .... Operational Reactor Safeguard Examination (NVT)
ORSE .... Otherwise
ORSEP .... Operational Reentry Systems Evaluation Program (SAA)
ORSER .... Office for Remote Sensing of Earth Resources [*Pennsylvania State University*] [*Research center*]
OrSh .... Sherwood Public Library, Sherwood, OR [*Library symbol Library of Congress*] (LCLS)
OrShe .... Sheridan Public Library, Sheridan, OR [*Library symbol Library of Congress*] (LCLS)
OrSi .... Sisters Public Library, Sisters, OR [*Library symbol Library of Congress*] (LCLS)
OrSibyll .... Sibylline Oracles (Pseudepigrapha) (BJA)
OrSil .... Silverton Public Library, Silverton, OR [*Library symbol Library of Congress*] (LCLS)
ORSIP .... Office of Research, Statistics, and International Policy [*Later, ORS*] [*Social Security Administration*] (IID)
ORSL .... Order of the Republic of Sierra Leone
ORSoc .... Operational Research Society [*British*] (DBA)
ORSociety... Operational Research Society (ACII)
ORSON .... Orient, Spell Out, Nail Down [*Method for organizing and communicating information, proposed by Barry Tarshis in his book "How to Write without Pain"*]
ORSORT ...... Oak Ridge School of Reactor Technology [*Department of Energy*]
OrSp .... Springfield Public Library, Springfield, OR [*Library symbol Library of Congress*] (LCLS)
ORS(S) .... Operational Research Section (Singapore) [*Military*]
ORSSA .... Office of Regulatory Support and Scientific Analysis [*Environmental science*] (COE)
OrSt .... Stayton Public Library, Stayton, OR [*Library symbol Library of Congress*] (LCLS)
OR St B ...... Operation Rescue Saint Bernard [*Test given to Junior Woodchucks in Donald Duck comic by Carl Barks*]
Or St B Bull... Oregon State Bar Bulletin [*A publication*] (DLA)
OrStbM .... Mount Angel College, Mount Angel Abbey, St. Benedict, OR [*Library symbol Library of Congress*] (LCLS)
OrStf .... Stanfield Public Library, Stanfield, OR [*Library symbol*] [*Library of Congress*] (LCLS)
OrSthDH ...... Columbia District Hospital, Medical Library, St. Helens, OR [*Library symbol Library of Congress*] (LCLS)
ORSTOM ...... Office de la Recherche Scientifique et Technique Outre-Mer (USDC)
ORSV .... Odontoglossum Ringspot Virus [*Plant pathology*]
ORT .... Northway, AK [*Location identifier FAA*] (FAAL)
ORT .... Oak Ridge [*Tennessee*] [*Seismograph station code, US Geological Survey*] (SEIS)
ORT .... Object Relations Technique [*Psychology*]
ORT .... Ooty Radio Telescope [*India*]
ORT .... Operating Room Technician [*Medicine*]
ORT .... Operationally Ready Time
ORT .... Operational Readiness Test
ORT .... Operational Readiness Training [*Army*]
ORT .... Optical Relay Tube (MCD)
ORT .... Optical Rotary Table
ORT .... Optimum Resolution Technique
ORT .... Oral Rehydration Therapy
ORT .... Orbital Rendezvous Technique (AAG)
ORT .... Orbit Readiness Test [*NASA*] (NASA)
ORT .... Order of Railroad Telegraphers [*Later, Transportation-Communication Employees Union*] (EA)
ORT .... Ordnance Repair Truck [*British*]
ORT .... Organization for Rehabilitation through Training [*Acronym is used in names of several Jewish social welfare organizations*]
ORT .... Orient-Avia [*Former USSR*] [*FAA designator*] (FAAC)
ORT .... Original Running Time [*Movies*] (CDAI)
Ort .... Ortho Diagnostics
ORT .... Overhaul RADAR Technology
ORT .... Overland RADAR Technology (MCD)
ORT .... Registered Occupational Therapist (STED)
ORTA .... Office of Research and Technology Applications [*Berkeley, CA*] [*Lawrence Berkeley Laboratory*] [*Department of Energy*] (GRD)
ORTA .... Office of Research and Technology Applications [*Army*] (RDA)
ORTA .... Office of Research and Technology Applications [*Gaithersburg, MD*] [*National Institute of Standards and Technology*] (GRD)
ORTA .... Optical Relay Tube Assembly (MCD)
ORTAG .... Operations Research Technical Assistance Group [*Army*] (PDAA)
ORTAI .... Orbit-to-Air Intercept (IAA)
ORTC .... Organized Reserve Training Center [*Military*]
ORTC .... Ortec International, Inc. [*NASDAQ symbol*] (SAG)
ORTC .... Ortec Intl. [*NASDAQ symbol*] (TTSB)
ORTC .... Ortec Intl. Wrrt'B' [*NASDAQ symbol*] (TTSB)

ORT/CTL ...... Operational Readiness Training - Combat Training Launch [*Military*] (SAA)
ORTCW .... Ortec Intl. Wrrt'A' [*NASDAQ symbol*] (TTSB)
ORTE .... Operational Readiness Training Equipment [*Military*] (SAA)
ORTEC .... Oak Ridge Technical Enterprises Corp.
OR tech .... Operating Room Technician (DAVI)
OrtecInt. .... Ortec International, Inc. [*Associated Press*] (SAG)
Ortel .... Ortel Corp. [*Associated Press*] (SAG)
ORTF .... Office de la Radio et de la Television Francaise [*State-owned radio and television network*] [*France*]
ORTF .... Office de Radiodiffusion-Television Francaise [*National Broadcasting Organization*] [*France*] (NTCM)
ORTF .... Organization Radio Television France (IAA)
ORTH .... Orthodox
Orth .... Orthodox (WDAA)
ORTH .... Orthography
ORTH .... Orthopedic
ORTH .... Orthopedic Technology, Inc. [*NASDAQ symbol*] (SAG)
Orthfx. .... Orthofix International [*Associated Press*] (SAG)
orthg .... Orthogonals (VRA)
Ort Hist .... Ortolan's History of the Roman Law [*A publication*] (DLA)
Orthlog .... Orghologic Corp. [*Associated Press*] (SAG)
ORTHO .... American Orthopsychiatric Association (EA)
ORTHO .... Orthochromatic [*Photography*] (ROG)
ORTHO .... Orthopedic
Orthodon ..... Orthodontic Centers of America, Inc. [*Associated Press*] (SAG)
ORTHOG ...... Orthagonal
ORTHOG ...... Orthogonal (NASA)
Ortho-K .... Orthokeratology [*Medicine*]
orthop .... Orthopnea [*Medicine*] (DAVI)
orthopod ...... Orthopedist [*Orthopedic Physician*] (DAVI)
OrthopT .... Orthopedic Technology, Inc. [*Associated Press*] (SAG)
OrTig .... Tigard Public Library, Tigard, OR [*Library symbol Library of Congress*] (LCLS)
Ort Inst .... Ortolan's Justinian's Institutes [*A publication*] (DLA)
OrtInt .... Ortec International, Inc. [*Associated Press*] (SAG)
ORTL .... Ortel Corp. [*NASDAQ symbol*] (SAG)
ORTN .... Officie Radiodiffusion Television du Niger [*Radio and television network*] [*Niger*]
ORTO .... Olympics Radio and Television Organization [*Organisme de Radio-Television des Olympiques*] [*Canada*]
ORTP .... Operational Readiness Training Program [*Military*] (AABC)
Or TR .... Oregon Tax Reporter [*A publication*] (DLA)
Or T Rep ...... Oregon Tax Reporter [*A publication*] (ILCA)
Or T Rep. ..... Orleans Term Reports [*1, 2 Martin*] [*Louisiana*] [*A publication*] (DLA)
Ort Rom Law... Ortolan's History of the Roman Law [*A publication*] (DLA)
ORTS .... Operational Readiness Test System [*Military*] (CAAL)
ORTS .... Optional Residential Telephone Service [*Telecommunications*] (TEL)
ORTT .... Operational Readiness Training Test [*Army*] (AABC)
ORTT .... Overreaching Transfer Trip (IAA)
ORTU .... Organized Reserve Training Unit [*Military*]
OrTua .... Tualatin Public Library, Tualatin, OR [*Library symbol Library of Congress*] (LCLS)
ORTUAG ...... Organized Reserve Training Unit, Vessel Augmentation [*Military*]
OrTuaM .... Meridian Park Hospital, Medical Library, Tualatin, OR [*Library symbol Library of Congress*] (LCLS)
ORTUAM ...... Organized Reserve Training Unit, Administration of Mobilization [*Military*]
ORTUAV ...... Organized Reserve Training Unit, Aviation Support [*Military*]
ORTUEL .... Organized Reserve Training Unit, Electronics [*Military*]
ORTUF .... Organized Reserve Training Unit, Coastal Force [*Military*]
ORTUPS ...... Organized Reserve Training Unit, Port Security [*Military*]
ORTUPS(O)... Organized Reserve Training Unit, Port Security (Operational) [*Military*]
ORTUR .... Organized Reserve Training Unit, Rescue Coordination Center [*Military*]
OrTW .... Wasco County Library, The Dalles, OR [*Library symbol Library of Congress*] (LCLS)
ORTX .... Ortner Air Service [*Air carrier designation symbol*]
ORU .... On-Line Replacement Unit [*Computer science*] (MCD)
ORU .... Operational Readiness Unit
ORU .... Optical Reference Unit
ORU .... Optimal Replaceable Unit (IAA)
ORU .... Oral Roberts University [*Oklahoma*]
ORU .... Orange & Rockland Utilities, Inc. [*NYSE symbol*] (SPSG)
ORU .... Orange/Rockland Util [*NYSE symbol*] (TTSB)
ORU .... Orbital Replaceable Unit (SSD)
ORU .... Orbital Replacement Unit (MCD)
oru .... Oregon [*MARC country of publication code Library of Congress*] (LCCP)
ORU .... Organization for Rebirth of Ukraine (EA)
ORU .... Oruro [*Bolivia*] [*Airport symbol*] (AD)
ORU .... Other than Ship or Squadron Reinforcement Unit [*Naval Reserve*] (DNAB)
ORU .... Russell Branch, Russell Township Public Library, Ontario [*Library symbol National Library of Canada*] (BIB)
OrU .... University of Oregon, Eugene, OR [*Library symbol Library of Congress*] (LCLS)
ORU .... University of Oregon Library, Eugene, OR [*OCLC symbol*] (OCLC)
OrU-C .... University of Oregon, Computing Center, Eugene, OR [*Library symbol Library of Congress*] (LCLS)
OrU-D .... University of Oregon, Dental School, Portland, OR [*Library symbol Library of Congress*] (LCLS)
ORUEF .... Oral Roberts University Educational Fellowship (EA)
ORUFE .... Operational Research Unit, Far East

OrUk .... Ukiah Public Library, Ukiah, OR [*Library symbol*] [*Library of Congress*] (LCLS)
OrU-L .... University of Oregon, Law Library, Portland, OR [*Library symbol Library of Congress*] (LCLS)
OrU-M .... University of Oregon, Medical School, Portland, OR [*Library symbol Library of Congress*] (LCLS)
OrUma .... Umatilla Public Library, Umatilla, OR [*Library symbol*] [*Library of Congress*] (LCLS)
OrUmaH .... Umatilla Hospital, Umatilla, OR [*Library symbol*] [*Library of Congress*] (LCLS)
OrUmH .... Umatilla Hospital, Umatilla, OR [*Library symbol Library of Congress*] (LCLS)
OrUn .... Carnegie Public Library, Union, OR [*Library symbol Library of Congress*] (LCLS)
O/RUNN .... Overrunning [*Automotive engineering*]
OrU-O .... University of Oregon, Ocean and Coastal Law Center, Eugene, OR [*Library symbol*] [*Library of Congress*] (LCLS)
OrU-Or .... University of Oregon, Oriental Museum, Portland, OR [*Library symbol Library of Congress*] (LCLS)
ORUP .... Ocean Resource Utilization Program (ASF)
ORUS .... Official Register of the United States
OrU-S .... University of Oregon, Science Division Library, Eugene, OR [*Library symbol Library of Congress*] (LCLS)
ORuss .... Old Russian [*Language*] (BARN)
OrV .... Fern Ridge Community Library, Veneta, OR [*Library symbol Library of Congress*] (LCLS)
ORV .... Noorvik [*Alaska*] [*Airport symbol*] (OAG)
ORV .... Oceanographic Research Vessel
ORV .... Ocean Range Vessel [*Air Force*]
ORV .... Off-Road Vehicle
ORV .... Orbital Reentry Vehicle [*NASA*] (IAA)
ORV .... Orbital Rescue Vehicle [*NASA*] (KSC)
ORV .... Orbital Return Vehicle [*NASA*] (IAA)
ORV .... Oroville [*California*] [*Seismograph station code, US Geological Survey*] (SEIS)
ORVAT .... Organizational Vehicle Automatic Tester
ORVC .... River Valley Community Library, Ontario [*Library symbol National Library of Canada*] (NLC)
ORVID .... Online X-ray Evaluation over Video-Display Including Documentation (PDAA)
ORVR .... On-Board Refueling Vapor Recovery [*Automotive engineering*]
ORVX .... OraVax, Inc. [*NASDAQ symbol*] (SAG)
ORW .... Norwich, CT [*Location identifier FAA*] (FAAL)
ORW .... Orange Walk [*British Honduras*] [*Airport symbol*] (AD)
ORW .... Orwell Resources Ltd. [*Vancouver Stock Exchange symbol*]
ORW .... Orwex [*Poland ICAO designator*] (FAAC)
ORW .... Outstanding Resource Waters [*Water quality standards*] [*Environmental Protection Agency*]
ORW .... Owner's Risk of Becoming Wet [*Shipping*]
ORW .... Raymond Walters General and Technical College, Blue Ash, OH [*OCLC symbol*] (OCLC)
OrWe .... Weston Public Library, Weston, OR [*Library symbol*] [*Library of Congress*] (LCLS)
OrWel .... West Linn Public Library, West Linn, OR [*Library symbol Library of Congress*] (LCLS)
OrWelH .... West Linn High School, West Linn, OR [*Library symbol Library of Congress*] (LCLS)
ORWG .... Operational Requirements Working Group (DOMA)
ORWH .... Office of Research on Women's Health [*National Institutes of Health*]
OrWi .... Willamina Public Library, Willamina, OR [*Library symbol Library of Congress*] (LCLS)
ORWISE .... Otherwise (ROG)
OrWo .... Woodburn Public Library, Woodburn, OR [*Library symbol Library of Congress*] (LCLS)
ORWP .... Optical Radiation Weapon Program (AAG)
ORX .... Oriximina [*Brazil*] [*Airport symbol*] (AD)
ORX .... Oryx Aviation [*South Africa ICAO designator*] (FAAC)
ORX .... Oryx Energy Co. [*NYSE symbol*] (SPSG)
ORY .... Paris [*France*] Orly Airport [*Airport symbol*] (OAG)
Oryx .... Oryx Energy Co. [*Associated Press*] (SAG)
ORYX .... Oryx Technology [*NASDAQ symbol*] (TTSB)
ORYX .... Oryx Technology Corp. [*NASDAQ symbol*] (SAG)
OryxTc .... Oryx Technology Corp. [*Associated Press*] (SAG)
ORYXW .... Oryx Technology Wrrt [*NASDAQ symbol*] (TTSB)
ORZ .... Omnirange Zero (IAA)
ORZ .... Omnirange Zone
ORZ .... Orange Walk [*Belize*] [*Airport symbol Obsolete*] (OAG)
ORZ .... Outer Radiation Zone
OS .... Austrian Airlines [*ICAO designator*] (AD)
OS .... By Mouth [*Pharmacy*] (DAVI)
OS .... Obese Strain [*White leghorn*]
OS .... Object-Subject [*Education of the hearing-impaired*]
OS .... Oblique Sounding [*Telecommunications*] (OA)
OS .... Observation-Scouting Plane [*When first two letters in Navy designation*]
OS .... Observing Station [*Marine science*] (MSC)
OS .... Occupational Safety (DAVI)
OS .... Oceanic Society (EA)
OS .... Ocean Station [*Maps and charts*]
OS .... Octavian Society (EA)
OS .... Oculus Sinister [*Left Eye*] [*Ophthalmology*]
OS .... Odd Symmetric
OS .... Office of Systems [*NASA*] (KSC)
OS .... Office of the Secretary

OS .... Officers' Steward [*Ranking title*] [*British Women's Royal Naval Service*]
OS .... Office System
OS .... Official Station
OS .... Off Scale (IAA)
OS .... Off Screen [*or Stage*]
OS .... Offset
OS .... Ohio State Reports [*A publication*] (DLA)
OS .... Oil Solenoid
OS .... Oil Switch
OS .... Old Saxon [*Language, etc.*]
OS .... Old School
OS .... Old Series
OS .... Old Side
OS .... Old Standard [*Currency*] (ROG)
OS .... Old Style [*Calendar, previous to 1752*]
OS .... Old Style [*Printing*] (NTCM)
OS .... Omega Society [*Defunct*] (EA)
OS .... Omnibus Society [*British*]
OS .... One Shot
OS .... One Side
OS .... One-Stop [*Aviation*]
OS .... Only Son
os .... Only Son (WDAA)
OS .... On-Orbit Station [*NASA*] (MCD)
os .... On-Orbit Station [*NASA*] (NAKS)
OS .... On Sale
OS .... On Sample
OS .... On Schedule
O/S .... On Sea [*In place names*] [*British*] (ROG)
OS .... On Sheet (WGA)
OS .... On Side
OS .... On-Site
OS .... On Spot (ROG)
OS .... On Station [*Military*]
OS .... On Switch
OS .... Opening Snaps [*Cardiology*]
OS .... Operating Schedule [*Field stations*] (MCD)
OS .... Operating Software (MCD)
OS .... Operating System [*Computer science*] (BUR)
O/S .... Operational Assist Project/Shipborne Application
OS .... Operational Sequence (KSC)
OS .... Operational Sheets
OS .... Operational Specialist [*Navy*]
OS .... Operational Suitability
OS .... Operational Supplements [*Air Force*] (MCD)
OS .... Operation Sandstone [*Atomic weapons testing*]
OS .... Operation Smile (EA)
OS .... Operation Snapper [*Atomic weapons testing*]
OS .... Operations Specialist [*Navy*] (DNAB)
OS .... Operations Support [*Office of U.S. Foreign Disaster Assistance*]
OS .... Operation Suburbia [*Defunct*] (EA)
OS .... Operator's Set
OS .... Optical Scanning [*Computer science*]
OS .... Optical Society (NADA)
OS .... Optics Subsystem
OS .... Option Spreading [*Investment term*]
OS .... Oral Surgery
OS .... Oral Suspension [*Pharmacy*]
OS .... Orbiter CEI [*Contract End Item*] Specification [*NASA*] (NASA)
OS .... Order of Servites
OS .... Order Sheet
OS .... Ordinary Seaman [*British*]
OS .... Ordnance School [*Army*] (MCD)
OS .... Ordnance Services [*Military British*]
OS .... Ordnance Specifications [*Navy*]
OS .... Ordnance Survey
OS .... Oregon Steel Mills [*NYSE symbol*] (SPSG)
OS .... Organizational Source [*Online database field identifier*] [*Computer science*]
OS .... Organizations System (IAA)
OS .... Original Series
OS .... Ornamental Stitching (DNAB)
OS .... Oro Sellado [*Standard Gold*] [*Business term Spanish*]
O/S .... Orthopaedic Surgery [*Medical Officer designation*] [*British*]
OS .... Orthopedics (DAVI)
OS .... Orthopedic Surgery (DAVI)
OS .... Orton Society [*Later, ODS*] (EA)
OS .... Osgood-Schlatter's Disease [*Medicine*]
Os .... Osmium [*Chemical element*]
OS .... Osmotic Shock
OS .... Osteogenic Sarcoma [*Medicine*]
OS .... Osteosarcoma [*Oncology*]
OS .... Osteosclerosis [*Medicine*] (DAVI)
OS .... Other Side [*A publication*] (BRI)
OS .... Other Sources
OS .... Otherwise Specified (MSA)
OS .... Outer Sheath [*Botany*]
OS .... Outlaw Shark [*RADAR surveillance*] [*Naval Electronic Systems Command*]
OS .... Outline Square Condition [*Vision*]
O/S .... Out of Service (AFM)
O/S .... Out-of-Shot [*Photography*]
OS .... Out of Stock (NTCM)
OS .... Output Secondary [*Electronics*]

OS...............	Outside
OS...............	Outside Sentinel
OS...............	Outsize [*Of clothes*]
O/S.............	Outstanding
OS...............	Outstation (MCD)
OS...............	Out Stealing [*Baseball*]
OS...............	Overlong Sentence [*Used in correcting manuscripts, etc.*]
OS...............	Overscene [*Films, television, etc.*]
OS...............	Oversea [*Military*]
O/S.............	Overshipped (MCD)
OS...............	Oversize (AAG)
OS...............	Overspecificity [*Psychometrics*]
OS...............	Over-the-Horizon Targeting System (MCD)
OS...............	Over-the-Shoulder Cinematography (NTCM)
OS...............	Over the State [*Regarding distribution*]
OS...............	Own Ship [*Navy*] (CAAL)
OS...............	Oxygen Saturation (DB)
OS...............	Oxygen Sensor [*Automotive engineering*]
OS...............	Oxygen Service (DNAB)
OS...............	Sarnia Public Library, Ontario [*Library symbol National Library of Canada*] (NLC)
OS...............	Shell Development Co. [*Research code symbol*]
OS...............	Test Oscilloscope [*JETDS nomenclature*] [*Military*] (CET)
OS...............	Warder Public Library of Springfield and Clark County, Springfield, OH [*Library symbol Library of Congress*] (LCLS)
OS/2...........	Operating System 2 [*Computer science*]
OS 2d.........	Ohio State Reports, Second Series [*A publication*] (DLA)
OSA	Aero Astra [*Mexico ICAO designator*] (FAAC)
OSA	Augustinian Nuns of Contemplative Life (TOCD)
OSA	[*The*] Augustinians (TOCD)
osa..............	[*The*] Augustinians (TOCD)
OSA	Augustinian Sisters of Our Lady of Consolation (TOCD)
OSA	Congregation of Augustinian Sisters Servants of Jesus and Mary (TOCD)
OSA	Obstructive Sleep Apnea [*Medicine*]
OSA	Occupational Safety Aid
OSA	Office of Savings Associations [*Formerly, FHLIC*]
OSA	Office of Services to the Aging (DAVI)
OSA	Office of Special Activities (CINC)
OSA	Office of State Administration [*Australia*]
OSA	Office of the Secretary of the Army
OSA	Office of the Special Assistant to the Ambassador
OSA	Official Secrets Act [*British*]
OSA	Offshore Acquisition [*Army*] (AABC)
OSA	Oklahoma Statutes Annotated [*A publication*] (DLA)
OSA	Old South Arabic (BJA)
OSA	Old Style Antique [*British*]
OSA	Omnibus Society of America (EA)
OSA	Ontario Society of Artists [*Canada*] (BARN)
OSA	Open Systems Architecture [*Computer science*]
OSA	Operational Support Aircraft [*or Airlift*]
OSA	Operational Support Airlift [*Air Force*] (DOMA)
OSA	Operational Support Area
OSA	Operation Sciences Appliquees [*Quebec*]
OSA	Optical Society of America (EA)
OSA	Optimization by Simulated Annealing [*Mathematics*]
OSA	Order for Simple Alert (NATG)
OSA	Order of St. Anne [*Anglican religious community*]
OSA	Order of St. Augustine [*See also OFSA*] [*Rome, Italy*] (EAIO)
OSA	Order-Sorting Aperture [*Instrumentation*]
OSA	Ormec Serro Analyst (NITA)
OSA	Orthodox Society of America
osa..............	Osage [*MARC language code Library of Congress*] (LCCP)
OSA	Osaka [*Japan*] [*Seismograph station code, US Geological Survey*] (SEIS)
OSA	Osaka [*Japan*] [*Airport symbol*] (OAG)
OSA	Ossa Resources, Inc. [*Vancouver Stock Exchange symbol*]
OSA	Outfit Supply Activity (MCD)
OSA	Ovarian Sectional Area [*Medicine*] (DMAA)
OSA	Overseas Supply Agency [*Military*]
OSA	Overspenders Anonymous (EA)
OSa..............	Sabina Public Library, Sabina, OH [*Library symbol Library of Congress*] (LCLS)
OSA	Sisters of St. Augustine (TOCD)
OSA	Sisters of St. Rita (TOCD)
OSAA	Operational Satellite Active Archive [*Marine science*] (OSRA)
OSA (ABCMR)...	Office, Secretary of the Army (Army Board for Correction of Military Records)
OSAC	Orifice Spark Advance Control [*Valve*] [*Automotive technology*]
OSAC	Overseas Schools Advisory Council [*Department of State*] [*Washington, DC*] (EGAO)
OSAC	Overseas Security Advisory Council [*Department of State*] [*Washington, DC*] (EGAO)
OSACI	Ecumenical Study and Action Centre on Investment [*Netherlands*]
OSAD A & L...	Office of the Secretary of the Army for Development / Acquisition and Logistics
OSADBU	Office of Small and Disadvantaged Business Utilization (AAGC)
OS/AEL	Operating Space/Allowance Equipage List
OSAF	Office of the Secretary of the Air Force
OSAFO	Office of the Special Assistant for Field Operations [*Formerly, CORDS*] (VNW)
OSAFU	Oromo Students Association of Finfine Univeristy [*Ethiopia*]
OSAH	Health Sciences Library, Sudbury Algoma Hospital, Sudbury, Ontario [*Library symbol National Library of Canada*] (NLC)

OSAHRC	Occupational Safety and Health Review Commission [*Department of Labor*]
OSAI	Office of Systems Analysis and Information [*Department of Transportation*]
OSAIS	Oil Spillage Analytical and Identification Service [*Laboratory of the Government Chemist*] (PDAA)
OSAIS	Oil Spillage Analytical Information Service (NITA)
OSAK	OSI [*Open Systems Interconnection*] Applications Kernel [*Computer science*] (TNIG)
Osaka Pref Bull...	Osaka Prefecture. University. Bulletin [*A publication*] (DLA)
Osaka ULR...	Osaka University. Law Review [*A publication*] (DLA)
Osaka UL Rev...	Osaka University. Law Review [*A publication*] (DLA)
Osaka Univ L Rev...	Osaka University. Law Review [*Osaka, Japan*] [*A publication*] (DLA)
OSAL	Opening of Salivary [*Gland*]
OSal............	Salem Public Library, Salem, OH [*Library symbol Library of Congress*] (LCLS)
OSALC	Savant Lake Community Library, Ontario [*Library symbol National Library of Canada*] (NLC)
OSalK	Kent State University, Columbiana Regional Campus, Salem, OH [*Library symbol Library of Congress*] (LCLS)
OSALSAA	Office, Special Assistant for Logistical Support of Army Aircraft (AABC)
OSALSTC	Office, Special Assistant for Logistical Support of Tactical Communications (AABC)
OSAM	Overflow Sequential Access Method [*Computer science*]
OSAMM	Optimum Supply and Maintenance Model [*Army*] (RDA)
OSAMS	Synod Office, Diocese of Moosonee, Anglican Church of Canada, Schumacher, Ontario [*Library symbol National Library of Canada*] (NLC)
OSand..........	Sandusky Library Association, Sandusky, OH [*Library symbol Library of Congress*] (LCLS)
OS & CP Dec...	Ohio Superior and Common Pleas Decisions [*A publication*] (DLA)
OS & D	Over, Short, and Damaged [*Report*] [*Shipping*] (MSA)
OS & DR......	Over, Short, and Damaged Report [*Shipping*]
OS & FM	Office of Systems and Financial Management [*DoD*]
OS & RP	On-Board Spares and Repair Parts [*Navy*] (DNAB)
OS & TD	Ocean Science and Technology Division [*Office of Naval Research*] (DNAB)
OS & W	Oak, Sunk, and Weathered [*Construction*]
OS & Y	Outside Screw and Yoke
OSAP	Aleppo/Neirab [*Syria*] [*ICAO location identifier*] (ICLI)
OSAP	Ocean Surveillance Air Patrol (CINC)
OSAP	Ocean Survey Advisory Panel [*Marine science*] (MSC)
OSAP	Office of Substance Abuse Prevention [*Department of Agriculture*] (EGAO)
OSAP	Office Space Allocation Plan (MCD)
OSAPI	Operating System/Application Program Interface [*Computer science*]
OSAR	Operations Suitability Assessment Report (SSD)
OSAR	Optical Storage and Retrieval [*Computer science*]
OSAR	Overhead Systems Apprearance Research (IAA)
OSarS	Southern State Community College, Sardinia, OH [*Library symbol Library of Congress*] (LCLS)
OSART	Operational Safety Review Team [*International Atomic Energy Agency*]
OSAS	Obstructive Sleep Apnea Syndrome [*Medicine*] (DMAA)
OSAS	Ohio Social Acceptance Scale (EDAC)
OSAS	Open Systems Accounting Software [*Computer science*]
OSAS	Overseas Service Aid Scheme
OSASF	Overseas Supply Agency, San Francisco [*Military*] (CINC)
OSASN	Office of Special Assistant, Secretary of the Navy
OSAT	Office for the Study of Automotive Transportation [*Department of Transportation*]
OSAT	Office of the Special Assistant for Training [*Army*] (RDA)
OSAT	Optical Sensor and Tracker
OSAT	Optimized Sustained Action Technology (DB)
OSATA	Order of Saint Andrew the Apostle (EA)
OSAY	Outside Screw and Yoke (IAA)
OSB	Benedictine Congregation of Our Lady of Monte (TOCD)
OSB	Benedictine Monks (TOCD)
osb.............	Benedictine Monks, Olivetan Benedictines, Sylvestrine Benedictines (TOCD)
OSB	Benedictine Nuns (TOCD)
OSB	Benedictine Nuns of the Congregation of Solesmes (TOCD)
OSB	Benedictine Nuns of the Primitive Observance (TOCD)
OSB	Benedictine Sisters (TOCD)
OSB	Benedictine Sisters of Liberty (TOCD)
OSB	Benedictine Sisters of Pontifical Jurisdiction (TOCD)
OSB	Benedictine Sisters of Sacred Heart (TOCD)
OSB	Congregation of Jesus Crucified (TOCD)
OSB	Congregation of the Benedictine Sisters of Perpetual Adoration of Pontifical Jurisdiction (TOCD)
OSB	Congregation of the Benedictine Sisters of the Sacred Heart (TOCD)
OSB	Contemplative Sisters of St. Benedict (TOCD)
OSB	Missionary Benedictine Sisters (TOCD)
OSB	Ocean Sciences Board [*NASA*] (MSC)
OSB	Office of Savings Bonds [*Navy*]
OSB	Office of Surveillance and Biometrics [*U.S. Food and Drug Administration*]
OSB	Officer Selection Battery [*Military*]
OSB	Officer Selection Board
OSB	Olivetan Benedictine Sisters (TOCD)
OSB	One-Statement Banking (MHDB)
OSB	Operational Status BIT [*Binary Digit*]
OSB	Operations Stations Book [*Navy*]

OSB .... Operations Support Building [*NASA*] (KSC)
OSB .... Operative Society of Bricklayers [*A union*] [*British*]
OSB .... Orangeburg [*South Carolina*] [*Seismograph station code, US Geological Survey*] (SEIS)
OSB .... Orbital Solar Observation (IAA)
OSB .... Order of Shepherds of Bethlehem (EA)
OSB .... Order of the Stars and Bars [*Later, MOSB*] (EA)
OSB .... Ordinis Sancti Bernardi [*Order of St. Bernard*] [*Latin*] (ROG)
OSB .... Ordnance Supply Bulletin
OSB .... Ordo Sancti Benedicti [*Order of St. Benedict*] [*Roman Catholic religious order*]
OSB .... Oriented-Strand Board [*A plywood panel composition*]
OSB .... Osage Beach [*Missouri*] [*Airport symbol Obsolete*] (OAG)
OSB .... Overseas Brats
OSB .... Sauble Beach Branch, Bruce County Public Library, Ontario [*Library symbol National Library of Canada*] (NLC)
OSBA .... Outlet and Switch Box Association [*Defunct*] (EA)
OSBA Bull... Ohio State Bar Association. Bulletin [*A publication*] (DLA)
OSBC .... Old Second Bancorp [*NASDAQ symbol*] (TTSB)
OSBC .... Old Second Bancorp, Inc. [*NASDAQ symbol*] (SAG)
OSBCam ..... Camaldolese Benedictine Sisters (TOCD)
OSBCam ..... Camaldolese Hermits (TOCD)
osbcam ...... Camaldolese Hermits (TOCD)
OSBF .... Damascus [*Syria*] [*ICAO location identifier*] (ICLI)
OSBF .... OSB Financial [*NASDAQ symbol*] (SAG)
OSBF Fn .... OSB Finl Corp. [*NASDAQ symbol*] (TTSB)
OSB Fn ...... OSB Financial [*Associated Press*] (SAG)
OSBL .... Outside Battery Limits [*Chemical engineering*]
OSBM .... Morrison Library Outpost, Severn Bridge, Ontario [*Library symbol National Library of Canada*] (NLC)
OSBM .... Office of Space Biology and Medicine [*Proposed for NASA*]
osbm .... Order of St. Basil the Great (TOCD)
OSBM .... Ordo Sancti Basil Magni [*Order of St. Basil the Great*] [*Roman Catholic religious order*]
OSBM .... Sisters of the Order of St. Basil the Great (TOCD)
OSBN .... Osborn Communications [*NASDAQ symbol*] (TTSB)
OSBN .... Osborn Communications Corp. [*NASDAQ symbol*] (NQ)
Osborn........ Osborn Communications [*Associated Press*] (SAG)
Osborn........ Osborne Communications Corp. [*Associated Press*] (SAG)
OSBR .... Seeley's Bay Branch, Rideau Lakes Union Library, Ontario [*Library symbol National Library of Canada*] (BIB)
OSBRD........ Office of Small Business Research and Development [*National Science Foundation*] (GRD)
OSBS .... Oblate Sisters of the Blessed Sacrament [*Roman Catholic religious order*]
OSBT .... Officer Selection Battery Test [*Military*]
OSC .... Canonici Regulares Ordinis Sanctae Crucis [*Canons Regular of the Order of the Holy Cross*] [*Crosier Fathers*] [*Roman Catholic religious order*]
osc............. Canons Regular of the Order of the Holy Cross, Crosier Fathers (TOCD)
OSC .... Clan Grant No. 17, Order of Scottish Clans (EA)
OSC .... Clark County Technical Institute, Springfield, OH [*Library symbol Library of Congress*] (LCLS)
OSC .... Complete Operational Software [*Telecommunications*] (TEL)
OSC .... Oak Satellite Corp. (NITA)
OSC .... Obedience Stewards Club (EA)
OSC .... Objective Supply Capability [*Army*] (RDA)
OSC .... Oblate Spherical Coordinates
OSC .... Oblati Sancti Caroli [*Oblate Fathers of St. Charles*] [*Roman Catholic religious order*]
OSC .... Occupational Standards Council (AIE)
OSC .... Ocean Science Committee [*National Academy of Sciences/Ocean Affairs Board*] (NOAA)
OSC .... Ocean Sciences Center [*Memorial University of Newfoundland*] [*Canada*]
OSC .... Office of Space Communications [*NASA*] (BARN)
OSC .... Office of Special Counsel [*Federal agency*]
OSC .... Office of the Security Council
OSC .... Officer Specialty Code [*Army*] (INF)
OSC .... Offshore Survival Centre [*Robert Gordon's Institute of Technology*] [*British*] (CB)
OSC .... Ogden [*Utah*] Service Center [*IRS*]
O-SC .... Ohio Supreme Court, Columbus, OH [*Library symbol Library of Congress*] (LCLS)
OSC .... One Shoe Crew [*An association*] (EA)
OSC .... On-Scene Commander [*Navy*] (NVT)
OSC .... On-Scene Coordinator [*Environmental Protection Agency*] (FFDE)
OSC .... On-Site Safety Committee (IAA)
OSC .... Ontario Securities Commission (HGAA)
OSC .... Operational Simulator Console
OSC .... Operational Summary Console
OSC .... Operational Support Center (NRCH)
OSC .... Operational Support Chart [*Nuclear energy*] (NUCP)
OSC .... Operational Switching Cabinet
OSC .... Operations Sequence Chart (MCD)
OSC .... Operator Services Complex [*Telecommunications*] (TEL)
OSC .... Optical Sciences Center [*University of Arizona*] [*Research center*] (RCD)
OSC .... Optical Signature Code
OSC .... Optical String Switch Controller (NITA)
OSC .... Options Selection Committee (COE)
OSC .... Orangeburg [*South Carolina*] [*Seismograph station code, US Geological Survey Closed*] (SEIS)
OSC .... Orbital Sciences Corp.

OSC .... Orbit Shift Coil
OSC .... Order of St. Clare [*Roman Catholic women's religious order*]
OSC .... Order to Show Cause
OSC .... Ordnance Store Corps [*British military*] (DMA)
OSC .... Ordnance Systems Command [*Formerly, Bureau of Naval Weapons; later, Naval Sea Systems Command*]
OSC .... Oregon State College [*Later, OSU*]
OSC .... Organic Solderability Coating [*Electronics*] (AAEL)
OSC .... Organic Sulfur Compound [*Organic chemistry*]
OSC .... Organizational Structure Code [*Air Force*] (AFIT)
OSC .... Organizational Supply Code [*Army*] (AABC)
OSC .... Oscillate [*or Oscillation, Oscillator, Oscillograph, Oscilloscope*] (KSC)
osc............. Oscillator (IDOE)
OSC .... Oscoda, MI [*Location identifier FAA*] (FAAL)
OSC .... Osmotically Sensitive Cell
OSC .... Outer Space Contact
OSC .... Out of Stock, Canceled [*Business term*]
OSC .... Output State Check [*Electronics*]
OSC .... Out, See Copy [*Proofreader's note*]
OSC .... Overlapping Spreading Centers [*Geology*]
OSC .... Overlap Slotted Container [*Packaging*]
OSC .... Overseas Settlement Committee [*World War I*] [*British*]
OSC .... Overseas Staff College [*British*]
OSC .... Overseas Supply Committee [*World War II*]
OSC .... Own Ship's Course [*Navy*]
OSC .... Oxidatively Solubilized Coal [*Fuel technology*]
OSC .... Oxygenated Sterol Compound [*Biochemistry*]
OSC .... Royal Clan, Order of Scottish Clans [*Later, Independent Order of Foresters*] (EA)
OSC .... Scugog Public Library, Ontario [*Library symbol National Library of Canada*] (NLC)
OSC .... Sisters of St. Clare (TOCD)
OSC .... Southern State Community College, Wilmington, OH [*OCLC symbol*] (OCLC)
OSCA .... Office of Saver and Consumer Affairs [*Federal Reserve Board*]
OSCA .... Office of Senior Citizens Affairs (NADA)
OSCA .... Office of State Corporate Affairs [*Western Australia*]
OSCA .... Optical Sensors Collaborative Association [*British*] (DBA)
OSCA .... Out-of-School Childcare Association (WDAA)
OSCAA .... Oil Spill Control Association of America [*Later, SCAA*] (EA)
oscam .... Camillian Fathers and Brothers (TOCD)
OS Cam ..... Order of St. Camillus [*Camillians*] [*Roman Catholic religious order*]
OSCAND .... Old Scandinavian [*Language, etc.*]
OSCAP .... Operating System Communication Application Program [*Computer science*]
OSCAR....... Observation Schedule and Records
OSCAR....... Online Serials Control at Ratcliffe (NITA)
OSCAR....... On-Site Computer Assisted Research [*Oscar, Inc.*] [*Information service or system*] (IID)
OSCAR....... Operating Sequence Control Array [*NASA*]
OSCAR....... Operational System Characteristics
OSCAR....... Operations, Scheduling, Control, and Reporting (MCD)
OSCAR....... Optically Scanned Character Automatic Reader [*Computer science*] (DIT)
OSCAR....... Optical Submarine Communications by Aerospace Relay
OSCAR....... Optimum Survival Containment and Recovery (AAG)
OSCAR....... Optimum System for the Control of Aircraft Retardation
OSCAR....... Optimum Systems Covariance Analysis Results (IEEE)
OSCAR....... Orbiting Satellite Carrying Amateur Radio [*Telecommunications*] (TEL)
OSCAR....... Order Status Control and Reporting [*Telecommunications*] (TEL)
OSCAR....... Oregon State Conversational Aid to Research [*Computer science*] (CSR)
OSCAR....... Organisation for Sickle Cell Anemia Research [*British*]
OSCAR....... Organization for Scientific Coordination in AIDS [*Acquired Immune Deficiency Syndrome*] Research, Inc. [*New York, NY*]
OSCAR....... Oscillogram Scan and Recorder System (PDAA)
OSCAR....... Overnight Statewide Customer Accounting Reporting (IAA)
OSCAR II .... Outside Cable Rehabilitation II [*Army*] (RDA)
OSCARS...... Order Status Control and Reporting System [*Telecommunications*]
OSCB .... College Bibliocentre, Scarborough, Ontario [*Library symbol National Library of Canada*] (BIB)
OSCCap ..... Capuchin Poor Clares (TOCD)
OSCCB .... On-Site Change Control Board [*Military*] (CAAL)
OSCCJA ...... Casimir, Jennings, and Appleby Public Library, St. Charles, Ontario [*Library symbol National Library of Canada*] (NLC)
OSCD .... Ohio Supreme Court Decisions, Unreported Cases [*A publication*] (DLA)
OSCD .... Ontario Securities Commission Decisions [*QL Systems Ltd.*] [*Information service or system Canada*] (CRD)
OSCE .... Office of Child Support Enforcement (USGC)
OSCE .... Office Statistique des Communautes Europeennes [*Statistical Office of the European Communities - EUROSTAT*] [*Commission of the European Communities*]
OSCE .... Organisation for Security and Co-Operation in Europe (ECON)
OSCER........ Offshore Survival Craft Emergency Radiotelephone [*Telecommunications*] (PDAA)
OSCF .... Operations Support Computing Facility (MCD)
OSCG .... Information Resource Centre, Consumers Gas, Scarborough, Ontario [*Library symbol National Library of Canada*] (NLC)
OSCG .... Oscillating
OSCG .... Oscillograph, String
OSCGRM..... Oscillogram [*Engineering*]
OSCH .... Schreiber Public Library, Ontario [*Library symbol National Library of Canada*] (NLC)

OSCILAB...... Ocean Science Laboratory [*Oceanography*]
OSCILLOSC.. Oscilloscope (IAA)
OSCL .... Operating System Control Language (NITA)
OSCL .... Own Ship's Centerline [*Navy*]
OSCMF .... Oxygen Scavenging Cell Membrane Fragment [*Biochemistry*]
OSCMIS ...... Operating and Support Costs Management Information System
(MCD)
OSC-MULT... Oscillator-Multiplier [*Telecommunications*] (TEL)
OSCO .... Organizational Source Code (NITA)
OSCOM .... Oslo Commission (EAIO)
OSCOT........ Overall Systems Combat Operability Test [*Navy*] (ANA)
OSCP .... Ocean Sediment Coring Program [*National Science Foundation*]
OSCP .... Oscilloscope (AAG)
OSCP .... Oscilloscope Panel
OSCPS........ Oxygen Supply and Cabin Pressurization Section [*Apollo*] [*NASA*]
OSCR .... Ocean Surface Current RADAR
OSCR .... Operating and Support Cost Reduction [*Army*]
OSCR .... Operations and Sustainment Cost Reduction Strategy (RDA)
OSCRL .... Operating System Command and Response Language
OSCRN........ Oil Screen
OSCUT .... Oil Spill Clean-Up Technology (ASF)
OSD .... Dow Chemical Co., Sarnia, Ontario [*Library symbol National Library
of Canada*] (NLC)
OSD .... Office of Standards Development [*Abolished*] [*Nuclear Regulatory
Commission*]
OSD .... Office of Student Detachment [*Navy*]
OSD .... Office of Systems Development [*Social Security Administration*]
OSD .... Office of the Secretary of Defense
OSD .... Officer Service Date [*Air Force*] (AFM)
OSD .... Officers Service Dress [*British military*] (DMA)
OSD .... Online System Drivers [*NCR Corp.*]
OSD .... On Screen Display [*Computer science*] (AAEL)
OSD .... Open Shelter Deck [*Shipping*] (DS)
OSD .... Open Software Description [*Computer science*]
OSD .... Operational Sea Vehicle Diagram (MCD)
OSD .... Operational Sequence Diagram (IEEE)
OSD .... Operational Support Directive [*Military*] (AFM)
OSD .... Operational Systems Development (MCD)
OSD .... Operations Subdirective
OSD .... Optical Scanning Device [*Computer science*]
OSD .... Ordinis Sancti Dominici [*Order of St. Dominic*] [*Latin*] (ROG)
OSD .... Ordnance Safing Device
OSD .... Ordnance Store Department [*British*] (ROG)
OSD .... Ordnance Supply Depot
OSD .... Osgood Semantic Differential [*Occupational therapy*]
OSD .... Ostersund [*Sweden*] [*Airport symbol*] (OAG)
OSD .... Out of Stock for the Duration [*Business term*] (DGA)
OSD .... Overseas Duty
OSD .... Overseas Settlement Department [*World War I*] [*British*]
OSD .... Overseas Standards Digest [*A publication*] (ADA)
OSD .... Overseas Supply Division [*Military*]
OSD .... Over, Short, and Damaged [*Report*] [*Shipping*] (MCD)
OSD .... Overside Drainage [*Medicine*] (DAVI)
OSD .... Own Ship's Distance [*Navy*] (MCD)
OSD .... Oxygen Selective Detector [*Chromatography*]
OSDA........... Oceanic System Development and Support [*FAA*] (TAG)
OSDBMC...... Office of the Secretary of Defense, Ballistic Missile Committee
OSDBU........ Office of Small and Disadvantaged Business Utilization [*See also
SDBU/CR*] [*Agency for International Development*]
OSD/CSD ..... Open Shelter Deck/Closed Shelter Deck [*Shipping*] (DS)
OSD/DSAA ... Office of the Secretary of Defense, Defense Security Assistance
Agency (MCD)
OSDH.......... Optical Shubnikhov-de Haas [*Effect*] (AAEL)
OSDH.......... Orbiter System Definition Handbook [*NASA*] (NASA)
OSDI .... Damascus/International [*Syria*] [*ICAO location identifier*] (ICLI)
OSDIDBAD... Office of the Secretary of Defense Identification Badge [*Military
decoration*] (GFGA)
OSDIdentBad... Office of the Secretary of Defense Identification Badge (AABC)
OSD/ISA....... Office of the Secretary of Defense for International Security Affairs
OSDIT .... Office of Software Development and Information Technology [*General
Services Administration*]
OSDIU.......... Over-the-Horizon Targeting System Digital Interface Unit
OSDM .... Optical Space-Division Multiplexing (EECA)
OSDMT........ Organization for the Support of Democratic Movement of Taiwan
(EA)
OSDOC........ Offshore Discharge of Container-Ships (RDA)
OSDOC........ Over-the-Shore Discharge of Cargo [*Navy*] (CAAL)
OS/DOS....... Operating System/Disk Operating System [*Software*]
OSDP.......... On-Site Data Processing [*or Processor*] [*NASA*]
OSDP.......... Operational System Development Program
OSDP.......... Operations System Development Program [*Marine science*] (OSRA)
OSD(PA & E)... Office of the Secretary of Defense for Program Analysis and
Evaluation (MCD)
OSDPT........ Optimization of Systems for Data Processing and Transmission
(PDAA)
OSDR.......... Oil Slick Detection RADAR
OSD-SA....... Office of the Secretary of Defense - Systems Analysis
OSDSAC...... Office of the Secretary of Defense, Scientific Advisory Committee
OSDT .... Damascus [*Syria*] [*ICAO location identifier*] (ICLI)
OSDU.......... Output Signal Distribution Unit (MCD)
OSDV.......... Oat Sterile Dwarf Virus [*Plant pathology*]
OSDZ.......... Deir Ez Zor [*Syria*] [*ICAO location identifier*] (ICLI)
OSE............. Bethel, AK [*Location identifier FAA*] (FAAL)
OSE............. Edwardsburg Township Public Library, Spencerville, Ontario [*Library
symbol National Library of Canada*] (BIB)

OSE......... Occupational Supplies and Equipment [*Red Cross*]
OSE......... Ocean and Science Engineering Inc.
OSE......... Oceanic Society Expeditions (EA)
OSE......... Office of Systems Engineering [*Social Security Administration*]
OSE......... Officer Scheduling the Exercise [*Navy*] (NVT)
OSE......... Olefin Strain Energy [*Organic chemistry*]
OSE......... Omniforce Spatial Environment (AAG)
OSE......... On Scene Endurance [*Environmental science*] (COE)
OSE......... Open Systems Environment [*Computer science*] (CIST)
OS/E......... Operating System/Environment [*Computer science*] (BYTE)
OSE......... Operational Security Evaluation (MCD)
OSE......... Operational Support Equipment
OSE......... Operation Status Equipment
OSE......... Orbital Sequence of Events [*NASA*] (IAA)
OSE......... Orbiter Support Equipment [*NASA*] (NASA)
OSE......... Order of the Star in the East [*A theosophical organization*]
OSE......... Organizational Support Equipment [*Army*]
OSE......... Osaka Stock Exchange [*Japan*]
OSE......... Osec Petroleum [*Vancouver Stock Exchange symbol*]
OSE......... Overall System Effectiveness (IAA)
OSE......... Overseas Security Eligibility [*DoD*]
OSE......... Salem Public Library, Salem, OR [*OCLC symbol*] (OCLC)
OSE......... Union Mondiale pour la Protection de la Sante des Populations
Juives et Oeuvres de Secours aux Enfants
OSEAP .... Oil Shale Environmental Advisory Panel [*Department of the Interior*]
OSEAS .... Ocean Sampling and Environmental Analysis System (PDAA)
O/SEAS .... Overseas
OSEC .... Office of the Secretary
OSEC .... Office Systems Education and Counseling (HGAA)
OSECCA ...... Old Sleepy Eye Collectors' Club of America (EA)
OSECY .... Office of the Secretary to the Staff [*NATO*] (NATG)
OSEDS .... Operational Support Equipment Design Specification
OSEE .... Optically Stimulated Electron Emission [*Also, PEE*] [*Physics*]
O/SEER .... Overseer
OSEH .... Order of St. Elizabeth of Hungary [*Anglican religious community*]
OSEM........... Office of Systems Engineering Management [*Department of
Transportation*]
OSEOS .... Operational Synchronous Earth Observatory Satellite
[*Telecommunications*] (TEL)
OSEP .... Office of Scientific and Engineering Personnel [*National Academy of
Sciences*] [*Information service or system*] (IID)
OSEP .... Office of Special Education Programs [*Also, SEP*] [*Department of
Education*]
OSERS.......... Office of Special Education and Rehabilitative Services [*Department
of Education*]
OSES .... Operations Systems Engineering Support (MCD)
OSESG......... Oil Sands Environmental Study Group [*Canada*]
OSF............. Bernardine Sisters of the Third Order of St. Francis (TOCD)
OSF............. Congregation of the Religious Brothers of the Third Order Regular of
St. Francis (TOCD)
OSF............. Congregation of the Sisters of the Third Order of St. Francis
Oldenburg, IN (TOCD)
OSF............. Congregation of the Third Order of St. Francis of Mary Immaculate,
Joliet IL (TOCD)
OSF............. Franciscan Brothers of Christ the King (TOCD)
osf............. Franciscan Brothers of Christ the King (TOCD)
osf............. Franciscan Brothers of the Third Order Regular (TOCD)
OSF............. Franciscan Missionaries of Our Lady (TOCD)
OSF............. Franciscan Missionary Brothers of the Sacred Heart of Jesus (TOCD)
osf............. Franciscan Missionary Brothers of the Sacred Heart of Jesus (TOCD)
OSF............. Franciscan Missionary Sisters for Africa (TOCD)
OSF............. Franciscan Missionary Sisters of Our Lady of Sorrows (TOCD)
OSF............. Franciscan Missionary Sisters of the Immaculate Conception (TOCD)
OSF............. Franciscan Sister, Daughters of the Sacred Hearts of Jesus and
Mary (TOCD)
OSF............. Franciscan Sisters of Allegany, New York (TOCD)
OSF............. [*The*] Franciscan Sisters of Baltimore (TOCD)
OSF............. Franciscan Sisters of Chicago (TOCD)
OSF............. Franciscan Sisters of Christian Charity (TOCD)
OSF............. Franciscan Sisters of Christ the Divine Teacher (TOCD)
OSF............. Franciscan Sisters of Little Falls, Minnesota (TOCD)
OSF............. Franciscan Sisters of Our Lady of Perpetual Help (TOCD)
OSF............. Franciscan Sisters of St. Paul (TOCD)
OSF............. Franciscan Sisters of the Immaculate Conception (TOCD)
OSF............. Franciscan Sisters of the Immaculate Conception and St. Joseph for
the Dying (TOCD)
OSF............. Franciscan Sisters of the Sacred Heart (TOCD)
OSF............. Franciscan Brothers of the Third Order Regular (TOCD)
OSF............. Hospital Sisters of the Third Order of St. Francis (TOCD)
OSF............. Missionary Franciscan Sisters of the Immaculate Conception (TOCD)
OSF............. Obtain Service From [*Navy*] (NVT)
OSF............. Ocean Simulation Facility [*Naval Coastal Systems Laboratory*]
(DNAB)
OSF............. Odd Side Flat
OSF............. Office of Space Flight [*NASA Washington, DC*] (NASA)
OSF............. Office Systems Family (HGAA)
OSF............. Open Software Foundation
OSF............. Open Systems Foundation
OSF............. Operational Service Fee (WDAA)
OSF............. Operation Support Facility [*National Weather Service*] (USDC)
OSF............. Optically-Shaped Film
OSF............. Order of St. Francis [*Franciscans*] [*Roman Catholic religious order*]
OSF............. Ordinary Shareholders Fund (WDAA)
OSF............. Ordnance Storage Facility (KSC)
OSF............. Organ System Failure [*Medicine*]

OSF............ Osaka Stock Futures [*Japan*] (ECON)
OSF............ Outer Spiral Fibers [*Ear anatomy*]
OSF............ Out of Stock, To Follow [*Business term*]
OSF............ Overgrowth Stimulating Factor [*Cancer cause*]
OSF............ Oxidation-Induced Stacking Fault (PDAA)
osf............ Religious Brothers of the Third Order Regular of St. Francis (TOCD)
OSF............ School Sisters of St. Francis (TOCD)
OSF............ School Sisters of the Third Order of St. Francis (Bethlehem, PA) (TOCD)
OSF............ School Sisters of the Third Order of St. Francis (Panhandle, TX) (TOCD)
OSF............ School Sisters of the Third Order of St. Francis (Pittsburgh, PA) (TOCD)
OSF............ Servants of the Holy Infancy of Jesus (TOCD)
OSF............ Sisters of Saint Francis, Clinton, Iowa (TOCD)
OSF............ Sisters of Saint Francis of Milvale, Pennsylvania (TOCD)
OSF............ Sisters of Saint Francis of the Providence of God (TOCD)
OSF............ Sisters of St. Francis (TOCD)
OSF............ Sisters of St. Francis of Christ the King (TOCD)
OSF............ Sisters of St. Francis of Penance and Christian Charity (TOCD)
OSF............ Sisters of St. Francis of Perpetual Adoration (TOCD)
OSF............ Sisters of St. Francis of Savannah, MO (TOCD)
OSF............ Sisters of St. Francis of the Congregation of Our Lady of Lourdes, Sylvania, Ohio (TOCD)
OSF............ Sisters of St. Francis of the Holy Cross (TOCD)
OSF............ Sisters of St. Francis of the Holy Eucharist (TOCD)
OSF............ Sisters of St. Francis of the Holy Family (TOCD)
OSF............ Sisters of St. Francis of the Immaculate Conception (TOCD)
OSF............ Sisters of St. Francis of the Immaculate Heart of Mary (Hankinson, North Dakota) (TOCD)
OSF............ Sisters of St. Francis of the Martyr St. George (TOCD)
OSF............ Sisters of St. Francis of the Third Order Regular (Williamsville, New York) (TOCD)
OSF............ Sisters of the Third Franciscan Order (TOCD)
OSF............ Sisters of the Third Order of St. Francis of Penance and Charity (TOCD)
OSF............ Sisters of the Third Order of St. Francis (Peoria, IL) (TOCD)
OSF............ Sisters of the Third Order Regular of St. Francis of the Congregation of Our Lady of Lourdes (TOCD)
OSF............ St. Francis Mission Community (TOCD)
OSF............ The Sisters of St. Francis of Assisi (TOCD)
OSF............ The Sisters of St. Francis of Philadelphia (TOCD)
OSFA.......... Office of Student Financial Assistance [*Department of Education*] (GFGA)
OSFA.......... Offshore Shrimp Fisheries Act of 1973
OSFAR........ Sturgeon Falls Branch of the Algonquin Regional Library System, Ontario [*Library symbol National Library of Canada*] (NLC)
OSFC.......... Fiberglas Canada, Inc., Sarnia, Ontario [*Library symbol National Library of Canada*] (NLC)
OSFC.......... Ordinis Sancti Francisci Capuccini [*Franciscan Capuchins*] [*Roman Catholic men's religious order*]
OSFCO........ Office of Solid Fuels Coordinator [*Military*] (DNAB)
OSFCSR...... Rideau Regional Centre, Ministry of Community and Social Services, Smiths Falls, Ontario [*Library symbol National Library of Canada*] (NLC)
OSFCW....... Office of Solid Fuels Coordinator for War [*World War II*]
OSFD.......... Office of Space Flight Development [*Obsolete NASA*]
OSFI........... Office of the Superintendent of Financial Institutions [*Department of Insurance*] [*Ottawa, ON*] [*Information service or system*] (IID)
OSFI........... Open Steel Flooring Institute [*Defunct*]
OSFM.......... Office of Spacecraft and Flight Missions [*NASA*]
OSFP.......... Office of Space Flight Programs [*Obsolete NASA*]
OSFS.......... Oblates of St. Francis de Sales (TOCD)
osfs........... Oblates of St. Francis de Sales (TOCD)
OSFS.......... Oblati Sancti Francisci Salesii [*Oblate Fathers or Sisters of St. Francis of Sales*] [*Roman Catholic religious orders*]
OSFT.......... ObjectSoft Corp. [*NASDAQ symbol*] (SAG)
OSG........... Occupations Study Group [*British*]
OSG........... Office of Sea Grant [*National Oceanic and Atmospheric Administration*]
OSG........... Office of the Secretary General [*United Nations*]
OSG........... Office of the Solicitor General [*Department of Justice*]
OSG........... Office of the Surgeon General [*of Public Health Service; later, absorbed by office of Assistant Secretary for Health and Scientific Affairs*]
OSG........... Operand Select Gate [*Computer science*]
OSG........... Operations Support Group [*Nuclear energy*] (NRCH)
OSG........... Organization and Staffing Guide [*Department of Labor*] (OICC)
OSG........... Osphradial Ganglion [*In mollusks*]
OSG........... Otosclerosis Study Group (EA)
OSG........... Overseas Shipldg [*NYSE symbol*] (TTSB)
OSG........... Overseas Shipholding Group, Inc. [*NYSE symbol*] (SPSG)
OSG........... South Gillies Library, Ontario [*Library symbol National Library of Canada*] (BIB)
OSGB.......... Orchid Society of Great Britain (EAIO)
OSGD.......... Office of Sea Grant Development [*National Oceanic and Atmospheric Administration*] (MSC)
OSGLI......... Office of Servicemen's Group Life Insurance
OSGP.......... Office of Sea Grant Programs [*National Oceanic and Atmospheric Administration*]
OSGR.......... Oscillator Single Gain Region (PDAA)
OSGS.......... Office of the Secretary of the General Staff
OSGS.......... Stittsville Branch, Goulbourn Township Public Library, Ontario [*Library symbol National Library of Canada*] (NLC)

OSH............ Community Hospital of Springfield, Springfield, OH [*Library symbol Library of Congress*] (LCLS)
OSH............ National Institute for Occupational Safety and Health, Cincinnati, OH [*OCLC symbol*] (OCLC)
OSH............ Occupational Safety and Health [*Department of Labor*]
OSH............ Office on Smoking and Health Database [*Centers for Disease Control*] [*Information service or system*] (CRD)
OSH............ Omni Singula Hora [*Every Hour*] [*Pharmacy*]
OSH............ Ordo Sancti Hieronymi [*Hieronymites*]
OSH............ Oshawa Group Ltd. [*Toronto Stock Exchange symbol*]
OSH............ Oshima [*Japan*] [*Seismograph station code, US Geological Survey*] (SEIS)
OSH............ Oshkosh [*Wisconsin*] [*Airport symbol*] (OAG)
OSH............ Oshman's Sporting Gds [*AMEX symbol*] (TTSB)
OSH............ Oshman's Sporting Goods, Inc. [*AMEX symbol*] (SAG)
OSH............ Own Ship's Heading [*Navy*]
OSh............ Shaker Heights Public Library, Shaker Heights, OH [*Library symbol Library of Congress*] (LCLS)
OSH............ Shelburne Public Library, Ontario [*Library symbol National Library of Canada*] (NLC)
OSHA.......... Occupational Safety and Health Act [*1970*]
OSHA.......... Occupational Safety and Health Administration [*Department of Labor*] [*Washington, DC*]
OSHA.......... Occupational Safety Hazards Act (AAEL)
OSHA.......... Office of Special Housing Assistance [*HUD*]
Oshap......... OSHAP Technologies Ltd. [*Associated Press*] (SAG)
OSHB.......... One-Sided Height Balanced [*Telecommunications*]
OshB.......... Oshkosh B'Gosh, Inc. [*Associated Press*] (SAG)
OSHB.......... Sheshegwaning Band Public Library, Ontario [*Library symbol National Library of Canada*] (NLC)
OSHC.......... Orchard Supply Hardware Stores Corp. [*NASDAQ symbol*] (SAG)
OSHC.......... Outside School Hours Care
OSHC.......... Overseas Student Health Coverage
OSH Cas..... Occupational Safety and Health Cases [*A publication*] (DLA)
OSHD.......... Occupational Safety and Health Decisions [*A publication*] (DLA)
OSH Dec..... Occupational Safety and Health Decisions [*A publication*] (DLA)
OSheIS........ Sacred Heart Seminary, Shelby, OH [*Library symbol Library of Congress*] (LCLS)
OSHI.......... Occupational, Safety, and Health Institute [*University of Houston*] [*Research center*] (RCD)
OSHJ.......... Oblate Sisters of the Sacred Heart of Jesus [*Roman Catholic religious order*]
OshkT......... Oshkosh Truck Corp. [*Associated Press*] (SAG)
OShL.......... Shaker Heights Public Library, Shaker Heights, OH [*Library symbol Library of Congress*] (LCLS)
Oshmn........ Oshman's Sporting Goods, Inc. [*Associated Press*] (SAG)
OSHR.......... Occupational Safety and heal Review Commission (EBF)
OSHRC........ Occupational Safety and Health Review Commission [*Department of Labor*]
OSHS.......... Occupational Safety and Health Statistics [*Bureau of Labor Statistics*] (GFGA)
OSHS.......... OSHAP Technologies Ltd. [*NASDAQ symbol*] (NQ)
OShS.......... Shaker Heights City School District, Shaker Heights, OH [*Library symbol Library of Congress*] (LCLS)
OSHSF........ Oshap Technologies Ltd. [*NASDAQ symbol*] (TTSB)
OSHT.......... Grand Lodge Order of the Sons of Hermann in Texas [*San Antonio, TX*] (EA)
OSHT.......... Sharon Temple, Sharon, Ontario [*Library symbol National Library of Canada*] (NLC)
OSI............ Aerosi SA de CV [*Mexico ICAO designator*] (FAAC)
OSI............ National Institute for Occupational Safety and Health, Rockville, MD [*OCLC symbol*] (OCLC)
OSI............ Office of Samoa Information [*Press agency*]
OSI............ Office of Scientific Information [*National Science Foundation*] (MCD)
OSI............ Office of Scientific Integrity [*National Institutes of Health*]
OSI............ Office of Scientific Intelligence [*Fictitious government agency on TV series "The Six Million Dollar Man"*]
OSI............ Office of Seniors' Interests [*Australia*]
OSI............ Office of Special Investigation [*Air Force*]
OSI............ Office of Strategic Information [*DoD*]
OSI............ Office of Strategic Intelligence [*Air Force*] (INF)
OSI............ Office of Systems Integration [*Social Security Administration*]
OSI............ Officer Skill Identifiers [*Army*]
OSI............ Office Systems Interconnection [*Telecommunications*] (TSSD)
OSI............ Offshore Islands (CINC)
OSI............ On-Site Inspection
OSI............ Open Society Institute [*Russia*]
OSI............ Open Space Institute (EA)
OSI............ Open Standards Interconnection [*International Standards Organisation*]
OSI............ Open System Interconnections [*Networking technique*]
OSI............ Open Systems Interconnect
OSI............ Operating Space Item [*Military*] (CAAL)
OSI............ Operating System Interface
OSI............ Operating Systems, Inc. (MCD)
OSI............ Operational Status Indicator (MUGU)
OSI............ Operation Smile International (EA)
OSI............ ORDALT [*Ordnance Alterations*]/SHIPALT Inspector [*Ship Alteration*] (MCD)
OSI............ Organic Sign Index [*Psychology*]
OSI............ Oriental Shorthairs International (EA)
OSI............ Osijek [*Former Yugoslavia*] [*Airport symbol*] (OAG)
OSI............ Other Support Items
OSI............ Out of Stock, Indefinite [*Business term*]
OSI............ Overhead Supply Inventory (MCD)

OSI	Oyster Shell Institute (EA)
OSI	Ozark Society (EA)
OSI	Research Technical Information Centre, ESSO Petroleum Canada, Sarnia, Ontario [*Library symbol National Library of Canada*] (NLC)
OSI	Woodside, CA [*Location identifier FAA*] (FAAL)
OSIA	Office, Services and Information Agency [*Military*] (AABC)
OSIA	On-Site Inspection Agency [*DoD*]
OSIA	Order Sons of Italy in America (EA)
OSIA	Outdoor Systems [*NASDAQ symbol*] (TTSB)
OSIA	Outdoor Systems, Inc. [*NASDAQ symbol*] (SAG)
OSIASL	Order Sons of Italy in America Supreme Lodge [*Later, OSIA*] (EA)
OSIC	Ocean Science Information Center [*University of Hawaii*] (NOAA)
OSIC	Oil Spill Information Center [*Santa Barbara, CA*]
OSIC	Optimization of Subcarrier Information Capacity
OSICOM	Open Systems Interconnections Division [*Now Open Systems Interconnection Division*]
Osicom	Osicom Technologies, Inc. [*Associated Press*] (SAG)
OSICS	Commission Scolaire de Sept-Iles, Quebec [*Library symbol National Library of Canada*] (NLC)
OSID	Open Systems Interconnection Division (ACII)
OSID	Operational System Interface Document (MCD)
OSIDM	Eva Brook Donly Museum, Simcoe, Ontario [*Library symbol National Library of Canada*] (NLC)
OSIE	Office of Software Improvement and Engineering [*Social Security Administration*]
OSIE	Open Systems Interconnection Environment [*Telecommunications*] (OSI)
OSIE	Operational Support Integration Engineering
OS/IES	On-Site Integrated Energy System
OSIGA	Ohio State Inventory of Guidance Awareness
OSIGO	Office of the Chief Signal Officer
OSII	Objective Sys Integrators [*NASDAQ symbol*] (TTSB)
OSII	Objective Systems Integrators, Inc. [*NASDAQ symbol*] (SAG)
OSIL	Lynwood Arts Centre, Simcoe, Ontario [*Library symbol National Library of Canada*] (NLC)
OSIL	Operating System Implementation Language
OSINH	Norfolk Historical Society, Simcoe, Ontario [*Library symbol National Library of Canada*] (NLC)
OSI/NMF	Open Systems Interconnect Network Management Forum [*Computer science*] (BTTJ)
OSIP	Operational and Safety Improvement Program (NVT)
OSIP	Operational Suitability Improvement Program [*Aviation*]
OSIP	OSI Pharmaceuticals [*NASDAQ symbol*] [*Formerly, Oncogene Science*] (SG)
OSIP	Simcoe Public Library, Ontario [*Library symbol National Library of Canada*] (NLC)
OS/IPC	Operating System/Inter-Process Communications (DOMA)
OSIQ	Offer Self-Image Questionnaire
OSIQA	Offer Self-Image Questionnaire for Adolescents (EDAC)
OSIR	Office of Scientific Integrity Review [*US Secretary of Health*]
OSIR	Oil Spill Intelligence Report
Os-Ir	Osmiridium (IDOE)
OSIR	Out of Service in Reserve [*Military*] (CINC)
OSIRIS	Online Search Information Retrieval Information Storage [*Computer science*] (PDAA)
OSIS	Ocean Surveillance Information System [*Navy*] (MCD)
OSIS	Office of Science Information Service [*National Science Foundation*]
OSITOP	Open Systems Interconnection Technical and Office Protocols [*Telecommunications*] (OSI)
OSJ	Oblates of St. Joseph [*Roman Catholic religious order*]
osj	Oblates of St. Joseph (TOCD)
OSJ	Office of Supervisory Jurisdiction [*Investment term*]
OSJ	Sovereign Order of Saint John of Jerusalem (EA)
OSJD	Ordinis Sancti Joannis de Deo [*Order of St. John of God*]
OSK	Osaka [*Takayasuyama*] [*Japan*] [*Seismograph station code, US Geological Survey*] (SEIS)
OSK	Oskarshamn [*Sweden*] [*Airport symbol*] (OAG)
OSKAR	Outstanding Superior Kitchen All-Rounder [*Trademark of Sunbeam Corp.*]
OSKL	Kamishly [*Syria*] [*ICAO location identifier*] (ICLI)
OSKL	Swastika Branch, Kirkland Lake Public Library, Ontario [*Library symbol National Library of Canada*] (BIB)
OSKNC	Skead Branch, Nickel Centre Public Library, Ontario [*Library symbol National Library of Canada*] (NLC)
OSKY	Mahaska Investment [*NASDAQ symbol*] (TTSB)
OSKY	Mahaska Investment Co. [*NASDAQ symbol*] (SAG)
OSL	International Order of Saint Luke the Physician (EA)
OSL	Oil Seal
OSL	Old [*Church*] Slavonic [*Language, etc.*]
OSL	Old Style Latin (ADA)
OSL	Open/Short Locator
OSL	Operating System Language
OSL	Operator Set Loop [*Electronics*] (ECII)
OSL	Optically Stimulated Luminescence [*Analytical Chemistry*]
OSL	Optical Storage Ltd.
OSL	Orbiting Space Laboratory
OSL	Order of St. Luke the Physician of America (EA)
OSL	Ordnance Sub-Lieutenant [*British military*] (DMA)
OSL	Oregon Short Line Railroad [*of Union Pacific Railroad Co.*]
OSL	Organic Semiconductor LASER [*Materials science*]
OSL	Osgood-Schlatter Lesion [*Medicine*] (STED)
OSL	Osler Resources, Inc. [*Vancouver Stock Exchange symbol*]
OSL	Oslo [*Norway*] [*Airport symbol*] (OAG)
OSL	O'Sullivan Corp. [*AMEX symbol*] (SPSG)
OSL	Outstanding Leg [*NASA*] (KSC)
OSL	Sioux Lookout Public Library, Ontario [*Library symbol National Library of Canada*] (NLC)
OSL	University of Oregon, School of Librarianship, Eugene, OR [*OCLC symbol*] (OCLC)
OSLA	Stella Branch, Lennox and Addington County Library, Ontario [*Library symbol National Library of Canada*] (NLC)
O Slav	Old [*Church*] Slavic [*Language*] (BARN)
OSLB	Operational Search Lower Bound [*RADAR*]
OSLC	Lambton College of Applied Arts and Technology, Sarnia, Ontario [*Library symbol National Library of Canada*] (NLC)
OSLEAS	Association Sectorielle de Fabrication d'Equipement de Transport et de Machines, St.-Leonard, Quebec [*Library symbol National Library of Canada*] (NLC)
OSLFC	Sharbot Lake Branch, Frontenac County Library, Ontario [*Library symbol National Library of Canada*] (BIB)
OSLI	Office of Servicemen's Life Insurance (OICC)
OSLJ	Law Journal. Student Bar Association. Ohio State University [*A publication*] (DLA)
OSLK	Latakia/Latakia [*Syria*] [*ICAO location identifier*] (ICLI)
OSLM	Operations Shop/Laboratory Manager [*NASA*] (MCD)
OSLR	Intergovernmental Committee for Ocean Science and Living Resources [*Marine science*] (OSRA)
OSLT	On-Site Logistics Team (MCD)
OSM	Mantellate Sisters, Servants of Mary of Blue Island (TOCD)
OSM	Mental Health Services for Clark County, Springfield, OH [*Library symbol*] [*Library of Congress*] (LCLS)
OSM	Mosul [*Iraq*] [*Airport symbol*] (AD)
OSM	Oblates of St. Martha (TOCD)
OSM	Office of Spectrum Management [*US National Telecommunications and Information Administration*] (TSSD)
OSM	Office of Surface Mining [*Department of the Interior*] (AAGC)
OSM	Office of Surface Mining Reclamation and Enforcement [*Department of the Interior*]
OSM	Off-Screen Model [*Computer science*]
OSM	Omnispectra Miniature
OSM	Oncostatin [*Antibiotic*]
OSM	On-Screen Manager [*Computer science*]
OSM	On-Site Maintenance
OSM	On Station Mode
OSM	Operating Service Month
OSM	Operating System Manual (MCD)
OSM	Operating System Monitor
OSM	Operator's Service Manual
OSM	Opisu Struktur Mikroprogramow.nych [*Programming language*] (CSR)
OSM	Optical Section Microscope
OSM	Option Select Mode [*Computer science*] (OA)
OSM	Orbital Service Module [*NASA*] (MCD)
osm	Orbital Service Module [*NASA*] (NAKS)
OSM	Ordnance Safety Manual [*Military*]
OSM	Ordo Servorum Mariae [*Order of Servants of Mary*] [*Servites*] [*Roman Catholic religious order*]
OSM	Orr-Schelen-Mayeron & Associates (EFIS)
OSM	Oscillating Secondary Mirror [*Telescope*]
osM	Osmolar [*Chemistry*] (DAVI)
OSM	Osmolarity (STED)
Osm	Osmole [*Physical chemistry*]
OSM	Osmonics, Inc. [*NYSE symbol*] (SPSG)
OSM	Osmotic
osm	Osmotic (STED)
OSM	Output Switch Module [*Automotive engineering*]
OSM	Outside Mail (AFM)
OSM	Outside of Metal
OSM	Ovine Submaxillary Mucin [*Medicine*] (DMAA)
OSM	Oxygen Saturation Meter (MAE)
OSM	Oxygen Steel Making
OSM	Schumacher Memorial Library, Ontario [*Library symbol National Library of Canada*] (BIB)
OSM	Servants of Mary (TOCD)
osm	Servite Fathers (TOCD)
OSM	Servites (TOCD)
OSMA	Occidental Society of Metempiric Analysis (EA)
OSMA	Office of Small Manufacturers Assistance [*FDA*]
OSMA	Optical Spectrometric Multichannel Analyzer [*Instrumentation*]
OSMA	Orthopedic Surgical Manufacturers Association (EA)
OSMA	Overseas Sales and Marketing Association of America [*Lake Bluff, IL*] (EA)
OSME	Open Systems Message Exchange [*Computer science*] (CIST)
OSME	Oral Speech Mechanism Screening Examination [*Educational test*]
OSME	Ornithological Society of the Middle East (EAIO)
OSMED	Otospondylomegaepiphyseal Dystrophy [*Medicine*] (DAVI)
OSMF	Oral Submucous Fibrosis [*Medicine*] (STED)
OSMF	Smith Falls Public Library, Ontario [*Library symbol National Library of Canada*] (NLC)
OS/MFT	Operating System/Multiprogramming Fixed Task (NITA)
OS/MFT	Operating System/Multiprogramming with a Fixed Number of Tasks [*IBM Corp.*] [*Computer science*]
OSML	McNeil Laboratories (Canada) Ltd., Stouffville, Ontario [*Library symbol National Library of Canada*] (NLC)
OSMM	Mercy Medical Center, Springfield, OH [*Library symbol Library of Congress*] (LCLS)
OSMM	Office of Safeguards and Materials Management [*AEC*]
OSMM	Optimum Supply and Maintenance Model
osmo	Osmolality [*Chemistry*]
osmol	Osmole [*Measurement*] (DAVI)

Osmonic	Osmonics, Inc. [*Associated Press*] (SAG)
OSMOS	Own Ship's Motion Simulator [*Navy*]
OSMOS	Own Ship's Motion System [*Navy*]
OSMP	Operational Support Maintenance Plan [*NASA*] (MCD)
OSMR	Office of Systems Modernization Requirements [*Social Security Administration*]
OSMRE	Office of Surface Mining Reclamation and Enforcement [*Also, OSM*] [*Department of the Interior*]
OSMS	Organizational Supply Management System [*Army*] (INF)
OSM S	Osmolarity Serum [*Biochemistry*] (DAVI)
OSMSE-R	Oral Speech Mechanism Screening Examination-Revised [*St. Louis and Ruscello*] (TES)
OSMU	Oesterreichische Schuhmusterschau [*Austrian Footwear Exhibition*] [*Wiener Messen und Kongress GmbH*] (TSPED)
OSM U	Osmolarity Urine [*Biochemistry*] (DAVI)
OSMV	Oat Striate Mosaic Virus [*Plant pathology*]
OSMV	One Shot Multivibrator (MSA)
OS/MVS	Operating System/Multiprogramming with Virtual Storage [*Computer science*]
OS/MVT	Operating System/Multiprogramming with a Variable Number of Tasks [*Computer science*]
OSN	Ocean Science News [*Marine science*] (OSRA)
OSN	Office of the Secretary of the Navy
OSN	Off Service Note [*Medicine*] (DAVI)
OSN	Osphradial Nerve [*In mollusks*]
OSN	Output Sequence Number
OSN	Sioux Narrows Public Library, Ontario [*Library symbol National Library of Canada*] (NLC)
OSNAP	Object Snap [*Auto CAD*] [*Computer science*]
OSNC	Sarnia Northern Collegiate, Ontario [*Library symbol National Library of Canada*] (NLC)
OSNLR	Ocean Science in Relation to Non-Living Resources [*Marine science*] (OSRA)
OSNS	Shedden Public Library, Spanish, Ontario [*Library symbol National Library of Canada*] (NLC)
OSNSW	Office of the Sheriff of New South Wales [*Australia*]
OSO	Ocean Systems Operation [*NASA*]
oso	Ocean Systems Operation [*NASA*] (NAKS)
OSO	Office of Systems Operations [*Social Security Administration*]
OSO	Officer Selection Office (DNAB)
OSO	Offshore Suppliers Office [*British*]
OSO	Onsala Space Observatory [*Sweden*]
OSO	Operations Scheduling Office (SSD)
OSO	Orbiting Satellite Observer (IEEE)
OSO	Orbiting Scientific Observatory (IAA)
OSO	Orbiting Solar Observatory [*A satellite*]
OSO	Ordnance Supply Office
OSO	Oregon State Library, Salem, OR [*OCLC symbol*] (OCLC)
O/S/O	Ore/Slurry/Oil [*Supertanker*]
OSO	Origination Screening Office [*Telecommunications*] (TEL)
OSO	Southampton Branch, Bruce County Public Library, Ontario [*Library symbol National Library of Canada*] (NLC)
OSOB	Old Senate Office Building [*Also, RSOB*] [*Washington, DC*] (DLA)
OSOC	Off-Site Originated Change (AAG)
OSOCC	On-Site Operations Coordination Center
OSODS	Office of Strategic Offensive and Defensive Systems [*Navy*]
OSOG	Office Systems Owners Group (HGAA)
OSOIPB	Ordnance Supply Office Illustrated Parts Breakdown [*Navy*]
OSol	Odes of Solomon (BJA)
OSOL	Office of the Solicitor [*Department of Labor*]
OS/OLM	On-Site/On-Line Maintenance
OSOM	Bruce County Museum, Southampton, Ontario [*Library symbol National Library of Canada*] (BIB)
OSOP	Off-Site Operations Plan (SSD)
OSOP	Orbiter Systems Operating Procedures [*NASA*] (NASA)
OSOR	Operational Standoff Range (NVT)
OSoSJ	Saint Joseph's Priory, Somerset, OH [*Library symbol Library of Congress*] (LCLS)
OSOT	Oakland Township Public Library, Scotland, Ontario [*Library symbol National Library of Canada*] (BIB)
OSOTM	Sombra Township Museum, Ontario [*Library symbol National Library of Canada*] (BIB)
OSP	Obiit sine Prole [*Died without Issue*] [*Latin*]
OSP	Oblate Sisters of Providence [*Roman Catholic religious order*]
OSP	Ocean Surveillance Product (DOMA)
OSP	Ocean Survey Plan [*or Program*] [*Navy*]
OSP	Office of Science Policy [*National Science Foundation*]
OSP	Office of Scientific Personnel [*NAS-NRC*]
OSP	Office of Special Projects (COE)
OSP	Office of Special Technology [*Formerly, Office of Special Projects*] [*Washington, DC Department of Energy*] (GRD)
OSP	Office of Staffing Policy [*Office of Personnel Management*] [*Washington, DC*] (GRD)
OSP	Office of Surplus Property [*Superseded by War Assets Corporation*] [*World War II*]
OSP	Office of the Special Prosecutor [*Queensland, Australia*]
OSP	Offshore Procurement [*Army*]
O-SP	Off-Street Parking (WDAA)
OSP	Oficina Sanitaria Panamericana [*Pan-American Sanitary Bureau - PASB*] [*Washington, DC*]
OSP	Oil Suction Pump (MSA)
OSP	On Station Position (MUGU)
OSP	Operating Steam Pressure (MSA)
OSP	Operating System Plan (SAA)
OSP	Operational Safety Procedures (COE)
OSP	Operational Surveillance Program [*Nuclear Regulatory Commission*] (NRCH)
OSP	Operational Survival Plan [*Civil Defense*]
OSP	Operations Support Plan [*Navy*] (NG)
OSP	Optical Signature Program [*Military*] (CAAL)
OSP	Optimum Sustainable Population [*Marine science*] (MSC)
OSP	Optoelectronic Systems Programme [*British*]
OSP	Orbital Support Plan (MCD)
OSP	Order of St. Paul [*Anglican religious community*]
OSP	Order of St. Paul the First Hermit [*Pauline Fathers*] [*Roman Catholic religious order*]
OSP	Ordinary Superphosphate (EDCT)
OSP	Organic Solderability Perservative [*Electronics*] (AAEL)
OSP	Original Set Pattern [*Ice dancing*]
OSP	Outer Surface Protein [*Cytology*]
OSP	Outfitting Stock Point
OSP	Outside Plant [*Telecommunications*] (TEL)
OSP	Outside Procured Stores (AAG)
OSP	Outside Purchase (WDAA)
OSP	Own Ship's Position [*Navy*] (MCD)
OSP	Polysar Ltd., Sarnia, Ontario [*Library symbol National Library of Canada*] (NLC)
OSP	Slupsk [*Poland*] [*Airport symbol*] (OAG)
OSPA	Open Signal Coprocessing Architecture [*Computer science*]
OSPAAAL	Organization of Solidarity of the Peoples of Africa, Asia, and Latin America
OSPC	Options Service of Project Concern [*An association*] (EA)
OSPCS	Charles M. Shields Centennial Library, South Porcupine, Ontario [*Library symbol National Library of Canada*] (BIB)
OSPD	Office of Sponsored Program Development [*State University of New York at Binghamton*] [*Research center*] (RCD)
OSPD	Official Scrabble Players Dictionary [*A publication*]
OSPE	Organizational Spare Parts and Equipment [*Army*]
OSPES	Outer Shell Photoelectron Spectroscopy
OSPF	Open Shortest Path First [*Communications routing protocol*]
OSPG	Original Society of Painters and Glaziers [*A union*] [*British*]
OS-PIF	Office of the Secretary of Defense Productivity Investment Funding
OSPIRG	Oregon State Public Interest Research Group [*Research center*] (RCD)
OSPJ	Offshore Procurement, Japan
OSpM	Mental Health Services for Clark County, Springfield, OH [*Library symbol Library of Congress*] (LCLS)
OSPNC	Porcupine Campus, Northern College of Applied Arts and Technology, South Porcupine, Ontario [*Library symbol National Library of Canada*] (NLC)
OSPPE	Pauline Fathers (TOCD)
osppe	Pauline Fathers (TOCD)
OSPR	Office of Oil Spill Prevention and Response
OSPR	Palmyra [*Syria*] [*ICAO location identifier*] (ICLI)
OSPRDS	Oblate Spheroid (PDAA)
OSPREY	Ocean Swell Powered Renewable Energy [*United Kingdom*]
OSPRO	Ocean Shipping Procedures
OSPTM	Timmins Museum, South Porcupine, Ontario [*Library symbol National Library of Canada*] (BIB)
OSQ	Officer Separation Questionnaire (DNAB)
OSQ	Officer Student Quarters (DNAB)
OSQ	San Antonio, TX [*Location identifier FAA*] (FAAL)
OSR	Occupational Survey Report
OSR	Office of Scientific Research [*AFSC*]
OSR	Office of Security Review [*Obsolete DoD*]
OSR	Office of Sport and Recreation [*Australian Capital Territory*]
OSR	Office of Standards and Regulations [*Environmental Protection Agency*] (GFGA)
OSR	Office of Systems Requirements [*Social Security Administration*]
OSR	Ohio State Reports [*A publication*] (DLA)
OSR	Old Style Roman (ADA)
OSR	Onsite Review [*Military*]
OSR	Operand Storage Register [*Computer science*]
OSR	Operational Safety Requirements (COE)
OSR	Operational Scanning Recognition
OSR	Operational Status Release [*Navy*] (NG)
OSR	Operational Support Readiness
OSR	Operational Support Requirement [*Military*]
OSR	Operations Support Room [*NASA*]
OSR	Optical Scanning Recognition [*Computer science*]
OSR	Optical Solar Reflector
OSR	Optical Sound Recorder
OSR	Optical Still Recorder [*LASER-disc technology*]
OSR	Optimum Ship Routing [*Obsolete*]
OSR	Ordnance Status Report (NG)
OSR	Originators Status Report [*Army*]
OSR	Oscar Resources Ltd. [*Vancouver Stock Exchange symbol*]
OSR	Ostrava [*Former Czechoslovakia*] [*Airport symbol*] (OAG)
OSR	Output Shift Register
OSR	Output Signal Range
OSR	Output Status Register
OSR	Oversea Returnee [*Military*]
OSR	Overseas Service Ribbon [*Military decoration*]
OSR	Over-the-Shoulder Rating
OSR	Own Ship's Roll [*Navy*]
OSR	Oxide-Stable Resin
OSRA	Office Systems Research Association [*Cleveland, OH*] (EA)
OSRAC	Ocean Shipping Requirements and Capabilities
OSRADP	Oil Spill Research and Development Program [*Louisiana*]
OSRC	Oil Sands Research Centre [*Alberta*]

OSRD.......... Office of Scientific Research and Development [*World War II*]

OSRD.......... Office of Standard Reference Data [*Gaithersburg, MD*] [*National Institute of Standards and Technology*]

OSRDB........ Office of Standard Reference Data Bibliography [*National Institute of Standards and Technology*]

OS Rep........ Ohio State Reports [*A publication*]   (DLA)

OSREPL....... Oversea Replacement [*Army*]

OSRET......... Oversea Returnee [*Army*]

OSRF.......... Smooth Rock Falls Public Library, Ontario [*Library symbol National Library of Canada*]   (NLC)

OSRI........... Originating Station Routing Identifier

OSRL.......... Organizations and Systems Research Laboratory [*Army*]   (RDA)

OSRM.......... Office of Standard Reference Materials [*Gaithersburg, MD*] [*National Institute of Standards and Technology*]

OSRM.......... South River-Machar Union Public Library, South River, Ontario [*Library symbol National Library of Canada*]   (NLC)

OSRO.......... Office for the Sahelian Relief Operation [*UN Food and Agriculture Organization*]

OSRO.......... Operations Support Requirements Office [*NASA*]   (KSC)

OSRP.......... Occupant Safety Research Partnership

OSRP.......... Oil Spill Response Plan [*Pollution prevention*]

OSRPA........ Offices, Shops, and Railway Premises Act [*1963*] [*British*]

OSRR.......... Spanish River Reserve Band Public Library, Ontario [*Library symbol National Library of Canada*]   (NLC)

OSRS.......... Operational Status Recording Subsystem

OSRTN........ Office of the Special Representative for Trade Negotiations [*Later, Office of the United States Trade Representative*] [*Executive Office of the President*]

OSRU.......... Optical Sensors Research Unit   (NITA)

OSRV.......... Outside Rear View [*Mirrors*] [*Automotive features*]

OSS............. Los Angeles, CA [*Location identifier FAA*]   (FAAL)

OSS............. Objective Supply System [*Army*]

OSS............. Object Services Standard   (AAEL)

OSS............. Object Sorting Scales [*Psychology*]

OSS............. Observing Simulation System   (USDC)

OSS............. Observing Stimulation System [*Marine science*]   (OSRA)

OSS............. Occupational Superannuation Standard

OSS............. Oceanic Scanning Spectrophotometer

OSS............. Oceanic Space Subcommittee [*Congressional committee*]   (MSC)

OSS............. Ocean Surveillance Satellite   (MCD)

OSS............. Ocean Surveillance System [*Navy*]   (SAA)

OSS............. Ocean Survey Ship   (NOAA)

OSS............. OEX [*Orbiter Experiments*] Support System [*NASA*]

OSS............. Office of Safeguards and Security [*Department of Energy Washington, DC*]   (GRD)

OSS............. Office of Senate Security [*Congress*]

OSS............. Office of Space Science [*NASA*]

oss............. Office of Space Science [*NASA*]   (NAKS)

OSS............. Office of Space Systems [*Air Force*]

OSS............. Office of Statistical Standards [*Bureau of the Budget; later, OMB*]

OSS............. Office of Strategic Services [*Facetiously translated as "Oh So Social" because some of its staff were socially prominent*] [*World War II*]

OSS............. Office of Support Services [*Army*]

OSS............. Office of Systems Operations [*National Weather Service*]   (USDC)

OSS............. Office Skills Series [*Test*]   (TMMY)

OSS............. Offshore Surveillance System

OSS............. Old Submarine [*Navy symbol*]

OSS............. One Stop Shop [*Small business advice*] [*British*]   (ECON)

OSS............. Ontario Secondary School Teachers' Federation [*UTLAS symbol*]

OSS............. Operating System Software [*Personal computers*]

OSS............. Operating System Supervisor

OSS............. Operating System Support   (NITA)

OSS............. Operational Storage Site [*Army*]

OSS............. Operational Support System [*Computer science*]

OSS............. Operations Support System   (DOMA)

OSS............. Optical Sensor Subsystem [*Military*]   (CAAL)

OSS............. Optical Sight System

OSS............. Optical Subsystem   (KSC)

OSS............. Optical Surveillance System   (AAG)

OSS............. Optimized Systems Software [*San Jose, CA*]

OSS............. Orbital Space Station Study [*NASA*]   (IAA)

OSS............. Orbital Stabilization System   (MCD)

oss............. Orbiting Space Station [*NASA*]   (NAKS)

OSS............. Orbiting Space Station [*NASA*]

OSS............. Ordnance Safety Switch [*Military*]   (IAA)

OSS............. Organised Science Series [*A publication*]

OSS............. Organization for Cooperation of Socialist Countries in the Domain of Posts and Telecommunications [*Defunct*]   (EAIO)

OSS............. Osisko Lake Mines Ltd. [*Toronto Stock Exchange symbol*]

oss............. Ossetic [*MARC language code Library of Congress*]   (LCCP)

OSS............. Ossory [*Ireland*]   (ROG)

OSS............. Outer Solar System

OSS............. Overhead Speaker System [*Automotive engineering*]

OSS............. Overseas Switch [*Military*]

OSS............. Over-the-Shoulder Shot [*Photography*]   (WDMC)

OSS............. Over-the-Shoulder Strap   (DMAA)

OSS............. Own Ship's Speed [*Navy*]

OSS............. Oxygen Sleep Starvation

OSS............. Religious of the Order of the Blessed Sacrament and Our Lady [*Sacramentine Nuns*] [*Roman Catholic religious order*]

OSS............. Sacramentine Nuns   (TOCD)

OSS............. Shawnee State Community College, Portsmouth, OH [*OCLC symbol*]   (OCLC)

OSSA.......... Office of Space Science and Applications [*Washington, DC NASA*]

OSSA.......... Order Scheduled Shipment Analysis   (MCD)

OSSA.......... Order Secular of St. Augustine [*See also ASAS*] [*Rome, Italy*]   (EAIO)

OSSC.......... Oblati Sacratissimi Cordis [*Oblate Fathers of the Sacred Heart*] [*Roman Catholic religious order*]

OSSC.......... Office of Stationary Source Compliance   (COE)

OSSC.......... Ordnance Storage and Shipment Chart [*Army*]   (MCD)

OSSD.......... Office of Space Systems Development [*NASA*]

OSSD.......... Off-Site Surveillance Data [*Military*]

OSSE.......... Object/Surface/Special Effect

OSSE.......... Observing Systems Simulation Experiments [*National Center for Atmospheric Research*]

OSSE.......... Oriented Scintillation Spectrometer Experiment [*Instrumentation in Gamma Ray Observatory*] [*NASA*]

OSSF.......... Operating System Support Facility   (MHDI)

OSSF.......... Overseas Services Storage Facility

OSShD........ Organisation fur die Zusammenarbeit der Eisenbahnen [*Organisation for the Collaboration of Railways - OCR*]   (EAIO)

OSSI........... Outback Steakhouse [*NASDAQ symbol*]   (TTSB)

OSSI........... Outback Steakhouse, Inc. [*NASDAQ symbol*]   (SPSG)

OSSJ........... St. Joseph's Hospital, Sarnia, Ontario [*Library symbol National Library of Canada*]   (BIB)

OSSKC........ Operative Society of Spring Knife Cutlers [*A union*] [*British*]

OSSL.......... Operating System Simulation Language [*1971*] [*Computer science*]   (CSR)

OSSM.......... Office of Safety Surface Mining [*Department of the Interior*]   (COE)

OSSM.......... Oil Spill Simulation Model

OSSMJ........ Order of the Societies of Mary and Joseph   (ROG)

OSSN.......... Operational Specialist Supervisor, Night [*Navy*]

OSSN.......... Other Specialty Serial Numbers [*Air Force*]

OSSNSS...... Ordnance Supply Segment of the Navy Supply System

OSSO.......... Office of State Systems Operations [*Social and Rehabilitation Service, HEW*]

OSSP.......... Operational Supply Support Plan   (MCD)

OSSP.......... Outer Solar System Probe

OS-SPT....... Osmolality Urin-Spot [*Test*] [*Biochemistry*]   (DAVI)

OSSR.......... Oblates [*or Order*] of the Most Holy Redeemer [*Roman Catholic women's religious order*]

OSSR.......... Order of the Most Holy Redeemer   (TOCD)

OSSR.......... Own Ship's Speed Repeater [*Navy*]

OSSRH........ Orbiter Subsystem Requirements Handbook [*NASA*]   (NASA)

OSSRS........ Optimum Step Size Random Search [*Computer science*]   (IAA)

osss........... Brigittine Monks   (TOCD)

OSSS.......... Damascus [*Syria*] [*ICAO location identifier*]   (ICLI)

OSSS.......... Optical Space Surveillance Subsystem   (AAG)

OSSS.......... Optical Space Surveillance System [*or Subsystem*]   (IAA)

OSSS.......... Orbital Space Station Study

OSSS.......... Orbital Space Station System [*of NASA*]

OSSS.......... Order of the Most Holy Savior [*Bridgettine Sisters*] [*Roman Catholic religious order*]

OSSS.......... The Brigittine Sisters   (TOCD)

OSST.......... Ocean Ship Surveillance Training

OSST.......... Official Summary of Security Transactions and Holdings

OSST.......... Offshore Storage Tank

OSST.......... Order of the Holy Trinity   (TOCD)

osst........... Order of the Most Holy Trinity, Trinitarian Fathers   (TOCD)

OSsT.......... Ordo Sanctissimae Trinitatis Redemptionis Captivorum [*Order of the Most Holy Trinity*] [*Trinitarians*] [*Roman Catholic religious order*]

OSST.......... Sisters of the Most Holy Trinity   (TOCD)

OSSU.......... Operator Services Switching Unit [*Telecommunications*]   (TEL)

OSSU.......... Sundridge & Strong Union Public Library, Sundridge, Ontario [*Library symbol National Library of Canada*]   (NLC)

OS Supp...... Oklahoma Statutes, Supplement [*A publication*]   (DLA)

OST............ Austria Fund [*NYSE symbol*]   (SPSG)

OST............ Objectives, Strategy, and Tactics [*Management system*]

OST............ Objective Start Time

OST............ Object Sorting Test [*Psychology*]

OST............ Observation Skills Test

OST............ Observatoire des Sciences et des Techniques [*France*]

OST............ Ocean Surface Temperature [*Marine science*]   (OSRA)

OST............ Office of Science and Technology [*Terminated 1973, functions transferred to National Science Foundation*] [*Later, CSTD*]

OST............ Office of Systems Operations [*Marine science*]   (OSRA)

OST............ Office of the Secretary of Transportation [*Department of Transportation*]

OST............ Office of the Special Trustee

O St............ Ohio State Reports [*A publication*]   (DLA)

OST............ One-Station Training

OST............ On Same Terms   (WDAA)

OST............ On-Shift Test   (IEEE)

OST............ On-Site Test   (IAA)

OST............ Operational Suitability Test [*Aviation*]

OST............ Operational System Test   (KSC)

OST............ Operations Support Team [*NASA*]   (MCD)

OST............ Optical Sensing Trigger

OST............ Optical Star Tracker

OST............ Optic Support Table

OST............ Orbiter Support Trolley [*NASA*]   (NASA)

OST............ Orbit Stay Time

OST............ Order Ship Time [*DoD*]

OST............ Ordinary Spring Tides

OST............ Ordnance Shock Test [*Military*]

OST............ Ordnance Special Training   (AAG)

OST............ Ordnance Suitability Test

OST............ Organisation Socialiste des Travailleurs [*Socialist Workers' Organization*] [*Senegal*] [*Political party*]   (PPW)

OST Organizacion Socialista de los Trabajadores [*Socialist Workers' Organization*] [*Costa Rica*] [*Political party*] (PPW)
OST Organizacion Socialista de los Trabajadores [*Socialist Workers' Organization*] [*Bolivia*] [*Political party*] (PPW)
OST Originating Station Treatment [*Telecommunications*] (TEL)
OST Ostend [*Belgium*] [*Airport symbol*] (OAG)
OST Osteopathic (WGA)
Ost Osteotomy [*Orthopedics*] (DAVI)
OST Osterhout Free Library, Wilkes-Barre, PA [*OCLC symbol*] (OCLC)
OST Out of Stock, Temporary [*Business term*]
OST Overseas Students Trust [*British*] (AEBS)
OST Over Stress Testing
OST Oxford Superconductive Technology [*Manufacturing company*] [*British*]
OST Stratford Public Library, Ontario [*Library symbol National Library of Canada*] (NLC)
OSTA Office of Space and Terrestrial Applications [*NASA*] (GRD)
OSTA Optical Storage Technology Association (CDE)
OSTA Stayner Public Library, Ontario [*Library symbol National Library of Canada*] (NLC)
OSTAC Bibliotheque Publique Cambridge-St.-Albert, St.-Albert, Ontario [*Library symbol National Library of Canada*] (NLC)
OSTAC Ocean Science Technology Advisory Committee [*Terminated, 1976*] [*National Security Industrial Association*] (MSC)
OSTAG Gallery Stratford, Ontario [*Library symbol National Library of Canada*] (NLC)
OSTAR Observer Single-Handed Transatlantic Race [*Sailing*]
OSTARE Old Scientific Technical Aerospace Reports Extended
OSTARS Orbiting Surveillance and Target Acquisition Relay [*Army*] (RDA)
OSTASDG St. Andrews Branch, Stormount, Dundas, and Glengarry County Library, Ontario [*Library symbol National Library of Canada*] (BIB)
O State Ohio State Reports [*A publication*] (DLA)
OSTB Office of the State Training Board [*Australia*]
OSTC Open Systems Testing Consortium (TELE)
OSTC St. Catharines Public Library, Ontario [*Library symbol National Library of Canada*] (NLC)
OStcB Belmont Technical Institute, St. Clairsville, OH [*Library symbol Library of Congress*] (LCLS)
OSTCB Brock University, St. Catharines, Ontario [*Library symbol National Library of Canada*] (NLC)
OSTCBG Department of Geography, Brock University, St. Catharines, Ontario [*Library symbol National Library of Canada*] (NLC)
OSTCG Grantham High School, St. Catharines, Ontario [*Library symbol National Library of Canada*] (NLC)
OSTCGL Genaire Ltd., St. Catharines, Ontario [*Library symbol National Library of Canada*] (NLC)
OSTCH Hotel-Dieu Hospital, St. Catharines, Ontario [*Library symbol National Library of Canada*] (BIB)
OSTCM St. Catharines Historical Museum, Ontario [*Library symbol National Library of Canada*] (BIB)
OSTCMEC Monenco Consultants Ltd., St. Catharines, Ontario [*Library symbol National Library of Canada*] (NLC)
OSTCOOP Office of the Secretary of Transportation Continuity of Operations Plan
OSTCT St. Catharines Teachers' College, Ontario [*Library symbol National Library of Canada*] (NLC)
OSTCTR St. Catharines Teachers' Reference Library, Ontario [*Library symbol National Library of Canada*] (NLC)
OStcU Ohio University, Belmont County Branch Campus, St. Clairsville, OH [*Library symbol Library of Congress*] (LCLS)
OSTD Office of Supersonic Transport Development [*Department of Transportation*] [*Obsolete*]
OSTD Off-Site Technical Director (MHDI)
OSTD Ontario Society for Training and Development [*Canada*] (EDAC)
OSTD Ordnance Standards
OSTD Ordnance Standard Technical Directives [*Obsolete*]
OSTDS Office of Space Tracking and Data Systems [*NASA*] (NASA)
OSTE Osteotech, Inc. [*NASDAQ symbol*] (SAG)
OSte Public Library of Steubenville and Jefferson County, Steubenville, OH [*Library symbol Library of Congress*] (LCLS)
OSteC College of Steubenville, Steubenville, OH [*Library symbol Library of Congress*] (LCLS)
osteo Osteoarthritis [*Medicine*]
OSTEO Osteomyelitis [*Medicine*]
Osteo Osteomyelitis [*Orthopedics*] (DAVI)
OSTEO Osteopathic
OSTEOPTH Osteopath
Osteotch Osteotech, Inc. [*Associated Press*] (SAG)
OSTEST Operating System Test [*Telecommunications*] (TEL)
Ostex Ostex International, Inc. [*Associated Press*] (SAG)
OSTF Operational Silo Test Facility
OSTF Operational Suitability Test Facility [*Aviation*]
OSTF Operational System Test Facility [*Air Force*]
OSTFC Storrington Branch, Frontenac County Library, Ontario [*Library symbol National Library of Canada*] (BIB)
OSTG Ocean Science and Technology Group [*Navy*] (MCD)
OSTG St. Georges Branch, South Dumfries Public Library, Ontario [*Library symbol National Library of Canada*] (BIB)
OSTI Bibliotheque Publique de St.-Isidore, Ontario [*Library symbol National Library of Canada*] (NLC)
OSTI Office of Scientific and Technical Information [*Later, BLR & DD*] [*British Library*]
OSTI Office of Scientific and Technical Information [*Department of Energy*] [*Information service or system*] (IID)
OSTI Organization for Social and Technical Innovation
OSTIR Stirling Public Library, Ontario [*Library symbol National Library of Canada*] (BIB)
OSTIV Organisation Scientifique et Technique Internationale du Vol a Voile [*International Technical and Scientific Organization for Soaring Flight*]
OStJ Officer of the Order of St. John of Jerusalem [*British*]
OStJ Officer, Venerable Order of St. John of Jerusalem [*Decoration*] (CMD)
ostk Oilstick (VRA)
OSTL Operating System Table Loader [*Telecommunications*] (TEL)
OSTL Ovary Style Length [*Botany*]
OSTM Sault Ste. Marie Public Library, Ontario [*Library symbol National Library of Canada*] (NLC)
OSTMA Algoma College, Sault Ste. Marie, Ontario [*Library symbol National Library of Canada*] (NLC)
OSTMAAS Synod Office, Diocese of Algoma, Anglican Church of Canada, Sault Ste. Marie, Ontario [*Library symbol National Library of Canada*] (NLC)
OStmaC Chatfield College, St. Martin, OH [*Library symbol Library of Congress*] (LCLS)
OSTMAS Research Library, Algoma Steel Corp. Ltd., Sault Ste. Marie, Ontario [*Library symbol National Library of Canada*] (NLC)
OSTMB Batchewana Indian Band, Sault Ste. Marie, Ontario [*Library symbol National Library of Canada*] (NLC)
OSTMEF Sea Lamprey Control Centre, Fisheries and Oceans Canada [*Centre de Controle des Lamproies de Mer, Peches et Oceans Canada*] Sault Ste. Marie, Ontario [*Library symbol National Library of Canada*] (NLC)
OSTMF Great Lakes Forest Research Centre, Canadian Forestry Service [*Centre de Recherches Forestieres des Grands Lacs, Service Canadien des Forets*] Sault Ste. Marie, Ontario [*Library symbol National Library of Canada*] (NLC)
OSTMFF Forest Pest Management Institute, Canadian Forestry Service [*Institut pour laRepression des Ravageurs Forestiers, Service Canadien des Forets*], Sault-Ste .-Marie, Ontario [*Library symbol National Library of Canada*] (NLC)
OSTMGH General Hospital, Sault Ste. Marie, Ontario [*Library symbol National Library of Canada*] (NLC)
OSTMH Sault Ste. Marie and 49th (SSM) Field Regiment RCA Historical Society, Ontario [*Library symbol National Library of Canada*] (NLC)
OSTMM Strathroy Middlesex Museum, Strathroy, Ontario [*Library symbol National Library of Canada*] (BIB)
OSTMNA Aviation and Fire Management Centre, Ontario Ministry of Natural Resources, Sault Ste. Marie [*Library symbol National Library of Canada*] (BIB)
OSTMPH Plummer Public Hospital, Sault Ste. Marie, Ontario [*Library symbol National Library of Canada*] (NLC)
OSTMSC Sault College of Applied Arts and Technology, Sault Ste. Marie, Ontario [*Library symbol National Library of Canada*] (NLC)
OSTMY St. Mary's Public Library, Ontario [*Library symbol National Library of Canada*] (NLC)
OSTMYM St. Mary's District Museum, St. Mary's, Ontario [*Library symbol National Library of Canada*] (BIB)
OSTO Office of Space Transportation Operations [*NASA*] (NASA)
OST-ONA Office of the Secretary of Transportation Office of Noise Abatement
OSTP Office of Science and Technology Policy [*Executive Office of the Presiden t*] [*Washington, DC*]
OSTP On-Site Test Procedure
OSTP Orbiting System Test Plan [*NASA*] (NASA)
OSTP Strathroy Public Library, Ontario [*Library symbol National Library of Canada*] (NLC)
OSTPA Stratford-Perth Archives Board, Ontario [*Library symbol National Library of Canada*] (BIB)
O St R Ohio State Reports [*A publication*] (DLA)
OSTR Streetsville Public Library, Ontario [*Library symbol National Library of Canada*] (NLC)
O St Rep Ohio State Reports [*A publication*] (DLA)
OSTRO Stroud Branch, Township of Innisfil Public Library, Ontario [*Library symbol National Library of Canada*] (NLC)
OSTS Office of Space Transportation System [*NASA*]
OSTS Office of Space Transportation Systems [*NASA*] (GRD)
OSTS Office of State Technical Services [*Also, STS*] [*Abolished, 1970 Department of Commerce*]
OSTS Official Seed Testing Station (WDAA)
OSTS Operational Suitability Test Site [*Aviation*] (AAG)
OSTT Damascus [*Syria*] [*ICAO location identifier*] (ICLI)
OSTT Open Systems Technology Transfer Programme [*British*]
OSTT St. Thomas Public Library, Ontario [*Library symbol National Library of Canada*] (NLC)
OSTTE Elgin County Public Library, St. Thomas, Ontario [*Library symbol National Library of Canada*] (NLC)
OSTTP St. Thomas Psychiatric Hospital, Ontario [*Library symbol National Library of Canada*] (NLC)
OSTV Operational Support Television [*Military*] (AFM)
OSTX Ostex International, Inc. [*NASDAQ symbol*] (SAG)
OSTX Ostex Intl. [*NASDAQ symbol*] (TTSB)
OSU Columbus, OH [*Location identifier FAA*] (FAAL)
OSU Irish Ursuline Union (TOCD)
OSU Ohio State University [*Columbus*]
OSU Ohio State University, Columbus, OH [*OCLC symbol*] (OCLC)
O Su Ohio Supplement [*A publication*] (DLA)
OSU Ohio Supreme Court Decisions, Unreported Cases [*A publication*] (DLA)

OSU .... Oklahoma State University
OSU .... Older-Worker Service Unit [US Employment Service] [Department of Labor]
OSU .... Open Systems Unit [British]
OSU .... Operational Switching Unit
OSU .... Operation Sisters United (EA)
OSU .... Optical Scanning Unit (DNAB)
OSU .... Optical Service Unit [Telecommunications]
OSU .... Order of St. Ursula [Roman Catholic women's religious order]
OSU .... Oregon State University [Formerly, OSC]
OSU .... O'Sullivan Industries Hldg [NYSE symbol] (TTSB)
OSU .... O'Sullivan Industries Holding [NYSE symbol] (SPSG)
OSU .... Own Ship's Use [Navy] (DNAB)
OSU .... Sudbury Public Library, Ontario [Library symbol National Library of Canada] (NLC)
OSU .... Ursuline Nuns of the Congregation of Paris (Cincinnati, OH) (TOCD)
OSU .... Ursuline Nuns of the Congregation of Paris (Cleveland, OH) (TOCD)
OSU .... Ursuline Nuns of the Congregation of Paris (Kansas City, KS) (TOCD)
OSU .... Ursuline Nuns of the Congregation of Paris (Louisville, KY) (TOCD)
OSU .... Ursuline Nuns of the Congregation of Paris (Owensboro, KY) (TOCD)
OSU .... Ursuline Nuns of the Congregation of Paris (St. Martin, OH) (TOCD)
OSU .... Ursuline Nuns of the Congregation of Paris (Toledo, OH) (TOCD)
OSU .... Ursuline Nuns of the Congregation of Paris (Youngstown, OH) (TOCD)
OSU .... Ursuline Sisters of Belleville (TOCD)
OSU .... Ursuline Sisters of the Congregation of Tildonk, Belgium (TOCD)
OSUBE .... Educational Media Centre, Sudbury Board of Education, Ontario [Library symbol National Library of Canada] (NLC)
OSUC .... Cambrian College, Sudbury, Ontario [Library symbol National Library of Canada] (NLC)
OSUCS .... Civic Square, Information and Reference, Sudbury Public Library, Ontario [Library symbol National Library of Canada] (NLC)
OSUE .... On-Site User Evaluation (MCD)
OSUGH .... Sudbury General Hospital, Ontario [Library symbol National Library of Canada] (NLC)
OSUK .... Ophthalmological Society of the United Kingdom
OSUL .... Laurentian University [Universite Laurentienne] Sudbury, Ontario [Library symbol National Library of Canada] (NLC)
OSUL .... Ohio State University Libraries (NITA)
OSULH .... Medical Library, Laurentian Hospital, Sudbury, Ontario [Library symbol National Library of Canada] (BIB)
OSullvnC..... O'Sullivan Corp. [Associated Press] (SAG)
OSulvInd..... O'Sullivan Industries Holdings [Associated Press] (SAG)
OSUM .... Ohio State University Museum of Zoology [Research center] (RCD)
OSUME .... Ontario Ministry of Education, Sudbury, Ontario [Library symbol National Library of Canada] (BIB)
OSUN .... North Central Regional Library, Sudbury, Ontario [Library symbol National Library of Canada] (NLC)
OSUN .... Ontario Library Service - Voyageur, Sudbury, Ontario [Library symbol National Library of Canada] (NLC)
OSUNB .... Brock Township Public Library, Sunderland, Ontario [Library symbol National Library of Canada] (NLC)
OSUOP .... Northeastern Ontario Oncology Program [Programme d'Oncologie du Nord-Est de l'Ontario], Sudbury, Ontario [Library symbol National Library of Canada] (NLC)
OSUP .... Ohio State University Press (DGA)
OSUPE .... Ohio State University Psychological Exam (EDAC)
O Supp .... Ohio Supplement [A publication] (DLA)
OSUR .... Ohio State University Reactor
OSUREP........ Overseas Unit Replacement System [Military] (AFIT)
OSURF........ Ohio State University Research Foundation
OSURO .... Ohio State University Radio Observatory
OSUT .... One-Station-Unit Training [Army]
OSUT .... On-Site User Test
OSUT .... On-Site User Training
OSUT .... Ordinary Seamen Under Training [Canadian Navy]
OSUT-COFT... One-Station-Unit Training - Conduct of Fire Trainer [Army] (MCD)
OSUU .... University of Subury [Universite de Sudbury] Ontario [Library symbol National Library of Canada] (NLC)
OSV .... Ocean Station Vessel
OSV .... Office of Space Vehicles
OSV .... Offscreen Voice [Films, television, etc.]
OSV .... Offset Scan Voting (AAEL)
OSV .... Offshore Supply Vessel [Coast Guard] (GFGA)
OSV .... On Station Vehicle (MCD)
OSV .... Orbital Support Vehicle
OSV .... Order of St. Vincent (EA)
OSV .... Oriented Space Vehicle
OSV .... Output Serving Voltage
OSV .... Over-Sand Vehicle
OSVA .... Off-Site Vital Area (MCD)
OS/VS .... Operating Schedule/Virtual System
OS/VS .... Operating System/Virtual Storage [Computer science] (MDG)
OSW .... Oblique Shock Wave
OSW .... Office of Saline Water [Later, OWRT] [Department of the Interior]
OSW .... Office of Secretary of War [Obsolete]
OSW .... Office of Solid Waste [Environmental Protection Agency] (EPA)
OSW .... Old Swedish [Language, etc.]
OSW .... Operational Switching Unit
OSW .... Operations Support Wing [NASA]
OSW .... Order of the Sacred Word [Affiliate of the magical society, Aurum Solis]
OSW .... Oswego, KS [Location identifier FAA] (FAAL)
OSW .... Oswestry [British depot code]

OSW .... Wittenberg University, Springfield, OH [Library symbol Library of Congress] (LCLS)
OSWA .... Off-Shift Work Authorization (AAG)
OSWA .... Orchid Society of Western Australia
OSWA .... Organ Society of Western Australia
OSWAC......... Ordnance Special Weapons Ammunition Command [Later, Weapons Command]
OSWC .... Ordnance Special Weapons Command [Merged with Missile Command] [Army]
OSWD .... Office of Special Weapons Development [Army]
OSWER .... Office of Solid Waste and Emergency Response [Environmental Protection Agency Washington, DC]
OSWG.......... Optical Systems Working Group (MUGU)
OSWI .... Old Spaghetti Warehouse, Inc. (MHDW)
OSWMP .... Office of Solid Waste Management Programs [Environmental Protection Agency]
OSWS .... Operating System Workstation [Computer science]
OSWS .... Whitchurch-Stouffville Public Library, Stouffville, Ontario [Library symbol National Library of Canada] (NLC)
OSWV .... Osteryoung Square Wave Voltammogram [Electrochemistry]
OSX .... Kosciusko, MS [Location identifier FAA] (FAAL)
OSY .... Namsos [Norway] [Airport symbol] (OAG)
OSY .... National Institute for Occupational Safety and Health, Morgantown, WV [OCLC symbol] (OCLC)
OSY .... Odyssey Resources Ltd. [Vancouver Stock Exchange symbol]
OSYC .... Officer Supervising Yardcraft [Canadian Navy]
OSYFC .... Sydenham Branch, Frontenac County Library, Ontario [Library symbol National Library of Canada] (BIB)
OSYS .... OccuSystems, Inc. [NASDAQ symbol] (SAG)
OSyS .... Sylvania Schools, Sylvania, OH [Library symbol] [Library of Congress] (LCLS)
OSZ............ Koszalin [Poland] [Airport symbol] (OAG)
OSZ............ Offshore Surf Zone
OSZ............ Washington, DC [Location identifier FAA] (FAAL)
OSzK........... Orszagos Szechenyi Konyvtar [National Szechenyi Library] [Information service or system] (IID)
OT............. Evergreen Helicopters of Alaska [ICAO designator] (AD)
OT............. Objective Test [Psychology]
OT............. Object Technology [Computer science] (CDE)
OT............. Observer Target [Army]
OT............. Occipitotransverse [Obstetrics]
OT............. Occlusion Time (MAE)
OT............. Occupational Therapist [or Therapy] [Medicine]
OT............. Occupational Therapy Technician [Navy]
OT............. Occupational Training (AIE)
OT............. Occupied Territories (BJA)
OT............. Ocean Systems Technician [Navy] (DNAB)
OT............. Ocean Transportation [Military]
OT............. Ocular Tension [Medicine]
OT............. Oedipus Tyrannus [of Sophocles] [Classical studies] (OCD)
OT............. Oesterreicher-Turner [Syndrome] [Medicine] (DB)
OT............. Offensive Tackle [Football]
OT............. Office of Telecommunications [Department of Commerce]
OT............. Office of Territories [Department of the Interior]
OT............. Office of Transportation [Department of Agriculture]
OT............. Off Time (WDAA)
OT............. Oil Temperature [Automotive engineering]
OT............. Oil-Tempered (IAA)
OT............. Oil-Tight
OT............. Old Term
OT............. Old Terminology
OT............. Old Testament [of the Bible]
OT............. Old Timer [Communications operators' colloquialism]
OT............. Old Tom [British slang term for gin] (ROG)
OT............. Old Top [Communications operators' colloquialism]
OT............. Old [or Original] Tuberculin [Also, TO] [Medicine]
OT............. Olfactory Threshold
OT............. Olfactory Tubercle [Neuroanatomy]
OT............. On a Track [Rail] [Shipping] (DCTA)
OT............. Once-Through [Nuclear reactor technology]
OT............. One Time
OT............. On Target [Military] (CAAL)
O/T............. On Thames [In place names] [British] (ROG)
OT............. On Time
O/T............. On Trent [In place names] [British] (ROG)
OT............. On Truck [Shipping]
OT............. Open Topped [Container] [Packaging] (DCTA)
OT............. Open Transport [Computer science]
OT............. Operating Temperature [Nuclear energy]
OT............. Operating Theater
OT............. Operating Time
OT............. Operational Instrumentation Tank [NASA] (NAKS)
OT............. Operational Technology [Nuclear energy] (NRCH)
OT............. Operational Test (AFM)
OT............. Operational TIROS [NASA]
OT............. Operational Training (MCD)
OT............. Operational Trajectory [Aerospace] (KSC)
OT............. Operations Team (MCD)
OT............. Optatam Totius [Decree on Priestly Formation] [Vatican II document]
OT............. Optical Tool
OT............. Optical Tracker [NASA] (NAKS)
OT............. Optical Tracking [NASA] (KSC)
OT............. Optical-Transient [Astronomy]
OT............. Optic Tectum [Anatomy]
O/T............. Oral Temperature (DAVI)

OT	Oral Testimony (BJA)
OT	Oral Thrush [*Medicine*] (MEDA)
OT	Oregon Territory [*Prior to statehood*]
OT	Oregon Trunk Railway [*AAR code*]
OT	Organizational Table
OT	Organization Table
OT	Orienteering Tasmania [*Australia An association*]
OT	Orifice Tube [*Automobile air conditioning system*]
OT	Original Tuberculin [*Medicine*] (DMAA)
OT	Orotracheal [*Medicine*]
O-T	Orthohombic-Tetragonal [*Temperature transition*]
OT	Ortho Tolidine (PDAA)
OT	Oscillation Transformer [*Radio*]
OT	Osmium Tetroxide [*Inorganic chemistry*]
OT	Other Than
OT	Other Time
OT	Otis Test [*Psychiatry*] (DAVI)
OT	Otolaryngology [*Medicine*]
OT	Otology [*Medicine*]
OT	O'Toole's Group, Inc. [*Toronto Stock Exchange symbol*]
Ot	Otto Papiensis [*Flourished, 12th century*] [*Authority cited in pre-1607 legal work*] (DSA)
Ot	Otto's United States Supreme Court Reports [*91-107 United States*] [*A publication*] (DLA)
OT	Ought (ROG)
OT	Outer Table (MCD)
OT	Outer Tube
OT	Outfit
OT	Out of Tolerance
OT	Output [*Computer science*] (IAA)
OT	Output Terminal
OT	Out Temperature (MCD)
OT	Overall Test (KSC)
OT	Overhead Transparencies
OT	Overlap Technician
OT	Overlap Telling (MCD)
OT	Overseas Territories (MCD)
OT	Overseas Trade
OT	Overseas Trading [*A publication*]
O/T	Overtemperature (KSC)
OT	Over There (ADA)
OT	Overtime
OT	Overtone
OT	Ovotransferrin [*Biochemistry*]
OT	Oxytocin [*Endocrinology*]
OT	Stations Open Exclusively to Operational Traffic of the Services Concerned [*ITU designation*] (CET)
OT	Tara Branch, Bruce County Public Library, Ontario [*Library symbol National Library of Canada*] (NLC)
OT	Toledo-Lucas County Public Library, Toledo, OH [*Library symbol Library of Congress*] (LCLS)
OTA	Academy of Medicine, Toronto, Ontario [*Library symbol National Library of Canada*] (NLC)
OTA	Mota [*Ethiopia*] [*Airport symbol*] (AD)
OTA	Occupational Therapists Association (NADA)
OTA	Occupied Territory Administration [*World War II*]
OTA	Office of Tax Analysis [*Department of the Treasury*]
OTA	Office of Technical Assistance (USGC)
OTA	Office of Technology Assessment [*Congressional study group*] [*Washington, DC*]
OTA	Office of Technology Assistance [*General Services Administration*]
OTA	Office of Telecommunications Applications [*US National Telecommunications and Information Administration*] (TSSD)
OTA	Officer Training Allowance [*Naval Reserve*]
OTA	Off-the-Air Record Club [*Record label*]
OTA	Oil Trades Association of New York (EA)
OTA	Old Testament Abstracts [*A publication*] (BJA)
OTA	Omnidirectional Transmitter Antenna
OTA	Open Test Assembly [*Nuclear energy*] (NRCH)
OTA	Operational Test Agency (DOMA)
OTA	Operational Transconductance Amplifier (IEEE)
OTA	Operation Town Affiliations [*An association*] (EA)
OTA	Operation-Triggered Architecture [*Computer science*]
OTA	Optical Telescope Assembly [*NASA*]
OTA	Optical Tracking Aid [*Deep Space Instrumentation Facility, NASA*]
OTA	Organic Trade Association
OTA	Organisation Mondiale du Tourisme et de l'Automobile [*World Touring and Automobile Organization*]
OTA	Ornithine Transaminase (DB)
OTA	Orthodontic Technicians Association [*British*] (DBA)
OTA	Ortho-Tolidine Arsenite [*Organic chemistry*]
OTA	Other Talk Address (IAA)
OTA	Other than Air (CINC)
ota	Ottoman Turkish [*MARC language code Library of Congress*] (LCCP)
OTA	Outer Transport Area
OTA	Output Transformerless Amplifier (DICI)
OTA	Outside-Wheel Turning Angle [*Automotive engineering*]
OTAA	AASTRA Aerospace, Inc., Downsview, Ontario [*Library symbol National Library of Canada*] (BIB)
OTAA	Office of Trade Adjustment Assistance [*Department of Labor*]
OTAC	Acres Consulting Services Ltd., Toronto, Ontario [*Library symbol National Library of Canada*] (NLC)
OTAC	Oceanic Trade Alliance Council International
OTAC	Ordnance Tank-Automotive Command [*Merged with Weapons and Mobility Command*] [*Army*]

OTACS	Old Timer Assay Commissioners Society [*Defunct*] (EA)
OTAD	Addiction Research Foundation, Toronto, Ontario [*Library symbol National Library of Canada*] (NLC)
OTAD	Office of Tributary Area Development [*Tennessee Valley Authority*]
OTAD	Oversea Terminal Arrival Date [*Army*] (AABC)
OTADA	Office of Tracking and Data Acquisition [*NASA*]
OTADL	Outer Target Azimuth Datum Line
OTAE	Atomic Energy of Canada [*L'Energie Atomique du Canada*] Toronto, Ontario [*Library symbol National Library of Canada*] (NLC)
OTAE	[*The*] Old Testament in the Light of the Ancient East [*A publication*] (BJA)
OTAF	Office of Technology Assessment and Forecast [*Patent and Trademark Office*] [*Washington, DC*]
OTAF	Ontario Ministry of Agriculture and Food, Toronto, Ontario [*Library symbol National Library of Canada*] (NLC)
OTAF	Operating Time at Failure (MCD)
OTAF Data Base	Office of Technology Assessment and Forecasts Data Base (NITA)
OTAG	Art Gallery of Ontario, Toronto, Ontario [*Library symbol National Library of Canada*] (NLC)
OTAG	Office of the Adjutant General [*Military*]
OTAG	Ozone Transport Assessment Group
OTAGAV	Audiovisual Library, Art Gallery of Ontario, Toronto, Ontario [*Library symbol National Library of Canada*] (NLC)
Otago Pol Gaz	Otago Police Gazette [*1861-64*] [*New Zealand*] [*A publication*] (DLA)
OTAL	Arts and Letters Club, Toronto, Ontario [*Library symbol National Library of Canada*] (NLC)
OTAN	Organisation du Traite de l'Atlantique Nord [*North Atlantic Treaty Organization - NATO*] [*Brussels, Belgium*]
OTAN	Organizacao do Tratado do Atlantico Norte [*North Atlantic Treaty Organization*] [*Portuguese*]
OT & E	Operational Test and Evaluation [*Military*] (AFM)
OT&E	Operational Testing and Evaluation (USDC)
OTANY	Oil Trades Association of New York (EA)
OTAP	Alternative Press Centre, Toronto, Ontario [*Library symbol National Library of Canada*] (NLC)
OTAQ	Offer Therapist-Adolescent Questionnaire [*Personality development test*] [*Psychology*]
OTAR	Archives of Ontario, Toronto, Ontario [*Library symbol National Library of Canada*] (NLC)
OTAR	Overseas Tariffs and Regulations (DS)
OTARC	Centennial College of Applied Arts and Technology, Scarborough, Ontario [*Library symbol National Library of Canada*] (NLC)
OTAS	Observer Target Acquisition Subsystem (MCD)
OTAS	On Top and Smooth [*NWS*] (FAAC)
OTASO	Organizacao do Tratado da Asia Sul-Oriental [*South-East Asia Treaty Organization*] [*Portuguese*]
O T AUTIC	Other than Automatic [*Freight*]
OTAWA	Occupational Therapy Association of Western Australia
Otb	October (CDAI)
OTB	Off the Board [*Investment term*]
OTB	Off-Track Betting
OTB	Old Tired Broads
OTB	On the Bow [*Nautical*]
OTB	Open to Buy
OTB	Orbiting Tanker Base [*NASA*] (NASA)
OTB	Ordnance and Terminal Ballistics
OTB	Ortho-Toluidine Boric Acid [*Organic chemistry*]
OTB	Overseas Trust Bank [*Hong Kong*]
OTB	Waverly Resource Library, Thunder Bay Public Library, Ontario [*Library symbol National Library of Canada*] (NLC)
OTBA	Ocean Thermal Boundary Analysis Charts [*Marine science*] (MSC)
OTBA	Owners, Traders, Breeders Association (NADA)
OTBA	Terrace Bay Public Library, Ontario [*Library symbol National Library of Canada*] (NLC)
OTBBR	Brodie Resource Library, Thunder Bay, Ontario [*Library symbol National Library of Canada*] (NLC)
OTBC	Canadian Broadcasting Corp. [*Societe Radio-Canada*] Toronto, Ontario [*Library symbol National Library of Canada*] (NLC)
OTBCC	Confederation College, Thunder Bay, Ontario [*Library symbol National Library of Canada*] (NLC)
OTBCG	Blake, Cassels & Graydon, Toronto, Ontario [*Library symbol National Library of Canada*] (NLC)
OTBCGC	Staff Library, Baycrest Centre for Geriatric Care, Toronto, Ontario [*Library symbol National Library of Canada*] (BIB)
OTBCIR	Bell Canada Information Resource Centre, Toronto, Ontario [*Library symbol National Library of Canada*] (NLC)
OTBCO	Technical Information Facility, Canadien Imperial Bank of Commerce, Toronto, Ontario [*Library symbol National Library of Canada*] (NLC)
OTBCP	Program Archives, Canadian Broadcasting Corp. [*Archives des Emissions, Societe Radio-Canada*] Toronto, Ontario [*Library symbol National Library of Canada*] (NLC)
OTBD	Doha/International [*Qatar*] [*ICAO location identifier*] (ICLI)
OTBD	Outboard (ADA)
OTBDHC	Thunder Bay District Health Council, Thunder Bay, Ontario [*Library symbol National Library of Canada*] (NLC)
OTBE	Ontario Ministry of Education, Thunder Bay, Ontario [*Library symbol National Library of Canada*] (NLC)
OTBE	Out of the Body Experiences [*Parapsychology*] (ECON)
OTBE	Overtaken by Events [*Military*]
OTBGH	General Hospital of Port Arthur, Thunder Bay, Ontario [*Library symbol National Library of Canada*] (NLC)

OTBH .... Thunder Bay Historical Museum Society, Ontario [*Library symbol National Library of Canada*] (NLC)

OTBHS .... Hammarskjold High School, Thunder Bay, Ontario [*Library symbol National Library of Canada*] (NLC)

OTBLA .... Audio Library Services of Northwestern Ontario, Lakehead University, Thunder Bay, Ontario [*Library symbol National Library of Canada*] (NLC)

OTBLL .... School of Library Technology, Lakehead University, Thunder Bay, Ontario [*Library symbol National Library of Canada*] (NLC)

OTBLP .... Staff Library, Lakehead Psychiatric Hospital, Thunder Bay, Ontario [*Library symbol National Library of Canada*] (NLC)

OTBM .... Technical Information Centre, Bank of Montreal, Willowdale, Ontario [*Library symbol National Library of Canada*] (NLC)

OTBMB .... Mary J. L. Black Library, Thunder Bay, Ontario [*Library symbol National Library of Canada*] (NLC)

OTBMBI .... Business Information Centre, Bank of Montreal, Toronto, Ontario [*Library symbol National Library of Canada*] (BIB)

OTBMC .... Medical Library, McKellar General Hospital, Thunder Bay, Ontario [*Library symbol National Library of Canada*] (NLC)

OTBML .... Music Library, Canadian National Institute for the Blind, Toronto, Ontario [*Library symbol National Library of Canada*] (BIB)

OTBNL .... National Library Division, Canadian National Institute for the Blind, Toronto, Ontario [*Library symbol National Library of Canada*] (NLC)

OTBNR .... Learning Resource Centre, BNR Ltd., Toronto, Ontario [*Library symbol National Library of Canada*] (NLC)

OTBNS .... Bell Northern Software Research, Toronto, Ontario [*Library symbol National Library of Canada*] (NLC)

OTBOC .... Ontario Cancer Treatment and Research Foundation, Thunder Bay, Ontario [*Library symbol National Library of Canada*] (NLC)

OTBP .... Blaney, Pasternak, Smela, Eagleson & Watson, Toronto, Ontario [*Library symbol National Library of Canada*] (NLC)

OTBQ .... Occupational Therapists' Board of Queensland [*Australia*]

OTBR .... Barringer Research Ltd., Rexdale, Ontario [*Library symbol National Library of Canada*] (NLC)

OTBS .... On-the-Bottom Sonobuoy (MCD)

OTBSL .... Bassel, Sullivan & Leake, Toronto, Ontario [*Library symbol National Library of Canada*] (NLC)

OTBSSC .... Over Thirty but Still Swinging Club

OTBV .... Oxidizer Turbine Bypass Valve (KSC)

OTBV .... Victoriaville Branch, Thunder Bay Public Library, Ontario [*Library symbol National Library of Canada*] (BIB)

OTC .... Bol [*Chad*] [*Airport symbol*] (AD)

OTC .... Faculty of Education, University of Toronto, Ontario [*Library symbol National Library of Canada*] (NLC)

OTC .... Objective, Time, and Cost

OTC .... Office of Technical Cooperation [*United Nations*]

OTC .... Office of Temporary Controls

OTC .... Officer in Tactical Command [*Air Force*]

OTC .... Officers' Training Camp [*World War I*]

OTC .... Officers' Training Corps

OTC .... Officers Transit Camp [*British military*] (DMA)

OTC .... Officer Training Center [*Navy*]

OTC .... Offshore Technology Conference

OTC .... Ohio Motor Freight Tariff Committee Inc., Columbus OH [*STAC*]

OTC .... Old Testament Commentary [*A publication*] (BJA)

OTC .... Old Timers' Club (EA)

OTC .... Once-Through Cooling [*Nuclear energy*] (NRCH)

OTC .... One-Stop Tour Charter [*Airline fare*]

OTC .... One-Time Carbon [*Paper*] (PDAA)

OTC .... Open Tubular Column [*For gas chromatography*]

OTC .... Operado de Terminal de Contenedores [*Container Terminal Operator*] [*Shipping*] [*Spanish*]

OTC .... Operador de Transporte Combinado [*Combined Transport Operator*] [*Spanish Business term*]

OTC .... Operating Telephone Co. [*Bell System*] (TEL)

OTC .... Operational Techniques Conference

OTC .... Operational Test Center [*NASA*] (KSC)

OTC .... Operational Test Coordinator [*Military*] (CAAL)

OTC .... Operational Training Capability [*Air Force*] (AFM)

OTC .... Operational Training Command (MCD)

OTC .... Operatore di Trasporto Combinato [*Combined Transport Operator*] [*Italian Business term*]

OTC .... Orbiter Test Conductor [*NASA*] (NASA)

OTC .... Orbiting Trajectory Computations

OTC .... Order of Three Crusades (EA)

OTC .... Ordnance Technical Committee [*Military*] (MUGU)

OTC .... Ordnance Training Command [*Army*]

OTC .... Organization for Trade Cooperation [*GATT*]

OTC .... Organize Training Center (EA)

OTC .... Organotin Compound [*Organic chemistry*]

OTC .... Original Trenton Cracker Co. [*Maker of Chowder & Oyster Crackers, claimed by some to be the oldest continuously manufactured American food product*]

OTC .... Originating Toll Center [*Telecommunications*] (TEL)

OTC .... Originating Toll Circuit [*Telecommunications*] (IAA)

OTC .... Originating Trunk Center [*Telecommunications*] (IAA)

OTC .... Ornithine Transcarbamoylase [*Also, OCT*] [*An enzyme*]

OTC .... Ornithine Transcarbamylase [*An enzyme*] (DAVI)

OTC .... Oshkosh Truck Corp.

OTC .... Otterbein College, Westerville, OH [*OCLC symbol*] (OCLC)

OTC .... Outer Tube Centerline

OTC .... Oval Target Cell (DMAA)

OTC .... Overseas Telecommunications Commission (NITA)

OTC .... Overseas Telecommunications Commission of Australia (BARN)

OTC .... Over-the-Calf [*Women's fashions*] (IIA)

OTC .... Over-the-Capacitor [*Sockets*]

OTC .... Over-the-Counter [*Pharmacy*]

OTC .... Over-the-Counter [*Also, O/C*] [*Stock exchange term*]

OTC .... Oxygen Transfer Compressor

OTC .... Oxytetracycline [*Antibiotic*]

OTC .... Ozone Transport Commission [*State environmental agencies*]

OTCA .... Olson 30 Class Association (EA)

OTCA .... Ontario College of Art, Toronto, Ontario [*Library symbol National Library of Canada*] (NLC)

OTCA .... Oxothiazolidinecarboxylic Acid [*Biochemistry*]

OTCAG .... Canada Arctic Gas Study Ltd., Toronto, Ontario [*Library symbol National Library of Canada*] (NLC)

OTCAS .... Canadian Association in Support of the Native Peoples, Toronto, Ontario [*Library symbol National Library of Canada*] (NLC)

OTCBS .... Central Baptist Seminary and Bible College, Toronto, Ontario [*Library symbol National Library of Canada*] (NLC)

OTCC .... Operator Test Control Console (MCD)

OTCC .... Organic Thermal Control Coating

OTCC .... United Church of Canada Archives, Toronto, Ontario [*Library symbol National Library of Canada*] (NLC)

OTCCC .... Cross Cultural Communication Centre, Toronto, Ontario [*Library symbol National Library of Canada*] (NLC)

OTCCC .... Open Type Control Circuit Contacts (MSA)

OTCCL .... Currie, Coopers & Lybrand Ltd., Toronto, Ontario [*Library symbol National Library of Canada*] (NLC)

OTCCP .... Canadian Centre for Philanthropy, Toronto, Ontario [*Library symbol National Library of Canada*] (NLC)

OTCCRT .... Technical Standards Division, Ontario Ministry of Consumer and Commercial Relations, Toronto, Ontario [*Library symbol National Library of Canada*] (NLC)

OTCD .... Ornithine Carbomoyltransferase Deficiency (DMAA)

OTCD .... Over-the-Counter-Drug (MEDA)

OTCE .... Central Library, North York, Ontario [*Library symbol National Library of Canada*] (NLC)

OTCEA .... [*The*] Canadian Education Association [*L'Association Canadienne d'Education*] Toronto, Ontario [*Library symbol National Library of Canada*] (NLC)

OTCF .... H. Ward Smith Library, Centre of Forensic Sciences, Toronto, Ontario [*Library symbol National Library of Canada*] (NLC)

OTCFA .... Occupational Therapy Comprehensive Functional Assessment

OTCFX .... Price T. Rowe: Small-Cap Stock [*Mutual fund ticker symbol*] (SG)

OTCGL .... Campbell, Godfrey & Lewtas, Toronto, Ontario [*Library symbol National Library of Canada*] (NLC)

OTCGR .... Canadian Gas Research Institute, Don Mills, Ontario [*Library symbol National Library of Canada*] (NLC)

OTCGW .... Clarkson, Gordon, Woods, Gordon, Toronto, Ontario [*Library symbol National Library of Canada*] (NLC)

OTCH .... Anglican Church House, Toronto, Ontario [*Library symbol National Library of Canada*] (NLC)

OTCH .... Obedience Trial Champion [*Dog training*]

OTCh .... Obedience Trial Champion [*Prefix*]

OTCHA .... Canadian Hospital Association [*Association des Hopitaux du Canada*] Toronto, Ontario [*Library symbol National Library of Canada*] (NLC)

OTCHAR .... Anglican Church of Canada Archives, Toronto, Ontario [*Library symbol National Library of Canada*] (NLC)

OTCI .... OTC [*Overseas Telecommunications Commission*] International Ltd. [*Australia Telecommunications service*] (TSSD)

OTCIA .... Canadian Institute of International Affairs [*Institut Canadien des Affaires Internationales*] Toronto, Ontario [*Library symbol National Library of Canada*] (NLC)

OTCIB .... Canadian Imperial Bank of Commerce, Toronto, Ontario [*Library symbol National Library of Canada*] (NLC)

OTCIL .... Central Library, C-I-L, Inc., North York, Ontario [*Library symbol National Library of Canada*] (NLC)

OTCILL .... Law Library, C-I-L, Inc., North York, Ontario [*Library symbol National Library of Canada*] (NLC)

OTCIXS .... Officer in Tactical Command Information Exchange Subsystem [*Navy*] (ANA)

OTCJC .... Genealogical Society Library, Church of Jesus Christ of Latter-Day Saints, Etobicoke, Ontario [*Library symbol National Library of Canada*] (NLC)

OTCL .... Connaught Laboratories Ltd., Willowdale, Ontario [*Library symbol National Library of Canada*] (NLC)

OTCLA .... Confederation Life Association, Toronto, Ontario [*Library symbol National Library of Canada*] (NLC)

OTCLANT ..... Fleet Operational Training Command, Atlantic [*Usually, COTCLANT*]

OTCLH .... Research and Information Library, Canadian Life and Health Insurance Association, Toronto, Ontario [*Library symbol National Library of Canada*] (BIB)

OTCM .... Canadian School of Missions and Ecumenical Institute, Toronto, Ontario [*Library symbol National Library of Canada*] (NLC)

OTCM .... Ocean Systems Technician, Master Chief [*Navy rating*] (DNAB)

OTCM .... Orbiter Thermal Control Model [*NASA*]

OTCM .... Ordnance Technical Committee Minutes [*Military*]

OTCM .... Royce Micro-Cap Tr [*NASDAQ symbol*] (TTSB)

OTCM .... Royce OTC [*Over the Counter*] Micro Capital Fund [*NASDAQ symbol*] (SAG)

OTCMC .... Canadian Memorial Chiropractic College, Toronto, Ontario [*Library symbol National Library of Canada*] (NLC)

OTCMCC ...... Old Time Country Music Club of Canada (EA)

OTCMH .... Saul A. Silverman Library, C. M. Hincks Treatment Centre, Toronto, Ontario [*Library symbol National Library of Canada*] (BIB)

OTCMHA ...... Canadian Mental Health Association, Toronto, Ontario [*Library symbol National Library of Canada*] (BIB)

OTCMLA ...... Canadian Music Library Association [*Association Canadienne des Bibliotheques Musicales*] Toronto, Ontario [*Library symbol National Library of Canada*] (NLC)

OTCMS .... Operations Training Certification Management System [*NASA*]

OTCOM .... Cominco Ltd., Toronto, Ontario [*Library symbol National Library of Canada*] (NLC)

OTCOP .... Olympic Training Center Outreach Program

OTCOS .... Concord Scientific Corp., Downsview, Ontario [*Library symbol National Library of Canada*] (NLC)

OTCOU .... Council of Ontario Universities, Toronto, Ontario [*Library symbol National Library of Canada*] (NLC)

OTCP .... Canada Packers Ltd., Toronto, Ontario [*Library symbol National Library of Canada*] (NLC)

OTCPAC .... Fleet Operational Training Command, Pacific [*Usually, COTCPAC*]

OTCPB .... Toronto City Planning Board Library, Ontario, [*Library symbol National Library of Canada*] (NLC)

OTCQM .... Office of the Theater Chief Quartermaster [*World War II*]

OTCR .... Office of Technical Cooperation and Research [*Department of State*]

OTCR .... Ontario Ministry of Culture and Communications, Toronto, Ontario [*Library symbol National Library of Canada*] (NLC)

OTCRC .... National Office Library, Canadian Red Cross Society [*Bibliotheque du Siege Social, Societe Canadienne de la Croix-Rouge*] Toronto, Ontario [*Library symbol National Library of Canada*] (NLC)

OTCRx .... Over-the-Counter Drug (MEDA)

OTCS .... Ocean Systems Technician, Senior Chief [*Navy rating*] (DNAB)

OTCS .... Ontario Ministry of Correctional Services, Toronto, Ontario [*Library symbol National Library of Canada*] (NLC)

OTCS .... Operational Teletype Communications Subsystem

OTCS .... Optical Transient Current Spectroscopy

OTCSA .... Canadian Standards Association, Rexdale, Ontario [*Library symbol National Library of Canada*] (NLC)

OTCSAO .... Construction Safety Association of Ontario, Toronto, Ontario [*Library symbol National Library of Canada*] (NLC)

OTCSC .... Civil Service Commission of Ontario, Toronto, Ontario [*Library symbol National Library of Canada*] (NLC)

OTCSE .... Canadian Selection, Toronto, Ontario [*Library symbol National Library of Canada*] (NLC)

OTCSS .... CANEBSCO Subscription Service Ltd., Toronto, Ontario [*Library symbol National Library of Canada*] (NLC)

OTCT .... Canadian Tax Foundation [*Association Canadienne d'Etudes Fiscales*] Toronto, Ontario [*Library symbol National Library of Canada*] (NLC)

OTCTA .... Canadian Telebook Agency, Toronto, Ontario [*Library symbol National Library of Canada*] (NLC)

OTCTAR .... Division of Records and Archives, City of Toronto (NLC)

OTCTH .... Town Hall, Collins Canada, Toronto, Ontario [*Library symbol National Library of Canada*] (NLC)

OTCTVN .... CTV News Research Library, CTV Television Network, Toronto, Ontario [*Library symbol National Library of Canada*] (NLC)

OTCW .... Canada Wire & Cable Co. Ltd., Toronto, Ontario [*Library symbol National Library of Canada*] (NLC)

OTCWB .... Welding Institute of Canada, Oakville, Ontario [*Library symbol National Library of Canada*] (NLC)

OTCWT .... Canadian Waste Technology, Inc., Toronto, Ontario [*Library symbol National Library of Canada*] (NLC)

OTD .... Contadora [*Panama*] [*Airport symbol*] (OAG)

OTD .... Doctor of Occupational Therapy (PGP)

OTD .... Ocean Travel Development (DS)

OTD .... Oculotrichodysplasia (DMAA)

OTD .... Office of Technology Development (COE)

OTD .... Official Table of Distances (AFM)

OTD .... Offset, Tilted Dipole [*Model of Uranus' magnetic field*]

OTD .... Oil Turbine Drive

OTD .... On the Deck

OTD .... Operational Technical Documentation [*NASA*] (NASA)

OTD .... Operational Test Director [*Navy*]

OTD .... Operations and Technical Data [*Engineering*]

OTD .... Optical Time Domain (EECA)

OTD .... Optical Tracking Device

OTD .... Optical Transient Detector

OTD .... Optimal Terminal Descent (PDAA)

OTD .... Oral Temperature Device (MCD)

OTD .... Orbiter Test Director [*NASA*] (NASA)

OTD .... Orbit Test Direction [*or Directive*] (IAA)

OTD .... Organ Tolerance Dose [*Medicine*] (DMAA)

OTD .... Original Transmission Density (OA)

OTD .... Ortho-Toluenediamine [*Organic chemistry*]

OTD .... Out the Door (DAVI)

OTD .... Overseas-Trained Doctors

OTDA .... DSMA Acton Ltd., Toronto, Ontario [*Library symbol National Library of Canada*] (NLC)

OTDA .... Office of Tracking and Data Acquisition [*NASA*]

OTD&C .... Offshore Technology Development & Consulting (EFIS)

OTDAR .... Alexander Raxlen Memorial Library, Doctors Hospital, Toronto, Ontario [*Library symbol National Library of Canada*] (NLC)

OTDC .... Dominion Colour Ltd., Toronto, Ontario [*Library symbol National Library of Canada*] (NLC)

OTDC .... Observational Test and Development Center [*National Weather Service*] (NOAA)

OTDC .... Optical Target Designation Computer

OTDCB .... Dictionary of Canadian Biography, Toronto, Ontario [*Library symbol National Library of Canada*] (BIB)

OTDD .... Optical Target Detecting Device

OTDE .... Ontario Ministry of Education, Toronto, Ontario [*Library symbol National Library of Canada*] (NLC)

OTDH .... Ontario Ministry of Health, Toronto, Ontario [*Library symbol National Library of Canada*] (NLC)

OTDHA .... De Havilland Aircraft of Canada Ltd., Downsview, Ontario [*Library symbol National Library of Canada*] (NLC)

OTDHC .... Oceanographic Technical Data Handling Committee

OTDHL .... Laboratory Services, Ontario Ministry of Health, Toronto, Ontario [*Library symbol National Library of Canada*] (NLC)

OTDL .... Ontario Ministry of Labour, Toronto, Ontario [*Library symbol National Library of Canada*] (NLC)

OTDM .... Mines Library, Ontario Ministry of Natural Resources, Toronto, Ontario [*Library symbol National Library of Canada*] (NLC)

OTDO .... Donwood Institute, Toronto, Ontario [*Library symbol National Library of Canada*] (BIB)

OTDR .... Optical Fiber Time-Domain Reflectometer [*Computer science*]

OTDR .... Optical Time Domain Reflectometer (NITA)

OTDR .... Outdoor

OTDR .... Scientific Information Centre, Defence and Civil Institute of Environmental Medicine, Canada Department of National Defence [*Centre d'Information Scientifique, Institut Militaire et Civil de Medecine de l'Environnement, Ministere de la Defense Nationale*] Downsview, Ontario [*Library symbol National Library of Canada*] (NLC)

OTDRE .... Ontario Ministry of Treasury and Economics, Toronto, Ontario [*Library symbol National Library of Canada*] (NLC)

OTDT .... Ontario Ministry of Transportation and Communications, Toronto, Ontario [*Library symbol National Library of Canada*] (NLC)

OTDT .... Operational Test, Development Test

OTDT .... Operations Training Development Team [*Air Force*]

OTDU .... Ontario Ministry of Colleges and Universities, Toronto, Ontario [*Library symbol National Library of Canada*] (NLC)

OTDW .... Day-Wilson-Campbell, Toronto, Ontario [*Library symbol National Library of Canada*] (BIB)

OTE .... Emmanuel College, Victoria University, Toronto, Ontario [*Library symbol National Library of Canada*] (NLC)

OTE .... On-Target Earnings [*Sales industry*] (ODBW)

OTE .... Ontario Ministry of Treasury and Economics Library [*UTLAS symbol*]

OTE .... Operational Test and Evaluation [*Army*] (AABC)

OTE .... Operational Test Equipment [*NASA*] (KSC)

OTE .... Optically Transparent Electrode

OTE .... Optical Tracking Electronics

OTE .... Organismos Tilepikoinonion Ellados [*Hellenic Telecommunications Organization*] [*Greek*]

OTE .... Other Technical Effort

OTE .... Outer Tube Equipment

OTE .... Overtaken by Events [*US Congress*]

OTE .... Oxalyl Thiolester [*Biochemistry*]

OTEA .... Operational Test and Evaluation Agency [*Army*]

OTEA .... Oval Track Equipment Association (EA)

OTEAOW ...... Atmospheric Environment Service (ODIT Ontario Weather Centre), Environment Canada [*Service de l'Environnement Atmospherique (Centre Meteorologique de l'Ontario), Environnement Canada*] Toronto, Ontario [*Library symbol National Library of Canada*] (NLC)

OTEBE .... Resource Library, Board of Education for the City of Etobicoke, Ontario [*Library symbol National Library of Canada*] (NLC)

OTEC .... Education Centre, Toronto Board of Education, Ontario [*Library symbol National Library of Canada*] (NLC)

OTEC .... Ocean Thermal Energy Conversion

OTEC .... Operational Test and Evaluation Command [*Army*] (AAGC)

OTEC .... Osage Tribal Education Committee [*Department of the Interior*] [*Muskogee, OK*] (EGAO)

OTECA .... Ocean Thermal Energy Conversion Act of 1980

OTECS .... Ocean Thermal Energy Conversion Systems [*Department of Energy*]

OTECU .... Colleges and Universitites, Ontario Ministry of Education, Toronto, Ontario [*Library symbol National Library of Canada*] (NLC)

OTEE .... Teeswater Branch, Bruce County Public Library, Ontario [*Library symbol National Library of Canada*] (NLC)

OTEF .... Operational Training and Evaluation Facility

OTEM .... ESSO [*Standard Oil*] Minerals of Canada, Toronto, Ontario [*Library symbol National Library of Canada*] (NLC)

OTEMAC ...... Temagami Community Library, Ontario [*Library symbol National Library of Canada*] (NLC)

OTEMAS ...... Osaka International Textile Machinery Show

OTEMC .... Elizabeth McRae Associates, Toronto, Ontario [*Library symbol Obsolete National Library of Canada*] (NLC)

OTEMP .... Overtemperature (NASA)

OTEMPO ..... Operating Temporaries

OTEMR .... Conservation and Renewable Energy Office, Energy, Mines, and Resources Canada [*Bureau de la Conservation de l'Energie et de l'Energie Renouvelable, Energie, Mines, et Ressources Canada*] Toronto, Ontario [*Library symbol National Library of Canada*] (NLC)

OTEP .... Office of Transportation Energy Policy [*Department of Transportation*]

OTEP .... Operational Test and Evaluation Plan [*Military*] (AFM)

OTEPL .... Etobicoke Public Library, Ontario [*Library symbol National Library of Canada*] (NLC)

OTEPS .... Environmental Protection Service, Environment Canada [*Service de la Protection de l'Environnement, Environnement Canada*] Toronto, Ontario [*Library symbol National Library of Canada*] (NLC)

OTEPSE....... Environmental Emergency Library, Environmental Protection Service, Environment Canada [*Bibliotheque des Incidences Environnementales, Service de la Protection de l'Environnement, Environnement Canada*] Toronto, Ontario [*Library symbol National Library of Canada*] (NLC)

OTER .... Ontario Institute for Studies in Education, Toronto, Ontario [*Library symbol National Library of Canada*] (NLC)

OTES........... Operational Test and Evaluation Squadron [*Military*]

OTES........... Optical Technology Experiment System

OTES........... Orbiter Thermal Effects Simulator [*NASA*]

OTET........... Ontario Educational Communications Authority, Toronto, Ontario [*Library symbol National Library of Canada*] (NLC)

OTET........... TVOntario, Toronto, Ontario [*Library symbol National Library of Canada*] (NLC)

OTEU .... Office and Technical Employees (International) Union

O TEUT .... Old Teutonic [*Language, etc.*] (ROG)

OTEX........... Open Text Corp. [*NASDAQ symbol*] (SAG)

OTEXA .... Office of Textiles and Apparel [*Department of Commerce*] (GFGA)

OTEXF......... Open Text [*NASDAQ symbol*] (TTSB)

OTEY........... East York Public Library, Toronto, Ontario [*Library symbol National Library of Canada*] (NLC)

OTEYBE....... Professional Library, Board of Education for the Borough of East York, Toronto, Ontario [*Library symbol National Library of Canada*] (NLC)

OTF............. Institute of Environment Studies, University of Toronto, Ontario [*Library symbol National Library of Canada*] (NLC)

OTF............. Octamer Transcription Factor [*Genetics*]

OTF............. Off-the-Film [*Photography*] (WDMC)

OTF............. Off-the-Film Metering [*Olympus cameras*]

OTF............. Ontario Teachers Federation (AEBS)

OTF............. On the Floor [*Computer language*] [*Computer science*]

OTF............. On-the-Fly [*Computer compression program*] (PCM)

OTF............. Open Token Foundation (BTTJ)

OTF............. Optical Transfer Function

OTF............. Optimum Traffic Condition [*Radio*] (IAA)

OTF............. Optimum Traffic Frequency [*Radio*]

OTF............. Oral Transfer Factor [*Virology*]

OTF............. Orbital Test Flight (MCD)

OTF............. Other than Flat [*Freight*]

OTFC........... Official 3 Stooges Fan Club [*Defunct*] (EA)

OTFC........... Ontario Ministry of Consumer and Commercial Relations, Toronto, Ontario [*Library symbol National Library of Canada*] (NLC)

OTFC........... Overflight Traffic [*Aviation*] (FAAC)

OTFCS......... On-Target Fire Control System (MCD)

OTFE........... Optical Terminal Flight Evaluation

OTFEC........ Fenco Consultants Ltd., Toronto, Ontario [*Library symbol National Library of Canada*] (NLC)

OTFH .... Forest Hill Public Library, Toronto, Ontario [*Library symbol National Library of Canada*] (NLC)

OTFM.......... Fire Marshal of Ontario, Toronto, Ontario [*Library symbol National Library of Canada*] (NLC)

OTFN .... Information Centre, Falconbridge Nickel Mines Ltd., Toronto, Ontario [*Library symbol National Library of Canada*] (NLC)

OT/FOT .... Operational Test/Follow-On Operational Test

OTFP........... Fisons Corp. Ltd., Markham, Ontario [*Library symbol National Library of Canada*] (NLC)

OTFP........... Octylthio(trifluoro)propanone [*Biochemistry*]

OTFP........... Operational Traffic Flow Planning (GAVI)

OTFP........... Other than Full Paid [*IRS*]

OTFR .... Overall Transfer Function Response

OTFT........... Financial Times, Don Mills, Ontario [*Library symbol National Library of Canada*] (NLC)

OTFT........... Observer Tit for Tat [*Gene theory*]

OT/FT.......... Operational Test/Follow-On Test [*Missiles*] (DOMA)

OTFTS......... Outfits

OTG .... Information Centre, Glaxo Canada, Inc., Toronto, Ontario [*Library symbol National Library of Canada*] (BIB)

OTG .... Oil Temperature Gauge (MSA)

OTG .... OPTEVFOR [*Operational Test and Evaluation Force*] Tactics Guide [*Navy*] (CAAL)

OTG .... Option Table Generator

OTG .... Otolith Test Goggles [*NASA*] (KSC)

OTG .... Worthington [*Minnesota*] [*Airport symbol*] (OAG)

OTGA .... Information Centre, Giffels Associates Ltd., Rexdale, Ontario [*Library symbol National Library of Canada*] (NLC)

OTGAR........ Engineering Library, Garrett Canada, Rexdale, Ontario [*Library symbol National Library of Canada*] (BIB)

OTGB .... Library and Audio-Visual Services, George Brown College of Applied Arts and Technology, Toronto, Ontario [*Library symbol National Library of Canada*] (BIB)

OTGFM .... Management Science Department, General Foods, Inc., Don Mills, Ontario [*Library symbol National Library of Canada*] (NLC)

OTGG .... Goodman & Goodman, Toronto, Ontario [*Library symbol National Library of Canada*] (BIB)

OTGH .... Fudger Medical Library, Toronto General Hospital, Ontario [*Library symbol National Library of Canada*] (NLC)

OTGHPP...... Ocean Thermal Gradient Hydraulic Power Plant

OTGM .... Globe and Mail, Toronto, Ontario [*Library symbol National Library of Canada*] (NLC)

OTGMC .... Gulf Minerals Canada Ltd., Toronto, Ontario [*Library symbol National Library of Canada*] (NLC)

OTGOH .... Gowling & Henderson, Toronto, Ontario [*Library symbol National Library of Canada*] (NLC)

OTGS .... Gore & Storrie Ltd., Toronto, Ontario [*Library symbol National Library of Canada*] (NLC)

OTGS .... Ocean Thermal Gradient System [*National Science Foundation*]

OTGSB .... Bibliographic Centre, Ontario Ministry of Government Services, Toronto, Ontario [*Library symbol National Library of Canada*] (NLC)

OTGSI .... CTS Information Resource Centre, Ontario Ministry of Government Services, Toronto [*Library symbol National Library of Canada*] (BIB)

OTH .... Independent Institute, NAD, Dublin, OH [*OCLC symbol*] (OCLC)

OTH .... North Bend [*Oregon*] [*Airport symbol*] (OAG)

OTH .... Oil-Tight Hatch [*Shipfitting*]

OTH .... Ontario Hydro, Toronto, Ontario [*Library symbol National Library of Canada*] (NLC)

OTH .... Optical Time History (MCD)

Oth............. Othello [*Shakespearean work*]

OTH............. Othello [*Washington*] [*Seismograph station code, US Geological Survey*] (SEIS)

OTH .... Other (DAVI)

oth .... Other (VRA)

OTH .... Other than Hand [*Freight*]

OTH .... Other than Honorable Conditions [*Military*] (AABC)

OTH .... Over-the-Horizon [*RADAR*]

OTHA .... Hatch Associates Ltd., Toronto, Ontario [*Library symbol National Library of Canada*] (NLC)

OTHB .... Over-the-Horizon Back-Scatter [*RADAR*]

OTHB .... Toronto Historical Society, Ontario [*Library symbol National Library of Canada*] (BIB)

OTHC .... Humber College of Applied Arts and Technology, Rexdale, Ontario [*Library symbol National Library of Canada*] (NLC)

OTH/DA .... Over-the-Horizon/Damage Assessment [*Navy*] (CAAL)

OTHDC & T... Over-the-Horizon Detection, Classification, and Targeting (NVT)

OTH-E .... Over-the-Horizon - Expanded

OTHE .... Thessalon Union Public Library, Ontario [*Library symbol National Library of Canada*] (NLC)

OTHER .... Open Tubular Heterogeneous Enzyme Reactor [*Biochemical engineering*]

OTH-F .... Over-the-Horizon - Forward Scatter

OTHL .... Advanced Technology Centre, Honeywell Ltd., Willowdale, Ontario [*Library symbol National Library of Canada*] (NLC)

OTHMC .... Information Resources, Hay Management Consultants, Toronto, Ontario [*Library symbol National Library of Canada*] (NLC)

OTHMH....... Humber Memorial Hospital, Weston, Ontario [*Library symbol National Library of Canada*] (NLC)

OTHO .... Thornbury Public Library, Ontario [*Library symbol National Library of Canada*] (NLC)

OTHOP........ Quebec & Ontario Paper Co. Ltd., Thorold, Ontario [*Library symbol National Library of Canada*] (NLC)

OTHOR........ Thornhill Public Library, Ontario [*Library symbol National Library of Canada*] (NLC)

OTHORF...... Metallurgical Laboratory, Falconbridge Nickel Mines Ltd., Thornhill, Ontario [*Library symbol National Library of Canada*] (NLC)

OTHORO ..... Thorold Public Library, Ontario [*Library symbol National Library of Canada*] (BIB)

OTHR .... Ontario Hydro Research, Toronto, Ontario [*Library symbol National Library of Canada*] (NLC)

OTHR .... Over-the-Horizon RADAR (MCD)

OTHSA .... Orphan Train Heritage Society of America (EA)

OTHSC........ Hospital for Sick Children, Toronto, Ontario [*Library symbol National Library of Canada*] (NLC)

OTHSSM ...... Over-the-Horizon Ship-to-Ship Missile

OTHT .... Over-the-Horizon Targeting (NVT)

OTHU .... Huntec Ltd., Toronto, Ontario [*Library symbol National Library of Canada*] (NLC)

OTI............. Morotai Island [*Indonesia*] [*Airport symbol*] (OAG)

OTI............. Newport, RI [*Location identifier FAA*] (FAAL)

OTI............. Office of Technical Information (MUGU)

OTI............. Office of Trade and Investment [*Victoria, Australia*]

OTI............. Office of Treatment Improvement [*U.S. Public Health Service*] (BARN)

OTI............. Official Test Insecticide

OTI............. Optimum Time Invariant (IAA)

OTI............. Ordnance Technical Instructions [*Navy*]

OTI............. Oregon Technical Institute

OTI............. Original Title [*Online database field identifier*]

OTI............. Otiai [*Former USSR Seismograph station code, US Geological Survey Closed*] (SEIS)

OTI............. OT Industries, Inc. [*Vancouver Stock Exchange symbol*]

OTI............. Ovomucoid Trypsin Inhibitor [*Medicine*] (DMAA)

OTI............. Oxide Throat Insert

OTI............. Timmins Public Library, Ontario [*Library symbol National Library of Canada*] (NLC)

OTIA .... Office of Technical Information Agency [*Army*] (MCD)

OTIA .... Ordnance Technical Intelligence Agency (AAG)

OTIAP .... IAPA [*Industrial Accident Prevention Association*] Library, Toronto, Ontario [*Library symbol National Library of Canada*] (NLC)

OTIBI .... IBI Group, Toronto, Ontario [*Library symbol National Library of Canada*] (BIB)

OTIC........... Idea Corp., Toronto, Ontario [*Library symbol National Library of Canada*] (NLC)

OTIC........... Innovation Ontario Corp., Toronto, Ontario [*Library symbol National Library of Canada*] (NLC)

OTICA .... Institute of Chartered Accountants of Ontario, Toronto, Ontario [*Library symbol National Library of Canada*] (NLC)

OTID .... Industrial Disease Standards Panel, Toronto, Ontario [*Library symbol National Library of Canada*] (BIB)

OTID .... Office of Talented Identification and Development [*Johns Hopkins University*] (EDAC)

OTID .... Office of Talented Indentification and Development [*Johns Hopkins Institute*] (WDAA)

OTIEP .... Office of Technical Information and Educational Programs [*Terminated NASA*]

OTIF .... Organisation Intergouvernementale pour les Transports Internationaux Ferrovaires [*Intergovernmental Organization for International Carriage by Rail*] (EAIO)

OTif .... Tiffin Seneca Public Library, Tiffin, OH [*Library symbol Library of Congress*] (LCLS)

OTifH .... Heidelberg College, Tiffin, OH [*Library symbol Library of Congress*] (LCLS)

OTIG .... Office of the Inspector General [*Army*] (AABC)

OTIHM .... Tillsonburg and District Historical Museum Society, Tillsonburg, Ontario [*Library symbol National Library of Canada*] (NLC)

OTII .... Our Torah Institutions of Israel (EA)

OTIL .... Tilbury Public Library, Ontario [*Library symbol National Library of Canada*] (NLC)

OTIM .... Pontifical Institute of Mediaeval Studies, University of Toronto, Ontario [*Library symbol National Library of Canada*] (NLC)

OTIN .... International Nickel Co. of Canada Ltd., Toronto, Ontario [*Library symbol National Library of Canada*] (NLC)

OTINF .... Infomart, Toronto, Ontario [*Library symbol National Library of Canada*] (NLC)

OTINP .... Information Plus Library, Toronto, Ontario [*Library symbol National Library of Canada*] (BIB)

OTIO .... United Kingdom Information Office, Toronto, Ontario [*Library symbol National Library of Canada*] (NLC)

OTIOL .... Imperial Oil Ltd., Toronto, Ontario [*Library symbol National Library of Canada*] (NLC)

OTIP .... Occupational Therapist in Independent Practice

OTIP .... Tillsonburg Public Library, Ontario [*Library symbol National Library of Canada*] (NLC)

OTIR .... Operational Test Incident Report (MCD)

OTIS .... Observer's Thermal Imaging System (PDAA)

OTIS .... Occupational Training Information System

OTIS .... Offset Target Indicator System (MCD)

OTIS .... Oklahoma Teletype Interlibrary System [*Library network*]

OTIS .... Once-Through Integral System [*Nuclear energy*] (NRCH)

OTIS .... One Term In-Service Course (AIE)

OTIS .... Online Telecommunications Information Service [*Connections Telecommunications, Inc.*] [*West Bridgewater, MA*] [*Telecommunications service*] (TSSD)

OTIS .... Operational Test Instrumentation Ship [*Navy*]

OTIS .... Operation, Transport, Inspection, Storage (MHDB)

OTIS .... Ordnance Telemetry Instrumentation Station [*Army*] (AABC)

OTIS .... Oregon Total Information System [*Eugene*] [*Information service or system*] (IID)

OTIS .... Other than Iron or Steel [*Freight*]

OTIS .... Overstayer Tracing and Intelligence System [*British*]

Otis Art Inst ... Otis Art Institute of Parsons School of Design (GAGS)

OT/ITS .... Office of Telecommunications Institute for Telecommunication Sciences [*Boulder, CO*] [*Department of Commerce*]

OTIU .... Overseas Technical Information Unit [*Department of Trade*] [*British*]

OTIV .... Tiverton Branch, Bruce County Public Library, Ontario [*Library symbol National Library of Canada*] (NLC)

OTJ .... Off-the-Job

OTJ .... On the Job

OTJ .... Toronto Regional Office, Department of Justice Canada [*Bureau Regional de Toronto, Ministere de la Justice du Canada*] Toronto, Ontario [*Library symbol National Library of Canada*] (NLC)

OTJAE .... John Arpin Enterprises, Inc., Toronto, Ontario [*Library symbol National Library of Canada*] (NLC)

OTJAG .... Office of the Judge Advocate General [*Army*] (AABC)

OTJFM .... James F. MacLaren Ltd., Willowdale, Ontario [*Library symbol National Library of Canada*] (NLC)

OTJL .... Judges Library, Ontario Ministry of the Attorney General, Toronto, Ontario [*Library symbol National Library of Canada*] (NLC)

OTJPS .... Sands Pharmaceutical Division, Jerram Pharmaceuticals Ltd., Toronto, Ontario [*Library symbol National Library of Canada*] (NLC)

OTJT .... On the Job Training

OTJWT .... Information Centre, J. Walter Thompson Co. Ltd., Toronto, Ontario [*Library symbol National Library of Canada*] (NLC)

OTK .... Knox College, University of Toronto, Ontario [*Library symbol National Library of Canada*] (NLC)

OTK .... Oil Tank

OTK .... Oxidizer Tank (MCD)

OTKC .... Kidd Creek Mines Ltd., Toronto, Ontario [*Library symbol National Library of Canada*] (NLC)

OTKDF .... Other than Knocked Down Flat [*Freight*]

OTKE .... Kilborn Engineering Ltd., Toronto, Ontario [*Library symbol National Library of Canada*] (NLC)

OTL .... Boutilimit [*Mauritania*] [*Airport symbol*] (AD)

OTL .... Legislative Library of Ontario, Toronto, Ontario [*Library symbol National Library of Canada*] (NLC)

OTL .... Libbey-Owens-Ford Glass Co., Technical Library, Toledo, OH [*Library symbol Library of Congress*] (LCLS)

OTL .... Observer Target Line (NVT)

OTL .... Office Technology Ltd. (NITA)

OTL .... Ogden Technology Laboratories [*NASA*] (KSC)

OTL .... Ohio Theological Librarians [*Library network*]

OTL .... Oil-Tight Light

OTL .... [*The*] Old Testament Library [*A publication*] (BJA)

OTL .... Online Task Loader

OTL .... Operating Temperature Limit

OTL .... Operating Time Log (AAG)

OTL .... Oracle Teletext Ltd. (NITA)

OTL .... Order Trunk Line [*Telecommunications*] (OA)

OTL .... Ordnance Test Laboratory (NASA)

OTL .... Outer Tube Limit [*Chemical engineering*]

OTL .... Outland Resources [*Vancouver Stock Exchange symbol*]

OTL .... Output-Transformerless (SAA)

OTL .... Out to Lunch

OTL .... Over the Line (WDAA)

OTL .... Ovine Testicular Lymph [*Endocrinology*]

OTL .... Oxidizer Topping Line (AAG)

OTLAC .... Tamworth Branch, Lennox and Addington County Library, Ontario [*Library symbol National Library of Canada*] (BIB)

OTLC .... Information Section, Ontario Ministry of Natural Resources, Toronto, Ontario [*Library symbol National Library of Canada*] (NLC)

OTLC .... Open Tubular Liquid Chromatography

OTLC .... Orbiter Timeline Constraints [*NASA*] (NASA)

OTLCC .... Lummus Co. Canada Ltd., Willowdale, Ontario [*Library symbol National Library of Canada*] (NLC)

OTLF .... Natural Resources Library, Ontario Ministry of Natural Resources, Toronto, Ontario [*Library symbol National Library of Canada*] (NLC)

OTLH .... Laventhol & Horwath, Toronto, Ontario, [*Library symbol National Library of Canada*] (BIB)

OTLK .... Outlook [*NWS*] (FAAC)

OTLMO .... Orde des Technologistes de Laboratoire Medical de l'Ontario (AC)

OTLO .... Libbey-Owens-Ford Glass Co., Corporate Library, Toledo, OH [*Library symbol Library of Congress*] (LCLS)

OTLP .... Ledbury Park Junior High School, Toronto, Ontario [*Library symbol National Library of Canada*] (NLC)

OTLR .... Research Branch, Ontario Ministry of Natural Resources, Toronto, Ontario [*Library symbol National Library of Canada*] (NLC)

OTLS .... Law Society of Upper Canada, Toronto, Ontario [*Library symbol National Library of Canada*] (NLC)

OTLSC .... Litton Systems Canada Ltd., Rexdale, Ontario [*Library symbol National Library of Canada*] (NLC)

OTM .... Atmospheric Environment Service, Environment Canada [*Service de l'Environnement Atmospherique, Environment Canada*] Downsview, Ontario [*Library symbol National Library of Canada*] (NLC)

OTM .... Odd Transversal Magnetic (IAA)

OTM .... Office of Telecommunications Management [*Later, OTP*] [*FCC*]

OTM .... Once-through-Methanol [*Fuel technology*]

OTM .... On the Mark - Mark Hamill Fan Club (EA)

OTM .... On-Time Marker [*Computer science*]

OTM .... Optical Tool Master (MCD)

OTM .... Organo-Transition-Metal (PDAA)

OTM .... Original Turkey Mill [*Paper*] (DGA)

OTM .... Ortho-Tolidine Manganese Sulphate

OTM .... Other than Mexican [*Term applied by US Border Patrol to certain illegal immigrants*]

OTM .... Ottumwa [*Iowa*] [*Airport symbol*] (OAG)

OTM .... Out of the Money [*Options*] [*Investment term*] (NUMA)

OTM .... Timken Co., Research Library, Canton, OH [*OCLC symbol*] (OCLC)

OTM .... Toledo Museum of Art, Toledo, OH [*Library symbol Library of Congress*] (LCLS)

OTMA .... Office Technology Management Association [*Defunct*] (EA)

OTMA .... Oilfield Tank Manufacturers Association (EA)

OTMAG .... Ontario Ministry of the Attorney General [*Ministere du Procureur-General*], Toronto [*Library symbol National Library of Canada*] (BIB)

OTMB .... McMillan, Binch, Toronto, Ontario [*Library symbol National Library of Canada*] (NLC)

OTMC .... Massey College, Toronto, Ontario [*Library symbol National Library of Canada*] (NLC)

OTMC .... Medical College of Ohio at Toledo, Toledo, OH [*Library symbol Library of Congress*] (LCLS)

OTMCL .... Metropolitan Toronto Library, Ontario [*Library symbol National Library of Canada*] (NLC)

OTME .... Ontario Ministry of Energy, Toronto, Ontario [*Library symbol National Library of Canada*] (NLC)

OTMEN .... Ontario Ministry of the Environment, Toronto, Ontario [*Library symbol National Library of Canada*] (NLC)

OTMENL .... Laboratory, Ontario Ministry of the Environment, Rexdale, Ontario [*Library symbol National Library of Canada*] (NLC)

OTMF .... McIntyre-Falconbridge Library, Toronto, Ontario [*Library symbol National Library of Canada*] (NLC)

OTMH .... Financial Post, Toronto, Ontario [*Library symbol National Library of Canada*] (NLC)

OTMI .... Royal Canadian Military Institute, Toronto, Ontario [*Library symbol National Library of Canada*] (NLC)

OTMIO .... Employment and Immigration Canada [*Emploi et Immigration Canada*] Toronto, Ontario [*Library symbol National Library of Canada*] (NLC)

OTMIO .... Ontario Region Library, Employment and Immigration Canada [*Bibliotheque de laRegion de l'Ontario, Emploi et Immigration Canada*], North York, Ontario [*Library symbol National Library of Canada*] (NLC)

OTMIP .... One-Time Mortgage Insurance Premium (GFGA)

OTMIS .... Medical Information Services, Toronto, Ontario [*Library symbol National Library of Canada*] (BIB)

OTMJ .... Outgoing Trunk Message Junction [*Telecommunications*] (OA)

OTML.......... Law Library, Manufacturers Life Insurance Co., Toronto, Ontario [*Library symbol National Library of Canada*] (BIB)
OTML.......... Oatmeal [*Freight*]
OTMM.......... Mary Manse College, Toledo, OH [*Library symbol Library of Congress*] (LCLS)
OTMM.......... McCarthy & McCarthy, Barristers & Solicitors, Toronto, Ontario [*Library symbol National Library of Canada*] (NLC)
OTMMB........ Ontario Milks Marketing Board, Toronto, Ontario [*Library symbol National Library of Canada*] (NLC)
OTMML........ Micromedia Ltd., Toronto, Ontario [*Library symbol National Library of Canada*] (NLC)
OTMMM........ Marshall-Macklin-Monaghan Library, Don Mills, Ontario [*Library symbol National Library of Canada*] (NLC)
OTMN.......... Oxotremorine [*Cholinergic agent*]
OTMO.......... Monopros Ltd., Toronto, Ontario [*Library symbol National Library of Canada*] (BIB)
OTMOF .... MacDonald Ophthalmic Foundation, Toronto, Ontario [*Library symbol National Library of Canada*] (NLC)
OTMS.......... Mount Sinai Hospital, Toronto, Ontario [*Library symbol National Library of Canada*] (NLC)
OTMS.......... [*The*] Old Testament and Modern Study [*A publication*] (BJA)
OTMS.......... Operational Technical Managerial System (NVT)
OTMSM........ Management Services Department Library, Municipality of Metropolitan Toronto, Ontario [*Library symbol National Library of Canada*] (BIB)
OTMSS .... Professional Library, Metropolitan Separate School Board, Willowdale, Ontario [*Library symbol National Library of Canada*] (NLC)
OTMT.......... Monetary Times, Toronto, Ontario [*Library symbol National Library of Canada*] (NLC)
OTMTC........ Economic Development Division, Metro Toronto Chairman's Office, Toronto, Ontario [*Library symbol National Library of Canada*] (BIB)
OTMTS........ Metropolitan Toronto School Board, Ontario [*Library symbol National Library of Canada*] (NLC)
OTMTSS ...... Secondary Schools, Metropolitan Toronto School Board, Ontario [*Library symbol National Library of Canada*] (NLC)
OTMW .... Department of Works, Municipality of Metropolitan Toronto, Ontario [*Library symbol National Library of Canada*] (BIB)
OTN .... Lastp-Linhas Aereas de Sao Tome e Principe [*ICAO designator*] (FAAC)
OTN .... Newtonbrook Secondary School, Willowdale, Ontario [*Library symbol National Library of Canada*] (NLC)
OTN .... Oaktown, IN [*Location identifier FAA*] (FAAL)
OTN .... Octal Track Number [*Computer science*]
OTN .... Operational Teletype Network
OTN .... Operational Test, Non-Major Systems (MCD)
OTN .... Over the Nose [*Aviation*]
OTN .... Own-the-Night [*Technology*] [*Army*] (INF)
OTNA .... Ontario Ministry of Northern Development and Mines, Toronto, Ontario [*Library symbol National Library of Canada*] (NLC)
OTNC .... International Council for Adult Education, Toronto, Ontario [*Library symbol National Library of Canada*] (BIB)
OTNG .... Observer Training [*Army*] (AABC)
OTNGH........ Health Sciences Library, Northwestern General Hospital, Toronto, Ontario [*Library symbol National Library of Canada*] (BIB)
OTNH .... National Heritage Ltd., Toronto, Ontario [*Library symbol National Library of Canada*] (NLC)
OTNHH........ Health Protection Branch, Canada Department of National Health and Welfare [*Direction Generale de la Protection de la Sante, Ministere de la Sante Nationale et du Bien-Etre Social*] Toronto, Ontario [*Library symbol National Library of Canada*] (NLC)
OTNI .... Industrial Development Office, National Research Council Canada [*Bureau du Developpement Industriel, Conseil National de Recherches Canada*], Scarborough, Ontario [*Library symbol National Library of Canada*] (NLC)
OTNIMR....... G. Allan Roeher Institute, Downsview, Ontario [*Library symbol National Library of Canada*] (NLC)
OTNIMR....... National Institute on Mental Retardation [*Institut National pour la Deficience Mentale*] Toronto, Ontario [*Library symbol National Library of Canada*] (NLC)
OTNM .... Northern Mines, Toronto, Ontario [*Library symbol National Library of Canada*] (NLC)
OTNM .... Over-Thirty-Never-Married [*Lifestyle classification*]
OTNP .... Other than New Procurement [*Navy*] (DNAB)
OTNR .... Survey Records Branch, Ontario Ministry of Natural Resources, Toronto, Ontario [*Library symbol National Library of Canada*] (BIB)
OTNS .... Bank of Nova Scotia [*Banque de Nouvelle-Ecosse*], Toronto, Ontario [*Library symbol National Library of Canada*] (NLC)
OTNY .... North York Public Library, Willowdale, Ontario [*Library symbol National Library of Canada*] (NLC)
OTNYE .... F. W. Minkler Library, North York Board of Education, Willowdale, Ontario [*Library symbol National Library of Canada*] (NLC)
OTO .... Oil Temperature Out
OTO .... One-Time-Only
OTO .... Operator-to-Operator [*Military*] (CAAL)
OTO .... Optical Tracker Operator (MUGU)
OTO .... Ordo Templi Orientis [*Order of the Oriental Templars*] [*A mystical lodge*] [*Latin*] (ADA)
Oto............. Otolaryngology [*Medicine*]
OTO .... Otology [*Medicine*]
oto .... Otomian [*MARC language code Library of Congress*] (LCCP)
OTO .... Otorhinolaryngology [*Medicine*] (DHSM)
OTO .... Otto, NM [*Location identifier FAA*] (FAAL)

OTO .... Out-to-Out (AAG)
OTO .... Owens-Illinois, Inc., Technical Information Service-NTC, Toledo, OH [*Library symbol Library of Congress*] (LCLS)
OTO .... Tottenham Public Library, Ontario [*Library symbol National Library of Canada*] (NLC)
OTOB .... Tobermory Branch, Bruce County Public Library, Ontario [*Library symbol National Library of Canada*] (NLC)
OTOC .... Ontario Cancer Institute, Toronto, Ontario [*Library symbol National Library of Canada*] (NLC)
OTOCTA ...... Optimum Technical Operational Concept to Accomplish
OTOD .... Organization of Teachers of Oral Diagnosis (EA)
OTOE .... Omnispace Environments Ltd., Toronto, Ontario [*Library symbol National Library of Canada*] (NLC)
OTOEB .... Ontario Energy Board, Toronto, Ontario [*Library symbol National Library of Canada*] (NLC)
OTO EPROM... One-Time-Only Erasable Read-Only Memory [*Computer science*] (MED)
OTOGR........ Canadian Geriatrics Research Society, Toronto, Ontario [*Library symbol National Library of Canada*] (NLC)
OTOH .... Ontario Ministry of Municipal Affairs and Housing, Toronto, Ontario [*Library symbol National Library of Canada*] (NLC)
OTOH .... On the Other Hand [*Internet language*] [*Computer science*]
OTOHCR ...... Central Records, Ontario Hydro, Toronto, Ontario [*Library symbol National Library of Canada*] (NLC)
OTOL .... Ontario Lottery Corporation, Toronto, Ontario [*Library symbol National Library of Canada*] (BIB)
Otol............. Otologist (STED)
OTOL .... Otology [*Medicine*]
Otolar .... Otolaryngology [*Medicine*] (DAVI)
OTOLR .... Ontario Labour Relations Board [*Commission des Relations de Travail de l'Ontario*], Toronto, Ontario [*Library symbol National Library of Canada*] (NLC)
OTOLRC....... Ontario Law Reform Commission, Toronto, Ontario [*Library symbol National Library of Canada*] (BIB)
OTOMA .... Ontario Medical Association, Toronto, Ontario [*Library symbol National Library of Canada*] (NLC)
OTOME .... Information Resource Centre, Ontario Municipal Employees Retirement Board, Toronto [*Library symbol National Library of Canada*] (BIB)
OTOMR .... Ontario Ministry of Revenue, Toronto, Ontario [*Library symbol National Library of Canada*] (NLC)
OTONA .... Ontario Nurses Association, Toronto, Ontario [*Library symbol National Library of Canada*] (NLC)
OTO NAVSUPPACT... Overseas Transportation Office, Naval Support Activity (DNAB)
O to O .... Out to Out [*Technical drawings*]
OTOPC .... Ortho Pharmaceutical Canada Ltd., Don Mills, Ontario [*Library symbol National Library of Canada*] (NLC)
OTOPCT ...... Planning and Research Library, Technical Services Branch, Ontario Police Commission, Toronto, Ontario [*Library symbol National Library of Canada*] (NLC)
OTOS .... Orbit-to-Orbit Stage [*NASA*] (MCD)
OTOSC .... Ontario Securities Commission, Toronto, Ontario [*Library symbol National Library of Canada*] (NLC)
OTOSS .... Ontario Secondary School Teachers Federation, Toronto, Ontario [*Library symbol National Library of Canada*] (NLC)
OTOW .... Resource Centre, Ontario Women's Directorate [*Library symbol National Library of Canada*] (BIB)
OTP............. Ocean Test Platform [*Marine science*] (MSC)
OTP............. Office of Telecommunications Policy [*Terminated, 1978*] [*Executive Office of the President*]
OTP............. Office of Territorial Programs (COE)
OTP............. Office of Trade Promotion [*Department of Commerce*]
OTP............. Office Technology Plus [*General Services Administration*]
OTP............. Of This Parish
OTP............. Of True Position (MSA)
OTP............. One-Time Pad [*Navy British*]
OTP............. One-Time Programmable [*Computer science*]
OTP............. On Top [*Aviation*]
OTP............. Open Top [*Freight*]
OTP............. Operational Test Plan
OTP............. Operational Test Procedure (KSC)
OTP............. Operations Turnaround Plan (NASA)
OTP............. Oscillation Test Point [*British military*] (DMA)
OTP............. Otepa [*Tuamotu Archipelago*] [*Seismograph station code, US Geological Survey*] (SEIS)
OTP............. Other than Portable [*Freight*]
Ot P .... Otto Papiensis [*Flourished, 12th century*] [*Authority cited in pre-1607 legal work*] (DSA)
OTP............. Outline Test Plan [*Army*]
OTP............. Overhead Trickle Purification (PDAA)
OTP............. Overtime Premium (MCD)
OTP............. Ovine Trophoblast Protein [*Biochemistry*]
OTP............. Oxidizer Tanking Panel (AAG)
OTP............. Ozone Trends Panel [*NASA*]
OTP............. Toronto Public Libraries, Ontario [*Library symbol National Library of Canada*] (NLC)
OTPA .... Institute of Public Administration of Canada [*Institut d'Administration Publique du Canada*] Toronto, Ontario [*Library symbol National Library of Canada*] (NLC)
OTPAL......... PAL Reading Service, Toronto, Ontario [*Library symbol National Library of Canada*] (NLC)
OTPEC .... Officer Training Program Examining Center [*Air Force*]
OTPFA .... Fine Arts Library, Northern District, Toronto Public Libraries, Ontario [*Library symbol National Library of Canada*] (NLC)

OTPG .... Polar Gas Library, Toronto, Ontario [*Library symbol National Library of Canada*] (NLC)

OTPH .... History Section, Metropolitan Toronto Library, Ontario [*Library symbol National Library of Canada*] (NLC)

OTPHC .... Prentice Hall Canada, Inc., Scarborough, Ontario [*Library symbol National Library of Canada*] (NLC)

OTPHR .... Resource Centre, Department of Public Health, City of Toronto, Ontario [*Library symbol National Library of Canada*] (BIB)

OTPI .... On Top Position Indicator [*Navy*] (NG)

OTPI .... Operational Test Program Instruction (MCD)

OTPM .... Peat, Marwick & Partners, Toronto, Ontario [*Library symbol National Library of Canada*] (NLC)

OTPMG .... Office of the Provost Marshal General [*Army*]

OTPNL .... Outer Pane [*Aerospace*] (IAA)

OTPP .... Ocean Thermal Power Plant

OTPP .... Office of Transport, Policy and Planning [*South Australia*]

OTPP .... Ontario Provincial Police, Toronto, Ontario [*Library symbol National Library of Canada*] (NLC)

Ot Pp .... Otto Papiensis [*Flourished, 12th century*] [*Authority cited in pre-1607 legal work*] (DSA)

OTPPC .... Ontario Provincial Police College, Toronto, Ontario [*Library symbol National Library of Canada*] (NLC)

OTPR .... Proctor & Redfern Group, Don Mills, Ontario [*Library symbol National Library of Canada*] (NLC)

OTPROM ...... One-Time Programmable Read Only Memory [*Computer science*]

OTP/RS .... Outline Test Plan/Resume Sheet (MCD)

OTPRW .... National Office Library, Price Waterhouse & Co., Toronto, Ontario [*Library symbol National Library of Canada*] (BIB)

OTPS .... Oceanic Traffic Planning System [*FAA*] (TAG)

OTPS .... Operational Test Program Set (MCD)

OTPT .... Operational Test Program Tape (MCD)

OTPT .... Output (KSC)

OTPW .... Ontario Ministry of Community and Social Services, Toronto, Ontario [*Library symbol National Library of Canada*] (NLC)

OTPWC .... Ontario Regional Library, Public Works Canada [*Bibliotheque Regionale de l'Ontario, Travaux Publics Canada*] Toronto, Ontario [*Library symbol National Library of Canada*] (NLC)

OTQ .... On the Quarter

OTQE .... Queen Elizabeth Hospital, Toronto, Ontario [*Library symbol National Library of Canada*] (NLC)

OTQL .... Quaere Legal Resources Ltd., Toronto, Ontario [*Library symbol National Library of Canada*] (NLC)

OTQRM .... [*The*] Queen's Own Rifles of Canada Regimental Museum, Toronto, Ontario [*Library symbol National Library of Canada*] (NLC)

OTQSM .... Queen Street Mental Health Centre, Toronto, Ontario [*Library symbol National Library of Canada*] (NLC)

OTR .... Coto 47 [*Costa Rica*] [*Airport symbol*] (OAG)

OTR .... [*The*] Oakland Terminal Railway [*Formerly, OKT*] [*AAR code*]

OTR .... Observed Temperature Rise

OTR .... Occupational Therapist, Registered

OTR .... Oceanic Transition Route [*FAA*] (TAG)

OTR .... Office of Technical Resources

OTR .... Office of Testing and Research [*Drug evalution*]

OTR .... Off-the-Road

OTR .... Old Time Radio

OTR .... One Touch Recording

OTR .... Open-Tubular Reactor

OTR .... Operating Temperature Range

OTR .... Operational Time Record (AAG)

OTR .... Optical Tracking [*NASA*] (KSC)

OTR .... Optical Transition Radiation [*Physics*]

OTR .... Oregon Tax Reports [*A publication*] (DLA)

OTR .... Organic Test Reactor [*Nuclear energy*]

OTR .... Orotek Resources Corp. [*Vancouver Stock Exchange symbol*]

OTR .... Outer (MSA)

OTR .... Ovarian Tumor Registry [*Medicine*]

OTR .... Over-the-Road [*Automotive engineering*]

OTR .... Oxygen Transfer Rate [*Chemical engineering*]

OTR .... Oxytocin Receptor [*Endocrinology*]

OTR .... Ryerson Polytechnical Institute, Toronto, Ontario [*Library symbol National Library of Canada*] (NLC)

OTr .... Troy-Miami County Public Library, Troy, OH [*Library symbol Library of Congress*] (LCLS)

OTRA .... Other than Regular Army (AABC)

OTRA .... Oversea Theater Requisitioning Authority [*Military*]

OTRA .... Royal Astronomical Society [*Societe Royale d'Astronomie*] Toronto, Ontario [*Library symbol National Library of Canada*] (NLC)

OTRAC .... Oscillogram Trace Reader [*Non-Linear Systems, Inc.*] [*Computer science*]

OTRAG .... Orbital Transport- und Raketen-Aktiengesellschaft [*Rocket company*] [*Germany*]

OTRAL .... Rio Algom Ltd., Toronto, Ontario [*Library symbol National Library of Canada*] (NLC)

OTRAN .... Ocean Testing Ranges and Instrumentation Conference

OTRAR .... Other than Regular Army

OTRBI .... Information Resources, Royal Bank of Canada, Toronto, Ontario [*Library symbol National Library of Canada*] (NLC)

OTRBSA .... Occupational Therapists' Registration Board of South Australia

OTRC .... Canadian Forces College, Toronto, Ontario [*Library symbol National Library of Canada*] (NLC)

OTRCF .... Royal Commission on the Future of the Toronto Waterfront, Toronto, Ontario [*Library symbol National Library of Canada*] (BIB)

OTRCL .... Reichhold Chemicals Ltd., Weston, Ontario [*Library symbol National Library of Canada*] (NLC)

OTRCR .... Trout Creek Community Library, Ontario [*Library symbol National Library of Canada*] (NLC)

OTRCS .... Canadian Forces Staff School, Canada Department of National Defence [*College d'Etat-Major des Forces Canadiennes, Ministere de la Defense Nationale*] Toronto, Ontario [*Library symbol National Library of Canada*] (NLC)

OTRE .... Trenton Public Library, Ontario [*Library symbol National Library of Canada*] (NLC)

OTREC .... Regis College, Toronto, Ontario [*Library symbol National Library of Canada*] (NLC)

OTReg .... Occupational Therapist Registered [*Canada*] (DAVI)

OTREN .... Northumberland County Public Library, Warkworth, Ontario [*Library symbol National Library of Canada*] (NLC)

OTREX .... Canada Department of Regional Industrial Expansion [*Ministere de l'Expansion Industrielle Regionale*] Toronto, Ontario [*Library symbol National Library of Canada*] (NLC)

OTR Ex .... OTR Express, Inc. [*Associated Press*] (SAG)

OTRF .... Ontario Research Foundation, Sheridan Park, Mississauga, Ontario [*Library symbol National Library of Canada*] (NLC)

OTRG .... Office Technology Research Group [*Defunct*] (EA)

OTRG .... Old Testament Reading Guide [*Collegeville, MN*] [*A publication*] (BJA)

OTRHNLRGYNGY... Otorhinolaryngology

OTRIC .... Collins Canada Division, Rockwell International, Toronto, Ontario [*Library symbol National Library of Canada*] (NLC)

OTRK .... Oshkosh Truck Corp. [*Oshkosh, WI*] [*NASDAQ symbol*] (NQ)

OTRKB .... Oshkosh Truck'B' [*NASDAQ symbol*] (TTSB)

OTRL .... Reed Ltd., Toronto, Ontario [*Library symbol National Library of Canada*] (NLC)

OTrL .... Troy-Miami County Public Library, Troy, OH [*Library symbol*] [*Library of Congress*] (LCLS)

OTRM .... Royal Ontario Museum, Toronto, Ontario [*Library symbol National Library of Canada*] (NLC)

OTRMC .... Canadiana Department, Royal Ontario Museum, Toronto, Ontario [*Library symbol National Library of Canada*] (NLC)

OTRMF .... Far Eastern Department, Royal Ontario Museum, Toronto, Ontario [*Library symbol National Library of Canada*] (NLC)

OTRO .... Overhaul Test Requirement Outline

OTROT .... Corporate Information Centre, Royal Trust, Toronto, Ontario [*Library symbol National Library of Canada*] (BIB)

OTRPM .... Rothmans of Pall Mall Ltd., Don Mills, Ontario [*Library symbol National Library of Canada*] (NLC)

OTRR .... Operation Test Readiness Review [*Army*]

OTRS .... Operational Test Readiness Statement

OT/RT .... Occupational Therapy/Recreational Therapy (STED)

OTRT .... Operating Time Record Tag (AAG)

OTRT .... Rose Technology Group Ltd., Toronto, Ontario [*Library symbol National Library of Canada*] (NLC)

OTRX .... OTR Express [*NASDAQ symbol*] (TTSB)

OTRX .... OTR Express, Inc. [*NASDAQ symbol*] (SAG)

OTS .... Object Time System (MHDB)

OTS .... Occipital Temporal Sulcus [*Medicine*] (DMAA)

OTS .... Octadecyltrichlorosilane [*Organic chemistry*]

OTS .... Office of Technical Services [*Later, CFSTI, NTIS*] [*National Institute of Standards and Technology*]

OTS .... Office of Technical Support [*US Employment Service*] [*Department of Labor*]

OTS .... Office of Thrift Supervision [*Department of the Treasury*] [*Superseded Federal Home Loan Bank Board, 1989*]

OTS .... Office of Toxic Substances [*Environmental Protection Agency*]

OTS .... Office of Transportation Security [*Department of Transportation*]

OTS .... Officers' Tactical School [*Navy*] (NVT)

OTS .... Officers' Training School

OTS .... Off the Shelf

OTS .... Ohio Carriers Tariff Service Inc., Cleveland OH [*STAC*]

OTS .... Omega Tau Sigma [*An association*] (NTPA)

OTS .... One-Time Source (MCD)

OTS .... On-Line Terminal System [*Computer science*] (MHDB)

OTS .... Open Two Seater [*Style of automobile*]

OTS .... Operational Test Site (AAG)

OTS .... Operational Time Sync

OTS .... Operational Training Squadron (MCD)

OTS .... Operational Training System [*HAWK*]

OTS .... Opportunities to See [*Business term*]

OTS .... Optical Technology Satellite

OTS .... Optical Tracking Satellite [*NASA*] (IAA)

OTS .... Optical Transport Systems (IEEE)

OTS .... Orbital Test Satellite [*Communications satellite*] [*European Space Agency*]

OTS .... Orbital Transport Systems (MCD)

OTS .... Organization for Tropical Studies (EA)

OTS .... Organized Track System [*Aviation*]

OTS .... Orotracheal Suction [*Medicine*] (DAVI)

OTS .... Ortho-Toluenesulfonamide [*Used in manufacture of saccharin*]

OTS .... Outside Temperature Sensor [*Automotive engineering*]

OTS .... Overlap Technician Supervisor (SAA)

OTS .... Overlap Telling and Surveillance (SAA)

OTS .... Overseas Telephone Services (DAS)

OTS .... Over-the-Shoulder [*Cinematography*]

OTS .... Over-the-Side [*Navy*] (CAAL)

OTS .... Ovonic Threshold Switch

OTS .... Own Time Switch [*Connection or call*] [*Telecommunications*] (TEL)

OTS .... Oxford Text System (NITA)

OTS .... Oxygen Test Stand (KSC)

OTS.............	Statistics Canada [*Statistique Canada*] Toronto, Ontario [*Library symbol National Library of Canada*] (NLC)
OTSA	Ocean Systems Technician, Seaman Apprentice [*Navy rating*] (DNAB)
OTSA	Orthodox Theological Society in America (EA)
OTSA	Salvation Army, Toronto, Ontario [*Library symbol National Library of Canada*] (NLC)
OTSAA	Officer Training School Alumni Association (EA)
OTSAC	Sanco Consultants Ltd., Toronto, Ontario [*Library symbol National Library of Canada*] (NLC)
OTS-AES	Optical Technology Satellite - Apollo Extension System (DNAB)
OTSAP	Spar Aerospace Products, Toronto, Ontario [*Library symbol National Library of Canada*] (NLC)
O/TSC	Other than Special Consultants [*Military*]
OTSC	Seneca College, Willowdale, Ontario [*Library symbol National Library of Canada*] (NLC)
OTSCC	Scarborough College, Ontario [*Library symbol National Library of Canada*] (NLC)
OTSCI	Sulzer Canada, Inc., Toronto, Ontario [*Library symbol National Library of Canada*] (NLC)
OTSCL	Shell Canada Ltd., Toronto, Ontario [*Library symbol National Library of Canada*] (NLC)
OTSCLT........	Library Techniques, Seneca College of Applied Arts and Technology, Willowdale, Ontario [*Library symbol National Library of Canada*] (NLC)
OTSD	Operational Test Supportability Demonstration
OTSE...........	Toronto Stock Exchange Library, Ontario [*Library symbol National Library of Canada*] (BIB)
OTSED	Scarborough Borough Board of Education, Toronto, Ontario [*Library symbol National Library of Canada*] (NLC)
OTSG	Office of the Surgeon General [*Public Health Service*]
OTSG	Once-Through Steam Generator [*Nuclear energy*]
OTSGS.........	Once-Through Steam Generating System [*Nuclear energy*] (IEEE)
OTSLI	Sun Life of Canada, Toronto, Ontario [*Library symbol National Library of Canada*] (NLC)
OTSM..........	St. Michael's Hospital, Toronto, Ontario [*Library symbol National Library of Canada*] (NLC)
OTSMC	Sunnybrook Medical Centre, Toronto, Ontario [*Library symbol National Library of Canada*] (NLC)
OTSMG	St. Mary's General Hospital, Timmins, Ontario [*Library symbol National Library of Canada*] (NLC)
OTSML.........	Selco Mining Corp., Toronto, Ontario [*Library symbol National Library of Canada*] (NLC)
OTSN	Ocean Systems Technician, Seaman [*Navy rating*] (DNAB)
OTSO	Office of Telecommunications Systems Operations [*Social Security Administration*]
OTSOA	Overseas Telegraph Superintending Officers' Association [*A union*] [*British*]
OTSOG.........	On the Shoulders of Giants [*Literature*]
OTSP	Office of Technology Support Programs [*Washington, DC Department of Energy*] (GRD)
OTSP	Office of Transportation Systems and Planning [*Battelle Memorial Institut e*] [*Department of Energy Also, an information service or system*] (IID)
OTSP	Scarborough Public Library, Ontario [*Library symbol National Library of Canada*] (NLC)
OTSPA	Albert Campbell Branch, Scarborough Public Library, Ontario [*Library symbol National Library of Canada*] (NLC)
OTSPC	Cedarbrae Branch, Scarborough Public Library, Ontario [*Library symbol National Library of Canada*] (NLC)
OTS-PST	Orbiting Transition State-Phase Space Theory [*Physical chemistry*]
OTSQ	Offer Teacher-Student Questionnaire [*Personality development test*] [*Psychology*]
OTSR	Once-Through Superheat Reactor [*Nuclear energy*]
OTSR	Optimum Track Ship Routing [*Navy*] (NVT)
OTSS	Office of Technical and Special Services [*Office of Field Operations*] [*Department of Labor*]
OTSS	Off-the-Shelf System [*Bell System*]
OTSS	Ontario Regional Library, Secretary of State Canada [*Bibliotheque Regionale de l'Ontario, Secretariat d'Etat*], Toronto, Ontario [*Library symbol National Library of Canada*] (NLC)
OTSS	Open Transport and Session Support (NITA)
OTSS	Operational Test Support System
OTSS	Optical Tracking Servo
OTS SB	Office of Technical Service, Selective Bibliographies [*US government*]
OTST...........	Ontario Science Centre, Toronto, Ontario [*Library symbol National Library of Canada*] (NLC)
OTSTA	St. Augustine's Seminary, Toronto, Ontario [*Library symbol National Library of Canada*] (NLC)
OTSTB	St. Basil's Seminary [*Collection transferred to OTSTM*] Ontario [*Library symbol National Library of Canada*] (NLC)
OTSTF.........	Ontario Film Institute, Ontario Science Centre Library, Don Mills, Ontario [*Library symbol National Library of Canada*] (NLC)
OTSTG	St. George's College, Toronto, Ontario [*Library symbol National Library of Canada*] (NLC)
OTSTJ.........	George Pennal Library, St. Joseph's Health Centre, Toronto, Ontario [*Library symbol National Library of Canada*] (BIB)
OTSTM........	University of Saint Michael's College, Toronto, Ontario [*Library symbol National Library of Canada*] (NLC)
OTSZH	Other than Steel or Zinc Heads [*Freight*]
OTT	Nottingham, MD [*Location identifier FAA*] (FAAL)
OTT.............	Ocean Transport and Trading [*British*]
OTT.............	Office of Technology Transfer [*University of Illinois*]
OTT.............	One-Time Tape
OTT	Operational Training Test (NVT)
OTT.............	Operator Tactics Trainer [*Patriot air defense system*] (MCD)
OTT.............	Optional Team Targeting (MCD)
OTT.............	Oral Trade Tests [*Department of Labor*]
OTT.............	Orotracheal Tube [*Medicine*] (DAVI)
OTT.............	Ottava [*Octave*] [*Music*]
OTT.............	Ottawa [*Ontario*] [*Seismograph station code, US Geological Survey*] (SEIS)
OTT.............	Ottery Saint Mary [*Urban district in England*]
Ott.............	Otto's United States Supreme Court Reports [*91-107 United States*] [*A publication*] (DLA)
OTT.............	Outgoing Teletype
OTT.............	Outgoing Trunk Terminal [*Telecommunications*] (IAA)
OTT.............	Outside Trim Template (MSA)
OTT.............	Over the Top [*British Slang*]
OTT.............	Over-the-Top [*Marshall-MacIntosh knee operation*]
OTT.............	Oxygen Tolerance Test
OTT.............	Teledyne CAE Engineering Library, Toledo, OH [*Library symbol Library of Congress*] (LCLS)
OTT.............	Toronto Transit Commission, Ontario [*Library symbol National Library of Canada*] (NLC)
OTT.............	University of Ottawa Library [*UTLAS symbol*]
OttawFn........	Ottawa Financial Corp. [*Associated Press*] (SAG)
OTTB...........	Optically-Thin Thermal Bremsstrahlung [*Astrophysics*]
OTTC...........	University of Trinity College, Toronto, Ontario [*Library symbol National Library of Canada*] (NLC)
OTTCA	University of Trinity College Archives, Toronto, Ontario [*Library symbol National Library of Canada*] (NLC)
OTTDB	Toronto-Dominion Bank, Toronto, Ontario [*Library symbol National Library of Canada*] (NLC)
OTTE	Operational Testing, Training, and Evaluation
OTTEC	Toronto Teachers' College, Ontario [*Library symbol National Library of Canada*] (NLC)
OTTER	Operational Training, Test, and Evaluation RADAR
OTTEX	Texaco Canada, Inc., Don Mills, Ontario [*Library symbol National Library of Canada*] (NLC)
OTTFC.........	Official Tim Topper Fan Club [*Defunct*] (EA)
OTTI...........	Ontario Ministry of Industry and Trade, Toronto, Ontario [*Library symbol National Library of Canada*] (NLC)
OTTLE.........	Optically Transparent Thin-Layer Electrode
OTTO	Olympic Technology Trailer Operations
OTTO	Once Through, Then Out [*Fuel management system*]
OTTO	Optical-to-Optical (IAA)
Otto...........	Otto's United States Supreme Court Reports [*91-107 United States*] [*A publication*] (DLA)
OTTOA	Ontario Region, Canadian Air Transportation Administration, Transport Canada [*Region de l'Ontario, Administration Canadienne des Transports Aeriens, Transports Canada*] Toronto, Ontario [*Library symbol National Library of Canada*] (NLC)
OTTR	Otter Tail Power [*NASDAQ symbol*] (TTSB)
OTTR	Otter Tail Power Co. [*NASDAQ symbol*] (NQ)
OTTR	Thomson, Rogers, Barristers & Solicitors, Toronto, Ontario [*Library symbol National Library of Canada*] (NLC)
OTTRAC	Travelers Canada, Toronto, Ontario [*Library symbol National Library of Canada*] (BIB)
OTTRC	Thistletown Regional Centre for Children and Adolescents, Rexdale, Ontario [*Library symbol National Library of Canada*] (NLC)
OTTRC	Touche Ross & Co., Toronto, Ontario [*Library symbol National Library of Canada*] (NLC)
OttrTP.........	Otter Tail Power Co. [*Associated Press*] (SAG)
OTTS...........	Operations Training and Technical Services [*Nuclear Regulatory Commission*] (NRCH)
OTTS...........	Organisation of Teachers of Transport Studies [*British*]
OTTS...........	Outgoing Trunk Testing System [*Telecommunications*] (TEL)
OTTST.........	Toronto School of Theology, Toronto, Ontario [*Library symbol National Library of Canada*] (NLC)
OTTSU	Open Tech Training Support Unit (AIE)
Ott's US Sup Ct R...	Otto's United States Supreme Court Reports [*91-107 United States*] [*A publication*] (DLA)
OTTT...........	Tory, Tory, DesLauriers & Binnington, Toronto, Ontario [*Library symbol National Library of Canada*] (BIB)
OTTW..........	Optical Telescope Technology Workshop [*NASA*] (PDAA)
OTTWH	Health Sciences Library, Toronto Western Hospital, Ontario [*Library symbol National Library of Canada*] (NLC)
OTU	Office of Technology Utilization [*NASA*]
OTU	Officers' Training Unit [*Air Force British*]
OTU	Ogden Test Unit (SAA)
OTU	Olfactory Tubercle (STED)
OTU	One-Time Use
OTU	Operating Time Update
OTU	Operational Taxonomic Unit [*Numerical taxonomy*]
OTU	Operational Test Unit (KSC)
OTU	Operational Training Unit [*Military*]
OTU	Opetus-ja Tutkimusalan Unioni [*Teaching and Research Employees Union*] [*Finalnd*] (EY)
OTU	Orthopedic Transcription Unit
OTU	Otu [*Colombia*] [*Airport symbol*] (OAG)
OTU	Output Terminal Unit (SSD)
OTU	University of Toledo, Toledo, OH [*Library symbol·Library of Congress*] (LCLS)
OTU	University of Toronto, Ontario [*Library symbol National Library of Canada*] (NLC)
OTUA	Institute for Aerospace Studies, University of Toronto, Ontario [*Library symbol National Library of Canada*] (NLC)

OTUAN......... Department of Anatomy, University of Toronto, Ontario [*Library symbol National Library of Canada*] (NLC)

OTUAP......... Department of Applied Physics, University of Toronto, Ontario [*Library symbol National Library of Canada*] (NLC)

OTUAR......... University of Toronto Archives, Ontario [*Library symbol National Library of Canada*] (NLC)

OTUAV......... Audio-Visual Library, University of Toronto, Ontario [*Library symbol National Library of Canada*] (NLC)

OTUB......... Department of Biochemistry, University of Toronto, Ontario [*Library symbol National Library of Canada*] (NLC)

OTUBP......... Banting-Best Physiology Library, University of Toronto, Ontario [*Library symbol National Library of Canada*] (NLC)

OTUC......... Department of Chemistry, University of Toronto, Ontario [*Library symbol National Library of Canada*] (NLC)

OTUCC......... Institute of Computer Science, University of Toronto, Ontario [*Library symbol National Library of Canada*] (NLC)

OTUCE......... Department of Chemical Engineering and Applied Chemistry, University of Toronto,Ontario [*Library symbol National Library of Canada*] (NLC)

OTUCI......... Department of Civil Engineering, University of Toronto, Ontario [*Library symbol National Library of Canada*] (NLC)

OTUCR......... Centre of Criminology, University of Toronto, Ontario [*Library symbol National Library of Canada*] (NLC)

OTUCS......... Institute of Child Study, University of Toronto, Ontario [*Library symbol National Library of Canada*] (NLC)

OTUD......... David Dunlap Observatory, University of Toronto, Ontario [*Library symbol National Library of Canada*] (NLC)

OTUDB......... Department of Botany, University of Toronto, Ontario [*Library symbol National Library of Canada*] (NLC)

OTUDM......... Department of Mathematics, University of Toronto, Ontario [*Library symbol National Library of Canada*] (NLC)

OTUDP......... Clarke Institute of Psychiatry, University of Toronto, Ontario [*Library symbol National Library of Canada*] (NLC)

OTUE......... Engineering Library, University of Toronto, Ontario [*Library symbol National Library of Canada*] (NLC)

OTUEE......... Department of Electrical Engineering, University of Toronto, Ontario [*Library symbol National Library of Canada*] (NLC)

OTUFA......... Department of Fine Art, University of Toronto, Ontario [*Library symbol National Library of Canada*] (NLC)

OTUFD......... Faculty of Dentistry, University of Toronto, Ontario [*Library symbol National Library of Canada*] (NLC)

OTUFM......... Faculty of Music, University of Toronto, Ontario [*Library symbol National Library of Canada*] (NLC)

OTUFP......... Faculty of Pharmacy, University of Toronto, Ontario [*Library symbol National Library of Canada*] (NLC)

OTUG......... Department of Geological Sciences, University of Toronto, Ontario [*Library symbol National Library of Canada*] (NLC)

OTUGL......... Geophysics Laboratory, University of Toronto, Ontario [*Library symbol National Library of Canada*] (NLC)

OTUH......... Science and Medicine Library, University of Toronto, Ontario [*Library symbol National Library of Canada*] (NLC)

OTUHO......... Occupational & Environment Health Unit, Science and Medicine Library, Universityof Toronto, Ontario [*Library symbol National Library of Canada*] (NLC)

OTUINC......... Innis College, University of Toronto, Ontario [*Library symbol National Library of Canada*] (NLC)

OTUIRN......... [*The*] Jean and Dorothy Newman Industrial Relations Library, Center for Industrial Relations, University of Toronto, Ontario [*Library symbol National Library of Canada*] (NLC)

OTUL......... Faculty of Law, University of Toronto, Ontario [*Library symbol National Library of Canada*] (NLC)

OTU-L......... University of Toledo, Law Library, Toledo, OH [*Library symbol Library of Congress*] (LCLS)

OTULAS......... UTLAS [*University of Toronto Library Automation System*] International Canada, Toronto, Ontario [*Library symbol National Library of Canada*] (NLC)

OTULS......... Faculty of Library Science, University of Toronto, Ontario [*Library symbol National Library of Canada*] (NLC)

OTUM......... Department of Mechanical Engineering, University of Toronto, Ontario [*Library symbol National Library of Canada*] (NLC)

OTUMA......... Map Library, University of Toronto, Ontario [*Library symbol National Library of Canada*] (NLC)

OTUME......... Department of Metallurgical Engineering, University of Toronto, Ontario [*Library symbol National Library of Canada*] (NLC)

OTUMI......... Department of Mining Engineering, University of Toronto, Ontario [*Library symbol National Library of Canada*] (NLC)

OTUMS......... Faculty of Management Studies, University of Toronto, Ontario [*Library symbol National Library of Canada*] (NLC)

OTUN......... Faculty of Nursing, University of Toronto, Ontario [*Library symbol National Library of Canada*] (NLC)

OTUNC......... Union Carbide Canada Ltd., Toronto, Ontario [*Library symbol National Library of Canada*] (NLC)

OTUNWC......... New College, University of Toronto, Ontario [*Library symbol National Library of Canada*] (NLC)

OTUP......... Department of Physics, University of Toronto, Ontario [*Library symbol National Library of Canada*] (NLC)

OTUPA......... Department of Pathology, Banting-Best Institute, University of Toronto, Ontario [*Library symbol National Library of Canada*] (NLC)

OTUPG......... Information Centre, Programme in Gerontology, University of Toronto, Ontario [*Library symbol National Library of Canada*] (NLC)

OTUS......... Office of the Treasurer of the United States

OTUSA......... School of Architecture, University of Toronto, Ontario [*Library symbol National Library of Canada*] (NLC)

OTUSP......... School of Physical and Health Education (Women), University of Toronto, Ontario [*Library symbol National Library of Canada*] (NLC)

OTUSW......... School of Social Work, University of Toronto, Ontario [*Library symbol National Library of Canada*] (NLC)

OTUTD......... Urban Transportation Development Corp., Toronto, Ontario [*Library symbol National Library of Canada*] (NLC)

OTUTF......... Thomas Fisher Rare Book Library, University of Toronto, Ontario [*Library symbol National Library of Canada*] (NLC)

OTUTP......... University of Toronto Press, Ontario [*Library symbol National Library of Canada*] (NLC)

OTUUC......... University College, University of Toronto, Ontario [*Library symbol National Library of Canada*] (NLC)

OTUZ......... Department of Zoology, University of Toronto, Ontario [*Library symbol National Library of Canada*] (NLC)

OTV......... Operational Television (KSC)

OTV......... Operational Test Vehicle (IAA)

OTV......... Optimum Time Varying (IAA)

OTV......... Orbiter Transfer Vehicle [*NASA*]

OTV......... Otavi [*South-West Africa*] [*Airport symbol*] (AD)

OTV......... Victoria University, Toronto, Ontario [*Library symbol National Library of Canada*] (NLC)

OTVC......... Open Top Vapor Cleaner [*Engineering*]

OTVCT......... Outer Tube Vertical Centerline Target

OTVL......... V & L Enterprises, Downsview, Ontario [*Library symbol National Library of Canada*] (NLC)

OTW......... Off the Wall [*Slang*]

OTW......... Over the Wing [*Aircraft*]

OTW......... Owner's Tank Wagons [*Shipping*]

OTW......... Owning the Weather [*Army*] (RDA)

OTW......... Wycliffe College, Toronto, Ontario [*Library symbol National Library of Canada*] (NLC)

OTWC......... Ontario Workmen's Compensation Board, Toronto, Ontario [*Library symbol National Library of Canada*] (NLC)

OTWCA......... Ontario Workers' Compensation Appeals Tribunal, Toronto, Ontario [*Library symbol National Library of Canada*] (NLC)

OTWCH......... Medical Library, Women's College Hospital, Toronto, Ontario [*Library symbol National Library of Canada*] (NLC)

OTWE......... Tweed Public Library, Ontario [*Library symbol National Library of Canada*] (BIB)

OTWEN......... Ontario Ministry of Northern Development and Mines, Tweed [*Library symbol National Library of Canada*] (BIB)

OTWFC......... Old Time Western Film Club (EA)

OTWH......... Wellesley Hospital, Toronto, Ontario [*Library symbol National Library of Canada*] (NLC)

OTWL......... William Lyon Mackenzie Collegiate Institute, Downsview, Ontario [*Library symbol National Library of Canada*] (NLC)

OTWLC......... Warner-Lambert Canada Ltd., Scarborough, Ontario [*Library symbol National Library of Canada*] (NLC)

OTWM......... William M. Mercer Ltd., Toronto, Ontario [*Library symbol National Library of Canada*] (NLC)

OTWR......... Oblique Tape Wound Refrasil

OTWRC......... Weston Research Centre, Toronto, Ontario [*Library symbol National Library of Canada*] (NLC)

OTWY......... Medical Library, Wyeth Ltd., Downsview, Ontario [*Library symbol National Library of Canada*] (BIB)

OTX......... Oiltex International Ltd. [*Toronto Stock Exchange symbol*]

OTXRA......... X-Ray Assay Laboratories Ltd., Don Mills, Ontario [*Library symbol National Library of Canada*] (NLC)

OTY......... Oria [*Papua New Guinea*] [*Airport symbol Obsolete*] (OAG)

OTY......... York University, Toronto, Ontario [*Library symbol National Library of Canada*] (NLC)

OTYA......... York University Archives, Toronto, Ontario [*Library symbol National Library of Canada*] (NLC)

OTYBE......... Professional Library, Board of Education for the City of York, Toronto, Ontario [*Library symbol National Library of Canada*] (NLC)

OTYBE......... York Borough Board of Education, Toronto, Ontario [*Library symbol National Library of Canada*] (NLC)

OTYBES......... Schools, Board of Education for the City of York, Toronto, Ontario [*Library symbol National Library of Canada*] (NLC)

OTYF......... Hospital Library, York-Finch General Hospital, Downsview, Ontario [*Library symbol National Library of Canada*] (BIB)

OTYL......... Law Library, York University, Toronto, Ontario [*Library symbol National Library of Canada*] (NLC)

OTYLR......... Listening Room, York University, Toronto, Ontario [*Library symbol National Library of Canada*] (NLC)

OTYP......... City of York Public Library, Toronto, Ontario [*Library symbol National Library of Canada*] (NLC)

OTZ......... Kotzebue [*Alaska*] [*Airport symbol*] (OAG)

OTZ......... Ortiz [*New Mexico*] [*Seismograph station code, US Geological Survey*] (SEIS)

OTZ......... Oxothiazolidine [*Biochemistry*]

OU......... City Express [*ICAO designator*] (AD)

OU......... Object Unit (NITA)

OU......... Observation Unit

OU......... Oculi Unitas [*Both Eyes Together*] [*Ophthalmology*]

OU......... Oculus Uterque [*Each Eye*] [*Ophthalmology*]

OU......... Odor Unit [*Air pollution*]

OU......... Official Use (WDAA)

OU......... Ohio State University, Columbus, OH [*Library symbol Library of Congress*] (LCLS)

OU......... Ohio University [*Athens*]

OU......... Oklahoma University

OU......... Open University [*British*]

OU	Operable Unit (BCP)
OU	Operation Unit
OU	Oppenheim-Urbach [*Disease*] [*Medicine*] (DB)
OU	Opposition Unie [*United Opposition*] [*The Comoros*] [*Political party*] (EY)
OU	Otonabee Airways [*ICAO designator*] (AD)
ou	Ounce [*Unit of weight*] (CDAI)
OU	Output Unit [*Computer science*] (IAA)
OU	Oxford University [*England*]
OU	University of Oklahoma, Norman [*USA*] [*Marine science*] (OSRA)
OUA	Office of University Affairs [*NASA*]
OUA	Order of United Americans (NADA)
OUA	Organisation de l'Unite Africaine [*Organization of African Unity - OAU*] (EAIO)
OUA	Ouagadougou [*Burkina Faso*] [*Airport symbol*] (OAG)
OUA	Ouanaham [*Loyalty Islands*] [*Seismograph station code, US Geological Survey*] (SEIS)
OUa	Upper Arlington Public Library, Upper Arlington, OH [*Library symbol Library of Congress*] (LCLS)
OUAM	Order of United American Mechanics
OUAS	Oxford University Air Squadron [*British*] (DI)
OUAT	Once upon a Time (The Prisoner Fan Club) (EA)
OUBD	Outbound [*ICAO designator*] (FAAC)
OU-BP	Ohio State University, Byrd Polar Research Center, Goldthwait Polar Library, Columbus, OH [*Library symbol*] [*Library of Congress*] (LCLS)
OUBS	Open University Business School [*British*]
OUC	Ocracoke, NC [*Location identifier FAA*] (FAAL)
OUC	Ohio University, Chillicothe Branch Campus, Chillicothe, OH [*OCLC symbol*] (OCLC)
OUCA	Chemical Abstracts, Ohio State University, Columbus, OH [*Library symbol Library of Congress*] (LCLS)
OUCC	Ohio University Cartographic Center [*Research center*] (RCD)
OUCH	Off-Line Universal Command History [*Computer science*] (KSC)
OUCTA	Order of United Commercial Travelers of America (EA)
OUD	AMOCO Production Co., Library, Tulsa, OK [*OCLC symbol*] (OCLC)
OUD	Operational Use Data
OUD	Oujda [*Morocco*] [*Airport symbol*] (OAG)
Oud C	Oudh Code [*India*] [*A publication*] (DLA)
Oudh C	Oudh Code [*India*] [*A publication*] (DLA)
Oudh LJ	Oudh Law Journal [*India*] [*A publication*] (DLA)
Oudh LR	Oudh Law Reports [*India*] [*A publication*] (DLA)
Oudh Rev Sel Cas...	Revised Collection of Selected Cases Issued by Chief Commissioner and Financial Commissioner of Oudh [*A publication*] (DLA)
Oudh Wkly N...	Oudh Weekly Notes [*India*] [*A publication*] (DLA)
Oudh WN	Oudh Weekly Notes [*India*] [*A publication*] (DLA)
OUDP	Officer Undergraduate Degree Program [*Army*] (AABC)
OUDS	Oxford University Dramatic Society [*British*] (AIE)
OUE	National Oceanic and Atmospheric Administration, National Severe Storms Laboratories, Norman, OK [*OCLC symbol*] (OCLC)
OUE	Operational Utility Evaluation
OUE	Orbital Uncertainty Estimate
OUE	Ouesso [*Congo*] [*Airport symbol*] (OAG)
OUE	Ouvriers Unis de l'Electricite, de la Radio, et de la Machinerie d'Amerique [*United Electrical, Radio, and Machine Workers of America - UE*]
OUF	Northwestern Oklahoma State University, Library, Alva, OK [*OCLC symbol*] (OCLC)
OUF	Optimum Usual Frequency Radio (IAA)
OUF	Order of Use File (MCD)
OUF	Oxygen Utilization Factor
OUG	Oklahoma Children's Memorial Hospital, Library, Oklahoma City, OK [*OCLC symbol*] (OCLC)
OUG	Organisation de l'Unite Guineenne [*Organization of Guinean Unity*] (PD)
OUG	Ouahigouya [*Upper Volta*] [*Airport symbol*] (AD)
Ought	Oughton's Ordo Judiciorum [*Order of Judgments*] [*A publication*] (DLA)
OUG/I	Online Users' Group/Ireland (EAIO)
OU-H	Ohio State University, Health Sciences Library, Columbus, OH [*Library symbol Library of Congress*] (LCLS)
OUH	Oklahoma College of Osteopathic Medicine and Surgery, Library, Tulsa, OK [*OCLC symbol*] (OCLC)
OUH	Oudtshoorn [*South Africa*] [*Airport symbol*] (OAG)
OUHK	Open University of Hong Kong
OUHSC	Oklahoma University Health Sciences Center
OUI	Ban Houei Sai [*Laos*] [*Airport symbol*] (AD)
OUI	Office of Unemployment Insurance [*Employment and Training Administration*] [*Department of Labor*]
OUI	Oklahoma Osteopathic Hospital, Library, Tulsa, OK [*OCLC symbol*] (OCLC)
OUI	Organisation Universitaire Interamericaine [*Inter-American Organization for Higher Education*] (EAIO)
OUI	Outdoors Unlimited (EA)
OUI	Outer Integument [*Botany*]
OUIL	Operating a Vehicle while under the Influence of Liquor [*Traffic offense charge*]
OUJ	Oklahoma State University, Technical Institute Library, Oklahoma City, OK [*OCLC symbol*] (OCLC)
OUK	Operation Upshot-Knothole [*Atomic weapons testing*]
OUK	Oscar Rose Junior College Library, Midwest City, OK [*OCLC symbol*] (OCLC)
OUL	Air Atonabee Ltd. [*Canada ICAO designator*] (FAAC)

OU-L	Ohio State University, College of Law, Columbus, OH [*Library symbol Library of Congress*] (LCLS)
OUL	Ohio University, Lancaster Branch Campus, Lancaster, OH [*OCLC symbol*] (OCLC)
OUL	Orbital Utility Light
OUL	Oulu [*Finland*] [*Seismograph station code, US Geological Survey*] (SEIS)
OUL	Oulu [*Finland*] [*Airport symbol*] (OAG)
OULCS	Ontario University Libraries Cooperative System (NITA)
Oult Ind	Oulton's Index to Irish Statutes [*A publication*] (DLA)
Oult Laws Ir...	Oulton's Laws of Ireland [*A publication*] (DLA)
OUM	Philbrook Art Center Library, Tulsa, OK [*OCLC symbol*] (OCLC)
OUMC	Otago University Medical Corps [*British military*] (DMA)
OUN	Norman, OK [*Location identifier FAA*] (FAAL)
OUN	Ohio University, Athens, OH [*OCLC symbol*] (OCLC)
OUNPSA	Office of United Nations Political and Security Affairs [*Department of State*]
OUNS	Office of Urban Neighborhood Services [*HUD*]
OUNSAF......	Office of the Under Secretary of the Air Force
OUO	Official Use Only
OUO	United States Army, Morris Swett Library, Fort Sill, OK [*OCLC symbol*] (OCLC)
OUP	Official Unionist Party [*Northern Ireland*] (PPW)
OUP	OFS [*Orbiter Functional Simulator*] Uplink Processor [*NASA*]
OU-P	Ohio State University, Pharmacy and Bacteriology Library, Columbus, OH [*Library symbol Library of Congress*] (LCLS)
OUP	Operative United Painters [*A union*] [*British*]
OUP	Operative United Plumbers [*A union*] [*British*]
OUP	Oxford University Press (NADA)
OUP	Oxford University Press, Inc. [*New York, NY*]
OUP	University of Portland, Portland, OR [*OCLC symbol*] (OCLC)
OUPT	Output (AAG)
OUQ	United States Army, Nye Library, Fort Sill, OK [*OCLC symbol*] (OCLC)
OUR	Batouri [*Cameroon*] [*Airport symbol*] (OAG)
OUR	Organizacion de Unidad Revolucionaria [*Organization of Revolutionary Unity*] [*Bolivia*] [*Political party*] (PPW)
OUR	Oxygen Uptake Rate [*Biochemistry*]
OUR	Oxygen Utilization Rate [*Photosynthesis*]
OUR	United States Federal Aviation Administration, Aeronautical Center Library, Oklahoma City, OK [*OCLC symbol*] (OCLC)
OUrC	Urbana College, Urbana, OH [*Library symbol Library of Congress*] (LCLS)
OURD	[*The*] Ogden Union Railway & Depot Co. [*AAR code*]
OURI	Oklahoma University Research Institute
Our Lady Lake U...	Our Lady of the Lake University (GAGS)
OURQ	Outer Upper Right Quadrant [*Anatomy*]
OURS	Orangutan Recovery Service [*Later, IUCN*]
OURS	Organization for United Response [*Later, AFA (Adoptive Families of America)*] (PAZ)
OURTEL	Our Telegram (NATG)
OUS	Oklahoma Union List of Serials Project, Stillwater, OK [*OCLC symbol*] (OCLC)
OUS	Ourinhos [*Brazil*] [*Airport symbol*] (OAG)
OUS	Outdoor Unit Substation
OUSA	Office of the Under Secretary of the Army
OUSA	OMNI U.S.A. [*NASDAQ symbol*] (TTSB)
OUSA	Omni USA, Inc. [*NASDAQ symbol*] (SAG)
OUSA	Open University Students' Association [*British*]
OUSA	Operation USA [*An association*] (EA)
OUSA	Organisation de l'Unite Syndicale Africaine [*Organisation of African Trade Union Unity - OATUU*] [*Accra, Ghana*] (EAIO)
OUSAF	Office of the Under Secretary of the Air Force
OUSAIRA	Office of the United States Air Attache (CINC)
OUSARMA ...	Office of the United States Army Attache
OUSCS	Office of Urban Studies and Clearinghouse Services [*HUD*]
OUSD	Office of the Under Secretary of Defense (MCD)
OUSDA	Office of the Under Secretary of Defense for Acquisition
OUSD(A & T)...	Office of the Under Secretary of Defense (Acquisition and Technology) (RDA)
OUSD(P)	Office of the Under Secretary of Defense (Policy) (MCD)
OUSDRE	Office of the Under Secretary of Defense for Research and Engineering
OUSH	Uxbridge-Scott Historical Society, Uxbridge, Ontario [*Library symbol National Library of Canada*] (BIB)
OUSN	Office of the Under Secretary of the Navy
OUSOFA	Office of the Under Secretary of the Army
OUST	Office of Underground Storage Tanks [*Environmental Protection Agency*]
OUSW	Office of the Under Secretary of War [*Obsolete*]
OUT	Bousso [*Chad*] [*Airport symbol*] (AD)
OUT	Orbiter Utilities Tray [*NASA*] (NASA)
OUT	Organizacao Unida de Trabalhadores [*United Organization of Workers*] [*Portugal Political party*] (PPE)
OUT	Organization for Unemployed Teachers
OUT	Organization for Use of the Telephone (EA)
Out	Outerbridge's State Reports [*97, 98 Pennsylvania*] [*A publication*] (DLA)
OUT	Outgoing
OUT	Outing (ROG)
OUT	Outlet [*Hawaii*] [*Seismograph station code, US Geological Survey*] (SEIS)
OUT	Output (NASA)
OUT	Outsize Cargo (COE)

OUT .... United States Federal Aviation Administration, CAMI Library, Oklahoma City, OK [*OCLC symbol*] (OCLC)

OUT .... Uxbridge Township Public Library, Uxbridge, Ontario [*Library symbol National Library of Canada*] (NLC)

OUTA .... Ouvriers Unis des Textiles d'Amerique [*United Textile Workers of America - UTWA*]

OUTBD .... Outboard

OUTBD .... Outbound

OutbdM .... Outboard Marine Corp. [*Associated Press*] (SAG)

OUTBGS ...... Outbuildings (ROG)

OutbkStk ..... Outback Steakhouse, Inc. [*Associated Press*] (SAG)

OUTC .... Ordnance Unit Training Center [*Military*]

OUTCONUS... Outside Continental Limits of the United States [*Military*] (DNAB)

OUTG .... Outage (KSC)

OUTHO .... Outhouse (ROG)

OUTL .... Outlet

outl .... Outline (VRA)

OUTL .... Outlook Group [*NASDAQ symbol*] (TTSB)

OUTL .... Outlook Group Corp [*NASDAQ symbol*] (SPSG)

Outlet.......... Outlet Communications, Inc. [*Associated Press*] (SAG)

OUTLIM .... Output Limiting Facility [*Computer science*] (MDG)

OutlkGrp ...... Outlook Group Corp. [*Associated Press*] (SAG)

OUTLT .... Outlet

OUTPUTM .... Output Measures for Public Libraries [*Clarion University of Pennsylvania*] [*Information service or system*] (IID)

OUTRAN ...... Outlet

OUTRAN ...... Output

OUTRAN ...... Output Translator [*IBM Corp.*]

OUTREG ...... Output Register (IAA)

OUTS .... Operational Unit Transportable System (MCD)

OUTSTDG .... Outstanding [*Business term*]

Outstdg .... Outstanding (EBF)

outstg .... Outstanding [*Business term*] (MHDW)

OUTUS .... Outside the United States

OUTWATS .... Outgoing Wide-Area Telephone Service [*Telecommunications*] (TEL)

OUTWD .... Outward (ROG)

OUTXLTR ..... Output Translator [*IBM Corp.*] (MSA)

OUU .... University of Oklahoma, Tulsa Medical College Library, Tulsa, OK [*OCLC symbol*] (OCLC)

OUUI............ Decisions Given by the Office of the Umpire (Unemployment Insurance) Respecting Claims to Out-of-Work Donation [*England*] (DLA)

OUUIBD .... Benefit Decisions of the British Umpire [*A publication*] (DLA)

OUUID .... Umpire Decisions, Benefit Claims [*England*] [*A publication*] (DLA)

OUUISD .... Benefit and Donation Claims, Selected Decisions of Umpire [*England*] [*A publication*] (DLA)

OUV .... University of Science and Arts of Oklahoma Libraries, Chickasha, OK [*OCLC symbol*] (OCLC)

OUVB .... Oxford University Volunteer Battalion [*British military*] (DMA)

OUVS .... Orbiter Ultraviolet Spectrometer [*NASA*]

OUW .... Elkins, WV [*Location identifier FAA*] (FAAL)

OUW .... Western Oklahoma State College, Library, Altus, OK [*OCLC symbol*] (OCLC)

OUZ .... Zouerate [*Mauritania*] [*Airport symbol*] (OAG)

OV.............. Observed Vehicle (WDAA)

OV.............. Obvious (AAMN)

OV.............. Offense Variable [*Criminal sentencing*]

OV.............. Office of Volunteers [*Red Cross*]

OV.............. Office Visit [*Medicine*]

OV.............. Ohio Valley

OV.............. Oil of Vitriol

OV.............. One Village [*An association*] (EAIO)

OV.............. One Voice: a Magazine about Church Music [*A publication*] (APTA)

OV.............. Open Ventilated (MSA)

OV.............. Open Visit (WDAA)

OV.............. Operation Venus (EA)

OV.............. Orbital [*or Orbiter*] Vehicle [*NASA*]

ov.............. Orbiter Vehicle [*NASA*] (NAKS)

OV.............. Orphan Voyage (EA)

OV.............. Osler-Vaquez [*Disease*] [*Medicine*] (DB)

OV.............. Output Voltage

OV.............. Oval

OV.............. Ovalbumin [*Also, OA, OVA, OVAL*] [*Biochemistry*]

OV.............. Ovarian Volume [*Gynecology*]

OV.............. Ovary (ADA)

OV.............. Oven [*Refers to the open space below the stage in a theater*] [*Slang*] (DSUE)

OV.............. Over (AAG)

ov.............. Over (VRA)

OV.............. Overflow

OV.............. Overruled [*Legal shorthand*] (LWAP)

OV.............. Overseas National Airways (GAVI)

OV.............. Overture (ROG)

OV.............. Overventilation [*Medicine*]

OV.............. Overvoltage

OV.............. Ovid [*Roman poet, 43BC-17AD*] [*Classical studies*] (ROG)

OV.............. Ovulate [*Gynecology*] (DAVI)

OV.............. Ovum [*Egg*] [*Latin*]

OV.............. Owner's Vans [*Shipping*]

OV.............. Oxygen Vent (NASA)

ov.............. Oxygen Vent (NAKS)

OVA .... Bekily [*Madagascar*] [*Airport symbol*] (OAG)

OVA .... Office of Veterans' Affairs

OVA .... Offshore Valve Association (EA)

OVA .... Organic Vapor Analyzer [*Chromatography*]

OVA .... Ottava [*Octave*] [*Music*]

OVA .... Ovalbumin [*Also, OA, OV, OVAL*] [*Biochemistry*]

OVA .... Overhead Value Analysis (ADA)

OVAB .... Orbiting Vehicle Assembly Building [*Later, OVSB*]

OVAC .... Organisation Value Analysis Chart (PDAA)

OVAC .... Overseas Visual Aids Centre [*British*]

OVAE .... Office of Vocational and Adult Education [*Department of Education*] (OICC)

OVAG .... Horticultural Research Institute of Ontario Ministry of Agriculture and Food, Vineland Station, Ontario [*Library symbol National Library of Canada*] (NLC)

OVAGR .... Research Station, Agriculture Canada [*Station de Recherches, Agriculture Canada*] Vineland Station, Ontario [*Library symbol National Library of Canada*] (NLC)

OVAL .... Oval [*Postal Service standard*] (OPSA)

OVAL .... Ovalbumin [*Also, OA, OV, OVA*]

OVAL .... Ovalocytes [*Laboratory science*] (DAVI)

OVAL .... Overalls [*Freight*]

OVALO .... Ovalocytosis [*Laboratory science*] (DAVI)

OVAM .... Orbital Vehicle Assembly Mode [*NASA*]

OVAMS .... Office of Vulnerability Assessment and Management Services [*Department of Commerce*]

OVAN .... Vanier Public Library, Ontario [*Library symbol National Library of Canada*] (NLC)

OVAS .... Offshore Vessels Availability System [*Alpha Asia Systems Pte. Ltd.*] [*Defunct Information service or system*] (CRD)

OVATE .... Okumenische Vereinigung der Akademien und Tagungzentren in Europa [*Ecumenical Association of Laity Centres and Academies in Europe - EALCAE*] [*Bad Boll, Federal Republic of Germany*] (EAIO)

OVAX .... Ovariectomized [*Gynecology*]

OVB .... Novosibirsk [*Former USSR Airport symbol*] (OAG)

OVB .... Overseas Visitors Bureau [*Department of Trade*] [*British*]

OVBC .... Ohio Valley Banc Corp. [*NASDAQ symbol*] (SAG)

OVBD .... Overboard (AAG)

OVC .... Office for Victims of Crime [*Department of Justice*]

OVC .... Ohio Valley Conference [*Collegiate sports*]

OVC .... Ontario Veterinary College

OVC .... Optimized Valence Configuration [*Air Force*]

ovc .... Other Valuable Considerations [*Commerce*] (BARN)

OVC .... Overcast

OVC .... Oxidizer Vent Control

OVC .... Valley East Public Library, Val Caron, Ontario [*Library symbol National Library of Canada*] (NLC)

OVCA .... Ovarian Carcinoma [*Oncology*]

OVCO .... Operational Voice Communication Office [*NASA*] (MCD)

ovco .... Operational Voice Communication Office [*NASA*] (NAKS)

OVCP .... Orbiting Vehicle Checkout Procedure

OVCS .... Operational Voice Communication Subsystem

OVCSEL ...... Organic Vertical-Cavity Surface-Emitting LASER [*Materials science*]

OVCST .... Overcast (AFM)

OVCT .... Caldwell Township Public Library, Verner, Ontario [*Library symbol National Library of Canada*] (NLC)

OVD .... Occlusal Vertical Dimension [*Dentistry*]

OV/D .... Operational Verification/Demonstration

OVD .... Optically Variable Device

OVD .... Optical Video Disk

OVD .... Outer Vapor Phase Deposition [*Coating technology*]

OVD .... Outside Vapor Deposition [*Coating technology*]

OVD .... Oviedo [*Spain*] [*Airport symbol*] (OAG)

OVDED .... Overdeduction

OVDF .... Official Visitors to Departmental Facilities [*New South Wales, Australia*]

OVDR .... Observed Vertical Detection Range

OVE .... Ohio Valley Electric Railroad

OVE .... On Vehicle Equipment

OVE .... Optimum Value Engineered (Home)

OVE .... Orator Verbis Electric (IAA)

OVE .... Oroville, CA [*Location identifier FAA*] (FAAL)

OVE .... Overton [*Nevada*] [*Seismograph station code, US Geological Survey Closed*] (SEIS)

OVE .... Owen Vapor Engine

OVEATP ...... Ohio Vocational Education Achievement Test Program (EDAC)

OVEN .... Italian Oven [*NASDAQ symbol*] (TTSB)

OVEN .... [*The*] Italian Oven, Inc. [*NASDAQ symbol*] (SAG)

OVER .... Optimum Vehicle for Effective Reconnaissance [*Air Force*] (PDAA)

OVER .... Oversize Cargo (COE)

Over............ Overtone [*Record label*]

Over............ Overton's Tennessee Supreme Court Reports [*1791-1816*] [*A publication*] (DLA)

Overl........... Overland [*A publication*]

OVERPASS... Overpass [*Commonly used*] (OPSA)

Overr........... Overruled In [*or Overruling*] [*Legal term*] (DLA)

OVERS .... Orbital Vehicle Reentry Simulator [*NASA*]

OVERS .... Overplus (DGA)

Overt........... Overton's Tennessee Supreme Court Reports [*1791-1816*] [*A publication*] (DLA)

Overt Pr ...... Overton's Iowa and Wisconsin Practice [*A publication*] (DLA)

OVF .... Overfill (NASA)

OVF .... Overflow [*Computer science*]

OVF .... Overvoltage Factor (IAA)

OVF............ Oxygen Vent Fill

OVFL .... Overflow (AAG)

ovflo .... Overflow (HGAA)

OVG .... Oberverwaltungsgericht [*Provincial Administrative Court of Appeal*] [*German*] (DLA)

OVG .... Office of the Valuer-General [*Northern Territory, Australia*]

OVH .... Vankleek Hill Public Library, Ontario [*Library symbol National Library of Canada*] (NLC)

OVHD .... Oval Head

OVHD .... Overhead (AAG)

OVHDLD .... Overhandled [*Freight*]

OVHD PWR CAB... Overhead Power Cable [*Nautical charts*]

OVHG .... Overhanging

OVHL .... Overhaul (AAG)

OVHT .... Overheat (NASA)

OVHT .... Tay-Victoria Harbour Union Library, Victoria Harbour, Ontario [*Library symbol National Library of Canada*] (BIB)

OVI .... Office of Volunteerism Initiatives (BARN)

OVI .... Operational Validation Inspection (MCD)

ovi .... Operational Validation Inspection (NAKS)

OVIC .... Orbiting Vehicle Integrating Contractor

OVID .... Ovid Technologies [*NASDAQ symbol*] (SAG)

OvidTec ...... Ovid Technoloiges [*Associated Press*] (SAG)

OVIR .... Office of Visas and Registrations [*Former USSR*]

OVIS .... Ohio Vocational Interest Survey [*Vocational guidance test*]

OVL .... Office of Volunteer Liaison [*ACTION*]

OVL .... Optically Void Liquid

OVL .... Oval [*Commonly used*] (OPSA)

OVL .... Overlap (IAA)

OVL .... Overlay (IAA)

OVL .... Overlay File [*Computer science*]

OVLAY .... Overlay

OVLBI .... Orbital Very-Long Baseline Interferometer [*Communications satellite*] [*Telecommunications*] (IEEE)

OVLD .... Overload (AAG)

OVLMA .... Orbiting Vehicle Limited Maintenance Area

OVLO .... Over-Voltage Lock-Out (CIST)

OVLP .... Overvoltage Load Protection

OVLT .... Organum Vasculosum of the Lamina Terminalis [*Medicine*]

OVM .... Congregation of the Oblates of the Virgin Mary [*Rome, Italy*] (EAIO)

OVM .... McGarry Public Library, Virginiatown, Ontario [*Library symbol National Library of Canada*] (BIB)

OVM .... Online Vacation Mall [*Computer site*]

OVM .... On Vehicle Materiel [*Military*]

OVM .... Orbiting Velocity Meter

OVNGT .... Overnight (FAAC)

OVO .... North Vernon, IN [*Location identifier FAA*] (FAAL)

OVON .... OIS Optical Imaging Sys [*NASDAQ symbol*] (TTSB)

OVON .... OIS Optical Imaging Systems, Inc. [*NASDAQ symbol*] (SAG)

OVONIC .... Ovshinsky and Electronic [*Excitation processing term formed by combining name of Stanford Ovshinsky, energy researcher, and "electronic"*]

OVOT .... Vernon Branch, Osgoode Township Library, Ontario [*Library symbol National Library of Canada*] (NLC)

OVP .... Oesterreichische Volkspartei [*Austrian People's Party*] [*Political party*] (PPW)

OVP .... Office of the Vice-President

OVP .... Oil-Vapor Pump

OVP .... Outside Vendor Personnel

OVP .... Oval Paint

OVP .... Ovarian Vein Plasma [*Endocrinology*]

OVP .... Overseas Private Investment Corp., Washington, DC [*OCLC symbol*] (OCLC)

OVP .... Overvoltage Protection

OVPC .... Ovary Pubescence - Curly [*Botany*]

OVPD .... Overpaid (AFM)

OVPG .... Ovary Pubescence, Glandular [*Botany*]

OVPO .... Outside Vapor Phase Oxidation [*Glass technology*]

OVPR .... Over-Voltage Protection Relay [*Electrical engineering*]

OVPRESS ..... Overpressurized

OVPU .... Over-Voltage Protection Unit [*Computer science*] (EECA)

OVPUS .... Office of the Vice President of the United States (BARN)

OVPWR .... Overpower

OVR .... Office of Vocational Rehabilitation [*Later, Vocational Rehabilitation Administration*] [*HEW*]

OVR .... Orbiting Vehicle Requirements

OVR .... Oudtshoorn Volunteer Rifles [*British military*] (DMA)

OVR .... Overlay File [*Computer science*]

OVR .... Overvoltage Relay

OVRA .... Organizzazione Vigilanza Repressione Antifascismo [*Italian Organisation for Vigilance & Repression of Anti-Fascism*] [*Political party*] (WDAA)

OVRD .... Override (AAG)

OVRH .... Val Rita-Harty Public Library, Val Rita, Ontario [*Library symbol National Library of Canada*] (BIB)

OVRHD .... Overhead

OVRN .... Overrun (AFM)

OVRN .... Overrun Standard Approach Lighting System [*Aviation*] (DA)

OVRNG .... Overrunning (DA)

OVRO .... Owens Valley Radio Observatory [*California Institute of Technology*] [*Research center*] (RCD)

OVRP .... Organizacion de Voluntarios para la Revolucion Puertorriquena [*Organization of Volunteers for the Puerto Rican Revolution*] (PD)

OVRR .... Office of Veterans Reemployment Rights [*Department of Labor*]

OVRS .... Operational Voice Recording Subsystem

OVRSGHT ..... Oversight

OVS .... Official Visitors' Scheme

OVS .... Online Version Storage [*Computer science*] (PDAA)

OVS .... Operational Voice System (MCD)

ovs .... Operational Voice System (NAKS)

OVS .... Optical Viewing System

OVS .... Orbiting Vehicle System

OVS .... Ovarian Vein Serum [*Endocrinology*]

OVS .... Overhaul Specification (NG)

OVS .... Oversize

OVS .... Overvoltage Sensing (MCD)

OVSB .... Orbiting Vehicle Support Building [*Formerly, OVAB*]

OVSEA .... Overseas [*Aviation*] (FAAC)

OvShip .... Overseas Shipholding Group, Inc. [*Associated Press*] (SAG)

OVSP .... Overspeed (AAG)

OVSR .... Office of Vehicle Systems Research [*Later, Safety System Laboratory*] [*National Institute of Standards and Technology*]

OVSTFD .... Overstuffed [*Freight*]

OVT .... Occupational-Vocational-Technical Training

OVT .... Operational Verification Test

OVT .... Optical Van Trailer

OVTK .... Overtake (FAAC)

OVTR .... Operational Video Tape Recorder [*Air Force*] (MCD)

OVTR .... Overtravel

OVUIL .... Operating Vehicle under Influence of Liquor or Narcotic Drugs [*FBI standardized term*]

OVUREP .... Overseas Unit Replacement [*System*] [*Army*]

O/V-U/V .... Over Voltage - Under Voltage (MCD)

OVV .... Optically Violently Variable [*QUASAR*]

OVV .... Overvoltage

ovv .... Overvoltage (NAKS)

OVV .... Ovvero [*Otherwise*] [*Music*]

OVWA .... On-Line Voltammetric Wastewater Analyzer [*Biochemistry*]

OVWD .... Operating Vehicle while Drunk [*Traffic offense charge*]

OVWV .... One Valley Bancorp [*NASDAQ symbol*] (TTSB)

OVWV .... One Valley Bancorp of West Virginia, Inc. [*NASDAQ symbol*] (NQ)

OVX .... Ovariectomized [*Gynecology*] (DAVI)

OW .... Obere Winkelgruppe [*Angles above 45*] [*German military - World War II*]

OW .... Observation Ward [*British*]

OW .... Ocellus Width

OW .... Offer Wanted

OW .... Office of Water [*Environmental Protection Agency*] (GFGA)

OW .... Officer's Writer [*British military*] (DMA)

OW .... Ohne Wert [*Without Value*] [*German*]

O/W .... Oil-dispersed-in-Water [*Emulsion*]

OW .... Oil-Immersed Water-Cooled [*Transformer*] (IEEE)

O/W .... Oil in Water

O/W .... Oil-Water [*Ratio*] [*Laboratory science*] (DAVI)

OW .... Older Worker

OW .... Old Wellingtonian [*Wellington College*] [*British*]

OW .... Old Welsh [*Language, etc.*]

OW .... Old Woman [*A wife*] [*Slang*]

OW .... One Way [*Fare*]

OW .... Open Wedge [*Osteotomy*] [*Orthopedics*] (DAVI)

OW .... Open Wheel [*A publication*]

OW .... Open Wire (NATG)

OW .... Optical Window (NASA)

ow .... Optical Window (NAKS)

O/W .... Optional With [*Automotive engineering*]

OW .... Options for Women [*Later, Options*] (EA)

OW .... Order Wire [*Military*] (AABC)

OW .... Order Writing (IAA)

OW .... Ordinary Warfare

O-W .... Ordinary Wave (MCD)

OW .... Ordinary Welfare (BABM)

OW .... Outer Wing

OW .... Out of Wedlock

OW .... Over-Achieving Women

OW .... Overall Width [*of the Vehicle*] [*TII*] (TAG)

OW .... Overseas Writers (EA)

OW .... Over Water (WDAA)

Ow .... Owen's English Common Pleas Reports [*A publication*] (DLA)

Ow .... Owen's English King's Bench Reports [*1556-1615*] [*A publication*] (DLA)

OW .... Owner's Wagons [*Shipping*]

OW .... Trans Mountain Airlines [*ICAO designator*] (AD)

OW .... Warren Public Library, Warren, OH [*Library symbol Library of Congress*] (LCLS)

OW .... Windsor Public Library, Ontario [*Library symbol National Library of Canada*] (NLC)

OWA .... Optical Wholesalers Association [*Later, OLA*] (EA)

OWA .... Organics-in-Water Analyzer [*Instrumentation*]

OWA .... Owase [*Japan*] [*Seismograph station code, US Geological Survey*] (SEIS)

OWA .... Owatonna, MN [*Location identifier FAA*] (FAAL)

OWA .... University of Windsor, Ontario [*Library symbol National Library of Canada*] (NLC)

OWAA .... Anderson Associates Ltd., Willowdale, Ontario [*Library symbol National Library of Canada*] (NLC)

OWAA .... Outdoor Writers Association of America (EA)

OWAAD .... Organisation of Women of Asian and African Descent [*British*] (DI)

OWAB .... Wasaga Beach Public Library, Ontario [*Library symbol National Library of Canada*] (BIB)

OWAEC .... Organization for West African Economic Co-operation

OWAG .... Art Gallery of Windsor, Ontario [*Library symbol National Library of Canada*] (NLC)

OWAIT .... Airy Township Public Library, Whitney, Ontario [*Library symbol National Library of Canada*] (NLC)

OWAL .... Law Library, University of Windsor, Ontario [*Library symbol National Library of Canada*] (NLC)

OWALK .... Walkerton Branch, Bruce County Public Library, Ontario [*Library symbol National Library of Canada*] (NLC)

OWALL .... Wallaceburg Public Library, Ontario [*Library symbol National Library of Canada*] (NLC)

OWAP .... Overhead Warning Annunciator Panel (MCD)

OWaP .... Pike County Free Public Library, Waverly, OH [*Library symbol Library of Congress*] (LCLS)

OWAP .... Waterford Public Library, Ontario [*Library symbol National Library of Canada*] (NLC)

OWAR .... Warkworth Public Library, Ontario [*Library symbol National Library of Canada*] (NLC)

OWARNP ..... Percy Township Branch, Northumberland County Public Library, Warkworth, Ontario [*Library symbol National Library of Canada*] (BIB)

OWas .... Carnegie Public Library, Washington Court House, OH [*Library symbol Library of Congress*] (LCLS)

OWASU .... Old World Archaeological Study Unit (EA)

OWAT .... Wainfleet Township Library, Ontario [*Library symbol National Library of Canada*] (NLC)

OWAV .... OneWave, Inc. [*NASDAQ symbol*] (SAG)

OWAVE .... Ordinary Wave (MSA)

OWay .... Mary L. Cook Public Library, Waynesville, OH [*Library symbol Library of Congress*] (LCLS)

OWB .... Oppenheimer World Bond Fund [*NYSE symbol*] (SAG)

OWB .... Owensboro [*Kentucky*] [*Airport symbol*] (AD)

OWB .... West Bay Public Library, Ontario [*Library symbol National Library of Canada*] (NLC)

OWBA .... Office of Women's Business Ownership (EBF)

OWBC .... Health Sciences Library, Bloorview Children's Hospital, Willowdale, Ontario [*Library symbol National Library of Canada*] (BIB)

OWBE .... Office of Women's Business Enterprise [*Federal government*]

OWBE .... Windsor Board of Education, Ontario [*Library symbol National Library of Canada*] (NLC)

OWBL .... Beaver Lake Branch, Walden Public Library, Ontario [*Library symbol National Library of Canada*] (NLC)

OWBL .... Office of Work-Based Learning [*U.S. Department of Labor*] (BARN)

OWBMS .... Manitoulin Secondary School Library, West Bay, Ontario [*Library symbol National Library of Canada*] (NLC)

OWBO .... Office of Women's Business Ownership [*Small Business Administration*]

OWBPA .... Older Workers Benefit Protection Act of 1990 (WYGK)

OWBR .... Bartlet & Richardes, Windsor, Ontario [*Library symbol National Library of Canada*] (BIB)

OWC .... Centennial Secondary School, Windsor, Ontario [*Library symbol National Library of Canada*] (NLC)

OWC .... Officers' Wives Club [*Military*]

OwC .... Omniwest Corporation, Salt Lake City, UT [*Library symbol Library of Congress*] (LCLS)

OWC .... Ontario Workers' Compensation Appeals Tribunal [*UTLAS symbol*]

OWC .... Order of Woodcraft Chivalry [*British*] (DBA)

OWC .... Ordinary Wave Component

OWC .... Ordnance Weapons Command [*Later, Weapons Command*]

OWC .... Outline of World Cultures [*Human Relations Area Files*] [*Information retrieval*]

OWC .... Owner Will Carry [*Banking*]

OWC .... Owning Work Center [*Military*] (AFIT)

OWC .... Wood County District Public Library, Bowling Green, OH [*OCLC symbol*] (OCLC)

OWCA .... Canadian Automobile Workers Union, Willowdale, Ontario [*Library symbol National Library of Canada*] (BIB)

OWCC .... Cape Croker Public Library, Wiarton, Ontario [*Library symbol National Library of Canada*] (NLC)

OWCF .... Canadian Federation of Independent Business, Willowdale, Ontario [*Library symbol National Library of Canada*] (BIB)

OWCL .... Octane Weekly Cost Ledger (MCD)

OWCP .... Office of Workers' [*formerly, Workmen's*] Compensation Programs [*Formerly, Bureau of Employees' Compensation*] [*Department of Labor*]

OWCS .... Outer Wing Canted Station (MCD)

OWCSC .... Old Water Colour Society's Club (EA)

OWD .... Norwood, MA [*Location identifier FAA*] (FAAL)

OWD .... Oil-in-Water Dispersion [*Pollution*]

OWD .... One-Way Doppler (MCD)

OWD .... On-Line Wholesale Distribution System [*Computer science*] (BUR)

OWDC .... Office of Water Data Coordination [*US Geological Survey*] [*Reston, VA*]

OWDE .... One-Way Doppler Extraction

OWE .... Eagle, CO [*Location identifier FAA*] (FAAL)

OWE .... Office of Water Enforcement [*Environmental Protection Agency*] (ERG)

OWE .... Operating Weight Empty [*of space shuttle*] [*NASA*]

OWE .... Optimum Working Efficiency

OWE .... Outer Window Envelope [*Business stationery*]

OWE .... Welland Public Library, Ontario [*Library symbol National Library of Canada*] (NLC)

OWE .... Western Plains Library System, Clinton, OK [*OCLC symbol*] (OCLC)

OWe .... Westerville Public Library, Westerville, OH [*Library symbol Library of Congress*] (LCLS)

OWEB .... Webbwood Public Library, Ontario [*Library symbol National Library of Canada*] (NLC)

OWEC .... Centennial Secondary School, Welland, Ontario [*Library symbol National Library of Canada*] (NLC)

OWel .... Sylvester Memorial Wellston Public Library, Wellston, OH [*Library symbol Library of Congress*] (LCLS)

OWEL........... Wellington Public Library, Ontario [*Library symbol National Library of Canada*] (BIB)

OWEN .... Niagara College of Applied Arts and Technology, Welland, Ontario [*Library symbol National Library of Canada*] (NLC)

OWEN .... Owen Healthcare, Inc. [*NASDAQ symbol*] (SAG)

Owen .... Owen's English King's Bench Reports [*1556-1615*] [*A publication*] (DLA)

Owen Bankr... Owen on Bankruptcy [*A publication*] (DLA)

OwenC........ Owens-Corning Fiberglas Corp. [*Associated Press*] (SAG)

OWENC........ Westport-North Crosby Public Library, Westport, Ontario [*Library symbol National Library of Canada*] (NLC)

OwenHlt....... Owen Healthcare, Inc. [*Associated Press*] (SAG)

OWENL........ Library Technician Program, Niagara College of Applied Arts & Technology, Welland, Ontario [*Library symbol National Library of Canada*] (NLC)

OwensIll ...... Owens Illinois [*Associated Press*] (SAG)

OwensM....... Owens & Minor Inc. Holding Co. [*Associated Press*] (SAG)

OWeO .... Otterbein College, Westerville, OH [*Library symbol Library of Congress*] (LCLS)

OWEP .... Office of Water Enforcement and Permits [*Environmental Protection Agency*] (GFGA)

OWESBC ...... Borden Chemical, Westhill, Ontario [*Library symbol National Library of Canada*] (NLC)

OWEST .... Asphodel Township Public Library, Westwood, Ontario [*Library symbol National Library of Canada*] (BIB)

OWF .... Oceania Weightlifting Federation [*Australia*] (EA)

OWF............. On Weight of Fiber

OWF............. Optimum Working Facility (NITA)

OWF............. Optimum Working Frequency [*Telecommunications*]

OWF............. Orbital, Weightless Flight (IAA)

OWG .... Oil, Water, Gas

OWG .... Washington, DC [*Location identifier FAA*] (FAAL)

OWGL .... Obscure Wire Glass

OWH .... Herman Collegiate Institute, Windsor, Ontario [*Library symbol National Library of Canada*] (NLC)

OWH .... Warren General Hospital, Warren, OH [*Library symbol*] [*Library of Congress*] (LCLS)

OWHA .... Oliver Wendell Holmes Association

OWHD .... Medical Library, Hotel-Dieu of St. Joseph Hospital, Windsor, Ontario [*Library symbol National Library of Canada*] (NLC)

OWHM .... Hiram Walker Historical Museum, Windsor, Ontario [*Library symbol National Library of Canada*] (BIB)

OWHM .... Office of Water and Hazardous Materials (OICC)

OWHP.......... Whitby Public Library, Ontario [*Library symbol National Library of Canada*] (NLC)

OWI .... Ocellus Width Index

OWI .... Office of War Information [*World War II*]

OWI .... Office of Waste Isolation [*Department of Energy*]

OWI .... OneWorld Internet [*Global Village Communication*] [*Internet gateway service*]

OWI .... Open Work Items (KSC)

OWI .... Operating Vehicle while Intoxicated [*Traffic offense charge*]

OWI .... Ottawa, KS [*Location identifier FAA*] (FAAL)

OWI .... Owens-Illinois, Inc., Technical and Business Information Services, Toledo, OH [*OCLC symbol*] (OCLC)

OWI .... Wiarton Branch, Bruce County Public Library, Ontario [*Library symbol National Library of Canada*] (NLC)

OWIB .... Wikwemikong Band Public Library, Ontario [*Library symbol National Library of Canada*] (NLC)

OWibfC .... Central State University, Wilberforce, OH [*Library symbol Library of Congress*] (LCLS)

OWibfP .... Payne Theological Seminary, Wilberforce, OH [*Library symbol Library of Congress*] (LCLS)

OWibfU .... Wilberforce University, Wilberforce, OH [*Library symbol Library of Congress*] (LCLS)

OWicB .... Borromeo Seminary of Ohio, Wickliffe, OH [*Library symbol Library of Congress*] (LCLS)

OWIFC .... Wolfe Island Branch, Frontenac County Public Library, Ontario [*Library symbol National Library of Canada*] (NLC)

OWIJC .... International Joint Commission [*Commission Mixte Internationale*] Windsor, Ontario [*Library symbol National Library of Canada*] (NLC)

OWil .... Willard Memorial Library, Willard, OH [*Library symbol Library of Congress*] (LCLS)

OWillo .... Willoughby-Eastlake Public Library, Willowick, OH [*Library symbol Library of Congress*] (LCLS)

OWilm .... Wilmington Public Library, Wilmington, OH [*Library symbol Library of Congress*] (LCLS)

OWilmC .... Wilmington College, Wilmington, OH [*Library symbol Library of Congress*] (LCLS)

OWilmH .... Clinton Memorial Hospital, Health Resource Center, Wilmington, OH [*Library symbol Library of Congress*] (LCLS)

OWilm-O...... Southwestern Ohio Rural Library, Wilmington, OH [*Library symbol Library of Congress*] (LCLS)

OWilmS .... Southern State Community College, Wilmington, OH [*Library symbol Library of Congress*] (LCLS)

OWin .... Adams-Brown County Bookmobile, Winchester, OH [*Library symbol Library of Congress*] (LCLS)

OWIN........... Office of Work Incentive Program [*Office of Comprehensive Employment Development*] [*Department of Labor*]

OWINF .... F. E. Madill Secondary School, Wingham, Ontario [*Library symbol National Library of Canada*] (NLC)

OWISDG ...... Williamstown Branch, Stormount, Dundas, and Glengarry County Library, Ontario [*Library symbol National Library of Canada*] (NLC)

OWIT .... Organization of Women in International Trade (NTPA)

OWIU .... Oil Workers International Union [*Later, OCAW*]

OWK .... Kent State University, Trumbull Regional Campus, Warren, OH [*Library symbol Library of Congress OCLC symbol*] (LCLS)

OWK .... Norridgewock, ME [*Location identifier FAA*] (FAAL)

OWL .... Lowe Technical School, Windsor, Ontario [*Library symbol National Library of Canada*] (NLC)

OWL .... Maui Airlines, Inc. [*ICAO designator*] (FAAC)

OWL .... National Order of Women Legislators (EA)

OWL .... Object Windows Library [*Borland International*] [*Computer science*] (PCM)

OWL .... Office Workstations Ltd. (NITA)

OWL .... Older Women's Dialogue (EA)

OWL .... Older Women's Liberation [*Feminist group*] [*Defunct*]

OWL .... Olympic-Wallowa Lineament [*Geology*]

OWL .... Online without Limits

OWL .... Online Writing Lab [*Purdue University*] [*Computer science*]

OWL .... Other Woman Limited [*An association*]

OWL .... Westerville Public Library, Westerville, OH [*OCLC symbol*] (OCLC)

OWLA .... Organization of Women for Legal Awareness (EA)

OWLaw .... Trumbull County Law Library, Warren, OH [*Library symbol Library of Congress*] (LCLS)

OWLB .... Wunnummin Lake Band Library, Ontario [*Library symbol National Library of Canada*] (BIB)

OWL/D .... Optical Warning Locator/Detector (MCD)

OWLEF .... Older Women's League Educational Fund (EA)

OWIGS .... Church Jesus Christ of Latter-Day Saints, Genealogical Society Library, Cleveland Branch, Westlake, OH [*Library symbol*] [*Library of Congress*] (LCLS)

OWIGS .... Church of Jesus Christ of Latter-Day Saints, Genealogical Society Library, Cleveland Branch, Westlake, OH [*Library symbol Library of Congress*] (LCLS)

OWLI .... Lively Branch, Walden Public Library, Ontario [*Library symbol National Library of Canada*] (NLC)

OWLS .... Office Workers Link Shift [*After-hours production workers*] [*World War II*]

OWLS .... Operation Work Load Scheduling (MCD)

OWLS .... Outagamie-Waupaca Counties Federated Library System [*Library network*]

OWLS .... Overseas Weapons, Logistically Supported (MCD)

OWLS .... Oxford Word and Language Service [*A service of the Oxford English Dictionary group*]

OWM .... Office of War Mobilization [*Succeeded by OWMR, 1944*]

OWM .... Office of Weights and Measures [*National Institute of Standards and Technology*]

OWM .... Office Work Measurement (CIST)

OWMMD ...... M. M. Dillon Ltd., Willowdale, Ontario [*Library symbol National Library of Canada*] (NLC)

OWMR .... Office of War Mobilization and Reconversion [*Succeeded OWM, 1944; became part of Office of Temporary Controls, 1946*]

OWMR .... Other War Materiel Requirements [*Army*]

OWMT .... Michipicoten Township Public Library, Wawa, Ontario [*Library symbol National Library of Canada*] (NLC)

OWN .... Naughton Branch, Walden Public Library, Ontario [*Library symbol National Library of Canada*] (NLC)

OWN .... Ontario Weekly Notes [*A publication*] (DLA)

OWN .... Oudh Weekly Notes [*India*] [*A publication*] (DLA)

OWN .... Overwintered Nest [*Ornithology*]

OWN .... Owen Healthcare [*NYSE symbol*] (TTSB)

OWN .... Owensboro [*Diocesan abbreviation*] [*Kentucky*] (TOCD)

OWN .... Owens Group Ltd. [*New Zealand*] [*ICAO designator*] (FAAC)

OWN .... Owen Ventures Ltd. [*Vancouver Stock Exchange symbol*]

OWN .... Owner (MCD)

OWN .... Sunterra Corp. [*NYSE symbol*] [*Formerly, Signature Resorts*]

OWN .... Wise, VA [*Location identifier FAA*] (FAAL)

OWNR .... Owner

OWO .... On Work Order [*Military*] (AFIT)

OWo .... Wayne County Public Library, Wooster, OH [*Library symbol Library of Congress*] (LCLS)

OWO .... Woodstock Public Library, Ontario [*Library symbol National Library of Canada*] (NLC)

OWoA .... Ohio Agricultural Research and Development Center, Wooster, OH [*Library symbol Library of Congress*] (LCLS)

OWOBC .... J. William Horsey Library, Ontario Bible College, Ontario Theological College, Willowdale, Ontario [*Library symbol National Library of Canada*] (NLC)

OWoC .... College of Wooster, Wooster, OH [*Library symbol Library of Congress*] (LCLS)

OWOH .... Huron Park Secondary School, Woodstock, Ontario [*Library symbol National Library of Canada*] (NLC)

OWoH .... Wooster Community Hospital, Wooster, OH [*Library symbol*] [*Library of Congress*] (LCLS)

OWOL .... Ontario Library Co-Operative, Wyoming, Ontario [*Library symbol National Library of Canada*] (NLC)

OWOM .... Woodstock Museum, Ontario [*Library symbol National Library of Canada*] (BIB)

OWOO .... Oxford County Public Library, Woodstock, Ontario [*Library symbol National Library of Canada*] (NLC)

OWor .... Worthington Public Library, Worthington, OH [*Library symbol*] [*Library of Congress*] (LCLS)

OWorNW ...... National Water Wall Association, Ground Water Library/Information Center, Worthington, OH [*Library symbol*] [*Library of Congress*] (LCLS)

OWorP .... Pontifical College Josephinum, Worthington, OH [*Library symbol Library of Congress*] (LCLS)

OWOS .... Owosso Corp. [*NASDAQ symbol*] (SAG)

Owosso .... Owosso Corp. [*Associated Press*] (SAG)

OWOW .... Office of Wetlands, Oceans, and Watersheds (WPI)

OWoWCL ..... Wayne County Law Library, Wooster, OH [*Library symbol Library of Congress*] (LCLS)

OWP .... Oboz Wielkiej Polski [*Camp of Great Poland*] (PPE)

OWP .... Office of Water Policy [*Department of the Interior*]

OWP .... Office of Water Programs [*Abolished*] [*Environmental Protection Agency*]

OWP .... Office of Wetlands Protection [*Office of Water*] (COE)

OWP .... One-Way Polar [*Telegraph*]

OWP .... One-Write Plus [*Computer software*]

OWP .... Operations Work Procedure [*Nuclear energy*] (NRCH)

OWP .... Orange Washed Pulp [*Citrus processing*]

OWP .... Organization of Wildlife Planners (EA)

OWP .... Outer Wing Panel

OWP .... Warner Pacific College, Portland, OR [*OCLC symbol*] (OCLC)

OWpAR .... United States Air Force, Aerospace Research Laboratories, Wright-Patterson Air Force Base, OH [*Library symbol Library of Congress*] (LCLS)

OWpDI .... United States Air Force, Defense Institute of Security Administration Management, Wright-Patterson Air Force Base, OH [*Library symbol Library of Congress*] (LCLS)

OWPE .... Office of Waste Programs Enforcement [*Environmental Protection Agency*] (EPA)

OWPH .... Whitby Psychiatric Hospital, Ontario [*Library symbol National Library of Canada*] (NLC)

OWpIT .... United States Air Force Institute of Technology, Wright-Patterson Air Force Base, OH [*Library symbol Library of Congress*] (LCLS)

OWpL .... United States Air Force, Air Force Logistics Command, Wright-Patterson Air ForceBase, OH [*Library symbol Library of Congress*] (LCLS)

OWpM .... United States Air Force, Medical Center Library, SGEL, Wright Patterson AFB, OH [*Library symbol Library of Congress*] (LCLS)

OWPO .... Office of Water Program Operations [*Environmental Protection Agency*] (EPA)

OWPP .... Office of Welfare and Pension Plans [*Department of Labor*]

OWPR .... Ocean Wave Profile Recorder (IEEE)

OWPS .... Offshore Windpower System [*Proposed system to generate electricity by wind turbines mounted on offshore platforms*]

OWpT .... United States Air Force, Wright-Patterson Technical Library, Wright-Patterson Air Force Base, OH [*Library symbol Library of Congress*] (LCLS)

OWR .... Obligated War Reserves [*Army*] (AABC)

OWR .... Office of Worship Resources [*Later, WRO*] (EA)

OWR .... Omega West Reactor [*Los Alamos, NM*] [*Department of Energy*]

OWR .... Ontario Weekly Reporter [*A publication*] (DLA)

OWR .... Order of the White Rose of Finland (DD)

OWR .... Riverside Secondary School, Windsor, Ontario [*Library symbol National Library of Canada*] (NLC)

OWR .... Worthington Public Library, Worthington, OH [*OCLC symbol*] (OCLC)

OWRAP .... Office of Worker Retraining and Adjustment Programs [*U.S. Department of Labor*] (BARN)

OWRB .... RC Reid-Bicknell Eng. Ltd., Woodbridge, Ontario [*Library symbol National Library of Canada*] (NLC)

OWRC .... Office of Water Resource Center [*Environmental Protection Agency*] (AEPA)

OWRC .... Old West Regional Commission [*Department of Commerce*]

OWRC .... White River Community Library, Ontario [*Library symbol National Library of Canada*] (NLC)

OWRD .... Ratter and Dunnet Public Library, Warren, Ontario [*Library symbol National Library of Canada*] (NLC)

OWRHS .... Ontario and Western Railroad Historical Society (EA)

OWRL .... One-Way Radio Link [*Telecommunications*] (LAIN)

OWRM .... Office of Weather Research and Modification [*National Oceanic and Atmospheric Administration*] (GRD)

OWRM .... Other War Reserve Materiel

OWRMR .... Other War Reserve Materiel Requirement (AFIT)

OWRMS .... Other War Materiel Reserve Stocks [*Army*] (AABC)

OWRR .... Office of Water Resources Research [*Later, OWRT*] [*Department of the Interior*]

OWRRI .... Oklahoma Water Resources Research Institute [*Stillwater, OK*] [*Department of the Interior*] (GRD)

OWRS .... Office of Water Regulations and Standards [*Environmental Protection Agency*] (GFGA)

OWRT .... Office of Water Research and Technology [*Formerly, OSW, OWRR*] [*Abolished, 1982 Department of the Interior*]

OWS .... Cargosur [*Spain ICAO designator*] (FAAC)

OWS .... Occupational Wage Survey

OWS .... Ocean Weather Ship

OWS .... Ocean Weather Station (MCD)

OWS .... Oil Water Separator [*Navy*] (CAAL)

OWS .... Old West Saxon [*Language, etc.*] (ROG)

OWS .... Oliphant Washington Service [*Information service or system*] (IID)

OWS .... Operational Weather Support

OWS .... Orbital Weapon System (AAG)

OWS .... Orbital Workshop [*NASA*]

OWS .... Ordnance Weapon Systems [*Army*]

OWS .... Outerwear Syndrome [*Medicine*] (DMAA)

OWS .... Outer Wing Station (MCD)

OWS .... Overload Warning System (MCD)
OWS .... Overwear Syndrome [*Of contact lens*]
OWS .... Southwestern Regional Library, Windsor, Ontario [*Library symbol Obsolete National Library of Canada*]
OWS .... Willamette University, Salem, OR [*OCLC symbol*] (OCLC)
OWSA .... Spar Aerospace Ltd., Weston, Ontario [*Library symbol National Library of Canada*] (NLC)
OWSAH .... Salvation Army Grace Hospital, Windsor, Ontario [*Library symbol National Library of Canada*] (BIB)
OWSC .... Old West Scandinavian [*Language, etc.*]
OWSC .... St. Clair College, Windsor, Ontario [*Library symbol National Library of Canada*] (NLC)
OWSCC .... Simon-Carves of Canada Ltd., Willowdale, Ontario [*Library symbol National Library of Canada*] (NLC)
OWSCL .... Senes Consultants Ltd., Willowdale, Ontario [*Library symbol National Library of Canada*] (NLC)
OWSDG .... Winchester Branch, Stormount, Dundas, and Glengarry County Public Library, Ontario [*Library symbol National Library of Canada*] (NLC)
OWSE .... Otherwise
OWSG .... Older Worker Specialists Group
OWSJ .... Off the Wall Street Journal [*Parody of the Wall Street Journal*]
OWSM .... Seagram Museum, Waterloo, Ontario [*Library symbol National Library of Canada*] (BIB)
OWT .... Organic Weather Team
OWT .... Waterloo Public Library, Ontario [*Library symbol National Library of Canada*] (NLC)
OWT .... Willamette University, Law Library, Salem, OR [*OCLC symbol*] (OCLC)
OWTA .... Kitchener-Waterloo Academy of Medicine, Kitchener, Ontario [*Library symbol National Library of Canada*] (NLC)
OWTAI .... Airworthiness Library, Ontario Region, Transport Canada [*Bibliotheque de la Navigabilite Aerienne, Region de l'Ontario, Transports Canada*], Willowdale, Ontario [*Library symbol National Library of Canada*] (NLC)
OWTG .... Kitchener-Waterloo Hospital, Kitchener, Ontario [*Library symbol National Library of Canada*] (NLC)
OWTL .... Wilfrid Laurier University [*Formerly, Waterloo Lutheran University*] Waterloo, Ontario [*Library symbol National Library of Canada*] (NLC)
OWTM .... Legal Reference Centre, Manufacturers' Life Insurance Co., Waterloo, Ontario [*Library symbol National Library of Canada*] (BIB)
OWTML .... Corporate Library, Mutual Life of Canada, Waterloo, Ontario [*Library symbol National Library of Canada*] (BIB)
OWTO .... Ontario Library Services Center, Waterloo, Ontario [*Library symbol National Library of Canada*] (NLC)
OWTS .... St. Mary's General Hospital, Kitchener, Ontario [*Library symbol National Library of Canada*] (NLC)
OWTU .... University of Waterloo, Ontario [*Library symbol National Library of Canada*] (NLC)
OWTUE .... Environmental Studies Library, University of Waterloo, Ontario [*Library symbol National Library of Canada*] (NLC)
OWU .... Office of War Utilities [*War Production Board*]
OWU .... Ohio Wesleyan University [*Delaware, OH*]
OWU .... Ohio Wesleyan University, Delaware, OH [*OCLC symbol*] (OCLC)
OWU .... Open-Window Unit (MSA)
OWU .... Overload Warning Unit (MCD)
OWU .... Woodward, OK [*Location identifier FAA*] (FAAL)
OW-USS ...... Our World-Underwater Scholarship Society (EA)
OWV .... Ocean Weather Vessel [*Shipping*] (AIA)
OWVM .... Vincent Massey Secondary School, Windsor, Ontario [*Library symbol National Library of Canada*] (NLC)
OWW .... Walkerville Collegiate Institute, Windsor, Ontario [*Library symbol National Library of Canada*] (NLC)
OWWA .... Waters Branch, Walden Public Library, Ontario [*Library symbol National Library of Canada*] (NLC)
OWWH .... Whitefish Branch, Walden Public Library, Ontario [*Library symbol National Library of Canada*] (NLC)
OWWM .... Office of Water and Waste Management (ERG)
OWX .... Office of the Assistant for Weather [*Air Force*]
OWX .... Ottawa, OH [*Location identifier FAA*] (FAAL)
OWY .... Owyhee, NV [*Location identifier FAA*] (FAAL)
OWYL .... Lambton County Public Library, Wyoming, Ontario [*Library symbol National Library of Canada*] (NLC)
OW/YM .... Older Woman / Younger Man (WDAA)
OX .... Air Atlantic Airlines [*ICAO designator*] (AD)
OX .... Optic Chiasm (STED)
OX .... Orthopedic Examination (STED)
OX .... Oxacillin [*Antibacterial compound*]
Ox .... Oxford [*Record label*]
OX .... Oxford [*England*]
OX .... Oxidant [*Photochemical*] (ERG)
OX .... Oxide [*or Oxidizer*] (AAG)
ox .... Oxides (VRA)
ox .... Oxidizer (NAKS)
Ox .... Oxygen (STED)
Ox .... Oxygen [*Chemical element*] (IAA)
ox .... Oxygen (IDOE)
OX .... Oxymel [*Syrup of vinegar and honey*] [*Pharmacy*]
OXA .... Oxalic Acid [*Organic chemistry*]
OXA .... Oxaprotiline (DMAA)
OXB .... Baldwin-Wallace College, Berea, OH [*OCLC symbol*] (OCLC)
OxboroM .... Oxboro Medical International, Inc. [*Associated Press*] (SAG)
OXBRIDGE ... Oxford/Cambridge [*England*]

OXC .... Oxford, CT [*Location identifier FAA*] (FAAL)
OXC .... Oxidizing Catalyst [*Automotive engineering*]
OXC .... Waterbury [*Connecticut*] [*Airport symbol*] (AD)
OXCI .... Oxford Consolidated, Inc. [*NASDAQ symbol*] (NQ)
OXD .... Oxford [*England*] [*Seismograph station code, US Geological Survey Closed*] (SEIS)
OXD .... Oxford, OH [*Location identifier FAA*] (FAAL)
OXD .... Oxide (NAKS)
OXD .... Oxidized (MSA)
OXDZR .... Oxidizer (NASA)
OXe .... Greene County District Library, Xenia, OH [*Library symbol Library of Congress*] (LCLS)
OXE .... OEC Medical Sys [*NYSE symbol*] (TTSB)
OXE .... OEC Medical Systems [*Formerly, Diasonics, Inc.*] [*NYSE symbol*] (SPSG)
OXE .... Oxaero [*British*] [*FAA designator*] (FAAC)
OXEA .... Ox Erythrocyte Antibody [*Medicine*] (STED)
OXeGH .... Greene Memorial Hospital, Health Resource Library, Xenia, OH [*Library symbol Library of Congress*] (LCLS)
OXERA .... Oxford Economic Research Associates Ltd
OXF .... Oxford [*England*]
OXF .... Oxford [*British depot code*]
OXF .... Oxford [*Mississippi*] [*Seismograph station code, US Geological Survey Closed*] (SEIS)
OXF .... Oxford [*England*] [*Airport symbol*] (AD)
OXF .... Oxford Properties Canada Ltd. [*Toronto Stock Exchange symbol*]
OXFAM .... Oxford Committee for Famine Relief [*Acronym is now organization's official name British*] (EA)
OXFD .... Oxford Resources Cl'A' [*NASDAQ symbol*] (TTSB)
OXFD .... Oxford Resources Corp. [*NASDAQ symbol*] (SAG)
OxfdHlt .... Oxford Health Plans, Inc. [*Associated Press*] (SAG)
OxfdRsc ...... Oxford Resources Corp, [*Associated Press*] (SAG)
Oxf Lawy .... Oxford Lawyer [*1958-61*] [*A publication*] (DLA)
Oxford .... Oxford Industries, Inc. [*Associated Press*] (SAG)
Oxford Law... Oxford Lawyer [*1958-61*] [*A publication*] (DLA)
OxfrdC .... Oxford Consolidated, Inc. [*Associated Press*] (SAG)
OXGN .... Oxigene, Inc. [*NASDAQ symbol*] (SAG)
OXGNW .... OXIGENE Inc. Wrrt [*NASDAQ symbol*] (TTSB)
OXH .... Oxygen Heat Exchanger (KSC)
OXHP .... Oxford Health Plans [*NASDAQ symbol*] (SPSG)
OXI .... Knox, IN [*Location identifier FAA*] (FAAL)
OXI .... Orbex Industries, Inc. [*Vancouver Stock Exchange symbol*]
Oxi .... Oximeter (STED)
OXID .... Oxidizer (AAG)
OXIDN .... Oxidation
Oxigene ...... Oxigene, Inc. [*Associated Press*] (SAG)
Oxign .... Oxigene, Inc. [*Associated Press*] (SAG)
OXIM .... Oxide-Isolated Monolith
OXINE .... Oxyquinoline [*Organic chemistry*]
OXIS .... Oxide Isolated (NITA)
OXIS .... Oxide Isolation (IAA)
OXIS .... OXIS International [*NASDAQ symbol*] (TTSB)
OXIS .... Oxis International, Inc. [*NASDAQ symbol*] (SAG)
OXK .... Belleville, IL [*Location identifier FAA*] (FAAL)
OXLAT .... Oxalate [*Laboratory science*] (DAVI)
Oxley .... Oxley's Railway Cases [*1897-1903*] [*A publication*] (DLA)
Oxley .... Young's Nova Scotia Vice-Admiralty Decisions, Edited by Oxley [*A publication*] (DLA)
OXM .... Oxford Indus [*NYSE symbol*] (TTSB)
OXM .... Oxford Industries, Inc. [*NYSE symbol*] (SPSG)
OXM .... Oxtotitlan [*Mexico*] [*Seismograph station code, US Geological Survey*] (SEIS)
OXN .... Oxin Industries Ltd. [*Vancouver Stock Exchange symbol*]
OXO .... Million Air, Inc. [*ICAO designator*] (FAAC)
OXO .... Orbiting X-Ray Observatory [*NASA*]
OXO .... Orientos [*Queensland*] [*Airport symbol*] (AD)
OXON .... Oxfordshire [*County in England*]
Oxon .... Oxoiensis [*Academic degree*] (WDAA)
OXON .... Oxonia [*Oxford University*] [*Latin*]
OXON .... Oxoniensis [*Of Oxford University*] [*Latin*]
OXP .... Oxford Poets [*A publication*]
OXP .... Oxprenolol [*Vasodilator*]
OXP .... Oxypressin (STED)
OXPHOS ..... Oxidative Phosphorylation [*Medicine*]
OXR .... Oxnard [*California*] [*Airport symbol*] (OAG)
OXRB .... Oxygen Replacement Bottles
OXT .... Oxytocin (STED)
OXV .... Knoxville, IA [*Location identifier FAA*] (FAAL)
OXY .... Occidental Petroleum Corp. [*NYSE symbol Toronto Stock Exchange symbol*] (SPSG)
OXY .... Occidental Petrol'm [*NYSE symbol*] (TTSB)
OXY .... Oxley [*British depot code*]
OXY .... Oxygen [*Chemical element*] [*Symbol is O*] (AAG)
OXY .... Oxytocin [*Endocrinology*]
OXYG .... Oxygen [*Chemical element*] [*Symbol is O*]
OXYM .... Oxymel [*Syrup of vinegar and honey*] [*Pharmacy*] (ROG)
OXYPrA .... Occidental Petr $3 Cv Pfd [*NYSE symbol*] (TTSB)
OY .... Denmark [*International civil aircraft marking*] (ODBW)
OY .... New Jersey Airways [*ICAO designator*] (AD)
OY .... Operating Year (COE)
OY .... Optimum Yield
OY .... Orange Yellow
Oy .... Osakeyhtioe [*Limited Company*] [*Finland*]
OY .... Public Library of Youngstown and Mahoning County, Youngstown, OH [*Library symbol Library of Congress*] (LCLS)

OYA	Goya [*Argentina*] [*Airport symbol*] (OAG)
OYA	Orthodox Youth of America [*Later, SOYO*]
OYAP	Outstanding Young American Pianist
OYAS	Abbs [*Yemen*] [*ICAO location identifier*] (ICLI)
OYBI	Al-Beida [*Yemen*] [*ICAO location identifier*] (ICLI)
OYBO	Al-Bough [*Yemen*] [*ICAO location identifier*] (ICLI)
OYBT	Barat [*Yemen*] [*ICAO location identifier*] (ICLI)
OYC	Conair AS [*Denmark ICAO designator*] (FAAC)
OYC	Corpus Christi, TX [*Location identifier FAA*] (FAAL)
OYC	Out Year Costs (MCD)
OYCV	Optimum Yaw Control Vertical (SAA)
OYD	Rome, GA [*Location identifier FAA*] (FAAL)
OYDV	Onion Yellow Dwarf Virus [*Plant pathology*]
OYE	Old Yellow Enzyme [*Biochemistry*]
OYE	Oyem [*Gabon*] [*Airport symbol*] (OAG)
OYesA	Antioch College, Yellow Springs, OH [*Library symbol Library of Congress*] (LCLS)
OYesF	Fels Research Institute, Yellow Springs, OH [*Library symbol Library of Congress*] (LCLS)
OYesK	Charles F. Kettering Foundation, Research Laboratory Library, Yellow Springs, OH [*Library symbol Library of Congress*] (LCLS)
OYG	Operating Year Guidance (GFGA)
OYHD	Hodeidah [*Yemen*] [*ICAO location identifier*] (ICLI)
OYK	Oiapoque [*Brazil*] [*Airport symbol*] (AD)
OYKM	Kamaran [*Yemen*] [*ICAO location identifier*] (ICLI)
OYM	Outstanding Young Man (DICI)
OYM	Oyama [*Japan*] [*Seismograph station code, US Geological Survey*] (SEIS)
OYM	St. Mary's, PA [*Location identifier FAA*] (FAAL)
OYMB	Marib [*Yemen*] [*ICAO location identifier*] (ICLI)
OYMC	Mokha [*Yemen*] [*ICAO location identifier*] (ICLI)
OYMHi	Mahoning Valley Historical Society, Arms Museum, Youngstown, OH [*Library symbol Library of Congress*] (LCLS)
OYMV	Ononis Yellow Mosaic Virus [*Plant pathology*]
OYO	Tres Arroyos [*Argentina*] [*Airport symbol*] (OAG)
OYOG	OYO Geospace Corp. [*NASDAQ symbol*] (SAG)
OYOGeo	OYO Geospace Corp. [*Associated Press*] (SAG)
OYP	Office of Youth Programs [*Department of Labor*]
OYP	Opportunities for Youth Program [*Canada*]
OYS	Otsar Yehude Sefarad (BJA)
Oys	Oysters [*Quality of the bottom*] [*Nautical charts*]
OYS	Yosemite National Park [*California*] [*Airport symbol Obsolete*] (OAG)
OYSH	Saada [*Yemen*] [*ICAO location identifier*] (ICLI)
OYSN	Sanaa/International [*Yemen*] [*ICAO location identifier*] (ICLI)
OYSREA	Office of Youth, Sport, Recreation and Ethnic Affairs [*Northern Territory, Australia*]
OYTZ	Taiz/Ganad [*Yemen*] [*ICAO location identifier*] (ICLI)
OYU	Youngstown State University, Youngstown, OH [*Library symbol Library of Congress*] (LCLS)
OYY	Columbus, OH [*Location identifier FAA*] (FAAL)
OYZM	Al-Hazm [*Yemen*] [*ICAO location identifier*] (ICLI)
Oz	Ooze [*Quality of the bottom*] [*Nautical charts*]
OZ	Ounce [*Unit of weight*] (AAG)
oz.	Ounce (IDOE)
OZ	Ozark Airlines, Inc. [*ICAO designator*] (OAG)
OZ	Ozone
oz.	Ozone (IDOE)
OZA	Ozark (MCD)
OZA	Ozark Airlines (MHDB)
OZA	Ozona, TX [*Location identifier FAA*] (FAAL)
OZ AP	Apothecaries' Ounce (WDAA)
oz apoth	Apothecaries Ounce (BARN)
OZAR	Ozark National Scenic Riverways [*National Park Service designation*]
OZARC	Ozone ARCAS [*All-Purpose Rocket for Collecting Atmospheric Soundings*] [*Navy*]
OZav	John McIntire Public Library, Zanesville, OH [*Library symbol Library of Congress*] (LCLS)
OZavU	Ohio University, Zanesville Branch Campus, Zanesville, OH [*Library symbol Library of Congress*] (LCLS)
OZC	Cleveland Heights-University Heights Public Library, Cleveland Heights, OH [*OCLC symbol*] (OCLC)
OZC	Ozamis City [*Philippines*] [*Airport symbol*] (OAG)
OZD	Observed Zenith Distance [*Navigation*]
OZE	Outer Zone Electron
OZEM	OzMail Ltd. [*NASDAQ symbol*] (SAG)
OzEmail	OZEmail Ltd. [*Associated Press*] (SAG)
OZEMY	OzEmail Ltd ADR [*NASDAQ symbol*] (TTSB)
OZEP	Outer Zone Electron Precipitation
OZ-FT	Ounce Foot (AAG)
OZ/FT²	Ounces per Square Foot
OZ/GAL	Ounces per Gallon
OZH	Zaporozh'ye [*Former USSR Airport symbol Obsolete*] (OAG)
OZ-IN	Ounce Inch (AAG)
oz-in	Ounce-Inch (IDOE)
oz-in	Ounce-Inches (IDOE)
OZ/IN²	Ounces per Square Inch
OZ/IN³	Ounces per Cubic Inch
OZIPP	Ozone Isopleth Plotting Package (GFGA)
OZIPPM	Ozone Isopleth Plotting Package, Modified (GFGA)
OZN	St. George, UT [*Location identifier FAA*] (FAAL)
OZO	Orbiting Zoological Observatory to Track Animals
OZON	Cyclc3PSS Corp. [*NASDAQ symbol*] (SAG)
OZON	Cyclopss Corp. [*NASDAQ symbol*] (TTSB)
OZ/PT	Ounces per Pint
OZR	Ozark, Fort Rucker, AL [*Location identifier FAA*] (FAAL)
OZRF	Opposed Zone Reheating Furnace (PDAA)
OZT	Ounces Troy [*Unit of weight*]
OZX	Oneonta, NY [*Location identifier FAA*] (FAAL)
OZ/YD²	Ounces per Square Yard
OZZ	Ouarzazate [*Morocco*] [*Airport symbol*] (OAG)
OZZ	Ozark, AR [*Location identifier FAA*] (FAAL)